The Far East and Australasia 2012

43rd Edition

Routledge
Taylor & Francis Group
LONDON AND NEW YORK

First published 1969
Forty-third Edition 2012

2 Park Square, Milton Park, Abingdon, Oxon, OX14 4RN
(Routledge is an imprint of the Taylor & Francis Group, an Informa business)

ISBN13: 978-1-85743-630-3
ISSN: 0071-3791

Editor: Lynn Daniel

Regional Organizations Editors: Helen Canton, Catriona Holman
Senior Editor, Statistics: Philip McIntyre

Statistics Researchers: Abhinav Srivastava (Lead Researcher), Mohd Khalid Ansari (Senior Researcher), Anuj Aggarwal, Charu Arora, Sasha Sadh, Akshay Sharma, Varun Wadhawan

Directory Researchers: Arijit Khasnobis (Lead Researcher), Surmeet Kaur, Tessy Margaret Rajappan

Contributing Editors, Commodities: Gareth Wyn Jones, Gareth Vaughan

Publisher and Series Editor: Joanne Maher

Typeset in New Century Schoolbook

FSC
www.fsc.org
MIX
Paper from responsible sources
FSC® C006021

Typeset by Data Standards Limited, Frome, Somerset

Printed and bound in Great Britain by Polestar Wheatons, Exeter

FOREWORD

Events in Japan for much of 2011 were dominated by the repercussions of the devastating earthquake and tsunami in March. Following criticism of the Prime Minister's response to the disaster and the continuing nuclear crisis at the Fukushima power plant, Prime Minister Naoto Kan resigned in August and was replaced by Yoshihiko Noda. A detailed account of the environmental disaster is given in Part One of this 43rd edition of THE FAR EAST AND AUSTRALASIA. Australia and New Zealand also suffered natural disasters in 2010/11: flooding in the former and earthquakes in the latter. Analyses of the economic impact of these major regional disasters is provided in Part Two.

A comprehensive assessment of the situation on the Korean peninsula is presented for the first time in Part One. In late 2010 tensions were further exacerbated by a North Korean assault on the island of Yeonpyeong, in which four South Koreans were killed. Part One also includes introductory essays on the remarkable rise of China, the USA's relations with the Asia-Pacific region, the security challenges of East and South-East Asia, human rights, and environmental issues.

In Myanmar opposition leader Aung San Suu Kyi was released from house arrest in November 2010, shortly after the holding of the country's first legislative elections for more than 20 years. In early 2011, however, outgoing Prime Minister Thein Sein was chosen as President of Myanmar, and the Cabinet continued to be dominated by former military officers. Bouasone Bouphavanh, the Prime Minister of Laos, unexpectedly resigned in December 2010 and was replaced by Thongsing Thammavong. In July 2011 Truong Tan Sang replaced Nguyen Minh Triet as President of Viet Nam, while Nguyen Tan Dung remained as Prime Minister. Although the People's Action Party was returned to office at elections conducted in Singapore in May, support for the governing party declined to its lowest level since independence. An early test for Thailand's first female Prime Minister, Yingluck Shinawatra, who took office in August, was the extensive flooding of Bangkok in October.

Frequent government changes continued to characterize the Pacific Islands. Vanuatu received its sixth Prime Minister, Sato Kilman, in almost as many months at the end of June 2011. In response to repeated transfers of political allegiance in Solomon Islands, Prime Minister Danny Philip was obliged to reorganize his Cabinet several times during 2011. In April the pro-independence Oscar Temaru assumed the French Polynesian presidency for the fifth time. Following a number of unsuccessful attempts to form a government, Harold Martin was finally confirmed as President of New Caledonia in mid-2011, thus ending a protracted crisis. Also in mid-2011 it was announced that, owing to ill health, Sir Michael Somare, who had dominated the politics of Papua New Guinea for several decades, was to resign as Prime Minister. The elections held in Tonga in November 2010 were the first to return a popularly elected majority to the country's legislature; however, in the subsequent contest for the premiership, democracy activist 'Akilisi Pohiva was defeated by Lord Tu'ivakano. At legislative elections in the Cook Islands in November 2010, Henry Puna defeated the incumbent Prime Minister. In Tuvalu in December, after only three months in office, Prime Minister Maatia Toafa was defeated in a parliamentary motion of no confidence and replaced by Willie Telavi. An entire section of the volume is dedicated to the Pacific Islands. Specially commissioned essays on the contemporary politics and on the security issues of the Pacific Islands examine topical subjects. Other detailed articles survey the general history, the current economic trends, the specific environmental concerns and the health issues of the Pacific Islands.

A calendar of the main political events between November 2010 and October 2011 provides a convenient reference guide to recent developments in the Far East and Australasia. All essays are updated annually by specialist authors and researchers. The statistical surveys, directories and bibliographies have also been extensively revised. Detailed coverage of international organizations and their recent activities in the Far East and Australasia is provided, along with a directory of research institutes and a general bibliography. Information on the region's major commodities is also incorporated.

The editors are once again grateful to all the contributors for their articles and advice, and to the numerous governments and organizations that have provided statistical and other information.

October 2011

ACKNOWLEDGEMENTS

The editors gratefully acknowledge the co-operation, interest and advice of all the authors who have contributed to the volume. We are also indebted to the many organizations that have provided information, particularly national statistical offices.

We are especially grateful for permission to reproduce material from the following sources: the United Nations' statistical databases and *Demographic Yearbook*, *Statistical Yearbook*, *Statistical Yearbook for Asia and the Pacific*, *Monthly Bulletin of Statistics*, *Industrial Commodity Statistics Yearbook* and *International Trade Statistics Yearbook*; the United Nations Educational, Scientific and Cultural Organization's *Statistical Yearbook* and Institute for Statistics database; the *Human Development Report* of the United Nations Development Programme; the Food and Agriculture Organization of the United Nations' statistical database; the statistical databases of UNCTAD/WTO International Trade Centre; the statistical databases of the World Health Organization; the International Labour Office's statistical database and *Yearbook of Labour Statistics*; the World Bank's *World Bank Atlas*, *Global Development Finance*, *World Development Report* and World Development Indicators database; the International Monetary Fund's statistical database, *International Financial Statistics* and *Government Finance Statistics Yearbook*; the World Tourism Organization's *Compendium* and *Yearbook of Tourism Statistics*; the Asian Development Bank's *Asian Development Outlook* and *Key Indicators for Asia and the Pacific*; the US Geological Survey; and the International Telecommunication Union. We are also grateful to the International Institute for Strategic Studies, Arundel House, 13–15 Arundel Street, London WC2R 3DX, for the use of defence statistics from *The Military Balance 2011*.

The following publications have been of special value: *IMF Survey*, Washington, DC, USA; and *Keesing's Record of World Events*, Cambridge, United Kingdom.

HEALTH AND WELFARE STATISTICS: SOURCES AND DEFINITIONS

Total fertility rate Source: WHO Statistical Information System (part of the Global Health Observatory). The number of children that would be born per woman, assuming no female mortality at child-bearing ages and the age-specific fertility rates of a specified country and reference period.

Under-5 mortality rate Source: WHO Statistical Information System. Defined by WHO as the probability of a child born in a specific year or period dying before reaching the age of five, if subject to the age-specific mortality rates of that year or period.

HIV/AIDS Source: UNAIDS. Estimated percentage of adults aged 15 to 49 years living with HIV/AIDS. < indicates 'fewer than'.

Health expenditure Source: WHO Statistical Information System.

US $ per head (PPP)

International dollar estimates, derived by dividing local currency units by an estimate of their purchasing-power parity (PPP) compared with the US dollar. PPPs are the rates of currency conversion that equalize the purchasing power of different currencies by eliminating the differences in price levels between countries.

% of GDP

GDP levels for OECD countries follow the most recent UN System of National Accounts. For non-OECD countries a value was estimated by utilizing existing UN, IMF and World Bank data.

Public expenditure

Government health-related outlays plus expenditure by social schemes compulsorily affiliated with a sizeable share of the population, and extrabudgetary funds allocated to health services. Figures include grants or loans provided by international agencies, other national authorities, and sometimes commercial banks.

Access to water and sanitation Source: WHO/UNICEF Joint Monitoring Programme on Water Supply and Sanitation (JMP) (Progress on Drinking Water and Sanitation, 2010 Update). Defined in terms of the percentage of the population using improved facilities in terms of the type of technology and levels of service afforded. For water, this includes house connections, public standpipes, boreholes with handpumps, protected dug wells, protected spring and rainwater collection; allowance is also made for other locally defined technologies. Sanitation is defined to include connection to a sewer or septic tank system, pour-flush latrine, simple pit or ventilated improved pit latrine, again with allowance for acceptable local technologies. Access to water and sanitation does not imply that the level of service or quality of water is 'adequate' or 'safe'.

Carbon dioxide emissions Source: World Bank, World Development Indicators database, citing the Carbon Dioxide Information Analysis Center (sponsored by the US Department of Energy). Emissions comprise those resulting from the burning of fossil fuels (including those produced during consumption of solid, liquid and gas fuels and from gas flaring) and from the manufacture of cement.

Human Development Index (HDI) Source: UNDP, *Human Development Report* (2010). A summary of human development measured by three basic dimensions: prospects for a long and healthy life, measured by life expectancy at birth; knowledge, measured by adult literacy rate and a combination of mean years of schooling and expected years of schooling; and standard of living, measured by GNP per head (PPP US $). The index value obtained lies between zero and one. A value above 0.8 indicates high human development, between 0.5 and 0.8 medium human development, and below 0.5 low human development. A centralized data source for all three dimensions was not available for all countries. In some cases other data sources were used to calculate a substitute value; however, this was excluded from the ranking. Other countries, including non-UNDP members, were excluded from the HDI altogether. In total, 169 countries were ranked for 2010.

CONTENTS

PART THREE

Regional Information

List of Maps

THE CONTRIBUTORS

Tilak Abeysinghe. Associate Professor, Singapore Centre for Applied and Policy Economics, Department of Economics, National University of Singapore, Singapore.

Rokiah Alavi. Associate Professor and Head, Department of Economics, International Islamic University, Kuala Lumpur, Malaysia.

Bryant J. Allen. Visiting Fellow, State Society & Governance in Melanesia Program, School of International, Political & Strategic Studies, College of Asia and the Pacific, The Australian National University, Canberra, Australia.

Donna Amoroso. Late Associate Professor of Southeast Asian Studies, National Graduate Institute for Policy Studies, Tokyo, Japan.

Robert F. Ash. Professor, Department of Economics, School of Oriental and African Studies, University of London, United Kingdom.

Michael D. Barr. Senior Lecturer, Department of International Relations, School of Political and International Studies, Flinders University, Adelaide, Australia.

Mark Beeson. Winthrop Professor in Political Science and International Relations, The University of Western Australia, Crawley, Australia.

Volker Boege. Visiting Fellow, Australian Centre for Peace and Conflict Studies, The University of Queensland, Brisbane, Australia.

Shaun Breslin. Professor of Politics and International Studies, University of Warwick, United Kingdom.

M. Anne Brown. Senior Research Fellow, Australian Centre for Peace and Conflict Studies, The University of Queensland, Brisbane, Australia.

Ian Brown. Professor of the Economic History of South East Asia, Department of History, School of Oriental and African Studies, University of London, United Kingdom.

Kerry Brown. Senior Fellow, Royal Institute of International Affairs, Chatham House, London, United Kingdom.

Jenny J. Bryant. Former Reader, Geography Department, University of the South Pacific, Suva, Fiji.

Ian Campbell. Former Professor, School of Social Sciences, University of the South Pacific, Suva, Fiji.

William F. Case. Professor and Acting Head, Southeast Asia Research Centre, Department of Asian and International Studies, City University of Hong Kong, Kowloon, Hong Kong.

Kenneth Christie. Professor and Head of Program, Master of Arts in Human Security and Peacebuilding, School of Peace and Conflict Management, Royal Roads University, Victoria, Canada.

Joseph S. Chung. Former Professor of Economics, Stuart School of Business, Illinois Institute of Technology, Chicago, USA.

Lesley Connors. Former Lecturer, Department of Political Studies, School of Oriental and African Studies, University of London, United Kingdom.

Robert Cribb. Professor, School of Culture, History and Language, College of Asia and the Pacific, The Australian National University, Canberra, Australia.

Harvey Demaine. Former Associate Professor of Regional, Rural and Agricultural Development Planning, Asian Institute of Technology, Bangkok, Thailand.

Chris Dixon. Professor of International Development, Global Policy Institute, London Metropolitan University, London, United Kingdom.

Jörn Dosch. Professor of Asia Pacific Studies, Department of East Asian Studies, University of Leeds, United Kingdom.

Chris Edwards. Former Senior Lecturer, School of Development Studies, University of East Anglia, Norwich, United Kingdom.

Greg Fealy. Fellow and Senior Lecturer in Indonesian Politics, Associate Dean for Higher Degree Research, Department of Political and Social Change, School of International, Political and Strategic Studies, College of Asia and the Pacific, The Australian National University, Canberra, Australia.

Stewart Firth. Visiting Fellow, School of International, Political and Strategic Studies, College of Asia and the Pacific, The Australian National University, Canberra, Australia.

C. P. Fitzgerald. Late Emeritus Professor, The Australian National University, Canberra, Australia.

Aidan Foster-Carter. Honorary Senior Research Fellow in Sociology and Modern Korea, University of Leeds, United Kingdom.

Michael Freeberne. Former Lecturer in Geography, School of Oriental and African Studies, University of London, United Kingdom.

Nick Freeman. Former Senior Fellow, Institute of Southeast Asian Studies, Singapore.

Volker Grabowsky. Professor, Asia-Africa Institute, University of Hamburg, Germany.

Jeanine Graham. Former Senior Lecturer in History, University of Waikato, Hamilton, New Zealand.

Geoffrey C. Gunn. Professor, Faculty of Economics, Nagasaki University, Nagasaki, Japan.

Lok Sang Ho. Professor of Economics, Centre for Public Policy Studies, Lingnan University, Hong Kong.

James E. Hoare. Former Research Analyst, Foreign and Commonwealth Office, London, United Kingdom.

Sarwar O. H. Hobohm. Former Senior Economist/Editor, Asia-Pacific, Country Analysis and Forecasting Division, The Economist Intelligence Unit, London, United Kingdom.

Edith Hodgkinson. Economic journalist specializing in developing countries, London, United Kingdom.

A. V. M. Horton. Former Honorary Fellow of the Centre for South-East Asian Studies, University of Hull, and Specialist in Brunei History, United Kingdom.

Kenneth E. Jackson. Associate Professor and Director, Centre for Development Studies, Anthropology Department, University of Auckland, New Zealand.

T. K. Jayaraman. Associate Professor, School of Economics, Faculty of Business and Economics, University of the South Pacific, Suva, Fiji.

Patrick Jory. Former Lecturer, Regional Studies Program (Southeast Asia), School of Liberal Arts, Walailak University, Nakhon Si Thammarat, Thailand.

Frank H. H. King. Former Professor of Economic History, The University of Hong Kong, Hong Kong.

Roger Lawrey. Associate Professor and Deputy Dean, Faculty of Business, Economics and Policy Studies, Universiti Brunei Darussalam, Brunei.

Suiwah Leung. Adjunct Associate Professor of Economics and Finance, Crawford School of Economics and Government, College of Asia and the Pacific, The Australian National University, Canberra, Australia.

Stuart Macintyre. Professor and Dean of the Faculty of Arts, School of Historical Studies, University of Melbourne, Australia.

Stephen McCarthy. Research Fellow, Griffith Asia Institute, Griffith University, Queensland, Australia.

A. E. McQueen. Former Assistant General Manager, New Zealand Government Railways, New Zealand.

Ruth McVey. Emeritus Reader in Politics with reference to South-East Asia, School of Oriental and African Studies, University of London, United Kingdom.

N. J. Miners. Former Reader in Political Science, Department of Politics and Public Administration, The University of Hong Kong, Hong Kong.

Andrew C. Nahm. Former Professor Emeritus of History and Consultant to the Office of International Education and Programs, Western Michigan University, USA.

Bhanupong Nidhiprabha. Associate Professor, Faculty of Economics, Thammasat University, Pathumthani, Thailand.

Anna Nolan. Research Officer, Australian Centre for Peace and Conflict Studies, The University of Queensland, Brisbane, Australia.

Neville Norman. Professor, Department of Economics, University of Melbourne, Australia.

Sorpong Peou. Professor and Chair of the Department of Politics, University of Winnipeg, Winnipeg, Canada.

Michael Pinches. Professor and Chair, Discipline of Anthropology and Sociology, School of Social and Cultural Studies, The University of Western Australia, Crawley, Australia.

Jirawat Saengthong. Specialist in Thai Social History, Institute of Liberal Arts, Walailak University, Nakhon Si Thammarat, Thailand.

J. W. Rowe. Former Director-General, New Zealand Employers' Federation, New Zealand.

Alan J. K. Sanders. Former Lecturer in Mongolian Studies, School of Oriental and African Studies, University of London, United Kingdom.

John Sargent. Former Reader in Geography, School of Oriental and African Studies, University of London, United Kingdom.

Josef Silverstein. Former Professor Emeritus of Political Science, Rutgers University, New Brunswick, USA.

Michael Smitka. Professor of Economics and Acting Director, Williams School of Commerce, Washington and Lee University, Lexington, Virginia, USA.

Sok Hach. Director, Economic Institute of Cambodia, Phnom-Penh, Cambodia.

Ross Steele. Former Lecturer and Director, Graduate Program in Population and Human Resources, School of Geography, Population and Environmental Management, Flinders University, Adelaide, Australia.

Richard Storry. Late Director of the Far East Centre, Oxford, United Kingdom.

Martin Stuart-Fox. Former Professor and Head of Department, Department of History, The University of Queensland, Brisbane, Australia.

Laura Summers. Former Lecturer, Department of Politics and Asian Studies, University of Hull, United Kingdom.

Robert Sutter. Professor of Practice of International Affairs, The Elliott School of International Affairs, Georgetown University, Washington, DC, USA.

Andrew T. H. Tan. Associate Professor and Convenor for International Studies, Faculty of Arts, The University of New South Wales, Sydney, Australia.

James Tang. Dean of the School of Social Sciences, Singapore Management University, Singapore.

John Taylor. Professor and Course Director of Development Studies, London South Bank University, London, United Kingdom.

Htwe Htwe Thein. Senior Lecturer in International Business Studies, School of Management, Curtin Business School, Curtin University of Technology, Perth, Australia.

C. M. Turnbull. Honorary Research Fellow, Centre for Asian Studies, and Former Professor of History, The University of Hong Kong, Hong Kong.

David A. K. Watters. Professor, Department of Surgery, Geelong Hospital, Geelong, Victoria, Australia.

Michael Yahuda. Former Visiting Scholar, Sigur Center, Elliott School of International Relations, George Washington University, Washington, DC, USA.

Akira Yamazaki. Former Editorial Writer, *Nihon Keizai Shimbun* (Japan Economic Journal), Tokyo, Japan.

ABBREVIATIONS

Acad.	Academician; Academy
ACP	African, Caribbean and Pacific (States)
ACT	Australian Capital Territory
AD	Anno Domini
ADB	Asian Development Bank
Adm.	Admiral
Admin.	Administration, Administrative, Administrator
AFTA	ASEAN Free Trade Area
AG	Aktiengesellschaft (limited company)
a.i.	ad interim
AIDS	acquired immunodeficiency syndrome
Alt.	Alternate
AM	Amplitude Modulation
ANZUS	Australia, New Zealand and the United States
Apdo	Apartado (Post Box)
APEC	Asia-Pacific Economic Cooperation
approx.	approximately
Apt	Apartment
AR	Autonomous Region
ARF	ASEAN Regional Forum
ARV	advanced retroviral
ASEAN	Association of South East Asian Nations
Asscn	Association
Assoc.	Associate
Asst	Assistant
ATM	automated teller machine
Aug.	August
auth.	authorized
Av.	Avenida (Avenue)
Ave	Avenue
BC	Before Christ
Bd	Board
b/d	barrels per day
Bhd	Berhad (public limited company)
BIS	Bank for International Settlements
Bldg(s)	Building(s)
Blk	Block
Blvd	Boulevard
BOT	build-operate-transfer
BP	Boîte Postale (Post Box)
br.(s)	branch(es)
Brig.	Brigadier
BSE	bovine spongiform encephalopathy
Btu	British thermal unit
C	Centigrade
c.	circa
cap.	capital
Capt.	Captain
CCP	Chinese Communist Party
Cdre	Commodore
Cen.	Central
CEO	Chief Executive Officer
cf.	confer (compare)
CFC	chlorofluorocarbon
CFP	Communauté française du Pacifique
Chair.	Chairman/Chairwoman
CIA	(US) Central Intelligence Agency
Cie	Compagnie
c.i.f.	cost, insurance and freight
C-in-C	Commander-in-Chief
circ.	circulation
CIS	Commonwealth of Independent States
cm	centimetre(s)
CMAG	Commonwealth Ministerial Action Group on the Harare Declaration
CMEA	Council for Mutual Economic Assistance (COMECON)
cnr	corner
c/o	care of
Co	Company
Col	Colonel
Comm.	Commission
Commdr	Commander
Commdt	Commandant
Commr	Commissioner
Conf.	Conference
Confed.	Confederation
COO	Chief Operating Officer
Corpn	Corporation
CP	Case Postale, Caixa Postal (Post Box)
CPO	Central Post Office
CPOB	Central Post Office Box
cres.	crescent
Cttee	Committee
cu	cubic
cwt	hundredweight
Dec.	December
Dem.	Democratic
Dep.	Deputy
dep.	deposit(s)
Dept	Department
Devt	Development
Dir	Director
Div.	Division
DNA	deoxyribonucleic acid
DPRK	Democratic People's Republic of Korea
Dr	Doctor
Dr.	Drive
Dra	Doutora (Doctor)
DRAM	dynamic random access memory
Drs	Doctorandus (Netherlands doctor's degree)
DVD	digital versatile disc
dwt	dead weight tons
E	East, Eastern
EAEC	East Asia Economic Caucus
EAGA	East ASEAN Growth Area
EC	European Community
ECF	Extended Credit Facility
Econ.	Economic
ECU	European Currency Unit(s)
Ed.(s)	Editor(s)
Edif.	Edifício (Building)
edn	edition
e.g.	exempli gratia (for example)
Eng.	Engineer; Engineering
EPZ	Export Processing Zone
ESCAP	Economic and Social Commission for Asia and the Pacific
ESPO	Eastern Siberia–Pacific Ocean
est.	established; estimate, estimated
etc.	etcetera
EU	European Union
excl.	excluding
Exec.	Executive
exhbn(s)	exhibition(s)
Ext.	Extension
F	Floor
f.	founded
FAO	Food and Agriculture Organization
FBI	Federal Bureau of Investigation
FDI	foreign direct investment
Feb.	February
Fed.	Federal, Federation
Feds	Federations
Flt	Flight
FM	Frequency Modulation
fmr(ly)	former(ly)
f.o.b.	free on board
Fr	Father
Fri.	Friday
ft	foot (feet)
FTA	free trade agreement/area
g	gram(s)
gall(s)	gallon(s)
GATT	General Agreement on Tariffs and Trade
GDP	gross domestic product
GEF	Global Environment Facility
Gen.	General
GMO	genetically modified organism(s)
GNI	gross national income
GNP	gross national product
Gov.	Governor
Govt	Government
GPO	General Post Office
GPOB	General Post Office Box
grt	gross registered tons
GSM	Global System for Mobile Communications
GSP	gross state product
GWh	gigawatt hour(s)
ha	hectare(s)
HD	high-definition
HDI	Human Development Index
HDTV	high-definition television

HE	His (or Her) Excellency; His Eminence
HH	His (or Her) Highness; His Holiness
HI	Hawaii
HIV	human immunodeficiency virus
hl	hectolitre(s)
HLTF	High Level Task Force
HM	His (or Her) Majesty
HMS	His (or Her) Majesty's Ship
HMSO	Her Majesty's Stationery Office
Hon.	Honorary
HPAI	highly pathogenic avian influenza
HQ	Headquarters
hr(s)	hour(s)
HRH	His (or Her) Royal Highness
HS	harmonized system
HSC	harmonized system classification
Hwy	Highway
HYV	high-yielding variety
ibid.	ibidem (from the same source)
IBRD	International Bank for Reconstruction and Development (World Bank)
ICT	information and communication technology
IDPs	internally displaced persons
i.e.	id est (that is to say)
ILO	International Labour Organization
IMF	International Monetary Fund
in	inch(es)
Inc	Incorporated
incl.	include(s); including
Ind.	Independent
Inst.	Institute
Int.	International
IP	intellectual property
IPCC	Intergovernmental Panel on Climate Change
IPO	initial public offering
Ir	Insinyur (Engineer)
IRF	International Road Federation
Is	Islands
ISIC	International Standard Industrial Classification
IT	information technology
ITC	information and communication technology
ITUC	International Trade Union Confederation
IUU	illegal,unreported and unregulated
Jan.	January
Jr	Junior
Jt	Joint
Jtly	Jointly
K	kina (Papua New Guinea currency)
Kav.	Kaveling (Plot)
kg	kilogram(s)
kHz	kilohertz
KK	Kaien Kaisha (limited company)
kl	kilolitre
km	kilometre(s)
kW	kilowatt(s)
kWh	kilowatt hour(s)
lb	pound(s)
LCD	liquid crystal display
LDC	less-developed country
LED	light-emitting diode
LNG	liquefied natural gas
LPG	liquefied petroleum gas
Lt	Lieutenant
Ltd	Limited
m	metre(s)
m.	million
M & A	mergers and acquisitions
Maj.	Major
Man.	Manager, Managing
MCPO	Manila Central Post Office
MDG	Millennium Development Goal
mem.	member
mfg	manufacturing
mfr(s)	manufacturer(s)
mg	milligram
Mgr	Monseigneur, Monsignor
MHz	megahertz
MIA	Missing in Action
Mil.	Military
Mlle	Mademoiselle
mm	millimetre(s)
Mme	Madame
Mon.	Monday
MOU	memorandum of understanding
MP	Member of Parliament
Mt	Mount
MV	Motor Vessel
MW	megawatt(s)
MWh	megawatt hour(s)
N	North, Northern
n.a.	not available
NAFTA	North American Free Trade Agreement
Nat.	National
NCD	National Capital District
NCO	Non-Commissioned Officer
n.e.s.	not elsewhere specified
NGO	non-governmental organization
No.	number
Nov.	November
NPL	non-performing loan(s)
NPT	Non-Proliferation Treaty
nr	near
nrt	net registered tons
NSW	New South Wales
NT	Northern Territory
NV	Naamloze Vennootschap (limited company)
NZ	New Zealand
Oct.	October
OECD	Organisation for Economic Co-operation and Development
OER	official exchange rate
OPEC	Organization of the Petroleum Exporting Countries
opp.	opposite
ORB	OPEC Reference Basket
Ord.	ordinary
Org.(s)	Organization(s)
oz	ounce(s)
p(p).	page(s)
p.a.	per annum
Parl.	Parliament(ary)
PB	Private Bag
PC	personal computer
PCL	Public Company Limited
Perm.	Permanent
PICTA	Pacific Island Countries Trade Agreement
PICTs	Pacific Island countries and territories
PLC	Public Limited Company
PMB	Private Mail Bag
PNG	Papua New Guinea
PO	Post Office
POB	Post Office Box
PPP	purchasing-power parity
PR	proportional representation
Pres.	President
Prin.	Principal
Prof.	Professor
Propr	Proprietor
Prov.	Province, Provincial
PRSP	Poverty Reduction Strategy Paper
PSI	Policy Support Instrument, Poverty Strategies Initiative
PT	Perseroan Terbatas (limited company)
Pt	Point
Pte	Private
Pty	Proprietary
p.u.	paid up
publ.(s)	publication(s); published
Publr	Publisher
Pvt	Private
QIP	Quick Impact Project
Qld	Queensland
q.v.	quod vide (to which refer)
R & D	research and development
Rd	Road
regd	registered
Rep.	Representative
Repub.	Republic
res	reserves
retd	retired
Rev.	Reverend
Rm	Room
RM	Ringgit Malaysia
RMB	renminbi
ro-ro	roll-on roll-off
Rp.	Rupiah (Indonesian currency)
Rt	Right
S	South, Southern
SA	South Australia; Société anonyme, Sociedad Anónima (limited company)
SAARC	South Asian Association for Regional Co-operation
SAR	Special Administrative Region
SARL	Sociedade Anônima de Responsibilidade Limitada (limited company)
SARS	Severe Acute Respiratory Syndrome
Sat.	Saturday
Sdn Bhd	Sendirian Berhad (private limited company)

SDR	Special Drawing Right(s)
SEATO	South-East Asia Treaty Organization
Sec.	Secretary; Section
Secr.	Secretariat
Sept.	September
SEZ	Special Economic Zone
SIM	Subscriber Identification Module
SIS	Small(er) Island States
SITC	Standard International Trade Classification
SMEs	small and medium-sized enterprises
SMS	short message service
Soc.	Society
SOE	State-Owned Enterprise
SPR	strategic petroleum reserve
Sq.	Square
sq	square (in measurements)
Sr	Senior
SRSG	Special Representative of the UN Secretary-General
St	Street; Saint, San, Santo
STI(s)	sexually transmitted infection(s)
subs.	subscribed
Sun.	Sunday
Supt	Superintendent
SUV	sports utility vehicle
Tas	Tasmania
tech.	technical
tel.	telephone
TEU	20-foot equivalent unit
Thur.	Thursday
trans.	translator, translated
Treas.	Treasurer
Tue.	Tuesday
TV	television
UHF	ultra-high frequency
UK	United Kingdom
UN	United Nations
UNCTAD	United Nations Conference on Trade and Development
UNDP	United Nations Development Programme
UNEP	United Nations Environment Programme
UNESCO	United Nations Educational, Scientific and Cultural Organization
UNFPA	United Nations Population Fund
UNHCHR	United Nations High Commissioner of Human Rights
UNHCR	United Nations High Commissioner for Refugees
UNIDO	United Nations Industrial Development Organization
UNMISET	United Nations Mission of Support in East Timor
UNMIT	United Nations Integrated Mission in East Timor
UNODC	United Nations Office on Drugs and Crime
UNTAC	United Nations Transitional Authority in Cambodia
UNTAET	United Nations Transitional Administration in East Timor
UNWTO	World Tourism Organization
US	United States
USA	United States of America
USAID	United States Agency for International Development
USSR	Union of Soviet Socialist Republics
VAT	value-added tax
Ven.	Venerable
VHF	very high frequency
Vic	Victoria
Vol(s)	Volume(s)
W	West, Western
WA	Western Australia
Wed.	Wednesday
WHO	World Health Organization
WSSD	World Summit on Sustainable Development
WTO	World Trade Organization
yd	yard
yr(s)	year(s)

INTERNATIONAL TELEPHONE CODES

To make international calls to telephone and fax numbers listed in *The Far East and Australasia*, dial the international code of the country from which you are calling, followed by the appropriate country code for the organization you wish to call (listed below), followed by the area code (if applicable) and telephone or fax number listed in the entry.

	Country code	+ or − GMT*
American Samoa	1 684	−11
Australia	61	+8 to +10
Brunei	673	+8
Cambodia	855	+7
China, People's Republic	86	+8
Christmas Island	61	+7
Cocos (Keeling) Islands	61	$+6\frac{1}{2}$
Cook Islands	682	−10
Fiji	679	+12
French Polynesia	689	−9 to −10
Guam	1 671	+10
Hong Kong	852	+8
Indonesia	62	+7 to +9
Japan	81	+9
Kiribati	686	+12 to +13
Korea, Democratic People's Republic (North Korea)	850	+9
Korea, Republic (South Korea)	82	+9
Laos	856	+7
Macao	853	+8
Marshall Islands	692	+12
Malaysia	60	+8
Micronesia, Federated States	691	+10 to +11
Mongolia	976	+7 to +9
Myanmar	95	$+6\frac{1}{2}$
Nauru	674	+12
New Caledonia	687	+11
New Zealand	64	+12
Niue	683	−11
Norfolk Island	672	$+11\frac{1}{2}$
Northern Mariana Islands	1 670	+10
Palau	680	+9
Papua New Guinea	675	+10
Philippines	63	+8
Pitcairn Islands	872	−8
Samoa	685	+13
Singapore	65	+8
Solomon Islands	677	+11
Taiwan	886	+8
Thailand	66	+7
Timor-Leste (East Timor)	670	+9
Tokelau	690	+13
Tonga	676	+13
Tuvalu	688	+12
Vanuatu	678	+11
Viet Nam	84	+7
Wallis and Futuna Islands	681	+12

* Time difference in hours + or − Greenwich Mean Time (GMT). The times listed compare the standard (winter) times. Some countries may adopt Summer (Daylight Saving) Times—i.e. + 1 hour—for part of the year. Samoa and Tokelau were to enter the above time zones at the end of 2011.

Note: Telephone and fax numbers using the Inmarsat ocean region code 870 are listed in full. No country or area code is required, but it is necessary to precede the number with the international access code of the country from which the call is made.

EXPLANATORY NOTE ON THE DIRECTORY SECTION

The Directory section of each chapter is arranged under the following headings, where they apply:

THE CONSTITUTION

THE GOVERNMENT
- HEAD OF STATE
- CABINET/COUNCIL OF MINISTERS
- MINISTRIES

LEGISLATURE

ELECTION COMMISSION

STATE GOVERNMENTS

POLITICAL ORGANIZATIONS

DIPLOMATIC REPRESENTATION

JUDICIAL SYSTEM

RELIGION

THE PRESS

PUBLISHERS

BROADCASTING AND COMMUNICATIONS
- TELECOMMUNICATIONS
- RADIO
- TELEVISION

FINANCE
- CENTRAL BANK
- STATE BANKS
- COMMERCIAL BANKS
- DEVELOPMENT BANKS
- INVESTMENT BANKS
- SAVINGS BANKS
- FOREIGN BANKS
- STOCK EXCHANGE
- INSURANCE

TRADE AND INDUSTRY
- GOVERNMENT AGENCIES
- DEVELOPMENT ORGANIZATIONS
- CHAMBERS OF COMMERCE AND INDUSTRY
- INDUSTRIAL AND TRADE ASSOCIATIONS
- EMPLOYERS' ORGANIZATIONS
- UTILITIES
- MAJOR COMPANIES
- CO-OPERATIVES
- TRADE UNIONS

TRANSPORT
- RAILWAYS
- ROADS
- INLAND WATERWAYS
- SHIPPING
- CIVIL AVIATION

TOURISM

DEFENCE

EDUCATION

CALENDAR OF POLITICAL EVENTS IN THE FAR EAST AND AUSTRALASIA, NOVEMBER 2010–OCTOBER 2011

NOVEMBER 2010

1 **Nauru:** following the appointment of Ludwig Scotty as Speaker of Parliament, thereby ending a protracted impasse, President Marcus Stephen was re-elected as the country's Head of State, defeating Milton Dube by 11 parliamentary votes to six.

1 **Papua New Guinea:** the Minister for Internal Security, Sani Rambi, exchanged portfolios with the Minister for Labour and Industrial Relations, Mark Maipakai, in what was described as a demotion for the former owing to increasing concerns with regard to the country's law-and-order situation.

1 **Singapore:** in a minor cabinet reorganization, the Deputy Prime Minister and Minister of Home Affairs, Wong Kan Seng, was appointed Co-ordinating Minister for National Security, while retaining his post as Deputy Prime Minister; the former holder of the national security portfolio, Prof. Shanmugam Jayakumar, remained as Senior Minister in the Prime Minister's Office.

2 **American Samoa:** incumbent Congressman Eni F. Hunkin Faleomavaega was re-elected as Delegate to the US House of Representatives for a record 12th two-year term; in a concurrent referendum, 70.2% voted against proposed changes to the islands' Constitution.

2 **Guam:** in a gubernatorial election, Edward B. Calvo, candidate of the Republican Party, defeated the Democrat Carl Gutierrez; in concurrent polls, Madeleine Z. Bordallo was re-elected as Delegate to the US House of Representatives, and the Democratic Party secured a majority of seats in the 15-member Guam Legislature.

2 **Northern Mariana Islands:** incumbent Congressman Gregorio K. C. Sablan was re-elected as Delegate to the US House of Representatives for a two-year term.

5 **Mongolia:** at its 26th congress the governing Mongolian People's Revolutionary Party voted to revert to its original name of Mongolian People's Party; Prime Minister Sükhbaataryn Batbold was re-elected as Chairman of the party.

6 **Democratic People's Republic of Korea:** Jo Myong Rok, member of the Political Bureau of the ruling Korean Workers' Party (KWP) and First Vice-Chairman of the National Defence Commission, died.

7 **Myanmar:** the first multi-party legislative elections since 1990 were won by the military-aligned Union Solidarity and Development Party; 25% of the seats in the national legislature were reserved for representatives of the military; the polls were boycotted by the the opposition National League for Democracy, led by Aung San Suu Kyi.

9 **Indonesia:** US President Barack Obama began a 10-day tour of Asia with his first official visit to Indonesia (a country in which he had lived during his childhood).

12 **New Zealand:** the Minister for Ethnic Affairs and of Women's Affairs, Pansy Wong, resigned; her departure from the Cabinet followed the revelation of her alleged misuse of a parliamentary travel allowance relating to an overseas trip by her husband in 2008; she was replaced by Hekia Parata.

13 **Myanmar:** opposition leader Aung San Suu Kyi was released after seven years under house arrest.

16 **Fiji:** the Minister for Defence, National Security and Immigration, Ratu Epeli Ganilau, tendered his resignation for unspecified reasons; Minister for Primary Industries Joketani Cokanasiga replaced Ganilau in an acting capacity.

17 **Cook Islands:** the governing Democratic Party was defeated at the legislative election, winning only eight of the 24 seats in Parliament; the Cook Islands Party, led by Henry Puna, took 16 seats; former Deputy Prime Minister Sir Terepai Maoate lost his seat (having been dismissed in December 2009, he stood as an independent candidate); in a concurrent referendum, voters failed to endorse proposals for a reduction in the number of parliamentary seats.

22 **Japan:** Minoru Yanagida, the Minister of Justice and Minister of State for the Abduction Issue, announced his resignation, thus pre-empting an opposition motion of censure instigated in response to public comments by the Minister in which he appeared to deride his role.

23 **Democratic People's Republic of Korea/Republic of Korea:** in an apparent artillery attack by North Korea, two civilians and two soldiers were killed on the South Korean island of Yeonpyeong, located to the west of the Korean peninsula and adjacent to the disputed maritime border.

25 **Tonga:** elections were held for the Legislative Assembly; the number of seats determined by direct popular election was increased from nine to 17, of which 12 were won by the recently established Democratic Party of the Friendly Islands, (DPFI) led by veteran pro-democracy activist 'Akilisi Pohiva; five seats were taken by independent candidates; nine seats were to be occupied by hereditary nobles (as previously).

26 **Republic of Korea:** following the resignation on the previous day of Kim Tae-Young as Minister of National Defence owing to the perceived inadequacy of his response to the North Korean attack on Yeonpyeong, Kim Kwan-Jin, a former Chairman of the Joint Chiefs of Staff, was nominated to replace him.

26 **Norfolk Island:** the Territories Law Reform Act 2010 was approved by the Australian Parliament; changes included the introduction of federal law in areas such as freedom of information, in exchange for federal funding and access for islanders to welfare facilities and other services.

27 **Australia:** after 11 years in office the Labor Government of Victoria was ousted at state elections; Premier John Brumby was replaced by Ted Baillieu, at the head of a Liberal-National administration.

29 **Solomon Islands:** Jimmy Lusibaea, the Minister for Fisheries and Marine Resources, was sentenced to 33 months' imprisonment on charges of assault and the wounding of a police officer during civil unrest in 2000; supporters of Lusibaea were involved in violent clashes with security forces in Honiara.

DECEMBER 2010

2 **Australia:** it was announced that the First Nations Political Party, led by veteran Aboriginal activist

Maurie Japarta Ryan, had applied for official registration; the new party hoped to campaign not only on indigenous rights but also on wider issues.

2 **Vanuatu:** during his absence from the country Prime Minister Edward Natapei was ousted from office in a parliamentary vote of no confidence and replaced by Sato Kilman, Deputy Prime Minister and leader of the People's Progressive Party; the motion to remove Natapei reportedly arose from his attempted suspension of five opposition MPs from Parliament and from his failure to agree to Fiji's assumption of the rotating chairmanship of the Melanesian Spearhead Group.

4 **Cook Islands:** following the formal appointment of Henry Puna on 30 November, the incoming Prime Minister announced details of the new Cabinet; Tom Marsters became Deputy Prime Minister, assuming responsibility inter alia for the portfolio of foreign affairs.

7 **Vanuatu:** the composition of a new coalition Government was announced; Ham Lini, leader of the National United Party, was appointed as Deputy Prime Minister, also receiving the trade portfolio; George Wells, hitherto the Speaker of Parliament, assumed responsibility for foreign affairs, and Moana Carcasses Kalosil was allocated the finance portfolio.

8 **Solomon Islands:** following his recent dismissal from the post of Minister for Forestry, Bodo Dettke was reinstated in the Cabinet as Minister for Fisheries and Marine Resources, a position left vacant by the recent imprisonment of Jimmy Lusibaea.

9 **Papua New Guinea:** it was announced that Minister for Foreign Affairs Samuel Abal had replaced Don Polye as Deputy Prime Minister; Abal also became Minister for Works, while Polye took responsibility for the portfolios of foreign affairs and immigration; other cabinet changes included the appointment of Sir Arnold Amet as Attorney-General and Minister for Justice.

10 **Papua New Guinea:** the Supreme Court ruled that the re-election in June 2010 of Governor-General Sir Paulias Matane had been unconstitutional; on 13 December Jeffery Nape, the Speaker of the National Parliament, was appointed acting Governor-General pending the election of a permanent replacement.

11 **Cambodia:** after an absence of two years Prince Norodom Ranariddh, the former Prime Minister, officially returned to politics with his election to the post of President of the renamed Norodom Ranariddh Party (the Nationalist Party reverting to its former name).

13 **Papua New Guinea:** pending an investigation into allegations of financial misconduct, Sir Michael Somare temporarily relinquished the premiership; Deputy Prime Minister Samuel Abal was appointed acting Prime Minister.

14 **New Zealand:** having been replaced by Hekia Parata, and despite her exoneration of serious misuse of her parliamentary travel entitlements, Pansy Wong, the former Minister for Ethnic Affairs and of Women's Affairs, resigned from the House of Representatives, in order to end the distractions caused by the ongoing debate of the issue.

16 **Malaysia:** the House of Representatives voted to suspend opposition leader Anwar Ibrahim from his parliamentary seat for a period of six months.

16 **Vanuatu:** during the Prime Minister's absence from the country, Deputy Prime Minister Ham Lini was reported to have dismissed Willie Lop, the newly appointed Minister of Internal Affairs; Lop was replaced by Dunstan Hilton, whose justice portfolio was reallocated to Alfred Carlot.

21 **Tonga:** in the contest for the country's premiership the leader of the DPFI, 'Akilisi Pohiva, was defeated by Lord Tu'ivakano, a member of the nobility and former cabinet minister; having secured the support of the five independent members of the newly elected Legislative Assembly, Lord Tu'ivakano received 14 parliamentary votes, while Pohiva was able to muster only 12.

21 **Vanuatu:** as discontent over the allocation of ministerial portfolios continued, Prime Minister Sato Kilman effected a further cabinet reorganization, this time incorporating members of the Union of Moderate Parties (UMP) in the coalition Government; new appointments included that of UMP leader Serge Vohor, who became Minister of Infrastructure and Public Utilities; Minister of Justice Alfred Carlot was among the recent appointees removed from office.

22 **Tuvalu:** Prime Minister Maatia Toafa was removed from office following his defeat, by eight votes to seven, in a parliamentary motion of no confidence; the Minister of Home Affairs, Willie Telavi, had withdrawn his support for Toafa.

23 **Laos:** the unexpected resignation of Prime Minister Bouasone Bouphavanh was announced; he was replaced by Thongsing Thammavong, hitherto the President (Speaker) of the National Assembly; Pany Yathotou, a Vice-President of the National Assembly and the only female member of the Political Bureau (Politburo) of the ruling Lao People's Revolutionary Party (LPRP), replaced Thongsing as Speaker.

24 **Tuvalu:** Willie Telavi was sworn in as Prime Minister, having received eight of the 15 parliamentary votes to defeat the other contender for the country's leadership, Deputy Prime Minister Enele Sopoanga; it was reported that Telavi had defected to the opposition in exchange for support for his candidacy for the premiership.

JANUARY 2011

4 **Tonga:** Lord Tu'ivakano announced the composition of his new Cabinet; the incoming Prime Minister took personal responsibility for several portfolios, including those of foreign affairs and of defence; Samiu Kuita Vaipulu was appointed Deputy Prime Minister, also being allocated the justice and transport portfolios; Sulia Fili became Minister of Finance; 'Akilisi Pohiva was offered the position of Minister of Health.

10 **Democratic People's Republic of Korea:** it was reported that Yi Kyong Sik had recently returned to the post of Minister of Agriculture (a portfolio he had held between 2003 and 2008), replacing Kim Chang Sik.

13 **Tonga:** following his nomination only in the previous week, opposition leader 'Akilisi Pohiva resigned as Minister of Health, citing his disappointment with the allocation of only two cabinet portfolios to members of the DPFI; he was subsequently replaced by Uliti Uata, also of the DPFI.

13 **Tuvalu:** the imposition of emergency rule, limiting meetings to a maximum of 10 people, was declared, following a demonstration by dozens of residents on the island of Funafuti; the protesters, members of the Nukufetau community, demanded the resignation of

their parliamentary representative, Lotoala Metia, recently appointed as Minister of Finance.

14 **Japan:** a reallocation of cabinet portfolios was announced; Yukio Edano was appointed Chief Cabinet Secretary and Minister of State for Okinawa and Northern Territories Affairs; having resigned from the Sunrise Party and stated his intention to join the governing Democratic Party of Japan (DPJ), Kaoru Yosano entered the Cabinet, assuming responsibility inter alia for economic and fiscal policy; other newcomers included Satsuki Eda, who became Minister of Justice; Banri Kaieda was appointed Minister of Economy, Trade and Industry.

14 **Papua New Guinea:** in a brief sitting of the National Parliament Michael Ogio, the candidate favoured by the ruling National Alliance, was elected as the country's Governor-General, defeating Sir Pato Kakaraya by 65 votes to 23; Ogio took office on 25 February.

17 **Papua New Guinea:** amid increased uncertainty with regard to the constitutionality of his decision in mid-December temporarily to step down, Sir Michael Somare resumed the premiership.

18 **Taiwan:** King Pu-tsung, Secretary-General of the governing Kuomintang (KMT), resigned in order to lead President Ma Ying-jeou's campaign for re-election in 2012; King was replaced by Liao Liao-yi.

19–20 **Tokelau:** Kelisiano Kalolo was elected Faipule of the atoll of Atafu on 19 January and Salesio Lui was chosen by voters on Nukunonu on the following day.

19 **Viet Nam:** on the closing day of the 11th National Congress of the ruling Communist Party of Viet Nam Nguyen Phu Trong, Chairman of the country's National Assembly, was elected as the General Secretary of the party Central Committee, in place of the retiring Nong Duc Manh; the incoming 14-member Political Bureau (Politburo), elected by the newly appointed Central Committee, incorporated several new entrants.

23 **Solomon Islands:** a cabinet reorganization was reported to have been effected, following the resignation of several ministers.

24 **Australia:** Lara Giddings replaced David Bartlett as Premier of Tasmania, following the latter's unexpected resignation for personal reasons.

24 **French Polynesia:** Richard Didier took office as France's High Commissioner in the territory, replacing Adolphe Colrat.

31 **Thailand:** it was reported that a complaint against Abhisit Vejjaviva, accusing the Prime Minister of criminal liability in relation to the deaths of 92 supporters of the United Front for Democracy against Dictatorship (UDD or Red Shirts) during the protests of 2010, had been lodged with the International Criminal Court.

FEBRUARY 2011

1 **Taiwan:** a minor cabinet reorganization was announced; the four new appointments included that of Chiu Wen-ta as Minister of the Department of Health, in place of Yaung chi-liang who had resigned in early January.

4 **Myanmar:** the incoming legislature elected Thein Sein, hitherto the Prime Minister, as the country's President; Tin Aung Myint Oo, First Secretary of the State Peace and Development Council, and Sai Mauk Kham, a relatively unknown doctor, were chosen as Vice-Presidents.

10 **Brunei:** Pehin Isa Ibrahim was appointed Speaker of the Legislative Council.

10 **Vanuatu:** three cabinet ministers, Serge Vohor and Charlot Salwai, respectively President and Vice-President of the UMP, and Marcellino Pipite, Secretary-General of the Vanuatu Republikan Pati, resigned in protest against the failure of Prime Minister Sato Kilman to allocate additional cabinet posts to their parties.

17 **New Caledonia:** owing to a protracted dispute relating to the role of the Kanak flag, the pro-independence Union Calédonienne (UC) withdrew from the Council of Ministers, automatically resulting in the removal from office of the governing coalition led by Philippe Gomès.

17 **Solomon Islands:** following weeks of political instability during which various cabinet members had resigned and transferred their allegiance to the opposition before rejoining the Government (some having crossed the floor several times), the ruling National Coalition for Reform and Advancement re-established its position with the swearing-in of four ministers (three of whom resumed their previous portfolios).

18 **Vanuatu:** pre-empting a forthcoming parliamentary vote of no confidence in his administration, Sato Kilman completed a reorganization of the Council of Ministers; while the UMP declared its intention to rejoin the opposition, Marcellino Pipite, hitherto the Minister of Agriculture, returned to the Government as Minister of Education.

24 **Philippines:** Albert del Rosario was appointed acting Secretary of Foreign Affairs, in place of Alberto Romulo; on the same day Edcel Lagman was elected as National Chairperson of Lakas-Kampi-CMD, replacing Gloria Arroyo, and Ramon Bong Revilla Jr was chosen as the minority party's National President.

25 **People's Republic of China:** the Minister of Railways, Liu Zhijun, was dismissed from his cabinet portfolio, following allegations of corruption, reportedly involving the acceptance of bribes totalling more than 800m. yuan; Liu was replaced by Sheng Guangzu.

27 **Brunei:** it was reported that, owing to ill health, Yasin Affendy had resigned as the President of the Parti Pembangunan Bangsa, the only remaining political party; he was replaced on an acting basis by Malai Hassan Othman.

MARCH 2011

1 **French Polynesia:** following their failure to support his proposed budget for 2011, President Gaston Tong Sang dismissed Vice-President Edouard Fritch and five cabinet ministers belonging to coalition party Tahoera'a Huiraatira; Tong Sang appointed Tearii Alpha, Minister for Land Affairs, Planning, Housing and Public Works, as Vice-President and redistributed the vacant portfolios among the remaining members of the Council of Ministers.

2 **Fiji:** the Minister for Lands, Mineral Sources and Environment, Netani Sukanaivalu, resigned; responsibility for his portfolio was assumed by Prime Minister Frank Bainimarama.

3 **New Caledonia:** minutes after its election by the Congress, the new Government collapsed upon the

resignation of a member of the anti-independence Calédonie Ensemble, led by Philippe Gomès; meanwhile, Harold Martin, President (Speaker) of Congress and leader of the anti-independence Avenir Ensemble, was elected to replace Gomès as the territory's President, with Gilbert Tyuienon of the UC as Vice-President.

4 **Samoa:** the ruling Human Rights Protection Party was returned to office at the general election, winning the support of 36 of the 49 members of the Fono (including seven independents); however, three cabinet ministers were reported to have lost their parliamentary seats; the Tautua Samoa Party won 13 seats.

6 **Japan:** the Minister for Foreign Affairs, Seiji Maehara, resigned, following the revelation that he had accepted illicit donations from a supporter who was not a Japanese citizen, in contravention of the regulations governing political funding; on 9 March Maehara was replaced by Takeaki Matsumoto.

8 **Federated States of Micronesia:** congressional elections were held for all 14 senators' seats.

11 **Japan:** a tsunami caused by the most powerful earthquake ever recorded in Japan inundated the north-eastern coast of the country, killing many thousands of people and obliterating entire communities; reactors at a nuclear power plant malfunctioned, leading to the release of radioactive material.

11 **Vanuatu:** after only three weeks in the position Ralph Regenvanu was replaced as Minister of Lands and Natural Resources by Alfred Carlot; however, Regenvanu was instead appointed to the post of Minister of Justice and Social Affairs.

16 **Democratic People's Republic of Korea:** it was announced that the Minister of People's Security, Ju Sang Song, had been removed from his post, ostensibly owing to ill health; he was replaced by Ri Myong Su.

17 **New Caledonia:** the ongoing political crisis intensified when a Government comprising six anti-independence and five pro-independence members was again appointed, only to disintegrate immediately upon the withdrawal of Calédonie Ensemble.

21 **Laos:** following the election of a new Central Committee, on the final day of the Ninth Congress of the ruling LPRP Choummaly Sayasone was re-elected as Secretary-General of the party; former Prime Minister Bouasone Bouphavanh was removed from the Politburo; the incoming 11-member body incorporated three new members.

24 **Papua New Guinea:** a leadership tribunal found Sir Michael Somare guilty of 13 charges of official misconduct, in relation to his failure to submit proper financial statements, as a result of which the Prime Minister was suspended from office for two weeks from 4 April.

26 **Australia:** the Labor administration of Kristina Keneally was defeated at state elections in New South Wales; Barry O'Farrell of the Liberal Party was subsequently appointed as the state's Premier.

30 **Myanmar:** Thein Sein was sworn in as the country's President, whereupon the ruling State Peace and Development Council (SPDC) was dissolved; Senior-Gen. (Field Marshal) Than Shwe, hitherto the Chairman of the SPDC, was replaced as Commander-in-Chief of the Defence Services by Gen. Min Aung Hlaing; the incoming Cabinet, which was dominated by former military officers, included Maj.-Gen. Hla Min as Minister of Defenceand Wunna Maung Lwin as Minister of Foreign Affairs.

APRIL 2011

1 **French Polynesia:** President Gaston Tong Sang was removed from office following his defeat in a parliamentary motion of no confidence, which was supported by 29 of the French Polynesian Assembly's 57 members; Oscar Temaru, leader of the pro-independence Tavini Huiraatira, thus returned to the position of President.

6 **French Polynesia:** the composition of the new Council of Ministers was announced; President Temaru assumed personal charge of the portfolios of international and regional relations, tourism and international air transport; the incoming Vice-President, Antony Géros, was allocated responsibility for budget and community development, while Pierre Frébault was appointed Minister for Economy, Finance, Labour and Employment.

8 **Australia:** Alex Chernov took office as Governor of the state of Victoria.

8 **Hong Kong:** owing to health issues, the Secretary for Commerce and Economic Development, Rita Lau, tendered her resignation; she was subsequently replaced by Gregory So.

16 **Malaysia:** the ruling Barisan Nasional was returned to office at state elections in Sarawak, albeit with a reduced majority, winning 55 of the 71 seats.

18 **Solomon Islands:** Prime Minister Danny Philip effected a cabinet reorganization, in order to accommodate several former members of the opposition who had recently transferred their allegiance; a total of six ministers were replaced.

19 **Papua New Guinea:** it was announced that, following the completion of his two-week suspension from office, Sir Michael Somare was to take indefinite medical leave; Samuel Abal thus remained as acting Prime Minister.

24 **Vanuatu:** the Government of Sato Kilman was removed from office following its defeat in a parliamentary motion of no confidence; Serge Vohor of the UMP replaced Kilman as Prime Minister.

25 **Vanuatu:** incoming Prime Minister Vohor announced the composition of the new Council of Ministers; Joshua Kalsakau of the Vanuatu Labour Party was appointed Deputy Prime Minister, also assuming responsibility for the portfolios of infrastructure and public utilities; Joe Natuman became Minister of Foreign Affairs.

27 **People's Republic of China:** following the Dalai Lama's formal announcement of his decision to relinquish his political responsibilities (while retaining the role of spiritual leader), it was announced that Lobsang Sangay, an academic at an eminent US university, had won 55% of the votes cast by the Tibetan diaspora to defeat two other candidates in the election for the premiership of the Tibetan government-in-exile.

27 **Taiwan:** incumbent President Ma Ying-jeou of the KMT was confirmed as the party's candidate for the 2012 presidential election; on the same day Tsai Ing-wen was chosen as the island's first female presidential candidate by the opposition Democratic Progressive Party (DPP).

30 **Laos:** elections for the expanded National Assembly were conducted, following which it was announced that the ruling LPRP had taken 128 of the 132 seats and that four independent candidates had won the remainder.

MAY 2011

6 **Republic of Korea:** in a major cabinet reorganization, President Lee Myung-Bak replaced five ministers; Bahk Jae-Wan, hitherto Minister of Employment and Labour, was nominated for the post of Minister for Strategy and Finance.

7 **Niue:** a legislative election was held, following which Prime Minister Tofe Talagi was reappointed as Prime Minister; in the subsequent reallocation of cabinet portfolios, Niue's first female minister was appointed, namely Joan Viliamu as Minister of Health, Community Affairs, Justice, Lands and Survey.

7 **Singapore:** the governing People's Action Party (PAP) was returned to office at the general election, winning 81 of the 87 parliamentary seats but with a much reduced percentage of the vote; the Workers' Party raised its representation to six seats.

11 **Federated States of Micronesia:** President Immanuel Mori was re-elected for a further four-year term by the members of the incoming Congress.

13 **Vanuatu:** the Court of Appeal overruled Serge Vohor's election as Prime Minister and restored Sato Kilman to the premiership; the reinstated Kilman then effected a number of cabinet changes, which included the appointment of Alfred Carlot as Minister of Foreign Affairs; Steven Kalsakau of the UMP replaced Carlot as Minister of Lands and Natural Resources.

18 **Singapore:** an extensive cabinet reorganization was announced; Tharman Shanmugaratnam was appointed Deputy Prime Minister, also being allocated the manpower portfolio, while retaining that of finance; Teo Chee Hean remained as Deputy Prime Minister, also taking the post of Co-ordinating Minister for National Security and Minister for Home Affairs; George Yeo was replaced as Minister for Foreign Affairs by K. Shanmugam, who retained the law portfolio.

16 **Australia:** Katy Gallagher was elected as Chief Minister of the Australian Capital Territory, following the resignation of Jonathan Stanhope.

22 **Viet Nam:** elections for the 500 seats of the National Assembly were held; more than 90% of those elected were reported to be members of the ruling Communist Party of Viet Nam.

31 **Democratic People's Republic of Korea:** it was reported that the Minister of Chemical Industry, Ri Mu Yong, had been appointed a Vice-Premier.

31 **Philippines:** having replaced Alberto Romulo on an acting basis in February, Albert del Rosario was confirmed in the position of Secretary of Foreign Affairs.

JUNE 2011

1 **Singapore:** Khaw Boon Wan replaced Lim Boon Heng as Chairman of the ruling PAP.

6 **Papua New Guinea:** citing issues of discipline, acting Prime Minister Samuel Abal dismissed two senior cabinet members, namely Don Polye, Minister for Foreign Affairs and Immigration, and William Duma, Minister for Petroleum and Energy.

16 **Indonesia:** following his rearrest in August 2010, Abu Bakar Bashir was found guilty of charges of supporting a training camp for Islamist militants in the province of Aceh; the cleric was sentenced to 15 years' imprisonment (subsequently reduced to nine years).

16 **Laos:** following the re-election by the National Assembly of President Choummaly Sayasone and Prime Minister Thongsing Thammavong on the previous day, the composition of the new Council of Ministers was announced; Phouphet Khamphounvong, hitherto Governor of the central bank, replaced Somdy Douangdy as Minister of Finance; four new ministries were established.

16 **New Caledonia:** following several attempts to form a new government (most recently on 10 June), the French Senate approved changes to the territory's electoral law whereby an incoming administration would be given a grace period of 18 months; Harold Martin was confirmed as President.

16 **Vanuatu:** owing to the parliamentary Speaker's failure to conduct a secret ballot as constitutionally required, the country's Chief Justice declared the election of Sato Kilman in late 2010 to have been null and void; the administration of Edward Natapei was thus reinstated, pending the election of a new Prime Minister.

20 **Vanuatu:** interim Prime Minister Edward Natapei appointed six new cabinet ministers, including Patrick Crowby as Minister of Internal Affairs; Joe Natuman, who resumed the foreign affairs portfolio, was among the ministers reappointed.

21 **Papua New Guinea:** as part of a major cabinet reorganization, Ano Pala was appointed to the vacant post of Minister for Foreign Affairs and Immigration, and Francis Potape became Minister for Petroleum and Energy; amid some controversy owing to allegations of his involvement in financial irregularities, Patrick Pruaitch was reappointed as Minister for Finance and Treasury in place of Peter O'Neill.

22 **People's Republic of China:** his whereabouts having remained unknown since his detention in April, Ai Weiwei, the internationally renowned artist and critic of the Government, was released on bail; he was reported to have pleaded guilty to charges of tax evasion.

26 **People's Republic of China:** human rights activist Hu Jia, convicted of subversion in 2008, was released from prison, reportedly being placed under conditions of house arrest.

26 **Vanuatu:** having secured 29 of the 52 votes to defeat Serge Vohor in the parliamentary ballot, Sato Kilman was reinstated as Prime Minister, thus assuming the premiership for the third time since late 2010.

27 **Cambodia:** the initial hearings of four former Khmer Rouge hearings opened in Phnom-Penh, pending their trial on charges of war crimes.

28 **Papua New Guinea:** following three major operations in a Singapore hospital, it was announced that with immediate effect Sir Michael Somare was permanently to relinquish the premiership and retire from politics.

30 **Taiwan:** former President Lee Teng-hui was indicted on charges of embezzling NT $238m. from public funds; similar to the charges upon which former President Chen Shui-bian had been convicted in 2009, the allegations related to the operation of a

clandestine account supposedly used to finance covert diplomatic initiatives.

JULY 2011

1 **Australia:** Malcolm McCusker was sworn in as Governor of Western Australia.

1 **Papua New Guinea:** pending the investigation of allegations of misconduct, the Minister for Finance and Treasury, Patrick Pruaitch, was suspended from office by the Supreme Court; however, acting Prime Minister Samuel Abal refused to recognize the court's ruling.

1 **Philippines:** Manuel Roxas II assumed the post of Secretary of Transportation and Communication.

2 **New Zealand:** the Waitangi Tribunal released its report on the so-called Wai262 claim, lodged 20 years previously in the hope of protecting Maori rights.

3 **Thailand:** Yingluck Shinawatra, prime ministerial candidate of Puea Thai and sister of exiled former Prime Minister Thaksin Shinawatra, secured an unexpectedly large majority at elections for the House of Representatives; outgoing Prime Minister Abhisit Vejjajiva swiftly conceded defeat and resigned as leader of the Democrat Party.

4 **Republic of Korea:** at a convention of the Grand National Party (GNP), Hong Joon-Pyo received 36.4% of the valid votes cast by delegates to defeat his nearest rival, Yoo Seong-Min, and five other candidates in the election for the chairmanship of the governing party.

5 **Japan:** after only a week in his new post, Ryu Matsumoto, the Minister for Reconstruction Measures from the Great East Japan Earthquake and Minister of State for Disaster Management, resigned following remarks deemed offensive by victims of the disaster of March; he was replaced by Tatsuo Hirano.

10 **Taiwan:** the Taiwanese National Party was formally established; its objectives included the promotion of Taiwanese identity and the holding of a referendum on the issue of self-determination.

13 **Fiji:** Jokapeci Koroi, President of the Fiji Labour Party since 2002, died.

20 **Tuvalu:** the Minister of Works and Natural Resources, Isaia Italeli Taeia, was found dead in his hotel room in Samoa, where he had been due to attend a regional fisheries conference.

22 **Democratic People's Republic of Korea/Republic of Korea:** amid international efforts to revive the six-party talks on the North Korean nuclear programme, for the first time since December 2008 representatives of the two countries resumed discussions, convening on the Indonesian island of Bali.

25 **Viet Nam:** at the first session of the newly elected National Assembly Truong Tan Sang was chosen as the country's President, receiving 487 of the 500 votes; he formally nominated incumbent Prime Minister Nguyen Tan Dung for a second term of office, the latter's appointment being confirmed on the following day.

AUGUST 2011

2 **Papua New Guinea:** the premiership was officially declared to be vacant, after a large number of disaffected MPs defected to the opposition; Peter O'Neill (erstwhile Minister for Finance and Treasury but recently demoted to the portfolio of works and transport) was elected as Prime Minister, having received 70 of 94 parliamentary votes.

3 **Viet Nam:** the incoming Cabinet was endorsed by the National Assembly; Pham Binh Minh was appointed Minister of Foreign Affairs, and Vuong Dinh Hue became Minister of Finance; Gen. Phung Quang Thanh retained the portfolio of national defence.

5 **Thailand** following her establishment of a coalition with the support of several other parties, Yingluck Shinawatra was formally appointed as the country's first female Prime Minister.

8 **Papua New Guinea:** Don Polye, incoming Minister for Finance and Treasury, was chosen to replace Sir Michael Somare as Parliamentary Leader of the National Alliance.

9 **Papua New Guinea:** the full membership of the new National Executive Council was confirmed; Belden Namah, leader of the Papua New Guinea Party, was appointed as Deputy Prime Minister and Minister for Forestry and Climate Change; having defected from the former Government, Ano Pala, Minister for Foreign Affairs and Immigration in the outgoing administration, was one of two ministers who retained their portfolios; John Boito became Minister for Internal Security, and William Duma was reinstated as Minister for Petroleum and Energy.

10 **Thailand:** details of the new Cabinet, which included representatives of the various coalition parties, were announced; Yongyuth Wichaidit, leader of the Puea Thai party, assumed the post of Deputy Prime Minister and Minister of the Interior; Thirachai Phuvanatnaranubala, was appointed as Minister of Finance, and Gen. Yutthasak Sasiprapha, a former army general, became Minister of Defence; the foreign affairs portfolio was unexpectedly allocated to Surapong Towijakchaikul.

12 **Republic of Korea:** the appointment of Kwon Jae-Jin as Minister of Justice was confirmed.

19 **New Caledonia:** following the annulment in July by the French Supreme Court of his election as Speaker of Congress, the pro-independence Roch Wamytan was reinstated in the position.

26 **Japan:** Prime Minister Naoto Kan announced his resignation, amid continued criticism of his response to the tsunami disaster and ongoing nuclear crisis at the Fukushima power station.

27 **Singapore:** in the first such contest since 1993, Dr Tony Tan Keng Yam defeated three other candidates narrowly to secure election as the country's President, having received 35.2% of the valid votes cast; he assumed office on 1 September

30 **Japan:** Yoshihiko Noda, hitherto the Minister of Finance, was elected to the presidency of the governing DPJ and duly confirmed in the post of Prime Minister.

31 **Republic of Korea:** amid continuing tensions with North Korea, Hyun In-Taek was replaced as Minister of Unification by Yu Woo-Ik; three other ministers were also to be replaced in the cabinet reorganization.

31 **New Zealand:** Lt-Gen. Sir Jerry Mateparae was sworn in as Governor-General, replacing Sir Anand Satyanand.

SEPTEMBER 2011

2 **Japan:** the composition of the new Cabinet was announced; among the new appointments was that

of Koichiro Genba as Minister for Foreign Affairs and Jun Azumi as Minister of Finance.

7 **Tonga:** it was revealed that a cabinet reorganization had been implemented on 1 September; the various changes included the transfer of the justice portfolio from Deputy Prime Minister Samiu Kuita Vaipulu to Clive Edwards (who retained responsibility for public enterprises) and the appointment of Viliami Latu as Minister of Tourism.

7 **Vanuatu:** after three previous unsuccessful attempts by the legislature, the Speaker of Parliament, Maxime Carlot-Korman, was removed from office; he was replaced by Dunstan Hilton.

10 **Japan:** following insensitive remarks relating to the Fukushima nuclear disaster and after only eight days in office, Yoshio Hachiro resigned from the Cabinet; he was replaced as Minister of Economy, Trade and Industry and for Nuclear Incident Economic Countermeasures by Yukio Edano, who in turn was replaced as Chief Cabinet Secretary by Osamu Fujimura.

20 **Papua New Guinea:** while the case relating to the constitutionality of the dismissal of his Government in early August continued, the Supreme Court rejected an appeal by Sir Michael Somare to regain his parliamentary seat, from which he had been removed on the grounds that, without permission, he had failed to attend three consecutive sessions of Parliament.

21 **Democratic People's Republic of Korea/Republic of Korea:** convening in Beijing, envoys of the two countries failed to agree on terms for the resumption of the six-party talks regarding the North Korean nuclear programme.

26 **Democratic People's Republic of Korea:** it was revealed that Kim Sok Jun had replaced Pae Tal Jun as Minister of Land Development and Construction Affairs, amid reports that a major house-building programme was progressing at an unacceptably slow pace.

28 **Hong Kong:** in advance of the election in 2012 for the new Chief Executive of Hong Kong, Henry Tang announced that he had submitted his resignation from the post of Chief Secretary.

28 **Tuvalu:** the critical shortage of fresh water led to the declaration of a state of emergency.

30 **Hong Kong:** it was announced that Stephen Lam had been appointed Chief Secretary, being replaced in turn as Secretary for Constitutional and Mainland Affairs by Raymond Tam.

30 **Democratic People's Republic of Korea/Republic of Korea:** in an unusual development and in what was regarded as an attempt to revive bilateral economic relations, Hong Joon-Pyo, Chairman of the GNP, the South Korean governing party, travelled over the border into North Korea to visit a joint industrial complex.

OCTOBER 2011

5 **French Polynesia:** former President Gaston Flosse was sentenced to four years' imprisonment, having been found guilty of abuse of public funds; he immediately submitted an appeal against the sentence.

11 **Myanmar:** following appeals for greater media freedom, it was announced that 6,359 prisoners were to be released under an amnesty; however, it was not immediately clear how many of these were political detainees; Zarganar, a popular comedian, was among those freed.

19 **Indonesia:** a major reorganization of the Cabinet was announced; Gita Wirjawan, hitherto Chairman of the Investment Co-ordinating Board, replaced Mari Pangestu as Minister of Trade; Dahlan Iskan, head of the state electricity company, was allocated responsibility for state-owned enterprises.

21 **Australia:** Jay Weatherill replaced Mike Rann as Premier of South Australia, following the latter's resignation.

21 **Kiribati:** the first stage of legislative elections took place, with a second round of voting held on 28 October; several cabinet ministers lost their parliamentary seats.

19 **Indonesia:** a major reorganization of the Cabinet was announced; Gita Wirjawan, hitherto Chairman of the Investment Co-ordinating Board, replaced Mari Pangestu as Minister of Trade; Dahlan Iskan, head of the state electricity company, was allocated responsibility for state-owned enterprises.

24 **Philippines:** in the first such government offensive for three years following a resumption of violence in the southern Philippines, several members of the rebel Moro Islamic Liberation Front were reported to have been killed during air strikes on Zamboanga.

25 **Democratic People's Republic of Korea:** as efforts to resume the stalled six-party talks continued, bilateral discussions in Switzerland between representatives of North Korea and the USA were reported to have made some progress.

27 **Solomon Islands:** a minor cabinet reorganization included the transfer of the fisheries portfolio to Bradley Tovosia, whose previous responsibility for forestry was allocated to Dickson Mua.

PART ONE

General Survey

CHINA'S RISE: EVOLUTION AND IMPLICATIONS

ROBERT SUTTER

In the first decade of the 21st century the rising power and prominence of the People's Republic of China in world affairs received increasing attention from government officials, international media and foreign affairs specialists. Commentators in China and elsewhere debated the substance, scope and significance of the country's rising international influence. Many Chinese and foreign observers perceived China as growing steadily to reach a position where it increasingly challenged the USA as the leading power in Asian and world affairs, while others were more reserved in their projections of Chinese power.

As China gained international economic and strategic influence at a time of US and international economic recession, beginning in 2008, it initiated some more assertive policies concerning territorial, economic and other disputes, notably with the USA and many of China's Asian neighbours. Contrasting sharply with China's generally more moderate and peaceful foreign approach in recent years, the new pattern was seemingly influenced by ongoing foreign policy debates in China. Some policy-making élites, supported by nationalistic public opinion, argued that rising Chinese power, and decline in the USA and Western-aligned countries, had reached a point where China could and should be more firm and active in protecting and furthering its interests. The results of the initiatives proved counter-productive, notably strengthening the resolve and unity of the USA and its Asia-Pacific allies and associates in opposing Chinese demands. Although China gave no ground on issues in dispute, Chinese leaders at the turn of the decade re-established a foreign policy stressing reassurance, peaceful development and dealing with differences through dialogue.

This essay reviews the evolution and importance of China's rising prominence in Asian affairs and the broader implications for China and the world. The periphery of China in Asia encompasses world areas where China has always exerted greatest influence. Other world regions, even when affected by increasing Chinese trade and other Chinese policies and practices, are geographically more remote; their relevance to Chinese interests is generally less than neighbouring countries and international powers, notably the USA, that are directly involved along China's periphery. According to this line of thinking, the global prominence of China shows first in Asia. Thus, after reviewing the context and salient features of China's rise in Asia, this essay discerns the country's increasing importance with regard to other Asian governments, to the USA's relations with Asia, and to Chinese and US relations with other world areas, in order to provide a forecast of how powerful China is likely to be in Asia and the world, and what this may mean for broader global concerns.

EVOLUTION

In the years that followed the Cold War (the protracted period of mutual hostility between the USA and the USSR) the People's Republic advanced Chinese interests and influence markedly in all neighbouring areas, with greatest success in South-East Asia and, for a time, on the Korean peninsula. Burgeoning economic exchanges, adroit diplomacy and steady expansion of Chinese military power propelled China into an increasingly prominent and favourable position with most neighbouring governments. Prevailing circumstances in 2009 suggested a continuation of generally moderate and pragmatic Chinese approaches to neighbouring areas, with China refraining from the more assertive policies and practices that had been prevalent throughout the first decades of the People's Republic.

Following the establishment of the People's Republic in 1949, those first decades of Chinese foreign relations were far from moderate and pragmatic. They left an impression on many Asian and other world leaders that sustains to this day a continuing wariness about Chinese intentions. Mao Zedong and his communist insurgents took power with revolutionary determination to support armed struggle against the USA and its allies and associates and to free China from the power and influence of the USA, its allies and other hostile powers.

China miscalculated US resolve when it supported the communist Kim Il Sung's assault on South Korea in June 1950. The USA miscalculated in turn when it disregarded China's warnings and sought to reunify Korea by force after defeating the North Korean assault later in that year. More than two years of bitter combat and confrontation ensued. The USA established a ring of defence arrangements with allies around China, which were supported by large-scale US military deployments in order to contain China and the spread of communist influence in East Asia.

Maoist China resisted in ways that were often aggressive, although China carefully avoided actions that would provoke a US nuclear attack or renewed direct combat with the USA. The USA was similarly wary of direct combat with the Chinese military. China increased military support for the communist forces that defeated US-backed French troops in Indo-China. Following the death of Stalin (Iosif Dzhugashvili) in the previous year, in 1954 Chinese leaders joined with the new Soviet leadership in supporting a compromise settlement at the peace conference in Geneva, Switzerland. Later in 1954, however, China resorted to force in confronting Taiwan and US troops in islands along its south-eastern coast.

In 1955 China's leaders adopted moderate diplomacy at the conference of Afro-Asian leaders held in Bandung, Indonesia. This brief interlude of 'peaceful co-existence' ended with shifts towards radicalism in Chinese domestic and foreign affairs later in the decade that resulted in renewed military tensions in the Taiwan Strait, tens of millions of deaths within China in the country's so-called Great Leap Forward and the public disintegration of the Sino-Soviet alliance. By the early 1960s China was competing actively with the USSR for influence among developing countries, including the Democratic People's Republic of Korea (North Korea), and among governments and groups in South-East Asia and South Asia. It supported North Viet Nam and communist forces in Laos as they confronted greater US military involvement in Indo-China. It challenged and defeated India in a border war over disputed territory. For several years China developed close relations with the left-leaning Sukarno administration in Indonesia before the military suppression and massacre of hundreds of thousands of communists and ethnic Chinese in 1965. China also began more active support for communist groups and insurgencies directed against various South-East Asian governments, some of which were aligning with the USA in its military involvement in Indo-China.

The turbulent influence of China in Asia took a bizarre turn as Mao focused inwards to destroy the existing Chinese Communist Party (CCP) and government leadership in the Cultural Revolution, begun in 1966. Chinese foreign policy was fixed in radical opposition to the USA, the USSR and their respective allies and associates. China's uncompromising truculence alienated even those regional leaders inclined to co-operate with or accommodate China, notably North Korea's leader, Kim Il Sung, North Viet Nam's Ho Chi Minh, Cambodia's Norodom Sihanouk and Burma's Ne Win. China lost ground to the USSR in North Korea and North Viet Nam as Soviet leader Leonid Brezhnev devoted more attention to Asia and to competition with China in the region. India allied itself increasingly with the USSR. China's emphasis on armed struggle and support for insurgencies against various non-communist administrations in South-East Asia emphasized its image as a major threat to the region.

The danger of a full-scale Soviet military invasion of China, including the use of nuclear weapons, in 1969 forced Mao and Chinese leaders to reconsider. The subsequent pragmatic Chinese shift to opening to the USA came only after bitter leadership debate and the death of the Minister of Defence, Lin Biao, and his family, and the arrest of many of the Chinese high command. The realignment among the USA, China, and the

USSR in the 1970s featured an overlap in Asia of international struggles for influence between the USA and the USSR on the one hand and China and the USSR on the other hand. These struggles generally undermined Asian stability.

The convolutions in China's behaviour and regional developments led to the country's support, at the end of the war in Viet Nam, for the compromise between the USA and North Viet Nam at the peace conference convened in the French capital of Paris, in 1973; however, the agreement rapidly faltered as the Vietnamese communists went on the offensive. China differed with regard to North Viet Nam's greater reliance on Soviet assistance and its assault on South Viet Nam in 1975. Chinese leaders publicly reassured US allies Thailand and the Philippines, which sought to improve relations with China in response to Viet Nam's expansion. China also strongly supported the radical Khmer Rouge leaders in Cambodia who opposed Viet Nam, while pursuing their violent consolidation of power, a situation that resulted in numerous deaths in Cambodia, estimated at more than 1m. China also eschewed support for Kim Il Sung in his reported bid to use the US defeat in South-East Asia to expand North Korean power through coercion or attack against the US-supported Republic of Korea (South Korea).

Deng Xiaoping rose to lead China at the beginning of the current era of economic reform in 1978, following Mao's death in 1976 and an intense struggle for power among divided Chinese leaders. Ideological radicalism ended at home and abroad, as Chinese leaders sought legitimacy through pragmatic pursuit of economic development and nation-building. Forecasts would have been for smoother Chinese relations with Asia, had it not been for the intense Sino-Soviet competition for influence around China's periphery. For 10 years Deng's focus in Asia was to preserve and develop a favourable environment, in response to Soviet expansion and pressure along China's borders. China competed with the USSR for influence in North Korea through aid and other means. In deference to its important links with North Korea, under Deng China only slowly developed compatible trade and investment relations with the advanced economy of South Korea. China strongly supported US and Japanese efforts to build military, diplomatic and other means to contain the spread of Soviet power in Asia.

China took the lead against the expansion of Soviet-aligned Viet Nam in South-East Asia. Viet Nam, supported by the USSR, invaded Cambodia in December 1978, ousted the Chinese-backed Khmer Rouge leadership and occupied the country. In 1979 China reacted with a massive but temporary military invasion of Vietnamese territory adjoining China, followed by years of large-scale artillery shelling and other hostilities placing pressure on the Vietnamese Government and its Soviet supporters. China also supported the Khmer Rouge insurgents who resisted the Vietnamese occupiers and the Vietnamese-backed regime in Cambodia. It joined with the USA, the non-communist South-East Asian countries in the Association of Southeast Asian Nations (ASEAN) and others in a united front supporting insurgents and pressing Viet Nam to withdraw from Cambodia. China gradually reduced its support for communist insurgents targeted against non-communist South-East Asian states; the latter were now seen as important allies in the struggle against Soviet-supported expansion in South-East Asia. Once the reformist Soviet leadership of Mikhail Gorbachev withdrew support from Viet Nam's occupation of Cambodia, and met other Chinese demands on the withdrawal of Soviet forces from Afghanistan, Mongolia and along the Sino-Soviet border, Deng Xiaoping's administration was willing to welcome the Soviet leader at a summit meeting in the Chinese capital of Beijing. That meeting unexpectedly coincided with the mass demonstrations in Tiananmen Square immediately prior to the Chinese military suppression of opposition in June 1989.

Priorities and Approaches after the Cold War

The Chinese Government's action of June 1989 prompted the Western-led isolation of China, which was reinforced by the disintegration of communism in Europe and developing countries and the eventual demise of the USSR in 1991. Soviet expansion ended. On the whole, this represented a positive development for China's security along its border and around its periphery, but it also meant that the USA and other powers had less interest in developing relations with China in order to counter Soviet power and influence.

China's efforts to end its international isolation were eventually successful. Over the next two decades China fostered ever-expanding interaction with neighbouring Asia and much of the rest of the outside world, through economic exchanges and broadening Chinese involvement with most foreign governments and with international organizations dealing with security, economic, political, cultural and other matters. In the years after the suppression of the Tiananmen protests, China established diplomatic relations with Indonesia, Singapore, the Republic of Korea and the former Soviet republics of Central Asia. It restored normal relations with Viet Nam and with the new Government of Cambodia, installed as a result of a UN-brokered peace agreement. China began participation in such regional groups as the Asia Pacific Economic Cooperation (APEC) forum. It worked more closely with ASEAN and its security grouping, the ASEAN Regional Forum (ARF). China was a formal, albeit generally passive, participant in four-party talks following the signing of the Agreed Framework by the USA and North Korea in 1994, which dealt with the issue of North Korea's nuclear weapons development. China participated much more actively in the three- and six-party talks (the latter involving China, the USA, Japan and Russia, as well as North and South Korea), which addressed crises caused by North Korea's advancing nuclear weapons development, beginning in 2003. China was a leader in creating and sustaining the Shanghai Co-operation Organization, the main sub-regional body dealing with issues involving Central Asian countries.

Chinese leaders were determined that the CCP administration would be an exception to the pattern of collapsing communist regimes at the end of the Cold War, and they strove to reinvigorate and sustain one-party rule in China. Foreign policy served these objectives by fostering an international environment that supported economic growth and stability in China. This was done partly through active and, over time, generally moderate Chinese diplomacy, intended to reassure neighbouring countries and other concerned powers, eventually including the USA, the dominant world power in Chinese foreign policy calculations. Chinese diplomacy gave ever greater emphasis to engagement and conformity with the norms of regional and other multilateral organizations as a means to reassure those concerned about the possible negative implications of China's increased power and influence.

Chinese foreign policy also placed great importance on international economic exchange beneficial to China's development. A large influx of foreign direct investment (FDI), as well as foreign aid, technology and expertise, was critically important in China's economic growth in the post-Mao period. Japan, South Korea, Taiwan and some advanced South-East Asian countries invested heavily in China. China also became the centre of a variety of intra-Asian and other international manufacturing and trading networks, from which China emerged as the world's leading exporter and second largest trader and the largest or second largest trade partner of most of its neighbours.

Chinese nationalism and security priorities were also important determinants in contemporary foreign policy that sometimes worked against Chinese efforts to sustain moderation and reassure neighbouring countries. The CCP administration placed greater emphasis on promoting nationalism among Chinese people, as communism weakened as a source of ideological unity and legitimacy, following the disintegration of the USSR and other communist regimes, along with China's shift towards free market economic practices. Nationalism supported the high priority given by the CCP administration to preventing Taiwanese independence and restoring this and other territory taken from China by foreign powers, when China was weak and vulnerable during the 19th and 20th centuries. Nationalism exacerbated ongoing Chinese disputes with North and South Korea, Japan, India, and several South-East Asian nations, regarding territorial and symbolically important historical questions. China's neighbours also showed varying degrees of concern over Chinese leaders' efforts to build advanced military power and to take coercive measures to achieve nationalistic goals, especially regarding Taiwan and the contested territorial claims in the East China Sea and the South China Sea. More broadly, Chinese leaders built what they called 'comprehensive national power', particularly economic, military, and political power, as China sought a leading role, as yet not clearly defined, as a great power in Asian and world affairs.

Shifts in policy and practice showed distinct phases in Chinese foreign relations with Asian neighbours from 1989. The first phase, from 1989 to 1996, witnessed strong Chinese efforts to emerge from the post-Tiananmen isolation and to address the pressure imposed by the USA and Western-aligned countries by means of more active Chinese diplomacy. Chinese leaders and diplomats focused on neighbouring countries and other developing states, which were more inclined to deal with China pragmatically and without pressure regarding China's political system or other internal affairs. The Chinese administration's emphasis on sovereignty and nationalism at this time also led in 1992 to the country's enactment of a territorial law asserting strong claims to disputed territories, especially along China's eastern and southern maritime borders. The military worked in tandem with Chinese oil companies, fishing enterprises and others to advance China's claims to the Spratly Islands, located in the South China Sea, against the expansion of such activities by Viet Nam, the Philippines, Malaysia and other claimants. Following a major incident in 1995, the leading states of ASEAN stood against Chinese territorial expansion, and the USA also publicly intervened, supporting peaceful resolution of regional disputes.

While trying to sustain a workable economic relationship with the USA and other developed countries that were critical of China's communist political system, human rights practices and other policies, Chinese leaders and official media responded sharply to the pressure exerted by the USA and its allies and associates, denouncing the perceived domineering nature of US foreign policy actions throughout many parts of the world. China used the international importance of its rapidly growing economy to force US President Bill Clinton (who held office between 1993 and 2001) to reverse his policy linking the USA's trade with China to human rights and other considerations. China was subsequently outmanoeuvred by the Taiwanese President, Lee Teng-hui, who, to the surprise of the Chinese Government, effectively exerted pressure on Clinton to reverse policy and allow Lee to visit the USA. This challenge to Chinese sovereignty and to nationalistic determination to reunify Taiwan with China led to a serious military confrontation, with broad implications for Asian stability. Nine months of intermittent large-scale Chinese military exercises followed. The exercises did not end until the USA dispatched two aircraft carrier battle groups to the Taiwan area in early 1996 for the first such US–Chinese military confrontation in the region since the 1960s. Few of China's neighbours explicitly supported China or the USA in the dispute, but many were seriously concerned by China's assertiveness and ambitions.

Subsequently, Chinese leaders moved to a second phase in 1996–2001, when they demonstrated more concern to reassure neighbours in Asia and other countries that China was not a threat. They propounded a 'new security concept' that consolidated the moderate approach that China had sometimes adopted in the past regarding peaceful co-existence in international affairs. Chinese diplomacy was very active in bilateral relations, establishing various types of special partnerships and fostering good neighbour policies. China also increased interaction with ASEAN, the ARF and other Asian regional organizations. The Shanghai Co-operation Organization was established under China's leadership in 2001. Chinese trade relations with neighbouring countries generally expanded at twice the rate of China's rapidly growing economy.

Asian investment in China grew, with South Korea, Taiwan, Japan and Singapore among the largest investors. The Chinese economy remained stable amid the Asian economic crisis of the late 1990s. China did not devalue its currency, it sustained economic growth and it supported some international efforts to assist failing regional economies—developments that raised China's stature in the region. The Chinese Government and the Clinton Administration held two summit meetings and improved relations, under the rubric of 'engagement', while seeking a constructive strategic partnership. However, both sides also highlighted serious differences. The US Congress, media and various interest groups continued sharply to condemn Chinese policies and to criticize the moderation of the Clinton Administration in view of perceived Chinese infractions regarding a long list of political, security and economic issues. The Chinese Government displayed strong opposition to what it regarded as US efforts to weaken China, and there was much public opposition to perceived US domination and pressure in various world areas. China informed neighbouring states that its 'new security concept' was in opposition to the archaic 'Cold War thinking' seen in US efforts to sustain and strengthen relations with allies, including the USA's alliances or closer military relations in Asia, notably with Japan, South Korea, Australia, and some South-East Asian nations. China indicated that these states would be wise to align with its approach and to eschew closer alliance and military links with the USA. The bombing by US aircraft of the Chinese embassy in the Yugoslav capital of Belgrade in 1999 prompted mass demonstrations that resulted in the destruction of US diplomatic properties in China and also led to a major strategic debate in China regarding whether peaceful development or opposition to US domination or 'hegemonism' should be the main trend in Chinese foreign relations in Asian and world affairs.

The third phase began after the coming to power of US President George W. Bush in January 2001. It was striking to observers at the time that the initially uncompromising approach of the Bush Administration regarding support for Taiwan and opposition to China's military build-up and proliferation practices, as well as other US initiatives on sensitive issues such as the strengthening of the US-Japanese alliance and the development of ballistic missile defences in Asia and the USA, did not elicit strident criticism from Chinese officials and in official Chinese media. In the recent past, even less serious US measures against Chinese interests had routinely been denounced as perceived manifestations of US hegemonism and Cold War thinking.

Over time, it became clear that the Chinese Government was endeavouring to broaden the scope of its ongoing efforts to reassure neighbouring countries that China was not a threat. The wider initiatives now included and focused on the USA. The previous Chinese efforts, critical of US policies and alliance structures in order to prompt Asian governments to choose between closer relations with China, under the rubric of its new security concept, and closer relations with the USA, were put aside. In their place emerged a new and evolving Chinese emphasis focused on the USA, as well as on Asian and other powers, that China's 'rise' would be a peaceful one that represented many opportunities and no threat to concerned powers.

Chinese officials were realistic in explaining the shift. They wanted to ensure that China's growing economic, military and other power and related international influence did not prompt the US superpower and other concerned governments to align together in ways that would thwart or oppose China's rise. In private briefings, authoritative Chinese spokespersons reiterated the rationale seen in the official media that China was well aware of the hostile international reactions to the rise of Imperial Japan and Nazi Germany in the 20th century and was striving to avoid such an outcome for China in the 21st century.

China's initial emphasis on 'peaceful rise' was eventually transformed into the even less threatening rubrics focused on 'peaceful development' and seeking 'harmony' in relations with all powers. Public opposition to 'hegemonism', a word used in the post-Cold War period to refer to the USA, had been one of China's two principal foreign policy objectives in authoritative pronouncements for more than 20 years, but it declined to a point where it was no longer a major stated aim of Chinese foreign policy. In its place was the reassuring emphasis of the Chinese administration on following an international path of peaceful development.

The shift in China's approach reinforced the positive momentum in China's relations with Asian neighbours. Progress was especially notable in South-East Asia and in relations with South Korea. The shift also helped to persuade the Bush Administration to adopt a more co-operative and less confrontational posture towards China over salient Asian and other issues. The crisis caused by North Korea's breaking of existing restrictions on its nuclear programme in late 2002, and that country's progression towards the development of nuclear weapons, led the US and Chinese Governments to co-operate closely in managing the various crises and in endeavouring to reach a negotiated solution. The perceived provocative acts of Chen Shui-bian, the Taiwanese President who held office from 2000 until 2008, in relations with China also prompted closer convergence of US and Chinese positions on the so-called Taiwan issue.

After the coming to office of President Barack Obama in January 2009, the US Administration sought greater co-operation with China and other powers in dealing with the international problems posed by the global economic recession, climate change, nuclear proliferation and conflicts with terrorists, notably in Afghanistan and Pakistan. Although Chinese leaders still spoke of seeking co-operation with and of reassuring the USA, China at this time adopted more assertive positions on differences with the USA, China's neighbours, and other countries regarding various issues: these included territorial claims in waters near China, economic and trade disputes, Taiwan, Tibet and human rights. The USA responded with firmness as it strengthened security and related links with countries around China's periphery that were concerned about Chinese intentions. The US-led response proved counter-productive for Chinese interests. By 2011 senior Chinese leaders had strongly reaffirmed policies of positive engagement, reassurance and peaceful development in relations with the USA and China's neighbours, muting public attention to continued generally uncompromising positions on various issues in dispute. Analysts in China and abroad were optimistic, but far from certain, that the moderate trend in China's foreign relations would persist.

IMPLICATIONS: CHINA'S INFLUENCE IN ASIA

At the start of the second decade of the 21st century, it was clear that China had made major advances in expanding its influence in Asia, although the record showed some serious limitations and set-backs. It was also clear that on the one hand the USA, Asian powers and a number of other regional governments generally sought to co-operate with China, while on the other hand they prepared for contingencies in case the recent Chinese moderation in Asia shifted to a more aggressive or disruptive course. These governments remained determined to preserve their interests and independence of action in view of changing Asian power dynamics characterized by China's increasing influence, thereby preserving an Asian order where China remained far from dominant. The implication for the future role of China in world affairs was that it would remain preoccupied with addressing complicated power dynamics in Asia, along with many difficult domestic issues, thereby reducing its ability to exert powerful influence in more distant regions of the world.

China's Advances and Limitations

China's advances in Asia depended heavily on the growth of Chinese trade with the neighbouring states of Asia, which made China the leading trading partner, or one of the leading partners, of most Asian countries. Asian producers of energy and raw materials found China to be a ready market for their goods. Asian manufacturers of consumer products and industrial goods often found it difficult to compete in international and domestic markets with Chinese manufactured goods of low cost and good quality. They tended to integrate their enterprises with China by joining the influx of foreign investors that each year made the country the largest, or one of the largest, recipients of FDI in the world.

What resulted were webs of trading relationships characterized by so-called processing trade, which accounted for one-half of China's overall trade each year. Led by foreign-invested enterprises in China, which similarly accounted for one-half of China's foreign trade, consumer and industrial goods were produced in China with components imported from foreign enterprises abroad, often in other parts of Asia. It was usually the case that the developing product and its components would cross the Chinese border, sometimes several times, before it was completed. Also, China was often the final point of assembly and the value added in China was relatively small in relation to the total value of the product. The final product would frequently be exported to advanced Asian economies, or even more frequently to China's largest export markets, the USA and the European Union. Overall, the result was that China's importance as a recipient of Asian investment, a leading trading partner and an engine of economic growth rose dramatically in Asia.

The weight of Chinese economic growth and importance was particularly strong in China's south-eastern periphery. Along land borders with South-East Asian states, China built, often with the support of international financial institutions, networks of roads, railways, waterways, hydroelectric dams and electric power transmission grids, as well as pipelines that linked China ever more closely with these nations. Such interchange was geographically challenged by high mountains in South Asia, but the pattern was followed to some degree in Chinese economic relations with Central Asian states. A similar close integration developed between China and Taiwan, with the strength of the Taiwanese economy becoming increasingly determined by the island's interchange with mainland China.

Adroit diplomacy that followed the lines of China's evolving 'good neighbour' policy towards Asian countries greatly improved Chinese relations with most adjacent Asian countries. Senior Chinese leaders were very active and attentive in frequent bilateral and multilateral meetings with Asian counterparts. Their 'win-win' diplomacy maintained that China and its Asian partners should seek mutual benefit by focusing on developing areas of common ground while putting aside differences. Apart from requiring support for China's stance on Taiwan, Tibet and such nationalistic issues, China made few demands on Asian countries. China's approach was greeted positively by Asian countries, many of which remembered and sought to avoid repetition of the assertive and disruptive Chinese policies of the past.

China's diplomacy emphasized willingness to trade with and to provide some aid, investment, and military support to countries with 'no strings attached'. This approach was well received by Asian governments in Myanmar (Burma), Cambodia and elsewhere. Another feature of China's diplomacy was emphasis on Chinese language, culture and personal exchanges. This included support for Confucius Institutes and other organizations promoting student exchanges, the teaching of Chinese language and culture, and facilitating ever larger numbers of Chinese tourist groups travelling to other countries.

Public statements of Chinese officials and those of most Asian states attempted to minimize the significance of China's impressive military build-up. None the less, it was obvious to all concerned that China was building the strongest military forces in Asia and developing a growing capability to impede and deny access to strategic areas along China's periphery (notably Taiwan) to US military forces, should they attempt to intervene.

The most notable example of limitations and shortcomings in relations with Asia was China's relationship with Japan, Asia's richest country and the principal ally of the USA. The record of recent years showed that China was usually unsuccessful in winning greater support, despite many positive economic and other connections linking China and Japan. India's interest in accommodation with China was very mixed and became overshadowed by a remarkable upward trend in strategic co-operation with the USA. Russian and Chinese interest in close alignment fluctuated and appeared to remain secondary to their respective relationships with the West.

Until recently, China had a very negative record in relations with Taiwan. The Taiwanese Government continued to move towards greater separation from China, despite extensive economic connections. That course changed in 2008 with the coming to power in Taiwan of a new Government, which was determined to reassure the Chinese Government. China's economic, diplomatic and military influence over Taiwan grew. The main obstacle was Taiwan's political opposition, which was due to challenge the incumbent Government in elections in January 2012.

Strong Chinese nationalism and territorial claims complicated efforts to improve relations with Asia. South Korean opinion of China declined sharply from a high point in 2004 because of nationalist disputes over whether an historic kingdom controlling much of Korea and north-east China had been Chinese or Korean. China's influence in South Korea diminished sharply in 2010, as a result of Chinese support for North Korean interests following North Korean military attacks against South Korea, which caused military and civilian casualties.

Chinese nationalism and territorial claims emphasized a strong position regarding differences with Japan. Chinese diplomacy endeavoured to reduce the significance of territorial disputes in South-East Asia, and with India and South Korea, but clear differences remained unresolved and became more prominent with China's more assertive foreign policy approach in 2008–10. On balance, the continued disputes served to impede Chinese efforts to improve relations with these countries. China's remarkable military modernization and its sometimes secretive and authoritarian political system raised suspicions and wariness on the part of a number of neighbouring states along with the USA, Australia and Western-aligned governments, which sought greater transparency regarding Chinese military intentions.

China's past record of aggression and intimidation towards many Asian countries remained hard to overcome. It also meant that China had few positive connections on which to build cordial relations. As a result, and also reflecting the state-led pattern of much of Chinese foreign relations, China's interchange with Asian countries depended heavily on the direction and leadership of the Chinese Government. Non-government channels of communication and influence were very limited. An exception was the so-called Overseas Chinese communities in South-East Asian countries. These people provided important investment and technical assistance to China's development and represented political forces supportive of their home country's good relations with China. At the same time, however, the dominant ethnic, cultural and religious groups in South-East Asia often had a long history of wariness of China and sometimes promoted violent actions and other discrimination against the perceived rising economic and political power and influence of ethnic Chinese.

The areas of greatest Chinese strength in Asia—economic relations and diplomacy—also showed limitations and weaknesses. Chinese trade figures were exaggerated because of the double-counting associated with processing trade. Double-counting such as this was estimated to represent 30% of China's reported trade with South-East Asia. The fact that one-half of Chinese trade was conducted by foreign-invested enterprises in China, that the country usually added only a small amount to the products of the resultant processing trade and that the finished product often depended on sales to the USA or the European Union also appeared to diminish China's image in Asia as a powerful trading country.

The large amount of Asian and international investment that went to China thus did not go to other Asian countries, thereby curbing their economic development. China invested little in Asia apart from in Hong Kong, a renowned tax haven and source of 'round-trip' funds leaving China and then returning as foreign investment. Chinese aid to Asia was very small, especially in comparison with other donors, with the exception of Chinese aid to North Korea and Myanmar. China continued to receive large amounts of foreign aid, including loans or other assistance valued at US $1,500m. annually from the World Bank, $1,300m. from the Asian Development Bank, and $2,000m.–3,000m. from developed countries. Presumably, these funds might have been allocated to other developing countries had they not gone to China. China's large foreign-exchange reserves served many purposes for the authoritarian Chinese administration, which was trying to maintain stability amid massive internal needs. They did not translate into big Chinese grants of assistance abroad. China's attraction to Asian producers of raw materials was not shared by Asian manufacturers. These entrepreneurs tended to relocate and invest in China where they appeared to do well, but their workers could not relocate to China and seemed to be adversely affected.

By definition, China's 'win-win' diplomacy did not lead the country to act in ways in which it would not have behaved ordinarily. The sometimes overwhelming array of meetings, agreements and pronouncements accompanying China's active policy of diplomacy in Asia did not obscure the fact that China remained reluctant to undertake significant costs, risks or commitments in dealing with difficult regional issues. The inability of Chinese officials to pursue a consistent line of reassurance toward its neighbours and other countries in 2008–10 tarnished China's image with regard to effective and reliable diplomacy.

The issue of North Korea demonstrated an unusual combination of Chinese strengths and weaknesses in Asia. On the one hand, China provided considerable food aid, petroleum and other material support to North Korea, was its largest trading partner and repeatedly endeavoured to protect North Korean interests in the face of US-led efforts at the UN to impose sanctions on the country, as a result of North Korea's development of nuclear weapons and ballistic missiles, nuclear proliferation activities, and military attacks on South Korea. The USA and other participants came to rely on China during the intermittent six-party talks to use its standing as the foreign power with the most influence in North Korea to persuade that country to engage in negotiations over its weapons development and proliferation activities. On the other hand, North Korea repeatedly rejected Chinese advice and warnings. Chinese leaders were loath to sever their aid or otherwise increase pressure on North Korea to conform to international norms, for fear of repercussions from the Pyongyang regime, which might undermine Chinese interests in preserving stability in north-eastern Asia. The net effect of these contradictions was that, while China's influence in North Korea was greater than that of other major powers, it was encumbered and limited.

The Role of the US and Asian Governments

China's rise in Asia did not take place in a vacuum. It was dependent upon an Asian environment heavily influenced by the power, policies and practices of the USA and the governments of Asia. Assessment of US strengths and weaknesses showed that the USA would remain the leading power in the Asian region for the foreseeable future. Meanwhile, Asian powers and other governments concerned with preserving independence in view of China's rise often worked closely with the USA in developing contingency plans to offset adverse implications of Chinese policies and behaviour.

Media and specialist commentary, as well as popular and élite sentiment in Asia, tended to emphasize the shortcomings of US policy and leadership in Asia throughout the early 21st century. Foremost were widespread complaints concerning the Bush Administration's uncompromising policy for many years towards North Korea, its military invasion and occupation of Iraq, and assertive and seemingly unilateral US approaches on wide-ranging issues including terrorism, climate change, the UN and Asian regional organizations. The USA appeared alienated and isolated, increasingly mired in the consequences of its invasion of Iraq and its perceived excessive emphasis on the so-called 'war on terror'. The slow pace of the USA's recovery from the economic recession that had begun in 2008 added to perceived US weakness and decline.

This emphasis on the negative aspects with regard to the USA's position in Asia overshadowed, but failed to obscure, four sets of US strengths in the region, far exceeding those of China and other nations. Those strengths endured and many grew in the recent period, providing a solid foundation for US leadership in 21st century Asia. The Obama Administration built on these strengths in improving US diplomacy and presenting a more attractive image of the USA in Asia at the beginning of the second decade of the 21st century.

First, security considerations were paramount among the US strengths and influence in Asia. In general, Asian governments are strong, viable and make the decisions that determine direction in foreign affairs. Popular, élite, media and other opinion may influence government officials in policy towards China, the USA and other countries, but ultimately the officials make decisions on the basis of their own calculus. For the most part, the officials see their governments' legitimacy and success resting on nation-building and economic development, which require a stable and secure international environment. Unfortunately, Asia is not particularly stable, and most Asian governments are privately wary of, and tend not to trust, each other. As a result, they look to the USA to provide the security they need to pursue goals of development and nation-building in an appropriate environment. They recognize that the US security role is very expensive and involves great risk, including large-scale casualties if necessary, for the sake of preserving Asian security. They also recognize that neither rising China, nor any other Asian power or coalition of powers, is able or willing to undertake even a fraction of these risks, costs and responsibilities.

Economic factors are also important determinants of enduring US influence and leadership in Asia. The nation-building priority of most Asian governments depends importantly on export-orientated growth. Chinese officials recognize this, and officials in other Asian countries acknowledge the rising importance of China in their trade; however, they all also recognize that Chinese and Asian trade heavily depends upon exports to developed countries, notably the USA. In recent years the USA has recorded a massive and growing trade deficit with China; the total trade deficit with Asia in 2008 was estimated at more than US $350,000m. at a time when the USA's overall trade deficit exceeded $700,000m. Asian government officials recognize that China, which registers a large overall trade surplus, and other trading partners of Asia are unwilling and unable to bear even a fraction of the cost of such large trade deficits, which none the less are very important for Asian governments.

Obviously, from 2008 the global economic recession had an enormous impact on trade and investment. Some Asian officials are considering the possibility of placing greater reliance on domestic consumption, but tangible progress seems slow, as they appear to be focusing on an eventual revival of world trade that would restore previous levels of export-orientated growth involving continued heavy dependence on the US market. Despite sometimes strident Chinese complaints about US economic policies and leadership, evidence appears to show great care on the part of the Chinese administration to avoid pressing ahead with controversial policies that would further undermine international confidence in the existing economic system and thwart meaningful efforts at economic recovery. Sustaining co-operation with the USA appears to remain central to China's economic development.

A third set of factors working to sustain US influence and leadership in Asia involves extensive and ongoing US government engagement in the region and the tendency of Asian governments to engage more closely with the USA as they develop contingency plans (so-called 'hedging') in response to changing power relations in Asia prompted by the rise of China. The Obama Administration inherited a US position in Asia buttressed by the Bush Administration's generally effective interaction with Asia's powers. It is very rare for the USA to enjoy good relations with Japan and China at the same time, but the Bush Administration carefully managed relations with both powers effectively. It is unprecedented for the USA to be the leading foreign power in South Asia and to sustain active relations with both India and Pakistan, but that has been the case since relatively early in the Bush Administration. Furthermore, it is unprecedented for the USA to have good relations with China and Taiwan at the same time, but that situation emerged during the Bush years and strengthened following the election of Ma Ying-jeou as President of Taiwan in 2008.

The US Pacific Command, along with other US military commands and security organizations, has led the way with regard to wide-ranging and growing US efforts to build and strengthen networks of military and other security relationships throughout the region. In an overall Asian environment where the USA remains on good terms with major powers and most other governments, the development of military and other security links through education programmes, on-site training, exercises, intelligence sharing and other means enhances US influence in generally quiet, but effective, ways. Part of the reason for the success of these efforts relates to active contingency planning by many Asian governments. As power relationships change in the region, notably on account of China's rise, Asian governments generally seek to work positively and pragmatically with China on the one hand; but on the other hand they seek the reassurance of close security, intelligence and other links with the USA, in case China shifts from its current generally benign approach to one of greater assertiveness or dominance. The US Government sees its interests well served by balancing US engagement with China with active contingency planning involving a wide variety of partners in the Asia-Pacific region.

A source of enduring US influence in Asia that is sometimes overlooked is non-governmental interaction with the region, and the role that Asian immigrants to the USA play in that process. For much of its history, the USA exerted influence in Asia much more through business, religious, educational, media and other interchange than through channels dependent on government leadership and support. Active non-government US interaction with Asia continues today, putting the USA in a unique position where the non-government sector has such a strong and usually positive impact on the influence the USA exerts in the region. Meanwhile, more than 40 years of generally 'colour-blind' US immigration policy since the ending of discriminatory restrictions on Asian immigration in 1965 has resulted in the influx of millions of Asian migrants who regard the USA as their home and who interact with their countries of origin in ways that generally support and reflect well on the US position in Asia. No other country, with the exception of Canada, has such an active and powerfully positive channel of influence in Asia.

OUTLOOK AND IMPLICATIONS BEYOND ASIA

The above examination of the salient strengths and limitations of China's rising influence in Asia, of the significant strengths and limitations of the USA and of the contingency planning of Asian governments shows continued Chinese advance. However, the USA remains the region's leading power, and other governments are wary of the implications of China's rise as they seek mutual benefit in greater economic and other interaction with China. Asia is the international area where China has always exerted greatest influence, but that does not mean that China will come to dominate the region. Prevailing conditions do not appear conducive to China's emergence in a dominant position in Asia. After a period of assertiveness in 2008–10, Chinese leaders have returned to an approach involving careful and incremental efforts and adjustments to overcome existing and unforeseen obstacles in order to improve China's influence, interests and status. The task has been, and is likely to remain, complicated and difficult to manage. Combined with the long array of domestic challenges and other preoccupations, it requires continued reserve in foreign policies and practices, as Chinese leaders take account of the sustained growth but substantial limits of China's international power and influence.

The complicated and often encumbered Chinese rise in Asia shares similar features with Chinese relations in other world areas. In the first decade of the 21st century Chinese influence increased remarkably in Africa, Latin America and the Middle East. As in the case of Asia, the major Chinese strengths have been growing trade and investment and adroit diplomacy. Ironically, an important factor in China's increasing involvement in developing countries in Asia and elsewhere has been a shortcoming in China's economic growth: Chinese leaders have had mediocre results in curbing the grossly wasteful use of energy and other resources in the heavy industries that have become a pillar of Chinese manufacturing in the 21st century. They have been compelled to purchase massive amounts of energy and other resources abroad, leading to large increases in Chinese trade and other economic interaction with resource producers in developing countries. The Chinese economic strategists have successfully linked their increased purchases with efforts encouraging China's prominent role in constructing infrastructure and Chinese exports of manufacturers' goods to these markets, resulting in overall balanced trade between China and developing countries.

However, China's rapidly growing economic links do not translate into a position of dominance. In the Middle East, challenges to Chinese influence include US military dominance of sea lanes controlling oil flows from the Persian (Arabian) Gulf, intense rivalry between China's two main oil suppliers, Saudi Arabia and Iran, and China's unwillingness to take sides on important regional questions regarding peace in the Middle East and terrorism directed at Israel. The Chinese Government was placed on the defensive by the mass demonstrations and armed resistance against authoritarian rule throughout the Middle East and North Africa in 2011, fearing that these events would encourage opposition to one-party rule in China. In Latin America, China is a growing but still secondary economic protagonist in comparison with the USA and the European powers, and it poses a major negative challenge to various manufacturers in the region. China also appears loath to be seen to challenge US leadership in the Western hemisphere. Apparent Western fatigue in dealing with failures of development in Africa suggests that China confronts fewer immediate obstacles to its economic advance there, which is generally well received by African governments. Nevertheless, the reception of China's growing 'footprint' in Africa is mixed and often negative at the levels of society below that of the governments and business élites.

Chinese relations with Europe remain very important economically. China records a massive trade surplus with Europe; investment and other assistance from the advanced European countries provide important support for Chinese economic development. Nevertheless, discussion of European alignment with China against US international leadership and the creation of a 'multi-polar' world has faded. The consolidation of US relations with European allies by the Obama Administration stands in contrast with repeated disputes between European powers and China over trade imbalances, currency policies, human rights and the status of Tibet. European opinion viewed unfavourably China's role in the international climate change conference in Copenhagen in December 2009. China's large-scale economic involvement in Africa undermines norms of development adopted by countries belonging to the Organisation for Economic Co-operation and Development (OECD), norms that are taken seriously by some European governments, adding to friction in relations with China.

BIBLIOGRAPHY

Brautigam, Deborah. *The Dragon's Gift: The Real Story of China in Africa*. New York, Oxford University Press, 2009.

Cassarini, Nicola. *Remaking Global Order: The Evolution of Europe-China Relations and Its Implications for East Asia and the United States.* New York, Oxford University Press, 2009.

Cooney, Kevin. J., and Sato, Yoichiro (Eds). *The Rise of China and International Security: America and Asia Respond.* Routledge, Abingdon, 2009.

Deng, Yong, and Wang Fei-Ling (Eds). *China Rising: Power and Motivation in Chinese Foreign Policy.* Lanham, MD, Rowman & Littlefield, 2005.

Dittmer, Lowell and Yu, George T. (Eds). *China, the Developing World and the New Global Dynamic.* Boulder, CO, Lynne Rienner Publishers, 2010.

Eisenman, Joshua, Heginbotham, Eric, and Mitchell, Derek (Eds). *China and the Developing World: Beijing's Strategy for the Twenty-first Century.* Armonk, NY, M. E. Sharpe, 2007.

Ellis, R. Evan. *China in Latin America: The Whats and Wherefores.* Boulder, CO, Lynne Rienner Publishers, 2009.

Fravel, M. Taylor. *Strong Borders, Secure Nation: Cooperation and Conflict in China's Territorial Disputes.* Princeton, NJ, Princeton University Press, 2008.

Garver, John. *Protracted Contest: Sino-Indian Rivalry in the Twentieth Century.* Seattle, WA, University of Washington Press, 2001.

Gill, Bates. *Rising Star: China's New Security Diplomacy.* Washington, DC, Brookings Institution Press, 2007.

Goh, Evelyn. *Meeting the China Challenge: The United States in Southeast Asian Regional Security Strategies. Policy Studies 21.* Washington, DC, East-West Center, 2006.

Goldstein, Avery. *Rising to the Challenge: China's Grand Strategy and International Security.* Stanford, CA, Stanford University Press, 2005.

Holslag, Jonathan. *China and India: Prospects for Peace.* New York, Columbia University Press, 2009.

Johnston, Alastair Iain. *Social States: China in International Institutions: 1980-2000.* Princeton, NJ, Princeton University Press, 2007.

Johnston, Alastair Iain, and Ross, Robert (Eds). *Engaging China: The Management of an Emerging Power.* New York, Routledge, 1999.

Kang, David C. *China Rising: Peace, Power, and Order in East Asia.* New York, Columbia University Press, 2007.

Kim, Samuel S. *The Two Koreas and the Great Powers.* New York, Cambridge University Press, 2006.

Kurlantzick, Joshua. *Charm Offensive: How China's Soft Power Is Transforming the World.* New Haven, CT, Yale University Press, 2007.

Lampton, David M. *The Three Faces of Chinese Power: Might, Money, and Minds.* Berkeley, CA, University of California Press, 2008.

Lo, Bobo. *Axis of Convenience: Moscow, Beijing, and the New Geopolitics.* Washington, DC, Brookings Institution Press, 2008.

Medeiros, Evan S. et al. *Pacific Currents: The Responses of US Allies and Security Partners in East Asia to China's Rise.* Santa Monica, CA, RAND Corporation, 2008.

Percival, Bronson. *The Dragon Looks South: China and Southeast Asia in the New Century.* Westport, CT, Praeger Publishers, 2007.

Ross, Robert S., and Zhu Feng (Eds). *China's Ascent: Power, Security, and the Future of International Politics.* Ithaca, NY, Cornell University Press, 2008.

Shambaugh, David (Ed.). *Power Shift: China and Asia's New Dynamics.* Berkeley, CA, University of California Press, 2005.

Shambaugh, David, and Yahuda, Michael (Eds). *International Relations of Asia.* Lanham, MD, Rowman & Littlefield, 2008.

Shirk, Susan L. *China: Fragile Superpower.* New York, Oxford University Press, 2007.

Simon, Sheldon W., and Goh, Evelyn (Eds). *China, the United States, and South-East Asia: Contending Perspectives on Politics, Security, and Economics.* Routledge, Abingdon, 2009.

Snyder, Scott. *China's Rise and the Two Koreas: Politics, Economics, Security.* Boulder, CO, Lynne Rienner Publishers, 2009.

Steinfeld, Edward. *Playing Our Game: Why China's Rise Doesn't Threaten the West.* New York, Oxford University Press, 2010.

Wan, Ming. *Sino-Japanese Relations: Interaction, Logic, and Transformation.* Stanford, CA, Stanford University Press, 2006.

Womack, Brantly (Ed.). *China's Rise in Historical Perspective.* Lanham, MD, Rowman & Littlefield, 2010.

Yee, Herbert, and Storey, Ian (Eds). *The China Threat: Perceptions, Myths, and Reality.* London, Routledge, 2002.

Yee, Herbert S. *China's Rise—Threat or Opportunity?* Abingdon, Routledge, 2010.

Zhang Yunling (Ed.). *Making New Partnership: A Rising China and Its Neighbors.* Beijing, Social Sciences Academic Press, 2008.

Zhang Yunling. *Rising China and World Order.* Singapore, World Scientific Publishing Co, 2010.

THE KOREAN PENINSULA: CONFLICT AND DIALOGUE

AIDAN FOSTER-CARTER

INTRODUCTION

Two-thirds of a century after the ancient nation of Korea was 'temporarily' partitioned by the victorious allies at the end of the Second World War in 1945, the peninsula has remained a major flashpoint. The two fatal attacks carried out by the Democratic People's Republic of Korea (North Korea) against the Republic of Korea (South Korea) in 2010 served as a stark reminder that in North-East Asia the Cold War is not yet over: the sinking of the South Korean navy corvette *Cheonan* in March, in which the North denied any involvement; and the shelling of Yeonpyeong island in November (see below). The risk that tensions might rise to dangerous levels therefore remains very real.

Korea is one of the world's older nations, unlike many other post-colonial states, in Asia and elsewhere, which were imperialist constructs at variance with previous boundaries and identities, thus creating a challenge for national integration and independent state-building. Most of the peninsula was unified in 668 AD, when the south-eastern kingdom of Silla (Shilla) conquered its larger northern rival, Goguryeo (Koguryo). Despite owing much of its civilization to China, to which it was long a formal vassal, Korea is ethnically and linguistically quite distinct and was in practice largely allowed to be self-governing.

Few countries have experienced a more difficult passage to modernity. The imperialist age found the last Chosun (or Yi) dynasty in dire decay. Its determined efforts to exclude the wider world earned it the sobriquet 'hermit kingdom', but its stubborn refusal to reform rendered it prey to whichever power achieved regional dominance. That proved to be Meiji Japan, which annihilated the fading Chinese and Russian empires to occupy Korea for 40 years from 1905 (formally 1910), repressing the Korean people, while ruthlessly mobilizing the peninsula's resources for the imperial war machine.

The last of many bitter legacies left by Japan was inadvertent. Following the swift Japanese collapse in 1945, the USA proposed the peninsula's 'temporary' partition in order more effectively to handle the local Japanese surrender. (With the Soviet army already crossing the border into Korea, the US Government had feared that the USSR would soon occupy the entire peninsula.) The hastily chosen line of division, which the USSR accepted, was the 38th parallel, the line being determined by two young US colonels, Dean Rusk (who was later appointed US Secretary of State) and Charles Bonesteel. This almost casual but fateful sundering would soon precipitate a devastating war, and thereafter shape the fates of more than three generations of Koreans, with no end yet in sight. In time the people of South Korea would come to enjoy prosperity and freedom; at the end of the first decade of the 21st century, those in the North had yet to experience either.

Predictably, US and Soviet zones hardened into separate regimes, proclaimed in 1948: first the Republic of Korea, in the south, and then the Democratic People's Republic of Korea, in the north. Border skirmishes across the 38th parallel were commonplace, and tensions erupted into full-scale war in June 1950 when the North's young ex-guerrilla leader, Kim Il Sung, invaded South Korea; he would have prevailed had a US-led UN force not intervened. The UN force, under Gen. Douglas MacArthur, swept north and might have reunified Korea as the Republic of Korea if Mao Zedong had not dispatched Chinese 'volunteers' to the aid of Kim. The Korean War ended in 1953 with an armistice, not a peace treaty (and South Korea did not even sign the armistice). The conflict left both sides utterly ravaged: cities in ruins, forests razed by napalm, and several million people dead.

Subsequent relations (or the lack thereof) between North and South Korea must be understood in the context of these traumatic origins, the effects of which have proved enduring. Constitutionally and legally, each still defines the other as an enemy, and both sides still claim, as they have done ever since their founding in 1948, to be the sole legitimate government on the peninsula.

Against that background, for most of the subsequent half-century both regimes not only eschewed all mutual contacts but also forced their citizens, on pain of draconian penalties, to do likewise. Quite unlike former East and West Germans, ordinary North and South Koreans have never been permitted to write to or telephone one another, nor to visit freely. Several million people have thus spent almost 60 years utterly cut off from close relatives, mostly not knowing if they are alive or dead. Each regime has also suppressed all but negative information about the other. As a result, over the years the two Koreas (unlike the two former Germanys) have become strangers as well as enemies, a fact that has added to the already huge incubus of mutual mistrust.

ACCORDS AND DISCORD

Only in the early 1990s did real signs of change begin to emerge. Previously there had been several attempts at dialogue, all abortive. The first began with secret visits in 1971, at which time both Korean states were alarmed by the recent US-Chinese rapprochement. This led to a joint statement on 4 July 1972, and the establishment of a South-North Co-ordinating Committee (SNCC). Red Cross talks also began, with the aim of arranging family reunions. Although SNCC meetings continued until 1975 and Red Cross talks until 1978, neither produced any result. The same was true of a further brief round of dialogue in 1979–80, during the democratic interlude in South Korea between the assassination of President Park Chung-Hee and Chun Doo-Hwan's coup (see the chapter on The Republic of Korea).

Meanwhile, North Korea did nothing to enhance its trustworthiness, committing regular acts of aggression against the South. In August 1974 a North Korean resident of Japan shot at President Park, killing his wife. In the late 1970s South Korea discovered the existence of several tunnels, dug under the demilitarized zone (DMZ) separating the two countries, large enough for an invading force from the North. In October 1983, while on a visit to Rangoon, Burma (now Yangon, Myanmar), President Chun Doo-Hwan narrowly escaped an assassination attempt: 17 members of his entourage, including four cabinet ministers, were killed. Two of the North Korean agents who planted the bomb were captured alive: one was hanged; the other, Kang Min Chul, died of cancer in a Myanma prison in May 2008.

Perhaps because of the opprobrium incurred by the Rangoon bombing incident, North Korea subsequently adopted a different approach. What may have been intended only as a propagandist offer of 'aid' to South Korea, after severe floods occurred there in late 1984, was shrewdly accepted by the South Korean Government. This led to a year of three-tiered dialogue in 1985, comprising economic, parliamentary and Red Cross talks. Only the last session yielded results, in the first reunion of separated families, which took place in September.

North Korea suspended all dialogue in early 1986 in protest against the annual 'Team Spirit' US-South Korean military exercises, and resumed its duplicitous policy: negotiating (unsuccessfully) with the International Olympic Committee to host part of the 1988 Seoul Olympic Games, only to bomb a South Korean civilian airliner in November 1987, causing the loss of 115 lives. None the less, South Korea's growing economic and diplomatic strength (symbolized by the full participation in the 1988 Olympics by the People's Republic of China, the USSR and the communist countries of Eastern Europe, even though, at that point, none formally recognized the legitimacy of South Korea) brought the North back into the negotiating process, albeit sporadically. Red Cross talks resumed in 1988, although planned family reunions in late 1989 failed to take place. Nevertheless, there was some progress in the sporting arena. The first ever inter-Korean football matches were held in Pyongyang and Seoul in late 1990, and in the following year joint Korean teams participated in two international sporting events. However, North and South Korea sent separate teams to Spain to participate in the 1992 Barcelona Olympics.

Meanwhile, although there was no resumption of economic talks, in 1988 South Korea initiated indirect trade with the North. Direct inter-Korean trade, which began in late 1990, increased rapidly in 1991, and was equivalent to some US $210m. annually by 1992, when the South became the North's fourth largest trading partner (after China, Russia and Japan).

In the political arena, the first ever talks between the countries' heads of government finally took place in September 1990. The three such meetings in that year were largely symbolic, and the premiers did not meet again until October 1991. However, progress was made in mid-1991, when North Korea withdrew its long-standing objection to both Korean states joining the UN as separate entities (if only because it became clear that neither the USSR (itself soon to dissolve) nor China would any longer veto South Korea's unilateral application). Both Koreas were thus admitted to the UN in September 1991. (They were already members of most of its specialized agencies, including FAO, UNESCO and the World Health Organization.)

At the resumption of the premier-level talks in October 1991, both parties agreed on the title, and envisaged provisions, of an accord governing future inter-Korean relations. Under the 'Agreement on Reconciliation, Non-aggression and Exchanges and Co-operation', which was signed in December and ratified in February 1992, North and South pledged, *inter alia*, to desist from mutual slander and sabotage, and to promote economic and other co-operation, as well as the reunion of separated family members. The accord was widely hailed as a milestone, and subsequent premiers' meetings, in May and September, resulted in agreements to fulfil its provisions, as well as to establish several joint commissions.

However, thereafter relations worsened and the agreement remained largely unimplemented. In late 1992 South Korea was angered by the discovery on its territory of a large-scale North Korean espionage operation, while North Korea criticized the South's decision to resume in 1993 the 'Team Spirit' exercises (which had been suspended in 1992). The projected ninth meeting of premiers in December 1992 was cancelled, and such meetings were not subsequently resumed.

The main impediment to a real improvement in inter-Korean relations was the question of suspected nuclear ambitions (see below, and the chapter on The Democratic People's Republic of Korea). Although the accord of December 1991 omitted any reference to nuclear issues, a separate agreement was signed later in that month to create a bilateral Joint Nuclear Control Committee (JNCC). However, this made no progress, with North Korea opposing the South's demand for unannounced inspections, while South Korea resisted the North's demand to open all the US bases stationed on its territory to North Korean scrutiny.

The visit to South Korea of Kim Tal Hyon, the North Korean Vice-Premier in charge of trade and investment, who toured a range of factories and met prominent business leaders as well as the then President, Roh Tae-Woo, in July 1992, brought hopes of a breakthrough. While North Korea desperately needed South Korean aid and investment, it still seemed reluctant or unable to convince the South (and indeed the world) that it had unequivocally abandoned any nuclear ambitions; moreover, prior to October 2002, it always denied ever having had a military nuclear programme. Such suspicions were only enhanced by North Korea's announced intention, in March 1993, of withdrawing from the Treaty on the Non-Proliferation of Nuclear Weapons, which it had signed in 1985. The nuclear issue continued to blight inter-Korean relations throughout the remainder of 1993, not least because of North Korea's insistence on negotiating with the USA rather than with South Korea. There were contacts in the 'peace village' of Panmunjom (in the DMZ) in October 1993 and March 1994, but both proved abortive.

In June 1994 former US President Jimmy Carter returned from Pyongyang, having defused a growing nuclear crisis between North Korea and the USA, bearing an offer from Kim Il Sung for a summit meeting with his South Korean counterpart. Kim Young-Sam accepted with alacrity, and two highly successful planning meetings were held at Panmunjom. However, following the sudden death of Kim Il Sung on 8 July, the summit (which had been arranged for 25–27 July) was postponed. Not only did the summit not take place in the ensuing months (technically North Korea remained without a head of state), but North-South relations became markedly worse. North Korea professed outrage when the South Korean Government failed to issue any condolence on the death of Kim Il Sung and acted harshly against the few South Korean radicals who did sympathize. North Korean denunciations of Kim Young-Sam, former dissident though he was, were, if anything, more virulent than they had ever been against the generals who preceded him.

The new bilateral relationship with the USA, created by the Agreed Framework signed in Geneva, Switzerland, in October 1994 (see the chapter on the Democratic People's Republic of Korea), had the advantage, from North Korea's viewpoint, of excluding South Korea—at least formally. Although this remained the North's official position, in practice by mid-1995 North Korea had accepted South Korean light-water reactors (LWRs) and engineers to build them under the Korean Peninsula Energy Development Organization (KEDO) consortium. The North also continued business links with South Korean companies (if not with their Government), and in July 1995 13 technicians of the Daewoo conglomerate became the first South Koreans since 1953 to settle in the North with both Governments' approval. The technicians were to supervise Daewoo's new export factory at the port of Nampo, a pioneer venture that other South Korean firms were thought likely to emulate.

Yet the North's policy of ignoring or bypassing the South Korean Government was hardly sustainable as a long-term strategy, particularly in the light of the agreements signed in 1991–92 (albeit hardly implemented). In June 1995 North Korea appeared to have changed its tactics, accepting an offer of rice aid from the South, having made a request for similar aid from Japan in the previous month (see below). However, the first South Korean ship was forced to fly the North Korean flag on its arrival in the port of Chongjin (for which North Korea later apologized), while in August another South Korean vessel was detained on spying charges. South Korea was aggrieved that its generosity did not elicit a similar spirit on the part of the North. Furthermore, North Korea's continuous denigration of former President Kim Young-Sam was unacceptable practice by international standards.

The issues of spies and of refugees continued to enliven inter-Korean relations in the mid-1990s, while doing nothing to improve them. The report of Kim Dong Sik, a North Korean agent captured after a gun battle in October 1995, was noteworthy; he landed by midget submarine after a decade of training. In July 1996 another alleged spy was arrested after living for more than a decade in South Korea disguised as a Lebanese-Filipino history professor. Two dramatic incidents affected inter-Korean relations during 1996–97. In September 1996 a North Korean submarine ran aground off South Korea's east coast. In the ensuing manhunt, all but two of its crew of 26 died (some by their own hands, apparently; one was captured alive and one escaped). South Korea's fury was only assuaged in December when, pressed by the USA, North Korea perfunctorily apologized for what, it still claimed, was an accident caused by engine trouble. Then, in February 1997, Hwang Jang Yop, one of North Korea's most senior leaders, sought asylum in the South Korean embassy in the Chinese capital, Beijing, while returning from a visit to Japan. Ranked 25th in the hierarchy, Hwang was the main theorist of North Korea's official ideology of Juche (self-reliance), and was currently serving as party secretary and Chairman of the Supreme People's Assembly (SPA) foreign affairs committee. This defection was awkward for China, but the situation was eventually resolved by sending Hwang initially to a third country, the Philippines, before allowing him to enter South Korea. Once in Seoul, Hwang warned that his former comrades were serious in threatening to attack the South. Even before Hwang's arrival, an earlier high-ranking defector had been assassinated near Seoul by unknown gunmen. As late as 2010, in which year the elderly Hwang died of natural causes, South Korea intercepted two Korean People's Army (KPA) majors, masquerading as defectors, who confessed that they had been sent to assassinate him.

Amid these set-backs for inter-Korean relations, there were also more positive signs. In particular, nuclear co-operation through KEDO reached the stage where ground-breaking for construction of the new LWRs began in mid-August 1997. Several dozen South Korean engineers were already on site at Shinpo, South Korean ships had delivered machinery and materials, and a telephone link with South Korea was in service. KEDO's office at Shinpo included the first South Korean diplomats ever to be based in North Korea. The South Korean Government also appeared to be easing its restrictions on businesses wishing to invest in North Korea. In May five more companies received permission to explore joint ventures. Negotiations concerning the opening of North Korean airspace to flights to and from Seoul finally yielded results in April 1998, when the tiny numbers of North and South Koreans in regular contact with one another began to include the countries' air traffic controllers.

THE 'SUNSHINE' POLICY

The prospects for inter-Korean relations improved markedly with the election of Kim Dae-Jung as South Korea's President in December 1997. Kim Dae-Jung had long advocated, and once in office immediately began to implement, a so-called 'sunshine' policy towards North Korea, involving consistent openness towards the North (while maintaining a strong security posture), in the belief that this would eventually elicit a positive response. The policy entailed a distinction between governmental and private (including business) contacts, and a much more relaxed attitude towards the latter, whatever the vicissitudes of the former. The acknowledged model here was that of relations between China and Taiwan. The first official North-South talks since the death of Kim Il Sung (there had been others that were quasi-governmental) took place in April 1998. Held in Beijing to discuss a North Korean request for fertilizer, the talks failed when South Korea linked this issue to its own demands for progress on family reunions. Yet, in a change of stance, the South Korean Government made no effort to prevent the transfer of private aid to the North. The pace of civilian and business contacts thus increased in 1998, even though the South's economic crisis took its toll on inter-Korean trade, which declined in the first half of the year by almost 50%.

During mid-1998 there were dramatic, if contradictory, developments in inter-Korean relations. In mid-June Chung Ju-Yung, the founder of the Hyundai group, South Korea's largest conglomerate, crossed the normally impenetrable DMZ at Panmunjom, bringing 500 cattle as a gift for his home town near Wonsan. During his week-long visit, Chung Ju-Yung also discussed a wide range of potential joint ventures between Hyundai and North Korean interests. The most dramatic involved a plan to run daily tour boats to Mount Kumgang, just north of the DMZ; this scheme commenced in November 1998 and represented the first opportunity for South Korean tourists to set foot in the North. However, this progress appeared to be in jeopardy when, during Chung Ju-Yung's visit to North Korea, a South Korean fishing boat caught a small Northern spy submarine in its nets. When the submarine was eventually towed to port, its crew of nine were found to have killed themselves (or each other). Then in July, a dead North Korean frogman was found on a beach in South Korea. In the past such provocations would certainly have led the South Korean Government to forbid Hyundai to continue with its plans. It was indicative of Kim Dae-Jung's imagination and courage that on this occasion no such linkage was made, and, after a short delay, Hyundai was allowed to proceed.

During 1999 Hyundai's tourism project proved a major advancement for the 'sunshine' policy, with more than 80,000 South Korean tourists making the journey north in the first eight months alone. However, there was criticism that Hyundai's payments to North Korea—which were set to total almost US $1,000m. over six years, although the North later reduced its fees—might be funding the North's military. The growing scepticism in Seoul reflected the failure of 'sunshine' to generate wider warmth. In June fresh talks in Beijing on fertilizer and family reunions broke down, even though South Korea modified its stance and sent fertilizer without preconditions. Meanwhile, on 15 June the two Koreas' navies fought a brief gun battle for the first time since the Korean War. North Korean boats were fishing for crab in the Yellow Sea (known as the West Sea in Korea) in an area south of the Northern Limit Line (NLL—a maritime boundary unilaterally set by the UN in 1953, which was never formally accepted by the North) and, unusually, held their positions when challenged by South Korean patrol boats. After several days of confrontation the South resorted to ramming, and the North opened fire; however, one of its boats was sunk (with a reported 80 dead) and three others were badly damaged. Remarkably, both the Beijing talks and fertilizer deliveries—by sea, close to the combat area—continued throughout, and despite, this contretemps. The gun battle may have reassured Kim Dae-Jung's domestic critics that 'sunshine' did not mean appeasement, and the policy remained in place. In August a workers' team from the militant Korean Confederation of Trade Unions was allowed to travel north to play football with North Korean counterparts.

The 'sunshine' policy finally achieved results in 2000. In March Kim Dae-Jung's offer in his 'Berlin Declaration' of Southern aid to rebuild infrastructure in North Korea led to secret talks in China, and the announcement in April of the first ever North-South summit meeting. This momentous event duly took place on 13–15 June, after an unexpected 24-hour delay. Kim Dae-Jung made the first ever official direct flight between Seoul and Pyongyang. Kim Jong Il met him at the airport with a full honour guard of the KPA's three services. South Korean television viewers—but not their Northern counterparts, who saw only the formalities—marvelled at the friendly demeanour of a figure hitherto demonized as utterly malign. After two days of public affability and private tough negotiations, the two leaders signed a brief declaration pledging further progress. The document's only substantive stipulation was the reunion of separated families, duly held on 15–18 August when two sets of 100 elderly Koreans flew in each direction to meet relatives whom they had not seen for 50 years. Two further reunions took place in December 2000 and February 2001 (but a third, scheduled for October, was cancelled). In the following month the first exchange of personal mail in over 50 years—involving some 300 letters from each side—was permitted between North and South Korean families.

The bilateral summit meeting and family reunions ushered in a wider inter-Korean peace process. Ministerial meetings to follow the summit began in Seoul at the end of July 2000, with a second round held in Pyongyang at the end of August and two further sessions thereafter. The first session agreed to reconnect railway lines across the DMZ: a goal endorsed by Kim Jong Il soon afterwards, with work inaugurated by Kim Dae-Jung in September. In a related development, Hyundai won Kim Jong Il's approval to build a vast industrial estate in, and run tour buses to, Kaesong, the ancient Korean capital just north of the DMZ. The project was envisaged as being comparable to the relationship between Shenzhen Special Economic Zone, in the People's Republic of China, and Hong Kong: serving both to link the two economies and as a basis for growth in the North. There were positive security implications too if the DMZ were to become a thoroughfare, instead of an all but impassable barrier. Economic talks were also held, during which a basic framework for business co-operation was agreed. North Korea's Minister of the People's Armed Forces, Vice-Marshal Kim Il Chol, visited Seoul in September, but would only discuss railways (the relinking of which was being carried out by the army on both sides), rather than military matters; no return visit was arranged.

These promising beginnings came to a halt in 2001. In January economic talks broke down when the South refused a technically unfeasible North Korean demand for the immediate supply of electricity. In the following month North Korea agreed, but failed to ratify, a protocol on joint railway building within the DMZ; construction work on its side had barely begun. In March the North withdrew from the fifth ministerial talks only hours before they were due to start. Thereafter it refused all official contact with South Korea for six months, seemingly as a corollary of its annoyance with the new Administration of President George W. Bush in the USA, except for sending a condolence delegation on the death of the Hyundai patriarch, Chung Ju-Yung. A further South Korean donation of fertilizer in May did not modify this stance. Indeed, in June there was a reversion to provocation, when several North Korean merchant ships took short cuts through Southern waters. The restrained response of the South Korean navy angered 'hard-liners' in the South; as did a later incident, when a few members of a South Korean unification activists' delegation, allowed to visit Pyongyang for Liberation Day celebrations on 15 August, appeared to support North Korean positions. The controversy that this generated brought down South Korea's ruling coalition (see the chapter on the Republic of Korea).

All this gravely weakened the position of Kim Dae-Jung. By late 2001 most South Koreans endorsed the opposition's criticism of the 'sunshine' policy as appeasement. North Korea's erratic behaviour did not help matters. It accepted a fifth round of ministerial talks in September, only to cancel family reunions, at short notice in October, on the pretext of South Korea's heightened state of alert after the 11 September terrorist attacks on the USA. A sixth round of ministerial talks in November, held (at the North's insistence) at Mount Kumgang, ended with no agreement to meet further; the South's Minister of Unification was dismissed soon after. Official relations thus remained suspended, although, in a major change from past policy, business and private contacts continued. So did links through KEDO: an unpublicized North Korean team inspected South Korean nuclear facilities in December, and other delegations followed in 2002. In December 2001 also, Hyundai sharply reduced its Mount Kumgang tours because of falling demand.

In February 2002 North Korea cancelled a joint celebration of the Lunar New Year, for which the South Korean civic delegates had already arrived at Mount Kumgang. President Bush's designation in January of North Korea as part of an 'axis of evil' alarmed Kim Dae-Jung; in April he sent his adviser Lim Dong-Won, the 'sunshine' policy's *éminence grise*, to try to persuade Kim Jong Il to agree to talks with the USA. This visit also revived North-South dialogue: April witnessed a fourth round of family reunions, this time at Mount Kumgang (on the North's insistence, again) rather than in the two capitals. In May, however, North Korea withdrew from economic discussions at a day's notice. It also disregarded all entreaties to share in the football World Cup co-hosted by South Korea and Japan, but did broadcast highlights of some matches held in the South.

Meanwhile, however, private and semi-official contacts burgeoned. Official subsidies revived Mount Kumgang tourism. South Korean firms established several business and educational joint ventures in information technology, including a college and Pyongyang's first internet café. In June 2002 South Korea's Assistant Minister of Information and Communication led a delegation from major companies to Pyongyang; however, North Korea later denied reports that agreement had been reached to install mobile telephone services in Pyongyang and Nampo, and no further detail emerged from this. Provincial links continued: Jeju sent a consignment of oranges to the North, and Gangwon (divided by the DMZ, and later to be badly hit by Typhoon Rusa in late August) jointly sprayed against pine pests. In June 320 members of a South Korean Christian aid non-governmental organization (NGO), when denied a promised church service in Pyongyang, held their own impromptu worship in a hotel; they were not impeded. In May Kim Jong Il hosted a dinner for Park Chung-Hee's daughter, Park Geun-Hye, herself a possible presidential candidate. Kim also agreed to a friendly football match in September.

In June 2002 relations sharply deteriorated when North Korean warships, seemingly without warning, fired on and sank a South Korean patrol boat in the Yellow Sea, killing six crew members. As in the 1999 incident, for which this may have been revenge, this occurred in disputed maritime border seas during the crab-fishing season. Yet it was wholly unexpected, prompting further criticism of the 'sunshine' policy and of the South Korean navy's lack of preparedness; the South Korean Minister of National Defence was dismissed a fortnight later. Within a month, however, North Korea expressed 'regret', and this sufficed for dialogue to resume. The seventh ministerial talks, held in Seoul in August 2002, arranged a full roster of further meetings in specific areas. Economic discussions later in that month set a timetable to open two cross-border road and rail links: not only the previously agreed route near Seoul, work on which had stalled, but a second corridor near the east coast. On 18 September ceremonies were held on both sides of the DMZ to mark the beginning of reconstruction of the two rail links between the Koreas. North Korea also agreed to take part in the Asian Games to be staged in Busan in October—the first time it had ever participated in an international event held in South Korea—in contrast to its eschewal of the football World Cup. Nearly 700 North Korean athletes and supporters went to Busan; however, speculation that Kim Jong Il might attend the opening ceremony proved unfounded.

From October 2002 the growing nuclear crisis cast a pall over inter-Korean relations, but did not derail them. North Korea firmly refused to discuss nuclear matters with the South, and on 12 May 2003 even declared null and void the North-South agreement on a nuclear-free peninsula signed in 1991. Yet most of the now established post-summit channels continued to operate, with some interruptions. Thus, regular ministerial talks reached their 11th round in July 2003, with repeated pledges to expedite substantive co-operation. The other major change in 2003 was the appointment of a new Government in Seoul. President Roh Moo-Hyun, who took office in February (when North Korea upstaged his inauguration by testing a 'cruise missile') pledged to continue Kim Dae-Jung's 'sunshine' policy; however, first indications suggested that in practice he might take a tougher line, or a more erratic one.

Tallying the results of 'sunshine', the South's Ministry of Unification found 2002 to be the most intensive year for North-South interaction since regular contacts began in 1989. Of a cumulative 39,433 South Koreans who had travelled to the North since 1989, nearly one-third did so in 2002. (This excluded tourists to Mount Kumgang, whose total number since tours began in 1998 had exceeded 500,000.) By category, the largest group (31%) was involved in KEDO's LWRs, followed by non-Kumgang tourism (24%). Aid workers made up 11%, business people 9%, and family reunions just 5%. Travel in the opposite direction was less brisk, but, similarly, of 2,568 North Koreans to visit the South since 1989, 40% went in 2002 alone. A total of 34 sets of North-South talks were held in 2002, or 9% of the cumulative total of 400. Unlike in the past, when inter-Korean contacts often took place outside the peninsula, almost all were now held in Korea: either in Seoul or Pyongyang, or at Mount Kumgang. However, for many in Seoul the pace was too slow, and the results disappointing. Thus, family reunions stalled in the last quarter of 2002, as North Korea took umbrage at the South raising the issue of South Koreans abducted to the North (who might number as many as 80,000, mainly taken during the Korean War). Reunions for a fortunate few resumed in 2003, with a sixth and seventh round (since the 2000 summit) in February and June. Yet these isolated encounters had no follow-up, and with a mere 100 from each side meeting each time, most of those affected would die without ever being reunited with their long-lost kin. Plans to build a permanent reunion centre at Mount Kumgang raised hopes of the pace quickening.

CROSS-BORDER LINKS

A significant development in 2003 was the partial opening to civilians of the long-sealed North–South border. Here again, progress was intermittent, as North Korea delayed matters by denying the jurisdiction of the UN Command (UNC) in the two new road and rail corridors through the DMZ. In February a temporary road to Mount Kumgang in the eastern (Donghae) corridor was used for the sixth round of family reunions and by a few tourists, before North Korea abruptly closed it for unspecified repairs, and then suspended tours altogether as part of stringent quarantine measures against Severe Acute Respiratory Syndrome (SARS). Work continued on linking railways in both corridors, and on 14 June both were ceremonially joined in the DMZ: a merely symbolic gesture, thus far, as gaps remained in both lines on the North Korean side. With genuine completion expected in the western (Kyongui) corridor by 2004, the prospect arose, politics permitting, of trains running for the first time in half a century from Seoul to Pyongyang, and on into China or Russia. However, for regular service to be possible, North Korea's decrepit internal rail network would need massive and costly repairs and upgrading. The Kyongui corridor was also crucial for the viability of the industrial zone at Kaesong. After many delays, ground-breaking took place on 30 June 2003: South Korean attendees crossed for the day from Seoul. Such cross-border commuting, unthinkable previously, had thus become normal for railway work and some other meetings, such as economic talks held in Kaesong in July. Yet, at these, North Korea baulked at making such access—essential if South Korean business was to invest in Kaesong as planned—routine. However, it did agree finally to implement four basic business accords arranged in December 2000, but never subsequently ratified, only to fail to send officials as promised to Panmunjom on 18 August 2003 to exchange the documents (they were eventually exchanged on 20 August). This seemed to indicate renewed displeasure with South Korea; a day earlier, the North withdrew from the Daegu Universiade (world student games) in protest at the burning of its flag—not a rare event—at a conservative rally in Seoul. It relented after an apology from President Roh Moo-Hyun, which in turn drew right-wing wrath at home. In the event the North Korean team did take part in the games, but they were marred by an assault by North Korean 'journalists' on peaceful human rights protesters.

Meanwhile, the 'sunshine' policy was now tarnished for many South Koreans by allegations that the June 2000 North-South summit had, in effect, been paid for by South Korea. In June 2003 a special counsel, appointed by the opposition-controlled legislature, confirmed that the previous Kim Dae-Jung administration had secretly sent US $100m. to North Korea just before the summit via the Hyundai group, which itself remitted a further $400m., supposedly as a business fee. Kim Dae-Jung was not questioned, but those charged included the former Minister of Unification, Lim Dong-Won, and the Chairman of Hyundai, Chung Mong-Hun, Chung Ju-Yung's son. In August Chung jumped to his death at Hyundai's headquarters. In September Lim and four others were convicted, but received suspended sentences as they were found to have acted in the national interest. However, Park Jie-Won, a former presidential chief of staff, was later sentenced to 12 years in prison, since his case involved corruption.

In the event, despite these set-backs and the continuing nuclear crisis, the Roh Moo-Hyun Government persisted with a 'sunshine' approach, now renamed as 'policy for peace and prosperity'; the more so after the pro-Roh Uri Party won a majority in legislative elections on 15 April 2004. In late 2003 it was estimated that on any given day up to 1,000 South Koreans were visiting the North: tourists, divided families, business people, NGOs and aid workers, civic organizations, educators and other professionals, journalists, cultural figures, government officials, railway inspectors and technicians, nuclear engineers and others. What was once newsworthy and exceptional—direct flights between Seoul and Pyongyang or land travel across the DMZ—was becoming regular, even mundane. A gradual de facto normalization of North-South links was gathering pace, even though the broader political and security context remained anything but normal. Most South Koreans, especially younger people, increasingly saw the North more as a younger (perhaps delinquent) brother, in need of guidance and succour, than a mortal enemy to be guarded against.

Thus, by late 2003 and into 2004, inter-Korean dialogue seemed institutionalized. Its highest normal level was that of so-called ministerial meetings (although North Korea described its own delegates as 'cabinet counsellors'), held quarterly in each capital alternately. The 12th, 13th and 14th sessions since the June 2000 summit meeting took place in October 2003 and February and May 2004, respectively. On each occasion South Korea sought to raise the nuclear issue but was rebuffed.

The other regular senior-level meeting was of the Economic Co-operation Promotion Committee (ECPC). This, too, met quarterly, alternating between Pyongyang and Seoul. Its sixth session, in August 2003, had a typically wide agenda: pledging to expedite cross-border transport, the Kaesong Industrial Zone, Mount Kumgang tourism, direct trade and processing on commission, Imjin river flood control, mutual economic visits, food aid and inspections, and more. Crucially, unlike in the past, these were not mere aspirations, but projects actually under way, if not always very rapidly. Most were the subject of less senior-level working meetings, which were increasingly held in towns near the border (Kaesong or Mount Kumgang in the North; Munsan, Paju or Sokcho in the South) with the visiting side commuting daily across the DMZ, a development that had previously been unimaginable.

Family reunions were another regular event: held at Mount Kumgang in September 2003 and in March–April and July 2004. In each case, 100 elderly Koreans from each side met briefly and publicly with relatives from across the DMZ. By late 2003, however, of 122,000 South Koreans who had originally applied for reunions, more than 20,000 had already died.

In September 2003 a total of 114 South Korean tourists flew from Seoul to Pyongyang for a five-day tour on the first ever direct flight. Presented as the first trip of many, this programme was suspended after just one month. In October a large bus convoy drove from Seoul to Pyongyang for the dedication of a new gymnasium, built by Hyundai. In the same month the first private sector truck delivery was made across the DMZ when Korea Express, South Korea's largest logistics operator, took 100,000 roof tiles to Kaesong: the first batch of 400,000 was donated by South Korean Buddhists, to help restore a temple in this ancient capital city located just across the border.

The Kaesong Industrial Zone made slow progress. In December 2003 North Korea published detailed regulations for the zone. Some were restrictive, and South Korea continued to demand an investment pact, plus free passage for South Korean business executives and equipment. Practically, this would also entail completion of road and rail links, which were ready on the South Korean side. A 50-year lease for the first full phase of development was signed in April 2004, and a first pilot mini-zone with 15 South Korean firms opened in December. A business complex covering 3.3 sq km was due to open in 2007, accommodating 250 South Korean firms. Henceforth, Hyundai would share the role of developer with Korea Land, a South Korean parastatal enterprise. The USA pressed South Korea to ensure no breach of the Wassenaar Arrangement, an export control regime restricting exports of sensitive technology to communist regimes (to which both nations were signatories).

South Korea was encouraged in August 2003 by the fact that North Korea's newly elected SPA included at least five officials prominent in inter-Korean dealings. These were: Kim Ryong Song, the North's chief delegate to inter-Korean ministerial talks; Song Ho Kyong, who, as Vice-Chairman of the Asia-Pacific Peace Committee, was in charge of projects with Hyundai; Pak Chang Ryon, head of the North Korean side in the ECPC; Jung Un Up, chief of another North-South co-operation body; and Choi Seung Chol, in charge of inter-Korean Red Cross contacts.

In an important development, in May 2004 North Korea accepted a long-standing South Korean demand for bilateral military talks. After just two meetings, the two sides agreed in June that their Yellow Sea fleets would maintain daily radio contact, to avoid any risk of fatal firefights like those of 1999 and 2002. In return, South Korea accepted a Northern demand to dismantle all propaganda at the DMZ. Loudspeakers fell silent after half a century on 15 June 2004, and all structures were initially due to come down by Liberation Day (15 August). However, dismantling was suspended by North Korea in July following an incident in which a South Korean ship fired warning shots at a North Korean vessel after the latter crossed the NLL. (It was subsequently revealed that information regarding radio communication with the North Korean ship had been intentionally withheld by the South Korean navy; the incident led to the resignation of the South Korean Minister of National Defence, Cho Young-Kil.) North Korea resumed removal of its propaganda facilities in August.

A major rail explosion in April 2004 at Ryongchon, near the North Korean border with China, led through tragedy to some progress in North Korea's opening, including southwards. South Korea at once offered an aid convoy by road, but the

North rejected this, insisting that relief goods come by sea; the first boat reached Nampo a week after the disaster. However, a South Korean cargo plane flew to the North with 70 metric tons of aid, in the first ever inter-Korean humanitarian direct flight. Not until the following month was a land convoy permitted; it had to unload just across the border in Kaesong. By then, the cargo was equipment and materials to rebuild schools and other facilities. Useful as these were, the North's initial delay meant that the chance to save more burns victims had been lost.

North Korean human rights were a perennially difficult issue, which South Korea had now become reluctant to raise for fear of undermining the 'sunshine' policy. In April 2003 it absented itself from a vote (which was carried) on this at the UN Commission on Human Rights in Geneva; a year later it was present, but abstained. Yet, the plight of refugees from North Korea continued to draw attention. In October South Korea twice temporarily closed its consulate in Beijing to clear a backlog of about 100 North Korean refugees camping there. After a spate of incidents involving North Koreans seeking sanctuary, China had increased security around embassies in Beijing, but any who successfully ran this gauntlet eventually gained safe passage to Seoul. However, many more were forced to pass through China to seek refuge elsewhere. In late July 2004 no fewer than 468 North Korean refugees were flown to Seoul from Viet Nam (not officially named, for reasons of protocol), which had reportedly threatened to repatriate them. This was by far the largest group of defectors ever to reach South Korea, which some saw as a portent of things to come.

Despite the general progress, North Korea on occasion reverted to previous tactics. In March 2004 it missed a meeting in the South, later claiming (by radio) that Roh Moo-Hyun's impeachment meant South Korea was in anarchy. In August the North failed to organize the scheduled 15th ministerial meeting, seemingly for two reasons: anger at the Viet Nam refugee airlift; and displeasure at the South Korean refusal to let pro-North activists attend joint Liberation Day celebrations (which it cancelled) due to be held in Pyongyang on 15 August. None the less, in August the two Koreas' athletes marched together, as agreed, at the opening of the Olympic Games in Athens, as they had in Sydney in 2000; however, once again they competed separately.

South Korea also could be negative. In January 2004 it revoked the licence of a South Korean firm, Hoonnet, which had installed Pyongyang's first internet café and public server, with online gaming sites (illegal in the South) and an informal North-South internet chat room. Despite the 'sunshine' policy, telephone, fax and e-mail contact with the North remained technically illegal in the South under the still-unrepealed National Security Law.

The fourth anniversary of the first ever North-South summit meeting in Pyongyang was celebrated on both sides of the DMZ in June 2004. To mark the anniversary, a senior North Korean emissary made a rare visit to Seoul. Ri Jong Hyok's bland title—Vice-Chairman of the Asia-Pacific Peace Committee—belied his role as a close confidant of Kim Jong Il. He met President Roh Moo-Hyun, and gave him a message from Kim Jong Il, prompting speculation that the 'Dear Leader' might at last fulfil his promised but long-delayed return visit southwards. This seemed unlikely while the nuclear crisis persisted

South Korea's Ministry of Unification used this anniversary to sum up and quantify progress. If including the summit meeting, in the previous four years there had been 111 official inter-Korean meetings: 47 economic, 27 military (but usually about cross-border road and rail links), 19 political, and 18 'humanitarian and athletic'. Visitors from South to North, excluding Hyundai's tours to Mount Kumgang, which had brought some 680,000 visitors since 1998, more than doubled, from 7,280 in 2000 to 15,280 in 2003. Traffic in the other direction was smaller, predictably, and more erratic, decreasing sharply from 706 in 2000 to 191 in 2001, rising to 1,052 in 2002, then back to 1,023 in 2003. (None of this was remotely on the scale of interchange between, for example, China and Taiwan.)

From the second half of 2004 North Korea chose to eschew formal contact with the South, apparently angered by the mass airlift of its defectors from Viet Nam to Seoul (see above). This boycott lasted until mid-2005, thus leaving the normal channels of inter-Korean dialogue suspended for a whole year. Civilian contacts continued, and the North took care also to exempt the Kaesong Industrial Zone. Even here complications arose: in September 2004 the official opening of a South Korean office in the zone was postponed when the North refused to admit 11 legislators of the South's conservative opposition Grand National Party (GNP); North Korea relented three days later. Meanwhile, Hyundai began a daily shuttle bus service to transport its employees from Seoul to the Kaesong zone: a significant breach in the once impermeable DMZ. The first goods manufactured in the zone went on sale in Seoul in December. A ceremony in Kaesong in mid-December to mark this occasion was attended by the South Korean Minister of Unification, Chung Dong-Young, on his first visit to North Korea. The North Korean media did not report his presence, while the Government sent a far less senior official as its representative, who berated the South for allegedly hindering the pace of progress and even walked out during Chung's speech. South Korea refrained from protesting (at least publicly) at such behaviour. In January 2005 North Korea barred South Korean doctors who had established a clinic in the zone, rejected coal briquettes and heaters that it had earlier requested, and postponed talks on a telephone service to Kaesong. Some in Seoul speculated that this was a reflection of disputes in Pyongyang on how far or fast to open up, with the KPA fighting a rearguard action.

Despite his experience during his recent visit to North Korea, Chung Dong-Young sought to reassure the North that there would be no more mass defections. In December 2004 South Korea tightened its screening of would-be North Korean refugees and reduced grants for new arrivals, who in 2004 totalled 1,890: an increase from 1,281 in 2003, but still surprisingly small-scale. In February 2005 South Korea's first defence 'white paper' for four years abandoned the designation of North Korea as the main enemy (controversy over this change had caused the delay). In April South Korea again abstained when the UN Commission on Human Rights approved a resolution condemning human rights abuses in North Korea.

In March 2005 South Korea began the first cross-border electricity supplies (to Kaesong) since 1947. In April 2005 it granted North Korea US $26m. to help complete cross-border railways, and sent veterinary aid to combat an outbreak of avian influenza ('bird flu') in the North. However, when in January North Korea demanded 500,000 metric tons of fertilizer, twice as much as usual, the South insisted that the North must first return to dialogue. Urgent need for fertilizer, plus the impending fifth anniversary of the Pyongyang summit meeting of June 2000 (which could hardly be celebrated unilaterally), combined to persuade Kim Jong Il to end what had all along been a curious boycott.

INCREASING CO-OPERATION

From April 2005 inter-Korean relations improved. While visiting the Indonesian capital of Jakarta for the 50th anniversary of the Bandung conference (which had ultimately led to the establishment of the Non-aligned Movement), Kim Yong Nam, Chairman of the SPA Presidium and thus the titular head of state of North Korea, twice met South Korea's Prime Minister, Lee Hae-Chan, and agreed that inter-Korean dialogue should resume. Vice-ministerial talks in Kaesong in mid-May resulted in an agreement to send 200,000 metric tons of fertilizer to the North. Days later, the first North Korean merchant ships to enter South Korean ports since the 1984 flood aid (from North to South) arrived to take delivery of the fertilizer. Some was also sent overland.

Contacts between North and South accelerated in June 2005. Having invited a huge South Korean delegation for the summit anniversary, at a late stage North Korea reduced the number of invitations in protest at the deployment of US Stealth fighter aircraft to the South. Nevertheless, 40 officials led by Chung Dong-Young, plus a 295-strong NGO group, flew to Pyongyang. On the day of his departure, Chung was suddenly summoned for an unscheduled lunch with an affable Kim

Jong Il. This positive tone continued in the following week, when, after a year's hiatus, the 15th round of ministerial talks was held in Seoul. This produced a 12-point joint statement that not only restored prior channels of communication but also committed to a significant expansion of co-operation. These provisions were further expanded at the 10th ECPC meeting in July, also in Seoul, which likewise resulted in a 12-point agreement.

Co-operation initiatives increased rapidly from mid-2005; moreover, most were promptly implemented. General-level military talks were agreed, albeit with no date set and in an odd location: Mount Paekdu, a sacred peak on North Korea's border with China. This was also the venue for the 16th round of ministerial talks in September. In August working-level talks agreed to finish dismantling propaganda apparatus along the DMZ and to open a 'hotline' to allow emergency communication between the militaries of the two sides and prevent accidental armed confrontations; the 'hotline' came into operation on 13 August, just before a senior North Korean team led by Kim Ki Nam, a KWP secretary close to Kim Jong Il, visited Seoul for the 60th anniversary of Korea's liberation from Japanese rule in 1945. (These celebrations were notable for the distinct anti-Japanese sentiment on display.) During the visit Kim Ki Nam and his party met President Roh Moo-Hyun and his predecessor, Kim Dae-Jung. In an unprecedented gesture, they also briefly paid respects to South Korea's war dead in Seoul's national cemetery; South Korean conservatives condemned this, criticizing the absence of an apology for the Korean War. Another difficult subject, the fate of South Korean prisoners of war and others abducted to the North (which had hitherto denied the existence of such abductees), was raised (without success) in Red Cross talks in late August 2005 at Mount Kumgang, which also hosted an 11th round of North-South family reunions. For those too infirm to travel, a new cross-border fibre-optic cable laid in July permitted brief video reunions. There was as yet no plan to expand such brief, isolated events by allowing wider visits, or contact by telephone or e-mail.

Economic links, less contentious, looked set to expand. A planned joint fishing zone in the Yellow Sea was supposed to prevent border clashes similar to the armed skirmishes of 1999 and 2002 (see above). A new committee on agriculture, co-chaired by vice-ministers from each side, agreed in August 2005 on a wide range of co-operation initiatives, whereby from 2006 South Korea was to aid several North Korean collective farms, as well as helping generally with reafforestation, seedlings, pest control and more. It was also resolved to expedite nine sets of regulations on business co-operation, already drawn up but not yet implemented. South Korea consented to send its usual 500,000 metric tons of rice, and a further 150,000 tons of fertilizer. More innovatively, the ECPC agreed that in exchange for supplying urgently needed materials to make soap, clothing and shoes, South Korea might invest in and export such Northern minerals as zinc, coal and apatites; the details were worked out in August 2005. With an exchange of economic inspection teams scheduled for November, it seemed that all this might mark the long overdue start of broad North-South business collaboration for mutual gain.

South Korea also considered providing larger-scale assistance. Chung Dong-Young had reportedly offered Kim Jong Il help in seven specific fields: energy, rivers, railways, harbours, tourism, farming and reafforestation. Hints of a further 'special proposal' by the South—a quasi-Marshall Plan of major reconstruction, conditional on a nuclear settlement—were clarified in July 2005 when it emerged that Chung had also offered to supply the North with 2m. kW of South Korean electricity per year (a figure thought to be equivalent to North Korea's entire annual production of electricity), starting in 2008.

Neither the ongoing nuclear dispute nor the North's boycott of official meetings deterred South Korean tourists. In April 2005 alone Hyundai took 31,330 people to Mount Kumgang, and in June the North Korean resort welcomed its one millionth South Korean visitor since trips began (by sea) in 1998. The number of vehicles crossing the DMZ—an idea unimaginable until recently—rose rapidly, from 3,814 in January 2005 to 10,893 in April. Plans for South Koreans to be able to drive their own cars to Mount Kumgang were delayed by misgivings in Seoul (rather than Pyongyang) about insurance and the like, rather than military risk. Hyundai also claimed that it had been granted permission to develop more than 100 km of coast north from Mount Kumgang to Wonsan for tourism. The Group's Chairwoman, Hyun Jeong-Eun (Chung Mong-Hun's widow), met Kim Jong Il in July and secured approval for new tours to Kaesong (the old city) and Mount Paekdu, where the South Korean National Tourism Organization (KNTO) had agreed to give US $3m. to upgrade roads. However, pilot tours to both were delayed in August, amid speculation of disapproval in Pyongyang at the dismissal of Kim Yun-Kyu, CEO of Hyundai Group's North Korean business operation, Hyundai Asan, who was accused of misappropriating funds. This dispute was resolved in time to celebrate the seventh anniversary of Kumgang tours in November.

Furthermore, North Korea agreed to hold opening ceremonies for two recently built cross-border roads, which were already in use by Hyundai. Rail links in the same two corridors, where progress had been slower, were to begin trial runs in October 2005 and an opening ceremony was to be held by the end of the year. Although physical tracks already linked Pusan and Seoul to Pyongyang and Beijing, it was unclear how soon services would actually commence. Meanwhile, South Korea agreed that from August North Korean merchant vessels would be allowed to pass between its island province of Jeju and the South Korean mainland.

Cultural co-operation also grew, including the production of joint television programmes. A popular South Korean television quiz show purported to show North and South Korean elementary school pupils competing, but in fact the Pyongyang segments were recorded separately and later interwoven (controversially) with studio shots in Seoul. The Kaesong zone functioned as a social as well as an economic 'laboratory'. In May 2005 it was the location for North Korea's first Western-style fashion show, staged by the South Korean clothing manufacturer Shinwon, which operated a factory in the zone. While 500 South Koreans crossed the DMZ to see the show, none of Shinwon's 280 North Korean workers was able to watch it. By mid-2005 3,200 North and 600 South Koreans were working at Kaesong; by mid-2006 the former number had more than doubled to 6,700.

At the end of 2005 summary statistics released from Seoul revealed that in 2005 more than 80,000 South Koreans, a record number, had visited the North, including 7,000 who in October had taken short trips by daily charter flight to see the Arirang festival in Pyongyang; a further 284,000 tourists visited Mount Kumgang. During the course of the year a total of 34 official inter-Korean meetings took place, and more than 3,000 South Koreans had experienced brief family reunions. For the first time North-South trade exceeded US $1,000m. Less publicized figures from the South's National Statistical Office in December quantified the vast and ever widening economic disparity between the two Koreas. In 2004 the South's gross national income was $681,000m., 32 times the North's $21,000m. The per caput gap was narrower (the South has double the population of the North) but nevertheless striking: $14,162 against $914. In trade, the difference was even more remarkable: the value of South Korea's trade reached $478,000m. and was therefore 167 times the North's $2,860m.

TESTING TIMES

A significant period in inter-Korean relations ended in January 2006 when the last South Korean workers were withdrawn from KEDO's LWR site at Kumho; they left equipment worth US $45m. The LWR project was formally closed down in May, and KEDO itself appeared to have no future. Whatever one's view of the 1994 Agreed Framework, it was hard to deny KEDO's pioneering role in creating a context in which for the first time the two Koreas could—and had to—learn to work together practically

In early 2006 a wide range of contacts continued, but with growing irritation in Seoul at North Korea's intransigence. In December 2005 the 17th ministerial talks, held for the first time on the island of Jeju, had made no progress. In the following month South Korea appointed Lee Jong-Seok as Minister of Unification, a North Korea specialist who was influential on policy. In March 2006 North Korea unilaterally postponed the 18th ministerial talks, due in Pyongyang later that month, in protest at two routine joint military exercises between the USA and South Korea. Also in March, the first inter-Korean military talks since 2004 became stalled, since North Korean officials would discuss nothing but redrawing the de facto marine border, the NLL, which the South would not countenance. The same issue stymied progress at a further round of generals' talks in May 2006.

At the ministerial talks, eventually held in April 2006, the South pressed on a sensitive issue: that of the South Korean prisoners of war and post-war abductees, allegedly held in the North and estimated to number more than 1,000. North Korea continued to deny the allegations, and no progress was made, despite a promise by Lee Jong-Seok of 'bold' aid should this matter be resolved. This affected two family reunions scheduled to take place at Mount Kumgang. In March the North expelled a South Korean TV reporter for referring to one 'Northern' family member—a Southern fisherman seized in 1969—as an abductee; the entire Seoul press corps decamped in solidarity. More riskily, in June 2006 the North produced Kim Young-Nam, a South Korean abducted as a schoolboy from a west coast island in 1978 and largely forgotten until April 2006 when Japan stated that DNA evidence had revealed that he had married Megumi Yokota: she was the best-known of Japan's far fewer, but higher-profile, kidnap victims, who later reportedly took her own life. Kim insisted that he had in fact drifted out to sea on a raft, had been rescued by a North Korean vessel, and had stayed in Pyongyang to take advantage of a free education. While South Koreans did not believe this version of events, the abduction issue continued to arouse little public concern; this apparent lack of interest was in sharp contrast to the deep anger felt in Japan, where it remained at the head of the bilateral agenda.

Official economic dealings also remained frustrating for South Korea, with the North reluctant to implement matters agreed earlier (often its own initiatives). At the 11th meeting of the ECPC, held in October 2005 at Kaesong, North Korea focused on a single deal: the procurement of raw materials for clothes and other goods in exchange for vague mining rights. Working-level talks failed to narrow the gap, and six months passed before the next ECPC meeting in May 2006. Curiously, it seemed easier for South Korean private firms and parastatals, such as Korea Resources Corpn, to negotiate their own deals. At ministerial talks in April, the two sides agreed in principle on joint extraction of sand in the Han river estuary at their border, for use by both sides' construction industries.

Planning for the long term, in March 2006 South Korea opened lavish border offices at the two trans-DMZ corridors. However, in May North Korea caused fury in Seoul when at short notice it cancelled the already oft-postponed test train runs on the two cross-border railways, citing alleged political instability in South Korea. The feeling grew that the 'sunshine' policy was one-sided, with little North Korean reciprocity. Yet the long-delayed 12th ECPC meeting, held in June on Jeju, resulted in a nine-point agreement on a range of joint projects, including light industries and minerals. These projects were only to be instituted once 'conditions are met', a phrase that the South explicitly presented as meaning railway test runs. North Korean media reports, by contrast, omitted this proviso.

North Korea's missile tests on 5 July 2006 effectively ended hopes that any of these projects were likely to proceed in the near future. Even before the event, the very prospect of the tests had prompted former President Kim Dae-Jung to cancel a planned return visit to Pyongyang in June, although a large North Korean delegation went to Gwangju as planned for the sixth anniversary of the Pyongyang summit meeting. The missile tests were a rebuff for the weak Government of President Roh Moo-Hyun, which felt obliged to react. Its choice of action was unexpected: to suspend food aid. By 2006 300,000 metric tons of fertilizer had already been sent, but the equally customary (and needed) 500,000 tons of rice had yet to be agreed and were now suspended. This news prompted the North Korean delegation to the 19th cabinet level talks, held in mid-July in Busan, to leave for home a day early; they did not deign to discuss the South's nuclear or missile concerns. Yet the Kaesong and Kumgang projects continued, on the grounds that these were private ventures—a contestable view—meant to promote reunification in the long term. The tactic of suspending food aid caused controversy, especially when in July North Korea suffered floods which appeared likely to affect its forthcoming autumn harvest. In reprisal for the loss of food aid, the North suspended family reunions; it also cited the floods as reason to cancel the usual celebrations of Liberation Day on 15 August. In mid-August South Korea agreed to give the North emergency aid worth US $60m., but this in turn was suspended after North Korea's nuclear test on 9 October, which was, *inter alia*, an affront to the 'sunshine' policy.

Yet the nuclear test by no means curtailed inter-Korean links. Both the Kaesong and Kumgang projects continued, and in late October 2006 a delegation of the left-wing Democratic Labour Party of South Korea proceeded with a planned visit to Pyongyang, where delegates met Kim Yong Nam, the President of the SPA Presidium. The delegation returned in early November to much criticism, partly for not revealing (until it emerged in the North Korean media) its visit to Mangyongdae, the birthplace of and shrine to Kim Il Sung. Similarly, the first inter-Korean meetings of writers and journalists since the peninsula was divided in 1945 went ahead at Mount Kumgang in October and November 2006.

In a change of policy, in November 2006 South Korea for the first time supported a UN resolution condemning North Korea's human rights record. Co-sponsored by the European Union, this was approved by the UN's Third Committee by 91 votes to 21, with 60 abstentions. Besides direct abuses, the resolution accused the North Korean Government of responsibility, through mismanagement, for a dire humanitarian situation, particularly with regard to infant malnutrition. South Korea had abstained from four previous such votes; its support on this occasion was thought to be linked to the election of Ban Ki-Moon, latterly South Korea's Minister of Foreign Affairs and Trade, as UN Secretary-General and was weakened by the plea of the South Korean Ministry of Unification for North Korea's understanding of a 'painful decision'.

The nuclear test of October 2006 gave South Korea's Ministry of National Defence, where resentment continued at no longer being allowed to designate North Korea as the 'main enemy', licence to upgrade the North Korean challenge to a 'grave threat' (from the 'direct military threat' established in 2004); this was published in the Ministry's biennial 'white paper', released in December 2006. Besides nuclear and other weapons of mass destruction (including chemical and biological weapons, which remained wholly unaddressed), the Ministry of National Defence cited North Korea's massive and offensively deployed conventional forces, whose 4,800 multiple rocket-launchers had increased by 200 since 2004. What the Ministry of National Defence did not mention was that South Korea's own defence spending by then exceeded North Korea's entire national income.

In January 2007 the South Korean Ministry of Unification issued its annual tally of North-South visits, trade and so on. In 2006 inter-Korean visits (excluding tourists to Mount Kumgang) had exceeded 100,000 for the first time, reaching 101,708, a 15% increase on 2005. The Ministry of Unification credited most of this to economic co-operation, with commuting by South Korean managers across the DMZ to the Kaesong zone boosting the figures. Yet, as the Ministry conceded, this flow remained highly unbalanced: a mere 870, or fewer than 1%, of these visits were by North Koreans entering South Korea. Over 1m. passenger journeys were made using the two relinked cross-border roads, the vast majority being tourists to Mount Kumgang. By contrast, the parallel railway lines continued to languish, unused. It was also a record year for inter-Korean trade, which rose by 28% to reach US $1,350m. While in the past, much so-called trade had in reality been South Korean aid, the Ministry of Unification noted that in 2006 the truly commercial proportion had risen by more than one-third (34.6%) to reach $928m.

Contact between the two states continued in 2007, despite the nuclear confrontation. In January doctors from both Koreas began working side by side for the first time, in a small NGO-managed hospital in the Kaesong zone. In the same month South Korea's new Minister of Unification, Lee Jae-Joung, led a 100-strong delegation to the Kaesong zone. The visitors were also allowed to tour Kaesong city, Korea's ancient capital, the first South Korean group to do so since the North banned this in July 2006, in reprisal for the South's suspension of aid. Days later, as had become the custom, the two Koreas marched together in the opening ceremony of the sixth Asian Winter Games in Changchun, China—but went on to compete separately. In February 2007 the South Korean island province of Jeju sent a shipload of local tangerines and carrots to the North, as it had been doing since 1998.

There were further developments after the six-party talks accord of mid-February 2007. At the end of February Lee Jae-Joung flew to Pyongyang for ministerial talks, the 20th session since the North-South summit meeting of June 2000. In early March 2007 this meeting produced a six-point statement, which was encouragingly precise in setting dates and deadlines for a range of further events. These included reunions of separated families: a fifth video-link session was held in late March, with the 15th round of 'face-to-face' reunions following at Mount Kumgang in May. Yet at Red Cross talks held in April, North Korean officials still angrily denied holding any of the thousands of alleged Southern abductees.

The 13th ECPC meeting, held in Pyongyang later in the month, began with discord but ended on a positive note. The start was delayed by almost a full day after North Korea made an unprecedented demand to see drafts not only of the final joint statement (it was revealing that the South had already prepared this) but also of the South Korean delegation's opening speech; it also sought a commitment in advance to the provision of rice aid. South Korea remained steadfast, and later the North's chief delegate rapidly departed from the meeting after the South sought to link rice aid to compliance with February's six-party agreement. Despite such difficulties, an agreement was finally reached: its 10 points covered previous issues, reflecting North Korea's reluctance to implement decisions on matters supposedly agreed already. Prior to this, in March the South Korean Government had agreed to send fertilizer aid worth US $115m., but on rice aid it continued to vacillate, as the six-party deadlines in April were not met as a result of the Banco Delta Asia (BDA) dispute (see the chapter on The Democratic People's Republic of Korea).

At military talks held at Panmunjom in May 2007, South Korea's main agenda was to secure a military guarantee for long-delayed cross-border train tests and avoid a repetition of the unexpected cancellation at a very late stage in 2006. However, North Korea insisted on raising the NLL issue (see above), as it did again at a sixth round in July, which ended in rancour when the North Korean general abruptly abandoned the proceedings. In mid-May, however, trains did finally cross the DMZ in both the Kyongui and Donghae (west and east coast) corridors for the first time in half-a-century, albeit just once and briefly, for a short distance. With no prospect as yet of the North allowing regular services, South Korean jubilation seemed somewhat premature; Lee Jae-Joung spoke of the crossings as 'reconnecting the severed bloodline of the Korean nation'.

In mid-2007 inter-Korean relations were strained in several areas. The 21st ministerial talks, held in Seoul in late May, failed to make any progress: South Korea urged North Korea to shut its Yongbyon nuclear site, while the North demanded the immediate dispatch of supplies of rice from the South. The meeting was adjourned without agreement on a schedule for forthcoming talks. Tensions continued in June, when a 284-strong South Korean delegation visited the North for the anniversary of the 2000 summit meeting; the hosts took umbrage both at a speech that mentioned a possible second summit (much rumoured since late 2006) and at a lawmaker of the South Korean conservative opposition GNP, who they claimed showed disrespect at a shrine to Kim Il Sung. (In July 2007, in a major policy shift, the GNP stated that it now favoured the holding of an inter-Korean summit meeting, and more generally an engagement approach; despite this repositioning, the party's regular vilification by the North Korean media suggested that relations would deteriorate at least temporarily if, as appeared quite probable, the GNP were to regain power in 2008, after a decade in opposition.) North Korea in turn boycotted planned joint Liberation Day celebrations in Busan in August, in protest against routine US-South Korean military exercises, code-named Ulchi Focus Lens. In the same month a brief exchange of fire took place across the DMZ, the first in over a year.

Meanwhile, supplies of both rice and oil were resumed. With the BDA affair resolved, at the end of June 2007 South Korea dispatched an initial consignment of 400,000 metric tons of rice. Under the six-party accord, in slightly premature recognition of the closure of Yongbyon, 50,000 tons of heavy fuel oil followed in July. Even the long-delayed scheme to exchange light industry materials for mining rights, first mooted in 2005, commenced: in July 2007 South Korea sent a first batch of 500 tons of polyester fibre, while South Korean geologists began a fortnight's inspection of three zinc and magnesite mines, among East Asia's largest. South Korea was keen to secure a presence in the North's extensive minerals sector, not least out of alarm that many mines had reportedly been already taken by Chinese firms.

THE NORTH-SOUTH SUMMIT OF 2007

Far larger joint economic ventures, such as the restoration of infrastructure and factories, were being canvassed in Seoul after the announcement that President Roh Moo-Hyun would visit Pyongyang in late August 2007 for a summit meeting with Kim Jong Il. Months of rumours, staunchly denied by the South Korean Government, thus proved to be true. The GNP denounced this as a ploy to influence the forthcoming elections, while unofficial speculation in Washington, Tokyo and elsewhere arose that Roh, an increasingly ineffectual President approaching the end of his term, might make too many concessions to Kim and thus risk delaying North Korea's further denuclearization. Kim Jong Il's lack of reciprocity was also criticized, as by rights it was his turn to travel to Seoul. The onset of severe flooding in North Korea in mid-August, which led to some 600 fatalities, resulted in the postponement of the inter-Korean summit meeting to October.

In the event the summit appeared successful. Roh drove rather than flew to Pyongyang, alighting at the border, in a symbolic gesture, to cross the DMZ on foot. Once arrived, he comported himself with dignity, astutely declining an invitation by Kim Jong Il to stay an extra day. Their eventual eight-point agreement, by no means one-sided, included practical measures for co-operation on both business and security issues.

For a brief period it thus seemed that inter-Korean relations would make a substantial advance. The summit's most striking proposal was to create a peace zone centred on the port city of Haeju in south-western North Korea. This would resolve a long-standing marine border dispute by creating a joint fishing zone, as well as facilitate co-operation in other areas, such as dredging sand for construction in the Han river estuary, which forms the bilateral border. Both Koreas agreed to upgrade their existing ECPC to a Commission at deputy premier level. This body duly met in Seoul in December 2007 to discuss details of new and expanded co-operation. Overall North-South relations were henceforth to be handled by the two heads of government, who were to meet in late 2008 in Seoul. (This was reminiscent of the early 1990s when the two sides' premiers met regularly, alternating between each capital.)

The North at last consented to let reconnected railways be used by cross-border freight trains, if only as far as the Kaesong Industrial Zone. More ambitiously, it was agreed to discuss repair of the Kaesong–Pyongyang highway, and of the railway all the way to Sinuiju on the Chinese border, 'for joint use'. It was specifically agreed that in mid-2008 a combined supporters' squad was to take the first train in more than 50 years to travel from Seoul to Beijing, to cheer on both Koreas in that year's Olympic Games.

In November 2007 Kim Yong Il visited Seoul as agreed, travelling on from an equally business-orientated visit to Indo-China and Malaysia. This was the first meeting of the two Koreas' premiers for 15 years. He and his South Korean counterpart, Prime Minister Han Duck-Soo, who had assumed office in April and who, like Kim, was an experienced technocrat, signed an agreement that was unprecedented in its detail.

This amplified October's summit accord, with 2,500 words, eight chapters, 45 clauses, and (crucially) more than 20 deadlines for specialized working groups to meet again on specific aspects. The result was a brief but intense phase of the 'sunshine' policy, and the densest interaction hitherto witnessed between the two Korean states. With numerous new committees working on specific areas of co-operation, hardly a day passed in December without an inter-Korean meeting somewhere. Specific areas of focus included joint shipbuilding, roads, railways, agriculture (especially seeds), reafforestation, fisheries, mining, public health, pharmaceuticals, environmental protection and weather-forecasting.

As agreed, a daily cross-border rail freight service began in December 2007, although this was largely symbolic: not even reaching Kaesong, and with trains so often empty that in January 2008 the service was reduced at the North's suggestion. Roads were busier, the more so from early December when Hyundai Asan, which to the chagrin of competitors continued to monopolize South Korean tourism to the North and, despite occasional differences with the authorities in Pyongyang, began day trips by coach from Seoul to the ancient capital city of Kaesong. This was a remarkable development: allowing well-fed, prosperous South Koreans to see (but not meet) lean, shabby North Koreans, and to reflect upon their respective situations.

A meeting of defence ministers (only the second ever held, and the first since 2000), convened in Pyongyang at the end of November 2007 to discuss the proposed Haeju peace zone, stalled on the NLL issue, the very problem that the zone was intended to solve; and a subsequent generals' meeting at Panmunjom in mid-December could not revive this. The North insisted that the joint fishing area be wholly south of the NLL, but the South suggested that it comprise an equal area on each side. Nevertheless, this did not impede progress elsewhere. A seven-point accord included security guarantees for cross-border economic projects, while a new joint military committee, to be headed by deputy defence ministers, would look at ways to reduce tensions. Defence ministers' talks were to be institutionalized, with another session to be held in 2008. Meanwhile, in late November 2007 Kim Yang Gon, the North's chief of intelligence, in his capacity as head of the KWP's Democratic Front for the Reunification of the Fatherland, visited the South, where he toured a range of economic facilities; in past decades his South Korean counterparts would have regarded it as their mission to prevent him from scrutinizing such facilities. In January 2008 the South reported that inter-Korean trade in 2007 had reached US $1,790m., an increase of one-third in comparison with the total for 2006, and with South Korea overtaking China as the North's main export market.

THE END OF THE 'SUNSHINE' ERA

On 19 December 2007 South Korean voters elected by a large majority Lee Myung-Bak of the conservative GNP as their next President. While the election issues were largely domestic, Lee (a former chief executive officer of Hyundai and ex-mayor of Seoul) stated that he would review the new agreements signed by Roh, and would link any fresh inter-Korean co-operation to the North's compliance on nuclear issues. Although President Lee did not take office until 25 February, by the beginning of 2008 the number of inter-Korean meetings was decreasing abruptly. Another omen was the incoming South Korean President's attempt to abolish the Ministry of Unification, as part of an initiative to reduce the number of government departments. This failed, owing to resistance by the outgoing centre-left ruling party, which controlled the National Assembly until the GNP won a narrow majority in separate parliamentary elections held on 9 April.

None the less, for more than three months North Korea, which in the past had regularly excoriated the GNP as a party of traitors and flunkeys, was unexpectedly silent with regard to Lee Myung-Bak. Nor did North Korea submit its customary request at this season, normally granted, for fertilizer. In late March 2008 11 South Korean officials (but not managers or engineers) were expelled from the Kaesong Industrial Complex (KIC—a joint development within the Kaesong Industrial Zone). The KPA accused Southern warships of violating Northern waters in the Yellow Sea; it also test-fired several short-range sea-to-sea missiles off the port of Nampo, having first warned shipping in the area. North Korea threatened that, if the South made a pre-emptive strike on its nuclear facilities, it would 'not merely plunge everything (in the South) into flames but reduce it to ashes'.

The trend was clear, and at the beginning of April 2008 the North launched a tirade of criticism of Lee. A long article in Rodong Sinmun described the South Korean President as 'a vicious political charlatan and impostor' and pro-US sycophant, for subordinating inter-Korean ties to wider diplomacy and linking co-operation to denuclearization. This outburst was the first of many such diatribes, which continued on an almost daily basis throughout mid-2008. South Korea asked the North to desist, and refrained from responding in kind. All official dialogue came to a halt, but business and private contacts continued.

Critics in Seoul feared a loss of the progress made during a decade of the 'sunshine' policy. President Lee himself was thought to be reconsidering the situation, after his domestic popularity declined dramatically from April 2008 during two months of street protests against his removal of a ban on beef imports from the USA. In July, in what was seen as a concessionary gesture, he urged that all inter-Korean accords be honoured. However, this was overshadowed by the fatal shooting by a North Korean soldier of a South Korean tourist at Mount Kumgang, after the woman apparently strayed into a military area. This incident further worsened relations: South Korea suspended all tourism to Mount Kumgang, while the North refused Southern investigators entry to the zone. In early August the North threatened to expel 'unnecessary' South Koreans from the area, presumably a reference to those who staffed the tourist facilities. In August a brief encounter between the North's titular Head of State, Kim Yong Nam, and President Lee Myung-Bak, during the opening of the Olympic Games in Beijing, did little to remedy matters. With North Korea also restricting Southern movement across the DMZ to the Kaesong industrial zone, there were fears that the dispute might extend to affect this also, with no signs of an early revival of the 'sunshine' policy. Ironically, a policy shift that the new South Korean administration intended to improve relations with the USA threatened to rebound: a North–South confrontation was unhelpful while President George W. Bush was seeking to conclude a nuclear accord with Kim Jong Il; and progress in that area might enable the North to reject any overtures from the South while gaining rewards from the USA, China and other parties.

Relations deteriorated further in late 2008 and 2009. In the first official inter-Korean meeting of Lee Myung-Bak's presidency, military discussions were held at the beginning of October 2008. It subsequently transpired that the North had requested the holding of these talks in order to demand that South Korean NGOs stop sending propaganda leaflets by balloon across the DMZ. The South Korean Government did ask those responsible for the leaflets to desist, but they robustly declined to do so.

Meanwhile, in July 2008 Won Jeong Hwa, an apparent defector from North Korea, was arrested on suspicion of being a secret agent; she was the first alleged North Korean spy to have been arrested in the South since 2006. Since arriving in Seoul in 2001, Won was alleged to have seduced at least four army officers, with one of whom she had a long-standing relationship, obtaining classified military information from the officers, including the location of strategic military installations and the personal details of South Korean military personnel, information that she was accused of subsequently relaying to the North Korean authorities. She was also accused of plotting to assassinate South Korean intelligence agents with poisoned needles. At an initial hearing in September, Won pleaded guilty to the charges against her and in October she was convicted on all counts and sentenced to five years' imprisonment. South Korean conservatives claimed that under the past 'sunshine' policy the National Intelligence Service had been instructed not to pursue the North's espionage and other malefactions, thus jeopardizing national security. In December the North announced that it had captured a

South Korean spy and would-be assassin of Kim Jong Il; the South Korean authorities firmly denied the accusation.

Visiting Russia in late September 2008, President Lee Myung-Bak signed an agreement with Russian President Dmitrii Medvedev to link the inter-Korean and trans-Siberian railways, and to build a gas pipeline between Russia and South Korea. Neither party saw fit to consult North Korea, without whose compliance neither project was feasible. Plans being made by others purportedly on behalf of North Korea were unlikely to be well received in Pyongyang.

From the latter part of 2008 North Korea increasingly threatened to impede the development of the KIC. At a second round of military talks in late October, the North warned that the KIC might be suspended if the delivery of hostile leaflets by South Korean NGOs continued. In early November the KIC received an unprecedented and unannounced KPA inspection, led by Gen. Kim Yong Chol, the North's chief delegate to inter-Korean military talks and policy chief of the NDC. The uniformed KPA team was reported to have asked several Southern firms how long it would take them to vacate their premises within the KIC. Meanwhile, North Korea's Red Cross announced that it was to close its liaison office in Panmunjom and cut off telephone lines to the South.

In mid-November 2008 Gen. Kim Yong Chol stated that from 1 December trans-DMZ trains would be 'disallowed'; tourist visits to Kaesong city would be 'totally suspended'; South Korean staff would be 'selectively expelled' from both the Kaesong and Kumgang zones; and border opening would be subject to 'more strict order and discipline'. The threatened measures were duly enforced, amid protests that the halving of the number of South Koreans permitted to remain at the two zones would impair business operations at the KIC.

Meanwhile, a record 2,809 North Korean defectors reached the South in 2008, 10% more than in 2007, although this rate of increase was far smaller than the 26% and 46% rises recorded in 2007 and 2006, respectively. The declining rate was attributed to more stringent Chinese border controls. (Very few defectors crossed the heavily armed DMZ directly; almost all made the long and hazardous journey across China to seek asylum at South Korean embassies in South-East Asia.)

In January 2009 a spokesman of the KPA General Staff appeared on television in full uniform, declaring that 'a war... can neither be averted nor avoided' and threatening 'the puppet military warhawks' with 'a strong military retaliatory step to wipe them out'. Such rhetoric became increasingly common. The more positive tone of Kim Jong Il's condolences in May following the suicide of former South Korean President Roh Moo-Hyun amid corruption allegations (see the chapter on the Republic of Korea) was cancelled out not only by the North's nuclear test on the same day, but also by North Korean accusations in early June that Lee Myung-Bak had murdered his predecessor.

Another target of North Korean wrath was Hyun In-Taek, an uncompromising academic who as an adviser had helped to formulate Lee Myung-Bak's policy approach to the North. In mid-January 2009 Hyun was appointed Minister of Unification in place of Kim Ha-Joong, a career diplomat reportedly perceived to be too lenient. In late January North Korea's Committee for the Peaceful Reunification of the Fatherland declared all past inter-Korean agreements 'nullified'. Specific mention of the Yellow Sea border caused unease in Seoul. Despite and during these tensions, South Korea's deputy envoy for nuclear issues spent five days in North Korea in mid-January, to discuss the possible purchase of the North's 14,800 unused nuclear fuel rods; however, no agreement was reached.

Rumours relating to Choe Sung Chol in 2009 highlighted the repercussions of failure in the North. As Vice-Chairman of North Korea's Asia-Pacific Peace Committee, Choe had hosted Roh Moo-Hyun during the then South Korean President's visit to Pyongyang in October 2007. However, as inter-Korean relations deteriorated, Choe was reported to have been dismissed in January 2009. By April he was said to be undergoing 'severe revolutionary training' at a chicken farm, and in May it was claimed that he had been executed. None of this was confirmed.

Harassment of the KIC continued into 2009. As a protest against the routine annual US-South Korean military exercises in March, the North three times shut the border without warning, stranding hundreds of South Koreans in Kaesong. At the end of March the North Korean authorities arrested Yu Song-Jin, a Hyundai Asan engineer at the KIC, accusing him of criticizing the regime and of urging a Northern female worker to defect.

Meanwhile, in May 2009 North Korea unilaterally declared 'null and void the rules and contracts on land rent, wages and all sorts of taxes' at the KIC. Insisting that the South accept the changes unconditionally, the North added that 'we do not care about them leaving'. A representative of the 106 mostly small South Korean firms operating in the KIC warned a few days later that they risked bankruptcy, as their orders declined amid mounting tension. In mid-June the two sides met and North Korea announced its new terms, demanding a four-fold increase in monthly wages, to US $300, for its workers in the KIC, plus a 30-fold increase in the 50-year land lease fee from $16m. to $500m. At a subsequent meeting in the same month, the North unexpectedly offered to remove the curbs that it had imposed with effect from December 2008 on cross-border traffic and on the number of South Koreans permitted to stay at the KIC.

Opinion in Seoul differed as to whether North Korea was driving a hard bargain or was genuinely prepared to sacrifice the KIC and revenues from its South Korean firms. In June 2009 a South Korean leather goods manufacturer became the first of the companies operating in the KIC (which together employed more than 40,000 North Korean workers) to quit the complex. Meanwhile, South Korea's response to the North's nuclear test in May was to forbid its citizens to visit North Korea, with the exception of travel to the KIC, thus undermining more than 600 Southern firms operating within the North (mostly as traders) outside the KIC. At a time when cross-Straits relations between mainland China and Taiwan, already pragmatic and buoyant in the area of business, were growing ever closer, the reverse process between the two Koreas was all the more disappointing.

Relations appeared to improve in August 2009, when a meeting between Kim Jong Il and the chairperson of the Hyundai group, Hyun Jeong-Eun, resulted in the announcement by North Korea that it would reopen the border and permit tourism and family reunions to resume, as well as release Yu Song-Jin. The engineer was duly released later that month, and the first family reunions since 2007 took place in September, at the Mount Kumgang resort. However, the North continued to refuse entry to representatives of the South seeking to investigate the fatal shooting of a South Korean tourist in July 2008 (see above).

Following the death of former President Kim Dae-Jung in August 2009, South Korea allowed two senior North Korean emissaries, KWP secretary Kim Ki Nam and chief of intelligence Kim Yang Gon, to fly to Seoul later that month in order to offer their condolences. The two officials met with Hyun In-Taek and President Lee, whom the North's media promptly stopped lambasting as a traitor; in Seoul the Office of the President (known as the Blue House) spoke of a 'paradigm shift'. In early September, however, six South Korean campers drowned after water was discharged from a dam on the Imjin river; North Korea admitted to having done this, but claimed that it had had no time to warn the authorities in Seoul; however, Hyun In-Taek contended that the action had been committed knowingly. Although the first family reunions for two years took place at the end of September (see above), the two sides subsequently disagreed on the terms under which such encounters were to continue, and the reunions were again suspended. Meanwhile, in mid-September North Korea suddenly moderated its wage demands at the KIC.

In November 2009, in the first inter-Korean naval skirmish for seven years, a North Korean patrol boat crossed the NLL and responded to South Korean warning shots with live fire. The South retaliated with several volleys of live rounds, setting the vessel ablaze and forcing it to retreat; one North Korean was reported to have been killed and a further three were injured. Rodong Sinmun claimed that the exchange of gunfire 'was not some simple, accidental incident but a deliberate, planned provocation by the South Korean military' intended to escalate bilateral tensions. Nevertheless, in December South

Korea swiftly sent medical aid when the North confirmed an outbreak of the H1N1 virus ('swine flu'), although President Lee still refused to resume aid on the scale of that provided during the 'sunshine' era. In the same month secret discussions were held in Singapore with regard to a potential summit meeting, but the two sides could not reach consensus on the agenda.

INCREASING AGGRESSION

On 1 January 2010 North Korea's regular New Year joint editorial in the three main daily newspapers struck a more placatory tone, appealing for 'national reconciliation and co-operation'. However, such rhetoric was not matched by the conduct of the North, which renewed its demands for significant wage increases at the KIC and fired volleys of artillery shells into the Yellow Sea in January and February. Discussions regarding the Kaesong and Kumgang projects continued sporadically.

A defining event in North-South relations was the sinking in March 2010 of the *Cheonan* following an explosion aboard the South Korean navy vessel. Of the 104 crew members on board, 46 were killed. The incident took place off the coast of the north-westernmost South Korean island of Baengnyeong, in waters disputed by the North. South Korea initially responded with caution, fearful of a wider conflict and of alarming investors. However, a joint investigation group (JIG) of experts, comprising military personnel as well as civilians, Koreans together with international representatives, was formed in order to examine the circumstances surrounding the incident. In the following weeks, information 'leaked' from the group suggested that the explosion had been caused by a KPA torpedo fired from a submarine. The JIG's final summary report, published in May, did indeed reach this conclusion, insisting that there could be no other possible explanation. (Alternative hypotheses had included routine wear and tear, a collision with a reef or an old mine, and 'friendly fire'.) The North denied any culpability.

South Korea responded to the findings of the JIG reports by adopting a firm stance, threatening military retaliation and the resumption of propaganda broadcasts across the DMZ, were such an attack to be repeated, as well as introducing a ban on North-South trade. However, the KIC, which accounted for more than one-half of all inter-Korean commerce, was exempted from the trade ban, continuing to operate normally throughout the crisis, despite North Korean threats to close the border and sever all links. The North maintained that it had had no involvement in the sinking of the *Cheonan*, and was supported in its claims by Russia and China, both of which queried the JIG's findings, as did one-quarter of South Koreans, prompting angry debates in Seoul and elsewhere.

No such ambiguity surrounded an attack on the South later in 2010. Without warning on 23 November North Korean coastal artillery batteries fired more than 150 artillery shells and rockets on Yeonpyeong, one of five South Korean-occupied islands in the Yellow Sea close to the North Korean mainland. A military base was targeted, but the majority of the areas damaged in the attack were civilian sites. Two marines and two civilians were killed and 18 others were injured, with severe fire damage to property, as well as to tree cover. South Korea returned artillery fire as best it could, but did not otherwise retaliate. Many of the island's 1,700 civilian inhabitants were evacuated during the days that followed.

Unlike its response to the sinking of the *Cheonan*, North Korea did not deny responsibility for the shelling of Yeonpyeong, but claimed that it had been merely responding to provocation in the form of artillery shells fired into its waters by the South during joint naval exercises with the USA. By any standards this pretext was specious, although notably the Chinese press reproduced it uncritically. The South Korean-US 'Hoguk' manoeuvres continued to be held annually, and the South's artillery fire was in waters to the south-west of Yeonpyeong—a considerable distance from North Korean territory. The North did not even claim that any of its ships were a target or in the vicinity, merely that these coastal waters were somehow its own. In a communiqué published by the official news agency, the KPA leadership stated unequivocally: 'There is in the West Sea of Korea only the maritime military demarcation line set by the DPRK.'

The attack on Yeonpyeong, which was the first shelling of South Korean territory since the 1953 armistice, appeared to have been a dramatic and deliberate escalation by North Korea, and, as with the sinking of the *Cheonan*, prompted accusations of weakness against the administration of President Lee for its perceived failure properly to address the issue of Northern aggression. The resignation of South Korean Minister of National Defence, Kim Tae-Young, initially submitted in May 2010, was abruptly accepted on 25 November; he was subsequently replaced by Kim Kwan-Jin. South Korea promptly banned its citizens from travelling to North Korea, suspended further deliveries of flood aid that had been agreed upon in August (when relations had briefly seemed to be improving) and broke off discussions with the North over family reunions and the resumption of tourism. The entry ban at first included the KIC, but protests from South Korean firms operating therein soon led to a gradual easing of the restriction. (In April 2010 the North had declared that it would freeze South Korean property at the zone—reported to be collectively worth some US $300m.; as of mid-2011 this dispute was still ongoing; despite threats, North Korea had not yet acted to dispose irrevocably of the South Korean assets that it had seized.)

The shelling of Yeonpyeong also prompted much speculation as to Kim Jong Il's motives, and the balance between domestic and external goals. Possible motivations included a wish to elevate the prestige of Kim's third son and appointed successor, Kim Jong Un, among a military that remained sceptical of the untested youth, who, despite possessing no known military experience, was promoted to the rank of a four-star general in September 2010. Kim Jong Un and the 'Dear Leader' were both reported by some sources to have been in the vicinity at the time of the shelling.

Inter-Korean relations were typically variable during the first half of 2011. In early January the North declared itself 'ready to meet anyone, anytime, and anywhere'; the South demanded that the North first admit responsibility, and apologize, for the two attacks in 2010. In February 2011 the two sides held the first bilateral cross-border talks since the shelling of Yeonpyeong, at the border town of Panmunjom; however, the North Korean delegation walked out on the second day owing to 'differences over the agenda for high-level talks', according to the South Korean Ministry of National Defence. A dispute emerged in early February when 31 North Koreans drifted into Southern waters near Yeonpyeong in a fishing vessel. Following lengthy questioning by the South Korean authorities, the group was released in the following month; most elected to return home, which they were allowed to do at the end of March, but four defected to the South, to the fury of the North. Meanwhile, a massive earthquake and tsunami that caused huge devastation in north-eastern Japan (q.v.) in mid-March prompted North Korea's earthquake bureau to propose joint research with South Korea on volcanic activity at Mount Paektu. Talks were held, but no substantive results were announced.

In late April 2011 Jimmy Carter visited Pyongyang, as part of The Elders, an independent group of global leaders established by former South African President Nelson Mandela to support international peace-building. Also there as part of the delegation were Ireland's former President Mary Robinson, former Norwegian Prime Minister Gro Harlem Brundtland and former Finnish President Martti Ahtisaari, the 2008 Nobel Peace Prize laureate. The group pressed for a resumption of dialogue on the Korean peninsula, but it was not granted a meeting with either Kim Jong Il or Lee Myung-Bak. At the end of the three-day visit, Carter angered many in Seoul by describing the refusal by South Korea and the USA to give food aid to North Korea as a human right violation. He also stated that officials in Pyongyang had pronounced themselves ready for dialogue, a message of which the South was outwardly dismissive.

In reality, the two Koreas were about to hold secret talks in Beijing, in May 2011, aimed at opening the way for a fresh bilateral summit meeting. With the intention of embarrassing the Lee administration, North Korea publicly revealed this fact in early June, claiming that the South had 'begged' for talks and tried to bribe it to attend, and adding that it was no longer prepared to have dealings with 'the Lee Myung-Bak group of traitors'. However, at the Association of Southeast Asian Nations (ASEAN) Regional Forum, held in mid-July on the Indonesian island of Bali, Wi Sung-Lac and Vice-Marshal Ri Yong Ho, the respective chief nuclear negotiators of both Koreas, unexpectedly held a two-hour meeting, during which they agreed to make joint efforts to resume the six-party talks as soon as possible. Both sides described the talks as serious and constructive. Given North Korea's usual refusal to discuss the nuclear issue bilaterally with the South, this was an unexpected development. On the following day the two Koreas' respective ministers responsible for foreign affairs also met, briefly, and their discussions were reported to have been cordial.

PROSPECTS FOR A RETURN TO ENGAGEMENT

It is hard to detect progress or even any pattern in inter-Korean relations over the years. Hopes that the 'sunshine' era marked an irreversible movement towards détente were severely set back by the election of President Lee Myung-Bak in December 2007, and were definitively ended by the two North Korean attacks on the South in 2010. At mid-2011 it might appear that the two Koreas are as hostile now as they ever were; however, the underlying situation has changed enormously since 1945, and even in the last 20 years, in ways that afford some cautious predictions. By any standards, South Korea has won the inter-Korean contest. North Korea has at its disposal only its military might and its mineral endowment, and hopes that it will curb the former and develop the latter have so far been in vain. The North Korean economy is in ruins, while politically the task of establishing Kim Jong Un as successor to his father is a very delicate one, with no guarantee of success. This ongoing state of transition is likely to render North Korea even more unpredictable in the coming years.

The events chronicled in this essay can bear more than one interpretation. Critics of the 'sunshine' policy cite North Korea's grudging, erratic and often curmudgeonly behaviour, above all, its development of nuclear capabilities during this very period, as proof that the Kim regime has not changed its stance but remains implacably hostile towards South Korea, which therefore, they argue, would be naive to lower its guard. Conversely, supporters of engagement with the North note that the West German policy for the normalization of relations with East Germany (Ostpolitik) was equally contentious at the outset, but prepared the way for an astonishingly peaceful reunification, wholly without bloodshed, two decades later.

In this insoluble debate as to what works best with North Korea, it should be noted that, while the 'sunshine' policy may have been one-sided, Lee Myung-Bak's uncompromsing approach has surely made matters worse. Even if the governing GNP retains power after legislative elections due in 2012, South Korea's next leader will almost certainly revert to engagement on some level. This will be no easier a task than previously, but it may well make the peninsula safer in the short term.

The longer term is harder to predict. South Koreans tend to assume, abstractly, that reunification with the North in some form is both inevitable and desirable. Both assumptions are questionable. One result of Lee Myung-Bak's rejection of the 'sunshine' policy has been to create a political and economic vacuum in the North, which China has hastened to occupy, appearing to have taken a strategic decision to support North Korea unconditionally. While anathema to Kim Jong Il, the surest way for the Kim dynasty to survive will be as a client state of China: the record of German unification suggests that this would be a much safer option than to rely on the tender mercies of a vengeful South. In that case Korea may remain divided for at least another generation, with relations between North and South experiencing as many convolutions as ever. That is a depressing prospect. The young Colonels Rusk and Bonesteel could never have imagined, as they hastily drew their 'temporary' line across the map of an obscure peninsula in North-East Asia, how lasting and devastating an effect their action would prove to have.

BIBLIOGRAPHY

Armstrong, Charles K. *The Koreas.* New York, Routledge, 2007.

Bleiker, Roland. *Divided Korea: Toward a Culture of Reconciliation.* Minneapolis, MN, University of Minnesota Press, 2005.

Bluth, Christoph. *Korea (Hot Spots in Global Politics).* Cambridge, Polity Press, 2008.

Center for U.S.-Korea Policy. *North Korea Contingency Planning and U.S.-ROK Cooperation.* Washington, DC, The Asia Foundation, 2009.

Cha, Victor, and Kang, David. *Nuclear North Korea: A Debate on Engagement Strategies.* New York, Columbia University Press, 2003.

Cha, Victor, and Kang, David. *Approaching Korean Unification: What We Learn from Other Cases.* Washington, DC, Center for Strategic and International Studies (CSIS), 2010.

Clough, Ralph N. *Embattled Korea: The Rivalry for International Support.* Boulder, CO, Westview Press, 1987.

Cumings, Bruce. *Korea's Place in the Sun: A Modern History.* New York, W. W. Norton, Revised edn, 2005.

The Korean War: A History. New York, Modern Library, 2010.

Dong, Wonmo. *The Two Koreas and the United States: Issues of Peace, Security, and Economic Cooperation.* Armonk, NY, M. E. Sharpe, 2000.

Dudley, William (Ed.). *North and South Korea: Opposing Viewpoints.* Farmington Hills, MI, Greenhaven Press, 2003.

Eberstadt, Nicholas. *Korea Approaches Reunification.* Armonk, NY, M. E. Sharpe, 1995.

Policy and Economic Performance in Divided Korea during the Cold War Era: 1945–91. Washington, DC, American Enterprise Institute Press, 2010.

Eberstadt, Nicholas, Lee Young-sun and Ahn Choon-yong (Eds). *A New International Engagement Framework for North Korea? Contending Perspectives.* Washington, DC, Korea Economic Institute, 2004.

Feffer, John. *North Korea / South Korea: U.S. Policy at a Time of Crisis.* New York, Seven Stories Press, 2003.

Flake, L. Gordon, and Snyder, Scott A. *Paved with Good Intentions: The NGO Experience in North Korea.* Westport, CT, Praeger, 2003.

Foley, James A. *Korea's Divided Families: Fifty Years of Separation.* London, RoutledgeCurzon, 2003.

Foster-Carter, Aidan. 'Standing Up: The Two Korean States and the Dependency Debate—A Bipartisan Approach', in Kim Kyong-dong (Ed.), *Dependency Issues in Korean Development.* Seoul, Seoul National University Press, 1987.

'Inter-Korean Relations'. Chapter 8 in Koh Byung Chul (Ed.), *North Korea and the World: Explaining Pyongyang's Foreign Policy.* Seoul, Kyungnam University Press for Institute for Far Eastern Studies, 2004.

'Scrapping the Second Summit: Lee Myung Bak's Fateful Mis-step.' 20 January 2011, http://38north.org/2011/01/lee-myung-bak-fateful-misstep/.

Frank, Rüdiger and Burghart, Sabine (Eds). *Driving Forces of Socialist Transformation: North Korea and the Experience of Europe and East Asia.* Vienna, Praesens, 2009.

Glaser, Bonnie, Snyder, Scott, and Park, John S., *Keeping an Eye on an Unruly Neighbor: Chinese Views of Economic Reform and Stability in North Korea.* Washington, DC, Center for Strategic and International Studies (CSIS) and United States Institute of Peace (USIP), 2008.

Grinker, Roy Richard. *Korea and Its Futures: Unification and the Unfinished War.* London, Macmillan, 2000.

Haggard, Stephan, and Noland, Marcus. *Witness to Transformation: Refugee Insights into North Korea.* Washington, DC, Peterson Institute for International Economics, 2011.

Harrison, Selig S. *Korean Endgame: A Strategy for Reunification and U.S. Disengagement.* Princeton, NJ, Princeton University Press, 2003.

Henriksen, Thomas H., and Lho, Kyongsoo (Eds). *One Korea?: Challenges and Prospects for Reunification.* Stanford, CA, Hoover Institution Press, 1994.

Hoare, James, and Pares, Susan. *Conflict in Korea: An Encyclopedia.* Santa Barbara, CA, ABC-CLIO, 1999.

Hwang, Eui-Gak. *The Korean Economies: A Comparison of North and South.* Oxford and New York, Oxford University Press, 1993.

International Institute for Strategic Studies, *North Korean Security Challenges: A Net Assessment.* London, International Institute for Strategic Studies, 2011, Chapter 9, 'Korean Reunification: Conditions, Dynamics and Challenges'.

Jonsson, Gabriel. *Towards Korean Reconciliation: Socio-cultural Exchanges and Cooperation.* Aldershot, Ashgate, 2006.

Jonsson, Gabriel, and Soffronow, Katharina (Eds). *Korea: A Stocktaking.* Stockholm University, Center for Pacific Asia Studies, 2000.

Kang, Man-gil. *A History of Contemporary Korea.* Folkestone, Global Oriental, 2005.

Kihl, Young Whan (Ed.). *Korea and the World: Beyond the Cold War.* Boulder, CO, Westwood Press, 1994.

Kim, Dae Hwan and Kong, Tat Yan (Eds). *The Korean Peninsula in Transition.* London, Macmillan, 1996.

Kim, Dong-choon. *The Unending Korean War: A Social History.* Larkspur, CA, Tamal Vista Publications, 2009.

Kim, Ilpyong J. *Two Koreas in Transition: Implications for U.S. Policy.* Rockville, ND, In Depth Books, 1998.

Kim, Samuel S. (Ed.). *Inter-Korean Relations: Problems and Prospects.* New York, Palgrave Macmillan, 2004.

Kim, Samuel S. *The Two Koreas and the Great Powers.* New York, Cambridge University Press, 2006.

Kim, Sun Joo (Ed.). *The Northern Region of Korea: History, Identity, and Culture.* Seattle, WA, University of Washington Press, 2010.

Lee, Chae-Jin. *A Troubled Peace: U.S. Policy and the Two Koreas.* Baltimore, MD, Johns Hopkins University Press, 2006.

Lee Si-woo. *Life on the Edge of the DMZ.* Folkestone, Global Oriental, 2008.

Levin, Norman D., and Han, Yong-Sup. *Sunshine in Korea: The South Korean Debate over Policies Toward North Korea.* Santa Monica, CA, Rand Corporation, 2002.

Lim, Eul-chul. *Kaesong Industrial Complex: History, Pending Issues, and Outlook.* Seoul, Haenam, 2007.

Lynn, Hyung Gu. *Bipolar orders: the two Koreas since 1989.* London, Zed Books, 2007.

McCormack, Gavan, and Selden, Mark. *Korea North and South: the Deepening Crisis.* New York, Monthly Review Press, 1978.

McCormack, Gavan, with Lone, Stewart. *Korea Since 1850.* New York, St Martin's Press, 1993.

McEachern, Patrick. *Inside the Red Box: North Korea's Post-Totalitarian Politics.* New York, Columbia University Press, 2010.

Michishita, Narushige. *North Korea's Military-Diplomatic Campaigns, 1966–2008.* Abingdon, Routledge, 2010.

Noland, Marcus (Ed.). *Economic Integration of the Korean Peninsula.* Washington, DC, Institute for International Economics, 1998.

Noland, Marcus. *Avoiding the Apocalypse: The Future of the Two Koreas.* Washington, DC, Institute for International Economics, 2000.

Oberdorfer, Don. *The Two Koreas: A Contemporary History.* New York, Basic Books, Revised edn, 2001.

Park, Kyung-Ae (Ed.). *New Challenges of North Korean Foreign Policy.* New York, Palgrave Macmillan, 2010.

Pollack, Jonathan D., and Lee, Chung Min. *Preparing for Korean Unification: Scenarios and Implications.* Santa Monica, CA, Rand, 1999.

Pollack, Jonathan D. (Ed.). *Korea: The East Asian Pivot.* Newport, RI, Naval War College Press, 2006.

Rozman, Gilbert. *Strategic Thinking about the Korean Nuclear Crisis: Four Parties Caught between North Korea and the United States.* New York, Palgrave Macmillan, 2007.

Ryang, Sonia (Ed.). *North Korea: Toward a Better Understanding.* Lanham, MD, Lexington Books, 2009.

Sakong, Il, and Kim, Kwang Suk (Eds). *Policy Priorities for the Unified Korean Economy.* Seoul, Institute for Global Economics, 1998.

Seth, Michael J. *A History of Korea: From Antiquity to the Present.* Lanham, MD, Rowman & Littlefield, 2010.

Shin, Gi-Wook. *Ethnic Nationalism in Korea: Genealogy, Politics, and Legacy.* Stanford, CA, Stanford University Press, 2006.

Smith, Hazel (Ed.). *Reconstituting Korean Security: A Policy Primer.* Tokyo, United Nations University Press, 2007.

Snyder, Scott. *China's Rise and the Two Koreas: Politics, Economics, Security.* Boulder, CO, Lynne Rienner Publishers, 2009.

Son, Key-young. *South Korean Engagement Policies and North Korea: Identities, Norms and the Sunshine Policy.* Abingdon, Routledge, 2006.

Stares, Paul B., and Wit, Joel S. *Preparing for Sudden Change in North Korea.* New York, Council on Foreign Affairs, 2009.

Suh, Jae-Jean. *The Lee Myung-Bak Government's North Korea Policy: a study on its historical and theoretical foundation.* Seoul, Korea Institute for National Unification, 2009.

Yang, Sung Chul. *The North and South Korean Political Systems: A Comparative Analysis.* Seoul, Hollym, Revised edn, 2001.

THE USA'S RELATIONS WITH THE ASIA-PACIFIC REGION

MARK BEESON

The USA remains the most important power in the Asia-Pacific region, but it is no longer quite the power it once was. Less than a decade ago, there was much talk of a new era of 'unipolarity' in which the USA was set to bestride the entire globe in the way that Rome once dominated parts of Europe and North Africa. Now the focus is more frequently on the USA's budget deficits and its reliance on foreigners to fund them, than on possible imperial ambitions. Neither the long-term potential of the USA's economy nor the entrepreneurial energy of its people should be underestimated, but it is quite remarkable how expectations about the USA's position and potential have changed in such a short time. It is all the more remarkable that this should have happened during the Administration of Barack Obama (who took office in January 2009), a President about whom great hopes were held both inside and outside the USA.

Yet if the current Administration is to be put into perspective, previous events should be remembered. The Administration of George W. Bush (2001–09) was not only associated with the beginning of unpopular, bloody, ruinously expensive conflicts in Iraq and Afghanistan, but it was also one that was overwhelmingly unilateral in its approach to foreign policy. This style of diplomacy was most dramatically visible in the so-called 'war on terror', and it had implications for friends and foes across the world. What was most noteworthy about the incoming Obama Administration, by contrast, was a rhetorical commitment to multilateralism and an ostensible willingness to engage other nations in dialogue. It was an approach that promised to restore the standing and authority of the USA, which had been significantly undermined during the Bush era.

Unfortunately for Obama in particular and Americans more generally, the material circumstances that might have allowed the new Administration to fulfil the hopes of its supporters were simply absent. The economic crisis that confronted the incoming Obama Administration has continued to intensify, a problem that is exacerbated by the increasingly partisan and polarized nature of domestic politics. This is not simply a problem for disappointed supporters of the Obama Administration in the USA itself: countries across the world are having to come to terms with a diminished USA, nowhere more so than in the Asia-Pacific region, which continues to underwrite the USA's deficits while relying on that country's military to maintain regional stability. The USA is already having to make difficult and substantial reductions in defence spending, raising serious questions about its ability to continue playing its customary geopolitical role. This underlying—possibly unsustainable—confluence of economic and strategic imperatives provides the backdrop against which the USA's relations with the Asia-Pacific region are unfolding.

The following discussion focuses primarily on the East Asian part of the more encompassing Asia-Pacific region, because this is where some of the USA's most important relationships are to be found. A focus on East Asia is also justified because the region is assuming a greater coherence and identity, in part because of China's increasing importance. In addition to considering the USA's relationship with China and the evolving nature of regional institutions, bilateral relations with Japan, the Democratic People's Republic of Korea (DPRK—North Korea), the Republic of Korea (South Korea), South-East Asia and Australia are analysed. East Asia is a famously heterogeneous and unpredictable region, but whatever its future may hold, one thing is safe to predict: it will remain the most important focus of foreign policy concern for any US administration for the foreseeable future.

THE CONTEXT OF THE USA'S RELATIONSHIP WITH EAST ASIA

In order to understand the USA's contemporary relationship with countries like China and Japan, it is necessary to examine the USA's historical interaction with the region and the nature of US foreign policy. Not only is the USA uniquely powerful, but its own trajectory of history and development has been unlike that of other nations, giving a distinctive quality to its foreign policy and national identity. A sense of 'exceptionalism' and 'special providence' has permeated national life and given rise to the concept that the USA has a unique role to play in international affairs. While US foreign policy has undoubtedly had many positive effects, it has frequently led to misunderstandings and even outright conflict as a consequence of its expansionary dynamism and, at times, missionary zeal. Nowhere have these contradictory qualities been more evident than in the USA's dealings with East Asia.

The USA has been actively attempting to influence the course of events in East Asia since the 19th century. The forceful 'opening' of a hitherto insular Japan in the 1850s was the most dramatic and historically important example of this influence, and it confirmed the USA as a Pacific power. The USA's most significant experience as a colonial power occurred in South-East Asia, when it inherited the Philippines in the aftermath of the Spanish–American War of 1898. Likewise, the most dramatic and far-reaching direct impact of US military power in Asia was, of course, the Second World War (1939–45), which established the USA's position at the core of regional affairs. Two aspects of this process were especially important and merit emphasis, as they had long-term implications for the region, which continue to influence outcomes to this day.

First, in the aftermath of the Second World War, the USA occupied Japan and established a series of 'hub and spoke' security relationships across the region. The USA's centrality to the region was further reinforced by the rapid escalation of the mutual hostility between the USA and the USSR in what became known as the Cold War. This development further divided the East Asian region along ideological lines, and entrenched countries like Japan and South Korea even more firmly into the USA's strategic sphere of influence. For allies of the USA this was, paradoxically enough, a positive development. The second major consequence of the USA's heightened post-war involvement in East Asia was to give a dramatic impetus to economic development in, first, Japan, and subsequently in the other 'miracle' economies of North-East Asia.

Divisive as the USA's involvement in the wars in Korea and Viet Nam may have been, both conflicts provided a major boost to development in the region—among the USA's allies, at least. The remarkable economic transformation that has occurred in much of East Asia cannot be understood without taking into account the somewhat inadvertent beneficial impact that US aid and military spending had on the region. Ironically, support for Japan's economic reconstruction would ultimately prove to be all too successful and help to create a formidable economic competitor and the world's second largest economy within a very short period of time. However, for those Asian countries on the other side of the ideological divide the outlook was less encouraging: even those countries that were not affected by direct military intervention found their development constrained by Cold War tensions and by their marginalized position in the expanding international economy. Nowhere were the material benefits of a close alliance with the USA more obvious than in Japan.

JAPAN

Although it is currently China that attracts most attention in discussions of the USA's relations with East Asia, Japan remains of paramount importance to the USA. Not only has it been the USA's single most important strategic partner in the region, but until 2010 Japan was the world's second largest economy, and therefore a potentially major force in regional affairs. The most striking and remarkable aspect of Japan's foreign policy is that the country has never played a role in regional or international affairs that matches its undoubted underlying economic strength. The fact that Japan has recently lost second place in the global economic league tables to arch-rival China, and also, from March 2011, suffered a massive, earthquake-induced shock to its economy, makes any change in this situation even more unlikely. Much of the diffidence of Japanese policy-makers can be explained by the legacy of the Second World War. In part, this has been a result of the inability of generations of Japanese policy-makers to disregard the past; but it is also partly a consequence of Japan's continuing dependency on, and deference to, the USA.

It is frequently observed by the Japanese themselves that Japan is not a 'normal' country. Certainly, its strategic reliance on the USA is highly unusual, possibly unique. Yet this has not prevented Japan from benefiting economically from close bilateral links, and until the 1990s many observers considered that Japan would eventually surpass the USA economically. As a result of a long-term shift in the relative economic standing of the USA and Japan, the 1980s and 1990s were punctuated by seemingly interminable trade disputes between the two countries, as US policy-makers once again attempted to force Japan to open up its economy. Despite the stagnation that overwhelmed the Japanese economy from the late 1990s, many of the country's companies are still formidably competitive, and Japan remains a crucial source of capital and investment for the USA itself. Indeed, many commentators feel that the USA has much to learn from Japan's frequently mismanaged attempts to address its own economic crisis of the 1990s—problems that may yet be repeated in the USA itself. Concern about the threat of Japanese economic competition has largely dissipated, owing to the combined impact of the apparent decline of Japan itself, which has been badly affected by the global financial crisis, and because of the remarkable rise of China.

China's ascendance also helps to explain the strategic dynamic in relations between the USA and Japan. US attitudes towards China have been characterized by ambivalence at best, outright hostility at worst. As far as Japan is concerned, this has meant that US policy-makers have placed increasing pressure on the Japanese Government to play a more prominent role in the region's strategic framework. The consequences of expectations about 'burden sharing' have been most visibly manifest in the USA's continuing military presence in Japan. The US base in Okinawa is deeply unpopular with the local people, but remains a central component in the USA's overall East Asian military structure. The base has been controversial owing to a number of highly publicized incidents, including the rape of local females by US service personnel, and because it has been revealed that successive Japanese governments lied about the highly sensitive presence of nuclear weapons there.

Just how sensitive an issue the presence of US troops in Okinawa remains can be seen in the rise and rapid fall of Yukio Hatoyama, the Japanese Prime Minister who took office in September 2009 and resigned in June 2010. As leader of the Democratic Party of Japan (DPJ), Hatoyama had promised to adopt a more independent policy with regard to the USA, which would be symbolized by the relocation of the Futenma Marine Corps Air Base. Despite this commitment, he ultimately decided to abandon the effort, owing to US opposition and a significant increase in tension on the Korean peninsula. His successor as leader of the DPJ and Prime Minister, Naoto Kan, promised to restore the strategic relationship with the USA as the 'cornerstone' of Japan's security position. However, it needs to be borne in mind that, given the Liberal-Democratic Party's long dominance of Japanese politics, the DPJ is still something of an aberration. None the less, relations with the USA remain the major foreign policy priority, regardless of who is in power in Japan, and the strategic dimension of the relationship remains both critical and potentially divisive. This possibility was especially evident during the 'war on terror' (following the attacks on the USA in September 2001, for which the Islamist fundamentalist organization, al-Qa'ida, was believed to be responsible) and the pressure that was placed on Japan to participate.

In view of Japan's history and the widespread hostility towards militarism that now exists there, the USA's desire for allies to provide visible assistance in Iraq (after the removal of that country's Government by US-led forces in 2003) was bound to be controversial. Despite the inherent sensitivity of the subject and the exhaustive analysis that inevitably accompanies domestic debates about Japan's security stance, a significant shift in favour of greater international activism has occurred, a development that culminated in Japan sending troops to Iraq and agreeing to be part of the USA's still-controversial and unproven missile defence system. One of the main reasons for the successful realization of this change in policy was undoubtedly the role played by Prime Minister Junichiro Koizumi, who held office from 2001 until 2006. Koizumi made the reinforcing of the alliance with the USA a major priority of his administration, an aim facilitated by his own good personal relationship with President George W. Bush. Proposals to change Japan's pacifist Constitution (a product of the USA's wartime occupation) may have the rather ironic effect of consolidating this change.

None of Japan's subsequent Prime Ministers has enjoyed the authority and longevity of Koizumi, and this has made the formation of both domestic and foreign policies difficult. Appointed to replace Koizumi as Prime Minister in September 2006, Shinzo Abe promised to put in place such a new constitution within six years of taking office (although in the event he was obliged to resign after only 12 months). Abe was also quick to start implementing the missile defence system, an issue that was given added urgency by North Korea's testing of a nuclear device in October. Whatever the merits of such a system, the practical effect was to entrench Japan ever more closely in the alliance with the USA. As a further illustration of the way in which the USA's principal allies in the Asia-Pacific region were part of a wider network of strategic relationships, Japan signed a security agreement with Australia, the other 'anchor' of regional stability as far as the USA is concerned. Although both signatories made strenuous attempts to assure China that such a pact was not directed against it, the Chinese Government was predictably uneasy with this development and concerned at the prospect of being contained by a US-led alliance.

Despite the fact that by the end of 2010 Japan had had six different Prime Ministers within five years, the country's relationship with the USA remains profoundly important to both sides. Indeed, the Obama Administration has made a special effort to send positive signals to Japan about the continuing importance of the relationship: not only was Japan the first stop on the inaugural overseas tour by the Secretary of State, Hillary Clinton, in February 2009, but Prime Minister Taro Aso was the first foreign leader to meet President Obama in the White House in Washington, DC. Even more significantly, when Obama visited Japan in November 2009, he described himself as 'America's first Pacific President', emphasizing the importance of the region to the USA, and charming his hosts by bowing to the Japanese Emperor. Yet the Obama Administration's efforts to assuage Japan's insecurities cannot disguise the underlying reality that the region is changing remarkably rapidly, as is Japan's place within it. The principal source of Japan's importance and influence has been further undermined by the economic crisis; the dysfunctional nature of Japanese domestic politics exacerbates the decline in power by making the country an even less effective diplomatic force. The tsunami of March 2011, and the rather inept handling of its aftermath, appeared likely to leave Japan and its people preoccupied with domestic matters for some time. The contrast with China, its long-standing regional rival, could hardly be more striking—a reality that is increasingly reflected in the USA's foreign policy priorities in the region.

The history of animosity between Japan and China complicates intra- and inter-regional relations and creates difficulties for the Obama Administration. Some observers regard the continuing rivalry between Japan and China as an outcome that is broadly beneficial to the USA: as long as regional rivalry and tension exist, there is no possibility that East Asia will coalesce against US interests, and the USA will continue to play a decisive role. The one country that really has the potential to disrupt the status quo is China.

CHINA

If Japan is not a 'normal' country, then the People's Republic of China is a country like no other. It is not simply the scale of China that sets it apart, but the fact that it has played such a pivotal role at the centre of what is now regarded as East Asia for thousands of years. Even more so than Japan, China's relations with the USA have been influenced by history, especially the 100 years of humiliation it suffered as a result of European imperialism. The USA also played a part in forcing open China in the 19th century; but it played an even larger role in China's 20th century integration into the international system, although one that occurred at a distance via international institutions such as the World Trade Organization (WTO). In retrospect, China's reintegration into the world economy and the abandonment of socialism in all but name may prove to be one of the most important developments of the 20th century. A remarkable aspect of this transformation was that it occurred peacefully and voluntarily; it was consolidated by institutional reform, rather than by force of arms.

Although it is China's spectacular, historically unprecedented economic rise that captures most attention, equally important has been the regulatory revolution that has occurred alongside it. In order to qualify for admission to the WTO, for example, China was required to change aspects of its domestic Constitution. This was formal recognition of an even more profound underlying structural change in which China shifted from a centrally planned to a market-based economic system. The results of this transformation are clear and have provided a vital impression of legitimacy for the increasingly anachronistic and somewhat contradictory Chinese Communist Party. It should be emphasized that this represents a significant 'victory' for the USA: a hitherto substantial ideological opponent has effectively capitulated and joined the capitalist camp, eliminating a profoundly important source of formerly non-negotiable ideological tension. Moreover, this peaceful development has been of tangible benefit both to the Chinese Government and to US consumers. However, one of the great ironies of this apparent triumph for the USA is that it has helped to transform China into one of the world's most important and dynamic economic powers.

China's extraordinary economic expansion has had a major impact on the international economy generally and on the USA in particular. China has rapidly become the USA's largest trade partner and a source of cheap consumer goods. Although this has been a positive development for individual consumers and until recently for international inflation rates, its impact on the long-term position of the US economy is more complex and debatable. One important feature of the bilateral economic relationship has been China's massive trade surplus and its very rapid accumulation of foreign-exchange reserves. There is a major, increasingly acrimonious debate about the causes and consequences of China's accumulation of foreign reserves, with US policy-makers claiming that China is manipulating the value of its currency and keeping it 'artificially' low. Given the importance of the US market to the Chinese economy as a whole, there is some merit in this. However, the Chinese leadership is unwilling to do anything that is likely to cost jobs or undermine the economy more generally in a country where regime survival depends on continuing economic expansion. The global financial crisis that started in 2008 reduced the USA's trade deficit somewhat, but it remains a politically sensitive issue in both countries, and one that could become the focus of further tension if the economic downturn persists.

Thus far, China has obligingly recycled much of its trade surplus back to the USA; without China's willingness to purchase US Treasury bonds, interest rates in the USA would probably have been much higher. This underlying structural reality places limits on the influence that US policy-makers can exert on China, as the country's steadfast refusal to devalue its currency, despite increasingly urgent requests for action and pressure from the US Congress, demonstrates. In any case, many economic commentators believe that such a devaluation would do little to address underlying problems of competitiveness and fiscal profligacy on the part of the USA. Equally importantly, many US companies with large economic investments in, or trade links with, China would also be uneasy about the prospect of economic friction. In the economic sphere at least, there is clear evidence of an emerging shift in the relative balance of power between the USA and China, a development that will be confirmed when, as most expect, China becomes the world's largest economy at some point within the next couple of decades.

The possible implications of this change, and the evolving balance of power between the USA and China, became apparent as a consequence of the financial crisis that had its origins in the USA in 2008. Ironically, the willingness of China to lend to the USA had helped to inflate real estate prices and stock market 'bubbles'. More recently, however, Chinese investment has become less passive, and some of the USA's most important financial institutions were rescued by China's increasingly powerful sovereign wealth funds. Some of these investments subsequently went awry, and some in strategically sensitive resource industries were blocked, but there is little doubt that the crisis reflected the growing power of China's state-dominated form of capitalism and the relative decline of the USA's market-orientated model. Indeed, in a telling sign of the changing respective status of the USA and China, the Chinese Premier, Wen Jiabao, has become increasingly outspoken in his criticism of the USA's form of capitalism and the failings of its domestic economic policy. China's demands for the US dollar to become a less important part of the global economic system will, if they are heeded, mark a fundamentally important reconfiguration of the international order.

As far as the more conventional balance of power is concerned, the situation is even more complex. US foreign policy towards China has been characterized by a continuing tension between those who consider that China should be 'contained' and those who think that it should be engaged. This was especially true during the Administration of George W. Bush, when elements of both opinions were evident. Although China was initially seen as a 'strategic competitor', such uncompromising views gave way to a more co-operative approach in the aftermath of the events of 11 September 2001. Indeed, there was a noticeable moderation in the rhetoric concerning China, despite the continuation of the sort of human rights problems that had formerly attracted such criticism. Concerns about China's military potential remained uppermost in the minds of officials of the Bush Administration. As a consequence, Chinese attitudes toward the Obama Administration have been ambivalent at times: on the one hand China sent positive, conciliatory messages to the new President upon his inauguration in January 2009, but on the other it aggressively confronted what it regarded as US intrusion into its exclusive economic zone in the South China Sea. China's failure to criticize or influence the behaviour of its North Korean ally has also been a source of frustration for the USA and its allies in the region.

China is plainly still coming to terms with its own spectacular rise and the diplomatic expectations that others have of it as a consequence. However, one area in which China is beginning to assert itself is in the modernization of its armed forces, which has direct implications for the regional balance of power and for the USA's relationship with East Asia as a whole. When seen from the viewpoint of Beijing, of course, the desire to use China's improved economic position to strengthen its armed forces is entirely understandable. Even with increases in spending and modernization, China's military capacities are comparatively modest, but recent developments may have important consequences for the conventional balance of military power. China's construction of a 'blue water' navy and its acquisition of cruise missiles capable of threatening US aircraft carriers operating in the region are changing the strategic balance, some analysts believe. In mid-2010 China declared that it sees the disputed South China Sea area as a 'core interest', a position that has alarmed some of its neighbours and led the USA to respond in kind by asserting that it has vital national interests at stake there. The net effect has been to strengthen a number of the USA's key alliance relationships in the region and to renew US interest in engaging with the region's evolving institutions.

From China's perspective it is vital that its armed forces have a substantial military capacity, if for no other reason than to curb any ideas that Taiwan's leaders may have about pursuing independence. Whether such a military capacity is likely to be actually used in anger is another question. Although China continues to assert its right to use force to reunify the country *in extremis*, such a possibility appears increasingly remote. The reality is that both China and its 'renegade province' of Taiwan have too much to lose, as their economies have become deeply integrated and interdependent. Taiwan is no different from most of the rest of the region in that China is its biggest single trading partner. In Taiwan's case, this growing interdependence is manifest in rapidly expanding flows of capital and even people as the two economies become ever more integrated. The declining prospect of conflict between Taiwan and the mainland is strategically advantageous for the USA, and is in large part a consequence of China's successful integration into a global capitalist economy that is dominated by US-inspired norms and values. The fact that the USA and China have agreed to hold a series of defence talks and inaugurate a bilateral military-to-military dialogue in the early 21st century suggests that, in the longer term, the relationship has the potential to be less confrontational and difficult than in the past.

However, one area in which China is beginning to demonstrate a surprising capacity to challenge the USA is in what was formerly a sphere of US dominance: 'soft power'. The Bush Administration often opted for confrontation and unilateralism, and seemed indifferent to regional sensitivities, so it is unsurprising that the USA's influence and standing were undermined. The Obama Administration may be better-intentioned and more attuned to regional sensitivities, but the loss of authority engendered by the financial crisis may constrain its options. By contrast, Chinese policy-makers have made considerable efforts to assure potentially nervous neighbours that China's rise is peaceful and unthreatening—a policy that had seemed to be making good progress until recently. Despite the development of a more assertive diplomatic stance on the part of the Chinese, the underlying economic reality is that for much of the region, including Japan, China has rapidly become the major trade partner, and coming to terms with China is essential. Indeed, for some countries, China's diplomatic overtures have become increasingly difficult to resist. The emergence of a 'Beijing consensus' of pragmatic development, in opposition to the familiar but increasingly discredited US-sponsored 'Washington consensus', is one of the most unexpected and potentially important manifestations of the emerging international order. Paradoxically, therefore, the policy of 'socializing' China into good behaviour by incorporating it into regional and global institutions has been all too successful, and China's diplomatic efforts in the early 21st century have appeared shrewd, far-sighted and sophisticated in comparison with those of the USA. Indeed, from being an awkward and sensitive outsider, China has rapidly transformed itself into an important diplomatic force in regional affairs. Nowhere was this transformation more obvious than in its attempts to resolve the continuing crisis on the Korean peninsula.

THE KOREAN PENINSULA

The Korean peninsula has long been regarded as one of the world's most potentially volatile 'flashpoints'. It is not hard to see why. The peninsula is an anachronistic reminder of the earlier Cold War period and remains divided, highly militarized and seemingly immune to the influences of reform that have permeated other parts of the region. In March 2010 the sinking of a South Korean warship, apparently by a North Korean torpedo, in flagrant violation of international law, brought the peninsula to the brink of resuming a war that has never officially ended. In November North Korea and South Korea engaged in a brief artillery exchange following the North's shelling of South Korean territory. These events provided a reminder of just how unpredictable, uncontrollable and potentially destabilizing the North Korean regime can be. China, the North's chief protector and ally, seems unable or unwilling to influence its behaviour, although there are signs that even China is beginning to lose patience with its unpredictable ally. For the USA, North Korea represents a continuing reminder of its limited ability to determine strategic outcomes in the region since the end of the Cold War.

The Bush Administration's depiction of North Korea as part of an 'axis of evil' was emblematic of the USA's frustration and limited policy traction. Indeed, it is striking just how dependent US policy-makers have become upon China to facilitate dialogue with North Korea and its eccentric leader, Kim Jong Il, despite the occasionally bellicose rhetoric. For the Bush Administration in particular, its attempts to deal with the North had the unfortunate effect of complicating relations with South Korea. The Obama Administration is not finding it any easier to deal with the North. Despite a direct warning from President Obama urging restraint, in April 2009 North Korea provocatively launched its *Taepo Dong-2* rocket, withdrew from the six-party talks concerning its nuclear programme (involving Japan and Russia, as well as North and South Korea, China and the USA) and expelled all UN personnel monitoring the country's compliance with earlier commitments to abandon its nuclear activities. Despite the North's increased belligerence and lack of co-operation, the USA has been able to do little more than threaten renewed sanctions and engage in verbal condemnation.

While the USA's relationship with North Korea is one of its most difficult anywhere, its relationship with South Korea is also challenging and prone to misunderstanding. The situation ought not to have evolved in this way. After all, South Korea, like Japan, is very much a product of US grand strategy during the Cold War, and a direct beneficiary of aid and assistance from the USA. Without this help, and a willingness to disregard the excesses of authoritarian rule, it is most unlikely that South Korea would have developed in the manner in which it did, or at such a speed. As in Japan, therefore, there are deeply entrenched links between the USA and South Korea, most visibly manifest in the presence of thousands of US troops who remain in bases around the country. Nevertheless, the policy agendas of South Korea and the USA have been noticeably at variance in recent years, and relations have often been fraught. Ironically, the North's recent behaviour has reminded policy-makers in South Korea and the USA of the potential importance of their alliance.

Prior to this, however, relations had been difficult at times. One major irritant for South Korea had been the USA's disruption of the policy of 'sunshine' diplomacy, implemented by President Kim Dae-Jung following his assumption of office in early 1998 and which had been intended to improve relations with the North. The repeated denunciations of North Korea as 'untrustworthy' and 'evil' by the Bush Administration were regarded as an unconstructive and humiliating rebuff to the South's diplomatic overtures, to say nothing of the impact on the North's already paranoid leadership. Compounding this sense of not being taken seriously, or fully consulted on matters that directly affected South Korea's welfare, was the USA's unilateral decision in 2004 to withdraw one-third of its 37,500 troops from the peninsula. In view of the importance of these troops to South Korea as a real and psychological deterrent, their withdrawal was heavy with symbolism and raised concerns about the possibility of pre-emptive US strikes against the North. South Korea has begun to urge a bilateral approach to the North, despite the Obama Administration's continuing support for multilateral dialogue.

Another factor that had made South Koreans increasingly and understandably uneasy was the revelation in 2006 that the North had successfully tested a nuclear weapon. The lesson that North Korea seemed to have derived from being denounced as part of the 'axis of evil' was that if it wanted to avoid the fate of fellow axis member Iraq, it needed to develop a nuclear capacity as rapidly as possible. Coincidentally or not, US policy has subsequently been characterized by negotiation rather than outright confrontation, with no recourse to the air strikes that occurred in Afghanistan and Iraq. However, the limited ability of the USA to influence North Korea's policies was clearly revealed by the latter's decision in 2009 to restart its nuclear programme.

A significant consequence of the long-term shift to diplomacy rather than confrontation under the Obama Administration is that the USA has found itself increasingly reliant on China. China is possibly the only country with any significant influence over the North Korean regime, should it choose to exercise it, and the multilateral auspices of the six-party talks seem to be the only way of making even limited progress with North Korea. It appears increasingly unlikely that the North Korean regime will honour any of the agreements into which it has entered in the past. Indeed, many think that its increasingly belligerent and unpredictable behaviour may be part of a consciously pursued policy of testing the Obama Administration to see whether any concessions can be extracted from a seemingly less aggressive US Government. It may represent an internal struggle for power as the ageing Kim Jong Il nears the end of his reign. If the North Korean regime were to undergo an abrupt collapse, this might well add to the short-term problems and tensions on the peninsula, no matter how welcome its longer-term consequences might be.

One area in which the USA initially appeared to be having more success, and going some way to repairing the damage caused by earlier diplomatic initiatives, was in its bilateral trade policy. In April 2007 South Korea and the USA signed a bilateral free trade agreement, thus consolidating the economic links between the USA and its seventh largest trade partner. From a US perspective, this may help to mitigate some of the negative sentiment that developed in the aftermath of the Asian economic crisis of the late 1990s, which affected South Korea very badly; the actions of the USA and the US corporations that bought up distressed Korean assets were widely resented. Significantly, however, the agreement has proved contentious in both South Korea and the USA itself at a time of growing trade protectionism internationally and doubts about the agreement's impact on powerful economic sectors in both countries. As a consequence, by mid-2011 neither country had ratified the treaty, despite a new version of the agreement being signed amid much publicity in late 2010. Given the level of hostility towards the deal on the part of many Koreans, especially in the agricultural sector, the agreement may prove difficult to implement, despite Obama's active support.

In some ways, therefore, US relations with South Korea appeared to be improving, especially while the threat from the North seemed as unpredictable and ungovernable as ever. However, while the tensions between North Korea and the USA continue to be characterized by mutual incomprehension and the rhetoric of the Cold War, it is difficult to see how the confrontation will be easily resolved unless, or until, the North Korean regime disintegrates. Even if this were to occur, a reunified Korea may well eventually provide another significant challenge to US influence in a region that seems to be moving slowly but surely out of the direct sphere of US domination.

SOUTH-EAST ASIA

There are, of course, a number of very different countries subsumed under the rubric of South-East Asia, nations that have had very different historical relationships with the USA. However, it is logical to consider them as a group because as part of the Association of Southeast Asian Nations (ASEAN) they have a collective identity, and because alone or together they simply do not have the same degree of importance to US policy-makers as the countries of North-East Asia. This is slightly surprising in view of the fact that the Bush Administration declared that South-East Asia was the 'second front' in the 'war on terror', and because the region contains a number of countries that may yet assume greater strategic significance.

Two countries in South-East Asia merit particular attention as far as the USA is concerned. As recently as the 1970s the USA was embroiled in its most traumatic and protracted modern conflict in the region, in Viet Nam. This war culminated in the USA's ignominious retreat from South-East Asia and partly accounts for the region's subsequent diminished importance for US strategists. Relations with Viet Nam have become increasingly cordial, partly because the country appears to have the potential eventually to become South-East Asia's largest capitalist economy. Again, there is no small irony in the way in which history has developed; the USA has ultimately achieved the very result it wanted through the indirect use of 'soft' rather than 'hard' power.

The other country in which the USA has a long-standing direct involvement is the Philippines, its former colony and—perhaps not coincidentally—the economic laggard among the region's larger countries. The Philippines' greatest claim to attention at present is the continuing insurrection by Islamist separatists, mainly on the southern island of Mindanao. Independence movements have emerged and retreated for decades in the Philippines. They have been led by groups such as the Moro National Liberation Front (MNLF) and its offshoots, the Moro Islamic Liberation Front (MILF) and the Abu Sayyaf group. These protracted conflicts were given new prominence as a consequence of the 'war on terror' and the claim by the Bush Administration that Abu Sayyaf in particular had links to al-Qa'ida. Therefore, military co-operation between the Philippines and the USA was rapidly increased from the low levels that followed the closure of the US base at Subic Bay in 1992. However, in view of the reputation of the Philippines' own armed forces as a threat to the stability of the country, owing to their repeated coup attempts, and the involvement of some military elements in supplying weapons to the Islamists, such co-operation was a strategically and morally contentious policy that was reminiscent of the Cold War period. Significantly, in January 2011 the USA promised to help the Philippines develop its naval capacity, allowing it to patrol the waters around the Spratly Islands—which are also claimed by China.

A similar strategy towards possible terrorist threats was adopted in relation to Indonesia, the world's largest Muslim country and the scene of a number of conspicuous terrorist attacks. After having severed links with Indonesia's powerful and often brutal military for a number of years, the USA pragmatically restored support and co-operation as part of its attempt to combat terrorism. The impact of such a strategy in Indonesia has yielded even fewer tangible advantages than it has in the Philippines, and it has had a negative effect on popular opinion. However, the situation has begun to improve, partly because of the Obama Administration's very different approach to foreign policy generally, and partly, no doubt, because of President Obama's close personal links with Indonesia, having lived there as a child. Significantly, nearly one-half of the Indonesian population thought that the Obama Administration would change US foreign policy for the better. After twice cancelling planned visits to Indonesia, Obama finally made a very brief stop there in late 2010. The fact that Indonesia has a democratically elected President in Susilo Bambang Yudhoyono is an advantage as far as the USA is concerned. Yudhoyono, by contrast, must maintain good relations with the world's most powerful nation while simultaneously not appearing too weak from the perspective of the Indonesian population, large sections of which have been uneasy about US conduct and pressure.

The pressure applied to Indonesia to take action against potential Islamist radicals is not the only source of tension for many Indonesians. The role played by the USA in the aftermath of the financial crisis of 1997/98 was widely resented in Indonesia, as the USA was seen as directing the stringent reformist agenda imposed by the IMF; these policies eventually brought down the Government and cast millions of Indonesians back into grinding poverty. While the departure from office of President Suharto may be regarded as a positive aspect of this period, it emphasized to many in Indonesia their vulnerability to changes in the international economic environment and to the intervention of powerful external protagonists such as the USA and the IMF. This realization has played a major part in the development of indigenous regional institutions, which do not include the USA.

It is no coincidence that one of the prime forces in the region for the development of such institutions has been Malaysia. Under Prime Minister Mahathir Mohamad, Malaysia had notoriously uneasy relations with the USA, accusing the country of using its power and influence to force unwelcome and inappropriate economic reforms on the region. While much of this rhetoric may have been self-serving and directed at a domestic audience, it made relations between Malaysia and the USA difficult and acrimonious at times. However, Mahathir's departure from politics and the prominence attached to strategic issues subsequently improved relations between the two countries. Significantly, much of this improvement occurred because the Bush Administration, unlike its predecessor under Bill Clinton, was willing to overlook aspects of Malaysia's authoritarian style of government that formerly caused such concern. Now, by contrast, Malaysia is frequently regarded as a model for successful modernization in a majority Muslim country. The visit of the US Secretary of State, Hillary Clinton, in late 2010 was the first such visit for over 15 years and an indication of improving relations.

Thailand has also benefited from improved relations with the USA, despite an increasingly authoritarian approach to dealing with domestic opposition and the overthrow of the democratically elected Government of Thaksin Shinawatra in September 2006. The brutal suppression of Thaksin's 'Red Shirt' supporters by the military in May 2010 did nothing to ensure the country's long-term stability. Ironically, it was Thaksin's harsh tactics in dealing with Thailand's predominantly Islamic provinces in the south that were partly responsible for the Prime Minister's downfall. Thaksin's often brutal policies clearly made the situation worse rather than better; but his approach can be explained, in part, by the expectation that such suppression might be welcomed by the USA, and make it more likely that Thailand would secure a preferential trade agreement as a result. Indeed, the other noteworthy aspect of US policy in the region generally has been an increasing propensity for bilateral trade agreements, a trend that enhances its economic and strategic influence. There are few signs that policy is likely to change significantly as far as US-Thai relations are concerned: the US ambassador to Thailand assured his hosts that neither the domestic political crises in Thailand nor the apparent return to authoritarian rule would make any difference to the overall bilateral relationship.

The South-East Asian countries' relations with the USA are influenced by their relative strategic and economic importance and by their development. Some, like Singapore, are enthusiastic supporters of a continuing strategic presence in the region. Indeed, many South-East Asians regard continuing US engagement as one way of offsetting China's growing power, but Singapore has also benefited economically from its successful integration into a post-war international order that was largely created by US power. It is no coincidence that Singapore's rapid economic development has also made it a supporter of a bilateral, rather than a multilateral, approach to the sort of trade agreements that seem difficult to achieve between the region's very diverse economies. For all of South-East Asia the future challenge will be the negotiation of a course between the increased economic importance of China, with its growing diplomatic influence, and the continuing desire to retain a US strategic presence in the region. As an indication of the extent to which the region has changed and of how US influence may not be as decisive as it once was, such pressures are affecting even the USA's most stalwart regional allies.

AUSTRALIA

Since the Second World War and the fall of Singapore to the Japanese in 1942, policy-makers in Australia have considered the USA to be the primary, indispensable guarantor of Australia's security. This fact is the principal reason for the effort that Australian leaders of all political persuasions have made to maintain very close links with the USA. Despite the significant costs that this has entailed at times, as Australian troops were deployed in Korea, Viet Nam and more recently in Afghanistan and Iraq, such involvement has always been judged worthwhile. Although the relationship has recently been subjected to some unusual and critical scrutiny, there is no suggestion that this underlying reality is likely to change. Indeed, one of the first acts of Kevin Rudd when he took office as Prime Minister in late 2007 was to assure the Bush Administration that Australian policy towards the USA would remain essentially unchanged. Julia Gillard, who replaced Rudd in June 2010, acted swiftly to assure President Obama of the continuation of Australia's support for the USA's military campaign in Afghanistan. Indeed, Gillard's speech to the US Congress in March 2011 went to extraordinary lengths to reassure her listeners about the strength of ties between the two countries and Australia's commitment to the strategic alliance.

US policy-makers need not have worried: two earlier important developments in the bilateral relationship had confirmed the extent and durability of the relations between the two countries. The most dramatic expression of Australia's commitment to the USA came in the immediate aftermath of the attacks of 11 September 2001, when Australian Prime Minister John Howard was the first foreign leader to offer support. The extent of this support was quite remarkable, even by Australian standards, as Howard invoked the ANZUS Treaty (signed by Australia, New Zealand and the USA in 1951) for the first time and promised an open-ended commitment to assist in the USA's response to the attacks—even before it was clear what form US policy might take. It subsequently became obvious that the primary component of this response was the ill-conceived invasion and occupation of Iraq.

Fortunately for the Howard Government, perhaps, Australia's involvement in Iraq proved to be relatively modest and did not result in any combat deaths. Nevertheless, Australian participation was undertaken in spite of widespread public opposition, and the longer the conflict lasted the more negative the domestic attitude towards the USA became. This partly explained Rudd's commitment to withdraw combat troops from Iraq. It rapidly became clear that the end of Australia's commitment in Iraq and the election of a new US President had a major impact on Australian sentiment toward the USA. A remarkable 73% of Australians reportedly preferred Obama to John McCain in the presidential election, and the USA was once again considered to be a more responsible country than China—the opposite of the situation during the final years of the Bush Administration. More predictably, perhaps, the ANZUS treaty is still regarded by 86% of Australians as fairly or very important for Australia's security. As part of the country's ongoing commitment to the alliance, Australian troops remained in Afghanistan, despite its negligible strategic importance to Australia and the increasing flow of asylum-seekers who sought to escape the seemingly endless conflict there.

While politicians from both of Australia's major political parties generally offer continuing support for the alliance, at times this has rendered diplomatic relations difficult for the Australian Government. Although some observers in Asia believe that Australia lacks an independent foreign policy and is little more than the USA's regional 'deputy sheriff'—an impression that the Howard Government sometimes reinforced—more recently Australia has been obliged to adopt a more independent approach. The reality is that Australia's current economic expansion is being sustained to an increasingly significant extent by rapidly rising demand from China. Consequently, Australia has tried to give the impression of impartiality in its dealings with the two countries. Indeed, the principal foreign policy challenge for the Rudd and Gillard Governments has proved to be balancing the potentially competing pressures from China and the USA, which are, respectively, Australia's most important economic and strategic partners.

Australia's situation highlights the impact that long-term changes in the relative influence of different countries are having within the region, and on the very definition of the region itself. For the USA and Australia, questions about regional identity and modes of institutionalization have revolved around the 'Asia-Pacific'. The principal institutional manifestation of this possibility was the Asia-Pacific Economic Cooperation (APEC) forum, an organization that Australia played a large part in initiating in 1989. However, APEC's influence and importance have steadily declined, mainly because of an absence of consistent support from the USA. This is not only a set-back to Australia's diplomatic standing. More importantly, in the longer term, it represents a significant downgrading of the sort of multilateral international order that the USA did so much to create, and from which Australia has derived substantial benefit. Prime Minister

Rudd responded to the apparent decline of APEC and the growth of alternative institutions from which Australia and the USA may be excluded by proposing his own Asia Pacific Community (APC) concept. Significantly, this proposal included the USA and was designed to address security and economic issues in one forum. Although the initial reception of the APC meant that it had little chance of success, the concept re-emerged in the form of the East Asia Summit (EAS), which held its first meeting in December 2005. Whether this organization will prove to be capable of assuming a dominant position among the region's growing number of competing institutions remains to be seen, but the fact that the USA was to be included in the EAS with effect from 2011, as part of that country's effort to re-engage with a region it was generally thought to have neglected, suggests that the EAS might succeed.

THE RISE OF EAST ASIA AND THE DECLINE OF US INFLUENCE

A number of forces have come together to alter the Asia-Pacific region and the USA's place in it—in the Asian part of that broadly defined region, at least. Perhaps the most important long-term factor in this context has been the rise of China, a development that may eventually transform the global balance of power and influence, but which is already having a profound effect on East Asia. In some ways, this is a return to an older regional order that existed long before America was even 'discovered'. Although China's renewed prominence will undoubtedly be accompanied by geopolitical pressures and tensions, it is a reality that neighbouring countries are already beginning to accommodate—even those, such as Australia, that have very close strategic, political and cultural links with the USA.

One of the potentially most important consequences of this rapidly evolving regional order with regard to the USA is that it is being accompanied by the development of new institutions. Although it is difficult to be sure which, if any, of these institutions are likely to play a decisive role in influencing the future intra-regional relations of East Asia, their emergence has potentially important implications. Although the USA currently favours the EAS, this is not the only organization trying to assert itself and define the region. For example, one of the most noteworthy features of the ASEAN + 3 grouping, which includes China, Japan and South Korea in addition to the member countries of ASEAN, is that it excludes the USA. Indeed, it also excludes other 'Anglo-American'-style economies such as those of Australia and New Zealand, making it an exclusively Asian grouping and one that is likely to reflect the kind of approach and objectives that distinguished the original ASEAN grouping.

The East Asian region has a rather unimpressive record of developing indigenous institutions, and this is clearly one reason why the USA has until recently seemed unconcerned about the emergence of a major regional grouping from which it is excluded. This is in contrast to the attitude of US policy-makers in the mid-1990s when Malaysia proposed a similar 'Asians only' grouping, only to see it suppressed by a combination of US opposition and an unwillingness on the part of Japan to take the lead in view of such opposition. However, with the rise of China the situation may be changing, as the recent interest in the EAS indicates. Clearly, for a number of countries, including the USA, such a grouping offers a potential method of containing Chinese influence.

There is no doubt that China is assiduously working to improve its regional standing. Unlike Japan, it is not encumbered by historical issues and the sense of deference that has made Japan incapable of taking a regional leadership role. On the contrary, many Chinese regard this reassertion of national power and regional leadership as being critical in restoring China to its rightful place at the forefront of great powers. In view of how much depends on China's ability to maintain its remarkable rate of economic expansion to fulfil this political ambition, it is far from clear that such a restoration will occur at all, much less without making alterations in the standing of various powers in the region and beyond. The dramatic impact of China's growth on its own environment, and on that of the world more generally, is becoming increasingly apparent. There are real doubts about its long-term sustainability.

From a US perspective it is difficult to determine which is the less attractive prospect: a China that continues to grow and increase its power and standing; or one that collapses into unpredictable chaos. The only apparent certainty is that whatever happens in China will have profound implications both for the region and for the foreign policy of the USA. There are likely to be many potential sources of friction for the USA as regards its attitude to China in particular: competition for diminishing resources is likely to intensify; tension over the USA's rising trade deficit and growing economic exposure to China will probably increase; and anxiety about China's military modernization is bound to heighten concerns about the USA's strategic vulnerability and declining power. All of these are potentially major problems, and there is clearly the potential for misunderstanding and even conflict. Yet the underlying reality is that both the USA and China have too much to lose by mismanaging their relationship. The relationship is a pivotal part of the future international order. It must be hoped that China can rapidly grow into its new global role and that the USA can come to terms with the idea that the era of unchallenged unipolarity and dominance may be well and truly over.

BIBLIOGRAPHY

Aggarwal, V. K. 'Look West: The Evolution of US Trade Policy Toward Asia', *Globalizations* 7 (4), pp. 455–473. Abingdon, Routledge, 2011.

Beeson, Mark. 'Hegemonic transition in East Asia? The dynamics of Chinese and American power', *Review of International Studies,* 35 (01), pp. 95–112. Cambridge, Cambridge University Press, 2009.

Regionalism and Globalization in East Asia: Politics, Security and Economic Development. Basingstoke, Palgrave Macmillan, 2006.

Beeson, M., and Stubbs, R. (Eds). *The Routledge Handbook of Asian Regionalism.* Abingdon, Routledge, 2011.

Chan, Steve. *China, the US, and the Power-Transition Theory.* Abingdon, Routledge, 2007.

Christensen, T. J. 'Fostering stability or creating a monster?: The rise of China and US policy toward East Asia', *International Security 31 (1)* pp. 81–126, 2006.

Chung, Jae Ho. *Between Ally and Partner: Korea-China Relations and the United States.* New York, Columbia University Press, 2008.

Cossa, Ralph A. 'Evolving US Views on Asia's Future Institutional Architecture', in M. Green and B. Gill, *Asia's New Multilateralism: Cooperation, Competition, and the Search for Community,* pp. 33–54. New York, Columbia University Press, 2009.

Foot, R., and Walter, A. *China, the United States, and Global Order.* Cambridge, Cambridge University Press, 2011.

Funabashi, Yoichi. 'Keeping Up with Asia: America and the New Balance of Power', in *Foreign Affairs* 87 (5), pp. 110–125. New York, Council on Foreign Relations, 2008.

Hemmer, C., and Katzenstein, P. J. 'Why is there no NATO in Asia? Collective identity, regionalism, and the origins of multilateralism', *International Organization 56 (3),* pp. 575–607, 2002.

Ikenberry, G. John. *The United States and Northeast Asia: Old Issues, New Thinking.* Lanham, MD, Rowman & Littlefield, 2007.

Iriye, Akira. *Across the Pacific: An Inner History of American-East Asian Relations.* Harbinger, New York, 1967.

Johnson, Chalmers. *Blowback: The Costs and Consequences of American Empire.* London, Little, Brown & Co, 2000.

Katzenstein, Peter J. *A World of Regions: Asia and Europe in the American Imperium.* Ithaca, NY, Cornell University Press, 2005.

Mahbubani, Kishore. *The New Asian Hemisphere: The Irresistible Shift of Global Power to the East.* New York, Public Affairs, 2008.

McMahon, Robert J. *The Limits of Empire: The United States and Southeast Asia Since World War II.* New York, Columbia University Press, 1999.

Pempel, T. J. 'How Bush bungled Asia: militarism, economic indifference and unilateralism have weakened the United States across Asia', in *The Pacific Review* 21 (5), pp. 547–581, 2008.

Sutter, Robert G. 'China's Rise: Implications for US Leadership in Asia', in *Policy Studies 21.* Washington, DC, East-West Center, 2006.

The United States in Asia. Lanham, MD, Rowman & Littlefield, 2008.

U.S.-Chinese Relations: Perilous Past, Pragmatic Present. Lanham, MD, Rowman & Littlefield, 2010.

Tao Xie. *US-China Relations: China Policy on Capitol Hill.* Abingdon, Routledge, 2010.

Tay, Simon S. C. *Asia Alone: The Dangerous Post-Crisis Divide from America.* Singapore, John Wiley & Sons, 2010.

Wade, R. 'The US role in the long Asian crisis of 1990–2000', in A. Lukanskas and F. Rivera-Batiz, *The Political Economy of the East Asian Crisis and Its Aftermath: Tigers in Distress,* pp. 195–226. Cheltenham, Edward Elgar Publishing, 2001.

Weatherbee, Donald E. *Historical Dictionary of United States-Southeast Asia Relations.* Lanham, MD, Scarecrow Press, 2008.

Woo-Cumings, M. 'Back to basics: Ideology, nationalism, and Asian values in East Asia', in E. Helleiner and A. Pickel, *Economic Nationalism in a Globalizing World,* pp. 91–117. Ithaca, NY, Cornell University Press, 2005.

Zhao Suisheng (Ed.). *China-US Relations Transformed.* Abingdon, Routledge, 2009.

Zhu Zhiqun. *US-China Relations in the 21st Century—Power Transition and Peace.* Abingdon, Routledge, 2009.

THE SECURITY CHALLENGES OF EAST AND SOUTH-EAST ASIA

ANDREW T. H. TAN

INTRODUCTION

East and South-East Asia continue to confront significant security challenges. In particular, the rise of the People's Republic of China has been accompanied by growing strategic rivalry with the USA, as China challenges the USA's dominant position, especially in East and South-East Asia. The erratic regime that rules the nuclear-armed Democratic People's Republic of Korea (DPRK—North Korea) has also remained a serious security concern for the region and for the international community. These two major security challenges increased considerably in the course of 2010–11.

In South-East Asia, fears of terrorism and concerns over maritime security were intensified following the July 2009 bombings of two Western-linked hotels in Jakarta, the discovery of a militant training camp in Aceh province in Indonesia in early 2010, and the warning issued by the Singapore navy in March 2010 over possible maritime attacks in the Straits of Melaka (Malacca).

Armed separatist movements have continued to trouble a number of countries in the region, such as Myanmar, Thailand, Indonesia, the Philippines and China. The majority of these armed separatist movements are Muslim in nature, thus raising concerns about possible links with the global *jihad* ('holy war') and with al-Qa'ida (the militant Islamist organization held responsible for the attacks on the USA on 11 September 2001 and led, until his death in May 2011, by Osama bin Laden).

Several countries in the region have also witnessed serious domestic instability, for example in Timor-Leste, Myanmar, and the autonomous region of Tibet in China. Non-traditional security challenges have also become much more prominent in recent years. Apart from health threats, natural disasters such as earthquakes, tsunamis and cyclones have attracted global attention. In Japan in March 2011 a major earthquake (measuring 9.0 on the scale of magnitude) and the resulting tsunami killed more than 15,000 people. The earthquake and tsunami also caused a partial meltdown of the Fukushima nuclear plant, north of Tokyo, as well as the radioactive contamination of soil, air, water and the seas around the area.

THE RISE AND CHALLENGE OF CHINA

China's rise as a global power has become the most significant issue in contemporary international relations, arguably eclipsing the threat of global terrorism. The ascendancy of China has led to evidently growing strategic competition with the USA, as the latter's global standing is increasingly challenged by China. The rise of China has prompted a debate about whether this constitutes a threat or an opportunity. In particular, the USA has repeatedly expressed concern over China's military capabilities, citing the lack of transparency and uncertainty over its intentions. In 2009 China declared that it would acquire aircraft carriers, in line with its status as a major global power. This coincided with reports that China would soon complete modifications to the former Russian aircraft carrier, the *Varyag*, although it was believed that the vessel would serve as a training ship, as China intended to build its own aircraft carriers in the near future. The release in 2010 of pictures of China's first stealth fighter, the J20, which was undergoing testing, caused both excitement and apprehension in Western defence circles, as hitherto only the USA had deployed such advanced aircraft. In recent years China's navy has also steadily expanded its maritime activities, such as making port calls around the world, as well as building ports, bases and surveillance facilities to patrol and defend its sea lines of communications (SLOCs) and to safeguard access to energy resources in the Middle East. In December 2008 China began anti-piracy patrols off the coast of Somalia in response to the problem of the growing incidence of piracy in East African waters, a development that indicated its increasingly global reach.

The financial and economic problems that affected the USA from 2007 contrasted with China's continuing economic growth, which has averaged around 10% annually for the past three decades. In 2010 China became the world's second largest economy, overtaking Japan. Furthermore, according to an estimate by investment bank Goldman Sachs, China is on course to surpass the USA as the world's largest economy by 2027. Indeed, the massive World Exposition in Shanghai in 2010 appeared designed to highlight to the world China's arrival as a global power.

China's rise, in contrast to the economic problems confronted by the USA and Western Europe, has been accompanied by growing confidence and assertiveness, which was evident throughout 2009–10. In March 2009 an unarmed US naval surveillance vessel, the *USNS Impeccable,* was surrounded and harassed by Chinese vessels in the South China Sea. China alleged that the ship was operating in Chinese territorial waters and that it was conducting spying activities. The USA asserted that the ship had the right of innocent passage in what it regarded as international waters, and responded by sending a destroyer to accompany the *USNS Impeccable.* China then dispatched more armed fishery vessels to the area to assert its claim to what it considers to be its exclusive economic zone (EEZ). In July 2010 regional concerns were further heightened when China declared that it now considered the South China Sea to be part of its core territorial interests, which put the disputed area on a par with Tibet and Taiwan. In response, US Secretary of State Hillary Clinton asserted that the South China Sea is pivotal to regional security and part of the US national interest.

In September 2010 the collision of a Chinese trawler with Japan Coast Guard vessels near the disputed Senkaku islands, which are claimed by both China and Japan, and the subsequent detention of the trawler's captain, led to a major diplomatic dispute between the two countries. This was resolved after public pressure by China, which led to the captain being released without charge. However, the incident heightened Japan's fears concerning a resurgent and increasingly assertive China, especially in the context of growing nationalism in China. Unfortunately, this nationalism has been profoundly anti-Japanese, as Japanese atrocities in China before 1945 form a prominent theme in the nationalistic propaganda used by the Chinese Communist Party to boost its legitimacy. The future prospects for Japan-China relations are therefore poor, with popular negative images on both sides.

In this context, the visit of US President Barack Obama to China in November 2009 was significant in that it demonstrated, for the first time, a relationship between equals. Obama struck a conciliatory note, focusing on common burdens and joint efforts in addressing global problems. The Obama Administration has thus tried to emphasize engagement (or 'enmeshment') with China, instead of Cold War-style containment. Given the parlous state of the US economy and the many other challenges, such as those relating to Iran and the conflict in Afghanistan, this seemed a pragmatic policy to follow. However, President Hu Jintao's return visit to the USA in January 2011 was characterized by underlying tensions, with senior Congressional leaders refusing to attend the White House dinner in his honour, and Obama gently criticizing China on human rights. Key issues dividing the two countries include: China's undervalued currency, its allegedly non-transparent military spending, diplomatic support for North Korea and China's poor human rights record. However, at the centre of the evidently rising tensions between the two powers is the challenge that China poses to the present dominance of the USA.

China's growing economic strength and emerging military power have also heightened concerns in the USA and its regional allies in Asia over the erosion of Taiwan's ability to defend itself. Hostile relations between China and Taiwan during the tenure of the latter's pro-independence President, Chen Shui-bian, gave way to an easing of tensions under the presidency of Ma Ying-jeou of the nationalist Kuomintang (KMT) party, who took office in May 2008. Ma, a supporter of the 'One China' principle, presided over an improvement in cross-Straits relations. However, concerns over Taiwan's weakening defence capabilities led to the approval in early 2010 by the Obama Administration of a US $6,000m. sale of armaments, consisting of *Patriot* anti-ballistic missiles, communications equipment, *Black Hawk* helicopters, *Harpoon* anti-ship missiles and mine-hunting ships. China has been developing ballistic missile, air, naval and submarine capabilities that could be used to coerce Taiwan into reunification. It has also developed anti-satellite and anti-access capabilities, such as anti-ship ballistic missiles designed to target aircraft carriers, which could deny the USA the ability to deploy its naval and air forces to defend Taiwan in a crisis. These capabilities, as well as Taiwan's inability to access advanced military technology due to its diplomatic isolation, have resulted in a growing military imbalance on both sides of the Taiwan Straits. This could potentially encourage China to be more assertive towards Taiwan in its pursuit of reunification, a popular nationalist cause in China.

In South-East Asia, China has also been in direct conflict with Viet Nam, Malaysia, Brunei and the Philippines over the potentially oil-rich Spratly Islands in the South China Sea. In 1992 China enacted a 'Law on Territorial Waters', asserting its claims to the South China Sea and reserving the right to use military means to enforce them. However, China signed the Declaration on the Conduct of Parties in the South China Sea with the member states of the Association of Southeast Asian Nations (ASEAN) in November 2002, whereby it affirmed the use of peaceful means to resolve the dispute. This was followed by agreements with the Philippines and Viet Nam, in 2004 and 2005 respectively, to develop resources in the South China Sea jointly, with the question of sovereignty put into abeyance. The Philippines also signed a series of agreements in April 2005, under which China would provide development aid to the Philippines. The response of states in the region to China's rise has thus been a pragmatic one of accommodation, as China is in close geographical propinquity and represents enormous economic opportunities. However, the South China Sea issue remains a security challenge. The creation of a new Sansha county administrative region on Hainan Island by China in 2007, to administer the Paracels and Spratlys, led to public protests in Viet Nam, although the China-Viet Nam Steering Committee was able to contain the problem after meeting in 2008. China's declaration in 2010 asserting that the South China Sea represented a core territorial interest raised apprehensions throughout the region, leading to the issue being discussed at the ASEAN Regional Forum in July of that year. However, the ASEAN states ultimately desisted from challenging China as a bloc. Although the South China Sea dispute remains unresolved, its eventual resolution is likely to be on China's terms, given that no one state or combination of states in the region can counter China's growing power.

THE 'ROGUE STATE' OF NORTH KOREA

Until 2010, and contrary to popular perception in the West, China played an important role in helping to manage the North Korea issue. North Korea was dubbed a 'rogue state' by the USA, and the country was described as part of the 'axis of evil' by the Administration of President George W. Bush, who left office in early 2009. North Korea's deep insecurity, on account of its serious economic problems and fears that it might be a target of US pressure for regime change, has driven it to develop nuclear weapons, perceiving these to be the only realistic guarantee of its security.

China acted as mediator and helped to co-ordinate the six-party talks, which were initiated in August 2003 and have been attended by representatives of North Korea, South Korea, China, Japan, Russia and the USA. China also used coercive measures, such as the suspension of oil supplies and the shifting of troop deployments along its border, to exert pressure on the North to negotiate. However, North Korea withdrew from the Nuclear Non-Proliferation Treaty (NPT) in 2003, and shocked the world when it carried out a small underground nuclear test in October 2006. In February 2007 North Korea agreed to end its nuclear weapons programme and readmit weapons inspectors, in exchange for supplies of fuel. In July 2007 North Korea shut down its nuclear reactor at Yongbyon. The improvement in the country's relations with the USA was epitomized by the visit by the New York Philharmonic orchestra to the North Korean capital of Pyongyang in February 2008. In October 2007 South Korean President Roh Moo-Hyun made a symbolic visit to North Korea, in a gesture of reconciliation.

However, the election of a conservative President, Lee Myung-Bak, in South Korea in early 2008 led to a change in the relationship, as he insisted that economic aid would be linked to North Korea's willingness to relinquish its nuclear weapons. This led to the suspension of official contacts between the North and the South, and the halting of all cross-border tourism projects. In April 2009 North Korea carried out an unsuccessful rocket launch, which it claimed was a satellite test. However, the USA, Japan and South Korea charged that it was in fact a long-range missile that violated a UN Security Council resolution adopted in October 2006, banning the North from engaging in ballistic missile activity.

North Korea also withdrew from the six-party talks and carried out a nuclear test in May 2009. The escalation of tensions coincided with reports of the serious illness of North Korea's erratic leader, Kim Jong Il, and apparent attempts by him to ensure that his son, Kim Jong Un, would succeed him. These developments, together with serious economic difficulties and widespread famine within the country, led to fears in China over potential instability in the Korean peninsula. In 2009 the growing exasperation at North Korea led to an unusually open and vigorous debate in China over its policy options. The debate pitted those who favoured a more robust attitude towards North Korea against those who wanted to maintain China's traditional support for the regime.

Ultimately, China voted in favour of the imposition of sanctions by the UN Security Council in 2009, albeit directed at North Korea's missile and nuclear programmes, and not at its economy. However, this did not indicate a fundamental change in policy on the part of China, as its priority has been stability, not denuclearization. China's primary objective is to prevent a military confrontation between North Korea and the USA, one that might lead to the collapse of the North Korean regime, sending a massive influx of refugees into China and leading to the presence of US forces in the North. China has thus tried to balance support for sanctions against North Korea with allowing it enough resources to survive.

The future trajectory of North Korea is likely to depend on domestic developments within the country. The unexpected confiscatory currency reform introduced in November 2009, which was apparently intended to curb the developing free market, instead caused chaos, amid reports of acts of civil disobedience. The deepening economic crisis, growing disillusionment among North Koreans, and the apparent desire of Kim Jong Il to expedite the anticipated succession to leadership of his son, Kim Jong Un, provided the impetus for an aggressive foreign policy stance in order to bolster domestic legitimacy and strengthen the North's negotiating position with the outside world. In March 2010 a South Korean navy corvette, the *Cheonan*, was sunk, apparently by a North Korean torpedo, near the disputed maritime border with North Korea, killing 46 sailors. Although North Korea threatened an 'all-out war' should there be 'reckless counter-measures', the South imposed a ban on all trade with the North. This was followed by the open shelling in November 2010 of an island in South Korea, which killed two civilians and two soldiers. The events raised tension to its highest level since the Korean War, arousing fears of an outbreak of full-scale conflict in the Korean peninsula. This would have exposed the South to weapons of mass destruction, including the possible use of nuclear weapons by the North, the destruction of the capital, Seoul, by massive artillery assaults from the North and deadly attacks by the North's huge commando forces. Despite the North's openly provocative behaviour, China continued to maintain its support for the regime, although both China and the USA were instrumental in encouraging North and South Korea to return to the negotiating table in February 2011. However, the talks failed almost immediately, as the North Korean delegates blamed the South for the recent confrontations and then walked out. The events of 2010 demonstrated that South Korea and the USA have few options, especially given China's continued support for the erratic North Korean regime, except continued sanctions and joint US-South Korea military exercises to deter future provocation. The events had the effect of reaffirming the centrality of the USA to the security of South Korea and Japan, and its broader role in underpinning regional security, thus ironically strengthening US alliance relationships and the USA's position in the region.

THE CONTINUING CHALLENGE OF TERRORISM

Following the seminal terrorist attacks on the USA on 11 September 2001, the designation of South-East Asia, and especially the Malay archipelago, as the 'second front' in the global 'war on terror' was not unexpected. The region has the world's largest population of Muslims, which in the view of the USA might offer refuge to al-Qa'ida terrorists fleeing world-wide security action against them.

In South-East Asia, the al-Qa'ida-linked Jemaah Islamiah (JI) network was exposed in late 2001 following the failure of its ambitious bomb plots in Singapore, where it had planned co-ordinated terrorist attacks, targeting US and Western interests. JI has been active in Indonesia, Malaysia, Singapore, the Philippines, Thailand and Australia, and has plans to establish a pan-Islamic caliphate in the region. JI can trace its origins to the Darul Islam movement in Indonesia in the 1950s, which launched an armed struggle to establish an Islamic state, as both the alleged founders of JI, Abu Bakar Bashir and Abdullah Sungkar, regarded themselves as the ideological successors of that movement. Indeed, many JI operatives in fact came from families that had participated in the Darul Islam movement. The JI network itself was established in the early 1990s, through the development of linkages throughout the region via former Afghan *mujahidin* volunteers from South-East Asia, who had returned after fighting Soviet forces in Afghanistan in the 1980s. Through the Afghanistan connection, JI also developed close links with al-Qa'ida, receiving both funding and ideological training from it.

Two senior al-Qa'ida operatives, Fathur Rohman al-Ghozi and Jabarah Mohammad Mansour, were arrested in 2002, in the Philippines and Oman respectively, for their co-ordinating roles in the abortive Singapore bomb plots. Al-Ghozi later escaped from prison in the Philippines in 2003 and was killed in an exchange of gunfire with security forces in October of that year. Further arrests significantly weakened the al-Qa'ida-JI nexus in the region, particularly those of Omar al-Faruq, a Kuwaiti citizen of Iraqi descent, in Indonesia in 2002, and of Riduan Isamuddin (also known as Hambali), in Thailand in 2003. Both suspects were subsequently transferred to US custody. Al-Faruq provided the authorities with a much clearer view of al-Qa'ida and JI activities in the region, which included a plan to assassinate President Megawati of Indonesia. Al-Faruq subsequently escaped from detention in Afghanistan, but was killed by British forces in Iraq in September 2006. Hambali, dubbed the 'Osama bin Laden' of South-East Asia by US intelligence services, was the chief strategist of many attacks in the region. His arrest was so significant that both US President George W. Bush and the Australian Prime Minister, John Howard, publicly commented on it. Other significant counter-terrorism successes included the killing by security forces in Indonesia of senior JI bomb-makers and leaders, such as Azahari Husin in 2005, Noordin Mohammad Top in 2009 and Dulmatin in early 2010 (see below).

The JI organization has been responsible for some spectacular terrorist attacks in the region, including that on Kuta Beach on the Indonesian island of Bali in October 2002, which killed 202 people, mostly foreign nationals. This was followed by the Marriott Hotel suicide bombing in the capital of Jakarta in August 2003, when 12 people were killed. Another bomb attack, this time on the Australian embassy in Jakarta in September 2004, killed a total of 11 people. In October 2005 a second bomb attack on Bali resulted in 23 deaths. In July 2009 co-ordinated attacks on the Marriott and Ritz-Carlton hotels in Jakarta killed seven people, including a number of Australian businessmen. JI elements have also been involved in local Muslim militias responsible for violence in the Maluku islands (the Moluccas) in Indonesia, the scene of bitter Christian–Muslim clashes between 1999 and 2002, which resulted in the deaths of some 10,000 people. Despite the conclusion of a peace accord that has largely been adhered to, communal tensions as a result of that conflict remain.

Throughout 2007 operations carried out by the Indonesian police counter-terrorism unit, Densus 88, led to the arrest of a number of JI operatives and the seizure of weapons and explosives. As a result, JI's operational capabilities were believed to be have been significantly degraded. By 2008 security operations throughout South-East Asia had resulted in more than 400 alleged JI operatives being taken into custody by the authorities in the region. JI is also reported to have fragmented, with some members disapproving of the recourse to wanton violence, and others working hard to establish links with other jihadist groups in the region in order to continue terrorist attacks on Western targets. Until his death in a police operation in September 2009, Noordin Mohammad Top was the self-proclaimed leader of JI's military wing, which he named 'al-Qa'ida in the Malay Archipelago'. Successful counter-terrorism operations, particularly those in Indonesia in 2007, reduced, but did not eliminate, the threat from terrorism. By 2010 the problem was acknowledged to be broader, long-term and ideological in nature. While al-Qa'ida's direct operational links appear to have been severed with the arrest of its senior commanders in the region, local radicals and jihadist networks have taken their place. JI itself is estimated to have a solid core of about 900 members, and there have been new recruits from conflict zones such as Sulawesi and Maluku in Indonesia. The continued terrorist threat was demonstrated when a JI plot to bomb a café on the Indonesian island of Sumatra was disrupted with the arrest of 10 militants, led by a Singaporean, and the recovery of bombs in July 2008. The long-awaited execution of the three Bali bombers, Imam Samudra, Amrozi bin Nurhasyim and Ali Gufron, in November 2008, led to fears that their perceived martyrdom might inspire further attacks. Indeed, two further bomb attacks were carried out in July 2009 in Jakarta (see above). Police operations in Aceh in February 2010 also led to the discovery of a militant training camp, which resulted in the recovery of documents as well as terrorist plans to carry out attacks throughout the region. This led to a series of police operations and gun battles with militants, resulting in the death or arrest of more than 70 suspected militants, including the death of the JI operational commander, Dulmatin, an event so significant that it was announced by President Yudhoyono. These more recent attacks and events have drawn attention to the continuing threat of terrorism in South-East Asia.

In the Philippines various radical Islamist groups continue to pose a serious threat to security, resulting in high and visible security measures throughout the country. Apart from elements of JI sheltering there, the activities of the Abu Sayyaf group continue to trouble the authorities. Founded in 1991 by former *mujahidin* who had returned from the conflict in Afghanistan, Abu Sayyaf established strong connections with al-Qa'ida, which sent Ramzi Yousef (responsible for the World Trade Center bombing in New York in 1993) to train members of Abu Sayyaf in the use of explosives. In April 2000 the group attracted world-wide attention when it kidnapped 21 hostages, including a number of Western tourists, during an assault on the Malaysian island resort of Sipadan. Abu Sayyaf and JI are also believed to have carried out the ferry bombing in Manila Bay in February 2004, which resulted in the deaths of more than 100 people. The authorities have also been troubled by the terrorist activities of a relatively new radical group, the Rajah Solaiman Movement, which has reportedly made progress in recruiting Catholic converts to Islam.

In short, the threat of terrorism remains a long-term security challenge. There is today a growing consensus among terrorism experts that the threat of global terrorism has gone well beyond al-Qa'ida, as most terrorist attacks since September 2001 have been carried out by local affiliates or associates of al-Qa'ida, acting independently and in response to local grievances.

MARITIME SECURITY

Since September 2001 concerns over maritime security in the environs of the busy and strategic Straits of Melaka have assumed urgency and priority. One-quarter of the world's trade, one-half of its oil and two-thirds of its natural gas trade pass through these waters. However, the high rates of piracy around Indonesian waters from the 1990s, the unregulated and insecure nature of the maritime trade, the threat of terrorist activity and the fact that any disruption of this sea-borne trade would have a devastating global impact, resulted in heightened concerns over maritime security.

Indeed, there was a dramatic increase in incidents of piracy in Indonesian waters after the crisis of governance that followed the downfall of the Suharto regime in 1998. In view of the trend of increasing links between transnational organized crime and terrorism, fears were expressed that vulnerable, high-risk and high-value shipping, such as cruise ships and chemical tankers, might be attractive terrorist targets. Ships, and particularly containers, could also be used to smuggle terrorists, as well as weapons of mass destruction.

One scenario might be the hijacking of a chemical tanker and its use as a floating bomb to devastate ports—a maritime version of the attacks of 11 September 2001. An assault on a supercontainer hub, such as Singapore or Hong Kong, would have devastating consequences in an age of globalization, with its increasing dependence on maritime trade and 'just-in-time' manufacturing processes. Moreover, al-Qa'ida appears to be aware of the vulnerability of sea-borne vessels and has carried out maritime attacks, such as the assault on the *USS Cole* in Aden harbour in 2000 and that on a French oil tanker, *The Lindberg*, off the coast of Yemen in 2002.

Apart from the Straits of Melaka, another area of growing concern has been the maritime trilateral border area of Malaysia, Indonesia and the Philippines. The waterways in the region, such as the Straits of Makassar, are increasingly being used by very large crude carriers (VLCCs). However, the potential for a link between piracy and terrorism exists in the area, owing to the presence of various illegal activities such as piracy and smuggling in the waters off Sulu and Celebes. Moreover, the area has become a logistical corridor for militants in the Malay archipelago, particularly those in the southern Philippines and Sulawesi island in Indonesia.

The threat of a maritime terrorist attack in South-East Asia is real, given JI's plans to attack US naval vessels in late 2001 as part of the failed Singapore bomb plots. Indeed, in 2004 JI and Abu Sayyaf succeeded in carrying out a major ferry bombing in Manila Bay, killing more than 100 people.

However, the problem with the maritime industry is vast, given that the entire logistical chain needs to be secured. This entails improving ship, container and port security. Ports in the region have therefore moved swiftly to implement the requirements of the International Ship and Port Security (ISPS) Code promulgated by the International Maritime Organization in December 2002, and the amendments to the Safety of Life at Sea (SOLAS) Convention, which took effect on 1 July 2004. Under these regulations, ships and ports are required to have improved security measures to ensure better control and monitoring of the movement of people and cargo. In October 2005 new Protocols were also added to the 1988 United Nations Convention for the Suppression of Unlawful Acts Against the Safety of Maritime Navigation (SUA). These protocols established, *inter alia*, the basis for boarding and inspecting ships in international waters.

The region has also responded, with varying degrees of enthusiasm, to US-led initiatives designed to improve port and container security as part of preventive measures against terrorism. These measures include the Container Security Initiative (CSI), the Customs-Trade Partnership Against Terrorism (C-TPAT), the US Coast Guard's International Port Security Program and the Proliferation Security Initiative (PSI). The littoral states of the Straits of Melaka have also developed close co-operation over maritime security. Indonesia, Malaysia and Singapore have, since 2004, carried out co-ordinated year-round patrols (known as the Malacca Strait Patrol), linked by communications 'hotlines', as well as joint air patrols under the 'Eye in the Sky' programme. Thailand joined these three countries in conducting air patrols, and also began participating in the Malacca Strait Patrol in 2009. The four countries have established a Joint Coordinating Committee, as well as an information exchange group comprising naval intelligence agencies. The littoral states have also developed the Malacca Strait Patrol Information System, which shares information about shipping in the Straits of Melaka.

As a result of security measures implemented since September 2001, the incidence of piracy in South-East Asian waters has declined significantly. In the first quarter of 2008, for example, there were 11 incidents, the lowest number for five years. The decrease has been most apparent in the ports and anchorages of Indonesia. Increased patrols in the Straits of Melaka have instead forced pirates to transfer their operations to the South China Sea, where the number of attacks on ships had reached a five-year high point by late 2009. However, the danger of a maritime terrorist attack has not disappeared. In March 2010 the Singapore Navy issued a warning over a possible attack by terrorists on maritime shipping in the Straits of Melaka, resulting in a heightened state of alert. This warning coincided with operations by security forces in Indonesia in Aceh province, in the northern tip of Sumatra, which led to the uncovering of a militant training camp.

The threat of terrorism and rising concerns about maritime security in the Malay archipelago have attracted the attention of extra-regional powers with deep interests in the security of vital waterways in the region. The USA and its allies in East Asia, namely Japan and Australia, have co-ordinated their efforts, strategy and approach. There thus emerged a trilateral security nexus linking the three countries. An unspoken objective was also to counter the emergence of China. Indeed, in the USA proponents have openly promoted the idea of a concert of democracies aimed at containing China. Thus, concerns over terrorism and maritime security have become conflated with traditional great power rivalries.

The idea of a Trilateral Security Dialogue was initially mooted in 2001 as a forum for security officials of the three countries to discuss security issues in Asia. The Dialogue process is based on the strong relationship, founded on their respective alliances, that both Japan and Australia have with the USA. In 2007 the last stage of the trilateral arrangement was completed when Japan and Australia signed a security co-operation agreement.

For its part, Australia has readily encouraged Japan to commit more resources to countering terrorism, as it believes that the latter has at its disposal expertise and resources that would be useful. Australia has placed enormous strategic importance on the Malay archipelago, not only because of its geographical propinquity but also because Australia is a prime terrorist target, on account of its close alliance with the USA and its active participation in the global 'war on terror'. The terrorist threat to Australia has emanated principally from the north, as demonstrated by Australia's inclusion in JI's sphere of operations and the Australian targets and casualties in various terrorist attacks in Indonesia. Australia therefore furnished Indonesia with forensic and other police assistance in investigating the various JI bombings. It also helped to establish the Jakarta Center for Law Enforcement Co-operation, which is partially staffed by Australian police officers.

Japan, too, has increasingly been drawn into multilateral security co-operation with the region. Indeed, any prolonged disruption or instability would imperil Japanese economic interests, as the Straits of Melaka are vital to its access to resources and markets. Al-Qa'ida had also publicly threatened Japan on account of its identification with the USA on security and political issues, and its dispatch of troops to Iraq. Japan's increasing rivalry with a rising China has also been a major force behind Japan's expanding strategic and security roles in South-East Asia. There has thus been a growing realization in Japan since September 2001 that the country needs to abandon its passive foreign and defence policy and instead play an active role in addressing the increasing international terrorist threat, as well as the challenge of China.

Japan's evolving role in South-East Asia has concentrated on capacity-building for counter-terrorism, given the country's constitutional and historical constraints on the deployment of military forces. This capacity-building approach has taken the form of the provision of training and equipment in the areas of immigration control, aviation security, customs co-operation, export control, law enforcement co-operation and measures against terrorism financing. Regional anti-piracy and counter-terrorism co-operation has been undertaken by the Japanese Coast Guard, which has provided training, equipment, and funding to all the coastal states of the region. Japan has conducted joint counter-terrorism training exercises with a number of South-East Asian states. It also sponsored a regional initiative in 2001 that subsequently became the Regional Cooperation Agreement on Combating Piracy and Armed Robbery Against Ships in Asia (ReCAAP), which was signed by 16 countries in 2004 and entered into force in September 2006. The Agreement provides mechanisms for international co-operation, establishes the obligations of member states to prevent piracy and also supports capacity-building initiatives.

The evolving Trilateral Security Dialogue partnership of Japan, Australia and the USA appeared to reach a culmination in the 'Malabar' naval exercises in the Indian Ocean in September 2007. This involved the three Trilateral partners and India, a prospective member of the alliance, as well as the partnership's closest South-East Asian regional ally, Singapore. The exercise was preceded by talks among the Trilateral partners and India, which led to China expressing its concerns over a possible US-led containment alliance designed to curb its rise. Indeed, China has increasingly been concerned about the so-called 'Malacca Dilemma,' whereby the USA and its allies could threaten its vital energy and trade supply lines in the Straits of Melaka. This has led to China building port facilities in the Indian Ocean, as well as the construction of an oil pipeline from Sittwe in Myanmar to southern China.

Recent developments suggest that a US-led containment alliance is not likely to eventuate. Australia has developed a complementary economic relationship with China, on account of the latter's voracious demand for resources. Indeed, in 2007 China became Australia's largest trading partner.The Obama Administration has also explicitly rejected using containment against China, preferring instead to pursue a policy of engagement in order to manage its rise. However, regional allies and non-traditional allies such as Viet Nam would be likely to look to the USA to contain China if it were to become increasingly aggressive in pursuing its national interests instead of utilizing diplomacy and working through regional institutions. Events since 2009 indicate that the tensions between China and the USA have clearly been extended into the maritime realm, underscoring the fact that the emerging strategic rivalry between the two powers will have significant security implications for East and South-East Asia.

ARMED SEPARATIST REBELLIONS

South-East Asia has experienced a number of ethno-nationalist insurgencies since decolonization after 1945. Their persistence and severity are symptomatic of deep, underlying local grievances and the lack of national legitimacy. Ethnic minorities in Burma (now Myanmar) rose in rebellion in 1948. The Hmong of Laos and Montagnards of Viet Nam have fought bitterly for autonomy, while Indonesia's invasion of East Timor (now Timor-Leste) in 1975 provoked a long insurgency that concluded only in 1999 with East Timor's vote in favour of independence. In China the problem of the separatist Muslim rebellion in the Xinjiang region has been exacerbated by the fundamentalist resurgence in Central Asia, as well as by the emerging links with radical elements in the Middle East.

Of significant concern have been the Muslim separatist rebellions in various parts of South-East Asia, notably in Mindanao in the southern Philippines, in the Indonesian province of Aceh and in Pattani in southern Thailand. These rebellions predated both JI and al-Qa'ida, which is indicative of the local nature of Muslim alienation and rebellion. Global jihadist elements, in the form of al-Qa'ida and its local affiliates such as JI, have attempted to establish linkages with these separatist groups, as the presence of local Muslim grievances appeared to offer tantalizing possibilities in terms of recruitment into a wider pan-Islamic radical revolution. However, the results have been mixed, owing to the competing strength of local nationalist sentiments, which have so far remained ascendant.

The most serious of these Muslim separatist rebellions has been the Moro rebellion in the southern Philippines. Its roots are deeply historical, as the Muslim south has never fully integrated with the predominantly Catholic Philippine state. Indeed, by the 1960s the Muslim Moros had become a minority in many parts of their traditional southern homeland, owing to an influx of immigrant Catholic settlers from the north. In addition to landlessness and discrimination, much poverty and unemployment exists among Muslim Moros, contributing to a very strong sense of alienation. The armed rebellion was instigated in 1972 by the Moro National Liberation Front (MNLF) led by Nur Misuari. After the MNLF signed a peace accord in 1996, the separatist cause was assumed by the more overtly religious MILF, led by Hashim Salamat, a Muslim cleric. The MILF established links with militant elements in the Middle East, and Osama bin Laden provided it with financial and training assistance.

The events of 11 September 2001, however, prompted the MILF leadership to re-evaluate its relationship with al-Qa'ida. Confronted with having to join the global *jihad* against the West, the MILF leadership distanced itself from al-Qa'ida and instead reiterated its nationalist credentials and the objective of an independent Moro homeland. Hashim Salamat's death through natural causes in August 2003 and his succession by Murad Ebrahim strengthened the nationalist orientation of the movement and opened the way for negotiations with the Government. An International Monitoring Team from Malaysia, Brunei, Libya and Japan helped to maintain the cease-fire, thereby providing favourable conditions for negotiations to take place. A peace agreement was to have been formally signed in August 2008, but the Philippine Supreme Court ruled that the demarcation of what constituted the ancestral domains of the Moros was unconstitutional, thus blocking the agreement's ratification. This prompted renewed fighting between the MILF and government forces, leading to the displacement of more than 400,000 people. For its part, the Government restructured its counter-insurgency and counter-terrorism strategy in order better to contain the ongoing Moro and communist insurgencies. It replaced the previous military-orientated 14-point plan to combat terrorism with a new 16-point counter-terrorism programme in 2005, and the legislature adopted the Human Security Act in 2007. Together, these measures constituted a new comprehensive strategy using political, diplomatic and economic means, in addition to the provision of security by the armed forces, a strategy that focused on addressing the fundamental causes underlying the recourse to armed rebellion. An Anti-Terrorism Council has also been established to co-ordinate the new 'whole-of-government' approach. However, the problem is the lack of resources, and serious governance issues such as corruption, which would hinder the effective implemention of the new comprehensive approach.

On the political front, the electoral victory of Benigno Aquino in 2010 provided a fresh start to the stalled peace process, as he pledged in his inaugural speech to seek a 'peaceful and just settlement of the conflict.' Talks have since resumed, with the MILF leadership becoming wary of fighting and prepared to seek a negotiated settlement. However, even if a final peace agreement is signed, major security challenges would remain. The presence of younger, extremist elements within the MILF, as well as in the extremist Abu Sayyaf, and the opposition of many Catholics to a peace agreement perceived as giving too many concessions to the Muslims, are likely to result in the continuation of violence.

Another protracted Muslim separatist insurgency, in southern Thailand, has shown signs of worsening. Since 1909, when the Anglo-Siamese Treaty confirmed Thailand's control of four Malay Muslim provinces in the south, the Malays have always viewed the Government in the Thai capital of Bangkok as an occupying colonial power. The insurgency movement is heavily fragmented, although the four major groups are: Barisan Revolusi Nasional—Coordinate (BRN—C); Pemuda, a separatist youth movement; Gerakan Mujahidin Islam Patani (GMIP), which was established by former Afghan *mujahidin* in the 1990s; and the New Patani United Liberation Organization (New PULO), created in 1995 by dissident members of one of the oldest insurgent groups in the south.

After years of sporadic violence in Thailand, from 2001 a series of attacks took place in which the insurgents targeted the security forces, government officials, school-teachers and Buddhist monks. There have been numerous allegations of links with international terrorism, a not implausible charge, as the scale and co-ordinated nature of the attacks appeared to suggest a new level of training, leadership and sophistication hitherto unseen among the Thai separatists. Three prominent southern Muslim community leaders were also arrested in 2003 on suspicion of planning major bomb attacks against foreign embassies and tourist spots. Members of JI, including Hambali, its operations leader, are also known to have sheltered in Thailand.

Nevertheless, this spate of attacks did not bear the hallmarks of al-Qa'ida and JI. The many foreigners in beach resorts in southern Thailand were not targeted, nor have there been mass-casualty attacks involving the use of ammonium nitrate and car bombs, as has happened in JI-linked attacks elsewhere, such as on Bali. Indeed, Hambali, who remained in US custody in early 2011, was reported to have told his interrogators that while al-Qa'ida and JI had approached southern Thai separatists for assistance in attacking Westerners, they were rebuffed, indicating that the nationalist momentum, as in the case of the MILF in Mindanao, had remained stronger.

However, two major incidents exacerbated tensions in southern Thailand. In April 2004 the Thai security forces killed 108 Muslim rebels in a single day, including a number who had been sheltering in an historic mosque. In October of the same year 78 unarmed Muslim demonstrators died after they suffocated while being transported in overcrowded police vans, several other demonstrators having been shot dead by the security forces. The extraordinary mishandling of these incidents by the Government of Thaksin Shinawatra, which had taken a military-orientated approach to the insurgency, deeply angered Muslims. The level of violence thus increased sharply from January 2004.

The coup against the Thaksin Government in September 2006 and its replacement by an interim administration led by Surayud Chulanont appeared to offer fresh prospects for resolving the insurgency. Surayud made an unprecedented apology to the Muslims of southern Thailand for past abuses, announced an end to the 'blacklisting' of suspected insurgents and expanded efforts at reconciliation. However, the Government's unco-ordinated approach and lack of a strategic plan led to uneven implementation and the alienation of the local Buddhist population. The separatists responded by intensifying their campaign of random violence against civilians in order to undermine the efforts towards conciliation, resulting in increased communal tensions and vigilante action against Muslims by Buddhists. The subsequent political conflict between the populist pro-Thaksin forces and the conservative royalist-military camp, exemplified by the civil disturbances in 2008 that resulted in the closure of Bangkok airport, led to a lack of central leadership and of any coherence in strategy towards the southern provinces. The Government of Abhisit Vejjajiva, who held office between December 2008 and July 2011, was preoccupied with political survival, in view of concerted challenges mounted by the supporters of Thaksin, and did not make any substantial policy shifts towards the south. For example, it failed to empower the civilian-led Southern Border Provinces Administrative Centre, which had functioned with relative effectiveness in reconciling the Muslims in the south prior to its disbandment by the Thaksin Government. More seriously, the continued failure to remedy the fundamental grievances of the Malay Muslims and address past abuses, such as the events of 2004, could transform the separatist insurgency by providing opportunities for radical groups seeking to link the problems in the south with the global jihad. Indeed, there are some fears that the situation in southern Thailand could yet become comparable to that prevailing in the separatist Russian republic of Chechnya.

Another serious armed insurgency that has bedevilled East Asia has been the Uygur (Uighur) Muslim separatist movement in the Xinjiang region of China. Like the other Muslim separatist movements in Asia, the cause of this separatist insurgency lies with political, economic and social grievances that have fundamental historical origins. The Uygurs have never accepted Chinese rule and have resisted Chinese attempts at assimilation, while China takes the view that (as with Tibet) it has an historical claim to sovereignty over the region, which it annexed in 1759. The problem has been exacerbated by massive Chinese migration to Xinjiang. This has resulted in communal tensions, which have been compounded by deep religious and cultural differences, as exemplified by the riots in Urumqi, the capital of Xinjiang, in July 2009, when nearly 200 people were killed.

The disintegration of the Soviet Union after the end of the 'Cold War', the world-wide Islamic revival and China's post-Mao 'open door' policy provided fresh impetus to the desire for a separate state, as other Central Asian republics achieved their long-desired independence. In view of the harsh political situation, the aspirations for Uygur independence have been carried by a number of clandestine terrorist groups. In the early 1990s they united under the banner of the Eastern Turkestan Islamic Movement (ETIM), a terrorist insurgent network consisting of 13 organizations, the objective of which is the secession of Xinjiang (or Eastern Turkestan) from China.

Since the early 1990s ETIM has carried out numerous terrorist attacks in China, with most of these being perpetrated in the Xinjiang region, although they have operated in neighbouring Central Asian states. According to the Chinese authorities, the low-level insurgency led to some 200 attacks between 1990 and 2001, resulting in the deaths of 162 people. The response of the Chinese Government has been harsh, with summary executions, torture and detention without trial.

The treatment of the separatists attracted criticism, but this became muted following the events of 11 September 2001. ETIM is believed to have strong connections with al-Qa'ida, having received financial and training assistance from it. Indeed, US-led forces in Afghanistan captured a number of Uygurs during operations there after September 2001. In 2002, therefore, the USA designated ETIM as a terrorist organization. To address the Islamist threat in Central Asia, in June 2001 China helped to found the Shanghai Co-operation Organization (SCO), grouping China, Russia, Kazakhstan, Kyrgyzstan, Tajikistan and Uzbekistan. However, an unspoken objective of the SCO has also been to contain US influence in Central Asia. The SCO established a counter-terrorism agency located in the Uzbek capital of Tashkent, and co-ordinated counter-terrorism exercises among the partners. The terrorist threat from ETIM is significant, as a reported attempt to hijack and blow up a passenger aircraft in March 2008 by two potential suicide bombers revealed. An attack carried out by two disaffected Uygurs in Kashgar in August of that year resulted in the deaths of 16 policemen. This was followed by other fatal attacks in Kuqa and Yamanya. These incidents heightened fears of attacks against the Olympic Games, which opened in Beijing in August 2008. A massive security operation was therefore mounted by the Chinese authorities to ensure that the event took place peacefully.

DOMESTIC SECURITY CHALLENGES

South-East Asia's newest state, Timor-Leste (formerly East Timor) gained independence on 20 May 2002. However, in 2006 it became evident that all was not well politically in the new nation. Almost 600 disaffected soldiers from the former Fretilin guerrilla force were dismissed, prompting street clashes that resulted in the deaths of more than 20 people. Much of the police force disintegrated, with many joining the rebels, and street gangs took part in the rioting and looting that ensued. The deployment of troops from Australia, New Zealand, Malaysia and Portugal was required to quell the riots and restore order. Prime Minister Mari Alkatiri was forced to resign, and President Xanana (also known as Kay Rala) Gusmão appointed José Ramos Horta as his replacement in

July 2006. In May 2007 Ramos Horta won a resounding mandate in the presidential election. In turn, he appointed Gusmão as Prime Minister.

The riots were the culmination of a combination of factors, including a power struggle between the President and the Prime Minister, regional differences and widespread discontent over serious social and economic problems. Indeed, unemployment remains at a very high level, despite the inflow of substantial aid since 1999 and of revenues that are becoming available from oil and gas production. The events of 2006 proved that the withdrawal of UN peace-keeping forces in June 2005 had been premature. This prompted the establishment in August 2006 of a new UN peace-keeping mission, the UN Integrated Mission in Timor-Leste (UNMIT). However, a renegade officer, Maj. Alfredo Reinado Alves, continued to lead rebel elements. A fresh crisis arose in February 2008 when Reinado attempted to assassinate President Ramos Horta. Reinado was shot and killed, and Ramos Horta was seriously injured. A separate attempt either to kill or kidnap Gusmão failed. In March 2010 a court sentenced 23 defendants to prison terms for the attempted assassinations. Despite early optimism about its prospects, Timor-Leste has been beset by corruption, crime and fatal ethnic and political rivalries. It was obvious that the country would have to address major challenges before it could achieve stability.

Domestic instability has also threatened the military regime in Myanmar, where the popular opposition leader, Aung San Suu Kyi, has remained under house arrest. Unannounced fuel price rises of as much as 500% led to sharp increases in the prices of goods and costs of transport, as a result of which protests began in August 2007. In September hundreds of monks descended on the home of Suu Kyi in Yangon. Monks in the city established an Alliance of All Burmese Buddhist Monks and asked followers throughout the country to refuse offerings from military personnel. Led by thousands of monks, the demonstrations soon attracted the participation of the wider public and spread to other cities such as Sittwe and Mandalay. By late September 2007 as many as 100,000 people were protesting in Yangon against the Government, which reacted by imposing a curfew and occupying Buddhist temples. Demonstrations were violently suppressed, leaving up to 200 people dead and thousands in detention, including many monks.

The violent suppression drew an unprecedented public rebuke from ASEAN, which had hitherto always avoided any interference in the domestic affairs of member states. The European Union enacted sanctions against 1,207 firms in Myanmar and expanded visa bans and asset freezes on the country's military leaders. The UN special envoy to Myanmar, Ibrahim Gambari, made several visits in an attempt to expedite the Government's own 'roadmap' to democracy, which was supposed to lead to elections in 2010, but he was shunned by the senior military leadership. Indeed, the military regime banned Suu Kyi from participating in the planned elections. In August 2009 the military regime also sentenced her to a further 18 months of house arrest for violating her detention rules after an uninvited US citizen swam across a lake to her compound in a bizarre incident. Although the Government indicated in January 2010 that Suu Kyi would be released in November, it did not divulge the terms of the release. In February, however, it did release the Vice-Chairman of the National League for Democracy (NLD), Tin Oo, who had been imprisoned for over a decade and was now 82 years old. The NLD announced that it would boycott the 2010 elections, citing unjust electoral laws that would ban thousands of political prisoners from taking part. Suu Kyi was released from house arrest in November.

In China, as the Olympic Games approached in 2008, the protests that took place in Tibet in March were a serious embarrassment to the Government. Initially led by monks, the demonstrations rapidly escalated into violence, with Tibetans attacking Chinese-owned shops and businesses in the regional capital of Lhasa, and the authorities responding harshly. More than 100 people were reportedly killed in the violence. Despite the implementation of many development projects in the region, ordinary Tibetans feel that their unique Buddhist culture is under threat; they perceive these projects as benefiting the many Han Chinese migrants who now live there. The authorities' forceful suppression of the protests prompted global condemnation of China, which was expressed in demonstrations along the route of the Olympic torch being carried around the world. The response of most Chinese was to defend their Government in a display of nationalism, against what they felt was biased Western reporting and interference in China's territorial integrity (a sensitive national issue in China on account of its historical humiliation by Western powers). Although discussions were subsequently held with representatives of the Dalai Lama, they were not productive, owing to mutual suspicion and recrimination. In March 2009 about 100 monks were detained after hundreds of Tibetans attacked a police station. The Tibet issue also contributed to new tensions between China and India in 2009, stimulated by press reports in India of incursions by China along the disputed border between the two countries. China also criticized visits in late 2009 by both the Dalai Lama and the Indian Prime Minister, Manmohan Singh, to the Indian state of Arunachal Pradesh, which China claims as its territory. At the centre of the new tensions is thus the Tibet issue, as China disapproves of India's sheltering of the Dalai Lama and keeping alive Tibetan culture and political identity.

In Thailand, bitter political divisions between the populist Prime Minister Thaksin Shinawatra and those in the military and bureaucratic establishment led to his removal from office in September 2006, in a military coup. In December 2008 Abhisit Vejjajiva, leader of the Democrat Party, was chosen to become the new Prime Minister. However, this was opposed by the United Front for Democracy against Dictatorship (UDD or 'Red Shirts'), a loose coalition of left-wing activists and pro-democracy campaigners, which also included the rural poor from the north and north-east provinces who supported Thaksin and had benefited from his policies. The 'Red Shirts' viewed the Abhisit Government as illegitimate and demanded fresh elections. However, they were opposed by another political force in Thailand, the 'Yellow Shirts', comprising royalists, business people and the urban middle class, grouped within the People's Alliance for Democracy (PAD). In March 2010 the 'Red Shirts' launched protests aimed at bringing down the unelected Abhisit Government. The protesters barricaded themselves into an encampment in central Bangkok and, after a two-month stand-off, were forcibly evicted by the armed forces. At least 50 people were killed in the protests, mostly by troops using live ammunition. Although the protests in Bangkok were suppressed, the political divisions within the country between the privileged military and bureaucratic élite, and the populist forces surrounding the now-exiled Thaksin, remain acrimonious and unresolved. Thailand thus entered a protracted period of political instability, exacerbated by the advancing years of its respected and long-reigning monarch, King Bhumibol Adulyadej, who reached the age of 84 in 2011.

NON-TRADITIONAL SECURITY ISSUES

In recent years various non-traditional security challenges have emerged in East and South-East Asia. These challenges have been so serious that they have assumed almost apocalyptic proportions, attracting global attention.

Significant health issues have included the outbreak of Severe Acute Respiratory Syndrome (SARS) in southern China in 2002, which by the following year had affected the entire region. By the time the viral disease had apparently run its course in mid-2003, more than 8,000 cases had been recorded throughout the region, with the number of deaths exceeding 700. The SARS crisis was surpassed by growing concerns over a potential regional pandemic of avian influenza ('bird flu'). The lethal H5N1 virus demonstrated its ability to infect humans if they came into contact with sick birds. Should the virus mutate to transmit more easily among humans, a repetition of the devastating world-wide influenza pandemic of 1918–19, when at least 40m. people died, might be possible. In 2006 the World Health Organization (WHO) ranked bird flu as the most significant danger to global health. As of mid-May 2011 there were 553 confirmed cases world-wide; the countries affected included Cambodia, China, Egypt, Indonesia, Thailand, Viet Nam, Laos and Myanmar. Of these, 323 people had died, a disturbing mortality figure; 148 deaths had occurred in Indonesia, raising concerns over the spread of the disease there. The disease appeared to be spreading fastest in Egypt and Indonesia, with 143 and 177 confirmed cases of infection, respectively, by mid-May 2011. There thus remained genuine concern over an impending pandemic.

However, environmental issues and serious natural disasters have become more prominent. The severity of natural disasters in the region was confirmed in a report released by the UN in October 2010, which estimated that people in the Asia-Pacific region are four times more likely to be affected by natural disasters than those in Africa and 25 times more likely than those in Europe or North America. Over the past three decades, the region had accounted for 85% of world-wide deaths due to natural disasters.

Indeed, various natural disasters in Asia have attracted international attention. A massive tsunami caused by an earthquake off the coast of Sumatra in December 2004 killed an estimated 226,400 people throughout the Indian Ocean region. The majority of the dead were in Indonesia, mainly in Aceh.

In early May 2008 a massive cyclone devastated the delta region of southern Myanmar. The Red Cross reported that as many as 128,000 people had been killed and 2.5m. made homeless. The response of the Government was one of indifference and outright obstructiveness towards international aid relief. Instead, the military junta proceeded with a referendum on the issue of a new constitution that would entrench its power. Eventually, after much pressure, particularly from ASEAN and the UN, the junta accepted limited relief aid from India, China, Bangladesh, Thailand, the USA and the UN, although it remained reluctant to allow large-scale international relief operations to take place. It was only in late May that the junta permitted the first foreign aid team, from Thailand, to visit the affected region.

The cyclone crisis in Myanmar was rapidly followed by the devastating earthquake that struck Sichuan Province in China later in May 2008. With a magnitude of 8.0, the earthquake destroyed many homes and institutions, including hospitals, factories and schools. The region's infrastructure, notably roads, bridges and railways, was badly damaged. This was the worst earthquake to occur in China since that of 1976, when perhaps 300,000 people were killed in Tangshan. The final death toll was 87,476., and 5m. people were made homeless. In contrast to Myanmar (and, as some pointed out, to the US Government's tardy and disorganized response to Hurricane Katrina in 2005), the Chinese Government acted swiftly, mobilizing tens of thousands of troops and emergency workers in urgent rescue and relief efforts, with Premier Wen Jiabao flying to the scene and personally directing operations. Local and international media provided very extensive coverage, for a global audience, of the rescue efforts. Ironically, amid the expressions of international sympathy, this natural disaster shifted attention from the Tibet issue and diminished tensions in advance of the Olympic Games in Beijing.

Elsewhere, an earthquake in the South Pacific in September 2009 caused a tsunami that devastated a number of islands, notably Samoa, American Samoa and Tonga, killing nearly 200 people. At around the same time, a major earthquake in West Java, Indonesia, killed 79 people, injured more than 1,250 and displaced over 200,000 people. In the same month another earthquake, off the southern coast of Sumatra, killed about 1,300 people. A year later, in October 2010, another earthquake in Sumatra resulted in a tsunami, and the deaths of over 400 people. This was after another major earthquake in China in April 2010, in the remote western province of Qinghai, where the final death toll was officially put at 2,698, with more than 12,000 injured.

Apart from earthquakes, massive storms and flooding have affected a number of countries. In Fiji, storms and flooding in January 2009 led to about a dozen deaths. At the end of September 2009 a 'super-typhoon' struck the Philippines, Viet Nam, Cambodia and Laos. Typhoon Ketsana led to the heaviest rainfall in the Philippines for 40 years, flooding the capital, Manila. In total, several million people in all the affected countries were displaced and more than 400 were killed. In August 2010 heavy rainfall and flooding resulted in a disastrous mudslide in Gansu Province, in north-west China, which killed over 1,500 people. There have also been major volcanic eruptions. In Indonesia the eruptions of Mount Merapi in Central Java in October 2010 caused more than 300 deaths, and the evacuation of over 350,000 people. In January 2011 the eruption of Mount Bromo in East Java disrupted commercial aviation on the tourist resort island of Bali.

These natural disasters were overshadowed by the devastating earthquake off the coast of Japan in March 2011, an event that led to a massive tsunami, which was witnessed, through television broadcasts, by a global audience. The tsunami devastated the Sendai region, north of Tokyo, destroying coastal towns and villages. By July 2011 the Japanese authorities had listed more than 15,500 people as dead, while more than 7,000 others were recorded as missing and presumed dead. The tsunami also damaged the cooling systems of the Fukushima nuclear power plant, north of Tokyo, leading to major radiation leakage that contaminated adjacent soil, air, inland water and seas. The event was classified as a Level 7 incident on the International Nuclear and Radiological Event Scale, on a par with the 1986 Chornobyl (Chernobyl) disaster in Ukraine. The earthquake and tsunami were clearly the most devastating disasters to affect Japan since the end of the Second World War, prompting a rare public address by Emperor Akihito to reassure the general populace. The Japanese Government estimated that the cost of reconstruction would be more than US $309,000m. The USA responded by carrying out Operation Tomodachi ('Friends') which involved relief and rescue operations by 22 ships, 132 aircraft and more than 15,000 personnel. Other countries, including China, sent rescue teams to assist. The events in Japan were followed by a major earthquake in Myanmar in late March 2011, measuring 6.8 on the scale of magnitude, which killed more than 120 people.

BIBLIOGRAPHY

Abuza, Zachary. *Militant Islam in Southeast Asia: Crucible of Terror.* Boulder, CO, Lynne Rienner Publishers, 2003.

Acharya, Amitav. *Constructing a Security Community in Southeast Asia—ASEAN and the Problem of Regional Order.* Abingdon, Routledge, 2nd Edn, 2009.

Ayson, Robert, and Ball, Desmond (Eds). *Strategy and Security in the Asia-Pacific.* St Leonards, NSW, Allen and Unwin, 2006.

Banlaoi, Rommel. *Philippine Security in the Age of Terror—National, Regional and Global Challenges in the Post-9/11 World.* Pennsauken, NJ, Auerbach Publications, 2009.

Barton, Greg. *Jemaah Islamiyah: Radical Islamism in Indonesia.* Singapore, Singapore University Press, 2005.

Bateman, Sam, and Emmers, Ralf (Eds). *Security and International Politics in the South China Sea.* Abingdon, Routledge, 2008.

Bisley, Nick. *Building Asia's Security.* Abingdon, Routledge, 2010.

Buszynski, Leszek. *Asia Pacific Security: Values and Identity (RoutledgeCurzon Security in Asia Studies).* London, RoutledgeCurzon, 2004.

Chalk, Peter. *The Malay Muslim Insurgency in Southern Thailand—Understanding the Conflict's Evolving Dynamic.* Santa Monica, RAND Corpn, 2008.

Chan, Jane, and Ho, Joshua. *Report on Armed Robbery and Piracy in Southeast Asia: First Quarter, 2008.* Rajaratnam School of International Studies, Singapore, 2008.

Cliff, Roger, and Shlapak, David A. *U.S.-China Relations After Resolution of Taiwan's Status.* Santa Monica, CA, RAND Corpn, 2007.

Cole, Bernard. *Taiwan's Security—History and Prospects.* Abingdon, Routledge, 2008.

Collins, Alan. *The Security Dilemmas of Southeast Asia.* Singapore, Institute of Southeast Asian Studies, 2001.

Security and Southeast Asia: Domestic, Regional and Global Issues. Boulder, CO, Lynne Rienner Publishers, 2003.

Cooney, Kevin. *Japan's Foreign Policy Since 1945.* Armonk, NY, M. E. Sharpe, 2006.

Cooney, Kevin J., and Sato, Yoichiro. *The Rise of China and International Security—America and Asia Respond.* Abingdon, Routledge, 2009.

Cronin, Patrick M. (Ed.). *Double Trouble—Iran and North Korea as Challenges to International Security.* Westport, CT, Praeger Publishers, 2008.

Dupont, Alan. *Unsheathing the Samurai Sword: Japan's Changing Security Policy.* Sydney, Lowy Institute, 2004.

Edmonds, Martin, and Tsai, Michael M. (Eds). *Taiwan's Maritime Security.* London, Routledge, 2003.

Emmers, Ralf. *Geopolitics and Maritime Territorial Disputes in East Asia.* Abingdon, Routledge, 2009.

Emmers, Ralf, Caballero-Anthony, Mely, and Acharya, Amitav (Eds). *Studying Non-Traditional Security In Asia: Trend and Issues.* Singapore, Marshall Cavendish, 2006.

Fuqua Jr, Jacques L. *Nuclear Endgame: The Need for Engagement with North Korea.* Westport, CT, Praeger Publishers, 2007.

Ganguly, Sumit, Scobell, Andrew, and Liow, Joseph (Eds). *The Routledge Handbook of Asian Security Studies.* Abingdon, Routledge, 2009.

Graham, Euan. *Japan's Sea Lane Security—A Matter of Life and Death.* Abingdon, Routledge, 2005.

Gunaratna, Rohan. *Inside Al Qaeda: Global Network of Terror.* London, Hurst, 2002.

Holslag, Jonathan. *Trapped Giant—China's Troubled Military Rise.* London, International Institute of Strategic Studies, 2010.

Hsiung, James C. *Comprehensive Security: Challenge for Pacific Asia.* Indianapolis, Indianapolis University Press, 2004.

Huxley, Tim. *Disintegrating Indonesia?: Implications for Regional Security.* Abingdon, Routledge, 2005.

Jacques, Martin. *When China Rules the World: The Rise of the Middle Kingdom and the End of the Western World.* London, Allen Lane, 2009.

Johnson, Derek, and Valencia, Mark (Eds). *Piracy in Southeast Asia.* Singapore, Institute of Southeast Asian Studies, 2005.

Jones, David Martin. (Ed.). *Globalization and the New Terror: The Asia Pacific Dimension.* Cheltenham, Edward Elgar Publishing, 2004.

Kapur, Ashok. *Regional Security Structures in Asia.* Abingdon, RoutledgeCurzon, 2007.

Kihl Young Whan and Kim Hong Nack (Eds). *North Korea: The Politics of Regime Survival.* Armonk, NY, M. E. Sharpe, 2005.

Kwak Tae-Hwan and Olsen, Edward A. (Eds). *The Major Powers in Northeast Asia: Seeking Peace and Security.* Boulder, CO, Lynne Rienner, 1996.

Li, Rex. *A Rising China and Security in East Asia—Identity Construction and Security Discourse.* Abingdon, Routledge, 2008.

Lovell, David W. (Ed.). *Asia-Pacific Security: Policy Challenges.* Singapore, Institute of Southeast Asian Studies, 2003.

McCargo, Duncan (Ed.). *Rethinking Thailand's Southern Violence.* Singapore, National University of Singapore Press, 2007.

Michishita, Narushige. *North Korea's Military-Diplomatic Campaigns, 1966–2008: A Case of Calculated Adventurism.* Abingdon, Routledge, 2009.

Nishikawa, Yukiko. *Human Security in Southeast Asia.* Abingdon, Routledge, 2010.

Odgaard, Liselotte. *The Balance of Power in Asia-Pacific Security: US-China Policies of Regional Order.* Abingdon, Routledge, 2006.

Ong, Russell. *China's Security Interests in the 21st Century.* Abingdon, Routledge, 2007.

Ong-Webb, Graham Gerard (Ed.). *Piracy, Maritime Terrorism and Securing the Malacca Straits.* Singapore, Institute of Southeast Asian Studies, 2006.

Parashar, Swati (Ed.). *Maritime Counter Terrorism: A Pan-Asian Perspective.* New Delhi, Dorling Kindersley, 2008.

Peou, Sorpong (Ed.). *Human Security in East Asia.* Abingdon, Routledge, 2008.

Shirk, Susan L. *China: Fragile Superpower.* New York, Oxford University Press, 2007.

Shlapak, David A., et al. *A Question of Balance—Political Context and Military Aspects of the China–Taiwan Dispute.* Washington, DC, RAND Corpn, 2009.

Sidel, John T. *Riots, Pogroms, Jihad: Religious Violence in Indonesia.* Singapore, National University Press, 2007.

Tan, Andrew T. H. *Security Perspectives of the Malay Archipelago: Security Linkages in the Second Front in the War on Terrorism.* Cheltenham, Edward Elgar Publishing, 2004.

Tan, Andrew T. H. (Ed.). *The Global Arms Trade.* Abingdon, Routledge, 2009.

A Handbook of Terrorism and Insurgency in Southeast Asia. Cheltenham, Edward Elgar Publishing, 2007.

The Politics of Terrorism—A Survey. Abingdon, Routledge, 2006.

Tien Hung-mao and Cheng Tun-jen (Eds). *The Security Environment in the Asia-Pacific.* Armonk, NY, M. E. Sharpe, 2000.

Togo, Kazuhiko. *Japan's Foreign Policy, 1945–2003.* Leiden, Brill, 2005.

Tow, William (Ed.). *Security Politics in the Asia-Pacific—A Regional-Global Nexus?* Cambridge, Cambridge University Press, 2009.

Tucker, Nancy Bernkopf (Ed.). *Dangerous Strait: The U.S.–Taiwan–China Crisis.* New York, Columbia University Press, 2005.

Umegaki, Michio, Thiesmeyer, Lynn, and Watabe, Atsushi (Eds). *Human Insecurity in East Asia.* Tokyo, United Nations University Press, 2009.

Vicziany, Marika, Wright-Neville, David, and Lentini, Pete (Eds). *Regional Security in the Asia Pacific: 9/11 and After.* Cheltenham, Edward Elgar Publishing, 2004.

Weeks, Donna. *The East Asian Security Community.* Abingdon, Routledge, 2009.

Yee, Herbert. *The China Threat; Perceptions, Myth and Reality.* London, RoutledgeCurzon, 2002.

Young, Adam. J. *Contemporary Maritime Piracy in Southeast Asia—History, Causes and Remedies.* Singapore, Institute of Southeast Asian Studies, 2007.

Yuan, Jing-Dong. *China-ASEAN Relations: Perspectives, Prospects and Implications for US Interests.* Carlisle, PA, Strategic Studies Institute, US Army War College, 2006.

Yuan Peng.*The Taiwan Issue in the Context of New Sino-US Strategic Cooperation.* Washington, DC, The Brookings Institution, 2004.

Zhu Zhiqun. *US-China Relations in the 21st Century—Power Transition and Peace.* Abingdon, Routledge, 2009.

HUMAN RIGHTS IN THE ASIA-PACIFIC REGION

KENNETH CHRISTIE

BACKGROUND

This essay examines the general and the specific state of human rights in the Asia-Pacific region. It is divided into three sections. The first part provides a general overview of the problem of, and views on, human rights in this vast geographical region, even though there are huge differences in the ways that human rights are perceived in different parts of the region, and also variations among individual states. Secondly, specific information on the current state of human rights in selected countries in the region (particularly on the most pressing issues) is provided. Lastly, a summary of the prospects and challenges for human rights throughout the Asia-Pacific region will be offered. Overall, there is no single, uniform version of human rights in the region. The area will always contain multi-faceted versions of what human rights constitute in theory, how they are implemented and what occurs in practice. Any attempt to superimpose a system of rights appears to be a difficult, if not impossible, task, given the variety of regimes and states, ranging from dictatorships to democracies and beyond, in this diverse and complex region.

The Context

One of the most dramatic changes affecting global human rights took place in the aftermath of the attacks on the USA on 11 September 2001, perpetrated by the Islamist fundamentalist organization al-Qa'ida. The subsequent reaction of the US Government against terrorism (the so-called 'war on terror') generated a crisis for human rights prospects in many parts of the Asia-Pacific region, as neo-conservative, authoritarian regimes were reinvigorated in their pursuit of long-standing agendas against domestic oppositions. The stance claiming that 'you're either for us or against us', heavily promoted by US President George W. Bush following the attacks, enabled states in Asia that previously were seen to be improving their human rights records to suppress dissent by 'securitizing' the argument. That is, in view of acts of terrorism, the issue of national security acquired a new political significance. This resulted in the restriction and the abolition of many civil liberties, a policy adopted by many governments in the region. These governments further increased repressive internal security measures, many of which had been inherited from former colonial masters.

From 2005 this 'securitization' intensified; the dominant theme remained the US 'war on terror', which had extremely negative connotations for human rights in the Asia-Pacific region. There seemed to be no end in sight to this 'war' during President Bush's second term of office (which ended in early 2009), and the situation appeared to change little with regard to the protection of rights across the region. This was particularly so in the People's Republic of China, Indonesia, Singapore, Malaysia and Thailand. These 'hard' and 'soft' authoritarian governments seized much of the context of the attacks of 11 September 2001 as a means of increasing suppression of internal dissent against their particular rule and as a way of bolstering their own legitimacy. This followed the disappearance of the debate on Asian values, which was made redundant in the aftermath of the regional financial crisis of 1997/98. These trends reflect a far more anxiety-driven notion that human rights can be completely discarded on account of 'internal' and 'external' threats. There has been a revival of the nation-state in terms of the assertion of sovereignty, as cosmopolitan claims to rights confront state security needs. The region was also severely affected by the Indian Ocean tsunami disaster of December 2004, which killed at least 230,000 people, the worst affected area being Aceh, in Indonesia. Although natural disasters of this magnitude cannot be equated with violations of human rights, they do tend to highlight the nature of some of these societies. For example, the 2004 disaster showed precisely how unwilling the Indonesian Government initially was to grant freedom of movement to relief agencies in areas like Aceh. In May 2008 another devastating natural disaster occurred when Cyclone Nargis struck Myanmar (formerly Burma), leaving an estimated 140,000 people dead and affecting nearly 2.4m. others. Despite the massive scale of the destruction and natural disaster, the country's junta was slow to react, denying entry visas to humanitarian workers and preventing the delivery of aid. These instances must be regarded as cases of human rights abuse, and they serve to highlight the nature of these undemocratic regimes. The tragedy drew attention to the complete lack of human security for individuals and the utter lack of regard and contempt by the regime for the safety of the country's people.

The election of Barack Obama as US President in late 2008 appeared to mark a radical change in the USA's policy towards human rights and democratization. In early 2009 Obama ordered the closure of the Guantánamo Bay detention centre in Cuba and also of secret prisons operated by the Central Intelligence Agency (CIA), the existence of which had significantly tarnished the human rights policy of the previous Administration. The rhetoric of the 'war on terror' was seemingly abandoned in favour of a more flexible policy, attempting to communicate with the Islamic world and to reach out with greater understanding and empathy to Muslims. Moreover, President Obama acted to implement a ban on torture, which was practised under the Bush Administration against terrorism suspects. This approach aligns itself with a new moral and ethical agenda for US foreign policy. The death of Osama bin Laden, the leader of al-Qa'ida, in an operation by US special forces in Pakistan in May 2011, while claimed as a major victory in the 'war on terror', did not mean that human rights issues were going to disappear. In fact many were predicting an increase in terrorist attacks. However, in the short term a more sympathetic Obama did initiate change, which bodes well for human rights in the region, but it will need some time to take effect. In the mean time, human rights abuses remain fairly constant across the region, and rogue states like Myanmar continue to violate the rights of their populations. Overall, areas of South-East and North-East Asia seem beset by issues of poor, weak, or simply bad, governance. Thailand's political system was seriously jeopardized in 2009/10, when political violence and mass demonstrations threatened to overthrow the Government. The Philippines continues to be adversely affected by corruption and weakness, as does Indonesia. The Democratic People's Republic of Korea (North Korea) is simply a rogue state, which adheres to no international conventions and does not heed the opinions of the wider world. Although elections were held in late 2010, Myanmar's rulers remain dictatorial. It would appear that regional mechanisms such as the Association of Southeast Asian Nations (ASEAN) have been unable and essentially unwilling to exercise much influence in terms of procuring change in human rights. Reports also suggest that human rights defenders and advocates have been targeted by regimes with poor human rights records, in clear efforts to deflect criticism. This is a worrying trend for the reporting of human rights abuses, not just in the region but on a global scale.

The 'Arab Spring' of early 2011 has yet to make a full impact on many of the regimes in Asia. The pro-democracy uprisings in much of the Middle East may in time serve as a model for would-be aspirants to change the power structures in Asia, but at mid-2011 it was too early to tell what sort of impact the events might have. In China, for example, there appeared to be little overall change by the Government in response to global events.

OVERVIEW

Theoretical Context

Some observations offer a context for the discussion of human rights in the Asia-Pacific region. It has been argued that there is no history of 'human rights' in Asia as understood in Western, liberal terms. Human rights in their original conception not only apply to all groups of people in all societies, regardless of status, but are also basic entitlements, which eclipse other considerations that may arise from an individual's relationship to social networks or to the state. However, in Asia there is no tradition or political history of such entitlements. Citizens are believed to have 'basic duties', not 'basic rights', because such societies did not adhere to the same liberal trajectory of Western modernization whereby rights were won from the state in political struggle. 'Asian' duties in this sense arise from a person's status or group affiliation. For many Asian governments, the priority of second-generation (economic and social) rights has always featured heavily in political agendas, much more so than the first-generation civil and political rights. In some ways the relationship is the opposite of that found in the West, where individuals are highly prioritized. Asian governments have been seen to value the group more than the individual; if the group means the nation-state, then of course individual rights can be abrogated in defence of the larger national community.

A 'Growth Industry'

The subject of human rights in East Asia became a 'growth industry' from the late 1980s, in part because of the region's dynamic economic expansion, the resultant 'East Asian miracle' and the subsequent failure of that phenomenon in 1997. The region witnessed, over time, the development of a substantial disparity between the levels of economic growth and the dual processes of democratization and human rights; this despite a standard hypothesis in political science that an increasing rate of economic growth leads to political liberalization. In fact, the reverse seems to be the case for some states in the region: the richer they become, the more they have to lose; and the more they have to lose then the greater the suppression of essential, individual rights. Some have argued that the region is 'recalcitrant' to the practice of democracy and human rights agendas. While paths of democratization and market freedoms may appear universal to Western political scientists, a very different approach was being adopted by some of the authoritarian governments of the Asia-Pacific region. In terms of the Asian values debate used to justify the anti-human rights position of 'soft' authoritarian rule, this disintegrated when the Asian economic crisis began in 1997. The concept that Asian values were inherently superior to Western values was discarded extraordinarily quickly, as it appeared that the much-heralded 'Asia-Pacific century' would not materialize after all. The whole point of the Asian values movement was to maintain the high rates of economic growth to which the region had become accustomed, without developing the social pathologies that followed increased affluence in the West; or, to enjoy the positive aspects of modernization without the social problems. This debate more or less ceased with the debilitating effects of the Asian financial crisis in 1997, as the less appealing aspects of modernization, such as unemployment, crime, decline in social welfare and many others, came to the region. This caused erstwhile *nouveaux riches* Asian states to abandon the moral high ground in the values debate, although Lee Kuan Yew, the then Prime Minister of Singapore who sponsored much of this argument, still retained the idea of Confucian values as one of the driving forces behind economic success in East Asia.

Human Rights and Globalization

Although the size and diversity of the region induce caution in making generalizations, it seems reasonable to posit that Asian authoritarian states tend to view human rights as a threat to national security, at least in comparison with the perspective of Western states.

The promotion of a security agenda in the aftermath of the attacks of September 2001, and the response to those attacks, could not have come at a worse time for defenders of human rights in the East Asian region if the belief that human rights are vital for a country's well-being was to be sustained. This time the antagonists represented 'security' versus 'civil liberties'. Although Western governments and Asian activists long ago rejected the Asian values argument, after the events of 11 September some Western governments expressed sympathy for, and even encouraged, the prioritizing of security over human rights. For Asians who had struggled for many years abroad against excessive national security laws and anti-crime campaigns aimed at quelling political dissent, this was a major set-back. The constant focus on terrorism and security overshadowed human rights developments that in other times might have made headlines. In the name of the 'war on terror', the USA attempted to increase its national security through direct or indirect intervention in the political and military frameworks of countries in Asia. It has actively sought to pre-empt terrorism through various measures, while at the same time asserting its national duty to spread democracy, freedom and liberty.

This region is a crucial battleground in the 'war on terror', owing to the activities of a minority of the significant number of Muslims, totalling more than 200m., who live there. Islamic believers reside in Malaysia, Brunei and Indonesia and other areas of the Malay archipelago. Levels of terrorist activity have remained very high in the region, and senior US officials have been concerned that in its transition to democracy South-East Asia has become susceptible to terrorism and instability. Most countries in the region have experienced a relatively high degree of political violence and terrorism in recent years. The Bali bombing of October 2002 killed more than 200 people, and Indonesia has subsequently witnessed many acts of terrorism, including the bomb attack on the Marriott Hotel in Jakarta in August 2003, that on the Australian embassy in September 2004, and a second attack on the Marriott in July 2009. This made South-East Asia a priority for the USA in terms of the 'war on terror', and the implications of this for human rights will be explored. While the 'war on terror' may or may not have assumed less importance in terms of the Obama Administration's impetus, the consequences of the policy in terms of its human rights implications will take years to become evident. For one thing, it enabled the nation-state in the region to reassert itself. Globalization has also affected the status of women, children and everyone who constitutes a migrant worker in the period after 1990. Millions of women have opted around the globe to seek domestic work in other countries in order to support themselves and their families. The patterns of migration in Asia shifted dramatically in the late 1970s, but the numbers had reached their peak by the mid-1990s, with an estimated 800,000 women migrating annually. This has led to systematic abuse and exploitation by receiving countries in the Asia-Pacific region where labour laws have been less than adequate. Human trafficking, prostitution and poor working conditions are only some of the problems confronting these groups and are worth examination.

Human rights in the region have undergone change in terms of the agendas pursued. From the neo-conservative emphasis on Asian values and their political implications in the early 1990s to the hegemonic imposition of the 'war on terror' in the new millennium, it seems certain that these issues will remain contentious for some time to come. However, it does appear that there has been a general degradation of human rights in favour of state (often meaning regime) security.

COUNTRY ANALYSES

China

The People's Republic of China is generally cited as one of the worst abusers of human rights by Western governments and international non-governmental organizations (NGOs). One of the reasons for this is its size and the dominating structure of the communist Government. According to the 2010 census, China is home to nearly 1,340m. people, the world's largest national population. The main concern in China is how to balance the prospect of individual rights with the overwhelming need for economic and social stability, and China has always focused on second-generation economic rights at the expense of political and civil liberties. The country's leadership, under President Hu Jintao and Prime Minister Wen Jiabao, who took office in 2003, has continued China's transition from a command economy to the free-market system initiated by Deng Xiaoping in the late 1970s. Recently, however, the consequences of the economic 'miracle' have attracted increasing scrutiny in terms of their effects on human rights. Millions of migrant labourers from the countryside have borne the brunt of human rights abuses at the economic and social levels. These groups tend to be outside the health care system, receive no state education and live in difficult, often overcrowded and insanitary conditions. The Government discriminates against migrant workers, whose numbers in Chinese cities are estimated to have reached 150–200m. There is little reason to make the argument in this case that economic and social rights might receive priority, as these workers clearly obtain no representation in any of these categories. In political terms, in March 2007, during the annual session of the National People's Congress (NPC), concerted action was taken across the country against protesters, petitioners and rights activists in what the US-based organization Human Rights Watch described as the largest 'clean-up' operation in recent years. The use of excessive force to disperse demonstrations and meetings has become increasingly common. Moreover, China has been criticized with regard to two major issues: that of religious freedom and freedom of speech; and that of Tibet. The Chinese Government has long conducted campaigns against 'heretical' organizations, such as Falun Gong, a religious group that was banned in 1999 and which the Government regards as a threat to social and political stability. Tens of thousands of Falun Gong members have been arrested, detained and allegedly mistreated in custody by the police for short and long periods. Their persecution by the Chinese authorities has attracted world-wide attention. More recently, activists in the area of human rights have been treated with severity. Prison terms are imposed with increasing frequency on those suspected of subversion or violations of secrecy, and this is in accordance with the country's draconian laws. Fabricated charges are also common if the requisite evidence is not available.

Furthermore, the authorities have also continued to restrict and repress minorities within China's borders. Tibet's ancient identity has been suppressed and marginalized since the invasion and annexation of its territory in 1950 and 1951. Tens of thousands of Tibetans were killed in the period following this intervention, dissidents were imprisoned, and Tibet's spiritual leader, the Dalai Lama, was forced into exile. Over time the restrictive practices of the Chinese mainland have also been implemented in Tibet. There is no freedom of expression, the internet is strictly controlled and Tibetans in urban areas are subject to rigid family-planning restrictions in a manner similar to the controls applicable to the majority Han Chinese. Tibet has always been a major issue in the context of international relations, but the global 'war on terror' announced by the Bush Administration allowed the Chinese Government (like many other authoritarian governments) to repress its own citizenry. In 2008 the issue re-emerged, with massive protests in Tibet and around the world coinciding with the 49th anniversary of the failed 1959 uprising against Chinese rule and the attention given to Beijing's role as the host city of the 2008 Olympic Games. In March 2008 there were serious rights violations in Tibet when demonstrators engaging in peaceful protest were violently suppressed. This was followed by violent protest, which was in turn countered by further violence. Estimates of the number killed in these events ranged from 80 to 140, with between 1,200 and 2,000 being detained and at least 100 people having disappeared. The impact of globalization was thus highlighted, with awareness of the issues having been raised, and opponents have put pressure on the Chinese Government to change its policy. To date, however, the authorities have refused to meet with the Dalai Lama. The major World Expo held in Shanghai in 2010 resulted in the silencing of dissidents and subjugation of any dissent. While this suppression was less obtrusive than that undertaken before and during the Olympics, it nevertheless reflected the rigid, 'no-nonsense' approach taken by the Chinese authorities, and the determination to remain firmly in control.

The Chinese Government has deliberately obscured the differences between terrorism and demands for independence by ethnic Uygurs (Uighurs). In the Xinjiang region of western China the authorities increased many restrictions, alleging that Uygurs were in collaboration with al-Qa'ida. The Xinjiang Uygur Autonomous Region constitutes nearly 17% of the territory of the People's Republic of China. Amnesty International has reported gross violations of the rights of the Uygurs, who represent the majority ethnic group among the predominantly Muslim population. In China this led to the development of a campaign against Muslims and ethnic separatists. These violations include executions, arbitrary detention and arrest, imprisonment and detention without trial, and unfair trials. In July 2009 nearly 200 people were killed in ethnic violence.

The lack of transparency in China is an issue, and 'saving face' is clearly more important to the Chinese Government than the violation of free speech and information. China has 1.3m. registered drug addicts, with at least 170,000 receiving treatment in rehabilitation centres. Former addicts have claimed that they suffered human rights abuses there, such as confinement and forced labour. Freedom of information is also a crucial problem. The struggle to control information flows relating to this and other subjects, such as the HIV/AIDS epidemic, has meant that human rights are severely compromised. There are reportedly at least 1m. people living with HIV/AIDS in China, but the true figure could be much higher. In 2008–09 China initiated a campaign of suppression of the media, as the Government imposed restrictions on news assistants working with foreign correspondents and created a 'blacklist' of Chinese journalists (those who engaged in 'independent' reporting). Since March 2008, by the Chinese Government's own accounts, there have been thousands of arbitrary arrests, and more than 100 trials were swiftly instigated under a judicial system that is widely held to be unfair and lacking impartiality. China has also increased restrictions on artists, perhaps fearing their political and social power. The most high-profile case in 2011 was that of Ai Weiwei, who was detained between April and June. This detention prompted outrage in the international art world, but again China seemed immune to criticism or moral persuasion in the pursuit of its goals. Since early 2011 many of the country's senior defence lawyers have virtually disappeared, and activists for village rights and the environment have been subjected to stricter measures. Demands on the internet for a 'jasmine revolution', in part prompted by the 'Arab Spring', have led to more censorship of the internet and of speech, and a general stifling of debate.

China, therefore, remains a serious violator of rights. The number of executions is extraordinarily high and increasing. In April 2004 Amnesty International reported that at least 726 people had been executed in China in the previous year, but as death sentences and executions remain a state secret, the number could be much higher. Amnesty International estimated that in 2005 at least 1,770 executions had taken place in China, while 3,900 people had been sentenced to death, and in 2006 more than 1,000 executions were confirmed. Figures such as these contrast with a senior delegate's statement at the 2004 session of the NPC that about 10,000 people are executed annually in China. The death penalty is roughly applicable to about 68 offences in Chinese criminal law, and the frequency of executions shows no sign of abating. In Zhejiang, a coastal province of China, a prominent businesswoman was given a death sentence on 'fraud' charges in April 2011, a punishment regarded as harsh even by Chinese standards. In November 2005, when the UN High Commissioner for Human Rights, Mary Robinson, visited China and expressed concern about separatist groups in Xinjiang and Tibet, the Chinese authorities declared that anti-human rights strategies were part of the global anti-terror battle and that 'no double standards should be pursued here'.

China also operates along a path of neutrality with regard to issues of abuse of human rights abroad. There is no question of interference in trade relations when it comes to assisting friendly tyrants or countries with poor records on human rights, such as Myanmar, Sudan or Zimbabwe. China has supplied weapons and training to many repressive dictatorships in Asia. The Chinese authorities are very keen to emphasize the principle of 'non-intervention', for example in Sudan, where massive rights violations and genocide have taken place. In 2008 the annual report of the US Department of State severely criticized rights in China, concluding that they had worsened, despite promises to improve them in view of the holding of the Olympic Games in Beijing in that year. Following international criticism of its record, China released a human rights action plan in April 2009, but continued to assert that economic and social rights would be given priority over individual civil and political rights.

North Korea

Any analysis of human rights in North Korea must be treated with caution, as the country is one of the most closed and secretive in the world. It is extremely difficult to enter North Korea, and the Government monitors all tourists and development workers. The regime denies the existence of any human rights violations and exercises total control over all activities. In essence, the political system is a totalitarian dictatorship, and the situation of human rights is exactly as generally expected of such dictatorships. A description of the rights situation is one largely obtained through the narratives of refugees and defectors, who endure enormous hardships to escape the system. The situation is compounded by the fact that North Korea regularly engages in international criminal activity, including nuclear proliferation, large-scale kidnapping and the smuggling of weapons and drugs, to mention a few of its alleged activities, which also include the abduction of citizens from other countries and its refusal to allow stranded people to leave. The Committee for Human Rights in North Korea, a lobby organization in the USA, has stated that the number of stranded people in North Korea is roughly 180,000, many of them South Koreans but also including a large proportion of ethnic Korean residents of Japan who have ended up there. Freedom House, the US-based human rights group, has given the country its lowest ratings in terms of civil liberties and political rights. In 2006 it was rated as 'Not Free' (and was ranked last of 194 countries) in terms of media independence. Furthermore, any notional claim that the regime has provided economic rights is easily dismissed, in view of the deaths of hundreds of thousands of North Koreans as a result of famine in recent decades. North Koreans are regularly on the brink of starvation, and if the regime breaks down and collapses the humanitarian disaster will be of epic proportions. In the 1990s more than 1m. people died as a result of famine.

Although North Korea's proposals for the eventual closure of its nuclear facilities attracted renewed attention in 2007, this development was overshadowed by a worrying aspect of its anti-human rights policies. The state abolished a decree issued in 2000 that allowed for lenient treatment of those who had 'illegally' crossed the border (in effect any citizen who leaves the country). This is a fundamental violation of freedom of movement. Chronic food shortages and natural disasters have also taken a heavy toll on the population of North Korea. For example, in 2006 the World Food Programme estimated that North Korea would be short of 800,000 metric tons of food, a serious problem for the vulnerable such as children, the elderly and pregnant women. This situation has had an impact on human rights, as the North Korean élite tends to take priority. In November 2005 the UN General Assembly adopted a resolution expressing serious concern about the 'systematic, widespread and grave violations of human rights' in North Korea. For example, those who were accused of crime had little or no access to a fair legal system. Prisoners are subjected to torture or mistreatment, and forced labour is common. Many testimonies of North Koreans reveal executions for lesser misdemeanours than serious anti-state crimes. North Korea appears increasingly desperate and isolated from the outside world. In the first few months of 2010 the value of the currency suffered a sharp decline; rice increased in price by nearly 50 times, and the exchange mechanisms for buying and selling seemingly disintegrated. There is an Orwellian level of control over the citizenry: the Government controls all the media and tolerates no dissent. In addition, the North Korean Government has caused tensions with South Korea to escalate to highly dangerous levels. It is impossible to predict what will happen next in this rogue state. In short, not only does North Korea operate outside the accepted rules of the international system, but the regime also clearly represents one of the worst violators of human rights on all accounts, political, social and economic, on a global scale.

Myanmar

The situation in Myanmar has been a consistent priority in terms of human rights agendas, but there has been little real progress since 1990 when the junta nullified the clear election victory of the National League for Democracy (NLD). From 1988 the country was ruled by a ruthless dictatorship, which initially called itself the State Law and Order Restoration Council (SLORC). This was later renamed the State Peace and Development Council (SPDC), in a cynical attempt to improve its image. Human rights conditions then appeared to improve slightly. However, subsequent reports suggested that the country had taken a marked turn for the worse. There remained the problematic issue of the detention of several thousand political prisoners. There is little that is more revealing about the situation of human rights in a country than the existence of political prisoners. Such prisoners embody the denial of the most basic freedoms, such as freedom of expression, assembly and association. The SPDC (which was dissolved in March 2011 upon the inauguration of President Thein Sein) repeatedly denied the existence of political prisoners, arguing that there were only criminals in the country's prisons. In reality, there were more than 2,000 people behind bars, without access to due process, for exercising their basic civil and political rights. The judicial system, far from affording individuals basic standards of justice, has been used by the regime as an instrument of repression to silence dissent. The USA has failed to establish any significant engagement with the Government, and President Obama has given support to efforts to establish an official UN Commission to investigate allegations of war crimes. Not only do the authorities deny the existence of political prisoners, but they also repudiate claims of torture and ill-treatment in places of detention, practices that are in fact widespread. There are 42 prisons in Myanmar, 109 labour camps and an unknown number of interrogation centres. The horrific conditions in these places are well documented: incommunicado detention, a poor diet, a complete denial of adequate medical attention and the use of torture. There are minimum conditions for being a 'political' or even a 'security' threat. Simply owning a copy of the Universal Declaration of Human Rights can result in a five-year prison sentence, as can handing out leaflets for an independent student union. Some political prisoners were not directly involved in politics before their arrest.

Furthermore, the regime is believed to have been responsible for the deaths of more than 70 supporters of Aung San Suu Kyi, the opposition leader. There is also the difficult question of ethnic minorities (a common theme to most discussions of human rights in the overall region). Ethnic minorities in Myanmar, such as the Karen and the Shan, and also the country's Muslims (the Rohingya, a Bengali-speaking ethnic group), are frequent targets of state repression and violations, the most common abuse being forced labour. Men, women and children are forced to work for the regime, repeatedly carrying heavy loads in order to construct railways, roads, dams and other projects the regime deems necessary for development. Often these labourers endure beatings, torture and widespread malnutrition; many hundreds have died in the process. Proposals for the construction of gas pipelines have heightened concerns that this abuse will continue and be exacerbated. It is argued that force will be used to displace villagers and confiscate land. These brutal measures, it is feared, will entrench the military. The use of child soldiers is prevalent in Myanmar. The country is reported to have the largest number of child soldiers in the world. There have also been reports of labourers being used as human mine-sweepers. Moreover, ethnic populations, particularly the Shan, are often subjected to rape and sexual violence carried out by Myanmar's military. In some cases women have been held in sexual slavery.

This systematic abuse has created hundreds of thousands of ethnic refugees, who have been forced to leave their villages because of a government strategy to prevent support for opposition groups. The refugees have tried to flee to neighbouring countries such as Thailand and Malaysia, often only to be repatriated by authoritarian governments. The treatment of the Karen, one of Myanmar's largest ethnic groups, has become particularly severe, resulting in displacement and severe hardship. A policy of burning homes and planting land-mines in civilian areas (commonly regarded as a 'scorched earth' policy to terrorize the Karen) has been systematically executed by the military. In 2011 reports suggested that the 140,000 Karen refugees who were sheltering just inside Thailand's border with Myanmar remained under threat from the low-intensity guerrilla war that had forced them to flee. At least nine camps, which were established in 1984, accommodate these vulnerable people.

Other reports indicated that by mid-2006 about 650,000 people had been displaced in eastern Myanmar alone since late 2004. In 2007 the Myanmar military and proxy militias were conducting raids on refugee camps in Thailand, in an extension of Myanmar's policy against Karen civilians across borders. Many Rohingya whose families have lived in Myanmar for centuries are not recognized as citizens by the Government and are not permitted to own property. In early 2009 thousands of the minority Rohingyas left Myanmar on boats bound for Thailand and Malaysia, and again hundreds disappeared, feared drowned. The Thai Government expelled nearly 1,000 of these refugees who had arrived in south-western Thailand. The refugees' situation remained uncertain. With the slow easing of Myanmar's isolation, the Karen refugees were concerned that they would be forced to return and would endure the regime's wrath. Eastern Myanmar is still a very unsafe place, with some of the world's worst health statistics. Land mines, malaria and appalling maternal mortality are just some of the hazards that the Karen would risk if they were to return.

ASEAN has been divided over how to deal with the country's continuing reluctance to reform its status with regard to rights and democracy; this represents a departure from the usual ASEAN policy of 'constructive engagement', which tends to limit criticism of member nations. However, ASEAN has been broadly ineffective in dealing with the crises that beset Myanmar, a country that has failed almost every expectation from its population, except the supposition that their rights will be violated. In May 2009 a bizarre incident occurred when a US citizen, John Yettaw, swam across a lake and entered the residence of Suu Kyi, subsequently staying at her house without official permission. On this pretext the junta detained Suu Kyi and put her on trial for breaching the terms of her house arrest. This happened shortly before she was due to be released and was widely regarded as a ploy to prevent her from participating in the political process (legislative elections having been scheduled for late 2010).

During August–September 2007 various democracy activists, monks and ordinary citizens tried again peacefully to challenge the dictatorship. This outburst of frustration, similar to the protests of 1988, was brutally suppressed by the regime. Unarmed demonstrators were beaten, mass arbitrary arrests were made and monks were detained. At one point hundreds of thousands of monks refused to receive alms from the military, a severe rebuff in such a religious country. The Government, of course, denounced the events. Following this action, the junta brought the full weight of the military to intimidate the opposition, harass protest leaders and defrock the monks involved. At least 20 people were reportedly killed in Yangon (Rangoon), but Human Rights Watch believed the total to be far higher, while hundreds remained in detention. Furthermore, the continued extra-judicial executions, rape, torture and compulsory relocation of villagers and the use of forced labour in Myanmar seem to have increased, rather than decreased, following the country's accession to ASEAN.

This trend illustrated not only the unwillingness to reform but the weakness and vacillation of ASEAN as an organization in enforcing basic standards of human rights among its members. Western countries have criticized ASEAN (which celebrated its 40th anniversary in 2007) for its 'soft' approach to rights, particularly in relation to Myanmar. This appeared to have little effect. In March 2008 three people were sentenced to prison for giving water to monks on the street; the junta clearly regarded this as a terrorist act. The devastation resulting from the cyclone of May 2008, which killed at least 140,000 people in Myanmar, demonstrated another failure of political will on the part of the junta and of ASEAN. The regime simply did not want experienced aid workers to help alleviate the crisis and assist with the distribution of food and other supplies. Subsequently the regime unfairly tried and incarcerated at least 21 community aid workers who tried to help survivors of the natural disaster, including the country's most famous comedian, Zarganar.

In a slightly more positive development, the regime released 24 political prisoners; however, it continued to incarcerate more than 2,100 people accused of various political crimes. In November 2010 the ruling junta held an election, the first in two decades. However, the NLD decided to boycott the election process, as a result of which there was no participation by the party of Suu Kyi. The electoral process was therefore regarded as flawed, and it was severely criticized by the USA. Any moderation in the country's dictatorship appears unlikely, and human rights prospects for Myanmar remain extremely unfavourable, alleviated only by the fact that members of the leadership are ageing and perhaps becoming weary of their continued control; this may allow for some change in the system. In May 2011 the Government began to free about 14,000 prisoners in an effort to improve its international image, while all death sentences were commuted to life imprisonment. However, this was seen as a token gesture to improve the regime's image. Virtually none of those released were 'political' prisoners, according to human rights groups. Meanwhile, international and regional pressure appears to have diminished somewhat following the election of 2010. ASEAN has also considered giving Myanmar the chair of its organization in 2014, which would represent a dramatic rehabilitation of this pariah state.

Indonesia and Timor-Leste

Indonesia is the world's largest Muslim nation and a country of strategic and political importance to the USA and to the 'war on terror'. It has only relatively recently begun to progress towards democracy and the respect of human rights. Nationwide legislative elections were held in April 2004, followed by two stages of voting at Indonesia's first-ever direct presidential elections in July and September, thus clearly illustrating the country's movement towards democracy, confirmed by the subsequent legislative and presidential elections that were held in 2009. In February 2006 the country acceded to two UN human rights agreements: the International Covenant on Civil and Political Rights (ICCPR) and the International Covenant on Economic, Social and Cultural Rights (ICESCR). In a number of ways, Indonesia is regarded as a front-line state in the global 'war on terror' and, to some extent, for good reason. During 2002–04 more than 200 civilians were killed in bomb attacks, mainly directed at Western institutions. Among the targets were the Australian embassy, the Marriott Hotel in Jakarta and a night-club in Bali; victims included Indonesian citizens as well as Australian and other tourists. In response to Western pressure, Indonesia acted to address the problem of terrorism; new anti-terrorist laws that curbed fundamental human rights were approved, and these laws were used to justify repressive action in Aceh and Papua. This had serious repercussions in these provinces, which were both engaged in protracted campaigns for independence. The Indonesian Government enacted harsh security measures and repressed separatism (easily categorized as part of its 'war on terror'). In addition to the separatist conflicts in Aceh (where a peace agreement was signed in 2005—see below) and Papua, both of which witnessed gross human rights violations, religious and ethnic conflict has been precipitated between Christian and Muslim factions in Maluku (the Moluccas) and Poso.

In Timor-Leste (formerly East Timor, which acceded to independence in May 2002) there remained an overall failure to bring to justice those responsible for human rights abuses, despite efforts by the Indonesian Government to appoint more judges and prosecutors. In September 1999 the majority of Timorese voted in favour of independence, following which the Indonesian army embarked upon a campaign of murder, arson and forced expulsion. A total of 1,000–2,000 people were killed and a further 500,000 forced from their homes. The notion of an amnesty for past abuses (based on work conducted by a truth commission for East Timor) was not resolved in any satisfactory manner. The question of justice for the atrocities perpetrated under Indonesian rule (recent and in the more distant past) continues to dominate much of the Timorese political scene. On the other hand, mainland human rights commissions, such as the Indonesian National Human Rights Commission (Komisi Nasional Hak Asasi Manusia—Komnas, HAM), became more and more ineffective and marginalized from the process of human rights activities, a pattern reflected in the treatment of human rights advocates across the region.

Nearly a decade after independence in 2002 Timor-Leste remains fragile, experiencing recurrent violence. An estimated 50% of the population live on less than 88 US cents a day. However, this belies the considerable progress in many areas of human development since independence. For example, the country's under-five and infant mortality rates have improved substantially, as has its literacy rate. Health campaigns have brought major successes in dealing with diseases prevalent during the period of Indonesian rule. In relation to income and consumption, Timor-Leste has undoubtedly benefited from the substantial increase in oil revenues since 2007, which have been managed better than those of other oil-rich developing countries; the revenue has been used to improve livelihoods, particularly in the rural sector.

In Aceh after the events of September 2001 the conflict between the Indonesian military and the Gerakan Aceh Merdeka (GAM—Free Aceh Movement) intensified. The Indonesian Government declared a state of military emergency in Aceh and a state of martial law in May 2003, after the failure of peace talks, and launched full-scale military operations in the province. Nearly 40,000 troops were sent to counter an estimated 5,000 members of GAM. Aceh was then devastated by the Indian Ocean tsunami disaster in December 2004, when more than 125,000 Acehnese were killed and an estimated 600,000 were forced to flee their homes. The immediate situation in Aceh remained uncertain, and there were concerns that humanitarian aid workers would be prevented from gaining access to the affected areas. However, as the reconstruction process began, an informal cease-fire was declared, and in August 2005 a peace agreement was signed. Some progress followed, with the establishment of a human rights court and a plan to establish a reconciliation commission. In July 2006 legislation granting Aceh greater autonomy, with a commitment of substantial subsidies, was approved.

However, in Papua (formerly Irian Jaya) the security situation has worsened, and civilians and human rights advocates have borne the brunt of this deterioration, confronting a heightened level of violence and insecurity, despite the approval of a 'special autonomy' law for Papua in October 2001. US proposals to spend millions of dollars to equip a 'domestic peace-keeping force' were criticized by human rights advocates as yet another way of repressing human rights, and may be attributed to the global anti-terror agenda. More than 100,000 West Papuans have been killed since Indonesia took control of the province from the Dutch in 1963. In March 2006 there were clashes between the police and students after security forces were attacked. Dozens of people were subsequently arrested and convicted in circumstances that failed to meet international legal standards. Both peripheries continue to be subject to widespread violence, random killings and human rights abuses, corresponding to the general internal security concerns for the Indonesian Government that resulted from the events of 11 September 2001. Furthermore, senior Indonesian officials have used the term 'terrorism' in their rhetoric when referring to domestic groups that are seen to be a threat to the overall unity of Indonesia. Impunity is still prevalent in the Indonesian context. There has been little effort to bring closure or justice for the victims of human rights crimes perpetrated during the 31 years of President Suharto's rule, which ended in 1998. With the country regarded as one of the front-line states in the 'war on terror', partly because Indonesia contains the largest Islamic population of any country in the world, these events do not augur well for the positive development of human rights in this South-East Asian archipelago.

Reports suggest that Indonesia has introduced laws that allow criminal charges to be brought against critics of the regime, a development that is reminiscent of Singapore's approach to dissidents. Criminal defamation law has been used against individuals involved in public demonstrations, people who have written critical letters to newspaper editors and even those who have registered official complaints with the authorities. This attempt to silence criticism is a worrying trend for the nascent democracy.

Indonesia's alleged abuse and exploitation of child domestic workers has also attracted attention. A report released by Human Rights Watch in early 2009 revealed that hundreds of thousands of girls in Indonesia, some as young as 11 years old, were being employed in menial domestic work, many of them working 14–18 hours a day, with some being physically, psychologically and sexually abused. Indonesia's policies on economic rights are seen as inadequate by human rights NGOs.

Viet Nam and Cambodia

Human rights conditions in Viet Nam, which could be described as 'poor at best', have deteriorated in recent years, with severe restrictions on freedom of speech, but with the greatest violations being in the area of religious freedom. Human rights problems in Viet Nam emanate from the authorities' treatment of ethnic minorities, again a common theme in the region as a whole. Documents show that the Montagnards of Viet Nam are one of the main minorities subjected to such violations. The abuses committed against them include assaults on church leaders by police and other officials, the destruction of churches, the banning of night-time gatherings and of travel outside villages and the large-scale appropriation of farmland by the authorities. This systematic campaign against what are termed 'illegal religious organizations' bears some resemblance to the Chinese authorities' suppression of Falun Gong and other movements within China. Montagnard Christians have been the principal targets of the attacks and persecution, many of them fleeing or going into hiding when asylum proved impossible to obtain in Cambodia. Numerous Montagnards have been imprisoned for involvement in church activity and demonstrations. A report in 2007 cited the wife of a Christian pastor in Dak Nong province who stated that people were being arrested and interrogated for supporting unauthorized religions in the most innocuous of circumstances, such as receiving money from overseas or talking on a mobile phone. The Vietnamese Government has also acted to suppress an ethnic group known as the Khmer Krom, who come from the Mekong Delta. The state has banned Khmer Krom human rights publications, as well as suppressing peaceful dissent. Many of these Buddhist monks and land activists have been incarcerated for peaceful expressions of their political and religious beliefs. Police have continued to use pressure tactics and physical violence in this suppression of religion. The status of ethnic minorities and refugees is a recurring theme throughout this essay, once again because the situation corresponds to a general renewal of state repression following the attacks on the USA in 2001.

Viet Nam has also witnessed a sharp rise in the imposition of the death penalty, mainly for drug offences and economic-related crimes. A total of 103 people were sentenced to death in 2003, and 64 were executed, many of them in public. In 2004 at least 64 people were executed. Clearly, this is a worrying trend, not only in Viet Nam but also in Thailand (see below), where there is a determined policy of addressing drug-related crime. Viet Nam also claims (much like China) to be a strong sponsor of economic rights; yet in 2008 more than 650 strikes took place, 20% more than in 2007. These strikes are not considered legal by the Vietnamese Government, despite its assertion that the Communist Party is loyal to the interests of the working class and the nation. All trade unions must be officially approved and affiliated to the Vietnam General Confederation of Labour, which is controlled by the Communist Party. The latter has pursued a repressive campaign against independent trade unions, often resulting in arrests and the intimidation of labour activists; essentially, the Vietnamese Government has tried to eradicate the independent trade union movement. More recent violations of human rights include Viet Nam's laws against freedom of speech. Professors, lawyers and entrepreneurs have been arrested and questioned about their activities in an operation aimed at suppressing any form of dissent. In January 2010 a Vietnamese court sentenced Le Cong Dinh, a lawyer, and Nguyen Tien Trung, an activist, to prison terms of five and seven years, respectively, for promoting multi-party democracy. These are not isolated incidents; some have argued that they are the result of a power struggle within the Political Bureau (Politburo) of the Communist Party.

Cambodia, meanwhile, recorded only minor improvements in its human rights record following the legislative elections of July 2003, whereupon the country witnessed an 11-month deadlock over the formation of a new government. Public demonstrations were banned, while politicians and journalists risked state violence if critical of the status quo. Hun Sen was reappointed Prime Minister following the elections of July 2008. Meanwhile, women and children have often been trafficked for the purposes of sexual exploitation through corrupt official channels. In keeping with a worrying trend throughout South-East Asia, those who use drugs in Cambodia are more likely to be subjected to arbitrary detention and torture or physical punishment. Some detainees have suffered beatings, been raped or been forced to donate blood. Such detention is often illegal and the victims have little, if any, access to legal counsel. On the positive side, the first trial of the notorious Khmer Rouge leaders opened in 2009. Kaing Guek Eav appeared in court in March; also known as Duch, the former director of the Tuol Sleng detention centre, where 16,000 detainees had been tortured and executed during the Democratic Kampuchean regime of the late 1970s, was charged with crimes against humanity and war crimes. In July 2010 Duch was sentenced to 35 years' imprisonment, of which he was expected to serve 19 years.

Singapore and Malaysia

The major human rights issue in both Singapore and Malaysia remains the lack of freedom of expression. Despite their 'developed' status (Singapore more so than Malaysia), these countries have continued to restrict freedom of speech and have effectively curbed and weakened opposition activists either by imprisoning them (as in the case of Malaysia) or by issuing defamation suits against opponents (as in Singapore). Malaysia experienced its first change of leadership for more than two decades in October 2003, when Abdullah Badawi replaced Dr Mahathir Mohamad as Prime Minister. Anwar Ibrahim, the former Deputy Prime Minister, who in 1999/2000 had been convicted on charges of corruption and sodomy, was released from prison in September 2004, and an attempt at some openness followed. However, in a demonstration of the official policy that continues to dominate human rights efforts in Malaysia, Anwar was again placed on trial, on similar charges, in 2009 (see below).

Meanwhile, restrictions remained in place. Scores of Islamists and suspected terrorists were arrested in the aftermath of the events of September 2001; few, if any, were brought to trial. The death penalty continues to be implemented. Following their conviction on charges of drugs-smuggling, a Nigerian citizen and a South African were hanged in Singapore in January 2007, despite appeals from the Nigerian Government and the UN Special Rapporteur. The Singapore Government uses the Internal Security Act (ISA) to counter potential espionage and international terror threats, as well as a range of other potential threats. In 2005 a total of 36 men were being held under the ISA; about 20 suspected Islamist militants were reported to be in detention in 2010. Moreover, instruments such as the Criminal Law (Temporary Provisions) Act (CLA), the Misuse of Drugs Act (MDA) and the Undesirable Publications Act are all methods of inflicting legal penalties on critics. In December 2009 Chee Soon Juan, Chee Siok Chin and Gandhi Ambalam were put on trial for distributing leaflets critical of the Government; they were sentenced to short prison terms after refusing to pay the fines imposed.

Freedom of speech continues to be one of Singapore's human rights issues. In November 2010 a British author was sentenced to six weeks' imprisonment and fined S $20,000 for having written a book that was critical of the Singapore judiciary. Critics of the Singaporean Government and its institutions are generally taken to court (if they are in Singapore) and typically prosecuted on the grounds that they are in 'contempt' of court.

Singapore's reputation for being a developed country that is an oasis of stability in South-East Asia is also problematic if the conditions of its migrant labour force, many of whom work as domestic maids, are taken into account. There are nearly 160,000 migrant domestic workers in Singapore and almost 300,000 in Malaysia. Conditions are often harsh, with low pay and long hours. Between 1995 and 2005 at least 147 migrant workers in Singapore died in workplace accidents or committed suicide, many of them jumping from high-rise residential buildings. Human Rights Watch has argued that poor working conditions, anxiety about debts and social isolation (including, for many, confinement indoors for long periods of time) have led to these occurrences. Globalization has produced a world-wide trade in domestic workers, but often to their detriment. If any country still adheres to the Asian values debate of the 1990s, then Singapore must be regarded as its chief defender. Human rights activists and spokespersons have argued that Singapore is a 'textbook example' of a repressive state. While this is true in terms of levels of political freedom, economic and social conditions for the majority are nevertheless admirable. There is much positive news concerning the development of democracy and human rights in Singapore, largely owing to the changing demographic situation. The People's Action Party (PAP), which has ruled the country since independence in 1965, recorded its worst ever electoral result in May 2011 when it won only 60.1% of the votes cast at the general election, its share of the vote having decreased by more than 15% in comparison with 10 years previously. Slowly young Singaporeans are ceasing to rely on the past as a guide to voting behaviour, and this is changing their habits.

Similarly, the situation in Malaysia is also changing. At a general election in March 2008 the incumbent coalition, Barisan Nasional (BN—National Front), won the majority of parliamentary seats. However, the ruling coalition recorded one of its worst results ever, with opposition parties winning large numbers of seats in the legislature, demonstrating what some argued was a major transformation in Malaysian politics. The election result proved to be a set-back for the BN, but it remained to be seen if this would lead to a concomitant increase in levels of rights. Harsh treatment of asylum-seekers and refugees served to reflect the global trend. From 2001 Malaysia enacted strict laws against illegal immigrants, which prompted an exodus of at least 300,000 workers to Indonesia, while a further 400,000 remained in Malaysia, with no financial support. The Malaysian Government at the time agreed to a one-month extension of the departure deadline, but those who remained still risked huge fines, prison sentences and even punishment by caning. In May 2003 thousands of Indonesians fled from the violence in the province of Aceh to Malaysia, but they did not receive the status or treatment normally granted to refugees as a result of conflict and persecution. If they did manage to avoid deportation, many were then subject to harsh conditions and poverty

During the first decade of the 21st century Malaysia succeeded in avoiding terrorist attacks on its soil. The Government attributed this success to the country's ISA, which allows suspects to be held incommunicado for 60 days and subsequently for two years without trial. Unless the judiciary intervenes, this can be renewed and extended indefinitely by the authorities. In a report issued by Amnesty International in April 2005, the Malaysian police force was accused of human rights abuses, including a 'pattern of torture and ill-treatment' of detainees in custody. The Malaysian Government stated that a total of 39 suspects had died in police custody between 2000 and 2003. Furthermore, according to Amnesty 'the local outcome of the war against terrorism has therefore been to entrench illiberal forces' in Malaysia. The testimony about terrorism in Malaysia and Singapore depends on evidence gained through their respective ISAs. These Acts were originally introduced by the British during the period of colonial rule to counter the activities of communist insurgents. They have been used more recently against political opponents and against those in particular who disagree with the Government.

One of the most prominent cases was that of Malaysia's former Deputy Prime Minister, Anwar Ibrahim, who was convicted of corruption and sodomy on very dubious grounds (see above). In May 2011 a Malaysian judge ordered the trial of Anwar Ibrahim on a new charge of sodomy to proceed, thus confirming the continuation of a lengthy trial that might increase support for Prime Minister Najib Razak's Government prior to a possible early election in 2011. Sodomy carries a maximum penalty of 20 years' imprisonment. The trial was to commence in June but was postponed to August 2011. Anwar pledged to contest the charges, declaring that the case represented a political plot aimed at vilifying the opposition. The decision to prosecute was widely condemned by human rights organizations and was clearly politically motivated.

According to some analysts, there have been numerous civil liberties violations in Malaysia since September 2001. Specifically, on the pretext of involvement in terrorist-related crimes, the Government has arrested suspects, claiming that they were members of militant Islamist groups. The Prime Minister, Abdullah Badawi, in fact argued that the 2001 attacks on the USA illustrated the value of Malaysia's ISA, which was revitalized following the events of 11 September. However, several of those arrested were members of the Parti Islam se Malaysia (PAS—Islamic Party of Malaysia). This pan-Malaysian grouping seeks the establishment of an Islamic state and constitutes the main opposition to the ruling United Malays National Organization (UMNO, the principal member of the BN). Mahathir Mohamad successfully used the events of September 2001 to turn opinion against the PAS, thus producing a tactical gain for UMNO, and against religious-based politics in Malaysia. Citing evidence from credible human rights reports, one international relations expert has argued that Malaysia's ISA has 'led to the arrest of more than a hundred individuals on terror-related grounds. However, the government has not shown that any of those detained has engaged in illegal activity. While in custody, family members and others report that those arrested have suffered serious abuse'. Detainees have been subjected to various forms of abuse, including sexually humiliating interrogations (a common occurrence in the 'war on terror'), beatings and sleep deprivation. Due process rights have also been denied, according to Human Rights Watch. Certainly the USA praised the Malaysian Government for its efforts. Now the USA values the country as a steadfast ally in the fight against terror. Malaysia has continued to use measures denying freedom of expression. In March 2009, for example, the Government notified opposition parties such as Parti Keadilan Rakyat (PKR—People's Justice Party) and its coalition partner, Parti Islam se Malaysia (PAS—Islamic Party of Malaysia) that they would be prohibited from publishing their respective party newspapers for three months. With by-elections taking place in April of that year, this action effectively allowed the silencing of the opposition.

Ostensibly in the interests of national security, refugees and migrant workers have also been confronted by the newly resurgent Malaysian nation state. Malaysia has approximately 2.5m. migrants, who in early 2007 became the subject of legislation proposing to restrict foreign employees to their workplace or living quarters, in a clear violation of the right to freedom of movement. The issue of the basic rights of these migrants, working long hours for little pay and subject to abuse, in particular the lot of 300,000 domestic workers, has long tarnished the Malaysian Government's record. Former Prime Minister Mahathir also argued that although in the past the USA had criticized the human rights policy of Malaysia, the former was now studying Malaysian methods of combating terrorism. In turn, the USA moderated its criticism of Malaysia's policies and began actively co-operating with the Southeast Asia Regional Center for Counter-Terrorism, which was established in Kuala Lumpur in 2003.

The Philippines

The Philippines has done little in recent years to improve its human rights situation. According to one member of a Philippine human rights alliance: 'the painful scenario of the human rights situation in the Philippines today only proves that the "war against terrorism" being waged by Arroyo's strong republic is an all out war against the Filipino people'. In February 2006 President Gloria Arroyo declared a state of emergency for one week. Public assembly was banned in this period, and many soldiers, left-wing sympathizers and politicians were arrested. According to a committee on human rights based in Canada, in the Philippines there were, on average, 19 cases of human rights violations every week, in which at least two people were killed. In the majority (almost 70%) of these cases the violations were perpetrated by the army and Special Forces. Extra-judicial killings (a common feature of Philippine human rights violations) and disappearances continued throughout 2006, aimed at human rights supporters, journalists, clergy and left-wing groups. Cris Hugo, a student leader, was shot dead in March 2006, and Bishop Alberto Ramento of the Philippine Independent Church was stabbed to death in October of the same year, in what were regarded as politically motivated killings. Rodolfo Stavenhagen, the UN envoy for the rights of indigenous people, has also argued that there are reports of natives being accused of and prosecuted for terrorist activity, simply because of their involvement in legitimate protest or the defence of their rights, and this shows an extension of the counter-terrorism policies pursued by the Philippine Government.

Like the USA in some ways, the Philippines is moving towards becoming a militarized society. The 'war on terror' has had a disproportionate effect on civilians there. According to Luis H. Francia, a Philippine writer, their lives have become worse as a result: 'the war itself can be regarded as terroristic, particularly in Mindanao, where the army has aggressively engaged the MILF (the secessionist Moro Islamic Liberation Front) and where the number of internal refugees at its peak rose as high as half a million'. In particular, the Philippine Government has demonstrated very strong support for the global 'war on terror'. In January 2007 the Philippine armed forces announced that a senior leader of Abu Sayyaf, a group of armed Islamist terrorists seemingly more interested in banditry than self-determination, had been killed. His death was a further example of how the 'war on terror' appears to be misguided and manipulated within these societies. However, there is serious evidence of local government involvement in death squad murders in Mindanao, and there has been little condemnation of these at an official level. In Davao City, Mindanao, for example, the number of murders rose from only two in 1998 to 98 in 2003 and to 124 in 2008; 33 killings were reported in January 2009 alone. Human rights reports have detailed the involvement and collusion of police and local government officials in the targeted killings of drug dealers, petty criminals and street children. There seems to have been a resort to vigilantism in this lawless area of the Philippines. In early 2011 the Mayor of Manila was involved in some controversial 'shoot to kill' orders, most notably against five policemen who were accused of stealing 12m. pesos of a ransom, which was recovered from the kidnappers of a Malaysian national. The sense of general lawlessness and gangland killings are pervasive in the Philippines. Developments such as this may have damaging effects in future years for human rights policies in a society that prides itself on being one of the most democratic countries within ASEAN.

In a positive development in June 2006, however, President Arroyo ratified legislation that abolished the death penalty. The Philippines continues to export millions of people who are employed as domestic workers in various countries (such as Singapore—see above). These workers are regarded as 'local heroes' by the Philippine population, but often they are subjected to ill-treatment, long working hours and low wages. In May 2010 there appeared to be some hope that the situation might change. Benigno Aquino, the son of former President Corazon Aquino (who led the 'people power' revolution that ousted the dictator, Ferdinand Marcos, in 1986), was elected to the country's presidency. The elections were very peaceful by any standards, and in his electoral campaign Aquino undertook to combat the corruption that has permeated the governance of the Philippines.

Thailand

In Thailand in 2010 political developments were directly linked to the events affecting politics in 2006, when a military coup removed the elected Government of Thaksin Shinawatra in September of that year. Thaksin had been accused of corruption on an extensive scale, and was subsequently sighted in a wide variety of locations throughout the world, apparently attempting to effect his return to Thai politics. The absence of violence in 2006 meant that there was no overt military repression of the type typically associated with coups. Nevertheless, the coup represented a retrograde development in terms of the country's democratic and human rights, a situation that has continued to dominate the country's politics. In 2010 Thailand experienced violence and strife, involving two main protagonists: one group, the United Front for Democracy against Dictatorship, known as the 'Red Shirts', represented Thailand's rural poor from the north-east of the country and were broadly supported by Thaksin; the other group, the 'Yellow Shirts', were drawn from the Bangkok urban élite and received support from the military and the monarchy. By mid-2010 clashes between protesters and government forces had left dozens dead and many seriously injured. Thailand slowly returned to normal over the ensuing year, but the threat of violence remained. According to Brad Adams, Asia Director at Human Rights Watch, 'Human rights in Thailand suffered a sharp and broad reverse in 2010', not only with regard to levels of violence but also in terms of the increasing use of censorship and ill-treatment of detainees.

Meanwhile, widespread violence has continued in southern Thailand, where there is a relatively high concentration of the country's ethnic Malay Muslim population. Several Muslim lawyers and human rights defenders have been intimidated and harassed by the security forces. Bombings, shootings and the theft of weapons had become commonplace by 2005, and the Thai Government became convinced that this was the result of the influence of al-Qa'ida on networks that were also operating in Malaysia, Indonesia and the Philippines. Muslims account for about 6m. of Thailand's population of 65m., and tensions have escalated gradually. At the end of March 2005 15 people were injured in bomb attacks and shooting incidents in southern Thailand. This prompted Brad Adams to argue that 'Thailand has gone from being a beacon of freedom and respect for human rights in the region to being a country of high concern. Much of the steady progress Thailand had made in the last decade was rolled back under Thaksin's tenure'. Thai security forces appeared to have been responsible also for the alarming rate of 'enforced disappearance' from early 2005. A report released by Human Rights Watch in March 2007 detailed 22 cases of unresolved disappearances during this period alone. Furthermore, thousands of Thai women, often enduring slave-like conditions, have been 'trafficked' every year into Japan to service the country's sex industry. This issue is clearly a problem for Japanese human rights standards as well as for Thailand. In response, the Governments of both countries have been involved in attempts to draft a UN anti-trafficking protocol. However, rights were not significantly improved by the accession to the position of Prime Minister of Samak Sundaravej, who took office following the legislative election held in December 2007.

Thailand has also encountered problems with migrant rights. In April 2008 37 women and 17 men, among a group of 121 illegal immigrants travelling in an unventilated container vehicle from Myanmar to southern Thailand where they hoped to find work, suffocated to death. Since the beginning of 2008 large numbers of Rohingya Muslims, fleeing from the repressive regime in Myanmar, have drowned in the Andaman Sea as they tried to reach Thailand. The Thai Prime Minister reacted by stating that, in order to deter similar attempts, such Rohingya migrants would be detained on a deserted island. Again, the attempts of people to flee poverty and political persecution lead to them being denied rights of any kind, sometimes with tragic results. The problem of migrants' rights is unlikely to be solved in the near future: 3m. migrants, most of them undocumented and the vast majority from Myanmar, will continue to be exploited. The Thai Government's plans to register this work-force have been largely unsuccessful, compelling the administration to adopt a 'carrot and stick' approach. Its attitude that unregistered foreign workers constitute a threat to domestic security is typical of opinions adopted in reaction to the events of September 2001.

Australia

Australia is not typically viewed as a country that is responsible for gross human rights violations, despite a history in which Aboriginal groups have been treated unfavourably, discriminated against and have become an impoverished underclass. Australia has often been seen in a positive light, as a society that generally respects the rights of its citizens, and in general is regarded as allowing people to have a 'fair go'. However, recent indications suggest that Aboriginal leaders are concerned about a deterioration of human rights. There is a view that the situation has become worse for Aboriginal people in the Northern Territory, for example, since the intervention of John Howard's conservative Government in their affairs in 2007. UN human rights commissioners have expressed concern at the discrimination against Aboriginal and Torres Straits Islanders and the mandatory detention of people. Without detailing the treatment of indigenous people in the past, indications were that Australia had been affected by the global repercussions of the events of 11 September 2001. The reaction against migrants, refugees and asylum-seekers attracted the attention of human rights groups around the world. Many governments adopted punitive and restrictive measures against these categories of displaced people. Under the Government of John Howard there was a particularly harsh turn of events in Australia, as major efforts to prevent and punish 'secondary' movements of asylum-seekers took place. A secondary movement is one in which refugees and asylum-seekers try to move away from the first country they reach (for example, Indonesia) and on to a second (and hopefully, in their view, permanent) country, in this case Australia. In April 2009 the incoming administration of Kevin Rudd reversed the policy of detaining all asylum-seekers upon arrival in Australia. From 2001 the Australian Government had enacted measures such as the interdiction at sea of boats carrying asylum-seekers, diverting them to offshore camps in third countries (such as the Pacific nations of Nauru and Papua New Guinea, and also the Australian territory of Christmas Island), and mandatory detention of persons applying for asylum within Australia, as well as the granting of temporary protection instead of refugee status. Many of these refugees, particularly those from Afghanistan, Iraq and Iran, were subjected to repression and human rights abuses within their countries of origin and had little choice but to flee their respective situations and circumstances. Numerous asylum-seekers (including many children) were detained in very poor conditions for lengthy periods of time; some attempted to commit suicide. In remote desert detention centres children were held with adults for up to two years in insanitary, hot conditions, and there were reports that some had been sexually assaulted.

The option of seeking asylum appeared to have been closed. If relocated to a territory such as Christmas Island, the right to apply for protection in Australia was effectively removed. Despite recognition as 'real' refugees under the 1951 UN Convention relating to the Status of Refugees, many of these persons could be denied a secure legal status indefinitely, resulting in a sort of permanent 'Temporary Protection Visa' status. They were, in other words, permanently stateless, hardly an attractive proposition. Australia was heavily criticized by NGOs for its 'uniqueness' in granting only this temporary status to Afghan refugees. Australia, like many developed countries involved in the 'war on terror', has also been criticized for the various measures it has taken against terrorism and which threaten civil liberties.

The Australian Security Intelligence Organisation Legislation Amendment (Terrorism) Act 2003 (ASIO Act) was to allow security organizations to detain terrorist suspects and criminalize the withholding of information. The new law was strongly opposed by civil liberties and human rights groups, as well as legislators. Despite a difficult passage through Parliament, the final version of the legislation continued to allow those between 16 and 18 years of age to be detained for up to a week. However, by reducing the complexity of the situation to the need to achieve security, the Howard Government was forgoing its human rights credentials as a liberal democracy. In terms of its powers to expel terrorist suspects, owing to relatively stringent border controls Australia was deporting only between 100 and 200 people a year. Australia has ratified international human rights conventions and will not deport people to countries where they will not be given assurances that they will not be tortured. Various measures proposed by the Prime Minister in late 2005 included the introduction of preventive detention for up to 14 days, following the practice of the United Kingdom, and the authorization of 'control orders' such as house arrest, electronic tracking devices and severe limitations on the movements of terrorist suspects. However, there was opposition to these measures, forcing changes in the legislation. The broad definition of terrorism proposed by the Howard administration was qualified to require some element of intentional intimidation or coercion. Following much criticism, the Government's view that suspected terrorists would have to prove themselves not to be terrorists was abandoned. Australia is a long-standing liberal democracy, but its record of human rights and civil liberties was called into question after the events of September 2001. Once again the State came to the fore, asserting the sovereignty of the nation over universal principles of human rights.

CONCLUSION

Prospects for Human Rights

The prospects for establishing a human rights culture following the terrorist attacks on the USA in September 2001 appear unclear and problematic in the Asia-Pacific region. The death of Osama bin Laden in May 2011 may diminish some of the capacity of terrorist organizations such as al-Qa'ida in the short term, but it is uncertain if this will lead to an improvement in the human rights situation. The countries of Australasia, notably Australia and New Zealand (the latter not reviewed here), are of course much more firmly rooted in the Western tradition of individual rights. Yet even they have their problems, as evinced by Australia's treatment of refugees arriving from Afghanistan via Indonesia and by the draconian measures that have interfered with domestic civil liberties and rights of ordinary Australians, imposed in response to the 'war on terror'. Moreover, Australia incurred some very negative press comments during 2009 and 2010 concerning its treatment of immigrants and ethnic minorities, who have suffered attacks and other demonstrations of xenophobic tendencies. The Australian tradition of tolerance towards outsiders has been severely compromised by these incidents. These patterns of intolerance towards foreigners are not limited to one or two countries but have international repercussions. The US response to the events of September 2001 led to the establishment of a unilateral, uncompromising stance on terrorism, a policy that was to have serious consequences for domestic security and one with dramatic implications for local populations in parts of Asia. 'Soft' authoritarian states like Singapore, Malaysia, Indonesia and others could now once again justify internal repression with reference to the threat of terrorism. The Philippines could suppress internal dissent with the aid of the US military by fighting the 'war on terror' and had its own Islamist movement, namely Abu Sayyaf, to justify its tactics. For example, US President George W. Bush gave an unqualified endorsement to the Philippine Government's counter-terrorism measures against Muslim insurgents, while some US officials warned that the southern Philippines could become the 'next Afghanistan' because of the proliferation of insurgents. Clearly, the stakes have been raised, with greater military aid being made available to repressive regimes. The USA declared that it wanted an active role in hunting terrorists in South-East Asia. China also sought to justify its repression of Muslim ethnic minorities, on the grounds that they posed a terrorist threat to the nation's stability. In other words, human rights were not so much a priority for the USA and the West as fighting the 'war on terror'; therefore, the USA could disregard internal human rights abuses, while states with problematic human rights records no longer needed to acquiesce to demands for rights reforms. Indeed, this encouraged many developing states with less than adequate rights records to enhance and 'securitize' their country's reaction to internal dissent.

It is difficult to discuss the development of human rights in the Asia-Pacific region without reference to globalization, which not only played its part in the region's dramatic economic growth but was a factor in its rapid downfall, with the onset of the Asian economic crisis in mid-1997. Globalization made national state borders increasingly porous, with the result that economies and populations have become much more interdependent. Studying the role of multinational corporations in the movement of capital, goods, services and labour around the world has become a growth industry in itself. One of the many effects of globalization has been the accompanying increase in poverty and in disparities on an economic and social scale; globalization is at once, paradoxically, an advantage and a disadvantage. The phenomenon helps to provide economic growth, but much of that growth is economically unbalanced and uneven. Financial crises occur more often and have severe, damaging effects on local populations, causing social disintegration and maldevelopment in poor and vulnerable countries.

The financial crisis and the attendant currency turmoil of the late 1990s simply brought these issues into sharp focus. There are serious questions of illegal (and legal) migration, labour standards, prostitution, child labour, child prostitution and discrimination against ethnic minorities, to name just a few. However, globalization has also had positive effects in that at least these debates have started to take place, and a consciousness of rights is developing. Indigenous groups have now become more assertive in their claims to political and economic rights. The tension between economic development, rapid growth and the state of governance is an important one. The protracted conflict in Timor-Leste testified to this; in part, globalization helped to highlight the case of severe human rights abuses there.

Another debate that dominates human rights in the region concerns nation-building. The question remains whether authoritarian government is necessary for successful economic and social development. Those who posit this view argue that national development requires discipline, austerity and obedience to measures that may be unpopular in the short term but will yield great dividends in the future. In such circumstances, effectively national emergencies, governments cannot ensure the successful prosecution of policies without limiting civil liberties such as freedom of speech and the press, the right of accused criminals to a fair trial, freedom from physical abuse by the police and so on. As a society becomes wealthier, more orderly and more educated, it is debatable whether civil and political privileges will naturally increase. Yet if the basic goals of development are not achieved, all subsequent aspirations, including human rights, are doomed. It is therefore unfair of the West, where human rights have evolved within a particular political and historical context, to demand that poor, politically unstable, underdeveloped countries immediately guarantee as broad a range of individual freedoms as exists in the developed world. The problem with this, in the view of human rights advocates, is the uncertainty over the point at which a society becomes developed enough to embrace human rights; at what stage does it determine that human rights are not expedient and are elevated to a different level in terms of priority? As noted above, the issue of human rights (at least as an individual interpretation of the term) has been downgraded in many of these countries.

In many parts of Asia, the problem of child labour, much sought after in the neo-liberal development model as cheap labour, continues to be an enduring issue, along with persistent encroachments in terms of women's rights. Women in South-East Asia and East Asia have been vulnerable to trafficking. The issue of the 'comfort women' of Korea, who were forced into prostitution by the Japanese army during the Second World War, has never been fully resolved in terms of acknowledgement, recognition or compensation. The decline in political rights has continued in Myanmar, Malaysia, the Philippines and Solomon Islands.

After September 2001 the global 'war on terror' produced a more difficult and complex world than ever before. The counter-terrorist measures used by the USA and its allies around the world can definitely be seen to have yielded counter-productive results, as governments often use these measures to perpetuate widespread abuse against people with legitimate grievances. Thus, ethnic groups in the Philippines and Indonesia (among others) can be targeted by governments determined to avert any threat to their country's unity and integrity. Furthermore, during the Bush Administration there were clear indications throughout the region that the USA was planning to escalate the 'war on terror' and initiate drastic measures to accomplish this. More often than not, such efforts are at the expense of individual human rights. Global repression and rights abuses have increased and are likely to assume a more intensive element than previously. In the ongoing 'war on terror', the USA has continued to support countries like the

Philippines and Indonesia. The accession of Barack Obama as US President might have raised hopes for a gentler policy, reversing these trends; unfortunately this does not seem to have been the case. The 'war on terror' has continued and, most importantly for human rights, this 'war' has allowed states to reinvigorate their internal security mechanisms and justify repression. They can be assured that they will suffer little criticism or adverse measures from the USA as a result. The 'war on terror' has given these countries a new opportunity to exploit the security nexus of the state in violating human rights. This trend appears likely to continue.

BIBLIOGRAPHY

See also Select Bibliography at the end of the volume

General

Avonius, Leena, and Kingsbury, Damien (Eds). *Human Rights in Asia: A Reassessment of the Asian Values Debate.* Basingstoke, Palgrave Macmillan, 2008.

Bauer, Joanne, and Bell, Daniel A. (Eds). *The East Asian Challenge for Human Rights.* Cambridge, Cambridge University Press, 1999.

Bell, Daniel A. *East Meets West: Human Rights and Democracy in East Asia.* Princeton, NJ, Princeton University Press, 2000.

Boudreau, Vincent. *Resisting Dictatorship: Repression and Protest in Southeast Asia.* Cambridge, Cambridge University Press, 2004.

Burdekin, Brian. *National Human Rights Institutions in the Asia-Pacific Region (The Raoul Wallenberg Institute Human Rights Library).* Leiden, Brill/Martinus Nijhoff, 2006.

Callaway, Rhonda L. 'The Rhetoric of Asian Values' in Rhonda L. Callaway and Julie Harrelson-Stephens (Eds) in *Exploring International Human Rights: Essential Readings.* Boulder, CO, Lynne Rienner Publishers, 2007.

Castellino, Joshua, and Dominguez Redondo, Elvira. *Minority Rights in Asia—A Comparative Legal Analysis.* Oxford, Oxford University Press, 2006.

Christie, Kenneth. *America's War on Terrorism: The Revival of the Nation-State versus Universal Human Rights.* New York, Edwin Mellen Press, 2008.

'Regime Security and Human Rights in Southeast Asia' in *Political Studies (UK),* 1995, XL 111.

Christie, Kenneth, and Roy, Denny. *The Politics of Human Rights in East Asia.* London, Pluto Press, 2001.

Close, Paul, and Askew, David. *Asia Pacific and Human Rights.* Aldershot, Ashgate, 2004.

Davis, Thomas, and Galligan, Brian (Eds). *Human Rights in Asia.* Cheltenham, Edward Elgar Publishing, 2011.

Donnelly, Jack. *International Human Rights.* Boulder, CO, Westview Press, 3rd Edn, 2006.

Eldridge, Philip J. *Politics of Human Rights in Southeast Asia.* London, Routledge, 2001.

Espirit, Caesar. *Law and Human Rights in the Development of ASEAN: with Special Reference to the Philippines.* Singapore, Friedrich-Naumann-Stiftung, 1986.

Frank, Thomas M. *Human Rights in Third World Perspective,* 3 vols. New York, Oceana, 1982.

Freeman, Michael. *Human Rights: An Interdisciplinary Approach.* Cambridge, Polity Press, 2002.

Gready, P. (Ed). *Fighting for Human Rights.* London, Routledge, 2004.

Haas, Michael. *International Human Rights: A Comprehensive Introduction.* Abingdon, Routledge, 2008.

Hashimoto, Hidetoshi. *The Prospects for a Regional Human Rights Mechanism in East Asia.* London, Routledge, 2003.

Hsiung, J. *Human Rights in East Asia: A Cultural Perspective.* New York, Paragon House, 1985.

Kingsbury, Damien. *South-East Asia—A Political Profile.* Oxford, Oxford University Press, 2nd Edn, 2005.

Langlois, Anthony J. *The Politics of Justice and Human Rights: Southeast Asia and Universalist Theory.* Cambridge, Cambridge University Press, 2001.

Lawrence, James T. (Ed.). *Human Rights in Asia and the Pacific.* Nova Publishers, 2004.

Nasu, Hitoshi, and Saul, Ben (Eds). *Human Rights in the Asia-Pacific Region: Towards Institution Building.* Abingdon, Routledge, 2011.

Neary, Ian. *Human Rights in Japan, South Korea and Taiwan.* London, RoutledgeCurzon, 2006.

Oraa, Jaime. *Human Rights in States of Emergency in International Law.* Oxford Monographs in International Law (Ed. Ian Brownlie), Oxford, Clarendon Press, 1992.

Peerenboom, Randall (Ed.). *Asian Discourses of Rule of Law.* London, Routledge, 2003.

Peerenboom, Randall, Petersen, Carole J., and Chen, Albert H. Y. (Eds). *Human Rights in Asia.* Abingdon, Routledge, 2006.

Robertson, Geoffrey. *Crimes Against Humanity. The Struggle for Global Justice.* London, Penguin Books, 3rd Edn, 2006.

Welch, Claude E., Jr, and Leary, Virginia A. (Eds). *Asian Perspectives on Human Rights.* Boulder, CO, Westview Press, 1990.

Women

Ehrenreich, Barbara, and Hochschild, Arlie Russell (Eds.) *Global Woman: Nannies, Maids and Sex Workers in the New Economy.* Henry Holt, New York, 2002.

Hazou, Winnie. *The Social and Legal Status of Women: A Global Perspective.* New York, Praeger Press, 1990.

Heyzer, Noeleen. *Working Women in South-East Asia: Development, Subordination, and Emancipation.* Milton Keynes, Open University Press, 1986.

Hilsdon, Anne-Marie, et al (Eds). *Human Rights and Gender Politics: Asia-Pacific Perspectives.* London, Routledge, 2000.

Jahan, Rounaq (Ed.). *Women in Asia* (revised edn). London, Minority Rights Group, 1982.

Kerr, Joana (Ed.). *Ours by Rights: Women's Rights as Human Rights.* London and Ottawa, Zed Books, in association with the North-South Institute, 1993.

Li Yu-ning (Ed.). *Chinese Women: Through Chinese Eyes.* New York, East Gate Books, 1992.

Shiva, Vandana. *Staying Alive: Women, Ecology, and Development.* Atlantic Highlands, NJ, Zed Books, 1988.

Selected Countries

See also the following websites: www.amnesty.org (Amnesty International); www.freedomhouse.org (Freedom House); and www.hrw.org (Human Rights Watch).

Australia

Amnesty International. *Australia, a Criminal Justice System Weighted against Aboriginal People.* New York, Amnesty International USA, 1993.

Bailey, Peter H. *Human Rights: Australia in an International Context.* Sydney, Butterworths, 1990.

Hocking, Barbara (Ed.). *International Law and Aboriginal Rights.* Sydney, Law Book Company, 1988.

Poynton, Peter. *Aboriginal Australia: Land, Law and Culture.* London, Institute of Race Relations, 1994.

Cambodia

Duffy, Terence. 'Toward a Culture of Human Rights in Cambodia', in *Human Rights Quarterly*, pp. 82–104, 1994.

Marks, Stephen P. 'Forgetting the Policies and Practices of the Past: Impunity in Cambodia' in *The Fletcher Forum of World Affairs,* pp. 17–43, 1994.

Pokempner, Dinah. *Cambodia at War.* New York, Human Rights Watch, 1995.

China

Amnesty International. *China, Punishment without Crime: Administrative Detention.* New York, Amnesty International USA, 1991.

Asia Watch. *Continuing Religious Repression in China*. New York, Asia Watch, 1993.

People's Republic of China: Repression in Tibet, 1987–1992. New York, Asia Watch, 1992.

Punishment Season: Human Rights in China after Martial Law. New York, Asia Watch Committee, 1990.

Ching, Frank. *China: The Truth About Its Human Rights Record*. New York, Crown Publishing Group, 2008.

Cohen, Roberta. *People's Republic of China: the Human Rights Exception*. London, Parliamentary Human Rights Group, 1988.

Davis, Michael C. (Ed.). *Human Rights and Chinese Values: Legal, Philosophical, and Political Perspectives*. Hong Kong and New York, Oxford University Press, 1995.

Edwards, R. Randle, Henkin, Louis, and Nathan, Andrew J. *Human Rights in Contemporary China*. New York, Columbia University Press, 1986.

Human Rights Watch. *Merciless Repression: Human Rights in Tibet*. New York, Human Rights Watch, 1990.

Young, Stephen B. *The Tradition of Human Rights in China and Vietnam*. New Haven, CT, Council on Southeast Asia Studies, Yale Center for International and Area Studies, 1990.

Indonesia and East Timor

Aspinall, Edward, and Mietzner, Marcus (Eds.) *Problems of Democratisation in Indonesia: Elections, Institutions and Society*. Singapore, Institute of Southeast Asian Studies, 2010.

Barton, Greg. *Indonesia's Struggle: Jemaah Islamiyah and the Soul of Islam*. Sydney, UNSW Press, 2004.

Budiardjo, Carmel. *West Papua: the Obliteration of a People*. Surrey, TAPOL, 1988.

Davies, Matthew N. *Indonesia's War over Aceh: Last Stand on Mecca's Porch*. Abingdon, Routledge, 2006.

Jones, Sydney. *Injustice, Persecution, Eviction: a Human Rights Update on Indonesia and East Timor*. New York, Asia Watch Committee, Human Rights Watch distributor, 1990.

The Limits of Openness: Human Rights in Indonesia and East Timor. New York, Human Rights Watch, 1994.

Kingsbury, Damien. *East Timor—The Price of Liberty*. Basingstoke, Palgrave Macmillan, 2009.

Orentlicher, Diane. *Human Rights in Indonesia and East Timor*. New York, Asia Watch Committee, 1989.

Stanley, Elizabeth. *Torture, Truth and Justice—The Case of Timor-Leste*. Abingdon, Routledge, 2008.

Tanter, Richard, Ball, Desmond, and Van Klinken, Gerry (Eds). *Masters of Terror: Indonesia's Military and Violence in East Timor*. Lanham, MD, Rowman and Littlefield, 2006.

Taylor, J. G. *Indonesia's Forgotten War: The Hidden History of East Timor*. London, Zed Books, 1991.

North Korea

Hassig, Ralph C., and Oh, Kongdan. *The Hidden People of North Korea: Everyday Life in the Hermit Kingdom*. Lanham, MD, Rowman and Littlefield, 2009.

Malaysia

Eldridge, Philip. 'Human Rights and Democracy in Indonesia and Malaysia' in *Contemporary Southeast Asia*, Vol. 18, No. 3, 1996.

Myanmar

Amnesty International. *Myanmar: the climate of fear continues, members of ethnic minorities and political prisoners still targeted*. New York, Amnesty International USA, 1993.

Goldston, James. *Human Rights in Burma (Myanmar)*. New York, Asia Watch Committee, Human Rights Watch, 1990.

Guyon, Rudy. 'Violent Repression in Burma: Human Rights and the Global Response' in *UCLA Pacific Basin Law Journal*, Vol. 10, pp. 409–459, 1992.

Human Rights Watch. *Crackdown: Repression of the 2007 Popular Protests in Burma*. New York, Human Rights Watch, 2007.

Smith, Martin. *Burma: Insurgency and the Politics of Ethnicity*. London, Zed Books, 1991.

US Department of State. Fact Sheet, Bureau of Democracy, Human Rights and Labour, *Rape by the Burmese Military in Ethnic Regions*, 17 December 2002.

Philippines

Hedman, Eva-Lotta E. *In the Name of Civil Society: From Free Election Movements to People Power in the Philippines*. Honolulu, HI, University of Hawaii Press, 2005.

Singapore

Asia Watch. *Silencing All Critics: Human Rights Violations in Singapore*. New York, Asia Watch, 1990.

Seow, Francis. *To Catch a Tartar*. New Haven, CT, Yale University Press, 1994.

Thailand

See www.hrw.org.

Viet Nam

Amnesty International. *Vietnam: 'Renovation' (doi moi), the Law and Human Rights in the 1980s*. New York, Amnesty International USA, 1990.

Kolko, Gabriel. *Vietnam: Anatomy of a Peace*. London, Routledge, 1997.

Ta Van Tai. *The Vietnamese Tradition of Human Rights*. Berkeley, CA, Institute of East Asian Studies, University of California, 1988.

ENVIRONMENTAL ISSUES OF THE ASIA-PACIFIC REGION

ROSS STEELE

INTRODUCTION

The Asia-Pacific region illustrates the stark reality that 'environmental' issues cannot be considered independently of issues of human and economic resource development. In mid-2011 this diverse and immense region, excluding South Asia, was home to more than 2,194m. people, representing about 31% of the world's population, and their numbers are growing by more than 13m. annually. This region is also the location of the industrialized economies of Japan, Australia and New Zealand, of the emerging economic superpower of the People's Republic of China and of the 'tiger economies' of East and South-East Asia. In addition, the Asia-Pacific region contains some of the world's poorer and smallest nations where development capital is scarce and large minorities lack the most basic human needs, such as sufficient food, adequate supplies of clean drinking water, minimal shelter, and access to health care and education. Governance in these circumstances is weak and undeveloped; immediate concerns dominate the political agenda, with governments and citizens taking the view that economic growth must be the first priority, even if it leads to serious environmental damage. In this context, 'environmental' strategies not concerned with the economic and political realities of development and with satisfying legitimate human aspirations will prove to be ineffectual.

Given that the Asia-Pacific region's population will continue to grow significantly for the foreseeable future and that the level of affluence, and therefore consumption, of the rapidly growing middle classes will rise even more quickly, total environmental impact must inevitably increase greatly. In order to achieve the rise in affluence demanded by their growing populations, with minimal environmental damage, the developing nations of the region must receive massive transfers of new, ecologically appropriate technology from the developed nations. Many of the attempts at rapid industrialization have made use of outmoded 'dirty' technology, which has only served to exacerbate environmental damage.

The Asia-Pacific region experiences a great variety of environmental problems, commensurate with its enormous size and extreme diversity of physical and human environments. The problems that are most serious over large geographic areas include deforestation and loss of biodiversity, depletion and degradation of agricultural land, pollution of the ground, water and air, global warming and rising sea levels. The region is also confronting rapidly growing urban environmental problems, with polluted air and difficulties of water supply and waste disposal. Encouraged by economic success and by the immense needs of their burgeoning populations, the countries of East and South-East Asia have launched a disproportionately high number of megaprojects. The environmental consequences of projects such as the Three Gorges Dam in China and the proposed construction of additional dams along the Mekong River have attracted much international attention. Concern has also risen about the impact of events such as chemical leaks and the disappearance of farmland and water reserves in China, as land is converted to non-agricultural uses at an increasing rate. A powerful Indian Ocean earthquake and resultant tsunami in December 2004, and also an earthquake in the Indonesian city of Yogyakarta in May 2006, caused large-scale loss of life. Again in Indonesia, a major gas leak and mud flow that began in East Java in May 2006 caused serious ongoing environmental damage. Two major natural disasters affected the region in May 2008: a tropical cyclone struck the low-lying delta region of the Ayeyarwady (Irrawaddy) River in southern Myanmar, and later in the month a powerful earthquake brought massive destruction and loss of life to Sichuan Province in south-western China.

In February 2009 serious flooding occurred in the Indonesian capital of Jakarta, while at the same time the state of Victoria in Australia experienced its worst ever bushfires. At first sight both events appear to be natural disasters, but detailed investigation suggests that human actions were major contributory factors. Certainly the consequences for residents in both areas were exacerbated by human settlement and human behaviour that failed to appreciate the environmental hazards present in both locations. Unfortunately, in an increasingly overcrowded world, driven by short-term economic imperatives and the need to exploit resources, events of this nature are becoming more frequent. Further evidence of the adverse impact of these pressures on the environment emerged in late 2009 and early 2010. In August 2009, in a relatively minor portent of the 2010 oil leak in the Gulf of Mexico, a mobile oil rig off the northern coast of Western Australia began leaking oil into the Timor Sea, with the leak not being successfully plugged until November 2009. In April 2010 an earthquake in the county of Yushu, in a remote, mainly Tibetan, area of Qinghai Province in north-western China, again revealed the lethal impact of China's inadequate construction standards: more than 2,000 people were killed, many of them in school buildings that collapsed.

In December 2010 and January 2011 the Australian states of Queensland and Victoria experienced a series of severe floods, which affected at least 70 towns and more than 200,000 people, culminating in the inundation of the Queensland capital of Brisbane. Subsequent investigation focused on the management of flood mitigation measures and the capacity of the emergency services to cope with disasters. Queensland was struck by another major weather event on 2 February 2011 when the massive Tropical Cyclone Yasi crossed the far north Queensland coast at Tully and totally destroyed the local banana and sugar cane crops, as well as housing and infrastructure. Both of these recent extreme weather events in Australia caused serious economic damage, but fortunately only limited loss of life.

On 22 February 2011 the city of Christchurch and the surrounding Canterbury region in New Zealand's South Island were struck by a magnitude 6.3 earthquake, which caused widespread devastation and 181 deaths. Damage to buildings and loss of life were exacerbated by the fact that the infrastructure had already been weakened by a deeper, more severe earthquake of 7.1 magnitude, which struck the city on 4 September 2010. Investigations were launched to review building collapses and the adequacy of general building standards and codes in this earthquake-prone area of New Zealand.

International attention was abruptly diverted from Christchurch to Japan on 11 March 2011 when a magnitude 9.0 earthquake and an accompanying huge tsunami struck the east coast of the country in the vicinity of Sendai. The earthquake and tsunami caused more than 15,000 deaths, with another 9,500 people missing. The tsunami also resulted in the failure of the back-up cooling systems in all six reactors at the Fukushima nuclear power plant, with nuclear fuel in three reactors possibly melting through several pressure vessels and into the earth below. This was the most serious nuclear accident since the Chornobyl (Chernobyl) disaster in Ukraine in 1986. It led to an ongoing radiation alert and the evacuation of all residents within a 20-km radius of the power plant. The event also exacerbated international concerns about the safety of nuclear power generation, with the Japanese Government acting to cease operations at several undamaged plants in the earthquake-prone region as a precautionary measure, while other countries such as Germany and Switzerland planned permanently to close down their nuclear power industries when existing plants became obsolete.

Since 2007, despite the holding of several international conferences to enhance global co-operative action to address the threat of climate change, only limited immediate action has been forthcoming. The most disappointing failure to establish an effective global accord was in December 2009, at the widely anticipated UN Climate Change Conference of world leaders, held in the Danish capital of Copenhagen (see below), which was intended to establish a set of binding and enforceable national carbon emission reduction targets after the expiry of the Kyoto Protocol in 2012. Salinization of water and land, combined with a long-term forecast of a drying climate in the principal agricultural regions of south-eastern Australia, have remained a major cause of concern, along with damage inflicted on coral reefs in South-East Asia and the Pacific, including Australia's Great Barrier Reef, by global warming, coastal development, overfishing and other human activity.

LOSS AND DEGRADATION OF ARABLE LAND

The most critical environmental issue confronting the Asia-Pacific region today is the continual loss and degradation of its most highly productive arable land, which, if allowed to continue at the present rates, will threaten the ability of the region's most populous countries to feed their own people. Land is lost to agricultural production by many processes, such as conversion to non-agricultural uses or by erosion and pollution of the topsoil. These processes can convert hitherto productive arable land, capable of producing food crops, into unproductive wasteland, which then requires expensive rehabilitation before production can be resumed. More serious than the absolute loss of land to agricultural production is what has been termed the 'quiet crisis', whereby the productivity of agricultural land is gradually, but insidiously, reduced by the dual processes of degradation and pollution. The term 'degradation' can be used to define the processes that lead to the loss of productivity in soils and to a decline of surface and underground storages and flows of water. Pollution is described as the contamination of air, water and soil by human activity. These two processes have had their most damaging impact on agricultural productivity in the most populous country in the region, China. However, the ecologically fragile semi-arid environments of Australia, and the steeply sloping uplands of Java, the Philippines, New Guinea and New Zealand have also been seriously eroded and degraded by ecologically unsuited land-management practices driven by economic and population pressures.

China

The cumulative loss of farmland in China since the late 1950s and the serious degradation of the fertility and quality of the remaining arable soils, owing to increased soil erosion and the spread of less environmentally sustainable management practices, pose doubts about the ability of China to feed itself in future decades. China is required to feed a major portion of the world's population on a disproportionately small share of the earth's arable land. For 2,000 years the Chinese people have been exhorted to subjugate nature. From pre-modern times China has converted extensive areas of natural ecosystems to crop fields, but this trend intensified during the 'grain first' policy of the 1960s, when the country's leadership was belatedly forced to give priority to increased food production after the famine of 1959–61. The environmental consequences soon became apparent, and the early 1960s witnessed a greatly accelerated degradation of China's farm soils, grasslands, forests and wetlands. Chinese sources put the total losses of arable land for 1957–77 at a conservative 29.3m. ha, equivalent to 26% of the nation's total arable area in 1957.

Official estimates of arable land in China have seriously miscalculated its extent. In the late 1980s and early 1990s official sources estimated the total area at about 96m. ha. However, country-wide sample surveys and satellite images suggested a total of at least 130m. ha in 1996, but the Ministry of Land and Resources claimed that this had declined to 122m. ha in 2005 and to 121.8m. ha in 2007, just above the 120m. ha set by the Government as the minimum area of arable land required to feed China's population. (See previous editions of *The Far East and Australasia* for further details.) The total area of arable land was estimated at 122m. ha in 2009.

Much of the lost arable land has included some of the most productive agricultural land, on rich alluvial soils close to major towns and cities. Increasing population, rapid industrialization and extension of transport links will make continued losses inevitable in future years. In 2008 the largest soil conservation survey since 1949 revealed that almost 40% of China's territory, or 3.57m. sq km of land, suffered from soil erosion, 1.61m. sq km from erosion by water and 1.96m. sq km from erosion by wind. To offset the losses of agricultural land, Chinese farming has become much more intensive, and China has become the world's largest producer and consumer of synthetic fertilizers. To combat the increased pressure on arable land, in mid-2009 the Government announced that it would not permit any new large-scale projects to return marginal farmland to woodland. Official sources have acknowledged that illegal land acquisition and use resulted in 40m. farmers losing their land between 1995 and 2005; a further 15m. were expected to have lost their land by 2010. In 2011 it was announced that the 12th Five-Year Plan would establish a permanent arable land protection zone, in an attempt to guarantee the country's food security.

DEFORESTATION

From the 1980s deforestation received far more attention than any other environmental issue in the Asia-Pacific region. Much of the initial concern was limited to ecologists, but this is no longer the case, with citizens increasingly aware of the importance of natural forests in protecting soil from erosion, maintaining soil productivity, preventing flooding and providing valuable timbers for national revenue. The deforestation and degradation of the tropical rain forests of South-East Asia are of greatest concern to environmentalists for a number of reasons. First, South-East Asia still contains very large areas of primary tropical rain forest. Second, if measured in terms of hectares of forest deforested per hectare of national territory, the rate of deforestation in South-East Asia has probably been the highest in the world since 1980. Third, the forests of this area are the habitat of millions of indigenous people, many of whom still practise traditional lifestyles. Fourth, this region, especially the western part of insular South-East Asia (sometimes termed Malesia, and comprising Sumatra, Peninsular Malaysia and the island of Borneo), is renowned for its exceedingly rich biodiversity. There are estimated to be at least 25,000 species of flowering plants in Malesia, along with 350 species of the dipterocarp family. The dense, tall forests have provided the tropical timber trade with some of its most valuable hardwood species. Borneo, for example, as well as being a centre of diversity of plant species, contains an immense array of animal and insect species with very high rates of endemism. Fifth, Indonesia has become one of the world's largest emitters of carbon dioxide, most of which originates from deforestation as the felled trees burn or rot. The loss of these forests will also have a deleterious effect on future global climate change, as their role as vast 'carbon sinks' is lost. Finally, the forests of South-East Asia have been regarded by local political leaders as one of their last untamed resources and as an appropriate site of megaprojects to dam rivers, construct commercial plantations of rubber and oil palm, and as settlement destinations for landless citizens from more densely populated regions.

Research has revealed wide discrepancies in estimates of deforestation rates in South-East Asia. The area of forest lost shows great variation by country and by data source, with the largest absolute losses in the period 1980–2000, according to the FAO Forest Resources Assessment (FRA), occurring in Indonesia, Thailand, the Philippines, Cambodia and Malaysia. Significant deforestation has also probably continued in Myanmar, with most of the large areas lost being closed broadleaf forests, the most valuable of all forest types in terms of biodiversity. Since the mid-1990s China has become the world's largest importer of tropical timber, with one-half of all tropical trees logged globally ending up in that country, where it is used in the manufacture of furniture, flooring and plywood for both domestic consumption and export to markets in the USA, Europe and Japan, to satisfy rising demand for cheap wood products.

Indonesia

Since the early 1980s the absolute scale of deforestation in Indonesia has surpassed that of any other South-East Asian country, with forest cover decreasing from an estimated 67% in 1980 to 47% in 2005. In 2002 a report entitled *The State of the*

Forest: Indonesia by Forest Watch Indonesia and Global Forest Watch concluded that 40% of the forests existing in Indonesia in 1950 had been cleared by 2000, with forest cover having declined from 162m. ha to 98m. ha. It was of even greater concern that the rate of forest loss appeared to be accelerating. During the 1980s the area of forest lost was about 1.2m. ha per year, rising further in the early 1990s, and then increasing to 2m. ha from 1996. The *State of the Environment Report 2005*, issued by the office of the Indonesian Minister of State for the Environment, estimated that rampant illegal logging increased the deforestation rate even further, to 3.5m. ha in 2005. The FAO Global FRA for 2010 suggested that Indonesia had significantly reduced its rate of net loss of forest since 2000, in comparison with the rate that prevailed in the 1990s. However, the FRA country report indicated that between 2000 and 2005 Indonesia's forest cover decreased from 99.4m. ha to 97.8m. ha, a decline of 1.55m. ha or 1.56%, whereas between 2005 and 2010 forest cover contracted by a further 3.42m. ha or 3.5%, suggesting that in the period 2005–10 the rate of deforestation accelerated. In May 2010 the President of Indonesia announced that his country would introduce a two-year moratorium on deforestation and the conversion of peat land and forest into plantations, as part of an agreement with Norway, which undertook to contribute up to US $1,000m. to help preserve Indonesian forests.

In June 2007 representatives of the European Union (EU) and the USA at a meeting of the Group of Eight (G8) industrialized nations on illegal logging, held in the German capital of Berlin, reported that a number of Malaysian business people had been involved in illicit logging practices in Kalimantan (the Indonesian part of the island of Borneo) and in Papua (formerly Irian Jaya) in 2003. Further deforestation of 31,000 ha of Indonesia's hitherto protected forest was also predicted as mining companies took advantage of exploration permits already granted in conservation areas. According to Greenpeace China, a significant proportion of this illegally felled timber is exported to China (see above). Indonesia's lowland tropical forests, the richest in timber resources and biodiversity, are those most at risk. By 2010 they had almost entirely disappeared in Sulawesi and were predicted to be completely cleared in Sumatra and Kalimantan in the near future, if current trends continued.

A report published by the World Bank and the British Government in 2007 emphasized the profound global impact of deforestation. It indicated that deforestation, which releases a significant amount of carbon dioxide, was so extensive in Indonesia in 2003 that the country ranked as the world's third largest emitter of greenhouse gases, after the USA and China. The report estimated that Indonesia's yearly emissions from energy, agriculture and waste combined were relatively small, at around 451m. metric tons of carbon dioxide equivalent (although increasing rapidly), whereas change of land use and forestry alone released an annual 2,563m. tons of carbon dioxide equivalent. (See previous editions of *The Far East and Australasia* for further details of the above issues.)

WATER AVAILABILITY AND POLLUTION

Obtaining sufficient supplies of unpolluted water is an increasing problem for the rural and urban populations of the Asia-Pacific region. Much of the contamination of water supplies is caused by the improper disposal of human waste, chemicals and other hazardous materials from both manufacturing and agricultural activities. The quality of surface and groundwater supplies has deteriorated as the pace of industrialization has accelerated and as farmers have attempted to maximize their returns with increased applications of fertilizers and pesticides. Growing populations and improved living standards have at the same time raised the demand for clean water for agricultural, industrial and domestic use, power generation and even recreational uses. A brief examination of the situation in China will highlight current and future problems of water availability.

China

The combined pressures placed on China's water resources from rising demand and limited supplies, along with severe water pollution, are the greatest in the region. Between 1950 and 1990 the population of China doubled, urban population increased five-fold, industrial output rose about 80-fold and the area of irrigated land tripled. These trends have continued, with China's cities being required to absorb more than 100m. additional residents in the 1990s. The Worldwatch Institute, a US research organization, has estimated that by 2030 China's total annual water demand will have increased from 483,000m. metric tons in 1995 to 1,068,000m. tons. The most dramatic increases in demand will be for industrial (417%) and residential (330%) uses, but the demand for agricultural water is also projected to increase, by 66%. China's total water resources may be enough to meet these quantitative demands, but they are very unevenly distributed. The humid south, with four-fifths of the water and 700m. people, is dominated by the vast Yangtze River (Changjiang—the world's third longest river) which will probably continue to supply an adequate quantity of water, even if industrial pollution may limit its use. However, some Chinese experts have warned that certain stretches of even the Yangtze may be dry by 2020. The arid north, comprising the four basins of the Yellow (Huanghe) River, Liao, Hai and Huai Rivers, is home to 550m. people and two-thirds of the nation's cropland. All four of these northern basins have suffered acute water shortages, which can only become more desperate as demand increases.

In 1998 it was predicted that unless China could significantly curtail its projected demand for non-agricultural water, by 2030 water shortages will have reduced China's ability to feed itself to such an extent that the country's increasing demand for grain imports would pose a threat to the world's food security. One solution proposed by the World Bank in 2009 to promote more efficient water use and water-saving technologies was to raise prices to reflect its full scarcity value. In 2007 water shortages were reported in 400 of China's 667 largest cities, including Beijing and Tianjin, where overexploitation of underground aquifers has caused widespread surface subsidence.

A prolonged dry spell in late 2010 in China's northern grain-growing regions was followed by a protracted drought, from January to June 2011, in the Yangtze Basin that affected 35m. people. The drought was so severe that it halted shipping along a 224-km stretch of the Yangtze River, severely limited hydro-electric power generation and reduced early crops of rice and irrigated vegetables. The Three Gorges Dam was forced to release record amounts of water for downstream irrigators, thereby limiting its power-generation capacity, with water levels at the worst of the drought reaching 4m below the minimum required to operate the turbines efficiently. According to rainfall records, the south of China is becoming drier, which will further reduce the amount of water available for irrigation and power generation. China's increasing water shortages call into question the capacity of the country to continue growing water-intensive wheat in some of the driest provinces such as Hebei and Shandong if it also requires more water for other higher-value uses. This, in turn, raises doubts regarding the ability of China to remain self-sufficient in food production, which will, in the long term, have an impact on world food supplies and prices. In an attempt to overcome its water shortages, in 2002 China began a massive project to divert water from its (usually) well watered and flood-prone south, to its water-needy agriculture and water-deficient cities in the north. The water diversion project consists of three south-to-north canals, each running more than 1,200 km across the eastern, middle and western parts of China at an estimated total cost of US $60,000m., twice the cost of the Three Gorges Dam. By 2050 it is intended that 45,000m. cu m of water a year will be diverted north along the three canals. The project was originally intended to start supplying water to Shandong Province by 2007 and to Beijing by 2010, but completion was delayed. However, recent droughts in the south of the country suggest that climatic conditions may limit the project's potential to alleviate the water shortages in the north.

Water pollution in China is serious and further limits the supply of clean water available for drinking and irrigation. Surveys in the 1980s revealed that more than 20% of the 878 major rivers examined had water so badly polluted that it could not be used for irrigation. In November 2005 it was revealed at a national symposium that a recent survey had found that 70%

of the country's rivers were contaminated with industrial pollutants and 75% excessively enriched with nitrogen leached from fertilizers. The Yangtze had more than 25,000m. metric tons of effluent discharged into it each year along its 6,300-km length, most of which was untreated. In urban areas 80% of China's surface water was contaminated, and only six of the country's 27 largest cities had drinking water within state standards.

In the Yellow River Basin abnormally high rates of stunting, mental retardation and developmental diseases are linked to high concentrations of arsenic and lead in the water and food. In Henan, the incidence of intestinal cancer has risen sharply owing to industrial pollution, and settlements such as Wang Gou are now referred to as 'cancer villages' by local environmentalists. To date, pollution of fresh water with nitrates has not been a problem in China, but the experience of the USA has suggested that, in view of China's extremely extensive usage of nitrogen fertilizers, high nitrate loadings will begin to appear in the country's drinking water and result in increased risks to human health. In addition, continued growth in energy consumption will involve greater use of coal, which in the case of China is high in sulphur content. This will lead to heavier acid deposition on water bodies from acid rain, which will degrade water quality even further and pose threats to aquatic life and humans in both China and Japan.

ENVIRONMENTAL PROBLEMS IN URBAN AREAS

Although, in terms of global impact and the number of people immediately affected, rural environmental problems have hitherto been of most significance, it is now recognized that 'brown' environmental issues in the cities of the Asia-Pacific region will be of greater importance to local residents in the 21st century. There are several reasons for this. First, the number and proportion of the region's inhabitants resident in urban areas will increase dramatically over the next 25 years or so. In 2008 the urban population totalled 1,067m., some 49% of the total population; by 2030 it is projected to reach at least 1,494m., an increase of some 40% in just 22 years, and to comprise 62% of the region's total inhabitants. Second, by 2015, it is expected that there will be 22 megacities world-wide (cities with more than 10m. inhabitants) and that seven of these will be in East and South-East Asia. Probably as much as 80% of the region's economic growth will be generated by that urban population, with the world's largest 20 megacities using an estimated 75% of the world's total energy in 2008. Clearly, the megacities will be at the forefront of the challenge of determining if this growth can be sustained environmentally. Third, most of the major cities are sited on or near river estuaries, some of the most productive natural ecosystems in the region. Any serious environmental pollution in these locations has the potential to damage fertile agricultural land, surrounding aquaculture and productive marine environments. These relatively low-lying coastal sites, especially the densely populated Asian megadeltas of the Mekong and Yangtze, will also be exposed to increased risks of flooding, local water pollution and coastal erosion as sea levels rise as a result of climate change. As noted in the Fourth Assessment Report (AR4) of the UN Intergovernmental Panel on Climate Change, developing nations will be much more vulnerable to these threats than a developed nation in an identical coastal setting. Fourth, these large cities are characterized by rapidly growing middle classes who, unlike the environmentalists of the West, are relatively indifferent to deforestation, global warming, wildlife issues and endangered species, but instead are increasingly concerned that their politicians address the environmental problems that create threats to their health, such as air pollution, traffic accidents, contaminated or insufficient water supplies, and inadequate waste treatment and disposal systems.

In very poor cities (Category 1) such as Hanoi, Ho Chi Minh City, Vientiane and Yangon (Rangoon), and also in the poorest slum areas of Manila and Jakarta, traditional problems such as inadequate access to clean drinking water, pollution of drinking water by human waste and poor community sanitation have increased the incidence of water-borne disease. In the Philippine capital of Manila, untreated or poorly treated domestic water accounts for 40% of water pollution, followed by industrial waste water (38%) and domestic solid waste (22%). Less than 15% of Metro Manila is served by sewers, and there has been an increase in water-borne diseases such as diarrhoea, typhoid, paratyphoid and salmonella infections. A report published in Indonesia in 2008 revealed that, in terms of pollutants affecting the biochemical oxygen demand (BOD), the total oxygen required by micro-organisms to decompose organic substances in sewage could not be met and that water in most rivers was no longer suitable as drinking water. Kalimalang canal in East Jakarta, Kali Surabaya in central Surabaya and Yogyakarta's Progo River were among those with the highest BOD pollutant concentrations.

In middle-income cities (Category 2) such as Bangkok, Kuala Lumpur, Beijing, Shanghai, Jakarta and Surabaya, more modern problems, such as air pollution, are a major concern. This pollution is caused by the rapid growth in the number of motorized vehicles, combined with antiquated road systems and heavy concentrations of industry. Improved living standards have increased the production of solid waste in these cities, and the safe disposal of domestic and industrial waste is now a major problem. The poorer neighbourhoods of these cities are concurrently exposed to high traditional health risks from water-borne disease, which probably means that the overall risk to their health from this overlap and possible synergism of traditional and modern risk factors may be greater than that confronted by inhabitants of Category 1 cities. A study prepared by the United Nations Environment Programme (UNEP) and the World Health Organization (WHO) revealed that all of the cities surveyed in the region (Bangkok, Beijing, Jakarta, Manila, Seoul and Shanghai) had air quality that was seriously affected by suspended particulate matter; Beijing, Seoul and Shanghai have serious to moderate sulphur dioxide pollution; Bangkok, Manila and Jakarta have a moderate lead problem; Jakarta has a moderate carbon monoxide problem; Beijing and Jakarta have a moderate ozone problem; while none of the cities had excessive concentrations of nitrogen dioxide in their air. Virtually all of the major cities of China, along with Bangkok and Jakarta, experience more than 100 days annually during which suspended particulate matter concentrations exceed the WHO standard of 230 micrograms/cu m. This compares with major cities in Japan and Australia, which do not suffer any days above the standard. Air quality in Indonesia's major cities has decreased further in recent years, and in 2005 there were only 29 clean-air days in Jakarta, 21 in Surabaya and 24 in Medan. In China sulphur dioxide concentrations are believed to be largely responsible for lung cancer mortality rates three to seven times higher in the nation's cities than in the country as a whole. In 2007 a WHO report estimated that diseases precipitated by indoor and outdoor air pollution killed 656,000 Chinese residents annually. In cities where there is a large concentration of heavy industry, people living near the congested industrial areas suffered from a much higher incidence of diseases such as chronic bronchitis, tuberculosis, skin allergies, anaemia and eye irritations than residents in cleaner suburbs.

In high-income cities (Category 3) such as Tokyo, Singapore, Osaka, Sydney and Melbourne, urban environmental health risks are much lower and confined to hazardous wastes (biological and toxic wastes associated with advanced technology), indoor air pollution and occasional but usually minor problems with localized water contamination. Amenity issues are of more concern to the relatively affluent residents, as they demand high-quality design, landscaping, green space and recreational facilities.

Most urban environmental problems are a result of the failure of governance, which in some cases, but by no means in all, is due to weaknesses in the national economy. It is obvious that strategies designed to improve environmental conditions in the major urban centres of the region must concentrate explicitly on the problems of the poor. In particular, they must focus on public health and environmental measures to prevent or limit the transmission of diarrhoeal diseases, typhoid, cholera and other water-borne or water-based diseases, acute respiratory infections, such as tuberculosis, and vector-borne diseases, such as malaria, dengue fever and yellow fever.

GLOBAL WARMING AND RISING SEA LEVELS

There is now widespread agreement among scientists that the world's climate warmed during the 20th century and will warm further over the 21st century, owing to a more pronounced greenhouse effect caused by the huge amounts of carbon dioxide and other gases, such as methane, being released into the atmosphere as a result of modern human activities. The major contributing activities have been greater energy use, in particular the increased burning of fossil fuels since the advent of the industrial revolution in the 18th century, the expansion of more intensive agricultural land uses, deforestation, and the manufacture of particular chemicals such as the now widely banned chlorofluorocarbons (CFCs). The Asia-Pacific region already contributes more than one-quarter of the global emissions of carbon dioxide. The rapid industrial growth and greater energy use predicted for populous countries such as China and India over the 21st century, and the fact that at least for the next 30 years this growth will be driven by a huge rise in the use of fossil fuels, will increase this share dramatically. According to the IPCC, a doubling of carbon dioxide in the atmosphere will make the climate warmer by approximately 3.0°C. What is not known is how rapidly this doubling will occur and what effect it will have on future temperatures. The World Meteorological Organization has suggested that a rise of 3.0°C may occur as early as 2030 if the effects of other greenhouse gases are included. However, the Third Assessment Report (TAR) of the IPCC, released in 2001, projected globally averaged surface temperature increases of between 1.4°C and 5.8°C over the period 1990–2100, greater than those predicted by the Second Assessment Report (SAR) of 1996.

By June 2007 the IPCC had released the reports of the three working groups of the AR4 (see previous editions of *The Far East and Australasia* for full details). The report of Working Group I, which examined the science of climate change, noted among its many observations that in the Qinghai-Tibet high plateau in western China mountain glaciers appeared to be receding faster than elsewhere, with scientists reporting that the overall area occupied by glaciers in China had contracted by about one-third over the past century. These glaciers are the source of the biggest rivers in Asia, the Yangtze, Yellow River, Indus and Ganges, which together provide water to around 2,000m. people. Working Group II examined the potential impact of climate changeand projected that by 2080 between 300m. and 1,200m. persons in Asia would be confronting a rise in water stress. Working Group III, which evaluated possible mitigation policies and practices, cited evidence that between 1970 and 2004 global greenhouse gas emissions had increased by 70%, with carbon dioxide the largest contributor. It therefore recommended the establishment of a carbon market to set a price per metric ton on carbon emissions to penalize large fossil fuel emitters, such as coal-fired electricity plants, and to encourage greater use of renewable energy resources in individual countries and globally.

The signatories to the Kyoto Protocol (1997) to the UN Framework Convention on Climate Change (UNFCCC) of 1992 (see Regional Organizations—UN Environment Programme) urging industrial nations to reduce greenhouse gas emissions, did not include the USA and the world's rapidly growing developing nations, such as China and India, with the former already overtaking the USA as the world's leading greenhouse gas emitter. In June 2007 the G8 summit meeting of the world's wealthiest countries overcame US resistance and agreed to 'substantial' reductions in emissions in an effort to address climate change. No mandatory target was set for the decreases, but the preference of the EU, Canada and Japan for a 50% emissions reduction by 2050 was included in the agreed statement. It was also agreed that the G8 would negotiate within a UN framework to seek a replacement to the Kyoto Protocol by the end of 2009, that developing nations should also reduce emissions and that 'strong and early action' was required. The September 2007 meeting of member countries of Asia-Pacific Economic Cooperation (APEC) in Sydney agreed to long-term goals regarding emissions, but no binding targets were set.

The Synthesis Report (SYR), the final report of the AR4, was adopted in Valencia, Spain, in November 2007. It summarized the findings of the three Working Group reports described above. The SYR concluded that stabilization of climate change is achievable 'by deployment of a portfolio of technologies that are either currently available or expected to be commercialised in coming decades, assuming appropriate and effective incentives are in place for their development, acquisition, deployment and diffusion. . . '.

At the meeting of parties to the UNFCCC, held on the Indonesian island of Bali in December 2007, participants acknowledged the conclusions of the AR4 and agreed upon a so-called Bali Road Map to guide negotiations on post-Kyoto policies, which culminated in a conference of treaty partners in December 2009 in Copenhagen (see below). The Bali Road Map established four basic negotiating groups to focus on: mitigation (i.e. reduction in emissions), adaptation, technology transfer and financing of measures. Its most significant element was an agreement by all parties, including the USA, to contribute with measurable emission liabilities to the global reduction in greenhouse gases, and the understanding that no one should be freed of responsibility for climate change.

The impact of the AR4 on public perceptions and on political leadership was profound, and was reinforced by observable changes in climatic events around the world. It was now deemed politically unacceptable in most developed democracies for leaders to ignore the likely consequences of climate change. The election of a new Government in Australia in late 2007 and of President Barack Obama in the USA in late 2008 reinforced the chances of real action being taken to address the issue, as both had campaigned on a platform of emissions reduction targets. By 2009, however, only the 27-member EU had a legislated emissions trading scheme (ETS) in operation to achieve the carbon pollution reduction targets (at least a 20% reduction on 1990 levels by 2020, and a 30% decrease if other advanced economies followed suit).

In 2008 the Garnaut Climate Change Review recommended that the state and territory governments in Australia adopt an ETS and commit to reductions of 25% on 2000 emission levels by 2020, and 90% by 2050. An ETS sets a limit on the amount of pollutants that companies can emit and then forces heavy polluters to buy credits from companies that pollute less, thus creating financial incentives to combat global warming. The Australian Government committed itself to a minimum reduction of 5% below 2000 levels by 2020, up to a conditional target of 25% (equivalent to a decrease of between 4% and 24% from 1990 levels), provided that the higher target was part of an ambitious international agreement, involving comprehensive global action capable of stabilizing atmospheric greenhouse gases at 450 parts per million or lower by 2050. In 2010 the incumbent Australian Labor Party Government, led by Julia Gillard, included promises in its electionl manifesto to introduce an ETS but not a carbon tax. However, after losing her parliamentary majority in the federal election in August and becoming dependent on the support of the Australian Greens to remain in government, Prime Minister Gillard abruptly changed course. She committed her minority Government to the introduction of a tax on carbon emissions by the largest 1,000 emitters, with the price to be decided by July 2011 and the scheme to become operational by July 2012. However, the implementation of an ETS was postponed for three to five years. Opposition political parties in Australia subsequently undertook a successful 'scare campaign' to highlight the adverse impact of the tax on employment through the relocation of jobs overseas, although it was also pointed out that their own alternative programme would impose a major burden on the budget without effectively limiting carbon emissions.

The Obama Administration's emissions reduction targets were equivalent to decreases of between 0% and 15% in comparison with 1990 emissions. The American Clean Energy and Security Act (ACES), known as the Waxman-Markey Bill, which was narrowly approved by the House of Representatives in June 2009, recommended reductions of 20% and 30% compared with 2005 levels of emissions, by 2020 and 2030, respectively. This would offer 100% protection for US exporters and import-competing industries until 2025. Environmentalists suggest that the legislation is seriously weakened by its reliance on offset credits to substitute for actual emission reductions by large emitters. Their core criticism is that it is not possible to ensure that every credit represents real and measurable reductions in emissions. However, with the Obama Administration losing its Democratic majority in the House of Representatives in 2010, any significant initiatives on climate change in the near future in the USA now appear to depend on action by individual states.

In December 2009 the UN Climate Change Conference was held in Copenhagen, with the aim of establishing a framework for climate change mitigation to follow the expiry in 2012 of the Kyoto Protocol. Expectations of conference outcomes and the intentions of the participant countries appear to have varied widely. The EU and several developed countries attempted to lead by example by making a commitment to implement binding carbon emission reductions under their own trading schemes, in the hope of thereby persuading the USA and China to take stronger action. Major developing countries such as China, India and Brazil, often in association with poorer African client countries, appeared intent on resisting their inclusion in any binding limits on carbon emissions, on the grounds that the developed countries, as the principal per caput polluters, should accept most of the burden, and that their own future economic development would be unfairly curtailed if they were to agree to binding targets. On the other hand, many non-governmental organizations (NGOs) representing some of the world's poorest peoples and the representatives of small island nations saw the acceptance of binding targets by the planet's biggest emitters (including China and India) as the only way in which their poor communities and small nations could survive. After several years of preparatory work, the conference witnessed 12 days of often acrimonious negotiations, stalemate and disagreement between rich countries and the large emerging economies, with neither block dominant nor sufficiently united to prevail. At the end of the conference an agreement known as the Copenhagen Accord was 'noted', with the conference delegates unwilling to endorse it as a binding agreement, leaving its exact legal status uncertain. The agreement, compiled by the USA and the so-called 'Basic Group' of China, India, Brazil and South Africa, was merely an expression of aims. The accord recognized the scientific case for limiting the rise in global temperatures to 2°C, but did not contain commitments for reduced emissions necessary to achieve that aim. It urged developed countries to provide US $30,000m. to the developing world over the following three years, rising to US $100,000m. annually by 2020, to help poor countries adapt to climate change, but failed to state who would pay what to whom, and, in short, appeared to commit none of the signatories to anything. Previous proposals aimed at limiting temperature rises to 1.5°C and at decreasing emissions by 80% by 2050 were abandoned. The Accord also encouraged developed countries to pay developing countries to reduce emissions from deforestation and land degradation.

While there was a general consensus that developing countries should retain the right to economic growth, there was suspicion that China was prepared to disregard the offer of binding targets from most of the developed world so that China itself would not be expected to agree to any legally enforceable targets. Mark Lynas, a British environmental activist and author, acknowledged that some developing countries wanted both China and India to do more to combat climate change, but he asserted that China hoped to weaken the climate regime in order to avoid the risk that it might be required to accept more ambitious targets in a few years' time. Nevertheless, this does not mean that China is not serious about global warming; its commitment to wind and solar industries refute this. However, China's growth and concomitant increase in global political and economic dominance are based on cheap coal, and the country was not willing to alter this successful formula unless forced to do so.

One major problem with the Accord is that it was not formally accepted by the Copenhagen conference and therefore it 'can easily be sidelined', an impression reinforced by the attitudes of most participants at the UNFCCC meeting held in Bonn, Germany, in April 2010. If this happens, then the world will, in effect, be without a global framework to combat climate change, which raises questions as to whether or not the UN, with processes vulnerable to delays and 'grandstanding' by voting blocs such as the G77, is the appropriate forum in which to reach a meaningful treaty. A second problem, emphasized by the unsuccessful outcome at Copenhagen, is that China views multilateral environmental governance as of little importance, particularly if it threatens this new superpower's freedom of action and its decision to base its future economic growth on the proven formula of cheap coal. A third major problem or danger arising from the failure of the Copenhagen conference is that it carried the hopes of many of the world's people of a sustainable future for their children, and with its failure political momentum is lost. This was clearly evident in Australia, where the lack of a binding agreement at the conference emboldened the opposition to discredit the ETS proposed by the Government of Kevin Rudd. Owing to the failure of the Copenhagen conference and to growing political opposition, the Australian Government under the new leadership of Gillard decided that action on a carbon tax would be postponed for at least another three years (see above), leaving the country with what Professor Ross Garnaut, an eminent Australian economist, deemed an unsustainable vacuum in its policy to combat climate change. An alternative view of the outcome of the conference was suggested by Bjørn Lomborg, a Danish academic, who asserted that it should serve as a 'wake-up call' to alert us to the fact that policies formulated drastically to reduce carbon emissions in a world that obtains 80% of its energy from carbon-emitting fossil fuels have failed dismally to achieve their objectives since the Rio 'Earth Summit' in 1992. This is particularly the case for China and India and other developing countries that have no affordable alternatives to fossil fuels if they wish to advance economically. The failure of policies to reduce carbon emissions should alert world leaders to the need for alternative policies that are technologically more advanced, politically more feasible and economically more efficient. If the demand for global energy doubles, as predicted, by 2050, the only alternative will be to increase reliance on 'green energy' by several orders of magnitude. However, research cited by Lomborg has indicated that, based on current rates of progress, alternative energy sources, if taken together and if hugely increased in scale, will meet less than one-half of the requirements for achieving stable carbon emissions by 2050, and will go only a fraction of the way towards stabilization by 2100. The technology will simply not be ready.

The Copenhagen Accord attempted to address this problem by committing developed countries to contribute up to US $100,000m. a year to help poor countries mitigate climate change (but by April 2011 little progress had been made). This implies that the funds will be used to subsidize carbon reductions, a pointless exercise, according to Lomborg, which would do nothing to improve the living standards of the poor and would result in only a marginal decrease in temperatures a century from now. Instead, Lomborg suggests, these funds should be devoted to 'green energy' research and development, designed to encourage technological innovations that will make 'green energy' cheaper and more efficient than carbon-emitting fuels. If this can be achieved by massive investment over the next 20–40 years, then there would no longer be a need to force or subsidize anyone to stop burning carbon-emitting fuels. Every country, including China and India, would shift to the cheaper and cleaner alternatives, and the problem of global warming would be solved. This approach would be more politically acceptable to all governments than carbon reductions.

As regards the question of the way forward, the Copenhagen Accord required countries to submit emissions targets by the end of January 2010; by early February 67 countries had registered their targets. The mid-year climate talks in Bonn in 2010 resumed negotiations on a global climate agreement, and acted as a process of reconciliation after the acrimonious and traumatic Copenhagen conference. Reports from Bonn suggested that all countries except the USA now viewed the Copenhagen Accord as having little relevance, insisting that the UNFCCC is the only agreed decision-making forum. The Bonn discussions concluded that the way forward would be to pursue a number of less ambitious partial agreements on such issues as the mode of transferring climate-friendly technologies and funds for climate change from richer to poorer countries, as well as an arrangement that would compensate countries for preserving their forests. The more difficult decisions on ambitious targets for countries to reduce their greenhouse gas emissions, and a legally binding agreement, were thus delayed, until the UNFCCC conference in Durban, South Africa, at the end of 2011, or later. However, by June 2011 climate envoys from the EU and the USA were stating that no conclusive agreement on emission reductions would be signed in Durban, but that there was now, at least, general recognition of the necessity of a legally binding agreement. There were also suggestions that the Durban talks might attempt to address shipping and aviation emissions for the first time. As political decisions were postponed and decisive action delayed, the International Energy Agency estimated that in 2010 global carbon dioxide emissions had reached a record 30.6 gigatons (Gt), a rise of 1.6 Gt on 2009, despite the most serious global economic recession for 80 years. Lord (Nicholas) Stern, a British economist and academic, suggested that this was close to the 'business as usual' path described by the IPCC, which would mean a 50% chance of an increase in global temperature of more than 4°C by 2100 and disastrous consequences for the planet.

The major likely effect of global warming is a rise in the mean sea level, as a result of the thermal expansion of ocean water and the melting of the ice caps. Oceans have absorbed more than 80% of heat added to the climate system owing to global warming. AR4 has projected that mean sea levels will rise by approximately 0.65m by 2100. This will seriously threaten the very existence of low-lying developing countries such as Tuvalu, Tonga, Kiribati and Vanuatu, where the vast majority of the population lives along the coasts. Flooding during cyclones and king tides (exceptionally high tides that prevail at certain times of year) will increase, affecting soils and salinizing freshwater supplies. Water tables will rise, and coastal farmland will be abandoned, forcing inhabitants to cultivate steeper slopes, leading to soil erosion. Tourism, which is the mainstay of many small island economies, will also be adversely affected, as beaches and sea walls are destroyed. Coral reefs, which protect tropical islands, will also be severely affected, and there will be fewer fish and shellfish. Coastal vegetation, particularly mangroves, will be lost, along with the protection from wave erosion that they provide and their fish-breeding environments. This may well lead to significant local human migration and the loss of cultural heritages.

Model simulations also suggest that the frequency of cyclones will increase as a result of global warming and that this may have catastrophic effects for the rural populations located in low-lying coastal areas. The impact of several large cyclones on northern Queensland in early 2011 was seen by some experts as evidence of climate warming, but others argued that data quality is inadequate to draw this conclusion. Predictions include a general reduction in crop yields in most tropical, subtropical and mid-latitude regions, decreased water availability for populations in many water-scarce regions, particularly in the subtropics, an increase in the number of people exposed to vector-borne and water-borne diseases, such as malaria, dengue fever and diarrhoeal disease, and to heat-stress mortality, a widespread rise in the risk of flooding for many human settlements, and an escalation in energy demand for space cooling, owing to higher summer temperatures.

Perhaps one of the most underestimated effects of global warming is that it will bring about shifts in major climatic zones and in vegetation types. Many animal and plant species may be able to follow these shifts in habitat, provided the changes are relatively slow. However, rapid changes in habitat, combined with artificial barriers such as agricultural land use or urban development, may make it impossible for many species to relocate to more favourable ecological sites, and this may pose a serious threat to future biodiversity in the most densely settled countries of the region.

OTHER DEVELOPMENTS

The problems confronting the region must be robustly addressed by both its developed and less developed countries. Some of the recent events that have caused environmental concern in the Asia-Pacific region have been analysed in previous editions of *The Far East and Australasia*. These include the major flooding in China and Indonesia in 1998, 2002 and 2006; the disastrous earthquake in Central Java, Indonesia, in May 2006; and the major chemical spill in north-eastern China in November 2005. Two serious natural disasters that struck the region in May 2008, Cyclone Nargis in Myanmar and the earthquake in Sichuan Province, were described in the 2009 edition.

One long-term, very difficult environmental problem, that of the threat of wet and dry land salinization and water toxicity to the Murray-Darling Basin in south-east Australia, was examined in the 2010 edition. However, between August 2010 and May 2011 Australia experienced one of the most formidable episodes on record of the effects of La Niña (a periodic oceanic/atmospheric phenomenon that lowers the sea-surface temperature). Rainfall records of 100 years were broken, unparalleled levels of flooding struck central and southern Queensland, western and southern New South Wales and northern Victoria, and near-record flows were registered at the mouth of the River Murray in South Australia. Despite such extensive precipitation, expert opinion is of the view that periods of prolonged and severe drought will become more frequent in the Murray-Darling Basin as a result of climate change and that continuing over-commitment of the Basin's water resources must be reversed. An independent report released in June 2010 recommended that, for the river system to be environmentally sustainable, some 39% (between 3,000 and 4,000 gigalitres) of the water currently allocated to irrigators would need to be returned to the river to meet environmental requirements. Political opposition to these recommendations has been so strong that there are now real doubts as to whether they will ever be adopted. This is because the floods of 2011 have removed the sense of urgency and the federal election of 2010 resulted in the reduction of the incumbent Australian Labor Party to a minority administration. A revised draft plan of the Murray-Darling Basin Authority was to be released by late 2011 and finalized in early 2012. However, a group of independent scientific advisers had already withdrawn from the process because of their concerns that less than 3,000 gigalitres would be returned to the river system and that their demand for an independent scientific review of the plan would be ignored. Doubts about the political commitment to serious reductions in water allocations were confirmed in late May 2011 when it was decided that all jurisdictions would be given until 2019 to meet conditions drawn up in the final plan, several years later than originally planned. The 2010 edition of *The Far East and Australasia* also analysed causes of serious flooding in Jakarta in early 2009 and issues associated with the disastrous bushfires in Australia in February of the same year. Both were natural events, the impact of which was exacerbated by human behaviour. Environmental management issues that came to the fore as a result of a major oil leak in the Timor Sea, off the northern coast of Western Australia, were briefly discussed in the 2011 edition. Environmental and hazard management issues arising from the near-record flooding of Brisbane in January 2011, the Christchurch earthquake of February 2011 and the March 2011 earthquake and tsunami, along with associated damage to nuclear power stations, in eastern Japan are all analysed below.

Earthquake, Tsunami and Nuclear Crisis in Japan

On 11 March 2011 a magnitude 9.0 megathrust earthquake struck eastern Japan. The epicentre of the earthquake was located 70 km east of the Oshika Peninsula at an underwater depth of 32 km. It was one of the five most powerful earthquakes to have been recorded in the world since 1900 and the most forceful known earthquake ever to have hit Japan (although Japanese scientists suggest that a more severe earthquake may have occurred in 869 AD when the Sendai area was swept by a large tsunami). The earthquake elevated the seabed off the coast of Miyagi prefecture by 3m and moved sections of north-eastern Japan up to 2.4m closer to North America. The nearest major city to the epicentre of the earthquake was Sendai, on the main island of Honshu, 130 km away. The earthquake led to extremely destructive tsunami waves, up to 38.9m in height, which struck the eastern coast between 26 and 90 minutes after the eartquake, in some cases travelling up to 10 km inland. This part of Honshu's Pacific coast is particularly vulnerable to tsunamis, as the coastline has many deep embayments that amplify tsunami waves and cause great wave inundations. Owing to the frequency of tsunamis along this coastline, most major towns had built substantial 10-m high anti-tsunami seawalls in an attempt to protect themselves, but most of these were breached by the sheer height and force of the waves. However, the city of Fudai, where the 15-m high seawall had been regarded as excessive by the neighbouring townships, was saved by its seemingly over-cautious defence structure.

As was the case with the Indian Ocean earthquake and tsunami of 2004, the damage caused by the huge waves and localized flooding was far more deadly and destructive than the actual earthquake, with waves of 60 km per hour crashing through the top floors of four-storey buildings. Entire towns were destroyed by the tsunami, and in the town of Minamisanriku alone 9,500 people were reported as missing, presumed dead. The most severe effects of the tsunami were manifested along a 670-km stretch of coastline from Erimo in the north to Oarai in the south, with the majority of the destruction occurring in the hour that followed the earthquake. The Japanese authorities confirmed 15,148 deaths, 5,304 injured and 8,881 people missing; 92% of the 13,000 fatalities recovered had drowned. The intensity and extent of the damage caused by the earthquake and resulting tsunami were enormous. Images of the worst-affected towns showed little more than piles of rubble, with almost no structures left standing. The Japanese police estimated that 190,000 buildings had been destroyed or damaged, combined with major destruction to roads and railways, the outbreak of fires in many areas and the collapse of an irrigation dam in Sukagawa city. Approximately 4.4m. households in north-eastern Japan were left without electricity and 1.5m. without water. Many electrical generators were destroyed, and at least three nuclear reactors suffered explosions caused by a build-up of hydrogen gas within their outer containment buildings after the failure of their cooling systems. Residents within a 20-km radius of the Fukushima I nuclear power plant and a 10-km radius of the Fukushima II plant were evacuated. The Japanese Prime Minister, Naoto Kan, described the catastrophe as the most serious crisis for Japan since the end of the Second World War. The Japanese Government estimated that US $184,000m. would be needed for reconstruction purposes, with the disaster pushing the Japanese economy into recession in the first two quarters of 2011 as a result of power shortages and supply-chain disruptions to factory output.

In the context of environmental management issues, the factor causing most concern was the damage inflicted on the nuclear power plants by the earthquake and tsunami, with the subsequent discovery that nuclear fuel in three of the six reactors at the Fukushima I nuclear power plant had possibly melted through several pressure vessels and into the earth below. It later appeared that dangerous levels of radioactive iodine and caesium had already contaminated the sea, the soil, groundwater and the air. Three months after the accident plutonium was detected for the first time outside the plant, and strontium-90, which can cause bone cancer and leukaemia, was found 60 km beyond the perimeters of the facility. The Fukushima I plant comprised six separate boiling-water reactors maintained by the Tokyo Electric Power Company (TEPCO), with a combined power of 4.7 gigawatts, making it one of the 25 largest nuclear power stations in the world. The magnitude 9.0 earthquake shook the six reactors above the design tolerances of three of the units. When the earthquake struck, reactor units 1, 2 and 3 were operating, while units 4, 5 and 6 had been shut down for periodic inspection. The operating units underwent an automatic shutdown, thus stopping electricity generation used to power the plant's cooling systems. TEPCO reported that one of the two connectors to the off-site power for reactors 1–3 had also failed, so 13 on-site emergency diesel generators began powering the plant's cooling and control systems.

Less than 45 minutes after the earthquake occurred, a 14-m tsunami struck, breaching the plant's 5.7-m seawall, flooding the entire plant and disabling the emergency diesel generators. All power for cooling was lost and the reactors started to overheat, owing to the natural decay of the fission products created before shutdown and the lack of sufficient cooling water. Evidence soon emerged of core meltdown in reactors 1, 2 and 3, hydrogen explosions in reactors 1, 3 and 4, an explosion damaging the containment inside reactor 2, and the outbreak of multiple fires in reactor 4. Despite being initially shut down, reactors 5 and 6 began to overheat as water levels dropped in the fuel rod storage pools. Fear of radiation leaks led to the official declaration of a 20-km radius evacuation around the plant, and workers suffering from radiation exposure were also withdrawn.

Scientific measurements taken by the Japanese authorities in areas of northern Japan 30–50 km from the plant revealed radioactive caesium levels high enough to cause concern. The sale of locally grown produce and locally caught fish was banned. and it later became evident that contamination had entered the food chain. International measurements of iodine-131 and caesium-137 suggested that the releases of those isotopes from Fukushima were of the same order of magnitude as those from Chornobyl in 1986. Plutonium contamination was detected in the soil at two sites in the Fukushima I plant. Japanese officials initially assessed the accident at level 4 on the International Nuclear Event Scale (INES), but the level was subsequently raised to 7, the maximum on the scale, with experts considering it to be the second worst nuclear accident after the Chornobyl disaster, but more complex as multiple reactors were involved. The authorities predicted that it could take a work-force of hundreds, or even thousands, several years or decades to clean up the area and a permanent exclusion zone could ultimately extend well beyond the plant's perimeter, with seriously exposed workers being at increased risk of cancers for the rest of their lives. Contrary to certain comments made by the Japanese Government, the aftermath of the earthquake/tsunami is not a temporary situation, with international health experts suggesting caesium-contaminated areas may be uninhabitable for about 200 years.

At mid-2011 the crisis was still very much ongoing. TEPCO proposed a plan to regain control of the reactors, but there were doubts about the company's ability to achieve its planned timetable; and on 3 June the radiation reading in the reactor building in unit 1 was the highest detected in the air at the plant thus far. On 20 March the Japanese Government announced that the Fukushima I plant would be decommissioned once the crisis was over, and on 6 May, in order to avoid a possible repetition of the disaster, Prime Minister Kan ordered the shutting down of the Hamaoka nuclear power plant, as an earthquake of magnitude 8.0 or higher is likely to strike the area within the next 30 years or so.

Given its long history of earthquakes and tsunamis, Japan was prepared for the events of 11 March 2011; most local communities had evacuation plans and seawalls. However, it was the sheer severity of this extreme natural phenomenon that caused the huge loss of life and damage, a degree of severity that could not have been precisely predicted. However, lessons will be learned from the disaster, particularly the need to prepare for the recurrence of such an event (which is estimated to happen once every several hundred years or so) by the construction of even taller seawalls than the existing 7–10-m high structures that are common in this area of coastal Japan. However, what was not foreseen was the way in which a natural disaster of this severity could have an impact on the Fukushima nuclear power plant, exposing weaknesses in design and regulatory supervision and in the responses of the Japanese Government. Indeed, the events of March 2011 had profound implications for the future of the nuclear industry world-wide.

When questioning what can be learned from the Fukushima natural disaster and the associated nuclear emergency, perhaps the most salient comment was made by Mike Weightman, leader of the International Atomic Energy Agency (IAEA) fact-finding team in Japan when he stated 'We cannot predict natural disaster precisely, but you can try to predict the consequence of it'. Prior to the Fukushima disaster some of the major consequences of a large-scale earthquake and tsunamis on a nuclear power plant had indeed been predicted, but no action had been taken. For example, as long ago as 1990 a report by the US Nuclear Regulatory Commission identified earthquake-induced diesel generator failure and power outage leading to failure of cooling systems as one of the 'most likely causes' of nuclear accidents from an external event. In 2004 Dr

Kiyoo Mogi, former chairman of the Japanese Coordinating Committee for Earthquake Prediction, stated that the impact of an earthquake and tsunami on a nuclear facility could 'bring a catastrophe to Japan through a man-made disaster'. Hidekatsu Yoshii, a member of the Japanese House of Representatives, twice warned in 2006 about the possibility of the severe damage that might be caused to a nuclear power plant by a tsunami or earthquake. Leading seismologist Professor Katsuhiko Ishibashi, a member of the 2006 subcommittee that reviewed the earthquake-resistance design standards of nuclear power plants, resigned from that body, claiming that the review process was 'unscientific' and the outcome contrived to suit the interests of the nuclear power industry. He subsequently asserted that the standards adopted in the review were seriously flawed as they underestimated the earthquake ground motion standards required.

In 2008 the IAEA warned that a strong earthquake of a magnitude above 7.0 could pose a serious problem for Japan's nuclear power stations. In the following year the Japanese Ministry of Economy, Trade and Industry (METI), which oversees the nuclear power industry, dismissed evidence from geologists that the stretch of coast on which the Fukushima power plants was located was overdue for a strike by a giant wave. As recently as May 2010, Yoshii, in a very prescient comment, warned that the cooling systems of a Japanese nuclear reactor might be destroyed by a landslide or an earthquake. In response, the head of the Japanese Nuclear and Industrial Safety Agency (NISA, the body responsible for monitoring the country's nuclear safety) replied that the country's plants were so well designed that such a situation was practically impossible. Part of the problem is a lack of regulatory independence within the nuclear industry. The METI manages the nuclear power industry and administers NISA, but at the same time encourages, for economic reasons, the expansion of domestic and international nuclear energy. According to some experts, relationships between the regulators and the commercial operators of the power stations, such as TEPCO, have also become too close and complacent. In June 2011 the Japanese Government gave an undertaking that it would separate NISA from METI after an IAEA report recommended that 'Nuclear regulatory systems should address extreme external events adequately, including their periodic review, and should ensure that regulatory independence and clarity of roles are preserved in all circumstances in line with IAEA safety standards'. The Japanese Government was criticized for its inadequate response to the disaster and its subsequent public understatement of the resultant risks to public health. It was revealed that the Government had obtained detailed atmospheric data shortly after the disaster indicating that the radioactive discharges were of Chornobyl levels; however, this was denied. The Government's failings resulted in the adoption of inadequate public health precautions and the establishment of an exclusion zone that was too small and did not correspond to the shape of the plume of contamination that extended north-west of the plant for up to 40–50 km.

Soon after the disaster it emerged that a number of the Fukushima reactors, built 40 years previously, were due to have been replaced in 1996 at the end of their design life of 25 years, but had been kept operational by TEPCO for economic reasons. Unlike more modern reactors that have better and more numerous back-up systems, the Fukushima plants had only one back-up system, the secondary generators. When these generators failed as a result of the tsunami breaching the seawall and destroying the fuel tanks of diesel, there was no further back-up. Observers familiar with similar plants in the USA make the point that the diesel fuel tanks for the auxiliary generators that keep the water pumping are all buried at these plants. However, at Fukushima the fuel tanks essential to keeping the last-resort diesel generators running in an emergency were above ground. According to former employees of the company, TEPCO was well aware of the dangers, but had failed to relocate the emergency diesel generators because of the costs involved. The reasons for this inaction are difficult to understand in a seismically active area such as Japan (the country that coined the term tsunami), but TEPCO is a company with a history of 'cover-ups': 10 years previously it had concealed the existence of cracks in its reactor facilities, and a few years later it had falsified data on its nuclear plants. In the context of the specific details of the Fukushima nuclear disaster, the age and design of the reactors and their ineffective back-up systems are critical factors.

Large developing countries such as China, where there is a huge demand for increased supplies of energy, have given no indication that they will abandon plans to expand dramatically the number of their nuclear plants, despite the incidence of some domestic anti-nuclear protests. Although pledging to boost its use of renewable energy to 20% of the country's total power supply by 2020 and to learn from the mistakes of the Fukushima accident, Japan has at the same time stated that nuclear power will remain one of the 'pillars' of national energy policy. Clearly, however, in some parts of the world such as the Nordic countries or even in Australia where there is well-established political resistance to the nuclear industry, the continued use or possible expansion of nuclear energy will be more strongly resisted henceforth. None the less, it is likely that the overall market for nuclear power generation and development will remain little changed in the 'post-Fukushima' world, with governments arguing that they have little choice but to support the expansion of the nuclear industry and attempting to convince their populations that the Fukushima accident was an exceptional, rare event and that the benefits of nuclear energy as a clean source of power make it a relatively safe alternative to the construction of new fossil fuel power stations. However, many densely populated developing nations in South-East Asia that are not as technologically advanced as Japan, and that lack the 'relatively' strong governance and regulatory traditions of that country, need to question whether nuclear energy is really the best alternative, if, like Japan, they are persuaded to build nuclear power plants at sea level on earthquake- and tsunami-prone sites with high population densities in Java, Sumatra, the Philippines, Thailand or Malaysia. The history of nuclear accidents reveals that we have learned little from past disasters and the Fukushima disaster may prove not to be very different, as it is the economic and political constraints imposed on human behaviour that are the real problem, rather than the nuclear technology itself.

Earthquake in Christchurch, New Zealand

At lunch-time on 22 February 2011 a magnitude 6.3 earthquake shook the Canterbury region of New Zealand's South Island. The epicentre of the earthquake was just 10 km south-east of the centre of Christchurch, New Zealand's second city. The earthquake occurred almost six months after the magnitude 7.1 earthquake of September 2010 that had caused major damage, but no fatalities, to the city and the Canterbury region. The 2011 earthquake also caused major devastation to Christchurch, especially to the central business district, with the damage exacerbated by the fact that the earlier earthquake had already weakened buildings and infrastructure. Significant liquefaction affected the eastern suburbs, making the rebuilding of parts of the city on their present site problematic, especially given the trauma caused by the frequent aftershocks that were still continuing four months after the major quake. The earthquake resulted in the deaths of 181 people and was the second most serious natural disaster recorded in New Zealand. Two six-storey buildings in Christchurch, the Canterbury Television (CTV) building and the Pyne Gould Corporation House, collapsed; most of the confirmed dead were recovered from these two sites. About 1,000 of the 4,000 buildings within the central city were so badly damaged that they were expected to have to be demolished. Unfortunately, many of the destroyed buildings were heritage buildings that had given Christchurch its distinctive character. The total cost of rebuilding, which was to be borne by insurers, was forecast to total around US $12,000m. making the earthquake one of the country's costliest natural disasters.

Peak ground acceleration during the earthquake was extremely high, with simultaneous vertical and horizontal ground movement making it unlikely that buildings would survive intact. Increased liquefaction simultaneously undermined foundations and destroyed infrastructure. Despite the severity of the earthquake, all of the buildings in Christchurch that had been erected since the last major update of the city's building code survived and performed as expected. The New

Zealand Society for Earthquake Engineering claimed that authorities throughout the country had for many years failed to act on warnings from experts that the country's earthquake building regulations were inadequate and that more should be done to reinforce older buildings that pre-dated new standards. Engineers had recommended that older earthquake-prone buildings be upgraded to the level of 67% of the standard for new buildings.

Instead, however, the Government had enacted legislation in 2004 requiring only 33% of the modern standard. Local engineers asserted that such a level was too low and that a building of this standard was still 20 times more likely than a modern building to collapse in an earthquake. A building that had been upgraded to a level of 67%, on the other hand, was only around three times as likely to fall. At the time of the earthquake Christchurch had 7,600 earthquake-prone commercial buildings, most of which were constructed before 1976. The city council had in the past developed plans to reinforce such buildings, but, because of the high costs involved and the potential risk of bankruptcy for many businesses, the owners were given long lead times (of 10, 20 or 30 years) to comply with the new regulations. After the September 2010 earthquake, the council strengthened its policy to raise the upgrade target to 67% for old buildings; however, if the building had not been damaged by the earthquake then the owner was permitted 10–15 years (from July 2012) to complete the reinforcement work. (In the event, the 2011 earthquake obviously pre-empted this deadline.) The lengthy time scale for carrying out the upgrade work was implemented owing to the fact that the cost of retrofitting old buildings is extremely expensive and there were concerns that the viability of many businesses located in such buildings would be threatened by earlier deadlines. A Royal Commission of Inquiry was established in March 2011 to examine the earthquake devastation. The remit of this body, which was to complete a preliminary report by September, was to cover the building collapses and consequent loss of life, damage to major structures, and general building standards and codes.

Floods in Queensland, Australia

Between November 2010 and January 2011 a series of floods devastated the state of Queensland in north-eastern Australia and its capital city of Brisbane. The floods were caused by Tropical Cyclone Tasha, which, in combination with a monsoonal trough that crossed the coast from the Coral Sea, brought torrential rainfall to a broad band of the country from the Gulf of Carpentaria to the Gold Coast in south-eastern Queensland. Communities along the Fitzroy and Burnett Rivers in central Queensland were subjected to heavy flooding, while the Condamine, Balonne and Mary Rivers, the next river systems to the south, also experienced substantial flooding. An unexpected flash flood killed several people in Toowoomba's central business district before devastating communities east of the city in the Lockyer Valley, where an inland tsunami of surging water 7–8m high carried away families, houses and cars in the small towns of Murphy's Creek and Grantham, about 100 km west of Brisbane. A total of 14 deaths occurred in these towns.

On 11 January 2011 the Brisbane River broke its banks and began to flood the state capital's central business district and other inner-city suburbs. Although the flood reached its height at almost 4.5m, a lower level than expected, it nevertheless inundated 14,200 homes, and a number of suburbs were cut off for three days until the arrival of the army with food supplies. The central business district of Ipswich, a city located 30 km west of Brisbane on the Bremer River, was also inundated, along with 3,000 houses; local reports estimated that one-third of the city was submerged. In total, the 2010/11 floods killed 35 people in Queensland and nine were still reported as missing as of January 2011. The floods forced the evacuation of thousands of people from towns and cities and affected at least 70 towns and 200,000 people. Three-quarters of the state was declared a disaster area. Initially, damage was conservatively estimated at around US $1,050m.; but, because of the severe damage caused by the flooding of the state's coal mines (a lucrative source of export earnings), Australia's annual GDP was likely to be reduced by about $32,000m. GDP was forecast to register negative growth in the first quarter of 2011. Four months after the floods coal production had still not fully recovered, with open-cut mines continuing to face dewatering issues.

The Queensland floods were followed by the severe flooding of more than 50 communities in the state of Victoria in January–February 2011. The federal Government announced a flood levy to fund reconstruction works, but this entailed a political compromise that all member states should henceforth take out disaster insurance. The most exposed communities in the flooded areas of Australia were those small councils that were left with massive bills for local road and bridge reconstruction well beyond their resources, particularly at a time when their ratepayer base was already itself left devastated by flood damage.

In mid-January 2011 the Queensland Premier, Anna Bligh, who had been widely admired for her efficient handling of the disaster, established an independent commission of inquiry to conduct a thorough examination of the chain of events leading up to the 2010/11 floods, all aspects of the response and the aftermath of the disaster. This inquiry heard claims that, owing to overly rigid management guidelines, Wivenhoe Dam, the major storage and flood mitigation facility on the Brisbane River, was kept excessively full just prior to the Brisbane flood, and that the necessity to release 645,000 megalitres of water on 11 January 2011 in order to protect dam safety was a major contributory factor in the inundation of Brisbane over the following few days. The river reached its peak flood level in Brisbane on 13 January and, as a release of water from the dam normally takes around 36 hours to reach the city, this argument appeared to have some validity. Hydrologist Andrew Dragun argued that the operating guidelines used to manage dam water levels were too inflexible and not proactive enough to deal with the likely risks posed by future weather patterns. His argument was supported by the fact that, as late as just one week before the Brisbane floods, water levels in the Wivenhoe Dam were maintained at the full supply level and were not reduced, seemingly regardless of warnings from the Bureau of Meteorology of a heavy rain incident in south-eastern Queensland and an increasingly high risk of floods. Even after the floods and following the end of the phase of king tides, no action was taken to reduce water levels in the dam, despite the fact that the threat of further rain had not diminished.

Perhaps the prolonged droughts of previous years, during which the Wivenhoe Dam reached a low point of about 15% capacity, influenced perceptions that the water supply should be safeguarded at all costs; yet, as Dragun pointed out, by March 2010 the dam was at 98% of its full supply level. At this point in time the perception that the major risk was that of again running out of water was justifiable. By July the Bureau of Meteorology was advising that a very strong La Niña occurrence had been established over eastern Australia and it was then that water levels should have been reduced, since at that stage there was a low risk to supply and a high risk of future floods. However, the management of the dam remained rigidly unchanged, despite the radically altered weather outlook, supply situation and flood predictions. The expert consultant to the Queensland floods inquiry refuted some of these arguments by claiming that, in his opinion, the trigger point for the emergency releases reached on 11 January would still have been met during the floods that month, even if the dam's capacity had been reduced to 75% of the full supply level in the lead-up to summer. However, no detailed modelling was carried out to prove this point, and the consultant proceeded to recommend changes to the dam's operating manual, including a review of the use of forecast rainfall in flood modelling.

FUTURE CONCERNS

This essay has served to emphasize the nexus between environmental issues and the demographic, economic and political realities of development in the Asia-Pacific region. This linkage will become even stronger in the future as the people of the region strive to achieve their legitimate aspirations to a better lifestyle. Governments in the region will be placed under increased pressure to allow developers to take environmental 'shortcuts' in the interests of rapid economic development.

Land shortages are forcing many new projects and drilling sites to be located either in already densely settled agricultural areas, on environmentally unsuited urban sites or in pristine offshore locations. Looking ahead to later this century, it is clear that environmental issues will increasingly be international, rather than national or local, in their significance. Efforts to minimize the environmental 'footprint' of development must inevitably involve technology transfer, financial support and compensation mechanisms that are at least multinational, if not global, in scale, if they are to succeed.

BIBLIOGRAPHY

See also the following websites: www.fao.org (Food and Agricultural Organization); www.ipcc.ch (Intergovernmental Panel on Climate Change); www.undp.org (United Nations Development Programme); and www.unep.org (United Nations Environment Programme).

General

Brookfield, H., and Byron, Y. (Eds). *South-East Asia's Environmental Future: The Search for Sustainability*. Kuala Lumpur, United Nations University Press and Oxford University Press, 1993.

Burnett, A. *The Western Pacific: Challenge of Sustainable Growth*. Aldershot, Edward Elgar Publishing, 1992.

Ehrlich, P. R., and Holdren, J. P. 'Impact of population growth', *Science*, Vol. 171, pp. 1212–17, 1971.

Hardjono, J. (Ed.). *Indonesia: Resources, Ecology, and Environment*. Singapore, Oxford University Press, 1991.

Harrison, P. *The Third Revolution: Population, Environment and A Sustainable World*. London, Penguin Books, 1992.

Howard, M. C. *Asia's Environmental Crisis*. Boulder, CO, Westview Press, 1993.

McDowell, M. A. 'Development and the environment in ASEAN', *Pacific Affairs*, Vol. 62, No. 3, pp. 307–329, 1989.

Meyer, W. B. *Human Impact on the Earth*. Cambridge, Cambridge University Press, 1996.

Parnwell, M. J. G., and Bryant, R. L. (Eds). *Environmental Change in South-East Asia: People, Politics and Sustainable Development*. London, Routledge in association with the ESRC Global Environmental Change Programme, 1996.

Ramphal, S., and Sinding, S. W. (Eds). *Population Growth and Environmental Issues*. Westport, CT, Praeger Publishers, 1996.

Loss and Degradation of Agricultural Land

Huang Jikun. 'Land Degradation in China: Erosion and Salinity'. A report submitted to the World Bank. Beijing, Center for Chinese Agricultural Policy, Chinese Academy of Agricultural Sciences, March 2000.

Smil, Vaclav. 'Land degradation in China: an ancient problem getting worse' in P. Blaikie and H. Brookfield. *Land Degradation and Society*, pp. 214–222. London, Methuen, 1987.

'Environmental problems in China: estimates of economic costs', *East-West Center Special Reports*, No. 5, pp. 1–62. Honolulu, HI, East-West Center, 1996.

Deforestation

Angelsen, A. 'Shifting cultivation and 'deforestation': A study from Indonesia', *World Development*, Vol. 23, No. 10, pp. 1713–29, 1995.

Angelsen, A., and Resosudarmo, D. P. 'Krismon, Farmers and Forests: the Effects of the Economic Crisis on Farmers' Livelihoods and Forest Use in the Outer Islands of Indonesia'. Bogor, Center for International Forest Research, 1999.

Brookfield, H., Potter, L., and Byron, Y. *In Place of the Forest: Environmental and Socio-economic Transformation in Borneo and the Eastern Malay Peninsula*. Tokyo, United Nations University Press, 1995.

Collins, N. M., Sayer, J. A., and Whitmore, T. C. (Eds). *The Conservation Atlas of Tropical Forests: Asia and the Pacific*. London, Macmillan, 1991.

Matthews, E. 'Understanding the FRA 2000', World Resources Institute, Forest Briefing No. 1. Washington, DC, March 2001.

Potter, L. 'Environmental and social aspects of timber exploitation in Kalimantan, 1967–1989' in J. Hardjono (Ed.). *Indonesia: Resources, Ecology, and Environment*, pp. 177–211. Singapore, Oxford University Press, 1991.

'The onslaught on the forests in South-East Asia' in H. Brookfield and Y. Byron (Eds). *South-East Asia's Environmental Future: The Search for Sustainability*, pp. 103–123. Tokyo, United Nations University Press, 1993.

Rudel, T., and Roper, J. 'The paths to rainforest destruction: Crossnational patterns of tropical deforestation, 1975–90'. *World Development*, Vol. 25, No. 1, pp. 53–65, 1997.

Tole, L. 'Sources of deforestation in tropical developing countries' in *Environmental Management*, Vol. 22, No. 1, pp. 19–33, 1998.

World Bank. *Sustaining Indonesia's Forests: Strategy for the World Bank, 2006–2009*. Working Paper. Jakarta, The World Bank Office, 2006.

World Bank, Environment and Social Development Unit. *Indonesia: Environment and Natural Resource Management in a Time of Transition*. New York, The World Bank, 2001.

World Resources Institute, in collaboration with the United Nations Environment Programme and the United Nations Development Programme. *World Resources 1994–95*. New York, Oxford University Press, 1994.

Water Availability and Pollution

Brown, L. R., and Halweil, B. 'China's water shortage could shake world food security', *Worldwatch*, pp. 10–21, July/August 1998.

Gleik, P. 'China and Water', in P. Gleik et al (Eds). *The World's Water 2008–09*. Washington, DC, Island Press, 2009.

Environmental Problems in Urban Areas

Bartone, C., Bernstein, J., Leitmann, J., and Eigen, J. *Toward Environmental Strategies for Cities: Policy Considerations for Urban Environmental Management in Developing Countries*. Strategic Options for Managing the Urban Environment, No. 18, Washington, DC, The World Bank, 1994.

Douglass, M. 'Planning for environmental stability in the extended Jakarta metropolitan region', in N. Ginsburg, B. Koppel and T. G. McGee (Eds). *The Extended Metropolis: Settlement Transition in Asia*, pp. 239–273. Honolulu, HI, University of Hawaii Press, 1991.

Firman, T. 'Land conversion and urban development in the Northern Region of West Java, Indonesia', *Urban Studies*, Vol. 34, No. 7, pp. 1027–46, 1997.

Firman, T., and Dharmapatni, I. A. I. 'The challenges to sustainable development in Jakarta metropolitan development', *Habitat International*, Vol. 18, No. 3, pp. 79–94, 1994.

Hardoy, J. E., Mitlin, D., and Satterthwaite, D. *Environmental Problems in Third World Cities*. London, Earthscan Publications, 1992.

McKee, D. L. *Urban Environments in Emerging Economies*. Westport, CT, Praeger Publishers, 1994.

Parai, A., Benhart, J. E., and Rense, W. C. 'Water Supply in Selected Mega Cities of Asia' in A. K. Dutt, F. J. Costa, S. Aggarwal and A. G. Noble (Eds). *The Asian City: Processes of Development, Characteristics and Planning*, pp. 205–212. Dordrecht, Kluwer Academic Publishers, 1994.

Smith, K. R., and Lee, Y. F. 'Urbanisation and the Environmental Risk Transition', in J. D. Kasarda and A. M. Parnell (Eds). *Third World Cities: Problems, Policies and Prospects*, pp. 161–179. London, Sage, 1993.

Webster, D. 'The Urban Environment in Southeast Asia: Challenges and Opportunities', *Southeast Asian Affairs 1995*. Singapore, Institute of Southeast Asian Studies, 1995.

Global Warming and Rising Sea Levels

Harvey, Fiona. 'Worst ever carbon emissions leave climate on the brink', guardian.co.uk, 29 May 2011.

Lomborg, Bjørn. 'We should change tack on climate after Copenhagen', in *Financial Times*, 22 December 2009.

Lynas, Mark. 'How do I know China wrecked the Copenhagen deal? I was in the room', in *The Guardian*, 22 December 2009.

World Bank, Department for International Development (United Kingdom) and Pelangi Energi Abadi Citra Enviro (PEACE—State Ministry of Environment, Indonesia). *Indonesia and Climate Change: Current Status and Policies, 2007*; internet siteresources.worldbank.org/INTINDONESIA/Resources/Environment/ClimateChange_Full_EN.pdf.

Other Developments

Dragun, Andrew. 'Bligh leaves the dam too full', in *The Australian,* 4 February 2011.

Kissane, Karen. 'Politicians warned on building standards', in *The Age,* 3 March 2011.

McCurry, Justin. 'Fukushima nuclear plant may have suffered 'melt-through', Japan admits'; internet guardian.co.uk. 8 June 2011.

Moore, Ali. 'Japan 'concealed' data during nuclear crisis', Lateline, Australian Broadcasting Corporation, 10 June 2011.

PART TWO

Country Surveys

AUSTRALIA

Physical and Social Geography

A. E. McQUEEN

With revisions by the editorial staff

The Commonwealth of Australia covers an area of 7,692,024 sq km (2,969,907 sq miles). Nearly 39% of its land mass lies within the tropics; Cape York, the northernmost point, is only 10° S of the Equator. At the other extreme, the southern limit of the mainland lies at 39° S or, if Tasmania is included, at 43° S, a distance on the mainland alone of 3,134 km from north to south. From east to west, Australia spans a distance of 3,782 km.

CLIMATE AND VEGETATION

Australia's climatic differences can be generally attributed to the wide latitudinal range. The average elevation of the land surface is only about 275 m; nearly three-quarters of Australia is a great central plain, almost all of it at 185 m–460 m above sea-level, with few high mountains. The Dividing Range, running parallel to most of the east coast, is the most notable; the highest peak, Mt Kosciuszko, reaches 2,228 m. Owing to the lack of mountains and to the moderating effects of the surrounding oceans, there are fewer abrupt regional climatic changes than would be found on land masses in comparable latitudes elsewhere.

The northern part of the continent, except the Queensland coast, comes under the influence of summer tropical monsoons. This produces a wet summer as the moist air flows in from the north-west; but winter is dry, with the prevailing wind coming from the south-east across the dry interior. Both the north-east and north-west are liable to experience tropical cyclones between December and April, as exemplified in early 2011 by Cyclone Yasi, one of the most severe ever recorded in Australia.

In the southern part of Australia winter is the wet season. Winter rainfall in the south-east and south-west corners of Australia and Tasmania can be particularly high. Rainfall decreases rapidly inland with distance from the coast. Parts of central Australia record some very low annual average rainfall figures; the area of lowest average annual rainfall is that around Lake Eyre in South Australia, which receives less than an average of 125 mm per year. At the other extreme lies Tully, on the east coast of Queensland, with an annual average of more than 4,000 mm. Overall, few parts of Australia enjoy abundant rainfall; and even where occasional heavy falls are recorded, the unreliability of its seasonal distribution may well lessen its value in terms of pasture growth. Exceptionally heavy rains, sometimes attributed to the recurrent weather phenomenon known as La Niña, may lead to severe flooding, as demonstrated by the devastation of parts of Queensland in early 2011.

Very high temperatures, sometimes exceeding 50°C (122°F), are experienced during the summer months over the central parts of the country and for some distance to the south, as well as during the pre-monsoon months in the north. In much of the interior, xerophytic plant species, such as spinifex, salt bush, blue bush and dwarf eucalyptus, adapted to very dry and variable conditions, are capable of supporting a limited cattle population. Between these arid areas and the zones of higher rainfall lie the semi-arid plains on which the main vegetation is mulga (*Acacia*) and mallee scrub (*Eucalyptus* spp.), in which several stems rise from a common woody base. It is this type of land that carries most of the sheep in New South Wales and Western Australia; it is also here, as well as in the even drier interior, that the major effects of drought are seen. In 2007–08 several consecutive years of dry conditions resulted in the country's worst drought for more than a century, causing severe losses in the agricultural sector. Water levels in the Murray River, which forms part of the vital Murray-Darling river system in south-eastern Australia, fell to the lowest ever recorded. In the semi-arid parts of Australia underground water supplies are fairly widespread, including the resources of the Great Artesian Basin, fed from inland slopes of the mountain range to make one of the largest such catchments in the world. In some areas, notably the Barkly Tableland, stock-raising is largely dependent upon bore water.

Australia is highly susceptible to bushfires, which are often exacerbated by extremely high temperatures and very strong winds. The fires of February 2009, in which 173 people were killed in Victoria, caused the largest loss of life ever recorded in such an Australian disaster.

SOILS AND LAND USE

Soils are very diverse in both type and origin, and are of low natural fertility over large areas, owing to the great geological age of Australia and the subsequent poor qualities of the parent materials. Climate has a marked effect on soil type, with seasonal desiccation and surface erosion coinciding with the extreme dry and wet seasons which affect much of the continent. Salinity and alkalinity are also problems, especially in arid southern Australia.

The generalized pattern of land use falls into three broad zones. The first comprises some 70% of the land area, and covers all central Australia, reaching the coast along the shores of the Bight and in north-west Australia. About one-third of the area is desert, useless for farming; the rest is of only marginal value for pastoral activities, and then only in the areas close to the rather more favourable conditions of the second zone. This second zone covers only some 17% of Australia, and contains a wide variety of climate and soil types; it is included within a broad belt over 300 km wide extending from the Eyre peninsula paralleling the east coast, and across the northern part of Australia to the Kimberleys. In this zone most farming is practised in the temperate part of the area, with activities including the growing of wheat and the rearing of sheep, beef cattle and dairy cattle.

The third general zone comprises a belt of land along the east coast from Cairns southward and then westward to south-east South Australia, all of Tasmania, south-west Western Australia and a small part of the Northern Territory around Darwin. Much of this zone (which covers some 13% of the continent) is of broken relief; in the remaining areas the pattern of land use is quite complex. In the northern parts beef grazing dominates, but in the remainder most forms of cropping and livestock production are found. Nearly all Australia's forests are within this zone, as are almost all of the dairying, sugar, fat-lamb, horticulture and high-producing beef cattle areas.

POPULATION AND RESOURCES

Although there has been much immigration from Asia since the 1970s, the majority of Australia's population is still of European stock. The total population at the census of August 1996 was 17,892,423, of whom 386,049 were enumerated as Aboriginal and Torres Strait Islanders. At the census of 8 August 2006 the population had reached 19,855,288 (of whom 437,215 were enumerated as Aboriginal and Torres Strait Islanders), giving a density of only 2.6 inhabitants per sq km, one of the lowest national figures in the world. The population was estimated at 22,477,378 in December 2010, density having reached 2.9 inhabitants per sq km. In terms of population, as well as land use, Australia can be divided into three broad zones, corresponding, in many respects, to those outlined in the last section: one part almost unpopulated, another sparsely populated and the final part containing the great majority of the people. This distribution pattern means that any discussion of 'averages', in terms of population densities, is of only limited value; this is specially so when the proportion of each state's population living in the respective state capitals is revealed (see Statistical Survey). The concentration of population within each state is matched by a concentration, on a national scale, in the south-east of Australia. New South Wales and Victoria contained more than 57% of the nation's population in 2010; if the population of Tasmania is added, the figure approaches 60%. Over the country as a whole, settlement is closely related to the areas of moderate rainfall and less extreme temperatures, a pattern initiated by the early growth of towns and cities based on a predominantly pastoral farming community dependent upon farm exports for a livelihood. The result was the rapid growth of settlement around major ports on which state railway systems were centred, and a subsequent development of manufacturing industry at these port centres where imported raw materials were available, where a skilled labour force could be found and where distribution facilities to all parts of the respective states were readily available. Only in Queensland and Tasmania did this basic pattern vary to any extent; in Queensland because of the widespread distribution of intensive farming (especially the cultivation of sugar cane) along a coast well serviced with ports, and in Tasmania because the more dispersed distribution of agricultural and other resources called into being a number of moderate-sized towns and commercial centres.

Australia possesses major deposits of coal. Other important mineral resources include iron ore, gold, silver and magnesite. Bauxite, zinc, copper, titanium, nickel, tin, lead, zirconium and diamonds are also mined. Production of crude petroleum is important, and the Gorgon gas project, being developed off the country's north-western coast, was expected to commence production in 2014.

History

STUART MACINTYRE

ABORIGINAL AUSTRALIA

The human settlement of Australia began at least 40,000 years ago. The settlers came from the north-west, by means of the chain of islands that extends from Indo-China to the Timor Sea, and they spread rapidly over the island continent. As hunter-gatherers, these settlers met their needs without resort to agriculture or domesticated animals, and adapted their practices to a highly diverse environment. The primary social unit was the extended family group, with links of kinship, language and territory to larger aggregations. At the time of European arrival there were about 250 language groups, and population estimates vary between 200,000 and 750,000. They are now known as Aboriginals, although many of them also use localized names from these indigenous languages.

Aboriginal life was characterized by rhythms of work and leisure, aggregation and dispersal. Sex and age were the main forms of differentiation in a highly egalitarian social structure where kinship defined obligations and elaborate systems of religious belief regulated behaviour. Through many millennia Aboriginals evolved complex relationships with the country in which they lived, expressed in mythologies that explained its creation by spiritual beings and the continuing spiritual presence within it.

The Aboriginal Australians adapted to changing environmental conditions and also contributed to them. Through periodic burning, for example, they created grasslands for the animals they hunted, although the larger marsupial species became extinct during their occupation. They acquired dogs some 5,000 years before the present, and improved their technology with nets, hafted axes and specialized stone implements. They also extended their trading networks.

BRITISH COLONIZATION

There was contact with Aboriginal Australia from the north before the European arrival. Traders from South-East Asia brought pottery, cloth and metal tools, and took timber and sea produce. Spanish navigators sailed through the Torres Strait that separates Australia from Papua New Guinea at the end of the 16th century, and Portuguese vessels may have landed further south. The Dutch trade route to the East Indies took their ships east after rounding the Cape of Good Hope, then north up the western coast of Australia; and in 1642 Abel Tasman proceeded further east to the island of Tasmania, which lies at the south-east corner of the continent. Tasman's return through the Torres Strait demonstrated the limits of what had previously been designated as the Great South Land and was henceforth known as New Holland.

None of these contacts led to settlement, which followed James Cook's Pacific voyage of 1768 to 1771 and his navigation of the eastern coast. Subsequent British and French expeditions, impelled by scientific investigation and strategic rivalry, completed the mapping of the island continent. Matthew Flinders, the first to make a full circumnavigation, suggested the name Australia, and it was subsequently adopted.

Cook declared British sovereignty over the Australian continent in 1770. The British took possession in 1788 when Capt. Arthur Phillip established a colonial settlement at Sydney. Although Cook had been instructed to obtain the consent of the inhabitants, he had not done so; and while Phillip was instructed to 'open an intercourse with the natives, and to conciliate their affections', the British made no recognition of the indigenous peoples' independent rights. The failure to pursue a formal agreement with them distinguished this British settlement from others, with consequences that still exercise the Australian nation state.

The settlement of New South Wales was designed as a penal colony, a place for the transportation of felons, but it was also expected to become a useful acquisition. Influenced by the reports of Cook and his companion, the botanist Joseph Banks, the British Government intended to establish agriculture in New South Wales and to use the timber and native flax on Norfolk Island (1,700 km to the east of Sydney) for naval supplies. These expectations proved ill-founded: the first crops failed and livestock died, while the trees and flax on Norfolk Island were found to be unsuitable for masts, spars or sails. After initial difficulties, the main settlement at New South Wales achieved viability and, to forestall French ambitions, an additional settlement was established in Tasmania in 1803.

The conclusion of the Napoleonic Wars in 1815 brought increased numbers of convicts. It coincided with the finding of a passage across the mountain range that had confined the Sydney colony to the coastal region, and the spread of settlement onto inland plains suitable for pastoralism. With the growing demands of British manufacturers for wool, sheep numbers rose rapidly and the Australian colonies found a durable staple export. The prospect of wealth attracted increasing numbers of free settlers, who were able to acquire land cheaply and to draw on convict labour. European settlement spread through the south-east corner of the continent and exacerbated conflict with Aboriginal landowners, who were driven from their hunting grounds. While Aboriginals were officially protected from assault, their resistance was suppressed by military action and unofficial massacres. The numbers killed in frontier violence remain the subject of controversy.

New mainland colonies were founded in Western Australia in 1829 and South Australia in 1836, both outside the convict system, while unofficial settlement in Victoria led to official recognition in the same year. The growth of the eastern colonies led to demands for the abolition of convict transportation, which was suspended on the mainland in 1840. The British Government's attempt to revive it in 1849 led to protest movements and demands for greater local consultation. The absolute authority of the governors had been qualified in the 1840s by partly elected legislatures, and in 1852 the British Government invited the colonies to draft constitutions for representative self-government. New South Wales, Tasmania and Victoria created bicameral legislatures and systems of responsible government by 1855; South Australia followed in 1856, and in 1859 the north-eastern colony of Queensland was separated from New South Wales and similarly endowed. Western Australia did not become self-governing until 1890.

The advent of self-government coincided with the discovery of gold, which brought a rapid influx of newcomers: the non-Aboriginal population increased from 430,000 in 1851 to 1.15m. in 1861. The richest finds were in Victoria, and mining laws allowed 'fossickers' to stake a small claim and work it with little capital. Attracting adventurers drawn from around the world, including British Chartists and continental Europeans who had participated in the revolutionary movements of 1848, the goldfields were a crucible of vigorous democracy. High charges for the miner's licence and arbitrary administration caused a rebellion at Ballarat in 1854, which was suppressed with the loss of 28 lives, but juries acquitted the leaders who were tried for treason. The egalitarian mood quickly spread to the new parliaments, which adopted manhood suffrage and the secret ballot. A further aspect of this popular radicalism was racial violence directed against the Chinese immigrants on the goldfields.

The Victorian gold rush was followed by subsequent movements to new fields in New Zealand and New South Wales during the 1860s; then Queensland in the 1870s and 1880s, and finally Western Australia during the 1890s. The moving frontier of mining settlement was characterized by youthful energy, personal ambition and collective endeavour that were channelled into civic buildings, voluntary societies, churches, schools and families. As the initial rush slowed, the colonies turned their attention to consolidating their new wealth. Using their political power, popular movements agitated for reform to land tenure, so that the miners could become farmers, and large pastoral holdings were broken up into agricultural selections. Tariffs were imposed to develop and protect local industry. The colonial Governments raised public loans in the United Kingdom to construct railways and ports, to build and operate public utilities and to create a system of compulsory education.

Australia enjoyed a high standard of living during this phase of sustained economic growth. Improvements in the pastoral industry increased output, while export prices for wool, minerals and a growing range of agricultural products were high. Assisted passages, better prospects and comparatively good wages attracted further waves of immigrants. With natural increase they brought the population to 3m. at the end of the 1880s, and provided a further stimulus to the construction and service sectors. The overwhelming majority were from the United Kingdom, with which the colonies retained close ties of kinship; the free movement of people, capital, knowledge and ideas assisted their rapid progress. Ethnic and religious differences were contained with a low degree of friction.

Urban concentration was a marked feature of this phase of rapid growth. One-half of the population lived in towns by the 1880s. Each of the colonies was dominated by its seat of government, which also served as the financial, commercial and administrative centre; these capital cities used their political influence to augment control over the hinterland. The Victorian capital of Melbourne expanded to 420,000 inhabitants and Sydney to 360,000. Adelaide, the capital of South Australia, had 115,000 residents and Brisbane, the capital of Queensland, 86,000.

The prosperity ended in 1890 as export prices declined and foreign lenders refused further advances. The pressure on production costs led to the formation of unions among workers in the important sectors of pastoralism, mining and transport, matched by the formation of national combinations of employers. A confrontation in 1890 brought strikes and lock-outs that paralysed the economy. The unions were broken by the use of volunteer labour, supported by the colonial Governments and protected by the volunteer militia, but the Australian economy rapidly declined into financial crisis and subsequent depression. This was followed later in the decade by a severe drought that had halved livestock numbers by the turn of the century.

NATIONAL RECONSTRUCTION

From these misfortunes arose some of the most powerfully formative principles of Australian national life. The industrial conflict gave rise to a labour movement that entered Parliament to make good the losses it had suffered and has remained ever since a force in politics. The colonies came together to create a federal nation state with responsibility for defence and external affairs, trade and national development. The new Commonwealth Government devised institutions designed to insulate Australia from economic disturbance, to safeguard living standards and to bridge social divisions. The national ethos was expressed in art, literature and popular culture.

The movement to federate Australia began in 1890 with a meeting in Melbourne of colonial statesmen, which was called by Sir Henry Parkes, the Premier of New South Wales, and stimulated by a recent report on the country's defence capacity; imperial rivalry had come closer to Australia with German and French activity in the South-West Pacific. A Federal Convention in Sydney in the following year drafted a Constitution, but the colonial Parliaments quibbled over its implications. The federal movement was revived in 1893 with an unofficial conference that proposed a new and directly elected convention, which met from 1897 to 1898. Its revised draft was submitted to popular referendums and finally enacted by the Imperial Parliament, so that the new Commonwealth of Australia was declared on the first day of the 20th century. The Constitution combined the principles of responsible government and federalism, with a Parliament consisting of a people's House of Representatives and a Senate made up of equal numbers of representatives of each of the six states (the name now given to the colonies). The rivalry between New South Wales and Victoria was resolved by the provision that Melbourne should be the temporary national capital until a new one was found within New South Wales but at least one hundred miles from Sydney; the federal Parliament moved to Canberra in 1927.

The federal movement was led by middle-class liberals, who saw no inconsistency in their combination of national ardour and imperial loyalty. Republican sentiment receded with the defeat of the unions and the decline of radicalism in the early 1890s. The unions turned to parliamentary activity in response to their defeat and made immediate gains, and as they directed their attention to electoral politics they moderated their policies. In the Commonwealth elections of 1910 the Labor Party achieved an absolute majority; previous Governments had lacked a majority and therefore shared office, except for a brief interregnum, between the protectionist Liberals and Labor, each depending upon the parliamentary support of the other.

The initial Commonwealth elections retained the voting arrangements of the states. The first parliament extended the franchise to women. South Australia and Western Australia had already granted voting rights to women, and Australia was a pioneer in the suffrage movement as well as in the emancipation of women from other restrictions. Like the labour movement, the feminist movement regarded Australia as a land of freedom and opportunity that had to be safeguarded from the evils of exploitation. Campaigns for women's rights of education, employment and public participation ran in parallel with campaigns for temperance and against gambling, prostitution and domestic violence. A maternalist conception of citizenship treated emancipation from masculine tyranny as a necessary condition of women's contribution to national life.

The same Commonwealth Franchise Act of 1902 denied the vote to Aboriginal Australians, despite the fact that they already voted in several of the states. This was in keeping with the exclusion of Aboriginals from most rights of citizenship at this time and with the increasing restriction of their lives by the states, which retained legislative power over them. There was a widespread perception that the indigenous peoples were doomed to extinction because they were incapable of bridging the gulf that separated them from civilization. Some of mixed parentage might succeed, and to this end Aboriginals were confined to designated settlements as wards of the State, while children of mixed descent were removed and expected to assimilate. In contrast to other white supremacist settler societies, Australia created no absolute barrier between black and white, but its own mixture of segregation and assimilation was designed to eliminate Aboriginality. The motives of those who devised the policy and the consequences for its victims have remained subjects of controversy.

Among the first acts of the new Parliament was the approval of immigration legislation whereby Asians could be denied entry to the country. To meet British concerns, it did not explicitly discriminate against Asians but rather allowed the Commonwealth to impose a test in any European language. Frequently modified and gradually relaxed, this White Australia policy lasted until the 1960s. Additional legislation repatriated Pacific islanders who had been introduced to Queensland as plantation labourers. The fear of aliens was expressed in the language of national purity. Asians were perceived as a threat to living standards, a cause of 'miscegenation' and moral decay, and a danger to territorial integrity. As the United Kingdom felt the strain of naval competition and withdrew most of its squadron from the Far East, this insecurity increased, and was further exacerbated by the British naval treaty with Japan of 1902. Thwarted in his attempts to restore the British naval presence in the Pacific, Deakin invited the US fleet to visit Australia in 1908 and in the following year commenced a building programme for the Australian navy. Compulsory military training was introduced in 1910.

Protection of local industry by the imposition of tariff duties on competing imports was a further policy of the new Commonwealth. In 1906 the Government of Alfred Deakin, who had become the country's second Prime Minister in 1903, linked the price advantage created for local employers to their payment of 'a fair and reasonable wage' to employees. It fell to the new Arbitration Court to determine whether the employers complied with this condition. The Court had been established in 1904 to provide a remedy for industrial conflict, and it had compulsory powers to settle disputes and make awards specifying wages and conditions that were binding on the parties. In 1907 the Court considered the meaning of a fair and reasonable wage, and its president determined that such a wage should be sufficient to cover the needs of a man, a wife and three children. Although the High Court struck down the Government's legislation, this 'basic wage', regularly adjusted for changes in the cost of living, was gradually extended across the workforce as a legal minimum. The basic wage confirmed the role of the male as the family breadwinner: women were restricted in employment opportunities and their minimum wage was designed to support a single person only. Around these arrangements a system of social welfare was created: an old-age pension from 1908, an invalidity pension from 1910 and a maternity benefit from 1912 to assist mothers with the expenses of childbirth.

This period of conscious nation-building was accompanied by an exploration of local forms in art and literature. The artists of the Heidelberg school revealed a landscape of dazzling light. Popular verse and fiction celebrated the independence, egalitarianism and irreverence for authority of the bushman. Australian flora and fauna became common decorative motifs in architecture and advertising. The green of the Australian eucalypt and the gold of the wattle were adopted first by the national cricket team and then by other sporting representatives. The national coat of arms featured a kangaroo and an emu, against a background of sprays of wattle. Australians thought of their country as an advanced democracy and took pride in the innovative public policies that earned it the reputation of a social laboratory.

WAR AND DEPENDENCE

Australia entered the First World War (1914–18) along with the other British Dominions in support of the United Kingdom. An Australian Imperial Force was formed by voluntary enlistment, and a first contingent fought alongside New Zealand in the Dardanelles and the Middle East. The unsuccessful attempt of this Australian and New Zealand Army Corps (better known by its acronym of ANZAC) to storm the Turkish peninsula of Gallipoli became a formative legend of heroic endeavour; with Australia Day on 26 January, marking the first white settlement, Anzac Day on 25 April remains the country's principal public anniversary. After evacuation from Gallipoli at the end of 1915, the main Australian force was deployed on the Western Front, and mounting casualties persuaded the Labor Prime Minister, William Morris Hughes, to propose conscription for overseas service. Referendums on the proposal in 1916 and 1917 failed narrowly and split the Labor Party; the pro-conscriptionists joined with the non-Labor forces to establish the Nationalist Party, which kept Hughes in office.

Hughes' vigorous prosecution of the war and liberal use of his emergency powers caused deep division. The instigation of legal proceedings against industrial militants, the internment of enemy aliens (there was a substantial German community) and vilification of anti-conscriptionists brought a new tone of acrimony to public life. The Prime Minister's conflict with the Irish-born Daniel Mannix, who was Catholic Archbishop of Melbourne, widened sectarian divisions. At the peace conference in Paris, France, at the end of the war Hughes antagonized the US President, Woodrow Wilson, with his insistence on heavy reparations, and offended the Japanese delegates with his determination to retain control of Pacific territory and reject a declaration of racial equality. The war resulted in the loss of 60,000 Australian lives and left a large debt. It also gave rise to lingering fears for Australia's security and deep suspicions of national loyalty. Ex-service organizations were formed to safeguard the country from sedition. The Nationalist Party affirmed a more conservative patriotism that was resistant to further experiment in social policy and hostile to alien influences.

A post-war slump was accompanied by renewed industrial unrest. The Hughes Government responded by raising tariffs and extending public enterprises, a policy that offended the farmers, who formed their own Country Party. This new party held the balance of power after the 1922 election, and Hughes lost the leadership of the Nationalist Party to a Melbourne businessman, S. M. Bruce (later Lord Bruce), who formed a coalition with the Country Party. The coalition sought to resume the policies of national development by extending government assistance to the farmers. Australia's population increased from 5,412,000 in 1920 to 6,336,000 in 1929. Further loans were raised to settle 200,000 British migrants on the land and create new farms for ex-servicemen. A wider range of agricultural products, including dairy produce, meat, fruit and sugar, as well as wheat and wool, were produced for the British market. Heavy industry followed the establishment of major steelworks at Newcastle during the war, and local manufacturers also expanded to meet the growing domestic market for consumer durables. The construction of the Sydney Harbour Bridge between 1926 and 1932 symbolized this triumph of urban modernity. Yet the city factories and offices remained heavily dependent on tariff protection, and their high cost structure imposed an increasing burden on the rural export sector.

Even before the Wall Street Crash of October 1929, the Nationalist-Country Party Government attempted to rectify the growing trade imbalance by reducing wage costs. A series of protracted strikes followed. Bruce's attempt to abandon industrial arbitration led to a party rebellion, and Labor won the ensuing election at the end of 1929, thus assuming responsibility for the Australian response to the Depression. With the collapse of export earnings and foreign investment, Australia's reliance on the traditional methods of protecting the economy proved futile and the unemployment rate rose to more than 20% of the labour force. Denied further credit by the banks, the federal and state Governments were forced to curtail their expenditure. The Arbitration Court reduced the basic wage by

10% in early 1931, while the currency was devalued by 30%. These economic measures caused widespread distress and political unrest. The Labor Government fell at the end of 1931 and the former Labor Treasurer, J. A. Lyons, took office at the head of a newly formed United Australia Party. The Government relied heavily on the resumption of trade with the United Kingdom, and an agreement concluded in Ottawa, Canada, in 1932 gave reciprocal preference to British imports. This arrangement caused particular difficulties with Japan, which retaliated in 1937 with damaging sanctions against Australian wool-growers. In foreign as well as trade policy, Australia followed the United Kingdom closely and therefore found itself again at war in 1939.

Australian troops were once more sent overseas, to North Africa, and fought in campaigns there, as well as in the unsuccessful defence of Greece in 1941. The entry of Japan into the Second World War (1939–45) at the end of 1941 and its rapid advance down the South-East Asian archipelago forced a concentration on home defence and a realization that Australia could no longer depend upon British assurances. A Labor Government took office and sought a closer relationship with the USA, which established its regional headquarters in Australia and led the Allied campaign to repulse the Japanese. The same circumstances forced a greater degree of national self-sufficiency: the Government assumed unprecedented controls to manage the war economy and supply the Allied forces; military conscription for overseas service was introduced in 1943. Australian losses in the Second World War, at 37,000, were lower than in the First, although the maltreatment of prisoners of war by the Japanese left bitter resentment (of 22,000 taken into captivity, only 14,000 returned). There was a greater spirit of unity in support of the war effort, encouraged by the Labor Government's insistence on equality of sacrifice, as well as its ambitious programme of post-war reconstruction.

POST-WAR EXPANSION

Again in contrast to the settlement of the First World War, Australia was fully committed to the international principles that led to the formation of the UN in 1945. It placed special emphasis on the democratic political imperative of full employment, and was quick to adopt the Keynesian techniques of economic management that expanded the government's role. Despite the backlog of consumer demand and shortages of essential materials, it introduced a programme of housing construction and major public works, created a range of welfare measures and set ambitious immigration targets. Few of the personnel who returned from the armed services after 1945 were placed on the land; many more undertook university education and training, as the aim was to harness science, foster expertise and increase national capacity. As part of this endeavour, a local car-manufacturing industry was established in agreement with General Motors.

While the Labor Government had secured control of income taxation and confirmed the Commonwealth's primacy in welfare provision, it failed in a series of constitutional referendums to extend its wartime economic powers, and was particularly concerned that full employment in a period of shortages would lead to inflation. The reluctance to allow wage increases and delays in the hearing by the Arbitration Court of an application for a 40-hour working week strained relations with the trade unions, while the onset of the period of hostility between the USA and the USSR known as the Cold War caused an open breach with the Communist Party, which had grown rapidly during the Second World War and held leading positions in major unions. A series of strikes in essential industries increased the dissatisfaction of an electorate weary of controls and shortages. A Liberal Party had been formed during the war and it won office in coalition with the Country Party in 1949.

Under Robert (later Sir Robert) Menzies, the Coalition established political dominance. Its initial attempt to outlaw the Communist Party failed when the High Court declared the Government's legislation to be unconstitutional, and a referendum in 1951 failed to win popular approval for the necessary constitutional amendment. Yet the new Government was able to link the Cold War with the long-standing fear of invasion from the north. Australia therefore dispatched troops to fight in Korea in 1950, and in 1951 entered into the ANZUS treaty with the USA and New Zealand, as well as the South-East Asia Treaty Organization, arranged by the USA after communist forces defeated France in Viet Nam in 1954. The Menzies Government emphasized that communist influence in trade unions compromised the Labor Party, a claim that was strengthened when a Soviet diplomat and his wife defected and in 1954 told a royal commission of their links with members of the staff of the Labor leader, Dr H. V. Evatt. An anti-communist organization had been formed in the unions under Catholic leadership, and was extending its influence into the Labor Party. When Evatt denounced this organization, the Labor Party split in 1955, and a breakaway Democratic Labor Party directed its preferences to the Coalition parties at subsequent elections. Labor was destined to languish in opposition in the federal Parliament until 1972.

The Menzies Government benefited from two decades of sustained economic growth, aided by the liberalization of world trade and increased demand for Australian exports. A trade treaty with Japan in 1957 indicated a reorientation of trade from the United Kingdom and Europe towards East Asia, as that region began to recover from war and to industrialize; minerals joined wool and agricultural products as major sources of export earnings. Australian manufactures expanded rapidly with the advantage of tariffs and import quotas. The service sector grew even faster as mechanization released blue-collar workers to join the white-collar salariat. An annual economic growth rate of 4% was maintained throughout the 1950s and into the 1960s. While Menzies condemned socialism and continued to proclaim his commitment to private enterprise, his Government maintained controls over foreign exchange and investment, regulated the banks and retained the Arbitration Court (restructured in 1956 as the Arbitration Commission) to determine wages. It increased public revenue and provided annual grants to the states for their operation of hospitals, schools, public transport and other services; but relied increasingly on private provision for its own schemes of subsidized medical insurance and assistance to home-buyers.

The rate of home ownership increased to 70% by 1961, while the rapid spread of car ownership and television supported suburban patterns of consumerism. Women had enjoyed new opportunities during the Second World War, both as members of the auxiliary forces and as workers in war industries; but with the advent of peace they were expected to revert to their roles of wives and mothers. Most did so, and the post-war 'baby boom' caused a rapid expansion of the education sector. However, full employment allowed a growing minority to undertake paid employment, and in 1950 the Arbitration Court increased women's pay to 75% of the male rate.

The population rose from 7,579,000 in 1947 to 11,550,000 by 1971, and more than one-half of the increase came from migration. The Labor Government tried initially to find migrants from the traditional source of the United Kingdom and Ireland. Unable to fill its annual quota, it turned to continental Europe and took in 170,000 from the refugee camps there. Agreements were made, initially with the governments of north-west Europe, and later with Italy, Greece and other Mediterranean countries, for assisted passage and settlement. Two-thirds of the 1m. settlers during the 1950s were non-British, a reorientation recognized in 1948 with the creation of Australian citizenship (previously Australians had the official status of British subjects). With this came the designation of immigrants as 'new Australians' and procedures designed to assimilate them into 'the Australian way of life'. There was no immediate relaxation of the White Australia policy, which was enforced by the repatriation of wartime refugees and became a growing embarrassment to Australia in its dealings with Asian neighbours, especially as the Colombo Plan (a post-war scheme for co-operative development of British Commonwealth countries in the region) brought South and South-East Asian students to Australia for university study. The dictation test was quietly abandoned in 1958, naturalization facilitated in 1966 and by the end of the decade 10,000 non-white immigrants were arriving annually.

Menzies gave little recognition of this growing diversity. While he presided over the transfer of Australia's primary alliance from the United Kingdom to the USA, he remained a romantic monarchist and champion of British links. His attempt to intervene in support of the homeland during the Suez crisis in 1956 only revealed that the United Kingdom was no longer a world power. Menzies was most relaxed during visits to London for meetings of the leaders of the white Commonwealth, ill at ease with the non-white leaders of the former colonies, and his defence of the apartheid regime in South Africa damaged Australia's international reputation. It was the United Kingdom's decision to seek membership of the European Economic Community (EEC, subsequently the European Union) in the early 1960s that finally ended the illusion of a special relationship.

Menzies committed Australia to support the USA in the Viet Nam War; his successors were left to deal with the consequences. Harold Holt, who became Liberal leader and Prime Minister in 1966, told the US President, Lyndon B. Johnson, that Australia would go 'all the way with LBJ' and sent conscripts to Viet Nam; but Holt's initial popularity waned before he died while swimming at the end of 1967. His successor, John Gorton, pursued a more independent foreign policy, but was overthrown two years later and replaced by William McMahon. By this time the war in Viet Nam had become a disadvantage for the Coalition Government. Labor won the election at the end of 1972 and immediately implemented its commitment to withdraw all troops.

UNCERTAINTY

The new Labor Prime Minister, Gough Whitlam, came to power with an ambitious programme of reform. He set aside the party's preoccupation with trade union concerns so that it could appeal to the mood for change among the educated middle class. With great speed he initiated a more independent stance for the country by establishing diplomatic relations with the People's Republic of China, announcing independence for Australia's colony of Papua New Guinea, ratifying international conventions on nuclear weapons, labour rights and racism, and abolishing imperial honours. Among Whitlam's domestic initiatives were the creation of a Department of Aboriginal Affairs and recognition of Aboriginal land rights; the abandonment of migrant assimilation in favour of multiculturalism; equal pay for women along with reform of family law and programmes to promote affirmative action; social welfare reform; a public health system; expansion of educational provision; environmental protection and urban renewal.

It was Whitlam's misfortune to take office just as the circumstances to support such an expansive policy ended. His Government doubled public expenditure in just three years. Prices and wages were increasing rapidly, despite a reduction of 25% in the tariff level, even before the Yom Kippur war of 1973 and the subsequent embargo imposed by the Arab petroleum producers that disrupted the world economy. While the Labor Government delivered a contractionary budget in early 1975, it was in serious trouble. The non-Labor parties used their majority in the Senate to refuse supply to the Government, and on 11 November 1975 the Governor-General took the extraordinary step of dismissing Whitlam from office. The Liberal and Country parties, led by Malcolm Fraser, won a decisive victory in the subsequent election. The Dismissal, as it was known, was the most serious constitutional crisis in Australian history, which weakened the next Prime Minister's legitimacy as he attempted to address new problems.

Malcolm Fraser searched for a solution to the novel combination of high inflation and high unemployment, dual scourges that had been regarded as alternatives in the preceding period of economic management. His Government determined to tackle inflation in order to reduce wage costs and restore profits, and to decrease government expenditure in order to ease interest rates and encourage private investment. While inflation declined, unemployment rose from 250,000 in 1975 to 400,000 by 1978. Australia's difficulties were compounded by a long-term decline in the price of its export commodities, setting at risk its traditional role as a producer of raw materials for overseas manufacturers. The best prospects seemed to be minerals, oil and gas, but these were capital-intensive industries that created few jobs and increased the pressure on domestic industries through their effect on the exchange rate.

Fraser won fresh elections in 1978 and 1980, although he lacked control of the Senate and was hampered by ministerial scandals. Forthright in his anti-communist foreign policy, he was at the same time a strong critic of white supremacy in southern Africa, and a supporter of both multiculturalism and Aboriginal land rights at home. These sympathies were criticized by some of his colleagues, while his abrasive industrial relations policy and insistence on uranium exports aroused protest. As the mineral boom suddenly ended in 1982, the Government relaxed its tight control of public expenditure and the money supply, bringing increases in wages, renewed inflation and a further rise in unemployment. No sooner was Fraser defeated at the 1983 election than those who had served under him dissociated themselves from his legacy.

The new Labor Prime Minister was Bob Hawke, previously the leader of the Australian Council of Trade Unions, and he came to office with an agreement by the unions to co-operate in economic reconstruction. Under the terms of a Prices and Income Accord, workers would accept wage restraint in return for job creation. The Government helped reconstruct vital industries such as steel and vehicle construction, and restored health care and other welfare benefits. As an employment strategy, the Accord was successful: 1.5m. jobs were created during the remainder of the decade, and the unemployment rate declined from 10% of the work-force to 6% by 1989. With subsequent revisions that included a national superannuation scheme, the Accord was maintained. Industrial disputes were brief and infrequent.

However, these arrangements alone did not restore competitiveness, and the Labor Treasurer, Paul Keating, implemented a series of further changes. The Australian dollar was floated, exchange controls were removed, the financial sector was deregulated, tariffs were lowered and other forms of protection were dismantled. This exposure of the Australian economy to market forces brought high borrowings, speculative investments, persistent trade deficits and rapid currency fluctuations. Traditional industries declined, and with them disappeared the job security that Australians had once expected; there was a rapid rise in part-time and casual employment. The rural sector struggled to adjust, and country towns lost the banks, public agencies and professional services that had sustained them. A rapid increase in interest rates at the end of the 1980s brought recession and renewed unemployment. The Government responded with further instalments of economic reform, including the privatization of public enterprises, and moved away from national wage determination by introducing enterprise agreements.

THE NEW ORDER

These changes completed the Government's abandonment of the institutions that had guided national life for most of the 20th century. The protection of local industry, the regulation of wages, the construction of welfare provision around the entitlements of the male breadwinner, the maintenance of full employment and the recourse to public enterprise were all designed to meet the needs and expectations of the inhabitants of a small, trading nation located on the opposite side of the world from its main sources of trade, finance, technology and culture. The institutions were dismantled because they were no longer effective in the changed circumstances that prevailed by the end of the century. Paul Keating, who drove the economic reforms, warned in 1986 that without them Australia was doomed to become a 'banana republic'. The Government therefore searched for greater competitive efficiency in the new global economy by embracing economic liberalism.

In contrast to similar reforms in the USA and the United Kingdom, those in Australia were undertaken by Labor Governments. The Hawke Ministry's willingness to embrace deregulation outflanked the Liberal and National parties (this change of name to the latter by the Country Party was an indication of the decline of the rural constituency); they found it harder to break free of their attachment to industrial interests that were accustomed to receiving government support. Labor's appeal to the national interest brought victories at federal elections in 1984, 1987 and 1990, while a similar reforming zeal enabled the party to hold office in five of the six states by 1990. Labor's programme retained vestiges of social democracy. While the Treasurer sought a more flexible labour market through enterprise agreements, the Government maintained wage levels. While income inequality increased, social welfare and employment programmes preserved the living standards of the lowest income earners.

After Keating replaced Hawke as Prime Minister at the end of 1991, the Liberal and National Coalition parties turned to John Hewson, an economist who offered a bold programme of tax reform, further labour market deregulation and reduction of government activity in favour of the principle of 'user pays'. Keating now reinvented himself as a defender of what he called the 'social fabric' and insisted that prosperity was greatest in 'social democracies where the government is involved in making societies tick'. He embraced a landmark decision by the High Court in 1992 that found native title survived on Crown land, and in the same year he addressed an Aboriginal audience in inner Sydney with a frank admission of the wrongs that had been committed against them. He argued that Hewson's policies would penalize the poor, marginalize indigenous and ethnic groups, and imperil the hard-won advances of the previous decade.

Keating was himself an abrasive polemicist, but the electorate was weary of change and reluctant to embark on a further round of radical reform. The Prime Minister mistakenly interpreted his victory in the March 1993 election as a vindication of what he called his 'big picture' of a 'competitive, outward-looking, phobia-free' society. His republican enthusiasms, his lavish patronage of the arts, his legislation to give effect to the High Court judgment on native title and his own weariness with the complexities of political management gave the impression of a Government that was out of touch. The Coalition parties turned to John Howard, a political veteran of great stamina and discipline, who took advantage of the growing discontent. Howard appealed to the 'battlers', as he called them, the ordinary men and women whose interests had been subordinated to the 'noisy minority groups' of feminists, environmentalists, the ethnic lobby, the Aboriginal 'industry' and the intellectuals. Juxtaposing the practical concerns of his battlers with the indulgences of Labor's pampered 'élites', he emphasized the national interest. Howard's promise at the March 1996 election was that he would govern 'for all of us', and he made major advances into Labor's heartland to win a decisive victory.

THE HOWARD ADMINISTRATION (1996–2007)

The Howard Government pursued a policy of economic liberalism and social conservatism. It embarked on a further phase of economic reform with renewed attention to trade liberalization, changes in the labour market to eliminate inefficiencies and uncompetitive practices, the partial sale of the telecommunications corporation Telstra (the largest of the remaining public enterprises), a retrenchment in government services and reduction of the public service in order to restore the budget to surplus. The collapse of stock exchanges in South-East Asia in 1997 and the deep recession that followed in the Asian region provided further justification for these policies. Reduced demand from Asian customers for Australian exports was partially offset by new markets, where the declining value of the Australian dollar gave a competitive advantage. Despite a persistent trade imbalance, interest rates remained low. Productivity gains allowed Australia to enjoy low inflation, low unemployment and sustained growth.

The Howard Government also pursued liberalization of the labour market. Its Workplace Relations Act of 1996 encouraged the establishment of individual contracts in addition to enterprise agreements, and restricted the scope of the Industrial Relations Commission's awards. Howard would have liked to extend the deregulation of industrial relations, but for his first eight years in office he lacked a majority in the Senate. The Government therefore had to negotiate a compromise with the smaller parties that held the balance of legislative power. Union membership had declined, to just 31% of the work-force by 1996, but remained strong in important industries such as maritime transport. In 1997 the Government drew up a plan with the National Farmers' Federation and one of the principal stevedoring companies to destroy the power of the Maritime Union of Australia. New workers were recruited from the Army and flown to Dubai, in the United Arab Emirates, for training. On the evening of 7 April 1998 security guards moved into the nation's ports to dismiss all members of the union who worked there. While pickets prevented the movement of cargo, and the courts ordered the reinstatement of the workers, negotiations brought major concessions from the union.

The new Government abolished the principal multicultural agencies and reduced the scope of the office for women's affairs. It decreased funding for Aboriginal programmes, legislated to circumscribe Aboriginal land rights and rejected the findings of an inquiry into the removal from their families of Aboriginal children that had been commissioned by the previous Government. The Prime Minister refused to make a formal apology to the 'stolen generation' or to support the programme for reconciliation that had begun under the previous administration. His Government dismissed reports issued by the UN in 2000 that were critical of Australia's policies.

This rift with the indigenous community was the most heavily contested of the ideological battles that were fought following the conservative accession to office. Census figures revealed a dramatic increase in indigenous numbers, from 156,000 in 1976 to 517,000 by 2006, and with the rebuilding of population came a renaissance of both traditional culture and new cultural forms in music, theatre, dance, art and literature. The Aboriginal flag, a striking arrangement of black, gold and ochre, was one of them. It became increasingly common in the 1990s for public meetings to begin with an Aboriginal elder giving a 'welcome to country' and a non-Aboriginal Australian to respond with an acknowledgement of the original inhabitants of the land on which they were meeting. There was a revival of Aboriginal languages, and a return to Aboriginal names.

However, there were few advantages in being Aboriginal. Those who identified themselves as such in the census had a higher rate of unemployment and lower income levels than the rest of the population. A much higher proportion of them were arrested and imprisoned. Their life expectancy was 15 years below the national average, despite a quarter-century of government activity that was intended to overcome their disadvantages. In 1991 the Hawke Government had initiated a formal process of reconciliation led by a statutory body of indigenous and non-indigenous Australians, who embarked on a process of consultation and discussion that was intended to culminate on the centenary of the Australian Commonwealth in 2001. It was at a convention of this Council for Aboriginal Reconciliation in 1997 that Howard dismissed what he regarded as symbolic gestures and exaggerated promises. The suppression of Aboriginal aspirations was accompanied by a denunciation of their moral legitimacy, both by denial of past wrongs and refusal of responsibility for their lasting effects. Historians who wrote of violence against Aboriginals on the colonial frontier were accused of scholarly malpractice and malevolent denigration of the national honour.

On the other hand, the Coalition Government was in a stronger position in seeking greater accountability in public expenditure and emphasizing health, housing, education and employment programmes with practical outcomes. The representative Aboriginal and Torres Strait Islander Commission lost much of its credibility and was abolished in 2005 in favour of an unelected National Indigenous Council. Noel Pearson, one of a younger generation of Aboriginal activists, spoke out on the need to tackle the problems of alcohol, violence and family breakdown in Aboriginal communities; he condemned welfare dependency as a threat to the very survival of his people and urged them to take greater responsibility for their own circumstances.

The Government's rebuff to Aboriginal aspirations was assisted by an independent member of the federal Parliament, Pauline Hanson. The proprietor of a small business, she had been endorsed as a Liberal candidate in 1996 for an electorate based on the Queensland industrial town of Ipswich, and then lost that endorsement after she alleged that excessive public funding was being provided for Aboriginals. In her maiden speech six months later she promised to end the 'reverse racism' of multiculturalism, Asian migration and 'the Aboriginal industry'. Hanson's rapid rise to prominence divided Labor's support base: she affronted its tertiary-educated, cosmopolitan, middle-class progressive citizens, while she appealed to older, less mobile, manual workers. Labor condemned her statements, while John Howard insisted that she was articulating the feelings of many people.

Assisted by a former Liberal organizer, Hanson formed her own One Nation party. Its threat became apparent in elections for the state of Queensland in June 1998. One Nation candidates won nearly one-quarter of the votes, pushing the Liberals into third place and allowing Labor to gain office. Fear of a similar result in the imminent federal election opened divisions in the Coalition. Although John Howard began criticizing Hanson's views, he resisted Labor's proposal that the major parties direct their preferences (the electoral system requiring voters to order candidates in terms of preference) away from One Nation, until the disastrous outcome for the Coalition in the Queensland election forced him to act. In the event, Hanson conducted a poor federal campaign and attracted just 10% of the national vote, but Howard was under pressure during the election in October 1998. It was a mark of his leadership that he made tax reform the principal feature of his campaign, with an undertaking to introduce a goods and services tax (GST). The election was closely contested, and a narrow majority of voters indicated a preference for Labor; but the distribution of electorates favoured the Coalition and it was returned with a safe parliamentary majority.

During its second term the Howard Government pressed ahead with the economic measures it had promised: tax reform, the full sale of Telstra, further deregulation of industrial relations and further conditions on welfare beneficiaries. The Government's lack of control of the Senate necessitated protracted negotiations with the smaller parties and independent senators, leading to substantial compromises. The implementation of the GST proceeded, with exemptions and compensation. The sale of Telstra was restricted to just one further tranche, leaving 50.1% still in public ownership.

The second term of the Howard Government also witnessed the defeat of the republican movement. Republican sentiment had been steadily increasing. The Whitlam Government had abandoned imperial honours in 1975. In 1984 the Hawke Government proclaimed 'Advance Australia Fair' as the national anthem, to the chagrin of many monarchists, and in 1986 the supremacy of the Australian Parliament was formalized. To neutralize the republican issue during the 1996 election, Howard had undertaken to provide an opportunity for the country to decide. He skilfully exploited the prominence of republican celebrities by suggesting that they were part of the 'élites', and he also arranged that the Constitutional Convention that met in Canberra during 1998 to settle on a republican model was composed of equal numbers of appointees and elected representatives. The model proved to be remarkably timid and was not enhanced by the new constitutional preamble that Howard himself drafted to accompany it. Both proposals were rejected by referendum in November 1999. The country thus hosted the Olympic Games in 2000 and celebrated the centenary of the Commonwealth early in the following year as a constitutional monarchy.

The 2001 election campaign was dominated by the issue of asylum-seekers who travelled by boat from South-East Asia and entered Australia or landed on island territories off the north-western coast. The Government devised what it called 'the Pacific solution', detaining asylum-seekers in facilities created on these islands or in adjoining countries. Labor initially refused to support the legislation required to make these arrangements, but then capitulated. The Government took advantage of its position and claimed that a boatload of illegal immigrants had thrown children overboard when approached by a naval vessel. The fears and uncertainties arising from the terrorist attacks on the USA of 11 September augmented the issue of border control. Full-page newspaper advertisements appeared on the morning of the November election showing John Howard with his fists clenched and the declaration '*We* decide who comes to this country'. He was returned to office with a slightly increased majority. After a third electoral victory John Howard was less troubled by ministerial mishaps and more adept in managing problems in troublesome policy areas.

At the October 2004 election the Howard Government won an increased majority in the House of Representatives and also took control of the Senate. The Government was thus able to complete the sale of Telstra, strengthen anti-terrorism measures, loosen controls on media ownership, impose work requirements on additional categories of welfare recipients and force radical changes to industrial relations. The last of these measures brought most workers covered by state provisions under a national system of industrial relations which the Government described as 'Work Choices'. This transferred the power to set minimum wages from the Industrial Relations Commission to a new and circumscribed tribunal; reversed safeguards against unfair dismissal; removed overtime, penalty rates and leave provisions from the requirements of the individual contracts that it promoted; and introduced new restrictions on trade unions.

As it implemented these measures during its fourth term, the Howard Government appeared to be in a strong position. After the recession of the early 1990s, the country had enjoyed 15 years of uninterrupted growth. China's seemingly insatiable demand for Australian minerals and energy led to a surge in exports. Gross domestic product (GDP) increased by more than 3% per annum, inflation and interest rates remained low, and unemployment declined to just 4% of the labour force. The growth in revenue from income and company tax allowed the Government to eliminate public debt, reduce marginal tax rates and still direct funding to interest groups.

However, the Government soon began to encounter difficulties. A report published in October 2005 by the UN's chief investigator, Paul Volcker, revealed that Australian wheat sales to Iraq had provided $A300m. in irregular payments to Saddam Hussain's regime. A judicial inquiry was established to investigate the conduct of the Australian Wheat Board (now AWB), and received evidence that the Government had been given repeated warnings of impropriety but had chosen not to investigate them. The Deputy Prime Minister and Minister for Trade, Mark Vaile, the Minister for Foreign Affairs, Alexander Downer, and the Prime Minister all appeared before the inquiry and denied any knowledge of breaching the UN sanctions; the Government was subsequently exonerated. During the course of the inquiry the opposition spokesman for foreign affairs, Kevin Rudd, provided a constant and effective commentary on the apparent failure of accountability, and within a week of the presentation of the inquiry's report in November 2006, he successfully challenged Kim Beazley for the leadership of Labor.

Kevin Rudd was a moderate former diplomat and senior public servant. As with previous changes of Labor leadership, the party benefited from an immediate improvement in public opinion polls, and once again the Government sought to reassert its superiority in the crucial policy areas of economic management and national security. This proved difficult, as the Reserve Bank of Australia, concerned about the inflationary dangers of a housing boom and capacity constraints, began raising interest rates, while Rudd took advantage of his expertise in international relations. When Howard sought to exploit popular concerns on sensitive issues, Rudd would render such tactics ineffective by means of agreement, refusing to be diverted from the policy areas where Labor held an advantage: industrial relations, health, education and climate change.

The perils of unfettered power were demonstrated by the Government's changes to industrial relations. Determined to deregulate the labour market, the administration prepared prescriptive legislation replete with prohibitions and penalties. The cumbrous bill extended to more than 750 pages and was forced through Parliament in late 2005. When the programme of Work Choices was implemented in the following year, there was a series of incidents embarrassing to the Government, as companies demanded that their workers accept salary reductions and the loss of elementary safeguards or risk dismissal. The Government was unprepared for the publicity given to these consequences by the Australian Council of Trade Unions and belatedly responded with an advertising campaign that proved unsuccessful: by 2007 legislation to modify Work Choices was necessary.

There was increasing criticism also of the treatment of David Hicks, an Australian who had served with the Taliban in Afghanistan. Hicks was captured at the end of 2001 and transferred to the US authorities. For some years the Australian Government had dismissed allegations of abusive treatment and justified his detention in Guantánamo Bay on the grounds that he had committed no crime that could be prosecuted under Australian law. By 2006 public opinion was becoming impatient at the long delay in bringing Hicks before a tribunal. The Howard Government belatedly urged that charges against him be heard, and after negotiating with the special military commission he pleaded guilty in March 2007 to providing material support for terrorism, was sentenced to seven years' imprisonment and returned to Australia to serve a gaol term of nine months, having agreed to have no contact with the media, among other conditions. The Government was also accused of mishandling the case of Mohamed Haneef, an Indian-born doctor who was arrested in July and charged with providing support for a terrorist organization after he lent a mobile phone SIM card to relatives in the United Kingdom who were thought to have been involved in a bomb attack at Glasgow airport. When Haneef was released on bail, the Minister for Immigration and Citizenship, Kevin Andrews, revoked his visa and returned him to prison. However, the case against him quickly foundered and the charges were withdrawn.

Opinion turned against the Government in other areas of public policy. In 2002 John Howard had joined the US President, George W. Bush, in refusing to ratify the Kyoto Protocol to the UN Framework Convention on Climate Change, negotiated in Japan in December 1997, which urged industrialized nations to reduce 'greenhouse gas' emissions. While business leaders had previously resisted any restrictions on carbon emissions, they were now urging the introduction of a trading scheme, and among them was Rupert Murdoch, whose News Corporation continued to dominate the print media in Australia. The Howard Government belatedly began an inquiry into global warming, and in May 2007 accepted its recommendation to establish a scheme for emissions trading, but insisted that further work was needed before setting targets for reduction. The possibility of nuclear power generation was also raised.

A related initiative responded to the prolonged and severe drought, which had reduced farm production and imposed severe restrictions on water use in Australian cities. In January 2007 John Howard announced a $A10,000m. plan to restore the river system of south-eastern Australia, which required the states to relinquish control of water management. The scheme failed owing to the refusal of one state, Victoria, to do so. Relations between the federal and state governments were a long-standing problem because the states retained responsibility for health, education, transport and other services, but possessed limited taxation powers. The growing fiscal imbalance made the states reliant on federal assistance to discharge their responsibilities. From the 1990s the states agreed to a national competition policy with incentives to increase efficiency in service provision and, as part of its tax reform in 2000, the Howard Government allocated the new GST to the states in return for their elimination of many of their own taxes and charges. However, the initial results proved disappointing.

By 2002 Labor held office in all six states, as well as in the Northern Territory and the Australian Capital Territory (which also have elected governments). The Liberals had traditionally maintained a strong commitment to the federal system, but after achieving control of both houses of the federal Parliament in 2004, had shown an increasing willingness to assert national control. The consequent arguments over responsibility for government activities distracted attention from a failure to invest in the nation's infrastructure. At a time when its revenue was growing strongly, the federal Government offered tax reductions and welfare benefits but was less willing to fund public investment in transport, communications, skills formation and innovation. The deficiencies of road, rail and telecommunications facilities, shortages of skilled labour and a low level of expenditure on research were identified as some of the fundamental constraints on the economy.

As the 2007 election approached, the Howard Government intervened in another emerging crisis. The Government of the Northern Territory had commissioned an inquiry into allegations of sexual abuse of children among Aboriginal communities, which found evidence of widespread abuse accompanied by violence, drug dependency, gambling, truancy, illiteracy and child neglect. In June Prime Minister Howard described the situation as a national emergency and announced that the federal Government would discontinue the permit system (whereby Aboriginal communities controlled entry), ban the consumption of alcohol and withhold 50% of welfare payments in the Territory to ensure that they were spent on necessities. Police and the armed services were to secure law and order, while health officials would check all Aboriginal children for signs of abuse. The federal Government was able to overrule the Government of the Northern Territory as its system of self-government was based on federal legislation and there was widespread concern for the welfare of these communities; but the emergency measures were imposed without consultation, and there was much scepticism with regard to the federal Government's motives in an election year.

Howard had failed to damage Kevin Rudd's popularity, and his own leadership was being subjected to increasing scrutiny. The deputy leader of the Liberals, Peter Costello, who had served as Treasurer since 1996, reportedly aspired to the position of Prime Minister, and in 2006 he revealed that Howard had originally agreed to serve two terms (or less) as Prime Minister. As Howard approached the end of his fourth term, the Prime Minister canvassed the views of his senior colleagues, who were doubtful that he could secure a fifth electoral victory but were no more confident of their prospects under Costello's leadership. The Prime Minister's announcement that he would transfer the leadership to Costello should he win a fifth term did nothing to reassure the electorate. Moreover, these discussions occurred while Howard was hosting a meeting of the Asia-Pacific Economic Cooperation (APEC) forum in Sydney in September 2007. Although the event was expected to serve as a display of Howard's stature among international counterparts, attention instead turned to Rudd, who demonstrated his language skills by addressing the Chinese President, Hu Jintao, in fluent Mandarin.

The election date was announced soon afterwards, and the poll was duly held on 24 November 2007. There was a substantial transfer of support from the governing Liberal and National parties to Labor, which won 83 of the 150 seats in the House of Representatives, thus securing a parliamentary majority. John Howard was defeated in his own constituency and retired from politics. In the concurrent elections for the Senate, Labor won 18 of the 40 seats being contested in the 76-member chamber.

THE RUDD ADMINISTRATION (2007–10)

Kevin Rudd and his new administration were sworn into office in early December 2007. The Deputy Prime Minister, Julia Gillard, assumed responsibility for a large portfolio, comprising education, employment, workplace relations and social inclusion, areas of government that she described as 'all ultimately about the same thing: productivity'. With Wayne Swan, the Treasurer, and Lindsay Tanner, the Minister for Finance and Deregulation, Rudd and Gillard worked closely on Australia's response to the global financial crisis that developed in the latter part of 2008. Rudd led a tightly controlled Government that was preoccupied with the news cycle. The Prime Minister placed inordinate demands on his staff: he wanted to be in control of every aspect of government but took advice from a narrow range of colleagues. Although Rudd attached great importance to his election commitments, he was preoccupied by the immediacy of the impending economic crisis. He came to office promising to rectify the previous underinvestment in infrastructure, and commissioned inquiries across the range of national policy. It was said that his Government 'hit the ground reviewing', but the plans that resulted were hindered by changed economic circumstances.

The Liberal and National parties found it difficult to adjust to their loss of office. Brendan Nelson, previously Minister for Defence, was elected Leader of the Liberal Party, defeating Malcolm Turnbull by a narrow majority, while Julie Bishop, formerly Minister for Education, Science and Training, became his deputy. Nelson sought to strike a balance between defending the record of the previous Government and adjusting to the new political situation, but failed to make an impression; in another election to the party leadership in September 2008, he was challenged and narrowly defeated by Turnbull. The new Liberal leader had been a lawyer, a merchant banker and the leader of the republican movement before entering Parliament in 2004.

In the first half of 2008 Australia experienced increasing inflation and rising interest rates. The Government sought to reduce public expectations when its first budget was announced in May, but it was committed to reducing taxes and to instigating new spending programmes. Strong revenue growth allowed the creation of three sovereign wealth funds for infrastructure, education and health. However, the international banking crisis four months later had an immediate effect, and the Reserve Bank began to reduce interest rates. Similarly, a large budget surplus allowed the Government to provide substantial stimulus measures. The first instalment came into effect in October, and included lump sum payments to middle- and low-income earners, as well as grants to first-home buyers. The second, in February 2009, provided further payments of $A12,700m. and a building programme of $A28,800m. The third was provided by the budget in May, which proceeded with tax reductions, increased old age pensions and made major commitments to transport and communications infrastructure. Strong demand from Asia for mineral and energy exports assisted with the economic recovery, and the rate of unemployment continued to decline in early 2010.

While criticized by the Opposition for wasting the surplus that the new Government had inherited, the stimulus measures were supported by industry and were popular with the public. However, problems began to emerge with the implementation of spending programmes. In June 2009 the Opposition alleged that the Prime Minister's office had intervened in the operation of a government scheme providing credit to car dealers in order to assist a businessman who, it said, had provided the Prime Minister with a vehicle for use in his constituency. The Leader of the Opposition, Malcolm Turnbull, used information from a Treasury official to press these allegations, but was discomfited when the official admitted that he had forged the e-mail that purportedly demonstrated the intervention by the Prime Minister's office. More serious difficulties beset a scheme to insulate houses for greater energy efficiency, since inadequate supervision of the contractors who undertook the work compromised safety standards. In February 2010 the scheme was abandoned and responsibility for energy efficiency was transferred to a different minister.

Problems in a third stimulus programme were slower to emerge. More than $A14,000m. was allocated at the beginning of 2009 for building better school facilities, part of the Rudd Government's 'Education Revolution' to improve school results and increase participation in higher education. This policy included the distribution of computers to schools, the preparation of a national curriculum and publication of school performance attainments. Its principal feature was the allocation of funds for construction projects, and here again the hasty negotiation of contracts provided inadequate oversight. By the end of 2009 the Opposition was alleging wasteful expenditure on government schools, and during 2010 there were numerous complaints from teachers and parents about poorly planned and unsuitable outcomes.

In its swift and emphatic response to the global economic crisis, the Government was determined to allocate expenditure to families, housing and construction in order to boost consumer demand, sustain house prices and maintain employment. Larger-scale infrastructure projects were delayed. After its election the Government had invited tenders for a high-speed National Broadband Network, but none was acceptable, so in 2009 it announced that it would establish a new company and contribute one-half of the $A43,000m. required to build the network. The obstacle here was Telstra, which owned the existing cable and copper network and was reluctant to upgrade it without assurances to protect its investment. Agreement was finally reached in 2010 for Telstra to transfer its network services to the new fibre network.

The Government pledged to limit future increases in recurrent expenditure, constraining latitude for further initiatives. The 2010 budget revealed an improvement in revenue, but the Treasurer was determined to return the budget to surplus by 2012/13, so that the limit on expenditure remained. To resolve the impasse, a new resource tax was announced. This was one of the recommendations made in a comprehensive review of the tax system conducted by the Treasury, but the Government was wary of the political consequences, delayed taking action on the findings of the review for as long as it could and finally singled out this measure for implementation. Royalties constituted a decreasing proportion of the record profits that Australian producers continued to enjoy from the mining and energy boom. The proposed Resource Super Profits Tax (RSPT) was intended to replace the existing royalties and charge companies 40% of profits in excess of the standard cost of capital, and provide offsets for losses incurred in exploration and development. The new revenue would be used to increase superannuation, reduce company tax and finance infrastructure in the resource-rich states of Queensland and Western Australia, where private development was already outstripping public provision. Having announced the new tax, the Government undertook a process of consultation to guide its implementation, and encountered vociferous opposition from the resource sector, as well as from the state governments that were affected by the tax.

This was not the first time that the Government had encountered strong opposition from the resource sector. It had been elected in 2007 after promising to take action on climate change. Immediately following its assumption of office it ratified the Kyoto Protocol, thereby committing Australia to a reduction in its greenhouse gas emissions. The Government relied on a senior economist, Ross Garnaut, to prepare a report on ways of reducing emissions, and in September 2008 Garnaut recommended an emissions trading scheme, for implementation in 2010, with the aim of achieving a reduction of 20% in emissions by 2020. The Government established a lower target, and encountered opposition in the Senate, where it lacked a majority, from both the Australian Greens, who wanted firmer action, and the National Party, which argued that the scheme would place export producers at a disadvantage. As public support for the trading scheme waned, a series of concessions was offered to miners and farmers. In November 2009, with the UN Climate Conference due to take place in Copenhagen, Denmark, in the following month, a legislative compromise was presented to the Opposition. By this time resistance had become more resolute, so that Malcolm Turnbull was unable to persuade his colleagues to accept the compromise. His leadership of the Liberal Party was challenged and on 1 December he narrowly lost a vote for the leadership to Tony Abbott, a former supporter of Howard and an opponent of the trading scheme. The Government subsequently abandoned the proposed scheme and announced that it would take no further action on the matter during its first term of office.

Climate change was only one of the areas where the new Government encountered difficulty in fulfilling the expectations that it had raised. Among the first public events following the 2007 election was an apology to the 'stolen generation' of Aboriginal Australians. Broadcast on television and watched at many public gatherings, the action promised a new start in the Government's relations with Aboriginal citizens, in contrast to Howard's resolute refusal to make an official apology. Yet the Government maintained many of the policies introduced by its predecessor with regard to indigenous people, especially the federal intervention in the Northern Territory. Debate continued on the effectiveness of the emergency measures: some Aboriginal leaders supported the prohibitions on alcohol and the campaign against welfare dependency, while others denounced their discriminatory implications. The Government demanded greater compliance as it launched new initiatives in indigenous education, employment, health and housing, but the results were disappointing.

Another election commitment was to replace the previous Government's draconian industrial relations system, Work Choices, with a more equitable arrangement. Julia Gillard, whose portfolios included responsibility for employment and workplace relations, had represented trade unions in her previous career as an industrial lawyer, but she proved a strong negotiator on the Government's behalf. The legislation that she prepared, the Fair Work Act, restored collective bargaining and provided for national pay awards with minimum conditions of employment covering hours of work, leave and redundancy; it also revived restrictions on unfair dismissal. However, the adoption of the legislation, which took effect on 1 July 2009, required concessions to those employers warning of loss of employment, and the new measures failed to meet the unions' expectations.

A further undertaking was to improve the hospital system, which was administered by the states. Following the publication in 2009 of a report by the Health and Hospitals Reform Commission, the Rudd Government announced in March 2010 that it would take over responsibility for hospitals and create a system of regional networks to administer them. Several states were critical of the proposal, as it would require them to surrender one-third of their revenue from the GST, and argued that the new arrangements would create another layer of bureaucracy. Rudd toured the country's hospitals, proclaiming that he would end the 'blame game', but in April he arranged a compromise. The state of Western Australia, where Labor had lost office to the Liberal Party in September 2008, refused to participate in the new arrangements.

The Rudd Government had greater freedom to initiate measures that did not incur additional costs. In April 2008 the Prime Minister announced that the Governor-General, Michael Jeffery, a former military officer appointed by John Howard, was to be replaced by Quentin Bryce, a former academic and federal commissioner on sex discrimination. In September, therefore, she became Australia's first female representative of the Head of State.

The previous Government's severe treatment of asylum-seekers was modified: overseas detention camps were closed and adult internees held instead on the Australian territory of Christmas Island, with access, after a defined period of detention, to an independent tribunal with the power to grant permanent protection visas. In 2009 an increase in the number of boats intercepted in northern waters, containing mainly Tamils from Sri Lanka and Afghans, led to fresh allegations of people-smuggling. In October an armed patrol vessel brought 78 asylum-seekers to Indonesia, for transfer to an Australian-funded detention centre on the island of Bintan, and their refusal to disembark aroused controversy. With the facilities at Christmas Island full and opinion polls indicating disapproval of official policy, the Government suspended processing of new claims by Afghans and Sri Lankans and revived the previous Government's practice of detaining refugees in remote Australian centres. There was growing debate also over the high rate of immigration as the population increased to 22,387,000 by June 2010, exacerbating problems of urban congestion.

Until the end of 2009 the Government maintained a lead in opinion polls. By this time approval of the successful response to the global financial crisis was giving way to dissatisfaction with Labor's failures of administration. After state elections in early 2010, Labor was narrowly returned to office in South Australia and relied on the support of the Greens in Tasmania. There was increasing criticism of the Prime Minister's failure to take advice from colleagues and his inability to communicate the Government's policies to voters. A federal election was due by early 2011, and Rudd's declining popularity precipitated a sudden challenge to his leadership from the Deputy Prime Minister, Julia Gillard, in June 2010. When it became clear that Rudd lacked support he stood aside, and Gillard was elected leader of the Labor Party, thus becoming the new Prime Minister on 24 June. This was the first time that a Labor leader had been ousted from prime ministerial office.

THE GILLARD ADMINISTRATION (2010–)

Julia Gillard thus became the first woman to hold the post of Australian Prime Minister. Seeking to benefit from a rise in the public opinion polls, in mid-July 2010 she announced the holding of an early election. However, hampered by criticism of the way in which she had supplanted Kevin Rudd, her campaign failed to achieve momentum, while Tony Abbott conducted a carefully measured campaign on behalf of the Liberal-National Coalition. The election on 21 August resulted in a shift away from the governing Labor Party, which won only 72 of the 150 seats in the House of Representatives. Although the Coalition attracted the largest number of votes, there was an increase in support for the Greens. Under Australia's system of preferential voting, the majority of votes for the Greens returned to the Labor Party, with the result that the Coalition parties also won 72 seats. The balance of power thus rested with five independent members and the lower chamber's first Green member, who had been elected to a Melbourne seat. Julia Gillard was able to negotiate an agreement with the Green member and three of the independent members, and she was sworn back into office on 14 September. Her deputy, Wayne Swan, remained as Treasurer, with Kevin Rudd as the Minister for Foreign Affairs.

Gillard sought acceptable solutions to the problems that had created such difficulty for her predecessor. In advance of the election she had renamed the RSPT, reduced the incidence of the tax, and restricted its application to coal and iron ore. The details of the new Minerals Resource Rent Tax were worked out after the election, and draft legislation was released for comment in June 2011. In place of the emissions trading scheme, also abandoned by the Government before the election, Gillard announced in February 2011 that Australia would adopt a carbon tax. Details of this tax were the subject of protracted negotiation between the Government, the Greens and independent members of the federal Parliament. Since Gillard had given a commitment during the election campaign that she would not introduce a carbon tax, the proposal encountered strong opposition. In July the Government released details of the carbon tax, which was to operate as a transitional measure for a future trading scheme. The tax burden was to fall on the 500 largest companies, and its effect on the cost of living was to be offset by tax reform and household assistance.

The Prime Minister sought to neutralize the contentious issue of illegal immigration prior to the election, with an announcement that negotiations were under way for the offshore processing of asylum-seekers. She specifically ruled out reopening the Howard Government's detention centre on the small Pacific island of Nauru and indicated that Timor-Leste (formerly East Timor) was a preferred destination. After the Government of Timor-Leste rejected the proposal, it was announced in late July 2011 that Australia and Malaysia had signed an agreement whereby the latter country would take 800 asylum-seekers over a period of four years and, in return, Australia would take 4,000 persons assessed as being refugees from Malaysia. This proposal was criticized on the grounds that Malaysia was not a signatory to the UN Convention relating to the Status of Refugees, adopted in 1951. Meanwhile, the Government announced the establishment of two detention centres in Western Australia and South Australia for women and children, and a further centre in Tasmania for single men. Similarly, the Government scaled back the immigration programme. Net overseas immigration declined from 264,000 people in 2009 to just 171,000 in 2010.

The budget that was delivered in May 2011 maintained the Government's commitment to restore a fiscal surplus by 2012/13. After the heavy outlays on stimulus measures in previous years, it did so by reducing some programmes and relying on future revenue estimates. In health policy, the Gillard Government renegotiated the earlier arrangement with the states. It no longer required them to surrender a portion of their revenue from the GST, but reduced its own contribution to 50% of the cost of the hospital system. Similarly, with regard to industrial relations and Aboriginal intervention, the Prime Minister employed her considerable skills of negotiation to reach an outcome that was acceptable to all those involved in the discussions. She maintained good relations with the Greens and the independent parliamentarians on whom she relied, but was constrained by the need to obtain their support for crucial government measures. Under the leadership of

Tony Abbott, meanwhile, the Opposition kept up its relentless criticism of the Government. As a result, the Government found itself occupying the middle ground, and it had great difficulty in articulating a persuasive explanation for the compromises it arranged.

Support for the Labor Party had decreased to 38% in the federal election of August 2010, and it continued to decline. In Victoria in November the Labor Government led by John Brumby, generally acknowledged to be the most competent of the state governments, attracted only 36% of the primary vote and lost office to the Coalition parties led by Ted Baillieu. Few were surprised in March 2011 when the Labor Government in New South Wales was swept from power, for it was beset by chronic instability and the Coalition leader, Barry O'Farrell, was studiously moderate. Yet Labor's primary vote, at just 24%, confirmed the party's national predicament. In Queensland the floods that struck in late December 2010 and claimed 44 lives brought a temporary boost of support for the Labor Premier, Anna Bligh, although this was short-lived. In South Australia and Tasmania Labor held onto office under Mike Rann and Lara Giddings respectively; in Western Australia Liberal Premier Colin Barnett continued to enjoy a substantial lead in the polls. With the next election due in 2013, Julia Gillard had just two years in which to recover lost ground.

The Prime Minister's political fortunes were somewhat enigmatic. Australia had escaped the consequences of the global recession; it continued to enjoy strong demand for its commodity exports and achieved a record trade surplus in 2010. Admittedly, the strength of the currency had a detrimental effect on manufacturing, tourism and other service industries, but the level of unemployment, at less than 5% in mid-2011, remained well below that of other countries of the Organisation for Economic Co-operation and Development. Australia continued to prosper, but there was a noticeable lack of agreement on how the country might build on its good fortune.

FOREIGN RELATIONS

Australia came late to the conduct of foreign policy. While the British colonies were granted powers of domestic self-government from the 1850s, they continued to follow the Imperial Government in external affairs. The Commonwealth, established in 1901, had power over defence and external relations but still conducted these through the United Kingdom; Australia did not establish its own diplomatic representation until the Second World War. Then, as now, Australians were conscious that they occupied a large land mass and possessed a limited capacity for independent action. They therefore sought a close relationship with a powerful protector. In the middle decades of the 20th century that process entailed a transfer of allegiance from the United Kingdom to the USA. The process occurred despite the strong pro-British sentiment of Sir Robert Menzies, and was marked by the establishment of the ANZUS Treaty in 1951 and the subsequent integration of Australia into the global military and diplomatic strategies of the USA. The transfer was completed with the entry of the United Kingdom into the EEC and the Australian support of the USA in the Viet Nam War.

Australia's relationship with the USA remained the cornerstone of its foreign policy, but there were significant changes in the manner in which the relationship was reconciled with other aspects of the national interest. Between 1972 and 1975 the Labor Government of Gough Whitlam attempted to take a more independent stance and relations deteriorated. From 1975 to 1983 Malcolm Fraser was concerned with strengthening the ANZUS alliance as tensions between the USA and the USSR mounted, but he paid significant attention to relations in the region, as well as to wider human rights issues.

The Hawke and Keating Governments maintained the US alliance, but acted to realign diplomacy, trade and migration; the merger in 1987 of the previously separate Departments of Foreign Affairs and Trade was a sign of this new orientation. By the end of the decade one-half of Australia's trade was conducted within the region, and the policies of the European and North American blocs threatened Australia's foothold in the markets of East and South-East Asia. The Australian Government played a leading role in forming the Cairns Group of agricultural exporting countries in preparation for a new round of international trade negotiations in 1986, and in 1989 it also promoted the creation of APEC as a regional trading bloc. Closer Economic Relations with New Zealand had been formalized in 1983 and brought increasing integration. However, this relationship became more problematic in 1986, when the New Zealand Government refused access to US warships carrying nuclear weapons; the USA subsequently suspended its obligations to New Zealand under the ANZUS treaty. Australia aligned itself firmly with its more powerful ally both then and during the Gulf War of 1991. Immigration policy allowed for substantial intakes based on economic, humanitarian and family reunion criteria, increasing the numbers of migrants from the Asian region. More generally, Australia encouraged multilateral strategies and was active in the settlement of the conflict in Cambodia, efforts to encourage nuclear disarmament and the peace-keeping activities of the UN.

During its first term in office the Howard Government sought to expunge Labor's record both at home and abroad. It had been particularly critical of Paul Keating's attempts to establish closer relations in the region and decried the suggestion that Australia's destiny lay in Asia, preferring to emphasize the distinctive character of Australian culture and traditions. It eschewed the former Labor Government's idea of Australia as a 'good international citizen', reiterating instead a 'hard-headed' pursuit of the national interest. The multilateral component of Labor policy gave way to bilateral strategies, and the regional defence policy that had been promulgated by the review of Australia's defence capabilities (known as the Dibb report) in 1986 to a more forward defence orientation. There was less support for the UN and other international agencies, and greater emphasis was placed on the US alliance. The Howard Government joined with the USA in rejecting the greenhouse gas emission targets set at the Kyoto conference on global warming in 1997.

The 1997 Asian economic crisis forced Australia into a more active regional engagement. It was drawn into the rescue programmes organized by the IMF for affected countries in the region, and also supported the strict conditions imposed by the Fund when it provided financial assistance. Those conditions increased poverty and unrest in Indonesia, forced the resignation of President Suharto and aggravated communal violence and violent repression by the armed forces in Indonesian provinces, including East Timor. Indonesia had agreed to a referendum on the future of East Timor, and its military assisted local militias in inflicting punitive reprisals on the population after they voted overwhelmingly for independence. In September 1999 an international force of 10,000 troops, under the authority of the UN, landed to restore order; Australia provided the Commander-in-Chief and the majority of the force.

Indonesia's continuing resentment of Australian involvement in East Timor had a further significant consequence. The Indonesian authorities did little to stem the flow of refugees who made their way by boat through South-East Asia to Australia. The numbers were relatively small—3,300 in 1999 and 2,900 in 2000—but the Australian Government none the less regarded the refugees as 'queue jumpers' and treated 'people smuggling' as a threat to Australian sovereignty and security. A solution required international co-operation, but Australia was increasingly at variance with the agencies of the UN with regard to issues of domestic human rights, as well as of refugees. In 2000 the Government announced that it would adopt a more economical and selective approach to requests for information from the UN, and a more robust and strategic approach to Australia's interaction with the treaty system.

The suicide attacks on the USA on 11 September 2001 precipitated the declaration of US President George W. Bush's 'war on terror', and Howard's immediate support for the invasion of Afghanistan. Australia had been involved in a dramatic incident two weeks previously when a Norwegian container vessel, the *Tampa*, came to the rescue of a drifting Indonesian fishing vessel loaded with 433 passengers, mostly from Afghanistan. The *Tampa* sailed for nearby Christmas Island, an Australian territory to the south of the Indonesian island of Java, but the Australian Government ordered the captain not to land. With the distressed passengers outnumbering his crew by a ratio of 16 to one, the captain dropped anchor off shore, allowing a detachment of Australia's élite Special Air Service (SAS) force to seize control of the *Tampa*. Some of the asylum-seekers were accepted by New Zealand, most were dispatched to a specially constructed internment centre on Nauru, and some went later to another camp in Papua New Guinea.

The US-led 'war on terror' began with the invasion of Afghanistan and broadened in scope after President Bush denounced the so-called 'axis of evil' (comprising Iran, Iraq and the Democratic People's Republic of Korea—North Korea) in his State of the Union address at the beginning of 2002. Howard supported the new US doctrine of pre-emptive defence, and disregarded regional sensitivities when he announced at the end of the year that Australia also would consider sending troops to a neighbouring country to strike at terrorist cells if they threatened its homeland security.

In October 2002 a terrorist cell was believed to be responsible for a bomb attack on a night-club on the Indonesian island of Bali; 88 Australians were among the 202 casualties of the blast. Australia and Indonesia co-operated in their response, and did so once again when terrorists bombed the Australian embassy in Jakarta, the Indonesian capital, in September 2004. Australia was also prominent in the international response to the devastating tsunamis that affected several countries in South and South-East Asia in December, and Howard travelled to Indonesia in January 2005 to pledge $A1,000m. of government aid for the rebuilding of the province of Aceh in northern Sumatra, the region most seriously affected by the disaster. A return visit to Australia by Indonesian President Susilo Bambang Yudhoyono in April, after Howard had attended his inauguration ceremony in the previous year, confirmed the improved relationship. However, in May the controversy surrounding the arrest and conviction in Indonesia on drugs-trafficking charges of a young Australian woman, Schapelle Corby, revealed a legacy of popular antagonism, as some Australians threatened to boycott Indonesian products. The arrival in Australia of a boat carrying 43 refugees from the Indonesian province of Papua (formerly Irian Jaya) in January 2006 created further animosity, as Indonesia regarded Australia's issue of temporary protection visas to the asylum-seekers as tacit support for Papuan independence. Indonesia responded by withdrawing its ambassador from Canberra, prompting the Australian Government to announce that no further asylum-seekers would be allowed to enter the country.

Relations with the People's Republic of China became more important as that country bought more Australian resources to support industrialization, while asserting its own expanding capacity. However, China's disputes with Taiwan and Japan threatened to destabilize the region, disrupt the strategic alliances of the USA and impair Australia's own trading relations with those countries. Howard's visit to the Chinese capital, Beijing, in April 2004 suggested that his Government's earlier neglect of Asia no longer applied. While Australia has sought to maintain good relations with China, it has also strengthened links with Japan. In March 2007 Howard signed a security co-operation agreement with Shinzo Abe, his Japanese counterpart, and the two countries proposed to join with the USA to develop missile defence capabilities.

Australia was already an active participant, with China, Japan, the USA and other countries, in the Regional Forum of the Association of Southeast Asian Nations (ASEAN), which began annual meetings on security matters in 1994. The Labor Government had aspired to closer involvement in ASEAN, but was prevented by the Prime Minister of Malaysia, Dr Mahathir Mohammad. With Mahathir's retirement in October 2003, the Howard Government sought to be included in ASEAN's discussions concerning a regional free trade agreement, and also in the proposed expansion of ASEAN into an East Asian Community; however, the condition that Australia subscribe to ASEAN's Treaty of Amity and Co-operation (pledging non-interference in the internal affairs of member countries) remained an obstacle, since Australia deemed it incompatible with its ANZUS obligations. In July 2005 the Government accepted this requirement, and Australia was a participant in the East Asian Summit (EAS) meeting at the end of the year. Australia has remained an active member of APEC, which has expanded from the original 12 members to 21, with which Australia conducts 70% of its international trade. Australia hosted the forum of national leaders in September 2007.

A similar shift of policy has been apparent in Australia's relations with the small island states of the Pacific. After achieving independence in the 1960s and 1970s, the islands receded from attention, except when Australian interests were affected. It was New Zealand that led the peace-keeping operations on Bougainville in 1997, when the movement for secession from Papua New Guinea descended into civil war; and it was New Zealand that took a more forceful stand against the coup in Fiji in 2000.

More recently, the problems of poverty, violence and HIV/AIDS have engendered a stronger response in Australia, as concerns arose that the problems of these 'failed states' might make them into a potential base for terrorist operations. Australia led the Regional Assistance Mission to Solomon Islands, designed to restore order there in 2003, and reinforced its presence in 2006 after violent protests followed the election of a Prime Minister widely regarded as corrupt. Australia also provided substantial assistance to Solomon Islands following an earthquake and tsunami in April 2007. In 2004 Australia provided for the deployment of police and public servants to Papua New Guinea, an arrangement that was suspended in the following year, after the Supreme Court of that country ruled it to be unconstitutional. A reduced commitment was subsequently agreed as part of Australia's aid programme, but the issue remained a source of contention. Australian troops were dispatched once more to Timor-Leste after communal violence broke out in the capital, Dili, in May 2006, and were involved again in 2007 when the country's presidential election of March–April precipitated further violence.

Australia maintained an absolute commitment to the alliance with the USA. The Howard Government thus joined the USA and the United Kingdom in the intervention in Iraq in March 2003, and repeatedly invoked the common values and shared outlook of the allies. The failure to locate the weapons of mass destruction allegedly possessed by the Iraqi Government, the continued insurgency and the human rights abuses of detainees proved less controversial in Australia than elsewhere, partly because Australia contributed only a small contingent to the forces that participated in the overthrow of the Iraqi leader, Saddam Hussain. US President Bush declared that Labor's commitment to bring Australian troops home from Iraq by the end of 2004—a policy that the Australian Government denounced as 'cut and run'—would be disastrous, and in the election in October of that year the Australian electorate expressed a similar view. Shortly afterwards, the Government dispatched additional forces to Iraq. Australia later extended its commitment to Afghanistan, and an additional contingent was deployed in mid-2007.

Australian prime ministers have typically begun their term of office by concentrating on domestic policy, until they are attracted subsequently to the sphere of international affairs. However, Kevin Rudd swiftly embarked upon an extended overseas tour in March and April 2008, and continued to travel frequently. His choice for the position of Minister for Foreign Affairs, Stephen Smith, was consistent with the Australian practice of entrusting the portfolio to a politician with little prior experience. Accordingly, the Prime Minister exercised an unusual measure of control over Australia's foreign relations.

Rudd stated repeatedly that his Government's international policy had three pillars: close relations with the USA, strong support for the UN and active engagement with the Asia-Pacific region. Thus his first international tour took him to Washington, DC, and he returned to the USA in February 2009 to meet the newly inaugurated President Barack Obama. The Rudd Government was committed to the withdrawal of Australian troops from Iraq and unwilling to increase the Australian deployment in Afghanistan. However, in response to further requests from the Obama Administration, Australia provided a small additional contingent in Afghanistan in April 2009 and supported the President's augmented deployment at the end of the year. Since Australia was only one of many allies operating in that country, and the fight against the Taliban insurgency was just one of the new US President's pressing concerns, it was difficult to engage Obama's full attention. A planned visit by the US President to Australia in 2010 was twice postponed.

The Labor Party has traditionally given greater attention to the UN and other multilateral bodies than the Liberal-National Party coalition, and the Howard Government was often at variance with agencies of the UN. Rudd restored multilateralism to Australian foreign policy at an opportune juncture and announced during his first visit to the USA that Australia would seek a non-permanent seat on the UN Security Council. Simon Crean, the Minister for Trade, similarly revived Australian involvement in the negotiations of the World Trade Organization. In June 2008 the Prime Minister proposed, with Japan, a new international commission on nuclear non-proliferation and disarmament.

Within the Asia-Pacific region, similarly, the Rudd Government reverted to the previous Labor Government's practice of promoting stronger organizational links. In a telephone conversation with President Bush in October 2008, Rudd reportedly urged the US President to include the Group of 20 leading industrial nations (G20) in plans for an international response to the global financial crisis, and played an active role in G20 meetings in Pittsburgh, USA, and London during 2009. This not only allowed Australian involvement in decision-making, but also the inclusion of China and India. Relations with both these countries proved challenging. In a speech given in Beijing in 2008 Rudd raised the issue of human rights in Tibet. In the following year the Government prevented Chinese acquisition of Australian mining ventures and refused to allow Chinalco, the Chinese aluminium company, to increase its stake in the mining company Rio Tinto. In July 2009 Stern Hu, an Australian national working for Rio Tinto in China, was arrested, with three Chinese colleagues, and subsequently sentenced to a 10-year term of imprisonment for stealing commercial secrets and receiving bribes. There was widespread criticism in India during 2009 of assaults on nationals studying in Australia, and the apparent reluctance of the Australian authorities to accept racism as a reason for this violence. Since education had expanded to become the country's third largest 'export industry', the damage was costly and Rudd attempted to repair it on a visit to India in November. Yet a month later Australia was at variance with both countries as it negotiated unsuccessfully for an agreement at the Copenhagen climate conference.

The Rudd Government participated fully in APEC, ASEAN and the EAS. In June 2008 Rudd proposed the formation of an enlarged Asia Pacific Community that would embrace the USA, China and India, and Australia hosted a preliminary conference in Sydney in December 2009, but the response to the proposal was not encouraging. There was greater success with an agreement in 2009 on an ASEAN-Australia and New Zealand Free Trade Area covering goods, services, investment and intellectual property. Australia and New Zealand also worked towards the goal of a Single Economic Market.

Finally, the Rudd Government sought to improve Australia's relations with its closer northern neighbours. In 2006 Brendan Nelson, as Minister for Defence, had referred to the island states that extended from Timor-Leste to Fiji as forming an 'arc of instability', and the leaders of both Papua New Guinea and Solomon Islands criticized Australia for what they perceived as its neo-colonial stance in its dealings with them. Rudd appointed a Parliamentary Secretary for Pacific Island Affairs, and he attended the Leaders' Meeting of the Pacific Islands Forum in Niue in August 2008, when new assistance measures were negotiated; the Australian town of Cairns hosted the Leaders' Meeting of August 2009.

By her own admission, Julia Gillard had little prior experience in foreign relations. Following the federal election of August 2010, she embarked on a series of international meetings. The first of these, the Asia-Europe Meeting in Brussels, Belgium, in October, enabled her to visit Australian troops in Afghanistan, and in November she attended a meeting of the North Atlantic Treaty Organization in Portugal to discuss the Afghanistan mission. In the same month she participated in the EAS meeting in Hanoi, Viet Nam; the G20 Summit in the South Korean capital of Seoul; and a meeting of APEC in the Japanese city of Yokohama. In 2010 Gillard also undertook visits to Malaysia and Indonesia, and in 2011 to New Zealand, the USA (where she addressed the US Congress), South Korea and Japan. In November 2010 she hosted a visit to Australia by Hillary Clinton, the US Secretary of State.

Gillard's predecessor, Kevin Rudd, who became Minister for Foreign Affairs in September 2010, was even more active in foreign travel and on several occasions seemed to pre-empt the Government's foreign policy. When travelling to Israel in December, he urged that Israeli nuclear facilities be subject to monitoring by the International Atomic Energy Agency, and in March 2011 he took a leading position on international action to enforce an air exclusion zone in Libya. Moreover, Rudd continued to urge other countries to take a robust stance towards China and was embarrassed in December 2010 when WikiLeaks, an organization publishing leaked private and classified content, revealed that he had advised Secretary of State Clinton that the USA should be in a position to use force against China if necessary.

However, neither the Prime Minister nor the Minister for Foreign Affairs was as prominent in handling the difficulties that arose within the region. Indonesia was reluctant to accept responsibility for the increased flow of asylum-seekers, while neither Timor-Leste nor Malaysia was as immediately willing to assist Australia in dealing with the problem as statements made in Australia suggested. Similarly, the decision by the Australian Government in June 2011 to suspend shipments of livestock to Indonesia, after Australian television revealed the cruel methods of slaughter, was followed by a lengthy hiatus in Australian diplomacy.

Economy

NEVILLE NORMAN

The Australian economy was the only developed economy to avoid recession in the two years to the end of June 2010. However, by June 2011 more than 30 developed nations had exceeded Australia's rate of annual economic growth; indeed, a negative movement for the first quarter of 2011 in Australia had been recorded. Quite quickly, the image of Australia's economy changed adversely, perhaps much more radically than was justified. A major theme of this essay is to look beyond simply stated short-term economic statistics and events, and to judge the position and more medium-term prospects for advanced modern economies like that of Australia.

Australia's financial year ends on 30 June each year. During the year that ended in June 2011 Australia followed closely behind Japan and New Zealand in terms of the intensity of natural disasters adversely affecting economic activity. In addition, some domestic political uncertainties seemed to have damaged business confidence and prospects for economic growth. The ongoing positive stimulus from close dependence on the People's Republic of China appeared to have been temporarily offset at the end of June 2011.

While every other economically advanced country exhibited at least two consecutive quarters of negative economic growth during the period from mid-2008 to the end of 2010, encompassed by the global financial crisis, Australia's national production continued to rise, albeit at a reduced pace. Within the Australian economy some sectors, notably international tourism, recorded various adverse effects arising from the crisis. To appreciate both the disparity of experiences within an economy and to explain why Australia seemed relatively immune to the effects of the global financial crisis, it is important to gain a close and detailed understanding of the structure and operation of the economy. It is one of the dominant purposes of this essay to provide the essential requirements for such an understanding, as well as offering a chronicle of recent events, policy considerations and relevant data.

AUSTRALIA IN THE GLOBAL FINANCIAL CRISIS

Despite Australia's good fortune throughout the global financial crisis, some economic policy inconsistencies and arguably preventable policy errors damaged confidence in the nation's leadership and probably caused the defeat of Prime Minister Kevin Rudd, who in June 2010 was replaced by his deputy, Julia Gillard. The moral would seem to have been that, even in a sound economy that was leading the developed world in growth in economic activity at the time, poor leadership could only have adverse consequences relating to business and economic policy, and would not be tolerated. Consequentially, the Australian Labor Party (ALP), now led by Gillard, did not succeed in obtaining a parliamentary majority at the general election of August 2010; it required the support of the Australian Greens and independents to form a minority Government. There was widespread speculation from the latter part of 2010 that the Gillard administation would not long survive. Indeed, at June 2011 survey measures of Australian voter intentions gave the Gillard Government little chance of being re-elected if a general election were to be held at that time. It is important to document how Australia came through the main phase of the global financial crisis so well, before experiencing the slowdown that emerged in early 2011.

The economic fundamentals of a country tend to be obscured when short-term economic crises dominate policy actions and public discussions. This was especially true in relation to the Australian economy over the two financial years that ended in June 2010. It was probably so for almost every economy, as the global financial crisis developed from mid-2008. There will be frequent references to this two-year epoch in this essay. The starting point for the specific consideration of these 'recent events' is given as late June 2008, because the financial crisis began to take effect from that time. Some other developed nations were still suffering the repercussions of the global crisis at mid-2011.

The global financial crisis can be defined as the world-wide extension from seemingly confined difficulties in the USA's sub-prime housing finance markets, commencing in mid-2006, through subordinated loans, which then implicated and damaged financial institutions throughout much of the world from 2008. As financial analysts and economic commentators realized that the difficulties were more severe than they had previously anticipated and that the problems were not going to be confined to the USA's own markets, asset values started to decrease, and equity prices began to weaken considerably, from late 2007. Prestigious financial institutions started to experience difficulty and to fail, with pressures emerging for governments to develop and finance various rescue programmes. Two dominant economic policy responses were subsequently seen, almost universally. First, fiscal stimulus programmes, meaning public spending or cash hand-outs to individuals, began to be adopted world-wide from about September 2008; second, official interest rates were radically reduced almost everywhere.

At mid-2009 there was little sign that any interest rate that had been reduced over the preceding year in any country was expected generally to rise, nor was any stimulus plan already in place likely to be diminished in its application or intensity. Australia was no exception: cash payments and capital works were announced as stimulus measures in November 2008, and official interest rates were reduced from 7.25% in late 2008 to 3.0% in mid-2009. In the year to the end of June 2010 the Australian economy recovered from a non-recessionary slowing of growth, and then continued to rebound, with six separate small upward interest rate adjustments being effected by the central bank, the Reserve Bank of Australia. Unemployment rates hardly rose above 5% of the Australian labour force. In fact, by May 2011 the proportion of the labour force recorded as unemployed had declined to 4.9%, despite a slowdown in the Australian economy in early 2011.

In every respect, Australia managed to record a more positive economic performance than any other developed nation in the two years to mid-2010. It therefore remains important to note that the negative factors that caused the dramatic change in the political leadership of Australia in June of that year cannot be traced to, or explained by, endemic economic difficulty as occurred elsewhere, for example in the United Kingdom.

Australia's experience of being implicated in and managing the global financial crisis shares some similarities with other countries. It also has several points of difference. A major similarity is that Australia and almost every other economy adopted financial sector support arrangements and stimulus measures from around mid-2008, in order to mitigate the adverse effects of diminished confidence and reduced purchasing power. These matters are covered in detail below, because a comparison of the similarities and the differences between the economies of Australia and other nations, especially those in the Asia-Pacific region, helps to explain the policy response and statistical economic outcomes.

In June 2008 most major economies were expanding at, or close to, the rates of real growth exhibited in previous trends. However, events moved rapidly from July, after which 'stimulus packages' and official interest rate reductions were both widely implemented by numerous countries. Relative to the countries' national incomes, China pursued the most aggressive stimulus programme, implemented in November at a cost of US $720,000m. From December Australia implemented its allocations of individual cash payments to citizens, infrastructure spending and some industry support measures; a supplementary stimulus programme followed in April 2009, although further stimulus expected from the annual federal budget in May was not forthcoming. The aggregate Australian stimulus programmes, extending over a period of about three years from December 2008, amounted to the equivalent of US $19,000m., according to official budget figures, which in relation to national incomes was smaller than the US programmes. Meanwhile, Australia's interest rates remained higher than elsewhere, its cash rate being reduced to 3.0% in April 2009, before subsequently rising. During the first half of 2010 two further interest rate increases in Australia were accompanied by minor adjustments upwards in the USA and in New Zealand, a sign that the global financial crisis was passing into history.

By mid-2009 the Rudd Government had accepted that a contractionary economy was in prospect. Accordingly, in May it announced a federal budget predicated on very pessimistic assumptions about economic growth, business spending on plant and equipment, and exports. Yet in June official data confirmed that a slight positive growth had taken place in the real national income as measured by gross domestic product (GDP) during the first quarter of 2009. There was a general, and at times grudging, agreement among Australian economists at mid-2009 that the stimulus programmes and lower interest rates had combined to limit recessionary pressures and to halt the collapse of aggregate purchasing power in Australia.

During 2009 and 2010 some critics of the Australian public policy response to the global crisis were questioning whether the stimulus programmes and interest rate reductions would succeed in preventing Australia from entering a deep recession or would facilitate any recovery from it. The technical definition of a recession is two successive quarters of negative growth in real national income. At the end of June 2011 Australia had continued to avoid a technical recession, although negative growth was recorded for the quarter ended in December 2008 and again for the three months to March 2011. The December 2008 result was followed by small positive growth in the first quarter of 2009. Critics of the Rudd Government's approach to economic management tended to assume (with the Government) that recession in Australia during 2009 was inevitable, and many doubted that the policies adopted by the Rudd administration from mid-2008 would have any beneficial effect on the country's economic position. It was argued that aggressive fiscal stimulus programmes were more likely to 'crowd out' private sector spending than to replace or overcome it, or to be wasted by those receiving them, and that the theory supporting such policy emanated from 1930s depression-era economics, which were not relevant to the contemporary situation.

In contrast to these critics, other economists (including this writer) had argued in mid-2009 that the measures would limit the recessionary influences and work positively to stimulate overall spending. It does seem that such 'positivists' interpreted events correctly; even the Rudd Government, in its May 2010 federal budget, conceded that it had misread the economic scene a year before, and it markedly revised estimates of economic growth and revenue to reflect the economic outlook which the positivists had already predicted 12 months previously. The Government radically amended the pessimistic expectations that it had propounded in May 2009 and claimed that a balanced budget would be achieved three years earlier than it had then expected. The Government's attempt to claim credit for this providential achievement rebounded, as it was widely observed that the only significant change was a correction by the same Government in relation to its own economic forecasts.

The striking reflection upon this important epoch of short-term economic management in Australia is that the relatively new Rudd Government acted quickly and capably, before performing quite obversely in relation to the introduction and management of longer-term policies concerning taxation, mining and the environment from about May 2010. Consequently, in the second of the two years of global financial crisis, as defined here, the Rudd Government lost support, initially within its own ranks and then generally, by executing a large number of avoidable economic policy errors and inconsistencies. These included the cancellation of its proposed carbon trading emissions reduction scheme; a poorly planned programme to support home insulation installations that was inadequately monitored; and, most damaging of all, the manner in which plans to impose a tax on resource sector profits above a certain level (the Resources Super Profits Tax—RSPT) were initiated, without community consultation, in May 2010. The Prime Minister was removed from office by his own political party in June, following intense criticism by industrial interests and the public.

Short-term economic indicators available at June 2010 confirmed that economic activity and business confidence had both been rising rapidly during the financial year 2009/10. Retail sales grew in Australian dollar terms by 4.2% in the year to May 2010, motor vehicle sales (by number of registrations) increased by 8.5%, and the number of dwelling approvals rose by 17.6% in the same period. Moreover, the Westpac-Melbourne Institute indicator of confidence rose by 32% in the year to June 2010.

In the financial year that ended on 30 June 2011 the ALP was not well supported in the general election, as seldom before had an incoming Government failed to be re-elected; floods affected much of eastern Australia in January 2011, and the economic public policy uncertainties documented here compounded the pressures already emerging for an economic downturn. Thus, in the year to March 2011 annual economic growth declined to 1.2%, consumer price inflation remained at an annual rate close to 3%, and interest rates remained high by world standards.

To understand Australia's response to the global financial crisis and assessments of the country's economic prospects, it is important to appreciate the nation's economic history, the impact of its endowed natural resources, its past economic policies and experiences, the demography, the political and institutional structure and the structure of economic activity in Australia in some detail.

FEATURES OF THE AUSTRALIAN ECONOMY

The Australian economy is advanced and mature, with features that distinguish it from other economies within its region or from those that have achieved similar levels of economic advancement. In the Asia-Pacific region only Japan exhibits a higher national income per caput than Australia. In the period from 1991 to mid-2011 Australia achieved high economic growth with low inflation, while continuing to avoid recession. Many institutional and regulatory procedures were reformed and improved, and a high reliance was retained on primary and mineral exports. Australia is sparsely populated by world standards: the population density was just 2.8 per sq km in December 2010. However, the proportion of the Australian population living in remote areas was only 1.5% at March 2011, while the proportion living in major cities was 66.9%. From 1996, when it took office, the administration of John Howard (1996–2007) acted to liberalize financial markets and superannuation (retirement income) systems and also to bring market forces more fully into the industrial relations system. Personal income tax rate scales were adjusted, and the Government attempted to maintain firm control of the economy by means of active monetary and fiscal policies. Australia also negotiated free trade agreements with the USA and with China. In all these respects the Australian economy had become more liberalized by late 2007 than it had been 10 years previously. The general thrust of these measures was subsequently pursued in similar form by the Rudd and Gillard administrations. However, after a confident start in its first federal budget in May 2008, the sharp reduction in economic activity, particularly the decline in company profits, caused a significant erosion of Australian taxation revenues and a dramatic turn from budget surplus to deficit in the year preceding the Rudd Government's presentation of its second federal budget in May 2009. Ironically, in the year to June 2010 the Australian economy improved markedly, while the popularity of the Government and its leader diminished.

In the two years to June 2011 the international economic and strategic challenges detailed above became prominent; however, many of the issues that the Australian economy confronted were of a domestic origin and were not caused by the global financial crisis. Many areas of southern Australia remained formally in drought throughout the decade to mid-2010, causing water restrictions to remain widespread. Some pressures for further increases in interest rates also arose as economic growth was expected to return to rates of expansion in excess of 3% a year. Yet some economic policy errors and reversals of policy remained inexplicable in the context of an expanding Australian economy that had clearly survived the global crisis, while the ruling political party had commanded a significant majority in the legislature before the instability set in from mid-2010 and continued a year later.

There are many criteria used by economists to measure the performance of an economy. These include indicators of economic activity, prices and price movements, measures of efficiency and competitiveness, and broader indicators covering income and wealth equality and also socio-environmental factors. Australia's economy has performed well in terms of most of these criteria. However, it has relinquished the position, gained earlier in the 2000s, of the world's fastest-growing developed economy. The country's ranking on a respected international index of competitiveness has also declined somewhat. Australia clearly led the Western world in terms of rates of real economic growth from around 1999 until 2003. In the year to March 2008 the growth rate of Australia's GDP, at 3.6% in real terms, was creditable by comparison with other developed nations. No other developed country achieved a level of economic growth as high as Australia's recorded average annual rate of more than 3.0% in the first three years of the 21st century. Only China and a limited number of developing or recovering economies grew more quickly than the Australian economy at that time. However, with the onset of the global financial crisis in 2008, Australia resumed its former status as the leading growth economy in the developed world, being the only such country, at June 2010, to have avoided recession. The slowdown in growth in the year to March 2011 has been documented above.

Good economic performance requires that an economy does much more than achieve high and sustained rates of material economic growth. In this essay a broader dimension of industries, technology, products and related economy-wide and industry-based data is analysed and reviewed. Geographically, and in some ways economically, Australia can be regarded as an Asian country. Its setting against spectacular and recent changes in Asian economies requires careful analysis.

The Australian economy is distinguished from other economies in the Asia-Pacific region, and from other advanced economies. Australia remains reliant on primary and mining activities to a greater degree than most other advanced economies; however, its government sector is relatively small and the nation remains sparsely populated. Many institutional and legal features of the Australian economy stand firmly in contrast to other countries. Recently, Australia's relative degree of reliance upon traditional primary and manufacturing activities has been substantially reduced. For some years up to mid-2011 much of Australia continued to operate successfully, notwithstanding the longest-ever drought in the nation's recorded history. In the period from June 2006 until June 2011 Australian military forces were in action in sensitive locations. Australia was also one of only a few countries to have joined with the USA and the United Kingdom in military involvements in Iraq and Afghanistan. There were substantial economic costs associated with these military exercises, whatever their justification on other grounds.

Despite the restraints on economic activity arising from the Asian financial crisis that began in 1997, from the terrorist attacks on the USA in September 2001 and from the opening of the Iraq conflict of 2003, the Australian economy had not experienced a recession over this period. Indeed, by mid-2010 Australia had recorded its 18th consecutive year of positive economic growth, accompanied by a low rate of inflation. No period in Australia's history from 1901, or of the Australian colonies before that, had displayed such a sustained span of recession-free economic activity. Few Western-style economies could boast the 3.8% growth rate that Australia had achieved in the fiscal year 2001/02. However, Australia's economic performance was subsequently exceeded by a number of other developed economies. (Such a growth rate remained low by comparison with a number of emerging countries. In the year to December 2009 the Chinese economy, for example, recorded real economic growth of 8.9%, accompanied by much reduced rates of consumer price inflation.) However, even in the period 1999–2010, when Australia was again in the ascendancy, strong growth was accompanied by structural weaknesses and by many significant corporate failures. Indeed, the years 2001–11 especially witnessed the demise of some large companies in the airline, telephony and insurance sectors. There were also concerns arising from Australia's external dependence (with the current account deficit on the balance of payments more than doubling between 2001 and 2010), some ongoing tax tensions, major contentious domestic regulatory policy reviews and, at times, the risk of higher inflation and interest rates.

In the year to March 2011 the national income of Australia, in current prices, totalled $A1,365,405m. (or approximately US $1,447,329m., using exchange rates applying at June 2011). From this national aggregate of gross household income, Australian households paid $A1,150m. in income tax, $A79,950m. in interest payments and consumed almost all of the disposable income remaining, leaving national household saving in the year to March 2011 at $A78,120m.

The revenue from exports provided by Australian producers was $A294,361m. in the year to the end of March 2011. Of this total, some 26% was derived from metal ores and minerals, 18% from coal and just 7% from manufactures. Australian spending on (foreign-provided) imports was $A271,937m. in the same period, recovering from the 11% decrease that occurred in the previous year because of stonger economic growth. That reduction, narrowing the negative external trade balance of Australia, was almost certainly due to the international financial crisis. Australian consumers then postponed or curtailed discretionary expenditures, and Australian companies significantly reduced their orders of capital equipment. (About one-third of the value of Australian imports was composed of intermediate, partly processed products.)

In the 1950s and 1960s the average annual rate of economic growth was 5.8%. In the 1970s Australia witnessed a deceleration in both population growth and productivity growth, resulting in a historically low average annual rate of economic growth for the decade of just 1.2%. The country's growth rate recovered to an annual average of 2.7% in the 1980s and further, to 3.7%, in the 1990s. Australia did not experience the extent of growth in equity values that occurred in the USA when the US stock markets surged upwards in the 1990s, nor the degree of equity market downturn that took place in the USA from mid-2002.

By early 2011 some significant regional disparities in economic growth had emerged within Australia. New South Wales (where about one-third of Australia's population resides) had been bordering on recession during early 2006, but had recovered by early 2007, with growth reaching 3.2% in the year to March 2008, the same as the growth rate achieved in Victoria. New South Wales exhibited no growth in 2008. Meanwhile, economic growth in resource-rich Western Australia (with about 10% of the national population in more than one-third of the land area) expanded at a rate of 5.2% in the same period, with that of Queensland increasing by 6.8%. The economies of most other states and territories in Australia grew within the range of 2.0%–3.5% over that period.

The trends in some overall ratios give a useful impression of the Australian economy. The share of government spending at all levels in national income rose from just less than 20% in 1948 to more than 30% in 1984. Since then the government share of economic activity in Australia has stabilized or declined slightly. The ratio of imports to domestic product sales increased gradually from 17% in 1948 to 25% in 1990. This share of imports in domestic-market sales then rose rapidly, from 25.2% in March 1992 to 30.7% in March 1996 and to 33.2% in March 2000, increasing further, to 34.2%, in March 2011. In some market sectors (such as motor vehicles) imports had progressed from comprising minority shares of 20%–25% in the 1980s to being the dominant market suppliers by June 2011. This conspicuous trend can be interpreted as confirmation of a substantially open Australian economy. Meanwhile, household saving in Australia had been declining systematically between the early 1970s and mid-2006, both in absolute terms and as a ratio to household income after tax. This ratio decreased from just over 20% in 1973 to 8.2% in the first quarter of 1990, to 2.7% in the March quarter of 1998, and to 0.2% for the first three months of 2002. Thereafter, the ratio recorded negative values, implying that Australian households were spending more than their available incomes. Between March 2006 and March 2011 household saving returned to a small positive ratio, reaching a share of household income of 9.5% in the year to March 2011.

In the half-century from 1950 Australia became less dependent on agricultural exports, and the country developed an advanced industrial and technological base with world-standard transport and communications networks, despite its low population density. As external perceptions about the structure and performance of the Australian economy can be distorted by false impressions, it will be important to document how far Australia had moved from its image, and the reality, of the 1950s, by the end of the first decade of the new millennium.

PERCEPTIONS, REALITY AND POLICY

The external perception of Australia is often formed through its tradition of primary-product exports, its films and its sporting achievements. These visions of Australia can easily differ from the reality of a modern economy, where the majority of people reside in cities, use computers actively and exhibit one of the highest comparative standards of educational and training achievement in the world. This is not to say that Australia has not sought to gain advantage from its image as a primary-product exporter. After the Havana Conference of 1947 that established the General Agreement on Tariffs and Trade, which was subsequently superseded by the World Trade Organization, there was much pressure from the contracting parties, as they were known, to reduce tariffs and other trade barriers multilaterally. Australia sought dispensation from this process on the grounds that it was a 'midway' country. By this it was meant that Australia was in many ways similar to a developed country, in terms of national income per head (indeed, in the later 20th century it led the world on this test). However, in relation to the structure of its exports and its exposure to large inherited fluctuations in economic activity arising from significant dependence on the global economy, it was more akin to the developing world. Images of outback Australia in films and tourism promotions appear to have perpetuated this perception. Yet from the earliest days of Western-style settlement the majority of the population lived in cities relatively close to the coast. Even in the early 21st century about 40% of the national population resided in just two cities—Sydney and Melbourne.

In the high-technology area, it is true that relatively little of the 'innovation' aspect of scientific advancement takes place in Australia, notwithstanding that several major inventions in electronic technology, aircraft navigation, agricultural chemicals, agricultural harvesting, materials processing and logistics have been made there. This is because large companies find it to be to their comparative advantage to focus the development side of these inventions in huge research establishments in North America and Europe in particular. However, Australian consumers, businesses and governments remain advanced users of high-technology products. Research and development policy continues to be a major focus of attention.

Australia has moved a considerable distance from the 'quarry and farm' image it had acquired and which still features prominently in some international perceptions. Australia remained in the leading 20 countries in the world on the basis of gross national product (GNP) per head of population from 1960 to 2011. Various international bodies and consultancy groups rank Australia between 15th and 18th place on this measure of GNP per caput, just above Germany, France and Sweden.

Economics and International Diplomacy

There is a complex connection between Australia's international political stance and material developments in trade and economic activity. For example, Australian merchandise export trade with Japan, the Republic of Korea (South Korea) and Viet Nam became prominent relatively soon after Australia ceased hostilities against these countries in the 1940s, 1950s and 1960s, respectively. In 1973 Australia became one of the first countries to recognize the sovereignty of, and to establish formal diplomatic relations with, the People's Republic of China. Very considerable trade and educational links then followed between the two countries. There was some lapse in this connection when Australia became a leading critic of the massacre in Tiananmen Square in the Chinese capital of Beijing in 1989. However, the economic and cultural links were little affected and had again become extremely strong by mid-2002, when a huge long-term contract for supplies of natural gas to China was won by the Australian north-west-shelf energy supplier, Woodside. Since that time, the continued rapid economic growth of China has granted substantial export and profit opportunities to Australian mineral exploration and processing companies, manifesting itself in labour shortages and pressure on transport and port facilities. At the same time China has been the source of a rapid influx of overseas students undertaking school, and especially tertiary-level, studies in Australian educational institutions. During 2005 Australia assumed a leading role in opposition to Japanese whaling ambitions, placing at risk the strongest economic relationship that it had formed in the post-war period. In May 2007 Australia led a number of nations at the annual conference of the International Whaling Commission, held in Alaska. The Rudd Government intensified this opposition to whaling. Relations with China improved in 2008, helped undoubtedly by a visit of the Chinese President, Hu Jintao, to Australia in September 2007 and by the visit of the Australian Prime Minister to Beijing in April 2008, Rudd being a fluent speaker of Mandarin.

The Question of Planning or the Market

As regards the philosophy of economic policy, Australia maintains a commitment to national budgets that are balanced or in surplus, to significant growth in living standards and to low inflation. The eagerness with which the federal Government seized the chance to proclaim an earlier than expected return to budget surplus from positively revised economic data in May 2010 affirmed this policy proclivity. In May 2011 the much-pressured Gillard Government, in the context of a decelerating economy, still made the imminent return to budget balance and surplus the focus of its federal budget statement.

The Australian Government as such does not make or accept formal plans or targets for the population size and structure and for the main national economic variables. There are frequent requests from within Australia for formal population targets and for economic planning agencies to be given official status. During the period 2002–11 several conferences convened by state governments and industrial bodies took place, at which many delegates supported the establishment of targets relating to population size, structure and growth. The matters were discussed and debated by a wide range of representative groups. However, successive Australian Governments have not embraced these proposals.

From 1996 to 2011 a policy target inflation zone was regularly announced and confirmed by successive Australian Governments in office and by the national monetary authority, the Reserve Bank of Australia; this provided that consumer price inflation rates should remain within the range of 2%–3% per year. This target zone was proposed and maintained by the central bank. Based in Sydney, the Reserve Bank of Australia has, since its creation in 1959, also carried formal responsibility for stability of the currency and overall supervision of the financial system. In 1965 a Committee for Economic Inquiry (Vernon Committee) proposed a more formal economic planning mechanism, a Council of Economic Planning. That notion was roundly condemned by the Government of the day, and an aversion to central-planning concepts has been part of the written and unwritten Australian political ethos ever since. During the tenure of Prime Minister Bob Hawke (1983–91) an Economic Planning and Advisory Council did operate, until its functions were absorbed into other bodies; it had effectively disappeared by 1996, when the Government of John Howard took office.

In relation to industrial policy, for decades the Australian approach has been to follow a monitored market course; that is, there are regulations to oversee the workings of the market with regard to mergers, corporate affairs, trade practices, construction proposals, consumer protection, the environment, foreign investment, financial transactions, insurance and banking. In the 1980s and 1990s some of these regulations were eased, especially in relation to the labour market and to financial transactions. In March 2003 the official response to an inquiry on regulatory policy (by the Dawson Committee) was to affirm the principle of light regulation based on case-by-case inquiries. After considerable debate, the Howard Government introduced legislation in June 2004 to give effect to the liberal approach to abuse of 'market power', as proposed by the Dawson Committee. A fierce and unresolved debate had developed by mid-2004, with many smaller businesses arguing that an opportunity for embracing more rights of action against aggressive larger companies was being missed. In June 2010 a new competition law replaced the long-standing Trade Practices Act (initiated in 1974). Apart from much stricter treatment of cartel arrangements, including price fixing, little change to the substance of anti-trust regulation in Australia was anticipated. However, during 2010 and 2011 regulatory officials pressed for more aggressive control of price signalling, meaning measures taken by firms to communicate to competitors its prices and price intentions. By mid-2011 the proposals had become controversial and seemed to have become a departure from the Australian policy ethic of awaiting research to establish that such heavy regulation might be required.

Controversial market-orientated regulations for employment conditions and employee dismissal were introduced by the Howard Government. In April 2005 contentious proposals concerning industrial relations challenged the primacy of unions and offered greater choice to individual workers (although by June 2008 the Rudd Government had acted to reverse most of these initiatives and procedures). From July 2005 workers were also given the option to place their superannuation (retirement income) funds apart from their industry or employer funds. The common name for this new approach to retirement planning was given as 'choice of fund'. In the federal budget of May 2006 the Howard Government announced further liberalization of the superannuation rules to permit greater preserved deposit by fund members approaching 60 years of age and the elimination of all previous taxes applying to withdrawals from these funds once members had reached the age of 60. During 2006 the Howard Government began to embrace a free trade agreement with China, to which it made fuller commitments in March 2007. Australia had already signed such agreements with New Zealand and the USA, and had markedly reduced its trade barriers generally. Hence, by 2006 a more liberal approach had been emerging in many aspects of Australian policy with regard to the economy, tax, retirement income, international trade and industrial relations. Despite some speculation that the Rudd and Gillard Governments would make major changes to industrial and trade policies, little effective change had been made by mid-2011.

Policy changes initiated by the Rudd Government that did attract attention in early 2010 included: the sudden termination of a home insulation support scheme after injury and death occurred; the development and sudden cessation of a carbon emissions trading scheme; and the announcement in May 2010 of a tax on 'excessive' profits made by companies in Australia's resources sector, the RSPT, which, more than any other single factor, appeared to bring about the abrupt removal of Rudd in June. The cancellation of the proposed RSPT and its reintroduction in 2011 as a Minerals Resource Rent Tax (MRRT) did not encourage much enthusiasm for the hope that policy execution uncertainties had been confined to the previous year.

The traditional Australian approach in many areas of economic policy, as practised in the 1950s and 1960s, had been to limit certain activities by formal regulation, and to intervene substantially in the market place. This was nowhere more evident than in relation to Australia's labour market and external economic policies. In the conduct of its external economic policy, Australia had tended (from Federation in 1901 until the 1970s) to limit international transactions at the point of entry into Australia: substantial barrier protection, mainly in the form of tariff duties, was erected against foreign supplies of goods; foreign investment was examined and restricted; and immigration was strictly controlled. Through a series of reductions in tariffs and the elimination of most non-tariff means of border protection, Australia has liberalized its trading policy. It has been prominent in the international arena in demanding and securing the removal of agricultural trade barriers multilaterally. Banking regulations that in the 1950s limited the deposit structure, entity ownership and asset allocation of the main banks and financial institutions have been liberalized. Prudential supervision and control of the financial sector has since 1998 been predominantly the responsibility of the Australian Prudential Regulation Authority. Competition policy generally prohibits few transactions absolutely. Practices of firms that mislead consumers or that are deemed unfair are illegal, as are various trade practices, arrangements and mergers that substantially lessen competition.

TRENDS IN POPULATION AND VITAL STATISTICS

It says much about Australia that, as the sixth largest country by land area and the 14th largest in terms of its economic transactions, Australia is the 55th most populous nation. At the time of the national census of 8 August 2006 Australia had a population of almost 19.86m. A further census was scheduled to take place in August 2011. By December 2010 the population was estimated by the Australian Bureau of Statistics to have exceeded 22.48m., the equivalent of just 0.32% of the world's population, living on a continent occupying one-12th of the world's land mass. While the rate of population growth from both natural increase and immigration has been reduced when compared with most periods since 1947, recorded population growth stood at 1.9% annually in 2009/10, a rate that exceeded the recorded population growth for recent previous years, which stood at around 1.5% annually in the period 2007–09. Although this is a higher rate of population growth than that exhibited by most advanced economies, it remained lower than the rate found in most countries in the Asia-Pacific region. The natural increase was supplemented by long-term immigration from overseas, equivalent in 2009/10 to 65.4% of the population increase itself. However, a downward trend in net rates of migration intake had set in from late 2009. The relative contributions of long-term immigration and natural increase to population growth represented a return to the conditions experienced in the 1960s, when natural increase and immigration were each relatively higher than the levels recorded for 2009. In the year to December 2010 immigration from overseas, measured as total permanent and long-term arrivals net of long-term and permanent departures overseas, reached 432, 600 persons. While this number was some 15% lower than the net migration gain during the calendar year 2009, it still contributed significantly to the growth of population in Australia. During the 1980s the share of population growth attributed to international migration was just less than 30%, as compared with 66% in 2009. The overseas-born component of the Australian population in March 2011 was 26.2%.

Australia's decline in fertility appears also to have been arrested from about 2004, with fertility rates increasing in each of the years 2005 to 2010. All Australian states and territories recorded increases in total fertility rates in the years between 2004 and 2010 inclusive, with Tasmania reaching replacement level fertility (2.1 babies per woman) in 2005 and maintaining it to December 2010. The median age of mothers giving birth in March 2011 was 32.0 years, 4.7 years older than first-mothers in 1985 (when the average age was 27.3 years). The median age of fathers was 34.3 years, 3.2 years older than fathers in 1985 (30.1 years).

As in most Western-style economies, the rates of marriage and childbirth have been declining significantly, while the average age at marriage has been rising, as has the ratio of aged dependants to the total working population. The median age of the Australian resident population was 36.8 years in December 2010, having risen from 31.2 years in 1986 to 34.2 years in 1996. The proportion of the Australian population aged 65 years and over at census night on 7 August 2001 increased to 12.6%, compared with 12.1% in 1996 and 10.2% in 1986. At the census of 8 August 2006, 13.3% of Australia's population were aged 65 years or older. Some 11.2% of the Australian population at December 2010 were in the age range of 55–64 years, 42.1% were in the range of 25–54 years, 13.5% were aged 15–24 and 19.8% were aged younger than 15 years. Official estimates placed the proportion of the population aged 65 and over at 14.1% at January 2011. This so-called aged population ratio is similar to the rise in aged shares of populations found in the USA and New Zealand. It remains considerably less than aged percentages found in 2010 in Japan (23%), but well above those that were found in developing countries in 2010, such as China (11%) and Malaysia (7.5%). According to official population projections released in Australia in April 2003, the aged population ratio for Australia is expected to be just over 17.5% in 2020, using plausible assumptions of fertility, mortality and immigration. There are considerable commercial, housing and social implications resulting from this rapidly ageing population, as experienced in several other countries for some time. A total of 51.0% of the population in the (latest available) December 2006 census was female. There is a tendency for the female proportion of the total Australian population to rise over time as the slight majority of males at birth is overtaken by a tendency for females to live longer in an ageing population.

English was the only language spoken in 79.1% of the homes at the Australian national census of August 1996, while Italian was the most common other language. However, by the census of 2001 Chinese languages had become the most common non-English spoken language. This trend remained evident in the results of the August 2006 census, with Chinese languages accounting for 2.3% (Cantonese 1.2%; Mandarin 1.1%) of languages spoken at home, while English accounted for 78.5%. Some 47.0% of the homes in 1991 contained families without children, a proportion that, despite the image of an increasing incidence of childless couples, had remained stable since the early 1990s. There has been an increasing proportion of adult persons living alone in Australian homes. Some 11.3% of the resident Australian population in 2006 was divorced (and not then remarried), as compared with 1.9% of the Australian population being of this status in 1971. Lone persons living in an Australian dwelling overall accounted for 22.9% of the population in the 2006 population census, compared with 18.1% in 1971.

Projections made by the Australian Bureau of Statistics indicated that the proportion of adults who would never marry would continue to rise in the years from 2006 to 2020, being 31% for men and 25% for women, compared with equivalent percentages at 1986 of 21% and 14%, respectively. Using the same methodology, the likelihood of marriages ending in divorce was 32%. The crude divorce rate in 2006 was 2.9 persons per 1,000 of national population, compared with 4.4 for the USA and 2.9 for the United Kingdom. The crude marriage rate in Australia in that year was 5.5 per 1,000 of national population, compared with 8.8 in the USA and 5.3 in the United Kingdom.

According to the Australian Government Actuary, life expectancy in Australia at December 2010 was 78.2 years at birth for males and 83.8 years for females. These figures were higher than in the USA (74 and 79 years, respectively) and the United Kingdom (74 and 80 years), and they are similar to life expectancy data for Japan. The main causes of death in Australia at December 2010 were cancer (29.5% of all deaths), heart disease (20.3%) and strokes (9.5%). At the rates of childbirth prevailing at October 2010, 26.0% of Australian women would remain childless at the end of their reproductive lives. During the 1990s the proportion of the Australian population aged 25–64 years with a professional, vocational or higher educational qualification rose from 46.5% to 51.0%. The figure had reached 57.8% by December 2010.

Reflecting the country's position as a favoured and rapidly growing tourist destination, a total of 5,912,100 persons arrived in Australia as short-term visitors in the year ending April 2011. With an average stay of just over one month, these temporary residents comprised an average of 3.1% of the Australian population during 2010/11. This figure represented an annual increase of 4.6% on the previous year. There had been a similar recovery in short-term arrivals following the Asian financial crisis of 1997/98, the terrorist attacks on the USA of 11 September 2001 and the widespread epidemic of avian influenza ('bird flu'). In addition to the global financial crisis of 2008, for many years the overall situation for tourist inflows into Australia had been affected by a combination of economic and strategic factors, including increased international uncertainties arising from the Iraq conflict and the perceived health risks associated with Severe Acute Respiratory Syndrome (SARS) in 2003, and by perceptions about Australia's role in the transmission of swine flu in 2009. Increased uncertainties documented here arose during 2010/11, despite the rise in both confidence and purchasing power as countries emerged from the financial crisis.

AGRICULTURE, MINING AND MANUFACTURING

Agriculture

Agriculture has remained an important source of export earnings for Australia. While farming activities may have accounted for just 1.4% of Australia's GDP in the year ending in March 2011, and for only 4.0% of its employment, the agricultural sector nevertheless contributed 18.0% of export earnings. Historically, the share of Australian export earnings arising from agriculture declined from a range of 29%–35% during the 1980s to 12%–16% in the decade 2000–09. In the year to March 2010 this contribution was 16.4%. This farm-product share of Australia's exports compared with as much as 49.0% in 1970. The proportion of the Australian total employment base engaged in agriculture decreased from 7.8% in 1960 to 2.6% in 2009. However, in the year to March 2011 real growth of 21% occurred in agricultural production, demonstrating its typically large growth fluctuations.

Agricultural activities occupy a high proportion of the arable land in Australia, although they offer relatively little employment. This is due to the rapid productivity growth achieved in agriculture's production processes, and declining relative demand for agricultural products. In the year to June 2011 crops accounted for 57% of the total value of farm production. Some 76% of the crop production by value and 72% of the livestock production of Australia was exported in the same year. Within the aggregate value of crop and livestock products, the most prominent contributors were beef (17%), wheat (12%), fruit and nuts (9%), milk (11%), wool (4%) and vegetables (4%). In the first half of the 20th century wool alone dominated Australian export earnings, leaving aside some periods of intensive gold-mining activity. Beef, lamb and wheat have also been traditionally the main export-earners. The erosion of preferential entry into the United Kingdom in the 1970s, the emergence of mineral and, more recently, manufacturing exports, and competition from new international suppliers have diminished the relative position of these traditional exports.

In the year to June 2011 Australia produced 22,140m. metric tons of wheat, 0.518m. tons of cotton, 7.290m. tons of barley, 1.783m. tons of wine grapes and 4.64m. tons of sugar. In the same period, Australia produced 2.126m. tons of beef and veal, 0.412m. tons of wool, 0.593m. tons of mutton and lamb, 0.91m. tons of poultry and 9.16m. tons of milk.

From the mid-1990s wool suffered the specific difficulties of competition from synthetic products, declining demand and prices, compounded by the Asian financial crisis of the late 1990s. In the aftermath of an unsuccessful attempt at policy intervention in Australia to maintain wool prices, a huge stockpile of wool had emerged by 1996, but this had been completely sold by 2002. The number of sheep in Australia had stabilized at around 75m. in the period 2004–06, about one-half of the number observed in the 1960s. Further reductions since 2004–06 reflect both the incidence of drought and market conditions. At June 2011 the number of sheep in Australia was 68.5m.

In the year to March 2011 the share of wool in Australia's total value of exports had declined to just 0.78%, with beef and veal accounting for 1.6% and wheat for 2.3%. A privatized Australian Wheat Board undertook the marketing of Australian-grown wheat until late 2005, when allegations of improper conduct were made against the company and its marketing practices in the Middle East. In the period from December 2005 to June 2011 Australia moved away from the 'single desk' approach to marketing its wheat crop. Indeed, the direct role of government itself in the overseas marketing of Australian agricultural products in general had become very limited. Traditional primary-product exports now appear as a stable and efficient, if smaller, component of the economy. None the less, wheat production and wheat export values increased markedly in the two years to March 2011. Some 13.51m. ha were planted to wheat at mid-2011, and production in the year to June totalled 22.14m. metric tons, some 75% higher than in the same period of 2009. This high rate of wheat production remains below Australia's highest ever rate of wheat output in 2005/06, when production of 25.1m. tons was recorded.

Intensive production of fruit and vegetables takes place in Australia around urban settlement areas in every state and on land areas that are relatively close to the coastline. However, the major broad-acre developments are located further inland. For example, the sheep-wheat belt is located in an ellipse on the eastern and southern part of the Australian land mass, some 150 km–1,300 km from the coast. Dairy production has moved further from the cities with the development of irrigation and water-storage facilities. These facilities were severely tested in the 1999–2010 droughts, although some rains began to fall again between mid-2007 and mid-2011. Wine-producing areas are found close to Adelaide, Melbourne and Perth, and in low-rainfall zones in every state. About two-thirds of the Australian continent is classified as low-rainfall desert, being the central, northern and western zones. Little economic activity, except for mining operations and large-scale grazing activities, is conducted in these inland zones, with some tourism locations interspersed.

From mid-2005 to mid-2011 the dairy industry confronted adverse conditions caused by water shortages, long-term competition from margarine and greatly increased competition from New Zealand, in cheese production especially, since freer market access to New Zealand producers was granted in the early 1990s. Aggressive competition in wheat markets from 1999 caused difficulty when Australia, as in its response to declining sugar prices in the 1970s, failed to follow market prices fully downwards. There are also some notable successes, including greatly increased penetration of Australian beef and rice in Japan and other Asian markets.

Australia has also reached considerable prominence as a premium exporter of table wines. However, from about 2007 Australian wine producers anxiously observed the huge worldwide wine surplus, which had been emerging for some time, as it began to curb the industry's prospects for high growth. In Australia, as in many wine-producing regions of the world, grape growers experienced price reductions in the period between mid-2004 and mid-2011, suggesting that crops had been overplanted. In 2006/07 some 38% of Australian wine was exported, mainly to Europe, compared with 12% in 1980. By 2010 this share had declined to 31%. About 1.78m. metric tons of grapes were crushed in 2010/11.

Australia benefits from its providential endowment of agricultural resources and a reputation for high quality in processing. These advantages are tempered by the long-term trend of declining relative prices of agricultural staples in world markets. Australia has been prominent in seeking freer access for primary products in protected world markets, using overt and other forms of diplomatic pressure to make its position known. In June 2002 the Australian Prime Minister addressed the US Congress, combining unequivocal endorsement for the USA's position on international terrorism with firm disagreement on the protectionist aspects of that country's trade policy. Australia is also particularly subject to the vagaries of climatic conditions. Thus, in December 2002, before the protracted Australian drought had appeared to have partially broken (in mid-2003), the office of the Australian Statistician presented estimates to the effect that the drought (since about 1999) had had the impact, through the reduction in potential agricultural production, of taking some 0.7% from the country's real GDP between 2001/02 and 2002/03. It was judged that there were few drought effects in the year 2003/04. During 2005 drought conditions re-emerged, and only in mid-2010 were there signs of further significant rain in southern Australia. At that time substantial water restrictions remained in place throughout most of Australia, being generally more severe in rural than in urban areas, affecting agricultural producers as well as town dwellers. In January 2011 significant floods occurred in Queensland and Victoria, causing damage not only for agricultural businesses, but also for mining and service sector operations. This led significantly to the negative growth of real national income in the first quarter of 2011.

Mining

Some $A87,820m., or 6.5% of Australian GDP, was derived directly from mining activities in the year to March 2011. A high proportion of all major minerals (other than brown coal) was exported. In the case of uranium oxide, the entire mineral output was exported because of domestic consumption prohibitions. About 42% of Australian export earnings was derived from mineral exports in the year to March 2011: 26% from metal ores alone and 18% from coal. Much environmental attention was given to the conditions of mineral exploration, production and handling. Legal issues arising from land-rights claims with traditional landowners remain controversial in some areas of the industry. Proposed resource rent taxes to apply only to mining activities and carbon taxes proposed more generally remained the most controversial of all policy matters being debated in Australia at mid-2011.

There is a considerable disparity between the location of the major valuable mineral deposits and the areas desired for habitation. Coal and valuable mineral deposits occur mainly inland and in low-rainfall areas. This potential problem has been addressed in three ways. First, some major settlements have developed at mine sites, such as: Broken Hill, about 800 km west of Sydney; Newcastle, 160 km north of Sydney; Wollongong, 130 km south of Sydney; and Ballarat and Bendigo, both around 160 km north-west of Melbourne on slightly different arcs. Second, the development of high-productivity extraction techniques and the availability of concentrate ores and their transport have limited the need for workers to be at the location of the major deposits. Third, there is a well-developed system of moving workers to mine sites. There is also the capacity to take workers into temporary locations. Quite commonly, workers will be engaged for periods of two to three weeks working intensively, followed by two weeks off site.

Historically, Australia has experienced pronounced booms associated with specific mineral products, especially gold. Since the late 1960s, commencing with iron ore, bituminous coal and bauxite, a long-sustained phase of mineral development has been evident. Both Australian and foreign-owned companies have developed huge resources of natural gas, coal, uranium, copper, lead, zinc and petroleum. There was no sign in the early 21st century that this long phase of mineral development was ending. Government financial support for mining development through state and federal budgets has been reduced significantly since 1990. Industrial relations have generally improved, although the 86% reduction in working days lost per employee between October 1984 and March 2011 conceals continuing tensions over pay and conditions that cause international buyers of coal, in particular, to be ready to substitute alternative suppliers should Australian sources prove unreliable.

Australia has impressive endowments of the world's proven mineral reserves, with more than 80% of the world's reserves of rutile and beach sands, over 40% of the uranium oxide, around 45% of brown coal (lignite) and 24% of black (bituminous) coal. While Australia has substantial petroleum resources, mostly beyond its south-eastern and north-western coastlines, it still needs to import about one-third of its domestic oil and petroleum needs.

The following data relating to production and exports of mineral products were seriously affected by heavy rains that limited mining production and distribution. In the year to June 2011 Australia mined 67.7m. metric tons of bauxite, processing this into 17.6m. tons of alumina, of which more than 85% was exported, mostly to Japan and South Korea. This export trade represented 9% of the world trade in aluminium. In the 12 months to March 2011 509m. tons of black coal were produced, mostly from Queensland (56%) and New South Wales (42%). After washing, the figure for coal was reduced to a net 392m. tons, of which 263m. tons were exported. Meanwhile, Australia produced 436m. tons and exported 399m. tons of iron ore in 2010/11, the world's largest exporter thereof, accounting for 39% of global iron ore exports. In the year to June 2011 Australia also mined 270 tons of gold and, through destocking, exported 302 tons of the commodity. In the same year Australian output of crude petroleum reached 28.26m. litres, of which 17.4m. litres were exported, together with 2.88m. litres of liquefied petroleum gas (LPG). Australian rutile production was just over one-half of the world's supply. In 2010/11 Australia produced 10,100 tons of uranium, some 30% of the world's aggregate uranium production and similar to the Canadian production level. In the year to June 2011 Australian mines produced 938,000 tons of copper ore and 471,000 tons of refined copper. Australian production of silver was 1,790 tons, while 1.42m. tons of zinc were produced in this period.

The prominent and rapid sustained growth of China is a substantial reason for the prosperity of the mineral sector in Australia as assessed at June 2011. The country's mineral sector appeared to have suffered no adverse effects from the global financial crisis in the three years to June 2011, and prospects remained good, provided that China's slight deceleration in growth did not lead to reduced demand for Australian minerals. The floods of early 2011 had receded by June. There are other issues for mining in Australia to address. The supply constraints arising from limitations of skilled labour, mineral supplies and transport have meant that price rather than volume gains have been the main factor in mineral revenue growth, since 2002 especially. Indeed, the aggregate volume of Australian exports, including mineral exports, hardly increased between 2000 and 2011, while import volumes rose by 69%. It is a risky strategic decision process to put in place the rail and port-handling facilities that would fully accommodate the strong volume demand as seen at mid-2011.

Rationalization and consolidation in Australia's mineral industries took place substantially in the 1990s. This was partly caused by the ending of decades of income tax exemption for gold-mining operations and by the mergers of larger operators. Mergers and take-overs have been closely monitored and often prevented. In late 2001 the (Royal Dutch) Shell company was blocked by a Treasury decree on 'public interest' grounds from taking over the operations of the Australian north-west-shelf gas producer, Woodside, although it retained significant interests therein. Seldom are gold producers out of the news concerning financial reconstruction and policy agitation. Some of the policy guidelines remain unclear or inconsistent as viewed by investors, explorers and producers. During 2008 and the first half of 2009 some companies within the Australian oil and mining sector became concerned at the prospective introduction of a carbon emissions trading scheme proposed by the Rudd Government. In the May 2009 budget it was envisaged that this scheme would begin to apply from 2012, a year later than had previously been anticipated. Somewhat dramatically, the Rudd Government abandoned these plans in April 2010. In May the Government announced proposals for the controversial RSPT which, within eight weeks, had brought about the replacement of the Prime Minister.

Serious public policy proposals affecting specific industries can have adverse economic consequences, even if they are never introduced as such. Moreover, there are ways to introduce new industry policies with understanding and consultation that create less harmful side-effects. By June 2010 many mining companies had postponed developments. They also supported their objections to the proposed tax with powerful public and media campaigns. In consultation with the newly appointed Prime Minister, in late June the media campaigns ceased, and it seemed that the new resource tax was destined to be abandoned. Soon after the general election of August 2010, which resulted in a hung Parliament, plans emerged for the reintroduction of a more confined RSPT and a generic carbon tax applied to a wide range of carbon dioxide emitters. It was plain that the market-based system adopted during the Rudd administration was not acceptable to the smaller parties that were dominated by green issues and to the independents who had enabled Julia Gillard to form a minority Government in 2010. In May 2011 some details of an MRRT accompanied the delivery of that year's federal budget. Concerns arising from the impact of such a tax on mining sector business investment and of the carbon tax on petroleum retail prices lay behind a sharp decline in the Gillard Government's electoral prospects. No further details were immediately divulged, except that the Government remained determined to press ahead with both measures. Combined with several uncertainties in other policy fields, such as competition (see Competition Policy Reform, below), these policy uncertainties quite clearly added to the forces restraining economic activity in Australia in mid-2011.

Manufacturing

As in many Western-style economies, there has been a declining trend in the relative position of the manufacturing sector since the early 1970s. This decrease has resulted from a combination of reduced import-duty protection, the emergence of low-cost foreign suppliers in textiles, clothing, footwear and metal manufactures, especially from Asia, and declining household budget shares devoted to manufactured goods. A considerable proportion of manufacturing activity is geared to serving the needs of the mining and agricultural sectors, which are relatively larger than in countries with a similar degree of economic development. In the year to March 2011 manufacturing value added totalled $A96,809m., a moderate decline as compared with the previous year; this represented 7.5% of national GDP, only the third year since reliable records have been kept that the manufacturing share of national income has been below 10%. Food, beverages and tobacco provided some 19% of manufacturing employment in the year to March 2009, 19% of value added and 24% of exports within the manufacturing sector. The contribution of the machinery and equipment sectors was similar. A further 17% of manufacturing added value was contributed by metal product manufacturing, while petroleum and chemical products provided 14%, printing and publishing 12%, wood products 7%, and textiles, clothing and footwear 3%.

There are several areas of policy uncertainty that impinge especially on the goods-producing sectors of the Australian economy, notably the large variations in the approach to research and development, export promotion and certain taxation issues. However, the manufacturing sector has arguably gained in relation to other sectors of the Australian economy from the introduction of the New Tax System (NTS) on 1 July 2000. This is because that tax initiative involved the elimination of wholesale sales taxation, which applied only to manufactured goods, and its replacement at the substantially lower rate of 10% by the goods and services tax (GST—see Economic Development and Government Policy, below).

Within the manufacturing sector there is considerable interest in the Australian motor vehicle industry, in which the major international vehicle builders have long been represented. No sector of Australian manufacturing was more adversely affected by the economic downturn of 2008/09 than vehicles, especially parts production. Motor vehicle registrations rose at an average annual rate of 2.6% in 1999–2002, that rate increasing to 4.2% in the year to June 2003. In the calendar year 2003 total vehicle registrations exceeded 900,000 units for the first time. Registrations grew rapidly again in the 12 months to May 2005, total vehicles registered being 975,985, of which 601,484 were passenger motor vehicles, 181,253 were sports or utility vehicles and 193,248 were other vehicles. In the year to March 2008 vehicle registrations totalled 101,200 units, showing a stabilization and a high level in motor vehicle sales in Australia. The market remained strong, although price discounting suggested that vehicle builders were anticipating some reductions in sales volumes. In the first five months of 2009 vehicle sales volumes decreased significantly, reflecting, *inter alia*, the impact of rising interest rates and the lack of confidence that was emerging from negative reports of the US economy. Vehicle registrations decreased by some 31% in the year to April 2009, compared with the previous 12 months. One year later a form of 'echo effect' arising from delayed motor vehicle replacements was observed, and registration advanced by 8.5% in the 12 months to May 2010. In the year to May 2011 motor vehicle registrations in Australia totalled 1,013,212 units, a slight decline on the previous year; of these, 572,759 were passenger motor vehicles and 233,726 were sports or utility vehicles. Some 65% of all vehicles are purchased by governments and business firms, rather than by households.

It was believed that the release of accumulated savings among younger people for whom residential property prices had become prohibitive had benefited the motor vehicle industry in the period from 1996 to 2011. The average age of cars on the road in Australia was 9.9 years, as recorded in an official motor vehicle census taken at March 2006, having risen from 6.1 years in 1971 to over 11 years in 1999. The fleet of motor vehicles in Australia at March 2006 was estimated at almost 14.4m. vehicles, of which 11.2m. were passenger motor vehicles, with 2.1m. being light commercial vehicles (a rising proportion of the market). Almost 60% of the passenger motor vehicles were of three brands: Holden (General Motors), Toyota and Ford. Public policy support for domestic economic activity in this sector was reduced, although in April 1998 the Howard Government announced a pause in the programmed reduction of motor vehicle import duties, based on agreement with the leading vehicle builders that cost-reducing plant and equipment investment would take place. Considerable modernization and extension of facilities subsequently followed. On the supply side of the motor vehicles sector there were further difficulties in early 2007 when Ajax, a fastener and metal products supplier, came under pressure until a rescue programme was announced in April of that year. In June 2008 a major Australian producer of automotive tyres announced plans for closure after decades of local production. It appeared likely that automotive parts would be one of the most sensitive production sectors to encounter such difficulties, with further trade liberalization measures arising from free trade agreements to be implemented with both the USA and China.

The future of the Australian manufacturing industry seemed uncertain on the basis of some indicators in the mid-1990s. Tariff rates assisting manufacturing production against import competition declined sharply from 15% in 1990 to just 5% by 2010, while those on imported cars and clothes decreased from 45% to 10%. This import-subsidy effect has been compounded since 2001 by movements in the exchange rate of the US dollar to the Australian dollar, which had risen substantially from 47 US cents to 109 US cents by mid-2011, and by the erosion of government support for local industry. Final buyers were devoting relatively less of their 'spending dollar' to manufactured goods, and the items that they did buy were increasingly sourced from imports rather than from domestic production.

The pronounced relative decline in manufacturing was not necessarily disastrous, although it was indeed damaging for many manufacturers, large and small, who tried to ignore these trends by continuing with the 'old' products made in the 'old ways'. From 2000, despite negative signals and strident import competition, Australian manufacturing unexpectedly increased its capital equipment outlays by around 80%: from $A10,000m. a year to just over $A19,000m. in 2009/10. Accompanying this pronounced capital intensification was a dramatic doubling in annual research and development outlays, from $A1,900m. to $A4,600m. In the same period, the investment was realized in profitability, the nominal value of manufacturing profits in Australia rising from $A14,000m. in 1999/2000 to $A36,200m. in 2009/10. The surviving manufacturing activities in Australia therefore became leaner, more capital-intensive, research-based and demonstrably more profitable than a decade previously, despite the barriers and the seemingly unfavourable background.

The underlying reality emerges from close inspection of individual industry sectors, ranging from steel to scientific instruments, from chemicals to cars, from paper to pharmaceuticals and from fashion goods to footwear. Many firms and product categories have disappeared. This is frequently the result of multinational company decisions to relocate outside Australia. The reduction of product ranges, adoption of advanced technology and widespread replacement of family managerial structures by modern managers all contribute to the success. Many of the materials and part-processed goods used in Australian manufacturing are themselves imported; therefore, the surging value of the country's currency helps as well as hinders. Some manufacturers even distribute imported products with their own wares. It is notable that some Australian manufacturing companies survived the global economic downturn of 2008/09 more capably than their foreign parent organizations. Nevertheless, in 2011 there remained many challenges for the manufacturing sector.

TRANSPORT, COMMUNICATIONS AND ENERGY

Transport

There are clearly difficulties in covering a land area similar to that of the USA with advanced transport networks, given Australia's small population. However, through significant government involvement and an active private sector there has been substantial coverage by road, rail, air and shipping facilities. From the late 1980s the domestic and international airline operations controlled by the federal Government were combined into Qantas, which was then sold to the private sector, a significant share being acquired by British Airways. In addition, the main airport infrastructure was divided into lots for sale by auction. Similarly, port and rail systems were exposed to greater competition by the removal of legislation requiring carriage of selected goods by designated modes, by privatization of some of these operations, and the introduction of corporatization principles into management and performance procedures. In the period 1999–2011 negotiations and disputes concerning the access arrangements and pricing of these facilities occasioned much activity in the area of competition law.

Since the mid-1990s Australia has followed a more 'open-skies' policy in permitting a wider range of international airline operators to participate in the Australian passenger airlines market. In domestic operations the traditional concept was for a 'two-airline policy' to operate. This involved one carrier being government-owned and one (Ansett, with its origins in the 1930s) being privately owned, with entry by any other potential provider being made impossible through bans on aircraft imports. Heavily monitored 'rationalization agreements' ensured that the two carriers had equal traffic, timetables, aircraft, facilities and profits. From the 1980s liberalization proceeded rapidly. The entry of third carriers and their failure in the 1990s provided warnings that competition might have become 'excessive'. Just three days after the terrorist attacks of 11 September 2001 in the USA, Ansett suddenly collapsed. The failed carrier had previously been sold to international trucking and news operators TNT and News Corp and then was acquired by Air New Zealand. Two further attempts at entry were more successful, the sustained entrant, Virgin Blue, occupying a significant role alongside Qantas from mid-2005 until June 2011. In response to the emergence of other entrants in the market, Qantas introduced Jetstar, a low-cost affiliated airline, which began domestic operations in mid-2004 and during 2006 commenced international services. In the period March–May 2007 Qantas received takeover offers from equity consortia. Although the board assented to the offer, the bidder was not able to meet the takeover conditions. The move exposed the now-privatized operator to market forces. Again, the image was one of rapid change and highly competitive business conditions. The transport sector accounted for almost 5% of Australia's GDP in 2010/11. By June 2011 the airlines in Australia had dealt with both the global financial crisis and constrictions on passenger volumes that resulted from volcanic eruptions; therefore, prospects were for stronger volumes of passenger carriage to emerge in 2011/12.

Communications

As in the transport sector of Australia, the traditional dominant role in the communications sector was played by a government-owned and government-controlled enterprise that has since been privatized. With responsibilities formerly for both post and telephony, this operation was divided in the 1970s, and in 1993 Telecom was renamed Telstra and partly privatized. New entrants subsequently appeared, a major operator being Optus. Many smaller operators exist in specialist areas, particularly suppliers of telephonic services using Telstra's network. From around 2005, and actively at mid-2011, a significant dispute arose between Telstra and the main competition regulator, especially in relation to access conditions and access prices. During 2002 a government review of the five-year process of telecommunications deregulation was carried out. Australia Post is the corporatized principal supplier of postal services. It is also exposed to competition and in turn has widened its functions to provide stationery sales and bill-paying services. The communications sector accounted for 2% of Australia's GDP in the year 2010/11.

Information Technology

During the world-wide technology boom of 1995–2001 in particular, Australia was commonly classified as an old-technology economy. The country's continuing substantial dependence on agricultural and mineral exports may have encouraged this perception. However, there was almost complete coverage of basic telephony in Australia, and advanced information technology (IT) had been widely adopted by mid-2011. Some 10.4m., or approximately 97%, of Australian households, had fixed residential telephone lines connected at March 2011. The number of mobile cellular telephones in use rose from 5.9m. in 1995 to 11.1m. in 2000 and to 19.7m. by March 2011, equivalent to 88% of the Australian resident population. Home computers numbered 3.2m. in 1995 and, according to official data, had reached 8.5m. by March 2011, the percentage of Australian households possessing a computer having risen from 44% in 1995 to 75% in 2011. There were some 560 internet service providers (ISPs) in Australia at March 2011, this number having declined from 720 providers in March 2004, owing to the difficulties that the technology industries were experiencing world-wide. Six of the larger ISPs each serviced in excess of 100,000 subscribers. Domestic broadband cable installations stood at 2.5m. in 2000 (35% of Australian households), rising to 6.1m. services installed by March 2008 (53% of households).

Some 1.93m. Australian households were Pay TV subscribers in March 2011, constituting 26% of Australian households, compared with 0.91m. subscribers in 1995. The figure at 2000 was similar to that in 2006, indicating that there was little growth in this sector during the intervening period. The percentage of businesses with internet access increased from 29% in 1997/98 to 87% in March 2011. The incidence of internet usage increased significantly with household income and where children under 18 years of age were in the household complement (55%, compared with 38% in households without youngsters); internet usage was greater in metropolitan areas than in rural areas (49% compared with 39%), in all cases for official data recorded as at March 2011. The information, media and telecommunications sector reported value added amounting to $A35,629m. in the year to March 2011, representing 2.7% of Australia's national income; the sector had 177,000 employees (1.5% of Australia's total employment).

Energy Supply and Distribution

Energy and gas supplies were traditionally provided by state-owned and state-operated monopolies with considerable fiscal support. Privatization of most of these services was accompanied by debate and by efforts to improve efficiency, which increased the accountability of the enterprises concerned and generally reduced or restrained consumer energy prices. Each of the energy-sector enterprises is subject to new 'access' regulations relating both to the conditions on which supplies are made available and to the prices charged. The dominant source of energy is electricity, which in turn is generated from (black and brown) coal and natural gas. Including the domestic energy component of coal and natural gas, the energy sector accounted for 2.5% of Australia's GDP and 0.9% of its employment in the year to March 2011.

The responsibility for energy provision and distribution has traditionally rested with state governments. Each state government tended to permit gas and electricity boards to assume quasi-monopoly positions in the entire production chain, from energy extraction to production and distribution to consumers. For legal and logistical reasons, there was no possibility of trade or exchange of energy products between the separate Australian states until recent times. The emergence of gas pipelines that crossed state boundaries in the 1970s and the 1991 facilitation of electricity sales between the states typify the liberalization that has taken place. In addition, the main electricity and gas providers have been split up, the common arrangement being for distribution systems in each state to be divided into some three to six regional areas sold to private interests that were by 2003 free to compete with each other. Even where government ownership was maintained, as in New South Wales, the component businesses were subject to stringent profit-making requirements combined with consumer service monitoring. In 2010 per head energy use by Australians was 283 gigajoules, within which the per head electricity use was 84 gigajoules. By mid-2011 financial markets, electors and energy observers were anticipating further proposed sales of Australian energy and public sector utilities, despite the global economic downturn and the sharp decline of equity prices. The sector itself was at that time preparing for the direct impact of the proposed carbon tax and the indirect effects arising from the MRRT, each discussed above.

OTHER SERVICES

Despite the image of rural and mining production traditionally associated with Australia, the majority of residents since British occupation over the last two centuries have lived in towns and cities and engaged in service activities. Australia has an advanced network of personal and business service industries, including legal, finance, education, medical, health and community services, leisure and sporting service activities. Banking, insurance and accounting services are predominantly controlled by large companies with international operations. Retail distribution activities involve both large and small operators. After correction for price movements, the value of retail sales in Australia has remained particularly constant on a per head basis since 1980. Within the aggregate there has been substitution against some food groups (meat and sugars) and an increasing trend towards processed food not prepared in the home. Shopping hours became progressively longer and more liberal from 1980, and internet purchasing of services, especially travel services, rose rapidly.

The tertiary sector can be usefully divided into the wholesaling (4.8% of employment and 4.3% of national income, at March 2011), storage and retailing of products (11.3% of employment and 4.9% of national income); community and charitable services (2.3% and 2.9%, respectively); health and medical services (7.7% and 3.8%); education (2.8% and 3.1%); tourism and leisure activities (7.7% and 2.4%); legal, accounting and business services (2.2% and 2.4%); and financial services (6.8% and 7.3%). In the past the retail sector featured two prominent chain-store entities: Coles Myer, established in 1985 by a merger of two successful family companies, which were involved in more than 40% of the retail transactions in Australia; and Woolworth-Safeway, which had been sharing the market more evenly. However, from 2006 Coles and Myer became separate entities, Myer being sold to a consortium and Coles being sold to Wesfarmers in October 2007. Within the retail sector, food and drink retailing comprised 44% of the total in 2008, household products 15% and department stores 9%. The health services sector featured a hospital system shared between government and private ownership, supported by national and private insurance arrangements; independent medical practitioners; and a large network of pharmaceutical retailers supplied by production and importing companies featuring most of the world's leading pharmaceutical manufacturers.

From 2003 there were many contentious issues and pressures within the tertiary or services sector, including debates about education funding, retrenchments in the finance and accounting sector, and pressures in support of and opposition to an informal 'four pillars' policy to prevent mergers among the leading banks. In addition, from July 2000 the services sector sustained significantly increased tax burdens with the introduction of the NTS (see Tax Reform and Tax Trends, below). Arguably, the tax burden became more uniformly spread under the NTS. Before the release of the Rudd Government's second budget in May 2009, it was regarded as likely that these issues would be prominent in the tax reform process initiated in its first budget, of May 2008. However, this did not occur, and by mid-2009 no actions of tax reform in the area had been announced. The Rudd Government's response to the Henry tax report proposals in May 2010 did not indicate any further ambitions in this area. By June 2011 no major tax changes, and few that were recommended in the Henry process, had been embraced by the Gillard Government.

Education

The education sector's value added constituted 3.1% of Australia's gross national income in the year ended March 2011 and 2.8% of national employment. An advanced, internationally focused education sector exists in Australia. Private (mostly church-based) and government (taxpayer-funded) primary and secondary schools operate in competition with each other. Universities and tertiary technical training institutes are mainly government-owned. There are some private tertiary institutions. From the mid-1990s full fee-paying tertiary students, many of them from other countries, became an increasing part of the educational intake. Australian universities began to market their services by website, promotional visits to other (mainly Asian) countries and in some cases by setting up establishments in other countries. For example, Monash University (Melbourne) established a campus in Malaysia in the mid-1990s.

At August 2010 there were 9,468 schools in Australia. The number of schools had been declining over the period from about 1990, when it stood at 9,600, as consolidations and closures took place. Some 3.486m. full-time students attended these schools, 68% in the government-provided (non-fee-paying) sector, compared with 72% in 1990. In 2010 the student-teacher ratio was 16.3 in primary schools and 12.0 in secondary schools, each having decreased from 20.8 and 13.1, respectively, in 1982. However, on the supply side, the number of people completing a university qualification in teacher education declined by 15% between 1991 and 2009. There were 286,000 full-time equivalent teachers in Australian schools in 2010, comprising 82,000 males and 204,000 females. The female proportion of this total was 71% and rising. There has been a significant increase in the age-specific participation rates in education in Australia. For example, 72% of 17-year-olds were full-time students in 2009, compared with 59% in 1992. The data also show a higher retention rate among female students aged 15–19 years than for male students in Australian schools.

A much greater commercial focus has come upon all aspects of education in Australia from the mid-1980s: schools and universities are managed more like businesses, with leaders actively promoting their institutions; fees have been widely reintroduced into the tertiary sector, while the overseas-born student population has risen rapidly in response to opportunities in Australia and some active marketing campaigns. In 1996 there were some 650,000 students in 36 Australian universities, with more than 625,000 students being classified as domestic students. By the end of 2009 there were some 1,105,000 students in 43 Australian universities, with the non-domestic category accounting for 36%, but over 50% in most commercial faculties. Between 2006 and 2010 some 33% of all university students were foreign-born (in comparison with 6.1% in 1992). Significant numbers of these students were provided with temporary student visas and were obliged to pay full fees, despite often coming from countries with low national per caput incomes. By mid-2005 there were signs of some significant slowing in the overall growth in numbers of foreign students entering Australian universities, leading to increases in marketing efforts to attract them. The deceleration was particularly acute for regional universities and for those with specialties in the IT areas.

In the May 2007 federal budget the Government set aside a fund of $A5,000m. as the capital base for future higher education funding, and liberalized the conditions under which universities could apply fees. In addition, some universities embarked on structural course design changes to meet new international challenges. A highly significant change in federal funding of education was announced in the May 2008 federal budget, with the creation of a separate education fund, supported by the mounting budget surpluses that had accrued since 2000. These funds were further enhanced as part of the Rudd Government's stimulus measures announced between November 2008 and May 2009. By 2011 it was clear that the global financial slowdown had resulted in surprisingly little adverse impact on the number of non-domestic students coming to Australia to undertake tertiary education.

Legal, Accounting and Business Services

Legal firms underwent a process of merger in the 1990s to establish some large firms, mainly serving government and major companies, not least with the work required in association with the privatization of the power and telephony sectors. Small-scale service providers are found in every main town offering legal, accounting or financial services. In both legal and accounting firms a dominant tendency emerged from mid-2008 to request staff to work fewer hours, a trend that remained pronounced at mid-2011 and which tended to conceal the extent of the economic downturn when measured simply by unemployment rates. In the accounting area, all major international firms are prominent in Australia. In the banking sector there are four major banks, each private or privatized. An unlegislated 'four pillars' policy operates to ensure that the 'big four' cannot merge further, although it was rumoured that attempts were to be made to test this policy through the courts. Insurance services are provided by major international underwriters, supported by affiliated agents and independent brokers, each subject to increasingly onerous regulations. In every one of these service areas, large and small firms co-exist, serving different parts of the market. Between 2002 and 2011 there were no further major mergers or major failures in this professional services area. The enhanced power of the Howard Government in the Senate between July 2005 and July 2008 did not lead to the reopening of merger policy in relation to banks and other significant financial services operators. At mid-2011 the direction of the Gillard administration on merger policy was unclear, despite the circulation of new merger guidelines by the competition policy regulator in 2009.

Tourism and Leisure Industries

The number of international visitors to Australia totalled 5.92m. in the year to April 2011. This figure reflected a slightly below-trend increase of just 2.0% in comparison with arrivals in the previous 12 months; this relative stability in numbers contrasted with a decline of 1.9% in the year to April 2009. Before this, strong positive annual growth rates in tourist numbers in the 1980s of more than 20% per annum took place, such high-growth trends having remained evident until 2001. The global economic slowdown, the stronger Australian dollar, the association of Australia with swine flu from April 2009 and international economic uncertainties clearly accounted for this decline, the image of Australia as a desirable tourist destination having been adversely affected. Tourist numbers form an excellent case study of the manner in which important economic variables can be affected by real and perceived causative influences, both domestic and global. In 2002–03 the visitor intake was adversely affected by threats of international terrorist action, SARS, a regional outbreak of avian influenza, and the global decrease in tourism. This temporary decline was an uncharacteristic interruption in a sustained period of rapid growth: the number of international tourist arrivals rose from 1.1m. in 1984 to 2.1m. in 1988 alone, and the sector then maintained an average annual compound growth rate of 6.3% between 1988 and 2001.

During 2003, however, international visits to Australia returned to the levels experienced in 2001, although the growth in numbers had decreased. The 2004 visitor total represented the first time that tourist intake numbers had clearly exceeded 5.0m. persons annually. Between 2004 and December 2007 the annual-equivalent number of tourists arriving in Australia resumed a moderate yearly trend growth pattern of 3.5%–7.0%. The main source of international tourists to Australia in recent years has been New Zealand (20.2% of the total in the year to December 2010), followed by the United Kingdom (12.1%), with China having risen rapidly to exceed 13.0% of the arrivals, now surpassing Japan (9.5%), and the USA (7.0%).

Tourism services comprised some 3.4% of the Australian GDP in the year to March 2011, having increased from 2.4% in 1990. Around 24% of this activity is attributed to serving international tourists. At March 2011 there were 227,129 rooms in hotels, motels and other tourist accommodation facilities in Australia. In the same month the hotel and general tourist accommodation occupancy rate was 64.3%. The average takings in these facilities as revenue from tourists was $A158 per room at March 2011 (or about US $170). The average stay in Australian hotels in 2010 was 2.3 nights. Occupancy rates in Australian hotels varied from 77% for 5-star hotels to 49% for 2-star hotels and caravan parks in 2010. Results from the Bureau of Tourism Research showed that some 55% of international tourist arrivals land initially in Sydney, although only about 34% of visitor nights are spent by them in New South Wales, the state in which Sydney is located. Considerable statistical information is available in relation to the events and theme parks that tourists attend and for data on satisfaction rates from surveys completed by tourists to Australia. Several tourist destinations were adversely affected in the year ended June 2011 by disruptions caused by volcanoes, earthquakes and floods.

FOREIGN TRADE AND THE BALANCE OF PAYMENTS

Since December 1983 Australia has operated a freely floating currency regime with little interference either directly or indirectly from Parliament or the monetary authorities. This means that all overseas monetary inflows will match the overseas outflows in aggregate, although at various stopping points in the statistics of external accounts imbalances can be, and are, evident. Throughout Australia's history the gap between exports and imports by value, the merchandise trade balance, has moved significantly from surplus to deficit. However, the overall external accounts exhibit a pronounced and permanent strong long-term capital inflow, alongside persistent current account outflows of freight payments and interest and debt-servicing payments. Undoubtedly this situation reflects the combination of huge natural resources and development potential with the limited population and savings base within Australia. It also means that Australia is significantly influenced by world interest rates. It has, therefore, gained much from the epoch of relatively low interest rates since the mid-1990s. In principle, the adjustments that once took place through movements in Australia's level of international reserves have in the years since 1983, or even since 1977, been absorbed through exchange rate changes. In the period from early 2001 to mid-2011 significant exchange rate volatility was evident, with the Australian dollar trading as low as 47 US cents and rising to above parity with the US dollar for the first time in three decades, reaching 110 US cents during this relatively short period. Owing to its diminished reliance on primary export staples and to greater economic flexibility, not least through the exchange rate mechanism described below, the Australian economy is now less likely to suffer from the cyclical behaviour of world markets that once took it quickly from boom conditions to slump.

Merchandise Trade

A significant deficit in Australia's balance of merchandise trade emerged in the seven years from 2003/04 to 2009/10. Ironically, a side-effect of the first full year of the global economic slowdown was that this external trade deficit narrowed in 2008/09 and 2009/10, because Australian import values decreased more significantly than did export values, as the country's discretionary consumer and business spending diminished. Whereas exports and imports of goods alone were each worth almost exactly $A120,000m. in the year to June 2002, in the year to March 2009 exports were valued at $A237,898m., while imports had risen to only $A229,597m. This trade surplus of $A8,300m. reflected the weakness of the Australian and world economies, as reductions in spending in Australia on imports were more dramatic than any curtailment in world demand for the country's exports. This was the first positive trade balance for many years in Australia. In the year to March 2010 exports were valued at $A186,538m. and imports at $A200,592m., resulting in a trade deficit of $A14,055m. In the year to April 2011 the trade balance increased further: merchandise export values rose to $A241,200m. and imports to $A214,100m., resulting in a trade surplus of $A27,100m.

The main export destinations in the year to March 2011 were China (which purchased 24.0% of total Australian exports by value in that period, a share rising from 9.7% five years previously), Japan (16.0%), South Korea (8.3%), India (6.5%) and the USA (5.2%). Exports to the United Kingdom, which accounted for 10% of Australia's exports in 1993, declined to less than 5% in the year to March 2011. Collectively, 11% of merchandise by value was exported by Australia to the countries of the Association of Southeast Asian Nations and 10% to the European Union in the year to March 2011. Overall, the rural component of exported goods had declined from 30% in 1981 to 13% by mid-2011. By type of product, metal ores accounted for 26% of the total in the year to December 2010 (largely exported to Japan, China and South Korea); the other main exported products were meat, wool, wheat and machinery and transport equipment. The traditionally dominant beef and wool products each accounted for about 3%, thereby emphasizing the substantial transformation of the Australian export structure away from staple products. It also reflects the increasing relative reliance of Australian exports on economic conditions in other Asian countries, especially China. The trade pattern by source and destination is also changing rapidly, with substantial growth in exports to India and of motor vehicle exports to the Middle East, especially Saudi Arabia.

The dominant product category in imports is machinery, including office and telecommunications equipment, which accounted for 45% of total import values in the year to March 2011; crude oil and petroleum products are also significant imports. In the same period the main sources of imports were Japan (which supplied 16.3% of all Australia's imported merchandise), China (15.6%), the USA (12.5%), Singapore (6.1%) and Thailand (5.2%).

Invisibles and Internationally Traded Services

Despite the movement to a net surplus in relation to international tourism activity since 1994, the non-merchandise current external account between Australia and other countries had remained significantly in deficit. This category is dominated by a small number of net deficit items, especially freight and insurance outgoings and the repatriation of interest payments and dividends abroad. In 2009/10 the main destinations for exports of services were the USA (which purchased 18%), Japan (11%), the United Kingdom (10%) and New Zealand (7%). Travel and tourism services comprised 47% of the total, with transport and freight services 25% and communications 5%.

Non-merchandise transactions ('invisibles') between Australia and other countries entail freight and other services (a net expenditure or deficit from Australia's perspective) and interest and other income or expense items crossing national borders. In the year to April 2011 the invisible credits were some $A52,200m, with debits of $A58,200m., leaving a net debit on non-merchandise items in Australia's external accounts of $A6,000m. This deficit has narrowed in recent years, as has the trade balance. Taking both visible and invisible international financial flows into consideration, the current account deficit had expanded to a level not encountered hitherto in the year to March 2008, but had been reduced slightly, to $A61,483m., in the year to March 2010. This statistic declined markedly in the year ended March 2011, to just $A28,715m. This figure is a difference variable and thus can be subject to huge fluctuations when relatively minor variations in its components take place; furthermore, under flexible exchange rate regimes there is no need to take corrective policy action when these movements actually occur.

At 31 March 2011 Australia's net foreign debt stood at $A724,756m., equivalent to 53% of Australia's GDP. The fact that some 93% of this debt was privately incurred and was secured on prime, often export-orientated, assets caused independent international assessments by analysts and credit-rating agencies to offer a confident view of Australia's financial future. Moreover, while GDP is used as a scaling device here, it is not implied that the debt must be funded, or repaid soon, out of the GDP itself. However, any significant increase in world interest rates would immediately raise the invisible debit component of the balance of payments. This is perhaps a more relevant risk factor than the traditional concerns about primary product export dependence, which are largely confined to history. Indeed, the servicing ratios of Australia's foreign debt seemed quite manageable at mid-2011, with net interest payments being around 9% of export revenue, net (foreign debt) interest payments representing 1.9% of GDP and net (overseas) income payments being just 3.5% of GDP. In each case these ratios were at low values by historical standards, undoubtedly reflecting, and relying upon, the continuance of low global interest rates.

Exchange Rates

Given the structural changes detailed above in relation to trade and other international economic dealings and the enhanced role for the exchange rate mechanism, it is not surprising that significant movements in exchange rates involving the Australian dollar have taken place. From around 1980 to 2002 the tendency was for a long-term decline of the Australian dollar in the cross rates associated with almost every major currency. In the period from 31 May 1980 to 31 July 2002 the Australian dollar decreased in value by 39% on a trade-weighted basis against other currencies, including a depreciation of 53% against the US dollar, 76% against the Japanese yen and 23% against the pound sterling. In September 2001 the Australian dollar reached a low point of just over 47 US cents, from which it had recovered to 66 US cents by July 2003. Thereafter, a strong recovery raised the Australian dollar to 80 US cents in February 2004 before the value of the Australian currency declined to around 70 US cents in mid-2004. There was some recovery during the latter part of that year, and in the period from October 2005 to June 2006 the rate traded in the range of 73–76 US cents. From late 2006 the rate strengthened further, at first on the basis of weakness of the US dollar against other currencies, and then with the momentum of positive expectations about the Australian economy as the US and European economies weakened from 2007. By June 2008 the cross rate was around 96 US cents to the Australian dollar. Despite the significant weakness of the US economy, the cross rate subsequently declined from 96 US cents in July 2008 to around 70 US cents in November 2008, before recovering to 81 US cents in June 2009. In February 2010 the rate stood close to 97 US cents again, before declining to 81 cents in May. At the end of June 2010 the rate stood at 85 US cents. In subsequent months most cross rates with the Australian dollar decreased markedly, thus taking the Australian currency past parity with the US dollar. At June 2011 the cross rate was US $1.06. The sterling rate had risen from just over 40 pence to 64 pence in about three years. These substantial movements require fuller explanation.

From 1949 to 1967 the Australian dollar was fixed to the pound sterling and followed the IMF practice of maintaining fixed rates in the absence of a 'fundamental disequilibrium' in the balance of payments. That rule was tested many times, in both directions, including a strong surplus position in 1972 that moved quickly into deficit in 1974. From 1977 a managed float achieved some flexibility, until the Hawke Government in December 1983 adopted the free float. Significant currency depreciation took place from January 1985. It is not credible to argue that the floating dollar 'caused' the pronounced long-term decline in the value of the Australian dollar. It is arguable that the adjustments would have taken place under any exchange rate system, and that under the free-float arrangements they have been smoother than otherwise and form part of a much better-managed Australian economy. The Howard and Rudd Governments were resolute in following the Hawke Government's free-float initiative of 1983. The fluctuations noted above are the result.

ECONOMIC DEVELOPMENT AND GOVERNMENT POLICY

Labour Market Trends

At May 2011 the Australian labour force (available for work but not necessarily in employment) totalled 12,016,600 persons, just over one-half of the Australian total population. Of these workers and potential workers, 11,428,800 were employed, 3,440,300 (or 30.1%) of these on a part-time basis. Within the total employment, there were 6,229,400 men and 5,196,400 women. However, males formed 65.1% of full-time workers, but only 30.0% of part-time workers. The unemployment rate had in the late 1990s been in the range of 7%–9%, although in the 1960s it was seldom above 2%. In late 1992 the rate reached a post-war peak of 10.7%.The unemployment rate, which in mid-2006 declined to below 5% for the first time in many years, had decreased in almost every month since mid-2001, when it was near 7.0%, until the trend was reversed in September 2008. By May 2007 the rate of unemployment had reached a 30-year low point of 4.2%, where it remained for a further full year, following which it rose, more slowly than in most other Western-style economies, to reach 5.7% at May 2009, the height of the global financial crisis. Many analysts were surprised that from this point the Australian unemployment rate did not rise, in contrast to most other Western economies that were suffering the effects of the international crisis. In fact, the rate remained at 4.9% in May 2011. Predictably, as has been evident in many countries, the unemployment rates of more fully qualified workers are demonstrably lower than for those less qualified or less experienced. In Australia in mid-2011 the rate among those with at least a first university degree was 1.9%, compared with 9.9% for those who had not completed Year 12 of their schooling. The labour force comprised 65.1% of the total Australian population at May 2011. This work-force participation rate has, as in many countries, grown markedly since the 1960s, especially with the increasing propensity of women, particularly married women, to work outside the home.

Economic Management

The Australian experience provides a useful case study for debates about the merits of short-term policy intervention to manage the economy. The country's history contains some classic mistakes of policy where demand management actually intensified cyclical economic fluctuations, as in 1961, when boom-curbing tax increases and monetary restraints deepened the recession that was already in train. More recently, problems in interpreting the movements in the economy and the delayed effects of monetary policy already initiated caused cyclical intensification at the end of the 1980s. Since that time, the demand management record has tended to support the view that active short-term policy intervention can be beneficial. The experience from July 2008 tended to silence the critics of 'fine-tuning' as stimulus programmes were introduced around the world from the latter part of 2008 with relatively little objection from classical economists, most of whom had tended in the period 1970–2007 to deride such measures. The short-term experience in Australia during this first year of the global financial crisis tended to favour such 'fine-tuning', as supported then by heterodox economists alone. Looking globally, it is difficult to identify any economy that did not adopt some form of stimulus 'package' of government deficit-increasing measures and then benefit from it. It is also difficult to find any generally adopted economics textbook in tertiary education courses that actually supports such measures. The obvious warning that conventionally trained economists are likely again to mislead is pertinent, but beyond the realm of this essay.

The economy-wide management performance of the Rudd Government of 2007–10 was thus exemplary. The administration took clear and deliberate actions, as described above, despite being a new Government and having been in opposition for more than a decade; its bold intervention policies assisted without doubt in avoiding a recession. It will be a challenging exercise in applied political economy to explain why a Government that started so well and had the advantage of a strong economy from 2010 developed approaches to industry-specific and longer-term economic policy, especially tax, mining industry and environmental policy, that reflected quite obversely a number of imperfectly considered strategies.

By the year 2009/10 annual economic growth in Australia since 1992 had averaged 3.3%. Few Western nations had experienced faster economic growth, although both India and China had achieved annual average growth rates that were more than double those recorded by Australia. During that time span quarterly real GDP growth rates had been negative on only two occasions: September 1993 and December 2000. At mid-2010 Australia had already been recession-free for about 19 years. No other period of its history boasted this record of unbroken economic growth. No other Western nation was recession-free in the period from July 2008 to June 2010. None the less, during the decade to June 2011 there remained pressures and tensions, arising from continued (or resumed) drought, other natural disasters at home and abroad, the delayed effects of international conflict and SARS, which presented challenges for both the economy and policy-makers.

The resumption of greater confidence from mid-2004 was assisted by the ending of the SARS concerns and of the initial conflict in Iraq, by the relatively subdued level of industrial-relations discord and by strong economic leadership by an increasingly politically dominant Commonwealth Government. It was necessary, in the view of the monetary authorities, to restrain the housing market; hence 12 separate small increases in official cash interest rates were pronounced between December 2001, when the previous rate reduction had been made, and mid-2008, leaving the Reserve Bank of Australia's cash rate at 7.25% at June 2008. It could be argued that the combination of controlled and predicted budget surpluses and timely small adjustments in interest rates worked well for the macroeconomic policy officials, keeping the short-term movements in real economic activity within tolerable bounds. Between July 2008 and June 2009, as a reaction to the onset of the global financial crisis, Australian monetary authorities joined those of almost every Western economy in reducing interest rates: over this period official cash rates in Australia decreased from 7.25% to 3.0%. Thereafter, Australia acted in advance of other Western-style economies, effecting no fewer than five interest rate increases between September 2009 and June 2010. Two further rates rises had been announced by December 2010, and more were anticipated in 2011. In the six months to June 2011, however, no further rate rises or decreases were announced by the central bank.

Australia recorded high inflation rates in the 1970s, both in relation to its own past and in comparison with most other Western-style economies. Wage surges, including movements to correct huge gender-based pay discrepancies, the sensitivity to world oil prices and currency depreciation can be cited as the main causative factors. Between 1996 and the March quarter of 2009, the general index of consumer prices (CPI) rose from

100 to 159, using 1996 as a base set to 100 index points. This inflation experience compares poorly with most other advanced nations, including analogous index data for Japan (100.3), Hong Kong (102.1), the United Kingdom (123.9), the USA (138.8) and even the euro zone (129.9), all in comparison to the same 1996 base value. The prices of individual products subject to technological change, such as household appliances (119) and communications (108), rose less quickly, while areas subject to tax and public policy intervention on pricing, such as alcohol and tobacco products (251) and education (283), rose most rapidly. Taking into account these latter categories, in which microeconomic policy requirements caused substantial price increases, the general rise in consumer prices from 1996 reflected significantly upon overall economic management. The compound average 2.7% annual average CPI increase was the result. These data also incorporated the exceptional 6.1% annual inflation rate of 2000/01 experienced with the fundamental policy switch both among and towards indirect taxes under the NTS. In the year to March 2009 the overall CPI rose by 2.5%, which was clearly similar to the underlying average inflation rate experienced throughout this period despite the global financial crisis. Within the inflation aggregate there are some variations in individual product components. The consumer cost of education rose by 5.0% in the year to March 2010, health services by 5.3% and housing by 1.9%, while alcohol and tobacco prices increased by 5.7%. Transport costs declined by 4.6%, and the prices of food, communications services, household furnishings, supplies and services increased by around 1.9%. In the same period clothing and footwear prices rose by only 2.1%. Such disparities in consumer product price movements are common in modern economies.

Underlying the lower inflation regime that had prevailed in Australia since 1990 was a commitment in policy manifesto and action to budgetary restraint that avoided the excesses of government witnessed in Australia in the 1970s. Formal budgetary targets were tried and removed in the 1970s and early 1980s. However, the commitment to fiscal discipline was reflected in policy pledges and speeches by the Treasurer and budget documents. When the Labor Government of Bob Hawke assumed office in 1983 it demonstrated a commitment to economic deregulation and financial liberalization, freer trade and budgetary responsibility. It also executed its undertakings. That tradition was continued by both political parties: the Labor administration until March 1996, the Liberal-National coalition until November 2007 and the Rudd Labor Government in the period immediately after its election in that month. The Howard Government, from March 1996, turned the headline (federal) budget deficit of $A5,001m. of 1995/96 into a surplus of $A22,100m. in 1999/2000. However, the net operating balances of all levels of government in Australia declined from $A14,365m. in 1999/2000 to $A3,264m. in 2000/01. The federal Government remained a net lender in 2000/01, allocating $A5,459m., while the states were new borrowers of $A2,350m. For the year ending in June 2008 Australia's underlying budget surplus was $A16,185m., despite significant 'tax cuts' in the five successive federal budgets from May 2004. These large and rising annual budget surpluses implied ongoing debt reduction from the public authorities and were a tribute to good economic management.

Prior to the federal election of October 2004, the Howard Government pressed ahead with income tax reductions and increased welfare support, thereby expending some of the substantial surplus. It was a sign of the extent of fiscal drag (the effect of inflation on government tax receipts) that personal income tax revenues continued to increase sharply despite these tax reductions. This feature of the Australian tax system is so pronounced that, even after these tax decreases, and further and equally substantial adjustments that were presented as reductions, there was little risk to revenue. In the 2009 budget, as in five previous years, further adjustments were made to the bracket limits on the Australian personal income tax scale and some of the marginal tax rates. It had been reassuring that both major political parties have been committed to strong and disciplined economic management. This was realized in the first federal budget of the Rudd administration in May 2008, with the underlying surplus for 2008/09 projected to rise to more than $A22,000m. Unfortunately, the outcome was very different from this projection because of the direct and world-wide effects of the global financial crisis.

The erosion of tax revenue, especially from companies, significantly damaged the basis of the federal budgets. In three separate revisions of budget figures between May 2008 and May 2009 the Rudd Government gradually revealed that the strong surplus had been eroded and that a budget deficit of significant proportions had emerged. From the perspective of mid-2009, it became evident that the Rudd Government's first budget in May 2008 was optimistic in raising the Howard administration's forward projections for corporate tax revenue by as much as 15%. This was the beginning of a new twist in economic management practices in Australia: the Government lost confidence in its own predictions and policies, and that loss of confidence began to extend to business and the Australian community. By late 2009 the first signs of political instability were in evidence.

In the May 2009 budget the tax revenue and budget balance projections mentioned above were revised sharply downwards, even to below the figures projected for tax revenues for the same future periods by the former Howard Government. For the fiscal year ending in June 2010, a budget that had been projected to yield a surplus of $A22,000m. was amended to a deficit of $A58,000m. While the Rudd Government introduced spending measures such as cash allocations to taxpayers, the revenue erosion contributed far more to the budget reversal than these spending initiatives. At mid-2010, therefore, with economic recovery already evident, there was the prospect of a Government having denied recession, taking steps to avoid it, then losing any confidence in those stimulus measures, propounding recession and reflecting it in budget figures, when all the relevant signs were that recession in Australia was going to be avoided. In addition, the same Government compounded these business uncertainties by introducing, in mid-2010, plans for resource-sector and environmental policies that had been poorly planned, created havoc and then did not eventuate.

In May 2009 the Rudd Government issued projections that federal budgets would not return to surplus for a further five years, causing widespread concern about the emerging debt to be financed in those years. The projections were predicated on almost no economic growth in Australia in the financial year 2009/10 and only moderate recovery in 2010/11. Some conventional Australian economists reacted by pronouncing these gloomy projections to be unduly optimistic, predicting even deeper deficits and higher debt scenarios. In 2008/09 this writer publicly criticized the pessimists, who were reformed optimists who had seen no prospect of a global financial crisis, and offered a different outlook: that the recovery in equity prices from February 2009, the stimulus measures, lower interest rates and a return to greater confidence would foster significant economic recovery in 2009/10 and beyond. Under this alternative, more optimistic scenario, interest rates would rise in 2009/10, not decline, and budgets would return to surplus within three years.

In mid-2009 active debate continued on these issues, with a further challenge ahead for the Rudd Government: if the optimistic scenario was correct, stimulus programmes would need to be adjusted to avoid inflationary pressures. In June 2009, with the US debt funding having forced longer-term bond rates to double from 2% to 4% since January 2009, banks in Australia started to raise their longer-term fixed rate loan rates, showing again the global connectedness of financial markets in driving events that had no apparent domestic cause. This was the first sign of rising interest rates that only a minority of observers had been predicting for the latter part of 2009; it raised further questions about whether businesses and governments in Australia were really ready for the recovery. It was into this environment that the Rudd Government introduced more and poorly considered detail in relation to its otherwise plausible carbon emissions trading scheme. The management of this proposal, and later of plans for the introduction of a super-profit tax for the resources sector, defied belief, caused businesses to lose confidence in the capacity of the Rudd Government to manage any aspect of the economy, and, after mining projects were cancelled or deferred, ultimately led to the end of the administration itself.

With the termination of Rudd's commission as Prime Minister in mid-2010, there followed a period of intensified political instability. Besides allegations of foul play within the Government, there was an inconclusive result at the federal election in August and a general belief that a minority Government would not last for very long, forcing yet another election. By late 2010, however, the feared adverse outcomes had not eventuated, and the Gillard Government showed strength.

The early months of 2011 did not help business confidence or the electoral position of the Gillard Government: natural disasters in New Zealand and in Japan were accompanied by floods in Queensland and Victoria, the main direct manifestions being the cessation of tourism and mining operations in those states. The negative real national income growth for the first quarter of 2011 was in some senses an aberration unlikely to be repeated; but it also reflected a sharp decline in business confidence as the Gillard Government reintroduced most of the controversial policies that had caused it political damage in 2010.

During the whole of the phase that followed the global financial crisis, the Reserve Bank of Australia continued to pursue its mandate of protection against inflation, raising interest rates six times when most other nations left such rates unchanged. Having failed to see the prospect of any interest rate increases in the period 2008/09, most market-based forecasters predicted that at least one or two interest rate rises would take place in the calendar year 2011, as seen from the perspective of late 2010. Once again, the market forecasters' track record was seriously damaged: no further rate rises had occurred by the end of June 2011. It is a fair reflection that the monetary side of economic policy management performed better than the fiscal side from 2009 to mid-2011. Indeed, the government-based planners of budgets came in for sharp criticism for their misreading of the Australian economy, after correctly placing the stimulus programmes in 2008. However, the May 2011 budget was based on realistic premises and played its part in helping the second quarter of economic activity to reverse the unexpected negative result of the first.

Competition Policy Reform

In the circumstances of the global financial crisis, long-term policies and issues concerning the structure of institutions, environmental intervention, tax reform and industry policy tend to be overlooked, and any debates on these issues receive little attention. In the period 1985–2008 Australia had introduced significant changes to its personal income tax and company tax systems. However, there were political pressures, from consumer groups and smaller business organizations especially, for major amendments also to be made to the Trade Practices Act (TPA), the principal organ of competition policy. In April 2003 the Australian Government released both the Dawson Committee report into the operation of the TPA and its own response. Both statements proposed that no major changes should be made to appease smaller businesses by creating uncertainty in the application of competition law. The existing form of the TPA had been in operation since 1974 and was modelled more on the US approach of court-based litigation than on the British system of investigation and examination in a more neutral setting. There are limited exemptions for any specific entity or trade practice, although immunity through authorization is available for potentially illegal agreements between corporations on the grounds of public interest justification. The central provisions are subject to an economic-based test of 'substantial lessening of competition in a market for goods and services', and this is the principal test for assessing proposed mergers and horizontal and vertical arrangements. Among the per se offences not subject to a test of competition as such, the Act contains strictures against misleading consumers and price fixing. These provisions have been clarified by case law and by clear legal drafting. One further area of per se offence concerns corporations that abuse their 'market power' by taking advantage thereof for the purpose of damaging competitors, preventing entry or deterring competitive behaviour. It was this section of the TPA that generated most controversy and prompted some agitation for it to be strengthened.

By mid-2003 a further parliamentary process had begun, under some political pressure, to determine whether the TPA was operating to the disadvantage of smaller businesses. After some delays and intense political and lobbying activity, some minor changes in merger evaluation procedures were proposed in legislation introduced by the Howard Government in June 2004. However, it was that Government's decision not to accept smaller business proposals for more aggressive regulation of larger companies. In early 2008 the Rudd Government endorsed some important amendments to the 'abuse of market power' section of the TPA, supposed to help smaller businesses. Similarly, the Rudd administration's introduction in 2010 of legislation against cartels and so-called creeping acquisitions (the gradual acquisition of a number of individual assets or businesses that may collectively raise competition concerns, but which individually were unlikely to contravene the TPA) caused considerable controversy. The main effect was to damage the internal consistency of the legislation and to cause confusion for practitioners. There is some history of new governments in Australia being moved to make changes that might better be the subject of fuller contemplation. One example was the Howard Government's swift reduction, in its first budget in 1996, of tax support for research and development.

During the financial year 2010/11 the competition regulator had cause to reflect upon a court case in which it did not succeed, reacting by proposing new laws to curtail 'price signalling'. The general policy intention is to restrain or prohibit practices of larger companies seeking to coerce rival firms to follow their proposed price movements by communicating or sending price lists, or otherwise seeking to gain concurrence. In the early 1980s it was accepted that no such coercion is proved in law without direct evidence, which if found leads to punitive consequences for the offending corporation. E-mail established that without such evidence, firms may simply be following market movements. The new proposed price signalling laws appeared to be encouraged by the Gillard Government at mid-2011, but had not been proclaimed, adding further instability to the business decision-making environment.

Tax Reform and Tax Trends

There are distinctive features of both the Australian taxation system and the process that has led to its current structure and administration. The Australian Taxation Office administers the system, collects the dominating federal taxes and handles rulings, objections and appeals. Massive legislation and case law supports the system, especially in relation to income and deductions definitions applying to persons and companies. Controversial areas also include international company transfer pricing, fringe benefits (for which a special tax exists) and anti-avoidance provisions.

With overall (federal, state and local) taxes comprising just under 30% of its GDP at June 2011 and for several years previously, Australia is one of the least-taxed countries among the members of the Organisation for Economic Co-operation and Development. With nearly 60% of the federal taxes collected coming from taxes on personal income alone, few other countries have tax jurisdictions that rely so prominently on any one tax type or tax base. This is despite the introduction in July 2000 of a value-added tax, the goods and services tax (GST), at the general rate of 10%. The personal income tax rate schedule is also steeply progressive, with high marginal tax rates applying at relatively low taxable incomes. The highest marginal tax rate from July 2006 was set at 47.5%. For the tax year 2004/05 the top marginal rate applied to taxable incomes at or above $A70,000 (or around US $54,000, using exchange rates that applied typically during the fiscal year 2004/05). In the Australian annual federal budget of May 2003 an unexpected but minor revision in income-tax bracket limits (taxable income values at which the four main marginal tax rates commence) was announced. This policy initiative was presented to the electorate as a 'tax cut'. However, it was in effect the first adjustment in the Australian personal income tax system since the introduction of the NTS in July 2000. The May 2003 initiative amounted to delivering only about one-third of the tax relief which automatic inflation-based indexation of these taxable income bracket limits would have provided. The 'surprise' was that there was no apparent political need for this measure, even though regular indexation of the bracket limits is technically justified as a standing policy measure.

In the May 2004 federal budget more substantial changes were made to the personal tax rate structure. These were achieved entirely by changing the income levels (brackets) at which the relatively high marginal tax rates applied. The adjustments were also confined to the upper end of the scale, and thus to the benefit of higher-income earners. In compensation, lower-income earners were offered welfare concessions. In some ways, the Howard Government was able in this budget to achieve the type of tax restructuring it sought (and could not achieve) with the introduction of the NTS. The tax rate changes made in the May 2005 budget applied throughout the range of incomes, with the standard marginal tax rate being reduced from 17% to 15% and the income boundary at which the top marginal tax rate applied being shifted from $A70,000 to $A95,000 from July 2005 and then raised again sharply, to $A125,000 and then to $A180,000 by July 2008, as approved by the Rudd Government. Despite the global financial crisis, the Australian Government continued with minor tax changes introduced in its first federal budget in 2008, amounting to reductions in personal tax in nominal but not real (price-corrected) terms. In many ways these changes are similar to those that the Howard Government sought with the introduction of the NTS programme in 2000. Further changes made in the May budgets of 2006–10 gave the appearance of tax reductions, but a proportion of the apparent concession effectively restored some of the fiscal drag arising from the interaction of rising nominal taxable personal incomes in Australia and the steeply progressive personal tax rate structure.

In a break from recent tradition, the Gillard Government made no attempt to present tax changes as tax reductions in its first budget of May 2011; indeed, it raised some tax rates as a special floods tax. Reflecting the tradition established under the Hawke Government in the 1980s, Gillard and Treasurer Wayne Swan delivered a responsible and even conservative budget that won considerable support, not least because of its prominent objective of seeking to return the budget to surplus, but at a future time reflecting balance in its approach. One side-effect was the deferral of nearly all tax reforms proposed in the Henry process, which remained unadopted at mid-2011. In Australia high rates of excise taxes are levied on alcoholic drinks (with wine treated much more lightly). High excise rates also apply to petroleum products, tobacco and cigarettes. Nevertheless, the excise component of petroleum products is considerably lower than the tax component of motor fuels prevailing in most European countries—the Australian motorist pays less than one-half of the petrol-pump prices found in most of Europe. There is no excise tax on wine, although a specific wine tax to take the place of a former wholesale sales tax has operated since July 2000. The broadly based GST applies widely to all purchases, with zero-rating (called in Australia 'GST-free') treatment awarded to food and exports and exemption ('input-taxed' is the Australian term) given for financial transactions and rent. With effect from July 2002 companies were taxed at a standard rate on company profits of 30.0%, with allowances (tax imputation method) in dividend distributions to tax-paying persons for tax already paid by companies. State governments rely on transfers from federal authorities for at least one-half of their revenues. Thus, there existed considerable vertical fiscal imbalance: the federal authority raising far more revenue than it requires for its own expenditures, the states being dependent on the intergovernmental transfers, supplementing them with taxes on share and land transactions and on gambling. Local authorities levy rates related to property values.

This description of the Australian tax system as at mid-2011 does not reveal the controversies and dynamic aspects of tax reform that lay behind the system. Some seven separate rounds of tax reform debates and proposals commenced in 1960 and carried through to 1993. They predated the introduction of the NTS, which involved as its centrepiece the GST. The NTS was implemented by the federal Government of John Howard from July 2000. It was accompanied by significant 'price exploitation provisions' to limit price increases, despite which Australia's annual inflation rate increased sharply, from an underlying rate of 2.3% in June 2000 to 6.1% in the year following its introduction. The price exploitation provisions involved price monitoring, heavy fines and public exposure for companies breaching the guidelines. These provisions ended in June 2002.

Prominent politicians of each major political party had previously promoted the structural shift towards GST or its equivalent, in all cases without success until the Howard initiative put the issue to the federal electorate in October 1998. Economists generally supported the reform proposals. Underlying them was a wartime initiative in 1942 to pass control of income tax 'as a temporary measure' from the states to the Commonwealth. These powers have not since been returned. In the mean time, the steeply progressive personal tax structure adopted and developed in the high inflation years of the 1950s meant that by the 1970s relatively low-income persons were incurring marginal tax rates designed many years previously for high-income persons. Opponents in each round of reform proposals objected to the administrative burdens resulting from any change on businesses, to the adverse effects of GST-type taxes on low-income households (despite proposals of generous compensation measures at each stage), and to the repercussions for inflation levels and for industry. Even when the Howard Government was returned to office at the 1998 election, with the issue of GST dominating the debates and differences between the parties, political difficulties required it to make many concessions and in several ways to increase the administrative complexity of the system. In the period since the November 2001 election there has been no serious proposal to change the essential structure of the Australian taxation system.

The NTS itself, applying in two stages from July 1999, but mainly from July 2000, involved repealing other indirect taxes, notably a wholesale sales tax that applied at rates of up to 30% on manufactured goods alone. The NTS thus caused prices in general, but especially of services, to rise at rates well above the pre-NTS annual inflation rate of around 2.3%, while some manufactured goods experienced price reductions, for example motor vehicles and jewellery. The short-term dynamics of effecting these changes caused disruption, especially in housing and vehicle sales. One curiosity of the NTS is that the federal Government that created it does not classify any GST revenue as its own. Instead, it collects GST as an 'agency function', passing the proceeds to the states in compensation for the loss of some of their fiscal transfer supports. Students of tax and government trends in Australia thus need to be careful in drawing inferences from the downward trend in the ratio of federal taxes and outlays to GDP from the fiscal year 2000/01 onwards. In the financial year 2005/06 collection of GST revenue by the federal Australian Government for and on behalf of the Australian states amounted to about $A42,200m. This is the agency-function sum that the federal Government did not absorb into its revenue estimates until the Rudd Government in its 2008 and 2009 budgets explicitly recorded it alongside other federal revenues and reworked past data for GST inclusion. During 2006 and 2007 further pressures had emerged, from both within and outside the Howard Government, for more action with regard to tax reform, owing to the realization that the tax changes that had been made since 2000 did not amount to any significant reform of the tax system itself. During the campaign for the 2007 general election, the Labor Party committed itself to tax reform; having taken office, it announced a process of tax reform under the guidance of the Secretary to the Treasury, the economist Ken Henry. The Government sought to limit any discussion of the rates and base definition of GST (where it had previously attempted to prevent the introduction of the GST system and the superannuation arrangements for older workers and retirees). In June 2009 a leading large-business lobby group pressed its case within the Henry review for the company tax rate to be halved, from 30% of company profits to 15%, with a revenue-preserving increase in GST rates. The Rudd Government swiftly and vigorously rejected this suggestion, reaffirming that the definition and rates of GST in Australia were not debatable. There remained many other tax issues to be debated during 2009, including the treatment of trusts as companies, the individual or family bases of personal tax, the issue of whether deductions perform any useful purpose, international aspects of tax (especially transfer pricing), environmentally based taxes, the taxation of superannuation funds and the tax treatment of fund contributions and, above all, the huge difficulties for tax collection posed by developing electronic commerce.

In addition to the efforts to change the longer-term structure of the tax system, there remain short-term economic management tensions reflected in annual budgets and other fiscal policies. The date for the delivery of the federal budget and most state budgets has settled on May, the convention until the mid-1990s having been for budgets to be announced in August. After the experience of fiscal neglect in the mid-1970s, during which government outlays rose by 46% in one year alone (in 1974/75), successive Australian Governments have shown disciplined commitment to fiscal responsibility. For a number of years, up to mid-2008, the federal budget surplus remained at around 1% of GDP, despite varying economic conditions and several tax policy adjustments, as detailed above. Interestingly, the tax share of GDP was 24.3% when the Howard Government took office in March 1996 and, despite various claims of tax reform and tax reductions, when the Rudd Government came to power in late 2007, the contribution of tax receipts to GDP remained at exactly 24.3% of GDP. The working assumption of most technical analysts and economists at mid-2011 was that there was no prospect of major change in the relative importance of government outlays and tax revenue, despite ongoing debate about whether those shares should be raised or lowered.

The Henry report relating to taxation reform was delivered to the Rudd Government in December 2009. Without any apparent consultation with independent experts or industry sectors likely to be affected by changes proposed or adopted, the Rudd administration delayed the release of the report, and its response to it, until May 2010. This delay, and the official response to the review, provoked widespread criticism, which either coincided with or caused the Prime Minister's removal from office less than two months after the release of the report, as detailed previously in this essay.

FUTURE CHALLENGES

The challenges for the main decision-makers in the Australian economy are a combination of issues that confront most advanced economies and some challenges that are specific to the country's economic structures and its own particular legal and political environment. Foremost is the need to continue economic growth, avoiding any recurrence of recession or unacceptable inflationary pressures, especially in view of the recent adverse developments in world oil markets and in the economy of the USA. In some ways, the real economy moves disparately from the financial sector, although profit expectations, which drive financial values, cannot for long be separated from the position and prospects in real terms of underlying economic activity. This point was emphasized by the manner in which sharply declining equity prices pre-dated economic downturns in real aggregate demand in 2008. As in the USA, share price indices rose spectacularly in the late 1990s, at a time when the real economy grew only moderately. Between 31 December 1996 and 31 December 1999 the USA's Dow Jones industrial share price index rose by 78.3%. The ASX200, the Australian stock market price index, also rose substantially, but by the much more modest rate of 29.9%. Subsequently, and until March 2003, the US equity price index declined by 15%, while the Australian index rose slightly. In the period between March 2003 and March 2006 there were substantial signs of equity market price recoveries in both the USA and Australia, although these were not supported by a stronger US real economy until later in 2004. Since late 2006 the reality of, and the perceptions arising from, the US subprime lending developments have damaged confidence, profit expectations and thus share prices. A challenge is for policymakers in all countries to ensure that these are equilibrium corrections in financial markets and not the portents of sharp equity market declines from equilibrium values. There is little that rising domestic Australian interest rates can do to curtail the inflationary trend of rising world oil prices. As 2008 progressed, a debate also emerged in Australia on whether the budget remained too accommodating to inflation, despite the large surplus outcomes. In May 2009 it became evident that the Rudd administration's first budget had been predicated on overly optimistic economic conditions, which the Government only slowly and reluctantly admitted in the year to June 2009. Several mistakes had been made: denying the downturn in economic conditions and budget balance, and then over-reacting to it; adding significantly to former company tax revenue estimates in 2008, before drastically reducing the same estimates a year later. That was confirmed by the Rudd administration itself in its May 2010 budget addresses.

Without doubt, the fiscal and monetary authorities maintained a strong and stable policy leadership from about 1976 until mid-2011, which clearly supported the Australian position in 2002–03 as the leading nation among advanced countries in terms of economic growth. Equally, beyond the challenges for short-term economic management, there is a medium-term imperative for Australia to maintain the trend of national productivity growth at above 2% per year and closer to 3%. For long periods underlying productivity growth has fallen short of both expectations and that of other advanced countries. The higher rate of economic growth has been due to population (more accurately work-force) growth in a country that is one of the few in the world to experience a positive and significant net migration gain. Policy reversals in relation to science and technology have not assisted this objective of maintaining high rates of productivity growth. Even in the period from 1996 to 2010 uncertainties over the application of laws on property rights, research incentives and research tax supports have been destabilizing.The unfortunate manner in which the Government introduced insulation support schemes and proposals for carbon emissions trading, together with radical changes in mining taxation, compounded the difficulty unnecessarily.

Overall, Australia can claim to have exhibited an excellent comparative record of short-term economic management between 1984 and mid-2011. It has been documented through this essay that Australia was the only Western-style economy to have avoided technical recession between 2008 and 2011. The country has also achieved much calmer industrial relations (with radical reductions in working days lost through industrial disputes), a fuller adoption of market-based influences in the labour market, a more open and flexible economy, and much less reliance on exports of primary products. Australia has a modern economy that has embraced advanced IT. The country is arguably underpopulated from an economic viewpoint. However, as the above data and descriptions confirm, the image of Australia as little more than a primary-product exporter, with huge fluctuations in the external payments balances limiting its growth potential, is long outdated. In so far as political leadership is involved in addressing future challenges, by mid-2011 it had become apparent that, while the Labor leadership would be addressing such issues similarly, despite differences in political affiliation, there had been mistakes in interpreting the economic and fiscal outlook, in denying the downturn and then over-reacting to it. The biggest challenge at mid-2011 was not in avoiding recession, which Australia had succeeded in doing, but in managing longer-term economic policy development.

Statistical Survey

Source (unless otherwise stated): Australian Bureau of Statistics, POB 10, Belconnen, ACT 2616; tel. (2) 6252-7983; fax (2) 6251-6009; internet www.abs.gov.au.

Area and Population

AREA, POPULATION AND DENSITY

Area (sq km)	7,692,024*
Population (census results)†	
7 August 2001	18,769,249
8 August 2006	
Males	9,799,252
Females	10,056,036
Total	19,855,288
Population (official estimate at 31 December)‡	
2008	21,730,585
2009§	22,151,909
2010§	22,477,378
Density (per sq km) at 31 December 2010§	2.9

* 2,969,907 sq miles; including Jervis Bay Territory.
† Population is *de jure*.
‡ Including Jervis Bay Territory, Christmas Island and the Cocos (Keeling) Islands.
§ Preliminary.

POPULATION BY AGE AND SEX

(estimated population at 30 June 2010, preliminary)

	Males	Females	Total
0–14	2,170,273	2,059,932	4,230,205
15–64	7,570,198	7,520,377	15,090,575
65 and over	1,376,633	1,631,434	3,008,067
Total	11,117,104	11,211,743	22,328,847

STATES AND TERRITORIES

(estimated population at 31 December 2010, preliminary)

	Area (sq km)	Population	Density (per sq km)
New South Wales (NSW)	800,642	7,272,158	9.1
Victoria	227,416	5,585,566	24.6
Queensland	1,730,648	4,548,661	2.6
South Australia	983,482	1,650,377	1.7
Western Australia	2,529,875	2,317,064	0.9
Tasmania	68,401	509,292	7.4
Northern Territory	1,349,129	229,874	0.2
Australian Capital Territory (ACT)	2,358	361,914	153.5
Other territories*	73	2,472	—
Total	7,692,024	22,477,378	2.9

* Area refers to Jervis Bay Territory only, but population also includes data for Christmas Island and the Cocos (Keeling) Islands.

PRINCIPAL TOWNS

(estimated population at 30 June 2010, preliminary)*

Sydney (capital of NSW)	4,575,532	Wollongong	292,190
Melbourne (capital of Victoria)	4,077,036	Sunshine Coast	251,081
Brisbane (capital of Queensland)	2,043,185	Hobart (capital of Tasmania)	214,705
Perth (capital of W Australia)	1,696,065	Geelong	178,650
Adelaide (capital of S Australia)	1,203,186	Townsville	172,316
Gold Coast-Tweed	591,473	Cairns	150,920
Newcastle	546,788	Toowoomba	131,258
Canberra (national capital)	358,222	Darwin (capital of N Territory)	127,532

* Figures refer to metropolitan areas, each of which normally comprises a municipality and contiguous urban areas.

BIRTHS, MARRIAGES AND DEATHS*

	Registered live births		Registered marriages		Registered deaths	
	Number	Rate (per 1,000)	Number	Rate (per 1,000)	Number	Rate (per 1,000)
2002	250,988	12.8	105,435	5.4	133,707	6.7
2003	251,161	12.6	106,394	5.3	132,292	6.5
2004	254,246	12.6	110,958	5.5	132,508	6.3
2005	259,791	12.7	109,323	5.4	130,714	6.0
2006	265,949	12.8	114,222	5.5	133,739	6.0
2007	285,213	13.6	116,322	5.5	137,854	6.0
2008	296,621	13.8	118,756	5.5	143,946	6.1
2009	295,738	13.5	120,118	5.5	140,760	5.7

* Data are tabulated by year of registration rather than by year of occurrence.

Life expectancy (years at birth, WHO estimates): 82 (males 80; females 84) in 2009 (Source: WHO, *World Health Statistics*).

IMMIGRATION AND EMIGRATION

(year ending 30 June)*

	2007/08	2008/09	2009/10
Permanent immigrants	149,365	158,021	140,610
Permanent emigrants	76,923	81,018	86,277

* Figures refer to persons intending to settle in Australia, or Australian residents intending to settle abroad.

ECONOMICALLY ACTIVE POPULATION

(annual averages, '000 persons aged 15 years and over, excluding armed forces)

	2006	2007	2008
Agriculture, hunting and forestry	340.2	339.7	343.5
Fishing	10.1	11.4	11.2
Mining and quarrying	116.7	119.0	133.0
Manufacturing	1,074.3	1,092.2	1,102.1
Electricity, gas and water	85.3	86.2	98.5
Construction	914.4	946.3	987.0
Wholesale and retail trade; repair of motor vehicles, motorcycles and personal and household goods	1,785.3	1,823.4	1,847.1
Hotels and restaurants	667.0	704.4	708.3
Transport, storage and communications	641.2	678.6	695.6
Financial intermediation	387.1	407.1	401.5
Real estate, renting and business activities	1,279.6	1,291.8	1,326.3
Public administration and defence; compulsory social security	626.0	641.6	644.5
Education	741.7	771.0	807.5
Health and social work	1,078.1	1,097.6	1,129.6
Other community, social and personal service activities	470.7	500.1	502.5
Private households with employed persons	0.5	1.8	2.1
Total employed	10,218.3	10,512.3	10,740.5
Unemployed	517.7	487.5	470.9
Total labour force	10,736.0	10,999.8	11,211.4
Males	5,883.1	6,015.6	6,116.1
Females	4,852.9	4,984.1	5,095.3

Source: ILO.

Health and Welfare

KEY INDICATORS

Total fertility rate (children per woman, 2009)	1.8
Under-5 mortality rate (per 1,000 live births, 2009)	5
HIV/AIDS (% of persons aged 15–49, 2007)	0.2
Physicians (per 1,000 head, 2001)	2.5
Hospital beds (per 1,000 head, 2005)	4.0
Health expenditure (2008): US $ per head (PPP)	3,365
Health expenditure (2008): % of GDP	8.5
Health expenditure (2008): public (% of total)	65.4
Total carbon dioxide emissions ('000 metric tons, 2007)	373,739.0
Carbon dioxide emissions per head (metric tons, 2007)	17.7
Human Development Index (2010): ranking	2
Human Development Index (2010): value	0.937

For sources and definitions, see explanatory note on p. vi.

Agriculture

PRINCIPAL CROPS
('000 metric tons)

	2007	2008	2009
Wheat	13,569.4	21,420.2	21,656.0
Rice, paddy	163.0	190.0	270.0
Barley	7,160.2	7,996.5	8,098.0
Maize	239.9	387.0	375.7
Oats	1,502.3	1,160.0	1,244.0
Millet	36.0*	37.0*	38.0†
Sorghum	1,283.0	3,789.9	2,691.8
Triticale (wheat-rye hybrid)	450.0	362.8	545.0
Potatoes	1,212.0	1,400.2	1,178.5
Sugar cane	36,397.0	32,621.1	31,456.9
Beans, dry	28.6	30.0†	50.6
Broad beans, dry	138.0	217.0	192.0
Peas, dry	268.0	238.1	356.0
Chick-peas	313.0	442.5	445.0
Lentils	131.0	64.2	143.0
Lupins	661.9	708.0	614.0
Soybeans (Soya beans)	32.0	35.0	80.1
Sunflower seed	15.6	73.0	55.3
Rapeseed	1,214.0	1,844.2	1,910.0
Seed cotton	720.6	304.0	801.7*
Lettuce and chicory	271.3	168.7	164.5
Tomatoes	296.0	381.8	440.1
Cauliflower and broccoli	69.8	64.3	70.3
Pumpkins, squash and gourds	102.5	114.4	103.7
Onions, dry	246.5	254.4	283.8
Peas, green	34.0	39.3	19.2
Carrots and turnips	271.5	272.6	263.5
Watermelons	136.9	152.1	131.1
Cantaloupes and other melons	71.6	66.9	75.6
Bananas	213.2	207.1	270.4
Oranges	470.7	409.3	347.7
Tangerines, mandarins, clementines and satsumas	104.4	94.4	90.3
Apples	270.5	265.5	295.1
Pears	134.8	130.5	120.4
Peaches and nectarines	130.9	128.0†	117.2
Grapes	1,530.4	1,956.8	1,797.0
Pineapples	164.7	162.0†	157.7

* Unofficial figure.
† FAO estimate.

Aggregate production ('000 metric tons, may include official, semi-official or estimated data): Total cereals 24,427.8 in 2007, 35,368.5 in 2008, 34,943.4 in 2009; Total roots and tubers 1,261.1 in 2007, 1,438.6 in 2008, 1,220.9 in 2009; Total vegetables (incl. melons) 1,882.0 in 2007, 1,868.4 in 2008, 1,892.7 in 2009; Total fruits (excl. melons) 3,270.7 in 2007, 3,600.1 in 2008, 3,439.9 in 2009.

Source: FAO.

LIVESTOCK
('000 head at 30 June)

	2007	2008	2009
Horses	264.9	260.0*	256.4
Cattle	28,036.6	27,321.0	27,906.8
Pigs	2,604.7	2,411.5	2,301.7
Sheep	85,711.2	79,937.6	72,739.7
Goats*	3,000.0	3,000.0	3,200.0
Chickens	97,386	88,629	95,409
Ducks	906	1,200*	1,473
Turkeys	1,975	1,500*	1,203

* FAO estimate(s).

Source: FAO.

LIVESTOCK PRODUCTS
('000 metric tons)

	2007	2008	2009
Cattle meat	2,226.0	2,154.9	2,147.9
Sheep meat	684	694	658
Goat meat*	16.3	16.3	16.3
Pig meat	381.9	377.4	324.0
Horse meat*	25.5	25.8	25.8
Chicken meat	811.6	802.4	832.5
Duck meat*	11.4	11.3	11.7
Turkey meat*	36.4	50.8	52.7
Cows' milk	9,583	9,223	9,388
Hen eggs	161.7†	160.0*	159.3
Honey*	18.0	17.1	16.6
Wool, greasy	450.5	407.9	370.6

* FAO estimate(s).
† Unofficial figure.

Note: Figures for meat and milk refer to the 12 months ending 30 June of the year stated.

Source: FAO.

Forestry

ROUNDWOOD REMOVALS
('000 cubic metres, excl. bark)

	2007	2008	2009
Sawlogs, veneer logs and logs for sleepers	12,530	12,654	11,195
Pulpwood	13,815	14,908	13,549
Other industrial wood	738	648	560
Fuel wood	5,181	5,059	4,828
Total	32,264	33,269	30,132

Source: FAO.

SAWNWOOD PRODUCTION
('000 cubic metres, incl. railway sleepers)

	2007	2008	2009
Coniferous (softwood)	3,929	4,263	3,740
Broadleaved (hardwood)	1,135	1,109	990
Total	5,064	5,372	4,730

Source: FAO.

Fishing

('000 metric tons, live weight, year ending 30 June)

	2006/07	2007/08	2008/09
Capture	188.1	181.8	172.8
Blue grenadier	3.9	3.6	2.3
Clupeoids	33.0	33.6	31.5
Australian spiny lobster	8.7	9.0	7.6
Penaeus shrimps	9.2	10.2	10.0
Scallops	10.6	10.3	7.5
Aquaculture*	55.8	58.9	64.5
Atlantic salmon	25.3	25.7	29.6
Total catch*	243.9	240.7	237.3

* FAO estimates.

Note: Figures exclude aquatic plants ('000 metric tons, capture only): 2.2 in 2006/07; 1.9 in 2007/08; 1.9 in 2008/09 (FAO estimate). Also excluded are crocodiles, recorded by number rather than by weight. The number of estuarine crocodiles caught was: 21,314 in 2006/07; 28,626 in 2007/08; 26,990 in 2008/09. Also excluded are whales, recorded by number rather than weight. The number of Baleen whales caught was: 1 in 2006/07; 2 in 2007/08–2008/09. The number of toothed whales (incl. dolphins) caught was: 66 in 2006/07; 45 in 2007/08; 33 in 2008/09. Also excluded are pearl oyster shells (metric tons, estimates): 200 each year in 2006/07–2008/09.

Source: FAO.

Mining

(year ending 30 June, '000 metric tons, unless otherwise indicated)

	2007/08	2008/09	2009/10
Black coal	421,181	446,174	471,089
Brown coal*	66,000	68,000	69,000
Crude petroleum (million litres)	25,789	26,950	25,572
Natural gas (million cu metres)	39,283	41,499	43,767
Iron ore: gross weight*	324,693	353,163	423,393
Copper ore*†	863	890	819
Nickel ore*†	190	185	160
Bauxite: gross weight	63,463	64,055	67,810
Bauxite: alumina content	19,359	19,597	20,057
Lead ore*†	641	596	617
Zinc ore*†	1,571	1,411	1,362
Tin ore (metric tons)*†	1,631	4,045	19,829
Manganese ore (metallurgical): gross weight*	5,412	3,730	5,795
Ilmenite*	2,208	1,932	1,394
Leucoxene*	157	117	123
Rutile*	327	285	361
Zirconium concentrates*	562	485	408
Silver (metric tons)*†	1,867	1,764	1,809
Uranium (metric tons)†	10,114	10,311	7,156
Gold (metric tons)*†	230	218	240
Salt (unrefined)*†‡	11,243	11,311	11,745
Diamonds ('000 carats, unsorted)	16,528	15,169	11,138

* Estimated production.

† Figures refer to the metal content of ores and concentrates.

‡ Excludes production in Victoria.

Source: Australian Bureau of Agricultural and Resource Economics, *Australian Mineral Statistics* and *Australian Commodity Statistics*.

Industry

SELECTED PRODUCTS

(year ending 30 June, '000 metric tons, unless otherwise indicated)

	2007/08	2008/09	2009/10
Raw steel	8,151	5,568	6,886
Aluminium—unwrought*	1,964	1,974	1,920
Copper—unwrought*	444	499	395
Lead—unwrought*	203	213	189
Zinc—unwrought*	507	506	515
Automotive gasoline (million litres)	17,079	17,159	16,771
Fuel oil (million litres)	979	872	846
Diesel-automotive oil (million litres)	12,177	12,231	11,720
Aviation turbine fuel (million litres)	5,182	5,494	5,341

* Primary refined metal only.

Pig Iron ('000 metric tons): 6,765 in 2005/06.

Tin (unwrought, '000 metric tons): 321 in 2006/07.

Sources: mainly Australian Bureau of Agricultural and Resource Economics, *Australian Mineral Statistics*, *Australian Commodity Statistics* and *Energy in Australia*.

Finance

CURRENCY AND EXCHANGE RATES

Monetary Units

100 cents = 1 Australian dollar ($A).

Sterling, US Dollar and Euro Equivalents (31 May 2011)

£1 sterling = $A1.541;
US $1 = $A0.934;
€1 = $A1.343;
$A100 = £64.89 = US $107.09 = €74.45.

Average Exchange Rate (Australian dollars per US $)

2008	1.1922
2009	1.2822
2010	1.0902

COMMONWEALTH GOVERNMENT BUDGET

($A million, year ending 30 June)

Revenue	2009/10	2010/11*	2011/12*
Tax revenue	268,000	290,298	329,247
Income taxes	187,016	206,040	240,630
Individuals	122,820	136,330	150,890
Taxes on fringe benefits	3,523	3,670	3,760
Superannuation taxation	6,182	7,220	9,330
Companies	53,193	57,880	74,600
Petroleum resource rent tax	1,297	940	2,050
Sales taxes	47,800	49,400	51,900
Excise and customs	30,295	32,100	33,850
Excise duty revenue	24,547	26,060	26,330
Other taxes	2,889	2,758	2,867
Non-tax revenue	24,767	20,480	20,714
Total	292,767	310,779	349,961

Expenditure	2009/10	2010/11*	2011/12*
Defence	20,150	20,136	21,277
Education	34,889	32,555	29,938
Health	51,426	57,240	59,858
Social security and welfare	109,197	116,739	121,907
Other services	44,090	38,204	40,009
General purpose inter-governmental transactions	47,157	48,919	51,152
General public services	19,203	21,239	20,887
Public-debt interest	6,303	9,286	11,632
Total (incl. others)	339,239	350,803	365,817

* Budget estimates.

Source: Government of Australia.

OFFICIAL RESERVES
(US $ million at 31 December)

	2008	2009	2010
Gold (national valuation)	2,233	2,792	3,608
IMF special drawing rights	174	4,856	4,764
Reserve position in IMF	649	1,092	1,102
Foreign exchange	29,867	33,002	32,793
Total	32,923	41,742	42,267

Source: IMF, *International Financial Statistics*.

MONEY SUPPLY
($A million at 31 December)

	2008	2009	2010
Currency outside banks	45,063	46,056	47,907
Demand deposits at trading and savings banks	312,367	326,830	364,196
Total money (incl. others)	357,864	372,907	412,152

Source: IMF, *International Financial Statistics*.

COST OF LIVING
(Consumer Price Index*; base 2000 = 100)

	2006	2007	2008
Food	129.2	132.3	138.5
Clothing	98.9	99.8	100.0
Rent†	116.5	122.9	132.4
Electricity, gas and other fuels	129.4	135.4	148.2
All items (incl. others)	120.2	123.1	128.3

* Weighted average of eight capital cities.
† Including expenditure on maintenance and repairs of dwellings; excluding mortgage interest charges and including house purchase and utilities.

2009: Food 143.6; All items (incl. others) 130.7.

2010: Food 145.8; All items (incl. others) 134.4.

Source: ILO.

NATIONAL ACCOUNTS
($A million, current prices, year ending 30 June)

National Income and Product

	2007/08	2008/09	2009/10
Compensation of employees	583,565	604,463	617,382
Gross operating surplus	386,416	432,883	440,549
Gross mixed income	92,714	98,592	102,528
Total factor incomes	1,062,695	1,135,938	1,160,459
Taxes, less subsidies, on production and imports	123,045	119,303	123,807
Statistical discrepancy	—	—	403
GDP in market prices	1,185,740	1,255,241	1,284,670
Net primary incomes from abroad	–49,496	–45,406	–49,224
Statistical discrepancy	—	—	–403
Gross national income	1,136,244	1,209,835	1,235,042
Current taxes on income, wealth, etc.	1,788	1,485	1,188
Other current transfers (net)	–1,693	–2,480	–2,102
Gross disposable income	1,136,339	1,208,840	1,234,128

Expenditure on the Gross Domestic Product

	2007/08	2008/09	2009/10
Government final consumption expenditure	201,617	220,868	234,336
Private final consumption expenditure	656,187	672,036	697,943
Gross fixed capital formation	346,668	355,315	360,341
Change in inventories	6,120	–602	–748
Total domestic expenditure	1,210,592	1,247,617	1,291,872
Exports of goods and services	233,061	284,441	254,331
Less Imports of goods and services	257,913	276,819	259,482
Statistical discrepancy	—	—	–2,051
GDP in market prices	1,185,740	1,255,241	1,284,670

Gross Domestic Product by Economic Activity

	2007/08	2008/09	2009/10
Agriculture, hunting, forestry and fishing	26 700	27,721	27,358
Mining and quarrying	83 727	114,462	100,231
Manufacturing	110,497	109,403	111,654
Electricity, gas and water	24,681	25,286	25,340
Construction	84,734	90,087	94,237
Wholesale and retail trade	103,755	109,039	111,208
Hotels and restaurants	26,162	26,574	27,324
Transport, storage and communications	95,234	98,404	101,338
Finance and insurance	128,249	128,151	127,008
Rental, hiring and real estate services	33,758	33,370	32,668
Professional, scientific and technical services	68,533	75,097	86,988
Ownership of dwellings	79,734	91,795	100,718
Public administration and defence	57,350	61,437	62,602
Education	47,116	50,797	53,085
Health and community services	66,686	70,548	74,679
Cultural and recreational services	9,429	9,798	9,896
Administrative and support services	29,825	28,964	29,880
Personal and other services	19,630	20,968	21,567
Gross value added at basic prices	1,095,800	1,171,901	1,197,780
Taxes, less subsidies, on products	89,940	83,340	86,486
Statistical discrepancy	—	—	403
GDP in market prices	1,185,740	1,255,241	1,284,670

BALANCE OF PAYMENTS
(US $ million)

	2007	2008	2009
Exports of goods f.o.b.	142,421	189,057	154,788
Imports of goods f.o.b.	–160,205	–193,972	–159,195
Trade balance	–17,784	–4,915	–4,406
Exports of services	40,496	45,240	41,807
Imports of services	–39,908	–48,338	–42,108
Balance on goods and services	–17,196	–8,013	–4,707
Other income received	32,655	37,320	27,917
Other income paid	–73,202	–76,719	–65,965
Balance on goods, services and income	–57,743	–47,412	–42,755
Current transfers received	4,402	4,431	5,049
Current transfers paid	–4,690	–4,805	–6,129
Current balance	–58,032	–47,786	–43,836
Capital account (net)	1,632	1,994	–312
Direct investment abroad	–19,966	–38,110	–15,525
Direct investment from abroad	41,076	47,281	25,951
Portfolio investment assets	–77,304	3,035	–70,990
Portfolio investment liabilities	60,227	30,397	145,255
Financial derivatives assets	673	2,289	39,021
Financial derivatives liabilities	–13,931	–2,167	–45,407
Other investment assets	–11,107	–55,611	–27,455
Other investment liabilities	40,580	62,000	4,080
Net errors and omissions	1,004	370	–4,839
Overall balance	–35,148	3,692	5,943

Source: IMF, *International Financial Statistics*.

External Trade

PRINCIPAL COMMODITIES
(distribution by HS, US $ million)

Imports c.i.f.	2008	2009	2010
Mineral fuels, oils, distillation products, etc.	30,098	20,136	25,926
Crude petroleum oils	15,146	9,760	14,576
Petroleum oils, not crude	12,756	8,142	8,962
Pharmaceutical products	6,726	7,089	8,280
Pearls, precious stones, metals, coins, etc.	9,942	8,839	8,043
Gold, unwrought, or in semi-manufactured forms	8,252	7,286	6,330
Nuclear reactors, boilers, machinery, etc.	27,864	24,977	28,104
Automatic data processing machines; optical readers, etc.	4,933	4,429	5,862
Electrical, electronic equipment	19,032	17,754	20,265
Vehicles other than railway, tramway	22,979	16,471	24,028
Cars (incl. station wagons)	12,507	9,253	14,300
Trucks, motor vehicles for the transport of goods	5,317	3,392	5,352
Optical, photo, technical, medical, etc. apparatus	6,116	5,733	6,557
Total (incl. others)	191,584	158,941	188,741

Exports f.o.b.	2008	2009	2010
Meat and edible meat offal	5,986	5,141	5,958
Ores, slag and ash	35,264	31,195	55,840
Iron ores and concentrates; including roasted iron pyrites	25,379	23,573	44,290
Mineral fuels, oils, distillation products, etc.	59,868	45,372	59,753
Coal; briquettes, ovoids and similar solid fuels manufactured from coal	39,253	30,942	38,572
Crude petroleum oils	8,709	5,629	9,385
Petroleum gases	8,783	6,771	9,452
Inorganic chemicals, precious metal compounds, isotopes	5,910	4,064	5,067
Aluminium oxide (incl. artificial corundum); aluminium hydroxide	5,373	3,732	4,687
Pearls, precious stones, metals, coins, etc.	12,965	12,667	13,909
Gold, unwrought, or in semi-manufactured forms	12,030	11,760	12,816
Aluminium and articles thereof	5,221	3,465	4,367
Unwrought aluminium	4,415	2,881	3,750
Nuclear reactors, boilers, machinery, etc.	5,019	4,233	5,044
Total (incl. others)	186,853	153,767	206,705

Source: Trade Map-Trade Competitiveness Map, International Trade Centre, www.intracen.org/marketanalysis.

PRINCIPAL TRADING PARTNERS
(US $ million)

Imports c.i.f.	2008	2009	2010
Canada	2,203	1,478	1,561
China, People's Republic	29,896	28,351	35,261
France	4,241	3,239	3,434
Germany	9,624	8,411	9,424
India	1,553	1,609	1,767
Indonesia	4,449	3,612	4,773
Ireland	1,895	1,852	2,075
Italy	4,523	3,873	4,395
Japan	17,155	13,223	16,327
Korea, Republic	5,450	5,252	6,416
Malaysia	7,595	5,985	8,196
New Zealand	6,447	5,201	6,469
Papua New Guinea	2,478	2,313	2,711
Singapore	13,721	8,853	9,597
Sweden	2,204	1,698	1,967
Switzerland	1,920	1,952	1,978
Taiwan	3,746	2,633	3,252
Thailand	8,608	9,213	9,887
United Arab Emirates	1,964	1,701	2,003
United Kingdom	8,441	4,908	5,213
USA	23,014	18,005	20,947
Viet Nam	4,399	2,471	2,808
Total (incl. others)	191,584	158,941	188,741

Exports f.o.b.	2008	2009	2010
China, People's Republic	27,225	33,360	52,314
Hong Kong	2,528	2,255	2,824
India	11,380	11,354	14,694
Indonesia	3,587	3,247	4,021
Japan	42,732	29,988	39,137
Korea, Republic	15,486	12,271	18,329
Malaysia	3,362	2,455	3,263
Netherlands	3,051	1,580	2,343
New Zealand	7,867	6,216	7,179
Saudi Arabia	2,099	1,353	1,404
Singapore	5,154	4,199	4,331
South Africa	2,061	1,174	1,615
Taiwan	6,947	5,089	7,501
Thailand	4,489	3,323	5,250
United Arab Emirates	3,291	1,649	1,913
United Kingdom	7,844	7,071	7,456
USA	10,184	7,461	8,232
Total (incl. others)	186,853	153,767	206,705

Source: Trade Map-Trade Competitiveness Map, International Trade Centre, www.intracen.org/marketanalysis.

Transport

RAILWAYS
(traffic)*

	1997/98	1998/99	1999/2000
Passengers carried (million)	587.7	595.2	629.2
Freight carried (millon metric tons)	487.5	492.0	508.0
Freight ton-km ('000 million)	125.2	127.4	134.2

* Traffic on government railways only.

Passengers carried (million): 610 in 2003/04; 616 in 2004/05.

Freight carried (million metric tons): 557.3 in 2001/02; 589.1 in 2002/03.

Freight ton-km ('000 million): 150.7 in 2001/02; 161.8 in 2002/03.

ROAD TRAFFIC
('000 vehicles registered at 31 March)

	2008	2009	2010
Passenger vehicles	11,804	12,023	12,269
Light commercial vehicles	2,288	2,371	2,461
Trucks*	557	572	585
Buses	81	84	86
Motorcycles	568	624	660

* Including camper vans, previously classified as passenger vehicles.

SHIPPING

Merchant Fleet
(registered at 31 December)

	2007	2008	2009
Number of vessels	696	693	719
Total displacement ('000 grt)	1,911.2	1,828.2	1,836.5

Source: IHS Fairplay, *World Fleet Statistics*.

International Sea-borne Traffic
('000 metric tons, year ending 30 June)

	2000/01	2001/02	2002/03
Goods loaded	496,204	506,317	540,570
Goods unloaded	54,579	58,041	62,459

CIVIL AVIATION
(traffic)*

	2006	2007	2008
International services ('000):			
Passenger arrivals	10,835.7	n.a.	11,881.1
Passenger departures	10,644.3	n.a.	11,584.1
Domestic services:			
Passengers carried ('000)	43,674	46,745	49,857
Passenger-km (million)	46,933	50,315	54,132

* Includes estimates for regional airline data.

1999 (metric tons): International freight carried 680,458; International mail carried 25,316; Domestic freight and mail carried 192,326.

Tourism

VISITOR ARRIVALS BY COUNTRY OF ORIGIN
('000)*

	2006	2007	2008
Canada	109.7	114.6	124.6
China, People's Republic	308.5	357.6	356.4
Germany	148.3	151.6	160.7
Hong Kong	154.6	147.0	144.0
Japan	651.0	573.0	457.3
Korea, Republic	260.8	253.3	218.3
Malaysia	150.3	159.4	171.0
New Zealand	1,075.8	1,138.0	1,113.3
Singapore	253.4	263.8	270.9
Taiwan	93.8	92.7	77.6
United Kingdom	732.6	687.7	670.9
USA	456.1	459.7	454.4
Total (incl. others)	5,532.4	5,644.1	5,585.8

* Visitors intending to stay for less than one year.

Receipts from tourism (US $ million, excl. passenger transport): 22,308 in 2007; 24,756 in 2008; 25,594 in 2009 (provisional).

Source: World Tourism Organization.

Communications Media

	2008	2009	2010
Telephones ('000 main lines in use)	9,370	9,020	8,660
Mobile cellular telephones ('000 subscribers)	22,120	22,200	22,500
Internet subscribers ('000)	6,450	6,100	n.a.
Broadband subscribers ('000)	5,150	5,400	5,165

Personal computers: 13,720,000 in 2005.

Television receivers ('000 in use): 14,168 in 2001.

Source: International Telecommunication Union.

Radio receivers ('000 in use): 25,500 in 1997 (Source: UNESCO, *Statistical Yearbook*).

Book production (1994): 10,835 titles (Source: UNESCO, *Statistical Yearbook*).

Newspapers (2004): 49 dailies (estimated combined circulation 3,114,000); 435 non-dailies (circulation 433,000) (Source: UNESCO, *Statistical Yearbook*).

Education

(August 2010 unless otherwise indicated)

	Institutions	Teaching staff*	Students
Government schools	6,802	163,698	2,282,357†
Non-government schools	2,725	87,724	1,187,567†
Universities‡	39	86,624	1,066,095

* Full-time teaching staff and full-time equivalent of part-time teaching staff.

† Primary and secondary students. In 2010 the total at both government and non-government schools comprised 2,010,327 primary and 1,476,552 secondary students.

‡ 2008 (Source: Department of Education, Science and Training).

Directory

The Constitution

The Federal Constitution was adopted on 9 July 1900 and came into force on 1 January 1901. Its main provisions are summarized below:

PARLIAMENT

The legislative power of the Commonwealth of Australia is vested in a Federal Parliament, consisting of HM the Queen (represented by the Governor-General), a Senate and a House of Representatives. The Governor-General may appoint such times for holding the sessions of the Parliament as he or she thinks fit, and may also from time to time, by proclamation or otherwise, prorogue the Parliament, and may in like manner dissolve the House of Representatives. By convention, these powers are exercised on the advice of the Prime Minister. After any general election Parliament must be summoned to meet not later than 30 days after the day appointed for the return of the writs.

THE SENATE

The Senate is composed of 12 senators from each state, two senators representing the Australian Capital Territory and two representing the Northern Territory. The senators are directly chosen by the people of the state or territory, voting in each case as one electorate, and are elected by proportional representation. Senators representing a state have a six-year term and retire by rotation, one-half from each state on 30 June of each third year. The term of a senator representing a territory is limited to three years. In the case of a state, if a senator vacates his or her seat before the expiration of the term of service, the houses of parliament of the state for which the senator was chosen shall, in joint session, choose a person to hold the place until the expiration of the term or until the election of a successor. If the state parliament is not in session, the Governor of the state, acting on the advice of the state's executive council, may appoint a senator to hold office until parliament reassembles, or until a new senator is elected.

The Senate may proceed to the dispatch of business notwithstanding the failure of any state to provide for its representation in the Senate.

THE HOUSE OF REPRESENTATIVES

In accordance with the Australian Constitution, the total number of members of the House of Representatives must be as nearly as practicable double that of the Senate. The number in each state is in proportion to population, but under the Constitution must be at least five. The House of Representatives is composed of 150 members, including two members for the Australian Capital Territory and two members for the Northern Territory.

Members are elected by universal adult suffrage and voting is compulsory. Only Australian citizens are eligible to vote in Australian elections. British subjects, if they are not Australian citizens or already on the rolls, have to take out Australian citizenship before they can enrol and before they can vote.

Members are chosen by the electors of their respective electorates by the preferential voting system.

The duration of the Parliament is limited to three years.

To be nominated for election to the House of Representatives, a candidate must be 18 years of age or over, an Australian citizen, and entitled to vote at the election or qualified to become an elector.

THE EXECUTIVE GOVERNMENT

The executive power of the Federal Government is vested in the Queen, and is exercisable by the Governor-General, advised by an Executive Council of Ministers of State, known as the Federal Executive Council. These ministers are, or must become within three months, members of the Federal Parliament.

The Australian Constitution is construed as subject to the principles of responsible government and the Governor-General acts on the advice of the ministers in relation to most matters.

THE JUDICIAL POWER

See Judicial System, below.

THE STATES

The Australian Constitution safeguards the Constitution of each state by providing that it shall continue as at the establishment of the Commonwealth, except as altered in accordance with its own provisions. The legislative power of the Federal Parliament is limited in the main to those matters that are listed in section 51 of the Constitution, while the states possess, as well as concurrent powers in those matters, residual legislative powers enabling them to legislate in any way for 'the peace, order and good Government' of their respective territories. When a state law is inconsistent with a law of the Commonwealth, the latter prevails, and the former is invalid to the extent of the inconsistency.

The states may not, without the consent of the Commonwealth, raise or maintain naval or military forces, or impose taxes on any property belonging to the Commonwealth of Australia, nor may the Commonwealth tax state property. The states may not coin money.

The Federal Parliament may not enact any law for establishing any religion or for prohibiting the exercise of any religion, and no religious test may be imposed as a qualification for any office under the Commonwealth.

The Commonwealth of Australia is charged with protecting every state against invasion, and, on the application of a state executive government, against domestic violence.

Provision is made under the Constitution for the admission of new states and for the establishment of new states within the Commonwealth of Australia.

ALTERATION OF THE CONSTITUTION

Proposed laws for the amendment of the Constitution must be passed by an absolute majority in both Houses of the Federal Parliament, and not less than two or more than six months after its passage through both Houses the proposed law must be submitted in each state to the qualified electors.

In the event of one House twice refusing to pass a proposed amendment that has already received an absolute majority in the other House, the Governor-General may, notwithstanding such refusal, submit the proposed amendment to the electors. By convention, the Governor-General acts on the advice of the Prime Minister. If in a majority of the states a majority of the electors voting approve the proposed law and if a majority of all the electors voting also approve, it shall be presented to the Governor-General for Royal Assent.

No alteration diminishing the proportionate representation of any state in either House of the Federal Parliament, or the minimum number of representatives of a state in the House of Representatives, or increasing, diminishing or altering the limits of the state, or in any way affecting the provisions of the Constitution in relation thereto, shall become law unless the majority of the electors voting in that state approve the proposed law.

STATES AND TERRITORIES

New South Wales

The state's executive power is vested in the Governor, appointed by the Crown, who is assisted by an Executive Council composed of cabinet ministers.

The state's legislative power is vested in a bicameral Parliament, composed of the Legislative Council and the Legislative Assembly. The Legislative Council consists of 42 members directly elected for the duration of two parliaments (i.e. eight years), 21 members retiring every four years. The Legislative Assembly consists of 93 members and sits for four years.

Victoria

The state's legislative power is vested in a bicameral Parliament: the Upper House, or Legislative Council, of 40 members, elected for one term of the Legislative Assembly; and the Lower House, or Legislative Assembly, of 88 members, elected for a minimum of three and maximum of four years. One-half of the members of the Council retires every three–four years.

In the exercise of the executive power the Governor is assisted by a cabinet of responsible ministers. Not more than six members of the Council and not more than 17 members of the Assembly may occupy salaried office at any one time.

The state has 88 electoral districts, each returning one member, and eight electoral regions.

Queensland

The state's executive power is vested in the Governor, appointed by the Crown, who is assisted by an Executive Council composed of Ministers. The state's legislative power is vested in the Parliament comprising the Legislative Assembly (composed of 89 members who are elected at least every three years to represent 89 electoral districts) and the Governor, who assents to bills passed by the Assembly. The state's Constitution anticipates that Ministers are also members of the Legislative Assembly and provides that up to 18 members of the Assembly can be appointed Ministers.

South Australia

The state's Constitution vests the legislative power in a Parliament elected by the people and consisting of a Legislative Council and a House of Assembly. The Council is composed of 22 members, one-half of whom retire every three years. Their places are filled by new members elected under a system of proportional representation, with the whole state as a single electorate. The executive has no authority to dissolve this body, except in circumstances warranting a double dissolution.

The 47 members of the House of Assembly are elected for four years from 47 electoral districts.

The executive power is vested in a Governor, appointed by the Crown, and an Executive Council consisting of 10 responsible ministers.

Western Australia

The state's administration is vested in the Governor, a Legislative Council and a Legislative Assembly.

The Legislative Council consists of 34 members, two of the six electoral regions returning seven members on a proportional representation basis, and four regions returning five members. Election is for a term of four years.

The Legislative Assembly consists of 57 members, elected for four years, each representing one electorate.

Tasmania

The state's executive authority is vested in a Governor, appointed by the Crown, who acts upon the advice of his premier and ministers, who are elected members of either the Legislative Council or the House of Assembly. The Council consists of 15 members who sit for six years, retiring in rotation. The House of Assembly has 25 members elected for four years.

Northern Territory

On 1 July 1978 the Northern Territory was established as a body politic with executive authority for specified functions of government. Most functions of the Federal Government were transferred to the Territory Government in 1978 and 1979, major exceptions being Aboriginal affairs and uranium mining.

The Territory Parliament consists of a single house, the Legislative Assembly, with 25 members. The first Parliament stayed in office for three years. As from the election held in August 1980, members are elected for a term of four years.

The office of Administrator continues. The Northern Territory (Self-Government) Act provides for the appointment of an Administrator by the Governor-General charged with the duty of administering the Territory. In respect of matters transferred to the Territory Government, the Administrator acts with the advice of the Territory Executive Council; in respect of matters retained by the Commonwealth, the Administrator acts on Commonwealth advice.

Australian Capital Territory

On 29 November 1988 the Australian Capital Territory (ACT) was established as a body politic. The ACT Government has executive authority for specified functions, although a number of these were to be retained by the Federal Government for a brief period during which transfer arrangements were to be finalized.

The ACT Parliament consists of a single house, the Legislative Assembly, with 17 members. The first election was held in March 1989. Members are elected for a term of three years.

The Federal Government retains control of some of the land in the ACT for the purpose of maintaining the Seat of Government and the national capital plan.

Jervis Bay Territory

Following the attainment of self-government by the ACT (see above), the Jervis Bay Territory, which had formed part of the ACT since 1915, remained a separate Commonwealth Territory, administered by the then Department of the Arts, Sport, the Environment and Territories. The area is governed in accordance with the Jervis Bay Territory Administration Ordinance, issued by the Governor-General on 17 December 1990.

The Government

Queen: HM Queen ELIZABETH II (succeeded to the throne 6 February 1952).

Governor-General: QUENTIN BRYCE (assumed office 5 September 2008).

THE MINISTRY

(October 2011)

The Government is formed by the Australian Labor Party.

Cabinet Ministers

Prime Minister: JULIA GILLARD.

Deputy Prime Minister and Treasurer: WAYNE SWAN.

Minister for Foreign Affairs: KEVIN RUDD.

Minister for Defence: STEPHEN SMITH.

Minister for Agriculture, Fisheries and Forestry: Senator JOE LUDWIG.

Minister for Regional Australia, Regional Development and Local Government, and for the Arts: SIMON CREAN.

Minister for Broadband, Communications and the Digital Economy, and Minister Assisting the Prime Minister on Digital Productivity: Senator STEPHEN CONROY.

Minister for Finance and Deregulation: Senator PENNY WONG.

Minister for Tertiary Education, Jobs, Skills and Workplace Relations: Senator CHRIS EVANS.

Minister for Health and Ageing: NICOLA ROXON.

Minister for Families, Housing, Community Services and Indigenous Affairs: JENNY MACKLIN.

Minister for School Education, Early Childhood and Youth: PETER GARRETT.

Minister for Infrastructure and Transport: ANTHONY ALBANESE.

Minister for Innovation, Industry, Science and Research: Senator KIM CARR.

Minister for Climate Change and Energy Efficiency: GREG COMBET.

Minister for Immigration and Citizenship: CHRIS BOWEN.

Minister for Sustainability, Environment, Water, Population and Communities: TONY BURKE.

Minister for Resources and Energy, and for Tourism: MARTIN FERGUSON.

Minister for Trade: CRAIG EMERSON.

Attorney-General: ROBERT MCCLELLAND.

Other Ministers

Minister for Home Affairs and Justice, and for Privacy and Freedom of Information: BRENDAN O'CONNOR.

Minister for Human Services and for Social Inclusion: TANYA PLIBERSEK.

Minister for Defence Materiel: JASON CLARE.

Minister for Veterans' Affairs, for Defence Science and Personnel, and for Indigenous Health: WARREN SNOWDON.

Special Minister of State and Special Minister of State for the Public Service and Integrity: GARY GRAY.

Minister for Small Business, Minister Assisting on Deregulation and Public Sector Superannuation, and Minister Assisting the Minister for Tourism: Senator NICK SHERRY.

Minister for Employment Participation and Childcare and for the Status of Women: KATE ELLIS.

Minister for Mental Health and Ageing: MARK BUTLER.

Assistant Treasurer and Minister for Financial Services and Superannuation: BILL SHORTEN.

Minister for Indigenous Employment and Economic Development, for Sport, and for Social Housing and Homelessness: Senator MARK ARBIB.

DEPARTMENTS

Department of the Prime Minister and Cabinet: 1 National Circuit, Canberra, ACT 2600; tel. (2) 6271-5111; fax (2) 6271-5414; internet www.dpmc.gov.au.

Department of Agriculture, Fisheries and Forestry: GPOB 858, Canberra, ACT 2601; tel. (2) 6272-3933; internet www.daff.gov.au.

Attorney-General's Department: Central Office, 3–5 National Circuit, Barton, ACT 2600; tel. (2) 6141-6666; internet www.ag.gov.au.

Department of Broadband, Communications and the Digital Economy: GPOB 2154, Canberra, ACT 2601; tel. (2) 6271-1000; fax (2) 6271-1901; e-mail patricia.scott@dbcde.gov.au; internet www.dbcde.gov.au.

Department of Climate Change and Energy Efficiency: GPOB 854, Canberra, ACT 2600; tel. (2) 6159-7000; e-mail communications@climatechange.gov.au; internet www.climatechange.gov.au.

Department of Defence: Russell Offices, Russell Dr., Campbell, Canberra, ACT 2600; tel. (2) 6265-9111; e-mail public.enquiries@defence.gov.au; internet www.defence.gov.au.

Department of Education, Employment and Workplace Relations: GPOB 9880, Canberra, ACT 2601; tel. (2) 6240-8111; fax (2) 6240-8571; e-mail feedback@deewr.gov.au; internet www.deewr.gov.au.

Department of Families, Housing, Community Services and Indigenous Affairs: POB 7576, Canberra Business Centre, ACT 2610; tel. (2) 6244-6385; fax (2) 6244-7919; e-mail enquiries@fahcsia.gov.au; internet www.fahcsia.gov.au.

Department of Finance and Deregulation: John Gorton Bldg, King Edward Tce, Parkes, ACT 2600; tel. (2) 6215-2222; fax (2) 6273-3021; e-mail feedback@finance.gov.au; internet www.finance.gov.au.

Department of Foreign Affairs and Trade: R. G. Casey Bldg, John McEwen Cres., Barton, ACT 0221; tel. (2) 6261-1111; fax (2) 6261-3111; internet www.dfat.gov.au.

Department of Health and Ageing: GPOB 9848, Canberra, ACT 2601; tel. (2) 6289-1555; e-mail enquiries@health.gov.au; internet www.health.gov.au.

Department of Human Services: POB 3959, Manuka, ACT 2603; tel. (2) 6223-4000; fax (2) 6223-4499; e-mail enquiries@humanservices.gov.au; internet www.humanservices.gov.au.

Department of Immigration and Citizenship: POB 25, Belconnen, ACT 2616; tel. (2) 6264-1111; fax (2) 6225-6970; internet www.immi.gov.au.

Department of Infrastructure and Transport: GPOB 594, Canberra, ACT 2601; tel. (2) 6274-7111; fax (2) 6257-2505; e-mail publicaffairs@infrastructure.gov.au; internet www.infrastructure.gov.au.

Department of Innovation, Industry, Science and Research: GPOB 9839, Canberra, ACT 2601; tel. (2) 6213-6000; fax (2) 6213-7000; e-mail inquiries@innovation.gov.au; internet www.innovation.gov.au.

Department of Regional Australia, Regional Development and Local Government: GPOB 803, Canverra, ACT 2601; tel. (2) 6274-7977; fax (2) 6257-2505; e-mail enquiries@regional.gov.au; internet www.regional.gov.au.

Department of Resources, Energy and Tourism: GPOB 1564, Canberra, ACT 2601; tel. (2) 6276-1000; fax (2) 6243-7037; e-mail ret@ret.gov.au; internet www.ret.gov.au.

Department of Sustainability, Environment, Water, Population and Communities: GPOB 787, Canberra, ACT 2601; tel. (2) 6274-1111; fax (2) 6274-1666; internet www.environment.gov.au.

Department of the Treasury: Langton Cres., Parkes, ACT 2600; tel. (2) 6263-2111; fax (2) 6273-2614; e-mail department@treasury.gov.au; internet www.treasury.gov.au.

Department of Veterans' Affairs: POB 21, Woden, ACT 2606; tel. (2) 6289-6736; fax (2) 6289-6257; e-mail generalenquiries@dva.gov.au; internet www.dva.gov.au.

Legislature

FEDERAL PARLIAMENT

Senate

President: JOHN HOGG.

Projected distribution of seats following election, 21 August 2010

Party	Seats*
Liberal-National Coalition	34
Australian Labor Party	31
Australian Greens	9
Others	2
Total	76

* The election was for 36 of the 72 seats held by state senators, who serve a six-year term, and for the two senators representing the Northern Territory and the two representing the Australian Capital Territory. With the exception of the four Territory representatives, whose three-year term of office commenced immediately, the newly elected Senators were not due to take office until 1 July 2011.

House of Representatives

Speaker: HARRY JENKINS.

Distribution of seats following election, 21 August 2010

Party	Seats
Australian Labor Party	72
Liberal Party of Australia	44
Liberal National Party of Queensland	21
National Party of Australia	7
Australian Greens	1
Country Liberals	1
Independents	4
Total	150

State and Territory Governments

(October 2011)

NEW SOUTH WALES

Governor: Prof. MARIE BASHIR, Level 3, Chief Secretary's Bldg, 121 Macquarie St, Sydney, NSW 2000; tel. (2) 9242-4200; fax (2) 9242-4266; internet www.nsw.gov.au.

Premier: BARRY O'FARRELL (Liberal), GPOB 5341, Sydney, NSW 2001; tel. (2) 9228-5555; fax (2) 9228-3522; e-mail thepremier@www.nsw.gov.au; internet www.dpc.nsw.gov.au.

VICTORIA

Governor: ALEX CHERNOV, Government House, Melbourne, Vic 3004; tel. (3) 9655-4211; fax (3) 9650-9050; internet www.governor.vic.gov.au.

Premier: EDWARD (TED) BAILLIEU (Liberal), 1 Treasury Place, Melbourne, Vic 3000; tel. (3) 9651-5000; fax (3) 9651-5054; e-mail premier@dpc.vic.gov.au; internet www.premier.vic.gov.au.

QUEENSLAND

Governor: PENELOPE WENSLEY, GPOB 434, Brisbane, Qld 4001; tel. (7) 3858-5700; fax (7) 3858-5701; e-mail govhouse@govhouse.qld.gov.au; internet www.govhouse.qld.gov.au.

Premier: ANNA BLIGH (Labor), POB 15185, City East, Qld 4002; tel. (7) 3224-2111; fax (7) 3229-2900; e-mail premiers.master@premiers.qld.gov.au; internet www.premiers.qld.gov.au.

SOUTH AUSTRALIA

Governor: KEVIN SCARCE, GPOB 2373, Adelaide, SA 5001; tel. (8) 8203-9800; fax (8) 8203-9899; e-mail governors.office@sa.gov.au; internet www.governor.sa.gov.au.

Premier: JAY WEATHERILL (Labor), GPOB 2343, Adelaide, SA 5001; tel. (8) 8463-3166; fax (8) 8463-3168; e-mail premier@dpc.sa.gov.au; internet www.premier.sa.gov.au.

WESTERN AUSTRALIA

Governor: MALCOLM MCCUSKER, Government House, St George's Terrace, Perth, WA 6000; tel. (8) 9429-9199; fax (8) 9325-4476; e-mail enquiries@govhouse.wa.gov.au; internet www.govhouse.wa.gov.au.

Premier: COLIN BARNETT (Liberal), 24th Floor, 197 St George's Terrace, Perth, WA 6000; tel. (8) 9222-9888; fax (8) 9322-1213; e-mail wa-government@dpc.wa.gov.au; internet www.premier.wa.gov.au.

TASMANIA

Governor: PETER UNDERWOOD, Government House, Lower Domain Rd, Hobart, Tas 7000; tel. (3) 6234-2611; fax (3) 6234-2556; internet www.govhouse.tas.gov.au.

Premier: LARA GIDDINGS (Labor), GPOB 123, Hobart, Tas 7001; tel. (3) 6233-3464; fax (3) 6234-1572; e-mail premier@dpac.tas.gov.au; internet www.premier.tas.gov.au.

NORTHERN TERRITORY

Administrator: TOM PAULING, GPOB 497, Darwin, NT 0801; tel. (8) 8999-7103; fax (8) 8999-5521; e-mail governmenthouse.darwin@nt.gov.au; internet www.nt.gov.au/administrator.

Chief Minister: PAUL HENDERSON (Labor), GPOB 3146, Darwin, NT 0801; tel. (8) 8901-4000; fax (8) 8901-4099; e-mail chiefminister.nt@nt.gov.au; internet www.nt.gov.au.

AUSTRALIAN CAPITAL TERRITORY

Chief Minister: KATY GALLAGHER (Labor), GPOB 158, Canberra, ACT 2601; tel. (2) 6205-0104; fax (2) 6205-0433; e-mail stanhope@act.gov.au; internet www.cmd.act.gov.au.

Election Commission

Australian Electoral Commission (AEC): West Block Offices, Queen Victoria Terrace, Parkes, ACT 2600; POB 6172, Kingston, ACT 2604; tel. (2) 6271-4411; fax (2) 6271-4558; e-mail info@aec.gov.au; internet www.aec.gov.au; f. 1984; statutory body; administers federal elections and referendums; Chair. PETER HEEREY; Electoral Commr ED KILLESTEYN.

Political Organizations

Australians for Constitutional Monarchy (ACM): GPOB 9841, Sydney, NSW 2001; tel. (2) 9251-2500; fax (2) 9261-5033; e-mail acmhq@norepublic.com.au; internet www.norepublic.com.au; f. 1992; also known as No Republic; Nat. Convener Prof. DAVID FLINT.

Australian Democrats Party: 711 South Rd, Black Forest, SA 5035; tel. (8) 8371-1441; e-mail inquiries@democrats.org.au; internet www.democrats.org.au; f. 1977; comprises the fmr Liberal Movement and the Australia Party; Nat. Pres. JULIA MELLAND; Nat. Exec. BRUCE CARNWELL.

Australian Greens: GPOB 1108, Canberra, ACT 2601; tel. (2) 6140-3217; fax (2) 6247-6455; e-mail greens@greens.org.au; internet www.greens.org.au; f. 1992; Parl. Leader Senator BOB BROWN; Nat. Convener ADAM BANDT.

Australian Labor Party (ALP): POB 6222, Kingston, ACT 2604; tel. (2) 6120-0800; fax (2) 6120-0801; e-mail info@cbr.alp.org.au; internet www.alp.org.au; f. 1891; advocates social democracy; trade unions form part of its structure; Fed. Parl. Leader JULIA GILLARD; Nat. Pres. MICHAEL WILLIAMSON; Nat. Sec. KARL BITAR.

Australian Republican Movement (ARM): GPOB 611, Canberra, ACT 2601; tel. (2) 6257-3705; fax (2) 6257-3670; e-mail republic@republic.org.au; internet www.republic.org.au; f. 1991; Chair. MICHAEL KEATING.

Communist Party of Australia: 74 Buckingham St, Surry Hills, NSW 2010; tel. (2) 9699-8844; fax (2) 9699-9833; e-mail cpa@cpa.org.au; internet www.cpa.org.au; f. 1971; fmrly Socialist Party; advocates public ownership of the means of production, working-class political power; Pres. Dr VINNIE MOLINA; Gen. Sec. HANNAH MIDDLETON.

First Nations Political Party (FNPP): e-mail firstnationspoliticalparty@hotmail.com; internet www.firstnationspoliticalparty.org; f. 2010; represents interests of Aboriginal people; Leader MAURIE JAPARTA RYAN.

Liberal Party of Australia: POB 6004, Kingston, ACT 2604; tel. (2) 6273-2564; fax (2) 6273-1534; e-mail libadm@liberal.org.au; internet www.liberal.org.au; f. 1944; advocates private enterprise, social justice, individual liberty and initiative; committed to national devt, prosperity and security; Fed. Dir BRIAN LOUGHNANE; Fed. Parl. Leader TONY ABBOTT; Fed. Pres. ALAN STOCKDALE.

Liberal National Party of Queensland (LNP): POB 5156, West End, Qld 4101; tel. (7) 3844-0666; fax (7) 3844 0388; e-mail info@lnp.org.au; internet lnp.org.au; f. 2008; est. by merger of Qld Liberals and Qld Nationals; aims to provide prosperity and security for Queensland; Pres. BRUCE MCIVER; Vice-Pres. GARY SPENCE.

National Party of Australia: POB 6190, Kingston, ACT 2604; tel. (2) 6273-3822; fax (2) 6273-1745; e-mail federal.nationals@nationals.org.au; internet www.nationals.org.au; f. 1916 as the Country Party of Australia; adopted present name in 1982; advocates balanced national devt based on free enterprise, with special emphasis on the needs of people outside the major metropolitan areas; Fed. Pres. JOHN TANNER; Fed. Parl. Leader WARREN TRUSS; Fed. Dir BRAD HENDERSON.

Diplomatic Representation

EMBASSIES AND HIGH COMMISSIONS IN AUSTRALIA

Afghanistan: POB 155, Deakin West, ACT 2600; tel. (2) 6282-7311; fax (2) 6282-7322; e-mail ambassador@afghanembassy.net; internet www.afghanembassy.net; Ambassador NASIR AHMAD ANDISHA.

Algeria: 9 Terrigal Cres., O'Malley, ACT 2606; tel. (2) 6286-7355; fax (2) 6286-7037; e-mail info@algeriaemb.org.au; internet www.algeriaemb.org.au; Ambassador HADI BROURI.

Argentina: POB 4835, Kingston, ACT 2604; tel. (2) 6273-9111; fax (2) 6273-0500; e-mail info@argentina.org.au; internet www.argentina.org.au; Ambassador PEDRO VILLAGRA DELGADO.

Austria: POB 3375, Manuka, ACT 2603; tel. (2) 6295-1533; fax (2) 6239-6751; e-mail canberra-ob@bmeia.gv.at; internet www.austria.org.au; Ambassador Dr HANNES PORIAS.

Bangladesh: 43 Culgoa Circuit, O'Malley, ACT 2606; tel. (2) 6290-0511; fax (2) 6290-0544; e-mail hoc@bhcanberra.com; internet www.bhcanberra.com; High Commissioner Lt-Gen. MASUD UDDIN CHOWDHURY.

Belgium: 19 Arkana St, Yarralumla, ACT 2600; tel. (2) 6273-2501; fax (2) 6273-3392; e-mail canberra@diplobel.fed.be; internet www.diplomatie.be/canberra; Ambassador PATRICK RENAULT.

Bosnia and Herzegovina: 5 Beale Cres., Deakin, ACT 2600; tel. (2) 6232-4646; fax (2) 6232-5554; e-mail embassy@bih.org.au; internet www.bih.org.au; Ambassador DAMIR ARNAUT.

Botswana: POB 3812, Manuka, ACT 2603; tel. (2) 6234-7500; fax (2) 6282-4140; e-mail botaus-info@gov.bw; internet www.botswanahighcom.org.au; High Commissioner MOLOSIWA SELEPENG.

Brazil: GPOB 1540, Canberra, ACT 2601; tel. (2) 6273-2372; fax (2) 6273-2375; e-mail brazilemb@brazil.org.au; internet www.brazil.org.au; Ambassador RUBEM CORRÊA BARBOSA.

Brunei: POB109, Curtin, ACT 2605; tel. (2) 6285-4500; fax (2) 6285-4545; e-mail canberra.australia@mfa.gov.bn; internet brunei.org.au; High Commissioner ADNAN JAAFAR.

Bulgaria: POB 6096, Mawson, ACT 2607; tel. (2) 6286-9711; fax (2) 6286-9600; e-mail embassy@bulgaria.org.au; internet www.bulgaria.org.au; Ambassador KRASSIMIR STEFANOV.

Cambodia: 5 Canterbury Cres., Deakin, ACT 2600; tel. (2) 6273-1259; fax (2) 6273-1053; e-mail cambodianembassy@ozemail.com.au; internet www.embassyofcambodia.org.nz/au.htm; Ambassador CHUM SOUNRY.

Canada: Commonwealth Ave, Canberra, ACT 2600; tel. (2) 6270-4000; fax (2) 6270-4081; e-mail cnbra@international.gc.ca; internet www.canadainternational.gc.ca/australia-australie; High Commissioner MICHAEL SMALL.

Chile: POB 5023, Garran, ACT 2605; tel. (2) 6286-2430; fax (2) 6286-1289; e-mail echileau@embachile-australia.com; internet chileabroad.gov.cl/australia/en/; Ambassador PEDRO PABLO DÍAZ HERRERA.

China, People's Republic: 15 Coronation Dr., Yarralumla, ACT 2600; tel. (2) 6273-4780; fax (2) 6273-5848; e-mail chinaemb_au@mfa.gov.cn; internet au.china-embassy.org/eng; Ambassador CHEN YUMING.

Colombia: POB 227, Civic Sq., ACT 2608; tel. (2) 6230-4203; fax (2) 6230-4209; e-mail embassyofcolombia@bigpond.com; internet www.cancilleria.gov.co/wps/portal/embajada_australia; Ambassador DIEGO BETANCUR.

Croatia: 14 Jindalee Cres., O'Malley, ACT 2600; tel. (2) 6286-6988; fax (2) 6286-3544; e-mail croemb.canberra@mvpei.hr; Ambassador VICENCIJE BIUK.

Cuba: 1 Gerogery Place, O'Malley, ACT 2606; tel. (2) 6290-2151; fax (2) 6286-9354; e-mail embajada@cubaus.net; internet embacuba.cubaminrex.cu/australiaing; Ambassador PEDRO MONZÓN BARATA.

Cyprus: 30 Beale Cres., Deakin, ACT 2600; tel. (2) 6281-0832; fax (2) 6281-0860; e-mail info@cyprus.org.au; internet www.cyprus.org.au; High Commissioner YANNIS IACOVOU.

Czech Republic: 8 Culgoa Circuit, O'Malley, ACT 2606; tel. (2) 6290-1386; fax (2) 6290-0006; e-mail canberra@embassy.mzv.cz; internet www.mzv.cz/canberra; Ambassador Dr HYNEK KMONICEK.

Denmark: 15 Hunter St, Yarralumla, ACT 2600; tel. (2) 6270-5333; fax (2) 6270-5324; e-mail cbramb@um.dk; internet www.oceanien.um.dk; Ambassador SUSANNE HOFFMANN SHINE.

Ecuador: 6 Pindari Cres., O'Malley, ACT 2606; tel. (2) 6286-4021; fax (2) 6286-1231; e-mail embassy@ecuador-au.org; Ambassador RAÚL GANGOTENA RIVADENEIRA.

Egypt: 1 Darwin Ave, Yarralumla, ACT 2600; tel. (2) 6273-4437; fax (2) 6273-4279; e-mail egyembassy@bigpond.com; Ambassador OMAR MUHAMMAD T. METWALLY.

Fiji: POB 159, Deakin West, ACT 2600; tel. (2) 6260-5115; fax (2) 6260-5105; e-mail admin@aus-fhc.org; internet www.fijihighcom.com; High Commissioner (vacant).

Finland: 12 Darwin Ave, Yarralumla, ACT 2600; tel. (2) 6273-3800; fax (2) 6273-3603; e-mail sanomat.can@formin.fi; internet www.finland.org.au; Ambassador MAIJA LÄHTEENMÄKI.

France: 6 Perth Ave, Yarralumla, ACT 2600; tel. (2) 6216-0100; fax (2) 6216-0127; e-mail info@ambafrance-au.org; internet www.ambafrance-au.org; Ambassador MICHEL FILHOL.

Germany: 119 Empire Circuit, Yarralumla, ACT 2600; tel. (2) 6270-1911; fax (2) 6270-1951; e-mail info@canberra.diplo.de; internet www.canberra.diplo.de; Ambassador CHRISTOPH MUELLER.

Ghana: 13 Numeralla St, O'Malley, ACT 2606; tel. (2) 6290-2110; fax (2) 6290-2115; e-mail gh57391@bigpond.net.au; internet www.ghanahighcom.org.au; High Commissioner PAUL YAW ESSEL.

Greece: 9 Turrana St, Yarralumla, ACT 2600; tel. (2) 6273-3011; fax (2) 6273-2620; e-mail gremb.can@mfa.gr; Ambassador ALEXIOS CHRISTOPOULOS.

Holy See: POB 3633, Manuka, ACT 2603 (Apostolic Nunciature); tel. (2) 6295-3876; fax (2) 6295-3690; e-mail nuntius@cyberone.com.au; Apostolic Nuncio Most Rev. GIUSEPPE LAZZAROTTO (Titular Archbishop of Numana).

Hungary: 17 Beale Cres., Deakin, ACT 2600; tel. (2) 6282-3226; fax (2) 6285-3012; e-mail mission.cbr@kum.hu; internet www.mfa.gov.hu/kulkepviselet/au; Ambassador ANNA SIKÓ.

India: 3–5 Moonah Pl., Yarralumla, ACT 2600; tel. (2) 6273-3999; fax (2) 6273-1308; e-mail hco@hcindia-au.org; internet www.hcindia-au.org; High Commissioner SUJATHA SINGH.

Indonesia: 8 Darwin Ave, Yarralumla, ACT 2600; tel. (2) 6250-8600; fax (2) 6273-6017; e-mail indonemb@kbri-canberra.org.au; internet www.kemlu.go.id/canberra; Ambassador PRIMO ALUI JOELIANTO.

Iran: POB 705, Mawson, ACT 2607; tel. (2) 6290-2430; fax (2) 6290-2825; e-mail amb.office@iranembassy.org.au; internet www.iranembassy.org.au; Ambassador MAHMOUD BABAEE.

Iraq: 48 Culgoa Circuit, O'Malley, ACT 2606; tel. (2) 6286-2744; fax (2) 6286-8744; e-mail iraqembcnb@hotmail.com; internet www.iraqembassyaustralia.org; Ambassador MOUAYED SALEH.

Ireland: 20 Arkana St, Yarralumla, ACT 2600; tel. (2) 6273-3022; fax (2) 6273-3741; e-mail canberraembassy@dfa.ie; internet www.embassyofireland.au.com; Ambassador MÁIRTÍN O'FAINNÍN.

Israel: 6 Turrana St, Yarralumla, ACT 2600; tel. (2) 6215-4500; fax (2) 6215-4555; e-mail info@canberra.mfa.gov.il; internet canberra.mfa.gov.il; Ambassador YUVAL ROTEM.

Italy: 12 Grey St, Deakin, ACT 2600; tel. (2) 6273-3333; fax (2) 6273-4223; e-mail ambasciata.canberra@esteri.it; internet www.ambcanberra.esteri.it; Ambassador GIAN LUDOVICO DE MARTINO DI MONTEGIORDANO.

Japan: 112 Empire Circuit, Yarralumla, ACT 2600; tel. (2) 6273-3244; fax (2) 6273-1848; e-mail cultural@japan.org.au; internet www.au.emb-japan.go.jp; Ambassador SHIGEKAZU SATO.

Jordan: 20 Roebuck St, Red Hill, ACT 2603; tel. (2) 6295-9951; fax (2) 6239-7236; e-mail jordan@jordanembassy.org.au; internet www.jordanembassy.org.au; Ambassador RIMA AHMAD ALAADEEN.

Kenya: GPOB 1990, Canberra, ACT 2601; tel. (2) 6247-4788; fax (2) 6257-6613; e-mail khc-canberra@kenya.asn.au; internet www.kenya.asn.au; High Commissioner STEPHEN K. TARUS.

Korea, Republic: 113 Empire Circuit, Yarralumla, ACT 2600; tel. (2) 6270-4100; fax (2) 6273-4839; e-mail info@korea.org.au; internet www.korea.org.au; Ambassador CHO TAE-YONG.

Kuwait: POB 26, Woden, ACT 2606; tel. (2) 6286-7777; fax (2) 6286-3733; e-mail Kuwaitcan_2002@yahoo.com.au; internet www.kuwaitemb-australia.com; Ambassador KHALED AL-SHAIBANI.

Laos: 1 Dalman Cres., O'Malley, ACT 2606; tel. (2) 6286-4595; fax (2) 6290-1910; e-mail laoemb@bigpond.net.au; internet www.laosembassy.net; Ambassador RANGSY KONGSAYSY.

Lebanon: 27 Endeavour St, Red Hill, ACT 2603; tel. (2) 6295-7378; fax (2) 6239-7024; e-mail lebanemb@tpg.com.au; internet www.lebanemb.org.au; Ambassador JEAN DANIEL.

Libya: 50 Culgoa Circuit, O'Malley, ACT 2606; tel. (2) 6290-7900; fax (2) 6286-4522; Ambassador a.i. MUSBAH A. A. ALLAFI.

Macedonia, former Yugoslav republic: POB 1890, Canberra, ACT 2601; tel. (2) 6282-6220; fax (2) 6282-6229; e-mail info@macedonianemb.org.au; internet www.missions.gov.mk/canberra; Ambassador PERO STOJANOVSKI.

Malaysia: 7 Perth Ave, Yarralumla, ACT 2600; tel. (2) 6120-0300; fax (2) 6273-2496; e-mail malcanberra@malaysia.org.au; internet www.malaysia.org.au; High Commissioner SALMAN AHMAD.

Malta: 38 Culgoa Circuit, O'Malley, ACT 2606; tel. (2) 6290-1724; fax (2) 6290-2453; e-mail highcommission.canberra@gov.mt; internet www.foreign.gov.mt/australia; High Commissioner FRANCIS TABONE.

Mauritius: 2 Beale Cres., Deakin, ACT 2600; tel. (2) 6281-1203; fax (2) 6282-3235; e-mail mhccan@cyberone.com.au; High Commissioner MARIE FRANCE LISIANNE MIRELLA CHAUVIN.

Mexico: 14 Perth Ave, Yarralumla, ACT 2600; tel. (2) 6273-3963; fax (2) 6273-1190; e-mail embamex@mexico.org.au; internet www.mexico.org.au; Ambassador MARÍA LUISA BEATRIZ LÓPEZ GARGALLO.

Mongolia: 1/44 Dalman Cres., O'Malley, ACT 2606; tel. (2) 6286-2947; fax (2) 6286-6381; e-mail mngemb@bigpond.com; internet www.canberra.mfat.gov.mn; Ambassador TSERENDORJ JAMBALDORJ.

Morocco: POB 3531, Manuka, ACT 2603; tel. (2) 6290-0755; fax (2) 6290-0744; e-mail sifmacan@moroccoembassy.org.au; internet www.moroccoembassy.org.au; Ambassador MOHAMED MAEL-AININ.

Myanmar: 22 Arkana St, Yarralumla, ACT 2600; tel. (2) 6273-3811; fax (2) 6273-3181; e-mail mecanberra@bigpond.com; internet www.myanmarembassycanberra.com; Ambassador PAW LWIN SEIN.

Nepal: Suite 2.02, AAPT Bldg, 24 Marcus Clarke St, Canberra, ACT 2601; tel. (2) 6162-1554; fax (2) 6162-1557; e-mail info@necan.gov.np; internet www.necan.gov.np; Ambassador YOGENDRA DHAKAL.

Netherlands: 120 Empire Circuit, Yarralumla, ACT 2600; tel. (2) 6220-9400; fax (2) 6273-3206; e-mail can@minbuza.nl; internet www.netherlands.org.au; Ambassador WILLEM ANDREAE.

New Zealand: Commonwealth Ave, Canberra, ACT 2600; tel. (2) 6270-4211; fax (2) 6273-3194; e-mail nzhccba@bigpond.net.au; internet www.nzembassy.com/australia; High Commissioner Maj.-Gen. (retd) MARTYN DUNNE.

Nigeria: POB 241, Civic Sq., ACT 2608; tel. 0424757698 (mobile); fax (2) 6282-8471; e-mail chancery@nigeria-can.org.au; internet www.nigeria-can.org.au; High Commissioner AYOOLA LAWRENCE OLUKANNI.

Norway: 17 Hunter St, Yarralumla, ACT 2600; tel. (2) 6273-3444; fax (2) 6273-3669; e-mail emb.canberra@mfa.no; internet www.norway.org.au; Ambassador SIREN GJERME ERIKSEN.

Pakistan: POB 684, Mawson, ACT 2607; tel. (2) 6290-1676; fax (2) 6290-1073; e-mail parepcanberra@internode.on.net; internet www.pakistan.org.au; High Commissioner ABDUL MALIK ABDULLAH.

Papua New Guinea: POB E6317, Kingston, ACT 2604; tel. (2) 6273-3322; fax (2) 6273-3732; e-mail kunducbr@netspeed.com.au; internet www.pngcanberra.org; High Commissioner (vacant).

Peru: POB 106, Red Hill, ACT 2603; tel. (2) 6273-7351; fax (2) 6273-7354; e-mail embassy@embaperu.org.au; internet www.embaperu.org.au; Ambassador LUIS FELIPE QUESADA INCHAUSTEGUI.

Philippines: 1 Moonah Place, Yarralumla, ACT 2600; tel. (2) 6273-2535; fax (2) 6273-3984; e-mail cbrpe@philembassy.org.au; internet www.philembassy.org.au; Ambassador BELEN F. ANOTA.

Poland: 7 Turrana St, Yarralumla, ACT 2600; tel. (2) 6272-1000; fax (2) 6273-3184; e-mail canberra.amb.sekretariat@msz.gov.pl; internet www.canberra.polemb.net; Ambassador ANDRZEJ JAROSZYŃSKI.

Portugal: 23 Culgoa Circuit, O'Malley, ACT 2606; tel. (2) 6290-1733; fax (2) 6290-1957; e-mail embportcanb@internode.on.net; Ambassador RUI QUARTÍN SANTOS.

Romania: 4 Dalman Cres., O'Malley, ACT 2606; tel. (2) 6286-2343; fax (2) 6286-2433; e-mail roembcbr@cyberone.com.au; internet www.canberra.mae.ro; Ambassador MIHAI STEFAN STUPARU.

Russia: 78 Canberra Ave, Griffith, ACT 2603; tel. (2) 6295-9033; fax (2) 6295-1847; e-mail rusembassy.australia@rambler.ru; internet www.australia.mid.ru; Ambassador VLADIMIR MOROZOV.

Samoa: POB 3274, Manuka, ACT 2603; tel. (2) 6286-5505; fax (2) 6286-5678; e-mail samoahcaussi@netspeed.com.au; High Commissioner LEMALU TATE SIMI.

Saudi Arabia: POB 9162, Deakin, ACT 2600; tel. (2) 6250-7000; fax (2) 6282-8911; e-mail amb.auemb@mofa.gov.sa; internet www.saudiembassy.org.au; Ambassador HASSAN TALAT NAZER.

Serbia: POB 728, Mawson, ACT 2607; tel. (2) 6290-2630; fax (2) 6290-2631; e-mail serbembau@optusnet.com.au; Ambassador NEDA MALETIĆ.

Singapore: 17 Forster Cres., Yarralumla, ACT 2600; tel. (2) 6271-2000; fax (2) 6273-9823; e-mail singhc_cbr@sgmfa.gov.sg; internet www.mfa.gov.sg/canberra; High Commissioner MICHAEL TEO.

Slovakia: 47 Culgoa Circuit, O'Malley, ACT 2606; tel. (2) 6290-1516; fax (2) 6290-1755; e-mail emb.canberra@mzv.sk; internet www.mzv.sk/canberra; Ambassador EVA PONOMARENKOVÁ.

Slovenia: 26 Akame Circuit, O'Malley, ACT 2606; tel. (2) 6290-0000; fax (2) 6290-0619; e-mail vca@gov.si; internet canberra.veleposlanistvo.si; Ambassador MILAN BALAZIĆ.

Solomon Islands: POB 256, Deakin West, ACT 2600; tel. (2) 6282-7030; fax (2) 6282-7040; e-mail info@solomonemb.org.au; High Commissioner BERAKI JINO.

South Africa: cnr State Circle and Rhodes Place, Yarralumla, ACT 2600; tel. (2) 6272-7300; fax (2) 6273-3203; e-mail info.canberra@foreign.gov.za; internet www.sahc.org.au; High Commissioner KOLEKA ANITA MQULWANA.

Spain: POB 9076, Deakin, ACT 2600; tel. (2) 6273-3555; fax (2) 6273-3918; e-mail emb.canberra@maec.es; internet www.maec.es/embajadas/canberra; Ambassador CARLOS SÁNCHEZ DE BOADO Y DE LA VÁLGOMA.

Sri Lanka: 35 Empire Circuit, Forrest, ACT 2603; tel. (2) 6239-7041; fax (2) 6239-6166; e-mail admin@slhcaust.org; internet www.slhcaust.org; High Commissioner Adm. (retd) THISARA SAMARASINGHE.

Sweden: 5 Turrana St, Yarralumla, ACT 2600; tel. (2) 6270-2700; fax (2) 6270-2755; e-mail sweden@iimetro.com.au; internet www.swedenabroad.com/canberra; Ambassador SVEN-OLOF PETERSSON.

Switzerland: 7 Melbourne Ave, Forrest, ACT 2603; tel. (2) 6162-8400; fax (2) 6273-3428; e-mail can.vertretung@eda.admin.ch; internet www.eda.admin.ch/australia; Ambassador DANIEL WOKER.

Syria: 41 Culgoa Circuit, O'Malley, ACT 2606; tel. (2) 6218-5200; fax (2) 6218-5250; e-mail info@syrianembassy.org.au; internet www.syrianembassy.org.au; Ambassador MOHAMMED KHADDOUR.

Thailand: 111 Empire Circuit, Yarralumla, ACT 2600; tel. (2) 6206-0100; fax (2) 6206-0123; e-mail thaican@mfa.go.th; internet canberra.thaiembassy.org; Ambassador KRIANGSAK KITTICHAISAREE.

Timor-Leste: 7 Beale Cres., Deakin, ACT 2600; tel. (2) 6260-4833; fax (2) 6232-4075; e-mail timor.embassy@bigpond.com; Ambassador ABEL GUTERRES.

Tonga: 7 Newdegate St, Deakin, ACT 2600; tel. (2) 6232-4806; fax (2) 6232-4807; e-mail info@tongahighcom.com.au; High Commissioner Crown Prince TUPOUTO'A LAVAKA.

Tunisia: POB 229, Civic Sq., ACT 2608; tel. (2) 6162-0534; fax (2) 6246-0300; e-mail canberra@embassytunisia.com; Ambassador RAOUF CHATTY.

Turkey: 6 Moonah Place, Yarralumla, ACT 2600; tel. (2) 6234-0000; fax (2) 6273-4402; e-mail turkemb.canberra@mfa.gov.tr; internet www.canberra.emb.mfa.gov.tr; Ambassador OĞUZ ÖZGE.

Uganda: POB 34, Woden, ACT 2606; tel. (2) 6286-1234; fax (2) 6286-1243; e-mail ugandahc@velocitynet.com.au; High Commissioner ENOCH NKURUHO (acting).

Ukraine: Level 12, St George Centre, 60 Marcus Clarke St, Canberra, ACT 2601; tel. (2) 6230-5789; fax (2) 6230-7298; e-mail ukremb@bigpond.com; internet www.mfa.gov.ua/australia; Ambassador VALENTYN ADOMAYTIS.

United Arab Emirates: POB 5173, Garran, ACT 2605; tel. (2) 6286-8802; fax (2) 6286-8804; e-mail uaeembassy@bigpond.com; internet www.uaeembassy.org.au; Ambassador ALI NASSER AL-NUAIMI.

United Kingdom: Commonwealth Ave, Canberra, ACT 2600; tel. (2) 6270-6666; fax (2) 6273-3236; e-mail PPA.Canberra@fco.gov.uk; internet ukinaustralia.fco.gov.uk; High Commissioner PAUL MADDEN.

USA: Moonah Place, Yarralumla, ACT 2600; tel. (2) 6214-5600; fax (2) 6214-5970; e-mail usrsaustralia@state.gov; internet canberra.usembassy.gov; Ambassador JEFFREY L. BLEICH.

Uruguay: POB 5058, Kingston, ACT 2604; tel. (2) 6273-9100; fax (2) 6273-9099; e-mail urucan@iimetro.com.au; Ambassador ALBERTO L. FAJARDO KLAPPENBACH.

Vanuatu: Canberra; High Commissioner KALVAU KALORIS (designate).

Venezuela: POB 37, Woden, ACT 2606; tel. (2) 6290-2968; fax (2) 6290-2911; e-mail embaustralia@venezuela-emb-org.au; internet www.venezuela-emb.org.au; Ambassador NELSÓN DÁVILA-LAMEDA.

Viet Nam: 6 Timbarra Cres., O'Malley, ACT 2606; tel. (2) 6286-6059; fax (2) 6286-4534; e-mail vembassy@webone.com.au; internet www.vietnamembassy.org.au; Ambassador HOANG VINH THANH.

Zimbabwe: 7 Timbarra Cres., O'Malley, ACT 2606; tel. (2) 6286-2700; fax (2) 6290-1680; e-mail zimbabwe1@iimetro.com.au; Ambassador JACQUELINE NOMHLE ZWAMBILA.

Judicial System

The judicial power of the Commonwealth of Australia is vested in the High Court of Australia, in such other Federal Courts as the Federal Parliament creates, and in such other courts as it invests with Federal jurisdiction.

In March 1986 all remaining categories of appeal from Australian courts to the Queen's Privy Council in the United Kingdom were abolished by the Australia Act.

HIGH COURT OF AUSTRALIA

The High Court consists of a Chief Justice and six other Justices, each of whom is appointed by the Governor-General in Council, and has both original and appellate jurisdiction.

The High Court's original jurisdiction extends to all matters arising under any treaty, affecting representatives of other countries, in which the Commonwealth of Australia or its representative is a party, between states or between residents of different states or between a state and a resident of another state, and in which a writ of mandamus, or prohibition, or an injunction is sought against an officer of the Commonwealth of Australia. It also extends to matters arising under the Australian Constitution or involving its interpretation, and to many matters arising under Commonwealth laws.

The High Court's appellate jurisdiction has, since June 1984, been discretionary. Appeals from the Federal Court, the Family Court and the Supreme Courts of the states and of the territories may now be brought only if special leave is granted, in the event of a legal question that is of general public importance being involved, or of there being differences of opinion between intermediate appellate courts as to the state of the law.

Chief Justice: ROBERT S. FRENCH, POB 6309, Kingston, Canberra, ACT 2604; tel. (2) 6270-6811; fax (2) 6270-6868; e-mail enquiries@hcourt.gov.au; internet www.hcourt.gov.au.

Justices: WILLIAM MONTAGUE CHARLES GUMMOW, KENNETH MADISON HAYNE, JOHN DYSON HEYDON, SUSAN MAREE CRENNAN, SUSAN MARY KIEFEL, VIRGINIA MARGARET BELL.

FEDERAL COURT OF AUSTRALIA

Chief Justice: PATRICK ANTHONY KEANE, Law Courts Bldg, Level 17, Queens Sq., NSW 2000; tel. (2) 9230-8535; fax (2) 9230-8295; e-mail query@fedcourt.gov.au; internet www.fedcourt.gov.au.

In 2010 there were 43 other judges.

FAMILY COURT OF AUSTRALIA

Chief Justice: DIANA BRYANT, GPOB 9991, Parramatta, NSW 2150; tel. (2) 8892-8578; fax (2) 8892-8585; e-mail enquiries@familylawcourts.gov.au; internet www.familycourt.gov.au.

In 2010 there were 33 other judges, as well as two judicial registrars.

STATE SUPREME COURTS

Chief Justices: JAMES JACOB SPIGELMAN (New South Wales), MARILYN WARREN (Victoria), PAUL DE JERSEY (Queensland), JOHN JEREMY DOYLE (South Australia), WAYNE MARTIN (Western Australia), EWAN CRAWFORD (Tasmania), TERENCE JOHN HIGGINS (Australian Capital Territory), TREVOR JOHN RILEY (Northern Territory).

Religion

CHRISTIANITY

According to the provisional results of the population census of August 2006, Christians numbered 12,685,834.

National Council of Churches in Australia: Locked Bag 199, Sydney, NSW 1230; tel. (2) 9299-2215; fax (2) 9262-4514; e-mail secretariat@ncca.org.au; internet www.ncca.org.au; f. 1946; est. as Australian Council of Churches; assumed present name in 1994; 19 mem. churches; Pres. Most Rev. MICHAEL PUTNEY; Gen. Sec. Rev. TARA CURLEWIS.

The Anglican Communion

The constitution of the Church of England in Australia, which rendered the church an autonomous member of the Anglican Communion, came into force in January 1962. The body was renamed the Anglican Church of Australia in August 1981. The Church comprises five provinces (together containing 22 dioceses) and the extra-provincial diocese of Tasmania. According to the 2006 population census there were 3,718,248 adherents.

Anglican Church of Australia—General Synod Office: Suite 2, Level 9, 51 Druitt St, Sydney, NSW 2000; tel. (2) 8267-2700; fax (2) 8267-2727; e-mail reception@anglican.org.au; internet www.anglican.org.au; Primate Most Rev. Dr PHILLIP ASPINALL; Gen. Sec. MARTIN DREVIKOVSKY.

Archbishop of Adelaide and Metropolitan of South Australia: Most Rev. JEFFREY DRIVER, 18 King William Rd, North Adelaide, SA 5006; tel. (8) 8305-9350; fax (8) 8305-9399; e-mail diocesanoffice@adelaide.anglican.com.au; internet www.adelaide.anglican.com.au.

Archbishop of Brisbane and Metropolitan of Queensland, Primate of Australia: Most Rev. Dr PHILLIP JOHN ASPINALL, Bishopsbourne, GPOB 421, Brisbane, Qld 4001; tel. (7) 3835-2222; fax (7) 3832-5030; e-mail info@anglicanbrisbane.org.au; internet www.anglicanbrisbane.org.au.

Archbishop of Melbourne and Metropolitan of Victoria: Most Rev. Dr PHILIP FREIER, The Anglican Centre, 209 Flinders Lane, Melbourne, Vic 3000; tel. (3) 9653-4220; fax (3) 9653-4268; e-mail archbishop@melbourne.anglican.com.au; internet www.melbourne.anglican.com.au.

Archbishop of Perth and Metropolitan of Western Australia: Most Rev. ROGER ADRIAN HERFT, GPOB W2067, Perth, WA 6846; tel. (8) 9325-7455; fax (8) 9221-4118; e-mail diocese@perth.anglican.org; internet www.perth.anglican.org; also has jurisdiction over Christmas Island and the Cocos (Keeling) Islands.

Archbishop of Sydney and Metropolitan of New South Wales: Most Rev. Dr PETER F. JENSEN, POB Q190, QVB PO, Sydney, NSW 1230; tel. (2) 9265-1555; fax (2) 9261-4485; e-mail reception@sydney.anglican.asn.au; internet www.sydneyanglicans.net.

The Roman Catholic Church

Australia comprises five metropolitan archdioceses, two archdioceses directly responsible to the Holy See and 24 dioceses, including one diocese each for Catholics of the Maronite and Melkite rites, and one military ordinariate. At 31 December 2007 there were an estimated 5,340,466 adherents in the country.

Australian Catholic Bishops' Conference: GPOB 368, Canberra, ACT 2601; tel. (2) 6201-9845; fax (2) 6247-6083; e-mail gensec@catholic.org.au; internet www.acbc.catholic.org.au; f. 1979; Pres. Most Rev. PHILIP WILSON (Archbishop of Adelaide); Sec. Rev. BRIAN LUCAS.

Archbishop of Adelaide: Most Rev. PHILIP WILSON, GPOB 1364, Adelaide, SA 5001; tel. (8) 8210-8108; fax (8) 8223-2307; e-mail archbishop3@adelaide.catholic.org.au; internet www.adelaide.catholic.org.au.

Archbishop of Brisbane: Most Rev. JOHN ALEXIUS BATHERSBY, 790 Brunswick St, New Farm, Brisbane, Qld 4005; tel. (7) 3336-9361; fax (7) 3358-1357; e-mail archbishop@bne.catholic.net.au; internet www.bne.catholic.net.au.

Archbishop of Canberra and Goulburn: Most Rev. MARK BENEDICT COLERIDGE, GPOB 3089, Canberra, ACT 2601; tel. (2) 6201-9800; fax (2) 6257-7410; e-mail archbishop@cg.catholic.org.au; internet www.cg.catholic.org.au.

Archbishop of Hobart: Most Rev. ADRIAN DOYLE, GPOB 62, Hobart, Tas 7001; tel. (3) 6208-6222; fax (3) 6208-6292; e-mail vicar.general@aohtas.org.au; internet www.hobart.catholic.org.au.

Archbishop of Melbourne: Most Rev. DENIS JAMES HART, POB 146, East Melbourne, Vic 3002; tel. (3) 9926-5677; fax (3) 9926-5617; e-mail info@cam.org.au; internet www.cam.org.au.

Archbishop of Perth: Most Rev. BARRY J. HICKEY, Catholic Church Office, 25 Victoria Ave, Perth, WA 6000; tel. (8) 9223-1351; fax (8) 9221-1716; e-mail enquiries@perthcatholic.org.au; internet www.perthcatholic.org.au.

Archbishop of Sydney: Cardinal GEORGE PELL, Polding Centre, 133 Liverpool St, Sydney, NSW 2000; tel. (2) 9390-5100; fax (2) 9261-8312; e-mail chancery@sydneycatholic.org; internet www.sydney.catholic.org.au.

Orthodox Churches

Greek Orthodox Archdiocese of Australia: 242 Cleveland St, Redfern, Sydney, NSW 2016; tel. (2) 9690-6100; fax (2) 9698-5368; e-mail webmaster@greekorthodox.org.au; internet www.greekorthodox.org.au; f. 1924; 700,000 mems; Primate Archbishop STYLIANOS HARKIANAKIS.

The Antiochian, Coptic, Romanian, Serbian and Syrian Orthodox Churches are also represented.

Other Christian Churches

Baptist Union of Australia: 1 Francis Ave, Broadview, SA 5083; tel. (8) 8261-1844; e-mail bua@baptist.org.au; internet www.baptist.org.au; f. 1926; 61,409 mems; 868 churches; Nat. Dir Rev. Dr JOHN BEASY.

Churches of Christ in Australia: 1st Floor, 582 Heidelberg Rd, Fairfield, Vic 3078; tel. (3) 9488-8847; fax (3) 9481-8543; e-mail eo.nc@churchesofchrist.org.au; internet cofcaustralia.org/cofc-cms; 36,000 mems; Pres. Rev. RICHARD MENTEITH; Exec. Officer Rev. NIGEL PEGRAM.

Lutheran Church of Australia: National Office, 197 Archer St, North Adelaide, SA 5006; tel. (8) 8267-7300; fax (8) 8267-7310; e-mail president@lca.org.au; internet www.lca.org.au; f. 1966; 70,000 mems; Pres. Rev. Dr M. P. SEMMLER.

United Pentecostal Church of Australia: POB 60, Woden, ACT 2606; tel. (2) 6291-7885; fax (2) 6281-2330; e-mail contact@upca.org.au; internet www.upca.org.au; f. 1952; over 3,000 adherents in 2008; associated with United Pentecostal Church Int. in North America; Gen. Superintendent JOHN DOWNS.

Uniting Church in Australia: POB A2266, Sydney South, NSW 1235; tel. (2) 8267-4428; fax (2) 8267-4222; e-mail enquiries@nat.uca.org.au; internet uca.org.au; f. 1977; est. as a union of Methodist, Presbyterian and Congregational Churches; 300,000 mems; Pres. Rev. ALISTAIR MACRAE; Gen. Sec. Rev. TERENCE CORKIN.

ISLAM

At the census of August 2006, the Muslim community was estimated to number 340,390.

The Australian Federation of Islamic Councils: 932 Bourke St, Zetland, Sydney, NSW 2017; tel. (2) 9319-6733; fax (2) 9319-0159; e-mail admin@afic.com.au; internet www.afic.com.au; Pres. IKEBAL PATEL; Vice-Pres. HAFEZ KASSEM.

JUDAISM

The Jewish community numbered 88,826 at the census of August 2006.

Great Synagogue: 166 Castlereagh St, Sydney, NSW; tel. (2) 9267-2477; fax (2) 9264-8871; e-mail admin@greatsynagogue.org.au; internet www.greatsynagogue.org.au; f. 1878; Sr Rabbi JEREMY LAWRENCE; Pres. MICHAEL GOLD.

OTHER FAITHS

According to the August 2006 census, Buddhists numbered 418,757 and Hindus 148,127.

The Press

The total circulation of Australia's daily newspapers is relatively high, but in the remoter parts of the country weekly papers are even more popular. Most of Australia's newspapers are published in sparsely populated rural areas where the demand for local news is strong.

ACP Publishing Pty Ltd: 54–58 Park St, Sydney, NSW 2000; tel. (2) 9282-8000; fax (2) 9267-4361; internet www.acp.com.au; publishes 60 magazines, incl. *Australian Women's Weekly*, *Cleo*, *Cosmopolitan*, *Woman's Day*, *Dolly*, *Ralph* and *Wheels*; Man. Dir PHIL SCOTT.

APN News and Media Ltd: Level 4, 100 William St, Sydney, NSW 2011; tel. (2) 9333-4999; fax (2) 9333-4900; e-mail info@apn.com.au; internet www.apn.com.au; publishes 14 daily newspapers, incl. *The Chronicle*, *Daily Mercury*, *Northern Star* and over 75 community publs; Chair. GAVIN O'REILLY; Chief Exec. BRENDAN M. A. HOPKINS.

Fairfax Media: GPO 506, Sydney, NSW 2001; tel. (2) 9282-2833; fax (2) 9282-3133; internet www.fxj.com.au; f. 1987; fmrly known as John Fairfax Holdings Ltd; merged with Rural Press Ltd 2007; Chair. ROGER CORBETT; Chief Exec. GREG HYWOOD; publs include *The Sydney Morning Herald*, *The Australian Financial Review* and *Sun-Herald* (NSW), *The Age* and *BRW Publications* (Victoria), and *The Canberra Times*; also provides online and interactive services.

News Ltd: Level 23, 175 Liverpool St, Sydney, NSW 2001; tel. (2) 9288-3000; fax (2) 9288-2300; e-mail newsroom@news.com.au; internet www.news.com.au; Australian subsidiary of US News Corpn; Chair. and CEO JOHN HARTIGAN; controls *The Australian* and *The Weekend Australian* (national), *Daily Telegraph* , *Sunday Telegraph* (NSW), *The Herald Sun* and *Sunday Herald Sun* (Victoria), *Northern Territory News* (Darwin), *Sunday Times* (WA), *Townsville Bulletin*, *Courier Mail*, *Sunday Mail* (Queensland), *The Mercury* (Tasmania), *The Advertiser*, *Sunday Mail* (South Australia).

West Australian Newspapers Holdings Ltd: Newspaper House, 50 Hasler Rd, Osborne Park, WA 6017; tel. (8) 9482-9047; fax (8) 9482-9051; e-mail westinfo@wanews.com.au; internet www.thewest.com.au; Chair. KERRY STOKES; CEO CHRIS WHARTON.

NEWSPAPERS

Australian Capital Territory

The Canberra Times: POB 7155, Canberra Mail Centre, ACT 2610; tel. (2) 6280-2122; fax (2) 6280-2282; e-mail letters.editor@canberratimes.com.au; internet www.canberratimes.com.au; f. 1926; daily and Sun.; morning; Editor-in-Chief JACK WATERFORD; Editor ROD QUINN; circ. 32,116 (Mon.–Fri.), 53,051 (Sat.), 33,439 (Sun.).

New South Wales

Dailies

The Australian: POB 4245, Sydney, NSW 2001; tel. (2) 9288-3000; fax (2) 9288-2250; e-mail letters@theaustralian.com.au; internet www.theaustralian.com.au; f. 1964; distributed nationally; edited in Sydney, simultaneous edns in Sydney, Melbourne, Perth, Townsville, Adelaide and Brisbane; Editor-in-Chief CHRIS MITCHELL; Editor PAUL WHITTAKER; circ. 136,268 (Mon.–Fri.); *The Weekend Australian* (Sat.) 300,079.

Australian Financial Review: GPOB 55, Melbourne, Vic 3001; tel. (2) 9282-1547; e-mail afreditor@afr.com.au; internet www.afr.com; f. 1951; distributed nationally; Publr/Editor-in-Chief MICHAEL GILL; Editor GLENN BURGE; circ. 75,339 (Mon.–Fri.), 72,898 (Sat.).

The Daily Telegraph: News Ltd, 2 Holt St, Surry Hills, NSW 2010; tel. (2) 9288-3000; fax (2) 9288-2300; e-mail news@dailytelegraph.com.au; internet www.dailytelegraph.com.au; f. 1879; merged in 1990 with *Daily Mirror* (f. 1941); 24-hour tabloid; Editor GARRY LINNELL; circ. 363,399 (Mon.–Fri.), 325,000 (Sat.).

The Manly Daily: 26 Sydney Rd, Manly, NSW 2095; tel. (2) 9976-1909; fax (2) 9977-1203; e-mail editor@manlydaily.com.au; internet www.manlydaily.com.au; f. 1906; Tue.–Sat.; Editor LUKE MCILVEEN; circ. 91,816.

The Newcastle Herald: 28–30 Bolton St, Newcastle, NSW 2300; tel. (2) 4979-5000; fax (2) 4979-5588; e-mail news@theherald.com.au; internet www.theherald.com.au; f. 1858; morning; 6 a week; Editor ROGER BROCK; Gen. Man. JULIE AINSWORTH; circ. 48,000.

The Sydney Morning Herald: GPOB 506, Sydney, NSW 2001; tel. (2) 9282-2833; fax (2) 9282-3253; e-mail newsdesk@smh.com.au; internet www.smh.com.au; f. 1831; morning; Editor-in-Chief PETER FRAY; circ. 204,421 (Mon.–Fri.), 332,066 (Sat.).

Weeklies

Bankstown Canterbury Torch: 47 Allingham St, Condell Park, NSW 2200; tel. (2) 9795-0000; fax (2) 9795-0096; e-mail torch@torchpublishing.com.au; internet www.torchpublishing.com.au; f. 1920; Wed.; owned by Torch Publishing Co Pty Ltd; Editor MARK KIRKLAND; circ. 91,335 (Oct. 2009).

Northern District Times: Suite 2, 3 Carlingford Rd, Epping, NSW 2121; tel. (2) 9024-8716; fax (2) 9024-8788; e-mail editor@northerndistricttimes.com.au; internet www.northerndistricttimes.com.au; f. 1921; Wed.; Editor COLIN KERR; circ. 58,450.

The Parramatta Advertiser: 142–154 Macquarie St, Parramatta, NSW 2150; tel. (2) 9689-5323; fax (2) 9689-5388; e-mail editor@parramattaadvertiser.com.au; internet www.parramattaadvertiser.com.au; f. 1933; Wed.; Editor RICK ALLEN; circ. 82,677.

St George and Sutherland Shire Leader: 633 Princess Hwy, Rockdale, NSW 2216; tel. (2) 9588-8888; fax (2) 9588-8887; e-mail leaderenquiries@fairfaxmedia.com.au; internet www.theleader.com.au; f. 1960; Tue. and Thur.; Editor ALBERT MARTINEZ; circ. 148,713.

Sun-Herald: GPOB 506, Sydney, NSW 2001; tel. (2) 9282-2833; fax (2) 9282-2151; e-mail newsdesk@smh.com.au; internet www.smh.com.au; f. 1953; Sun.; Editor RICK FENELEY; circ. 429,199.

Sunday Telegraph: 2 Holt St, Surry Hills, NSW 2010; tel. (2) 9288-3000; fax (2) 9288-2300; e-mail letters@sundaytelegraph.com.au; f. 1938; Editor NEIL BREEN; circ. 635,269.

Northern Territory

Daily

Northern Territory News: Printers Place, GPOB 1300, Darwin, NT 0801; tel. (8) 8944-9900; fax (8) 8981-6045; e-mail ntnmail@ntnews.com.au; internet www.ntnews.com.au; f. 1952; morning; Editor-in-Chief JULIAN RICCI; Gen. Man. EVAN HANNAH; circ. 22,989 (Mon.–Sat.); *The Sunday Territorian*, circ. 22,624.

Weekly

Centralian Advocate: 2 Gap Rd, Alice Springs, NT 0871; tel. (8) 8950-9777; fax (8) 8950-9740; e-mail ceneditorial@aliceadvocate.com.au; f. 1947; Tue. and Thur.; Editor DALLAS FRAKKING; circ. 6,992 (Sept. 2009).

Queensland

Daily

The Courier-Mail: Cnr Mayne Rd and Campbell St, Bowen Hills, Qld 4001; tel. (7) 3666-6775; fax (7) 3666-6696; e-mail crutcherm@gnp.newsltd.com.au; internet www.thecouriermail.com.au; f. 1933; morning; Editor MICHAEL CRUTCHER; Man. Editor ANNA REYNOLDS; circ. 206,110 (Mon.–Fri.), 278,982 (Sat.).

Gold Coast Bulletin: 385 Southport Nerang Rd, Molendinar, Qld 4214; tel. (7) 5584–2000; internet www.goldcoast.com.au; f. 1885; 6 a week; Editor DEAN GOULD; circ. 39,128 (Mon.–Fri.), 64,915 (Sat.).

Weekly

The Sunday Mail: cnr Mayne Rd and Campbell St, Bowen Hills, Qld 4001; tel. (7) 3666-6276; fax (7) 3666-6767; e-mail mcanenya@qnp.newsltd.com.au; internet www.thesundaymail.com.au; f. 1953; Editor SCOTT THOMPSON; circ. 1,200,000.

South Australia

Daily

The Advertiser: 31 Waymouth St, Adelaide, SA 5000; tel. (8) 8206-2000; fax (8) 8206-3669; e-mail tiser@adv.newsltd.com.au; internet www.adelaidenow.com.au; f. 1858; morning; Editor MELVIN MANSELL; circ. 180,807 (Mon.–Fri.), 242,903 (Sat.).

Weekly

Sunday Mail: Level 2, 31 Waymouth St, GPOB 339, Adelaide, SA 5000; tel. (8) 8206-2000; fax (8) 8206-3646; e-mail mailedit@sundaymail.com.au; internet www.adelaidenow.com.au; f. 1912; Editor MEGAN LLOYD; circ. 294,930.

Tasmania

Dailies

The Advocate: POB 63, Burnie, Tas 7320; tel. (3) 6440-7409; fax (3) 6440-7340; e-mail news@theadvocate.com.au; internet www.theadvocate.com.au; f. 1890; morning; Editor JASON PURDIE; circ. 22,786.

Examiner: 71–75 Paterson St, POB 99, Launceston, Tas 7250; tel. (3) 6336-7111; fax (3) 6334-7328; e-mail admin@examiner.com.au; internet www.examiner.com.au; f. 1842; 6 a week; Editor MARTIN GILMOUR; Gen. Man. PHIL LEERSEN; circ. 31,144.

Mercury: 93 Macquarie St, Hobart, Tas 7000; tel. (3) 6230-0622; fax (3) 6230-0711; e-mail mercury.news@dbl.newsltd.com.au; internet www.themercury.com.au; f. 1854; morning; Man. Dir REX GARDNER; Editor GARRY BAILEY; circ. 44,221 (Mon.–Fri.), 60,082 (Sat.); *Sunday Tasmanian*, circ. 57,868.

Weeklies

Sunday Examiner: 71–75 Paterson St, Launceston, Tas 7250; tel. (3) 6336-7111; fax (3) 6334-7328; e-mail mail@examiner.com.au; internet www.examiner.com.au; f. 1924; Editor MARTIN GILMOUR; circ. 38,826.

Victoria

Dailies

The Age: 655 Collins St, Docklands, Melbourne, Vic 3008; tel. (3) 8667-2250; e-mail newsdesk@theage.com.au; internet www.theage.com.au; f. 1854; morning; Editor-in-Chief PAUL RAMADGE; Chief Exec. DON CHURCHILL; circ. 190,100 (Mon.–Fri.), 273,700 (Sat.).

Geelong Advertiser: 191–195 Ryrie St, Geelong, Vic 3220; tel. (3) 5227-4300; fax (3) 5227-4330; internet www.geelongadvertiser.com.au; f. 1840; morning; Editor STEELE TALLON; circ. 25,586 (Mon.–Fri.), 44,319 (Sat.).

Herald Sun: HWT Tower, 40 City Rd, Southbank, Vic 3006; tel. (3) 9292-2000; fax (3) 9292-2112; e-mail news@heraldsun.com.au; internet www.heraldsun.com.au; f. 1840; Editor-in-Chief PETER BLUNDEN; Editor SIMON PRISTEL; circ. 500,800 (Mon.–Fri.), 495,600 (Sat.).

Weekly

The Sunday Age: 655 Collins St, Docklands, Melbourne, Vic 3008; tel. (3) 8667-2250; e-mail newsdesk@theage.com.au; internet www.theage.com.au; f. 1989; Editor GAY ALCORN; circ. 226,700.

Sunday Herald Sun: HWT Tower, 40 City Rd, Southbank, Vic 3006; tel. (3) 9292-2963; fax (3) 9292-2080; e-mail sundayhs@heraldsun.com.au; internet www.heraldsun.com.au; f. 1991; Editor SIMON PRISTEL; circ. 593,700.

Western Australia

Daily

The West Australian: GPOB D162, Perth, WA 6840; tel. (8) 9482-3111; fax (8) 9482-9080; internet www.thewest.com.au; f. 1833; morning; Editor BRETT MCCARTHY; circ. 192,230 (Mon.–Fri.), 316,062 (Sat.).

Weekly

Sunday Times: 34 Stirling St, Perth, WA 6000; tel. (8) 9326-8326; fax (8) 9221-1121; e-mail editorial@sundaytimes.newsltd.com.au; internet www.perthnow.com.au; f. 1897; Man. Dir DAVID MAGUIRE; Editor SAM WEIR; circ. 293,136.

PRINCIPAL PERIODICALS

Weeklies and Fortnightlies

Business Review Weekly (BRW): GPOB 55, Melbourne, Vic 3001; tel. (2) 9282-1111; fax (2) 9282-1779; e-mail brweditor@brw.fairfax.com.au; internet www.brw.com.au; f. 1981; Editor-in-Chief SEAN AYLMER; Editor KATE MILLS; circ. 45,467.

Computerworld Australia: Level 22, 8–20 Napier St, North Sydney, NSW 2060; tel. (2) 9902-2700; fax (2) 9439-5512; e-mail editor@idg.com.au; internet www.computerworld.com.au; weekly; information technology news; Editor MATT RODGERS.

The Countryman: GPOB D162, Perth, WA 6840; tel. (8) 9482-3327; fax (8) 9482-3314; e-mail countryman@wanews.com.au; internet countryman.thewest.com.au; f. 1885; Thur.; farming; Editor CAMERON MORSE; circ. 10,500.

The Medical Journal of Australia: Locked Bag 3030, Strawberry Hills, NSW 2012; tel. (2) 9562-6666; fax (2) 9562-6699; e-mail medjaust@ampco.com.au; internet www.mja.com.au; f. 1914; fortnightly; Editor Dr MARTIN VAN DER WEYDEN; circ. 27,532.

New Idea: 35–51 Mitchell St, McMahons Point, NSW 2060; tel. (2) 9464-3200; fax (2) 9464-3203; e-mail letters@newidea.com.au; internet www.newidea.com.au; weekly; women's; Editor KIM WILSON; Publr SUZANNE MONKS; circ. 327,649.

News Weekly: 35 Whitehorse Rd, POB 251, Balwyn, Vic 3103; tel. (3) 9816-0800; fax (3) 9816-0899; e-mail nw@newsweekly.com.au; internet www.newsweekly.com.au; f. 1943; publ. by Nat. Civic Council; fortnightly; Sat.; political, social, educational and trade union affairs; Editor PETER WESTMORE; circ. 9,000.

NW: 54 Park St, Sydney, NSW 2000; tel. (2) 9282-2000; e-mail nw@acp.com.au; internet www.nwonline.com.au; weekly; entertainment news; Editor LISA SINCLAIR; circ. 143,302.

People: Level 18, 66–68 Goulburn St, Sydney, NSW 2000; tel. (2) 9282-8388; fax (2) 9283-7923; e-mail mvine@acpmagazines.com.au; internet www.acpmagazines.com.au/people.htm; weekly; men's interest; Editor SHANE CUBIS; circ. 40,045.

Picture: GPOB 5201, Sydney, NSW 2001; tel. (2) 9288-9686; fax (2) 9267-4372; e-mail picture@acp.com.au; internet www.acp.com.au/the_picture.htm; weekly; men's interest; Editor SHAYNE BUGDEN; circ. 56,559.

Queensland Country Life: cnr Finucane Rd and Delancey St, Ormiston, Qld 4160; tel. (7) 3826-8200; fax (7) 3821-1236; e-mail editorialsec.qcl@ruralpress.com; internet qcl.farmonline.com.au; f. 1935; Thur.; Editor MARK PHELPS; Gen. Man. JOHN WARLTERS; circ. 29,823.

Stock and Land: Unit 6, 99–101 Western Ave, Tullamarine, Vic 3043; tel. (3) 9344-9999; fax (3) 9338-1044; e-mail stockandland@ruralpress.com; internet sl.farmonline.com.au; f. 1914; weekly; agricultural and rural news; Editor TOM DAWKINS; circ. 7,354 (2008).

Take 5: 54–58 Park St, Sydney, NSW 2000; tel. (2) 9282-8000; fax (2) 9267-4361; e-mail take5@acpmagazines.com.au; internet www.take5mag.com.au; weekly; Editor BELINDA WALLIS; circ. 221,033.

That's Life!: 35–51 Mitchell St, McMahons Point, NSW 2060; tel. (2) 9464-3300; fax (2) 9464-3480; e-mail thatslife@pacificmags.com.au; internet www.thatslife.com.au; f. 1994; weekly; features; Editor LINDA SMITH; circ. 305,607.

Time South Pacific: Level 10, 32 Walker St, North Sydney, NSW 2060; tel. (2) 9925-2500; fax (2) 9954-0828; e-mail letters@time.com; internet www.time.com/time/magazine/pacific; weekly; current affairs; Editor STEVE WATERSON; circ. 76,514.

TV Week: 54 Park St, Sydney, NSW 2000; tel. (2) 9288-9611; fax (2) 9283-4849; e-mail tvweek@acp.com.au; internet www.tvweek.ninemsn.com.au; f. 1957; Wed.; colour national; Editor EMMA NOLAN; circ. 226,832.

The Weekly Times: POB 14999, Melbourne, Vic 8001; tel. (3) 9292-2672; fax (3) 9292-2697; e-mail wtimes@theweeklytimes.com.au; internet www.theweeklytimes.com.au; f. 1869; farming, regional issues, country life; Wed.; Editor ED GANNON; circ. 78,900.

Woman's Day: POB 5245, Sydney, NSW 2001; tel. (2) 9282-8000; fax (2) 9267-4360; e-mail womansday@acp.com.au; internet womansday.ninemsn.com.au; weekly; circulates throughout Australia and NZ; Editor FIONA CONNOLLY; circ. 406,825.

Monthlies and Others

Architectural Product News: Architecture Media Pty Ltd, Level 6, 163 Eastern Rd, South Melbourne, Vic 3205; tel. (3) 8699-1000; fax (3) 9696-2617; e-mail apn@archmedia.com.au; internet www

.architecturemedia.com; 6 a year; Editorial Dir CAMERON BRUHN; Editor PETER DAVIES; circ. 24,584.

Australian Geographic: 54 Park St, Sydney, NSW 2000; tel. (2) 9263-9813; fax (2) 9263-9810; e-mail editorial@ausgeo.com.au; internet www.australiangeographic.com.au; f. 1986; every 3 months; Man. Dir RORY SCOTT; Editor IAN CONNELLAN; circ. 140,724.

Australian Good Taste: Locked Bag 5030, Alexandria, NSW 2015; tel. (2) 9353-6666; fax (2) 9353-6699; e-mail goodtaste@newsmagazines.com.au; internet www.taste.com.au/good+taste; monthly; food and lifestyle; Editor BRODEE MYERS-COOKE; circ. 134,003.

Australian Gourmet Traveller: GPOB 4088, Sydney, NSW 2001; tel. (2) 9282-8758; fax (2) 9264-3621; e-mail gourmet@acpmagazines.com.au; internet gourmettraveller.com.au; monthly; food and travel; Editor ANTHEA LOUCAS; circ. 74,292.

Australian Home Beautiful: 35–51 Mitchell St, McMahons Point, NSW 2060; tel. (2) 9464-3218; fax (2) 9464-3263; e-mail homebeautiful@pacificmags.com.au; internet www.homebeautiful.com.au; f. 1925; monthly; Editor WENDY MOORE; circ. 70,480.

Australian House and Garden: 54 Park St, Sydney, NSW 2000; tel. (2) 9282-8456; fax (2) 9267-4912; internet www.houseandgarden.com.au; f. 1948; monthly; design, decorating, renovating, gardens, food, travel, health and beauty; Editor-in-Chief LISA GREEN; circ. 96,554.

Australian Journal of Mining: Informa Australia Pty Ltd, Level 2, 120 Sussex St, Sydney, NSW 2000; tel. (2) 9080-4443; e-mail charles.macdonald@informa.com.au; internet www.theajmonline.com; f. 1986; bi-monthly; mining and exploration throughout Australia and South Pacific; Editor CHARLES MACDONALD; circ. 5,875.

Australian Journal of Pharmacy: Level 5, 8 Thomas St, Chatswood, NSW 2067; tel. (2) 8117-9500; fax (2) 8117-9511; e-mail david.weston@appco.com.au; internet www.ajp.com.au; f. 1886; monthly; journal of the associated pharmaceutical orgs; Publr and Man. Editor DAVID WESTON; Editor MATTHEW ETON; circ. 16,553.

Australian Law Journal: 100 Harris St, Pyrmont, NSW 2009; tel. (2) 8587-7000; fax (2) 8587-7104; e-mail lta.alj@thomsonreuters.com; internet www.thomsonreuters.com.au; f. 1927; monthly; Gen. Editor Justice P. W. YOUNG; circ 4,500.

Australian Photography: 17–21 Bellevue St, Surry Hills, NSW 2010; tel. (2) 9281-2333; fax (2) 9281-2750; e-mail robertkeeley@yaffa.com.au; f. 1950; monthly; Editor ROBERT KEELEY; circ. 9,099.

The Australian Women's Weekly: 54–58 Park St, Sydney, NSW 2000; tel. (2) 9282-8000; fax (2) 9267-4459; e-mail womensweekly@acpmagazines.com.au; internet www.aww.ninemsn.com.au; f. 1933; monthly; Editor-in-Chief HELEN MCCABE; circ. 493,301.

Belle: 54 Park St, Sydney, NSW 2000; tel. (2) 9282-8000; fax (2) 9267-8037; e-mail belle@acp.com.au; internet www.acpmagazines.com.au/belle.htm; f. 1975; every 2 months; interior design and architecture; Editor-in-Chief NEALE WHITAKER; circ. 35,190.

Better Homes and Gardens: 35–51 Mitchell St, McMahon's Point, NSW 2060; e-mail bhgmagenquiries@pacificmags.com.au; internet au.lifestyle.yahoo.com/better-homes-gardens; f. 1978; 13 a year; Editor JULIA ZAETTA; circ. 370,000.

Cleo: 54 Park St, Sydney, NSW 2000; tel. (2) 9282-8617; fax (2) 9267-4368; internet www.cleo.com.au; f. 1972; women's monthly; Editor NATALIE POOL; circ. 134,286.

Cosmopolitan: 54 Park St, Sydney, NSW 2000; tel. (2) 9282-8039; fax (2) 9267-4457; e-mail cosmo@acp.com.au; internet www.cosmopolitan.com.au; f. 1973; monthly; women's lifestyle; Editor BRONWYN MCCAHON; circ. 166,208.

Delicious: Locked Bag 5030, Alexandria, NSW 2015; tel. (2) 9353-6666; fax (2) 9353-6699; e-mail delicious@newsmagazines.com.au; internet www.taste.com.au/delicious; 11 a year; food and lifestyle; Editor TRUDI JENKINS; circ. 129,626.

Dolly: 54–58 Park St, Sydney, NSW 2000; tel. (2) 9282-8437; fax (2) 9126-3715; internet dolly.ninemsn.com.au/dolly; f. 1970; monthly; for young women; Editor TIFFANY DUNK; circ. 103,131.

Family Circle: Pacific Magazines, Media City, 8 Central Ave, Eveleigh, NSW 2015; tel. (2) 9394-2866; fax (2) 9394-2481; internet www.pacificmagazines.com.au; 2 a year; Editor-in-Chief JULIA ZAETTA; circ. 87,301.

FHM: EMAP Australia, Level 6, 187 Thomas St, Haymarket, Sydney, NSW 2000; tel. (2) 9581-9400; fax (2) 9581-9570; e-mail incoming@emap.com.au; internet www.fhm.com.au; monthly; men's interest; Editor GUY MOSEL; circ. 51,063.

Financial Review Smart Investor: 201 Sussex St, GPOB 506, Sydney, NSW 2000; tel. (2) 9282-2822; fax (2) 9603-3137; e-mail smartinvestor@afr.com.au; internet www.afrsmartinvestor.com; monthly; Editor NICOLE PEDERSEN-MCKINNON.

Gardening Australia: POB 199, Alexandria, NSW 1435; tel. (2) 9353-6666; fax (2) 9317-4615; e-mail ga@newsmagazines.com.au; internet www.gardeningaustralia.com.au; f. 1991; monthly; Editor JENNIFER STACKHOUSE; circ. 94,868.

Girlfriend: 35–51 Mitchell St, McMahons Point, NSW 2060; tel. (2) 9464-3300; fax (2) 9464-3483; e-mail girlfriend@pacificmags.com.au; internet www.girlfriend.com.au; monthly; for teenage girls; Editor SARAH CORNISH; circ. 108,119.

Good Health and Medicine: 54 Park St, Sydney, NSW 2000; tel. (2) 9282-8000; fax (2) 9267-4361; internet health.ninemsn.com.au/goodmedicine/goodmedicine.aspx; monthly; fmrly Good Medicine; health and beauty; Editor CATHERINE MARSHALL; circ. 66,115.

Houses: Architecture Media Pty Ltd, Level 6, 163 Eastern Rd, South Melbourne, Vic 3205; tel. (3) 8699-1000; fax (3) 9696-2617; e-mail houses@archmedia.com.au; internet www.architecturemedia.com/houses; f. 1989; 6 a year; Publisher/Editorial Dir SUE HARRIS; Editoral Dir CAMERON BRUHN; circ. 19,877.

K-Zone: Media City, 8 Central Ave, Eveleigh, NSW 2015; tel. (2) 9394-2760; fax (2) 9464-3483; e-mail kzone@pacificmags.com.au; internet www.kzone.com.au; monthly; gaming and entertainment; Editor DANIEL FINDLAY; circ. 50,272.

Marie Claire: Media City, 8 Central Ave, Eveleigh, NSW 2015; tel. (2) 9394-2000; e-mail marieclaire@pacificmags.com.au; internet www.marieclaire.com.au; f. 1995; owned by Pacific Magazines Pty Ltd; monthly; fashion and lifestyle; Editor and Publr JACKIE FRANK; circ. 112,682 (2010).

Motor: POB 4088, Sydney, NSW 2001; tel. (2) 9288-9172; fax (2) 9263-9777; e-mail motor@acpmagazines.com.au; f. 1954; monthly; Editor ANDREW MACLEAN; circ. 50,085.

Open Road: NRMA Publishing, Level 1, 9 George St, North Strathfield, NSW 2137; tel. (2) 8741-6675; fax (2) 8741-6697; e-mail open.road@mynrma.com.au; internet www.openroad.com.au; f. 1927; every 2 months; journal of Nat. Roads and Motorists' Asscn (NRMA); Publr BERNADETTE BRENNAN; Editor-in-Chief NEEDRA D'SOUZA; circ. 1,555,917.

Ralph: 54–58 Park St, Sydney, NSW 2000; tel. (2) 9282-8000; fax (2) 9267-4361; internet ralph.ninemsn.com.au; monthly; men's lifestyle; Editor SANTI PINTADO; circ. 68,061.

Reader's Digest: GPOB 5030, Sydney, NSW 2001; tel. (2) 9690-6111; fax (2) 9690-6211; e-mail editors.au@readersdigest.com; internet www.readersdigest.au.com; monthly; Editor-in-Chief SUE CARNEY; circ. 325,028.

Street Machine: Locked Bag 756, Epping, NSW 2121; tel. (2) 9868-4832; fax (2) 9869-7390; e-mail streetmachine@acpaction.com.au; internet www.acpmagazines.com.au/street_machine.htm; monthly; motoring magazine; Editor GEOFF SEDDON; circ. 50,840.

Super Food Ideas: Locked Bag 5030, Alexandria, NSW 2015; tel. (2) 9353-6666; fax (2) 9353-6699; e-mail superfoodideas@newsmagazines.com.au; internet www.taste.com.au/super+food+ideas; 11 a year; Editor REBECCA COX; circ. 271,376.

TV Soap: Level 5, 55 Chandos St, St Leonards, NSW 2065; tel. (2) 9901-6132; fax (2) 9901-6116; e-mail tvsoap@next.com.au; internet www.tvsoap.com.au; f. 1983; monthly; Editor VESNA PETROPOULOS; circ. 103,000.

Vogue Australia: 180 Bourke Rd, Alexandria, NSW 2015; tel. (2) 9353-6666; fax (2) 9353-0935; e-mail vogue@vogue.com.au; internet www.vogue.com.au; f. 1959; monthly; fashion; Editor KIRSTIE CLEMENTS; circ. 50,752.

Wheels: GPOB 4088, Sydney, NSW 2001; tel. (2) 9263-9732; fax (2) 9263-9702; e-mail wheels@acp.com.au; internet motoring.ninemsn.com.au/wheelsmag; f. 1953; monthly; international motoring magazine; Editor GED BULMER; circ. 55,338.

Your Garden: Media City 8, Cen. Ave, Eveleigh, NSW 2015; tel. (2) 9394-2381; fax (2) 9394-4206; e-mail yg@pacificmags.com.au; internet pacificmagazines.com.au/Pages/Magazines; f. 1947; every three months; owned by Pacific Magazines; Editor PAUL URQUHART; circ. 53,824.

NEWS AGENCY

AAP: 3 Rider Blvd, Rhodes Waterside, Rhodes, NSW 2138; tel. (2) 9322-8000; fax (2) 9322-8888; e-mail customerservice@aap.com.au; internet www.aap.com.au; f. 1983; owned by major daily newspapers of Australia; Chair. MICHAEL GILL; CEO BRUCE DAVIDSON.

PRESS ASSOCIATIONS

Australian Press Council: Suite 10.02, 117 York St, Sydney, NSW 2000; tel. (2) 9261-1930; fax (2) 9267-6826; e-mail info@presscouncil.org.au; internet www.presscouncil.org.au; Chair. Prof. JULIAN DISNEY.

Community Newspapers of Australia Pty Ltd: POB 234, Auburn, NSW 1835; tel. (2) 8789-7362; fax (2) 8789-7387; e-mail kim@cna.org.au; internet www.cna.org.au; Fed. Pres. GENE SWINSTEAD; Exec. Sec. ROBYN BAKER.

Country Press Association of SA Inc: 198 Greenhill Rd, Eastwood, SA 5063; tel. (8) 8373-6533; fax (8) 8373-6544; e-mail countrypsa@bigpond.com; internet www.sacountrypress.com.au; f. 1912; represents South Australian country newspapers; Pres. T. McAuliffe; Admin. Officer Marilyn McAuliffe.

Country Press Australia: 163 Epsom Rd, Flemington, Vic 3031; tel. (3) 8387-5580; fax (3) 9372-2427; internet www.countrypress.net.au; f. 1906; 420 mems.

Queensland Country Press Association: POB 229, Kelvin Grove DC, Qld 4059; tel. (7) 3356-0033; fax (7) 3356-0027; e-mail nmclary@qcpa.com.au; internet www.qcpa.com.au; Pres. David Richardson; Exec. Dir Neal McLary; 26 mems.

Tasmanian Press Association Pty Ltd: 71–75 Paterson St, Launceston, Tas 7250; tel. (3) 6336-7111; Sec. Tom O'Meara.

Victorian Country Press Association Ltd: 1st Floor, 163 Epsom Rd, Flemington, Vic 3031; tel. (3) 8387-5500; fax (3) 9371-2792; internet www.vcpa.com.au; f. 1910; Pres. Ken Jenkins; Exec. Dir J.E. Ray; 110 mems.

Publishers

Allen and Unwin Pty Ltd: 83 Alexander St, Crows Nest, NSW 2065; tel. (2) 8425-0100; fax (2) 9906-2218; e-mail info@allenandunwin.com; internet www.allenandunwin.com; fiction, trade, academic, children's; Exec. Chair. and Publishing Dir Patrick A. Gallagher; Man. Dir Paul Donovan.

Australasian Medical Publishing Co Pty Ltd: AMPCo House, 277 Clarence St, Sydney, NSW 2000; tel. (2) 9562-6666; fax (2) 9562-6699; e-mail ampco@ampco.com.au; internet www.ampco.com.au; f. 1913; scientific, medical and educational; Gen. Man. Jackie Gambrell.

Black Inc: 37–39 Langridge St, Collingwood, Vic 3066; tel. (3) 9654-0288; fax (3) 9654-0244; e-mail enquiries@blackincbooks.com; internet www.blackincbooks.com; f. 2000; literary fiction and non-fiction; an imprint of Schwartz Publishing; Man. Dir Sophy Williams.

Cambridge University Press (Australia): 477 Williamstown Rd, PB 31, Port Melbourne, Vic 3207; tel. (3) 8671-1411; fax (3) 9676-9966; e-mail enquiries@cambridge.edu.au; internet www.cambridge.org/aus; scholarly and educational; Chief Exec. Stephen Bourne.

Cengage Learning Australia Pty Ltd: Level 7, 80 Dorcas St, South Melbourne, Vic 3205; tel. (3) 9685-4111; fax (3) 9685-4199; e-mail anz.customerservice@cengage.com; internet www.cengage.com.au; fmrly Thomson Learning Australia, name changed as above 2007; educational; Gen. Man. Paul Petrulis.

Commonwealth Scientific and Industrial Research Organisation (CSIRO Publishing): 150 Oxford St, POB 1139, Collingwood, Vic 3066; tel. (3) 9662-7500; fax (3) 9662-7595; e-mail publishing@csiro.au; internet www.publish.csiro.au; f. 1926; scientific and technical journals, books, magazines, videos, CD-ROMs; Gen. Man. P. W. Reekie.

Elsevier Australia: Level 12, Tower 1, 475 Victoria Ave, Chatswood, NSW 2067; tel. (2) 9422-8500; fax (2) 9422-8501; e-mail customerserviceau@elsevier.com; internet www.elsevier.com.au; a division of Reed Int. Books Australia Pty Ltd; health sciences, science and medicine; Man. Dir Rob Kolkman.

Encyclopaedia Britannica Australia Ltd: Locked Bag 927, North Sydney, NSW 2060; tel. (2) 9923-5600; fax (2) 9929-3753; e-mail feedback@britannica.com.au; internet www.britannica.com.au; reference, education, art, science and commerce; Man. Dir James Buckle.

Harlequin Enterprises (Australia) Pty Ltd: Locked Bag 7002, Chatswood, NSW 2067; tel. (2) 9415-9200; fax (2) 9415-9292; internet www.eHarlequin.com.au; Man. Dir Michelle Laforest.

Hyland House Publishing Pty Ltd: POB 1116, Carlton, Vic 3053; tel. (3) 9818-5700; fax (3) 9818-5044; e-mail info@hylandhouse.com.au; internet www.hylandhouse.com.au; f. 1977; Aboriginal and children's literature, gardening, pet care; Rep. Michael Schoo.

Lansdowne Publishing: POB 1669, Crows Nest, NSW 1585; tel. and fax (2) 9436-2974; e-mail info@lansdownepublishing.com.au; internet www.lansdownepublishing.com.au; cookery, new age, interior design, gardening, health, history, spirituality; Chief Exec. Steven Morris.

LexisNexis: Tower 2, 475–495 Victoria Ave, Chatswood, NSW 2067; tel. (2) 9422-2174; fax (2) 9422-2405; e-mail customer.relations@lexisnexis.com.au; internet www.lexisnexis.com.au; f. 1910; div. of Reed Elsevier; legal and commercial; CEO T. J. Viljoen.

McGraw-Hill Australia Pty Ltd: Level 2, The Everglade Bldg, 82 Waterloo Rd, North Ryde, NSW 2113; tel. (2) 9900-1800; fax (2) 9900-1980; e-mail cservice_sydney@mcgraw-hill.com; internet www.mcgraw-hill.com.au; f. 1964; educational, professional and technical; Man. Dir Murray St Leger.

Melbourne University Publishing Ltd: 187 Grattan St, Carlton, Vic 3053; tel. (3) 9342-0300; fax (3) 9342-0399; e-mail mup-info@unimelb.edu.au; internet www.mup.com.au; f. 1922; scholarly non-fiction, Australian history and biography; CEO Louise Adler.

Murdoch Books: GPOB 4115, Sydney, NSW 2001; tel. (2) 8220-2000; fax (2) 8220-2558; e-mail inquiry@murdochbooks.com.au; internet www.murdochbooks.com.au; cooking, gardening, DIY, craft, gift, general leisure and lifestyle, narrative, history, non-fiction, travel memoirs and business; CEO Matt Handbury; Publishing Dir Chris Rennie.

National Library of Australia: Parkes Place, Canberra, ACT 2600; tel. (2) 6262-1111; fax (2) 6257-1703; e-mail media@nla.gov.au; internet www.nla.gov.au; f. 1968; produces trade and library-related publs; Chair. James J. Spigelman.

Oxford University Press: 253 Normanby Rd, South Melbourne, Vic 3205; tel. (3) 9934-9123; fax (3) 9934-9100; e-mail cs.au@oup.com; internet www.oup.com.au; f. 1908; general non-fiction and educational; Man. Dir Marek Palka.

Pan Macmillan Australia Pty Ltd: Level 25, BT Tower, 1 Market St, Sydney NSW 2000; tel. (2) 9285-9100; fax (2) 9285-9190; e-mail pansyd@macmillan.com.au; internet www.panmacmillan.com.au; general, reference, children's, fiction, non-fiction; Chair. R. Gibb.

Pearson Education Australia Pty Ltd: Unit 4, Level 3, 14 Aquatic Dr., Frenchs Forest, NSW 2086; tel. (2) 9454-2200; fax (2) 9453-0089; e-mail customer.service@pearson.com.au; internet www.pearson.com.au; f. 1957; mainly educational, academic, computer, some general; CEO Marjorie Scardino.

Penguin Group (Australia): POB 701, Hawthorn, Vic 3122; tel. (3) 9811-2400; fax (3) 9811-2620; internet www.penguin.com.au; f. 1946; general; Man. Dir Gabrielle Coyne; Publishing Dir Robert Sessions.

Random House Australia Pty Ltd: Level 3, 100 Pacific Highway, North Sydney, NSW 2060; tel. (2) 9954-9966; fax (2) 9954-4562; e-mail random@randomhouse.com.au; internet www.randomhouse.com.au; fiction, non-fiction and children's; Man. Dir Margaret Seale.

Reader's Digest (Australia) Pty Ltd: GPOB 5030, Sydney, NSW 2001; tel. (2) 9018-6000; fax (2) 9018-7000; e-mail customerservice.au@readersdigest.com; internet www.readersdigest.com.au; general; Man. Dir Paul Heath.

Scholastic Australia Pty Ltd: 76–80 Railway Cres., Lisarow, NSW 2250; tel. (2) 4328-3555; fax (2) 4323-3827; e-mail customer_service@scholastic.com.au; internet www.scholastic.com.au; f. 1968; educational and children's; Man. Dir David Peagram.

Schwartz Publishing (Victoria) Pty Ltd: 37–39 Langridge St, Melbourne, Vic 3000; tel. (3) 9486-0288; fax (3) 9486-0244; e-mail admin@blackincbooks.com; internet www.blackincbooks.com; non-fiction; Dir Morry Schwartz.

Simon and Schuster (Australia) Pty Ltd: Suite 19A, Level 1, Bldg C, 450 Miller St, Cammeray, NSW 2062; tel. (2) 9983-6600; fax (2) 9988-4232; e-mail cservice@simonandschuster.com.au; internet www.simonandschuster.com.au; non-fiction incl. anthropology, cooking, gardening, house and home, craft, parenting, health, history, travel, biography, motivation and management; Man. Dir Lou Johnson.

Thames and Hudson Australia Pty Ltd: 11 Central Boulevard, Portside Business Park, Fishermans Bend, Vic 3207; tel. (3) 9646-7788; fax (3) 9646-8790; e-mail enquiries@thaust.com.au; internet www.thamesandhudson.com.au; art, history, archaeology, architecture, photography, design, fashion, textiles, lifestyle; Man. Dir Jamie Camplin.

Thomson Reuters Australia Ltd: Level 5, 100 Harris St, Pyrmont, NSW 2009; tel. (2) 8587-7980; fax (2) 8587-7981; e-mail LTA.Service@thomsonreuters.com; internet www.thomsonreuters.com.au; legal, professional, tax and accounting; CEO Tony Kinnear.

Thorpe-Bowker: Level 1, 607 St Kilda Rd, Melbourne, Vic 3004; tel. (3) 8517-8333; fax (3) 8517-8399; e-mail yoursay@thorpe.com.au; internet www.thorpe.com.au; bibliographic, library and book trade reference; Gen. Man. Gary Pengelly.

UNSW Press Ltd: University of New South Wales, Sydney, NSW 2052; tel. (2) 9664-0900; fax (2) 9664-5420; e-mail enquiries@newsouthpublishing.com.au; internet www.unswpress.com.au; f. 1962; scholarly, general and tertiary texts; Chief Exec. Kathy Bail.

University of Queensland Press: POB 6042, St Lucia, Qld 4067; tel. (7) 3365-7244; fax (7) 3365-7579; e-mail uqp@uqp.uq.edu.au; internet www.uqp.uq.edu.au; f. 1948; scholarly and general cultural interest, incl. Black Australian writers, adult and children's fiction; Gen. Man. Greg Bain.

University of Western Australia Press: 35 Stirling Highway, Crawley, WA 6009; tel. (8) 6488-3670; fax (8) 6488-1027; e-mail admin-uwap@uwa.edu.au; internet uwap.uwa.edu.au; f. 1935; literary fiction, natural history, history, literary studies, Australiana, general non-fiction; Dir Assoc. Prof. TERRI-ANN WHITE.

John Wiley & Sons Australia, Ltd: POB 3065, Stafford BC, Qld 4053; tel. (7) 3859-9755; fax (7) 3859-9715; e-mail brisbane@wiley.com; internet au.wiley.com; f. 1954; educational, reference and trade; Pres. and CEO STEPHEN SMITH.

PUBLISHERS' ASSOCIATION

Australian Publishers Association Ltd: 60/89 Jones St, Ultimo, NSW 2007; tel. (2) 9281-9788; fax (2) 9281-1073; e-mail apa@publishers.asn.au; internet www.publishers.asn.au; f. 1948; over 210 mems; Pres. STEPHEN MAY; Chief Exec. MAREE MCCASKILL.

Broadcasting and Communications

TELECOMMUNICATIONS

In 2009 175 licensed telecommunications carriers were in operation.

AAPT Ltd: 680 George St, Sydney, NSW 2000; tel. (2) 8314-1700; fax (2) 9009-9999; internet www.aapt.com.au; f. 1991; part of Telecom New Zealand Group; long-distance telecommunications carrier; CEO PAUL BROAD.

Hutchison Telecoms Australia: Level 7, 40 Mount St, NSW 2060; tel. (2) 8579-8888; fax (2) 8904-0457; e-mail investers@hutchison.com.au; internet www.hutchison.com.au; f. 2003; mobile services; owns 50% share in Vodafone Hutchison Australia; Chair. CANNING FOK KIN-NING.

Optus Ltd: POB 1, North Sydney, NSW 2059; tel. (2) 9342-7800; fax (2) 9342-7100; internet www.optus.com.au; f. 1992; division of Singapore Telecommunications Ltd; general and mobile telecommunications, data and internet services, pay-TV; Chair. Sir RALPH ROBINS; Chief Exec. PAUL O'SULLIVAN.

Telstra Corpn Ltd: Level 41, 242 Exhibition St, Melbourne, Vic 3000; tel. (3) 9634-6400; e-mail companysecretary@team.telstra.com; internet www.telstra.com.au; general and mobile telecommunication services; Chair. CATHERINE LIVINGSTONE; CEO DAVID THODEY.

Vodafone Hutchison Australia: Level 7, 40 Mount St, NSW 2060; tel. (2) 8579-8888; fax (2) 8904-0457; internet www.three.com.au; third generation (3G) mobile services; est. following merger between Hutchison Whampoa and Vodafone Australia Ltd in 2009; CEO NIGEL DEWS.

Regulatory Authority

Australian Communications and Media Authority (ACMA): POB 13112, Law Courts, Melbourne, Vic 8010; tel. (3) 9963-6800; fax (3) 9963-6899; e-mail candinfo@acma.gov.au; internet www.acma.gov.au; f. 2005; Commonwealth regulator for telecommunications, broadcasting, internet and radiocommunications; Chair. CHRIS CHAPMAN.

BROADCASTING

Many programmes are provided by the non-commercial statutory corporation, the Australian Broadcasting Corporation (ABC). Commercial radio and television services are provided by stations operated by companies under licences granted and renewed by the Australian Communications and Media Authority (ACMA). They rely for their income on the broadcasting of advertisements. In late 2009 there were about 274 commercial radio stations in operation, and 59 commercial television stations.

Australian Broadcasting Corporation (ABC): 700 Harris St, Ultimo, POB 9994, Sydney, NSW 2001; tel. (2) 8333-1500; fax (2) 8333-5344; internet www.abc.net.au; f. 1932; est. as Australian Broadcasting Comm; became corpn in 1983; one national television network operating on about 961 transmitters, one international television service broadcasting via satellite to Asia and the Pacific and nine radio networks operating on more than 6,000 transmitters; Chair. MAURICE NEWMAN; Man. Dir MARK SCOTT.

Radio Australia: GPOB 428, Melbourne 3001; tel. (3) 9626-1500; fax (3) 9626-1899; international service broadcast by short wave and satellite in English, Burmese, French, Indonesian, Standard Chinese, Khmer, Tok Pisin and Vietnamese; CEO MIKE MCCLUSKEY.

Radio

Commercial Radio Australia Ltd: Level 5, 88 Foveaux St, Surry Hills, NSW 2010; tel. (2) 9281-6577; fax (2) 9281-6599; e-mail mail@commercialradio.com.au; internet www.commercialradio.com.au; f. 1930; represents the interests of Australia's commercial radio broadcasters; CEO JOAN WARNER.

Major Commercial Broadcasting Station Licensees

Associated Communications Enterprises (ACE) Radio Broadcasters Pty Ltd: Level 8C, 18 Albert Rd, South Melbourne, Vic 3205; tel. (3) 9645-9877; fax (3) 9645-9866; e-mail headoffice@aceradio.com.au; internet www.aceradio.com.au; operates six stations; Chair. ROWLY PATERSON; Man. Dir S. EVERETT.

Austereo Pty Ltd: Ground Level, 180 St Kilda Rd, St Kilda, Vic 3182; tel. (3) 9230-1051; fax (3) 9593-9007; e-mail peter.harvie@austereo.com.au; internet www.austereo.com.au; operates 15 stations; Chair. PETER HARVIE; CEO GUY POBSON.

Australian Radio Network Pty Ltd: 3 Byfield St, North Ryde, NSW 2113; tel. (2) 8899-9999; fax (2) 8899-9811; e-mail webmaster@arn.com.au; internet www.arn.com.au; operates 12 stations; jt venture between APN News & Media and Clear Channel Communications Inc, Texas; CEO BOB LONGWELL.

Capital Radio Network: POB 1206, Mitchell, ACT 2911; tel. (2) 6452-1521; fax (2) 6452-1006; operates seven stations; Man. Dir KEVIN BLYTON.

DMG Radio Australia: Level 5, 75 Hindmarsh St, Adelaide, SA 5000; tel. (8) 8419-5000; fax (8) 8419-5062; e-mail enquiries@dmgradio.com.au; internet www.dmgradio.com.au; operates 11 stations; Chair. LACHLAN MURDOCH; CEO CATHY O'CONNOR.

Grant Broadcasting Pty Ltd: Suite 303, 10–12 Clarke St, Crows Nest, NSW 2065; tel. (2) 9437-8888; fax (2) 9437-8881; e-mail web@grantbroadcasters.com.au; internet www.grantbroadcasters.com.au; operates 31 stations; Gen. Man. JANET CAMERON.

Greater Cairns Radio Ltd: Virginia House, Abbott St, Cairns, Qld 4870; tel. (7) 4050-0800; fax (7) 4051-8060; e-mail cnssales@dmgradio.com.au; Gen. Man. ROD COUTTS.

Prime Radio: N. A. B. Bldg, 17 Carnaby St, Maroochydore, Qld 4558; tel. (7) 5475-1911; fax (7) 5475-1961; e-mail info@primeradio.com.au; internet www.primeradio.com.au; operates 10 stations.

Regional Broadcasters (Australia) Pty: McDowal St, Roma, Qld 4455; tel. (7) 4622-1800; fax (7) 4622-3697; Chair. G. MCVEAN.

Rural Press Ltd: 159 Bells Line of Rd, North Richmond, NSW 2754; tel. (2) 4570-4444; fax (2) 4570-4663; internet www.ruralpress.com; f. 1911; operates six stations; Man. Dir and CEO B. K. MCCARTHY.

Southern Cross Media Pty Ltd: Level 2, 70 Park St, South Melbourne, Vic 3205; tel. (3) 9922-2121; fax (3) 9922-2199; e-mail corporate@scmedia.com.au; internet www.scmediagroup.com.au; operates 68 stations; Exec. Chair. MAX MOORE-WILTON; CEO RHYS HOLLERAN.

RadioWest: 89 Egan St, Kalgoorlie, WA 6430; tel. (8) 9021-2666; fax (8) 9091-2209; e-mail rhutchinson@radiowest.com.au; internet theradio.com.au; f. 1931; operates 10 stations along with HOT FM in Western Australia.

SEA FM Pty Ltd: Level 2, Seabank Bldg, 12–14 Marine Parade, Southport, Qld 4215; tel. (7) 5591-5000; fax (7) 5591-6080; operates 28 stations.

Super Radio Network: POB 1269, Pyrmont, NSW 2009; owned by Broadcast Operations Pty Ltd; operates 33 stations; Chair. BILL CARALIS.

Radio 2SM Gold 1269: Level 3, 8 Jones Bay Rd, Pyrmont, NSW 2009; tel. (2) 9660-1269; fax (2) 9552-2979; e-mail admin@2sm.com.au; internet www.2sm.com.au; f. 1931.

Tamworth Radio Development Company Pty Ltd: POB 497, Tamworth, NSW 2340; tel. (2) 6765-7055; fax (2) 6762-0008; e-mail traffic@2tn.com.au; operates two stations; acquired by Super Radio Network in 1993; Man. W. A. MORRISON.

Tasmanian Broadcasting Network (TBN): POB 665G, Launceston, Tas 7250; tel. (3) 6431-2555; fax (3) 6431-3188; operates three stations; Chair. K. FINDLAY.

Tasmanian Radio Network: 109 York St, Launceston, Tas 7250; tel. (3) 6331-4844; fax (3) 6334-5858; internet www.bestmusicmix.com.au; operates six radio stations and part of Macquarie Regional Radioworks; Man. MATT RUSSELL.

Wesgo Ltd: POB 234, Seven Hills, NSW 2147; tel. (2) 9831-7611; fax (2) 9831-2001; operates eight stations; CEO G. W. RICE.

Television

Free TV Australia: 44 Avenue Rd, Mosman, NSW 2088; tel. (2) 8968-7100; fax (2) 9969-3520; e-mail contact@freetv.com.au; internet www.freetv.com.au; f. 1960; fmrly Commercial Television Australia; represents all commercial free-to-air broadcasters in Australia; Chair. WAYNE GOSS; CEO JULIE FLYNN.

Commercial Television Station Licensees

Channel 9 South Australia Pty Ltd: 202 Tynte St, North Adelaide, SA 5006; tel. (8) 8267-0111; fax (8) 8267-3996; internet www.nws9.com.au; f. 1959; Gen. Man. MARK COLSON.

General Television Corporation Pty Ltd: 22–46 Bendigo St, POB 100, Richmond, Vic 3121; tel. (3) 9429-0201; fax (3) 9429-3670; internet www.ninemsn.com.au; f. 1957; operates one station; Man. Dir GRAEME YARWOOD.

Golden West Network Pty Ltd: Roberts Cres., Bunbury, WA 6230; tel. (8) 9721-4466; fax (8) 9792-2932; e-mail gwn.bunbury@gwn.com.au; internet www.gwn.com.au; f. 1967; subsidiary of Prime Television Ltd; operates three stations (SSW10, VEW and WAW); CEO W. FENWICK.

Imparja Television Pty Ltd: POB 52, Alice Springs, NT 0871; tel. (8) 8950-1411; fax (8) 8950-1422; e-mail imparja@imparja.com.au; internet www.imparja.com.au; CEO ALISTAIR FEEHAN.

NBN Television Ltd: 11–17 Mosbri Cres., Newcastle, NSW 2300; tel. (2) 4929-2933; fax (2) 4926-2936; internet www.nbntv.com.au; f. 1962; operates one station; Man. Dir DENIS LEDBURY.

Network Ten Ltd: GPOB 10, Sydney, NSW 2000; tel. (2) 9650-1010; fax (2) 9650-1111; internet www.ten.com.au; f. 1964; operates Australian TV network and commercial stations in Sydney, Melbourne, Brisbane, Perth and Adelaide; Exec. Chair. NICK FALLOON; CEO GRANT BLACKLEY.

Nine Network Australia Pty Ltd: Level 7, Tower Bldg, Australia Sq., 264–278 George St, Sydney, NSW 2000; tel. (2) 9383-6000; fax (2) 9383-6100; e-mail sales@ninemsn.com.au; internet www.ninemsn.com.au; f. 1956; division of Publishing and Broadcasting Ltd; operates three stations: TCN Channel Nine Pty Ltd (Sydney), Queensland Television Ltd (Brisbane) and General Television Corpn Ltd (Melbourne); CEO JOE POLLARD.

Prime Television (Holdings) Pty Ltd: POB 878, Dickson, ACT 2602; tel. (2) 6242-3700; fax (2) 6242-3889; e-mail primetv@primetv.com.au; internet www.primemedia.com.au; part of Prime Media Group Ltd; Chair. PAUL RAMSAY; CEO IAN AUDSLEY.

Queensland Television Ltd: GPOB 72, Brisbane, Qld 4001; tel. (7) 3214-9999; fax (7) 3369-3512; f. 1959; operated by Nine Network Australia Pty Ltd; Gen. Man. CHRIS TAYLOR.

Seven Network Ltd: 38-42 Pirrama Rd, Pyrmont, NSW 2009; tel. (2) 8777-7777; internet www.sevencorporate.com.au; owns Amalgamated Television Services Pty Ltd (Sydney), Brisbane TV Ltd (Brisbane), HSV Channel 7 Pty Ltd (Melbourne), South Australian Telecasters Ltd (Adelaide) and TVW Enterprises Ltd (Perth); Exec. Chair. KERRY STOKES; CEO DAVID JOHN LECKIE.

Channel Seven Adelaide Pty Ltd: 40 Port Rd, Hindmarsh, SA 5007; tel. (8) 8342-7777; fax (8) 8342-7717; f. 1965; mem. of Seven Network; Man. Dir TONY DAVISON.

Channel Seven Brisbane Pty Ltd: Sir Samuel Griffith Dr., Mt Coot-tha, Qld 4006; tel. (7) 3369-7777; fax (7) 3368-7410; f. 1959; operates one station; mem. of Seven Network; Man. Dir MAX WALTERS.

Channel Seven Melbourne Pty Ltd: 160 Harbour Esplanade, Docklands Melbourne, Vic 3008; tel. (3) 9697-7777; fax (3) 9697-7747; e-mail daspinall@seven.com.au; f. 1956; operates one station; Gen. Man. LEWIS MARTIN.

Channel Seven Perth Pty Ltd: POB 77, Tuart Hill, WA 6939; tel. (8) 9344-0777; fax (8) 9344-0670; e-mail traffic@7perth.com.au; internet www.7perth.com.au; f. 1959.

Channel Seven Queensland Pty Ltd: 140–142 Horton Parade, Maroochydore, Qld 4558; tel. (7) 5430-1777; fax (7) 5430-1760; f. 1965; fmrly Sunshine Television Network Ltd.

Southern Cross Media Pty Ltd: (see above) operates two stations: Southern Cross Ten and Southern Cross Television.

Special Broadcasting Service (SBS): Locked Bag 028, Crows Nest, NSW 1585; tel. (2) 9430-2828; fax (2) 9430-3047; e-mail comments@sbs.com.au; internet www.sbs.com.au; f. 1980; national multi-cultural broadcaster of TV and radio; Chair. JOSEPH SKRZYNSKI; Man. Dir SHAUN BROWN.

Spencer Gulf Telecasters Ltd: POB 305, Port Pirie, SA 5540; tel. (8) 8632-2555; fax (8) 8633-0984; e-mail dweston@centralonline.com.au; f. 1968; operates two stations; Chair. P. M. STURROCK; Chief Exec. D. WESTON.

Swan Television & Radio Broadcasters Pty Ltd: POB 99, Tuart Hill, WA 6939; tel. (8) 9449-9999; fax (8) 9449-9900; Gen. Man. P. BOWEN.

Territory Television Pty Ltd: POB 1764, Darwin, NT 0801; tel. (8) 8981-8888; fax (8) 8981-6802; f. 1971; operates one station; Gen. Man. A. G. BRUYN.

WIN Corpn Pty Ltd: Television Ave, Mt St Thomas, NSW 2500; tel. (2) 4227-3682; fax (2) 4223-4199; internet www.wintv.com.au; f. 1962; Man. Dir DAVID BUTORAC; CEO JOHN HATCHER.

Satellite, Cable and Digital Television

Digital television became available in metropolitan areas in January 2001 and was available in all major regional areas by 2004.

Austar United Communications: Locked Mailbag A3940, Sydney South, NSW 1235; tel. (2) 9251-6999; fax (2) 9251-0134; e-mail corporate@austar.com.au; internet www.austarunited.com.au; began operations in 1995; 740,000 subscribers (2009); Chair. MICHAEL T. FRIES; CEO JOHN C. PORTER.

Australia Network: GPOB 9994, Sydney, NSW 2001; tel. (2) 8333-5598; fax (2) 8333-1558; internet australianetwork.com; international satellite service; broadcasts to countries and territories in Asia and the Pacific; owned by Australian Broadcasting Corpn; Chief Exec. BRUCE DOVER.

Foxtel: 5 Thomas Holt Dr., North Ryde, NSW 2113; tel. (2) 9813-6000; fax (2) 9813-7303; e-mail corporateaffairs@foxtel.com.au; internet www.foxtel.com.au; owned by News Corpn, Telstra Corpn and Consolidated Media Holdings Ltd; over 1,630,000 subscribers; Chair. BRUCE AKHURST; CEO KIM WILLIAMS.

Optus Television: Tower B, Level 15, 16 Zenith Centre, 821–841 Pacific Highway, Chatswood, NSW 2067; provides Foxtel cable television under the Optus brand as part of its broader services.

Finance

(cap. = capital; p.u. = paid up; res = reserves; dep. = deposits; m. = million; brs = branches; amounts in Australian dollars)

Australian Prudential Regulation Authority (APRA): GPOB 9836, Sydney, NSW 2001; tel. (2) 9210-3000; fax (2) 9210-3411; internet www.apra.gov.au; f. 1998; responsible for regulation of banks, insurance cos, superannuation funds, credit unions, building societies and friendly societies; Chair. Dr JOHN LAKER.

BANKING

Central Bank

Reserve Bank of Australia: 65 Martin Place, Sydney, NSW 2000; tel. (2) 9551-8111; fax (2) 9551-8000; e-mail rbainfo@rba.gov.au; internet www.rba.gov.au; f. 1911; est. as Commonwealth Bank of Australia; assumed functions of central bank in 1959; responsible for monetary policy, financial system stability, payment system development; cap. 40m., res 10,154m., dep. 20,987m., total assets 85,652m. (June 2010); Gov. GLENN STEVENS.

Development Bank

Rabobank Australia Ltd: GPOB 4577, Sydney, NSW 2001; tel. (2) 8115-4000; e-mail sydney.webmaster@rabobank.com; internet www.rabobank.com.au; f. 1978 as Primary Industry Bank of Australia Ltd; name changed as above 2003; Chair. WILLIAM P. GURRY; CEO THEODORUS GIESKES; 219 brs.

Trading Banks

Arab Bank Australia Ltd: Suite 1A, 200 George St, Sydney, NSW 2000; tel. (2) 9377-8917; fax (2) 9221-5428; e-mail service@arabbank.com.au; internet www.arabbank.com.au; cap. 55.0m., res 8.0m., dep. 1,051.7m. (Dec. 2009); Chair. SAMIR KAWAR; Man. Dir JAMES WAKIM.

Australia and New Zealand Banking Group Ltd: ANZ Centre, 833 Collins St, Docklands, Vic 3008; tel. (3) 8654-7682; fax (3) 8654-9977; e-mail investor.relations@anz.com; internet www.anz.com; f. 1835; present name adopted in 1970; cap. 20,757m., res –2,587m., dep. 369,210m. (Sept. 2010); Chair. JOHN MORSCHEL; CEO PHILIP CHRONICAN; 748 domestic brs, 204 overseas brs.

Bank of America Australia Ltd: Level 63, MLC Centre, 19–29 Martin Place, Sydney, NSW 2000; tel. (2) 9931-4200; fax (2) 9221-1023; f. 1964; Man. Dir JOHN LILES.

Bank of Queensland Ltd: 229 Elizabeth St, POB 898, Brisbane, Qld 4001; tel. (7) 3212-3463; fax (7) 3212-3399; internet www.boq.com.au; f. 1874; cap. 2,057m., res 86.6m., dep. 28,415.8m. (Aug. 2010); Chair. NEIL SUMMERSON; Man. Dir DAVID P. LIDDY; 162 brs.

Bank of Tokyo-Mitsubishi UFJ Ltd: Level 25, Gateway, 1 Macquarie Place, Sydney, NSW 2000; tel. (2) 9296-1111; fax (2) 9247-4266; f. 1985; Gen. Man. K. TSUSHIMA.

Bank of Western Australia Ltd (BankWest): Level 47, BankWest Tower, 108 St George's Terrace, Perth, WA 6000; tel. (8) 9449-2840; fax (8) 9449-2570; internet www.bankwest.com.au; f. 1895 as Agricultural Bank of Western Australia, est. 1945 as Rural and Industries Bank of Western Australia; present name adopted in 1994; 100% owned by HBOS Australia; cap. 872.3m., res 300,000, dep. 16,436.9m. (Dec. 2002); Chair. HARVEY COLLINS; Man. Dir JON SUTTON; 87 brs.

Bankers' Trust Financial Group: 275 Kent St, Sydney, NSW 2000; tel. (2) 8253-2999; fax (2) 9274-5786; internet www.btfg.com.au; f. 1986; wealth management division of Westpac Banking Corpn; CEO BRAD COOPER.

Bendigo and Adelaide Bank Ltd: The Bendigo Centre, Bendigo, Vic 3550; tel. (3) 5485-7873; fax (3) 5485-7660; e-mail oncall@bendigobank.com.au; internet www.bendigobank.com.au; f. 1995; cap. 3,522.5m., res 29.5m., dep. 33,918.8m. (June 2010); Chair. ROBERT N. JOHANSON; Man. Dir MIKE HIRST; 373 brs.

Citigroup Pty Ltd: GPOB 40, Sydney, NSW 2001; tel. (2) 8225-0615; fax (2) 8225-5306; internet www.citibank.com.au; f. 1954; fmrly Citibank Pty Ltd, name changed as above in 2005; cap. 460.0m, res 387.0m., dep. 12,978m. (Dec. 2009); CEO STEPHEN ROBERTS; 6 brs.

Commonwealth Bank of Australia: Ground Floor, Tower 1, 201 Sussex St, Sydney, NSW 2000; tel. (2) 9378-2000; fax (2) 9118-7192; internet www.commbank.com.au; f. 1912; merged with Colonial Ltd in 2000; cap. 24,020m., res 1,089.0m., dep. 427,497.0m. (June 2010); Chair. DAVID TURNER; CEO and Man. Dir RALPH NORRIS; more than 1,200 brs world-wide.

HSBC Bank Australia Ltd: Level 32, HSBC Centre, 580 George St, Sydney, NSW 2000; tel. (2) 9006-5888; fax (2) 9255-2647; e-mail pr@hsbc.com.au; internet www.hsbc.com.au; f. 1985; fmrly Hongkong Bank of Australia; cap. 811.0m., res 1.0m., dep. 15,921.0m. (Dec. 2009); Chair GRAHAM BRADLEY; CEO PAULO MAIA; 35 brs.

ING DIRECT (Australia) Ltd: 140 Sussex St, Sydney, NSW 2001; tel. (2) 9028-4077; fax (2) 9028-4708; internet www.ingdirect.com.au; f. 1994; fmrly known as ING Bank; name changed as above 2007; cap. 1,334m., res 40.5m., dep. 43,644.6m. (Dec. 2009); CEO DON KOCH.

Investec Bank (Australia) Ltd: Level 31, Chifley Tower, 2 Chifley Sq., Phillip St, Sydney, NSW 2000; tel. (2) 9323-2000; fax (2) 9323-2002; e-mail australia@investec.com.au; internet www.investec.com.au; fmrly N. M Rothschild & Sons; acquired by Investec Bank in July 2006; Chair. DAVID GONSKI; CEO DAVID CLARKE; 3 brs.

JPMorgan Australia: Level 32, Grosvenor Place, 225 George St, Sydney, NSW 2000; tel. (2) 9250-4111; internet www.jpmorgan.com/australia; formed through merger of Ord Minnett, Chase Manhattan Bank, JPMorgan and Bank One; Head (Asia-Pacific) GABY ABDELNOUR.

Macquarie Group Ltd: 1 Martin Place, Sydney, NSW 2000; tel. (2) 8232-3333; fax (2) 8232-3350; internet www.macquarie.com.au; f. 1969 as Hill Samuel Australia Ltd; present name adopted in 1985; cap. 6,990m., res –26.0m., dep. 109,653m. (March 2010); Chair. DAVID S. CLARKE; Man. Dir NICHOLAS MOORE; 4 brs.

National Australia Bank Ltd (NAB): 800 Bourke St, Melbourne, Vic 3008; tel. (3) 8641-9083; fax (3) 8641-4912; e-mail feedback@nab.com.au; internet www.nab.com.au; f. 1858; cap. 23,551m., res –639m., dep. 509,618m. (Sept. 2010); Chair. MICHAEL CHANEY; Group CEO CAMERON CLYNE; 2,349 brs.

RBS Group (Australia) Pty Ltd: RBS Tower, 88 Phillip St, Sydney, NSW 2000; tel. (2) 8259-5000; fax (2) 8259-5444; e-mail mailbox.au@rbs.com; internet www.rbs.com.au; f. 1971; fmrly ABN AMRO Australia Pty Ltd, rebranded as above in 2009; CEO STEPHEN WILLIAMS.

SG Australia Ltd: Level 23, 400 George St, Sydney, NSW 2000; tel. (2) 9210-8000; fax (2) 9231-2196; internet www.sgcib.com.au; f. 1981; fmrly Société Générale Australia Ltd; CEO JOHN HARVEY.

St George Bank Ltd: Locked Bag 1, St George House, 4–16 Montgomery St, Kogarah, NSW 2217; tel. (2) 9553-5173; fax (2) 9952-1000; internet www.stgeorge.com.au; f. 1937 as building society; purchased by Westpac Group in Dec. 2008; Chair. JOHN CURTIS; CEO ROB CHAPMAN; 409 brs.

Standard Chartered Bank Australia Ltd: Level 1, 345 George St, Sydney, NSW 2000; tel. (2) 9232-9333; fax (2) 9232-9334; internet www.standardchartered.com/au; f. 1986; Chair. JOHN PEACE; CEO (Asia) JASPAL SINGH BINDRA.

Westpac Banking Corporation: 275 Kent St, Sydney, NSW 2000; tel. (2) 9293-9270; fax (2) 8253-4128; internet www.westpac.com.au; f. 1817; merged with St George Bank Ltd in Dec. 2008; cap. 24,496m., res –57m., dep. 545,508m. (Sept. 2010); Chair. TED EVANS; CEO GAIL KELLY; 825 domestic brs, 197 brs in New Zealand, 48 other brs.

STOCK EXCHANGE

Australian Securities Exchange (ASX): Level 7, 20 Bridge St, Sydney, NSW 2000; tel. (2) 9227-0000; fax (2) 9347-0005; e-mail info@asx.com.au; internet www.asx.com.au; Australian Stock Exchange f. 1987 by merger of the stock exchanges in Sydney, Adelaide, Brisbane, Hobart, Melbourne and Perth, to replace the fmr Australian Associated Stock Exchanges; demutualized and listed Oct. 1998; Australian Securities Exchange formed through merger of Australian Stock Exchange and Sydney Futures Exchange July 2006; ASX group operates under the brand Australian Securities Exchange; spans markets for corporate control, capital formation and price discovery; operator, supervisor, central counter-party clearer and payments system facilitator; Chair. DAVID GONSKI; Man. Dir and CEO ROBERT ELSTONE.

Supervisory Body

Australian Securities and Investments Commission (ASIC): GPOB 9827, Sydney, NSW 2001; tel. (2) 9911-2000; fax (2) 9911-2414; internet www.asic.gov.au; f. 1990; corpns and financial products regulator; Chair. TODO D'ALOISIO.

PRINCIPAL INSURANCE COMPANIES

Allianz Australia Ltd: GPOB 4049, Sydney, NSW 2001; tel. (7) 3023-9322; e-mail corporate_communications@allianz.com.au; internet www.allianz.com.au; f. 1914; workers' compensation; fire, general accident, motor and marine; Chair. J. S. CURTIS; Man. Dir T. TOWELL.

AMP Ltd: AMP Bldg, Level 24, 33 Alfred St, Sydney, NSW 2000; tel. (2) 9257-5000; fax (2) 9257-7178; internet www.amp.com.au; f. 1849; fmrly Australian Mutual Provident Society; life insurance; Chair. PETER MASON; CEO and Man. Dir CRAIG DUNN.

AXA Asia Pacific Holdings Ltd: 750 Collins St, Melbourne, Vic 3008; tel. (3) 8688-3911; fax (3) 9614-2240; e-mail investor.relations@axa.com.au; internet www.axaasiapacific.com.au; f. 1869; fmrly The Nat. Mutual Life Asscn of Australasia Ltd; financial advice, funds management, superannuation, retirement and savings products, life and trauma insurance, income protection; Chair. R. H. ALLERT; CEO ANDREW PENN.

Calliden Insurance Ltd: Level 7, 100 Arthur St, North Sydney, NSW 2060; tel. (2) 9551-1111; fax (2) 9551-1155; e-mail feedback@calliden.com.au; internet www.calliden.com.au; general insurance products; CEO NICHOLAS KIRK.

Catholic Church Insurances Ltd: Level 8, 485 La Trobe St, Melbourne, Vic 3001; tel. (3) 9934-3000; fax (3) 9934-3464; e-mail info@ccinsurances.com.au; internet ww1.ccinsurances.com.au; f. 1911; Chair. PAUL A. GALLAGHER; CEO PETER RUSH.

General Reinsurance Australia Ltd: Level 24, 123 Pitt St, Sydney, NSW 2000; tel. (2) 8236-6100; fax (2) 9222-1540; e-mail lifesydney@genre.com; f. 1961; reinsurance, life and health, fire, accident, marine; Chair. F. A. MCDONALD; Man. Dir C. J. CROWDER.

GIO Australia Holdings Ltd: GPOB 1453, Brisbane, Qld 4001; tel. (3) 8650-4196; fax (3) 8650-4552; e-mail emailus@gio.com.au; internet www.gio.com.au; f. 1926; CEO PETER CORRIGAN.

Guild Insurance Ltd: 5 Burwood Rd, Hawthorn, Vic 3122; tel. (3) 9810-9820; fax (3) 9810-9810; internet www.guildinsurance.com.au; f. 1963; Chair. JOHN BARRINGTON; CEO MARIO J. PIRONE.

Insurance Australia Group Ltd: Level 26, 388 George St, Sydney, NSW 2000; tel. (2) 9292-9222; fax (2) 9292-8485; e-mail investor.relations@iag.com.au; internet www.iag.com.au; f. 1926; fmrly NRMA Insurance Ltd; name changed as above 2002; Chair. BRIAN SCHWARTZ; CEO MIKE WILKINS.

Lumley General Insurance Ltd: Level 9, Lumley House, 309 Kent St, Sydney, NSW 2000; tel. (2) 9248-1111; fax (2) 9248-1122; e-mail general@lumley.com.au; internet www.lumley.com.au; owned by Westfarmers General Insurance Ltd; Man. Dir ROBERT SCOTT.

MLC Wealth Management Ltd: POB 200, North Sydney, NSW 2059; tel. (3) 8634-4721; fax (3) 9964-3334; e-mail contactmlc@mlc.com.au; internet www.mlc.com.au; f. 2000; est. as CGNU following merger of CGU and Norwich Union, renamed as Aviva Australia Holdings Ltd in 2003; renamed as above after acquisition by National Australia Bank in 2009; CEO STEVE TUCKER.

QBE Insurance Group Ltd: Level 2, 82 Pitt St, Sydney, NSW 2000; tel. (2) 9375-4193; fax (2) 9231-6104; e-mail corporate@qbe.com; internet www.qbe.com; f. 1886; general insurance; Chair. BELINDA HUTCHINSON; CEO F. M. O'HALLORAN.

RAC Insurance Pty Ltd: 228 Adelaide Terrace, Perth, WA 6000; tel. (8) 9436-4444; fax (8) 9421-4593; internet rac.com.au; f. 1947; Chair. ALDEN HALSE.

RACQ Insurance: POB 4, Springwood, Qld 4127; tel. (7) 3361-2444; fax (7) 3361-2140; e-mail racq@racq.com.au; internet www.racq.com.au; f. 1971; Chair. RICHARD PIETSCH; CEO IAN GILLESPIE.

Suncorp Ltd: Level 18, 36 Wickham Tce, Brisbane, Qld 4000; tel. (7) 3362-1222; fax (7) 3836-1190; e-mail direct@suncorp.co.au; internet www.suncorp.com.au; f. 1996; Chair. JOHN STORY; CEO PATRICK SNOWBALL.

Swiss Reinsurance Co Ltd: Level 29, 363 George St, Sydney, NSW 2000; tel. (2) 8295-9500; fax (2) 8295-9600; internet www.swissre.com; f. 1956; Head of Australia and New Zealand operations MARK SENKEVICS.

Vero Insurance Ltd: GPOB 3999, Sydney, NSW 2001; tel. (8) 8205-5878; e-mail veroinformation@vero.com.au; internet www.vero.com.au; fmrly RSA Insurance Australia Ltd; name changed as above 2003; CEO ANTHONY DAY.

Wesfarmers Insurance Ltd (WFI): 184 Railway Parade, Bassendean, WA 6054; tel. (8) 9273-5333; fax (8) 9378-2172; e-mail info@wfi.com.au; internet www.wfi.com.au; Man. Dir ROBERT SCOTT.

Westpac Life Insurance Services Ltd: 275 Kent St, Sydney, NSW 2000; tel. (2) 9293-9270; fax (2) 8253-4128; e-mail online@westpac.com.au; internet www.westpac.com.au; f. 1986; CEO Gail Kelly.

Zurich Financial Services Australia Ltd: 5 Blue St, North Sydney, NSW 2060; tel. (2) 9995-1111; fax (2) 9995-3797; e-mail client.service@zurich.com.au; internet www.zurich.com.au; Chair. Terence John Paradine; CEO David Smith.

Insurance Associations

Australian and New Zealand Institute of Insurance and Finance: Level 8, 600 Bourke St, Melbourne, Vic 3000; tel. (3) 9613-72080; fax (3) 9642-4166; e-mail customerservice@theinstitute.com.au; internet www.theinstitute.com.au; f. 1884; provider of education, training, and professional devt courses across the region; 15,000 mems; 8,500 students; Pres. and Chair. of the Bd Duncan West; CEO Joan Fitzpatrick.

Financial Services Council (FSC): Level 24, 44 Market St, Sydney, NSW 2000; tel. (2) 9299-3022; fax (2) 9299-3198; e-mail info@fsc.org.au; internet www.fsc.org.au; f. 1997; est. following merger of Australian Investment Managers' Asscn, Investment Funds Asscn and Life, Investment and Superannuation Asscn of Australia Inc; fmrly Investment and Financial Services Association (IFSA); non-profit org.; Chair. Peter Maher; CEO John Brogden.

Insurance Council of Australia Ltd: Level 4, 56 Pitt St, Sydney, NSW 2000; tel. (2) 9253-5100; fax (2) 9253-5111; e-mail comms@insurancecouncil.com.au; internet www.insurancecouncil.com.au; f. 1975; Pres. T. R. Towell; CEO R. W. Whelan.

Trade and Industry

GOVERNMENT AGENCY

Austrade: Level 23, Aon Tower, 201 Kent St, Sydney, NSW 2000; tel. (2) 9390-2000; fax (2) 9390-2024; e-mail info@austrade.gov.au; internet www.austrade.gov.au; f. 1931; export promotion agency; CEO Peter Grey.

CHAMBERS OF COMMERCE

Australian Chamber of Commerce and Industry (ACCI): POB 6005, Kingston, ACT 2604; tel. (2) 6273-2311; fax (2) 6273-3286; e-mail info@acci.asn.au; internet www.acci.asn.au; Pres. David Michaelis; CEO Peter Anderson.

Chamber of Commerce and Industry of Western Australia (CCIWA): POB 6209, East Perth, WA 6892; tel. (8) 9365-7627; fax (8) 9365-7550; e-mail info@cciwa.com; internet www.cciwa.com; f. 1890; 5,200 mems; Chief Exec. Peter Hood; Pres. Dr Penny Flett.

Commerce Queensland: Industry House, 375 Wickham Terrace, Brisbane, Qld 4000; tel. (7) 3842-2244; fax (7) 3832-3195; e-mail contact@cciq.com.au; internet www.cciq.com.au; f. 1868; operates World Trade Centre, Brisbane; 5,500 mems; Pres. David Goodwin; Gen. Man. Nick Willis.

South Australian Employers' Chamber of Commerce and Industry Inc: Enterprise House, 136 Greenhill Rd, Unley, SA 5061; tel. (8) 8300-0103; fax (8) 8300-0204; e-mail enquiries@business-sa.com; internet www.business-sa.com; f. 1839; 4,700 mems; Pres. Vincent Tremaine; CEO Peter Vaughan.

Sydney Chamber of Commerce: Level 12, 83 Clarence St, Sydney, NSW 2000; tel. (2) 9350-8100; fax (2) 9350-8199; e-mail enquiries@thechamber.com.au; internet www.thechamber.com.au; f. 1825; offers advice to and represents over 70,000 businesses; Pres. Roger Hood; Exec. Dir Patricia Forsythe.

Tasmanian Chamber of Commerce and Industry: GPOB 793, Hobart, Tas 7001; tel. (3) 6236-3600; fax (3) 6231-1278; e-mail admin@tcci.com.au; internet www.tcci.com.au; Chair. Troy Harper; CEO Robert Wallace.

Victorian Employers' Chamber of Commerce and Industry: Industry House, 486 Albert St, Melbourne, Vic 3002; tel. (3) 8662-5333; fax (3) 8662-5462; e-mail vecci@vecci.org.au; internet www.vecci.org.au; f. 1851; Pres. Peter McMullin; CEO Wayne Kayler-Thomson.

AGRICULTURAL, INDUSTRIAL AND TRADE ASSOCIATIONS

Australian Business Ltd: Locked Bag 938, North Sydney, NSW 2059; tel. (2) 9458-7500; fax (2) 9923-1166; e-mail customerservice@australianbusiness.com.au; internet www.australianbusiness.com.au; f. 1885; fmrly Chamber of Manufactures of NSW; Man. Dir and CEO Kevin MacDonald.

Australian Manufacturers' Export Council: POB E14, Queen Victoria Terrace, ACT 2600; tel. (2) 6273-2311; fax (2) 6273-3196; f. 1955; Exec. Dir G. Chalker.

Australian Wine and Brandy Corporation (AWBC): POB 2733, Kent Town Business Centre, Kent Town, SA 5071; tel. (8) 8228-2000; fax (8) 8228-2022; e-mail awbc@awbc.com.au; internet www.wineaustralia.com; f. 1981; Chair. James Dominguez; Chief Exec. Andrew Cheesman.

Australian Wool Innovation Ltd: Level 30, HSBC Centre, 580 George St, Sydney, NSW 2000; tel. (2) 8295-3100; fax (2) 8295-4100; e-mail info@wool.com; internet www.wool.com; f. 2001; est. following privatization of Australian Wool Research and Promotion Org; owner of The Woolmark Co; Chair. Walter B. Merriman; CEO Stuart McCullogh.

Business Council of Australia (BCA): GPOB 1472, Melbourne, Vic 3001; tel. (3) 8664-2664; fax (3) 8664-2666; e-mail info@bca.com.au; internet www.bca.com.au; public policy research and advocacy; governing council comprises chief execs of Australia's major cos; Pres. Graham Bradley; Chief Exec. Katie Lahey.

Cotton Australia: 247 Coward St, Suite 4.01, Mascot, NSW 2020; tel. (2) 9669-5222; fax (2) 9669-5511; e-mail talktous@cottonaustralia.com.au; internet www.cottonaustralia.com.au; Chair. Andrew Watson; CEO Adam Kay.

Meat and Livestock Australia: Level 1, 165 Walker St, North Sydney, NSW 2060; tel. (2) 9463-9333; fax (2) 9463-9393; e-mail info@mla.com.au; internet www.mla.com.au; producer-owned co; represents, promotes, protects and furthers interests of industry in both the marketing of meat and livestock and industry-based research and devt activities; Chair. Arthur (Don) Heatley; Man. Dir David Palmer.

National Farmers' Federation: POB E10, Kingston, ACT 2604; tel. (2) 6273-3855; fax (2) 6273-2331; e-mail nff@nff.org.au; internet www.nff.org.au; Pres. Jock Laurie; CEO Ben Fargher.

Natural Resource Management Ministerial Council (NRMMC): NRMMC Secretariat, GPOB 858, Canberra, ACT 2601; tel. (2) 6272-3076; fax (2) 6272-4772; e-mail nrmmc@daff.gov.au; internet www.mincos.gov.au; f. 2002; replaced the Agricultural and Resource Management Council of Australia and New Zealand; promotes the conservation and sustainable use of Australia's natural resources; mems comprising the Commonwealth/state/territory and New Zealand ministers responsible for environment, water and natural resources.

Primary Industries Ministerial Council (PIMC): Dept of Agriculture, Fisheries and Forestry, GPOB 858, Canberra, ACT 2601; tel. (2) 6272-5216; fax (2) 6272-4772; e-mail pimc@daff.gov.au; internet www.mincos.gov.au; f. 2002; develops and promotes sustainable, innovative and profitable agriculture, fisheries, food and forestry industries; mems comprising the state/territory and New Zealand ministers responsible for agriculture, fisheries, food and forestry.

Winemakers' Federation of Australia (WFA): National Wine Centre, Botanic Rd, POB 2414, Kent Town, SA 5071; tel. (8) 8222-9255; fax (8) 8222-9250; e-mail wfa@wfa.org.au; internet www.wfa.org.au; f. 1990; Pres. Peter Schulz; Chief Exec. Stephen Strachan.

WoolProducers Australia: POB E10, Kingston, Canberra, ACT 2604; tel. (2) 6273-2531; fax (2) 6273-1120; e-mail woolproducers@nff.org.au; internet www.woolproducers.com.au; f. 2001; fmrly Wool Council Australia; represents wool-growers in dealings with the Federal Govt and industry; Pres. Donald Hamblin.

EMPLOYERS' ORGANIZATIONS

Australian Industry Group: 51 Walker St, North Sydney, NSW 2060; tel. (2) 9466-5566; fax (2) 9466-5599; e-mail helpdesk@aigroup.asn.au; internet www.aigroup.asn.au; f. 1998 through merger of MTIA and ACM; 11,500 mems; Nat. Pres. Lucio di Bartolomeo; CEO Heather Ridout.

Australian Meat Industry Council: POB 1208, Crows Nest, NSW 1585; tel. (2) 9086-2200; fax (2) 9086-2201; e-mail admin@amic.org.au; internet www.amic.org.au; f. 1928; represents meat retailers, processors and small goods mfrs; Chair. Terry Nolan; CEO Kevin Cottrill.

NSW Farmers' Association: GPOB 1068, Sydney, NSW 2001; tel. (2) 8251-1700; fax (2) 8251-1750; e-mail emailus@nswfarmers.org.au; internet www.nswfarmers.org.au; f. 1978; Pres. Charles Armstrong; CEO Matt Brand.

UTILITIES

Australian Institute of Energy: POB 193, Surry Hills, Vic 3127; fax (3) 9898-0249; e-mail aie@aie.org.au; internet www.aie.org.au; f. 1977; Pres. Tony Vassallo.

Australian Water Association: POB 222, St Leonards, NSW 1590; tel. (2) 9436-0055; fax (2) 9436-0155; e-mail info@awa.asn.au; internet www.awa.asn.au; f. 1962; c. 5,500 mems; Pres. Peter Robinson; CEO Tom Mollenkopf.

Energy Supply Association of Australia: GPOB 1823, Melbourne, Vic 3001; tel. (3) 9670-0188; fax (3) 9670-1069; e-mail info@esaa.com.au; internet www.esaa.com.au; Chair. TONY CONCANNON; CEO BRAD PAGE.

Electricity Companies

Country Energy: POB 718, Queanbeyan, NSW 2620; tel. (2) 6338-3628; fax (2) 6589-8695; internet www.countryenergy.com.au; f. 2001; est. following merger of Advance Energy, Great Southern Energy and NorthPower; state-owned; electricity and gas distributor; Chair. BARBARA WARD; Man. Dir TERRY BENSON.

Delta Electricity: Level 20, 175 Liverpool St, Sydney, NSW 2000; tel. (2) 9285-2700; fax (2) 9285-2777; e-mail raymond.madden@de.com.au; internet www.de.com.au; f. 1996; Chief Exec. GREGORY EVERETT.

ENERGEX: GPOB 1461, Brisbane, Qld 4001; tel. (7) 3664-4000; fax (7) 3025-8301; e-mail enquiries@energex.com.au; internet www.energex.com.au; spans Queensland and New South Wales; Chair. JOHN DEMPSEY; Gen. Man. MICHAEL RUSSELL.

EnergyAustralia: GPOB 4009, Sydney, NSW 2001; tel. (2) 9269-4200; fax (2) 9269-2830; internet www.energyaustralia.com.au; supplies customers in NSW; Chair. JOHN CONDE; Man. Dir GEORGE MALTABAROW.

Ergon Energy: POB 1090, Townsville, Qld 4810; tel. (7) 4921-6001; fax (7) 3228-8118; e-mail customerservice@ergon.com.au; internet www.ergon.com.au; national retailer of electricity; Chair. RALPH CRAVEN; Chief Exec. IAN MCLEOD.

Power and Water Corpn: Mitchell Centre, Level 2, 55 Mitchell St, Darwin, NT 0800; tel. (8) 8923-4681; fax (8) 8924-7730; e-mail customerservice@powerwater.com.au; internet www.powerwater.com.au; state-owned; supplier of electricity, water and sewerage services in NT; Chair. JUDITH KING; Man. Dir ANDREW MACRIDES.

Powercor Australia Ltd: Locked Bag 14-090, Melbourne, Vic 8001; fax (3) 9683-4499; e-mail info@powercor.com.au; internet www.powercor.com.au; Chair. PETER TULLOCH; CEO SHANE BREHENY.

Snowy Hydro Ltd: AMP Centre, Level 37, 50 Bridge St, Sydney, NSW 2000; tel. (2) 9278-1888; fax (2) 9278-1879; e-mail info@snowyhydro.com.au; internet www.snowyhydro.com.au; Chair. RICK HOLLIDAY-SMITH; Man. Dir TERRY V. CHARLTON.

United Energy Ltd: Locked Bag 7000, Mount Waverley, Vic 3149; tel. (3) 8544-9000; internet www.ue.com.au; f. 1994; est. following division of State Electricity Comm. of Victoria; transferred to private sector; distributor of electricity and gas; CEO HUGH GLEESON.

Western Power Corpn: 363 Wellington St, Perth, WA 6000; tel. (8) 9326-4911; fax (8) 9326-4595; e-mail info@westernpower.com.au; internet www.westernpower.com.au; f. 1995; principal supplier of electricity in WA; Chair. MARK BARNABA; CEO DOUG ABERLE.

Gas Companies

APA Group: HSBC Bldg, Level 19, 580 George St, Sydney, NSW 2000; tel. (2) 9693-0000; fax (2) 9693-0093; e-mail feedback@pipelinetrust.com.au; internet www.apa.com.au; f. 2000; Chair. LEONARD BLEASEL; CEO MICHAEL MCCORMACK.

Australian Gas Light Co: AGL Centre, Level 22, 101 Miller St, North Sydney, NSW 2060; tel. (2) 9921-2999; fax (2) 9957-3671; e-mail aglmail@agl.com.au; internet www.agl.com.au; f. 1837; Chair. JEREMY MAYCOCK; Man. Dir and CEO MICHAEL FRASER.

Envestra: 10th Floor, 81 Flinders St, Adelaide, SA 5000; tel. (8) 8227-1500; fax (8) 8277-1511; e-mail des.petherick@envestra.com.au; internet www.envestra.com.au; f. 1997 by merger of South Australian Gas Co, Gas Corpn of Queensland and Centre Gas Pty Ltd; purchased Victorian Gas Network in 1999; Chair. JOHN GEOFFREY ALLPASS; Man. Dir IAN BRUCE LITTLE.

Epic Energy: Level 8, 60 Collins St, Melbourne, Vic 3000; tel. (3) 8626-8400; fax (3) 8626-8454; internet www.epicenergy.com.au; f. 1996; privately owned gas transmission co; Chair. BRUCE MCKAY; Man. Dir and CEO STEVE BANNING.

Origin Energy: Level 45, Australia Sq., 264–278 George St, Sydney, NSW 2000; tel. (2) 8345-5000; fax (2) 9252-9244; e-mail enquiry@originenergy.com.au; internet www.originenergy.com.au; Chair. H. KEVIN MCCANN; Man. Dir GRANT KING.

TRUenergy: Locked Bag 14060, Melbourne Mail Centre, Vic 8001; tel. (3) 8628-1000; fax (3) 9299-2777; internet www.truenergy.com.au; formed through merger of TXU, Yallourn Energy and Auspower; owned by CLP Power Asia; Man. Dir RICHARD MCINDOE.

WestNet Infrastructure Group: GPOB W2030, Perth, WA 6846; tel. (8) 6213-7000; e-mail info@wng.com.au; internet www.wng.com.au; fmrly AlintaGas; acquired in 2007 by consortium comprising Singapore Power Int., Babcock & Brown Infrastructure and Babcock & Brown Power; CEO JOHN CLELAND.

Water Companies

Melbourne Water Corpn: POB 4342, Melbourne, Vic 3001; tel. (3) 9235-7100; fax (3) 9235-7200; internet www.melbournewater.com.au; state-owned; Chair. ELEANOR UNDERWOOD; Man. Dir ROB SKINNER.

Power and Water Corpn: see Electricity, above.

South Australian Water Corpn: SA Water House, Ground Floor, 250 Victoria Sq., Adelaide, SA 5000; tel. (8) 8204-1000; fax (8) 7003-3329; e-mail customerservice@sawater.com.au; internet www.sawater.com.au; state-owned; Chair. PHILIP PLEDGE; Chief Exec. JOHN RINGHAM.

South East Water Ltd: Locked Bag 1, Moorabbin, Vic 3189; tel. (3) 9552-3000; fax (3) 9552-3001; e-mail info@sewl.com.au; internet www.southeastwater.com.au; f. 1995; state-owned; Chair. DOUG SHIRREFS; Man. Dir SHAUN COX.

Sydney Water Corpn: POB 399, Parramatta, NSW 2124; internet www.sydneywater.com.au; state-owned; Chair. Dr THOMAS PARRY; Man. Dir Dr KERRY SCHOTT.

Water Corpn: 629 Newcastle St, Leederville, WA 6007; tel. (8) 9420-2420; fax (8) 9423-7722; e-mail customer@watercorporation.com.au; internet www.watercorporation.com.au; state-owned; Chair. PATRICK O'CONNOR; CEO SUE MURPHY.

Yarra Valley Water Ltd: Private Bag 1, Mitcham, Vic 3132; tel. (3) 9874-2122; fax (3) 9872-1353; e-mail enquiry@yvw.com.au; internet www.yvw.com.au; f. 1995; state-owned; Chair. PETER WILSON; Man. Dir TONY KELLY.

MAJOR COMPANIES

Mining and Metals

Alcoa World Alumina Australia: POB 252, Applecross, WA 6953; tel. (8) 9316-5111; fax (8) 9316-5228; internet www.alcoa.com/australia; f. 1961; 60% owned by Alcoa Inc, 40% by Alumina Ltd; sales $A26,901m. (2008); producer of aluminium, bauxite, etc.; Chair. and Man. Dir ALAN CRANSBERG; 87,000 employees (2008).

AngloGold Ashanti Australia Ltd: Level 13, 44 St George's Terrace, Perth, WA 6000; tel. (8) 9425-4624; fax (8) 9425-4650; e-mail kvlahov@anglogoldashanti.com.au; internet www.anglogold.com.au; gold mining; Exec. Vice-Pres., Australasia GRAHAM EHM.

BHP Billiton Ltd: Level 27, 180 Lonsdale St, Melbourne, Vic 3000; tel. (3) 9609-3333; fax (3) 9609-3015; e-mail investor.relations@bhpbilliton.com; internet www.bhpbilliton.com.au; f. 2001; est. by merger of BHP (f. 1885) and Billiton (UK); cap. and res US $36,831m., revenue US $50,211m. (2008/09); mining of iron ore, coal, copper, silver and diamonds; iron and steelmaking; oil and natural gas production; operates in every state, the NT and in many foreign countries; has 165 subsidiaries and nine major associated cos; Chair. JACQUES NASSER; CEO MARIUS KLOPPERS; 40,990 employees (2009).

BlueScope Steel Ltd: Level 11, 120 Collins St, Melbourne, Vic 3000; tel. (3) 9666-4000; fax (3) 9666-4111; e-mail steeldirect@bluescopesteel.com; internet www.bluescopesteel.com; revenue $A10,328.7m. (2008/09); fmrly BHP Steel Ltd; name changed as above 2003; mfr of steel; Chair. GRAHAM KRAEHE; Man. Dir and CEO PAUL O'MALLEY.

Fortescue Metals Group Ltd: 87 Adelaide Terrace, Level 2, East Perth, WA 6004; tel. (8) 6218-8888; fax (8) 6218-8880; e-mail fmgl@fmgl.com.au; internet www.fmgl.com.au; f. 1987; revenue US $1,830m. (2008/09); mining of iron ore; Chair. ANDREW FORREST; CEO NEV POWER.

Newcrest Mining Ltd: Level 9, 600 St Kilda Rd, Melbourne, Vic 3004; tel. (3) 9522-5333; fax (3) 9525-2996; e-mail corporateaffairs@newcrest.com.au; internet www.newcrest.com.au; f. 1990; mining of gold and other minerals; cap. and res $A3,284.2m., sales $A2,530m. (2008/09); Chair. DONALD MERCER; Man. Dir and CEO GREG ROBINSON; 5,100 employees.

Newmont Australia Ltd: 100 Hutt St, Adelaide, SA 5000; tel. (8) 8303-1700; fax (8) 8303-1900; internet www.newmont.com; f. 1921; acquired Normandy Mining Ltd 2002; mining of gold, diamonds and base metals; Chair. VINCENT A. CALARCO; 1,900 employees.

OneSteel Ltd: Level 40, 259 George St, Sydney, NSW 2000; tel. (2) 9239-6666; fax (2) 9251-3042; e-mail OneSteelDirect@OneSteel.com; internet www.onesteel.com; sales $A7,241.5m. (2008/09); mining, steel manufacturing, distribution of steel and other metal products; merged with Smorgon Steel in 2007; Chair. PETER SMEDLEY; Man. Dir and CEO GEOFF PLUMMER; 10,000 employees.

OZ Minerals Ltd: Level 10, 31 Queen St, Melbourne, Vic 3000; tel. (3) 9288-0333; fax (3) 9288-0300; e-mail info@ozminerals.com; internet www.ozminerals.com; f. 2008; formed through merger of Oxiana Ltd and Zinifex Ltd in 2008; cap. and res $A5,227.5m., revenue $A1,373.4m. (2009); base and precious metal mining; Chair. NEIL HAMILTON; Man. Dir and CEO TERRY BURGESS; 5,000 employees.

Rio Tinto Ltd: 120 Collins St, Melbourne, Vic 3000; tel. (3) 9283-3333; fax (3) 9283-3707; internet www.riotinto.com; f. 1962; fmrly CRA; cap. and res US $19,180m., sales US $41,825m. (2009); acquired Alcan Inc in 2007; subsidiaries include Rio Tinto Aluminium; exploration and mining group, principally iron ore, aluminium, coal, salt, gold, silver and diamonds; Chair. JAN DU PLESSIS; Chief Exec. TOM ALBANESE; 36,000 employees.

Santos Ltd: 60 Flinders St, Adelaide, SA 5000; tel. (8) 8116-5000; fax (8) 8116-5050; e-mail investor.relations@santos.com; internet www.santos.com; cap. and res $A4,704m., sales $A2,181m. (2009); gas and petroleum exploration and production; Chair. PETER ROLAND COATES; CEO and Man. Dir DAVID KNOX; 2,200 employees.

Motor Vehicles

Ford Motor Company of Australia Ltd: 1735 Sydney Rd, PMB 6, Campbellfield, Vic 3061; tel. (3) 9359-8211; fax (3) 9359-8200; internet www.ford.com.au; f. 1925; mfrs of passenger and commercial motor vehicles and parts and accessories; Pres. JOSEPH HINRICHS; 5,000 employees.

Holden Ltd: 191 Salmon St, Port Melbourne, Vic 3207; tel. (3) 9647-1111; fax (3) 9647-2550; internet www.holden.com.au; f. 1986; subsidiary of General Motors Corpn; mfrs of passenger and commercial vehicles; Chair. and Man. Dir MIKE DEVEREUX; 6,336 employees (2009).

Iveco Trucks Australia Ltd: Princes Hwy, POB 117, Dandenong, Vic 3175; tel. (3) 9238-2200; fax (3) 9238-2387; e-mail iveco@iveco.com.au; internet www.iveco.com.au; f. 1912; cap. and res $A81.3m. (2001), sales $A377.5m. (2003); designers, mfrs and marketers of trucks; Man. Dir GIORGIO GALLIA; 800 employees.

Mitsubishi Motors Australia Ltd: 1284 South Rd, Clovelly Park, SA 5042; tel. (8) 8275-7111; fax (8) 8275-6841; internet www.mitsubishi-motors.com.au; issued cap. $A279.3m., sales $A2,694m. (2001); mfrs of cars, service parts, accessories, automotive components, engines; Pres. and CEO MASAHIKO TAKAHASHI; 4,100 employees.

Petroleum

BP Australia: Durham St, Rosehill, NSW 2142; tel. (2) 8868-0444; fax (2) 8868-0548; internet www.bp.com.au; f. 1952; refining, marketing, exploration, transport of petroleum products; 30 subsidiaries; 2 refineries; Pres. PAUL WATERMAN; 6,083 employees.

Caltex Australia Ltd: Level 24, 2 Market St, Sydney, NSW 2000; tel. (2) 9250-5000; fax (2) 9250-5742; internet www.caltex.com.au; cap. and res $A536m., total revenue $A17,984m. (2009); petroleum refining and marketing; Chair. ELIZABETH BRYAN; Man. Dir and CEO JULIAN SEGAL; 4,000 employees.

Chevron Australia Pty Ltd: QV1 Bldg, 250 St George's Terrace, Perth, WA 6000; tel. (8) 9216-4000; fax (8) 9216-4444; e-mail ask@chevron.com; internet www.chevronaustralia.com; fmrly West Australian Petroleum, later known as ChevronTexaco Australia Pty Ltd; exploration and production of petroleum and natural gas; 50% interest in Caltex Australia Ltd; Man. Dir ROY KRZYWOSINSKI.

ExxonMobil Australia: 12 Riverside Quay, Southbank, Vic 3006; tel. (3) 9270-3333; fax (3) 9270-3995; internet www.exxonmobil.com.au; Australian subsidiaries incl. Esso, ExxonMobil Australia Pty Ltd and Mobil Oil Australia; active in the upstream oil and gas business; Chair. JOHN DASHWOOD; 3,194 employees.

Shell Australia Ltd: POB 872K, Melbourne, Vic 3000; tel. (3) 9666-5444; fax (3) 8823-4800; internet www.shell.com.au; inc. 1958; total revenue $A17,647m. (2005); petroleum refining and marketing; Country Chair. ANN PICKARD; 3,200 employees.

Woodside Energy Ltd: GPOB D188, Perth, WA 6840; tel. (8) 9348-4000; fax (8) 9214-2777; e-mail companyinfo@woodside.com.au; internet www.woodside.com.au; f. 1954; operations include Woodside Petroleum; sales $A4,352m. (2009); exploration and production of petroleum and natural gas; Chair. MICHAEL CHANEY; Man. Dir and CEO PETER J. COLEMAN; 3,500 employees.

Rubber and Textiles

Ansell Ltd: 678 Victoria St, Level 3, Richmond, Vic 3121; tel. (3) 9270-7270; fax (3) 9270-7300; internet www.ansell.com; sales $A1,350m. (2008/09); fmrly Pacific Dunlop Ltd; name changed as above 2002; marketing and manufacture of surgical, industrial and examination gloves and condoms; Man. Dir MAGNUS NICOLIN.

Paper and Pulp

Amcor Ltd: 109 Burwood Rd, Hawthorn, Vic 3122; tel. (3) 9226-9000; fax (3) 9226-9050; internet www.amcor.com.au; f. 1926; est. as Australian Paper Manufacturers (APM) Ltd; cap. and res $A4,824m. (2005/06), sales $A14,364m. (2008/09); afforestation; production of woodpulp, paper and paperboard and associated goods; manufacture and sale of metal, paper, plastic and corrugated packaging products; trading of industrial and consumer products; 300 locations worldwide, operating in 43 countries; Chair. CHRIS ROBERTS; Man. Dir KEN MACKENZIE; 35,000 employees.

Visy Ltd: Level 11, 2 Southbank Boulevard, Southbank, Vic 3006; tel. (3) 9247-4777; fax (3) 9247-4747; e-mail info@visy.com.au; internet www.visy.com.au; f. 1948; paper, pulp and packaging mfr; printing and recycling services provider; operations in New Zealand and Malaysia; Chair. RICHARD PRATT; 5,600 employees.

Food and Drink, etc.

Accolade Wines: Reynell Rd, Reynella, SA 5161; tel. (8) 8392-2222; fax (8) 8392-2154; e-mail corporate@accolade-wines.com; internet www.accolade-wines.com; production and distribution of wine; CEO TROY CHRISTENSEN.

Arnotts Ltd: 11 George St, Homebush, NSW 2160; tel. (2) 9394-3555; fax (2) 9394-3500; e-mail croberts@arnotts.com; internet www.arnotts.com.au; manufacture of biscuits and snacks; Chair. D. M. McDONALD; Man. Dir and CEO C. I. ROBERTS; 2,600 employees.

AWB Ltd: 380 La Trobe St, Melbourne, Vic 3000; tel. (3) 9209-2000; fax (3) 9670-2782; e-mail awb@awb.com.au; internet www.awb.com.au; f. 1939; fmrly Australian Wheat Board; national and international marketing of grain, financing and marketing of wheat and other grains for growers; 12 mems; Chair. PETER POLSON.

British American Tobacco Australasia Holdings Ltd: Virginia Park, Westfield Dr., Eastgardens 2036, NSW; tel. (2) 9370-1500; fax (2) 9370-1188; internet www.bata.com.au; Chair. TIM EVERY-BURNS; Man. Dir DAVID CROW; 1,200 employees.

Cadbury Pty Ltd: 636 St Kilda Rd, Melbourne, Vic 8008; tel. (3) 9520-7444; fax (3) 9520-7400; e-mail consumer.services@ap.csplc.com; internet www.cadbury.com.au; f. 1971; mfrs and distributors of chocolate and sugar confectionery; fmrly Cadbury Schweppes Australia Ltd; name changed as above in 2009; owned by Kraft Foods Australia Pty Ltd since 2010; Man. Dir for Australia and New Zealand (vacant); 5,000 employees.

Coca-Cola Amatil Ltd: 40 Mount St, Sydney, NSW 2060; tel. (2) 9259-6159; fax (2) 9259-6623; e-mail aus_contactus@anz.ccamatil.com; internet www.ccamatil.com; f. 1904; manufacturing and distribution of beverages in Asia-Pacific; 24 plants, of which 18 are overseas; cap. and res $A2,058.4m., revenue $A4,546.8m. (2009); Chair. DAVID M. GONSKI; Man. Dir WARWICK WHITE; 31,800 employees.

Foster's Group Ltd: 77 Southbank Boulevard, Southbank, Vic 3006; tel. (3) 8626-2000; fax (3) 8626-2002; e-mail corporate.affairs@fostersgroup.com; internet www.fostersgroup.com; f. 1962; sales revenue $A4,684.5m. (2008/09); production and distribution of beer, wine, cider and non-alcoholic beverages; operates in Australia, Asia-Pacific and the UK; Chair. DAVID A. CRAWFORD; CEO JOHN POLLAERS; 6,997 employees.

Goodman Fielder Ltd: T2, 39 Delhi Rd, North Ryde, NSW 2113; tel. (2) 8899-7000; fax (2) 8026-4200; e-mail corporate.affairs@goodmanfielder.com.au; internet www.goodmanfielder.com.au; revenue $A2,848.6m. (2008/09); manufacture, sale and export of foods; Chair. MAX OULD; CEO CHRIS DELANEY; 14,299 employees.

Lion Nathan Ltd: Level 7, 68 York St, Sydney, NSW 2000; tel. (2) 9320-2200; fax (2) 9320-2264; internet www.lion-nathan.com.au; cap. and res $A435.5m., total revenue $A2,094.2m. (2007/08); production and distribution of beer and wine; Chair. GEOFF RICKETTS; CEO ROB MURRAY; 3,200 employees.

National Foods Ltd: 737 Bourke St, Docklands, Vic, 3008; tel. (3) 9188-8000; e-mail Geoff.Lynch@natfoods.com.au; internet www.natfoods.com.au; wholly owned subsidiary of Lion Nathan National Foods Pty Ltd; Man. Dir PETER KEAN; 5,000 employees.

Philip Morris (Australia) Ltd: 252 Chesterville Rd, POB 1093, Moorabbin, Vic 3189; tel. (3) 8531-1000; fax (3) 8531-1900; internet www.philipmorrisinternational.com; f. 1954; mfrs of tobacco products; Pres. MATTEO PELLEGRINI; approx. 700 employees.

George Weston Foods Ltd: Level 1, Tower B, 799 Pacific Hwy, Chatswood, NSW 2067; tel. (2) 9415-1411; fax (2) 9419-2907; internet www.gwf.com.au; subsidiary of Associated British Foods plc; CEO ANDREW REEVES; approx. 8,000 employees.

Miscellaneous

Boral Ltd: AMP Centre, Level 39, 50 Bridge St, Sydney, NSW 2000; tel. (2) 9220-6300; fax (2) 9233-6605; e-mail info@boral.com.au; internet www.boral.com.au; total assets $A1,648.2m., revenue $A4,875.1m. (2008/09); quarrying, sand extraction, premixed concrete, fly ash, lightweight aggregate producer, clay and concrete products, road surfacing, road transport, marketing and distribution of cements and industrial lime, windows, doors, timber, plasterboard, bricks, etc.; Chair. Dr BOB EVERY; CEO MARK SELWAY; 14,700 employees.

Brambles Industries Ltd: Level 40, Gateway Bldg, 1 Macquarie Place, Sydney, NSW 2000; tel. (2) 9256-5222; fax (2) 9256-5299;

e-mail info@brambles.com; internet www.brambles.com.au; f. 1875; sales revenue US $4,018.6m. (2008/09); materials movement and distribution, incl. industrial plant hire, equipment pools, scheduled freight forwarding by road, rail, sea and air, heavy haulage, logistical support programmes for major projects, marine towage and transport, pollution control services, security services, records management, shipping and travel agencies; operations in over 45 countries; Chair. Graham Kraehe; CEO Tom Gorman; 13,283 employees.

Brookfield Multiplex Group: Level 22, 135 King St, NSW 2000; tel. (2) 9322-2000; fax (2) 9322-2001; e-mail information@brookfieldmultiplex.com; internet www.brookfieldmultiplex.com; f. 1962; revenue $A2,833.8m. (2007/08); wholly owned subsidiary of Brookfield Asset Management Inc; construction and funds management; Chair. Allan McDonald; approx. 1,500 employees.

CSL Ltd: 45 Poplar Rd, Parkville, Vic 3052; tel. (3) 9389-1911; fax (3) 9389-1434; e-mail customerservice@csl.com.au; internet www.csl.com.au; f. 1916; sales $A4,622m. (2008/09); development, manufacture and marketing of pharmaceutical and biotechnology products; Chair. Elizabeth A. Alexander; Man. Dir and CEO Brian A. McNamee.

CSR Ltd: Triniti 3, 39 Delhi Rd, North Ryde, NSW 2113; tel. (2) 9235-8000; fax (2) 8362-9013; internet www.csr.com.au; f. 1855; cap. and res $A1,732.4m., trading revenue $A3,754.9m. (2009/10); manufacture of building materials, sugar milling, and investments in aluminium; Chair. Jeremy Sutcliffe; Man. Dir Rob Sindel; 4,500 employees.

Downer EDI Ltd: Triniti Business Campus, 39 Delhi Rd, North Ryde, NSW 2113; tel. (2) 9648-9700; fax (2) 9813-8915; e-mail info@downeredi.com.au; internet www.downeredi.com; cap. and res $A993.6m., total revenue $A5,861.4m. (2008/09); engineering and infrastructure management services; Chair. Michael Harding; CEO Grant Fenn; 24,000 employees.

Elders Ltd: Level 3, 27 Currie St, Adelaide, SA 5000; tel. (8) 8425-4999; fax (8) 8410-1597; e-mail information@elders.com.au; internet www.elders.com.au; sales revenue $A2,853.9m. (2008/09); provision of services to rural sector, financial services, forestry operations, automotive components, etc.; acquired Futuris in 1996 and merged companies under name of Elders in 2009; Chair. John Ballard; CEO and Man. Dir Malcolm Geoffrey Jackman; approx. 4,600 employees.

The GPT Group: Level 52, MLC Center, 19 Martin Place, Sydney, NSW 2000; tel. (2) 8239-3555; e-mail gpt@gpt.com.au; internet www.gpt.com.au; revenue $A1,053.9m. (2007/08); real estate; Chair. Rob Ferguson; CEO and Man. Dir Michael Cameron.

Hewlett-Packard Australia Pty Ltd: 353 Burwood Hwy, Forest Hill, Vic 3131; tel. (3) 8833-5000; fax (3) 8833-5901; internet www.hp.com.au; total revenue US $114,552m. (2008/09); machinery and equipment wholesaling; Man. Dir (South Pacific) Paul Brandling; 2,807 employees.

James Hardie Industries Ltd: Level 3, 22 Pitt St, Sydney, NSW 2000; tel. (2) 8274-5239; fax (2) 8274-5217; e-mail info@jameshardie.com.au; internet www.ir.jameshardie.com.au; net sales US $1,124.6m. (2009/10); mfrs of fibre cement building products and building systems, supply and installation of insulated panel systems; Chair. Michael Hammes; CEO Louis Gries; 2,300 employees.

Kodak (Australasia) Pty Ltd: 181 Victoria Parade, Collingwood, Vic 3066; tel. (3) 8417-8000; fax (3) 9350-2416; internet www.kodak.com.au; mfrs of sensitized photographic materials, photographic chemicals and equipment; distributors and retailers; Man. Dir Stephen Green; 500 employees.

Leighton Holdings Ltd: 472 Pacific Highway, St Leonards, NSW 2065; tel. (2) 9925-6666; fax (2) 9925-6000; e-mail leighton@leighton.com.au; internet www.leighton.com.au; cap. and res $A2,339.3m., total revenue $A18,315.3m. (2008/09); construction, infrastructure development, contract mining, property development, telecommunications, waste management; Chair. S. P. Johns; CEO H. G. Tyrwitt; 21,270 employees.

Lend Lease Corpn Ltd: The Bond, 30 Hickson Rd, Millers Point, NSW 2000; tel. (2) 9236-6111; fax (2) 9252-2192; internet www.lendlease.com.au; cap. and res $A1,230.2m., total revenue $A14,785m. (2008/09); property management, etc.; Chair. David A. Crawford; Man. Dir and CEO Steve McCann; 4,627 employees.

Metcash Trading Ltd Australasia: 50 Waterloo Rd, Macquarie Park, NSW 2113; tel. (2) 9751-8200; fax (2) 9889-1557; e-mail josie.ianni@metcash.com; internet www.metcash.com; total assets 3,286.5m., revenue 11,067.5m. (2008/09); marketing and distribution of food and other products; Chair. Peter Barnes; CEO Andrew Reitzer.

Mirvac Group: Level 26, 60 Margaret St, Sydney, NSW 2000; tel. (2) 9080-8000; fax (2) 9080-8111; e-mail webmaster@mirvac.com; internet www.mirvac.com; f. 1972; total assets $A7,373.8m., total revenue $A1,675.7m. (2008/09); property investment and management, hotel ownership and management, property development; Chair. James MacKenzie; Man. Dir Nicholas Collishaw.

Myer Group Ltd: Level 7, 275–295 Lonsdale St, Melbourne, Vic 3000; tel. (3) 9661-1111; fax (3) 9661-3770; internet www.myer.com.au; f. 1900; total sales $A3,260m. (2008/09); retailer; Chair. Howard McDonald; CEO Bernie Brookes.

Orica Ltd: 1 Nicholson St, East Melbourne, Vic 3002; tel. (3) 9665-7111; fax (3) 9665-7937; e-mail companyinfo@orica.com; internet www.orica.com; cap. and res $A1,457.6m., sales $A7,411m. (2008/09); mfrs of fertilizers, chemicals, plastics, etc.; Chair Peter Duncan; CEO Graeme R. Liebelt; 13,000 employees.

PBL Media Pty Ltd: e-mail contact@pblmedia.com.au; internet www.pblmedia.com.au; f. 2006; owned by CVC Asia Pacific Ltd (75%) and Consolidated Media Holdings (25%); media and entertainment; interests in broadcasting, publishing and websites; businesses incl. ACP Magazines and Nine Network Australia; Chair. Tim Parker; CEO David Gyngell.

Stockland: Level 25, 133 Castlereagh St, Sydney, NSW 2000; tel. (2) 9035-2000; fax (2) 8988-2000; e-mail geninfo@stockland.com.au; internet www.stockland.com.au; f. 1952; cap. and res $A7,925.5m., total revenue $A1,847.4m. (2008/09); property development and management, etc.; Chair. Graham Bradley; Man. Dir Matthew J. Quinn.

Wesfarmers Ltd: 11th Floor, Wesfarmers House, 40 The Esplanade, Perth, WA 6000; tel. (8) 9327-4211; fax (8) 9327-4216; e-mail info@wesfarmers.com.au; internet www.wesfarmers.com.au; total revenue $A50,982m. (2008/09); mfrs of fertilizers and chemicals; gas-processing and distribution; coal mining; building materials and hardware; insurance; acquired Coles Group 2007; Chair. Bob Every; Man. Dir Richard Goyder; 30,000 employees.

Westfield Group: Westfield Towers, 100 William St, Sydney, NSW 2011; tel. (2) 9358-7000; fax (2) 9358-7079; e-mail investor@au.westfield.com; internet westfield.com; f. 1960; retail property; total revenue $A4,123m. (2009); Chair. Frank P. Lowy; Group Man. Dirs Steven M. Lowy, Peter S. Lowy; 4,000 employees.

Woolworths Ltd: 1 Woolworths Way, Bella Vista, NSW 2153; tel. (2) 8885-0000; fax (2) 8888-1068; internet www.woolworthslimited.com.au; f. 1924; sales $A49,595m. (2008/09); retail; Chair. James Strong; Man. Dir and CEO Grant O'Brien; 191,000 employees.

TRADE UNIONS

Australian Council of Trade Unions (ACTU): Level 6, 365 Queen St, Melbourne, Vic 3000; tel. (3) 9664-7333; fax (3) 9600-0050; e-mail help@actu.org.au; internet www.actu.org.au; f. 1927; br. in each state, generally known as a Trades and Labour Council; 45 affiliated trade unions; Pres. Ged Kearney; Sec. Jeff Lawrence.

Principal Affiliated Unions

Association of Professional Engineers, Scientists & Managers, Australia (APESMA): GPOB 1272, Melbourne, Vic 8060; tel. (3) 9695-8800; fax (3) 9695-8902; e-mail info@apesma.asn.au; internet www.apesma.asn.au; Nat. Pres. Dario Tomat; Nat. Sec. Robyn Porter; 25,000 mems.

Australasian Meat Industry Employees' Union (AMIEU): Level 1, 39 Lytton Rd, East Brisbane, Qld 4169; tel. (7) 3217-3766; fax (7) 3217-4462; e-mail federal@amieuqld.asn.au; internet amieu.net; Fed. Pres. Grant Courtney; Fed. Sec. Brian Crawford; 20,484 mems.

Australian Education Union (AEU): Ground Floor, 120 Clarendon St, Southbank, Vic 3006; tel. (3) 9693-1800; fax (3) 9693-1805; e-mail aeu@aeufederal.org.au; internet www.aeufederal.org.au; f. 1984; Fed. Pres. Angelo Gavrielatos; Fed. Sec. Susan Hopgood; 175,000 mems.

Australian Manufacturing Workers' Union (AMWU): POB 160, Granville, NSW 2142; tel. (2) 9897-9133; fax (2) 9897-9274; e-mail info@amwu.asn.au; internet www.amwu.org.au; Nat. Pres. Paul Bastian; Nat. Sec. Dave Oliver; 170,000 mems.

Australian Services Union (ASU): Ground Floor, 116–124 Queensberry St, Carlton South, Vic 3053; tel. (3) 9342-1400; fax (3) 9342-1499; e-mail info@asu.asn.au; internet www.asu.asn.au; f. 1885; amalgamated in present form in 1993; Nat. Sec. Paul Slape; 125,000 mems.

Australian Workers' Union (AWU): Level 10, 377-383 Sussex St, Sydney, NSW 2000; tel. (3) 8005-3333; fax (3) 8005-3300; e-mail members@nat.awu.net.au; internet www.awu.net.au; f. 1886; Nat. Pres. Bill Ludwig; Nat. Sec. Paul Howes; 135,000 mems.

Communications, Electrical and Plumbing Union of Australia (CEPU): Suite 701, Level 7, 5–13 Rosebery Ave, Rosebery, NSW 2018; tel. (2) 9663-3699; fax (2) 9663-5599; e-mail edno@nat.cepu.asn.au; internet www.cepu.asn.au; Nat Pres. (vacant); Nat. Sec. Peter Tighe; 180,000 mems.

Community and Public Sector Union (CPSU): Level 5, 191–199 Thomas St, Haymarket, NSW 2000; tel. (2) 9334-9200; fax (2) 8204-6902; e-mail members@cpsu.org.au; internet www.cpsu.org.au; Nat. Pres. MICHAEL TULL; Nat. Sec. NADINE FLOOD; 200,000 mems.

Construction, Forestry, Mining and Energy Union (CFMEU): Box Q235, QVB PO, Sydney, NSW 1230; tel. (2) 8524-5850; fax (2) 8524-5851; e-mail queries@fed.cfmeu.asn.au; internet www.cfmeu.net.au; f. 1992 by amalgamation; Nat. Pres. TONY MAHER; Nat. Sec. JOHN SUTTON; 120,000 mems.

Finance Sector Union of Australia (FSU): GPOB 9893, 341 Queen St, Melbourne, Vic 3001; tel. 1300-366378; fax 1300-307943; e-mail fsuinfo@fsunion.org.au; internet www.fsunion.org.au; f. 1991; Nat. Pres. CAROL GORDON; Nat. Sec. LEON CARTER; 50,000 mems.

Health Services Union (HSU): 208-212 Park St, South Melbourne, Vic 3205; tel. (3) 9341-3328; fax (3) 9341-3329; e-mail hsu@hsu.net.au; internet www.hsu.net.au; Nat. Pres. MICHAEL WILLIAMSON; Nat. Sec. KATHY JACKSON; 90,000 mems.

Independent Education Union of Australia (IEU): POB 177, Deakin West, ACT 2600; tel. (3) 6273-3107; fax (3) 6273-3710; e-mail ieu@ieu.org.au; internet www.ieu.org.au; Fed. Sec. CHRIS WATT; Fed. Pres. RICHARD SHEARMAN; 63,000 mems.

Maritime Union of Australia (MUA): 2nd Floor, 365–367 Sussex St, Sydney, NSW 2000; tel. (2) 9267-9134; fax (2) 9261-3481; e-mail muano@mua.org.au; internet www.mua.org.au; f. 1993; Nat. Sec. PADDY CRUMLIN; 10,012 mems.

Media, Entertainment & Arts Alliance (MEAA): POB 723, Strawberry Hills, NSW 2012; tel. (2) 9333-0999; fax (2) 9333-0933; e-mail mail@alliance.org.au; internet www.alliance.org.au; Pres. PATRICIA AMPHLETT; Fed. Sec. CHRISTOPHER WARREN; 30,000 mems.

National Union of Workers (NUW): POB 343, North Melbourne, Vic 3051; tel. (3) 9287-1850; fax (3) 9287-1818; e-mail nuwnat@nuw.org.au; internet www.nuw.org.au; Gen. Sec. CHARLES DONNELLY; Gen. Pres. DOUG STEVENS; 100,000 mems.

Rail, Tram and Bus Union (RTBU): 83–89 Renwick St, Redfern, NSW 2016; tel. (2) 9310-3966; fax (2) 9319-2096; e-mail rtbu@rtbu-nat.abn.au; internet www.rtbu-nat.asn.au; Nat. Pres. KEN MASON; Nat. Sec. ALLEN BARDEN; 35,000 mems.

Shop, Distributive & Allied Employees Association (SDA): 6th Floor, 53 Queen St, Melbourne, Vic 3000; tel. (3) 8611-7000; fax (3) 8611-7099; e-mail general@sda.org.au; internet www.sda.org.au; f. 1908; Nat. Pres. GERARD DWYER; Nat. Sec. JOE DE BRUYN; 214,029 mems.

Textile, Clothing and Footwear Union of Australia (TCFUA): 359 Exhibition St, Melbourne, Vic 3000; tel. (2) 9639-2955; fax (2) 9639-2944; e-mail nationaloffice@tcfvic.org.au; f. 1919; Pres. BARRY TUBNER; Nat. Sec. MICHELE O'NEIL; 21,354 mems.

Transport Workers' Union of Australia (TWU): POB 47, Parramatta, NSW 2124; tel. (2) 8114-6500; fax (2) 8114-6515; e-mail twu@twu.com.au; internet www.twu.com.au; Nat. Pres. WAYNE MADER; Nat. Sec. TONY SHELDON; 82,000 mems.

United Voice: Locked Bag 9, Haymarket, NSW 1240; tel. (2) 8204-3000; fax (2) 9281-4480; e-mail info@unitedvoice.org.au; internet www.unitedvoice.org.au; f. 1915; Nat. Pres. BRIAN DALEY; Nat. Sec. LOUISE TARRANT; 126,916 mems.

Transport

Australian Transport Council: POB 594, Canberra, ACT 2601; tel. (2) 6274-7462; fax (2) 6274-8090; e-mail atc@infrastructure.gov.au; internet www.atcouncil.gov.au; f. 1993; mems include Australian and New Zealand ministers responsible for transport; Sec. TONY MAZZER.

Adelaide Metro: Dept of Transport, Energy and Infrastructure, Public Transport Div., POB 1, Walkerville, SA 5081; fax (8) 8303-0849; e-mail dtei-ptd@saugov.sa.gov.au; internet www.adelaidemetro.com.au; f. 1999; operates metropolitan bus, train and tram services; CEO BOB STOBBE.

State Transit Authority of New South Wales: 219–241 Cleveland St, Strawberry Hills, NSW 2010; tel. (2) 9245-5777; e-mail info@sydneybuses.nsw.gov.au; internet www.sydneybuses.info; operates government buses and ferries in Sydney and Newcastle metropolitan areas; Chair. BARRLE UNSWORTH; CEO PETER ROWLEY.

RAILWAYS

In December 2009 there were 42,048 km of railways in Australia. In 2003 the construction of a 1,400-km railway between Alice Springs and Darwin was completed. The rail link was to be used principally for transporting freight. The development of a high-speed network for the country's east coast was under consideration in 2011.

Pacific National: Level 6, 15 Blue St, North Sydney, NSW 2060; tel. (2) 8484-8000; fax (2) 8484-8151; e-mail communication@pacificnational.com.au; internet www.pacificnational.com.au; freight; fmrly Nat. Rail Corpn Ltd; CEO MARK ROWSTHORN.

QR (Queensland Rail): GPOB 1429, Brisbane, Qld 4001; tel. (7) 3235-2180; fax (7) 3235-1373; e-mail ceoffice@qqr.com.au; internet www.qr.com.au; f. 1863; passenger commuter and long-distance services, freight and logistic services, track access and rail-specific expert services; Chair. JOHN B. PRESCOTT; CEO LANCE HOCKRIDGE.

RailCorp: POB K349, Haymarket, NSW 1238; tel. (2) 8202-2000; fax (2) 8202-2111; internet www.railcorp.info; f. 1980; responsible for passenger rail and associated coach services in NSW; Chair. ELIZABETH CROUCH; CEO ROB MASON.

Victorian Rail Track (VicTrack): Level 8, 1010 LaTrobe St, Docklands, Vic 3008; tel. (3) 9619-1111; fax (3) 9619-8851; e-mail victrack@victrack.com.au; internet www.victrack.com.au; f. 1997; Chair. BRUCE COHEN; Chief Exec. JOHN SUTTON.

ROADS

In 2007 there were 815,074 km of roads open for general traffic. This included 18,773 km of highways and national roads, 122,082 km of regional roads and 672,118 km of other roads.

Austroads: Suite 2, Level 9, 287 Elizabeth St, Sydney, NSW 2000; tel. (2) 9264-7088; fax (2) 9264-1657; e-mail austroads@austroads.com.au; internet www.austroads.com.au; f. 1989; asscn of road transport and traffic authorities; Chair. ALAN TESCH; Chief Exec. MURRAY KIDNIE.

SHIPPING

In December 2009 the Australian merchant fleet comprised 719 vessels, with a total displacement of 1,836,500 grt.

ANL Ltd (Australian National Line): GPOB 2238, Melbourne, Vic 3001; tel. (3) 8842-5555; fax (3) 9257-0619; e-mail webmaster@anl.com.au; internet www.anl.com.au; f. 1998; shipping agents; coastal and overseas container shipping and coastal bulk shipping; container management services; overseas container services to Asia; extensive transshipment services; Chair. JACQUES SAADE; Man. Dir JOHN LINES.

BHP Transport Pty Ltd: 27th Level, 600 Bourke St, Melbourne, Vic 3001; tel. (3) 9609-3333; fax (3) 9609-2400; Chair. D. ARGUS; Man. Dir P. ANDERSEN.

Svitzer Australasia: Level 23, 201 Elizabeth St, Sydney, NSW 2000; tel. (2) 9369-9200; fax (2) 9369-9277; e-mail ausydinfo@svitzer.com; internet www.svitzer.com; f. 1875; fmrly Adelaide Steamship Co; later known as Adsteam Marine Ltd, until acquisition by Svitzer (Denmark); Man. Dir ANDERS EGEHUS.

CIVIL AVIATION

Jetstar Airways Pty Ltd: GPOB 4713, Melbourne, Vic 3001; tel. (3) 9347-0091; internet www.jetstar.com.au; f. 2004; owned by Qantas Airways Ltd; low-cost domestic passenger services and flights to New Zealand, Fiji, Singapore, Indonesia, Japan and other Asia-Pacific destinations; Chief Exec. BRUCE BUCHANAN.

National Jet Systems: National Dr., Adelaide Airport, SA 5950; tel. (8) 8154-7000; fax (8) 8154-7019; internet www.nationaljet.com.au; f. 1989; chartered flights; CEO PETER NOTTAGE; Group Gen. Man. MATTHEW LANG.

Qantas Airways Ltd: Qantas Centre, 203 Coward St, Mascot, NSW 2020; tel. (2) 9691-3636; fax (2) 9691-3339; internet www.qantas.com; f. 1920; est. as Queensland and Northern Territory Aerial Services; Australian Govt became sole owner in 1947; merged with Australian Airlines in Sept. 1992; British Airways purchased 25% in March 1993; remaining 75% transferred to private sector in 1995; services throughout Australia and to 36 countries, including destinations in Europe, Africa, the USA, Canada, South America, Asia, the Pacific and New Zealand; Chair. LEIGH CLIFFORD; CEO ALAN JOYCE.

Virgin Blue: 56 Edmondstone Rd, Bowen Hills Qld 4006; tel. (7) 3295-3000; e-mail customercare@virginblue.com.au; internet www.virginblue.com.au; domestic services; CEO JOHN BORGHETTI.

Tourism

The main attractions are the cosmopolitan cities, the Great Barrier Reef, the Blue Mountains, water sports and also winter sports in the Australian Alps, notably the Snowy Mountains. The town of Alice Springs, the Aboriginal culture and the sandstone monolith of Uluru (also known as Ayers Rock) are among the attractions of the desert interior. Much of Australia's wildlife is unique to the country. Australia received nearly 5.9m. foreign visitors in 2010, an increase of more than 5% in comparison with the previous year. New Zealand, the United Kingdom, Japan, the USA and the People's Republic of

China are the principal sources of visitors. Receipts from international tourism totalled approximately $A23,000m. in 2009/10. Tourist accommodation facilities comprised 227,129 rooms in March 2011.

Tourism Australia: GPOB 2721, Sydney, NSW 1006; tel. (2) 9360-1111; fax (2) 9331-6469; e-mail corpaffairs@tourism.australia.com; internet www.tourism.australia.com; f. 2004; government authority responsible for marketing of international and domestic tourism; Chair. Rick Allert.

Defence

As assessed at November 2010, Australia's active armed forces numbered 56,552: army 28,246, navy 14,250, air force 14,056. There were also reserve forces of 20,440. Military service is voluntary. All restrictions on the deployment of women in combat roles were ended in September 2011. Australia is a member of the ANZUS Security Treaty (with New Zealand and the USA), and of the Five Power Defence Arrangements (with Singapore, Malaysia, the United Kingdom and New Zealand). In November 2010, in support of peace-keeping efforts, 1,550 Australian troops were stationed in Afghanistan, with 35 personnel remaining in Iraq. A total of 404 Australian military personnel were present in Timor-Leste, while 80 remained in Solomon Islands.

Defence Expenditure: Estimated at $A25,900m. for 2011.

Chief of the Defence Force: Gen. David Hurley.

Chief of Navy: Vice-Adm. Ray Griggs.

Chief of Army: Lt-Gen. David Morrison.

Chief of Air Force: Air Marshal Geoffrey Brown.

Education

Education is the responsibility of each of the states and the Federal Government. It is free of charge and compulsory for all children from the ages of six to at least 16 years (in most states) or 17 if not going into training. Primary education generally begins with a preparatory year commencing at five years of age, followed by six or seven years of schooling. Secondary education, beginning at the age of 12, usually lasts for five or six years. In 2007/08 enrolment at primary schools included 97% of pupils in the relevant age group, while enrolment at secondary schools included an estimated 88% of pupils in the relevant age group. In August 2010 there were 2,010,327 children enrolled in primary schools (including those attending non-government schools, the majority being Catholic institutions) and 1,476,552 in secondary schools. A total of 1,066,095 students were attending 39 universities in 2008. Public expenditure on education under the federal budget for the financial year 2011/12 was projected at $A29,938m.

Although the six states and two territories are responsible for providing education services for their own residents, the Australian Constitution empowers the Federal Government to make special-purpose financial grants to the states for education in both government and non-government schools.

GOVERNMENT SCHOOLS

In August 2010 there were 6,802 government primary and secondary schools, with a total enrolment of 2,282,357 full-time pupils and 163,698 teachers. Primary schools are generally mixed and cater for children up to the age of 11 or 12. The co-educational high school offers a wide range of subjects. Most have modern facilities for teaching sciences, information technology and general technology, including woodwork and metal fabrication. Many schools are beginning to focus on vocational education, which prepares students for work. Some states also have separate high schools and colleges specializing in the agricultural, commercial and vocational/technical fields.

INDEPENDENT SCHOOLS

The majority of primary and secondary students at independent schools attend Roman Catholic schools. Most other independent schools are under the auspices of, or are administered by, other religious denominations. The teaching staff at independent schools in August 2010 totalled 87,724. A total of 1,187,567 full-time students were enrolled in the 2,725 non-government or independent schools.

EDUCATION FOR CHILDREN IN ISOLATED AREAS

Australia has developed some innovative approaches to delivering education to overcome the challenges confronting children who live in remote areas. A long-standing example is that of the Schools of the Air, which began broadcasting lessons for remote primary and secondary school children, using two-way radio equipment, in 1950. Rapid changes in technology have improved this type of educational support. Schools can make use of satellite and television broadcasting and use computer networks to provide material for their students.

HIGHER EDUCATION

The majority of higher education institutions offer courses to both internal and external students, and have postgraduate research facilities. Most students contribute to the cost of their courses, which last between three and six years.

TAFE

Technical and Further Education (TAFE) is the major provider of post-secondary vocational education and training. There are more than 7,000 courses (including non-vocational courses) available at almost 1,500 locations throughout Australia. Most TAFE courses are developed in consultation with the industry concerned. TAFE award courses can be studied both full time and part time, by internal study at campuses, by external studies and also through flexible delivery (open learning).

ADULT AND COMMUNITY EDUCATION

Adult and Community Education (ACE) centres include neighbourhood centres, non-government adult education providers, community centres and SkillShare centres. They provide recreational, pre-vocational and vocational training to local communities focusing particularly on mature students and long-term unemployed people. Much of the training is in subjects such as arts and humanities, health and community services, office administration and English as a second language. SkillShare centres provide access to training courses and employment-related services to disadvantaged job-seekers. There are more than 1,500 ACE centres around Australia.

EDUCATION NETWORK AUSTRALIA (EDNA)

The Education Network Australia (EdNA) is a multi-faceted process of co-operation and consultation among representatives of all sectors of the education community, including Federal, State and Territory governments, non-government schools, the vocational education and training sector, the higher education sector and the adult and community education sectors. Its principal aim is to maximize the benefits of information technology for all.

Bibliography

General

Anderson, Warwick. *The Cultivation of Whiteness: Science, Health and Racial Destiny in Australia.* New York, Basic Books, 2003.

Brennan, Geoffrey, and Castles, Francis G. (Eds). *Australia Reshaped: 200 Years of Institutional Transformation.* Cambridge, Cambridge University Press, 2002.

Burke, Anthony. *Fear of Security: Australia's Invasion Anxiety.* Sydney, UNSW Press, 2008.

Chesterman, John. *Civil Rights: How Indigenous Australians Won Formal Equality.* St Lucia, University of Queensland Press, 2005.

Crase, Lin. *Water Policy in Australia: The Impact of Change and Uncertainty.* Washington, DC, Resources for the Future, 2008.

Curran, James, and Ward, Stuart. *The Unknown Nation: Australia After Empire.* Carlton, Melbourne University Publishing, 2010.

Dalrymple, Rawdon. *Continental Drift: Australia's Search for a Regional Identity.* Burlington, VT, Ashgate, 2003.

Fernandes, Clinton. *Reluctant Saviour: Australia, Indonesia and the Independence of East Timor.* Carlton North, Scribe Publications, 2005.

Germov, R., and Motta, M. *Refugee Law in Australia.* South Melbourne, Oxford University Press, 2003.

Gothard, J., Jayasuriya, L., and Walker, D. (Eds). *Legacies of White Australia: Race, Culture and Nation.* Perth, University of Western Australia Press, 2003.

Greig, A., Lewins, F., and White, K. *Inequality in Australia.* Melbourne, Cambridge University Press, 2003.

Hammerton, A. James, and Thomson, Alistair. *'Ten Pound Poms': Australia's Invisible Migrants.* Manchester, Manchester University Press, 2005.

Hinton, Martin, Rigney, Daryle, and Johnston, Elliott (Eds). *Indigenous Australians and the Law.* Abingdon, Routledge, 2nd Edn, 2008.

Hiscock, Peter. *Archaeology of Ancient Australia.* Abingdon, Routledge, 2007.

Howe, B., and Hughes, P. (Eds). *Spirit of Australia II: Religion in Citizenship and National Life.* London, Sheldon Press, 2003.

Jupp, James. *From White Australia to Woomera: The Story of Australian Immigration.* Melbourne, Cambridge University Press, 2nd Edn, 2007.

Khoo, Tseen. *Locating Asian Australian Cultures.* Abingdon, Routledge, 2007.

Mares, Peter. *Borderline: Australia's Treatment of Refugees and Asylum Seekers in the Wake of the Tampa.* Sydney, UNSW Press, 2003.

McManus, Phil. *Vortex Cities to Sustainable Cities: Australia's Urban Challenge.* Sydney, UNSW Press, 2004.

Neumann, Klaus. *Refuge Australia: Australia's Humanitarian Record.* Sydney, UNSW Press, 2004.

O'Brien, Anne P. *God's Willing Workers: Women and Religion in Australia.* Sydney, UNSW Press, 2005.

Russell, Peter. *Recognizing Aboriginal Title: The Mabo Case and Indigenous Resistance to English-Settler Colonialism.* Toronto, University of Toronto Press, 2005.

Simone, Dennis. *Christmas Island: An Anthropological Study.* Amherst, NY, Cambria Press, 2008.

Smith, Babette. *Australia's Birthstain: The Startling Legacy of the Convict Era.* Sydney, Allen and Unwin, 2008.

Smith, Claire. *Country, Kin and Culture: Survival of an Australian Aboriginal Community.* Kent Town, Wakefield Press, 2005.

Sutton, Peter. *Native Title in Australia: An Ethnographic Perspective.* Melbourne, Cambridge University Press, 2003.

History and Politics

Atkinson, Alan. *The Europeans in Australia: The Beginning* (Vol 1). Melbourne, Oxford University Press, 1997.

The Europeans in Australia: Democracy (Vol 2). Melbourne, Oxford University Press, 2005.

Attwood, Bain. *Possession: Batman's Treaty and the Matter of History.* Melbourne, Melbourne University Press, 2009.

Attwood, Bain, and Markus, Andrew (Eds). *The Struggle for Aboriginal Rights: A Documentary History.* Sydney, Allen and Unwin, 2000.

Aulich, Chris, and Wettenhall, Roger (Eds). *Howard's Second and Third Government: Australian Commonwealth Administration, 1998–2004.* Sydney, UNSW Press, 2005.

Aulich, Chris, and Wettenhall, Roger (Eds). *Howard's Fourth Government: Australian Commonwealth Administration 2004-2007.* Sydney, UNSW Press, 2008.

Australian Dictionary of Biography (12 vols). Melbourne University Press, 1966–90.

Barns, Greg. *Selling the Australian Government: Politics and Propaganda from Whitlam to Howard.* Sydney, UNSW Press, 2005.

Benwell, Philip. *In Defense of Australia's Constitutional Monarchy.* New York, Edwin Mellen Press, 2003.

Blainey, Geoffrey. *The Tyranny of Distance.* Melbourne, Sun Books, 2nd Edn, 1976.

Bramble, Tom. *Trade Unionism in Australia: A History from Flood to Ebb Tide.* Melbourne, Cambridge University Press, 2008.

Bramble, Tom, and Rick Kuhn. *Labor's Conflict—Big Business, Workers and the Politics of Class.* Melbourne, Cambridge University Press, 2010.

Brett, Judith. *Australian Liberals and the Moral Middle Class: From Alfred Deakin to John Howard.* Melbourne, Cambridge University Press, 2003.

Broome, R. *Aboriginal Australians—the Black Response to White Dominance, 1788–1980.* Sydney, Allen and Unwin, 1982.

The Other Side of the Frontier: Aboriginal Resistance to the Invasion of Australia. Sydney, UNSW Press, 2nd Edn, 2006.

Cavalier, Rodney. *Power Crisis—The Self-Destruction of a State Labor Party.* Melbourne, Cambridge University Press, 2010.

Chappell, Louise, Chesterman, John, and Hill, Lisa. *The Politics of Human Rights in Australia.* Melbourne, Cambridge University Press, 2009.

Clark, Manning. *A History of Australia* (6 vols). Carlton, Melbourne University Press, 1962–87. (Abridgement by Michael Cathcart, 1994.)

A Short History of Australia. Melbourne, Pan Books, 1999.

Cocklin, Chris, and Dibden, Jacqui (Eds). *Sustainability and Change in Rural Australia.* Sydney, UNSW Press, 2004.

Curran, James. *Curtin's Empire.* Melbourne, Cambridge University Press, 2011.

Davison, Graeme, et al. (Eds). *The Oxford Companion to Australian History.* Oxford, Oxford University Press, 2002.

Dawkins, Peter, and Steketee, Mike (Eds). *Reforming Australia: New Policies for a New Generation.* Carlton, Melbourne University Press, 2004.

Edwards, Peter, and Goldsworthy, David (Eds). *Facing North: A Century of Australian Engagement with Asia* (2 vols). Carlton, Melbourne University Press, 2001 and 2004.

Firth, Stewart. *Australia in International Politics: An Introduction to Australian Foreign Policy.* Sydney, Allen and Unwin, Revised Edn, 2011.

Garran, Robert. *True Believer: John Howard, George Bush and the American Alliance.* St Leonards, Allen and Unwin, 2005.

Goot, Murray, and Rowse, Tim (Eds). *Make a Better Offer: The Politics of Mabo.* Leichhardt, Pluto Press, 1994.

Grey, Jeffrey. *A Military History of Australia.* Melbourne, Cambridge University Press,3rd Edn, 2008.

Hubbard, Christopher. *Australian and US Military Cooperation: Fighting Common Enemies.* Burlington, VT, Ashgate, 2005.

Hughes, Robert. *The Fatal Shore: A History of the Transportation of Convicts to Australia, 1787–1868.* London, Harvill, 2nd Edn, 1996.

Isaacs, Jennifer. *Australian Dreaming: 40,000 Years of Aboriginal History.* Frenchs Forest, Hew Holland Publishers, 2005.

Keating, Paul. *Engagement: Australia Faces the Asia-Pacific.* Sydney, Pan Macmillan, 2000.

Kelly, Paul. *The End of Certainty: The Story of the 1980s.* Sydney, Allen and Unwin, 1993.

One Hundred Years. Sydney, Allen and Unwin, 2001.

The March of Patriots: The Struggle for Modern Australia. Carlton, Melbourne University Publishing, 2010.

Kelton, Maryanne. *'More than an Ally'? Contemporary Australia-US Relations.* Farnham, Ashgate, 2008.

Kemp, Rod, and Stanton, Marion (Eds). *Speaking for Australia: Parliamentary Speeches that Shaped the Nation.* St Leonards, Allen and Unwin, 2005.

Keneally, Tom. *The Commonwealth of Thieves: The Story of the Founding of Australia.* London, Vintage, 2007.

Knightley, Phillip. *Australia—A Biography of a Nation.* London, Jonathan Cape, 2000.

Macintyre, Stuart. *A Concise History of Australia*. Cambridge, Cambridge University Press, 3rd Edn, 2009.

Marr, D., and Wilkinson, M. *Dark Victory*. St Leonards, Allen and Unwin, 2003.

McAllister, Ian. *The Australian Voter: 50 years of change*. Sydney, UNSW Press, 2011.

Moon, J., and Sharman, C. (Eds). *Australian Politics and Government: The Commonwealth, The States and The Territories*. Melbourne, Cambridge University Press, 2003.

Moran, Albert. *Australia: Nation, Belonging, and Globalization*. London, Routledge, 2004.

Nugent, Maria. *Captain Cook Was Here*. Melbourne, Cambridge University Press, 2009.

Parker, Derek. *Outback: The Discovery of Australia's Interior*. Stroud, Sutton Publishing Ltd, 2007.

Perkins, Rachel, and Langton, Marcia. *First Australians*. Melbourne, Melbourne University Press, 2008.

Rhodes, R. A. W. (Ed.). *The Australian Study of Politics*. Melbourne, Palgrave Macmillan, 2009.

Rumley, D. *The Geopolitics of Australia's Regional Relations*. Kluwer Academic Publishers, 1999.

Schreuder, Deryck M., and Ward, Stuart (Eds). *Australia's Empire*. Oxford, Oxford University Press, 2008.

Rusden, George William. *History of Australia*. (3 Vols). Melbourne, Cambridge University Press, 2011.

Sharp, C. A. *The Discovery of Australia*. London, Oxford University Press, 1963.

Shaw, A. G. L. *The Story of Australia*. London, Faber and Faber, 5th Edn, 1983.

Shaw, A. G. L., and Nicolson, H. D. *Australia in the Twentieth Century*. Sydney, Angus and Robertson, 1967.

Sheridan, Greg. *Living with Dragons: Australia Confronts its Asian Destiny*. St Leonards, Allen and Unwin, 1995.

The Partnership: the Inside Story of the US-Australian Alliance under Howard and Bush. Sydney, UNSW Press, 2006.

Smith, Rodney, Vromen, Ariadne, and Cook, Ian. *Keywords in Australian Politics*. Cambridge University Press, 2006.

Smyth, Paul, Reddel, Tim, and Jones, Andrew (Eds). *Community and Local Governance in Australia*. Sydney, UNSW Press, 2005.

Statham-Drew, P. *James Stirling: Admiral and Founding Governor of Western Australia*. Perth, University of Western Australia Press, 2003.

Sutton, Peter. *The Politics of Suffering: Indigenous Australia and the End of the Liberal Consensus*. Carlton, Melbourne University Publishing, 2010.

Taffe, Sue. *Black and White Together, FCAATSI: The Federal Council for the Advancement of Aborigines and Torres Strait Islanders 1958–1973*. St Lucia, University of Queensland Press, 2005.

Taylor, Brendan (Ed.). *Australia as an Asia Pacific Regional Power: Friendships in Flux?* Abingdon, Routledge, 2007.

Trembath, Richard. *A Different Sort of War: Australians and the Korean War 1950–1953*. Melbourne, Australian Scholarly Publishing, 2005.

Uhr, John. *Terms of Trust: Arguments over Ethics in Australian Government*. Sydney, UNSW Press, 2005.

Ungerer, Carl (Ed.) *Australian Foreign Policy in the Age of Terror*. Sydney, UNSW Press, 2007.

Van Schoubroeck, Lesley. *The Lure of Politics: Geoff Gallop's Government 2001–2006*. Perth, University of Western Australia Press, 2010.

Wanna, John, and Williams, Paul (Eds). *Yes, Premier: Political Leadership in Australia's States and Territories*. Sydney, UNSW Press, 2005.

Ward, R. *A History of Australia: The Twentieth Century 1901–1975*. London, Heinemann, 1978.

Waterhouse, Richard. *Vision Splendid: A Social and Cultural History of Rural Australia*. Fremantle, Fremantle Arts Centre Press, 2005.

Weller, Patrick. *Cabinet Government in Australia, 1901–2006*. Sydney, UNSW Press, 2007.

Welsh, Frank. *Great Southern Land: A New History of Australia*. London, Allen Lane, 2004.

Wesley, M. and Gyngell, A. *Making Australian Foreign Policy*. Melbourne, Cambridge University Press, 2003.

Williams, John M. *The Australian Constitution: A Documentary History*. Carlton, Melbourne University Press, 2005.

Economy

Beer, Andrew. *Developing Australia's Regions*. Sydney, UNSW Press, 2003.

Bell, Stephen. *Australia's Money Mandarins: The Reserve Bank and the Politics of Money*. Melbourne, Cambridge University Press, 2004.

Bell, Stephen (Ed.). *The Unemployment Crisis in Australia: Which Way Out?* Melbourne, Cambridge University Press, 2000.

Blainey, Geoffrey. *The Rush That Never Ended: A History of Australian Mining*. Carlton, Melbourne University Press, 2003.

Brown, Douglas M. *Market Rules: Economic Union Reform and Intergovernmental Policy-Making in Australia and Canada*. Montréal, QC, McGill-Queen's University Press, 2003.

Capling, Ann. *Australia and the Global Trade System*. Cambridge University Press, 2001.

Charlton, Andrew. *Ozonomics: Inside the Myth of Australia's Economic Superheroes*. Milson's Point, NSW, Random House, 2007.

Conley, Tom. *The Vulnerable Country: Australia and the Global Economy*. Sydney, UNSW Press, 2009.

Davis, Mark. *The Land of Plenty: Australia in the 2000s*. Carlton, Melbourne University Publishing, 2008.

Edwards, Lindy. *How to Argue with an Economist: Reopening Political Debate in Australia*. Melbourne, Cambridge University Press, 2007.

Emerson, Craig. *Vital Signs, Vibrant Society: Securing Australia's Economic and Social Wellbeing*. Sydney, NSW, UNSW Press, 2006.

Higgins, V. J. G. *Constructing Reform: Economic Expertise and the Governing of Agricultural Change in Australia*. Canberra, ACT, Nova Science Publishers, 2003.

Jayasuriya, Sisira, Maclaren, Donald, and Magee, Gary (Eds). *Negotiating a Preferential Trading Agreement: Issues, Constraints and Practical Options*. Cheltenham, Edward Elgar Publishing, 2009.

Leigh, Andrew, Madden, David, and Macgregor, Duncan (Eds). *Imagining Australia: Ideas for our Future*. St Leonards, Allen and Unwin, 2004.

McMichael, Philip. *Settlers and the Agrarian Question: Capitalism in Colonial Australia*. Melbourne, Cambridge University Press, 2003.

McNeil, Ben. *The Clean Industrial Revolution*. Sydney, Allen and Unwin, 2009.

Meredith, David, and Dyster, Barrie. *Australia in the Global Economy: Continuity and Change*. Cambridge, Cambridge University Press, 2000.

Okamoto, Jiro. *Australia's Foreign Economic Policy and ASEAN*. Singapore, Institute of Southeast Asian Studies, 2010.

Painter, Martin. *Collaborative Federalism: Economic Reform in Australia in the 1990s*. Cambridge, Cambridge University Press, 2nd Edn, 2009.

Peter, P., Dawkins, P., and Kelly, P. (Eds). *Hard Heads, Soft Hearts: A New Reform Agenda for Australia*. St Leonards, Allen and Unwin, 2003.

Pigram, John J. *Australia's Water Resources: From Use to Management*. Collingwood, CSIRO Publishing, Revised Edn, 2007.

Pusey, Michael. *The Experience of Middle Australia: The Dark Side of Economic Reform*. Melbourne, Cambridge University Press, 2003.

Saunders, Peter. *The Ends and Means of Welfare: Coping with Economic and Social Change in Australia*. Melbourne, Cambridge University Press, 2003.

Shaw, A. G. L. *The Economic Development of Australia*. Melbourne, 7th Edn, 1980.

Stilwell, Frank, and Jordan, Kirrily. *Who Gets What? Analysing Economic Inequality in Australia*. Melbourne, Cambridge University Press, 2007.

AUSTRALIAN DEPENDENCIES IN THE INDIAN OCEAN

Australia's 'non-self-governing' territories in the Indian Ocean comprise the Ashmore and Cartier Islands, Christmas Island and the Cocos (Keeling) Islands. Heard Island and the McDonald Islands are not permanently inhabited

ASHMORE AND CARTIER ISLANDS

The Ashmore Islands (known as West, Middle and East Islands) and Cartier Island are situated in the Timor Sea, about 850 km and 790 km west of Darwin respectively. The Ashmore Islands cover some 93 ha of land and Cartier Island covers 0.4 ha. The islands are small and uninhabited, consisting of sand and coral, surrounded by shoals and reefs. Grass is the main vegetation. Maximum elevation is about 2.5 m above sea-level. The islands abound in birdlife, sea-cucumbers (*bêches-de-mer*) and, seasonally, turtles.

The United Kingdom took formal possession of the Ashmore Islands in 1878, and Cartier Island was annexed in 1909. The islands were placed under the authority of the Commonwealth of Australia in 1931. They were annexed to, and deemed to form part of, the Northern Territory of Australia in 1938. On 1 July 1978 the Australian Government assumed direct responsibility for the administration of the islands; this rests with a parliamentary secretary appointed by the Attorney-General. Periodic visits are made to the islands by the Royal Australian Navy and aircraft of the Royal Australian Air Force, and the Civil Coastal Surveillance Service makes aerial surveys of the islands and neighbouring waters. The oilfields of Jabiru and Challis are located in waters adjacent to the Territory.

In August 1983 Ashmore Reef was declared a national nature reserve. An agreement between Australia and Indonesia permits Indonesian traditional fishermen to continue fishing in the territorial waters and to land on West Island to obtain supplies of fresh water. In 1985 the Australian Government extended the laws of the Northern Territory to apply in Ashmore and Cartier, and decided to contract a vessel to be stationed at Ashmore Reef during the Indonesian fishing season (March–November) to monitor the fishermen.

From 2000 increasing numbers of refugees and asylum-seekers attempted to land at Ashmore Reef, hoping to gain residency in Australia. The majority had travelled from the Middle East via Indonesia, where the illegal transport of people was widespread. Consequently, in late 2000 a vessel with the capacity to transport up to 150 people was chartered to ferry unauthorized arrivals to the Australian mainland. In September 2001 the Australian Government introduced legislation to Parliament excising Ashmore Reef and other outlying territories from Australia's migration zone. However, in March 2004 a group of nine women and six men, believed to be seeking asylum in Australia, was discovered on Ashmore Reef. A government spokesperson reiterated the Territory's exclusion from Australia's migration zone, stating that this would preclude the group from seeking any form of residency in the country. In December 2008 it was reported that a vessel carrying suspected asylum-seekers had been apprehended by the Australian authorities in the vicinity of the Ashmore Islands. A total of 35 passengers and five crew members were taken into custody, pending the processing of their claims. Such interceptions by the authorities continued in 2009. Suspected asylum-seekers continued to be transferred to Christmas Island for processing. In a major incident off Ashmore Reef in April 2009, a boat carrying 47 asylum-seekers, which had been intercepted by the Australian Navy, caught fire and sank following an explosion. Five of the asylum-seekers were killed in the incident, and the survivors were taken to Darwin for medical treatment.

In April 2005 the Australian Government invited petroleum exploration companies to bid for a number of leases which it had made available in an area covering some 920 sq km near the islands. In mid-2006 two permits were granted for exploration to take place in the territory's Bonaparte Basin. Two more offshore petroleum exploration permits were issued in April 2007, with further permits being granted subsequently.

CHRISTMAS ISLAND

Introduction

Christmas Island lies 360 km south of Java Head (Indonesia) in the Indian Ocean. The nearest point on the Australian coast is North West Cape, 1,408 km to the south-east. Christmas Island has no indigenous population. The population was estimated at 1,349 at the census of August 2006 (compared with 1,906 in 1996). The population comprises mainly ethnic Chinese (some 70%), but there are large minorities of Malays (about 10%) and Europeans (about 20%). Since 1981 all residents of the island have been eligible to acquire Australian citizenship. A variety of languages are spoken (more than 60% of the population spoke a language other than English in 2001), but English is the official language. The predominant religious affiliation is Buddhist (55% in 1991). The principal settlement and only anchorage is Flying Fish Cove. The other settlements are Drum Site, Silver City and Poon Saan.

Christmas Island was first sighted by English sailors in the early 17th century. Following annexation by the United Kingdom in 1888, Christmas Island was incorporated for administrative purposes with the Straits Settlements (now Singapore and part of Malaysia) in 1900. Japanese forces occupied the island from March 1942 until the end of the Second World War, and in 1946 Christmas Island became a dependency of Singapore. Administration was transferred to the United Kingdom on 1 January 1958, pending final transfer to Australia, effected on 1 October 1958. The Australian Government appointed Official Representatives to the Territory until 1968, when new legislation provided for an Administrator, appointed by the Governor-General. Responsibility for administration lies with the Attorney-General. In 1980 an Advisory Council was established for the Administrator to consult. In 1984 the Christmas Island Services Corporation was created to perform those functions that are normally the responsibility of municipal government. This body was placed under the direction of the Christmas Island Assembly, the first elections to which took place in September 1985. Nine members were elected for one-year terms. In November 1987 the Assembly was dissolved, and the Administrator empowered to perform its functions. The Corporation was superseded by the Christmas Island Shire Council in 1992.

In May 1994 an unofficial referendum on the island's status was held concurrently with local government elections. At the poll, sponsored by the Union of Christmas Island Workers, the islanders rejected an option to secede from Australia, but more than 85% of voters favoured increased local government control.

From the 1990s increasing numbers of illegal immigrants, hoping to reach Australia, began arriving on Christmas Island. International attention was focused on the island in August 2001 when the *MV Tampa*, a Norwegian container ship carrying 433 refugees whom it had rescued from a sinking Indonesian fishing boat, was refused permission to land on the island. As the humanitarian crisis escalated, the Australian Government's steadfast refusal to admit the (mostly Afghan) refugees prompted international condemnation and led to a serious diplomatic dispute between Australia and Norway. Hundreds of Christmas Island residents attended a rally urging the Australian Government to reconsider its uncompromising stance. In September the refugees were transferred (via Papua New Guinea and New Zealand) to Nauru, where their applications for asylum were to be processed. In the same month the Senate in Canberra approved new legislation that excised Christmas Island and other outlying territories from Australia's official migration zone. The new legislation also imposed stricter criteria for the processing of asylum-seekers and the removal of their right to recourse to the Australian court system. Meanwhile, increasing numbers of asylum-seekers continued to attempt to reach Christmas Island via Indonesia. According to Australian Immigration Department figures, 146 asylum-seekers were turned away from Christmas Island and Ashmore Reef in December 2001. In January 2002 211 asylum-seekers remained on Christmas Island awaiting transferral. In March the Government announced plans to establish a permanent detention centre on the island to accommodate an anticipated total of 18,000 illegal immigrants who were expected to arrive at Christmas Island during 2002–06. However, plans to scale down the project were announced in February 2003. Some 42 Indonesian refugees from Papua province arrived at Christmas Island in January 2006. They were granted temporary visas in March, while awaiting transfer to Melbourne. The construction of the 800-bed detention centre began in February 2005; some 100 construction workers were engaged on the project. By late 2007 the estimated cost had reportedly increased to $A396m., and the centre opened in early 2008. Meanwhile, in February 2007 more than 80 Sri Lankan refugees, en route from Indonesia, were intercepted by a ship of the Australian navy and detained on Christmas Island, prior to being transferred to Nauru.

The Government of Kevin Rudd relaxed Australia's policy on the treatment of refugees in July 2008, when it announced that the automatic incarceration of asylum-seekers upon arrival was to be ended. In January 2009 28 refugees from Afghanistan and Iran, who had been intercepted off Western Australia in the latter part of 2008 and detained on Christmas Island, were granted permanent residence in Australia. The members of this group, which included 10 children, were thus the first beneficiaries of the Labor Government's 'more humane' approach to the issue.

In 2009 the number of asylum-seekers arriving in Australian waters increased dramatically, reportedly owing to the deteriorating security situation in countries such as Afghanistan and Sri Lanka. These asylum-seekers were taken to Christmas Island for processing, and in October the Government announced plans to increase the detention centre's capacity beyond 1,400, in order to accommodate the growing numbers. Representatives of Amnesty International were permitted to visit the detention centre in August 2008 and again in December 2009, when the human rights organization reiterated its concerns with regard to the facilities and described the Australian Government's policy as 'unviable and inhumane'. By January 2010, according to the Australian Department of Immigration, the detention centre held a total of 1,628 asylum-seekers. In February, with numbers at the centre again approaching capacity, the Government announced plans for a further extension of the facility, to hold 2,200 inmates. In June, in an attempt to ease the overcrowding, the authorities commenced the transfer of dozens of asylum-seekers from the centre to a disused mining camp on the mainland, located at Leonora in Western Australia. Meanwhile, asylum-seekers on Christmas Island continued to be processed and resettled in mainland Australia. In April, however, the Government imposed moratoriums of six and of three months respectively on applicants who had travelled from Afghanistan and from Sri Lanka, in response to 'changing conditions' in those countries.

In November 2010, in a unanimous ruling that was expected to have extensive implications for government policy, the Australian High Court found in favour of two unsuccessful Sri Lankan seekers of asylum. The two Tamil migrants had been detained on Christmas Island and had argued that legislation that prevented them from appealing against the rejection of their asylum claims was unfair. The dispute centred on the official distinction made between asylum-seekers who arrived by sea and those who travelled by air: the latter category was not subject to automatic detention and had the right of appeal in the event of the rejection of a claim for asylum.

In a major incident in rough seas in December 2010 dozens of asylum-seekers, mainly from Iraq and Iran, perished when their wooden vessel disintegrated on rocks off Christmas Island. A parliamentary inquiry into the disaster was to be held in Australia. In January 2011 three Indonesian members of the ship's crew were indicted on charges of illegally transporting people to Australia. Also, an Australian citizen of Iranian descent was arrested in Indonesia in connection with various allegations of immigration offences, including arrangements for the dispatch of the boat that had foundered off Christmas Island in the previous month; in May, following his deportation from Indonesia, Ali Khorram Heydakhani appeared in court in the Australian city of Sydney, whereupon he was charged with 89 counts of people smuggling. His trial was to be held in Western Australia.

In March 2011 about 170 asylum-seekers were recaptured following a mass escape from the detention centre. In a protest against the slow processing of their applications for asylum, detainees were reported to have set fire to the facility and to have assaulted security personnel. The authorities resorted to the use of tear gas to quell the disturbances. In June riot police were drafted in to curb further protests, and there was renewed unrest in July when as many as 100 inmates were involved in a confrontation during which medical records were destroyed.

The health implications of the United Kingdom's nuclear experiments on Christmas Island in the 1950s were brought to the fore in 2007. Some 700 former military service personnel from the United Kingdom, Fiji and New Zealand instigated legal action against the British Government in an attempt to gain compensation for the significant deterioration in health that had allegedly resulted from their presence at the nuclear tests carried out on Christmas Island during the period of the Territory's administration by the United Kingdom. A parliamentary inquiry into the possibility of a link opened in the United Kingdom in October 2007. In December the inquiry acknowledged that there was a link between the nuclear tests and the health problems subsequently experienced. The British parliamentarians recommended the award of an interim compensation payment of $A10,000 to each claimant. In January 2009 a hearing began at the High Court in London to rule on the validity of the veterans' case. Lawyers for the Ministry of Defence argued that the Limitation Act 1980 required the instigation of proceedings within three years of an injury being sustained and that this thus precluded legal action by the nuclear test veterans now. In June 2009, with more than 1,000 cases pending, the High Court declared that the former service personnel be allowed to claim compensation from the British Government, ruling that 10 test cases could proceed. In November 2010, however, the Court of Appeal ruled against the continuation of nine of these 10 cases on the grounds that they had been instigated after the expiry of the legal time limit. Although the judges also cited the issue of lack of evidence that illnesses had been caused by radiation exposure, the veterans and their families were expected to take their claims for compensation to the Supreme Court. The one case permitted to proceed to trial was that of a former serviceman who had died in 2007. In July 2011 it was announced that the Supreme Court was to give further consideration to the issue of compensation for the veterans.

The economy of Christmas Island has been based on the recovery of phosphates. Reserves were estimated to be sufficient to enable production to be maintained until the mid-1990s, but in November 1987 the Australian Government announced the closure of the phosphate mine, owing to industrial unrest. Although mining activity ceased in December 1987, in 1990 the Government allowed private operators to recommence phosphate extraction, subject to certain conditions. A new 21-year lease, drawn up by the Government and the owner of the mine, Phosphate Resources Ltd, took effect in February 1998. The agreement incorporated environmental safeguards and provided for a conservation levy, based on the tonnage of phosphate shipped, which was to finance a programme of rainforest rehabilitation. In mid-2007 Phosphate Resources instigated a legal challenge against the federal Government's refusal in April to allow access to nine areas of vacant land on Christmas Island. The company argued that, if these new leases were not granted, it would be obliged to cease its mining operations, thus jeopardizing 200 jobs and the island's entire economy. In October 2008, declaring that the decision of the Minister for the Environment and Water Resources had been flawed, the Federal Court of Australia ruled against the Government, thereby permitting the company's expansion of its mining operations to proceed.

Efforts have been made to develop the island's considerable potential for tourism. However, prospects for the development of eco-tourism have been curtailed by the negative publicity surrounding the detention centre. In 1989, in an attempt to protect the natural environment and many rare species of flora and fauna (including the Abbott's Booby and the Christmas frigate bird), the National Park was extended to cover some 70% of the island. Christmas Island possesses more than 20 species of crab. These include the robber (or coconut) crab, the largest land invertebrate in the world. In 2010, however, local reports suggested that increasing numbers of this protected native species were being killed by road vehicles driven at undue speed by personnel from the mainland.

Between 1992 and 1999 the Australian Government invested an estimated $A110m. in the development of the island's infrastructure, as part of the Christmas Island Rebuilding Programme. The main areas of expenditure under the programme included the construction of a new hospital, the upgrading of port facilities and the improvement of the island's roads. The closure of a casino resort in 1998, opened only in 1993, had serious economic and social repercussions for Christmas Island. A project to develop a communications satellite launching facility on the island received government approval in 2000, but the scheme was subsequently postponed indefinitely. In April 2004 the Australian Government announced that it was to provide $A2.5m. to finance a new mobile telephone network for the Territory. It was hoped that enhanced communications would facilitate new business prospects for the island. A major issue for the local population has been the substantial rise in the cost of living on the island, largely owing to the presence of 2,800 mainland personnel, including immigration officials, security guards and medical staff.

Statistical Survey

AREA AND POPULATION

Area: 136.7 sq km (52.8 sq miles).

Population: 1,508 at census of 7 August 2001; 1,347 (males 765, females 582) at census of 8 August 2006. *2007* (estimate): 1,400 (Source: Commonwealth Secretariat).

Density (2007): 10.2 per sq km.

Population by Age and Sex (2006 census): *0–14:* 314 (males 152, females 162); *15–64:* 967 (males 570, females 397); *65 and over:* 66 (males 43, females 23); *Total* 1,347 (males 765, females 582).

Country of Birth (2006 census): Australia 609; Malaysia 412; United Kingdom 41; Singapore 39; Indonesia 21; New Zealand 20.

Births and Deaths (1985): Registered live births 36 (birth rate 15.8 per 1,000); Registered deaths 2.

Economically Active Population (persons aged 15 years and over, excl. overseas visitors, 2006 census): Agriculture, forestry and fishing 4; Mining 96; Manufacturing 23; Electricity, gas and water 14; Construction 101; Wholesale and retail trade, restaurants and hotels 91; Transport, storage and communications 41; Financing, insurance, real estate and business services 16; Government administration and defence 96; Community, social and personal services 165; Activities not stated or not adequately defined 34; *Total employed* 681 (males 442, females 239); Unemployed 36 (males 20, females 16); *Total labour force* 717 (males 462, females 255).

MINING

Natural Phosphates ('000 metric tons, official estimates): 285 in 1994; 220 in 1995. Note: By 2007 it was estimated that 600,000 metric tons of phosphates were being mined each year.

FINANCE

Currency and Exchange Rates: Australian currency is used.

Budget ($A, year ending 30 June 2011): Operating revenue 10,102,249 (General purpose funding 4,573,132; Welfare 235,215; Community amenities 1,215,431; Recreation and culture 1,379,485; Transport 2,489,946); Operating expenditure 8,987,719 (Governance 500,441; Law and order and public safety 164,869; Health 105,292; Welfare 491,889; Housing 148,194; Community amenities 1,231,064; Recreation and culture 2,251,135; Transport 3,808,906); Capital expenditure 1,667,261 (Community amenities 365,094; Recreation and culture 222,502; Transport 942,777).

EXTERNAL TRADE

Exports: An estimated 600,000 metric tons of phosphates are exported each year to mainland Australia and markets in South-East Asia.

Principal Trading Partners (phosphate exports, '000 metric tons, year ending 30 June 1984): Australia 463; New Zealand 332; Total (incl. others) 1,136.

2006/07 ($A million): *Imports:* Australia 5. *Exports:* Australia 26. Source: Australian Bureau of Statistics, *Year Book Australia*.

2006/07 ($NZ million): *Exports:* New Zealand 9. Source: Ministry of Foreign Affairs and Trade, New Zealand.

TRANSPORT

International Sea-borne Shipping (estimated freight traffic, '000 metric tons, 1990): Goods loaded 1,290; Goods unloaded 68. Source: UN, *Monthly Bulletin of Statistics*.

TOURISM

Visitor Arrivals and Departures by Air: 14,513 in 1996; 3,895 in 1997; 2,712 in 1998. Source: *Year Book Australia*.

COMMUNICATIONS MEDIA

Radio Receivers (1997): 1,000 in use.

Personal Computers (home users, 2001 census): 506.

Internet Users (2006 census): 480.

EDUCATION

Pre-primary (August 2008): 38 pupils.

Primary (August 2008): 124 pupils.

Secondary (August 2007): 88 pupils.

Source: Education Department of Western Australia.

Directory

The Government

The Administrator, appointed by the Governor-General of Australia and responsible to the Attorney-General, is the senior government representative on the island.

Administrator: BRIAN JAMES LACY (non-resident).

Attorney-General's Department: Pantai St, POB 868, Christmas Island 6798, Indian Ocean; tel. (8) 9164-7901; fax (8) 9164-8245.

Shire of Christmas Island: George Fam Centre, POB 863, Christmas Island 6798, Indian Ocean; tel. (8) 9164-8300; fax (8) 9164-8304; e-mail kelvin@shire.gov.cx; internet www.christmas.shire.gov.cx; CEO KELVIN MATTHEWS; Pres. GORDON THOMSON.

Judicial System

Judicial services on Christmas Island are provided through the Western Australian Department of the Attorney-General. Western Australian Court Services provides a Magistrate's Court, District Court, Supreme Court, Family Court, Children's Court and Coroner's Court.

Managing Registrar: JEFFREY LOW, c/o Dept of Infrastructure, Transport, Regional Development and Local Government, POB 868, Christmas Island 6798, Indian Ocean; tel. (8) 9164-7901; fax (8) 9164-8530; e-mail jeffrey.low@dotars.gov.cx.

Religion

According to the census of 2006, a total of 407 Christmas Island residents were Buddhists (about 30%), 266 (20%) were Muslims and 238 (18%) were Christians, of whom 157 were Roman Catholics and 81 were Anglicans. Within the Christian churches, Christmas Island lies in the jurisdiction of both the Anglican and Roman Catholic Archbishops of Perth, in Western Australia.

The Press

The Islander: Shire of Christmas Island, George Fam Centre, POB 863, Christmas Island 6798, Indian Ocean; tel. (8) 9164-8300; fax (8) 9164-8304; e-mail chong@shire.gov.cx; newsletter; fortnightly; Editor KELVIN MATTHEWS.

Broadcasting and Communications

BROADCASTING

Radio

Christmas Island Community Radio Service: f. 1967; operated by the Administration since 1991; daily broadcasting service by Radio VLU-2 on 1422 KHz and 102 MHz FM, in English, Malay, Cantonese and Mandarin; Station Man. WILLIAM TAYLOR.

Christmas Island Radio VLU2–FM: POB 474, Christmas Island 6798, Indian Ocean; tel. (8) 9164-8316; fax (8) 9164-8315; daily broadcasts on 102.1FM and 105.3FM in English, Malay, Cantonese and Mandarin; Chair. and Station Man. TONY SMITH.

Television

Christmas Island Television: POB AAA, Christmas Island 6798, Indian Ocean.

Finance

BANKING

Commercial Bank

Westpac Banking Corpn (Australia): Flying Fish Cove, Christmas Island, Indian Ocean; tel. (8) 9164-8221; fax (8) 9164-8241.

Trade and Industry

In April 2001 there were 67 small businesses in operation.

Administration of Christmas Island: POB 868, Christmas Island 6798, Indian Ocean; tel. (8) 9164-7901; fax (8) 9164-8245; operates power, public housing, local courts; Dir of Finance JEFFERY TAN.

Christmas Island Chamber of Commerce: POB 510, Christmas Island 6798, Indian Ocean; tel. (8) 9164-8856; fax (8) 9164-8322; e-mail info@cicommerce.org.cx; Pres. JOHN RICHARDSON; Vice-Pres. PHILLIP OAKLEY.

Shire of Christmas Island: see The Government.

Union of Christmas Island Workers (UCIW): Poon Saan Rd, POB 84, Christmas Island 6798, Indian Ocean; tel. (8) 9164-8471; fax (8) 9164-8470; e-mail uciw@pulau.cx; fmrly represented phosphate workers; Pres. FOO KEE HENG; Gen. Sec. GORDON THOMSON.

Transport

There are good roads in the developed areas. National Jet Systems operates a twice-weekly flight from Perth, via the Cocos (Keeling) Islands, and a private Christmas Island-based charter company operates services to Jakarta, Indonesia. The Australian National Line (ANL) operates ships to the Australian mainland. Cargo vessels from Fremantle deliver regular supplies to the island. The Joint Island Supply System, established in 1989, provides a shipping service for Christmas Island and the Cocos Islands. The only anchorage is at Flying Fish Cove.

Tourism

Tourism has the potential to be an important sector of the island's economy. Much of the unique flora and fauna is found in the national park, which covers about 70% of the island and contains large tracts of rainforest. Other attractions are the waterfalls, beaches, coves and excellent conditions for scuba-diving and game-fishing. In 2000 there were approximately 90 hotel rooms on the island.

Christmas Island Tourism Association/Christmas Island Visitor Information Centre: POB 63, Christmas Island 6798, Indian Ocean; tel. (8) 9164-8382; fax (8) 9164-8080; e-mail cita@christmas.net.au; internet www.christmas.net.au.

Christmas Island Travel: Christmas Island 6798, Indian Ocean; tel. (8) 9164-7168; fax (8) 9164-7169; e-mail xch@citravel.com.au; internet www.citravel.com.au; Dir TAN SIM KIAT.

Island Bound Holidays: tel. (8) 9381-3644; fax (8) 9381-2030; e-mail info@islandbound.com.au.

Parks Australia: POB 867, Christmas Island 6798, Indian Ocean; tel. (8) 9164-8055; fax (8) 9164-8755; internet www.environment.gov.au/parks/christmas/index.html.

Education

The Christmas Island District High School, operated by the Western Australia Ministry of Education, provides education from pre-school level up to Australian 'Year 12'. In August 2008 enrolment totalled 38 in pre-primary and 124 in primary institutions. Secondary pupils totalled 88 in August 2007.

COCOS (KEELING) ISLANDS

Introduction

The Cocos (Keeling) Islands are 27 in number and lie 2,768 km north-west of Perth, in the Indian Ocean. The islands have an area of 14 sq km (5.4 sq miles) and form two low-lying coral atolls, densely covered with coconut palms. The climate is equable, with temperatures varying from 21°C (70°F) to 32°C (90°F), and rainfall of 2,000 mm per year. The population comprises mainly a Cocos Malay community and a European community. The Cocos Malays are descendants of the people brought to the islands by Alexander Hare and of labourers who were subsequently introduced by the Clunies-Ross family (see below). English is the official language, but Cocos Malay and Malay are also widely spoken. Most of the inhabitants are Muslims (75% in 2006). The Cocos Malay community is based on Home Island. The only other inhabited island is West Island, where most of the European community lives, the administration is based and the airport is located. The total population of the islands was 572 at the 2006 censuses, in comparison with 621 at the census of 2001.

The islands were uninhabited when discovered by Capt. William Keeling, of the British East India Company, in 1609, and the first settlement was not established until 1826, by Alexander Hare. The islands were declared a British possession in 1857 and came successively under the authority of the Governors of Ceylon (now Sri Lanka), from 1878, and the Straits Settlements (now Singapore and part of Malaysia), from 1886. Also in 1886 the British Crown granted all land on the islands above the high-water mark to John Clunies-Ross and his heirs and successors in perpetuity. In 1946, when the islands became a dependency of the Colony of Singapore, a resident administrator, responsible to the Governor of Singapore, was appointed. Administration of the islands was transferred to the Commonwealth of Australia on 23 November 1955. The agent of the Australian Government was known as the Official Representative until 1975, when an Administrator was appointed. A designated Australian cabinet minister is responsible for the governance of the islands. The Territory is part of the Northern Territory Electoral District.

In June 1977 the Australian Government announced new policies concerning the islands, which resulted in its purchase from John Clunies-Ross of the whole of his interests in the islands, with the exception of his residence and associated buildings. The purchase for $A6.5m. took effect on 1 September 1978. An attempt by the Australian Government to acquire Clunies-Ross' remaining property was deemed by the Australian High Court in October 1984 to be unconstitutional. The Clunies-Ross family was declared bankrupt in mid-1993, following unsuccessful investment in a shipping venture, and the Australian Government took possession of its property.

In July 1979 the Cocos (Keeling) Islands Council was established, with a wide range of functions in the Home Island village area (which the Government transferred to the Council on trust for the benefit of the Cocos Malay community) and, from September 1984, in the greater part of the rest of the Territory.

On 6 April 1984 a referendum to decide the future political status of the islands was held by the Australian Government, with UN observers present. A large majority voted in favour of integration with Australia. As a result, the islanders were to acquire the rights, privileges and obligations of all Australian citizens. In July 1992 the Cocos (Keeling) Islands Council was replaced by the Cocos (Keeling) Islands Shire Council, comprising seven members and modelled on the local government and state law of Western Australia. The first Shire Council was elected in 1993. The Territories Law Reform Bill 2010 included provision for the comprehensive application of the laws of Western Australia to the Cocos Islands.

In September 2001, following an increase in the numbers of illegal immigrants reaching Australian waters (see Christmas Island), legislation was approved removing the Cocos Islands and other territories from Australia's official migration zone. In October of that year the Australian Government sent contingency supplies to the islands as a precaution, should it be necessary to accommodate more asylum-seekers. This development provoked concern among many Cocos residents that the former quarantine station used as a detention centre might become a permanent asylum-processing facility under the order of the Australian Government. In December 123 Sri Lankan and Vietnamese asylum-seekers were housed at the station, which was built to accommodate only 40. They were transferred to Christmas Island in February 2002.

In July 2009 an edict reportedly issued by the Shire Council banning employees and students from speaking Cocos Malay caused considerable consternation among the Malay residents. Those found speaking languages other than English in the workplace or at school were liable to receive a penalty. The ban exacerbated the growing tensions between the majority Cocos Malay population and Australian public servants, deployed from the mainland, with regard to pay claims and cultural attitudes.

Although local fishing is good, some livestock is kept and domestic gardens provide vegetables, bananas and papayas (pawpaws), the islands are not self-sufficient; other foodstuffs, fuels and consumer items are imported from mainland Australia. Industrial activity on the islands is limited, and the majority of those working in this area are engaged in the utilities sector. A Cocos postal service (including a philatelic bureau) came into operation in September 1979, and revenue from the service is used for the benefit of the community. In early 2000 the islands' internet domain name suffix, '.cc' was sold to Clear Channel, a US radio group, thus providing additional revenue. An estimated 19% of the total labour force were unemployed in 2001, 60% of whom were under the age of 30. The islands have a small tourist industry. According to census data, the services sector engaged 83% of the employed population in 2006. By 2002 the Cocos Islands had ceased to export any goods or produce. A clam farm had been established in 2000 but had not progressed sufficiently to yield any export revenue. Coconuts, grown throughout the islands, are the sole cash crop. In 2001/02 the Administration and the Shire provided support for a study investigating the potential economic benefits of various coconut products, including the production of high-quality carbon from coconut kernels, and the manufacture of furniture from coconut palm wood.

The Territory is important as a habitat for various species of flora and fauna. In December 1995 a national park (the Pulu Keeling National Park) was designated on North Keeling Island, an isolated island on an atoll 24 km to the north of the main island group, which is renowned for its populations of seabirds. The area has one of the largest breeding colonies of red-footed boobies in the world and is also important for frigate birds, common noddies and white terns, as well as an endangered sub-species, the Cocos buff-banded rail. Public access to the Park is strictly controlled.

Statistical Survey

AREA AND POPULATION

Area: 14.1 sq km (5.4 sq miles).

Population: 621 at census of 7 August 2001; 572 (males 274, females 298) at census of 8 August 2006. *2007* (estimate): 600 (Source: Commonwealth Secretariat).

Density (2007): 42.6 per sq km.

Country of Birth (2006 census): Australia (incl. Cocos Islands) 512; Malaysia 22; Singapore 11; Kenya 3; Netherlands 3.

Births and Deaths (1986): Registered live births 12 (birth rate 19.8 per 1,000); Registered deaths 2.

Economically Active Population (persons aged 15 years and over, excl. overseas visitors, 2006 census): Agriculture, forestry and fishing 3; Manufacturing 4; Electricity, gas and water 15; Construction 13; Wholesale and retail trade, restaurants and hotels 29; Transport, storage and communications 25; Government administration and defence 39; Community, social and personal services 61; Activities not stated or not adequately defined 21; *Total employed* 210 (males 133, females 77).

AGRICULTURE

Production (metric tons, 2006, FAO estimate): Coconuts 7,600. Source: FAO.

INDUSTRY

Production (metric tons, 2006, FAO estimates): Copra 1,000; Coconut (copra) oil 650. Source: FAO.

FINANCE

Currency and Exchange Rates: Australian currency is used.

EXTERNAL TRADE

Principal Commodities (metric tons, year ending 30 June 1985): *Exports:* Coconuts 202. *Imports:* Most requirements come from Australia. The trade deficit is offset by philatelic sales and Australian federal grants and subsidies. *2006/07* ($A '000, imports from Australia): 6,000.

Source: *Year Book Australia*.

COMMUNICATIONS MEDIA

Radio Receivers (1992): 300 in use.

Personal Computers (home users, 2001 census): 142.

Internet Users (2001 census): 171.

EDUCATION

Pre-primary (August 2008): 15 pupils.

Primary (August 2008): 83 pupils.

Secondary (August 2008): 31 pupils.

Teaching Staff (2004): 17 (10 primary, 7 secondary).

Source: Education Department of Western Australia.

Directory

The Government

The Administrator, appointed by the Governor-General of Australia and responsible to the Attorney-General, is the senior government representative in the islands.

Administrator: BRIAN JAMES LACY (non-resident).

Administrative Offices: Administration Bldg, Morea Close, Cocos (Keeling) Islands 6799, Indian Ocean; tel. (8) 9162-6600; fax (8) 9162-6691; e-mail cocosadmin@afp.gov.au.

Cocos (Keeling) Islands Shire Council: POB 1094, Home Island, Cocos (Keeling) Islands 6799, Indian Ocean; tel. (8) 9162-6649; fax (8) 9162-6668; e-mail info@cocos.wa.gov.au; internet www.shire.cc; f. 1992 by Territories Law Reform Act; Pres. AINDIL MINKOM; CEO PETER CLARKE.

Judicial System

Judicial services in Cocos (Keeling) Islands are provided through the Western Australian Department of the Attorney-General. Western Australian Court Services provide a Magistrates Court, District Court, Supreme Court, Family Court, Children's Court and Coroner's Court.

Court Services: c/o Australian Federal Police, Cocos (Keeling) Islands 6799, Indian Ocean; tel. (8) 9162-6600; fax (8) 9162-6691; e-mail cocosadmin@afp.gov.au.

Religion

According to the census of 2006, of the 572 residents, 431 (some 75%) were Muslims and 73 (13%) Christians. The majority of Muslims live on Home Island, while most Christians are West Island residents. The Cocos Islands lie within both the Anglican and the Roman Catholic archdioceses of Perth (Western Australia).

Broadcasting and Communications

BROADCASTING

Radio

As well as a local radio station, Radio 6CKI (see below), the Cocos (Keeling) Islands receive daily broadcasts from ABC regional radio and the Western Australian station Red FM.

Radio 6CKI Voice of the Cocos (Keeling) Islands: POB 1084, Cocos (Keeling) Islands 6799, Indian Ocean; tel. and fax (8) 9162-6666; e-mail 6cki@cki.cc; non-commercial, run by volunteers; daily broadcasting service in Cocos Malay and English; Chair. KELLY EDWARDS.

Television

Four television stations, ABC, SBS, WIN and GWN, are broadcast from Western Australia via satellite.

Industry

Cocos (Keeling) Islands Co-operative Society Ltd: POB 1058, Home Island, Cocos (Keeling) Islands 6799, Indian Ocean; tel. (8) 9162-6708; fax (8) 9162-6764; e-mail admin@CocosCoOp.com; internet www.cocoscoop.com; f. 1979; conducts the business enterprises of the Cocos Islanders; activities include boat construction and repairs, copra and coconut production, sail-making, stevedoring and airport operation; owns and operates a supermarket and tourist accommodation; Chair. MOHAMMED SAID CHONGKIN; Gen. Man. RONALD TAYLOR.

Transport

An airport is located on West Island. Virgin Blue Airlines operates a twice-weekly service from Perth (Western Australia), via Christmas Island, for passengers to and from the airport on West Island. Cargo vessels from Singapore and Perth deliver regular supplies. The islands have a total of 10 km of sealed and 12 km of unsealed roads.

Zentner Shipping Pty Ltd: tel. (8) 9337-5911; e-mail zentner1@iinet.au; operate sea freight service from Fremantle (WA) every 4–6 weeks.

Tourism

Tourism is relatively undeveloped. However, the Cocos Islands possess unique flora and fauna, along with pristine beaches and coral reefs that offer excellent opportunities for scuba-diving and snorkelling. In 2009 there was one 28-room hotel on West Island, as well as several self-catering villas.

Cocos Island Tourism Association: Admiralty House, POB 1030, Cocos (Keeling) Islands 6799, Indian Ocean; tel. (8) 9162-6790; fax (8) 9162-6696; e-mail info@cocos-tourism.cc; internet www.cocos-tourism.cc.

Parks Australia: POB 1043, Cocos (Keeling) Islands 6798, Indian Ocean; tel. (8) 9162-6678; fax (8) 9162-6680; internet www.environment.gov.au/about/structure/pa/index.html.

Education

Pre-primary and primary education is provided at the schools on Home and West Islands. Secondary education is provided to the age of 16 years on West Island. In August 2008 pre-primary pupils totalled 15. Primary pupils numbered 83, and there were 31 secondary students. A bursary scheme enables Cocos Malay children to continue their education on the Australian mainland.

HEARD ISLAND AND THE McDONALD ISLANDS

These islands are situated about 4,000 km (2,500 miles) south-west of Perth, Western Australia. The Territory, consisting of Heard Island, Shag Island (8 km north of Heard) and the McDonald Islands, is almost entirely covered in ice and has a total area of 369 sq km (142 sq miles). Sovereignty was transferred from the United Kingdom to the Commonwealth of Australia on 26 December 1947, following the establishment of a scientific research station on Heard Island (which functioned until March 1955). The islands are administered by the Antarctic Division of the Australian Department of Sustainability, Environment, Water, Population and Communities. There are no permanent inhabitants. However, in 1991 evidence emerged of a Polynesian community on Heard Island some 700 years before the territory's discovery by European explorers. The island is of considerable scientific interest, as it is believed to be one of the few Antarctic habitats uncontaminated by introduced organisms. Heard Island is about 44 km long and 20 km wide and possesses an active volcano, named Big Ben. In January 1991 an international team of scientists travelled to Heard Island to conduct research involving the transmission of sound waves, beneath the surface of the ocean, in order to monitor any evidence of the 'greenhouse effect' (melting of polar ice and the rise in sea-level as a consequence of pollution). The pulses of sound, which travel at a speed largely influenced by temperature, were to be received at various places around the world, with international co-operation. Heard Island was chosen for the experiment because of its unique location, from which direct paths to the five principal oceans extend. The McDonald Islands, with an area of about 1 sq km (0.4 sq miles), lie some 42 km west of Heard Island. Only two successful landings by boat have been recorded since the discovery of the McDonald Islands in the late 19th century. In late 1997 Heard Island and the McDonald Islands were accorded World Heritage status by UNESCO in recognition of their outstanding universal significance as a natural landmark.

In 1999 concern was expressed that stocks of the Patagonian toothfish in the waters around the islands were becoming depleted as a result of over-exploitation, mainly by illegal operators. (The popularity of the fish in Japan and the USA, where it is known as Chilean sea bass, increased significantly during the early 21st century.) This problem was highlighted in August 2003 when a Uruguayan fishing vessel was seized, following a 20-day pursuit over 7,400 km by Australian, South African and British patrol boats. The trawler had been fishing illegally in waters near Heard and McDonald and had a full cargo of Patagonian toothfish worth some US $1.5m. Experts feared that, if poaching continued at current rates, the species would become extinct by 2007. In response to this situation, the Australian Government announced in December 2003 that it was to send an ice-breaking patrol vessel with deck-mounted machine guns to police the waters around Heard and McDonald Islands. It was hoped that this action might serve to deter illegal fishing activity in the area, much of which was believed to involve international criminal organizations. However, it was reported that many vessels continued fishing in protected waters, including operations on the Banzare Bank, a plateau in the Southern Ocean, which in February 2005 was closed to fishing by the Convention for the Conservation of Arctic Marine Living Resources Commission. (An anomaly of international law meant that vessels flying flags of non-member countries of the Commission could not be evicted by Australian forces.) In August the Australian customs department announced that it was to train commandos to patrol the protected waters around Heard and McDonald for vessels fishing illegally. In September 2006 conservation groups petitioned the USA, a major importer of Patagonian toothfish, urging the Government to impose sanctions on Spain for failing to comply with laws governing fishing activities in the region.

In 2001 the Australian Government's Antarctic Division conducted a five-month scientific expedition to Heard Island. It claimed that glacial cover had retreated by 12% since 1947 as a result of global warming. In October 2002 the Australian Government declared the establishment of the Heard Island and McDonald Islands Marine Reserve. Covering 6.5m. ha, the marine reserve was to be one of the largest in the world, strengthening existing conservation measures and imposing an official ban on all fishing and petroleum and mineral exploitation. Among the many species of plant, bird and mammal to be protected by the reserve were the southern elephant seal, the sub-Antarctic fur seal and two species of albatross. Limited scientific research and environmental monitoring were to be allowed in the Marine Reserve. The Marine Reserve draft management plan, announced in 2005, proposed measures further to restrict human activity on the islands, in an attempt to protect their unique flora and fauna from damage and from introduced organisms. The islands remained the only unmodified example of a sub-Antarctic island ecosystem in the world.

BRUNEI

Physical and Social Geography

HARVEY DEMAINE

PHYSICAL FEATURES AND CLIMATE

The Sultanate of Brunei (Negara Brunei Darussalam) covers an area of 5,765 sq km (2,226 sq miles) and faces the South China Sea along the north-west coast of the island of Borneo, most of which comprises the Indonesian territory of Kalimantan. On its landward side, Brunei is both surrounded and split into two separate units by Sarawak, part of Malaysia. Brunei is divided into four districts: Brunei/Muara, Tutong and Seria/Belait, in the western section of Brunei, and Temburong, forming the eastern section.

The greater part of Brunei's small territory consists of a low coastal plain, and only on its southern margins does it attain heights of more than 300 m above sea-level. Brunei's highest point is Bukit Pagon, in the east of the country, which reaches 1,841 m above sea-level. Situated only 4°–5° N of the Equator, Brunei has a consistently hot and humid climate, with mean monthly temperatures of around 27°C and a heavy annual rainfall, well distributed throughout the year, of more than 2,500 mm. Except for those areas that have been cleared for permanent cultivation in the coastal zone, about three-quarters of the country is covered by dense equatorial forest, although this has deteriorated in places as a result of shifting cultivation.

POPULATION AND RESOURCES

At the census of August 2001 the population of Brunei was 332,844, compared with 260,482 at the August 1991 census. In 2009 the population was estimated to have reached 406,200. In 2006 an estimated 66.7% of the population were Malay and 11.1% Chinese. Indigenous races, which comprised 3.4% of the population, are mainly Muruts, Kedayans and Dusuns. More than 50% of the population were less than 20 years of age in 2000. The Chinese reside mainly in Bandar Seri Begawan (formerly Brunei Town), the capital, and Seria. Bandar Seri Begawan, which occupies an impressive site overlooking the large natural inlet of Brunei Bay, had a population of 27,285 at the census of 2001.

Brunei's natural resources consist almost exclusively of petroleum and natural gas. In the 1980s new petroleum reserves were discovered at Seria, the first significant onshore oilfield in Brunei. Further reserves were subsequently discovered in new and existing offshore fields. At the end of 2010 proven petroleum reserves amounted to 1,100m. barrels, sufficient to maintain output at that year's levels (averaging 172,000 barrels per day) for more than 17 years.

Brunei's proven reserves of natural gas totalled 300,000m. cu m at the end of 2010. Reserves of gas were estimated to be sufficient to maintain output for nearly 25 years, assuming current rates of production. Production of natural gas, which in 2010 totalled 12,200m. cu m, is mainly destined for export to Japan under long-term contracts.

History

C. M. TURNBULL

Revised by A. V. M. HORTON

EARLY HISTORY

Brunei was once the centre of a great maritime empire. Its origins are obscure, but there is a suggestion that it was founded in the late seventh century by a refugee prince fleeing from the Khmer conquest of Funan. From that time until the 16th century it was the centre of three successive empires, which at their height held sway over much of coastal Borneo and the Philippines. Known to the Chinese as P'o-ni, the port lay on the main trading route between China, the western part of the Indonesian archipelago and the Indian Ocean. There was extensive trade between the area and China during the period of the Tang and Song dynasties.

Brunei became an independent sultanate at an unknown date; estimates vary between 1368 and 1514/15, although there was a report in 1992 that a tombstone dating from 1301 of an otherwise unknown Muslim ruler had been discovered. Brunei profited from trade with Melaka (Malacca) but supposedly achieved even greater prosperity after the great Malay port was conquered by the Portuguese in 1511, when many Muslim traders diverted their custom to Brunei.

The first recorded European visitor to the city of Brunei was Ludovico Varthema in 1505, or late 1504. He was followed in 1521 by members of the Spanish expedition that had been led by the Portuguese navigator, Fernão de Magalhães (Magellan). They arrived in 1521, popularly believed, although historically unlikely, to have been during the reign of Bolkiah, one of the most illustrious of Brunei's sultans; they described the capital as a large and wealthy city allegedly comprising some 25,000 households, with an impressive and cultivated royal court. Brunei established cordial relations with Portugal. In 1526 the two countries concluded a commercial arrangement, and the Portuguese established a trading post at Brunei. As Portuguese trade with China and Japan expanded, Brunei became a regular port of call on the route between Melaka and Macao, and the Chinese community expanded greatly. Brunei already had a considerable Chinese community; indeed, a Chinese person married into the Brunei royal family.

The first half of the 16th century was Brunei's 'golden age', when it claimed suzerainty over the whole coast of Borneo, the Sulu archipelago and Mindanao, and its sphere of influence extended as far as what is now the Philippine capital of Manila. The empire was not a centralized polity but comprised a group of individual river states ruled by vassals, who paid obeisance to the Sultan and secured revenue through river tolls and poll taxes. The empire depended almost entirely on its ability to control regional trade.

Brunei came into conflict with the Spaniards, who established themselves in the northern Philippines in the latter part of the 16th century. The rivals clashed over trade and religion, and in 1578 the Spaniards seized Brunei for a short period and attempted unsuccessfully to impose Christianity. Eventually the Spaniards abandoned attempts to subdue the southern Philippines, and vassal chiefs in Mindanao and the Sulu archipelago took advantage of Brunei's weakness to break away and establish their own independence. Sulu was an aggressive state, the home of the infamous Balanini pirates, who ravaged the Borneo coasts and even ventured as far as the Straits of Melaka. As recompense for its intervention in a civil war in Brunei in the mid-17th century, Sulu claimed the whole of North Borneo (present-day Sabah), a claim that remains unresolved to this day.

Brunei continued to decline, and by the early 19th century the Sultan could lay claim only to the district centring on Brunei Town itself, the Sarawak River and the western coast of northern Borneo. Even here he exerted only weak control along the coastal strip and the lower reaches of the main rivers. Pirates operated along the coast of North Borneo, and Brunei Town became little more than a trading centre for their plunder and slaves. The stability of the sultanate was also threatened by disputed successions and rebellious chiefs. When antimony was discovered in the Sarawak valley in 1824, Brunei officials were sent to organize local Dayaks to mine the ore. In 1835 the corruption of the Brunei Governor drove the local chiefs and Dayaks to revolt. The province was still in a state of armed rebellion when an English gentleman adventurer, James (later Sir James) Brooke, arrived four years later. In 1841, in return for his help in settling the revolt, Brooke was granted the Sarawak River district and the title of Raja, which was confirmed by the Sultan in the following year when Brooke paid the customary tribute at the Brunei court.

BRITISH INTERVENTION

The British connection was to lead to the dissolution of most of Brunei's empire, but was arguably responsible for the continued existence of the sultanate. When Brooke's position at the Brunei court was threatened, the British Navy intervened. The Sultan was compelled to confirm Brooke's tenure at Sarawak for himself and his successors in perpetuity, to give the island of Labuan to the United Kingdom and to sign a treaty, in 1847, undertaking not to cede any further territory without British approval. In 1853, as a result of conflict with pirates, the Sultan ceded to Brooke the troublesome Saribas and Skrang districts, which later constituted the Second Division of Sarawak. Eight years later further piracy, which threatened the profitable sago trade of the Mukah and Oya valleys, compelled the Sultan to cede to Brooke the vast Rejang River basin, which became the Third Division of Sarawak.

James Brooke's successor, his nephew Charles (later Sir Charles) Brooke, wished to extend Sarawak's rule over the 'lawless' upper Baram area, the scene of recurrent friction between the people of Sarawak and Brunei, but for many years the British Government opposed this. In 1874 the British Government rejected Charles Brooke's proposal to place Brunei under the protection of either the United Kingdom or Sarawak. However, in 1877 the Sultan granted the northern part of Borneo (present-day Sabah) to a Hong Kong-based company owned by a British businessman, Alfred Dent, and the Austrian Consul, Gustavus, Baron von Overbeck. Four years later, Dent purchased the Austrian share, and in the same year the British Government granted him a royal charter to form the British North Borneo Company.

Fears of rival foreign ambitions in the region, inspired by Sultan Abdul Mumin's advancing years and uncertainty concerning the succession, prompted the United Kingdom to give approval in 1882 for Charles Brooke to obtain cession of the Baram basin, which became the Fourth Division of Sarawak. In 1884 he also acquired the Trusan valley. Now only the heartland of Brunei remained, under growing pressure from both Sarawak and the British North Borneo Company. In 1885 Sultan Mumin persuaded the *pengiran* (holders of hereditary titles used by relatives of the royal family) to join him in swearing a solemn oath, or *amanah*, not to cede any further territory. He was succeeded shortly afterwards as Sultan by Hashim Jalilul Alam, and in 1888 the United Kingdom made Brunei, Sarawak and North Borneo protectorates, thus assuming paramountcy over the whole of north-western Borneo. The Governor of the Straits Settlements was appointed High Commissioner for Brunei, but the British Government did not appoint a Resident at the Brunei court, and Sarawak continued to present a threat to the sultanate. In 1890 the chiefs of Limbang, which had been in a state of rebellion for some years, asked Raja Brooke to assume responsibility for their district, which was then joined with Trusan to form the Fifth Division of Sarawak. This deprived Brunei of a valuable food-producing area and divided it into two parts. The British Government offered to pay compensation to the Sultan but the offer was never formally accepted, and therefore this came to be regarded as a cession by default. After the death of the second Raja in 1917, the High Commissioner, Sir Arthur Young, recommended that an effort be made to secure the restitution of Limbang to Brunei. The new Raja, Vyner Brooke, was adamantly opposed to the suggestion, on account of the damage it would cause to Sarawak's prestige. However, even in 1919 the Colonial Office did not give up hope of restoring Limbang to Brunei; the Sultans of Brunei never acknowledged the cession, and the status of Limbang remains controversial to this day.

By the early 20th century the Tutong and Belait districts were in revolt, many people were migrating into adjoining Sarawak, and the sultanate had contracted to little more than 2,000 sq miles. The United Kingdom considered dividing what remained of Brunei between Sarawak and the British North Borneo Company, but decided against this after considering a detailed report by Stewart McArthur, an officer of the Straits Settlements' civil service, who in 1904 spent six months investigating the situation in Brunei. In the following year the British Government signed an agreement with the Sultan and senior chiefs, establishing Brunei as a full protectorate, under the terms of which all matters relating to administration, legislation and taxation were to be conducted on the advice of a British Resident. McArthur was appointed as first incumbent of this post in 1906, and, apart from the period of Japanese occupation, the British Resident remained the effective ruler of Brunei, certainly until the 1950s. The administration was modelled on that of the (British) Federated Malay States, and until 1948 the Resident was always seconded from Malaya. A modern civil service was created, a land code was introduced and the state revenues were organized. The traditional State Council was formalized, with the Sultan presiding but with the Resident as the dominant influence. Despite some dissatisfaction, quasi-colonial rule brought peace and stability to the country and guaranteed Brunei's survival. Brunei's future economic prosperity was also foreshadowed in this period when petroleum, albeit a minimal amount, was first discovered. However, a major oilfield was located at Seria in 1929. By the 1930s Brunei's debts had been discharged, and revenues from petroleum exports helped to finance modest programmes in education and social services.

THE POST-WAR PERIOD AND INDEPENDENCE

Brunei was occupied by Japanese forces from December 1941, shortly after Japan entered the Second World War, until it was liberated by Australian troops in July 1945. The immediate post-war years were devoted to rehabilitation and the resumption of petroleum production, which had been interrupted by the war.

The United Kingdom envisaged an eventual self-governing confederation embracing all the British dependencies in South-East Asia, namely the Malay Peninsula, Singapore and Borneo. As a first step, it planned to abolish protectorate status, bringing all the territories under the direct rule of the British crown. Sarawak and British North Borneo did become crown colonies, but the transition in Brunei was deferred, following difficulties encountered in abrogating the Malay States' treaties. In 1948 the Governor of Sarawak was appointed High Commissioner for Brunei, in place of the Governor of the now defunct Straits Settlements, but this did not alter the protectorate's status or the Resident's powers. Nevertheless, political changes in the region and the prospect of ultimate British withdrawal presented new threats to Brunei's security. These problems dominated Brunei politics for the next 20 years, producing two rival forms of nationalism: an enlightened paternalism, propounded by the Sultan and his supporters, and a form of popular democracy.

In 1953 Sultan Omar Ali Saifuddin III established a commission to help to formulate a written constitution for Brunei. District Councils, nominated by the Sultan, were created in 1954, but little progress was made in devising a constitution.

Meanwhile, Brunei's first political party, the Parti (or Partai) Rakyat Brunei (PRB—Brunei People's Party), was formed in 1956, modelled on the left-wing Malayan Parti Rakyat. Its charismatic President, Sheikh Ahmad Azahari (born in Labuan of Arab-Malay parentage), had studied in Java during the Japanese occupation and taken part in the Indonesian struggle for independence against the Dutch. He spent some time in Singapore in the early 1950s, and was imprisoned briefly for organizing the first political demonstration in Brunei. While remaining loyal to the sultanate, the party advocated democratic self-government for Brunei as part of a federation of the three Borneo states. The PRB attracted considerable popular support and in 1957 petitioned the Sultan and the Colonial Office for independence. Leaders of the PRB were angered by their exclusion from the delegation that the Sultan led to London, United Kingdom, in 1958 for constitutional talks. Under the Brunei Constitution, which was promulgated in 1959, the United Kingdom retained responsibility for Brunei's defence and foreign relations but transferred internal government to the Sultan, who was to preside over an Executive Council and rule with the help of a Legislative Council and District Councils, the latter being elected by universal adult suffrage. The PRB pressed for immediate elections, for independence in Brunei by 1963 and for a merger with the other Borneo states. The Sultan preferred a closer association with the Federation of Malaya, which had gained its independence in 1957. He welcomed the proposal made by Tunku Abdul Rahman, the Malayan Prime Minister, in May 1961, mooting a Malaysian federation to include Malaya, Singapore and the three Borneo territories. This led to an intense confrontation between the Sultan's supporters and the PRB.

At district council elections, which were eventually held in August 1962 after many delays, the PRB won all but one of the 55 seats, which also gave its candidates all the indirectly elective legislative council seats. The PRB's campaign had advocated internal democratic reform and rejection of the Malaysia proposal, in favour of a Borneo federation. In September the party united with politicians in Sarawak and North Borneo to form an Anti-Malaysia Alliance, for which Azahari tried to rouse international support. In December, after failing in an attempt to present to the Legislative Council a proposal in favour of independence from Malaysia, Azahari resorted to force and staged a rebellion through the North Borneo Liberation Army, which had strong links with the Indonesian Communist Party and with left-wing extremists in Singapore. The rebels proclaimed a Revolutionary State of North Kalimantan, with Azahari as Prime Minister. However, the Sultan quickly suppressed the revolt, with the aid of British forces from Singapore, and most of Azahari's former supporters in Sarawak and North Borneo disowned his use of force. A state of emergency was declared, the PRB was banned, Azahari went into exile in Indonesia, and his supporters fled or were imprisoned. The Sultan subsequently ruled by decree, with the emergency laws being renewed every two years.

The rebellion initially strengthened Sultan Omar's resolve to join Malaysia, as a means of ensuring Brunei's permanent security. However, in June 1963 negotiations collapsed, owing mainly to disputes concerning petroleum revenues but also to disagreement regarding the Sultan's precedence among Malay rulers. Two meetings between the Tunku and Sultan Omar failed to resolve the issue, and Brunei withdrew from the final negotiations that led to the establishment of Malaysia in September 1963. Brunei's decision not to join Malaysia resulted in a deterioration in relations with Kuala Lumpur, and allegations about Indonesia's involvement in the December 1962 revolt strained relations with Jakarta. Brunei was isolated, increasingly dependent upon the United Kingdom, and its autocratic Government and semi-colonial status exposed it to international criticism.

Following the 1962 revolt, the ban on the PRB had removed the most articulate opposition, and most other parties united to form a Brunei Alliance Party (BAP), which supported entry to Malaysia. The Sultan ignored the BAP's demand for a fully elected legislature, although he agreed to elections in 1965 for some legislative council seats and replaced the Executive Council with a Council of Ministers. The British Government exerted pressure on Sultan Omar to quicken the pace of constitutional reform, but he insisted upon an appointed cabinet. In August 1966 two small political groups united to form the Barisan Kemerdeka'an Rakyat (BAKER—Brunei People's Independence Front), which demanded responsible government, a full ministerial system and a fully elected legislature. The British Government was impatient at the slow progress of constitutional reform, at a time when it was preparing to withdraw most of its forces 'east of Suez'. In 1967 Sultan Omar abdicated in favour of his 21-year-old son, Hassanal Bolkiah, but the ex-Sultan retained effective power. The BAKER failed to gain support at district council elections held in 1968, which were overshadowed by the young Sultan's forthcoming talks in London about the future defence of Brunei. Under a new treaty, which was signed with the United Kingdom in 1971, the 1959 Constitution was amended to give the Sultan full control of all internal matters, with the United Kingdom retaining responsibility for foreign affairs. A separate agreement provided for the stationing of a British battalion of Gurkhas in Brunei.

Brunei developed close links with Singapore following the latter's secession from the Federation of Malaysia in 1965, but relations with Malaysia continued to be strained for many years. Malaysia offered political asylum to PRB leaders, permitted the illegal party to open an office in Kuala Lumpur, and in 1975 sponsored a PRB delegation, which presented a case for independence to the UN Committee on Decolonization. Brunei recalled all its students from Malaysia for fear that they might become a focus for dissidence, and it officially revived the Limbang claim, with former Sultan Omar crossing the border to incite Limbang villagers against Malaysia.

In 1977 the UN General Assembly adopted a Malaysian-sponsored resolution proposing free elections in Brunei, the end of the ban on political parties and the return of all political exiles to Brunei. While the British Labour Government (whose representative abstained from voting on the UN resolution) was prepared to sever its links with Brunei, the Sultan regarded the association as a protection against the possible encroachment of neighbouring governments, secessionists and political opponents within Brunei itself. The sultanate was reluctant to revise the terms of its 1971 treaty with the United Kingdom until it received assurances that Malaysia and Indonesia would respect Brunei's independence. In June 1978 Sultan Sir Hassanal Bolkiah and his father visited London in an unsuccessful attempt to resist separation from the United Kingdom. In 1979, however, they were compelled to sign an agreement whereby Brunei would become a sovereign independent state on 1 January 1984. In September 1983 Brunei concluded a new defence agreement with the United Kingdom whereby Brunei would continue, at its own expense, to employ the battalion of Gurkhas under British command.

Meanwhile, on 4 October 1970 (the anniversary of the 1967 abdication) the capital city, Brunei Town, had been renamed Bandar Seri Begawan (loosely translatable as 'Old Kingston'); this was a signal to the world that the sultanate was starting to regain full control of its internal affairs.

Some of the leading davisierships were filled by brothers of the Sultan. Prince Mohamed Bolkiah became Pengiran Temenggong in 1967, before being promoted to the position of Pengiran Perdana Wazir (Premier Vizier), an office specially created for him in February 1970. The two youngest brothers, namely Prince Sufri Bolkiah and Prince Jefri Bolkiah, became Pengiran Bendahara and Pengiran Di-Gadong respectively in 1979.

SUBSEQUENT DOMESTIC AFFAIRS

When Brunei became independent, henceforth being officially known as Negara Brunei Darussalam (the Nation-State of Brunei, Abode of Peace), the Council of Ministers was abolished in favour of a seven-member Cabinet, headed by the Sultan and including his father and two brothers. *Melayu Islam Beraja* (MIB—Malay Islamic Monarchy) was proclaimed as the state ideology, promoting Islamic values, an emphasis on the unique nature of Brunei-Malay culture and the importance of the role of the monarchy.

In the 1980s new laws were adopted to increase the share of petroleum revenue accruing to the State. While the demarcation between state revenue and the Sultan's personal wealth was not clearly defined and much was spent on royal prestige projects, all citizens enjoyed free medical care and education, and government housing loans. Indigenous, mainly Malay, inhabitants, *bumiputras* (sons of the soil), received preferential treatment. Even Brunei-born non-*bumiputras* were subject to stringent requirements with respect to residence and language when applications for citizenship were considered. In 1985 90% of the ethnic Chinese, who at that time constituted about one-third of the population, were classified as non-citizens excluded from state benefits. Although they still dominated the private sector, many Chinese began to emigrate.

Increasingly, Brunei's modernization and exposure to the rest of the world were regarded as a potential threat to its moral, cultural and religious traditions. At the same time rising unemployment and, more particularly, a shortage of non-manual jobs (menial work was generally undertaken by immigrant labourers) led to the emergence in the early 1990s of social problems, including drug and alcohol abuse. There was concern at the prospect of the situation deteriorating since more than one-half of the Bruneian population were aged under 20, and educational standards and employment expectations were rising. Partly in response to these incipient problems, from 1990 MIB was promoted more vigorously. Muslims were encouraged to adhere more closely to the tenets of Islam, with greater emphasis on Islamic holiday celebrations, and in January 1991 the import of alcohol was banned. In December of that year the public celebration of Christmas, the Christian festival, was forbidden. The state Mufti was brought under the direct control of the Sultan rather than the Ministry of Religious Affairs and in that same year the first Islamic bank was established. Under the Seventh National Development Plan (1996–2000) more resources were devoted to building mosques, religious schools and an Islamic college. An Islamic radio station began broadcasting in 1997.

After former Sultan Omar's death in 1986, the Cabinet was enlarged to 11 ministers, incorporating members of the educated élite. However, the royal family remained the dominant force in the Government, with the Sultan as Prime Minister and Minister of Defence, and his brothers, Mohamed and Jefri, responsible for foreign affairs and finance, respectively. In 1985 the Sultan considered permitting the introduction of a party political system and agreed to the formation of the Parti Kebangsaan Demokratik Brunei (PKDB—Brunei National Democratic Party). The PKDB advocated greater participation in the administration of the Government, democratization and a more equitable distribution of wealth. It attracted an alleged membership of some 3,000, comprising mainly Malay professionals and business executives, but it aroused little public support. Within a year a breakaway faction had formed a new party, the Parti Perpaduan Kebangsaan Brunei (PPKB—Brunei National Solidarity Party), which emphasized greater co-operation with the Government. In 1988, however, the President and the Secretary-General of the PKDB, Abdul Latif Hamid and Abdul Latif Chuchu, were arrested and detained for two years under the provisions of the Internal Security Act. The party was dissolved after it had demanded the Sultan's resignation as head of government (although not as head of state), the holding of democratic elections and the ending of the 26-year state of emergency. Meanwhile, at the beginning of 1988 a number of political detainees of the former PRB were released in a general amnesty. In 1990 the last six PRB men were set free, and in 1996 the few remaining PRB members were permitted to return from exile, on condition that they refrained from political activity. Azahari himself died in Bogor, Indonesia, in May 2002. In any event, radical politicians found it difficult to attract popular support while most Bruneians continued to enjoy a high standard of living.

In October 1992 Brunei celebrated Sultan Hassanal's Silver Jubilee, but hopes of liberal political concessions were dispelled when the Sultan marked the occasion by reaffirming the central role of the monarchy in a Malay Islamic nation. He assumed a more paternal stance, as 'the People's Sultan', distancing himself from the extravagant lifestyle of earlier days to stress diligence and mutual responsibility to Brunei as a country with 'its own firm identity and image among the non-secular nations of the world'. District and village councils were established in 1993 and held their first general assembly in May 1996. In 1994 a constitutional committee, chaired by Prince Mohamed, which had been appointed by the Sultan to review the 1959 constitutional arrangements, submitted a new draft constitution to the Sultan for consideration. In February 1995 the PPKB was permitted to hold its first national assembly, at which its newly elected President, Abdul Latif Chuchu, reaffirmed support for the monarchy and the national ideology. However, he also urged the holding of democratic elections, and was soon forced to resign by the Government, which renewed the emergency laws. Following an inactive period of three years, in May 1998 the PPKB held an annual general meeting, at which a business executive, Hatta Zainal Abidin, was elected President. The party briefly voiced concern at allegations of official corruption during the Amedeo court case in May 2000 (see below), but soon lapsed into infighting in attempts to oust its President.

The anachronistic political system remained firmly entrenched, and the dominance of the monarchy was reaffirmed in August 1998 when the Sultan's eldest son, Al-Muhtadee Billah Bolkiah, was formally installed as the heir to the throne in a lavish ceremony. The royal family enjoyed a monopoly of power, but maintained its popularity by enabling all citizens to share to some extent in the wealth of the State. There was no personal income tax, while housing, fuel and other essentials were subsidized and until 1995, when nominal charges were introduced for medical and dental treatment, both health services and education remained free for citizens. The populace, as well as foreign dignitaries, were involved in extravagant royal festivities, and at his birthday celebrations in 1998 the Sultan pledged salary increases for lower-paid civil servants and greater state support for pensioners and the destitute.

The economic crisis that beset South-East Asia from late 1997, together with scandals in Brunei itself, provided the catalyst for economic and, potentially, political change. Initially, Brunei provided assistance to other countries of the region; the sultanate contributed to an IMF emergency programme for Thailand, the state-owned Brunei Investment Agency (BIA) helped to stabilize currencies by buying Singapore dollars and Malaysian ringgit, and Brunei promised to invest in Malaysia to assist its recovery. However, Brunei itself was adversely affected by a sharp decline in the international price of petroleum and by pollution from forest fires in Indonesia and Malaysia in 1997 and 1998, which threatened the development of tourism. The downturn was compounded in July 1998 with the collapse of the Amedeo Development Corporation, Brunei's largest investment and construction firm, which Prince Jefri controlled through his son and which had benefited from numerous lucrative government contracts.

Relations between the Sultan and his younger brother Jefri were already severely strained. Lawsuits were brought against Prince Jefri in the USA in 1997 and 1998 by US and British beauty queens alleging sexual misconduct, and in February 1998 two former business associates sued the Prince for £80m. in London, claiming that he had reneged on property agreements. The first case was withdrawn when Prince Jefri was granted diplomatic immunity, and the other two lawsuits were settled out of court for undisclosed sums. The cases were unreported in Brunei but attracted wide international publicity and drew attention to Prince Jefri's extravagant and profligate lifestyle. In February 1998 the Sultan removed the finance portfolio from Prince Jefri, assuming responsibility for it himself, in the first major cabinet change for 10 years. In the following month the Minister of Health was dismissed, reportedly owing to his inadequate response to the haze over Brunei caused by forest fires in Indonesia and Malaysia, and in June the Sultan accepted the resignation of the Attorney-General and of the Solicitor-General. In July the Sultan appointed international accountants as executive managers of Amedeo, removed Prince Jefri from the boards of seven telecommunications companies and dismissed him as Chairman of the BIA, which controlled much of Brunei's overseas investment.

For a long time the Brunei Government made no official comment about the collapse of the Amedeo group, the misappropriation of BIA funds or the role played by Prince Jefri. In August 1999, however, Abdul Aziz Umar, the Minister of Education, who was Chairman of the government task force appointed to investigate the missing BIA funds, admitted that there had been mismanagement. After the failure of private negotiations, the Government and the BIA began civil proceedings against Prince Jefri in Brunei and the United Kingdom, alleging misappropriation of more than US $28,000m. while he was Minister of Finance and Chairman of the BIA. A total of 71 others were named in the action, including Prince Jefri's eldest son, Prince Muda Abdul Hakeem, along with his private secretary, and more than 60 overseas companies believed to be controlled by Prince Jefri. In April 2000 the Brunei court dismissed an appeal against disclosure of his assets, which were frozen world-wide, and rejected his plea for an independent judge from outside Brunei. The court case, which opened in May, dominated the local press, but Prince Jefri and his son reached confidential out-of-court settlements, in which the case against them was abandoned when they agreed to return all assets purchased with BIA funds. In October, however, Haji Awang Kassim, Jefri's former confidential secretary, who had virtually been responsible for the management of Amedeo and was deputy managing director of the BIA, was arrested after being extradited from Manila. The State and the BIA also began civil proceedings to recover funds from six other former associates of Prince Jefri, including the former managing directors of two state-owned corporations. Meanwhile, there were angry scenes at meetings of Amedeo creditors in November when they refused the BIA's settlement terms, and in May 2001 the liquidators sued a former senior official.

In September 1998 the Brunei Darussalam Economic Council (BDEC), chaired by Prince Mohamed, was established to seek ways of improving the economy. The Sultan approved the BDEC's report, released in February 2000, which warned that Brunei's economy was becoming increasingly unsustainable, and appointed Prince Mohamed to oversee the recommended economic recovery plan. There were no proposals to match economic modernization with political reform. The aim was to create a corporate system of government presided over by a traditional monarchy and to transform the bureaucracy into a 'technocracy'. To this end, in February 2004, during the celebrations of the 20th anniversary of independence, the Sultan announced the establishment of a special task force to update and streamline the 'National Vision', along with the formation of a long-term development planning body, which would prepare the framework and formulate plans for a 30-year period, beginning in the financial year 2006. The aim was to involve the people as 'stakeholders' in the country's development. These themes of development, adaptation and involvement recurred in the Sultan's speeches. The Wawasan Brunei 2035 programme was finally published in January 2008. This ambitious plan envisaged that by 2035 Brunei would rank within the 10 leading countries of the world in terms of quality of life, income per head and educational attainment. The first phase (2007–12) of the programme involved no fewer than 826 projects at a budgeted cost of B $9,500m. (see Economy).

In mid-1999 Prince Mohamed announced that the report on the Constitution had been completed, and in March 2000 seminars on modern management were organized for village headmen, but the Sultan, in his capacity as Prime Minister and Minister of Defence and of Finance, continued to rule by decree under the state of emergency. Modernization was led by the Sultan, who carried out random checks on government departments. He continued to visit rural *kampong*, making himself accessible to his people, and holding open days every year during the three-day Hari Raya festivities, when thousands of people would visit the palace. Crown Prince Al-Muhtadee Billah played an increasing role in public life, and in March 2004 he was bestowed with the rank of four-star General. In this capacity he made visits to installations of the Royal Brunei Armed Forces. In June Prince Billah spent a full day visiting factories at Muara, while the Sultan was distributing land titles and house keys to the landless, as part of the Kampong Ayer Resettlement Scheme. Prince Billah's marriage in September, to Dayangku Sarah binte Pengiran Haji Salleh Abdul Rahaman, was lavishly celebrated, and was attended by dignitaries from around the world. His status was further enhanced by his elevation to the position of Deputy Inspector-General of Police in May 2005 and by his appointment in the cabinet reorganization at the end of that month as Senior Minister at the Prime Minister's Office.

In a speech celebrating his 54th birthday in July 2000, the Sultan urged the development of a new mindset to counter antiquated regulations, with a view to making Brunei a financial hub for the region. He also repeatedly insisted that the economy should be strengthened in line with Islamic teaching in order to preserve social and moral values. In October, as Chancellor of the Universiti Brunei Darussalam (UBD), the Sultan urged that Islamic studies be upheld as the most important field of education, and in the following month he officially launched the Islamic Development Bank of Brunei, seven years after the opening of the country's first Islamic bank. Following the attacks on the USA on 11 September 2001, Brunei aligned itself with the other member states of the Association of Southeast Asian Nations (ASEAN) and Asia-Pacific Economic Cooperation (APEC), closing ranks against terrorism. The Sultan continued to exhort young people to follow the teachings of the Koran, and he himself went regularly on pilgrimage to Mecca, in Saudi Arabia. Meanwhile, the State was determined to eradicate so-called deviant or extremist teachings among Muslims. In 2000 a Malay martial arts group, which planned armed attacks on what it held to be 'un-Islamic' institutions, was uncovered, and in December three men, including one retired senior police officer and two Malay businessmen, were arrested for allegedly supporting subversive Christian practices, with close links to groups in the Malaysian states of Sabah and Sarawak.

The broadcast media and the press remained closely controlled. Legislation enacted in 1997 required all journalists to register, and prohibited 'undesirable' foreign broadcasts, criticism of the royal family and objectionable religious or cultural material. Until 1999 television was state-owned, but the first commercial television channel was introduced in that year. The Government began to adopt a slightly more relaxed attitude to the press, paying heed to mildly critical letters about administrative shortcomings; these began to appear from 1999 in the correspondence pages of the English-language newspaper *Borneo Bulletin*, which was owned by Prince Mohamed. A second English-language newspaper, *News Express*, which was partly owned by the former Attorney-General, was established in August, and was later permitted to publish Brunei's first Chinese-language newspaper and a Malay daily. While official willingness to accept restrained criticism marked a substantial advance, the press exerted self-censorship, avoiding any questioning of the sultanate or national philosophy, and in March 2000 the Government warned newspapers to focus on national development, social well-being and character-building, instead of 'negative news'. In October 2001 a Local Newspapers (Amendment) Order introduced more stringent measures, requiring newspapers to obtain an annual permit, increasing deposit fees and fines and permitting the authorities to suspend any local newspaper without appeal and to ban foreign newspapers from entering the country. *News Express* had to suspend publication temporarily in order to meet the new financial requirements; it finally closed down in September 2002. Although more open than previously, comment in the press remained cautious. A new daily newspaper, the *Brunei Times*, was officially launched in June 2006 with the motto 'fresh ideas, new options and global vision'. In April 2007, however, journalists were given a stern warning; one Deputy Minister cautioned that freedom of the press needed to be exercised responsibly, particularly with regard to issues involving public security.

Meanwhile, the repercussions of the Amedeo crisis continued. In September 2001 about 300 creditors remained unpaid, with no settlement in prospect. The Government was engaged in disputes with Prince Jefri concerning the assets covered by the out-of-court settlement that he had made, while the case was generating huge costs in fee payments to foreign liquidators, lawyers and accountants. In October the Government intervened and established Global

Evergreen Sdn Bhd—a government-owned corporation under the chairmanship of the Minister of Education, a former Chairman of the BIA. Within two months Global Evergreen had settled 97% of all claims and dispensed with the services of overseas consultants. However, in May 2002 it emerged that several of the overseas consultants employed by Global Evergreen had allegedly been prevented from leaving Brunei owing to visa irregularities. The consultants had been investigating the reported embezzlement of an estimated B $10,000m. from Sultan Hassanal and had made inquiries into the conduct of the Minister of Home Affairs, Pehin Dato' Haji Isa, following which the immigration authorities had forcibly searched the company's offices and uncovered the alleged visa errors. The Government claimed that the consultants had been subjected only to normal immigration procedures, and those involved were finally permitted to depart. By August 2002 litigation over Amedeo had almost been completed. After a decent interval Prince Jefri was publicly rehabilitated, appearing at the end of July 2003 along with the Sultan and other members of the royal family at a concert. However, the reconciliation was brief, and in October 2004 the BIA sought High Court intervention to enforce the settlement reached in 2000, under the terms of which Prince Jefri had agreed to return to the State the personal assets he had acquired using BIA funds.

In May 2004 the former Minister of Development, Pengiran Indera Wijaya Ismail bin Pengiran Haji Damit, who had been replaced in May 2001, was charged with corruption, along with businessman Wong Tim Kai, and went on trial in February 2005. One of the multiple charges was abandoned in February 2007, but court proceedings for the remaining charges were subsequently delayed by the ill health of the original trial judge, who was replaced in March 2009. The case was further delayed by the ill health of the Chief Justice, Dato' Mohammed Saied, who was replaced by Dato' Seri Paduka Haji Kifrawi Kifli (the first indigenous holder of the post) in August, and by Wong's failure to attend the rescheduled court hearing in September. However, the proceedings finally resumed, and Pengiran Damit and Wong were both convicted of corruption in February 2010, after the longest court proceedings in the sultanate's history. Both men were sentenced to seven years' imprisonment and fined heavily. In December the Court of Appeal dismissed the case brought by the former Minister, both against his conviction and against the length of his prison sentence.

In July 2004 the Sultan announced that by the end of the year he intended to reinstate the country's Legislative Council, which had been formally disbanded in 1984 (the relevant constitutional provision having been in abeyance since the revolt of 1962). However, its members were to be elected by a governmental committee, and the Sultan confirmed his intention to continue ruling by decree. The Council was to comprise a speaker (to be a member of the royal family nominated by the Sultan), 15 elective members and up to 30 others nominated by the Sultan. By the end of the year 21 councillors had been named, including the Sultan and other cabinet ministers, the Attorney-General, permanent secretaries, leading public figures, business representatives and community leaders. Elections for the elective seats were to be held in the indefinite future. Nevertheless, the promise of some elective element had been given, and the perception of Brunei as an absolute monarchy had been slightly modified. However, the nominated members included no women and only one non-Malay; thus the concept of the Malay Muslim monarchy had hardly been breached. The two extant political parties, the Parti Kesedaran Rakyat (PAKAR—People's Consciousness Party—formed in May 2000 and subsequently split into two opposing factions) and the PPKB remained of little significance.

In May 2005 a government reorganization introduced important changes. Removed from the Cabinet were Pehin Dato' Haji Isa, hitherto the Minister of Home Affairs and Special Adviser to the Prime Minister; Pehin Dato' Haji Aziz, the Minister of Education; Pehin Dato' Haji Zakaria, the Minister of Communications; and Pehin Dato' Haji Hussein, the Minister of Culture, Youth and Sports. In addition to the inclusion of Prince Al-Muhtadee Billah as the Senior Minister at the Prime Minister's Office, Pehin Dato' Lim Jock Seng, previously a Permanent Secretary at the Ministry of Foreign Affairs, was appointed Minister of Foreign Affairs II (Prince Mohamed Bolkiah remaining Minister of Foreign Affairs), the first ethnic Chinese official to be raised to cabinet rank. Another departure from tradition was the appointment of two ministers from the corporate sector: Dato' Haji Hamdillah bin Haji Abdul Wahab, hitherto managing director of Brunei LNG, as Deputy Minister of Industry and Primary Resources; and Dato' Dr Haji Mat Suny bin Haji Mohd Hussein, a former deputy managing director of Brunei Shell, as Deputy Minister of Development. A new Ministry of Energy was created within the Prime Minister's Office. The cabinet reorganization and the appointment of 10 new Deputy Ministers was welcomed as a progression towards a government more representative of Brunei society. The Ministry of Foreign Affairs was renamed the Ministry of Foreign Affairs and Trade in August 2005.

Meanwhile, international concern about the human rights record of Brunei continued. The US Department of State's annual survey for 2005 reported that citizens 'did not have the right to change their Government peacefully' and that civil servants were not permitted to join political parties. It was alleged that the Government 'employed an informer system as part of its internal security apparatus to monitor suspected dissidents'. Freedom of speech and of the press were 'significantly' confined. Furthermore, the regime 'routinely restricted' the practice of non-Muslim religions and Muslims who wished to change their religion experienced 'considerable difficulties'. The Ministry of Education required courses on Islam and the values of MIB (under the Sedition Act, as amended in May 2005, it became an offence to denigrate 'directly or indirectly' the MIB concept) but prohibited the teaching of other religions, with the Government regularly censoring the press, removing photographs of crucifixes and other non-Islamic religious symbols. The report also stated that the regime lacked transparency; civil society was poorly developed; and the State might suspend the activities of a registered non-governmental organization (NGO) 'if it deems such an act in the public interest'. Other issues giving rise to international concern included limited labour rights and the exploitation of foreign workers. The US Department of State's concerns about the human rights situation in the sultanate were not significantly altered in its 2007 report, which was released in March 2008.

In August 2005 a third political organization, the Parti Pembangunan Bangsa (PPB—National Development Party, NDP), was formally established. More than 100 people attended the PPB's initial gathering at Gadong in the following month, and by the time of the party's first congress in April 2006 the number of official members had reached 700. Headed by the octogenarian Muhammad Yasin Affendy bin Abdul Rahman, a former stalwart of the defunct PRB, the PPB, the activities of which were regularly reported in the press, appeared to be well organized and quickly established a presence in all four districts, attracting activists and support from middle-ranking and retired personnel. Profoundly conservative, its projected mission was to partner the Government in nation-building and in upholding MIB.

Meanwhile, both of the pre-existing political parties were struggling to maintain their influence. PAKAR, in particular, was in crisis. In March 2005 there were two factions, both of which held separate meetings to choose their own officials. The split attracted the attention of the Commissioner of the Royal Brunei Police Force and threatened the party's legal existence. By late August the contending factions had agreed to settle their differences and to elect a new committee, recognizing in the interim the board in place prior to the breach. In the same month, in obscure circumstances, the PAKAR Secretary-General, Haji Hamzah Rahman, ceased to be a member of the party. The significance of PAKAR subsequently appeared to diminish, despite an attempt to launch the party in Belait District in November 2005, and in March 2007 PAKAR was deregistered.

On 1 September 2005 the Sultan dissolved the 21-member Legislative Council and appointed an enlarged Council of 29 members with effect from the following day. A total of 15 members were retained, and the 14 newcomers comprised predominantly cabinet ministers appointed in May (including the Crown Prince) and persons involved in district administration. At mid-2011, however, the promised elections for 15 of the eventual 45 seats on the Legislative Council had yet to be held.

The Legislative Council held a six-day session in March 2006 to endorse the national budget for 2006/07, which it approved unanimously. Having executed its duty, the Council was adjourned until the following March, when the procedure was more or less repeated. In his opening *titah* (royal address) at the Council session, the Sultan spoke of the need to diversify the economy, to develop sectors such as agriculture and to achieve self-sufficiency.

The Sultan's various *titah* in 2005–06 afforded an insight into some of his principal concerns. Recurring themes included the need to meet the challenges of globalization, to boost national development, to improve competitiveness, to reduce unemployment and to diversify the economy. Corruption and bureaucratic obstacles to business success needed to be eradicated. In a *titah* given in September 2005, the Sultan envisaged the establishment of a second, explicitly Islamic university in the sultanate. In November he announced that the Government planned to establish an Islamic capital bond market in the country, and by May 2009 30 issues of *sukuk* (short-term Islamic bonds) had been sold.

Responsibility for religious education was returned to the Ministry of Religious Affairs (from the Ministry of Education) at the start of the 2006 school year. In January 2007 Sultan Hassanal announced plans for the foundation of the Universiti Islam Sultan Sharif Ali (UNISSA), Brunei's first Islamic university. It was hoped that this second university would play a role in producing the Muslim intellectuals required by the nation. UNISSA accepted its first intake of students in August, but was strongly criticized by the Sultan in a *titah* in November 2009 for placing too little emphasis on the teachings of the Koran. Meanwhile, the Seri Begawan Training College for Teachers of Islamic Religion was upgraded to become the Seri Begawan University College for Teachers of Islamic Religion, with effect from August 2007. In April 2008 it was announced that the Princess Rashidah College of Nursing, founded in 1986, was to merge with UBD's Institute of Medicine. The Sistem Pendidikan Negara Abad Ke-21 (SPN 21—National Education System for the 21st Century) programme was introduced in 2008.

In March 2007 the Crown Princess gave birth to her first child, a son, who was generally regarded as being second in line to the throne (the succession, in theory, not being hereditary; her third child was born in January 2011). When the annual Open House was held at the Istana Nurul Iman (the principal palace in Bandar Seri Begawan) during the three-day post-Ramadan holiday in October 2006, no fewer than 102,599 members of the public, equivalent to almost one-quarter of the country's entire population, queued up to greet members of the royal family.

At the opening session of the Legislative Council in March 2007 Sultan Hassanal insisted that government programmes should not simply focus on enhancing the country's economy but should also encompass cultural aspects of life. The 'socialization' of youth had become a particular concern, and in April the Sultan urged young people to remain consistent with Islamic religious practice.

In early 2008, and again in early 2009, the US Department of State noted in its annual report on Brunei that although the parties criticized administrative deficiencies 'their few activities received limited publicity, and they were hindered by membership restrictions'. Nevertheless, several members and former members of political parties were consulted informally about the programme of the Legislative Council. During 2007, however, there were credible reports that government officials had advised members of political parties not to discuss certain politically sensitive issues during their congresses.

The PPKB, Brunei's oldest extant political party, was deregistered in November 2007, owing to its failure to furnish annual reports to the Registrar of Societies. The dissolution became final in February 2008, after the party's appeal against the ruling was rejected by the Minister of Home Affairs, thus leaving the PPB as the only active party. Also in February, a membership of 2,000 persons was claimed when 500 PPB members attended the National Day gathering in Bandar Seri Begawan. The PPB pledged to support the Sultan and the Government. Yasin Affendy, the PPB President, issued an appeal for party unity prior to its third congress, which was held in July. The PPB subsequently made little impact. The fifth party congress was held in June 2010; issues discussed included the importance of the Wawasan Brunei 2035 economic programme.

Meanwhile, the legal dispute between the Sultan and Prince Jefri, reputed to have become the most expensive family feud in legal history, showed no signs of abating. In a ruling in March 2006 the Brunei High Court had upheld the enforceability of the May 2000 out-of-court settlement; and this decision was endorsed, in turn, by the Privy Council in London during 2007. In March 2008 it was reported that the Brunei Government had wrested control, by means of a local US court order, of the New York Palace Hotel (although the Prince was disputing the transfer of control and further legal proceedings were likely). Prince Jefri was already reported to have relinquished property to the value of thousands of millions of pounds sterling, including a hotel in Paris, a yacht, a car collection and more than 100 paintings by artists such as Picasso, Renoir and Modigliani, as well as a set of rare diamonds valued at £100m. However, the Government deemed the surrender of these assets insufficient. High Court proceedings were in progress in London, where the Prince was accused of breaching a court order that required him to surrender more than £3,000m. in cash and assets to the BIA. In June, when Prince Jefri failed to appear at the hearing, a warrant was issued for his arrest on charges of alleged contempt of court. The Prince was believed to have fled to Paris.

The Legislative Council convened for its fourth annual meeting of the series in March 2008 at its new building in Jalan Kebangsaan, near the capital. Built at a cost of B $70m., the Dewan Majlis was officially inaugurated by the Sultan, who in his opening address to the week-long session focused on the need to eliminate poverty from Brunei and to improve standards in rice production. Issues subsequently capturing the attention of legislators included improvements in the government media, larger bonuses for civil servants and the defence budget (which in comparison with the previous financial year was slightly reduced in 2008/09). On the question of the outstanding election, the Sultan preferred to focus on the consolidation of the existing system.

In his New Year address for 2008 Sultan Hassanal envisaged a further 12 months of peace and prosperity. With oil prices already at record levels, with the prospect of success in the legal dispute with Prince Jefri, with the USA perceived as having lost the moral authority to put pressure on Brunei for further democratization owing to its prolonged involvement in the conflicts in Iraq and in Afghanistan, and with little or no sign of any domestic opposition, there appeared to be sound reasons for the Sultan's optimism. Nevertheless, he felt obliged to impress upon the public the need for hard work and to warn of the dangers of corruption.

The Cabinet underwent a minor reorganization in August 2008, when Pehin Ahmad Jumat, Minister of Industry and Primary Resources, became Minister of Culture, Youth, and Sports, in succession to Pehin Maj.-Gen. Mohammad Haji Daud, who was appointed Minister of Energy in the Prime Minister's Office. Pehin Yahya Bakar, hitherto the Minister of Energy, was transferred to the industry and primary resources portfolio. It was also announced that Pehin Abu Bakar Apong, Minister of Communications, would serve concurrently as Chairman of the BIA. The post of managing director of the BIA was elevated to Deputy Permanent Secretary status at the Ministry of Finance in January 2008.

When opening the fifth annual session of the revived Legislative Council on 12 March 2009, the Sultan announced the formation of a Sustainability Fund to consolidate the nation's financial position in the long term. He also announced an allocation of B $30m. to accelerate improvements to flood defences, following flash flooding and landslide disasters earlier in the year.

A new law established 31 March as Adat Istiadat Day (Ceremonial Customs Day), to be celebrated annually. In April 2009 the Academy of Brunei Studies at UBD held a series of activities designed to promote Brunei's culture. In May the

Sultan urged the revival of the MIB National Council, which had been formed in 2001 but had been in abeyance in recent years. In the same month the 26th annual Adau Gayoh carnival was held, a harvest festival combined with a celebration of art and culture. This annual event was designed to foster solidarity within the beleaguered non-Muslim Dusun community of Borneo.

Although the judiciary was largely composed of indigenous Bruneians, the Court of Appeal continued to be staffed by expatriates. In May 2009 24 lawyers received accreditation to practise in local *Shari'a* (Islamic law) courts. The liberalization of legal services was becoming an important issue, as ASEAN intended to implement a single market in goods, services and investment by 2015, as a result of which foreign lawyers might be allowed to practise in the sultanate.

In June 2009 the Ministry of Home Affairs contested an earlier report by the US Department of State that Brunei was failing to take effective action to combat human-trafficking in the sultanate. Also in June the Global Corruption Barometer, a survey commissioned by the anti-corruption organization Transparency International, ranked Brunei as second only to Singapore in the Asia-Pacific region with regard to freedom from corruption and third for government effectiveness in countering the problem. The public was increasingly willing to report cases of alleged corruption, adding substantially to the Anti-Corruption Bureau's workload in 2009–10.

Meanwhile, the National Council for Social Issues convened in September 2008. Its members included several cabinet ministers, with Pehin Ahmad Jumat, the Minister of Culture, Youth and Sports, as Chairman. The Council was responsible for detecting emergent social issues, establishing causes and developing solutions. A special committee on poverty held its first meeting in December, again under the chairmanship of Pehin Ahmad.

In his national address marking New Year 2009 the Sultan noted that Brunei had enjoyed 'peace and tranquillity' and had been largely spared from the economic downturn, social controversies, environmental deterioration and political instability that were affecting much of the world. A sum of B $5m. had originally been allocated to the forthcoming National Day celebrations on 23 February, but the budget was subsequently scaled back to only B $2m., an indication perhaps that the deterioration in the global financial situation was in fact having some impact on the sultanate. On 29 September the sultanate celebrated the 50th anniversary of the end of the Residential Era, marking the recovery of internal autonomy. The celebrations were relatively muted, with the emphasis placed on the enshrinement of Malay as the national language in the 1959 Constitution.

Further efforts were made to promote the MIB ideology and to improve Islamic religious education in the sultanate. The MIB National Council was restyled as the Supreme Council in mid-2009 and convened in October; members of the Council, appointed for three-year terms from August, comprised government ministers, senior civil servants, members of the royal household and senior law officers. Chaired by the Minister of Education, the Council was designed to strengthen understanding of the national philosophy by all levels of society.

Environmental conservation was a prominent consideration, along with the need for more efficient land use, and a master plan was to be drawn up for Bandar Seri Begawan. Housing was also an issue; in an attempt to meet demand, thousands of houses were to be constructed under the 2007–12 National Development Plan. Meanwhile, in his birthday *titah* in July 2009 the Sultan announced the establishment of a supplementary contributory pension and the raising, from 55 years to 60, of the standard age of retirement; both measures duly took effect on 1 January 2010.

In August 2009 Datin Hayati Salleh, a High Court judge since January 2001, was promoted to the position of Attorney-General, becoming the first woman to hold the post, which had been upgraded to cabinet rank in 2005; consequently, she also became only the second woman to attain ministerial status in Brunei, following in the footsteps of Princess Hajah Masna, Brunei's ambassador-at-large and frequently acting Minister of Foreign Affairs. A further notable development during the second half of 2009 was the apparent rehabilitation of Prince Jefri, who returned to the sultanate and was regularly seen in the company of other senior members of the royal family.

The country's human rights record remained an outstanding issue. Brunei was ranked only 163rd in the world on the 2010 index of press freedom compiled by Freedom House, and was categorized by this US-based NGO as 'not free'. The lack of accountability was perceived by some to have led to inefficiency, delays, waste and corruption. In his 2010 New Year *titah* the Sultan reiterated his Government's determination to eradicate poverty in the sultanate. The Sultan also noted with concern that, according to the World Bank's *Doing Business 2010* report, Brunei currently ranked only 96th out of 183 countries in terms of ease of doing business. In his televised address on the eve of National Day 2010 the Sultan insisted that an orderly economic policy and a conducive investment climate were required in order to promote overall economic growth; that plans should be executed according to timetable; and that, since the nation could not progress if the environment were damaged, the Environmental Impact Assessment procedure must be strengthened. An anti-corruption campaign was under way in 2010, coupled with an emphasis on the importance of integrity within the civil service.

In late May 2010 the Sultan announced the formation of the fifth post-independence Cabinet, which was to serve for a five-year term. Four senior ministers departed from the public arena after decades of service, most notably Pehin Abdul Rahman Taib, who had served continuously in the Cabinet since independence in 1984 (most recently as Minister of Education), and Pehin Zain Serudin, the Minister of Religious Affairs, who had held that portfolio since October 1986. Notable appointments included that of Pehin Dato' Haji Badaruddin bin Haji Othman, hitherto Deputy Minister of Religious Affairs, as the Minister of Home Affairs; Pengiran Dato' Dr Mohammad bin Haji Abdul Rahman, previously Deputy Minister of Education, as Pehin Zain's replacement at the head of the Ministry of Religious Affairs; and Pehin Dato' Haji Col (retd) Mohammad Yasmin bin Haji Umar, formerly Deputy Minister of Defence, as Minister of Energy at the Prime Minister's Office. Datin Adina Othman, hitherto Director of the Community Development Department within the civil service, was installed as Deputy Minister of Culture, Youth and Sports, thereby becoming the third woman to achieve ministerial status in Brunei.

In a national address in July 2010, the Sultan announced the intention to establish a monetary authority, equivalent to a central bank, with the aim of strengthening financial stability. The Monetary Authority of Brunei Darussalam duly came into existence on 1 January 2011 under the chairmanship of the Crown Prince. Mohd Rosli bin Haji Sabtu was appointed Managing Director. There was no desire to undermine the existing currency agreement under which the Brunei dollar remained at par with its Singapore counterpart.

In his *titah* for New Year 2011, the Sultan announced that maternity leave for civil servants was to be increased from 56 days to 105. As the country entered a new decade, the Government pledged to continue to strengthen efforts to improve the welfare of the people and the stability of the nation. There remained many challenges, notably relating to financial issues, oil, food, health and climate.On the eve of National Day in February the Sultan reminded the people to value the country's independence by living within their means, avoiding waste and appreciating the provision of services such as free medical care and education, as well as subsidies on essential products such as rice, sugar, fuel, electricity and water. The importance of attracting foreign investment was also stressed.

In March 2011 the Sultan ordered the country's laws to be aligned more closely with Muslim teachings. The intervention of the British during the colonial era had undermined Islamic jurisprudence. A working committee was to be established, therefore, to ensure that criminal justice was structured according to the requirements of Koranic teachings; and any discrepancy between existing civil legislation and the Law of Allah was to be eradicated.

A protracted legal dispute developed between Prince Jefri and Thomas Derbyshire, who had formed a legal team with his wife, Faith Zaman. Prince Jefri had been a client of the two lawyers between 2004 and 2006, and in December 2010 they were awarded US $21m. after convincing a New York jury that they had been underpaid by Prince Jefri. However, a spokesman for the Sultan's brother was confident that the verdict would be overruled on appeal.

Within the sultanate itself, Prince Jefri's rehabilitation continued. He was regularly photographed at major national events, but the rapprochement did not extend as yet to his being restored to government office or to some other prominent national role. In April 2011, in a sign that a new generation was coming to the fore, three princes (Abdul Azim, Abdul Malik and Abdul Mateen) were appointed as members of the Privy Council by the Sultan. Two former cabinet ministers were also drafted on to the Council, namely Pehin Abdul Aziz Umar and Pehin Mohd Zain Serudin. Meanwhile, the Crown Prince continued to act as deputy for the Sultan during the latter's absences from Brunei.

The popular uprisings in the 'Arab Spring' of 2011 affected some of the sultanate's closest allies (such as Bahrain and Jordan), but the movement appeared to have little discernible impact in the sultanate itself (although some Brunei students required evacuation from Egypt). There were no public demonstrations in the Sultanate, nor overt signs of popular discontent; any undercurrents of dissent remained to be seen. The MIB ideology certainly continued to be promoted.

The sole remaining political organization, the PPB, remained quiescent. Veteran politician Yasin Affendy resigned as its President in February 2011, owing to ill health. A successor was to be elected by a special congress of the party in due course, but at mid-2011 Malai Hassan Othman, a journalist, was reported to be the party's acting President.

In February 2011 Pehin Isa Ibrahim, a distinguished former government minister who was believed to be the first local person to have been awarded a university degree, was appointed Speaker of the Legislative Council, in succession to Pengiran Anak Kemaludin, the elderly uncle of the Sultan. In his keynote address to the Legislative Council on 1 March the Sultan urged the nation to increase economic diversification activities. The existing Council was dissolved on 15 March, and a new membership, once again entirely nominated, was announced on 1 June. The eight district representatives were chosen on the basis of nomination and election by their fellow *penghulu* (village heads) in March. There was also representation for women, including Datin Paduka Hajjah Salbiah binti Haji Sulaiman, a former Permanent Secretary at the Prime Minister's Office, and Datin Paduka Ustazah Hajjah Zasia binti Sirin. Otherwise, the Council continued to comprise largely members of the royal family, government ministers and one or two others chosen because of their acknowledged distinction in their own sphere of activity. In an unexpected development in November 2010, Dato' Timothy Ong ceased to be Chairman of the Brunei Economic Development Board, which along with the Department of Economic Planning and Development, was placed under the aegis of the Prime Minister's Office.

With regard to environmental issues, Brunei planned to establish marine protected areas in order to ensure the conservation of the near-shore marine environment, with particular emphasis on coral, fisheries and food security. In June 2011 the Government was reported to be drafting three environmental laws.

Military Affairs

In his birthday address of July 2008 the Sultan stated that challenges to security were unpredictable and that the ability of the nation to overcome them was crucial. On his return from the APEC summit meeting in November, he visited Honolulu, taking the opportunity to tour the US Pacific Command Headquarters. While in Hawaii the Sultan made an informal agreement with the USA to exchange military information.

The Crown Prince, Gen. Al-Muhtadee Billah, on this occasion acting as 'Deputy Sultan', opened the Officer Cadet School at Sungai Akar Camp in August 2008, when the first intake commenced the 42-week training course. The aim was to inculcate leadership values and forge common bonds among officer cadets of the three services. It was also hoped to encourage young people to pursue a military career, and to attract foreign trainees as a means of developing closer relations with other countries.

Military exercises were another example of defence co-operation with foreign nations. In December 2008 the Royal Brunei Navy hosted its Indonesian counterpart in the five-day operation *Helang Laut*, the 11th such operation since it was first staged in 1995. Two Indonesian warships docked at Muara in April 2009 for a three-day visit. In May two ships of the Pakistan Navy made a goodwill visit to the sultanate; the Royal Brunei Navy was invited to participate in joint naval exercises with its Pakistani counterpart. In June the United Kingdom sent two of its largest naval ships, and various other vessels, to Brunei to lead a multinational land and maritime exercise.

At the end of October 2008 five personnel of the Royal Brunei Armed Forces (Angkatan Bersenjata Diraja Brunei—ABDB) were assigned to serve for nine months, under Malaysian command, with the UN Interim Force in Lebanon. In September six soldiers returned to Brunei from Mindanao, in the southern Philippines, after participating for a year in the International Monitoring Team based at Cotabato City; a replacement contingent of personnel from Brunei had already departed for the Philippine island. During 2009–11 the ABDB continued to participate in peace-keeping missions in Lebanon and Mindanao.

In August 2009 the Sultan granted a royal audience to the Pakistan Armed Forces' Chairman of Joint Chiefs of Staff Committee, Gen. Tariq Majeed, who was paying a five-day visit to the sultanate, primarily to attend the second Brunei International Defence Exhibition and Conference (BRIDEX), which was held in the sultanate in mid-August. Those displaying their military hardware at the event included ASEAN, Commonwealth and EU nations, as well as Canada, Japan, Jordan, the Republic of Korea (South Korea), Norway, Turkey and the USA, while some 250 companies from 60 countries were reported to have participated.

Meanwhile, in May 2008 Col Dato' Joharie Matussin was succeeded as Commander of the Royal Brunei Navy by Col Abdul Halim bin Haji Mohamed Hanifah. In the following month Pengiran Hajjah Saliza Ibrahim was promoted to the rank of Special Commissioned Full Lieutenant, thus becoming the armed forces' first female paramedical officer. In August 2009 Brig. Mahmud Saidin retired as Commander of the Royal Brunei Air Force and was replaced by Col Jofri bin Haji Abdullah, and in December Maj.-Gen. Aminuddin Ihsan Abidin was appointed Commander of the Royal Brunei Armed Forces, replacing Maj.-Gen. Pehin Halbi Yussof. In his inaugural speech, Maj.-Gen. Ihsan stressed the importance of maintaining the international credibility of the Royal Brunei Armed Forces. Maj.-Gen. Halbi was subsequently appointed High Commissioner to Malaysia, in March 2010; however, in the cabinet reorganization of May, Maj.-Gen. Halbi was recalled to Brunei to assume the position of Deputy Minister of Home Affairs. In mid-2010 proposals for the formation of a fourth battalion of the Royal Brunei Land Forces were under consideration.

In July 2010 the Sultan approved the formation of a Research and Development Centre for Defence Science and Technology (Pusat Penyelidikan dan Perkembangan Sains dan Teknologi Pertahanan), which was to play a role in strategic planning and the modernization of the ABDB. The ABDB Staff College at Sungai Akar Camp, officially opened by the Sultan in November, was regarded as the 'final pillar' in the formation of a defence academy in the sultanate. The first course, for 22 officers from both Brunei and overseas, commenced in the same month. On Armed Forces Day 2011, observed on 31 May, the Sultan announced a reform of terms of service and career development structure for all levels of the ABDB, and expressed the hope that the forthcoming changes in remuneration arrangements would 'enhance the quality of excellence and bring added value to the military profession'. The Royal Brunei Navy, which celebrated its 46th anniversary in mid-2011, continued to act as one of the most important government law enforcement agencies at sea, and two offshore patrol vessels were commissioned in May. Adm. Patrick M. Walsh, Commander of the US Pacific Fleet, visited the sultanate in January 2011.

RECENT FOREIGN RELATIONS

After independence in 1984 Brunei began to develop extensive international links. It became a member of the UN, ASEAN, the Commonwealth and the Organization of the Islamic Conference (OIC). In 1992 it joined the Non-aligned Movement (NAM) and established diplomatic relations with Russia and the People's Republic of China. In the same year diplomatic links were formally established with Viet Nam, and in 1993 with Myanmar (formerly Burma). In 1995 Brunei entered the World Bank and the IMF. Brunei remained heavily dependent on the United Kingdom and Singapore for defence, but the sultanate also forged defence links with Australia and the USA. Sultan Hassanal played an active part, presiding over regional and international meetings in Brunei and travelling widely to consolidate good relations with other countries.

The most immediate foreign policy objective was to establish cordial relations with ASEAN partners. Brunei was closest to Singapore, which was to remain an important trading partner, a major source of skilled labour and a repository of Brunei's petroleum revenues, with the two currencies 'pegged' under an interchangeability agreement dating from 1967. As small states, Brunei and Singapore shared a concern to promote peace and stability in the region, working closely together in bodies such as the ASEAN Regional Forum (ARF—established to address security issues) and APEC. They co-operated in offering training facilities for their armed forces, officials exchanged regular visits, and in November 2002 the Port of Singapore Authority Corporation and Brunei Archipelago Development Corporation signed a joint venture contract to manage and develop Muara Container Terminal for the next 25 years.

From the late 1980s Brunei provided generous aid and investment to promote economic development in Indonesia and the Philippines, and in 1994 the ministers responsible for foreign affairs of Brunei, Indonesia, Malaysia and the Philippines (BIMP) agreed to establish an East ASEAN Growth Area (EAGA). At its first meeting held on the Indonesian island of Bali in October 2003, the Sultan joined with the Presidents of Indonesia and the Philippines and Prime Minister Mahathir Mohamad of Malaysia in resolving to revitalize business activities in the region.

Meanwhile, relations with Malaysia showed the most dramatic improvement. In 1993 Mahathir headed a delegation to Brunei, and the two countries agreed to resolve all border disputes, including the Limbang question (see above), through bilateral negotiations. In 1994 Brunei signed an agreement with Malaysia establishing a joint commission to promote co-operation in trade, industry, finance, education, culture and religion. Despite occasional friction, relations remained cordial. Senior officials exchanged frequent visits, Sultan Hassanal held annual consultations with Mahathir in Brunei or Kuala Lumpur, and in August 2002 the Malaysian head of state paid a visit to Brunei. In May 2003, however, a dispute began concerning the offshore boundary between the two countries, when Malaysia and Brunei granted conflicting oil exploration licences. The Sultan immediately flew to Penang to meet Mahathir, and both countries suspended their drilling operations pending a compromise. On Mahathir's departure, Sultan Hassanal quickly established cordial relations with his successor, Abdullah Badawi, and in April 2005 undertook a state visit to Malaysia.

At the third unofficial ASEAN summit meeting, held in Manila in November 1999, the Sultan urged greater openness to achieve economic integration, strengthen economies and attract foreign investment. At the same time he argued for closer but more gradual co-operation with Japan, China and the Republic of Korea (South Korea). In February 2000 Brunei hosted its first APEC Senior Officials' Meeting, attended by 3,000 delegates from 21 countries, and in the following month ASEAN ministers responsible for finance met in Brunei to discuss a proposal for an Asian monetary fund. In November Brunei played host to the annual APEC meeting, the largest international event hitherto staged in Brunei: 6,000 delegates attended, including Presidents Clinton of the USA, Jiang Zemin of China and Putin of Russia. Brunei lobbied intensively for APEC unity, but its hopes of achieving a major breakthrough in obtaining consensus for a new round of World Trade Organization (WTO) talks encountered resistance from some delegates, notably Malaysia, and a compromise was reached.

Three ASEAN leaders visited Brunei in swift succession in August 2001: the Prime Minister of Thailand, the President of the Philippines and the new President of Indonesia, Megawati Sukarnoputri. In the same month Brunei and the Philippines agreed to establish a Bilateral Commission for Co-operation. Brunei was particularly eager to improve regional co-operation to protect the environment. The sultanate celebrated World Forestry Day in 2000, introduced a total ban on open burning and illegal logging, as agreed by ASEAN, and inaugurated 'ASEAN Environment Year 2000'. In January 2001 the Sultan launched both 'Visit Brunei Year 2001' and 'Visit ASEAN Year 2002'.

Brunei hosted the seventh ASEAN summit meeting in November 2001, with representatives from China, Japan and South Korea also in attendance. At the meeting of the so-called 'ASEAN + 3' the national leaders declared 'war on terrorism' and agreed to form an ASEAN + 3 secretariat. In July 2002 Brunei hosted a meeting of ASEAN ministers responsible for foreign affairs and also staged the ninth meeting of the ARF, which was attended by delegates from the 10 member nations, together with representatives of 13 dialogue partners. These included US Secretary of State Colin Powell, who, with the Sultan, signed a US-ASEAN Joint Declaration for Co-operation to Counter Terrorism; this provided for the exchange of information and intelligence and made a commitment to suppress all forms of terrorism, but without creating any new US bases in the region. The issue of terrorism dominated the meeting of ASEAN ministers of foreign affairs and the ARF. However, in opening the 34th meeting of ASEAN ministers responsible for economic affairs, which was held in Brunei in September with representatives from Australia, New Zealand and India, the Sultan stressed economic development as being integral to ASEAN's progress. In October 2003 the annual summit meeting of ASEAN leaders, held in Bali, endorsed plans to accelerate the creation of an ASEAN Economic Community. While in Bali, the ASEAN leaders met representatives from China, Japan, South Korea and India for bilateral talks. In December the Sultan joined other ASEAN leaders in Tokyo, Japan, to sign a declaration for an enduring ASEAN-Japan partnership. In his speech the Sultan endorsed the ASEAN + 3 policy as a mechanism for the promotion of co-operation between ASEAN and Japan, China and South Korea.

Following the conclusion of the US-led operation to remove the regime of Saddam Hussain, in April 2003 the Government of Brunei established a humanitarian fund for Iraq. In May Prince Mohamed publicly expressed concern at the post-war situation in Iraq. Brunei welcomed the transfer of power to the interim Iraqi regime in 2005. Meanwhile, Brunei had made clear its support for reform of the UN Security Council in a speech by Prince Mohamed Bolkiah, Minister of Foreign Affairs, to the UN General Assembly in September 2003. This was reiterated a year later by Princess Masna, Brunei's ambassador-at-large, who supported reform of the UN, including an expanded and more representative Security Council. In October 2004, attending the Fifth Asia-Europe Meeting (ASEM) in Hanoi, Viet Nam, Sultan Hassanal strongly supported the initiative for the UN to lead the struggle against terrorism and urged that more be done to eliminate the root causes of terrorist violence. APEC was another forum in which Brunei actively participated. In October 2003 the Sultan met APEC leaders at the forum's annual summit meeting in Bangkok, Thailand. Immediately prior to this he had attended the 10th session of the OIC in Kuala Lumpur. In November 2004 he attended the APEC summit meeting in Chile where he reiterated his support for the fight against terror. These international meetings illustrated Brunei's determination to confirm its role as an independent protagonist in world affairs.

Meanwhile, Sultan Hassanal made state visits to Thailand in August 2002 and to the Philippines in January 2003. In May 2003 Brunei and the Philippines held their first joint naval exercise. In February 2004 the first Commission for Bilateral Co-operation between Brunei and the Philippines met in Manila; agreements were signed relating to defence co-operation and technical and trade co-operation in fisheries and air services. In October Brunei sent a small peace-keeping contingent to join the International Monitoring Team in the troubled region of Mindanao, in the southern Philippines. Relations with Indonesia remained cordial. In December 2003 three Indonesian warships visited Brunei, and the Sultan attended the inauguration of Indonesian President Susilo Bambang Yudhoyono in October 2004. Brunei provided generous aid to Indonesia following the tsunami disaster in December of that year; the Sultan attended the international summit meeting on the disaster in January 2005 and visited the Indonesian province of Aceh in February. Brunei retained its close relations with Singapore, holding bilateral talks with the country's new Prime Minister, Lee Hsien Loong, in Singapore in October 2004. In April of that year the Vietnamese Minister of National Defence, Lt.-Gen. Pham Van Tra, led a delegation of officials from his ministry on a four-day visit to the sultanate, during which the strengthening of military links was discussed.

Perhaps the most significant development in foreign relations was Brunei's increasing rapport with China, following Sultan Hassanal's first state visit to the country in November 1993. His second visit, in August 1999, was followed by President Jiang Zemin's visit to Brunei in November 2000. Both leaders met again at APEC meetings in China in May and October 2001 and in Brunei at the ASEAN + 3 Summit in November. In October 2003 an agreement was signed for the sale of Brunei's crude petroleum to China, and the first goodwill visit of two Chinese warships followed in November. In September 2004 the Sultan again travelled to China for talks with President Hu Jintao, who in April 2005 made a state visit to Brunei *en route* to the Asia-Africa summit meeting in Bandung, Indonesia. These and meetings between other representatives led to increased economic links, including energy sales to China, bilateral economic investment and improved relations, with both sides seeking a diplomatic solution to disputed territorial claims in the South China Sea.

Brunei continued to maintain a wide range of diplomatic, commercial and defence relationships, in addition to its longstanding links with countries such as Jordan, Saudi Arabia and the Gulf states. In September 2002 the Sultan undertook a three-day working visit to Syria, shortly after the establishment of diplomatic relations. In November the Sultan made a two-day goodwill trip to Bahrain, and in 2004 Brunei drew upon Bahrain's expertise in Islamic banking and international finance. In May 2004 the Sultan paid a three-day visit to Pakistan, during which the two Governments signed memoranda of understanding (MOUs) relating to counter-terrorism, defence and co-operation. In December 2002 the Sultan had met US President George W. Bush in Washington, DC, and relations with the USA remained cordial. Brunei retained its defence links, but distanced itself from events in Iraq. In February 2005 the Sultan made a state visit to Australia, where counter-terrorism issues were among the matters discussed. Defence links were also retained with the United Kingdom, the Sultan visiting London in June 2004. During that year Brunei also established diplomatic relations with Eritrea, Guatemala and Tajikistan, and hosted visits by the Kings of Sweden and Jordan, the Presidents of Singapore and Ukraine and the Prime Minister of Bangladesh.

In July 2002 Sultan Hassanal had stressed the importance of the quest for peace, stability, good regional relations and firmness in condemning terrorism in co-operation with other countries. By mid-2004 he had become increasingly concerned with Brunei's security. In March of that year three people, a former high-ranking soldier, a senior police officer and a leading businessman, were detained for subversion and treason for allegedly 'leaking' official government secrets on the internet. The Sultan addressed broader regional security concerns in a national broadcast at the end of May, when he outlined the strategic and economic significance of the South China Sea and the threat from international terrorism. The Sultan continued to stress the importance of Islamic principles and observance. In March 2004, addressing the opening session of the 39th South-East Asian Ministers of Education Organization (SEAMEO), held in Brunei, the Sultan revealed his desire that students gaining an ever-increasing amount of technological, scientific and electronic information would also acquire tolerance and respect for others.

In August 2005, in his capacity as Minister of Foreign Affairs and Trade, Prince Mohamed Bolkiah visited Singapore where an Avoidance of Double Taxation Agreement was signed. He also represented the sultanate at the Commonwealth Heads of Government meeting in Malta, held in November, at the World Trade talks in Hong Kong in December, and at a meeting in Kuala Lumpur of the NAM's Co-ordinating Bureau in May 2006. Meanwhile, the Sultan attended several major multilateral gatherings in 2005–06, including the 'Group of 77 plus China' meeting in Doha, and the APEC, OIC and ASEAN summits. In September 2005 the Sultan addressed the UN General Assembly and stressed the need for the organization to be reformed and revitalized. The sultanate joined UNESCO in March 2005 and the Asian Development Bank (ADB) in April 2006.

In April 2006 the Sultan made his first state visits to Qatar and the United Arab Emirates. In June he visited Bangkok for the diamond jubilee celebrations of Thailand's King Bhumibol Adulyadej. Indonesian President Yudhoyono paid a two-day state visit to Brunei at the end of February 2006, and expressed his desire further to strengthen the bilateral relationship. Malaysian Prime Minister Abdullah Badawi visited Bandar Seri Begawan in August 2005 to explore new areas of co-operation between the two countries, with particular regard to education and Islamic finance; and in May 2006 his predecessor, Mahathir Mohamad, had met with the Sultan in Jerudong.

Diplomatic relations were established with Venezuela in July 2005, with Samoa in February 2006, with Iceland in April of that year and with Estonia in May. Brunei's diplomatic outreach thus extended to around 150 states. Brunei's adherence to the 'one China' policy (whereby formal recognition of Taiwan was withheld) was praised by the Vice-Premier of the People's Republic, Wu Yi, during her three-day visit to Bandar Seri Begawan in September 2005.

In June 2006, during a meeting in the Chinese capital of Beijing with the Bruneian Minister of Foreign Affairs and Trade II, Lim Jock Seng, Chinese State Councillor Tang Jiaxuan reaffirmed his country's commitment to enhancing co-operation with Brunei in political, economic and cultural fields; Lim Jock Seng stated that Brunei would join China in pressing for an ASEAN-China strategic partnership and for increased co-operation among the nations of East Asia. Meanwhile, in February 2006 officials from Japan and Brunei convened in Tokyo, with a view to commencing negotiations on an economic partnership agreement.

Diplomatic relations were established with Moldova and Angola (both in October 2006), with Afghanistan (in February 2007), and with Macedonia (in August 2007). At March 2007 Brunei maintained a total of 31 embassies and high commissions overseas, as well as four consulates. Owing to a shortage of personnel Bruneian diplomats tend to be accredited to more than one country. In 2007 Brunei became a member of the International Labour Organization; and on 1 May Labour Day was observed for the first time in the sultanate's history.

Sultan Hassanal continued to attend major international conferences, such as regular meetings of APEC, ASEAN, ASEM and the OIC. In April 2007 he paid a state visit to Cambodia; later in the same month he was present at festivities in Kuala Lumpur to celebrate the installation of the new Malaysian head of state, although at the coronation itself Brunei was represented by the Crown Prince. The previous king (the Raja of Perlis) had visited the Istana Nurul Iman in November 2006. Other important visitors to Brunei included Gen. Surayud Chulanont, Prime Minister of Thailand, in November 2006; the Laotian Prime Minister, Bouasone Bouphavanh, in January 2007; Donald McKinnon, Commonwealth Secretary-General in April; and various other officials, particularly from ASEAN countries. The Japanese Minister of Economy, Trade and Industry, visited in May 2007; Japan remained one of the sultanate's leading export markets. The Saudi Arabian Minister of Awqaf (Religious Endowments), Dawa, Mosques and Guidance Affairs visited Bandar Seri Begawan in March.

Relations with China continued to be given a high priority. The Sultan attended a conference in Nanning in October 2006, marking 15 years of ASEAN-China dialogue. In the previous month, the Minister of Foreign Affairs and Trade had paid an eight-day official visit to Beijing, where Prince Mohamed Bolkiah signed a tourism co-operation agreement with Shanghai and Hong Kong. He held meetings with his Chinese counterpart, Li Zhaoxing, and also with Prime Minister Wen Jiabao. In November the Minister of Home Affairs, whose brief on this occasion concerned municipal matters, also visited China. In August 2007 the Chinese Chief of General Staff, Gen. Chen Bingde, visited Bandar Seri Begawan in order to explore areas of military co-operation, and in January 2008 Gen. Cao Gangchuan, the Chinese Minister of National Defence, paid a three-day visit.

In May 2007 a group of senior officials from mainland China paid a three-day visit; the delegation to Brunei was led by Wu Guanzheng, a member of the Standing Committee of the Political Bureau (Politburo) of the Central Committee of the Chinese Communist Party, and was received in separate audiences by both the Crown Prince (on this occasion acting in the capacity of 'Deputy Sultan') and by the Perdana Wazir.

Brunei has become more active in humanitarian activities, notably in Indonesia where projects included the post-tsumani redevelopment programme in Aceh, and also in peace-keeping initiatives, for example in Mindanao, in the southern Philippines. At the 10th annual bilateral discussions with Malaysia, held in Terengganu in August 2006, Sultan Hassanal and Malaysian Prime Minister Abdullah Badawi expressed satisfaction with the state of relations between the two countries, particularly with regard to economic relations, science, broadcasting, education and defence. The two leaders also discussed maritime border issues.

The 12th ASEAN Ministerial Meeting on Haze and the Second Meeting of the Conference of the Parties to the ASEAN Agreement on Trans-Boundary Haze Pollution took place in Bandar Seri Begawan in March 2007. In the same month Prince Mohamed Bolkiah attended the meeting in Germany that gave rise to the Nuremberg Declaration on an EU-ASEAN Enhanced Partnership: among other commitments, the two sides pledged to co-operate closely with regard to combating terrorism, human-trafficking and organized crime. Following the 13th ASEAN Economic Ministers' Retreat and Related Meetings held in Bandar Seri Begawan in May, ASEAN and the EU agreed to begin negotiations with the objective of concluding a free trade agreement between the two organizations.

Nearly 80% of Brunei remains forest-clad; this is stated to be the highest percentage in Asia. The Ulu Temburong National Park (upriver in the isolated eastern area of the sultanate), which attracted 270,000 visitors in 2005, has been recognized by the World Wide Fund for Nature as part of the transnational Heart of Borneo (HOB) area. The HOB initiative, involving Brunei in partnership with neighbouring areas of Malaysia and Indonesia, was officially inaugurated in March 2006 and was endorsed by BIMP-EAGA heads of government at their meeting in Cebu, in the Philippines, in January 2007. Comprising approximately 85,000 sq miles of equatorial rainforest in the three countries, the HOB accounts for some 6% of the world's total biodiversity. In February the three Governments signed a Declaration in Bali reiterating their agreement to conserve almost one-third of the island of Borneo for the benefit of future generations. Following additions to the HOB area, nearly three-quarters of the entire land area of the sultanate had been encompassed by the project by December 2007. In July of that year Brunei offered to host a 'Heart of Borneo centre', which would co-ordinate implementation of the scheme. Financial support was being contributed by the USA and by the Brunei Shell Petroleum Company.

In his *titah* for New Year 2008 Sultan Hassanal declared that Brunei's relations with international bodies needed to be strengthened. BIMP-EAGA was one such entity identified; one way in which BIMP-EAGA might help was in the joint promotion of tourism. At a meeting in July 2007 preparations were finalized for the BIMP-EAGA Roadmap to Development 2006–2010, which incorporated the promotion of tourism, and its associated Action Plan. In November 2007, furthermore, Brunei was admitted to the World Tourism Organization, an agency of the UN.

The Sultan continued to stress the importance of achieving the UN's Millennium Development Goals (MDGs), and in October 2007 it was reported that Brunei was making excellent progress towards the attainment of these targets, having gained 'early achiever' status in no fewer than 12 of the 21 categories. At the 61st World Health Assembly, held in Switzerland in May 2008, the Bruneian Minister of Health, Pehin Suyoi Osman, confirmed that the sultanate was one of the first countries to fulfil some of the MDGs, including universal primary education, gender equality, empowerment of women, reduction in child mortality, and the combating of AIDS, malaria and other diseases. However, much remained to be done, as the country confronted challenges such as the increasing costs of health care, natural disasters and non-communicable diseases, including diabetes, heart disease and cancer.

The Sultan attended the 13th ASEAN Summit meeting, held in Singapore in November 2007, when the ASEAN Charter, committing the region to promoting human rights and democratic ideals, was adopted. In mid-February 2008 Brunei became one of the first countries to ratify the Charter. In May Brunei hosted a three-day meeting of the ASEAN Police Federation. Opened by Crown Prince Al-Muhtadee Billah, the conference aimed at enhancing police professionalism in countering transnational crime, weapons-smuggling and commercial fraud, and at fostering closer links among the police forces of ASEAN. It was also announced that the Royal Brunei Police Force would host an ASEANAPOL training programme, with help from the Australian Federal Police, to address the issue of human-trafficking.

The Yang di-Pertuan Agong (Paramount Ruler) of Malaysia undertook an official visit to Brunei in July 2007, at which time it was reported that 30,000 Malaysians were working in the sultanate. The Sultan visited the Malaysian city of Kuala Lumpur at the end of August to attend celebrations for the 50th anniversary of the country's independence, returning to the peninsula for a two-day working visit in May 2008.

The Prime Minister of Viet Nam, Nguyen Tan Dung, visited the sultanate in August 2007 to celebrate the 15th anniversary of the establishment of diplomatic relations between the two countries. An official visit to Brunei by Gen. Thein Sein, the Prime Minister of Myanmar, followed in January 2008. The Sultan noted the good working relationship between the two countries, especially co-operation in health, education and technical assistance.

The year 2008 was designated 'Visit Brunei Year', in an attempt both to raise the sultanate's international profile and to diversify the economy. It was hoped to increase annual tourist arrivals, to improve hotel occupancy rates, to organize more conferences and exhibitions and to boost eco-tourism. Meanwhile, Bruneians were encouraged by the Director of Industrial Promotion and Tourism Development to spend their holidays locally.

Following a state visit to Brunei by King Norodom Sihamoni of Cambodia in March 2008, Sultan Hassanal paid a state visit to Indonesia in April. He expressed satisfaction at the existing state of bilateral relations, emphasizing the close co-operation between the two countries over the previous 20 years in the areas of investment, culture, education and defence.

Hosting a state visit by the Sultan in May 2008, India expressed interest in continuing to import crude petroleum from Brunei and also in starting to buy liquefied natural gas (LNG). Both sides identified the need for co-operation in the defence sector. India agreed to share with Brunei its experience in 'e-governance'. Trade and investment would be facilitated, and Brunei also undertook to support India's bid for permanent membership of the UN Security Council. A significant MOU intended to increase bilateral co-operation in the field of information and communications technology (ICT) was signed by the two countries in February 2010.

Meanwhile, in his birthday *titah* of July 2007, Sultan Hassanal touched on security matters. He reiterated that government agencies would continue to enhance regional and international co-operation for the benefit of all. In recent years the Royal Brunei Armed Forces had established several new departments and institutions, notably the Institute of Defence and Strategic Studies, a Strategic Management Office, a Performance Optimization Centre and an Excellence and

Evolution Centre. Furthermore, the country's armed forces also participated in peace-monitoring operations. The annual Cooperation Afloat Readiness and Training (CARAT) drill between the Brunei and US navies was held in August. The sultanate carried out similar military drills (on land, at sea and in the air) with allies such as the Philippines and Singapore.

In June 2008 the Sultan had discussions in Paris with French President Nicolas Sarkozy. Both leaders expressed satisfaction with progress in bilateral defence and investment co-operation and agreed to strengthen links in the areas of education and culture. The Sultan also expressed interest in French expertise in the fields of counter-terrorism and hostage-rescue operations.

In December 2008 the Russian Prime Minister, Vladimir Putin, signed an order to open a Russian embassy in Brunei (the Russian ambassador having previously been non-resident), thereby ensuring that henceforth his country would have a permanent diplomatic presence in all 10 ASEAN capitals. At the invitation of Russian President Dmitrii Medvedev, the Sultan paid a six-day official visit to Russia in October 2009. The Sultan met with Putin and Medvedev, and both sides reiterated their commitment to the establishment of an embassy in Bandar Seri Begawan, which opened in the following year.

Meanwhile, in his birthday *titah* in July 2008 the Sultan reiterated Brunei's commitment to regional peace and security. In October he travelled to Beijing for the ASEM conference. Addressing the media on behalf of ASEAN member states, the Sultan stated that valuable discussions had been held on many global subjects, and declared: 'In view of the current situation in the financial markets, we in ASEAN feel that this is probably the most important meeting of ASEM that we have ever had.' In the following month the Sultan flew to the Peruvian capital of Lima for the annual APEC gathering. He reiterated the importance of accelerating recovery by restoring public confidence through efforts that were global in scale and by the need to reach agreement in the Doha Round of free trade talks, which continued in 2009 under the auspices of the WTO.

The Sultan travelled to Thailand in April 2009 to attend the 14th ASEAN Summit meeting, which was postponed owing to internal unrest. The Sultan welcomed the completion of the ASEAN-Korea Free Trade Area. In a bilateral meeting with South Korean President Lee Myung-Bak at the beginning of June, the Sultan expressed concern about North Korea's nuclear ambitions. In May the Perdana Wazir represented Brunei at the ninth ASEM Foreign Ministers' Meeting in Hanoi. ASEM members exchanged views on the global financial crisis and other matters. In the Indonesian capital of Jakarta in June Pengiran Hajjah Basmillah binti Pengiran Hajjah Abbas presented her credentials as Brunei's first Permanent Representative (with the rank of 'Ambassador') to ASEAN.

The sultanate continued to enjoy good relations with Malaysia. In a statement issued in August 2008, at the end of the 12th annual Malaysia-Brunei Consultation (held in the Malaysian city of Johor Bahru), the Sultan and Abdullah Badawi agreed that the two countries needed to continue to work together to facilitate a more conducive business environment. Both leaders expressed satisfaction with the launch of the Frequent Travellers' Card in 2007 to facilitate travel between Brunei and Malaysia; they also agreed that an increase in flight frequencies between the two countries could promote tourism. It was announced that a team of officers from the BIA would be sent to explore opportunities in the Iskandar Malaysia corridor in Johor, a development zone established in 2006; among the main industries being promoted there was the processing of *halal* food. In March 2009 Brunei and Malaysia initialled an Exchange of Letters that included the final delimitation of maritime boundaries between the two countries; the establishment of Commercial Agreement Areas in oil and gas exploration; and modalities for the final demarcation of the land border; however, no solution could yet be found to the contentious Limbang issue (see above). At the end of April the new Prime Minister of Malaysia, Dato' Seri Najib Razak, received a warm welcome when he paid his first official visit to the sultanate, as did the Malaysian Minister of Foreign Affairs, Datuk Anifah bin Haji Aman, and Minister of Defence, Dato' Seri Dr Ahmad Zahid bin Hamidi, when they visited Brunei in March 2010.

The ambassador of Japan to Brunei, Itsuo Hashimoto, noted that the two countries had recorded several significant achievements in their economic relations, namely the Japan-Brunei Darussalam Economic Partnership Agreement, which entered into force on 31 July 2008, the methanol plant and the Microbial Resources Exploration Project. In March 2009 a two-day workshop was held at Sungai Liang as part of the five-year Brunei-Japan MOU under the Heart of Borneo project, aimed at discovering micro-organisms that could be used to produce new materials such as pharmaceuticals.

Long-standing relationships in the Middle East were not neglected. In May 2008 the King and Queen of Jordan were guests at the Istana Nurul Iman. In July Brunei and Kuwait signed a pact on economic and technical co-operation. In April 2009 Sultan Hassanal paid state visits to Kuwait and Oman. Consolidating the achievements of a visit to Brunei by the Prime Minister of Kuwait in July 2008, several further bilateral agreements were concluded, involving the reciprocal promotion and protection of investment; the avoidance of double taxation; the prevention of fiscal evasion; oil and gas co-operation; and the provision of air services. Also in April 2009 Brunei and Oman signed an MOU providing for the establishment of a joint investment company which was to direct funds towards infrastructure, tourism, health, telecommunications and utilities in both countries and elsewhere.

In June 2008 the British Prime Minister, Gordon Brown, received the Sultan in London, where they discussed bilateral relations in education, defence and trade. The United Kingdom remained the most popular destination for Brunei students furthering their studies overseas. The Sultan expressed gratitude for the support given by the British Government to the Heart of Borneo project. In June 2009 it was agreed that the British army's battalion of Gurkhas would continue to be stationed in the sultanate for a further five years from September. Gen. Sir David Richards, the British Chief of General Staff, visited the sultanate for four days in February 2010, when he met with the Sultan in his capacity as Commander-in-Chief of the Royal Brunei Armed Forces, further consolidating the long-standing close military links between the two countries.

At the 63rd annual session of the UN General Assembly in New York in September 2008, the Crown Prince expressed the need jointly to address the challenges of climate change, citing the Heart of Borneo initiative as Brunei's contribution to the endeavour. At a NAM ministerial meeting held in Cuba in April 2009 the Perdana Wazir, as Minister of Foreign Affairs and Trade, urged countries to work together to overcome the current global economic crisis.

Princess Masna, on this occasion acting as Minister of Foreign Affairs and Trade, visited Kampala, Uganda, in June 2008 to attend the 35th session of the OIC's Council of Foreign Ministers. The Princess expressed a fear that political, economic and environmental factors might hinder the achievement of the MDGs; she supported the emphasis on increasing food production and reducing trade restrictions. In July the Princess represented Brunei at a conference of NAM ministers in the Iranian capital of Tehran.

In September 2009 the Perdana Wazir represented Brunei at the 64th annual session of the UN General Assembly in New York. At the seventh WTO Ministerial Meeting in Geneva, Switzerland, in November–December, he appealed for efforts to be made to ensure that the Doha Round of free trade talks was brought to a successful conclusion.

The sultanate continued to establish diplomatic relations with several states, including Trinidad and Tobago (in November 2009), Antigua and Barbuda (in December), Montenegro and Grenada (both in January 2010), Georgia (in March), the Dominican Republic (in August), Fiji (in April 2011), and Andorra, Jamaica and Monaco (in June).

Brunei continued to express its views at regional and global conferences, including the 15th annual summit of ASEAN in Thailand (in October 2009) and the 21st APEC annual summit meeting in Singapore (in November), with an overriding goal of ensuring the security of the country and striving for regional and international stability. Brunei's leaders also sought to enhance co-operation with regional neighbours and other countries further afield, with foreign workers in the sultanate helping to strengthen bilateral relations, particularly with ASEAN and South Asian states.

The Sultan remained active in regional affairs, attending the ASEAN summit meetings in Hanoi in October 2010 and in Jakarta in May 2011. He also attended the APEC summit meeting held in the Japanese city of Yokohama in November 2010 and the Bali Democracy Forum convened in the following month. At the meeting in October 2010 the Sultan urged ASEAN to display strong political will and thereby influence the direction of economic affairs, both regionally and globally. In Yokohama he highlighted the importance of co-ordinating economic, social and environmental policies to ensure that growth would be balanced, inclusive, sustainable, innovative and secure. In Bali the Sultan declared that lasting peace and stability had to emerge from the people themselves.

With the 20th anniversary of the establishment of diplomatic relations between Brunei and China falling in 2011, the year was designated by the two countries a friendship year. In June Princess Masna, Ambassador-at-large, paid a five-day official visit to the People's Republic, where she received the award of 'Friendship Ambassador' in recognition of her contribution to bilateral ties. Various Chinese dignitaries visited the sultanate, including Hua Jianmin, Deputy Chairman of the Standing Committee of the Chinese People's Congress, who was received in March, and Ma Biao, Governor of Guangxi Zhuang Autonomous Region, who arrived in May). Meanwhile, the strong expansion in bilateral relations continued, reaching record levels.

During a three-day state visit to Brunei by the Laotian President, Choummaly Sayasone, in November 2010 the sultanate pledged to support attempts by Laos to join the WTO. State Visits to the sultanate were also undertaken by the Presidents of Indonesia, in February 2011, and of the Philippines in June 2011. During his visit the President of Ukraine was accompanied by a 60-member delegation. In April of the same year the Sultan paid an official visit to Indonesia, where he had discussions with President Yudhoyono. The Sultan also travelled to the Netherlands in January and to Germany in June 2011. Najib Razak, Prime Minister of Malaysia, visited Bandar Seri Begawan in December 2010, when the Sultan welcomed the signing of a joint petroleum exploration agreement. Crown Prince Al-Muhtadee Billah, accompanied by his cousin, Prince Abdul Qawi, paid a four-day official visit to Kuwait in August 2010. This was followed by a three-day official visit to the emirate by the Perdana Wazir in January 2011.

Having served as the sultanate's Minister of Foreign Affairs and Trade since 1984, the Perdana Wazir also remained busy with ASEAN affairs. He represented Brunei at the 43rd ASEAN Ministerial Meeting convened in Hanoi in July 2010; he attended the ASEAN Foreign Ministers' Retreat on the Indonesian island of Lombok in January 2011; and in April he participated in the Special ASEAN Informal Foreign Ministers' Meeting on the East Asia Summit held in Bangkok. He revisited the Thai capital for the Asia-Middle East Dialogue in December 2010; and in May 2011 he flew to Bali for the NAM Ministerial Conference.

The Perdana Wazir also attended the ninth Asia Co-operation Dialogue Ministerial Meeting held in Tehran in November 2010; the forum, which Brunei joined at its inception in 2002, was playing an 'important role' in the future of the entire Asian continent. The Prince also had a bilateral meeting with President Ahmadinejad, and later in the month he travelled to Marrakech in order to attend the Moroccan Tourism Forum at the invitation of King Mohammad VI. In April 2011 the Perdana Wazir attended the Plenary Session of the International Renewable Energy Agency at the Abu Dhabi National Exhibition Centre.

In March 2011 the Perdana Wazir emphasized the importance of 'defence diplomacy', the two areas being complementary. International relations were regarded as 'a chance to build friendship and co-operation between all people, no matter what their background, culture or belief'.

Economy

ROGER LAWREY

INTRODUCTION

Brunei Darussalam is a small, oil- and gas-dependent economy, which is continuing to strive for economic diversification and attempting to reduce its dependence on non-renewable resources. The Sultanate has good physical infrastructure; free high-quality health care and education for its citizens; no personal income tax or sales taxes; heavily subsidized retail prices for petrol, diesel, electricity, rice and sugar that have remained unchanged for many years; and a relatively high material standard of living.

However, the hydrocarbon resources that provide this wealth are non-renewable, within a human planning horizon, and therefore provision must be made for the time when such resources will no longer be able to support the economy in the traditional manner. By the end of the first decade of the 21st century that point in time appeared to be approaching for Brunei, and the debates about the requisite action intensified. Access to the deep offshore oil and gas areas, which had involved Brunei in a dispute with Malaysia regarding overlapping maritime claims since 2003, was resolved when the leaders of the two countries met in Brunei in March 2009. Following the surveying, delimiting and demarcating of the land and maritime boundary between Brunei and Malaysia, in September 2010 it was announced that a deed of amendment had been signed with the Brunei National Petroleum Company, or PetroleumBrunei, that changed the original production-sharing contract for what had previously been known as Block J (see below). However, for production from this block to be economically viable sufficient volumes would be needed to have a significant impact on Brunei's economy.

Having reached record levels, exceeding US $147 per barrel in mid-2008, international oil prices declined to less than $34 in March 2009. The average price received for Brunei's oil exports in that year was $64.54, and with export revenue, nominal gross domestic product (GDP) and government revenue so dependent on oil and gas prices, such fluctuations emphasize the need for economic diversification in Brunei.

GDP CONCEPTS, ISSUES AND STATISTICS

For some years it had been clear that the published figures for GDP in current prices were not fully reflecting changes in the prices of oil and natural gas, even though these price changes were manifested in export figures. In 2005 the Department of Economic Planning and Development (Jabatan Perancangan Dan Kemajuan Ekonomi) completed an overall revision of the system of national accounts for Brunei, which included adopting a new base year of 2000 = 100 for constant price calculations, thus restating GDP for the period 2000–04 using the production approach and estimating GDP using the expenditure approach.

This resulted in a substantial upward revision of GDP estimates and a corresponding upward revision of the oil and gas sector within GDP. The previously published nominal GDP for 2004 of B $9,270m. was revised upwards by 44%, to B $13,306m. The oil and gas sector was subsequently shown to account for some 62% of GDP in 2004, compared with the previous estimate of approximately 45%. For 2005 GDP was stated to be B $15,864m., and in 2008 GDP was estimated at B $20,397.9m., or B $51,300 per caput, more than double the previous 2004 figure. In 2008 the oil sector accounted for nearly 65% of GDP. These figures gave a much more accurate measure of the importance of oil and gas to the Brunei economy than the previous GDP series.

However, the system of national accounts as used by Brunei was designed primarily for diversified economies with an industrial base. Since Brunei's economy is highly dependent on oil and gas production, this results in some problems in interpreting GDP statistics. There are four particular issues.

First, for diversified economies, price increases across the whole economy are basically inflation. Inflation does not make a country better off. Thus, if incomes rise by 10% and prices go up by 10%, real incomes are unchanged. Accordingly, it is usual to report changes in GDP by factoring out price changes and reporting constant dollar GDP growth. This reflects changes in production. Changes in production in diversified economies are important because more production means more jobs, higher real incomes, more consumption and generally more economic activity. However, in Brunei there are two problems with considering constant dollar GDP. When the price of oil rises, this is not in itself inflation, although it may lead to some increase in the rate of inflation. In fact, increased oil prices result in more revenue for the country, which is, of course, beneficial. Two scenarios may be considered: in one case the production of oil goes down by 10% and the price received goes up by 50%; in the other case the production of oil goes up by 10% and prices go down by 50%. In the first case, GDP in terms of constant dollar prices has declined, apparently indicating that the economy is in a worse condition than before. However, it is clearly better to produce less oil at a higher price than more oil at a lower price. The average annual price received for Brunei's oil has varied between US $13.46 per barrel in 1998, $30.17 in 2003 and $128.90 in the second quarter of 2008. To deflate these prices would be misleading, since the change in price was not due to inflation in Brunei. Higher US dollar prices do translate into greater real value of production. The second problem with regard to calculations in constant dollar GDP concerns economic activity. In diversified economies, higher constant dollar GDP means more economic activity. In an oil- and gas-based economy like that of Brunei, higher GDP in the oil sector (in constant or current dollars) generally means more revenue for the oil companies, their shareholders and the government. Oil and gas production is very capital-intensive and does not directly employ many people (fewer than 4,000 in Brunei). Therefore, oil and gas production can be increased, or decreased, without directly changing the employment situation. Accordingly, changes in GDP owing to the oil and gas sector do not directly affect economic activity as they would do in more diversified economies.

The second issue with regard to applying the conventional method of calculating GDP in Brunei concerns the reserves of oil and gas. In industrialized economies, production can, at least theoretically, be increased every year indefinitely. However, oil and gas reserves are physically finite. Although reserves can be increased by new discoveries, and recovery rates from existing reserves can be increased, every barrel of oil produced is still one barrel fewer that is left in the ground. Therefore, if Brunei increases its current production of oil and gas, constant dollar GDP will increase but at the expense of future production. This complicates the interpretation of increasing constant dollar GDP. This may appear positive at present, but without detailed information on reserve changes it could be misleading.

The third point concerns the timing of changes in GDP affecting the economy. In diversified industrial economies, changes in GDP have an impact on the economy almost immediately. In fact, GDP is actually measuring what has already happened. Thus, if GDP has increased this means that production, incomes and probably employment have also increased. In Brunei, increases in GDP resulting from the oil and gas sector enter the economy through higher spending by the oil companies and the Government. Therefore, there is likely to be a hiatus between the time that the revenues are received and the time that some of them are spent. Indeed, development expenditure from previously accrued oil revenues might occur at any time, not particularly at the time of GDP increases. This implies that GDP may be reported to have increased, but businesses do not experience any sign of increased economic activity.

Finally, the Brunei economy can be considered to have two distinct sectors, and is reported as such by the Department of Economic Planning and Development: the oil and gas sector and the non-oil and gas sector. Basically, with few exceptions, the non-oil and gas industries, such as wholesale and retail trade, communications, banking and finance, insurance, real estate, etc, are recirculating the revenues that are earned from oil and gas. It is these industries for which the measurement of constant dollar GDP is particularly suitable.

One implication of the above analysis is that targeting a rate of GDP growth for the future can be problematic. If that rate is achieved by increasing oil and gas production, Brunei might be simply reducing its reserves of oil and gas, leading to increased problems in the future. However, if this growth rate is targeted at the non-oil and gas sector, the result, if achievable, could be sustainable. In the case of Brunei, it is important to examine closely the GDP figures for sectoral composition. Reviewing simply the headline constant dollar figure might give misleading indications of the state of the economy.

The above discussion was particularly pertinent in 2007 and 2008, when petroleum production declined at the same time as international oil prices began to increase substantially. The sector of 'mining' in the constant dollar GDP accounts, which is the term that captures upstream oil and gas production, contracted by 8% in the fourth quarter of 2007 in comparison with the corresponding period of the previous year. However, the same entry in the current dollar GDP accounts increased by 33%, reflecting higher oil and gas prices. In the second quarter of 2008 this trend continued. The oil and gas sector continued to expand in current dollar terms, while contracting in constant dollar terms, reflecting reduced oil and gas production. Whether this indicates a problem for the economy or not depends upon the reasons for the decline in production. If it is planned, for example for oil field maintenance or even for conservation purposes, it is clearly not a problem. However, if it is due to declining production capability then it is a cause for concern.

In nominal terms, GDP totalled B $20,398m. in 2008, declining to B $15,611m in 2009. This decline was entirely due to continuing reductions in both oil and gas production and export prices, with the oil and gas sector's contribution to nominal GDP decreasing from B $14,300 to B $9,417. In real terms, GDP contracted by 1.9% in 2008 and by 1.8% in 2009. However, according to the IMF, oil and gas production recovered in the first half of 2010, and real GDP increased by 5.5% compared with the corresponding period of the previous year. Oil and gas prices also increased in 2010 from their 2009 levels, indicating that nominal GDP could be expected to show a substantial increase when official figures are released.

OIL AND GAS SECTOR DEVELOPMENTS

Petroleum was first discovered in Brunei in 1929, on shore at Seria, but the more productive offshore reserves were discovered in 1963 at South West Ampa. Since then there has been considerable exploration and development in the same shallow water; numerous other fields, including Fairley, Fairley-Baram, Champion, Magpie, Iron Duke, Jurajan, Perdana, Gannet and Egret, have been discovered.

Crude petroleum and condensate production ranged from 254,000 barrels per day (b/d) in 1979 to 150,000 b/d in 1988 and 1989. More recently, output has declined steadily, from about 219,000 b/d in 2006 to 194,000 b/d in 2007, 174,000 b/d in 2008 and 167,000 b/d in 2009. In 2009 about 149,000 b/d were exported at an average price of US $64.54 per barrel, to give annual oil export revenue of $3,510m.

Natural gas is liquefied and then exported to Japan and the Republic of Korea (South Korea) by tanker under long-term contracts. Production and exports of liquefied natural gas (LNG) also declined, from 999,622m. British thermal units per day (Btu/day) in 2008 to 920,240m. Btu/day in 2009. Over the same period LNG prices declined from an average of US $12.93 per million Btu to $10.46 per million Btu. LNG export revenues declined from $4,716m. in 2008 to $3,514m. in 2009. Output of natural gas declined from 1,202m. standard cu ft (scf) per day in 2008 to 1,140m. scf per day in 2009.

Brunei Shell Petroleum (BSP) is the primary oil and gas company in Brunei. It is owned 50% by the Brunei Government and 50% by Shell International. Until recently it was the only producer of oil and gas in Brunei. Other related companies with the same ownership are Brunei Shell Tankers, which transports the LNG to overseas markets, and Brunei Shell Marketing, which sells petroleum products at petrol stations in Brunei. Brunei Liquefied Natural Gas (BLNG), which liquefies the gas produced by BSP and Total, is owned 50% by the Brunei Government, 25% by the United Kingdom-based Shell International and 25% by the Mitsubishi Corporation of Japan. Brunei Gas Carriers was formed in 1998 to build and manage LNG vessels. It is owned 80% by the Brunei Government, 10% by Shell International and 10% by the Mitsubishi Corporation.

Apart from the old shallow fields, there are two deeper, further offshore blocks, which were previously called J and K. However, since the resolution of the border dispute with Malaysia in the latter part of 2010, these blocks are now called CA-1 and CA-2, respectively, reflecting their positions in the new commercial arrangement area. The agreement with Malaysia allowed two new participants, PETRONAS Carigali Overseas of Malaysia and Canam Brunei (a wholly owned subsidiary of the US-based Murphy Oil Corporation), to join the existing consortium of Total of France, Australia's BHP Billiton and Hess of the USA. Total remains the operator of the block, with a 54% interest. The original shares in the block were reduced as follows: Total 60.0% to 54.0%; BHP Billiton 25.0% to 22.5%; and Hess 15.0% to 13.5%. This rearrangement released a 10% share, which was to be divided equally between Murphy and PETRONAS. With the signing of the deed of amendment to the original production-sharing contract, exploration work was resumed and drilling was expected to commence based on previously conducted seismic studies. Industry sources stated that for production to be economically feasible from this block, volumes of oil and/or gas would have to be large enough to make a substantial impact on Brunei's GDP and government revenue.

The original Block K group comprised Shell (50%), ConocoPhillips (USA—25%) and Mitsubishi (25%). In December 2010 a new agreement was signed for the renamed Block CA-2, which added Murphy, through its subsidiary Canam Brunei, and PETRONAS to the group. Murphy was to have a 30% share of this block. Details of changes to the other shares were not publicly released.

In 2006 mineral rights were also granted to two onshore blocks, L and M. The partners in Block L changed over time and became AED South East Asia Ltd (50%), Kulczyk Oil Brunei Ltd (40%) and QAF Brunei Sdn Bhd (10%). Survey work started on Block L in 2008, and the Lempuyang-1 exploratory well was drilled in 2010. Possible gas-charged reservoirs were indicated, but the well was suspended in April 2011 owing to mechanical difficulties.

In Block M the partners are KOV Borneo Ltd (36%), Tap Energy (Borneo) Pty Ltd (39%), China Sino Oil Co Ltd (21%) and Jana Corporation Sdn Bhd (4%). KOV Borneo Ltd is an indirect, wholly owned subsidiary of Kulczyk Oil. Drilling of the Markisa-1 exploratory well began in 2010. This is the second of a minimum of three wells to be drilled on Block M by Kulczyk Oil and its joint venture partners during the Phase 1 exploration period ending in August 2011. In March of that year Tap Oil announced its intention to sell its stake in Block M as it concentrated on its other core asset areas.

The other oil company with production interests in Brunei is Total. Total has been active in Brunei since 1986. It operates the Maharaja Lela/Jamalulalam field, which produced gas equivalent to 29,000 barrels of oil per day in 2009. The gas is sold to BLNG for liquefaction and export. In October 2010 Total announced a significant new offshore discovery of gas and condensate from Well ML-5 in Block B, in a water depth of 65 m, approximately 50 km from the coast. Total stated that 10m. cu ft of gas and 220 b/d of condensate were produced during the test at a depth of 5,350 m. This was the deepest successful test in South-East Asia. The gross thickness of the hydrocarbon-bearing formation exceeds 800 m. Furthermore, ML-5 is the third positive well of an exploration campaign that started in 2007, targeting the deep, high-pressure, high-temperature horizons of the Maharaja Lela structure. Total is the operator of this block, with a 37.5% interest, in association with Shell (35.0%) and local partners (27.5%).

Despite the resolution of the border dispute, BSP continued working on increasing recovery rates from its established fields. In January 2006 BSP delivered the first oil from its Champion West Phase 3 development using snake wells (which undulate through the sea-bed) and so-called smart field technology. The snake well can be directed through chambers in the reservoir, and the technology is 'smart' in that it includes variable inflow control valves, pressure gauges and fibre-optic sensors. BSP also produced the first petroleum from the Mampak field in 2009. This field was officially announced as a discovery in 1997. Current production is from an unmanned and fully remotely operated platform.

PetroleumBrunei was established in 2002. It is registered under the Companies Act as a private limited liability company wholly owned by the Government of Brunei through the Prime Minister's Corporation. PetroleumBrunei was originally granted the mineral rights to Blocks J, K, L and M, and with the Brunei Economic Development Board (BEDB) it is actively involved in promoting the Sungai Liang petrochemical projects, in which it is expected to be the local partner.

Other important institutional developments have included the creation of the post of Minister of Energy and the Energy Division at the Prime Minister's Office in May 2005. Prior to that, energy-related issues were handled by the Petroleum Unit of the Prime Minister's office; this unit was transferred to the Energy Division. Subsequently, in December, the Department of Electrical Services was placed under the responsibility of the Energy Division. The Minister of Energy is the Chairman of PetroleumBrunei.

It is recognized that energy subsidies and relatively high domestic energy use are inefficient, despite the substantial energy reserves in Brunei. Accordingly, a substantial amount of research and development of renewable energy sources is being funded in the country. Universiti Brunei Darussalam has a multi-million dollar research grant to investigate the potential for generating solar and wind power, while the Centre for Strategic and Policy Studies has funded two large research studies undertaken by international consultants on improving the efficiency of energy production and use and alternative sources of energy. Moreover, the Tenaga Suria Brunei Photovoltaic Power Generation Demonstration Project's Plant, which is fully funded by Mitsubishi Corporation, began operations in 2010. This facility is the largest solar power demonstration plant in South-East Asia and produces sufficient power for about 200 homes, generating some 1,344 MW-hours of electricity per year.

AGRICULTURE, FORESTRY AND FISHING

The areas of agriculture, forestry and fisheries are small but significant parts of the economy. The sector contributed B $141.9m. to GDP in 2009, compared with B $129.7m. in 2008. The fishery sector has recorded notable success in Brunei in recent years and has grown strongly. In the capture industry, production increased steadily, from 13,833.7 metric tons in 2002 to 16,964.9 tons in 2008. Small-scale fishing output declined from 4,864 tons in 2004 to 3,371 tons in 2008, but commercial-scale fishing output gradually expanded, from 10,818 tons to 12,205 tons, over that period. Commercial-scale fishing is defined as trawlers, purse-seiners and longliners, while small-scale fishermen are those who use outboard engines and fishing gear such as trammel nets, pots, and hook and line.

At the same time, imports of marine fish from neighbouring Malaysia declined, from 2,116 metric tons in 2002 to just 604 tons in 2008. However, this apparent success has had repercussions, and it appears that fishing activities in Zone 1 (i.e. the area extending from Brunei's shore to a distance of three nautical miles) have been conducted at an unsustainable level, thus resulting in dangerously low levels of fish stocks. The Fishery Department subsequently took action, and a moratorium was imposed on fishing in this Zone in January 2008. All commercial and small-scale fishing must now be conducted in Zone 2 (between three and 20 nautical miles off shore) or in Zones 3 and 4, which extend out to the 200-mile (370-km) limit of Brunei's territorial waters. The coastline is only 130 km in total and, with a marine territorial area of 38,600 sq km, it was estimated that the maximum annual sustainable, economic yield was 21,300 tons.

Other fisheries-related economic activities include aquaculture and the fish-processing industry. Aquaculture has been quite successful, with farmed (Rostris) prawn output increasing from 304.5 metric tons in 2002 to 573.3 tons in 2007, although it declined to 438.4 tons in 2008. The Fisheries Department, under the Ministry of Industry and Primary Resources, supports the local fish farmers by providing land and basic infrastructure as well as research and advice. In 2006 the Department signed an agreement with Integrated Aquaculture International to assist with new technology and niche marketing. Brunei's prawns have been exported to Japan, South Korea and the USA. The fish-processing industry has also expanded substantially in recent years, with output increasing from 439.4 tons in 2002 to 822.6 tons in 2008.

Brunei imports the vast majority of its food, and 12.3% of imports were food and live animals in 2008. However, the country is self-sufficient in chicken meat and eggs, producing 19,485 metric tons of chicken and 123m. eggs in 2008. Brunei has continued to import most of its rice from Thailand, and the Brunei Government heavily subsidizes rice and sugar consumer prices. In 2009, however, a new plan for self-sufficiency in rice production was announced, with the aim of increasing self-sufficiency from some 3% in 2007 to 20% in 2010 and 60% by 2015. In order to achieve this, the Ministry of Industry and Primary Resources gave land grants for paddy farming, developed agricultural infrastructure such as irrigation systems and roads, planned more systematic farming methods and introduced the use of mechanized rice planting. Rice production is relatively expensive in Brunei, and this initiative was accompanied by 50% rebates on fertilizers, chemicals and seeds, as well as a support price of B $1,600 per metric ton of rice. In addition to promoting the high-yielding Laila variety of rice, the Department of Agriculture and Agrifood (formerly the Department of Agriculture) has been working with South Korea, the People's Republic of China and the Philippines to test the suitability of other varieties for their cultivation in Brunei. At mid-2011 figures for rice production in 2010 had yet to be published; however, it was announced that the 20% target had not been met because only about 1,300 ha of land were opened for planting, while about 2,300 ha were actually needed; the yield per ha was only 1.4 metric tons, whereas 3 tons per ha was required.

Brunei's agricultural sector has been targeted as a source of economic diversification, as a means of increasing food security and as a potential buffer against rural poverty. The Agriculture Strategic Plan envisages agricultural output (as opposed to sectoral GDP) increasing from B $225m. in 2008 to B $612m. in 2013 and to B $2,700m. in 2023. The bulk of the growth is anticipated to come from the processed food sector (agrifood), with output reaching B $1,870m. in 2023. This sector contributed only B $52,500m. in 2008. Of the remaining B $830m. output projected for 2023, B $600m. is expected from livestock and B $230m. from other farm output such as crops. Annual compound growth rates required to achieve these ambitious targets are 10.6% for livestock and 12.1% for crops. In addition to the expansion of output using conventional farming practices, there is considerable potential for expansion of the Brunei Halal brand, which has been developed under the auspices of the Ministry of Industry and Primary Resources with private sector participation.

Although the forestry sector as such is not significant in Brunei, the forests are. The Forestry Act of Brunei (enacted in 1934 and revised in 1984) provides the legal framework for the conservation of forests in the country. Timber is produced only as required by the local market. Production of round timber totalled 99,240 cu m in 2008, compared with 94,836 cu m in 2007. In February 2007 the Heart of Borneo declaration was signed by the ministers of the three countries concerned, namely Brunei, Malaysia and Indonesia. This declaration aims to conserve the last large expanse of contiguous forests on Borneo, which covers 240,000 sq km of rainforest straddling the border highlands of Brunei, Indonesia and Malaysia. The Brunei Government has committed 60% of the land of Brunei to the Heart of Borneo initiative (see History).

LABOUR FORCE, EMPLOYMENT AND INFLATION

The population in mid-2010 was estimated at 414,400, comprising 219,100 males and 195,300 females. The number of young people entering the labour force clearly exceeds the number of old people leaving it: in 2010 34.1% of the population were below 20 years of age and only 8.4% above 54 years. In the past, the government sector would have easily absorbed these additional workers, but in 2010 the Government was looking to reduce its economic influence and was considering the possibility of corporatizing and privatizing some departments. Looking forward, this partly explains the need to diversify the economy, to create private sector jobs and to reduce the relative, if not the absolute, size of government.

Official data on the labour force, employment and unemployment are somewhat limited in Brunei. A population census is conducted every 10 years, most recently in 2001 and a 2011 census was being undertaken; a labour force survey was conducted in 1995 and another was carried out in 2008; the Labour Department also conducts an annual census on employers, and the Immigration Department has data on temporary resident workers. The Department of Economic Planning and Development publishes estimates of population and the labour force annually, but there are no official estimates of unemployment other than the register of job-seekers at the Labour Department, within the Ministry of Home Affairs.

Brunei became a member of the International Labour Organization (ILO) in January 2007. In June 2008 Brunei ratified ILO's Convention 182 on Worst Forms of Child Labour. This convention is one of eight core Conventions, which concern four general areas: forced labour, freedom of association, discrimination and child labour. Prior to this ratification, Brunei was one of only five countries that had not ratified any of the core Conventions. Brunei is addressing child labour and other labour-related issues under new labour laws: the Employment Order and the Workplace Safety and Health Order. As a member of ILO, Brunei may be obliged to continue to address issues concerning the protection and safety of workers in accordance with ILO ideals, for example in the areas of minimum wage and working conditions.

The labour force in mid-2010 was estimated to total 198,800, of whom 121,200 were males and 77,600 were females. However, the most recent analysis of employment figures was at the 2001 census. The Report on the 2001 Population Census showed a labour force (aged 15 years and above) in that year of 157,594. Of the 146,254 in this age group who were in employment, 91,389 were engaged in the private sector and 54,865 in the public sector. The data on employment by residential status is for the age group of 15–64 years. In this group, there were 145,554 employed people: 67,655 employed foreign workers (temporary residents) and 77,899 employed Brunei citizens and permanent residents. The vast majority of temporary residents work in the private sector. In 2008 the number of temporary residents working in the private sector alone was estimated at 87,867, out of a total private sector work-force of 127,410. By industry sector, in 2008 37% worked in construction, 16% in mining, manufacturing and quarrying, and 14% in wholesale and retail trade. By occupational classification, at the 2001 census 43% of the temporary resident labour force worked in 'elementary occupations', while 23% were engaged in the field of 'craft and related trades'.

There are currently only two ways of estimating unemployment in Brunei using secondary data: the 2001 census and the list of registered job-seekers from the Labour Department. At the 2001 census, unemployment (among those aged between 15 and 64 years) was estimated at 11,339 persons. All foreign workers in Brunei hold work permits for specific jobs, and therefore there should be no unemployment among legally resident foreign workers. Nevertheless, some 725 temporary residents did claim to be unemployed at the time of the census. Unemployment among Bruneians in 2001 totalled 10,614 persons out of a Bruneian (citizen and permanent resident) work-force of 88,513, the rate thus reaching 12%.

Regarding the specific question on activity status for the reference week, 15–21 August 2001, six check boxes were given: working, actively looking for work, housewife, student, retired and others. The census is not specifically designed to estimate unemployment, and the questions are not as specific as they would be in a labour force survey. Presumably, respondents in the 'working' category would have been classified as employed; 'actively looking for work' would have been classified as unemployed; and the others would have been classified as not in the labour force. It is likely that the census data overstate unemployment as defined by ILO, since those actively looking for work may have done one hour or more of work during the reference period. Moreover, 725 temporary residents were classified as unemployed (actively looking for work) when temporary residents would either generally be on working visas, and therefore working, or on dependant or student visas, and therefore not allowed to work. Moreover, the reference week was in August, which would have captured new school leavers and graduates who were seeking employment for the first time. Most of the unemployed in Brunei are young people, and many are looking for their first jobs. It is unusual for established government workers to lose their jobs, although there does appear to be voluntary unemployment whereby Bruneians leave private sector jobs because of perceived low pay and poor benefits.

An alternative measure of unemployment used by the Department of Economic Planning and Development is to take the people registered as seeking work with the Labour Department as a percentage of the total labour force. In 2010 there were 5,300 registered job seekers and a total labour force estimated at 198,800, so by this definition the unemployment rate was a mere 2.7%. However, this is unlikely to give a realistic measure of true unemployment for three reasons: first, many job-seekers will not be unemployed, as they may simply be looking for a better job; second, with no unemployment benefits in Brunei and only generally unskilled and clerical jobs on the books of the Labour Department, there is little incentive for many people to register; finally, those who have registered and subsequently found work have no incentive to have their names removed from the list. In conclusion, there is currently no accurate measure of unemployment in Brunei; however, membership of ILO means that efforts to compile more accurate statistics in this area will continue.

A consumer price index (CPI) is estimated monthly, quarterly and annually. Inflation has usually been relatively benign in Brunei, with the CPI in 2007 at only 0.3% above the 2006 figure. In 2008, however, consumer prices rose by 2.7%, with the rate of inflation easing to 1.8% in 2009, according to official figures.

BEDB INITIATIVES

The BEDB was created in November 2001 through the Brunei Economic Development Board (Amendment) Order 2001. It is a state-owned statutory body and has autonomy to carry out its mandate to stimulate the growth and development of the economy by attracting foreign direct investment. The BEDB is the branch of government that can enter into joint ventures with foreign investors. The Board is also responsible for implementing certain government economic policies, particularly with regard to attracting foreign investment in industries with good export potential.

From 2008 the focus and priority of the Board was on the development of the Sungai Liang Industrial Park (SPARK), Pulau Muara Besar port development, and the facilitation of industrial development as a whole, including supporting the development of small and medium enterprises (SMEs).

Sungai Liang Development

The SPARK is located on a 271-ha site that was gazetted to the BEDB by the Brunei Government in October 2004. Located about 100 km south-west of the capital of Bandar Seri Begawan, the park was to be developed into a world-class site for industrial development associated with the downstream processing of hydrocarbons, particularly natural gas. Potential projects include production of ammonia/urea, methanol, elastomers and possibly aluminium smelting. The Sungai Liang Authority handles the administration of the Park, such as the granting of licences and approvals, entering into contracts, building infrastructure, such as roads and a marine terminal, and providing utility services, such as electricity, and operating and managing common services.

The first project to proceed at Sungai Liang was the methanol plant. Methanol can be used in a variety of ways to produce value-added products, such as formaldehyde for use in the polymer industries. The methanol project was undertaken by a joint-venture company, Brunei Darussalam Methanol Project Consortium (BMC), consisting of PetroleumBrunei (50%), Mitsubishi Gas Chemical of Japan (MGC—25%) and Itochu Corporation (25%). Construction began in February 2008, and the plant commenced commercial operation in May 2010. The project was managed by the newly established Brunei Methanol Company. Construction was being undertaken by Mitsubishi Heavy Industries under an engineer, procure, construct basis. The cost of construction of the new facility was estimated at US $400m. The plant has an output capacity of 2,500 metric tons of methanol per day (850,000 tons annually). It was also anticipated that the plant would produce a range of products from the methanol it produces, including resins, adhesives, polymers, paint and gasoline (petrol) additives. In late 2005 MGC signed a memorandum of understanding (MOU) with the consortium, enabling it to buy the entire production of the plant upon completion. PetroleumBrunei signed an MOU to supply approximately 500,000m. cu ft of gas to the plant over a 22-year period. Brunei Shell Petroleum also agreed to supply gas for the new plant. The financing for the project was partially secured by a further MOU signed by PetroleumBrunei and the Japan Bank for International Cooperation in October 2006.

The BEDB has selected a consortium comprising Incitec Pivot (an Australian fertilizer company), the Mitsubishi Corporation, and privately owned WestSide Ltd (majority Australian shareholding) jointly to study a US $600m. ammonia-urea project. The plant is expected to produce 3,500 metric tons of urea per day for export throughout the Asian region.

Pulau Muara Besar Development

Another major development initiative being investigated and marketed by the BEDB is a US $1,500m. transshipment port and container terminal, possibly with an export processing zone on a small island, namely Pulau Muara Besar, at the northern end of the country. Transshipment is based on the 'hub and spoke' principle. As container ships become bigger in order to capture all available economies of scale, long-distance routes are conducted by the biggest ships, which call at very few 'hub' ports. At these ports, cargoes are transferred to smaller vessels for shipment to feeder ports in regional countries. The reverse system also applies.

Given the strategic location of Brunei in central South-East Asia, naturally occurring deep water in the area of the island and the growing trend in transshipment globally, it appears that Brunei may have a comparative advantage in this area, and one that is not associated with oil and gas.

Various engineering and economic studies have been undertaken, and marketing efforts to find investors are under way. The Government of Brunei is anticipating the provision of 70% of the required investment and the infrastructure, and it is hoping to form a consortium with established port operators and shipping lines. However, there is considerable competition to be a major hub port from existing regional facilities in Singapore and Hong Kong, as well as from former feeder ports such as Port Klang in Malaysia, which are located on direct shipping routes.

In July 2011 the BEDB announced that the Sultan had approved plans for the construction of a petroleum refinery and aromatics cracker project on Pulau Muara Besar. The first stage of the project was to cost US $2,500m. and provide more than 800 employment opportunities. To be built by a Chinese company, the new refinery was to have a production capacity of 135,000 b/d. Upon successful completion of the first phase, further investment of $3,500m. was to be allocated to the expansion of the refinery, to permit the production of olefins (used in the manufacture of plastics). The creation of an additional 1,200 jobs was anticipated in the second stage of the project.

Small and Medium Enterprises

The BEDB is also involved in promoting many other areas to stimulate economic growth in the country. For example, it is funding the Infocomms Tech Incubation Centre, the vision of which is to be a centre of excellence for supporting and developing entrepreneurship in information and communication technology (ICT) start-up operations. The BEDB is also actively promoting 'clusters' of development in areas that have been identified in an influential consulting report. Four areas were regarded as being of particular potential: hospitality and tourism; financial services; business services; and transport and logistics. In addition, education and knowledge creation were identified as important in enabling the achievement of success in all these clusters.

The BEDB has since focused on some of these areas and expanded others. It is now actively marketing Brunei and negotiating with potential overseas investors in the areas of eco-tourism, aquaculture, renewable energy and Islamic finance, also aiming to establish Brunei as a *halal* processing hub. *Halal* certification applies traditionally to food prepared in an approved way, but there is also the possibility of expanding this to such items as medicines and cosmetics.

DEVELOPMENT PLANS

In the area of more formal planning, the Ninth Five-Year National Development Plan (2007–12) was released in January 2008, as part of a new 30-year development framework that extends to 2035. This ambitious plan is based on the National Vision, or Wawasan Brunei 2035, which envisages Brunei's quality of life and per caput income being ranked within the leading 10 countries of the world by 2035. In addition to the National Vision, the plan contains the Outline of Strategies and Policies for Development (OSPD) and the National Development Plan (Rancangan Kemajuan Negara). Although this is the country's ninth development plan, it is the first to be based explicitly on a formal national vision. The OSPD (2007–17) contains eight main strategies and 50 policy directions. The strategies concern education, economy, security, institutional development, local business development, infrastructure, social security and environment.

The total budget for the Ninth National Development Plan was B $9,500m., and during the period 2007–12 the Government envisaged spending approximately B $1,700m. per year. It was planned to implement 826 projects, under 257 programmes, with expenditure being 30% higher than the budget for the previous five-year plan. It was hoped that this would result in average annual growth in GDP of 6%. The plan noted that, in the past, one of the problems with development planning had been the country's inability to spend its development budgets. Accordingly, a crucial initiative was to strengthen institutions and streamline bureaucratic processes. There were three other specific development objectives: widening the economic base and developing a knowledge-based economy; consolidating social progress and political stability; and developing a highly skilled work-force.

The 2007–12 plan was wide-ranging. In the industrial and commercial sector, which was allocated 11% of the total budget, the focus was on food security and food safety, development of the Brunei Halal brand and also tourism. In the tourism sector three specific targets were set: to increase tourist arrivals by 7% annually; to raise hotel occupancy rates to 50%–60% by 2008; and to increase employment in the tourism sector by 50% by 2010. In mid-2011, however, Royal Brunei Airlines (RBA) unexpectedly announced that it was to suspend its services to several destinations. The carrier's flights from the New Zealand city of Auckland and from the Australian cities of Brisbane and Perth were among the routes to be discontinued. RBA's decision to retrench was regarded as a major set-back for Brunei's tourism sector.

The social service sector was allocated 32% of the budget, and the focus here was on improvements in health care and management, as well as on greater construction of public housing. As regards human resources, the plan emphasized research and development, particularly in the areas of science, technology and innovation. The plan was to fund various aspects of the development of human resources, scholarship, skills development and entrepreneurial development programmes.

Public utilities were to receive 16% of the budget, with the focus on increasing the generating capacity of the electricity grid and interconnecting the three existing systems. Water supply, sewerage and drainage were to be improved. A new Environment Act remained under consideration in 2010.

National security was allocated 6% of the budget for building new infrastructure and improving existing infrastructure and facilities. In the ICT area, e-government and e-business initiatives were to be expanded in order to improve customer service in government departments and to assist the development of SMEs. At the end of the second quarter of 2008 only 191 projects had been completed, representing 8.1% of the total scheme outlay. All other projects were either being implemented or were at the tender or planning stage.

Despite the very heavy involvement of government in this development framework, private sector financing was to be sought through public-private partnerships; plans for privatization and corporatization were to be accelerated. In this regard, a Privatization Master Plan was to be developed, which was to include guide-lines on the planning, co-ordination, implementation and monitoring of privatization programmes.

Privatization and the removal of subsidies are regarded as important measures in the invigoration of the Brunei economy, but they raise difficult social issues. In 2010 the most expensive petrol in Brunei was B $0.53 per litre (US $0.38 per litre), and regular petrol cost B $0.36 per litre (US $0.26 per litre). Electricity is charged on a declining rate block for post-paid, with a flat rate for pre-paid, and averages about B $0.06/kWh (US $0.04/kWh), the lowest in the region (compared with approximately B $0.18/kWh in neighbouring Singapore). As international energy prices increase, the forgone revenue from maintaining these subsidies and the other social benefits that could be financed with that revenue, combined with the lack of incentives to conserve precious resources, become more obvious. However, with no formal social 'safety net' and with so many Bruneians in receipt of government salaries that have not increased in many years, it would not be politically straightforward to remove these subsidies.

PUBLIC FINANCE AND FINANCIAL SERVICES

Another indicator of the degree of dependence on oil and gas can be seen from government revenues. For the fiscal year ending 31 March 2010 total government revenues were B $6,392.9m. and expenditures were B $6,638.8m., giving a deficit of B $245.9m. This compares with 2009 revenues of B $11,378m., expenditures of B $5,974.6m. and thus a surplus of B $5,403.4m. Government revenue is very highly dependent on the oil and gas industry. For the period January to December 2009 government revenue totalled B $6,583.8m., of which B $5,740.3m., or 87%, was from the oil and gas sector in the form of corporate taxes on oil and gas companies, oil and gas royalties, and dividends paid by oil and gas companies. The remaining B $839m. of revenue was derived largely from utilities, corporate taxes on non-oil and gas companies and import duties. However, this other revenue was not entirely independent of oil and gas. For example, the money used to buy the imported cars on which duty was paid was the oil and gas revenue that was being recirculated via the salaries of government servants and others.

This approach to the economy of Brunei is quite insightful. In 2009 combined oil and gas exports totalled B $10,023.5m. In paying their staff of approximately 4,000, their domestic suppliers and their contractors, BSP, BLNG and Total, all recirculated these revenues into the local economy. By spending B $6,638.8m. in the fiscal year 2009/10 on the salaries of government servants, suppliers and contractors among other costs, the Government also recirculated oil and gas revenues.

Brunei's financial reserves from the surpluses created by oil and gas revenues are invested by the Brunei Investment Agency (BIA). This body was established in July 1983, with a balance of B $12,000m. transferred from the British Crown Agents. The BIA invests in international markets. Income from these investments is not in the public domain (also see History).

A new development in the financial sector was the establishment of the Autoriti Monetari Brunei Darussalam (AMBD) and the Deposit Protection Scheme on 1 January 2011. AMBD is a corporate body that acts as the country's central bank; it is responsible for the formulation and implementation of monetary policies, supervision of financial institutions and currency management. The establishment of the AMBD required the amendment of the Currency and Monetary Order (2004) by the Currency and Monetary (Amendment) Order (2010), which took effect on 1 January 2011. This provided for the transfer of the Brunei Currency and Monetary Board's powers to the AMBD, including its assets and liabilities. In addition, the Order also provided for the establishment of the Currency Fund for the purpose of currency management.

The Brunei dollar is subject to a one-for-one interchangeability arrangement with the Singapore dollar. The two currencies circulate together and are repatriated to their respective countries annually. There are no currency restrictions on the inflow or outflow of money in Brunei. However, in February 2007 the Ministry of Finance established the Finance Intelligence Unit, which is responsible for gathering information regarding potential money-laundering activities or terrorist financing.

In the third quarter of 2009 the total assets of the banking industry were B $16,400m. and total deposits stood at B $13,000m. Total loans reached B $6,039.7m., of which 38%, or B $2,308.0m. were in the form of personal loans. With a labour force estimated at 198,800 in 2010, this gave an average personal loan of B $11,610 for every member of the labour force, a substantial decline from the figure of nearly B $16,000 in 2007. In 2008 temporary residents in the private sector labour force were estimated to total 87,867; as the majority of these people would not qualify for a personal loan, the figure for Brunei citizens and permanent residents in the labour force is likely to be closer to B $21,800 each. Personal loans, both in aggregate and per caput, continued to decline, largely as a result of the directive by the Ministry of Finance for personal loans to be limited in relation to a borrower's salary. The second largest category for lending was the mortgage sector, which accounted for 20% of the total loans portfolio in the third quarter of 2009.

In addition to the 2005 directive to reduce consumers' personal loans, in December 2009 the Ministry of Finance issued new credit card regulations that forbade the use of credit cards to repay loans, set a minimum monthly repayment that became 8% of the outstanding balance from June 2010, linked credit card accounts to payroll accounts only, and set credit limits based on salary ranges. The Brunei International Financial Centre (BIFC) was established in July 2000, with the aim of stimulating more finance-related activity in Brunei. The BIFC offers services such as registration of international business companies and international limited partnerships, issuing international banking, insurance and mutual fund licences and trust administration. In 2005 there were more than 4,000 international business companies registered in Brunei. The Royal Bank of Canada was the first bank to open an international branch under the International Banking Order 2000. In 2008 there were 11 retail banks operating in Brunei.

With a view to greater participation in international financial markets, Brunei began the issuance of Islamic bonds or *sukuk* in April 2006. In 2010 it issued series 43 to 46 of the Government's short-term Sukuk Al-Ijarah (91 days' maturity) bonds to the value of B $158m., bringing the total issued since April 2006 to B $2,304m. These bonds are based on a property-leasing arrangement whereby property rental payments are used for the payment of dividends to bond investors. Islamic finance principles do not allow the payment of interest as such.

The Insurance Order was introduced in March 2006. Among other requirements, it specified the need for all insurance companies to have minimum capital of B $8m., rather than the previous requirement of B $1m. All existing insurance companies were to re-register in order to show that they had met the requirements of the order. By the first quarter of 2007 six companies were operating in Brunei. The assets of all insurance companies increased from B $1,016.7m. in 2008 to B $1,038.5m. in the second quarter of 2010.

Provision for *Shari'a*-compliant practices was to be extended to other areas of the economy, including business activities and trade. In this regard it was reported in September 2010 that some laws had already been amended and that new legislation was in the process of being drafted. The Ministry of Religious Affairs was to supply legal experts to advise on the principles of Islamic finance.

In March 2010 it was announced that the Ministry of Finance was to enter into partnership with a Japanese financial services enterprise, SBI Holdings, in order to establish a fund management company. The new company was expected to handle private equity funds, including *Shari'a*-compliant facilities. The Hong Kong Government was also reported to be considering the establishment of a similar operation in Brunei.

The Brunei dollar strengthened from B $1.63 = US $1.00 in the first quarter of 2006 to approximately B $1.38 = US $1.00 in mid-2008; however, it subsequently weakened, reaching B $1.46 = US $1.00 in mid-2009. In 2011 the value of the Brunei dollar rose strongly against the US dollar, standing at approximately B $1.24 = US $1.00 in June of that year.

BALANCE OF TRADE

In 2009 exports totalled B $10,431.7m., and the petroleum sector accounted for B $10,023.5m., or 96%, of those exports. The largest markets for Brunei's crude petroleum in 2010 were Indonesia, South Korea and Australia. Nearly 93% of Brunei's exports of LNG are shipped to Japan under long-term contracts, with the remainder being bought by South Korea. The only other major source of export revenue is the garment industry, which was established to take advantage of the international quota system agreed under the terms of the Multi-Fibre Arrangement (MFA). However, following the expiry of the MFA on 31 December 2004 and in view of the increasing competition from China and India, the future of the garment industry in Brunei appeared uncertain at best. The garment sector accounted for approximately 0.5% of exports in 2009, having declined from 5.2% in 2003. The remaining 3.5% of exports comprised mainly re-exports of machinery and transport equipment, manufactured goods, fuels, and food, beverages and tobacco.

Imports in 2009 totalled B $3,491.9m., giving a trade surplus of nearly B $6,939.9m. In that year the largest category of imports other than services was that of machinery and transport equipment (B $1,382.6m.), followed by manufactured goods (B $781.1m.) and food (B $422.5m.). The leading sources of imports in 2009 were Singapore (26%), Malaysia (19%), the USA (13%) Japan (9%) and China (6%). Brunei's trade, notably the country's imports of fresh produce, was expected to be affected by RBA's decision to reduce its network, with Melbourne becoming the only Australian city to be served by Brunei's national airline from the latter part of 2011.

CONCLUSION

The contraction in Brunei's GDP in 2009 was attributed both to the weakening of international oil and gas prices and to constraints in crude petroleum and LNG production. However, according to the IMF, oil and gas production rebounded in the first half of 2010, and real GDP increased by 5.5% in comparison with the corresponding period of the previous year. Oil and gas prices also increased in 2010 from their 2009 levels, indicating that nominal GDP might be expected to show a substantial increase when official figures are released.

Despite recent fluctuations, in 2009 Brunei's GDP per caput remained among the highest in the world, at B $38,400, although this represented a substantial decline from the 2008 figure of B $51,300. Nevertheless, the country continued its drive for diversification of the economy, both by adding value to oil and gas through downstream developments, such as petrochemicals, and by developing new, non-oil and gas industries. The BEDB, in conjunction with the new National Vision and Ninth National Development Plan, is aggressively marketing Brunei as a profitable destination for foreign direct investment.

While there is some debate about the appropriate role of government in the future Brunei economy, it seems that public-private partnerships and the promotion of SMEs may lead to successful outcomes. However, despite the inauguration of the Brunei Methanol Company at the Sungai Liang Industrial Park in 2010, a project that is nevertheless dependent on natural gas, there were still no potential large-scale employers that might replace oil and gas as the driving force of the economy and absorb the rapidly growing work-force. Nevertheless, the resolution of the maritime border dispute with Malaysia in 2009 greatly improved the prospects for future oil and gas production from offshore Blocks CA-1 and CA-2, which could extend the life of Brunei's hydrocarbon reserves and reduce the urgency of the need for diversification. The establishment of a new petroleum refinery complex on Pulau Muara Besar, plans for which were confirmed in mid-2011, was expected to provide numerous employment opportunities for local workers.

An important element of the Government's diversification strategy was the advancement of the Brunei Halal brand on international markets. In addition to the area of Islamic financial services, the Government hoped to extend the programme beyond food products to items such as pharmaceuticals. However, the Sultanate's lack of the raw materials required for such undertakings remained a major obstacle, and analysts warned of the difficulties that Brunei was likely to experience in its attempts to become competitive in this area. The relatively slow progress in the implementation of government programmes appeared to be largely due to weaknesses in Brunei's institutional capacity. In 2010 the IMF and other international institutions continued to urge Brunei to give greater encouragement to the private sector through the promotion of more favourable business conditions.

Statistical Survey

Sources (unless otherwise stated): Department of Economic Planning and Development, Prime Minister's Office, Block 2A, Jalan Ong Sum Ping, Bandar Seri Begawan BA 1311; tel. 2244433; fax 2230236; e-mail info@jpke.gov.bn; Brunei Economic Development Board, Block 2K, Bangunan Keraajan, Jalan Ong Sum Ping, Bandar Seri Begawan BA 1311; tel. 2230111; fax 2230063; e-mail info@bedb.com.bn; internet www.bedb.com.bn.

AREA AND POPULATION

Area: 5,765 sq km (2,226 sq miles); *By District:* Brunei/Muara 570 sq km (220 sq miles), Seria/Belait 2,725 sq km (1,052 sq miles), Tutong 1,165 sq km (450 sq miles), Temburong 1,305 sq km (504 sq miles).

Population (excluding transients afloat): 260,482 at census of 7 August 1991; 332,844 (males 168,925, females 163,919) at census of 21 August 2001; 406,200 (males 215,000, females 191,200) in 2009 (official estimate, preliminary). *By District* (2009, provisional): Brunei/Muara 283,300; Seria/Belait 67,100; Tutong 45,700; Temburong 10,100; Total 406,200.

Density (at mid-2009): 70.5 per sq km.

Population by Age and Sex (UN estimates at mid-2011): *0–14:* 105,021 (males 54,439, females 50,582); *15–64:* 285,960 (males 143,026, females 142,934); *65 and over:* 14,957 (males 7,533, females 7,424); *Total* 405,938 (males 204,998, females 200,940) (Source: UN, *World Population Prospects: The 2010 Revision*). *Population by Age* ('000 persons in 2009, official estimates, preliminary): *0–19:* 141.1; *20–64:* 251.3; *65 and over:* 13.8; *Total* 406.2.

Ethnic Groups (2009, provisional): Malay 269,400, Chinese 44,600, Others 92,200, Total 406,200.

Principal Towns: Bandar Seri Begawan (capital): population 27,285 at 2001 census; Kuala Belait: population 21,200 at 1991 census; Seria: population 21,100 at 1991 census; Tutong: population 13,000 at 1991 census. *Mid-2009* (incl. suburbs, UN estimate): Bandar Seri Begawan 22,228 (Source: UN, *World Urbanization Prospects: The 2009 Revision*).

Births, Marriages and Deaths (2008): Live births 6,424 (birth rate 16.1 per 1,000); Marriages 2,391; Deaths 1,091 (death rate 2.7 per 1,000).

Life Expectancy (years at birth, WHO estimates): 77 (males 76; females 77) in 2009. Source: WHO, *World Health Statistics*.

Economically Active Population (persons aged 15 years and over, 2001 census, provisional): Agriculture, hunting, forestry and fishing 1,994; Mining and quarrying 3,954; Manufacturing 12,455; Electricity, gas and water 2,639; Construction 12,301; Trade, restaurants and hotels 20,038; Transport, storage and communications 4,803; Financing, insurance, real estate and business services 8,190; Community, social and personal services 79,880; *Total employed* 146,254 (males 85,820, females 60,434); Unemployed 11,340 (males 6,734, females 4,606); *Total labour force* 157,594 (males 92,554, females 65,040). *2008:* Total employed 181,800; Unemployed 7,000; Total labour force 188,800 (Source: Asian Development Bank).

HEALTH AND WELFARE

Key Indicators

Total Fertility Rate (children per woman, 2009): 2.1.

Under-5 Mortality Rate (per 1,000 live births, 2009): 7.

HIV/AIDS (% of persons aged 15–49, 2005): <0.1.

Physicians (per 1,000 head, 2002): 1.1.

Hospital Beds (per 1,000 head, 2005): 3.0.

Health Expenditure (2008): US $ per head (PPP): 1,131.

Health Expenditure (2008): % of GDP: 2.3.

Health Expenditure (2008): public (% of total): 85.5.

Total Carbon Dioxide Emissions ('000 metric tons, 2007): 7,599.1.

Carbon Dioxide Emissions Per Head (metric tons, 2007): 19.7.

Human Development Index (2010): ranking: 37.

Human Development Index (2010): value: 0.805.

For sources and definitions, see explanatory note on p. vi.

AGRICULTURE, ETC.

Principal Crops ('000 metric tons, 2009): Rice, paddy 1.4 (unofficial figure). *Aggregate Production* ('000 metric tons, may include official, semi-official or estimated data): Total vegetables (incl. melons) 10.0; Total fruits (excl. melons) 7.6.

Livestock ('000 head, 2009, FAO estimates): Cattle 1.0; Buffaloes 4.6; Sheep 3.8; Goats 3.0; Pigs 1.3; Chickens 16,000.

Livestock Products ('000 metric tons, 2009): Cattle meat 0.6 (FAO estimate); Chicken meat 18.9 (FAO estimate); Hen eggs 6.8.

Forestry ('000 cubic metres, 2009, FAO estimates): *Roundwood Removals:* Sawlogs, veneer logs and logs for sleepers 101.1; Other industrial roundwood 11.0; Fuel wood 11.7; Total 123.8. *Sawnwood Production:* Total (all broad-leaved) 50.9.

Fishing (metric tons, live weight, 2009, FAO estimates): Capture 2,358; Aquaculture 433 (Blue Shrimp 320); *Total catch* 2,791.

Source: FAO.

MINING

Production (2009, estimates): Crude petroleum ('000 barrels, incl. condensate) 61,000; Natural gas (million cu m, gross) 12,100. Source: US Geological Survey.

INDUSTRY

Production ('000 metric tons, 2007, unless otherwise indicated): Motor spirit (petrol) 217; Distillate fuel oils 189; Residual fuel oil 97; Cement 220 (2009, estimate); Electric energy (million kWh) 3,071 (2008). Sources: mainly UN Industrial Commodity Statistics Database; and US Geological Survey.

FINANCE

Currency and Exchange Rates: 100 sen (cents) = 1 Brunei dollar (B $). *Sterling, US Dollar and Euro Equivalents* (31 May 2011): £1 sterling = B $2.034; US $1 = B $1.233; €1 = B $1.773; B $100 = £49.15 = US $81.11 = €56.39. *Average Exchange Rate* (Brunei dollars per US $): 1.4172 in 2008; 1.4546 in 2009; 1.3635 in 2010. Note: The Brunei dollar is at par with the Singapore dollar.

Budget (B $ million, year ending 31 March 2011, projected figures): *Revenue:* Tax revenue 2,841 (Oil and gas sector 2,530); Non-tax revenue 1,790 (Oil and gas sector 1,324); Total 4,631. *Expenditure:* Current expenditure 4,074 (Wages and salaries 1,819, Other annual recurrent charges 1,586, Charged expenditure 669); Capital expenditure 1,581 (Special expenditure charges 531; Development expenditure 1,050); Total 5,655. Source: IMF, *Brunei Darussalam: Statistical Appendix* (June 2011).

International Reserves (excl. gold, US $ million at 31 December 2009): IMF special drawing rights 339.14; Reserve position in IMF 21.44; Foreign exchange 996.69; *Total* 1,357.27. *2010* (US $ million at 31 December): IMF special drawing rights 333.23; Reserve position in IMF 21.06. Source: IMF, *International Financial Statistics*.

Money Supply (B $ million at 31 December 2010): Currency outside depository corporations 824.5; Transferable deposits 2,992.6; Other deposits 8,755.9; Securities other than shares 0.0; *Broad money* 12,573.0. Source: IMF, *International Financial Statistics*.

Cost of Living (Consumer Price Index; base: 2005 = 100): All items 101.2 in 2007; 103.3 in 2008; 104.4 in 2009. Source: IMF, *International Financial Statistics*.

Gross Domestic Product (B $ million at constant 2000 prices): 11,986 in 2007; 11,754 in 2008; 11,546 in 2009.

Expenditure on the Gross Domestic Product (B $ million in current prices, 2009): Government final consumption expenditure 3,635.5; Private consumption expenditure 3,803.0; Changes in inventories 1.2; Gross fixed investment 2,739.6; *Total domestic expenditure* 10,179.3; Exports of goods and services 11,362.4; *Less* Imports of goods and services 5,587.2; Statistical discrepancy –343.1; *GDP in purchasers' values* 15,611.4 (Source: IMF, *Brunei Darussalam: Statistical Appendix* —June 2011).

Gross Domestic Product by Economic Activity (B $ million in current prices, 2009): Agriculture, hunting, forestry and fishing 141.9; Mining and quarrying 7,389.7; Manufacturing 2,180.8; Electricity, gas and water 122.0; Construction 518.1; Wholesale and retail trade 591.2; Transport and communications 556.0; Finance 573.8; Public administration 2,189.7; Others 1,348.2; *GDP in purchasers' values* 15,611.4 (Source: IMF, *Brunei Darussalam: Statistical Appendix*—June 2011).

Balance of Payments (US $ million, 2009): Exports of goods 7,171.9; Imports of goods –2,282.4; *Trade balance* 4,889.5; Exports of services 914.9; Imports of services –1,434.2; *Balance on goods and services* 4,370.2; Other income received 316.3; Other income paid –264.2; *Balance on goods, services and income* 4,422.2; Current transfers (net) –444.8; *Current balance* 3,977.4; Capital account (net) –10.9; Direct investment (net) 325.6; Portfolio investment (net) 139.3; Other investment assets 644.4; Other investment liabilities 498.1; Net errors and omissions –5,420.0; *Overall balance* 153.7. Source: IMF, *International Financial Statistics*.

EXTERNAL TRADE

Principal Commodities (US $ million, 2009): *Imports c.i.f.:* Food and live animals 290; Chemicals 192; Basic manufactures 537; Machinery and transport equipment 950; Miscellaneous manufactured articles 246; Total (incl. others) 2,400. *Exports f.o.b.:* Mineral fuels 6,888; Machinery and transport equipment 152; Miscellaneous manufactured articles 78; Total (incl. others) 7,169 (Source: IMF, *Brunei Darussalam: Statistical Appendix*—June 2011).

Principal Trading Partners (US $ million, 2009): *Imports:* China, People's Republic 140; Japan 214; Malaysia 465; Singapore 614; Thailand 95; USA 312; Total (incl. others) 2,400. *Exports:* Australia 524; Indonesia 772; Japan 3,305; Republic of Korea 829; Singapore 184; Thailand 138; Total (incl. others) 7,169 (Source: IMF, *Brunei Darussalam: Statistical Appendix*—June 2011).

TRANSPORT

Road Traffic (registered vehicles, 2007): Passenger cars 252,679; Lorries and vans 16,744; Buses 1,522; Motorcycles and mopeds 12,177. Source: IRF, *World Road Statistics*.

Merchant Fleet (displacement, '000 grt at 31 December): 483.2 in 2007; 494.0 in 2008; 500.0 in 2009. Source: IHS Fairplay, *World Fleet Statistics*.

International Sea-borne Shipping (freight traffic, '000 freight tons, 2008): Goods loaded 26.6; Goods unloaded 919.8. Note: One freight ton equals 40 cu ft (1.133 cu m) of cargo.

Civil Aviation (2006): Kilometres flown (million) 30; Passengers carried ('000) 1,041; Passenger-km (million) 4,058; Total ton-km (million) 497. *2008:* Passengers carried ('000) 1,554.9. Source: mainly UN, *Statistical Yearbook*.

TOURISM

Foreign Visitor Arrivals by Nationality (tourist arrivals at national borders, 2008): Australia 25,732; Canada 2,244; China, People's Republic 27,652; Germany 2,056; India 3,402; Japan 4,489; Korea, Republic 17,548; New Zealand 9,427; United Kingdom 16,192; USA 3,408; Total (incl. others) 225,757.

Tourism Receipts (US $ million, excl. passenger transport): 224 in 2006; 233 in 2007; 241 in 2008.

Source: World Tourism Organization.

COMMUNICATIONS MEDIA

Radio Receivers (2000, estimate): 362,712 in use.

Television Receivers (2000, estimate): 216,223 in use.

Telephones (2010): 79,900 main lines in use. Source: International Telecommunication Union.

Mobile Cellular Telephones ('000 subscribers, 2010): 435.1. Source: International Telecommunication Union.

Personal Computers: 33,000 (89.2 per 1,000 persons) in 2005. Source: International Telecommunication Union.

Internet Subscribers ('000, 2009): 100.1. Source: International Telecommunication Union.

Broadband Subscribers ('000, 2010): 21.7. Source: International Telecommunication Union.

Book Production (1992): 25 titles; 56,000 copies. *1998:* 38 titles. Source: UNESCO, *Statistical Yearbook*.

Newspapers (2002 unless otherwise indicated): Daily 2 (with total circulation of 25,000 copies) in 2004; Non-daily: English 2 (with circulation of 22,000 copies); Malay 3 (with circulation of 39,500 copies); Malay and English 1 (with circulation of 10,000 copies) (Source: partly UNESCO Institute for Statistics).

Other Periodicals (1998): 15 (estimated combined circulation 132,000 copies per issue).

EDUCATION

Pre-primary and Primary (2008): 203 schools (incl. some schools also offering secondary education), 4,232 teachers and 57,902 pupils.

General Secondary (2008): 34 schools (excl. schools offering primary education also), 3,687 teachers and 38,693 pupils.

Nursing/Technical/Vocational (2008): 13 colleges, 563 teachers and 3,406 students.

Teacher Training (2008): 1 college, 37 teachers and 437 students.

Higher Education (2008): 3 institutes (incl. 1 university); 496 teachers and 4,021 students.

Pupil-teacher Ratio (primary education, UNESCO estimate): 11.9 in 2008/09. Source: UNESCO Institute for Statistics.

Adult Literacy Rate (UNESCO estimates): 95.3% (males 96.8%; females 93.7%) in 2009. Source: UNESCO Institute for Statistics.

Directory

The Constitution

Note: Certain sections of the Constitution relating to elections and the Legislative Council were in abeyance between 1962 and 2004.

A new Constitution was promulgated on 29 September 1959 (and amended significantly in 1971 and 1984). Under its provisions, sovereign authority is vested in the Sultan and Yang Di-Pertuan (Head of State), who is assisted and advised by five Councils: the Religious Council, the Privy Council, the Council of Cabinet Ministers, the Legislative Council and the Council of Succession. Power of appointment to the Councils is exercised by the Sultan.

The 1959 Constitution established the Chief Minister as the most senior official, with the British High Commissioner as adviser to the Government on all matters except those relating to Muslim and Malay customs.

In 1971 amendments were introduced reducing the power of the British Government, which retained responsibility for foreign affairs, while defence became the joint responsibility of both countries.

In 1984 further amendments were adopted as Brunei acceded to full independence and assumed responsibility for defence and foreign affairs.

In 2004 further amendments were approved by the newly reconvened Legislative Council, allowing for an expanded Council of 45 members, including 15 directly elected members.

THE RELIGIOUS COUNCIL

In his capacity as head of the Islamic faith in Brunei, the Sultan and Yang Di-Pertuan is advised on all Islamic matters by the Religious Council, whose members are appointed by the Sultan and Yang Di-Pertuan.

THE PRIVY COUNCIL

This Council, presided over by the Sultan and Yang Di-Pertuan, is to advise the Sultan on matters concerning the Royal prerogative of mercy, the amendment of the Constitution and the conferment of ranks, titles and honours.

THE COUNCIL OF CABINET MINISTERS

Presided over by the Sultan and Yang Di-Pertuan, the Council of Cabinet Ministers considers all executive matters.

THE LEGISLATIVE COUNCIL

The role of the Legislative Council is to scrutinize legislation. However, following political unrest in 1962, provisions of the Constitution relating, *inter alia*, to the Legislative Council were amended, and the Legislative Council did not meet between 1984 and 2004. In the absence of the Legislative Council, legislation is enacted by royal proclamation.

In July 2004 the Sultan announced that the Legislative Council would be reinstated by the end of that year. It was duly reconvened in September. Its 21 members were appointed by a governmental committee. However, the state of emergency that had been declared in 1962 was to remain in force and the Sultan was to continue to rule by decree.

In September 2005 the Sultan dissolved the existing Legislative Council and appointed a new Council comprising 29 members.

THE COUNCIL OF SUCCESSION

Subject to the Constitution, this Council is to determine the succession to the throne, should the need arise.

ADMINISTRATIVE DISTRICTS

The State is divided into four administrative districts, in each of which is a District Officer responsible to the Prime Minister and Minister of Home Affairs.

The Government

HEAD OF STATE

Sultan and Yang Di-Pertuan: HM Sultan Haji HASSANAL BOLKIAH (succeeded 5 October 1967; crowned 1 August 1968).

COUNCIL OF CABINET MINISTERS
(October 2011)

Prime Minister, Minister of Defence and of Finance: HM Sultan Haji HASSANAL BOLKIAH.

Senior Minister at the Prime Minister's Office: HRH Prince Haji AL-MUHTADEE BILLAH BOLKIAH.

Minister of Energy at the Prime Minister's Office: Pehin Dato' Haji Col (retd) MOHAMMAD YASMIN BIN Haji UMAR.

Minister of Foreign Affairs and Trade: HRH Prince Haji MOHAMED BOLKIAH.

Minister of Home Affairs: Pehin Dato' Haji BADARUDDIN BIN Haji OTHMAN.

Minister of Education: Pehin Dato' Haji ABU BAKAR BIN Haji APONG.

Minister of Industry and Primary Resources: Pehin Dato' Paduka Haji YAHYA BIN Haji BAKAR.

Minister of Religious Affairs: Pengiran Dato' Dr MOHAMMAD BIN Haji ABDUL RAHMAN.

Minister of Development: Pehin Dato' Paduka Haji SUYOI BIN Haji OSMAN.

Minister of Health: Pehin Dato' Haji ADANAN BIN Pehin Dato' Haji MOHAMMAD YUSOF.

Minister of Culture, Youth and Sports: Pehin Dato' Haji HAZAIR BIN Haji ABDULLAH.

Minister of Communications: Pehin Dato' Paduka Haji ABDULLAH BIN Haji BAKAR.

Minister of Finance II: Pehin Dato' Paduka Haji ABDULLAH RAHMAN BIN Haji IBRAHIM.

Minister of Foreign Affairs and Trade II: Pehin Dato' Seri Paduka LIM JOCK SENG.

MINISTRIES

Prime Minister's Office (Jabatan Perdana Menteri): Blk 2D, Ong Sum Ping Complex, Bandar Seri Begawan BA 1000; tel. 2223626; fax 2233743; e-mail info.jpm@jpm.gov.bn; internet www.jpm.gov.bn.

Ministry of Communications (Kementerian Perhubungan): Jalan Menteri Besar, Bandar Seri Begawan BB 3910; tel. 2383838; fax 2380127; e-mail info@mincom.gov.bn; internet www.mincom.gov.bn.

Ministry of Culture, Youth and Sports (Kementerian Kebudayaan, Belia dan Sukan): Simpang 336-17, Jalan Kebangsaan, Bandar Seri Begawan BA 1210; tel. 2382911; fax 2380652; e-mail info@kkbs.gov.bn; internet www.kkbs.gov.bn.

Ministry of Defence (Kementerian Pertahanan): Bolkiah Garrison, Bandar Seri Begawan BB 3510; tel. 2386352; fax 2382110; e-mail info@mindef.gov.bn; internet www.mindef.gov.bn.

Ministry of Development (Kementerian Pembangunan): Old Airport, Jalan Berakas, Bandar Seri Begawan BB 3510; tel. 2383222; fax 2380298; e-mail info@mod.gov.bn; internet www.mod.gov.bn.

Ministry of Education (Kementerian Pendidikan): Old Airport, Jalan Berakas, Bandar Seri Begawan BB 3510; tel. 2381133; fax 2380050; e-mail feedback@moe.edu.bn; internet www.moe.edu.bn.

Ministry of Energy: Office of the Prime Minister, Tingkat 5, Bahirah Bldg, Jalan Menteri Besar, Bandar Seri Begawan BB 3910; tel. 2384488; fax 2384444; e-mail energy@jpm.gov.bn; internet www.energy.gov.bn.

Ministry of Finance (Kementerian Kewangan): Tingkat 15, Bangunan Kementerian Kewangan, Commonwealth Dr., Jalan Kebangsaan, Bandar Seri Begawan BB 3910; tel. 2383950; fax 2226132; e-mail administration@mof.gov.bn; internet www.mof.gov.bn.

Ministry of Foreign Affairs and Trade (Kementerian Hal Ehwal Luar Negeri dan Perdagangan): Jalan Subok, Bandar Seri Begawan BD 2710; tel. 2261293; fax 2262904; e-mail info@mfa.gov.bn; internet www.mfa.gov.bn.

Ministry of Health (Kementerian Kesihatan): Jalan Menteri Besar, Commonwealth Dr., Bandar Seri Begawan BB 3910; tel. 2381640; fax 2381440; e-mail prohealth@moh.gov.bn; internet www.moh.gov.bn.

Ministry of Home Affairs (Kementerian Hal Ehwal Dalam Negeri): Jalan James Pearce, Bandar Seri Begawan BS 8610; tel. 2223225; fax 2241367; e-mail info@home-affairs.gov.bn; internet www.home-affairs.gov.bn.

Ministry of Industry and Primary Resources (Kementerian Perindustrian dan Sumber-sumber Utama): Jalan Menteri Besar, Bandar Seri Begawan BB 3910; tel. 2380599; fax 2382474; e-mail helpdesk@bruneimipr.gov.bn; internet www.bruneimipr.gov.bn.

Ministry of Religious Affairs (Kementerian Hal Ehwal Ugama): Jalan Menteri Besar, Jalan Berakas, Bandar Seri Begawan BB 3910; tel. 2382525; fax 2382330; e-mail info@religious-affairs.gov.bn; internet www.religious-affairs.gov.bn.

Legislature

THE LEGISLATIVE COUNCIL

In September 2005 the Sultan dissolved the existing Legislative Council and appointed a new Council comprising 29 members. The Council usually convenes annually, in March.

Speaker: Pehin ISA IBRAHIM.

Political Organizations

At mid-2011 there was only one legally registered political organization in Brunei.

Parti Pembangunan Bangsa (PPB) (National Development Party): Limbaruh Hijau, Simpang 323, Jalan Jerudong, Kampong Jerudong, Brunei Muara, BG 3122; tel. 2610703; fax 2610701; e-mail aspirasi@aspirasi-ndp.com; internet www.aspirasi-ndp.com; f. 2005; 2,000 mems; Pres. MALAI HASSAN OTHMAN (acting); Gen. Sec. Haji RAMLI.

Political organizations that have officially ceased activities include: Parti Rakyat Brunei (PRB—Brunei People's Party), banned in 1962 and leaders all exiled; Barisan Kemerdeka'an Rakyat (BAKER—People's Independence Front), f. 1966 but no longer active; Parti Perpaduan Kebangsaan Rakyat Brunei (PERKARA—Brunei People's National United Party), f. 1968 but no longer active; Parti Kebangsaan Demokratik Brunei (PKDB—Brunei National Democratic Party—BNDP), f. 1985 and dissolved by government order in 1988; Parti Kesedaran Rakyat (PAKAR—People's Consciousness Party), f. 2000 and subsequently split into two opposing factions, prior to being deregistered in 2007; and Parti Perpaduan Kebangsaan Brunei (PPKB—Brunei National Solidarity Party—BNSP), f. 1986 but deregistered in 2008.

Diplomatic Representation

EMBASSIES AND HIGH COMMISSIONS IN BRUNEI

Australia: Level 6, DAR Takaful IBB Utama, Jalan Pemancha, Bandar Seri Begawan BS 8711; tel. 2229435; fax 2221652; e-mail austhicom.brunei@dfat.gov.au; internet www.bruneidarussalam.embassy.gov.au; High Commissioner MARK SAWERS.

Bangladesh: 10 Simpang 83-20, Jalan Sungai Akar, Kampong Sungai Akar, Bandar Seri Begawan BC 3915; tel. 2342420; fax 2342421; e-mail bdoot@brunet.bn; internet www.hcbangladesh.org.bn; High Commissioner M. SHAMEEM AHSAN.

Cambodia: 7 Simpang 1444-14, Jalan Beribi, Gadong, Bandar Seri Begawan BE 1118; tel. 2426450; fax 2426452; e-mail cambodia@brunet.bn; Ambassador NAN SY.

Canada: 5th Floor, Jalan McArthur Bldg, 1 Jalan McArthur, Bandar Seri Begawan BS 8711; tel. 2220043; fax 2220040; e-mail bsbgn@international.gc.ca; internet www.canadainternational.gc.ca/brunei_darussalam; High Commissioner WENDELL SANFORD.

China, People's Republic: 1, 3 & 5 Simpang 462, Kampong Sungai Hanching, Jalan Muara, Bandar Seri Begawan BC 2115; tel. 2339609; fax 2335710; e-mail chinaemb_bn@mfa.gov.cn; internet bn.chineseembassy.org/eng; Ambassador MIN YONGNIAN.

France: Kompleks Jalan Sultan, Units 301–306, 3rd Floor, 51–55 Jalan Sultan, Bandar Seri Begawan BS 8811; tel. 2220960; fax 2243373; e-mail france@brunet.bn; internet www.ambafrance-bn.org; Ambassador LOUIS LE VERT.

Germany: Kompleks Yayasan Sultan Haji Hassanal Bolkiah, Blk A, 2nd Floor, Unit 2.01, Jalan Pretty, Bandar Seri Begawan BS 8711; tel. 2225547; fax 2225583; e-mail prgerman@brunet.bn; internet www.bandar-seri-begawan.diplo.de; Ambassador Dr THOMAS BRUNS.

India: Baitussyifaa, Simpang 40-22, Jalan Sungai Akar, Bandar Seri Begawan BC 3915; tel. 2339947; fax 2339783; e-mail hicomind@brunet.bn; internet www.hcindiabrunei.org.bn; High Commissioner LALDUHTHLANA RALTE.

Indonesia: Simpang 528, Lot 4498, Kampong Sungai Hanching Baru, Jalan Muara, Bandar Seri Begawan BC 2115; tel. 2330180; fax 2330646; e-mail kbribsb@brunet.bn; internet www.kemlu.go.id/bandarseribegawan; Ambassador HANDRIYO KUSUMO PRIYO.

Iran: 2 Jalan Dato Ratna, Kampong Kiarong BE 1318; tel. 2424873; fax 2424875; e-mail iranemb1@brunet.bn; Ambassador MOHAMMAD REZA HAVASELI ASTIANI.

Japan: 1 & 3 Jalan Jawatan Dalam, Lot 37355, 33 Simpang 122, Kampong Kiulap, Bandar Seri Begawan BE 1518; tel. 2229265; fax 2229481; e-mail embassy@japan.com.bn; internet www.bn.emb-japan.go.jp; Ambassador NORIKI HIROSE.

Korea, Republic: 17 Simpang 462, Kampong Hancing Baru, Jalan Muara, Bandar Seri Begawan BC 2115; tel. 2330248; fax 2330254; e-mail brunei@mofat.go.kr; internet brn.mofat.go.kr; Ambassador KIM DAE-SIK.

Kuwait: Lot 4144, 21 & 25 Simpang 40, Jalan Elia Fatimah, Kampong Kiarong, Gadong BE 1318; tel. 2457176; fax 2457179; e-mail kuwait@brunet.bn; Ambassador GHASSAN MOHAMMED ABDURRAHMAN AL-DUWAISAN.

Laos: 159 Simpang 336, Kampong Sungai Akar, Jalan Kebangsaan, Bandar Seri Begawan BB 4313; tel. 2384382; fax 2384381; e-mail laosemba@brunet.bn; Ambassador SOUVANNA PHOUYAVONG.

Malaysia: 61 Simpang 336, Jalan Kebangsaan, Kampong Sungai Akar, Bandar Seri Begawan BA 1211; tel. 2381095; fax 2381278; e-mail malbrnei@kln.gov.my; internet www.kln.gov.my/perwakilan/seribegawan; High Commissioner Dato' ABDULLAH SANI BIN OMAR.

Myanmar: 14 Lot 2185/46292, Simpang 212, Jalan Kampong Rimba, Gadong, Bandar Seri Begawan BE 3119; tel. 2451960; fax 2451963; e-mail myanmar@brunet.bn; Ambassador THURA THET OO MUANG.

Oman: 35 Simpang 100, Kampong Pengkalan, Jalan Tungku Link, Gadong, Bandar Seri Begawan BE 3719; tel. 2446953; fax 2446956; e-mail omnembsb@brunet.bn; Ambassador SAYYID FAKHRI MOHAMMED AL-SAID.

Pakistan: 8 Simpang 31, Jalan Bunga Jasmine, Kampong Beribi, Gadong, Bandar Seri Begawan BE 1118; tel. 2424600; fax 2424606; e-mail hcpak@brunet.bn; internet www.mofa.gov.pk/brunei; High Commissioner (vacant).

Philippines: 17 Simpang 126, Km 2, Jalan Tutong, Bandar Seri Begawan BA 2111; tel. 2241465; fax 2237707; e-mail bruneipe@brunet.bn; internet www.philippineembassybrunei.net; Ambassador NESTOR Z. OCHOA.

Qatar: Lot 188897, Simpang 898, Kampong Jangsak, Gadong, Bandar Seri Begawan; tel. 2447777; fax 2443333; Chargé d'affaires AHMAD IBRAHIM AL-ABDULLAH.

Russia: The Holiday Lodge Hotel, 97192, Kampong Jerudong, Jalan Palau Kubu, Bandar Seri Begawan; tel. 2611413; fax 2411424; e-mail ruembr@yandex.ru; Ambassador VIKTOR A. SELEZNEZ.

Saudi Arabia: 1 Simpang 570, Jalan Muara, Kampong Salar, Bandar Seri Begawan BU 1429; tel. 2792821; fax 2792826; e-mail saudibru@brunet.bn; Ambassador MOHAMMED JAMIL ABDUL JALEEL HASHIM.

Singapore: 8 Simpang 74, Jalan Subok, Bandar Seri Begawan; tel. 2262741; fax 2262752; e-mail singhc_bwn@sgmfa.gov.sg; internet www.mfa.gov.sg/brunei; High Commissioner JOSEPH K. H. KOH.

Thailand: 2 Simpang 682, Jalan Tutong, Kampong Bunut, Bandar Seri Begawan BF 1320; tel. 2653108; fax 2653032; e-mail thaiemb@brunet.bn; Chargé d'affaires THAWAT SUMITMOR.

United Kingdom: Kompleks Yayasan Sultan Haji Hassanal Bolkiah, Blk D, 2nd Floor, Unit 2.01, Bandar Seri Begawan BS 8711; tel. 2222231; fax 2234315; e-mail brithc@brunet.bn; internet ukinbrunei.fco.gov.uk; High Commissioner ROBERT FENN.

USA: Simpang 336-52-16-9, Jalan Kebangsaan, Bandar Seri Begawan; tel. 2384616; fax 2384606; e-mail amembassy_bsb@state.gov; internet brunei.usembassy.gov; Ambassador DANIEL L. SHIELDS, III.

Viet Nam: 9 Simpang 148-3, Jalan Telanai, Bandar Seri Begawan BA 2312; tel. 2651580; fax 2651574; e-mail vnembassy@yahoo.com; internet www.vietnamembassy-brunei.org; Ambassador PHAM BINH MAN.

Judicial System

SUPREME COURT

The Supreme Court consists of the Court of Appeal and the High Court. Syariah (*Shari'a*) courts coexist with the Supreme Court and deal with Islamic laws.

Office of the Supreme Court

Km 11/2, Jalan Tutong, Bandar Seri Begawan BA 1910; tel. 2243939; fax 2241984; e-mail judiciarybn@hotmail.com; internet www.judicial.gov.bn.

Chief Registrar: Haji ROSTAINA Pengiran Haji DURAMAN.

The Court of Appeal

Composed of the President and two Commissioners appointed by the Sultan. The Court of Appeal considers criminal and civil appeals against the decisions of the High Court and the Intermediate Court. The Court of Appeal is the highest appellate court for criminal cases. In civil cases an appeal may be referred to the Judicial Committee of Her Majesty's Privy Council in London if all parties agree to do so before the hearing of the appeal in the Brunei Court of Appeal.

President: JOHN BARRY MORTIMER.

The High Court

Composed of the Chief Justice and judges sworn in by the Sultan as Commissioners of the Supreme Court. In its appellate jurisdiction, the High Court considers appeals in criminal and civil matters against the decisions of the Subordinate Courts. The High Court has unlimited original jurisdiction in criminal and civil matters.

Chief Justice: Dato' Seri Paduka Haji KIFRAWI KIFLI.

OTHER COURTS

Intermediate Courts: have jurisdiction to try all offences other than those punishable by the death sentence and civil jurisdiction to try all actions and suits of a civil nature where the amount in dispute or value of the subject/matter does not exceed B $100,000.

The Subordinate Courts

Presided over by the Chief Magistrate and magistrates, with limited original jurisdiction in civil and criminal matters and civil jurisdiction to try all actions and suits of a civil nature where the amount in dispute does not exceed B $50,000 (for Chief Magistrate) and B $30,000 (for magistrates).

Chief Magistrate: ABDULLAH SOEFRI BIN Pengiran Haji ABIDIN.

The Courts of Kathis

Deal solely with questions concerning Islamic religion, marriage and divorce. Appeals lie from these courts to the Sultan in the Religious Council.

Chief Kathi: Dato' Seri Setia Haji SALIM BIN Haji BESAR.

Attorney-General: Datin Paduka Hajah HAYATI Dato' Seri Paduka Haji MOHD SALLEH, Attorney-General's Chambers, The Law Bldg, Km 1, Jalan Tutong, Bandar Seri Begawan BA 1910; tel. 2244872; fax 2223100; e-mail info@agc.gov.bn; internet www.agc.gov.bn.

Solicitor-General: Datin Paduka MAGDALENE CHONG.

Religion

The official religion of Brunei is Islam, and the Sultan is head of the Islamic community. The majority of the Malay population are Muslims of the Shafi'is school of the Sunni sect; at the 1991 census Muslims accounted for 67.2% of the total population. The Chinese population is either Buddhist (accounting for 12.8% of the total population at the 1991 census), Confucianist, Daoist or Christian. Large numbers of the indigenous ethnic groups practise traditional animist forms of religion. The remainder of the population are mostly Christians, generally Roman Catholics, Anglicans or members of the American Methodist Church of Southern Asia. At the 1991 census Christians accounted for 10.0% of the total population.

ISLAM

Supreme Head of Islam: HM Sultan Haji HASSANAL BOLKIAH (Sultan and Yang Di-Pertuan).

CHRISTIANITY

The Anglican Communion

Within the Church of the Province of South East Asia, Brunei forms part of the diocese of Kuching (Malaysia).

The Roman Catholic Church

Brunei comprises a single apostolic vicariate. At 31 December 2007 there were an estimated 18,427 adherents in the country, equivalent to 5.0% of the population.

Prefect Apostolic: Rev. CORNELIUS SIM, Church of Our Lady of the Assumption, Jalan Kumbang Pasang, Bandar Seri Begawan BS 8670; tel. 2222261; fax 2238938; e-mail frcsim@brunet.bn.

The Press

NEWSPAPERS

Borneo Bulletin: Locked Bag No. 2, MPC (Old Airport, Berakas), Bandar Seri Begawan BB 3510; tel. 2451468; fax 2451461; e-mail borneobulletin@brunet.bn; internet www.brunet.bn/news/bb; f. 1953; daily; English; independent; owned by QAF Group; Editor-in-Chief CHARLES REX DE SILVA; circ. 20,000 (weekdays), 25,000 (Sat.), 20,000 (Sun.).

Brunei Darussalam Newsletter: Dept of Information, Prime Minister's Office, Istana Nurul Iman, Berakas, Bandar Seri Begawan BB 3510; tel. 2383400; fax 2382012; e-mail bd.newsletter@information.gov.bn; internet www.information.gov.bn/bdnewsletter; monthly; English; govt newspaper; distributed free; Editor SASTRA SARINI BINTI Haji JULAINI; circ. 3,000.

The Brunei Times: Wisma Haji Mohd Taha, 3rd Floor, Jalan Gadong, Bandar Seri Begawan BE 4119; tel. 2428333; fax 2454752; e-mail theeditor@bruneitimes.com.bn; internet www.bruneitimes.com; f. 2006; daily; English; Editor-in-Chief Haji BUJANG BIN MASU'UT.

Daily News Digest: Dept of Information, Prime Minister's Office, Istana Nurul Iman, Bandar Seri Begawan BA 1000; English; govt newspaper.

Media Permata: Locked Bag No. 2, MPC (Old Airport, Berakas), Bandar Seri Begawan BB 3510; tel. 2451468; fax 2451461; e-mail mediapermata@brunet.bn; internet www.brunei-online.com/mp; f. 1995; daily (not Sun.); Malay; owned by QAF Group; Editor MUHAMMAD NOOR; circ. 10,000.

Pelita Brunei: Dept of Information, Prime Minister's Office, Old Airport, Berakas, Bandar Seri Begawan BB 3510; tel. 2383941; fax 2381004; e-mail e.pelita@yahoo.com; internet www.pelitabrunei.gov.bn; f. 1956; 3 a week (Mon., Wed. and Sat.); Malay; govt newspaper; distributed free; Editor Haji JAAFAR BIN Haji IBRAHIM; circ. 27,500.

Salam: c/o Brunei Shell Petroleum Co Sdn Bhd, Jalan Utara, Panaga, Seria KB 3534; tel. 3374184; fax 3374189; e-mail editorial@shell.com; internet www.bsp.com.bn/main/mediacentre/publications.asp; f. 1953; monthly; Malay and English; distributed free to employees and shareholders of the Brunei Shell Petroleum Co Sdn Bhd; Editor JUSTIN JAAPAR; circ. 46,000.

Publishers

Borneo Printers & Trading Sdn Bhd: POB 2211, Bandar Seri Begawan BS 8674; tel. 2651387; fax 2654342; e-mail bptl@brunet.bn.

Brunei Press Sdn Bhd: Lots 8 & 11, Perindustrian Beribi II, Jalan Gadong, Bandar Seri Begawan BE 1118; tel. 2451468; fax 2451462; e-mail brupress@brunet.bn; internet www.bruneipress.com.bn; f. 1953; Gen. Man. REGGIE SEE.

Capital Trading & Printing Pte Ltd: POB 1089, Bandar Seri Begawan; tel. 2244541.

Leong Bros: 52 Jalan Bunga Kuning, POB 164, Seria; tel. 322381.

Offset Printing House: Lot Q37, 4 Simpang 5, Lambak Kanan Industrial Area, Berakas, Bandar Seri Begawan BB 1714; tel. 2390797; fax 2390798; e-mail offset@brunei.bn; f. 1980; Gen. Man. KENNY TEO.

GOVERNMENT PUBLISHING HOUSES

Dewan Bahasa dan Pustaka (Language and Literature Bureau): c/o Ministry of Culture Youth and Sports, Berakas BB 3510; tel. 2382511; fax 2381817; e-mail pengarahdbp@brunet.bn; internet www.dbp.gov.bn; f. 1961; publs incl. children's books, textbooks, novels, poetry and translations of foreign works; promotion and preservation of Malayan literature and folklore; library services; Dir-Gen. Datuk TERMUZI ABDUL AZIZ.

Jabatan Percetakan Kerajaan (Government Printing Dept): Prime Minister's Office, Bandar Seri Begawan BB 3510; tel. 2382541; fax 2381141; e-mail info@printing.gov.bn; internet www.printing.gov.bn; f. 1975; Dir Haji DAUD BIN Haji AHMAD.

Broadcasting and Communications

TELECOMMUNICATIONS

Authority for Info-Communications Technology Industry (AITI): Blk B14, Simpang 32–35, Kampong Anggrek Desa, Jalan Berakas, Bandar Seri Begawan BB 3713; tel. 2323232; fax 2382447; e-mail info@aiti.gov.bn; internet www.aiti.gov.bn; f. 2003; assumed responsibility for regulating and representing telecommunications industry following corporatization of Dept of Telecommunications of Brunei in April 2006; also entrusted with devt of ICT industry; Chair. ALAIHUDDIN BIN Haji MOHAMMED TAHA.

B-Mobile Communications Sdn Bhd (b-mobile): Old Airport, Berakas, Bandar Seri Begawan BB 3510; tel. 2221010; fax 2384040; e-mail contact@bmobile.com.bn; internet www.bmobile.com.bn; f. 2005; 3G mobile service provider; jt venture between Telekom Brunei Bhd (TelBru) and QAF Comserve.

DST Communications Sdn Bhd: Jalan Tungku Link, Bandar Seri Begawan BE 3619; tel. 2410888; fax 2410142; e-mail dstmarketing@simpur.net.bn; internet www.dst-group.com/dstcom; mobile and internet broadband services provider; mem. of DST Group; signed agreement with Alcatel in 2003 to improve provision of mobile services in Brunei; Chief Operating Officer (DST Group) Haji MARSAD BIN Haji ISMAIL.

Telekom Brunei Bhd (TelBru): Jalan Lapangan Terbang Lama, Berakas, Bandar Seri Begawan BB 3510; tel. 2321321; fax 2382444; e-mail info@telbru.com.bn; internet www.telbru.com.bn; fmrly Jabatan Telekom Brunei (Dept of Telecommunications of Brunei); name changed as above upon corporatization in April 2006; telecommunications services provider; Chair. Dato' Paduka Haji OTHMAN BIN Haji YAAKUB; Man. Dir SONG KIN KOI.

BROADCASTING

Radio

KRISTALfm: Jalan Tungku Link, Bandar Seri Begawan BE 3619; tel. 2410888; fax 2411788; e-mail kristalfm@dst-group.com; internet simpur.net.bn/kristalfm; f. 1999; subsidiary of Kristal Media Sdn Bhd; mem. of DST Group; two networks; Malay and English.

Radio Televisyen Brunei (RTB): Prime Minister's Office, Jalan Elizabeth II, Bandar Seri Begawan BS 8610; tel. 2243111; fax 2241882; e-mail gts@rtb.gov.bn; internet www.rtb.gov.bn; f. 1975; five radio networks; Malay, Chinese (Mandarin), English and Arabic;

also broadcasts on the internet; Dir Haji IDRIS BIN Haji MUHAMMAD ALI (acting).

Television

Kristal Astro Sdn Bhd: Unit 1-345, 1st Floor, Gadong Properties Centre, Gadong, Bandar Seri Begawan BE 4119; tel. 2456828; fax 2420682; f. 2000; jt venture between Kristal Sdn Bhd and Malaysian Measat Broadcast Network Systems Sdn Bhd; provides more than 30 digital satellite subscription channels.

Kristal TV: DST Network Sdn Bhd, Unit 1-345, 1st Floor, Gadong Properties Centre, Gadong, Bandar Seri Begawan BE 4119; tel. 2456828; fax 2420682; f. 1999; 14 TV channels.

Radio Televisyen Brunei (RTB): Prime Minister's Office, Jalan Elizabeth II, Bandar Seri Begawan BS 8610; tel. 2243111; fax 2241882; e-mail director@rtb.gov.bn; internet www.rtb.gov.bn; f. 1975; five TV channels; five radio channels; Dir Haji IDRIS BIN Haji MUHAMMAD ALI (acting).

Finance

(cap. = capital; res = reserves; dep. = deposits; brs = branches; amounts in Brunei dollars unless otherwise stated)

BANKING

In 2008 there were 11 banks in operation, including six foreign and two 'offshore' banks. In January 2011 the Monetary Authority of Brunei Darussalam formally assumed responsibility for the functions of the Brunei Currency and Monetary Board.

Autoriti Monetari Brunei Darussalam (AMBD) (Monetary Authority of Brunei Darussalam): Bandar Seri Begawan; f. 2011; performs functions of central bank; responsible for monetary policy, supervision of financial institutions and currency management; Chair. HRH Prince Haji AL-MUHTADEE BILLAH BOLKIAH; Man. Dir Haji MOHD ROSLI bin Haji SABTU.

Commercial Banks

Baiduri Bank Bhd: Blk A, Units 1–4, Kiarong Complex, Lebuhraya Sultan Hassanal Bolkiah, Bandar Seri Begawan BE 1318; tel. 2268300; fax 2455599; e-mail bank@baiduri.com; internet www.baiduri.com; f. 1994; cap. 100m., res 14.8m., dep. 1,795.5m. (Dec. 2008); Chair. Pengiran Anak ISTERI Pengiran Anak Hajjah ZARIAH; Gen. Man. PIERRE IMHOF; 11 brs.

Bank Islam Brunei Darussalam: Lot 159, Bangunan IBB, Jalan Pemancha, POB 2725, Bandar Seri Begawan BS 8711; tel. 2235687; fax 2235722; internet www.bibd.com.bn; f. 1981; est. as Island Devt Bank; fmrly Islamic Bank of Brunei; merged with Islamic Devt Bank of Brunei Bhd in 2006; practises Islamic banking principles; Chair. Dato' Seri Setia Haji ABDULLAH BIN BEGAWAN MUDIM Dato' Paduka Haji BAKAR; Man. Dir JAVED AHMED (acting); 14 brs.

Foreign Banks

Citibank NA (USA): Darussalam Complex, 12–15 Jalan Sultan, Bandar Seri Begawan BS 8811; tel. 2243983; fax 2237344; e-mail glen.rase@citi.com; Country Head GLEN RASE; 2 brs.

The Hongkong and Shanghai Banking Corpn Ltd (HSBC) (Hong Kong): Jalan Sultan, cnr Jalan Pemancha, Bandar Seri Begawan BS 8670; tel. 2252252; fax 2241316; e-mail hsbc@hsbc.com.bn; internet www.hsbc.com.bn; f. 1947acquired assets of Nat. Bank of Brunei in 1986; CEO TAREQ MUHMOOD; 10 brs.

Maybank (Malaysia): 1 Jalan McArthur, Bandar Seri Begawan BS 8711; tel. 2242494; fax 2225404; e-mail maybank@brunet.bn; f. 1960; Country Man. GEOFFREY LIM CHEE TIONG; 3 brs.

RHB Bank Bhd (Malaysia): Kompleks Yayasan Sultan Haji Hassanal Bolkiah, Blk D, Unit G.02, Jalan Pretty, Bandar Seri Begawan BS 8711; tel. 2222515; fax 2237487; e-mail apandi_klompot@rhbbank.com.myfmrly Sime Bank Bhd; Country Man. APANDI BIN KLOMPOT; 1 br.

Standard Chartered Bank (United Kingdom): Kompleks Jalan Sultan, 1st Floor, 51–55 Jalan Sultan, POB 186, Bandar Seri Begawan BS 8811; tel. 2228400; fax 2220103; e-mail scb.brunei@bn.standardchartered.com; internet www.standardchartered.com/bn; f. 1958; CEO TIEW SIEW CHUEN; 7 brs.

United Overseas Bank Ltd (Singapore): Units 10–11, Bangunan D'Amin Jaya, Lot 54989, Kampong Kiarong, Bandar Seri Begawan BE 1318; tel. 2225477; fax 2240792; f. 1973; Gen. Man. GEORGE LAI TED MIN; 2 brs.

'Offshore' Banks

The Brunei International Financial Centre (BIFC—see Government Agencies), under the Ministry of Finance, supervises the activities of the 'offshore' banking sector in Brunei.

Royal Bank of Canada: 1 Jalan McArthur, 4th Floor, Unit 4A, Bandar Seri Begawan BS 8711; tel. 2224366; fax 2224368; Gen. Man. SUHAILA KANI.

Sun Hung Kai International Bank (Brunei) Ltd (Hong Kong): Bandar Seri Begawan; e-mail cs@shkf.com; f. 2004; Dir PAK HUNG MAK.

STOCK EXCHANGE

International Brunei Exchange Ltd (IBX): The Empire, Muara-Tutong Highway, Jerudong BG 3122; tel. 2611222; fax 2611020; e-mail info@ibx.com.bn; f. 2001; CEO B. C. YONG.

INSURANCE

General Companies

Audley Insurance Co Sdn Bhd: Ministry of Finance Bldg, 9th Floor, Commonwealth Dr., Jalan Kebangsaan, Bandar Seri Begawan BB 3910; tel. 2383535; fax 2383548; e-mail audley@bia.com.bn; Man. Dir Datuk HAJAH UMI SALAMAH Haji ISMAIL.

Etiqa Insurance Bhd: B7, Ground Floor, Shakirin Kompleks, Kampong Kiulap, Bandar Seri Begawan BE 1518; tel. 2443393; fax 2427451; e-mail tsangpy@brunet.bn; fmrly known as Malaysia National Insurance Bhd; Man. TSANG POH YEE.

MBA Insurance Sdn Bhd: First Floor, Units 15–17, Lot 9784, Bangunan Haji Hassan Abdullah, Kampong Menglait, Jalan Gadong, Bandar Seri Begawan BE 3978; tel. 2441535; fax 2441534; e-mail mbabrunei@brunet.bn; Gen. Man. SHIM WEI HSUING.

Mitsui Sumitomo Insurance (Malaysia) Bhd: Unit 311, 3rd Floor, Kompleks Mohamad Yussof, Km 4, Jalan Tutong, Bandar Seri Begawan; tel. 2223632; fax 2220965; Sr Exec. DAVID ENG.

National Insurance Co Bhd: Units 12 and 13, Blk A, Regent Sq., Simpang 150, Kampong Kiarong BE1318; tel. 2226222; fax 2429888; e-mail insurance@national.com.bn; internet www.national.com.bn; f. 1969; Gen. Man. KOLJA KLAWUNN.

South East Asia Insurance (B) Sdn Bhd: Unit 2, Blk A, Abdul Razak Complex, 1st Floor, Jalan Gadong, Bandar Seri Begawan BE 3919; tel. 2443842; fax 2420860; Gen. Man. SHIM WEI HSIUNG.

Standard Insurance (B) Sdn Bhd: 2 Bangunan Hasbullah I, Ground Floor, Bandar Seri Begawan BE 3719; tel. 2450077; fax 2450076; e-mail feedback@standard-ins.com; internet www.standard-ins.com; Man. PAUL KONG.

Tokio Marine Insurance Singapore Ltd: Unit A1 & A2, 1st Floor, Blk A, Bangunan Hau Man Yong, Simpang 88, Kampong Kiulap, Bandar Seri Begawan BE 1518; tel. 2236100; fax 2236102; e-mail davidwong@tmasiainsurance.com; f. 1929; Br. Man. DAVID WONG KOK MIN.

Life Companies

American International Assurance Co Ltd: Unit 509, Wisma Jaya Bldg, 5th Floor, 85–94 Jalan Pemancha, Bandar Seri Begawan BS 8811; tel. 2239112; fax 2221667; e-mail Kenneth-WC.Ling@aia.com; Gen. Man. PETER LIM.

The Great Eastern Life Assurance Co Ltd: Unit 18, Blk B, Bangunan Habza Simpang 150, Kampong Kiarong, Bandar Seri Begawan BA 1318; tel. 2233118; fax 2238118; e-mail helenyeo@lifeisgreat.com.bn; Man. HELEN YEO.

TM Asia Life Singapore Ltd: Unit 2, 1st Floor, Blk D, Abdul Razak Complex, Jalan Gadong, Bandar Seri Begawan BE 4119; tel. 2423755; fax 2423754; e-mail tmasialife@brunet.bn; fmrly Asia Life Assurance Society Ltd; Br. Man. JOSEPH WONG SIONG LION.

Takaful (Composite Insurance) Companies

Insurans Islam TAIB Sdn Bhd: Perbadanan TAIB, Jalan Sultan, Bandar Seri Begawan BS 8811; tel. 2232222; fax 2237729; e-mail ict@insuranstaib.com.bn; internet www.insuranstaib.com.bn; f. 1993; provides Islamic insurance products and services; Gen. Man. OSMAN MOHAMAD JAIR.

Takaful Bank Pembangunan Islam Sdn Bhd (TBPISB): Unit 10, Komplex Seri Kiulap, Kampong Kiulap, Gadong, Bandar Seri Begawan BE 1518; tel. 2237220; fax 2237045; internet www.takafulbpisb.com; f. 2001; fmrly Takaful IDBB Sdn Bhd; name changed as above in 2003; Islamic life and non-life insurance products; Chair. Pehin Dato' Haji AHMAD WALLY SKINNER; Man. Dir Haji AISHATUL AKMAR SIDEK.

Takaful IBB Bhd: Levels 2 & 7–8, Dar Takaful IBB Utama, Jalan Pemancha, Bandar Seri Begawan BS 8711; tel. 2239338; fax 2451808; e-mail takaful@brunet.bn; f. 1993; Chair. Pehin Dato' Haji ABU BAKAR BIN Haji APONG DAUD.

Insurance Association

General Insurance Association of Negara Brunei Darussalam (GIAB): Unit C2-2, Blk C, Shakirin Complex, Kampong Kiulap, Bandar Seri Begawan BE 1518; tel. 2237898; fax 2237858; e-mail giab@brunet.bn; internet www.giab.com.bn; f. 1986; 15 mems; Chair. HELEN YEO.

Trade and Industry

GOVERNMENT AGENCIES

Brunei International Financial Centre (BIFC): Tingkat 14, Ministry of Finance, Commonwealth Dr., Jalan Kebangsaan, Bandar Seri Begawan BB 3910; tel. 2383747; fax 2383787; e-mail bifc@mof.gov.bn; internet www.mof.gov.bn/english/bifc; f. 2000; regulates international financial sector and encourages devt of Brunei as investment destination; Dir MOHAMED ROSLI SABTU.

Brunei Investment Agency (BIA): Tingkat 11, Bangunan Kementerian Kewangan, Commonwealth Dr., Jalan Kebangsaan, Bandar Seri Begawan BB 3910; tel. 2383535; fax 2383539; e-mail dramin.abdullah@bia.com.bn; f. 1983; Chair. Pehin Dato' Haji ABU BAKAR BIN Haji APONG; Man. Dir Haji MOHAMMAD AMIN LIEW ABDULLAH.

DEVELOPMENT ORGANIZATIONS

Brunei Economic Development Board (BEDB): Blk 2K, Bangunan Kerajaan, Jalan Ong Sum Ping, Bandar Seri Begawan, BA 1311; tel. 2230111; fax 2230063; e-mail info@bedb.com.bn; internet www.bedb.com.bn; f. 2001; promotes Brunei as an investment destination; facilitates and assists industrial devt; under control of Prime Minister's Office since late 2010; Chair. Dato' Paduka Haji ALI Haji BIN APONG; CEO Dato' Paduka VINCENT CHEONG.

Brunei Industrial Development Authority (BINA): Ministry of Industry and Primary Resources, Km 8, Jalan Gadong, Bandar Seri Begawan BE 1118; tel. 2444100; fax 2423300; e-mail bruneibina@brunet.bn; internet www.bina.gov.bn; f. 1996; Dir Pengiran SHARIFUDDIN BIN Pengiran Haji METALI.

Brunei Islamic Trust Fund (Tabung Amanah Islam Brunei): Bangunan Kewangaan Utama, Jalan Sultan, Bandar Seri Begawan BS 8811; tel. 2232222; fax 2240316; e-mail administration@taib.com.bn; internet www.taib.com.bn; f. 1991; promotes trade and industry; Chair. Dato' Paduka Dr Haji MAT SUNY Haji MUHAMMAD HUSSEIN.

Semaun Holdings Sdn Bhd: Unit 10, Blk B, Warisan Mata-Mata Complex, Kampong Mata-Mata, Gadong, Bandar Seri Begawan BE 1718; tel. 2456064; fax 2456070; e-mail semaun@brunet.bn; internet www.semaunholdings.com; f. 1994; promotes industrial and commercial devt through direct investment in key industrial sectors; 100% govt-owned; bd of dirs is composed of ministers and senior govt officials; chaired by Minister of Industry and Primary Resources; Man. Dir Hajah ASMAH Binti Haji SAMAN.

CHAMBERS OF COMMERCE

Brunei Darussalam International Chamber of Commerce and Industry: Unit 401–403A, 4th Floor, Wisma Jaya, Jalan Pemancha, Bandar Seri Begawan BS 8811; tel. 2236601; fax 2228389; Chair. Haji AHMAD BIN Haji ISA; Sec. Haji SHAZALI BIN Dato' Haji SULAIMAN; 30 mems.

Brunei Malay Chamber of Commerce and Industry: Suite 301, 2nd Floor, Bangunan Guru-Guru Melayu Brunei, Jalan Kianggehi, Bandar Seri Begawan 1910; tel. 2227297; fax 2227278; f. 1964; Pres. Haji RAZALI BIN Haji JOHARI; 160 mems.

Chinese Chamber of Commerce: Chinese Chamber of Commerce Bldg, 4th Floor, 72 Jalan Roberts, Bandar Seri Begawan BS 8711; tel. 2235494; fax 2235493; e-mail ccc@brunet.bn; Pres. Dr CHAN SUI KIAT.

Indian Chamber of Commerce: Unit 13–15, Blk B, Delima Jaya Complex, Kampong Serusop, Jalan Muara, Bandar Seri Begawan BB 2313; tel. and fax 2340972; fax 2340976; Pres. NAZEER AHMAD.

National Chamber of Commerce and Industry of Brunei Darussalam (NCCIBD): Unit 1, Blk D, Beribi Industrial Complex 1, Jalan Gadong, Bandar Seri Begawan BE 1118; tel. 2421840; fax 2421839; e-mail nccibd@brunet.bn; internet www.nccibd.com; Pres. Haji RAZALI BIN Haji JOHARI; Sec.-Gen. Haji ABDUL SAMAN AHMAD.

STATE HYDROCARBON COMPANIES

Brunei LNG Sdn Bhd (BLNG): Lumut, Seria KC 2935; tel. 3236901; fax 3236892; e-mail enquiry@bruneilng.com; internet www.blng.com.bn; f. 1969; natural gas liquefaction; owned jtly by the Brunei Govt (50%), Shell and Mitsubishi Corpn; operates LNG plant at Lumut, which has a capacity of 7.2m. metric tons per year; Man. Dir and CEO Haji SALLEH BOSTAMAN Haji ZAINAL ABIDIN.

Brunei National Petroleum Co Sdn Bhd (PetroleumBrunei): Unit 1.01, 1st Floor, Blk D, Kompleks Yayasan Sultan Haji Hassanal Bolkiah, Jalan Pretty, Bandar Seri Begawan BS 8711; tel. 2230720; fax 2230654; e-mail pb@pb.com.bn; internet www.pb.com.bn; f. 2001; wholly govt-owned; CEO MOHAMMED JA'AFAR BIN Haji BAKAR.

Brunei Shell Marketing Co Bhd: Ground & 12th Floor, PGGMB Bldg, Jalan Kianggeh, Bandar Seri Begawan BS 8811; tel. 2229304; fax 2240470; e-mail edyzurina.awang@shell.com; internet www.bsm.com.bn; f. 1978; est. from Shell Marketing Co of Brunei Ltd as jt venture between Shell and the Bruneian Govt; markets petroleum and chemical products throughout Brunei; Man. Dir MAT SUNY Haji MOHD HUSSEIN.

Brunei Shell Petroleum Co Sdn Bhd (BSP): Jalan Utara, Panagia, Seria KB 3534; tel. 3373999; fax 3372040; internet www.bsp.com.bn; f. 1957; the largest industrial concern in the country; 50% state holding; Man. Dir GRAHAEME HENDERSON.

Jasra International Petroleum Sdn Bhd: RBA Plaza, 2nd Floor, Jalan Sultan, Bandar Seri Begawan; tel. 2228968; fax 2228929; petroleum exploration and production; Man. Dir ROBERT A. HARRISON.

MAJOR COMPANIES

Ath Garments Sdn Bhd: Simpang 245, Plot 18, Serambangan Industrial Estate, Tutong TA 1141; tel. 4261383; fax 4261390; e-mail athgmt_gm@brunet.bn; f. 1998; mfr of textiles and garments; Man. Dir Hajah SAADATENA A. BAKAR; 879 employees.

BlueScope Lysaght (B) Sdn Bhd: Industrial Complex, Beribi, Phase 1, 6 Km, Jalan Gadong, Bandar Seri Begawan BE 1118; tel. 2447155; fax 2447154; e-mail bluescope@brunet.bn; f. 1993; fmrly BHP Steel Lysaght (B) Sdn Bhd; supplier of steel building solutions; CEO SANJAY DAYAL.

Brunei Methanol Company Sdn Bhd: Sungai Liang Industrial Park, Kampong Sungai Liang Daerah Belait KC 1135; tel. 3229300; fax 3230890; e-mail enquiries@brunei-methanol.com; internet www.brunei-methanol.com; f. 2006; jt venture est. by Brunei Nat. Petroleum Co (50%), Mitsubishi Gas Chemical Co (25%) and Itochu Corpn (25%); CEO KINYA TSUJI; 170 employees.

Brunei Oxygen Sdn Bhd: Lot 5761, Tapak Perindustrian, Pekan Belait, Kuala Belait KA 3131; tel. 3332861; fax 3333466; e-mail qaf@brunet.com; internet www.qaf-brunei.com.bn/industrial/brunox.htm; f. 1962; owned by QAF Brunei Sdn Bhd; mfr of industrial gases; Gen. Man. CHRISTOPHER LEE TIAN YAU.

Butra HeidelbergCement Sdn Bhd (Brunei Cement): Lot 3, Serasa Industrial Area, POB 153, Muara BT 1128; tel. 2771395; fax 2771404; e-mail bhz@bruneicement.com; internet www.bruneicement.com; f. 1993; jt venture between local co Butra and the international Heidelberg Cement Group; mfr and distributor of cement; cap. and res B $30m. (1999); Man. Dir JEAN-CLAUDE JAMAR; 115 employees.

Hunt Concrete Industries Sdn Bhd: Rm 302, 1st Floor, Blk C, Chandrawaseh Complex, Mile 1, Jalan Tutong, Bandar Seri Begawan; tel. 2229249; fax 2226596; e-mail hunt@brunet.bn; f. 1983; Chair. LIM MING SIONG; Man. Dir KOH MING SHAM; 180 employees.

Jati Freedom Textile Sdn Bhd: Jalan Perusahaan, Simpang 15, Pekan Muara, Muara Negara BT 1728; tel. 2770010; fax 2770017; e-mail jatiinvest@brunet.bn; f. 1988; mfr of garments; Station Man. ALICE LEE; 420 employees.

Mulaut Abattoir Sdn Bhd: Lot 20354, Jalan Mulaut Kilanas, Sengkurong BG 1121; tel. 2670678; fax 2670800; f. 1990; supply and marketing of livestock and meat products; Chair. Haji ABDUL RAHMAN BIN Haji KASIM; 100 employees.

QAF Brunei Sdn Bhd: QAF Centre, Lot 65–66, Perindustrial Beribi II, Bandar Seri Begawan BE 1118; tel. 2453388; fax 2452152; e-mail qaf@brunet.com; internet www.qaf-brunei.com.bn; f. 1982; investment holding co with interests in wholesale and retail trade, investment, engineering, offshore services and publishing; subsidiary of Baiduri Holdings Bhd; Chair. HRH Pengiran Anak ISTERI Pengiran Anak Haji ZARIAH; CEO HRH Prince ABDUL QAWI.

Supercrete Sdn Bhd: Supercrete Complex, LTS 42/92, Simpang 99, Bengkurong, Bandar Seri Begawan BF 1920; tel. 2654744; fax 2654731; e-mail firstmix@brunet.bn; internet www.supercretebrunei.com; f. 1978; incorporated in 1995; mfr and supplier of pre-mixed concrete; Dir WONG NYEN FOOK.

VSL Systems (N) Sdn Bhd: POB 291, MPC-Old Airport, Bandar Seri Begawan BB 3577; tel. 2380153; fax 2381954; e-mail vsl@brunet.bn; f. 1984; mfr of ready-mixed concrete and concrete products; Man. Dir CHUAH MENG HU; 60 employees.

TRADE UNIONS

All trade unions must be registered with the Government. Authorization for affiliation with international trade union organizations is required. In 2008 the three officially registered trade unions were all in the petroleum sector, which collectively represented about 1,500 workers (less than 1% of the total work-force). Two of the unions, representing the sector's office workers, were reported to be inactive.

Brunei Oilfield Workers' Union: XDR/11, BSP Co Sdn Bhd, Seria KB 3534; f. 1964; 470 mems; Pres. SUHAINI Haji OTHMAN; Sec.-Gen. ABU TALIB BIN Haji MOHAMAD.

Transport

RAILWAYS

There are no public railways. The Brunei Shell Petroleum Co Sdn Bhd maintains a 19.3-km section of light railway between Seria and Badas.

ROADS

In 2005 there were 3,650 km of roads in Brunei, of which 77.2% were paved. The main highway connects Bandar Seri Begawan, Tutong and Kuala Belait.

Land Transport Department: Jalan Beribi Gadong, Bandar Seri Begawan BE 1110; tel. 2451979; fax 2424775; e-mail latis@brunet.bn; internet www.land-transport.gov.bn; f. 1962; Dir MOHAMMAD RIZA BIN Haji MOHAMMAD YUNOS.

SHIPPING

Most sea traffic is handled by a deep-water port at Muara, 28 km from the capital. It has a container terminal, warehousing, freezer facilities and cement silos. In September 2007 a cruise ship centre was opened at Muara. The port at Kuala Belait takes shallow-draught vessels and serves mainly the Shell petroleum field and Seria. The jetty at Lumut handles liquefied natural gas (LNG) carriers.

Four main rivers, with numerous tributaries, are an important means of communication in the interior. Water taxis operate daily to the Temburong district.

Shipping Association of Brunei Darussalam (SABD): POB 476, Bandar Seri Begawan BS 8670; tel. 2421572; fax 2421453; e-mail seatradefang@brunet.bn; Pres. Haji RAZALI BIN Haji JOHARI; Sec.-Gen. FANG TECK SIONG.

Bee Seng Shipping Co: 7 Blk D, Sufri Complex, Km 2, Jalan Tutong, POB 1777, Bandar Seri Begawan; tel. 2220055; fax 2221815; e-mail beeseng@beeseng.com.

Brunei Gas Carriers Sdn Bhd (BGC): Setia Kenangan Office Blk, 7th Floor, Setia Kenangan Complex, Kampong Kuilap, Bandar Seri Begawan BE 1518; e-mail bgc@brunet.bn; internet www.syarikatbgc.com; f. 1998; LNG shipping co; owned jtly by the Prime Minister's Corpn (80%), Shell Gas BV (10%) and Mitsubishi subsidiary Diamond Gas Carriers BV (10%); one vessel operated by Shell Int. Trading and Shipping Co Ltd; Man. Dir KOH HUI LING (acting).

Brunei Shell Tankers Sdn Bhd: Seria KB 3534; tel. 3372722; f. 1986; owned jtly by the Prime Minister's Corpn (50%), Shell Petroleum Ltd (25%) and Diamond Gas BV (25%); seven vessels operated by Shell Int. Trading and Shipping Co Ltd; delivers LNG to domestic customers; Man. Dir Dr GRAHAEME HENDERSON.

Harper Wira Sdn Bhd: B2, 1st Floor, Bangunan Pehin, Simpang 27, Lot 12284, Km 3, Jalan Gadong, Bandar Seri Begawan 3180; tel. and fax 2448529.

IDS Borneo Sdn Bhd: Bangunan Inchcape Borneo, Km 4, Jalan Gadong, Bandar Seri Begawan; tel. 2422396; fax 2232537; f. 1856; Gen. Man. LO FAN KEE.

Pansar Co Sdn Bhd: Unit A6, 2nd Floor, Bangunan Urairah, Kampong Kiulap Mukim, Jalan Gadong, Bandar Seri Begawan BE 1518; tel. 2233641; fax 2233643; e-mail pscbwn-admin@pansar.com.my.

Seatrade Shipping Co: POB 476, Bandar Seri Begawan BS 8670; tel. 2421457; fax 2425824; e-mail seatradefang@brunet.bn.

Silver Line (B) Sdn Bhd: 2nd Floor, 6 Abdul Razak Complex, Simpang 137, Jalan Gadong, Bandar Seri Begawan BE 4119; tel. 2445069; fax 2430276; e-mail silvline@brunet.bn.

Tri-Star Shipping and Trading Co Sdn Bhd: Unit 16, Simpang 584, Jalan Tutong, Bandar Seri Begawan; tel. 2653013; fax 2652685; e-mail enquiry@tristarbrunei.com; internet www.tristarbrunei.com.

CIVIL AVIATION

There is an international airport at Berakas, near Bandar Seri Begawan. The Brunei Shell Petroleum Co Sdn Bhd operates a private airfield at Anduki for helicopter services.

Department of Civil Aviation: Brunei International Airport, Bandar Seri Begawan BB 2513; tel. 2330142; fax 2340971; e-mail info@civil-aviation.gov.bn; internet www.civil-aviation.gov.bn; Dir Haji OMARALI BIN Haji MOHAMMED JA'AFAR.

Royal Brunei Airlines (RBA) Ltd: RBA Plaza, Jalan Sultan, POB 737, Bandar Seri Begawan BS 8671; tel. 2212222; fax 2244737; e-mail feedback@rba.com.bn; internet www.bruneiair.com; f. 1974; operates services within the Far East and to the Middle East, Australia and Europe; Chair. Dato' LIM JOCK SENG; CEO ROBERT YANG.

Syabas Aviation Services Sdn Bhd: Unit 47, 1st Floor, Haji Uthman Kompleks, Simpang 13, Jalan Lapangan Terbang Antarabangsa, Bandar Seri Begawan BB 2513; tel. 2342657; fax 2342658; e-mail info@syabasaviation.com; internet syabasaviation.com; f. 2009; Chair. ABAS MOHAMMED.

Tourism

Tourist attractions in Brunei include the flora and fauna of the rain forest and the national parks, as well as mosques and water villages. In 2008 the number of tourist arrivals was estimated at 225,757, and international tourist receipts totalled US $241m.

Brunei Tourism: c/o Ministry of Industry and Primary Resources, Jalan Menteri Besar, Bandar Seri Begawan BB 3910; tel. 2382822; fax 2382824; e-mail info@tourismbrunei.com; internet www.tourismbrunei.com; Chair. Dato' HAMDILLAH WAHAB.

Defence

As assessed at November 2010, the total strength of the Royal Brunei Malay Regiment was 7,000 (including 700 women): army 4,900; navy 1,000; air force 1,100. Military service (for which only ethnic Malays are eligible) is voluntary. Paramilitary forces comprise an estimated 2,250, of whom an estimated 400–500 belong to the Gurkha Reserve Unit and 1,750 are members of the Royal Brunei Police. A Gurkha battalion of the British army guards the petroleum and gas fields. Singaporean troops operate a training school in Brunei.

National defence has been the responsibility of the Brunei Government since 1971. The Gurkha battalion, comprising about 550 men in November 2009, is not responsible for internal security. In mid-2009 it was agreed that the Gurkha unit would continue to be stationed in the sultanate for a further five years.

Defence Expenditure: B $512m. in 2010.

Commander of the Royal Brunei Armed Forces: Maj.-Gen. Haji AMINUDDIN IHSAN ABIDIN.

Commander of the Royal Brunei Land Force: Col YUSSOF BIN Haji ABD RAHMAN.

Commander of the Royal Brunei Navy: Col Haji ABDUL HALIM BIN Haji MOHAMED HANIFAH.

Commander of the Royal Brunei Air Force: Col JOFRI BIN Haji ABDULLAH.

Education

Education is free and is compulsory for 12 years from the age of five years. Islamic studies form an integral part of the school curriculum. There are three official languages of instruction, Malay, English and Chinese (Mandarin), with schools being divided accordingly. In 2007/08 enrolment at pre-primary level included 65% of children in the relevant age-group (males 63%; females 66%), while enrolment at primary level included 93% of children in the relevant age group (males 93%; females 93%). Enrolment at secondary level included 88% of pupils in the relevant age-group (males 87%; females 90%). In 2008 there were 203 pre-primary and primary schools, 34 secondary schools, 13 vocational colleges, one teacher-training college and three higher education institutions. In the budget for 2007/08 the Government allocated B $546m. to the Ministry of Education.

All Malay schools are state-administered and are, in general, co-educational. Pre-primary education begins at the age of five years. Primary education in the Malay schools lasts for six years from the age of six years; it is divided into two cycles of three years, lower primary and upper primary. At lower primary level all instruction is in Malay but at upper primary certain subjects, e.g. mathematics, geography and science, are taught in English. Pupils sit for the Penilaian Sekolah Rendah (PSR—Primary School Assessment) examination at the end of primary education.

Secondary education lasts for seven years. The first five years are divided into lower secondary, lasting for three years, at the end of which pupils sit the Penilaian Menengah Bawah (PMB—Lower Secondary Assessment) examination, and upper secondary, which lasts for two or three years. After the PMB some pupils follow the Program Menengah Vokasional (PMV—Secondary Vocational Programme) where courses last for two years, leading to the National Trade Certificate or National Vocational Certificate. More able students follow a two-year course leading to the Brunei-Cambridge General Certificate of Education Ordinary Level (BC-GCE 'O' Level) examinations. Students with the requisite 'O' Level results proceed to the pre-university level to pursue a two-year course leading to the

BC-GCE Advanced Level ('A' Level) examination. Students with adequate 'A' Level passes may be eligible for entry to the University of Brunei Darussalam (UBD) or other tertiary institutions, or be awarded scholarships to study abroad. The Institut Teknologi Brunei provides courses leading to a Higher National certificate (part-time) or a National Diploma (full-time). A second national university, the Universiti Islam Sultan Sharif Ali (UNISAA), was established in 2007. In the same year the status of the Seri Begawan Training College for Teachers of Islamic Religion was upgraded when it became the Seri Begawan University College for Teachers of Islamic Religion. In April 2008 it was announced that the Princess Rashidah College of Nursing, founded in 1986, was to merge with UBD's Institute of Medicine. A review of the country's secondary school curriculum in 2007 resulted in the implementation of the Sistem Pendidikan Negara Abad Ke-21, or SPN 1, the National Education System for the 21st Century. This programme aimed to raise the number of pupils proceeding to university level.

Chinese schools are privately managed and do not receive government assistance. They cater for pupils at both primary and secondary levels..

Bibliography

(See also Malaysia Bibliography)

Anaman, Kwabena Asomanin, and Duraman, Ismail (Eds). *Applied Economic Analysis in Brunei Darussalam: Evaluation of Economic Growth and Trade, Microeconomic Efficiency, and Analysis of Socio-Economic Problems.* Bandar Seri Begawan, Universiti Brunei Darussalam, 2003.

Bartholomew, James. *The Richest Man in the World: The Sultan of Brunei.* London, Viking, 1989.

Blomqvist, Hans C. 'Brunei's Strategic Dilemmas'. *The Pacific Review,* Vol. 6, No 2, 1993.

Bolkiah, Prince Mohamed. *Time and the River*. Brunei, 2000.

Remember, Remember . . . The 8th of December. Brunei, 2007.

Borneo Bulletin. *Brunei Yearbook Key Information on Brunei.* Bandar Seri Begawan.

Braighlinn, G. *Ideological Innovation under Monarchy: Aspects of Legitimisation Activity in Contemporary Brunei.* Amsterdam, V U University Press, 1992.

Brown, D. E. *Brunei, The Structure and History of a Bornean Malay Sultanate.* Brunei, Brunei Museum, 1970.

Brunei Currency Board. *Brunei Darussalam Financial Structure, Functions and Policies.* Bandar Seri Begawan, 1996.

Chalfont, Lord. *By God's Will: A Portrait of the Sultan of Brunei.* London, Weidenfeld and Nicolson, 1989.

Cleary, Mark, and Shuang Yann Wong. *Oil, Economic Development and Diversification in Brunei Darussalam.* London and New York, Macmillan and St Martin's Press, 1994.

Hamzah, B. A. *The Oil Sultanate: Political History of Oil in Brunei Darussalam.* Kuala Lumpur, Mawaddan Enterprise, 1991.

Horton, A. V. M. *The British Residency in Brunei, 1906–1959.* Hull, Centre for South-East Asian Studies, 1984.

'Negara Brunei Darussalam: Economic Gloom and the APEC Summit.' in *Southeast Asian Affairs.* Singapore, Institute of Southeast Asian Studies/Heinemann, 2001.

Hussainmiya, B. A. *Sultan Omar Ali Saifuddin III and Britain: The Making of Brunei Darussalam.* Kuala Lumpur, Oxford University Press, 1995.

Brunei: Revival of 1906: A Popular History. Bandar Seri Begawan, Brunei Press, 2006.

Ibrahim, Haji Abdul Latif Haji. *Issues in Brunei Studies.* Bandar Seri Begawan, Universiti Brunei Darussalam, 2003.

Information Department, Prime Minister's Office. *Brunei Darussalam In Brief 1995.* Bandar Seri Begawan, Revised Edn, 2003.

International Business Publications. *Brunei Foreign Policy and Government Guide.* USA, 2004.

Krausse, Sylvia C. Engelen, and Gerald, H. *Brunei* (An annotated bibliography.) Oxford, Clio Press, 1988.

Lawrey, Roger, Pillarisetti, J. R., and Siddiqui, S. A. 'Commercialisation of Brunei's Electricity Sector: Efficiency and Distributional Consequences of Following a Global Trend', in Tisdell, Clem (Ed.), *Globalisation and World Economic Policies: Effects and Policy Responses of Nations and their Groupings.* New Delhi, Serials Publications, 2005.

Leake, David, Jr. *Brunei: The Modern Southeast Asian Islamic Sultanate.* Jefferson, McFarland and Co, 1990.

McArthur, M. S. H. *Report on Brunei in 1904.* Athens, OH, 1987.

Majid, Harun Abdul. *Rebellion in Brunei: The 1962 Revolt, Imperialism, Confrontation and Oil.* London, I. B. Tauris, 2007.

Metra Consulting. *Handbook of National Development Plans*. London, Graham and Trotman, 1986.

Ministry of Communications. *Brunei Darussalam: Service Hub for Trade and Tourism (SHuTT) 2000 and Beyond.* Bandar Seri Begawan.

Ministry of Industry and Primary Resources. *Brunei Darussalam Investment Guide.* Bandar Seri Begawan.

Saunders, Graham. *Bishops and Brookes.* Singapore, Oxford University Press, 1992.

A History of Brunei. London, RoutledgeCurzon, 2nd Edn, 2002.

Siddique, Sharon. 'Brunei Darussalam 1991: the Non-secular State'. *Southeast Asian Affairs 1992.* Singapore, Institute of Southeast Asian Studies/Heinemann, 1992.

Sidhu, Jatswan S. *Historical Dictionary of Brunei Darussalam.* London, Scarecrow Press, 2nd Edn, 2009.

Singh, D. S. Ranjit. *Brunei, 1839–1983, The Problems of Political Survival.* Singapore, Oxford University Press, 1984.

Statistics Division, Economic Planning Unit, Ministry of Finance. *Brunei Darussalam Statistical Yearbook.* Bandar Seri Begawan.

Tan Siew Ee and Ismail Haji Duraman, Haji (Eds). *Readings on the Economy of Brunei Darussalam.* Gadong, Universiti Brunei Darussalam, 2002.

Tan Siew Ee and Opai, Rosnah (Eds). *The Economy of Brunei Darussalam: Perspectives and Insights.* Bandar Seri Begawan, HBJ Education, 2008.

Tarling, Nicholas. *Britain, the Brookes and Brunei.* Kuala Lumpur, Oxford University Press, 1971.

Turnbull, C. M. *A History of Malaysia, Singapore and Brunei.* Sydney, Allen and Unwin, 1989.

Zaini Haji Ahmad, Haji. *The People's Party of Brunei, Selected Documents.* Kuala Lumpur, Insan, 1988.

CAMBODIA

Physical and Social Geography

HARVEY DEMAINE

Cambodia comprises a relatively small and compact territory on the Indo-Chinese peninsula and covers an area of 181,035 sq km (69,898 sq miles), bordered by Thailand to the west, by Laos to the north and by Viet Nam to the east.

PHYSICAL FEATURES

Apart from the Cardamom and related mountains in the south, which divide the country's interior from its short southern coastline, the greater part of Cambodia consists of a shallow lacustrine basin, centred on Tonlé Sap ('the Great Lake'), which was historically of far greater extent than it is today. This lowland drains eastwards, via the Tonlé Sap River, to the Mekong, which flows through the eastern part of the lowlands from north to south before turning eastwards into Viet Nam and to the South China Sea.

Throughout its course across Cambodia, the Mekong River averages about 2 km in width, but it is interrupted by precipitous rapids at Kratié, and by falls at Khone along the border with Laos. Moreover, its flow fluctuates widely from season to season; during the period of greatest volume between June and October, a substantial portion of its flood-waters is diverted up the Tonlé Sap River (the flow of which is thus reversed) into the Great Lake itself. The lake therefore comes to occupy an area at least twice as great as that encompassed during the dry season in the early months of the year. The temperature is generally between 20°C and 36°C (68°F and 97°F), and the annual average in Phnom-Penh is 27°C (81°F).

RESOURCES AND POPULATION

Cambodia has some good alluvial soils, abundant water for irrigation and a tropical monsoon climate without excessive rainfall. Such favourable agricultural conditions could support both a wider area and a greater intensity of cultivation. Rice is the principal crop. The country's rich forest resources have been seriously depleted, much timber having been illegally felled.

Significant offshore reserves of petroleum and natural gas have been identified. It was envisaged that Cambodia would commence the exploitation of its petroleum reserves in late 2012. Deposits of commercially viable mineral ores include iron ore and manganese, as well as bauxite, phosphates, gemstones such as sapphires and rubies, silicon, manganese and gold.

In 1975 Cambodia had an estimated 7.1m. inhabitants and an average population density of 39 per sq km. By 1981, according to a census, the country's population had declined to 6.7m., owing to warfare, famine and migration, reducing the density to 36.9 per sq km. At the census of 3 March 2008 the population totalled 13,395,682, and density had increased to 74.0 per sq km. By mid-2011 the country's population had risen to an estimated 14,666,053, with density reaching 81.0 per sq km. The capital city, Phnom-Penh, had an estimated population of only 20,000 in 1978, but by mid-2010 the city's population was estimated to have risen to 1,562,498.

History

SORPONG PEOU

Based on an earlier article by LAURA SUMMERS

Early Khmer civilization, owing to its situation on major Chinese and Indian trade routes, was greatly affected by foreign cultural influences. The assimilation of Indian Brahmans into Khmer society encouraged the adoption of Hindu cults, including the recognition of the supremacy of the god Siva (Shiva) in the 'Funan' period (which extended from the first to the sixth century AD). Archaeological discoveries indicate the existence, at that time, of a highly pluralistic, peninsular political system containing a number of Khmer princely families, each of which supported and promoted family cults. Religious syncretism in the sixth century signalled the beginning of military competition for ascendancy in the Mekong delta. The ensuing wars between the cult-based principalities eventually gave rise to the highly centralized Angkorian empires during the ninth–14th centuries. The rejection of established religious cults and the rise of a moral tradition that united images of royalty, divinity and fertility corresponded to a massive intensification of rice production in the area surrounding the modern city of Siem Reap (Siem Reab). A complex system of hydraulics, which diverted the water of highland streams and retained flood waters from the Tonlé Sap (a natural reservoir of the Mekong), permitted year-round agriculture and hitherto unthinkable concentrations of population. Much of the labour required for the building of the irrigation system and its associated, extraordinary temple complexes was provided by slaves, most of whom were prisoners of war or captured tribespeople from the highlands. With each succeeding century, the political influence of Angkor expanded, as did its agrarian economy and artistic achievements. At its greatest extent in the 12th century, during the reign of Jayavarman VII (1181–1218), the Angkorian empire embraced the Chao Phraya plain and parts of the Malay peninsula as well as all principalities and populations south of the Annamite chain in present-day Viet Nam, including the powerful Cham state of Champa. Jayavarman VII was also the first Buddhist King of Angkor. By the late 13th century the Angkorian civilization displayed unmistakable signs of decadence. In 1431 the declining economic power and military capacity of Cambodia were further eroded when the ascendant Thai civilization, based at Sukothai, sacked Angkor and its surrounding sites. Succeeding monarchs abandoned all efforts to continue state-controlled rice cultivation, permanently renounced Hindu cults and shifted their capitals southward to Lovek and Oudong, to the north of the riparian crossroads of Phnom-Penh.

PRE-COLONIAL CAMBODIA

Historians differ significantly in their assessment of society and politics from the 16th to the 19th century. Most French historians, focusing on the dramatic decrease in royal military power after the collapse of the empire, argue that Khmer civilization went into decline. By contrast, US scholars, reacting critically to the socially oppressive features of Angkorian centralization and the construction of monuments (especially since the failed socialist revolution in the 1970s), have argued that the 16th century gave rise to a pluralistic, dispersed, village-centred political order, in which communities, organized around Buddhist temples (*wat*), were able to avoid some of the earlier tyrannical excesses. Nevertheless, it is recognized that these communities were under the control of royally appointed governors who collected taxes and demanded labour service (*corvée*) in the name of the still revered monarch.

By the end of the 18th century the Khmer kingdom had contracted in geographical size to approximately two-thirds of its present area. The rise of the powerful Chakri dynasty, to the west, and the southward expansion of the demographically buoyant Vietnamese nation, resulted in the need to pay tribute to both foreign courts in order to solicit royal respect and paternalist protection. This period of dual Siamese-Vietnamese suzerainty came to an abrupt end after an unsuccessful Vietnamese attempt to annex Cambodia. An indigenous, Buddhist-led rebellion, discreetly encouraged by the monarch and supported by timely military intervention from Siam (Thailand), ultimately defeated the Vietnamese plan, but inevitably led to near-total subordination to the Siamese court. Although, unlike the Vietnamese, the Siamese did not insist on cultural assimilation or commence settling on Khmer land, King Ang Duang approached the French in the hope of signing a treaty of protection. The treaty, signed in 1863 by his son King Norodom, gave France complete control over Cambodia's foreign policy and required the royal court to accept a permanent Resident-General. France proceeded almost immediately to assume colonial control.

COLONIAL CAMBODIA

Inevitably, colonialism had a profound impact on the development of the Cambodian state and its politics. By 1884 a second, far-reaching treaty, imposed on Norodom, established French control over the royal administration, royal treasury and foreign trading. Cambodia was incorporated into the Indo-Chinese Union in 1887. The Union's budgetary resources were used to reinforce the near-sacred regard for the Khmer monarch, in an attempt to counter discontent among the populace and the élite (following the successful suppression of a national uprising in 1884–86).

The colonial order was undermined only by the war in the Pacific. Vichy French collaboration with Japan after 1940, combined with Thailand's alliance with the Japanese, resulted in the Japanese-approved Thai annexation of Battambang province in 1941. King Monivong died and was replaced soon afterwards by King Norodom Sihanouk, who was only 18 years of age. King Sihanouk initially displayed sympathy for the emergent nationalist sentiments forcefully articulated by Son Ngoc Thanh and Buddhist monks, among others. (Thanh was appointed Prime Minister in an 'independent' Cabinet hastily established by the Japanese in 1945.) However, alarmed by the increasingly anti-royalist tendencies of the nationalist movement, Sihanouk subsequently initiated secret discussions with France, arranging the arrest and exile of Thanh, the resumption of French colonial rule in 1946 and the promulgation of a new Constitution in 1947. The post-war Constitution permitted the formation of political parties and provided for the holding of legislative elections. These reforms satisfied the aspirations of some of the élite nationalists.

France, meanwhile, used Cambodia as a rear military staging area in its war against the Viet Minh (see the chapter on Viet Nam), a strategic manoeuvre that was also attempted by the USA after 1970. The resumption of colonial rule and the exile of Thanh divided the nascent nationalist movement. Some nationalists, responding partly to Viet Minh urgings, formed resistance groups seeking to overthrow both colonialism and monarchy, which was finally seen as a French instrument of repression. These *Issaraks*, or freedom fighters, displayed little internal unity. The mainstream of the nationalist movement (represented by the Democrat Party of Prince Yutevong), although anti-royalist, eschewed violence and opted to remain in Phnom-Penh, seeking to gain power through the parliamentary process. The Democrats were highly successful in the legislative elections, but encountered strong opposition from the powerful Liberal Party, which represented royalist and land-owning families, and the smaller, ultra-conservative Khmer Renovation Party, a movement led by Lt-Gen. (later Marshal) Lon Nol and other high-ranking state functionaries and their families. The nationalist threat prompted Sihanouk to suspend the Constitution in June 1952 and to assume governmental powers. Fearing French defeat in Viet Nam as well as Democrat and *Issarak* ascendancy, Sihanouk undertook a diplomatic mission to France and the USA, pleading for his country's right to independence. This 'Royal Crusade for Independence' succeeded. France conceded independence on 9 November 1953, and Cambodia's independence was ratified by the Geneva Conference on Indo-China in July 1954.

THE SIHANOUK, LON NOL AND POL POT YEARS

The Sihanouk years of 1954–70 brought the restoration of limited constitutional rights to Cambodians, but were also characterized by Sihanouk's efforts to achieve stability, while being confronted by renewed challenges from the socialist left, the liberal-democratic and reformist centre and extreme right-wing parties and interests. In foreign policy, Sihanouk constantly renewed his nationalist credentials by steadily opposing US imperialism in Viet Nam. In 1955 he abdicated in favour of his father, Norodom Suramarit, to circumvent the limitations of his role as constitutional monarch and thus to play a more direct role in politics and government. He founded the Sangkum Reastr Niyum (Popular Socialist Community), which decisively defeated the Democrats at the polls. Prince Sihanouk also created a biannual National Congress, effectively a mass meeting at which the public was invited to present its complaints. Thus, the power of the elected National Assembly was steadily eroded, and the mass media were also increasingly subject to state control and repression. In response to severe economic problems after 1966, Sihanouk resorted to arbitrary arrests and to some public executions, especially of 'pro-American' Thanists, who were known in this period as *Khmer Serei*. The political repression and economic disorder that marred the late 1960s affected nearly every well-placed family. The appointment of an emergency Government of National Salvation in 1969, under the leadership of Lon Nol, resulted in a carefully co-ordinated *coup d'état* in March 1970. The ostensible motive for the coup was Sihanouk's alleged collaboration with the Vietnamese communist revolutionaries who used Cambodian territory for sanctuary and who seemingly presented a new threat to Cambodia's independence. The organizers of the coup comprised remnants of the old Democrat and Khmer Renovation Parties. In October 1970 Lon Nol proclaimed the Khmer Republic, of which he was elected President in 1972. Thanh became Prime Minister once again briefly in 1972. However, the Khmer Republic administration was rapidly overwhelmed by the corruption attendant upon a war economy.

Informed of the coup while on a diplomatic mission and convinced of the involvement of the US Central Intelligence Agency (CIA), Sihanouk formed an alliance with North Viet Nam and with an underground Marxist insurgency group, the Khmers Rouges, led by Saloth Sar, who later became known as Pol Pot. The Khmers Rouges had initiated an armed struggle against Sihanouk in 1968 and already had a guerrilla force of 3,000 by the time of the coup. Following organized mass demonstrations opposing the coup, there were fears in South Viet Nam and in the USA that Lon Nol's administration might rapidly be overthrown. A joint US-South Vietnamese invasion of some 50,000 troops, officially for the purpose of clearing communist Vietnamese forces out of their Cambodian sanctuaries, served only to drive an estimated 30,000 Vietnamese revolutionary troops deeper into the country, where they systematically assisted the Khmers Rouges in raising support and troops for their new, Sihanouk-led United National Front of Cambodia—FUNC. Despite massive US military and economic assistance, the armed forces of Lon Nol were effectively defeated by the end of 1972. The US Air Force engaged in nine months of round-the-clock saturation bombings in 1973, until the US Congress terminated funding. Between 1973 and 1975 the Khmers Rouges gradually assumed control of ministerial portfolios in Sihanouk's Royal Government of National Union of Cambodia (in exile) and put pressure on Vietnamese armed forces and advisers to leave Cambodia. Party cadres who were judged to be too loyal to the Vietnamese or to their revolutionary traditions and ideology were secretly removed from office; many were killed rather than demoted. By early 1975 Phnom-Penh was completely isolated from all overland and river communications and was dependent on US airlifts. Lon Nol was flown to Hawaii on 1 April 1975, in advance of a revolutionary occupation of the capital on 17 April. In the following weeks the entire populations of Phnom-Penh and other refugee-swollen cities were evacuated and resettled in rural areas in agricultural collectives under Khmer Rouge control. Over the next three years an estimated 1.7m. people died as a result of hard labour, inadequate food and medical supplies, harsh treatment and executions. The Khmers Rouges' campaign to transform Cambodia so rapidly was partly stimulated by fears that Viet Nam and the USA would not respect Cambodia's right to independence, especially its right to an 'independent' socialist revolution.

Although he returned to Phnom-Penh, Sihanouk was rapidly eclipsed in the post-war revolutionary turmoil. A new Constitution renamed the state 'Democratic Kampuchea' (DK). National elections were held in March 1976 for a legislative body, the People's Representative Assembly, with the franchise restricted to full member-supporters of the state collectives (approximately one-half of the adult population). In a typical gesture, calculated to initiate bargaining over terms and conditions, Sihanouk declined to serve as Head of State in April. The Assembly elected Khieu Samphan to the Chairmanship of the State Presidium, while the relatively unknown Pol Pot was named Prime Minister. In September 1977, as border conflicts with Viet Nam increased, Pol Pot revealed that the ruling organization was the Communist Party of Kampuchea (CPK). His revised version of party history eliminated all reference to early Vietnamese involvement in the Cambodian communist movement, a clear indication that international solidarity had been permanently ruptured. Social tensions, arising from catastrophic shortfalls in production and the outbreak of a full-scale border war with Viet Nam at the end of 1977, provoked the removal of numerous officials from within the CPK and the urgent reorganization of rural collectives, in an attempt to support the armed forces. Diplomatic relations with Viet Nam were severed at the end of December, after an unsuccessful invasion attempt appeared to confirm CPK fears that Viet Nam intended to incorporate the Kampuchean revolution into a Vietnamese-dominated, communist federation of Indo-China. During 1978 relations between the two countries continued to deteriorate. Viet Nam feared that the harsh conditions and instability in Cambodia would make the fiercely independent but increasingly beleaguered CPK dependent upon and vulnerable to the will of the People's Republic of China. On 25 December Viet Nam invaded Democratic Kampuchea, with a force estimated at more than 200,000 men, supported by the newly formed Kampuchean National United Front for National Salvation (KNUFNS) led by Heng Samrin and comprising CPK dissidents. (In 1981 the KNUFNS was renamed as the United Front for the Construction and Defence of the Kampuchean Fatherland; in April 2006 the movement became the Solidarity Front for Development of the Cambodian Motherland.) The rebel forces occupied Phnom-Penh on 7 January 1979. By the beginning of 1980 the defeated Democratic Kampuchean army, which numbered 70,000 prior to the assault, had been forced to retreat into remote mountain redoubts along the frontier, with troops estimated at fewer than 30,000.

THE PEOPLE'S REPUBLIC OF KAMPUCHEA

The Vietnamese-supported People's Republic of Kampuchea (PRK) failed to secure widespread international recognition, despite its efforts to portray its installation as the result of an indigenously supported revolutionary uprising against the violations of human rights by the Democratic Kampuchean Government. China and members of the Association of South-east Asian Nations (ASEAN) viewed Viet Nam's intervention in Kampuchea as another manifestation of traditional Vietnamese expansionism, which constituted a threat to their own security. The USA responded to the invasion by strengthening its economic embargoes on aid and trade with Indo-China, persuading Japan and most member countries of the European Community (now European Union—EU) to join the embargo. Between 1979 and 1981 the dislodged Pol Pot Government continued to be recognized by the UN in view of Viet Nam's open violation of the UN Charter. From 1982 the Government of Democratic Kampuchea had taken the form of a coalition Government-in-exile comprising the Party of Democratic Kampuchea (PDK—the CPK was officially disbanded in 1981), a royalist movement known as FUNCINPEC (a French acronym for United National Front for an Independent, Neutral, Peaceful and Co-operative Cambodia), led by Sihanouk, and the Khmer People's National Liberation Front (KPNLF), led by a former Prime Minister under Sihanouk, Son Sann. An anti-communist republican movement, the KPNLF embraced many important personalities from the Khmer Republic regime and the old Democrat Party. Sihanouk agreed to serve as President in the new Coalition Government of Democratic Kampuchea (CGDK). Although united by their opposition to the Vietnamese occupation of Cambodia and to the communist Government headed by Heng Samrin, which had been installed in Phnom-Penh, the parties that formed the CGDK were unable to function as a political alliance in view of their mutually hostile political visions. Each of the three parties fielded its own army, and periodic attempts by the foreign supporters of the CGDK to encourage more than sporadic military co-operation were largely unsuccessful. China supplied nearly all of the weapons required by each of the three armies, while smaller amounts of military, humanitarian and 'non-lethal' aid were supplied to the non-communist FUNCINPEC and the KPNLF by the ASEAN countries, the USA, France and the United Kingdom. The USSR, its allies in Eastern Europe and Cuba supplied and financed the PRK.

By 1988 fighting between the CGDK and the PRK armed forces was of low intensity. The stalemate extended to the political arena. Although Viet Nam formally ignored UN resolutions appealing for a full and unconditional withdrawal and steadfastly rejected appeals from the CGDK and ASEAN for a negotiated end to the occupation, it tacitly responded to international criticism after 1983 by reducing its troop levels during annual rotations. Following reductions in military and economic aid from the USSR in 1987, rapid Sino-Soviet rapprochement in 1988 and Soviet pressure to seek a settlement in Cambodia based on 'national reconciliation' and the restoration of the monarchy, Viet Nam made increasingly firm unilateral pledges to withdraw all of its forces from Cambodia by the end of September 1989. The leadership of the ruling Kampuchean People's Revolutionary Party (KPRP) in Phnom-Penh issued an appeal for 'national reconciliation', urging the formation of a broad coalition government embracing all nationalist forces. The appeal made clear that the envisaged coalition would be guided by the KPRP communists and be based on the legal and administrative framework that had been established in Phnom-Penh in 1979. The KPRP also proposed to offer a senior position in the PRK to Sihanouk.

Mindful of the need to widen its social base, the KPRP announced in 1988 that it would reform its state-controlled economy and proceeded to award managerial autonomy to nationalized industries. In 1989 peasants were informed that traditional usufruct titles to land would be reintroduced and tenants in state-supplied housing were promised property deeds, an act which simultaneously dispossessed pre-1975 owners of urban housing stock. In April 1989 the KPRP-controlled National Assembly voted to change the official name of the PRK to the State of Cambodia (SOC). Sihanouk, who had requested the change as a concessionary gesture, refused nevertheless to join the reformed SOC, and continued to urge the creation of an interim, quadripartite coalition government to replace both the CGDK and SOC governmental frameworks, UN supervision of the Vietnamese troop withdrawal, a cease-fire and UN-supervised, national elections. In spite of SOC reluctance to form a coalition, the collapse of communist power elsewhere in the world encouraged Sihanouk as well as France to believe that the situation in Cambodia was evolving towards a settlement. Thus, aided by Indonesia (acting on behalf of the ASEAN countries), France convened an international conference on Cambodia in Paris at the end of July. By this time, the USSR had lent its approval to proposals for an interim, quadripartite coalition government to be led by Sihanouk, but in Paris the delegations representing Viet Nam, Laos and the KPRP continued to oppose an all-party interim government, advocating instead a coalition of 'national reconciliation' excluding the PDK, which was denounced as 'genocidal' and 'anti-national'. They also rejected all proposals for UN intervention in Cambodia, accusing the UN of being politically biased. The communist states also insisted that the SOC deserved legal recognition because it controlled most of the population and administered most of Cambodia's territory. It was further asserted that the SOC alone possessed the sovereign rights to negotiate a solution to Cambodia's internal conflict and to organize national elections.

The Paris Conference deliberations were suspended after one month, one obstacle having been the failure of the major powers to present a unified view to the Cambodian parties. US delegates reinforced the tendency of each of the two Cambodian sides to resist compromise; while the USA accepted that peace required the awarding of political roles to all four parties, its diplomats made no secret of their personal preference for a solution excluding the PDK, as demanded by the SOC. Despite the diplomatic stalemate and encouraged by the open US hostility towards the PDK, Viet Nam proceeded unilaterally to withdraw its regular armed forces from the country at the end of September. Its appeals for reciprocal withdrawals of foreign military support for other Cambodian parties were discounted by foreign intelligence sources. Reports noted that hundreds, and perhaps thousands, of Vietnamese cadres remained in Cambodia in advisory roles and that as many as 3,000 rapid-intervention troops had been reintroduced to Cambodian battlefields within a matter of weeks.

The retreat of Vietnamese regular forces prompted a dramatic increase in fighting in several parts of Cambodia, but especially in the west, with the National Army of Democratic Kampuchea (NADK), the army of the PDK, making the most significant advances. Responding to the Cambodian failure to agree on how to form an interim coalition government, a US Congressman, Stephen Solarz, proposed the establishment of an interim UN administration in Cambodia, a proposal that circumvented debate about which Government, the SOC or the CGDK, should form the basis for an interim state authority. Solarz also favoured a UN role as a means of promoting human rights education in Cambodia. The Australian Government, acting on Solarz's proposal, undertook the difficult task of persuading Viet Nam, as well as the KPRP, that support for a UN administrative role, UN monitoring of a cease-fire and UN-supervised elections were not incompatible with KPRP desires to retain power. Viet Nam in January 1990 and the KPRP in February cautiously agreed to a 'limited' UN role. Concurrently, at the initiative of the USA, the five permanent members of the UN Security Council began monthly meetings to establish a mutually acceptable and practical framework for a settlement, which could then be recommended to the Cambodian parties. Since the USA and the USSR had already agreed on the desirability of a non-communist, neutral administration led by Sihanouk, the concern in the first half of 1990 was to persuade China to abandon its continuing diplomatic and military support for the PDK, which remained the principal obstacle to a settlement of the conflict.

The comprehensive political settlement negotiated by the permanent members of the UN Security Council, which was finally presented in September 1990, envisaged: free and fair elections to be conducted under direct UN administration; the verified withdrawal of foreign forces; the cessation of all military assistance to Cambodia; the repatriation of refugees and displaced persons from Thailand under the auspices of the office of the UN High Commissioner for Refugees (UNHCR); the rehabilitation and reconstruction of Cambodia's economy; the formation of a Supreme National Council (SNC) by the four Cambodian parties (none being treated as a government); and the creation of a UN Transitional Authority in Cambodia (UNTAC), which would have special powers of administration and supervision during a transitional period and which would be headed by a Special Representative of the UN Secretary-General. The SNC would represent Cambodian sovereignty externally during a transitional period and would occupy Cambodia's seat in the UN General Assembly; UNTAC was to have powers of control or supervision over wide areas of national government (especially all agencies responsible for defence, internal security, finance and public information), primarily for the purpose of creating a neutral political environment for the holding of free elections. The UN plan envisaged a substantial reduction in the power wielded by the existing administrative structures, especially the SOC ministries in Phnom-Penh. Sihanouk, the President of the resistance coalition, and Hun Sen, the Chairman of the Council of Ministers of the SOC, had informally agreed in June to an equal division of the SNC seats between the two rival Governments (rather than among the four parties). In September the four parties agreed to a 12-member SNC comprising six representatives from the KPRP, two from FUNCINPEC, two from the KPNLF and two from the PDK. It was further agreed that SNC decisions would be taken by consensus, a procedure that awarded each party the power of veto. These compromises were influenced by Chinese diplomats, who quietly informed the PDK, the KPNLF and FUNCINPEC that all military aid to their armies would be gradually reduced and then cease altogether, perhaps from the beginning of 1991, and by Soviet diplomats, who reciprocated by advising Viet Nam and Phnom-Penh, to which aid had effectively ceased, to abandon demands for the exclusion of the PDK from a settlement.

The first meeting of the SNC in September 1990 finished acrimoniously with no agreement on who should assume the chairmanship of the SNC or who would represent it in the UN General Assembly. The permanent members of the UN Security Council intervened by proposing that Sihanouk head the SNC, a proposal initially unacceptable to the SOC side, which had been seeking joint chairmanship, rotating chairmanship or the compensatory appointment of Hun Sen as Sihanouk's deputy, together with an additional, compensatory seat for the SOC to rebalance the numbers at seven members each. The SOC also raised objections to proposals for the full disarmament of all four Cambodian armies, insisting upon the need to have access to weapons both during and after the proposed transitional period as a guarantee against attempts by the PDK (whose troops and weapons caches might escape UN monitoring) to seize power. Still seeking to portray the UN role as indirect diplomatic recognition, the KPRP also objected to UN plans to exercise control over its ministries. Neither the SOC nor the resistance coalition was reassured when in December the UN Secretary-General's Special Representative for Cambodia explained that the UN's draft agreement for a settlement was based on 'full respect' for Cambodia's existing administrative structures and that the UN accepted that there would be 'three categories of entities exercising powers' during the transitional period: the SNC; UNTAC, which would assume control of all administrative agencies concerned with foreign affairs, national defence, finance, public security and information; and the existing administrative structures in the zones controlled by the four parties, which would continue to function either under UNTAC control or supervision or with no control or supervision. With each side seeking to promote its claim for leadership of the SNC and both anxious (for opposed reasons) about the administrative influence of the KPRP state apparatus on the population, diplomatic progress ceased in early 1991. Military activity intensified during the dry season, rapidly increasing the number of refugees housed in holding centres in Thailand. The UN Secretary-General, Javier Pérez de Cuéllar, appealed in April for a cease-fire.

The diplomatic impasse was broken by Sihanouk, who was irritated by the lack of progress at the informal discussions that had resumed in the Indonesian capital of Jakarta. In June 1991 Sihanouk announced the resignation of one of the FUNCINPEC representatives in the newly formed, but inoperative, SNC, and appointed himself to the empty seat as a 'simple member'. He then convened and presided, unappointed, over a meeting of the SNC held in Pattaya, Thailand. At the June SNC meeting in Pattaya, and two others subsequently held in the Chinese capital of Beijing (in July) and again in Pattaya (in August), delegates representing the four Cambodian parties finally agreed that Sihanouk would assume the chairmanship of the SNC, that the SNC would be based in Phnom-Penh and that it would commence functioning in November. The accession of the Prince to the chairmanship of the SNC was achieved without compensation to the SOC because China, in a clear change of foreign policy, concurrently ceased to extend diplomatic recognition to the resistance Government and began to accord equal recognition to all Cambodian parties, and their representatives, specifically to Hun Sen, head of the SOC delegation in the SNC. Adding to the momentum, China also reportedly conceded secretly to Viet Nam that military demobilization, fixed at 100% in the UN draft plan, did not have to be total. The Cambodian parties then agreed at their second meeting in Pattaya to a mutual reduction of 70% in their force levels and weapons stocks, a compromise forced on the PDK by Thailand. The guerrilla-based PDK favoured 100% disarmament, as originally recommended in the UN draft.

The final significant dispute among the parties involved the modalities of the free and fair elections envisaged by the UN. Under a compromise negotiated within the SNC in September 1991, the SOC abandoned its demands for single-member constituencies with simple plurality elections, a formula favouring the largest, nationally organized parties, and agreed to a system of proportional representation for each of 21 constituencies, these being the existing SOC provinces (19) and municipalities (two). Comprehensive political agreements and treaties were formally signed by the UN Secretary-General, the four Cambodian parties, Viet Nam and 17 other states at a reconvened Paris Conference on 23 October. Although no announcements were made, China halted weapons shipments to its three former allies; Viet Nam, equally, recalled its advisers and ceased to intervene militarily in Cambodia.

THE 1991 PARIS PEACE AGREEMENT, UN INTERVENTION AND DEMOCRATIC TRANSITION

UN intervention in Phnom-Penh accelerated the liberalizing trends which the KPRP had set in motion in 1988, but also exposed, albeit inadvertently, the profoundly illiberal and authoritarian character of Cambodian politics. Anticipating the arrival of the UN, at an extraordinary party congress the KPRP formally abandoned its one-party state on 18 October 1991. The congress changed the name of the KPRP to the Cambodian People's Party (CPP) and abandoned its Marxist-Leninist ideology. The veteran leader of the KPRP, Heng Samrin, was retired to an honorary role in the party, and replaced as Chairman of the Central Committee by the lesser-known Chea Sim, who named the youthful Hun Sen as his deputy and principal party spokesman. Hun Sen declared his support for Sihanouk as an elected President in a new constitutional order to be elaborated following the national elections. Sihanouk returned to Phnom-Penh in November to establish the SNC in its national headquarters and negotiated a plan for co-operation between the CPP and FUNCINPEC with Prince Norodom Ranariddh, Sihanouk's son and the leader of FUNCINPEC. The vaguely worded agreement was renounced in December. The approach to FUNCINPEC from the CPP served to emphasize its continuing opposition to a political role for the PDK. Khieu Samphan's return to Phnom-Penh in November provoked a violent demonstration. The villa that housed the PDK delegation to the SNC was besieged, and Khieu Samphan and Son Sen (the former DK Commander-in-Chief) were forced to flee to Thailand. A third SNC meeting in Pattaya, at which security arrangements for the PDK were discussed, finally permitted the SNC to begin functioning in Phnom-Penh at the end of December.

In the mean time, civic order in Phnom-Penh had collapsed. Former state employees, dispossessed of their jobs as a result of SOC 'privatizations', began to picket their former workplaces; people dispossessed of their assigned, cheaply leased housing as the result of the now lawful, but often corrupt, sale of state-owned buildings, or evicted from squatter settlements, demonstrated in support of demands for compensation and new homes. Students protested against corruption among senior officials. Public order was only slowly restored by the imposition of a curfew, the assassination of one prominent critic, the use of armed police and security services and the detention of a large number of demonstrators.

Cambodian expectations from the UN could not be satisfied. UNTAC was the largest multi-functional mission ever attempted, involving 16,000 troops, 3,600 civilian police, 2,400 civilian administrators and approximately 5,000 local employees, and there were delays linked to fund-raising and the recruitment of appropriate personnel. Yasushi Akashi, the most senior Japanese diplomat at the UN, was named Special Representative of the UN Secretary-General in Cambodia and Head of UNTAC. Maj.-Gen. John Sanderson, an Australian, was chosen to head UNTAC's vital military component. UNTAC was not formally established in Phnom-Penh until mid-March 1992, and then with only limited staff. By this time the cease-fire agreed in October had disintegrated, and the four factions had become determined to secure further territorial gains. The PDK refused to comply with the peace process, and in April the UN condemned the party for its failure to co-operate and particularly for its refusal to allow UNTAC officials free access to PDK-controlled territory. The PDK army, the NADK, engaged the CPP army in Kampong Thom, accusing the 'Vietnamese' forces of initiating the offensive. Concurrently, PDK spokesmen accused UNTAC of ignoring its responsibilities under the Paris agreement to control and supervise the withdrawal of all 'foreign forces', claiming the existence of thousands of concealed Vietnamese troops in Cambodia. By June the PDK had announced that its army would not regroup or disarm, in compliance with the demands of the incomplete military contingent of UNTAC. The PDK strongly criticized provisions of the election law introduced by Akashi, which permitted Vietnamese residents to vote providing that the intending voter was born in Cambodia, with at least one parent who was also born in Cambodia, or, wherever born, able to prove that at least one parent was a Cambodian person by the place of birth principle.

As the election campaign advanced, a total of 20 political parties met UNTAC requirements for a place on the ballot paper. Most of the parties were poorly organized and lacked financial resources; the majority were vehicles for prominent individuals who in some cases had returned from long periods of overseas exile. Excluding the parties forged during the 1978–91 war, namely the CPP, FUNCINPEC (which altered its title to the FUNCINPEC Party when adopting political status in February 1992) and the political party formed by the KPNLF, the Buddhist Liberal Democratic Party (BLDP) led by Son Sann, the parties lacked the capacity to campaign effectively in every province. Difficulties of access to voters were further compounded by the SOC's refusal to allow access to state-controlled media to any party but the CPP, in clear violation of the Paris agreement. UNTAC quickly installed its own radio station in order to educate the Cambodian public about free and fair elections.

Hun Sen pledged that the CPP would outlaw the PDK and defeat its forces militarily. The BLDP, together with the majority of parties formed on the basis of bonds of personal loyalty, judged the major issue to be the need to defend Cambodia from Vietnamese immigration and annexation. Provincial CPP leaders systematically threatened anti-CPP party workers and candidates, discouraging many from campaigning; among those who persisted, a large number were murdered. The PDK brutally encouraged the rising sentiments of anti-Vietnamese nationalism by massacring Vietnamese civilians in long-established fishing communities on the Tonlé Sap, provoking a mass exodus of more than 20,000 Cambodian Vietnamese to Viet Nam in April–May 1993. Ranariddh, leading the FUNCINPEC Party's campaign, warned that a CPP election victory would result in renewed civil war between the CPP and the PDK.

Despite an increase in fighting between Phnom-Penh forces and the PDK, UNTAC's voter registration campaign was extremely successful; by the end of the process in February 1993 4.7m. Cambodians (constituting 97% of the estimated eligible electorate) had been registered. The repatriation of refugees from camps on the Thai border also proceeded on schedule; all 360,000 had been returned to Cambodia by the end of April. Despite fears of PDK assaults against polling stations, 89.6% of all eligible registered voters participated in the elections, which took place on 23–28 May. The PDK offered its support to the FUNCINPEC Party in the hope of securing a role in government. Amid allegations of electoral malpractice, UNTAC rejected CPP requests for fresh elections in at least four provinces. Sihanouk, supposedly advised of an imminent coup as troops surrounded the Royal Palace, agreed to an interim FUNCINPEC-CPP coalition Government, following discussions with the CPP Chairman, Chea Sim. The proposal was vetoed, unexpectedly, by Ranariddh, who was out of the country.

The official results of the election were released on 5 June 1993. The FUNCINPEC Party secured 58 of the 120 seats in the Constituent Assembly and the CPP 51. The CPP carried 11 of the 21 constituencies, with most of its votes coming from the smaller, rural provinces in which many opposition parties had failed to campaign. The BLDP finished a distant third, securing 10 seats, while the only other party to gain representation was MOLINAKA (National Liberation Movement of Cambodia, a breakaway faction from FUNCINPEC), which took one seat. The CPP refused to transfer power to the FUNCINPEC Party. Some senior CPP officials formed a secession movement led by one of Sihanouk's sons, Norodom Chakrapong, who had been appointed Vice-Chairman of the Council of Ministers following his defection from FUNCINPEC to join the CPP shortly after the signing of the Paris agreement. The movement, which sought to force the formation of a coalition government, was unsuccessful and Chakrapong fled to Viet Nam, although he was subsequently permitted to return. Hun Sen arranged for the Constituent Assembly to endorse special powers for Sihanouk at its inaugural meeting on 14 July 1993. Sihanouk's spokesmen announced in July 1993 that Ranariddh and Hun Sen would be co-chairmen of the Provisional National Government of Cambodia, pending the drafting of a new constitution. Although the formation of an interim government and the resumption of powers by Sihanouk were outside the terms of the Paris agreement, UNTAC was powerless to intervene in these developments. In July and August, as Sihanouk attempted to organize 'round-table' talks with the PDK, the USA continued to object to any role for the PDK in the coalition. Excluded from the coalition, the Khmers Rouges continued their armed rebellion, but, with no foreign government willing to recognize them, the group lost national and international political legitimacy.

Although Sihanouk's attempts to arrange a political settlement between the PDK and CPP at meetings in 1993 and 1994 failed, the Prince exerted considerable influence in determining his role, and the role of future Kings, in the new constitutional order. On 21 September 1993 the Constituent Assembly adopted a new Constitution. This was signed and promulgated by Sihanouk on 24 September (in his newly resumed, extra-legal role of 'Head of State' and as Chairman of the SNC, a legal but non-functioning entity), and on the same day Sihanouk acceded to the throne of the new Kingdom of Cambodia. The promulgation of the Constitution coincided with the first public acknowledgements that Sihanouk was seriously ill with cancer. Although prevented by the Constitution from identifying a crown prince, Sihanouk awarded royal titles to three sons, a half-brother and one relative from the Sisowath line. The Constituent Assembly duly became the National Assembly, and Chea Sim was subsequently re-elected as its Chairman, replacing Son Sann, leader of the BLDP (who had held the post during the period of provisional national government between June and October).

THE ROYAL GOVERNMENT OF CAMBODIA

At the end of October 1993 the National Assembly approved the composition of the new Royal Government of Cambodia (RGC), which had been endorsed by Sihanouk. Ranariddh was named First Prime Minister and Hun Sen Second Prime Minister. Paradoxically, the restoration of constitutional government to Cambodia led to serious factional disputes within the ruling CPP and the FUNCINPEC Party. King Sihanouk's personal agenda was at variance with the predominantly bureaucratic and militarist impulses within the CPP as well as anti-communist, technocratic tendencies within the royalist movement. After 25 years of political turmoil, Cambodia was no longer self-sufficient in cereal production, had little modern infrastructure, and supported excessively large and ill-disciplined security forces. The use of patronage to secure political support during the PRK era had also led to an oversized bureaucracy staffed by a highly politicized corps of civil servants. Disputes relating to policy and supremacy within the CPP revolved around Chea Sim, who represented the deeply authoritarian and traditional element of the party. Hun Sen, by contrast, spoke for a younger generation of cadres who had been recruited to the revolutionary cause during the 1970s. In his role as Chairman of the National Assembly, Chea Sim ignored Sihanouk's initiatives, defended the corporate interests of the army and of the state administration (which were broadly indistinguishable from the organizational interests of the CPP) and urged uncompromising policies towards the PDK. The most significant such policy was the adoption in July 1994 of a law that declared the PDK to be 'an illegal and criminal group', thereby proscribing the party.

Despite its impressive electoral success, the FUNCINPEC Party, in contrast to the CPP, lacked a nation-wide organization of disciplined cadres and supporters, although at a ministerial level FUNCINPEC was stronger, displaying a pronounced technocratic orientation. Serious differences of opinion on how best to resolve the PDK issue continued to divide party intellectuals; with the PDK being in control of 5%–10% of the population and around 10% of national territory, the issue had become one of partitioning the country. The conciliatory position of Sihanouk towards the PDK commanded most support. The Minister of Finance, Sam Rainsy, a FUNCINPEC member of the National Assembly, regarded economic growth, rather than political unity, as crucial to the Government's stability. As a former banker and advocate of free market development, Rainsy favoured co-operation with foreign donors in the drafting of reconstruction plans.

By mid-1994 Ranariddh had begun openly to support the CPP election pledge to ban the PDK. Once introduced in the National Assembly, the law to ban the PDK was initially opposed by a group of approximately 15 legislators, led by Rainsy. However, most members of the National Assembly, including Rainsy, subsequently voted in favour of the legislation, after various amendments were agreed. The proposed legislation was quickly signed into law by the acting Head of State, Chea Sim, and it eventually received the assent of Sihanouk (who had been undergoing chemotherapy in China at the time of the vote).

Political co-operation between Ranariddh and Hun Sen grew considerably from July 1994, following a coup attempt allegedly instigated by Norodom Chakrapong. With the support of ex-FUNCINPEC army generals and units loyal to Ranariddh, Hun Sen succeeded in arresting Chakrapong, who protested his innocence and appealed successfully to his father to be allowed to go into exile. Sihanouk announced that he would no longer intervene in the affairs of the RGC. Former CPP general Sin Song was also arrested, but escaped to Thailand in September before he could be brought to trial. A new press law, adopted by the National Assembly in July 1995, made defamation a criminal offence and codified governmental rights to suspend publication of newspapers that carried articles deemed disruptive of 'national security' and 'political stability'.

The adoption of the law proscribing the PDK, the political eclipse of Sihanouk and the restrictions imposed on the press signalled an end to the era of political transition. Having neutralized the role of Sihanouk, the two Prime Ministers succeeded in removing the popular Rainsy from the Ministry of Finance during a cabinet reorganization in October 1994. Rainsy was expelled from the FUNCINPEC Party in May 1995 and excluded from his FUNCINPEC seat in the Assembly in June.

As the leaders of the CPP-FUNCINPEC coalition Government continued to consolidate their power and as the demise of most other political parties occurred, in July 1995 Son Sann, the President of the BLDP, and Ieng Mouly, the party's Secretary-General and the Minister of Information and the Press in the coalition Government (and a long-standing rival of Son Sann), convened an extraordinary unofficial congress of the party. Although the two leaders were ostensibly in dispute over the allocation of public appointments offered to the party (one list prepared by Son Sann had been disregarded by the Government and a shorter list prepared by Mouly had been accepted), Mouly claimed that his strategic concern was party political: to determine decisively whether the BLDP was part of the RGC of which he was a member, or whether, as Son Sann believed, the party was part of the parliamentary opposition. The congress elected Mouly's candidates as new party officers and approved a vote of no confidence in four of the BLDP members of the National Assembly, including Son Sann. Contrary to expectation, the four were not immediately expelled from the Assembly.

The formation in November 1995 of the Khmer Nation Party (KNP) by Rainsy was highly significant, as it challenged the organizational viability of Rainsy's former party. In rapid succession a planned FUNCINPEC party congress was postponed until March 1996; Prince Norodom Sirivudh, the party's General Secretary and a personal friend of Rainsy, was arrested for allegedly expressing a wish to assassinate Hun Sen; and in December 1995, following international and domestic protests over political abuse of the legal system, another intervention from Sihanouk secured Sirivudh's release from prison and exile to France.

The arrest of Sirivudh, organized by Hun Sen, which ultimately deprived FUNCINPEC of its leading organizational personality just as the party risked major defections to the KNP, disrupted the CPP-FUNCINPEC alliance. However, the Second Prime Minister's leading role in the CPP did not remain unchallenged. In January 1996 Hun Sen insisted on the reintroduction of 7 January as a public holiday in commemoration of the Vietnamese 'liberation' of 1979. For supporters of the former non-communist resistance of 1979–91, which included FUNCINPEC, this holiday was an affront, even though the regime installed by the Vietnamese in Phnom-Penh on 7 January 1979 had replaced that of Pol Pot. Ranariddh retaliated in January 1996 by denouncing Vietnamese encroachments on Cambodian border territory as a 'full invasion'. The CPP-controlled judiciary proceeded in February with the trial *in absentia* of Sirivudh, who was found guilty of criminal conspiracy and of possession of unlicensed firearms and sentenced to 10 years' imprisonment. In March Ranariddh accused the CPP of reneging on power-sharing agreements at district *(srok)* level. Hun Sen demanded a public apology from Ranariddh, and in June he instructed CPP provincial governors not to facilitate visits of the First Prime Minister to their provinces.

The dispute between the two Prime Ministers was communicated through the ranks of their parties, paralysing public administration, obstructing decisions relating to foreign investment and making it impossible to set an agenda for meetings of the National Assembly. Political and ideological tensions were exacerbated by an economic downturn, and especially by the suspension by the IMF of aid to the budget, the devaluation of the national currency in US dollar exchanges and labour unrest.

International consultants recommended that both the forthcoming *khum* (sub-district or commune) headship elections and the legislative elections be held concurrently in 1998 and that a national election commission, to include non-governmental organizations (NGOs), be established. CPP representatives were steadily seeking to limit international expectations of involvement in the elections, beyond the provision of funding, technical assistance and a modest number of observers. CPP officials and local CPP-controlled security forces also forced the closure of many provincial party offices opened by the KNP in the second half of 1996. Police harassment, and the assassination of several party officials, signalled a refusal to allow opposition parties to challenge the existing political configuration. Sam Rainsy, with tacit support from FUNCINPEC, emphasized the need for the widest possible international involvement in the forthcoming elections. In June Hun Sen proclaimed his support for political pluralism and the formation of new parties, while denying that the CPP had any aspirations to integrate all parties into one and thereby restore the one-party state of the 1980s. While conflict between the CPP and FUNCINPEC increased, and the repression of the KNP continued, the CPP lent support to small or newly formed parties and also encouraged defections from the KNP and FUNCINPEC.

Following the military set-backs of 1995 and the substantial losses suffered as a result of defections and self-demobilizations in 1995–96, the PDK leadership was perturbed by the near-loss of its economic capital at Pailin in April–May 1996. Deprived of Chinese military assistance in 1991, the Khmers Rouges had financed their armed struggle by selling logging and gem concessions to entrepreneurs in neighbouring Thailand and by purchasing weapons and ammunition in private markets. Inadequate or poor agricultural land in zones under the movement's control pushed many communities in the interior to offset revenue shortfalls by resorting to banditry, extortion and theft. The appropriation of goods and wealth and the coercive treatment of civilians undermined the historically good social relations between the PDK/NADK and the peasantry. War-weariness was compounded by Phnom-Penh's adoption of the law proscribing the movement in 1994; by January 1995 more than 7,000 fighters had taken advantage of an offer of amnesty made by the RGC. The PDK formed a Provisional Government of National Union and National Salvation of Cambodia (PGNUNSC) in July 1994 and, in early 1995, launched an assault on villages in the north-west, leaving more than 40,000 civilians temporarily displaced. By mid-1996 negotiators from FUNCINPEC, led by the royalist Gen. Nhiek Bun Chhay and assisted by the Thai authorities, had initiated secret contacts with several DK commanders based near the border with Thailand.

Independent of the FUNCINPEC initiative, policy disputes within the PDK led younger military leaders in the movement's commercial regions of Pailin and Phnom Malai into open confrontation with senior civilian leaders in Anlong Veng, in the north-west of the country. In August 1996 the Pol Pot-controlled clandestine radio denounced several field commanders and Ieng Sary, the former DK Minister of Foreign Affairs, as 'traitors' and ordered their immediate arrest. Rejecting the charges, Commanders Y Chhien at Pailin and Sok Pheap at Phnom Malai revealed that they had been unwilling to carry out instructions to recollectivize the economy, starting with the confiscations of means of transport. Once effectively expelled from the movement, the dissident Khmers Rouges indicated their willingness to recognize the authority of the Royal Government and their respect for the Constitution, but made clear their refusal either to surrender or to defect to Phnom-Penh. The Democratic National Union Movement (DNUM), founded by Ieng Sary, was quickly established as a channel for negotiating a union with the Government, while resisting integration by either side and carefully asserting the political and territorial autonomy of the breakaway region. Subsequently, the DNUM and generals from FUNCINPEC and the CPP competed for brokering opportunities and political influence. Together, they ultimately garnered support from 11 other DK divisions and fronts during late 1996. At the joint request of the two Prime Ministers, a royal amnesty was granted to Ieng Sary for the death sentence given *in absentia* by a PRK tribunal in 1979 and also for criminal penalties arising from the 1994 law that outlawed the DK group. Breakaway troops associated with the DNUM were formally inducted into the command structure of the Royal Cambodian Armed Forces (RCAF) in November, although most refused reassignment. In official appointments and commissions announced in January 1997, Y Chhien was appointed Governor of Pailin, while retaining control of the lucrative gem and logging activities, the principal source of income for the DK movement after 1991. Although the CPP initially welcomed the dissolution of the DK movement, and acquired the political loyalty of some breakaway DK military commanders, the renewal of resistance era comradeship among many dissident Khmers Rouges and pro-BLDP and FUNCINPEC military leaders, together with military confrontations between pro-FUNCINPEC and pro-CPP forces in Battambang, gave rise to suspicions that FUNCINPEC hoped to establish a new political alliance.

Senior CPP officials asserted that their party was in full control and would win most or all of the approaching 1,453 *khum* headship elections. In an attempt further to marginalize their royalist allies and opponents, many of whom, like Ranariddh and Sam Rainsy, held dual French and Cambodian nationality, the quinquennial congress of the CPP proposed to require candidates for all public offices in Cambodia, including *khum* headships, to hold Cambodian nationality only. Royalist officials began overtly to supply military protection and political assistance to the KNP at the opening of its party offices in Battambang, and to seek negotiations with the last of the insurgent, Pol Pot-led PDK forces in Anlong Veng.

Alongside the KNP, a new electoral National United Front (NUF) was established in February 1997, to which the BLDP-Son Sann faction and the small Khmer Neutral Party quickly rallied. This revitalization of the historic nationalist front, which had propelled the royalists to power in the 1993 elections, coincided with the publication of an interview with King Sihanouk, in which he revealed his unhappiness with the way in which the governing parties had restored some respectability to the Khmers Rouges, his concerns about the country's future in view of the suspension of IMF assistance and about deforestation. He also suggested that he might abdicate the throne, as he had done in 1955. Clearly alarmed by the prospect of the King usurping CPP state power, Hun Sen announced that he would cancel the local and national elections if Sihanouk should abdicate. He added that if the King did not refrain from interfering in politics, he would seek to amend the Constitution to prohibit all members of the royal family from participating in politics. The King, though silenced, had successfully exposed the gradual realignment of the royalist movement as well as the authoritarian orientations of the Second Prime Minister. The FUNCINPEC-CPP discussions of March 1997 produced little reconciliation.

The decline in public order in the second quarter of 1997 was rapid and seemingly irreversible, despite attempts made by a bipartisan FUNCINPEC-CPP Commission for Abnormal Conflict Resolution to uphold the neutrality of national policing and of the army. As the CPP began in earnest to form a new ruling alliance, it secured support from Ieng Mouly of the BLDP, the Democrat Party (In Tam), the Free Development Republican Party (Ted Ngoy), the Khmer Citizens' Party (Nguon Soeur), and the Liberal Democratic Party (LDP—Chhim Om Yon), and abandoned its demand for electoral candidates to be Cambodian nationals. Hun Sen lent support to a rebellion against Ranariddh's leadership of the FUNCINPEC Party promoted by eight FUNCINPEC members of the National Assembly, thus beginning the process of the accumulation of the necessary parliamentary votes for the removal of the First Prime Minister by constitutional means. A party congress organized by the rebels in June resulted in the formation of FUNCINPEC II and the election of Toan Chhay, a former resistance commander and the FUNCINPEC Governor of Siem Reap, as Chairman. At the same time, the attempt by the exiled Prince Sirivudh (still a seated FUNCINPEC legislator) to return to Phnom-Penh was blocked in Hong Kong. Equally concerned about political realignments and the possible disintegration of FUNCINPEC, PDK-Anlong Veng radio broadcasts urged public support for the Ranariddh-led NUF, even though the movement continued to detain 15 FUNCINPEC Party negotiators who had been taken hostage in mid-February. DNUM leaders expressed fears that inter-party disputes were undermining aspirations for national reconciliation and peace: their former leader, Pol Pot, was held responsible.

THE REMOVAL OF PRINCE RANARIDDH AND SUBSEQUENT ELECTIONS

One final attempt at reconciling the personal and political disputes dividing the two Prime Ministers occurred in May 1997; within 24 hours, however, Prince Ranariddh had accused Hun Sen of planning to restore a communist dictatorship if the CPP won the elections. The Prince urged the dissolution of the National Assembly and the holding of early elections but, as a means of delaying a confrontation in the legislature, the FUNCINPEC Party General Secretary and acting Chairman of the National Assembly, Loy Simchheang, postponed conflict on the issue of the FUNCINPEC-Ranariddh proposal to expel renegade FUNCINPEC deputies from the Assembly via the procedural device of suspending steering committee meetings. Polarization of party politics was further accentuated at the end of May, when containers of weapons, destined for the First Prime Minister's 1,500-strong bodyguard unit, were seized by CPP officials, and when Ranariddh revealed that Khieu Samphan, the nominal leader of the PDK, had communicated to him a desire to return to mainstream Cambodian politics. Controversy over the treatment to be accorded to Pol Pot and the last of his close associates increased in early June, when speculation that the FUNCINPEC Party was on the verge of reaching an agreement with Khieu Samphan intensified. FUNCINPEC's senior military adviser, Gen. Nhiek Bun Chhay, announced that Pol Pot, Ta Mok (Pol Pot's Chief of Staff) and Son Sen would go into voluntary exile in exchange for immunity from prosecution; it was indicated by FUNCINPEC that the exile of these individuals would constitute acceptable grounds for the return to the mainstream political arena of Khieu Samphan, with reports suggesting that there were plans for him to form a new political alliance with FUNCINPEC and Sam Rainsy's KNP. However, Pol Pot apparently vetoed the agreement with FUNCINPEC and then reportedly ordered the assassination of Son Sen, his wife and nine relatives in retaliation for Son Sen's suspected secret dealings with Hun Sen and a CPP spy network. The news of Son Sen's death was later confirmed by Ranariddh. Pol Pot then reportedly fled in a 10-vehicle convoy, which included Khieu Samphan. The convoy was intercepted by troops wanting to defect to the Government, led by Ta Mok. The surrounding of Pol Pot by mutinous NADK soldiers gave rise to international, and some national, appeals for him to be transferred to the Cambodian Government and brought to justice. These appeals were supported by the two Prime Ministers, but produced no lessening of strife between the two coalition parties. Ranariddh reaffirmed his willingness, in principle, to accept the defection of nearly all Anlong Veng guerrillas, barring only Pol Pot and Ta Mok, and to welcome Khieu Samphan and his National Solidarity Party into the NUF provided that he received the necessary royal amnesty. However, disregarding his previous negotiations with Ieng Sary, Hun Sen began insisting, *inter alia*, that negotiations with the DK were illegal.

In June 1997, after denouncing the fleeing Pol Pot for acts of treason in an extraordinary public criticism of the former leader, a radio broadcast made on Anlong Veng radio in Khieu Samphan's name pledged the loyalty of the latter's National Solidarity Party to the FUNCINPEC-led NUF and urged all national forces to unite in a struggle against Hun Sen, stigmatized as a 'lackey' of Viet Nam. Within hours, the military bodyguard units of the two Prime Ministers and other high officials clashed on the streets of Phnom-Penh. Characterizing a personal meeting between Ranariddh and Khieu Samphan as an intolerable betrayal, Hun Sen then issued an ultimatum to the Prince giving him a few days in which to decide whether he wished to work with the coalition Government or with Khieu Samphan. Anlong Veng radio announced triumphantly that Pol Pot had surrendered. As the Consultative Group on Cambodia, (CG—comprising bilateral and multilateral donors) met in Paris in early July, Hun Nheng, the CPP Governor of Kampong Thom province and a brother of Hun Sen, forcibly disarmed 70 of Ranariddh's security guards as the Prince completed a tour of the province. As the DK defector Keo Pong, allegedly acting upon orders from the Second Prime Minister, positioned his troops for an assault on Gen. Nhiek Bun Chhay's garrison, the Prince boarded a flight to France.

The airport and large parts of Phnom-Penh were cordoned off and looted by marauding troops during 4–6 July 1997, and the FUNCINPEC and KNP party offices were ransacked. Hun Sen denied that he was staging a coup or aiming to govern on his own; however, he insisted that the First Prime Minister be replaced. He attributed the outbreak of violence in the capital to a criminal conspiracy mounted by Ranariddh, together with the outlawed Khmers Rouges, and accused Ranariddh of having broken the law by negotiating with the DK, by unlawfully smuggling ex-DK troops into Phnom-Penh to strengthen his own forces and by secretly importing weapons to arm those forces. Denouncing Ranariddh's actions, Hun Sen ordered the two factions in FUNCINPEC to replace the Prince, and thereby to restore stability to the ruling FUNCINPEC-CPP coalition, protecting the 1993 Constitution and providing the basis for democratic elections in May 1998. Furthermore, Hun Sen revealed that he had already asked both the Co-Minister of Defence, Tie Chamrath, and the leader of FUNCINPEC II, Toan Chhay, if they would serve as First Prime Minister, but each had declined. Only three FUNCINPEC leaders—Nhiek Bun Chhay, Chau Sambath and Serei Kosal—were unacceptable to Hun Sen. Troops loyal to the CPP and Keo Pong were ordered to locate and eliminate these three; other FUNCINPEC leaders were also similarly named as targets. In total, approximately 40 people, including Sambath, were murdered during the week beginning 4 July 1997; tens of thousands of civilians associated with the royalist, democratic or human rights movements and parties went into temporary hiding, and approximately one-half of the FUNCINPEC Party members in the legislature fled overseas, fearing for their lives. Hun Sen pledged that all FUNCINPEC ministers, legislators and cabinet officials who agreed to withdraw their support from Ranariddh as party leader and Prime Minister would be allowed to retain their government positions; he also promised to amend the Constitution to create more positions, allowing individuals belonging to parties not represented in the National Assembly to hold government portfolios.

However, the politics of armed resistance continued. From France, Ranariddh announced his intention to resist his expulsion from the Government, vowing to employ military force if necessary. Although five FUNCINPEC generals had been killed, Gen. Nhiek Bun Chhay and others escaped, and proceeded to establish resistance bases in the north-west. At the UN and in the USA, Ranariddh continued to be recognized as Prime Minister. The US Government expressed strong opposition to the use of force to change the results of the 1993 election and effectively to rupture the Paris Peace Agreement of 1991. Sam Rainsy, leader of the KNP but acting on behalf of the NUF, issued an appeal to the international community to suspend economic assistance to Cambodia, excluding essential humanitarian aid; Germany and the USA obliged, while Australia suspended military assistance. Both Sam Rainsy and Prince Ranariddh rushed to the Thai-Cambodian border to make contact with the more than 20,000 people fleeing the country, many of whom were their supporters, and quickly agreed with more than 20 temporarily exiled BLDP and FUNCINPEC legislators to establish a Union of Cambodian Democrats (UCD) for the purpose of restoring the legitimate Royal Cambodian Government by peaceful means. ASEAN members agreed at a ministerial conference in July 1997 to postpone indefinitely Cambodia's accession to the organization, originally scheduled for that month, and formally requested Cambodia to take measures to preserve, until the forthcoming elections, the power-sharing arrangement agreed following the elections of 1993. ASEAN also agreed to send mediators to Beijing, the Thai capital of Bangkok and Phnom-Penh in an attempt to facilitate a peaceful solution to the crisis, despite Hun Sen's initial rejection of previous offers of mediation. Hun Sen's decision in mid-July 1997 to ask the FUNCINPEC Minister of Foreign Affairs, Ung Huot, to serve concurrently as First Prime Minister provoked international criticism. In the first DNUM comment regarding the events of 5–6 July, Gen. Y Chhien of Pailin stated that his party opposed the ousting of Ranariddh and regarded the nomination of Ung Huot as inappropriate.

The CPP stayed the course. In August 1997 the National Assembly voted on the nomination of Ung Huot as First Prime Minister, replacing Prince Ranariddh: 86 members of the 120-seat National Assembly voted in favour of his appointment. Ung Huot was formally elected when acting Head of State Chea Sim signed a royal decree approving the appointment after King Norodom Sihanouk reportedly gave his authorization; Ung Huot and Hun Sen agreed that a legislative election would be held in May 1998 as scheduled, and that the winner of that election would become Cambodia's sole Prime Minister. Meanwhile, Hun Sen gave National Assembly members who had left the country three months in which to return before being replaced. However, Hun Sen insisted that if Prince Ranariddh returned he would stand trial for attempting to negotiate an alliance with remaining Khmer Rouge rebels. A further significant development in Cambodia in July 1997, meanwhile, was the denunciation and trial of the former Khmer Rouge leader, Pol Pot, by his own comrades: an announcement broadcast on the PDK radio station stated that Pol Pot had been sentenced to life imprisonment at the Anlong Veng guerrilla base for 'betraying the Khmer Rouge movement'. (See below for subsequent developments.)

The events of 5–6 July 1997 resulted not only in the removal of Prince Ranariddh as First Prime Minister, but more fundamentally they were regarded as an attempt by Hun Sen to re-establish CPP control of the State and to put an end to the parallel FUNCINPEC structure in the armed forces, police and bureaucracy that had developed since 1993. The killing of several of Ranariddh's senior army and police commanders (a sixth general, Thach Kim Sang, was assassinated in March 1998) and the sentencing *in absentia* of two others (Nhiek Bun Chhay and Serei Kosal) to long prison terms severely weakened Ranariddh's capacity to mount a military challenge. In the immediate aftermath of the fighting, FUNCINPEC forces either agreed to be disarmed or retreated rapidly to their pre-1993 bases on the Thai border, from where they sought to link up with the remaining Khmer Rouge insurgents. Within a month, Nhiek Bun Chhay's forces retained only one stronghold, the border village of O Smach in Oddar Meanchey province. Total military control of the country evaded Hun Sen, owing to the failure of repeated government offensives against O Smach and the persistence of FUNCINPEC and PDK activity in other remote areas of the north and west; an internationally sponsored cease-fire was implemented on 27 February 1998.

However, achieving total control of the state apparatus proved less difficult for the CPP. Ung Huot, Ranariddh's replacement as First Prime Minister, served Hun Sen's purposes faithfully: the principle of 'consensus' and equality between the two parties, on which the coalition Government had been founded, was retained in form but not in substance. With the exception of Ranariddh, Hun Sen left almost all FUNCINPEC appointees in place; his priority was to retain international legitimacy. Hun Sen thus invited FUNCINPEC and BLDP ministers and members of the National Assembly to return from exile to their former positions, and even permitted a small UN team to monitor their safety. Hun Sen did attempt to reorganize the Cabinet in September 1997, with a view to rewarding Ieng Mouly, Toan Chhay and others, but this initiative was unexpectedly obstructed by internal disagreements within the remnants of FUNCINPEC and by opposition from the Chea Sim faction of the CPP, whose suspicion of Hun Sen's intentions had reached new heights. Hun Sen did successfully exploit his newly obtained parliamentary majority to ensure that the CPP would control the preparations for the elections due in 1998 and would retain judicial, as well as bureaucratic and military, power during and after the polls. The National Election Committee (NEC), the Supreme Council of Magistracy (SCM) and the Constitutional Council (CC)—the bodies mandated under the Constitution to organize elections, to appoint and supervise judges, and to monitor the constitutionality of laws and judge electoral disputes—were finally established with clear CPP majorities in each.

One obstacle confronting Hun Sen was the international opposition to his violent seizure of power. The UN decided in September 1997 to leave Cambodia's seat in the organization vacant until the elections. Foreign investment in Cambodia decreased sharply. Hun Sen consistently rejected offers from ASEAN, Thailand, the USA and King Sihanouk to mediate between him and Ranariddh, but his need for international recognition and aid ultimately proved too great. In February 1998 a 'four-pillar' peace plan, proposed by Japan and strongly supported by the 'Friends of Cambodia' (an informal grouping of countries involved in the Paris agreement), was accepted by both sides. The 'four pillars' were: a cease-fire, to be followed by the reintegration of Ranariddh's forces into the RCAF; the end of links between the Prince's forces and the PDK; a prompt trial and pardoning of Ranariddh; and his participation in the elections. A cease-fire was declared and was largely adhered to, but reintegration failed to take place and both sides continued to exchange accusations of links with the Khmers Rouges. In March two peremptory trials were held, at which Ranariddh was found guilty *in absentia* of smuggling weapons, causing instability, disobeying the orders of superiors and complicity with the Khmers Rouges. He was sentenced to a total of 35 years' imprisonment and ordered, together with his senior military commanders, to pay compensation of more than

US $54m. to cover the damage caused in the fighting. With the prospect of Japan, ASEAN and the EU withdrawing their support for the elections, Hun Sen wrote to the King requesting a full pardon for Ranariddh. The Prince was finally allowed to return to Cambodia at the end of March.

Between the violent removal of Prince Ranariddh from power and mid-2008 six major elections took place in Cambodia: the National Assembly election in 1998; the *khum* elections in 2002 and 2007; the National Assembly election in 2003; the first-ever Senate election in 2006; and the National Assembly election in 2008. All of these elections gave rise to a further consolidation of power by Hun Sen, thus putting electoral democracy in Cambodia at greater risk.

During the 1998 legislative election (which had been postponed from 23 May to 26 July to allow sufficient time for the NEC to complete preparations), the opposition's ability to compete for power had been severely weakened. As well as losing their headquarters during the events of July 1997, the opposition had been deprived of all access to the electronic media: the FUNCINPEC-aligned television and radio stations and the radio station operated by the BLDP had been taken over by the Government. Opposition and UN demands that past political violence be investigated went unheeded. Both the KNP and the BLDP were forced to change their names (to the Sam Rainsy Party (SRP) and Son Sann Party, respectively) owing to ongoing legal disputes. The uncertainty over Ranariddh's participation also exacerbated the split within FUNCINPEC. Three breakaway parties with close connections to the CPP registered for the elections: they were led by Toan Chhay, Ung Huot and Loy Simchheang. Meanwhile, the opposition was adversely affected by internal tensions within the UCD (particularly between Ranariddh and Rainsy).

None the less, under strong international pressure and despite grave reservations about the entire electoral process, the opposition did compete. The election proceeded unexpectedly smoothly. In spite of widespread low-level intimidation and an estimated 12 killings of their members, the FUNCINPEC Party and the SRP managed to attract significant crowds to their campaign rallies. Officially, 93.7% of the 5,395,024 registered went to vote on 26 July 1998, and on the next day the UN-co-ordinated Joint International Observation Group expressed its confidence that the elections had been 'free and fair'. However, the situation quickly deteriorated. Official preliminary results awarded the CPP 64 of the 122 seats in the National Assembly, the FUNCINPEC Party 43 and the SRP 15, under a complex system of proportional representation, although combined support for the FUNCINPEC Party and the SRP, which had won 31.7% and 14.3% of the votes respectively, represented a majority of the popular vote; the CPP secured 41.4%. The 36 other participating parties failed to obtain a single seat. The results gave the CPP a parliamentary majority but not the two-thirds' majority needed to form a government; Hun Sen thus offered to form a 60:40 coalition government with FUNCINPEC, with the provision that he be appointed premier and that the CPP retain all the important ministries. He also suggested the formation of a tripartite coalition, with the SRP being given 10% of ministerial positions and the FUNCINPEC Party 30%. These offers were rejected as premature by FUNCINPEC and the SRP, which alleged massive electoral irregularities. Both parties' leaders refused to recognize the election results until their complaints were investigated by the NEC. They also announced their intention to boycott the new National Assembly, which was scheduled to convene in September. FUNCINPEC and the SRP lodged nearly 900 complaints of election irregularities. In mid-August the Constitutional Council rejected all but one of the complaints lodged by the SRP, and this concerned a vote recount. In October the NEC issued a report, which concluded that there were no discrepancies in the vote count and that the results would stand.

In September 1998, amid steadily rising politically motivated violence, King Sihanouk convened unsuccessful negotiations in Siem Reap province, involving representatives from the CPP, FUNCINPEC, the SRP and the Constitutional Council. Accusing Sam Rainsy of responsibility for a grenade attack on his residence, Hun Sen sought refuge in a UN office. The police subsequently cleared 'Democracy Square', an area near the National Assembly that had been occupied by opposition supporters, precipitating street violence. Groups loyal to Sam Rainsy clashed with supporters of the CPP. Two monks were shot dead, and the Government banned members of the National Assembly from leaving the country. In mid-September Thomas Hammarberg, the UN Secretary-General's Special Representative for Human Rights in Cambodia, announced that, since the police action, 16 bodies (including those of the two monks) had been found. This figure was later revised to 26.

External diplomatic pressures resulted in the resumption of political negotiations among party leaders. Ranariddh announced that he was cancelling street demonstrations and would meet with the King. He also stated that FUNCINPEC would attend the first session of the National Assembly on 24 September 1998. Sam Rainsy made a similar public announcement. The King convened a summit meeting in Siem Reap involving Chea Sim, Hun Sen, Ranariddh and Sam Rainsy. The ban on foreign travel was removed. None the less, the tripartite discussions broke down in late September, and Ranariddh and Rainsy fled abroad in October.

In early October 1998 the King travelled to Phnom-Penh to renew his efforts to break the political impasse. In November the King hosted discussions attended by Hun Sen, Chea Sim and Ranariddh, which resulted in a protocol on power-sharing: Hun Sen would remain in office as Prime Minister, while Ranariddh would become the President of the National Assembly, replacing Chea Sim. A full amnesty was granted to Princes Norodom Sirivuth and Norodom Chakrapong and Generals Nhiek Bun Chhay, Serei Kosal and Sin Song. A second parliamentary chamber, a senate, was to be created under the chairmanship of Chea Sim, who would also serve as acting Head of State when the King was out of the country. Sam Rainsy, who had not been present at these discussions, was highly critical of them. He nevertheless returned to Cambodia from Paris; Prince Sirivuth also returned to Cambodia in early 1999.

On 30 November 1998 Hun Sen was approved as Prime Minister by a vote of 99 to 13 in the National Assembly. Of the 29 cabinet posts, 15 were accorded to the CPP and the remainder to FUNCINPEC. Both parties shared control of the Ministry of Interior and the Ministry of Defence. The new Government began drafting legislation for the conduct of 'free and fair' local elections, which were not held until February 2002 (see below).

By 2000 there were signs of greater political stability. Within the CPP, Hun Sen's power base appeared to have been consolidated. The Deputy Prime Minister and Co-Minister of the Interior, Sar Kheng, was apparently perceived by observers to represent the greatest threat to Hun Sen's leadership; it was also alleged that a rift existed between Sar Kheng and Hun Sen's closest ally, Sok An, Minister in charge of the Council of Ministers. FUNCINPEC, meanwhile, remained under the leadership of Ranariddh. At its congress in March it was acknowledged that the party would need to regroup if it were to become an effective political force. Ranariddh was subject to criticism for his ambivalence regarding the return to FUNCINPEC of former party members who were alleged to have abandoned the party after the events of July 1997. Hun Sen, while retaining FUNCINPEC as his coalition partner in the Government, sought to improve domestic security by adopting severe measures to control weapons and by seeking to reform the armed forces. Although repressive violence against members of the SRP by elements allied with the Government appeared to decline during 1999–2000, Rainsy continued to challenge the Government, voicing the concerns of groups such as protesting garment workers and the landless. In October 1999 a member of the legislature belonging to the SRP was abducted.

However, the royalists became increasingly accommodating. As leader of FUNCINPEC and Chairman of the National Assembly, Ranariddh did not want his ministers and royalist members of the legislature to be in conflict with the Hun Sen-dominated CPP; he thus assumed a secondary role in the Government. During its annual congress in March 2001 FUNCINPEC reaffirmed its commitment to working closely with the CPP in the interests of peace and reconciliation. After he had taken up the position of FUNCINPEC Secretary-General in July, Prince Sirivudh also advocated the politics of non-confrontation. This accommodating tone was motivated more by practical considerations than by goodwill: the royalists could no longer afford to risk another violent confrontation with Hun Sen, who had previously 'exiled' Prince Sirivudh after the latter had been accused of plotting a coup against the Prime Minister and had also ousted Ranariddh in 1997. Nevertheless, increasing political stability was being gained at the expense of democracy. Hun Sen acted as a stabilizing force within the Government, although the death of the Minister of Agriculture, Forestry, Hunting and Fisheries, Chhea Song, in April 2001 precipitated the need for a cabinet reorganization.

Local elections for the 1,621 *khum* headships took place on 3 February 2002. While the opposition political parties did participate, they failed to make any serious progress. The CPP retained approximately 98% of *khum* seats, leaving only 11 for the SRP and 10 for FUNCINPEC. Although the monopoly of power exercised by the CPP over the *khum* was broken, the participation of the SRP and FUNCINPEC appeared to contribute to the legitimacy of elections that were regarded by many as being far from 'free and fair', contrary to the testimony of the EU Election Observation Mission. Moreover, about 1.75m. of the 6.2m. eligible voters did not turn out to vote. Although the reason for the lower than expected turn-out was unclear, the campaign period had been characterized by intimidation and violence. At least 22 *khum* candidates and political activists belonging to FUNCINPEC and the SRP were reported to have been murdered. The Election Monitoring Organizations—comprising NGOs—issued a joint statement rejecting claims that the elections had been 'free and fair' and citing several instances of irregularities.

Relations between the CPP and FUNCINPEC remained stable for a while, as the CPP continued to consolidate its control over the country and the royalists found it hard to resist. Political stability was promoted both by FUNCINPEC's new commitment to a non-confrontational style of politics and by the weakened ability of the royalists to challenge the CPP. Internal frictions among the royalists intensified when they were forced to take sides between those who supported the Deputy Commander-in-Chief of the RCAF, Khan Savoeun (a FUNCINPEC member), and supporters of the Co-Minister of the Interior, You Hockry (another FUNCINPEC member), who was accused of nepotism and corruption. Under growing pressure from the party to resign from his cabinet post, You Hockry finally announced in May 2002 that he would accept the party's decision. (The National Assembly later rejected the efforts of Savoeun's supporters to remove You Hockry from his post.) At the same time Hang Dara, a senior member of FUNCINPEC, announced that he intended to create a new party. In late May he registered the Hang Dara Movement Democratic Party with the Ministry of the Interior, citing his dissatisfaction with FUNCINPEC's performance as his motivation. Another setback to FUNCINPEC came when Prince Chakrapong (the half-brother of Prince Ranariddh) chose to create a new royalist party—the Prince Norodom Chakrapong Khmer Soul Party; its members included Toan Chhay. Chakrapong sought permission to contest the legislative election, scheduled for July 2003, and offered to form a political alliance with the SRP.

The CPP continued to restrict civil liberties. In December 2002 the Government formed the Central Bureau for Security (CBS), most of the members of which were powerful CPP leaders. The decision to pursue more repressive measures against potential trouble-makers came in January 2003, after demonstrators protesting against comments made by a Thai actress regarding ownership of the temples at Angkor Wat burned down the Thai embassy and looted Thai business interests in Phnom-Penh. In February the National Police Commissioner, Gen. Hok Lundy, claimed that the police force was now prepared to demonstrate its strength by taking action against any demonstrators who refused to accept the election results. In March about 200 armed riot police dispersed a group of demonstrators loyal to the SRP, injuring 13 of them. In June the police opened fire on around 300 workers staging a protest at a garment factory, leaving two protesters dead and more than 20 policemen injured.

As campaigning for the national election of 2003 got under way, the CPP maintained its political dominance. In August 2002 the National Assembly approved amendments to the Election Law that allowed the Ministry of the Interior to nominate five 'dignitaries' to the NEC, allowing the CPP to exercise greater control over the electoral process. The amendments were adopted without any debate in the Senate. Three of the five new NEC members reportedly enjoyed close links with the CPP, while the other two belonged to FUNCINPEC. Tensions between King Sihanouk and the CPP did not help FUNCINPEC. The King's position on national issues was challenged by CPP officials, in particular Hun Sen. On several occasions the King threatened to abdicate unless the Government convened the Royal Council of the Throne to be entrusted with the power to elect a new king, but this threat was disregarded by Hun Sen, who declared that the 2003 election was of more importance. Meanwhile, the royalists still found themselves unable to co-operate with the SRP. Members of the two parties engaged in a campaign of defections. In March it was reported that about 20 royalist generals intended to defect to the SRP. By May six royalists had defected to the SRP, and seven SRP members had joined FUNCINPEC.

On 27 July 2003 a total of 23 political parties contested elections to the 123-seat National Assembly. The CPP secured victory, obtaining 73 seats and 47.35% of all votes cast, an improvement on its performance at the 1998 poll, followed by FUNCINPEC with 26 seats (20.75% of votes) and the SRP with 24 (21.87%). However, as in the 1998 elections, the CPP failed to obtain the two-thirds' majority of National Assembly seats that would enable it to form a single-party government, raising the prospect of further political instability.

When assessed in terms of its free nature and fairness, the 2003 national election appeared to bear testament to the country's democratic progress. Between the *khum* elections of early 2002 and the commencement of the 2003 election campaign, 12 acts of lethal violence (including the murder of Om Rasady, one of Prince Ranariddh's senior advisers) were committed against political activists. The polling period itself was relatively free from violence. However, the Government took repressive action after the election. Restrictions on political freedoms continued, and post-election demonstrations were prohibited. In November 2003 garment factory workers staged a demonstration but were confronted by armed riot police, who used excessive force to disperse them. Any serious opposition to the CPP regime continued to risk violent repression. In October a Ta Prohm Radio editor and journalist, Chour Chetharith, was shot dead outside his office, the first time that a journalist had been killed in the country since 1996. In January 2004 Chea Vichea, the leader of a major trade union, a founding member of the SRP and a member of the Alliance of Democrats (comprising supporters of FUNCINPEC and the SRP), was also shot dead. Even monks remained subject to control. In October 2003 12 Buddhist monks were threatened with expulsion from their pagoda because they allegedly supported the SRP. In May 2005 the Ministry of the Interior's ban of a workers' march planned for International Labour Day was regarded by observers as further evidence of Hun Sen's increased power.

Another arena for the consolidation of Hun Sen's power was the Senate, where he also managed to expand CPP domination. On 4 March 1999 the National Assembly finally voted by 106 to five to amend the Constitution and create a Senate with the power to scrutinize and amend bills before returning them to the National Assembly for affirmation and final royal assent. Chea Sim was duly elected Chairman of the Senate. Prince Sisowath, Chivoun Monirak and Nhiek Bun Chhay were chosen as Deputy Chairmen. Representation in the 61-member Senate was proportional to party strength in the lower house: 31 seats were allocated to the CPP; 21 seats to FUNCINPEC; seven seats to the SRP; and two members were nominated by the King. The inaugural session of the Senate was held on 25 March. Only the 123 members of the National Assembly and some 13,000 commune councillors (most of whom were loyal to the CPP) would be allowed to cast ballots at the election for the 57 senators for the next six-year term, to take place in early 2006. In late 2005 Hun Sen ordered the arrest of several leading activists critical of his policies (including prominent

NGO activists in the field of human rights, most notably Kem Sokha), but released them after the election and prior to the meeting of international donors of March 2006. In January the CPP secured 45 of the 57 elective seats in the Senate, while FUNCINPEC won 10 seats and the SRP obtained the remaining two. (A further four seats were filled by appointees of the National Assembly and the King.) Several of the new CPP senators were business tycoons who had developed close links with Hun Sen over the years.

The second *khum* elections, held on 1 April 2007, helped to maintain the CPP's political power at the local level. The Norodom Ranariddh Party (NRP), under the leadership of the Prince following his departure from FUNCINPEC in late 2006 (see below), won no commune chief positions, having secured only 425 sub-district councillor positions, compared with the 7,993 won by the CPP and 2,660 by the SRP. Overall, the election was conducted in an atmosphere of less violence, political intimidation and confrontation than had prevailed at previous polls.

The only two non-CPP parties—FUNCINPEC and the SRP—that had any chance of gaining popular support in future elections could not form a credible united front capable of challenging the CPP. The SRP and FUNCINPEC had formed the Alliance of Democrats in August 2003, demanding that Hun Sen relinquish the post of Prime Minister. In mid-2004, however, the interim Government remained in power, as the CPP, FUNCINPEC and the SRP had failed to agree on the composition of the next administration. The CPP was unwilling to meet several of the demands of the Alliance of Democrats, including the formation of a tripartite government incorporating FUNCINPEC and the SRP, an increase in salary for public servants from US $30 to $100 per month and a commitment to combating corruption through the promotion of good governance. Hun Sen rejected the concept of any coalition government that would include the SRP. The idea of a 'two-and-a-half party' government was entertained, but the post-election crisis remained unresolved for almost a year. After the 2007 *khum* elections the SRP again considered the possibility of a 'Democratic Movement' that would include all the challengers to the CPP, but any new pragmatic alliance between the SRP and FUNCINPEC (and possibly also the NRP) was likely to lack cohesion. By mid-2007 the opposition to the CPP was in complete disarray. FUNCINPEC was weakened by internal divisions, and the SRP was still in search of new political allies.

As the 2008 legislative election approached, the CPP appeared to be in a strong position. The number of political parties registered to contest the election had been reduced to 11, and the prospect of a serious challenge to the CPP's dominance was unlikely. The NRP had become largely dysfunctional, with its leader, Prince Ranariddh, reportedly experiencing financial problems, along with allegations of corruption and scandals in his personal affairs. The royalists remained deeply divided; some joined the CPP, and many were under pressure to follow in the same direction. Leading members of FUNCINPEC, such as Prince Chakrapong, Prince Sirivudh, Princess Norodom Vacheara and Prince Sisowath Sireirath Phanara, were driven out of active politics. There was an ongoing debate among FUNCINPEC members about the possible return of Ranariddh, but resistance to the possibility remained strong because some still regarded him as a liability rather than an asset. Meanwhile, the perception that Cambodians benefited from fewer limits to civil liberties than other countries in the region was challenged by evidence that basic entitlements such as freedom of speech and the right to strike and to protest had been eroded by ongoing political intimidation. In May 2008, for example, Hun Sen threatened an independent station, Beehive Radio, after it had broadcast programming from opposition parties. A week later, a new radio station, Angkor Ratha, had its licence revoked after only six months, having offered air time to the political opposition. Observers suggested that, rather than indicating greater freedom, the decrease in protests and vocal criticism showed that the opposition had been increasingly silenced.

At the legislative election held on 27 July 2008, the CPP won 90 seats, leaving the SRP with 26 seats, the Human Rights Party with three, and FUNCINPEC and the NRP with two seats each. Female representation in the National Assembly increased to 22% (in comparison with 5% in 1993). Although the election was conducted in far more peaceful circumstances than previous polls, the distribution of seats caused some controversy: the four opposition parties rejected the results, claiming that they had been subject to manipulation by the CPP, accusing both the NEC and the Constitutional Council of having dismissed their requests for fresh polls or vote recounts, and urging the international community not to recognize the CPP's overwhelming victory. The overall trend indicated that the CPP was becoming increasingly successful in consolidating its political power, while, to some, the future of democracy remained uncertain. As analysed below, the process of democratization that began in the early 1990s had, by mid-2010, been reversed by the process of autocratization or personalization of power by Prime Minister Hun Sen.

HUN SEN'S CONSOLIDATION OF POWER

In addition to its electoral successes between 1998 and 2008, the CPP continued to consolidate its power by coercive means such as dividing or weakening the opposition, taking advantage of other parties' internal frictions, and controlling state institutions, the economy, civil society and the media.

The CPP actively sought to undermine FUNCINPEC. In September 2003 Prime Minister Hun Sen reportedly dismissed 17 senior FUNCINPEC government officials, accusing them of failing to carry out their duties. In June 2004 the political stalemate was exacerbated by FUNCINPEC's unreasonable demand that it be given one-half of all senior government-appointed posts; the CPP was reportedly prepared to give the royalist party only 40% of them. However, the two parties finally signed a deal that would increase the number of cabinet posts by 150%: from 89 in the previous Government to 207 (with 136 to be allocated to the CPP and 71 to FUNCINPEC).

After almost a year of political deadlock, a coalition Government was finally formed in mid-July 2004. The cabinet was reported to be the largest in the world: the total number of political appointees in government was 332, including 146 Under-Secretaries of State. At the same time, Hun Sen put pressure on members of the legislature to approve the 'package vote' that would facilitate his re-election as Prime Minister and enable him to maintain power. He sought to amend the Constitution and the Internal Rules of the National Assembly (requiring a vote by secret ballot) by introducing a new rule that would allow legislators to vote instead by a show of hands.

Hun Sen succeeded in strengthening his position by relying also on the strategy of direct condemnation of his opponents as well as on 'divide and conquer' tactics. Initially, he and Ranariddh co-operated, as coalition partners, to weaken the SRP. For example, after the coalition Government was formed in July 2004, 60 SRP members defected to FUNCINPEC and received assurances from Ranariddh that 90% of them would obtain new positions, mainly as secretaries or under-secretaries of state. In August CPP and FUNCINPEC legislators agreed, in a majority vote, to exclude the opposition SRP members from positions on the nine commissions of the National Assembly. In February 2005 Hun Sen and Ranariddh finally succeeded in removing three SRP legislators' parliamentary immunity by means of a show of hands, which violated the procedural rule of secret ballot. One of the three SRP members, Cheam Channy, was arrested and imprisoned at the Military Police Headquarters in Phnom-Penh, while Sam Rainsy and Chea Poch fled the country. Hun Sen and Ranariddh then filed defamation lawsuits against Rainsy and intensified their criticism of his party. In March Ranariddh remained conciliatory toward the SRP legislators, but then hardened his position by refusing to engage in any dialogue with Rainsy. In May Hun Sen also threatened to arrest Rainsy if the latter returned to Cambodia. Additionally, between January and August 2004 11 SRP members were reportedly assassinated by unidentified gunmen.

Owing to the political support that he received from Hun Sen, Ranariddh allowed himself to become more subservient to the Prime Minister's political interests, intensified his criticism of his former democratic alliance partner, the SRP, and even turned against his father. The Prince was also perceived to have become corrupt, and consequently he saw the need to rely to a greater degree upon protection by the CPP. He even proposed that the National Police, dominated by the Hun Sen faction within the CPP, be removed from the jurisdiction of the Ministry of the Interior (the CPP Co-Minister of the Interior belonging to the Chea Sim camp) and placed under Hun Sen's direct control. In early 2005 he offered his support for Hun Sen as the prime ministerial candidate in the 2008 national election. The Prince's growing support for the CPP came about after he had been implicated in a number of corruption scandals, such as his approval of a US $27m. contract to construct a new National Assembly building following his rejection of an offer by another construction company to build it for $13m.; the Prince was accused by the opposition of having retained approximately $14m. for himself.

Together Hun Sen and Ranariddh also successfully marginalized King Sihanouk's political influence. The Prime Minister became more publicly critical of the monarch and even offered his support for Ranariddh, who became increasingly estranged from his father. In October 2004 Sihanouk unexpectedly announced his decision to abdicate and selected one of his sons, Sihamoni, as his successor to the throne. Following his appointment by the Royal Council of the Throne, Sihamoni's coronation ceremony was held on 29 October. Sihanouk subsequently spent much of his time overseas, including a five-month stay in Beijing in the first half of 2005, and became increasingly critical of the Cambodian Government, particularly of its failure to address the unresolved border disputes with neighbouring countries. He accused Cambodia's neighbours of annexing its territory and Cambodian leaders of selling it. In June, however, Hun Sen took a much more aggressive stance against Sihanouk, accusing him of endorsing a 'plot' against him and threatening to punish the 'plotters'. Moreover, the Prime Minister reportedly sought to weaken or abolish the Supreme National Council on Border Affairs (SNCBA), which was chaired by Sihanouk. Prince Ranariddh apparently objected to any attempts to enhance his father's power over the SNCBA, instead supporting Hun Sen's stance on border issues.

Meanwhile, Ranariddh continued to lose political credibility within his party, and FUNCINPEC became increasingly fragmented. Members of FUNCINPEC, such as Princess Norodom Vacheara, seemed to have lost confidence in his ability to lead the party. In August 2004 Mu Sochua, former FUNCINPEC Minister for Women's Affairs and Veterans, defected to the SRP. Even the pro-FUNCINPEC newspaper, *Voice of Khmer Youth*, accused the Prince of accepting bribes (alleged to total US $30m.) from a pro-CPP businessman, Ly Yong Phat. Prince Sirivudh (who continued to hold the post of FUNCINPEC Secretary-General, as well as that of Deputy Prime Minister and Co-Minister of the Interior in the coalition Government) also proved to be increasingly unpopular, because of his alleged corruption and 'cronyism'. Prominent royalists, such as Deputy Prime Minister and Co-Minister of National Defence Nhiek Bun Chhay and Senior Minister without Portfolio Serei Kosal, were part of the anti-Sirivudh faction. Although he had become more subservient to Hun Sen, Ranariddh was hardly popular among CPP supporters. The pro-CPP newspaper, *Rasmei Kampuchea*, urged the Prince to resign. Following the National Assembly's decision to change the voting rule from the requirement of a two-thirds' majority to a simple majority, FUNCINPEC was weakened further after Ranariddh resigned from the post of Chairman in March 2006.

FUNCINPEC was no longer a major protagonist in national politics. Although he had initially favoured the new rule, Ranariddh appeared to realize that the CPP would no longer need the support of his party. The Prince then left the country, returning for a brief visit to Phnom-Penh in September 2006. This turn of events troubled many royalists, who preferred to work with the CPP and wished to restore the credibility of their party prior to the *khum* elections in April 2007. In October 2006 FUNCINPEC held an extraordinary congress in the absence of Ranariddh, who was removed from the presidency of the party and given the title of 'historic leader'. Several reasons were cited for the decision, which was regarded by the Prince and his supporters as a coup. The Prince had spent the previous six months overseas, mostly in France, where he held a teaching position at a university. Royalist leaders who supported the decision to remove him, such as Prince Sisowath Sireirath and the party's Secretary-General, Nhiek Bun Chhay (FUNCINPEC's former senior general), complained that Ranariddh was no longer in a position to perform his duty. According to a report, Nhiek (regarded as close to Hun Sen) had expressed the need for 'a leader who is regularly at work with the party in the country'. The Prince was accused of being obsessed with his own personal power rather than with the survival of FUNCINPEC, having allegedly planned to form a new party or, alternatively, to join the Ronakse Samgkum Cheat Niyum (Social National Front Party), recently founded by another prince. He was also reported to have stated that he would even be prepared to relinquish his royal surname of 'Norodom' if the Government were to ban royal family members from politics, and might thus be willing to renounce FUNCINPEC if the party no longer proved useful to him. In March 2007 Prince Ranariddh was found guilty of having defrauded FUNCINPEC; also, he was formally charged with contravening a recently introduced monogamy law. Following his removal from FUNCINPEC, he formed the NRP. Neither FUNCINPEC nor the NRP was powerful enough to challenge the CPP, as demonstrated by the results of the *khum* elections in April. Some royalists therefore sought to revive FUNCINPEC by suggesting that the party restore the Prince to his former position. By mid-2007 reconciliation among the royalists had not been achieved: Ranariddh remained reluctant to consider this option unless FUNCINPEC agreed to take action against leading 'rebels' such as Gen. Nhiek. He failed to regain his influence, chose to retire from politics and was subsequently appointed as adviser to the King. The new President of FUNCINPEC, Keo Puth Rasmey, also had to contend with growing challenges from senior party members, some of whom were alleged to have tried to oust him. Furthermore, royalist defections to the CPP continued unabated. In December 2008 some 20 senior FUNCINPEC officials were reported to have decided to defect to the CPP. In January 2009 it was also reported that 35 FUNCINPEC officials had planned to join the ruling party. The royalist defectors included Serei Kosal (a former fierce critic of Hun Sen and a royalist commander who had fought against the forces of Hun Sen after the coup in 1997), Kassie Neou (a former secretary of state in the Ministry of Justice), Pou Sothirak (a former minister and a former ambassador to Japan), and Sun Chanthol (a former Minister of Transport and Public Works). With the former King and current King, as well as all the princes, politically marginalized, some observers believed that Hun Sen now regarded himself as the new 'monarch', who had succeeded in deposing the royal family. Prince Sirivudh even disparagingly branded FUNCINPEC as 'HUNSENPEC', apparently deeming the party to have 'sold out' to the CPP.

The SRP emerged as the strongest opposition party but continued to encounter challenges both from within the party and from the CPP leadership. Sam Rainsy himself remained a divisive figure, perceived as unable to co-operate with others, including many members of his own party. Rainsy could not work well with the newly established Human Rights Party (HRP) led by Kem Sokha, founder and former head of the Cambodian Center for Human Rights (CCHR), an NGO that had been officially launched in November 2002.

Hun Sen also continued to consolidate power by seeking to weaken the SRP. He ensured that any members of the party who attempted to take legal action against him would suffer the consequences. After accusing Hun Sen of corruption, Rainsy was stripped of his parliamentary immunity from prosecution in February 2009, thereby allowing the Prime Minister to file a criminal defamation lawsuit against the SRP leader. Rainsy's immunity was restored only after his party paid a fine of US $2,500, but his immunity was again removed in November; in the previous month he had been charged with racial incitement and the destruction of public property, having allegedly encouraged his supporters to uproot border demarcation posts that he claimed had been illegally positioned by Viet Nam and constituted Vietnamese encroachment upon Cambodian territory. In January 2010 Rainsy was convicted *in absentia* of the charges, ordered to pay approximately $2,000, and sentenced to two years' imprisonment.

Rainsy was subsequently accused of manipulating a map that he had publicized in order to demonstrate the alleged Vietnamese border encroachment. In September Rainsy received a further 10-year prison sentence following his conviction *in absentia* on charges of misinformation and falsifying documents.

Meanwhile, Hun Sen had instigated a counter-lawsuit against Mu Sochua, another SRP member of the National Assembly: following derogatory references to her in a public speech made by the Prime Minister in April 2009, she had filed a defamation lawsuit against Hun Sen. The Phnom-Penh Municipal Court initially agreed to register their respective complaints, but Hun Sen then took action to remove Mu Sochua's parliamentary immunity (which had prevented criminal charges being brought against her), while leaving intact his own immunity. In June the removal by the National Assembly of Mu Sochua's immunity, in particular the peremptory manner in which the parliamentary vote on the matter had been conducted, was condemned by human rights groups. The Phnom-Penh Municipal Court rejected Mu Sochua's lawsuit, dismissing it as 'groundless', and proceeded with the Prime Minister's counter-lawsuit for criminal defamation. In August Mu Sochua was convicted of defaming Hun Sen and ordered to pay fines totalling 8.5m. riels, in addition to compensation of 8m. riels. A subsequent appeal lodged by Mu Sochua against the conviction was dismissed by the Court of Appeals in October, and her final appeal was similarly rejected in June 2010, when the Supreme Court upheld the original verdict. The legal immunity of another SRP parliamentarian, Ho Vann, was also removed in June 2009. On the grounds of defamation and disinformation, he was sued by 22 senior military officers after he apparently questioned the value of academic awards that they had received from a Vietnamese military institute. Ho Vann claimed to have been misquoted by the newspaper concerned, and, owing to a lack of sufficient evidence, he was acquitted in September.

External and internal party opposition to Hun Sen's rule was increasingly diminished. The anti-CPP parties proved unable to form an alliance in preparation for the legislative election scheduled to take place in 2012. The SRP and the HRP, for instance, had agreed in principle on a merger but failed to implement this agreement. Power within the CPP also shifted in favour of Hun Sen. As party Vice-Chairman, he attempted to undermine the position of the party members who belonged to the rival faction led by CPP Chairman Chea Sim and to defend party members who were loyal to him. Hun Sen reportedly presided over an extraordinary meeting of the party's standing committee in early July 2005 in the absence of Chea Sim and his brother-in-law, Sar Kheng, CPP Minister of the Interior. In mid-July, after Chea Sim (who remained Chairman of the Senate) had refused to approve the Government's proposed amendment to the Constitution and the Internal Rules of the National Assembly, Hun Sen attempted to arrest him and reportedly even threatened to kill him, but succeeded only in forcing him to leave the country for Thailand. However, Chea Sim returned to Cambodia after 14 days. The CPP had thus become more openly divided, but the balance of power between Chea Sim (supported by the Commander-in-Chief of the armed forces, Gen. Ke Kimyan) and Hun Sen (favoured by Gen. Hok Lundy) helped to stabilize the tense situation. Hun Sen and Ke Kimyan had not been on good terms since the coup of July 1997, because the general at the time refused to take orders from the Prime Minister to attack the FUNCINPEC forces. In more recent years Hun Sen had threatened to dismiss the general. In 2005, for example, the Prime Minister publicly stated that he would dismiss Ke Kimyan if he refused to take his orders and would replace him with Gen. Kun Kim (the Deputy Commander-in-Chief). In January 2009 Hun Sen finally succeeded in removing Ke Kimyan from his senior military position; the latter was then appointed as 10th Deputy Prime Minister and head of the National Authority for Combating Drugs. More noteworthy was the fact that the Prime Minister replaced Ke Kimyan with his deputy, Gen. Pol Saroeun, another long-standing loyalist. Pol Saroeun reportedly then sent back to their barracks the 507 soldiers who had served as bodyguards to Chea Sim. In addition, Hun Sen appointed seven new Deputy Commanders-in-Chief (including Generals Chea Dara, Mol Roeu, Hing Bun Heang, Kun Kim, Ung Samkhan, and Sao Sokha, all of whom were known for their staunch loyalty to the Prime Minister).

Hun Sen successfully consolidated his power by increasing control over the police and military élites. He personally commanded his own bodyguard unit. Numbering approximately 4,000, these soldiers were well trained, well equipped and apparently well funded. He also had a support force of 2,000 soldiers, known as Brigade 70, under the leadership of Gen. Hak Mao, who owned 16 trucks and two depots in Phnom-Penh and was allegedly involved in illegal logging. One of his strongest allies was the four-star general Hok Lundy, who first rose to prominence as the Governor of Phnom-Penh in 1990, and who in 1994 was appointed National Police Commissioner reporting directly to Hun Sen; he was subsequently related by marriage to the Prime Minister. To his supporters, Gen. Hok Lundy was a man who had helped to bring peace during some of the country's most difficult times. However, to his critics he was a 'thug' who inspired fear and was directly responsible for much bloodshed, notably his alleged involvement in the killings of numerous opposition politicians and soldiers during the violent coup in 1997. He was also alleged to have been engaged in drugs-trafficking. When Gen. Hok Lundy died in a helicopter crash in November 2008, Hun Sen lost a close ally, but he acted quickly to restore his control over the national police. Deputy Police Commissioner Gen. Neth Savoeun (who was married to the daughter of provincial Governor Hun Neng, the brother of the Prime Minister) was appointed the new National Police Commissioner.

Cambodia's legal and judicial system, which was subject to CPP control, also remained highly under-institutionalized and continued to be largely instrumental in hegemonic politics. Almost all of the judges and prosecutors were appointed by the CPP and remained members of the party. The director of the Phnom-Penh Municipal Court was Chiev Keng, an appointed adviser to Sok An, a Deputy Prime Minister and member of the CPP, who was also President of the Council of Jurists of the Council of Ministers. The President of the Supreme Court, Dith Munty, was a member of the CPP's standing and central committees. The SCM, dominated by CPP members, could hardly guarantee and protect the independence of the judiciary and did not respect the irremovability of judges and prosecutors. The Minister of Justice, Ang Vong Vathna, also of the CPP, controlled the SCM secretariat and appointed judges and prosecutors. The King simply formalized their appointment, while the SCM approved it. The CC, tasked by the Constitution with the responsibility to uphold the separation of powers and the independence of the judiciary, also lacked independence. Like the SCM, the CC remained dominated by the CPP: almost all of its nine members were affiliated with the ruling party. Even members of the Bar Association of the Kingdom of Cambodia (BAKC) became politicized and remained under threat from the ruling élite. For instance, Kong Sam Onn, Mu Sochua's lawyer during her ill-fated criminal defamation lawsuit against Hun Sen in mid-2009 (see above), was threatened with disbarment, forced to apologize to the Prime Minister and coerced into formally joining the CPP in return for the withdrawal of charges that he had breached the Bar's professional code of ethics and defamed Hun Sen.

Not only did the CPP, under the political leadership of Hun Sen, seek to consolidate political and military power, but it also sought to dominate politics by means of increased control over civil society. With approximately 95% of the population professing faith in Buddhism, Cambodia now had more than 57,500 Buddhist monks in more than 4,000 pagodas. The ruling party thus had an interest in depoliticizing anti-CPP Buddhist monks. The ruling party installed and promoted Tep Vong (who had served as a deputy for Siem Reap province after the 1981 National Assembly election and as Vice-Chairman of the National Assembly in July 1981), as a Monk Superior in 1988, as Supreme Patriarch of the Maha Nikaya Order in 1992, as a member of the Throne Council (with the power to select the King) in September 1993, and, subsequently, as Great Supreme Patriarch. In addition, the CPP sought to subordinate the other Buddhist sect, the Thammayut Nikaya—which was pro-royalist, had been banned until 1993 and was led by the Venerable Bou Kry, who had close links to Sihanouk—to

Tep Vong's Maha Nikaya. The balance of religious power between the two Buddhist sects shifted in favour of Maha Nikaya, which now controlled nearly 4,000 pagodas (compared with about 150 that followed Thammayut Nikaya). Throughout this period, the Venerable Tep Vong also served as a political instrument of the CPP, which reportedly played a role in suppressing monks' right to vote. During the 2003 election, for example, a number of monks became politically active, and their leader was disrobed and expelled. One year later Tep Vong ordered all monks who had arrived in Phnom-Penh to return to their home pagodas. He was reported to be politically 'aligned with the CPP' and to have close links with Hun Sen. The Great Supreme Patriarch did not avoid declaring publicly that the CPP was the only party that could protect Buddhism as part of the country's national identity, and that the other opposition parties sought only to destroy it. The Government also sought to restrict the activities of NGOs: draft legislation to this end was announced in December 2010, with a revised version made public in March 2011; the proposed law elicited widespread criticism from domestic and international commentators alike, who viewed it as the 'most significant threat to civil society'.

The Government continued to increase its control over the media by keeping defamation laws under the criminal code; imposing financial penalties ranging from US $24 to $2,394; and bringing to court journalists who had been critical of the State. As well as owning television and radio stations, the CPP also limited the provision of television broadcasting licences to individuals loyal to the ruling party. A new Penal Code, which came into existence in November 2010, continued to make disinformation and defamation offences punishable by substantial fines and imprisonment. However, there were some signs that civil society and media organizations were prepared to fight back. In 2009, for example, the CCHR announced that it was to establish a media legal defence group in conjunction with Legal Aid of Cambodia, the Cambodian Justice Initiative, the Cambodian Association for the Protection of Journalists and the Cambodian Center for Independent Media.

In short, Prime Minister Hun Sen had succeeded in consolidating his power, not only within his political party but also beyond. There were various other reasons for his political successes and increasing confidence. The country's generally impressive economic growth convinced more Cambodians, especially unemployed young people, that the CPP had become the party most capable of maintaining the strength of the economy. Second, the discovery of offshore petroleum reserves and the national wealth that this was expected to generate might serve to minimize pressures from donors urging further political liberalization. Third, the CPP's political strategy was still proving successful: members of other political parties were given no choice but to abandon their struggle for power, either out of self-interest or under growing pressure. Opposition parties were divided and conquered, beginning with the disintegration of the Coalition Government of Democratic Kampuchea (CGDK), the 'delegitimization' and disintegration of the Khmer Rouge movement, the seemingly irreversible decline of FUNCINPEC, the rise of Hun Sen within the CPP at the expense of other CPP party leaders, a weak civil society and the international support enjoyed by the Hun Sen Government (see The Restoration of Foreign Relations—below). Moreover, Hun Sen continued to marginalize the King. The power of Cambodia's monarch had thus declined, with the State providing him with a minimum budget to help cover his living expenses. Hun Sen's consolidation of power afforded him the semblance of a higher degree of political legitimacy as no credible political or military threats had emerged. However, his authoritarian regime still confronted other challenges. Cambodians continued to question the legitimacy of state institutions, such as the judiciary and police, their doubts often being exacerbated by mob killings and the failure of the police to intervene, as well as the police's alleged role in instigating some attacks. Corruption remained a serious issue, further threatening the Government's political legitimacy; even Hun Sen himself acknowledged the seriousness of corruption within the military and security apparatus.

KHMER ROUGE TRIALS AND SECURITY ISSUES

The military sources of threats to security diminished dramatically from the late 1990s. The dissolution of the Khmers Rouges entered its final stage in late March 1998, when five divisions of its army rebelled against the leadership of Ta Mok and defected to Hun Sen. Within weeks Anlong Veng was in government possession, and the ever-dwindling Khmer Rouge forces had been almost entirely forced into Thailand. Although Hun Sen embraced Keo Pok (a 68-year-old former DK zonal secretary during the Pol Pot period) as the leader of the rebels, in fact some were Pol Pot and Son Sen loyalists, others were resentful that Ta Mok had reneged on his promises of liberalization, while almost all were weary of the war and realized that defeat was inevitable. Pol Pot himself died on 14 April, only a day after a desperate Ta Mok had offered to surrender Pol Pot to the international community. Pol Pot's death (which was later reliably reported to have been suicide, following a radio broadcast describing Ta Mok's plans) deprived the PDK of its last opportunity to negotiate.

Throughout the last quarter of 1998 the remaining Khmer Rouge leaders negotiated an end to their armed resistance and their re-entry into Cambodian society. A ceremony was held in February 1999, at which time more than 1,500 troops were reintegrated into the ranks of the RCAF. The Khmer Rouge officials, Nuon Chea (the former Chairman of the National Assembly and the second most senior member of the PDK) and Khieu Samphan, left the jungle in December 1998 under an agreement with the Government. They were received warmly by Hun Sen in Phnom-Penh. In March 1999 Ta Mok was captured along the Thai border and placed in detention. In the following month Duch (also known as Kang Khek Ieu or Kaing Guek Eav), the former director of Tuol Sleng prison (where at least 17,000 prisoners had been tortured and executed), was discovered working in Battambang province; he was arrested in May and charged with violating a 1994 law outlawing the Khmers Rouges. The presence of senior Khmer Rouge leaders in Cambodian society prompted appeals from within Cambodia, and especially from the international community, for their trial and punishment for crimes committed under the PDK regime. In May 2002 Gen. Sam Bith, a former Khmer Rouge commander, was arrested, ostensibly for his participation in a train ambush in 1994 in which 16 people, including three foreign tourists, died. The most senior of the three former Khmer Rouge commanders (the others being Gen. Nuon Paet and Col Chhouk Rin) to stand trial for the killings, he was convicted of the charges against him in December 2002 and sentenced to life imprisonment, pending an appeal. The appearance of former Khmer Rouge leader Nuon Chea as a witness at his trial provoked criticism that the Government had made no effort to detain him. Meanwhile, pressure from Australia and the United Kingdom had resulted in the arrest of Gen. Nuon Paet in August 1998. Paet was also implicated in the ambush of 1994. In June 1999 he was convicted and sentenced to life imprisonment, and in September 2002 the Supreme Court confirmed his life sentence. Ten other Khmer Rouge leaders, including two former commanders and eight subordinates, were also charged. In July 2000 Col Chhouk Rin was freed after it was decreed that he was covered by the amnesty granted to Khmer Rouge cadres who surrendered to the Cambodian Government. (He had been appointed a colonel in the Cambodian army after his surrender; however, following strong formal protests at the acquittal from the British, French and Australian Governments, the Cambodian Government subsequently announced that it was to appeal against the court's decision, and in September 2002 Chhouk Rin received a sentence of life imprisonment.) Hun Sen resisted external pressures to try senior Khmer Rouge leaders, arguing that such action would undermine his attempts to reach national reconciliation with the Khmer Rouge rank and file and prompt a renewal of insurgency.

None the less, momentum continued towards some sort of international accounting, and in August 1998 a Commission of Experts, appointed by the UN Secretary-General, was established. In March 1999 a team of three legal experts commissioned by the UN recommended that 20–30 Khmer Rouge leaders be brought to trial and reparations be made to their victims. Hun Sen was reported to have considered the possibility of a 'truth and reconciliation commission' modelled on that of South Africa. However, the UN Secretary-General, Kofi Annan, argued in a letter to Hun Sen that a tribunal for the Khmers Rouges should be international in character. After several leaders were captured, Hun Sen announced that they would be tried under the jurisdiction of the Kingdom of Cambodia. Both China and Thailand endorsed his stance; however, when Hun Sen met Thomas Hammarberg in May, he accepted the UN envoy's offer of assistance in refining draft legislation to create a domestic tribunal using international standards, prior to its submission to the National Assembly. This tribunal would include both Cambodian and foreign judges and prosecutors. However, in August it was clear that Hun Sen was still resisting pressures to form a tribunal for this purpose. The National Assembly approved a law extending the period of detention without trial for those who were accused of 'genocide, crimes against humanity or war crimes' from six months to three years. The effect of this law was to postpone the trials of Ta Mok and Duch, who nevertheless were both charged with genocide (under a 1979 decree) in September 1999.

International concern over the culture of judicial impunity that pervaded the country's legal system remained high. More than 20 years after the collapse of the PDK regime, none of the leaders of the Khmers Rouges had been brought to trial for the atrocities committed, and several Khmer Rouge leaders continued to live openly in Pailin. Although, in the late 1990s, the CPP was believed to have largely opposed any compromise with the UN on the issue of Khmer Rouge trials, external pressure eventually forced the Government to take action. In April 2000 Hun Sen agreed to co-operate with the UN over a US proposal for the establishment of a UN-sponsored court, which would include both Cambodian and foreign judges and would uphold international standards of justice, as well as maintain Cambodia's national sovereignty. In July the Government and the UN finalized the details of a draft accord on the establishment of a special tribunal to try former Khmer Rouge leaders.

Legislation to establish the tribunal gave rise to serious controversy, domestically and internationally, as it allegedly failed to meet international standards of justice. In June 2001, however, Hun Sen accused the UN of violating Cambodia's sovereignty, reaffirming his desire to conduct a trial without UN participation. His criticism of the organization followed the departure of Peter Leuprecht, Hammarberg's successor as UN Special Representative. Leuprecht expressed misgivings about the way in which the tribunal law had been formulated and stated that the legislation would benefit from further scrutiny. Reiterating the views of Hun Sen, Ranariddh declared that he was no longer prepared to conform to UN stipulations. In July the legislation was approved by 86 of the 88 members of the National Assembly who supported the proposals to bring Khmer Rouge leaders to justice. The legislation, which was endorsed by King Sihanouk in August, specified that life imprisonment would be the heaviest penalty that the tribunal could mete out to convicted Khmer Rouge leaders. Meanwhile, Hun Sen stated that he expected only about 10 former Khmer Rouge commanders to stand trial and reassured the others that they should have nothing to fear. Cambodia still failed to satisfy the UN. In February 2002 the UN Secretary-General decided to terminate negotiations with the Cambodian Government, having failed to gain its support for the establishment of a court that would conform to international standards of independence, impartiality and objectivity. The Hun Sen Government responded by stating that it would proceed with the planned trials, with or without UN support.

A UN press release issued in Phnom-Penh in August 2002 indicated that the UN was prepared to restart discussions on the Khmer Rouge trials, that it would allow the Cambodian Government to conduct them and that it would only provide assistance to help ensure that the future tribunal would observe international standards of justice. In June the UN and the Cambodian Government finally signed an agreement providing for the establishment of one Pre-Trial Chamber of five judges (three appointed by the SCM and two appointed by the Council upon nomination by the UN Secretary-General) and two Extraordinary Chambers (the Trial Chamber composed of three Cambodian judges and two international judges, and the Supreme Court Chamber comprising four Cambodian judges and three international judges). The Chambers would have jurisdiction over those 'senior (Khmer Rouge) leaders of Democratic Kampuchea' who were considered to be 'most responsible for the crimes and serious violations of Cambodian penal law, international humanitarian law and custom and international conventions recognized by Cambodia that they had committed during the period from 17 April 1975 to 6 January 1979'. The Tribunal was officially known as the 'Extraordinary Chambers in the Courts of Cambodia for the Prosecution of Crimes Committed During the Period of Democratic Kampuchea' (ECCC, or simply EC). The ECCC was composed of three Chambers (the Pre-trial Chamber, the Trial Chamber, and the Supreme Court Chamber) and the Co-Prosecutors' Office. In addition to their agreement on the ECCC, which would operate within the existing Cambodian court structure, the UN and the Government of Cambodia also agreed to create two posts for co-investigating judges (one Cambodian and one international) and a Prosecutors' Office.

Various obstacles were subsequently raised. The Government had initially agreed to contribute at least US $13.3m. to the estimated $56.3m. budget for a three-year period, but later took the position that it could not afford to fulfil that obligation. Although UN Secretary-General Kofi Annan announced at the end of April 2005 that enough funding had been pledged for the tribunal to begin its proceedings, the Government then stated that the tribunal could not move forward until the full $56.3m. had been secured. Only then did Cambodian leaders agree that the tribunal could finally proceed. Ta Mok died in July 2006, but Duch remained in custody, awaiting trial. Controversies continued. By mid-2006 the UN and the Government had together appointed 30 judges and prosecutors, 17 of whom were Cambodian. The other 13 international judges and prosecutors were to come from Australia, Austria, Canada, France, Japan, Sri Lanka, the Netherlands, Poland and the USA. In July of that year the 17 Cambodian appointees and 10 of the international judicial officials were formally sworn in during a ceremony in Phnom-Penh. The inauguration of the remaining international officials was scheduled for a later date. Preliminary investigations commenced later in July. However, critics argued that free and fair trials were impossible because the Cambodian judiciary was alleged to be corrupt. Furthermore, Cambodian judges were regarded by many as professionally incompetent. Of the 17 ECCC Cambodian judges, four had received their legal education in Cambodia, four had studied in Kazakhstan and three in the former Soviet Union. One of the Cambodian judges was Ney Thol, President of Cambodia's military court and a member of the CPP's Central Committee. He was responsible for sentencing Prince Ranariddh (after the coup in 1997) to 30 years in prison and Cheam Channy (an SRP legislator) to seven years' imprisonment. Another judge, Thou Mony, overruled a lower court's guilty verdict against Hun Sen's nephew for his involvement in a shooting incident in 2003 in which two people were killed and two others wounded.

The judicial process remained contentious and slow. Cambodian judges and their international counterparts were engaged in disputes over Internal Rules of Procedures for the ECCC. International judges and their supporters took issue with Cambodian judges and other national legal bodies, most notably the BAKC, over procedural matters. When the BAKC sought to impose a membership application or registration fee of US $500 and a monthly fee of $200 for foreign lawyers wishing to take part in the trials, several international judges threatened to boycott preparations for the trials, demanding the exclusion of the BAKC from the ECCC process on the grounds that the BAKC's proposal would severely limit the rights of both the accused and victims to select lawyers of their choice. International organizations such as the Asian Human Rights Commission and Amnesty International were also critical of the BAKC's proposal. Although ECCC judges finally announced an agreement on their Internal Rules in June 2007, other challenges remained, such as the conclusion of referrals of cases from the co-prosecutors for formal investigation, the conducting of investigations that would meet international standards and the creation of transparent administrative procedures.

The main points of contention between the Cambodian side and members of the international community originated in the lack of mutual trust. International judges sought to make the process comply with international legal standards, whereas their Cambodian counterparts and the BAKC reportedly viewed the global effort as an external attempt to control all aspects of the criminal justice process in their country and to force them into a subordinate role. They regarded foreign lawyers and judges as having no understanding of Cambodian laws and culture, as taking advantage of the weakness of Cambodia's legal profession and as seeking to gain financial benefits from ECCC funds. More importantly, they tended to perceive the international community as seeking to impinge upon Cambodian sovereignty.

By late 2008, therefore, the progress of the Khmer Rouge trials was limited in scope, and further challenges were yet to be addressed. Ultimately, only five senior Khmer Rouge leaders (Khieu Samphan, Nuon Chea, Ieng Sary, his wife Ieang Thirith and Duch) were to stand trial. (Duch was formally indicted in August.) Furthermore, the ECCC experienced significant financial problems and needed additional funds: the original budget of US $56.3m. had run out, and an additional $114m. was required to meet a mandate now extended until 2011. In March 2008 200 Cambodian staff members of the ECCC were informed that their positions were in doubt owing to the depletion of the Cambodian portion of the funds. The ECCC subsequently lowered its proposed total budget from $170m. to $143m.; despite further pledges during 2008–09 from members of the international donor community, financing concerns remained. Political tensions also caused delays in the judicial process. Nuon Chea's two Dutch lawyers demanded that Ney Thol, a Cambodian judge in the court's pre-trial chamber, be removed owing to his role as an army general heading the country's military court and as a member of the CPP. One of Khieu Samphan's defence lawyers, Jacques Vergers (a French national), caused a delay when he angrily protested against the ECCC's failure to translate thousands of pages of documents into French, one of three official languages used in the court (along with Khmer and English). Ieng Sary's lawyer, Ang Udom, contended that the trial of his client would be illegitimate because he had already obtained a royal pardon and an amnesty from the then monarch, King Sihanouk. Moreover, it was far from clear that the judicial process was helping to consolidate the democratic gains that Cambodia had made. Evidence suggested that members of the CPP élite remained wary of such legalistic efforts, partly because they had no real interest in making the Cambodian judiciary more independent and more effective and partly because they feared that the politicization of the Khmer Rouge trials might implicate them in the future; early in 2008 Chea Sim himself had warned against this politicization. It was reported in June that Dam Sith, a candidate of the SRP and editor of the *Khmer Conscience* newspaper, had been arrested because he had questioned the role that the Deputy Prime Minister and Minister of Foreign Affairs and International Co-operation, Hor Nam Hong of the CPP, had allegedly played during the Khmer Rouge period.

Although the scope of the ECCC remained limited, progress was made from 2009. The trial of Duch, on charges of war crimes, crimes against humanity and torture, finally commenced in March of that year. During the proceedings, Duch acknowledged responsibility for the crimes committed, expressed remorse for his actions and asked his victims for their forgiveness. However, on the final day of his trial in November, Duch unexpectedly asked to be acquitted as he had co-operated with the ECCC, thus casting doubt on the sincerity of his stated remorse for his past actions. A verdict in the trial was originally expected to have been announced in early 2010; in the event, this was delayed until July, when the ECCC finally convicted Duch: he was sentenced to 35 years' imprisonment, although this was reduced to 30 years, on account of the time that he had already served in detention prior to the establishment of the tribunal. Meanwhile, in December 2009 the ECCC charged Nuon Chea, Ieng Sary and Khieu Samphan with genocide owing to their alleged atrocities against Cambodia's Cham Muslim minorities and ethnic Vietnamese minorities; they were also charged with, *inter alia*, war crimes and crimes against humanity. Their trials began in June 2011, but were not expected to be concluded before the second half of 2012.

Whether pursuit of international criminal justice helped, or would help, to strengthen the process of peace-building and democratic institutionalization remained to be seen, but the evidence hitherto suggested that it did not and would not. The end of the war resulted from the democratic process that discredited the Khmers Rouges. The pursuit of justice was made possible after the movement disintegrated in 1998 and after a series of formal and informal amnesties was granted to its leaders, rather than because of the process of international criminal justice. In fact, the pursuit of retributive justice gave rise to authoritarianism as the Khmer Rouge trials also made the CPP leadership uneasy. For example, Hun Sen declared that he saw no need to try more than five defendants charged with war crimes and crimes against humanity, and he warned that placing more Khmer Rouge cadres on trial would take the country back into civil war. He remarked: 'I would prefer to see this tribunal fail instead of seeing war return to my country.' In February 2009 Hun Sen even suggested that the UN should be tried because it had supported the CGDK, which included the Khmer Rouge leadership, in the 1980s. This position also reflected the fact that the Cambodian and international prosecutors continued to disagree openly on the issue of whether the ECCC should pursue other suspects, and the fact that there was considerable opposition to the Cambodian investigating judge's continued refusal to summon senior government officials as witnesses.

As of mid-2011 action taken against other Khmer Rouge leaders had still received no support from the State. For instance, complaints filed against five other former Khmer Rouge officials who were still at large (namely former Khmer Rouge navy commander Meas Mut, former air force commander Sou Met, former district chief Im Chaem, and former zone deputy secretaries Ta Tith and Ta An) received no support from the Cambodian ECCC co-prosecutor, Chea Leang, or the Cambodian ECCC co-investigating judge, You Bunleng. In June 2011 You Bunleng and the international co-investigating judge, Siegfried Blunk, rejected the request for further investigation by the international co-prosecutor, Andrew Cayley of the United Kingdom, on the grounds that he had failed to register a disagreement on the issue that he had with Chea Leang, who was accused by some observers of serving the Hun Sen Government's agenda owing to his refusal to investigate new cases. Hun Sen continued to resist the idea of bringing charges against more former Khmer Rouge leaders and insisted that no member of his Government was under any obligation to provide testimony to the ECCC. Indeed, in late 2009 several senior government officials—including Deputy Prime Minister and Minister of Foreign Affairs and International Co-operation Hor Nam Hong, Deputy Prime Minister and Minister of Economy and Finance Keat Chhon, CPP Chairman and Senate President Chea Sim and National Assembly Chairman Heng Samrin—refused to testify in court when Marcel Lemonde of France, the international co-investigating judge at the time, attempted to summon them, a refusal that was supported by Hun Sen. The ongoing process of successful power consolidation by the CPP, particularly within the judicial system and the armed forces (the latter strengthened in recent years by the acquisition of new military equipment), thus did not seem to validate the theory that retributive justice would ensure peace and democratization.

Meanwhile, as the Khmers Rouges no longer posed a politico-military threat to Cambodia in general, and to the Hun Sen regime in particular, the overall security situation throughout the country improved. Efforts were made to reform the security sector, particularly the military and police. As a result of the protocol on power-sharing between them after the 1998 election, Hun Sen and Ranariddh agreed to rationalize and reform the RCAF. Cambodia's military was still widely viewed as overstaffed, underpaid, unruly and heavily engaged in illegal logging activities. The exact size of the armed forces was unknown, owing to the large numbers of 'ghost soldiers' on the payroll (soldiers who had either been killed or had returned to their villages but whose pay continued to be collected by senior officers). In late 1999 it was estimated that these soldiers constituted at least one-third of the military's approximate total of 155,000 personnel. The military was regularly implicated in armed robberies, kidnapping for ransom and drugs-trafficking. In January 1999, as agreed, Hun Sen resigned as Commander-in-Chief of the RCAF; Gen. Ke Kimyan, the former Chief of the General Staff, was elevated to that position. Of 26 senior positions within the armed forces, FUNCINPEC representatives were given only three posts. Hun Sen urged that the armed forces be reduced by 55,000 and the police by 24,000 over the next few years. Germany, the Asian Development Bank (ADB) and the World Bank pledged financial assistance for this programme. Attempts at reforming the RCAF were generally unsuccessful. In 1999 the Government identified 15,551 'ghost soldiers' and 163,346 'ghost dependants'. The process of demobilization started in May 2000. The first phase resulted in the demobilization of 1,500 soldiers in 2000 and a further 15,000 in 2001. By the end of 2003, however, efforts to demobilize an additional 15,000 troops had failed and the programme was suspended. The armed forces remained unprofessional and deeply politicized.

Armed politics continued until the early 2000s. In July 2001 two bombs exploded in separate hotels in Phnom-Penh, killing three people. A man later admitted to the bombings, claiming that he had acted to extort money. In August two explosions in the main offices of FUNCINPEC in Phnom-Penh injured three people. The Cambodian Freedom Fighters (CFF) initially posed a military threat to the Hun Sen regime, but disintegrated soon afterwards. In November 2000 a group of CFF members carried out an armed attack on government buildings in Phnom-Penh, leaving at least eight people dead. In total, 47 people, including three US citizens, were charged in connection with the coup attempt. Members of the CFF were arrested, prosecuted and imprisoned. In June 2001 a court tried 32 coup plotters. Of the 15 defence lawyers, 12 abandoned the proceedings after the start of the trial because the court was perceived to be subject to government pressure. In March 2002 a further 18 men were sentenced to prison terms of between seven and 18 years. Some of those convicted were also said to have been members of FUNCINPEC. In June 2005 their leader, Chhun Yasith, was arrested in the USA, at his home in California; Chhun's arrest brought an end to the CFF's attempts forcibly to overthrow Hun Sen.

The Government made efforts to improve the security situation by reducing the proliferation and misuse of small arms and light weapons. According to a survey conducted by the Working Group for Weapons Reduction in Cambodia (WGWR), Cambodians increasingly relied on weapons as a means of protecting property and ensuring their personal safety. In August 1998, therefore, the Government began a national weapons collection programme. (Similar programmes in 1989 and 1993 had achieved little success.) In April 1999 a law aimed at cancelling all existing gun licences was also approved. The Phnom-Penh municipal authorities initiated a weapons 'buy-back' and confiscation scheme (offering US $7.50 for an AK-47 rifle and $5 for an M-16). These initiatives were relatively successful, but no such monetary incentives were provided after April 1999. Decades of conflict had left the country with an estimated 500,000–1m. small arms and light weapons, and WGWR data suggested that there remained a considerable problem. By mid-2007 the Government had collected 210,000 such weapons, most of which had been destroyed.

The trafficking of drugs remained a significant human security problem. The UN Office on Drugs and Crime (UNODC) reported that illegal drugs-trafficking in the country had 'skyrocketed' in 2004 compared with 2003. Estimates of the amount of amphetamine-type stimulants entering the country increased 10-fold, prompting UNODC staff to declare the drugs situation in Cambodia to be 'out of control'.

Cambodia was also described as a major destination and transit country for human-trafficking, for the purposes of forced labour (such as street begging) and sexual exploitation, and the Government was often accused of not taking effective action to curb this phenomenon. Furthermore, the incidence of rape and domestic violence continued to be major concerns. In the first half of 2004 a human rights NGO investigated 109 cases of rape in 14 provinces; it then reported 153 rapes, 246 incidents of domestic violence and 29 human-trafficking offences involving children. Women and children continued to fall victim to human-trafficking across the country's borders, although the number of those returning from Thailand and Viet Nam increased. Pornographic videos and fear of HIV infection were also reported to have increased the incidence of rape against children. At the end of 2004 157,000 Cambodians were said to be living with HIV/AIDS; however, at the end of 2008, according to UNAIDS, the number had declined to 75,000 (of whom 20,000 were women and 4,400 children).

Political violence and human rights violations continued. Human Rights Watch, an international NGO based in New York, USA, reported that during 2000 the most serious incidents of violence since 1997 had occurred in Phnom-Penh, including numerous attacks against *khum* leaders, mostly directed at members of the SRP. Cambodia's record on human rights remained questionable. In June 1998 Cambodia established a Human Rights Committee, to respond to concerns expressed by the Office of the UN High Commissioner for Human Rights (UNHCHR) regarding 80 unresolved deaths following the events of July 1997. More than a year after its formation the committee had yet to acknowledge that any politically motivated killings had taken place, and there had been no arrests or prosecutions in connection with these murders. In early 2002 Human Rights Watch issued a review of developments in Cambodia. The report criticized the rise of political violence prior to the *khum* headship elections, the lack of improvement in prison conditions and the ongoing use of torture by police and prison officials, who continued to act with impunity. Human Rights Watch also accused the Government of violating the fundamental principle of non-refoulement (under which refugees are protected from returning to any country where they might be subjected to inhumane treatment) when deporting more than 100 asylum-seekers (who complained of persecution and repression by the Vietnamese Government) back to Viet Nam. In March a senior UN official stated that Cambodia had violated international law by deporting 63 Vietnamese refugees against their will. In December 2009 the Government deported 20 ethnic Uygur (Uighur) asylum-seekers to China before allowing their asylum claims to be heard, allegedly following coercion from the Chinese Government and despite strong objections from the UN, Western states and international human rights organizations. The members of the Turkic-speaking Muslim minority group had fled to Cambodia in the previous month, claiming that they were being persecuted by the Chinese Government following violent clashes in July between Uygur and Han Chinese in Urumqi, in the Xinjiang region of China (see the chapter on The People's Republic of China).

Poor socio-economic conditions remained a threat to democracy and to the overall security situation, while the gap between rich and poor continued to widen. Ordinary people still lacked health care and could not afford to live comfortably in Phnom-Penh. The problem of landlessness remained largely unresolved, and was so serious an issue that the UN Secretary-General's Special Representative for Human Rights in Cambodia, Peter Leuprecht, had declared the issue to be a threat to social stability. The continuation of forced evictions also constituted a violation of human rights, with thousands of people being removed from their homes to make way for new developments. In June 2009, for example, the authorities evicted a further 31 families affected by HIV/AIDs from their homes in Borei Keila, an area of prime land in central Phnom-Penh. The families were transferred to an area on the outskirts of the capital, where they were given insufficient compensation and the arrangements for their permanent rehousing remained uncertain. The problem of forced evictions appears to have become more prevalent. Human rights activists estimated that some 150,000 Cambodians, of whom 80,000 were in Phnom-Penh, would be evicted from their homes during 2011, furthering concerns that the issue of such evictions might precipitate widespread social unrest. In June 2011 at least 11 people were injured when 250 residents from several communes armed themselves and clashed with 300 police and military police officers attempting to enforce a 2009 Supreme Court order, which awarded a private company a 65-ha plot of land occupied by villagers.

Overall, at mid-2011 Cambodia's authoritarian stability had become more evident. Hun Sen's domestic political legitimacy had not diminished to any significant degree, and no credible political, military or legal challenges had emerged within the country (especially after the disintegration of the Khmers Rouges in 1998). As shall be seen below, the international donor community continued to provide assistance, which helped to enhance the Prime Minister's legitimacy. However, various forms of threat to human security remained. The Government seemed prepared to use force to silence dissent and continued to boost its military capacity by acquiring additional weaponry. In September 2010, for instance, Cambodia purchased 94 military vehicles (including 50 tanks and 44 armoured personnel carriers) from Russia. Cambodia also received significant military aid from China.

THE RESTORATION OF FOREIGN RELATIONS

Cambodia's relations with the international community were steadily strengthened after the country's elections in 1993. Most remarkable was the fact that Cambodia was able to develop positive relations with its former enemies. Throughout the 1980s and until the signing of the Paris Peace Agreement in 1991, the country had belonged to the Soviet-led socialist bloc and remained internationally isolated, even within its own region. During this period ASEAN did not recognize the Hun Sen regime. However, after the formation of its first coalition Government in 1993, Cambodia developed positive relations with ASEAN and individual states in South-East Asia. The improvement in political stability and domestic security prompted ASEAN officials to agree at their informal summit meeting in the Vietnamese capital of Hanoi in late 1998 to admit Cambodia as the 10th member; Cambodia formally acceded to the organization on 30 April 1999. The prospect of ASEAN membership effectively ended Cambodia's diplomatic isolation, and normal foreign relations were restored. In July 1999 Cambodia attended a meeting of the ASEAN Ministers of Foreign Affairs, its first attendance as a full member of the association. The Cambodian Minister of Foreign Affairs pledged the Government's commitment to political and economic reforms as Cambodia sought to integrate itself with its South-East Asian neighbours. Hun Sen, meanwhile, maintained that the main reasons for his Government's decision to join ASEAN in 1999 were related to Cambodia's interest in regional security and stability, the ASEAN norm of consensus and the principle of non-interference, the economic growth experienced by ASEAN states over the previous 30 years, and the possibility of ASEAN serving as a gateway for trading relations with the outside world.

Cambodia also contributed to regional stability and security in South-East Asia. As a new member of ASEAN, Cambodia was initially perceived as a potential challenge to the unity of the regional group. In October 1999, for example, Cambodia and the other two most recent entrants to ASEAN—Laos and Viet Nam—held their first unofficial Indo-China summit meeting, which prompted concern across the region. At the meeting, Hun Sen and his Laotian and Vietnamese counterparts expressed their joint opposition to outside intervention in the newly independent territory of East Timor (now Timor-Leste), hitherto part of Indonesia. There were several other positive developments, which facilitated Cambodia's more active role within and outside South-East Asia. In 2002–03 the Government hosted three major international meetings. In November 2002 Cambodia was the venue for the eighth ASEAN Summit meeting, which was attended by the leaders of the 10 member countries, as well as those of China, Japan, India, the Republic of Korea (South Korea) and South Africa. Hun Sen reaffirmed his support for ASEAN's commitment to the 'Initiative for ASEAN Integration'. In June 2003 Cambodia, as Chair of ASEAN, organized both the 36th ASEAN meeting of ministers responsible for foreign affairs and the 10th ASEAN Regional Forum (ARF), attended by ministers for foreign affairs and senior officials from its 22 members, including the USA, China, Russia, Japan and India. In September 2003 Cambodia hosted the 35th ASEAN meeting of ministers responsible for economic affairs, discussing regional economic integration among member states in South-East Asia. However, subsequent territorial disputes between Cambodia and Thailand resulting in armed clashes (see below) engendered a loss of confidence within Cambodia in ASEAN's ability to settle such disagreements.

After the ASEAN summit meeting in Hanoi in December 1998, the Cambodian Government made a concerted attempt to improve its bilateral relations with ASEAN member states. Malaysia was an advocate of Cambodia's membership of ASEAN long before the country was formally admitted to the association. In February 1999 Hun Sen paid an official three-day visit to Kuala Lumpur, where he discussed Cambodia's proposed new Senate with Malaysian Prime Minister Mahathir Mohamad. At the conclusion of the visit both countries signed an agreement further to expand trade, economic and industrial co-operation. Cambodia and Indonesia also improved their bilateral relations. In March 2001 Hun Sen paid an official visit to Indonesia, where he held discussions with the President, B. J. Habibie. At the end of the visit an agreement on the protection of investments, trade and tourism was signed. Indonesia also agreed to provide training assistance to the Cambodian police. In August 2001 Indonesia's new President, Megawati Sukarnoputri, arrived in Phnom-Penh for an official visit. Cambodia also sought to improve relations with Singapore. In June 1999 Hun Sen visited Singapore, where he asserted that peace and political stability had returned to his country, which would strive to fulfil its commitments to achieving ASEAN's 2020 vision and Hanoi's Plan of Action. Cambodia-Laos relations were positive. The Prime Minister of Laos, Sisavat Keobounphan, visited Cambodia in April 2000 and the new Prime Minister, Boungnang Volachit, also visited in August 2001. In general, Cambodian relations with these ASEAN states remained positive in the decade that followed.

Cambodia's bilateral relations with Viet Nam were generally stable and increasingly co-operative. In March 1999 Cambodia formally established a joint Cambodia-Viet Nam border committee, the first meeting of which was held in the same month. In May Prince Ranariddh, in his capacity as Chairman of the National Assembly, met his Vietnamese counterpart, Nong Duc Manh, to draw up a programme of co-operation between the two legislatures. In July Chea Sim, the new Chairman of the Senate, also visited Viet Nam. Meanwhile, in June 1999 Viet Nam's party Secretary-General, Le Kha Phieu, made an official visit to Phnom-Penh, during which he met King Sihanouk, and held discussions with Hun Sen, Ranariddh and Chea Sim. Although this visit provoked anti-Vietnamese demonstrations, the leaders of the two countries consolidated bilateral relations, agreeing to resolve outstanding border demarcation issues before the end of 2000, and signing co-operation agreements for education and energy. In February 2000 the Chairman of the Vietnamese National Assembly visited Cambodia; Vietnamese Minister of Foreign Affairs Nguyen Dy Nien visited the country in the following month. In May the two countries signed an agreement allowing Viet Nam to search for the remains of its soldiers listed as missing in action. The two countries continued to exchange senior-level official visitors, including visits to Hanoi by Hun Sen in November 2008 and by Heng Samrin in January 2009, and visits to Phnom-Penh by Vietnamese President Nguyen Minh Triet in August 2010 and by Prime Minister Nguyen Tan Dung in November 2010 and April 2011.

Disputes over border issues featured prominently in relations with Viet Nam, but subsequently became less tense. The Cambodian Government's decision to allow Montagnard refugees from Viet Nam to enter Cambodia in 2001 strained relations, and issues of border demarcation remained unresolved. It was reported in August 2000 that Prince Ranariddh had urged Hun Sen to negotiate with Viet Nam following the latter's violation of a border agreement signed in 1995. In June 2001 King Sihanouk urged Hun Sen to 'save the sovereignty' of Cambodia. This was in response to Buth Rasmei Kongkea, the director of the Khmer Border Protection Organization, who accused both Viet Nam and Thailand of having illegally entered all 15 Cambodian provinces that border the two neighbouring countries. In May 2002 a group of Cambodian protesters travelled to Phnom-Penh to complain about land encroachment by Vietnamese authorities. Cambodian leaders, including the Governor of Svay Rieng province (the brother of Hun Sen), as well as officials and legislators from FUNCINPEC and the SRP, voiced their concerns. In May the King requested again that the Government investigate this matter and employ harsher measures to prevent border encroachment by neighbouring countries. Tensions inside Cambodia mounted after the signing in October 2005 of a border treaty with Viet Nam, supplementary to the controversial existing border agreement (signed in 1985), which was regarded as illegal by Cambodian critics; according to the terms of the new treaty, the final demarcation of the border was to be agreed upon by the two countries by 2009. In September 2006 Prime Ministers Hun Sen and Nguyen Tan Dung officially witnessed the planting of the first border pillar on the Viet Nam–Cambodia frontier, which was placed at Moc Bai on the side of Viet Nam and Ba Vet in Cambodia. In 2007 further progress included the defining of 49 landmark positions, the planting of markers at four of seven border gates, the review of 29 out of 40 map fragments and the identification of 176 out of 314 positions on the revised map. In early 2008 representatives from both countries met to review the implementation process, endorsing the demarcation and marker-planting plan for 2008 and extending to 2012 the mandate to complete the demarcation process.

Cambodia's bilateral relations with Thailand have long been affected by intermittent tensions but have become increasingly hostile, with tensions giving way to armed clashes several times (see below). In February 1999 the Supreme Commander of the Royal Thai Armed Forces visited Phnom-Penh to discuss co-operation on the repatriation of 30,000 refugees from Thailand to Cambodia, which constituted the major issue in bilateral relations. Later in that month the Thai Deputy Minister of Foreign Affairs, Sukhumbhand Paribatra, visited Phnom-Penh to attend the tripartite meeting of Cambodia, Thailand and UNHCR concerning the final repatriation of Cambodian refugees. In his meeting with Hun Sen, Sukhumbhand also discussed border issues and Cambodia's impending membership of ASEAN. In June the Prime Minister of Thailand, Chuan Leekpai, visited Phnom-Penh, where representatives of the Thai and Cambodian Governments pledged to resolve the territorial disputes between their respective countries 'in the spirit of friendship and neighbourliness'. In March a senatorial delegation from Thailand visited Cambodia, seeking ways to settle land- and sea-border disputes between the two countries. In June 2001 Thai Prime Minister Thaksin Shinawatra also visited Cambodia. In January 2003 relations between the two countries were tested when Cambodian demonstrators burned down the Thai embassy in Phnom-Penh and looted Thai-owned business properties (see above). The Thai Government evacuated its citizens resident in Cambodia, recalled its ambassador, ordered the Cambodian ambassador in Bangkok to leave and demanded that the Cambodian Government pay an estimated US $47m. in compensation for the damage inflicted on Thai interests. However, relations were normalized following the reopening of the border in March. In April the Cambodian ambassador returned to Bangkok and the Thai ambassador went back to Phnom-Penh, where he declared that the two countries should 'let bygones be bygones'. Cambodia had paid Thailand $5.9m. in compensation.

Nevertheless, border tensions between Cambodia and Thailand remained unresolved. Disputes concerning ownership of the 11th-century Khmer temple of Preah Vihear (which led to a suspension of diplomatic relations between the two countries in 1958 and, in 1962, to the ruling by the International Court of Justice (ICJ) that it belonged to Cambodia) continued. This territorial dispute re-emerged after the Governments of the two countries signed a joint communiqué in June 2008 allowing the temple to be listed as a UNESCO World Heritage site, provoking criticism in both countries. In July the decision of the UNESCO World Heritage Committee to list the temple as a World Heritage site was not universally welcomed, and the two countries subsequently deployed their troops in the border areas adjacent to the temple. Thailand's territorial claim covered most of the disputed areas, leaving Cambodia only with access to the temple. In a serious border confrontation in October 2008 it was reported that two Cambodian soldiers had been killed and two wounded, with five Thai casualties. In April 2009 two Thai soldiers were reportedly killed and several injured on both sides. Both countries pledged to enter into discussions in the hope of preventing any further armed clashes. However, further confrontations in February 2010 left at least 10 soldiers dead, and at least 18 more were killed in clashes in April. The Cambodian Government regarded the Thai military presence near the temple as an act of aggression and a violation of Cambodia's sovereignty, and in April it submitted a request to the ICJ, requesting that it order Thailand to withdraw its troops from the contentious areas near the temple and to ban all Thai military activity in the vicinity of Cambodian territory. In May 2011 representatives of the two countries appeared before the ICJ in connection with the dispute, with Thailand's spokesperson for the Ministry of Foreign Affairs, Thani Thongphakdi, stating that Thailand would respect the decision of the ICJ, although in mid-June the Thai Government formally denounced the 1972 UNESCO World Heritage Convention. The ICJ issued its ruling in July 2011, ordering both countries to withdraw all troops from the areas surrounding the disputed temple and to establish a demilitarized zone along the border, which was to be monitored by ASEAN observers. The Cambodian Government welcomed the ruling, but Thai officials insisted that their Government would not have to observe any ruling that might constitute a violation of Thai sovereignty.

Meanwhile, bilateral tensions were further exacerbated in November 2009 when Hun Sen appointed as his economic adviser former Thai Prime Minister Thaksin Shinawatra (who had been removed from power in a military coup in September 2006 and was convicted *in absentia* of corruption and sentenced to two years' imprisonment by the Thai Supreme Court in October 2008). The Thai Government was incensed when Hun Sen rejected its request to extradite the fugitive Thaksin back to Thailand. Relations worsened in early 2010, when the Cambodian Prime Minister denounced his Thai counterpart, Abhisit Vejjajiva, as 'stupid'. Abhisit had criticized Hun Sen's visit to the border area, during which he had worn military clothing and told the Cambodian troops that they had his support for the defence of their national border against potential 'invasion' from 'the enemy'. However, the situation seemed to have improved after Hun Sen assured Thailand that he would not allow Thaksin to use Cambodia as a base from which to launch attacks against Thailand, and relations were further improved when Hun Sen and Abhisit had discussions at a summit meeting later in 2010 (attended by the leaders of Cambodia, Laos, Thailand and Viet Nam). In August 2010, following the announcement that Thaksin had resigned from his advisory position in Cambodia, diplomatic relations between Cambodia and Thailand, which had been suspended in November 2009, were restored, raising hopes of a rapprochement between the two countries. However, tension re-emerged after a Cambodian court convicted two members of a Thai nationalist movement on espionage charges and, in February 2011, sentenced them both to eight years in prison.

Relations between Cambodia and the UN remained uneasy. As a result of the formation of a second coalition Government in November 1998, Cambodia regained its seat at the UN General Assembly in December, following an absence of 15 months. Cambodia subsequently contributed troops to UN peace-keeping operations, including 135 de-mining specialists who were dispatched to Sudan in 2006 and a further 139 sent to replace them in June 2007; and in July 2010 Cambodia hosted a field training exercise in which more than 20 countries participated; the exercise formed part of the Global Peace Operations Initiatives, a UN-US peace-keeping training programme that aimed to build and maintain capability, capacity and effectiveness of peace operations. However, relations between Cambodia and the UN were intermittently strained. For example, relations deteriorated when the UN Drug Control Programme concluded in February 2001 that Cambodia was fast becoming the most attractive country in South-East Asia for transnational criminals. Yet the most contentious issue that constantly strained relations between Cambodia and the UN was that of the country's human rights record. In December 1999 the office of the UN Secretary-General's special envoy to Cambodia had been closed at the Government's request, despite UN pleas for it to remain open for a further year. The

Cambodian Government had agreed in August to extend the mandate of the UN Special Representative for Human Rights in Cambodia, Thomas Hammarberg. The issue of the Khmer Rouge trials constituted a persistent source of tension, as the UN continued to urge Hun Sen's Government to bring Khmer Rouge leaders to justice (see above). During her visit to Cambodia in August 2002 the UN High Commissioner for Human Rights, Mary Robinson, criticized the country for its pervasive human rights abuses and urged the Government to promote judicial independence and to reform the SCM.

However, the country's relations with the UN improved after the two sides reached an agreement on the Khmer Rouge trials in 2003. At the end of 2003 the UN General Assembly removed from its agenda its annual discussion of the human rights situation in Cambodia. In April 2004 the UN Commission on Human Rights also approved a resolution on Cambodia, which critics viewed as weak. Hun Sen, meanwhile, contended that the UN should focus more on providing assistance in areas such as the drafting of laws and judicial reform. Hammarberg's successors, Peter Leuprecht and Yash Ghai, also seemed to be on poor terms with the Hun Sen Government, which often threatened to close down the UN human rights office in Cambodia. Leuprecht became increasingly critical of the Hun Sen regime, arguing that the latter was becoming more authoritarian as it consolidated its political power. In April 2005, at the 61st session of the UN Human Rights Commission in the Swiss city of Geneva, for example, he testified that there was a correlation between an 'increasingly autocratic form of government' and 'growing concentration of power (in the hands of Hun Sen) behind a shaky façade of democracy'. In March 2006 Yash Ghai also accused Hun Sen of ruling with an 'iron fist'; the Cambodian leader responded by dismissing UN human rights workers as 'long-term tourists'. (In May the new UN High Commissioner for Human Rights, Louise Arbour, also criticized the Cambodian judiciary, claiming that it had 'very serious' problems.) Ghai continued to write reports critical of Cambodia's government institutions, especially the judiciary. Relations between Ghai and the Hun Sen Government remained uneasy, as members of the latter refused to meet with him. During his visit to Cambodia in May 2007, Ghai was able to meet only with Sar Kheng (the CPP Deputy Prime Minister and Minister of the Interior); other senior government officials were unavailable. The Prime Minister became impatient with Ghai, despite the latter's praise for recent legal reforms such as the introduction of the Code of Penal Procedure. Ghai remained critical of state institutions, most notably the judiciary, which he regarded as lacking independence and as ineffective. Hun Sen, for his part, repeatedly refused to meet Ghai, and his various criticisms of the envoy further strained relations. Following Ghai's resignation in September 2008, Surya Subedi was appointed UN Special Rapporteur for Human Rights in Cambodia in March 2009. Subedi offended Hun Sen when he criticized the Cambodian judiciary for a lack of political independence and stated that he was 'disappointed' at having been unable to meet with the Cambodian Prime Minister during a 10-day visit to the country in June 2010. Hun Sen, who was said to have been unwell, accused Subedi of being disrespectful, stating that he had met with Subedi on all of his previous visits, accusing him of wanting to 'colonize' Cambodia, and announcing that henceforth he would be willing to meet with the UN envoy only once, rather than three times, a year. When UN Secretary-General Ban Ki-Moon visited Cambodia in October 2010, Hun Sen reiterated his threats and demands for the closure of the UN human rights office in Cambodia.

Cambodia's relations with members of the international donor community (especially those that remained largely uncritical of Hun Sen's policies) continued to improve. Donors first made their pledge to provide the country with assistance in 1992. At the annual Consultative Group (CG) meetings—subsequently superseded by the Cambodia Development Cooperation Forum (CDCF)—the donor community continued to make regular pledges to assist Cambodia (the exceptions having been 1998, owing to the coup of the previous year, and 2003, as a result of the political deadlock that followed the election of July). Between 1993 and 2006 the total amount pledged was thought to have been in excess of US $6,000m. In June 1999 the CG carried out its first review, identifying as priority areas the end of illegal logging and the reform of the armed forces, the civil service and the financial sector. At subsequent meetings of the CG the aid pledged was subject to the fulfilment of various conditions. These included the honouring of the Cambodian Government's commitments to reduce military spending; to suppress trafficking in illegal drugs; to take appropriate measures to combat corruption; to improve legal and judicial institutions; to adopt the tribunal law (see above); and to promote human rights. In 2007 the donor community increased its assistance to Cambodia, despite the recent political trend toward a hegemonic party system and the release of a report by Global Witness, an advocacy group, on CPP officials' involvement in illegal logging activities. At the CG meeting held in Phnom-Penh in June, the donor community pledged $690m. in aid to Cambodia for the coming year, thus bolstering the Hun Sen regime's international legitimacy. The donor community subsequently raised its level of aid to Cambodia still further, with the CDCF pledging $951.5m. and $1,100.0m. for 2009 and 2010, respectively. Donors were reported to have pledged close to $3,000m. for 2010–12, despite criticism of the Hun Sen Government, which continued to be regarded as politically repressive and abusive of human rights.

However, relations between the Cambodian Government and the international donor community were not without problems. The corruption scandal of the early 2000s that resulted in the ending of military reform led the World Bank to ask the Cambodian Government to pay back a sum of US $2.8m. Tensions between the Government and the World Bank continued, especially after the latter discovered that its funds were being diverted by senior Cambodian officials, and then considered the possibility of asking the Government to repay $7.6m. This time Hun Sen made it clear that his Government would not return the funds in question. Meanwhile, donors continued to express frustration at the lack of reform with regard to land, judicial and anti-corruption issues. However, the Government felt sufficiently confident to resist international pressure. In September 2009, for instance, Hun Sen terminated a land registry project funded by the World Bank when the multilateral organization and other donors requested that his Government halt its policy of forced evictions (see above). In March 2010 the Deputy Prime Minister and Minister of Foreign Affairs and International Co-operation, Hor Nam Hong, threatened to expel Douglas Broderick, the UN Resident Co-ordinator and UNDP Resident Representative, who had suggested that the Government should devote more attention to drafting anti-corruption legislation, comments that Hor Nam Hong argued constituted 'unacceptable interference in the internal affairs of Cambodia'. As noted above, Hun Sen also accused UN Special Rapporteur Surya Subedi of wanting to 'colonize' Cambodia. Part of the problem was that international donors still proved unable to ensure effectiveness of aid co-ordination and continued to lend support to the Hun Sen regime despite its lack of tangible progress towards democratization.

The problem was exacerbated by the fact that some major state donors in the Asia-Pacific region continued to pursue their own interests by co-operating with the Hun Sen Government. China emerged as a major force in the provision of international assistance to the countries of South-East Asia, and from 1997 continued to provide political and financial support to the Hun Sen Government. The Chinese Government vehemently criticized what it perceived as external attempts to interfere in Cambodia's internal affairs. In January 1999 it was announced that China would supply agricultural equipment to Cambodia and construct a building to accommodate the new Senate. Hun Sen visited Beijing in February, when he held discussions with the Chinese Premier, Zhu Rongji, and met President Jiang Zemin. Following Hun Sen's reiteration of an earlier pledge by the Cambodian Government that the country would not engage in political relations with Taiwan, Cambodia's 'one China' policy was further reaffirmed in March 2000 during Hun Sen's meeting with a visiting Chinese government delegation, and in November President Jiang Zemin visited Cambodia, the first visit by a Chinese head of state since 1966. In November 2002 Hun Sen also met with Premier Zhu Rongji in Phnom-Penh and announced subsequently that the Chinese Government had agreed to relieve Cambodia of its debt to China, which amounted to approximately US $200m. In April 2004 Hun Sen led a large group of CPP officials on a trip to China, where they met with Chinese President Hu Jintao.

Chinese influence in Cambodia continued to grow, and China rapidly became the leading investor in Cambodia, investing US $4,300m. in 2008 alone, and with accumulative investment standing at some $8,000m. by the end of 2010. Between 1997 and 2005 China provided loans and grants to Cambodia totalling about $600m. In April 2006 Chinese Premier Wen Jiabao visited Phnom-Penh, where he pledged to loan Cambodia a further $600m., equivalent to the total amount pledged by the entire international donor community for that year. Cambodian leaders appeared likely to co-operate increasingly closely with the Chinese Government. Cambodia praised Chinese leaders for respecting its state sovereignty by not imposing any conditions on the Government. Although in June 2007 China made its first public pledge (of $91.0m.) at the meeting of the CG and in December 2008 it pledged a further $256.7m., it was possible that unofficially China had offered Cambodia larger amounts of assistance. More notably, China also became the biggest source of military aid to Cambodia. Beginning in 1999, Chinese military aid totalled about $5m. annually, apparently with no conditions attached. In 2006, at an inauguration ceremony for two Chinese-financed bridges, Hun Sen praised China, noting that as a donor it 'talked less but did a lot' and that its aid to Cambodia had 'no strings attached'. However, in December 2009 the two countries signed various agreements worth in excess of $1,000m., just two days after Cambodia had deported 20 ethnic Uygur asylum-seekers to China (see above), prompting widespread speculation that the deals had been secured as a result of Cambodian compliance with Chinese demands that the Uygurs be repatriated. In 2009 the Chinese Government pledged $256m. in assistance to Cambodia, making China the biggest donor to the South-East Asian country. In June 2010 China delivered to the Cambodian armed forces 257 military trucks, and this was followed, in May 2011, by the provision of 50,000 military uniforms. The development followed an announcement made by the USA in April 2010 stating that it was to suspend a military aid programme that included the provision of about 200 military trucks and trailers to Cambodia, reportedly owing to the latter's deportation of the Uygurs. China's increasing influence over Cambodia suggested that the latter might be part of the newly emerging 'Beijing Consensus', an alternative approach to development based on the belief that political authoritarianism is crucial to good governance.

Hun Sen led a high-ranking Cambodian delegation, which included Hor Nam Hong and Minister of Commerce Cham Prasidh, on a five-day visit to China in December 2010, when they met with President Hu Jintao and China's most senior legislator, Wu Bangguo. Hor Nam Hong was reported to have stated that no country in the world could prevent China's development and that Sino-Cambodian relations had moved from an initial phase of good neighbourly co-operation to a comprehensive strategic partnership based on mutual trust. In June 2011 Hun Sen met with Du Qinglin, Vice-Chairman of the 11th National Committee of the Chinese People's Political Consultative Conference, during the latter's visit to Phnom-Penh. Cambodia's Deputy Prime Minister and Minister of National Defence, Gen. Tea Banh, visited China in June 2011, during which he held meetings with Chinese Vice-President Xi Jinping and the Chinese Minister of National Defence, Liang Guanglie, in a bid further to enhance bilateral co-operation in the field of defence, as well as in social and economic development. These meetings took place despite the US Administration having warned Cambodia against aligning itself too closely with China (see below).

Cambodia's closer relations with China may also have encouraged Japan to continue to strengthen its own relations with the Hun Sen regime. In January 2000 the Prime Minister of Japan, Keizo Obuchi, made an official visit to Cambodia, the first by a Japanese head of government for more than 40 years. During his visit, Obuchi met with King Norodom Sihanouk and Hun Sen. Obuchi declared his Government's intention to assist Cambodia's development over the coming decade. The Japanese leader also expressed his readiness to send Japanese financial experts to Cambodia to assist in the areas of taxation and debt management, and was reported to be considering providing the Cambodian Government with non-project grants valued at 2,000m. yen. In return, Hun Sen pledged his Government's support for Japan's bid for permanent membership of the UN Security Council. During the same month Japan's Prince Akishino and his wife, Princess Kiko, made the first visit to Cambodia by members of the Japanese royal family. Japan remained the biggest donor in Cambodia, giving the latter more than US $100m. per year. Between April 2004 and March 2005 alone Japan contributed $159m. to the country, and between April 2005 and March 2006 the Japanese contribution amounted to $115m. At the donor meeting in March 2006, the Japanese delegation confirmed its willingness to work in conjunction with the Hun Sen Government and pledged to give the latter $114m. The Japanese Government also allocated an additional $22m. for the financing of the Khmer Rouge trials. In 2008 Japan made a further pledge to Cambodia of $112.3m., emphasizing that this level of annual aid would be maintained until 2011. In the event, the amount pledged for 2010 was increased to $130m.

Japan also sought to strengthen diplomatic relations and, to a lesser extent, security links with the Cambodian Government. In June 2007 Hun Sen made his first state visit to the Japanese capital, Tokyo, at the invitation of the Japanese Government (although this was his 15th trip; the previous 14 had been working visits). This official visit was arranged after Cambodia had agreed to support Japan's resolution to impose economic sanctions on the Democratic People's Republic of Korea (North Korea), following the first test of a North Korean nuclear device in October 2006. Notably, Hun Sen did not consult former King Sihanouk, who had always considered North Korea one of his few close allies; nor did he consult any other ASEAN states that did not extend formal support for the Japanese resolution. Apparently as a token of appreciation to Hun Sen, Japan implemented a number of measures, including the signing of an agreement to promote investment in Cambodia. Japan also pledged to send a business mission to Cambodia in July as part of its strategy to promote Japanese investment in the country, to provide Cambodia with 3,000m. yen in official development assistance over the next three years and to build a second major bridge over the Mekong River. In April 2008 Japan invited Cambodia's Deputy Prime Minister and Minister of National Defence, Gen. Tea Banh, to Tokyo for an official visit. The Minister was unprepared when Japanese officials enquired about small battleships that Cambodia had received from China. Japanese officials apparently regarded these ships as obsolete, stating that superior vessels would have been available from Japan.

The Cambodian Government appeared relatively less successful in promoting relations with Western democracies, but used its stronger links with China as a means to minimize pressure for political liberalization, most notably from the USA. Hun Sen's requests to make official visits to several countries, including Australia and the United Kingdom, were unsuccessful. In August 2004 Hun Sen travelled to France, but only in a private capacity, risking the possibility of being summoned by a French court with regard to a lawsuit that Sam Rainsy (who remained a French citizen) had filed against the Prime Minister in 2000. In October 2004 he attended the ASEAN-Europe Meeting in Viet Nam, but found himself embarrassed by questions concerning King Sihanouk's decision to abdicate without having first consulted him in his prime ministerial capacity. The Hun Sen Government's continued repressive actions against members of the opposition often provoked criticism from foreign leaders. Members of legislatures in many democratic states, such as Australia, Canada, France, Germany, Norway and the USA, together with the EU, put pressure on their leaders to protest against the removal in February 2005 of the three SRP legislators' parliamentary immunity and to ensure their safety. Political leaders in these countries continued to express concern about the Cambodian Government's repressive actions against the opposition. Meanwhile, Cambodian leaders became more resistant to foreign pressure. In March 2005 Ranariddh accused the European Parliament and the Australian and US Senates of being 'under Sam Rainsy's influence'. Nevertheless, countries such as Australia and France continued to consolidate their relations with Cambodia. Australia allocated annual financial assistance to the Cambodian armed forces. France also provided military aid to Cambodia's 7,800-strong gendarmerie, and its military commitment to Cambodia remained the largest in Asia. Each year about 40 Cambodian soldiers travelled to France for military training. French Prime Minister François Fillon led a high-ranking delegation to Phnom-Penh in July 2011, becoming the first French leader to make an official visit to Cambodia in almost two decades. During the two-day visit Fillon met with Hun Sen, as well as with King Norodom Sihamoni.

The USA remained a major source of irritation to, but still appeared to seek to co-operate with, the Hun Sen Government. In October 1998 the US House of Representatives approved a resolution accusing Hun Sen of genocide and other crimes. In March 1999 it was indicated that a resumption of US assistance was dependent upon democratic reforms and Cambodia's agreement to the establishment of an international tribunal to try Khmer Rouge leaders. In July a US official paid a brief visit to Phnom-Penh for discussions with Hun Sen and Ranariddh regarding the trial of Khmer Rouge leaders, democratic reforms and human rights. While little progress was made on these matters, Cambodia had earlier agreed to host a regional conference on the issue of US soldiers listed as missing in action during the Viet Nam War. Overall, the US strategy of combining pressure with reward was aimed at prompting Cambodia to accelerate the process of bringing Khmer Rouge leaders to justice and at curbing growing Chinese influence in Cambodia. The USA had not officially committed itself to funding the ECCC, owing to its concerns that the court would not operate as an independent institution, until 2010 when it finally pledged US $5m. to the ECCC, following progress made by the latter, and it expressed its intention to help Cambodia to build a society based on the rule of law. In May 2009, speaking at a concert to promote the campaign against corruption, the US ambassador to Cambodia, Carol Rodley, alleged that Cambodia was losing as much as $500m. annually as a result of corruption, funds that the country might otherwise have used for development purposes. The Hun Sen Government responded by stating that the allegation was politically motivated, unsubstantiated and not in keeping with the generally good relations that prevailed between Cambodia and the USA.

Meanwhile, in June 2002 the US Department of State released its second annual Trafficking in Persons Report, which described Cambodia as a 'Tier 3' country (owing to its failure to comply fully with the minimum standards for the elimination of trafficking and to make sufficient efforts to do so) and warned that it might be subjected to aid sanctions by the USA. In June 2003 the Department of State upgraded Cambodia's ranking to 'Tier 2', which meant that the country no longer risked the imposition of US sanctions. Hitherto, US politicians had remained highly critical of the Hun Sen Government, and in September 2002 US Senator Mitch McConnell had even appealed for 'regime change' in Cambodia. A US Department of State report described the Cambodian Government's handling of the anti-Thai riots in January 2003 as 'irresponsible' and 'incompetent'. Although the US Administration pledged US $8m. to Cambodia for its national elections, eminent US lawmakers continued to criticize the country's electoral process. In February 2005 five prominent US senators urged the Administration of US President George W. Bush to review its assistance programmes for Cambodia and to encourage other donors and international financial institutions to do the same. In 2005 the USA placed Cambodia on 'Tier 3', owing to the latter's failure to take effective action against human-trafficking between 2004 and May 2005. In both 2006 and 2007 the USA placed Cambodia back on 'Tier 2', largely because of the country's efforts to meet US standards for combating human-trafficking. Cambodia was subsequently placed on the 'Tier 2 Watchlist', but in 2010 the USA again upgraded Cambodia to Tier 2 (where it remained in 2011), based on evidence of a noted improvement from the previous year.

The USA remained a major bilateral donor in Cambodia, still seeking to strengthen diplomatic, political and military relations with the country, as Chinese influence over Cambodia continued to deepen. The Hun Sen Government continued to welcome US officials to Cambodia, despite continuing resentment. At the CG meeting in Tokyo in June 2001 the USA finally announced that it would resume direct aid to Cambodia, subsequently pledging US $45m. at the donor conference in June 2002. At the donor meeting in March 2006, the US Administration pledged to give Cambodia nearly $62m.; in that year the USA also decided to provide Cambodia with $1m. of military assistance. In 2008 the US Government justified better relations with Cambodia on the grounds that the country had taken positive measures towards strengthening civil society and democratic processes, maintaining rapid economic growth, countering human-trafficking and supporting democratic reforms in Myanmar. Although it suspended a military aid programme for Cambodia in April 2010, the USA continued to provide aid to Cambodia, pledging $68.5m. and $79.3m. for 2010 and 2011, respectively.

The improvement in bilateral relations between Cambodia and the USA was due in some measure to recent domestic developments in Cambodia, although a more important factor was the Hun Sen Government's commitment to helping advance US security interests in the region. For example, Cambodia signed the Article 19 Agreement with the USA that contained a Cambodian commitment not to send any US citizens to the International Criminal Court (ICC). The USA's fears of Islamist militancy in Cambodia also tempered its criticism of the Hun Sen Government. The arrests of foreign Muslims in Cambodia (later charged with terrorist offences) and Cambodia's plan to expel other Muslims from the country prior to the holding of the 2003 ARF conference gratified the US Government. In comparison with the other ASEAN member states, Cambodia was gradually regarded as the most willing to co-operate in the USA's efforts to combat global terrorism. In 2006 the US Federal Bureau of Investigation (FBI) awarded Gen. Hok Lundy a medal for his support in efforts to combat terrorism. In April 2007 Gen. Hok Lundy held discussions on counter-terrorism with officials of the FBI in Washington, DC. Senior US officials also met with the Cambodian National Police Commissioner at the Department of State. The meetings took place amid criticism from human rights activists and others that the US Administration had changed its policy by granting Gen. Hok Lundy a visa to enter the USA (it had refused to do so in 2005 because of his alleged complicity in human-trafficking and involvement in unresolved political killings). In early February 2007 a US warship paid a visit to a Cambodian seaport for the first time in more than 30 years; in mid-February President Bush formally signed a congressional appropriations resolution containing 'no restrictions on direct US government funding of Cambodian government facilities'. There was some speculation with regard to the possibility of the establishment of a US military base on Cambodian territory. In June 2008, in the first such direct supply since the events of 1997, the USA donated 31 trucks (part of a consignment of 60) and US $7m. in military aid to Cambodia. In January 2009 the two countries signed an agreement to strengthen Cambodia's military capacity to combat organized crime, such as terrorism and drugs-smuggling, as well as human-trafficking, and agreed to exchange military attachés.

A series of confidential diplomatic cables dating back to December 2008 and published online by WikiLeaks (an organization releasing leaked private and classified content) in July 2011 revealed the concerns of the US ambassador in Phnom-Penh, Carol Rodley, over China's growing influence in Cambodia and her observations on the high number of official Chinese visitors to the country. Meanwhile, the USA continued in its efforts to court Cambodia. During a visit to Phnom-Penh in late October–early November 2010, US Secretary of State Hillary Clinton expressed the desire of her Government to broaden and deepen relations with Cambodia. Clinton also warned Cambodia against becoming 'too dependent on any one country' and urged the Hun Sen Government to seek 'partnerships that cut across regional geographical lines', thereby making clear the US Administration's desire to affirm its influence in Asia and to serve as a counterpoint to the rise of China.

Economy

SOK HACH

Based on an earlier article by LAURA SUMMERS

Revised for this edition by the editorial staff

INTRODUCTION

Following the country's recovery from many years of conflict, the political unrest of July 1997 (see History) had a major impact on the Cambodian economy. Several international lenders and donors (including the USA, the IMF and the World Bank) withheld aid, stating that its resumption was dependent upon the successful completion of free and fair national elections. A decrease in receipts from customs duties (caused by a decline in imports) and from income taxes resulted in a significant shortfall in government revenue. The shortages of certain goods that followed the unrest prompted public anxiety and, in turn, led to large-scale purchasing, causing inflation to increase. Furthermore, the Asian financial crisis, which intensified in the latter part of 1997, led to a reduction in investment from neighbouring countries.

The withdrawal of aid in 1997 and the substantial decline in foreign investment resulted in the loss of an estimated 40,000 jobs in Cambodia, mostly within the services sector. Nevertheless, the economy was sustained by the forestry sector, which witnessed a significant expansion in logging activity. However, this expansion was largely uncontrolled, and the rapacious nature of timber-logging operations, much of it by foreign interests, further undermined confidence in the country's economic future and jeopardized the provision of external loans.

The garment industry grew rapidly from the late 1990s. The sharp increase in exports of clothing were largely attributable to the granting to Cambodia by the USA of the trading status of Most Favoured Nation (MFN—now Normal Trade Relations), accorded in September 1996, and to Cambodia's admission to the USA's Generalized System of Preferences (GSP) in August 1997. The development of the garment sector was further encouraged by similar concessions from the European Union (EU). Thereafter, the economy grew strongly, expanding in real terms at an estimated average annual rate of just under 10% during 2000–07. The recovery was partly due to improved consumer confidence and renewed aid pledges, being driven also by the robust performance of the agricultural sector and the continued growth in garment exports and tourism.

The strong rates of annual growth that prevailed until 2008 were aided by favourable world economic conditions, by Cambodia's accession to the World Trade Organization (WTO) in October 2004 and by the discovery of substantial reserves of petroleum and gas in the offshore region south of the country. From the last quarter of 2008, however, the effects of the global financial crisis, which had originated in the USA in the previous year, began to emerge in Cambodia. Many large projects, especially in the real estate and tourism sectors, were deferred. Actual investment in Cambodia declined significantly in 2009, before partially recovering in 2010. Although the country had achieved strong growth during the previous 10 years, the global economic crisis revealed that the Cambodian economy remained fragile and vulnerable to external factors. Growth in gross domestic product (GDP) decelerated to 6.7% in 2008 and to just 0.1% in 2009, according to the National Institute of Statistics (NIS). However, according to the Asian Development Bank (ADB), growth recovered to 5.9% in 2010 and was forecast to increase to 6.5% and 6.8% in 2011 and 2012, respectively.

One effect of the decline in investment from the late 1990s was that it became increasingly difficult for new entrants to be absorbed into the labour market. The number of new job-seekers exceeded 250,000 per year by 2010, and was projected to reach 400,000 in the near future, as more young people reached working age. Although household incomes in rural areas grew moderately between 2000 and 2007, World Bank studies showed that poverty reduction in Cambodia was slow in comparison with neighbouring countries, and inequality significantly increased. The poverty rate in Cambodia was estimated to have decreased only moderately, from 47.0% in 1993/94 to 30.1% in 2007, with rural poor comprising about 90% of the total. According to official data, the total poverty rate was projected to decline to 25.0% in 2010, in line with a target included in the National Strategic Development Plan for 2006–10. Meanwhile, many urban poor were evicted from their homes to make way for development projects, and the Government's various measures to reduce this social problem had limited results. Thousands of young workers were expected to have become jobless and the poverty rate was expected to have increased in both rural and urban areas as a result of the global economic crisis of 2008/09.

AGRICULTURE

After many years of political instability and the neglect of economic development, agriculture (including forestry and fishing) continued to provide employment for more than two-thirds of the population, with 72.3% of the employed labour force engaged within the sector in 2010. About 80% of the poor derive their main source of income from agriculture. Agricultural GDP growth averaged 4.2% per annum, in real terms, during 1995–2009, about twice the rate of growth of the population during the same period; the sector expanded by 5.4% in 2009 and by 4.0% in 2010. Despite this relatively strong performance, the contribution to GDP of agriculture significantly declined, from 47.7% in 1995 to 36.0% in 2010, reflecting the continuing poverty in rural areas. The agricultural sector has been characterized by a sharp decline of natural resources, including forestry and fish stocks, and erratic growth of paddy production. An efficient irrigation system, as well as regulation enforcement, would reduce Cambodia's vulnerability to the effects of extreme environmental conditions. In addition to the problems of poor soils, sporadic rainfall and irregular flooding, along with inadequate fertilization (by silt or appropriate chemicals) or use of pesticides, farmers have also had to contend with the presence of landmines over an estimated 300,000 ha, including 55,000 ha of prime rice-growing land in the provinces of Siem Reap, Banteay Meanchey and Battambang, the country's traditional grain-growing region. In 2009 the total area under cultivation reached an estimated 2.63m. ha, in comparison with 1.8m. ha in 1994, as some land previously containing landmines was reclaimed.

Following the sharp increases in global prices for agricultural commodities and the concomitant food crisis in 2008, Cambodia became a more attractive place for agricultural investment. From 2008, in an attempt to improve their food security, several Arabian Gulf countries (which lack agricultural land), including Qatar and Kuwait, were reported to be providing substantial concessional loans for rural infrastructure development in Cambodia, in exchange for land concessions. The Republic of Korea (South Korea) was also reported to be engaged in such negotiations with the Cambodian Government. Rice mills equipped with modern technology started to be installed in the country, and exports of milled rice, especially to Europe, began. Investors argued that private and foreign agricultural investment would create jobs and help to improve farming methods within Cambodia's vital, but hitherto undeveloped, agriculture sector. However, human rights organizations and other critics contended that such arrangements have historically yielded scant reward for ordinary, impoverished Cambodians, owing to corruption, poor governance and forced land evictions (for which compensation is not always offered).

The world market is more or less open to Cambodia. As a WTO member, Cambodia can export its products to more than 150 other member countries under MFN tariff rates. Similarly, Cambodia is able to export goods to other members of the Association of Southeast Asian Nations (ASEAN) under the rates of Common Effective Preferential Tariff (CEPT—a system of reciprocal tariff reductions) owing to its membership of the ASEAN Free Trade Agreement. In addition, Cambodia has preferential market access to the EU under the 'Everything but Arms' initiative and to the People's Republic of China under the 'Early Harvest' programme.

Despite the improved market access for Cambodian products and favourable weather during 2005–09, exports of agricultural products were of little significance according to official figures, accounting for only 8% of total exports in the latter year, seemingly as a result of supply inconsistency and poor trade-related institutional support. Cambodia has one of the most inefficient export services in the region. However, most Cambodian agricultural products are unofficially exported in a non-processed state to neighbouring countries, reflecting the very low value added of the sector.

Marketing problems also blight the sector. Farmers do not have access to information concerning prices and demand—information comes only from traders, either directly or via their neighbours—and they do not have much bargaining power owing to financial constraints. Moreover, there is a strong fluctuation in prices. Extraordinary daily fluctuations seem to be the consequence of Cambodia's redundant role as a supplier of last resort to neighbouring countries. Farmers also find their commodity prices unacceptably low. Almost one-half of the farmers interviewed for one survey stated that they were being offered unreasonably low prices for their crops. However, exploitation by local traders does not appear to be an issue: their prices seem to be largely dictated by the levels set by foreign traders and they make only a modest profit.

In Cambodia's present context, where both forward and backward market linkages are lacking and government support is practically non-existent, plantation and contract farming seem to be suitable choices. Theoretically, both types of agrarian structures provide better market linkages and are more suited to the task of commercializing agriculture. Case studies prove the viability of such structures in Cambodia. However, great care must be taken in order to ensure that there is no exploitation, and that contracts are fairly enforced between partners with unequal bargaining power. Moreover, a balance between economic growth and poverty reduction must also be taken into account.

Draught animal stocks were severely depleted during the conflicts of the 1970s. Herds subsequently recovered, and by early 1991 there were 2.9m. head of cattle, including 1.5m. draught animals, representing a sufficient number to plough 2.1m. ha of paddy by traditional, manual means. During the 1990s livestock numbers increased further, owing to a rising consumption of meat. According to FAO estimates, there were 3.55m. head of cattle and 2.20m. pigs in 2009. The livestock sector's contribution to GDP increased by about 5% per year during 2003–09. Livestock production increased by an estimated 5.5% in 2010, according to the ADB. However, local meat production remained insufficient to meet the rapid increase in local demand resulting from strong economic growth (with the exception of 2009) and the sharp rise in the number of foreign tourist arrivals in Cambodia. The main exporters of meat to Cambodia were Viet Nam and Thailand.

Paddy production attained self-sufficiency levels in 1995, rising to 3.5m. metric tons, owing both to the expansion of the area under cultivation and to improvements in productivity. Thereafter, paddy production continued to increase steadily, reaching 4.7m. tons in 2003, and about 7.9m. tons in 2010. About 500,000 tons of unmilled rice were exported in 2003, and this figure rose to more than 2m. tons in 2009. Productivity rose from 1.3 tons per ha in the early 1980s to 1.8 tons per ha in 1995, and then to 2.3 tons per ha in 2003. In 2004 productivity declined to 1.9 tons per ha because of severe drought, but recovered to 2.4 tons per ha in 2005, rising to 2.77 tons per ha in 2009; this was forecast to increase slightly to 2.80 tons per ha in 2010, with productivity of 3.00 tons per ha expected to be reached by 2013. As a result of the 'Everything but Arms' initiative, from September 2009 exports of milled rice from Cambodia to the EU became exempt from import duties and export quotas. This preferential measure, together with the removal of licence requirements for milled rice exporters and a doubling of Rural Development Bank capital to US $36m., led to an extraordinary increase in the level of exports. According to the Ministry of Commerce, during the first six months of 2010 milled rice exports totalled 107,291 tons, an increase of some 2,356% from the 4,369 tons exported during the first half of 2009; over the same period, the value of exports increased from $2.2m. to $13.4m. Thus encouraged, in mid-2010 the Government adopted an ambitious seven-point plan intended to make Cambodia the world's third largest exporter of rice (regarded as the country's 'white gold'), behind Thailand and Viet Nam, by 2015, in which year the Government was targeting milled rice exports of some 1m. tons, compared with just 13,000 tons for 2009. The scheme included strategies intended to improve the irrigation system, to upgrade rice-milling and storage facilities, and to enhance existing, and develop new, farming communities and institutions.

Vegetables and other secondary food crops feature prominently in household consumption and income generation in Cambodia. Vegetables are grown largely on homestead lands and their cultivation is considered to constitute a small-scale production practice. The size of the area under cultivation and levels of production have fluctuated from year to year owing to pest and disease outbreaks, natural disasters and price fluctuations. Daily vegetable consumption per caput in Cambodia has been estimated to average about one-half of the standard 200 g recommended by FAO. Forestry and lakes are the source of about 25% of all vegetables consumed, while local cultivation accounts for another 25%. The remaining 50% is imported from neighbouring countries. There are more than 40 local and international non-governmental organizations (NGOs) that work to improve food security for rural people through the promotion of vegetable growing for both self-consumption and income generation. As a consequence of these activities, the productivity of some areas has increased significantly, especially since 2001. Moreover, the horticulture and livestock sectors should benefit from the increased demands of the tourism sector (hotels and restaurants). However, poor infrastructure in rural areas and the inability of local products to compete with imported vegetables, in terms of both quality and price, cause problems for the growers. In addition, improved distribution of land resources, and the clear definition of rights and responsibilities over them, are of fundamental importance to the sector's development. The country's lack of clear land tenure rights has discouraged potential investors. Nevertheless, the enactment of a new Land Law in 2001 created a legal framework for the management of land in Cambodia.

Exports of rubber were traditionally an important source of foreign exchange, but production became increasingly affected by the ageing of trees. Although neglected plantations were rehabilitated with the replanting of rubber trees during the 1980s, they required time to mature. Plans for the eventual privatization of the seven state-owned plantations (the majority of which are in Kampong Cham Province) were agreed with the Caisse Française de Développement (now Agence Française de Développement) in January 1995, and involved the introduction of foreign managerial control. All seven plantations had been privatized by early 2009. Meanwhile, annual production of rubber continued to fluctuate. According to FAO estimates, production decreased from 21.4m. tons in 2006 to 17.9m. tons in 2007, but increased to 31.7m. tons in 2008 and further to 38.7m. tons in 2009.

Measures to improve and diversify agricultural production were outlined in the National Strategic Development Plan (NSDP) for 2006–10. Nevertheless, owing to higher land prices and to an unclear land titling system, the number of land disputes increased dramatically. In June 2010 it was announced that the time-frame of the NSDP was to be altered so as to synchronize its duration with that of the legislative term, 'in order to ensure that the actions, programmes, and projects of all ministries and agencies are aligned to implement [the Government's] prioritised policies'. Consequently, an updated version of the NSDP was drafted, to cover the period 2009–13. As well as reiterating the Government's commitment to improving and diversifying agricultural production, the updated NSDP also identified land reform, the clearing of land mines, and reform of the fisheries and forestry sectors as key priorities.

FORESTRY

In 1969 the area under forest cover was 13.2m. ha, which accounted for 73% of the national land area. By 1997, however, forest cover had been reduced to about 10.6m. ha, representing only 58% of total land area. Subsequently, the rate of forest cover has remained relatively stable and stood at 57.59% in 2009, with a modest increase to 57.99% projected for 2010. Provincial authorities were engaged in widespread illegal logging activities, despite bans on felling and efforts to centralize revenue collection. Much of the exploitation of Cambodia's forests was carried out by Thai companies following the granting of concessionary areas, with rights of exploitation, either directly by the Phnom-Penh authorities, or indirectly by local provincial authorities or opposition party leaders and military officials. Timber concessions incorporating transport across disputed zones often involved payments to more than one party.

As environmental concerns increased, with hardwoods being irreplaceable and with no reafforestation programme in place, various attempts to enforce restrictions on logging activities were made during the 1990s. A new ban on logging took effect in April 1995, but a timber concession granted to Malaysia's Samling Corporation in August 1994, which awarded rights to exploit 805,509 ha (about 12% of the remaining forest area) over a 60-year period, was not rescinded. Thai companies received renewed authorization to remove previously felled logs from May 1995, but this concession was rapidly and openly abused. In March 1996 it was revealed that the two co-Prime Ministers of Cambodia had personally authorized 20 Thai companies to remove up to 1,079,300 cu m of logs, when accounts showed that felled, lying timber inside Cambodia following the ban on cutting amounted to only 330,648 cu m. The revelations precipitated the suspension of IMF loans and protests from the country's co-premiers that the contracts were being misinterpreted.

Seeking to avert criticism at the July 1996 donors' meeting in Tokyo, Japan, the Government announced that the rights of Thai firms to remove felled timber would expire, definitively, on 31 December 1996. By June 1997 environmentalist groups revealed that illegal logging continued without disruption, with companies often securing protection and labour from regional military commanders. However, official revenue yields were limited and continued to decline sharply from 2001, reaching a low point of about US $0.5m. annually during 2004–06. Reafforestation projects were not properly implemented, and the deforestation of recent years would continue to cause disruptions to seasonal rainfall patterns.

Meanwhile, an intensified campaign against illegal logging was ordered in January 1999 prior to the meeting of multilateral and bilateral aid donors in February. The donors reiterated their stance that aid was to be dependent, among other conditions, on Cambodia's implementation of a sustainable forestry management programme to halt the rapid environmental degradation caused by deforestation. By mid-1999 the Government had revoked logging concessions totalling 2,173,041 ha and made this area into forest reserves. In mid-1999, according to official sources, 4,739,153 ha of land was being worked by 14 companies. The World Bank estimated that 4.2m. cu m of commercial timber were illegally felled in 1997 (costing the Government US $100m. in lost revenue), compared with an estimated sustainable yield of 1.5 cu m, and that at this rate Cambodia's timber resources would be depleted within five years. To protect the forests from further deterioration, reforms have been initiated with the support of donors, and remedial measures have been implemented. To ease access to the country's common property, and as part of the reforms, the Government allowed local populations access to some forest land (about 5% of the total forest land). Assisted by NGOs, an estimated 210 community forests were established in over 16 provinces in 2009, and this was projected to have increased to 350 by the end of 2010. However, the role played by the village communities in the management of forestry remained in need of enhancement. The decline in forestry stocks has posed serious concerns. Government efforts to halt illegal logging and strengthen forest concession practices have thus far been insufficient. Small-scale, community-based forests with strict adherence to technical standards might be good enough to cover demand for domestic wood consumption, but any continuance of large-scale commercial logging would require transparent and credible management, and would need to show compliance with environmental, and regard for social, impact assessments.

FISHING

Fish is the primary source of protein in the national diet. Historically, freshwater catches from the Mekong-Tonlé Sap basin satisfied most of the country's requirements, with marine products accounting for less than 20% of the total catch. Fish farming, introduced by foreign aid agencies and the Vietnamese, supplied about 10% of the freshwater catch in 1990. Ecological changes, such as falling water levels, heavy and rapid flooding, and loss of the forested regions once completely inundated by seasonal flooding in the Tonlé Sap, have disrupted fish migration, breeding and feeding patterns. The forested area around the Tonlé Sap was the main breeding ground for the lake's fish. By 1998 only 39% of the original 10,000 sq km of flooded forest remained under natural vegetation. The repercussions of deforestation therefore present a serious challenge to inland fishing, with the Tonlé Sap at risk of ultimately being silted over, as the mean depth of the lake continues to decline. Nevertheless, the total fishing catch increased from 471 metric tons in 2008 to an estimated 515 tons in 2009, and this was projected to increase further, to 617 tons, in 2010.

Fishing was transferred to the private sector in late 1993. Leases, or 'concessions' as they were called in colonial times, for lots on the Tonlé Sap and inland rivers were sold on a two-yearly basis to the highest bidders. However, sales were organized by provincial governors, with arrangements being open to manipulation and abuse at several stages and levels. Successful bidders for one or more of the 280 leases available were required to pay 40% of their bid as a deposit for exploitation rights, the balance falling due at the end of the lease period. Public revenues from sales of leases increased sharply to US $3.7m. in 1995, from $1.2m. in 1993 and $1.9m. in 1994, but subsequently declined steadily to less than $2.0m. a year during 2003–09, owing to high levels of corruption within the sector and to the decline of valuable fish stocks.

The fishery sector contributed about 7.0% of total GDP in 2009, compared with 16.7% in 1993. The question of the sector's sustainability has now become a matter of public debate. As the available fish supply has become scarcer, prices have risen sharply. Fisheries management practices are inadequate at both the central and community government levels. Incomplete regulations and a lack of enforcement of those that are in place have led to high levels of inefficiency. Although, ideally, individual fishermen and farmers could be educated about resource management, on a practical level they would likely find that their own poverty leaves them no alternative but to fish illegally during the banned season or to clear inundated forests for cultivation in order to survive.

INDUSTRY

Investment in industry decelerated following the political instability of July 1997. Some factories were damaged or looted during the violence, and many expatriate staff left the country. The industrial sector was also adversely affected by the regional financial crisis of 1997/98, which caused a decline in investment from countries in the region and increased competition in the domestic market in some industries, as the weakening of the Thai currency led to an influx of cheap imports from Thailand. Industrial GDP increased by 17% in 1997, but the growth rate decelerated to 5% in 1998 before registering a strong recovery, to reach an average annual rate of about 15% during 1999–2007. Growth slowed significantly to 8.4% in 2007 and further to 4.0% in 2008, before declining by 9.5% in 2009. However, largely sustained by a strong recovery in the garment industry (see below), the industrial sector expanded by 13.5% in 2010.

The industrial sector was traditionally dominated by rice mills (of which there were approximately 1,500) and by 80–100 state industries or factories, including the state-owned latex-processing plant in Kampong Cham. From the mid-1990s there was significant industrial growth in areas such as textiles, garments, beer and soft drinks, food-processing and construction materials, and in early 1998 a consumer electronics plant started production.

However, many factories operated at low levels of efficiency, being constrained by outdated and virtually unserviceable equipment, frequent interruptions to the power supply and difficulties in securing supplies. Many industries were unable to record profits, and by July 1991 about 25 state factories, in financial difficulty, had been leased to private entrepreneurs. By the end of 1998 the Government had privatized 73 industrial enterprises, of which 68 were leased to the private sector and five were joint ventures. The total contribution of industry to GDP was estimated at 15% in 1994 (around the same level as its contribution in the 1960s), but by 2010 this contribution to GDP had increased to 22.95%.

The increased importance of industry to the economy was largely due to the rapid development of the garment industry. Prior to being subject to international quotas, Cambodia received considerable foreign direct invesment (FDI) from Malaysia, Hong Kong, Taiwan, South Korea, China and Singapore. Garment exports, which were negligible in 1994, increased to US $378m. in 1998. About 70% of the garments were exported to the USA, and the rest to Europe. In January 1999 the USA introduced quantitative restrictions on imports of 12 categories of garment products from Cambodia, necessitating an increased focus on European markets. Nevertheless, in 1999 garment exports increased by 46%, and were valued at $553m. Despite the US quota and less favourable global economic conditions, expansion of the sector remained robust in 2000, with an increase in production of 78% compared with the previous year. However, garment exports were hindered both by the normalization of trade relations between Viet Nam and the USA and by the accession of China to the WTO in late 2001. Cambodian garment exports continued to increase, but at a slower rate of 20% annually, during 2001–06. By the end of 2007 there were about 350 garment factories operating in Cambodia, compared with 184 in 2002 and just 13 in 1995. However, the rate of growth of the garment sector continued to decelerate, to about 10% in 2007 and 2% in 2008, before contracting by 15% in 2009. This significant decline was caused mainly by the world-wide economic downturn, especially in the USA. In 2009 production declined by 20% year-on-year, while Cambodian garment exports to the USA decreased by 21%. However, sectoral output and garment exports both recovered in 2010: according to official data, output was forecast to have increased by 18.8%; according to the ADB, garment exports increased by 19% in US dollar terms, primarily owing to a strong recovery in exports to the USA and the EU. Official estimates indicated that the garment industry employed 335,000 workers at the end of 2009, and this was forecast to have increased to 340,000 by the end of 2010.

The Better Factories programme, a labour compliance project introduced in 2001, provided for regular, independent reports on working conditions. Monitored by the International Labour Organization, the programme was regarded as a major advantage in the sourcing strategies of foreign buyers and assisted Cambodia in creating a niche market for its garments. Membership of the WTO and the reduction of the bureaucracy surrounding export transactions also helped maintain growth in the sector. Despite these efforts, unit prices for Cambodian garments continue to decrease (by more than 7.0% in 2008 and 2009), as a result of aggressive competition, particularly from China, Viet Nam and Bangladesh. Furthermore, growth margins in the garment industry were expected to become even narrower as a result of the expiry, at the end of 2008, of safeguarding measures imposed on China by the USA and the EU, as Cambodia was not regarded as internationally competitive. In September 2010 around 20,000 workers from the Cambodian garment industry staged a four-day strike in protest at a recently announced increase to the minimum monthly wage, from US $50 to $61—far below what some union leaders had sought, with some unions demanding an increase to more than $90. Government officials had argued that increasing wages beyond the stipulated level would render Cambodia an unattractive destination for foreign investment. More than 200 union representatives were suspended by factory owners in the days immediately following the strike, on the grounds that the industrial action was deemed to have been illegal. Later in September several thousand garment workers were reported to have staged a protest at these suspensions, and at least 12 people were injured in clashes with police officers in the capital and in Kandal province.

Like other sectors, that of construction was also affected by the loss of external funding and factional fighting in 1997. The construction sector's GDP declined by about 10% in both 1997 and 1998, before growing by 27.4% in 1999. In 2000–07 construction activity remained relatively buoyant (registering an average annual increase of 18% in real terms), as a result of significant inflows of foreign aid and of rapidly expanding hotel construction in Siem Reap/Angkor Town. Nevertheless, the construction sector experienced difficulties in 2008–09, owing to the sharp deterioration in global economic conditions, and remained subdued in 2010, reflecting declining foreign investment in the sector and a decrease in property prices of 15% year-on-year; at the end of 2010 property prices were reported to have fallen by as much as 50% since their peak at mid-2008. According to some sources, recovery of the residential sector would take at least five years, before the existing housing stock surplus would be absorbed by the market. In view of this, the Government planned a significant increase in spending on road and other public infrastructure works in order to stimulate the construction sector. Draft legislation was being discussed from 2010 that, if approved, would lead to a relaxation in the laws governing property ownership by foreign individuals and companies, in a bid to counter the depressed property prices and to boost weakening foreign investment.

Mining

Mining contributed an estimated 0.7% of GDP in 2010, up from 0.4% in 2009. The sector expanded at an average annual rate of 18% during 2000–09, and by some 45.0% in 2010. According to a study funded by the United Nations Development Programme (UNDP) and released in January 2006, the successful exploration for petroleum and gas in Cambodia's territorial waters, along with the identification of abundant mineral resources in the eastern and northern parts of the country, will enable Cambodia to become an industrialized country. An initial estimate has revealed that, within the 37,000 sq km of Cambodian waters, offshore reserves may amount to as much as 2,000m. barrels of petroleum and 10,000,000m. cu ft of gas; in the 27,000 sq km of the Overlapping Claims Area that lies between Cambodia and Thailand, petroleum reserves may total about 3,000m. barrels. The Cambodia National Petroleum Authority divided the offshore petroleum exploration zones in Cambodia into six blocks from A to F. Among those blocks, very limited information on the reserves was initially available only for Block A, and subsequently for Block D, while exploration in the other blocks continued. In 2002 Chevron-Texaco (now Chevron) of the USA gained a concession right over the exploration in part of Block A, and in a preliminary estimate in 2005 the company announced that in that block alone there were approximately 400m.–500m. barrels of recoverable petroleum and as much as 2,000,000m.–3,000,000m. cu ft of gas, although these figures would not be confirmed pending completion of exploratory drilling. Furthermore, in early 2007 China Petrotech estimated there to be about 227m. barrels of recoverable petroleum and 496,000m. cu ft of natural gas in Block D. By mid-201023 firms had been awarded rights to explore for petroleum in Cambodia. The Government hoped to commence the exploitation of its offshore petroleum reserves by the end of 2012. Nevertheless, experts from the World Bank regarded this objective as very ambitious, since the necessary infrastructure and services to support all the activities were not yet in place. In particular, Cambodia still needed to enact legislation on petroleum and sectoral taxes. Preliminary forecasts suggested that production in Block A alone might reach 12,000 barrels per day within 20 years.

In addition to these offshore petroleum and gas resources, Cambodia has large proven reserves of mineral ore. About 2.5m.–4.8m. metric tons of iron ore have been identified in the northern part of the country, and 5.2m. tons in Kampong Thom. Moreover, there are about 120,000 tons of manganese ore in Kampong Thom alone. Also, the eastern part of Cambodia, particularly Mondul Kiri, is believed to possess large reserves of bauxite, thus showing much potential for aluminium refining. In this regard, the agreement signed in October 2006 by the Government of Cambodia, the Mitsubishi Corporation of Japan and BHP Billiton of Australia allowed for the exploration of up to 1m. ha of land for bauxite. However, the results of the exploration were disappointing, and in August 2009 it was reported that the two companies were withdrawing from the project. Furthermore, the issue of transparency in the sector has become subject to increased scrutiny. Concerns regarding extractive resource revenues were prompted when BHP Billiton announced in April 2010 that it was under investigation by the US Securities and Exchange Commission on suspicion of having violated anti-corruption laws; this was widely interpreted as being related to the company's operations in Cambodia.

Phosphate deposits are processed for use as fertilizer. Other mineral reserves include deposits of silver, tin and silicon. The commercial mining of sapphires and rubies in the Pailin district of Battambang increased dramatically after 1991 when the Khmers Rouges used revenues from this source to offset lost aid from China. In common with the timber trade, Thai companies profited the most. Although the Khmers Rouges were effectively defunct by 1999, many of the gem-mining areas remained under the control of former Khmer Rouge leaders, and exploitation of these resources was largely uncontrolled by the central Government. Use of the Bavel River for the industrial sifting of excavated soil for gems has contaminated water supplies in Battambang Province. There is some gold-mining—at a household level—in the eastern provinces. Various Australian, Canadian and Malaysian companies have signed agreements to prospect in this region.

Energy

Most commercial energy used in Cambodia is imported. Domestic energy is principally derived from timber. In 2003 electrification rates in Cambodia were among the lowest in the region; only 17% of Cambodian households had access to electricity, compared with 84%, 81% and 41% in Thailand, Viet Nam and Laos, respectively. By 2010 Cambodia's electrification rate had increased only slightly, to about 24%, with the figure remaining much lower in rural areas. The peak demand of electricity in 2004 was 246 MW, of which 70% was consumed by users in Phnom-Penh; by 2010 peak demand was estimated to have increased to 437 MW. A US $30m. credit agreement secured in principle with the ADB in November 2010 would, if confirmed, fund a rural electrification project intended to improve electrification in rural areas, by enhancing the grid electricity supply infrastructure in conjunction with private rural electricity enterprises.

According to the ADB, in 2009 total installed electricity generation capacity stood at 372 MW (compared with 190 MW in 2004), of which diesel and heavy fuel oil power plants accounted for 91.4%, hydropower 3.6%, coal 3.5% and biomass and wood fuel 1.6%. Production of electricity in Cambodia increased by about 12% a year in the early 2000s. Official data indicated that Cambodia generated 1,882.0m. kWh of electricity in 2009, and this was forecast to increase to 2,164.3m. kWh in 2010 and further to 2,488.9m. kWh in 2011. Cambodia experienced an electricity shortfall of an estimated 100m. kWh in 2010, a deficit that was largely met by supplies from Thailand and Viet Nam, as a result of power sector co-operation agreements between Cambodia and its two neighbours. Electricity tariffs in Cambodia remained very high compared with those of neighbouring countries; this was due not only to high fuel prices but also to the inefficient management and operation of power plants and of transmission and distribution systems. In 2010 the average electricity tariff for residential consumers supplied by the state-owned Electricité du Cambodge was estimated at US $0.17 per kWh; the corresponding average tariff for those supplied by private rural electricity enterprises was estimated at $0.66 per kWh.

Nevertheless, Cambodia has substantial hydropower potential, and considerable efforts were being made from the early 2000s to develop further projects, owing to the potential importance of revenue from sales of electricity to Thailand and Viet Nam. In late 2002 the Government signed an agreement with China, Laos, Myanmar, Thailand and Viet Nam to establish a regional power distribution system, facilitating hydropower development in the Mekong River area. In late 2005 the Government awarded a contract to China's state-owned Sinohydro Corporation for the construction of a hydroelectric dam in Kamchay, and in February 2006 the Chinese company secured the rights to develop the hydroelectric project on a build-operate-transfer (BOT) basis for 44 years, following which the project would be transferred to the control of the Cambodian Government. Upon completion the project was to have a total installed capacity of 193.2 MW and provide 498m. kWh of energy annually, which was to be distributed to Phnom-Penh through Kampot, Takeo and Kandal Provinces. The first phase of the project was inaugurated by Prime Minister Hun Sen in December 2009, with an initial capacity of 10 MW. An agreement with another Chinese company, Huadian Corporation, was signed in January 2010 providing for the development of a US $558m., 338-MW hydropower plant in Cambodia's south-western Koh Kong province on a 30-year BOT basis. Construction work on the project, one of nine new hydropower plants that the Government planned to build between 2010 and 2019, commenced in April 2010 and was scheduled to be completed in 2013. According to a preliminary strategy drafted in the mid-2000s by Electricité du Cambodge, with assistance from the World Bank, almost all of Cambodia was to be electrified by 2015; however, despite the Government's increasingly apparent commitment to strengthening the country's energy industry, it appeared unlikely that this objective would be met.

FINANCE

Following the elections of 1993, and with stabilization programmes in place to address the volatility that had prevailed in recent years, the Cambodian currency recovered and maintained its position on foreign exchanges at 2,200–2,600 riels to US $1. From early 1994 official market exchange rates were kept in line with free market exchanges and adjustments were made on a daily basis. The Law on Investment, approved by the National Assembly in August 1994, removed all foreign exchange restrictions that had previously applied to investors. New bank notes in larger denominations were issued in April 1995. Following the 1997–98 Asian financial crisis, combined with domestic political problems, the riel significantly depreciated against the US dollar, trading at about 3,800 riels to $1 at mid-1998, in comparison with 2,500 riels before the regional crisis. However, the riel depreciated less than other regional currencies in the initial period of the financial crisis, owing to the widespread use of the US dollar in the Cambodian economy. This dependence on the US dollar also mitigated the impact of the depreciation by 27% against the US dollar and the appreciation by 4% against the Thai baht in 1998, which, despite the use of dollars, resulted in an increase in inflation. A new foreign exchange law was enacted in 1997, formalizing the liberal exchange structure. As a result, the riel remained basically stable against the US dollar during 1998–2008, trading within a range of 3,800–4,100 riels to $1.

A major problem for Cambodia was the poor rate of revenue generation as a result of weak management. Fiscal revenue remained equivalent to only about 8% of GDP during 1994–98, while official foreign reserves to support the local currency were relatively low. Additional fiscal measures were subsequently implemented. The introduction of value-added tax (VAT), levied at 10%, and competitive bidding for garment export quotas in 1999 substantially raised government revenue (a 40% increase compared with the previous year). Although significantly lower than forecast, revenue collection in 1999–2006 improved slightly, fluctuating at around 10% of GDP, largely as a result of the enforcement of VAT regulations and non-tax revenue collection. Owing to strong economic growth, revenue collection from domestic activities increased significantly in 2007–08. As a result, overall budget revenue rose from 11.4% of GDP in 2006 to 13.3% of GDP in 2008. Gross official reserves increased from the equivalent of 2.2 months of imports in 1996 to 3.3 months at the end of 2007, owing to the release by the Bank for International Settlements of gold reserves that had been frozen since the 1970s. This increase in reserves permitted the authorities greater flexibility in exchange rate management.

Nevertheless, the global economic crisis had a significant impact on the national account in 2009: government revenue declined to 11.9% of GDP, owing to a slowdown of economic activity, while government expenditure increased from 15.9% of GDP in 2008 to 20.5% in 2010. For the first time since 1998 the Ministry of Finance printed additional bank notes in order to fund its budget deficit. As a result, the position of the riel became more fragile, requiring repeated interventions from the central bank to prevent the value of the riel from declining beyond 4,300 to US $1. During 2010 the riel appreciated by 2.4% against the US dollar, and at mid-August 2011 it was trading at 4,098 riels to $1. Government revenue and expenditure were both estimated to have increased relative to GDP in 2010, to 13.4% and 20.7%, respectively.

Having risen from 9.1% in 1997 to 12.6% in 1998, the rate of inflation began to decelerate in mid-1998, reaching zero in 1999, despite the introduction of VAT and a 30% increase in the salaries of public sector workers in that year. Inflation remained very low during 1999–2003. However, the annual average rate of inflation then rose sharply from 1.1% in 2003 to 5.8% in 2005, declining to 4.7% in 2006 before increasing to 5.9% in 2007. Inflation reached a high point in mid-2008 when the rate exceeded 35%, owing to the scarcity of some food items and to the rapid increase in world oil prices. The inflation rate then decelerated significantly, to 12.5% in December 2008, with the annual average for 2008 standing at 19.7% and annual average food price growth at 29.9%. The consumer price index declined by 0.7% in 2009, but increased by 4.0% in 2010. Inflation was projected to increase further, to 5.5% in both 2011 and 2012.

BANKING

A Law on the Management of Foreign Exchange, adopted in August 1991, and a Law on the State Bank of Cambodia, adopted in March 1992, gave the former socialist State Bank the powers of a central bank, including the authority to issue money. The ability of the National Bank of Cambodia (NBC, as it was restyled in 1992) to implement monetary policy was severely limited by the widespread use of the US dollar. Although the riel was not convertible in international exchanges, it was freely exchanged. Figures for the end of 2009 showed that total liquidity recorded by the NBC was approximately 38% of GDP, a sharp increase from the end of 2001 (when it stood at about 14%). This rise was due to a rapid increase in foreign currency deposits, as a result of significant improvement in the business environment and the regional economic recovery. Liquidity in riels increased to 7.0% of GDP in 2009 (from 3.5% at the end of 2001), while the amount of US dollars circulating through the banking system rose to 29.8% of GDP (from 10.0% at the end of 2001), or as much as 95% of all currency in circulation, according to some estimates. Foreign currencies circulating outside the banking system were estimated to be at least twice as high as the total liquidity recorded by the NBC. The use of riels remained confined to small transactions and low-wage payments, while larger transactions were conducted in foreign currencies such as the US dollar and the Thai baht. Meanwhile, Cambodia's banking sector developed rapidly. Credit to the private sector grew dramatically, increasing by 52% in 2006, by 76% in 2007 and by 103% in the first six months of 2008. However, this rate of growth decreased to 56% by December 2008, and to virtually nil during 2009. The global financial crisis severely restricted the country's credit supply, as Cambodian banks sourced their loans from international financial institutions. Nevertheless, the financial sector appeared to recover from the crisis relatively swiftly, with deposits increasing by 35%–40% during the first half of 2010.

According to NBC figures, by 2009 Cambodia had 25 commercial banks, six specialized banks (most of them small private ventures) and 17 microfinance institutions. The non-performance loan ratio of Cambodian banks was one of the lowest in the world, at about 0.2% in early 2008. Nevertheless, this ratio was estimated to have increased to 1%–2% by mid-2009, as a result of global economic difficulties, but remained stable at mid-2011.

The NBC increased reserve requirements for banks from 5% to 8% and the capital guarantee deposit from 5% to 10% with effect from 1 January 1998, to ensure liquidity and solvency in the banking system following the onset of the Asian financial crisis in 1997. In order further to strengthen the credibility of the sector, the NBC also requested in May 2000 that all commercial banks apply for a new licence. As a result, several non-viable banks shut down, unable to comply with the required increase of registered capital to US $13m. from $5m. To ease inflationary pressures, the NBC again increased the reserve requirement for banks from 8% to 16% in May 2008, but lowered it to 12% in early 2009 to facilitate credit to the private sector. Furthermore, in order to promote foreign investment, the Government launched Cambodia's inaugural stock exchange in July 2011, two years later than initially planned and with trading not expected to commence until late 2011. The Cambodian Stock Exchange was 55% owned by the Cambodian Government and 45% owned by the South Korean stock exchange. In accordance with the Financial Sector Development Strategy 2006–2015, a plan funded by the ADB, the Government hoped to strengthen the banking sector with the installation of an automated payment and cheque-clearing system and with the creation of a national electronic payment system for supporting inter-bank market transactions. The Government also planned to improve supervision of the banking sector.

TOURISM

Tourism is regarded as one of the most important immediate and long-term sources of foreign exchange. Tours of Phnom-Penh and Angkor Wat, via Ho Chi Minh City, were made available from 1986, but Cambodia attracted fewer than 1,000 visitors in 1987. Foreign visitor arrivals subsequently increased considerably, but then declined as a result of the political unrest of mid-1997, the difficulties being compounded by the onset of the regional financial crisis in that year.

The Government developed a plan for the tourism industry that focused on the Angkor temples, the beaches of Sihanoukville, and 'eco-tourism' in Ratanak Kiri. Furthermore, the significant decline in the number of visitors to Cambodia in 1997 prompted the Government to initiate an 'open skies' policy, in accordance with which direct flights from overseas would be permitted to land in Siem Reap. Many tour and hotel operators in Phnom-Penh opposed this policy, arguing that it would directly affect their business and other enterprises in the capital. Hitherto tourists tended to stay only for short periods, usually no more than two days, and it was unclear whether the 'open skies' policy would benefit the entire economy in the longer term. According to a study prepared by a group of NGOs, only 30% of the income generated by foreign tourists in Siem Reap benefited business within Cambodia, the remaining 70% returning to foreign countries, as most of the assets in the tourism sector (airlines, hotels and even airports) were owned by foreign interests. The number of foreign visitors arriving on direct flights to Siem Reap almost trebled in 1999 in relation to 1998, and continued to increase significantly during 2000–02, representing 35% of the total number of arrivals by air in Cambodia in 2002.

The outbreak of Severe Acute Respiratory Syndrome (SARS) in the region in 2003 contributed to a decline in foreign tourist arrivals in that year. The number of tourist arrivals sharply increased in 2004–07, reaching 2.0m. visitors in 2007, and exceeded 2.12m. in 2008, when receipts increased to more than US $1,595m. By the onset of the global financial crisis of 2008–09, the tourism sector had become one of the main sources of economic growth and had attracted a high proportion of foreign capital investment. Despite the economic slowdown, in 2009 tourism arrivals and receipts both continued to record positive growth, albeit at a slow rate, according to Ministry of Tourism data; the number of foreign visitors increased to 2.16m., while tourism income increased to $1,617m. In 2010 there 2.33m. visitors, and receipts reached $1,750m. The number of people employed within the tourism industry was forecast to increase from an estimated 305,000 in 2009 to 315,000 in 2010, while the number of rooms available in hotels and guest houses was forecast to increase from an estimated 37,191 to 40,910.

TRADE AND THE BALANCE OF PAYMENTS

From 1997 traditional exports like logs, sawn timber and rubber were increasingly superseded by sales of garments, which accounted for 44% of domestic exports (excluding re-exports) in that year and for about 92% in 2003. Logs, sawn timber and rubber accounted for only 3% of domestic exports in the latter year and for less than 5% in 2005. Imports were dominated by investment-related products, durable consumer goods and petroleum products. Re-exports represented a significant feature of external trade, prompted by the differences in import tariffs between Cambodia and its neighbours, and included cigarettes, motorcycles, beer and electric equipment (which were re-exported to Viet Nam) and gold (which was principally re-exported to Thailand). In the late 1990s, however, re-exports declined sharply. Re-exports accounted for 62% of total exports in 1995, but declined to an estimated 5% of the total in 2009.

Despite the decline of timber exports, the volume of Cambodia's external trade continued to grow steadily, reaching US $3,343m. in 2001, exceeding the nominal GDP for the first time in Cambodia's history. In 2002–08 exports of goods increased by an average annual rate of about 18%; imports of goods rose by about the same rate. In terms of the balance of trade, the trade surplus in agriculture was very significant owing to the increase in production of paddy and higher prices for rubber exports. The trade surplus in the garment sector remained relatively strong. However, the trade deficit in the energy and non-garment manufacturing sectors increased significantly, owing to the expansion in economic activity and to high oil prices. As a result, in 2008 the trade deficit rose to $1,800.4m., the equivalent of 17.4% of GDP, compared with $522.8m., or 13.1% of GDP, in 2001; the trade deficit declined to $1,634.2m. (15.7% of GDP) in 2009, before increasing to $1,714.8m. (15.6% of GDP) in 2010. The balance in the service sector was largely in surplus (about 6% of GDP), owing to the sharp increase in receipts from tourism. The outflow of income owed by expatriates (including salaries and profits generated by FDI) was broadly balanced by the inflow of money repatriated by Cambodians residing overseas. Overall, Cambodia's current account deficit increased to $1,061.5m. (equivalent to 10.3% of GDP) in 2008, compared with $43.0m. (1.1% of GDP) in 2001; the deficit decreased to $930.9m. (8.9% of GDP) in 2009 and further to $897.1m. (8.2% of GDP) in 2010.

Cambodia's relations with ASEAN improved significantly following the 1993 elections, although Cambodia was not formally admitted to the organization until April 1999. ASEAN membership required the implementation of the CEPT (see above). However, Cambodia experienced difficulties in reducing tariffs for customs duties, which provided a substantial proportion of non-aid revenues to the national budget. The Government envisaged increasing domestic taxes, principally excise duties, to offset the decline in customs duties. In addition, Cambodia's accession to the WTO in 2004 required the country to adopt 47 items of legislation, of which 14 pieces had already been approved in 2001–03; all 47 essential laws had been endorsed by the Cambodian legislature by mid-2010.

In November 2010 an agreement was signed by Cambodia, Laos, Myanmar, Thailand and Viet Nam with a view to bolstering economic co-operation among the five South-East Asian countries. The so-called Phnom-Penh Declaration incorporated measures intended to boost trade and investment (including a proposal to exempt nationals of the five countries from visa requirements when visiting any of the other signatory states for up to 30 days), as well as enhancing co-operation in the fields of, *inter alia*, agriculture, industry, energy, tourism and human resource development.

DEBT, FOREIGN AID AND INVESTMENT

The exact level of Cambodia's outstanding external debt remained unclear at mid-2011, although World Bank documents showed that at the end of 2008 Cambodia's overall foreign debt totalled about US $3,000m. (or 30% of GDP), most of which was owed to Russia. These debts were contracted during four different periods: at the end of the 1960s Cambodia's outstanding external debt amounted to about $50m., all of which was already rescheduled or partly cancelled in 1995, according to the procedure of the 'Paris Club' of creditor nations, and which by mid-2006 had been reduced to about $20m.; however, it appeared that Cambodia also owed at least $300m. to the USA during 1970–75, and about 800m. convertible roubles (equivalent to $1,400m.) to Russia during 1980–91. At mid-2011 the Cambodian Government had not yet recognized these two debts, although discussions with Russia continued, and in November 2010 Cambodia and the USA agreed to resume negotiations on the issue that had remained dormant since 2006. According to a joint IMF/World Bank assessment, these two debts could be reduced to about $600m., if the 'Paris Club' procedure were applied.

After 1993 the Cambodian Government resumed borrowing from the World Bank and the ADB in order to finance the rehabilitation of the country's public infrastructure. By 2009 these debts were estimated to have reached about US $1,000m. China and South Korea have also become major creditors of Cambodia, their credit disbursements totalling about $300m. by the end of 2008. In sum, the total outstanding external debt recognized by the Cambodian Government at the end of 2009 amounted to about $2,000m., while pending debt was estimated at $1,700m.

Aid for economic rehabilitation and infrastructural development amounting to US $880m. was pledged by approximately 30 donors, including ASEAN, at a conference in Tokyo in June 1992. At subsequent donor meetings between 1992 and 2007, pledges rose to more than $7,000m. Disbursements for the repatriation and resettlement of refugees, community development, agriculture, health and sanitation, education and training, public utilities, industry and public administration were spread over several years, and by 1996 were behind schedule, owing to problems of absorption. However, the political unrest of July 1997 prompted several lenders and donors to reduce their aid programmes. The USA, Germany, the IMF and the World Bank suspended all non-humanitarian aid. Other donors made more modest reductions, or continued providing assistance. Australia only ceased providing military assistance, and Japan briefly delayed the release of some funds, while China made no decreases in aid. Nevertheless, the aid decreases forced the Government to reduce its budget and to take measures to increase revenue collection, which mitigated but did not prevent an increase in the budget deficit.

Following Cambodia's achievement of political progress, Japan (Cambodia's leading aid donor) resumed yen-denominated loans in 1999, for the first time in 30 years. The IMF resumed assistance to Cambodia in late 1999, following its approval in October of a three-year arrangement under the Enhanced Structural Adjustment Facility for Cambodia to support the Government's economic programme for 1999–2000; however, the organization remained critical of Cambodia's fiscal performance. Relative political stability in Cambodia, and the cessation of formal armed resistance following the disintegration of the Khmers Rouges, augured well for Cambodia's ambitions of achieving rapid economic development. Donors hoped that the importance of external aid in the Government's budget would provide impetus for political and financial reform. Meanwhile, the Consultative Group (CG), comprising 16 countries and six international financial institutions, pledged an assistance grant and loan of US $470m. for Cambodia, at a meeting held in Tokyo in February 1999. The CG promised a further $548m. in May 2000 and another $615m. in June 2001. During 2002–07 annual foreign assistance ranged between $600m. and $700m.

The release of funds by the CG and other institutions was dependent upon the Cambodian Government's commitment to implement reforms, including: military demobilization; administrative and fiscal reforms; the reduction of corruption; and the elimination of illegal logging. Donors regularly requested that budgetary procedures and transparency be improved, and that greater priority be given to basic needs through the expansion of health and education services and the promotion of rural development (the latter of which necessarily required protection of the environment by means of effective regulation of logging and reafforestation). In pursuing their reform agenda, lending institutions and countries increasingly attempted to make aid conditional upon improved performance and accountability from the Government, and to transfer aid directly to local areas, thereby circumventing central ministries. A significant number of functions that were traditionally the responsibility of central government, such as the organization and management of credit associations, have been assumed by NGOs. (At mid-2011 there were about 2,000 national and international NGOs operating in Cambodia.)

The Cambodia Development Cooperation Forum (CDCF), which superseded the CG, held its first meeting in June 2007, when foreign donors pledged a total of US $689m. for the coming year. The Financial Sector Development Strategy 2006–2015 was also officially inaugurated. At the CDCF's second meeting, convened in December 2008, a total of $951.5m. in foreign assistance was pledged; the amount pledged at the third meeting, convened in June 2010, increased to $1,100.0m. A fourth meeting of the CDCF was scheduled to be held in November 2011; however, in August of that year the Cambodian Government announced the indefinite suspension of the meeting, owing to ongoing global economic uncertainty and a number of development partners remaining 'mired in crisis' as a result. Official data forecast a decline in official development assistance from $1,044.6m. in 2010 to $707.0m. in 2011 and further to $459.6m. in 2012. In February 2011 it was announced that Japan was to provide a grant of $1.9m. to fund a four-year programme—to be administered by the ADB—intended to support rural entrepreneurs in the central Cambodian province of Kampong Thom.

The 1994 Law on Investment in Cambodia provided for a low corporate taxation rate of 9%, tax exemptions of up to eight years, five-year loss carried forward, no taxation of reinvested profits, the free repatriation of profits, the leasing of land for up to 70 years and tariff exemptions on imported capital goods destined for use in export-orientated production. In 1994 a newly created Council for the Development of Cambodia (CDC) approved investments worth US $465m. (of which $285m. were domestic); more than one-half of the total was for tourism and other service industries. Cambodia's attempts to secure foreign investment in the following years were hindered by: investor anxiety about political and budgetary stability; a lack of banking regulations and legal guarantees; and the slow implementation of projects as a result of ministerial or local government bureaucracy. The CDC approved investments totalling about $2,250m. in 1995, and more than $1,000m. in 1996 but, according to the IMF, actual investments remained substantially lower; net foreign investment was estimated at $151m. in 1995 and at $294m. in 1996. Meanwhile, in addition to the granting by the USA of MFN trading status and Cambodia's admission to the GSP, the country joined the International Finance Corporation of the World Bank in December 1996, thereby gaining access to multilateral sources of finance for private sector interests.

Prior to the discovery of petroleum and gas reserves, the majority of investment was concentrated within the three main sectors of garments, construction and tourism, which together represented more than 80% of total capital registered. Investment approved by the CDC declined sharply during 1999–2004. Having reached US $474m. in 1999, it fluctuated between $200m. and $300m. per year thereafter. Such potential investment totalled $209m. in 2004, while actual investment reached only $121m. in the same year (or 2.2% of GDP). Nevertheless, the amount of approved investment subsequently increased significantly, rising from $695m. in 2005 to $4,451m. in 2006, declining to $2,667m. in 2007 before reaching $10,891m. in 2008. According to the IMF, actual investment increased from $375m. in 2005 to more than $800m. in 2007 and 2008, before declining to an estimated $506m. in 2009, although this was projected to have recovered to $632m. in 2010.

CONCLUSION

Cambodia's long-term development requires major investment in infrastructural improvements. Significant resources need to be allocated to education so as to provide the skilled personnel essential to the improvement of the country's administrative, legal and educational institutions. The health sector also requires substantial investment, in order to improve general health care and in particular to address the relatively high rates of HIV/AIDS in Cambodia.

Although Cambodia's efforts towards economic integration have made great progress, notably with its entry to ASEAN in 1999 and its accession to the WTO in 2004, the country will derive real benefits from the open market only if it is able to offer more competitive products for export. This is dependent upon the Government's ability to institute other reforms, such as trade facilitation and the elimination of burdensome informal transaction costs. The improvement of administrative accountability and transparency will be possible only through radical, structural public administrative reforms. While progress has been made in recent years, civil servants' wages have remained unacceptably low, which merely encourages the practice of corruption. Public reform must also include military demobilization, decentralization of power and efficient diffusion of administrative tasks. To accelerate reform, clear guidelines urgently need to be drawn up and to be strongly enforced. Indeed, any progress in this regard depends heavily on the willingness of line ministries to delegate responsibilities to provincial and district administrations.

Effective and reliable legal and judicial improvements are crucial to the proper implementation of any of the aforementioned reforms. A council of legal and judicial reform has been established and long-awaited anti-corruption legislation was approved by the National Assembly in March 2010 and implemented later in the year; the first conviction under the new legislation was secured in May 2011, with a senior official in Pursat province being sentenced to 19 years' imprisonment, having been found guilty of extortion and accepting bribes from timber smugglers. The restructuring of the Supreme Council of Magistracy (the country's highest judicial body) and the creation of a credible court of law would also crucially enhance judicial integrity. Such reforms are vital if the system of influence that has long impeded Cambodia's progress is to be eroded.

Statistical Survey

Source (unless otherwise stated): National Institute of Statistics, Ministry of Planning, Sangkat Boeung Keng Kang 1, blvd Monivong, Phnom-Penh; tel. (23) 216538; fax (23) 213650; e-mail census@camnet.com.kh; internet www.nis.gov.kh.

Area and Population

AREA, POPULATION AND DENSITY

Area (sq km)	181,035*
Population (census results)†	
3 March 1998	11,437,656
3 March 2008	
Males	6,516,054
Females	6,879,628
Total	13,395,682
Population (UN estimates at mid-year)‡	
2009	14,261,565
2010	14,464,739
2011	14,666,053
Density (per sq km) at mid-2011	81.0

* 69,898 sq miles; figure includes Tonlé Sap lake (approx. 3,000 sq km).
† Excluding adjustments for underenumeration.
‡ Source: UN, *World Population Prospects: The 2010 Revision*.

POPULATION BY AGE AND SEX

(UN estimates at mid-2011)

	Males	Females	Total
0–14	2,239,393	2,151,623	4,391,016
15–64	4,671,441	4,670,026	9,341,467
65 and over	432,891	500,679	933,570
Total	7,343725	7,322,328	14,666,053

Source: UN, *World Population Prospects: The 2010 Revision*.

PROVINCES

(population at 2008 census)

	Area (sq km)*	Population	Density (per sq km)
Banteay Meanchey	6,679	677,872	101.5
Battambang	11,702	1,025,174	87.6
Kampong Cham	9,799	1,679,992	171.4
Kampong Chhnang	5,521	472,341	85.6
Kampong Spueu	7,017	716,944	102.2
Kampong Thom	13,814	631,409	45.7
Kampot	4,873	585,850	120.2
Kandal	3,568	1,265,280	354.6
Koh Kong	11,160	117,481	10.5
Kratie	11,094	319,217	28.8
Mondul Kiri	14,288	61,107	4.3
Phnom-Penh	290	1,327,615	4,578.0
Preah Vihear	13,788	171,139	12.4
Prey Veng	4,883	947,372	194.0
Pursat	12,692	397,161	31.3
Ratanak Kiri	10,782	150,466	14.0
Siem Reap	10,299	896,443	87.0
Sihanoukville (Preah Sihanouk)	868	221,396	255.1
Stung Treng	11,092	111,671	10.1
Svay Rieng	2,966	482,788	162.8
Takeo	3,563	844,906	237.1
Oddar Meanchey	6,158	185,819	30.2
Kep	336	35,753	106.4
Pailin	803	70,486	87.8
Total	178,035	13,395,682	75.2

* Excluding Tonlé Sap lake (approx. 3,000 sq km).

PRINCIPAL TOWNS

(population at 1998 census)

Phnom-Penh (capital)	999,804	Bat Dambang (Battambang)	139,964
Preah Sihanouk (Sihanoukville)*	155,690	Siem Reab (Siem Reap)	119,528

* Also known as Kampong Saom (Kompong Som).

Mid-2010 ('000, incl. suburbs, UN estimate): Phnom-Penh 1,562,498 (Source: UN, *World Urbanization Prospects: The 2009 Revision*).

BIRTHS AND DEATHS

(annual averages, UN estimates)

	1995–2000	2000–05	2005–10
Birth rate (per 1,000)	30.3	25.1	25.3
Death rate (per 1,000)	10.2	9.1	8.3

Source: UN, *World Population Prospects: The 2010 Revision*.

2004: Live births 384,267; Deaths 124,391 (Source: UN, *Population and Vital Statistics Report*).

Life expectancy (years at birth, WHO estimates): 61 (males 57; females 65) in 2009 (Source: WHO, *World Health Statistics*).

EMPLOYMENT

('000 persons)

	2005	2006	2007
Agriculture, forestry and fishing	4,655	4,619	4,670
Mining and quarrying	19	20	22
Manufacturing	789	870	944
Electricity, gas and water	17	19	21
Construction	234	260	299
Wholesale and retail trade	1,104	1,140	1,196
Restaurants and hotels	43	61	86
Transport and communications	206	217	228
Financial intermediation	23	32	32
Real estate and renting	16	18	20
Public administration	185	184	185
Education	113	120	128
Health and social work	43	49	57
Other social services	89	108	123
Other services	341	336	343
Total employed	7,878	8,053	8,354

Source: IMF, *Cambodia: Statistical Appendix* (February 2009).

2008 ('000 persons): Agriculture 4,813.1; Manufacturing 694.7; Mining 16.4; Others 2,620.6; Total employed 8,144.8 (Source: Asian Development Bank).

Health and Welfare

KEY INDICATORS

Total fertility rate (children per woman, 2009)	2.9
Under-5 mortality rate (per 1,000 live births, 2009)	88
HIV/AIDS (% of persons aged 15–49, 2007)	0.8
Physicians (per 1,000 head, 2000)	0.2
Hospital beds (per 1,000 head, 2004)	0.1
Health expenditure (2008): US $ per head (PPP)	118
Health expenditure (2008): % of GDP	5.7
Health expenditure (2008): public (% of total)	23.8
Access to water (% of persons, 2008)	61
Access to sanitation (% of persons, 2008)	29
Total carbon dioxide emissions ('000 metric tons, 2007)	4,437.1
Carbon dioxide emissions per head (metric tons, 2007)	0.3
Human Development Index (2010): ranking	124
Human Development Index (2010): value	0.494

For sources and definitions, see explanatory note on p. vi.

Agriculture

PRINCIPAL CROPS

('000 metric tons)

	2007	2008	2009
Rice, paddy	6,727.0	7,175.5	7,586.0*
Maize	523.0	611.9	924.0*
Sweet potatoes	38.0	39.6	40.0†
Cassava (Manioc)	2,215.0	3,676.2	3,497.0*
Beans, dry	54.5	38.6	38.0†
Soybeans (Soya beans)	117.0	108.4	137.0*
Groundnuts, with shell	30.0	25.5	30.0†
Sesame seed	31.0	27.3	31.0†
Coconuts	71.0*	71.0*	71.0†
Sugar cane*	286.8	385.2	350.0
Tobacco, unmanufactured	13.6	17.4	18.6†
Natural rubber*	17.9	31.7	38.7
Oranges†	63.0	55.7	50.4
Guavas, mangoes and mangosteens†	57.6	59.0	58.6
Pineapples†	27.4	22.9	22.6
Bananas†	142.1	152.7	160.8

* Unofficial figure(s).

† FAO estimate(s).

Aggregate production ('000 metric tons, may include official, semi-official or estimated data): Total cereals 7,250.0 in 2007, 7,787.3 in 2008, 8,510.0 in 2009; Total roots and tubers 2,288.8 in 2007, 3,753.1 in 2008, 3,576.7 in 2009; Total vegetables (incl. melons) 487.0 in 2007; 460.4 in 2008; 468.7 in 2009; Total fruits (excl. melons) 371.4 in 2007; 370.6 in 2008; 374.6 in 2009.

Source: FAO.

LIVESTOCK

('000 head, year ending September)

	2007	2008	2009*
Horses*	28	28	28
Cattle	3,368	3,458	3,550
Buffaloes	773	746	750
Pigs	2,389	2,216	2,200
Chickens	15,825	16,928	17,000
Ducks*	7,000	7,000	7,000

* FAO estimates.

Source: FAO.

LIVESTOCK PRODUCTS

('000 metric tons, FAO estimates)

	2007	2008	2009
Cattle meat	60.7	62.4	64.1
Buffalo meat	10.7	10.4	10.4
Pig meat	120.0	110.0	105.0
Chicken meat	18.0	19.0	19.0
Cows' milk	23.1	23.8	24.4
Hen eggs	17.0	16.8	15.8
Other poultry eggs	5.7	6.4	6.3

Source: FAO.

Forestry

ROUNDWOOD REMOVALS

('000 cubic metres, excl. bark, FAO estimates)

	2007	2008	2009
Sawlogs, veneer logs and logs for sleepers	105	105	105
Other industrial wood	13	13	13
Fuel wood	8,891	8,735	8,586
Total	9,009	8,853	8,704

Source: FAO.

SAWNWOOD PRODUCTION

('000 cubic metres, incl. railway sleepers)

	2006	2007	2008
Total (all broadleaved)	2	4	10

2009: Production assumed to be unchanged from 2008 (FAO estimate).

Source: FAO.

Fishing

('000 metric tons, live weight)

	2007*	2008	2009
Capture	458.5	431.0	465.0
Freshwater fishes	394.5	364.6	389.7
Marine fishes	41.5	45.3	55.4
Natantian decapods	12.4	11.0	7.0
Aquaculture*	35.3	40.0	50.0
Total catch*	493.7	471.0	515.0

* FAO estimates.

Note: Figures exclude crocodiles, recorded by number rather than by weight. The total number of estuarine crocodiles caught was: 128,945 in 2007; 156,500 in 2008; 185,000 in 2009. Also excluded are aquatic plants.

Source: FAO.

Mining

('000 metric tons)

	2007	2008	2009
Gravel	36.3	37.5*	41.8
Limestone*	1,000.0	1,000.0	1,000.0
Sand (construction material)	329.0	6,581.5	14,035.8
Salt (unrefined)	76.7	78.0*	n.a.

* Estimate(s).

Source: US Geological Survey.

Industry

SELECTED PRODUCTS

	2007	2008	2009
Plywood ('000 cu m)*†	4.5	4.5	4.5
Electric energy (million kWh)‡	1,349.3	1,484.1	1,234.6

* Source: FAO.

† FAO estimate.

‡ Source: Electricity Authority of Cambodia.

Finance

CURRENCY AND EXCHANGE RATES

Monetary Units
100 sen = 1 riel.

Sterling, Dollar and Euro Equivalents (29 April 2011)
£1 sterling = 6,702.0 riels;
US $1 = 4,024.0 riels;
€1 = 5,979.7 riels;
10,000 riels = £1.49 = $2.49 = €1.67.

Average Exchange Rate (riels per US $)
2008 4,054.17
2009 4,139.33
2010 4,184.92

BUDGET
('000 million riels)

Revenue	2006	2007	2008*
Tax revenue	2,372	3,343	3,241
Direct taxes	331	480	486
Trade tax	644	903	858
Value-added tax	836	1,093	1,120
Excise duties	418	617	587
Non-tax revenue	681	705	710
Forestry	2	0	10
Quota auction/garment licences, etc.	88	118	90
Tourism income	59	78	118
Casino royalties	77	75	69
Posts and telecommunications	83	78	61
Passports and visas	95	122	132
Capital revenue	377	117	157
Total	3,431	4,165	4,109

Expenditure	2006	2007	2008*
Current expenditure	2,527	3,043	3,569
Salaries	975	1,058	1,242
Operating costs	974	1,129	945
Economic transfers	137	65	73
Social transfers	34	501	441
Interest	50	70	75
Provincial expenditure	220	220	207
Other current expenditure	176	1	586
Statistical discrepancy	−39	—	—
Capital expenditure	1,716	2,121	2,111
Locally financed	381	436	711
Externally financed	1,336	1,682	1,400
Total	4,244	5,164	5,680

* Budget projections.

Source: IMF, *Cambodia: Statistical Appendix* (February 2009).

2008 ('000 million riels): *Revenue:* Tax revenue 4,494 (Direct taxes 654, Indirect taxes 3,433, Provincial taxes 259, Other 148); Non-tax revenue 769; Capital revenue 200; Total 5,463. *Expenditure:* Current expenditure 4,097 (Wages 1,438, Non-wage 2,311, Provincial expenditure 347); Capital expenditure 2,654; Total 6,751 (Source: IMF, *Cambodia: 2010 Article IV Consultation—Staff Report; Staff Supplement; Public Information Notice on the Executive Board Discussion; and Statement by the Executive Director—February 2011*).

2009 ('000 million riels, budget figures): *Revenue:* Tax revenue 4,177 (Direct taxes 746, Indirect taxes 3,300, Provincial taxes 131); Non-tax revenue 870; Capital revenue 135; Total 5,182. *Expenditure:* Current expenditure 4,663 (Wages 1,730, Non-wage 2,577, Provincial expenditure 357); Capital expenditure 2,759; Total 7,422 (Source: IMF, *Cambodia: 2010 Article IV Consultation—Staff Report; Staff Supplement; Public Information Notice on the Executive Board Discussion; and Statement by the Executive Director—February 2011*).

INTERNATIONAL RESERVES
(US $ million at 31 December)

	2008	2009	2010
Gold (national valuation)	349.01	437.32	547.01
IMF special drawing rights	0.11	107.39	105.43
Foreign exchange	2,291.44	2,743.74	3,149.68
Total	2,640.56	3,288.45	3,802.12

Source: IMF, *International Financial Statistics*.

MONEY SUPPLY
('000 million riels at 31 December)

	2008	2009	2010
Currency outside depository corporations	2,305.00	3,008.57	3,103.56
Transferable deposits	2,241.74	2,572.67	3,030.17
Other deposits	7,355.51	10,556.17	13,440.93
Broad money	11,902.26	16,137.41	19,574.66

Source: IMF, *International Financial Statistics*.

COST OF LIVING
(Consumer Price Index for Phnom-Penh at January; base: October-December 2006 = 100)

	2008	2009	2010
Food and non-alcoholic beverages	123.5	137.6	148.4
Clothing and footwear	102.8	109.5	112.8
Housing and utilities	114.0	113.4	118.8
Household furnishings, etc.	107.4	115.2	120.8
Medical care and health expenses	107.4	109.7	115.1
Transport	114.0	101.8	116.1
Communication	85.2	76.3	72.9
Recreation and culture	99.9	104.0	103.9
Education	106.5	131.6	139.4
All items	116.1	125.4	134.1

NATIONAL ACCOUNTS
('000 million riels at current prices)

Expenditure on the Gross Domestic Product

	2006	2007	2008
Government final consumption expenditure	1,574.8	2,008.2	2,268.0
Private final consumption expenditure	24,166.8	27,384.8	28,754.1
Change in stocks	359.5	499.7	506.7
Gross fixed capital formation	5,774.7	6,783.7	6,898.4
Total domestic expenditure	31,875.8	36,676.3	38,427.2
Exports of goods and services	20,474.7	22,891.6	23,482.9
Less Imports of goods and services	22,691.9	25,560.5	33,711.8
Statistical discrepancy	190.7	1,031.9	16,331.4
GDP in purchasers' values	29,849.1	35,039.3	44,529.8
GDP at constant 2000 prices	24,379.7	26,867.6	28,667.5

Gross Domestic Product by Economic Activity

	2006	2007	2008
Agriculture, hunting, forestry and fishing	8,972.4	10,406.3	13,593.3
Mining and quarrying	114.8	133.2	164.6
Manufacturing	5,541.4	6,072.6	6,441.1
Electricity, gas and water	164.2	194.6	211.9
Construction	1,995.0	2,337.8	2,571.5
Trade, hotels and restaurants	3,968.2	4,645.1	5,618.8
Transport, storage and communications	2,115.0	2,423.4	3,102.0
Finance, real estate and other business activities	2,324.2	2,688.4	5,805.2
Public administration	515.1	667.7	767.8
Other services	2,634.0	3,068.8	3,559.8
Sub-total	28,344.3	32,637.9	41,836.0
Less Imputed bank service charge	290.5	386.2	442.6
GDP at factor cost	28,053.8	32,251.7	41,393.4
Indirect taxes, *less* subsidies	1,795.2	2,787.6	3,136.3
GDP in purchasers' values	29,849.1	35,039.3	44,529.8

Source: Asian Development Bank.

BALANCE OF PAYMENTS
(US $ million)

	2007	2008	2009
Exports of goods f.o.b.	4,088.5	4,708.0	4,301.8
Imports of goods f.o.b.	–5,438.9	–6,508.4	–5,875.8
Trade balance	–1,350.4	–1,800.4	–1,573.9
Exports of services	1,547.5	1,645.1	1,624.9
Imports of services	–915.4	–1,035.8	–1,022.4
Balance on goods and services	–718.3	–1,191.1	–971.5
Other income received	112.2	108.4	55.6
Other income paid	–476.2	–583.0	–523.8
Balance on goods, income and services	–1,082.2	–1,665.7	–1,439.7
Current transfers received	620.3	642.8	595.5
Current transfers paid	–25.8	–27.9	–21.3
Current balance	–487.7	–1,050.8	–865.6
Capital account (net)	258.3	232.7	311.6
Direct investment abroad	–1.1	–20.5	–18.8
Direct investment from abroad	867.3	815.2	530.2
Portfolio investment assets	–6.5	–11.6	–7.6
Other investment assets	–780.6	312.4	–346.7
Other investment liabilities	602.4	290.8	533.9
Net errors and omissions	–28.9	–45.9	–34.7
Overall balance	423.2	522.4	102.2

Source: IMF, *International Financial Statistics*.

External Trade

PRINCIPAL COMMODITIES
(US $ million)

Imports c.i.f.	2005	2006	2007
Cigarettes	80	103	108
Petroleum products	164	212	273
Motorcycles	55	93	108
Vehicles	90	105	172
Clothing	45	47	55
Cement	44	53	54
Total (incl. others)	4,230	5,123	5,874

Exports f.o.b.	2005	2006	2007
Crude rubber	119	175	157
Logs and sawn timber	16	18	21
Clothing	2,261	2,727	2,943
Fish	76	90	105
Rice	177	332	411
Total (incl. others)	2,910	3,694	4,089

Note: Totals include imports for re-export and estimates for unrecorded items.

Source: IMF, *Cambodia: Statistical Appendix* (February 2009).

PRINCIPAL TRADING PARTNERS
(US $ million)

Imports c.i.f.	2007	2008	2009
China, People's Republic	1,145.2	1,573.8	987.7
France	83.2	89.2	n.a.
Hong Kong	673.3	669.2	517.4
Indonesia	134.0	191.4	124.5
Japan	122.6	204.2	123.7
Korea, Republic	309.6	323.8	286.0
Malaysia	147.5	181.5	168.4
Singapore	482.2	570.9	791.5
Thailand	1,491.1	2,221.4	1,732.6
USA	152.7	169.5	139.9
Viet Nam	1,145.2	1,573.8	1,390.1
Total (incl. others)	6,536.7	8,212.6	6,987.4

Exports f.o.b.	2007	2008	2009
Canada	189.2	252.1	253.8
France	51.0	52.9	52.8
Germany	298.3	329.1	302.4
Hong Kong	17.1	8.7	11.6
Israel	0.1	1,151.7	n.a.
Japan	126.2	109.6	129.7
Singapore	76.7	105.5	380.3
Spain	115.1	140.5	129.8
United Kingdom	211.7	232.0	284.2
USA	2,363.1	2,314.3	1,822.5
Viet Nam	186.8	190.9	168.6
Total (incl. others)	4,073.3	4,252.8	4,022.8

Note: Data reflect the IMF's direction of trade methodology and, as a result, the totals may not be equal to those presented for trade in commodities.

Source: Asian Development Bank.

Transport

RAILWAYS
(traffic)

	1997	1998	1999
Freight carried ('000 metric tons)	16	294	259
Freight ton-km ('000)	36,514	75,721	76,171
Passengers ('000)	553	438	431
Passenger-km ('000)	50,992	43,847	49,894

Source: Ministry of Economy and Finance, Phnom-Penh.

2000: Passenger-km (million) 15; Freight ton-km (million) 91 (Source: UN, *Statistical Yearbook*).

2005: Passenger-km (million) 45 (Source: World Bank, World Development Indicators database).

ROAD TRAFFIC
(estimated number of motor vehicles in use)

	2002	2003	2004
Passenger cars	209,128	219,602	235,298
Buses and coaches	3,196	3,269	3,502
Trucks	29,968	30,448	31,946
Other vehicles	421	428	440
Motorcycles and mopeds	586,278	619,748	646,944

Sources: Ministry of Public Works and Transport, Phnom-Penh, and Phnom-Penh Municipal Traffic Police.

SHIPPING

Merchant Fleet
(registered at 31 December)

	2007	2008	2009
Number of vessels	881	939	963
Displacement ('000 grt)	2,059.8	2,096.2	1,963.9

Source: IHS Fairplay, *World Fleet Statistics*.

International Sea-borne Freight Traffic
(estimates, '000 metric tons)

	1988	1989	1990
Goods loaded	10	10	11
Goods unloaded	100	100	95

Source: UN, *Monthly Bulletin of Statistics*.

Tourism

FOREIGN TOURIST ARRIVALS BY COUNTRY OF RESIDENCE

Country of residence	2008	2009	2010
Australia	99,087	96,678	98,986
Canada	36,891	36,340	36,251
China, People's Repub.	129,626	128,210	138,012
France	97,517	105,437	104,270
Germany	59,903	59,916	60,303
Japan	163,806	146,286	143,820
Korea, Republic	266,525	197,725	274,817
Malaysia	80,738	77,759	83,914
Philippines	39,294	49,079	49,927
Singapore	40,945	41,273	43,211
Taiwan	83,000	72,119	82,848
Thailand	109,020	102,018	79,148
United Kingdom	98,093	106,837	97,298
USA	145,079	148,482	132,959
Viet Nam	209,516	316,202	454,091
Total (incl. others)	2,125,465	2,161,577	2,330,578

Source: Ministry of Tourism, Phnom-Penh.

Tourism receipts (US $ million, excl. passenger transport): 1,135 in 2007, 1,219 in 2008, 1,185 in 2009 (provisional) (Source: World Tourism Organization).

Communications Media

	2008	2009	2010
Telephones ('000 main lines in use)	43.1	54.2	358.8
Mobile cellular telephones ('000 subscribers)	4,237.0	6,268.0	8,150.8
Internet subscribers ('000)	19.1	n.a.	n.a.
Broadband subscribers ('000)	16.6	30.0	35.7

Personal computers: 52,000 (3.6 per 1,000 persons) in 2007.

Television receivers ('000 in use): 98 in 1999; 99 in 2000.

Radio receivers ('000 in use): 1,120 in 1995; 1,300 in 1996; 1,340 in 1997.

Sources: UNESCO, *Statistical Yearbook* and International Telecommunication Union.

Education

(2008/09 unless otherwise indicated)

			Students		
	Institutions*	Teachers	Males	Females	Total
Pre-primary	n.a.	5,211†	88,645	89,938	178,583
Primary	5,915	48,223†	1,204,094	1,085,665	2,289,759
Secondary	594	30,258‡	488,683‡	386,437‡	875,120‡
General	411	27,856‡	498,656	420,052	918,708
Vocational	183	2,402‡	10,080‡	8,840‡	18,920‡
Tertiary†	n.a.	6,086	80,505	42,128	122,633

* 2002/03 data.
† 2007/08 data.
‡ 2006/07 data.

Sources: IMF, *Cambodia: Statistical Appendix* (October 2004); UNESCO Institute for Statistics.

Pupil-teacher ratio (primary education, UNESCO estimate): 49.1 in 2008/09 (Source: UNESCO Institute for Statistics).

Adult literacy rate (UNESCO estimates): 77.6% (males 85.1%; females 70.9%) in 2008 (Source: UNESCO Institute for Statistics).

Directory

The Constitution

The Constitution was promulgated on 21 September 1993; various amendments were approved in March 1999 and in March 2006. The main provisions of the Constitution are summarized below:

GENERAL PROVISIONS

The Kingdom of Cambodia is a unitary state in which the King abides by the Constitution and multi-party liberal democracy. Cambodian citizens have full right of freedom of belief; Buddhism is the state religion. The Kingdom of Cambodia has a market economy system.

THE KING

The King is Head of State and the Supreme Commander of the Khmer Royal Armed Forces. The monarchist regime is based on a system of selection: within seven days of the King's death the Royal Council of the Throne (comprising the Chairman of the Senate, the Chairman of the National Assembly, the Prime Minister, the Supreme Patriarchs of the Maha Nikaya and Thammayut Nikaya sects, the First and Second Vice-Chairmen of the Senate and the First and Second Vice-Chairmen of the National Assembly) must select a King. The King must be at least 30 years of age and be a descendant of King Ang Duong, King Norodom or King Sisowath. The King appoints the Prime Minister and the Cabinet. In the absence of the King, the Chairman of the Senate assumes the duty of acting Head of State.

THE LEGISLATURE

Legislative power is vested in the National Assembly (the lower chamber) and the Senate (the upper chamber). The National Assembly has 123 members who are elected by universal adult suffrage. A member of the National Assembly must be a Cambodian citizen by birth, over the age of 25 years, and has a term of office of five years, the term of the National Assembly. The National Assembly may not be dissolved except in the case where the Royal Government (Cabinet) has been dismissed twice in 12 months. The National Assembly may dismiss cabinet members or remove the Royal Government from office by passing a censure motion through a two-thirds' majority vote of all the representatives in the National Assembly. The Senate comprises 61 members (the number not exceeding one-half of all of the members of the National Assembly). Two Senators are nominated by the King, two are elected by majority vote in the National Assembly and 57 are chosen by an electoral college comprising the 123 members of the National Assembly and more than 11,000 local councillors. A member of the Senate has a term of office of six years. The Senate reviews legislation passed by the National Assembly and acts as a co-ordinator between the National Assembly and the Royal Government. In special cases, the National Assembly and the Senate can assemble as the Congress to resolve issues of national importance. In March 2006 a constitutional amendment reduced the threshold required to form a government from a two-thirds' majority of the members of the National Assembly to a formula of 50% plus one of the votes of the Assembly.

THE CABINET

The Cabinet is the Royal Government of the Kingdom of Cambodia, which is led by a Prime Minister, assisted by Deputy Prime Ministers, with state ministers, ministers and state secretaries as members. The Prime Minister is designated by the King at the recommendation of the Chairman of the National Assembly from among the representatives of the winning party. The Prime Minister appoints the members of the Cabinet, who must be representatives in the National Assembly or members of parties represented in the National Assembly.

THE CONSTITUTIONAL COUNCIL

The Constitutional Council's competence is to interpret the Constitution and laws passed by the National Assembly and reviewed completely by the Senate. It has the right to examine and settle disputes relating to the election of members of the National Assembly and the Senate. The Constitutional Council consists of nine members with a nine-year mandate. One-third of the members are replaced every three years. Three members are appointed by the King, three elected by the National Assembly and three appointed by the Supreme Council of Magistracy.

The Government

HEAD OF STATE

King: HM King NORODOM SIHAMONI (appointed by the Royal Council of the Throne on 14 October 2004).

ROYAL GOVERNMENT OF CAMBODIA
(October 2011)

A coalition of the Cambodian People's Party (CPP) and the FUNCINPEC Party.

Prime Minister: HUN SEN (CPP).

Permanent Deputy Prime Minister and Minister of National Assembly-Senate Relations and Inspection: MEN SAM ON (CPP).

Deputy Prime Minister and Minister of Economy and Finance: KEAT CHHON (CPP).

Deputy Prime Minister and Minister of the Interior: SAR KHENG (CPP).

Deputy Prime Minister and Minister of National Defence: Gen. TEA BANH (CPP).

Deputy Prime Minister and Minister of Foreign Affairs and International Co-operation: HOR NAM HONG (CPP).

Deputy Prime Minister and Minister in Charge of the Council of Ministers: SOK AN (CPP).

Deputy Prime Minister and Minister of Royal Palace Affairs: KONG SAM OL (CPP).

Deputy Prime Ministers without Portfolio: Gen. NHIEK BUN CHHAY (FUNCINPEC), YIM CHHAY LY (CPP), BIN CHHIN (CPP), KE KIMYAN.

Senior Ministers: CHAM PRASIDH (CPP), CHHAY THON (CPP), KEAT CHHON (CPP), IM CHHUN LIM (CPP), Dr MOK MARETH (CPP), NHIM VANNDA (CPP), TAV SENGHUO (CPP), OM YINTIENG (FUNCINPEC), KHUN HAING (FUNCINPEC), NUTH SOKHOM (CPP), KOL PHENG (FUNCINPEC), SUN CHANTHOL (FUNCINPEC), VENG SEREIVUTH (FUNCINPEC), LY THUCH (FUNCINPEC), SEREI KOSAL (FUNCINPEC).

Minister of Agriculture, Forestry and Fisheries: Dr CHAN SARUN (CPP).

Minister of Commerce: CHAM PRASIDH (CPP).

Minister of Culture and Fine Arts: HIM CHAEM (CPP).

Minister of Education, Youth and Sport: IM SITHY (CPP).

Minister of Environment: Dr MOK MARETH (CPP).

Minister of Health: MAM BUN HENG (CPP).

Minister of Industry, Mines and Energy: SUY SEM (CPP).

Minister of Information: KIEU KANHARITH (CPP).

Minister of Justice: ANG VONG VATHNA (CPP).

Minister of Labour and Vocational Training: VORNG SOTH (CPP).

Minister of Land Management, Urban Planning and Construction: IM CHHUN LIM (CPP).

Minister of Planning: CHHAY THAN (CPP).

Minister of Posts and Telecommunications: SO KHUN (CPP).

Minister of Public Works and Transport: TRAM EAV TOEK (CPP).

Minister of Religions and Cults: MIN KHIN (CPP).

Minister of Rural Development: CHEA SOPHARA (CPP).

Minister of Social Affairs, Veterans and Youth Rehabilitation: ITH SAM HENG (CPP).

Minister of Tourism: THONG KHON (CPP).

Minister of Water Resources and Meteorology: LIM KEAN HOR (CPP).

Minister of Women's Affairs: OENG KANTHA PHAVY (FUNCINPEC).

Secretary of State for Public Functions: PECH BUN THIN (CPP).

Secretary of State for Civil Aviation: MAO HAS VANNAL (FUNCINPEC).

MINISTRIES

Office of the Council of Ministers: 41 blvd Confédération de la Russie, Sangkat Toeuk Thla, Khan Sen Sok, Phnom-Penh; tel. (12) 804442; fax (23) 880624; e-mail ocm@cambodia.gov.kh; internet www.cambodia.gov.kh.

Ministry of Agriculture, Forestry and Fisheries: 200 blvd Norodom, Sangkat Tonle Bassac, Khan Chamkarmon, Phnom-Penh 12301; tel. (23) 211351; fax (23) 217320; e-mail info@maff.gov.kh; internet www.maff.gov.kh.

Ministry of Commerce: blvd Confédération de la Russie, Sangkat Toeuk Thla, Khan Sen Sok, Phnom-Penh; tel. (23) 866088; fax (23) 866188; e-mail moccab@moc.gov.kh; internet www.moc.gov.kh.

Ministry of Culture and Fine Arts: 227 blvd Norodom, Phnom-Penh; tel. and fax (23) 218148; e-mail info@mcfa.gov.kh; internet www.mcfa.gov.kh.

Ministry of Economy and Finance: 60 rue 92, Sangkat Wat Phnom, Khan Duan Penh, Phnom-Penh; tel. (23) 724664; fax (23) 427798; e-mail admin@mef.gov.kh; internet www.mef.gov.kh.

Ministry of Education, Youth and Sport: 80 blvd Preah Norodom, Phnom-Penh; tel. (23) 217253; fax (23) 212512; e-mail info@moeys.gov.kh; internet www.moeys.gov.kh.

Ministry of Environment: 48 blvd Sihanouk, Sangkat Tonle Bassac, Khan Chamkarmon, Phnom-Penh; tel. (23) 427894; fax (23) 427844; e-mail moe-cabinet@camnet.com.kh; internet www.camnet.com.kh/moe.

Ministry of Foreign Affairs and International Co-operation: 3 rue Samdech Hun Sen, Sangkat Tonle Bassac, Khan Chamkarmon, Phnom-Penh; tel. (23) 214441; fax (23) 216144; e-mail mfaic@mfa.gov.kh; internet www.mfaic.gov.kh.

Ministry of Health: 151–153 blvd Kampuchea Krom, Phnom-Penh; tel. (23) 722873; fax (23) 426841; e-mail webmaster@moh.gov.kh; internet www.moh.gov.kh.

Ministry of Industry, Mines and Energy: 45 blvd Preah Norodom, Khan Duan Penh, Phnom-Penh; tel. (23) 211141; fax (23) 428263; e-mail info@mime.gov.kh; internet www.mime.gov.kh.

Ministry of Information: 62 blvd Monivong, Phnom-Penh; tel. and fax (23) 430514; e-mail info@information.gov.kh; internet www.information.gov.kh.

Ministry of the Interior: 275 blvd Norodom, Khan Chamkarmon, Phnom-Penh; tel. (23) 721190; fax (23) 726052; e-mail info@interior.gov.kh; internet www.interior.gov.kh.

Ministry of Justice: 240 blvd Sothearos, Phnom-Penh; tel. (23) 360327; fax (23) 364119; e-mail moj@cambodia.gov.kh; internet www.moj.gov.kh.

Ministry of Labour and Vocational Training: 3 blvd Confédération de la Russie, Sangkat Toeuk Thla, Khan Sen Sok, Phnom-Penh; tel. (23) 884375; e-mail mlv@cambodia.gov.kh; internet www.mlv.gov.kh.

Ministry of Land Management, Urban Planning and Construction: 771–773 blvd Monivong, Boeung Trabek, Khan Chamkarmon, Phnom-Penh; tel. (23) 880780; e-mail mlmupc@camnet.com.kh; internet www.mlmupc.gov.kh.

Ministry of National Defence: blvd Confédération de la Russie, cnr rue 175, Sangkat Toeuk Thla, Khan Sen Sok, Phnom-Penh; tel. and fax (23) 883184; e-mail info@mond.gov.kh; internet www.mond.gov.kh.

Ministry of National Assembly-Senate Relations and Inspection: rue Jawaharlal Nehru 215, Phnom-Penh; tel. (23) 884261; fax (23) 884264; e-mail mnasrl@cambodia.gov.kh.

Ministry of Planning: 386 blvd Monivong, Sangkat Boeung Keng Kang 1, Phnom-Penh; tel. (23) 212049; fax (23) 210698; e-mail mop@cambodia.gov.kh; internet www.mop.gov.kh.

Ministry of Posts and Telecommunications: Sangkat Wat Phnom, cnr rues 13 & 102, Phnom-Penh; tel. (23) 426510; fax (23) 426011; e-mail mptc@cambodia.gov.kh; internet www.mptc.gov.kh.

Ministry of Public Works and Transport: cnr blvd Norodom, rue 106, Phnom-Penh; tel. (23) 427845; e-mail mpwt@online.com.kh; internet www.mpwt.gov.kh.

Ministry of Religions and Cults: Preah Sisowath Quay, cnr rue 240, Phnom-Penh; tel. (23) 725099; fax (23) 725699; e-mail morac@cambodia.gov.kh; internet www.morac.gov.kh.

Ministry of Rural Development: blvd Confédération de la Russie, cnr rue 169, Sangkat Toeuk Thla, Khan Sen Sok, Phnom-Penh; tel. and fax (23) 880007; e-mail mrd@cambodia.gov.kh; internet www.mrd.gov.kh.

Ministry of Social Affairs, Veterans and Youth Rehabilitation: 788B blvd Monivong, Phnom-Penh; tel. (23) 726103; fax (23) 726086; internet www.mosvy.gov.kh.

Ministry of Tourism: 3 blvd Monivong, Phnom-Penh 12258; tel. (23) 213741; fax (23) 220704; e-mail admin@mot.gov.kh; internet www.mot.gov.kh.

Ministry of Water Resources and Meteorology: 47 blvd Norodom, Phnom-Penh; tel. (23) 724289; fax (23) 426345; e-mail mowram@cambodia.gov.kh; internet www.mowram.org/temp.

Ministry of Women's Affairs: rue 47, Sangkat Sras Chork, Khan Daun Penh, Phnom-Penh; tel. (23) 430992; e-mail mwva@online.com.kh.

Legislature

PARLIAMENT

National Assembly

blvd Samdech Sothearos, cnr rue 240, Phnom-Penh; tel. (23) 214136; fax (23) 217769; e-mail kimhenglong@cambodian-parliament.org; internet www.national-assembly.org.kh.

Chairman: HENG SAMRIN.

Election, 27 July 2008

	% of votes	Seats
Cambodian People's Party	58.11	90
Sam Rainsy Party	21.91	26
Human Rights Party	6.62	3
FUNCINPEC Party	5.05	2
Norodom Ranariddh Party	5.62	2
Total	100.00*	123

* Including others.

Senate

Chamkarmon State Bldg, blvd Norodom, Phnom-Penh; tel. (23) 211441; fax (23) 211446; e-mail info@senate.gov.kh; internet www.senate.gov.kh.

President: CHEA SIM (CPP).

First Vice-President: HRH Samdech Sisowath CHIVAN MONIRAK (FUNCINPEC).

Second Vice-President: TEP NGORN (CPP).

Election, 22 January 2006

	Seats
Cambodian People's Party	45
FUNCINPEC Party	10
Sam Rainsy Party	2
King's appointees	2
National Assembly's appointees	2
Total	61

Note: 57 of the 61 Senators were chosen by means of an electoral college system.

Election Commission

National Election Committee (NEC): blvd Preah Norodom, Khan Chamkarmon, Phnom-Penh; tel. (12) 855018; fax (23) 214374; e-mail necinfo@forum.org.kh; internet www.necelect.org.kh; independent body, appointed by royal decree; Chair. IM SUOSDEY.

Political Organizations

Cambodian People's Party (CPP) (Kanakpak Pracheachon Kampuchea): 203 blvd Norodom, Sangkat Tonle Bassac, Khan Chamkarmon, Phnom-Penh; tel. and fax (23) 215801; e-mail cpp@camnet.com.kh; internet www.thecpp.org; f. 1951; known as the Kampuchean People's Revolutionary Party (KPRP) 1979–91; name changed as above in 1991; 30-mem. Standing Cttee of the Cen. Cttee; Cen. Cttee of 268 full mems; Hon. Chair. of Cen. Cttee HENG SAMRIN; Chair. of Cen. Cttee CHEA SIM; Vice-Chair. HUN SEN; Chair. of Permanent Cttee SAY CHHUM.

Solidarity Front for Development of the Cambodian Motherland (SFDCM): Phnom-Penh; f. 1978; est. as Kampuchean National United Front for National Salvation (KNUFNS); name changed to Kampuchean United Front for National Construction and Defence (KUFNCD) in 1981, and to United Front for the Construction and Defence of the Kampuchean Fatherland (UFCDKF) in 1989; present name adopted in 2006; mass org. supporting policies of the CPP; an 89-mem. Nat. Council and a seven-mem. hon. Presidium; Chair. of Nat. Council HENG SAMRIN; Gen. Sec. of Nat. Council MIN KHIN.

Farmers' Party: 21 rue 528, Sangkat Boeung Kak I, Khan Chamkarmon, Phnom-Penh; tel. (16) 333200; Pres. PON PISITH.

FUNCINPEC Party (United National Front for an Independent, Neutral, Peaceful and Co-operative Cambodia Party): 11 blvd Monivong (93), Sangkat Sras Chak, Khan Daun Penh, BP 1444, Phnom-Penh; tel. (23) 428864; fax (23) 218547; e-mail funcinpec@funcinpec.org; FUNCINPEC altered its title to the FUNCINPEC Party when it adopted political status in 1992; the party's military wing was the National Army of Independent Cambodia (fmrly the Armée Nationale Sihanoukiste—ANS); merged with the Son Sann Party in Jan. 1999; Pres. KEO PUTH RASMEY; Sec.-Gen. Gen. NHIEK BUN CHHAY.

Hang Dara Movement Democratic Party: 16 rue 430, Sangkat Phsar Doeum Thkov, Khan Chamkarmon, Phnom-Penh; tel. (12) 672007; f. 2002; breakaway faction of the FUNCINPEC Party; Pres. HANG DARA.

Human Rights Party (HRP): 72–74 rue 598, Sangkat Boeung Kak II, Khan Tol Kok, Phnom-Penh; tel. (23) 884649; e-mail hrpcambodia@yahoo.com; internet www.hrpcambodia.info; f. 2007; Pres. KEM SOKHA.

Indra Buddra City Party: Commune, Chbarmon District, Kampong Spueu; tel. (12) 710331; Pres. NOREAK RATANAVATHANO.

Khmer Democratic Party (Kanakpak Pracheathippatei Khmer): 79A rue 186, Sangkat Touek Laak III, Khan Tuol Kok, Phnom-Penh; tel. (12) 842947; Pres. OUK PHURIK.

Khmer M'chas Srok (Khmer Sovereign): 14A rue Keo Chea, Phnom-Penh; tel. (23) 62365; fax (23) 27340; e-mail khmer.mchas.srok@gmail.com; internet www.khmer-mchas-srok.org; fmrly Khmer Neutral Party; Pres. SAKHONN CHAK.

Khmer Republican Party (KRP): 282 rue 371, Phoum Obekaam, Sangkat Taek Thla, Khan Russey Keo, Phnom-Penh; tel. (23) 350842; e-mail krp2005@gmail.com; f. 2006; Pres. LON RITH.

League for Democracy Party: 61A rue 608, Sangkat Boeung Kak II, Khan Tuol Kok, Phnom-Penh; tel. (12) 897600; e-mail info@leadparty.org; internet www.camldp.org; f. 2006; Pres. KHEM VEASNA; Sec.-Gen. OK VETH.

Norodom Ranariddh Party (NRP): 27 blvd Mao Tse Toung, Khan Chamkarmon, Phnom-Penh; tel. and fax (11) 559088; fax (23)

218795; e-mail skpstaff@yahoo.com; f. 2002; est. as Khmer Front Party; present name adopted 2006; renamed Nationalist Party late 2008; reverted to present name Dec. 2010; Pres. Prince NORODOM RANARIDDH; Vice-Pres. Prince NORODOM CHAKRAPONG.

Rice Party (Svor): 69 blvd Sothearos, Sangkat Tonle Bassac, Khan Chamkarmon, Phnom-Penh 12301; tel. (11) 860060; e-mail riceparty@asia.com; f. 1992; Pres. NHOUNG SEAP.

Sam Rainsy Party (SRP): 71 blvd Sothearos, Sangkat Tonle Bassac, Khan Chamkarmon, Phnom-Penh; tel. (23) 217452; fax (23) 211336; e-mail srphq@online.com.kh; internet www.samrainsyparty.org; f. 1995; est. as Khmer Nation Party; present name adopted 1998; Pres. SAM RAINSY; Sec.-Gen. KE SOVANNROTH.

Sangkum Jatiniyum Front Party: 40 rue 566, Boeung Kak II, Khan Tuol Kok, Phnom-Penh; tel. (12) 762207; internet sjfparty.free.fr; f. 1997; fmrly the Khmer Unity Party; Delegate-Gen. HRH Samdech SISOWATH THOMICO; Sec.-Gen. SUTHER DINA.

Diplomatic Representation

EMBASSIES IN CAMBODIA

Australia: 16B rue Nat. Assembly, Sangkat Tonle Bassac, Khan Chamkarmon, Phnom-Penh; tel. (23) 213470; fax (23) 213413; e-mail australian.embassy.cambodia@dfat.gov.au; internet www.cambodia.embassy.gov.au; Ambassador PENNY RICHARDS.

Brunei: 237 rue Pasteur 51, Sangkat Boeung Keng Kang 1, Khan Chamkarmon, Phnom-Penh; tel. (23) 211457; fax (23) 211456; e-mail brunei@online.com.kh; Ambassador Pengiran Dato' Paduka Haji ABU BAKAR BIN Pengiran Seri Indera Pengiran Haji ISMAIL.

Bulgaria: 227–229 blvd Norodom, Phnom-Penh; tel. (23) 217504; fax (23) 212792; e-mail bulgembpnp@online.com.kh; internet www.mfa.bg/en/39; Chargé d'affaires IVAN PETKOV.

China, People's Republic: 156 blvd Mao Tse Toung, Phnom-Penh; tel. (23) 720920; fax (23) 720922; e-mail chinaemb_kh@mfa.gov.cn; internet kh.china-embassy.org/chn; Ambassador PAN GUANGXUE.

Cuba: 96–98 rue 214, Sangkat Veal Vong, Khan 7 Makara, Phnom-Penh; tel. (23) 213965; fax (23) 217428; e-mail embacambodia1@online.com.kh; internet embacuba.cubaminrex.cu/cambodia; Ambassador (vacant).

France: 1 blvd Monivong, BP 18, Phnom-Penh; tel. (23) 430020; fax (23) 430037; e-mail ambafrance.phnom-penh-amba@diplomatie.gouv.fr; internet www.ambafrance-kh.org; Ambassador CHRISTIAN CONNAN.

Germany: 76–78 rue Yougoslavie (rue 214), BP 60, Phnom-Penh; tel. (23) 216381; fax (23) 427746; e-mail info@phnom-penh.diplo.de; internet www.phnom-penh.diplo.de; Ambassador Dr WOLFGANG MOSER.

India: 5 rue 466, Phnom-Penh; tel. (23) 210912; fax (23) 210914; e-mail embindia@online.com.kh; internet www.indembassyphnompenh.org; Ambassador RAJESH K. SACHDEVA.

Indonesia: 1 rue 466, cnr blvd Norodom, BP 894, Phnom-Penh; tel. (23) 216148; fax (23) 217566; e-mail indoembassy-phnompenh@clickmail.com.kh; internet www.kemlu.go.id/phnompenh; Ambassador SOEHARDJONO SASTROMIHADJO.

Japan: 194 blvd Preah Norodom, Sangkat Tonle Bassac, Khan Chamkarmon, BP 21, Phnom-Penh; tel. (23) 217161; fax (23) 216162; e-mail eojc@online.com.kh; internet www.kh.emb-japan.go.jp; Ambassador MASAFUMI KUROKI.

Korea, Democratic People's Republic: 39 blvd Samdech Suramarith, Phnom-Penh; tel. and fax (15) 217013; Ambassador RI IN SOK.

Korea, Republic: 50–52 rue 214, Sangkat Boeung Raing, Khan Daun Penh, BP 2433, Phnom-Penh; tel. (23) 211900; fax (23) 219200; e-mail cambodia@mofat.go.kr; internet khm.mofat.go.kr; Ambassador CHANG HO-JIN.

Laos: 15–17 blvd Mao Tse Toung, Khan Chamkarmon, BP 19, Phnom-Penh; tel. (23) 982632; fax (23) 720907; e-mail laoembpp@camintel.com; Ambassador YASENG LAO.

Malaysia: 5 rue 242, Sangkat Chaktomouk, Khan Daun Penh, Phnom-Penh; tel. (23) 216176; fax (23) 426101; e-mail malppenh@kln.gov.my; internet www.kln.gov.my/web/khm_phnom-penh; Ambassador Datuk Pengiran Haji MOHD TAHIR NASRUDDIN.

Myanmar: 181 blvd Preah Norodom, Sangkat Boeung Keng Kang 1, Khan Chamkarmon, Phnom-Penh; tel. (23) 223761; fax (23) 223763; e-mail mephnompenh@yahoo.com; Ambassador CHO HTUN AUNG.

Pakistan: 45 rue 310, Sangkat Boeung Keng Kang 1, Phnom-Penh; tel. (23) 996890; fax (23) 992113; e-mail parep.cambodia@yahoo.com; internet www.mofa.gov.pk/cambodia; Ambassador (vacant).

Philippines: 15 rue 422, Khan Chamkarmon, Sangkat Tonle Bassac, Phnom-Penh; tel. (23) 222203; fax (23) 215143; e-mail phnompenhpe@ezecom.com.kh; Ambassador NOE A. WONG.

Russia: 213 blvd Samdech Sothearos, Phnom-Penh; tel. (23) 210931; fax (23) 216776; e-mail russemba@gmail.com; internet www.embrusscambodia.mid.ru; Ambassador ALEKSANDR IGNATOV.

Singapore: 129 blvd Preah Norodom, Phnom-Penh; tel. (23) 221875; fax (23) 210862; e-mail singemb_pnh@sgmfa.gov.sg; internet www.mfa.gov.sg/phnompenh; Ambassador S. PREMJITH.

Sweden: POB 68, Phnom-Penh; tel. (23) 212259; fax (23) 212867; e-mail ambassaden.phnompenh@sida.se; Ambassador ANNE HÖGLUND.

Thailand: 196 blvd Preah Norodom, Sangkat Tonle Bassac, Khan Chamkarmon, Phnom-Penh; tel. (23) 726306; fax (23) 726303; e-mail thaipnp@mfa.go.th; internet www.thaiembassy.org/phnompenh; Ambassador SOMPONG SANGUANBUN.

United Kingdom: 27–29 rue 75, Sangkat Srah Chak, Khan Daun Penh, Phnom-Penh; tel. (23) 427124; fax (23) 427125; e-mail britemb@online.com.kh; internet ukincambodia.fco.gov.uk/en; Ambassador ANDREW MACE.

USA: 1 rue 96, Sangkat Wat Phnom, Khan Daun Penh, Phnom-Penh; tel. (23) 728000; fax (23) 728600; e-mail ACSPhnomPenh@state.gov; internet cambodia.usembassy.gov; Ambassador CAROL A. RODLEY.

Viet Nam: 436 blvd Monivong, Khan Chamkarmon, Phnom-Penh; tel. (23) 726274; fax (23) 726495; e-mail banbientap@mofa.gov.vn; internet www.vietnamembassy-cambodia.org; Ambassador NGO ANH DUNG.

Judicial System

An independent judiciary was established under the 1993 Constitution. A council for legal and judicial reform was created in 2003 to co-ordinate the implementation of reforms. A new criminal law code took effect in December 2010, replacing the penal code implemented by the UN Transitional Authority in Cambodia in 1992. The highest judicial body is the Supreme Council of Magistracy.

Supreme Court: 222 blvd Trasak Phaem, Sangkat Boeung Keng Kang I, Khan Chamkarmon, Phnom-Penh; tel. and fax (23) 212828; Pres. DITH MUNTY.

Religion

The Government of Democratic Kampuchea banned all religious activity in 1975. Under a constitutional amendment of 1989, Buddhism was reinstated as the national religion and was retained as such under the 1993 Constitution.

BUDDHISM

The principal religion of Cambodia is Theravada Buddhism (Buddhism of the 'Tradition of the Elders'), the sacred language of which is Pali. In 2010 about 93% of the population were Buddhists.

Great Supreme Patriarch: Ven. Patriarch TEP VONG.

Supreme Patriarchs: Ven. Patriarch BOU KRY (Thammayut Nikaya sect), Ven. Patriarch NON NGET (Maha Nikaya sect).

CHRISTIANITY

The Roman Catholic Church

Cambodia comprises the Apostolic Vicariate of Phnom-Penh and the Apostolic Prefectures of Battambang and Kampong Cham. At December 2010 the Christian community constituted 2% of the population.

Vicar Apostolic of Phnom-Penh: Rev. OLIVIER SCHMITTHAEUSLER (Titular Bishop of Catabum Castra), 787 blvd Monivong (rue 93), BP 123, Phnom-Penh; tel. and fax (23) 212462; e-mail evecam@forum.org.kh.

ISLAM

Islam is practised by a minority in Cambodia; in 2010 there were an estimated 464,000 Muslims.

The Press

According to Cambodia's Press Law, newspapers, magazines and foreign press agencies are required to register with the Department of Media at the Ministry of Information.

NEWSPAPERS

Areyathor (Civilization): 52 rue Lyuk Lay, Sangkat Chey, Chummneah, Phnom-Penh; tel. (23) 913662; f. 1994; 2 a week; Editor LEANG HI.

Business News: 28B rue 75, Sangkat Sraas Chak, Khan Daun Penh, Phnom-Penh 12201; tel. and fax (23) 990110; e-mail editor@businessnews-bd.com; weekly; English; Editor-in-Chief BALA CHANDRAN.

Cambodge Nouveau: 58 rue 302, Sangkat Boeung Keng Kang 1, Khan Chamkarmon, Phnom-Penh 12302; tel. (23) 214610; e-mail cn@forum.org.kh; internet www.cambodgenouveau.com; f. 1994; monthly; French; politics, economics and business; Editor-in-Chief ALAIN GASCUEL.

Cambodge Soir: 26CD rue 302, Sangkat Boeung Keng Kang 1, Khan Chamkarmon, Phnom-Penh 12302; tel. and fax (23) 362654; e-mail cambodgesoirpnh@online.com.kh; f. 1994; daily; French and Khmer; publ. suspended Sept. 2010; Editor-in-Chief PIERRE GILLETTE.

Cambodia Daily: 129 rue 228, Phnom-Penh; tel. (23) 426602; fax (23) 426573; e-mail aafc@camnet.com.kh; internet www.cambodiadaily.com; f. 1993; Mon.–Sat.; English and Khmer; distributed free of charge within Cambodia; Editor-in-Chief KEVIN DOYLE; Publr BERNARD KRISHER; circ. 3,500.

Cambodia New Vision: BP 158, Phnom-Penh; tel. (23) 219898; fax (23) 360666; e-mail cabinet1b@camnet.com.kh; internet www.cnv.org.kh; f. 1998; official newsletter of the Cambodian Govt.

Cambodia Sin Chew Daily: 107 blvd Josep Broz Tito, rue 214, Sangkat Boeung Prolit, Khan 7 Makara, Phnom-Penh 12258; tel. (23) 212628; fax (23) 211728; e-mail sinchew_daily@online.com.kh; internet www.sinchew-i.com/cambodia; f. 2000; daily; Chinese; Editor CHARLES SHAW.

Chakraval: 3 rue 181, Sangkat Tumnop Teuk, Khan Chamkarmon, Phnom-Penh; tel. (12) 669629; fax (23) 720141; e-mail chakraval@hotmail.com; f. 1992; daily; Khmer; Publr KEO SOPHORN; Editor NGOUN CHANMUNY.

The Commercial News: 394 blvd Preah Sihanouk, Phnom-Penh; tel. (23) 721665; fax (23) 721709; e-mail tcnews@online.com.kh; internet www.tcnewscambodia.com; f. 1993; Chinese; Chief Editor LIU XIAO GUANG; circ. 8,000.

Jian Hua Daily: 116–118 blvd Kampuchea Krom, Sangkat Monorom, Khan 7 Makara, Phnom-Penh 12251; tel. (23) 883801; fax (23) 883797; e-mail jianhuadaily@hotmail.com; internet www.jianhuadaily.com; daily; Chinese; Editor-in-Chief XENG ZUANG RONG.

Kampuchea Thmey (New Cambodia): 805 blvd Kampuchea Krom, rue 128, Sangkat Tuk Laak 1, Khan Tuol Kok, Phnom-Penh 12156; tel. (23) 6624141; fax (23) 726617; e-mail kampucheathmey@mail2world.com; internet www.kampucheathmey.com; daily; Editor-in-Chief KEV NAVY.

Kampuchea Thnai Nes (Cambodia Today Newspaper): 21 rue 163, Sangkat Veal Vong, Khan 7 Makara, Phnom-Penh 12253; tel. and fax (23) 364882; e-mail cambodiatoday@online.com.kh; daily; Editor-in-Chief HONG NARA.

Koh Santepheap (Island of Peace): 41E rue 338, Sangkat Boeung Tumpun, Khan Meanchey, Phnom-Penh 12351; tel. (23) 211818; fax (23) 220155; e-mail kohdaily@gmail.com; internet www.kohsantepheapdaily.com.kh; daily; Khmer; Dir THONG UY PANG.

Mekong News: POB 623, 576 National Rd 2, Sangkat Chak Angre Krom, Khan Menachey, Phnom-Penh; tel. (23) 425353; fax (23) 425363; e-mail mrcs@mrcmekong.org; f. 2005; quarterly; English and Khmer; publ. by Mekong River Commission Secretariat, distributed free of charge; Editor and Publr M. NOOR ULLAH.

Neak Chea: 1 rue 158, Oukghna Toeung Kang, Beng Raing Daun Penh, Phnom-Penh; tel. (23) 218653; fax (23) 217229; e-mail adhoc@forum.org.kh; 2 a month; Khmer; bulletin of Cambodia Human Rights and Devt Assen.

Phnom Penh Post: 888 Bldg F, 8th Floor, Phnom Penh Center, cnr Sothearos & Sihanouk Blvd, Sangkat Tonle Bassac, Khan Chamkarmon, Phnom-Penh; tel. (23) 214311; fax (23) 214318; e-mail bernie.leo@phnompenhpost.com; internet www.phnompenhpost.com; f. 1992; fortnightly; English; Editor-in-Chief BERNIE LEO.

Pracheachon (The People): 101 blvd Norodom, Phnom-Penh; tel. (23) 723665; f. 1985; 2 a week; organ of the CPP; Editor-in-Chief SOM KIMSUOR; circ. 50,000.

Raja Bori News: 76 rue 57, Sangkat Boeung Kak II, Khan Tuol Kok, Phnom-Penh 12152; tel. (12) 840993; weekly; Editor-in-Chief KIM SOMLOT.

Rasmei Angkor (Light of Angkor): 25/25Z rue 372, Sangkat Boeung Salang, Khan Tuol Kok, Phnom-Penh 12160; tel. (11) 637609; e-mail raksmeiangkor@yahoo.com; f. 1992; 3 a week; Editor-in-Chief EN CHAN SIVUTHA.

Rasmei Kampuchea (Light of Cambodia): T. B. R. Printing Co Ltd, 474 blvd Preah Monivong, Sangkat Tonle Bassac, Khan Chamkarmon, Phnom-Penh 12301; tel. and fax (23) 7266555; e-mail rasmei_kampuchea@yahoo.com; daily; f. 1993; local newspaper in northern Cambodia; Editor PEN SAMITHY.

Sahasavat Thmey (New Millennium): 48AE blvd Oknha Chun, Sangkat Chaktomuk, Khan Daun Penh, Phnom-Penh 12207; tel. (16) 719551; e-mail sahasawatthmey@mail2world.com; f. 2004; 3 a week; Editor-in-Chief MANN BUNTHOEUN.

Samleng Thmei (New Voice): 91 rue 139, Sangkat Veal Vong, Khan 7, Phnom-Penh; tel. (15) 920589; Khmer; Editor KHUN NGOR.

Samleng Yuvachun (Voice of Khmer Youth): 251 rue 261, Sangkat Tuk Laak 2, Khan Tuol Kok 12200, Phnom-Penh 12309; tel. (12) 859142; fax (23) 997470; e-mail khmeryouthnews@yahoo.com; f. 1993; Editor-in-Chief UK SUN HENG.

Udomkate Khmer (Khmer Ideal): 17 blvd Samdech Sothearos, Sangkat Tuk Laak 3, Khan Tuol Kok, Phnom-Penh 12158; tel. (12) 851478; daily; Editor-in-Chief HOR SOK LEN.

PERIODICALS

Angkor Thom: 105 rue 324, Sangkat Boeung Salang, Khan Tuol Kok, Phnom-Penh 12253; tel. (23) 996421; fax (23) 996441; e-mail vuthyrith@angkorthommagazine.com; internet ekhmermagazines.com; f. 1998; 3 a month; Khmer; news, current affairs, arts and sport; Editor-in-Chief SING VUTHYRITH; circ. 30,000.

Bayon Pearnik: 3 rue 174, Sangkat Phsar Thmei 3, Khan Daun Penh, Phnom-Penh 312210; tel. (12) 803968; e-mail bp@forum.org.kh; internet www.bayonpearnik.com; f. 1996; monthly; English; news for expatriates and tourists; Publr and Editor-in-Chief ADAM PARKER.

Cambodian Scene: 41 blvd Sang Kreach Tieng, rue 222, Sangkat Boeung Raing, Khan Daun Penh, Phnom-Penh 12211; tel. (23) 224488; fax (23) 222266; e-mail publisher@cambodianscene.com; internet www.cambodianscene.com; every 2 months; English; tourism, culture and entertainment guide; Publr and Editor-in-Chief MOEUN NHEAN.

L'Echo du Cambodge: 42 blvd Preah Norodom, Sangkat Phsar Thmei 2, Khan Daun Penh, Phnom-Penh 12206; e-mail echoducambodge@yahoo.fr; monthly; English and French; Editor-in-Chief MARCEL ZARCA.

Indradevi: 167 blvd Mao Tse Toung, Sangkat Tuol Svay Prey 2, Khan Chamkarmon, Phnom-Penh 12309; tel. and fax (23) 215808; e-mail indradevi@camnet.com.kh; f. 2000; Editor-in-Chief CHHEM SARITH.

Kambuja: Kambuja Dept, Agence Kampuchea Presse, Ministry of Information, 62 blvd Preah Monivong, Sangkat Wat Phnom, Khan Daun Penh, Phnom-Penh 12202; tel. and fax (23) 427945; e-mail akp@camnet.com.kh; monthly; Khmer; publ. by the AKP; devt, education and int. affairs; Editor-in-Chief NERK SARAT.

Khmer Apsara: 143A Khum Pring Kang Cheung, Sangkat Chom Chao, Khan Dangkor, Phnom-Penh 12405; tel. (17) 391087; e-mail khmer_apsara01@yahoo.com; internet www.khmerapsaramagazine.com; f. 2005; monthly; Khmer; entertainment, fashion, technology, health and culture; Editor-in-Chief EN SOPHANNA.

Pracheaprey (Popular): 71–73 rue 70, Sangkat Sras Chak, Phnom-Penh; tel. (12) 890613; fax (12) 890614; e-mail popularmagazine@online.com.kh; f. 2000; 3 a month; Khmer; news, current affairs, politics, arts, science and sport; Editor-in-Chief PRACH SIM.

Samay Thmei (Modern): 127 rue 357, Sangkat Chbar Ampheou 2, Khan Meanchey, Phnom-Penh 12355; tel. (23) 359969; fortnightly; Khmer; fashion, contemporary living, sports and entertainment; Editor-in-Chief EK SAMAT.

Suorsadey Magazine: 13A rue 222, Sang Kreach Tieng, Phnom-Penh; tel. (23) 224488; fax (23) 222266; f. 2009; quarterly; tourism, culture and entertainment guide; Editor MOEN NHEAN.

NEWS AGENCY

Agence Kampuchea Presse (AKP): 62 blvd Monivong, Phnom-Penh; tel. (23) 430564; fax (23) 427945; e-mail akp@camnet.com.kh; internet www.camnet.com.kh/akp; f. 1978; Dir-Gen. KIT-KIM HUON.

ASSOCIATIONS

Cambodian Association for the Protection of Journalists (CAPJ): BP 816, 58 rue 336, Sangkat Phsar Doeum Kor, Khan Tuol Kok, Phnom-Penh; tel. (15) 997004; fax (23) 215834; e-mail umsarin@hotmail.com; Pres. UM SARIN.

Club of Cambodian Journalists: 226 rue 155, Sangkat Tuol Tumpong 1, Khan Chamkarmon, Phnom-Penh; tel. and fax (23) 224094; e-mail ccj@online.com.kh; internet www.ccj.com.kh; f. 2000; Pres. PEN SAMITTHY; Sec.-Gen. PRACH SIM.

Khmer Journalists' Association: 170C rue 167, Sangkat Tuol Tom Poung 2, Khan Chamkarmon, Phnom-Penh 12311; tel. (23) 987622; e-mail mondulkeo@yahoo.com; f. 1979; Pres. TATH LY HOK.

Press Council of Cambodia: 127 blvd Norodom, Sangkat Tonle Bassac, Khan Chamkarmon, Phnom-Penh; tel. (12) 910425; f. 2008;

est. as an umbrella body for more than 15 journalists' asscns; Pres. SOK SOVANN.

Broadcasting and Communications

TELECOMMUNICATIONS

Applifone Co Ltd (Star-Cell): 173 rue 215, Sangkat Phsar Doeum Kor, Khan Tuol Kok, Phnom-Penh; tel. (855) 98202 888; fax (855) 98202 098; e-mail info@star-cell.net; internet www.star-cell.net; f. 2006; operates GSM mobile services; CEO DAMIR KARASSAYEV.

Cambodia Advance Communications Co Ltd (CADCOMMS): 825ABC blvd Preah Monivong, Sangkat Phsar Damthkov, Khan Chamkarmon, Phnom-Penh; tel. (13) 300313; fax (13) 300317; e-mail info@qbmore.com; internet www.qbmore.com; f. 2006; operates mobile services; Chief Information Officer SANDOS NONG.

Camintel: 1 cnr Terak Vithei Sisowath & Vithei Phsar Dek, Phnom-Penh; tel. (23) 986986; fax (23) 986277; e-mail support@camintel.com; internet www.camintel.com; f. 1995; jt venture between the Ministry of Posts and Telecommunications and Indonesian co Indosat; operates domestic telephone network and internet; CEO KANG NAM KOOK; Man. Dir CHOI DEUG MAN.

Mfone Co Ltd: 721 blvd Preah Monivong, Sangkat Boeung Keng Kang 3, Khan Chamkarmon, Phnom-Penh; tel. (23) 307777; e-mail sales@mfone.biz; internet www.mfone.com.kh; f. 1993; fmrly Cambodia Shinawatra Co Ltd; subsidiary of Shenington Investments Pte Ltd and Asia Mobile Holdings Pte Ltd; provides both fixed line and mobile services; CEO WAI KHEE YAP.

MobiTel: 33 blvd Preah Sihanouk, BP 2468, Phnom-Penh; tel. (12) 800800; fax (12) 801801; e-mail helpline@mobitel.com.kh; internet www.mobitel.com.kh; f. 1998; wholly owned by The Royal Group since Nov. 2009; operates national GSM 900 mobile network under trade name Cellcard; CEO DAVID SPRIGGS.

Telekom Malaysia International (Cambodia) Co Ltd: cnr Sihanouk & Sothearos, Sangkat Tonle Bassac, Khan Chamkarmon, Phnom-Penh; tel. (16) 880002; internet www.hello.com.kh; f. 1992; est. as Cambodia Samart Communication; name changed as above following acquisition by Telekom Malaysia Bhd in 2006; operates a national mobile network under trade name Hello; CEO MUHAMMED YUSOFF ZAMRI.

BROADCASTING

Radio

Apsara Radio (FM 97 MHz): 69 rue 57, Sangkat Boeung Keng Kang 1, Khan Chamkarmon, Phnom-Penh; tel. (23) 303002; fax (23) 214302; internet www.apsaratv.com.kh; f. 1996; linked to Cambodian People's Party; Khmer; Dir-Gen. SOK EYSAN.

Bayon Radio (FM 95 MHz): 3 rue 466, Sangkat Tonle Bassac, Khan Chamkarmon, Phnom-Penh; tel. (12) 682222; fax (23) 363795; internet www.bayontv.com.kh; f. 1998; linked to Prime Minister Hun Sen; Dir-Gen. HUN MANA; Deputy Dir-Gen. HUOT KHEANGVENG.

Beehive Radio (Sambok Khmoum): 44G rue 360, Sangkat Boeung Keng Kang 1, Khan Chamkarmon, Phnom-Penh; tel. (23) 210401; fax (23) 210439; e-mail sbk@online.com.kh; internet www.sbkcambodia.org; f. 1996; broadcasts incl. news programmes from Voice of America and Radio Free Asia; Dir-Gen. MAM SONANDO.

Family FM 99.5 MHz (Krusa FM): Phnom-Penh; e-mail febcam@bigpond.com.kh; internet www.febc.org; f. 2002; controlled by Far East Broadcasting Co; religious and educational programmes from a Christian perspective; Dir SAMOEUN INTAL.

FM 90 MHz: 65 rue 178, Phnom-Penh; tel. (16) 709090; fax (23) 368623; news, music and educational programmes; affiliated to the FUNCINPEC Party; Dir-Gen. NHIM BUN THON; Dep. Dir-Gen. TUM VANN DET.

FM 107 MHz: 18 rue 562, Boeung Kak 1, Khan Toul Kork, Phnom-Penh; tel. (23) 880874; fax (23) 368212; e-mail info@tv9.com.kh; internet www.tv9.com.kh; news and music; Dir-Gen. KHUN HANG.

National Radio of Cambodia (RNK) (Radio National Kampuchea): Bldg 6, Sangkat Wat Phnom, cnr rues 19 & 102, Phnom-Penh; tel. (23) 722869; fax (23) 427319; internet www.rnk.gov.kh; f. 1978; fmrly Vithyu Samleng Pracheachon Kampuchea (Voice of the Cambodian People); controlled by the Ministry of Information; domestic service in Khmer; broadcasts on both AM and FM frequencies; daily external services in English, French, Lao, Vietnamese and Thai; Dir-Gen. TAN YAN.

Phnom-Penh Municipality Radio (103 MHz): 2 blvd Confédération de la Russie, Phnom-Penh; tel. (23) 725205; fax (23) 360800; Gen. Man. KHAMPUN KEOMONY.

Royal Cambodian Armed Forces Radio (RCAF Radio) (FM 98.0 MHz): c/o Borei Keila, rue 169, Sangkat Vealvong, Phnom-Penh; tel. (23) 306064; fax (23) 884245; f. 1994; Dir THA TANA; News Editor SENG KATEKA.

Ta Prohm Radio (FM 90.5 MHz): 27B rue 472, Phnom-Penh; tel. (23) 993206; e-mail taprohm@yahoo.com; f. 2003; launched by FUNCINPEC Party as opposition radio station; broadcasts news programmes in Khmer to Phnom-Penh and surrounding area; Propr EAR LIMSUOR.

Women's Radio FM 102 MHz: 30 rue 488, Sangkat Phsar Demthkov, Khan Chamkarmon, Phnom-Penh; POB 497, Phnom-Penh; tel. (23) 212264; fax (23) 364882; e-mail fm102@wmc.org.kh; independent; radio station of Women's Media Centre of Cambodia; Dir CHEA SUDANETH.

There are also several private local radio stations.

Television

Apsara Television (TV11): 69 rue 57, Sangkat Boeung Keng Kang 1, Khan Chamkarmon, Phnom-Penh; tel. (23) 303002; fax (23) 214302; e-mail tv11@camnet.com.kh; internet www.apsaratv.com.kh; broadcasts for 14 hours per day on weekdays, and for 16 hours per day at weekends, in Khmer; linked to Cambodian People's Party; Dir-Gen. SOK EYSAN.

Bayon Television (TV27): 3 rue 466, Sangkat Tonle Bassac, Khan Chamkarmon, Phnom-Penh; tel. (12) 682222; fax (23) 363795; e-mail bayontv@camnet.com.kh; internet www.bayontv.com.kh; linked to Prime Minister Hun Sen; Dir-Gen. HUN MANA.

Cambodian Television Network (CTN): POB 2468, Phnom-Penh 12104; tel. (12) 999434; e-mail tv@ctn.com.kh; internet www.ctn.com.kh; f. 2003; wholly owned by The Royal Group; operates two free-to-air stations, CTN and MYTV; CTN International available internationally via satellite; Propr KITH MENG; Gen. Man. GLEN FELGATE.

Cambodian Television Station Channel 9 (TV9): 18 rue 562, Phnom-Penh; tel. (23) 880874; fax (23) 368212; e-mail info@tv9.com.kh; internet www.tv9.com.kh; f. 1992; Dir-Gen. KHOUN ELYNA; News Editor PHAN TITH.

National Television of Cambodia (TVK): 62 blvd Preah Monivong, Phnom-Penh; tel. and fax (12) 554535; e-mail tvk@camnet.gov.kh; internet www.tvk.gov.kh; f. 1983; broadcasts in Khmer, 24 hours per day (TVK) and 12 hours per day (TVK2); Dir-Gen. (Head of Television) KEM GUNAWADH.

Phnom-Penh Municipality Television (TV3): 2 blvd Confédération de la Russie, Phnom-Penh; tel. (12) 814323; fax (23) 360800; e-mail tv3@kcsradio.com; internet www.tv3.com.kh; jt venture between Phnom Penh Municipality and KCS Cambodia Co Ltd (Thailand); Dir-Gen. KHAMPHUN KEOMONY.

Royal Cambodian Armed Forces Television (TV5 Cambodia): Prek Tloeng Village, Prek Kampoes, Kandal Stoeng, Kandal; tel. (23) 303925; fax (23) 994385; e-mail info@ch5cambodia.com; internet www.ch5cambodia.com; f. 1995; jt venture between Royal Cambodian Armed Forces and MICA Media Co; also operates an FM radio service.

Finance

(cap. = capital; res = reserves; dep. = deposits; brs = branches; amounts in US dollars unless otherwise stated)

BANKING

In 2009 there were 35 banks (excluding the central bank) operating in Cambodia, comprising: six specialized banks; 27 locally incorporated private banks; and two branches of foreign banks.

Central Bank

National Bank of Cambodia (NBC): 22–24 blvd Preah Norodom, BP 25, Phnom-Penh; tel. (23) 722563; fax (23) 426117; e-mail info@nbc.org.kh; internet www.nbc.org.kh; f. 1954; est. as National Bank of Cambodia; name changed to People's National Bank of Cambodia in 1979; name reverted to above in 1992; cap. 100,000m. riels, res 6,537,600m. riels, dep. 3,875,862m. riels (June 2007); Gov. CHEA CHANTO; Dep. Gov. NEAV CHANTHANA.

Specialized Banks

First Investment Specialized Bank (FISB): 72 blvd Preah Sihanouk, Sangkat Tonle Bassac, Khan Daun Penh, Phnom-Penh; tel. (23) 222281; fax (23) 221112; e-mail service@fibank.com.kh; internet www.fibank.com.kh; f. 2005; cap. 12m. (Dec. 2009); Chair. and CEO NEAK OKNHA; Gen. Man. YIP SOREIYOS.

Peng Heng SME Bank: 74 blvd Norodom, Sangkat Chey Chumneas, Khan Daun Penh, Phnom-Penh; tel. (23) 219243; fax (23) 219185; e-mail pengheng@camnet.com.kh; f. 2001.

Rural Development Bank: 9–13 rue 7, Sangkat Chaktomouk, Khan Daun Penh, BP 1410, Phnom-Penh; tel. (23) 220810; fax (23)

224628; e-mail admin@rdb.com.kh; internet www.rdb.com.kh; f. 1998; state-owned; provides credit to rural enterprises; Chair. and CEO SON KOUN THOR.

Private Banks

ACLEDA Bank PLC: 61 blvd Monivong, Sangkat Srah Chork, Khan Duan Penh, BP 1149, Phnom-Penh; tel. (23) 430999; fax (23) 430555; e-mail acledabank@acledabank.com.kh; internet www .acledabank.com.kh; f. 1993; became specialized bank Oct. 2000; awarded commercial banking licence Dec. 2003; provides financial services to all sectors; cap. 68.1m., res 28.0m., dep. 702.0m. (Dec. 2009); Chair. CHEA SOK; Pres. and CEO IN CHANNY; 232 brs.

Advanced Bank of Asia Ltd: 148 blvd Preah Sihanouk, Sangkat Boeung Keng Kang 1, Khan Chamkarmon, Phnom-Penh; tel. (23) 225333; fax (23) 216333; e-mail info@ababank.com; internet www .ababank.net; f. 1996; CEO MADI AKMAMBET.

Cambodia Asia Bank Ltd: 439 blvd Monivong, Ground Floor, Phnom-Penh; tel. (23) 220000; fax (23) 426628; e-mail cab@cab.com .kh; internet www.cab.com.kh; incorporated in 1992; cap. 13.0m., dep. 13.9m. (Dec. 2009); Man. WONG TOW FOCK.

Cambodia Mekong Bank: 6 blvd Monivong, Khan Daun Penh, Phnom-Penh; tel. and fax (23) 217122; e-mail ho.mailbox@ mekongbank.com; f. 1994; cap. 37.0m., dep. 18.2m. (Dec. 2009); Chair. MICHAEL C. STEPHEN; Pres. and CEO KHOV BOUN CHHAY.

Cambodian Commercial Bank Ltd: 26 blvd Preah Monivong, Sangkat Phsar Thmei 2, Khan Daun Penh, Phnom-Penh; tel. (23) 426145; fax (23) 426116; e-mail ccbpp@online.com.kh; f. 1991; cap. 13m., dep. 115.2m. (Dec. 2009); Chair. NABHENGBHASANG KRISHNAMRA; Dir and Gen. Man. NATTHAWUT CHAKANAN; 4 brs.

Cambodian Public Bank (Campu Bank): Campu Bank Bldg 23, rue Kramoun Sar 114, Sangkat Phsar Thmei 2, Khan Daun Penh, Phnom-Penh; tel. (23) 222880; fax (23) 222887; e-mail campuhoe@ campubank.com.kh; internet www.campubank.com.kh; f. 1992; cap. 90m., dep. 751m. (Dec. 2009); wholly owned subsidiary of Public Bank Bhd, Malaysia; Chair. (non-exec.) Tan Sri Dato' Sri Dr HONG PIOW TEH; Country Head PHAN YING TONG.

Canadia Bank PLC: 315 rue Preah Ang Duong, cnr blvd Monivong, Khan Daun Penh, Phnom-Penh; tel. (23) 868222; fax (23) 222830; e-mail canadia@canadiabank.com.kh; internet www.canadiabank .com; f. 1991; est. as Canadia Gold and Trust Corpn Ltd; present name adopted 2004; cap. 50.6m. riels, res 32.3m. riels, dep. 411.6m. riels (2001); Pres. and CEO PUNG KHEAV SE; 26 brs.

Foreign Trade Bank: 3 rue Kramoun Sar, Sangkat Phsar Thmei 1, Khan Daun Penh, Phnom-Penh; tel. (23) 724466; fax (23) 426108; e-mail info@ftbbank.com; internet www.ftbbank.com; f. 1979; removed from direct management of Nat. Bank of Cambodia in 2000; scheduled for privatization; Chair. OKNHA PUNG KHEAV SE; Gen. Man. LOK ONUMTEAV OUK MALY.

Singapore Banking Corporation Ltd: 68 rue Samdech Pan 214, Sangkat Boeung Raing, Khan Daun Penh, BP 688, Phnom-Penh; tel. (23) 211211; fax (23) 212121; e-mail info@sbc-bank.com; internet www.sbc-bank.com; f. 1992; cap. 17m., dep. 32.8m. (Dec. 2009); Pres. ANDY KUN SWEE TIONG; Chair. KUN KAY HONG.

Union Commercial Bank PLC: UCB Bldg, 61 rue 130, Sangkat Phsar Chas, Khan Daun Penh, Phnom-Penh; tel. (23) 427995; fax (23) 427997; e-mail ucbhq@ucb.com.kh; internet www.ucb.com.kh; f. 1994; cap. 14.1m., res 2.0m., dep. 114.1m. (Dec. 2009); Chair. and Pres. YUM SUI SANG; 4 brs.

Vattanac Bank: 89 blvd Preah Norodom, Sangkat Boeung Raing, Khan Daun Penh, Phnom-Penh; tel. (23) 212727; fax (23) 216687; e-mail service@vattanacbank.com; internet www.vattanacbank .com; f. 2002; cap. 13m., dep. 102.7m. (Dec. 2007); Chair. SAM ANG; Pres. CHHUN LEANG.

Bankers' Association

The Association of Banks in Cambodia: 1 rue Kramuon Sar (rue 114), Sangkat Phsar Thmei 1, Khan Daun Penh, Phnom-Penh; tel. (23) 218610; fax (23) 224310; e-mail secretariat@abc.org.kh; internet www.abc.org.kh; f. 1994; Chair. PUNG KHEAV SE.

STOCK EXCHANGE

The Cambodia Stock Exchange, a joint venture between the Government and the Korea Exchange (KRX—Republic of Korea), commenced operations in July 2011.

Stock Exchange

Cambodia Stock Exchange (CSX): Phnom-Penh; f. 2011; 55% govt-owned and 45% owned by Korea Exchange; CEO HONG SOK HOUR.

Supervisory Body

Securities and Exchange Commission of Cambodia (SECC): 99 rue 598, Sangkat Phnom-Penh Thmei, Khan Sen Sok, Phnom-Penh; tel. (23) 885611; fax (23) 885622; e-mail sovy_va@secc.gov.kh; internet www.secc.gov.kh; f. 2007; govt-owned; Gen. Dir MING BANKOSAL; Dir SOVY VA.

INSURANCE

Asia Insurance (Cambodia) Ltd: 5 rue 13, Sangkat Wat Phnom, Khan Daun Penh, Phnom-Penh 12201; tel. (23) 427981; fax (23) 216969; e-mail email@asiainsurance.com.kh; internet www .asiainsurance.com.kh; f. 1996; Gen. Man. PASCAL BRANDT-GAGNON.

Cambodia National Insurance Company (CAMINCO): cnr rues 106 & 13, Sangkat Wat Phnom, Khan Daun Penh, Phnom-Penh; tel. (23) 722043; fax (23) 427810; e-mail info@caminco.com.kh; internet www.caminco.com.kh; f. 1990; fmrly 100% state-owned; since 2008 75% owned by Viriyah BVB Insurance PLC (Cambodian co est. by local businessman Duong Vibol), 25% state-owned; Chair. LOK CHHUM TEV OKNHA SAT NAVY; Man. Dir DUONG VIBOL.

Forte Insurance (Cambodia) PLC: 325 blvd Mao Tse Toung, BP 565, Phnom-Penh; tel. (23) 885077; fax (23) 986922; e-mail info@ forteinsurance.com; internet www.forteinsurance.com; f. 1996; Man. Dir CARLO CHEO; Gen. Man. YOUK CHAMROEUNRITH.

Infinity General Insurance PLC: 126 blvd Preah Norodom, Phnom-Penh; tel. (23) 999888; fax (23) 999123; e-mail cs@infinity .com.kh; internet www.infinityinsurance.com.kh.

Trade and Industry

DEVELOPMENT ORGANIZATIONS

Council for the Development of Cambodia (CDC): Government Palace, quai Sisowath, Sangkat Wat Phnom, BP 1225, Phnom-Penh; tel. (23) 981241; fax (23) 981161; e-mail cdc-cmb@camnet.com.kh; internet www.cdc-crdb.gov.kh; f. 1994; Chair. HUN SEN; Sec.-Gen. SOK CHENDA.

Cambodian Investment Board (CIB): Government Palace, quai Sisowath, Sangkat Wat Phnom, Phnom-Penh; tel. (23) 981156; fax (23) 428426; e-mail cdc.cib@bigpond.com.kh; internet www .cambodiainvestment.gov.kh; f. 1993; part of CDC; sole body responsible for approving foreign investment in Cambodia; Chair. HUN SEN; Sec.-Gen. SUON SITTHY.

Cambodian National Petroleum Authority (CNPA): 13–14 blvd Confédération de la Russie, Sangkat Toeuk Thla, Khan Sen Sok, Phnom-Penh; tel. (23) 890569; fax (23) 890569; internet cnpa-cambodia.com; f. 1999; Chair. SOK AN; Dir-Gen. TE DUONG TARA.

National Information Communications Technology Development Authority (NiDA): 113 rue 214, Sangkat Bong Prolet, Khan 7 Makara, Phnom-Penh; tel. (12) 812282; fax (23) 216793; e-mail info@ nida.gov.kh; internet www.nida.gov.kh; f. 2000; promotes IT and formulates policy devt; Chair. HUN SEN; Sec.-Gen. Dr PHU LEEWOOD.

CHAMBER OF COMMERCE

Cambodia Chamber of Commerce: 7D blvd Confédération de la Russie, Khan Tuol Kok, Phnom-Penh; tel. (23) 880795; fax (23) 881757; e-mail info@ppcc.org.kh; internet www.ppcc.org.kh; f. 1995; Pres. KITH MENG; Dir-Gen. NGUON MENG TECH.

INDUSTRIAL AND TRADE ASSOCIATIONS

Garment Manufacturers' Association in Cambodia (GMAC): 175 blvd Jawaharlal Nehru (rue 215), Sangkat Phsar Doeum Kor, Khan Tuol Kok 12159, Phnom-Penh; tel. (23) 882860; fax (23) 331183; e-mail info@gmac-cambodia.org; internet www .gmac-cambodia.org; Chair. VAN SOU IENG; Sec.-Gen. KEN LOO.

Trade Promotion Department: Ministry of Commerce, 65–69 rue 136, Sangkat Phsar Kandal 2, Khan Daun Penh, Phnom-Penh; tel. (23) 216948; fax (23) 211745; e-mail info@tpd.gov.kh; internet www .tpd.gov.kh; Dir SEUN SOTHA.

UTILITIES

Electricity

Electricité du Cambodge (EDC): EDC Bldg, rue 19, Sangkat Wat Phnom, Khan Daun Penh, Phnom-Penh; tel. (23) 723971; fax (23) 426018; e-mail edchq@edc.com.kh; internet www.edc.com.kh; f. 1996; state-owned; Chair. TUN LEAN; Man. Dir KEO ROTTANAK.

Electricity Authority of Cambodia (EAC): 2 rue 282, Sangkat Boeung Keng Kang 1, Khan Chamkarmon, Phnom-Penh; tel. (23) 217654; fax (23) 214144; e-mail admin@eac.gov.kh; internet www .eac.gov.kh; f. 2001; regulatory authority; Chair. Dr TY NORIN.

Water

Phnom-Penh Water Supply Authority (PPWSA): rue 108, Phnom-Penh 12201; tel. (23) 724046; fax (23) 428969; e-mail eksonnchan@ppwsa.com.kh; f. 1996; autonomous public enterprise; Dir-Gen. EK SONN CHAN.

MAJOR COMPANIES

Asia Flour Mill Corpn: 228 blvd Preah Norodom, Sangkat Tonle Bassac, Khan Chamkarmon, Phnom-Penh; tel. (23) 301228; fax (23) 366928; e-mail info@asiaflourmill.com; flour mfr; Man. IGOR HENRI.

British American Tobacco Cambodia Ltd: 1121 rue Nationale 2, Sangkat Chak Ang Re Leu, Phnom-Penh; tel. (23) 722555; fax (23) 726555; f. 1996; jt venture between British American Tobacco, a leading Cambodian businessman and Singapore United Tobacco Ltd; Man. Dir DAVID FELL.

Cambodia Beverage Co Ltd: 287 rue Nationale 5, Khan Russei Keo, Phnom-Penh; tel. (23) 428995; fax (23) 428992; f. 1993; majority owned by Coca-Cola Sabco; mfr and retailer of soft drinks; Country Man. DENISE LAUWENS; 298 employees.

Cambodia Brewery Ltd: 438 Monivong, Phnom-Penh; tel. (23) 722683; fax (23) 723106; f. 1994; subsidiary of Asia Pacific Breweries Ltd; production of beer; Gen. Man. TAI HONG KOH.

Cambrew Ltd: 215 blvd Norodom, Sangkat Tonle Bassac, Khan Chamkarmon, Phnom-Penh 12301; tel. (23) 987663; fax (23) 997408; e-mail info@angkorbeer.com.kh; internet www.angkorbeer.com.kh; f. 1991; 50% owned by Carlsberg (Denmark); mfr of beer.

Chevron (Cambodia) Ltd: 4/F, Phnom Penh Center, rue 274, Sangkat Tonle Bassac, Khan Chamkarmon, Phnom-Penh; tel. (23) 223355; fax (23) 223599; e-mail hengs@chevrontexaco.com; f. 1995; retail service station operator; distribution and marketing of fuels and lubricants; Country Chair. and Gen. Man. KHOO TENG CHYE.

Continental Indochine Import/Export Co Ltd: 139 blvd Monivong, Phnom-Penh; tel. (23) 366602; fax (23) 366604; e-mail cil@bigpond.com.kh; f. 1992; aviation fuel supply and bulk fuel distribution; mfr of knitwear and woven garments; bar, restaurant and hotel management; Group Chair. CLIVE MCLEOD FAIRFIELD.

Goodhill Enterprise (Cambodia) Ltd: 214/216 Goodhill Bldg, blvd Preah Sihanouk, Phnom-Penh; tel. (23) 217888; fax (23) 213688; e-mail main_acc@goodhill.com.kh; internet www.goodhill.com.kh; f. 1989; distributor of consumer products, stationery, office equipment, lubricants, beverages and fertilizer.

Hung Hiep (Cambodia) Co Ltd: 230A blvd Preah Norodom, Khan Chamkarmon, Phnom-Penh; tel. (23) 213527; fax (23) 216659; e-mail hunghiep@online.com.kh; dealers in passenger and commercial vehicles; Exec. Dir PILY WONG.

JIT Service Ltd: 50 rue 139, Sangkat Veal Vong, Khan Makara 7, Phnom-Penh; tel. (15) 830031; fax (23) 721197; e-mail jitcambodia@bigpond.com.kh; f. 1996; jt venture with Singapore; export of frozen seafood; freight forwarding services; automotive repairs; Chair. RAMADY MOUN.

JMK Group: 6 blvd Monivong, BP 112, Phnom-Penh; tel. (23) 217366; fax (23) 218884; e-mail jmkt@camnet.com.kh; f. 1992; architectural services; computer sales and maintenance.

Kampot Cement Co Ltd: 100 rue Nationale 2, Phnom-Penh 12354; tel. (23) 996839; fax (23) 996849; e-mail khr@kampotcement.com; internet www.scg.co.th; f. 2005; suppliers and mfrs of cement and limestone; subsidiary of SCG Cement (Thailand).

Khaou Chuly MKK Co Ltd: 15 rue 306, Boeung Keng Kang 1, Khan Chamkarmon, Phnom-Penh; tel. (23) 218080; fax (23) 217036; e-mail info@khaouchuly.com; internet www.khaouchuly.com; f. 1955; infrastructure construction; Chair. Oknha KHAO CHULY; Pres. Oknha KHAO PHALLABOTH; 400 employees.

Khmer Cement Industry Co Ltd: 9 rue 80, cnr rue 75, Phnom-Penh 12201; tel. (23) 430902; fax (23) 430817; e-mail sinith@online.com.kh; internet www.holcim.com; f. 2004; subsidiary of Siam City Cement Public Co Ltd (Thailand); suppliers, mfrs and importers of cement; CEO KUCH SINITH.

KT Pacific Group: 315 blvd Mao Tse Toung, Sangkat Phsar Damkor, Khan Tuol Kok, Phnom-Penh; tel. (23) 882423; fax (23) 883407; e-mail ktpacific@camnet.com.kh; f. 1990; 7 jt-venture cos and 6 subsidiaries; manufacturing, engineering, construction, land devt, trading and entertainment; Chair. Neak Oknha KONG TRIV.

Men Sarun Import and Export Co Ltd: Bldg 12, blvd Mao Tse Toung, Sangkat Tonle Bassac, Khan Chamkarmon, Phnom-Penh; tel. (23) 218505; fax (23) 364238; e-mail mensarun@camnet.com.kh; internet www.mensarun.com.kh; f. 1994; import and export of rice, rubber tree products, wheat flour, pesticides and fertilizers; Pres. Oknha MEN SARUN.

Mong Reththy Group Co Ltd: 152S blvd Preah Norodom, Phnom-Penh; tel. (23) 211065; fax (23) 216496; e-mail mrtgroup@mongreththy.com; internet www.mongreththy.com; f. 1989; and agro-industrial products, construction, import and export; Pres. Dr Oknha MONG RETHTHY.

Muhibbah Engineering (Cambodia) Pte Ltd: 313–315 blvd Mao Tse Toung, POB 2488, Phnom-Penh; tel. (23) 367988; fax (23) 366888; e-mail admin.mec@muhibbah.com.kh; civil engineering, general contracting, real estate development, architectural services; Man. CHEAH SOON LYE.

The Royal Group: 246 blvd Monivong, Phnom-Penh; tel. (12) 900977; fax (23) 426415; e-mail opportunities@royalgroup.com.kh; internet www.royalgroup.com.kh; investment and development; interests in telecommunications, finance, media, hotels and property devt; Chair. and CEO Neak Oknha KITH MENG.

The Shell Co of Cambodia Ltd: 216 blvd Norodom, Phnom-Penh; tel. (23) 215180; fax (23) 215170; e-mail nestor.tan@shell.com.kh; f. 1920; oil storage and retailing; Country Man. NESTOR A. TAN.

Sok Kong Import-Export Group (SOKIMEX): Villa 22, rue Kramuonsar, Sangkat Phsar Thmei 2, Khan Daun Penh, Phnom-Penh; tel. (23) 427207; fax (23) 217867; e-mail info@sokimex.com.kh; internet www.sokimex.com.kh; f. 1990 under the name Sok Kong Import-Export Co Ltd; sales US $155m. (2000); multi-divisional matrix company dealing predominantly with petroleum distribution; also controls ventures within wide range of other sectors, including finance, textiles and garments, tourism and pharmaceuticals; Pres. and CEO Neak Oknha SOK KONG; Vice-Chair. SORN SOKNA.

Tela Petroleum Group Investment Co: 9 rue Jawaharlal Nehru, Sangkat Toul Kork, Phnom-Penh; tel. (23) 428739; fax (23) 725559; e-mail tela@telapetroleum.com; internet www.telapetroleum.com; f. 1995; supplies petroleum products to Cambodian armed forces and civil administration; Chair. CHHUN ON; Dir-Gen. MUONG KOMPHEAK.

Total E&P Cambodia: 108–112 blvd Preah Sothearos, Hong Kong Centre, 2nd Floor, BP 600, Phnom-Penh; tel. (23) 218630; fax (23) 217662; e-mail total.cambodge@total.com.kh; sales US $30m. (2003); international petroleum co; Chair. CHRISTOPHE DE MARGERIE.

TRADE UNIONS

Cambodia Federation of Independent Trade Unions (CFITU): 45 rue 63, Sangkat Boeung Keng Kang 1, Khan Chamkarmon, Phnom-Penh; tel. (23) 213356; e-mail cfitu@online.com.kh; f. 1979 as Cambodia Fed. of Trade Unions; changed name as above in 1999; Chair. ROS SOK.

Cambodia Labour Union Federation (CLUF): 78 rue 474, Sangkat Boeung Trabek, Khan Chamkarmon, Phnom-Penh; tel. (23) 866682; f. 1999; Pres. SOM AUN.

Cambodian Independent Teachers' Association (CITA): 54E rue 95, Sangkat Boeung Keng Kang 3, Khan Chamkarmon, Phnom-Penh; tel. and fax (23) 217544; e-mail cita@online.com.kh; internet www.the-ccu.org; f. 2000; Pres. RONG CHHUN; Gen. Sec. CHEA MUNI.

Cambodian Labor Organization (CLO): 425 rue 310, Sangkat Boeung Keng Kang 2, Khan Chamkarmon, Phnom-Penh; tel. and fax (23) 218132; e-mail clo@forum.org.kh; f. 1995.

Cambodian Labour Confederation: No. 2, 3G rue 26BT, Tnotchrum Village, Sangkat Boeung, Tompun, Khan Meanchey, Phnom-Penh; tel. (12) 998906; e-mail c.l.ccambodia@online.com.kh; internet clccambodia.org; f. 2006; Pres. ATH THORN.

Cambodian Union Federation (CUF): 16 rue 11 (New World City), Phoum Tropaintling, Sangkat Chomchao, Khan Dongkor, Phnom-Penh; tel. (12) 837789; fax (23) 884329; e-mail CUF@online.com.kh; internet cuf-cctu.org; f. 1997; est. with CPP support in response to formation of FTUWKC; Pres. CHUON MOMTHOL.

Cambodian Union Federation of Building and Wood Workers: 18A rue 112, Sangkat Phsar Depo 3, Khan Tuol Kok, Phnom-Penh; tel. (23) 842382; fax (23) 882453; f. 2001; Pres. SOK SOVANDEITH; Sec.-Gen. KEN CHENGLANG.

Coalition of Cambodia Apparel Workers' Democratic Union: 6C rue 476, Sangkat Tuol Tompoung 1, Khan Chamkarmon, Phnom-Penh; tel. and fax (23) 210481; e-mail c.cawdu@online.com.kh; f. 2001; Pres. ATH THUN.

Free Trade Union of Workers of the Kingdom of Cambodia (FTUWKC): 16A rue 360, Sangkat Boeung Keng Kang 3, Khan Chamkarmon, Phnom-Penh; tel. and fax (23) 216870; e-mail contact@ftuwkc.org; internet www.ftuwkc.org; f. 1996; fmrly Free Trade Union of Khmer Workers; Pres. CHEA MONY; Gen. Sec. SREY KIM HENG.

National Independent Federation Textile Union of Cambodia (NIFTUC): 120AE rue 432, Sangkat Toul Tompoung 2, Khan Chamkarmon, Phnom-Penh; tel. (12) 994908; e-mail niftuc_2006@yahoo.com; f. 1999; Pres. MORM NHIM.

Transport

RAILWAYS

Toll Royal Railways: Central Railway Station, Railway Sq., Sangkat Srach Chak, Khan Daun Penh, Phnom-Penh; tel. (23) 992379; fax (23) 992353; e-mail sonyka.bunny@tollgroup.com; internet www.tollroyalrailway.com; two single-track lines: the original 385-km Phnom-Penh to Poipet line (incl. 48-km Sisophon–Poipet link); and a redeveloped 254-km line between Phnom-Penh and Sihanoukville, a 117-km section of which, linking Phnom-Penh and Kampot, reopened in late 2010; jt venture between Toll (55%) and Royal Group (45%) under 30-year concession agreement with Cambodian govt; Pres. and Dir-Gen. SOKHOM PHEAKAVANMONY; CEO DAVID KERR.

ROADS

In 2004 the total road network was 38,257 km in length, of which 4,757 km were highways and 5,700 km were secondary roads; about 6.3% of the road network was paved. A road bridge across the Mekong River opened in 2001.

INLAND WATERWAYS

The major routes are along the Mekong River, and up the Tonlé Sap River into the Tonlé Sap (Great Lake), covering, in all, about 2,400 km. The inland ports of Neak Luong, Kampong Cham and Prek Kdam have been supplied with motor ferries.

SHIPPING

The main port is Sihanoukville, on the Gulf of Thailand, which has 11 berths and can accommodate vessels of 10,000–15,000 tons. Phnom-Penh port lies some distance inland. Koh Kong port, near the border with Thailand, serves as a docking bay for vessels entering Cambodia from Singapore, Malaysia and Thailand.

Phnom Penh Autonomous Port: Preah Sisowath, Sangkat Sras Chak, Khan Daun Penh; tel. and fax (23) 427802; e-mail ppapmpwt@online.com.kh; internet www.ppap.com.kh; state-owned; Chair. and CEO HEI BAVY.

Sihanoukville Autonomous Port (PAS): Terak Vithei Samdech Akka Moha Sena Padei Techo HUN SEN Sangkat No 3, Sihanoukville, Preah Sihanouk; tel. (34) 933416; fax (34) 933693; e-mail pasplan@pas.gov.kh; internet www.pas.gov.kh; Chair. and CEO LOU KIM CHHUN.

CIVIL AVIATION

There are international airports at Pochentong, serving nearby Phnom-Penh, and at Siem Reap. Plans for the construction of a new US $1,000m. international airport at Siem Reap were under discussion in mid-2010.

State Secretariat of Civil Aviation (SSCA): 62 blvd Norodom, Phnom-Penh; tel. and fax (23) 211019; e-mail sengvany@camnet.com.kh; internet www.civilaviation.gov.kh; Dir-Gen. MAO HAS VANNAL.

Cambodia Angkor Air: 1–2, 294 blvd Mao Tse Tong, Phnom-Penh; tel. (23) 6666786; fax (23) 424496; internet www.cambodiaangkorair.com; f. 2009; national carrier; jt venture with Viet Nam Airlines; Chair. and CEO TRINH NGOC THANH.

PMT Air: 118 rue 2013, Sangkat Kakab, Khan Dong Kar, Phnom-Penh; tel. and fax (23) 23890322; e-mail tiket@pmtair.com; internet www.pmtair.com; f. 2003; domestic and international services.

Royal Khmer Airlines: 36B, 245 blvd Mao Tse Toung, Sangkat Boeung Trabek, Khan Chamkarmon, Phnom-Penh; tel. (23) 994888; fax (23) 994508; e-mail rudy@royalkhmerairlines.com; internet www.royalkhmerairlines.com; f. 2000; jt venture with Indonesia; domestic and international services; CEO RUDYANTO WIDJAJA.

Royal Phnom-Penh Airways: 209 rue 19, Sangkat Chey Chumneah, Khan Daun Penh, Phnom-Penh; tel. (23) 215565; fax (23) 217420; e-mail ppenhairw@bigpond.com.kh; f. 1999; scheduled and charter passenger flights to domestic and regional destinations; Chair. Prince NORODOM CHAKRAPONG.

Siem Reap Airways International: 65 rue 214, Sangkat Boeung Raing, Khan Daun Penh, Phnom-Penh; tel. (23) 723962; fax (23) 720522; internet www.siemreapair.com; f. 2000; scheduled domestic and international passenger services; CEO PRASERT PRASARTTONG-OSOTH.

Tourism

Cambodia's attractions include the ancient temples of Angkor and the beaches of Sihanoukville. Receipts from tourism totalled US $1,750m. in 2010. In that year visitor arrivals reached 2.3m. Major sources of visitors included Viet Nam, South Korea, China and Japan. The number of rooms available in hotels and guest houses was estimated to have exceeded 40,000 in 2010.

Directorate-General of Tourism: 3 blvd Monivong, Phnom-Penh; tel. (23) 427130; fax (23) 426107; f. 1988; Dir-Gen. THITH CHANTHA.

Defence

As assessed at November 2010, the total strength of the Royal Cambodian Armed Forces was estimated to be 124,300 (including provincial forces): army 75,000, navy 2,800, air force 1,500 and provincial forces about 45,000. Paramilitary forces are organized at village level and numbered some 67,000 men and women in 2010. The defence budget for 2011 was estimated at 1,220,000m. riels.

Supreme Commander of the Royal Cambodian Armed Forces: King NORODOM SIHAMONI.

Commander-in-Chief: Gen. POL SAROEUN.

Education

In 2003/04 there were 1,345 pre-primary institutions. In 2002/03 there were 5,915 primary schools, 411 general secondary schools and 183 vocational secondary schools. In 2008/09 a total of 178,583 children were attending pre-primary schools, and primary pupils totalled 2,289,759. Secondary students totalled 875,120 in 2006/07. In 2007/08 enrolment at pre-primary level included 12% of children in the relevant age group (males 12%; females 13%). Primary education is compulsory for nine years between the ages of six and 15. Enrolment at primary level included 89% of children in the relevant age group (males 90%; females 87%) in 2007/08. Secondary education comprises two cycles, each lasting three years. Enrolment at secondary level included 34% of children in the relevant age group (males 36%; females 32%) in 2006/07.

Institutions of higher education include Phnom-Penh University, an arts college, a technical college, a teacher-training college, a number of secondary vocational schools and an agricultural college.

The budget for 2003 allocated 300,000m. riels (10.3% of total expenditure) to the Ministry of Education, Youth and Sport.

Bibliography

(See also Laos and Viet Nam)

Ayres, David M. *Anatomy of a Crisis: Education, Development and the State in Cambodia, 1953–1998.* Honolulu, HI, University of Hawaii Press, 2001.

Becker, Elizabeth. *When the War Was Over: Cambodia and the Khmer Rouge Revolution.* New York, PublicAffairs, 1998.

Bizot, François. *The Gate.* London, Harvill Press, 2003.

Brinkley, Joel. *Cambodia's Curse: The Modern History of a Troubled Land.* New York, PublicAffairs, 2011.

Chandler, David P. *A History of Cambodia.* Boulder, CO, Westview Press, 4th Edn, 2007.

The Tragedy of Cambodian History: Politics, War and Revolution since 1945. New Haven, CT, Yale University Press, 1992.

Brother Number One: A Political Biography of Pol Pot. Boulder, CO, Westview Press, 1992.

Voices from S-21: Terror and History in Pol Pot's Secret Prison. Berkeley, CA, University of California Press, 2000.

Chandler, David P., and Kent, Alexandra. *People of Virtue: Reconfiguring Religion, Power and Moral Order in Cambodia Today.* Copenhagen, NIAS Press, 2009.

Chandler, David P., Kiernan, Ben, and Boua, Chanthou (Eds). *Pol Pot Plans the Future: Confidential Leadership Documents from Democratic Kampuchea.* New Haven, CT, Yale University Press, 1988.

Clymer, Kenton. *The United States and Cambodia, 1969–2000: A Troubled Relationship.* London, RoutledgeCurzon, 2004.

Coates, Karen J. *Cambodia Now: Life in the Wake of War.* Jefferson, NC, McFarland & Co, 2005.

Corfield, Justin J., and Summers, Laura. *Historical Dictionary of Cambodia.* Oxford, Rowman and Littlefield Publrs, 2003.

Cummins, Nick. *The 1997 Coup in Cambodia: the Prince, the Comrade and the Revolutionary.* Clayton, Vic, Monash University Press, 2008.

Deedrick, Tami. *Khmer Empires (Ancient Civilisations).* London, Raintree Steck-Vaughn, 2001.

Derks, Annuksa. *Khmer Women on the Move: Exploring Work and Life in Urban Cambodia.* Honolulu, HI, University of Hawaii Press, 2008.

Dunlop, Nic. *The Lost Executioner: A Story of the Khmer Rouge.* London, Bloomsbury Publishing, 2005.

Dy, Khamboly. *A History of Democratic Kampuchea (1975-1979).* Phnom-Penh, Documentation Center of Cambodia, 2007.

Edwards, Penny. *Cambodge: The Cultivation of a Nation, 1860–1945.* Honolulu, HI, University of Hawaii Press, 2007.

Etcheson, Craig. *The Rise and Demise of Democratic Kampuchea.* Boulder, CO, Westview Press, 1984.

After the Killing Fields: Lessons from the Cambodian Genocide. London, Greenwood Publishing Group, 2005.

Fawthrop, Tom, and Jarvis, Helen. *Getting Away with Genocide: Cambodia's Long Struggle Against the Khmer Rouge.* London, Pluto Press, 2004.

Gottesman, Evan R. *Cambodia After the Khmer Rouge: Inside the Politics of Nation Building.* New Haven, CT, Yale University Press, 2nd Edn, 2004.

Guy, John. *Sanctuary: The Temples of Angkor.* London, Phaidon Press, 2002.

Harris, Ian. *Buddhism under Pol Pot.* Phnom-Penh, Documentation Center of Cambodia, 2007.

Higham, Charles. *The Civilization of Angkor.* Berkeley, CA, University of California Press, 2002.

Him, Chanrithy. *When Broken Glass Floats: Growing Up Under the Khmer Rouge.* New York, W. W. Norton & Co, 2001.

Hinton, Alexander Laban. *Why Did They Kill? Cambodia in the Shadow of Genocide.* Berkeley, CA, University of California Press, 2004.

Hughes, Caroline. *UNTAC in Cambodia: The Impact on Human Rights.* Singapore, Institute of Southeast Asian Studies, 1996.

The Political Economy of the Cambodian Transition. London, RoutledgeCurzon, 2002.

Dependent Communities: Aid and Politics in Cambodia and East Timor. Ithaca, NY, Cornell University Press, 2009.

Hughes, Caroline, and Kiernan, Chris C. (Eds). *Conflict and Change in Cambodia.* Abingdon, Routledge, 2006.

Hughes, Caroline, and Kheang Un (Eds). *Cambodia's Economic Transformation.* Copenhagen, NIAS Press, 2011.

Kamm, Henry. *Cambodia: Report from a Stricken Land.* London/New York, Arcade Publishing, 2011.

Kerbo, Harold R. *The Persistence of Cambodian Poverty: From the Killing Fields to Today.* Jefferson, NC, McFarland, 2011.

Kiernan, Ben. *How Pol Pot Came to Power.* New Haven, CT, Yale University Press, 2nd Edn, 2004.

The Pol Pot Regime: Race, Power and Genocide in Cambodia under the Khmer Rouge, 1975–79. New Haven, CT, Yale University Press, 3rd Edn, 2008.

Genocide and Resistance in Southeast Asia: Documentation, Denial, and Justice in Cambodia and East Timor. Piscataway, NJ, Transaction Publishers, 2007.

Lafreniere, Bree. *Music Through The Dark: A Tale of Survival in Cambodia.* Honolulu, HI, University of Hawaii Press, 2000.

Lilja, Mona. *Power, Resistance and Women Politicians in Cambodia: Discourses of Emancipation.* Honolulu, HI, University of Hawaii Press, 2006.

Maguire, Peter H. *Facing Death in Cambodia.* New York, Columbia University Press, 2005.

Marston, John, and Guthrie, Elizabeth (Eds). *History, Buddhism and New Religious Movements in Cambodia.* Honolulu, HI, University of Hawaii Press, 2004.

Matthews, Verghese. *Cambodia: Wasted Time and Lost Opportunities.* Singapore, Institute of Southeast Asian Studies, 2006.

Mehta, Harish. *Warrior Prince: Norodom Ranariddh, Son of Sihanouk of Cambodia.* Singapore, Graham Brash, 2001.

Mehta, Harish, and Mehta, Julie. *Hun Sen—Strongman of Cambodia.* Singapore, Graham Brash, 2000.

Morris, Stephen J. *Why Vietnam Invaded Cambodia.* London, Cambridge University Press, 2001.

Muller, Gregor. *Colonial Cambodia's 'Bad Frenchmen'.* Abingdon, Routledge, 2006.

Ngor, Haing, and Warner, Roger. *Survival in the Killing Fields.* London, Constable and Robinson, 2003.

Norodom Sihanouk. *War and Hope: the Case for Cambodia.* London, Sidgwick and Jackson, 1980.

Öjendal, Joakim, and Lilja, Mona (Eds). *Beyond Democracy in Cambodia: Political Reconstruction in a Post-Conflict Society.* Copenhagen, NIAS Press, 2009.

Ollier, Leakthina Chau-Pech, and Winter, Tim. *Expressions of Cambodia: The Politics of Tradition, Identity and Change.* Abingdon, Routledge, 2006.

Osborne, Milton E. *Sihanouk: Prince of Light, Prince of Darkness.* St Leonards, NSW, Allen and Unwin, 1994.

Before Kampuchea: Preludes to Tragedy. Bangkok, Orchid Press, 2003.

Peou, Sorpong. *Conflict Neutralization in the Cambodia War: From Battlefield to Ballot-Box.* Kuala Lumpur, New York & Singapore, Oxford University Press, 1997.

Intervention and Change in Cambodia: Towards Democracy? Singapore, Institute of Southeast Asian Studies, 2000.

International Democracy Assistance for Peacebuilding: Cambodia and Beyond. London and New York, Palgrave Macmillan, 2007.

Peou, Sorpong (Ed.). *Cambodia: Change and Continuity in Contemporary Politics.* Aldershot, Ashgate Publishing, 2001.

Picq, Laurence. *Beyond the Horizon: Five Years with the Khmer Rouge.* New York, St Martin's Press, 1989.

Pran, Dith, and DePaul, Kim (Eds). *Children of Cambodia's Killing Fields: Memoirs by Survivors.* New Haven, CT, Yale University Press, 1997.

Quigley, John, and Robinson, Kenneth (Eds). *Documents from the Trial of Pol Pot and Ieng Sary.* Philadelphia, PA, University of Pennsylvania Press, 2000.

Richardson, S. *China, Cambodia and the Five Principles of Peaceful Coexistence.* New York, Columbia University Press, 2009.

Roberts, David. *Political Transition in Cambodia 1991–1999: Power, Elitism and Democracy.* Richmond, Surrey, Curzon Press, 2001.

Shawcross, William. *Sideshow: Kissinger, Nixon and the Destruction of Cambodia.* London, André Deutsch, 1979.

The Quality of Mercy: Cambodia, Holocaust and Modern Conscience. London, André Deutsch, 1984.

Cambodia's New Deal. Washington, Carnegie Endowment for International Peace, 1994.

Short, Philip. *Pol Pot: The History of a Nightmare.* London, John Murray, 2004.

Slocomb, Margaret. *People's Republic of Kampuchea, 1979–1989: The Revolution after Pol Pot.* Seattle, WA, University of Washington Press, 2004.

An Economic History of Cambodia in the Twentieth Century. Honolulu, University of Hawaii Press, 2010.

Springer, Simon. *Cambodia's Neoliberal Order: Violence, Authoritarianism, and the Contestation of Public Space.* Abingdon, Routledge, 2010.

Stuart-Fox, Martin, and Ung, Bunhaeng. *The Murderous Revolution.* Bangkok, Tamarind Press, 1986.

Tully, John A. *France on the Mekong: A History of the Protectorate in Cambodia, 1863–1953.* Oxford, Rowman and Littlefield Publrs, 2003.

A Short History of Cambodia: From Empire to Survival. Sydney, Allen and Unwin, 2006.

Tyner, James A. *The Killing of Cambodia: Geopolitics, Genocide, and the Unmaking of Space.* Burlington, VT, Ashgate, 2008.

Vickery, Michael. *Cambodia: 1975–1982.* Sydney, Allen and Unwin, 1984.

Kampuchea: Politics, Economics and Society. Sydney, Allen and Unwin, 1987.

Widyono, Benny. *Dancing in Shadows: Sihanouk, the Khmer Rouge, and the United Nations in Cambodia.* Lanham, MD, Rowman and Littlefield Publrs, 2007.

Winter, Tim. *Post-conflict Heritage, Postcolonial Tourism: Culture, Politics and Development at Angkor.* Abingdon, Routledge, 2007.

Yimsut, Ronnie. *Facing the Khmer Rouge: A Cambodian Journey.* Piscataway, NJ, Rutgers University Press, 2011.

THE PEOPLE'S REPUBLIC OF CHINA

Physical and Social Geography

MICHAEL FREEBERNE

With additions by the editorial staff

The People's Republic of China covers an area of 9,572,900 sq km (almost 3.7m. sq miles) and extends about 4,000 km from north to south and 4,800 km from east to west. China's land frontiers extend for a total of 20,000 km, and have been the source of some tension. China shares frontiers with the Democratic People's Republic of Korea (North Korea), Mongolia, Russia, Kazakhstan, Kyrgyzstan, Tajikistan, Afghanistan, Pakistan, India, Nepal, Bhutan, Myanmar (formerly Burma), Laos and Viet Nam. The dispute over the boundary between China and India resulted in the border war of 1962. Negotiations regarding the settlement of the dispute by peaceful means have continued. The two sections of the Sino-Russian border (in the north-east and the north-west of China) total more than 4,300 km. Various boundary incidents occurred after 1960, but subsequent negotiations resulted in the demarcation of large parts of both sections in the mid-1990s. Discussions concerning the shorter western section and the status of two islands continued. An agreement regarding the delimitation of the eastern section (some 4,300 km) was signed in July 2008. China's eastern seaboard is 14,000 km in length. Its territorial waters are dotted with some 5,000 islands, ranging from provincial-sized Hainan down to minute atolls, which include the strategically significant but disputed Xisha (Paracel) and Nansha (Spratly) Islands. Rich in fish (and also petroleum reserves), these waters make a significant contribution to the output of marine and fresh water aquatic products. China's relatively smooth coastline is largely without good natural harbours.

PHYSICAL FEATURES

The geographical environment has presented considerable obstacles to development. According to official figures, in the early 21st century 13% of China's surface was cultivated, 18% was forest and almost 42% was grassland. Less than 33% of the area was classified as usable. In practice, China has been required to feed more than 20% of the world's population on just 7% of its arable land and with only 8% of its fresh water. Farming land has been lost, not only through increasing urbanization and industrial development, but also through drought and flooding. In an attempt to address the issue of soil erosion, the felling of trees has been banned in some areas. In 2000 it was calculated that 27% of China's total land area was affected by desertification. A national survey conducted between 2005 and 2009 revealed little improvement in the situation: 2.62m. sq km of land were degraded and 1.73m. sq km were affected by sand encroachment.

Relief, configuration and climate have been critical in suggesting possible settlement areas and zones suitable for economic development. For the most part high in the west and relatively low in the east, China has been compared to a three-section staircase. The Qinghai-Tibet (Xizang) plateau, at over 4,000 m, is the highest flight; next is an arc of plateaux and basins lying at 1,000 m–2,000 m, extending eastwards from the Tarim Basin, across Inner Mongolia (Nei Monggol) and the loess lands, then turning south to include the immensely fertile Sichuan Basin and the Yunnan-Guizhou plateau; much of the land that constitutes the lowest flight lies below 500 m and covers the most densely settled areas, such as the middle and lower Yangtze (Changjiang) Basin, the North China plain and the north-eastern plain. About 33% of China's total area comprises mountains; 26% is plateau land; 10% is hill country; 19% is occupied by basins; but only 12% of the surface is composed of plains.

Watering these plains are rivers that in some years bring good agricultural conditions and rich harvests, but in other years may cause flooding or dry up altogether. In terms both of regional and of seasonal distribution, water supplies are inconsistent and uneven. In the north, the Yellow River (Huanghe) is 5,464 km in length and has a drainage basin of 752,443 sq km. In central China, the Yangtze is 6,300 km long with an annual flow of 9,513,000m. cu m, and a massive drainage basin of 1.8m. sq km, covering one-fifth of the country. The Zhujiang (2,214 km) flows through southern China. Water conservation is actively pursued, and flood control, irrigation, navigation and power generation have all been emphasized in numerous multi-purpose projects.

China experienced exceptionally severe flooding of the Yangtze in mid-1998: more than 240m. people were affected, some 14m. people were forced to leave their homes, more than 3,000 people lost their lives and damage costing in excess of US $20,000m. was caused by the worst floods since 1954 (when 30,000 were killed). The authorities conceded that soil erosion, resulting from extensive deforestation, was largely responsible, and acknowledged the need for an accelerated tree-planting programme. In southern China torrential rains in mid-2010 killed several hundred people and forced millions of citizens to be evacuated from their homes. In August, furthermore, a landslide caused by heavy rain in Gansu Province killed more than 1,200 people. About 550,000 citizens were evacuated from their homes in southern China in June 2011 when heavy rains broke what was described as the worst drought for 50 years.

In 1994 work commenced on the Three Gorges scheme, the world's largest civil engineering project, in Hubei Province. Comprising a 1,983-m hydroelectric dam across the Yangtze, the plant was to have an annual generating capacity of 84,700m. kWh of electricity. The scheme involved the submerging of 17,000 ha of farmland and the displacement of more than 1m. people (see Environmental Issues of the Asia-Pacific Region). In October 2007 it was announced that a further 4m. people were to be relocated. With the Three Gorges project scheduled to become fully operational in 2011, work on various other major hydroelectric schemes was also progressing.

The Three Gorges project incorporates a massive water-conservancy programme. Increasingly, many Chinese cities, including Beijing and Tianjin, are suffering from acute water shortages. In the 1990s scientists began to warn of a serious shortage of drinking water by the early 21st century. Furthermore, the rapid degradation of the quality of water supplies through industrial pollution has become a cause of grave concern, leading the Government to implement stricter regulations. In mid-2001 the most severe drought for more than a decade was reported to have left millions of Chinese citizens without adequate drinking water, the most seriously affected areas being Shandong and Liaoning Provinces. By 2004 it was being reported that 400 of China's 670 largest cities were suffering serious water deficits. In August 2009 as many as 4.6m. people and more than 4m. head of livestock were thought to be affected by shortages of drinking water as a result of prolonged drought in northern areas of China. In March 2010 it was reported that 18m. people and 11m. head of livestock were affected by drought conditions in southern China, necessitating the Government's dispatch of 1.4m. metric tons of emergency supplies of grain to the region. In early 2011 drought conditions across northern China were reported to be jeopardizing the winter wheat crop.

In 2002 work began on a major project to transport water, via three channels, from the south of the country to the drier

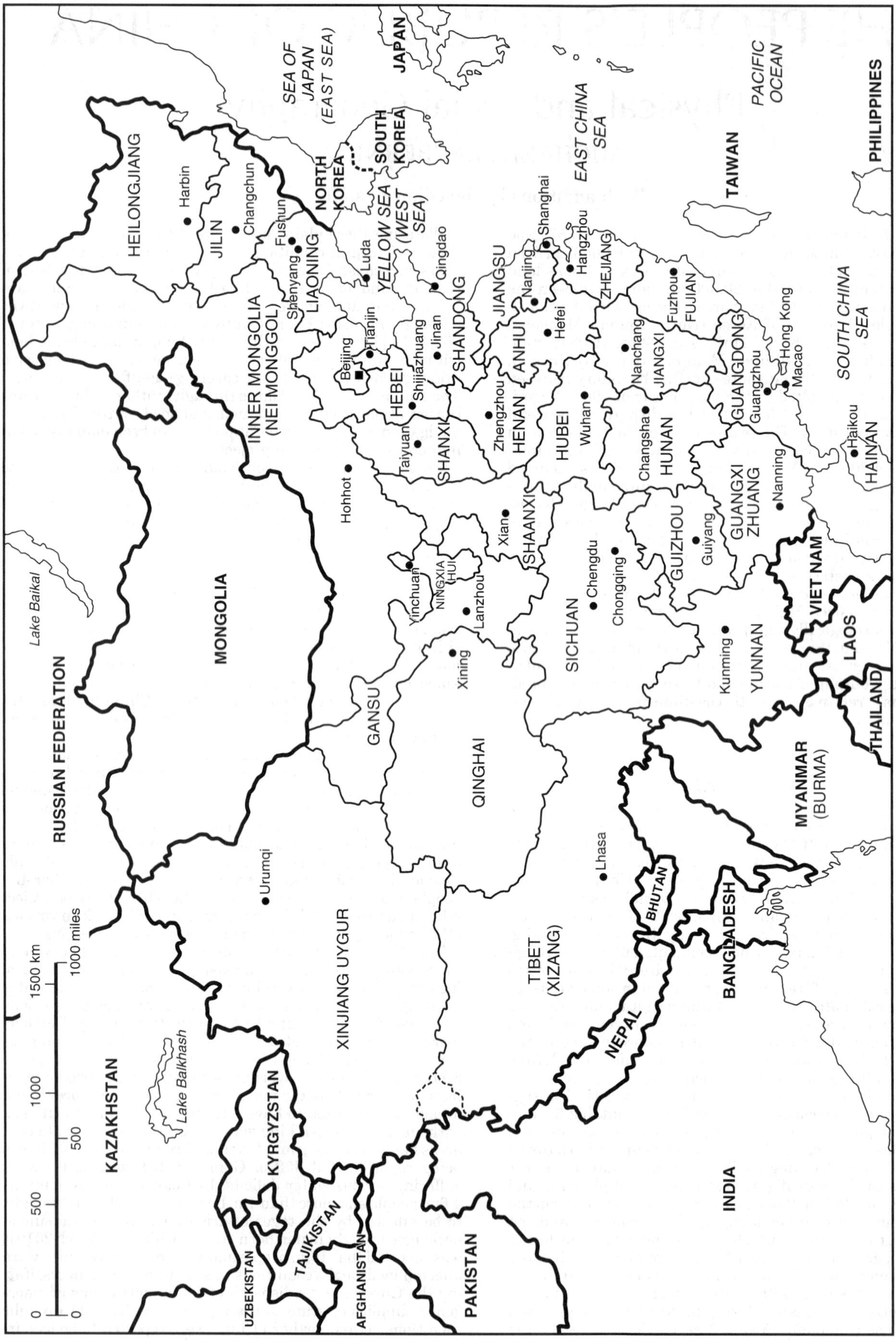

The People's Republic of China

northern regions. As part of the South–North Water Diversion Project, which was to take water from the Yangtze to the cities of Beijing and Tianjin, the first stage in the relocation of a total of 330,000 residents took place in August 2010 when 499 residents were transferred from their homes in a village in Hubei Province in central China. By 2014 about 180,000 people were to be relocated from Hubei and 150,000 from Henan. Meanwhile, the Chinese Government's plans to divert water from Tibet to the Yellow River over a 300-km network of pipes and tunnels, first revealed in 2006, were reported to have raised serious concerns in neighbouring India.

CLIMATE

China is dominated by a monsoonal regime. Cold air masses build up over the Asian land mass in winter, and the prevailing winds are offshore and dry. In summer there is a reversal of this pattern, and the rainy season is concentrated in the summer months over the most densely settled parts of the country in the east and the south. Running from south to north there are six broad temperature zones: tropical and subtropical, warm-temperate and temperate, cold-temperate and the Qinghai-Tibet plateau area, which has its own characteristic regime. January is generally the coldest month and July the hottest. There is a great range in winter temperatures—as much as 15°C between the average for Guangzhou in the south and Harbin in the north. South of the Nanling mountains January temperatures average around 8°C, but they fall to between −8°C and −15°C over much of the north-east, Nei Monggol and the north-west. In summer the temperature difference between Guangzhou and Harbin narrows to 12°C and summer temperatures over much of the country average above 20°C.

The summer monsoon brings abundant rain to coastal China, especially in the south and east, but amounts decrease drastically to the north and west. A humid zone covers much of south-eastern China and the average annual rainfall is above 750 mm. In the semi-humid zone, extending across the north-east, the North China plain and the south-eastern region of the Qinghai-Tibet plateau, the average falls to less than 500 mm. The remainder of the Qinghai-Tibet plateau, the loess, and the Inner Mongolia plateaux receive only about 300 mm, while western Inner Mongolia and Xinjiang, where there are extensive deserts, get less than 250 mm. About 80% of China's precipitation usually falls between May and October, with July and August being the wettest months.

VEGETATION AND NATURAL RESOURCES

Over hundreds of years much of China's natural vegetation has been stripped. The basic contrast is between the forests and woodlands of the eastern half of the country and the grassland-desert complex of the western half. Tree types vary from the tropical rain forests in the south, through evergreen broadleaved forests, mixed mesophytic forests, temperate deciduous broadleaved forests, and mixed northern hardwood and boreal coniferous forests in the north. The eastern Mongolian plateau, the Xiao Hinggan Ling and Da Hinggan Ling (the Lesser and Greater Khingan mountains), and the Changbaishan massif contain 60% of China's forest reserves. Other natural forests are located in Yunnan, Jiangxi, Fujian, Guizhou, Sichuan, Hainan and in the Qinling mountains and along the eastern edge of the Qinghai-Tibet plateau. However, most of China's forests are largely inaccessible, and there is a serious shortage of workable timber.

Owing to the widespread destruction of natural vegetation, soil erosion is a major problem. Sheet and gully erosion are common; water and wind erosion do great damage in the north, while water erosion is the chief enemy in the south; also, farming malpractices, such as deep ploughing, have aggravated the situation. It has been estimated that about 40% of the total cultivated area comprises 'poor' soils: red loams, saline-alkaline soil and some of the rice paddy soils.

The Daqing oilfield, China's largest, has provided a substantial percentage of China's petroleum output since the 1960s. At the end of 2010 China's total petroleum reserves were estimated by industry sources at 14,800m. barrels and natural gas reserves at 2,800,000m. cu m. Major petroleum and gas reserves lie in the Tarim Basin, in Xinjiang. China is extremely rich in coal and iron ore. The country is also a major producer of natural graphite, antimony, tungsten and zinc. Other important minerals include molybdenum, tin, lead, mercury, bauxite, phosphate rock, diamonds, gold and manganese.

POPULATION

At the first national census conducted in 1953 China's population totalled 582,603,417. The preliminary results of the census of 1 November 2010 revealed that the population had increased to an estimated 1,339,724,852 (thus giving a density of 139.9 persons per sq km), compared with 1,242,612,226 at the time of the previous census in 2000. These figures, which represent more than one-fifth of the world's population, are formidable in view of both the pressures that population growth has exerted historically and the contemporary problems in the physical environment already outlined. There is, for instance, a striking imbalance in the distribution of population, which is heavily concentrated in the plain and riverine lands of the south-eastern half of the country, while most of the north-western half is, by comparison, thinly populated.

According to the census of 2000 91.53% of the population are Han Chinese. The remaining 8.47% belong to one of the national minority groups. Altogether there are more than 106m. non-Chinese living within China, chiefly in the peripheral areas beyond the Great Wall, in the north, the north-west and the south-west. There are 55 different minorities scattered throughout 60% of the country. According to the 2000 census, 18 minorities numbered more than 1m. each (see Statistical Survey). Between 1982 and 1990, while the Han Chinese population increased by 102m., or 10.80% (1.29% annually), the national minorities grew by 24m., or 35.52% (3.87% per year). However, between 1990 and 2000 the Han Chinese population increased by 116.92m., or 11.22% (1.07% annually), while the national minorities grew by 15.23m., or 16.7% (1.56% annually), the latter thus recording a faster rate of growth than the Han, but significantly slower than in the previous decade. Linguistic differences among the seven main Chinese dialects, as well as between Chinese and minority languages, have proved a difficult issue, despite the adoption of Mandarin (Putonghua) as the national language

China has become an increasingly urbanized society. In 2009 almost 621.9m. people, or 46.6% of the population, resided in cities or towns, with 53.4% living in the countryside (compared with almost 88% in 1952). The inequalities in living standards between urban and rural areas have become a major issue.

In 2009 China's birth rate was estimated at 12.13 per thousand and the death rate at 7.08 per thousand, thus giving a natural growth rate of 5.05 per thousand. Family-planning programmes from the mid-1950s failed to make any substantial difference to the increase in Chinese numbers. In 1979, therefore, the Government issued further directives favouring couples with only one child and penalizing those who practised 'anarchism in parenthood'. However, rural parents are now allowed to have two children if the first is a girl. Furthermore, as the Chinese population continued to age and as the relative size of the labour force began to decrease, the one-child policy was reported to be under review in some areas. In July 2009 it was announced that Shanghai (where those aged more than 60 years had already exceeded 3m. or 21.6% of registered residents) was to relax the policy for many couples living in China's most populous city: husbands and wives who had themselves both been only children were to be encouraged to have a second child.

Despite improved grain harvests in the 1970s and the 1980s, significant declines in the production of grain were recorded in the late 1990s and in the early years of the 21st century. None the less, after four consecutive years of decline, during which many farmers switched to more profitable crops such as fruit and vegetables, in 2004 the Government reported the achievement of an excellent grain harvest of 469.5m. metric tons. According to official sources, the grain harvest rose steadily in subsequent years, to reach 546.6m. tons in 2010. A record harvest of 550m. tons was anticipated in 2011.

History up to 1966

C. P. FITZGERALD

PREHISTORY AND CLASSICAL PERIOD

The earliest Chinese written records, recovered by archaeological excavation at the site of what was the capital of the Shang kingdom in Henan Province, date from approximately 1500 BC. Legendary history, for which there is as yet no archaeological evidence, records a previous kingdom, Xia, and a golden age of the rule of Sages, for at least 1,000 years earlier. The agreement between the king list of Shang, as found on the oracle bones discovered at Anyang, and the list preserved in Chinese official history, which are wholly independent of each other, shows that the official history must be treated with some respect. Shang culture included the making of bronze vessels of great beauty, some of which are briefly inscribed. The succeeding period, the Zhou dynasty, from 1100 to 221 BC, continued the Shang culture, but a more elaborate literature appeared, and in the second part of the Zhou rule, from about 800 BC onwards, the feudal system instituted at the foundation broke down. China became a land of contending kingdoms. At the same time there arose the various schools of philosophy (Confucian, Daoist, Moist and Legalist), whose contention matched the military conflict between the kingdoms.

UNIFICATION OF CHINA

From about the date of the death of Confucius (479 BC) until 221 BC China was constantly subjected to the wars of the contending kingdoms, of which the western state of Qin and the southern state of Chu, in the Yangtze (Changjiang) valley, were the chief protagonists. The history of Chu provides all that is known of south China in the earlier period. The struggle was won by Qin in 221 BC. The ruler of that kingdom then assumed the new title of *Huang Di*, translated as 'emperor', and imposed on his new dominions the harsh Legalist code of laws and administration, which had been in force in his country. Qin law despised art and literature, glorifying war and promoting agriculture as the foundation of military power. To suppress the opposition of the literate class in the new empire, the emperor ordered the burning of all books on history and philosophy not included in his own library. Although much was hidden and preserved, this policy did great damage to the recorded literature of China. A few years after his death, a general revolt overthrew the Qin and they were replaced by the Han dynasty, which ruled from 206 BC to AD 221.

THE FIRST EMPIRE AND PERIOD OF PARTITION

The Han dynasty consolidated the new empire, but ruled with moderation. A civil service, filled with educated men recommended by patrons, replaced the feudal system. Free tenure of land created both a landlord and a tenant system, which endured until recent times. Confucianism became the established orthodoxy. The empire was expanded to include the Guangzhou (Canton) region, and later, in central Asia, as far as the Caspian Sea. Contact with the Roman empire, although slight, is recorded. In art the Han developed mural painting and bas-reliefs, and in literature history was highly esteemed and developed in a systematic and accurate form. Paper and ink replaced bamboo strips and the stylus for writing. After 400 years the Han empire fell in confusion. Contending states were briefly suppressed by a reunion under the Jin dynasty, which itself soon lost North China to the invading Tartar tribes. China was divided from AD 316 to 589. Tartar rulers held the north, and Chinese dynasties the south (Yangtze valley). Both in north and south the dynasties were brief, and internal conflict frequent. However, although an 'Age of Confusion', this was not a 'Dark Age'. Literature flourished in both north and south. Buddhism was introduced and spread widely. The majority of the population being Chinese, the Tartar invaders were soon absorbed, both ethnically and culturally.

THE SECOND EMPIRE, TANG AND SONG DYNASTIES

The Tang dynasty, founded in AD 618, reunited the empire on a lasting basis. The aristocratic military class gave way to a bureaucracy recruited by public examination open to all literates. The administration of government was developed to a degree unknown elsewhere for several centuries to come. Art and literature, especially poetry, flourished. The population recorded by an apparently accurate census in AD 754 was 52,880,488. Archaeological discovery of a census return shows that this figure included women and children. The Song dynasty, which succeeded the Tang in AD 907, continued the civil service system which now controlled the government. The Song were unassertive, and failed to recover north-eastern territory lost to nomad invasion at the fall of the Tang. In AD 1127 the Song lost North China to an invasion of the Jin Tartars. A century later the Song were conquered, after a long war, by the Mongols. The new Confucian philosophy was the main development in literature; in art Song painting is still the most esteemed. Technical developments include printing, porcelain, the maritime compass, gunpowder and primitive cannon, advances in silk spinning and the development of maritime trade with South and West Asia.

THE LATE EMPIRE AND SUBSEQUENT DYNASTIES

The Mongol conquest of China in 1280 was most destructive, especially in the northern half of the country. Huge depopulation occurred, and great areas of fertile land became wilderness. Song culture, though damaged, survived. Mongol rule was oppressive and largely exercised through foreign officials from West Asia and even Europe (Marco Polo). It was also brief. After less than a century the Chinese revolt ended in the foundation of the Ming dynasty and the expulsion of the Mongols in 1368. The development of drama, written by unemployed Chinese scholars, is the significant cultural development of the Mongol period.

However, the Ming dynasty not only restored Chinese rule, but it also expanded the limits of the empire. South Manzhou (Manchuria) was settled and incorporated, as was Yunnan, at the opposite extremity of the empire. The Ming aimed to restore the style of Tang and Song government, but their rule was much more autocratic. In early Ming (1405–33) expeditions were sent by sea to South-East Asia, the Indian coast, the Persian Gulf, the Red Sea and East Africa, but this naval activity was abandoned only a few years before the Portuguese first appeared in Far Eastern waters. In late Ming contact with Europeans increased, and the first Roman Catholic missionaries reached China.

From the middle of the 15th century China was threatened, to an increasing extent, by the growth of a new power in what is called Manzhou (Manchuria), or the Three Eastern Provinces. The Manzhou tribes, kindred of the Jin Tartars who had ruled northern China in the late Song period, were at first tributary to the Ming. From China, through this contact, they acquired a knowledge of governing techniques, literacy and organization. Late in the 16th century they coalesced into a new kingdom, which threw off allegiance to the Ming, and before long began to encroach on the Ming territory of South Manzhou, or modern Liaoning Province. By the middle of the 17th century they had seized this region and were raiding the Great Wall frontier of China proper. The Ming fell in 1644 to an internal rebellion, which gave the Manzhous (Manchus) the opportunity to enter China and, after nearly 40 years, control the whole empire.

The Qing (Manzhou) dynasty ruled until 1912. The first 150 years, under the three very competent emperors Kang Xi, Yong Zheng and Qian Long, were prosperous and peaceful. At the end of the 18th century the dynasty began to decline. The growth of trade with Europe was at first very profitable to China, but the Manzhous distrusted the foreign traders and imposed restrictions on their activities. The discovery of opium smuggling by British traders brought about the Opium War of 1842; China, unable to match the strength of the British fleet, was defeated. The Treaty of Nanjing, the first of the 'Unequal Treaties' as they came to be called, which followed this defeat, established the system of Treaty Ports, concession areas and the right of extraterritorial jurisdiction. Shanghai was claimed as a British Treaty Port, and by the end of the century had become an International Settlement, guarded by its own multinational troops.

The unsuccessful war, and the internal rebellions that swept the country in the 1850s, weakened the authority of a dynasty always considered alien in the south. Moreover, in the 1870s China began to suffer the encroachment of the European powers. Russia took advantage of the rebellions in China to obtain territory in the north, while in the 1880s France seized Indo-China and forced Beijing to renounce its suzerainty. The United Kingdom and France together waged war with China in 1858 and actually occupied Beijing, exacting a further 'Unequal Treaty'. Towards the end of the century Japan became involved, and in the war of 1894–95 drove the Chinese out of Korea. At home the young intellectuals, inspired by Western education and thinking, adopted revolutionary ideas under the leadership of Dr Sun Yat-sen. In 1911, three years after the death of the empress dowager Ci Xi (who had ruled from 1862), a revolt of the army at Wuhan led to the fall of the dynasty and the abolition of the monarchy.

REPUBLICAN CHINA

Sun Yat-sen was a native of Guangzhou, who had been educated from childhood in Hawaii and then taken a degree at the medical school of Hong Kong. His formation was thus largely foreign and Western. Finding that radical reform was unacceptable to the official world of China, he turned revolutionary and republican, and for more than 10 years maintained an unceasing effort to incite rebellion in China. He was for long unsuccessful; but his influence grew steadily among the young Chinese studying abroad, particularly in Japan, where the majority of them went. He built up a nationalist party and a secret organization, obtained funds from the overseas Chinese of South-East Asia, and finally his followers were able to infiltrate the army—the new model army whose officers had also studied abroad.

Thus, when the revolution started in 1911, it was dominated by the army, a servitude from which it was not to escape for many years. The court had lost further prestige in 1900 by supporting the peasant anti-foreign movement known as the Boxer Rebellion, which for a time threatened to massacre the diplomatic corps in Beijing; the Rebellion was finally crushed by an international expedition, which took Beijing and drove the court to retreat to the west of China. The southern provinces under their great viceroys refused to follow court policy over the Boxers, and virtually concluded a separate peace with the foreign powers. After signing a further humiliating peace agreement, the court returned to Beijing, and belatedly attempted to implement reforms. When Ci Xi died in 1908, there was no competent successor to continue the regency in the name of the next infant emperor, Xuan Tong or Pu Yi. Within three years the revolution had broken out and the dynasty was doomed.

In its last extremity, the imperial regime appealed to the former commander-in-chief of the imperial army, Yuan Shikai, who was out of favour with the new regent, to save it. The northern troops would obey only their old commander; the southern army had transferred its allegiance to the revolution. Yuan took command, but he did not intend to save the dynasty; he hoped to establish his own. First he showed by a brief campaign that he was a serious contender, then began to negotiate with the republicans. A plan was soon arranged. Yuan would bring about the peaceful abdication of the dynasty, which would, in return, be granted very favourable terms, and the republic would elect Yuan to be president. When the first parliament was convened (under conditions of flagrant corruption), Yuan had some of the more able members assassinated, and soon, having obtained a loan from the foreign powers without the assent of parliament, dissolved that body and ruled by decree. Futile and ineffective resistance in the south was rapidly suppressed. In 1914 Yuan acted to obtain support for a new dynasty with himself as emperor.

The outbreak of the First World War in 1914 was a factor that worked against this programme. It divided the foreign powers, and left Japan comparatively unfettered in Asia. Japan bribed and armed Yuan's secret opponents, his own generals, who resented his pretensions to the throne. On 25 December 1915 a revolt broke out, and within a few months it was evident that the generals had turned against him, and the projected monarchy was impossible. He renounced his plans and tried to retain the presidency, but he died in June 1916. His death was soon followed by contests among his former generals who controlled the provinces. The 'warlord era' from 1917 to 1927 was marked by a series of short civil wars fought entirely between rival militarists to gain control of revenues, and above all control of the impotent Government in Beijing, which could dispense the customs revenue collected under foreign supervision to service external loans, but which still left a valuable residue for whichever general could dominate Beijing. Within the country there was an increasing breakdown of law and order, banditry, and rural distress.

Nationalism and Communism

In May 1919 the students of Beijing had rioted against the Government's acceptance of the secret arrangement whereby Japan was to acquire the former German-leased port of Qingdao in Shandong. It was generally known that the corrupt politicians and their militarist master had received large sums from Japan for this virtually treasonable decision. The 'May Fourth Movement', as it became known, spread widely; it was the first sign of a new phase of the revolution, a revolt against Western dictation of China's affairs and fate, the first overt reaction of the generation who had grown up since the fall of the empire. The Communist Government subsequently commemorated it as the opening of a new era.

In May 1925 another violent outbreak followed upon the shooting by International Settlement police of student demonstrators in Shanghai. This time the wave of anger, directed against the United Kingdom and Japan, was nation-wide. There was a total boycott of British and Japanese trade and enterprise. Hong Kong's labour was withdrawn and its life all but paralysed. Further riots and shootings occurred in Guangzhou, and missionaries were compelled to leave the interior of China. Boycott pickets were established in the Treaty Ports and became an extra-legal militia.

Dr Sun Yat-sen, having failed to obtain any help from the Western powers to reinstate his Government—which he and his followers regarded as the only legal one—had turned to the USSR, which gave him the necessary support in arms, advisers and possibly finance. He regained control of Guangzhou in 1923 and swiftly set about the organization of an efficient government and a new model army. In 1921 the Chinese Communist Party (CCP) had been formally established at a meeting attended by 11 members, one of whom was Mao Zedong. At almost the same time a CCP had been formed in France by students living in Paris. One of its founders was Zhou Enlai. The two parties in China, the CCP still very small, and the Nationalists (Kuomintang—KMT) already gaining wide support, co-operated on the basis that members of the CCP might join the KMT as individuals, but there was no affiliation of the two parties. Aided by the repercussions of May 1925, revolutionary agitation increased rapidly.

After Dr Sun's death in 1925 all hope of peaceful reunion ended, and the KMT Government in Guangzhou prepared for war, which was launched in 1926 against the southern warlords. Success was rapid, and by early 1927 the whole of the middle Changjiang region had fallen to the KMT, whose armies, commanded by Jiang Jieshi (Chiang Kai-shek), were approaching Shanghai. Alarmed, the Treaty Powers sent troops to defend the International Settlement. The Shanghai workers and boycott pickets, organized by the Communists, rose and seized the Chinese-governed part of Shanghai, expelling the warlord army. When Jiang's forces arrived, they found Chinese Shanghai already under the control of the revolutionaries and confronting the acute danger of war with the foreign powers. Jiang had close connections with Chinese big business and finance in Shanghai. These people, good Nationalists, and no friends of the plundering warlords, were equally very fearful of social revolution and the Communist-controlled workers. Jiang, knowing that he had their support, carried out a sudden coup and massacre of the Communists (from which Zhou Enlai narrowly escaped) and broke with the CCP. For several months the situation was confused. Jiang formed a right-wing KMT Government at Nanjing; the former Guangzhou Government was now established at Wuhan, further up the Changjiang, and did not at first break with the CCP. In much of South China, particularly Hunan Province, social revolution, inspired by rural agitators led by Mao Zedong, was rapidly spreading through the country.

The two Nationalist Governments coalesced at Nanjing, and Jiang could turn his attention to combating the Communists. From 1929 to 1935 Jiang launched successive extermination campaigns against the Communists, who had now, under the leadership of Mao Zedong and Zhu De, established a Soviet area in the hill country on the Hunan–Jiangxi border. Jiang's campaigns failed until he devised, on the advice of his German staff officers, the plan of blockading the Jiangxi Soviet and thus forcing the Communists to break out or be starved into submission.

In 1935 the Communists set out on what came to be known as the 'Long March', with about 100,000 men and many of their dependants. A year later they reached Yanan, in north Shaanxi, after marching and counter-marching for more than 9,500 km, with 30,000 fighting men. However, they had not been defeated and, during that epic march, Mao Zedong had emerged as the unquestioned leader of the CCP, a position he retained until his death in 1976. The CCP, also, was fully emancipated from long-distance control by Moscow, which had proved uniformly disastrous for several years. Yanan, in the far north-west, was difficult to attack, almost impossible to blockade, and close to the areas soon to be threatened by the impending Japanese invasion.

The Japanese Invasion

In China it was widely recognized that the Japanese had embarked upon an all-out effort to conquer the country. Japan feared that, if it waited, China's power would increase, and it was also fearful of the rise of Communist influence. However, the Nanjing Government was still determined to destroy the CCP before resisting the Japanese. It was not until December 1936, when Jiang's own army, confronting the Communists at Xian in Shaanxi, mutinied and held him prisoner until he agreed to end the civil war, that he was forced to concede to the slogans 'Chinese do not fight Chinese' and 'unite to resist Japanese aggression'. The Japanese acted swiftly: in July 1937 they struck near Beijing, and the fighting soon escalated into a large-scale, but still undeclared, war.

In the early stages KMT resistance, as at Shanghai and the battle of Taierzhuang in Shandong, had been, at times, effective. However, Japanese armaments were far superior and Japan had almost unchallenged air power and complete control of the sea. The KMT forces were driven back from the coast to the mountainous interior of western China, losing nearly two-thirds of the provinces. The difficulties of forcing the Changjiang gorges halted the Japanese at that point, and the added challenge of holding vast conquered territories prevented any further advance. In those conquered territories, particularly northern China, the CCP was organizing the guerrilla resistance, which was soon to challenge Japanese authority.

The hope of a Chinese military collapse had faded; by early 1942 Japan was involved in the Second World War in the Pacific, and here, too, early victories were proving inconclusive and presaging Japan's eventual defeat. The CCP steadily expanded its guerrilla war until large areas were liberated, in which the CCP set up its own administration, gaining essential experience in social, economic and political reform, including the major problems of land reform. Japanese retaliation was brutal and ruthless, forcing the Chinese peasantry to rely on guerrilla groups for their protection. It roused the national consciousness of an indifferent apolitical peasantry, and was the main factor in building the power of the CCP to national level.

COMMUNIST CHINA

The war was ended neither by the still-passive resistance of the KMT in western China, nor by the activity of the guerrillas, but by the Japanese surrender in August 1945. The termination of the Japanese occupation left China deeply divided. The KMT took over from the Japanese in the southern and eastern provinces. The CCP controlled the rural north, and cut the communications when the KMT flew in men to take over the Japanese-held cities. Civil war threatened. The USA sent Gen. George C. Marshall to mediate, and to establish, if possible, a coalition government. He failed; neither side trusted the other, and the demands made by the KMT would have resulted in the demise of the CCP. Early in 1946 the foreshadowed civil war began, but the conflict proved to be neither as long nor as destructive as most Chinese had feared. It soon became evident that the CCP was going to win. Its troops fought well under firm discipline; the KMT forces had no will to war, and plundered wherever they went. Gross inflation was ruining the economy and alienating those to whom the KMT looked for support; corruption was rife in the KMT Government and army, and business was almost paralysed. There was nothing that the KMT could offer to enlist the support of any social class, not even the capitalists of Shanghai.

Therefore, despite massive US arms supplies, full control of the air, and vastly superior numbers, the KMT armies were wholly routed within three years. Vast numbers surrendered; relatively few were killed in battle. By the end of 1948 the Communists already held all of northern China, including the north-eastern provinces that formed Manzhou; they were on the banks of the Changjiang opposite Nanjing. The KMT was no longer united. A large group that favoured peace and negotiation compelled Jiang to renounce his presidency, but was unable to reduce his covert control over many units of the army. The Nanjing Government tried to secure peace, and nearly did so, but this effort was sabotaged by the agents of Jiang at the last moment, and the acting President, Li Zongren (Li Tsung-jen), was forced into exile. The war resumed, the Communists crossed the Changjiang, took Nanjing, then Shanghai, and swept on into the south and west. By late 1949, with the People's Republic of China having been proclaimed on 1 October in Beijing, the Communists ruled China. Jiang and his remnant forces retreated to Taiwan, where they and their successors have since remained (see the chapter on Taiwan for the subsequent history of the island and reunification initiatives).

Yet the failure to end the war by negotiation damaged China and the Communists: the continuity of the legitimate internationally recognized Government was destroyed. If the Nanjing regime had made peace—any sort of peace—it would have remained the legal Government, even if it were now led by the CCP. By failing to win this diplomatic victory, the Communists found their new regime subject to recognition, or non-recognition, at the will of foreign states, and their claim to China's seat at the UN disputed by the KMT protégés of the USA.

This situation continued to be one of the main causes of friction between the People's Republic and the Western powers, which, in their attitudes to the new China, were also deeply divided. To many of the Western, in particular the European, countries the fate of China was settled; the KMT on Taiwan was no longer significant. To the USA, on the other hand, the KMT regime was the 'real China' and the CCP considered to be Soviet 'puppets'. Thus, the CCP regime started out with the open ill will of the USA, the doubtful and wary acceptance of the United Kingdom and other smaller Western powers, and the unenthusiastic, cautious approval of the USSR. Only two years previously Stalin had assured the USA that he recognized only Jiang Jieshi as the legitimate ruler of China.

China's political affairs were now dominated by Mao Zedong, who was Chairman of the CCP from 1935 until his death in 1976. Chairman Mao, as he was known, also became Head of State in October 1949, but he relinquished this post in December 1958. His successor was Liu Shaoqi, First Vice-Chairman of the CCP, who was elected Head of State in April 1959. The first Premier (head of government) was Zhou Enlai, who held this office from October 1949 until his death in 1976. Zhou was also Minister of Foreign Affairs from 1949 to 1958.

Economic and Social Reform

The early policy of the new regime in Beijing was necessarily one of national renewal. The economy was at a standstill, communications were seriously interrupted, inflation was rampant and public utilities had deteriorated as a result of years of neglect. Even foreign trade was deflected into the supply of quick-selling consumer goods, largely useless to the economy, while valuable exports could not be moved and necessary imports could not be paid for. Nevertheless, the new regime, headed by men who had had no experience of urban life for more than 25 years, addressed these tasks with skill and expedition. Within weeks, the railways were running, and supplying coal to Shanghai in place of the normal seaborne supplies which were under a KMT naval blockade. Inflation was brought under steady control and ended, with the introduction of a new currency, in the following year. Thereafter, the Chinese currency, subjected to violent fluctuations for longer than living memory, remained stable. Foreign trade began to revive, cautiously, being limited to imports of essential goods, and to exports that would earn foreign exchange. The restoration of the cities, some of which were still in partial ruins from wartime bombing, and all neglected, insanitary and decaying, was made a high priority. This improvement brought widespread popular support for the CCP regime, and served to offset other policies that were less immediately appealing to many people. Land reform was the first major socialist, or communist, policy implemented. It was at first a simple redistribution of land in equal lots to all cultivators, including the families of former landlords.

The CCP did not intend to leave the matter at the level of peasant proprietorship of tiny plots. From the outset, mutual aid teams were organized to manage the busy agricultural period. Later these were developed into the two stages of co-operative farming, and still later the co-operatives were grouped together into communes. In this way, private ownership of agricultural land was abolished and replaced by the communal system under which each former owner had a share of the commune's revenue allotted by 'work points', based on hours worked. State-owned collective farms were confined to newly opened lands or reclaimed land not previously privately owned. Whatever other defects and difficulties the new land system encountered, owing to bad weather or administrative over-centralization, it can be said with certainty to have made two major advances: the constant threat of starvation in bad times receded; and water control and supply were made more possible by the new institutional units that replaced the smallholdings.

The Korean War and Relations with the USSR

The Korean War of 1950–53 gave rise to much debate with regard to its origins. Chinese intervention, after UN forces began to move northwards into the Democratic People's Republic of Korea (DPRK) in a counter-offensive, was forewarned, but the warnings were not heeded. To the Chinese this movement was a direct threat to their vital industrial area of south Manzhou (Liaoning Province), bordering on the DPRK. It was also widely feared in China to be the preliminary move to an invasion of China itself. The extent to which the Chinese intervention was intended to reassert Chinese authority, rather than Soviet influence, in Manzhou and in Korea, remains conjectural. Later developments seem to indicate that this consideration was important. It was certainly a consequence of the war, because, after the cease-fire, the USSR soon renounced the special position that the Chinese had conceded to it in the port of Dalian and over the railways across Manzhou.

In China the effect of the war was to strengthen the prestige of the Government, which had, for the first time for more than a century (if ever), shown itself able to counter a large-scale Western army. In the years that followed the signing of the truce to end the war in Korea, Chinese relations with the DPRK were not always smooth. The pretensions of President Kim Il Sung to be a major ideological leader were not appreciated in Beijing. The DPRK's attitude of neutrality in the Sino-Soviet dispute, although undoubtedly very wise, tempered relations with China. On the other hand, foreign observers drew the conclusion that China exercised a restraining influence on the adventurism of President Kim (and subsequently Kim Jong Il) in respect of the Republic of Korea. However, the DPRK was certainly not a Chinese satellite.

In 1957, in the 'Hundred Flowers' movement, the Government permitted open criticism of its methods, if not its basic policies. The extent of the resulting criticisms was probably disconcerting to the authorities, yet much of what was said made its mark and led to some change of style in the CCP. The 'Hundred Flowers' movement was almost contemporary with the first phase of the Sino-Soviet dispute, which grew over the years until the two countries became completely estranged. The original disagreement over ideology developed into a dispute more concerned with national interests, especially after the USSR withdrew its technical aid and experts from China in 1960. This was a severe reverse to the developing Chinese industrialization, but the set-back was overcome. Meanwhile, the economic and social initiative known as the 'Great Leap Forward', which began in 1958, had major repercussions for China (see Recent History). After a series of border clashes in 1969, negotiations for a settlement of Sino-Soviet differences concerning the border regions opened in Beijing in October 1969. Subsequent relations between the two countries long remained under strain. The fear of a possible Soviet attack, using either conventional or nuclear weapons, strongly influenced China's military and diplomatic planning. The expectation entertained by the Soviet leaders that, after the death of Mao Zedong, China would prove willing to renew the former friendship, or at least to modify its criticisms of the USSR, was not realized until mid-1989, when relations between the two countries were officially normalized.

The Tibet Issue and Relations with India

All Chinese Governments since the fall of the Qing dynasty have continued to assert rights of sovereignty over Tibet (Xizang), although the western two-thirds of the territory were, in practice, independent after 1912. Tibet was occupied in 1950 by Chinese Communist forces. In March 1959 there was an unsuccessful armed uprising by Tibetans opposed to Chinese rule. As a result, the Dalai Lama, the head of Tibet's Buddhist clergy and thus the region's spiritual leader, fled with some 100,000 supporters to northern India, where a government-in-exile was established. The Chinese ended the former dominance of the lamas (Buddhist monks) and destroyed many monasteries. Tibet became an 'Autonomous Region' of China in September 1965, but the majority of Tibetans have continued to regard the Dalai Lama as their 'god-king', and to resent the Chinese presence, leading to intermittent unrest.

In 1962 the establishment of Chinese forces on the Indian border with Tibet led to disputes about the position of the undefined and unmarked boundary. China proposed negotiations, but the Indian side rejected them, asserting that the frontier had been established by the United Kingdom before Indian independence. The tension escalated into a border war when Indian forces attempted to expel Chinese troops from some disputed positions. The confrontation resulted in a Chinese victory, which could have led to an invasion of Indian Assam (now known as Asom), but China unilaterally terminated the operations and withdrew to the positions already established before the conflict. Soviet verbal support for the Indian claim considerably embittered relations between China and the USSR. The frontier dispute remained unsettled.

Recent History

SHAUN BRESLIN

Based on an earlier article by MICHAEL YAHUDA

Revised for this edition by KERRY BROWN

THE CULTURAL REVOLUTION

Political Background

Many aspects of the Cultural Revolution of 1966–76 remain controversial, but few dispute that its origins may be traced to political developments that began in the late 1950s. The upheavals in Eastern Europe in 1956, and Mao Zedong's growing doubts about the Soviet leadership, led him to the view that, even after the revolution and the establishment of a socialist society on the Leninist model, it was possible that a restoration of capitalism could take place. By 1965 he had convinced himself that this was indeed happening in the USSR, where a complacent party élite had become isolated from the Soviet people on whose behalf it supposedly ruled, a development akin to the emergence of a new ruling class that exercised a dictatorship over, rather than of, the proletariat. If action were not taken, so Mao believed, it might occur in China too and the whole revolution would be compromised.

Mao's theory stressed the importance of leadership and of the values that were espoused and institutionalized by those leaders. Rather than arguing that economic reform would alter the way people thought, and consequently lead to political revolution, he instead maintained that after the political revolution, citizens might be persuaded to change their ideas and attitudes, thereby engendering economic change. In other words, the best way of promoting economic change was first to win the 'hearts and minds' of the people and convince them of the superiority of (his) socialist ideas. Just as Mao had regarded the peasantry as a potential revolutionary force before 1949, he similarly saw the countryside as a source of continued revolutionary zeal and both political and economic change after the revolution.

In contrast, a numerically larger group of senior leaders was more inspired, rather than forewarned, by the experience of the Communist Party of the Soviet Union. While these leaders did not agree on all aspects of policy, they shared a common desire to construct a stable political structure underpinned by a strong professional cadre of party officials. They also believed that economic growth strategies should focus on industrialization in the towns and cities, to be achieved by organization, expertise and capital, rather than by revolutionary enthusiasm. In addition to these conflicting positions, Mao's increasing antipathy to the USSR and a growing frustration with his colleagues resulted in the political conflicts that punctuated Chinese history at regular intervals during the first three decades of the People's Republic of China, established in 1949.

The first major division within the hierarchy of the Chinese Communist Party (CCP) emerged in 1954, with the removal of Gao Gang and Rao Shushi. Both officials had been leading protagonists of the revolution, having occupied important positions in the new post-1949 political order—notably in establishing party and government structures in Manchuria (Manzhou) and East China respectively. Both were transferred to the central Government in Beijing in 1953, with some analysts suggesting that these were not the promotions that they initially appeared to be, but instead constituted a ploy to separate them from their local power bases. It is certainly true that Gao Gang, in particular, had developed a strong personal relationship with Stalin, the Soviet leader, much closer than approved by Mao, raising the suspicion that he was attempting to construct an independent Manchurian power base or even to turn Manchuria into an autonomous, Soviet-satellite, state. Yet it also appears that Gao and Rao emerged unsuccessfully from the factional disputes over the designation of Mao's successor. Gao committed suicide in 1954, and Rao formally lost his party membership and was imprisoned in the following year. Whatever the exact cause of their downfall, this was not to be the last time that relations with the USSR were to form at least part of the cause of internal conflict.

The Gao-Rao affair was conducted largely in secret and restricted to an intra-party issue. By contrast, the 'Hundred Flowers' movement was very much a public affair. That campaign, undertaken in the spring of 1957, urged professionals and intellectuals to criticize the confined autocracy of the CCP, but it was resisted by some of the other, more orthodox, Leninist leaders. Although originally instigated by Mao to use the people to censure his opponents in the Party, criticism was not simply restricted to their policies, and Mao himself was criticized. The movement was called to a close and replaced by an 'anti-rightist' movement which was to plunge hundreds of thousands who had simply done what they were asked to do into a disgrace from which they were not to be rehabilitated for another 20 years.

In the aftermath of the 'anti-rightist' movement, party officials across China were keen to display their 'leftist' revolutionary credentials. In this situation, Mao's proposals for rapid economic development built on the revolutionary enthusiasm of the masses were widely embraced by local leaders, even though the proposals had previously been rejected by the Party's senior leadership. Initially, relatively cautious calls for a faster transition towards real communism were put aside, as the peasantry was first encouraged and cajoled, and later often forced, into communal living. The 'Great Leap Forward' of 1958 at first appeared to be successful: not only had the process of communization seemingly confirmed the masses' revolutionary enthusiasm, but industrial and agricultural output had also apparently increased. However, this ostensible success proved to be a serious misrepresentation. While peasants laboured to produce worthless steel from backyard furnaces, the fields remained ill-attended and grain rotted before it could be harvested. As production targets were repeatedly raised, cadres increasingly inflated output statistics to prove their loyalty to the revolution and to Mao. The result was the erroneous impression that the population was embracing communism and that grain supplies were plentiful. Furthermore, central leaders used the supposed excess production to accelerate the process of repaying loans to the USSR. There is now evidence that Mao was perfectly aware of the terrible consequences of his policies, but he believed that these were merely short-term costs in order to achieve a greater longer-term political objective.

The 'Great Leap' proved to be an unmitigated disaster, marking the most tragic period of Maoist rule. Chinese historian Yang Jisheng in his epic study from 2008, 'Tombstone', estimated that up to 45m. people died in this era. Although most of the leaders had initially supported the 'Great Leap' programme, the leadership that met to review the situation in August 1959 was divided. The Minister of Defence, Marshal Peng Dehuai, severely criticized the 'Great Leap' and, at Mao's insistence, he was dismissed. Mao had construed Peng's disapproval of the programme as a personal criticism. The episode may be regarded as a break with those norms of CCP procedure that allowed for open debate (at the highest levels at least) and as the beginning of the elevation of Mao to a higher authority than the collective wisdom of the CCP. Peng was replaced by Marshal Lin Biao, one of the great heroes of the Civil War of 1945–49 against the nationalists, who soon ingratiated himself with Mao by elevating the study of Mao Zedong Thought in the armed forces and by emphasizing the latter's role as a 'people's army', rather than fulfilling the more professional role inspired by the Soviet example. To aid this study of Mao, Marshal Lin oversaw the production of a new collection of his greatest works, 'The Highest Targets', which was to become compulsory reading for all good revolutionaries, being more popularly known as 'the little red book'.

Much of this was not immediately apparent, as Mao retreated from the daily management of domestic affairs, relinquishing responsibility for this to senior leaders such as Liu Shaoqi, Deng Xiaoping and Zhou Enlai. Chen Yun, whose original proposals for economic growth had been superseded by the 'Great Leap', returned to plan the country's economic recovery, which included a massive reduction in targets, allowing peasants more autonomy to use their land as they thought best, and interaction with the capitalist global economy to import much-needed food (these policies were to have haunting parallels with those introduced after 1978—see below). While these leaders directed China's recovery from the effects of the three difficult years of 1959–61 through a focus on stability, professionalism and expertise, Mao apparently confined himself to foreign affairs and ostensibly ideological questions related to the Sino-Soviet conflict. He later complained that he had felt like a 'Buddha placed on the shelf' in this period.

The Initial Phase, 1966–69

Mao's thinking was a complex combination of ruthless political pragmatism and lofty idealism. He himself celebrated contradictions, writing some of his most accomplished theoretical works about this. His greatest fear was to see the Party, which he had done so much to bring to power, slide into revisionism, forsaking its Utopian ideals in order to become a mundane bureaucracy. The human catastrophe of the 'Great Leap' did not cause Mao to question the fundamental basis of his ideas. Instead, he focused on the organizational and ideological failings that had prevented the concepts from working in reality. Mao made his first attempt to reassert his ideas by launching a Socialist Education Movement in 1962 (also often referred to as the 'Four Clean-ups Movement'). The aim was to remove from politics, economy, organization and ideology those reactionary elements that were preventing the adoption of his revolutionary line. According to Mao's thinking, once the process was complete and cadres and masses alike were re-imbued with his correct ideas, then the goals of the 'Great Leap' could be reintroduced and the transition to communism would be attainable.

Rather than oppose the movement outright, Liu Shaoqi and Deng Xiaoping (and probably also Zhou Enlai, although his position was much more ambiguous and nuanced) instead decided to adopt and thus control it. Mao increasingly urged that party members be subject to the scrutiny of the masses and be removed if they were not considered to be serving the people (the idea of 'new democracy', which he had articulated in the 1940s). In contrast, Liu and Deng argued that the Party was obliged to lead and that, rather than becoming another mass movement, socialist education should remain an intra-party affair. As a result, Mao's goal of socialist education was reduced to a relatively minor campaign that had more or less ended by 1965.

Thwarted in his attempts to reassert a dominant role in 1962, Mao embarked on a more ambitious (and some would argue desperate) campaign to restore his authority by launching the 'Great Proletarian Cultural Revolution' in 1966. The movement was directed against those 'party leaders in authority taking the capitalist road': namely Liu Shaoqi, Deng Xiaoping and the other leaders regarded as obstructive. Mao's shock troops were to be rebellious groups (subsequently nicknamed 'Red Guards'), principally composed of middle-school and university students who were to draw inspiration from Mao himself—now the supreme authority in all matters. They were to be guided by the newly established Cultural Revolution Group of the Central Committee, a prominent member of which was Mao's wife, Jiang Qing. Having been denied a political role for more than 25 years at the behest of Mao's political peers, she sought to gain revenge against those who had slighted her. Even more tragic than this were her narrow, dogmatic views on art and culture, as a result of which these areas were effectively suppressed to such an extent that they were non-existent during the decade of the Cultural Revolution.

The Red Guards initially focused their attacks on teachers and CCP leaders in schools and universities. The campaign quickly extended to criticism of anybody who was thought to have bad class ancestry, links with the West, bourgeois ideas or feudal thoughts, or indeed anything that the specific team of Red Guards deemed to be anti-revolutionary at the time. These 'enemies' were typically paraded in public and subjected to fierce verbal and often physical attacks (called 'struggle meetings'). Ad hoc executions and deaths through beatings and suicides were not uncommon. Historical, cultural and religious sites were attacked, and many all but destroyed, as they represented old feudal beliefs rather than the modern socialist Maoist belief. However unpalatable it may be to state this now, the Cultural Revolution was a popularist movement, with vast social mobilization and enthusiastic following from a major segment of at least the urban population that existed then. Its impact in the rural areas was much more modest. However, questions remain over the extent to which Mao was cynically manipulating youthful fervour and whether he actually saw real revolutionary potential in this area.

This popular mass movement ran concurrently with an élite-level purge of those who opposed the Maoist path, which removed government ministers and important members of the CCP's Political Bureau (Politburo). This is the other crucial aspect of the movement. Even those who had already been removed, such as Peng Dehuai, were brought back into the public arena for a second stage of vilification. Such leaders were typically condemned at mass meetings before being subjected to ad hoc punishment. The number of people who died as a result of the Cultural Revolution is unclear; estimates range from 1m. to 4m. However, as the writer Ba Jin, who lived through this period, stated several years later, it was more as a spiritual holocaust than a physical one that the movement made the deepest impression, shaping the thinking of a generation.

As with the Socialist Education Movement, Liu Shaoqi initially tried to comply with the Cultural Revolution in order to control it. In April 1966 he presided over a meeting of the Political Bureau at which it was announced that an anti-Party clique of senior leaders (Lu Dingyi, Yang Shangkun, Peng Zhen and Luo Ruiqing) had been suppressed. However, the Cultural Revolution was not to be confined to a limited purge. Mao himself had singled out Liu Shaoqi—the official whom he had once described as his eventual successor—as the leading 'capitalist roader' responsible for preventing the return to Mao's correct socialist road. Crowds massed outside Liu's offices in Beijing, effectively placing him under house arrest. He was formally dismissed as Head of State in October 1968; denied medical treatment, he died in prison in 1969. Deng Xiaoping was also forced to undergo self-criticism and disgrace (in 1966), and few other senior leaders survived unscathed.

Moreover, by the end of 1966 the CCP itself had virtually ceased to operate as a national organization, and the state administration was barely functioning. The one truly national organization, with an effective chain of command from the centre down to the localities, was the army. Chinese politics became highly polarized and factionalized. This was to be its predominant character for the ensuing 10 years. The Cultural Revolution itself lacked coherence. Mao's theory of how to avoid what he regarded as a counter-revolution was seriously flawed, as he had not articulated a clear vision of the political system to replace the one that was seen to have gone awry. All groups and factions in China claimed to be the true followers of Mao Zedong Thought, and each one stigmatized its opponents as revisionists. When the two radicals, Yao Wenyuan and Zhang Chunqiao (who had been so useful to Mao in launching the 'Revolution' and who were later to be condemned as members of the notorious 'Gang of Four'), reported to Mao in January 1967 about the establishment of a Shanghai Commune, modelled on the Paris Commune of 1871, Mao turned against them, dismissing the new institution as anarchist and insisting on the need for leaders. Meanwhile, the army had been brought in to restore order, and it soon began to play a greater role in public life. Rejecting the Commune, Mao turned to the so-called 'three-way revolutionary committees' as the solution to China's absence of organization. These were largely dominated by the army, and also included representatives of surviving older cadres and of the 'revolutionary masses'.

By 1968 Red Guard factions, reduced to their hard-core members, were engaged in internecine armed struggles. Finally, on Mao's insistence, the organizations were disbanded and, alongside millions of educated young Chinese, their members were sent to the countryside. Mao urged a reconstruction of the CCP. In early 1969, as fighting took place on the riverine border with the USSR, the Ninth Party Congress was convened. The newly elected Central Committee was dominated by men in military uniform (well over one-half of the members of the former Committee were either in prison, or dead), but it also included people who had been promoted during the Cultural Revolution, as well as a small proportion of surviving senior leaders. A new Constitution was proclaimed, in which Lin Biao was designated as Mao's successor—an unusual and irregular constitutional provision. The Congress also reviewed the Cultural Revolution.

Factional Conflicts, 1969–76

Many in the West initially interpreted the CCP Congress of 1969 as signalling the end of the Cultural Revolution. The events of mid-1968 certainly brought about its end at street level. Henceforth the Cultural Revolution took the form of increasingly ruthless power struggles at the highest level of the leadership, and clashes between those, on the one side, who tried to institutionalize the so-called 'new-born things' of the 'Revolution' (principally in education and culture, but also in resisting allegedly revisionist economic practices) and those, on the other, who stressed the need for modernization. Underlying all these disputes were the questions of the succession to the ageing Mao and the future direction of China.

The official account of the episode that led to Lin Biao's rapid demise from heir apparent to counter-revolutionary described him as plotting the assassination of Mao after having been denied the position of Head of State. Having failed to kill Mao in August–September 1971, Lin allegedly escaped in a requisitioned aircraft, but died when it crashed in neighbouring Mongolia. Whatever the truth, Lin's death resulted in a realignment of factional powers. Lin was initially accused of having been an 'ultra-leftist' when news of what he had done was released almost a year after his death, but this designation was problematic for other leaders, such as Mao's wife, who had also benefited from the Cultural Revolution. To solve this problem, Lin was redesignated as a 'rightist' who had only been pretending to be a 'leftist', with the intention of restoring capitalism. The fact that he died trying to flee to the USSR showed where his real revisionist loyalties lay.

With Lin now denounced as a counter-revolutionary, of either the left or right, the revolutionary credentials of those whom he had previously opposed and criticized required reconsideration. As Lin's followers were removed from power across the country, many of the leaders who had been disgraced earlier in the Cultural Revolution and accused by Lin and his supporters, were now regarded as having been erroneously criticized. Over the next five years many officials who had been denounced as counter-revolutionaries only a few years previously were brought back to office. The most notable and important of these rehabilitated officials was Deng Xiaoping, who had been reviled in 1966 as China's 'No. 2 capitalist roader' but re-emerged in April 1973. Unbeknown to the outside world, Premier Zhou Enlai was terminally ill, and Deng rapidly assumed many of Zhou's responsibilities.

Deng's rehabilitation brought about a new phase of political struggles between the uncompromising 'leftist' Cultural Revolutionaries led by Jiang Qing, on the one side, and the modernizers headed by Zhou and Deng on the other. Much of this struggle took the form of highly confusing debates on abstruse historical allegories that few beyond the protagonists themselves genuinely understood at the time. An uneasy balance between the two sides existed for almost three years, reaching a climax when Zhou Enlai died in January 1976. Deng Xiaoping delivered the funeral address and promptly disappeared from public view. At the Qing Ming Festival—the traditional time for honouring the dead—in April, public demonstrations in memory of Zhou took place in the major cities. These were the first truly spontaneous demonstrations to have occurred in the history of the People's Republic. The principal demonstration was in Beijing, where hundreds of thousands of people laid wreaths that pointedly eulogized the late Premier, with some even condemning Jiang Qing and criticizing Mao's rule. On 5 April 1976 this escalated into a serious public disturbance, known as the 'Tiananmen incident', which led to hundreds of arrests and the deaths of some of the demonstrators. The episode was condemned as counter-revolutionary at a tense meeting of the CCP's Central Committee, and Deng Xiaoping was denounced as the instigator. Deng was removed from his official posts, but he was allowed to retain party membership. The little-known Hua Guofeng, hitherto the Minister of Public Security, was appointed Premier and First Vice-Chairman of the CCP. As Mao was becoming increasingly incapacitated, the radicals frantically sought to bolster their position in a final bid to denigrate Deng and his supporters. The country was in a chaotic state, and was later said to have been on the verge of civil war.

Mao died, aged 82, on 9 September 1976. With Deng in supposed disgrace, the path should have been clear for those positioned on the left of the Cultural Revolution to assert themselves as the new 'second generation' of Chinese leaders in succession to Zhou and Mao. However, one of Hua Guofeng's first acts in power was to arrest Jiang Qing and her three associates, possibly because they had been manoeuvring to oust Hua, or possibly because the new Premier wanted to dissociate himself from them. They were quickly condemned as the 'Gang of Four', the cause of all the radical excesses of the previous decade, and the Cultural Revolution was declared to be at an end.

TOWARDS A NEW POLITICAL ORDER

Hua Guofeng and Deng Xiaoping

Hua Guofeng, as Mao's chosen successor and as the man who instigated the arrest of the 'Gang of Four', assumed the post of Chairman of the CCP, alongside his premiership of the State Council (cabinet). As he now notionally succeeded both Mao Zedong and Zhou Enlai, Hua was theoretically more powerful than any other communist leader, including Mao himself. However, this power was more institutional than real. A relative newcomer to central politics, he and a number of undistinguished members of the Political Bureau were beneficiaries of the Cultural Revolution. They did not have the prestige, the seniority, the experience or the wide range of contacts of the pre-revolutionary senior leaders who had either survived the purges or who had been removed and then rehabilitated after 1971. Moreover, neither Hua nor his fellow beneficiaries could wholly criticize the Cultural Revolution or reverse the verdict of the 'Tiananmen incident' without undermining their own position. They wanted to attribute the worst excesses of the Cultural Revolution to the 'Gang of Four', but had been active proponents of the movement themselves. Ultimate responsibility for suppressing the demonstration of 5 April 1976 lay with Hua himself, as Minister of Public Security. Moreover, while they were committed to modernizing China, the modernization programme had been initiated not by them but by Zhou Enlai and subsequently influenced by Deng Xiaoping and other rehabilitated victims of the Cultural Revolution.

By 1977 Deng had returned to prominence again, and in August he was restored to his former posts. Hua and his fellow beneficiaries from the Cultural Revolution sought in vain to retain power by adhering to Mao's fading prestige. They advanced the slogan of following whatever Mao had said and whatever he had done, and thus became known as the 'whateverist faction'. In early 1978 Hua Guofeng announced a grandiose plan to modernize the country by 1985 (an extension of the 10-Year Plan advocated by Deng in 1975). The economy, already seriously out of balance, was soon dangerously overextended. The situation culminated at the third plenary session of the 11th CCP Central Committee in December 1978, which marked Deng's de facto return to power.

The Significance of the Third Plenum

The Third Plenum of the 11th Congress of late 1978 is rightly regarded as one of the major turning points in the history of the

People's Republic. It set in motion a series of reforms that brought about a fundamentally new political and economic order. Although Mao had died two years previously, Hua Guofeng had retained elements of the Mao period. Consequently, the Third Plenum in many respects marked the beginning of the post-Mao era in China. It also brought new members into the Political Bureau, notably Hu Yaobang, hitherto director of the CCP's organization department and prior to that a provincial official in Sichuan. Above all, the Third Plenum set the stage for a soundly based programme of economic reforms, which could take place against a background of greater institutional regularity, legality and freedom from the fear of chaotic political campaigns. This also entailed a re-examination of CCP history, a rehabilitation of past leaders and, indeed, a reconsideration of hundreds of thousands of unjust verdicts on people of humbler status.

The political changes that took place at the Third Plenum occurred within a wider context of popular pressure for political reform. Groups of young people, many of whom were former Red Guards, displayed wall posters in the centre of Beijing at a specially designated 'Democracy Wall' and circulated their own unofficial magazines, demanding the rectification of the wrongs committed during the Cultural Revolution. With the excesses of the past officially acknowledged following the arrest of the 'Gang of Four', a new strand of literature emerged cataloguing the many injustices that citizens had endured: 'scar literature' or 'literature of the wounded'. Both developments proved useful to Deng and his reformers in the period prior to the Third Plenum, recalling darker political days from which Hua was unable to dissociate himself. Yet when the 'Democracy Wall' activists began to demand Western-style pluralist democracy and legality, the movement became an embarrassment that had to be suppressed in the name of order. Deng issued a statement outlining the limits of tolerance: any action that challenged the primacy of the socialist road, the dictatorship of the proletariat, the leadership of the CCP and Marxism-Leninism-Mao Zedong Thought was deemed illegitimate. However, the true interpretation of Mao Zedong Thought at this stage was increasingly what Deng and his followers wanted it to be, not necessarily what Mao himself had said and believed.

This redefinition of Mao Zedong's thoughts and actions formed a crucial part of the Party's verdict on its own history that it revealed in September 1981. While the Soviet leadership was able to denounce Stalin's excesses and draw inspiration and legitimacy from the preceding revolutionary generation, this was not possible in China. As the main figurehead of the revolution and the founder of modern China, Mao was both the primary source of revolutionary legitimacy and, through the 'Great Leap Forward' and the Cultural Revolution, simultaneously the main problem. Thus, the official resolution on party history gave a very positive assessment of Mao, emphasizing his many great successes in leading the CCP to power. Nevertheless, the Party was critical of his excessive personal power and regarded him as having been too 'leftist' in his final 20 years, stating that this was because of the evil effects of bad-intentioned and exploitative people around him. The Cultural Revolution was condemned as an unmitigated disaster, based on a theory by Mao that bore no relation to reality. As Mao Zedong Thought was now redefined to equate to the collective wisdom of party leaders rather than simply Mao's ideas, by disregarding collective leadership and embarking on his radical 'adventures', Mao himself was deemed to have contravened what was considered to be Mao Zedong Thought.

While Mao's mistakes provided the basis for the Cultural Revolution, the terrible excesses carried out under its name were attributed to alleged plotters such as the Lin Biao group and the 'Gang of Four', members of which had been put on trial in the previous year and sentenced to long periods of imprisonment. Jiang Qing and Zhang Chunqiao had been sentenced to death, unless they repented within two years. Although no evidence was presented suggesting their repentance, their sentences were eventually commuted to life imprisonment. Meanwhile, some of those of lesser rank who had been found responsible for the persecution and, indeed, for the deaths of fewer people during the Cultural Revolution, were in fact executed.

By the 12th CCP Congress in September 1982, Deng had succeeded in bringing to an end the practice of life-long tenure of senior CCP positions. A new Central Advisory Commission was established for those of at least 40 years' standing as CCP members. Much emphasis was placed on the need to promote more professional, young and middle-aged party members to positions of high responsibility. In December 1982 a new Constitution was promulgated, which, while reinforcing the limits to legitimate criticism of the Party and the Government, contained more detailed provisions than ever before on citizens' rights and the specific functions of organizations. In short, the Third Plenum ushered in a period of political change aimed at promoting China's economic development without sacrificing the Party's monopoly of power. Despite the continual tension between the ensuing economic transformations and the unyielding political dominance of the Party, the system introduced by the plenary session in December 1978 was to endure for longer than any previous period in the history of the People's Republic.

Modernization under Deng Xiaoping: Aims and Achievements

The purpose of the economic modernization of the new order was defined as the development of the productive forces in order to raise the standard of living of the Chinese people, and to ensure the long-term security of China in accordance with its status as a world power. The ultimate purpose of the reforms was to transform the country into a 'modern socialist state with Chinese characteristics'. The process of reform, described by Deng Xiaoping in 1979 as China's 'second revolution', lacked any coherent theoretical framework. It proceeded intermittently in a pragmatic accommodation to changing circumstances. Nevertheless, the economic achievements were remarkable, with an average annual growth rate from 1978 of nearly 10%. Foreign trade expanded rapidly, as did China's engagement with the international economy. However, this success was uneven. The state-owned enterprises (SOEs) that employed the bulk of the urban labour force stagnated, while the rural-based industries and the foreign-orientated sectors showed strong growth.

The reforms began in the agricultural sector, as peasants were allowed to revert to family farming at the expense of the collective. Starting in the poorer areas, peasant households were permitted to contract for the use of land for 15 years or more. After fulfilling certain production quotas for the State, they were allowed to cultivate almost any crops they wished, and either sell them to state agencies at above-quota prices or market the produce themselves. In terms of removing the State from the economy, these reforms were relatively minor, particularly compared with later liberalizing reforms. However, their importance in commencing the process of reform and the transition from socialism cannot be exaggerated. The reforms also led to a phenomenal growth in agricultural output.

However, as the ratio of land to population inevitably continued to decrease, there remained a need to combine greater efficiency in farming with the provision of better employment prospects for the millions of unemployed or underemployed peasants in the countryside. Concerned that the campaign for rural efficiency might lead to a flood of migrants to the cities, the Government encouraged peasants to 'leave the land but not the countryside': to stop farming and move into industrial activity in the countryside. Up to 100m. people found employment in these small Township and Village Enterprises (TVEs) from 1984 to 1997, when the sector began to contract as a result of overcapacity and increased competition. In addition to being a very useful means of absorbing surplus rural labour, TVEs proved to be one of the main engines of economic growth during this period and also made substantial contributions to China's growing international economic profile.

Reform of the urban industrial sector proved more difficult by far. Following a three-year period of readjusting structural imbalances between the different sectors of the economy, in October 1984 the Government announced an ambitious programme to revitalize the planning system and the state-run industries. With the exception of a few strategic economic categories, mandatory planning was to be replaced for the bulk of industry by 'guidance planning' or by the macro-economic

controls of market forces. The SOEs were to be responsible for marketing their products and for their profitability. Accordingly, the programme envisaged that enterprise managers would have greater authority to reward and, if necessary, to dismiss workers. It also anticipated that loss-making enterprises might even be at risk of bankruptcy. Managers were given the right to sell above-quota production at higher prices. However, unlike other parts of the economy, the SOEs proved very difficult to reform as they provided life-long employment, social services and housing.

These economic and political developments were accompanied by social changes with far-reaching implications. In 1979 Deng Xiaoping finally removed the stigma attendant upon intellectuals for the previous 30 years, by declaring them to be members of the working class. Former business executives and industrialists, and even former landlords and rich peasants, were also, in the main, redefined as members of the working populace. Positive encouragement was extended to overseas Chinese communities to contribute to China's modernization. The 'compatriots' of Hong Kong were the most active element in the development of the various Special Economic Zones (SEZs) located on the southern coast, accounting for up to 80% of joint ventures and other forms of economic co-operation. The adjoining province of Guangdong also benefited from the association with Hong Kong. Indeed, the 'open door' policy was deemed so successful that, beginning with the Seventh Five-Year Plan (1986–92), China's economic strategy was orientated to give priority to the development of its southern and eastern coastal regions. At the same time, the 'twenty-two regulations' were enacted to create a more favourable business environment for external investors, including allowing wholly foreign-owned enterprises to operate in the SEZs, rather than insisting on joint venture partnerships with Chinese factories. These regulations represented a major change in China's relationship with the global economy, providing the basis for increased foreign investment to produce exports to third markets.

Thus, rural society was transformed, as the family unit gained at the expense of collectivism and as the significance of the market and rural-based industries increased sharply. The capitalist global economy, so recently the epitome of all that China opposed, was embraced as a source of capital, investment, expertise and employment. The social role of the CCP declined even as its political role was rearticulated and focused. Many party members and officials drew on their administrative experience and extensive personal networks to benefit from the rural reform that they were implementing by establishing themselves as 'specialized households', the start of a process of creating a non-state sector in the economy.

At the same time rural unemployment, or underemployment, became more evident, while the long-standing provisions against the mobility of the population remained. In the cities tension grew between the traditionally favoured state enterprises and the numerous bureaucracies on the one hand, and the newer collective and private operators on the other. The impetus for money-making and consumerism replaced Maoist orthodoxy, while corruption, nepotism and official racketeering became more visible and widespread. Most urban residents and a growing number of rural dwellers gained access to the 'global village' of international television and radio transmissions. Traditional pre-communist beliefs and customs re-emerged, particularly in the countryside. Official injunctions, designed to inculcate the values of 'socialist spiritual civilization', were less than successful. The more conservative, veteran leaders initiated brief campaigns against reformist CCP leaders and intellectuals. The first, against 'spiritual pollution' in 1983–84, rapidly went to excess and was brought to a premature end. The others, against 'bourgeois liberalization' in early 1987 and mid-1989, involved the dismissals of the General Secretaries of the CCP, Hu Yaobang and his replacement, Zhao Ziyang. These could all be seen as related to the social tensions engendered by the reforms, as they involved the problem of upholding the identity of China as a socialist country under CCP rule, while simultaneously reforming the economy along quasi-capitalist lines and opening it up to foreign influence.

ISSUES OF POLITICAL REFORM

By the mid-1980s there was evidence of major divisions within the Chinese élite about the direction and pace of economic reform and, above all, about the extent to which political reform should be a necessary component of economic change. Traditional communist values, at least as they had been articulated in the Maoist period, no longer held sway. Indeed, the lack of belief in socialism and in the CCP itself, which was a legacy of the Cultural Revolution, became a crisis for the system. This crisis was intensified by the corruption and nepotism that were prevalent in the Party at all levels. Intellectuals who had hitherto been relatively quiescent under party rule became increasingly critical and independent in their thinking.

Although it was not immediately apparent, the sixth plenary session of the 12th CCP Central Committee, held in September 1986, signalled the onset of an ideological struggle between contending factions within the Chinese leadership, which finally culminated in the Beijing massacre of 4 June 1989. On the one side were those who favoured greater ideological diversity, democratization and structural reform as necessary for long-term economic modernization. On the other was a more conservative group supported by many of the long-serving revolutionary veterans, who held a more doctrinaire concept of the political role of the CCP and who feared the potentially disruptive effects of some of the proposed reforms. Underlying the struggle was the question of the choice of a successor to Deng Xiaoping. Indeed, as the post-Mao leadership had replaced many of the younger generation who had risen to power in the Cultural Revolution with an older generation that had previously been in power in the early 1960s, there arose the wider question of finding successors to a whole generation of octogenarian revolutionary veterans.

In December 1986 demonstrations by students, demanding a greater measure of democracy, took place in Hefei, and then in Shanghai, Beijing and other major cities. By January 1987 the CCP had condemned these demonstrations as a threat to public order, and new municipal laws were enacted to prohibit them. Conservative leaders of the CCP and the army initiated a campaign against 'bourgeois liberalization' (defined, at the sixth plenary session of the 12th CCP Central Committee, as 'the negation of the socialist system in favour of capitalism'). On 16 January it was announced that Hu Yaobang had submitted his resignation as General Secretary of the CCP, having been compelled to undergo 'self-criticism', following accusations that he had allowed 'bourgeois liberalization' to spread. Following the departure of Hu Yaobang, Premier Zhao Ziyang assumed the additional duties of acting General Secretary of the CCP. Although he, too, had been a protégé of Deng Xiaoping and was a leading reformer, Zhao had not taken a public stand in the ideological dispute, and was widely respected as an effective administrator and economic manager.

The 13th National Congress of the CCP, convened in October 1987, provided a major platform for Zhao, who still enjoyed the support of Deng. His report, which had undergone some drafting and redrafting within the Party, put forward the idea that China was in 'the primary stage of socialism'. The biggest challenge confronting China was that of economic underdevelopment, not class struggle. As development was now designated the primary challenge, the class struggle could be deferred until the most urgent challenge of development had been accomplished. Furthermore, there was no problem in abandoning the command economy (which by implication had been introduced prematurely) in favour of the market and of co-operation with Western countries, provided, of course, that the Party retained its leading role. The slogan was that the State would regulate the market and the market would regulate the enterprises. Zhao also went on to argue that party and state functions should be separated: that is, the CCP should withdraw from the direct administration of the State and from the direct management of enterprises, leaving those tasks to professional civil servants and trained managers respectively.

In early 1988, with the public support of Deng Xiaoping, Zhao Ziyang pursued a policy of rapid price reform, which had immediate inflationary consequences. The official annual inflation rate (considered to be a gross underestimate) rose from 7% in 1987 to more than 13% in the first quarter of 1988

(22% in urban areas, including 44% for fresh vegetables). By July the rate had reached 24%. Zhao remained committed to pressing ahead with reform. However, having assumed the position of party leader in succession to Hu Yaobang, Zhao had been forced to relinquish his position as Premier to the more economically cautious and politically conservative Li Peng. Li believed that the best way of dealing with inflation was not to proceed further with reform but to retreat, and he used his position as Premier to challenge Zhao's reforms. After highly contentious meetings of the senior leaders throughout mid-1988, the State Council announced its decision to defer any further reform of prices until 1990. Meanwhile, social tensions had been exacerbated, and the economy was showing alarming signs of 'overheating'. A policy of retrenchment was announced.

The Tiananmen Massacre

On 15 April 1989 the former party General Secretary, Hu Yaobang, died. In a reflection of the protests that had followed Zhou Enlai's death in 1976, students made their way to the memorial for revolutionary martyrs in Tiananmen Square in Beijing to pay homage to a man whom they considered to be a symbol of political reform. Although their demand for Hu's posthumous rehabilitation over his forced resignation in January 1987 embarrassed the party elders, they were nevertheless tolerant of the students. As protests persisted beyond Hu's funeral ceremony, at the instigation of Li Peng, Deng Xiaoping authorized the issuing of a condemnatory editorial in the *People's Daily*. Unlike the student protests of 1986/87, these demonstrations were relatively restrained in demanding only a dialogue with state leaders and the ending of party corruption. However, they also demanded a retraction of the editorial and the truthful reporting of their demonstrations.

The protesters were soon joined by the ordinary citizens of the capital, by workers, intellectuals, teachers, civil servants, journalists, staff of ministries and members of the security forces. At one stage, more than 1m. people congregated in Tiananmen Square and its main approaches. Similar demonstrations took place in 81 other cities in China, disrupting the official visit of the Soviet leader, Mikhail Gorbachev, in mid-May 1989, while some 3,000 students began a hunger strike to give further impetus to their demands. Although the General Secretary of the Party, Zhao Ziyang, appeared to show a degree of sympathy to the demonstrators, on 20 May martial law was declared by Premier Li Peng and President Yang Shangkun. However, the soldiers dispatched to the centre of Beijing were stopped by crowds of people. The demonstrators now demanded the resignations of Li Peng, Yang Shangkun and Deng Xiaoping. On 30 May they erected a 30-m replica of the US Statue of Liberty, called the Goddess of Democracy.

On the night of 3–4 June 1989 heavily armed troops, accompanied by tanks and armoured personnel carriers, opened fire and forced their way into Tiananmen Square. The Chinese authorities claimed that no one had been killed in the square itself, but initially stated that 300 civilians and up to 400 soldiers had died in fighting elsewhere. This was later revised downwards to about 200 deaths (although the claim that more soldiers than protesters had died was reiterated). Non-party eyewitness accounts reported a total of 1,000 students, workers and bystanders killed, and also acknowledged that a considerably smaller number of the troops had been attacked and killed by the crowd. Initial figures from the China Red Cross Society, of 2,600 civilian deaths, were later denied. While the exact number remains unknown to this day, the fact that both the demonstrations and the killings were witnessed by a global television audience had a significant influence on popular conceptions of China around the world.

It was officially stated that a counter-revolutionary rebellion had been taking place and that the main victims had been soldiers. At this stage of events, following the suppression of the uprising, the principal decision-makers were the revolutionary veterans, now in their eighties and late seventies. On 23–24 June 1989 a plenary session of the CCP's Central Committee was held. It dismissed Zhao Ziyang from all his party posts, as well as other prominent reformers, and it established an inquiry to examine his case further. Although never formally tried, Zhao remained under effective house arrest until his death in January 2005. Jiang Zemin, hitherto secretary of the Shanghai municipal party committee, was chosen as the new General Secretary of the CCP, and the Standing Committee of the Political Bureau was enlarged to six members. However, it was clear from the official accounts of the proceedings, and of the enlarged Political Bureau meeting that preceded it, that the effective rulers of China were the veteran revolutionary leaders. All of this was reinforced by the memoirs of Zhao, which were secretly smuggled out of China and published in 2009, revealing that the final responsibility for the order to suppress the students lay with Deng.

The fifth plenary session of the CCP's Central Committee was convened at the end of October 1989. An attempt was made to prepare for the impending political succession with the resignation of Deng Xiaoping from the chairmanship of the Party's Central Military Commission in favour of Jiang Zemin. Although Deng no longer held any official posts, he was more than simply the ordinary retired citizen and CCP member that he claimed to be. He remained the country's effective paramount leader.

Deng Xiaoping's Final Years

In his final years Deng carried out two major endeavours of lasting significance for the development of China. First, he arranged for his succession in such a way as to provide for a smooth transition and to strengthen the institutionalization of Chinese political life. Second, he propelled China fully down the road of 'marketization' and rapid economic growth so as to end the control that the remnant command sector had over the economy.

In the absence of an effective legal system, let alone one that could constrain the senior political leaders, China could still be characterized by what was called 'rule by men instead of rule by law'. However, one of the striking legacies of Deng Xiaoping was the attempt to institutionalize important areas of political life. Thus, the functions of the main central political organizations were more clearly specified, and meetings were henceforth held at regular intervals according to proper procedures, particularly the all-important Party Congresses, which from 1982 were held regularly every five years. More importantly, Deng established a system whereby office holders were obliged to retire upon reaching a particular age. Even the senior leaders were technically not allowed to put their names forward for re-election at national congresses once they had reached the age of 70. This development was strengthened by the transition of leadership from the old guard of the revolutionary veterans to the bureaucratic technocrats who had been trained in the Soviet-influenced era of the 1950s. If the former drew their authority from their personal stature as founders who had achieved so much, the standing of the latter emanated from their institutional positions. The link between these two sources of authority was that the technocrats had been selected by the veterans as their successors. Although political succession might be regarded as a fundamental weakness in the Chinese political system, the transition from Deng to Jiang Zemin proceeded remarkably smoothly. Jiang emerged as a political leader in his own right, who, none the less, was constrained by the need to compromise with other major leaders and to foster powerful constituencies such as the military.

Although Deng Xiaoping had technically retired in 1989, he continued to dominate Chinese politics until, in late 1994, he declined into inactivity, eventually dying on 19 February 1997, at the age of 92. By living to such an age, he succeeded in surviving most of the other revolutionary veterans, many of whom were less enthusiastic about his reforms and who might well have been able to upstage the younger Jiang Zemin. Notable among these was the austere Chen Yun, the most important of the conservative reformers, who died in April 1995. By the time of Deng's death, his successors, the seven-member Standing Committee of the Political Bureau, headed by Jiang Zemin, whom Deng had designated the 'core leader', had been in charge of daily affairs for a considerable time, with the result that Deng's passing was marked by a singular calmness.

Deng Xiaoping's legacy was a country that had begun to recover from the traumas of the Tiananmen killings, the collapse of the European communist regimes in 1989 and the demise of the USSR, 'the motherland of socialism', two years later. His response to these critical events, which deepened the crisis of communism in China, was to emphasize rapid economic growth, in order to increase prosperity and elicit popular support for the stability provided by communist rule. Influenced by the example of Singapore, Deng saw no contradiction between maintaining authoritarian rule and encouraging rapid economic expansion and the attendant socio-economic changes. The alternative to communist rule, according to Deng, was the chaos and poor economic growth that became evident in the former USSR as the 1990s progressed. Thus, he strengthened the forces of order while simultaneously stimulating economic reforms and the opening up of China to the outside world.

In early 1992, in the course of a quasi-imperial tour of southern China, Deng challenged the conservative retrenchment in place since 1988. He envisaged a dramatic increase in the rate of economic growth and the intensification of the policies of economic reform and openness. He urged Guangdong Province to emulate the newly industrialized economies of East Asia, in order to serve as a model for the rest of China. Deng argued that the distinction between capitalist and socialist practices was insignificant, and that capitalist and foreign forms of ownership were all to be embraced to promote economic growth. China was now a 'socialist market economy'. This was effectively written into the country's Constitution at the Congress held later in that year.

Jiang Zemin as the Core Leader

At the time of his nomination in 1989 many observers inside and outside China regarded Jiang Zemin as lacking in political authority and as possibly being an interim appointment. An engineer by training, he had been Party Secretary in Shanghai in the late 1980s, and was chosen as national leader as much because of his calm handling of the demonstrations that occurred there in 1989 as for any other political skills that he possessed. In the event, Jiang had more than seven years to ease himself into the most senior post. Within a year of his appointment as CCP General Secretary, Jiang had inherited the positions of Chairman of the CCP Central Military Commission and Chairman of the State Central Military Commission from Deng Xiaoping, and in March 1993 he was elected President of the People's Republic at the first session of the Eighth National People's Congress (NPC). By the time of Deng's death in 1997, Jiang had cleverly manoeuvred some members of his so-called 'Shanghai faction' into leading positions in both the state and party organizations. Perhaps even more significantly, Jiang also made extensive new appointments to the senior military ranks. Although some of these were no more than reshuffles of regional leaders, it meant that leading military members owed their appointment to him; he proved able to retain the loyalty of the army, despite being its first civilian leader with no experience of military service.

Thus, by the time of the 15th Party Congress in September 1997, Jiang was well placed to consolidate his position as the 'core leader' of what was known as the third generation (Mao being leader of the first and Deng of the second). He was able to remove troublesome opponents, including Qiao Shi, the former minister and Chairman of the NPC, who had challenged some of Jiang's positions from an apparently more liberal perspective, and the 81-year-old Gen. Liu Huaqing. Although Jiang did not entirely succeed in determining the new appointments to the Political Bureau and its Standing Committee, he emerged from the Congress with his personal authority considerably enhanced. The new Central Committee of 193 full and 151 alternate members could be said to reflect Jiang's experience and outlook. Only 43% of the previous Central Committee's members were re-elected, with most of the remainder being excluded on account of their age. Yet the new Committee's average age of 55.9 years was not even six months lower than the previous average at the time of selection. Similarly, the membership remained largely technocratic, with more than 90% educated to college standard, and the vast majority having bureaucratic experience. These developments were taken a stage further at the Ninth NPC, which convened in March 1998, when Li Peng displaced Qiao Shi as Chairman of the NPC Standing Committee and Zhu Rongji, the former Mayor of Shanghai, became the new Premier of the State Council. Zhu announced that the ministries of the State Council would be reduced in number from 40 to 29, with about one-half of these to be headed by ministers who were aged in their fifties.

Jiang and Zhu confronted two major challenges that were undermining the Party's legitimacy at this time. First, corrupt local officials were becoming the target of increasingly vociferous, and sometimes violent, popular protests. In response, the senior leadership embraced limited village democracy as a means to constrain official corruption, on the principle that villagers were unlikely to elect those who had cheated them. This approach built on experiments in rural democracy carried out after the enactment of the first Organic Village Election Law in 1988. The outcome was mixed as far as democratic accountability was concerned, since the election results needed confirmation by authorities at the next highest level (townships). Nor was the problem of corruption solved—far from it. Nevertheless, the limited democratization at village level was a sign of progress in itself, and it attracted much interest in the West, particularly among analysts searching for signs of the beginnings of a long-term transition to democracy. It managed, in particular, to restore stability to a crucial area of the country, at a time of rapid and disruptive change, and is a process continuing to this day.

Second, by the time Jiang and Zhu took office, economic deceleration was becoming a problem. This was partly because, during his term in power as Vice-Premier, Zhu Rongji had been charged with contriving a successful 'soft landing' for the economy after rapid and largely uncontrolled growth between 1993 and 1995. Following the regional economic crisis that began in July 1997, China lost the Asian market that had hitherto accounted for nearly one-fifth of the value of its exports, and the amount of foreign direct investment coming into the country began to decline sharply.

Furthermore, the long-standing difficulties of the SOEs suddenly became more acute, leading to a precipitate fall in central government revenues. Economically, the SOEs received huge subsidies that in one form or another accounted for one-third of central budgetary expenditure. Yet they were also massively in debt to each other and were consuming vast loans from the banking sector that were not realistically expected to be repaid. The post-Deng leadership decided to address the situation by undertaking a fundamental restructuring of the SOEs, despite the rapid rise in unemployment that they knew would ensue. Accordingly, it was announced at the 15th Party Congress in September 1997 that apart from some 500–1,000 large strategic SOEs, the remaining 150,000 would be restructured by means of amalgamations, share flotations and even bankruptcies. This was known as the 'letting go of the small, controlling the big' policy. The decision was reaffirmed at the following NPC in March 1998, when the new Premier, Zhu Rongji, also announced that the number of civil servants in the central bureaucracies would be reduced by one-half.

Zhu promised to complete the reforms within three years, thereby suggesting that he did not fully appreciate the severity of the deceleration of domestic demand, which continued to decline during the following two years. While official figures claimed annual growth rates of 7%–8%, many, perhaps even most, of the extra goods that were being produced were languishing unsold in warehouses. Consequently, the pace of reform slowed as the Government attempted to promote expansion through massive state investment in infrastructure (principally transport, communications, energy and water conservation). Nevertheless, the authorities continued to press the SOEs to restructure in order to reduce financial losses; this inevitably entailed laying off workers. Overall, from 1995 until China's entry into the World Trade Organization (WTO) at the end of 2001, around 100m. workers either lost their jobs or were laid off from state and collectively-owned urban enterprises; some 40% of these people reportedly found new jobs.

As far as President Jiang was concerned, a new and entirely unexpected challenge to the status quo emerged with a demonstration in April 1999 surrounding the central government compound in Beijing by an ostensibly quietist sect encompassing Buddhist and Daoist elements and composed largely of the middle-aged: Falun Gong (also known as Falun Dafa). Shocked to find that the sect had adherents in the highest circles of the élite, Jiang hastily had it condemned as a 'cult' and prosecuted it with the full coercive force of the regime. However, these alleged subversives continued their quiet demonstrations, and they appeared not to be intimidated by harassment and the arrest of thousands of practitioners, including government and party officials. The President's inability to control the spiritual movement entirely was indicative of how much authority, as opposed to power, the CCP had lost. It was not until mid-2001 that the Chinese authorities began to overcome the challenge of Falun Gong, at least to the extent that its followers were no longer able to mount public demonstrations. Adherents of the sect were frequently reported by human rights organizations to have been subjected to horrendous treatment in prisons and detention camps, which sometimes resulted in mass suicides. In the final two years of Jiang's period as Party Secretary the Chinese authorities were especially active in suppressing open dissent, showing great nervousness as they undertook a crucial leadership transition from the third to the fourth generation of leaders. Religious groups, indigenous human rights campaigners and democracy activists were subject to direct attacks by the security organs. Attempts to register a China Democracy Party in 1998–99 in Hangzhou and other provincial centres resulted in a major offensive of suppression. Unrest in Xinjiang Autonomous Region grew, with riots in Yili and Kashgar in the mid-1990s, provoked by clashes between Uygur (Uighur) and Han Chinese living there. This culminated, after the attacks of 11 September 2001 on the USA, in the placing by the US authorities of two Uygur groups on an international terrorist list. Yet during this period of egregious infringements of basic human rights, the Chinese Government signed the two main UN Conventions on Human Rights and even ratified the one concerning economic and social rights. However, the CCP was remorseless and unforgiving towards anyone who dared to establish an organization or to publicly challenge the Party's legitimacy and its right to a monopoly on power. The CCP depicted its programme as the only one providing stability and unity to China. Its ability to deliver rapid economic growth meant that the vast majority of people were either supporters of the Party, or were apolitical.

The Jiang era resulted in perhaps two main legacies for China, both of which were brought about by the senior leadership despite considerable opposition. First, Jiang, and particularly Zhu Rongji, moved to resolve discussions with the WTO on China's entry to that body, which had been ongoing since 1985. Some party members were sceptical about the wisdom of pressing for entry, on the grounds that a communist party should not embrace WTO principles of free-market capitalism. Many more, including a number of senior officials, were concerned about the practical implications of allowing foreigners greater and freer access to the Chinese economy, most clearly with regard to the impact on employment. Despite this opposition, Zhu visited Washington, DC, in the USA, in March 1999 and offered a wide range of concessions in the hope of gaining US approval for Chinese entry to WTO. The extent of the concessions offered took many in China, including senior officials, by surprise. When Zhu's offers were rejected by US President Bill Clinton because of pressure from Congress, and he returned home without an agreement, his position seemed to be in danger. However, a change in US policy, combined with offers of even more concessions from China, led to the conclusion of a bilateral agreement in November. After two years of further negotiation over the specific terms of Chinese entry, with accords reached with the USA, Japan, the European Union (EU) and other existing WTO members, China finally acceded to the organization in late 2001. Entry to WTO released forces of productivity and growth, as well as deepening internationalization, which continues to this day. It is from this period that China can truly be said to have become the major manufacturer for the world, and has been able to record huge surpluses with leading trading partners such as the EU and the USA, while also accruing vast reserves of foreign currency.

The second main legacy of the Jiang era was the abandonment, in ideational terms, of the pretence that the CCP was a proletarian party. Although individual entrepreneurs had been joining the Party in the 1980s, they were formally barred from membership after the unrest of 1989 because of alleged links between some private business people and the student leaders. Jiang's proposals to formalize the situation and establish a new basis for party rule on the 80th anniversary of the creation of the CCP in 2001, by allowing entrepreneurs to be readmitted to the Party, raised concern and bitter opposition among many party members. Despite these protests, the CCP Constitution was amended at the 16th Party Congress in November 2002 to include Jiang's theory of the 'Three Represents' (*sange daibiao*) alongside Marxism-Leninism-Mao Zedong Thought as the Party's guiding principle. Subsequently, the CCP formally represented not only the Chinese proletariat, but also China's advanced productive forces, China's culture and 'the fundamental interests of the overwhelming majority of the Chinese people'; the Communist Party was no longer simply the vanguard of the proletariat, but of 'Chinese People and the Chinese nation', and membership was open to 'any advanced element', including private entrepreneurs.

For the average Chinese citizen, the way in which the CCP theoretically justified its management of economic reform was not as important as the resulting clear benefits. The Party's statements were of less significance than the delivery of tangible results, and this conditioned popular attitudes to the CCP's continued tenure of power. However, the 'Three Represents' theory was important in that it marked the official recognition that the fundamental basis of CCP rule, and thus the foundation of the Chinese political regime, had changed.

The Leadership of Hu Jintao

In addition to establishing a new theoretical foundation for party rule, the 16th Party Congress in November 2002 elected Hu Jintao, the country's Vice-President, as the new General Secretary of the CCP, in succession to Jiang Zemin. Hu had been regarded as a likely successor for more than a decade, after successfully handling the unrest of the late 1980s while serving as Party Secretary of Tibet Autonomous Region. He had a diverse background as both a provincial and central leader, and had attracted Deng Xiaoping's attention in the 1980s during his leadership of the China Youth League. Hu subsequently replaced Jiang as China's President at the NPC in March 2003, when Wen Jiabao succeeded Zhu Rongji as Premier. Initially, however, the transition to the fourth generation of CCP leadership was far from complete. Jiang Zemin's determination not to relinquish his power and influence led to his retention of the chairmanship of the Central Military Commission, responsible for the operational command of the armed forces. Jiang also ensured that his supporters retained a majority on the Standing Committee of the Political Bureau, which by this time had expanded to nine members. The trend was repeated at the NPC held in March 2003, when Jiang's stalwarts were allocated significant positions on the State Council. Zeng Qinghong, Jiang's most able and ambitious associate, was appointed as the country's Vice-President.

However, before the new leadership was firmly in place, the incoming administration was confronted with a crisis arising from the outbreak of the highly infectious Severe Acute Respiratory Syndrome (SARS). This hitherto unknown pneumonia-like illness, which was sometimes fatal, first appeared in the southern province of Guangdong in November 2002, but the news was suppressed by local and national officials lest it disrupt New Year travel and thereby damage the economy. Consequently, the disease spread more rapidly both within China and to neighbouring Hong Kong, Taiwan and Viet Nam. Signifying the advent of a more globalized era, the virus was carried by air travellers to Toronto, in Canada.

International exposure played a major role in highlighting the true extent of the epidemic. So too did Jiang Yanyong, a retired doctor from Beijing whose e-mails and faxes to the Chinese media questioning the official figures on SARS infections were 'leaked' to the foreign media. With the actual extent of the outbreak becoming ever more apparent, the Minister of Public Health and the Mayor of Beijing were dismissed, and a strict quarantine regime, monitored by the World Health

Organization (WHO), was imposed in affected areas of the country. By the time that China was declared to be clear of SARS by WHO in June 2003, globally more than 800 people had died from the infection, with 80% of the deaths having occurred in China and Hong Kong. The crisis led to demands that the Government become more open and allow the media greater freedom, so as to provide better and earlier warnings of future threats to public health. However, the spirit and practice of media freedom that briefly flourished in response to Jiang Yanyong's revelations did not last long. While the CCP leadership envisaged greater accountability and more honesty, this was considered to be a matter for the Party to address internally, and free from external scrutiny. Indeed, the Party soon reverted to its previous policy of discouraging informants, dismissing editors of investigative newspapers and even closing down offending journals.

However, Premier Wen Jiabao in particular did make efforts to respond to the popular mood. In November 2003 he became the first Chinese leader officially to discuss the extent of HIV/AIDS infections in China, drawing attention to the particularly high rates of infection in the provinces of Yunnan and Henan. Wen subsequently also highlighted the extent of drug addiction in China, and made numerous visits to meet people living with AIDS and recovering addicts. Wen's adoption of public health issues was part of a wider attempt to promote a fresh style of leadership. Hu and Wen sought to portray themselves as more open to new ideas and more willing than their predecessors to heed the views of others. While part of this 'listening mode' entailed encouraging academics to discuss their ideas with the leadership in an open and plural manner, they also wanted to avoid being perceived as an élitist party.

This involved the establishment in April 2007 of a more transparent mode of governance with new regulations requiring all levels of government to adopt 'Government Information Openness' from May 2008 (partly modelled on freedom of information legislation in the West). These regulations required the publication of all government data and decisions, as well as information on administrative procedures and dispute resolution mechanisms. In addition to publishing an annual report on its activities, each level of government was henceforth to be responsible for making itself accessible to the public, with many establishing websites and publicizing relevant e-mail addresses well in advance of the 2008 deadline.

In the aftermath of the devastating earthquake that struck Sichuan Province in May 2008, the Chinese leadership went to great lengths to show a new openness and transparency, in sharp contrast to the initial closed and defensive response to the outbreak of SARS five years previously. The media were allowed to give a full and open account of the extent of the disaster, in which at least 80,000 people died, with nearly 20,000 registered as missing and about 5m. people left homeless. A period of national mourning resulted in not only the greatest display of mass sorrow since the death of Mao, but also the donation of millions of yuan for the bereaved, injured and homeless. There was a particular focus on the number of schools that had collapsed while adjacent buildings had fared much better. Accusations of poor construction standards, sometimes allied with allegations of corruption, were aired in the media, and the leadership initiated an investigation into these apparent shortcomings. Hu Jintao, Wen Jiabao and other senior leaders visited the earthquake area to demonstrate their support and sympathy. The army was swiftly mobilized to assist those affected by the disaster (in contrast to the first reaction to SARS, when the focus had apparently been on helping officials to protect their own reputations). Nevertheless, the extent of some of the protests and critical writings resulted in a number of protesters being removed and some arrested. One of the main activists, Tan Zuoren, who had been compiling a list of those whose children had died as a result of the earthquake, was imprisoned for five years in 2010 on subversion charges.

As China moved into the second decade of the 21st century, the exceptionally rapid growth of the economy was accompanied by signs of increasing political conservatism on the part of the leadership of the CCP under Hu Jintao. Discussions regarding what political form best suited the country continued unabated, largely because of the major social problems that had emerged and developed as the economy prospered. A general awareness of the lack of inherent flexibility in the system as it stood remained widespread. However, there was no consensus over how best to address these issues, particularly those concerning rule of law and the role of civil society. The latter part of the Hu-Wen era was highly repressive, with concerted action against lawyers and civil rights activists ongoing from 2009. In 2010 and 2011 the discordant voices within the party élite on the question of political reform were very apparent. Wen Jiabao became associated with the more reformist wing of the Party. In a speech celebrating the 30th anniversary of the establishment of the Shenzhen SEZ in August 2010 he insisted on the need for faster and deeper political reform. This contrasted with a speech made by Hu Jintao in the same SEZ only a few days later, in which he maintained that stability was essential and that only the CCP was able to guarantee this. At the annual session of the NPC held in March 2011, the same contrast in viewpoints was evident. Wu Bangguo, Chairman of the Standing Committee of the NPC and second in the party hierarchy, not only made a powerful rebuttal of attempts to adopt 'Western-style bicameral multi-party systems' but also alluded to the need for firm control of the private sector. On the following day Wen repeated his comments in support of the need for greater political reform. However, these seemingly contradictory remarks were accompanied by universal support, at least within the political élite, for the Party's retention of full leadership in all areas of political, social and economic life. Furthermore, it was stressed that only changes that did not threaten this party monopoly were open for discussion. Hu's concept of 'intra party' democracy, therefore, remained the accepted norm.

Whatever liberal and reformist aspirations might be imputed to the central leaders, actions spoke more powerfully than words, and the highly controlling, risk-averse nature of the Hu era was typified by the angry and resentful response of the Chinese authorities to the award, in late 2010, of the Nobel Peace Prize to imprisoned dissident and academic Liu Xiaobo. The announcement of this award in September was met with initial silence from Beijing, but was soon followed by a forceful rebuttal and an active campaign by Chinese diplomats to prevent countries from sending official representatives to the award ceremony in Oslo, Norway, on 9 December. While a number of countries, including Russia, Viet Nam and Saudi Arabia, refused to attend, the majority did, despite strong protests from China. The suppression of rights lawyers (including those dealing with China's human rights issues, representing sensitive cases such as those involving Falun Gong practioners or petitioners) intensified from late 2010, leading to the detention of even academic lawyers such as Teng Biao of Beijing University. China's assertiveness in this area destroyed much of the global goodwill that it had accumulated as a result of its successful hosting of the 2008 Olympic Games. However, observing the developments of the 'Arab Spring', a series of popular demonstrations and protests that commenced in the Middle East and North Africa in December 2010, in whatever the clear differences between the situations in Arab countries and in China may have been, it remained clear that disturbances in unexpected areas were always possible and that governments could not afford to become complacent. In March 2011 the Chinese Government announced that it planned, for the first time, to allocate a greater proportion of budgetary expenditure to internal security than the amount to be assigned to the army.

Meanwhile, in 'Storming the Fortress: A Research Report on China's Political System Reform after the 17th Party Congress', published in early 2008, researchers from the Central Party School promoted a 'comprehensive political system reform plan', proposing the restoration of fundamental authority to the people and an increasing tolerance of diverse opinions and beliefs; not only tolerance of social groups, but also of religious alternatives. Other influential academics such as Yu Keping and Xie Tao, who were closely associated with important political leaders, also urged greater political reform. Xie praised the Swedish model of democracy, in contrast to the Marxist-Leninist system that had 'cheated' the Soviet people (which, by extension, could be interpreted as having deceived the Chinese people too, although this was left unsaid). Hu Jintao himself also envisaged more democracy. However, in all of these cases democracy and democratization did not equate to multi-party democracy. In this context, democratization was to be regarded in terms of the 'new three principles of the people' outlined by Hu in 2003: ultimate power to the people, concern to be shown for the people and the benefits of policy to be enjoyed by the people. Such a process of democratization would entail exposing more officials to popular scrutiny through the extension of local level elections. It would also involve other forms of encouraging participation.

An oft-cited example in China related to experiments in Wenling in Zhejiang Province, where citizens were widely consulted on a range of government policies at local meetings. In Sichuan Province villages experimented in choosing one of their own residents as a form of 'political manager' to co-ordinate and oversee political issues, while competitive elections permitted non-CCP members to seek and win representative office. Increasing numbers of non-party members also began to occupy senior positions, including the Ministers of Health and of Science and Technology, both of whom were appointed in 2007. Perhaps a clearer statement of élite conservative thinking could be found in a short document published by the People's Daily in mid-2009: 'The Six Whys', listed a number of bold reform proposals, such as the introduction of Western-style bicameral parliamentary systems and the granting of fully free courts, but then dismissed them all as not being in the interests of stability and good governance in China. Elite CCP leaders, in particular, noted the huge social and economic repercussions in the post-communist era in countries such as the former USSR and used this observation to justify their own refusal to change. When Chinese leaders spoke of democratization (and in his major speech at the 17th Party Congress in 2007 Hu used the word 'democracy' more than 60 times), in reality they were referring to proposals to make existing one-party rule more democratic by promoting transparency, increasing predictability and strengthening the legal system, particularly within the Party. Democratization in this context occurred through popular surveillance of policy and officials. An administrative litigation law was implemented in 1990, allowing individuals to use the law courts against local governments and officials to claim their rights and to protest against abuses. The impact of the internet on communication between government, party and people has been significant, with users increasing from only a few million in 1998 to almost 600m. by 2011 (including those who could access the internet on their mobile phones).

The unruliness of the internet remained an issue of deep concern, with Hu Jintao insisting to a closed group of party leaders in early 2011, shortly after the outbreak of unrest in the Middle East and North Africa, on the need resolutely to control internet content and to recognize the serious risks that such technology posed in linking aggrieved and potentially hostile groups together. Facebook, Twitter and other social networking sites remained under constant surveillance, with some being permanently blocked, and others, such as LinkedIn, being restricted during sensitive times (for example, during the convening of major conferences). In response to the continuing imposition of censorship through the Government's so-called 'Great Firewall of China' (a censorship and surveillance project launched in 2003), the leading internet facility Google withdrew its search engine capacity from China in January 2010. None the less, the internet remained a resource full of diversity, energy and creativity and one that the government propaganda chiefs found extremely challenging to control. In February 2011 Chen Guangcheng, a blind civil rights activist who had been released from prison in September 2010, posted an hour-long recording of his life at home under intense police surveillance on the video-sharing website YouTube; this subversive action led to Chen suffering a further assault by the police and security personnel who surrounded his house. Like President Jiang and Premier Zhu before them, Hu and Wen repeatedly confirmed their commitment to combating corruption. In addition to undermining faith in the Party's leadership, corruption had resulted in severe economic losses and jeopardized the leadership's ability to attain developmental objectives. Hu Angang of the Chinese Academy of Social Sciences found that between 1999 and 2001 the economic losses caused by corruption averaged nearly 15% of gross domestic product (GDP), while national auditors estimated that 10% of targeted poverty alleviation funding was lost to corruption. Misuse of funds allocated to develop the pension system was one of the reasons for the dismissal in September 2006 of Chen Liangyu, Secretary of the Shanghai Municipal Committee of the CCP and member of the Political Bureau.

However, two other factors appeared to have prompted this intervention. First, Chen's dismissal was perceived as a warning to other local leaders who had flouted central directives to reduce certain types of investment and curb growth in some economic sectors. The Hu-Wen leadership was attempting to restore more central control over local leaders by exerting stronger fiscal supervision and, from 2006, by restricting local leaders' control over land. As Chen had previously openly opposed central government plans to restrain economic growth in 2004 and in early 2006, his dismissal was regarded as criticism of the de facto provincial resistance to the central Government.

Second, it appeared to be part of a wider struggle within the élite to lay the foundation for the succession to Hu and Wen, an issue prevailing at the 17th Party Congress, held in October 2007. Owing to the new stipulation that leaders were to serve for only two five-year periods and had to retire after they reached 68 years of age, the intervening party congress after the first five-year term would entail both the consolidation of the existing leadership and simultaneously the starting point of the transition to the next leadership. As such, the appointments and dismissals made at the 17th Party Congress, and at the 11th NPC held in March 2008, together prepared the way for a new leadership to replace that of Hu and Wen during 2012–13. The fifth generation, as it would be known, had five years in which to prepare for a major transition of power at the 18th Party Congress, which would probably be held in late 2012. Observers noted various unique features in this forthcoming transition. There was no major political 'godfather' acting in a role similar to that of Deng Xiaoping in his ability to legitimize both Jiang Zemin and Hu Jintao. Leadership choices would need to be made as a result of consensus, and would have to satisfy complex constituents in the Party and in society. The factionalism of the past, with élite groups linked, for instance, to the Shanghai Group, or the China Youth League, had broken down. The likely new leaders were from more diverse backgrounds (the fourth generation being dominated by technocrats), with some having family links to former élite leaders ('princelings') and others coming from a more 'grassroots' background. Of the Political Bureau members of 2011, it was expected that all but two would need to stand down in 2012. This would represent one of the largest turnovers ever experienced by the CCP at this level, and its handling was expected to have an immense impact on the political direction of China in the years ahead.

Of the members of the Standing Committee of the Political Bureau elected in 2007, Li Keqiang seemed to carry the approval of Hu Jintao and was widely thought to be Hu's choice to replace him at the head of the CCP in 2012. However, the same could not be said so definitively for Xi Jinping, He Guoqiang and Zhou Yongkang, all of whom had different levels of relationships with Zeng Qinghong (and therefore to some extent with Jiang Zemin). Moreover, with Li Keqiang lower than Xi Jinping in the rankings of the Standing Committee, the latter was the leading contender to replace Hu Jintao as General Secretary of the party in 2012, with Li widely expected to replace Wen Jiabao as Premier in 2013, a theory that was reinforced when Xi Jinping was appointed a Vice-Chairman of the Central Military Commission in October 2010. This had been the same path followed by Hu Jintao more than a decade earlier, and was regarded as a powerful sign that, barring disaster, Xi would be Hu's replacement as leader of the CCP in 2012.

The Scientific Concept of Development

One of the great criticisms of the Jiang Zemin-Zhu Rongji era was the increasing inequality in society. In 1984, according to the Gini coefficient measure of income inequality, China was one of the world's most equal societies. By 2000, however, it had become one of the most unequal. Its export-orientated, energy-inefficient, but manufacturing-intense economy had created huge environmental problems. This was the background of the addition at the 17th Party Congress of the 'scientific concept of development' to the party Constitution, defined as a 'major strategic thought' to guide economic and social development. The 'scientific' nature of this thought emanated from the application of guiding principles to develop strategies that start from the consideration of the true impact on people, rather than simply the contribution to raising gross national income—a policy of 'putting people first'. For example, policies that might result in the achievement of a higher national income but that might also lead to environmental degradation, and perhaps exacerbate inequality, were not scientifically derived. In contrast to the undirected growth policies that had characterized earlier periods, the new scientific development strategy was to emphasize co-ordination of various policies to create a rational, scientific entity. In addition, development strategies were to be economically and socially sustainable, not simply environmentally sustainable (although this remained an important issue in itself). Thus, the new scientific strategy emphasized co-ordination and balance between town and country, and among China's various regions, with the aim of reducing inequality. It was also necessary to find a balance between the search for economic growth and the provision of social welfare (health care, pensions, education, etc.), between 'man and nature', and between developing the domestic economy and opening to the outside world. This last issue was a reference to a growing unease that Chinese development had become too dependent upon the global economy—upon foreign investment and, in particular, upon external demand. As such, domestic consumption and demand needed to be raised in order to ensure long-term growth and sustainability, and also to reduce vulnerability and economic insecurity.

As well as looking forward, official ideology increasingly looked to the past to find historical precedents that legitimated the contemporary system. Through the eclectic and selective use of thinkers like Sun Zi, Mencius, Confucius and others, China's lack of Western-style democracy was explained as a continuation of a unique state-society relationship that had emerged over centuries. There was also a new emphasis on harmony as the basis of Chinese society, often linked to ideas of social responsibility and the need to maintain social order. While officials were instructed to study the basics of scientific development, the call to 'construct a harmonious society' was more targeted at the general public through poster campaigns and propaganda. The new high-speed train between Beijing and Tianjin was named 'harmonious' (*hexie hao*) when it commenced operations in 2008.

Although the scientific concept of development was formally adopted only in 2007, the policy of 'putting people first' had been in place from mid-2004, when official speeches and media reports increasingly began to criticize the economic strategy of the previous leadership. With its emphasis on greater economic efficiency and profits, the previous policy (which was never associated with any named individual) had not only neglected developmental concerns but had in fact increased inequality. The ability of the leadership to promote the new agenda was further facilitated when Jiang Zemin finally relinquished control of the Central Military Commission to Hu Jintao in September 2004.

The Hu-Wen leadership (rhetorically at least) promoted the cause of those who had been overlooked in the transition from socialism. Public holidays were spent visiting the poor and the sick in China's interior provinces, and official speeches emphasized the need to redress the many imbalances in Chinese society. In some respects, this new polity reflected the agenda of a group of intellectuals and scholars who were broadly termed the New Left. The New Left argued that China's leaders had placed too much emphasis on generating economic growth and that insufficient attention had been paid to distributing the benefits of that growth or to caring for those whom reform had not yet benefited. These emerging underclasses, the New Left contended, were being neglected by the Government, while individual CCP members continued to make personal fortunes either through outright corruption or simply by using their insider knowledge and contacts to become successful entrepreneurs in the new private sector.

For some of these thinkers, China had also gone too far in restructuring the domestic economy to comply with the interests of the global economy. The specific terms of China's WTO entry were criticized as giving foreign companies too much access to the Chinese economy, to the detriment of domestic producers, while not guaranteeing the same access for Chinese producers to foreign markets (particularly the USA and the EU). Others argued that the Chinese economy had become overly dependent upon foreign investments and markets, resulting in patterns of development that favoured external, rather than internal, needs and interests. To varying degrees, most of these thinkers believed the origin of the problem to be the adoption of neo-liberalism; they argued for a strong and active government to rebalance the relationship between endogenous and exogenous growth, and to redirect economic activity to benefit those domestic groups that had previously formed the sound basis of CCP rule.

Economic policy was also revised to address the issue of inequality, with investment targeted at the cities in north-east and central China that had suffered the biggest job losses as a result of SOE reform, and at rural China in general. In February 2006 the Government announced that its principal and urgent objective was now to build a 'new socialist countryside'. Spending on the rural regions of China was to increase and the tax burden on the peasantry was to be reduced, with the agricultural tax abolished, in an attempt to redress the significant imbalances between urban and rural dwellers. Local governments in rural China were to be placed under closer surveillance from above, by the central administration, and from below, by the people through local elections, in order to combat corruption and to ensure that government spending reached its intended targets. New reforms were also to be developed to ensure basic access to health care, welfare and education for China's poorest. These were increasingly supported through the 600,000m.-yuan fiscal stimulus programme introduced from 2009, which was intended to start building some of the critically necessary social infrastructure in China's less developed areas. The 'Opening up the West' (sometimes called 'Go West') campaign that started in the late 1990s to improve the less developed, impoverished vast hinterland of China, was remodulated from the mid-2000s also to address issues in central China. There remained the huge challenge of balancing a rapidly growing coastal region, with all the manufacturing, wealth and prosperity it was enjoying, against the vast swathes of China that were still dominated by state-owned industry and had millions of impoverished people. While élite leaders talked of 'harmony', therefore, as leading Chinese social scientist Yu Jianrong noted in December 2009, they were challenged by a society in which there were an estimated 90,000 demonstrations each year and in which, over the period 2006–09, a total of 10m. petitions had been submitted by disgruntled citizens to the central Government.

While some initiatives gave the impression of increased state control, others appeared to suggest a greater role for the market. For example, in addition to promoting the socialist countryside, the Government had recommitted itself to maintaining ownership of SOEs in strategic industries, most of which, after years of 'restructuring', were beginning to make a profit. However, under the leadership of Hu and Wen, reforms also deliberately weakened the State's control over the economy. In 2003 administrative reforms were undertaken which, in combination, established a governmental structure designed to regulate the economy rather than control it through planning. The word 'planning' no longer appeared in the name of any central agency. In addition, WTO entry commitments resulted in the further reduction of government controls over the economy, an ever greater role for the market and increased access for foreign companies. Although new restrictions were sometimes introduced to offset the impact of these reforms, they only limited the pace of liberalization and did not fully negate or reverse the programme.

The Twelfth Five-Year Plan (2011–15) contained a number of new development measures aimed at addressing the issue of quality of growth rather than quantity of growth. More funding was to be allocated from the central budget to health care, to environmental measure and to the development of social infrastructure. One of the programme's targets was to increase life expectancy for men and women by one year. It was also planned to allocate greater funding to education and to address the increasing disparities between the countryside and the cities, between the western and eastern regions, and between the north and the south. An indication of just how diverse Chinese society had become, was the fact that a number of billionaires were invited to attend the annual session of the NPC in March 2011. In that month the 'rich list' compiled by Forbes, a US publishing and media company, revealed that China had 115 US dollar billionaires, second only to the number in the USA.

The Social Impact of the Reforms

Much attention has rightly been paid to China's economic successes. Near double-digit growth rates from the early 1990s resulted in a more than two-fold increase in average personal incomes. The gradual establishment of an urban middle class became evident in the coastal belt and other major cities. Millions of Chinese began to enjoy prosperous or relatively affluent lifestyles that were inconceivable two or three decades previously. Around 20% of the population could be considered part of the 'consumer class', with around 13%, or 170m., able to afford branded luxury items. Official figures also showed that the number of people living in dire poverty declined from some 250m. in 1978 to around 25m. in 2006, although the World Bank estimated that as many as 200m. lived under the generally accepted measure of absolute poverty and that there were as many as 24m. malnourished people. Premier Wen Jiabao himself admitted in his government work report at the NPC in 2010 that there were 150m. people still living in poverty in China.

One of the most profound impacts of the reforms from 1978 was the creation of an entire new group in society: the migrant workers (*mang liu*, literally 'blind masses' in Chinese). As a result of the increased efficiency of the agricultural sector, by the 2000s there was a huge movement of people from rural areas to the cities to work in new sectors such as manufacturing, construction or the entertainment industry. By 2009, therefore, China had become a society in which the population was almost equally balanced between those who lived in cities and towns, and those who lived in the countryside. The household registration system, which had been a mainstay of social control under Mao, had largely broken down, although repeated discussions at the NPC had never resulted in a consensus to abandon it completely. By 2010 as many as 200m. people fell into this mobile category, but had to live with major hindrances to gaining access to education, health care and property rights.

Migrant workers thus became the unrecognized heroes of the whole reform era. China's great new cities and much of its manufacturing have been achieved through their toil. However, by 2010 they had been receiving depressed wages for several years; as a result of the global economic crisis many simply returned to their villages, in order to start businesses there. The impact of the low rate of renumeration was a number of significant unofficial strikes by workers at largely foreign-owned factories in mid-2010. Some international companies, such as Kentucky Fried Chicken, addressed the problem of low wages by offering a 25% increase. In 2010 a spate of suicides at the Taiwan-owned Foxconn Factory in Shenzhen, near the border with Hong Kong, highlighted the plight of many migrant labourers, who had to endure long working hours in confined conditions. The simple fact was that after years of rapid development and 'sweat-shop' conditions, Chinese workers wanted more. The prospect of the end of a cheap labour market in China was increasingly being discussed, and, indeed, in the latter part of 2010 a number of wage rises were sanctioned. These increases were also partly necessitated by the large rises in consumer prices over this period. By early 2011 the annual rate of inflation had exceeded 5%, causing many Chinese employees to complain that the value of their wages had stagnated or even declined in recent years.

Environmental issues, furthermore, represented a major negative impact of the type of economic growth witnessed in China. Although China had introduced a full range of environmental laws, there was a problem of implementation at the local level, where governments charged with applying environmental legislation were also often the owners of polluting enterprises. Failure to address the growing environmental concerns of the population undermined faith in the ability of both Party and Government to act on behalf of the people (although the focus primarily appeared to be on the failings of specific local authorities, rather than the systemic failing of the regime itself). As with other societal concerns, the Government responded by visibly promoting itself as deeply committed to addressing these problems. However, with the Global Climate Change Summit held in Copenhagen, Denmark, in December 2009, the Chinese Government confronted the challenge of combining increasing GDP growth with sustainability. Having overtaken the USA as the world's largest carbon dioxide emitter in 2006, expectations that China would sign up to specific emissions targets were disrupted by the demand from its negotiating team, led by Premier Wen Jiabao, that the Western developed nations accept the greatest responsibility there. The severe floods in Gansu Province in August 2010 highlighted how vulnerable the Chinese environment remained. In recognition of the importance of addressing environmental concerns, the Government included further targets for reducing energy inefficiency and carbon emissions in the Twelfth Five-Year Plan.

Reflecting the changed dynamics within society between the Government and those governed, from the early 1980s wide opportunities opened up for NGOs. Many of these had been established with a focus on the environment, and in the 1990s a whole movement protested against the construction of huge hydroelectric power projects, in particular the vast Three Gorges Dam. Civil society groups began to work in areas ranging from gender and ethnic minority rights, along with legal aid, to the provision of services on behalf of the Government, and the elderly and the poor. Estimates of the numbers of these organizations varied from 3,000 to more than 300,000, but all legitimate NGOs were required to have a government partner, as a result of which they remained under strict political supervision and control. Those that strayed into sensitive territory were shut down, usually for reasons such as alleged non-payment of taxes, where the regulations were highly ambiguous. In studies of the 'colour revolutions' that occurred in Eastern Europe and Central Asia after the disintegration of the USSR in 1991, Chinese academics noted in particular the role of the NGO sector. There was particular anxiety among the Chinese authorities about both these groups and lawyers challenging the legitimacy of the Party; while they were allowed to exist, they did so within carefully monitored parameters.

The lack of data about public opinion in China (surveys are required to be undertaken with Chinese partners and there are restrictions on the questions asked, how they are asked and of whom) can only really be remedied by surveying the vast domain of the internet. Here opinions range from those who are hugely proud of what the country has achieved since 1978, to those who are sickened by official corruption. A number of bloggers, such as Liu Di, known as the 'Stainless Steel Rat', have irritated officials to such a degree that they have been imprisoned. However, in other moves, cyberspace phenomena such as 'human flesh searches' and internet lynchings have actually unsettled local officials to such an extent that they have been forced to resign. For example, a young girl working in an entertainment parlour in 2009, who had stabbed an official to death for harassing her, had her initial sentence overruled and was freed as a result of an enormous, angry public reaction on the internet. The dynamics between the rulers and those ruled, therefore, is changing, and in radical ways. Public opinion surveys carried out by an international research organization based in the USA immediately after the 2008 Olympics held in Beijing showed that the Government enjoyed strong support and that as many as 86% of Chinese people felt that their country was on the right course. In perhaps a more telling survey undertaken in mid-2009 by a Chinese magazine, of the most trusted figures in society, farmers came top, followed by doctors and lawyers, and then sex workers; the perceived trustworthiness of central government officials had declined by more than 10% compared with the previous year, with local government officials being the least trusted. Anger over rising property prices in 2010 and dissatisfaction with the continuing uncertainty regarding property rights were offset against an economy that continued to boom.

China's Border Regions

China's restive border regions have been a constant concern for central government since 1949. Tibet was fully annexed, after a period of loose central rule, in 1959. The area suffered greatly during the Cultural Revolution, when many of the Buddhist temples were closed down and monks were forced to renounce their faith. The new leadership under Deng Xiaoping from 1979 resumed discussions with Tibetan groups in exile, but only on condition that any mention of independence was absolutely forbidden. By 2011 more than 10 sessions of these discussions had been held. A large uprising in Tibet in 1989, coinciding with the unrest in Beijing, was suppressed on the orders of Hu Jintao, who was then CCP Secretary in the region. From the 1990s the Government's main priority was to integrate the area into the Chinese State more closely by building transport links, the most prominent of which was the train line from Qinghai across the Tibetan plateau and into Lhasa, the capital of the Tibetan (Xizang) Autonomous Region. However, throughout this period, there remained credible reports of widespread imprisonment of Tibetans who were accused of being separatists and demanding full independence. The Chinese Government became increasingly aggressive in its actions against foreign governments that allowed their leaders to meet with the Dalai Lama, the Tibetan spiritual leader, who remained in exile in India. One particularly sensitive issue was the central Government's appointment in 1995 of its own choice for the second most important position in the Buddhist hierarchy, the reincarnation of the Panchen Lama; the original nominee, selected by the Dalai Lama, was placed under house arrest.

If the Government believed that economic development alone would suffice to placate its critics in Tibet, it was wrong. As Beijing prepared to host the 2008 Olympic Games, violence unexpectedly broke out in Lhasa in late March of that year. It was unclear how the violence started, but within two days it had spread from the Tibetan capital to other urban centres of Chinawhere there were significant concentrations of ethnic Tibetans. The provinces of Sichuan and Gansu, in particular, witnessed large protests. Only in April was full order restored, after the central Government committed huge resources to pacifying the affected areas, attributing the unrest to unruly elements. In 2009 the 50th anniversary of the annexation of Tibet, which occurred almost a year to the day after the huge protests, was greeted with great anxiety by the local and national authorities. The continuing international sympathy for the Dalai Lama was best shown when he was able to meet with US President Barack Obama in early 2010, provoking the usual angry denunciations by the Chinese Government, and giving rise to a series of indignant comments by bloggers and observers within China. The Dalai Lama announced his retirement as Tibet's political leader in March 2011 (while retaining the role of spiritual leader), and it was revealed that an elected leader was subsequently to carry this function forward. Part of the reason for the Dalai Lama's resignation may have been to avoid the possibility that, on his eventual death, his replacement would be appointed from within China (as was the case with the Panchen Lama in 1995). In April it was announced that Lobsang Sangay, an academic at Harvard University in the USA, had defeated two other candidates to secure election as Prime Minister of the Tibetan government-in-exile.

The Xinjiang Autonomous Region has presented equally complex and contentious problems as those experienced in Tibet. Partially independent between 1945 and 1949, Xinjiang accounts for 18% of China's landmass and is rich in unexploited energy resources and minerals. Dominated by Muslim Uygur in the 1950s, in subsequent decades the area received great influxes of inward migration from largely Han Chinese. This phenomenon intensified in the 1990s, as a result of which by 2010 the area was balanced almost equally between Han and Uygur, with about 20 other ethnic minorities also living there. In the 1990s a number of local groups linked up with others across the border in Pakistan and other Central Asian states, creating a worrying, potentially international force. Some of these dissident groups were responsible for detonating two bombs in buses in Beijing during 1997, but, as in Tibet, the central Government responded by concentrating on developing the economy of the area, building airports and a train link between the capital, Urumqi, and the far western border town of Kashgar. Following the attacks on the USA in September 2001, the Chinese Government also secured US agreement to place two Xinjiang groups on an international terrorist list. Wang Lequan, Party Secretary of the region until 2010, had a reputation as a hardliner who was willing to crush any form of opposition. The treatment of Uygur businesswoman Rebiya Kadeer typified this. One of the region's most respected entrepreneurs in the 1990s, she sat on the national consultative body for the CCP until her name was linked with separatists and she was imprisoned in 1999. As a result of international pressure, Kadeer was released and exiled to the USA in 2005.

Events in Xinjiang in July 2009 eerily reflected those in Tibet of the previous year. A film posted on YouTube, showing the assault of two Uygur workers involved in a factory dispute in Guangdong Province provoked demonstrations in Urumqi. The disturbances escalated into major rioting. About 200 people died in the ensuing violence, most of them Han Chinese; Uygur were attacked in subsequent reprisals. The Party Secretary of Urumqi resigned and, almost a year later, the much-disliked long-standing regional Party Secretary, Wang Lequan, was removed and transferred to a position in the central Government. In July 2010, on the anniversary of the riots, the region once again witnessed huge security surveillance as nervous officials, both locally and in Beijing, watched for any signs of attempts to repeat the events of the previous year. Xinjiang also endured widespread restrictions on the internet for much of 2009 and 2010, with access allowed only to government websites, for fear that other material might spread and incite anger and protest.

The central Government's response to both of these problems of regional unrest was to convene major meetings in January and May 2010, for Tibet and Xinjiang respectively, both chaired by President Hu Jintao, in an attempt to set out a sustainable plan for the development of the regions and avoid future agitation. It was recognized that short-term repression (many Tibetan and Uygur activists having been executed or sentenced to lengthy prison terms) should be replaced by a longer-term strategy. Increased spending on infrastructure and economic development was announced, with efforts made to address the crucial issue, in Xinjiang, of very high levels of unemployment among young male Uygur. In both areas there were claims that economic development was focused on the Han settlers, rather than on local Tibetans or Uygur. Conversely, Han were resentful of what they regarded as beneficial policies extended to ethnic minorities; for example, lowering their educational requirements for university entrance and granting them social benefits such as the right to have two children, rather than being restricted to the usual one. However, the far more contentious issues of greater autonomy for ethnic minorities remained largely unaddressed. No leading members of the CCP were non-Han, and in both Tibet and Xinjiang the important post of Party Secretary continued to be held by a Han. However, the central Government's one concession was the replacement of the unpopular Party Secretary of Xinjiang, Wang Lequan, with a slightly more consensual appointee, Zhang Chunxian, in April 2010. The central Government had also demanded the resignation of the Party Secretary of Urumqi in the previous year. None the less, the continuing imposition of harsh sentences against those accused of being supportive of independence for Tibet or Xinjiang in 2010–11 indicated that the central Government was not yet ready for any form of compromise in this respect.

CHINA AND THE WORLD

As noted in the preceding essay (History up to 1966), the initial post-1949 foreign policy of emphasis on close relations with the USSR was soon strained. Diverging ideological positions provide a partial explanation for the Sino-Soviet rift. As already noted, Mao perceived the ossification, routinization and bureaucratization of the Soviet revolution as a negative example of what might happen in China if the momentum and zeal of the revolution were not carried on into the post-revolutionary state. While some CCP leaders looked to the USSR as a model for political and economic construction in China, Mao perceived or depicted such a view as at best folly, and at worst, during the Cultural Revolution, as counter-revolutionary. When Soviet leader Nikita Khrushchev denounced Stalinism in 1956, Mao and his followers interpreted this as an implicit and unwarranted criticism of Mao's own leadership in China. While Stalin had possessed credibility as leader of the communist world, Mao did not believe that Khrushchev had any revolutionary credentials or any right to criticize China. When Khrushchev criticized Mao's 'Great Leap' policies, the path to a complete ideological schism between Mao and the USSR was set firmly in place.

There was also a degree to which Chinese leaders were disappointed by the extent of Soviet fraternity. The financial support that the USSR provided was in the form of loans that had to be repaid, not free aid. Furthermore, the benefits of this support were all but eradicated when China was left to finance its role in the Korean War of 1950–53. Although the USSR did send experts to build new factories in China, these were 'turn key' plants where the Soviets retained the plans, thus ensuring continued Chinese dependence on Soviet expertise and often spare parts. In addition, the USSR had repatriated millions of US dollars worth of goods and resources in war reparations from Manchuria after the Japanese surrender, even though they had been at war with Japan for only a short time, compared with the eight years of Sino-Japanese warfare (and indeed, the Soviets maintained control of the Chinese city of Port Arthur/Dalian until as late as 1955).

National security considerations were also clearly very important. The Chinese experience in the Korean War had highlighted the clear technological superiority of the USA. Remaining under Soviet nuclear protection was deemed essential for China's security by leading military figures such as Peng Dehuai. Yet the extent to which the USSR could be relied upon to defend China's national security was increasingly questioned. For example, the USSR refused to support an attempt to seize several small islands off the south-east coast that were part of Kuomintang (KMT)-controlled Taiwan, and increasingly gave support to one of China's principal rivals, India. The fact that the USSR had used force to restore its preferred form of socialism in Poland and, most dramatically, Hungary in 1956 (with no response from the Western world) also showed that the USSR was prepared to use military intervention in its own 'sphere of influence' if the need arose.

At the same time, Chinese leaders, and particularly Zhou Enlai, came to reject the idea that the West constituted a single unified bloc. Zhou returned from the Geneva Conference in 1954 (convened to settle the post-colonial situation in Indo-China) aware that there were important schisms in the Western world, including divisions over how to deal with China. Despite the US-led trade and diplomatic embargo on the People's Republic, and the fact that Taiwan retained the China seat at the UN, a number of Western countries had defied the USA and formally recognized the People's Republic. Others developed closer relations with the mainland while still formally recognizing Taiwan.

At the Bandung Conference of non-aligned states held in Indonesia in 1955, Premier Zhou affirmed China's commitment to recognizing the principles of sovereignty and declared that China would not become involved in the domestic politics of other developing states. Towards the end of the decade, however, China's stance changed as it increasingly became involved in supporting wars of liberation and revolutionary movements in the 'Third World'. Notably, rather than consolidating the socialist bloc in collective revolutionary action, China and the USSR typically supported different revolutionary groups as China attempted to curb the spread of Soviet influence.

These ideas evolved into a 'Theory of the Three Worlds' that became associated with Mao, but owed much to Zhou's earlier thinking and practice (and was first formally enunciated by Deng Xiaoping at the UN in 1974). The 'First World', according to the Chinese designation, consisted of the USSR and the USA, which had different political and economic systems, but were nevertheless imperialistic and hegemonic. The 'Second World' was composed of those states allied to and dependent on the superpowers—Japan, Australia, Canada and both halves of Europe. The 'Third World' comprised the remainder of non-aligned, independent developing states. China's role, as leader of this 'Third World', was to build a counter-hegemonic global alliance, and, where possible, to form alliances with 'Second World' countries in order to separate them from their 'First World' superpower.

The 'Cold War'

While the protracted period of mutual hostility between the USSR and the USA that became known as the 'Cold War' continued, China's growing international role was largely suspended during the Cultural Revolution, when the People's Republic deliberately chose a policy of isolationism, even though a global superpower was embroiled in a revolutionary war on China's borders. In 1965, when the USA first bombed North Viet Nam and then introduced combat troops in the South, there was serious discussion over whether China should join in united action with the USSR to help North Viet Nam. Yet, not least because Sino-Soviet relations had now deteriorated to the extent that the USSR itself was increasingly considered a threat to China's national security, Mao decided instead only to continue to aid North Viet Nam independently and allow the USSR to channel weapons through China to Viet Nam. Mao also urged the Vietnamese communists to adopt a low-level guerrilla strategy in the South—advice that was not followed at the time.

By 1966 any fear that the USA might launch an attack on China was subsiding, and by 1968 the anxieties had diminished. The Vietnamese communist offensive during the *Tet* (lunar New Year) festival of that year marked the limits of the USA's intervention in South-East Asia, embroiling the US army in a war that made escalation into conflict with China impossible. Conversely, the USSR was viewed with increasing suspicion: the Soviet invasion of Czechoslovakia in August 1968 clearly demonstrated the regime's readiness to intervene overseas to impose the USSR's preferred brand of socialism on recalcitrant, subordinate socialist states. Increased military deployments to the north of China only heightened the perceived threat in Beijing.

As a result, China abandoned its diplomatic isolation and sought to restore relations with countries bordering the USSR, including Yugoslavia. Since Marshal Tito's brand of socialism had previously been officially designated as 'heretic', China's new diplomatic initiatives towards Yugoslavia represented revolutionary ideals and purity being put aside in the more pragmatic search for national security. This pragmatism was soon to become manifest in the search to restore working relations with developing countries, including small and medium-sized capitalist powers.

The military tension with the USSR led to clashes on the Ussuri river border in March 1969. These conflicts were not resolved until a Soviet armoured column penetrated into Xinjiang, and Aleksei Kosygin, the Chairman of the USSR Council of Ministers, held a meeting with Zhou and Mao at Beijing airport in September. As fears of a Soviet nuclear strike grew, the initiatives of US President Richard Nixon and his national security adviser, Dr Henry Kissinger, culminated in the latter's unscheduled visit to Beijing in July 1971. It was then announced that Nixon would visit China in the early part of the following year. In October the UN General Assembly expelled representatives of Taiwan and invited the People's Republic to take China's seat. In February 1972 Nixon duly visited China, to be received by Mao and later to sign the famous Shanghai communiqué, pledging to work towards the improvement of relations, with Zhou Enlai. In effect, China had helped to change the central balance between the two superpowers by its shift from alliance with the USSR in the 1950s to alignment with the USA in the 1970s.

For the remainder of the 1970s China sought to build an anti-Soviet coalition against what it regarded as the major expansionist power in the world. During this time the closer relations that China forged with the USA were tempered by concern that, in the era of *détente*, the USA was insufficiently vigilant in confronting the alleged Soviet threat, and by anxiety that the US Government was too dilatory over the Taiwan issue. China's new Western-orientated foreign policy included the restoration of normal relations with Japan; moreover, in sharp contrast with the earlier period of the Cultural Revolution, interaction with the capitalist global economy—supposedly the source of counter-revolutionary evil—increased in terms of both trade and inward investment.

In the aftermath of the final victory of the revolutionary forces in Indo-China in 1975, Chinese fears of Soviet encirclement, following the US withdrawal, increased. These fears were exacerbated by what were perceived as Soviet advances in Africa and in the People's Democratic Republic of Yemen. Events in Indo-China brought matters to a culmination. The rapid deterioration of Sino-Vietnamese relations, accompanied by the exodus of Hoa Chinese from Viet Nam, was centred mainly on the issue of Cambodia, where China was aligned with the country's infamous leader, Pol Pot, as part of a long-standing policy to deny to Viet Nam dominance over the whole of Indo-China. As Viet Nam consolidated its links with the USSR in 1978, China signed a treaty of peace and friendship with Japan and, in December (during the course of the vital Third Plenum of the CCP—see above), restored normal relations with the USA. Towards the end of December Viet Nam duly invaded Cambodia and, within a fortnight, had occupied most of the country and established a subservient regime in the capital of Phnom-Penh. In February–March 1979 China attacked Viet Nam in an exercise that was announced in advance to be of limited duration and penetration. The campaign did not go well for the Chinese forces. Nevertheless, after the capture of the provincial capital of Long Son, the Chinese army withdrew. This was perhaps a salutary episode for both China and Viet Nam, but, importantly from the Chinese point of view, the USSR did not directly intervene.

For the next 10 years the result was an impasse in Indo-China, leaving Viet Nam in a parlous economic condition, politically isolated and dependent upon the USSR. China, meanwhile, acting in parallel with the USA, forged an alliance with Thailand and a diplomatic partnership with the countries of the Association of Southeast Asian Nations (ASEAN), despite the misgivings of at least two of the member countries. The collapse of the USSR left Viet Nam economically bereft and totally incapable of sustaining its occupation of Cambodia. China, therefore, was able to impose its terms for an accommodation with Viet Nam, which was achieved in 1991, and at the same time to co-sponsor a UN Security Council Resolution for settling the Cambodian problem. Accordingly, China was able to attain its main objectives in Indo-China through the UN. In this way Chinese leaders could portray themselves as important and responsible members of the international community—a significant consideration in view of the international disapprobation still attached to China after the Tiananmen massacre.

Since embarking upon the policies of reform in the late 1970s, economic considerations have become an increasingly important component of China's foreign relations. As China's leaders put it, they sought a tranquil international environment in which to concentrate on domestic economic tasks. To this end, they were quick to seize upon the perceived decline of the Soviet threat, and in 1982, at the 12th Congress of the CCP, it was announced that China was to pursue a foreign policy of independence and would adopt a more balanced approach to the two superpowers. Indeed, China still gravitated towards the USA, but Chinese leaders sought to manoeuvre more freely. China's problems with the USSR were epitomized by the reiterated demands that it remove the so-called 'three obstacles' (withdraw from Afghanistan, reduce the military threat from the north and end the support to Viet Nam that had enabled the latter to occupy Cambodia). Following the accession of Mikhail Gorbachev to the Soviet leadership, the USSR developed new approaches to foreign policy that met Chinese demands and prepared the way for a summit meeting between Gorbachev and Deng Xiaoping in May 1989. However, this meeting was overshadowed by the student-led demonstrations in Beijing, and hopes that the two reforming communist powers might develop new relations were thwarted in part by the bloodshed in Tiananmen Square. Yet China's leaders were also concerned about the implications for themselves of the collapse of communism in Eastern Europe, for which the Chinese leadership privately held Gorbachev responsible to a considerable degree. The failure of the Soviet coup of August 1991 disappointed China's leaders, but they reacted with unusual aplomb to the collapse of the USSR itself, moving quickly to establish formal diplomatic relations with the successor states, including those of Central Asia.

China's relations with the West in general, and the USA in particular, have been marked by ambivalence. On the one hand, China's leaders recognize the importance of the West for China's modernization as a supplier of technology, managerial expertise and capital; on the other hand, they fear the possibility of 'Westernization' and the erosion of the Chinese communist system that may follow. These concerns have focused especially upon relations with the USA. For much of the 1980s China's leaders were able to manoeuvre within the so-called 'strategic triangle' involving both the USSR and the USA. As a result, they were able to take advantage of a quasi-alignment with the USA without paying what they would have regarded as excessive costs in terms of loss of independence. Thus, China and the USA pursued parallel policies regarding the Cambodian and Afghan conflicts. They were separately allied with Thailand and Pakistan, and they both gave material and diplomatic support to the armed resistance to the Vietnamese and Russian invaders respectively. The Chinese were also able to gain access to advanced technology of military significance. At the same time the existence of the USSR as a counterweight to the USA enabled China's leaders to pursue in principle an independent foreign policy. Despite the continuation of the Taiwan issue as a problem between the two sides, China won favour within the USA because of its economic reforms and its open-door policies. Its poor record on human rights proved to be no obstacle to gaining US support for accession to international economic organizations, such as the World Bank and the IMF, from which China gained greatly. Unlike the USSR, China was also allowed entry into the domestic US market on the basis of most favoured nation trading status (MFN, now known as normal permanent trading relations—NPTR).

After 1989 much of this changed. In the short term, the Tiananmen killings brought international condemnation. Although pragmatic self-interest soon ensured that most countries began to re-engage with China, the unduly favourable image of Chinese reformist leaders in the West changed instantly. More significantly, the importance of gaining the support of China, with its crucial position between the USSR and the USA, was fundamentally altered by the end of the 'Cold War'.

China's Changing Position

China's geo-strategic importance during the 'Cold War' was soon replaced by considerations of China's geo-economic position as a result of rapid economic growth after 1992. From the mid-1990s the idea that China was not simply a growing power but a potential superpower that would eventually challenge the USA and the liberal world order, became increasingly widespread. That view, combined with the fact that the USA no longer needed to invoke the issue of China with regard to the USSR, contributed to the US-led insistence that China conform better to what were presented as universal norms of state conduct. In particular, the USA emphasized observance of human rights, agreements about the non-proliferation of weapons of mass destruction and medium-range missiles, and greater transparency in military matters and various trade practices, including observance of intellectual property rights (IPRs).

In 1994 US President Bill Clinton yielded on the MFN issue by dissociating it from that of human rights. In February 1995, after tense negotiations, the Chinese eventually acceded to US demands on IPRs. However, by this stage Chinese strategists had come to the conclusion that the USA was imposing various constraints upon China in a concerted attempt to maintain its weakness. Matters came to a head when President Lee Teng-hui of Taiwan was granted a visa to visit the USA in a private capacity in April 1995. The USA was consequently accused of seeking to divide China. Beijing denounced President Lee in the most virulent terms for allegedly seeking independence, and in late 1995 initiated a series of intimidatory military manoeuvres. These culminated in March 1996 with the firing of missiles into the sea within less than 100 km of Taiwan's two major ports.

If anything, these tactics produced the opposite of the effect intended, as in an overwhelming victory Lee was returned to office in Taiwan's first direct presidential election. Moreover, the USA responded to the Chinese military aggression by sending two aircraft carrier battle groups. The crisis of March 1996 ironically opened the way for an improvement in Sino-US relations, as both sides sought to avoid similar confrontations in the future. Meanwhile, the USA upgraded its strategic alliance with Japan by agreeing new guidelines that widened the scope of the support that Japan might give to US forces engaged in a conflict in the region. A closer Sino-US dialogue developed, in part to assuage Chinese concerns about the possible implications of these guidelines for the Taiwan Strait. These developments culminated in important reciprocal presidential visits, by Jiang Zemin to the USA in late 1997, and by Bill Clinton to China in mid-1998. The two Presidents agreed to establish a 'strategic partnership', and Clinton's visit was notable for his address to the Chinese people, broadcast live on television and radio, in which he denounced the Tiananmen killings and urged a progression to greater democracy. However, Clinton also praised Jiang's personal qualities and the 'moral' worth of China's reform programmes.

This improvement in relations was tested by the election of George W. Bush to the US presidency. After his assumption of office in January 2001, there was no more talk of strategic partnerships; instead China was viewed as a potential 'strategic competitor' in some respects and as a country with which the USA had important economic links in other respects. In practice, relations were strained initially by an accident on 1 April, involving a US surveillance aircraft and a Chinese jet that was monitoring it. The collision, which killed the pilot of the Chinese aircraft and forced the US aeroplane to make an emergency landing on Hainan Island, led to a crisis that was not resolved until the 24 US crew members were released 12 days later. Meanwhile, relations had not been improved by a decision by the new US Administration to accede to requests from Taiwan for the provision of most of the modern weaponry required by the island. However, officials in both Beijing and Washington recognized that it was not in their interests to allow their relationship to deteriorate unduly, and they thus ensured that their economic links were unaffected. The Chinese leadership nevertheless objected to what it regarded as US hegemonic attempts to prevent China's rise. It favoured the development of multi-polarity among the world's great powers as a means to constrain the unilateralism of the single superpower. The Chinese objected especially to aspects of the anti-ballistic-missile systems supported by the Bush Administration, as they feared that these would undermine the Chinese deterrent force and promote Taiwanese independence by providing protection for Taiwan against China.

The terrorist attacks on the USA on 11 September 2001 led to a major improvement in the all-important relationship with that country. China was quick to join the US-led coalition against international terrorism. Although the Chinese leadership did not contribute directly to the campaign against al-Qa'ida, the organization held responsible for the attacks on the USA, and the Taliban of Afghanistan, it did begin to share intelligence and undertook to deny financial assets and services to international terrorists. China managed to elicit formal US support against alleged Uygur terrorists in Xinjiang in return for greater legal explicitness on the part of China in restricting the export of weapons of mass destruction and related technologies. Much to Jiang's satisfaction, President Bush visited China twice within six months (in October 2001 and again in February 2002). Bush also appeared to have established a good rapport with President Hu Jintao at the first appearance of a Chinese leader at a G8 meeting of advanced industrialized nations in Evian, France, in June 2003. Although outstanding differences remained, neither pressed the other unduly on any particular issue. In April 2006, during Hu's first official presidential visit to the USA, a protester shouted at Bush to stop Hu killing and persecuting members of Falun Gong. The protester was forcefully removed. Bush later apologized to Hu for the incident, which was in many ways symbolic of the manner in which the Administration of George W. Bush had reduced its criticism of Chinese human rights violations. Instead, Bush sought a more pragmatic bilateral relationship in an era when economic considerations appeared to have transcended the rhetoric of the promotion of human rights.

Nevertheless, these economic issues remained a source of considerable bilateral tension. The principal concern was the growing size of an already large US trade deficit with China. US criticisms focused on residual protection of the Chinese economy and the lack of full implementation of WTO reforms, the subsidizing of Chinese companies, including exporters (for example, by extending loans that were never repaid), and, in particular, exchange rate controls that kept the Chinese currency undervalued (and as a result, continued to render the value of Chinese exports to the US 'artificially' low). The Chinese authorities responded by arguing that much of this deficit was caused by foreign (including US) firms having closed their factories elsewhere and transferred to China and was therefore not simply a 'Chinese' surplus. In addition, they pointed out that an end to the US embargo on high-technology exports to China would significantly reduce the imbalance. Other major issues included continued complaints about the enforcement of IPR legislation in China and the extent to which cheap Chinese goods were being produced by means of the violation of workers' rights. Although this latter question related to the issue of human rights, it was equally important both for US producers and employees, who were unable to compete as a result, and for Chinese workers and their treatment.

However, the balance of power in this economic relationship appeared to change with the onset of the global economic crisis in late 2008. China's increasing trade surplus had resulted in the accumulation of massive foreign exchange reserves. In addition, from 2007 Chinese organizations began to increase their purchases of stakes in major foreign financial institutions. While there was considerable concern at the growth of Chinese ownership of financial assets in the USA (and elsewhere), as the global economic crisis began to develop, Chinese finance seemed to provide an important and welcome source of capitalization. The consequences for US-Chinese financial relations were far from clear. In the USA and elsewhere, there was concern (and in some places hope) that Chinese institutions would see the crisis as an opportunity to buy ever greater numbers of shares at low prices and thus increase their overseas holdings. However, there was also concern that, if political relations were to deteriorate, China might decide to dispose of US-dollar holdings and thus substantially weaken the dollar. Notwithstanding considerable opposition within China to increasing contributions to the IMF to support rich Western states in crisis, there was a recognition that a stable global financial order and a recovery in global demand were in China's own economic interest.

With both sides in a position of mutual mistrust but also mutual dependency, debates over how to handle the future relationship remained very much ongoing in both countries. However, the pragmatic acceptance of this dependency resulted in an apparent increase in China's economic power. As perhaps best epitomized by China's presence at the G20 summit meeting of leading industrial nations held in London, United Kingdom, in April 2009, China had become an essential element of any form of global financial governance. In June President Hu Jintao attended the first leaders' summit meeting of the BRIC states—Brazil, Russia, India, China; the first BRIC meeting, in 2008, had been attended by ministers responsible for foreign affairs. The 2009 summit's official communiqué urged a greater role for emerging economic powers in global financial governance. Thus, the desire for a new global order that reflected the changing balance of international economic activity and power was not simply a Chinese aspiration.

Although bilateral tensions largely focused on economic issues, there remained concern in the USA about the nature of China's rise and whether this would undermine the global power and influence of the USA, and perhaps even lead to future conflict. Early enthusiasm about President Obama in

China was rapidly replaced by anger and disappointment on both sides in late 2009. Obama's visit to China in November puzzled many because of the way in which his itinerary was carefully controlled; during his tour, Obama met mainly with politicians and was allowed very little contact with ordinary Chinese people. Despite issuing a comprehensive joint statement reiterating their major acts of co-operation and joint interests, the Copenhagen Climate Change Summit in December marked a far less well-tempered period, with both sides accusing the other of responsibility for the lack of a clear agreement. Chinese anger at being forced into an unwelcome position was held up against US criticism that China was refusing to accept its responsibilities. In early 2010 confirmation of the sale to Taiwan by the USA of defence equipment worth several thousand million US dollars only deepened Chinese displeasure. It was equalled in the USA by protests against the large trade deficit and by claims that China was manipulating its own currency to secure an advantage. Some economists claimed that this was causing the loss of as many as 2m. jobs in the USA. Political arguments over what pressure to exert on Iran through the UN regarding its nuclear programme, how to deal with the Democratic People's Republic of Korea (DPRK—North Korea), and the repercussions of the withdrawal of Google from the Chinese market were only partially dispelled in April when President Hu Jintao attended a global non-proliferation conference in Washington, DC. However, the Chinese Government remained highly resistant to any notion of a global 'G2', with the USA and China as vital partners in a modern global structure. Hu Jintao and Wen Jiabao were both vociferous in their resistance to this prospect, stating that China had enough internal problems without having to assume some kind of global policing role akin to that of the USA. The impact of the mid-term elections in the USA in November 2010 on that country's political scene, with a distinct shift to the right, meant that Obama was forced further to strengthen his position even with regard to Hu Jintao's state visit to the USA in January 2011. While Hu was accorded full formal treatment, considerable pressure was imposed on him during discussions on the value of the Chinese currency and on China's human rights record, with the US Administration displaying an impressive coherence. At a press conference held at the White House, Hu was openly confronted about the human rights situation; he responded by asserting that China fully supported universal human rights. Perhaps one of the greatest problems in Sino-US relations that became more evident during 2010–11 was the restatement of strategic interest in the South China Sea by the USA and the attendant awareness on the part of US policy-makers of China's increased influence and power in that region. The USA's concern over this situation appeared to be exacerbated by the substantial military technological advances that China had made in recent years.

However, the unresolved status of Taiwan, (de facto independence, but still regarded by the Chinese Government as part of the People's Republic) could not be underestimated, no matter what other issues came to the fore in China's foreign relations. The election of Nationalist Party (KMT) leader Ma Ying-jeou in March 2008 reduced some of the tension. By 2010 his more conciliatory approach to relations across the straits had resulted in the establishment of direct air, shipping and postal links. More mainland tourists were permitted to visit Taiwan, and the Economic Co-operation Framework Agreement (ECFA—see below) was ratified in June 2010. In addition, from 2009, following the withdrawal of long-held Chinese objections, Taiwan had been allowed to assume observer status at meetings of WHO. However, China maintained more than 1,000 missile launchers on the coast facing the island, and continued to assert its rights over how Taiwan operated internationally. The USA remained politically and, through the 1979 Taiwan Relations Act, legally committed to helping the island defend itself, in case of any military attack (see below).

China's engagement with Africa was another source of potential misunderstanding and conflict. This engagement was primarily driven by Chinese resource requirements and was supported by senior-level diplomatic initiatives, such as Premier Wen Jiabao's official visits to seven African states in June 2006 and President Hu Jintao's 12-day visit to eight African countries in February 2007. In addition, China hosted a special Sino-African summit meeting in Beijing in November 2006, with a subsequent meeting in 2009.

While immediate external attention focused on the repercussions for the prices and distribution of resources, considerations of the political implications soon emerged. China not only offered an alternative market and source of finance for African states, but an alternative that did not insist on democratization and/or economic liberalization in return for increased trade relations. Despite repeated official statements that China was not seeking hegemony in Africa, some scholars and policymakers argued that this engagement would diminish the existing US dominance and undermine the liberal order through the replacement of the 'Washington consensus' with an illiberal 'Beijing consensus'. Indeed, much to the annoyance of many Chinese officials, China was criticized not only for providing economic support to the Sudanese Government, but also for not using its influence to halt the conflict in the province of Darfur. Similarly, when Buddhist monks took to the streets in anti-Government demonstrations in Myanmar in 2007, China came under scrutiny and again attracted criticism for providing economic and diplomatic support to the country's military rulers while not taking firmer action to bring the crisis to a positive conclusion.

In April 2008 there was strong international condemnation of China when it became clear that the Chinese ship *An Yue Jiang* was carrying weapons for the Zimbabwean Government at a time when the result of the Zimbabwean election was still being disputed. After South African dockers refused to unload the ship, it was formally recalled to China. However, the weapons were reported eventually to have found their way to Harare via the Republic of the Congo with the help of the Angolan Government, which not only remained friendly towards Zimbabwe, but was also China's biggest trade partner on the African continent and was itself a subject of international criticism in relation to its own human rights record.

With international pressure on China to act responsibly and to influence its allies to act accordingly, Chinese policy did seem to moderate. Rather than simply rejecting the Western global order, China's position in Darfur and its relations with 'pariah' states such as Zimbabwe and Myanmar were increasingly defended in terms of China's contribution to peace, security and wealth and the maintenance of the existing global order. Officials also emphasized China's increasing contribution to UN peace-keeping operations: by 2009 a total of 12,744 Chinese peace-keepers had been dispatched to assist on 18 UN operations since the first Chinese participation as observers to truce supervision in 1990. Nevertheless, the Chinese leadership appeared to be caught in a dilemma with regard to how to promote the image of the country as a protagonist in the global order: on one side, a responsible status quo stakeholder in the existing order; on the other, the promoter of an alternative to the dominant liberal world order, and an alternative economic partner with no conditions of liberalization attached to economic relations.

However, a possible shift in policy was evident in China's response to the deteriorating situation in Libya in February and March 2011, when that country was convulsed first by protests and then by full-scale rebellion against the regime of Col Muammar al-Qaddafi. China supported UN resolutions in condemning the Libyan Government's brutal suppression of the uprising and evacuated more than 36,000 Chinese nationals from the troubled country. What remained less clear, however, was whether China would support the imposition of a 'no-fly' zone, and the extent to which it had moved away from its traditional position of 'non interference' in the affairs of other countries.

China's new approach to Africa was symbolic of the way in which the end of the 'Cold War' and the requirements of economic modernization had become even more important in the country's foreign policy. Better relations had been forged with China's neighbours, including the newly established states of Central Asia and Russia itself. Relations between Russia and China were described by both sets of leaders as better than ever. With the USSR no longer in existence, Viet Nam and India, both former Soviet allies, have accommodated themselves more to Chinese interests. Indeed, as a result of increasing convergence on economic issues, Sino-Indian relations have become better than at any time since 1949, and were officially described as a 'strategic and co-operative partnership for peace and prosperity' in a statement signed by Premier Wen Jiabao and Indian Prime Minister Manmohan Singh in April 2005. This was renewed during Singh's visit to China in January 2008 when the two leaders issued a joint communiqué which was officially described as a 'shared vision for the 21st century'. Even so, the two countries remain wary of each other, with their ongoing border dispute still unresolved (one of the few land-border issues that China still has). China has maintained an ambiguous position towards many other countries in Asia, sometimes presenting itself as a fellow developing country doing its best to emerge from poverty, and at other times as a true regional superpower, able to flex its diplomatic and economic power over almost the whole region. On the positive side, despite the Asian financial crisis of the late 1990s, China was acknowledged to have assumed a significant role in enhancing the economy of the region as a whole. It forged closer links with Japan, which became a major trading partner, and economic relations deepened with the Republic of Korea (South Korea), Taiwan and the ASEAN countries. China's adjacent provinces of Fujian and Guangdong became increasingly integrated with the economies of Taiwan and Hong Kong, collectively being recognized as 'Greater China' and representing one of the USA's largest trading partners. The objective of economic growth, it was suggested, meant that China needed a peaceful international environment and would become an ever more responsible power desirous of maintaining the status quo.

On the more negative side, some observers suggested that China's expanding international economic relations were having an adverse impact on other regional economies. Investment that might once have gone to Malaysia, Thailand or the Philippines was instead being drawn to China, while Japanese, South Korean and Taiwanese producers also transferred labour-intensive productive capacity to take advantage of China's lower wage costs. As the Chinese economy grew, jobs were lost elsewhere in the region, and other countries' economic fortunes became increasingly dependent on developments in China.

To this end, China attempted to show that it took the interests of neighbouring countries into account. At the 2003 meeting of the Boao Forum for Asia, Zheng Bijian, the Chairman of the China Reform Forum, promoted the 'Peaceful Rise of China' thesis, which subsequently became a quasi-official ideology: rather than leading to the threat to international security that some had predicted, China's rise would instead not only be peaceful but act as a positive force for development.

On a more practical level, Chinese leaders began to take a pro-active role in pressing for greater regional economic integration. Following the Asian financial crisis of the late 1990s, the concept of economic security (based on the recognition that events elsewhere in the region had important domestic consequences) became increasingly important for Chinese policy-makers. Thus, following its instigation in 2001, China participated in the Chiang Mai Initiative, whereby regional states agreed to support each others' currencies against speculative action (such as that undertaken in 1997). China became an active advocate of the ASEAN + 3 process, which brought together the leaders of ASEAN states and those of China, Japan and South Korea. China was also working individually with ASEAN, and, in 2004, it agreed to establish an ASEAN-China Free Trade Area, which took effect in January 2010. At a meeting of the ADB in 2006, the Chinese Minister of Finance agreed with his Japanese and South Korean counterparts to start work on the feasibility of a single Asian currency. Within a decade, therefore, Chinese policy-makers had progressed from viewing multilateral regional organizations as a threat to not only accepting them but actively promoting the further consolidation of such regional co-operation.

The global economic crisis that quickly escalated from September 2008 provided another opportunity for Chinese financial diplomacy in the region. One week after the cancellation of a scheduled summit meeting in Thailand of ASEAN + 6 (the ASEAN states plus China, Australia, Japan, India, South Korea and New Zealand) owing to domestic political violence in the host town of Pattaya, Chinese Premier Wen Jiabao used the Boao Forum for Asia conference in April 2009 to promote not only deeper regional co-operation to cope with the crisis, but also the idea that China was at the centre of this regional effort. China announced the creation of a US $10,000m. investment fund to support infrastructure projects in ASEAN states to help them withstand the global crisis. The promotion of the fund by the Chinese Government was regarded as a material sign of the East Asian country's increasing regional influence.

China has revealed a more ruthless side in the assertion of its territorial claims, involving nearly all of its maritime neighbours. No way has been found of settling the competing claims, and China appears to have difficulty in deciding between the nationalist urge to claim control over the disputed islands and territorial seas, on the one hand, and the economic necessity of establishing stable relations with the same disputants on the other. While competing claims in South-East Asia have remained unresolved, China has at least agreed (for the moment anyway) not to settle the issues by force. However, clashes between Chinese fishing trawlers and Japanese and South Korean coastguard vessels in September 2010 and March 2011 respectively emphasized just how contentious such issues could become. China was the first non-ASEAN country to sign the Association's Treaty of Amity and Co-operation in South-East Asia, which committed members to settle conflicts by non-military means. It also signed a declaration of a code of conduct concerning the South China Sea that required it to desist from making unilateral bids to expand its presence in the contested Spratly chain of islands.

In April 1996 an unprecedented multilateral treaty was signed with Russia and the three Central Asian Republics of Kazakhstan, Kyrgyzstan and Tajikistan, the countries becoming known as the Shanghai Five. This document went beyond agreement about the demarcation of the members' long-disputed borders to include commitments to undertake military measures to enhance confidence and a pledge to refrain from exacerbating ethnic or religious tensions in each others' countries. In June 2001 these links were reaffirmed with the establishment of the Shanghai Co-operation Organization (SCO), and the number of participating states was increased to six with the accession of Uzbekistan. The SCO established a Regional Anti-Terrorism Structure in 2004, and annual summit meetings also consider other forms of co-operation (economy, technology, transport, energy, culture and education) as well as the original security agenda. At the 2009 summit in the Russian city of Yekaterinburg, observer states (Pakistan, Iran, India and Mongolia) were allowed to participate in closed-door discussions for the first time, and the President of Afghanistan also took part as a specially invited guest. The summit extended dialogue-partner status to Sri Lanka and Belarus, and it was agreed to work towards a formal mechanism for expanding membership in the future. In addition to China's co-operation with Russia within the SCO, direct bilateral exchanges between the two countries have continued. A new treaty of partnership and friendship was signed in July 2001.

As a symbol of the new relationship, 2006 was designated the official 'Year of Russia' in China and 2007 the 'Year of China' in Russia. After a meeting between Presidents Putin and Hu in July 2005, the two countries issued a 'Joint Declaration on the International Order in the 21st Century', outlining their common concerns about US hegemony and threats to territorial integrity from separatist ethnic groupings. Following his election as Russian President in March 2008, Dmitrii Medvedev chose China as the destination for his first official foreign visit. The two sides used the occasion to repeat their shared concern about the global order, this time focusing on missile defence systems (although not specifically referring to the USA). This shared objection to US dominance was not merely rhetorical. China and Russia had started engaging in large-scale joint military exercises for the first time in August 2005. Moreover, as China continued the process of upgrading and modernizing its own military-industrial complex (and since the US-EU embargo on sales of weaponry to the People's Republic, introduced in 1989, remained in force), Russia had become the main supplier of a new generation of military hardware. The different levels of military co-operation formed a very important part of the new Sino-Russian partnership, as did economic relations. The need to secure access to energy resources either in or through (via new pipelines) the former Soviet Union, and through Russian support for China's nuclear energy programme, highlighted the importance of economic security in general, and energy security in particular, as a determinant of Chinese foreign policy.

North Korea also found itself more dependent upon China and, under Chinese pressure, it joined the UN, together with South Korea, in 1991. Yet it did not follow China in reforming its troubled economy and in opening up to the outside world. North Korean leaders were greatly angered by China's formal recognition of the South in 1992. North Korea then began to use its perceived nuclear potential in a desperate diplomatic bid to ensure its survival. China skilfully manoeuvred between its own conflicting interests of seeking to avoid the collapse of North Korea, while at the same time striving to prevent the proliferation of nuclear weapons in North-East Asia. In reaching the Framework Agreement with North Korea in 1994, the US Government acknowledged that the Chinese had been crucially helpful behind the scenes. China continued to play a role in facilitating US diplomacy with North Korea and in encouraging North-South interactions. China was pleased with the first North-South summit meeting, which was held in the North Korean capital of Pyongyang in mid-2000, and with the exchange of senior officials between North Korea and the outgoing Clinton Administration.

From 2001, however, the Administration of George W. Bush took an unaccommodating approach to North Korea and ended this phase of active diplomatic engagement. Chinese interests were not best served by an escalation of tension, and China favoured the resumption of US-DPRK negotiations and the establishment of a mode of co-existence between the two Koreas, as that would allow the North to remain as an unofficial buffer state. Preoccupied with Iraq, the Bush Administration, like its predecessor, soon came to realize the advantage of using China as an interlocutor with North Korea. Tension increased after North Korea's admission in October 2002 that it was engaged in the use of enriched uranium. China started to play a more active diplomatic role, particularly as North Korea began to carry out its threat of building nuclear weapons amid fears of a possible US attack, especially following the onset of the conflict in Iraq in early 2003. Beijing subsequently hosted six-party talks, encompassing China, North and South Korea, the USA, Russia and Japan. Following North Korea's statement in February 2005 that it now possessed nuclear weapons, in September of that year a draft joint agreement on the dismantling of the DPRK's nuclear programme was signed by all six participants in the talks, an achievement for which Chinese diplomacy received considerable credit. Although that agreement was compromised almost immediately by North Korean demands to receive a light-water reactor before any disarmament could take place, China remained the country believed to be the most capable of influencing the North Korean regime, as shown by an incognito visit to the People's Republic in January 2006 by the North Korean leader, Kim Jong Il, during which he undertook a tour of the Shenzhen SEZ. Reports of North Korea's first test of a nuclear weapon in October aroused much international concern and led to the imposition of UN sanctions, which, as a permanent member of the Security Council, China endorsed, despite expressing some reservations.

Tensions increased in April 2009 when North Korea tested an intermediate-range missile that flew over Japan and landed in the sea off the east coast. A statement issued by the Chinese Ministry of Foreign Affairs declared that 'we strongly urge the DPRK to honour its commitment to denuclearization, stop relevant moves that may further worsen the situation and return to the six-party talks'. The language of the statement suggested considerable anger within the Chinese Government over North Korea's actions and frustration at its inability to influence the leadership in Pyongyang. However, the six-party talks were effectively suspended in April when North Korea announced that it was no longer willing to participate. After a further nuclear test in May, the UN issued a new resolution (No. 1874), which condemned the testing 'in the strongest terms' and strengthened existing sanctions. (See the chapter on the Democratic People's Republic of Korea.) Reports of increasing poverty owing to a mishandled currency revaluation in North Korea in late 2009, and problems over the succession plans for an ailing Kim Jong Il, only served to make the regime even more erratic in 2010. A torpedo attack on a South Korean ship in international waters in March, which resulted in 46 deaths, was, after an international investigation, attributed to North Korea. Kim Jong Il made his first visit in five years to Beijing in late April. He returned in August of the same year, arousing keen interest in the purpose behind a second visit within a matter of a few months (an unprecedented occurrence). Unconfirmed reports stated that Kim Jong Il was accompanied by his third son, Kim Jong Un, perhaps hoping to gain China's support in nominating him as his successor. In November an attack by North Korea on the South Korean island of Yeonpyeong led to more international pressure being exerted on China to curb its increasingly erratic and isolated neighbour. Chinese frustrations at North Korea's behaviour were perhaps best expressed by material published in November 2010 by WikiLeaks (an organization disseminating leaked private and classified content), which quoted a senior Chinese official as stating that the country frequently acted like a spoiled child and suggesting that China increasingly favoured Korean reunification. Meanwhile, however, China's leaders continued publicly to support their neighbour, with Wu Bangguo expressing 'eternal affection' for visiting North Koreans only one week after the fatal artillery attacks on the island of Yeonpyeong.

On 1 July 1997 Hong Kong was returned to China under the terms of the Sino-British Joint Declaration that had been agreed in September 1984. The Chinese Government undertook to allow Hong Kong to enjoy a high degree of autonomy as a Special Administrative Region (SAR), in order to maintain its economic system and way of life for a further 50 years. (This arrangement of 'one country, two systems' is regarded in China as a potential model for the eventual reunion of Taiwan with the mainland.) The negotiations between the United Kingdom and China were often acrimonious, and Chinese leaders were particularly displeased with the last British Governor, Chris Patten, whom they vilified for his attempts to broaden democracy in the territory without first securing their consent. Consequently, in 1997 they replaced the legislature elected in 1995 with a provisional body. Elections to a new legislative body were held in May 1998, under a mixed system of voting in which the number of people eligible to vote was severely reduced and, despite apprehensions on all sides, the transition to Chinese sovereignty proceeded smoothly. In April 2004 the Chinese Government announced from Beijing that it had 'interpreted' the Basic Law (Hong Kong's Constitution) and that, regardless of the desires of the Hong Kong people, universal suffrage would not be permitted either to elect the Chief Executive in the following year or in the legislative elections scheduled for 2007/08. Popular demonstrations against the policies of the mainland Government continued in Hong Kong. Hu Jintao publicly criticized Tung Chee-hwa' s leadership of Hong Kong, and in March 2005 the SAR's Chief Executive resigned, ostensibly owing to ill health. Tung was replaced by his Chief Secretary, Donald Tsang, who, despite having been honoured as a Knight Commander of the Order of the British Empire, was considered to be close to the Government in Beijing. Constitutional arguments continued in 2010 over the plans to introduce full universal suffrage for elections to the Chief Executive position by 2018, and for the Legislative Council by 2022. On 20 December 1999 Macao, the first and last Western possession in Asia, reverted from Portuguese to Chinese sovereignty on a similar basis to that of Hong Kong. (See the chapters on Hong Kong and Macao for further details.)

The Prospects for China's Future Relations

China's international relations have changed considerably in the post-'Cold War' era. There remain major concerns about the global role of the USA, particularly the Administration's ability to circumvent the UN and pursue US interests through military force when deemed necessary. However, the direct military threat that the superpowers once posed to China has now ended, and the previously uneasy relationships with Russia, Viet Nam and India have been transformed into varying degrees of partnership and collaboration. Relations with ASEAN have moved from being characterized by suspicion to active engagement, symbolized by the China-ASEAN summit meeting held in Nanning in October 2006, commemorating 15 years of formal dialogue. Followed a week later by the Sino-African summit in Beijing, the two meetings combined to promote a vision of a China that is an increasing force in international relations, and a leading power in the 'non-West'—if not yet the world as a whole. China's leaders might be reconciled to the global predominance of the USA as the world's sole superpower, but they still seek to encourage movement towards a more multi-polar world that would enable China better to balance the power of the USA. This is manifest not only in Chinese initiatives in South-East Asia, the former USSR, and Africa, but elsewhere as well.

Chinese relations with the EU as a whole and with individual EU states have also improved. While these relations are primarily based on expanding economic relations (and resolving bilateral economic problems such as access to the EU market), there is a suspicion in some quarters in the USA that China is trying to develop a strategic relationship with the EU that, although perhaps not directly challenging US hegemony, would at least go some way towards undermining US power in relation to China. The implementation of the Lisbon Treaty, creating an EU president and a high representative for external affairs, in November 2009 aroused expectations by some in China that this would give EU foreign policy greater coherency. Although the EU had become China's largest single trading partner, issues such as the failure of the Union to confer market economy status on China (despite having done so for Russia), its refusal to remove the arms embargo imposed in 1989, and meetings between the presidents of countries such as Germany and France with the Dalai Lama, continued to cause immense irritation in the Chinese Government. By 2010, however, even despite the Lisbon Treaty, there was much greater realism about what the EU was able to deliver collectively. The failure of the Greek economy in mid-2010 resulted in China's purchasing of significant investments and assets in Greece, and even working to stabilize the euro. In January 2011 China bought a substantial amount of Spanish Eurobonds. The Chinese Government also began to purchase more European debt, in order to diversify away from US Treasury bills. While China remained rightly sceptical, therefore, of the EU's political cohesiveness, it understood clearly the Union's economic importance.

China wishes to maintain good relations with the USA largely because it is a major export market and because it is a guarantor of security in the Asia-Pacific region. The conditions of US predominance have served Chinese interests well by providing a peaceful environment in which, since the late 1970s, China has been able to develop its economy so successfully. The US strategic presence has ensured the absence of full-scale war on the Korean Peninsula since 1953 and the containment of possible Japanese militarism. The main practical issue is the question of Taiwan. Beyond that, the Chinese appear to have learned how to balance their practical need to work with the USA against their principled opposition to much of what the USA stands for. The Iraq conflict, which began in 2003, showed how China could maintain a principled opposition without antagonizing the USA. However, China's foreign policy has become increasingly a product of the primary domestic concern: to maintain economic growth and social stability as the prerequisites for maintaining CCP rule.

There remains considerable anxiety in many parts of the world that China will prove to be a, if not the, major challenge to global security. New publications appear on a regular basis (primarily, but not exclusively, in the USA) indicating how economic growth, resource needs, nationalism, territorial claims and increasing military capabilities put China on the road towards superpower status and, according to some observers, inevitable conflict with the USA. Yet in many areas, China appears to be increasingly moderating its ambitions and policies and is now engaging the international community in a pro-active and largely peaceful manner. However, there remain exceptions to this general policy. In addition to the above-mentioned engagement of Africa, the biggest challenges to security lie in China's relations with two territories with which it has extensive economic relations: Japan and Taiwan.

The Chinese authorities have consistently complained that the Japanese have not acknowledged their aggression in the recent past, as demonstrated by the failure of the Japanese authorities to make a full apology for atrocities committed during 1937–45. The Chinese have also claimed that there remains a latent tendency towards militarism in Japan, and the Chinese leadership has quietly appreciated the fact that the US security alliance kept the Japanese from returning to the military path (while publicly often condemning the relationship). From 2001 repeated visits by Japanese Prime Minister Junichiro Koizumi to the Yasukuni Shrine—a controversial memorial honouring Japan's war dead—antagonized China, which continued to fear a resurgence of nationalist sentiment in Japan. Notwithstanding massive Japanese investment in China and extensive bilateral trade relationships, economic interdependence has continued to co-exist alongside sometimes acrimonious political relations.

Ironically, the election of Shinzo Abe, who was previously perceived as holding 'revisionist' views of history, as Japan's Prime Minister in September 2006 immediately resulted in a moderate improvement in relations. Abe engendered concern in Beijing by repeating assertions that no government coercion had been involved in the recruitment by Japanese troops of 'comfort women' for sexual purposes during the Second World War, by urging the EU to maintain its weapons embargo on China and by envisaging closer collaboration between those countries with 'common values' in the region: not with China, but with Australia, India and the USA. However, notwithstanding Abe's views of Japan's past, the Chinese and Japanese authorities regarded the appointment of a new Prime Minister as an opportunity to end the diplomatic confrontation of the Koizumi era. Abe's first international act as Prime Minister was to visit China in October 2006, followed by further discussions with President Hu Jintao and Premier Wen Jiabao at ministerial meetings of Asia-Pacific Economic Cooperation (APEC) and ASEAN respectively in Viet Nam and the Philippines. Wen Jiabao reciprocated the official visit at premier level in April 2007. Although Abe's premiership lasted for only one year, this conciliatory trend continued after Yasuo Fukuda became Prime Minister in September 2007. Most notably, in May 2008 Hu Jintao visited the Japanese capital of Tokyo in his capacity as Head of State (a higher level of diplomacy than Wen's visit as Premier), meeting not only Fukuda and other politicians, but also the Emperor and Empress. In addition to formal discussions regarding competing territorial claims, Hu Jintao promised to lend Japan two pandas, offering to replace the recently deceased Ling Ling in Tokyo Zoo.

The disjuncture between official language and popular commentary is very strong in the relations between China and Japan. On his visit to Japan in 2008 President Hu Jintao talked of a 'new spring' in bilateral relations. Premier Wen Jiabao followed this by emphasizing the good trade and economic links between the two countries in May 2010, when he met in Tokyo with Prime Minister Yukio Hatoyama. However, the memory of the Second World War and Japan's role in destroying so much of China remains strong, with huge museums in Nanjing and other locations in China commemorating the atrocities committed. The perceived failure of Japanese leaders to apologize correctly or, for that matter, to be willing to pay compensation, and the treatment of the war in official Japanese textbooks, where some of the worst events are simply disregarded, all feature highly in popular blogs and complaints in China. This is set against the enormous amounts of economic and development aid that China has received from Japan since the 1980s.

One of the most significant events in 2010 was the ascent of China over Japan as the world's second largest economy in terms of market size. This hugely important development may well force the Japanese to reflect more deeply on their relationship with China. One outstanding issue, in particular, is China's continuing opposition to any reform of the UN Security Council that might allow Japan to occupy a permanent seat. Disputes over sea borders have also continued. Officially, the two countries remain co-operative and enjoy good diplomatic links. On the more popular level, there are constant tensions between the two countries, for example as demonstrated at football matches between the two sides.

Popular nationalism came to the fore in 2008 during preparations for the Olympic Games. The hosting of the Games became an important symbol of national pride, being promoted as international recognition of China's increasing maturity. The association of the hosting of a successful event with patriotism was used to justify some unpopular policies; for example, complaints about the diversion of water sources to Beijing for the Olympics were denounced as unpatriotic. Nevertheless, the Games became a source of national cohesion when the procession of the Olympic torch through Europe and the USA was disrupted by protesters—primarily, but not only, supporters of Tibetan independence—which resulted in discussions in the West about human rights in China and about whether politicians should boycott the opening ceremony. Chinese citizens overseas responded by organizing their own counter-demonstrations in support of the torch relay and by defending China's treatment of Tibet, proclaiming that the region 'was, is and always will be part of China' in the traditional media and also through postings on YouTube, MySpace and other online communities. Within China itself, the protests were perceived either as part of a concerted international effort to condemn China or as the result of Western ignorance or duplicity (and often both). Suggestions of a partial Olympic boycott by France resulted in an embargo of French goods in China and a substantial reduction in the number of Chinese tourists applying for French visas.

With anti-Japanese nationalism in China in turn giving rise to increasing anti-Chinese sentiment in some sectors of the Japanese population, the prospect of competing nationalist movements in each country being inspired by the other remains high. However, the possibility of political conflict developing into military action remains relatively low. The Chinese response to the devastating earthquake and tsunami disaster in Japan in March 2011 was largely sympathetic, with the popular daily newspaper *Renmin Ribao* even carrying an editorial stating that, ultimately, people of all countries were members of one race and needed to respect and have compassion for each other. In the case of relations with Taiwan, conflict remains possible, but again, less so than previously. Since Taiwan is regarded as the last obstacle to attaining the complete unity of the Chinese State and as a remnant of the civil war that has been kept apart from the mainland solely because of US intervention, China's leaders are determined to use any means to prevent the island from declaring itself independent. In mid-2003 China's leaders objected strenuously to a proposal by Chen Shui-bian, the elected President of Taiwan, to change the Constitution by a referendum, as this would have given the sovereignty of the island to the people of Taiwan rather than to the people of China as a whole—a development that would be regarded by Beijing as tantamount to a declaration of Taiwanese independence. Following threats of military action by China if Chen's reform proposals were to be realized, in December 2003 US President Bush warned Chen against seeking to change the status quo unilaterally. Chen nevertheless won the presidential election of March 2004, to the consternation of officials in Beijing. China continued to press the USA on the issue of weapons sales to the island, which in its view only encouraged the untrustworthy Chen to pursue his unilateralist path towards formal independence, and claimed that it would prevent such a development at all costs. China mustered sufficient military force to make these threats credible, and it deployed medium-range ballistic missiles across the Taiwan Strait in the Nanjing Military Region.

In March 2005 the NPC approved a new anti-secession law mandating a military response in the event of any move to establish an independent Taiwan. Although the law added little to existing Chinese national defence commitments to preventing any declaration of Taiwanese independence, it acted as a clear reaffirmation of those commitments (and reinforced the nationalist credentials of the leadership of Hu Jintao and Wen Jiabao). Highly publicized visits to mainland China by Taiwanese nationalist leaders, including that of KMT Chairman Lien Chan in April–May 2005, could be regarded as an attempt by Beijing to persuade the Taiwanese electorate to support a 'one China' party rather than risk provoking war by voting for Chen Shui-bian's pro-independence Democratic Progressive Party (DPP). In January 2006 Chen announced that the National Reunification Council, established in 1991 to plan Taiwan's strategy of eventual unification with the mainland, was no longer in operation (and had reportedly not met since 2000). This development was portrayed by the mainland Chinese Government as another stage in the island's progression to independence, and when it became clear that the Council had been abolished rather than simply suspended, the USA also criticized Chen for destabilizing cross-straits relations. In May 2006 Chen requested an overnight stop in the USA en route to official engagements in Panama and Costa Rica, as he had done prior to previous visits to Latin America. When he was granted only a brief refuelling stop in Alaska shortly before his aircraft was due to depart from Taiwan, Chen decided to fly west via the Lebanese capital of Beirut instead. However, when news of Chen's decision was made public in the USA, the Chinese authorities contacted the Lebanese Government, which, with the plane already airborne, retracted permission to land. Chen finally arrived in Paraguay after 36 hours and refuelling stops in Abu Dhabi and Amsterdam. The nature of Chen's trip stood in stark contrast to President Hu Jintao's first formal state visit to the USA in the previous month, conducted with all the accoutrements of official diplomacy.

The congruence of the US and Taiwanese presidential elections with the holding of the Olympic Games in Beijing in 2008 led to some concern regarding the possibility of any progression towards Taiwanese independence resulting in a military response from the mainland. However, in the event, the pro-independence movement suffered significant set-backs in 2008. At Taiwan's legislative election in January the KMT won the majority of seats. Although the DPP chose the pragmatic former Premier, Frank Hsieh, as its candidate for the island's presidential election, held in March, the KMT candidate, Ma Ying-jeou, secured victory, winning a large majority of the votes cast. While not advocating immediate reunification, Ma's support for the diplomatic status quo removed the threat of conflict arising from any movement towards independence. Moreover, the incoming KMT Government repeatedly stressed its desire to improve relations with the mainland, as demonstrated by Vice-President Vincent Siew's highly significant meeting with President Hu Jintao at the quasi-official Boao Forum in China, held shortly before the official presidential inauguration. Somewhat ironically, while the KMT's establishment of political authority on Taiwan might have been the original cause of cross-straits difficulties, the re-emergence of the KMT as the dominant political authority on Taiwan significantly reduced the immediate sources of tension. Ma Ying-jeou's ability finally to sign an Economic Co-operation Framework Agreement with China in June 2010, effectively creating a free market with hugely reduced tariffs across the Straits, and the establishment of direct air and postal links, were all seen as having a stabilizing influence. However, the major issue of how finally to settle the status of the island is no nearer a solution and, with stronger political identity in Taiwan following its successful democratic development, in many ways the situation appears ever more intractable. (See the chapter on Taiwan for further details of bilateral relations.)

Economy

ROBERT F. ASH

INTRODUCTION

China's traditional economy was dominated by agriculture. Before 1949 more than 90% of the population lived in the countryside and drew a living from farming. The dominance of agriculture is easily explained: from earliest times until as recently as the 1980s the central economic problem for China was how to maintain a favourable balance between food production and population. The scale of this challenge is captured in the finding that during almost 2,000 years of imperial history, a seven-fold increase in population was accompanied by a mere doubling in the area of arable land. Throughout this period there is abundant evidence of frequent local famines caused by natural disasters. At times, neglect of the agricultural infrastructure associated with political upheavals and dynastic decline resulted in even more severe food shortages affecting wider areas. Overall, however, the most remarkable historical achievement of China's farmers was their ability to maintain sufficient output growth to meet the needs of a rising population, and to produce a surplus sufficient to support one of the greatest urban civilizations in the world.

During the 19th century, as serious resource constraints and challenges from the West and from Japan increased, the traditional economy began to falter. According to estimates made by analyst Angus Maddison, between 1820 and 1913 China's share of global gross domestic product (GDP) decreased from 32% to just 9%. During the same period average GDP per caput declined from 90% of the world average to less than 40%. By 1913 the last imperial Chinese Dynasty—the Qing—had fallen and been replaced by a Republican Government. Yet far from this change having heralded a reversal of China's economic fortunes, during the Republican period on the mainland (1912–49) political and military upheavals militated against sustained economic growth. Above all, the war against Japan (1937–45) and the civil war between the ruling Kuomintang (KMT—Nationalist Party) and the Chinese Communist Party (CCP) of 1946–49 had a hugely dislocating effect upon the economy. The impact of these 13 years of war was two-fold. First, it caused massive economic disruption, reflected in depressed levels of agricultural and industrial production, large-scale unemployment, hyperinflation and financial collapse. Second, it devastated China's economic infrastructure through the physical destruction of industrial capital and damage to the all-important irrigation and drainage network, on which agriculture was critically dependent. Such was the economic legacy of the Government of the newly established People's Republic of China in 1949.

ECONOMIC DEVELOPMENT UNDER MAO ZEDONG

When it assumed power in October 1949, the Chinese Government under the leadership of the CCP sought to fulfil the same long-term goal as that of virtually all post-war developing countries. This goal was to transform a poor, backward, traditional and overwhelmingly agricultural economy into a modern, industrial economic power, and to bring substantial improvements in welfare for its citizens. However, the Chinese approach involved the formulation of specific policies to achieve this broad objective. Under Mao Zedong, these reflected the aspirations of a country in pursuit of a socialist-orientated development strategy that borrowed heavily from the CCP's own Marxist-Leninist origins, as well as from the development experience of the USSR.

In 1949 the immediate economic aims of the Chinese Government were defined by the dislocated nature of the economy that it had inherited from 13 years of war. The challenges were three-fold: to curb inflation through the establishment of strict control over the budget and money supply; to restore levels of industrial and farm output to their previous pre-war peaks; and to return the unemployed to work. In addition, the Government sought to lay the foundation for the institutional transformation that would facilitate the subsequent (post-recovery) socialization of the economy.

Owing to the accommodating nature of CCP policies, economic recovery was swift, and by the end of 1952 all major goals had been fulfilled. In the urban sector, small-scale capitalist entrepreneurs were encouraged to continue their operations. Many planners and scientists who had served the KMT Government were found jobs working for the new regime. Only in the agricultural sector did the CCP show its radical credentials through the implementation of a land reform. This increasingly violent campaign eliminated the political power of the landlords in the countryside and made possible the redistribution of more than 40% of all arable land, as well as other farm assets, to the benefit of millions of poor farmers and landless peasants. For the time being, however, land continued to be privately owned and households remained the locus of all major decisions in respect to farming.

The First Five-Year Plan (1953–57)

China's economic strategy between 1953 and 1957 was based on the Soviet model of development. Inherent in this was the imperative of heavy industrialization, which was to be achieved through the establishment of a command economy. The primacy of central planning was reflected in the establishment of a huge bureaucratic apparatus of planning bodies and economic ministries, which formulated and oversaw annual and five-year plans. By this means, strict adherence to the economic priorities of the Government was guaranteed. In particular, by controlling the production and supply of consumer goods, the planners made sure that investment funds were directed to priority heavy industries (industry absorbed 58% of all capital construction investment during the First Five-Year Plan, with transport and communications accounting for a further 19%). The focus of the First Plan was the construction of 156 modern, capital-intensive Soviet 'aid' projects, designed to provide a balanced programme of basic industrial facilities (including iron and steel, energy, machine-building and armaments). However, Soviet assistance extended to more than the provision of capital. In addition to plant and machinery—much of it embodying advanced technology—the USSR provided designs and specifications, and hosted training programmes for large numbers of Chinese engineers and technicians. Some 6,000 Soviet advisers also travelled to China to help with its industrial construction programme. Foreign trade was dominated by the USSR, too, with Chinese primary goods and raw materials being exchanged for Soviet industrial equipment.

In contrast to the industrial sector, and despite its developmental role, agriculture was largely deprived of investment for its needs. Moreover, the imposition of farm quotas at prices fixed by the State was the source of a net financial outflow from the farm sector that helped fund industrial construction, albeit to the detriment of agriculture. Investment neglect of agriculture was justified by the belief that institutional change would be a sufficient condition for farm output growth. Accordingly, in 1955–56 a 'high tide' of accelerated collectivization transformed the organizational framework of agriculture. Private ownership in the farm sector was almost entirely eliminated, and all major agricultural decisions and activities were transferred from households to fully socialist collectives. The collectivist thrust of farm policy remained in place for the remainder of the Mao era. Indeed, not until the early 1980s was the collective framework finally dismantled.

In terms of industrial growth, the First Five-Year Plan was a great success. In constant prices, industrial GDP growth averaged 19.8% annually during 1953–57, as a result of which the industrial sector's share of national GDP rose from 20.9% to 29.7%. By contrast, annual agricultural growth increased by only 3.8%, and by only 3.5% for grain (barely fulfilling the 3.4% target). On its merchandise trade account, China suffered a cumulative deficit of US $6m.

The 'Great Leap Forward' and its Aftermath (1958–65)

The highly unbalanced nature of economic growth under the First Plan was the source of the first 'Maoist adventure'. By 1956 excessive industrial growth, combined with increasing factory wages, was already giving rise to the first episode of serious inflationary pressures since the establishment of the People's Republic in 1949. In addition, intermittent constraints of supplies of food, agricultural raw materials and exports caused by disappointing growth in farm output threatened to impede the overall growth momentum. This was the background against which the leadership began to question the suitability of existing economic policies. Out of this process emerged in 1958 a more indigenous radical strategy, the 'Great Leap Forward', thought to be more appropriate to Chinese conditions. More a vision than a plan, the new strategy advocated a policy of technological dualism ('walking on two legs'), whereby budgetary investment would continue to be focused on heavy industry (the modern leg), while unprecedented mass mobilization of the supposedly under-utilized rural labour force within large-scale communes (the traditional leg) would help promote more rapid agricultural growth, as well as support industry through the establishment of rural factories (especially back-yard steel furnaces). Meanwhile, Mao advocated decentralization of decision-making in order to overcome bureaucratic rigidities and introduce a greater degree of flexibility in planning. A major institutional innovation was the creation of 'people's communes' throughout the countryside. These enormous units, each comprising an average of 5,000 households, were far more ambitious in scope than the collectives they replaced and had no precedent in the collectivization experience of the USSR. They embodied political and military functions, as well as an economic role. Their large size reflected the intention that, in addition to promoting agricultural growth, they should provide essential social services and be used to mobilize labour into non-agricultural capital formation (including the development of small-scale rural industries).

The origins of the catastrophic failure of the 'Leap' lay in economic mismanagement in agriculture, fatally exacerbated by a failure of the statistical reporting system. As ideological fervour replaced objective economic judgement, the Government was convinced that China was poised to make an unprecedented economic advance. In particular, in the belief that the 1958 harvest had doubled, it sanctioned a withdrawal of almost 30m. workers from agriculture to support urban and rural industries. At the same time, it raised peasants' grain procurement quotas in order to increase urban workers' rations and generate higher export earnings. However, the Government's perception of farm conditions was very different from reality. In contrast to grossly inflated early harvest reports, in 1958 there was only a marginal rise in grain output, followed during the next three years by a steady decline in production. By the end of 1961 rural per caput food availability had contracted by at least 25%. The result was unprecedented starvation and the deaths of at least 30m. people during 1959–61. The situation was made more serious by growing ideological differences between China and the USSR, which in mid-1960 reached a point of crisis, prompting the latter to withdraw aid to China. What started as an agricultural crisis became a deep depression affecting the entire economy. Part of the cost of the 'Leap' is highlighted in the finding that in 1961 agricultural GDP was more than 38% below the previous peak of 1958. The lagged response of industry was even greater: in 1962 its GDP had decreased by almost 50% compared with the 1959 peak. The low point of China's foreign trade was also in 1962, when the value of exports and imports was 20% below the previous peak (also 1959).

By 1961 the Government finally responded to the crisis. The most dramatic evidence of the severity of the situation lay in the decision to reverse economic policy in favour of prioritizing agriculture. Some 20m. workers were sent back to the countryside to support the agricultural front. Within the rural sector itself, the industrialization programme was downgraded. The remarkable pragmatism of recovery policies extended to the restructuring of the communes and the delegation of decision-making responsibility down to individual households. Free markets were re-opened in the countryside and material incentives revived. By such means, which bore a marked resemblance to the earliest post-1978 rural reform initiatives, economic recovery was eventually (in 1965) secured. The economy seemed poised, once more, for renewed growth.

The Decade of the Cultural Revolution (1966–76)

Despite the profound impact of this crisis, such was Mao's antipathy towards what he regarded as the capitalistic and 'revisionist' nature of the recovery policies after 1961 that in 1962 he initiated the 'anti-rightist' Socialist Education Movement. In 1966 this was transformed into a new national experiment, which became known as the 'Great Proletarian Cultural Revolution'. Although not primarily an economic phenomenon, the accompanying political upheavals resulted in temporary periods of serious economic dislocation. This was especially evident in China's cities during 1967–69, when revolutionary Red Guards entered planning offices and factories, disrupting production and policy formulation. In general, however, the economic impact of the Cultural Revolution was not as severe as that of the 'Leap'. Reductions in investment limited new initiatives, but, except in 1967–68 and 1976, the momentum of industrial growth was maintained. Meanwhile, the agricultural sector was hardly affected at all.

The most serious economic indictment of the Cultural Revolution is perhaps illustrated by the disproportionate emphasis placed on self-sufficiency, which caused serious structural distortions within the economy. The most extraordinary manifestation of this was the 'Third Front': a gigantic development initiative designed to create a self-sufficient industrial base deep in the interior of China. The region's isolation was considered a crucial means of safeguarding China's economy from attack by either US or Soviet forces—or even by both simultaneously. The 'Third Front' involved massive investment in the construction of large-scale industrial facilities and associated infrastructure in western provinces of China (especially Sichuan and Guizhou). Between the mid-1960s and mid-1970s, such was the scale of this undertaking that it absorbed about one-half of the entire central budget. However, its economic returns were disappointing and there is overwhelming evidence that the 'Third Front' entailed serious inefficiency, resource waste and economic losses.

From Mao Zedong to Deng Xiaoping: the Interregnum of Hua Guofeng (1976–78)

Following Mao's death in September 1976, political power was rapidly transferred from the radical faction that had overseen the Cultural Revolution to a new administration under former Vice-Premier Hua Guofeng (Mao's chosen successor), who rehabilitated disgraced former pragmatic officials and reintroduced more orderly economic planning. Hua sought to maintain his authority by sanctifying the Maoist legacy (hence his advocacy of the 'two whatevers'—i.e., whatever Mao had decided should remain valid, and whatever Mao had instructed should be obeyed). Hua also revived the idea of the 'four modernizations' (of agriculture, industry, science and technology, and national defence), which had first been articulated by Premier Zhou Enlai in 1964. Finally, in February–March 1978, he revealed an ambitious strategy for China's long-term development in the form of an ill-conceived Ten-Year Plan (1976–85), based on the implementation of 120 large-scale projects geared mainly towards heavy industrialization. However, it was China's good fortune that this grandiose Plan did not materialize. By the end of 1978 Hua had been eclipsed by the return to supreme political power of the previously disgraced Deng Xiaoping, thus opening the way for radical new departures in economic policy.

China's Economic Performance during the Mao Era (1949–78)

China's economic record under Mao had been uneven. Heavy industry expanded rapidly, but at a high cost in terms of agricultural and light industrial growth. Between 1952 and 1978 GDP growth averaged 6.1% annually in constant price terms. Concealed within this figure were rates of expansion of 11.0% for industry (manufacturing and construction), but only 5.5% for services and a mere 2.1% for the farm sector. During the same period the average annual rate of natural increase of total population was 2%, so that average GDP per caput grew by 4% per year. There is strong evidence that this growth record—by no means unimpressive compared with that of many, but not all, developing countries—was driven by massive inputs of physical capital, unaccompanied by efficiency improvements. For example, it is significant that the average rate of fixed capital formation during 1952–78 was 10.5% annually. In short, alongside only modest improvements in labour productivity, capital productivity showed hardly any improvement. Indeed, the calculations of one authoritative analyst indicates that between 1952 and 1978 there was no increase at all in total factor productivity, growth being sustained entirely by physical increases in the inputs of capital and labour. China's relative isolation within the international economy also resulted in a widening gap between its own industrial technology levels and best-practice techniques available not only in the USA, Japan and Western Europe but also in the first-echelon Asian newly industrializing economies (ANIEs), such as Taiwan and the Republic of Korea (South Korea). Nor, finally, was economic growth translated into corresponding improvements in material living standards. On the contrary, the disproportionate emphasis on heavy industry constrained rises in consumption, which increased on average by only 2.3% annually (3.0% for urban residents, but a mere 1.8% in the rural sector).

Rapid industrial growth had a significant impact on the structure of the economy. Between 1952 and 1978 the contribution of manufacturing industry to GDP increased from less than 18% to more than 44%. This was mainly offset by a contraction in the share of agriculture (from 51% to 28%), although the contraction of retail commerce was responsible for a parallel contraction in the share of tertiary industry from 29% to 24%.

THE IMPACT OF POST-1978 REFORM

Since 1978—first under Deng Xiaoping, subsequently under Jiang Zemin and from 2003 under Hu Jintao—China's broad development goal has become increasingly market-orientated (the aim being to establish and perfect, in Chinese parlance, a 'socialist market economy'). In the intervening years (incidentally, now an even longer period than that of Maoist socialization), despite occasional retreats and serious systemic problems, major progress has been made towards the fulfilment of this goal.

In July 2005 Ma Kai, then Minister of the National Development and Reform Commission, declared that China's transition to a socialist market system had been basically completed. In support of this claim, he pointed out that, at the end of 2004, more than one-half of all state-owned or state-controlled large industrial enterprises had become joint-stock companies, while the private sector provided 80% of all new jobs and contributed one-third of GDP. He added that the prices of 96% of retail commodities, 97% of agricultural and 'sideline' goods and 87% of capital goods were determined by market forces. The scale of the privatization process that has taken place is demonstrated by the finding that in 2007 more than one in every three Chinese urban workers was either self-employed or working for a domestically owned private company (including limited liability and share-holding corporations). If foreign-owned companies were included, the share rose to more than 40%. More than 10% of national tax revenue now comes from privately owned companies, excluding those financed through foreign direct investment (FDI) or from Hong Kong, Macao and Taiwan.

The Rationale of Post-1978 Reforms

The political victory in 1978 of a group of pragmatic leaders centred around Deng Xiaoping was a turning point that was to have profound consequences not only for China's own growth trajectory, but also for political, social and economic development in the Asia-Pacific region and throughout the world. For the Chinese people, its significance was immense, for it marked a seismic shift away from the primacy of the ideological imperative (i.e. pursuit of class struggle), characteristic of the Maoist developmental thrust, towards a new ethos in which economic construction and growth were placed at the core of the national agenda. In domestic economic terms, it also signalled the abandonment of the Maoist system of central control over resource use and allocation in favour of a new orthodoxy of reform and experimentation.

In December 1978 the Third Plenum of the 11th CCP Central Committee took place. Out of this seminal meeting came a sober and objective reappraisal of China's development level and capacity. Unprecedentedly, it contained a critique of Mao himself that generated the orthodoxy that his policies had been 70% right, 30% wrong. The Third Plenum's communiqué acknowledged that the Chinese economy suffered major imbalances, as well as 'some disorder in production, construction, circulation, and distribution'. It also referred to the long-standing failure to improve mass living standards. Hence, the need for 'comprehensive balance' as the first step towards establishing a firm foundation upon which longer-term economic growth could take place.

The years of poor efficiency, slow productivity growth, increasing technological backwardness and stagnant living standards inherited from the Mao era made the case for economic reform overwhelming. The direction of reform was also clear: away from interventionist central planning towards greater reliance on prices and markets as the arbiters of production, consumption and distribution. The more difficult challenge was how to formulate an appropriate transition strategy. The history of Communism's rise and fall had been compressed into little more than 70 years (1917–89), and there was no accepted model of how to reform a command economy. Rather, there were two contrasting views about the most effective way to achieve reform and transition: the 'big bang' and the 'incremental' approaches.

Proponents of a 'big bang' argued that the most effective approach was to implement a single, comprehensive reform programme. To this end, they advocated simultaneous political and economic reform. The former would facilitate the withdrawal of the State and its replacement by a representative democracy. Meanwhile, economic reforms would free prices, dismantle restrictive institutions in favour of privatization and facilitate integration with the global economy through the removal of protective devices and distorted price regimes. Such 'shock therapy' would cause considerable hardship, not least as a result of declining output and rising unemployment, as loss-making enterprises were closed down, but, it was argued, these short-term difficulties would be offset by longer-term gains.

Advice, especially from outside, that China should follow the 'big bang' approach were firmly rejected by Deng Xiaoping and his colleagues. Deng's view was that democratization in China would generate chaos. He was also one of the generation of Chinese leaders who shared in the collective responsibility for the 'Great Leap Forward' and the subsequent terrible famine. This episode formed part of the mindset of the Chinese leaders, and their awareness of its dislocation no doubt predisposed them against pursuing a 'big bang' strategy that could be interpreted as a latter-day variant of the earlier venture. Instead, they chose an alternative way forward, which they likened to 'crossing the river by feeling for the stones'. This Chinese phrase vividly captured the gradualism, experimentation and incrementalism that lay at the heart of the new approach. These characteristics reflected not only the continuing influential role of the CCP, but also its cautious attitude towards sudden change for fear of precipitating instability.

The new strategy sought to decentralize economic decision-making to local government, departmental and eventually even lower levels, to increase regional autonomy, to encourage competitiveness and to facilitate the establishment of an increasingly market-driven economic system (albeit one that left a significant residual role for the State in managing the economy—hence the later reference to a 'socialist market economy'). A cornerstone of the new approach was also the implementation of an 'open door' policy, the radical nature of which was exemplified in China's willingness to accept foreign capital (including increasing inflows of FDI) in order to help fund investment and upgrade its obsolete industrial technology.

The First Phase of Reform (1978–92)

China's domestic economic reform programme began in the countryside, where early initiatives encompassed the decollectivization of agricultural production, the raising of purchase prices for farm products and the encouragement of increasing economic diversification. Such was the impact of these policies that by 1983 the previous collectivist thrust of farming had disappeared. Decollectivization led to the dismantlement of the previous three-tier structure of commune, production brigade and production team, and its replacement by variants of so-called contract-based 'production responsibility systems', which returned a high degree of autonomy and decision-making power to individual farm households. As rural markets reopened, China's farming system began increasingly to resemble that of the early 1950s, except that land remained under collective rather than private ownership. Meanwhile, the transformation of former commune and brigade industry into township and village enterprises (TVEs) became the basis of a process of rapid rural industrialization. By 1987 rural industries had already surpassed agriculture as the main source of rural GDP, and they were to become one of the most dynamic growth sectors of the entire economy.

Another radical departure was the establishment, in 1980, of four Special Economic Zones (SEZs) in two southern provinces (Guangdong and Fujian). Not coincidentally, these were located next to Hong Kong and Taiwan, and they were to become the catalyst for the increasing integration of those economies with that of the mainland. Intended to be 'windows' on the global economy, the SEZs were bases for economic experimentation (technical and institutional), as well as channels for inflows of foreign investment. By the end of the 1980s other coastal cities and provinces had been opened to foreign investment.

Reform of the state-owned enterprises (SOEs), the mainstay of the industrial sector, began by focusing on improvements in management. The underlying aim was to increase the autonomy and decision-making powers of enterprises in order to enhance incentives and thereby increase profitability. Vital to the success of these initiatives were various progressive profit-sharing schemes and the creation of more direct links between rewards and profitability. For the time being, however, privatization was not part of the industrial reform agenda.

The success of these policies laid the foundation for a gradual transformation of China's planned economy during and after the 1980s. Price reform was at the core of the first stage of macro-economic reform and addressed the irrationality of a system in which prices had previously been set administratively merely in order to accommodate plan priorities, but without reflecting the reality of market-orientated demand-supply relations. It was a system that favoured producers at the expense of consumers, and industrial producers at the expense of farmers and other primary producers. In the first stage of price reform, from 1979, purchase prices for agricultural and rural 'sideline' products were raised to increase incentives for farmers and to create markets for light industrial goods. In the early 1980s an increasing number of transactions began to take place at market prices. In 1985 market exchange of producer goods outside the plan was, for the first time, also sanctioned. Implicit in these developments was the emergence of a dual ('two-track') pricing system, characterized by two co-ordinating mechanisms—plan and market. The underlying aim was, in the interests of maintaining stability and facilitating fulfilment of priority goals, to allow the retention of a significant degree of control by the centre, while enabling the economy gradually to move towards a market system, with an increasing share of goods being produced and sold at market prices. It was believed that in this way ('growing out of the Plan', as Barry Naughton, a US expert on the Chinese economy, described it) mandatory prices would gradually give way to a market-based pricing system, but without generating significant inflationary pressures. The dual track was defined in terms of prices, not ownership. For example, once a state-owned enterprise had fulfilled its output quota within the plan, any surplus capacity could be used to produce goods for sale at market prices. It was an innovative system that encouraged enterprises to adapt their production to market demand. However, on the debit side two-track pricing also gave rise to corruption, by enabling officials to make windfall profits by buying goods at low prices under the planned system and subsequently reselling them at higher market prices.

China's dual-track transition strategy made possible the co-existence of the planned economy with an increasing number of unregulated sectors, of which the most notable were the rural collective enterprises or TVEs. The outcome was continued economic growth within a framework in which the scope of price controls and economic planning was gradually reduced. Owing to the faster development of the private and non-state sectors, the Chinese economy was indeed 'growing out of the Plan'. In overseeing these developments, the CCP was aware of the increasing loss of control by the Communist Party of the Soviet Union in the aftermath of its sanctioning of political, as well as economic, reform. By rejecting even minor political changes, let alone democratization, the Chinese Government retained significant control over macro-economic policies and reform ideology. In general, it maintained social stability by avoiding the abrupt and wholesale dismantling of the institutional framework of the command economy, particularly of the dominant SOE sector, which traditionally afforded substantial social service benefits to its workers and their families. However, one disadvantage of this approach was the severe fiscal drain associated with making available huge state subsidies in order to sustain inefficient sectors.

Although the reforms of the 1980s were overwhelmingly successful, they were not unqualifiedly so. In particular, there is evidence of a cyclical pattern of macro-economic instability having characterized China's development during the first decade of reform. Excess aggregate demand, encouraged by monetary expansion, was a significant element in several episodes of quite serious inflationary pressure, although excessive wage increases and structural imbalances were also important contributory factors. The most serious of these occurred in 1988–89 and culminated in massive demonstrations in Tiananmen Square (April–June 1989). The immediate cause of students taking to the streets was the death of the former reformist Party leader, Hu Yaobang. However, the demonstrations were not simply politically inspired. In addition to widespread anger at growing corruption among officials, a major factor in the increasing scale of the protests was the anxiety felt by many ordinary urban residents as rising inflation threatened to erode their living standard. Following the subsequent tragic mishandling of the demonstrations, a new Government under Premier Li Peng introduced a period of retrenchment, which temporarily halted the momentum of economic reforms and marked the end of their first phase.

The Second Phase of the Reforms (1993–2003)

The events of 1989 damaged both the domestic and international standing of the CCP and the Chinese leadership. The Government's economic reaction to them was to re-emphasize central control and curb the pace of reform. The subsequent years of retrenchment were marked by a leadership struggle for power over the direction of economic policy. The urgency of the issue was emphasized by the collapse of the USSR in 1991, which shocked Chinese leaders. A conservative faction of senior officials was led by Chen Yun, one of the protagonists of economic construction in the 1950s and 1960s and an advocate of economic pragmatism after 1978. These officials now favoured a retreat from reform in order to re-establish administrative and party control over the economy. However, this approach was decisively rejected by Deng Xiaoping, who reaffirmed his commitment to the establishment of a market economy with a strong private sector, in which the role of the CCP would be restricted to political and social control. In a manoeuvre typical of traditional Chinese politics, Deng rallied support from provincial leaders during his 'Southern Tour' (*nanxun*) in early 1992, which took him to Shanghai, Shenzhen SEZ and other parts of Guangdong. In speeches during these visits he repeatedly endorsed the reformist ethos and urged accelerated market-orientated reform. As Deng put it, 'Development is the only hard truth. It doesn't matter whether policies are called 'socialist' or 'capitalist' as long as they promote development'. In October 1992 the 14th Party Congress officially sanctioned Deng's proposals for accelerated reform and economic liberalization through its formal advocacy of the creation of a 'socialist market economy'.

By the early 1990s the two-track system had become increasingly redundant and when, in 1993, material-balances planning was abolished, its usefulness effectively disappeared. By the end of the 1990s more than 90% of retail prices and about 80% of prices of raw materials and agricultural products had been liberalized. However, the final removal of central planning mechanisms highlighted the central Government's need to identify a way of establishing sufficient financial authority to fulfil its regulatory and macro-economic responsibilities. Ironically, given the decentralizing thrust of the first decade of reform, it was to find this through financial recentralization. Fiscal reforms, instituted in 1994, sought to halt the serious decline in budgetary revenues (which had decreased from 31.1% of GDP in 1978 to 10.8% in 1994). By broadening the tax base, revenues recovered strongly and in 2009 constituted 20.4% of GDP.

Central to the policy focus of the second phase of China's economic reforms was the accelerated restructuring of its SOEs. A major constraint on progress in this area was an awareness that a costly precondition of SOE reform was a programme of urban social reform that would put in place an effective urban social security network in order to provide workers and their families with basic social services (including pensions, unemployment insurance, health care and housing), formerly provided by the state enterprise sector. Through a combination of closures, mergers and downsizing, in the second half of the 1990s a fundamental rationalization of the state enterprise sector was effected. At their peak, in 1995, urban SOEs had employed more than 112m. workers; by 2010 this total had declined to about 65.2m. Even more striking were the changes in governance that accompanied the restructuring process. These have embraced privatization, often through management buy-outs, and the transformation of SOEs into limited liability corporations. The radical nature of industrial reform was perhaps most dramatically illustrated at the end of the 1990s, when various SOEs were listed on the Shanghai and Shenzhen stock markets. From a wider perspective, China's progress as a result of such reform was highlighted by the fact that between 1990 and 2005 the contribution of shareholding and foreign-owned firms (including those of investors in Hong Kong, Macao and Taiwan) to total industrial value-added rose from less than 10% to more than 75%. The pace of change in the ownership composition of industry was encapsulated by the finding that in just five years (2000–05), the nominal annual growth rates of value-added in share-holding and foreign-funded firms were 34.3% and 25.5%, respectively, compared with only 13.6% for their state-owned counterparts. Most remarkable of all was the growth of the private industrial sector, 55% annually, during the same period. Such developments explain why the degree of central control over China's economy, as measured by the share of GDP produced by state-owned firms, has fallen below that of France, Italy and Singapore.

Reform of the state enterprises has been inextricably linked to reform of China's financial system, which has been burdened with the accumulated debt of SOEs. During the 1990s significant restructuring took place in the banking system. Between 1993 and 1998 the People's Bank of China was given increasing authority and independence, which greatly facilitated the implementation of monetary policy in its role as China's central bank. Important too has been the imposition of more stringent budget constraints, designed to encourage the state-owned commercial banks to exercise greater discretion in extending credit and handling debt. Meanwhile, considerable success has been achieved in reducing the major economic burden associated with a preponderance of loss-making SOEs, which were traditionally dependent on state investment and supported by loans from an increasingly heavily indebted banking sector. The establishment in 1999 of four state asset management corporations signalled the Government's determination to address the problems associated with this huge overhang of non-performing loans.

The institution of the 'open door' policy was one of the earliest post-1978 reform initiatives and the Chinese Government has been consistent in its commitment to playing a greater role in the international economy. In 1993 important foreign trade reforms were introduced. The effect of these was to devalue the currency, unify the foreign-exchange regime and establish current (but not capital) account convertibility. However, the culmination of China's efforts towards integration with the global economy was its admission, in December 2001 and after many years of protracted negotiations, to membership of the World Trade Organization (WTO). The repercussions of this momentous event have continued.

The Third Phase of the Reforms: the Shift towards Development Sustainability (2004–)

Under Deng Xiaoping and the subsequent ('Third Generation') leadership of Jiang Zemin, growth maximization was the ultimate economic goal to which all others were subordinated. In many ways, this approach served China well. China's remarkable growth record since 1978 is the foundation on which its subsequent economic and social development achievements have been built. By the early 2000s, however, it was increasingly clear that the differentiated pace and distribution of development associated with the strategy of growth maximization was the source of economic, social and environmental strains within China. Basic natural and economic resources—for example, land, water energy and some minerals—were being subjected to what many regarded as unsustainable pressure. Environmental degradation, particularly soil, air and water pollution, as well as climate change, posed serious challenges. Most alarming of all to the Government, increasing discontent in the form of demonstrations and protests (sometimes violent) drew attention to the existence of an extensive urban and rural malaise that had resulted from widening economic and social disparities. It is reported that between 1993 and 2008 the annual number of 'incidents of social unrest' increased from 8,700 to 127,000. In September 2006 the official Xinhua News Agency commented that social unrest had become 'the most destabilizing factor in the country' and even threatened the authority of the CCP itself. Three months later the same source reported that 'major group actions continue to occur, and are becoming broader and broader...the degree of violence in the confrontations is clearly stepping up, and there exists the potential for bloody incidents to develop'. The loss of jobs and income resulting from the global economic crisis of 2008/09 added to the threat of social instability.

That the 'Fourth Generation' leadership under President Hu Jintao and Premier Wen Jiabao has remained committed to rapid economic growth as an essential precondition of China's broader development and the maintenance of stability is not in doubt. However, against the background of emerging resource, environmental and social problems, the Chinese leadership has acknowledged that growth maximization is no longer regarded as a sufficient condition of continuing progress. In any case, since 2003–04 a new official orthodoxy of sustainability ('harmonious development') has become the criterion of success of China's development programme. The need for a new 'scientific development concept' was a central theme of Wen Jiabao's annual government work report in 2004. Subsequently, some sought to lend legitimacy to this approach by placing it in the context of programmatic documents, such as the 'Rio Declaration' and the '21st Century Agenda'. Others tried, not wholly convincingly, to do the same by citing Deng Xiaoping's supposed emphasis on the importance of 'stable, co-ordinated and sustainable' development.

The new concept rejects the idea that physical GDP growth ('seeing only material and not people') is the sole measure of successful development. Instead, it embodies a 'people-centred principle', which recognizes that the ultimate objective of growth should be to meet people's material and 'spiritual' needs. Fulfilment of this goal in turn demands the implementation of comprehensive and co-ordinated planning designed to achieve balance in five key areas: urban and rural development; inter-regional development; economic and social development; environmental development through attainment of a 'harmonious' relationship between man and nature; and finally domestic and international development.

To those familiar with current development orthodoxies, the emphasis on sustainability is unexceptional. In China, however, it signals a major intellectual departure from the previous preoccupation with the speed of GDP growth. It also conveys a message that in formulating development policies, attention must be given to both their short-term and long-term costs and gains from the perspective of all sections of society. The notion of sustainability also highlights the need to revisit China's GDP accounting system and re-evaluate official economic statistics and indicators of changes in living standards. There are signs too that greater attention is being given to the costs of environmental damage and resource use in implementing policies. Evaluation of local officials' performances also seeks to place a higher premium on success in meeting the needs of development sustainability than in the past. However effective such measures prove to be, there is one inescapable conclusion: that China's future social and economic trajectory will mainly be determined by the extent to which the previous pattern of rapid growth with inequality is replaced by one of sustained growth with equity. The onset of the global economic crisis and China's response to this have done nothing to change the validity of this conclusion, although they may make it more difficult to fulfil.

The attainment of a more sustainable trajectory of economic growth and creation of a 'harmonious society' (*hexie shehui*) was central to China's Eleventh Five-Year 'Programme' (the contemporary Chinese equivalent of 'Plan') for 2006–10. In order to fulfil this goal, the Programme envisaged a new developmental principle of 'scientific development' and articulated a new orthodoxy, which advocated that growth was meaningless unless it addressed problems such as social inequality and environmental degradation. To this end, it explicitly endorsed slower physical GDP growth as an acceptable price to pay for improvements in the quality of such growth.

The outcome of the Eleventh Programme was, at best, mixed. While it is true that most quantitative targets were met, the shift towards a more sustainable pattern of growth was not achieved. Far from GDP growth slowing, for example, it accelerated (from 9.8% annually in 2001–05 to 11.2% in 2006–10). Most worrying of all, the intended move towards more inclusive growth was not forthcoming: urban–rural income and consumption gaps continued to widen, as did inter-regional differentials. Nor did the process of environmental degradation appear to have been halted, let alone reversed. Indeed, in 2011 Premier Wen Jiabao was still warning, as he had done in 2007, that China's economic development was 'unbalanced, unco-ordinated and unsustainable'.

In March 2011 China's National People's Congress approved China's Twelfth Five-Year Development Programme for 2011–15. It shows clear policy continuity with the recent past, its main goals and guidelines overlapping closely with those of the Eleventh Programme. Like its predecessor, the Twelfth Programme endorses the idea that growth should translate into higher living standards based on a more equal and equitable distribution of national income. In particular, it envisages a rebalancing of the economy by making consumption a more potent force in GDP expansion—and, by implication, thereby reducing reliance on investment and exports as the main sources of growth. To this end, the Programme seeks to extend social welfare insurance cover for urban and rural residents, raise wages (the average minimum wage is set to increase by at least 13% per year during 2011–15), expand employment and accelerate urbanization. Other priority goals include a reduction in energy use, further enhancement of China's 'green' credentials (for example, by implementing stricter low-carbon regulations) and the promotion of seven so-called 'strategic emerging industries', designed to facilitate China's ascent of the value-added scale.

China and the Global Economic Crisis

As economic difficulties rapidly gathered pace in the USA from September 2008, there was a feeling in some quarters that China might be able to isolate itself sufficiently from such developments to emerge relatively unscathed from the crisis. In reality, however, there is no decoupling in the global economy, and the international crisis took a heavy economic toll on China, albeit one that has not been lasting. A collapse in the property market early in 2008, which led to a major reduction in demand for construction materials, was already taking a toll on China's economy in the first half of the year. However, the economic downturn was greatly exacerbated by the dramatic deceleration in export growth late in 2008 that resulted from the global crisis and the accompanying recession. In 2008 China's GDP growth slowed to its lowest rate since 2001, and in the first quarter of 2009 it declined sharply to 6.1% year-on-year (the lowest quarterly rate to be recorded for 10 years).

The essence of the Chinese Government's response to the global economic crisis was the introduction of a substantial stimulus programme, containing both fiscal and, especially, monetary elements. These initiatives were designed, above all, to fulfil the Government's target of 8% GDP growth in 2009—a figure apparently regarded as a minimum if economic buoyancy and social stability were to be maintained. The original fiscal stimulus programme, introduced in November 2008, was worth 4,000,000m. yuan. Its essential thrust was to implement, within just three or four years, infrastructural projects that the Government had previously planned to implement over a five- to 10-year period. Some questioned China's ability to finance this ambitious programme, but such fears proved to be groundless. In part, this was because the programme was financed from monetary, as well as fiscal, sources. These included: deficit-financing, which was expected to raise the government budget deficit to around 3% of GDP; the issue of corporate bonds; and expanded bank lending (in the first quarter of 2009 the value of new bank loans was equivalent to that of the whole of 2008). An authoritative estimate made by the *China Economic Quarterly* indicated that in 2009 the monetary and fiscal stimulus directed additional funds to the equivalent of more than 20% of GDP—considerably more than was originally announced in the programme of November 2008.

The consensus view at mid-2010 was that China's policies had already proved highly effective in addressing the repercussions of the global economic downturn. From the second quarter of 2009 recovery began to take place, and by the end of the year economic growth had reached double figures (11.4% in the fourth quarter). The annual rate of GDP growth in 2009 was 9.2%, easily exceeding the Government's target of 8.0%. As the year progressed there were signs of improving business confidence, the stock market proved resilient and property transactions increased sharply (eventually prompting the Government to intervene in an attempt to curb investor housing purchases). The main effect of the economic stimulus programme was an increase in fixed investment, which grew by 30% in 2009 (the highest rate of growth since 1994). However, efforts to stimulate a significant increase in household consumption were much less successful: official estimates of the National Bureau of Statistics (NBS) show that whereas fixed investment contributed 8.4 percentage points of GDP growth in 2009, the corresponding figure for consumption was only 4.4 percentage points (and for net exports this was negative, at –3.6 percentage points). In 2010 the corresponding figures were 5.6, 3.8 (the lowest figures since 1997) and 0.9 percentage points. Such figures partly explain why the Chinese Government has prioritized efforts to rebalance the economy under the current Five-Year Development Programme (see above).

Economic Performance under the Impact of Reform (1978–)

Viewed from its own historical perspective, China's growth performance since 1978 is unprecedented. Between 1978 and 2010 GDP increased, on average, by 9.9% annually (in constant price terms). Concealed in this figure is a slight acceleration in growth during the last two decades: whereas the rate of increase in GDP averaged 9.9% per annum during 1978–2010, between 2000 and 2010 the corresponding figure was 10.5%. In sharp contrast to the Mao era, GDP growth since 1978 has been accompanied by major improvements in material living standards, in which both the urban and rural population have shared. GDP per caput rose by 8.8% annually during 1978–2010 (but by 9.8% during 2000–10), a figure that incidentally highlights the very low rate of population increase during the same period. In nominal terms, GDP per caput in 2010 was 78 times that of 1978. Data published by the NBS show that between 1978 and 2010 both urban and rural per caput income grew, in constant price terms, by 7.3% a year. However, it is noteworthy that the most marked improvements in rural per caput income occurred in the early years of post-1978 reform, whereas income gains have accrued more disproportionately to urban residents in more recent years. Thus, NBS data show an average rate of per caput income growth of 9.7% per annum during 2000–10, compared with only 7% among the rural population. Post-1978 growth has also been translated into a massive reduction in absolute poverty, the number of the rural population living below the official Chinese poverty line having declined from 150m. in 1978 to fewer than 15m. However, China's official rural poverty criterion is low by international standards, and in 2008 it was raised by more than 50%, as a result of which the incidence of rural poverty rose, to encompass more than 40m. people (in 2010 it had declined to 27m., or 4% of the rural population). On the basis of estimates published by the World Bank as part of its International Comparison of Prices project (ICP—see also below), the proportion of China's total population living in poverty decreased from 64% in 1981 to 7% in 2007.

From international perspectives, China's growth record is no less remarkable. Since the early 1980s China has been the world's fastest-growing major economy. As a result, its economy is now one of the largest in the world. With China having previously overtaken Germany to become the third largest economy in the world, in August 2010 the Japanese Cabinet Office reported that in the second quarter of 2010 China's nominal GDP had overtaken that of Japan for the first time, making it the second largest economy after that of the USA. In terms of purchasing-power parity (PPP), having overtaken Japan in 2001, China already ranked second to the USA, even though its GDP is still smaller than that of the European Union (EU). It has also surpassed Germany to become the largest exporting country in the world. An indication of the global impact of recent developments is illustrated by the fact that from 2001 until the onset of the global financial crisis China accounted for around one-third of global economic growth (measured at PPP), or about twice that of the USA. In comparison with former socialist countries, the most notable of which is the former USSR, China's market-orientated reforms not only started earlier, but have also achieved greater success despite—some would argue because of—being implemented in the absence of accompanying political reform. China has also become a major industrial power, ranked alongside Japan within the Asia-Pacific Economic Cooperation (APEC) forum. It now possesses an independent, comprehensive and largely self-sufficient industrial system of considerable technological sophistication. From these perspectives, China's recent record is unmatched by any other country in the Asia-Pacific region.

China has become one of the largest markets for investment goods; it is the biggest purchaser of iron ore and copper, and the second biggest purchaser of crude petroleum. It has demonstrated strong potential for growth in new markets, such as automobiles (in 2009 it overtook the USA to become the world's largest market for cars), telecommunications and financial services. China is also a global manufacturing base and a leading supplier of cheap consumer items throughout the world (hence its sobriquet, 'factory of the world'). From such perspectives, its decisions have a significant bearing on the economic performance of other countries. Even allowing for the negative, as well as positive, impact of China's accession to the WTO, the steady integration of its domestic markets into the international economy is already increasing such influence. The predicted increase in unemployment resulting from greater competition among domestic enterprises, as well as between domestic and foreign firms, following accession to the WTO, has not materialized to any significant extent. The same may be said of inter-regional strains associated with the post-WTO restructuring of domestic markets, as successful efforts have been made to abolish provincial protectionism and trade barriers. Indeed, if China's buoyant GDP growth momentum is maintained, the employment-creation effects of WTO membership are likely to emerge even more clearly in the future.

Overall, China's economic record since 1978 is impressive and attests to the undoubted success of the country's reform strategy. Nevertheless, this positive assessment needs to be qualified in some important respects. The first is that China remains firmly in the ranks of less developed, lower middle-income countries of the world. Of more than 130 countries listed in the 2010 *World Development Report*, the World Bank ranks China 65th in terms of average per caput gross national income (GNI) on a PPP basis in 2008. It estimated China's average GDP per head to have been US $6,020 (on a PPP basis), 328% above the figure for low-income countries and 31% above the average for lower-middle income countries ($4,592), but 42% below the world average ($10,357). For the time being, the gap between China and the first echelon of ANIEs, let alone the USA and countries of Western Europe, remains huge. On a PPP basis, *World Development Report* estimates show China's per caput GNI to have been 12.8% of that of the USA in 2008. Previous extrapolations based on the two countries' average growth rates for the last decade had suggested that China's aggregate GDP would not overtake that of the USA until 2035, by which time there would still be a per caput income gap of 4:1. However, these figures have been called into question as a result of the publication by the World Bank's ICP of revised PPP GDP estimates for 2005. These price comparisons show China's per caput GDP to have been $4,091 in 2005—around 40% less than previously thought. If correct, the ICP data indicate that China's share of global GDP in 2005 was 9.7%, not 14% as previously believed. A further implication is that it would take China about a decade longer to catch up with the USA and become the largest economy in the world.

Another important finding that qualifies the positive assessment suggested by crude estimates of physical GDP growth is the extent to which China has become an increasingly unequal society under the impact of post-1978 reform. During the Mao era, although the gap between urban and rural incomes was quite large, within cities and countryside income was distributed fairly equally. In 1982 China's national Gini coefficient (a measure of income inequality) was estimated at 0.28, but a mere 0.166 in the urban sector, thus making it one of the most equal societies in the world. It is true that as a result of the first rural-based reforms (1978–84), farmers' incomes grew faster than those of their urban counterparts. However, after 1985 the income gap between cities and countryside once more widened (for example, during 1985–2005 real urban incomes grew by 7.1% annually, compared with only 4.4% for rural incomes). By 2010 the absolute urban–rural income gap had reached 13,190 yuan: close to 40 times greater, in nominal terms, than in 1985, and almost 63 times greater than in the period immediately preceding the reforms in 1978. Estimates suggest that 45% of total income is concentrated in the highest 10% of the population, while the lowest 10% of recipients have a mere 1.4% of income. At the end of 2006 the Chinese Academy of Social Sciences revealed that China's Gini coefficient had reached 0.496—well above the corresponding level of Western European countries and Japan, and also higher than that of the USA (0.41), where inequality in income distribution has also been rising. Even though it does not yet match that of some large Latin American countries, such as Brazil and Mexico, China's income distribution is more unequal than in many other Asian developing countries (India, for example, has a Gini level of 0.33). Not least, it is now significantly higher than the internationally recognized warning level of 0.4, above which the danger of social unrest is considered to pose a significant threat to stability. Official survey data reveal that in 2008 the average per caput disposable income of the lowest-income decile among urban households was barely 11% of that of the highest income decile.

Reference has already been made to the remarkable poverty alleviation impact of China's post-1978 reforms. However, estimates of poverty are sensitive to the choice of measure, and application of the international US $1-per-day criterion suggests that, even allowing for a recent upward adjustment in the rural poverty criterion, the number of poor is significantly greater than that indicated by official Chinese statistics: in 2006, for example, 24.8% of all rural households were recorded as having an average per caput income of 85 cents or less per day, although this had decreased to 14.5% by 2008. Household survey data show that in 2008 just over 60% of rural households had to survive on the equivalent of less than $2 per day (calculations were derived from official exchange rates). Nor do these figures take account of the numbers of urban poor, which have been increasing quite sharply in recent years. Furthermore, even accepting that material consumption is universally far higher today than it was in 1978, qualitative indicators of welfare, such as health, education, economic security and the environment, show quite unambiguously that there has been a significant deterioration in standards for hundreds of millions of Chinese citizens, especially (but not only) in the countryside.

Finally, there remain external misgivings about China's economic status as a 'true' market system. For example, although the EU has removed China from its list of non-market economies, the European Commission's programmatic document on EU-China relations, released in October 2006, reaffirmed the view that China had still not fulfilled all the necessary requirements to be granted market economy status. As such, it remains a market-transition economy. The USA also has yet to grant market economy status to China. Such exclusions and treatment continue to elicit protests from Chinese officials, not least because of their wish to avoid the penalties for alleged export 'dumping' to which the Chinese economy remains susceptible. According to WTO rules, China can expect to attain market economy status 15 years after its WTO accession—i.e. in 2016 at the latest.

Under the impact of reform, major structural changes have also taken place within the economy, as shown in the changing distribution of GDP and employment among primary, secondary and tertiary sectors. From a high point of 33.4% in 1982, agriculture's contribution to GDP had contracted to 10.2% by 2010. The most significant expansion has been that of the services sector, its output contribution having risen from 21.6% in 1980 to 43%. As for secondary sector activities, their share of GDP initially contracted from 48.2% in 1980 to 42.9% in 1985, but has since risen once more to reach 46.9% in 2010 (with 40.2% being derived from manufacturing alone). These figures embody a major readjustment of official GDP statistics, following the publication of the results of a national economic census in 2005. This revealed what many had long suspected: that the service sector's role in GDP growth had previously been seriously understated in official statistics. As a result of the census's findings, the tertiary sector's share of GDP was revised upwards by almost nine percentage points, while the primary and secondary sectors' contributions were adjusted downwards (by 2.1 and 6.7 percentage points, respectively). One of the principal targets contained in the Twelfth Five-Year Development Programme is that the contribution of services to GDP should rise by a further four percentage points by 2015.

The changes in the sectoral composition of output have inevitably been reflected in parallel changes in employment. Thus, since 1978 a contraction in the primary sector's share of total employment (from 70.5% in 1978 to 38.1% in 2009) has been offset by rises in the corresponding figures for industry (from 17.3% to 27.8%) and, above all, for services (from 12.2% to 34.1%). The fact that the primary sector engages almost 40% of employed labour but generates barely 10% of GDP emphasizes the relative inefficiency of agriculture vis-à-vis other sectors of the economy and highlights the continuing existence of massive surplus labour in farming.

Perhaps the most striking structural change of all has been the rapid expansion of the 'non-state' sector of the industrial economy. Unclear and indistinct ownership categories (for example, joint ownership enterprises) make it extremely difficult to measure the exact size of this sector. What is clear, however, is that it has rapidly overtaken the SOE sector in terms of the gross value of industrial output (GVIO). In 2009 SOEs accounted for only 8.3% of GVIO (10.1%, if collectively owned enterprises were included), compared with 29.6% from domestically funded private firms, 22.1% from non-state-funded limited liability corporations, 9.2% from domestic share-holding enterprises and 27.8% from foreign-funded enterprises (FFEs—including those sourced from Hong Kong, Macao and Taiwan—see below). However, SOEs' claims on domestic investment remain huge: in the same year they absorbed one-third of total domestic fixed capital formation (more than 37% when including collective-owned enterprises). Meanwhile, employment data dramatically show the rapid expansion of the non-state sector during recent years. In 1995 a total of 112.6m. workers were employed in urban SOEs, compared with 4.85m. in private enterprises and 5.13m. in FFEs. By 2010 the corresponding figures were 65.2m. (a reduction of 42%), 60.7m. (an average increase of 18.3% per annum) and 18.2m. (a rise of 255%). During the same period the numbers of individual self-employed almost doubled from 15.6m. to 44.7m. Such figures capture the extent to which a private market economy is emerging in China. Moreover, the non-state sector has played an increasingly important role in absorbing excess farm labour and surplus workers previously employed in overstaffed SOEs.

There is strong evidence that the Chinese economy has followed a cyclical pattern of growth since 1978. During this period there have been four phases in which the rate of GDP increase has been especially pronounced. The years of highest growth were: 1978 (11.7%), 1984–85 (14.3%), 1992–94 (13.8%) and 2003–07 (11.4%). Each of these periods gave rise to strains and, to varying degrees, inflationary pressures. In each case, rapid expansion gave way to retrenchment and slower growth, although slowing growth in 2008 and 2009 was largely due to the impact of external factors—namely, the effects of the global economic crisis. Two such episodes in China's post-1978 experience are of particular significance. The first was the retrenchment that followed the 'Tiananmen Incident' in 1989, when GDP growth decreased in a single year from 11.3% to 4.2%. The second took place over a longer period between 1992 and 1999, during which GDP growth declined from 14.2% to 7.6%. The fact that the most recent phase (2003–07) of strongest growth should have coincided with the shift towards a new strategy of development sustainability—a period when, according to the Government, fulfilment of associated qualitative targets was likely to entail a sacrifice in terms of physical growth—is also a source of concern. To what extent the Twelfth Five-Year Programme will result in China following a growth path that is more consonant with its continued pursuit of a sustainable path of expansion remains to be seen.

Given that China's rapid post-1978 growth has been due largely to the maintenance of very high rates of investment, periods of peak growth have often coincided with an increase in demand-led inflationary pressure. Thus, accelerating GDP growth in the mid-1980s was accompanied by a much sharper rise in the consumer price index (CPI), from 2.7% to 9.3% during 1984–85. With another period of particularly rapid growth, in 1988–89 consumer price inflation averaged 18.4%. Associated with the next phase of accelerated growth during 1992–94 was another increase in CPI growth, from 6.4% to 24.1%. The exception to this pattern was the most recent period of rapid growth: alongside average annual GDP expansion of 10.3% during 2003–06, the corresponding rate of increase in the CPI was a mere 2.1%. However, in 2007 mild inflationary pressure gave way to a significant acceleration in the CPI, which rose to 4.8% in 2007 and further, to 5.9%, in 2008 (5.6% in urban areas, 6.5% in rural areas). Concealed within the annual figure for 2008 is the finding that having reached a high point in the first half of the year, consumer price inflation declined sharply in the second half. Indeed, by the first quarter of 2009 consumer prices were declining, and for the year as a whole the CPI declined by 0.7%. The deflationary trend was, however, reversed in 2010, when the CPI rose by 3.3%; in the first half of 2011 it accelerated further, to 5% and 5.7%, respectively, in the first and second quarters. Rising food prices were the principal reason for the upward movement of the CPI in 2010 and 2011. The effect of the global recession on the producer price index (PPI) was marked: in contrast to 2008, when the PPI for manufactured goods rose by 6.9%, in 2009 it declined by 5.4%. Only in December 2009 did positive PPI growth resume, after which the rate of PPI growth accelerated to reach an average of 5.5% in 2010.

Accelerated GDP growth after 2003 once again gave rise to concerns about the potential destabilizing impact of excessive investment, especially in heavy industry. According to the NBS, between 2002 and 2003 the rate of fixed asset investment rose sharply from 16.9% to 27.7%; in 2004 and 2005 it averaged more than 26% and, despite declining modestly to 23.9% in 2006, it recovered to 24.8% in 2007 and further to 25.9% in 2008. There are domestic reasons, such as increased enterprise profitability, why fixed investment has maintained such a high rate of expansion in recent years, but an external factor has also been significant: China's huge and expanding global trade surplus has given rise to excess liquidity and resulted in high availability of funds for investment. In 2009 there was a major surge in fixed asset investment (FAI), which averaged 30% for the entire year—the highest figure to be recorded since the first half of the 1990s. This dynamic performance reflected the impact of the stimulus programme introduced in November 2008 to counter the effects of the global economic recession (see above), as well as lower construction and materials costs. However, it is telling that most investment growth in the first half of 2009 took place in the state sector, while private investment spending remained weak. Most FAI in 2009 was directed towards construction and infrastructural projects, while manufacturing capacity expanded more slowly. There was a strong consensus that the high rate of investment during 2009 was unsustainable, and in 2010 the expected contraction in growth took place, to 23.8% (the lowest figure since 2002). In the first half of 2011 slowing FAI in the state sector was offset by activity in manufacturing and real estate, generating year-on-year growth of between 17% and 18%.

Until 2007 China's economic growth record during the most recent past had been extraordinarily buoyant. Indeed, despite the shift towards a more sustainable growth path, NBS data showed that between 2001 and 2007 annual GDP growth in constant price terms accelerated from 8.3% to 14.2%. In 2008, however, the effect on growth of the global economic crisis was marked. The annual rate of GDP expansion decelerated to 9.6%—slower than in any year since 2002. By the final quarter of 2008 GDP growth had declined to its lowest rate for seven years, 6.8% year-on-year; it declined further in the first quarter of 2009, to 6.1% (its lowest level for 10 years), before recovering to reach 9.2% for the year as a whole. A slower rate of growth was a characteristic common to almost all major sectors in both 2008 and 2009. One exception to this pattern was agriculture, the GDP growth of which exceeded that of 2007 in both years (rising by 5.4% and 4.2%, respectively, compared with 3.7% in 2007). By contrast, manufacturing industry and services both suffered significant reductions in growth: in the case of the former, from 14.9% in 2007 to 9.9% in 2008 and 8.7% in 2009; in the case of the latter, from 16.0% to 10.4% in 2008 and 9.6% in 2009. Having declined from 16.2% to 9.5% between 2007 and 2008, under the impact of the stimulus programme construction growth rose sharply to 18.6% in 2009. One of the most marked effects of the global recession was to curb the momentum of foreign trade growth, especially in 2009. Between 2007 and 2008 the annual rate of increase of merchandise trade (exports plus imports) declined from 23.6% to 17.8%, although despite slightly faster import growth compared with that of exports, China's global trade surplus rose to a record US $298,130m. (almost 14% above the level of 2007—itself an historical peak). In 2009 the foreign trade impact of the global recession was much more in evidence. For the first time since 1978, merchandise trade growth was negative, decreasing from $2,563,260m. in 2008 to $2,207,540m. in 2009 (a decline of almost 14%). Within these figures was a 16% contraction in exports, and a decrease of just over 11% in imports. The further implication was that China's trade surplus was reduced by more than one-third to $195,690m. Alongside slowing trade growth, inflows of utilized FDI rose by 23.6% to reach $92,400m. (equivalent to 2.1% of GDP) in 2008, but decreased slightly to $90,030m. in 2009. Such figures confirm that among less-developed countries China remains by far the most attractive destination for overseas investors.

In the years immediately prior to 2008, China's GDP growth was driven by a combination of fixed capital formation, final consumption and net exports. In 2005–07, for example, consumption and investment each contributed around 40% of growth, with the remaining 20% coming from net exports. However, according to NBS estimates, in 2008 the growth contribution of net exports was a mere 0.8 of a percentage point, compared with 4.6 and 4.2 percentage points for FAI and consumption, respectively. The sharp decline of foreign trade meant that in 2009 net exports' contribution to GDP growth was a negative 3.6 percentage points. Thus, China's GDP growth of 9.6% in 2009 was wholly sustained by consumption (which contributed 4.4 percentage points) and, above all, gross fixed investment (8.4 percentage points). In 2010 trade recovery transformed the net export contribution to growth to 0.9 percentage points, compared with 5.6 percentage points and 3.8 percentage points for FAI and consumption. Looking further ahead, the prospects for strong and sustained export recovery are likely to remain constrained by continuing depressed demand from what have previously been important markets for Chinese goods (especially the USA and EU member states), although this effect has been partly offset by China's success in diversifying the geographical pattern of trade. The Government is also seeking to attach much greater importance to consumption as a source of future GDP growth. This is problematic, since consumption growth hitherto has been primarily dependent on the Government sector. In other words, a pressing need is to increase urban and rural household consumption growth. Raising wages, expanding urban employment, reforming the tax system and extending social welfare insurance cover are among the means through which the Government is seeking to increase the share of household consumption in GDP under the Twelfth Five-Year Development Programme.

For the time being, it is clear that the momentum of recovery, well under way by the end of 2009, has been maintained. In 2010 annual GDP growth was 10.3%, and averaged a little more than 9.5% year-on-year in the first half of 2011. In response to growing inflationary pressures, since the end of 2010 the Government has introduced a number of measures designed to slow down lending. Most external observers believe that such measures will remain in place, generating growth of approximately 9.5% for the entire year.

In the longer term, China confronts new challenges resulting from both internal and external factors. A serious internal problem relates to its demographic trajectory. For many years, China has benefited from a pattern of population change that has afforded it a significant demographic dividend—captured most obviously in the existence of low young and old age-dependency ratios (see also below). As population ageing accelerates, this dividend will disappear, with potentially serious economic and social consequences. Meanwhile, the global economic recession has generated two major external challenges to China's export growth: the slowdown in US personal consumption growth, and the deceleration of global trade growth. Collectively, these challenges are indicative of the emergence of significant constraints on China's future growth trajectory.

NON-ECONOMIC FACTORS

Political Reform

To argue that China's economic reforms have been unaccompanied by systemic political reform is not to suggest the complete absence of political change. One of the last major policy initiatives of the 'Third Generation' leadership under Jiang Zemin, taken in 2002, was to endorse the admission of private entrepreneurs to membership of the CCP. This decision was charged with political symbolism. It signalled in the most dramatic way possible the Government's endorsement of Deng Xiaoping's statement a decade earlier that 'socialist' or 'capitalist' credentials were irrelevant, as long as they served to promote development. Another important change was announced in 2004, when a revision to the wording of the country's Constitution, giving formal endorsement to state protection of the 'lawful rights and interests of individual and private economies', represented the first legal protection of private property rights in China since 1949.

The shift from administrative interventionism to more indirect methods of macro-economic control has effectively deprived the CCP of much of its former influence over the economy. What remains of the orthodox tradition is the Party's opposition to open public debate, individual rights and a democratic, parliamentary system, as well as its control over public security and strategic ('pillar') sectors of the economy and state. In view of the threat to the state monopoly on information posed by electronic media (such as the internet), the Government has sought to exercise strict control over the new technologies by making itself the leading provider of web-based information and taking selective action against the new media forms.

Nevertheless, economic issues are still linked to political developments and power struggles within a system that remains highly opaque. As it happened, the transition to the 'Fourth Generation' of leaders under Hu Jintao was relatively smooth. That same basic political stability was evident in the endorsement by the 17th National Congress of the CCP, in October 2007, of Hu's second term of office, although some interpreted the composition of the new Standing Committee of the Political Bureau (Politburo) as evidence of a weakening of Hu's authority and a threat to unambiguous policy formulation. The scale of the changes that have taken place since 1978 is such that, short of state collapse—an unlikely eventuality—it seems inconceivable that the reformist thrust and momentum of recent years can be reversed. However, events of mid-2006 provided a salutary reminder of the controversy that reform can still provoke. These followed the publication of a speech by Liu Guoguang, an influential economist and former Vice-President of the prestigious Chinese Academy of Social Sciences, in which he criticized the downgrading of Marxist economics in Chinese university curricula. Liu's remarks were interpreted as implicit criticism of China's market reforms, and there was speculation that they might presage a reassertion of 'leftist' influence, threatening the core of China's reformist developmental ethos. In the event, such speculation proved to be wholly unfounded. Nevertheless, these events were a reminder that ideological tensions within the CCP persist and that opposition to reform from advocates of a return to state interventionism has by no means completely disappeared. In the most recent past, what is most telling is that slowing growth and tensions (such as rising unemployment) occasioned by the global economic recession have produced no challenge either to the strategic thrust of the Government's policies or to its tactical efforts to address the specific challenges of the international downturn.

However, in a very real sense, the tension between pluralistic tendencies engendered by the market economy and the Party's tradition of ideological control of all political discourse has not yet been fully resolved. Indeed, the presumption is that as the nascent urban middle class grows, such tensions will become more pronounced. Meanwhile, in the absence of a strong institutional and legal framework, new protagonists (including bureaucratic and entrepreneurial élites at central and provincial levels) will no doubt also continue to emerge and will exert considerable power. In particular, as control over industries and enterprises is further devolved from central to regional and local authorities, protectionist and expansionist interests seem certain to remain potent influences shaping China's evolving development trajectory. For the foreseeable future, the State's retention of a strong role in preserving social stability and public confidence in the economy will almost certainly persist.

Legal and Administrative Reform

Not the least of the challenges confronting China is the need for the further strengthening of the legal, administrative and regulatory framework within which economic reform is taking place. The introduction of the 'rule of law' has already begun to transform the Chinese economy, as well as social and political life. Yet much remains to be done: for the time being, China's legal system is better described as 'rule by law' than 'rule of law'. Since 1979 legal reform has been driven by domestic and external pressures on China to establish procedural and other norms that accord with standard international practice, while meeting the needs of China's market-orientated path of development. As a result of such initiatives, economic activity is now regulated by a considerable body of economic and commercial legislation. Among the earliest economic legislation passed in the reform period was the Joint Venture Law (1979), which established the legal basis for foreign investment in China and was later used as a model for the development of parallel domestic legislation (for example, the Contract Law (1999), and the Company Law (1994), which for the first time introduced limited liability and share-issuing companies). Some progress too has been made towards the legal protection of intellectual property rights, although this has been limited by weaknesses in its implementation. There is also a Civil Procedure Law, and litigation has become an increasingly common (if not always effective) means of conflict resolution. Recent important legal initiatives affecting the economy include the adoption, in August 2006, of the long-awaited Bankruptcy Law. The enactment of this law, effective from 1 June 2007, was a significant development, which promised to facilitate further progress towards ongoing reforms of China's SOE and financial sectors. Two other significant events occurred in March 2007, when the National People's Congress (NPC) adopted a Property Law and an Enterprise Income Tax Law. The former for the first time provided for equal legal treatment for privately owned and state-owned property; through its imposition of a unified 25% corporate income tax rate on both domestically owned and foreign-owned firms, the latter ended previous preferential treatment for foreign capital in the form of a tax rate that was between 9% and 18% lower than the 33% levy on domestic enterprises. A more recent important piece of legislation is the Social Insurance Law, which took effect from 1 July 2011. This law seeks to provide universal access to medical, employment injury and unemployment insurance, as well as to pension cover. The law also undertakes to facilitate urbanization (an important government objective) by eliminating previous restrictions on the movement of would-be migrants.

Reforms of the central ministries and commissions have changed government administration. In 1998 a restructuring of the State Council resulted in a contraction in the number of central ministries and commissions from 40 to 29, as well as in the size of the central government civil service establishment by one-third (in some individual ministries, by more than one-half). By mid-2011 the number of ministries and commissions under the State Council had been further reduced to 27. Under the 1998 restructuring programme, industries such as coal, power, metallurgy, machine-building, electronics and chemicals were removed from central bureaucratic control and placed under the direction of more general supervisory organs, with their operational activities being administered by newly corporatized structures. Such changes, which are being extended to provincial and local levels, are intended to reduce remaining government monopolistic powers and introduce industries to competition.

THE REGIONAL DIMENSION OF DEVELOPMENT

The People's Republic has a unitary system of government that co-exists with strong and mostly informal federalist features. Under the central administration, there are four more levels of government, embracing 31 units at provincial level (22 provinces, five autonomous regions and four municipalities, excluding Hong Kong, Macao and Taiwan), 333 at prefectural level, 2,856 at county level, and 40,906 at township level. They are structured in the form of a 'nested' hierarchy in the sense that higher levels of government deal only with directly subordinate levels, with units at every level having independent budgetary authority.

Under the impact of reform and increasing provincial autonomy, regional economic disparities have widened significantly. In particular, coastal regions—above all, those constituting the three major growth hubs of the Zhujiang (Pearl) River and the Changjiang (Yangtze) River Deltas and the Bohai Gulf (centred on Beijing and Tianjin)—have benefited disproportionately from their more advanced industrial infrastructure and better access to overseas markets. As a result, GDP in these more developed, highly industrialized coastal areas has been much higher than in central or western regions. In 2010 the combined GDP of the four largest provincial economies (Guangdong, Shandong, Jiangsu and Zhejiang) accounted for 35.4% of national GDP, or for almost 40% if Shanghai is included. Guangdong contributed 10.5% of the total; Jiangsu's share was 9.5%; that of Shandong was 9.1%; and Zhejiang contributed 6.3%. By contrast, the 12 western provinces accounted for less than 19% of GDP (and a mere 13%, excluding Sichuan and Chongqing). There is a powerful urban bias within these figures. Thus, China's 2004 Urban Development Report underlined the continuing economic primacy of the three major coastal metropolitan areas, centred on the Bohai Bay, and the Yangtze and Pearl River Deltas. It predicted that they would remain the driving forces behind urbanization, industrial modernization and China's integration into the global economy, eventually accounting for two-thirds of national GDP.

Chinese provinces not only differ in terms of comparative and competitive advantages, but they have also pursued different privatization policies that have generated distinctive regulatory and business environments (for example, coastal provinces like Guangdong and Zhejiang have a much higher proportion of private enterprises than elsewhere). Competition for foreign investment has disproportionately favoured coastal regions: in 2004 four provinces (Guangdong, Jiangsu, Shandong and Zhejiang) and three municipalities (Shanghai, Beijing and Tianjin) absorbed 72.5% of all utilized FDI, while in 2009 they still attracted almost 60% of total FFE investment. Jiangsu and Shanghai together accounted for 30% of the total. In the early years of reform, labour-intensive manufacturing in the Pearl River Delta—based on major cities, such as Guangzhou, Shenzhen, Zhuhai and Dongguan—was the principal driving force of China's economic growth. More recently, higher value-added, more capital and skill-intensive activities in the Yangtze River Delta have become the prime focus of Chinese growth. In this respect, there was a major development in 2003, when for the first time Jiangsu replaced Guangdong as the single most important provincial recipient of FDI. The Yangtze River Delta now also accounts for well over one-third of China's foreign trade. The Bohai Bay region, with Beijing and Tianjin at its core, also has the potential for rapid scientific and technological development. The economic importance of Tianjin, which has sustained double-digit growth for more than a decade, has increased rapidly. In particular, through the development of the Binhai New Area (including the Binhai High-Tech Industrial Park), Tianjin aspires to become an international port city on a par with Shanghai.

Meanwhile, formal and informal trade barriers still impede inter-provincial economic exchange, although China's WTO membership is helping to reduce internal trade restrictions and expand domestic trade and competition. Significantly, there is evidence that the immediate interior neighbours of some coastal provinces are now beginning to benefit from increased FDI flows. In 2004, for example, the province of Jiangxi overtook Fujian as a recipient of FDI. In some cases, improvements in transport links have also enabled industrial plants to be transferred from the rapidly growing coastal areas, such as Guangdong, Zhejiang, Jiangsu and Shandong, to their inland neighbours in order to take advantage of lower labour costs.

Growing social and economic disparities between China's coastal regions and the interior have become a source of great concern to the central Government, not least because of their impact on social and political stability. The central Government's declining fiscal authority has limited its ability to enforce equalizing inter-regional revenue transfers between rich and poor regions. Under the Ninth Five-Year Plan (1996–2000), voluntary partnership schemes, involving capital transfers and cross-regional co-operation, sought to combat widening differentials, but to little effect. This was the background against which, during the Tenth Five-Year Plan (2001–05), the Government announced a strategic initiative to 'open up the West' in an attempt to strengthen economic integration, improve the ecological environment and raise the development level of China's 12 western provinces. The scope of this programme is reflected in the huge scale of projected infrastructural investment in improving road and rail links, building natural gas pipelines and strengthening communication links between less-developed western regions and prosperous coastal provinces. Under the Tenth Five-Year Plan, almost 20% of state investment was allocated to infrastructure projects in these western regions. However, such are the resource and infrastructural deficiencies of the West that fulfilment of the programme's development goals remains, at best, a long-term goal. An authoritative Chinese report in 2005 referred to the 'many difficulties, many problems and arduous tasks' still confronting planners in the region, a reference to continuing infrastructural and environmental constraints, persistent inefficiencies in SOEs (which still account for about two-thirds of industrial GDP in western regions) and pervasive rural poverty. The greatest challenge of all is how the West can overcome inherent resource deficiencies and other disadvantages in order to attract critically needed private investment from both domestic and overseas sources. Such problems are most dramatically highlighted in the north-west (Shaanxi, Gansu, Qinghai, Ningxia and Xinjiang), where rapid population growth, inadequate education, low labour productivity and a lack of employment opportunities have created a vicious circle of poverty. China's Twelfth Five-Year Development Programme (2011–15) has reiterated the importance of continuing to 'open up the West'.

A significant initiative was the State Council's announcement in June 2010 that a new economic zone had been approved in the Liangjiang district of Chongqing. The Liangjiang zone would enjoy the same status as the Pudong and Binhai zones in Shanghai and Tianjin. According to a report published by the Economist Intelligence Unit (EIU—a research and analysis organization based in the United Kingdom), it was expected to become a testing ground for financial and fiscal, investment, foreign trade and land policies to the particular benefit of the energy sector. The EIU predicted that Chongqing's real GDP would achieve average annual growth of 13.5% during 2010–14.

The difficulties inherent in 'opening up the West' are reflected in a shift in regional development priorities, since early 2005, towards central China (Shanxi, Henan, Anhui, Jiangxi, Hubei and Hunan). This region contains more than one-quarter of the Chinese population and contributes about one-fifth of national GDP. Its choice as a focus of China's regional strategy reflects inherent structural, geographical and resource advantages, as well as the region's susceptibility to positive 'trickle-down' effects of the more rapid growth that has been taking place in neighbouring coastal areas. The development of central China and its emergence as a national transport, commercial and distribution hub are expected to facilitate the creation of closer linkages between east and west. Meanwhile, individual central provinces are destined to fulfil distinctive economic roles: Hubei, as a centre of automobile, photoelectron, and iron and steel production; Anhui, as a labour-intensive manufacturing base; Henan and Jiangxi, as focuses for modern agricultural production.

Since 2003 another regional priority has been the revitalization of the economy of the North-east (Liaoning, Jilin and Heilongjiang). As the former heartland of China's centrally planned industrial economy, this region has been a major victim of SOE restructuring. For example, around one-quarter of the 30–40m. SOE redundancies have occurred in the north-east, where the unemployment rate is significantly higher than elsewhere in the country. Accordingly, social security initiatives designed to lessen the social impact of unemployment and maintain basic living standards for those laid off have been a particular priority. In the longer term, the principal efforts to revive the regional economy of the north-east lie in industrial diversification based on the extension of private sector activities. Some progress has been made towards fulfilling these goals, and the approval in April 2010 of the Shenyang Experimental Economic Zone in Liaoning as a focus of 'new industrialization' was likely further to facilitate this process. However, financial constraints remain a serious problem, and the transformation of the old industrial bases of Liaoning and other parts of the region will be a long-term process.

In general, the Twelfth Five-Year Programme seeks to reinforce the policy thrusts described above. The principal drivers of future growth in inland provinces will be infrastructural investment, improved and preferential tax treatment, and increased overseas investment. The intention is that development will be based on the comparative advantage of each major region. In particular, western provinces, such as Yunnan and Xinjiang, are likely to assume particular importance in China's pursuit of energy security, with government plans to construct oil and gas pipelines across land borders into South-East and Central Asia.

POPULATION, LABOUR AND SOCIAL SECURITY

The history of China's population growth since 1949 may be divided into two main periods. Between the early 1950s and the early 1970s total population expanded rapidly, with annual growth averaging more than 2%. By contrast, subsequent years, until the present day, have witnessed unprecedented success by the Government in limiting increases in population. Such trends reflect the vagaries of official policy on demographic change. Rapid population growth after 1949 reflected a sharp reduction in the death rate, associated with major improvements in basic health and hygiene, and an increase in the birth rate that was facilitated by a deliberately pro-natalist stance. Dislocation caused by the 'Great Leap Forward' and the early radical phase of the Cultural Revolution prevented the implementation of population control policies, and only in 1972 did the Government begin to put in place effective family-planning policies, designed to control the number of births. Early efforts sought to restrict family size through late marriages, less frequent births and fewer births, but these were overtaken, in 1979, by advocacy of the one-child family. This attracted strong resistance, especially in the countryside, where a marked cultural preference for boys persisted. Opposition to the policy took various forms, including the under-reporting of female births, the use of ultra-sound scans to facilitate abortion of female foetuses and female infanticide. The harsh nature of China's demographic policies is defended by government officials, who claim that, in the absence of such strategies, at least 400m. more births would have occurred in the 30 years that followed the introduction of the one-child policy.

China's gender ratio remains abnormally high, the 2000 census showing 120 males for every 100 females among the age group of 0–4 years, well above international norms of 103–107. In recent years there has been a relaxation of the one-child rule in the countryside; in urban areas, the rule is generally accepted and has been easier to uphold. In July 2009 it was announced that married couples with one child in Shanghai, who were themselves only children, were being encouraged to have a second child. It would be premature to interpret this as a signal that the one-child policy is about to be abandoned in cities, not least because Shanghai has a very high number of elderly people among its residential population. In any case, the response of married couples to the Shanghai initiative was unenthusiastic, most of them expressing no great desire to increase family size because of the cost of raising an extra child. In July 2011 it was reported that the authorities in Guangdong had also submitted a request to the central Government to be allowed to relax the one-child rule. In general, as the proportion of elderly dependants increases, the pressure to relax official guidelines in order to care for the aged can be expected to grow, not least in order to reduce the Government's fiscal burden of providing adequate social welfare cover.

Projections suggest that, even without any further decline in fertility, China's total population will have reached 1,350m. by 2012–13. At the end of 2010 the total population was officially estimated at 1,339.72m., of whom 49.7% were officially classified as 'urban'. Vital statistics for 2009 showed crude birth and death rates of 12.1 (marginally lower than in 2008) and 7.1 per thousand (marginally higher than the previous year), generating a rate of natural increase of 5.1 (i.e. 0.5%). According to projections published in the US-based Population Reference Bureau's 2010 Population Data Sheet, China's total population will be 1,476m. in 2025, but will have decreased to 1,437m. by 2060. These figures are in line with other estimates, which show China's total population reaching its highest level of between 1,500m. and 1,600m. in the 2030s or 2040s. Meanwhile, India's population will overtake that of China to become the largest in the world: Population Reference Bureau projections show that in 2050 India's population will number 1,748m., compared with China's 1,437m.

Since the 1950s the proportion of children in China's population has steadily declined, while the problem of an ageing population is only now beginning to emerge. Since 1990 the percentage of 65-year-olds and above has increased from 5.6% to 8.9%, a figure that is expected to reach 12% by 2020. During the same period the aged dependency ratio has risen from 8.0% to 12%. If those between the ages of 60 and 64 are also included, China's 'elderly' population is now significantly in excess of 140m., equivalent to well over one-tenth of the total population and about one-fifth of the global total of those aged 60 and above. By 2050 almost one in three of China's population will have reached the age of 60 or above. The rise in the percentages of elderly will place an increasing financial burden on the Government and the under-60s: from around 2030 onwards, every two people in 'young' age categories will in effect have to support one elderly person—a very high ratio by international standards. Meanwhile, the average age of the elderly is itself rising: since 2000 the cohort of over-80s has reached more than 20m. and is expected to increase to over 40m. by 2030 and 100m. by mid-century. This is a significant development, since the more elderly become increasingly susceptible to diseases and need extra care, with predictable implications in terms of health care provision and costs.

The rise in the proportion of working-age people (15–64 years) from 61.5% to 74.5% between 1982 and 2010 highlights the serious challenge for the Government in providing full employment, although recent projections indicating that the working population would reach a high point around 2015 suggest that the severity of this challenge will lessen over time. Overall, employment generation has decreased quite sharply since the early 1990s, as a result of declining GDP growth, efficiency improvements and economic structural change. Between 1980 and 1992 the rate of job creation increased annually by 3.8%; thereafter, the corresponding figure was closer to 1%. The most important employment contribution has been that of the expansion of the services sector, its share of total employment having risen from 12.2% in 1978 to more than one-third in 2010. In the urban sector, the Government's most serious employment challenge has been to find jobs for the tens of millions of workers laid off as a result of SOE restructuring. In 2010 the official rate of urban unemployment was 4.1%—marginally less than in 2009 and well below the peak of 5.4% recorded in 1979. However, this is a serious understatement of reality; the true figure was closer to 10% and may have been even higher. Urban unemployment is most severe in the north-east, the heartland of the former SOEs, where in some cities it has reached 15%–20% or more. The employment challenge in the rural sector is even greater, reflecting the existence of an 'overhang' of at least 130m. surplus farm labourers (despite the creation of more than 100m. jobs in rural industrial enterprises alone since 1978). This massive surplus of farm labour has been the source of huge rural–urban migration in recent years, although with most young, able-bodied men (and some women too) having already left the countryside, there are signs that such movements have slowed considerably in recent years. China's migrant population now numbers more than 150m. people, or about 12% of the total population.

Reports in 2008–09 suggested that the contraction in global demand for Chinese exports had taken a serious toll on employment, especially that of migrant workers. Although difficult to interpret, Chinese estimates of job losses in 2008 and early 2009 ranged from 18m. to 40m., affecting between 13% and 30% of the total migrant worker population. By mid-2009, however, there were signs that the stimulus spending programme was having a positive effect on employment. In August, for example, while acknowledging the continuing seriousness of the situation, a senior official in the Ministry of Human Resources and Social Security claimed that the migrant worker population had increased by some 10m. since the end of the previous year and that fewer than 3% of the 67m. migrant workers who had returned to cities in recent months had failed to find jobs. The Ministry's confident prediction that China would be able to keep the official urban unemployment rate below 4.5% during 2009 was indeed vindicated and it has since been further reduced (see above). However, one major issue that remained unresolved was the poor employment record among recent Chinese university graduates, one-third of whom are probably without work.

Raising the consumption share of GDP and resolving China's ageing and employment problems are closely linked to the continuing reform of the social security system (including old-age insurance, medical insurance and unemployment insurance). Social security provision has improved significantly in the urban sector. Participation in basic urban health insurance, based on shared contributions by government, enterprise and the individual, has risen from 19m. in 1998 to 432m. in 2010 (65% of the urban population—a sharp increase over 2007, when the corresponding figure was 37%), including 45.8m. rural migrant workers. Unemployment insurance has traditionally been the State's responsibility, exercised through SOEs, although the financial burden is now increasingly being shared by government, company and employee. At the end of 2010 a total of 133.8m. employees and workers participated in unemployment insurance programmes. In the same year 256.7m. people (including 193.7m. urban employees and 63m. retirees) were enrolled in basic pension programmes (9.2% more than in 2008). Almost 162m. people, including 63.3m. rural migrants, were insured against accidents at work. In recent years the incidence of urban poverty has risen markedly, and it is significant that in 2009 some 23.1m. urban residents were in receipt of minimum income relief from the Government; in addition, some 52m. rural residents received the Government's minimum living allowance.

Social insurance coverage is still seriously lacking in rural areas, although the Government has launched two major initiatives: the first, introduced in 2008, was a rural co-operative medical care system. This has rapidly expanded, and in 2010 reached 96% coverage, with expenditure totalling 83,200m. yuan, to the benefit of a reported 700m. people. The second initiative, announced and implemented on an experimental basis in 2009, was a rural pension scheme. By 2010 more than 100m. people were reported to have participated in the scheme, with pay-outs totalling 2.1m. yuan. The aim is to provide comprehensive pension coverage throughout the countryside by 2020. There is a strong consensus that China has experienced an increasingly serious health crisis, the cost of health care having been too high for most rural residents. From this perspective, the attempt to extend medical coverage in the countryside is an important initiative.

AGRICULTURE

In line with the changing nature of the Chinese economy since 1978, the role of the farming sector has contracted significantly, and agriculture's contribution to GDP growth has become increasingly marginalized. However, with a farm labour force that still numbers around 275m. (about 40% of total employment) and in view of the Government's continued insistence on maintaining 95% grain self-sufficiency, agriculture remains an important part of the economy. Under the impact of reform, farming has also become more diversified, as the growth of non-cropping activities, such as husbandry, fishing and fruit-farming, has outstripped that of grain-farming, which had previously dominated agriculture. However, in terms of employment the changes have been less profound: even today, most farmers are crop cultivators and the great majority of them are committed, even if unproductively and part-time, to grain cultivation. Emerging trends in agriculture reflect the demand for a more diversified diet by increasingly affluent consumers (especially in cities) and highlight the growing emphasis on grain for indirect uses (such as feed and inputs for processing).

The changes in China's agricultural economy are largely, but not solely, attributable to the implementation of reforms, which have freed farmers from the previous constraints of a rigid planning regime. Between the late 1950s and the end of the 1970s the three-tier collective institutional framework of communes, brigades and production teams had regulated agricultural production to the detriment of individual incentives and efficiency in resource use. As a result, food consumption levels remained low, and the margin above subsistence narrow. Post-1978 reforms addressed such problems by sanctioning de facto decollectivization through the introduction of a contract responsibility system, which required producers to deliver fixed-price quotas to the State, but enabled them to sell their surplus to the market at a higher price. Not only did farmers acquire increasingly long-term land use (although not ownership) rights, but by being given greater decision-making powers, they were also able to diversify their operations into cash-crop farming, animal husbandry, fishing or forestry. For example, by 2010 the contribution of crop farming to agriculture's gross value output (GVO) had contracted to just over 53%, compared with 80% in 1978. During the same period the corresponding figures for livestock farming, aquaculture and forestry had risen to 30%, more than 9% and almost 4%, respectively. Between 1979 and 1984 institutional change, accompanied by increases in purchase prices, generated unprecedented agricultural growth and resulted in a doubling of average per caput farm income. Private local and inter-regional markets for vegetables and other produce opened, and the prices of many products (including meat and fish) were also gradually liberalized. Under the impact of reforms designed to separate government administration from enterprise functions in the purchase, sale and storage of grain, the responsibility for grain procurement has also been decentralized.

Since the mid-1980s animal husbandry and aquaculture have registered consistently rapid and sustained growth, although the performance of the crucially important grain sector (including cereals, pulses, soybeans and tubers) has been more mixed. Total grain output rose from 305m. metric tons in 1978 to a then-record level of 407m. tons in 1984, although this level was not reattained until 1989. The first half of the 1990s showed no clear trend, leading some to argue that China would be forced to import increasingly large amounts of grain to feed its growing population, to the detriment of nutritional standards in sub-Saharan Africa. Such predictions appeared to be confounded by a series of fine harvests, which took average annual output to 505m. tons during 1996–99 (significantly above the critical level of 400 kg per head that is considered sufficient to meet the dietary demands of China's increasingly affluent population). However, this surge was not sustained, and grain production once again declined and stagnated, averaging only 451m. tons during 2000–03. The low point occurred in 2003, when the harvest totalled just 430.7m. tons, almost 78m. tons less than in 1999 (sufficient to feed around 195m. Chinese, at current rates of consumption), and left average grain output per head lower than in any year since 1981. This sequence of poor harvests affected both China's domestic economy and its foreign economic relations. In late 2003 grain shortages were finally translated into rising prices, especially of maize and wheat, and in 2004 grain prices rose by 26.4% compared with a mere 2.3% during the previous year. Such increases set off a chain reaction in farm product industries. The grain price rise had a major impact on the CPI, reversing five years of zero inflation. However, owing to a recovery in grain output, as well as the introduction of substantial imports (see below), the upward pressure on food prices subsequently moderated: in 2005 grain prices rose by a mere 1.4%, although by 2008 the rate of increase had accelerated to 7%. After falling back to a rate of 5.6% in 2009, grain prices once more rose sharply, by 11.8% in 2010, contributing more than any other factor to renewed upward pressure on consumer prices. Since 2003 grain production has recovered well, and in 2010 total output reached a new record of 546.5m. tons, 3% above the previous historical peak of the preceding year.

Despite declining grain production, China remained a net exporter of cereals (rice, wheat and maize) during 2000–03. In 2003, for example, with per caput grain output at its lowest level for more than two decades, its net exports nevertheless exceeded 10.5m. metric tons, earning more than US $1,000m. The maintenance of its status as a net exporter was made possible only through the massive depletion of domestic grain reserves: between 2000 and 2003 China's wheat stocks decreased by almost 60%, and its coarse grain reserves by almost two-thirds. However, this process was unsustainable, and in 2004 China purchased 7.26m. tons of wheat (1,500% more than in 2003), making it the largest importer in the world and incidentally contributing to a shift in its agricultural trade balance from a strong surplus to a deficit of $5,500m. Although it remained a sizeable net wheat importer in 2005, albeit at a significantly reduced level, a major recovery in maize exports helped move China's overall cereal trade balance back into surplus. Indeed, by 2006 trade in all three cereals had reverted to robust surplus. In 2007 a new phenomenon emerged in the form of sharp rises in the international prices of cereals. There was no evidence to suggest that China's involvement in international markets was a significant factor contributing to these price increases. Indeed, major increases in China's net exports of wheat and maize during 2007 (up by 230% and 61%, respectively) would appear to have endorsed the official view that Chinese overseas sales had in fact had a stabilizing effect on international cereal prices, although the Ministry of Agriculture acknowledged that some traders had sought to profit from surging international prices through illegal cereal exports. In 2007 China's net cereal exports totalled 14.5m. tons, compared with just 2.2m. tons in 2006. However, as a result of substantial reductions in wheat and maize shipments, in 2008 the corresponding figure decreased to 0.9m. tons. In 2009 the export surplus was transformed into a deficit of 0.3m. tons. Meanwhile, China has for some years been a purchaser of massive amounts of soya beans: in 2009, for example, it spent almost $19,000m. to import 42.6m. tons of soya beans.

Since the 1980s all three cereals—rice, wheat and corn—have experienced output growth. Given its role as a major animal feed and the basis of China's bio-fuel industry, the fact that corn has been the fastest-growing cereal would seem to be an encouraging sign. However, this buoyant performance is attributable more to an expansion of sown area—partly the result of reallocating land out of rice and wheat—than to rises in yields. If rice, wheat and maize outputs are to continue to rise, the burden on yield improvements will intensify. A report released in early 2011 pointed out that rice yields in China are approaching those of Japan, where yields have remained virtually unchanged for the last 14 years. If Chinese rice yields have reached a plateau, reallocating more land towards corn production may become increasingly difficult, unless China is prepared to increase its rice imports. The inference seems clear. The Chinese Government is likely to encounter increasing difficulties in the coming years in continuing to fulfil its long-held objective of maintaining 95% self-sufficiency in the provision of basic foodstuffs. As this target is abandoned, China's engagement in international grain markets will increase. The extent of the impact of this on world cereal prices and supplies remains to be seen.

Against the background of official government recognition of lagging economic and social development in many parts of the countryside, the role of agricultural and rural development in generating a prosperous society has become a priority focus of policy since 2004. Indeed, for the first time since 1986, in both 2004 and 2005 agricultural and rural issues were the subject of major policy documents, which explicitly placed the 'three rural issues' (agriculture, peasants and the rural sector) at the centre of the CCP's work agenda. To this end, new policy measures were introduced, designed to address lagging farm income growth by extending more support to the agricultural sector (especially to grain farmers). These initiatives included paying direct subsidies to grain farmers (for the first time since 1949), abolishing the 2,000-year-old agricultural tax, stopping illegal land acquisitions, reforming the grain distribution system, and introducing new rural health and pension insurance schemes (see above). The seriousness with which weakening farm income growth was viewed was illustrated by an official statement to the effect that 'if the peasants cannot increase their income and the rural areas are unstable, the development of the national economy and social stability will lose their essential meaning and motive force'. The impact of the 2004 policy initiatives was undoubtedly positive. Owing mainly to income from grain sales having increased by more than 60,000m. yuan, between 2003 and 2005 per caput farm income rose by 20%, to reach 1,844.5 yuan. This was a major advance, although one that is heavily qualified by the finding that farmers' average income remained well below that of the rural sector as a whole (the rural economy embracing industrial, construction and service activities in addition to farming 'proper'). Indeed, in 2010 the gap between urban disposable and rural net incomes—19,109.4 yuan and 5,919 yuan—was higher than ever before, at 3.3:1 (compared with a low point of 1.8:1 in 1984). It is a further salutary reminder of the difficulties confronting the rural sector that average per caput rural income in 2009 was, in terms of US dollar equivalent, only US $2.4 per day. Moreover, this figure is an average for those engaged in agricultural and better-paid non-agricultural work in the rural sector. The implication is that farmers' average per caput income was significantly less than the $2 per day equivalent, although it is an important qualification that, quite apart from problems associated with the use of official exchange rates as a basis for comparison, monetary measures understate welfare by failing to take account of consumption generated through non-market channels.

The most important recent policy initiative affecting agriculture occurred in the latter half of 2008, although its full effects have by no means yet fully materialized. In September, during a visit to Anhui Province, where China's rural reforms had started 30 years previously, President Hu Jintao indicated that small-scale farmers would in future be allowed to transfer their land lease rights, while retaining the ownership rights to their land. This was subsequently endorsed in a CCP Central Committee document, which sanctioned the right of farmers to 'transfer the right to operate on contracted land in the form of sub-contracting, leasing out, swap, transfer, shareholder co-operation, etc.'. The purpose of the proposal appeared to be to allow farmers to rent out their land to others, including companies, thereby providing new agricultural investment opportunities of a kind that had previously been impossible within the framework of small-scale household-based farming. Farmers who took advantage of such opportunities could seek employment outside the rural sector. Alternatively, if they so chose, they might continue to work as labourers for the company to which they had rented their land, thereby receiving both a wage and a rent.

The new arrangement promised to confer three main benefits: first, it would provide farmers with a higher and more secure income than had previously been available to them as owner-occupiers; second, it would facilitate the consolidation of land into larger, more efficient farms; and third, it appeared to offer farmers the chance to cash in their land use rights in order to pursue entrepreneurial careers outside farming. The main disadvantage of the initiative was its potential negative effect on employment, as a result of the displacement of farmers who failed to find alternative employment (land having previously been viewed as the ultimate form of social security for itinerant rural migrant workers). The enforced return of millions of laid-off migrant workers to their villages under the initial impact of the global financial crisis served precisely to highlight the social security role of migrants' residual claims to land. To what extent a new pattern of agricultural land use will emerge as China recovers from the effects of the global economic recession remains to be seen, although most observers believe that a shift towards the consolidation of small-scale farms into larger holdings is inevitable.

INDUSTRY

The origins of China's modern industrialization lie in developments along the coast and, later, in the north-east, driven by western imperialist powers and Japan. Starting in the second half of the 19th century, mainly light industries were established in the Treaty Ports, especially Shanghai and Tianjin. One-third of China's total manufacturing output was produced by foreign-owned factories in these coastal areas, although linkages between modern industry and the rest of the economy remained limited. Before the outbreak of war in 1937, modern industries produced less than 4% of net domestic product and employed fewer than 2m. workers. Two-thirds of the national industrial GVO was produced by handicraft industries and only one-third by industries that relied on machinery for production. Heavy industry on a larger scale developed in Manzhou (Manchuria) during the Japanese occupation after 1931. When the CCP assumed power in 1949, only 5% of all factories throughout China employed more than 500 people, and the weak industrial base was concentrated in the north-east and a few coastal centres.

This low industrial base facilitated the achievement of high growth rates after 1949. Industrialization was overwhelmingly orientated towards heavy industries, including mining, chemicals, machine-building and metallurgy. For both economic and defence reasons, investment in inland locations was prioritized, especially after the mid-1960s, when military and strategic factors encouraged the establishment of a self-sufficient industrial economy in inaccessible western regions (the so-called 'Third Front'). Such activities, and associated economic and social infrastructural construction, were hugely wasteful, absorbing around one-half of the central budget during the decade of the Cultural Revolution (1966–76). Moreover, as a result of increasingly isolationist policies, China's industrial technology and infrastructure became obsolete and outmoded. By the end of the Mao era the urgent need for industrial reform was clear. Hence post-1978 initiatives, involving the opening of China's economy to the outside world, implementation of technical modernization, relocation of industries closer to markets, reorientation of production towards consumer demand, and the reform of enterprise structures.

Industrial Reform, Enterprise Restructuring and Privatization

One of the stated priorities that emerged from the CCP's Third Plenum of December 1978 was the promotion of faster growth of light consumer goods industries in order to help raise levels of consumption that had stagnated since the 1950s. Although great progress has been made in meeting consumer aspirations (especially in cities), China's industrial structure is still dominated by heavy industry, even after more than 25 years of reform. Between 2003 and 2007 the annual rate of heavy industrial growth ranged from 17% to 19.6%, compared with 14%–16% for light industry; in 2008 and 2009 growth decreased sharply, although heavy industrial growth (13.2% and 11.5%, respectively) continued to outpace that of light industry (12.3% and 9.7%, respectively). In 2010 a degree of recovery took place, the corresponding figures being 16.5% and 13.6%. Heavy industry still accounts for almost two-thirds of industrial value-added. Industry's share of GDP (excluding the construction sector) in 2010 was 40.2%. State-owned industrial activities accounted for about one-third of industrial value-added (the corresponding figure in 2000 was 54%), although SOEs contributed significantly more to heavy than to light industry.

China has two broad categories of enterprises: state-owned and non-state. However, the latter is a heterogeneous grouping that comprises rural and urban collective enterprises, private enterprises and foreign-funded enterprises (including those funded by 'compatriots' in Hong Kong, Macao and Taiwan). Non-state enterprises operate in a market environment, while SOEs are still afforded a degree of protection by the State through preferential access to credit. Indeed, SOEs have been the main source of what until recently was a very high level of non-performing loans (NPLs) in China's banking sector. Distinguishing state and non-state sectors is not easy, the dividing line between them having become blurred, as local governments transformed and sold off enterprises under their control without always changing their ownership status. In general, development of the emerging non-state enterprise sector has been a consistent theme of China's market-orientated reform strategy. This process was strengthened by WTO accession, although under the impact of the global financial crisis there has been a reassertion of the role of state enterprises, which some have interpreted as a signal of a tightening of private sector activities.

The origins of China's SOE reform programme lie in experimental changes that began in the 1980s, when measures were introduced to encourage incentives for workers and management. Since then, SOE restructuring has often proceeded haltingly, sometimes for strategic and ideological reasons, but mainly because of the critically important social role traditionally played by such enterprises in providing employment and essential services (such as housing, health care and pensions) for urban workers and their families. The absence of a comprehensive social security system in the urban sector has made it difficult to downsize, let alone close down, SOEs, for fear of undermining social order. In short, SOE reform is inextricably linked to social security reforms and the extension of more effective social welfare provision for urban residents. 'Grasping the big and letting go the small' is the slogan that from 1997 guided efforts to limit state control to a relatively small number of large corporations concentrated in industrial sectors of strategic importance. In 1998 the Government initiated a three-year programme to reform the then 986,000 SOEs, two-thirds of which were still reporting losses. Policies focused on 6,600 large and medium-scale SOEs, and by 2000 70% of these were said to have broken even or become profitable. Further improvements in profitability subsequently took place, and by 2007 the NBS estimated that the profits of state-owned and state shareholding enterprises totalled almost 1,080,000m. yuan (about 40% of all industrial profits). In 2008, however, under the impact of deteriorating global economic conditions, the corresponding figure declined by 16% to a little over 906,000m. yuan (30% of total profits), before recovering to reach 1,192,410m. yuan in 2010. The broad goal is that some 1,000 large enterprises will eventually be managed on a commercial basis, but under state control, organized in enterprise groups loosely modelled on the Korean *chaebol*. Enterprises selected for inclusion in these groups will receive state support in settling their debt with the banking sector, if necessary through equity swaps (a process that began in 1999). As enterprises fulfil their financial and organizational commitments, so their shares will be listed on the stock market, as has been happening since the late 1990s.

Meanwhile, many medium- and small-scale SOEs have been restructured in order to reduce the State's economic and welfare burden in the industrial sector. This has been achieved by various means, including sale, privatization, conversion to joint ownership (with employees receiving shares in the enterprise) or leasing arrangements. A bankruptcy law was first promulgated on a trial basis in 1986, but because of the potential adverse social consequences of large-scale enterprise closures its legislative impact was quite slight. From this perspective, a highly significant event was the formal adoption, in August 2006, of a fully comprehensive Corporate Bankruptcy Law, embracing both domestic and foreign firms, and designed to give greater protection to creditors through recognition of their claims ahead of those of redundant workers. With special provision for SOEs removed from all but 2,000 enterprises, one authoritative source (*China Economic Quarterly*) suggested that some 100,000 'tottering' state enterprises were at risk of bankruptcy proceedings.

In the 1980s urban collective enterprises were a means for both local government institutions and private entrepreneurs to engage in commercial business activity. Many private entrepreneurs used the collective nomenclature to minimize the political risks associated with the operation of private enterprises. However, the most important manifestation of collective industry has been the rapid expansion of rural TVEs, more than 20m. of which have been established in rural areas since 1978. About one-third of these are engaged in manufacturing and construction, and a further two-thirds in service sector activities (especially wholesale and retail trade). In 2010 they employed a work-force of 158.9m. (one-third of the rural labour force); between 1980 and 1995 their output value increased, on average, by 36% annually, although subsequent growth has slowed to little more than 10%. Their contribution to exports has also become increasingly important, generating 3,588,800m. yuan in export deliveries in 2008.

Non-agricultural, rural industrialization has been a defining characteristic of the Chinese development 'model' since the late 1950s, when small-scale enterprises were set up in the countryside in order to produce simple farm tools, agricultural inputs (especially chemical fertilizers) and raw materials, such as cement. Since the 1980s the scope of rural industrial activities has broadened immeasurably and, in particular, TVEs have made a major contribution to industrial employment, production and exports. Almost one-half of all jobs in TVEs are in the service sector. Competition from the urban consumer industries has presented a major challenge to TVEs, to which they have responded unevenly: some have raised their productivity and efficiency successfully to meet the challenge, often through the use of more capital-intensive techniques, which has negated their labour-absorption capacity; other, less successful units have been forced to close.

The relative importance of the non-state sector varies considerably among regions. In a number of wealthy coastal provinces (most notably Jiangsu, Zhejiang and Guangdong), its weight, in terms of contribution to industrial GVO, is disproportionately greater than that of the state sector. Elsewhere (for example, in the west and north-east), the legacy of heavy industrialization under central planning is evident in SOEs' still high share of industrial production. A major economic contribution of the non-state sector has been its absorption of surplus urban and rural labour, thereby facilitating the downsizing of the state sector. Official figures show that in 2009 private enterprises and the individual economy provided jobs for 97.9m. people in the urban sector (31.5% of all urban employment), about 40% of whom worked in just seven provinces or municipalities (Beijing, Shanghai, Jiangsu, Zhejiang, Guangdong, Shandong and Liaoning). Inclusion of those engaged in rural TVEs and private enterprises, and the rural self-employed, would raise this figure to well over 300m. workers. Along with more than 75,000 foreign-funded enterprises—47% of them funded from Hong Kong, Macao and Taiwan—these activities form the basis of China's market economy.

Pillar Industries

Under central planning, core industries, such as machine-building, petrochemicals, and construction and building materials, benefited disproportionately from government investment allocations. Under reform, 'new' industries, including information technology (IT), electronics and automobiles, have become the fastest-growing branches and have replaced traditional heavy industries as the principal industrial pillars. The output of the machine-building industry almost halved between 1993 and 1998, although thereafter the downward trend was reversed, facilitating the attainment of a new record level of production in 2002. Within this sector, growth has been strongest in agricultural machinery, especially combine harvesters and tractors. It has also been quite buoyant in the production of numerically controlled machine tools and hydro-electric equipment.

China's IT sector has grown spectacularly in recent years. The output expansion of some high-technology products has been spectacular: in 2010, for example, production of integrated circuits, microcomputers and mobile telephones increased by 57.4%, 35% and 46.4%, respectively. The IT work-force is well over 6m. and has more than quadrupled since 1997. High-technology IT industries have particularly benefited from FDI and associated foreign technological expertise, especially from the USA and Taiwan. It is estimated that 85% of new high-technology products are produced by foreign-funded enterprises. This strong presence and role of FFEs should be kept in mind in assessing the true significance of China's emergence, since 2006, as the largest high-technology exporting country in the world (see also below). Thus, according to the *China Economic Quarterly*, the assembly of most globally produced laptop computers takes place in China, but only 10% of its value-added typically originates there, most of which accrues to subsidiaries of foreign companies. In particular, Taiwanese companies have played an extremely important role in helping to promote China's high-technology industrial development. By 2007 Taiwanese firms' laptop computer, motherboard, liquid crystal display (LCD) monitor and digital camera production capacities had been virtually wholly relocated to mainland China. US products dominate the software market for word-processing, spread-sheets and graphical user interfaces. China's own software industry has been most successful in adapting software written in English for the Chinese market. Illegally produced software remains a major problem for the future development of this industry. In 2005 a significant development, which highlighted Chinese companies' ambitions in pursuit of foreign assets, was the acquisition by a Chinese computer manufacturer, Lenovo, of IBM's personal computer operations for $1,750m.

Following the restructuring of China's state-owned petroleum industry in 1998, there now exist three oil corporations. The largest of these is China National Petroleum Corporation (CNPC), better known under the name of its listed subsidiary, PetroChina, which originally specialized in petroleum and gas exploration and production. CNPC is ranked seventh among the world's leading 50 oil companies. Between 2006 and 2007 its total profit increased from 186,640m. yuan to 206,870m. In 2008, however, difficult global conditions were reflected in a 30% decline in profits to 134,200m. yuan. Although the rate of contraction slowed, total profit decreased again in 2009 (to 128,420m. yuan). In 2010, however, CNPC experienced a sharp recovery, with profits rising by almost 35% to 172,657m. yuan. Second in importance among Chinese oil companies is China Petrochemical Corporation (Sinopec), the original focus of which was refining and distribution. Between 2005 and 2007 its pre-tax profits rose from 67,977m. to 85,864m. yuan, but in 2008 sharply declining prices and demand for petrochemical goods caused profits to decrease by two-thirds; however, a degree of recovery was visible in the first quarter of 2009 and by the end of the year operating profits had recovered to 81,691m. yuan. In 2010 there was a further sharp rise in profits to 105,216m. yuan. PetroChina and Sinopec have been transformed into all-embracing, regionally based oil companies, CNPC operating mainly in the north and west, and Sinopec in the south. The third, and smallest, producer is China National Offshore Oil Corporation (CNOOC), which is responsible for China's offshore exploration and production.

The motor vehicle (especially car) industry is another 'pillar sector' that has experienced very rapid growth under the impact of reform. Car production expanded by 27% annually between 1980 and 2000; during 2001–07 the corresponding figure was more than 34%, and although 2008 witnessed a sharp decline in annual output growth (from 24% to 5%), in the following two years production increased by a remarkable 90% to reach a record level of 9.6m. units in 2010. In 2009 China overtook the USA to become the biggest car producer and market in the world. However, despite a surge in sales in recent years, for the time being car ownership remains overwhelmingly an urban middle-class phenomenon enjoyed by the very few: for China as a whole, in 2009 access to cars was fewer than 10 per 100 urban households, but almost 30 in Beijing, where car ownership is the highest in the country (in Shanghai the corresponding figure was 14). Survey data show that almost 40% of households in the highest 10% of income recipients now own cars, compared with 1%–2% amongst those in the bottom 20%. What is clear is that although it will be many years before ownership reaches the levels currently prevailing in middle-income Asian countries such as Taiwan, Malaysia and South Korea, the potential for future growth in China is enormous. However, if China is to benefit fully from this expanding market it will need to consolidate its domestic industry, which currently comprises some 45 car producers. Foreign—especially Japanese—companies (such as Volkswagen, Peugeot and Citroën, BMW, General Motors (GM), Honda, Daihatsu, Nissan and Toyota) are also very active in China. The leading 10 manufacturers in 2009, accounting for about two-thirds of domestic car sales, were Shanghai Volkswagen Automotive Co, FAW-VW Automobile, Shanghai General Motors, Beijing Hyundai Motor, Dongfeng Nissan, BYD, Chery Automobile, Guangqi Honda Automobile, FAW Toyota Motor and Geely Holding Group. Although China has ambitious car export plans, production is overwhelmingly dependent on the domestic consumer market. By contrast, overseas sales remain quite modest: for example, exports rose from 610,000 to 670,000 between 2007 and 2008, but decreased by 45% to a mere 370,000 in 2009, declining further to 283,000 in 2010. China's leading exporter is Chery, with exports of 189,100 vehicles in 2005, or more than one-half of all overseas sales. In addition to its manufacturing plants in Iran and Russia, in August 2006 Chery opened another in Egypt in conjunction with South Korea's Daewoo Motors Egypt. Short-term exports are likely to be restricted to markets in Central Asia (where sales rose by 93% between January and April 2011), the Middle East, Latin America and Africa; but in the longer term Chinese companies are anxious to target North American, European and Japanese markets. A 2007 agreement between DaimlerChrysler's Chrysler Group and Chery, under the terms of which the Chinese company was to produce small cars for sales in international markets, was another sign of the global aspirations of the Chinese car industry.

Construction activity has benefited from state spending and government privatization of residential housing. Since the 1990s construction growth has been rapid: between 1995 and 2008, for example, the average annual rate of value-added output was 13.6% (in nominal terms). China's hosting of the Olympic Games in 2008 was a source of huge construction activity, with an associated budget estimated at US $40,000m., or the equivalent of almost one-third of the 2006 value of national construction. In recent years, increases in the price of land for residential use and in house prices themselves gave rise to concerns that a property market 'bubble' might be emerging, especially in some cities. In Beijing, for example, house prices rose by 8.8% and 11.4% in 2006 and 2007, respectively, compared with national average price increases of 5.5% and 7.6%, respectively. As prices accelerated, controls imposed in the latter stages of 2007 on loans to real estate developers and investors caused a sharp decline in property sales during 2008, and the average house price rise fell back to 6.5%, before once more accelerating to 7.8% in 2009. Concealed in these figures was a rise in absolute house prices in Beijing to $300,000 for a 100-sq m apartment—a figure comparable with that of Washington, DC (data from *China Economic Quarterly*). In 2010 investment in residential property surged by about one-third, although a consensus view was that as stimulus spending slowed and credit tightening continued, property investment would slow considerably in 2011. Meanwhile, owing to the worsening shortages of affordable housing for low- and middle-income households, the Government has sought to prioritize the construction of low-cost apartments. In particular, a priority under the Twelfth Five-Year Development Programme (2011–15) is the construction of 36m. units of social housing. If this target is fulfilled, by 2015 about one-fifth of the urban population will be accommodated in low-cost, subsidized housing. Between 2000 and 2009 investment in real estate development throughout China grew, on average, by 25% annually (25.5% for investment in residential buildings).

Environment

China's rapid industrialization since the early 1980s has led to serious environmental degradation. According to the World Bank, in the late 1990s particulate pollution in northern China and sulphur dioxide pollution in the south (reflecting the high sulphur content of coal in the region) accounted for some 300,000 premature deaths annually as a result of chronic pulmonary disease. Environmental problems include air pollution, acid rainfall, water shortages and worsening water quality, a contracting arable land base and land degradation (the area of desert and 'desertified' land reportedly now exceeds China's arable area). China's pollution problems are mainly energy-related. Coal remains the main source of primary energy in China and the widespread use of unwashed coal has generated very high emissions of greenhouse gases, sulphur dioxide and particulate matter. Although conversion from coal to natural gas for domestic fuel is helping to reduce urban pollution, coal will remain the cheapest form of generating energy for many years to come. Hence the importance of increasing investment in coal treatment plants and adopting desulphurization technologies. No less serious are water and land problems: Northern China, in particular, suffers from a chronic water shortage, while urban and industrial encroachment on arable land is a serious problem, especially in fertile coastal regions of the country.

The cost of this environmental degradation is enormous and the consequences are profound. The challenge it presents to the Chinese Government is a massive one and has serious implications for the region and for the world. Of the world's 20 most polluted cities, 16 are in China, and two-thirds of all large Chinese cities fail to meet World Health Organization (WHO) air standards. In 2006 an officially sponsored project found that damage caused by environmental pollution was costing the equivalent of 3% of the 2004 level of GDP and suggested that cleaning up the environment would entail spending 1,080,000m. yuan (around US $136,000m.), or about 7% of GDP. Such estimates are probably conservative, and other authoritative sources have put the cost of addressing environmental degradation at 9%–10% of GDP. The human cost, in terms of illness and death, is also huge. Less obvious is the political threat that environmental degradation poses, should social unrest associated with resource pressures and pollution begin to undermine the CCP's authority. In 2005 alone environmental pollution was the source of more than 50,000 public disputes, 30% more than in the previous year.

There is no doubting the Government's genuine commitment to improving China's environment. As host of the 2008 Olympic Games, Beijing was well aware of the importance of projecting an environmentally conscious agenda to the rest of the world. Environmental protection was a major investment priority of the Eleventh Five-Year Programme (2006–10), as it is in the new Twelfth Five-Year Programme. Underlining the recent strategic shift towards development sustainability have been important legislative initiatives. The Chinese Government first introduced environmental legislation in the 1980s, when it also began to establish links with international non-governmental organizations (NGOs), and bilateral and multilateral aid agencies. Since the mid-1990s more than 25 environmental protection laws have been adopted. The most important of these was the 2003 Environmental Impact Assessment Law, which requires not only that all construction and infrastructural projects be evaluated in terms of their environmental effect, but also that all environmental impact assessment reports be made publicly available. Such initiatives reflect the belief that the legal framework is just as important as economic and technological instruments in promoting more effective environmental protection.

All this is encouraging. However, the serious challenges that lie ahead must be recognized. For example, the weak sense of law that still characterizes China diminishes government efforts to address environmental issues by legislative means. Notwithstanding its explicitly wide mandate, the former State Environmental Protection Agency (SEPA) (now elevated to ministerial status as the Ministry of Environmental Protection) suffered severe funding and staffing shortages. At the end of 2004 it had only 300 full-time employees (compared with 6,000 working in the US Environmental Protection Agency). Most alarming of all, quantitative environmental indicators have offered only limited scope for optimism. There is evidence that the discharge of major pollutants has continued to rise, and earlier than expected China has become the largest emitter of both sulphur dioxide and carbon dioxide in the world. It is responsible for as much as one-quarter of global mercury emissions. Meanwhile, soil and water pollution is worsening, with serious consequences for public health. The Government's 2009 environmental report revealed that environmental protection investment in 2008 totalled 34,000m. yuan (3% more than in 2007). Many would argue that this sum is quite insufficient to address the environmental challenges confronted by China.

China is a significant contributor to the problem of global warming. Until quite recently, China's emissions of greenhouse gases were low. In 1950, for example, when the industrial sector accounted for barely 15% of GDP, China's carbon dioxide emissions from burning fossil fuels accounted for just 1.13% of the global total. Subsequently, with the impact of sustained energy-intensive industrialization, China's cumulative contribution rose substantially and accounted for 9.3% of global greenhouse gas emissions during 1959–2002. Within this figure is the increasing intensity in energy use associated with annual GDP growth in excess of 10% since the 1980s. Thus, between 1994 and 2004 China's emissions of carbon dioxide grew, on average, by 5.1% annually, while the corresponding figure for all emissions of greenhouse gases was 4.2%. International Energy Agency (IEA) statistics show that China's share of global carbon dioxide emissions rose from 5% to 9% between 1990 and 2007 (in average per caput terms from 2.0 to 4.6 tons), and will reach at least 13% by 2020.

Until 2005 China was the world's second largest emitter of greenhouse gases after the USA. It was widely believed that China would not overtake the USA to become the biggest single source of emissions of carbon dioxide and greenhouse gases until between 2015 and 2020. However, in June 2007 a report by the Netherlands Environmental Assessment Agency (NEAA) showed that as a result of a continuing rise in coal consumption and a surge in cement production, in 2006 China had already overtaken the USA to become the world's largest producer of carbon dioxide. An informed consensus view is that China has now become the largest emitter of greenhouse gases in the world. The alarming implications of such findings were highlighted in projections made by the IEA, which showed that, if current trends were to continue, Chinese emissions of greenhouse gases between now and 2030 would be double the cumulative total of all other industrialized countries.

The Twelfth Five-Year Development Programme has once again prioritized sustainable development. The Government has committed itself to reducing energy consumption and carbon emissions further by 2015. Targets include decreasing energy consumption per unit of GDP by 16% and raising the share of fossil fuels in total energy consumption by more than

3%. Carbon dioxide emissions per unit of GDP are to be reduced by 17%.

Energy

The energy sector remains a weak link in China's industrial development. China is the world's second largest producer and the largest consumer of energy, although domestic energy supplies have increasingly fallen behind the demands of industrial growth. During the 1980s and 1990s China's demand for primary energy grew significantly faster than that of the global average, and between 1980 and 1995 its share of global energy consumption rose from 6.5% to 10.3%. In 2008 the corresponding figure had reached 16.4%. NBS data show that in 2010 primary energy production (2,990m. tons of coal equivalent—TCE) was about 8% below consumption (3,250m. TCE). Centres of energy production and consumption in China are situated more than 1,000 km apart, and long-distance shipments of coal take up to 40% of railway freight capacity. This situation is not expected to improve in the short term. IEA projections show primary energy demand more than doubling between 2005 and 2030, implying an average annual rate of growth of 3.2% (but of 5.1% during 2005–15, before the structure of industrial output shifts towards less energy-intensive activities and production makes more use of energy-efficient technologies). Most of the increase will occur in coastal provinces, which are far from the centres of production in the north and north-west.

For many years dependence on coal has been a striking feature of China's energy industry. The contribution of coal in total energy consumption reached its highest point in 1990, when it exceeded 76%; it subsequently decreased, to a low point of 68.3% in 2001, but rose again, to reach 70.9% in 2010. The declining trend since the beginning of the 1990s has been offset by rises in the contributions of crude petroleum (the share of which reached 22.3% in 2002, but thereafter decreased to 16.5% in 2010), natural gas (4.3% in 2010), and other sources (hydroelectric power, nuclear energy and other renewables—8.3% in 2010). The contribution of nuclear energy on its own is negligible, but was expected to increase to between 2.5% and 4.5% of total installed generating capacity by 2010. Alternative and sustainable forms of energy have been of minor importance, although in October 2006 the Government announced that more funds would be allocated towards developing bio-energy, solar and wind energy projects, and such investment is planned to rise significantly under the new Five-Year Development Programme. In 2008 manufacturing accounted for 71.5% of total energy consumption; among other claims on energy resources were household consumption (11%), transport, storage, posts and telecommunications (7.7%), and farming (2%).

Electricity

China's electricity production in 2010 was 4,206,540m. kWh, 13.2% above the 2009 level—a significant re-acceleration of annual growth compared with 2007 and 2008, and close to the average rate of annual expansion during 2000–07 (13.5%). From a base of 294,000 MW in 2000, the Tenth Five-Year Programme aimed to raise capacity to 370,000 MW by 2005 and to 500,000 MW–550,000 MW by 2010. Industry absorbs about three-quarters of total electricity consumption, and households consume a further 11%. Thermal power accounts for a little over 80% of total electricity output, compared with a contribution of 16% from hydropower, and no more than 2% from nuclear power. Hydroelectric power is relatively abundant in China's southern provinces, but the sources are often located in remote areas. Accounting for 15.3% of global supply in 2007, China is the world's largest hydroelectricity producer, ahead of Canada, Brazil and the USA. The largest hydroelectric project in China is the Three Gorges Dam on the Changjiang (River Yangtze). On completion, its 32 main generators will have a total capacity of 22,500 MW; as of 2009 26 generators were in operation, with installed capacity of 18,300 MW. However, notwithstanding the immense financial and engineering challenges inherent in the Dam's construction, an authoritative Chinese source suggests that its contribution to meeting national power requirements will be no more than 2%–3%. The social implications of its construction have also been considerable, involving the displacement and resettlement of an estimated 1.3m. people; its environmental consequences have also come under increasing scrutiny. Another large-scale hydroelectric scheme is planned for the Huanghe (Yellow River) under the newly established Yellow River Water and Hydroelectric Development Corporation, which plans to achieve an installed capacity of 25 generating stations capable of generating 15.8 GW.

Small-scale power plants with a capacity of 125 MW or less account for 50% of installed capacity of coal-fired stations. These plants are relatively cheap to build, but they incur substantial transport costs for coal and emit high levels of carbon dioxide, sulphur dioxide and particles; hence official encouragement, where possible, of larger, more efficient plants. The development of larger grids is expected to facilitate the long-distance transport of electricity and to reduce the need for coal. China remains susceptible to power shortages. In mid-2004 China experienced the worst energy shortages since the 1980s, with street lighting being switched off, air conditioning turned down and some factories being forced to halt production. Although the situation subsequently improved (by the summer of 2006 only four provinces were experiencing power deficits) the underlying problem remains. In early 2008 severe winter weather forced some power stations to ration power supplies, as a result of which some 30m. people were reported to have been affected by power shortages. In July there were reports of further threats to power supplies caused by rising coal prices and low, subsidized electricity rates. The scale of the challenge for the power sector is captured in the finding that in order fully to accommodate demand, China needs to add to its existing electricity-generating capacity the equivalent of more than the total installed capacity of the USA.

The structure of the power sector was changed in 1997 when, in an attempt to separate power production and distribution and to make the industry more competitive, the operation of the State's power plants was transferred from the former Ministry of Power Industry to the State Power Corporation (SPC). The SPC was made responsible for the funding of energy development (state subsidies to the power industry being discontinued in favour of commercial funding from domestic and foreign sources) and for power distribution, through its control of national electricity grids. In October 2002 the SPC itself underwent restructuring, involving its transformation into five generating and two distributing companies.

Coastal provinces predictably account for most of China's electricity consumption. On their own, Shanghai and the two provinces of the Lower Yangtze Delta—Jiangsu and Zhejiang—accounted for 19% of national consumption in 2007, while Guangdong alone consumed a further 10.4%.

Coal

China is today the world's largest producer and consumer of coal and, at current levels of consumption, reserves are expected to last for 250 years (compared with only 50–70 years for proven petroleum and natural gas reserves). Recoverable coal reserves have been estimated by the US Energy Information Administration (EIA) to total 114,500m. short tons, placing China in third place behind Russia and the USA; its reserves account for 13% of global reserves. Official Chinese figures show that total domestic production decreased by 30% between 1996 and 2000, as the Government sought to rationalize production and, in particular, to address problems of surplus labour and inefficiency associated with the continuing operation of so many dangerous small-scale mines. Those same sources indicate that the previous peak level of production has now been reattained and surpassed, with total output reaching an historic high point of 3,240m. metric tons in 2010 (9% higher than in 2009—itself a record level). Despite the attainment of record output levels, China's overseas purchases of coal grew from 2002 and in the first half of 2007 the country became a net importer of coal, although for the entire year China's exports exceeded overseas sales by 2.15m. tons. In 2008, too, China's foreign trade balance in coal remained in surplus, with net exports of 5.03m. tons. In 2009, however, for the first time annual trade figures revealed China to be a net importer of coal, with a total of 103m. tons purchased. In 2010, owing to a 15% decline in exports and a 31% rise in imports, annual net imports increased to almost 146m. tons. Many observers have predicted that China's net import status will persist for some time. Meanwhile, coal remains China's major energy source, accounting for more than three-quarters of total energy production and 70.9% of consumption in 2010. According to the EIA, in 2008 China accounted for 47.4% of global coal consumption (in 1973 the corresponding figure was 18.7%). Coal utilization is divided roughly equally among electricity generation, industrial activities, and domestic heating and cooking. Problems arising from the use of coal (especially that mined in southern China, which has a high sulphur and ash content) include greenhouse gas emissions, air pollution and acid rain, and cities increasingly prohibit the burning of coal for heating and cooking. Environmental concerns have also encouraged technical advances designed to make coal cleaner and easier to transport through liquefaction or gasification.

Coal deposits are concentrated in the north and north-west of China, in the provinces of Shanxi (where most state-owned mines are located), Shaanxi and Inner Mongolia. In 2009 these three regions generated half of national production. From these regions coal must be carried, mainly by rail, to eastern coastal and southern provinces. The scale of this challenge is indicated by the fact that in 2009 1,327m. tons of coal were carried by railway. Limited rail capacity has added to the energy shortages along the Changjiang (Yangtze) valley and in southern regions, and hundreds of trucks make daily journeys from the coalfields of Shanxi Province in order to supply coal to Beijing. In 2004 a 70% deficiency in rail wagons needed to transport coal from the main producing regions contributed significantly to serious power shortages that affected much of China. Stocks of coal also had to be moved around railway yards in order to prevent spontaneous combustion. By the end of 2005 such transport difficulties had largely been brought under control, although other factors have caused continuing power shortages.

From the early 1980s demand for coal led central government to encourage the growth of small, decentralized coal mines, managed either by provincial or by local authorities, to supplement the bulk of output generated from fewer than 100 large-scale units. By the late 1990s small-scale mines (managed privately or by TVEs), each with an annual output of 30,000 metric tons or less, generated 44% of national production. However, many of these were highly inefficient, and in 1998 the Government announced the planned closure of some 26,000 small mines, with the expected loss of almost 1m. jobs. To what extent closures on this scale really have taken place is difficult to determine (deaths in the industry seem not to have declined significantly), although an EIA report confirmed the closure of 20,000–50,000 small mines. Meanwhile, against the background of high levels of inefficiency and poor management in a fragmented industry in which the three largest state-owned companies generate less than 15% of domestic output, in February 2006 the National Development and Reform Commission announced a plan to consolidate the coal sector through the closure, by 2015, of all remaining small-scale mines and the establishment of six huge conglomerates. The Government has sought to encourage foreign investment in the industry in an attempt to facilitate much-needed technological upgrading and modernization.

Petroleum and Natural Gas

In 2009 China's proven petroleum reserves were estimated by EIA to total some 16,000m. barrels. Since 2000 domestic crude petroleum output has grown, on average, by only 2.2% per annum—from 163m. tons to 203.01m. tons in 2010. Despite being the fifth largest oil producer in the world, such relatively slow growth in recent years has been insufficient to meet increasing demand, as a result of which China has had to resort increasingly to importing large quantities of oil. In 2007 China was the third largest net oil importer, after the USA and Japan; but the IEA has predicted that by 2025 China will have overtaken the USA to become the world's biggest overseas purchaser of petroleum and natural gas (a projection that some regard as unduly cautious). The same source has indicated that by 2030 China will account for about three-quarters of global oil consumption.

In 2009 domestic crude oil production of 189.5m. tons was supplemented by imports (net) of 198.72m. tons (almost 14% higher than in 2008). Imports thus accounted for more than one-half of China's total consumption of crude petroleum. China has also been a major importer of refined oil, although in 2009 its overseas purchases fell by 5% to 37m. tons. Sometimes owing to the sharp increase in international prices, the cost of oil imports has risen steeply—by a full two-thirds for crude in 2008 alone—leading to a deficit on both crude (US $126,355.5m. in 2008, or more than 60% above the 2007 level) and refined ($16,379.2m., more than twice the 2007 figure and about four times higher than in 2006) oil accounts. In 2009 the corresponding deficit on the crude account was $87,100m. China's transformation from a major oil exporter in the 1980s to an increasing importer since 1993 emphasizes the energy constraint that high GDP growth has imposed. China's annual petroleum production will not increase significantly in the near future, and one recent report indicated that oil dependence could rise to 65% by 2020. The impact of WTO membership on the oil sector is also significant, since its rules require China to allow foreign companies to import, distribute and sell oil products. About one-half of China's imported petroleum is from the Middle East, and a further 30% comes from African sources. The two most important sources of imports are Saudi Arabia and Angola, which together account for more than one-third of China's overseas purchases of crude petroleum.

For the time being, about three-quarters of total domestic production are extracted from older oilfields in eastern and north-eastern China. Since beginning production in 1963, CNPC's Daqing in north-eastern China has remained the country's largest oilfield and still accounts for about one-fifth of total output: around 801,000 barrels per day (b/d) in 2008. The second largest oilfield, owned by Sinopec, is Shengli, which generated about 553,000 b/d. About 85% of China's national oil output is from onshore production facilities. Offshore production, which in 2008 totalled some 680,000 b/d—but which the IEA predicts will rise to 980,000 b/d by 2014—is dominated by CNOOC. Onshore exploitation and new exploration are centred in western China (Xinjiang, Inner Mongolia, Gansu and Sichuan). Offshore centres, mostly based on consortia with international partners, include the Bohai Gulf, near Tianjin (where reserves are estimated at 1,500m. barrels), and the Zhujiang Delta region in southern China. China and Viet Nam have also agreed to undertake joint oil and gas production in the Beibu Gulf.

For some years, China has participated in international petroleum and gas prospecting and exploitation, involving oil projects in Peru, Canada, Sudan, Thailand, Venezuela and Kazakhstan. CNPC is reported to have a presence in Russia and 28 other countries in Africa, Central Asia, South America, the Middle East and the Asia Pacific. Since 2004 China has intensified its 'oil diplomacy' in an attempt to broaden the sources of its foreign oil supplies in order to meet economic, environmental and geo-strategic goals. Russia and Central Asia (especially Kazakhstan) have emerged as important suppliers. In 2006, for example, China's first transnational oil pipeline began operations, facilitating the supply of oil from Russia and Kazakhstan, and in 2011 oil began flowing from the Russian Far East via the Eastern Siberia-Pacific Ocean Pipeline (ESPO). There have been significant developments, too, in Latin America (in Ecuador and, most notably, Venezuela, where Chinese companies have a significant presence). Most noteworthy of all recent developments has been China's interest in increasing oil supplies from African countries. The significance of these efforts was dramatically highlighted in 2006, when Angola overtook Saudi Arabia to become the single most important source of overseas oil supplies (based on data for January–September). Other important African sources of petroleum shipments are the Republic of the Congo, Equatorial Guinea, Sudan, Kenya and Nigeria. Some projections have suggested that Africa's contribution to oil imports will reach 25% by 2015. Overall, China's increasing engagement in oil diplomacy is unprecedented in its global scope and has major implications—political and military, as well as economic—for the international economy.

It was reported in December 2007 that China's first national oil reserve base, located in Zhejiang Province and with a storage capacity of 5.2m. cu m, had been filled with oil. This was one of four such bases (two in Zhejiang and one each in Shandong and Liaoning) which became operational at the end of 2008, providing China with a strategic oil reserve of around 10m. tons, or the equivalent of about 30 days of imports. Construction of an oil base in Xinjiang is also believed to have been completed. Under the second phase of China's national oil reserve plan, scheduled for completion in 2020, a further eight oil bases will be constructed in Jiangsu, Guangdong, Gansu and Liaoning.

Natural gas consumption remains at a relatively low level. Between 1978 and 1995 its share of total primary energy consumption declined from 3.2% to 1.8%, although it has since recovered to reach a new high point of 4.3% in 2010. Recent estimates suggest that China's proven reserves of natural gas are about 80,000,000m. cu ft, half of which are located in the Tarim Basin in the north-west of the country. In 2008 China's natural gas production totalled 3,334,000m. cu ft, but consumption reached 3,768,000m. cu ft, as a result of which China was a net importer for the second consecutive year in almost 20 years. In some large cities, gas has already replaced coal as a household fuel. Intensified petroleum exploration is expected to generate further discoveries of natural gas. China's search for more diversified, as well as clean and efficient, energy sources means that natural gas features strongly in national energy planning, and the EIA expects demand to more than triple between 2009 and 2030. There have been important discoveries of new natural gas sources in western and north-eastern China, and a new gas pipeline from Xinjiang to Shanghai is a core project in the development of western China. Nevertheless, realization of the target of supplying 6% of primary energy consumption from natural gas by 2010 has not been fulfilled, and meeting the 8% target for 2020 will be dependent on increased imports from Central Asia, Russia and Australia. In April 2008 agreement was reached to establish a joint venture with Uzbekistan, whereby CNPC was to be involved in the construction of a gas pipeline from the Turkmenistan border through Uzbekistan and Kazakhstan to China. CNPC already had a 30-year gas import contract with Uzbekneftigas. In March 2009 CNPC signed an agreement with Myanmar to finance construction of a pipeline that will extend from two of Myanmar's offshore blocks to Kunming in China's Yunnan Province.

Nuclear Power

In 2003 nuclear power supplied just 2.3% of China's total electricity (the world average being about 16%) and was the third most important source of power after thermal and hydro power. In November 2007 the State Council approved plans to increase China's nuclear-generating capacity to 40,000 MW by 2020 (by which time the share of nuclear power in national energy output will have risen to 4%). The expansion plan is expected to cost about 450,000m. yuan. Meanwhile, the EIA has projected a 45-GW expansion in China's nuclear-generating capacity between 2005 and 2030, equivalent to two-thirds of total additional capacity expected of all non-Organisation for Economic Co-operation and Development (OECD) Asian countries. In mid-2009 the EIA reported that eight new nuclear plants were under construction in China, and plans were being made for construction of a further eight plants. The largest of these was a 4.4-GW complex, sited at Haiyang in Shandong Province, which was expected to begin commercial operations in 2014. China has been strongly reliant on imported foreign nuclear technology from France, Canada and Russia. Only the Qinshan Plant in Zhejiang, which is partly operational, has installed domestic generators. Future development will continue to involve plant imports and foreign co-operation alongside a greater role for independent domestic construction.

Transport and Communications

Like energy, transport and telecommunications are a weak link in China's infrastructure. Transport was designated a priority area under the Tenth Five-Year Programme (2001–05) (as it is again under the Twelfth Programme, 2011–15), associated projects including the Beijing–Shanghai Express rail project, the Shanghai International Shipping Center and major transport infrastructure projects in China's western regions. In order to meet infrastructural needs, roads, railways, airports, and ports and harbours are being upgraded, or new facilities built. Meanwhile, freight volume rose to 14,183,800m. freight ton-km in 2010 (an annual increase of 16.1% compared with trend growth of 12.3% per annum since 2000). Of this, 19.5% was carried by rail, 30.6% by road and 48.2% by water. Following a small decline in 2003 because of the crisis that arose from the outbreak of Severe Acute Respiratory Syndrome (SARS), since 2004 the volume of passenger traffic has risen steadily to reach 2,789,400m. person-km in 2010 (a year-on-year increase of 12.3%): 31.4% of this was carried by rail, 53.9% by road, and almost all of the rest by air.

The railway system plays a strategic role in China's infrastructure through its transport of grain from surplus to deficit regions (99.3m. tons in 2009, 13.5% less than in 2008), of coal (1,327m. tons) from north-western provinces to the high-demand eastern and southern provinces, and of other important materials, such as metal ores (356.8m. tons), iron, steel and non-ferrous metals (215.3m. tons), and fertilizers and pesticides (80.3m. tons). China's railways have no more than 6% of global track mileage, but carry about one-quarter of the world's freight and passenger traffic. New railway corridors are expected to invigorate the economies of adjoining regions, including provinces along the new line between Kowloon (Hong Kong) and Beijing, and the south-western line connecting Guangxi Zhuang Autonomous Region and Yunnan Province. The main trunk lines of Beijing–Guangzhou, Harbin–Dalian, Beijing–Shenyang and Lianyungang–Lanzhou carry a freight volume three times their official capacity. High-speed trains, capable of speeds of up to 140 km per hour (the average for long-distance routes is a mere 60 km per hour), are in service between Beijing, Shanghai, Harbin and Guangzhou. A magnetic levitation ('maglev') train, the first of its kind in the world, began passenger operations in 2003 and, at speeds of up to 400 km per hour, links central Shanghai with the city's airport. In August 2008 the Beijing–Tianjin Intercity Railway opened: with trains running at speeds of up to 350 km per hour, the link has reduced the travelling time between the two cities from 70 to 30 minutes. In June 2011 China inaugurated its latest high-speed railway link, between Beijing and Shanghai, which is reported to have reduced travelling time to less than five hours. Another important development was the opening in 2006 of the Qingzang railway, a 1,140-km line linking Beijing with Lhasa, the capital of Tibet (Xizang). The Government plans to extend this as far as the China–India border in the west, and to Dali in the east. Despite such developments, China's rail system is still able to meet only about one-third of demand and delays in freight shipments remain common. Plans to extend track length to 85,000 km by 2010 have been fulfilled (85,500 km in 2009), owing to a 67.5% increase in rail investment under the Government's stimulus programme. It was intended that rail track length would increase to 100,000 km by 2020, and with a total track length of 91,200 km in 2010, China has made good progress towards achieving this target. An institutional departure, which will also assist in upgrading the rail system, was the abolition of the State's previous monopoly role and a willingness to use private capital (including overseas funding) in order to help fulfil construction targets.

In July 2011, however, China's impressive record of high-speed railway construction was seriously undermined by a major accident in which two high-speed trains collided in Zhejiang Province (in eastern China), causing the deaths of 39 passengers. Initial reports attributed the accident to a lightning strike that had caused one of the trains to lose power, thereby allowing a second approach train to crash into its rear. However, subsequent reports spoke of a system failure, and 54 bullet trains were later recalled because of 'design flaws'. Meanwhile, the Chinese official in charge of the accident investigation admitted that the crash was 'completely avoidable'. The accident was widely considered to be a serious setback to China's hopes of selling high-speed trains abroad as part of its efforts to become a major high-technology exporter.

Since the 1980s highway construction has helped to create a long-distance network facilitating inter-regional road transport and replace what was previously a localized and province-orientated system. Between 1990 and 1995 China completed 130,000 km of highways, including 1,619 km of expressways and 9,328 km of wider and dual-carriage roads. Official NBS statistics show that between 2000 and 2010 the length of China's highways increased more than three-fold to total 4m. km. Moreover, between 1990 and 2010 high-speed expressway routes expanded from almost zero to 74,100 km (second only to the USA). Even so, the pressure on road use is intense: since the 1980s the number of vehicles (including, in recent years, cars) has increased 10 times faster than the expansion of the road system. Long-term plans seek to expand the total length of expressways to at least 85,000 km by 2020, and to construct a 35,000-km network of 12 national highways that will link Beijing to all provincial capitals and larger cities. In view of the inadequacy of roads in rural China, a major challenge is to link the farm and non-farm economies of towns and villages with the national road network, an objective that the Government had hoped to achieve by 2010.

China has 13 major ocean shipping ports, each with an annual capacity of more than 5m. metric tons. The four largest of these are Ningbo-Zhoushan (which handled 633m. tons of freight in 2010), Shanghai (563.2m. tons), Tianjin (413.25m. tons) and Guangzhou (411m. tons). The volume of freight handled at all major coastal ports in 2010 was 5,484m. tons (15.3% above the 2009 level, almost four and a half times that of 2000 and more than 11 times that of 1990). This remarkable rate of expansion reflects China's surging foreign trade. However, in technical terms Chinese ports do not match international standards: less than one-quarter of trade is containerized, compared with a world average of 50%. Turnaround times in Chinese ports are another major concern: for example, deliveries of coal and iron ore are sometimes delayed for up to three weeks because of the lack of unloading berths. Resolving such problems will take time, not least because it takes three–four years to construct a port.

Between 1978 and 1980 there was a sharp contraction in the length of inland shipping waterways, from 136,000 km to 108,500 km. Recovery subsequently took place, and in 2010 the corresponding figure was 124,200 km. In 2010 freight carried by inland waterways totalled 3,789.5m. metric tons (almost 19% more than in 2009). Inland river navigation is especially highly developed in southern and south-west China. Since 1997 upgrading of facilities on the Xijiang to accommodate 1,000-ton vessels has given Nanning, the capital of Guangxi, access to Hong Kong and Macao. New navigation networks have also been constructed and existing ones improved in the Zhujiang Delta, along the Changjiang/Yangtze and on the Beijing–Hangzhou Grand Canal. By far the most important future development will be the upgrading of port facilities in Chongqing, which will enable much heavier ocean-going vessels to penetrate deep into the western interior of the country.

The aviation sector grew at an annual rate of 20% during the 1990s and continues to expand rapidly. Since 1990 the number of international air routes has risen from 44 to 302, while that of domestic air transport routes increased from 385 to 1,578. Air passenger traffic rose from 23,000m. passenger-km in 1990 to 403,900m. passenger-km in 2010 (an average annual increase of over 15%). China now has the second largest volume of air traffic in the world. Lack of profitability is a problem that afflicts many of China's 135 civil airports; only the larger airports, such as Beijing, Shanghai and Guangzhou, are believed to be profitable. The challenge confronting the aviation sector is captured in the finding that in contrast to the global situation, in which general aviation aircraft constitute 97% of all civil aviation aircraft, in China the corresponding figure is well under one-half. In recent years China has emerged as one of the most important aircraft purchasers in the world. Since 2000, for example, its fleets of Boeing-737 and Airbus A-320 have expanded rapidly (to 593 and 219, respectively, by 2009). Overall, the number of Chinese civil aircraft increased from 503 in 1990 to 982 in 2000 and 2,181 in 2009. Official Chinese projections indicate a need for some 12,000 general aviation aircraft by 2012; authoritative non-Chinese sources suggest that actual availability will be 10,000 by 2020. Thus, development of general aviation was designated a priority under the Eleventh Five-Year Plan (2006–10). It also helps to explain China's intensified pursuit of foreign investment in order to facilitate industrial restructuring designed to merge China's 10 major airlines into three groups (Air China, China Eastern Airlines and China Southern Airlines). There has also been pressure on China from the EU and USA to liberalize its aviation sector. An important recent domestic initiative was the announcement, in May 2008, of plans for China's first jumbo jet passenger aircraft, a mid-range aircraft with 150 seats, to be manufactured by the Commercial Aircraft Corporation of China (CACC).

Since the early 1990s China's telecommunications industry has experienced a very rapid expansion, driven by huge demand for new technology. However, despite major initiatives undertaken by the Government, such as the accelerated development and expansion of a digital network, fibre-optic cables and satellite systems, and mobile communication facilities, the indigenous industry remains quite immature. The potential for growth is correspondingly huge, especially in terms of supplying indigenous innovative capacity. Between 1985 and 2008 the number of urban household fixed-line telephone subscribers rose from 41,000 to 156m., but had declined to 130m. in 2009, no doubt reflecting the universality of mobile telephone usage; in the countryside the number of fixed-line subscribers also reached a record 105m. in 2008, falling back to 102m. in 2009. Growth of the mobile telephone market has indeed been extraordinary. In 1990 there were a mere 18,000 mobile subscribers; in 2000 the corresponding figure was 84.5m., and by 2010 it had reached 859m. (of whom 12.3m. were 3G mobile subscribers). In 2010 alone there were more than 110m. new mobile phone subscribers. The length of long-distance fibre-optic cable has also risen dramatically: to 818,200 km by 2010. High fees and sophisticated efforts by the Government to control content continue to restrict access to data communication in China. In 2005 it was reported that some 4,000 'internet security police' would be appointed to monitor internet cafés and companies. However, the true figure is far higher: according to a 2005 source, numbering around 30,000. Despite attempts by the Government to tighten control over the internet, as well as other media forms, since 2000 the number of internet users has grown by 35% a year to reach 457m. in 2010 (giving China the second largest number of users in the world after the USA). However, access is disproportionately orientated towards commercial users in coastal provinces and major cities, such as Beijing, Guangzhou and Shanghai.

THE FINANCIAL SECTOR

Banking and Finance Reform

The State still plays a major role in China's financial and banking system. From 1949 to 1983 the People's Bank of China (PBC) was China's only bank. Its remit was all-embracing, ranging from the issue of currency to account settlement and foreign-currency transactions. In 1984 the PBC became the central bank, and its business functions were taken over by four newly established state-owned commercial banks (SOCBs): the Industrial and Commercial Bank of China (ICBC), the Agricultural Bank of China (ABC), the People's Construction Bank of China—subsequently China Construction Bank (CCB)—and the Bank of China (BOC). In 2005–06 three of the SOCBs—CCB, BOC and ICBC—undertook initial public offerings (IPOs), when they listed on the Hong Kong stock exchange. In July 2010 the long-awaited IPO of the ABC took place, raising US $22,100m. and making it the largest IPO on record.

Meanwhile, in support of the Government's macro-objectives, three new policy banks were established in 1994: the China Development Bank, Export-Import Bank and Agricultural Development Bank. In addition to these dominant institutions, there also exist a small number of joint-stock commercial banks, around 100 city banks (created out of the former urban credit co-operatives) and restructured rural credit co-operatives. Foreign banks have a small, but increasing presence. The domestic private banking sector has yet to be developed as a significant force. The China International Trust and Investment Corporation (CITIC) was established in 1979: its original *raison d'être* was to attract Overseas Chinese capital, although its remit subsequently came to include the provision of a wider range of financial services (including leasing and foreign investment). Most provinces subsequently established their own international trust and investment corporations (ITICs), but in the aftermath of the spectacular default and bankruptcy of Guangdong ITIC in 1998, they underwent retrenchment. Finally, in 2003 the Government established the China Banking Regulatory Commission (CBRC) in an attempt to enhance financial stability, improve the international competitiveness of the Chinese banking sector and exercise an independent supervisory and regulatory role within the sector. Legislative support for this important institutional initiative was forthcoming in the enactment of a Law on the Supervision of the Banking Industry.

Against the background of excessive domestic liquidity, the Government has sought to encourage investment overseas and/or the establishment of production overseas by domestic Chinese firms. In this regard, two important financial institutional initiatives took place in 2006. The first was the implementation of the Qualified Domestic Institutional Investment (QDII) scheme, designed to facilitate portfolio investment overseas by selected Chinese institutions; the second was the establishment of the China Council for International Investment Promotion (CCIIP), which offers advice and guidance on both inward and outward investment.

The essential fragility of China's banking system was not officially recognized until the late 1990s. Prior to this, the absence of hard budget constraints was reflected in the funding of unproductive projects and the extension of credit to inefficient SOEs. In order to protect savers, interest rates on deposits were also frequently significantly higher than on loans. The inevitable outcome was a reduction in banks' profitability, an erosion of their capital and the steady accumulation of NPLs. By the late 1990s bad loans represented about 40% of total lending, and the SOCBs' capital adequacy ratios (CARs) had decreased to around 5%. Thus, in 1998 major efforts got under way to recapitalize the banking system and reduce NPLs. The first initiative was a massive bond issue, designed to help the SOCBs raise their CARs. However, by far the most important event was the establishment, in 1999, of four state asset management corporations (AMCs), which undertook to purchase the SOCBs' pre-1996 NPLs at face value. The impact of the AMCs is highlighted by the fact that between 2002 and 2005 the NPLs of the SOCBs were almost halved, declining from 2,090,000m. to 1,070,000m. yuan (from 26.0% to 10.5% of all SOCB loans). Meanwhile, by the end of 2005 the AMCs themselves had disposed of an estimated two-thirds of their total NPLs and recovered 177,000m. yuan in cash. It is expected that as AMC activities are phased out, the State will assume responsibility for any remaining AMC debt. Of the four major banks, the CCB has been the most successful in reducing NPLs, with an NPL ratio of 3.8% in 2005. The ABC, with a ratio of 23.5% at the end of 2007, has been the least successful and was the focus of major restructuring efforts in preparation for its IPO. The success of such efforts was highlighted by the finding that ABC's NPL ratio had been reduced to around 3% by mid-2010. Overall, the recent record of success in addressing the problem of NPLs has been impressive, with China's NPLs amounting to US $55,500m. at the end of 2010 (84% below the 2002 level). However, there is concern that the massive credit expansion intended to address the consequences of the global economic recession may prove to be the source of further NPL pressure through having generated excessive low-return, low-multiplier loans to the state sector.

Fiscal and Monetary Policy

Fiscal reform, like price reform, was necessary to introduce market incentives into the enterprise sector. Until the first tax reform in 1983, government revenue consisted primarily of the financial surplus of the SOEs, which had to be remitted in full to the State. Tax reform in 1983, under the slogan 'tax for profit', introduced enterprise taxes and allowed enterprises to retain part of their profits as an economic incentive. However, taxation was not unified, and different tax rates applied to SOEs, collective enterprises and FFEs. Lower tax rates were used as an incentive to attract foreign investment in the 1980s. The fact that in the early 1990s the state sector accounted for only 40% of GDP but contributed 80% of tax revenues, highlighted the irrational nature of the tax system.

Between 1978 and 1995 fiscal revenues declined from 31.1% of GDP to 10.3%. Moreover, having increased from 1.5% to 38.4% during 1978–85, central government's share of total revenues subsequently contracted sharply, to 22% in 1993. In 1994 the Government introduced radical fiscal reforms, which provided a new system of revenue sharing whereby central and local governments were each given their own separate administration for the collection of central and local taxes. At the same time, new taxes were introduced: these included a uniform 33% profit tax on state, collective and private enterprises; a 17% value-added tax (VAT), levied on most manufactured goods, and shared between central and local government on the basis of a 75%: 25% ratio; and a new system of personal income taxes. An important institutional initiative was the establishment of a new tax collection body under the sole control of central government.

The impact of these reforms was dramatic. First, the process of fiscal erosion was halted and reversed: since 1995 revenue as a share of GDP has doubled, to reach 20.8% in 2010, the highest level for more than two decades. Second, central government's share of tax revenue increased dramatically, from 22.0% in 1993 to 51.1% in 2010. Central government takes the largest share of domestic VAT levies, as well as the entire proceeds of tariffs, consumption, import and cargo, and vehicle purchase taxes. Local governments are entitled to all, or almost all, of the receipts from taxes on urban and arable land, resources, urban maintenance and development taxes, contract taxes and other miscellaneous items. They also receive a significant share of the proceeds of local personal and corporate income tax, and VAT revenue. In short, most local government tax is derived from extra-budgetary items and administrative charges that are not part of regular government revenue. Personal income taxes, which remain underdeveloped (constituting a mere 5.8% of national government revenue in 2010), are divided between central and local governments on a 60:40 basis. However, China's tax-sharing system is complicated by the use of rebate schemes from central government to local governments and by inter-governmental transfer mechanisms. In 2008 the central Government disbursed 563,500m. yuan in VAT and consumption tax rebates on exports.

Under the Twelfth Five-Year Development Programme, there are plans to adjust the personal income tax threshold in order to stimulate consumption spending. Following a decision by the NPC Standing Committee, on 1 September 2011 the threshold below which income tax is not payable was raised from 2,000 yuan per month to 3,500 yuan. In addition, the minimum tax rate for low-income earners (i.e. those in receipt of between 3,500 and 4,500 a month) was reduced from 5% to 3%. These changes were expected to exempt an additional 60m. people (about one-fifth of the urban work force) from income tax.

A report by the World Bank in 2002 noted that the heavy expenditure responsibilities of local governments in China were at variance with international practice. The report drew special attention to China's highly decentralized fiscal system, under which sub-national governments accounted for more than 70% of total budgetary expenditure (in 2010 the figure was 82%) and more than two-thirds of extra-budgetary funds. The limited ability of central government to exercise control over the economy through budgetary tools and the unequalizing effects of inter-regional transfers remain unresolved problems of financial reform. Increasingly, fiscal policies have been used to raise domestic demand and exports in order to stimulate the economy. From 1999 such measures included reduced tax rates on capital and real-estate investments, tax exemptions for investment in western China, increased tax reimbursement for exports, and higher taxation of private savings deposits to encourage consumption. Such forms of deficit spending have persisted, although their impact on consumption has so far been quite modest, partly because of highly unequal income distribution.

Until the 1990s the budgetary deficit remained modest, never exceeding 1% of GDP. Subsequently, however, it steadily increased to reach 314,951m. yuan (2.6% of GDP) in 2002. From 2002 the deficit declined sharply, and by 2006 it had decreased to 166,253m. yuan, or 1.2% of GDP. For the first time for more than two decades, in 2007 the budget moved into surplus, which at 154,043m. yuan was equivalent to 0.7% of GDP. The underlying 32% increase in revenues was attributable to major increases in corporation tax and stamp duty, as well as to the impact of adjustments to the export-tax rebate scheme. However, this surplus was not sustained. In 2008 budgetary spending increased by one-quarter, while revenues rose by less than one-fifth. The outcome was the re-emergence of a deficit of more than 125,000m. yuan (0.4% of GDP). Increased spending associated with the Government's stimulus programme, as well as increasing expenditure on pensions and other social security payments for an increasingly ageing population, helped raise total budgetary expenditure by almost 22% in 2009—far higher than the 12% rise in revenue. As a result, the budget deficit increased more than six-fold to 778,160m. yuan (or 2.3% of GDP). In 2010 the deficit contracted to 649,510m. yuan, or 1.6% of GDP. Lack of transparency makes it extremely difficult to estimate China's sovereign debt: official figures indicated a government debt-to-GDP ratio of 17% in 2010. However, Dragonomics, an independent research company, estimated the true figure to be almost 90% of GDP.

Rapid monetization of the Chinese economy has accompanied post-1978 market-orientated economic reforms, and money supply expansion has generated bouts of inflationary pressures (see above). For example, between 1978 and 2000 M0 (the stock of notes and coins in circulation) grew, on average, by 21% a year, while during the same period retail price inflation was almost 6% annually. Meanwhile, annual expansion of M1 (M0 plus the value of current accounts) and M2 (M1 plus some deposit or interest-bearing accounts) was also rapid, averaging 20% and 24% growth, respectively. After 2000 monetary expansion slowed significantly: average annual rates of growth of M1 and M2 were 16.3% and 17.0%, respectively, during 2000–07. However, owing to the global economic crisis, towards the end of 2008 the rate of monetary expansion accelerated, and in 2009 M1 and M2 increased sharply by 33.2% and 28.4%, respectively (while in 2010 the corresponding figures were 20.4% and 18.9%). Although the acceleration in monetary growth in the aftermath of the global crisis eliminated any deflationary risk that otherwise might have emerged, inflationary pressures were mitigated by the low multiplier and short-term nature of much of the loan expansion. Throughout most of 2010 the Government pursued what it described as an 'appropriately loose' monetary policy, but at the end of the year this was adjusted to a 'prudent' stance in order to accommodate inflationary pressures. Inflationary concerns persisted during the first half of 2011, as rising food prices and wage increases exerted upward pressure on both consumer and producer price indexes.

It is noteworthy that in contrast to the direct administrative intervention of the past, efforts to influence the level of economic activity by monetary means have in recent years been characterized by a much greater role played by the central bank (the People's Bank of China)—for example, through adjustments in interest rates. Nevertheless, there is a perception that the PBC's monetary policy tools remain constrained, and recourse to direct intervention, such as raising banks' required reserve ratio, may continue to be a feature of China's macro-economic policies. Such considerations are a reminder that the Chinese economy is still in transition, as a result of which the relationship between orthodox monetary policy methods and economic activity remains quite tenuous.

The Chinese Stock Market

Stock exchanges were established in Shanghai and Shenzhen in 1990, since when they have shown spectacular growth. The number of domestically listed and Hong Kong-listed companies increased from 10 in 1990 to 1,088 in 2000, and numbered 1,718 in 2009. China's stock markets remain relatively immature, weak and highly speculative. Recent trends confirm their volatility. NBS estimates show China's total stock-market capitalization to have been 3,243,000m. yuan in 2005, the lowest level since 1999 and 33% below the peak level of 2000. One year later, the corresponding figure was 8,940,400m. yuan, the highest level in more than a decade or 43% of GDP; and in 2007 capitalization rose by a further 266% to reach 32,714,100m. yuan. The Shanghai 'A' share price index in the final quarter of 2005 had declined by 7.5% year-on-year; remarkably, by the same period of 2006 it had more than doubled. At the beginning of 2007 some 90,000 new trading accounts were being opened daily, a 35-fold increase in comparison with the same period a year earlier; the composite index for 2007 was 5,262, or virtually double that of 2006 (when it reached 2,675). This extraordinary growth was unlikely to be sustained, not least against the background of emerging domestic and international economic pressures. Thus, in 2008 total market capitalization decreased by more than 60% to 12,136,600m. yuan. This decline was reflected in sharp falls in both the Shanghai and Shenzhen stock market indexes: from 5,262 to 1,821 (Shanghai), and from 1,447 to 553 (Shenzhen). However, the volatility of China's stock market was once more in evidence in 2009 when total market capitalization rebounded strongly to reach 24,393,900m. yuan (more than twice as high as in the previous year), and 26,542,300m. yuan in 2010. The composite Shanghai and Shenzhen indexes in 2010 were 2,808 (14% below the 2009 level) and 1,291 (a rise of 7.5%).

Despite stricter regulations and some improvement in operational efficiency, the Chinese stock market continues to be tarnished by problems of mismanagement. A Code of Corporate Governance for Listed Companies was enacted by the China Securities Regulatory Commission in 2002 as part of an initiative to improve the reporting of inflated profits and the delisting of loss-making companies. Listed companies are required to undergo supplementary audits by the major international auditing firms. In general, opportunities for domestic firms and individuals to hold foreign-currency denominated stocks and bonds (the B share market) remain heavily circumscribed. Although still constrained, opportunities for foreign firms and individuals to purchase Chinese-currency denominated assets (the A share market) are gradually increasing. More than 100 of China's 500 largest companies, including China Telecom, Anshan Iron and Steel Company, and Handan Iron and Steel Company, have been publicly listed, although state institutions still hold around 60% of shares in such enterprises. Big state corporations, including the four SOCBs (see above), have also listed their shares in international markets. China's other capital markets remain underdeveloped, although the country's WTO accession is one factor that will help enhance bond, insurance and securities markets. Diversification within the interbank market has strengthened its role as a source of capital for domestic banks. Meanwhile, although the corporate bond market remains small, the National Financial Work Conference has signalled that the issue of corporate bonds would play an increasingly important role, as China's bond markets developed.

FOREIGN TRADE AND INVESTMENT

China's foreign trade and its absorption of foreign investment have represented an important part of the reform of its domestic economy and of strengthening its status as a regional and international economic power. China's increased international standing became evident during the Asian economic crisis of 1997–98, when the country received international praise for having resisted pressure to devalue its currency. The global economic crisis that began in late 2008 highlighted further China's role in influencing the world's future growth and development trajectories.

Ideological and historical factors have at times made China's involvement in the global economy a controversial issue. From the 1950s until the 1980s the country's reluctance to participate in international exchange reflected the adoption of a foreign trade regime that was modelled on that of the former USSR. Under this structure, 10 large foreign trade corporations (FTCs) under the Ministry of Foreign Economic Relations and Trade (later the Ministry of Foreign Trade and Economic Co-operation—itself reorganized under a new State Economic and Trade Commission in 2003), and some technical ministries, monopolized all foreign trade. Through their role as an independent intermediary between domestic producers or buyers and their foreign counterparts, they protected the domestic economy from competition, but more importantly isolated it from technical innovation. In essence, foreign trade performed no more than a 'gap-filling' role, exports serving merely to secure the foreign exchange needed to pay for the import of capital goods that could not be produced domestically. As a result of the dislocation caused by the 'Great Leap Forward' and the early phase of the Cultural Revolution, the 1959 peak level of trade was not subsequently reattained until 1970. Thereafter, however, rapid growth took place, although in 1978 merchandise trade accounted for less than 10% of GDP, with China ranked 32nd among world trading nations.

Deng Xiaoping's adoption of the 'open door' policy was a major development, marking a reorientation of China's official view of its role in the international economic community, henceforth to be characterized by a much more pro-active stance that owed a great deal to the export-led growth model of the first-echelon ANIEs. The most radical sign of the new approach was the Government's active encouragement of overseas involvement in economic construction through foreign investment (above all, FDI). The impact was profound. By the end of the 1990s China had become the 10th largest trading nation in the world and the second largest recipient (by far the largest among developing countries) of overseas capital, above all FDI. It had also become a pivotal force in the Asian economy and a major protagonist within the global system.

From the start, a major thrust of trade reform was the institutional decentralization of decision-making. Foreign trade monopolies were gradually reduced, as Chinese corporations and private enterprises, as well as Sino-foreign joint-venture companies, received foreign trading rights. Other initiatives took place, including tariff reductions. Not least important, a succession of devaluations took the official exchange rate to a more rational level, and in 1994 it was implicitly pegged to the US dollar at around 8.3 yuan to the dollar. Initially, a dual exchange rate was introduced (a lower rate applied to commercial transactions), but in 1994 this was replaced by a unified rate. The US dollar 'peg' remained in place, despite increasing pressure from overseas trading partners (above all, the USA) to revalue in order to restrain China's exports and stimulate its purchases overseas. Continuing large-scale inflows of FDI also put pressure on the currency. Although the Chinese Government rejects allegations that it has been engaged in 'exporting deflation', in July 2005 it adopted a new exchange rate regime replacing the dollar 'peg' with a managed floating exchange rate against a weighted basket of currencies. The new rate was set at US $1:8.11 yuan. Since then, there has been a steady appreciation of the Chinese currency, as a result of which it rose to $1:6.77 yuan in 2010. In 1996 China's currency was made fully convertible for current account transactions, although the Chinese Government has remained much more resistant to capital account convertibility in order to protect itself against destabilizing speculative activities.

One signal of China's commitment to joining the international economic community was its formal application, in 1986, to rejoin the General Agreement on Tariffs and Trade (GATT), the precursor of the WTO. Subsequent negotiations were protracted and WTO accession was not achieved until December 2001. In the process, China undertook to make major market access concessions, in particular, committing itself not only to a reduction in tariffs and removal of other quantitative restrictions, but also to opening up its services sectors (including insurance, banking, telecommunications, and wholesale and retail distribution). Since 2001 the average tariff has fallen from 15.3% to 9.8% (8.9% for industrial products, and 15.2% for agricultural products). Important too was the implementation of a foreign trade law in 2004, which gave unrestricted trading rights to all domestic and foreign private companies. The consequences of WTO accession will emerge only over the long term. The official Chinese orthodoxy is that even allowing for inevitable casualties, membership has had a major and positive impact on the economy, not least by facilitating the restructuring of large enterprises and enabling them to compete with global firms. It is a view for which there is already considerable supporting evidence. Trade liberalization, perhaps most dramatically illustrated by the abolition of textile quotas in 2004, has worked to China's strong advantage, and facilitated its attainment of a more open, dynamic and integrated trade regime. It has also helped fulfil China's global aspirations by attracting accelerated FDI flows (see below).

The value of China's foreign merchandise trade increased, in nominal terms, from US $20,640m. in 1978 to $165,530m. in 1992; by 2000 it had risen further to $474,290m., and in 2008 it reached $2,563,260m. (17.9% above the level of the previous year). The values of exports and imports in 2008 were $1,430,690m. and $1,132,560m., respectively. The aggregate figures indicate average annual growth of merchandise trade of 23.5% between 2000 and 2008, and of 17.4% annually since 1978. During 2000–08 exports increased by an annual average of 21.7% and imports by 22.4%. Within these figures is the transformation from a merchandise trade deficit, which reached a high point of $14,900m. in 1985, to a robust surplus, which had totalled $43,470m. by 1998. A sharp rise in imports caused the surplus subsequently to contract, to $25,470m., in 2003. However, it subsequently rebounded, and in 2008 reached a record $298,130m. (almost 14% above the 2007 level—the previous peak). According to EIU estimates, following a rise of more than 50% in 2007, China's current account balance increased by a further 14% to $360,700m. in 2008, equivalent to 8.2% of GDP. China's buoyant foreign trade performance has generated major increases in its foreign-exchange reserves. At the end of June 2011 they totalled $3,200,000m., almost three times that of Japan (the second largest holder of reserves).

The impact of the global economic recession on China's foreign trade was profound. In almost three decades between 1979, when economic reforms began, and 2008 China never once suffered a decline in its exports. However, owing to the dramatic slowdown in global trade—above all, in the USA, the EU and Japan (previously major markets for Chinese goods)—in 2009 export growth was, for the first time, negative. The value of overseas sales declined by 16% to US $1,201,610m. (although this was still the third highest figure on record). The potentially serious implications of this downturn were reflected in the fact that in 2008 China's foreign trade and net exports to GDP ratios were at unprecedentedly high levels: 57% and 32%, respectively. As a result, observers argued that deceleration in China's export growth would introduce a new constraint on the rate of GDP expansion—one that would place an even higher premium on increased household consumption as a catalyst for economic growth.

In the event, however, China's export sector displayed remarkable resilience. In the second half of 2009 exports showed strong recovery, and in the first half of 2010 they rose year-on-year by 35.2% to reach US $705,100m. Imports, meanwhile, increased by an even greater margin (of 52.7%), as a result of which the value of total merchandise trade rose by 43.1% to $1,354,900m. By the end of 2010 exports had risen year-on-year by 31%, to $1,577,930m., while imports reached $1,394,830m. (an increase of almost 39%). China's export surplus in 2010 was $183,100m.—the second highest on record. In the first half of 2011 the rate of increase of both exports and imports remained buoyant, although in both cases it decelerated between the first and second quarters (from 26% to 22% for exports, and from 33% to 23% for imports). EIU projections suggested that merchandise trade would continue to slow down in 2011, to growth rates of 8.6% for exports and 10.2% for imports.

A notable feature of China's foreign trade performance after the mid-1980s was the shift, in accordance with the dictates of comparative advantage, away from exports based on natural resources (for example, oil) to labour-intensive commodities, such as textiles, shoes, toys, electrical appliances, etc. In 1985 primary goods exports accounted for 51% of the value of all exports, 49% being manufactured goods; by 2010 the corresponding figures were 5.2% and 94.8%. Furthermore, high-technology goods have become an increasingly important export category: according to an OECD report, in 2006 China overtook the 27 EU nations, the USA and Japan to become the largest high-technology exporter in the world, with a global market share of 17%. The same source noted that between 1995 and 2008 China's high-technology exports grew, on average, by 33% per annum to reach US $415,600m. (i.e. about 29% of the total value of overseas sales). According to a World Bank report, in 2009 the value of high-technology exports was $381,000m. Some 90% of these high-technology exports comprised computer and telecommunications products. However, in interpreting these figures, it is important to keep in mind that almost 90% of such goods are produced in FFEs by multinational companies that have relocated their operations to China. In other words, China's main contribution has been that of assembly, a labour-intensive, semi-skilled activity. Indeed, one of the most important foreign trade developments under the impact of reform has been the increasingly important role of FFEs. In 2009 China's officially registered FFEs accounted for 55.2% of China's foreign merchandise trade: 55.9% ($672,230m.) of exports and 54.2% ($545,207m.) of imports.

In 2009 Chinese exports were dominated by machinery, transport and electrical equipment, the earnings from which (some US $590,274m.) accounted for 49% of the value of all exports, compared with 37% in as recently as 2000. The continued viability of traditional labour-intensive industries is most clearly highlighted in the apparel and clothing sector, although rising costs, currency appreciation and the reduction in export tax rebates have begun to erode the competitive advantage of Chinese producers, especially in relation to their counterparts in countries such as Cambodia, India and Viet Nam, where costs are lower. In 2010 the value of exports of clothing and textiles was $206,600m. Purchases of electrical machinery are the single most important category of imports, followed by oil and mineral products. Finally, trade in services has also grown rapidly: for example, from a negligible base in 1989, by 2005 services exports had far exceeded $30,000m.

Although China's foreign trade remains concentrated within Asia (with almost one-half of exports being transported to Asian destinations, and more than 60% of imports coming from Asian origins), in 2004 the EU supplanted the USA as China's single most important trading partner—a position it has since retained—while China is the EU's second largest partner. Between 2003 and 2008 Sino-EU trade grew by almost 28% per annum to reach US $425,800m., or 16.6% of China's global merchandise trade. Although in 2009 it contracted by 14.5% to $364,000m., in the following year it recovered and reach a new record of $479,700m. NBS data show that in 2010 China exported goods worth $311,200m. to the EU (32% more than in 2009), compared with imports of $168,500m. (also up 32%). Implied in these figures is a Chinese trade surplus of $165,388m. In 2007 the EU overtook the USA to become China's largest overseas market, and in 2010 exports to the EU accounted for 19.7% of all China's exports. Next in importance were the USA (18.0%), Hong Kong (13.8%), the Association of Southeast Asian Nations (ASEAN) (8.8%), Japan (7.7%), and South Korea (4.4%). Within the EU—and indeed Europe—the three most important export destinations are Germany, the Netherlands (its ranking owing mainly to the entrepôt role of Rotterdam) and the United Kingdom. The most important source of imports in 2010 was Japan (12.7%), followed by the EU (12.1%), ASEAN (11.1%), South Korea (9.9%), and Taiwan (8.3%); the USA's share was 7.3%.

Since its introduction in 1979, the use of foreign capital has been an important element of China's reform strategy and had a major impact on its economic development. Three features have characterized flows of overseas capital into China: first, the increasing dominance of FDI, which by 2010 contributed 97% of all inflows (including overseas loans); second, the very high share of FDI coming from East and South-East Asia (more than two-thirds in 2010, including Taiwanese investment via British Caribbean territories); third, the high proportion of FDI destined for manufacturing, which absorbed 52% of all such inflows in 2009, rather than resource-based industries and services (although services are likely to absorb increasing amounts of FDI in the future). NBS figures for 2010 showed Hong Kong to have been by far the single most important source of FDI, accounting for 57% of the total. Next in importance were Taiwan (including substantial volumes of FDI routed through the Cayman and British Virgin Islands), South Korea and the EU (led by France, Germany and the United Kingdom). It is noteworthy that the USA is not a significant source of FDI (in 2008 and 2009 FDI flows from South Korea exceeded those from the USA, although this trend was reversed in 2010), accounting for less than 3% of total inflows to China.

The Joint Venture Law of 1979 and other early legislation created the basis for inflows of FDI, primarily in the SEZs. Three of the first four SEZs were established in Guangdong in the vicinity of Hong Kong (the fourth was in Xiamen, Fujian Province, across the Taiwan Strait from Taiwan). By far the largest was that of Shenzhen, immediately across the Hong Kong border. In effect, the SEZs fulfilled the role of export processing zones (EPZs), offering preferential treatment to foreign investors in the form of low tax rates, duty-free imports of intermediate materials for assembly, and simplified administrative and customs procedures. In 1984 Economic and Technological Development Zones (ETDZs) were established in 14 new 'Open Cities' (including Shanghai), which were added to the original SEZs and became further areas of foreign investment activity; in the early 1990s more ETDZs were created, the most important of which was the Pudong Development Zone in Shanghai. The outcome of these developments is that there now exist well over 100 investment zones of various kinds, approved by central government and located throughout China, in interior, as well as coastal, areas. The economic contribution of FDI has been immense. Most obviously, it has boosted investment by supplementing domestic funding sources. One analyst estimated that during 1991–2001 FDI accounted for 11% of total capital formation, although as a share of GDP it has been in decline since the mid-1990s. However, more important than its physical impact on investment has been the qualitative contribution of FDI, as a source of technology transfer (patent applications overwhelmingly derive from the foreign-funded sector) and as the conduit for improvements in managerial and marketing expertise.

The cumulative value of inflows of all forms of utilized foreign capital during 1979–2010 was US $1,250,440m., of which FDI was $1,048,380m. (84%). From a base of $1,770m. (1979–82, cumulative), annual utilized FDI inflows grew steadily to $4,370m. in 1991, after which, in response to Deng Xiaoping's 'Southern Tour' (see above), they grew by a remarkable 98% annually to reach $33,770m. in 1994. Since 1994 FDI has risen on average by 6.8% annually to reach a record $105,730m. in 2010. Although there have been significant annual fluctuations (in 1999, 2005 and 2009 FDI experienced negative rates of growth), overseas confidence in China as an investment environment remains strong. In particular, even allowing for the modest contraction in 2009, there has been a marked acceleration in FDI inflows since 2005 (average annual growth was almost 12% during 2005–10). It is noteworthy that coastal provinces have benefited disproportionately from inflows of FDI: in 2004, for example, just five regions (in order of importance, Guangdong, Jiangsu, Shandong, Shanghai and Zhejiang) absorbed two-thirds of all FDI. As land and labour prices rise in these areas, a major challenge for the Government will be to overcome infrastructural (especially transport) constraints in order to attract more investment into interior regions. As yet, in western China only Sichuan and Chongqing have attracted significant overseas investment interest. Failure to maintain China's competitive advantage as an investment destination will have serious consequences, especially as cheaper destinations become available elsewhere in South and South-East Asia.

An aspect of China's international economic activities that has become increasingly important is its role as an overseas investor in its own right. The large scale of such outward investment is illustrated by the fact that in 2005 China was the 17th largest foreign investor in the world. NBS estimates show that in 2008 overseas direct investment by Chinese firms more than doubled to reach US $56,528.99m. Chinese FDI outflows aim to seek new markets, to secure resources and strategic assets, to obtain expertise and to enhance efficiency. Such motivations ensure that the rapid momentum of FDI growth will be maintained, and the UN Conference on Trade and Development (UNCTAD) has predicted that China, along with India and South Korea, will account for an increasing share of Asian outward FDI.

Statistical Survey

Source (unless otherwise stated): National Bureau of Statistics of China, 38 Yuetan Nan Jie, Sanlihe, Beijing 100826; tel. (10) 68515074; fax (10) 68515078; e-mail service@stats.gov.cn; internet www.stats.gov.cn/english/.

Note: Wherever possible, figures in this Survey exclude Taiwan. In the case of unofficial estimates for China, it is not always clear if Taiwan is included or excluded. Where a Taiwan component is known, either it has been deducted from the all-China figure or its inclusion is noted. Figures for the Hong Kong Special Administrative Region (SAR) and for the Macao SAR are listed separately. Transactions between the SARs and the rest of the People's Republic continue to be treated as external transactions.

Area and Population

AREA, POPULATION AND DENSITY

Area (sq km)	9,572,900*
Population (census results)	
1 November 2000	1,242,612,226
1 November 2010 (preliminary)	
Males	686,852,572
Females	652,872,280
Total	1,339,724,852
Density (per sq km) at 2010 census	139.9

* 3,696,100 sq miles.

Note: Data for population censuses do not include adjustment for under-enumeration; adjusted total for 2000 was 1,265,830,000.

POPULATION BY AGE AND SEX
('000, UN estimates at mid-2011)

	Males	Females	Total
0–14	140,631	116,399	257,030
15–64	505,505	472,244	977,749
65 and over	53,495	59,290	112,786
Total	699,631	647,934	1,347,565

Note: Totals may not be equal to the sum of components, owing to rounding.

Source: UN, *World Population Prospects: The 2010 Revision*.

Population by Age (at 2010 census, preliminary): *0–14* 222,459,737; *15–64* 939,616,410; *65 and over* 177,648,705; *Total* 1,339,724,852.

PRINCIPAL ETHNIC GROUPS
(at census of 1 November 2000)

	Number	%
Han (Chinese)	1,137,386,112	91.53
Zhuang	16,178,811	1.30
Manchu	10,682,262	0.86
Hui	9,816,805	0.79
Miao	8,940,116	0.72
Uygur (Uighur)	8,399,393	0.68
Tujia	8,028,133	0.65
Yi	7,762,272	0.63
Mongolian	5,813,947	0.47
Tibetan	5,416,021	0.44
Bouyei	2,971,460	0.24
Dong	2,960,293	0.24
Yao	2,637,421	0.21
Korean	1,923,842	0.16
Bai	1,858,063	0.15
Hani	1,439,673	0.12
Kazakh	1,250,458	0.10
Li	1,247,814	0.10
Dai	1,158,989	0.09
She	709,592	0.06
Lisu	634,912	0.05
Gelao	579,357	0.05
Dongxiang	513,805	0.04
Others	3,568,237	0.29
Unknown	734,438	0.06
Total	1,242,612,226	100.00

ADMINISTRATIVE DIVISIONS
(previous or other spellings given in brackets)

	Area ('000 sq km)	Population at 1 November 2010 (preliminary): Total	Density (per sq km)	Capital of province or region	Estimated population ('000) at mid-2000*
Provinces					
Sichuan (Szechwan)	487.0	80,418,200	165.1	Chengdu (Chengtu)	3,294
Henan (Honan)	167.0	94,023,567	563.0	Zhengzhou (Chengchow)	2,070
Shandong (Shantung)	153.3	95,793,065	624.9	Jinan (Tsinan)	2,568
Jiangsu (Kiangsu)	102.6	78,659,903	766.7	Nanjing (Nanking)	2,740
Guangdong (Kwangtung)	197.1	104,303,132	529.2	Guangzhou (Canton)	3,893
Hebei (Hopei)	202.7	71,854,202	354.5	Shijiazhuang (Shihkiachwang)	1,603
Hunan (Hunan)	210.5	65,683,722	312.0	Changsha (Changsha)	1,775
Anhui (Anhwei)	139.9	59,500,510	425.3	Hefei (Hofei)	1,242
Hubei (Hupeh)	187.5	57,237,740	305.3	Wuhan (Wuhan)	5,169
Zhejiang (Chekiang)	101.8	54,426,891	534.6	Hangzhou (Hangchow)	1,780
Liaoning (Liaoning)	151.0	43,746,323	289.7	Shenyang (Shenyang)	4,828
Jiangxi (Kiangsi)	164.8	44,567,475	270.4	Nanchang (Nanchang)	1,722
Yunnan (Yunnan)	436.2	45,966,239	105.4	Kunming (Kunming)	1,701
Heilongjiang (Heilungkiang)	463.6	38,312,224	82.6	Harbin (Harbin)	2,928
Guizhou (Kweichow)	174.0	34,746,468	199.7	Guiyang (Kweiyang)	2,533
Shaanxi (Shensi)	195.8	37,327,378	190.6	Xian (Sian)	3,123
Fujian (Fukien)	123.1	36,894,216†	299.7	Fuzhou (Foochow)	1,397
Shanxi (Shansi)	157.1	35,712,111	227.3	Taiyuan (Taiyuan)	2,415
Jilin (Kirin)	187.0	27,462,297	146.9	Changchun (Changchun)	3,093
Gansu (Kansu)	366.5	25,575,254	69.8	Lanzhou (Lanchow)	1,730
Hainan	34.3	8,671,518	252.8	Haikou	438‡
Qinghai (Tsinghai)	721.0	5,626,722	7.8	Xining (Hsining)	692
Autonomous regions					
Guangxi Zhuang (Kwangsi Chuang)	220.4	46,026,629	208.8	Nanning (Nanning)	1,311
Nei Monggol (Inner Mongolia)	1,177.5	24,706,321	21.0	Hohhot (Huhehot)	978
Xinjiang Uygur (Sinkiang Uighur)	1,646.9	21,813,334	13.2	Urumqi (Urumchi, Wulumuqi)	1,415
Ningxia Hui (Ninghsia Hui)	66.4	6,301,350	94.9	Yinchuan (Yinchuen)	592
Tibet (Xizang)	1,221.6	3,002,166	2.5	Lhasa (Lhasa)	134
Municipalities					
Shanghai	6.2	23,019,148	3,712.8	—	12,887
Beijing (Peking)	16.8	19,612,368	1,167.4	—	10,839
Tianjin (Tientsin)	11.3	12,938,224	1,145.0	—	9,156
Chongqing (Chungking)	82.0	28,846,170	351.8	—	4,900
Total	9,572.9	1,339,724,852§	139.9		

* UN estimates, excluding population in counties under cities' administration.
† Excluding islands administered by Taiwan, mainly Jinmen (Quemoy) and Mazu (Matsu), with 49,050 inhabitants according to figures released by the Taiwan authorities at the end of March 1990.
‡ December 1998 figure.
§ Including 2,300,000 military personnel and 4,649,985 persons with unregistered households.

PRINCIPAL TOWNS
(incl. suburbs, UN estimates, population at mid-2010)

Shanghai (Shang-hai)	16,575,110	Wenzhou	2,658,536
Beijing (Pei-ching or Peking, the capital)	12,385,263	Shijiazhuang (Shih-chia-chuang or Shihkiachwang)	2,486,936
Chongqing (Ch'ung-ch'ing or Chungking)	9,401,170	Zibo	2,455,566
Shenzhen	9,005,283	Changsha (Chang-sha)	2,414,920
Guangzhou (Kuang-chou or Canton)	8,883,865	Hefei	2,403,907
Tianjin (T'ien-chin or Tientsin)	7,884,473	Urumqi (Wulumuqi)	2,398,154
Wuhan (Wu-han or Hankow)	7,681,099	Suzhou	2,398,024
Dongguan	5,346,652	Lanzhou (Lan-chou or Lanchow)	2,284,587
Shenyang (Shen-yang or Mukden)	5,165,771	Ningbo	2,216,771
Chengdu (Chengtu)	4,960,893	Xiamen	2,206,840
Xian (Hsi-an or Sian)	4,746,755	Guiyang	2,153,908
Nanjing (Nan-ching or Nanking)	4,518,826	Xuzhou	2,141,789
Harbin (Ha-erh-pin)	4,251,063	Nanning	2,095,872
Hangzhou (Hang-chou or Hangchow)	3,860,094	Baotou	1,931,736
Changchun (Ch'ang-ch'un)	3,596,748	Jilin	1,888,374
Qingdao (Ch'ing-tao or Tsingtao)	3,323,062	Tangshan	1,870,384
Dalian (Ta-lien or Dairen)	3,305,864	Zaozhuang	1,175,057
Jinan (Chi-nan or Tsinan)	3,237,414	Anshan	1,662,528
Taiyuan (T'ai-yüan)	3,153,686	Hohhot	1,588,622
Kunming (K'un-ming)	3,115,793	Luoyang	1,539,243
Zhengzhou (Cheng-chou or Chengchow)	2,965,730	Yantai	1,526,309
Fuzhou	2,786,585	Linyi	1,426,549
Nanchang (Nan-ch'ang)	2,701,478	Datong	1,251,087
Wuxi	2,681,870		

Note: Wade-Giles or other spellings are given in parentheses.

Source: UN, *World Urbanization Prospects: The 2009 Revision*.

BIRTHS AND DEATHS
(sample surveys)

	2007	2008	2009
Birth rate (per 1,000)	12.10	12.14	12.13
Death rate (per 1,000)	6.93	7.06	7.08

2009 (rounded data): Births 16,150,000; Deaths 9,430,000.

Marriages (number registered, rounded data): 9,863,000 in 2007; 10,932,000 in 2008; 1,207,500 in 2009.

Life expectancy (years at birth, WHO estimates): 74 (males 72; females 76) in 2009 (Source: WHO, *World Health Statistics*).

EMPLOYMENT*
('000 persons at 31 December, official estimates)

	2000	2001	2002
Agriculture, forestry and fishing	333,550	329,740	324,870
Mining	5,970	5,610	5,580
Manufacturing	80,430	80,830	83,070
Electricity, gas and water	2,840	2,880	2,900
Construction	35,520	36,690	38,930
Geological prospecting and water conservancy	1,100	1,050	980
Transport, storage and communications	20,290	20,370	20,840
Wholesale and retail trade and catering	46,860	47,370	49,690
Banking and insurance	3,270	3,360	3,400
Real estate	1,000	1,070	1,180
Social services	9,210	9,760	10,940
Health care, sports and social welfare	4,880	4,930	4,930
Education, culture, art, radio, film and television broadcasting	15,650	15,680	15,650
Scientific research and polytechnic services	1,740	1,650	1,630
Government agencies, etc.	11,040	11,010	10,750
Others	56,430	58,520	62,450
Total	629,780	630,520	637,790

* In addition to employment statistics, sample surveys of the economically active population are conducted. On the basis of these surveys, the number of employed persons ('000 at 31 December) was: 744,320 (agriculture, etc. 365,460, industry 160,770, services 218,090) in 2003; 752,000 (agriculture, etc. 352,690, industry 169,200, services 230,111) in 2004; 758,250 (agriculture, etc. 339,700, industry 180,840, services 237,710) in 2005; 764,000 (agriculture, etc. 325,610, industry 192,250, services 246,140) in 2006; 769,900 (agriculture, etc. 314,440, industry 206,290, services 249,170) in 2007; 774,800 (agriculture, etc. 306,540, industry 211,090, services 257,170) in 2008; 779,950 (agriculture, etc. 297,080, industry 216,840, services 266,030) in 2009.

Health and Welfare

KEY INDICATORS

Total fertility rate (children per woman, 2009)	1.8
Under-5 mortality rate (per 1,000 live births, 2009)	19
HIV/AIDS (% of persons aged 15–49, 2007)	0.1
Physicians (per 1,000 head, 2003)	1.4
Hospital beds (per 1,000 head, 2006)	2.2
Health expenditure (2008): US $ per head (PPP)	265
Health expenditure (2008): % of GDP	4.3
Health expenditure (2008): public (% of total)	47.3
Access to water (% of persons, 2008)	89
Access to sanitation (% of persons, 2008)	55
Total carbon dioxide emissions ('000 metric tons, 2007)	6,533,018.3
Carbon dioxide emissions per head (metric tons, 2007)	5.0
Human Development Index (2010): ranking	89
Human Development Index (2010): value	0.663

For sources and definitions, see explanatory note on p. vi.

Agriculture

(FAO data are assumed to include Hong Kong, Macao and Taiwan; may include official, semi-official or estimated data)

PRINCIPAL CROPS
('000 metric tons)

	2007	2008	2009
Wheat	109,298	112,463	115,115
Rice, paddy	187,397	193,354	196,681
Barley	2,788	2,823	2,318
Maize	152,419	166,032	164,108
Rye*	700	650	630
Oats*	643	600	580
Millet	1,508	1,288	1,226
Sorghum	1,929	1,840	1,677
Buckwheat*	650	600	570
Triticale (wheat-rye hybrid)*	450	383	350
Potatoes	64,837	70,840	73,282
Sweet potatoes	75,800	78,453	76,773
Cassava (Manioc)*	4,362	4,409	4,506
Taro (Cocoyam)*	1,642	1,737	1,693
Sugar cane	113,732	124,918	116,251
Sugar beet	8,931	10,044	7,179
Beans, dry†	1,532	1,708	1,489
Broad beans, horse beans, dry†	1,620	1,800	1,650
Peas, dry†	1,080	1,100	960
Chestnuts*	925	1,000	1,085
Walnuts, with shell	630	829	979
Soybeans (Soya beans)	12,725	15,545	14,981
Groundnuts, with shell	13,079	14,341	14,765
Coconuts	271	298*	310*
Oil palm fruit*	665	668	670
Sunflower seed	1,187	1,792	1,956
Rapeseed	10,573	12,102	13,657
Sesame seed	558	586	623
Linseed	268	350	318
Cabbages and other brassicas	30,530*	30,918	30,215
Asparagus*	6,253	6,353	6,502
Lettuce and chicory*	12,006	12,505	12,855
Spinach	14,011*	16,640	17,550
Tomatoes	36,097*	39,939	45,365
Cauliflowers and broccoli*	8,068	8,268	8,427
Pumpkins, squash and gourds*	6,310	6,360	6,507
Cucumbers and gherkins	38,049*	42,241	44,250
Aubergines (Eggplants)	22,026*	23,748	25,913
Chillies and peppers, green*	14,026	14,274	14,520
Onions and shallots, green*	810	835	870
Onions, dry*	20,567	20,823	21,047
Garlic	16,065*	18,357	17,968
Beans, green	13,467*	14,470	14,688
Peas, green	8,907*	9,361	9,599
Carrots and turnips	12,086*	14,859	15,168
Mushrooms and truffles	4,069*	4,711	4,681
Watermelons	62,257	63,025	65,002
Cantaloupes and other melons	14,210	12,011	12,225
Grapes	6,787	7,236	8,039
Apples	27,866	29,851	31,684
Pears	13,045	13,676	14,416
Peaches and nectarines	9,080	9,564	10,170
Plums and sloes	4,826†	5,223*	5,373*
Oranges	3,689	4,191	4,865
Tangerines, mandarins, clementines and satsumas	7,810	8,948	9,746
Lemons and limes	842†	919†	1,014*
Grapefruit and pomelos	2,353	2,606	2,768
Guavas, mangoes and mangosteens	3,715†	3,977*	4,140*

—continued	2007	2008	2009
Pineapples	1,382	1,386	1,477
Persimmons	2,607	2,745	2,871
Bananas	8,038	8,043	9,006
Tea	1,183	1,275	1,376
Chillies and peppers, dry*	250	252	260
Ginger*	327	329	331
Other spices	76	77	86
Tobacco, unmanufactured	2,397	2,840	3,068
Jute†	56	48	44
Natural rubber	588	548	619

* FAO estimate(s).
† Unofficial figure(s).

Aggregate production ('000 metric tons, may include official, semi-official or estimated data): Total cereals 457,812.3 in 2007, 480,053.1 in 2008, 483,267.5 in 2009; Total vegetable fibres 8,367.2 in 2007, 8,142.4 in 2008, 7,006.7 in 2009; Total treenuts 1,738.5 in 2007, 2,022.1 in 2008, 2,273.0 in 2009; Total oilcrops (primary) 14,502.2 in 2007, 16,261.3 in 2008, 16,656.6 in 2009; Total pulses 4,482.9 in 2007, 4,895.9 in 2008, 4,331.1 in 2009; Total roots and tubers 146,658.1 in 2007, 155,455.5 in 2008, 156,271.5 in 2009; Total vegetables (incl. melons) 487,078.8 in 2007, 507,943.1 in 2008, 522,650.9 in 2009; Total fruits (excl. melons) 100,917.4 in 2007, 107,803.1 in 2008, 115,876.2 in 2009.

Source: FAO.

LIVESTOCK
('000 head at 31 December)

	2007	2008	2009
Horses	7,197	7,030	6,823
Asses	7,306	6,891	6,731
Cattle	82,067	82,815*	84,117*
Buffaloes	22,721	23,272*	23,279*
Camels	269	242	240
Pigs	425,265	446,463	450,880
Sheep	146,018	136,436	128,557
Goats	137,930	143,595	152,499
Chickens	4,505,479*	4,602,198†	4,702,670†
Ducks†	752,162	761,250	769,427
Geese and guinea fowls†	302,841	312,318	316,990

* Unofficial figure.
† FAO estimate(s).

Source: FAO.

LIVESTOCK PRODUCTS
('000 metric tons)

	2007	2008	2009
Cattle meat*	5,846	5,841	6,061
Buffalo meat*	307	306	309
Sheep meat*	2,070	1,978	2,090
Goat meat*	1,760	1,828	1,853
Pig meat	43,933	47,190	49,874
Horse meat†	192	198	198
Rabbit meat*	604	660	663
Chicken meat*	10,616	11,016	11,443
Duck meat*	2,328	2,509	2,644
Goose and guinea fowl meat*	2,092	2,235	2,326
Other meat†	671	695	708
Cows' milk	35,574	35,874	35,510
Buffaloes' milk†	2,900	2,950	3,000
Sheep's milk	1,072	1,096	1,150†
Goats' milk†	263	266	272
Hen eggs	21,833	23,292	23,634
Other poultry eggs	3,822	4,082	4,139
Honey	357	407	407
Wool, greasy	363	368	364

* Unofficial figures.
† FAO estimate(s).

Source: FAO.

Forestry

ROUNDWOOD REMOVALS
('000 cubic metres, excl. bark)

	2007	2008	2009
Sawlogs, veneer logs and logs for sleepers	52,227*	57,249	49,830
Pulpwood	4,444	5,134	4,839
Other industrial wood	34,260	38,460	38,460
Fuel wood*	199,735	196,028	192,390
Total	290,665	296,871	285,519

* FAO estimate(s).

Source: FAO.

Timber production (official figures, '000 cubic metres): 78,000 in 2006; 69,740 in 2007; 78,940 in 2008; 69,380 in 2009.

SAWNWOOD PRODUCTION
('000 cubic metres, incl. railway sleepers)

	2007*	2008	2009
Coniferous (softwood)	11,931	11,970	13,603
Broadleaved (hardwood)	16,845	16,915	19,180
Total	28,776	28,885	32,783

* Unofficial figures.

Source: FAO.

Fishing

('000 metric tons, live weight)

	2007	2008	2009
Capture	14,659.0	14,791.2	14,919.6
Freshwater fishes	1,574.0	1,615.3	1,526.3
Aquaculture*	31,415.1	32,731.4	34,779.9
Common carp	2,228.6	2,350.7	2,462.3
Crucian carp	1,937.1	1,955.5	2,055.5
Bighead carp	2,135.4	2,290.2	2,434.6
Grass carp (White amur)	3,556.0	3,707.1	4,081.5
Silver carp	3,075.6	3,193.3	3,484.4
Pacific cupped oyster	3,508.9	3,354.4	3,503.8
Japanese carpet shell	2,957.3	3,058.1	3,192.5
Total catch*	46,074.2	47,522.5	49,699.5

* FAO estimates.

Note: Figures exclude aquatic plants ('000 metric tons, wet weight): 10,081.2 (capture 328.6, aquaculture 9,752.6) in 2007; 10,299.9 (capture 366.1, aquaculture 9,933.8) in 2008; 10,775.5 (capture 276.2, aquaculture 10,499.3) in 2009.

Source: FAO.

Aquatic products (official figures, '000 metric tons): 47,475 (marine 25,509, freshwater 21,966) in 2007; 48,956 (marine 25,983, freshwater 22,973) in 2008; 51,164 (marine 26,816, freshwater 24,348) in 2009. The totals include artificially cultured products ('000 metric tons): 32,783 (marine 13,073, freshwater 19,710) in 2007; 34,128 (marine 13,403, freshwater 20,725) in 2008; 36,217 (marine 14,052, freshwater 22,165) in 2009. Figures include aquatic plants on a dry-weight basis ('000 metric tons): 1,388 in 2007; 1,423 in 2008; 1,484 in 2009. Freshwater plants are not included.

Mining

('000 metric tons unless otherwise indicated)

	2007	2008	2009
Coal*	2,526,000	2,802,000	2,973,000
Crude petroleum*	186,318	190,431	189,490
Natural gas (million cu m)*	69,240	80,299	85,269
Iron ore: gross weight	707,000	824,000	880,000
Copper ore†	928	940	970
Nickel ore (metric tons)†	67,000	72,000	81,000
Bauxite	30,000	35,000	40,000
Lead ore†	1,410	1,550	1,600
Zinc ore†	3,040	3,340	3,400
Tin concentrates (metric tons)†	149,000	140,000	135,000
Manganese ore†	2,000	2,200	2,400
Tungsten concentrates (metric tons)†	41,000	50,000	51,000
Molybdenum ore (metric tons)†	67,700	81,000	93,500
Vanadium (metric tons)†	45,200	46,000	52,000
Antimony ore (metric tons)†	147,000	158,000	168,000
Cobalt ore (metric tons)†	6,100	6,630	6,000
Mercury (metric tons)†	800	1,300	1,400
Silver (metric tons)†	2,700	2,800	2,900
Uranium (metric tons)†‡	712	769	750
Gold (metric tons)†	275	285	320
Magnesite	14,000	15,600	15,000
Phosphate rock§	15,100	15,200	18,000
Potash‖	2,600	2,750	3,000
Native sulphur	960	960	1,000
Fluorspar	3,200	3,250	3,200
Barite (Barytes)	4,400	4,600	3,000
Salt (unrefined)*	61,670	66,644	66,628
Gypsum (crude)	4,800	4,600	4,500
Graphite (natural)	800	800	780
Asbestos	390	380	380
Talc and related materials	2,000	2,200	2,300

* Official figures. Figures for coal include brown coal and waste. Figures for petroleum include oil from shale and coal. Figures for natural gas refer to gross volume of output.

† Figures refer to the metal content of ores, concentrates or (in the case of vanadium) slag.

‡ Data are estimates from the World Nuclear Association (London, United Kingdom).

§ Figures refer to phosphorous oxide (P_2O_5) content.

‖ Potassium oxide (K_2O) content of potash salts mined.

Source: mainly US Geological Survey.

Industry

SELECTED PRODUCTS

Unofficial Figures

('000 metric tons unless otherwise indicated)*

	2005	2006	2007
Plywood ('000 cu m)†‡	25,961	28,099	36,427
Mechanical wood pulp†‡§	565	790	907
Chemical and semi-chemical wood pulp†‡§	3,500	4,840	5,513
Other fibre pulp†‡	13,046	13,346	13,466§
Sulphur§‖¶(a)	2,800	3,000	3,300
Sulphur§‖¶(b)	4,010	3,810	4,200
Kerosene	10,065	9,755	11,533
Residual fuel oil	17,674	17,847	19,673
Paraffin wax	2,636	2,928	3,037
Petroleum coke	8,910	9,899	10,267
Petroleum bitumen (asphalt)	9,229	10,090	10,465
Liquefied petroleum gas	14,327	17,453	19,447
Refined aluminium (primary and secondary)‖	9,740	11,700	15,400
Refined copper (primary and secondary)‖	2,600	3,000	3,600
Refined lead (primary and secondary)‖	2,390	2,720	2,790
Tin (unwrought, Sn content)‖	122	132	149
Refined zinc (primary and secondary)‖	2,780	3,170	3,740

* Figures include Hong Kong and Macao SARs, but exclude Taiwan, except where otherwise specified.

† Data from FAO.

‡ Including Taiwan.

§ Provisional or estimated figure(s).

‖ Data from the US Geological Survey.

¶ Figures refer to (a) sulphur recovered as a by-product in the purification of coal-gas, in petroleum refineries, gas plants and from copper, lead and zinc sulphide ores; and (b) the sulphur content of iron and copper pyrites, including pyrite concentrates obtained from copper, lead and zinc ores.

Lubricating oils: 5,326,000 metric tons in 2004.

Source: mainly UN Industrial Commodity Statistics Database.

2008 ('000 metric tons unless otherwise indicated): Plywood ('000 cu m) 36,224; Mechanical wood pulp 1,005 (estimate); Chemical and semi-chemical wood pulp 6,085; Other fibre pulp 13,416 (unofficial figure); Refined aluminium (primary and secondary) 15,900; Refined copper (primary and secondary) 3,900; Refined lead (primary and secondary) 3,200; Tin (unwrought, Sn content) 110; Refined zinc (primary and secondary) 4,000 (Sources: FAO; US Geological Survey).

2009 ('000 metric tons unless otherwise indicated): Plywood ('000 cu m) 45,327; Mechanical wood pulp 755 (estimate); Chemical and semi-chemical wood pulp 4,640; Other fibre pulp 12,196 (unofficial figure); Refined aluminium (primary and secondary) 16,000; Refined copper (primary and secondary) 4,150; Refined lead (primary and secondary) 3,710; Tin (unwrought, Sn content) 115; Refined zinc (primary and secondary) 4,360 (Sources: FAO; US Geological Survey).

Official Figures

('000 metric tons unless otherwise indicated)

	2007	2008	2009
Edible vegetable oils	26,369.8	28,050.9	34,334.3
Refined sugar	12,713.8	14,326.1	13,383.5
Beer (million litres)	39,540.7	41,569.1	41,621.8
Cigarettes ('000 million)	2,143.9	2,219.9	2,290.2
Cotton yarn (pure and mixed)	20,682	21,709	23,935
Woven cotton fabrics (pure and mixed—million metres)	67,526	72,305	75,342
Chemical fibres	24,137.8	24,532.9	27,472.8
Paper and paperboard	77,924.3	84,043.0	89,651.3
Rubber tyres ('000)	558,329.7	519,569.4	656,015.6
Sulphuric acid	54,125.6	50,979.5	59,609.1
Caustic soda (Sodium hydroxide)	17,592.9	19,260.1	18,323.7
Soda ash (Sodium carbonate)	17,650.0	18,546.0	19,447.7
Insecticides	1,764.8	2,099.9	2,262.2
Nitrogenous fertilizers (a)*	42,331.3	43,924.2	45,533.6
Phosphate fertilizers (b)*	13,392.8	13,855.0	15,131.4
Potash fertilizers (c)*	2,525.7	2,501.3	3,185.1
Synthetic rubber	2,289.2	2,960.3	2,749.1
Plastics	31,845.4	36,802.3	36,299.7
Motor spirit (gasoline)	59,894.2	64,347.5	71,954.8
Distillate fuel oil (diesel oil)	123,591.1	134,583.0	141,270.0

—continued	2007	2008	2009
Coke	335,534.3	320,314.8	355,101.4
Cement	1,361,173	1,423,557	1,643,978
Pig-iron	476,516.3	478,244.2	552,834.6
Crude steel	489,288.0	503,057.5	572,182.3
Internal combustion engines ('000 kw)	566,419.0	936,439.9	848,925.2
Tractors—over 20 horse-power (number)	2,031,000	2,844,000	3,713,000
Railway freight wagons (number)	42,200	57,400	42,800
Road motor vehicles ('000)	8,888.9	9,305.9	13,795.3
Bicycles ('000)	74,752.0	71,851.8	57,576.5
Electric fans ('000)	154,400.4	158,668.5	159,550.5
Mobile telephones ('000 units)	548,578.6	559,451.0	619,244.7
Microcomputers ('000)	120,734	158,537	182,151
Integrated circuits (million)	41,162	43,877	41,440
Colour television receivers ('000)	84,780	91,871	98,988
Cameras ('000)	86,896.0	81,930.3	84,578.1
Electric energy (million kWh)	3,281,553	3,495,761	3,714,651

* Production in terms of (a) nitrogen; (b) phosphorous oxide; or (c) potassium oxide.

Finance

CURRENCY AND EXCHANGE RATES

Monetary Units

100 fen (cents) = 10 jiao (chiao) = 1 renminbiao (People's Bank Dollar), usually called a yuan.

Sterling, Dollar and Euro Equivalents (31 May 2011)

£1 sterling = 10.701 yuan;
US $1 = 6.485 yuan;
€1 = 9.328 yuan;
100 yuan = £9.34 = $15.42 = €10.72.

Average Exchange Rate (yuan per US $)

2008 6.9487
2009 6.8314
2010 6.7703

Note: Since 1 January 1994 the official rate has been based on the prevailing rate in the interbank market for foreign exchange.

STATE BUDGET

(million yuan)*

Revenue	2007	2008	2009
Taxes	4,562,197	5,422,379	5,952,159
Personal income tax	318,558	372,231	394,935
Company income tax	877,925	1,117,563	1,153,684
Tariffs	143,257	176,995	148,381
Business tax	658,217	762,639	901,398
Consumption tax	220,683	256,827	476,122
Value-added tax	1,547,023	1,799,694	1,848,122
Non-tax revenue	569,981	710,656	899,671
Total	5,132,178	6,133,035	6,851,830
Central government	2,774,916	3,268,056	3,591,571
Local authorities	2,357,262	2,864,979	3,260,259

Expenditure†	2004	2005	2006
Capital construction	343,750	404,134	439,038
Circulation of capital	1,244	1,817	1,658
Agriculture, forestry and water conservancy	169,379	179,240	216,135
Culture, education, science and health care‡	514,365	610,418	742,598
National defence	220,001	247,496	297,938
Administration	405,991	483,543	563,905
Social security	311,608	369,886	436,178
Subsidies to compensate price increases	79,580	99,847	138,752
Promotion of innovation, science and technology	124,394	149,459	174,456
Operating expenses of industry, transport and commerce	36,821	44,415	58,125
Geological prospecting	11,545	13,270	14,182
Total (incl. others)	2,848,689	3,393,028	4,042,273
Central government	789,408	877,597	999,140
Local authorities	2,059,281	2,515,431	3,043,133

* Figures represent a consolidation of the regular (current) and construction (capital) budgets of the central government and local administrative organs. The data exclude extrabudgetary transactions, totalling (in million yuan): Revenue 469,918 (central 35,069, local 434,849) in 2004; 554,416 (central 40,258, local 514,158) in 2005; 640,788 (central 46,711, local 594,077) in 2006. Expenditure 435,173 (central 38,950, local 396,223) in 2004; 524,248 (central 45,834, local 478,414) in 2005; 586,695 (central 37,772, local 548,923) in 2006. Note: Figures for extrabudgetary revenue and expenditure in 2007 were not available.

† Excluding payments of debt interest.

‡ Current expenditure only.

2007 (million yuan): General public services 851,424 (Interest payments on domestic and foreign debts 105,290); National defence 355,491; Public security 348,616 (Armed police 58,517); Education 712,232; Science and technology 178,304; Culture, sport and media 89,864; Social safety net and employment effort 544,716; Medical and health care 198,996; Environment protection 99,582; Urban and rural community affairs 324,469; Agriculture, forestry and water conservancy 340,470; Transportation 191,538 (Purchasing vehicles 84,913); Industry, commerce and banking 425,749; Total expenditure (incl. others) 4,978,135 (central government 1,144,206, local authorities 3,833,929).

2008 (million yuan): General public services 979,592 (Interest payments on domestic and foreign debts 130,509); Foreign affairs 24,072; National defence 417,876; Public security 405,976 (Armed police 66,413); Education 901,021; Science and technology 212,921; Culture, sport and media 109,574; Social safety net and employment effort 680,429; Medical and health care 275,704; Environment protection 145,136; Urban and rural community affairs 420,614; Agriculture, forestry and water conservancy 454,401; Transportation 235,400 (Purchasing vehicles 100,274); Industry, commerce and banking 622,637; Expenditure for post-earthquake recovery and reconstruction 79,834; Other expenditures 294,079; Total expenditure 6,259,266 (central government 1,334,417, local authorities 4,924,849).

2009 (million yuan): General public services 916,421; Foreign affairs 25,094; National defence 495,110; Public security 474,409 (Armed police 86,629); Education 1,043,754; Science and technology 274,452; Culture, sport and media 139,307; Social safety net and employment effort 760,668; Expenditure for affordable houses 72,597; Medical and health care 399,419; Environment protection 193,404; Urban and rural community affairs 510,766; Agriculture, forestry and water conservancy 672,041; Transportation 464,759 (Purchasing vehicles 108,508); Mining and quarrying, electricity and information technology 287,912; Expenditure for reserve for cereals and oils 221,863; Financial affairs 91,119; Expenditure for post-earthquake recovery and reconstruction 117,445; Interest payments on government bonds 149,128; Other expenditures 320,325; Total expenditure 7,629,993 (central government 1,525,579, local authorities 6,104,414).

INTERNATIONAL RESERVES

(US $ million at 31 December)

	2008	2009	2010
Gold (national valuation)	4,074	9,815	9,815
IMF special drawing rights	1,199	12,510	12,344
Reserve position in IMF	2,031	4,382	6,397
Foreign exchange*	1,946,030	2,399,152	2,847,338
Total*	1,953,334	2,425,859	2,875,894

* Excluding the Bank of China's holdings of foreign exchange.

Source: IMF, *International Financial Statistics*.

MONEY SUPPLY
(million yuan at 31 December)*

	2008	2009	2010
Currency outside banking institutions	3,421,900	3,824,700	4,462,820
Demand deposits at banking institutions	13,199,820	18,319,880	22,199,340
Total money (incl. others)	16,621,710	22,144,580	26,662,150

* Figures are rounded to the nearest 10 million yuan.

Source: IMF, *International Financial Statistics*.

COST OF LIVING
(General Consumer Price Index; base: previous year = 100)

	2007	2008	2009
Food	112.3	114.3	100.7
Clothing	99.4	98.5	98.0
Housing*	104.5	102.8	100.2
All items (incl. others)	104.8	105.9	99.3

* Including water, electricity and fuels.

NATIONAL ACCOUNTS
('000 million yuan at current prices)

Expenditure on the Gross Domestic Product

	2007	2008	2009
Government final consumption expenditure	3,590.0	4,175.2	4,439.7
Private final consumption expenditure	9,561.0	11,059.5	12,113.0
Increase in stocks	699.5	1,024.1	778.4
Gross fixed capital formation	10,394.9	12,808.4	15,668.0
Total domestic expenditure	24,245.3	29,067.2	32,999.0
Exports of goods and services *Less* Imports of goods and services	2,338.1	2,422.9	1,503.3
Sub-total	26,583.4	31,490.1	34,502.3
Statistical discrepancy*	–2.4	–85.6	–451.6
GDP in purchasers' values	26,581.0	31,404.5	34,050.7

* Referring to the difference between the sum of the expenditure components and official estimates of GDP, compiled from the production approach.

Gross Domestic Product by Economic Activity

	2007	2008	2009
Agriculture, forestry and fishing	2,862.7	3,370.2	3,522.6
Construction	1,529.7	1,874.3	2,239.9
Other industry*	11,053.5	13,026.0	13,524.0
Transport, storage and communications	1,460.1	1,636.3	1,705.8
Wholesale and retail trade	2,093.8	2,618.2	2,898.4
Hotels and restaurants	554.8	661.6	711.8
Financial intermediation	1,233.8	1,486.3	1,772.8
Real estate	1,381.0	1,473.9	1,865.5
Other services	4,411.8	5,257.7	5,809.9
Total	26,581.0	31,404.5	34,050.7

* Includes mining, manufacturing, electricity, gas and water.

BALANCE OF PAYMENTS
(US $ million)

	2008	2009	2010
Exports of goods f.o.b.	1,434,601	1,203,797	1,581,417
Imports of goods f.o.b.	–1,073,919	–954,287	–1,327,238
Trade balance	360,682	249,509	254,180
Exports of services	147,112	129,549	171,203
Imports of services	–158,924	–158,947	–193,321
Balance on goods and services	348,870	220,112	232,062
Other income received	101,615	108,582	144,622
Other income paid	–83,920	–101,321	–114,242
Balance on goods, services and income	366,565	227,372	262,442
Current transfers received	52,565	42,645	49,521
Current transfers paid	–6,766	–8,897	–6,588
Current balance	412,364	261,120	305,374
Capital account (net)	3,051	3,958	4,630
Direct investment abroad	–53,471	–43,898	–60,151
Direct investment from abroad	175,148	114,215	185,081
Portfolio investment assets	32,750	9,888	–7,643
Portfolio investment liabilities	9,910	28,804	31,681
Other investment assets	–106,074	9,365	–116,262
Other investment liabilities	–14,992	58,483	188,708
Net errors and omissions	20,868	–41,425	–59,760
Overall balance	479,553	400,508	471,659

Source: IMF, *International Financial Statistics*.

External Trade

PRINCIPAL COMMODITIES
(distribution by SITC, US $ million)

Imports c.i.f.	2007	2008	2009
Food and live animals	11,499.6	14,051.2	14,824.1
Crude materials (inedible) except fuels	117,915.3	166,695.1	140,821.8
Metalliferous ores and metal scrap	69,617.6	99,976.4	85,902.9
Mineral fuels, lubricants, etc.	104,930.1	169,242.0	123,962.8
Petroleum, petroleum products, etc.	99,150.5	162,374.4	109,350.7
Crude petroleum oils, etc.	79,857.5	129,330.9	89,255.6
Chemicals and related products	107,420.5	118,996.8	111,973.0
Organic chemicals	38,288.2	39,035.5	35,880.9
Basic manufactures	102,877.3	107,164.9	107,732.0
Textile yarn, fabrics, etc.	16,644.7	16,288.6	14,944.7
Iron and steel	24,144.4	27,149.0	26,476.3
Machinery and transport equipment	412,640.2	441,952.6	408,259.2
Machinery specialized for particular industries	30,597.5	31,781.1	24,885.7
General industrial machinery, equipment and parts	30,512.3	38,946.0	36,136.4
Office machines and automatic data-processing equipment	45,458.0	46,890.9	43,059.5
Telecommunications and sound equipment	35,737.9	36,896.6	34,065.2
Other electrical machinery, apparatus, etc.	209,224.7	216,810.9	199,042.8
Thermionic valves, tubes, etc.	145,263.5	148,120.6	136,924.3
Electronic microcircuits	127,901.2	129,457.3	120,164.6
Road vehicles and transport equipment *	34,928.5	39,606.8	42,798.7
Miscellaneous manufactured articles	87,330.8	97,458.0	84,935.0
Total (incl. others)	955,955.9	1,132,562.2	1,005,555.2

Exports f.o.b.	2007	2008	2009
Food and live animals	30,742.8	32,762.0	32,603.0
Mineral fuels, lubricants, etc.	19,950.9	31,772.9	20,382.8
Chemicals and related products	60,314.4	79,312.6	62,007.8
Basic manufactures	219,877.0	262,391.2	184,774.6
Textile yarn, fabrics, etc.	55,967.7	65,366.6	59,823.5
Machinery and transport equipment	577,751.4	674,065.0	591,127.5
Office machines and automatic data-processing equipment	165,880.3	176,839.1	157,320.7
Automatic data-processing machines and units	112,243.7	122,727.7	111,890.6
Telecommunications and sound equipment	146,267.5	161,947.7	148,799.0
Other electrical machinery, apparatus, etc.	128,803.9	153,398.8	134,672.5
Road vehicles and transport equipment*	53,868.6	69,151.6	59,006.5
Miscellaneous manufactured articles	296,139.2	335,235.9	298,986.2
Clothing and accessories (excl. footwear)	115,237.5	120,404.7	107,263.7
Footwear	25,305.6	29,720.4	28,016.3
Baby carriages, toys, games and sporting goods	29,019.8	34,948.8	28,166.7
Children's toys	8,485.8	8,644.0	7,783.6
Total (incl. others)	1,217,775.7	1,430,693.1	1,201,646.8

* Data on parts exclude tyres, engines and electrical parts.

Source: UN, *International Trade Statistics Yearbook*.

PRINCIPAL TRADING PARTNERS
(US $ million)*

Imports c.i.f.	2007	2008	2009
Angola	12,888.7	22,382.5	14,675.8
Australia	25,843.2	37,435.1	39,438.8
Brazil	18,339.5	29,863.4	28,281.0
Canada	10,979.1	12,673.4	12,026.2
Chile	10,280.4	11,172.8	12,790.5
France (incl. Monaco)	13,352.4	15,644.1	13,031.1
Germany	45,383.1	55,789.9	55,764.1
India	14,618.1	20,258.9	13,714.3
Indonesia	12,396.5	14,322.9	13,663.8
Iran	13,306.8	19,594.2	13,286.5
Italy	10,210.8	11,639.0	11,020.3
Japan	133,942.7	150,600.0	130,937.5
Korea, Republic	103,752.0	112,137.9	102,551.7
Malaysia	28,697.1	32,101.4	32,330.7
Philippines	23,117.8	19,504.7	11,946.6
Russia	19,688.6	23,832.8	21,283.0
Saudi Arabia	17,559.7	31,022.7	23,620.2
Singapore	17,523.7	20,171.3	17,796.6
Taiwan	101,027.2	103,338.1	85,723.0
Thailand	22,664.7	25,656.7	24,896.9
USA	69,528.7	81,585.6	77,755.1
Total (incl. others)	955,955.9	1,132,562.2	1,005,555.2

Exports f.o.b.	2007	2008	2009
Australia	17,989.7	22,247.3	20,645.6
Belgium	12,679.4	14,871.3	10,872.8
Brazil	11,398.5	18,807.5	14,118.5
Canada	19,355.7	21,795.9	17,675.1
France (incl. Monaco)	20,461.1	23,498.7	21,611.7
Germany	48,714.3	59,209.0	49,919.6
Hong Kong†	184,436.2	190,729.0	166,216.9
India	24,011.5	31,585.4	29,666.6
Indonesia	12,601.3	17,193.1	14,720.6
Italy	21,169.6	26,628.8	20,243.6
Japan	102,008.6	116,132.5	97,911.0
Korea, Republic	56,098.9	73,932.0	53,679.9
Malaysia	17,689.2	21,455.2	19,631.9
Mexico	11,717.7	13,866.5	12,299.0
Netherlands	41,417.8	45,918.6	36,682.2
Russia	28,466.2	33,075.8	17,513.8
Singapore	29,620.3	32,305.8	30,066.4
Spain	16,582.4	20,818.4	14,077.8
Thailand	12,032.9	15,636.4	13,307.1
United Arab Emirates	17,105.0	23,643.7	18,632.3
United Kingdom	31,656.3	36,072.7	31,277.4
USA	233,096.7	252,843.5	221,295.0
Viet Nam	11,895.0	15,122.1	16,300.9
Total (incl. others)	1,217,775.7	1,430,693.1	1,201,646.8

* Imports by country of origin; exports by country of consumption.
† The majority of China's exports to Hong Kong are re-exported.

Source: UN, *International Trade Statistics Yearbook*.

Transport

SUMMARY

	2007	2008	2009
Freight (million ton-km):			
railways	2,379,700	2,510,630	2,523,920
roads	1,135,470	3,286,820	3,718,880
waterways	6,428,480	5,026,270	5,755,670
Passenger-km (million):			
railways	721,630	777,860	787,890
roads	1,150,680	1,247,610	1,351,140
waterways	7,780	5,920	6,940

ROAD TRAFFIC
('000 motor vehicles in use)*

	2007	2008	2009
Passenger cars and buses	31,959.9	38,389.2	48,450.9
Goods vehicles	10,540.6	11,260.7	13,686.0
Total (incl. others)	43,583.6	50,996.1	62,806.1

* Excluding military vehicles.

SHIPPING

Merchant Fleet
(registered at 31 December)

	2007	2008	2009
Number of vessels	3,799	3,916	4,064
Total displacement ('000 grt)	24,918.5	26,811.1	30,077.1

Source: IHS Fairplay, *World Fleet Statistics*.

Sea-borne Shipping
(freight traffic, '000 metric tons)

	2007	2008	2009
Goods loaded and unloaded	3,882,000	4,295,990	4,754,810

CIVIL AVIATION

	2007	2008	2009
Passenger traffic (million)	185.8	192.5	230.5
Passenger-km (million)	279,172.6	288,279.9	337,523.5
Freight traffic ('000 metric tons)	4,018.5	4,076.4	4,455.3
Freight ton-km (million)	11,638.7	11,960.2	12,623.1
Total ton-km (million)	36,529.9	37,676.5	42,707.3

Tourism

FOREIGN VISITORS
(arrivals, '000)

Country of origin	2007	2008	2009
Australia	607.4	571.5	561.5
Canada	577.2	534.7	550.3
Germany	556.7	528.9	518.5
Indonesia	477.1	426.3	469.0
Japan	3,975.5	3,446.1	3,317.5
Korea, Republic	4,777.1	3,960.4	3,197.5
Malaysia	1,062.0	1,040.5	1,059.0
Mongolia	682.0	705.3	576.7
Philippines	833.0	795.3	748.9
Russia	3,003.9	3,123.4	1,743.0
Singapore	922.0	875.8	889.5
Thailand	611.6	554.3	541.8
United Kingdom	605.1	551.5	528.8
USA	1,901.2	1,786.4	1,709.8
Total (incl. others)*	26,109.7	24,325.3	21,937.5

* Excluding visitors from Hong Kong and Macao (1,011.4 in 2007, 1,013.2 in 2008 and 1,000.5 in 2009), and from Taiwan (46.3 in 2007, 43.9 in 2008 and 44.8 in 2009).

Tourism receipts (US $ million): 41,919 in 2007; 40,843 in 2008; 39,675 in 2009.

Communications Media

	2007	2008	2009
Telephones ('000 main lines in use)	365,637	340,359	313,732
Mobile cellular telephones ('000 subscribers)	547,306	641,245	747,214
Internet subscribers ('000)	85,889	95,214	111,522
Broadband subscribers ('000)	66,414	82,879	103,978
Book production:			
titles	248,283	275,668	301,719
copies (million)	6,293	6,936	7,037
Newspaper production:			
titles	1,938	1,943	1,937
copies (million)	438,000	442,922	439,113
Magazine production:			
titles	9,468	9,549	9,851
copies (million)	3,040	3,105	3,153

2010: Telephones ('000 main lines in use) 294,383; Mobile cellular telephones ('000 subscribers) 859,003; Broadband subscribers ('000) 126,337.

Television receivers ('000 in use): 380,000 in 2000**Personal computers:** 74,110,000 (56.5 per 1,000 persons) in 2006.

Radio receivers ('000 in use): 417,000 in 1997.

Sources: International Telecommunication Union; UNESCO, *Statistical Yearbook*; UN, *Statistical Yearbook*.

Education

(2009)

	Institutions	Full-time teachers ('000)	Students ('000)
Kindergartens	138,209	986	26,578
Primary schools	322,094	5,667	100,715
Secondary schools	87,639	5,889	86,536
Junior secondary schools	57,878	3,522	54,336
Senior secondary schools	15,360	1,498	24,343
Vocational secondary schools	14,401	869	7,857
Special schools	1,672	38	428
Higher education	2,305	1,295	21,447

Pupil-teacher ratio (primary education, UNESCO estimate): 17.2 in 2008/09 (Source: UNESCO Institute for Statistics).

Adult literacy rate (UN estimate): 94.0% (males 96.9%; females 90.9%) in 2009 (Source: UNESCO Institute for Statistics).

Directory

The Constitution

A new Constitution was adopted on 4 December 1982 by the Fifth Session of the Fifth National People's Congress. Its principal provisions, including amendments made in 1993, 1999 and 2004, are detailed below. The Preamble, which is not included here, states that 'Taiwan is part of the sacred territory of the People's Republic of China'. The seventh paragraph of the Preamble was amended in 1993 and 1999 to state: 'The basic task of the nation is to concentrate its efforts on socialist modernization by following the road of building socialism with Chinese characteristics. Under the leadership of the Communist Party of China and the guidance of Marxism-Leninism, Mao Zedong Thought and Deng Xiaoping Theory, the Chinese people of all nationalities will continue to adhere to the people's democratic dictatorship.' The paragraph was further amended in 2004 to refer to 'Chinese-style socialism' and to 'the important thought of the Three Represents'.

GENERAL PRINCIPLES

Article 1: The People's Republic of China is a socialist state under the people's democratic dictatorship led by the working class and based on the alliance of workers and peasants.

The socialist system is the basic system of the People's Republic of China. Sabotage of the socialist system by any organization or individual is prohibited.

Article 2: All power in the People's Republic of China belongs to the people.

The organs through which the people exercise state power are the National People's Congress and the local people's congresses at different levels.

The people administer state affairs and manage economic, cultural and social affairs through various channels and in various ways in accordance with the law.

Article 3: The state organs of the People's Republic of China apply the principle of democratic centralism.

The National People's Congress and the local people's congresses at different levels are instituted through democratic election. They are responsible to the people and subject to their supervision.

All administrative, judicial and procuratorial organs of the State are created by the people's congresses to which they are responsible and under whose supervision they operate.

The division of functions and powers between the central and local state organs is guided by the principle of giving full play to the initiative and enthusiasm of the local authorities under the unified leadership of the central authorities.

Article 4: All nationalities in the People's Republic of China are equal. The State protects the lawful rights and interests of the minority nationalities and upholds and develops the relationship of equality, unity and mutual assistance among all of China's nationalities. Discrimination against and oppression of any nationality are prohibited; any acts that undermine the unity of the nationalities or instigate their secession are prohibited.

The State helps the areas inhabited by minority nationalities speed up their economic and cultural development in accordance with the peculiarities and needs of the different minority nationalities.

Regional autonomy is practised in areas where people of minority nationalities live in compact communities; in these areas organs of self-government are established for the exercise of the right of autonomy. All the national autonomous areas are inalienable parts of the People's Republic of China.

The people of all nationalities have the freedom to use and develop their own spoken and written languages, and to preserve or reform their own ways and customs.

Article 5: The People's Republic of China shall be governed according to law and shall be built into a socialist country based on the rule of law.

The State upholds the uniformity and dignity of the socialist legal system.

No law or administrative or local rules and regulations shall contravene the Constitution.

All state organs, the armed forces, all political parties and public organizations and all enterprises and undertakings must abide by the Constitution and the law. All acts in violation of the Constitution and the law must be looked into.

No organization or individual may enjoy the privilege of being above the Constitution and the law.

Article 6: The basis of the socialist economic system of the People's Republic of China is socialist public ownership of the means of production, namely, ownership by the whole people and collective ownership by the working people.

The system of socialist public ownership supersedes the system of exploitation of man by man; it applies the principle of 'from each according to his ability, to each according to his work.'

In the initial stage of socialism, the country shall uphold the basic economic system in which the public ownership is dominant and diverse forms of ownership develop side by side, and it shall uphold the distribution system with distribution according to work remaining dominant and a variety of modes of distribution coexisting.

Article 7: The state-owned economy, namely the socialist economy under the ownership of the whole people, is the leading force in the national economy. The State ensures the consolidation and growth of the state-owned economy.

Article 8: The rural collective economic organizations shall implement a two-tier operations system that combines unified operations with independent operations on the basis of household contract operations and different co-operative economic forms in the rural areas—the producers', supply and marketing, credit, and consumers' co-operatives—are part of the socialist economy collectively owned by the working people. Working people who are all members of rural economic collectives have the right, within the limits prescribed by law, to farm plots of cropland and hilly land allotted for their private use, engage in household sideline production and raise privately-owned livestock.

The various forms of co-operative economy in the cities and towns, such as those in the handicraft, industrial, building, transport, commercial and service trades, all belong to the sector of socialist economy under collective ownership by the working people.

The State protects the lawful rights and interests of the urban and rural economic collectives and encourages, guides and helps the growth of the collective economy.

Article 9: Mineral resources, waters, forests, mountains, grassland, unreclaimed land, beaches and other natural resources are owned by the State, that is, by the whole people, with the exception of the forests, mountains, grassland, unreclaimed land and beaches that are owned by collectives in accordance with the law.

The State ensures the rational use of natural resources and protects rare animals and plants. The appropriation or damage of natural resources by any organization or individual by whatever means is prohibited.

Article 10: Land in the cities is owned by the State.

Land in the rural and suburban areas is owned by collectives except for those portions which belong to the State in accordance with the law; house sites and private plots of cropland and hilly land are also owned by collectives.

The State may, in the public interest and in accordance with the provisions of law, expropriate or requisition land for its use and shall make compensation for the land expropriated or requisitioned.

No organization or individual may appropriate, buy, sell or lease land, or unlawfully transfer land in other ways.

All organizations and individuals who use land must make rational use of the land.

Article 11: The non-public sector of the economy comprising the individual and private sectors, operating within the limits prescribed by law, is an important component of the socialist market economy.

The State protects the lawful rights and interests of the non-public sectors of the economy such as the individual and private sectors of the economy. The State encourages, supports and guides the development of the non-public sectors of the economy and, in accordance with the law, exercises supervision and control over the non-public sectors of the economy.

Article 12: Socialist public property is sacred and inviolable.

The State protects socialist public property. Appropriation or damage of state or collective property by any organization or individual by whatever means is prohibited.

Article 13: Citizens' lawful private property is inviolable.

The State, in accordance with the law, protects the rights of citizens to private property and to its inheritance.

The State may, in the public interest and in accordance with the law, expropriate or requisition private property for its use and shall make compensation for private property expropriated or requisitioned.

Article 14: The State continuously raises labour productivity, improves economic results and develops the productive forces by enhancing the enthusiasm of the working people, raising the level of their technical skill, disseminating advanced science and technology, improving the systems of economic administration and enterprise operation and management, instituting the socialist system of responsibility in various forms and improving organization of work.

The State practises strict economy and combats waste.

The State properly apportions accumulation and consumption, pays attention to the interests of the collective and the individual as well as of the State and, on the basis of expanded production, gradually improves the material and cultural life of the people.

The State establishes a sound social security system compatible with the level of economic development.

Article 15: The State practises a socialist market economy. The State strengthens economic legislation and perfects macro-control. The State prohibits, according to the law, disturbance of society's economic order by any organization or individual.

Article 16: State-owned enterprises have decision-making power in operations within the limits prescribed by law.

State-owned enterprises practise democratic management through congresses of workers and staff and in other ways in accordance with the law.

Article 17: Collective economic organizations have decision-making power in conducting economic activities on the condition that they abide by the relevant laws. Collective economic organizations practise democratic management, elect and remove managerial personnel, and decide on major issues in accordance with the law.

Article 18: The People's Republic of China permits foreign enterprises, other foreign economic organizations and individual foreigners to invest in China and to enter into various forms of economic co-operation with Chinese enterprises and other economic organizations in accordance with the law of the People's Republic of China.

All foreign enterprises and other foreign economic organizations in China, as well as joint ventures with Chinese and foreign investment located in China, shall abide by the law of the People's Republic of China. Their lawful rights and interests are protected by the law of the People's Republic of China.

Article 19: The State develops socialist educational undertakings and works to raise the scientific and cultural level of the whole nation.

The State runs schools of various types, makes primary education compulsory and universal, develops secondary, vocational and higher education and promotes pre-school education.

The State develops educational facilities of various types in order to wipe out illiteracy and provide political, cultural, scientific, technical and professional education for workers, peasants, state functionaries and other working people. It encourages people to become educated through self-study.

The State encourages the collective economic organizations, state enterprises and undertakings and other social forces to set up educational institutions of various types in accordance with the law.

The State promotes the nation-wide use of Putonghua (common speech based on Beijing pronunciation).

Article 20: The State promotes the development of the natural and social sciences, disseminates scientific and technical knowledge, and commends and rewards achievements in scientific research as well as technological discoveries and inventions.

Article 21: The State develops medical and health services, promotes modern medicine and traditional Chinese medicine, encourages and supports the setting up of various medical and health facilities by the rural economic collectives, state enterprises and undertakings and neighbourhood organizations, and promotes sanitation activities of a mass character, all to protect the people's health.

The State develops physical culture and promotes mass sports activities to build up the people's physique.

Article 22: The State promotes the development of literature and art, the press, broadcasting and television undertakings, publishing and distribution services, libraries, museums, cultural centres and other cultural undertakings that serve the people and socialism, and sponsors mass cultural activities.

The State protects places of scenic and historical interest, valuable cultural monuments and relics and other important items of China's historical and cultural heritage.

Article 23: The State trains specialized personnel in all fields who serve socialism, increases the number of intellectuals and creates conditions to give full scope to their role in socialist modernization.

Article 24: The State strengthens the building of socialist spiritual civilization through spreading education in high ideals and morality, general education and education in discipline and the legal system, and through promoting the formulation and observance of rules of conduct and common pledges by different sections of the people in urban and rural areas.

The State advocates the civic virtues of love for the motherland, for the people, for labour, for science and for socialism; it educates the people in patriotism, collectivism, internationalism and communism and in dialectical and historical materialism; it combats capitalist, feudalist and other decadent ideas.

Article 25: The State promotes family planning so that population growth may fit the plans for economic and social development.

Article 26: The State protects and improves the living environment and the ecological environment, and prevents and remedies pollution and other public hazards.

The State organizes and encourages afforestation and the protection of forests.

Article 27: All state organs carry out the principle of simple and efficient administration, the system of responsibility for work and the system of training functionaries and appraising their work in order constantly to improve quality of work and efficiency and combat bureaucratism.

All state organs and functionaries must rely on the support of the people, keep in close touch with them, heed their opinions and suggestions, accept their supervision and work hard to serve them.

Article 28: The State maintains public order and suppresses treasonable and other criminal activities that endanger national security; it penalizes activities that endanger public security and disrupt the socialist economy as well as other criminal activities; and it punishes and reforms criminals.

Article 29: The armed forces of the People's Republic of China belong to the people. Their tasks are to strengthen national defence, resist aggression, defend the motherland, safeguard the people's peaceful labour, participate in national reconstruction, and work hard to serve the people.

The State strengthens the revolutionization, modernization and regularization of the armed forces in order to increase the national defence capability.

Article 30: The administrative division of the People's Republic of China is as follows:

(1) The country is divided into provinces, autonomous regions and municipalities directly under the central government;

(2) Provinces and autonomous regions are divided into autonomous prefectures, counties, autonomous counties and cities;

(3) Counties and autonomous counties are divided into townships, nationality townships and towns.

Municipalities directly under the central government and other large cities are divided into districts and counties. Autonomous prefectures are divided into counties, autonomous counties, and cities.

All autonomous regions, autonomous prefectures and autonomous counties are national autonomous areas.

Article 31: The State may establish special administrative regions when necessary. The systems to be instituted in special administrative regions shall be prescribed by law enacted by the National People's Congress in the light of the specific conditions.

Article 32: The People's Republic of China protects the lawful rights and interests of foreigners within Chinese territory, and while on Chinese territory foreigners must abide by the law of the People's Republic of China.

The People's Republic of China may grant asylum to foreigners who request it for political reasons.

FUNDAMENTAL RIGHTS AND DUTIES OF CITIZENS

Article 33: All persons holding the nationality of the People's Republic of China are citizens of the People's Republic of China.

All citizens of the People's Republic of China are equal before the law.

Every citizen enjoys the rights and at the same time must perform the duties prescribed by the Constitution and the law.

The State respects and preserves human rights.

Article 34: All citizens of the People's Republic of China who have reached the age of 18 have the right to vote and stand for election, regardless of nationality, race, sex, occupation, family background, religious belief, education, property status, or length of residence, except persons deprived of political rights according to law.

Article 35: Citizens of the People's Republic of China enjoy freedom of speech, of the press, of assembly, of association, of procession and of demonstration.

Article 36: Citizens of the People's Republic of China enjoy freedom of religious belief.

No state organ, public organization or individual may compel citizens to believe in, or not to believe in, any religion; nor may they discriminate against citizens who believe in, or do not believe in, any religion.

The State protects normal religious activities. No one may make use of religion to engage in activities that disrupt public order, impair the health of citizens or interfere with the educational system of the state.

Religious bodies and religious affairs are not subject to any foreign domination.

Article 37: The freedom of person of citizens of the People's Republic of China is inviolable.

No citizen may be arrested except with the approval or by decision of a people's procuratorate or by decision of a people's court, and arrests must be made by a public security organ.

Unlawful deprivation or restriction of citizens' freedom of person by detention or other means is prohibited; and unlawful search of the person of citizens is prohibited.

Article 38: The personal dignity of citizens of the People's Republic of China is inviolable. Insult, libel, false charge or frame-up directed against citizens by any means is prohibited.

Article 39: The home of citizens of the People's Republic of China is inviolable. Unlawful search of, or intrusion into, a citizen's home is prohibited.

Article 40: The freedom and privacy of correspondence of citizens of the People's Republic of China are protected by law. No organization or individual may, on any ground, infringe upon the freedom and privacy of citizens' correspondence except in cases where, to meet the needs of state security or of investigation into criminal offences, public security or procuratorial organs are permitted to censor correspondence in accordance with procedures prescribed by law.

Article 41: Citizens of the People's Republic of China have the right to criticize and make suggestions to any state organ or functionary. Citizens have the right to make to relevant state organs complaints and charges against, or exposures of, violation of the law or dereliction of duty by any state organ or functionary; but fabrication or distortion of facts with the intention of libel or frame-up is prohibited.

In case of complaints, charges or exposures made by citizens, the state organ concerned must deal with them in a responsible manner after ascertaining the facts. No one may suppress such complaints, charges and exposures, or retaliate against the citizen making them.

Citizens who have suffered losses through infringement of their civic rights by any state organ or functionary have the right to compensation in accordance with the law.

Article 42: Citizens of the People's Republic of China have the right as well as the duty to work.

Using various channels, the State creates conditions for employment, strengthens labour protection, improves working conditions and, on the basis of expanded production, increases remuneration for work and social benefits.

Work is the glorious duty of every able-bodied citizen. All working people in state-owned enterprises and in urban and rural economic collectives should perform their tasks with an attitude consonant with their status as masters of the country. The State promotes socialist labour emulation, and commends and rewards model and advanced workers. The State encourages citizens to take part in voluntary labour.

The State provides necessary vocational training to citizens before they are employed.

Article 43: Working people in the People's Republic of China have the right to rest.

The State expands facilities for rest and recuperation of working people, and prescribes working hours and vacations for workers and staff.

Article 44: The State prescribes by law the system of retirement for workers and staff in enterprises and undertakings and for functionaries of organs of state. The livelihood of retired personnel is ensured by the State and society.

Article 45: Citizens of the People's Republic of China have the right to material assistance from the State and society when they are old, ill or disabled. The State develops the social insurance, social relief and medical and health services that are required to enable citizens to enjoy this right.

The State and society ensure the livelihood of disabled members of the armed forces, provide pensions to the families of martyrs and give preferential treatment to the families of military personnel.

The State and society help make arrangements for the work, livelihood and education of the blind, deaf-mute and other handicapped citizens.

Article 46: Citizens of the People's Republic of China have the duty as well as the right to receive education.

The State promotes the all-round moral, intellectual and physical development of children and young people.

Article 47: Citizens of the People's Republic of China have the freedom to engage in scientific research, literary and artistic creation and other cultural pursuits. The State encourages and assists creative endeavours conducive to the interests of the people that are made by citizens engaged in education, science, technology, literature, art and other cultural work.

Article 48: Women in the People's Republic of China enjoy equal rights with men in all spheres of life, political, economic, cultural and social, including family life.

The State protects the rights and interests of women, applies the principle of equal pay for equal work for men and women alike and trains and selects cadres from among women.

Article 49: Marriage, the family and mother and child are protected by the State.

Both husband and wife have the duty to practise family planning.

Parents have the duty to rear and educate their minor children, and children who have come of age have the duty to support and assist their parents.

Violation of the freedom of marriage is prohibited. Maltreatment of old people, women and children is prohibited.

Article 50: The People's Republic of China protects the legitimate rights and interests of Chinese nationals residing abroad and protects the lawful rights and interests of returned overseas Chinese and of the family members of Chinese nationals residing abroad.

Article 51: The exercise by citizens of the People's Republic of China of their freedoms and rights may not infringe upon the interests of the State, of society and of the collective, or upon the lawful freedoms and rights of other citizens.

Article 52: It is the duty of citizens of the People's Republic of China to safeguard the unity of the country and the unity of all its nationalities.

Article 53: Citizens of the People's Republic of China must abide by the Constitution and the law, keep state secrets, protect public property and observe labour discipline and public order and respect social ethics.

Article 54: It is the duty of citizens of the People's Republic of China to safeguard the security, honour and interests of the motherland; they must not commit acts detrimental to the security, honour and interests of the motherland.

Article 55: It is the sacred obligation of every citizen of the People's Republic of China to defend the motherland and resist aggression.

It is the honourable duty of citizens of the People's Republic of China to perform military service and join the militia in accordance with the law.

Article 56: It is the duty of citizens of the People's Republic of China to pay taxes in accordance with the law.

STRUCTURE OF THE STATE

The National People's Congress

Article 57: The National People's Congress of the People's Republic of China is the highest organ of state power. Its permanent body is the Standing Committee of the National People's Congress.

Article 58: The National People's Congress and its Standing Committee exercise the legislative power of the State.

Article 59: The National People's Congress is composed of deputies elected from the provinces, autonomous regions, municipalities directly under the Central Government, and the special administrative regions, and of deputies elected from the armed forces. All the minority nationalities are entitled to appropriate representation.

Election of deputies to the National People's Congress is conducted by the Standing Committee of the National People's Congress.

The number of deputies to the National People's Congress and the manner of their election are prescribed by law.

Article 60: The National People's Congress is elected for a term of five years.

Two months before the expiration of the term of office of a National People's Congress, its Standing Committee must ensure that the election of deputies to the succeeding National People's Congress is completed. Should exceptional circumstances prevent such an election, it may be postponed by decision of a majority vote of more than two-thirds of all those on the Standing Committee of the incumbent National People's Congress, and the term of office of the incumbent National People's Congress may be extended. The election of deputies to the succeeding National People's Congress must be completed within one year after the termination of such exceptional circumstances.

Article 61: The National People's Congress meets in session once a year and is convened by its Standing Committee. A session of the National People's Congress may be convened at any time the Standing Committee deems this necessary, or when more than one-fifth of the deputies to the National People's Congress so propose.

When the National People's Congress meets, it elects a presidium to conduct its session.

Article 62: The National People's Congress exercises the following functions and powers:

(1) to amend the Constitution;

(2) to supervise the enforcement of the Constitution;

(3) to enact and amend basic statutes concerning criminal offences, civil affairs, the state organs and other matters;

(4) to elect the President and the Vice-President of the People's Republic of China;

(5) to decide on the choice of the Premier of the State Council upon nomination by the President of the People's Republic of China, and to decide on the choice of the Vice-Premiers, State Councillors, Ministers in charge of Ministries or Commissions and the Auditor-General and the Secretary-General of the State Council upon nomination by the Premier;

(6) to elect the Chairman of the Central Military Commission and, upon his nomination, to decide on the choice of all the others on the Central Military Commission;

(7) to elect the President of the Supreme People's Court;

(8) to elect the Procurator-General of the Supreme People's Procuratorate;

(9) to examine and approve the plan for national economic and social development and the reports on its implementation;

(10) to examine and approve the state budget and the report on its implementation;

(11) to alter or annul inappropriate decisions of the Standing Committee of the National People's Congress;

(12) to approve the establishment of provinces, autonomous regions, and municipalities directly under the Central Government;

(13) to decide on the establishment of special administrative regions and the systems to be instituted there;

(14) to decide on questions of war and peace; and

(15) to exercise such other functions and powers as the highest organ of state power should exercise.

Article 63: The National People's Congress has the power to recall or remove from office the following persons:

(1) the President and the Vice-President of the People's Republic of China;

(2) the Premier, Vice-Premiers, State Councillors, Ministers in charge of Ministries or Commissions and the Auditor-General and the Secretary-General of the State Council;

(3) the Chairman of the Central Military Commission and others on the Commission;

(4) the President of the Supreme People's Court; and

(5) the Procurator-General of the Supreme People's Procuratorate.

Article 64: Amendments to the Constitution are to be proposed by the Standing Committee of the National People's Congress or by more than one-fifth of the deputies to the National People's Congress and adopted by a majority vote of more than two-thirds of all the deputies to the Congress.

Statutes and resolutions are adopted by a majority vote of more than one-half of all the deputies to the National People's Congress.

Article 65: The Standing Committee of the National People's Congress is composed of the following:

the Chairman;
the Vice-Chairmen;
the Secretary-General; and
members.

Minority nationalities are entitled to appropriate representation on the Standing Committee of the National People's Congress.

The National People's Congress elects, and has the power to recall, all those on its Standing Committee.

No one on the Standing Committee of the National People's Congress shall hold any post in any of the administrative, judicial or procuratorial organs of the State.

Article 66: The Standing Committee of the National People's Congress is elected for the same term as the National People's Congress; it exercises its functions and powers until a new Standing Committee is elected by the succeeding National People's Congress.

The Chairman and Vice-Chairmen of the Standing Committee shall serve no more than two consecutive terms.

Article 67: The Standing Committee of the National People's Congress exercises the following functions and powers:

(1) to interpret the Constitution and supervise its enforcement;

(2) to enact and amend statutes with the exception of those which should be enacted by the National People's Congress;

(3) to enact, when the National People's Congress is not in session, partial supplements and amendments to statutes enacted by the National People's Congress provided that they do not contravene the basic principles of these statutes;

(4) to interpret statutes;

(5) to examine and approve, when the National People's Congress is not in session, partial adjustments to the plan for national economic and social development and to the state budget that prove necessary in the course of their implementation;

(6) to supervise the work of the State Council, the Central Military Commission, the Supreme People's Court and the Supreme People's Procuratorate;

(7) to annul those administrative rules and regulations, decisions or orders of the State Council that contravene the Constitution or the statutes;

(8) to annul those local regulations or decisions of the organs of state power of provinces, autonomous regions and municipalities directly under the Central Government that contravene the Constitution, the statutes or the administrative rules and regulations;

(9) to decide, when the National People's Congress is not in session, on the choice of Ministers in charge of Ministries or Commissions or the Auditor-General and the Secretary-General of the State Council upon nomination by the Premier of the State Council;

(10) to decide, upon nomination by the Chairman of the Central Military Commission, on the choice of others on the Commission, when the National People's Congress is not in session.

(11) to appoint and remove the Vice-Presidents and judges of the Supreme People's Court, members of its Judicial Committee and the President of the Military Court at the suggestion of the President of the Supreme People's Court;

(12) to appoint and remove the Deputy Procurators-General and Procurators of the Supreme People's Procuratorate, members of its Procuratorial Committee and the Chief Procurator of the Military Procuratorate at the request of the Procurator-General of the Supreme People's Procuratorate, and to approve the appointment and removal of the Chief Procurators of the People's Procuratorates of provinces, autonomous regions and municipalities directly under the Central Government;

(13) to decide on the appointment and recall of plenipotentiary representatives abroad;

(14) to decide on the ratification and abrogation of treaties and important agreements concluded with foreign states;

(15) to institute systems of titles and ranks for military and diplomatic personnel and of other specific titles and ranks;

(16) to institute state medals and titles of honour and decide on their conferment;

(17) to decide on the granting of special pardons;

(18) to decide, when the National People's Congress is not in session, on the proclamation of a state of war in the event of an armed attack on the country or in fulfilment of international treaty obligations concerning common defence against aggression;

(19) to decide on general mobilization or partial mobilization;

(20) to decide on entering the state of emergency throughout the country or in particular provinces, autonomous regions, or municipalities directly under the Central Government; and

(21) to exercise such other functions and powers as the National People's Congress may assign to it.

Article 68: The Chairman of the Standing Committee of the National People's Congress presides over the work of the Standing Committee and convenes its meetings. The Vice-Chairmen and the Secretary-General assist the Chairman in his work.

Chairmanship meetings with the participation of the Chairman, Vice-Chairmen and Secretary-General handle the important day-to-day work of the Standing Committee of the National People's Congress.

Article 69: The Standing Committee of the National People's Congress is responsible to the National People's Congress and reports on its work to the Congress.

Article 70: The National People's Congress establishes a Nationalities Committee, a Law Committee, a Finance and Economic Committee, an Education, Science, Culture and Public Health Committee, a Foreign Affairs Committee, an Overseas Chinese Committee and such other special committees as are necessary. These special committees work under the direction of the Standing Committee of the National People's Congress when the Congress is not in session.

The special committees examine, discuss and draw up relevant bills and draft resolutions under the direction of the National People's Congress and its Standing Committee.

Article 71: The National People's Congress and its Standing Committee may, when they deem it necessary, appoint committees of inquiry into specific questions and adopt relevant resolutions in the light of their reports.

All organs of State, public organizations and citizens concerned are obliged to supply the necessary information to those committees of inquiry when they conduct investigations.

Article 72: Deputies to the National People's Congress and all those on its Standing Committee have the right, in accordance with procedures prescribed by law, to submit bills and proposals within the scope of the respective functions and powers of the National People's Congress and its Standing Committee.

Article 73: Deputies to the National People's Congress during its sessions, and all those on its Standing Committee during its meetings, have the right to address questions, in accordance with procedures prescribed by law, to the State Council or the Ministries and Commissions under the State Council, which must answer the questions in a responsible manner.

Article 74: No deputy to the National People's Congress may be arrested or placed on criminal trial without the consent of the presidium of the current session of the National People's Congress or, when the National People's Congress is not in session, without the consent of its Standing Committee.

Article 75: Deputies to the National People's Congress may not be called to legal account for their speeches or votes at its meetings.

Article 76: Deputies to the National People's Congress must play an exemplary role in abiding by the Constitution and the law and keeping state secrets and, in production and other work and their public activities, assist in the enforcement of the Constitution and the law.

Deputies to the National People's Congress should maintain close contact with the units which elected them and with the people, listen to and convey the opinions and demands of the people and work hard to serve them.

Article 77: Deputies to the National People's Congress are subject to the supervision of the units which elected them. The electoral units have the power, through procedures prescribed by law, to recall the deputies whom they elected.

Article 78: The organization and working procedures of the National People's Congress and its Standing Committee are prescribed by law.

The President of the People's Republic of China

Article 79: The President and Vice-President of the People's Republic of China are elected by the National People's Congress.

Citizens of the People's Republic of China who have the right to vote and to stand for election and who have reached the age of 45 are eligible for election as President or Vice-President of the People's Republic of China.

The term of office of the President and Vice-President of the People's Republic of China is the same as that of the National People's Congress, and they shall serve no more than two consecutive terms.

Article 80: The President of the People's Republic of China, in pursuance of decisions of the National People's Congress and its Standing Committee, promulgates statutes; appoints and removes the Premier, Vice-Premiers, State Councillors, Ministers in charge of Ministries or Commissions, and the Auditor-General and the Secretary-General of the State Council; confers state medals and titles of honour; issues orders of special pardons; proclaims entering the state of emergency; proclaims a state of war; and issues mobilization orders.

Article 81: The President of the People's Republic of China, on behalf of the People's Republic of China, engages in activities involving State affairs and receives foreign diplomatic representatives and, in pursuance of decisions of the Standing Committee of the National People's Congress, appoints and recalls plenipotentiary representatives abroad, and ratifies and abrogates treaties and important agreements concluded with foreign states.

Article 82: The Vice-President of the People's Republic of China assists the President in his work.

The Vice-President of the People's Republic of China may exercise such parts of the functions and powers of the President as the President may entrust to him.

Article 83: The President and Vice-President of the People's Republic of China exercise their functions and powers until the new President and Vice-President elected by the succeeding National People's Congress assume office.

Article 84: In case the office of the President of the People's Republic of China falls vacant, the Vice-President succeeds to the office of President.

In case the office of the Vice-President of the People's Republic of China falls vacant, the National People's Congress shall elect a new Vice-President to fill the vacancy.

In the event that the offices of both the President and the Vice-President of the People's Republic of China fall vacant, the National People's Congress shall elect a new President and a new Vice-President. Prior to such election, the Chairman of the Standing Committee of the National People's Congress shall temporarily act as the President of the People's Republic of China.

The State Council

Article 85: The State Council, that is, the Central People's Government, of the People's Republic of China is the executive body of the highest organ of state power; it is the highest organ of state administration.

Article 86: The State Council is composed of the following: the Premier; the Vice-Premiers; the State Councillors; the Ministers in charge of ministries; the Ministers in charge of commissions; the Auditor-General; and the Secretary-General.

The Premier has overall responsibility for the State Council. The Ministers have overall responsibility for the respective ministries or commissions under their charge.

The organization of the State Council is prescribed by law.

Article 87: The term of office of the State Council is the same as that of the National People's Congress.

The Premier, Vice-Premiers and State Councillors shall serve no more than two consecutive terms.

Article 88: The Premier directs the work of the State Council. The Vice-Premiers and State Councillors assist the Premier in his work.

Executive meetings of the State Council are composed of the Premier, the Vice-Premiers, the State Councillors and the Secretary-General of the State Council.

The Premier convenes and presides over the executive meetings and plenary meetings of the State Council.

Article 89: The State Council exercises the following functions and powers:

(1) to adopt administrative measures, enact administrative rules and regulations and issue decisions and orders in accordance with the Constitution and the statutes;

(2) to submit proposals to the National People's Congress or its Standing Committee;

(3) to lay down the tasks and responsibilities of the ministries and commissions of the State Council, to exercise unified leadership over the work of the ministries and commissions and to direct all other administrative work of a national character that does not fall within the jurisdiction of the ministries and commissions;

(4) to exercise unified leadership over the work of local organs of state administration at different levels throughout the country, and to lay down the detailed division of functions and powers between the Central Government and the organs of state administration of provinces, autonomous regions and municipalities directly under the Central Government;

(5) to draw up and implement the plan for national economic and social development and the state budget;

(6) to direct and administer economic work and urban and rural development;

(7) to direct and administer the work concerning education, science, culture, public health, physical culture and family planning;

(8) to direct and administer the work concerning civil affairs, public security, judicial administration, supervision and other related matters;

(9) to conduct foreign affairs and conclude treaties and agreements with foreign states;

(10) to direct and administer the building of national defence;

(11) to direct and administer affairs concerning the nationalities, and to safeguard the equal rights of minority nationalities and the right of autonomy of the national autonomous areas;

(12) to protect the legitimate rights and interests of Chinese nationals residing abroad and protect the lawful rights and interests of returned overseas Chinese and of the family members of Chinese nationals residing abroad;

(13) to alter or annul inappropriate orders, directives and regulations issued by the ministries or commissions;

(14) to alter or annul inappropriate decisions and orders issued by local organs of state administration at different levels;

(15) to approve the geographic division of provinces, autonomous regions and municipalities directly under the Central Government, and to approve the establishment and geographic division of autonomous prefectures, counties, autonomous counties and cities;

(16) in accordance with the provisions of law, to decide on entering the state of emergency in parts of provinces, autonomous regions, and municipalities directly under the Central Government;

(17) to examine and decide on the size of administrative organs and, in accordance with the law, to appoint, remove and train administrative officers, appraise their work and reward or punish them; and

(18) to exercise such other functions and powers as the National People's Congress or its Standing Committee may assign it.

Article 90: The Ministers in charge of ministries or commissions of the State Council are responsible for the work of their respective departments and convene and preside over their ministerial meetings or commission meetings that discuss and decide on major issues in the work of their respective departments.

The ministries and commissions issue orders, directives and regulations within the jurisdiction of their respective departments and in accordance with the statutes and the administrative rules and regulations, decisions and orders issued by the State Council.

Article 91: The State Council establishes an auditing body to supervise through auditing the revenue and expenditure of all departments under the State Council and of the local government at different levels, and those of the state financial and monetary organizations and of enterprises and undertakings.

Under the direction of the Premier of the State Council, the auditing body independently exercises its power to supervise through auditing in accordance with the law, subject to no interference by any other administrative organ or any public organization or individual.

Article 92: The State Council is responsible, and reports on its work, to the National People's Congress or, when the National People's Congress is not in session, to its Standing Committee.

The Central Military Commission

Article 93: The Central Military Commission of the People's Republic of China directs the armed forces of the country.

The Central Military Commission is composed of the following: the Chairman; the Vice-Chairmen; and members.

The Chairman of the Central Military Commission has overall responsibility for the Commission.

The term of office of the Central Military Commission is the same as that of the National People's Congress.

Article 94: The Chairman of the Central Military Commission is responsible to the National People's Congress and its Standing Committee.

Regional Administration

Two further sections, not included here, deal with the Local People's Congresses and Government and with the Organs of Self-Government of National Autonomous Areas, respectively.

The People's Courts and the People's Procuratorates

Article 123: The people's courts in the People's Republic of China are the judicial organs of the State.

Article 124: The People's Republic of China establishes the Supreme People's Court and the local people's courts at different levels, military courts and other special people's courts.

The term of office of the President of the Supreme People's Court is the same as that of the National People's Congress; he shall serve no more than two consecutive terms.

The organization of people's courts is prescribed by law.

Article 125: All cases handled by the people's courts, except for those involving special circumstances as specified by law, shall be heard in public. The accused has the right of defence.

Article 126: The people's courts shall, in accordance with the law, exercise judicial power independently and are not subject to interference by administrative organs, public organizations or individuals.

Article 127: The Supreme People's Court is the highest judicial organ.

The Supreme People's Court supervises the administration of justice by the local people's courts at different levels and by the special people's courts; people's courts at higher levels supervise the administration of justice by those at lower levels.

Article 128: The Supreme People's Court is responsible to the National People's Congress and its Standing Committee. Local people's courts at different levels are responsible to the organs of state power which created them.

Article 129: The people's procuratorates of the People's Republic of China are state organs for legal supervision.

Article 130: The People's Republic of China establishes the Supreme People's Procuratorate and the local people's procuratorates at different levels, military procuratorates and other special people's procuratorates.

The term of office of the Procurator-General of the Supreme People's Procuratorate is the same as that of the National People's Congress; he shall serve no more than two consecutive terms.

The organization of people's procuratorates is prescribed by law.

Article 131: People's procuratorates shall, in accordance with the law, exercise procuratorial power independently and are not subject to interference by administrative organs, public organizations or individuals.

Article 132: The Supreme People's Procuratorate is the highest procuratorial organ.

The Supreme People's Procuratorate directs the work of the local people's procuratorates at different levels and of the special people's procuratorates; people's procuratorates at higher levels direct the work of those at lower levels.

Article 133: The Supreme People's Procuratorate is responsible to the National People's Congress and its Standing Committee. Local people's procuratorates at different levels are responsible to the organs of state power at the corresponding levels which created them and to the people's procuratorates at the higher level.

Article 134: Citizens of all nationalities have the right to use the spoken and written languages of their own nationalities in court proceedings. The people's courts and people's procuratorates should provide translation for any party to the court proceedings who is not familiar with the spoken or written languages in common use in the locality.

In an area where people of a minority nationality live in a compact community or where a number of nationalities live together, hearings should be conducted in the language or languages in common use in the locality; indictments, judgments, notices and other documents should be written, according to actual needs, in the language or languages in common use in the locality.

Article 135: The people's courts, people's procuratorates and public security organs shall, in handling criminal cases, divide their functions, each taking responsibility for its own work, and they shall co-ordinate their efforts and check each other to ensure correct and effective enforcement of law.

THE NATIONAL FLAG, THE NATIONAL ANTHEM, THE NATIONAL EMBLEM AND THE CAPITAL

Article 136: The national flag of the People's Republic of China is a red flag with five stars.

The National Anthem of the People's Republic of China is the March of the Volunteers.

Article 137: The national emblem of the People's Republic of China is the Tiananmen (Gate of Heavenly Peace) in the centre, illuminated by five stars and encircled by ears of grain and a cogwheel.

Article 138: The capital of the People's Republic of China is Beijing (Peking).

The Government

HEAD OF STATE

President: HU JINTAO (elected by the 10th National People's Congress on 15 March 2003; re-elected by the 11th National People's Congress on 15 March 2008).

Vice-President: XI JINPING.

STATE COUNCIL
(October 2011)

The Government is formed by the Chinese Communist Party.

Premier: WEN JIABAO.

Vice-Premiers: LI KEQIANG, HUI LIANGYU, ZHANG DEJIANG, WANG QISHAN.

State Councillors: LIU YANDONG, LIANG GUANGLIE, MA KAI, MENG JIANZHU, DAI BINGGUO.

Secretary-General: MA KAI.

Minister of Foreign Affairs: YANG JIECHI.

Minister of National Defence: LIANG GUANGLIE.

Minister of National Development and Reform Commission: ZHANG PING.

Minister of Education: YUAN GUIREN.

Minister of Science and Technology: WAN GANG.

Minister of Industry and Information Technology: MIAO WEI .

Minister of State Ethnic Affairs Commission: YANG JING.

Minister of Public Security: MENG JIANZHU.

Minister of State Security: GENG HUICHANG.

Minister of Supervision: MA WEN.

Minister of Civil Affairs: LI LIGUO.

Minister of Justice: WU AIYING.

Minister of Finance: XIE XUREN.

Minister of Human Resources and Social Security: YIN WEIMIN.

Minister of Land and Resources: XU SHAOSHI.

Minister of Housing and Urban-Rural Construction: JIANG WEIXIN.

Minister of Railways: SHENG GUANGZU.

Minister of Transport: LI SHENGLIN.

Minister of Water Resources: CHEN LEI.

Minister of Agriculture: HAN CHANGFU.

Minister of Environmental Protection: ZHOU SHENGXIAN.

Minister of Commerce: CHEN DEMING.

Minister of Culture: CAI WU.

Minister of Health: CHEN ZHU.

Minister of National Population and Family Planning Commission: LI BIN.

Governor of the People's Bank of China: ZHOU XIAOCHUAN.

Auditor-General of the National Audit Office: LIU JIAYI.

MINISTRIES

Ministry of Agriculture: 11 Nongzhanguan Nanli, Chao Yang Qu, Beijing 100125; tel. (10) 59191830; fax (10) 59191831; e-mail webmaster_en@agri.gov.cn; internet www.agri.gov.cn.

Ministry of Civil Affairs: 147 Beiheyan Dajie, Dongcheng Qu, Beijing 100721; tel. (10) 58123114; fax (10) 65135332; internet www.mca.gov.cn.

Ministry of Commerce: 2 Dongchangan Dajie, Dongcheng Qu, Beijing 100731; tel. (10) 65284671; fax (10) 65599340; e-mail webmaster@mofcom.gov.cn; internet www.mofcom.gov.cn.

Ministry of Culture: 10 Chao Yang Men Bei Dajie, Chao Yang Qu, Beijing 100020; tel. (10) 59881114; fax (10) 65551433; e-mail webmaster@ccic.gov.cn; internet www.ccnt.gov.cn.

Ministry of Education: 37 Damucang Hutong, Xidan, Beijing 100816; tel. (10) 66096114; fax (10) 66011049; e-mail english@moe.edu.cn; internet www.moe.edu.cn.

Ministry of Environmental Protection: 115 Xizhimennei Nan Xiao Jie, Xicheng Qu, Beijing 100035; tel. (10) 66556006; fax (10) 66556010; e-mail mailbox@mep.gov.cn; internet www.mep.gov.cn.

Ministry of Finance: 3 Nansanxiang, Sanlihe, Xicheng Qu, Beijing 100820; tel. (10) 68551114; fax (10) 68551783; e-mail webmaster@mof.gov.cn; internet www.mof.gov.cn.

Ministry of Foreign Affairs: 2 Chao Yang Men, Nan Dajie, Chao Yang Qu, Beijing 100701; tel. (10) 65961114; fax (10) 65962146; e-mail webmaster@mfa.gov.cn; internet www.fmprc.gov.cn.

Ministry of Health: 1 Xizhinenwai Nan Lu, Xicheng Qu, Beijing 100044; tel. (10) 68792114; fax (10) 64012369; e-mail manager@moh.gov.cn; internet www.moh.gov.cn.

Ministry of Housing and Urban-Rural Construction: 9 Sanlihe Lu, Haidian Qu, Beijing 100835; tel. (10) 58934114; e-mail cin@mail.cin.gov.cn; internet www.cin.gov.cn.

Ministry of Human Resources and Social Security: 12 Hepinglizhong Jie, Dongcheng Qu, Beijing 100716; tel. (10) 84201114; fax (10) 64218350; internet www.mohrss.gov.cn.

Ministry of Industry and Information Technology: 13 Xichangan Dajie, Beijing 100804; tel. (10) 66014249; fax (10) 66034248; e-mail mail@miit.gov.cn; internet www.miit.gov.cn.

Ministry of Justice: 10 Chaoyangmen, Nan Dajie, Chao Yang Qu, Beijing 100020; tel. (10) 65205114; fax (10) 65205316; e-mail minister@legalinfo.gov.cn; internet www.moj.gov.cn.

Ministry of Land and Resources: 64 Funei Jie, Xisi, Beijing 100812; tel. (10) 66558407; fax (10) 66127247; e-mail webmaster@mail.mlr.gov.cn; internet www.mlr.gov.cn.

Ministry of National Defence: 20 Jingshanqian Jie, Beijing 100009; tel. (10) 66730000; fax (10) 65962146; e-mail mod@chinamil.com.cn; internet www.mod.gov.cn.

Ministry of Public Security: 14 Dongchangan Dajie, Dongcheng Qu, Beijing 100741; tel. (10) 66262114; fax (10) 65136577; e-mail gabzfwz@mps.gov.cn; internet www.mps.gov.cn.

Ministry of Railways: 10 Fuxing Lu, Haidian Qu, Beijing 100844; tel. (10) 51842281; fax (10) 63242150; internet www.china-mor.gov.cn.

Ministry of Science and Technology: 15B Fuxing Lu, Haidian Qu, Beijing 100862; tel. (10) 58881888; fax (10) 68515006; e-mail officemail@mail.most.gov.cn; internet www.most.gov.cn.

Ministry of State Security: 14 Dongchangan Dajie, Dongcheng Qu, Beijing 100741; tel. (10) 65244702.

Ministry of Supervision: 4 Zaojunmiao, Haidian Qu, Beijing 100081; tel. (10) 62114181; fax (10) 62217692; internet www.mos .gov.cn.

Ministry of Transport: Beijing 100736; tel. (10) 65292818; fax (10) 65292819; e-mail zhenglb@moc.gov.cn; internet www.mot.gov.cn.

Ministry of Water Resources: 2 Baiguang Lu, Xiang 2, Xuanwu Qu, Beijing 100053; tel. (10) 63202114; fax (10) 63202558; e-mail webmaster@mwr.gov.cn; internet www.mwr.gov.cn.

STATE COMMISSIONS

National Development and Reform Commission (NDRC): 38 Yuetannan Jie, Xicheng Qu, Beijing 100824; tel. (10) 68504409; fax (10) 68512929; e-mail ndrc@ndrc.gov.cn; internet www.ndrc.gov.cn.

National Population and Family Planning Commission: 14 Zhichun Lu, Haidian Qu, Beijing 100088; tel. (10) 62046622; fax (10) 62051865; e-mail sfpcdfa@public.bta.net.cn; internet www.npfpc .gov.cn.

State Ethnic Affairs Commission: 252 Taipingqiao Dajie, Xicheng Qu, Beijing 100800; tel. and fax (10) 66508000; fax (10) 66017375; e-mail webmaster@seac.gov.cn; internet www.seac.gov .cn.

People's Governments

PROVINCES

Governors: Wang Sanyun (Anhui), Shu Shulin (Fujian), Liu Weiping (Gansu), Huang Huahua (Guangdong), Zhao Kezhi (Guizhou), Jiang Dingzhi (acting—Hainan), Zhang Qingwei (acting—Hebei), Wang Xiankui (Heilongjiang), Guo Gengmao (Henan), Wang Guosheng (Hubei), Xu Shousheng (Hunan), Li Xueyong (Jiangsu), Lu Xinshe (Jiangxi—acting), Wang Rulin (Jilin), Chen Zhenggao (Liaoning), Luo Huining (Qinghai), Zhao Zhengyong (Shaanxi), Jiang Daming (Shandong), Wang Jun (Shanxi), Jiang Jufeng (Sichuan), Li Jiheng (acting—Yunnan), Xia Baolong (acting—Zhejiang).

SPECIAL MUNICIPALITIES

Mayors: Guo Jinlong (Beijing), Huang Qifan (Chongqing), Han Zheng (Shanghai), Huang Xingguo (Tianjin).

AUTONOMOUS REGIONS

Chairmen: Ma Biao (Guangxi Zhuang), Bagatur (Inner Mongolia—Nei Monggol), Wang Zhengwei (Ningxia Hui), Padma Choling (Tibet—Xizang), Nur Bekri (Xinjiang Uygur).

Legislature

QUANGUO RENMIN DAIBIAO DAHUI

(National People's Congress)

The National People's Congress (NPC) is the highest organ of state power, and is indirectly elected for a five-year term. The first plenary session of the 11th NPC was convened in Beijing in March 2008, and was attended by 2,967 deputies. The first session of the 11th National Committee of the Chinese People's Political Consultative Conference (CPPCC, www.cppcc.gov.cn, Chair. Jia Qinglin), a revolutionary united front organization led by the Communist Party, took place simultaneously. The CPPCC holds discussions and consultations on the important affairs in the nation's political life. Members of the CPPCC National Committee or of its Standing Committee may be invited to attend the NPC or its Standing Committee as observers.

Standing Committee

In March 2008 161 members were elected to the Standing Committee, in addition to the following:

Chairman: Wu Bangguo.

Vice-Chairmen: Wang Zhaoguo, Lu Yongxiang, Uyunqimg, Han Qide, Hua Jianmin, Chen Zhili, Zhou Tienong, Li Jianguo, Ismail Tiliwaldi, Jiang Shusheng, Chen Changzhi, Yan Junqi, Sang Guowei.

Secretary-General: Li Jianguo.

Political Organizations

COMMUNIST PARTY

Zhongguo Gongchan Dang (Chinese Communist Party—CCP): Zhongnanhai, Beijing; f. 1921; 80.3m. mems (Dec. 2010); at the 17th Nat. Congress of the CCP in Oct. 2007, a new Cen. Cttee of 204 full mems and 167 alternate mems was elected; at its first plenary session the 17th Cen. Cttee appointed a new Political Bureau.

Seventeenth Central Committee

General Secretary: Hu Jintao.

Political Bureau (Politburo)

Members of the Standing Committee: Hu Jintao, Wu Bangguo, Wen Jiabao, Jia Qinglin, Li Changchun, Xi Jinping, Li Keqiang, He Guoqiang, Zhou Yongkang.

Other Full Members: Bo Xilai, Gen. Guo Boxiong, Hui Liangyu, Li Yuanchao, Liu Qi, Liu Yandong, Liu Yunshan, Wang Gang, Wang Lequan, Wang Qishan, Wang Yang, Wang Zhaoguo, Xu Caihou, Yu Zhengsheng, Zhang Dejiang, Zhang Gaoli.

Secretariat: Xi Jinping, Liu Yunshan, Li Yuanchao, He Yong, Ling Jihua, Wang Huning.

OTHER POLITICAL ORGANIZATIONS

China Association for Promoting Democracy: 98 Xinanli Guloufangzhuangchang, Beijing 100009; tel. (10) 64033452; f. 1945; 103,000 mems, drawn mainly from literary, cultural and educational circles; 45-mem. Cen. Cttee; Chair. of Cen. Cttee Yan Junqi; Sec.-Gen. Zhao Guanghua.

China Democratic League: 1 Beixing Dongchang Hutong, Dongcheng Qu, Beijing 100006; tel. (10) 65232757; fax (10) 65232852; e-mail bwh@dem-league.org.cn; internet www.dem-league.org.cn; f. 1941; formed from reorganization of League of Democratic Parties and Organizations of China; 196,000 mems, mainly intellectuals active in education, science and culture; Chair. Jiang Shusheng; Sec.-Gen. Gao Shuanping.

China National Democratic Construction Association: 208 Jixiangli, Chaowai Lu, Chao Yang Qu, Beijing 100020; tel. (10) 85698008; fax (10) 85698007; e-mail bgt@cndca.org.cn; internet www .cndca.org.cn; f. 1945; 112,698 mems, mainly industrialists and business executives; Chair. Chen Changzhi; Sec.-Gen. Zhang Jiao.

China Zhi Gong Dang (Party for Public Interests): Beijing; e-mail czgpwz@zg.org.cn; internet www.zg.org.cn; f. 1925; reorg. 1947; 15,000 mems, mainly returned overseas Chinese and scholars; Chair. Wan Gang; Sec.-Gen. Qiu Guoyi.

Chinese Communist Youth League: 10 Qianmen Dong Dajie, Beijing 100051; tel. (10) 67018132; fax (10) 67018131; e-mail gqt@gqt .org.cn; internet www.gqt.org.cn; f. 1922; 68.5m. mems; First Sec. of Cen. Cttee Lu Hao.

Chinese Peasants' and Workers' Democratic Party: 55 An Wai Dajie, Beijing; tel. and fax (10) 84125629; e-mail info@ngdzy.org.cn; internet www.ngd.org.cn; f. 1930; est. as the Provisional Action Cttee of the Kuomintang; took present name in 1947; more than 102,000 mems, active mainly in public health and medicine; Chair. Sang Guowei.

Jiu San (3 September) Society: 14 Wan Quan Xinxin Jiayuan, Wanliu Donglu, Haidian Qu, Beijing 100089; tel. (10) 82552001; fax (10) 82552002; e-mail bwww@93.gov.cn; internet www.93.gov.cn; f. 1946; fmrly Democratic and Science Soc; more than 105,000 mems, mainly scientists and technologists; Chair. Han Qide; Sec.-Gen. Xu Guoquan.

Revolutionary Committee of the Chinese Kuomintang: 84 Donghuang Chenggen Nan Jie, Dongcheng Qu, Beijing 100006; tel. (10) 65595873; fax (10) 65125886; e-mail webmaster@minge .gov.cn; internet www.minge.gov.cn; f. 1948; over 53,000 mems, mainly fmr Kuomintang mems, and those in cultural, educational, health and financial fields; Chair. Zhou Tienong; Sec.-Gen. Qi Xuchun.

Taiwan Democratic Self-Government League: 20 Jingshan Dongjie, Beijing 100009; tel. and fax (10) 64043293; e-mail webmaster@taimeng.org.cn; internet www.taimeng.org.cn; f. 1947; 1,600 mems; recruits Taiwanese living on the mainland; Chair. Lin Wenyi; Sec.-Gen. Zhang Ning.

Diplomatic Representation

EMBASSIES IN THE PEOPLE'S REPUBLIC OF CHINA

Afghanistan: 8 Dong Zhi Men Wai Dajie, Chao Yang Qu, Beijing 100600; tel. (10) 65321582; fax (10) 65322269; e-mail afgemb_beijing@yahoo.com; Ambassador Sultan Ahmad Baheen.

Albania: 28 Guang Hua Lu, Jian Guo Men Wai, Beijing 100600; tel. (10) 65321120; fax (10) 65325451; e-mail embassy.beijing@mfa.gov .al; Ambassador Kujtim Xhani.

Algeria: 7 San Li Tun Lu, Beijing; tel. (10) 65321231; fax (10) 65321648; Ambassador Hassane Rabehi.

Angola: 1-8-1 Tayuan Diplomatic Office Bldg, Chao Yang Qu, Beijing 100600; tel. (10) 65326968; fax (10) 65326992; Ambassador JOÃO GARCIA BIRES.

Argentina: Bldg 11, 5 Dong Wu Jie, San Li Tun, Beijing 100600; tel. (10) 65322090; fax (10) 65322319; e-mail echin@mrecic.gov.ar; Ambassador GUSTAVO ALBERTO MARTINO.

Armenia: 4-1-61 Tayuan Diplomatic Office Bldg, Chao Yang Qu, Beijing 100600; tel. (10) 65325677; fax (10) 65325654; e-mail armchinaembassy@mfa.am; Ambassador ARMEN SARGSYAN.

Australia: 21 Dong Zhi Men Wai Dajie, San Li Tun, Beijing 100600; tel. (10) 51404111; fax (10) 51404204; e-mail pubaff.beijing@dfat.gov.au; internet www.china.embassy.gov.au; Ambassador FRANCES ADAMSON.

Austria: 5 Xiu Shui Nan Jie, Jian Guo Men Wai, Beijing 100600; tel. (10) 65322061; fax (10) 65321505; e-mail peking-ob@bmeia.gv.at; internet www.bmeia.gv.at/botschaft/peking; Ambassador MARTIN SAJDIK.

Azerbaijan: Qijiayuan Diplomatic Compound, Villa No. B-3, Beijing 100600; tel. (10) 65324614; fax (10) 65324615; e-mail mailbox@azerbembassy.org.cn; internet www.azerbembassy.org.cn; Ambassador YASHAR TOFIGI ALIYEV.

Bahamas: 2-4 Tayuan Diplomatic Office Bldg, 14 Liang Ma He Lu, Beijing 100600; tel. (10) 65322922; fax (10) 65322304; e-mail info@bahamasembassy.cn; internet www.bahamasembassy.cn; Ambassador ELMA CAMPBELL.

Bahrain: 10-06 Liang Ma Qiao Diplomatic Residence Compound, 22 Dong Fang Dong Lu, Chao Yang Qu, Beijing; tel. (10) 65326483; fax (10) 65326393; e-mail kingdombahrain@yahoo.cn; internet www.mofa.gov.bh/beijing; Ambassador BIBI SHARAF AL-ALAWI.

Bangladesh: 42 Guang Hua Lu, Beijing 100600; tel. (10) 65322529; fax (10) 65324346; e-mail bdemb@public3.bta.net.cn; internet www.bangladeshembassy.com.cn; Ambassador MUNSHI FAIZ AHMAD.

Barbados: Villa 09-02, Block A, Liang Ma Qiao Diplomatic Compound, 22 Dong Fang Dong Lu, Chao Yang Qu, 100600 Beijing; tel. (10) 85325404; fax (10) 85325437; e-mail beijing@foreign.gov.bb; Ambassador Sir LLOYD ERSKINE SANDIFORD.

Belarus: 1 Dong Yi Jie, Ri Tan Lu, Beijing 100600; tel. (10) 65321691; fax (10) 65326417; e-mail china@belembassy.org; internet www.china.belembassy.org; Ambassador VIKTOR BURYA.

Belgium: 6 San Li Tun Lu, Beijing 100600; tel. (10) 65321736; fax (10) 65325097; e-mail beijing@diplobel.fed.be; internet www.diplomatie.be/beijing; Ambassador PATRICK NIJS.

Benin: 38 Guang Hua Lu, Jian Guo Men Wai, Beijing 100600; tel. (10) 65322741; fax (10) 65325103; Ambassador SEDOZAN APITHY.

Bolivia: 2-3-2 Tayuan Diplomatic Office Bldg, Chao Yang Qu, Beijing 100600; tel. (10) 65323074; fax (10) 65324686; e-mail embolchin@public3.bta.net.cn; internet www.embolchina.com; Ambassador FERNANDO RODRÍGUEZ UREÑA.

Bosnia and Herzegovina: 1-5-1 Tayuan Diplomatic Office Bldg, Chao Yang Qu, Beijing 100600; tel. (10) 65326587; fax (10) 65326418; e-mail ambbhdip@public.bta.net.cn; Ambassador AMEL KOVAČEVIĆ.

Botswana: Unit 811, IBM Tower, Pacific Century Place, 2A Gong Ti Bei Lu, Beijing 100027; tel. (10) 65391616; fax (10) 65391199; e-mail info@botswanaembassy.com; internet www.embbiz.net/com/botswana; Ambassador SASARA CHASALA GEORGE.

Brazil: 27 Guang Hua Lu, Jian Guo Men Wai, Chao Yang Qu, Beijing 100600; tel. (10) 65322881; fax (10) 65322751; e-mail brasemb.pequim@itamaraty.gov.br; internet pequim.itamaraty.gov.br; Ambassador CLODOALDO HUGUENEY FILHO.

Brunei: 1 Liang Ma Qiao Bei Jie, Chao Yang Qu, Beijing 100600; tel. (10) 65329773; fax (10) 65324097; e-mail beb@public.bta.net.cn; Ambassador MAGDALENE TEO CHEE SIONG.

Bulgaria: 4 Xiu Shui Bei Jie, Jian Guo Men Wai, Beijing 100600; tel. (10) 65321946; fax (10) 65324502; e-mail bgembassybeijing@gmail.com; internet www.mfa.bg/en/43/; Ambassador GEORGI PEYCHINOV.

Burundi: 25 Guang Hua Lu, Jian Guo Men Wai, Beijing 100600; tel. (10) 65321801; fax (10) 65322381; e-mail ambbubei@yahoo.fr; Ambassador PASCAL GASUNZU.

Cambodia: 9 Dong Zhi Men Wai Dajie, Beijing 100600; tel. (10) 65321889; fax (10) 65323507; e-mail cambassy@public2.bta.net.cn; Ambassador KHEK CAI MEALY SYSODA.

Cameroon: 7 Dong Wu Jie, San Li Tun, Beijing 100600; tel. (10) 65321828; fax (10) 65321761; e-mail acpk71@hotmail.com; Ambassador MARTIN MPANA.

Canada: 19 Dong Zhi Men Wai Dajie, Chao Yang Qu, Beijing 100600; tel. (10) 51394000; fax (10) 51394454; e-mail beijing-pa@international.gc.ca; internet www.canadainternational.gc.ca/china-chine; Ambassador DAVID MULRONEY.

Cape Verde: 6-2-121 Tayuan Diplomatic Office Bldg, Chao Yang Qu, Beijing 100600; tel. (10) 65327547; fax (10) 65327546; e-mail ecvb@163bj.com; internet bio-visa.com/program/com/cape; Ambassador JULIO CESAR FREIRE DE MORAIS.

Central African Republic: 1-1-132 Tayuan Diplomatic Office Bldg, 1 Xin Dong Lu, Chao Yang Qu, Beijing; tel. 65327353; fax 65327354; e-mail ambrcapk@yahoo.fr; Ambassador EMMANUEL TOUABOY.

Chad: 1 Tayuan Diplomatic Office Bldg, Xin Dong Lu, Chao Yang Qu, Beijing 100600; tel. (10) 85323822; fax (10) 85322783; e-mail ambatchad.beijing@yahoo.fr; Ambassador AHMED SOUNGUI.

Chile: 1 Dong Si Jie, San Li Tun, Beijing 100600; tel. (10) 65321591; fax (10) 65323179; e-mail embachile@echilecn.com; internet chileabroad.gov.cl/china; Ambassador LUIS SCHMIDT MONTES.

Colombia: 34 Guang Hua Lu, Jian Guo Men Wai, Beijing 100600; tel. (10) 65323377; fax (10) 65321969; e-mail ebeijing@cancilleria.gov.co; internet www.embcolch.org.cn; Ambassador CARLOS URREA.

Congo, Democratic Republic: 6 Dong Wu Jie, San Li Tun, Beijing 100600; tel. (10) 65323224; fax (10) 65321360; Ambassador CHARLES MUMBALA NZANKU.

Congo, Republic: 7 Dong Si Jie, San Li Tun, Beijing 100600; tel. (10) 65321658; fax (10) 65322915; Ambassador RIGOBERT ITOUA.

Costa Rica: Jian Guo Men Wai, 1-5-41 Jiao Gong Lu, Beijing 100600; tel. (10) 65324157; fax (10) 65324546; e-mail info@embajadacrchina.org; internet www.embajadacrchina.org; Ambassador MARCO VINICIO RUIZ GUTIÉRREZ.

Côte d'Ivoire: 9 San Li Tun, Bei Xiao Jie, Beijing 100600; tel. (10) 65321223; fax (10) 65322407; Ambassador COFFIE ALAIN NICAISE PAPATCHI.

Croatia: 2-72 San Li Tun Diplomatic Office Bldg, Beijing 100600; tel. (10) 65326241; fax (10) 65326257; e-mail croemb.beijing@mvpei.hr; internet cn.mfa.hr; Ambassador ANTE SIMONIĆ.

Cuba: 1 Xiu Shui Nan Jie, Jian Guo Men Wai, Beijing 100600; tel. (10) 65321714; fax (10) 65322870; e-mail embajada@embacuba.cn; internet embacuba.cubaminrex.cu/china; Ambassador CARLOS MIGUEL PEREIRA.

Cyprus: 2-13-2 Tayuan Diplomatic Office Bldg, 14 Liang Ma He Nan Lu, Chao Yang Qu, Beijing 100600; tel. (10) 65325057; fax (10) 65324244; e-mail cyembpek@public3.bta.net.cn; Ambassador MARIOS IERONYMIDES.

Czech Republic: 2 Ri Tan Lu, Jian Guo Men Wai, Beijing 100600; tel. (10) 85329500; fax (10) 65325653; e-mail beijing@embassy.mzv.cz; internet www.mzv.cz/beijing; Ambassador LIBOR SEČKA.

Denmark: 1 Dong Wu Jie, San Li Tun, Beijing 100600; tel. (10) 85329900; fax (10) 85329999; e-mail bjsamb@um.dk; internet www.ambbeijing.um.dk; Ambassador FRIIS ARNE PETERSEN.

Djibouti: 1-1-122 Tayuan Diplomatic Office Bldg, Chao Yang Qu, Beijing; tel. (10) 65327857; fax (10) 65327858; Ambassador AHMED MOHAMED HASSAN.

Dominica: LA-06 Liang Ma Qiao Diplomatic Residence Compound, 22 Dong Fang Dong Lu, Chao Yang Qu, Beijing 100600; tel. (10) 65320848; fax (10) 65320838; e-mail dominica@dominicaembassy.com; Ambassador DAVID KING HSIU.

Ecuador: 2-62 San Li Tun Office Bldg, Chao Yang Qu, 100600 Beijing; tel. (10) 65320489; fax (10) 65324371; e-mail embecuch@public3bta.net.cn; Ambassador LEONARDO ARÍZAGA.

Egypt: 2 Ri Tan Dong Lu, Jian Guo Men Wai, Beijing 100600; tel. (10) 65321825; fax (10) 65325365; e-mail eg_emb_bj@yahoo.com; internet www.mfa.gov.eg/Beijing_Emb; Ambassador AHMED REZK.

Equatorial Guinea: 2 Dong Si Jie, San Li Tun, Beijing; tel. (10) 65323679; fax (10) 65323805; e-mail emguies@yahoo.com; Ambassador MARCOS MBA ONDO.

Eritrea: 2-10-1 Tayuan Diplomatic Office Bldg, Chao Yang Qu, Beijing 100600; tel. (10) 65326534; fax (10) 65326532; Ambassador TSEGGAI TESFATSION SEREKE.

Estonia: C-617–618 Office Bldg, Beijing Lufthansa Center, 50 Liang Ma Qiao Lu, Chao Yang Qu, Beijing 100125; tel. (10) 64637913; fax (10) 64637908; e-mail embassy.beijing@mfa.ee; internet www.peking.vm.ee; Ambassador ANDRES UNGA.

Ethiopia: 3 Xiu Shui Nan Jie, Jian Guo Men Wai, Beijing 100600; tel. (10) 65325258; fax (10) 65325591; e-mail ethchina@public3.bta.net.cn; internet www.ethiopiaemb.org.cn; Ambassador SEYOUM MESFIN.

Fiji: 1-15-2 Tayuan Diplomatic Office Bldg, 14 Liang Ma He Nan Lu, San Li Tun, Chao Yang Qu, Beijing 100600; tel. (10) 65327305; fax (10) 65327253; e-mail info@fijiembassy.org.cn; internet bio-visa.com/program/com/fiji; Ambassador Cdre ESALA TELENI.

Finland: Beijing Kerry Centre, 26/F South Tower, 1 Guanghua Lu, Beijing 100020; tel. (10) 85198300; fax (10) 85198301; e-mail sanomat.pek@formin.fi; internet www.finland.cn; Ambassador LARS BACKSTRÖM.

France: 3 Dong San Jie, San Li Tun, Chao Yang Qu, Beijing 100600; tel. (10) 85328080; fax (10) 85324841; e-mail presse@ambafrance-cn

.org; internet www.ambafrance-cn.org; Ambassador SYLVIE BERMANN.

Gabon: 36 Guang Hua Lu, Jian Guo Men Wai, Beijing 100600; tel. (10) 65322810; fax (10) 65322621; Ambassador EMMANUEL MBA-ALLO.

Georgia: LA-03-02, Section A, Liang Ma Qiao Diplomatic Compound, Beijing; tel. (10) 65327518; fax (10) 65327519; e-mail geobeijing@gmail.com; internet www.china.mfa.gov.ge; Ambassador KARLO SIKHARULIDZE.

Germany: 17 Dong Zhi Men Wai Dajie, Chao Yang Qu, Beijing 100600; tel. (10) 85329000; fax (10) 65325336; e-mail embassy@peking.diplo.de; internet www.peking.diplo.de; Ambassador Dr MICHAEL SCHAEFER.

Ghana: 8 San Li Tun Lu, Beijing 100600; tel. (10) 65321319; fax (10) 65323602; e-mail ghmfa85@yahoo.com; Ambassador HELEN MAMLE KOFI.

Greece: 17/F The Place Tower, 9 Guang Hua Lu, Jian Guo Men Wai, Chao Yang Qu, Beijing 100020; tel. (10) 65872838; fax (10) 65872839; e-mail gremb.pek@mfa.gr; internet www.grpressbeijing.com; Ambassador THEODOROS GEORGAKELOS.

Grenada: T5-2-52 Tayuan Diplomatic Office Bldg, Chao Yang Qu, Beijing 100600; tel. (10) 65321208; fax (10) 65321015; e-mail grenembbeijing@yahoo.com; Ambassador F. MARCELLE GAIRY.

Guinea: 2 Xi Liu Jie, San Li Tun, Beijing 100600; tel. (10) 65323649; fax (10) 65324957; Ambassador DIARE MAMADY.

Guinea-Bissau: 2-2-101 Tayuan Diplomatic Compound, Chao Yang Qu, Beijing; tel. (10) 65327393; fax (10) 65327106; Ambassador ARAFAN ANSU CAMARA.

Guyana: 1 Xiu Shui Dong Jie, Jian Guo Men Wai, Beijing 100600; tel. (10) 65321601; fax (10) 65325741; e-mail guyemb@public3.bta.net.cn; Ambassador DAVID DABYDEEN.

Hungary: 10 Dong Zhi Men Wai Dajie, San Li Tun, Beijing 100600; tel. (10) 65321431; fax (10) 65325053; e-mail mission.pek@kum.hu; internet www.mfa.gov.hu/kulkepviselet/CN; Ambassador SÁNDOR KUSAI.

Iceland: Landmark Tower 1, 802, 8 Dongsanhuan Bei Lu, Beijing 100004; tel. (10) 65907795; fax (10) 65907801; e-mail emb.beijing@mfa.is; internet www.iceland.org/cn; Ambassador KRISTIN ÁRNADÓTTIR.

India: 1 Ri Tan Dong Lu, Jian Guo Men Wai, Beijing 100600; tel. (10) 65321908; fax (10) 65324684; e-mail sscom@indianembassy.org.cn; internet www.indianembassy.org.cn; Ambassador S. JAISHANKAR.

Indonesia: 4 Dong Zhi Men Wai Dajie, Beijing 100600; tel. (10) 65325486; fax (10) 65325368; e-mail set.beijing.kbri@kemlu.go.id; internet www.kemlu.go.id/beijing; Ambassador IMRON COTAN.

Iran: 13 Dong Liu Jie, San Li Tun, Beijing 100600; tel. (10) 65322040; fax (10) 65321403; Ambassador MEHDI SAFARI.

Iraq: 25 Xiu Shui Bei Jie, Jian Guo Men Wai, Beijing 100600; tel. (10) 65323385; fax (10) 65321599; e-mail bknemb@iraqmofamail.net; Ambassador ABDUL KARIM HASHIM MUSTAFA.

Ireland: 3 Ri Tan Dong Lu, Jian Guo Men Wai, Beijing 100600; tel. (10) 65322691; fax (10) 65326857; e-mail beijing@dfa.ie; internet www.embassyofireland.cn; Ambassador DECLAN KELLEHER.

Israel: 17 Tian Ze Lu, Chao Yang Qu, Beijing 100600; tel. (10) 85320500; fax (10) 85320555; e-mail info@beijing.mfa.gov.il; internet beijing.mfa.gov.il; Ambassador AMOS NADAI.

Italy: 2 Dong Er Jie, San Li Tun, Beijing 100600; tel. (10) 85327600; fax (10) 65324676; e-mail ambasciata.pechino@esteri.it; internet www.ambpechino.esteri.it; Ambassador ATTILIO MASSIMO IANNUCCI.

Jamaica: 6-2-72 Jian Guo Men Wai Diplomatic Compound, 1 Xiu Shui Jie, Beijing 100600; tel. (10) 65320667; fax (10) 65320669; e-mail embassy@jamaicagov.cn; internet www.jamaicagov.cn; Ambassador EARLE COURTENAY RATTRAY.

Japan: 7 Ri Tan Lu, Jian Guo Men Wai, Beijing 100600; tel. (10) 65322361; fax (10) 65324625; e-mail info@eoj.cn; internet www.cn.emb-japan.go.jp; Ambassador UICHIRO NIWA.

Jordan: 5 Dong Liu Jie, San Li Tun, Beijing 100600; tel. (10) 65323906; fax (10) 65323283; e-mail beijing@fm.gov.jo; Ambassador ANMAR ABDULHALIM NAMIR HARMUD.

Kazakhstan: 9 Dong Liu Jie, San Li Tun, Beijing 100600; tel. (10) 65324189; fax (10) 65326183; e-mail kz@kazembchina.org; internet www.kazembchina.org; Ambassador IKRAM ADYRBEKOV.

Kenya: 4 Xi Liu Jie, San Li Tun, Beijing 100600; tel. (10) 65323381; fax (10) 65321770; e-mail info@kenyaembassy.cn; internet www.kenyaembassy.cn; Ambassador JULIUS LEKAKENY OLE SUNKULI.

Korea, Democratic People's Republic: 11 Ri Tan Bei Lu, Jian Guo Men Wai, Beijing 100600; tel. (10) 65321186; fax (10) 65326056; Ambassador JI JAE RYONG.

Korea, Republic: 20 Dong Fang Dong Lu, Chao Yang Qu, Beijing 100600; tel. (10) 85310700; fax (10) 85320726; e-mail chinawebmaster@mofat.go.kr; internet www.koreanembassy.cn; Ambassador LEE KYU-HYUNG.

Kuwait: 23 Guang Hua Lu, Jian Guo Men Wai, Beijing 100600; tel. (10) 65322216; fax (10) 65321607; e-mail beijing@mofa.gov.kw; Ambassador MUHAMMAD SALEH AL-THUWAIKH.

Kyrgyzstan: H-10–11 King's Garden Villas, 18 Xiao Yun Lu, Chao Yang Qu, Beijing 100125; tel. (10) 64681297; fax (10) 64681291; e-mail kyrgyz.embassy.china@gmail.com; internet www.kyrgyzstanembassy.net; Ambassador JEENBEK KULUBAYEV.

Laos: 11 Dong Si Jie, San Li Tun, Chao Yang Qu, Beijing 100600; tel. (10) 65321224; fax (10) 65326748; e-mail laoemcn@public.east.cn.net; Ambassador SOMDY BOUNKHOUM.

Latvia: Unit 71, Green Land Garden, 1A Green Land Rd, Chao Yang Qu, Beijing 100016; tel. (10) 64333863; fax (10) 64333810; e-mail embassy.china@mfa.gov.lv; internet www.latvianembassy.org.cn; Ambassador INGRIDA LEVRENCE.

Lebanon: 10 Dong Liu Jie, San Li Tun, Beijing 100600; tel. (10) 65323281; fax (10) 65322770; e-mail lebanon@public.bta.net.cn; Ambassador (vacant).

Lesotho: 302 Dong Wai Diplomatic Office Bldg, 23 Dong Zhi Men Wai Dajie, Chao Yang Qu, Beijing 100600; tel. (10) 65326843; fax (10) 65326845; e-mail lesotho-brussels@foreign.gov.ls; Ambassador RACHOBOKOANE ANTHONY THIBELI.

Liberia: Rm 013, Gold Island Diplomatic Compound, 1 Xi Ba He Nan Lu, Beijing 100028; tel. (10) 64403007; fax (10) 64403918; Ambassador NEH RITA SANGAI DUKULY TOLBERT.

Libya: 3 Dong Liu Jie, San Li Tun, Beijing 100600; tel. (10) 65323666; fax (10) 65323391; Ambassador TAHER E. A. JEHAIMI.

Lithuania: A-18 King's Garden Villas, 18 Xiaoyun Lu, Chao Yang Qu, Beijing 100125; tel. (10) 84518520; fax (10) 84514442; e-mail amb.cn@urm.lt; internet cn.mfa.lt; Ambassador LINA ANTANAVICIENE.

Luxembourg: 1701, Tower B, Pacific Century Place, 2A Gong Ti Bei Lu, Chao Yang Qu, Beijing 100027; tel. (10) 85880900; fax (10) 65137268; e-mail pekin.amb@mae.etat.lu; internet pekin.mae.lu; Ambassador CARLO KRIEGER.

Macedonia, former Yugoslav republic: 1-32 San Li Tun Diplomatic Office Bldg, Beijing 100600; tel. (10) 65327846; fax (10) 65327847; e-mail beijing@mfa.gov.mk; Ambassador OLIVER SAMBEVSKI.

Madagascar: 3 Dong Jie, San Li Tun, Beijing 100600; tel. (10) 65321353; fax (10) 65322102; e-mail ambpek@public2.bta.net.cn; Ambassador VICTOR SIKONINA.

Malawi: 503 Dong Wai Diplomatic Office Bldg, 23 Dong Zhi Men Wai Dajie, Beijing 100600; tel. (10) 65325889; fax (10) 65326022; Ambassador CHARLES ENOCH NAMONDWE.

Malaysia: 2 Liang Ma Qiao Bei Jie, Chao Yang Qu, San Li Tun, Beijing 100600; tel. (10) 65322531; fax (10) 65325032; e-mail mwbjing@kln.gov.my; internet www.kln.gov.my/web/chn_beijing; Ambassador Datuk ISKANDAR BIN SARUDIN.

Maldives: 1-5-31 Jian Guo Men Wai Diplomatic Compound, Jianwai Xiushui Lu, Chao Yang Qu, Beijing 100600; tel. (10) 85323847; fax (10) 85323746; e-mail admin@maldivesembassy.cn; internet www.maldivesembassy.cn; Ambassador AHMED LATHEEF.

Mali: 8 Dong Si Jie, San Li Tun, Beijing 100600; tel. (10) 65321704; fax (10) 65321618; e-mail ambamali@163bj.com; Ambassador N'TJI LAICO TRAORÉ.

Malta: 1-52 San Li Tun Diplomatic Compound, Gong Ti Bei Lu, Beijing 100600; tel. (10) 65323114; fax (10) 65326125; e-mail maltamembassy.beijing@gov.mt; internet www.mfa.gov.mt/china; Ambassador JOSEPH CASSAR.

Mauritania: 9 Dong San Jie, San Li Tun, Beijing 100600; tel. (10) 65321346; fax (10) 65321685; e-mail ambarim@ambarim-beijing.com; internet ambarim-beijing.com; Ambassador MOHAMED EL-HABIB BAL.

Mauritius: 202 Dong Wai Diplomatic Office Bldg, 23 Dong Zhi Men Wai Dajie, Chao Yang Qu, Beijing 100600; tel. (10) 65325695; fax (10) 65325706; e-mail mebj@public.bta.net.cn; Ambassador PAUL REYNOLD LIT FONG CHONG LEUNG.

Mexico: 5 Dong Wu Jie, San Li Tun, Beijing 100600; tel. (10) 65321717; fax (10) 65323744; e-mail embmxchn@public.bta.net.cn; internet www.sre.gob.mx/china; Ambassador JORGE EUGENIO GUAJARDO GONZÁLEZ.

Micronesia, Federated States: 1-1-11 Jian Guo Men Wai Diplomatic Compound, Chao Yang Qu, Beijing 100010; tel. (10) 65324738; fax (10) 65324609; e-mail embassy@fsmembassy.cn; Ambassador AKILLINO H. SUSAIA.

Moldova: 2-9-1 Tayuan Diplomatic Office Bldg, Chao Yang Qu, Beijing 100600; tel. (10) 65325494; fax (10) 65325379; e-mail beijing@mfa.md; Ambassador ANATOL URECHEANU.

Mongolia: 2 Xiu Shui Bei Jie, Jian Guo Men Wai, Beijing 100600; tel. (10) 65321203; fax (10) 65325045; e-mail mail@

mongolembassychina.org; internet www.mongolembassychina.org; Ambassador TSEDENJAVIIN SUKHBAATAR.

Montenegro: 3-1-12 San Li Tun Diplomatic Compound, Beijing 100600; tel. (10) 65327610; fax (10) 65327662; e-mail china@mfa.gov.me; Ambassador LJILJANA TOSKOVIĆ.

Morocco: 16 San Li Tun Lu, Beijing 100600; tel. (10) 65321489; fax (10) 65321453; e-mail sifama.beijing@moroccoembassy.org.cn; Ambassador JAAFAR ALJ HAKIM.

Mozambique: 1-7-2 Tayuan Diplomatic Office Bldg, Chao Yang Qu, Beijing 100600; tel. (10) 65323664; fax (10) 65325189; e-mail embamoc@embmoz.org; Ambassador ANTÓNIO INÁCIO JÚNIOR.

Myanmar: 6 Dong Zhi Men Wai Dajie, Chao Yang Qu, Beijing 100600; tel. (10) 65320351; fax (10) 65320408; e-mail info@myanmarembassy.com; internet www.myanmarembassy.com; Ambassador TIN OO.

Namibia: 2-9-2 Tayuan Diplomatic Office Bldg, Chao Yang Qu, Beijing 100600; tel. (10) 65324810; fax (10) 65324549; e-mail namemb@eastnet.com.cn; Ambassador LEONARD NAMBAHU.

Nepal: 1 Xi Liu Jie, San Li Tun Lu, Beijing 100600; tel. (10) 65322739; fax (10) 65323251; e-mail beijing@nepalembassy.org.cn; internet www.nepalembassy.org.cn; Ambassador TANKA KARKI.

Netherlands: 4 Liang Ma He Nan Lu, Beijing 100600; tel. (10) 85320200; fax (10) 85320300; e-mail pek@minbuza.nl; internet www.hollandinchina.org; Ambassador RUDOLF BEKINK.

New Zealand: 1 Ri Tan, Dong Er Jie, Chao Yang Qu, Beijing 100600; tel. (10) 85327000; fax (10) 65324317; e-mail beijing.enquiries@mft.net.nz; internet www.nzembassy.com/china; Ambassador CARL ROBINSON WORKER.

Niger: 1-21 San Li Tun, Beijing 100600; tel. (10) 65324279; fax (10) 65327041; e-mail nigerbj@public.bta.net.cn; Ambassador ADAMOU BOUBAKAR.

Nigeria: 2 Dong Wu Jie, San Li Tun, Beijing; tel. (10) 65323631; fax (10) 65321650; e-mail nigerianembassybj@yahoo.com; internet www.nigeriaembassy.cn; Ambassador AMINU BASHIR WALI.

Norway: 1 Dong Yi Jie, San Li Tun, Beijing 100600; tel. (10) 85319600; fax (10) 65322392; e-mail emb.beijing@mfa.no; internet www.norway.cn; Ambassador SVEIN OLE SÆTHER.

Oman: 6 Liang Ma He Nan Lu, San Li Tun, Beijing 100600; tel. (10) 65323692; fax (10) 65327185; Ambassador ABDULLAH SALEH AL-SAADII.

Pakistan: 1 Dong Zhi Men Wai Dajie, San Li Tun, Beijing 100600; tel. (10) 65322504; fax (10) 65322715; e-mail info@pakembassy.cn; internet www.pakembassy.cn; Ambassador MASOOD KHAN.

Papua New Guinea: 2-11-2 Tayuan Diplomatic Office Bldg, Chao Yang Qu, Beijing 100600; tel. (10) 65324312; fax (10) 65325483; e-mail kundu_beijing@pngembassy.org.cn; internet en.pngembassy.org.cn; Ambassador CHRISTOPHER SIAOA MERO.

Peru: 1-91 San Li Tun, Bangonglou, Beijing 100600; tel. (10) 65323477; fax (10) 65322178; e-mail embaperu-pekin@rree.gob.pe; internet bio-visa.com/program/com/peru; Ambassador HAROLD FORSYTH MEJÍA.

Philippines: 23 Xiu Shui Bei Jie, Jian Guo Men Wai, Beijing 100600; tel. (10) 65321872; fax (10) 65323761; e-mail beijing.pe@dfa.gov.ph; internet www.philembassychina.org; Ambassador DOMINGO LEE.

Poland: 1 Ri Tan Lu, Jian Guo Men Wai, Chao Yang Qu, Beijing 100600; tel. (10) 65321235; fax (10) 65321745; e-mail polska@public2.bta.net.cn; internet www.pekin.polemb.net; Ambassador TADEUSZ CHOMICKI.

Portugal: 8 San Li Tun Dong Wu Jie, Beijing 100600; tel. (10) 65323242; fax (10) 65324637; e-mail embport@public2.bta.net.cn; Ambassador JOSÉ SOARES.

Qatar: A-7 Liang Ma Qiao Diplomatic Compound, Chao Yang Qu, Beijing 100600; tel. (10) 6532231; fax (10) 65325274; e-mail beijing@mofa.gov.qa; Ambassador ABDULLA A. AL-MUFTAH.

Romania: Ri Tan Lu, Dong Er Jie, Beijing 100600; tel. (10) 65323442; fax (10) 65325728; e-mail ambasada@roamb.link263.com; internet www.beijing.mae.ro; Chargé d'affaires a.i. ION DICU.

Russia: 4 Dong Zhi Men Nei, Bei Zhong Jie, Beijing 100600; tel. (10) 65322051; fax (10) 65324851; e-mail embassy@russia.org.cn; internet www.russia.org.cn; Ambassador SERGEI SERGEEVICH RAZOV.

Rwanda: 30 Xiu Shui Bei Jie, Jian Guo Men Wai, Beijing 100600; tel. (10) 65322193; fax (10) 65322006; e-mail ambabeijing@minaffet.gov.rw; internet www.china.embassy.gov.rw; Ambassador FRANÇOIS XAVIER NGARAMBE.

Samoa: 2-7-2 Tayuan Diplomatic Office Bldg, 14 Liang Ma He Nan Lu, Chao Yang Qu, Beijing 100600; tel. (10) 65321673; fax 65321642; Ambassador TAPUSALAIA TOOMATA.

Saudi Arabia: 1 Bei Xiao Jie, San Li Tun, Beijing 100600; tel. (10) 65324825; fax (10) 65325324; Ambassador YAHYA AL-ZAID.

Senegal: 305 Dong Wai Diplomatic Office Bldg, 23 Dong Zhi Men Wai Dajie, Beijing 100600; tel. (10) 65325035; fax (10) 65323730; Ambassador Gen. PAPE KHALILOU FALL.

Serbia: 1 Dong Liu Jie, San Li Tun, Beijing 100600; tel. (10) 65323516; fax (10) 65321207; e-mail embserbia@embserbia.cn; internet www.embserbia.cn; Ambassador MIOMIR UDOVICKI.

Seychelles: Rm 1105, The Spaces International Center, 8 Dong Da Qiao, Chao Yang Qu, Beijing 100020; tel. (10) 58701192; fax (10) 58701219; e-mail amb.legall@yahoo.com; Ambassador PHILIPPE LE GALL.

Sierra Leone: 7 Dong Zhi Men Wai Dajie, Beijing 100600; tel. (10) 65322174; fax (10) 65323752; e-mail slbeijing@foreignaffairs.gov.sl; Ambassador JOSEPH M. KOROMA.

Singapore: 1 Xiu Shui Bei Jie, Jian Guo Men Wai, Chao Yang Qu, Beijing 100600; tel. (10) 65321115; fax (10) 65329405; e-mail singemb_bej@sgmfa.gov.sg; internet www.mfa.gov.sg/beijing; Ambassador CHIN SIAT-YOON.

Slovakia: Ri Tan Lu, Jian Guo Men Wai, Beijing 100600; tel. (10) 65321531; fax (10) 65324814; e-mail emb.beijing@mzv.sk; internet www.mzv.sk/peking; Ambassador FRANTIŠEK DLHOPOLČEK.

Slovenia: Block F, 57 Ya Qu Yuan, King's Garden Villas, 18 Xiao Yun Lu, Chao Yang Qu, Beijing 100016; tel. (10) 64681030; fax (10) 64681040; e-mail vpe@gov.si; internet beijing.embassy.si; Ambassador MARIJA ADANJA.

Somalia: 2 San Li Tun Lu, Beijing 100600; tel. and fax (10) 65321651; fax (10) 65321752; e-mail somaliaemb.beij@yahoo.com; Ambassador MOHAMMED AHMED AWIL.

South Africa: 5 Dong Zhi Men Wai Dajie, Chao Yang Qu, Beijing 100600; tel. (10) 85320000; fax (10) 65327319; e-mail embassy@saembassy.org.cn; internet www.saembassy.org.cn; Ambassador W. J. LANGA.

Spain: 9 San Li Tun Lu, Beijing 100600; tel. (10) 65323629; fax (10) 65323401; e-mail embespcn@mail.mae.es; internet www.mae.es/embajadas/pekin; Ambassador EUGENIO BREGOLAT OBIOLS.

Sri Lanka: 3 Jian Hua Lu, Jian Guo Men Wai, Beijing 100600; tel. (10) 65321861; fax (10) 65325426; e-mail lkembj@public3.bta.net.cn; internet www.slemb.com; Ambassador KARUNATILAKA AMUNUGAMA.

Sudan: 1 Dong Er Jie, San Li Tun, Beijing 100600; tel. (10) 65323715; fax (10) 65321280; Ambassador MIRGHANI MOHAMED SALIH.

Suriname: 2-2-22 Jian Guo Men Wai Diplomatic Compound, Beijing 100600; tel. (10) 65322938; fax (10) 65322941; e-mail surinamechina@gmail.com; Ambassador (vacant).

Sweden: 3 Dong Zhi Men Wai Dajie, San Li Tun, Beijing 100600; tel. (10) 65329790; fax (10) 65325008; e-mail ambassaden.peking@foreign.ministry.se; internet www.swedenabroad.com/peking; Ambassador LARS FREDÉN.

Switzerland: 3 Dong Wu Jie, San Li Tun, Beijing 100600; tel. (10) 85328888; fax (10) 65324353; e-mail bei.vertretung@eda.admin.ch; internet www.eda.admin.ch/beijing; Ambassador BLAISE GODET.

Syria: 6 Dong Si Jie, San Li Tun, Beijing 100600; tel. (10) 65321372; fax (10) 65321575; e-mail sy@syria.org.cn; internet www.syria.org.cn; Ambassador Dr KHALAF AL-JARAD.

Tajikistan: 5-1-41 Tayuan Diplomatic Office Bldg, Chao Yang Qu, Beijing 100600; tel. (10) 65322598; fax (10) 65323039; e-mail tjkemb@public2.bta.net.cn; Ambassador RASHID ALIMOV.

Tanzania: 8 Liang Ma He Nan Lu, San Li Tun, Beijing 100600; tel. (10) 65321719; fax (10) 65324351; e-mail beijing@tanzaniaembassy.org.cn; internet www.tanzaniaembassy.org.cn; Ambassador OMAR RAMADHAN MAPURI.

Thailand: 40 Guang Hua Lu, Jian Guo Men Wai, Beijing 100600; tel. (10) 65321749; fax (10) 65321748; e-mail thaibej@public.bta.net.cn; internet www.thaiembbeij.org; Ambassador PIAMSAK MILINTACHINDA.

Timor-Leste: Rm 156, Gold Island Diplomatic Compound, 1 Xi Ba He Nan Lu, Beijing 100028; tel. (10) 64403072; fax (10) 64403071; e-mail rdtlemb_beijing04@yahoo.com; Ambassador VICKY FUN HA TCHONG.

Togo: 11 Dong Zhi Men Wai Dajie, Beijing 100600; tel. (10) 65322202; fax (10) 65325884; Ambassador NOLANA TA-AMA.

Tonga: 1-2-11 Jian Guo Men Wai Diplomatic Compound, Beijing 100600; tel. (10) 65327203; fax (10) 65327204; Ambassador SIAMELIE LATU.

Tunisia: 1 Dong Jie, San Li Tun, Chao Yang Qu, Beijing 100600; tel. (10) 65322435; fax (10) 65325818; e-mail at_beijing@netchina.com.cn; Ambassador Dr MOHAMED ADEL SMAOUI.

Turkey: 9 Dong Wu Jie, San Li Tun, Beijing 100600; tel. (10) 65321715; fax (10) 65325480; e-mail embassy.beijing@mfa.gov.tr; internet beijing.emb.mfa.gov.tr; Ambassador MURAT SALIM ESENLI.

Turkmenistan: D-1 King's Garden Villas, 18 Xiao Yuan Lu, Beijing; tel. (10) 65326975; fax (10) 65326976; e-mail embturkmen@netchina.com.cn; Ambassador GRUBANNAZAR NAZAROV.

Uganda: 5 Dong Jie, San Li Tun, Beijing 100600; tel. (10) 65321708; fax (10) 65322242; Ambassador CHARLES MADIBO WAGIDOSO.

Ukraine: 11 Dong Liu Jie, San Li Tun, Beijing 100600; tel. (10) 65326359; fax (10) 65324014; e-mail gc_cnp@mfa.gov.ua; internet www.mfa.gov.ua/china; Ambassador YURII KOSTENKO.

United Arab Emirates: LA-10-04 Liang Ma Qiao Diplomatic Compound, 22 Dong Fang Dong Lu, Beijing; tel. (10) 65327651; fax (10) 65327652; e-mail beijing@mofa.gov.ae; Ambassador OMAR AHMED OUDAI NASEEB AL-BETAR.

United Kingdom: 11 Guang Hua Lu, Jian Guo Men Wai, Beijing 100600; tel. (10) 51924000; fax (10) 51924239; e-mail consular.beijing@fco.gov.uk; internet www.ukinchina.fco.gov.uk; Ambassador SEBASTIAN WOOD.

USA: 3 Xiu Shui Bei Jie, Jian Guo Men Wai, Beijing 100600; tel. (10) 85313000; fax (10) 85314200; e-mail ircacee@state.gov; internet beijing.usembassy-china.org.cn; Ambassador GARY LOCKE.

Uruguay: 1-11-2 Tayuan Diplomatic Office Bldg, Chao Yang Qu, Beijing 100600; tel. (10) 65324445; fax (10) 65327375; e-mail urubei@public.bta.net.cn; Ambassador ROSARIO PORTELL.

Uzbekistan: 11 Bei Xiao Jie, San Li Tun, Beijing 100600; tel. (10) 65326305; fax (10) 65326304; Ambassador ALISHER A. SALAHITDINOV.

Vanuatu: 3-1-11 San Li Tun Diplomatic Compound, Chao Yang Qu, Beijing 100600; tel. (10) 65320337; fax (10) 65320336; e-mail info@vanuatuembassy.org.cn; internet www.vanuatuembassy.org.cn; Ambassador WILLIE JIMMY TAPANGARARUA.

Venezuela: 14 San Li Tun Lu, Beijing 100600; tel. (10) 65321295; fax (10) 65323817; e-mail embvenez@public.bta.net.cn; internet www.venezuela.org.cn; Ambassador ROCÍO MANEIRO GONZÁLEZ.

Viet Nam: 32 Guang Hua Lu, Jian Guo Men Wai, Beijing 100600; tel. (10) 65321155; fax (10) 65325720; e-mail suquanbk@yahoo.com; internet www.vnemba.org.cn; Ambassador NGUYEN VAN THO.

Yemen: 5 Dong San Jie, San Li Tun, Beijing 100600; tel. (10) 65321558; fax (10) 65327997; e-mail info@embassyofyemen.net; internet www.embassyofyemen.net; Ambassador ABDULMALEK SULAIMAN M. AL-MUALEMI.

Zambia: 5 Dong Si Jie, San Li Tun, Chao Yang Qu, Beijing 100600; tel. (10) 65321554; fax (10) 65321891; e-mail admin@zambiaembassy-beijing.com; internet www.zambiaembassy-beijing.com; Ambassador JOYCE MWAKA CHEMBE MUSENGE.

Zimbabwe: 7 Dong San Jie, San Li Tun, Beijing 100600; tel. (10) 65323795; fax (10) 65325383; e-mail zimbei@163.bj.com; Ambassador FREDERICK M. SHAVA.

Judicial System

The general principles of the Chinese judicial system are laid down in Articles 123–135 of the 1982 Constitution.

PEOPLE'S COURTS

Supreme People's Court: 27 Dongjiaomin Xiang, Beijing 100745; tel. (10) 67550114; e-mail info@court.gov.cn; internet www.court.gov.cn; f. 1949; the highest judicial organ of the State; handles first instance cases of national importance; handles cases of appeals and protests lodged against judgments and orders of higher people's courts and special people's courts, and cases of protests lodged by the Supreme People's Procuratorate in accordance with the procedures of judicial supervision; reviews death sentences meted out by local courts, supervises the administration of justice by local people's courts; interprets issues concerning specific applications of laws in judicial proceedings; its judgments and rulings are final; Pres. WANG SHENGJUN (five-year term of office coincides with that of National People's Congress, by which the President is elected).

Local People's Courts: comprise higher courts, intermediate courts and basic courts.

Special People's Courts: include military courts, maritime courts and railway transport courts.

PEOPLE'S PROCURATORATES

Supreme People's Procuratorate: 147 Beiheyan Dajie, Beijing 100726; tel. (10) 65209114; e-mail web@spp.gov.cn; internet www.spp.gov.cn; acts for the National People's Congress in examining govt depts, civil servants and citizens, to ensure observance of the law; prosecutes in criminal cases; Procurator-Gen. CAO JIANMING (elected by the National People's Congress for a five-year term).

Local People's Procuratorates: undertake the same duties at the local level; ensure that the judicial activities of the people's courts, the execution of sentences in criminal cases and the activities of departments in charge of reform through labour conform to the law; institute, or intervene in, important civil cases that affect the interest of the State and the people.

Religion

The 1982 Constitution states that citizens enjoy freedom of religious belief and that legitimate religious activities are protected. Since 1994 all religious organizations have been required to register with the Bureau of Religious Affairs. In the late 1990s a new religious sect, Falun Gong (also known as Falun Dafa, and incorporating elements of Buddhism and Daoism) emerged and quickly gained new adherents. However, the authorities banned the group in 1999.

State Administration for Religious Affairs: 32 Beisantiao, Jiaodaokou, Dongcheng Qu, Beijing 100007; tel. (10) 64023355; fax (10) 66013565; Dir WANG ZUOAN.

ANCESTOR WORSHIP

Ancestor worship is believed to have originated with the deification and worship of all important natural phenomena. The divine and human were not clearly defined; all the dead became gods and were worshipped by their descendants. The practice has no code or dogma, and the ritual is limited to sacrifices made during festivals and on birth and death anniversaries.

BUDDHISM

Buddhism was introduced into China from India in AD 67, and flourished during the Sui and Tang dynasties (6th–8th century), when eight sects were established. The Chan and Pure Land sects are the most popular. The dominant religion of Tibet (Xizang) is Tibetan Buddhism or Lamaism, a branch of Vajrayana Buddhism.

Buddhist Association of China (BAC): f. 1953; Pres. YIN CHUAN; Sec.-Gen. XUE CHENG.

Tibetan Institute of Lamaism: Pres. BUMI JANGBALUOZHU; Vice-Pres. CEMOLIN DANZENGCHILIE.

14th Dalai Lama: His Holiness the Dalai Lama TENZIN GYATSO; spiritual leader of Tibet; fled to India following the failure of the Tibetan national uprising in 1959; resident at: Thekchen Choeling, McLeod Ganj, Dharamsala 176 219, Himachal Pradesh, India; tel. (91) 1892-21343; fax (91) 1892-21813; e-mail ohhdl@cta.unv.ernet.ind; internet www.tibet.com.

CHRISTIANITY

In the early 21st century there was a revival of interest in the Christian faith. The official Catholic Church in China operates independently of the Vatican. The 'underground' Catholic Church is recognized by the Vatican. Various Christian sects have continued to expand in China. By 2009 the number of Chinese Christians had reached an estimated 130m. Of these, 100m. were believed to be independent worshippers, with only 21m. adhering to the official Protestant Church and 5m. to the approved Catholic Church.

Three-Self Patriotic Movement Committee of Protestant Churches of China: 219 Jiujiang Lu, Shanghai 200002; tel. (21) 63210806; fax (21) 63232605; e-mail tspmccc@online.sh.cn; Chair. Rev. FU XIANWEI; Gen. Sec. Rev. XU XIAOHONG.

China Christian Council: 219 Jiujiang Lu, Shanghai 200002; tel. (21) 63210806; fax (21) 63232605; e-mail tspmccc@online.sh.cn; f. 1980; comprises provincial Christian councils; Pres. Rev. K. H. TING; Gen. Sec. Rev. KAN BAOPING.

The Catholic Church: Catholic Mission, Si-She-Ku, Beijing; Bishop of Beijing JOSEPH LI SHAN.

Chinese Patriotic Catholic Association: Pres. JOHN FANG XINGYAO; Sec.-Gen. LIU BAINIAN.

CONFUCIANISM

Confucianism is a philosophy and a system of ethics, without ritual or priesthood. The respect that adherents accord to Confucius is not bestowed on a prophet or god, but on a great sage whose teachings promote peace and good order in society and whose philosophy encourages moral living.

DAOISM

Daoism was founded by Zhang Daoling during the Eastern Han dynasty (AD 125–144). Lao Zi, a philosopher of the Zhou dynasty (born 604 BC), is its principal inspiration, and is honoured as Lord the Most High by Daoists. According to unofficial sources, there were 1,600 Daoist temples in China in 2005.

China Daoist Association: Temple of the White Cloud, Xi Bian Men, Beijing 100045; tel. (10) 63406670; e-mail chinadaosim@yahoo.com.cn; internet www.taoist.org.cn; f. 1957; Pres. REN FARONG; Sec.-Gen. YUAN BINGDONG.

ISLAM

Islam was introduced into China in AD 651. There were some 20.3m. adherents in China in 2000 according to official sources, mainly among the Wei Wuer (Uygur) and Hui people, although unofficial sources estimate that the total is far higher.

Beijing Islamic Association: Dongsi Mosque, Beijing; f. 1979; Chair. Imam Al-Hadji CHEN GUANGYUAN.

China Islamic Association: Beijing 100053; tel. (10) 63546384; fax (10) 63529483; internet www.chinaislam.net.cn; f. 1953; Chair. Imam Al-Hadji CHEN GUANGYUAN; Sec.-Gen. YU ZHENGUI.

The Press

In 2009 China had 1,937 newspaper titles (including those below provincial level) and 9,851 magazines. Each province publishes its own daily newspaper. The major newspapers and periodicals are listed below.

PRINCIPAL NEWSPAPERS

Anhui Ribao (Anhui Daily): 1469 Zhongshan Lu, Hefei, Anhui 230071; tel. (551) 5179860; fax (551) 2832534; e-mail ahch2005@163.com; internet www.anhuinews.com; Editor-in-Chief SUN BANGKUN.

Beijing Ribao (Beijing Daily): 20 Jian Guo Men Nei Dajie, Beijing 100734; tel. (10) 85201843; fax (10) 65136522; internet www.bjd.com.cn; f. 1952; organ of the Beijing municipal cttee of the CCP; Dir WAN YUNLAI; Editor-in-Chief LIU ZONGMING; circ. 700,000.

Beijing Wanbao (Beijing Evening News): 20 Jian Guo Men Nei Dajie, Beijing 100734; tel. 8008108440 (mobile); fax (10) 65126581; internet www.ben.com.cn; f. 1958; Editor-in-Chief REN HUANYING; circ. 800,000.

Beijing Youth Daily: Beijing; tel. (10) 65901655; e-mail jubao@ynet.com; internet bjyouth.ynet.com; national and local news; promotes ethics and social service; circ. 3m.–4m.

Changsha Wanbao (Changsha Evening News): 161 Caie Zhong Lu, Changsha, Hunan 410005; tel. (731) 4424457; fax (731) 4445167.

Chengdu Wanbao (Chengdu Evening News): Qingyun Nan Jie, Chengdu 610017; tel. (28) 664501; fax (28) 666597; circ. 700,000.

China Economic Times: Palace St, Changping Qu, Beijing 102209; tel. (10) 81785100; fax (10) 81785120; e-mail cesnew@163.com; internet www.jjxww.com; economic news; publ. by the Development Research Centre of the State Council.

China Times: Wanda Plaza, 93 Jianguo Lu, Chaoyang Qu, Beijing 100022; tel. (10) 59250005; internet www.chinatimes.cc; f. 1989; finance; weekly.

Chongqing Ribao (Chongqing Daily): Chongqing; Dir and Editor-in-Chief LI HUANIAN.

Chungcheng Wanbao (Chungcheng Evening News): 51 Xinwen Lu, Kunming, Yunnan 650032; tel. (871) 4144642; fax (871) 4154192.

Dazhong Ribao (Dazhong Daily): Dazhong News Bldg, 4/F, 6 Luoyuan Dajie, Jinan, Shandong 250014; tel. (531) 85193611; fax (531) 2962450; internet www.dzwww.com; f. 1939; Dir XU XIYU; Editor-in-Chief LIU GUANGDONG; circ. 2,100,000.

Fujian Ribao (Fujian Daily): 84 Hualin Lu, Fuzhou, Fujian; tel. (591) 87079319; e-mail fjnet.cn@163.com; internet www.fjdaily.com; daily; Dir HUANG SHIYUN; Editor-in-Chief HUANG ZHONGSHENG.

Gansu Ribao (Gansu Daily): Gansu; tel. (931) 8157213; fax (931) 8158955; e-mail gansudaily@163.com; internet www.gansudaily.com.cn.

Gongren Ribao (Workers' Daily): Dongcheng Qu, Beijing 100718; tel. (10) 84151567; fax (10) 84151516; e-mail news@workercn.cn; internet www.workercn.cn; f. 1949; trade union activities and workers' lives; also major home and overseas news; Dir LIU YUMING; Editor-in-Chief SHENG MINGFU; circ. 2,500,000.

Guangming Ribao (Guangming Daily): 5 Dong Lu, Chongwen Qu, Zhushikou, 100062; tel. (10) 67078856; fax (10) 67078854; e-mail webmaster@gmw.cn; internet www.gmw.cn; f. 1949; literature, art, science, education, history, economics, philosophy; Editor-in-Chief YUAN ZHIFA; circ. 920,000.

Guangxi Ribao (Guangxi Daily): Guangxi Region; tel. (771) 5690995; fax (771) 5690933; e-mail newgx@gxrb.com.cn; internet www.gxnews.com.cn; Dir and Editor-in-Chief CHENG ZHENSHENG; circ. 650,000.

Guangzhou Ribao (Canton Daily): 10 Dongle Lu, Renmin Zhonglu, Guangzhou, Guangdong; tel. (20) 81919191; fax (20) 81862022; internet gzdaily.dayoo.com; f. 1952; daily; social, economic and current affairs; Editor-in-Chief LI YUANJIANG; circ. 600,000.

Guizhou Ribao (Guizhou Daily): Guiyang, Guizhou; tel. (851) 6793333; fax (851) 6625615; internet gzrb.gog.com.cn; f. 1949; Dir GAO ZONGWEN; Editor-in-Chief GAN ZHENGSHU; circ. 300,000.

Hainan Ribao (Hainan Daily): News Bldg, 9/F, Haikou, Hainan 570001; tel. (898) 66810815; fax (898) 66810545; e-mail hnrb@hndaily.com.cn; internet hnrb.hinews.cn; Dir ZHOU WENZHANG; Editor-in-Chief CHANG FUTANG.

Harbin Ribao (Harbin Daily): Harbin; internet www.harbindaily.com.

Hebei Ribao (Hebei Daily): 210 Yuhuazhong Lu, Shijiazhuang, Hebei 050013; tel. (311) 88631054; fax (311) 6046969; e-mail webmaster@hebeidaily.com; internet hebnews.cn; f. 1949; Dir GUO ZENGPEI; Editor-in-Chief PAN GUILIANG; circ. 500,000.

Heilongjiang Ribao (Heilongjiang Daily): Heilongjiang Province; tel. (451) 84656368; e-mail hljnews@hljnews.cn; internet www.hljnews.cn; Dir JIA HONGTU; Editor-in-Chief AI HE.

Henan Ribao (Henan Daily): Henan Newspaper Network Center, 10/F, 28 East Agriculture Rd, Zhengzhou, Henan 450008; tel. and fax (371) 65795870; e-mail dahenews@dahe.cn; internet www.dahe.cn; f. 1949; Dir YANG YONGDE; Editor-in-Chief GUO ZHENGLING; circ. 390,000.

Huadong Xinwen (Eastern China News): f. 1995; published by Renmin Ribao.

Huanan Xinwen (South China News): Guangzhou; f. 1997; published by Renmin Ribao.

Hubei Ribao (Hubei Daily): Metropolis Media Bldg, 13/F, 181 Wuchang Dong Wu Lu, Wuhan, Hubei 430077; tel. (27) 88567711; e-mail webmaster@cnhubei.com; internet www.cnhubei.com; f. 1949; Editor-in-Chief YAN SITIAN; circ. 800,000.

Hulunbeir Ribao (Hulunbeir Daily): 28 Victory Ave, Hahilar, Hulunbeir; tel. (470) 8252039; fax (470) 8258035; e-mail hlbrdaily@163.com; internet www.hlbrdaily.com.cn.

Hunan Ribao (Hunan Daily): 18 Furong Zhong Lu, Changsha, Hunan 410071; tel. (731) 4312999; fax (731) 4314029; Dir JIANG XIANLI; Editor-in-Chief WAN MAOHUA.

Jiangxi Ribao (Jiangxi Daily): 175 Yangming Jie, Nanchang, Jiangxi; tel. (791) 6849868; fax (791) 6849008; internet www.jxnews.com.cn/jxrb; f. 1949; Dir ZHOU JINGUANG; circ. 300,000.

Jiefang Ribao (Liberation Daily): 300 Han Kou Lu, Shanghai 200001; tel. (21) 63521111; fax (21) 63516517; e-mail info@jfdaily.com; internet www.jfdaily.com.cn; f. 1949; Editor-in-Chief JIA SHUMEI; circ. 1m.

Jiefangjun Bao (Liberation Army Daily): 34 Fuchengmenwai Dajie, Xicheng Qu, Beijing 100832; tel. (10) 68577779; fax (10) 68577779; e-mail feedback@jfjb.com.cn; internet www.chinamil.com.cn; f. 1956; official organ of the Central Military Commission; Dir Maj.-Gen. ZHANG SHIGANG; Editor-in-Chief WANG MENGYUN; circ. 800,000.

Jilin Ribao (Jilin Daily): Changchun, Jilin Province; tel. (431) 88600621; fax (431) 88600622; e-mail news@chinajilin.com.cn; internet www.chinajilin.com.cn; Dir and Editor-in-Chief YI HONGBIN.

Jingji Ribao (Economic Daily): 2 Bai Zhi Fang Dong Jie, Xuanwu Qu, Beijing 100054; tel. (10) 83512266; fax (10) 83543336; e-mail en_feedback@mail.ce.cn; internet www.ce.cn; f. 1983; financial affairs, domestic and foreign trade; administered by the State Council; Editor-in-Chief TUO ZHEN; circ. 1.2m.

Jinrong Shibao (Financial News): 18 Zhongguancun Nan Dajie, 18–22/F, Blk D, Haidan Qu, Beijing 100081; tel. (10) 82198111; fax (10) 82198029; e-mail fnweb@126.com; internet www.financialnews.com.cn.

Liaoning Ribao (Liaoning Daily): Shenyang, Liaoning Province; tel. (10) 22698539; e-mail lnd@lndaily.com.cn; internet www.lndaily.com.cn; Dir XIE ZHENGQIAN.

Nanfang Ribao (Nanfang Daily): 289 Guangzhou Da Lu, Guangzhou, Guangdong 510601; tel. (20) 87373998; fax (20) 87375806; internet nf.nfdaily.cn; f. 1949; Nanfang Daily Group also publishes *Nanfang Dushi Bao* (Southern Metropolis Daily), *Ershiyi Shiji Jingji Baodao* (21st Century Economic Herald), and weekly edn *Nanfang Zhoumou* (Southern Weekend); Dir YANG XINFENG; Editor WANG FU; circ. 1m.

Nanjing Ribao (Nanjing Daily): 223 Nanjing Lu, Shanghai 210002; tel. (25) 84499000; internet njrb.njnews.cn.

Nongmin Ribao (Peasants' Daily): Shilipu Beili, Chao Yang Qu, Beijing 100029; tel. (10) 85831572; fax (10) 85832154; e-mail zbs@farmer.com.cn; internet www.farmer.com.cn/wlb/nmrb; f. 1980; 6 a week; circulates in rural areas nation-wide; Dir ZHANG DEXIU; Editor LIU ZHENYUN; circ. 1m.

Renmin Ribao (People's Daily): 2 Jin Tai Xi Lu, Chao Yang Qu, Beijing 100733; tel. (10) 65363470; fax (10) 65363689; e-mail info@peopledaily.com.cn; internet www.people.com.cn; f. 1948; organ of the CCP; also publishes overseas edn; Pres. ZHANG YANNONG; Editor-in-Chief WU HENGQUAN; circ. 2.15m.

Shaanxi Ribao (Shaanxi Daily): 1 East Ring Rd, Xian, Shaanxi Province 710054; tel. (29) 82267114; fax (29) 82267082; e-mail sxdaily@tom.com; internet www.sxdaily.com.cn; Dir LI DONGSHENG; Editor-in-Chief DU YAOFENG.

Shanxi Ribao (Shanxi Daily): 124 Shuangtasi Jie, Taiyuan, Shanxi; tel. (351) 4281494; fax (351) 4283320; internet www.sxrb.com; CEO LIU XINYU; Editor-in-Chief HU KAIMIN; circ. 300,000.

Shenzhen Tequ Bao (Shenzhen Special Economic Zone Daily): 4 Shennan Zhonglu, Shenzhen 518009; tel. (755) 83518877; e-mail sznews@sznews.com; internet www.sznews.com; f. 1982; reports on special economic zones, as well as mainland, Hong Kong and Macao; Editor-in-Chief HUANG YANGLUE.

Sichuan Ribao (Sichuan Daily): Sichuan Daily Press Group, 70 Hongxing Zhong Lu, Erduan, Chengdu, Sichuan 610012; tel. and fax (28) 86968000; e-mail 028@scol.com.cn; internet www.sichuandaily.com.cn; f. 1952; Chair. of Bd YU CHANGQIU; Editor-in-Chief LUO XIAOGANG; circ. 8m.

Tianjin Ribao (Tianjin Daily): Tianjin Bldg, 10/F, 873 Dagu Nan Lu, Heri Qu, Tianjin 300211; tel. (22) 28201063; fax (22) 28201064; e-mail tjw@tjrb.com.cn; internet www.tianjinwe.com; f. 1949; Editor-in-Chief WANG HONG; circ. 600,000.

Wenhui Bao (Wenhui Daily): 50 Huqiu Lu, Shanghai 200002; tel. (21) 63211410; fax (21) 63230198; internet wenhui.news365.com.cn; f. 1938; Editor-in-Chief WU ZHENBIAO; circ. 500,000.

Xin Jing Bao (The Beijing News): 37 Xingfu Bei Lu, Dongcheng Qu, Beijing 100061; tel. (10) 67106666; fax (10) 67106777; e-mail shepingbj@vip.sina.com; internet www.bjnews.com.cn; f. 2003 as jt venture by owners of Guangming Ribao and Nanfang Ribao; Editor-in-chief (vacant).

Xin Min Wan Bao (Xin Min Evening News): 839 Yan An Zhong Lu, Shanghai 200040; tel. (21) 62791234; fax (21) 62473220; e-mail newmedia@wxjt.com.cn; internet xmwb.news365.com.cn; f. 1929; specializes in public policy, education and social affairs; Editor-in-Chief HU JINGJUN; circ. 1.8m.

Xinhua Ribao (New China Daily): Dacheng Plaza, 20/F, 127 Xuanwumen Xi Lu, Beijing 100031; tel. (10) 63070950; fax (10) 63070938; e-mail xhszbs@xinhuanet.com; internet www.xinhuanet.com; Editor-in-Chief HE PING; circ. 900,000.

Xinjiang Ribao (Xinjiang Daily): Daily News Bldg, 11/F, Yangtze River Rd, Urumqi, Xinjiang 830051; tel. (991) 5593345; fax (991) 5859962; e-mail info@xjdaily.com; internet www.xjdaily.com; Editor-in-Chief HUANG YANCAI.

Xizang Ribao (Tibet Daily): Lhasa, Tibet; Editor-in-Chief LI ERLIANG.

Yangcheng Wanbao (Yangcheng Evening News): 733 Dongfeng Dong Lu, Yangcheng Wanbao Bldg, 7/F, Guangzhou, Guangdong 510085; tel. (20) 87319116; fax (20) 87133836; e-mail kefu@ycwb.net; internet www.ycwb.com; f. 1957; Editor-in-Chief PAN WEIWEN; circ. 1.3m.

Yunnan Ribao (Yunnan Daily): 51 Xinwen Lu, Kunming 650032; tel. (871) 4160447; fax (871) 4156165; e-mail ynrb-zbs@yndaily.com; internet www.yndaily.com; Editor-in-Chief LUO JIE.

Zhejiang Ribao (Zhejiang Daily): Zhejiang Province; tel. (571) 85310961; e-mail zjrb@zjnews.com.cn; internet zjdaily.zjol.com.cn; f. 1949; Pres. GAO HAIHAO; Editor-in-Chief YANG DAJIN.

Zhongguo Qingnian Bao (China Youth Daily): 2 Haiyuncang, Dong Zhi Men Nei, Dongcheng Qu, Beijing 100702; tel. (10) 64098088; fax (10) 64098077; e-mail cyd@cyd.net.cn; internet www.cyol.com; f. 1951; daily; aimed at 14–40 age-group; Dir XU ZHUQING; Editor-in-Chief CHEN XIAOCHUAN; circ. 1.0m.

Zhongguo Ribao (China Daily): 15 Huixin Dong Jie, Chao Yang Qu, Beijing 100029; tel. (10) 64995000; fax (10) 64918377; internet www.chinadaily.com.cn; f. 1981; English; China's political, economic and cultural developments; world, financial and sports news; also publishes *Business Weekly* (f. 1985), *Beijing Weekend* (f. 1991), *Shanghai Star* (f. 1992), *Reports from China* (f. 1992), *21st Century* (f. 1993), *China Daily Hong Kong Edition*; Editor-in-Chief ZHU LING; circ. 300,000.

Zhongguo Xinwen (China News): 12 Baiwanzhuang Nan Jie, Beijing 100037; tel. (10) 87826688; fax (10) 68327649; e-mail gaojian@chinanews.com.cn; internet www.chinanews.com; f. 1952; daily; current affairs; Editor-in-Chief WANG XIJIN.

SELECTED PERIODICALS

Ban Yue Tan (China Comment): Shijingshan Qu, Beijing 100043; tel. (10) 63074102; fax (10) 63074105; e-mail news_byt@xinhua.org; internet www.xinhuanet.com/banyt; f. 1980; in Chinese and Wei Wuer (Uygur); Editor-in-Chief DONG RUISHENG; circ. 6m.

Beijing Review: 24 Baiwanzhuang Lu, Xicheng Qu, Beijing 100037; tel. (10) 68996288; fax (10) 68328738; e-mail contact@bjreview.com.cn; internet www.bjreview.com.cn; f. 1958; weekly; English; also *Chinafrica* (monthly in English and French); Publr WANG GANGYI; Editor-in-Chief LII HAIBO.

BJ TV Weekly: 2 Fu Xing Men Wai Zhenwumiao Jie, Beijing 100045; tel. (10) 6366036; fax (10) 63262388; circ. 1m.

Caijing: 19th Floor, Prime Tower 22 Chaoyangmenwai Lu, Beijing 100020; tel. (10) 65885047; fax (10) 65885046; e-mail newsroom@caijing.com.cn; internet www.caijing.com.cn; f. 1998; business and finance; 2 a month; Editor WANG BOMING.

China TV Weekly: 15 Huixin Dong Jie, Chao Yang Qu, Beijing 100013; tel. (10) 64214197; circ. 1.7m.

Chinese Literature Press: 24 Baiwanzhuang Lu, Beijing 100037; tel. (10) 68326010; fax (10) 68326678; e-mail chinalit@public.east.cn.net; f. 1951; monthly (bilingual in English); quarterly (bilingual in French); contemporary and classical writing, poetry, literary criticism and arts; Exec. Editor LING YUAN.

Chinese National Geography: Rm 200, Jia 11, Datun Rd, Chaoyang Qu, Beijing 100101; tel. (10) 64865566; fax (10) 64859755; e-mail bjb@cng.com.cn; internet cng.dili360.com; f. 1950; monthly; world geography, anthropology and nature; Editor LI SHUAN.

Dianying Xinzuo (New Films): 796 Huaihai Zhong Lu, Shanghai; tel. (21) 64379710; f. 1979; bi-monthly; introduces new films.

Dianzi yu Diannao (Compotech China): Beijing; tel. (10) 82563704; fax (10) 82563744; e-mail jane_ma@compotech.com.cn; internet www.compotech.com.cn; f. 1985; popular information on computers and microcomputers; Editorial Man. MALAN JUAN.

Elle (China): 14 Lane 955, Yan'an Zhong Lu, Shanghai; tel. (21) 62790974; fax (21) 62479056; internet www.ellechina.com; f. 1988; monthly; fashion; Publr and Editor-in-Chief XIAO XUE; circ. 300,000.

Guoji Xin Jishu (New International Technology): Zhanwang Publishing House, Beijing; f. 1984; also publ. in Hong Kong; international technology, scientific and technical information.

Guowai Keji Dongtai (Recent Developments in Science and Technology Abroad): Institute of Scientific and Technical Information of China, 54 San Li He Lu, Beijing 100045; tel. (10) 58882491; fax (10) 58882288; e-mail kjdt@istic.ac.cn; internet www.wanfang.com.cn; f. 1962; monthly; scientific journal; Editor-in-Chief GUO YUEHUA; circ. 40,000.

Huasheng Monthly (Voice for Overseas Chinese): 12 Bai Wan Zhuang Nan Jie, Beijing 100037; tel. and fax (10) 68315039; internet www.chinaqw.com; f. 1995; monthly; intended mainly for overseas Chinese and Chinese nationals resident abroad; Editor-in-Chief FAN DONGSHENG.

Jianzhu (Construction): Baiwanzhuang, Beijing; tel. (10) 68992849; f. 1956; monthly; Editor FANG YUEGUANG; circ. 500,000.

Jinri Zhongguo (China Today): 24 Baiwanzhuang Lu, Beijing 100037; tel. (10) 68996376; fax (10) 68328338; e-mail chinatodaynews@yahoo.com.cn; internet www.chinatoday.com.cn; f. 1952; fmrly China Reconstructs; monthly; edns in English, Spanish, French, Arabic and Chinese; economic, social and cultural affairs; illustrated; Pres. and Editor-in-Chief HUANG ZU'AN.

Liaowang (Outlook): 57 Xuanwumen Xijie, Beijing; tel. (10) 63073049; internet news.sohu.com/liaowang; f. 1981; weekly; current affairs; Gen. Man. ZHOU YICHANG; Editor-in-Chief JI BIN; circ. 500,000.

Luxingjia (Traveller): Beijing; tel. (10) 6552631; f. 1955; monthly; Chinese scenery, customs, culture.

Meishu Zhi You (Chinese Art Digest): 32 Beizongbu Hutong, East City Region, Beijing; tel. (10) 65591404; f. 1982; every 2 months; art review journal, also providing information on fine arts publs in China and abroad; Editors ZONGYUAN GAO, PEI CHENG.

Nongye Zhishi (Agricultural Knowledge): 21 Ming Zi Qian Lu, Jinan, Shandong 250100; tel. (531) 88935267; fax (531) 88550734; e-mail sdnyzs@jn-public.sd.cninfo.net; internet www.sdny.com.cn; f. 1950; fortnightly; popular agricultural science; Dir YANG LIJIAN; circ. 410,000.

Puzhi (Reader's Digest): Reader's Digest (Shanghai) Advertising Co Ltd, Raffles City Tower, Tibet Rd, Shanghai 200021; tel. (21) 61030347; fax (21) 61030388; e-mail friends@puzhi.com.cn; internet www.readersdigest.cn; f. 2008; monthly; general interest; Editor-in-Chief WANG YOU-BU.

Qiushi (Seeking Truth): 83 Beiheyan Dajie, Dongcheng Qu, Beijing 100727; tel. (10) 64037005; fax (10) 64022727; e-mail qiushi@qstheory.com; internet www.qsjournal.com.cn; f. 1988; succeeded Hong Qi (Red Flag); 2 a month; theoretical journal of the CCP; Editor-in-Chief LI BAOSHAN; circ. 1.83m.

Renmin Huabao (China Pictorial): 33 Chegongzhuang Xilu, Haidian Qu, Beijing 100044; tel. (10) 88417467; fax (10) 68412601; e-mail cnpictorial@gmail.com; internet www.chinapictorial.com.cn; f. 1950; monthly; edns: two in Chinese, one in Tibetan and 12 in foreign languages; Dir and Editor-in-Chief ZHANG JIAHUA.

Shufa (Calligraphy): 81 Qingzhou Nan Lu, Shanghai 200233; tel. (21) 64519008; fax (21) 64519015; f. 1977; every 2 months; journal on ancient and modern calligraphy; Chief Editor LU FUSHENG.

Stories: 74 Shaoxing Lu, Shanghai 200020; tel. and fax (21) 64677160; e-mail storychina@gmail.com; internet www.storychina .cn; f. 1963; bi-monthly; short stories, fiction, comics; Editor HE CHENGWEI.

Tiyu Kexue (Sports Science): 11 Tiyuguan Lu, Beijing 100061; tel. (10) 87182588; fax (10) 67181293; f. 1981; sponsored by the China Sports Science Soc; monthly; in Chinese; summary in English; Chief Officer TIAN YE; circ. 5,000.

Wenxue Qingnian (Youth Literature Journal): 27 Mu Tse Fang, Wenzhou, Zhejiang; tel. (577) 3578; f. 1981; monthly; Editor-in-Chief CHEN YUSHEN; circ. 80,000.

Window of the South: Guangzhou; tel. (20) 61036188; fax (20) 61036195; e-mail window@vip.163.com; internet www.nfcmag.com; bi-monthly; politics and current affairs; Editorial Dir ZHAO LINGMIN.

Women of China English Monthly: Rm 814, 15 Jianguonei Dajie, Beijing, 100730; tel. (10) 65103411; fax (10) 65225376; e-mail womenofchina@gmail.com; internet www.womenofchina.com.cn; f. 1956; monthly; in English; administered by All-China Women's Federation; women's rights and status, views and lifestyle, education and arts, etc.; Editor-in-Chief PENGJU YUN.

Xian Dai Faxue (Modern Law Science): Southwest University of Political Science and Law, Chongqing, Sichuan 400031; tel. (23) 67258823; fax (23) 67258826; e-mail xiandaifaxue@126.com; internet www.swupl.edu.cn; f. 1979; bi-monthly; with summaries in English; Editor-in-Chief SUN CHANGYONG.

Zhongguo Sheying (Chinese Photography): South Tower Bldg, Rm 502, 67 Campbell St, Dongheng Qu, Dongdan, Beijing 100005; tel. (10) 65252277; fax (10) 65257623; e-mail cphotoeditor@sina.com; internet www.cphoto.com.cn; f. 1957; monthly; photographs and comments; Editor WEN DANQING.

Zhongguo Zhenjiu (Chinese Acupuncture and Moxibustion): China Academy of Traditional Chinese Medicine, 16 Nan Xiao Jie, Dongzhimen Nei, Beijing 100700; tel. (10) 84014607; fax (10) 84046331; e-mail zhenjiubj@vip.sina.com; internet www .cjacupuncture.com; f. 1981; monthly; publ. by Chinese Soc. of Acupuncture and Moxibustion; abstract in English; Editor-in-Chief Prof. DENG LIANGYUE.

Other popular magazines include *Gongchandang Yuan* (Communists, circ. 1.63m.) and *Nongmin Wenzhai* (Peasants' Digest, circ. 3.54m.).

NEWS AGENCIES

Xinhua (New China) News Agency: 57 Xuanwumen Xi Dajie, Beijing 100803; tel. (10) 63071114; fax (10) 63071210; e-mail xhszbs@xinhuanet.com; internet www.xinhuanet.com; f. 1931; offices in all Chinese provincial capitals, and about 100 overseas bureaux; news service in Chinese, English, French, Spanish, Portuguese, Arabic and Russian, feature and photographic services; CNC World (China Xinhua News Network Corporation) commenced television broadcasts in Jan. 2010; 24-hour English-language news channel began broadcasting in July; Pres. LI CONGJUN; Editor-in-Chief HE PING.

Zhongguo Xinwen She (China News Service): 12 Baiwanzhuang Nan Jie, Beijing 100037; tel. (10) 87826688; fax (10) 68327649; e-mail hezuo@chinanews.com.cn; internet www.chinanews.com; f. 1952; office in Hong Kong; supplies news features, special articles and photographs for newspapers and magazines in Chinese printed overseas; services in Chinese; Dir WANG SHIGU.

PRESS ORGANIZATIONS

All China Journalists' Association: Xijiaominxiang, Beijing 100031; tel. (10) 66023981; fax (10) 66014658; Chair. TIAN CONG MING.

China Newspapers Association: Beijing; Chair. WANG CHEN.

The Press and Publication Administration of the People's Republic of China (State Copyright Bureau): 85 Dongsi Nan Dajie, East District, Beijing 100703; tel. (10) 65124433; fax (10) 65127875; Dir SHI ZONGYUAN.

Publishers

A total of 301,719 books were published in 2009.

Beijing Chubanshe Chuban Jituan (Beijing Publishing House Group): 6 Bei Sanhuan Zhong Lu, Beijing 100011; tel. (10) 58572219; fax (10) 58572220; e-mail public@bphg.com.cn; internet www.bph .com.cn; f. 1956; politics, history, law, economics, geography, science, literature, art, etc.; Dir ZHU SHUXIN; Editor-in-Chief TAO XINCHENG.

Beijing Daxue Chubanshe (Peking University Press): 205 Chengfu Lu, Zhongguancun, Haidian Qu, Beijing 100871; tel. (10) 62752033; fax (10) 62556201; e-mail zpup@pup.cn; internet www .pup.cn; f. 1979; academic and general; Pres. WANG MINGZHOU.

China International Book Trading Corpn: 35 Chegongzhuang Xilu, Beijing 100044; tel. (10) 68412045; fax (10) 68412023; e-mail cibtc@mail.cibtc.com.cn; internet www.cibtc.com.cn; f. 1949; foreign trade org. specializing in publs, including books, periodicals, art and crafts, microfilms, etc.; import and export distributors; Pres. QI PINGJIN.

China Publishing Group (CPG): 55A Dajie, Dongcheng Qu, Beijing; tel. and fax (10) 59757238; e-mail zq@cnpubg.com; internet www.cnpubg.com; f. 2002; aims to restructure and consolidate publishing sector; comprises 29 major publishing houses, including the People's Publishing House, the Commercial Press, Zhonghua Book Co, Encyclopedia of China Publishing House, China Fine Arts Publishing Group, People's Music Publishing House, SDX Joint Publishing Co, China Translation and Publishing Corpn, Orient Publishing Centre; Pres. NIE ZHENNING.

CITIC Publishing House: 8–10/F, Fusheng Bldg Tower 2, Huixindong Jie 4, Chao Yang Qu, Beijing 100029; tel. (10) 84849555; fax (10) 84849000; e-mail liyinghong@citicpub.com; internet www .publish.citic.com; f. 1988; finance, investment, economics and business; Pres. WANG BIN.

Dianzi Gongye Chubanshe (Publishing House of the Electronics Industry—PHEI): 288 Jin Jia Cun, Wanshou Nan Lu, Beijing 100036; tel. (10) 88258888; fax (10) 68159025; internet www.phei .com.cn; f. 1982; electronic sciences and technology; Pres. LIANG XIANGFENG; Vice-Pres. WANG MINGJUN.

Dolphin Books: 24 Baiwanzhuang Lu, Beijing 100037; tel. (10) 68997480; fax (10) 68993503; e-mail dolphin_books@sina.cn; internet www.dolphin-books.com.cn; f. 1986; children's books in Chinese and foreign languages; Dir WANG YANRONG.

Falü Chubanshe (Law Publishing House): Lianhuachi Xili, Fengtai Qu, Beijing 100073; tel. (10) 63939796; fax (10) 63939622; e-mail info@lawpress.com.cn; internet www.lawpress.com.cn; f. 1980; current laws and decrees, legal textbooks, translations of important foreign legal works; Pres. MIN HUANG.

Foreign Languages Press: 19 Chegongzhuang Xi Lu, Fu Xing Men Wai, Beijing 100044; tel. (10) 68413344; fax (10) 68424931; e-mail wwdinggou@cipg.org.cn; internet www.flp.com.cn; f. 1952; books in 20 foreign languages reflecting political and economic devts in China and features of Chinese culture; Pres. HU BAOMIN; Editor-in-Chief LI ZHENGUO.

Gaodeng Jiaoyu Chubanshe (Higher Education Press): 4 Dewai Dajie, Xicheng Qu, Beijing 100011; tel. (10) 82085550; fax (10) 82085552; e-mail international@hep.edu.cn; internet www.hep.edu .cn; f. 1954; academic, textbooks; Pres. LIU ZHIPENG; Editor-in-Chief ZHANG ZENGSHUN.

Gongren Chubanshe (Workers' Publishing House): Liupukeng, Andingmen Wai, Beijing; tel. (10) 64215278; f. 1949; labour movement, trade unions, science and technology related to industrial production.

Guangdong Keji Chubanshe (Guangdong Science and Technology Press): 11 Shuiyin Lu, Huanshidong Lu, Guangzhou, Guangdong 510075; tel. and fax (20) 37607770; e-mail gdkjzbb@21cn.com; internet www.gdstp.com.cn; f. 1978; natural sciences, technology, agriculture, medicine, computing, English language teaching; Dir HUANG DAQUAN.

Heilongjiang Kexue Jishu Chubanshe (Heilongjiang Science and Technology Press): 41 Jianshe Jie, Nangang Qu, Harbin 150001, Heilongjiang; tel. and fax (451) 3642127; f. 1979; industrial and agricultural technology, natural sciences, economics and management, popular science, children's and general.

Huashan Wenyi Chubanshe (Huashan Literature and Art Publishing House): 45 Bei Malu, Shijiazhuang, Hebei; tel. (0311) 22501; f. 1982; novels, poetry, drama, etc.

Kexue Chubanshe (Science Press): 16 Donghuangchenggen Beijie, Beijing 100717; tel. (10) 64034313; fax (10) 64020094; e-mail webmaster@mail.sciencep.com; internet www.sciencep.com; f. 1954; books and journals on science and technology.

Lingnan Meishu Chubanshe (Lingnan Art Publishing House): 11 Shuiyin Lu, Guangzhou, Guangdong 510075; tel. (20) 87771044; fax (20) 87771049; f. 1981; works on classical and modern painting, picture albums, photographic, painting techniques; Pres. CAO LIXIANG.

Minzu Chubanshe (The Ethnic Publishing House): 14 Anwai Hepingli Beijie, Beijing 100013; tel. and fax (10) 64211126; e-mail e56@e56.com.cn; internet www.e56.com.cn; f. 1953; books and periodicals in minority languages, e.g. Mongolian, Tibetan, Uygur, Korean, Kazakh, etc.; Editor-in-Chief HUANG ZHONGCAI.

Qunzhong Chubanshe (Masses Publishing House): Bldg 15, Part 3, Fangxingyuan, Fangzhuan Lu, Beijing 100078; tel. (10) 67633344; f. 1956; politics, law, judicial affairs, criminology, public security, etc.

Renmin Chubanshe (People's Publishing House): 8 Hepinglidongjie, Andingmenwai, Beijing; tel. (10) 4213713; f. 1950; publishes works on Marxism-Leninism, Mao Zedong Thought and Deng Xiaoping Theory, collected works and biographies of Chinese leaders, academic works in philosophy, social sciences, arts and culture, biography etc.; Dir and Editor-in-Chief XUE DEZHEN.

Renmin Jiaoyu Chubanshe (People's Education Press): 17-1 Zhongguancun Nan Dajie, Haidian, Beijing 100081; tel. (10) 58758866; fax (10) 58758877; e-mail pep@pep.com.cn; internet www.pep.com.cn; f. 1950; school textbooks, guidebooks, teaching materials, etc.

Renmin Meishu Chubanshe (People's Fine Arts Publishing House): Beijing; tel. (10) 65122371; fax (10) 65122370; f. 1951; works by Chinese and foreign painters, sculptors and other artists, picture albums, photographic, painting techniques; Dir GAO ZONGYUAN; Editor-in-Chief CHENG DALI.

Renmin Weisheng Chubanshe (People's Medical Publishing House): 19 Panjia Yuan Xi Lu, Nan Li, Chaoyang Qu, Beijing 100021; tel. (10) 59780011; fax (10) 59787588; e-mail pmphsales@pmph.com; internet www.pmph.com; f. 1953; medicine (Western and traditional Chinese), pharmacology, dentistry, public health; Pres. HU GUOCHEN.

Renmin Wenxue Chubanshe (People's Literature Publishing House): 166 Chaoyangmen, Nei Dajie, Beijing 100705; tel. (10) 65287513; fax (10) 65138394; e-mail rwbq@sina.com; internet www.rw-cn.com; f. 1951; largest publr of literary works and translations into Chinese; Pres. PAN KAIXIONG; Editor-in-Chief GUAN SHIGUANG.

Shanghai Guji Chubanshe (Shanghai Classics Publishing House): 272 Ruijin Erlu, Shanghai 200020; tel. (21) 64370011; fax (21) 64339287; e-mail guji1@guji.com.cn; internet www.guji.com.cn; f. 1956; classical Chinese literature, history, art, philosophy, geography, linguistics, science and technology.

Shanghai Jiaoyu Chubanshe (Shanghai Education Publishing House): 123 Yongfu Lu, Shanghai 200031; tel. (21) 64377165; fax (21) 64339995; e-mail webmaster@seph.com.cn; internet www.seph.com.cn; f. 1958; academic; Dir and Editor-in-Chief BAO NANLIN.

Shanghai Yiwen Chubanshe (Shanghai Translation Publishing House): 193 Fujian Lu, Shanghai 200001; tel. (21) 53594508; fax (21) 63914291; e-mail info@yiwen.com.cn; internet www.yiwen.com.cn; f. 1978; translations of foreign classic and modern literature; philosophy, social sciences, dictionaries, etc.

Shangwu Yinshuguan (The Commercial Press): 36 Wangfujing Dajie, Beijing 100710; tel. (10) 65258899; fax (10) 65134942; e-mail xxzx@cp.com.cn; internet www.cp.com.cn; f. 1897; dictionaries and reference books in Chinese and foreign languages, translations of foreign works on social sciences; Editor HU LONGBIAO; Pres. YU DIANLI.

Shaonian Ertong Chubanshe (Juvenile and Children's Publishing House): 1538 Yan An Xi Lu, Shanghai 200052; tel. (21) 62823025; fax (21) 62821726; e-mail forwardz@public4.sta.net.cn; f. 1952; children's educational and literary works, teaching aids and periodicals; Gen. Man. ZHOU SHUNPEI.

Shijie Wenhua Chubanshe (World Culture Publishing House): Dir ZHU LIE.

Wenwu Chubanshe (Cultural Relics Publishing House): 2 Dongzhimen Bei Dajie, Beijing 100007; tel. (10) 64027424; fax (10) 64010698; e-mail web@wenwu.com; internet www.wenwu.com; f. 1956; books and catalogues of Chinese relics in museums and those recently discovered; Dir SU SHISHU.

Wuhan Daxue Chubanshe (Wuhan University Press): Luojia Hill, Wuhan, Hubei; tel. (27) 68756075; fax (27) 68754094; e-mail epd@whu.edu.cn; internet www.wdp.com.cn; f. 1981; reference books, academic works, maps, audio-visual works, etc.; Pres. Prof. CHEN QINGHUI.

Xiandai Chubanshe (Modern Press): 504 Anhua Li, Andingmenwai, Beijing 100011; tel. (10) 64263515; fax (10) 64214540; f. 1981; directories, reference books, etc.; Dir ZHOU HONGLI.

Xinhua Chubanshe (Xinhua Publishing House): 8 Jungyuan Lu, Shijingshan, Beijing 100000; tel. (10) 63074407; fax (10) 63073880; e-mail wjybox@xinhuanet.com; f. 1979; social sciences, economy, politics, history, geography, directories, dictionaries, etc.; Dir LUO HAIYUAN.

Xuelin Chubanshe (Scholar Books Publishing House): 120 Wenmiao Lu, Shanghai 200010; tel. and fax (21) 63768540; f. 1981; academic, including personal academic works at authors' own expense; Dir LEI QUNMING.

Zhongguo Caizheng Jingji Chubanshe (China Financial and Economic Publishing House): 28 Fu Cheng Lu, Haidian Qu, Beijing 100142; tel. (10) 64011805; e-mail cfeph@cfeph.cn; internet www.cfeph.cn; f. 1961; finance, economics, commerce and accounting.

Zhongguo Dabaike Quanshu Chubanshe (Encyclopaedia of China Publishing House): 17 Fu Cheng Men Bei Dajie, Beijing 100037; tel. (10) 68338370; fax (10) 88390680; e-mail jxh@ecph.com.cn; internet www.ecph.com.cn; f. 1978; specializes in encyclopaedias; Dir SHAN JIFU.

Zhongguo Ditu Chubanshe (SinoMaps Press): 57 Nan Lu, Xuanwu Qu, Beijing 100055; tel. (10) 63529243; fax (10) 63529403; e-mail webmaster@sinomaps.com; internet www.sinomaps.com; f. 1954; cartographic publr; Dir ZHAO XIAOMING.

Zhongguo Funü Chubanshe (China Women Publishing House): 24A Shijia Hutong, Beijing 100010; tel. (10) 65228814; fax (10) 65133162; e-mail service@womenbooks.com.cn; internet www.womenbooks.com.cn; f. 1981; women's movement, marriage and family, child care, etc.; Editor-in-Chief YANG GUANGHUI.

Zhongguo Qingnian Chubanzongshe (China Youth Publishing Group): 21 Dongsi Shiertiao, Beijing 100708; tel. (10) 84039659; fax (10) 64031803; e-mail cyp_webmaster@126.com; internet www.cyp.com.cn; f. 1950; state-owned; literature, social and natural sciences, youth work, autobiography; also periodicals; Pres. ZHANG JINGYAN; Editor-in-Chief WEN YUXIN.

Zhongguo Shehui Kexue Chubanshe (China Social Sciences Publishing House): 158A Gulou Xidajie, Beijing 100720; tel. (10) 84029453; fax (10) 84002041; e-mail duzhe-cbs@cass.org.cn; internet www.csspw.com.cn; f. 1978; Dir MENG ZHAOYU.

Zhongguo Xiju Chubanshe (China Theatrical Publishing House): 52 Dongsi Batiao Hutong, Beijing; tel. (10) 64015815; f. 1957; traditional and modern Chinese drama.

Zhongguo Youyi Chuban Gongsi (China Friendship Publishing Corpn): e-mail tmdoxu@public.east.cn.net; Dir YANG WEI.

Zhonghua Shuju (Zhonghua Book Co): 38 Taipingqiao Xili, Fenglai Qu, Beijing; tel. (10) 63458226; f. 1912; general; Pres. LI YAN.

PUBLISHERS' ASSOCIATION

Publishers' Association of China: Beijing; tel. (10) 65246062; internet www.pac.org.cn; f. 1979; arranges academic exchanges with foreign publrs; Chair. YU YOUXIAN.

Broadcasting and Communications

TELECOMMUNICATIONS

China Mobile Communications Corpn (China Mobile): 53A Xibianmen Nei Dajie, Xuanwu Qu, Beijing 100053; tel. (10) 63604988; fax (10) 63600364; internet www.chinamobile.com; controlling shareholder in China Mobile (Hong Kong) Ltd; f. 2000; Pres. WANG JIANZHOU.

China Satellite Communications Corpn Ltd (CHINA SATCOM): International Finance Centre, Haidian Qu, Beijing 100089; tel. (10) 59718188; fax (10) 59718199; internet www.chinasatcom.com; f. 2001; satellite telecommunications, radio and television services; Chair. RUI XIAOWU.

China Telecom Corpn Ltd: 31 Jinrong Jie, Xicheng Qu, Beijing 100032; tel. (10) 66428166; fax (10) 66010728; e-mail ir@chinatelecom.com.cn; internet www.chinatelecom-h.com; f. 1997; est. as a vehicle for foreign investment in telecommunications sector; restructured as a jt-stock limited company in 2002 with responsibility for fixed-line networks, via its subsidiaries, in 20 provinces, municipalities and autonomous regions; Chair. and CEO WANG XIAOCHU; Pres. SHANG BING.

China United Network Communications Co Ltd (China Unicom): 21 Financial St, Xicheng District, Beijing 100140; fax (10) 66110009; e-mail webmaster@chinaunicom.com.cn; internet www.chinaunicom.com.cn; f. 1994; fixed line and mobile telephone services; fmrly China United Telecommunications Corpn; above name adopted after merger with China Netcom Group in 2009; 273m. subscribers (2008); Chair. and CEO CHANG XIAOBING.

Netease.com: SP Tower D, 26th Floor, Tsinghua Science Park Bldg 8, 1 Zhongguancun Dong Lu, Haidan Qu, Beijing 100084; tel. (10) 82558163; fax (10) 82618163; e-mail bjsales@service.netease.com; internet corp.163.com; f. 1997; Nasdaq-listed internet portal; Founder and CEO WILLIAM DING LEI.

Sina.com: Jinmao Tower, 37th Floor, 88 Century Blvd, Pudong, Shanghai 200121; tel. (21) 50498666; fax (21) 50498806; e-mail ir@staff.sina.com.cn; internet www.sina.com.cn; Nasdaq-listed internet portal; Pres. and CEO CHARLES CHAO; Chair. YAN WANG.

Sohu.com: Sohu Internet Plaza, Park 1, Zhongguancun Dong Lu, Haidan Qu, Beijing 100084; tel. (10) 62726666; fax (10) 62726988; e-mail ir@contact.sohu.com; internet www.sohu.com; Nasdaq-listed internet portal; Chair. and CEO CHARLES ZHANG.

BROADCASTING

In 2007 there were 263 radio broadcasting stations and 11,384 radio transmitting and relay stations (covering 95.4% of the population). In the same year there were 287 television stations and 18,249 television transmitting and relay stations (covering 96.5% of the population).

Regulatory Authority

State Administration of Radio, Film and Television (SARFT): 2 Fu Xing Men Wai Dajie, POB 4501, Beijing 100866; tel. (10) 68513409; fax (10) 68512174; e-mail sarft@chinasarft.gov.cn; internet www.sarft.gov.cn; controls the Central People's Broadcasting Station, the Central TV Station, China Radio International, China Record Co, Beijing Broadcasting Institute, Broadcasting Research Institute, the China Broadcasting Art Troupe, etc.; Dir CAI FUCHAO.

Radio

China National Radio (CNR): 2 Fu Xing Men Wai Dajie, Beijing 100866; tel. (10) 86093114; fax (10) 63909751; e-mail cn@cnr.cn; internet www.cnr.cn; f. 1941; domestic service in Chinese, Zang Wen (Tibetan), Min Nan Hua (Amoy), Ke Jia (Hakka), Hasaka (Kazakh), Wei Wuer (Uygur), Menggu Hua (Mongolian) and Chaoxian (Korean); Dir-Gen. YANG BO.

Zhongguo Guoji Guangbo Diantai (China Radio International): 16A Shijingshan Lu, Beijing 100040; tel. (10) 68891123; fax (10) 68891232; e-mail crieng@cri.com.cn; internet www.cri.cn; f. 1941; fmrly Radio Beijing; foreign service in 61 languages and dialects incl. Arabic, Burmese, Czech, English, Esperanto, French, German, Hindi, Indonesian, Italian, Japanese, Lao, Malay, Polish, Portuguese, Russian, Spanish, Turkish and Vietnamese; Dir WANG GENGNIAN.

Television

China Central Television (CCTV): Media Centre, 11B Fuxing Lu, Haidian Qu, Beijing 100038; tel. (10) 68508381; fax (10) 68513025; e-mail cctv-9@cctv.com; internet www.cntv.com; operates under Bureau of Broadcasting Affairs of the State Council, Beijing; f. 1958; operates eight networks; 24-hour global satellite service commenced in 1996; Pres. JIAO LI.

Anhui Television (AHTV): 355 Tong Cheng Nan Lu, Hefei 230066; tel. (551) 2615582; fax (551) 2615582; e-mail webmaster@ahtv.cn; internet www.ahtv.cn; f. 1960; broadcasts eight television channels.

China Beijing Television Station (BTV): 98 Jianguo Lu, Chaoyang Qu, Beijing 100022; tel. (10) 68419922; fax (10) 68429120; e-mail btvsuggest@btv.com.cn; internet www.btv.com.cn; broadcasts 14 television channels; state-owned; Dir WANG XIAODONG.

Chongqing Television: tel. (23) 68812609; fax (23) 63850485; e-mail webmaster@ccqtv.com; internet www.ccqtv.com; f. 1961; broadcasts nine television channels.

Fujian Television: 2 Gu Tian Lu, Fuzhou 350001; tel. (591) 83310941; fax (591) 83311945; internet www.fjtv.net; f. 1960; broadcasts 10 television channels; part of the Fujian Media Group.

Gansu Television (GSTV): 226 Dong Gang Xi Lu, Lanzhou 370000; tel. (931) 8416419; fax (931) 8416499; internet www.gstv.com.cn; f. 1970; broadcasts three television channels.

Guangdong Television: Guangdong Television Centre, 331 Huan Shi Dong Lu, Guangzhou 510066; tel. (20) 83355188; e-mail gdtv@gdtv.com.cn; internet www.gdtv.com.cn; f. 1959; programmes in Mandarin, Cantonese and English; state-owned; broadcasts 14 channels.

Guangxi Television (GXTV): 73 National Rd, Nanning 530022; tel. (771) 2196666; fax (771) 5854039; e-mail gxtv@gxtv.com.cn; internet www.gxtv.cn; f. 1970; broadcasts six television channels.

Guizhou Television (GZTV): e-mail webmaster@gztv.com; internet www.gztv.com.cn; f. 1968; broadcasts three television channels.

Hainan Television (HNTV): f. 1982; broadcasts three television channels.

Hebei Television (HEBTV): internet www.hebtv.com.cn; f. 1969; broadcasts two television channels.

Henan Television (HNTV): 2 Jing Wu Lu, Zhengzhou 450008; tel. (371) 5726212; fax (371) 5726285; e-mail hntv@hntv.ha.cn; internet www.hntv.ha.cn; f. 1969; broadcasts three television channels.

Hubei Television (HBTV): 1 Zi Jin Cun Liang Dao Jie, Wuchang, Wuhan 430071; tel. (27) 7839223; fax (27) 7816130; e-mail webmaster@hbtv.com.cn; internet www.hbtv.com.cn; f. 1960; broadcasts two television channels.

Hunan Television (HNTV): Hunan International Convention & Exhibition Center, 4th Floor, Changsha 410003; tel. (731) 82871680; fax (731) 82871686; e-mail media@hunantv.com; internet www.hunantv.com; f. 1960; broadcasts two television channels; CEO ZHANG RUOBO.

Jiangsu Broadcasting Corpn: 4 East Beijing Rd, Nanjing, Jiangsu; tel. (25) 83188185; fax (25) 83188187; e-mail info@vip.jsbc.com; internet www.jstv.com/jsbc_en/index.shtml; f. 1960; broadcasts 14 television channels; Pres. ZHOU LI.

Liaoning Television (LNTV): 10 Guang Rong Jie, Shenyang 110003; tel. (24) 23232945; fax (24) 22913733; e-mail lntv@lntv.com.cn; internet www.lntv.com.cn; f. 1959; broadcasts two television channels.

Nei Monggol Television (NMGTV): 71 Xinhua Dajie, Hohhot 010058; tel. (471) 6630621; fax (471) 6630600; e-mail info@nmtv.cn; internet www.nmtv.cn; f. 1969; broadcasts two television channels; Dir FANG GUAN.

Ningxia Television (NXTV): 66 Ningxia Lu, Beijing 750001; tel. (951) 6130011; internet www.nxtv.com.cn; f. 1970; broadcasts two television channels.

Shaanxi Television (SXTV): 336 Chang An Nan Jie, Xian 710061; tel. (29) 85257538; fax (29) 5218553; e-mail webmaster@sxtvs.com; internet www.sxtvs.com; f. 1970; broadcasts seven television channels.

Shandong Television (SDTV): 81 Jingshi Lu, Jinan 250062; tel. (531) 2951295; fax (531) 2953809; e-mail webmaster@sdtv.com.cn; internet www.sdtv.com.cn; f. 1960; broadcasts six television channels.

Shanghai Media Group: 298 Weihai Lu, Shanghai; tel. (21) 62565899; internet www.smg.cn; f. 2001; est. by merger of Radio Shanghai, Eastern Radio Shanghai, Shanghai Television, Oriental Television Station and Shanghai Cable TV; broadcasts 15 television channels and 11 radio channels; Pres. LI RUIGANG.

Shanxi Television (SXTV): 318 Ying Chak Lu, Taiyuan, Shanxi 030001; tel. and fax (351) 4066178; e-mail mail@sxrtv.com; internet www.sxrtv.com; f. 1960; broadcasts two television channels.

Sichuan Television (SCTV): 40 Dong Sheng Jie, Chengdu 610015; tel. (28) 86636065; fax (28) 86635195; e-mail webmaster@sctv.com; internet www.sctv.com; f. 1960; broadcasts nine television channels.

Xinjiang Television (XJTV): Xinjiang Television Centre 84B, 8th Floor, Urumqi 830044; tel. (991) 2577531; fax (991) 2871947; e-mail XJTVS@96669.net; internet www.xjtvs.com.cn; f. 1970; broadcasts 15 television channels; broadcasts in Mandarin, Uygur and Kazakh.

Xizang Television (XZTV): 11 Xi Lu, Lhasa; tel. (891) 6814522; internet www.xztv.net.cn; f. 1993; broadcasts two television channels; Mandarin and Tibetan.

Yunnan Television: 182 Renmin Xi Lu, Kunmin, Yunnan 650031; tel. (871) 5357842; fax (871) 5350586; e-mail webmaster@yntv.com.cn; internet www.yntv.cn; f. 1969; broadcasts nine television channels.

Zhejiang Satellite Television (ZJSTV): 111 Mo Gan Shan Lu, Hangzhou 310005; internet www.zjstv.com; f. 1960; broadcasts two television channels.

Finance

(cap. = capital; auth. = authorized; p.u. = paid up; res = reserves; dep. = deposits; m. = million; amounts in yuan unless otherwise stated)

BANKING

Regulatory Authority

China Banking Regulatory Commission: 15 Financial St, Xicheng Qu, Beijing 100140; tel. (10) 66279749; e-mail cbrclib@cbrc.gov.cn; internet www.cbrc.gov.cn; f. 2003; Chair. LIU MINGKANG.

Central Bank

People's Bank of China (PBC): 32 Chengfang Jie, Xicheng Qu, Beijing 100800; tel. (10) 66194114; fax (10) 66195370; e-mail webbox@pbc.gov.cn; internet www.pbc.gov.cn; f. 1948; bank of issue; decides and implements China's monetary policies; Gov. ZHOU XIAOCHUAN; 2,204 brs.

Other Banks

Agricultural Bank of China: 69 Jianguomen Nei Dajie, Dongcheng Qu, Beijing 100005; tel. (10) 68216807; fax (10) 68297160; e-mail 95599bj@abchina.com; internet www.abchina.com; f. 1951; serves mainly China's rural financial operations, providing services for agriculture, industry, commerce, transport, etc. in rural areas; sale of shares commenced in mid-2010; cap. 260,000m., res 23,002m.,dep. 8,320,280m. (Dec. 2009); Pres. XIANG JUNBO; 28,111 brs (domestic).

Agricultural Development Bank of China: 2A Yuetanbei Jie, Xicheng Qu, Beijing 100045; tel. (10) 68081557; fax (10) 68081773; internet www.adbc.com.cn; f. 1994; cap. 165,800m. (2006); Pres. ZHENG HUI.

Bank of Beijing Co Ltd: 17C Financial St, Xicheng Qu, Beijing 100140, Beijing 100031; tel. (10) 66426928; fax (10) 66426691; internet www.bankofbeijing.com.cn; f. 1996; est. as Beijing City United Bank Corpn, changed name to Beijing City Commercial Bank Corpn Ltd in 1998, assumed present name in 2004; cap. 6,227.5m., res 22,716.4m., dep. 489,371.4m. (Dec. 2009); Chair. YAN BINGZHU; Pres. YAN XIAOYAN.

Bank of Changsha: 433 Furong Zhong Lu, Section 1, Changsha, Hunan 410005; tel. (731) 4305570; fax (731) 4305560; e-mail cscb@hncccb.com; internet www.cscb.cn; f. 1997; fmrly Changsha City Commercial Bank, name changed as above in 2008; cap. 1,173.2m., res 580.8m., dep. 60,457.9m. (Dec. 2009); Chair. ZHI YONG ZHANG; Pres. YU GUO ZHU.

Bank of China Ltd: 1 Fu Xing Men Nei Dajie, Beijing 100818; tel. (10) 66596688; fax (10) 66593777; internet www.boc.cn; f. 1912; handles foreign exchange and international settlements; operates Orient AMC (asset management corporation) since 1999; fmrly Bank of China; became shareholding co in Aug. 2004; 10% stake acquired in 2005 by a consortium headed by Royal Bank of Scotland PLC (UK); further 10% acquired by Temasek Holdings (Pvt) Ltd; cap. 253,839m., res 152,303m., dep. 7,953,385m. (Dec. 2009); Chair. XIAO GANG; Pres. LI LIHUI; 117 brs.

Bank of Chongqing: 153 Zou Rong Lu, Zou Rong Sq., Yu Zhong Qu, Chongqing 400010; tel. (23) 63836229; fax (23) 63792176; e-mail webmaster@cqcbank.com.cn; internet www.cqcbank.com.cn; f. 1996; fmrly Chongqing Commercial Bank; cap. 2,020.6m., res 640m., dep. 75,121.1m. (Dec. 2009); Pres. CHONG YI WANG; Chair. FU ZHANG.

Bank of Communications Ltd: 188 Yin Cheng Lu, Shanghai 200120; tel. (21) 58766688; fax (21) 58798398; e-mail investor@bankcomm.com; internet www.bankcomm.com; f. 1908; commercial bank; 19.9% stake was acquired by HSBC in Aug. 2004; cap. 48,994m., res 88,808m., dep. 3,034,602m. (Dec. 2009); Chair. HU HUAIBANG; Pres. NIU XIMING; 93 brs.

Bank of Hebei Co Ltd: 28 Ping An Bei Lu, Shijiazhuang, Hebei 050011; tel. (11) 88627003; fax (11) 88627075; internet www.hebbank.com; f. 1996; fmrly Shijiazhuang City Commercial Bank, name changed as above in 2009; cap. 2,000m., res 1,045.9m., dep. 50,713.6m. (Dec. 2009); Chair. QIAO ZHIQIANG.

Bank of Jiangsu Co Ltd: 55 Hongwu Lu, Nanjing, Jiangsu Province 210005; tel. (25) 58588050; fax (25) 58588055; internet www.jsbchina.cn; f. 2007; est. by merger of 13 banks; cap. 8,400m., res 5,599.1m., dep. 306,998m. (Dec. 2009); Chair. and Pres. HUANG ZHIWEI.

Bank of Ningbo Co Ltd: 294 Zhongshan Dong Lu, Ningbo 315040, Zhejiang; tel. (574) 87050028; fax (574) 87050027; e-mail inter@nbcb.cn; internet www.nbcb.com.cn; f. 1997; cap. 2,500m., res 4,978.3m., dep. 151,604m. (Dec. 2009); Chair. LU HUAYU; Pres. YU FENGYING.

Bank of Shanghai Co Ltd: 585 Zhongshan Lu (E2), Shanghai 200010; tel. (21) 68475888; fax (21) 68476111; e-mail webmaster@bankofshanghai.com.cn; internet www.bankofshanghai.com; f. 1995; est. as Shanghai City United Bank, assumed present name in 1998; cap. 2,600m., res 11,788.7m., dep. 420,059.5m. (Dec. 2009); Chair. JIANHUA FU; Pres. CHEN XIN; 209 brs.

Bank of Shaoxing Co Ltd: 20 Lao Dong Lu, Shaoxing, Zhejiang 312000; tel. (575) 85129734; fax (575) 85131190; e-mail sxsyyh@mail.sxptt.zj.cn; internet www.sxccb.com; f. 1997; fmrly Shaoxing City Commercial Bank Co Ltd, name changed as above in 2009; cap. 983.6m., res 628m., dep. 29,943m. (Dec. 2009); Pres. CHEN FANG XIAO; Chair. CHEN JUN QUAN.

Bank of Weifang Co Ltd: Shengli Lu, Weifang 261041; tel. (536) 8106161; internet www.wfccb.com; f. 1997; fmrly Weifang City Commercial Bank, name changed as above in 2009; cap. 1,396.8m., res 239.9m., dep. 28,746.9m. (Dec. 2009); Pres. WANG ZHONGUA.

BNP Paribas (China) Ltd: World Financial Center, 25/F, 100 Century Ave, Pudong Nan Lu, Shanghai 200120; tel. (21) 28962888; fax (21) 28962800; internet www.bnpparibas.com.cn; f. 1992; fmrly Int. Bank of Paris and Shanghai; name changed as above 2004; 100% owned by BNP Paribas SA (France); cap. US $520.4m., res US $40.6m., dep. US $3,452m. (Dec. 2009); Chief Exec. FRANÇOIS CRISTOFARI.

Changshu Rural Commercial Bank: 58 Century Blvd, Changshu, Jiangsu; tel. (512) 52909020; fax (512) 52962000; e-mail jscsxhc@sina.com; internet www.csrcbank.com; f. 1953; cap. 575.6m., res. 1,743.1m., dep. 36,834m. (Dec. 2009); Chair. WU JIANYA; Pres. SONG JIANMING.

China Bohai Bank: 201–205 Race Course Rd, Hexi 300204; tel. (22) 58316666; e-mail enquiry@cbhb.com.cn; internet www.cbhb.com.cn; f. 2004; 20% stake owned by Standard Chartered Bank; Chair. YANG ZILIN.

China Citic Bank Corpn Ltd: Block C, Fuhua Mansion, 8 Chao Yang Men Bei Dajie, Dongcheng Qu, Beijing 100027; tel. (10) 65558000; fax (10) 65550809; e-mail ir_cncb@citicbank.com; internet bank.ecitic.com; f. 1987; est. as Citic Industrial Bank; name changed as above in April 2007; cap. 39,033m., res 47,071m., dep. 1,632,012m. (Dec. 2009); Chair. KONG DAN; Pres. CHEN XIAOXIAN; 26 brs.

China Construction Bank Corpn (CCBC): 25 Jinrong Jie, Xicheng Qu, Beijing 100033; tel. (10) 67597114; fax (10) 66212862; e-mail ccb@bj.china.com; internet www.ccb.com; f. 1954; fmrly People's Construction Bank of China; makes payments for capital construction projects; issues loans to construction enterprises and others, incl. housing loans; handles foreign-exchange business; cap. 233,689m., res 187,674m., dep. 8,830,795m. (Dec. 2009); Chair. GUO SHUQING; Pres. ZHANG JIANGUO; 44 brs.

China Development Bank (CDB): 29 Fuchengmenwai Dajie, Xicheng Qu, Beijing 100037; tel. (10) 68306688; fax (10) 68306699; e-mail webmaster@cdb.com.cn; internet www.cdb.com.cn; f. 1994; merged with China Investment Bank 1998; handles low-interest loans for infrastructural projects and basic industries; Gov. JIANG CHAOLIANG; 32 brs.

China Everbright Bank: Everbright Bldg, 6 Fu Xing Men Wai Lu, Beijing 100045; tel. (10) 68098000; fax (10) 68561260; e-mail eb@cebbank.com; internet www.cebbank.com; f. 1992; est. as Everbright Bank of China; acquired China Investment Bank and assumed present name in 1999; cap. 33,434.7m., res 13,076.3m., dep. 1,078,898.3m. (Dec. 2009); Pres. GUO YOU; Chair. TANG SHUANGNING; 30 brs.

China International Capital Corporation (CICC): 28th Floor, China World Tower 2, 1 Jian Guo Men Wai Dajie, Beijing 100004; tel. (10) 65051166; fax (10) 65051156; e-mail info@cicc.com.cn; internet www.cicc.com.cn; f. 1995; international investment bank; 43.4% owned by China Jianyin Investment Ltd, 34.3% owned by Morgan Stanley; registered cap. US $100m.; Chair. LI JIANGE; CEO LEVIN ZHU.

China Merchants Bank: China Merchants Bank Tower, 49/F, 7088 Shennan Blvd, Shenzhen 518040; tel. (755) 83198888; fax (755) 83105109; e-mail office@cmbchina.com; internet www.cmbchina.com; f. 1987; cap. 19,119m., res 46,072m., dep. 1,879,231m. (Dec. 2009); Chair. FU YUNING; Pres. and CEO MA WEIHUA; 44 brs.

China Minsheng Banking Corporation: 8/F, 2 Fuxingmen Nei Dajie, Xicheng Qu, Beijing 100031; tel. (10) 58560666; fax (10) 58560635; internet www.cmbc.com.cn; first non-state national commercial bank, opened Jan. 1996; cap. 22,262m., res 54,129m., dep. 1,280,650m. (Dec. 2009); Chair. DONG WENBIAO; Pres. QI HONG; 29 brs.

China Zheshang Bank Co Ltd: 288 Qingchun Lu, Hangzhou, Zhejiang 310006; tel. (571) 95105665; fax (571) 87659108; e-mail zcbho@mail.nbptt.zj.cn; internet www.czbank.com; f. 1993; fmrly Zhejiang Commercial Bank; cap. 5,216.4m., res 3,031.9m., dep. 140,945m. (Dec. 2009); Chair. ZHANG DAYANG; Pres. GONG FANGLE.

Chinese Mercantile Bank: Ground and 23rd Floors, Dongfeng Bldg, 2010 Shennan Lu, Futian Qu, Shenzhen 518031; tel. (755) 83786833; fax (755) 83257955; e-mail service@cmbcn.com.cn; internet www.cmbcn.com.cn; f. 1993; wholly owned by ICBC (Asia) Ltd; cap. 1,650m., res 87.8m., dep. 5,721.7m. (Dec. 2009); CEO PANG KOON KWAI.

CITIC Group: Capital Mansion, 6 Xin Yuan Nan Lu, Chao Yang Qu, Beijing 100004; tel. (10) 64660088; fax (10) 64661186; e-mail g-office@citic.com.cn; internet www.citic.com; f. 1979; name changed from China International Trust and Investment Corporation in 2003; economic and technological co-operation; finance, banking, investment and trade; registered cap. 3,000m.; total assets 935,720m. (Dec. 2006); Chair. CHANG ZHENMING; Pres. TIAN GUOLI.

Export and Import Bank of China (China Exim Bank): 30 Fu Xin Men Nei Lu, Xicheng Qu, Beijing 100031; tel. (10) 83579988; fax (10) 66060636; internet www.eximbank.gov.cn; f. 1994; provides trade credits for export of large machinery, electronics, ships, etc.; Chair. and Pres. LI RUOGU.

Foshan Shunde Rural Commercial Bank Co Ltd: 38 Fengshan Zhong Lu, Guangdong, Shunde 528300; tel. (757) 22388888; fax (757) 22388226; e-mail lsbgs@sdebank.com; internet www.sdebank.com; fmrly The Rural Credit Cooperatives Union of Shunde, name changed as above in 2009; cap. 1,856.4m., res 5,144.9m., dep. 92,229.9m. (Dec. 2009).

Fujian Haixia Bank Co Ltd: 158 Liuyi Bei Lu, Fuzhou; tel. (591) 87593778; fax (591) 87585341; e-mail gyb@fuzhoubank.com; internet www.fjhxbank.com; fmrly Fuzhou City Commercial Bank Co Ltd, name changed as above in 2009; cap. 2,078.7m., res 1,568.2m., dep. 34,422.7m. (Dec. 2009); Chair. YUNLIAN GUO; Pres. JIEHONG JIANG; 30 brs.

Guangdong Development Bank: 83 Nonglinxia Lu, Dongshan Qu, Guangzhou, Guangdong 510080; tel. (20) 38322888; fax (20)

87310779; internet www.gdb.com.cn; f. 1988; 85% stake acquired by a consortium led by Citigroup Inc (USA) in Nov. 2006; cap. 11,978.8m., res 6,712.2m., dep. 630,134.9m. (Dec. 2009); Chair. DONG JIANYUE; Pres. MORRIS LI; 28 brs.

Guangxi Beibu Gulf Bank Co Ltd: 10 Qing Xiu Lu, Nanning, Guangxi Zhuang 530028; tel. (771) 6115338; fax (771) 6115383; internet www.bankofbbg.com; cap. 2,000m., res 1,038.8m., dep. 23,532.2m. (Dec. 2009); Chair. TENG CHONG; Pres. JIANPING LIU.

Hua Xia Bank: Hua Xia Bank Mansions, 22 Jianguomennei Dajie, Dongcheng Qu, Beijing 100005; tel. (10) 85238000; fax (10) 85239000; e-mail zhgjb@hxb.com.cn; internet www.hxb.com.cn; f. 1992; est. as part of Shougang Corpn; cap. 4,990.5m., res 21,469.5m., dep. 658,809.1m. (Dec. 2008); Chair. WU JIAN; Pres. FAN DAZHI; 47 brs.

Industrial and Commercial Bank of China: 55 Fu Xing Men Nei Dajie, Xicheng Qu, Beijing 100031; tel. (10) 66106070; fax (10) 66106053; e-mail webmaster@icbc.com.cn; internet www.icbc.com.cn; f. 1984; handles industrial and commercial credits and international business; operates Huarong AMC (asset management corporation) since 1999; cap. 334,019m., res 221,114m., dep. 10,834,047m. (Dec. 2009); Chair. JIANG JIANQING; Pres. YANG KAISHENG.

Industrial Bank Co Ltd: Zhong Shang Bldg, 154 Hudong Lu, Hualin, Fuzhou, Fujian 350003; tel. (591) 87839338; fax (591) 87841932; e-mail irm@cib.com.cn; internet www.cib.com.cn; f. 1982; fmrly Fujian Industrial Bank; cap. 5,000m., res 28,743.2m., dep. 1,256,140.6m. (Dec. 2009); Chair. GAO JIANPING; Pres. LI RENJIE; 48 brs.

Laishang Bank Co Ltd: 137 Longtan Dong Dajie, Laiwu, Shandong; tel. (634) 8861182; fax (634) 8681177; e-mail bgs@lsbankchina.com; internet www.lsbankchina.com; f. 1987; cap. 600m., res 703.7m., dep. 18,837.3m. (Dec. 2009); Chair LI MINSHI; Pres. TAN LEQING.

Linshang Bank Co Ltd: 336 Yimeng Lu, Linyi, Shandong; tel. (539) 8311353; fax (539) 8309052; e-mail lypfboy@sohu.com; internet www.lsbchina.com; f. 1998; fmrly Linyi City Commercial Bank Co Ltd, name changed as above in 2008; cap. 1,712m., res 214.8m., dep. 22,850.5m. (Dec. 2009); Chair. WANG JIAYU; Gen. Man. QIANG ZHAO.

Ping An Bank: Galaxy Development Centre, 15/F, 3 Fu Hua Lu, Guangdong, Futian Qu, Shenzhen; tel. (755) 82436179; fax (755) 82431019; e-mail IR@pingan.com.cn; internet bank.pingan.com; f. 1995; fmrly Shenzhen Commercial Bank; cap. 8,622.8m., res 4,481.9m., dep. 200,071.4m. (Dec. 2009); Chair. MA MINGHZE; Pres. SUN JIANYI; 45 brs.

QiLu Bank Co Ltd: 176 Shun He Lu, Jinan 250001; tel. (531) 86075850; fax (531) 81915514; e-mail boardoffice@qlbchina.com; internet www.qlbchina.com; f. 1996; fmrly Jinan City Commercial Bank Co Ltd, above name adopted in 2009; cap. 1,668.7m., res 813.1m., dep. 55,679.7m. (Dec. 2009); Chair. QIU YUNZHANG.

Shanghai Pudong Development Bank: 12 Zhongshan Dong Yi Lu, Shanghai 200002; tel. (21) 63296188; fax (21) 63232036; e-mail bdo@spdb.com.cn; internet www.spdb.com.cn; f. 1993; cap. 8,830m., res 41,907m., dep. 1,504,487.8m. (Dec. 2009); Chair. JI XIAOHUI; Pres. FU JIANHUA; 28 brs.

Shenzhen Development Bank Co Ltd: 5047 Shennan Dong Lu, Shenzhen 518001; tel. (755) 82088888; fax (755) 82081069; e-mail shudi@sdb.com.cn; internet www.sdb.com.cn; f. 1987; 18% acquired by Newbridge Capital (USA) in 2004; cap. 3,105.4m., res 12,977.3m., dep. 542,549.8m. (Dec. 2009); Chair. XIAO SUINING; Pres. FRANK NEWMAN.

Xiamen Bank Co Ltd: 101 Hubin Bei Lu, Siming, Xiamen 361012; tel. (592) 2275219; fax (592) 2275173; e-mail xmcbgc@public.xm.fj.cn; internet www.xmccb.com; f. 1996; cap. 607.5m., res 661.6m., dep. 21,149.3m. (Dec. 2009); Pres. GAO CHAOYANG.

Xiamen International Bank: 8–10 Jiang Lu, Xiamen, Fujian 361001; tel. (592) 2078888; fax (592) 2988788; e-mail xib@xib.com.cn; internet www.xib.com.cn; f. 1985; cap. 1,068m., res 1,017.8m., dep. 43,392.7m. (Dec. 2009); Chair. DING SHI DA; Pres. LU YAO MING; 3 brs.

Zhejiang Chouzhou Commercial Bank Co Ltd: Jiangbin Lu, Yiwu Leyuan, Zhejiang 322000; tel. (579) 85337701; fax (579) 85337706; e-mail intl@czcb.com.cn; internet www.czcb.com.cn; f. 2006; cap. 800m., res 1,072.7m., dep. 30,123.3m. (Dec. 2009); Chair. JIN ZIJUN; Pres. ZHOU RUIGU.

STOCK EXCHANGES

The number of companies listed on the Shanghai and Shenzhen Stock Exchanges rose from 323 in 1995 to 1,434 in 2006. A total of 1,625 Chinese companies were listed in 2008.

Stock Exchange Executive Council (SEEC): Beijing; tel. (10) 64935210; f. 1989; oversees the development of financial markets in China; mems comprise leading non-bank financial institutions authorized to handle securities; Vice-Pres. WANG BOMING.

Securities Association of China (SAC): Focus Plaza, 2/F, Tower B, 19 Financial St, Xicheng Qu, Beijing 100032; tel. (10) 66575800; fax (10) 66575827; e-mail bgs@sac.net.cn; internet www.sac.net.cn; f. 1991; 332 mems; Chair. HUANG XIANGPING.

Beijing Securities Exchange: 5 Anding Lu, Chao Yang Qu, Beijing 100029; tel. (10) 64939366; fax (10) 64936233.

Shanghai Stock Exchange: 528 Pudong Nan Lu, Shanghai 200120; tel. (21) 68808888; fax (21) 68804868; e-mail webmaster@secure.sse.com.cn; internet www.sse.com.cn; f. 1990; 870 listed cos (Dec. 2009); Chair. GENG LIANG; Pres. ZHANG YUJUN.

Shenzhen Stock Exchange: 5045 Shennan Dong Lu, Shenzhen, Guangdong 518010; tel. (755) 82083333; fax (755) 82083947; e-mail cis@szse.cn; internet www.szse.cn; f. 1991; 1,012 listed cos (June 2010); Chair. CHEN DONGZHENG; Pres. SONG LIPING.

Regulatory Authorities

Operations are regulated by the State Council Securities Policy Committee and by the following:

China Securities Regulatory Commission (CSRC): 19 Focus Plaza, Jinrong Lu, Xicheng Qu, Beijing 100033; tel. (10) 66210182; fax (10) 66210205; e-mail consult@csrc.gov.cn; internet www.csrc.gov.cn; f. 1993; Chair. SHANG FULIN.

INSURANCE

At the end of 2007 the number of insurance institutions operating in China totalled 120, of which eight were insurance group corporations, 43 were joint venture corporations and 59 were domestically funded insurance corporations. In 2007 total premiums reached 703,600m. yuan: property insurance accounted for 208,700m. yuan and life insurance for 494,900m. yuan.

Aegon-CNOOC Life Insurance Co Ltd: 15/F, Pufa Tower, 588 Pudong Nan Lu, Shanghai 200120; internet www.aegon-cnooc.com; f. 2002; jt venture between Aegon (The Netherlands) and China Nat. Offshore Oil Corpn.

Anbang Property and Casualty Insurance Co Ltd: Beijing; tel. (10) 65309999; e-mail webmaster@ab-insurance.com; internet www.ab-insurance.com; f. 2004.

AXA-Minmetals Assurance Co: 19/F China Merchants Tower, 166 Jia Zui Dong Lu, Pudong, Shanghai 200120; tel. (21) 58792288; fax (21) 58792299; internet www.axa-minmetals.com.cn; f. 1999; jt venture by Groupe AXA (France) and China Minmetals Group; CEO MA ZHEMING.

China Continent Property and Casualty Insurance Co Ltd: Shanghai; tel. (21) 58369588; internet www.ccic-net.com.cn; f. 2003; Chair. DAI FENGJU; CEO JIANG MING.

China Life Insurance Co: China Life Centre, 22–28/F, 17 Financial St, Xicheng Qu, Beijing 100140; tel. (10) 66009999; e-mail serve@e-chinalife.com; internet www.chinalife.com.cn; f. 1999; formed from People's Insurance (Life) Co, division of fmr People's Insurance Co of China—PICC; restructured into a parent company and a shareholding company Aug. 2003; initial public offering Dec. 2003; Chair. YANG CHAO; Exec. Dir WAN FENG.

China Pacific Insurance Co Ltd (CPIC): 1226 Zhongshan Lu (Bei 1), Shanghai; tel. (21) 58767282; fax (21) 68870791; e-mail ir@cpic.com.cn; internet www.cpic.com.cn; f. 1991; jt-stock co; Chair. GAO GUOFU; Pres. YANG XIANGHAI.

China Taiping Insurance Group Co: Beijing; tel. (10) 63600601; fax (10) 63600605; internet www.cntaiping.com; f. 1931; fmrly China Insurance (Holdings) Co Ltd; cargo, hull, freight, fire, life, personal accident, industrial injury, motor insurance, reinsurance, etc.; 20 subsidiaries; Chair. LIN FAN; CEO KENNETH NG YU LAM.

China United Property Insurance Co: 600 Chengdu Bei Lu, Shanghai; tel. (21) 53554600; fax (21) 63276000; internet www.cicsh.com; f. 1986; fmrly Xinjiang Corpn Property Insurance Co; Gen. Man. LU FENG YUAN.

Huatai Insurance Co of China Ltd: International Business Bldg, 18/F, Tower A, 35 Financial St, Xicheng Qu, Beijing 100033; tel. (10) 59371818; fax (10) 63370081; e-mail beijing@ehuatai.com; internet www.ehuatai.com; f. 1996; est. by 63 industrial cos; Chair. and CEO WANG ZIMU.

Manulife Sinochem Life Insurance Co Ltd: Jin Mao Bldg, 21/F, 88 Century Rd, Pudong, Shanghai 200121; tel. (21) 50492288; fax (21) 50491110; e-mail cs@manulife-sinochem.com; internet www.manulife-sinochem.com; f. 1996; jt venture between Manulife (Canada) and Sinochem; Chair. MARC STERLING.

New China Life Insurance: 12 Jian Guo Man Wai Dajie, Chaoyang Qu, Beijing 100073; e-mail e@newchinalife.com; internet www.newchinalife.com; f. 1996; Chair. KANG DIAN.

PICC Property and Casualty Co Ltd: 69 Dongheyan Jie, Xuanwu Men, Beijing 100052; tel. (10) 63156688; fax (10) 63033589; e-mail webmaster@piccnet.com.cn; internet www.picc.com.cn; f. 2003;

fmrly the People's Insurance Company of China; Chair. WU YAN; CEO YI WANG.

Ping An Insurance (Group) Co of China (Ping An): Galaxy Development Centre, 3 Fu Hua Lu, Futian District, Shenzhen; tel. (400) 8866338; fax (755) 82431019; e-mail IR@pingan.com.cn; internet www.pingan.com; f. 1988; 19.9% owned by HSBC Bank PLC (UK); total assets 292,519m. (June 2005); Chair. and CEO MA MINGZHE.

Sino Life Insurance: Yi Tian Rd, Fujian Qu, Shenzhen; internet www.sino-life.com; f. 2000; Chair. ZHANG JUN.

Sunlife Everbright Insurance Co Ltd: 37/F, Tianjin International Bldg, 75 Nanjing Lu, Heping Qu, Tianjin 300050; tel. (22) 23391188; fax (22) 23399929; internet www.sunlife-everbright.com; f. 1999; jt venture between Sunlife Financial (Canada) and China Everbright Group; Pres. and CEO JANET DE SILVA.

Sunshine Property and Casualty Insurance Co Ltd: 28/F, Kuntai International Mansion, 12B Chao Wai Dajie, Beijing 100020; tel. (10) 58289999; fax (10) 58289688; e-mail pinpaixuanchuan@ygbx.com; internet yangguang.sinosig.com; Pres. and Dir-Gen. ZHANG WEIGONG.

Taikang Life Insurance Co Ltd: Taikang Life Bldg, 156 Fu Xing Men Nei Dajie, Beijing 100031; tel. (10) 66429988; fax (10) 66426397; internet www.taikang.com; f. 1996; Chair. CHEN DONGSHENG.

Tianan Insurance Co Ltd: 1 Pudong Dajie, Shanghai 200120; tel. (21) 61017878; internet www.tianan-insurance.com; f. 1994; Chair. QIU QIANG.

Yongan Insurance: Jinqiao International Plaza, Tower C, 50 Keji Lu, Xian 710075; tel. (29) 87233888; fax (29) 88231200; internet www.yaic.com.cn; Chair. ZHANG DONG WU.

Regulatory Authority

China Insurance Regulatory Commission (CIRC): 15 Financial St, Xicheng Qu, Beijing 100140; tel. (10) 66286688; fax (10) 66018871; e-mail help@circ.gov.cn; internet www.circ.gov.cn; f. 1998; under direct authority of the State Council; Chair. WU DINGFU.

Trade and Industry

GOVERNMENT AGENCIES

China Council for International Investment Promotion (CCIIP): Rm 406–409, Jing Guang Centre, Hujia Lu, Chao Yang Qu, POB 8806, Beijing 100020; tel. (10) 65978801; fax (10) 65978210; e-mail msc@cciip.org.cn; internet www.cciip.org.cn; f. 2006; est. by State Council; aims to promote China's inward and outward investment; Pres. MIAO GENGSHU; Sec.-Gen. ZHOU MING.

China Investment Corpn (CIC): New Poly Plaza, 1 Chaoyangmen Bei Dajie, Dongcheng Qu, Beijing 100010; tel. (10) 64086277; fax (10) 64086908; e-mail pr@china-inv.cn; internet www.china-inv.cn; f. 2007; sovereign wealth fund; manages China's foreign-exchange reserves; Chair. LOU JIWEI; Pres. GAO XIQING.

China National Light Industry Council: 22B Fuwai Dajie, Beijing 100833; tel. (10) 68396613; fax (10) 68396264; e-mail webmaster@clii.com.cn; internet www.clii.com.cn; under supervision of State Council; Chair. CHEN SHINENG; Sec.-Gen. WANG SHICHENG.

China National Textile Industry Council (CNTIC): 12 Dong Chang An Jie, Beijing 100742; tel. (10) 65129545; under supervision of State Council; Chair. SHI WANPENG.

State Administration for Industry and Commerce: 8 San Li He Dong Lu, Xicheng Qu, Beijing 100820; tel. (10) 68013447; fax (10) 68010463; e-mail dfa@saic.gov.cn; internet www.saic.gov.cn; responsible for market supervision and administrative execution of industrial and commercial laws; functions under direct supervision of State Council.

State Administration of Foreign Exchange (SAFE): Huanrong Hotel, 18 Fucheng Lu, Haidan Qu, Beijing 100048; tel. (10) 68402265; internet www.safe.gov.cn; drafts foreign-exchange regulations, designs and implements balance of payments statistical system, manages foreign-exchange reserves; brs in Hong Kong, Singapore, London and New York; Administrator YI GANG.

State-owned Assets Supervision and Administration Commission: Beijing; tel. (10) 63192334; e-mail iecc@sasac.gov.cn; internet www.sasac.gov.cn; f. 2003; supervision and administration of state-owned assets, regulation of ownership transfers of state-owned enterprises; Chair. WANG YONG.

Takeover Office for Military, Armed Police, Government and Judiciary Businesses: Beijing; f. 1998; est. to assume control of enterprises fmrly operated by the People's Liberation Army.

CHAMBERS OF COMMERCE

All-China Federation of Industry and Commerce (All-China General Chamber of Industry and Commerce): 93 Beiheyan Dajie, Beijing 100006; tel. (10) 65136677; fax (10) 65131769; e-mail acfic@acfic.org.cn; internet www.acfic.com.cn (Chinese); www.chinachamber.org.cn (English); f. 1953; Chair. HUANG MENGFU.

China Chamber of Commerce for the Import and Export of Foodstuffs, Native Produce and Animal By-products (CFNA): Talent International Bldg, 80 Guanqumennei Jie, Chongwen Qu, Beijing 100062; tel. (10) 87109883; fax (10) 87109829; e-mail contact@cccfna.org.cn; internet www.cccfna.org.cn; f. 1988; over 5,400 mems; Pres. BIAN ZHENHU.

China Chamber of Commerce for Import and Export of Light Industrial Products and Arts-Crafts (CCCLA): 10/F, Pan Jia Yuan Da Sha Bldg, 12 Pan Jia Yuan Nanli, Chao Yang Qu, Beijing 100021; tel. (10) 67732707; fax (10) 67732698; e-mail xxb@cccla.org.cn; internet www.cccla.org.cn; f. 1988; over 6,000 mems; Chair. WANG ZHONGQI.

China Chamber of Commerce for Import and Export of Machinery and Electronic Products (CCCME): Rm 904, 9/F, Bldg 12, Pan Jia Yuan Nanli, Chao Yang Qu, Beijing; tel. (10) 58280863; fax (10) 58280860; e-mail international@cccme.org.cn; internet www.cccme.org.cn; f. 1988; more than 6,500 mems; Pres. and Sec.-Gen. ZHANG YUJING.

China Chamber of Commerce for Import and Export of Medicines and Health Products (CCCMHPIE): 11–12/F, Bldg 3, 6 Nanzhugan Hutong, Dongcheng Qu, Beijing 100010; tel. (10) 58036282; fax (10) 58036284; internet www.cccmhpie.org.cn; f. 1989; more than 1,500 mems; Pres. ZHOU XIAOMING.

China Chamber of Commerce for Import and Export of Textiles (CCCT): 12 Pan Jia Yuan Nanli, Chao Yang Qu, Beijing 100021; tel. (10) 67739246; fax (10) 67719235; e-mail info@ccct.org.cn; internet www.ccct.org.cn; f. 1988; Chair. WANG SHENYANG; over 6,300 mems.

China Council for the Promotion of International Trade (CCPIT)—China Chamber of International Commerce (CCOIC): 1 Fuxingmenwai Lu, Xicheng Qu, Beijing 100860; tel. (10) 88075000; fax (10) 68011370; e-mail webmaster@ccpit.org; internet www.ccpit.org; Chair. WAN JIFEI.

TRADE AND INDUSTRIAL ORGANIZATIONS

Beijing Urban Construction Group Co Ltd: 62 Xueyuannan Lu, Haidian, Beijing 100081; tel. (10) 62255511; fax (10) 62256027; e-mail cjp@mail.bucg.com; internet www.bucg.com; construction of civil and industrial buildings and infrastructure; Chair. LIU LONGHUA.

China Aerospace Science and Industry Corpn (CASIC): Aerospace Science and Industry Bldg 8, Fu Cheng Men Nei Dajie, Haidian Qu, Beijing 100048; tel. (10) 68373522; fax (10) 68383626; e-mail bgt@casic.com.cn; internet www.casic.com.cn; f. 1999; Gen. Man. XU DAZHE.

China Aerospace Science and Technology Corpn: 16 Fucheng Lu, Haidian Qu, Beijing 100048; tel. (10) 68767492; fax (10) 68372291; e-mail casc@spacechina.com; internet www.spacechina.com; f. 1999; Pres. MA XINGRUI.

China Aviation Industry Corporation I: AVIC1 Plaza, 128, Jianguo Lu, Beijing 100022; tel. (10) 65665922; fax (10) 65666518; e-mail lixm@avic1.com.cn; internet www.avic1.com.cn; f. 1999; Pres. LIN ZUOMING.

China Aviation Industry Corporation II: 67 Jiao Nan Dajie, Beijing 100712; tel. (10) 64094013; fax (10) 64032109; e-mail international@avic2.com; internet www.avic2.com.cn; Pres. ZHANG HONGBIAO.

China Aviation Supplies Holding Co (CASC): 3 Tianwei Si Jie, Airport Industrial Zone A, Shunyi, Beijing 101312; tel. (10) 89455000; fax (10) 89455018; internet www.casc.com.cn; f. 1980; fmrly China Aviation Supplies Import & Export Group Corpn; aviation equipment supply services; Pres. LI HAI.

China Certification and Inspection Group Co Ltd (CCIC): Sanyuan Bldg, 18 Xibahe Dongli, Chao Yang Qu, Beijing 100028; tel. (10) 84603456; fax (10) 84603333; e-mail ccic@ccic.com; internet www.ccic.com; fmrly China National Import and Export Commodities Inspection Corpn; inspects, tests and surveys import and export commodities for overseas trade, transport, insurance and manufacturing firms; Pres. WANG FENGQING.

China Civil Engineering Construction Corpn (CCECC): 4 Beifeng Wo, Haidian Qu, Beijing 100038; tel. (10) 63263392; fax (10) 63263864; e-mail zongban@ccecc.com.cn; internet www.ccecc.com.cn; f. 1979; general contracting, provision of technical and labour services, consulting and design, etc.; Chair. LIU ZHIMING; Pres. LI YUAN.

China Construction International Inc: 9 Sanlihe Lu, Haidian Qu, Beijing; tel. (10) 68394086; fax (10) 68394097; Pres. Fu Renzhang.

China Electronics Corpn: 27 Wanshou Lu, Haidian Qu, Beijing 100846; tel. (10) 68218529; fax (10) 68213745; e-mail webmaster@cec.com.cn; internet www.cec.com.cn; Chair. Xiong Qunli; Pres. Liu Liehong.

China Garment Industry Corpn: 9a Taiyanggong Beisanhuandong Lu, Chao Yang Qu, Beijing 100028; tel. (10) 64216660; fax (10) 64239134; Pres. Dong Binggen.

China General Technology (Group) Holding Ltd (Genertec): 23/F Genertec Plaza, 90 Xi San Huan Zhong Lu, Feng Tai Qu, Beijing 100055; tel. (10) 63348889; fax (10) 63348118; e-mail genertec@genertec.com.cn; internet www.genertec.com.cn; f. 1998; est. by merger of China Nat. Technical Import and Export Corpn, China Nat. Machinery Import and Export Corpn, China Nat. Instruments Import and Export Corpn and China Nat. Corpn for Overseas Economic Co-operation; total assets 16,000m. yuan; Chair. He Tongxin; Dir and Pres. Li Dang.

China Great Wall Computer Group: 18/F, Great Wall Technology Bldg, 66 East Rd, Haidian Qu, Beijing 100190; tel. (10) 59831188; fax (10) 59831133; e-mail cs@gwssi.com.cn; internet www.gwssi.com.cn; f. 1988; Pres. Du Heping.

China Great Wall Industry Corpn: 67 Beisihuan Xilu, Haidian Qu, Beijing 100080; tel. (10) 88102000; fax (10) 88102107; e-mail cgwic@cgwic.com; internet www.cgwic.com.cn; f. 1980; international commercial wing of China Aerospace Science and Technology Corpn (CASC); Pres. Yin Liming.

China Guangdong Nuclear Power Holding Co Ltd (CGNPC): Science Bldg, 1001 Shangbu Zhong Lu, Shenzhen 518028; e-mail webmaster_cgnpc@cgnpc.com.cn; internet www.cgnpc.com.cn; f. 1994; operates nuclear power plants; develops hydropower and wind power stations; more than 20 subsidiaries; Chair. He Yu.

China International Book Trading Corpn: see under Publishers.

China International Contractors Association: Dong Zhi Men Wai Dajie, Dongcheng Qu, Beijing 100007; tel. (10) 59765260; fax (10) 59765200; e-mail webmaster@chinca.org; internet www.chinca.org; f. 1988; Chair. Diao Chunhe.

China International Futures Co Ltd (CIFCO): Rong Chao Business Centre, 15/F, Bldg A, 6003 Yi Tian Lu, Futian Qu, Shenzhen 518000; tel. (755) 23818333; fax (755) 23818283; e-mail cifco996@hotmail.com; internet www.szcifco.com; f. 1992; Pres. Chen Donghua.

China International Telecommunication Construction Corpn (CITCC): 56 Nan Fang Zhuang, Fengtai Qu, Beijing 100079; tel. (10) 67668269; fax (10) 67668183; e-mail office@citcc.cn; internet www.citcc.cn; f. 1983; Chair. Wang Qi; Gen. Man. Xu Chuguo.

China International Water and Electric Corpn (CWE): 3 Liupukang Yiqu Zhongjie, Xicheng Qu, Beijing 100120; tel. (10) 59302288; fax (10) 59302900; e-mail headoffice@cwe.cn; internet www.cwe.cn; f. 1956; est. as China Water and Electric International Corpn, name changed 1983; imports and exports equipment for projects in the field of water and electrical engineering; undertakes such projects; provides technical and labour services; Pres. Lu Guojun.

China Iron and Steel Industry and Trade Group Corpn (Sinosteel): Sinosteel Plaza, 8 Hai Dian Lu, Beijing 100080; tel. (10) 62686689; fax (10) 62686688; e-mail info@sinosteel.com; internet www.sinosteel.com; f. 1999; formed by merger of China National Metallurgical Import and Export Corpn, China Metallurgical Raw Materials Corpn and China Metallurgical Steel Products Processing Corpn; Pres. Huang Tianwen.

China Minmetals Corpn (Minmetals): 5 San Li He, Haidian Qu, Beijing 100044; tel. (10) 68495888; fax (10) 68335570; e-mail support@minmetals.com.cn; internet www.minmetals.com.cn; f. 1950; fmrly China National Metals and Minerals Import and Export Corpn, current name adopted 2004; imports and exports steel, antimony, tungsten concentrates and ferro-tungsten, zinc ingots, tin, mercury, pig-iron, cement, etc.; Pres. Zhou Zhongshu.

China National Aerotechnology Import and Export Corpn: Catic Plaza, 18 Beichen Dong Lu, Chao Yang Qu, Beijing 100101; tel. (10) 84972255; fax (10) 84971088; e-mail master@catic.cn; internet www.catic.com.cn; f. 1979; exports signal flares, electric detonators, tachometers, parachutes, general purpose aircraft, etc.; Pres. Ma Zhiping.

China National Animal Breeding Stock Import and Export Corpn (CABS): 5/F Beijing News Plaza, 26 Jian Guo Men Nei Dajie, Beijing 100005; tel. (10) 65228866; fax (10) 85201555; e-mail cabs@cabs.com.cn; sole agency for import and export of stud animals including cattle, sheep, goats, swine, horses, donkeys, camels, rabbits, poultry, etc., as well as pasture and turf grass seeds, feed additives, medicines, etc.; Gen. Man. Liu Xiaofeng.

China National Arts and Crafts (Group) Corpn (CNACGC): Arts and Crafts Bldg, 103 Jixiangli, Chao Yang Men Wai, Chao Yang Qu, Beijing 100020; tel. (10) 85698808; fax (10) 85698866; e-mail info@cnacgc.com; internet www.cnacgc.com; deals in jewellery, ceramics, handicrafts, embroidery, pottery, wicker, bamboo, etc.; jointly est. by two central enterprises: China National Arts and Crafts Import & Export Corpn and China National Arts & Crafts (Group) Corpn; Pres. Zhou Zhengsheng.

China National Automotive Industry Corpn (CNAIC): 46 Fucheng Lu, Haidian Qu, Beijing 100036; tel. (10) 88123968; fax (10) 68125556; Pres. Chen Xulin.

China National Automotive Industry Import and Export Corpn (CAIEC): 265 Beisihuan Zhong Lu, Beijing 100083; tel. (10) 82379009; fax (10) 82379088; e-mail info@caiec.cn; internet www.caiec.cn; Pres. Zhang Fusheng; 1,100 employees.

China National Cereals, Oils and Foodstuffs Import and Export Corpn (COFCO): COFCO Fortune Plaza, 8 Chao Yang Men Wai Dajie, Chao Yang Qu, Beijing 100020; tel. (10) 85006688; fax (10) 65278612; e-mail cofcointo@cofco.com; internet www.cofco.com; f. 1952; imports, exports and processes grains, oils, foodstuffs, etc.; also hotel management and property development; Chair. Ning Gaoning; Pres. Yu Xubo.

China National Chartering Ltd (SINOCHART): Sinotrans Plaza A, Rm 818, 43 Xi Zhi Men Bei Dajie, Beijing 100044; tel. (10) 62295052; fax (10) 62296859; e-mail sinochart@sinochart.com; internet www.sinochart.com; f. 1950; subsidiary of SINOTRANS (see below); arranges chartering of ships, reservation of space, managing and operating chartered vessels; Gen. Man. Geng Chen.

China National Chemical Construction Corpn: Bldg No. 15, Songu, Anzhenxili, Chao Yang Qu, Beijing 100029; tel. (10) 64429966; fax (10) 64419698; e-mail cnccc@cnccc.com.cn; internet www.cnccc.com.cn; Pres. Chen Lihua.

China National Chemicals Import and Export Corporation (SINOCHEM): SINOCHEM Tower, 6–12/F, 28 Fu Xing Men Nei Dajie, Beijing 100031; tel. (10) 59568888; fax (10) 59568890; internet www.sinochem.com; f. 1950; import and export, domestic trade and entrepôt trade of oil, fertilizer, rubber, plastics and chemicals; Pres. Liu Deshu.

China National Coal Group Corpn: 1 Huangsi Lu, Chao Yang Qu, Beijing 100120; tel. (10) 82256688; fax (10) 82236023; e-mail zgzm@chinacoal.com; internet www.chinacoal.com; f. 1982; imports and exports coal and equipment for coal industry, joint coal development and compensation trade; fmrly known as China National Coal Industry Import and Export Corpn; Chair. and Pres. Wu Yaowen.

China National Coal Mine Corpn: 21 Bei Jie, Heipingli, Beijing 100013; tel. (10) 64217766; Pres. Wang Senhao.

China National Complete Plant Import and Export Corpn (Group) (Complant): 9 Xi Bin He Lu, An Ding Men, Beijing 100011; tel. (10) 64253388; fax (10) 64211382; e-mail info@complant.com; internet www.complant.com; Chair. Li Zhimin; Gen. Man. Tang Jianguo.

China National Electronics Import and Export Corpn: 8th Floor, Electronics Bldg, 23a Fuxing Lu, Beijing 100036; tel. (10) 68219550; fax (10) 68212352; e-mail webmaster@ceiec.com.cn; internet www.ceiec.com.cn; f. 1980; imports and exports electronics equipment, light industrial products, ferrous and non-ferrous metals; advertising; consultancy; Pres. and CEO Chen Xu.

China National Export Bases Development Corpn: Bldg 16–17, District 3, Fang Xing Yuan, Fang Zhuang Xiaoqu, Fengtai Qu, Beijing 100078; tel. (10) 67628899; fax (10) 67628803; Pres. Xue Zhao.

China National Foreign Trade Transportation Corpn (Group) (SINOTRANS): 12/F, Sinotrans Plaza A, 43 Xi Zhi Men Bei Dajie, Beijing 100044; tel. (10) 62295900; fax (10) 62295901; e-mail office@sinotrans.com; internet www.sinotrans.com; f. 1950; agents for China's import and export corpns; arranges customs clearance, deliveries, forwarding and insurance for sea, land and air transport; Chair. Zhao Huxiang; Pres. Liu Xihan.

China National Gold Group Corpn (China Gold): 1 South St, Liuyin Park, Dongcheng Qu, Beijing 100011; tel. (10) 84123635; fax (10) 84118355; e-mail cngc@chinagoldgroup.com; internet www.chinagoldgroup.com; gold mining, research and trade; Pres. Sun Zhaoxue.

China National Instruments Import and Export Corpn (Instrimpex): Instrimpex Bldg, 6 Xi Zhi Men Wai Jie, Beijing 100044; tel. (10) 68330618; fax (10) 68318380; e-mail cnic@cnic.genertec.com.cn; internet www.instrimpex.com.cn; f. 1955; imports and exports; technical service, real estate, manufacturing, information service, etc.; Pres. An Fengshou.

China National Light Industrial Products Import and Export Corpn: 910, 9th Section, Jin Song, Chao Yang Qu, Beijing 100021;

tel. (10) 67766688; fax (10) 67747246; e-mail info@chinalight.com.cn; internet www.chinalight.com.cn; imports and exports household electrical appliances, audio equipment, photographic equipment, films, paper goods, building materials, bicycles, sewing machines, enamelware, glassware, stainless steel goods, footwear, leather goods, watches and clocks, cosmetics, stationery, sporting goods, etc.; Pres. PAN WANG.

China National Machine Tool Corpn: World Trade Centre, 23/F, Blk A, Dong San Huan Bei Lu, Dongcheng Qu, Beijing; tel. (10) 58257788; fax (10) 64015657; e-mail zcb@cnmtc.net; internet www.cnmtc.net; f. 1979; imports and exports machine tools and tool products, components and equipment; supplies apparatus for machine-building industry; Pres. QUAN YILU.

China National Machinery and Equipment Import and Export Corpn (Group) (CMEC): 178 Guang An Men Wai Dajie, Beijing 100055; tel. (10) 63451188; fax (10) 63261865; e-mail cmec@mail.cmec.com; internet www.cmec.com; f. 1978; imports and exports machine tools, all kinds of machinery, automobiles, hoisting and transport equipment, electric motors, photographic equipment, etc.; Pres. JIA ZHIQIANG.

China National Medicine and Health Products Import and Export Corpn (Meheco): Meheco Plaza, 18 Guangming Zhong Jie, Chongwen Qu, Beijing 100061; tel. (10) 67116688; fax (10) 67121579; e-mail meheco@meheco.com.cn; internet www.meheco.cn; Pres. ZHANG BEN ZHI.

China National Native Produce and Animal By-Products Import and Export Corpn (TUHSU): COFCO Fortune Plaza, 8 Chao Yang Men Wai Dajie, Chao Yang Qu, Beijing 100020; tel. (10) 85018181; fax (10) 85615151; e-mail tuhsu@cofco.com; internet www.tuhsu.com.cn; f. 1949; imports and exports include tea, coffee, cocoa, fibres, etc.; 9 tea brs; 23 overseas subsidiaries; Pres. WANG ZHEN.

China National Non-Ferrous Metals Import and Export Corpn (CNIEC): 12B Fuxing Lu, Beijing 100814; tel. (10) 63975588; fax (10) 63964424; Chair. WU JIANCHANG; Pres. XIAO JUNQING.

China National Nuclear Corpn: 1 Nansanxiang, Sanlihe, Beijing 100822; tel. (10) 68512211; fax (10) 68533989; e-mail xxzx@cnnc.com.cn; internet www.cnnc.com.cn; Dir SUN QIN.

China National Oil and Gas Exploration and Development Corpn: 1 Fu Cheng Men Bei Dajie, Xicheng Qu, Beijing 100034; tel. (10) 58551114; fax (10) 58551000; e-mail master@cnpcint.com; internet www.cnpc.com.cn/cnodc; subsidiary of China National Petroleum Corpn (see below); Gen. Man. BO QILIANG.

China National Packaging Import and Export Corpn: Xinfu Bldg B, 3 Dong San Huan Bei Lu, Chao Yang Qu, Beijing 100027; tel. (10) 64616359; fax (10) 64611080; e-mail info@chinapack.net; internet www.chinapack.net; handles import and export of packaging materials, containers, machines and tools; contracts for the processing and converting of packaging machines and materials supplied by foreign customers; Pres. ZHENG CHONGXIANG.

China National Petroleum Corpn (CNPC): 9 Dong Zhi Men Bei Lu, Dongcheng Qu, Beijing 100007; tel. (10) 62094114; fax (10) 62094205; e-mail admin_eng@cnpc.com.cn; internet www.cnpc.com.cn; responsible for petroleum extraction and refining in northern and western China, and for setting retail prices of petroleum products; restructured mid-1998, transferring to PetroChina Co Ltd (a publicly listed subsidiary) domestic operations in the areas of petroleum and gas exploration and devt, petroleum refining and petrochemical production, marketing, pipeline transport, and natural gas sales and utilization; acquired PetroKazakhstan in 2005; Pres. JIANG JIEMIN.

China National Publications Import and Export (Group) Corpn: 16 Gongrentiyuguandong Lu, Chao Yang Qu, Beijing; tel. (10) 65066688; fax (10) 65067100; e-mail cnpeak@cnpiec.com.cn; internet www.cnpeak.com; imports and exports books, newspapers and periodicals, records, CD-ROMs, etc.; Pres. WU JIANGJIANG.

China National Publishing Industry Trading Corpn: POB 782, 504 An Hua Li, An Ding Men Wai, Beijing 100011; tel. (10) 64210403; fax (10) 64214540; e-mail cnpitc@cnpitc.com.cn; internet www.cnpitc.com.cn; f. 1981; imports and exports publications, printing equipment technology; holds book fairs abroad; undertakes joint publication; Pres. ZHOU HONGLI.

China National Seed Group Corpn: Sinochem Tower A, 15/F, 2 Fu Xing Men Wai Dajie, Beijing 100045; tel. (10) 88079999; fax (10) 88079998; e-mail chinaseeds@sinochem.com; internet www.chinaseeds.com.cn; f. 1978; imports and exports crop seeds, including cereals, cotton, oil-bearing crops, teas, flowers and vegetables; seed production for foreign seed companies etc.; Gen. Man. ZHANG WEI.

China National Silk Import and Export Corpn: 105 Bei He Yan Jie, Dongcheng Qu, Beijing 100006; tel. (10) 65123338; fax (10) 65125125; e-mail chinasilk@chinasilk.com; internet www.chinasilk.com; 22 subsidiaries and more than 40 domestic co-operative enterprises; Gen. Man. ZHANG WEIMING.

China National Technical Import and Export Corpn: 16/F, Genertec Plaza, 90 Xi San Huan Zhong Lu, Fengtai Qu, Beijing 100055; tel. (10) 63349206; fax (10) 63373713; e-mail cntic@cntic.genertec.com.cn; internet www.cntic.com.cn; f. 1952; imports all kinds of complete plant and equipment, acquires modern technology and expertise from abroad, undertakes co-production and jt ventures, and technical consultation and updating of existing enterprises; Pres. TANG YI.

China National Textiles Import and Export Corpn: Chinatex Mansion, 19 Jian Guo Men Nei Lu, Beijing 100005; tel. (10) 65281122; fax (10) 65124711; e-mail webmaster@chinatex.com; internet www.chinatex.com; f. 1951; imports synthetic fibres, raw cotton, wool and garment accessories; exports cotton yarn, cotton fabric, knitwear and woven garments; over 30 subsidiaries; Pres. ZHAO BOYA.

China National Tobacco Import and Export Group Corpn: 9 Guang An Men Wai Dajie, Xuan Wu Qu, Beijing 100055; tel. (10) 63605290; fax (10) 63605915; internet www.cntiegc.com.cn; Chair. ZHANG HUI.

China North Industries Group Corpn (CNGC): 44 Sanlihe Lu, Beijing 100821; tel. (10) 68594210; fax (10) 68594232; e-mail webmaster@cngc.com.cn; internet www.cngc.com.cn; exports vehicles and mechanical products, light industrial products, chemical products, opto-electronic products, building materials, military products, etc.; Pres. ZHANG GUOQING.

China Railway Construction Corpn: 40 Fuxing Lu, Beijing 100855; tel. (10) 51888114; fax (10) 68217382; e-mail webmaster@crcc.cn; internet www.crcc.cn; f. 1948; state-owned; over 30 subsidiaries; design, construction, equipment installation and maintenance of railways and highways; Pres. ZHAO GUANGFA.

China Railway Group Ltd: China Railway Tower 9, 69 Fuxing Lu, Haidian Qu, Beijing 100039; tel. (10) 51845225; fax (10) 51841757; e-mail webmaster@crec.cn; internet www.crec.cn; f. 2007; est. as jt stock co; 46 subsidiaries; infrastructure construction, design, survey and consulting services; mfr of engineering equipment; Chair. LI CHANGJIN; Pres. BAI ZHONGREN.

China Road and Bridge Corpn: Zhonglu Bldg, 88C, An Ding Men Wai Dajie, Beijing 100011; tel. (10) 64280055; fax (10) 64285686; e-mail crbc@crbc.com; internet www.crbc.com; overseas and domestic building of highways, urban roads, bridges, tunnels, industrial and residential buildings, airport runways and parking areas; contracts to do surveying, designing, pipe-laying, water supply and sewerage, building, etc., and/or to provide technical or labour services; Chair. ZHANG JIANCHU; Pres. WEN GANG.

China Shipbuilding Trading Co Ltd: 8–12/F, Bldg 1, 9 Shouti Nan Lu, Haidian Qu, Beijing 100048; tel. (10) 88573688; fax (10) 88573600; e-mail webmaster@cstc.com.cn; internet www.cstc.com.cn; f. 1982; Pres. LI ZHUSHI.

China State Construction Engineering Corpn: CSCEC Mansion, 15 San Li He Dajie, Haidian Qu, Beijing 100037; tel. (10) 88082888; fax (10) 88082789; e-mail ir@cscec.com.cn; internet www.cscec.com.cn; f. 1982; Pres. YI JUN.

China State Shipbuilding Corpn (CSSC): 9 Shouti Nan Lu, Haidian Qu, Beijing 100044; tel. (10) 68038833; fax (10) 68034592; e-mail cssc@cssc.net.cn; internet www.cssc.net.cn; f. 1999; naval and civil shipbuilding; Pres. TAN ZUOJUN.

China Tea Import and Export Corpn: South Gate, Chao Yang Qu, Beijing 100020; tel. (10) 64204127; fax (10) 64204101; e-mail info@teachina.com; internet www.chinatea.com.cn; Chair. ZHU FUTANG; Gen. Man. SUN YUEHUA.

China Xinshidai (New Era) Co: Xinshidai Plaza, 26 Ping An Xi Li Dajie, Xicheng Qu, Beijing 100034; tel. (10) 88009999; fax (10) 88009779; e-mail xsd@xsd.com.cn; internet www.xsd.com.cn; f. 1980; imports and exports defence industry and civilian products; Pres. WANG XINGYE.

Daqing Petroleum Administration Bureau: Sartu Qu, Daqing, Heilongjiang; tel. (459) 814649; fax (459) 322845; Gen. Man. WANG YONGCHUN.

Maanshan Iron and Steel Co (Masteel): 8 Hongqibei Lu, Maanshan 243003, Anhui Province; tel. (555) 2888158; fax (555) 2324350; internet www.magang.com.cn; sales 34,319.9m. yuan (2006); Chair. GU JIANGUO.

PetroChina International Co Ltd (China National United Oil Corporation—Chinaoil): 27 Chengfang Lu, Xicheng Qu, Beijing 100032; tel. (10) 66227001; fax (10) 66227002; internet www.chinaoil.com.cn; international trading subsidiary of PetroChina Co Ltd; imports and exports petroleum, natural gas and refined petroleum products; Chair. DUAN WENDE; Pres. WANG LIHUA.

Shanghai International Trust Trading Corpn: 201 Zhaojiabang Lu, Shanghai 200032; tel. (21) 64033866; fax (21) 64034722; f. 1979; present name adopted 1988; handles import and export business, international mail orders, processing, assembling, compensation, trade, etc.

State Bureau of Non-Ferrous Metals Industry: 12B Fuxing Lu, Beijing 100814; tel. (10) 68514477; fax (10) 68515360; Dir ZHANG WULE.

Xinxing Oil Co (XOC): Beijing; f. 1997; exploration, development and production of domestic and overseas petroleum and gas resources; Gen. Man. ZHU JIAZHEN.

UTILITIES

Regulatory Authority

State Electricity Regulatory Commission: 86 Xichangan Dajie, Beijing 100031; tel. (10) 66058800; e-mail serc_manager@serc.gov.cn; internet www.serc.gov.cn; f. 2003; Pres. WU XINXIONG.

Electricity

Anhui Province Energy Group Co Ltd (Wenergy): 76 Ma'anshan Lu, Hefei, Anhui 230001; tel. (551) 2225678; fax (551) 2225959; e-mail webmaster@wenergy.com.cn; internet www.wenergy.com.cn.

Beijing Electric Power Corpn: Qianmen Xi Dajie, Beijing 100031; tel. (10) 63129201; internet www.bjpsc.com.

Central China Electric Power Group Co: 47 Xudong Lu, Wuchang, Wuhan 430077; tel. (27) 6813398.

Changsha Electric Power Bureau: 162 Jiefang Sicun, Changsha 410002; tel. (731) 5912121; fax (731) 5523240.

China Atomic Energy Authority: Jia 8, Fucheng 100048; e-mail webmaster@caea.gov.cn; internet www.caea.gov.cn; Chair. CHEN QUIFA.

China Guodian Corpn: 6–8 Fu Cheng Men Bei Dajie, Xicheng Qu, Beijing 100034; tel. (10) 58682000; fax (10) 58553900; e-mail cgdcb@cgdc.com.cn; internet www.cgdc.com.cn; f. 2002; transfer of Jianbi power plant from fmr State Power Corpn completed Sept. 2003; Chair. ZHU YONGPENG.

China Power Grid Development (CPG): 4 Xueyuang Nanli, Haidan Qu, Beijing; manages transmission and transformation lines for the Three Gorges hydroelectric scheme; Pres. ZHOU XIAOQIAN.

China Power Investment Corpn: Bldg 3, 28 Financial St, Xicheng Qu, Beijing 100140; tel. (10) 66298000; fax (10) 66298095; e-mail engweb@cpicorp.com.cn; internet www.zdt.com.cn; f. 2002; formed from part of the constituent businesses of fmr State Power Corpn; parent company of China Power International; Pres. LU QIZHOU.

China Southern Power Grid Co: 6 Huasui Lu, Zhujiang Xincheng, Tianhe Qu, Guangzhou 510623, Guangdong Province; tel. (20) 38121080; fax (20) 38120189; e-mail international@csg.cn; internet eng.csg.cn; f. 2002; est. from power grids in southern provinces of fmr State Power Corpn; Chair. ZHAO JIANGUO; Pres. JUN ZHONG.

China Three Gorges Project Corpn (CTGPC): 1 Jianshe Dajie, Yichang 443002, Hubei Province; tel. (717) 6276666; fax (717) 6270088; e-mail webmaster@ctgpc.com.cn; internet www.ctgpc.com; Chair. CAO GUANGJING; Pres. FI CHEN.

China Yangtze Power Co Ltd: Block B, Focus Place, 19 Financial St, Xicheng Qu, Beijing 100032; tel. (10) 58688999; fax (10) 58688888; e-mail cypc@cypc.com.cn; internet www.cypc.com.cn; f. 2002; generation of power from the Yangtze river; manages power-generating assets on behalf of China Yangtze Three Gorges Project Development Corpn; initial public offering on the Shanghai Stock Exchange Nov. 2003; Gen. Man. ZHANG CHENG.

Chongqing Jiulong Electric Power Co Ltd: 15 Qianjinzhi Lu, Yangjiaping, Jiulongpo Qu, Chongqing 400050; tel. (23) 68787910; fax (23) 68787944; internet www.jiulongep.com; Chair. LIU WEIQING; Gen. Man. ZHENG WUSHENG.

Chongqing Three Gorges Water Conservancy and Electric Power Co Ltd: 85 Gao Suntang, Wanzhou Qu, Chongqing 400040; tel. (23) 87509622; fax (23) 58237588; internet www.cqsxsl.com; Chair. YE JIANQIAO.

Dalian Power Supply Co: 102 Zhongshan Lu, Dalian 116001; tel. (411) 2637560; fax (411) 2634430; Chief Gen. Man. LIU ZONGXIANG.

Datang Huayin Electric Power Co Ltd: 255, Third Section, Central Furong Lu, Changsha 410007; tel. (731) 5388028; internet www.hypower.com.cn; Gen. Man. WEI YUAN.

Datang International Power Generation Co Ltd: 9 Guang Ning Bo Lu, Xicheng Qu, Beijing 100140; tel. (10) 88008800; fax (10) 88008111; internet www.dtpower.com; independent power producer; Chair. ZHAI RUOYU; Pres. CAO JINGSHAN.

Fujian Electric Power Co Ltd: 4 Xingang Dao, Taijrang Qu, Fuzhou 350009; tel. and fax (591) 3268514; Gen. Man. LI WEIDONG.

Fujian Mindong Electric Power Co Ltd: 8–10/F, Hualong Bldg, 143 Huancheng Lu, Jiaocheng Qu, Ningde 352100; tel. (593) 2096666; fax (593) 2096993; internet www.mdep.com.cn; f. 2000; Chair. ZHOU DUNBIN.

Gansu Electric Power Co: Lanzhou 730050; tel. (931) 2334311; fax (931) 2331042; e-mail webmaster@gsepc.com; internet www.gsepc.com; Dir ZHANG MINGXI.

GD Power Development Co Ltd: 9/F, International Investment Plaza Tower B, 6–8 Fu Cheng Men Bei Dajie, Xicheng Qu, Beijing; tel. (10) 58682200; fax (10) 583553800; e-mail gdd1@600795.com.cn; internet www.600795.com.cn; manufacture and sale of electricity and heat, and the operation of power grids in northern, eastern, north-eastern and north-western China, as well as Yunnan and Sichuan Provinces; Chair. ZHU YONGFAN.

Guangdong Electric Power Bureau: 757 Dongfeng Dong Lu, Guangzhou 510600; tel. (20) 87767888; fax (20) 87770307.

Guangdong Electric Power Development Co Ltd: 23–26/F, South Tower, Yuedian Plaza, 2 Tian He Dong Lu, Guangzhou 510630; tel. (20) 87570251; fax (20) 85138004; internet www.ged.com.cn; Chair. LI PAN.

Guangdong Yudean Group: Yudean Plaza, 2 Tianhe Dong Lu, Guangzhou, Guangdong 510630; tel. (20) 85138888; fax (20) 85136666; e-mail ydbianjibu@gdyd.com; internet www.gdyd.com; Chair. LI PAN.

Guangxi Guiguan Electric Power Co Ltd: 126 Minzhu Lu, Nanning 530022; tel. (771) 6118880; fax (771) 6118899; e-mail ggep@ggep.com.cn; internet www.ggep.com.cn; Chair. YANG QING; Gen. Man. DAI BO.

Guangzhou Electric Power Co: 9th Floor, Huale Bldg, 53 Huale Lu, Guangzhou 510060; tel. (20) 83821111; fax (20) 83808559.

Guodian Changyuan Electric Power Co Ltd: Huazhong Electric Finance Bldg, 117 Xu Dong Jie, Wuchang Qu, Wuhan 430067, Hubei Province; tel. (27) 86610541; fax (27) 86610524; e-mail sec@cydl.com.cn; internet www.cydl.com.cn; Chair. LI QINGKUI.

Hainan Electric Power Industry Bureau: 34 Haifu Dadao, Haikou 570203; tel. (898) 5334777; fax (898) 5333230.

Huadian Energy Co Ltd: 209 Dacheng Jie, Harbin 150001; tel. (451) 53685938; fax (451) 53685915; internet www.hdenergy.com; Chair. SHUHUI REN.

Huadian Power International Corpn Ltd: 2 Xuanwumen Jie, Xicheng Qu, Beijing 100031; tel. (10) 83567888; fax (10) 83567963; e-mail hdpi@hdpi.com.cn; internet www.hdpi.com.cn; f. 1994; fmrly Shandong International Power Development, renamed as above 2003; Chair. DA HONGXING; Gen. Man. CHEN JIANHUA.

Huadong Electric Power Group Corpn: 201 Nanjing Dong Lu, Shanghai; tel. (21) 63290000; fax (21) 63290727; power supply.

Huaneng Power International: Huaneng Bldg 4, Fu Xing Men Nei Dajie, Xicheng Qu, Beijing 100031; tel. (10) 63226999; fax (10) 63226888; e-mail zqb@hpi.com.cn; internet www.hpi.com.cn; f. 1998; transfer of generating assets from fmr State Power Corpn completed Sept. 2003; Chair. CAO PEIXI; Pres. LIU GUOYUE.

Huazhong Electric Power Group Corpn: Liyuan, Donghu, Wuhan, Hubei Province; tel. (27) 6813398; fax (27) 6813143; electrical engineering; Gen. Man. LIN KONGXING.

Hunan Chendian International Development Share-holding Ltd Co: 15/F, Wanguo Bldg, Minsheng Lu, Intersection Qingnian Dajie, Chenzhou 423000; tel. (735) 2339233; fax (735) 2339269; internet www.chinacdi.com; f. 2000; electricity and gas supply and generation; Chair. FU GUO.

Inner Mongolia Electric Power Co: 28 Xilin Nan Lu, Huhehaose 010021; tel. (471) 6942222; fax (471) 6924863.

Jiangmen Electric Power Supply Bureau: 87 Gangkou Lu, Jiangmen 529030; tel. and fax (750) 3360133.

Jiangxi Electric Power Corpn: 13 Yongwai Zheng Jie, Nanchang 330006; tel. (791) 6224701; fax (791) 6224830; internet www.jepc.com.cn; f. 1993.

National Grid Construction Co: established to oversee completion of the National Grid.

North China Grid Company Ltd: 482 Guanganmen Nei Dajie, Xuanwu Qu, Beijing 100053; tel. and fax (10) 83583114; internet www.nc.sgcc.com.cn; Chair. MA ZONGLIN.

Northeast China Grid Co Ltd: 11 Shiyiwei Lu, Heping Qu, Shenyang 110003; tel. (24) 3114382; fax (24) 3872665; internet www.ne.sgcc.com.cn.

Northwest Power Construction Group Corpn: 3 Changle Xi Lu, Xian 710032; tel. (29) 82551370; fax (29) 83382405; e-mail nwepc_hr@163.com; internet www.nwepc.cn.

Shandong Electric Power Group Corpn: 150 Jinger Lu, Jinan 250001; tel. (531) 6911919; internet www.sd.sgcc.com.cn; Chair. LI TONG ZHI.

Shandong Rizhao Power Co Ltd: 1st Floor, Bldg 29, 30 Northern Section, Shunyu Xiaoqu, Jinan 250002; tel. (531) 2952462; fax (531) 2942561; subsidiary of Huaneng Power International.

Shanghai Electric Power Co Ltd: China Resource Plaza, Bldg 1, 36/F, 268 Zhongshou Nan Lu, Shanghai 200010; tel. (21) 51156666;

e-mail sepco@shanghaipower.com; internet www.shanghaipower.com; Chair. ZHOU SHIPING.

Shanghai Municipal Electric Power Co (SMEPC): 1122 Yuanshen Lu, Shanghai 200122; tel. (21) 28925222; fax (21) 28926512; e-mail smepc@smepc.com; internet www.smepc.com.cn.

Shantou Electric Power Development Co: 23 Zhuchi Lu, Shantou 515041; tel. (754) 8857191; Chair. LIN WEIGUANG.

Shanxi Zhangze Electric Power Co Ltd: 197 Wuyi Lu, Taiyuan 030001; tel. (351) 4265111; fax (351) 4265112; e-mail xww@zdthb.com.cn; internet www.zhangzepower.com; Chair. JIA BIN.

Shenergy Co Ltd: 1 Fuxing Zhong Lu, Shanghai 200021; tel. (621) 63900303; fax (621) 63900456; e-mail zhengquan@shenergy.com.cn; internet www.shenergy.com.cn; f. 1992; supply and distribution of electricity and natural gas; Chair. CHOU WEIGUO.

Shenzhen Power Supply Co: 2 Yanhe Xi Lu, Luohu Qu, Shenzhen 518000; tel. (755) 5561920.

Sichuan Electric Power Co: Room 1, Waishi Bldg, Dongfeng Lu, Chengdu 610061; tel. (28) 444321; fax (28) 6661888.

Sichuan Mingxing Electric Power Co Ltd: 88 Ming Yue Lu, Sui Ning 629000; tel. (825) 2210076; fax (825) 2210017; internet www.mxdl.com.cn; f. 1988; distribution of electric power and gas; Chair. ZHANG YOUCAI.

State Grid Corpn of China: 86 Chang'an Xi Lu, Xicheng Qu, Beijing 100031; tel. and fax (10) 66597205; e-mail sgcc-info@sgcc.com.cn; internet www.sgcc.com.cn; f. 1997 from holdings of Ministry of Electric Power; fmrly State Power Corpn of China; became a grid co following division of State Power Corpn into 11 independent companies (five generating companies, four construction companies and two transmission companies) in Dec. 2002; generating assets transferred to Huaneng Group, Huadian Group, Guodian Group, China Power Investment Corpn and Datang Group; Pres. and CEO LIU ZHENYA.

Tianjin Electric Power Corpn: 39 Jinbu Dao, Hebei Qu, Tianjin 300010; tel. (22) 24406031; fax (22) 24408615; e-mail tj.sgcc-info@sgcc.com.cn; internet www.tj.sgcc.com.cn; Gen. Man. ZHANG NING.

Top Energy Co Ltd: 272 Changzhi Jie, Taiyuan, Shanxi; tel. (351) 7021857; fax (351) 7021077; e-mail top600780@sina.com; internet www.600780.net; f. 1992; Chair. CHANG XIAOGANG.

Wuhan Power Supply Co: 1053 Jiefang Dadao, Hankou 430013, Wuhan Province; tel. (27) 82403109.

Wuxi Power Supply Bureau: 8 Houxixi, Wuxi 214001; tel. (510) 2717678; fax (510) 2719182.

Xiamen Power Transformation and Transmission Engineering Co: 67 Wenyuan Lu, Xiamen 361004; tel. (592) 2046763.

Xian Power Supply Bureau: Huancheng Dong Lu, Xian 710032; tel. (29) 7271483.

Xinjiang Tianfu Thermoelectric Co Ltd: 54 Hongxing Lu, Shihezi 832000; tel. (993) 2901108; fax (993) 2901121; e-mail yj@tfrd.com.cn; internet www.tfrd.com.cn; f. 1999; generation and distribution of electricity in Shihezi, Xinjiang Uygur Autonomous Region; Chair. WEI LU.

Zhejiang Southeast Electric Power Co: 152 Tianmushan Lu, Hangzhou, Zhejiang 310007; tel. (51) 85774567; fax (51) 85774321; internet www.zsepc.com; Chair. MAO JIANHONG.

Gas

Beijing Gas Group Co Ltd: Xicheng; tel. (10) 66205589; fax (10) 66205587; e-mail bjgas@bjgas.com; internet www.bjgas.com; owned by the Hong Kong-based Beijing Enterprises Holdings Ltd; Chair. SI ZHOU.

Beijing Natural Gas Co: Bldg 5, Dixingju, An Ding Men Wai, Beijing 100011; tel. (10) 64262244.

Changchun Gas Co: 421 Yan'an Jie, Changchun 130021; tel. (431) 5937850; fax (431) 5954646; internet www.ccrq.com.cn.

Changsha Gas Co: 18 Shoshan Lu, Changsha 410011; tel. (731) 4427246.

ENN Energy Holdings Ltd: Huaxiang Lu, Langfang Economic and Technical Development Zone, Hebei 065001; tel. (316) 2598100; fax (316) 2598585; e-mail xagas_news@enn.cn; internet yw.xinaogas.com; fmrly known as Xinao Gas Holdings Ltd; Chair. WANG YUSUO.

Qingdao Gas Co: 399A Renmin Lu, Qingdao 266032; tel. (532) 4851945; fax (532) 4858653; e-mail gasoffice@qdgas.com.cn; internet www.qdgas.com.cn.

Shanghai Dazhong Public Utilities: 8/F, 1515 Zhongshan Xi Lu, Shanghai 200235; tel. (21) 64288888; fax (21) 64288727; internet www.dzug.cn; Chair. YANG GUOPING.

Shenzhen Energy Group Co Ltd: 2068 Shennan Lu, Futian Qu, Shenzhen 518031; tel. (755) 83680288; fax (755) 83680298; e-mail IR@sec.com.cn; internet www.sec.com.cn; f. 1992; Chair. GAO ZIMIN.

Wuhan Gas Co: Qingnian Lu, Hankou, Wuhan 430015; tel. (27) 5866223.

Xiamen Gas Corpn: Ming Gong Bldg, Douxi Lukou, Hubin Nan Lu, Xiamen 361004; tel. (592) 2025937; fax (592) 2033290.

Water

Beijing Municipal Water Works Bureau: 83 Cuiwei Lu, Haidian Qu, Beijing 100036; tel. (10) 68213366; fax (10) 68130728.

Changchun Water Group Co Ltd: 53 Dajing Lu, Changchun 130000; tel. (431) 88974423; e-mail ccws@changchunwater.com; internet www.changchunwater.com.

Chengdu Municipal Waterworks Co Ltd: 16 Shierqiao Jie, Shudu Dadao, Chengdu 610072; tel. (28) 77663122; fax (28) 7776876; internet www.cdwater.chengdu.gov.cn.

Guangzhou Water Supply Co: 12 Zhongshan Yi Lu, Yuexiu Qu, Guangzhou 510600; fax (20) 87159099; internet www.gzwatersupply.com; Pres. WANG JIANPING.

Haikou Water Group Co Ltd: Haidian; tel. (898) 66269271; fax (898) 66269696; internet www.haikouwater.com.

Harbin Water Co: 49 Xi Shidao Jie, Daoli Qu, Harbin 150010; tel. (451) 4610522; fax (451) 4611726.

Jiangmen Water Supply Co Ltd: 44 Jianshe Lu, Jiangmen 529000; tel. (750) 3286358; fax (750) 3286368; e-mail jmwtof@163.com; internet www.jmwater.com.

Qinhuangdao Pacific Water Co: 71 West First St, Changli, Hebei 066600; tel. (335) 2022579; fax (335) 2986924; e-mail qpwc@sinofrench.com; internet www.sinofrench.com/Qinhuangdao.htm; f. 1998; Sino-US water supply project.

Sembcorp Utilities Investment Management (Shanghai) Ltd: Unit 503–506, Fortune Gate, 1701 Beijing West Rd, Jing'an, Shanghai 200040; tel. (21) 62880822; internet www.sembcorp.com; f. 1996; treatment of wastewater, industrial water, potable water and overall water management; fmrly The China Water Co, name changed as above after acquisition by Sembcorp (Singapore) in 2010; Pres. and CEO TANG KIN FEI.

Shanghai Water Authority: 389 Jiangsu Lu, Shanghai 200050; tel. (21) 52397000; e-mail webmaster@shanghaiwater.gov.cn; internet www.shanghaiwater.gov.cn; service provider for municipality of Shanghai; Dir-Gen. ZHANG JIAYI.

Shenzhen Water Supply Group Co: 7/F Water Bldg, 1019 Shennan Zhong Lu, Shenzhen 518031; tel. (755) 82137618; fax (755) 82137830; e-mail master@waterchina.com; internet www.waterchina.com.

Tianjin Waterworks Group: 54 Jianshe Lu, Heping Qu, Tianjin 300040; tel. (22) 3393887; fax (22) 3306720; e-mail sonic356@sohu.com; internet www.jinnanwater.com.

Xian Water Co: Huancheng Xi Lu, Xian 710082; tel. (29) 4244881.

Zhanjiang Water Co: 20 Renmin Dadaonan, Zhanjiang 524001; tel. (759) 2286394.

Zhongshan Water Supply Co: 23 Yinzhu Jie, Zhuyuan Lu, Zhongshan 528403; tel. (760) 8312969; fax (760) 6326429.

Zhoushan Water Supply Co Ltd: 263 Jiefang Xi Lu, Zhoushan 316000; tel. (580) 2022769; e-mail webmaster@zswater.com; internet www.zswater.com.

Zhuhai Water Group Co Ltd: 338 Meihua Dong Lu, Zhuhai 519000; tel. (756) 8899110; e-mail zhgsdnzx@pub.zhuhai.gd.cn; internet www.zhuhai-water.com.cn.

MAJOR COMPANIES

(cap. = capital; res = reserves; m. = million; amounts in yuan, unless otherwise stated)

Agriculture

Chaoda Modern Agriculture Group: No. 29 Tongpan Rd, Fuzhou 350003, Fujian Province; tel. (591) 28378888; fax (591) 28023860; e-mail english@chaoda.com; internet www.chaoda.com; organic agriculture; cap. 309.6m., res 16,444.1m., total revenue 6,127m. (2009); Chair. and CEO KWOK HO; 23,000 employees.

East Hope Group: East Hope Bldg, 15/F, 1777 Century Ave, Shanghai 200122; tel. (21) 58303333; fax (21) 68768746; e-mail postmaster@easthope.com.cn; internet www.easthope.com.cn; f. 1995; created from restructuring of Hope Group; feed production; sales 7,000m. (2001); Chair. LIU YONGXING; 11,843 employees.

New Hope Group Co Ltd: 9 Xin Yuan Lu, Chengdu 610041, Sichuan Province; tel. (28) 85224545; fax (28) 85234545; e-mail xuanchuan@newhopegroup.com; internet www.newhopegroup.com; f. 1983; 76 factories; animal feed, food, trade; sales 11,300m. (2001); Pres. LIU YONGHAO; 10,000 employees.

Shanghai Dajiang (Group) Stock Co Ltd: 7/F Huayi Plaza, 1555 Lianhua Lu, Shanghai 200233; tel. (21) 34225317; fax (21) 34225056; e-mail dajiang@dajiang.com; internet www.dajiang.com; f. 1985;

production and sale of animal feed and feed machinery; sales 754.3m. (2005); Chair. and Pres. YU NAIFEN; 1,277 employees.

Tongwei Group: POB 618, Hi-tech Development Zone, Chengdu, Sichuan 610041; tel. (28) 85188888; fax (28) 85199999; e-mail lill@tongwei.com; internet www.tongwei.com; feed production, bio-engineering, construction; sales 26,200m. (2009); Chair. LIU HANYUAN; approx. 10,000 employees.

Automobiles and Other Transport Equipment

Brilliance China Automotive Holdings Ltd: Suites 1602–05, Chater House, 8 Connaught Rd, Central, Hong Kong; tel. (852) 25237227; fax (852) 25268472; e-mail cba@brillianceauto.com; internet www.brillianceauto.com; f. 1992; mfr of light trucks; cap. and res 6,049.6m., total revenue 12,390m. (2009); Chair. WU XIAO AN; CEO QI YUMIN; 6,360 employees.

Chery Automobile Co Ltd: 8 Changchun Lu, Economic and Technological Development Zone, Wuhu 241006, Anhui Province; tel. (400) 8838888; fax (553) 5951289; e-mail chery_bd@mychery.com; internet www.chery.cn; f. 1997; manufactures and exports automobiles and components; Pres. YIN TONGYAO; 13,000 employees.

China Communications Construction Co Ltd: 85 Deshengmenwai Dajie, Xicheng Qu, Beijing 100088; tel. (10) 82016644; fax (10) 82016500; e-mail ir@ccccltd.cn; internet www.ccccltd.cn; f. 2006; construction and design of transport infrastructure and port machinery; 41 subsidiary cos and 16 jt stock cos; cap. and res 39,041m., revenue 226,920m. (2009); Chair. ZHOU JICHANG; Pres. LIU QITAO.

China FAW Group Corpn: 3025 Dong Feng Lu, Changchun 130011, Jilin Province; tel. (431) 5905407; fax (431) 87614780; e-mail xhg_wj@faw.com.cn; internet www.faw.com; f. 1953; mfr of trucks and automobiles; 28 wholly owned and 18 partially owned subsidiaries; total assets 109,850m., sales 218,400m. (2008); Chair. XU JIANYI; 133,000 employees.

Chongqing Chang'an Automobile Co Ltd: 260 Jianxin Dong Lu, Jiangbei Qu, Chongqing 400060; tel. (23) 67591349; fax (23) 67866055; e-mail cazqc@mail.changan.com.cn; internet www.changan.com.cn; manufactures and exports road vehicles and vehicle components; sales 6,703.2m. (2000); Chair. YIN JIA XU; 28,000 employees.

Commercial Aircraft Corpn of China Ltd: 25 Zhangyang Lu, Shanghai 200120; tel. (21) 38588888; fax (21) 38588800; e-mail zgsfgsxwzx@comac.cc; internet www.comac.cc; f. 2008; manufactures passenger aircraft; cap. 19,000m.; Chair. ZHANG QINGWEI; Pres. JIN ZHUANGLONG.

Dongfeng Motor Corpn: Dongfeng Lu, Wuhan Economic and Technology Development Zone, Wuhan, Hubei 430056; tel. (27) 84285041; fax (27) 84285288; e-mail wzgl@dfmc.com.cn; internet www.dfmc.com.cn; f. 1969; trucks and automobiles; has established jt ventures for the manufacture of passenger vehicles with Nissan Motor Co Ltd (Japan), Honda Motor Co Ltd (Japan) and Kia Motors Corpn (South Korea); total assets 73,250m., sales 197,000m. (2008); CEO XU PING; 120,000 employees.

First Tractor Co Ltd: 154 Jian She Jie, Luoyang City, Henan 471004; tel. (379) 64969135; fax (379) 64970771; e-mail msc0038@ytogroup.com; internet www.first-tractor.com.cn; production and sale of agricultural tractors; cap. and res 2,713.7m., revenue 8,971.2m. (2009); Chair. ZHAO YANSHUI; Gen. Man. QU DAWEI; 14,330 employees.

Jinan Qingqi Motorcycle Co Ltd: 34 Heping Lu, Jinan 250014; tel. (531) 86599882; fax (531) 86599889; e-mail sshwt@qingqi.com.cn; internet www.qingqi.com.cn; mfr of motorcycles; Chair. YU GUOHUA; Pres. HAN JINFU.

Liaoning SG Automotive Group Co Ltd (SG): 50 Shuguang Lu, Zhen An Qu, Dandong 118001, Liaoning Province; tel. (415) 4146825; fax (415) 4142821; e-mail dongban@sgautomotive.com; internet www.sgautomotive.com; design, manufacturing and marketing of automobile components, buses, SUVs and light trucks; Chair. LI JINDIAN.

Shanghai Automotive Industry Corpn (SAIC): 489 Weihai Lu, Shanghai; tel. (21) 22011688; fax (21) 22011188; e-mail saicgroup@saicgroup.com; internet www.saicgroup.com; acquired a 48.9% stake in South Korean company Ssangyong Motor in Oct. 2004; sales US $24,880m. (2008); Chair. HU MAOYUAN; Pres. SHEN JIANHUA; 70,374 employees (2006).

Shanghai GM: 1500 Shenjiang Lu Jinqiao, Pudong Qu, Shanghai 201206; tel. (21) 28902890; fax (21) 58997570; e-mail ct@shanghaigm.com; internet www.shanghaigm.com; f. 1997; jt venture between General Motors (USA) and Shanghai Automotive Industry Corpn; Pres. YE YONGMING.

Shanghai Volkswagen Automotive Company Ltd: 63 Antingluopu Lu, Shanghai 201805; tel. (21) 59561888; fax (21) 59572815; internet www.csvw.com; f. 1985; jt venture between Volkswagen (Germany) and Shanghai Automotive Industry Corpn to manufacture cars; total assets 29,935.4m., sales 36,265.3m. (2002); Pres. CHEN ZHIXIN; 10,957 employees (2002).

Wanxiang Group Corpn: Ningwei Town, Xiaoshan City, Zhejiang Province; tel. (571) 82832999; fax (571) 82833999; e-mail webmaster@wanxiang.com.cn; internet www.wanxiang.com.cn; major mfr of car parts; sales 8,600.0m. (2001); Pres. LIU GUANQIU; 6,500 employees.

Yuejin Motor (Group) Corpn (Nanjing Automobile Group Corpn): 331 Zhong Yang Bei Lu, Gulou Qu, Nanjing 210037; tel. (25) 83437788; fax (25) 83433526; e-mail nac@nanqi.com.cn; internet www.nanqi.com.cn; f. 1947; acquired MG Rover (United Kingdom) in 2005; Pres. CHEN ZHIXIN.

Zhonglu Co Ltd (Shanghai Forever Import & Export Co Ltd): 818 Nan Liu Lu, Shanghai 201300; tel. (21) 51087787; fax (21) 51087786; e-mail info@forever-bicycle.com; internet www.forever-bicycle.com; f. 1940; fmrly Shanghai Forever Co Ltd; name changed as above in 2008; design, manufacture and distribution of bicycles; Chair. CHEN RONG; Gen. Man. GENG WEI.

Zongshen Industrial Group: 25 Erlang Jie, Gaoxin Qu, Chongqing 400039; tel. (23) 66372255; fax (23) 66372338; e-mail zsgroup@zongshenmotor.com; internet www.zongshenmotor.com; f. 1992; manufactures motorcycles and engines; assets 4,000.0m. (2002); Chair. ZUO ZONGSHEN; 18,000 employees.

Electronics and Electrical Goods

Amoi Electronics Co Ltd: Software Park, 4/F, Xiamen, Fujian Province; tel. (592) 3663088; fax (592) 3663080; e-mail service@amoi.com.cn; internet www.amoi.com.cn; mfrs of telecommunications terminal products and consumer electronics; revenue 306.8m. (2009); Chair. WANG LONGCHU.

Beijing Huaqi Information Digital Technology Co Ltd: 10–11/F, Ideal Plaza, 58 West Rd, North 4th Ring Rd, Beijing 100080; tel. (10) 62606115; fax (10) 82607852; e-mail sales@aigo.com; internet www.aigo.com; f. 1993; mfr of consumer electronics; CEO JUN FENG.

Broad Air Conditioning: Broad Town, Changsha 410138; tel. (10) 84086688; fax (10) 82515208; e-mail css@broad.net; internet www.broad.com; manufactures air conditioning products; sales US $145.0m. (2001); Chair. ZHANG YUE; 2,000 employees.

BYD Electronic (International) Co Ltd: 3001 Hengping Lu, Pingshan, Longgang, Shenzhen 518118; tel. (755) 89888888; fax (755) 84202222; internet www.byd-electronic.com; mfrs of mobile telephone handset components; cap. and res 6,477m., revenue 11,198.6m. (2009); Dir LI KE; 45,000 employees (Dec. 2009).

Chint Group: Chint High-tech Industrial Park, North Baixiang, Wenzhou 325603, Zhejiang Province; tel. (577) 62777777; fax (577) 62875888; e-mail chint@chint.com; internet www.chint.com; f. 1984; specialized mfr of electrical appliances; sales US $2,000m. (2006); Chair. and CEO NAN CUNHUI; 16,000 employees (2007).

Delixi Group: Delixi Industrial Zone, Yueqing, Zhejiang Province, Wenzhou 325604; tel. (577) 62723888; fax (577) 62725559; e-mail info@delixi.com; internet www.delixi.com; f. 1984; manufactures electric power transmission and distribution appliances; sales US $790.0m. (2001); Chair. HU CHENGZHONG; 20,000 employees.

Galanz Group Co Ltd: 25 Ronggui Nan, Shunde, Foshan 528305, Guangdong Province; tel. (757) 28886389; fax (757) 28889628; e-mail info@galanz.com.cn; internet www.galanz.com; f. 1978; home appliances, incl. air conditioning equipment and microwave ovens; Chair. and CEO LEUNG QINGDE.

Gome Electrical Appliances Holding Ltd: 18/F, Block B, Eagle Plaza, 26 Xiaoyun Lu, Chao Yang Qu, Beijing; tel. (10) 59288915; fax (10) 59288925; e-mail info@gome.com.hk; internet www.gome.com.hk; f. 1987; retailers of electrical appliances and consumer electronics products; cap. and res 11,802.4m., revenue 42,667.5m. (2009); Chair. ZHANG DAZHONG; Pres. WANG JUNZHOU; 42,368 employees (Dec. 2009).

Gree Group Corp: Beijing Industrial Zone, Zhuhai 519020, Guangdong Province; tel. (756) 8614883; fax (756) 8614998; e-mail gree@gree.com.cn; internet www.gree.com; f. 1985; manufactures electronic and electrical goods and machinery; property and transport; operating revenue 42,637m. (2009); Chair. ZHU JIANGHONG; CEO DONG MINGZHU.

Guangdong Midea Electric Appliances Co Ltd: Midea Industrial City, Bei Jiao, Shunde 528311, Guangdong Province; tel. (757) 26338888; fax (757) 26650073; internet www.midea.com.cn; f. 1968; 42.86% owned by Midea Group; manufactures consumer electronics, incl. air-conditioning units, electric fans, microwave ovens, etc.; sales 75,000m. (2007); Chair. HE XIANGJIAN.

Haier Group: Inside Haier Garden, Haier Industrial Park, Haier Lu, Qingdao 266101; tel. (532) 88939999; fax (532) 88938666; e-mail info@haier.com; internet www.haier.com; f. 1991; household appliances, pharmaceuticals, air conditioners, refrigerators; cap. HK $996.4m., res HK $206.8m., sales HK $3,152.7m. (2004); Chair. and CEO ZHANG RUIMIN; 4,300 employees (June 2006).

Henan Star Hi-Tech Co Ltd: 38 Jinsuo Lu, Zhengzhou 450001, Henan Province; tel. (371) 67988282; fax (371) 67982830; e-mail starscb@126.com; internet www.stardc.com.cn; f. 1988; electric measurement equipment, telecommunication systems; 66.72% owned by Henan Star Science and Technology Group Ltd; revenue 772m. (2009); Chair. LIU SHUANGHE; 1,010 employees.

Hisense Electric Co Ltd: 22/F, Hisense Tower, 17 Donghaixi Jie, Qingdao 266071; tel. (532) 83878888; fax (532) 83872882; e-mail service@hisense.com; internet www.hisense.com; f. 1969; mfrs of televisions, mobile telephones, air conditioners and refrigerators; Chair. ZHOU HOUJIAN; Pres. and CEO YU SHUMIN.

Hisense Kelon Electrical Appliance Co (Kelon Group): 8 Ronggang Lu, Ronggui, Shunde 528303, Guangdong Province; tel. (757) 28362570; fax (757) 28361055; e-mail kelonsec@hisense.com; internet www.kelon.com; f. 1993; domestic electrical appliances, incl. refrigerators; sales 8,673.7m. (2009); Chair. TANG YEGUO; 18,132 employees.

Konka Group Co Ltd: East Industrial Zone, Overseas Chinese Town, Nanshan Qu, Shenzhen 518053; tel. (755) 26608866; fax (755) 26600082; e-mail hjzxgdsl@konka.com; internet www.konka.com; f. 1979; consumer electronics; cap. 602.0m., res 2,610.0m. (2005), revenue 13,983.8m. (2009); Chair. HOU SONGRONG; Pres. CHEN YUEHUA; 17,217.

Lenovo Group: 6 Chuang Ye Lu, Haidian Qu, Beijing 100085; tel. (10) 58868888; fax (10) 62570209; e-mail cmk@lenovo.com; internet www.lenovo.com; f. 1984; fmrly Legend Group Corpn; mfr of personal computers; acquired personal computing division of IBM in Dec. 2004; cap. and res US $1,605.8m., sales US $16,604.8m. (2009/10); Chair. LIU CHUANZHI; CEO YANG YUANQING; 22,205 employees.

Ningbo Bird Co Ltd: 999 Dacheng Dong Jie, Fenghua 315500, Zhejiang Province; tel. (0574) 88918812; fax (0574) 88927489; e-mail export@chinabird.com; internet www.chinabird.com; f. 1992; mfrs of mobile telephones, palm-held computers and system equipment; Chair. XU LIHUA; Gen. Man. ZHANG ZHANGXUAN; 1,998 employees (March 2008).

TCL Corp: 8/F, TCL Industrial Bldg, 6 Eling Nan Lu, Huizhou 516001, Guangdong Province; tel. (752) 2288333; fax (752) 2265428; e-mail 4008123456@tcl.com; internet www.tcl.com; f. 1981; mfrs of consumer electronics, home appliances. component products and mobile telephones; revenue 44,295m. (2009); Chair. and Pres. LI DONGSHENG; 50,000 employees.

Tengen Group: Tengen Mansion, Dongfeng Industrial Zone, Liushi, Wenzhou 325604; tel. (577) 62775688; fax (577) 62776888; e-mail ibd@tengen.com.cn; internet www.tengen.com.cn; manufactures low-voltage electrical appliances; sales 8,427m. (2009); Chair. GAO TIANLE; 7,100 employees.

Zhongshan Changhong Electric Co Ltd: 1 Xingye Bei Lu, Nantou, Zhongshan Qu 528427; tel. (760) 23138685; fax (760) 23830555; e-mail acexport@changhong.com; internet www.changhongac.com; f. 1988; manufactures electrical appliances, electronic components and computers; major television mfr; sales 15,028.3m. (2005); Chair. YANG XUEJUN; Pres. ZHAO YONG; 30,000 employees.

ZTE Corpn: ZTE Plaza, 55 Keji Nan Jie, Hi-Tech Industrial Park, Nanshan Qu, Shenzhen 518057; tel. (755) 26770282; fax (755) 26770286; e-mail fengjianxiong@zte.com.cn; internet www.zte.com.cn; f. 1985; telecommunications equipment; cap. and res 10,086.4m., revenue 60,272.6m. (2009); Chair. HOU WEIGUI; Pres. SHI LIRONG; 70,345 employees.

Food and Drink

China Yurun Food Group Ltd: 10 Yurun Jie, Jianye Qu, Nanjing, Jiangsu Province 210041; tel. (258) 66638888; e-mail ir@yurun.com.hk; internet www.yurun.com.hk; meat products; cap. and res HK $8,369.7m., sales HK $13,870.4m. (2009); Chair. ZHU YICAI; CEO ZHU YILIANG; 16,458 employees.

Hangzhou Wahaha Group Co Ltd: 160 Qingtai Lu, Hangzhou; tel. (571) 86846000; fax (571) 86951532; e-mail whh@wahaha.com.cn; internet www.wahaha.com.cn; f. 1987; beverage producer; revenue 43,214m. (2009); Chair. and CEO ZONG QINGHUO; 30,000 employees.

Huiyuan Group: Huiyuan Lu, Beixiaoying Town, Shunyi District, Beijing 101305; tel. (10) 60483388; fax (10) 60483366; internet www.huiyuan.com.cn; f. 1992; investment holding co; subsidiaries engaged in the manufacture and sale of juice products; Pres. ZHU XINLI.

Inner Mongolia Yili Industrial Group Co Ltd: 8 Jinsidao, Jinchuan Development Zone, Hohhot 010080; tel. (471) 3388888; fax (471) 3601621; e-mail info@yili.com; internet www.yili.com; mfrs of dairy products and mixed feed products; revenue 26,804.6m. (2009); Chair. PAN GANG; 15,218 employees (March 2008).

Kweichow Moutai Co Ltd: Moutai, Renhuai, Guizhou 564501; tel. (852) 2386002; fax (852) 2386005; e-mail fnp@moutaichina.com; internet www.moutaichina.com; f. 1999; production and sale of distilled spirits, mfr of beverages, food and food packaging; Pres. YUAN RENGUO.

People's Food Holding Ltd: Bancheng Town, Linyi 276036, Shandong; tel. (539) 8692888; fax (539) 8692875; internet www.peoplesfood.com.sg; f. 1994; meat products; cap. and res 4,896m., revenue 10,497.7m. (2009); Chair. MING KAM SING; CEO ZHOU LIAN KUI; 22,947 employees.

Tsingtao Brewery Co Ltd: Tsingtao Beer Tower, Hong Kong Lu, Central, Qingdao; tel. (532) 85713831; fax (532) 85713240; e-mail info@tsingtao.com.cn; internet www.tsingtao.com.cn; f. 1903; beer production; cap. and res 5,509m. (2007), sales 17,700m. (2009); Chair. JIN ZHIGUO; Pres. SUN MINGBO; 37,602 employees.

Zhongpin Inc (Henan Zhongpin Food Share Co Ltd): 21 Changshe Jie, Changge 461500, Henan Province; tel. (374) 6216633; fax (374) 6227818; e-mail zhongpin@zhongpin.com; internet www.zpfood.com; f. 1993; meat and food processing; sales 726m. (2009); Chair. and CEO XIANFU ZHU.

Machinery

Changchai Co Ltd: 123 Huaide Jie, Changzhou 213002, Jiangsu Province; tel. (519) 86603656; fax (519) 86670765; e-mail overseas@changchai.com; internet www.changchai.com.cn; f. 1913; production of diesel engines and agricultural product-processing machinery; 31.4% state-owned; assets 1,951m., revenue 1,543m. (2003); Chair. ZHANG JUNYUAN; 3,845 employees.

Dongfang Electric Co Ltd: 13 Huanghe Xi Jie, Deyang 618000, Sichuan Province; tel. (838) 2412144; fax (838) 2203305; e-mail info@dfem.com.cn; internet www.dongfang.com.cn; production and sale of power-generating equipment; total assets 8,462.0m., sales 3,047.9m. (2005); Chair. SI ZEFU; Pres. WEN SHUGANG; 15,981 employees (March 2008).

Jingwei Textile Machinery Co Ltd: 7/F, 1 Shanghai Centre, 39 Liangma Qiao Jie, Chao Yang Qu, Beijing; tel. (10) 84534078; fax (10) 84534135; e-mail jwgf@jwgf.com; internet www.jwgf.com; manufacture and sale of textile machinery; distribution of computers; cap. and res 2,827.9m. (2007), revenue US $4,007.7m. (2009); Chair. YE MAOXIN; Gen. Man. YAO YUMING; 13,346 employees.

SGSB Group Co Ltd: 12th Floor, Orient Mansion, No. 1500 Shiji Da Dao, Pudong New Area, Shanghai 200122; tel. (21) 68407700; fax (21) 63302939; e-mail sgsb@sgsbgroup.com; internet www.sgsbgroup.com/en; f. 1965; est. as Shanghai Industrial Sewing Machine Factory, renamed Shanggong Co Ltd in 1997; current name adopted following restructuring of assets with SMPIC Corpn in 2004; manufacture and sale of sewing machines; cap. 448.9m., res 116.9m., sales 1,480.9m. (2005); Chair. and CEO ZHANG MIN; 3,213 employees (2005).

Shanghai Automation Instrumentation Co Ltd (SAIC): 41 Hongcao Jie, Shanghai 200233; tel. (21) 54279898; fax (21) 62801680; e-mail office@saic.sh.cn; internet www.saic.sh.cn; f. 1993; manufacture of control systems and meters for industrial use; revenue 1,118m. (2009); Gen. Man. ZHU YUTAO; 2,351 employees (March 2008).

Shanghai Erfangji Co Ltd: 687 Chang Zhong Jie, Shanghai 200434; tel. (21) 65318888; fax (21) 65421963; e-mail shej@public7.sta.net.cn; f. 1944; manufacture and sale of textile machinery; sales US $124.4m. (2005); Chair. CUI LING (acting); 1,235 employees (March 2008).

Shenji Group Kunming Machine Tool Co Ltd: 23 Ciba Jie, Kunming 650203, Yunnan Province; tel. (871) 5150186; fax (871) 5150317; e-mail company@jkht.com; internet www.kmtcl.com.cn; f. 1936; est. as Central Machine Plant; fmrly Jiaoda Kunji High-Tech Co Ltd; design, devt and production of machine tools, precision-measuring equipment, etc.; cap. and res 1,206.8m., sales 1,366.8m. (2009); Chair. and Gen. Man. GAO MINGUI; 2,700 employees.

Wuxi Little Swan Co Ltd: 18 Changjiang Nan Lu, Wuxi 214028, Jiangsu Province; tel. (510) 83704003; fax (510) 83705002; e-mail info@littleswan.com.cn; internet www.littleswan.com; f. 1979; design, devt, manufacture and sale of domestic washing machines; cap. and res 725.3m., total revenue 4,375.2m. (2009); Chair. FANG HONGBO; Gen. Man. CHAI XINJIAN; 1,597 employees (2007).

Metals

Aluminium Corporation of China Ltd (CHALCO): 62 Xizhimen Bei Dajie, Haidian Qu, Beijing 100082; tel. (10) 82298080; fax (10) 82298081; e-mail webmaster@chalco.com.cn; internet www.chinalco.com.cn; f. 2001; est. as part of restructuring of state-owned aluminium industry; cap. 11,049.9m., res 10,242.6m. (2005), revenue 70,268m. (2009); Chair. and CEO XIONG WEIPING.

Anben Iron and Steel Group (ABIS): 258 Tai Ping Jie, Lishan Qu, Anshan; tel. (0412) 672 8573; internet absteelgroup.com; f. 2005 through merger of Anshan Iron and Steel Group (Angang) and Benxi Iron and Steel Group (Bengang); Chair. and Pres. LIU JIE.

Anyang Iron and Steel Inc: Meiyuan Village, Yindu Qu, Anyang 455004, Henan Province; tel. (372) 3120175; fax (372) 3120181; internet www.aysteel.com.cn; iron, steel and steel products; Chair. WANG ZILIANG; 20,865 employees (March 2008).

Baosteel Group Corpn (Baosteel): Baosteel Tower, 370 Pudian Lu, Shanghai 200122; tel. (21) 58350000; fax (21) 68404832; e-mail customer@baosteel.com; internet www.baosteel.com; f. 1988; incorporating Baoshan Iron and Steel Corpn, and absorption of Shanghai Metallurgical Holding Group Corpn and Shanghai Meishan Group Corpn Ltd; major iron and steel producer; 22 wholly owned subsidiaries, incl. 9 abroad; cap. and res 115,865m., sales 226,751m. (2007); Chair. XU LEJIANG; Pres. HE WENBO; 106,914 employees.

Baotou Iron and Steel (Group) Co: Gangtie Dajie, Kundulun Qu, Baotou 014010, Inner Mongolia; tel. (472) 2183163; fax (472) 5155484; e-mail shigh@public.hh.nm.cn; internet www.btsteel.com; f. 1954; Pres. and Chair. LIN DONGLU.

Chongqing Iron and Steel Co Ltd: 30 Gangtie Lu, Dadukou Qu, Chongqing 400084; tel. (23) 68845030; fax (23) 68849520; e-mail dms@email.cqgt.cn; internet www.cqgt.cn; manufacture and sale of iron and steel products; cap. and res 3,418m., revenue 10,654m. (2009); Chair. DENG QIANG; Gen. Man. CHEN HONG; 11,962 employees.

Handan Iron and Steel Group Co Ltd (Hebei Iron and Steel Group): 232 Fuxing Jie, Handan 056015, Hebei Province; tel. (310) 6072141; fax (310) 4041978; e-mail admin@mail.hgjt.cn; internet www.hdgt.com.cn; f. 1958; Chair. LI GUIYANG; Gen. Man. PENG ZHAOFENG.

Hunan Valin Steel Co Ltd: 20/F, Hualin Bldg, 111 Fu Rong Zhong Lu, Changsha 410011, Hunan Province; tel. (731) 82565997; fax (731) 84447112; e-mail valinsteel@163.com; internet www.valin.cn; 37.17% owned by Hunan Valin Iron and Steel Group Ltd, 37.17% owned by Mittal Steel Co; cap. and res 3,519.6m., revenue 41,503.2m. (2009); Chair. LI XIAOWEI; 31,458 employees (March 2008).

Jiangsu Shagang Group Ltd: Jinfeng, Zhangjiagang 215625, Jiangsu Province; tel. (512) 58568872; fax (512) 58551627; internet www.sha-steel.com; f. 1975; Chair. and Pres. SHEN WENRONG.

Panzhihua New Steel and Vanadium Co Ltd: New Steel and Vanadium Tower, Xiangyang Village, Dong Qu, Panzhihua 617067, Sichuan Province; tel. (812) 3394123; fax (812) 3392222; internet www.pgsv.com; f. 1993; metal (incl. high vanadium steel) manufacturing and exports; sales 15,156m. (2005); Chair. FAN ZHENGWEI; Gen. Man. ZHANG DADE; 21,915 employees (March 2008).

Shougang Group: Shijingshan, Beijing 100041; tel. (10) 88293520; fax (10) 88295578; e-mail bgt@mail.shougang.com.cn; internet www.shougang.com.cn; f. 1919; produces iron and steel; sales US $4,396.8m. (1999/2000); Pres. ZHU JIMIN.

Taiyuan Iron and Steel (Group) Co Ltd (TISCO): 2 Jian Cao Ping Lu, Taiyuan 030003, Shanxi Province; tel. (351) 3012615; fax (351) 3134170; internet www.tisco.com.cn; steel production; sales 51,800m. (2006); Chair. LI XIAOBO.

Shanxi Taigang Stainless Steel Co Ltd: 2 Jian Cao Ping Lu, Taiyuan 030003, Shanxi Province; tel. (351) 3017701; fax (351) 3014731; e-mail tgbxg@tisco.com.cn; internet www.tgbx.com; listed br. of Taiyuan Iron and Steel Co Ltd; stainless steel; Chair. LI XIAOBO; Gen. Man. LIU FUXING; 22,114 employees (March 2008).

Tangshan Iron and Steel Co Ltd: 9 Binhe Lu, Tangshan 063016, Hebei Province; tel. (315) 2702941; fax (315) 2702198; e-mail tgyang@ts-user.he.cninfo.net; f. 1995; manufacturing of ferrous metals; sales 27,587m. (2006); Chair. and Pres. WANG TIANYI; 23,942 employees (2006).

Western Mining Co Ltd: 52 Wusi Lu, Xining 810001, Qinghai Province; tel. (971) 6123888; fax (971) 6153149; e-mail wm@westmining.com; internet www.westmining.com; metal mining, smelting and trading; revenue 8,709.3m. (2007); Chair. WANG HAITAO; 6,993 employees (March 2008).

Wuhan Iron and Steel Co Ltd (WISCO): 3 Yangang Lu, Qingshan Qu, Wuhan 430083, Hubei Province; tel. (27) 86569436; fax (27) 86898888; internet www.wisco.com.cn; f. 1997; metals manufacturing; cap. and res 12,072m., revenue 53,714m. (2009); Pres. DENG QILIN; 29,181 employees.

Zijin Mining Group Co Ltd: Zijin Dajie, Shanghang, Longyan 364200, Fujian Province; tel. (597) 3833105; fax (597) 3883997; e-mail zjky@zjky.cn; internet www.zjky.cn; exploration, mining and smelting of non-ferrous metals; cap. and res 2,525m., revenue 20,215m. (2009); Chair. and Pres. CHEN JINGHE.

Petroleum

China National Offshore Oil Corpn (CNOOC): 25 Chaoyangmen Bei Dajie, Dongcheng Qu, Beijing 100010; tel. (10) 84521010; fax (10) 64602600; e-mail cnooc@cnooc.com.cn; internet www.cnooc.com.cn; f. 1982; offshore exploration and production of petroleum; cap. and res 97,258m., revenue 209,578m. (2009); Pres. WANG YILIN; 65,800 employees.

China Petroleum and Chemical Corporation (SINOPEC): 22 Chaoyangmen Bei Dajie, Chaoyang Qu, Beijing 100728; tel. (10) 59960114; fax (10) 59760111; e-mail ir@sinopec.com.cn; internet www.sinopec.com.cn; f. 2000; exploration, devt, production, refining, transport and marketing of petroleum and natural gas, production and sales of petrochemicals, chemical fibres, chemical fertilizers, and other chemicals, research, devt and application of technology and information; cap. and res 86,702m., revenue 1,345,052m. (2009); Chair. FU CHENGYU; Pres. WANG TIANPU.

SINOPEC Shanghai Petrochemical Co Ltd: 48 Jinyi Lu, Jinshan Qu, Shanghai 200540; tel. (21) 57941941; fax (21) 57942267; e-mail spc@spc.com.cn; internet www.spc.com.cn; processing of crude petroleum into synthetic fibres, resins and plastics, and other petroleum products; cap. and res 15,005m., sales 51,657.9m. (2009); Chair. RONG GUANGDAO; 17,131 employees.

SINOPEC Star Petroleum Co Ltd: 263 Bei Si Huan Xi Lu, Haidan Qu, Beijing 100083; tel. (10) 82335150; e-mail xxgs@sinopecstar.com.cn; internet www.cnspc.com.cn; f. 1997; fmrly China National Star Petroleum Corpn; merged with SINOPEC in 2000, fully acquired by latter in 2001; petroleum and gas exploration, devt and production; Gen. Man. ZHANG YAOCANG.

SINOPEC Yangzi Petrochemical Co Ltd (YPC Ltd): 777 Xinhua Lu, Yanjian Development Zone, Luhe Qu, Nanjing 210048; tel. (25) 57782200; fax (25) 57784389; e-mail yzshgs@ypc.com.cn; internet www.ypc.com.cn; f. 1998; processing of petroleum and production of petroleum products; sales 31,773.6m. (2004); Chair. and Pres. ZHANG DABEN.

SINOPEC Yizheng Chemical Fibre Co Ltd: Zhenzhou, Yizheng, Jiangsu 211900; tel. (514) 83232235; fax (514) 83233880; e-mail cso@ycfc.com; internet www.ycfc.com; f. 1993; chemical products; mfr of chemical fibre and polyester; cap. and res 4,176m., revenue 13,225m. (2009); Chair. QIAN HENGGE; 7,931 employees (March 2008).

SINOPEC Zhenhai Refining and Chemical Co Ltd: Zhenhai Qu, Ningbo 315207, Zhejiang Province; tel. (574) 86440114; fax (574) 86270077; internet www.zrcc.com.cn; f. 1974; privatized in 2006 through 'merger by absorption' with Ningbo Yonglian, a wholly owned subsidiary of Sinopec Corpn, established for the purpose of the merger; petroleum refining and production of related chemicals; cap. 2,523.8m., res 6,404.1m., sales 41,991.5m. (2004); Pres. JIANG ZHENGHONG.

PetroChina Co Ltd: 9 Dongzhimen Bei Dajie, Dongcheng Qu, Beijing 100007; tel. (10) 59986223; fax (10) 62099557; e-mail webmaster@petrochina.com.cn; internet www.petrochina.com.cn; f. 1999; est. in course of restructuring of China National Petroleum Corpn (CNPC); exploration, devt, and production of crude petroleum and natural gas, and refining, transport, storage, and trade of crude petroleum and its products; cap. and res 316,543m., sales 1,109,275m. (2009); Chair. JIANG JIEMIN; Pres. ZHOU JIPING; 539,168 employees.

Jilin Chemical Industrial Co Ltd: 9 Longtan Lu, Longtan Qu 132021, Jilin Province; tel. (432) 3903651; fax (432) 3028126; e-mail jcic@jcic.com.cn; internet www.jcic.com.cn; subsidiary of Petrochina Co Ltd; production and sale of petroleum and chemical products; total assets 14,392.8m., sales 31,857.4m. (2004); Chair. WANG JINJUN; 20,445 employees (Dec. 2004).

PetroChina Jinzhou Petrochemical Co Ltd: 7, Sec. 2, Chongqing Lu, Guta, Jinzhou 121001, Liaoning Province; tel. (416) 4153252; fax (416) 4167440; e-mail zhang.hongyan@chinaoil.com.cn; internet www.petrochinajzintl.com; f. 1997; petroleum processing and coking; subsidiary of Petrochina Co Ltd; revenue US $1,094.8m. (2000); Gen. Man. ZHANG HONGYAN; 10,500 employees.

Pharmaceuticals

Harbin Pharmaceutical Group Co Ltd: 94 Gongchang Lu, Harbin 150018, Heilongjiang Province; tel. and fax (451) 84608188; internet www.hayao.com; f. 1991; pharmaceuticals company; revenue US $778.4m. (2000); Chair. TIANFU YANG; Gen. Man. JIANG LINKUI; 18,025 employees (March 2008).

Shandong Xinhua Pharmaceutical Co Ltd: 19 Dongyi Jie, Zhangdian Qu, Zibo 255005, Shandong Province; tel. (533) 2166666; fax (533) 2287508; e-mail xhzy@xhzy.com; internet www.xhzy.com/en; f. 1943; manufacture and sale of pharmaceuticals; total assets 2,207.0m., sales 1,712.1m. (2005); Chair. GUO QIN; Gen. Man. ZHAO SONGGUO; 5,005 employees (March 2008).

Shanghai Fosun Pharmaceutical (Group) Corpn Ltd: 2 Fuxing Dong Lu, Shanghai 200010; tel. (21) 63323318; fax (21) 63325080; e-mail int@fosunpharma.com; internet www.fosun.com.cn; f. 1994; fmrly Shanghai Fosun Industries Ltd; drugs, active pharmaceutical ingredients, medical equipment and diagnostic products; cap. and res 3,639.8m. (2007), revenue 3,872.6m. (2009); Chair. CHEN QIYU; Pres. and CEO YAO FANG.

Shenyang Xiehe Group Co: 30 Gaoke Lu, Hunnan New & High Tech Industrial Development Zone, Shenyang 110179; tel. (24) 23784596; fax (24) 23787042; e-mail xiehe@xiehegroup.com.cn; internet www.xiehegroup.com.cn; f. 1988; pharmaceutical products, healthcare; Pres. CHEN JUYU; 350 employees.

Tasly Group: Tasly TCM Garden, 2 Pujihe Dong Lu, Beichen Qu, Tianjin 30042; tel. (22) 26736808; fax (22) 26736618; e-mail info@tasly.com; internet www.tasly.com; f. 1994; pharmaceutical enterprise engaged in scientific research and devt, production and marketing of medicines; 23 subsidiary cos, incl. Tianjin Tasly Pharmaceutical Co Ltd; Chair. YAN XI JUN.

Textiles

Hebei Qifa Textiles Co Ltd: New Developing Industry Zone, Baoding 071400, Hebei Province; tel. (312) 5399966; fax (312) 5399911; e-mail wang_cui2008@hotmail.com; internet www.qifagroup.com; f. 1988; producer of yarns, pure knitting wool, chemical fibres, worsted woollen products; cap. 200m., fixed assets 160m. (2002); Chair., Pres. and CEO WANG QIFA; 3,600 employees.

Shanghai Haixin Group Co Ltd: 688 Changxing Lu, Dongjing, Song Jiang Qu, Shanghai 201619; tel. (21) 56798100; fax (21) 57698200; e-mail haixin@haixin.com; internet www.haixin.com; f. 1986; manufacture and sale of plush and flannel materials; total assets 3,296.4m., sales 1,629.2m. (2002); Chair. YAN ZHENBO; Pres. YUAN YONGLIN; 7,500 employees.

Shenzhen Textile (Holdings) Co Ltd: 6th Floor, Shen Fang Bldg, 3 Hua Qiang Bei Lu, Shenzhen 518031; tel. (755) 23776043; fax (755) 23360139; e-mail sztext@szonline.net; f. 1994; manufacture of textiles, garments and related products; cap. 245.1m., res 107.9m., sales 448.4m. (2004); Chair. GUAN TONGKE; 1,000 employees.

Zhejiang Zhongda Group Co Ltd: 21/F, Tower A, Zhongda Plaza, Hangzhou 310003; tel. (571) 85155000; fax (571) 85777050; e-mail gufen@zhongda.com; internet www.zhongda.com; garments and textiles; diversifying into other consumer industries; revenue 24,691.8m. (2009); Chair. CHEN JIDA; Pres. XU YINGCHENG; 615 employees.

Miscellaneous

Baidu.com Inc: Baidu Campus, 10 Haidan Qu, Shangdi, Beijing 100085; tel. (10) 59928888; fax (10) 59920000; e-mail beixiaochao@baidu.com; internet www.baidu.com; internet search provider; cap. and res 2,021m., revenue 1,744.4m. (2007); Chair. and CEO ROBIN YANHONG LI; 6,252 employees (March 2008).

China Aoyuan Property Group Ltd: Hanxi Dajie, Panyu, Guangzhou 511495; tel. (8620) 23836368; fax (8620) 34719915; e-mail webmaster@aoyuan.net; internet www.aoyuan.com.cn; property devt, leasing and hotel operations; cap 24.9m., res 5,702m., sales 2,364m. (2009); Chair. GUO ZIWEN.

China Harbour Engineering Company Ltd (CHEC): 9 Chunxiu Lu, Dong Zhi Men Wai, Beijing 100027; tel. (10) 64154455; fax (10) 64168276; e-mail chec@chec.bj.cn; internet www.chec.bj.cn; f. 1980; re-est. in Dec. 2005; marine engineering, civil engineering, road and bridge, port machinery; sales US $1,000m. (2005/06); Chair. and Pres. SUN ZIYU.

China Shenhua Energy Co Ltd: 4th Floor, Zhouji Tower, 16 Ande Lu, Dongcheng Qu, Beijing 100011; tel. (10) 5813-3355; e-mail ir@shenhuachina.com; internet www.csec.com; revenue 121,312m. (2009); Chair. ZHANG XIWU.

China Vanke Co Ltd: 33 Huanmai Lu, Dameisha, Yantian Qu, Shenzhen; tel. (755) 25606666; fax (755) 25531696; e-mail IR@vanke.com; internet www.vanke.com.cn; devt and management of residential property; cap. and res 37,861m., revenue 46,047m. (2009); Chair. WANG SHI; Pres. YU LIANG; 17,616 employees.

Double Coin Holdings Ltd: 63 Sichuan Lu, Shanghai 200002; tel. (21) 63290433; fax (21) 63299609; e-mail company@cstarc.com; internet www.cstarc.com; tyres and machinery for production of rubber products; sales US $633.1m. (2005); Chair. LIU XUNFENG; 3,823 employees.

Guanghui Industry Co Ltd (Xinjiang Guanghui Stone Joint-Stock Co Ltd): No. 6 Shanghai Rd, Economic & Technology Development Zone, Urumqi, Xinjiang Province; tel. (991) 3715828; fax (991) 3735502; internet www.guanghui.com; f. 1988; liquefied natural gas, automobile trading, stone excavation, real estate; sales 2,237.1m. (2005); Chair. SUN GUANGXIN; 20,000 employees.

Haci Group Co Ltd: 169 Tongxiang Jie, Harbin 150046, Heilongjiang Province; tel. (451) 2688688; fax (451) 2686254; internet www.hacico.com; f. 1992; 12 corporate mems; magnetic health care products, food engineering; Pres. GUO LIWEN; 480 employees.

Hengdian Group (Zhejiang Hengdian Imp. & Exp. Co Ltd): Hengdian Industrialized Zone, Dongyang, Zhejiang; tel. (579) 6551511; fax (579) 6551220; e-mail hg@hengdian.com; internet www.hengdian.com; f. 1975; magnetic materials, electronics, chemicals and pharmaceuticals; sales 8,000.0m. (2001); Chair. XU YONGAN; 35,944 employees (2001).

Hongta Tobacco (Group) Co Ltd: Hongta Dadao Shangduan, Yuxi 653100, Yunnan Province; tel. and fax (877) 2968165; fax (877) 2968562; e-mail public@hongta.com; internet www.hongta.com; f. 1956; tobacco products; core enterprise is Yuxi Tobacco Factory, but controls other tobacco factories elsewhere in China, incl. Chuxiong, Dali and Changchun; Chair. LIU WANDONG; Pres. LIU SHUIMING.

Li Ning Co Ltd: Suite 3201, 32/F, China Merchants Tower, 161 Lujiazui Dong Lu, Pudong, Shanghai 200120; tel. (21) 58797298; fax (21) 58799009; internet www.lining.com; mfrs of sports footwear, apparel and accessories for sport and leisure use; revenue 8,386m. (2009); Chair. LI NING.

NetEase.com Inc: 26/F, SP Tower D, Tsinghua Science Park Bldg 8, 1 Zhongguancun Dong Lu, Beijing 100084; tel. (10) 82558163; fax (10) 82618163; e-mail ir@service.netease.com; internet www.netease.com; f. 1997; provider of internet portal, online games and wireless value-added services; revenue 3,823m. (2009); CEO WILLIAM DING.

Nine Dragons Paper Industries Co Ltd: Xinsha Port Industry Zone, Mayong Town, Dongguan 523147, Guangdong Province; tel. (769) 88234888; fax (769) 88824198; e-mail info_group@ndpaper.com; internet www.ndpaper.com; f. 1995; mfr of packaging and paperboard; sales 13,128.6m. (2008/09); Chair. CHEUNG YAN; Gen. Man. MING CHUNG LIU; 5,800 employees.

Orient Group Inc: 2nd Bldg of Science Industry and Trade, Nangang Qu, Harbin 150001, Heilongjiang Province; tel. (451) 3666036; fax (451) 3666030; e-mail master@china-orient.com; internet www.china-orient.com; f. 1988; finance, transport, construction, industry, real estate management; sales 2,945.7m. (2005); Chair. ZHANG HONGWEI.

Shanghai Chlor-Alkali Chemical Co Ltd: 47 Longwu Jie, Shanghai 200241; tel. (21) 64340000; fax (21) 64341341; e-mail public@styc.com; internet www.scacc.com; f. 1992; production of industrial chemicals; sales 4,120.3m. (2005); Chair. LI JUN; 3,995 employees.

Shanghai Huili Building Materials Co Ltd (Shanghai Huili (Group) Ltd): 299 Dongyi Lu, Kangqiao Pudong, Shanghai; tel. and fax (21) 68130988; internet www.huili.com; devt, production and sale of wall coatings and PVC flooring; sales 370.1m. (2004); Chair. XU ZEXIAN; Pres. FENG XINGHUA; 960 employees.

Shanghai Xin Gao Chao Group Co: 7635 Daye Lu, Fengxian Qu, Shanghai; tel. (21) 57559526; fax (21) 57559527; internet sxgcgcl.en.china.cn; manufactures flooring and furniture; sales 5,600.0m. (2001); Pres. TAO XIN KANG; 20,000 employees.

Shide Group: Dalian Shide Group, 38 Gao Er Ji Lu, Xi Gang Qu, Dalian, Liaoning 116011; tel. (411) 3622218; e-mail webmaster@shide-global.com; internet www.shide-global.com; f. 1992; home electrics, chemical building materials, automobile manufacturing; sales US $460.0m. (2001); Chair. XU MING; 5,000 employees.

Wumart Stores Inc: Yuquan Bldg, Shi Jing Shan Lu, Beijing 100049; tel. (10) 88259488; e-mail info@wu-mart.com; internet www.wumart.com; operates hypermarkets and supermarkets; cap. and res 2,262.1m., revenue 10,511m. (2009); Chair. WU JIANZHONG; 9,856 employees.

TRADE UNIONS

At the end of 2009 the 1.84m. trade unions comprised 226.3m. members.

All-China Federation of Trade Unions (ACFTU): 10 Fu Xing Men Wai Jie, Beijing 100865; tel. (10) 68592114; fax (10) 68562030; e-mail webmaster@acftu.org.cn; internet www.acftu.org.cn; f. 1925; organized on an industrial basis; 15 affiliated national industrial unions, 30 affiliated local trade union councils; 169.94m. mems (2007); Chair. WANG ZHAOGUO; First Sec. SUN CHUNLAN.

Principal affiliated unions:

All-China Federation of Railway Workers' Unions: f. 1924; Chair. GUO YIMIN; 3.1m. mems (2006).

Chinese Agricultural, Forestry and Water Conservancy Workers' Union: f. 1933; Chair. SHENG MINGFU; 10m. mems (2008).

Chinese Aviation Workers' Union: f. 2003; Chair. GAO HONGFENG; 360,000 mems.

Chinese Defence Industry, Postal and Telecommunications Workers' Union: f. 2001; Chair. DONG XUIBIN; 6.41m. mems (2007).

Chinese Educational, Scientific, Cultural, Health and Sports Workers' Union: f. 2001; Chair. WANG XIAOLONG; 25m. mems (2007).

Chinese Energy and Chemical Workers' Union.

Chinese Financial, Commercial, Light Industry, Textile and Tobacco Workers' Union: f. 2001; Chair. JIA YANMIN; 48m. mems (2007).

Chinese Financial Workers' Union: f. 1951; Chair. HE JIESHENG; 2m. mems (2007).

Chinese Machinery, Metallurgy and Building Materials Workers' Union: f. 2001; Chair. LIU HAIHUA; 35m. mems (2007).

Chinese Seamen and Construction Workers' Union: f. 2003; Chair. WU ZIHENG; 40m. mems (2008).

Transport

RAILWAYS

The total length of railways in operation in 2009 was 65,491 km, of which 30,243 km were electrified. A 1,142-km railway linking Tibet (Xizang) with other areas of China, via Qinghai Province, was completed in 2005. The magnetic levitation ('maglev') railway linking Shanghai to Pudong International airport entered into service in 2004, and work on a 200-km 'maglev' line from Shanghai to Hangzhou was expected to start in 2011, with completion scheduled for 2014. In mid-2008 a 114-km high-speed link between Beijing and Tianjin began operating. A high-speed line from Shanghai and Hangzhou was opened in October 2010. The construction of a high-speed 1,318-km line between Beijing and Shanghai was scheduled for completion by 2012.

Ministry of Railways: see under Ministries; controls most railways through regional divisions; major routes include Beijing–Guangzhou, Tianjin–Shanghai, Manzhouli–Vladivostok, Jiaozuo–Zhicheng and Lanzhou–Badou; also line to Tibet.

City Underground Railways

Beijing Mass Transit Railway Operation Corpn Ltd: 2 Beiheyan Lu, Xicheng, Beijing 100044; tel. (10) 62293820; fax (10) 62292074; e-mail service@bjsubway.com; internet www.bjsubway.com; f. 1969; total length 142 km; projected to expand to 440 km by 2012; Gen. Man. XIE ZHENGGUANG.

Chengdu Metro Co Ltd: Chengdu; internet www.cdmetro.cn; f. 2004; network comprises seven lines and 274 km of track.

Chongqing Metro: Yuzhong Qu, Chongqing; tel. (23) 68002222; e-mail cqmetro@cta.cq.cn; internet www.cqmetro.cn; f. 2005; China's first monorail system; one operating line of 19.15 km, with further devt planned.

Guangzhou Metro: 204 Huanshi Lu, Guangzhou 510010; tel. (20) 83289033; e-mail ServiceCenter@21cn.com; internet www.gzmtr.com; opened June 1997; total length 36.6 km; network expected to comprise 9 lines and 225 km of track by 2010; Gen. Man. DING JIANLONG.

Nanjing Metro: internet www.nj-dt.com; f. 2005; one line of 17 km; Line 2 completed in 2009.

Shanghai Shentong Metro Group Co Ltd: Level 31, Jiu Shi Bldg, 28 Zhongshan Nan Lu, Shanghai 200010; tel. (21) 58308595; fax (21) 63300065; internet www.shmetro.com; f. 1995; 228.4 km; network planned to exceed 500 km by 2010; Pres. ZHU HUSHENG; Gen. Man. GU CHENG.

Shenzhen Metro: 1016 Metro Bldg, Futian Qu, Shenzhen; tel. (755) 23992600; fax (755) 23992555; e-mail szmc@shenzhenmc.com; internet www.szmc.net; f. 2004; Chair. HUANG RUI; Gen. Man. LIN MAODE.

Tianjin Metro Group Ltd: 3 Harmony Jiayuan, Hankou Xi Lu, Heping, Tianjin 300051; tel. (22) 87811512; fax (22) 27825588; e-mail master@tjdt.cn; internet www.tjdt.cn; f. 2000; est as Tianjin Metro Corpn; name changed as above in 2008; total planned network 154 km; Gen. Man. WANG YUJI.

Wuhan Metro Group Co Ltd: tel. (27) 83749024; internet www.whrt.gov.cn; f. 2004; currently one 10.2-km line, with six more lines being planned; Chair. HEPING TU; Gen. Man. LIU YUHUA.

The first stage of an underground system in Xian opened in September 2011. An underground system was also planned for Qingdao.

ROADS

In 2009 China had 3,860,080 km of highways, including 65,100 km of expressways. The programme of expressway construction to link all main cities continued; the expressway network was projected to total 55,000 km by 2020. Construction work on a bridge connecting Zhuhai with Macao and Hong Kong commenced in December 2009. Spanning nearly 50 km and comprising a six-lane expressway, the project was scheduled for completion in 2016.

INLAND WATERWAYS

In 2009 there were some 123,700 km of navigable inland waterways in China. The main navigable rivers are the Changjiang (Yangtze River), the Zhujiang (Pearl River), the Heilongjiang, the Grand Canal and the Xiangjiang.

SHIPPING

China has a network of more than 2,000 ports, of which more than 130 are open to foreign vessels. With full operation scheduled for 2020, the third stage of the biggest container port in the world, sited on the Yangshan Islands off shore from Shanghai, was completed in 2010. Other major ports include Dalian, Qinhuangdao, Tianjin, Yantai, Qingdao, Rizhao, Lianyungang, Shanghai, Ningbo, Guangzhou and Zhanjiang. In December 2009 China's merchant fleet comprised 4,064 ships, totalling 30.1m. grt.

Bureau of Water Transportation: Beijing; controls rivers and coastal traffic.

China International Marine Containers (Group) Co Ltd (CIMC): 2 Gangwan Dajie, Shekou Industrial Zone, Shenzhen, Guangdong 518067; tel. (755) 26691130; fax (755) 26692707; e-mail email@cimc.com; internet www.cimc.com; f. 1980; jt venture between China Merchants Holdings, the East Asiatic Co Ltd (EAC) and China Ocean Shipping (Group) Co (COSCO); manufacture and supply of containers, trailers and airport equipment; cap. 2,017.0m., res 7,596.8m., sales 30,938.5m. (2005); Chair. FU YUNING; Pres. MAI BOLIANG.

China National Chartering Corpn (SINOCHART): see Trade and Industrial Organizations.

China Ocean Shipping (Group) Co (COSCO): 11th and 12th Floors, Ocean Plaza, 158 Fu Xing Men Nei, Xi Cheng Qu, Beijing 100031; tel. (10) 66493388; fax (10) 66492288; internet www.cosco.com.cn; reorg. 1993, re-est. 1997; head office transferred to Tianjin late 1997; br. offices: Shanghai, Guangzhou, Tianjin, Qingdao, Dalian; 200 subsidiaries (incl. China Ocean Shipping Agency—PENAVIC) and joint ventures in China and abroad, engaged in ship-repair, container-manufacturing, warehousing, insurance, etc.; merchant fleet of 800 vessels; 47 routes; Pres. WEI JIAFU.

China Shipping (Group) Co: 700 Dong Da Ming Lu, Shanghai 200080; tel. (21) 65966666; fax (21) 65966556; e-mail cscas@cnshipping.com; internet www.cnshipping.com/english; f. 1997; state-owned shipping conglomerate; incorporates five specialized shipping fleets of oil tankers, tramps, passenger ships, container vessels and special cargo ships respectively; a total of 440 vessels with an aggregate deadweight of 20.18m. metric tons; Pres. LI SHAODE.

China Shipping Container Lines Co Ltd: 5th Floor, Shipping Tower, 700 Dong Da Ming Lu, Shanghai 200080; tel. (21) 65966833; fax (21) 65966498; e-mail ir@cnshipping.com; internet www.cscl.com.cn; container shipping company; 135 vessels (July 2010); Chair. LI SHAODE; Gen. Man. HUANG XIAOWEN.

China Shipping Development Co Ltd: Shanghai Maritime Bldg, 16th Floor, 700 Dong Da Ming Lu, Shanghai 200080; tel. (21) 65967160; fax (21) 65966160; e-mail csd@cnshipping.com; internet www.cnshipping.com/cndev; 50.51% owned by China Shipping (Group) Co; operates oil tankers and dry bulk cargo vessels; Chair. LI SHAODE.

Fujian Shipping Co: 151 Zhong Ping Lu, Fuzhou 350009; tel. (591) 83259900; fax (591) 83259716; e-mail fusco@fusco.com.cn; internet www.fusco.com.cn; f. 1950; transport of bulk cargo, crude petroleum products, container and related services; subsidiary of Fujian Provincial Communication Transportation Group Co Ltd; Gen. Man. YANG JINCHANG.

Guangzhou Maritime Transport (Group) Co: 308 Binjiang Zhong Lu, Guangzhou 510220; tel. (20) 84102787; fax (20) 84102187; e-mail gzmaritime@gzmaritime.com; internet www.gzmaritime.com; f. 1949; Gen. Man. YAN ZHICHONG.

CIVIL AVIATION

Air travel has continued to expand very rapidly. Following the completion of six new facilities during 2009, China had a total of 166 airports. In 2004 the establishment of private airlines was approved. Plans for the construction of a further 45 airports were announced in early 2011.

Civil Aviation Administration of China (CAAC): POB 644, 155 Dongsixi Jie, Beijing 100710; tel. (10) 64014104; fax (10) 64016918; e-mail webmaster@caac.gov.cn; internet www.caac.gov.cn; f. 1949; restructured in 1988; subsidiary of Ministry of Transport; Dir LI JIAXIANG.

Air China Ltd: Beijing International Airport, POB 644, Beijing 100621; tel. (10) 61462799; fax (10) 61462805; e-mail ir@airchina.com; internet www.airchina.com.cn; 51% owned by state-owned China Nat. Aviation Holding Co (CNAC); international and domestic scheduled passenger and cargo services; Chair. KONG DONG; Pres. CAI JIANJIANG.

Chengdu Airways Ltd: Chengdu Shuangliu International Airport, Chengdu 610202, Sichuan Province; tel. (28) 66668888; fax (28) 85706199; internet www.chengduair.cc; f. 2004; privately owned; fmrly United Eagle Airlines; name changed as above in 2010; Chair. LI JINING.

China Eastern Airlines: 92 Hongqiao Rd, Hongqiao Airport, Shanghai 200335; tel. (21) 62686268; fax (21) 62686116; e-mail ir@ceair.com; internet www.ceair.com; f. 1987; domestic services; operates flights within Asia and to the USA, Europe and Australia; Chair. LIU SHAOYONG; Pres. MA XULUN.

China Eastern Airlines Wuhan (CEAW): 435 Jianshe Dajie, Wuhan 430030; tel. (87) 63603888; fax (87) 83625693; e-mail wuhanair@public.wh.hb.cn; f. 1986; fmrly Wuhan Air Lines; became China's first partly privately owned airline upon refounding in 2002; 96% owned by China Eastern Airlines; domestic services; Pres. CHENG YAOKUN.

China Eastern Xi Bei Airlines: Laodong Nan Lu, Xian 710082, Shaanxi Province; tel. (29) 88792299; fax (29) 84261622; e-mail webcnwa@mail.cnwa.com; internet www.cnwa.com; f. 1992; fmrly China Northwest Airlines; renamed following acquisition of assets by China Eastern Airlines in 2005; domestic services and flights to Macao, Singapore and Japan; Pres. GAO JUNQUI.

China Eastern Yunnan Airlines: Wujaba Airport, Kunming 650200; tel. (871) 7113007; fax (871) 7151509; internet www.c3q.com.cn; f. 1992; est. as Yunnan Airlines; renamed following acquisition of assets by China Eastern Airlines in 2005; 49 domestic services; also serves Thailand, Singapore, and Laos; Pres. XUE XIAOMING.

China General Aviation Corpn: Wusu Airport, Taiyuan 030031, Shanxi Province; tel. (351) 7040600; fax (351) 7040094; f. 1989; 34 domestic routes; Pres. ZHANG CHANGJING.

China Southern Airlines: 6 Airport Lu, Guangzhou Baiyun Int. Airport; tel. (20) 86134388; fax (20) 86137318; e-mail webmaster@csair.com; internet www.csair.com; f. 1991; merged with Zhong Yuan Airlines in 2000; acquired operations and assets of China Northern Airlines and China Xinjiang Airlines in 2004; domestic services; overseas destinations include Bangkok, Fukuoka, Hanoi, Ho Chi Minh City, Kuala Lumpur, Penang, Pyongyang, Singapore, Manila, Vientiane, Jakarta and Surabaya; Chair. SI XIANMIN; Gen. Man. TAN WENGENG.

Xiamen Airlines: 22 Dai Liao Lu, Xiamen 361006, Fujian Province; tel. (592) 5739888; fax (592) 5739777; e-mail info@xiamenair.com.cn; internet www.xiamenair.com.cn; f. 1992; 60% owned by China Southern Airlines, 40% owned by Xiamen Construction and Devt Corpn; domestic services; also serves Bangkok (Thailand); Pres. YANG GUANGHUA.

China United Airlines: Dong Lu, Fengtai Qu, Beijing 100076; tel. (10) 67978899; internet www.cu-air.com; f. 2005; est. in 1986 as part of the People's Liberation Army civil transport division; closed down in 2002; resumed operations in 2005; 80% owned by Shanghai Airlines; Pres. LAN DINGSHOU.

Hainan Airlines (HNA): HNA Development Bldg, 29 Haixiu Lu, Haikou 570206, Hainan Province; tel. (898) 66739801; fax (898) 66786273; e-mail webmaster@hnair.com; internet www.hnair.com; f. 1993; leading air transport enterprise of HNA Group; 300 domestic services; international services to Korea; 14.8% owned by financier George Soros; Chair. CHEN FENG; Pres. WANG YINGMING.

Changan Airlines: 16/F, Jierui Bldg, 5 South Er Huan Rd, Xian 710068, Shaanxi Province; tel. (29) 8378027; fax (29) 8707911; f. 1992; subsidiary of HNA Group; local passenger and cargo services; Pres. SHE YINING.

China Xinhua Airlines: 1 Jinsong Nan Lu, Chao Yang Qu, Beijing 100021; tel. (10) 66766027; fax (10) 67740126; e-mail infocxh@homeway.com.cn; internet www.chinaxinhuaair.com; f. 1992; subsidiary of HNA Group; Chair. LIU JIAXU; Pres. YANG JINGLIN.

Shanxi Airlines: Customs Bldg, Wusu Airport, Taiyuan 030031, Shanxi Province; subsidiary of HNA Group; Chair. QIN JIANMIN, LI QING.

Okay Airways: 16 Tianzhu Lu, Tianzhu Airport Industrial Zone, Shunyi Qu, Beijing 101312; tel. (10) 59237777; fax (10) 59237590; internet www.okair.net; f. 2004; inaugural flight 2005; China's first privately owned airline; Chair. WANG SHUSHENG.

Shandong Airlines: Shandong Aviation Mansion, 5746 Er Huan Dong Lu, Lixia Qu, Jinan 250014, Shandong Province; tel. (531) 85698666; fax (531) 85698668; e-mail webmaster@shandongair.com.cn; internet www.shandongair.com.cn; f. 1994; domestic services; Pres. SUN YUDE.

Shanghai Airlines: 212 Jiangning Lu, Shanghai 200041; tel. (21) 62558888; fax (21) 62558885; e-mail service@shanghai-air.com; internet www.shanghai-air.com; f. 1985; domestic services; also serves Phnom-Penh (Cambodia); Chair. ZHOU CHI; Pres. FAN HONGXI.

Shenzhen Airlines: Lingtian Tian, Lingxiao Garden, Shenzhen Airport, Shenzhen 518128, Guangdong Province; tel. (755) 7771999; fax (755) 7777242; e-mail wm@shenzhenair.com; internet www.shenzhenair.com; f. 1993; owned by Air China (51%), Total Logistics Co (25%) and Shenzhen Huirun Investment (24%); domestic services; Chair. CAI JIANJIANG.

Sichuan Airlines: Chengdu Shuangliu International Airport, Chengdu 610202, Sichuan Province; tel. (28) 85393566; fax (28) 85393045; e-mail scal@scal.com; internet www.scal.com.cn; f. 1986; domestic services; Pres. LAN XINGGUO.

Spring Airlines: 158 Ding Xi Lu, Shanghai; tel. (21) 62520000; fax (21) 62523734; e-mail webmaster@china-sss.com; internet www.china-sss.com; privately owned; low-cost airline; inaugural flight July 2005; Chair. and Pres. WANG ZHENGHUA.

Tourism

The tourism sector has continued to develop rapidly. Attractions include dramatic scenery and places of historical interest such as the Temple of Heaven and the Forbidden City in Beijing, the Great Wall, the Ming Tombs and the terracotta warriors at Xian. The 2008 Olympic Games were held in Beijing in August of that year. In 2009 there were 14,498 tourist hotels in operation. In 2010 China received a total of nearly 133.8m. visitors, of whom 26.1m. were foreign tourists; visitors from Hong Kong, Macao and Taiwan totalled 107.6m. Revenue from international tourism was estimated to have risen by 15.5% in 2010 to total US $45,800m., while receipts from domestic tourism increased by 23.5% to reach an estimated 1,258.0m. yuan.

China International Travel Service (CITS): 103 Fu Xing Men Nei Dajie, Beijing 100800; tel. (10) 85228888; fax (10) 65226855; e-mail support-enb@cits.com.cn; internet www.cits.net; f. 1954; makes travel arrangements for foreign tourists; 14 subsidiary overseas cos; Pres. YAO YUECAN.

China National Tourism Administration (CNTA): 9A Jian Guo Men Nei Dajie, Beijing 100740; tel. (10) 65201114; fax (10) 65137871; e-mail webmaster@cnta.gov.cn; internet www.cnta.gov.cn; parastatal org. charged with co-ordinating devt and regulation of the tourism industry; five subsidiary cos; Chair. SHAO QIWEI.

Chinese People's Association for Friendship with Foreign Countries: 1 Tai Ji Chang Dajie, Beijing 100740; tel. (10) 65122474; fax (10) 65128354; internet www.cpaffc.org.cn; f. 1954; Chair. QI HUAIYUAN.

Defence

China is divided into seven major military administrative units. All armed services are grouped in the People's Liberation Army (PLA). As assessed at November 2010, according to Western estimates the regular forces totalled 2,285,000, of whom 660,000 were paramilitary forces: the army numbered 1,600,000, the navy 255,000 (including a naval air force of 26,000), the air force approximately 300,000, and the strategic missile forces 100,000. Reserves numbered some 510,000, and the People's Armed Police comprised an estimated 660,000. Military service is usually by selective conscription, and is for two years in all services. In support of international peacekeeping efforts, 218 Chinese troops were stationed in the Democratic Republic of Congo in November 2010, 344 in Lebanon, 564 in Liberia and 756 in Sudan.

Defence Expenditure: Budgeted at 519,000m. yuan for 2010.

Chairman of the CCP Central Military Commission (Commander-in-Chief): HU JINTAO.

Vice-Chairmen: Gen. XU CAIHUO, Gen. GUO BOXIONG, XI JINPING.

Director of the General Political Department (Chief Political Commissar): LI JINAI.

Chief of General Staff: Gen. CHEN BINGDE.

Commander, PLA Navy: Adm. WU SHENGLI.

Commander, PLA Air Force: Gen. XU QILIANG.

Director, General Logistics Department: Gen. LIAO XILONG.

Commanders of Military Regions: Gen. FANG FENGHUI (Beijing), Gen. LI SHIMING (Chengdu), Gen. ZHANG QINSHENG (Guangzhou), Gen. FAN CHANGLONG (Jinan), Gen. WANG GUOSHENG (Lanzhou), Gen. ZHAO KESHI (Nanjing), Lt-Gen. ZHANG YOUXIA (Shenyang).

Education

Fees are charged at all levels. Much importance is attached to kindergartens. Primary education begins for most children at seven years of age and lasts for six years. Secondary education usually begins at 12 years of age and lasts for six years. In 2009 nearly 26.6m. children attended kindergartens, of which there were 138,209, and 100.7m. pupils were enrolled at the 322,094 primary schools. In 2007/08 enrolment at pre-primary school was equivalent to 44% of pupils in the relevant age group (males 44%; females 44%). In the same year enrolment in primary and secondary education was equivalent to 91% of the relevant age groups (males 90%; females 93%). In 2009 there were 87,639 secondary schools, at which a total of 86.5m. pupils were enrolled. In the same year 428,000 children attended one of 1,672 special schools, while a total of 21.4m. students were enrolled in one of 2,305 higher education institutions. Private education developed quickly from the 1980s when it was first permitted. By 2004 the number of private schools was estimated at 70,000. As the Government placed increasing emphasis on higher education, this sector expanded extremely rapidly in the early years of the 21st century. In 2006 there were 27.9m. students enrolled on internet-based courses. In the state budget for 2009 an allocation of 1,043,754m. yuan was made to education. In addition to the 39,240m. already allocated for the purposes of supporting nine years of compulsory education for students in rural areas, the release from the central budget of a further 7,930m. was announced in August 2011.

Bibliography

Adshead, S. A. M. *China in World History*. 3rd Edn, Basingstoke, Macmillan Press, 1999.

Alexandroff, Alan S., Ostry, Sylvia, and Gomez, Rafael (Eds). *China and the Long March to Global Trade—The Accession of China to the World Trade Organization*. London, Routledge, 2003.

Ambler, Tim, Witzel, Morgen, and Xi, Chao. *Doing Business in China*. Abingdon, Routledge, 2009.

Ash, Robert, Howe, Christopher, and Kueh, Y. Y. (Eds). *China's Economic Reform—A Study with Documents*. London, Routledge-Curzon, 2002.

Bailey, Paul J. *Gender and Education in China: Gender Discourses and Women's Schooling in the Early Twentieth Century*. Abingdon, Routledge, 2007.

Béja, Jean-Philippe (Ed.). *The Impact of China's 1989 Tiananmen Massacre*. Abingdon, Routledge, 2010.

Bell, Daniel. *China's New Confucianism: Politics and Everyday Life in a Changing Society*. Princeton, NJ, Princeton University Press, 2008.

Blasko, Dennis. *The Chinese Army Today: Tradition and Transformation for the 21st Century*. Abingdon, Routledge, 2005.

Blecher, Marc. *China Against the Tides: Restructuring Through Revolution, Radicalism and Reform*. 3rd Edn, London, Continuum, 2009.

Brahm, Laurence J. *China's Century: The Awakening of the Next Economic Powerhouse*. New York, John Wiley & Sons, 2001.

Zhu Rongji and the Transformation of Modern China. Singapore, John Wiley & Sons, 2002.

Brandt, Loren, and Rawski, Thomas G. (Eds). *China's Great Economic Transformation*. Cambridge, Cambridge University Press, 2008.

Brodsgaard, Kjeld Erik, and Yongnian, Zheng (Eds). *The Chinese Communist Party in Reform*. Abingdon, Routledge, 2006.

Brown, David, and MacBean, Alasdair (Eds). *Challenges for China's Development: An Enterprise Perspective*. Abingdon, Routledge, 2005.

Brownell, Susan. *Beijing's Games: What the Olympics Mean to China*. Lanham, MD, Rowman & Littlefield, 2008.

Carlson, Allen, et al (Eds). *Contemporary Chinese Politics: New Sources, Methods, and Field Strategies*. Cambridge, Cambridge University Press, 2010.

Chai, Joseph C. H. (Ed.). *The Economic Development of Modern China*. Cheltenham, Edward Elgar, 2000.

Chang, Jung, and Halliday, Jon. *Mao: the Unknown Story*. London, Jonathan Cape, 2005.

Cheek, Timothy (Ed.). *A Critical Introduction to Mao*. Cambridge, Cambridge University Press, 2010.

Cheng Li (Ed.). *China's Changing Political Landscape: Prospects for Democracy*. Washington, DC, Brookings Institution Press, 2008.

Cheung, Tai Ming. *Fortifying China: the Struggle to Build a Modern Defense Economy*. Ithaca, NY, Cornell University Press, 2009.

Chung, Chien-peng. *China's Multilateral Co-operation in Asia and the Pacific: Institutionalizing Beijing's 'Good Neighbour Policy'*. Abingdon, Routledge, 2010.

Chunghang, Liu. *Multinationals, Globalization and Indigenous Firms in China*. Abingdon, Routledge, 2009.

Conboy, Kenneth, and Morrison, James. *The CIA's Secret War in Tibet*. Lawrence, KS, University of Kansas Press, 2002.

Cunningham, Philip J. *Tiananmen Moon: Inside the Student Uprising of 1989*. Lanham, MD, Rowman & Littlefield, 2009.

Deng Xiliang. *Foreign Direct Investment in China: Spillover Effects on Domestic Enterprises*. Abingdon, Routledge, 2011.

Denoon, David B. H. (Ed.). *China: Contemporary Political, Economic, and International Affairs*. New York, New York University Press, 2007.

Dikötter, Frank. *Mao's Great Famine: The History of China's Most Devastating Catastrophe, 1958–62*. London, Bloomsbury Publishing, 2010.

Dillon, Michael. *Contemporary China: An Introduction*. Abingdon, Routledge, 2008.

Xinjiang—China's Muslim Far Northwest. Abingdon, Routledge, 2009.

China: A Modern History. London, I. B. Tauris, 2010.

Dillon, Michael (Ed.). *Key Papers on Islam in China*. Folkestone, Global Oriental, 2007.

Key Papers on Chinese Economic History up to the Modern Era. Folkestone, Global Oriental, 2007.

Ding Sheng. *The Dragon's Hidden Wings: How China Rises with Its Soft Power*. Lanham, MD, Rowman & Littlefield, 2008.

Dittmer, Lowell, and Yu, George T. (Eds). *China, the Developing World, and the New Global Dynamic*. Boulder, CO, Lynne Rienner Publishers, 2010.

Economy, Elizabeth C. *The River Runs Black: The Environmental Challenge to China's Future*. Ithaca, NY, Cornell University Press, 2004.

Eichengreen, Barry, Park, Yung Chul, and Wyplosz, Charles (Eds). *China, Asia and the New World Economy*. Oxford, Oxford University Press, 2008.

Eisenman, Joshua, Heginbotham, Eric, and Mitchell, Derek (Eds). *China and the Developing World: Beijing's Strategy for the Twenty-First Century*. Armonk, NY, M. E. Sharpe, 2007.

Elvin, Mark. *The Retreat of Elephants: An Environmental History of China*. New Haven, CT, Yale University Press, 2004.

Eshrick, Joseph W., Pickowicz, Paul G., and Walder, Andrew G. (Eds). *The Chinese Cultural Revolution as History*. Stanford, CA, Stanford University Press, 2006.

Europa Publications. *The Territories of the People's Republic of China*. London, Europa Publications, 2002.

Fairbank, John K. *The Great Chinese Revolution: 1800–1985*. New York, Harper and Row, 1986.

Fairbank, John K., et al. (Eds). *The Cambridge History of China*. 15 vols. Cambridge, Cambridge University Press, 1987–92.

Fairbank, John K., and Goldman, Perle. *China: A New History*. Cambridge, MA, Harvard University Press, 2005.

Fenby, Jonathan. *The Penguin History of Modern China: The Fall and Rise of a Great Power, 1850–2008*. London, Allen Lane, 2008.

Feng Hui. *The Politics of China's Accession to the World Trade Organization: The Dragon Goes Global*. Abingdon, Routledge, 2005.

Fernández-Stembridge, Leila, and Fisac, Taciana. *China Today: Economic Reforms, Social Cohesion and Collective Identities*. Abingdon, Routledge, 2010.

Fewsmith, Joseph. *Elite Politics in Contemporary China*. Armonk, NY, M. E. Sharpe, 2000.

China Today, China Tomorrow: Domestic Politics, Economy, and Society. Lanham, MD, Rowman & Littlefield, 2010.

Finkelstein, David M., and Gunness, Kristen (Eds). *Civil-Military Relations in Today's China: Swimming in a New Sea*. Armonk, NY, M. E. Sharpe, 2007.

Foot, Rosemary, and Walter, Andrew. *China, the United States, and Global Order.* Cambridge, Cambridge University Press, 2011.

Friedmann, John. *China's Urban Transition.* Minneapolis, MN, University of Minnesota Press, 2005.

Gamer, Robert E. (Ed.) *Understanding Contemporary China.* Boulder, CO, Lynne Rienner, 2008.

Garnaut, Ross G., and Ligang Song (Eds). *Private Enterprise in China.* London, RoutledgeCurzon, 2003.

Garnaut, Ross G., and Yiping Huang (Eds). *Growth Without Miracles: Readings on the Chinese Economy in the Era of Reform.* Oxford, Oxford University Press, 2000.

Gilley, Bruce. *China's Democratic Future: How It Will Happen and Where It Will Lead.* New York, Columbia University Press, 2004.

Gilmore, Fiona, and Dumont, Serge. *Brand Warriors China: Creating Sustainable Brand Capital.* London, Profile Books, 2003.

Gittings, John. *China Changes Face: The Road from Revolution 1949–1989.* Oxford, Oxford University Press, 1989.

Real China: From Cannibalism to Karaoke. London, Simon and Schuster, 1996.

The Changing Face of China: From Mao to Market. Oxford, Oxford University Press, 2005.

Goh, Esther. *China's One-Child Policy and Multiple Caregiving: Raising Little Suns in Xiamen.* Abingdon, Routledge, 2011.

Goodman, David S. G. *Deng Xiaoping and the Chinese Revolution: A Political Biography.* London, Routledge, 1995.

China's Provinces in Reform: Class, Community and Political Culture. London, Routledge, 1997.

The New Rich in China: Future Rulers, Present Lives. Abingdon, Routledge, 2008.

Gore, Lance. *The Chinese Communist Party and China's Capitalist Revolution: The Political Impact of Market.* Abingdon, Routledge, 2010.

Greenaway David, Milner, Chris, and Yao Shujie. *China and the World Economy.* Basingstoke, Palgrave Macmillan, 2010.

Gries, Peter Hays. *China's New Nationalism: Pride, Politics and Diplomacy.* Berkeley, CA, University of California Press, 2004.

Gries, Peter Hays, and Rosen, Stanley (Eds). *State and Society in 21st century China: Crisis, Contention and Legitimation.* London, RoutledgeCurzon, 2004.

Chinese Politics: State, Society and the Market. Abingdon, Routledge, 2010.

Guo Sujian and Deng Chenglai (Eds). *China's Search for Good Governance.* Basingstoke, Palgrave Macmillan, 2011.

Guo Yingjie. *Cultural Nationalism in Contemporary China.* London, RoutledgeCurzon, 2004.

Gustafsson, Björn A., Li Shi and Sicular, Terry (Eds). *Inequality and Public Policy in China.* Cambridge, Cambridge University Press, 2010.

Handberg, Roger, and Li, Zhen. *Chinese Space Policy: A Study in Domestic and International Politics.* Abingdon, Routledge, 2007.

Hassard, John, et al. *China's State Enterprise Reform: From Marx to the Market.* Abingdon, Routledge, 2007.

He, Kai. *Institutional Balancing in the Asia Pacific: Economic Interdependence and China's Rise.* Abingdon, Routledge, 2009.

Hoffman, W. John, and Enright, Michael. *China into the Future: Making Sense of the World's Most Dynamic Economy.* London, John Wiley & Sons, 2008.

Holslag, Jonathan. *Trapped Giant: China's Troubled Military Rise.* Abingdon, Routledge, 2010.

Hook, Brian, and Twitchett, Denis (Eds). *The Cambridge Encyclopedia of China.* Cambridge, Cambridge University Press, 1991.

Hsiao, Hsin-Huang Michael, and Lin, Cheng-Yi (Eds). *Rise of China: Beijing's Strategies and Implications for the Asia-Pacific.* Abingdon, Routledge, 2009.

Hsü, Immanuel C. Y. *The Rise of Modern China.* 6th Edn, Oxford, Oxford University Press, 2000.

Hu, Angang. *Economic and Social Transformation in China: Challenges and Opportunities.* Abingdon, Routledge, 2006.

Hsueh, Roselyn. *China's Regulatory State: A New Strategy for Globalization.* Ithaca, NY, Cornell University Press, 2011.

Huang, Xiaoming. *The Institutional Dynamics of China's Great Transformation.* Abingdon, Routledge, 2010.

Hughes, Christopher R. *Chinese Nationalism in a Global Era.* London, RoutledgeCurzon, 2004.

Hughes, Christopher R., and Wacker, Gudrun (Eds). *China and the Internet.* London, RoutledgeCurzon, 2003.

Huiyun Feng. *Chinese Strategic Culture and Foreign Policy Decision-Making.* Abingdon, Routledge, 2007.

Hutchings, Graham. *Modern China: A Guide to a Century of Change.* Cambridge, MA, Harvard University Press, 2001.

Jeffries, Ian. *Contemporary China: a Guide to Economic and Political Developments.* Abingdon, Routledge, 2009.

Political Developments in Contemporary China: A Guide. Abingdon, Routledge, 2010.

Jia Xinting and Tomasic, Roman. *Corporate Governance and Resource Security in China—The Transformation of China's Global Resources Companies.* Abingdon, Routledge, 2009.

Jocelyn, Ed, and McEwen, Andrew. *The Long March: The True Story Behind the Legendary Journey That Made Mao's China.* London, Constable & Robinson, 2006.

Johnston, Ian. *Wild Grass: China's Revolution from Below.* London, Penguin Books, 2005.

Joseph, William A. (Ed.). *Politics in China: An Introduction.* Oxford, Oxford University Press, 2010.

Ka Zeng (Ed.). *China's Foreign Trade Policy: The New Constituencies.* Abingdon, Routledge, 2007.

Kanbur, Ravi, and Zhang Xiaobu (Eds). *Governing Rapid Growth in China: Equity and Institutions.* Abingdon, Routledge, 2009.

Karrar, Hasan H. *The New Silk Road Diplomacy: China's Central Asian Foreign Policy Since the Cold War.* Vancouver, BC, University of British Columbia Press, 2009.

Keane, Michael. *Created in China: The Great New Leap Forward.* Abingdon, Routledge, 2007.

Keith, Ronald C. (Ed.). *China as a Rising World Power and its Response to 'Globalization'.* Abingdon, Routledge, 2007.

Kirby, William C., Ross, Robert S., and Li, Gong (Eds). *Normalization of US-China Relations: An International History.* Cambridge, MA, Harvard University Press, 2006.

Krug, Barbara. *China's Rational Entrepreneurs: The Development of the New Private Sector.* London, RoutledgeCurzon, 2004.

Kynge, James. *China Shakes the World: The Rise of a Hungry Nation.* London, Weidenfeld & Nicolson, 2006.

Lai Hongyi. *The Domestic Sources of China's Foreign Policy: Regimes, Leadership, Priorities and Process.* Abingdon, Routledge, 2011.

Laliberte, Andre, and Lanteigne, Marc (Eds). *The Chinese Party-State in the 21st Century: Adaptation and the Reinvention of Legitimacy.* Abingdon, Routledge, 2011.

Lam, Willy Wo-Lap. *The Era of Zhao Ziyang: Power Struggle in China, 1986–88.* Hong Kong, A. B. Books and Stationery (International) Ltd, 1989.

China after Deng Xiaoping: The Power Struggle in Beijing since Tiananmen. Singapore, John Wiley & Sons, 1995.

The Era of Jiang Zemin. Singapore, Prentice Hall, 1999.

Chinese Politics in the Hu Jintao Era: New Leaders, New Challenges. Armonk, NY, M. E. Sharpe, 2006.

Lampton, David M. *The Making of Chinese Foreign and Security Policy in the Era of Reform.* Stanford, CA, Stanford University Press, 2001.

Lanteigne, Marc. *Chinese Foreign Policy: An Introduction.* Abingdon, Routledge, 2009.

Lardy, Nicholas R. *China's Unfinished Economic Revolution.* Washington, DC, Brookings Institution Press, 1998.

Integrating China into the Global Economy. Washington, DC, Brookings Institution Press, 2002.

Laurenceson, James, and Chai, Joseph C. H. *Financial Reform and Economic Development in China.* Cheltenham, Edward Elgar Publishing, 2003.

Li Lanquing. *Breaking Through: The Birth of China's Opening-up Policy.* Oxford, Oxford University Press, 2010.

Li Mingjiang. *China's International Relations in Asia.* Abingdon, Routledge, 2009.

Li Nan (Ed.). *Chinese Civil-Military Relations: The Transformation of the People's Liberation Army.* Abingdon, Routledge, 2005.

Li, Rex. *A Rising China and Security in East Asia: Identity Construction and Security Discourse.* Abingdon, Routledge, 2009.

Liew, Yeong H., and Wang Shaoguang (Eds). *Nationalism, Democracy and National Integration in China.* London, RoutledgeCurzon, 2003.

Lilley, James, with Lilley, Jeffrey. *China Hands: Nine Decades of Adventure, Espionage and Diplomacy in Asia.* New York, Public Affairs, 2004.

Lin, George C. S. *Developing China: Land, Politics and Social Conditions.* Abingdon, Routledge, 2011.

Lin Shuanglin and Zhu Xiaodong (Eds). *Private Enterprises and China's Economic Development.* Abingdon, Routledge, 2011.

Liu, Lydia H. *The Clash of Empires: The Invention of China in Modern World Making*. Cambridge, MA, Harvard University Press, 2004.

Liu Xiaohui and Zhang Wei (Eds). *China's Three Decades of Economic Reforms*. Abingdon, Routledge, 2009.

Liu, Yong. *The Dutch East India Company's Tea Trade With China, 1757–1781*. Boston, Brill, 2007.

Lovell, Julia. *The Great Wall: China Against the World, 1000BC–AD2000*. New York, Atlantic, 2006.

Lu Caizhen. *Poverty and Development in China: Alternative Approaches to Poverty Assessment*. Abingdon, Routledge, 2011.

Lu Hong, and Miethe, Terance D. *China's Death Penalty: History, Law, and Contemporary Practices*. Abingdon, Routledge, 2007.

MacFarquhar, Roderick. *The Origins of the Cultural Revolution*. 2 vols. London, Oxford University Press, 1983, and New York, Columbia University Press, 1984.

The Politics of China: Sixty Years of The People's Republic of China. Cambridge, Cambridge University Press, 3rd Edn, 2011.

MacFarquhar, Roderick, and Schoenhals, Michael. *Mao's Last Revolution*. Cambridge, MA, Harvard University Press, 2006.

Mackerras, Colin (Ed.). *Ethnic Minorities in Modern China*. Abingdon, Routledge, 2011.

McGregor, Richard. *The Party: The Secret World of China's Communist Rulers*. London, Allen Lane, 2010.

McLaren, Ann. *Chinese Women—Living and Working*. Abingdon, Routledge, 2003.

McNally, Christopher A. *China's Emergent Political Economy: Capitalism in the Dragon's Lair*. Abingdon, Routledge, 2007.

Muhlhahn, Klaus. *Criminal Justice in China: a History*. Cambridge, MA, Harvard University Press, 2009.

Murphy, Rachel. *Labour Migration and Social Development in Contemporary China*. Abingdon, Routledge, 2008.

Ong, Russell. *China's Security Interests in the 21st Century*. Abingdon, Routledge, 2007.

Pei, Minxin. *China's Trapped Transition: The Limits of Developmental Autocracy*. Cambridge, MA, Harvard University Press, 2006.

Perry, Elizabeth J. *Patrolling the Revolution: Worker Militias, Citizenship, and the Modern Chinese State*. Lanham, MD, Rowman & Littlefield, 2006.

Roberts, John A. G. *A History of China*. Basingstoke, Palgrave Macmillan, 3rd Edn, 2011.

Rongxing Guo. *An Introduction to the Chinese Economy*. Hoboken, NJ, John Wiley and Sons Ltd, 2010.

Rose, Caroline. *Sino-Japanese Relations: Facing the Past, Looking to the Future*. London, Routledge, 2004.

Ross, Robert S. *Chinese Security Policy: Structure, Power and Politics*. Abingdon, Routledge, 2009.

Ross, Robert S., and Zhu Feng (Eds). *China's Ascent: Power, Security, and the Future of International Politics*. Ithaca, NY, Cornell University Press, 2008.

Rui Huaichuan. *Globalisation, Transition and Development in China*. London, RoutledgeCurzon, 2004.

Saee, John (Ed.) *China and the Global Economy in the 21st Century*. Abingdon, Routledge, 2011.

Saich, Tony. *Governance and Politics of China*. Basingstoke, Palgrave Macmillan, 3rd Edn, 2010.

Sanders, Richard, Chen Yang (Eds). *China's Post-Reform Economy: Achieving Harmony, Sustaining Growth*. Abingdon, Routledge, 2007.

Saw Swee-Hock and Wong, John (Eds). *Regional Economic Development in China*. Singapore, Institute of Southeast Asian Studies, 2010.

Schiere, Richard. *China's Development Challenges: Public Sector Reform and Vulnerability to Poverty*. Abingdon, Routledge, 2009.

Scotton, James F., and Hachten, William A. (Eds). *New Media for a New China*. Chichester, Wiley Blackwell, 2010.

Shakya, Tsering. *The Dragon in the Land of Snows: A History of Modern Tibet Since 1947*. London, Pimlico, 1999.

Shambaugh, David. *Is China Unstable? Assessing the Factors*. Armonk, NY, M. E. Sharpe, 2000.

The Modern Chinese State. Cambridge, Cambridge University Press, 2000.

Modernizing China's Military: Progress, Problems, and Prospects. Berkeley, CA, University of California Press, 2003.

Power Shift: China and Asia's New Dynamics. Berkeley, CA, University of California Press, 2006.

China's Communist Party: Atrophy and Adaptation. Berkeley, CA, University of California Press, 2008.

Shambaugh, David (Ed.). *Charting China's Future: Domestic and International Challenges*. Abingdon, Routledge, 2011.

Sheng, Yumin. *Economic Openness and Territorial Politics in China*. Cambridge, Cambridge University Press, 2010.

Shi, Chenxia. *The Political Determinants of Corporate Governance in China*. Abingdon, Routledge, 2011.

Shue, Vivienne, and Wong, Christine (Eds). *Paying for Progress in China: Public Finance, Human Welfare and Changing Patterns of Inequality*. Abingdon, Routledge, 2007.

Smil, Vaclav. *China's Past, China's Future*. London, RoutledgeCurzon, 2003.

Smith, Warren W., Jr. *China's Tibet? Autonomy or Assimilation*. Lanham, MD, Rowman & Littlefield, 2008.

Tibet's Last Stand?: The Tibetan Uprising of 2008 and China's Response. Lanham, MD, Rowman & Littlefield, 2009.

Starr, S. Frederick (Ed.). *Xinjiang, China's Muslim Borderland*. Armonk, NY, M. E. Sharpe, 2004.

Suettinger, Robert L. *Beyond Tiananmen: The Politics of US-China Relations, 1989–2000*. Washington, DC, Brookings Institution Press, 2003.

Sutter, Robert G. *U.S.-Chinese Relations: Perilous Past, Pragmatic Present*. Lanham, MD, Rowman and Littlefield, 2010.

Taylor, Ian. *China's New Role in Africa*. Boulder, CO, Lynne Rienner Publishers, 2009.

Teiwes, Frederick C., and Sun, Warren. *The End of the Maoist Era: Chinese Politics During the Twilight of the Cultural Revolution, 1972–1976*. Armonk, NY, M. E. Sharpe, 2007.

Tong, James W. *Revenge of the Forbidden City: The Suppression of the Falungong in China, 1999–2008*. Oxford, Oxford University Press, 2009.

Tubilewicz, Czeslaw (Ed.). *Critical Issues in Contemporary China*. Abingdon, Routledge, 2006.

Tyler, Christian. *Wild West China: The Taming of Xinjiang*. London, John Murray, 2003.

Urio, Paolo. *Reconciling State, Market and Society in China: The Long March Toward Prosperity*. Abingdon, Routledge, 2010.

Varum, Celeste Amorim, Huang, Can, and Gouveia, Joaquim Jose Borges. *China: Building an Innovative Economy*. Oxford, Chandos, 2007.

Veeck, Gregory, et al. *China's Geography: Globalization and the Dynamics of Political, Economic, and Social Change*. Lanham, MD, Rowman & Littlefield, 2011.

Vogel, Ezra F. *One Step Ahead in China: Guangdong Under Reform*. Cambridge, MA, Harvard University Press, 1989.

Deng Xiaoping and the Transformation of China.Cambridge, MA, Harvard University Press, 2011.

Wakeman, Carolyn, and Light, Ken (Eds). *Assignment Shanghai: Photographs on the Eve of Revolution*. Berkeley, CA, University of California Press, 2003.

Walter, Carl E., and Howie, Fraser J. T. *Privatizing China*. Singapore, John Wiley, 2003.

Wang Gungwu and Zheng Yongnian (Eds). *China and the New International Order*. Abingdon, Routledge, 2008.

Wang Hui. *China's New Order: Society, Politics and Economy in Transition*. Cambridge, MA, Harvard University Press, 2003.

Wang Xiaolu, Li Shi and Wang Sangui. *Eliminating Poverty Through Development in China*. Abingdon, Routledge, 2008.

Watson, James L. (Ed.) *Class and Social Stratification in Post-Revolution China*. Cambridge, Cambridge University Press, 2010.

Wayne, Martin I. *China's War on Terrorism: Counter-Insurgency, Politics and Internal Security*. Abingdon, Routledge, 2007.

Weatherley, Robert. *Politics in China Since 1949: Legitimizing Authoritarian Rule*. Abingdon, Routledge, 2006.

Mao's Forgotten Successor: The Political Career of Hua Guofeng. Basingstoke, Palgrave Macmillan, 2010.

Wei, Yehua Dennis. *Regional Development in China—State, Globalization and Inequality*. London, Routledge, 2000.

White, Tyrene. *China's Longest Campaign: Birth Planning in the People's Republic, 1949–2005*. New York, Cornell University Press, 2006.

Whyte, Martin King (Ed.). *One Country, Two Societies: Rural-Urban Inequality in Contemporary China*. Cambridge, MA, Harvard University Press, 2010.

Woetzel, Jonathan R. *Capitalist China*. Singapore, John Wiley & Sons, 2003.

Wu, Guoguang, and Lansdowne, Helen (Eds). *Socialist China, Capitalist China: Social Tension and Political Transition Under Economic Globalization*. Abingdon, Routledge, 2009.

Wu Jinglian. *Understanding and Interpreting Chinese Economic Reform.* Mason, OH, Texere, 2005.

Wu, Zhongmin. *China in the World Economy.* Abingdon, Routledge, 2009.

Xiaowei, Zang. *Ethnicity and Urban Life in China: A Comparative Study of Hui Muslims and Han Chinese.* Abingdon, Routledge, 2007.

Xu Yi-chong. *The Politics of Nuclear Energy in China.* Basingstoke, Palgrave Macmillan, 2010.

Yan Sun. *Corruption and Market in Contemporary China.* New York, Cornell University Press, 2004.

Yang, Dali L. *Calamity and Reform in China: State, Rural Society, and Institutional Change since the Great Leap Famine.* Stanford, CA, Stanford University Press, 1996.

Remaking the Chinese Leviathan: Market Transition and the Politics of Governance in China. Stanford, CA, Stanford University Press, 2004.

Yao Shujie and Liu Shaming (Eds). *Sustaining China's Economic Growth in the Twenty-first Century.* London, RoutledgeCurzon, 2003.

Yee, Herbert, and Storey, Ian (Eds). *The China Threat: Perceptions, Myths, and Reality.* London, RoutledgeCurzon, 2002.

Yin, Jason Z., Lin Shuanglin, and Gates, David F. (Eds). *Social Security Reform: Options for China.* River Edge, NJ, World Scientific Publishing, 2000.

Yu Hong. *Economic Development and Inequality in China: The Case of Guangdong.* Abingdon, Routledge, 2010.

Yueh, Linda. *The Economy of China.* Cheltenham, Edward Elgar, 2010.

Yusuf, Shahid, Perkins, Dwight H. and Nabeshima, Kaoru. *Under New Ownership: Privatizing China's Enterprises.* Stanford, CA, Stanford University Press, 2006.

Zang Xiaowei. *Elite Dualism and Leadership Selection in China.* London, RoutledgeCurzon, 2003.

Zarrow, Peter. *China in War and Revolution, 1895–1949.* Abingdon, Routledge, 2005.

Zhang Mei. *China's Poor Regions.* London, RoutledgeCurzon, 2003.

Zhang Wei (Ed.). *Economic Reform in Modern China.* Abingdon, Routledge, 2011.

Zheng Yongnian. *The Chinese Communist Party as Organizational Emperor.* Abingdon, Routledge, 2009.

Zheng Yongnian and Fewsmith, Joseph (Eds). *China's Opening Society: The Non-State Sector and Governance.* Abingdon, Routledge, 2008.

Zheng Yongnian, Lu Yiyi and White III, Lynn T. (Eds). *Politics of Modern China.* Abingdon, Routledge, 2009.

Zheng Yongnian and Tong, Sarah Y. (Eds). *China and the Global Economic Crisis.* Singapore, World Scientific Publishing, 2010.

Zhu, Zhiqun. *US-China Relations in the 21st Century: Power Transition and Peace.* Abingdon, Routledge, 2006.

Zweig, David, and Chen Zhimin (Eds). *China's Reforms and International Political Economy.* Abingdon, Routledge, 2007.

CHINESE SPECIAL ADMINISTRATIVE REGIONS

HONG KONG

Physical and Social Geography

MICHAEL FREEBERNE

With additions by the editorial staff

The population of the Special Administrative Region (SAR) of Hong Kong occupies a total land area of only 1,104 sq km (426.3 sq miles). The territory, which reverted from British to Chinese sovereignty in July 1997, is situated off the south-east coast of Guangdong Province of the People's Republic of China, to the east of the mouth of the Zhujiang (Pearl River), between latitudes 22° 9' and 22° 37' N and longitudes 113° 52' and 114° 30' E. The SAR comprises the island of Hong Kong, ceded to the United Kingdom by China in 1842, the Kowloon peninsula, ceded in 1860, and the New Territories, which are part of the mainland and were leased to the United Kingdom between 1898 and 1997, together with Deep Bay and Mirs Bay and some 236 outlying islands and islets. The fine anchorages between the northern shore of Hong Kong Island and Kowloon provided an ideal situation for the growth of one of the world's leading entrepôt ports.

PHYSICAL FEATURES

Hong Kong Island is approximately 17 km long and between 3 km and 8 km wide. An irregular range of hills rises abruptly from the sea; several peaks are over 300 m in height, and Victoria Peak reaches 554 m. Granites, basalt and other volcanic rocks account for the main geological formations. These rocks are most common, too, on Lantau and Lamma islands and in the Kowloon peninsula and New Territories, which are mostly hilly, rising to 957 m in Tai Mo Shan, and have rugged, deeply indented coastlines. The territory is poor in minerals and, apart from hillside areas of dense scrub, was largely stripped of natural vegetation by indiscriminate tree-felling during the Japanese occupation of 1941–45. The resultant erosion was extensively repaired under a vigorous programme of reafforestation. Flat land is scarce. Reclamation of land from the sea for building purposes is very important, and since 1945 much additional land has been made available for housing and commercial development, as well as for projects like the international airport at Chek Lap Kok, off Lantau Island, which was opened in 1998. In 1996 major reclamation work at West Kowloon, which included the extension of Stonecutters Island, was substantially completed. Reclamation has also continued to progress on Hong Kong Island and in the New Territories.

CLIMATE

The climate of Hong Kong is subtropical and governed by monsoons. Winter lasts from October to April, when the winds are from the north or north-east, while during the summer months, from May to September, south or south-westerly winds predominate. Average daily temperatures are highest in July with 29°C and lowest in January with 16°C. The wet summer is very humid. Annual rainfall averages 2,214 mm, some 80% of which falls between May and September. Devastating typhoons occasionally strike in summer.

Despite the high rainfall, it has proved increasingly difficult to supply sufficient domestic and industrial water, and most supplies are piped from the neighbouring Guangdong Province of China. The Plover Cove reservoir, inaugurated in 1969, trebled Hong Kong's reservoir capacity, and further reservoirs subsequently came into operation, including the world's first seabed reservoir. Nevertheless, in 2006 Hong Kong was dependent upon China for 80% of its water supply, compared with 45% in 1984. By 2006 a total of 1,100m. cu m of water was being supplied annually from China, following an upgrade of the Dongjiang-Shenzhen water supply project in 2003. Additional purchases may be made in years of low rainfall.

POPULATION

The population of Hong Kong at the census of July 2006 totalled 6,864,346, giving an average density of 6,217.7 persons per sq km. However, average density in the New Territories at the census of 2006 was 3,659 per sq km, whereas for Hong Kong Island and Kowloon it was 15,759 per sq km and 43,033 per sq km respectively, with a density of 52,123 persons per sq km being reached in the district of Kwun Tong, in Kowloon. The population totalled an estimated 7,120,200 in mid-2011, when density reached 6,449.5 persons per sq km. The figures for population density are among the highest in the world.

Hong Kong has experienced an extraordinary growth in population. Between 1841 (when only about 5,000 people lived on the island) and 1941 the colony received numerous migrants, following which the population was estimated at about 1.5m. There was a drastic reduction during the Japanese occupation of 1941–45, but by 1949 the population had increased to 1,857,000. After the establishment of the People's Republic of China in 1949, large numbers of refugees arrived in Hong Kong, where the rate of natural increase was already high. Hong Kong's crude birth rate in 2010 was estimated at 12.5 per 1,000 (compared with 18.3 in 1975). At an estimated 1.6 per 1,000 registered live births in 2007, the mortality rate among under-fives was one of the lowest in Asia. The crude death rate in 2009 was estimated at 5.7 per 1,000 (compared with 4.9 in 1975). The proportion of the population under 15 years of age declined from 23% in 1986 to 14% in 2006, while the proportion comprising those aged 65 years and over rose from 8% to 12%. About 95% of the territory's population are of predominantly Chinese descent. The Cantonese form the largest community.

History

JAMES TANG

Based on an earlier article by N. J. MINERS

EARLY DEVELOPMENT TO 1945

The colonial territory of Hong Kong was acquired by the United Kingdom in three stages. The First Opium War of 1840–42 began after the Chinese commissioner in Guangzhou (Canton) had seized and destroyed large stocks of opium held by the British traders there, who then left the city. The British Government demanded compensation and a commercial treaty, and an expedition was dispatched to enforce these demands. During the hostilities a naval force occupied the island of Hong Kong, which was ceded to the United Kingdom 'in perpetuity' by the Treaty of Nanjing (Nanking) of 1842. As soon as this was ratified, a colony was formally proclaimed in June 1843. Continuing disputes between the United Kingdom and China over trade and shipping led to renewed warfare in 1856. This was ended by the Convention of Beijing (Peking) of 1860, by which the peninsula of Kowloon on the mainland opposite the island was annexed.

Following China's defeat in the Sino-Japanese War of 1895, the Western powers seized the opportunity to extract further concessions. The United Kingdom demanded, and obtained in 1898, a 99-year lease on the mainland north of Kowloon, together with the adjoining islands. These New Territories increased the area of the colony from about 110 sq km to more than 1,000 sq km. The terms of the 1898 Convention of Beijing allowed the existing Chinese magistrates to remain in the old walled city of Kowloon, but in 1899 they were unilaterally expelled on the pretext that they had encouraged resistance to the British occupation. The Chinese Government protested at the time and reasserted a claim to jurisdiction over this small area in 1933, 1948 and 1962, although this was rejected by the Hong Kong courts. In 1994, with the agreement of China, the area was cleared, levelled and converted into a public park.

The main reason for the British occupation of Hong Kong in 1841 was its magnificent harbour. Attracted by its free port status, the entrepôt trade between the West and China grew steadily for the next 100 years. The great trading companies established their headquarters under the British flag; banks, insurance companies and other commercial enterprises were founded to serve the China traders as well as shipbuilding, ship-repairing and other industries dependent on the port. At the same time the population grew from about 5,000 in 1841 to more than 500,000 in 1916 and to exceed 1m. by 1939, of whom fewer than 20,000 were non-Chinese. Chinese were allowed free access; the flow of migrants increased whenever China was disturbed by wars or rebellions, the process being reversed when peaceful conditions had been restored on the mainland. Apart from the settled farming population of the New Territories, relatively few Chinese regarded Hong Kong as their permanent home until after the end of the Second World War in 1945. Most came to trade or seek employment and then returned to their home towns. Europeans were similarly transient, whether they were government officials or in private employment.

The colony's administration followed the usual crown colony pattern; power was held by a Governor, who was advised by nominated executive and legislative councils, on which government officials had an overall majority over the unofficial members. The first unofficial members were appointed to the Legislative Council in 1850, and the first Chinese in 1880; the first 'unofficials' in the Executive Council were appointed in 1896, and the first Chinese in 1926. In 1894, 1916 and 1922 the British residents pressed for an unofficial majority in the Legislative Council and the election of some or all of the 'unofficials' on a franchise confined to British subjects, citing the constitutional progress made in other colonies; but on all occasions the British Government was unwilling to allow the Chinese majority to be politically subjected to a small European minority. A sanitary board was set up in 1883 and this was made partly elective in 1887. In 1936 it was renamed the Urban Council.

There were large-scale strikes in the early 1920s, but otherwise anti-foreigner agitation in China had little effect on Hong Kong's prosperity. The growing threat of war in the late 1930s led to an increase in defence expenditure, which forced the imposition of income and profits taxes for the first time; this wartime expedient was made permanent in 1947. Japanese forces occupied most of the Chinese province of Guangdong, north of the colony, in 1938, and in December 1941 overran Hong Kong. In August 1945, as the Second World War drew to a close, the Japanese authorities restored power to the surviving colonial officials who had been interned with the rest of the British community throughout the occupation. A British naval force arrived in late August to install an interim military administration, thus forestalling pressures from the US Government for Hong Kong to be returned to China.

POST-WAR ISSUES

After the Japanese capture of Hong Kong in December 1941, a planning unit was formed in London to prepare for the post-war rehabilitation of the colony. Its members later staffed the interim military administration, which restored public services on a minimum basis. Civil government, on the traditional colonial pattern, was re-established in May 1946. Meanwhile, China was disrupted by civil war between the nationalist and communist armies, which ended with the communist victory in 1949. The United Kingdom recognized the new communist Government of China in 1950, having heavily reinforced the garrison in Hong Kong in 1949 to deter any possible Chinese attack. The only serious violation of the frontier occurred in 1967. The strength of the garrison was reduced at successive defence reviews. In 1992 special units of the Hong Kong Police Force assumed responsibility for the security of the border. All Gurkha troops left the territory in November 1996; one British battalion provided security until mid-1997, when it was replaced by soldiers of the Chinese People's Liberation Army.

During the Second World War the colony's population had declined to about 600,000, as a result of privation and mass deportations by the Japanese. The population quickly regained pre-war levels and rose to about 2m. in 1950, owing to a massive influx of refugees from the civil war in China. The pressures resulting from this inflow forced the colony to abandon its policy of free access, and the frontier was closed in 1950. Movement over the border was subsequently tightly controlled by the Chinese authorities, with the exception of a period during May 1962, when the frontier was unexpectedly opened and 120,000 refugees were allowed to leave. Individual escapees also attempted to enter clandestinely. From 1974 to 1980 any illegal immigrants who were apprehended in the frontier region were transferred to the Chinese authorities, but those who succeeded in reaching the urban areas were allowed to remain. This concession continued to encourage escape attempts. After a massive surge in illegal immigration in 1979–80 (when it was estimated that more than 200,000 people succeeded in settling in the colony in spite of the fact that 170,000 were captured and repatriated), it was announced in October 1980 that, in future, all illegal immigrants who were discovered anywhere in the colony would be repatriated. This announcement caused a sharp decline in illegal attempts to enter, but such immigration continued, and in 1997 an average of some 49 illegal immigrants were arrested daily and forcibly repatriated to China. The Chinese authorities permitted 150 people a day to cross the border, and more were entitled to settle in Hong Kong after China's resumption of sovereignty. From 1990 a total of 25,000 workers were allowed to enter Hong Kong each year on fixed-term contracts, to relieve the labour shortage.

Meanwhile, the problem of feeding the refugees and providing employment was exacerbated by the outbreak of the Korean War in 1950, which led to the imposition of an embargo on the export of strategic goods to China and gravely damaged Hong Kong's entrepôt trade. However, the refugees provided a pool of compliant, hard-working labour. Local businessmen and industrialists who had fled from Shanghai took advantage of this and, by making use of the colony's existing financial infrastructure and world-wide trading connections, they reorientated the economy towards manufacturing for export.

The refugees put an immense strain on all public services, and the newcomers were left to build themselves shanty towns, which spread over the hillsides. A devastating fire at one of these shanty towns in 1953 prompted the Government to initiate a resettlement programme; huge estates were built, with rooms allocated on the scale of 2.3 sq m for each adult. The early designs provided few amenities, as the main consideration was speed of construction. The housing programme continued steadily, with additional expansion from 1972, when a 10-year programme to house a further 1.5m. people, mainly in new towns in the New Territories, was announced. At the same time, various government housing agencies were amalgamated into a new housing authority to assume responsibility for the planning, construction and management of all public housing in Hong Kong. By 1991 more than 50% of the population were living in government-provided housing.

From 1976 many refugees from Viet Nam attempted to reach Hong Kong by sea. Initially, most were accepted for resettlement in the USA, Canada, Australia and Europe. However, in 1982, after the resettlement countries had reduced their immigration quotas, Hong Kong adopted a policy of confining all newly arrived Vietnamese in closed camps, in order to deter others from landing in the territory. Nevertheless, the numbers continued to increase. A large influx in 1988 led the Hong Kong Government to abandon its policy of automatically granting refugee status to newly arrived Vietnamese. All arrivals were subjected to a test, and those considered to be 'economic migrants' were classified as illegal immigrants and confined in detention centres, to await eventual repatriation to Viet Nam. Nevertheless, Vietnamese continued to arrive in increasing numbers, in the hope that they might ultimately secure passage to the USA, since the Government of Viet Nam refused to accept the forced repatriation of those who had been classified as economic migrants. At the end of 1991 Viet Nam finally agreed to accept a limited programme of mandatory repatriation. This significantly reduced the number of Vietnamese arriving in Hong Kong. About 12,000 of those at risk of mandatory repatriation volunteered to return to Viet Nam, and China demanded that all Vietnamese be removed before July 1997. Many of those remaining in Hong Kong were determined to resist forcible repatriation by any available means, and there were intermittent riots and demonstrations in the camps. From early 1998 it was announced that Hong Kong would no longer conduct a 'port of first asylum' policy, whereby refugees were permitted to apply for asylum upon arriving in the territory. Some 1,200 refugees, 659 migrants and 743 illegal immigrants from Viet Nam remained in Hong Kong in March, and negotiations took place between the Hong Kong and British Governments to determine responsibility for their repatriation. Hong Kong's last remaining camp for Vietnamese refugees was closed in May 2000, and inmates were granted residency in the territory.

Between 1945 and 1982 Hong Kong's stability was disturbed only three times: in 1956 there were faction fights between communist and nationalist supporters; in 1966 there were three nights of rioting, provoked by an increase in fares on the cross-harbour ferry; and for several months in 1967 there were disturbances and bomb attacks, led by communist sympathizers who were inspired by the example of the 'Cultural Revolution' in China. These had ended by late 1967, with the restoration of order in China itself.

In 1982 the start of negotiations on Hong Kong's future caused an upsurge in political activity. Anxiety at the prospect of rule by China after 1997 led to an increase in emigration and investment overseas. The massacre of students in Tiananmen Square in Beijing in June 1989 and the forcible suppression of the pro-democracy movement throughout China had a devastating impact on local confidence in the future. Demonstrations involving up to 1m. people were held in Hong Kong to protest against the massacre. The number of emigrants, mostly to Canada, Australia and the USA, reached a record 66,200 in 1992. The outflow fluctuated thereafter, and the number of departures declined to 30,900 in 1997. Many sought to obtain passports of foreign countries to enable them to leave Hong Kong before China's resumption of sovereignty in mid-1997. In an attempt to restore confidence, the British Government agreed in 1990 to grant full British passports with the right of abode in the United Kingdom to 50,000 business executives, administrators and professional people, together with their immediate family members, making a total of 225,000 individuals. It was hoped that this would encourage senior personnel to remain in Hong Kong. However, China denounced this initiative as a plot to entrench British influence in Hong Kong, and insisted that it would not recognize these passports after 1997.

In October 1989 the Governor announced plans to build a new international airport at Chek Lap Kok, near Lantau Island, a railway to link the airport to the city, and large new port facilities and container terminals in the west of the harbour. China objected strongly to the proposals. In July 1991 the United Kingdom and China signed a memorandum of understanding on the arrangements for building the new airport, but the Chinese Government continued to raise objections to the costs of the project, and tried to use its power to withhold consent in order to extract concessions on political issues. In particular, China opposed the proposals made by the new Governor, Chris Patten, to extend the franchise for the 1995 Legislative Council elections. In 1995 China finally agreed to the arrangements for the new airport, which opened in July 1998.

In June 1991 the Hong Kong Government enacted a Bill of Rights to give effect in local law to the relevant provisions of the UN International Covenant on Civil and Political Rights. These provisions remained in force following the territory's transfer to Chinese sovereignty in mid-1997.

POLITICAL AND ADMINISTRATIVE DEVELOPMENT

Following the restoration of civil government in May 1946, the returning Governor promised a greater measure of self-government and, after inviting suggestions from the public, proposed that an elected Municipal Council, with wide powers over local affairs in the urban area, should be established. These plans for major constitutional reform were deferred after the communist victory in China in 1949, and were finally abandoned in 1952. Thereafter, there were no further initiatives towards democratic government until 1985, largely in deference to China's dislike of any such changes. Instead, the number of appointed unofficial members on the Legislative Council was successively increased from eight in 1951 to 30 in 1984.

Under the terms of the 1984 Joint Declaration (see below), the future legislature of Hong Kong was to be constituted by election. Therefore, in 1985 the composition of the Legislative Council was substantially changed, to include 24 indirectly elected members, 12 chosen by the district boards, Urban Council and Regional Council, and 12 by 'functional constituencies', composed of the representatives of the commercial and industrial sectors, trade unions and various professional bodies. These 24 elected members were outnumbered by the 22 appointed members and the 10 officials. In deference to China's wishes, only minor constitutional changes were made in 1988. In 1990 the British Government agreed with China that the 1991 Legislative Council would consist of 21 functional constituency members, 18 directly elected by universal franchise, 18 members appointed by the Governor and three civil servants. Elections were held in September 1991. Of the 18 seats open to election by universal suffrage, 15 were won by the United Democrats (a liberal grouping led by Martin Lee—who subsequently became the Chairman of the Democratic Party of Hong Kong) and their allies. The new Legislative Council, inaugurated in October, had a majority of elected members for the first time in the territory's history, although most of the 21 members representing functional constituencies had been chosen by only a few hundred voters. Contrary to the normal constitutional practice in British colonies, none of the leaders of the United Democrats was invited to join the Executive Council.

In 1992 Sir David Wilson was replaced as Governor by Chris Patten, a Conservative politician who had lost his parliamentary seat in the recent British general election. Three months after his arrival he announced detailed proposals for the conduct of the 1995 elections, without first consulting China. He proposed that the Legislative Council should conform to the model laid down in the Basic Law (see below), with 30 members elected by functional constituencies, 20 directly elected by geographical constituencies and 10 by an electoral college, but that the electorate for the nine new functional constituencies should be enlarged to 2.7m. voters and that the electorate for the 10 electoral college seats should consist of all the elected members of the District Boards. China denounced this plan as an attempt to increase the number of directly elected seats beyond that laid down in the Basic Law. Negotiations were held with China during 1993, but no compromise could be found. Patten's original proposals were enacted into law by the Legislative Council in June 1994.

At the elections to the Legislative Council held in September 1995, for the first time all 60 seats were determined by election. A total of 920,567 people (36% of registered electors) voted for the 20 seats open to direct election on the basis of geographical constituencies. The Democratic Party of Hong Kong won 19 seats (12 by direct election, five by functional constituencies and two chosen by electoral college). About one-half of the members of the Council usually supported the Democratic Party of Hong Kong, but the Government was able to avoid any significant defeats in the legislature by vigorous lobbying for the support of smaller parties and independent members.

From 1896 to 1992 members of the Legislative Council who were not officials were appointed by the Governor to sit on the Executive Council. After 1946 the unofficial members outnumbered the officials. In 1992 Patten ended this practice, making the membership of the Executive Council entirely separate from the Legislative Council. The Governor was empowered to reject the advice given to him by the majority of the Executive Council (of which he also was a member) but, in practice, this never occurred.

In 1996 the Urban Council remained responsible for public health and sanitation, recreation, amenities and cultural services in the urban area. From 1995 the Council consisted entirely of elected members, with nine indirectly chosen by District Boards and 32 elected by all those over 18 years of age who had been resident in Hong Kong for at least seven years. A similar Regional Council served the New Territories. The Chinese Government objected strongly to the abolition of the seats for appointed members, and threatened to reconstitute both councils after 1997. Elections were held for the two councils in March 1995, at which 26% of registered voters cast their ballots. The Democratic Party of Hong Kong and its allies won 31 of the 59 directly elective seats.

Hong Kong comprised 18 districts. In each of these divisions there was a management committee of officials from various government departments working in the area, presided over by a senior administrative officer. This committee was assisted by an advisory district board. Between 1994 and mid-1997 all members of District Boards were elected by universal suffrage. However, in July 1997 the District Boards were replaced by Provisional District Boards, comprising members appointed by the Chief Executive of Hong Kong. The interests of the rural indigenous inhabitants of the New Territories were served by an elected advisory body, the Heung Yee Kuk. Advisory committees were attached to most government departments.

SOVEREIGNTY NEGOTIATIONS

After the communist victory in the Chinese civil war in 1949, the People's Republic asserted that all the unequal treaties, forced upon China, were no longer recognized as binding; however, the treaties of 1842, 1860 and 1898 were not formally abrogated. The Chinese Government was unwilling to clarify its intentions with regard to the arrangements after 1997, when the lease on the New Territories was due to expire, apart from giving intermittent assurances that the interests of investors would be protected.

In 1982 the United Kingdom decided to press China for a decision. Following the visit of the British Prime Minister, Margaret Thatcher, to China in September, negotiations commenced through diplomatic channels and continued for two years. In August 1984 agreement was reached on a Joint Declaration, which was subsequently approved by the British Parliament and ratified in May 1985. Under this agreement, the United Kingdom undertook to restore sovereignty over the whole of Hong Kong to China on 1 July 1997, upon the expiry of the lease on the New Territories. Until that date, the British Government was to continue to be responsible for the administration of the territory, but a Joint Liaison Group (JLG—see below), consisting of British and Chinese diplomatic representatives, was formed to consult on the implementation of the agreement, and also to ensure a smooth transfer of sovereignty in 1997.

China undertook that, after 1997, Hong Kong would be constituted as a Special Administrative Region (SAR, designated 'Hong Kong, China'), to be governed by its own inhabitants in accordance with its own legal code, except in matters of foreign affairs and defence, for a period of at least 50 years. The arrangement, known as 'one country, two systems', promised capitalist Hong Kong 'a high degree of autonomy'. It was to retain its status as a free port and separate customs territory, and the Hong Kong dollar was to remain a freely convertible currency. Hong Kong's social and economic systems were to remain unchanged, and freedom of speech, of the press, of association, of travel and of religion was to be guaranteed by law. Existing leases of land were to be recognized, and were to be extended to the year 2047.

From mid-1997 all existing Chinese residents of Hong Kong were to become citizens of the People's Republic of China. As such, they were forbidden by Chinese law to hold dual British nationality. Following approval of the Hong Kong agreement, the British Government announced a new form of nationality, to be effective from 1997, designated 'British National (Overseas)', which would entitle the holders to British consular protection when travelling outside China. This status conferred no right of abode in the United Kingdom and was not transferable to descendants. Non-Chinese residents of Hong Kong were not to be granted Chinese nationality after 1997. They were to be entitled to hold only the new British National (Overseas) passport, and there were fears that they might become, in effect, stateless. In September 1995 the Governor aroused much controversy when he urged the United Kingdom to give the right of abode to more than 3m. Hong Kong citizens.

A 59-member Basic Law Drafting Committee (BLDC) was established in Beijing in June 1985, with the aim of drawing up a new Basic Law (Constitution) for Hong Kong, in accordance with Article 31 of the Chinese Constitution, which provided for special administrative regions within the People's Republic. The BLDC included 25 representatives from Hong Kong itself. In April 1988 the first draft of the Basic Law for Hong Kong was published, and public comments were invited; the draft was further revised, and a second version was published in February 1989.

The final draft was adopted by the National People's Congress (NPC) of China in April 1990. The Basic Law gave China the right to declare a state of emergency in the territory and the right to station Chinese troops there. The SAR was also required to enact laws prohibiting any acts of subversion against the Government of China and forbidding any political groups in the SAR from establishing links with any foreign organizations. The Legislative Council adopted a motion expressing its disapproval of the Basic Law.

The JLG, consisting of five representatives each from China and the United Kingdom, was established to hold consultations on the implementation of the Joint Declaration and to oversee arrangements for a smooth transition to Chinese sovereignty. Agreement was reached on a number of issues between 1985 and 1989, including the clearance of the Kowloon Walled City. Following the Tiananmen massacre, and particularly after the arrival of Chris Patten, progress was much slower. China asserted its right to veto any policy decisions that encompassed 1997 and withheld its approval of proposals to adapt legislation and revise international agreements to take account of China's resumption of sovereignty. In 1994 China and the United Kingdom finally reached agreement on the disposal of the land occupied by the British garrison. More than one-half of the barracks sites were to be handed over to the Hong Kong Government for redevelopment. The remainder was to be used by the Chinese army and navy. In 1995 agreement was reached on the procedure for the establishment of a Court of Final Appeal (CFA), which after 1997 was to assume the role exercised hitherto by the Privy Council in London.

In September 1996 China and the United Kingdom agreed on the arrangements for the ceremony marking the transfer of sovereignty, which was to take place at midnight on 30 June 1997. In January the two Governments reached agreement on defining the borders of the territory of Hong Kong and formally signed a memorandum on the boundary in June.

PREPARATIONS FOR THE RESUMPTION OF CHINESE SOVEREIGNTY

Following the breakdown of the 1993 talks over Chris Patten's reform proposals, the Chinese Government declared that it would establish a 'second stove' in order to ensure a smooth political transition. This unilateral action to create new political institutions for the SAR, from the Chinese perspective, was to be consistent with the Joint Declaration, the Basic Law and the understanding reached in 1990 between the Chinese Minister of Foreign Affairs and the British Foreign Secretary. In July 1993 the Chinese Government established a Preliminary Working Committee (PWC) to advise on and formulate proposals for the transition. The PWC, chaired by the Vice-Premier and Minister of Foreign Affairs, Qian Qichen, comprised senior Chinese officials in charge of Hong Kong affairs, as well as prominent pro-Beijing government representatives. There were five sub-groups with responsibilities for economic, political, legal, cultural, and social and security matters. Since the Chinese Government refused to accept the Legislative Council elected in 1995, the PWC proposed the establishment of a provisional council in order to avoid a power vacuum.

In January 1996 a 150-member Preparatory Committee (PC) for the Hong Kong SAR was formally established, to succeed the PWC. The PC, also headed by Qian Qichen, included 94 members from Hong Kong and 56 members from the mainland. Most Hong Kong members were known to be sympathetic to the central Government's position on Hong Kong. While a number of legislative councillors were appointed to the PC, the Democratic Party of Hong Kong, the largest political party in the Legislative Council, was excluded. In March the PC decided that a 60-member Provisional Legislative Council (PLC) was to be established, which would commence operation after the election of the first Chief Executive of the SAR. It also decided that the PLC should cease operation upon the formation of the first Legislative Council of the SAR, while the term of the PLC was not to extend beyond 30 June 1998. All PLC members had to be permanent residents of Hong Kong, with up to 12 members holding non-Chinese nationality or the right of abode in foreign countries. Members of the PLC were to be chosen by a 400-member Selection Committee, which would also elect the SAR's first Chief Executive. The responsibilities of the PLC included: to enact, amend or appeal laws to ensure the proper functioning of the Hong Kong SAR; to examine and approve budgets proposed by the administration; to approve taxation and public expenditure; to receive and debate the Policy Address of the Chief Executive of the SAR; to endorse the appointment of the judges of the CFA and the Chief Judge of the High Court; and to deal with other necessary legislative matters before the formation of the first SAR Legislative Council. The President of the PLC also had to participate in the nomination of the six Hong Kong members of the Committee for the Basic Law of the Standing Committee of the NPC in Beijing.

In November 1996 the PC elected the 400-member Selection Committee from among 5,789 candidates. On 11 December Tung Chee-hwa, having defeated two other candidates (the former Chief Justice, (Sir) Yang Ti-liang, and businessman Peter Woo) in the final round of the selection process, was elected the first Chief Executive of the SAR Government by the Selection Committee. On 21 December the PLC's 60 members were elected from among 134 candidates. Thirty-three served concurrently in the existing Legislative Council, but the Democratic Party of Hong Kong boycotted the election. On 14 March 1997 the NPC approved a PC report on the establishment of the PLC. Soon after its establishment, the PLC began operation in parallel to the Legislative Council, in the neighbouring town of Shenzhen, scrutinizing and approving bills. In June the PLC introduced legislation to restore colonial restrictions and to impose new conditions on public demonstrations and the establishment of political organizations in the SAR. Under the legislation, public demonstrations and political organizations could be banned in the interests of national security, defined as 'the safeguarding of the territorial integrity and the independence of the People's Republic of China'. Political organizations were, moreover, not permitted to have connections with foreign political organizations or with Taiwan.

THE SAR GOVERNMENT

The Administration of Tung Chee-hwa

On 1 July 1997, following the handover ceremony at midnight, the SAR Government was inaugurated at 1.30 a.m. The ceremonies were attended by 4,000 dignitaries, including ministers of foreign affairs from more than 40 countries and senior representatives of more than 40 international organizations. However, the newly elected British Prime Minister and his Foreign Secretary, as well as the US Secretary of State, did not attend the inauguration, in an expression of their disapproval of the swearing-in of PLC members during the ceremony. Legislators from the Democratic Party of Hong Kong and a number of independent Legislative Councillors protested against the abolition of the Legislative Council on the balcony of the Council building, shortly after midnight, vowing to return by means of elections in 1998.

More than 4,000 People's Liberation Army troops were deployed to the Hong Kong garrison. With the consent of the British authorities, a small number of unarmed military personnel entered the territory in April and May 1997, and an advance party of some 500 troops crossed the border a few hours before the handover ceremony. Twenty-two of the 23 principal officials were retained by the SAR administration. The only new appointment was that of Elsie Leung as Secretary for Justice, who replaced a retired expatriate. The incoming Executive Council comprised 14 members, with a former senior Executive Council member as convener, three ex-officio members—the Chief Secretary, the Financial Secretary and the Secretary for Justice—and 10 unofficial members. In addition to the Chief Secretary and the Financial Secretary, two outgoing members of the previous Executive Council were reappointed. The Chief Executive also appointed a special adviser with close connections to Beijing. In March 1999 Anson Chan, regarded by the international media as representing Hong Kong's conscience, agreed to continue serving as Chief Secretary for Administration for two years beyond her normal retirement age, until 2002, when the term of office of the Chief Executive was to end. In June 1999 the Government appointed Dr Yeoh Eng-kiong, hitherto Chief Executive of the Hospital Authority, as Secretary for Health and Welfare. After the Secretary for Justice, Dr Yeoh was the second person from outside the civil service to be appointed to a senior position by the SAR Government. The convener of the Executive Council, Dr Chung Sze-yuen, retired in late June. He was replaced by a fellow member of the Executive Council, Leung Chun-ying. In May 2000 Elsie Leung was reappointed as Secretary for Justice, for a further two years. In January 2001 Anson Chan unexpectedly announced that for personal reasons she would relinquish her position at the end of April, well before the expiry of Tung's first term. She was replaced by Donald Tsang, hitherto the Financial Secretary. Antony Leung, a former banker and member of the Executive Council, was appointed Financial Secretary. In 1999, meanwhile, the Government announced a civil service reform programme, including the introduction of performance-based pay, new entry and exit procedures and a lower starting salary. In July 2002 thousands of civil servants took to the streets to demonstrate against the pay decreases, introduced in an effort to reduce civil service costs (as a measure to counter the SAR's budget deficit). While the public appeared to be supportive of the pay decreases, there were concerns that the administration had not handled the issue well and that as a result morale in the civil service had suffered.

The SAR Government replaced the existing local administration with the Provisional Urban Council, a Provisional Regional Council and 18 Provisional District Boards. While their responsibilities remained the same and all existing councillors and board members continued to serve, membership of these elected bodies was expanded with appointed members, many of whom had been unsuccessful in earlier elections. In April 1999 the SAR administration decided to restructure local government by abolishing the municipal and regional councils. The Government intended to assume responsibility for the public services offered by the councils. Existing district boards were to be replaced by district councils. While the public was dissatisfied with the performance of the two municipal councils, critics of the Government maintained that in terms of local democracy the restructuring was a retrograde measure. In November the Democratic Party of Hong Kong threatened legal action if the plan were not abandoned, as it contravened the Basic Law. The Hong Kong SAR's first district elections took place on 28 November. The Democratic Party of Hong Kong won the largest number of elected seats (86), but the pro-Beijing Democratic Alliance for the Betterment of Hong Kong (DAB) substantially increased its representation, from 37 seats to 83.

One of the first acts of the SAR administration was the introduction of legislation to prevent an influx of mainland-born children of Hong Kong residents. These children were granted the right of abode in the territory by the Basic Law, but the Government insisted that they could be admitted only upon verification of their identities and in an orderly manner, according to a quota system controlled by the mainland authorities.

Elections for the first Legislative Council of the SAR were held on 24 May 1998 and were conducted under new electoral arrangements. Of the 60 seats, 30 were elected by narrowly defined functional constituencies, 20 were elected by proportional representation in geographically based constituencies and 10 were chosen by an 800-member Election Committee. Pro-democracy parties criticized the reduction of the franchise under these new arrangements. With almost 1.5m. registered voters casting their ballots, the participation rate of 53.3% was the highest since the introduction of direct elections in Hong Kong. Most former Legislative Councillors who had boycotted the PLC were elected to the new body.

The Democratic Party of Hong Kong, led by Martin Lee, returned to the Legislative Council with 13 seats, of which nine were obtained in the geographical constituencies. Although the Democratic Party of Hong Kong and other pro-democracy parties received solid support from the electorate and won most seats in the geographical constituencies (14 of the 20 seats), their overall political strength in the legislature was reduced. Together with the Frontier and the Citizens' Party, and liberal independents, the pro-democracy camp secured a total of 19 seats. Another pro-democracy group, the Association for Democracy and People's Livelihood (ADPL), which had participated in the PLC, lost all of its seats on the Council.

Pro-Beijing supporters dominated the functional constituencies and the electoral committee ballot and also secured some seats in the geographical constituencies. The DAB, which won 10 seats, with five from geographical constituencies, benefited most from the new electoral system. The leader of the pro-business Liberal Party, Allen Lee, failed to win a seat in the geographical elections, but his party obtained 10 seats through the functional and election committee constituencies, while the Hong Kong Progressive Alliance managed to obtain five seats.

The powers of the new legislature were curbed by the Basic Law. Henceforth, Legislative Councillors were not permitted to introduce bills related to public expenditure, the political structure or the operation of the Government. The passage of private members' bills or motions also required the majority of votes of both groups of councillors—those elected through geographical constituencies, and those returned through functional constituencies and the election committee.

Although political forces in the first legislature were fragmented, the Legislative Council was more assertive than the PLC. Even before the new legislature convened, the seven major political parties, together with a number of like-minded independents, formed a temporary alliance in June 1998, demanding that the administration adopt new measures to address the economic downturn in Hong Kong. Tung Chee-hwa responded by announcing a series of initiatives, including the abolition of savings tax for commercial corporations, the postponement of the sale of land by auction and tender until 31 March 1999, an increase in loans to home-buyers, and allocation of additional government funding to assist small and medium enterprises. The coalition was not maintained over constitutional and political issues. Senior civil servants were often required to respond to questions presented by the Legislative Council. In June 2000 the legislature overwhelmingly approved a vote of no confidence in two senior officials, following a series of public housing scandals. One of the officials involved, the Secretary for Housing, Rosanna Wong, resigned shortly before the vote took place. The term of the Legislative Council ended on 30 June. All the major political parties presented candidates for the elections to the second post-1997 legislature, which were held on 10 September 2000. The number of directly elective seats was increased from 20 to 24, while the number of Council members selected by the Election Committee was reduced from 10 to six. (The ballot for Election Committee members, who were responsible for choosing those who were to occupy the Election Committee seats, had taken place in July.) Of the 60 seats in the Legislative Council, the Democratic Party of Hong Kong secured a total of 12 (including nine by direct election), the DAB won 11 seats (including eight by direct election), and the Liberal Party won eight seats. The level of voter participation was 43.6% of the electorate. Following the resignation from the incoming Legislative Council on 19 September of a newly elected member, Gary Cheng, the DAB's Vice-Chairman (owing to his admission of a conflict of interest between his role as a legislator and previously undeclared business assets), a by-election took place in December. The seat was won by Audrey Eu, an independent candidate and former chairperson of the Hong Kong Bar Association.

In March 2001 the Hong Kong Government introduced the Chief Executive Election Bill, interpreting the powers of the central Government in Beijing to remove the Chief Executive and providing detailed arrangements for the next election for the latter. Although the Government amended the Bill's provisions relating to the removal of the Chief Executive (after it was criticized by some legislators for giving unnecessary powers to the Chinese Government), following which the Bill was duly approved by the Legislative Council by 36 votes to 18 in July, the approval of the new legislation was widely regarded as a set-back for Hong Kong's democratic progress.

An economic recession followed the financial turmoil that affected the Asian region from mid-1997, leading to the collapse of the Hong Kong property market, rising unemployment and negative economic growth. In August 1998, in an attempt to counter manipulation by foreign speculators and to maintain the stability of the Hong Kong dollar and stock market, the Government undertook a massive intervention in the financial markets, spending more than US $15,000m. Although the intervention was supported by the local business community, it undermined Hong Kong's reputation as a free economy, and at the time was criticized by the international media. However, many observers later accepted as necessary the authorities' involvement in the financial markets, owing to the exceptional circumstances.

The issue of the right of abode raised questions with regard to the foundation of the rule of law and Hong Kong's autonomous status. In January 1999 the CFA ruled against the SAR Government's position that, according to Article 24 of the Basic Law, mainland children born of a Hong Kong permanent resident should be granted the right of abode in the territory only if at the time of their birth their parents had already become permanent residents. In delivering their verdict, the judges also maintained that the CFA had the authority to interpret the Basic Law. The ruling was questioned by mainland legal experts who had been involved in the drafting of the Basic Law and by other senior Chinese officials. In February, in response to a motion filed by the Department of Justice, the CFA declared that its ruling did not question the authority of the Standing Committee of the NPC. Human rights groups argued that the Government's action, in seeking clarification from the Court, undermined the rule of law and judicial independence in Hong Kong. Claiming that the decision would lead to the influx of more than 1.6m. people from the mainland, the SAR authorities suggested that the CFA had misinterpreted the Basic Law. Supported by opinion polls, in May the SAR Government requested the State Council (Cabinet) of China to ask the Ninth NPC to interpret the relevant articles of the Basic Law. Pro-democracy legislators walked out of the Legislative Council Chamber in protest at the Government's decision. In late June the Standing Committee of the Ninth NPC ruled that the CFA's interpretation of the Basic Law was wrong and provided a new interpretation, which reduced the number of mainland children with the right of abode in Hong Kong to about 200,000.

In April 2000 a deputy director of the Liaison Office of the Central People's Government, formerly part of the Hong Kong branch of the Xinhua News Agency, suggested that the Hong Kong media should not disseminate the views of those who advocated the independence of Taiwan. In June another official from the Liaison Office warned the local business community not to deal with Taiwanese companies that support independence for Taiwan. Following both incidents, the Hong Kong Government reaffirmed that the local media remained free to report and comment on public issues, and that businesses in the SAR were at liberty to choose their business partners.

In July 2001 Li Shaomin, a US national who had been convicted in China of spying for Taiwan and who had spent five months in a mainland prison, was permitted by the Hong Kong Government to return to the SAR, where he worked as an academic. His case was widely seen as a test of the 'one country, two systems' arrangement with China. Li's employer, the City University of Hong Kong, decided to permit him to resume his teaching and research duties. He later returned to the USA when his leave application was unsuccessful.

In December 2001 Tung Chee-hwa announced that he would stand for a second five-year term as Chief Executive, the election having been scheduled for 24 March 2002. The central Government in Beijing endorsed his candidacy. On the closing date for nominations at the end of February, however, Tung was the only candidate with overwhelming support, having received 714 nominations from the 794-strong Selection Committee. On 4 March, therefore, the central Government formally appointed Tung for a second term, beginning on 1 July.

The most important political change that Tung introduced was a new scheme for the appointment of senior officials. Under this scheme, all principal officials, defined as the Chief Secretary for Administration, the Financial Secretary, the Secretary for Justice, along with the 11 secretaries in charge of policy bureaux, were to become political appointees, with their terms of office not exceeding that of the Chief Executive who had appointed them. These senior officials, widely regarded as 'ministers', were also to be members of the Executive Council, thus turning it into a cabinet-style body. The principal officials would report directly to the Chief Executive and would have to accept total responsibility for their respective portfolios. The civil service remained a permanent service based on meritocracy. Amid criticisms that the 'ministers' were accountable only to the Chief Executive and not to the Legislative Council or to the public, in addition to concerns that the arrangements might not be consistent with the Basic Law, the new scheme was approved by the Legislative Council on 29 May 2002, less than six weeks after its first formal introduction there. In mid-June the Council approved the funding, and a government resolution transferring statutory powers to the principal officials was approved by a vote of 36 to 21.

The 14 principal officials appointed by Tung Chee-hwa included eight who had served under Tung in his first term. The three most senior officials, Donald Tsang (Chief Secretary), Antony Leung (Financial Secretary) and Elsie Leung (Secretary for Justice) remained unchanged. Tung appointed five new 'ministers' from business and the professions: the Secretary for Commerce, Industry and Technology, Henry Tang Ying-yen; the Secretary for Education and Manpower, Arthur Li Kwok-cheung; the Secretary for Home Affairs, Patrick Ho Chi-ping; the Secretary for the Environment, Transport and Works, Sarah Liao Sau-tung; and the Secretary for Financial Services and the Treasury, Frederick Ma Si-hang. In addition to the 14 principal officials, Tung appointed five non-official members to the Executive Council, including the leaders of two political parties—James Tien from the Liberal Party and Jasper Tsang Yok-sing from the DAB.

The Government tried to allay concerns about the political neutrality of the civil service under the new scheme by announcing that the Secretary for the Civil Service would be selected from within the civil service and would not lose civil servant status if he or she decided to return to the service upon the expiry of his or her term. The new scheme represented a significant political change. The accountability system was tested in mid-2002 when principal officials responsible for financial matters appeared to have underestimated the implications of a new proposal to eliminate stocks valued below HK $0.5. In September, after a review of the incident had been completed, the Secretary for Financial Services and the Treasury, Frederick Ma, apologized to the public. Following the introduction of the accountability system, the Chief Executive delivered his Policy Address in January 2003 instead of in October, as previously.

In early 2003 Hong Kong was badly affected by an outbreak of Severe Acute Respiratory Syndrome (SARS), a hitherto little-known form of pneumonia, which had originated in neighbouring Guangdong Province. By March the spread of the virus had become a global health crisis. In Hong Kong more than 1,750 people were infected and 298 died. As a result, the World Health Organization (WHO) listed Hong Kong as an infected area and issued a travel advisory against the city, which remained in place until June.

The Government's proposal to introduce a National Security Bill as stipulated by Article 23 of the Basic Law led to much disquiet. According to Article 23, the Hong Kong SAR 'shall enact laws on its own to prohibit any act of treason, secession, sedition, subversion against the Central People's Government or theft of state secrets, to prohibit foreign political organisations or bodies from conducting political activities in the Region, and to prohibit political organisations or bodies of the region from establishing ties with foreign political organisations or bodies'. In a consultation document released in September 2002, the SAR Government suggested that the proposed legislation was necessary to protect sovereignty and safeguard territorial integrity, unity and national security. It would meet the requirements of Article 23 but would also respect the fundamental rights and freedoms of the people of Hong Kong. While most people did not appear to question the constitutional responsibility of the Government to introduce a National Security Bill, concerns about specific provisions were expressed, and many demanded draft legislation in the form of a 'White Bill' to allow for more public discussion of the proposed legislation. In December 60,000 people demonstrated against the proposals.

In January 2003 the SAR Government announced a series of amendments, but rejected the demand for a 'White Bill'. The draft National Security Bill was presented to the Legislative Council in February. After discussion in the Bills Committee, the Government announced further amendments to the Bill in June, but those who opposed the proposals still believed that the amendments did not address major issues concerning the protection of fundamental rights and freedoms. The annual gathering to commemorate the anniversary of the Tiananmen Square tragedy of 4 June 1989 turned into a demonstration against the Government's proposals. When the Government rejected demands to delay the introduction of the Bill for a second reading in the Legislative Council, on 1 July 2003 about 500,000 people took to the streets of Hong Kong in a demonstration against Article 23. This developed into an anti-Government protest, with demonstrators demanding the resignation of the Chief Executive and of a number of principal officials. Among the officials targeted were the Secretary for Security, Regina Ip, who had been responsible for the legislative work of the draft National Security Bill, and Financial Secretary Antony Leung, who had purchased a luxury car prior to introducing new taxes for such vehicles in his budget in March. The protesters also objected to the appointment of the Secretary for Health, Welfare and Food, Yeoh Eng-kiong, as chair of the independent inquiry on the SARS outbreak in Hong Kong. (Yeoh resigned in July 2004—see below.) The size of the demonstration and the intensity of the anger of the protesters surprised the Government and many observers. The demonstration created a political crisis in Hong Kong, and the popularity of the Chief Executive and his team of principal officials declined to a new low point, as shown in a public opinion poll conducted by the University of Hong Kong.

In early July 2003 Tung Chee-hwa continued to refuse to delay the introduction of the Bill to the Legislative Council but agreed to address specific concerns by deleting provisions regarding the possible proscription of Hong Kong organizations subordinate to those proscribed in the mainland on national security grounds, as well as those regarding additional emergency investigation powers for the police and the introduction of a 'public interest' defence for disclosure of certain official information. The Chief Executive reversed his position when James Tien, Chairman of the Liberal Party (part of the 'ruling coalition'), resigned from the Executive Council, thus depriving the Government of the number of votes necessary in the Legislative Council for the approval of the Bill. The political crisis took another dramatic turn in mid-July when Tung Chee-hwa announced first that Secretary for Security Regina Ip had resigned, citing personal reasons, and then that Financial Secretary Antony Leung had also resigned. The Chief Executive pledged that he would reopen consultation on Article 23, improve dialogue with the public, remove Secretary Yeoh from the chair of the investigation panel on the outbreak of SARS and improve Hong Kong's economic performance. Later that month Tung Chee-hwa met senior Chinese leaders, including President Hu Jintao and Premier Wen Jiabao, during a visit to Beijing. (The new Chinese leaders had assumed power in March 2003.) Premier Wen Jiabao had recently returned from a successful visit to Hong Kong, where he had reaffirmed the principle of 'one country, two systems', leaving just hours prior to the demonstrations of 1 July. The Chinese leaders confirmed their support for Tung Chee-hwa, following his earlier indication that he had no intention of resigning. In early September, however, it was announced that the National Security Bill had been withdrawn, pending further public consultations.

In response to public pressure for the introduction of universal suffrage at the elections for the Chief Executive in 2007 and for the members of the Legislative Council in 2008, the Government suggested that a timetable for public consultations would be announced by the end of 2003. In November pro-democracy candidates gained new seats in Hong Kong's second post-1997 District Council election at the expense of candidates from the pro-Beijing DAB. The election attracted a record turn-out of 1m. voters. However, the Chief Executive subsequently exercised his power to appoint an additional 102 District Councillors.

During an official visit to Beijing in December 2003, Chief Executive Tung met President Hu Jintao and Premier Wen Jiabao. President Hu declared that Hong Kong's political system should be developed gradually, in accordance with the Basic Law and the 'actual situation' in Hong Kong.

The political atmosphere remained tense in 2004. The year began with a demonstration of 100,000 people demanding political reform. On 7 January, in his Policy Address, the Chief Executive announced the establishment of a three-member Task Force on Constitutional Development headed by the Chief Secretary, with the support of the Secretary for Constitutional Affairs and the Secretary for Justice. The aims of the Task Force were to examine the 'relevant principles and legislative process in the Basic Law' relating to constitutional development, to consult the central Government and to take account of the views of Hong Kong people. On the same day the Hong Kong and Macao Affairs Office in Beijing issued a statement expressing serious concerns over constitutional developments in Hong Kong and requesting that the central Government be consulted.

In addition to conducting public consultations on constitutional reform in Hong Kong, the Task Force visited Beijing in February 2004 to confer with the central Government. After the departure of the Task Force, the Xinhua News Agency published a series of commentaries on the principles governing the Basic Law and suggested that only 'patriots' should comprise the main body of the Government. The commentaries generated intense debates in Hong Kong when some pro-democracy figures were accused of being 'unpatriotic'. Chinese officials were particularly critical of the visit by former Democratic Party Chairman Martin Lee to the USA, where he testified at a congressional hearing on Hong Kong and met the US Secretary of State.

In March 2004 the central Government announced that the Standing Committee of the NPC would provide interpretations of Annexes I and II of the Basic Law on the methods for selecting the Chief Executive and Legislative Councillors. In April the Standing Committee of the NPC ruled that there should not be universal suffrage for the election of Hong Kong's Chief Executive in 2007, nor for all 60 members of the Legislative Council at the elections due by 2008. It also ruled that the number of functional seats for the Legislative Council should remain unchanged at 30 and that the procedure for voting on the motions and bills in the Council should not be altered.

Although both Beijing and the pan-democracy camp seemed interested in adopting a more conciliatory stance, a large number of people demonstrated again on 1 July 2004, demanding more democracy for Hong Kong. The organizers put the number of demonstrators at 530,000, whereas the police suggested a total of 200,000. The demonstration confirmed the people's aspiration for faster democratization in Hong Kong and a willingness to express that aspiration in public.

In July 2004 the Tung administration lost another member of the Executive Council, the third minister to resign since the introduction of the 'ministerial accountability system'. Following the release of a Legislative Council Select Committee report on the Government's management of the SARS outbreak, which criticized a number of senior government officials, Dr Yeoh Eng-kiong, the Secretary for Health, Welfare and Food, tendered his resignation on 7 July.

At the legislative elections of 12 September 2004, a record number of more than 1.78m. voters participated in the poll, resulting in the highest ever turn-out, of 55.6%. While popular support for the pan-democracy camp remained high, at 60%, the grouping won only 25 of the 60 seats in the Legislative Council. The pro-Government camp secured a total of 33 seats. The pro-Beijing and pro-Government parties, namely the DAB with 12 seats and the Liberal Party with 10 seats, became the largest party and second largest party, respectively, in the legislature. The Liberal Party, known also for its pro-business stance, succeeded in winning two directly elected seats in the geographical constituencies. However, the Hong Kong Progressive Alliance, a pro-Government party of which the members were elected by the Election Committee, failed to secure any seats following the abolition of the election committee constituency. The pro-democracy camp secured a modest 25 seats, gaining ground not only in the geographical seats but also in two functional constituencies, representing medical and accountancy interests. However, within the pro-democracy camp, the Democratic Party of Hong Kong failed to maintain its position as the largest party in the chamber. The Article 45 Concern group (consisting of lawyers who had come to the fore during the anti-Article 23 campaign) emerged as a significant political force. Several outspoken anti-Government critics, including Leung Kwok-hung, an anti-Beijing radical from April Fifth Action (widely known as 'Long Hair' because of his hairstyle), and Albert Cheng, a former radio talk-show host (who had resigned in May, citing political pressure), also won seats.

In December 2004 the Task Force on Constitutional Development released its fourth report, which summarized public views on constitutional reforms gathered over the course of a six-month consultation period. The report acknowledged that there was public demand for the election of the Chief Executive in 2007 and Legislative Council members in 2008 by universal suffrage, but emphasized that proposals in conflict with the decision of the Standing Committee of the NPC from April 2004 (see above) would not be accepted. The fifth report was expected to be released before the end of 2005.

The most dramatic political event of 2005 was the departure of Chief Executive Tung Chee-hwa, just three years into his second term. Tung announced his resignation in March, claiming ill health, although there was considerable speculation in the press that he had been forced to step down by the central Government and accept an appointment as Vice-Chairman of the Chinese Political Consultative Conference, owing to his unpopularity and perceived mishandling of the pro-democracy movement. Chief Secretary Donald Tsang assumed the role of Acting Chief Executive until late May, whereupon he resigned in order to present his candidacy for the election to the post of Chief Executive, which was due to be held in July.

In the aftermath of Tung's resignation, considerable dispute arose regarding the correct duration of the term of his successor. The pro-democracy camp and many in the local legal community held that, according to the Basic Law, the new Chief Executive should serve a full five-year term; however, the Secretary for Justice, citing the opinion of legal experts from the mainland, suggested that a Chief Executive returned through a by-election should only serve for the remainder of the term of the outgoing Chief Executive. Eventually, the Standing Committee of the NPC, asked by the central Government to provide an interpretation of the provisions of the Basic Law on this issue, declared that the new Chief Executive should serve only for the remaining two years of Tung's elected term of office. Many in the legal profession and elsewhere expressed concern that this interpretation undermined the rule of law and the judicial autonomy of Hong Kong, furthering instead the political interests of the central Government by the establishment of a two-year probationary period for the new Chief Executive.

In addition to Donald Tsang, the Chairman of the Democratic Party, Lee Wing-tat, and legislator Chim Pui-chung also declared their intention to stand in the election. During his election campaign, which emphasized the principle of 'people first' and the importance of good governance but avoided the issue of universal suffrage, Tsang was seen to focus on meeting ordinary Hong Kong residents, but did not engage in direct policy debates with the other potential candidates. In the event, however, the holding of the election was rendered unnecessary. The candidacies of Lee and Chim failed to receive the required endorsement of at least 100 members of the 800-member Election Committee, and were consequently rejected. At the close of the designated nomination period, in mid-June 2005, the returning officer announced that the candidacy of Tsang, which had received the support of 674 Committee members, was the only valid nomination, and that Tsang was therefore elected uncontested to the post of Chief Executive. On 21 June Tsang was officially appointed as Chief Executive by the central Government.

The Administration of Donald Tsang

Vastly experienced in public service, and credited with fending off international speculation against the Hong Kong currency when he was Financial Secretary in 1997 during the Asian financial crisis, Donald Tsang enjoyed a high level of popularity. According to a University of Hong Kong poll, his support rating at the end of June 2005 was 72.3 points out of 100, and 75% of the respondents in an opinion survey supported him as Chief Executive. On 30 June Raphael Hui, a close colleague of Tsang, who had served as Secretary of Financial Services before leaving the civil service in 2000, was appointed Chief Secretary for Administration, with the approval of the central Government.

Tsang began his term by assembling a new team, making efforts to address the political divide between the central Government and the pan-democracy camp, and pressing for limited constitutional reform. Soon after his inauguration, he restructured the office of the Chief Executive, giving the Commission on Strategic Development the task of advising the Government on proposals for political development and the strengthening of governance in the SAR. Tsang also appointed a respected lawyer, Wong Yan-lung, who had participated in marches against the interpretation of the Basic Law by the Standing Committee of the NPC in 2005, as the new Secretary for Justice. At the same time he appointed eight new members to the Executive Council, for the most part business and professional people. However, the appointees also included Anthony Cheung, former Vice-Chairman of the Democratic Party, who was well known for his pro-democracy stance. In late September Tsang organized a two-day visit to the Pearl River (Zhujiang) Delta in neighbouring Guangdong Province for all 60 members of the Legislative Council, who were permitted to meet the Provincial Secretary of the Chinese Communist Party, Zhang Dejiang. Tsang's stated priorities, outlined in his first Policy Address in October, were strong governance, social harmony and economic development.

Also in October 2005 the Task Force on Constitutional Development issued a Fifth Report. This contained a number of proposals, among which was an increase in the number of seats at the Legislative Council from 60 to 70. Of the 10 new seats, five would be determined by direct election from geographical constituencies and five members would be elected by all 529 District Councillors (of whom, at the time of this proposal, 427 were directly elected and 102 were appointed). Furthermore, the proposals envisaged the expansion of the membership of the Chief Executive Election Committee from 800 to 1,600, to include all District Councillors as well as an additional 100 representatives drawn from the commercial, social and professional sectors. Candidates for the post of Chief Executive, meanwhile, would be required to have received 200 nominations from the Committee in order to contest the second round of the election for the Chief Executive. However, these proposals were rejected by those in the pan-democracy camp who felt that they were superficial in nature and did not represent progress towards universal suffrage. Instead, they called for a timetable aimed at progression towards the establishment of full democracy. The question of constitutional reform returned to the political agenda in late November, when the Vice-Secretary-General of the Standing Committee of the NPC, Qiao Xiaoyang, invited the Chairs and Deputy Chairs of the Legislative Council Committees, District Council Chairs and community representatives to a meeting in Shenzhen to exchange views on the issue. This meeting took place in early December and was attended by a number of Legislative Council members belonging to the pan-democracy camp, including several who had not previously been permitted to travel to the mainland. The pan-democracy camp organized a mass rally in advance of the

Legislative Council debate on the proposals, which required approval by a two-thirds' majority of the members, in accordance with the Basic Law. Demanding that full democracy be implemented, the marchers described the proposals as a set-back to the democratic process.

Tsang responded to the rally, which was estimated by some sources to have attracted around 250,000 protesters, by insisting that change would have to be gradual. The Government appeared to make some concessions when it announced that it would instigate a gradual reduction in the number of appointed District Council seats prior to 2016, on the condition that the constitutional reform programme would be granted passage through the Legislative Council. The Government also pledged that the Commission on Strategic Development would consider additional institutional reforms, including a 'roadmap' for universal suffrage, and would report by early 2007. However, the pan-democracy members of the Legislative Council rejected these concessions, with 24 democrats voting against the Government. Opinion polls suggested that the people of Hong Kong blamed both the Government and the pan-democracy camp for the deadlock on constitutional reform and the lack of progress towards greater democracy.

In January 2006 Tsang announced his first reallocation of senior government posts. The Secretary for Commerce, Industry and Technology, John Tsang Chun-wah, was appointed to head the Chief Executive's office, being succeeded in his previous position by Joseph Wong Wing-ping, hitherto Secretary for the Civil Service. Denise Yue Chung-yee, formerly Permanent Secretary for Commerce, Industry and Technology, became Secretary for the Civil Service. Tsang made further changes in the following month when he appointed Lau Sai-leung, former Democratic Party member, journalist and political commentator, as a full-time member of the Central Policy Unit and Andy Ho, a former political editor of the *South China Morning Post*, became information co-ordinator. Gary Chang, a former district co-ordination officer of the DAB, was appointed as an aide in the Chief Executive's office. During the first half of 2006 one of the most important political developments was the formation of a new political party by the Article 45 Concern Group. With six seats in the Legislative Council, the Civic Party was established in March. Audrey Eu was appointed the leader of the new party, and a respected political scientist, Kuan Hsin-chi, assumed the chairmanship. The party declared that it would fight for democracy, social justice, universal suffrage and the introduction of a minimum wage and standard working hours. However, the democratic aspirations of the Hong Kong people received a set-back in April when prominent legal scholars from the mainland suggested that the population would not be ready for democracy until certain conditions were met. The conditions identified by the mainland legal experts included the introduction of controversial national security legislation, the emergence of a consensus among different sectors in Hong Kong, which would require endorsement by the central Government in Beijing, and the development of civic education to promote patriotism. Xu Chongde, a former member of the BLDC, stated that one condition for the introduction of universal suffrage was a guarantee that 'patriots' would be elected.

In May 2006 the Legislative Council approved by 31 votes to 21 a bill that made some technical changes to the methods of electing the Chief Executive and Legislative Council. The Chief Executive Election and Legislative Council Election (Miscellaneous Amendments) Bill 2006 stipulated that an election for the Chief Executive would be required even if there were only one candidate for the post and that the mandate of a Chief Executive elected mid-term would have to be limited to that term and to the following term. However, the Tsang administration was criticized for not using the opportunity to make the electoral system more democratic by supporting amendments to the Bill, which would have removed the legal impediments for party affiliation of the Chief Executive. The political situation none the less appeared to improve as the year progressed and the economy strengthened. In particular, the rate of unemployment reached a 57-month low point of 4.9% in the period March–May, the level of inflation decreased and the Hong Kong stock market recorded a strong performance. On 1 July, however, thousands of people took to the streets of Hong Kong, again demanding greater democracy.

The announcement by former Chief Secretary Anson Chan in September 2006 that she would not contest the forthcoming election for the post of Chief Executive removed any remaining doubts about the incumbent Donald Tsang's prospects of re-election. As the official with the widest experience in the administration of the SAR, the popular Chan had been regarded as a potentially strong contender. The pan-democratic camp subsequently decided to support the Civic Party's Alan Leong, who formally announced his candidacy in November. In December the poll to determine the membership of the Election Committee returned 114 pro-democracy candidates, thus indicating the strong desire for a contested election among members of the professional sub-sectors representing the various functional constituencies (373 of the 800 seats being uncontested). Leong was confident of securing the minimum 100 nominations required to contest the election for the post of Chief Executive, and he declared that his decision to enter the poll had been made in order to avert the possibility of an uncontested election, which would emphasize the undemocratic nature of the process. Leong also expressed his desire to work towards the introduction of universal suffrage, a common theme throughout the election period. Alan Leong's candidacy was confirmed in March 2007, when he received 132 nominations (compared with the 641 in favour of Donald Tsang).

In March 2007, prior to the election, the candidates took part in two televised debates. These were unprecedented in Hong Kong's electoral history and attracted millions of viewers. In opinion polls Donald Tsang consistently received a higher level of public support. He pledged to resolve the issue of universal suffrage during his second term in office. In the event, Tsang won 649 of the 789 votes cast and was re-elected for a second term; Leong received 123 votes. In declaring victory, Tsang reaffirmed the commitments that he had made during the campaign and praised the maturity of the people of Hong Kong. Leong also pledged that, despite having lost the election, he would continue to press for the introduction of universal suffrage in 2012. Tsang's appointment was officially confirmed on 2 April 2007, and he was sworn in for a five-year term on 1 July, as Hong Kong observed the 10th anniversary of the transition from British to Chinese rule.

Donald Tsang began his new term by reorganizing the Government, increasing the number of policy bureaux from 11 to 12, with the creation of a new development bureau to oversee planning, land use and conservation. Most of the new appointments made by Tsang were of former civil servants, with the addition of two others: one academic and one former journalist who had served in the Government's Central Policy Unit and who had previously enjoyed good relations with the central authorities in Beijing. The new team included: Henry Tang, the former Financial Secretary, who was appointed as Chief Secretary for Administration; John Tsang, former Director of the Chief Executive Office, as Financial Secretary; Wong Yan-lung, reappointed as Secretary for Justice; and Denise Yue, reappointed as Secretary for the Civil Service. Stephen Lam expanded his portfolio to become Secretary for Constitutional and Mainland Affairs. Tsang Tak-sing, a former editor-in-chief of the newspaper *Tai Kung Pao* and subsequently a member of the Central Policy Unit, became Secretary for Home Affairs. Professor Ka-Keung C. Chan, former Dean of the Faculty of Business at the Hong Kong University of Science and Technology, became Secretary for Financial Services and the Treasury, replacing Frederick Ma, who was appointed Secretary for Commerce and Economic Development. Tsang also appointed a new Commissioner for the Independent Commission Against Corruption to replace Fanny Law, a former Permanent Secretary for Education and Manpower, who resigned in June 2007 following the publication of a report by a Commission of Inquiry on alleged interference in the academic freedom of the Institute of Education; the report suggested that her complaints against two academics at the Institute to their superiors were improper.

The general aspiration for greater democracy was demonstrated once again when tens of thousands of people took to the streets of Hong Kong in the annual pro-democracy march on 1 July 2007. However, before the Green Paper was published Wu Bangguo, a member of the Standing Committee of the Political Bureau of the Central Committee of the Chinese Communist Party, remarked that the high degree of autonomy awarded to Hong Kong had in fact been granted by the central Government in Beijing. While the comment was true, some observers in Hong Kong interpreted this as a reminder that the central Government retained ultimate authority with regard to constitutional developments in Hong Kong. The implication, therefore, was that progression towards democracy in the SAR would continue at a gradual pace.

Elections for the District Council took place on 18 November 2007. A total of 1.15m. voters, equivalent to 38.8% of the registered electorate, participated in the poll, constituting the highest turnout ever recorded at a local election in Hong Kong. A total of 41 candidates were elected unopposed, and 866 candidates contested the remaining 364 seats. The pro-Government parties dominated the election, with the DAB winning 115 seats (increased from 62 in 2003) and the Liberal Party 14. The pan-democratic parties, which co-ordinated the seats for which they presented their candidates, won a total of 90 seats; the Democratic Party took 59, the ADPL 17 and the Civic Party eight; the League of Social Democrats (LSD), a new anti-corporations and pro-'grass roots' party formed in late 2006, won six seats. In mid-December 2007 the Chief Executive appointed a further 102 District Councillors.

The electoral contest between Anson Chan, the former Chief Secretary, and Regina Ip, the former Secretary for Security, attracted much public attention in 2007. The Legislative Council seat for Hong Kong Island became vacant in August as a result of the death of Ma Lik, Chairman of the DAB, following a long-term illness. The contest between the two women for the seat was widely regarded as one between pan-democratic and pro-government political forces. Anson Chan's candidature was endorsed by the pan-democratic camp, and she was nominated as the official candidate. Regina Ip, who in 2006 had founded the Savantas Policy Institute, was supported by the pro-Government DAB and the Liberal Party. Other candidates included barrister Lee Wing-kin, company directors Tandon Lal Chaing and Ling Wai-wan, worker Lau Yuk-shing, solicitor Siu See-kong and environmentalist Ho Loy. The by-election took place on 2 December, when 52% of the 618,350 registered voters turned out to vote. The poll was won by Anson Chan, who secured 55% of the votes cast (175,874 votes), while Regina Ip received 43% (137,550 votes). Although Chan's success was a convincing victory for the pan-democratic camp, the fact that Ip secured more than 40% of the votes cast represented a strong return to politics by the former Secretary for Security, who had resigned in 2003 following the protests against Article 23 (see above).

However, a political development of greater significance in the latter part of 2007 was the Beijing authorities' agreement to a timetable for the introduction of universal suffrage. The Hong Kong public was caught unprepared for the announcement of this schedule. In early July, soon after the 10th anniversary of the establishment of the SAR, the Hong Kong Government had produced a Green Paper on Constitutional Development, for public consultation. The document was based on discussions held by the Commission on Strategic Development. The Government then initiated a three-month public consultation period on the various options available for the future election of the Chief Executive and the Legislative Council by universal suffrage. In December the Hong Kong Government submitted the 'mainstream' views of the consultation exercise to the central Government in Beijing. The SAR Government reported: first, the general public expected universal suffrage as soon as possible and the production of a timetable; second, while half the population of Hong Kong expected universal suffrage for the post of Chief Executive in 2012, the implementation of this at the later date of 2017 would stand a better chance of being accepted by the majority; third, the election of the Chief Executive by universal suffrage, to be followed by that of the Legislative Council, had emerged as the consensus; and fourth, a timetable for implementing universal suffrage should be produced to resolve the question.

At the end of December 2007, a little over two weeks after the SAR Government had submitted its report, the Standing Committee of the NPC officially rejected the introduction of universal suffrage in Hong Kong for both the Chief Executive and all members of the Legislative Council in 2012, maintaining that the ratio of functional constituency seats to directly elected seats should remain at 50:50. However, the central Government stated that the people of Hong Kong might elect their Chief Executive in 2017 and all members of the Legislative Council at the earliest in 2020. In explaining this decision, the NPC Standing Committee's Vice-Secretary-General, Qiao Xiaoyang, made various suggestions: first, the Basic Law stated that the methods for the election of the Chief Executive and for the formation of the Legislative Council had to be specified in the light of 'actual conditions' in Hong Kong and according to the principle of 'gradual and orderly progress'; second, there was not enough support within the Legislative Council to elect the Chief Executive by universal suffrage before 2017; and third, to have balanced participation by various sectors and to ensure the smooth functioning of the system, it would not be appropriate to amend the existing electoral arrangement for functional constituency seats in 2012. On the issue of the timetable, Qiao maintained that the decision was progressive because by 2017, 20 years after its return to Chinese sovereignty, Hong Kong would have gained more election experience and would be approaching the mid-point of the 50-year period during which the 'capitalist system' of Hong Kong was to remain unchanged, as had been pledged by China.

Although this was a major advance in the democratization process, critics were disappointed by the delay in its implementation, and many continued to be sceptical about the sincerity of the Chinese Government in introducing full and fair universal suffrage. The pan-democrats remained suspicious of the Beijing leadership's commitment, suggesting that the future electoral arrangements might not be fully democratic. For example, one Beijing official in charge of Hong Kong affairs remarked that the functional constituencies should not automatically be excluded from proposals for universal suffrage. The Hong Kong public was also divided over the decision. An opinion poll conducted by the University of Hong Kong suggested that, while 43% of respondents welcomed the ruling, 41% wanted to continue to press for the introduction of universal suffrage in 2012. For his part, Chief Executive Donald Tsang's promise to resolve the question of universal suffrage had been delivered.

For most of the first half of 2008 the popularity rating of the Chief Executive remained high (at above 60, on a scale of 0–100) according to opinion polls conducted by the University of Hong Kong, reaching 66.4 in February after the Financial Secretary announced a number of tax reduction measures and other one-off tax benefits and special allowances for the aged and the poor in the 2008/09 budget. However, Tsang's popularity began to decline in May after his administration named officials for two new tiers of political appointees, first proposed by the Government in its Report on Further Development of the Political Appointment System in October 2007. The two new tiers of politically appointed officials included Deputy Directors of Bureau and Political Assistants to Directors of Bureau, these posts being created to support the political work of the administration's senior officials. In May 2008 the Government also named eight new Under-Secretaries and nine Political Assistants. The public became highly critical following media disclosure that a number of these appointees were of foreign nationality, and some questioned their political and professional experience; the public also demanded more transparency in the recruitment process and the level of pay awarded to such appointees.

In mid-July 2008, as the Hong Kong economy was increasingly affected by rising international fuel prices, the administration announced a programme of counter-inflationary measures, costing about HK $11,000m., to help the population. The programme included allowances for the aged, travel subsidies for school children and the extension of subsidies on electricity charges. However, one of the measures, a two-year suspension of the levy on new contracts for employers who were hiring new maids, or renewing the contracts of their foreign maids, became highly controversial when many employers sought to terminate existing contracts in order to benefit from the scheme. The Government was perceived to have introduced the measure with undue haste and without careful planning, as a result of which the administration's popularity rating declined to 54.5 in mid-July. In August the Government also mishandled the approval of the application for employment by the former Permanent Secretary for Housing, Planning and Lands, Leung Chin-man, who was named deputy managing director and executive director of New World China Land Ltd. As Leung was involved in a highly controversial project with New World Development (the parent company of New World China), there was widespread public concern that the appointment would be regarded as a reward for possible favours granted to the company during his tenure as a government official. While there was no evidence that Leung had granted any such favour to New World, Hong Kong's Chief Executive ordered the Civil Service Bureau, the body responsible for scrutinizing the employment of former civil servants for potential conflicts of interest, to submit a report on the case. The Secretary for the Civil Service, Denise Yue, apologized for failing to consider all relevant factors during the examination process. Leung's contract with New World China Land was terminated by the company as a result of the controversy. As the 2008 election for the Legislative Council approached, the Tsang administration obviously realized that it had to act decisively in order to limit the political damage.

Polling for the Legislative Council election was held on 7 September 2008. A total of 200 candidates contested the 60 seats, with 142 candidates from 53 lists standing for 30 seats in the five geographical constituencies; 14 candidates in the functional constituencies were returned unopposed. With 1.52m. votes being cast, turn-out was reported at 45.2% of the electorate, a lower rate of participation than had been recorded in the 2004 election. The pan-democratic camp unexpectedly secured 23 seats, winning 19 of the 30 directly elected seats and four seats from the 30 functional constituencies, with 59.0% of the popular vote, marginally less than in 2004 when it had secured 60.6% of the vote. Although the pan-democratic camp lost two seats, it maintained its vital one-third share of the total number of seats in the Legislative Council and, therefore, its critical role in Hong Kong's process of democratic change (any amendments to the selection methods of the Chief Executive and the legislature required the endorsement of a two-thirds' majority in the Legislative Council). Both Martin Lee and Anson Chan, the two prominent pan-democratic politicians, had decided not to seek re-election. Cyd Ho Sau-lan, whose narrow defeat in the 2004 elections had been attributed to a tactical error, secured election as a representative of Civic Act-up, a small pro-democracy group of young activists. Newcomers to the Legislative Council from the pan-democratic camp included Tanya Chan, who headed the list of candidates for the Civic Party, the leader of which, Audrey Eu, was re-elected. Another new member of the Legislative Council was Kam Lai-Wai, who secured a seat for the Democratic Party. However, Yeung Sum, a Democratic Party veteran who was ranked second on the party list after Kam, lost his seat and announced that he would not seek re-election again. Another prominent pan-democratic member, Fernando Cheung of the Civic Party, who had decided not to stand in the functional constituency that represented social workers, was defeated in a geographical constituency.

The pan-democrats were disadvantaged at the polls by the central Government's promise that a firm timetable would be drawn up for the introduction of universal suffrage for the election of both the Chief Executive and all Legislative Council members; this had made the demand for full democracy seem less urgent. The pro-establishment parties were further boosted by heightened patriotism following Beijing's successful hosting of the Olympic Games in August 2008, together with widespread sympathy for those affected by a devastating earthquake in Sichuan Province in May. The Democratic Party lost one seat, with its share of the popular vote declining to 19.4%, from 25.2% in 2004. The Civic Party, which had contested the 2004 elections as the Article 45 Concern Group, also lost one seat, although its share of the popular vote increased to 13.6%, from 9.2%

in 2004. The biggest advance within the pan-democratic camp was made by the more radical LSD. Under the leadership of Raymond Wong and Leung Kwok-hung, the LSD secured more than 10% of the votes and three of its five candidates won directly elective seats.

However, despite the fact that the pan-democrats had performed better than expected, the political reality was that the pro-establishment camp maintained its dominant political position, with 35 seats (11 directly elected from geographical constituencies and 24 from functional constituencies). Furthermore, the pro-establishment camp's share of the popular vote increased to 39.4%, from 37.3% in 2004. The DAB gained one additional seat and remained the largest political party in the Legislative Council with 13 seats (nine from geographical constituencies and four from functional constituencies), and it introduced younger and better-educated members to the legislature, including Starry Lee and Gary Chan, both of whom were under the age of 30.

Inter-party divisions between the DAB and the business-orientated Liberal Party partly undermined the success of the pro-establishment grouping. Although the Liberal Party won more than 4% of the popular vote, both the party Chairman, James Tien, and Vice-Chairwoman Selina Chow lost their seats in the geographical constituencies. The Liberal Party's pro-business agenda failed to secure it any seats in the geographical constituencies, and the party subsequently experienced serious difficulty when three of its members in the Legislative Council formed a splinter group.

The election of the DAB's Jasper Tsang as President of the Legislative Council, after he defeated Fred Li of the Democratic Party by 36 votes to 24, further emphasized the pro-establishment camp's dominance of the legislature. Frustrated by this dominance, the LSD employed highly controversial, aggressive tactics, challenging senior government officials with abusive language and menacing action. In October 2008, for example, LSD leader Raymond Wong threw a banana inside the chamber to protest against the Government's proposal to introduce means-testing for the payment of 'fruit money', a special allowance for the elderly; and in February 2009 Wong attempted to seize from the Financial Secretary's hands the text of his budget speech.

The Tsang administration's most urgent problem in the second half of 2008 and first half of 2009 was the global financial turmoil. Following the failures in the US financial sector, economic growth in Hong Kong declined significantly; export trade decreased sharply and unemployment rose. The Government proposed a number of measures to support the economy. However, more troubling for the Government were the political consequences of the collapse of US investment bank Lehman Brothers, as a result of which thousands of small investors who had bought securities backed by the company and sold by other financial institutions in Hong Kong suddenly lost their life-savings. These so-called minibond investors protested against what they regarded as the dishonest selling tactics of the banks and the failure of the regulators to protect their interests, staging demonstrations and mobilizing cross-party support for an independent investigation into the affair by the Legislative Council. Meanwhile, the political divide in the new legislature did not preclude the establishment of a Select Committee to conduct an independent investigation into the Government's granting of approval for Leung Chin-man, former Permanent Secretary for Housing, Planning and Lands, to take up his controversial appointment with New World China Land Ltd (see above).

Further public discontent was evident in mid-2009 when a record number of people (estimated at about 150,000) participated in a vigil in Victoria Park to mark the 20th anniversary of the Tiananmen Square tragedy. Many of those who took part were also upset by remarks made by the Chief Executive stating that his view—that the incident had happened many years ago and China had subsequently made significant economic progress that had also benefited Hong Kong—represented the opinion of many people in Hong Kong.

Hong Kong's relations with mainland China continued to be strengthened, especially over development in the Pearl River Delta, including co-operation in major cross-boundary infrastructural projects and boundary control points such as the Hong Kong–Zhuhai–Macao Bridge, the Hong Kong section of the Guangzhou–Shenzhen–Hong Kong Express Rail Link and the Liantang/Heung Yuen Wai Boundary Control Point. Progress was also made in improving bilateral co-operation on environmental protection, trade and tourism, including another supplement to the Closer Economic Partnership Arrangement (CEPA) between the mainland and Hong Kong.

Meanwhile, the local media reported concerns over a number of incidents that had prompted accusations against the mainland Chinese authorities of interference in Hong Kong's internal affairs. In July 2008 remarks by Chinese Vice-President Xi Jinping urging 'mutual understanding and support among the executive authorities, the legislature and the judiciary' prompted the Hong Kong authorities to issue a statement reiterating the importance of judicial independence in Hong Kong. In March 2009 Li Guikang, a deputy director of the Central Liaison Office, reportedly told Hong Kong members of the Chinese People's Political Consultative Conference (CPPCC), behind closed doors, that the Office had reached a 10-point agreement with the Government of the SAR to allow its CPPCC members to play a more active role in Hong Kong affairs. Both Li and the Hong Kong Government later denied the existence of such an agreement. In April the Hong Kong media drew attention to an article that had been written in the previous year by Cao Erbao, head of research at the Central Liaison Office, effectively stating that there were two ruling teams in Hong Kong: the SAR Government on the one hand, and mainland China's officials responsible for Hong Kong affairs on the other. The Central Liaison Office issued a statement in mid-April refuting such a notion, reiterating the policy of 'one country, two systems' and maintaining that Hong Kong enjoyed a high degree of autonomy. Another controversial incident towards the end of 2009 also attracted much attention. On 27 December, when four Hong Kong demonstrators who were involved in a protest at the Lo Wu border in support of a mainland activist, Liu Xiaobo, and two journalists were detained by Chinese police officers. The protesters claimed that they had been physically moved from the Hong Kong side of the border by plain-clothed mainland police.

A number of important public appointments were made by the Government in 2009. Justice Barnabas Fung replaced Justice Pang Kin-kee as Chairman of the Electoral Affairs Commission when Pang stepped down in August. In the same month Raymond Tam, the Under-Secretary for Constitutional and Mainland Affairs, was appointed Director of the Chief Executive's Office, replacing Norman Chan who took over from Joseph Yam as Chief Executive of the Hong Kong Monetary Authority in October. Adeline Wong, formerly the Deputy Director of Home Affairs, assumed the position of Under-Secretary for Constitutional and Mainland Affairs; and former Director of Immigration Lai Tung-kwok became Under-Secretary for Security. The highly respected Chief Justice of the CFA, Andrew Li, who announced his retirement in September 2009, was replaced by Geoffrey Ma, with effect from September 2010, following a recommendation made by the Judicial Officers Recommendations Commission in accordance with the standard procedure.

Public demand for democratic change remained strong, with as many as 70,000 demonstrators (28,000 according to police estimates) taking part in the annual pro-democracy march in mid-2009. The 60th anniversary of the establishment of the People's Republic of China fell in 2009, and the central Government invited a delegation of 212 people to attend the celebrations in Beijing; however, only two Legislative Council members from the pan-democratic camp were invited, leading to suggestions that an opportunity for dialogue between the two sides had been missed.

A major advance in the SAR's constitutional development took place in mid-2010 when the Hong Kong Government, with the support of the central Government, reached a compromise with the Democratic Party on future election arrangements for both the Chief Executive and Legislative Council. However, the negotiations for the compromise were characterized by political drama, and the pan-democratic camp split into two over the issue.

The consultation document for the 2012 elections (originally scheduled for release in the first half of 2009) was published in November 2009. The document proposed increasing the size of the Election Committee from 800 to 'not more than' 1,200 by adding 100 members to each of the four sectors (with most of the 100 seats in the fourth sector to be elected by elected District Council members) and maintaining the nomination threshold within the Election Committee at one-eighth of the total membership (150 votes out of 1,200) for the election of the Chief Executive. For the Legislative Council elections, the document proposed an increase in the number of seats from 60 to 70, with five new geographical constituency seats and five functional constituency seats to be determined by election among elected District Council members.

The pan-democratic camp expressed concerns that the proposed changes might in practice turn the functional constituencies into a permanent feature of the electoral system in Hong Kong and thus further delay the eventual introduction of universal suffrage. Although the Government dismissed such concerns and pointed out that the central Government had made a commitment to the introduction of universal suffrage for the election of the Chief Executive in 2017, and for the Legislative Council in 2012, the law providing for the reform programme needed the support of the pan-democrats because the favourable votes of a two-thirds' majority of the members of the Legislative Council would be required for the legislation to be approved.

In an attempt to exert more pressure on the Government to put forward better proposals, the 'radical' pan-democrats, led by the Civic Party and the LSD, announced in January 2010 that members of their parties (two from the Civic Party and three from LSD) would resign from each of the five geographical constituencies in Hong Kong in order to force the holding of territory-wide by-elections, which would become a de facto 'referendum' on the reform programme. The Government quickly announced that there were no provisions in the Basic Law for the holding of a referendum in Hong Kong. In Beijing the Hong Kong and Macao Affairs Office also issued a statement dismissing the 'referendum' plan as a violation of the Basic Law. The SAR's Secretary for Constitutional and Mainland

Affairs accused the two parties of wasting public resources by compelling the Government to organize the by-elections.

However, the pan-democrats were divided over the plan, which did not receive strong public support. When the Government went ahead with the arrangements for the by-elections, held on 16 May 2010, the more 'moderate' Democratic Party and the ADPL, like the pro-establishment parties including the DAB and the Liberal Party, declined to take part in the polls. The five Civic Party and LSD legislators were all re-elected, but at 17.1% the turn-out was very low. However, the Civic Party and the LSD claimed that the 579,000 votes that they had received none the less represented strong public demand for democracy.

The division in the pan-democratic camp led to the establishment of the Alliance for Universal Suffrage, a coalition of 'moderate' legislators, academics and political commentators who had not been involved in the by-election exercise; nor had they been involved in dialogues between the 'moderates' of the pan-democratic camp and the Hong Kong Government, as well as central government officials, on the issue of electoral reform and the 'roadmap' for the introduction of universal suffrage. In early June 2010 the Government announced that the original proposal would be presented to the Legislative Council, without change. The Government then launched a campaign to win public support for its proposal. Chief Executive Donald Tsang also entered into a televised debate with the leader of the Civic Party, Audrey Eu.

In a dramatic development towards the end of June 2010, the Government and the mainland authorities accepted the Democratic Party's proposed compromise: to open up the planned five new District Council functional seats to popular election (except the small number of registered voters of existing functional constituencies, on the grounds they should not be allowed to vote twice in functional constituencies) and therefore in practice transform the new seats into directly elected seats. The arrangements also effectively allowed each eligible voter in Hong Kong two votes: one in a geographical seat and one in a functional constituency seat, or 'one person, two votes'.

Also in June 2010, with the support of the Democratic Party, the Legislative Council approved the Government's proposals for changes to the method of electing the Chief Executive, by 46 votes to 13. On the following day the new election procedure for the Legislative Council itself was also approved, by 46 votes to 12. The 'radical' pan-democrats remained opposed to the plans and denounced the moderates for 'selling out', local opinion surveys suggested that the proposals had public support, while ratings for government performance in the promotion of democratic development improved.

The political landscape in Hong Kong underwent major changes from the end of 2010. In December 30 members of the Democratic Party (including seven district councillors who disagreed with the party's support for the Government's proposed electoral reforms and the refusal to participate in the by-elections of May) departed and formed the Neo Democrats. The solidarity among members of the pan-democratic camp was further weakened when the co-founder of the radical LSD, Raymond Wong, together with another senior member, Albert Chan, left the League in early 2011; they cited personal differences with Andrew To, the Chairman of the LSD, and launched People's Power. The Civic Party also witnessed its first leadership changes with the replacement of Audrey Eu as party leader and the election of Kenneth Chan as Chairman in place of Kuan Hsin-chi.

The pro-establishment camp also underwent changes, with two former leaders of the Liberal Party, James Tien and Selina Chow, returning to play important roles. However, Michael Tien, another senior Liberal Party member and brother of James, left to join the New People's Party (NPP). This new party was formally established in January 2011 by Regina Ip, the former Secretary for Security, who had been tasked with introducing the controversial legislation for the implementation of Article 23 of the Basic Law in 2002 (see above). Having left the Government after the legislation was withdrawn, Ip had won a Legislative Council seat in 2008. She became Chairperson of the NPP, with Michael Tien as a deputy chairman.

However, the question of the by-elections continued to generate political tensions. The Government described the by-elections as an abuse and waste of public funds and in early June 2011, keen to prevent another de facto referendum, it formally gazetted a bill to abolish by-elections altogether. The Government proposed that any Legislative Council seats determined by direct election and subsequently vacated would henceforth be filled by the next best placed candidates at the last poll. The proposal encountered strong criticism, not only from the pan-democratic camp but also from the pro-establishment camp. The proposed legislation, which was deemed unfair and impractical, was also criticized for depriving the people of Hong Kong of their constitutional rights to elect, and to be elected, with proper consultation. In response, in July the Government produced a consultation paper with a view to a public consultation period of two months.

Another important political development in 2011 was the Government's announcement in mid September that all appointed seats for the District Council were to be abolished. While the Government was willing only gradually to remove the appointed members in three phases by 2020, beginning with a reduction of one-third of such seats for the District Council elections in November 2011, the decision not to remove all the appointed seats simultaneously was clearly one small but crucial step towards greater democracy in Hong Kong.

Hong Kong's relationship with the mainland remained complex. While the SAR continued to rely on China for its economic well-being, issues of human rights and political freedom on the mainland remained politically sensitive in Hong Kong. With the appointment of China's former most senior diplomat to the UN, Wang Guangya, as Director of the Hong Kong and Macao Affairs Office, Beijing's Hong Kong policy team came under new leadership towards the end of 2010. Wang, who succeeded Liao Hui to become the second Director for the Office, was far more open and active than his predecessor, willing to engage with the media and the public in Hong Kong. He made a high-profile visit to Hong Kong in June 2011 which was largely regarded as sucessful. Nevertheless, he urged those in Hong Kong who were concerned about the sentencing of Zhao Lianhai, an advocate for the victims of the 2008 tainted milk powder scandal on the mainland (which had resulted in the deaths of several babies, with 300,000 infants being affected), to observe the principle that 'well water should not pollute the river water', a metaphor that Hong Kong should avoid interfering in mainland affairs. When in December 2010 the internationally renowned Chinese artist and activist Ai Weiwei was prevented from travelling to Norway to attend the Nobel Peace Prize award ceremony for the Chinese dissident Liu Xiaobo, and when in April 2011 Ai was arrested by the Chinese authorities as he was about to board a plane to Hong Kong (where he was due to attend a conference), protests demanding the release of Zhao Lianhai and Liu Xiaobo, as well as that of Ai Weiwei, took place in Hong Kong.

While such demonstrations took place without incident, the visit of Chinese Vice-Premier Li Keqiang in August 2011 became highly controversial when the police were accused of acting in an uncompromising manner in curbing the freedom of expression for those who wanted to stage demonstrations during Li's three-day visit, including a protest planned at the University of Hong Kong. The Hong Kong Journalists Association also complained against what its members considered to be repressive police action that prevented reporters from properly covering the Vice-Premier's. While rejecting accusations that it had curbed media coverage and freedom of expression, the Government agreed to review the security arrangements. However, journalists in Hong Kong were further dismayed when the Government decided to appoint as Head of Broadcasting, with responsibility for managing Radio Television Hong Kong, an administrative officer, Roy Tang, rather than a person with broadcasting experience. Radio Television Hong Kong remained a public broadcasting organization and an independent government department.

The issue that attracted most media coverage in 2011, however, was the forthcoming contest for the position of Chief Executive, scheduled for 2012. By August 2011 three likely candidates had emerged: Henry Tang, the incumbent Chief Secretary; Leung Chun-ying, the convenor of the Executive Council; and Rita Fan, former Legislative Council President and a Hong Kong delegate to the NPC in Beijing. At one point Rita Fan enjoyed the highest level of popular support, according to opinion polls conducted by the University of Hong Kong. However, Fan expressed support for Henry Tang in early September when she announced that she would not stand for the position of Chief Executive position if Tang were to be a candidate. In late September Leung declared that he would resign from the Executive Council in order to dedicate his efforts to the campaign for the Chief Executive election. Tang then announced his resignation from the position of Chief Secretary. At the end of September Stephen Lam was appointed Chief Secretary; he was replaced as Secretary for Constitutional and Mainland Affairs by Raymond Tam.

The path to full democracy in Hong Kong continued to be beset by obstacles: the longer-term political implications of the division between the radical and moderate camps of the pan-democrats were still not clear. The establishment of the New People's Party, as well as the probable contest for the Chief Executive position for the 2012 election by pro-establishment candidates, further complicated the political scene. Moreover, the actual implementation of the constitutional reforms would continue to be controversial. However, the constitutional reforms would broaden the base for popular elections in Hong Kong, while the creation of the additional seats in the Legislative Council would expand the pool of directly elected legislators, as well as introduce new dynamics into Hong Kong's political process. The year 2012 was therefore likely to be a watershed in the SAR's political development.

Economy

LOK SANG HO

Revised for this edition by the editorial staff

INTRODUCTION

Hong Kong's unique geographical location, political stability, industrious work-force, efficient civil service and excellent infrastructure have all contributed to its economic success. Other important factors in the strong competitiveness of this Special Administrative Region (SAR) of China are the adherence to the rule of law and relative freedom from corruption, the free markets and low tax rates. Hong Kong's role as a major financial centre is unlikely to change. The economy is market-driven rather than government-led, and its resilience has been repeatedly demonstrated. While the free market is Hong Kong's strength, prudent regulation of its financial markets, particularly its banks, is also a major advantage. Although there have been occasional complaints about regulatory lapses, the quality of Hong Kong's overall regulation is good.

The global recession that developed in the latter part of 2008 led to a marked deterioration in the economy of Hong Kong, largely owing to its heavy dependence on financial services and external trade. As the year elapsed the SAR was seriously challenged by the increasingly adverse economic conditions. Exports, consumption and investment all weakened significantly in the latter months of the year. Gross domestic product (GDP) contracted by 2.6% year-on-year in the final quarter of 2008.

The first three months of 2009 proved to be even more difficult for Hong Kong: a sharp decline in GDP of 7.8% was recorded, representing the largest quarterly contraction since the third quarter of 1998. Merchandise exports were severely affected, declining by 22.7% in relation to the first quarter of 2008, the biggest decrease since the second quarter of 1954; exports of services declined by 8.2%. In 2009 as a whole exports of goods decreased substantially, leading to a significant trade, while exports of services registered negligible growth. Private consumption expenditure was subdued by surging unemployment and faltering asset prices.

Following the decline in the annual growth rate of Hong Kong's GDP from 6.4% in 2007 to 2.2% in 2008, GDP contracted by 2.8% in 2009 as a whole. This contraction represented only the second full-year economic decline in Hong Kong's statistical record since 1962. Income in terms of GDP per head declined from HK $240,339 in 2008 to HK $231,638 in 2009.

By the latter part of 2009, however, improvement was in evidence; following four consecutive quarters of contraction, the economy resumed positive growth in the final three months of that year. As Hong Kong's recovery gathered momentum, aided largely by robust growth in mainland China and by the strengthening of export markets, in 2010 GDP grew by 7.0%, while GDP per head rose to HK $246,733. Sustained by strong domestic demand, overall GDP expanded by 7.5% in the first quarter of 2011 and by 5.1% in the second quarter. In August 2011 the Government projected a GDP growth rate for the year as a whole at 5%–6%.

GOVERNMENT MEASURES AND FISCAL POLICY

By the end of 2008 it was obvious that Hong Kong's trade and financial sectors had suffered serious set-backs. In December, in an effort to address the repercussions of the global downturn, the Government announced details of a major programme of fiscal stimulus. Notable measures included the provision of support for small and medium-sized enterprises (SMEs), with loan guarantees for businesses totalling HK $100,000m. It was envisaged that 60,000 employment opportunities would be created, and the recruitment of civil servants was to be brought forward. Work on various infrastructure projects was also to be accelerated. In February 2009, furthermore, in order to make additional resources available to Hong Kong banks, the establishment of a Contingent Bank Capital Facility was announced.

In response to the global financial turmoil, the Chief Executive of Hong Kong, Donald Tsang, had announced in his 2008/09 Policy Address that he was to create and head a task force. The new body was to propose measures to assist the Government and business community in addressing the problems arising from the global slowdown. In April 2009 the Task Force on Economic Challenges identified six areas that would benefit from government support as important potential areas of future growth: testing and certification; medical services; innovation and technology; cultural and creative industries; environmental industry; and educational services. This raised the question of whether Hong Kong should do more to diversify away from financial services. That Hong Kong had strengths in these six areas was beyond dispute. However, with perhaps the exception of the environment industry's recycling sub-sector, these areas were unlikely to create many jobs. In any case, they could not address the short-term problems presented by the global financial crisis.

In October 2008, in the aftermath of the failure of Lehman Brothers, a US-based investment bank that had declared bankruptcy, the Hong Kong Monetary Authority (HKMA) announced that it would provide liquidity assistance to licensed banks in Hong Kong. Five temporary measures were announced. These measures, which relaxed some restrictions on borrowing by banks, were to remain in place from early October until the end of March 2009. In addition, the HKMA announced that it would provide 100% bank deposit insurance, following the lead of several other countries, which were similarly attempting to address the crisis of investor confidence arising from the exceptional global economic conditions.

As the global recession deepened, the Hong Kong Government sought to conserve its fiscal reserves. Many argued that the 2009/10 budget did not provide enough help for Hong Kong's population, given the momentous nature of the crisis and the generally good fiscal position of the Government, which was further enhanced by the higher tax revenues derived from a substantial increase in the number of property transactions and the raising of stamp duty. With the fiscal outturn exceeding expectations and GDP data much worse than anticipated in the first quarter of 2009, the SAR Government boosted its relief effort. In late May the Government announced an additional HK $16,800m. of tax relief, transfer payments, exemption of fees and financial assistance for SMEs. The announcement included additional funds for export credit insurance and an expansion of the loan guarantee programme with the guarantee ratio raised from 70% to 80% and the maximum loan raised from HK $6m. to HK $12m. The guarantee period was extended from three years to five years. The most notable tax concession was the increase in tax relief from 50% to 100%, subject to an upper limit of HK $8,000, rather than the previously announced HK $6,000. Around 500,000 taxpayers were expected to receive a tax rebate by October 2009. Among other measures, the Government also pledged to pay two months' rent for public housing tenants and subsidize rent for an additional two quarters, subject to a limit of HK $1,500 per quarter. Those in receipt of the Comprehensive Social Security Allowance and those eligible for the elderly allowance would also benefit from an additional month's stipend.

Public expenditure as a percentage of GDP was to be reduced from 19.9% in 2008/09 to 19.4% in 2009/10. None the less, the Government maintained that the 2009/10 budget was expansionary, emphasizing the transfer nature of some of the public expenditure in the earlier year; these included the release of HK $6,000 into the retirement fund accounts of workers with an average monthly income at or below HK $10,000, as well as government contributions to the Public Works Fund. The 2009/10 budget was also unpopular with the public, owing to the widespread belief that the Government had been more generous in the previous year, when economic conditions had been significantly worse. The 2009/10 budget projected a consolidated surplus of HK $13,800m., equivalent to 0.8% of GDP.

The budget of 2010/11 placed greater emphasis on social welfare: in that year recurrent expenditure on education, health care and provision for the elderly and disabled was to be raised to HK $130,000m., a sum projected to account for 56% of total recurrent expenditure. A deficit on the consolidated account of HK $25,200m. (1.5% of projected GDP) was envisaged for 2010/11. Details of the draft budget for 2011/12 were announced in February 2011. However, the proposals incurred much criticism, mainly owing to the Government's perceived disregard for the needs of the disadvantaged members of Hong Kong society. In response to public protest, the Government was obliged to review its decision to channel surplus funds into workers' pension schemes. It was subsequently announced that all permanent residents were to receive immediate lump sum payments of HK $6,000 and that income tax was to be reduced.

THE FINANCIAL SERVICES SECTOR

With Hong Kong's transformation into a services-focused economy having accelerated from the early 1990s, by 2009 services accounted for more than 92% of GDP, in comparison with 75% in 1990. (In contrast, the manufacturing sector's contribution to GDP dwindled to less than 3%, from 17% in 1990.) Reflecting the transition towards a service-orientated economy is the changing composition of Hong Kong's total exports. Compared with 10 years previously, by 2007 Hong Kong's exports of services had increased by more than 140% in real terms. The value of these exports in 2008 stood at about HK $719,900m. and was equal to around 25.3% of total merchandise exports, up from 18.9% in 1995. By 2007 the contribution to GDP of financial services had reached 20%.

The profits of Hong Kong's banks declined substantially as a result of the global financial crisis. The Bank of East Asia experienced a 99% decrease in profits in 2008. HSBC, the leading global bank from Hong Kong, latterly domiciled in the United Kingdom, recorded a 62% decline. None the less, during the difficult conditions of 2008/09 not a single licensed bank in Hong Kong failed; indeed, most banks managed to remain in profit during the period of global recession.

However, several developments during 2008/09 raised concerns in relation to Hong Kong's status as a world-class financial centre. The Lehman Brothers minibond scandal added to the controversy over the various 'accumulator contracts' that led to huge losses among investors, suggesting that Hong Kong had perhaps been too permissive in terms of allowing risky products to be marketed at the retail level. More than 27,000 complaints were lodged with the Securities and Futures Commission (SFC) and the HKMA with regard to the Lehman Brothers minibonds. Accumulator contracts provided an opportunity for professional investors to buy designated shares at a lower price than the prevailing market price in a buoyant market, but required them to buy the shares at a much higher cost than the market price when the market was weakening; contractors were thus exposed to unlimited losses. In response to media enquiries following a series of complaints from investors who felt that they had been misled, the SFC issued a statement in April 2008 pointing out that the accumulator contracts, which were sold through private banks and licensed corporations, were intended for professional investors; therefore, no SFC approval had been necessary. Nevertheless, under the Code of Conduct for Licensed and Registered Persons, intermediaries were supposed to have explained to the clients the inherent risks of these products. The SFC would not intervene in the event of any other dispute between the investors and the issuers.

Furthermore, the various releases of minibonds that were sold to thousands of small investors were very unsuitable. Indeed, by the latter part of 2008 it had become evident that even elderly people, with little formal education and meagre life savings, were among the clients who had been persuaded by banks to buy such novel and risky financial products. The inter-relationships between the various institutions involved were very complicated, and the minibonds were nothing like the bonds issued by corporations that would have prior claims to the assets should the issuing corporations fail. A public outcry followed the release of the SFC statement; while acknowledging the complex nature of these financial products, the regulators adopted the position that, as long as proper disclosure of the associated risks was made, they would not approve or disapprove the products. However, the SFC reminded intermediaries that it was their responsibility to offer suitable products to their clients.

Although some settlements relating to the Lehman débâcle were reported, involving cases in which the victims had obviously been misled or were poorly positioned to take the attendant risks, a lengthy litigation process ensued, jeopardizing the reputation of Hong Kong as an international financial centre. In March 2011 it was announced that 16 Hong Kong banks had agreed to buy back financial instruments for up to 96.5% of their value (in contrast to the 60% previously offered) and to repay investors who had lost money as a result of the failure of Lehman Brothers. However, the conclusion of this settlement gave rise to a record number of bankruptcy claims in June 2011 when 1,809 transfers were made, thus surpassing Hong Kong's previous record of 1,530 transfers, reached in March 2010.

Hong Kong's stock market activity was seriously affected by the global downturn of 2008/09. As measured by the Hang Seng Index, the HKEx declined by 48% during the course of 2008, closing at 14,387 points at the end of December, before recovering to stand at 21,872 points on the closing day of 2009. In comparison with the previous year, the value of market turnover in securities decreased by 19% in 2008 and by 12% in 2009, reaching a total of HK $15,515,200m. in the latter year. None the less, in terms of market capitalization, by 2010 Hong Kong's stock market was reportedly ranked sixth in the world. Owing to international concerns related to sovereign debt issues in various European countries, a period of stock market volatility ensued in April–May during which the Hang Seng Index declined to a low point of 18,986; however, the index reached 23,035 points on the closing day of 2010, more than 5% higher than at the end of 2009. In comparison with the previous year, the value of market turnover in securities increased by 11% in 2010 to reach HK $17,210,100m. Following another period of instability on global markets, by early October 2011 the Hang Seng Index had declined to below 17,000 points.

The amount of capital raised through initial public offerings (IPOs) of shares decreased sharply from HK $292,400m. in 2007 to HK $65,800m. in 2008. Following a substantial increase in new listings, in 2009 the Hong Kong stock market was reported to have surpassed both New York and the mainland Chinese city of Shanghai to occupy the position of the world's leading centre for IPOs, the value of which rose to reach the equivalent of US $31,400m. Owing to adverse market conditions in the first half of 2010, however, a number of Hong Kong's IPOs were withdrawn or scaled down, notably that of Swire Properties in May, the potential value of which had been projected at US $2,700m. Such factors, combined with the forthcoming release of major IPOs in the mainland banking sector, were expected to place Shanghai in first position in that important segment in 2010.

OTHER SERVICES

To boost tourism the Hong Kong Government and the mainland authorities devised a new scheme under which qualified Shenzhen residents could apply for year-round multiple-entry visas to visit Hong Kong, while those with no registered household in Guangdong could apply for endorsement for individual visits in Shenzhen at a later date. This scheme took effect in April 2009, in which month the Hong Kong Tourism Board launched the 'Hong Kong Welcomes Shenzhen Visitors with Citywide Promotion' in Shenzhen. The promotion, which was in place until the end of 2009, extended a range of offers intended to encourage Shenzhen residents to make more frequent consumption trips to Hong Kong.

Although the total number of all categories of visitor arrivals rose only marginally in 2009 to reach 29.6m., the number of travellers from mainland China increased from 57% of the total to nearly 61% in 2009. In 2010 the number of visitors to Hong Kong rose by almost 22% to exceed 36.0m., of whom 63% were from mainland China.

The retail sector was relatively well sustained until January 2009. In February, however, the value of retail sales decreased substantially, by 12.6% year-on-year, the biggest decline in 10 years; this was largely attributable to poor performance by the automobile and auto-parts sub-sectors. Owing to lower prices, the decline in volume terms was even more severe, at 13.8%. By mid-2010, however, the situation had greatly improved: in the first six months of the year retail sales increased by 17.9% in terms of value and by 14.7% in volume in comparison with the first half of 2009. Sales of motor vehicles and parts demonstrated a particularly strong recovery, as did sales of electrical goods and photographic equipment.

The improvement in the retail sector was sustained in the first half of 2011: in June of that year the value of total sales reached HK $31,300m., representing an increase of 28.8% in comparison with June 2010, while the volume of sales expanded by 22.2%. Having declined by 0.4% in 2009, private consumption expenditure showed strong expansion in the first quarter of 2010, when it increased by 7.1%, before growth moderated to 4.6% in the second quarter. In comparison with the corresponding quarters of 2010, in real terms private consumption expenditure grew by 8.0% in the first three months of 2011 and by 9.2% in the second quarter of the year.

THE PROPERTY MARKET

The Hong Kong Government effectively reversed the policy of gradually excluding more affluent tenants from housing subsidies when it introduced the Tenants Purchase Scheme (TPS) in December 1997. The TPS offered sitting tenants in Hong Kong's public housing estates, including wealthier residents, the opportunity to purchase their rental units at only 12% of the estimated market price. Although well-off tenants were later denied the so-called 'discount upon discount' and were offered only a smaller discount, the TPS caused a sudden decline in the number of buyers of private housing as well as Home Ownership Scheme (HOS) housing. The extremely low prices being charged to sitting tenants served as a benchmark price for all homebuyers and sellers. If home-sellers could sell their homes only at low prices, they could also offer relatively low prices in trading up to better units; thus, the housing 'ladder' was distorted. After the launch of the TPS, housing market turnovers declined significantly, as did housing prices. Between the high point of 1997 and the low point of 2003 an extraordinary 67% decline in housing prices was recorded. The TPS remained a major impediment to a recovery in the housing market. In November 2002, however, the Secretary of Housing, Planning, and Land announced nine measures to stimulate the market, including the termination of the TPS after Phase 6, which had already been announced and could not be changed.

In 2007 some old stocks of HOS housing that had been held back in order to revive the housing market in the aftermath of the 1997/98 Asian financial crisis were released for sale. According to the Census and Statistics Department, in 2007 46,000 public housing tenants had monthly household incomes in excess of HK $30,000. At the same time, the Housing Authority reported that the number of wealthier tenants paying between 150% and 200% of the regular rent, or even market rent, had doubled from 12,000 in March 2003 to 24,000 in August 2007. Those who were so well off as to pay market rent were required to vacate their units within a year. In order that these more affluent tenants might move out and make room for poorer families, many observers urged the Government to resume HOS housing construction (the policy of subsidized building having been abandoned in 2001).

The housing market started a dramatic recovery that lasted until mid-2008, when the global financial crisis developed. The recovery had in fact resulted in the prices of some luxury homes surpassing their pre-1997 peaks. The opposite ends of the housing market behaved very differently. While luxury home prices soared, the prices of most other homes, and particularly those at the lower end of the market, rose at a much more subdued pace. Nevertheless, in the first eight months of 2008 some 30 TPS homes were sold at prices in excess of HK $1m., between three and five times the amount that the sitting tenants had paid in 1998. Some of the most expensive TPS home transactions occurred in Sha Tin's Pok Hong Estate and in Wong Tai Sin's Lower Estate, with prices in the region of HK $1.65m., and HK $1.54m., respectively. The tenants had not only enjoyed years of subsidized rent, but also earned more than HK $1.2m. in capital gains; this was at the expense of middle-class taxpayers, who had been required to pay high prices for their homes and who had thus suffered huge capital losses on account of the policy.

Cases of negative equity increased three-fold within the last three months of 2008, from 2,568 to 10,949 cases. However, the Hong Kong housing market was one of the first in the world to exhibit signs of a recovery from the low point reached at the end of 2008, with prices rising by about 10% by mid-2009. The number of transactions was also surging, helped by very low mortgage lending rates.

Residential property prices increased substantially in the latter part of 2009, as seemingly exemplified in October when a major property company, Henderson Land Development Co, was reported to have secured the sale of 25 luxury apartments in a new development in the desirable Mid-Levels area of Hong Kong Island. The complex included a penthouse costing US $57m., which was reported to be the most expensive property in Asia. In June 2010, however, amid suggestions of deliberate manipulation of the market with the intention of artificially raising prices, it was revealed that 20 of the 25 transactions had been cancelled and deposits refunded to the prospective buyers. It also emerged that the purported purchasers were in fact representatives of apparently bogus companies, all of which had engaged the same law firm to oversee the transaction. Meanwhile, a police investigation into the affair commenced, and members of Hong Kong's legislature renewed their demands for more stringent regulation of the property market.

Demand for housing strengthened in mid-2010 when land auctions for prime sites were reported to have exceeded expectations. Momentum was further encouraged by abundant liquidity in the banking system, the continuation of low mortgage rates and lack of new housing supply. Indeed, by the latter part of 2009 the immediate challenge for the Government was to curb renewed speculation in the property market. In October, therefore, the HKMA increased from 30% to 40% the minimum deposit required for mortgages on residential properties valued at more than HK $20m. For properties valued at less than HK $20m. the maximum loan available was set at HK $12m. In April 2010, furthermore, stamp duty on property transactions in the upper end of the market was raised.

During 2010, with public concern about the substantial increases in property prices rising and amid renewed demands for more stringent regulation of the sector, various measures to stabilize the housing market were announced; these included the implementation of restrictions on excessive mortgage lending. Nevertheless, intense speculative activity continued, and by 2011 residential property prices had reached their highest level for 13 years, having risen by 30% in 2009 and by 24% in 2010. Some apartments were reported to have been bought and immediately returned to the market at prices of as much as 20% above their previous cost of purchase. Furthermore, it was estimated that about 30% of the properties in the most expensive price range were being purchased by mainland Chinese buyers. In mid-2011 it was announced that the HKMA was to implement further measures to subdue the property market. Residential mortgages on homes valued at HK $10m. or more were to be restricted to 50% of the property's value. Mortgages on properties worth between HK $7m. and HK $10m. were to be limited to 60%, while loans for less expensive homes were to be restricted to HK $4.2m.

However, owing to the seemingly inexorable rise of residential property prices, financial pressure on the 'sandwich class', as middle-income earners were known, continued to increase. Many families in this income bracket could not afford to buy their own home, but failed to qualify for rental accommodation in the public housing sector. With property prices in Hong Kong having surpassed the heights reached in 1997 and with the number of mainland Chinese purchasers starting to decline, by the latter part of 2011 many analysts were warning that the situation had become unsustainable. Particular concern was expressed in relation to the position of first-time buyers, some of whom had borrowed excessively and thus placed themselves in an untenable situation.

Office rents in Hong Kong have been among the highest in the world since the 1970s, largely reflecting the city's competitive advantage, for which investors are often willing to pay a premium. According to a report released in March 2009 by Colliers International, a global real estate organization, Hong Kong occupied the top place among the world's cities in terms of the most expensive office accommodation in 2008, despite the decline in average rents for prime office space in that year. In tandem with the resurgence of commercial activities in 2010, office rental costs began to rise once more, as did shop rentals owing to increasing retail demand.

The resumption of the HOS scheme was announced by Chief Executive Donald Tsang in his 2011/12 Policy Address, delivered in October 2011. Tsang identified six major issues with regard to the residential property market: the difficulty of maintaining sufficient public rental housing; the escalation of private house prices beyond levels of affordability; the inadequate supply of suitable land; malpractice in the selling of properties; the ageing of buildings in Hong Kong's older urban areas; and the sub-division of units. With the intention of providing affordable homes to middle-income families, therefore, between 2016 and 2020 the Government planned to release for sale more than 17,000 apartments, at prices of betweeen HK $1.5m. and HK $2.0m. In addition to the resumption of the programme of subsidized sales, it was also announced that 75,000 public rental housing units would be completed within the next five years and made available to lower-income families.

EXTERNAL TRADE AND LOGISTICS

As a city economy with a large population, Hong Kong invariably relies heavily on its export and import trade. Trading and logistics activities remain the most important pillar industry in Hong Kong, but these were also badly affected by the impact of the global financial crisis of 2008/09. The ratio of the value of total exports to Hong Kong's GDP in 2008 was 1.68, while that of the value of imports to GDP was 1.80, emphasizing the importance of re-exports. In 2008 electrical machinery accounted for about one-quarter of Hong Kong's exports (including re-exports). The export of telecommunications equipment, office machines, clothing and chemicals is also significant.

Despite the difficult conditions of the recessionary period, Hong Kong's current account maintained a consistent surplus, although this decreased substantially, from US $29,494m. in 2008 to US $13,936m. in 2010. The value of total merchandise exports (including re-exports) declined from HK $2,824,151m. in 2008 to HK $2,469,089m. in 2009, but a strong recovery was recorded in 2010 when total export receipts reached HK $3,031,019m. Re-exports amounted to HK $2,411,347m. in 2009 and HK $2,961,507m. in 2010.

In the second quarter of 2011, however, there was a marked deceleration in trade in merchandise exports. Although this was partly due to the disruption of supply chains caused by the tsunami disaster and nuclear accident in Japan, slower growth in export demand elsewhere was also reported. Having decreased from HK $3,025,288m. in 2008 to HK $2,692,356m. in 2009, the cost of imports rose to HK $3,364,840m. in 2010. As imports of goods increased more quickly than exports, therefore, the visible trade deficit reached HK $125,600m. in the second quarter of 2011.

However, exports of services expanded more rapidly than imports of services. The value of exports of services was estimated to have increased by 24.6% in 2010, to reach HK $835.0m. In comparison with the corresponding period of the previous year, in real terms exports of services rose by 9.3% in the first quarter of 2011 and by 7.8% in the second quarter. In the second quarter of 2011 Hong Kong recorded a surplus of HK $19,6000m. on its balance of payments (equivalent to 4.4% of GDP), in comparison with a surplus of $18,700m. in the previous quarter.

Hong Kong's trade is orientated mainly towards China and the USA, although Singapore, Taiwan, Japan and the Republic of Korea (South Korea) are also important trading partners. The main destinations for Hong Kong's exports in 2010 were: mainland China (which purchased 52.7%), the USA, Japan, Germany, the United Kingdom, Singapore, Taiwan, India, South Korea and the Netherlands. In the same year Hong Kong's principal suppliers of imports were: mainland China (45.5%), Japan, Singapore, Taiwan, the USA, South Korea, Malaysia, Germany, Thailand and the Philippines.

Hong Kong is widely recognized as a strategic regional sourcing, supply chain management and logistics centre, notwithstanding concerns raised over the SAR's loss of competitiveness to such mainland ports as Shanghai and Yantian (in Guangdong Province). The transport and storage sector contracted considerably in 2008/09, as export trade weakened while shipping and aviation business stagnated. Cathay Pacific, one of the world's most successful airlines, lost HK $8,696m. in 2008, its first unprofitable year since 1998 (during the Asian financial crisis) and the carrier's first annual loss in its 63-year history. In 2009 Cathay Pacific's turnover declined by 22.6%, to reach HK $66,978m., and the carrier remained under great pressure, obliging it to take various measures to reduce operating costs and capital expenditure. These included the introduction of an unpaid leave scheme for staff, the reduction of capacity, thereby improving load factors, and the postponement of new deliveries from aircraft manufacturers. Cathay Pacific was able to register a profit of HK $4,694m. in 2009, rising to a record $14,048m. in 2010.

POPULATION AND EMPLOYMENT

In mid-2011 the population of Hong Kong was estimated at 7,120,200. The birth rate rose steadily during the first decade of the 21st century, increasing from 7.1 per 1,000 in 2002 to 12.5 per 1,000 in 2010. The number of births increased to 82,100 in 2009, rising to 88,600 in 2010. However, in recent years an increasing number of births have been to mothers from mainland China who had travelled to Hong Kong so that their babies would have the right of abode in the SAR (see below). Meanwhile, the number of deaths totalled an estimated 41,175 in 2009. Life expectancy in 2010 was estimated to have reached 80.0 years for men and 85.9 for women.

Hong Kong has a rapidly ageing population. The proportion of the population aged 65 years and over was projected to rise markedly, from 12% in 2006 to 26% in 2036, although the increase would be gradual until about 2016 (when the proportion was expected to reach 15%), accelerating to a much faster pace thereafter. Meanwhile, the proportion of the population aged under 15 was expected to decrease gradually, from 14% in 2006 to 12% by 2036. As a result, the tax base will be reduced, and the number of elderly, who will require more health care and will be more likely to need various forms of assistance, will continue to grow. Although the Government had implemented the Mandatory Provident Fund (MPF) in December 2000, it had become clear that many of the elderly would need further assistance.

The policy with regard to admitting foreign professionals to work in Hong Kong is very liberal. This is important if Hong Kong is to remain competitive as a global financial centre. However, Hong Kong is generally much stricter about immigration from the mainland. Of a total of 22,636 employment visas granted in 2006/07, only 5,296 were granted to mainland Chinese under the Admission Scheme for Mainland Talents and Professionals. The objective of this scheme, which was introduced in July 2003, was to fill obvious personnel needs in view of the increasing integration with the mainland. With effect from August 2001, mainland Chinese who had graduated from institutions funded by Hong Kong's University Grants Committee (UGC) in 1990 or afterwards, and who had received an offer of employment within Hong Kong, might be granted work visas. By the end of March 2007 a total of 1,078 mainland Chinese citizens had been admitted under this arrangement. From 2005/06 the policy of allowing non-local students to stay in Hong Kong to work was further liberalized and extended to holders of recognized degrees from non-UGC-funded institutions (see below).

Another programme intended to expand Hong Kong's talent pool was the Quality Migrant Admission Scheme, implemented in June 2006. Operating on a points-based system, there was no requirement to hold an offer of local employment before taking up residence in Hong Kong; all that was needed was the accumulation of sufficient merit points to secure one of a limited quota of places provided for under the scheme. Successful entrants could also bring in their spouse and unmarried dependent children below the age of 18. The scheme was intended to permit the entry of 1,000 'quality migrants' per year, but by 2008 hardly more than 700 such migrants had been admitted. After the onset of the global financial crisis in late 2008, there was a decline in the number of individuals migrating to Hong Kong who were skilled in finance. Despite a concomitant rise in the number of migrants working in the manufacturing industry, the total number of 'quality migrants' remained low. A further scheme offered resident status to those investing HK $6.5m. or more in the Hong Kong economy. Between October 2007 and March 2008 1,336 applications were received under this scheme; between October 2008 and March 2009 the number of applications declined to 1,124. The average amount of investment attributed to approved cases also declined over the same period, from HK $7.155m. to HK $6.995m.

These radical changes in policy were regarded as long overdue, as many of the mainland Chinese immigrants admitted to Hong Kong under the One-way Permit scheme were not well educated. This scheme provided for the admission of a daily quota of 150 mainlanders for family reunion reasons. Although the Hong Kong population consists predominantly of immigrants originally from the mainland, there had been a deep impression that recent immigrants from China were mostly welfare recipients who obtained undeserved benefits from the SAR Government at the expense of local people. This negative perception increased during the recession that resulted from the 1997/98 Asian financial crisis. Resentment towards mainlanders intensified when it emerged that many pregnant mainland Chinese women were travelling to Hong Kong expressly to give birth. Hong Kong-born babies have the right to live in the SAR and to receive free education. The number of babies born to mainland Chinese mothers began to rise sharply in 2006. Although non-locals had to pay much higher fees for care in a public hospital, the direct competition that they presented to local women for a place within a maternity ward, gave rise to considerable anger in Hong Kong. Furthermore, a sizeable number of these mainland mothers apparently left Hong Kong without paying their hospital bills. This prompted the authorities to change the rules. From February 2007 pregnant women from the mainland were required to pay HK $5,000 and book an appointment for their hospital care before being allowed to enter Hong Kong. Immigration officers were instructed to turn back any mainlander who appeared to be at least seven months pregnant and who did not have a pre-booked hospital appointment, or who had not already submitted payment. In October 2009, furthermore, the authorities suspended all maternity ward bookings for non-residents, a measure that remained in place until the following January. Nevertheless, in 2010 Hong Kong's birth rate reached a record level. In that year 45% of babies delivered in the SAR were born to mainland mothers, in comparison with 18% in 2002. In April 2011, in a further attempt to ease pressure on local medical facilities, additional measures were introduced by the Hong Kong authorities. These measures included action against illegal intermediaries and the imposition of annual quotas on the number of non-local women permitted to give birth in Hong Kong.

In order to address the shortage of skilled workers, in 2008 the Hong Kong Government introduced the Immigration Arrangements for Non-local Graduates, a scheme whereby non-local graduates who have obtained a degree or higher qualification in a full-time and locally accredited programme in Hong Kong are not required, for a six-month period after graduation, to secure an offer of employment upon application for an employment visa. After such time, non-local graduates may still apply for an employment visa, but need first to secure a job offer. With the number of non-local graduates rising, it was thought possible that the impending labour shortage might be alleviated.

When the economy entered recession, wages declined and some full-time workers were forced into part-time employment. The rate of unemployment increased from 3.6% of the work-force in 2008 to an estimated 5.4% in 2009. However, the level of unemployment decreased to 4.4% in 2010 and to 3.6% in the second quarter of 2011. Related to the problem of an ageing population is the possibility that in the medium to longer term Hong Kong may experience another labour shortage problem. With the generation of post-War 'baby boomers' approaching retirement by the end of the first decade of the 21st century, the number of retirees was expected to exceed the number of new entrants to the labour force. Upon the recovery of the Hong Kong economy, therefore, the attendant decline in the unemployment rate was expected by some analysts to lead to a severe labour shortage within just a few years.

Hong Kong is a major destination for foreign domestic helpers from around the region. Maids from the Philippines have traditionally dominated the market, but over the years Indonesian maids have become increasingly popular. Of the 223,394 foreign domestic helpers recorded in the city in 2005, 53% were from the Philippines and 43% from Indonesia. Hong Kong also imports significant numbers of Thai and Sri Lankan maids. From October 2003, however, employers of foreign domestic helpers were required to pay an Employees Retraining Levy of HK $400 per month for the entire contract period (HK $9,600) for each worker. Following the implementation of the levy, the Government reduced the minimum monthly wage applicable to such employees. As a result, there were various protests from the domestic helpers, who viewed the levy as an unfair tax on their labour.

Furthermore, in August 2011 a judicial review commenced in response to a legal challenge relating to the issue of permanent residency, instigated by a domestic worker from the Philippines. The Filipina maid had lived and worked in Hong Kong for 25 years but under a controversial legal provision was denied permanent residency, whereas other foreign workers were able to apply for permanent residency after seven years. The High Court's ruling at the end of September that the maid be permitted to apply for permanent residency was expected to have widespread repercussions. It was estimated that 120,000 such maids had lived and worked in Hong Kong for more than seven years. The Government announced its intention to appeal against the ruling, amid concerns that the granting of permanent residency to these large numbers of domestic workers would thereby permit them to bring their families to Hong Kong, thus placing additional strains on the SAR's housing and education facilities.

HOUSEHOLD POVERTY AND INCOME DISPARITY

With the onset of the global financial crisis in late 2008, unemployment rose across the world, and many Hong Kong workers who had been employed outside the SAR, the majority of them in Macao or on the mainland, lost their jobs and returned home. However, the Comprehensive Social Security Assistance (CSSA) scheme required at least one year of continuous residence in Hong Kong prior to the date of application. It was estimated that the number of such Hong Kong citizens unable to apply for CSSA as a result of this stipulation might total almost 30,000. While 1,502 people had been granted special exemption from this requirement in 2008, most were not so fortunate and, according to the Community Organization Association, the criteria for granting such exemptions were far from clear. As economic conditions continued to weaken in early 2009, the number of unemployment and low-income CSSA cases started to increase. By July 2010, however, these cases had declined to 31,379 in the former category and to 14,887 in the latter category.

With the recession deepening towards the end of 2008, household poverty in Hong Kong became a matter of even greater concern. According to the Census and Statistics Department, the number of households earning less than HK $4,000 a month had increased by 35,000 to reach 190,200 in the period November 2008–January 2009, as compared with the three months ending December 2008. The median household income decreased from HK $18,400 a month to HK $18,000. This was due in part to decreasing wages and in part to declining employment and working hours; fewer workers were employed and more workers were underemployed or working part-time. A study of pay trends conducted by the Pay Survey and Research Unit of the Joint Secretariat for the Advisory Bodies on Civil Service and Judicial Salaries and Conditions of Service found that average pay for employees in the surveyed companies between April 2008 and April 2009 declined by as much as 4.79% for the upper salary band and by 0.17%–1.34% for the lower and middle salary bands. These findings suggested a slight improvement in income disparity during the 2008/09 recession, with high-income earners appearing to bear the brunt of the wage reductions.

From the late 1990s evidence of growing income disparity began to increase. Some 31.6% of employees earned less than HK $8,000 a month in 2008, compared with 26.6% in 1998. On the other hand, 16.7% of employees earned more than HK $25,000 a month in 2008, compared with 13.4% in 1998. With the increasing disparity between rich and poor in Hong Kong thus becoming a major issue, the Government came under great pressure to introduce minimum wage legislation. Considering the statutory minimum wage to be the last resort, Chief Executive Donald Tsang announced in his Policy Address of October 2006 the launch of the Wage Protection Movement, whereby employers were to be persuaded to offer not less than the relevant average market rates as stipulated in the Census and Statistics Department's Quarterly Report of Wage and Payroll Statistics.

By 2008 it was widely acknowledged that the Wage Protection Movement had not been very effective, and in his 2008/09 Policy Address Tsang announced the intention to introduce a bill on a statutory across-the-board minimum wage. A Provisional Minimum Wage Commission was formed in February 2009 to advise the Chief Executive on the matter. The business sector hoped to postpone the legislative process, but the Government pressed ahead and in July 2010 the Minimum Wage Bill was approved by the Legislative Council. However, the Minimum Wage Commission did not immediately recommend the precise level of the statutory minimum wage, which remained the subject of much debate between employers' organizations and trades unions: the former demanded a rate of HK $24 per hour and the latter HK $33. An hourly rate of HK $28 was eventually set, and the legislation took effect in May 2011. The new law was likely to have the greatest impact on sectors such as catering, cleaning services and the security business. However, although intended to protect Hong Kong's most vulnerable workers from exploitation, critics argued that the legislation would distort the labour market and result in many job losses, which in turn would exert greater pressure on government programmes of unemployment insurance. The Minimum Wage Commission had estimated that as many as 40,000 jobs might be at risk and that about 1,700 enterprises might find it difficult to remain in profit. Furthermore, it was reported that some employers were attempting to circumvent the legislation by dismissing and re-engaging workers on new contracts whereby meal breaks and rest days were unpaid. Also, the legislation did not encompass domestic helpers, most of whom were from the Philippines and Indonesia.

INFRASTRUCTURE AND ENVIRONMENT

Several major projects were approved during 2007/08 that were expected substantially to accelerate the economic integration of Hong Kong with mainland China. One such project is the Hong Kong–Zhuhai–Macao Bridge, for which a financing agreement was reached in early 2007. Hong Kong was to be responsible for HK $6,750m. of the estimated total cost of HK $37,800m. Work on the project began in late 2009; however, the instigation of a legal challenge to the project appeared likely to jeopardize the originally scheduled completion date of 2016. Spanning almost 50 km and comprising a six-lane expressway, the bridge will greatly improve cargo flows to the container ports and the airport in Hong Kong. It was also expected to promote tourism across the three territories, as well as facilitate cultural and business exchanges. Meanwhile, the construction of a third runway at Hong Kong International Airport was under consideration in 2011.

A major railway project is a high-speed line to connect Hong Kong to Guangzhou. With construction scheduled for completion by 2015, the Guangzhou–Shenzhen–Hong Kong Express Rail Link will halve the journey time between Guangzhou and Hong Kong to just 48 minutes, while travel time between Shenzhen and Hong Kong will be reduced to a mere 14 minutes. Ultimately, the high-speed train will be able to travel from Hong Kong to Beijing in just 10 hours, reduced from about 24 hours. The publicly listed MTR Corporation of Hong Kong was to design, build and operate the Hong Kong section of the line, and it was to share the revenues with the Government. The new railway line will feed into the current Airport Express tracks and then branch off to a new terminus in West Kowloon. A 23-minute train journey will connect the Shenzhen airport with the Hong Kong International Airport, thereby allowing the latter to enter the Chinese market for passengers flying overseas. Some 120,000 passengers were expected to be using the service each day by 2030. The MTR Corporation inaugurated the Kowloon Southern Link service in August 2009, connecting the West Rail Line Nam Cheong Station with the East Rail Line East Tsim Sha Tsui Station, eventually ending in Hunghom where passengers will be able to transfer to the East Rail Line to form a complete loop.

Various other rail projects have been approved, including: the South Island Line, the Sha Tin–Central Link (to be completed between 2015 and 2019), the Hong Kong section of the Guangzhou–Shenzhen–Hong Kong Express Rail Link and the Northern Link. Construction of an extension to the West Island Line from Sheung Wan to Kennedy Town was ongoing. Upon completion of these rail links, Hong Kong's rail network would expand to over 270 km and the railways' share of the public transport system would be increased from 35% to about 40%. All of these projects were under the remit of the MTR Corporation, which took over the operations of the Kowloon–Canton Railway Corporation in December 2007. The merger facilitated transfers from one system to the other and resulted in a modest reduction in fares.

In an attempt to solve the increasing problem of road congestion on Hong Kong Island, in May 2009 the Chief Executive in Council gave approval for the controversial Central–Wanchai Bypass and the Wanchai Development Phase II projects. The Secretary for Development, Carrie Lam Cheung, stressed that the Government had made every effort to minimize the area to be reclaimed under the projects. The Government contended that the early completion of the bypass had the strong endorsement of the relevant District Councils on Hong Kong Island.

Since the mid-1990s Hong Kong has reconstructed its sewage treatment and disposal system under the Strategic Sewage Disposal Scheme. The Environment Protection Department reported that in 2007 the water quality at Hong Kong's beaches was the best on record. As regards air quality, as early as 1990 Hong Kong introduced a regulation that limited the sulphur content of industrial fuel. This led to an almost immediate decline in sulphur dioxide levels in the atmosphere. Other measures, such as more stringent fuel and vehicle emission standards and stricter enforcement of existing rules against vehicles with excessive emissions, also proved effective in reducing pollution from vehicle traffic. Roadside concentrations of the major air pollutant emissions from vehicles, namely respirable suspended particulates and nitrogen oxides, were reduced by 15% and 24%, respectively, between 1999 and 2007. Additional measures were adopted in 2007 and 2008 to strengthen the reduction of vehicle emissions. The Hong Kong and Guangdong Governments were also discussing a possible emission trading scheme to reduce the total amount of emissions within the Pearl River Delta region.

EXCHANGE RATES AND CONSUMER PRICES

Ever since the Hong Kong dollar was linked to the US dollar in October 1983, the Hong Kong economy has experienced severe oscillations, 'overheating' when the US dollar has been weak and experiencing recessionary conditions when the US dollar has been strong. Towards the end of 2008, as the financial market turmoil reached its height, the US dollar suddenly strengthened, reflecting an aversion towards risk. The strength of the US dollar was a factor in the reduction of inflation in 2009, but this was damaging to Hong Kong's exports, a plight compounded by the appreciation of the yuan against the US dollar. The strength of the yuan exacerbated the decline in overseas markets, thereby severely weakening the position of manufacturing concerns in the Pearl River Delta and other parts of China. Tens of thousands of factories failed, many of which were owned by Hong Kong citizens, and hundreds of thousands of migrant workers from poorer rural parts of China were forced to return home.

The mainland Government was well aware of the potential damage that a strong currency might cause to the economy and appeared to act to halt any further appreciation of the yuan. For several months the yuan was apparently pegged to the US dollar at an unofficial level of around 6.836 yuan to the US dollar. Since this was the case regardless of the strength or weakness of the US dollar, the notion that the yuan was tied to a basket of currencies, rather than to the US dollar, lost credibility. Seemingly owing to political pressures, the People's Bank of China (the mainland's central bank) opted not to allow the yuan to depreciate against the US dollar when the latter was strong, even though it prevented the yuan's rise when the US dollar was weak. The strength of both the yuan and the US dollar represented a double set-back to Hong Kong's economy in the final quarter of 2008 and the first quarter of 2009.

With the US dollar at a high point in April 2009 and subsequently entering into decline, evidently reflecting a reduction in risk aversion, the yuan actually depreciated noticeably against a basket of currencies, benefiting the trade sector and also Hong Kong. China confronts a clear dilemma: a strong US dollar would preserve the value of its reserve assets but, given the implicit link, would also indicate a strong yuan, which would undermine the competitiveness of Chinese exports. On the other hand, a weak US dollar that also brings down the exchange value of the yuan against other currencies would help to boost exports, but would erode the value of China's foreign-exchange reserves.

With the yuan implicitly tied to the US dollar and the Hong Kong dollar explicitly pegged to the US currency, the yuan and the Hong Kong dollar behave very much as if in one currency area. In 2011 the Hong Kong Government thus came under renewed pressure to review the currency peg to the US dollar. Although the arrangement had provided a large degree of stability, critics claimed that the SAR's effective lack of monetary independence, combined with the low level of interest rates that had prevailed in the USA and elsewhere in recent years, continued to have a negative impact on the Hong Kong economy.

The appreciation of the Chinese yuan against the US dollar, and thus also the Hong Kong dollar, compounded inflationary pressures in the SAR. By the beginning of 2008 the rate of inflation had reached 5%, and the economy showed clear signs of 'overheating'. However, inflationary pressures subsequently moderated, with the CPI rising by 4.3% in 2008 as a whole. The consumer price index declined sharply, by 6.4%, in 2009. Following this period of deflation, consumer prices rose by 2.4% in 2010. In early 2011, with inflationary pressures having re-emerged, partly as a result of increasing prices for essential commodities, the Government confirmed its intention to diversify the sources of Hong Kong's imports of food (domestic production being negligible). In comparison with the same month of the previous year, in July 2011 the annual rate of inflation, as measured by the composite consumer price index, reached 7.9%, before declining to 5.7% in August.

RELATIONS WITH MAINLAND CHINA

The opening up of China to the world in 1979 led to a new phase in Hong Kong's economic restructuring. Many manufacturing firms started to relocate to southern China, where costs were lower. The decline of Hong Kong's manufacturing sector has been dramatic: in 1987 some 875,932 people worked in the sector; by 1997 the number had decreased to 306,510; and by the end of 2008 only 149,957 workers out of a labour force of more than 3.68m. (about 4%) were employed in manufacturing. Yet it would be wrong to conclude that manufacturing is not important for the Hong Kong economy. Instead of carrying out processing locally, manufacturing operations have moved north into the Pearl River Delta region and have in fact expanded considerably. Today, Hong Kong manufacturers employ more than 5m. workers in the Pearl River Delta region, compared with fewer than 1m. in the 1980s. This 'outward processing activity' has led to a surge in related trade. For example, in 2007 35% of Hong Kong's total exports to mainland China were for outward processing; the corresponding figures for domestic exports and re-exports were 47% and 34%, respectively, while 59% of Hong Kong's imports from mainland China were related to outward processing; some 78% of Hong Kong's 2007 re-exports of mainland origin to other destinations were also produced through outward processing in the mainland. Generally speaking, re-exports have grown quite rapidly in recent years, while domestic exports have increased much more slowly. In this connection, a distinction should be made between re-exports and transshipments: the former usually carry a value-added content of over 20% attributable to Hong Kong, while the latter provide negligible value added, if any.

From the late 1980s, and increasingly in the 1990s, mainland China started investing heavily in Hong Kong across a wide spectrum of industries, in particular wholesale, trade and retail, business services, transport and related services, finance and banking, construction, architectural and civil engineering, and manufacturing. At the end of 2004 the cumulative value of the mainland's investment in Hong Kong exceeded US $130,000m., or 29% of Hong Kong's total externally owned capital stock. At the same time, Hong Kong has been the mainland's largest source of realized foreign direct investment (FDI), accounting for about 40% of the national total, with a cumulative value of HK $2,398,500m. (US $307,500m.) at the end of 2007. While the cumulative total of Hong Kong's investment in mainland China is greater than that of the mainland in Hong Kong, since the turn of the century the flow of FDI into Hong Kong from the mainland is thought to be at least equal to Hong Kong FDI flows into the mainland. Mainland China was the largest source of inward direct investment in Hong Kong. At the end of 2006 the cumulative value of such investment was estimated at HK $2,024,300m. (US $260,400m.), accounting for 35% of Hong Kong's total stock.

The appreciation of the Chinese yuan has been a major issue for Hong Kong's manufacturers that have operations in the Pearl River Delta. Furthermore, Hong Kong's position as a leading business centre is being increasingly challenged Shanghai. Located in the estuaries of the River Yangtze (Changjiang) in the heartland of mainland China, Shanghai has developed excellent infrastructure, including, inter alia, a highly efficient container port, a new airport and the world's first magnetic levitation train. Hong Kong's main advantage over Shanghai lies in its well-respected legal system, its strong governance and supervisory mechanisms, and its reputation as being relatively free from corruption. In January 2009 the HKEx and Shanghai Stock Exchange signed a Closer Co-operation Agreement, which committed the two exchanges to working together more closely, raising funds for the continued development of Chinese enterprises and contributing to the greater development of China's economy. In March 2010 it was reported that, in terms of GDP, the economy of Shanghai had surpassed that of Hong Kong in 2009; that of the Chinese city increased by 8.2% in relation to 2008 to reach US $218,300m., while the SAR contracted by 2.7% to US $210,700m.

Inflows of Chinese yuan into Hong Kong have continued to show strong expansion. According to the HKMA, in January 2011 local deposits totalled 370,600m. yuan, representing a six-fold increase in comparison with November 2009. In an attempt to make its currency more widely available on international markets and to reduce its dependence on the US dollar, China has permitted the development of yuan-denominated financial markets in Hong Kong. The sale in Hong Kong of yuan-denominated debt securities, known as 'dim sum' bonds, has proved popular with investors, and in 2010 bonds totalling 36,000m. yuan were issued by corporate institutions and banks. In April 2011 the release on the HKEx of a yuan-denominated initial public offering (IPO), the first such sale of shares on a stock exchange outside mainland China, proved disappointing when the sale of shares in Hui Xian, a property investment trust controlled by Hong Kong magnate Li Ka-shing, attracted much less interest than anticipated. However, some observers attributed the lack of interest to wider global issues, such as European sovereign debt concerns.

Closer Economic Partnership Arrangement

Hong Kong and China signed into agreement the Closer Economic Partnership Arrangement (CEPA) in June 2003, followed by six annexes to the accord in September of that year. Specific liberalization measures were set out in six supplements, which were signed between October 2004 and May 2009. Supplement VI to CEPA contained a total of 29 liberalization measures, covering 20 service sectors, including 18 existing CEPA service sectors and two new service sectors (see below). As a result, the total number of service sectors covered by CEPA was to expand from 40 to 42. Both sides also agreed to enhance financial co-operation and consolidate progress made with regard to mutual recognition of professional qualifications. CEPA was intended progressively to reduce, and in some case eliminate, tariff barriers in the trade of exports and services between Hong Kong and the mainland. According to the Department of Industry and Trade, a total of 42,751 Certificates of Hong Kong Origin had been approved under CEPA as of March 2009, of which 1,303 certificates were issued to Hong Kong service suppliers, focusing mainly on distribution, advertising, and logistics and transport.

Along with the Individual Visit Scheme, CEPA was widely regarded as a concession from China and some argued that it was the primary stimulant for Hong Kong's economic recovery in mid-2003. However, given the fact that any investment or new business ventures under CEPA could not have begun in 2003 or even in early 2004, these attributions had little empirical support. Under CEPA, residents of all of the 21 cities in the Guangdong Province and 23 other cities, including the capital Beijing, and Shanghai, were allowed to visit Hong Kong on an individual basis. From 2007 the scheme was further extended to five more cities, namely Shijiazhuang, Zhengzhou, Changchun, Hefei and Wuhan. Although the scheme brought in many more tourists from the mainland, it was unlikely to have a material effect on the economy, owing to the relatively minor contribution of tourism to Hong Kong's GDP.

Reform and Development of the Pearl River Delta

In January 2009 the National Development and Reform Commission released The Outline of the Plan for the Reform and Development of the Pearl River Delta for 2008–20. The Hong Kong and Macao SAR Governments, as well as the Guangdong provincial government, took the matter very seriously. A Liaison and Co-ordinating Meeting was held in Hong Kong in February. At the meeting, the three governments agreed: to establish a liaison and co-ordinating meeting mechanism; to confirm that the principal areas of co-operation among Hong Kong, Guangdong and Macao would include finance, industry (with strategic areas including the services industry, tourism, innovation technology, etc.), infrastructure and town-planning, environmental protection, as well as education and training; to conduct jointly specialized topical studies on regional co-operation; and to confirm the major co-operation initiatives jointly taken forward by Hong Kong, Guangdong and Macao. There had been eight recent major co-operation initiatives, including infrastructural and transport arrangements, which aimed to improve the three areas' connectivity, as well as agreements on greater co-ordination of regional development, town-planning, tourism and environmental protection.

The Chinese Government announced in December 2008 that trade between Hong Kong and Macao, and also between Guangdong and the Yangtze River Delta, could be settled in yuan-denominated payments. At the same time, the trade of member states of the Association of Southeast Asian Nations (ASEAN) with China's

Guangxi region and Yunnan Province could be settled in yuan, on a trial basis. These arrangements were intended to reduce exchange risks for traders, and over the longer term may threaten the role of the US dollar as the primary means of settlement, while promoting the internationalization of the Chinese currency. In June 2010, following the release in Hong Kong of the first yuan sovereign bond issue in the previous year, the HKMA announced that the SAR's banks were to be permitted to sell yuan-denominated investment products such as securities and insurance.

OTHER REGIONAL ECONOMIC RELATIONS

Hong Kong's economic relations with Taiwan have also expanded. The election of Hong Kong-born Ma Ying-jeou to the presidency of Taiwan in 2008 was seen to offer a unique opportunity to forge closer relations. Reflecting improved relations across the Taiwan Strait, the Hong Kong Secretary for Home Affairs, Tsang Tak-sing, led a delegation to the Second World Buddhist Forum, held jointly in the Chinese city of Wuxi and Taipei, in March–April 2009. The historic visit to Taiwan was the first by a senior Hong Kong government official. The Hong Kong Secretary for Constitutional and Mainland Affairs, Stephen Lam, stated that the SAR Government maintained a positive and pro-active attitude towards promoting Hong Kong-Taiwan exchanges and relations. In early June Lam visited Taipei at the invitation of the Taiwanese Mainland Affairs Council to discuss further enhancement of bilateral relations. Furthermore, in May the SFC signed an agreement with the Taiwanese authorities preparing the way for the mutual launch of Exchange Traded Funds (ETFs) in the stock exchanges of Hong Kong and Taipei. Financial Secretary John Tsang expressed the wish that ETFs from Hong Kong and Taiwan might soon be listed in both exchanges, and that further financial market bilateral co-operation might ensue.

Hong Kong is a favoured destination for FDI. Most of the investment has come from the Chinese mainland, the Asia-Pacific region (notably Japan and Australasia), Western Europe and North America, covering various sectors but primarily services, reflecting the nature of Hong Kong's economy, and including consumer products, retail and sourcing, business and professional services, and technology. In 2007 a total of 47 mainland companies established or expanded their businesses in Hong Kong. Total inflows of FDI were reported to have increased from US $52,394m. in 2009 to US $68,903m. in 2010. Hong Kong is also an important provider of FDI in the region and beyond. Traditionally, Hong Kong's investment has been concentrated in the Pearl River Delta area. However, with costs having risen, firms are increasingly moving further inland, while many others are preferring instead to invest in Viet Nam, Thailand and Cambodia.

Hong Kong has been a member of the Asia-Pacific Economic Cooperation (APEC) organization since 1991, and has been very supportive of countries in the region, many of which, particularly Japan, Thailand and South Korea, are popular with Hong Kong residents as tourist destinations. Following its transfer to Chinese sovereignty in 1997 Hong Kong remained a separate customs territory, within the World Trade Organization, which it joined in 1995.

CONCLUSION

The challenge posed by Shanghai notwithstanding, Hong Kong continues further to integrate with mainland China: physically, through additional and better transport links; and financially, through yuan settlement and the issuance of yuan-denominated bonds in Hong Kong. While there is no immediate prospect of the financial market 'through train' allowing mainland investors to open accounts for direct trading in Hong Kong shares, the expectation that Hong Kong ETFs will at some stage trade in Shanghai offers hope of a second channel for mainland investors to invest in the Hong Kong stock market. in the longer term, Hong Kong is expected to co-operate closely with Shanghai to enhance both the depth and the breadth of the Chinese financial markets.

Although Hong Kong was clearly not immune to the global financial crisis of 2008/09, in comparison with many of its regional counterparts (with the notable exception of mainland China) the SAR's economy withstood the difficulties of that period relatively well. Hong Kong's banks remained profitable, at a time when most banks were recording significant losses. Although the housing market contracted, the scale of the problem was minimal in relation to that experienced in 1998–2003. Recovery swiftly commenced, leading to renewed concerns about the unsustainable nature of the housing market. However, in contrast to the dramatic collapse of the housing market witnessed in 1998, any correction in property prices from the latter part of 2011 appeared likely to be gradual, while interest rates remained low and while the authorities' stricter borrowing criteria remained in place.

It was estimated that as many as 100,000 residents of the SAR were living in inadequate accommodation, and the results of a survey released by the University of Hong Kong in July 2011 indicated that popular dissatisfaction with the Government in relation to conditions of livelihood had reached its highest level for nearly 20 years. With many citizens encountering increasing difficulty in meeting their basic living costs, social discontent in Hong Kong was reported to be rising rapidly. In October the SAR's Chief Executive identified the wealth gap, the state of the housing market and the ageing of the population as the issues of greatest public concern. Various measures to address the problems of the residential property market were announced.

If Hong Kong cannot offer an attractive living environment to highly skilled professionals and senior managers, it will not be able to recruit or retain the personnel needed by the financial services industry. There has been a determined attempt by concerned citizens to prevent the 'concrete jungle' from further encroaching upon country parks. If Hong Kong is to continue to prosper as a global financial centre, it must preserve its parks and improve its air quality. If land costs were to rise even further because of the need for conservation and preservation, the prognosis for the re-establishment of low-cost manufacturing in Hong Kong would be even less promising. Although some high-technology industries have been established, such industries cannot offer many jobs to local workers. Therefore, the SAR's character as a service economy will not change in the foreseeable future, and the Hong Kong economy remains fundamentally sound.

Statistical Survey

Source (unless otherwise stated): Census and Statistics Department, 19/F, Wanchai Tower, 12 Harbour Rd, Hong Kong; tel. 25825073; fax 28271708; e-mail gen-enquiry@censtatd.gov.hk; internet www.censtatd.gov.hk.

Area and Population

AREA, POPULATION AND DENSITY

Land area (sq km)	1,104*
Population (census and by-census results)†	
15 March 2001	6,708,389
14 July 2006	
Males	3,272,956
Females	3,591,390
Total	6,864,346
Usual residents	6,645,220
Present at census	6,416,124
Absent at census	229,096
Mobile residents	219,126
Present at census	43,632
Absent at census	175,494
Population (official estimates at mid-year)	
2009	7,003,700
2010	7,063,300
2011	7,120,200
Density (per sq km) at mid-2011	6,449.5

* 426 sq miles.

† All residents (including mobile residents) on the census date, including those who were temporarily absent from Hong Kong. In 2006 the census recorded population by place of birth as follows: Hong Kong 4,138,844, China (other than Hong Kong) 2,298,956, Other 426,546.

POPULATION BY AGE AND SEX
('000, official estimates at mid-2011)

	Males	Females	Total
0–14	430.9	403.0	833.8
15–64	2,456.8	2,892.0	5,348.8
65 and over	434.3	503.4	937.7
Total	3,321.9	3,798.3	7,120.2

Note: Totals may not be equal to the sum of components, owing to rounding.

DISTRICTS AND DISTRICT COUNCILS
(2006 census)

	Area (sq km)*	Population	Density (per sq km)†
Hong Kong Island	80.47	1,268,112	15,759
Central and Western	—	250,064	20,102
Wanchai	—	155,196	15,788
Eastern	—	587,690	31,664
Southern	—	275,162	7,083
Kowloon	46.93	2,019,533	43,033
Yau Tsim Mong	—	280,548	40,136
Sham Shui Po	—	365,540	39,095
Kowloon City	—	362,501	36,178
Wong Tai Sin	—	423,521	45,540
Kwun Tong	—	587,423	52,123
New Territories	976.57	3,573,635	3,659
Kwai Tsing	—	523,300	22,421
Tsuen Wan	—	288,728	4,679
Tuen Mun	—	502,035	6,057
Yuen Long	—	534,192	3,858
North	—	280,730	2,055
Tai Po	—	293,542	2,156
Sha Tin	—	607,544	8,842
Sai Kung	—	406,442	3,135
Islands	—	137,122	783
Total	1,103.97	6,864,346‡	6,218

* Data at 31 December 2006.
† Data for district councils are not strictly comparable with the district aggregates and the territory total as calculations were based on area distribution at mid-2006.
‡ Including marine population (3,066).

PRINCIPAL TOWNS
(population at 1996 census)

Kowloon*	1,988,515	Tai Po	271,661
Victoria (capital)	1,011,433	Tseun Wan	268,659
Tuen Mun	445,771	Sheung Shui	192,321
Sha Tin	445,383	Tsing Yu	185,495
Kwai Chung	285,231	Aberdeen	164,439

* Including New Kowloon.

BIRTHS, MARRIAGES AND DEATHS
(numbers rounded to nearest 100 persons)

	Known live births*		Registered marriages*		Known deaths	
	Number	Rate (per 1,000)	Number	Rate (per 1,000)	Number	Rate (per 1,000)
2003	47,000	6.9	35,400	5.2	36,971	5.4
2004	49,800	7.2	41,400	6.0	36,918	5.3
2005	57,100	8.4	43,000	6.3	38,830	5.7
2006	65,600	9.6	50,300	7.3	37,457	5.5
2007	70,900	10.2	47,500	6.8	39,476	5.7
2008	78,800	11.3	47,300	6.8	41,796	6.0
2009	82,100	11.7	51,200	7.3	41,175	5.7
2010	88,600	12.5	52,600	7.4	n.a.	n.a.

* Numbers are rounded to the nearest 100 persons.

Life expectancy (years at birth, 2010, provisional): Males 80.0; Females 85.9.

ECONOMICALLY ACTIVE POPULATION
('000 persons aged 15 years and over, excl. armed forces)

	2006	2007	2008
Agriculture and fishing	8.2	6.4	8.3
Manufacturing	216.9	202.4	191.2
Electricity, gas and water	14.6	15.2	14.1
Construction	269.2	274.7	268.6
Wholesale, retail and import/export trades, restaurants and hotels	1,104.8	1,143.8	1,145.5
Transport, storage and communications	369.2	372.2	377.9
Financing, insurance, real estate and business services	525.7	548.0	580.0
Community, social and personal services	892.1	921.1	933.1
Total employed	3,400.8	3,483.8	3,518.8
Unemployed	171.1	145.7	130.1
Total labour force	3,571.9	3,629.5	3,648.9
Males	1,950.6	1,958.2	1,949.4
Females	1,621.2	1,671.3	1,699.5

Source: ILO.

2009 (million persons aged 15 years and over, excl. armed forces): Total employed 3.48; Unemployed 0.2; Total labour force 3.68 (Source: Asian Development Bank).

Health and Welfare

KEY INDICATORS

Total fertility rate (children per woman*, 2004)	0.9
Under-5 mortality rate (per 1,000 live births, provisional, 2007)	1.6
HIV/AIDS (% of persons aged 15–49, 2003)	0.1
Physicians (per 1,000 head, provisional, 2007)†	1.7
Hospital beds (per 1,000 head, provisional, 2007)	5.0
Total carbon dioxide emissions ('000 metric tons, 2006)	39,010.6
Carbon dioxide emissions per head (metric tons, 2006)	5.7
Human Development Index (2010): ranking	21
Human Development Index (2010): value	0.862

* Excluding female domestic helpers.
† Excluding practitioners of Chinese medicine.

For sources and definitions, see explanatory note on p. vi.

Agriculture

PRINCIPAL CROPS
('000 metric tons, FAO estimates)

	2000	2001	2002
Lettuce	5	5	5
Spinach	11	11	11
Onions and shallots (green)	4	4	4
Other vegetables	24	14	34
Fruit	4	4	4

2003–04: Figures assumed to be unchanged from 2001 (FAO estimates).

2005–09: Separate data not available for Hong Kong (see the chapter on the People's Republic of China).

Source: FAO.

Total vegetables ('000 metric tons): 25 in 2005; 21 in 2006; 19 in 2007 (Source: Asian Development Bank).

LIVESTOCK
('000 head unless otherwise indicated, year ending September, FAO estimates)

	2002	2003	2004
Cattle (head)	1,500	1,500	1,500
Pigs	100	100	100
Chickens	1,000	1,000	1,000
Ducks	250	230	250

2005–09: Separate data for Hong Kong not available (see the chapter on the People's Republic of China).

Source: FAO.

LIVESTOCK PRODUCTS
('000 metric tons)

	2002	2003	2004
Beef and veal*	14	13	13
Pig meat*	147	145	194
Poultry meat	61	58	29
Game meat†	6	6	6
Cattle hides (fresh)†	2	2	2

* Unofficial figures.
† FAO estimates.

2005–09: Separate data for Hong Kong not available (see the chapter on the People's Republic of China).

Source: FAO.

Chicken meat ('000 metric tons): 21 in 2005; 17 in 2006; 13 in 2007 (Source: Asian Development Bank).

Fishing

('000 metric tons, live weight)

	2007	2008	2009
Capture*	154.1	158.1	159.0
Lizardfishes*	5.7	5.9	5.9
Threadfin breams*	16.6	17.0	17.1
Shrimps and prawns*	4.6	4.7	4.7
Squids*	7.2	7.4	7.4
Aquaculture	4.5	4.8	4.8
Total catch*	158.7	162.9	163.8

* FAO estimates.

Source: FAO.

Industry

SELECTED PRODUCTS
('000 metric tons unless otherwise indicated)

	2005	2006	2007
Cotton yarn (other than sewing thread)	62.2	70.5	39.8
Cotton woven fabrics (million sq m)	199.8	n.a	n.a.
Women's and girls' blouses ('000)	29,706.0	2,077.0	7,401.0
Women's and girls' dresses, not knitted or crocheted ('000)	2,609.0	n.a.	n.a.
Women's and girls' skirts, slacks and shorts ('000)	43,426.0	83,756.0	45,504.0
Men's or boys' shirts, not knitted or crocheted ('000)	72,360.0	5,702.0	21,052.0
Watches ('000)	6,099.0	9,455.0	5,029.0

2008: Women's and girls' blouses ('000) 2,011.0; Women's and girls' skirts, slacks and shorts ('000) 42,922.0; Men's or boys' shirts, not knitted or crocheted ('000) 7,627.0.

Uncooked macaroni and noodle products (instant macaroni and noodles only, '000 metric tons): 62 in 2001; 20 in 2002; 99 in 2003.

Knitted sweaters ('000): 151,965 in 2001; 113,685 in 2002; 143,143 in 2003.

Men's and boys' jackets ('000): 1,838 in 2001; 1,285 in 2002; 1,087 in 2003.

Men's and boys' trousers ('000): 14,139 in 2001; 22,696 in 2002; 11,293 in 2003.

Source: UN, *Industrial Commodity Statistics Yearbook* and Industrial Commodity Statistics Database.

Cement ('000 metric tons): 1,005 in 2005; 1,255 in 2006; 1,300 in 2007 (Source: Asian Development Bank).

Electric energy (million kWh): 38,948 in 2007; 37,990 in 2008; 38,728 in 2009 (Source: Asian Development Bank).

Finance

CURRENCY AND EXCHANGE RATES

Monetary Units

100 cents = 1 Hong Kong dollar (HK $).

Sterling, US Dollar and Euro Equivalents (31 May 2011)

£1 sterling = HK $13.221;
US $1 = HK $8.011;
€1 = HK $11.524;
HK $100 = £7.56 = US $12.48 = €8.68.

Average Exchange Rate (HK $ per US $)

2008 7.7868
2009 7.7518
2010 7.7692

BUDGET
(HK $ million, year ending 31 March)

Revenue	2007/08	2008/09	2009/10
Direct taxes:			
Earnings and profits tax	133,729	146,143	123,184
Indirect taxes:			
Bets and sweeps tax	13,048	12,620	12,767
Duties on petroleum products, beverages, tobacco and cosmetics	7,059	6,047	6,465
General rates (property tax)	9,495	7,175	9,957
Motor vehicle taxes	5,553	4,981	4,816
Royalties and concessions	863	2,389	1,596
Others (stamp duties, hotel accommodation tax and air passenger departure tax)	53,670	34,011	44,000
Fines, forfeitures and penalties	997	1,006	1,183
Receipts from properties and investments	11,552	12,483	12,601
Loans, reimbursements, contributions and other receipts	2,826	3,305	3,277

Revenue—*continued*	2007/08	2008/09	2009/10
Operating revenue from utilities	3,344	3,320	3,438
Fees and charges	12,297	10,470	10,487
Investment income:			
General revenue account	12,005	23,352	17,893
Land Fund	9,876	14,183	11,196
Capital Works Reserve Fund (land sales and interest)	66,377	23,155	41,877
Capital Investment Fund	2,207	1,917	1,232
Loan Fund	2,098	2,101	2,276
Other capital revenue	11,469	7,904	10,197
Total government revenue	358,465	316,562	318,442

Expenditure	2007/08	2008/09	2009/10
Operating expenditure	204,734	258,007	234,367
Recurrent expenditure	120,331	129,745	134,669
Personal emoluments	46,658	49,726	50,794
Pensions	14,736	15,700	16,911
Departmental expenses	18,079	19,312	20,740
Other recurrent expenditure	40,858	45,007	46,224
Subventions	79,115	84,374	86,511
Education	26,518	28,465	29,195
Health	29,345	31,323	32,422
Universities and polytechnics	11,534	11,711	11,476
Other subventions	11,718	12,875	13,418
Non-recurrent operating expenditure	5,288	43,888	13,187
Capital expenditure	30,081	57,105	58,158
Plant, equipment and works	1,033	1,134	1,415
Subventions	1,252	1,303	1,454
Capital Works Reserve Fund	23,065	50,719	51,582
Loan fund	3,053	2,240	2,150
Other funds	1,678	1,709	1,557
Total government expenditure	234,815	315,112	292,525

INTERNATIONAL RESERVES

(US $ million at 31 December)

	2008	2009	2010
Gold (national valuation)	58	74	94
Foreign exchange*	182,469	255,768	268,649
Total	182,527	255,842	268,743

* Including the foreign-exchange reserves of the Hong Kong Special Administrative Region Government's Land Fund.

Source: IMF, *International Financial Statistics*.

MONEY SUPPLY

(HK $ '000 million at 31 December)

	2008	2009	2010
Currency outside banks	170.2	194.1	218.6
Demand deposits at banking institutions	265.1	391.1	420.4
Total money	435.3	585.2	639.0

Source: IMF, *International Financial Statistics*.

COST OF LIVING

(Consumer Price Index; base: 2000 = 100)

	2006	2007	2008
Food	100.1	104.4	115.0
Housing	86.4	88.1	91.7
Electricity, gas and other fuels	109.6	108.8	101.7
Clothing and footwear	102.5	106.8	107.7
All items (incl. others)	95.5	97.4	101.6

2009: Food 114.1; All items (incl. others) 95.1.

Source: ILO.

NATIONAL ACCOUNTS

(HK $ million at current prices)

Expenditure on the Gross Domestic Product

	2008	2009	2010
Government final consumption expenditure	139,262	142,853	147,209
Private final consumption expenditure	1,022,862	1,012,790	1,085,268
Change in stocks	8,480	22,899	38,945
Gross fixed capital formation	334,352	322,772	374,586
Total domestic expenditure	1,504,956	1,501,314	1,646,008
Exports of goods and services	3,562,628	3,164,575	3,888,108
Less Imports of goods and services	3,390,573	3,043,567	3,790,258
GDP in purchasers' values	1,677,011	1,622,322	1,743,858

Gross Domestic Product by Economic Activity

	2007	2008	2009
Agriculture, fishing, mining and quarrying	1,015	925	1,090
Manufacturing	31,729	30,993	28,227
Electricity, gas and water	40,685	39,585	34,961
Construction	40,611	48,357	50,146
Wholesale, retail and import/export trades, restaurants and hotels	423,441	447,510	414,667
Transport, storage and communications	170,601	146,503	145,856
Financing, insurance, real estate and business services	451,326	421,180	409,164
Community, social and personal services	254,391	269,601	279,453
Ownership of premises	166,352	188,244	187,286
Gross domestic product at factor cost	1,580,148	1,592,897	1,550,851
Taxes on production and imports	64,634	59,919	55,967
Statistical discrepancy	–29,208	24,195	15,504
GDP in purchasers' values	1,615,574	1,677,011	1,622,322

BALANCE OF PAYMENTS

(US $ million)

	2008	2009	2010
Exports of goods f.o.b.	365,236	321,836	394,015
Imports of goods f.o.b.	–388,353	–348,698	–436,980
Trade balance	–23,117	–26,862	–42,965
Exports of services	92,292	86,411	106,432
Imports of services	–47,062	–44,939	–50,869
Balance on goods and services	22,113	15,610	12,598
Other income received	118,546	100,773	116,536
Other income paid	–107,845	–95,243	–111,829
Balance on goods, services and income	32,814	21,139	17,305
Current transfers received	611	469	614
Current transfers paid	–3,931	–3,646	–3,983
Current balance	29,494	17,963	13,936
Capital account (net)	2,105	4,671	5,233
Direct investment abroad	–50,549	–63,994	–76,093
Direct investment from abroad	59,614	52,395	68,915
Portfolio investment assets	–25,353	–52,086	–66,663
Portfolio investment liabilities	–12,799	9,197	5,791
Financial derivatives assets	68,601	48,542	35,215
Financial derivatives liabilities	–60,474	–45,373	–31,462
Other investment assets	46,105	97,012	–63,297
Other investment liabilities	–23,006	454	113,823
Net errors and omissions	209	2,080	3,759
Overall balance	33,948	70,860	9,153

Source: IMF, *International Financial Statistics*.

External Trade

PRINCIPAL COMMODITIES

(HK $ million)

Imports c.i.f.	2006	2007	2008
Food and live animals	61,497	72,365	92,151
Chemicals and related products	155,536	167,117	171,261
Basic manufactures	372,067	386,973	383,315
Textile yarn, fabrics, made-up articles, etc.	108,552	105,775	95,880
Machinery and transport equipment	1,401,055	1,541,199	1,615,191
Office machines and automatic data-processing equipment	284,995	249,433	265,633
Telecommunications and sound recording and reproducing apparatus and equipment	335,208	385,444	407,160
Electrical machinery, apparatus and appliances n.e.s., and electrical parts thereof	629,143	740,115	764,417
Miscellaneous manufactured articles	496,257	570,078	603,091
Clothing (excl. footwear)	146,439	149,387	144,412
Photographic apparatus, equipment and supplies, optical goods, watches and clocks	61,433	71,966	78,806
Baby carriages, toys, games and sporting goods	79,157	97,651	109,477
Total (incl. others)	2,599,804	2,868,011	3,025,288

Exports f.o.b.*	2006	2007	2008
Chemicals and related products	121,060	133,169	135,743
Basic manufactures	297,018	310,941	314,139
Textile yarn, fabrics, made-up articles, etc.	108,052	104,674	95,435
Machinery and transport equipment	1,347,588	1,476,112	1,580,134
Office machines and automatic data-processing equipment	315,235	261,760	279,780
Telecommunications and sound recording and reproducing apparatus and equipment	358,948	436,004	467,734
Electrical machinery, apparatus and appliances n.e.s., and electrical parts thereof	554,495	650,489	691,867
Miscellaneous manufactured articles	643,537	708,087	721,935
Clothing (excl. footwear)	220,529	224,403	217,311
Photographic apparatus, equipment and supplies, optical goods, watches and clocks	82,311	88,894	92,202
Baby carriages, toys, games and sporting goods	90,631	109,924	120,078
Total (incl. others)	2,461,027	2,687,514	2,824,151

* Including re-exports (HK $ million): 2,326,500 in 2006; 2,578,392 in 2007; 2,733,394 in 2008.

2009: *Imports:* Food and live animals 100,440; Mineral fuels, lubricants and related materials 90,072; Chemicals and related products 140,935; Basic manufactures 313,220; Machinery and transport equipment 1,489,438; Miscellaneous manufactured articles 517,912; Total (incl. others) 2,692,356. *Exports* (incl. re-exports): Chemicals and related products 116,029; Basic manufactures 253,248; Machinery and transport equipment 1,425,941; Miscellaneous manufactured articles 606,823; Total (incl. others) 2,469,089 (re-exports 2,411,347).

2010: *Imports:* Food and live animals 117,661; Mineral fuels, lubricants and related materials 119,266; Chemicals and related products 180,317; Basic manufactures 381,267; Machinery and transport equipment 1,923,525; Miscellaneous manufactured articles 590,850; Total (incl. others) 3,364,840. *Exports* (incl. re-exports): Chemicals and related products 143,153; Basic manufactures 320,843; Machinery and transport equipment 1,823,214; Miscellaneous manufactured articles 663,583; Total (incl. others) 3,031,019 (re-exports 2,961,507).

PRINCIPAL TRADING PARTNERS

(HK $ million, excl. gold)

Imports	2008	2009	2010
China, People's Republic	1,410,735	1,249,374	1,529,751
Germany	53,438	50,103	57,660
India	58,015	52,599	71,794
Japan	297,552	236,369	308,161
Korea, Republic	118,084	103,046	133,714
Malaysia	66,137	68,016	84,705
Philippines	48,407	n.a.	n.a.
Singapore	194,951	174,659	237,407
Taiwan	192,041	175,649	224,761
Thailand	63,756	57,589	76,304
USA	150,738	142,137	179,160
Total (incl. others)	3,025,288	2,692,356	3,364,840

Domestic exports	2008	2009	2010
Australia	1,752	1,334	n.a.
China, People's Republic	34,758	26,672	31,223
Germany	1,931	n.a	n.a.
Japan	2,290	1,651	2,032
Korea, Republic	1,285	1,196	1,495
Netherlands	2,252	1,863	2,639
Singapore	3,025	2,225	2,866
Switzerland	1,395	1,095	1,683
Taiwan	3,863	1,918	2,815
United Kingdom	2,723	1,239	1,554
USA	18,860	7,317	8,356
Total (incl. others)	90,757	57,742	69,512

Re-exports	2008	2009	2010
China, People's Republic	1,335,687	1,236,577	1,566,999
France	36,804	n.a.	n.a.
Germany	92,011	78,830	79,776
India	51,268	51,473	73,481
Japan	118,663	107,218	125,615
Korea, Republic	48,279	41,937	52,174
Netherlands	43,076	35,403	41,482
Singapore	52,290	40,028	48,113
Taiwan	51,080	52,795	65,789
United Kingdom	72,665	58,432	59,226
USA	340,395	277,920	323,733
Total (incl. others)	2,733,394	2,411,347	2,961,507

Transport

RAILWAYS

(traffic)

	2008	2009	2010
Freight ('000 metric tons):			
loaded	19,000	16,000	7,000
unloaded	90,000	68,000	29,000

Passenger journeys ('000): 3,188 in 2003.

ROAD TRAFFIC

('000 registered motor vehicles at 31 December)

	2008	2009	2010
Private cars	383	394	415
Buses (private and public)	13	13	13
Light buses (private and public)	6	6	6
Taxis	18	18	18
Goods vehicles	109	107	109
Motorcycles	38	38	38
Government vehicles (excl. military vehicles)	6	6	6
Total (incl. others)	575	584	608

Note: Figures do not include tramcars.

SHIPPING

Merchant Fleet
(registered at 31 December)

	2007	2008	2009
Number of vessels	1,242	1,371	1,529
Total displacement ('000 grt)	35,816.2	39,100.5	45,338.3

Source: IHS Fairplay, *World Fleet Statistics*.

Traffic
(2010)

	Ocean-going vessels	River vessels
Total capacity (million nrt)	803*	194†
Cargo landed ('000 metric tons)*	113,300	39,200
Cargo loaded ('000 metric tons)*	65,900	45,000

* Provisional.
† 2007.

Passenger traffic ('000, arrivals and departures by sea, 2010): Passengers landed 12,209; Passengers embarked 13,653.

Note: Includes passengers travelling to and from Macao by helicopter.

CIVIL AVIATION

	2008	2009	2010
Passengers ('000):			
arrivals	15,350	14,936	17,030
departures	14,810	14,302	16 241
Freight ('000 metric tons):			
landed	1,327	1,263	1,480*
loaded	2,301	2,084	2,650*

* Provisional.

Tourism

TOURIST ARRIVALS BY COUNTRY OF RESIDENCE
(non-resident tourist arrivals at national borders)

	2006	2007	2008
Australia	451,300	507,100	509,900
Canada	254,700	296,300	281,900
China, People's Republic	8,434,300	9,092,700	9,379,700
Germany	162,800	177,000	170,800
Indonesia	255,200	276,900	261,900
Japan	874,100	846,000	816,800
Korea, Republic	457,600	592,400	637,800
Macao	223,000	241,100	256,200
Malaysia	327,400	370,200	372,300
Philippines	361,100	439,800	451,500
Singapore	444,000	478,900	479,500
Taiwan	676,800	694,800	649,400
Thailand	295,700	290,600	298,600
United Kingdom	431,000	496,900	467,200
USA (incl. Guam)	878,300	924,100	837,600
Total (incl. others)	15,821,400	17,153,900	17,319,400

Note: Figures are rounded to the nearest 100 persons.

Receipts from tourism (US $ million, excl. passenger transport): 13,754 in 2007; 15,304 in 2008; 16,463 in 2009 (provisional).

Source: World Tourism Organization.

2009: Total arrivals 29,591,000 (mainland China 17,957,000; Taiwan 2,010,000; Macao 671,000).

2010: Total arrivals 36,030,000 (mainland China 22,684,000; Taiwan 2,165,000; Macao 780,000).

Communications Media

	2008	2009	2010
Telephones ('000 in use)	4,183.0	4,277.3	4,345.3
Mobile cellular telephones ('000 subscribers)	11,580.1	12,597.2	13,416.0
Internet subscribers ('000)	2,932.7†	3,085.3	n.a.
Broadband subscribers ('000)	1,962.5	2,049.3	2,127.0

† Estimate.

Personal computers: 4,835,300 (693.0 per 1,000 persons) in 2008.

1997 ('000 in use): Radio receivers 4,450.

2000 ('000 in use): Television receivers 3,105.

2004 (unless otherwise indicated): Daily newspapers 46; Non-daily newspapers 23; Periodicals 864 (2003).

Sources: partly UNESCO, *Statistical Yearbook;* UN, *Statistical Yearbook*; International Telecommunication Union.

Education

(2010/11 unless otherwise indicated)

	Institutions	Teachers	Students
Kindergartens	951	10,454	148,940
Primary schools	572	21,902	331,112
Secondary schools	533	29,969	449,737
Special schools	61	1,476	7,803
Institute of Vocational Education	1†	2,135*	64,640†
Approved post-secondary college†	2	149	1,977
Other post-secondary colleges†	16	n.a	8,093
UGC-funded institutions	8†	5,813*‡	168,019†
Open University of Hong Kong	1†	130*	21,339†
Adult education institutions†	2,218	n.a.	273,640

* 2009/10.
† 2006/07.
‡ Provisional figure.

Pupil-teacher ratio (primary education, UNESCO estimate): 15.9 in 2008/09 (Source: UNESCO Institute for Statistics).

Adult literacy rate (UNESCO estimates): 94.6% in 2003 (Source: UN Development Programme, *Human Development Report*).

Directory

The Constitution

Under the terms of the Basic Law of the Hong Kong Special Administrative Region, the Government comprises the Chief Executive, the Executive Council and the Legislative Council. The Chief Executive must be a Chinese citizen of at least 40 years of age; is appointed for a five-year term, with a limit of two consecutive terms; is chosen by an 800-member Election Committee; is accountable to the State Council of the People's Republic of China, and has no military authority; appoints the Executive Council, judges and the principal government officials; makes laws with the advice and consent of the legislature; has a veto over legislation, but can be overruled by a two-thirds' majority; may dissolve the legislature once in a term, but must resign if the legislative impasse continues with the new body. The Legislative Council has 60 members; in September 2008 candidates for 30 seats were directly elected under a system of proportional representation and 30 seats were determined by elections within 'functional constituencies' (comprising professional and special interest groups). The Legislative Council is responsible for enacting, revising and abrogating laws, for approving the budget, taxation and public expenditure, for debating the Policy Address of the Chief Executive and for approving the appointment of the judges of the Court of Final Appeal and of the Chief Justice of the High Court.

The Government

Chief Executive: DONALD TSANG YAM-KUEN (elected unopposed 16 June 2005; re-elected 25 March 2007).

EXECUTIVE COUNCIL
(October 2011)

Chairman: The Chief Executive.

Ex-Officio Members (Principal Officials)

Chief Secretary for Administration: STEPHEN LAM SUI-LUNG.

Financial Secretary: JOHN TSANG CHUN-WAH.

Secretary for Justice: WONG YAN-LUNG.

Secretary for Education: MICHAEL SUEN MING-YEUNG.

Secretary for Commerce and Economic Development: GREGORY SO KAM-LEUNG.

Secretary for Constitutional and Mainland Affairs: RAYMOND TAM CHI-YUEN.

Secretary for Security: AMBROSE LEE SIU-KWONG.

Secretary for Food and Health: Dr YORK CHOW YAT-NGOK.

Secretary for the Civil Service: DENISE YUE CHUNG-YEE.

Secretary for Home Affairs: TSANG TAK-SING.

Secretary for Labour and Welfare: MATTHEW CHEUNG KIN-CHUNG.

Secretary for Financial Services and the Treasury: Prof. K. C. CHAN KA-KEUNG.

Secretary for Development: CARRIE LAM CHENG YUET-NGOR.

Secretary for the Environment: EDWARD YAU TANG-WAH.

Secretary for Transport and Housing: EVA CHENG.

In addition to the above ex-officio members of the Executive Council, in late 2011 there were also 13 non-official members.

GOVERNMENT OFFICES

Executive Council: 1/F, Main Wing, Central Government Offices, Lower Albert Rd, Central; tel. 28102581; fax 28450176; e-mail ceo@ceo.gov.hk; internet www.ceo.gov.hk/exco.

Office of the Chief Executive: 5/F, Main Wing, Central Government Offices, Lower Albert Rd, Central; tel. 28783300; fax 25090577; e-mail ceo@ceo.gov.hk; internet www.ceo.gov.hk.

Government Secretariat: Central Government Offices, Lower Albert Rd, Central; tel. 28102900; fax 28457895.

Information Services Department: 8/F, Murray Bldg, Garden Rd, Central; tel. 28428777; fax 28459078; e-mail internet@isd.gov.hk; internet www.isd.gov.hk.

Legislature

LEGISLATIVE COUNCIL

The fourth Legislative Council since Hong Kong's transfer to Chinese sovereignty was elected on 7 September 2008. The Legislative Council comprises 60 members: 30 chosen by functional constituencies and 30 by direct election in five geographical constituencies. The term of office is four years.

President: JASPER TSANG YOK-SING.

Election, 7 September 2008 (unofficial results)

Party	Directly elective seats	Functional Constituency seats	Total seats
Democratic Alliance for the Betterment and Progress of Hong Kong	9	4	13
Democratic Party	7	1	8
Liberal Party	—	6	7
Civic Party	4	1	5
The Alliance	—	3	3
League of Social Democrats	3	—	3
Association for Democracy and People's Livelihood	1	1	2
The Frontier*	1	—	1
Hong Kong Confederation of Trade Unions	1	—	1
Hong Kong Federation of Trade Unions	—	1	1
Neighbourhood and Worker's Service Centre	1	—	1
Civic Act-up	1	—	1
Independents and others	2	13	14
Total	30	30	60

* Merged with the Democratic Party in November 2008.

Election Commission

Electoral Affairs Commission: 10/F, Harbour Centre, 25 Harbour Rd, Wanchai; tel. 28911001; fax 28274644; e-mail eacenq@reo.gov.hk; internet www.eac.gov.hk; f. 1997; Chair. BARNABAS FUNG.

Political Organizations

Alliance for Universal Suffrage: Hong Kong; internet www.universalsuffrage.hk; f. 2010; coalition of 11 pro-democracy parties and groups (incl. the ADPL, Democratic Party, Hong Kong Confederation of Trade Unions and professional groups).

Association for Democracy and People's Livelihood (ADPL): Sun Beam Commercial Bldg, Rm 1104, 469–471 Nathan Rd, Kowloon; tel. 27822699; fax 27823137; e-mail info@adpl.org.hk; internet www.adpl.org.hk; advocates democracy; Chair. BRUCE LIU; Sec.-Gen. QIN SHAN.

Citizens' Party: GPOB 321, Central; tel. 28930029; e-mail enquiry@citizensparty.org; f. 1997; urges mass participation in politics; Chair. Dr JOE WONG.

Civic Party: Unit 202, 2/F, Blk B, Sea View Bldg, 4–6 Watson Rd, North Point; tel. 28657111; fax 28652771; e-mail contact@civicparty.hk; internet www.civicparty.hk; f. 2006; pro-democracy; Chair. KENNETH CHAN; Leader ALAN LEONG.

Democratic Alliance for the Betterment and Progress of Hong Kong (DAB): SUP Tower, 15/F, 83 King's Rd, North Point; tel. 35821111; fax 35821188; e-mail info@dab.org.hk; internet www.dab.org.hk; f. 2005; formed by merger of Democratic Alliance for the Betterment of Hong Kong (f. 1992, supported return of Hong Kong to the motherland and implementation of the Basic Law) and Hong Kong Progressive Alliance (f. 1994, supported by business and professional community); pro-Beijing; Chair. TAM YIU-CHUNG; Sec.-Gen. THOMAS PANG.

Democratic Party: Hanley House, 4/F, 776–778 Nathan Rd, Kowloon; tel. 23977033; fax 23978998; e-mail dphk@dphk.org; internet www.dphk.org; f. 1994; formed by merger of United Democrats of Hong Kong (UDHK—declared a formal political party in 1990) and Meeting Point; merged with The Frontier (f. 1996) in Nov. 2008; liberal grouping; advocates democracy; Chair. ALBERT HO CHUN-YAN; Sec.-Gen. CHEUNG YIN-TUNG.

Hong Kong Democratic Foundation: POB 35588, King's Road Post Office, North Point; tel. 28696443; fax 28696318; e-mail secretariat@hkdf.org; internet www.hkdf.org; advocates democracy and an open society; Chair. ALAN LUNG KA-LUN.

League of Social Democrats/April Fifth Action: A-78, 2/F, Kam Fai Court, Kimberley Rd, Tsim Sha Tsui, Kowloon; tel. 23755338; fax

23755732; e-mail lsd@lsd.org.hk; internet www.lsd.org.hk; socialist group; anti-Beijing; Leader ANDREW TO.

Liberal Party: 801–803 Manhattan Place, 23 Wang Tai Rd, Kowloon; tel. 28696833; fax 25334238; e-mail liberal@liberal.org.hk; internet www.liberal.org.hk; f. 1993; est. by mems of Co-operative Resources Centre (CRC); business-orientated; pro-Beijing; Chair. MIRIAM LAU KIN-YEE.

Neighbourhood and Worker's Service Centre: Unit 326, 3/F, West Wing, Central Government Offices, 11 Ice House St, Central; tel. 25372101; fax 25372102; e-mail legco@nwsc.org.hk; internet www.nwsc.org.hk; Chair. LEUNG YIU-CHUNG.

New Hong Kong Alliance: 4/F, 14–15 Wo On Lane, Central; tel. 27826111; fax 27706083; e-mail contact@alliance.org.hk; internet www.alliance.org.hk; pro-China; Chair. SZETO WAH.

New People's Party (NPP): Flats D–F, 11/F, China Overseas Bldg, 139 Hennessy Rd, Wanchai; tel. 31000079; fax 31000087; e-mail info@npp.org.hk; internet www.npp.org.hk; f. 2011; pro-Beijing; advocates universal suffrage, economic diversification and reduction in wealth gap; Chair. REGINA IP.

People Power: c/o The Legislative Council; e-mail admin@peoplepower.hk; internet www.peoplepower.hk; f. 2011; est. by fmr mems of League of Social Democrats; pro-democracy; Chair. LAU KA HUNG; Sec.-Gen. CHAN SO LING.

At the elections of September 2008, the Hong Kong Confederation of Trade Unions and The Hong Kong Federation of Trade Unions (see Trade and Industry), the Alliance and Civic Act-up also secured seats in the Legislative Council. A new grouping, the Neo Democrats, was established by former members of the Democratic Party in late 2010.

The Chinese Communist Party (based in the People's Republic) and the Kuomintang (Nationalist Party of China, based in Taiwan) also maintain organizations in Hong Kong.

Judicial System

The Court of Final Appeal was established on 1 July 1997 upon the commencement of the Hong Kong Court of Final Appeal Ordinance. It replaced the Privy Council in London as the highest appellate court in Hong Kong to safeguard the rule of law. The Court comprises five judges—the Chief Justice, three permanent judges and one non-permanent Hong Kong judge or one judge from another common-law jurisdiction.

The High Court consists of a Court of Appeal and a Court of First Instance. The Court of First Instance has unlimited jurisdiction in civil and criminal cases, while the District Court has limited jurisdiction. Appeals from these courts lie to the Court of Appeal, presided over by the Chief Judge or a Vice-President of the Court of Appeal with one or two Justices of Appeal. Appeals from Magistrates' Courts are heard by a Court of First Instance judge.

Chief Justice of the Court of Final Appeal: GEOFFREY MA TAO-LI.

Permanent Judges of the Court of Final Appeal: K. BOKHARY, PATRICK S. O. CHAN, R. A. V. RIBEIRO.

Chief Judge of the High Court: ANDREW CHEUNG KUI-NUNG .

Justices of Appeal: K. H. WOO, F. STOCK, D. LE PICHON, P. C. Y. CHEUNG, A. G. ROGERS, M. C. K. N. YUEN, W. C. K. YEUNG, R. C. TANG, R. A. HARTMAN, SUSAN KWAN.

Judges of the Court of First Instance: D. Y. K. YAM, V. S. BOKHARY, K. K. PANG, W. D. STONE, C. M. BEESON, A. R. SUFFIAD, A. H. SAKHRANI, A O. T. CHUNG, C. F. L. CHU, L. P. S. TONG, M. A. MCMAHON, J. M. H. LAM, A. K. N. CHEUNG, M. V. LUNN, A. T. BARMA, A. F. T. REYES, B. W. FUNG, J. W. L. BARNES, A. R. WRIGHT, S. C. POON, J. L. SAUNDERS, D. G. SAW, A. K. F. TO, P. J. LINE, M. M. K. POON, D. W. C. PANG, C. R. MACKINTOSH, H. C. AU, J. R. HARRIS, M. T. BHARWANEY, J. P. FOK, A. C. MACRAE.

OTHER COURTS

District Court: There are 32 District Judges headed by a Chief District Judge.

Magistrates' Courts: There are seven Principal Magistrates, 59 Magistrates and seven Special Magistrates, sitting in nine magistracies.

Religion

The population is predominantly Buddhist. The number of active Buddhists is estimated at between 650,000 and 700,000, and there were more than 600 temples in 2005. Confucianism and Daoism are widely practised. The three religions are frequently found in the same temple. In 2005 there were some 660,000 Christians, approximately 90,000 Muslims, 40,000 Hindus, and 8,000 Sikhs. Judaism, the Bahá'í faith and Zoroastrianism are also represented.

BUDDHISM

Hong Kong Buddhist Association: 1/F, 338 Lockhart Rd, Wanchai; tel. 25749371; fax 28340789; e-mail enquiry@hkbuddhist.org; internet www.hkbuddhist.org; Pres. Ven. KOK KWONG.

CHRISTIANITY

Hong Kong Christian Council: 9/F, 33 Granville Rd, Kowloon; tel. 23687123; fax 27242131; e-mail hkcc@hkcc.org.hk; internet www.hkcc.org.hk; f. 1954; 22 mem. orgs; Chair. Rev. NICHOLAS TAI HO-FAI; Sec. Rev. YUEN TIN-YAU.

The Anglican Communion

Primate of Hong Kong Sheng Kung Hui and Bishop of Hong Kong Island and Macao: Most Rev. PETER K. K. KWONG, Bishop's House, 1 Lower Albert Rd, Central; tel. 25265355; fax 25212199; e-mail office1@hkskh.org; internet www1.hkskh.org.

Bishop of Eastern Kowloon: Rt Rev. LOUIS TSUI, 4/F, Holy Trinity Bradbury Centre, 139 Ma Tau Chung Rd, Kowloon; tel. 27139983; fax 27111609; e-mail dek@hkskh.org; internet dek.hkskh.org.

Bishop of Western Kowloon: Rt Rev. THOMAS SOO, 15/F, Ultra Grace Commercial Bldg, 5 Jordan Rd, Kowloon; tel. 27830811; fax 27830799; e-mail dwk@hkskh.org; internet dwk.hkskh.org.

The Lutheran Church

Evangelical Lutheran Church of Hong Kong: 4/F, Lutheran Bldg, Waterloo Rd, Yau Ma Tei, Kowloon; tel. 23885847; fax 23887539; e-mail info@elchk.org.hk; internet www.elchk.org.hk; f. 1954; 16,000 mems (2011); Bishop Rev. JENNY CHAN.

Lutheran Church—Hong Kong Synod: 68 Begonia Rd, Yau Yat Chuen, Kowloon; tel. 23973721; fax 23974826; e-mail hksynod@lutheran.org.hk; internet www.lutheran.org.hk; Pres. Rev. ALLAN YUNG.

The Roman Catholic Church

For ecclesiastical purposes, Hong Kong forms a single diocese, nominally suffragan to the archdiocese of Canton (Guangzhou), China. According to Vatican sources, in December 2007 there were an estimated 352,939 adherents in the territory, representing more than 5% of the total population.

Bishop of Hong Kong: JOHN TONG HON, 12/F, Catholic Diocese Centre, 16 Caine Rd, Central; tel. 28434679; fax 25254707; e-mail bishophk@pacific.net.hk; internet www.catholic.org.hk.

The Press

At the end of 2005, according to Hong Kong government figures, there were 49 daily newspapers, including 23 Chinese-language and 13 English-language dailies, and 722 periodicals.

PRINCIPAL DAILY NEWSPAPERS

English Language

China Daily: internet www.chinadaily.com.cn/hkedition/hk.html; Hong Kong edn of China's official English-language newspaper; launched 1997; Editor-in-Chief RAY ZHOU; circ. 20,000.

International Herald Tribune: 1201 K Wah Centre, 191 Java Rd, North Point; tel. 29221188; fax 29221190; internet www.iht.com; Correspondent SYLVIA HUI; circ. 8,390 (2009).

South China Morning Post: 3/F, 1 Leighton Rd, Causeway Bay; tel. 25652222; fax 28111048; e-mail info@scmp.com; internet www.scmp.com; f. 1903; Editor-in-Chief CLIFF BUDDLE (acting); circ. 107,000.

The Standard: 3/F, Sing Tao News Corporation Bldg, 3 Tung Wong Rd, Shau Kei Wan; tel. 27982798; fax 23051765; e-mail editor@thestandard.com.hk; internet www.thestandard.com.hk; f. 1949; publ. as free newspaper since Jan. 2007; Editor-in-Chief IVAN TONG; circ. 231,018.

Target Intelligent Report: Suite 2901, Bank of America Tower, 12 Harcourt Rd, Central; tel. 25730379; fax 28381597; e-mail info@targetnewspapers.com; internet www.targetnewspapers.com; f. 1972; financial news, commentary, politics, property, litigations, etc.

Wall Street Journal Asia: 25/F, Central Plaza, 18 Harbour Rd, Wanchai; tel. 25737121; fax 28345291; e-mail wsj.ltrs@wsj.com; internet www.wsj-asia.com; f. 1976; business; Editor-in-Chief ALMAR LATOUR; circ. 80,393.

Chinese Language

Hong Kong Commercial Daily: 1/F, 499 King's Rd, North Point; tel. 25905322; fax 25658947; internet www.hkcd.com.hk; f. 1952; Chair. and CEO HUANG YANG LUE; Editor CHENG XI TIAN.

Hong Kong Daily News: 5/F, CWG Bldg, 3A Kung Ngam Village Rd, Shau Kei Wan; tel. 39216688; fax 39216686; e-mail edit@hkdailynews.com.hk; internet www.hkdailynews.com.hk; f. 1958; morning; CEO RODDY YU; Chief Editor K. K. YEUNG; circ. 120,000.

Hong Kong Economic Journal: 22/F, North Point Industrial Bldg, 499 King's Rd, North Point; tel. 28567567; fax 28111070; e-mail enquiry@hkej.com; internet www.hkej.com; Dir CHO CHI-MING; Chief Editor K. C. CHAN; circ. 30,000.

Hong Kong Economic Times: Kodak House, Block 2, 6/F, 321 Java Rd, North Point; tel. 28802444; fax 25169989; e-mail etp_info@hket.com; internet www.etpress.com.hk; f. 1988; Publr MAK PING LEUNG; Chief Editor CHAN CHO BIU; circ. 80,371.

Ming Pao Daily News: Block A, Ming Pao Industrial Centre, 15/F, 18 Ka Yip St, Chai Wan; tel. 25953111; fax 28982534; e-mail mingpao@mingpao.com; internet www.mediachinesegroup.com; f. 1959; morning; Chief Editor PAUL CHEUNG; circ. 78,258.

Oriental Daily News: Oriental Press Centre, 23 Dai Cheong St, Tai Po Industrial Estate, New Territories; tel. 36000000; fax 36001100; e-mail news@oriental.com.hk; internet orientaldaily.on.cc; Chair. C. F. MA; Editor-in-Chief LIU KOU CHOUAN; circ. 650,000.

Ping Kuo Jih Pao (Apple Daily): 8 Chun Ying St, Industrial Estate West, Tseung Kwan; tel. 29908388; fax 26239132; e-mail adnews@appledaily.com; internet appledaily.atnext.com; f. 1995; published by Next Media; Propr JIMMY LAI; Publr LOH CHAN; circ. 309,261.

Sing Pao Daily News: 3/F, CWG Bldg, 3A Kung Ngam, Village Rd, Shau Kei Wan; tel. 25702201; fax 28062091; e-mail dailynews@singpao.com.hk; internet www.singpao.com; f. 1939; morning; Chief Editor CHENG SI WEI; circ. 229,250.

Sing Tao Daily: 3/F, Sing Tao News Corpn Bldg, 3 Tung Wong Rd, Shau Kei Wan; tel. 27982323; fax 27518634; e-mail info@singtao.com; internet www.singtao.com; f. 1938; morning; Editor-in-Chief LUK KAM WING; circ. 60,000.

The Sun: Oriental Press Centre, 23 Dai Cheong St, Tai Po Industrial Estate, New Territories; tel. 36009911; fax 36009900; e-mail news@the-sun.com.hk; internet the-sun.on.cc; f. 1999; publ. by the Oriental Press Group.

Ta Kung Pao: 342 Hennessy Rd, Wanchai; tel. 25757181; fax 28345104; e-mail tkp@takungpao.com; internet www.takungpao.com; f. 1902; morning; supports People's Republic of China; Editor T. S. TSANG; circ. 150,000.

Wen Wei Po: 2–4 Hing Wai Centre, 3/F, 7 Tin Wan Praya Rd, Aberdeen; tel. 28738288; fax 28730657; e-mail editor@wenhuibao.com.hk; internet www.wenweipo.com; f. 1948; morning; Dir WANG SHUCHENG; Editor-in-Chief WONG BAK YAO; circ. 200,000.

SELECTED PERIODICALS

English Language

Asia Money: 27/F, 248 Queen's Rd East, Wanchai; tel. 29128074; fax 28656225; e-mail richard.morrow@asiamoney.com; internet www.asiamoney.com; 10 a year; Publr ANDREW COVER; Editor RICHARD MORROW.

Business Traveller Asia–Pacific: Suite 405, 4/F, Chinachem Exchange Square, 1 Hoi Wan St, Quarry Bay; tel. 25949300; fax 25196846; e-mail enquiry@businesstravellerasia.com; internet asia.businesstraveller.com; f. 1982; consumer business travel; 10 a year; Publr PEGGY TEO; Editor-in-Chief TOM OTLEY; circ. 32,439.

Electronics: 38/F, Office Tower, Convention Plaza, 1 Harbour Rd, Wanchai; tel. 28924672; fax 28240249; e-mail hktdc@hktdc.org; internet www.hktdc.com; f. 1985; 4 a year (April, June, Oct. and Dec.); publ. by the Hong Kong Trade Development Council; Chief Editor GEOFF PICKEN; circ. 90,000.

Enterprise: 38/F, Office Tower, Convention Plaza, 1 Harbour Rd, Wanchai; tel. 25844333; fax 28240249; e-mail hktdc@hktdc.org; internet www.hktdc.com; f. 1967; monthly; publ. by the Hong Kong Trade Devt Council; Chief Editor GEOFF PICKEN; circ. 150,000.

Houseware: 38/F, Office Tower, Convention Plaza, 1 Harbour Rd, Wanchai; tel. 25844333; fax 28240249; e-mail hktdc@hktdc.org; internet www.hktdc.com; f. 1983; publ. by the Hong Kong Trade Development Council; household and hardware products; 2 a year; Chief Editor GEOFF PICKEN; circ. 90,000.

Hong Kong Industrialist: Federation of Hong Kong Industries, 31/F, Billion Plaza, 8 Cheung Yue St, Cheung Sha Wan, Kowloon; tel. 27323188; fax 27213494; e-mail fhki@fhki.org.hk; internet www.industryhk.org; monthly; publ. by the Federation of Hong Kong Industries; Editor ANTHONY CHAN; circ. 6,000.

Hong Kong Special Administrative Region Government Gazette: Printing Division, Government Logistics Department, 10/F, Government Offices, 333 Java Rd, North Point; tel. 25649500; fax 28876591; e-mail info@gld.gov.hk; internet www.gld.gov.hk; weekly.

Official Hong Kong Guide (e-Newsletter): c/o HKTB, Citicorp Centre, 9–11/F, 18 Whitfield Rd, North Point; f. 1982; monthlyinformation on sightseeing, shopping, dining, etc. for overseas visitorspublished by the Hong Kong Tourism Board.

Orientations: 815, 8/F, Zung Fu Industrial Bldg, 1067 King's Rd, Quarry Bay; tel. 25111368; fax 25074620; e-mail omag@netvigator.com; internet www.orientations.com.hk; f. 1970; 8 a year; arts of East Asia, the Indian subcontinent and South-East Asia; Publr and Editorial Dir ELIZABETH KNIGHT.

Reader's Digest (Asia Edn): Reader's Digest Association Far East Ltd, 19/F, Cyber Centre, 3 Tung Wong Rd, Shau Kei Wan; tel. 25681117; fax 96906389; e-mail friends@rdasia.com.hk; internet www.readersdigest.com.hk; f. 1963; general topics; monthly; Editor DORA CHEOK; circ. 332,000.

Sunday Examiner: 11/F, Catholic Diocese Centre, 16 Caine Rd, Central; tel. 25220487; fax 25369939; internet sundayex.catholic.org.hk; e-mail sunday@examiner.org.hk; f. 1946; religious; weekly; Editor-in-Chief Sister TERESA YUEN; Deputy Editor-in-Chief Fr JIM MULRONEY; circ. 6,500.

Textile Asia: c/o Business Press Ltd, California Tower, 11/F, 30–32 D'Aguilar St, GPOB 185, Central; tel. 25233744; fax 28106966; e-mail texasia@biznetvigator.com; internet www.textileasia-businesspress.com; f. 1970; monthly; textile and clothing industry; Publr and Editor-in-Chief MAX W. SUNG; circ. 17,000.

Travel Business Analyst: GPOB 12761, Hong Kong; tel. 25072310; e-mail TBAoffice@gmail.com; internet www.travelbusinessanalyst.com; f. 1982; monthly; travel trade; Editor MURRAY BAILEY.

Chinese Language

Affairs Weekly: Hong Kong; tel. 28950801; fax 25767842; f. 1980; general interest; Editor WONG WAI MAN; circ. 130,000.

Cheng Ming Monthly: Hennessy Rd, POB 20370, Wanchai; tel. 25740664; e-mail editor.chengmingmag@gmail.com; internet www.chengmingmag.com; current affairs; Chief Editor WAN FAI.

City Magazine: 9/F, Zung Fu Industrial Bldg, 1067 King's Rd, Quarry Bay; tel. 22509188; fax 28919719; e-mail hk@modernmedia.com.hk; internet www.cityhowwhy.com.hk; f. 1976; monthly; fashion, wine, cars, society, etc.; Publr JOHN K. C. CHAN; Chief Editor PETER WONG; circ. 30,000.

East Touch: 3/F, Sing Tao News Corpn Bldg, 3 Tung Wong Rd, Shau Kei Wan; tel. 27074471; fax 27074554; e-mail easttouch@singtaonewscorp.com; internet www.easttouch.com.hk; f. 1995; weekly; fashion, celebrity and entertainment news.

East Week: 3/F, Sing Tao News Corpn Bldg, 3 Tung Wong Rd, Shau Kei Wan; tel. 31813588; fax 21104209; e-mail info@eastweek.com.hk; internet www.eastweek.com.hk; f. 1992; weekly; publication halted in 2002; relaunched in 2003; general interest; Chair. HE ZHUGUO.

Kung Kao Po (Catholic Chinese Weekly): 16/F, 11 Catholic Parish Centre, Caine Rd, Central; tel. 25220487; fax 25213095; internet kkp.catholic.org.hk; e-mail kkp@kkp.org.hk; f. 1928; religious; weekly; Editor-in-Chief Sister TERESA YUEN.

Ming Pao Monthly: Ming Pao Industrial Centre, 15/F, Block A, 18 Ka Yip St, Chai Wan; tel. 25953111; fax 28982691; e-mail mpmeditor@mingpao.com; internet www.mingpaomonthly.com; Chief Editor KOO SIU-SUN.

Next Magazine: 8 Chun Ying St, T. K. O. Industrial Estate West, Tseung Kwan O, Kowloon; tel. 27442733; fax 29907210; internet www.nextmedia.com; internet next.atnext.com; f. 1989; weekly; news, business, lifestyle, entertainment; Editor-in-Chief LEE CHI-HO; circ. 172,708.

Open Magazine: POB 20064, Hennessy Rd; tel. 28939197; fax 28915591; e-mail open@open.com.hk; internet www.open.com.hk; f. 1990; monthly; Chief Editor JIN ZHONG; circ. 15,000.

Oriental Sunday: 10/F, Johnson Bldg, 14–16 Lee Chung St, Chai Wan; tel. 29603504; fax 29605701; e-mail anniekwan@newmediagroup.com.hk; internet www.orientalsunday.hk; f. 1991; weekly; leisure magazine; Publr TSO SUET CHUNG; circ. 120,000.

Reader's Digest (Chinese Edn): Reader's Digest Association Far East Ltd, 19/F, Cyber Centre, 3 Tung Wong Rd, Shau Kei Wan; tel. 25681117; fax 25690370; internet www.readersdigest.com.hk; f. 1965; monthly; Editor-in-Chief JOEL POON; circ. 200,000.

Today's Living: 2207, 22/F, Westlands Center, 20 Westlands Rd, Quarry Bay; tel. 28822230; fax 28823949; e-mail magazine@todaysliving.com; internet www.todaysliving.com; f. 1987; monthly; interior design; Publr and Editor-in-Chief KENNETH LI; circ. 55,000.

Yazhou Zhoukan: Block A, Ming Pao Industrial Centre, 15/F, 18 Ka Yip St, Chai Wan; tel. 25155358; fax 25059662; e-mail yzzk@mingpao.com; internet www.yzzk.com; f. 1987; international Chinese news weekly; Chief Editor YAU LOP-POON; circ. 110,000.

Yuk Long TV Weekly: Hong Kong; tel. 25657883; fax 25659958; f. 1977; entertainment, fashion, etc.; Publr TONY WONG; circ. 82,508.

NEWS AGENCIES

International News Service: 2E Cheong Shing Mansion, 33–39 Wing Hing St, Causeway Bay; tel. 25665668; Rep. AU KIT MING.

Xinhua (New China) News Agency, Hong Kong SAR Bureau: 387 Queen's Rd East, Wanchai; tel. 28314126; f. 2000; est. from fmr news dept of branch office of Xinhua (responsibility for other activities assumed by Liaison Office of the Central People's Govt in the Hong Kong SAR); Dir ZHANG GUOLIANG.

PRESS ASSOCIATIONS

Chinese Language Press Institute: 3/F, Sing Tao News Corpn Bldg, 3 Tung Wong Rd, Shau Kei Wan; tel. 27982501; fax 27953017; e-mail clpi68@yahoo.com.hk; f. 1968; Pres. Sir TIONG HIEW KING.

Hong Kong Chinese Press Association: Rm 2208, 22/F, 33 Queen's Rd, Central; tel. 28613622; fax 28661933; 13 mems; Chair. HUE PUE-YING.

Hong Kong Journalists Association: Henfa Commercial Bldg, Flat 15A, 348–350 Lockhart Rd, Wanchai; tel. 25910692; fax 25727329; e-mail hkja@hkja.org.hk; internet www.hkja.org.hk; f. 1968; 413 mems; Chair. MAK YING-TING.

Newspaper Society of Hong Kong: Rm 904, 9/F, 75–83 King's Rd, North Point; tel. 25713102; fax 25712676; e-mail secretariat@nshk.com.hk; internet www.nshk.org.hk; f. 1954; Chair. KEITH KAM; Pres. LEE CHO-JAT.

Publishers

Asia 2000 Ltd: Rm 4, 26/F, Global Trade Centre, 15 Wing Kin Rd, Kwai Chung, New Territories; tel. 25301409; fax 25261107; e-mail sales@asia2000.com.hk; internet www.asia2000.com.hk; Asian studies, politics, photography, fiction; Man. Dir MICHAEL MORROW.

Chinese University Press: Units 1–3 and 18, 9/F, Sha Tin Galleria, 18–24 Shan Mei St, Fo Tan, New Territories; tel. 29465300; fax 26036692; e-mail cup@cuhk.edu.hk; internet www.chineseupress.com; f. 1977; studies on China and Hong Kong and other academic works; Dir QI GAN.

Commercial Press (Hong Kong) Ltd: Eastern Central Plaza, 8/F, 3 Yiu Hing Rd, Shau Kei Wan; tel. 25651371; fax 25645277; e-mail info@commercialpress.com.hk; internet www.commercialpress.com.hk; f. 1897; trade books, dictionaries, textbooks, Chinese classics, art, etc.; Chair. and Man. Dir CHAN MAN HUNG.

Excerpta Medica Asia Ltd: 1601, 16/F, Leighton Centre, 77 Leighton Rd, Causeway Bay; tel. 29651300; fax 29760778; e-mail emal@excerptahk.com; subsidiary of Elsevier; f. 1980; sponsored medical publications, abstracts, journals, etc.

Hoi Fung Publisher Co: 125 Lockhart Rd, 2/F, Wanchai; tel. 25286246; fax 25286249; Dir K. K. TSE.

Hong Kong University Press: Hing Wai Centre, 14/F, 7 Tin Wan Praya Rd, Aberdeen; tel. 25502703; fax 28750734; e-mail hkupress@hku.hk; internet www.hkupress.org; f. 1956; Publr MICHAEL DUCKWORTH.

Ling Kee Publishing Co Ltd: 14/F, Zung Fu Industrial Bldg, 1067 King's Rd, Quarry Bay; tel. 25616151; fax 28111980; e-mail admin@lingkee.com; internet www.lingkee.com; f. 1956; educational and reference; Chair. B. L. AU; Man. Dir K. W. AU.

Oxford University Press (China) Ltd: Warwick House East, 18/F, 979 King's Rd, Taikoo Place, Quarry Bay; tel. 25163126; fax 25658491; e-mail elt.china.hk@oup.com; internet www.oupchina.com.hk; f. 1961; school textbooks, reference, academic and general works relating to Hong Kong, Macao, Taiwan and China; Regional Dir SIMON LI.

Taosheng Publishing House: Lutheran Bldg, 3/F, 50A Waterloo Rd, Yau Ma Tei, Kowloon; tel. 23887061; fax 27810413; e-mail taosheng@elchk.org.hk; Dir CHANG CHUN WA.

Textile Asia/Business Press Ltd: California Tower, 11/F, 30–32 D'Aguilar St, GPOB 185, Central; tel. 25233744; fax 28106966; e-mail texasia@biznetvigator.com; internet www.textileasia-businesspress.com; f. 1970; textile magazine; Man. Dir KAYSER W. SUNG.

The Woods Publishing Co: Li Yuen Bldg, 2/F, 7 Li Yuen St West, Central; tel. 25233002; fax 28453296; e-mail tybook@netvigator.com; Production Man. TONG SZE HONG.

Times Publishing (Hong Kong) Ltd: Seaview Estate, Block C, 10/F, 2–8 Watson Rd, North Point; tel. 25668381; fax 25080255; e-mail abeditor@asianbusiness.com.hk; trade magazines and directories; CEO COLIN YAM; Executive Editor JAMES LEUNG.

GOVERNMENT PUBLISHING HOUSE

Government Information Services: see Government Offices.

PUBLISHERS' ASSOCIATIONS

Hong Kong Publishers' and Distributors' Association: Flat C, 4/F, 240–246 Nathan Rd, Kowloon; tel. 23674412; 45 mems; Chair. HO KAM-LING; Sec. HO NAI-CHI.

Hong Kong Publishing Federation Ltd: Room 904, SUP Tower, 75–83 King's Rd, North Point; tel. 25786000; fax 25786838.

Hong Kong Publishing Professionals Society Ltd: 8/F, Eastern Central Plaza, 3 Yiu Hing Rd, Shaukeiwan; tel. 29766804; fax 25645270; Chair. Dr CHAN MAN HUNG.

The Society of Publishers in Asia: Hang Seng North Point Bldg, 7/F, 341 King's Rd, North Point; tel. 28071212; fax 28877026; e-mail mail@sopasia.com; internet www.sopasia.com; f. 1982; Chair. DAVE SMITH.

Broadcasting and Communications

TELECOMMUNICATIONS

Asia Satellite Telecommunications Co Ltd (AsiaSat): 19/F, Sunning Plaza, 10 Hysan Ave, Causeway Bay; tel. 25000888; fax 25000895; e-mail as-mkt@asiasat.com; internet www.asiasat.com; f. 1988; CEO WILLIAM WADE.

China Mobile Ltd: 60/F, The Center, 99 Queen's Rd, Central; tel. 31218888; fax 25119092; internet www.chinamobileltd.com; f. 1997; leading mobile services provider in mainland China, operating through its 31 subsidiaries in all 31 provinces, autonomous regions and municipalities in the People's Republic; subsidiary of China Mobile Communications Corpn; 558.9m. subscribers (July 2010); Chair. and CEO WANG JIANZHOU.

China Unicom (Hong Kong) Ltd: 75/F, The Center, 99 Queen's Rd, Central; tel. 21262018; fax 21262016; e-mail info@chinaunicom.com.hk; internet www.chinaunicom.com.hk; f. 2000; internet and telephone service provider; operates throughout China; 57.8% shares held by Unicom Group; 303.5m. subscribers (July 2010); Chair. and CEO CHANG XIAOBING.

PCCW Ltd: 39/F, PCCW Tower, Taikoo Place, 979 King's Rd, Quarry Bay; tel. 28882888; fax 28778877; e-mail pr@pccw.com; internet www.pccw.com; fmrly Cable and Wireless HKT Ltd, acquired by PCCW in Aug. 2000; telecommunications, multimedia, information and communications technology services provider; Chair. RICHARD LI; Group Man. Dir ALEX ARENA.

Hutchison Telecom, New T and T Hong Kong Ltd, and New World Telecom also operate local services. At November 2007 there were five companies licensed to provide mobile telecommunications services, serving 10.5m. customers in Hong Kong.

Regulatory Authority

Office of the Telecommunications Authority: 29/F, Wu Chung House, 213 Queen's Rd East, Wanchai; tel. 29616333; fax 28035110; e-mail webmaster@ofta.gov.hk; internet www.ofta.gov.hk; f. 1993; statutory regulator, responsible for implementation of the Govt's pro-competition and pro-consumer policies; Dir-Gen. MARION LAI CHAN CHI-KUEN.

BROADCASTING

Regulatory Authority

Broadcasting Authority: 39/F, Revenue Tower, 5 Gloucester Rd, Wanchai; tel. 25945721; fax 25072219; e-mail ba@tela.gov.hk; internet www.hkba.hk; regulatory body; administers and issues broadcasting licences; Chair. AMBROSE HO.

Radio

Hong Kong Commercial Broadcasting Co Ltd: 3 Broadcast Drive, KCPOB 73000, Kowloon; tel. 23394810; fax 23380021; e-mail comradio@crhk.com.hk; internet www.881903.com; f. 1959; broadcasts in English and Cantonese on three radio frequencies; Chair. G. J. HO; Dir and CEO RITA CHING-HAN CHAN.

Metro Broadcast Corpn Ltd (Metro Broadcast): Basement 2, Site 6, Whampoa Garden, Hunghom, Kowloon; tel. 36988000; fax 21239889; e-mail prenquiry@metroradio.com.hk; internet www.metroradio.com.hk; f. 1991; broadcasts on three channels in English, Cantonese and Mandarin; Man. Dir BIANCA MA.

Radio Television Hong Kong: Broadcasting House, 30 Broadcast Drive, Kowloon; tel. 23369314; fax 23380279; e-mail ccu@rthk.org.hk; internet rthk.hk; f. 1928; govt-funded; 24-hour service in English, Cantonese and Mandarin on seven radio channels; Dir FRANKLIN WONG.

Television

Asia Television Ltd (ATV): 25–31 Dai Shing St, Tai Po Industrial Estate, Tai Po; tel. 29928888; fax 23380438; e-mail atv@atv.com.hk; internet www.hkatv.com; f. 1973; operates eight commercial television services (English and Chinese) and produces television programmes; Chair. WONG PO-YAN; Dir and CEO (vacant).

Hong Kong Cable Television Ltd: Cable TV Tower, 9 Hoi Shing Rd, Tsuen Wan; tel. 21126868; fax 21127878; e-mail info@i-cablecomm.com; internet www.i-cablecomm.com; f. 1993; subsidiary of i-CABLE Communications Ltd; 24-hour subscription service of news, sport and entertainment on 100 channels; carries BBC World Service Television; Chair. and CEO STEPHEN NG.

Phoenix Satellite Television: No. 9, Tower 1, Seashore Square, 18 Defeng St, Kowloon; tel. 26219888; fax 26219898; internet www.ifeng.com; f. 1995; partly owned by News Corpn (USA); Mandarin; three domestic and two international channels; CEO LIU CHANGLE.

Radio Television Hong Kong: see Radio; produces drama, documentary and public affairs programmes; also operates an educational service for transmission by two local commercial stations; Dir FRANKLIN WONG.

STAR Group Ltd: One Harbourfront, 8/F, 18 Tak Fung St, Hunghom, Kowloon; tel. 26218888; fax 26213050; e-mail corp_aff@startv.com; internet www.startv.com; f. 1990; subsidiary of News Corpn; broadcasts over 40 channels in English, Hindi, Tamil, Mandarin, Cantonese, Korean and Thai, including a range of sports programmes, music, movies, news, entertainment and documentaries; reaches more than 300m. people in 53 countries across Asia and the Middle East, with a daily audience of about 130m. people; has interests in cable systems in India and Taiwan; services also extend to terrestrial and cable TV, wireless and digital media platforms.

Television Broadcasts Ltd (TVB): TVB City, 77 Chun Choi St, Tseung Kwan O Industrial Estate, Kowloon; tel. 23352288; fax 23581300; e-mail external.affairs@tvb.com.hk; internet www.tvb.com; f. 1967; operates Chinese and English language television programme services; Chair. Sir RUN RUN SHAW.

Finance

(cap. = capital; res = reserves; dep. = deposits; m. = million; brs = branches; amounts in Hong Kong dollars unless otherwise stated)

BANKING

In 2010 there were 145 licensed banks operating in Hong Kong. There were also 21 restricted licence banks (formerly known as licensed deposit-taking companies) and 26 deposit-taking companies. There were 82 foreign banks' representative offices in September 2007.

Hong Kong Monetary Authority (HKMA): 55/F, Two International Finance Centre, 8 Finance St, Central; tel. 28788196; fax 28788197; e-mail hkma@hkma.gov.hk; internet www.hkma.gov.hk; f. 1993; est. by merger of Office of the Commr of Banking and Office of the Exchange Fund; govt authority responsible for maintaining monetary and banking stability; manages official reserves in the Exchange Fund; Chief Exec. NORMAN CHAN.

Banks of Issue

Bank of China (Hong Kong) Ltd (People's Repub. of China): Bank of China Tower, 1 Garden Rd, Central; tel. 28266888; fax 28105963; internet www.bochk.com; f. 1917; became third bank of issue in May 1994; merged in Oct. 2001 with the local branches of 11 mainland banks (incl. Kwangtung Provincial Bank, Sin Hua Bank Ltd, China and the South Sea Bank Ltd, Kincheng Banking Corpn, China State Bank, National Commercial Bank Ltd, Yien Yieh Commercial Bank Ltd, Hua Chiao Commercial Bank Ltd and Po Sang Bank Ltd), to form the Bank of China (Hong Kong); cap. 43,043m., res 49,049m., dep. 1,012,119m. (Dec. 2009); CEO HE GUANGBEI; 270 brs.

The Hongkong and Shanghai Banking Corporation Ltd (HSBC): 1 Queen's Rd, Central; tel. 28221111; fax 28101112; internet www.hsbc.com.hk; f. 1865; personal and commercial banking; cap. 22,494m., res 84,063m., dep. 3,681,436m. (Dec. 2009); Chair. STUART GULLIVER; CEO ANITA FUNG; more than 600 offices world-wide.

Standard Chartered Bank: Standard Chartered Bank Bldg, 4–4A Des Voeux Rd, Central; tel. 28203333; fax 28569129; internet www.standardchartered.com.hk; f. 1859; cap. 97m., res 38,626m., dep. 608,128m. (2009); Chair. C. K. CHOW; CEO BENJAMIN HUNG; more than 500 offices worldwide.

Other Commercial Banks

Bank of East Asia Ltd: Bank of East Asia Bldg, 16/F, 10 Des Voeux Rd, Central; tel. 36083608; fax 36086000; e-mail chengwcm@hkbea.com; internet www.hkbea.com; inc in Hong Kong in 1918, absorbed United Chinese Bank Ltd in Aug. 2001, and First Pacific Bank (FPB) in April 2002; cap. 4,623m., res 23,549m., dep. 358,681m. (Dec. 2009); Chair. and Chief Exec. DAVID K. P. LI; 91 domestic brs, 23 overseas brs.

Chiyu Banking Corpn Ltd: 78 Des Voeux Rd, Central; tel. 28430111; fax 28104207; e-mail chiyu@chiyubank.com; internet www.chiyubank.com; f. 1947; mem. of Bank of China (Hong Kong); cap. 300m., res 583.3m., dep. 34,450.3m. (Dec. 2009); Chair. HE GUANGBEI; 24 brs.

Chong Hing Bank Ltd: 17–18/F, Chong Hing Bank Centre, 24 Des Voeux Rd, Central; tel. 37681021; fax 37681383; e-mail info@chbank.com; internet www.chbank.com; f. 1948; fmrly Liu Chong Hing Bank; cap. 217.5m., res 6,924m., dep. 62,280.5m. (Dec. 2009); Chair. LIU LIT-MO; CEO LIU LIT-CHI; 51 domestic brs, 3 overseas brs.

CITIC Bank International Ltd: 232 Des Voeux Rd, Central; tel. 36036633; fax 36034000; e-mail info@citicbankintl.com; internet www.citicbankintl.com; f. 1922; cap. 7,283.3m., res 203.2m., dep. 101,908.7m. (Dec. 2009); acquired Hong Kong Chinese Bank Ltd Jan. 2002; fmrly CITIC Ka Wah Bank Ltd, name changed as above in 2010; Chair. DOU JIANZHONG; CEO DOREEN CHAN HUI DOR LAM; 30 domestic brs.

Dah Sing Bank Ltd: Dah Sing Financial Centre, 36/F, 108 Gloucester Rd, Central; tel. 25078866; fax 25985052; e-mail ops@dahsing.com.hk; internet www.dahsing.com; f. 1947; cap. 3,600.0m., res 102.9m., dep. 92,684.8m. (Dec. 2009); Chair. DAVID S. Y. WONG; Man. Dir DEREK H. H. WONG; 39 domestic brs.

DBS Bank (Hong Kong) Ltd: 11/F, The Center, 99 Queen's Rd, Central; tel. 22188822; fax 21678222; e-mail hkcs@dbs.com; internet www.dbs.com.hk; f. 1938; inc in 1954 as Kwong On Bank, name changed 2000; subsidiary of the Development Bank of Singapore; cap. 7,000m., res 13,677m., dep. 193,753.2m. (Dec. 2009); acquired Dao Heng Bank and Overseas Trust Bank July 2003; Chair. KWA CHONG SENG; CEO AMY YIP; 32 brs.

Hang Seng Bank Ltd: 83 Des Voeux Rd, Central; tel. 21983422; fax 28684047; e-mail ccdca@hangseng.com; internet www.hangseng.com; f. 1933; a principal member of the HSBC group, which has an ownership of 62.14%; cap. 9,559m., res 10,946m., dep. 687,163m. (Dec. 2009); Chair. RAYMOND C. F. CH'IEN; Vice-Chair. and CEO MARGARET LEUNG; 149 brs in Hong Kong, 17 in mainland China and 1 in Macao; also rep. office in Taipei.

Industrial and Commercial Bank of China (Asia): 33/F, ICBC Tower, 3 Garden Rd, Central; tel. 25881188; fax 28051166; e-mail enquiry@icbcasia.com; internet www.icbcasia.com; f. 1964; fmrly Union Bank of Hong Kong; cap. 2,636.6m., res 10,286m., dep. 185,296m. (Dec. 2009); Chair. JIANG JIANQING; 42 brs.

Mevas Bank: 33/F, Dah Sing Financial Centre, 108 Gloucester Rd, Wanchai; tel. 31013286; fax 31013298; e-mail contactus@mevas.com; internet www.mevas.com; cap. 400m., res. 1,646m., dep. 3,632.7m. (Dec. 2009); Chair. DAVID S. Y. WONG; CEO HO MAN-CHAN.

Nanyang Commercial Bank Ltd: 151 Des Voeux Rd, Central; tel. 28520888; fax 28153333; e-mail nanyang@ncb.com.hk; internet www.ncb.com.hk; f. 1949; cap. 700m., res 19,609.2m., dep. 131,306.2m. (Dec. 2009); Chair. ZHOU ZAIQUN; 41 brs, 2 overseas brs.

Public Bank (Hong Kong) Ltd: Public Bank Centre, 120 Des Voeux Rd, Central; tel. 25419222; fax 25452866; e-mail contact@publicbank.com.hk; internet www.publicbank.com.hk; f. 1934; fmrly Asia Commercial Bank; name changed as above June 2006; cap. 1,481.6m., res 3,114.7m., dep. 30,453.2m. (Dec. 2009); Chair. Tan Sri Dato' Sri Dr TEH HONG PIOW; CEO TAN YOKE KONG; 30 domestic brs, 1 overseas.

Shanghai Commercial Bank Ltd: 12 Queen's Rd, Central; tel. 28415415; fax 28104623; e-mail contact@shacombank.com.hk; internet www.shacombank.com.hk; f. 1950; cap. 2,000m., res 8,247.9m., dep. 95,086.6m. (Dec. 2009); Chair. LINCOLN CHU KUEN YUNG; CEO, Man. Dir and Gen. Man. DAVID SEK-CHI KWOK; 42 domestic brs, 5 overseas brs.

Standard Bank Asia Ltd: 36/F, Two Pacific Place, 88 Queensway, Central; tel. 28227888; fax 28227999; e-mail askbanking@standardbank.com.hk; internet www.standardbank.com; f. 1970; est. as Jardine Fleming & Co Ltd; renamed Jardine Fleming Bank Ltd in 1993; absorbed by Standard Bank Investment Corpn Ltd; current name adopted in July 2001; cap. US $72m., res US $62.5m., dep. US $788m. (Dec. 2009); Chair. ROB A. G. LEITH.

Tai Yau Bank Ltd: 29/F, Tai Tung Bldg, 8 Fleming Rd, Wanchai; tel. 25223296; f. 1947; cap. 300.0m., res 203.3m., dep. 1,597.5m. (Dec. 2009); Chair. KO FOOK KAU.

Wing Hang Bank Ltd: 161 Queen's Rd, Central; tel. 28525111; fax 28517127; e-mail whbpsd@whbhk.com; internet www.whbhk.com; f. 1937; cap. 295.0m., res 12,226.1m., dep. 127,416.2m. (Dec. 2009); acquired Chekiang First Bank Ltd in Aug. 2004; Chair. and Chief Exec. PATRICK Y. B. FUNG; 40 domestic brs, 13 overseas brs.

Wing Lung Bank Ltd: 45 Des Voeux Rd, Central; tel. 28268333; fax 28100592; e-mail wlb@winglungbank.com; internet www.winglungbank.com; f. 1933; cap. 1,160.9m., res 1,388.6m., dep. 98,686m. (Dec. 2009); Chair. MA WEIHUA; Exec. Dir and Chief Exec. ZHU QUI; 41 domestic brs, 4 overseas brs, 1 rep. office in China.

Principal Foreign Banks

ABN AMRO Bank NV (Netherlands): 37/F, Cheung Kong Center 2, Queens Rd, Central; tel. 37633700; fax 37633709; internet www.abnamroprivatebanking.com/hongkong; CEO (Asia) HANS DIEDEREN; 3 brs.

American Express International Inc (USA): 18/F, Cityplaza 4, 12 Taikoo Wan Rd, Taikoo Shing; tel. 22771010; internet www.americanexpress.com/hk; Senior Country Exec. DOUGLAS H. SHORT III; 3 brs.

Australia and New Zealand Banking Group Ltd: 17/F, One Exchange Square, 8 Connaught Place, Central; tel. 21768888; fax 39182211; internet www.anz.com.au/hongkong; CEO SUSAN YUEN.

Bangkok Bank Public Co Ltd (Thailand): Bangkok Bank Bldg, 28 Des Voeux Rd, Central; tel. 28016688; fax 28015679; e-mail bangkokbank@bbl.com.hk; Gen. Man. KHUN SITTHICHAI JIWATTANAKUL; 2 brs.

Bank of Communications, Hong Kong Branch: 20 Pedder St, Central; tel. 28419611; fax 28106993; e-mail enquiry@bankcomm.com.hk; internet www.bankcomm.com.hk; f. 1934; Gen. Man. FANG LIANKUI; 41 brs.

Bank of India: Ruttonjee Centre, 2/F, Dina House, 11 Duddell St, Central; tel. 25240186; fax 28771178; e-mail boihk@netvigator.com; internet www.bankofindia.com.hk; Chief Exec. B. G. KURUP.

Bank Negara Indonesia: G/F, Far East Finance Centre, 16 Harcourt Rd; tel. 28618600; fax 28656500; Gen. Man. BRAMONO DWIEDJANTO.

Bank of Tokyo-Mitsubishi UFJ Ltd (Japan): 8/F, AIG Tower, 1 Connaught Rd, Central; tel. 28236666; fax 25293821.

Barclays Capital Asia Ltd: Cheung Kong Center, 41/F, 2 Queen's Rd, Central; tel. 29032000; fax 29032999; internet www.barcap.com; f. 1972; Chair. and CEO ROBERT A. MORRICE.

BNP Paribas (France): 59–63/F, Two International Finance Centre, 8 Finance St, Central; tel. 29098888; fax 28652523; e-mail didier.balme@bnpgroup.com; internet www.bnpparibas.com.hk; f. 1958; Chief Exec. MIGNONNE CHENG; 2 brs.

Crédit Agricole Corporate and Investment Bank (France): 27/F, Two Pacific Place, 88 Queensway, Central; tel. 28267333; fax 28261270fmrly Calyon Bank, above name adopted in 2010; Country Officer FRANÇOIS RAMEAU; 1 br.

China Construction Bank (Asia) Corpn Ltd: 16/F, York House, The Landmark, 15 Queen's Rd Central, Central; tel. 27795533; fax 25218555; internet www.asia.ccb.com; fmrly Bank of America (Asia); wholly owned subsidiary of China Construction Bank Corpn; commercial banking and retail banking; cap. 6,511m., res 9,485.1m., dep. 64,859.8m. (Dec. 2009); Pres. and CEO MIRANDA KWOK; 41 brs in Hong Kong; 9 brs in Macao.

Citibank, NA (USA): Citibank Tower, 39–40/F and 44–50/F, Citibank Plaza, 3 Garden Rd, Central; tel. 28688888; fax 25230949; internet www.citibank.com.hk; CEO (Asia Pacific) SHIRISH APTE; 26 brs.

Commerzbank AG (Germany): 29/F, Two International Finance Centre, 8 Finance St, Central; tel. 39880680; fax 39880698; internet www.commerzbank.com.hk; Man. STEFAN GÖHMANN; 1 br.

Crédit Suisse (Switzerland): 23/F, Three Exchange Square, 8 Connaught Place, Central; tel. 28414888; fax 28400012; internet www.credit-suisse.com/hk; CEO (Asia-Pacific) OSAMA ABBASI.

Deutsche Bank AG (Germany): 52/F, International Commerce Centre, 1 Austin Rd West, Kowloon; tel. 22038888; fax 22037300; internet www.db.com/hongkong; Gen. Mans Dr MICHAEL THOMAS, REINER RUSCH; 1 br.

Indian Overseas Bank: 3/F, Ruttonjee House, 11 Duddell St, Central; tel. 25227157; fax 28451549; e-mail iobsm@netvigator.com; internet www.iobhongkong.com; f. 1955; CEO SRINIVASAN KRISHNAMACHARY; 2 brs.

JP Morgan Chase Bank (USA): 39/F, One Exchange Square, Connaught Place, Central; tel. 28431234; fax 28414396.

Malayan Banking Berhad (Malaysia): 21/F, Man Yee Bldg, 68 Des Voeux Rd, Central; tel. 35188888; fax 35188889; f. 1962trades in Hong Kong as Maybank; Gen. Man. AMOS ONG SEET JOON; 2 brs.

Mizuho Corporate Bank Ltd (Japan): 17/F, Two Pacific Place, 88 Queensway, Admiralty; tel. 21033040; fax 28101326; Man. Dir and CEO NOBORU AKATSUKA; 1 br.

National Bank of Pakistan: POB 99006, 1103 Fourseas Bldg, 208–212 Nathan Rd, Kowloon; tel. 23697355; fax 27245622; e-mail nbphkkm@netvigator.com; CEO GHULAM HUSSAIN AZHAR.

Oversea-Chinese Banking Corpn Ltd (Singapore): 9/F, 9 Queen's Rd, Central; tel. 28406200; fax 28453439; Gen. Man. BENJAMIN YEUNG; 3 brs.

Philippine National Bank: 26/F, Worldwide House, 19 Des Voeux Rd, Central; tel. 25431066; fax 25253107; e-mail pnbhkgrp@pnbhk.com; Gen. Man. RODEL BICOL; 1 br.

N. M. Rothschild and Sons (Hong Kong) Ltd: 16/F, Alexandra House, 16–20 Chater Rd, Central; tel. 25255333; fax 28106997; e-mail jackson.woo@rothschild.com.hk; cap. 308.8m., dep. 22.9m. (Dec. 2007); Chair. RUSSELL EDEY.

Société Générale Asia Ltd (France): Level 38, Three Pacific Place, 1 Queen's Rd East; tel. 21665388; fax 28682368; internet www.sgcib.hk; Head (Asia-Pacific) HIKARU OGATA.

Sumitomo Mitsui Banking Corpn (SMBC) (Japan): 7–8/F, One International Finance Centre, 1 Harbour View St, Central; tel. 22062000; fax 22062888; Gen. Man. TOSHIO MORIKAWA; 1 br.

UBAF (Hong Kong) Ltd (France): The Sun's Group Centre, 21/F, 200 Gloucester Rd, Wanchai; tel. 25201361; fax 25274256; e-mail larry.yap@ubaf.fr; cap. US $30.1m., dep. US $10.4m. (Dec. 2009); Man. Dir LARRY S. YAP.

United Overseas Bank Ltd (Singapore): 25/F, Gloucester Tower, The Landmark, 15 Queen's Rd, Central; tel. 29108888; fax 28105506; internet www.uobgroup.com/hk; Sr Vice-Pres. and CEO WEE EE CHEONG; 5 brs.

Banking Associations

The Chinese Banks' Association Ltd: South China Bldg, 5/F, 1–3 Wyndham St, Central; tel. 25224789; fax 28775102; 1,666 mems; chaired by Bank of East Asia.

The DTC Association (The Hong Kong Association of Restricted Licence Banks and Deposit-Taking Companies): Unit 2404, 24/F, Bonham Trade Centre, 50 Bonham Strand East, Sheung Wan; tel. 25264079; fax 25230180; e-mail dtca@dtca.org.hk; internet www.dtca.org.hk; f. 1981; Sec. PUI CHONG LUND; 50 mem. banks.

The Hong Kong Association of Banks: Rm 525, Prince's Bldg, Central; tel. 25211169; fax 28685035; e-mail info@hkab.org.hk; internet www.hkab.org.hk; f. 1981; est. to succeed The Exchange Banks' Asscn of Hong Kong; all licensed banks in Hong Kong are required by law to be mems of this statutory body, the function of which is to represent and further the interests of the banking sector; 132 mems; chaired by Bank of China (HK) Ltd; Sec. EVA WONG.

STOCK EXCHANGE

Hong Kong Exchanges and Clearing Ltd (HKEx): 12/F, One International Finance Centre, 1 Harbour View St, Central; tel. 25221122; fax 22953106; e-mail info@hkex.com.hk; internet www.hkex.com.hk; f. 2000; est. by merger of the Stock Exchange of Hong Kong, the Hong Kong Futures Exchange and the Hong Kong Securities Clearing Co; Chair. RONALD ARCULLI; CEO CHARLES LI.

SUPERVISORY BODY

Securities and Futures Commission (SFC): 8/F, Chater House, 8 Connaught Rd, Central; tel. 28409222; fax 25217836; e-mail enquiry@sfc.hk; internet www.sfc.hk; f. 1989; regulates the securities and futures markets; Chair. EDDY FONG; CEO ASHLEY ALDER.

INSURANCE

In December 2007 there were 178 authorized insurance companies, of which 112 were pure general insurers, 47 were pure long-term insurers and the remaining 19 were composite insurers. The following are among the principal companies:

ACE Insurance Ltd: 25/F, Shui On Centre, 6–8 Harbour Rd, Wanchai; tel. 31916800; fax 25603565; e-mail inquiries.hk@acegroup.com; internet www.aceinsurance.com.hk; Pres. and CEO (Asia-Pacific) DAMIEN SULLIVAN.

American Home Assurance Co: AIA Bldg, 1 Stubbs Rd, Wanchai; tel. 28321800; e-mail cs@aiu.com.hk; internet www.aiu.com.hk.

Asia Insurance Co Ltd: Worldwide House, 16/F, 19 Des Voeux Rd, Central; tel. 36069933; fax 28100218; e-mail mailbox@afh.hk; internet www.asiainsurance.com.hk; Chair. ROBIN CHAN.

Aviva Life Insurance Co Ltd: Suite 1701, Cityplaza One, 1111 King's Rd, Taikoo Shing; tel. 35509600; fax 29071787; e-mail enquiry@aviva-asia.com; internet www.aviva.com.hk; Gen. Man. ELBA TSE.

AXA General Insurance Hong Kong Ltd: 21/F, Manhattan Pl., 23 Wang Tai Rd, Kowloon Bay; tel. 25233061; fax 28100706; e-mail axahk@axa-insurance.com.hk; internet www.axa-insurance.com.hk; CEO BILLY CHAN.

Bank of China Group Insurance Co Ltd: 9/F, Wing On House, 71 Des Voeux Rd, Central; tel. 28670888; fax 25221705; e-mail info_ins@bocgroup.com; internet www.bocgroup.com/bocg-ins.

China Taiping Insurance (HK) Co Ltd: China Taiping Tower, 19/F, 8 Sunning Rd, Causeway Bay; tel. 28151551; fax 25416567; e-mail mai@mingan.com.hk; internet www.mingan.com; f. 1949; fmrly Ming An Insurance Co Ltd, name changed as above in 2009; Chair. LIN FAN; CEO CHENG KWOK PING.

Hong Kong Export Credit Insurance Corpn: South Seas Centre, Tower I, 2/F, 75 Mody Rd, Tsim Sha Tsui East, Kowloon; tel. 27329988; fax 27226277; internet www.hkecic.com; f. 1966; est. by govt to encourage and support trade; Commr RALPH LAI; Gen. Man. CYNTHIA CHIN.

HSBC Insurance (Asia) Ltd: 18/F, Tower 1, HSBC Centre, 1 Sham Mong Road, Kowloon; tel. 22886688; fax 28277636; e-mail insurance@hsbc.com.hk; internet www.insurance.asiapacific.hsbc.com; Man. Dir JASON SADLER.

MSIG Insurance (Hong Kong) Ltd: 9/F, Cityplaza One, 1111 King's Rd, Taikoo Shing; tel. 28940555; fax 28905741; e-mail hk_hotline@hk.msig-asia.com; internet www.msig.com.hk; CEO KENNETH REID.

Prudential Assurance Co Ltd: 23/F, One Exchange Square, Central; tel. 22811333; fax 29771233; e-mail service@prudential.com.hk; internet www.prudential.com.hk; life and general; CEO DEREK YUNG.

QBE Hongkong and Shanghai Insurance Ltd: 17/F, Warwick House, West Wing, Taikoo Place, 979 King's Rd, Quarry Bay; tel. 28778488; fax 36070300; e-mail info.hk@qbe.com.hk; internet www.qbe.com.hk; Gen. Man. JECKY LUI.

Royal and Sun Alliance (Hong Kong) Ltd: Dorset House, 32/F, Taikoo Place, 979 King's Rd, Quarry Bay; tel. 29683000; fax 29685111; e-mail hotline@hk.rsagroup.com; internet www.rsagroup.com.hk; Chief Exec. SIMON LEE.

Swiss Re Hong Kong Branch: 61/F, Central Plaza, 18 Harbour Rd, Wanchai; tel. 28274345; fax 28276033; acquired Mercantile and General Reinsurance in 1996; Head (Asia) MARTYN PARKER.

Zurich Insurance Group (Hong Kong): 24–27/F, One Island East, 18 Westlands Rd, Island East; tel. 29682222; fax 29680988; e-mail enquiry@hk.zurich.com; internet www.zurich.com.hk; CEO TED RIDGWAY.

Insurance Associations

Hong Kong Federation of Insurers (HKFI): 29/F, Sunshine Plaza, 353 Lockhart Rd, Wanchai; tel. 25201868; fax 25201967; e-mail hkfi@hkfi.org.hk; internet www.hkfi.org.hk; f. 1988; 87 general insurance and 47 life insurance mems; Chair. ALLAN YU.

Insurance Institute of Hong Kong: Rm 1705, Beverly House, 93–107 Lockhart Rd, Wanchai; tel. 25200098; fax 22953939; e-mail enquiry@iihk.org.hk; internet www.iihk.org.hk; f. 1967; Pres. MICHAEL HAYNES.

Trade and Industry

Hong Kong Trade Development Council: 38/F, Office Tower, Convention Plaza, 1 Harbour Rd, Wanchai; tel. 1830668; fax 28240249; e-mail hktdc@hktdc.org; internet www.hktdc.com; f. 1966; Chair. JACK SO CHAK-KWONG; Exec. Dir FREDERICK LAM.

Trade and Industry Department: Rm 908, Trade and Industry Department Tower, 700 Nathan Rd, Kowloon; tel. 23922922; fax 27877422; e-mail enquiry@tid.gov.hk; internet www.tid.gov.hk; Dir-Gen. MARIA KWAN.

DEVELOPMENT ORGANIZATIONS

Hong Kong Housing Authority: 33 Fat Kwong St, Homantin, Kowloon; tel. 27122712; fax 27114111; e-mail hkha@housingauthority.gov.hk; internet www.housingauthority.gov.hk; f. 1973; plans, builds and manages public housing; Chair. EVA CHENG; Dir of Housing D. W. PESCOD.

Hong Kong Productivity Council: HKPC Bldg, 78 Tat Chee Ave, Yau Yat Chuen, Kowloon Tong, Kowloon; tel. 27885678; fax 27885900; e-mail hkpcenq@hkpc.org; internet www.hkpc.org; f. 1967; promotes increased productivity and international competitiveness of industry; Council comprises a Chair. and 22 mems appointed by the Govt, representing managerial, labour, academic and professional interests, and govt depts associated with productivity matters; Chair. CLEMENT CHEN CHENG-JEN; Exec. Dir AGNES MAK TANG PIK-YEE.

CHAMBERS OF COMMERCE

Chinese Chamber of Commerce, Kowloon: 2/F, 8–10 Nga Tsin Long Rd, Kowloon; tel. 23822309; f. 1936; 234 mems; Chair. and Exec. Dir YEUNG CHOR-HANG.

The Chinese General Chamber of Commerce: 4/F, 24–25 Connaught Rd, Central; tel. 25256385; fax 28452610; e-mail cgcc@cgcc.org.hk; internet www.cgcc.org.hk; f. 1900; 6,000 mems; Chair. JONATHAN CHOI KOON-SHUM.

Hong Kong General Chamber of Commerce: United Centre, 22/F, 95 Queensway, POB 852. Admiralty; tel. 25299229; fax 25279843; e-mail chamber@chamber.org.hk; internet www.chamber.org.hk; f. 1861; 4,000 mems; Chair. ANTHONY WU; CEO ALEX FONG.

Kowloon Chamber of Commerce: KCC Bldg, 3/F, 2 Liberty Ave, Homantin, Kowloon; tel. 27600393; fax 27610166; e-mail kcc02@hkkcc.biz.com.hk; internet www.hkkcc.org.hk; f. 1938; 1,600 mems; Chair. CHENG KWAN SUEN; Sec. of Gen. Affairs CHENG PO-WO.

FOREIGN TRADE ORGANIZATIONS

Hong Kong Chinese Importers' and Exporters' Association: Champion Bldg, 7–8/F, 287–291 Des Voeux Rd, Central; tel. 25448474; fax 25814979; e-mail info@hkciea.org.hk; internet www.hkciea.org.hk; f. 1954; 3,000 mems; Pres. ZHUANG CHENG XIN.

Hong Kong Exporters' Association: Rm 825, Star House, 3 Salisbury Rd, Tsim Sha Tsui, Kowloon; tel. 27309851; fax 27301869; e-mail exporter@exporters.org.hk; internet www.exporters.org.hk; f. 1955; not-for-profit asscn; comprises leading merchants and manufacturing exporters; 598 mems (June 2011); Chair. TOM TANG; Exec. Dir SHIRLEY SO.

INDUSTRIAL AND TRADE ASSOCIATIONS

Chinese Manufacturers' Association of Hong Kong: CMA Bldg, 64 Connaught Rd, Central; tel. 25456166; fax 25414541; e-mail info@cma.org.hk; internet www.cma.org.hk; f. 1934; promotes and protects industrial and trading interests; operates testing and certification laboratories; 3,700 mems; Pres. Dr DAVID Y. K. WONG.

Communications Association of Hong Kong: GPOB 13461; tel. 25042732; fax 25042752; e-mail info@cahk.hk; internet www.cahk.hk; 108 mems; Chair. Dr HUBERT CHAN.

Federation of Hong Kong Garment Manufacturers: Unit 401–403, Cheung Lee Commercial Bldg, 25 Kimberley Rd, Tsim Sha Tsui, Kowloon; tel. 27211383; fax 23111062; e-mail info@garment.org.hk; internet www.garment.org.hk; f. 1964; 120 mems; Pres. YEUNG FAN; Sec.-Gen. MICHAEL LEUNG.

Federation of Hong Kong Industries (FHKI): 31/F, Billion Plaza, 8 Cheung Yue St, Cheung Sha Wan, Kowloon; tel. 27323188; fax 27213494; e-mail fhki@fhki.org.hk; internet www.industryhk.org; f. 1960; 3,000 mems; Chair. CLIFF SUN; Dir-Gen. DENNIS T. W. YAU.

Federation of Hong Kong Watch Trades and Industries Ltd: Peter Bldg, Rm 604, 58–62 Queen's Rd, Central; tel. 25233232; fax 28684485; e-mail hkwatch@hkwatch.org; internet www.hkwatch.org; f. 1947; 650 mems; Chair. JOSEPH CHU KAI TO.

Hong Kong Association for the Advancement of Science and Technology Ltd: 2A, Tak Lee Commercial Bldg, 113–117 Wanchai Rd, Wanchai; tel. 28913388; fax 28381823; e-mail info@hkaast.org.hk; internet www.hkaast.org.hk; f. 1985; 170 mems; Pres. YUNG QILIANG.

Hong Kong Biotechnology Association Ltd: Rm 1007, 10/F, Hang Seng Bldg, 77 Des Voeux Rd, Central; tel. 28770222; fax 26201238; e-mail secretary@hkbta.org.hk; internet www.hkbta.org.hk; f. 1999; 100 mems; Chair. FRANK WAN.

Hong Kong Chinese Enterprises Association: Rm 2104–2106, Harbour Centre, 25 Harbour Rd, Wanchai; tel. 28272831; fax 28272606; e-mail info@hkcea.com; internet www.hkcea.com; f. 1991; 960 mems; Pres. FENG HONGZHENG.

Hong Kong Chinese Textile Mills Association: 11/F, 38–40 Tai Po Rd, Sham Shiu Po, Kowloon; tel. 27778236; fax 27881836; f. 1921; 150 mems; Pres. Dr ROGER NG KENG-PO.

Hong Kong Construction Association Ltd: 3/F, 180–182 Hennessy Rd, Wanchai; tel. 25724414; fax 25727104; e-mail admin@hkca.com.hk; internet www.hkca.com.hk; f. 1920; 372 mems; Pres. CONRAD WONG.

Hong Kong Electronic Industries Association Ltd: Rm 1201, 12/F, Harbour Crystal Centre, 100 Granville Rd, Tsim Sha Tsui, Kowloon; tel. 27788328; fax 27882200; e-mail hkeia@hkeia.org; internet www.hkeia.org; 310 mems; Chair. Dr K. B. CHAN; Exec. Dir ALFRED WONG.

Hong Kong Footwear Association: Kar Tseuk Bldg, 2/F, Blk A, 185 Prince Edward Rd, Kowloon; internet www.hkfootwear.org; f. 1948; over 300 mems; Pres. TOMMY FONG.

Hong Kong Garment Manufacturers Association: Unit 401–403, Cheung Lee Commercial Bldg, 25 Kimberley Rd, Tsim Sha Tsui, Kowloon; tel. 23052893; fax 23052493; e-mail sec@textilecouncil.com; f. 1987; 40 mems; Chair. PETER WANG.

Hong Kong Information Technology Federation Ltd: KITEC, 1 Trademart Dr., Kowloon Bay, Kowloon; tel. 31018197; fax 30074728;

e-mail info@hkitf.com; internet www.hkitf.org.hk; over 300 mems; f. 1980; Pres. FRANCIS FONG.

Hong Kong Jewellery and Jade Manufacturers Association: Flat A, 12/F, Kaiser Estate Phase 1, 41 Man Yue St, Hunghom, Kowloon; tel. 25430543; fax 28150164; e-mail hkjja@hkjja.org; internet www.jewellery-hk.org; f. 1965; 227 mems; Pres. CHARLES CHAN; Chair. BILLY LAU.

Hong Kong Jewelry Manufacturers' Association: Unit G, 2/F, Kaiser Estate Phase 2, 51 Man Yue St, Hunghom, Kowloon; tel. 27663002; fax 23623647; e-mail enquiry@jewelry.org.hk; internet www.jewelry.org.hk; f. 1988; 345 mems; Chair. SUNNY CHAN.

Hong Kong Knitwear Exporters and Manufacturers Association: Unit 401–403, Cheung Lee Commercial Bldg, 25 Kimberley Rd, Tsim Sha Tsui, Kowloon; tel. 27552621; fax 27565672; f. 1966; 70 mems; Chair. LAWRENCE LEUNG; Exec. Sec. KARINA TSUI.

Hong Kong Optical Manufacturers' Association Ltd: 2/F, 11 Fa Yuen St, Mongkok, Kowloon; tel. 23326505; fax 27705786; e-mail hkoma@netvigator.com; internet www.hkoptical.org.hk; f. 1982; 111 mems; Pres. HUI LEUNG WAH.

Hong Kong Plastics Manufacturers Association Ltd: Rm 3, 10/F, Asia Standard Tower, 59–65 Queen's Rd, Central; tel. 25742230; fax 25742843; f. 1957; 200 mems; Chair. CLIFF SUN; Pres. JEFFREY LAM.

Hong Kong Printers Association: 1/F, 48–50 Johnston Rd, Wanchai; tel. 25275050; fax 28610463; e-mail printers@hkprinters.org; internet www.hkprinters.org; f. 1939; 400 mems; Chair. YEUNG KAM KAI.

Hong Kong Sze Yap Commercial and Industrial Association: Cosco Tower, Unit 1205–6, 183 Queen's Rd, Central; tel. 25438095; fax 25449495; e-mail gahk_ltd@hotmail.com; f. 1909; 1,082 mems; Chair. LOUIE CHICK-NAN; Sec. WONG KA CHUN.

Hong Kong Toys Council: 31/F, Billion Plaza, 8 Cheung Yue St, Cheung Sha Wan, Kowloon; tel. 27323188; fax 27213494; e-mail hktc@fhki.org.hk; internet www.toyshk.org; f. 1986; 200 mems; Chair. BERNIE TING WAI CHEUNG; Sec.-Gen. JOSEPH LI.

Hong Kong Watch Manufacturers' Association: Fu Hing Bldg, 2/F, 10 Jubilee St, Central; tel. 25225238; fax 28106614; e-mail hkwma@netvigator.com; internet www.hkwma.org; 650 mems; Pres. PAUL SO; Sec.-Gen. HUNG HAN SANG.

Information and Software Industry Association Ltd: China Overseas Bldg, 24B, 139 Hennessy Rd, Wanchai; tel. 26222867; fax 26222731; e-mail info@isia.org.hk; internet www.isia.org.hk; f. 1999; 76 mems; Chair. REGGIE WONG.

New Territories Commercial and Industrial General Association Ltd: Cheong Hay Bldg, 2/F, 107 Hoi Pa St, Tsuen Wan; tel. 24145316; fax 24934130; e-mail ntciga@netvigator.com; f. 1973; 2,663 mems; Pres. YU WAN; Chair. WAN HOK LIM; Sec.-Gen. HUANG JINHUI.

Real Estate Developers Association of Hong Kong: Worldwide House, Rm 1403, 19 Des Voeux Rd, Central; tel. 28260111; fax 28452521; f. 1965; 829 mems; Pres. Dr STANLEY HO; Chair. KEITH KERR; Sec.-Gen. LOUIS LOONG.

Textile Council of Hong Kong Ltd: 401–3, Cheung Lee Commercial Bldg, 25 Kimberley Rd, Tsim Sha Tsui, Kowloon; tel. 23052893; fax 23052493; e-mail sec@textilecouncil.com; internet www.textilecouncil.com; f. 1989; 11 mems; Chair. WILLY LIN; Exec. Dir MICHAEL LEUNG.

Toys Manufacturers' Association of Hong Kong Ltd: Rm 1302, Metroplaza, Tower 2, 223 Hing Fong Rd, Kwai Chung, New Territories; tel. 24221209; fax 31880982; e-mail info@tmhk.net; internet www.tmhk.net; f. 1996; 250 mems; Pres. SAMSON CHAM.

EMPLOYERS' ORGANIZATIONS

Employers' Federation of Hong Kong: Suite 2004, Sino Plaza, 255–257 Gloucester Rd, Causeway Bay; tel. 25280033; fax 28655285; e-mail info@efhk.org.hk; internet www.efhk.org.hk; f. 1947; 504 mems; Chair. JOHN CHAN; Exec. Dir LOUIS PONG.

Hong Kong Factory Owners' Association Ltd: Wing Wong Bldg, 11/F, 557–559 Nathan Rd, Kowloon; tel. 23882372; fax 23857129; f. 1982; 1,261 mems; Pres. HWANG JEN; Sec. CHA KIT YEN.

UTILITIES

Electricity

CLP Power Ltd: 147 Argyle St, Kowloon; tel. 26788111; fax 27604448; e-mail clp_info@clp.com.hk; internet www.clpgroup.com; f. 1918; fmrly China Light and Power Co Ltd; generation and supply of electricity to Kowloon and the New Territories; Chair. Sir MICHAEL D. KADOORIE; CEO ANDREW BRANDLER.

The Hongkong Electric Co Ltd: 44 Kennedy Rd; tel. 28433111; fax 28100506; e-mail mail@hec.com.hk; internet www.heh.com; generation and supply of electricity to Hong Kong Island, and the islands of Ap Lei Chau and Lamma; Chair. CANNING FOK KIN-NING; Man. Dir TSO KAI SUM.

Gas

Gas Authority: all gas supply cos, gas installers and contractors are required to be registered with the Gas Authority. At the end of 2003 there were seven registered gas supply cos.

Chinese People Holdings Co Ltd: Unit 2111, 21/F, China Merchants Tower, Shun Tak Centre, 168–200 Connaught Rd, Central; tel. 29022008; fax 28030108; e-mail info@681hk.com; internet www.681hk.com; distributes and supplies natural gas in mainland China; Chair. Dr MO SHIKANG; Man. Dir JIN SONG.

Hong Kong and China Gas Co Ltd (Towngas): Leighton Centre Basement, 77 Leighton Rd, Causeway Bay; tel. 25761535; fax 28948058; e-mail compsec@towngas.com; internet www.towngas.com; f. 1862; production, distribution and marketing of gas, water and related activities in Hong Kong and mainland China; operates two plants; Chair. LEE SHAU KEE; Man. Dir ALFRED CHAN WING KIM.

Water

Drainage Services Department: responsible for planning, designing, constructing, operating and maintaining the sewerage, sewage treatment and stormwater drainage infrastructures.

Water Supplies Department: 48/F, Immigration Tower, 7 Gloucester Rd, Wanchai; tel. 28294500; fax 28240578; e-mail wsdinfo@wsd.gov.hk; internet www.wsd.gov.hk; responsible for water supplies for some 7m. people living within 1,100 sq km of the Hong Kong SAR; Dir MA LEE TAK.

MAJOR COMPANIES

The following are among Hong Kong's leading companies. Capital, reserves and sales are given in HK dollars unless otherwise stated.

Brilliance China Automotive Holdings: jt ventures with several mainland vehicle manufacturers and Toyota (Japan); see Major Companies of the People's Republic of China.

Cheung Kong (Holdings) Ltd: Cheung Kong Centre, 7/F, 2 Queen's Rd, Central; tel. 21288888; fax 21288348; e-mail contactckh@ckh.com.hk; internet www.ckh.com.hk; cap. and res 234,268m., sales 24,293m. (2009); investment holding, project management, property devt; Chair. LI KA-SHING; Man. Dir VICTOR LI TZAR KUOI; 8,700 employees.

China Daye Non-Ferrous Metals Mining Ltd: Unit 2201, World Wide House, 19 Des Voeux Rd, Central; tel. 28682101; fax 28682302; e-mail info@hk661.com; internet www.hk661.com; cap. 257.5m., res 573.7m., revenue 20.2m. (2008/09); exploration and devt of non-ferrous mines; fmrly known as China National Resources Development Holdings Ltd, name changed as above in 2009; Chair. WAN BI QI; CEO CHEN XIANG.

China Resources Enterprise Ltd: Rm 3908, China Resources Bldg, 26 Harbour Rd, Wanchai; tel. 28271028; fax 25988453; e-mail info@cre.com.hk; internet www.cre.com.hk; f. 1992; cap. and res 25,847m., sales 71,629m. (2009); food and beverages, distribution and trading, retailing; Chair. QIAO SHIBO; Man. Dir CHEN LANG; approx. 152,000 employees.

Chow Sang Sang Holdings International Ltd: Chow Sang Sang Bldg, 4/F, 229 Nathan Rd, Kowloon; tel. 29910366; fax 27309683; e-mail tamsy@chowsangsang.com; internet www.chowsangsang.com; cap. 150m., res 3,621m., sales 9,463m. (2009); manufacturing, retailing and trading of jewellery, gold and other precious metals; Chair. CHOW KWEN LIM; Gen. Man. WING SING CHOW; 4,000 employees.

CITIC Pacific Ltd: CITIC Tower, 32/F, 1 Tim Mei Ave, Central; tel. 28202111; fax 28772771; e-mail contact@citicpacific.com; internet www.citicpacific.com; cap. and res 59,347m., sales 19,079m. (2009); investment holding, power generation, construction of roads, bridges and tunnels; Chair. CHANG ZHENMING; Man. Dir ZHANG JIJING; 24,319 employees (2007).

Crocodile Garments Ltd: Rm 1001, 10/F, Lai Sun Commercial Centre, 680 Cheung Sha Wan Rd, Kowloon; tel. 27853898; fax 27860190; e-mail corpadmin@crocodile.com.hk; internet www.crocodile.com.hk; cap. and res 446.3m., revenue 432m. (2009); manufacture and sale of garments; Chair. and CEO LAM KIN MING; 900 employees.

Crown Motors Ltd: 22/F, Citicorp Center, 18 Whitfield Rd, North Point; tel. 25622226; fax 28111060; internet www.crown-motors.com; subsidiary of Inchcape.

Dah Chong Hong Holdings Ltd: 8/F, DCH Bldg, 20 Kai Cheung Rd, Kowloon Bay, Kowloon; tel. 27683388; fax 27968838; e-mail dch@dch.com.hk; internet www.dch.com.hk; f. 1946; cap. and res 5,457m., sales 22,131m. (2009); subsidiary of CITIC Pacific Ltd; manufacture and retail of foods; distribution of motor vehicles; Chair. HUI YING BUN; CEO YIP MOON TONG; 12,070 employees.

Daido Concrete (HK) Ltd: Unit 1906, 19/F, West Tower, Shun Tak Centre, 168–200 Connaught Rd, Central; tel. 31078600; fax 21111438; e-mail general@daidohk.com; internet www.daidohk.com; cap. and res 382.7m., sales 155.2m. (2009); manufacture and sale of concrete piles; trading in construction materials; Chair. FUNG WA KO; 279 employees.

Dairy Farm International Holdings Ltd: Devon House, 7/F, Taikoo Place, 979 King's Rd, Quarry Bay; tel. 22991888; fax 22994888; internet www.dairyfarmgroup.com; cap. and res US $504.2m., sales US $7,028.5m. (2009); international food and drugstore retailing; Chair. SIMON KESWICK; CEO MICHAEL KOK; 77,000 employees.

Dickson Concepts (International) Ltd: East Ocean Centre, 4/F, 98 Granville Rd, Tsim Sha Tsui East, Kowloon; tel. 23113888; fax 23113323; internet www.dickson.com.hk; cap. 111.6m., res 1,963.4m., revenue 3,633.6m. (2010); investment holding; trading of luxury goods; Chair. DICKSON POON; CEO RAYMOND LEE; 2,553 employees.

Geely Automobile Holdings Ltd: 23/F, Rm 2301, Great Eagle Centre, 23 Harbour Rd, Wanchai; tel. 25983333; fax 25983399; e-mail general@geelyauto.com.hk; internet www.geelyauto.com.hk; cap. and res 6,375.6m. yuan, revenue 14,069m. yuan (2009); mfrs and distributors of automobiles, principally in the People's Republic of China; Chair. LI SHU FU; CEO GUI SHENG YUE; 12,282 employees.

Gold Peak Industries (Holdings) Ltd: Gold Peak Bldg, 8/F, 30 Kwai Wing Rd, Kwai Chung, New Territories; tel. 24271133; fax 24891879; e-mail gp@goldpeak.com; internet www.goldpeak.com; cap. and res 1,474m., sales 1,457.5m. (2009/10); manufacture and sale of batteries, car audio equipment, other electrical and electronic products; Chair. VICTOR C. W. LO; 12,700 employees.

Guangdong Investment Ltd: Guangdong Investment Tower, 28–29/F, 148 Connaught Rd, Central; tel. 28604368; fax 25284386; internet www.gdi.com.hk; cap. and res 16,657.2m., revenue 5,915.7m. (2009); holding company, activities incl. travel, hotels, property, industrial investment, water supply and energy; Chair. LI WENYUE; Man. Dir ZHANG HUI; 4,016 employees.

Hang Lung Properties Ltd: Standard Chartered Bank Bldg, 28/F, 4 Des Voeux Rd, Central; tel. 28790111; fax 28686086; e-mail CorpComm@hanglung.com; internet www.hanglung.com; f. 1949; cap. and res 68,037.5m., sales 4,172.6m. (2008/09); property investment and management, investment holding and car-park management; Chair. RONNIE CHICHUNG CHAN; Man. Dir PHILIP NAN LOK CHEN; 1,955 employees.

Henderson Land Development Co Ltd: Worldwide House, 6/F, 19 Des Voeux Rd, Central; tel. 28265222; fax 29088838; e-mail henderson@hld.com; internet www.hld.com; cap. and res 133,127m., revenue 15,230m. (June 2008–Dec. 2009); property devt and investment, investment holding; Chair. and Man. Dir Dr LEE SHAU KEE; 7,700 employees.

Hong Kong Land Holdings Ltd: 8/F, One Exchange Sq., 8 Connaught Place, Central; tel. 28428428; fax 28459226; e-mail gpobox@hkland.com; internet www.hkland.com; cap. and res US $12,756m., revenue US $1,322.6m. (2009); property investment and devt; part of Jardine Matheson group; Chair. SIMON KESWICK; Man. Dir A. J. L. NIGHTINGALE; CEO Y. K. PANG; 1,104 employees.

Hopewell Holdings Ltd: Hopewell Centre, 64/F, 183 Queen's Rd East, Wanchai; tel. 25284975; fax 28656276; e-mail ir@hopewellholdings.com; internet www.hopewellholdings.com; cap. and res 16,310m. (2005), sales 968m. (2009); property investment and management, road infrastructure and power station projects; Chair. Sir GORDON WU YING SHEUNG; Man. Dir THOMAS JEFFERSON WU; 1,170 employees.

Hutchison Whampoa Ltd: Hutchison House, 22/F, 10 Harcourt Rd; tel. 21281188; fax 21281705; e-mail info@hutchison-whampoa.com; internet www.hutchison-whampoa.com; cap. and res 283,531m., revenue 301,000m. (2009); investment holding and management company; Chair. LI KA-SHING; Man. Dir CANNING FOK; 220,000 employees.

Hysan Development Co Ltd: Manulife Plaza, 49/F, The Lee Gardens, 33 Hysan Ave, Causeway Bay; tel. 28955777; fax 25775153; e-mail hysan@hysan.com.hk; internet www.hysan.com.hk; cap. and res 33,668m., sales 1,680m. (2009); property investment, management and devt; Chair. Sir DAVID AKERS-JONES; CEO GERRY LUI FAI YIM; 487 employees.

Jardine Matheson Holdings Ltd: 48/F, Jardine House, GPOB 70; tel. 28438288; fax 28459005; e-mail jml@jardines.com; internet www.jardines.com; f. 1832; cap. and res US $11,094m., revenue US $22,501m. (2009); engineering and construction, transport services, insurance brokerage, property investment and development, retail, restaurants, hotels, motor vehicles and related activities, financial services, heavy equipment, mining and agribusiness; Chair. Sir HENRY KESWICK; Man. Dir A. J. L. NIGHTINGALE; 285,000 employees (world-wide).

Jardine Motors Group Ltd: Devon House, 25/F, Taikoo Place, 979 King's Rd, Quarry Bay; tel. 25792888; fax 28569674; e-mail jpl@jardines.com; internet www.jardines.com; revenue US $2,522m. (2009); sales and servicing of motor vehicles; Chair. ANTHONY NIGHTINGALE; 10,000 employees.

Jardine Pacific Ltd: Devon House, 25/F, Taikoo Place, 979 King's Rd, Quarry Bay; tel. 25792888; fax 28569674; e-mail jpl@jardines.com; internet www.jardines.com; f. 1997; revenue US $3,104m. (2009); marketing and distribution, engineering and construction, aviation and shipping, property and financial services; Chair. ANTHONY NIGHTINGALE; 53,000 employees.

Johnson Electric Holdings Ltd: 12 Science Park East Ave, 6/F, Shatin, New Territories; tel. 26636688; fax 28972054; e-mail sales@johnsonelectric.com; internet www.johnsonelectric.com; f. 1959; cap. and res US $1,091.4m., sales US $1,741m. (2009/10); design, manufacture and marketing of motors for automotive and commercial applications; Chair. and CEO PATRICK SHUI-CHUNG WANG; 38,000 employees (world-wide).

Kader Holdings Co Ltd: Kader Bldg, 11/F, 22 Kai Cheung Rd, Kowloon; tel. 27981688; fax 27961126; e-mail info@kader.com; internet www.kader.com.hk; f. 1989; cap. 66.5m., res 816.9m., revenue 1,537.6m. (2009); manufacture and sale of plastic and stuffed toys, electronic toys and model trains, property investment, investment holding and trading; Chair. KENNETH W. S. TING; Man. Dir IVAN T. L. TING; 19,763 employees.

Kerry Properties Ltd: 14/F, Cityplaza 3, 14 Taikoo Wan Rd, Taikoo Shing; tel. 29672200; fax 29679480; e-mail communication@kerryprops.com; internet www.kerryprops.com; f. 1996; cap. and res 13,893m., sales 12,938.2m. (2009); property management in Hong Kong and the People's Republic of China; Chair. KUOK KHOON CHEN; Man. Dir WONG SIU KONG; 7,663 employees.

Lai Sun Garment (International) Ltd: Lai Sun Commercial Centre, 11/F, 680 Cheung Sha Wan Rd, Kowloon; tel. 27410391; fax 27852775; e-mail advpr@laisun.com; internet www.laisun.com; cap. and res 164.8m., sales 14.5m. (2009); manufacture and sales of garments; Chair. and Man. Dir LAM KIN MING; 2,000 employees.

Lam Soon (Hong Kong) Ltd: 21 Dai Fu St, Tai Po Industrial Estate, New Territories; tel. 26803388; fax 26804069; e-mail webmaster@lamsoon.com; internet www.lamsoon.com; cap. and res 1,296m., sales 2,072m. (2008/09); investment holding co, its subsidiaries' activities incl. the processing and trading of edible oils, flour products, food products, detergents, electronic products and packaging; Chair. KWEK LENG HAI; Man. Dir LEUNG WAI FUNG; 1,300 employees.

Li & Fung Ltd: 11/F, Li Fung Tower, 888 Cheung Sha Wan Rd, Kowloon; tel. 23002300; fax 23002000; e-mail ir@lifung.com.hk; internet www.lifung.com; f. 1906; cap. and res 15,905.3m., sales 104,478.9m. (2009); manufacture and trade of consumer products; Chair. VICTOR K. FUNG; Man. Dir WILLIAM K. FUNG; 13,400 employees.

New World Development Co Ltd: New World Tower, 30/F, 18 Queen's Rd, Central; tel. 25231056; fax 28104673; e-mail newworld@nwd.com.hk; internet www.nwd.com.hk; cap. and res 73,600m., sales 24,415m. (2008/09); property investment, construction and hotels; Exec. Chair. Dato' Dr CHENG YU-TUNG; Man. Dir CHENG KAR-SHUN; 55,000 employees.

Shanghai Industrial Holdings Ltd: Harcourt House, 26/F, 39 Gloucester Rd, Wanchai; tel. 25295652; fax 25295067; e-mail enquiry@sihl.com.hk; internet www.sihl.com.hk; cap. and res 24,891.2m., sales 6,917.8m. (2009); manufacture, distribution and sale of cigarettes, packaging materials and printed products; Chair. TENG YI LONG; CEO CAI YU TIAN; 15,141 employees.

Shell Electric Mfg (Holding) Co Ltd: Shell Industrial Bldg, 1/F, 12 Lee Chung St, Chai Wan Industrial District; tel. 25580181; fax 28972095; e-mail group@smc.com.hk; internet www.smc.com.hk; cap. and res 3,008.6m., revenue 3,552.0m. (2007); manufacturing and marketing of electric fans and other household appliances; Chair. and Man. Dir BILLY YUNG KWOK KEE; 1,815 employees.

Shougang Concord International Enterprises Co Ltd: Bank of East Asia Harbour View Centre, 7/F, 51–57 Gloucester Rd, Wanchai; tel. 28612832; fax 25290126; e-mail info@shougang-intl.com.hk; internet www.shougang-intl.com.hk; cap. and res 8,581m., sales 11,357.6m. (2009); manufacture and sale of steel products; Chair. WANG QINGHAI; Man. Dir LI SHAOFENG; 3,900 employees.

Shui On Holdings Ltd: Shui On Centre, 34/F, 6–8 Harbour Rd, Wanchai; tel. 28791888; fax 28024396; e-mail corpcomm@shuion.com.hk; internet www.shuion.com; f. 1965; construction co, specializes in public sector projects; Chair. VINCENT H. S. LO; CEO FRANKIE Y. L. WONG.

Shun Tak Holdings Ltd: Penthouse 39/F, West Tower, Shun Tak Centre, 200 Connaught Rd, Central; tel. 28593111; fax 28577181; e-mail enquiry@shuntakgroup.com; internet www.shuntakgroup.com; f. 1972; cap. 505.9m., res 13,211.5m., sales 3,334m. (2009);

operates passenger ferries between Hong Kong and Macao; property devt; hotel investment and management in Macao; Chair. Dr STANLEY HO; Man. Dir PANSY HO; 2,300 employees.

Sime Darby Group Motors (HK) Ltd: East Wing, Hennessy Centre, 28/F, 500 Hennessy Rd, Causeway Bay; tel. 28950777; fax 28905896; internet www.simedarbymotors.com; distribution of motor vehicles and heavy construction equipment, industrial, electrical and mechanical contracting, etc.; Exec. Vice-Pres. Dato' LAWRENCE LEE; Man. Dir PETER GOH.

Sino Land Co Ltd: Tsim Sha Tsui Centre, 12/F, Salisbury Rd, Kowloon; tel. 27218388; fax 27235901; e-mail info@sino.com; internet www.sino.com; cap. and res 60,001m., sales 9,692.6m. (2008/09); investment holding, share investment, property devt and investment; Chair. ROBERT NG CHEE-SIONG; 5,800 employees.

Sun Hung Kai Properties Ltd: Sun Hung Kai Centre, 45/F, 30 Harbour Rd, Wanchai; tel. 28278111; fax 28272862; e-mail shkp@shkp.com; internet www.shkp.com; cap. and res 222,268m., revenue 34,234m. (2008/09); investment holding, property devt and management; Chair. KWONG SIU-HING; Man. Dir THOMAS KWOK; 31,000 employees.

Swire Group (John Swire and Sons (HK) Ltd): 35/F, Two Pacific Place, 88 Queensway, Central; tel. 28408888; fax 25269365; internet www.swire.com; shipping managers and agents, airline operators, aviation services, marine and aviation engineering, trading, China trade devt, property devt, operators of offshore oil drilling support equipment, mfrs of soft drinks and paints, packagers and distributors of sugar; also waste management; Chair. JAMES HUGHES-HALLETT.

Swire Pacific Ltd: Two Pacific Place, 35/F, 88 Queensway, Central; tel. 28408438; fax 25269365; internet www.swirepacific.com; cap. and res 15,443m., sales 24,909m. (2009); conglomerate; Chair. CHRISTOPHER D. PRATT; 43,000 employees.

Tse Sui Luen Jewellery (International) Ltd: Summit Bldg, Ground Floor, Block B, 30 Man Yue St, Hunghom, Kowloon; tel. 23334221; fax 27640753; internet www.tsljewellery.com; cap. and res 627.3m., sales 2,018m. (2009/10); investment holding co, its subsidiaries' activities incl. manufacturing and marketing of jewellery products; also property investment; Chair. ANNIE YEE; CEO ERWIN HUANG; 3,200 employees.

Tsim Sha Tsui Properties Ltd: Tsim Sha Tsui Centre, 12/F, Salisbury Rd, Kowloon; tel. 27218388; fax 27235901; e-mail info@sino.com; internet www.sino.com; cap. and res 5,355m. (2009); investment holding, property devt; Chair. ROBERT NG CHEE SIONG; 5,800 employees.

Unibros FE Ltd: Jardine House, Rm 2106, 1 Connaught Place, Central; tel. 25582306; fax 2582616; e-mail steel@unibros.com; internet www.unibros.com; sale of steel products.

Vitasoy International Holdings Ltd: 1 Kin Wong St, Tuen Mun, New Territories; tel. 24660333; fax 24651008; e-mail info@vitasoy.com; internet www.vitasoy.com; cap. and res 1,358m., sales 3,012m. (2009/10); manufacture and distribution of food and beverages; Chair. and Man. Dir WINSTON L. Y. LO; 3,200 employees.

A S Watson and Co Ltd: Watson House, 11/F, 1–5 Wo Lin Hang Rd, Fo Tan, Sha Tin, New Territories; tel. 26068833; fax 26953664; e-mail grouppr@aswatson.com; internet www.aswatson.com; mfr of mineral water, fruit juices and ice cream; Man. Dir DOMINIC LAI; 87,000 employees.

The Wharf (Holdings) Ltd: Ocean Centre, 16/F, Harbour City, Canton Rd, Kowloon; tel. 21188118; fax 21188018; e-mail ir@wharfholdings.com; internet www.wharfholdings.com; f. 1886; cap. and res 115,210m., sales 17,553m. (2009); property investment and devt, hotels, logistics, hotels, communications, media and entertainment, and transport; Chair. PETER K. C. WOO; Man. Dir STEPHEN NG; more than 10,000 employees.

Wheelock & Co Ltd: Wheelock House, 23/F, 20 Pedder St; tel. 21182118; fax 21182018; e-mail ir@wheelockcompany.com; internet www.wheelockcompany.com; f. 1857; cap. and res 68,691m., sales 18,957m. (2009); merchant house and property investment; Chair. PETER K. C. WOO; 13,400 employees.

Winsor Industrial Corpn Ltd: East Ocean Centre, 2/F, 98 Granville Rd, Tsimshatsui East, Kowloon; tel. 27311888; fax 28101199; e-mail ir@winsorindustrial.com; internet www.winsorindustrial.com; cap. and res 1,410.8m., sales 867.7m. (2005/06); investment holding co, its subsidiaries' activities incl. manufacture of textiles, knitwear and other garments; Chair. CHOU WEN HSIEN; Man. Dir CHOW CHUNG KAI; 3,400 employees.

TRADE UNIONS

In December 2005 there were 729 trade unions in Hong Kong, comprising 686 employees' unions, 21 employers' associations and 22 mixed organizations.

Hong Kong and Kowloon Trades Union Council (TUC): 11/F, On Cheong Bldg, 456 Nathan Rd, Kowloon; tel. 23845150; fax 27705396; e-mail hktuc@yahoo.com.hk; f. 1949; 66 affiliated unions, mostly covering the catering and building trades; 30,000 mems; supports Taiwan; affiliated to ITUC; Pres. TONG WOON FAI; Gen. Sec. LEE TAK-MING.

Hong Kong Confederation of Trade Unions: Wing Wong Commercial Bldg, 19/F, 557–559 Nathan Rd, Kowloon; tel. 27708668; fax 27707388; e-mail hkctu@hkctu.org.hk; internet www.hkctu.org.hk; f. 1990; registered Feb. 1990; 89 affiliated independent unions and federations; 170,000 mems; affiliated to ITUC and IFWEA; Pres. CHENG CHING FAT; Gen. Sec. LEE CHEUK-YAN.

The Hong Kong Federation of Trade Unions (HKFTU): 12 Ma Hang Chung Rd, Tokwawan, Kowloon; tel. 36525700; fax 27608477; e-mail info@ftu.org.hk; internet www.ftu.org.hk; f. 1948; 221 affiliated and associated unions, mostly in textiles, printing, insurance, construction, manufacturing, civil service, wholesale & retail, public transport and public utilities; approx. 341,000 mems; Pres. CHENG YIU-TONG; Chair. NG CHAU-PEI.

Also active are the Federation of Hong Kong and Kowloon Labour Unions (31 affiliated unions with 21,700 mems) and the Federation of Civil Service Unions (29 affiliated unions with 12,000 mems).

Transport

Transport Department: 41/F Immigration Tower, 7 Gloucester Rd, Wanchai; tel. 28042600; fax 28240433; e-mail tdenq@td.gov.hk; internet www.td.gov.hk; Commr JOSEPH LAI.

RAILWAYS

Kowloon–Canton Railway Corpn: 8/F, Fo Tan Railway House, 9 Lok King St, Fo Tan, New Territories; tel. 26881333; fax 31241073; e-mail admin@kcrc.com; internet www.kcrc.com; f. 1982; operated by the Kowloon–Canton Railway Corpn, a public statutory body; assets controlled by MTR Corpn since 2007; also provides passenger and freight services to and from various cities on the mainland; plans for 17-km railway to link Sha Tin and Central via a new cross-harbour tunnel and thus provide the first direct rail route from the Chinese border to Hong Kong Island; Chair. K. C. CHAN; CEO Ir JAMES BLAKE.

MTR Corporation: MTR Tower, Telford Plaza, 33 Wai Strip St, Kowloon Bay; tel. 28818888; fax 27959991; internet www.mtr.com.hk; f. 1975; first section of underground mass transit railway (MTR) system opened in 1979; merged operations with Kowloon–Canton Railway Corpn in 2007; nine railway lines serving Hong Kong Island, Kowloon and New Territories; 26-km Guangzhou–Shenzhen–Hong Kong Express Rail Link to be completed by 2015; CEO C. K. CHOW; Chair. Dr RAYMOND K. F. CH'IEN.

TRAMWAYS

Hong Kong Tramways Ltd: Whitty Street Tram Depot, Connaught Rd West, Western District; tel. 21186338; fax 21186038; e-mail enquiry@hktramways.com; internet www.hktramways.com; f. 1904; operates six routes and 161 double-deck trams between Kennedy Town and Shaukeiwan; Man. Dir BRUNO CHARRADE.

ROADS

In 2009 there were 2,050 km of public roads in Hong Kong. Almost all of them are concrete or asphalt surfaced. Owing to the hilly terrain, and the density of building development, the scope for substantial increase in the road network is limited. Work on a bridge linking Hong Kong's Lantau Island with Macao and Zhuhai City, in the Chinese province of Guangdong, commenced in late 2009. Spanning nearly 50 km and comprising a six-lane expressway, the project was scheduled for completion in 2016.

Highways Department: Ho Man Tin Government Offices, 5/F, 88 Chung Hau St, Ho Man Tin, Kowloon; tel. 29264111; fax 27145216; e-mail hydenquiry@1823.gov.hk; internet www.hyd.gov.hk; f. 1986; planning, design, construction and maintenance of the public road system; co-ordination of major highway and railway projects; Dir PETER LAU KA-KEUNG.

FERRIES

Conventional ferries, hoverferries, catamarans and jetfoils operate between Hong Kong, China and Macao. There is also an extensive network of ferry services to outlying districts.

Hongkong and Yaumati Ferry Co Ltd: 98 Tam Kon Shan Rd, Ngau Kok Wan, North Tsing Yi, New Territories; tel. 23944294; fax 27869001; e-mail hkferry@hkf.com; internet www.hkf.com; licensed routes on ferry services, incl. excursion, vehicular and dangerous goods; Chair. COLIN K. Y. LAM.

Shun Tak-China Travel Ship Management Ltd (TurboJET): 83 Hing Wah St West, Lai Chi Kok, Kowloon; tel. 23070880; fax 27865125; e-mail enquiry@turbojet.com.hk; internet www.turbojet

.com.hk; f. 1999; operates hydrofoil services between Hong Kong, Macao and Shenzhen.

The Star Ferry Co Ltd: Star Ferry Pier, Kowloon Point, Tsim Sha Tsui, Kowloon; tel. 23677065; fax 21186028; e-mail sf@starferry.com.hk; internet www.starferry.com.hk; f. 1898; operates 8 passenger ferries between Tsim Sha Tsui and Central, the main business district of Hong Kong; between Central and Hung Hom; between Tsim Sha Tsui and Wanchai; and between Wanchai and Hung Hom; also a licensed harbour tour ferry service at Victoria Harbour; Man. Dir FRANKIE YICK.

SHIPPING

Hong Kong is one of the world's largest shipping centres and among the busiest container ports. At the end of 2009 the shipping register comprised a fleet of 1,529 vessels, totalling 45.3m. grt. The container terminals at Kwai Chung are privately owned and operated. The construction of a ninth terminal (CT9) at Kwai Chung was completed in 2004, bringing the total number of berths to 24. Lantau Island has been designated as the site for any future expansion.

Marine Department, Hong Kong Special Administrative Region Government: Harbour Bldg, 22/F, 38 Pier Rd, Central, GPOB 4155; tel. 25423711; fax 25417194; e-mail mdenquiry@mardep.gov.hk; internet www.mardep.gov.hk; Dir ROGER TUPPER.

Shipping Companies

Anglo-Eastern Ship Management Ltd: 23/F, 248 Queen's Rd East, Wanchai; tel. 28636111; fax 28612419; e-mail commercial@angloeasterngroup.com; internet www.aesm.com.hk; f. 1974; merged with Denholm Ship Management in 2001; CEO PETER CREMERS; Man. Dir MARCEL LIEDTS.

COSCO (Hong Kong) Shipping Co Ltd (CHS): 52/F, Cosco Tower, 183 Queen's Rd, Central; tel. 28098865; fax 25485653; internet www.coscochs.com.hk; established by merger of former Ocean Tramping Co Ltd and Yick Fung Shipping and Enterprise Co; owned by COSCO (Hong Kong) Group Ltd; Chair. Capt. WEI JIAFU; Man. Dir LI ZHENYU.

Fairmont Shipping (HK) Ltd: Fairmont House, 21/F, 8 Cotton Tree Dr., Central; tel. 25218338; fax 28104560; e-mail vcrmnt@fairmontshipping.com; Pres. ROBERT HO.

Hong Kong Ming Wah Shipping Co: Unit 3701, China Merchants Tower, 37/F, Shun Tak Centre, 168–200 Connaught Rd, Central; tel. 25172128; fax 25473482; e-mail mwbs@hkmw.com.hk; internet www.hkmw.com.hk; f. 1980; subsidiary of China Merchants Group; Chair. QIN XIAO; Pres. FU YUNING.

Island Navigation Corpn International Ltd: Harbour Centre, 28–29/F, 25 Harbour Rd, Wanchai; tel. 28333222; fax 28270001; Man. Dir M. H. LIANG.

Jardine Shipping Services: 24/F, Devon House, Taikoo Place, 979 King's Rd; tel. 25793001; fax 28569927; e-mail Eric.van.der.Hoeven@jardineshipping.com; internet www.jardine-shipping.com; CEO ERIC VAN DER HOEVEN.

Oak Maritime (HK) Inc Ltd: 2301 China Resources Bldg, 26 Harbour Rd, Wanchai; tel. 25063866; fax 25063563; e-mail mail01@oakhk.com; Chair. STEVE G. K. HSU; Pres. FRED C. P. TSAI.

Orient Overseas Container Line Ltd: 31/F, Harbour Centre, 25 Harbour Rd, Wanchai; tel. 28333888; fax 25318122; e-mail hkgcsd@oocl.com; internet www.oocl.com; mem. of the Grand Alliance of shipping cos (five partners); Chair. C. C. TUNG; CEO PHILIP CHOW.

Teh-Hu Cargocean Management Co Ltd: Unit B, Fortis Bank Tower, 15/F, 77–79 Gloucester Rd, Wanchai; tel. 25988688; fax 28249339; e-mail tehhuhk@on-nets.com; f. 1974; Man. Dir KENNETH K. W. LO.

Wah Kwong Shipping Holdings Ltd: Shanghai Industrial Investment Bldg, 26/F, 48–62 Hennessy Rd, POB 283; tel. 25279227; fax 28656544; e-mail wk@wahkwong.com.hk; internet www.wahkwong.com.hk; Chair. GEORGE S. K. CHAO.

Wallem Shipmanagement Ltd: 12/F Warwick House East, Taikoo Place, 979 King's Rd, Quarry Bay; tel. 28768200; fax 28761234; e-mail wsmhk@wallem.com; internet www.wallem.com; Man. Dir JIM NELSON.

Associations

Hong Kong Cargo-Vessel Traders' Association: 21–23 Man Wai Bldg, 2/F, Ferry Point, Kowloon; tel. 23847102; fax 27820342; e-mail info@cvta.com.hk; internet www.cvta.com.hk; 978 mems; Chair. CHOW YAT-TAK; Sec. CHAN BAK.

Hong Kong Shipowners' Association: Queen's Centre, 12/F, 58–64 Queen's Rd East, Wanchai; tel. 25200206; fax 25298246; e-mail hksoa@hksoa.org.hk; internet www.hksoa.org.hk; f. 1957; 181 mems; Chair. KENNETH KOO; Man. Dir ARTHUR BOWRING.

Hong Kong Shippers' Council: Rm 2407, Hopewell Centre, 183 Queen's Rd East, Wanchai; tel. 28340010; fax 28919787; e-mail shippers@hkshippers.org.hk; internet www.hkshippers.org.hk; 63 mems; Chair. WILLY LIN; Exec. Dir SUNNY HO.

CIVIL AVIATION

A new international airport, on the island of Chek Lap Kok, near Lantau Island, opened in 1998. Construction of a third runway was under consideration in 2011. At the end of 2009 Hong Kong was served by 95 airlines.

Airport Authority of Hong Kong: HKIA Tower, 1 Sky Plaza Rd, Hong Kong International Airport, Lantau; tel. 21887111; fax 28240717; internet www.hongkongairport.com; f. 1995; scheduled for privatization; Chair. MARVIN CHEUNG KIN-TUNG; CEO STANLEY H. C. HUI.

Civil Aviation Department: 46/F, Queensway Government Offices, 66 Queensway, Admiralty; tel. 28674332; fax 28690093; e-mail enquiry@cad.gov.hk; internet www.cad.gov.hk; Dir-Gen. NORMAN LO SHUNG-MAN.

AHK Air Hong Kong Ltd: 4/F, South Tower, Cathay Pacific City, 8 Scenic Rd, Hong Kong International Airport, Lantau; tel. 27618588; fax 27618486; e-mail ahk.hq@airhongkong.com.hk; internet www.airhongkong.com.hk; f. 1986; regional cargo carrier; wholly owned subsidiary of Cathay Pacific Airways Ltd; COO RICHARD CATER.

Cathay Pacific Airways Ltd: 7/F, North Tower, Cathay Pacific City, 8 Scenic Rd, Hong Kong International Airport, Lantau; tel. 27477222; fax 27535751; internet www.cathaypacific.com; f. 1946; services to more than 40 major cities in the Far East, Middle East, North America, Europe, South Africa, Australia and New Zealand; Chair. CHRISTOPHER D. PRATT; CEO JOHN SLOSAR.

Hong Kong Airlines Ltd: 7/F, One Citygate, 20 Tat Tung Rd, Tung Chung, Lantau; tel. 31511800; fax 31511838; e-mail crd@hkairlines.com; internet www.hkairlines.com; f. 2004; flights to mainland China, Japan, Philippines, Singapore, Indonesia, Viet Nam, Taiwan, Thailand and Moscow; Pres. YANG JIANG HONG; CEO KALID RAZACK.

Hong Kong Dragon Airlines Ltd (Dragonair): Dragonair House, 11 Tung Fai Rd, Hong Kong International Airport, Lantau; tel. 31933888; fax 31933889; internet www.dragonair.com; f. 1985; scheduled and charter flights to destinations throughout mainland China and to Bangladesh, Thailand, Cambodia, Brunei, Malaysia, Taiwan and Japan; wholly owned subsidiary of Cathay Pacific Airways Ltd; CEO JAMES TONG.

Sky Shuttle Helicopters Ltd: Rm 1603, 16/F, China Merchants Tower, Shun Tak Centre, 200 Connaught Rd, Central; tel. 21089988; fax 21089938; e-mail info@skyshuttlehk.com; internet www.skyshuttlehk.com; f. 1990; fmrly East Asia Airlines; merged with Helicopters Hong Kong Ltd in 1998; renamed as Heli Express Ltd in 2005, and as above in 2008; operates helicopter services between Hong Kong, Macao and Shenzhen (China); CEO CHEYENNE CHAN.

Tourism

Tourism is a major source of foreign exchange. Receipts from tourism totalled HK $162,800m. in 2009. Visitor arrivals rose by nearly 22% in 2010 to exceed 36.0m. (of whom almost 22.7m. travelled from mainland China). In 2010 the 175 licensed hotels offered 60,428 rooms, while tourist guesthouses totalled 619, with 5,926 rooms available. The first phase of a new Disneyland theme park opened in September 2005.

Hong Kong Tourism Board (HKTB): 9–11/F, Citicorp Centre, 18 Whitfield Rd, North Point; tel. 28076543; fax 28060303; e-mail info@discoverhongkong.com; internet www.discoverhongkong.com; f. 1957; est. as Hong Kong Tourist Asscn; reconstituted as Hong Kong Tourism Bd in April 2001; co-ordinates and promotes the tourist industry; has govt support and financial assistance; up to 20 mems of the Bd represent the Govt, the private sector and the tourism industry; Chair. JAMES TIEN; Exec. Dir ANTHONY LAU.

Defence

In July 1997 a garrison of 4,800 troops belonging to the Chinese People's Liberation Army (PLA) was established in Hong Kong. The garrison can intervene in local matters only at the request of the Hong Kong Government, which remains responsible for internal security. A total of 7,000 Chinese troops were stationed in Hong Kong in 2007.

Defence Expenditure: Projected expenditure on internal security in 2006/07 totalled HK $92.7m.

Commander of the PLA Garrison in Hong Kong: Maj.-Gen. ZHANG SHIBO.

Education

Full-time education is free and compulsory in Hong Kong between the ages of six and 15. In 2008/09 the duration of free education was extended from nine to 12 years. In 2010/11 an estimated 148,940 children attended kindergartens, which totalled 951. A total of 331,112 children attended primary schools, while secondary school pupils totalled 449,737. There are three main types of secondary school in Hong Kong: grammar, technical and pre-vocational schools. In 2004/05 total enrolment at primary and secondary schools was equivalent to 90% of the school-age population. Primary enrolment in 2004/05 included 90.7% of children in the relevant age-group (males 92.8%, females 88.6%), while the comparable ratio for secondary enrolment in 2007/08 was 75% (males 74%, females 76%). An education reform programme was in progress from 2000, including reform of curriculum and education management, and the establishment of Project Yi Jin, a life-long learning initiative. Budgetary expenditure on general education was an estimated HK $29,195m. in the financial year 2009/10.

Schools fall into three main categories: those wholly maintained by the Government; those administered by non-governmental organizations with government financial aid; and those administered independently by private organizations. The adult literacy rate in 2002 was estimated at 93.5% (males 96.9%; females 89.6%). It rose to 94.6% in 2003.

PRE-PRIMARY AND PRIMARY SCHOOLS

Kindergartens are administered by private bodies without direct government assistance for children between the ages of three and five. The Government provides indirect assistance through rent and rate rebates to non-profit-making kindergartens, fee assistance for needy parents, etc. The age of entry into primary school is six, and the schools provide a six-year course of basic primary education. Compulsory primary education was first introduced in 1971 when fees were abolished in most of the primary schools in the public sector. There are nine government-subsidized primary schools and a number of private international schools catering for the education of English-speaking children. At the end of six years, every primary school-leaver is allocated a free place in a secondary school for three years. The method of allocation is based on parental choice and schools' internal assessments, monitored by an Academic Aptitude Test under the Secondary School Places Allocation scheme.

SECONDARY SCHOOLS

Junior secondary education (Secondary 1–3), which became compulsory in 1979, has been free since 1978. A centralized system of selection and allocation of subsidized school places for senior secondary education (Secondary 4–5), known as the Junior Secondary Education Assessment System, was first introduced in 1981, and was enhanced in 1988 by the adoption of the Mean Eligibility Allocation Method, which relieved all students from taking any public scaling test. Both the performance of students in the school internal assessments and parental choice form the basis for selection and allocation of Secondary 3 students to subsidized Secondary 4 places. Students may also choose to continue their studies in post-Secondary 3 craft courses offered by technical institutes and industrial training centres. The Hong Kong Certificate of Education Examination may be taken at the end of the fifth year of secondary education; a further course of two years leads to the Hong Kong Advanced Level Examination. Pre-vocational schools provide a five-year secondary course. Sixth-form classes were introduced in September 1992.

Following the resumption of Chinese sovereignty in mid-1997, Cantonese was gradually to replace English as the official medium of instruction. Some 100 schools were to be allowed to retain English as the medium of instruction, provided that they fulfil certain criteria (for example, language capability of the students).

HIGHER EDUCATION

There are eight institutions of higher education funded by the University Grants Committee: City University of Hong Kong (CUHK), Hong Kong Baptist University (HKBU), Hong Kong Polytechnic University (HKPU), Lingnan University (LU), the Chinese University of Hong Kong (CUHK), the Hong Kong University of Science and Technology (HKUST), the University of Hong Kong (HKU) and the Hong Kong Institute of Education. In addition, the Open University of Hong Kong (founded in 1989 as the Open Learning Institute of Hong Kong) offers sub-degree, degree and postgraduate courses via a system of distance learning.

Technological training is also provided by the Vocational Training Council (VTC), which operates the Hong Kong Institute of Vocational Education (IVE) and 24 training centres. The IVE was founded in 1999 and incorporated two technical colleges and seven government-funded technical institutes.

The four government-operated colleges of education and the Institute of Languages merged to form the Hong Kong Institute of Education in 1994. The Institute provides training for teachers of kindergartens, primary and secondary schools, and offers full- and part-time courses of two and three years' duration. The Government provides loans and grants for needy students.

Bibliography

General

Constable, Nicole. *Maid to Order in Hong Kong: Stories of Migrant Workers.* Ithaca, NY, Cornell University Press, 2007.

Forrest, Ray, La Grange, Adrienne, and Yip, Ngai Ming. *Cohesion and Community in Contemporary Hong Kong.* Abingdon, Routledge, 2011.

Gauld, Robin, and Gould, Derek. *The Hong Kong Health Sector: Development and Change.* Otago, Otago University Press, 2003.

Matthews, Gordon, Lui, Tai-lok, and Ma, Eric Kit-wai. *Hong Kong, China: Learning to Belong to a Nation.* Abingdon, Routledge, 2007.

McDonogh, Gary, and Wong, Cindy. *Global Hong Kong.* Abingdon, Routledge, 2005.

Scott, Ian. *The Public Sector in Hong Kong.* Hong Kong, Hong Kong University Press, 2010.

Yung, Betty. *Hong Kong's Housing Policy: A Case Study in Social Justice.* Hong Kong, Hong Kong University Press, 2008.

History and Politics

Ash, Robert F., Ferdinand, Peter, Hook, Brian, and Porter, Robin (Eds). *Hong Kong in Transition: One Country, Two Systems.* Richmond, Curzon Press, 2002.

Banham, Tony. *Not the Slightest Chance: The Defence of Hong Kong, 1941.* Hong Kong, Hong Kong University Press, 2003.

Beatty, Bob. *Democracy, Asian Values, and Hong Kong: Evaluating Political Elite Beliefs.* Westport, CT, Praeger, 2003.

Bickers, Robert, and Yep, Ray. *May Days in Hong Kong: Riot and Emergency in 1967.* Hong Kong, Hong Kong University Press, 2009.

Carroll, John M. *Edge of Empires: Chinese Elites and British Colonials in Hong Kong.* Cambridge, MA, Harvard University Press, 2005.

A Concise History of Hong Kong. Lanham, MD, Rowman & Littlefield, 2007.

Chan Chak Kwan. *Social Security Policy in Hong Kong: From British Colony to China's Special Administrative Region.* Lanham, MD, Lexington Books, 2011.

Chan, Joseph M., and Lee, Francis F. L. (Eds). *Media and Politics in Post Hand-over Hong Kong.* Abingdon, Routledge, 2008.

Chan, Ming K., and Lo, Shiu Hing. *Historical Dictionary of the Hong Kong SAR and the Macao SAR.* Lanham, MD, Rowman & Littlefield, 2006.

Cheng, Joseph Y. S. *The Hong Kong Special Administrative Region in Its First Decade.* Hong Kong, City University of Hong Kong Press, 2007.

Cheung, Anne S. Y. *Self-Censorship and the Struggle for Press Freedom in Hong Kong.* New York, Kluwer Law International, 2003.

Cheung, Gary Ka-Wai. *Hong Kong's Watershed: The 1967 Riots.* Hong Kong, Hong Kong University Press, 2009.

Chiu, Stephen W. K., and Wong Siu-lu (Eds). *Repositioning the Hong Kong Government: Social Foundations and Political Challenges.* Hong Kong, Hong Kong University Press, 2011.

Chu, Cindy Yik-Yi (Ed.). *Foreign Communities in Hong Kong, 1840s–1950s.* London, Palgrave Macmillan, 2006.

Chinese Communists and Hong Kong Capitalists: 1937–1997. Basingstoke, Palgrave Macmillan, 2010.

Fu Hualing, Petersen, Carole J., and Young, Simon N. M. (Eds). *National Security and Fundamental Freedoms: Hong Kong's Article 23 Under Scrutiny.* Hong Kong, Hong Kong University Press, 2005.

Hong Kong Journalists Association and Article 19. *False Security: Hong Kong's National Security Laws Pose a Grave Threat to Freedom of Expression.* Hong Kong, Hong Kong Journalists Association and Article 19, 2003.

Horlemann, Ralf. *Hong Kong's Transition to Chinese Rule: The Limits of Autonomy.* Richmond, Curzon Press, 2002.

Hsiung, James C. *Hong Kong the Super Paradox: Life After Return to China.* New York, St Martin's Press, 2000.

Ku, Agnes, and Ngai Pun (Eds). *Remaking Citizenship in Hong Kong: Community, Nation and the Global City.* London, RoutledgeCurzon, 2004.

Lai, Carine, and Loh, Christine. *Reflections of Leadership: Tung Chee Hwa and Donald Tsang, 1997–2007*. Hong Kong, Civic Exchange, 2007.

Lam Wai-man, et al (Eds). *Contemporary Hong Kong Politics: Governance in the Post-1997 Era*. Hong Kong, Hong Kong University Press, 2007.

Lau Siu-kai and Louie Kin-shuen. *The First Tung Chee-hwa Administration: The First Five Years of the Hong Kong Special Administrative Region*. Hong Kong, Chinese University Press, 2002.

Law Wing Sang. *Collaborative Colonial Power: The Making of the Hong Kong Chinese*. Hong Kong, Hong Kong University Press, 2009.

Lee, Francis L. F., and Chan, Joseph M. *Media, Social Mobilisation and Mass Protests in Post-colonial Hong Kong: The Power of a Critical Event*. Abingdon, Routledge, 2010.

Lee Pui Tak. *Colonial Hong Kong and Modern China: Interaction and Reintegration*. Hong Kong, Hong Kong University Press, 2006.

Hong Kong Reintegrating with China: Political, Cultural and Social Dimensions. Hong Kong, Hong Kong University Press, 2001.

Lindsay, Oliver. *Battle for Hong Kong, 1941–1945*. Montréal, McGill-Queens University Press, 2006.

Loh, Christine. *Underground Front: The Chinese Communist Party in Hong Kong*. Hong Kong, Hong Kong University Press, 2009.

Ma, Ngok. *Political Development in Hong Kong: State, Political Society, and Civil Society*. Hong Kong, Hong Kong University Press, 2007.

Meyer, David R. *Hong Kong as a Global Metropolis*. Cambridge, Cambridge University Press, 2000.

Miners, N. J. *Hong Kong under Imperial Rule 1912–1941*. Oxford University Press, 1987.

The Government and Politics of Hong Kong (with post-handover update by James T. H. Tang). 5th Edn, Oxford University Press, 1998.

Ortmann, Stephan. *Politics and Change in Singapore and Hong Kong: Containing Contention*. Abingdon, Routledge, 2010.

Poon, Kit. *The Political Future of Hong Kong: Democracy Within Communist China*. Abingdon, Routledge, 2008.

Postiglione, G. A., and Tang, J. T. H. *Hong Kong's Reunion with China: The Global Dimensions*. Armonk, NY, M. E. Sharpe, 1997.

Sing Ming. *Hong Kong's Tortuous Democratization*. London, RoutledgeCurzon, 2003.

Politics and Government in Hong Kong: Crisis Under Chinese Sovereignty. Abingdon, Routledge, 2009.

Snow, Philip. *The Fall of Hong Kong: Britain, China and the Japanese Occupation*. London, Yale University Press, 2003.

Tsang, Steve Y. S. *A Modern History of Hong Kong: 1841–1998*. London, Tauris, 2002.

Governing Hong Kong: Administrative Officers from the Nineteenth Century to the Chinese Takeover. Hong Kong, Hong Kong University Press, 2007.

Vickers, Edward. *In Search of an Identity: The Politics of History Teaching in Hong Kong, 1960s–2000*. London, Routledge, 2003.

Welsh, Frank. *A History of Hong Kong*. London, HarperCollins, Revised Edn, 1997.

Wesley-Smith, P. *Unequal Treaty 1898–1997*. Oxford University Press, 1980.

Wesley-Smith, P., and Chen, Albert (Eds). *The Basic Law and Hong Kong's Future*. London, Butterworth, 1988.

Wong Yiu-chung (Ed.). *One Country, Two Systems in Crisis: Hong Kong's Transformation Since the Handover*. Lanham, MD, Lexington Books, 2008.

Wong Yun-Bor. *Autonomy and Protection of Fundamental Rights in the Hong Kong Special Administrative Region*. Hong Kong, LexisNexis, 2007.

Yahuda, Michael. *Hong Kong: China's Challenge*. London, Routledge, 1996.

Young, Simon, and Cullen, Richard. *Electing Hong Kong's Chief Executive*. Hong Kong, Hong Kong University Press, 2010.

Economy

Ash, Robert, and Lok, Sang-ho (Eds). *China, Hong Kong and the World Economy: A Study of Globalisation*. London, Palgrave Macmillan, 2006.

Chiu, Stephen, and Lui Tai-Lok. *Hong Kong—Becoming a Chinese Global City*. Abingdon, Routledge, 2009.

Faure, David, and Lee Pui-tak (Eds). *A Documentary History of Hong Kong: Economy*. Hong Kong, Hong Kong University Press, 2004.

Fosh, Patricia, Chan, Andy W., and Chow, Wilson W. S. (Eds). *Hong Kong Management and Labour: Change and Continuity*. London, Routledge, 2000.

Genberg, H. *The Banking Sector in Hong Kong: Competition, Efficiency, Performance and Risk*. Basingstoke, Palgrave Macmillan, 2008.

Goodhart, Charles, and Lu, Dai. *Intervention to Save Hong Kong: The Authorities' Counter-Speculation in Financial Markets*. Oxford University Press, 2003.

Goodstadt, Leo. *Uneasy Partners: The Conflict Between Public Interest and Private Profit in Hong Kong*. Hong Kong, Hong Kong University Press, 2005.

Greenwood, John. *Hong Kong's Link to the US Dollar: Origins and Evolution*. Hong Kong, Hong Kong University Press, 2008.

Ho, Simon S. M., Scott, Robert Haney, and Wong, Kie Ann (Eds). *The Hong Kong Financial System*. Hong Kong, Oxford University Press China, 2003.

Lam, Pun-Lee, and Chan, Sylvia. *Competition in Hong Kong's Gas Industry*. Hong Kong, Chinese University Press, 2000.

Latter, Tony. *Hands On, Hands Off?: The Nature and Process of Economic Policy in Hong Kong*. Hong Kong, Hong Kong University Press, 2007.

Hong Kong's Money: The History, Logic and Operation of the Currency Peg. Hong Kong, Hong Kong University Press, 2007.

Lei, Chung Kwok, and Yao, Shujie. *Economic Convergence in Greater China: Mainland China, Hong Kong, Macau and Taiwan*. Abingdon, Routledge, 2011.

Lethbridge, David (Ed.). *The Business Environment in Hong Kong*. Oxford University Press, 4th Edn, 2000.

Low, C. K. (Ed.). *Financial Markets in Hong Kong*. Singapore, Springer-Verlag Singapore, 2003.

Rowley, Chris, and Fitzgerald, Robert (Eds). *Managed in Hong Kong*. Ilford, Frank Cass, 2000.

Schenk, Catherine R. *Hong Kong as an International Financial Centre: Emergence and Development, 1945–65*. London, Routledge, 2001.

Hong Kong SAR's Monetary and Exchange Rate Challenges: Historical Perspectives. Basingstoke, Palgrave Macmillan, 2009

MACAO

Physical and Social Geography

The Special Administrative Region (SAR) of Macao (or Macau as it was also known prior to its reversion from Portuguese to Chinese sovereignty in December 1999) is situated on the south-eastern coast of the People's Republic of China, at latitude 22°14' N and longitude 113°35' E. The territory comprises the narrow, hilly Macao peninsula of the Chinese district of Foshan, on which is situated the Cidade do Santo Nome de Deus de Macau, together with two small islands to the south, Taipa and Coloane. The highest peak, of 170.6 m, is situated on the island of Coloane. A major land reclamation programme continued to progress in the early 21st century. By 2009 the SAR covered an area of 29.5 sq km (11.39 sq miles) in 2009 (compared with 17.3 sq km in 1989). Of the 2009 total, the Cotai reclamation area accounted for 5.8 sq km. Macao lies some 64 km west of Hong Kong (across the Zhujiang—Pearl River—estuary), and 145 km south of the city of Guangzhou (Canton), the capital of Guangdong Province. In 1998 it was announced that Macao and the Pearl River Water Resources Committee (PRWRC) of China were to conduct a joint study on the realignment of local waters, the land reclamation projects having had a negative impact on water flow. In the same year Macao and the Land Department of Guangdong conducted a joint aerial land survey. The Macao peninsula is linked by three bridges (the first spanning 2.6 km, the second 4.4 km and the third 2.2 km) to the island of Taipa, which in turn is connected to Coloane by a 2.2-km causeway and, more recently, by a large area of reclaimed land. Another link with the mainland, the 1.5-km Lotus Bridge connecting Macao to Zhuhai (Guangdong Province), opened in December 1999. Work on a bridge linking Macao with Hong Kong's Lantau Island and

Zhuhai began in December 2009. The climate is subtropical, with temperatures averaging 15°C in January and 29°C in July. The average annual rainfall is between about 100 cm and 200 cm. The highest levels of humidity and precipitation occur between April and September.

The census of August 2001 enumerated the population at 435,235, of whom 414,200, or 95.2%, held Chinese nationality, while 8,793 (2.0%) were of Portuguese nationality. (About 60% of the population were between 15 and 50 years of age at the census of 1996.) At the by-census of August 2006 the population had increased to 502,113. By the end of 2009 the population had reached 542,200, according to official estimates. At 18,379.7 persons per sq km in December 2009, the territory's population density remained one of the highest in the world. The majority of the population reside on the Macao peninsula. In 2010 the birth rate rose to 9.4 per 1,000, and a death rate of 3.3 per 1,000 was recorded. The official languages are Chinese (Cantonese being the principal dialect) and Portuguese. English is also widely spoken, speakers of English outnumbering Portuguese-speakers. The predominant religions are Chinese Buddhism, Daoism, Confucianism and Roman Catholicism. The executive and legislative bodies of Macao are based in the city of Macao, which is situated on the peninsula.

History

FRANK H. H. KING

Revised by the editorial staff

The territory was established as one of several trading posts by the Portuguese as early as 1537, the first Portuguese sailors having anchored in the Zhujiang (Pearl River) in 1513. A permanent settlement was established in 1557. Motivated by trade and missionary zeal, the Portuguese developed Macao as a base for their operations both in China and Japan, and penetration during Japan's 'Christian century' from 1543 involved close relations with Macao. The first Portuguese Governor was appointed in 1680. However, sovereignty remained vested in China; the Chinese residents were subject to a Chinese official, and Macao's Portuguese administration, virtually autonomous for the first 200 years, concerned itself with the governance of the Portuguese and, until the establishment of Hong Kong, with the growing presence of other European trading nations. The Portuguese paid an annual rent to China.

Macao was an uncertain base from which to expand trade with China. The Roman Catholic administration was unfriendly to Protestants, the Chinese authority was too close and restrictive, and the opium question and growing restlessness of the 'private' merchants undermined a system that had developed during the years of controlled and relatively limited 'company' trade.

The ceding of Hong Kong to Britain in 1842 revealed China's weakness, and in 1845 Portugal declared Macao a free port. In the consequent disputes Portugal drove out the Chinese officials, and the settlement was proclaimed Portuguese territory. This unilateral declaration was recognized by China in 1887 in return for provisions intended to facilitate the enforcement of its customs laws, particularly in regard to opium, by the Imperial Maritime Customs.

However, Macao's establishment as a colony did not restore prosperity. With the silting of its harbour, the diversion of its trade to Hong Kong, and the opening of the treaty ports as bases of trade and missionary work, Macao was left to handle the local distributive trade, while developing a reputation as a base for smuggling, gambling and other unsavoury activities. With the closing of the Hong Kong–China border in 1938, Macao's trade boomed, but this prosperity declined after 1942, when the colony became isolated as the only European settlement on the China coast not occupied by the Japanese during the Second World War.

In 1951 Macao was declared an overseas province of Portugal and elected a representative to the Portuguese legislature in Lisbon. Macao's economy depended largely on the gold trade, at that time illegal in Hong Kong, on gambling and tourism, and on an entrepôt business with China.

Macao's tranquillity was disrupted by communist riots in 1966–67, inspired by the 'Cultural Revolution' in mainland China. These were contained only after the Macao Government signed an agreement with Macao's Chinese Chamber of Commerce outlawing the activities of Chinese loyal to the Taiwan regime, paying compensation to the families of Chinese killed in the rioting, and refusing entry to refugees from China. However, China wished the Portuguese administration to continue, and on admission to the UN the Beijing Government affirmed that it regarded the future of Macao as an internal matter.

SUBSEQUENT POLITICAL DEVELOPMENTS

After the military coup in Portugal in April 1974, the only Governor of an overseas territory to be retained in office was that of Macao. China refused to discuss the future of Macao with Portugal, and the revolutionary leaders became convinced that there was no demand for an independence which China would not, in any case, have tolerated. Nevertheless, the revolution caused considerable political activity in Macao. The Centro Democrático de Macau (CDM) was established to press for radical political reform and the removal of those connected with the former regime in Portugal. The conservative Associação para a Defesa dos Interesses de Macau (ADIM) was established, and in April 1975 defeated the CDM's candidate for Macao's representative to the Lisbon assembly. The Macao electorate reaffirmed its conservative bias when over 65% voted for right-wing parties in the Lisbon constituency.

Col Garcia Leandro, who succeeded Nobre de Carvalho at the end of his much-extended term as Governor in late 1974, correctly assessed China's position while being sufficiently flexible to recognize that Macao needed capitalism and was not ready for socialism. He initiated policies that, in effect, insulated Macao from the direct influence of a series of Portuguese governments which contained elements sympathetic to the USSR and which might have disrupted the delicate balance necessary for the continuation of Macao's existence. Thus, Leandro, who had at first dealt with the CDM, expelled many of its supporters, effectively assuring the success of the ADIM in elections to the Legislative Assembly in July 1976. Leandro also supported the enactment of legislation in Portugal (the Organic Law) which, in February 1976, appeared to give Macao virtual political autonomy.

Macao had thus become a special territory of Portugal with a Governor of ministerial rank appointed by the President of the Portuguese Republic, to whom he was responsible. The Governor was the executive authority and could issue decrees, a subject of continued controversy, and he remained independent of the Legislative Assembly with the right to veto legislation not endorsed by a two-thirds' majority. The composition of the Assembly reflected Macao's social and political structure, which was still divided into 'Chinese' and 'Portuguese', the latter self-determined on the basis of culture, language and religion—not on place of origin. Of the 17 members at that time, six were elected on a proportional basis, six were elected indirectly by designated organizations, and five were appointed by the Governor.

The 1976 elections confirmed Macao's conservative preference, with the ADIM receiving 55% of the 2,700 votes cast and winning four of the six seats. A group of young independents stood as the Grupo de Estudos para o Desenvolvimento Communitário de Macau (GEDEC), winning 17% of the vote, while the radical and once dominant CDM was less successful, but also elected a member. The Governor's appointees and those indirectly elected created an Assembly that was still recognizably Portuguese, confirming the Portuguese nature of the Government and avoiding the anomalous position of a Chinese population voting for non-communist parties on China's very borders.

Macao's international relations continued to be subject to the *de jure* approval of the President of Portugal and the de facto tolerance of China. In April 1978 the Chinese authorities acted on a long-standing request of Governor Leandro and invited him to visit several Chinese cities (excluding Beijing). It was the first visit by a Governor of Macao since the communist revolution but, while interpreted as confirmation of China's acceptance of Macao's status at that time, the visit was seen in the context of China's overall policy rather than as an endorsement of Leandro himself. Meanwhile, leaders of the Chinese community in Macao continued to participate in political events in China, including regular attendance at sessions of the National People's Congress (NPC) in Beijing. Portugal and China established diplomatic relations in February 1979.

Governor Leandro, who correctly appraised Macao's needs in 1974, was frustrated in his desire to obtain greater local Chinese political participation, and his efforts to have the Macao population involved in the nomination of his successor were ineffective. However, his four-year administration was marked by a more realistic planning orientation, marred in execution by administrative problems. Nevertheless, he was able to change patterns of thinking, set in motion basic economic reforms, and secured the passage of legislation that resulted in a more efficient taxation system and improvements to the local civil service.

The next Governor, Gen. Nuno de Melo Egídio, arrived in February 1979. Elections for the Legislative Assembly were due in late 1979, but in June the Assembly extended the term of the seven elected representatives for another year. This temporarily averted the constitutional crisis confronting the Governor in 1980, when the four-year-old Organic Law was due for review. A delegation of the representatives had visited Lisbon to discuss proposals to revise the 1976 Organic Law with politicians in the Portuguese legislature. Their proposals, which were to give the local population a greater influence in decisions concerning the administration of Macao, included plans to enlarge the Legislative Assembly from 17 to 21 members. All of these would, they proposed, be elected, thus reducing the Governor to a merely titular status. In March 1980, when Gen. Melo Egídio visited Beijing on the first 'official' visit by a Governor of Macao since its establishment as a Portuguese colony in 1557, the Chinese leader Deng Xiaoping, while expressing his approval of the stability of Macao, also made it clear that the Chinese Government opposed any change in the Organic Law. His views were reiterated by sections of the local population in Macao; 97% of the population did not speak Portuguese, participated very little in political life and were largely unaffected by the Portuguese administration.

The appointment in 1981 of Cdre (later Rear-Adm.) Vasco Almeida e Costa as Governor was evidence of an unspoken agreement between Beijing and Lisbon not to alter the legal status of Macao. Governor Almeida e Costa was determined to extend voting rights in Macao, to produce a more representative Assembly. Following a constitutional dispute in March 1984, after he had used his controversial authority to issue two administrative decrees without the approval of the Legislative Assembly (and had successfully introduced electoral reforms despite vigorous opposition), he requested that President Eanes of Portugal dissolve the Assembly. In August 1984 elections for a new Assembly were held, in which the Chinese majority were allowed to vote for the first time, regardless of their length of residence in the territory. Two of the six directly elected seats were won by Chinese candidates, while the six indirectly elected members, all Chinese, were returned unopposed. The Governor appointed four government officials and a Chinese businessman to complete the Assembly, which was thus, for the first time, dominated by ethnic Chinese deputies.

Governor Almeida e Costa resigned in January 1986. He was replaced as Governor by Joaquim Pinto Machado, who had hitherto been a professor of medicine and was little-known as a political figure. His appointment marked a break in the tradition of military governors for Macao, but his political inexperience placed him at a disadvantage. Within weeks of Pinto Machado's arrival, the likelihood of his departure was widely rumoured, and in May 1987, one year after his appointment, he resigned for reasons of 'institutional dignity'. He was replaced in August by Carlos Melancia, a former socialist deputy in the Assembly of the Republic, who had held ministerial posts in several Portuguese Governments led by Dr Mário Lopes Soares, Prime Minister and subsequently President of Portugal.

PREPARATIONS FOR THE RESUMPTION OF CHINESE SOVEREIGNTY

In May 1985 President Eanes visited Beijing and Macao, and it was announced that the Portuguese and Chinese Governments had agreed to hold formal talks about the territory's future. The first session of negotiations took place in June 1986, in Beijing, and further talks were held in September and October, when it was reported that 'broad agreement' had been reached. Portugal's acceptance of Chinese sovereignty greatly simplified subsequent negotiations, and on 13 April 1987, following the conclusion of the fourth round of talks, a joint declaration was formally signed in Beijing by the Portuguese and Chinese Governments, during an official visit to China by the Prime Minister of Portugal. According to the agreement, which was formally ratified in January 1988, Macao was to become a 'Special Administrative Region' (SAR) of the People's Republic, to be known as Macao, China, on 20 December 1999. Macao was thus to have the same status as that agreed (with effect from mid-1997) for Hong Kong, and was to enjoy autonomy in most matters except defence and foreign policy. A Sino-Portuguese Joint Liaison Group (JLG), established to oversee the transfer of power, held its inaugural meeting in Lisbon in April 1988.

Under the detailed arrangements for the transfer, a chief executive for Macao was to be appointed in 1999 by the Chinese Government, following 'elections or consultations to be held in Macao', and the territory's legislature was to contain 'a majority of elected members'. The inhabitants of Macao were to become Chinese citizens; the Chinese Government refused to allow the possibility of dual Sino-Portuguese citizenship, although Macao residents in possession of Portuguese passports were apparently to be permitted to retain them for travel purposes. The agreement provided for a 50-year period during which Macao would be permitted to retain its free-enterprise capitalist economy, and to be financially independent of China.

In August 1988 the establishment of a Macao Basic Law Drafting Committee was announced by the Chinese Government. Comprising 30 Chinese members and 19 representatives from Macao, the Committee was to draft a law determining the territory's future constitutional status within the People's Republic of China.

Triennial elections to the six directly elective seats in Macao's 17-seat Legislative Assembly were held in October 1988. In a low turnout (representing fewer than 30% of the 67,492 registered voters), an informally constituted 'liberal' grouping increased its representation from one seat in the previous Assembly to three seats. These gains were achieved at the expense of the long-dominant 'grand alliance' of pro-Beijing and Macanese business interests. The new members hoped to influence the administration's policies on housing, education and workers' welfare.

In January 1989 it was announced that Portuguese passports were to be issued to about 100,000 ethnic Chinese inhabitants, born in Macao before October 1981, and it was anticipated that as many as a further 100,000 would be granted before 1999. Unlike their counterparts in the neighbouring British dependent territory of Hong Kong, therefore, these Macao residents (but not all) were to be granted the full rights of a citizen of the European Community (EC, now European Union—EU). In February 1989 President Mário Soares of Portugal visited Macao, in order to discuss the transfer of the territory's administration to China.

Following the violent suppression of the pro-democracy movement in China in June 1989, as many as 100,000 residents of Macao participated in demonstrations in the enclave to protest against the Chinese Government's action. The events in the People's Republic gave rise to much concern in Macao, and it was feared that many residents would wish to leave the territory prior to 1999. However, in August 1989 China assured Portugal that it would honour the agreement to maintain the capitalist system of the territory after 1999.

In March 1990 the implementation of a programme to grant permanent registration to parents of 4,200 Chinese residents, the latter having already secured the right of abode in Macao, developed into chaos when other illegal immigrants demanded a similar concession. The authorities decided to declare a general amnesty, but were unprepared for the numbers of illegal residents who rushed to take advantage of the scheme, thereby revealing the true extent of previous immigration from China. In the ensuing stampede by 50,000 illegal immigrants, desperate to obtain residency rights, about 200 persons were injured and 1,500 arrested, as the police attempted to control the situation. Border security was increased, in an effort to prevent any further illegal immigration from China.

In late March 1990 the Legislative Assembly approved the final draft of the territory's revised Organic Law. The Law was approved by the Portuguese Assembly of the Republic in mid-April, and granted Macao greater administrative, economic, financial and legislative autonomy, in advance of 1999. The powers of the Governor and of the Legislative Assembly, where six additional seats were to be created, were therefore increased. The post of military commander of the security forces was abolished, responsibility for security being assumed by a civilian Under-Secretary.

In June 1990 the Under-Secretary for Justice, Dr Manuel Magalhães e Silva, resigned, owing to differences of opinion on the issues of Macao's political structure and Sino-Portuguese relations. In the same month, while on a visit to Lisbon for consultations with the President and Prime Minister, Carlos Melancia rebuked the Chinese authorities for attempting to interfere in the internal affairs of Macao. This unprecedented reproach followed criticism of the Governor's compromising attitude towards the People's Republic of China.

Meanwhile, in February 1990, Carlos Melancia had been implicated in a financial scandal. It was alleged that the Governor had accepted 50m. escudos from a Federal German company which hoped to be awarded a consultancy contract for the construction of the new airport in Macao. Although he denied any involvement in the affair, the Governor resigned, and was replaced on an acting basis by the Under-Secretary for Economic Affairs, Dr Francisco Murteira Nabo. In September 1991 it was announced that Melancia and five others were to stand trial on charges of corruption. In August 1993 the former Governor was acquitted on the grounds of insufficient evidence. However, in February 1994, it was announced that Melancia was to be retried, owing to irregularities in his defence case.

The ability of Portugal to maintain a stable administration in the territory had once again been called into question. Many observers believed that the enclave was being adversely affected by the political situation in Lisbon, as differences between the socialist President and centre-right Prime Minister were being reflected in rivalries between officials in Macao. In an attempt to restore confidence, therefore, President Soares visited the territory in November 1990. In January 1991, upon his re-election as Head of State, the President appointed Gen. Vasco Rocha Vieira (who had served as the territory's Chief of Staff in 1973/74 and as Under-Secretary for Public Works and Transport in 1974/75) to be the new Governor of Macao. In March 1991 the Legislative Assembly was expanded from 17 to 23 members. All seven Under-Secretaries were replaced in May.

Following his arrival in Macao, Gen. Rocha Vieira announced that China would be consulted on all future developments in the territory. The 10th meeting of the Sino-Portuguese JLG took place in Beijing in April 1991. Topics under regular discussion included the participation of Macao in international organizations, progress towards an increase in the number of local officials employed in the civil service (hitherto dominated by Portuguese and Macanese personnel) and the status of the Chinese language. The progress of the working group on the translation of local laws from Portuguese into Chinese was also examined, a particular problem being the lack of suitably qualified bilingual legal personnel. (The training of civil servants was duly improved: the University of Macao opened new courses in administration, law and translation; and hundreds of civil servants were dispatched to Beijing or Lisbon for training.) It was agreed that Portuguese was to remain an official language after 1999. The two sides also reached agreement on the exchange of identity cards for those Macao residents who would require them in 1999. Regular meetings of the JLG continued.

In July 1991 the Macao Draft Basic Law was published by the authorities of the People's Republic of China. Confidence in the territory's future was enhanced by China's apparent flexibility on a number of issues. Unlike the Hong Kong Basic Law, that of Macao did not impose restrictions on holders of foreign passports assuming senior posts in the territory's administration after 1999, the only exception being the future Chief Executive.

In November 1991 the Governor of Macao visited China, where it was confirmed that the 'one country, two systems' policy would operate in Macao from 1999. Following a visit to Portugal by the Chinese Premier in February 1992, the Governor of Macao stated that the territory was to retain 'great autonomy' after 1999. In March 1993 the final draft of the Basic Law of the Macao SAR was ratified by the NPC in Beijing, which also approved the design of the future SAR's flag. The adoption of the legislation was welcomed by the Governor of Macao, who reiterated his desire for a smooth transfer of power in 1999. The Chief Executive of the SAR was to be selected by local representatives. The SAR's first Legislative Council was to comprise 23 members, of whom eight would be directly elected. Its term of office would expire in October 2001, when it would be expanded to 27 members, of whom 10 would be directly elected.

Meanwhile, elections to the Legislative Assembly were held in September 1992. The level of participation was higher than on previous occasions, with 59% of the registered electorate (albeit only 13.5% of the population) attending the polls. Fifty candidates contested the eight directly elective seats, four of which were won by members of the main pro-Beijing parties, the União Promotora para o Progresso (UPP) and the União para o Desenvolvimento (UPD).

Relations between Portugal and China remained cordial. In June 1993 the two countries reached agreement on all outstanding issues regarding the construction of the territory's airport and the future use of Chinese air space. Furthermore, Macao was to be permitted to negotiate air traffic agreements with other countries. In October, upon the conclusion of a three-day visit to Macao, President Soares expressed optimism regarding the territory's smooth transition to Chinese administration. In November President Jiang Zemin of China was warmly received in Lisbon, where he had discussions with both the Portuguese President and Prime Minister.

In April 1994, during a visit to China, the Portuguese Prime Minister received an assurance that Chinese nationality would not be imposed on Macanese people of Portuguese descent, who would be able to retain their Portuguese passports. Speaking in Macao itself, the Prime Minister expressed confidence in the territory's future. Regarding the issue as increasingly one of foreign policy, he stated his desire to transfer jurisdiction over Macao from the Presidency of the Republic to the Government, despite the necessity for a constitutional amendment.

In July 1994 a group of local journalists dispatched a letter, alleging intimidation and persecution in Macao, to President Soares, urging him to intervene to defend the territory's press freedom. The journalists' appeal followed an incident involving the director of the daily *Gazeta Macaense*, who had been obliged to pay 300,000 escudos for reproducing an article from *Semanário*, a Lisbon weekly newspaper, and now awaited trial. The territory's press had been critical of the Macao Supreme Court's decision to extradite ethnic Chinese to the mainland (despite the absence of any extradition treaty) to answer criminal charges and risk the possibility of a death sentence.

Gen. Rocha Vieira embarked upon a second visit to China in August 1994. The Governor of Macao had discussions with the Chinese Minister of Foreign Affairs, who declared Sino-Portuguese relations to be sound but, as a result of a gaffe relating to the delegation's distribution to the press of a biography of Premier Li Peng containing uncomplimentary remarks, stressed the need for vigilance.

The draft of the new penal code for Macao did not incorporate the death penalty. In January 1995, during a visit to Portugal, Vice-Premier Zhu Rongji of China confirmed that the People's Republic would not impose the death penalty in Macao after 1999, regarding the question as a matter for the authorities of the future SAR. The new penal code, prohibiting capital punishment, took effect in January 1996.

On another visit to the territory in April 1995, President Soares emphasized the need for Macao to assert its identity. He stressed the importance of three issues: the modification of the territory's legislation; the rights of the individual; and the preservation of the Portuguese language. Travelling on to Beijing, accompanied by Gen. Rocha Vieira, the Portuguese President had successful discussions with his Chinese counterpart on various matters relating to the transition.

In November 1995, following the change of government in Lisbon, the incoming Portuguese Minister of Foreign Affairs, Jaime Gama, urged that the rights and aspirations of the people of Macao be protected. In December, while attending the celebrations to mark the inauguration of the territory's new airport, President Soares had discussions with the Chinese Vice-President, Rong Yiren. During a four-day visit to Beijing in February 1996, Jaime Gama met President Jiang Zemin and other senior officials, describing the discussions as positive. While acknowledging the sound progress of recent years, Gama and the Chinese Minister of Foreign Affairs agreed on an acceleration in the pace of work of the Sino-Portuguese JLG. In March 1996 Gen. Rocha Vieira was reappointed Governor of Macao by the newly elected President of Portugal, Jorge Sampaio. António Guterres, the new Portuguese Prime Minister, confirmed his desire for constitutional consensus regarding the transition of Macao. The JLG's 26th meeting took place in June 1996 in Macao.

At elections to the Legislative Assembly in September 1996, a total of 62 candidates from 12 electoral groupings contested the eight directly elective seats. The pro-Beijing UPP received 15.2% of the votes and won two seats, while the UPD won 14.5% and retained one of its two seats. The business-orientated groups were more successful: the Associação Promotora para a Economia de Macau took 16.6% of the votes and secured two seats; the Convergência para o Desenvolvimento de Macau (CODEM) and the União Geral para o Desenvolvimento de Macau each won one seat. The pro-democracy Associação de Novo Macau Democrático (ANMD) also won one seat. The level of voter participation was 64%. The 23-member legislature was to remain in place beyond the transfer of sovereignty in 1999.

During 1996 the rising level of violent criminal activity became a cause of increasing concern. Between January and December there were 14 bomb attacks, in addition to numerous brutal assaults. In November a Portuguese gambling inspector narrowly survived an attempt on his life by an unidentified gunman and, as attacks on local casino staff continued, three people were killed and three wounded in six separate incidents. Criminal violence continued to gather momentum in 1997, giving rise to fears for the future of the territory's vital tourism industry. Many attributed the alarming increase in organized crime to the opening of the airport in Macao, which was believed to have facilitated the entry of rival gangsters from mainland China, Taiwan and Hong Kong. In May, following the murder of three men believed to have associations with one such group of gangsters, the Chinese Government expressed its concern at the deterioration of public order in Macao and urged Portugal to observe its responsibility to maintain the enclave's social stability during the transitional period, while pledging the enhanced co-operation of the Chinese security forces in the effort to curb organized crime in Macao.

The freedom of Macao's press was jeopardized in June 1997, when several Chinese-language newspapers, along with a television station, received threats instructing them to cease reporting on the activities of the notorious 14K triad, a 10,000-member secret society to which much of the violence had been attributed. In July, during a night of arson and shooting, an explosive device was detonated in the grounds of the Governor's palace, although it caused no serious damage. In the following month China deployed 500 armed police officers to reinforce the border with Macao in order to intensify its efforts to combat illegal immigration, contraband and the smuggling of arms into the enclave. Despite the approval in July of a law further to restrict activities such as extortion and 'protection rackets', organized crime continued unabated. In early October the police forces of Macao and China initiated a joint campaign against illegal immigration. In late October Leong Kwok-hon, an alleged leader of the 14K triad, was shot dead.

Meanwhile, the slow progress of the 'three localizations' (civil service, laws and the implementation of Chinese as an official language) continued to concern the Government of China. In mid-1996 almost 50% of senior government posts were still held by Portuguese expatriates. In January 1997 the Governor pledged to accelerate the process with regard to local legislation, the priority being the training of the requisite personnel. In the same month, during a visit to Portugal, the Chinese Minister of Foreign Affairs reiterated his confidence in the future of Macao. In February President Sampaio travelled to both Macao and China, where he urged respect for Macao's identity and for the Luso-Chinese declaration regarding the transfer of sovereignty. In December details of the establishment in Macao of the office of the Chinese Ministry of Foreign Affairs, which was to commence operations in December 1999, were announced. In January 1998 the Macao Government declared that 76.5% of 'leading and directing' posts in the civil service were now held by local officials.

In March 1998 the murder of a Portuguese gambling official, followed by the killing of a marine police officer, prompted the Chinese authorities to reiterate their concern at the deteriorating situation in Macao. In the following month the driver of the territory's Under-Secretary for Public Security was shot dead. In April, by which month none of the 34 triad-related murders committed since January 1997 had been solved, the Portuguese and Chinese Governments agreed to co-operate in the exchange of information about organized criminal activities. Also in April 1998 the trial, on charges of breaching the gaming laws, of the head of the 14K triad, Wan Kuok-koi ('Broken Tooth'), was adjourned for two months, owing to the apparent reluctance of witnesses to appear in court. Following an attempted car-bomb attack on Macao's chief of police, António Marques Baptista, in early May Wan Kuok-koi was rearrested. However, the charge of the attempted murder of Marques Baptista was dismissed by a judge three days later on the grounds of insufficient evidence. Wan Kuok-koi remained in prison, charged with other serious offences. (In April 1999 he was acquitted of charges of the coercion of croupiers, but was to stand trial again on charges of triad membership, illegal gambling activities and money-laundering.) The renewed detention in May 1998 of Wan Kuok-koi led to a spate of arson attacks. The Portuguese Government was reported to have dispatched intelligence officers to the enclave to reinforce the local security forces. In June Marques Baptista travelled to Beijing and Guangzhou for discussions on the problems of cross-border criminal activity and drugs-trafficking.

In April 1998 the Portuguese Prime Minister, accompanied by his Minister of Foreign Affairs and a business delegation, paid an official visit to Macao, where he expressed confidence that after 1999 China would respect the civil rights and liberties of the territory. The delegation travelled on to China, where the Prime Minister had cordial discussions with both President Jiang Zemin and Premier Zhu Rongji.

The Preparatory Committee for the Establishment of the Macao SAR, which was to oversee the territory's transfer to Chinese sovereignty and was to comprise representatives from both the People's Republic and Macao, was inaugurated in Beijing in May 1998. Four subordinate working groups (supervising administrative, legal, economic, and social and cultural affairs) were subsequently established. The second plenary session of the Preparatory Committee was convened in July 1998, discussions encompassing issues such as the 'localization' of civil servants, public security and the drafting of the territory's fiscal budget for the year 2000. In July 1998, during a meeting with the Chinese Premier, the Governor of Macao requested an increase in the mainland's investment in the territory prior to the 1999 transfer of sovereignty.

In July 1998, as abductions continued and as it was revealed, furthermore, that the victims of kidnapping and ransom had included two serving members of the Legislative Assembly, President Jiang Zemin of China urged the triads of Macao to cease their campaign of intimidation. The police forces of Macao, Hong Kong and Guangdong Province launched 'S Plan', an operation aiming to curb the activities of rival criminal gangs. In August, in an apparent attempt to intimidate the judiciary, the territory's Attorney-General and his pregnant wife were shot and slightly wounded. In the following month five police officers and 10 journalists, who were investigating a bomb attack, were injured when a second bomb exploded.

In August 1998 representatives of the JLG agreed to intensify Luso-Chinese consultations on matters relating to the transitional period. In September, in response to the increasing security problems, China unexpectedly announced that, upon the transfer of sovereignty, it was to station troops in the territory. This abandonment of a previous assurance to the contrary caused much disquiet in Portugal, where the proposed deployment was deemed unnecessary. Although the Basic Law made no specific provision for the stationing of a mainland garrison, China asserted that it was to be ultimately responsible for the enclave's defence. By October, furthermore, about 4,000 soldiers of the People's Liberation Army (PLA) were on duty at various Chinese border posts adjacent to Macao. During a one-week visit to Beijing, the territory's Under-Secretary for Public Security had discussions with senior officials, including the Chinese Minister of Public Security. In mid-October the detention without bail of four alleged members of the 14K triad in connection with the May car-bombing and other incidents led, later in the day, to an outburst of automatic gunfire outside the courthouse.

In November 1998 procedures for the election of the 200 members of the Selection Committee were established by the Preparatory Committee. Responsible for the appointment of the members of Macao's post-1999 Government, the delegates of the Selection Committee were required to be permanent residents of the territory: 60 members were to be drawn from the business and financial communities, 50 from cultural, educational and professional spheres, 50 from labour, social service and religious circles and the remaining 40 were to be former political personages.

About 70 people were arrested in November 1998, when the authorities conducted raids on casinos believed to be engaged in illegal activities. In December an off-duty Portuguese prison warder was shot dead and a colleague wounded by a gunman, the pair having formed part of a contingent recently dispatched from Lisbon to improve security at the prison where Wan Kuok-koi was being held. At the end of December it was confirmed that Macao residents of wholly Chinese origin would be entitled to full mainland citizenship, while those of mixed Chinese and Portuguese descent would be obliged to decide between the two nationalities. In January 1999 protesters clashed with police during demonstrations to draw attention to the plight of numerous immigrant children, who had been brought illegally from China to Macao to join their legitimately resident parents and whose irregular status precluded entitlement to the territory's education, health and social services.

In January 1999 a grenade attack killed one person, and the proprietor of a casino, suspected to be member of 14K, was shot dead. In that month details of the composition of the future PLA garrison were disclosed. The troops were to comprise solely ground forces, totalling fewer than 1,000 soldiers and directly responsible to the Commander of the Guangzhou Military Unit. They would be permitted to intervene to maintain social order in the enclave only if the local police were unable to control major triad-related violence or if street demonstrations posed a threat of serious unrest. In March, during a trip to Macao (where he had discussions with the visiting Portuguese President), Qian Qichen, a Chinese Vice-Premier, indicated that an advance contingent of PLA soldiers would be deployed in Macao prior to the transfer of sovereignty. Other sources of contention between China and Portugal remained the unresolved question of the post-1999 status of those Macao residents who had been granted Portuguese nationality, and also the issue of the court of final appeal.

In April 1999 an alleged triad member was shot dead by a gunman on a motorcycle. Also in April, at the first plenary meeting of the Selection Committee, candidates for the post of the SAR's Chief Executive were elected. Edmund Ho received 125 of the 200 votes, while Stanley Au garnered 65 votes. Three other candidates failed to secure the requisite minimum of 20 votes. Edmund Ho and Stanley Au, both bankers and regarded as moderate pro-business candidates, thus proceeded to the second round of voting by secret ballot, held in May. The successful contender, Edmund Ho, received 163 of the 199 votes cast, and confirmed his intention to address the problems of law and order, security and the economy. The Chief Executive-designate also fully endorsed China's decision to deploy troops in Macao.

During 1999, in co-operation with the Macao authorities, the police forces of Guangdong Province, and of Zhuhai in particular, initiated a new offensive against the criminal activities of the triads. However, China's desire to deploy an advance contingent of troops prior to December 1999 reportedly continued to be obstructed by Portugal. Furthermore, the announcement that, subject to certain conditions, the future garrison was to be granted law-enforcement powers raised various constitutional issues. Some observers feared the imposition of martial law, if organized crime were to continue unabated. However, many Macao residents appeared to welcome the mainland's decision to station troops in the enclave. In a further effort to address the deteriorating security situation, from December 1999 Macao's 5,800-member police force was to be restructured.

In July 1999 the penultimate meeting of the JLG took place in Lisbon. In August, in accordance with the nominations of the Chief Executive-designate, the composition of the Government of the future SAR was announced by the State Council in Beijing. Appointments included that of Florinda da Rosa Silva Chan as Secretary for Administration and Justice. Also in August an outspoken pro-Chinese member of the Legislative Assembly was attacked and injured by a group of unidentified assailants. This apparently random assault on a serving politician again focused attention on the decline in law and order in the enclave. In September the Governor urged improved co-operation with the authorities of Guangdong Province in order to combat organized crime, revealing that more than one-half of the inmates of Macao's prisons were not residents of the territory. In the same month it was reported that 90 former Gurkhas of the British army were being drafted in as prison warders, following the intimidation of local officers. In September the Chief Executive-designate announced the appointment of seven new members of the Legislative Council, which was to succeed the Legislative Assembly in December 1999. While the seven nominees of the Governor in the existing Legislative Assembly were thus to be replaced, 15 of the 16 elected members (one having resigned) were to remain in office as members of the successor Legislative Council. (However, in practice, the new Legislative Council continued to be known by its former name.) The composition of the 10-member Executive Council was also announced.

In October 1999 President Jiang Zemin undertook a two-day visit to Portugal, following which it was declared that the outstanding question of the deployment of an advance contingent of Chinese troops in Macao had been resolved. The advance party was to be restricted to a technical mission, which entered the territory in early December. In November the 37th and last session of the JLG took place in Beijing, where in the same month the Governor of Macao held final discussions with President Jiang Zemin.

Meanwhile, in April 1999 Wan Kuok-koi had been acquitted of charges of coercing croupiers. In November the trial of Wan Kuok-koi on other serious charges concluded: he was found guilty of criminal association and other illegal gambling-related activities and sentenced to 15 years' imprisonment. Eight co-defendants, including Wan Kuok-koi's brother, received lesser sentences. In a separate trial Artur Chiang Calderon, a former police officer alleged to be Wan Kuok-koi's military adviser, received a prison sentence of 10 years and six months for involvement in organized crime. While two other defendants were also imprisoned, 19 were released on the grounds of insufficient evidence. As the transfer of the territory's sovereignty approached, by mid-December almost 40 people had been murdered in triad-related violence on the streets of Macao since January 1999.

THE SAR GOVERNMENT

In November 1999 representatives of the JLG reached agreement on details regarding the deployment of Chinese troops in Macao and on the retention of Portuguese as an official language. At midnight on 19 December 1999, therefore, in a ceremony attended by the Presidents and heads of government of Portugal and China, the sovereignty of Macao was duly transferred; 12 hours later (only after the departure from the newly inaugurated SAR of the Portuguese delegation), 500 soldiers of the 1,000-strong force of the PLA, in a convoy of armoured vehicles, crossed the border into Macao, where they were installed in a makeshift barracks in a vacant apartment building. However, prior to the ceremony it was reported that the authorities of Guangdong Province had detained almost 3,000 persons, including 15 residents of Macao, suspected of association with criminal gangs. The celebrations in Macao were also marred by the authorities' handling of demonstrations by members of Falun Gong, a religious movement recently outlawed in China. The expulsion from Macao of several members of the sect in the days preceding the territory's transfer and the arrest of 30 adherents on the final day of Portuguese sovereignty prompted strong criticism from President Jorge Sampaio of Portugal. Nevertheless, in an effort to consolidate relations with the EU, in May 2000 the first official overseas visit of the SAR's Chief Executive was to Europe, his itinerary including Portugal.

Meanwhile, a spate of arson attacks on vehicles in February 2000 was followed by the fatal shooting, in a residential district of Macao, of a Hong Kong citizen believed to have triad connections. In March, in an important change to the immigration rules, it was announced that children of Chinese nationality whose parents were permanent residents of Macao would shortly be allowed to apply for residency permits. A monthly quota of 420 successful applicants was established, while the youngest children were to receive priority.

In May 2000 hundreds of demonstrators took part in a march to protest against Macao's high level of unemployment. This shortage of jobs was attributed to the territory's use of immigrant workers, mainly from mainland China and South-East Asia, who were estimated to total 28,000. During the ensuing clashes several police officers and one demonstrator were reportedly injured. Trade unions continued to organize protests, and in July (for the first time since the unrest arising from the Chinese Cultural Revolution of 1966) tear gas and water cannon were used to disperse about 200 demonstrators who were demanding that the immigration of foreign workers be halted by the Government. In the same month it was announced that, in early 2001, an office of the Macao SAR was to be established in Beijing, in order to promote links between the two Governments. In Guangzhou in August 2000, as cross-border crime continued to increase, senior officials of Macao's criminal investigation unit met their counterparts from China and Hong Kong for discussions on methods of improving co-operation. It was agreed that further meetings were henceforth to be held twice a year, alternately in Beijing and Macao.

Celebrations to mark the first anniversary in December 2000 of Macao's reversion to Chinese sovereignty were attended by President Jiang Zemin, who made a speech praising the local administration, but warning strongly against those seeking to use either of the SARs as a base for subversion. A number of Falun Gong adherents from Hong Kong who had attempted to enter Macao for the celebrations were expelled. The same fate befell two Hong Kong human rights activists who had hoped to petition the Chinese President during his stay in Macao about the human rights situation in the People's Republic. A group of Falun Gong members in Macao held a protest the day before the President Jiang's arrival. They were detained in custody and subsequently alleged that they had suffered police brutality.

In January 2001 China urged the USA to cease interfering in its internal affairs, following the signature by President Bill Clinton of the US Macao Policy Act, which related to the control of Macao's exports and the monitoring of its autonomy. In the same month voter registration began in Macao, in preparation for the expiry of the first Legislative Council's term of office in October and the election of a new assembly. In his Chinese Lunar New Year address on 23 January, Edmund Ho urged new efforts to revitalize the economy and achieve social progress.

The Governor of Guangdong Province, Lu Ruihua, made an official visit to Macao in early February to improve links between the two regions. At the same time, the Legislative Council announced plans to strengthen relations with legislative bodies in the mainland, and the President of the Legislative Council, Susana Chou, visited Beijing and held talks with Vice-Premier Qian Qichen. Also in February, a Macao resident was charged with publishing online articles about Falun Gong.

Edmund Ho visited Beijing in early March 2001 to attend the fourth session of the Ninth NPC, and held talks with President Jiang Zemin, who praised the former's achievements since the reversion of Macao to Chinese rule. On returning to Macao, Ho received the President of Estonia, Lennart Meri, who was touring the mainland and who thus became the first head of state to visit the SAR since its return to China. The two leaders discussed co-operation in the fields of tourism, trade, information technology (IT), and telecommunications, with Ho apparently seeking to learn from Estonia's experience in opening the telecommunications market. The EU announced in mid-March that SAR passport holders would, from May 2001, no longer require visas to enter EU countries. In the same month Jorge Neto Valente, a prominent lawyer and reputedly the wealthiest Portuguese person in Macao, was kidnapped by a gang, but freed in a dramatic police operation.

The Macao, Hong Kong, and mainland police forces established a working group in mid-March 2001 to combat cross-border crime, with a special emphasis on narcotics, and in late March the Macao, Hong Kong, and Guangdong police forces conducted a joint anti-drugs operation, 'Spring Thunder', resulting in the arrest of 1,243 suspected traffickers and producers, and the seizure of large quantities of heroin, ecstasy, and marijuana. As part of the growing campaign against crime, a Shanghai court sentenced to death a Macao-based gangster, Zeng Jijun, on charges of running a debt-recovering group, members of which had committed murder. Three of Zeng's associates were given long prison sentences.

In May 2001 Macao and Portugal signed an agreement to strengthen co-operation in the fields of economy, culture, public security, and justice during the visit of the Portuguese Minister of Foreign Affairs, Jaime Gama, the most senior Portuguese official to visit Macao since its reversion to Chinese rule. In June Macao's Secretary for Security, Cheong Kuoc Va, visited Beijing and signed new accords aimed at reducing the trafficking of drugs, guns and people. In the same month Chief Executive Edmund Ho made his first official visit to the headquarters of the EU in Brussels, where he sought to promote contacts and exchanges between the SAR and the EU.

In July 2001 China's most senior representative in Macao, Wang Qiren, died of cancer. Later in the month, another major campaign against illegal activities related to the triads was conducted by the Macao, Hong Kong, and Guangdong police forces, and was part of ongoing attempts to eradicate organized crime. At the end of the month, the Secretary for Security, Cheong Kuoc Va, reported that cases of violent crime had declined by 37.3% year-on-year in the first half of 2001, and murders, robberies, arson, drugs-trafficking, and kidnapping had all decreased significantly over the same period. In a further sign of co-operation between Macao and the mainland against crime, the two sides signed an agreement on mutual judicial co-operation and assistance in late August, the first of its kind. In September José Proença Branco and Choi Lai Hang were appointed police commander and customs chief respectively.

Elections to the Legislative Council were held on 23 September 2001, the first since Macao's reversion to Chinese rule. The number of seats was increased from 23 to 27: seven members were appointed by the Chief Executive, 10 elected directly and 10 indirectly. Of the 10 directly elective seats, two seats each were won by the business-orientated CODEM, the pro-Beijing UPP and UPD and the pro-democracy ANMD. Two other factions won one seat each. Of the 10 indirectly elective seats, four were won by a group representing business interests. Two seats each were won by a group representing welfare, cultural, educational, and sports interests; by the Comissão Conjunta da Candidatura das Associações de Empregados (CCCAE—a group representing labour interests); and by a group representing professional people.

In October 2001 China appointed Bai Zhijian as director of its liaison office in Macao, and later in the month Cui Shiping was selected as Macao's representative in the NPC, replacing the late Wang Qiren. At the same time, Edmund Ho attended the summit meeting of Asia-Pacific Economic Cooperation (APEC) in Shanghai, and the EU-Macao Joint Committee held a meeting in the SAR, aimed at improving trade, tourism and legal co-operation between the two entities. During late 2001, meanwhile, Macao increased co-operation with Hong Kong and the mainland in fighting crime and combating terrorism, amid reports that Russian mafias were becoming increasingly active in the SARs, and in mid-November the three police departments held an anti-drugs forum in Hong Kong. Later in the month, Edmund Ho announced that personal income tax would be waived and industrial and commercial taxes reduced for 2002, in order to alleviate the impact of the economic downturn. Ho also pledged to create 6,000 new jobs and invest more in infrastructure, and urged employers to avoid staff reductions.

In December 2001 the Government finally acted to end the 40-year monopoly on casinos and gambling held by Stanley Ho and his long-established company, the Sociedade de Turismo e Diversões de Macau (STDM). Under the new arrangements, some 21 companies, none of which was Chinese-owned, were to be permitted to bid for three new operating licences for casinos in the SAR. Meanwhile, Stanley Ho's daughter Pansy was playing an increasingly prominent role in managing the family businesses (which included the shipping, property and hotel conglomerate, Shun Tak holdings).

Also in December 2001 Edmund Ho undertook a visit to Beijing, where he and President Jiang Zemin discussed the situation in Macao. In January 2002 Ho visited the mainland city of Chongqing, seeking to reinforce bilateral economic links, and stating that Macao would play a more active role in developing the region. Also in January, the Government granted permission to the Taipei Trade and Cultural Office (TTCO) to issue visas for Taiwan-bound visitors from Macao and the mainland. In February Li Peng, Chairman of the Standing Committee of the NPC, paid an official visit to Macao, where he held discussions with the Chief Executive of the SAR. During Li's visit, a leading Macao political activist, along with several activists from the Hong Kong-based 'April Fifth Action' group, were arrested for planning to stage protests against Li for his role in the Tiananmen Square suppression of 1989 and in favour of the release of mainland political dissidents. The Hong Kong activists were immediately deported. At the same time the Hong Kong media reported that a Hong Kong-based cameraman had been beaten and had his camera destroyed by a Macao policeman when he attempted to film the interception of the activists. Other journalists also claimed to have been treated aggressively.

In March 2002 a new representative office of the Macao SAR was established in Beijing, with the aim of enhancing links between the SAR and the mainland. Wu Beiming was named as its director. At its inaugural ceremony, Edmund Ho and Chinese Vice-Premier Qian Qichen praised the 'one country, two systems' model, and the director of the central government liaison office in Macao, Bai Zhijian, suggested that Macao might become a model for Taiwan's eventual reunification with the mainland.

On 1 April 2002 Stanley Ho's STDM formally relinquished its 40-year monopoly on casinos. However, Ho retained influence in the gambling sector after his Sociedade de Jogos de Macau (SJM—Macao Gaming Holding Company) won an 18-year licence to operate casinos. Also in early April, Edmund Ho attended the first annual conference of the Bo'ao Forum for Asia (BFA—a non-profit non-governmental organization), held on Hainan Island, China, where he met Hong Kong Chief Executive Tung Chee-hwa and Chinese Premier Zhu Rongji, as well as business leaders.

In December 2002 Macao selected its 12 candidates for the 10th NPC (convened in Beijing in March 2003). At the same time, Edmund Ho paid a routine visit to Beijing, where he held discussions with Jiang Zemin and Vice-President Hu Jintao.In March 2003 Edmund Ho held a meeting with the new Chinese Premier, Wen Jiabao, at which the future development of Macao under the policy of 'one country, two systems' was discussed. In October Chinese Vice-President Zeng Qinghong visited Macao to attend the signing ceremony of the Closer Economic Partnership Arrangement (CEPA) between Macao and the Chinese mainland. Also in October, Chinese Vice-Premier Wu Yi attended a trade forum in Macao relating to China's trade relations with Portuguese-speaking countries.

In November 2003 Edmund Ho outlined plans for administrative reform of Macao's Government, alongside legal reform, to begin in 2004. Also in November 2003, Xiao Yang, President of China's Supreme People's Court, delivered a speech emphasizing the importance of judicial co-operation between Macao and the mainland. Draft legislation detailing the procedure for the election of Macao's next Chief Executive, who was to be chosen in 2004 by a 300-member Election Committee, was approved by the Government in February 2004. In June it was announced that the re-election of the Chief Executive would take place in late August. Edmund Ho began his election campaign in mid-August, and was duly re-elected on 29 August, securing 296 of the 300 votes of the members of the Election Committee. In December Chinese President Hu Jintao visited Macao to mark the fifth anniversary of Macao's reunification with the People's Republic. During his visit Hu praised the successful implementation of 'one country, two systems' in Macao. In January 2005 President Sampaio of Portugal visited Macao, at the conclusion of an official visit to China.

In mid-2005 it was reported that the number of voters registered for the legislative elections scheduled for September had reached 220,653, almost one-half of the population of the SAR and an increase of some 35% compared with the number registered for the elections of 2001. During the period prior to the election, the Commission Against Corruption, established in 1999, announced that it had uncovered a series of schemes involving electoral malpractice. (Subsequently, in October 2005, it was reported that 36 residents of the SAR were being charged with electoral fraud.) At the elections, held on 25 September, the number of seats allocated by direct suffrage was increased from 10 to 12, bringing the total number of seats in the Legislative Council to 29. The pro-democracy ANMD received the highest proportion of votes cast (18.8%) and secured two of the 12 directly elective seats. The Associação dos Cidadãos Unidos de Macau (ACUM), a citizens' association that reportedly drew a large degree of its support from immigrants from Fujian Province and advocated support for the gaming industry, also obtained two seats, while the pro-Beijing UPD and UPP retained their representation of two seats each in the legislature. Angela Leong On Kei, wife of influential businessman and casino owner Stanley Ho, was elected on the list of the Aliança para o Desenvolvimento de Macau (AMD). The remaining three seats were divided among Nova Esperança (NE), supported by civil servants and the ethnic Portuguese community, the União Geral para o Bem-querer de Macau (UBM) and CODEM. The turn-out was evaluated at 58.4% of registered voters. The 10 indirectly elective seats, meanwhile, were distributed as in 2001: four were allocated to representatives of business interests, and two each to representatives of labour interests (CCCAE), to the interests of professionals and to welfare, cultural, educational and sports interests (União Excelente).

In September 2005 attention focused on Macao's financial sector when the US Administration asserted that the Government of the Democratic People's Republic of Korea (DPRK—North Korea) had been laundering and counterfeiting money through a Macao bank, Banco Delta Asia (BDA). The Macao authorities took control of the bank pending an inquiry into its activities, and the assets held within these accounts, believed to total US $25m., were 'frozen'. A three-month investigation by Chinese officials reportedly concluded in January 2006 that the allegations were accurate. In February it was announced that BDA was terminating its links with the DPRK and that independent accountants had been appointed to monitor the bank's clients. In October an independent audit conducted by Ernst and Young, an international accounting company, reported that it had found no evidence to suggest that the bank had knowingly facilitated money-laundering activities. However, following the completion of an 18-month investigation, in March 2007 US Treasury officials concluded that the bank had deliberately disregarded illicit activities and ordered US banks and companies to terminate all links with BDA. The Monetary Authority of Macao expressed deep regret at this conclusion. The North Korean assets in question were to be released and transferred to a mainland Chinese bank. A Russian bank subsequently agreed to act as intermediary for the transfer of the funds, which was carried out in late June (see the chapter on the Democratic People's Republic of Korea). In September the Monetary Authority of Macao announced that control of BDA was being restored to its Chairman, Stanley Au, partly because the bank had shown an improvement in its practices. The US Treasury's measures, despite a legal challenge filed by the bank, remained in effect.

In December 2006 a corruption scandal emerged in Macao when the Chief Executive ordered the arrest of Ao Man Long, Secretary for Transport and Public Works, and that of 11 others. Ao, who had served as a government official for 20 years, was accused of bribery and involvement in irregular financial activities, including the transfer of millions of patacas from bank accounts in Hong Kong to the United Kingdom. Various members of his family were also said to be involved in the affair. Ao was alleged to have collaborated with his relatives to register a number of bogus companies abroad in order to 'launder' the bribes that he had reportedly received. Ao was subsequently charged on 76 corruption-related counts, including accepting bribes and money-laundering; he was alleged to have misappropriated 800m. patacas and to have amassed a considerable personal fortune. The trial at the Court of Final Appeal, to which about 100 witnesses were summoned, began in November 2007. In January 2008, having been found guilty of 57 of the charges against him, Ao was sentenced to 27 years' imprisonment. In June Ao's wife, three members of his family and three businessmen were also convicted of various money-laundering and bribery charges. Ao's wife, Chan Meng-leng, received a prison sentence of 23 years. The three business associates of Ao received sentences ranging from seven to 10 years and were ordered to pay compensation to the Government. In February 2009 Ao appeared in court to answer 28 new charges, including abuse of power. In April he was convicted of 23 additional charges of taking bribes and of five charges of money-laundering, following which he was sentenced to a further 28 years in prison. In practice, however, owing to the limit of 30 years upon prison terms in Macao, Ao's sentence would be extended by a relatively short period.

At a May Day labour rally in 2007, demonstrators protesting against alleged corruption and the use of illegal workers in the SAR proceeded to demand the resignation of Edmund Ho as Chief Executive. In this unusual display of civil unrest, there were violent clashes between thousands of protesters and several hundred police officers, armed with batons and pepper spray. The police also fired blank shots into the air to disperse the demonstrators. However, one man was reportedly shot and injured during the clashes, although the police denied the use of live ammunition. A number of protesters were arrested by the authorities. Another demonstration took place in October. Amid increasing popular concern about the rapid pace of change and the perceived deterioration in the quality of life in Macao, in December hundreds attended a further protest against corruption, this time coinciding with the eighth anniversary of the establishment of the SAR. Meanwhile, in August 2007 it was alleged in the media that Edmund Ho owned shares in Many Town Company, a Hong Kong-based business with interests in STDM; the Government issued a denial, claiming that Ho's shares had been transferred to his brother in 1995. In April 2008 Edmund Ho introduced new measures that limited the number of gaming licences to six and ruled out the building of any new casinos, as the Chinese Government reportedly favoured a shift in emphasis to other areas of the economy. In July it was reported that the Macao Government had decided to regulate commission rates paid by casinos to promoters.

In January 2008 Macao conducted its election of deputies to the mainland Chinese legislature. The electoral conference, comprising more than 300 representatives of various sectors of Macao society, selected 12 deputies, who were to attend the 11th NPC, convened in Beijing in March. In May Lu Shumin was appointed as commissioner of the Ministry of Foreign Affairs in the Macao SAR, in place of Wan Yongxiang who had served in the post since 2002.

In December 2008 more than 20 Hong Kong activists, who had planned to attend a demonstration against proposed legislation relating to the security of Macao, were barred from entering the SAR. In February 2009 the Legislative Council overwhelmingly approved the National Security Bill, prohibiting acts of treason, secession, sedition or subversion against the Chinese Government and outlawing the theft of state secrets. The legislation provided for prison sentences of up to 30 years for those convicted of such crimes. Fearing that the law was open to abuse by the authorities, various human rights groups, including Amnesty International, criticized the ambiguous wording of the law, particularly the reference to ill-defined 'preparatory acts'. Furthermore, shortly after the promulgation of the law in early March, the dean of the faculty of law at the University of Hong Kong, who had been invited to deliver a speech at the University of Macao, was refused entry to the territory. As fears for freedom of expression in both Macao and Hong Kong grew, the authorities of the latter SAR requested clarification of Macao's denial of entry to the law professor. Various other Hong Kong residents, including pro-democracy politicians and a photographer, were similarly prohibited from entering Macao.

The election for the next Chief Executive of the SAR, who was to replace Edmund Ho in December 2009, took place in July of that year. Fernando Chui Sai On, former Secretary for Social Affairs and Culture, was elected unopposed to the post by the Election Committee, receiving 282 valid votes; 14 of the 300 members of the Election Committee were reported to have abstained, and three were absent from the proceedings.

Although the next elections for Macao's Legislative Council were not due to take place until the latter part of 2009, it was reported in 2006 that bogus associations were already being established in an apparent attempt to influence the outcome of the future poll. The majority of these newly founded nominal organizations were sports groups, part of the category representing culture, education and sporting interests, which together with local charities would form the constituency responsible for choosing two of the Legislative Council's 10 indirectly elected members. (The three constituencies of labour, employer and professional interests would be entitled to determine the remaining eight indirectly elective seats.) The legitimacy of the SAR's Election Committee, responsible for choosing Macao's next Chief Executive, was also believed to be in serious jeopardy, with 80 of its 300 members due to be selected by the constituency of culture, education and sport. Emphasizing the fact that 207 bogus associations had been created between January and April 2006 alone, compared with 234 for the whole of 2005, the Hong-Kong based *South China Morning Post* quoted a pro-democracy legislator as comparing the electoral contest to 'gangs fighting to control a larger number of factions'. Under electoral rules, such associations were required to have been established for at least three years in order to be eligible to vote, hence the proliferation of these organizations prior to the deadline in 2006.

The legislative election took place on 20 September 2009. The level of participation was reported to be 60% of the electorate. The pro-Beijing UPD won two of the 12 seats determined by direct election. The pro-gaming ACUM and the pro-democracy Associação de Próspero Macau Democrático (APMD) took two seats each. The remaining six seats were taken by: the pro-democracy ANMD; the pro-Beijing UPP; the Nova União para o Desenvolvimento de Macau (NUDM), representing the interests of the gaming sector; the NE, which continued to be supported by civil servants; the pro-business União Macau-Guangdong; and the Aliança para a Mudança, an alliance advocating public reform. Four of the 10 indirectly elective seats were taken by representatives of business interests; two by representatives of the professional sector; two by representatives of labour interests; and two by members of the social, cultural, educational and sports sector.

Fernando Chui's five-year term of office commenced on 20 December 2009. The incoming Chief Executive retained the four incumbent Secretaries, and Cheong U was appointed as Secretary for Social Affairs and Culture. As Macao celebrated the 10th anniversary of its reversion to Chinese sovereignty, President Hu Jintao praised the achievements of the previous decade, but suggested that the SAR be more 'creative' and work more closely with the Pearl River Delta region. The Chinese President also urged stronger management of the gambling industry, the diversification of the economy, the raising of living standards and the improvement of the education system.

In his first Policy Address, delivered in March 2010, the Chief Executive focused on issues of social welfare, announcing the continuation of various measures to provide financial support for the residents of Macao (see Economy), along with subsidies to assist disadvantaged families and other needy citizens, particularly the elderly. In an acknowledgement of increasing public concern with regard to the issue of corruption in Macao, Chui also pledged to improve the transparency and integrity of the civil service. The probity of public servants was to be more closely supervised by the Commission Against Corruption; in particular, details of the property transactions of government officials were to be made publicly available. The Commission Against Corruption subsequently agreed to establish a permanent working group with its counterparts in neighbouring Guangdong Province and in Hong Kong.

Police used water cannon and pepper spray to control the May Day demonstration of 2010, which was attended by as many as 1,500 protesters, whose grievances included the continued use of illegal labour in Macao. About a dozen people, in addition to two police officers, required hospital treatment for injuries sustained during the clashes.

In its annual Trafficking in Persons Report, issued in May 2010, the US Department of State continued to identify Macao as a jurisdiction that had yet to become fully compliant with minimum standards for the elimination of human trafficking. However, the report acknowledged the SAR's 'significant efforts' to address the issue of commercial sexual exploitation, the principal victims of which were reported to have travelled to Macao from mainland China, Mongolia, Russia and South-East Asia, in search of employment opportunities. Macao was also identified as a source territory for women and girls subjected to forced prostitution elsewhere in Asia. In the authorities' first conviction related to such activities (many similar cases having been closed on the grounds of lack of evidence), in November 2009 a local man was sentenced to more than seven years' imprisonment for his involvement in the trafficking in 2008 of two Macao females to Japan.

In June 2010 it was announced that, in order to assist the Chief Executive in the area of policy-making, a new government institute was to be established. This policy institute was to be responsible for conducting research on political, economic and legal issues, as well as various other matters.

During an official visit to Portugal in June 2010 Chui had discussions with President Aníbal Cavaco Silva and other senior government members. The Chief Executive's delegation included his Secretary for Economy and Finance, Francis Tam Pak Yuen, and the Secretary for Social Affairs and Culture, Cheong U, as well as representatives of Macao's business community. With the objective of revitalizing bilateral relations and of promoting co-operation in the areas of trade, investment in tourism, education and culture, it was confirmed that a joint summit meeting would take place in late 2010.

Amid much public criticism, draft legislation to provide civil servants with financial aid, either if being sued or if pursuing a lawsuit on a matter arising from the performance of their public duty, was under consideration in mid-2010. Critics of the proposed legislation included Susana Chou, former President of the Legislative Assembly, who denounced it as a serious violation of the Basic Law. Media organizations, in particular, expressed concern for the freedom of the press, fearing that such a law might be used to support legal action against newspaper reporters.

In policy address delivered in November 2010 the Chief Executive focused on the implementation of new measures in various areas, including the diversification of the SAR's economy, social welfare, transparency of government and regional co-operation. Chui announced that, following public consultation, the Government had decided to exclude the development of casino premises from the urban planning for newly reclaimed land and these strips areas would be used only for the purposes of the development of residential housing and local industries that would help to diversify the economy, Chui. During Fernando Chui's visit to Beijing in December Chinese Premier Wen Jiabao expressed the hope that Macao would work towards the improvement of its governance and promote the diversification of its economy.

In March 2011 the Chief Executive of Macao and the Governor of Guangdong Province signed a wide-ranging agreement providing for further bilateral co-operation in various fields, including economic matters, public welfare and culture. Under the Guangdong-Macao Cooperation Framework Agreement the two sides were to co-operate in the development of local industries, the construction of infrastructural facilities, the provision of public services and in development planning. In October it was announced that Hu Zhengyue had been appointed as China's commissioner of the Ministry of Foreign Affairs in the Macao SAR, replacing Lu Shumin.

Economy

Upon its return to Chinese sovereignty in December 1999, the Special Administrative Region (SAR) of Macao was permitted to retain its system of free enterprise for a period of 50 years. The economy is now based mainly on tourism and gambling. By 2009 the services sector accounted for nearly 90% of gross domestic product (GDP). In 2007, owing to the substantial growth of casino business in that year, real GDP expanded by 26.0%. GDP growth was 12.9% in 2008. In comparison with the first half of the previous year, however, GDP contracted by 14.8% in the first six months of 2009, Macao's worst result on record. Growth reached just 1.3% for 2009 as a whole, but a strong recovery followed in 2010, in which year GDP expanded by 26.2%. In the first six months of 2011, Macao's GDP increased by an estimated 22.9% in comparison with the corresponding period of the previous year.

Between 2000 and 2009 the population increased at an average annual rate of 2.2%. Rapid economic growth in the mid-2000s facilitated a stronger rate of increase in per caput income. GDP per head increased, in real terms, at an average annual rate of 11.8% during 2000–08. The results of the 2006 by-census revealed that the population had risen to 502,113, of whom 471,263 claimed Chinese nationality. A further 8,593 of Macao's resident population identified themselves as Portuguese. The population was projected to total 644,000 by December 2011.

Major infrastructural projects, along with the rapid expansion of the tourism industry, resulted in the creation of thousands of new jobs. None the less, in 2007 unemployment stood at 3.1%, decreasing slightly to 3.0% in 2008. By early 2009 unemployment (particularly in the construction and services industries) had begun to rise, reaching a high point of 3.8% later in the year. However, by mid-2010 the rate of unemployment had declined to 2.9%, decreasing to 2.6% in mid-2011. Non-resident workers totalled 88,740 in August 2011.

In 2000 the Macao Government introduced the Immigration Investment Scheme, which offered potential investors residency status in the Special Administrative Region (SAR) in exchange for capital investment. The provision of residency rights ensured that this scheme appealed greatly to citizens of the People's Republic of China, most of whom required permits to visit Macao. Applicants were required to purchase fixed assets in Macao to the value of 1m. patacas, as well as to make an initial deposit (a minimum of 500,000 patacas) in one of Macao's banking institutions. The programme proved very successful, attracting some 10,000m. patacas during 2000–05. According to the Macao Trade and Investment Promotion Institute, 2,337 applications were submitted to the fixed asset scheme in 2006.

Macao has attempted to present attractive prospects to foreign investors through other measures such as reforms of the taxation system and of the banking sector. The liberalization of the gambling industry in 2002 prompted greater competition and investment. In comparison with the previous year, foreign direct investment in the SAR was reported to have increased by 1,340m. patacas in 2009 to reach 22,120m. patacas, of which more than 70% was destined for the gaming sector. The principal sources of investment finance were Hong Kong, the USA and mainland China.

TOURISM AND GAMBLING

Despite various attempts to diversify, the economy of Macao has become increasingly dependent on tourism and the related gambling industry. By the end of 2009 six concessionaires were operating a total of 33 casinos in the SAR. By 2010 the Government's receipts from direct taxes on gambling accounted for more than 80% of the Government's total recurrent budget revenue, in comparison with about 40% in 1990 and 60% in 2000. The profitability of the gambling sector, and consequently the level of revenue received by the Government of the SAR from its taxes on gaming activities, increased sharply following the liberalization of the sector in 2002.

The inauguration of the Venetian casino complex in August 2007 (see below) significantly increased capacity in the sector; in that year revenue from games of fortune increased by 46.6% to total 83,022m. patacas—equivalent to 54.0% of GDP. Revenue from games of fortune increased by a further 31% in 2008, reaching 108,772m. patacas. Gross gaming revenue from games of fortune reached 119,369m. patacas in 2009, rising to a record 188,343m. patacas in 2010. The Government's revenue from gambling taxes reached an estimated 41,900m. patacas in 2008, representing almost 73% of total public revenue in that year.

In 2006 total visitors to Macao numbered almost 22.0m., representing a 17.6% increase in arrivals in comparison with 2005, and a further increase, of 12.2%, was recorded in 2007, when visitor arrivals totalled nearly 27.0m. In 2008 visitor arrivals rose by a further 11.9%, to reach nearly 30.2m. However, visitor arrivals declined by 27.8% in 2009, reaching just 21.8m., owing to the global recession. As general economic conditions improved, in 2010 visitor numbers rose to nearly 25.0m., of whom 29.9% came from Hong Kong.

The majority of tourists traditionally came from Hong Kong, but from the mid-1990s the number of visitors from mainland China increased rapidly. Following Macao's transfer of sovereignty in December 1999, passports remained necessary for incoming mainland Chinese visitors, along with special passes issued by the Ministry of Public Security of the People's Republic. Arrivals from China totalled 5.7m. in 2003, when for the first time the number of visitors from the mainland surpassed those from Hong Kong. Chinese numbers rose to almost 10.5m. in 2005, representing 55.9% of total visitors in that year. In 2007 nearly 14.9m. people (equivalent to 59.4% of all visitors to Macao) came from the Chinese mainland, compared with 12.0m. travellers in the previous year. In May 2008, however, the Chinese authorities announced plans to limit the allocation of individual travel permits to residents of Guangdong Province. As the mainland authorities became increasingly concerned by the extent of gambling activities by those travelling from the province, Guangdong residents were subsequently restricted to two trips to Macao per year. In 2008, therefore, the number of visitors from mainland China decreased to 11.6m. (or 56.4% of total visitors). In 2009 visitors from mainland China declined further, to under 11.0m. (or 56.1% of total visitors), before rising to 13.3m. (53.0%) in 2010.

Average visitor spending rose to 1,729 patacas per head in 2008, before declining to 1,616 in 2009. Having reached only 1,436 patacas in the second quarter of 2010, per caput expenditure increased to 1.482 patacas in the corresponding quarter of 2011. In the latter three-month period, average spending by tourists from mainland China totalled 1,868 patacas (compared with 3,571 patacas in 2008). The average expenditure by visitors from Hong Kong in the second quarter of 2011 was 906 patacas.

Efforts have been made to broaden the base of the tourist industry, to promote the territory's unique heritage and to encourage longer stays. Programmes to restore and develop Macao's historic and religious monuments have attempted to offer visitors opportunities for cultural insights perhaps lost in Hong Kong. The first preservation statutes were approved in 1976. Numerous sites have since been similarly protected, and in 2005 Macao was designated by UNESCO as a World Heritage Site. From the 1990s numerous new hotels were built, including many by leading international hotel chains. The hotel occupancy rate increased to 77.2% in 2007, but declined to 74.3% and 71.4% in 2008 and 2009, respectively. A total of 18,146 hotel rooms were available in September 2009. The average length of sojourn was only 0.9 days in the second quarter of 2011, while that of same-day visitors remained at 0.2.

By the mid-1990s a tourist activity centre was in operation, incorporating the Macao Grand Prix Museum, the Wine Museum, restaurants, conference halls, exhibition areas and other facilities. Other projects included a 360m.-patacas shopping centre (a joint venture with a major Japanese retailing company). In collaboration with a Taiwan-based enterprise, a 2,000m.-patacas complex, incorporating the territory's largest casino and office building, was constructed by the Sociedade de Turismo e Diversões de Macau (STDM). A new sports stadium, covering an area of 44,000 sq m on the island of Taipa, was inaugurated in early 1997. In 1998 plans for the redevelopment of the greyhound racecourse (which had a turnover of US $44m. in 1997) were announced. The construction of a 16,000-sq-m cultural centre, on a huge site of reclaimed land around the Outer Harbour, was completed in 1999. The complex comprises a museum block, housing the historical, archaeological and architectural collections of Macao, and a theatre block. A new 17-ha marine park, including a dolphin tank and aquarium, was planned for reclaimed land on Taipa Island. In July 2000 the SAR Government established the Macao 2005 East Asian Games Co-ordination Office to prepare Macao for the Fourth East Asian Games in 2005, which had been awarded to Macao in 1996 (the Games Co-ordination Office was replaced in January 2002 by the Macao Fourth East Asian Games Organising Committee). Several sporting venues were constructed to cater for the games, including the Macau East Asian Games Dome, which covered a total area of 139,960 sq m. In September 2001 construction began on a new 900m.-patacas (US $112m.) amusement park, Fisherman's Wharf. Opened in December 2005, the 140,000-sq-m park incorporates a seafood section (Dynasty Wharf), with the main amusements and rides area being located on 40,000 sq m of reclaimed land; the third section comprises a marina, restaurants, bars and a nightclub (Legend Wharf). Meanwhile, in December 2001 STDM opened the 338m-high Macao Tower Convention and Entertainment Centre, as part of plans to make the SAR more family-orientated and to dispel its unsavoury image. In an effort to attract more visitors, the Macao Government designated 2006 as 'Macao Heritage Year'.

The tourism sector was historically dominated by STDM, a syndicate to which the territory's gambling monopoly was transferred in 1962 (although STDM's monopoly was subsequently withdrawn—see below). The company has interests in the jetfoil service between Hong Kong and Macao, the local airport and Air Macau, various infrastructural operations and property projects, the electricity company, a television network and a supermarket chain. In June 1997 the Sino-Portuguese Joint Liaison Group (JLG—see History) reached agreement on the revision of Macao's gambling franchise. Under the revision, STDM was to pay tax of 31.8% on its revenues from casinos (increased from 30% and backdated to January 1996). In addition to an initial contribution of US $22.7m., STDM was also to contribute 1.6% of its annual gross takings to a new government-controlled Macao development foundation—see below (responsible for the operation of the cultural centre). In 1998 this annual contribution reached US $116m. Furthermore, the contract obliged STDM to guarantee marine transport operations and maintenance, to meet the cost of various public works and to match any government spending on tourism promotion.

In July 2000 it was announced that a special committee, chaired by the Chief Executive of the SAR, was to be established to study the future development and management of the gambling industry. STDM's gambling franchise had been renewed once in 1996. However, in December 2001 the Government decided against renewing STDM's monopoly, and the agreement finally expired in April 2002. Under the new arrangements, the Government announced in February 2002 that three companies had successfully bid for casino licences—the Las Vegas-backed Wynn Resorts (Macao) Ltd, the Galaxy Casino Co Ltd (a Hong Kong-Macao joint venture), and the Macao Gaming Holding Co (SJM—Sociedade de Jogos de Macau, a subsidiary of STDM), managed by Stanley Ho. The Gaming Industrial Regime, approved by the Legislative Assembly in August 2001, stipulated that casinos should contribute to the development of tourism, and that SJM was to pay 35% of its total income to the SAR Government annually—up from 31.8% previously. Despite the loss of his monopoly, Stanley Ho was expected to retain a strong influence in the gambling sector, as his competitors needed time to develop a presence in the SAR. (STDM employed more than 10,000 people in its 11 casinos in 2001, and contributed approximately 30% of Macao's GDP.) In late June 2002 the Government formally awarded Wynn Resorts (Macao) Ltd a 20-year contract to operate casinos. As a first step, Wynn was to invest 4,000m. patacas in Macao over seven years, and open its first casino and hotel complex in 2006. Also in June 2002, a similar contract was signed with Galaxy Casino Co Ltd. In May 2004 Las Vegas Sands Inc, operating under a sub-concession granted by Galaxy Casino, opened a new casino, The Sands, representing the effective end of Stanley Ho's monopoly on the gambling industry. An extension to this casino, opened in August 2006, made it reportedly the largest casino in the world, with more than 700 gaming tables and 1,000 slot machines, comprising 25% and 30%, respectively, of Macao's total. Meanwhile, in July 2004 Galaxy Casino commenced operation of their Galaxy Waldo Casino, within the Galaxy Waldo Hotel.

The Las Vegas Sands Venetian casino and hotel complex, extending to 980,000 sq m, opened in August 2007. Reported to be the world's largest hotel development and the biggest building in Asia, the complex provided the SAR with 3,000 luxury hotel rooms and suites. Some 20,000 workers were employed during the construction process, and an estimated 16,000 employees were needed to maintain operations following completion. The casino provided facilities for 15,000 visitors, including 870 gambling tables and 3,400 slot machines. In addition to gambling and hotel amenities, the Venetian provided a sports arena and retail space. A total of 1m. sq m of floor space was allocated for conventions and exhibitions. Elsewhere, Cyber One Agents Ltd announced plans to develop a major leisure and convention centre, Macao Studio City, near to the recently constructed Lotus Bridge immigration checkpoint. The project was originally scheduled for completion in 2009 but was subject to delays. To occupy 131,000 sq m., hotels, entertainment facilities and retail outlets would be incorporated in the new complex, which received an initial investment of US $2,000m. The US-based company Playboy Enterprises Ltd was to undertake the development in tandem with Cyber One and, in mid-2007, outlined plans to construct a 3,700 sq m entertainment centre, which would include hotel and dining facilities, as well as a speciality retail outlet. The extraordinary growth of the casino industry in 2007 enabled Macao to overtake the US city of Las Vegas as the world's biggest gaming market in terms of revenue.

Owing to concerns that the economy was becoming too specialized, in 2008 the Government outlined a number of measures aimed at limiting further expansion in the casino sector. In April the Chief Executive of Macao announced that new gaming licences would be limited to four and that no new applications for land use would be approved for gambling facilities.

Meanwhile, in June 1997 the JLG reached agreement on the establishment of a foundation, to be funded in part by a tax on gambling revenue (see above). The Macao Development and Co-operation Foundation, which replaced the Orient Foundation, became responsible for the promotion of academic research, science and technology, the arts, education and welfare, with particular emphasis on the preservation and development of the territory's cultural heritage. In August 2002 the Macao Foundation announced the construction of a new Macao Science Center, which would mainly serve educational purposes, but would also function as a convention centre and a tourist attraction. The Center, designed by renowned architect I. M. Pei, was to accommodate physics laboratories, an exhibition hall, a multi-media studio, a science ground for youngsters, an astronomical hall and a multi-purpose conference room. Reclamation work for the Center began in November 2005. The complex was completed in late 2009 and was expected to attract around 500,000 visitors annually.

In co-operation with the territory's large hotels, a tourism-training institute was established in the territory in 1995. Macao is a member of the Pacific Asia Travel Association (PATA) and of the World Tourism Organization.

INDUSTRY AND INFRASTRUCTURE

There has been a substantial contraction in Macao's manufacturing industry since the late 1990s. By 2009 the manufacturing sector had declined to account for less than 1.5% of GDP, engaging 5.4% of the employed labour force. Clothing, knitwear and textiles have traditionally been the most important manufacturing industries, but the number of employees in the manufacturing sector reportedly decreased by some 23% in the first quarter of 2010 compared with a year earlier. In 2010 the value of the manufacturing sector's output decreased by 24.6% in comparison with previous year. The production of clothing and textiles declined by 51.4% and 10.5%, respectively. However, the value of the production of foods and beverages rose by 33.9%, reflecting the increasing needs of the tourist sector. Other products have included footwear, toys, fireworks, plastics and electronics.

In 2003 the authorities of Macao and of the Chinese Special Economic Zone (SEZ) of Zhuhai jointly developed a new industrial zone, sited on 0.4 sq km of land between Macao and Zhuhai. The Macao-Zhuhai industrial project was officially inaugurated in December of that year. It was hoped that the new zone would bring benefits to both cities. A total of 23 Macao enterprises were to be based in the Macao part of the zone.

Macao possesses few natural resources. Mainland China provides part of the SAR's water supply.In 1984 Macao's electricity supply was linked to mainland China. The People's Republic was initially to supply 10% of Macao's power requirement. In April 2003 a new power plant with a capacity of 136 MW began operating on the island of Coloane. Total gross output of electricity reached 1,466.0m. kWh in 2009. Imports of petroleum and its products accounted for 5.9% of total import costs in 2010.

The shortage of land suitable for development purposes has presented a major challenge. Details of the Nam Van Lakes land reclamation scheme were announced in July 1993 by a prominent entrepreneur, following the project's approval by the Chinese authorities. Work on this major project, scheduled to be completed in four stages and eventually to enlarge the peninsular area by 20%, continued in 2010. The development was to incorporate hotels, offices, apartments and commercial malls, with residential and business accommodation along a six-lane waterfront highway. Between 1989 and 2009 Macao's land area was increased from 17.3 sq km to 29.5 sq km.

In the early 21st century work was under way on a reclamation scheme on both sides of an existing causeway joining Coloane and Taipa Islands. The Cotai strip was eventually to include a railway terminal serving a new planned passenger and freight route to Zhuhai and thence all the way to Guangzhou. In 2010 it was reported that just 60% of the Guangzhou–Zhuhai light railway project had been completed, meaning that it would not be ready in time for the scheduled Asian Games in November. Meanwhile, in July 2003 Las Vegas Sands Inc announced plans for a large tourist development on the Cotai strip, for which investment was expected to amount to between US $5,000m. and $10,000m. In late 2008, however, as global economic conditions deteriorated, Las Vegas Sands was reported to be heavily indebted and to have suspended its operations along the Cotai strip.

As a result of the establishment of diplomatic relations between Portugal and China in February 1979 and the subsequent growth of confidence in the future of the territory, there was a considerable rise in property prices in Macao. Land sold by the Portuguese administration a few years previously to encourage residential development had more than quadrupled in value by 1981. In March 2000 the transfer to the SAR's Government of the assets of the Sino-Portuguese Land Group, established in 1988 to handle land concession matters, was completed. The property market subsequently remained volatile. Following the global financial crisis and recession of 2008/09, property prices declined significantly in Macao, and the market remained depressed in 2010. Work on various major projects was temporarily suspended.

In 1993 Portugal and China reached agreement on all outstanding issues regarding the building of an airport in Macao. It was envisaged that the airport would not only enhance Macao's role as a point of entry to China and afford the enclave access to international transport networks, but also improve investment conditions and provide new opportunities for the development of industries such as tourism. A regional airline, Air Macau, was formally established in 1994, with investment from the Civil Aviation Administration of China (CAAC) and with Portuguese and Macao interests. Constructed on reclaimed land and off the island of Taipa, the airport was officially inaugurated in December 1995, at a final cost of 8,900m. patacas. In 2001 the airport's franchise was extended to 2039. The terminal has an annual capacity of 6m. passengers. By 2000 Air Macau was operating flights to several cities in China, Taiwan, Thailand, Japan, the Republic of Korea and the Philippines. Of particular significance was the opening by Air Macau of a direct route between Taiwan and mainland China, passengers no longer being required to change aircraft. The airport handled almost 3.8m. passengers in 2008, compared with just over 3.3m. in 2007. In 2010 the airport processed 45,958 metric tons of cargo.

The regular catamaran, jetfoil and high-speed ferry services between Macao and Hong Kong are complemented by a helicopter service, which commenced in 1990. A scheduled helicopter service between Macao and Shenzhen began operations in January 2003. In conjunction with the construction of the airport, a new 4.4-km four-lane bridge, providing an additional link between the island of Taipa and the peninsula of Macao, opened in April 1994, having been completed at a cost of more than 600m. patacas. Other completed development plans include the construction of a deep-water harbour. The new port of Kao-ho, on the island of Coloane, began operations in the early 1990s, handling both container and oil tanker traffic.

In mid-1997 a preliminary agreement was reached by the Sino-Portuguese Infrastructure Co-ordination Commission, which was established in April of that year, concerning the construction of a six-lane road bridge linking Macao with Zhuhai. The bridge, which was to cost US $12.29m. (financed equally by Macao and Zhuhai), was to extend from an area of reclaimed land between Taipa and Coloane to the island of Hengqin, situated off the coast of Zhuhai, and would provide a link with the planned Beijing–Zhuhai highway. Construction work began in June 1998, and the 1.5-km Lotus Bridge, Macao's second link to the Chinese mainland, duly opened to traffic in December 1999. The Chinese Government was to develop the island of Hengqin as an international free trade zone. In July 2003 detailed plans for the connection between the Beijing–Zhuhai highway and Macao's highway system were announced. In December 2009 construction of a new bridge linking Macao with Hong Kong's Lantau Island and Zhuhai City, Guangdong Province, began. To extend to nearly 50 km and comprising a six-lane expressway, the project was originally scheduled for completion in 2016. Work on the project began in December 2009, with completion originally scheduled for 2016, but progress was subsequently delayed by a legal challenge instigated in Hong Kong (see below).

In 2007 the Office for the Development of Infrastructure (GDI) appeared closer to finalizing plans for a light rail transit system (LRT). This project had formed part of Macao's infrastructure programme since 2001, but development had been hampered hitherto by financing problems. The system was projected to cover 20 km of tracks, incorporating 23 scheduled stops including: Macau Ferry Terminal, the Lotus Bridge and Macau International Airport. However, plans to extend the LRT circuit to the historic sites of Praia Grande Avenue and Almeida Ribeiro were abandoned following pressure from focus groups. In October 2007 it was announced that a new administrative unit, the Office for Transport Infrastructure (GIT), was to be established to oversee the development of the LRT, thereby allowing the GDI to focus on other infrastructure projects. In February 2008 the GIT invited seven international consultancy firms to tender proposals relating to the first phase of the LRT. Construction work commenced in 2009.

Macao's telecommunications network has been extensively modernized. Following Macao's transfer of sovereignty in December 1999, Portugal Telecom retained its 28% share in the Companhia de Telecomunicações de Macau (CTM). The former's management concession was renewed until 2001, thus granting CTM exclusive rights to provide fixed-line telephone services, data communications and leased lines. In June 2000 a new body, the Office for the Development of Telecommunications and Information Technology (GDTTI), was established, with a view to building a legal framework for the telecommunications sector, ensuring that services met the needs of the market, developing the communications infrastructure, issuing licences, and maintaining quality control, price regulation and standardization of the network. Internet broadband access became available in 2000. The liberalization of the mobile telecommunications market commenced in 2001. In October 2006 the Government awarded an eight-year licence for 3G operations to Hutchison Telephone (Macau) Co Ltd, and to China Unicom (Macao) Ltd, a subsidiary of the Hong Kong-based China Unicom Ltd. These services commenced in October 2007.

FOREIGN TRADE

In December 1999 the newly established SAR retained its status as a free port. Macao remained a separate customs territory, and its trade with China continued to be classified as foreign trade. The SAR retained its membership of the World Trade Organization (WTO). It also remained a 'privileged partner' of the European Union (EU).

Export-orientated manufacturing performed well in the 1980s and 1990s, when the value of merchandise exports increased sharply, but the sector subsequently weakened. Reflecting the global financial crisis and the attendant decline in external demand, in 2008 export receipts decreased by more than 20% in comparison with 2007. The ensuing global recession in 2009 had a further negative effect on export receipts, which declined by 52% in 2009. The value of exports decreased to 16,025.4m. patacas in 2008, declining to just 7,672.5m. patacas in 2009 and to 6,960.0m. patacas (including re-exports of 4,570.2m.) in 2010. Merchandise exports continued to decline in 2011, contracting by 7.0% in the first three months of the year and by 8.2% in the second quarter.With imports having risen substantially since 2001, large deficits on the trade balance have been regularly recorded. The cost of imports reached 44,118.4m. patacas in 2010. Imports rose sharply in the first half of 2011, increasing by 22.4% in the first quarter and by 26.4% in the second quarter.

During the 1990s many manufacturing operations were relocated from Macao to China and to South-East Asia, where labour costs were lower. From mid-1997 Macao's position was further weakened by the relative appreciation of the pataca against the currencies of its South-East Asian competitors. The garment and textile sectors subsequently entered into decline. In 2010 earnings from garment exports totalled only 1,118.4m. patacas. The toy-manufacturing sector showed strong growth in the late 1980s, providing 10% of all exports in 1989, but subsequently contracted, and the electronics sector demonstrated a similar trend.

In October 2003 the Closer Economic Partnership Arrangement (CEPA), a free trade agreement, was signed between Macao and mainland China.In August 2004 the first CEPA certificates were issued to Macao retailers, enabling them to take advantage of preferential policies when investing in the mainland. In mid-2005 the Chinese Ministry of Commerce announced that, as part of the ongoing CEPA, trade tariffs on all products from Macao would be abolished by 2006. A third supplementary agreement of CEPA was signed in June 2006, under which China pledged to take 13 new measures further to open up the mainland to Macao businesses. These measures were to take effect in January 2007.

China surpassed Hong Kong to become Macao's principal supplier of imports in 1997. In 2010 more than 31% of Macao's imports were supplied by China. Other major suppliers in that year were Hong Kong, France and Japan. Hong Kong was Macao's most important purchaser of merchandise exports, accounting for 43% of the total, followed by China and the USA.

FINANCE AND BANKING

From December 1999, upon its reversion to Chinese sovereignty, Macao began administering its own finances, and was to be exempt from taxes imposed by central government. Consumption taxes are levied on only a limited number of items, such as cigarettes and alcohol. The rates of income tax are lower than in the neighbouring SAR of Hong Kong.

Owing to the decline in Macao's export sector, significant deficits on the balance of trade have been recorded in recent years. In 2009 revenue from exports of goods reached only US $973m., while the cost of imports totalled $5,456m., thus resulting in a trade deficit of $4,483m. However, a surplus of US $6,238m. was recorded on the current account of the balance of payments.

Following several years of deflationary conditions, in 2004 the cost of living increased in real terms for the first time since 1998, with an inflation rate (excluding rents) of 1.0% being registered. The rate subsequently rose sharply, reaching 8.6% in 2008. The acceleration in inflation during 2007–08 was attributed partly to the robust growth engendered by the gambling industry, which stimulated massive investment and a rise in household consumption. Consumer prices rose by just 1.2% in 2009 and by 2.8% in 2010. With inflationary pressures re-emerging in 2011, in the first eight months of the year the composite consumer price index increased by 5.4% on a year-on-year basis.

Considerable increases in public expenditure have been made possible by the large revenues accruing from the gambling and property sectors. The Government's revenues from direct taxes on the gambling sector increased by 48.3% in 2007 to reach 29,341m. patacas (equivalent to 54.6% and 58.4% of total and current revenue, respectively). Revenues from the gaming sector rose to 39,564m. patacas in the following year, and in, late 2008 the Government confirmed that the 39% tax on gambling revenues was to remain in place. Gambling revenues continued to show strong growth, reaching 41,870m. patacas in 2009 and 65,004m. patacas in 2010. Furthermore, the Government's receipts from gambling taxes in the first nine months of 2011 alone reached 68.725m. patacas, again surpassing official expectations

Owing to the substantial increases in government revenue deriving from the gaming sector, large budget surpluses have been recorded in recent years. The Government's total budget revenue reached 79,635.8m. patacas in 2010, in which year public expenditure totalled 37,758.1m. patacas. The revised 2011 budget projected that government revenue would far exceed expenditure, to reach 70,165.7m. patacas, with spending expected to total 53,068.1m. patacas. Within the first nine months of 2011, however, the Government's revenue was estimated already to have exceeded projections

In April 1977 the local currency's link with the Portuguese escudo was ended and a new parity of 1.075 (subsequently 1.030) patacas = HK $1 was established, an appreciation of about 38%. Exporters of merchandise were required to surrender 50% (subsequently 40%) of their foreign-exchange earnings to the official Exchange Fund. The banking system therefore had sufficient resources to maintain the value of the pataca, which continues to float with the Hong Kong dollar. The latter currency also circulates widely in Macao. Upon the territory's transfer of sovereignty, the pataca was retained and remained freely convertible.

A state-owned institution responsible for currency issue, the Instituto Emissor de Macau (IEM), was founded in 1980, nominally taking over this function from the Banco Nacional Ultramarino, which remained the Government's banker for the territory. In 1989 the IEM was replaced by the Autoridade Monetária e Cambial de Macau (AMCM, Monetary and Foreign Exchange Authority of Macao), now the Autoridade Monetária de Macau (Monetary Authority of Macao). Banknotes will continue to be issued by the Banco Nacional Ultramarino, acting as the Government's agent, until at least 2020 (extended from the original date of 2010). Since October 1995 notes have also been issued by the Bank of China's branch in Macao. In August 2004 representatives of the Monetary Authority of Macao and the People's Bank of China signed a memorandum allowing business in Macao to be conducted in renminbi (the mainland Chinese currency).

Plans to revitalize the banking sector began in July 1982, when a new banking ordinance was approved, allowing for the establishment of development banks. The financial sector was declared open to competition, and six international and three Portuguese banks were granted full commercial licences. The aim was to establish an enlarged financial sector, providing a widening of financial services to support the growth of various business sectors. In 1987 legislation to permit offshore banking was introduced, allowing foreign companies to operate tax-free, apart from the payment of an annual fee. However, the level of offshore activity has been disappointing. Also in 1987 Macao's largest bank, the Nan Tung Bank, was acquired by the Bank of China, the official foreign-exchange bank of the People's Republic.

In 2009 a total of 26 registered banks were operating in Macao. In addition, a postal savings bank, established in 1935, is operated by the Government. According to provisional figures, by the end of 2007 the gross assets of the entire banking sector (including the offshore segment) totalled 328,104m. patacas, equivalent to 214% of GDP for that year.

Macao has no foreign-exchange controls or restrictions on capital flows. The Financial System Act, which aimed to improve the reputation of the territory's banks, took effect in September 1993. The legislation required banks to record the identity of those making unusually large transactions, in an attempt to curb the unauthorized acceptance of deposits. In June 1996, in an effort to combat organized crime, the first guidelines on the prevention of money-laundering operations were issued. These underwent revision in 1999. In May 2002 the Monetary Authority of Macao updated the Anti-Money Laundering Guideline for Credit Institutions, which was fully enforced in August of the same year. The revision required credit institutions to formulate clear policies and procedures, with customers being divided into different categories according to their risk levels. More stringent regulations to govern large cash transactions were also introduced.

The credibility of the SAR's financial institutions became subject to international scrutiny in 2005 as a result of allegations that one of Macao's banks, Banco Delta Asia (BDA), was processing 'laundered' money from the Democratic People's Republic of Korea (North Korea). Following a series of investigations carried out by the Chinese authorities, the US Treasury and an international accounting company, namely Ernst and Young, it was concluded that these allegations were true (although there remained disagreement with regard to the culpability of the BDA). In October 2006, however, an independent audit conducted by Ernst and Young reported that it had found no evidence to suggest that the bank had knowingly facilitated money-laundering activities. Nevertheless, an 18-month investigation by US officials concluded that the bank had deliberately disregarded these illicit activities, and in March 2007 the US Treasury issued a decree that forbade US firms and banking institutions to engage in transactions with the BDA (see History).

RECENT DEVELOPMENTS

By 2005, in terms of GDP per head, Macao was ranked third among 23 developing Asian countries in a survey conducted by the Asian Development Bank, by 2007 local residents were beginning to express fears for the quality of life in Macao, particularly with regard to issues such as rising property prices and increasing traffic congestion.

In November 2008, as the global credit crisis developed and as construction work at the sites of many of Macao's new hotels, shopping centres and casinos was suspended, the Government announced a range of measures to support the economy. Small and medium-sized businesses, in particular, were to receive assistance. An allocation of 10,200m. patacas was made to various new infrastructural projects, including public housing. Subsidies were to be made available to home-buyers, in an effort to stimulate the property market. Lump sum payments of 6,000 patacas and health care vouchers were to be distributed to all permanent residents of Macao, while non-permanent residents were to receive 3,600 patacas each.

In March 2010 the newly appointed Chief Executive announced the retention of the two schemes. Other initiatives announced by the new Chief Executive included further measures to reduce the tax obligations of small and medium businesses and, in order to address the lack of human resources in certain areas, plans to accelerate the granting of labour permits to foreign workers. The drafting of minimum wage legislation was also under consideration. With the extension of the Government's wealth-sharing scheme, in November 2010 it was announced that every permanent resident was to receive 4,000 patacas and a medical coupon worth 500 patacas, while non-permanent residents would be given 2,400 patacas each.

In its 2011 report the Heritage Foundation, an influential US institute, rated Macao as the 19th freest economy in the world, of the 179 listed. The SAR's favourable entrepreneurial environment, low rates of tax and sound property rights were among the positive factors cited in the report.

With Macao's revenue from gambling having overtaken that of the US city of Las Vegas several years previously, some analysts were forecasting that in 2011 the SAR's gaming receipts would be as much as five times those of its US counterpart. In early October, however, the Hong Kong-listed shares of SJM lost more than 25% of their value in a single day. The sharp market decline, which also affected the stocks of other gaming groups, was primarily attributed to an unexpected delay in the construction of the Hong Kong–Macao–Zhuhai bridge and the likelihood of its completion date being postponed. A local objection in Hong Kong to a 12-km road section had resulted in the need for a judicial review of the original assessment of the environmental impact of the project. The timely completion of the programme was crucial to Macao's plans for further expansion of the tourism industry. Other concerns included fears of a significant deceleration in the mainland Chinese economy, to which Macao was inextricably linked. Furthermore, the prospect of more concerted action against corruption in China and the mainland authorities' imposition of new restrictions on visits to the SAR were expected to have major repercussions in Macao. A report released in 2010 had suggested that government officials and senior executives of state enterprises accounted for almost one-half of mainland Chinese visitors to the SAR's casinos.

Statistical Survey

Source (unless otherwise indicated): Direcção dos Serviços de Estatística e Censos, Alameda Dr Carlos d'Assumpção 411–417, Dynasty Plaza, 17° andar, Macao; tel. 83995311; fax 28307825; e-mail info@dsec.gov.mo; internet www.dsec.gov.mo.

AREA AND POPULATION

Area (2009): 29.5 sq km (11.39 sq miles), comprising Macao peninsula 9.3, Taipa island 6.8, Coloane island 7.6, Cotai Reclamation Area 5.8.

Population: 435,235 (males 208,865, females 226,370) at census of 23 August 2001; 502,113 (males 245,167, females 256,946) according to results of by-census of 19 August 2006 (491,482 were classed as usual residents and 10,631 as mobile residents). *2011* (official estimate at 31 December, '000): 644.0 (male 319.8, female 324.2).

Density (at 31 December 2011): 21,830.5 per sq km.

Population by Age and Sex (population in '000, official estimate at 31 December 2011): *0–14:* 73.1 (males 37.7, females 35.4); *15–64:* 525.7 (males 261.4, females 264.4); *65 and over:* 45.1 (males 20.8, females 24.4); *Total* 644.0 (males 319.8, females 324.2). Note: Totals may not be equal to the sum of components, owing to rounding.

Population by Nationality (at by-census of August 2006): Chinese 471,484; Portuguese 8,536.

Population by Parish (official estimates at 31 December 2009, '000): Santo António 121.3; São Lázaro 32.8; São Lourenço 50.2; Sé 43.7; Nossa Senhora de Fátima 214.8; Taipa 74.2; Coloane 3.5; Maritime 1.6; Total 542.2.

Births, Marriages and Deaths (2010): Registered live births 5,114 (birth rate 9.4 per 1,000); Registered marriages 3,103 (marriage rate 5.7 per 1,000); Registered deaths 1,774 (death rate 3.3 per 1,000).

Life Expectancy (years at birth, 2007–10 average): 82.5 (males 79.4; females 85.2).

Economically Active Population (persons aged 16 years and over, 2009): Agriculture, forestry, fishing and mining 1,100; Manufacturing 17,000; Production and distribution of electricity, gas and water 1,000; Construction 32,700; Wholesale and retail trade, repair of motor vehicles, motorcycles and personal and household goods 41,500; Hotels, restaurants and similar activities 43,700; Transport, storage and communications 16,700; Financial services 7,500; Real estate, renting and services to companies 25,600; Public administration, defence and compulsory social security 20,300; Education 12,300; Health and social work 7,300; Other community, social and personal service activities 75,200; Private households with employed persons 15,700; *Total employed* 317,500; Unemployed 11,700; *Total labour force* 329,200. Note: Totals may not be equal to the sum of components, owing to rounding.

HEALTH AND WELFARE

Key Indicators

Under-5 Mortality Rate (per 1,000 live births, 2008): 3.6.

HIV/AIDS (% persons aged 15–49, 2008): 0.1.

Physicians (per 1,000 head, 2010): 2.4.

Hospital Beds (per 1,000 head, 2010): 2.1.

Human Development Index (2009): value 0.835.

For definitions, see explanatory note on p. vi.

AGRICULTURE, ETC.

(since 2004 no separate data available for livestock—see the chapter on the People's Republic of China)

Livestock ('000 head, 2004): Poultry 700 (FAO estimate).

Livestock Products ('000 metric tons, 2004): Beef and veal 1.1; Pig meat 9.6; Poultry meat 6.5 (FAO estimate); Hen eggs 1.0 (FAO estimate).

Fishing (metric tons, live weight, 2009, FAO estimates): Marine fishes 1,020; Shrimps and prawns 230; Other marine crustaceans 210; Total catch (incl. others) 1,500.

Source: FAO.

INDUSTRY

Production (2003, unless otherwise indicated): Wine 700,745 litres; Knitwear 36.18m. units; Footwear 12.13m. pairs; Clothing 230.73m. units; Furniture 5,253 units; Electric energy 1,466.0 million kWh (2009).

FINANCE

Currency and Exchange Rates: 100 avos = 1 pataca. *Sterling, Dollar and Euro Equivalents* (31 May 2011): £1 sterling = 13.221 patacas; US $1 = 8.011 patacas; €1 = 11.524 patacas; 100 patacas = £7.56 = $12.48 = €8.68. *Average Exchange Rate* (patacas per US dollar): 8.020 in 2008; 7.984 in 2009; 8.002 in 2010. Note: The pataca has a fixed link with the value of the Hong Kong dollar (HK $1 = 1.030 patacas).

Budget (million patacas, 2009, provisional): *Revenue:* Current revenue 60,634.1 (Direct taxes 45,190.3, Indirect taxes 1,491.4, Property income 3,801.1, Transfers 5,852.0, Other current revenue 4,371.3); Capital revenue 9,236.8; Total 69,870.9. *Expenditure:* Payroll 9,056.3; Goods and services 5,607.8; Current transfers 13,060.8; Other current expenditure 2,611.3; Capital expenditure 5,111.7; Total 35,447.9.

International Reserves (million patacas, 2009): Total (all foreign exchange) 146,578.7.

Money Supply (million patacas at 31 December 2010): Currency outside depository corporations 5,077.2; Transferable deposits 29,306.7; Other deposits 208,320.2; Securities other than shares 206.0; *Broad money* 242,910.1. Source: IMF, *International Financial Statistics*.

Cost of Living (Consumer Price Index; base: April 2008–March 2009 = 100): All items 100.23 in 2008; 101.40 in 2009; 104.25 in 2010.

Gross Domestic Product (million patacas at constant 2002 prices): 125,034.6 in 2007; 141,219.5 in 2008; 143,091.5 in 2009 (provisional).

Expenditure on the Gross Domestic Product (million patacas at current prices, 2010, provisional): Government final consumption expenditure 17,496.2; Private consumption expenditure 50,691.0; Changes in inventories 255.4; Gross fixed capital formation 27,471.4; *Total domestic expenditure* 95,914.1; Exports of goods and services 232,461.6; *Less* Imports of goods and services 111,051.5; *GDP in purchasers' values* 217,324.2.

Gross Domestic Product by Economic Activity (million patacas at current prices, 2009, provisional): Mining and quarrying 2.1; Manufacturing 1,680.8; Electricity, gas and water supply 1,464.9; Construction 9,401.4; Wholesale, retail, repair, restaurants and hotels 15,829.9; Transport, storage and communications 4,206.5; Financial intermediation, real estate, renting and business activities 26,350.4; Public administration, other community, social and personal services (incl. gaming services) 54,742.5; *GDP at basic prices* 113,678.5; Taxes on products (net) 47,295.9; Statistical discrepancy (representing the difference between the expenditure and production approaches) 4,483.1; *GDP at market prices* 165,457.5.

Balance of Payments (US $ million, 2009): Exports of goods f.o.b. 973; Imports of goods f.o.b. –5,456; *Trade balance* –4,483; Exports of services 18,316; Imports of services –4,930; *Balance on goods and services* 8,903; Other income received 1,132; Other income paid –2,993; *Balance on goods, services and income* 7,042; Current transfers received 104; Current transfers paid –908; *Current balance* 6,238; Capital account (net) 634; Direct investment abroad 708; Direct investment from abroad 1,797; Portfolio investment assets –1,674; Portfolio investment liabilities –1; Financial derivatives assets –15; Other investment assets –7,608; Other investment liabilities 4,193; Net errors and omissions –2,156; *Overall balance* 2,115. Source: IMF, *International Financial Statistics*.

EXTERNAL TRADE

Principal Commodities (million patacas, 2010): *Imports c.i.f.*(distribution by SITC): Live animals (excl. marine) 338.9; Vegetable and fruit 475.3; Beverages and tobacco 3,409.2 (Beverages 2,672.3); Petroleum, petroleum products, etc. 2,595.2; Textile yarn, fabrics, etc. 938.3; Iron and steel 439.3; Electrical machinery, apparatus, etc. 1,125.7; Road vehicles 2,206.2; Clothing and accessories 1,936.2; Total (incl. others) 44,118.4. *Exports f.o.b.:* Cotton garments (knitted and crocheted) 559.3; Cotton garments (excl. knitted and crocheted) 559.1; Radios, TV, image and sound recorders and reproducers 197.1; Machines and apparatus 449.0; Total (incl. others) 6,960.0 (incl. re-exports 4,570.2).

Principal Trading Partners (million patacas, 2010): *Imports c.i.f.:* Australia 421.4; China, People's Republic 13,718.3; France 4,039.8; Germany 1,321.55; Hong Kong 4,627.9; Italy 2,071.5; Japan 3,812.1; Korea, Republic 645.7; Singapore 838.6; Taiwan 1,078.3; United Kingdom 852.1; USA 2,619.0; Total (incl. others) 44,118.4. *Exports f.o.b.:* Canada 36.1; China, People's Republic 1,102.4; France 71.9; Germany 142.6; Hong Kong 3,002.6; Netherlands 77.3; United Kingdom 64.4; USA 782.1; Total (incl. others) 6,960.0 (incl. re-exports 4,570.2).

TRANSPORT

Road Traffic (motor vehicles in use, December 2010): Light vehicles 83,879; Heavy vehicles 6,335; Motorcycles 106,420.

Shipping (international sea-borne containerized freight traffic, '000 metric tons, 2010): Goods imported 147.0; Goods exported 19.5.

Civil Aviation (2010, unless otherwise indicated): Passenger arrivals 1,842,074 (2008 figure); Passenger departures 1,934,393 (2008 figure); Goods loaded (metric tons) 32,361; Goods unloaded (metric tons) 13,597.

TOURISM

Visitor Arrivals by Country of Residence (2010): China, People's Republic 13,229,100; Hong Kong 7,466,100; Taiwan 1,292,700; Total (incl. others) 24,965,400.

Receipts from Tourism (US $ million, incl. passenger transport): 9,755 in 2006; 13,404 in 2007; 17,093 in 2008 (Source: World Tourism Organization).

COMMUNICATIONS MEDIA

Radio Receivers (1997): 160,000 in use.

Television Receivers (2000): 125,115 in use.

Daily Newspapers (2008): 14.

Telephones (2010): 167,500 main lines in use.

Mobile Cellular Telephones (2010): 1,122,300 subscribers.

Personal Computers (2006): 192,000 (384.1 per 1,000 persons).

Internet Users (2010, estimate): 270,200.

Broadband Subscribers (2010): 131,200.

Sources: partly UNESCO, *Statistical Yearbook*; International Telecommunication Union.

EDUCATION

(2009/10)

Kindergarten: 57 schools; 597 teachers; 10,038 pupils.

Primary: 70 schools; 1,686 teachers; 25,705 pupils.

Secondary: 56 schools; 2,635 teachers; 39,298 pupils.

Vocational/Technical: 10 schools; 169 teachers; 1,752 pupils.

Higher: 10 institutions; 1,963 teaching staff; 23,562 students.

Pupil-teacher Ratio (primary education, UNESCO estimate): 17.3 in 2008/09 (Source: UNESCO Institute for Statistics).

Adult Literacy Rate: 93.5% (males 96.5%, females 90.7%) in 2006 (Source: UNESCO Institute for Statistics).

Notes: For non-tertiary education, figures for schools and teachers refer to all those for which the category is applicable. Some schools and teachers provide education at more than one level. Institutions of higher education refer to those recognized by the Government of Macao Special Administrative Region.

Directory

The Constitution

Under the terms of the Basic Law of the Macao Special Administrative Region (SAR), which took effect on 20 December 1999, the Macao SAR is an inalienable part of the People's Republic of China. The Macao SAR, which comprises the Macao peninsula and the islands of Taipa and Coloane, exercises a high degree of autonomy and enjoys executive, legislative and independent judicial power, including that of final adjudication. The executive authorities and legislature are composed of permanent residents of Macao. The socialist system and policies shall not be practised in the Macao SAR, and the existing capitalist system and way of life shall not be changed for 50 years. In addition to the Chinese language, the Portuguese language may also be used by the executive, legislative and judicial organs.

The Central People's Government is responsible for foreign affairs and for defence. The Government of Macao is responsible for maintaining social order in the SAR. The Central People's Government appoints and dismisses the Chief Executive, principal executive officials and Procurator-General.

The Chief Executive of the Macao SAR is accountable to the Central People's Government. The Chief Executive shall be a Chinese national of no less than 40 years of age, who is a permanent resident of the region and who has resided in Macao for a continuous period of 20 years. He or she is elected locally by a broadly representative Selection Committee and appointed by the Central People's Government.

The Basic Law provides for a 300-member Election Committee, which serves a five-year term. The Election Committee shall be composed of 300 members from the following sectors: 100 members from industrial, commercial and financial sectors; 80 from cultural, educational and professional sectors; 80 from labour, social welfare and religious sectors; and 40 from the Legislative Council, municipal organs, Macao deputies to the National People's Congress (NPC), and representatives of Macao members of the National Committee of the Chinese People's Political Consultative Conference (NCCPPCC). The term of office of the Chief Executive of the Macao SAR is five years; he or she may serve two consecutive terms. The Chief Executive's functions include the appointment of a portion of the legislative councillors and the appointment or removal of members of the Executive Council.

With the exception of the first term (which expired on 15 October 2001), the term of office of members of the Legislative Council (commonly known as the Legislative Assembly) shall be four years. The second Legislative Council shall be composed of 27 members, of whom 10 shall be returned by direct election, 10 by indirect election and seven by appointment. The third and subsequent Legislative Councils shall comprise 29 members, of whom 12 shall be returned by direct election, 10 by indirect election and seven by appointment.

The Macao SAR shall maintain independent finances. The Central People's Government shall not levy taxes in the SAR, which shall practise an independent taxation system. The Macao pataca shall remain the legal currency. The Macao SAR shall retain its status as a free port and as a separate customs territory.

The Government

Chief Executive: FERNANDO CHUI SAI ON (took office 20 December 2009).

SECRETARIES

(October 2011)

Secretary for Administration and Justice: FLORINDA DA ROSA SILVA CHAN.

Secretary for Economy and Finance: FRANCIS TAM PAK YUEN.

Secretary for Security: CHEONG KUOC VA.

Secretary for Social Affairs and Culture: CHEONG U.

Secretary for Transport and Public Works: LAU SI IO.

GOVERNMENT OFFICES

Office of the Chief Executive: Headquarters of the Government of the Macao Special Administrative Region, Av. da Praia Grande; tel. 28726886; fax 28725468; internet www.gov.mo.

Executive Council: Headquarters of the Government of the Macao Special Administrative Region, Av. da Praia Grande; tel. 28726886; fax 28726168; Sec.-Gen. HO VENG ON.

Office of the Secretary for Administration and Justice: Rua de S. Lourenço 28, Sede do Governo, 4º andar; tel. 28726886; fax 28726880; internet www.gov.mo.

Office of the Secretary for Economy and Finance: Rua de S. Lourenço 28, Sede do Governo, 3º andar; tel. 28726886; fax 28726665; internet www.gov.mo.

Office of the Secretary for Security: Calçada dos Quartéis, Quartel de S. Francisco; tel. 87997501; fax 28580702; internet www.gov.mo.

Office of the Secretary for Social Affairs and Culture: Rua de S. Lourenço 28, Sede do Governo, 2º andar; tel. 28726886; fax 28727594; internet www.gov.mo.

Office of the Secretary for Transport and Public Works: Rua de S. Lourenço 28, Edif. dos Secretários, 1° andar; tel. 28726886; fax 28727566; internet www.gov.mo.

Macao Government Information Bureau: Gabinete de Comunicação Social do Governo de Macau, Av. da Praia Grande 762–804, Edif. China Plaza, 15° andar; tel. 28332886; fax 28355426; e-mail info@gcs.gov.mo; internet www.gcs.gov.mo; Dir VICTOR CHAN CHI PING.

Economic Services Bureau: Direcção dos Serviços de Economia, Rua Dr Pedro José Lobo 1–3, Edif. Luso Internacional, 25° andar; tel. 28386937; fax 28590310; e-mail info@economia.gov.mo; internet www.economia.gov.mo; Dir SOU TIM PENG.

Legislature

LEGISLATIVE COUNCIL (LEGISLATIVE ASSEMBLY)

The Legislative Assembly was superseded by the Legislative Council under the terms of the Basic Law, implemented in 1999. In practice, however, the legislature continues to be referred to as the Legislative Assembly, which comprises 29 members: seven appointed by the Chief Executive, 12 elected directly and 10 indirectly. Members serve for four years. The Assembly chooses its President from among its members, by secret vote. At the election held on 20 September 2009 the pro-Beijing União para o Desenvolvimento (UPD) received the highest number of votes cast and secured two of the 12 directly elective seats. The Associação dos Cidadãos Unidos de Macau (ACUM), which supports the gaming industry, also took two seats, as did the pro-democracy Associação de Próspero Macau Democrático (APMD). The following six groupings each took one seat: the pro-democracy Associação de Novo Macau Democrático (ANMD); the pro-Beijing União Promotora para o Progresso (UPP); the Nova União para o Desenvolvimento de Macau (NUDM), which promotes the interests of the gaming sector; Nova Esperança (NE), supported by civil servants; the pro-business União Macau-Guangdong; and the Aliança para a Mudança, which advocates public reform. Four of the 10 indirectly elective seats were taken by representatives of business interests; two by representatives of the professional sector; two by representatives of labour interests; and two by members of the social, cultural, educational and sports sector.

Legislative Council (Legislative Assembly): Praça da Assembléia Legislativa, Edif. da Assembléia Legislativa, Aterros da Baía da Praia Grande; tel. 28728377; fax 28727857; e-mail info@al.gov.mo; internet www.al.gov.mo.

President: LAU CHEOK VA.

Political Organizations

There are no formal political parties, but various registered civic associations exist and may participate in elections for the Legislative Assembly by presenting a list of candidates (see Legislature). A total of 16 groupings contested the legislative election of September 2009.

Judicial System

Formal autonomy was granted to the territory's judiciary in 1993. A new penal code took effect in January 1996. Macao operates its own five major codes, namely the Penal Code, the Code of Criminal Procedure, the Civil Code, the Code of Civil Procedure and the Commercial Code. In 1999 the authority of final appeal was granted to Macao. The judicial system operates independently of the mainland Chinese system.

The judicial system has three tiers: the Court of Final Appeal, Intermediate Court and the First Trial Court.

President of the Court of Final Appeal: SAM HOU FAI, Praçeta 25 de Abril, Edif. dos Tribunais de Segunda Instância e Ultima Instância; tel. 83984117; fax 28326744; e-mail ptui@court.gov.mo; internet www.court.gov.mo.

Procurator-General: HO CHIO MENG.

Religion

The majority of residents profess Buddhism, and there are numerous places of worship, Daoism and Confucianism also being widely practised. The Christian community numbers about 30,000. There are small Muslim and Hindu communities.

CHRISTIANITY

The Roman Catholic Church

Macao forms a single diocese, directly responsible to the Holy See. At 31 December 2007 there were 28,242 adherents in the territory, comprising nearly 5.6% of the population.

Bishop of Macao: Rt Rev. JOSÉ LAI HUNG SENG, Paço Episcopal, Largo da Sé s/n, POB 324; tel. 28309954; fax 28309861; e-mail jesuitas@macau.ctm.net; internet www.catholic.org.mo.

The Anglican Communion

Macao forms part of the Anglican diocese of Hong Kong (q.v.).

The Press

A new Press Law, prescribing journalists' rights and obligations, was enacted in August 1990.

PORTUGUESE LANGUAGE

O Clarim: Rua Central 26A, 1° andar; tel. 28573860; fax 28307867; e-mail clarim@macau.ctm.net; internet www.oclarim.com.mo; f. 1948; weekly; Editor ALBINO BENTO PAIS; circ. 1,500.

Hoje Macau: Av. Dr Rodrigo Rodrigues 600E, Edif. Centro Comercial First National, 14° andar, Sala 1408; tel. 28752401; fax 28752405; e-mail hoje@macau.ctm.net; internet www.hojemacau.com; f. 2001; daily; Dir CARLOS MORAIS JOSÉ; circ. 1,200.

Jornal Tribuna de Macau: Av. Almeida Ribeiro 99, Edif. Comercial Nam Wah, 6° andar, Salas 603–05; tel. 28378057; fax 28337305; internet www.jtm.com.mo; f. 1998 through merger of Jornal de Macau (f. 1982) and Tribuna de Macau (f. 1982); daily; Dir JOSÉ FIRMINO DA ROCHA DINIS; circ. 1,000.

Ponto Final: Alameda Dr Carlos d'Assumpção; tel. 28339566; fax 28339563; e-mail editor@pontofinalmacau.com; daily; Publr RICARDO PINTO; Dir ISABEL CASTRO; circ. 1,500.

CHINESE LANGUAGE

Cheng Pou: Av. da Praia Grande 57–63, Edif. Heng Chang, 1° andar, Bloco E–F; tel. 28965972; fax 28965741; e-mail chengpou@macau.ctm.net; internet www.chengpou.com.mo; daily; Dir KUNG SU KAN; Editor-in-Chief LEONG CHI CHUN; circ. 5,000.

Correio de Macau: Estação Central, Largo do Senado; tel. 28574491; fax 28336603; e-mail macpost@macaupost.gov.mo; internet www.macaupost.gov.mo; f. 1989.

Jornal Informação (Son Pou): Rua de Francisco 22, Edif. Mei Fun, 1° andar; tel. 28561557; fax 28566575; e-mail sonpou@macau.ctm.net; internet www.sonpou.com.mo; weekly; Dir CHAO CHONG PENG; circ. 8,000.

Jornal San Wa Ou: Av. Venceslau de Morais 231, Edif. Industrial Nam Fong, 15° andar, Bloco E–F; tel. 28717569; fax 28717572; e-mail correiro@macau.ctm.net; internet www.waou.com.mo; daily; Dir LIN CHANG; circ. 1,500.

Jornal 'Si-Si': Av. Dr Rodrigues, Edif. Centro Comercial First National, 21° andar, Sala 2103; tel. and fax 28421333; e-mail sisinews@hotmail.com; internet www.jornalsisi.com; weekly; Dir and Editor-in-Chief CHEANG VENG PENG; circ. 3,000.

Jornal Va Kio: Rua da Alfândega 69; tel. 28345888; fax 28513724; e-mail vakiopou@macau.ctm.net; internet www.jornalvakio.com; f. 1937; daily; Publr ALICE CHIANG SAO MENG; Editor-in-Chief LEONG CHI SANG; circ. 28,000.

Ou Mun Iat Pou (Macao Daily News): Rua Pedro Nolasco da Silva 37; tel. 28371688; fax 28331998; internet www.macaodaily.com; f. 1958; daily; Dir LEI PANG CHU; Editor-in-Chief PO LOK; circ. 100,000.

O Pulso de Macau: Rua 1, 13°, Bloco B, Guang Dong Nan-Gui Jardim, Taipa; tel. 28400194; fax 28400284; e-mail pulsomacau@gmail.com; internet www.pulso.com.mo; weekly; Dir IEONG IAT FO.

Semanário Desportivo de Macau: Av. Venceslau de Morais 231, Edif. Industrial Nam Fong 7C; tel. 28354208; fax 28718285; e-mail macsport@macau.ctm.net; internet www.macausports.com.mo; weekly; sport; Dir FONG NIM LAM; Editor-in-Chief FONG NIM SEONG; circ. 2,000.

Semanário Recreativo de Macau: Av. Sidónio Pais 31D, 3° andar, Bloco A; tel. 28553216; fax 28516792; e-mail srm405@yahoo.com.hk; weekly; Dir IEONG CHEOK KUONG; Editor-in-Chief TONG IOK WA.

Seng Pou (Star): Travessa da Caldeira 9; tel. 28938387; fax 28388192; e-mail sengpou@macau.ctn.net; f. 1963; daily; Dir and Editor-in-Chief POLICARPO KOK; Deputy Editor-in-Chief TOU MAN KUM; circ. 6,000.

Si Man Pou (Jornal do Cidadão): Rua dos Pescadores, Edif. Indian Ocean, 2° Fase, Bloco 2B; tel. 28722111; fax 28722133; e-mail shemin@macau.ctm.net; internet www.shimindaily.com.mo; f. 1944; daily; Dir and Editor-in-Chief KUNG MAN; circ. 8,000.

Tai Chung Pou: Av. Leste do Hipódromo 25-69, Edif. Fok Tai, 6° andar; tel. 28939888; fax 28282322; e-mail taichung@macau.ctm.net; f. 1933; daily; Dir VONG U. KONG; Editor-in-Chief CHAN TAI PAC; circ. 8,000.

Today Macau Journal: Pátio da Barca 20, R/C; tel. 28215050; fax 28210478; e-mail todaymac@yahoo.com; internet www.todaymacao.com; daily; Dir LAM IONG CHONG; Editor-in-Chief IU VENG ION; circ. 6,000.

ENGLISH LANGUAGE

Macau Post Daily: Av. de Almeida Ribeiro 99, Edif. Nam Wah Centre, 10° andar; tel. 28331050; fax 28331104; e-mail macaupost@macau.ctm.net; internet www.macaupostdaily.com; f. 2004; Dir HARALD BRUNING.

SELECTED PERIODICALS

Agora Macau: Av. Dr Rodrigo Rodrigues 7B, Edif. Centro Comercial First National, 10° andar, Sala 1005; tel. 66283212; fax 28519236; e-mail agora28@macau.ctn.net; weekly; Chinese; Dir LAO TAT KAO.

Boletim Associação Budista Geral de Macau: Estrada de Lou Lim Ieok 2, Pou Tai Un, Ilha da Taipa; tel. 28811038; bi-monthly; Dir LEI SENG VO.

Business Intelligence: Av. da Amizade, Edif. Chong Yu 12 D; tel. 28331258; fax 28331487; e-mail admin@bizintelligenceonline.com; internet www.bizintelligenceonline.com; monthly; Chinese; Dir PAULO ALEXANDRE TEIXEIRA DE AZEVEDO.

Cáritas Ligação: Largo de Santo Agostinho 1A; tel. 28573297; bimonthly; Dir PUN CHI MENG.

Chinese Cross Currents: Macau Ricci Institute, Av. Cons. Ferreira d'Almeida 95E; tel. 28532536; fax 28568274; e-mail currents@riccimac.org; internet www.riccimac.org; f. 2004; quarterly; Chinese and English; cultural studies; Dir of Publs ARTUR WARDEGA; Editor YVES CAMUS.

Macau Business: Av. Dr Rodrigo Rodrigues 600E, Edif. Centro Comercial First National, 16° andar, Sala 1605; tel. 28331258; fax 28331487; e-mail editor@macaubusiness.com; internet www

.macaubusiness.com; f. 2004; monthly; Publr PAULO A. AZEVEDO; Editor-in-Chief EMANUEL GRAÇA; circ. 32,500.

Macau Manager: Rua de Santa Clara 9, Edif. Ribeiro, 6° andar; tel. 28323233; quarterly; Chinese; published by the Macau Management Asscn; Dir CHUI SAI CHEONG.

Macau Times: Rua Almirante Costa Cabral 11, Edif. Iau Fai, 11° andar A; tel. 28554978; fax 28552834; e-mail mail@macautimes.net; internet www.macautimes.net; f. 1994; monthly; Chinese; Dir WONG TAI WAI; circ. 10,000.

Revista Mensal de Macau: Av. Dr Rodrigo Rodrigues 600E, Edif. Centro Comercial First National, 14° andar, Sala 1404; tel. 28323660; fax 28323601; e-mail contacto@revistamacau.com; internet www.revistamacau.com; f. 1987; quarterly; Portuguese; govt publication; Dir VICTOR CHAN CHI PING; Editor FERNANDO SALES LOPES.

Saúde de Macau: Rua Ferreira do Amaral 9, 2° andar; tel. 28307271; quarterly; health issues; Dir KUOK HONG NENG.

x1 Week: Av. do Infante D. Henrique 43–53A, Edif. The Macau Square, 7° andar; tel. 28710566; fax 28710565; e-mail info@x1week.com; internet www.x1week.com; computing; Dir CHAN SAO SEONG.

NEWS AGENCIES

China News Service: Rua de Londres, Edif. Zhu Kuan, 14° andar, Y/Z; tel. 28594585; fax 28594586; Correspondent HUANG HONGBIN.

Xinhua (New China) News Agency Macao SAR Branch: Av. Gov. Jaime Silvério Marques, Edif. Zhu Kuan, 13° andar V; tel. 28727710; fax 28700548; e-mail xinhua@macau.ctm.net; Dir WANG HONGYU.

PRESS ASSOCIATIONS

Associação de Imprensa de Língua Portuguesa e Inglesa de Macau: Av. do Dr Rodrigo Rodrigues 600E, Centro Comercial First National, 14° andar, Sala 1408; tel. 28752401; fax 28752405; e-mail imprensamacau@gmail.com; f. 2005; Dir PAULO AZEVEDO.

Macao Media Workers Association: Travessa do Matadouro, Edif. 3, 3B; tel. and fax 28939486; e-mail mcju@macau.ctm.net; Pres. LEI PANG CHU.

Macao Journalists Association: Rua de Jorge Alvares 7–7B, Viva Court 17A; tel. and fax 28569819; e-mail macauja@gmail.com; internet hk.myblog.yahoo.com/macaujournalist; f. 1999; Pres. ZHENG YUEMING.

Macao Journalists Club: Estrada do Repouso, Edif. Tak Fai 18B; tel. and fax 28921395; e-mail cjm@macau.ctm.net; Pres. LO SONG MAN.

Macao Media Club: Rua de Santa Clara 5–7E, Edif. Ribeiro, 4B; tel. 28330035; fax 28330036; e-mail mmedia@macau.ctn.net; Pres. CHEONG CHI SENG.

Macao Sports Press Association: Estrada de D. Maria II 1-E, Edif. Kin Chit 2G; tel. 28838206, ext. 151; fax 28718285; e-mail macsport@macau.ctm.net; Pres. LAO IU KONG.

Publishers

Associação Beneficência Leitores Jornal Ou Mun: Nova-Guia 339; tel. 28711631; fax 28711630.

Fundação Macau: Av. República 6; tel. 28966777; fax 28968658; e-mail info@fm.org.mo; internet www.fmac.org.mo; Chair. WU ZHILIANG.

Instituto Cultural de Macau: publishes literature, social sciences and history; see under Tourism.

Livros do Oriente: Av. Amizade 876, Edif. Marina Gardens, 15E; tel. 28700320; fax 28700423; e-mail livros.macau@oriente.com; internet www.loriente.com; f. 1990; publishes in Portuguese, English and Chinese on regional history, culture, etc.; Gen. Man. ROGÉRIO BELTRÃO COELHO; Exec. Man. CECÍLIA JORGE.

Universidade de Macau—Centro de Publicações: Av. Padre Tomás Pereira, SJ, Taipa; tel. and fax 83978189; e-mail pub_enquiry@umac.mo; internet www.umac.mo/pub; f. 1993; art, economics, education, political science, history, literature, management, social sciences, etc.; Head Dr RAYMOND WONG.

GOVERNMENT PUBLISHER

Imprensa Oficial: Rua da Imprensa Nacional s/n; tel. 28573822; fax 28596802; e-mail info@io.gov.mo; internet www.io.gov.mo; Dir TOU CHI MAN.

Broadcasting and Communications

TELECOMMUNICATIONS

The Government initiated a liberalization of the mobile telecommunications market in 2001. In October 2006 the Government awarded an eight-year licence for 3G operations to Hutchison Telephone (Macau) Co Ltd, and to China Unicom (Macao) Ltd, a subsidiary of the Hong Kong-based China Unicom Ltd. These services commenced in October 2007.

Companhia de Telecomunicações de Macau, SARL (CTM): Rua de Lagos, Edif. Telecentro, Taipa; tel. 28833833; fax 88913031; e-mail comm@macau.ctm.net; internet www.ctm.net; f. 1981; holds local telecommunications monopoly; shareholders include Cable and Wireless (51%), Portugal Telecom (28%), and CITIC Pacific (20%); Chair. JAMES CHEESEWRIGHT; CEO VANDY POON; 806 employees.

Hutchison Telephone (Macau) Co Ltd (3 Macau): Av. Xian Xing Hai, Zhu Kuan Bldg, 8/F; tel. 8933388; fax 781282; e-mail feedback@three.com.mo; internet www.three.com.mo; f. 2001; mobile telecommunications operator; subsidiary of Hutchison Whampoa Group (Hong Kong); local capital participation; CEO HO WAI-MING.

SmarTone Mobile (Macau) Ltd: Macao; e-mail enquiry@smartone.com.mo; internet www.smartone.com.mo; f. 2001; mobile telecommunications provider; subsidiary of SmarTone Mobile Communications Ltd (Hong Kong); local capital participation; CEO PATRICK CHAN KAI-LUNG.

Regulatory Authority

Office for the Development of Telecommunications and Information Technology (GDTTI): Av. da Praia Grande 789, 3° andar; tel. 28356328; fax 83969166; e-mail ifx@gdtti.gov.mo; internet www.gdtti.gov.mo; f. 2000.

BROADCASTING

Radio and Television

Cosmos Televisão por Satélite, SARL: Av. Infante D. Henrique 29, Edif. Va Iong, 4° andar A; tel. 28785731; fax 28788234; satellite TV services; Chair. NG FOK.

Macau Cable TV Ltd: Av. Conselheiro Ferreira de Almeida 71B; tel. 28822866; e-mail enquiry@macaucabletv.com; internet www.macaucabletv.com; f. 2000; offers 70 channels from around the world; CEO ANGELA LAM.

Macau Satellite Television: c/o Cosmos Televisão por Satélite, Av. Infante D. Henrique 29, Edif. Va Iong, 4° andar A; commenced transmissions in 2000; operated by Cosmos Televisão por Satélite, SARL; domestic and international broadcasts in Chinese aimed at Chinese-speaking audiences world-wide.

Rádio Vilaverde: Macao Jockey Club, Taipa; tel. 28820338; fax 28820337; e-mail helpdesk@am738.com; internet www.am738.com; private radio station; programmes in Chinese; CEO. STANLEY LEI.

Teledifusão de Macau, SARL (TDM): Rua Francisco Xavier Pereira 157A, POB 446; tel. 28335888 (Radio), 28519188 (TV); fax 28520208; internet www.tdm.com.mo; f. 1982; owned by the Govt of the Macao SAR ; radio channels: Rádio Macau (Av. do Dr Rodrigo Rodrigues, Edif. Nam Kwong, 7° andar; tel. 28335888; fax 28343220; rmacau@tdm.com.mo), broadcasting 24 hours per day in Portuguese on TDM Canal 1 (incl. broadcasts from RTP International in Portugal) and 17 hours per day in Chinese on TDM Channel 2; Chair. Dr STANLEY HO.

Finance

(cap. = capital; res = reserves; dep. = deposits; m. = million; brs = branches; amounts in patacas unless otherwise indicated)

BANKING

Macao has no foreign-exchange controls, its external payments system being fully liberalized on current and capital transactions. The Financial System Act, aiming to improve the reputation of the territory's banks and to comply with international standards, took effect in September 1993. A total of 27 registered banks were in operation in 2009.

Issuing Authority

Autoridade Monetária de Macau (AMCM) (Monetary Authority of Macao): Calçada do Gaio 24–26, POB 3017; tel. 28568288; fax 28325432; e-mail general@amcm.gov.mo; internet www.amcm.gov.mo; f. 1989; est. as Autoridade Monetária e Cambial de Macau (AMCM), to replace the Instituto Emissor de Macau; cap. 8,324m., res 4,860m., dep. 132,183.1m. (Dec. 2009); govt-owned; Chair. ANSELMO L. S. TENG.

Banks of Issue

Banco Nacional Ultramarino (BNU), SA: Av. Almeida Ribeiro 22, POB 465; tel. 28335533; fax 28355653; e-mail markt@bnu.com .mo; internet www.bnu.com.mo; f. 1864; est. in Macao 1902; subsidiary of Caixa Geral de Depósitos (Portugal) since 2001; agent of Macao Govt; agreement whereby the Bank remains an agent of the treasury signed with the administration of the Macao SAR in 2000; to remain a note-issuing bank until 2020; cap. 400m., res 1,456.7m., dep. 24,550.4m. (Dec. 2009); Chair. Dr RODOLFO MASCARENHAS; CEO ARTUR SANTOS; 14 brs.

Bank of China: Av. Dr Mário Soares, Edif. Banco da China, R/C; tel. 28781828; fax 28781833; e-mail bocmo@bocmacao.com; internet www.bocmacau.com; f. 1950 as Nan Tung Bank, name changed 1987; authorized to issue banknotes from Oct. 1995; Gen. Man. YE YIXIN; 24 brs.

Other Commercial Banks

Banco Comercial de Macau, SA: Av. da Praia Grande 572, POB 545; tel. 87910000; fax 28332795; e-mail bcmbank@bcm.com.mo; internet www.bcm.com.mo; f. 1974; cap. 225m., res 188.3m., dep. 9,999.1m. (Dec. 2009); Chair. and Pres. DAVID SHOU-YEH WONG; CEO CHIU LUNG-MAN; 17 brs.

Banco Delta Asia (BDA), SARL: Largo de Santo Agostinho; tel. 87969600; fax 87969624; e-mail contact@bdam.com; internet www .delta-asia.com.mo; f. 1935; fmrly Banco Hang Sang; cap. 210.0m., res 173.2m., dep. 3,323.1m. (Dec. 2004); Chair. STANLEY AU; Exec. Dir DAVID LAU; 9 brs.

Banco Tai Fung, SARL: Av. Alameda Dr Carlos d'Assumpção 418, Edif. Sede Banco Tai Fung; tel. 28322323; fax 28570737; e-mail tfbsecr@taifungbank.com; internet www.taifungbank.com; f. 1971; cap. 1,000m., res 2,021m., dep. 38,472m. (Dec. 2010); Chair. HO HAO TONG; Pres. LIU DAGUO; 22 brs.

Banco Weng Hang, SA: Av. Almeida Ribeiro 241; tel. 28335678; fax 28576527; e-mail bwhhrd@whbmac.com; internet www.whbmac .com; f. 1973; subsidiary of Wing Hang Bank Ltd, Hong Kong; cap. 120m., res 1,274.3m., dep. 15,647m. (Dec. 2008); Chair. PATRICK YUK-BUN FUNG; Gen. Man. TAK LIM LEE; 11 brs.

China Construction Bank (Macau) Corpn Ltd: Av. Almeida Ribeiro 70–76, POB 165; tel. 83969611; fax 83969683; e-mail ccb .macau@asia.ccb.com; internet www.asia.ccb.com; f. 1937; fmrly Banco da América (Macau); cap. 500m., res 88.3m., dep. 3,563.1m. (Dec. 2008); Pres. and CEO (Asia) MIRANDA KWOK; 8 brs.

Industrial and Commercial Bank of China (Macau) Ltd (ICBC—Macau): Av. da Amizade 555, Macau Landmark, 18° andar, Torre Banco ICBC; tel. 28555222; fax 28338064; e-mail icbc@icbc .com.mo; f. 1972; est. as Seng Heng Bank Ltd; present name adopted 2009, following merger with Industrial and Commercial Bank of China; Exec. Dir PATRICK YUEN; 9 brs.

Luso International Banking Ltd: Av. Dr Mário Soares 47; tel. 28378977; fax 28711100; e-mail lusobank@lusobank.com.mo; internet www.lusobank.com.mo; f. 1974; cap. 315.6m., res 754.7m., dep. 15,030.0m. (Dec. 2009); Chair. LU YAO MING; Gen. Man. IP KAI MING; 11 brs.

Banking Association

Associação de Bancos de Macau (ABM) (The Macau Association of Banks): Av. da Praia Grande 575, Edif. 'Finanças', 15/F; tel. 28511921; fax 28346049; e-mail abm@macau.ctm.net; f. 1985; Chair. YE YIXIN.

INSURANCE

ACE Seguradora, SA: Rua Dr Pedro José Lobo 1–3, Luso Bank Bldg, 17° andar, Apt 1701–02; tel. 28557191; fax 28570188; Pres. and CEO (Asia-Pacific) DAMIEN SULLIVAN.

American International Assurance Co (Bermuda) Ltd: Unit 601, AIA Tower, Av. Comercial de Macau 251A–301; tel. 89881817; fax 28315900; e-mail salina-if.ieong@aig.com; life insurance; Rep. ALEXANDRA FOO CHEUK LING.

Asia Insurance Co Ltd: 762 Av. da Praia Grande, Edif. China Plaza, 10° andar, Apt C-D; tel. 28570439; fax 28570438; e-mail asiamc@macau.ctm.net; non-life insurance; Rep. S. T. CHAN.

AXA China Region Insurance Company: Av. do Infante D. Henrique 43–53A, 20° andar, The Macau Square; tel. 28781188; fax 28780022; life insurance; CEO (Asia) MICHAEL BISHOP.

Chartis Insurance Hong Kong Ltd: Av. Comercial de Macau 251A-301, Unit 6, AIA Tower, 5° andar; tel. 28355602; fax 28355299; internet www.chartisinsurance.com.hk/macau; f. 2010; non-life insurance.

China Life Insurance (Overseas) Co Ltd: Alameda Dr Carlos D'Assumpção 263, China Civil Plaza, 22° andar A-B; tel. 28787288; fax 28787287; e-mail info@chinalife.com.mo; Gen. Man. WANG JIAN GUO.

China Taiping Insurance (Macau) Co Ltd: Av. Alameda Dr Carlos d'Assumpção 398, Edif. CNAC, 10° andar; tel. 28785578; fax 28787218; e-mail info@mo.cntaiping.com; internet www.cicmacau .com.mo; non-life insurance.

Companhia de Seguros Delta Asia, SA: Rua do Campo 39–41; tel. 28559898; fax 28921545; e-mail contact@bdam.com; internet www .delta-asia.com/macau; Chair. STANLEY AU.

Companhia de Seguros Fidelidade: Av. da Praia Grande 567, Edif. BNU, 14° andar; tel. 28374072; fax 28511085; e-mail info@ fidelidademundial.com.mo; life and non-life insurance; Gen. Man. EDUARDO CLARISSEAU MESQUITA D'ABREU.

Crown Life Insurance Co: Av. da Praia Grande 287, Nam Yuet Commercial Centre, Bl. B, 8° andar; tel. 28570828; fax 28570844; Rep. STEVEN SIU.

HSBC Insurance (Asia) Ltd: Av. da Praia Grande 619, Edif. Comercial Si Toi, 1° andar; tel. 28212323; fax 28217162; non-life insurance; Rep. NORA CHIO.

Ing Life Insurance Co (Macao) Ltd: Av. Almeida Ribeiro 61, 11° andar, Unit C and D; tel. 9886060; fax 9886100; e-mail customerservice@ing.com.mo; internet www.ing.com.mo; Heads LENNARD YONG, WIM HEKSTRA.

Luen Fung Hang Insurance Co Ltd (Luen Fung Hang Life Ltd): Alameda Dr Carlos d'Assumpção 398, Edif. CNAC, 4° andar; tel. 28700033; fax 28700088; e-mail info@luenfunghang.com; internet www.luenfunghang.com; life (Luen Fung Hang Life Ltd) and non-life insurance; Rep. SI CHI HOK.

Macao Life Insurance Co (Macao Insurance Company): Av. da Praia Grande 594, Edif. BCM, 10–11° andar; tel. 28555078; fax 28551074; e-mail mic@bcm.com.mo; internet www.macauinsurance .com.mo; life and non-life insurance (Macao Insurance Company); Rep. SI CHI HOK.

Manulife (International) Ltd: Av. da Praia Grande 517, Edif. Comercial Nam Tung, 8° andar, Unit B & C; tel. 3980388; fax 28323312; internet www.manulife.com.hk; CEO MICHAEL HUDDART.

MassMutual Asia Ltd: Av. da Praia Grande 517, Edif. Nam Tung 16° andar, E1–E2; tel. 28322622; fax 28322042; life insurance; Pres. MANLY CHENG.

Min Xin Insurance Co Ltd: Rua do Dr Pedro José Lobo 1–3, Luso International Bank Bldg, 27° andar, Rm 2704; tel. 28305684; fax 28305600; non-life insurance; Rep. PETER CHAN.

MSIG Insurance (Hong Kong) Ltd: Av. da Praia Grande 693, Edif. Tai Wah, 13° andar A–B; tel. 28923329; fax 28923349; internet www .msig.com.hk; wholly owned subsidiary of Mitsui Sumitomo Insurance Group Holdings Inc; CEO KENNETH REID.

QBE Insurance (International) Ltd: Rua do Comandante Mata e Oliveira 32, Edif. Associação Industrial de Macau, 8° andar B-C; tel. 28323909; fax 28323911; e-mail sally.siu@mo.qbe.com; non-life insurance; Rep. SALLY SIU.

Insurers' Associations

Federation of Macao Professional Insurance Intermediaries: Rua de Pequim 244–46, Macao Finance Centre, 6° andar G; tel. 28703268; fax 28703266; Rep. DAVID KONG.

Macao Insurance Agents and Brokers Association: Av. da Praia Grande 309, Nam Yuet Commercial Centre, 8° andar D; tel. 28378901; fax 28570848; Rep. JACK LI KWOK TAI.

Macao Insurers' Association: Av. da Praia Grande 575, Edif. 'Finanças', 15° andar; tel. 28511923; fax 28337531; e-mail info@ mia-macau.com; internet www.mia-macau.com; 22 mems; Pres. SI CHI HOK.

Trade and Industry

CHAMBER OF COMMERCE

Associação Comercial de Macau (Macao Chamber of Commerce): Rua de Xangai 175, Edif. ACM, 5° andar; tel. 28576833; fax 28594513; internet www.acm.org.mo; Pres. MA IAO LAI.

INDUSTRIAL AND TRADE ASSOCIATIONS

Associação dos Construtores Civis e Empresas de Fomento Predial de Macau (Macao Association of Building Contractors and Developers): Rua do Campo 103, 5° andar; tel. 28573226; fax 28345710; e-mail info@macaudeveloper.com; internet www .macaudeveloper.com; 145 corp. mems; Pres. FONG CHI KEONG.

Associação dos Exportadores e Importadores de Macau (Macao Importers and Exporters Association): Av. Infante D. Henrique 60–62, Centro Comercial 'Central', 3° andar; tel. 28375859; fax

28512174; e-mail aeim@macau.ctm.net; internet www.macauexport.com; exporters' and importers' asscn; Pres. VITOR NG.

Associação dos Industriais de Tecelagem e Fiação de Lã de Macau (Macao Weaving and Spinning of Wool Manufacturers' Asscn): Av. da Amizade 271B, Edif. Kam Wa Kok, 6° andar A; tel. 28553378; fax 28511105; Pres. WONG SHOO KEE.

Associação Industrial de Macau (Industrial Association of Macao): Rua Dr Pedro José Lobo 34–36, Edif. AIM, 17° andar; tel. 28574125; fax 28578305; e-mail info@madeinmacau.net; internet www.madeinmacau.net; f. 1959; Pres. HO IAT SENG.

Centro de Produtividade e Transferência de Tecnologia de Macau (Macao Productivity and Technology Transfer Centre): Rua de Xangai 175, Edif. ACM, 6° andar; tel. 28781313; fax 28788233; e-mail cpttm@cpttm.org.mo; internet www.cpttm.org.mo; vocational or professional training; Pres. VITOR NG; Dir-Gen. VICTOR KUAN.

Instituto de Promoção do Comércio e do Investimento de Macau (IPIM) (Macao Trade and Investment Promotion Institute): Av. da Amizade 918, World Trade Center Bldg, 1°–4° andares; tel. 28710300; fax 28590309; e-mail ipim@ipim.gov.mo; internet www.ipim.gov.mo; Pres. JACKSON CHANG.

Ponto de Contacto da Rede Portuguesa da Enterprise Europe Network: Alameda Dr Carlos d'Assumpção 263, Edif. China Civil Plaza, 20°andar; tel. 28713338; fax 28713339; e-mail info@ieem.org.mo; internet een.ieem.org.mo; f. 1992; promotes trade with European Union; fmrly Euro-Info Centre Relay of Macao; Man. VIOLET NG; Pres. JOSÉ LUÍS DE SALES MARQUES.

SDPIM (Macao Industrial Parks Development Co Ltd): Av. da Amizade 918, World Trade Center Bldg, 13° andar A & B; tel. 28786636; fax 28785374; e-mail sdpim@macau.ctm.net; internet www.sdpim.com.mo; f. 1993; Pres. of the Bd PAULINA Y. ALVES DOS SANTOS.

World Trade Center Macao, SARL: Av. da Amizade 918, Edif. World Trade Center, 16° andar; tel. 28727666; fax 28727633; e-mail wtcmc@wtc-macau.com; internet www.wtc-macau.com; f. 1995; trade information and business services, office rentals, exhibition and conference facilities; Chair. PETER LAM; Man. Dir ALBERTO EXPEDITO MARÇAL.

UTILITIES

Electricity

Companhia de Electricidade de Macau, SARL (CEM): Estrada D. Maria II 32–36, Edif. CEM; tel. 28339933; fax 28308361; e-mail e-doc@cem-macau.com; internet www.cem-macau.com; f. 1972; sole distributor; 6% owned by China Power International Holding Ltd; Chair. MARQUES DA CRUZ; CEO FRANKLIN WILLEMYNS.

Water

Sociedade de Abastecimento de Aguas de Macau, SARL (SAAM) (Macao Water): Av. do Conselheiro Borja 718; tel. 28220088; fax 28234660; e-mail customer.info@macaowater.com; internet www.macaowater.com; f. 1985; jt venture with Suez Lyonnaise des Eaux; Chair. STEPHEN CLARK; Man. Dir CHIN CHEUNG.

MAJOR COMPANIES

Gambling is Macao's most significant economic activity. At the end of 2009 there were 33 casinos in operation. Capital, reserves and revenues are given in HK dollars.

Galaxy Entertainment Group: Av. da Amizade, StarWorld Hotel, 17/F; tel. 82906811; fax 28750922; internet www.galaxyentertainment.com; cap. and res 8,168m., revenue 12,233m. (2009); owns and operates Waldo Casino, Rio Casino, President Casino, Grand Waldo Casino and StarWorld Hotel and Casino through Galaxy Casino SA; signed a sub-concession contract in December 2002 with Venetian Macao Ltd, owner of the Sands Macao casino; Chair. Dr LUI CHE WOO; Pres. MICHAEL MECCA; 6,200 employees.

Sociedade de Jogos de Macau, SA (SJM) (Macao Gaming Company Ltd): Hotel Lisboa, 9F, Av. de Lisboa 2–4; tel. 28574266; fax 28562285; e-mail ir@macausjm.com; internet www.sjmholdings.com; cap. and res 8,454m., revenue 34,352m. (2009); subsidiary of Sociedade de Turismo e Diversões de Macau (STDM), which operated a monopoly on gaming in Macao prior to the expiry of its franchise in 2001; operates 17 casinos in Macao (2010); Man. Dir Dr STANLEY HO; CEO SO SHU FAI; 19,936 employees.

Venetian Macao Ltd: Largo de Monte Carlo 203; tel. 28883388; e-mail generalinquiries@sands.com.mo; internet www.sands.com.mo; operates Sands Macao, the first Western-owned casino in Macao when it opened in May 2004; subsidiary of Las Vegas Sands, Inc; operates on a sub-licence granted by Galaxy Resort & Casino in Dec. 2002; COO EDWARD M. TRACY.

Wynn Resorts (Macao), SA: Rua Cidade de Sintra, Nape; tel. 28889966; fax 28329966; e-mail inquiries@wynnmacau.com; internet www.wynnmacau.com; operates Wynn Macau hotel and casino complex; Chair. and CEO STEPHEN A. WYNN.

Two other concessionaires are Melco Crown Jogos (Macau) SA and MGM Grand Paradise SA.

Supervisory Body

Direcção de Inspecção e Coordenação de Jogos (DICJ) (Gaming Inspection and Coordination Bureau): Av. Praia Grande, Edif. China Plaza 762–804, 21° andar; tel. 28569262; fax 28370296; e-mail enquiry@service.dicj.gov.mo; internet www.dicj.gov.mo; monitors gambling activity in Macao and advises the SAR's Chief Executive on gaming policies; Dir MANUEL JOAQUIM DAS NEVES.

TRADE UNIONS

Macao Federation of Trade Unions: Rua Ribeira do Patane 2; tel. 28576231; fax 28553110; Chair. CHIANG CHONG SEK.

Macao Labour Union: Pres. HO HEN KUOK.

Transport

RAILWAYS

There are no railways in Macao. A plan to connect Macao with Zhuhai and Guangzhou (People's Republic of China) is under consideration. Construction of the Zhuhai–Guangzhou section was under way in mainland China in the early 21st century. In October 2006 the Government announced plans to invest 4,200,000m. patacas in the construction of an elevated light rail system. According to reports, the project would span around 22 km, with 26 stations.

ROADS

In 2007 the public road network extended to 401 km. The peninsula of Macao is linked to the islands of Taipa and Coloane by three bridges and by a 2.2-km causeway, respectively. The first bridge (2.6 km) opened in 1974. In conjunction with the construction of an airport on Taipa (see Civil Aviation), a 4.4-km four-lane bridge to the Macao peninsula was opened in April 1994. A third link between Macao and Taipa, a double-deck bridge, opened in early 2005. A second connection to the mainland, the 1.5-km six-lane road bridge (the Lotus Bridge) linking Macao with Hengqin Island (in Zhuhai, Guangdong Province), opened to traffic in December 1999. Construction of a new bridge linking Macao with Hong Kong's Lantau Island and Zhuhai City, Guangdong Province, commenced in December 2009. To extend to nearly 50 km and comprising a six-lane expressway, the bridge was originally scheduled for completion in 2016.

SHIPPING

There are representatives of shipping agencies for international lines in Macao. There are passenger and cargo services to the People's Republic of China. Regular services between Macao and Hong Kong are run by the Hong Kong-based New World First Ferry and Shun Tak-China Travel Ship Management Ltd companies. A new terminal opened in late 1993. The port of Kao-ho (on the island of Coloane), which handles cargo and operates container services, entered into service in 1991.

Agência de Navegação Ka Fung: Av. da Praia Grande 429, South Bay Centro Comercial, 11° andar, Rm 1101; tel. 28553311; fax 28569233; e-mail info@kafung-shipping.com; internet www.kafung-shipping.com; f. 1984.

CTS Parkview Holdings Ltd: Av. Amizade, Porto Exterior, Terminal Marítimo de Macau, Sala 2006B; tel. 28726789; fax 28727112; purchased by Sociedade de Turismo e Diversões de Macau (STDM) in 1998.

DHC Logistics (Macau) Ltd: Av. de Praia Grande 619, Edif. Comercial Si Toi, 7° andar B; tel. 28788063; fax 28788093; e-mail pollywong@dhclogistics.com; internet www.dhclogistics.com.

Macao Dragon: Terminal Ferry, Taipa; tel. 82968296; internet www.macaodragon.com; f. 2010; operates two catamarans between Hong Kong and Macao; owned by Giant Dragon Sea Transport Co Ltd; Chair. DAVID LIANG.

New Line Shipping Ltd: Av. do Dr Rodrigo Rodrigues, Centro Comercial First Int., 24° andar, Rm 2404; tel. 28710250; fax 28710252; e-mail newline@macau.ctm.net; internet www.newline.com.mo; f. 2001.

STDM Shipping Dept: Av. da Amizade Terminal Marítimo do Porto Exterior; tel. 28726111; fax 28726234; e-mail shpgdept@macau.ctm.net; affiliated to STDM; Gen. Man. ALAN HO; Office Man. ALAN LI.

Association

Associação de Agências de Navegação e de Logistica de Macau (Macau Shipping and Logistics Association): Rua de Xanghai

175, Edif. ACM, 8F; tel. 28528207; fax 28302667; e-mail secretary@logistics.org.mo; internet www.logistics.org.mo; f. 1981; Pres. VONG KOK SENG.

Port Authority

Capitania dos Portos de Macau: Rampa da Barra, Quartel dos Mouros, POB 47; tel. 28559922; fax 28511986; e-mail info@marine.gov.mo; internet www.marine.gov.mo; Dir WONG SOI MAN.

CIVIL AVIATION

Macau International Airport, constructed on the island of Taipa, was officially opened in December 1995. The terminal has the capacity to handle 6m. passengers a year. By 2007 a total of 14 airlines operated flights to 25 destinations, mostly in mainland China, but also to the Democratic People's Republic of Korea, the Philippines, Singapore, Taiwan and Thailand. Helicopter services between Hong Kong and Macao are available.

Autoridade de Aviação Civil (AACM) (Civil Aviation Authority of Macao): Alameda Dr Carlos d'Assumpção 336–342, Centro Comercial Cheng Feng, 18° andar; tel. 28511213; fax 28338089; e-mail aacm@aacm.gov.mo; internet www.aacm.gov.mo; f. 1991; Pres. SIMON CHAN WENG HONG.

Administração de Aeroportos, Lda (ADA): Macau International Airport, Taipa; tel. 28861111; fax 28862222; e-mail directoraeroporto@ada.com.mo; internet www.ada.com.mo; f. 1995; owned by China National Aviation Corpn (CNAC) and ANA—Aeroportos de Portugal SA; CEO JOSÉ CARLOS ANGEJA.

CAM (Sociedade do Aeroporto Internacional de Macau, SARL): CAM Office Bldg, 4/F, Av. Wai Long, Macao International Airport; tel. 5988888; fax 28785465; e-mail mkd@macau-airport.com; internet www.macau-airport.com; f. 1989; airport owner, responsible for design, construction, development and international marketing of Macao International Airport; Chair. DENG JUN.

Air Macau: Macao Unidos Praça, Alameda Dr Carlos d'Assumpção 398, 13°–18° andar; tel. 83966888; fax 83966866; e-mail airmacau@airmacau.com.mo; internet www.airmacau.com.mo; f. 1994; controlled by China National Aviation Corpn (Group) Macao Co Ltd; services to several cities in the People's Republic of China, the Republic of Korea, the Philippines, Taiwan and Thailand; other destinations planned; Chair. ZHAO XIAO HANG; CEO ZHOU GUANG QUAN.

Tourism

In addition to the casinos, Macao's attractions include the cultural heritage and museums, dog-racing, horse-racing, and annual events such as Chinese New Year (January/February), the Macao Arts Festival (February/March), Dragon Boat Festival (May/June), the Macao International Fireworks Festival (September/October), the International Music Festival (October), the Macao Grand Prix for racing cars and motorcycles (November) and the Macao International Marathon (December). In 2007 the opening of the Las Vegas Sands Venetian casino and hotel complex provided 3,000 luxury hotel rooms. A total of 18,146 hotel rooms were available in September 2009. Visitor arrivals rose from fewer than 21.8m. in 2009 to nearly 25.0m. in 2010, the majority of tourists travelling from mainland China and from Hong Kong. Receipts from tourism (including passenger transport) reached US $17,093m. in 2008.

Macao Government Tourist Office (MGTO): Alameda Dr Carlos d'Assumpção 335–341, Edif. Hot Line, 12° andar; tel. 28315566; fax 28510104; e-mail mgto@macautourism.gov.mo; internet www.macautourism.gov.mo; Dir Eng. JOÃO MANUEL COSTA ANTUNES.

Instituto Cultural de Macau: Praça do Tap Seac, Edif. do Instituto Cultural; tel. 83996699; fax 28366899; e-mail postoffice@icm.gov.mo; internet www.icm.gov.mo; f. 1982; organizes performances, concerts, exhibitions, festivals, etc.; library facilities; Pres. HEIDI HO.

Macau Hotel Association: Rua Luís Gonzaga Gomes s/n, Bl. IV, r/c, Centro de Actividades Turísticas, Cabinet A; tel. 28703416; fax 28703415; e-mail mhacmo@macau.ctm.net; internet www.macauhotel.org; f. 1985; aims to promote and support high quality standards and growth of tourism, in conjunction with MGTO; Dir ANTONIO SAMEIRO.

Sociedade de Turismo e Diversões de Macau (STDM), SA: Hotel Lisboa, 9th Floor, Avda de Lisboa; tel. 28574266; fax 28562285; e-mail stdmmdof@macau.ctm.net; f. 1962; operation of its casinos handled by subsidiary Sociedade de Jogos de Macau (SJM) after ending of STDM's monopoly franchise in 2002; other commercial interests include hospitality, real estate, transport, infrastructure and overseas investments; Man. Dir Dr STANLEY HO.

Defence

The budget for defence is allocated by the Chinese Government. Upon the territory's reversion to Chinese sovereignty in December 1999, troops of the People's Liberation Army (PLA) were stationed in Macao. The force comprises around 1,000 troops: a maximum of 500 soldiers are stationed in Macao, the remainder in Zhuhai, China, on the border with the SAR. The unit is directly responsible to the Commander of the Guangzhou Military Region and to the Central Military Commission. The Macao garrison is composed mainly of ground troops. Naval and air defence tasks are performed by the naval vessel unit of the PLA garrison in Hong Kong and by the air force unit in Huizhou. Subject to the request of the Macao SAR, the garrison may participate in law enforcement and rescue operations in the SAR.

Commander of the PLA Garrison in Macao: Col. ZHU QING-SHENG.

Education

The education system in Macao is structured as follows: pre-school education (lasting two years); primary preparatory year (one year); primary education (six years); and secondary education (five–six years, divided into junior secondary of three years and senior secondary of two–three years). Schooling is compulsory between the ages of five and 15, but normally lasts from the ages of three to 17. In 2009/10 schools enrolled a total of 10,038 children in kindergarten, 25,705 primary pupils and 39,298 secondary students. In 2008/09 enrolment at primary schools included 87% (males 88%, females 87%) of pupils in the relevant age-group, while enrolment at secondary level included 76% (males 76%, females 76%) of pupils in the relevant age-group. In 2009/10 23,562 students attended courses offered by tertiary institutions, ranging from the bacharelato (three-year courses) to doctorate programmes. The projected education budget for 2007 was 1,860m. patacas.

Free education was extended from government schools to private schools in 1995/96. Private schools provide education for more than 90% of children. Of these schools, 77% were reported to have joined the free education system, and together with the government schools they form the public school system, in which all pupils receive 10 years' free tuition (from the primary preparatory year up to the junior secondary level).

In 2008/09 there were 12 public and private universities, polytechnic institutes and research centres; these include the University of Macao and the Macao Polytechnic Institute. Other tertiary institutions are: the Institute for Tourism Studies, Macao Security Forces Academy, Inter-University Institute of Macao, Asia International Open University (Macao), Institute of European Studies of Macao, Kiang Wu Nursing College of Macao, United Nations University/International Institute for Software Technology, Macao University of Science and Technology, Macao Institute of Management, and Macao Millennium College.

The rate of literacy among the population aged 15 and over in Macao was 93.5% in 2006, illiteracy being confined mainly to elderly women.

Bibliography

Boxer, C. R. *The Portuguese Seaborne Empire*. London, Hutchinson and Co, 1969.

Braga, J. M. *O primeiro acordo Luso-Chinês*. Macao, 1939.

The Western Pioneers and their Discovery of Macau. Macao, 1949.

Bray, M., and Koo, Ramsey (Eds). *Education and Society in Hong Kong and Macao: Comparative Perspectives on Continuity and Change*. Springer-Verlag New York, 2006.

Breitung, Werner. *Overcoming Borders, Living with Borders: Macao and the Integration with China*. Macao, Instituto Cultural de Macau, 2007.

Brookshaw, D. *Visions of China: Stories from Macau*. Hong Kong, Hong Kong University Press, 2002.

Do Carmo, Maria Helena. *Os Interesses dos Portugueses em Macau, na Primeira Metade do Século XVIII*. Macao, University of Macau Publications Centre, 1999.

Chan, Ming K., and Lo, Shiu Hing. *Historical Dictionary of the Hong Kong SAR and the Macao SAR*. Lanham, MD, Rowman and Littlefield, 2006.

Chan, S. S. *The Macau Economy*. Macao, University of Macau Publications Centre, 2000.

Cheng, Christina Miu Bing. *Macau: A Cultural Janus.* Hong Kong, Hong Kong University Press, 1999.

Clayton, Cathryn H. *Sovereignty at the Edge: Macau and the Question of Chineseness.* Cambridge, MA, Harvard University Press, 2009.

Coates, Austin. *A Macao Narrative.* Hong Kong, Oxford University Press, 1998.

Macao and the British, 1637–1842: Prelude to Hong Kong. Hong Kong, Oxford University Press, 1989.

Gomes, L. G. *Bibliografia Macaense.* Macao, Imprensa Nacional, 1973.

Guillén Núñez, César, and Leong Kai Tai. *Macao Streets.* Hong Kong, Oxford University Press, 1999.

Gunn, Geoffrey C. *Encountering Macau: A Portuguese City-state on the Periphery of China, 1557–1999.* Boulder, CO, Westview Press, 1996.

Ieong Wan Chong and Chi Sen Siu, Ricardo. *Macau: A Model of Mini-Economy.* Macao, University of Macau Publications Centre, 1997.

Jesus, C. A. Montalto de. *Historic Macao.* Hong Kong, Kelly & Walsh Printers & Publishers, 1902.

Lam, Newman M. K., and Scott, Ian (Eds).*Gaming, Governance and Public Policy in Macao.* Hong Kong, Hong Kong University Press, 2011.

Lei, Chung Kwok, and Yao, Shujie. *Economic Convergence in Greater China: Mainland China, Hong Kong, Macau and Taiwan.* Abingdon, Routledge, 2011.

Leong Ka Tai, and Davies, S. *Macau.* Singapore, Times Editions, 1986.

Ljungstedt, A. *An Historical Sketch of the Portuguese Settlements in China.* Boston, 1936.

Lo, Shiu-Hing. *Political Change in Macao.* Abingdon, Routledge, 2008.

Lui Kwok Man. *Macau in Transition.* Macao, University of Macau Publications Centre, 2000.

Macau Research Group. *A Strategic Assessment of Macau, 2000 Edition.* Icon Group International, 2000.

McGivering, Jill. *Macao Remembers.* Hong Kong, Oxford University Press, 1999.

Mo, Timothy. *An Insular Possession.* London, Chatto and Windus, 1998.

Pons, Philippe. *Macao.* Paris, Le Promeneur, 2000.

Porter, Jonathan. *Macau: The Imaginary City.* Boulder, CO, Westview Press, 2000.

Ramos, Rufino, et al. (Eds). *Population and Development in Macau.* Macao, University of Macau Publications Centre, 1994.

Macau and its Neighbors in Transition. Macao, University of Macau Publications Centre, 1997.

Macau and its Neighbors Towards the 21st Century. Macao, University of Macau Publications Centre, 1998.

Shipp, Steve. *Macau, China: A Political History of the Portuguese Colony's Transition to Chinese Rule.* Jefferson, NC, McFarland & Co, 1997.

Da Silva Diaz de Seabra, Isabel Leonor. *Relações Entre Macau e O Sião (Séculos XVIII–XIX).* Macao, University of Macau Publications Centre, 1999.

Sit, Victor F. S., et al. *Entrepreneurs and Enterprises in Macao: A Study in Industrial Development.* Hong Kong, Hong Kong University Press, 1991.

USA International Business Publications. *Macau Country Study Guide.* International Business Publications, 2000.

Macao Government and Policy Guide. International Business Publications, 2000.

Van Dyke, Paul A. *Merchants of Canton and Macao: Politics and Strategies in Eighteenth-Century Trade.* Hong Kong, Hong Kong University Press, 2011.

Wesley-Smith, P. 'Macao' in Albert P. Blaustein (Ed.), *Constitutions of Dependencies and Special Sovereignties, Vol. III.* New York, Oceana Press, 1977.

Wong Hon Keung. *Economic Interaction Between Guangxi and Macau.* Macao, University of Macau Publications Centre, 1998.

Yee, Herbert S. *Macau in Transition: From Colony to Autonomous Region.* New York, St Martin's Press, 2001.

INDONESIA

Physical and Social Geography

HARVEY DEMAINE

With revisions by ROBERT CRIBB

The Republic of Indonesia, which today comprises the same area as the former Netherlands East Indies, lies along the Equator between the south-eastern tip of the Asian mainland and Australia. Its western and southern coasts abut on the Indian Ocean; to the north it faces the Straits of Melaka (Malacca) and the South China Sea; and the remote northern shore of Papua (formerly Irian Jaya) province has frontage on to the Pacific Ocean. Indonesia's only land frontiers are with Papua New Guinea, to the east of (West) Papua, with Timor-Leste (known as East Timor prior to independence in 2002), and with the Malaysian states of Sarawak and Sabah, which occupy northern Borneo; almost all of the remainder of Borneo comprises the Indonesian territory of Kalimantan.

Indonesia extends more than 4,800 km from east to west and 2,000 km from north to south. However, nearly four-fifths of the area between these outer extremities consists of sea, and the total land surface of Indonesia covers 1,910,931 sq km (737,814 sq miles).

PHYSICAL FEATURES

The country consists of about 17,500 islands of extremely varied size and character, of which about 6,000 are inhabited. The largest exclusively Indonesian island is Sumatra (Sumatera), covering 480,793 sq km, although this area is exceeded by that of Kalimantan, the Indonesian segment of Borneo, which occupies 544,150 sq km (about two-thirds) of the island. The other major island groups are: the Maluku (Moluccas) and Papua; Sulawesi (Celebes); and Java (Jawa) and Madura. The remaining areas are the smaller islands of Bali and the Nusa Tenggara group.

Differences in size also reflect fundamental differences in geological structure. All the large islands except Sulawesi stand on one of two great continental shelves: the Sunda Shelf, representing a prolongation of the Asian mainland, covered by the shallow waters of the Straits of Melaka, the Java Sea and the southernmost part of the South China Sea; and the Sahul Shelf, which is covered by the shallow Arafura Sea and links New Guinea with Australia. In Sumatra, Java, north-eastern Borneo and western Papua there are pronounced mountain ranges facing the deep seas along the outer edges of the shelves, and extensive lowland tracts, facing the shallow inner seas whose coastlines reveal evidence of recent submergence. In contrast to the larger islands of western and eastern Indonesia, most of those lying between the two shelves, including Sulawesi as well as those of the Nusa Tenggara and Maluku groups, rise steeply from deep seas on all sides, with only extremely narrow coastal plains.

The recent mountain building in most parts of the archipelago is related to widespread vulcanicity, much of which is still in the active stage. Except in Borneo and western Papua, the culminating relief normally consists of volcanic cones, many of which exceed 3,000 m in altitude, although the loftiest peaks of all are the non-volcanic Punjak Jaya (5,000 m) and Idenburg-top (4,800 m) in the Snow mountains of western Papua. The archipelago is also subject to earthquakes and associated tsunamis. In December 2004 an earthquake of 9.0 magnitude occurred in the Indian Ocean off the north-west coast of Sumatra, precipitating a series of devastating tsunamis and killing a total of more than 200,000 people, a large proportion of whom died in Indonesia, mainly in Aceh.

NATURAL RESOURCES

The volcanic soils of the eastern two-thirds of Java and nearby Bali are highly fertile and conducive to the cultivation of important crops such as coffee. The soils elsewhere, whether volcanically derived or not, are poorer in quality.

The country is rich in hydrocarbon deposits. Exploration and extraction of coal have been expanded, and sources of geothermal energy are being exploited. At the end of 2010 proven reserves of coal totalled 5,529m. metric tons. In the same year proven reserves of petroleum amounted to 4,200m. barrels. Indonesia is a leading exporter of liquefied natural gas. The country's proven gas reserves totalled 3,100,000m. cu m at the end of 2010. Tin, bauxite, copper, nickel, gold and silver are also extracted.

CLIMATE AND VEGETATION

Climatically the greater part of Indonesia may be described as maritime equatorial, with consistently high temperatures (except at higher altitudes) and heavy rainfall in all seasons, although in many parts of western Indonesia there are distinct periods of exceptionally heavy rain when either the north-east or the south-west monsoon winds are blowing on shore. However, the eastern half of Java, Bali, southern Sulawesi and Nusa Tenggara, which lie further to the south and nearer to the Australian desert, experience a dry season during the period of the south-east monsoon between June/July and September/October. The south-east monsoon subsequently changes direction, to become the south-west monsoon over western Indonesia. In Pontianak, situated almost exactly on the Equator on the west coast of Borneo, the monthly mean temperature varies only from 25.6°C in December to 26.7°C in July, and average monthly rainfall varies from 160 mm in July to 400 mm in December. The total annual rainfall is 3,200 mm. Surabaya, in eastern Java, shows even less variation in mean monthly temperature, which ranges between 26.1°C and 26.7°C throughout the year. It has four months (December–March) with over 240 mm of rain each, and four others (July–October) with less than 50 mm, out of an annual total of 1,735 mm.

Nearly all of Indonesia, in its natural state, supports very dense vegetation, with significant variations, including tidal swamps, normal lowlands, lower slopes, and higher altitudes. However, widespread illegal logging practices have resulted in a serious depletion of the country's natural forests. Forested areas declined from 118.5m. ha in 1990 to 94.4m. ha in 2010. None the less, the latter figure represented almost one-half of Indonesia's total area.

POPULATION

The census of May 2010 recorded a population of 237,556,363, in comparison with 206,264,595 at the 2000 census. Indonesia thus continued to rank as the fourth most populous country in the world (after the People's Republic of China, India and the USA). According to UN estimates, the population had risen to 242,325,637 by mid-2011, when density stood at 126.8 persons per sq km. This large, rapidly increasing population, spread over so vast and fragmented a territory, presents wide variations in ethnic type, religion and language. Java, Madura and Bali, which comprise about 8% of the total area of Indonesia, contain about 80% of its population. This situation has persisted, despite extensive efforts to shift population out of Java and Bali from as early as 1905 under colonization schemes, latterly known as transmigration.

Archaeological evidence suggests that the archipelago was sparsely populated from at least 50,000 years ago by people of Austromelanesian (Papuan) stock. In the western two-thirds of the archipelago, the Austromelanesians were later largely displaced by Austronesians, seafaring people from the island of Taiwan, who began to move southwards from about 4000 BC. The considerable physical differences between ethnic groups in Indonesia is now thought to be related to different levels of mixing between the two peoples, with the older Austromelanesian elements progressively stronger in the eastern part of the archipelago.

The peoples of the coastal regions of Western Indonesia are predominantly Muslim, although their religious practice varies considerably according to the influence of local custom or *adat*. The strongly Muslim Minangkabau of West Sumatra, for instance, maintain a matrilineal system of inheritance directly at variance with normal Islamic practice, and local customs are important even in Aceh (far northern Sumatra), which is traditionally regarded as the staunchest Muslim region. In the interior of Java, earlier Hindu and animist influences are strong, producing a belief system known as *Kejawen* which is only broadly recognizable as Muslim. In the interior of the other larger islands, some of the formerly animist ethnic groups have been converted to Islam (such as the Gayo and Alas in northern Sumatra) or Christianity (such as the neighbouring Bataks and the Minahasans of North Sulawesi). Christian missionary influence has been strongest in eastern Indonesia. Hinduism remains the religion of the island of Bali and of a few small enclaves in Java. The traditional religion of the Dayaks of Borneo has also been given official recognition as a form of Hinduism, although it bears only a passing resemblance to the religion practised in Bali. Christianity, Buddhism and Confucianism are strong amongst the Chinese minority. Small animist communities remain in many regions, but official policy requires all Indonesians in time to accept one of the larger religions.

Over 270 Austronesian languages and 180 Papuan languages have been recognized in Indonesia, but only 13 of these have more than 1m. speakers.The Indonesian nationalist movement formally adopted Malay as the national language in 1929, and called it 'Indonesian' (Bahasa Indonesia). The vocabulary of Indonesian subsequently expanded enormously. Indonesian is now used exclusively at all but the initial levels of the education system and is the only language of public affairs.

Besides its indigenous population, Indonesia has one of the largest Chinese communities in South-East Asia. This community may have totalled nearly 3m. Although a substantial proportion of the Chinese were born and brought up in Indonesia, accepted citizenship and became 'Indonesianized', many remained without citizenship. The Chinese and smaller non-indigenous groups, such as Arabs and Eurasians, are largely concentrated in the urban areas. The cities have grown rapidly, with the population of the capital, Jakarta, rising from 4.6m. in 1971 to an estimated 9.2m. in mid-2010.

History

ROBERT CRIBB

Revised by GREG FEALY

HISTORICAL BACKGROUND

From about AD 100 the rise of Asia's great maritime trade route, linking India and China through South-East Asia, drew the small hunting, fishing and agricultural communities of the Indonesian archipelago into a broader world of civilization and commerce. Newly rich local rulers, trading in spices, resins and fragrant woods, justified their acquired wealth by adopting Indian political ideology, turning themselves into Hindu god-kings and providing a conduit through which Hindu ideas spread unevenly to the mass of the people. Srivijaya on the Sumatra coast (c. 700–1200) and Majapahit in the interior of Java (c. 1300–1450) emerged as the greatest early states, their influence covering much of the western archipelago. Islam arrived on the trade routes from India in about 1100, and during subsequent centuries largely displaced Hinduism and Buddhism as the formal religion of the courts and of society, although in practice it fused with Indian and local religions into distinctive Indonesian forms.

Colonial Rule

European traders and raiders were present in the archipelago from the early 16th century, but only gradually did the Dutch East Indies Company turn its scattered forts and trading posts into a colonial empire. The company focused initially on trade and soon became involved in plantations, but it was finally unable to cope with the complexities of colonial administration and the metropolitan Dutch Government took over the colony in 1799. After a brief period of British occupation under Sir Stamford Raffles (1811–16), the Dutch authorities launched an era of intensive colonial exploitation on Java known as the Cultivation System. Many authorities have argued that this exploitation brought about the long-term impoverishment of the island, although empirical evidence is equivocal. From the 1870s Western private enterprise was allowed to operate in the colony, leading to a spectacular expansion of plantation agriculture outside Java (Jawa), especially in East Sumatra (Sumatera). Petroleum extraction in Sumatra and Borneo (Kalimantan) also became important. During the four decades to 1910, the Dutch largely completed their military conquest of the archipelago. The Dutch preserved many of the traditional rulers of the archipelago as agents of colonial rule, and established a complicated legal system under which the traditional native law (*adat*) in each region was codified and applied to indigenous people. The result was a form of racial classification in which the population was divided into Europeans, Natives and 'Foreign Orientals' (principally Chinese), with differing rights and duties. Only Natives were permitted to own land, but they had fewer political and legal rights. The Chinese community, which included both recent immigrants and locally born families with a long history in the archipelago, came to occupy a middle position in society, dominating small- and medium-scale commerce to the exclusion of indigenous Indonesians.

The disruption of indigenous society by Western economic penetration and the emergence of a small educated élite, trained especially to serve the increasingly complex government and private bureaucracies, led to the rise of a nationalist movement in the early 20th century. Islamic and communist influences were initially strong in this movement, but by the late 1920s the movement was dominated by 'secular' nationalists, notably Sukarno, Hatta and Sjahrir. The movement extracted few concessions from the colonial authorities and remained politically weak until the Japanese occupation (1942–45), which removed the Dutch and raised hopes of rapid independence.

INDEPENDENCE

In the confusion following the Japanese surrender, Sukarno and Hatta declared independence on 17 August 1945, becoming President and Vice-President, respectively, of the new Republic of Indonesia. However, more than four years of fighting and negotiation with the Dutch ensued before the formal transfer of sovereignty on 27 December 1949. By January 1949 the Dutch had reconquered most of the archipelago, but they were defeated by a combination of guerrilla resistance and foreign pressure; the USA, in particular, became convinced of the moderate credentials of the Indonesian nationalists, and wished to avoid a prolonged struggle that might encourage the growth of communism. The transfer of sovereignty left Indonesia with a federal system, devised by the Dutch to isolate radical forces on Java and Sumatra; the Republic of Indonesia declared in 1945 was thus a constituent state of the 14-member Republic of the United States of Indonesia. The other states were quickly dissolved, and in August 1950 Indonesia returned to a unitary structure. However, against Indonesian wishes the Dutch retained the territory of West New Guinea (later West Irian, renamed Irian Jaya and subsequently Papua) on the grounds that it was ethnically distinct from the rest of Indonesia.

Parliamentary Democracy, 1950–57

Under the 1950 Constitution, political power was vested in a legislature, with Prime Ministers and their cabinets responsible for executive government. Although the legislature was unelected (most members were present by virtue of their roles in one or other of the many deliberative bodies created by both sides during the war of independence), it was diverse and appears to have represented the main social forces and currents of political thought in the country. Because of this diversity, governments were invariably coalitions and were vulnerable to defections; few lasted longer than a year in office. Indonesia lacked the human and infrastructural resources to deal rapidly and effectively with the social and economic problems left by colonialism, and the performance of these governments was thus generally disappointing. Expectations had been raised by the independence struggle and could not easily be met. The political parties themselves undermined their own standing and performance by discord, corruption and partisan appointments to the civil service. The country also confronted rebellions: in South Maluku (the Moluccas) a conservative, largely Christian movement attempted to secede, while in parts of Java, Sumatra and Celebes (Sulawesi) the Darul Islam (DI) movement attempted to impose an Islamic state. Many people also resented the failure of successive governments to dislodge the Dutch from West New Guinea, although Indonesia's international status was heightened when it hosted the Afro-Asian Conference in Bandung in 1955.

At the first national elections in 1955 Java-based parties and those towards the left gained the greatest support, although no party came close to a majority. The continuing impasse in Jakarta, together with growing alarm in the islands outside Java, led in 1956 to local mutinies in Sumatra, an island that generated much of Indonesia's export revenue. The mutinies developed into full rebellions in 1957, although their aim was to recover central power, not to secede. In response to the crisis, President Sukarno declared martial law in 1957, and during the next two years gradually replaced the parliamentary system with authoritarian rule based on the original 1945 Constitution adopted at the beginning of the war for independence.

'Guided Democracy', 1959–65

Sukarno called his authoritarian system 'Guided Democracy', but for the most part it was a retreat from democracy. The elected legislature was purged of non-compliant members and a new assembly created in which many seats were filled by presidential appointees; cabinets were chosen by and responsible to the President. Political activity was restricted, and two parties were banned. The army, which had by then defeated the regional rebellions, became deeply involved in the administration under martial law, and also assumed a major role in the economy as managers of Dutch enterprises that had been nationalized in 1957. Although conservative in structure and social policy, 'Guided Democracy' was radical in rhetoric and ideology. Sukarno proclaimed a continuing revolution in the name of the poor and oppressed, and he increasingly incorporated Marxist elements into state ideology. Although he enjoyed unrivalled oratorical power over the Indonesian masses, he also made extensive use of the Partai Komunis Indonesia (PKI—Indonesian Communist Party) in mobilizing popular support. The communists had created by far the most effective party structure in the country and had won 16.4% of the vote in the 1955 elections, but probably enjoyed the support of between one-third and one-half of the population by 1965. 'Guided Democracy' delivered few tangible benefits to Indonesians. Sukarno showed little interest in day-to-day administration, and the fabric of the country gradually deteriorated; by 1965 Indonesia was one of the poorest countries in the world. The little radical legislation that he did sponsor (notably in the area of land reform) failed to be implemented, owing to bureaucratic inertia and the resistance of local powers. Sukarno's recovery of West New Guinea in 1963 by a mixture of bluff and shrewd international diplomacy won him enormous credit with Indonesians, but his confrontation with Malaysia (1963–66), which he regarded as an undemocratic and neo-colonial 'puppet' of the British, brought no such success.

Although the PKI held virtually no powers, there was widespread speculation that its broader ideological influence would lead to its control of Indonesia on the death of Sukarno, who by 1965 was suffering serious health problems and appeared at risk of losing political control. However, such a prospect provoked concern within the Muslim community and in the army, which remained the most powerful institution in the country. Deepening social and ideological conflict, exacerbated by declining economic conditions, led to a sense of impending crisis. On 30 September 1965 a group of left-wing middle-ranking army officers staged a limited coup against the more conservative High Command in order to forestall a rumoured army coup a few days later. PKI leaders, and possibly Sukarno, had some knowledge of the plot, although there was no reliable evidence that they took part in planning it. However, poor execution of the coup (most but not all of the targeted generals were killed) apparently led the plotters to expand it into a full-scale seizure of power, for which they were utterly unprepared. Their movement, therefore, was easily suppressed by one of the senior surviving army commanders, Maj.-Gen. Suharto.

Sukarno remained formally in office, but between October 1965 and March 1966 Suharto steadily eroded his power, preventing his exercise of authority in the Government and countering his still formidable oratorical skills by establishing what became known as the 'New Order' coalition of Muslims, students, economic managers and the armed forces, which demanded a radical change of policy direction towards economic recovery. During the same period the PKI was proscribed. Probably about 500,000 party members and sympathizers (from a claimed membership of 3m.) were killed, some by the armed forces, some by anti-communist vigilantes, and more than 1.5m. were detained for various periods. Suharto became acting President in March 1967 and full President a year later. Sukarno was held under house arrest until his death in 1970.

SUHARTO AND THE 'NEW ORDER'

Suharto's new regime presented itself as a managerial government, the primary task of which was to restore economic growth and political stability. Suharto left much of the management of the Indonesian economy to a team of US-trained economists, who worked closely with the Inter-Governmental Group for Indonesia (IGGI), an international consortium of aid donors to Indonesia. Although they maintained the large state sector of the economy inherited from the period of 'Guided Democracy', they opened the Indonesian economy to foreign investment, first in mining and forestry, and later in industrial manufacture. Indonesia benefited especially from the rapid increase in petroleum prices, and was able to finance a massive programme of infrastructural investment. The new Government also began programmes aimed at addressing the problems of rapid population growth. A major and effective family-planning campaign was launched. The long-standing policy of encouraging people from densely populated Java and Bali to move to less-populated regions in the other islands was expanded, with World Bank finance, into a massive population transfer that involved 1.5m. people between 1969 and 1982.

Suharto swiftly abandoned the left-wing rhetoric of 'Guided Democracy', and made the national ideology of *Pancasila*, literally 'five principles', the regime's main ideological instrument. These principles were: belief in Almighty God, national unity, humanitarianism, social justice and democracy. These had originally been set out in deliberately general terms by Sukarno on the eve of independence in 1945 in order to address ideological differences between secular nationalist and Islamic leaders. Suharto now used the *Pancasila* to dominate the central symbolic space in Indonesian politics, thereby marginalizing the perceived rival ideologies of the left (communism) and the right (fundamentalist Islam).

The armed forces played a crucial role in the new Government. They provided the main security and intelligence apparatus in the form of the Operational Command for the Restoration of Security and Order (Kopkamtib). Those who had been involved in the abortive 1965 coup were relentlessly pursued, and involvement was interpreted so broadly that most leftist dissent was encompassed. The armed forces also increased their role in administration through the doctrine of *dwi-fungsi* or dual function, which held that the concern of the armed forces was not simply national defence but also the actual conduct of government in the interests of good administration. A powerful myth began to develop that the armed forces had played the principal role in securing independence in the 1940s, that they had done so despite obstruction and betrayal by the civilian authorities and that they therefore retained a special right and duty to supervise and take charge of the conduct of government. Under *dwi-fungsi*, serving and retired army officers took a wide variety of posts, from the level of cabinet minister down to village head.

In order to meet domestic and international expectations of a restoration of democracy, elections took place in July 1971, but under conditions designed to ensure a government victory. During the preceding months and years, the authorities comprehensively undermined the surviving parties, often intervening directly in their internal affairs to ensure that they were controlled by groups sympathetic to the armed forces. More significantly, the Government introduced the doctrine of 'monoloyalty', under which government officials were permitted to support only the Government at election time; other political parties thus lost the influential backing they had previously received from various sections of the bureaucracy, especially in the countryside. At the same time, the Government decreed the so-called 'floating mass policy', under which the mass of Indonesians were not to be exposed to political campaigning except during the brief, defined campaign period before elections; this was ostensibly to avoid distracting people from the tasks of national development. For the election campaign itself, contestants were screened by security officials before being permitted to stand, and public questioning of government policy was not permitted (although the implementation of policy might be challenged). In addition, inter-ethnic, inter-religious or inter-'group' (i.e. class) issues were not permitted to be discussed publicly at any time. In 1973, after the elections, the Government further weakened the parties by forcing them to merge into two fractious amalgamations: the Partai Persatuan Pembangunan (PPP—United Development Party), comprising the four Muslim parties, and the Partai Demokrasi Indonesia (PDI—Indonesian Democratic Party), composed of the remaining five nationalist and Christian parties.

Government candidates contested the 1971 elections as the Partai Golongan Karya (Party of Functional Groups, also known as Golkar), an organization that had played a minor role under 'Guided Democracy' as an army-dominated co-ordinating body for anti-communist trade unions and other associations. According to the regime, Golkar was not a political party as it had no individual membership. It was thus exempt from most of the restrictions on the parties but gained great advantage from having the support of the bureaucracy and the armed forces. Golkar received 63% of the votes cast in the 1971 elections, and its share of the vote never fell below 61% at the remaining five elections of the 'New Order' period. However, serious discontent began to arise in Indonesia during the mid-1970s. Student groups, in particular, protested against the perceived lack of true democracy, the hardships being caused to ordinary Indonesians by the rapid modernization programme and the corruption of the ruling group. The President's wife, Siti Hartinah (Tien), was among those accused of appropriating funds from the Government and of abusing her position. Concern that the exceptionally high revenue derived from petroleum exports was being squandered was later vindicated when the state oil company, Pertamina, came close to bankruptcy in 1975–76, having recorded massive financial losses. There was much resentment, too, of the business relations between protagonists of the 'New Order' and Chinese Indonesian business-owners (*cukong*). Furthermore, in January 1974 a mass student protest during a visit to Jakarta by the Japanese Prime Minister, Kakuei Tanaka, developed into a riot, the so-called Malari (Malapetaka Lima Belas Januari or 15 January Disaster), in which 11 people were killed and hundreds of vehicles and buildings were set on fire.

Towards a 'Pancasila State', 1975–88

Disturbed by this dissent, Suharto intensified his programme to turn the *Pancasila* from a symbol into a national ideology. In a major programme of ideological construction, the vague unifying principles of *Pancasila* became a comprehensive ideology, with the Government exclusively responsible for formulation and interpretation. The *Pancasila* was held to prescribe a society modelled on the traditional family, in which parental authority was respected and in which individual interest was subordinate to the well-being of the community. *Pancasila* labour relations, for instance, implied that there could be no conflict of interests between workers and management and that strikes were inherently anti-social. In emphasizing submission to authority, the *Pancasila* also reinforced Suharto's position as president, and some observers began to liken his style to that of a traditional Javanese king.

Opposition to the new interpretation of the *Pancasila* came first from a group of older politicians associated with the parliamentary period and the early 'New Order'. In 1980 they signed the Petition of 50, objecting to Suharto's new doctrines and urging the legislature to review (i.e. reject) them; but the strongest reaction to the new *Pancasila* came from religious groups, when the Government insisted in the early 1980s that all social organizations adopt the *Pancasila* as their sole ideological principle (*azas tunggal*), placing it above even religious principles. There was great disquiet among major Islamic organizations; however, all but one eventually accepted *Pancasila*, for fear of being dissolved by the regime.

The years 1975–88 were a time of continued political repression. Muslim militants especially were often arrested and tried, but the Government maintained that the banned PKI remained a threat and periodically dismissed officials on the grounds of tenuous left-wing connections. None the less, these were also years in which the Suharto Government deftly refined economic and social policy. Pertamina was rehabilitated, and the regime reacted promptly and efficiently to the collapse of petroleum prices. As the impossibility of significantly diminishing Java's population by means of transmigration became apparent, the goals of the programme were shifted to economic development in the other islands, the resettlement of people displaced by development projects and natural disasters, and the establishment of politically reliable Javanese settler communities in potentially secessionist regions.

Suharto's Final Decade, 1988–98

From the late 1980s the question of the succession to President Suharto increasingly dominated the political agenda. Born in 1921, Suharto had long passed normal retirement age. During the approach to each of the successive five-yearly Majelis Permusyawaratan Rakyat (MPR—People's Consultative Assembly) sessions, at which the President was elected, Suharto indicated that he expected his next term to be his last; but once he was elected, such indications gradually gave way to expressions of willingness to stand for a further term, if that were the will of the people and of the MPR. The political order was commonly described as being in 'a state of waiting', and it was widely felt that policy-making was being seriously hampered by the efforts of senior politicians to position themselves in preparation for Suharto's eventual demise.

For a time during the 1990s it appeared as if Suharto was willing to allow moves towards a more liberal political order. On several occasions the regime eased restrictions on the media and permissible public discussion in what came to be known as *keterbukaan* (openness). In 1993 the formerly ineffective PDI elected to its chair Megawati Sukarnoputri (a daughter of the late President Sukarno), whose leadership appeared to attract greater public support for the party. Despite raising the prospect of reform, Suharto again took action against dissent; he also modified or withdrew new regulations or draft legislation originally intended to formalize greater freedom of expression and association.

These policy alterations reflected broader changes in Indonesian society under the 'New Order'. Growing prosperity and an increasingly complex economy and society had led to better education, improved living standards and greater international awareness for a substantial new middle class of bureaucrats, professionals and entrepreneurs. These groups were keen to obtain greater political influence and to see a more regularized economic and administrative order; without necessarily wanting a democracy that enfranchised the poor, they desired a political system in which power and influence were no longer reserved for a small civilian and military élite.

Another major development of the late 1980s and 1990s was a rapprochement between the regime and many sections of the Islamic community that had previously felt marginalized politically and economically. Suharto adopted the given name Mohamed after his pilgrimage to Mecca in 1991 and agreed to a number of new statutes as concessions to Muslim sentiment. More generally, the regime began to reflect a policy of 'proportionality'; whereas devout Muslims had previously been under-represented in the senior ranks of government and the military, they now gained appointment in large numbers to important positions, often displacing Christians and nominal Muslims.

Political calculation appeared to be a major reason for Suharto's closer relations with the Islamic community. From the mid-1980s the armed forces became uneasy about the growing favouritism and economic power of Suharto's family members and their business colleagues. Military enterprises often suffered as 'The Family' widened the scope of its activities, and there were also concerns that dynastic intentions on the part of Suharto might overshadow the armed forces politically. Thus, the military tried to apply pressure on Suharto to curtail his family's activities and safeguard the armed forces' role. In response, Suharto sought to purge the military of his critics, but also to cultivate the Islamic community in order to strengthen his own support base.

Not all Muslims supported these closer relations with the 'New Order'. The Chairman of the Nahdlatul Ulama (NU—Council of Scholars, Indonesia's largest Muslim organization), Abdurrahman Wahid (also known as Gus Dur), claimed that the Ikatan Cendekiawan Muslim Indonesia (ICMI—Association of Indonesian Muslim Intellectuals) was sectarian and founded the Democracy Forum, comprising 45 prominent Indonesian intellectuals, including a number of Christians.

As the 1997 legislative elections approached, the new PDI leader, Megawati Sukarnoputri, appeared to be the main beneficiary of this discontent. Taking advantage of somewhat romanticized memories of her father as a President who had cared for the underprivileged, she appeared likely to lead the PDI to win a record share of the votes. In June 1996 government supporters within the PDI contrived to convene a special party congress of dubious legality, which removed Megawati as leader and installed her predecessor, Soerjadi. However, as the congress met, Megawati mobilized her supporters in rallies in Jakarta and other cities, and prepared court cases to reclaim the party leadership. She also announced that her opponents had been expelled from the party, and refused to surrender the party headquarters to them. On 27 July 1996 armed vigilantes from the Soerjadi faction stormed the PDI headquarters in Jakarta, with military support, evicting Megawati's supporters and provoking two days of rioting in the capital.

The misfortunes of the PDI reinvigorated the PPP, which had suffered from internal division and lack of funds. The dour personality of the party Chairman, Ismael Hassan Metareum, once a liability, now enhanced the party's image as a serious contestant, but the PPP benefited most of all from growing signs that discontented PDI adherents were now supporting it.

The election, held on 29 May 1997, delivered an unprecedented victory to Golkar, which won every province and received 74.5% of the votes nationally; the outcome was widely regarded as an indication of the Government's forceful manipulation rather than a measure of popularity or approval. The PPP also improved its performance, winning 22.4% (up from almost 16.0% in 1992), while the PDI vote plummeted to 3.1% from its previous figure of 14.9%. Soerjadi himself failed to win a seat. The election victory appeared to leave President Suharto firmly in control of the political order, and the formal process leading to Suharto's nomination for a seventh term as President began in October. However, social tensions evident before the election resulted in serious unrest, including anti-Chinese violence in several parts of the country.

Meanwhile, Indonesia was being drawn steadily into the regional economic crisis that had begun in Thailand in mid-1997. Although the decline in the value of the rupiah was partly a consequence of 'contagion' from the rest of the region, it was also exacerbated by international concerns over the high levels of indebtedness among large Indonesian companies, many of which were associated with President Suharto's circle. The decline in the rupiah worsened the debt crisis, forcing Indonesia to request assistance from the IMF in October. However, the resulting IMF rescue programme was much more radical than the Government had expected, demanding a substantial limitation of the privileges enjoyed by Suharto's family and friends and also a reduction in government expenditure in areas that were an important source of patronage, both within and outside élite circles.

The crisis had immediate and extensive implications for the economy. External credit for Indonesian companies became unavailable, and firms were unable to obtain finance for routine operations. Factories and construction projects were closed down, forcing millions of workers out of employment. The price of imported goods (including staples such as wheat flour) rose dramatically, compounding the hardship. Unrest spread rapidly, precipitating riots in dozens of cities and towns across the archipelago. Shops and other businesses owned by members of the Chinese community were especially targeted. The crisis worsened as it became clear that the Suharto Government was resisting implementation of the IMF programme. In the last week of January 1998 the markets drove the rupiah down to an unprecedented 17,000 to the US dollar, after Suharto indicated that he would choose as his Vice-President the Minister of State for Research and Technology, Prof. Dr Ir Bucharuddin Jusuf (B. J.) Habibie, whose reputation as a proponent of economic nationalism and expensive technological projects ran directly counter to the IMF's insistence on economic austerity and openness.

There was hope that the President would respond to the obvious discontent with imaginative and responsible measures, but also fear of cataclysmic disorder if he were to step down. On 10 March 1998 Suharto was duly re-elected as President. Habibie was installed as Vice-President. Following his election victory, Suharto sought to strengthen his position by appointing a Cabinet that concentrated power in his immediate circle of friends and family, and promoting loyalists to senior positions within the military.

The composition of the new Cabinet, together with the fact that the main points of continuing dispute between the IMF and the Suharto Government concerned the economic privileges that continued to be enjoyed by Suharto's family members and associates, largely eliminated any hopes that Suharto himself might permit significant political and economic reforms in Indonesia. Evidence of widespread discontent was emerging, expressed first in a growing number of student demonstrations in the cities and subsequently in riots across the archipelago. Meanwhile, the political opposition to Suharto grew more confident, with Dr Amien Rais, Chairman of the modernist Muhammadiyah, the country's second largest Islamic organization, taking a particularly prominent role. In a process reminiscent of the events of 1965, disparate opposition groups attempted to disregard their differences and adopted a single slogan, *reformasi* (reform), as a code for the simple goal of removing Suharto from office. As the popular movement against Suharto gathered momentum, signs of disunity began to appear within the military.

On 5 May 1998, when the Government announced a 70% increase in fuel prices as part of its agreement with the IMF to reduce state subsidies, the violence escalated abruptly. As in January, the main targets of the violence were members of Indonesia's ethnic Chinese minority. In April and early May tens of thousands of Chinese Indonesians fled to neighbouring Singapore and Malaysia in search of refuge from the violence.

Within days of the riots of 5 May, members of the legislature and senior officials from within the regime began to demand immediate reform. Some military units were even seen greeting student protesters enthusiastically and protecting them from riot police. Street violence in Jakarta reached a peak on 14 May, when armed gangs took control of large parts of the city. An estimated 500 people died; 3,000 buildings were burnt and many thousands of vehicles were destroyed. A further 700 people were reported to have been killed in other centres.

On 18 May 1998, his former supporter, Harmoko, Golkar Chairman and Speaker of the Legislature, astounded observers by demanding the President's resignation and by then publicly threatening Suharto with impeachment if he failed to step down. Suharto endeavoured to recover the initiative by offering immediate political reforms, including the appointment of a new Cabinet, and the holding of an election in early 1999, followed by an MPR session to elect a new President; he also reversed the fuel price increase, the original announcement of which had precipitated the worst disturbances. Although these pledges won the apparent support of Gen. Wiranto, the Armed Forces' commander, and of Abdurrahman Wahid, both of whom feared that instability would ensue if Suharto were to resign abruptly, they failed to appease the protest movement. Finally, following the resignation from the Cabinet of 14 ministers with responsibility for various sectors of the economy on the evening of 20 May, Gen. Wiranto visited the President to inform him that the military could no longer guarantee security in Jakarta if he remained in office. On the following morning Suharto announced his resignation. Vice-President Habibie was sworn in immediately as his successor, and Gen. Wiranto promised to defend Suharto and his family.

PRESIDENT B. J. HABIBIE, 1998–99

Suharto's resignation certainly saved Indonesia from even greater turmoil; however, it also raised new uncertainties. President Habibie's relations with the armed forces were considered poor, and his capacity to manage the economy was doubted in view of his reputation for promoting prestigious but costly projects. He was also widely perceived as a protégé of his predecessor and possibly susceptible to continuing manipulation by Suharto. In the event, Habibie managed his first months in office rather astutely, balancing the continuing demand for reform against the power of entrenched interests. He at once dubbed his Government the 'Reform Order', and supported Gen. Wiranto in his dismissal of Suharto's son-in-law, Gen. Prabowo, from his command position in the army's strategic reserve, KOSTRAD (Prabowo was dismissed from the armed forces in August 1998 and spent several years in effective exile in Jordan). Habibie also released prominent political prisoners, encouraged government departments to sever their business links with enterprises owned by the Suharto family, and prepared the way for electoral reform, with the announcement that new elections would take place in 1999. In June the Government announced a liberalization of the censorship laws and an investigation into the wealth of state officials. However, both the extent and the timetable of most of these reforms fell short of the demands that students and others had made of the Suharto regime, and there was widespread impatience with the pace of change under Habibie.

In the early days of his presidency, Habibie announced that he would not serve out the remainder of Suharto's term (1998–2003), and he called a special session of the MPR on 10–13 November 1998 to authorize the holding of new legislative elections. The MPR amended the Constitution to limit future Presidents and Vice-Presidents to a maximum of two five-year terms of office each. It also decreed that the number of seats in the House of Representatives (Dewan Perwakilan Rakyat—DPR) held by nominated representatives of the military should be reduced, and provided for the establishment of an independent Commission on General Elections (Komisi Pemilihan Umum—KPU), within which all contesting parties would be represented, to oversee the poll. However, greatest attention focused on the revised election laws. Under these statutes, candidates were required to be 'loyal to the *Pancasila*' and the PKI remained banned. In contrast with previous elections, at which government employees had been compelled to support Golkar, the new laws prohibited Indonesia's 4.1m. civil servants on active duty from campaigning. In addition, the armed forces announced that they would maintain neutrality in the election.

Following intense debate and vehement student protests, the DPR agreed to reduce the number of seats in the legislature allocated to the military from 75 to 38; in addition, the military presence in provincial and district assemblies was reduced from 20% to 10%. It was also announced that the membership of the MPR was to be reduced from 1,000 to 700 (500 of whom would comprise the members of the DPR while, of the remainder, 135 were to be elected by the provincial assemblies and 65 appointed by the KPU to represent social and professional organizations).

Soon after May 1998, in anticipation of the new laws, political parties began to form on a wide variety of ideological, ethnic and religious bases. By early 1999 more than 200 new parties had been created; however, only 48 met the criteria for competing in the forthcoming election. Most observers agreed that Megawati's wing of the PDI, reconstituted as the PDI—Perjuangan (PDI—P; Indonesian Democratic Struggle Party) would perform well, and that the Partai Kebangkitan Bangsa (PKB—National Awakening Party) of Abdurrahman Wahid had a secure base among the traditionalist rural Muslims of East and Central Java; however, the potential of the other parties, including Golkar, remained uncertain. Particularly unclear was whether Golkar's prestige as the party of government would help it to survive the loss of military and civil service support and the defection of former supporters to new parties. This uncertainty bedevilled attempts by the parties to anticipate the kind of partners they might seek to work with after the election, in the likely event that no party won a majority. A semi-formal alliance of party leaders Megawati, Amien Rais, who now led the Partai Amanat Nasional (PAN—National Mandate Party, formed in 1998), and Abdurrahman Wahid soon showed signs of serious strains.

Meanwhile, serious violence broke out in several parts of the country, and sectarian tensions grew (see below). In Jakarta in mid-November 1998, in the worst violence since the riots of May, at least 16 people were killed and more than 400 injured when students and civilians clashed with soldiers outside the MPR building. Further riots occurred in Jakarta in late November, in which at least another 14 people died during confrontations between Muslims and Christians.

In an attempt to reduce the military's association with petty repression, the police force (part of the military since 1962) was formally separated from the armed forces on 1 April 1999. The armed forces also resumed their revolutionary-era name, Tentara Nasional Indonesia (TNI—the Indonesian National Defence Forces), in place of the Suharto-era name, ABRI (the Armed Forces of the Republic of Indonesia).

Although the election campaign dominated politics during the first half of 1999, the Habibie Government continued an extensive programme of reform. In April the DPR approved radical new decentralization laws. These provided for the election of district heads (*bupati*) by the district assemblies, rather than through appointment by Jakarta, transferred a wide range of administrative functions to the provinces and districts (*kabupaten* and *kotamadya*), and allocated to districts a much greater share of revenue from natural resources such as oil, gas, fisheries and timber.

The day on which the polls were held, 7 June 1999, was declared a public holiday in order to eliminate any potential intimidation of voters by their employers. Approximately 118m. people voted (a turn-out of 91%). The final results of the poll were not announced until mid-July. Foreign observers and most Indonesian monitoring groups pronounced the election itself fair, despite the delay in finalizing the outcome. The slow accumulation of voting tallies allowed the public to adjust to some unexpected results: although Megawati's PDI—P led the poll as expected, with 34% of the votes, its nearest rival proved to be Golkar, whose poor performance in much of Java was balanced by the achievement of impressive results in the outer islands, especially in eastern Indonesia. Although Golkar received 20% of the national vote, the weighting given to outer islands meant that the party won 120 seats (26% of the total) compared with the PDI—P's 154. Abdurrahman Wahid's

PKB did well in East Java, but the PAN of Amien Rais performed below expectations, receiving only 7% of the vote. In third place in the poll was the PPP, the principal Muslim party of the Suharto era, with 11% of the vote and 59 seats. Under its new chairman, Hamzah Haz, the party sought to adapt its image from one of being a largely compliant participant in the 'New Order' system to being a staunch advocate of Islamism and the implementation of Islamic law. In addition to these five parties, some 14 smaller parties won seats in the MPR (although their combined share of the vote was only about 7%). A number of small parties, some of which had failed to win a seat, withheld formal ratification of the election results, but they were subsequently overruled by President Habibie, who finally endorsed the results on 3 August.

During the election campaign, each of the parties nominated a preferred candidate for the presidency, which was originally scheduled to be decided by the MPR in November 1999. With the PDI—P and Golkar leading the polls, Megawati and Habibie initially emerged as the main candidates for the presidency. However, Habibie's prospects were seriously damaged by factionalism within Golkar and by allegations that he had helped to channel funds originally intended for the recapitalization of the struggling Bank Bali into his wing of Golkar. He was also widely perceived to have mishandled the issue of East Timor (now Timor-Leste): many Indonesians felt that the country had been humiliated by the overwhelming vote in favour of independence by the East Timorese in August 1999 and by the subsequent introduction of foreign peacekeeping troops into the territory. Megawati's prospects, meanwhile, were impaired by her apparent remoteness: she made few public speeches during the election campaign and showed no interest in lobbying other parties for support. Concealed threats from PDI—P members that there would be violence if she were not elected, and indications of 'money politics' in the PDI—P also raised doubts about Megawati's capacity to improve the standards of government if she were to come to power. Megawati's position was further weakened by the public statements of some Muslim leaders, including Abdurrahman Wahid, to the effect that a woman should not become President in a predominantly Muslim country.

Meanwhile, Amien Rais recovered from his electoral setback by assembling a coalition of Muslim parties called Poros Tengah (Central Axis), which aimed to give its member parties a powerful collective voice in the proceedings, as a means of exerting pressure with a view to increasing future influence in government. As the date of the MPR vote approached, both Habibie and Megawati appeared increasingly unlikely to succeed; however, no clear alternatives had emerged. On 20 October 1999, only hours before the rescheduled vote was due to take place, Habibie withdrew his candidacy, following the rejection of his presidential accountability speech by the MPR in a secret ballot. Poros Tengah and much of Golkar then transferred their support to Abdurrahman Wahid, even though Wahid's party, the PKB, was not part of the Poros Tengah coalition. Wahid was subsequently elected President by the MPR, securing a total of 373 votes; Megawati received 313 votes. The announcement of Wahid's victory provoked outrage among Megawati's supporters, leading to violence in Jakarta and elsewhere. On 21 October, however, the MPR voted to appoint Megawati as Vice-President.

PRESIDENT ABDURRAHMAN WAHID, 1999–2001

President Wahid's new Cabinet, announced on 26 October 1999, was large (consisting of 36 members) and was drawn from many parties, reflecting both Wahid's desire to include in the new political order all the major forces in Indonesian society and to discharge the political debts he had incurred in winning the presidency. However, Poros Tengah, with more than one-third of the seats in the DPR, secured half the posts in the Cabinet, whereas Golkar, which held one-quarter of the elected seats in the DPR, was allocated only four positions in the Cabinet. Many observers questioned whether such a diverse and unwieldy Cabinet, led by a President who was blind and in ill health, would be capable of effectively addressing the country's pressing economic problems. None the less, President Wahid's tolerant, inclusive style of leadership initially raised hopes for an easing of the political tensions that had developed during and after the Suharto era. Wahid's credentials as an opposition leader during the Suharto era were strong, but he made it clear that he had no interest in avenging the wrongs of the 'New Order'; as a pious Muslim he was acceptable to Islamic modernists, but he also had a strong record of respect and tolerance for other religious traditions. Habibie had removed a ban on the use of the Mandarin Chinese language in public places, and Wahid took further measures to reintegrate the Chinese community into Indonesian political and cultural life, ending restrictions on the public celebration of Chinese festivals. He also included a Chinese Indonesian, Kwik Kian Gie, in his Cabinet, in the senior post of Co-ordinating Minister for Economic Affairs. The President abolished the Ministries of Information and Social Affairs (both of which had been closely associated with the Suharto-era apparatus for the political control of society). While the new President attempted a radical reform of the notoriously corrupt judiciary, he achieved only limited success in reducing the political power of the military. Gen. Wiranto became Co-ordinating Minister for Political, Legal and Security Affairs, and six members of the new Cabinet had a military background, although a civilian, Juwono Sudarsono, held the post of Minister of Defence, and for the first time a naval officer, Adm. Widodo Adi Sutjipto, was appointed Commander-in-Chief of the Armed Forces. The number of military officers included in the presidential staff was also greatly reduced.

However, the President's commitment to regularizing the political order was undermined by his own idiosyncratic political style. His public statements were often impulsive, contradictory and made without consulting his advisers or Cabinet. In November 1999, only a month after installing the Cabinet, Wahid dismissed the Co-ordinating Minister for People's Welfare, and PPP leader, Hamzah Haz, on unspecified charges of corruption, which were never pursued. The President appeared to veer between detachment from the process of government and undue intervention in administrative detail. Meanwhile, those who had hoped that Vice-President Megawati would take a more active role than her predecessors were disappointed, as she continued her inactive approach to politics.

In early 2000 Wahid removed Gen. Wiranto from his powerful cabinet position after Indonesia's National Human Rights Commission at the end of January found him responsible for the violence that had followed East Timor's referendum on independence in August 1999. Travelling in Europe and Asia at the time, the President announced that he had asked Wiranto to resign. However, Wiranto resisted and, amid rumours of the possibility of a military coup, Wahid agreed in February 2000 to allow him to retain his post until the Attorney-General had investigated the issue. Nevertheless, the Cabinet Secretary announced that Wiranto had been suspended from his position. He was replaced by the Minister of Home Affairs, Gen. (retd) Suryadi Sudirja. Wiranto subsequently resigned in May.

Rivalry between ministers and lack of co-ordination between government departments became a serious problem. Moreover, allegations had begun to emerge of corruption and the abuse of power within the new Government. Many cabinet ministers appeared to be turning their departments into party fiefdoms, as had happened in the 1950s. In April 2000 President Wahid dismissed the Minister of State for Investment and Development of State Enterprises, Laksamana Sukardi of the PDI—P, and the Minister of Trade and Industry, Jusuf Kalla of the pro-Habibie wing of Golkar, later suggesting that both ministers were guilty of corruption. Such accusations had often been heard previously against Kalla. However, Sukardi was a respected and capable minister; his dismissal appeared to reflect the fact that he had pressed too hard for rapid reform and had thus lost support within his own party. Wahid shocked the legislature in July when he uncharacteristically refused to explain his reasons for dismissing the ministers. Misgivings also grew over the increasing business activities of Wahid's own organization, the NU, and of the President's brother, Hasyim Wahid, who, despite a lack of economic experience, had been secretly appointed adviser to the Indonesian Bank Restructuring Agency (IBRA). Still more disturbing was an affair in early 2000 in which the President's masseur,

Suwondo, was alleged to have solicited US $4.1m. from the deputy chief of the state logistical agency, BULOG. According to official accounts, the funds were a 'private' bribe paid to Suwondo by the deputy chief of the agency, who was subsequently dismissed from his post. The Sultan of Brunei was also reported to have illegally given $2m. to Wahid for unspecified purposes. Wahid's appointment of the NU Deputy Chairman, Rozy Munir, as Minister for State Enterprises also encouraged rumours that he intended to exploit those industries (traditionally a major source of corruption) for the PKB's use in future election campaigns.

By mid-2000 there was growing speculation over whether the forces unhappy with President Wahid's policies and style of leadership might combine to remove him from office. Wahid was summoned to give an account of his actions at the annual MPR session on 7–18 August, but escaped formal censure, as party leaders feared that action against him might precipitate mass unrest, and because they obtained what they believed was a promise from Wahid to relinquish some major policy-making powers to Megawati. However, with the MPR session safely over, he claimed that only 'administrative' duties, and not decision-making powers, were to be transferred to the Vice-President, and on 23 August 2000 he announced the formation of a new 26-member Cabinet. The incoming Cabinet included considerably fewer representatives of Megawati's PDI—P, reportedly resulting in serious tensions between the President and the Vice-President. Two of the most influential cabinet posts were allocated to Wahid loyalists: Gen. (retd) Susilo Bambang Yudhoyono was appointed Co-ordinating Minister for Political, Legal and Security Affairs, while Rizal Ramli was designated Co-ordinating Minister for Economic Affairs, replacing Kwik Kian Gie, who had previously resigned from the post.

During his first year in office Wahid attempted to establish greater control over the military by supporting the promotion of reforming officers, but these attempts generated a hostile reaction in military circles. The August 2000 session of the MPR was also perceived to have made a number of concessions to the military, including the introduction of a constitutional amendment that excluded military personnel from prosecution for crimes committed prior to the enactment of the legislation used to prosecute them; this particular amendment was feared by many international observers seriously to threaten the possibility of the prosecution of members of the Indonesian military believed responsible for recent human rights violations in the former province of East Timor. Legislation was also enacted to extend military representation in the MPR until 2009, four years after the date at which the military had been scheduled to lose its remaining 38 seats in the House.

However, even more important than reforms to the military was the process of administrative decentralization that took effect under Wahid's presidency. Planning for a greater delegation of authority to district and municipality governments (the administrative level below the provinces) had begun under Habibie. A specifically appointed State Minister for Regional Autonomy, Ryaas Rasyid, oversaw early preparations for decentralization. However, in one of Wahid's arbitrary changes of direction, Rasyid was transferred to an unrelated portfolio in August 2000. The decision to devolve authority to Indonesia's approximately 350 districts and municipalities, rather than to provinces, was taken to diminish the risk that the provinces might develop a desire for self-rule and attempt to secede, but it raised serious questions over the administrative capacity of such small units and over the likely social consequences for resource-poor districts. Popular aspirations, moreover, continued to focus on the provincial level, with public pressure leading to the establishment of three new provinces (Gorontalo, Banten and Bangka-Belitung) in late 2000, with strong campaigns under way for the creation of several more.

In early August 2000 former President Suharto was formally charged with corruption arising from his 30 years in power. However, in late September all corruption charges against him were dismissed after he was declared mentally and physically unfit to stand trial. In mid-September, meanwhile, President Wahid announced that he had ordered the arrest of Suharto's youngest son, Tommy. Supporters of the former President and his family were suspected of involvement in a series of bomb threats and explosions in Jakarta in August and September. In one attack in mid-September at least 15 people were killed when a bomb exploded at the Jakarta Stock Exchange. The police declined to arrest Tommy without evidence, whereupon President Wahid sought to dismiss the police chief. Tommy was later sentenced to 18 months' imprisonment on separate corruption charges, but disappeared before he could be detained. In July 2001 Syafiuddin Kartasasmita, the judge who had sentenced Tommy, was assassinated by apparently professional gunmen in Jakarta. The gunmen later admitted in custody that they had been paid by Tommy, who was subsequently placed on trial (see below).

In February 2001 the DPR formally censured Wahid over the BULOG and Brunei corruption allegations, thus initiating his formal dismissal. The dismissal process was accompanied by demonstrations by both opponents and supporters of Wahid. In May the DPR issued a second formal memorandum claiming unsatisfactory performance on the part of Wahid (just two days previously he had been cleared of corruption charges in the Brunei and BULOG scandals by the Attorney-General, Marzuki Darusman), and on this basis requested the MPR to convene a special session to impeach the President. Since the MPR was in practice a somewhat augmented DPR, the working body of the assembly agreed, calling the session for 1 August. Wahid responded by describing the DPR's action as unconstitutional and threatening that his supporters would resort to violence. He reorganized his Cabinet on 3 June and again on 12 June; the first reallocation of portfolios was a major reorganization that removed Yudhoyono and the second led to the replacement of his Minister for Finance, Prijadi Praptosuharjo. The President also attempted to dismiss the head of the national police, Gen. Surojo Bimantoro, although Wahid made no attempt to obtain the requisite approval of the DPR and Bimantoro subsequently refused to accept his dismissal.

The President announced on 9 July 2001 that he would declare a state of emergency on 20 July if a compromise were not reached. However, the declaration was not made on the latter date, and Wahid merely delayed the deadline for reconciliation to 31 July, the day before the impeachment hearing before the MPR. A special session convened on 21 July, but was boycotted by Wahid's PKB and the small Christian party, Partai Demokrasi Kasih Bangsa (PDKB). The assembly speaker, Amien Rais, requested the President to deliver an account of his actions, to which Wahid replied that the session was illegal and that he would not attend. He separately met military MPR representatives and threatened them with dismissal if they continued to support the session. In the early hours of 23 July Wahid declared a state of civil emergency, tried to suspend the MPR, the DPR, and Golkar, and announced that new elections would be held within a year. Later that morning, however, the Supreme Court issued an advisory opinion that the President's declaration was illegal, while the chief of the Jakarta police force announced that he would accept orders only from the Vice-President and would protect the security of the MPR session. The MPR itself then declared that the President had no constitutional authority to attempt to suspend it and that he had violated his oath of office in attempting to do so; Amien Rais demanded an immediate impeachment hearing. That afternoon the assembly formally voted unanimously to dismiss Abdurrahman Wahid and to elevate Megawati Sukarnoputri to the country's presidency. Three days later the PPP leader, Hamzah Haz, defeated four other candidates, including the Golkar leader, Akbar Tandjung, and former Co-ordinating Minister for Political, Legal and Security Affairs Yudhoyono, for election as Vice-President. Although Hamzah Haz had been among those rejecting a female president on Islamic principles in 1999, he appeared to be Megawati's preferred candidate and received strong PDI—P support in the ballot.

PRESIDENT MEGAWATI SUKARNOPUTRI, 2001–04

Delays in the announcement of the composition of the new Government led to widespread fears that Megawati was already being weakened by the bargaining among the various power groups. However, when the membership of the incoming

Cabinet was made public on 9 August 2001, it incorporated an impressive blend of technocratic skill and political connections. Yudhoyono returned as Co-ordinating Minister for Political, Legal and Security Affairs, with Dorodjatun Kuntjoro-Jakti as Co-ordinating Minister for Economic Affairs and Jusuf Kalla as Co-ordinating Minister for People's Welfare. However, many observers were disappointed with her selection as Attorney-General of M. A. Rachman, generally described as unremarkable. Reform of Indonesia's notoriously corrupt legal system was widely considered essential for the restoration of domestic and international confidence in the country.

None the less, Megawati's election brought with it a powerful sense of relief and hope for stability and reconciliation. Her placid personality appeared to satisfy a widespread desire that the President should play a moderating role after the tumult of the Wahid period. However, the Government was seriously constrained by a lack of revenue, as a result of which the implementation of many desirable measures remained beyond its capacity. The radical decentralization of 1 January 2001 had also succeeded in placing many important areas of policy beyond the reach of the central Government. In November the MPR agreed to amend the Constitution to provide for the direct election of the President and Vice-President, for a constitutional court to review legislation and for a bicameral legislature, with a new upper house representing the regions. In August 2002 the MPR finally approved more detailed plans providing for the direct election of the President: provision was made for the establishment of an electoral process whereby, if no candidate polled more than 50% of the votes, a second round of voting would be held. It was also decided that the 38 seats reserved for the military within the legislature would be abolished by 2004, five years ahead of the previously established schedule. The new electoral procedure removed the system of preferential weighting of seats in sparsely populated provinces outside Java; the representation of the province of Papua in the MPR would thus decline from 13 seats to five. However, requests for the introduction of Islamic law were rejected.

Early in her term, Megawati aroused fears that she would reverse some of the reforms made during the Habibie and Wahid presidencies. In January 2002 the Government announced that the payment period granted to major shareholders of failed banks—all of them associates of Suharto—would be extended to 10 years, meaning that these debts were unlikely ever to be repaid (this decision was reversed in March). The Ministry of Information, which had sought to manage public access to news under Suharto and which had been abolished by Habibie, was to some extent re-established in the form of the State Ministry of Communications and Information in August 2001. Shortly after Megawati came to power, moreover, the authorities arrested a number of activists under laws against 'sowing hatred' from the colonial era, which had not been used since the fall of Suharto. During 2003 several people were charged with the colonial-era offence of insulting the head of state, which Suharto had often invoked to protect his dignity. Megawati surprised observers in July 2001 by establishing ad hoc human rights tribunals to try TNI members for excesses in Tanjung Priok in 1984 and in East Timor between April and August 1999. Over time, however, her Government seemed to become less sympathetic to the ideals of an open society. A new Broadcasting Law, approved in November 2002, restored government censorship of films and advertisements, restricted foreign ownership and content, and required the fragmentation of private television companies into several local stations. A new armed forces bill, presented to the legislature in February 2003, gave the Commander-in-Chief of the Armed Forces the authority to deploy troops anywhere in the country to meet an emergency without previous approval from the President.

In August 2002 the Indonesian judiciary was subjected to widespread international condemnation when the special tribunal returned its first verdicts relating to the violence in East Timor. While Abílio Soares, the last Indonesian Governor of East Timor, was convicted and given a three-year prison term for gross human rights violations, a sentence criticized for its leniency, the former Chief of Police in East Timor, Timbul Silaen, and five other officers were acquitted of all the charges against them. A further four Indonesian security officials were acquitted of similar charges in November, whereas the East Timorese militia leader, Eurico Guterres, was found guilty of crimes against humanity and sentenced to 10 years in prison. The verdicts prompted criticism that only East Timorese were being found guilty and demands from human rights organizations for UN intervention in the process. In February 2003 the UN indicted 32 people, including 16 soldiers, for crimes against humanity in East Timor. (See the chapter on Timor-Leste for further details.)

Indonesia's dysfunctional legal system continued to be a major issue. Tommy Suharto remained at large for 12 months following his conviction on corruption charges. While a fugitive, he was declared to be the main suspect in the murder of Justice Syafiuddin Kartasasmita, one of the Supreme Court judges who had found him guilty. In October 2001, however, the Supreme Court overruled Tommy's conviction and, in the following month, Tommy was finally arrested. In March 2002 he stood trial, charged with possession of weapons and with ordering the murder of Kartasasmita. During the trial, which was broadcast on both television and radio, Tommy boasted that the police had helped him to visit his family regularly during his flight. One of Tommy's lawyers was herself charged with trying to bribe prosecution witnesses, and the Jakarta police officer who had arrested him was investigated for smuggling luxury cars into Indonesia. Tommy was found guilty in July and sentenced to 15 years in prison. (His sentence was subsequently reduced, and in November 2006 he was released on medical grounds, following which he returned to business activities.)

In March 2002 Akbar Tandjung, Speaker of the DPR and Chairman of Golkar, was arrested and put on trial on charges of sequestering funds for his party's election campaign from the state logistical agency, BULOG. During the course of the trial, it emerged that most of the parties had received a share of these illegal BULOG funds, said to amount to US $350m. In September Tandjung was found guilty of misusing state funds and sentenced to three years in prison, but in February 2004 the Supreme Court overruled his conviction. Meanwhile, the Governor of Bank Indonesia, the central bank, Syahril Sabirin, was sentenced to a three-year prison term in March 2002 for his role in the Bank Bali scandal (see above). However, many of these trials and investigations were criticized: in some cases, the defendants seemed to have been selected for political reasons; in others the charges appeared to have been chosen in order to increase the possibility of an acquittal or to minimize the severity of the eventual sentence. The criticism was to some extent borne out in August 2002 when the Court of Appeal overruled Sabirin's conviction for corruption. Sabirin had retained his position as Governor throughout the appeals process.

In December 2003 Megawati appointed a new Corruption Eradication Commission (Komisi Pemberantasan Korupsi—KPK), chaired by Taufiequrrachman Ruki. In its first six months the KPK received more than 500 complaints and began a number of major investigations, including one into allegations against the Governor of Aceh, Abdullah Puteh. Trials conducted on the basis of these investigations became possible only after Megawati installed an ad hoc corruption court in July 2004. However, the most noteworthy action against corruption was the conviction, in May 2004, of 43 members of the 55-seat West Sumatran provincial legislature on charges of embezzlement from the funds of the 2002 provincial budget; the defendants each received prison terms of up to two years and three months.

The 2004 legislative election took place on 5 April, and there was no indication of systematic fraud or manipulation. The island of Java, containing 59% of the 147m. eligible voters, elected just over one-half of the seats in the new legislature. Furthermore, one of the first decisions taken by the new Constitutional Court, which had been established in August 2003 following a constitutional amendment, was to rescind a regulation prohibiting those accused of 'direct or indirect involvement' in the 1965 coup from standing as candidates. This regulation, which encompassed the family members of people with connections to the former PKI and its associated organizations, was said to affect between 10m. and 20m.

people. The authorities announced that they had no intention of rescinding the 30 or so other regulations that discriminated against former communists and their families, and that the teaching of communism remained illegal.

The result of the legislative election significantly altered President Megawati's position. Her PDI—P received only 18.5% of the votes cast, to take 109 of the 550 seats in the DPR (down from 33.7% in 1999), and came second after Golkar, which secured 21.6% (a result similar to that which it had achieved at the previous election), taking 128 seats. The result both confirmed the public's loss of enthusiasm for Megawati and suggested that voters would turn instead to new parties, rather than revert to Golkar as a nostalgic representative of the stability and prosperity of the 'New Order'. Two new parties performed particularly well in the election. These were the Partai Demokrat (PD) of the former Co-ordinating Minister for Political, Legal and Security Affairs Yudhoyono, which obtained 7.5% of the votes, and the Partai Keadilan Sejahtera (PKS—Prosperous Justice Party), an Islamist party whose members took a strong stand against corruption, which received 7.4%. The PKS headed the poll in Jakarta, where the PD also did well. Golkar's strength remained in the outer islands, while the PDI—P performed best in Central and East Java and Bali. Other parties that had achieved a significant share of the vote in 1999—Abdurrahman Wahid's PKB, the PPP of Vice-President Hamzah Haz and the PAN of Amien Rais—all experienced a slight decline in votes.

The election of 2004 gave rise to a national legislature that was bestowed with a greater level of power than any witnessed since the 1950s. The legislature no longer included any members from East Timor (now Timor-Leste) and, for the first time, none of the bodies contained nominated members or representatives of the armed forces or police. The number of parties represented decreased from 32 to 25. Moreover, a new legislative chamber, the Dewan Perwakilan Daerah (DPD—House of Representatives of the Regions), which comprised four representatives from each of the country's provinces, was also established. Although having the form of a Senate, the DPD's functions were limited to proposing and reviewing legislation related to the position of the regions in national governance. The DPD subsequently became increasingly frustrated by its lack of specific powers and perceived marginalization by the DPR, pressing for constitutional amendments to allow it a greater legislative and monitoring role. The MPR, Indonesia's supreme decision-making body under the Constitution, was henceforth to be constituted by a joint sitting of the DPR and the DPD.

The result of the legislative election was rapidly overshadowed by the campaign for the forthcoming presidential election. Five teams of candidates for the posts of President and Vice-President competed in this election. (A sixth team, with former President Abdurrahman Wahid as a candidate, was ruled invalid by the KPU under a rule that required all candidates to pass a medical test.) Yudhoyono recruited as his vice-presidential candidate Jusuf Kalla, who had been one of the seven candidates for the Golkar nomination. Megawati chose the NU leader, Ahmad Hasyim, in place of Vice-President Hamzah Haz, who stood in his own right with the Minister of Transportation and Telecommunications, Lt-Gen. (retd) Agum Gumelar. Amien Rais was the candidate of the PAN, with Siswono Yudohusodo as his deputy. Gen. Wiranto, with Solahuddin Wahid (younger brother of Abdurrahman Wahid and former deputy chairman of the National Human Rights Commission), was Golkar's candidate.

The strong performance of the PD in the legislative election especially strengthened the presidential prospects of Yudhoyono. He had not been directly associated with either human rights abuses or corruption in the Suharto era and increasingly projected an image of competence and commitment to democracy. His candidacy had been confirmed when he resigned from his cabinet position as Co-ordinating Minister for Political, Legal and Security Affairs in March 2004, claiming that President Megawati had failed to include him in her decision-making. Most opinion polls soon showed Yudhoyono to be the leading contender, although his campaign was hampered by the lack of a strong party organization. In the first round of the presidential election, held on 5 July 2004, he received 33.6% of the votes cast, with Megawati in second place with 26.6%, while Wiranto received 22.2% of the votes. Some 32m. of those eligible failed to vote, a significant increase on the 23.5m. who had declined to vote in the legislative election of April. With no candidate securing more than the requisite 50% of the votes, the result necessitated a second round of voting, between Yudhoyono and Megawati, which was held on 20 September. In early October Yudhoyono was declared the winner of the country's first direct presidential election, having received 61% of the votes cast. Yudhoyono achieved this victory despite the formation of the Nationhood Coalition (Koalisi Kebangsaan), consisting of Golkar, the PDI—P, the PPP and a few smaller parties, to oppose him in the final stages of the campaign.

PRESIDENT SUSILO BAMBANG YUDHOYONO, 2004–

Megawati showed little grace as outgoing President, delaying her acknowledgement of Yudhoyono's victory, declining to cooperate in a smooth transfer and failing to attend the new President's inauguration on 20 October 2004. Megawati also allocated herself accommodation to the value of US $2m. just before stepping down. The composition of the new Cabinet was announced on the following day, although Megawati had preempted her successor by seeking to appoint the uncompromising Gen. Ryamizard Ryacudu as Commander-in-Chief of the Armed Forces in the final days of her presidency; the appointment was ultimately thwarted by Yudhoyono. There was praise for Yudhoyono's appointment of Muhammad Abdurrahman Saleh to the post of Attorney-General; as a Supreme Court judge, Saleh had been the sole member of the Court to uphold the conviction of Akbar Tandjung for misappropriating state funds. However, the new Co-ordinating Minister for Political, Legal and Security Affairs, Adm. (retd) Widodo Adi Sutjipto, was not known for progressive political views, and the incoming Co-ordinating Minister for Economic Affairs, Aburizal Bakrie, was a businessman who was reported to have a bad record of debt repayment.

Many observers were concerned that the Nationhood Coalition, which held exactly one-half of the seats in the legislature, would obstruct Yudhoyono's programme and undermine his administration. His own People's Coalition (Koalisi Kerakyatan), built around his DP, the PAN and the PKS, was considerably smaller (although after the election it was boosted by the defection of the PPP from the Nationhood Coalition in order to join Yudhoyono's side in the legislature). Within Golkar, there was growing unease at the oppositional role under Akbar Tandjung. Theirs being traditionally a party of government, the cadres of which had come to expect career and patronage opportunities from political service, some Golkar leaders began pressing for a change of direction. At the Golkar national congress held in Bali in December 2004, Kalla decisively defeated the pro-Megawati Akbar Tandjung in the contest for the party leadership. Kalla immediately steered Golkar into supporting the Yudhoyono Government, giving the ruling coalition a nominal majority in the legislature. As with most post-Suharto governing alliances, legislators from parties supporting Yudhoyono frequently criticized and sometimes voted against the Government, although this did not threaten its survival. An instance of this occurred in March 2005 when seven parliamentary parties joined forces to secure the passage of a motion summoning Yudhoyono to account for his decision to remove fuel price subsidies. The legislature was unable to bring about a change in government policy, but the motion indicated that members could combine effectively against the President on populist issues.

On 26 December 2004 an earthquake off the north-west coast of Sumatra, measuring 9.0 on the scale of magnitude, led to a series of tsunamis that devastated the northern and western coastal regions of Aceh province, including the capital, Banda Aceh. The number of resultant deaths in Indonesia was estimated conservatively at 132,000, with another 37,000 missing and some 100,000 injured. The number of people displaced by the tsunami disaster probably exceeded 700,000, some 60,000 of whom were still living in tents almost two years after the event. A relatively high proportion of the victims were children and the elderly, who were more vulnerable to the force of the waves. The tsunami disaster heightened a growing perception that President Yudhoyono was less active than his supporters had formerly hoped and that Vice-President Kalla was a man of greater initiative; observers were surprised that it was Kalla, who formally had no powers under the Constitution, rather than Yudhoyono, who was responsible for removing the state of civil emergency in Aceh following the tsunami.

Anti-corruption efforts gathered pace from 2005, particularly as a result of the investigations of the KPK, and prosecutions mounted in special ad hoc anti-corruption courts. Prominent cases included that of the former Minister of Religious Affairs, Prof. Said Agil Munawwar, who in May 2006 was found guilty of corruption and imprisoned for seven years; and Abdullah Puteh, the Governor of Aceh, who was convicted in April 2005 of corruption pertaining to a US $12m. helicopter deal and was sentenced to 10 years' imprisonment. Throughout much of 2007 a corruption scandal surrounding a former cabinet minister of the Megawati administration, Rokhman Dahuri, attracted much media attention. Revelations about his extensive payments to a wide range of political and community leaders provided insights into Indonesia's pervasive culture of 'money politics'. Four members of the National Election Commission were imprisoned for bribery and corruption, and the Chief Justice of the Supreme Court was investigated but eventually cleared of accusations that he had accepted payments from Suharto's half-brother, Probosutedjo, to enter a not-guilty verdict in a corruption trial. Anti-corruption efforts also gained momentum in the provinces, with more than 1,000 senior regional officials and local politicians being placed under investigation. Some 330 local legislators were found guilty of corruption, including the 43 members of the West Sumatra legislature sentenced in 2004.

President Yudhoyono's popularity remained high for much of 2005 and 2006. From late 2006, however, several issues affected the Government. First, there was widespread criticism of the role of two senior ministers, State Secretary Yusril Ihza Mahendra and the Minister of Justice and Human Rights Affairs, Hamid Awaluddin, in helping Tommy Suharto to repatriate several million US dollars from British bank accounts. (Tommy Suharto was, at that time, in prison after being found guilty of ordering the murder of a Supreme Court judge—see above.) Second, the Government's handling of the mud flow crisis in the Sidoarjo district of East Java was widely criticized. In May 2006 mud began gushing from an oil well operated by Lapindo Brantas, a company within the extensive business interests of the Co-ordinating Minister for Public Welfare, Aburizal Bakrie. By mid-2007 the 'mud volcano' had become an environmental, economic and social catastrophe for East Java, having necessitated the relocation of more than 3,500 families and having severely disrupted road and rail links. Critics claimed that Bakrie had used his position within government to avoid paying compensation to victims, and in June President Yudhoyono ordered an acceleration of the process of compensation for those displaced by the disaster. Third, a succession of major transport accidents on land, sea and air, resulting in the loss of hundreds of lives, attracted severe criticism of the Government in general, and of the Minister of Transportation and Telecommunication, Hatta Radjasa, in particular. Responding to these criticisms, in May 2007 Yudhoyono reorganized his Cabinet, removing Yusril, Hamid and several other poorly performing ministers. The President unexpectedly retained Hatta Radjasa, but transferred him to the position of State Secretary.

From early 2008 perceived economic mismanagement also eroded the standing of the President and his Government. In May the Government responded to the sharp rise in the price of crude oil by increasing fuel prices by an average of 28%, claiming that it could no longer maintain the increasing budgetary cost of fuel subsidies. Accompanying the price rises was a new range of compensation measures, including cash allocations for poor families and collateral-free credit for small businesses. The Government's policies drew widespread criticism and provoked some street protests.

Meanwhile, the administration of Yudhoyono had inherited embarrassment over the discovery by a Dutch autopsy that the human rights activist Munir, who had died aboard a flight to the Netherlands in September 2004, had been poisoned with arsenic. As head of the Commission for Missing Persons and Victims of Violence (Komisi untuk Orang Hilang dan Korban Tindak Kekerasan—Kontras), Munir had played a major role in publicizing the kidnapping and presumed murder of activists both during and after the fall of Suharto, a role for which he had received many death threats. Following a protracted investigation and trial process, Pollycarpus Budihari Priyanto, a former pilot for Garuda Indonesia, the state airline, and an undercover intelligence agent, was finally found guilty in January 2008 of murdering Munir and sentenced to 20 years' imprisonment. More sensationally, Muchdi Purwoprandjono, the former deputy head of the State Intelligence Agency (Badan Intelijen Negara—BIN), was arrested on suspicion of directing the murder plot and was formally charged in July. BIN had long denied any involvement in Munir's poisoning and the Muchdi case was regarded by many non-governmental organizations (NGOs) and commentators as being a test case for the legal system in prosecuting senior intelligence and military officials. At the end of 2008, however, Muchdi was acquitted, and the Supreme Court rejected an appeal by the Attorney-General's office for a new trial. Muchdi later played a major role in the vice-presidential election campaign of his former military commander, Prabowo Subianto.

In 2008 new corruption scandals affected the political élite. The most prominent of these was a bribery case involving US $11m. paid by a central bank foundation to members of a DPR committee dealing with financial issues. In April of that year the Governor of Bank Indonesia, Burhanuddin Abdullah, was found guilty of corruption and given a prison sentence of five years. The scandal led to the arrest of two legislators being arrested, and two cabinet ministers, M. S. Ka'ban, the Minister of Forestry, and Paskah Suzetta, the Minister of State for National Development Planning, were also implicated. The President stated that he would dismiss the ministers only if they were charged by the KPK. In June 2009 Aulia Pohan, the father of President Yudhoyono's son-in-law and also a Bank Indonesia board member, was sentenced to four-and-a-half years' imprisonment. Meanwhile, another prominent case involved large payments to members of the DPR by the local Government of Bintan, a regency in Riau Islands province, Sumatra. One legislator was arrested by KPK officials while in the process of receiving a bribe in a hotel in April 2008, and was subsequently sentenced to a prison term of four years. Although corruption remained prevalent in 2010, the sheer volume of anti-corruption investigations was expected to have a deterrent effect and to result in a modest improvement in standards of governance.

Suharto died in late January 2008, aged 86, after several years of poor health. Public sympathy for him proved surprisingly strong, given the widespread support over the past decade for his prosecution for corruption and human rights abuses. Most sections of the political élite and the media were generous in their assessments of his career and achievements as head of state, and few chose to dwell upon the negative aspects of his rule. Many of the nation's political, business and military leaders, including President Yudhoyono, attended his funeral at the lavish Suharto family mausoleum.

During 2005–08 more than 300 direct elections were successfully held for provincial and district heads. Despite fears of violence, most elections proceeded relatively smoothly. While many serious candidates spent vast sums of money on campaigning, the results suggested that in many areas voters had retaliated against candidates and incumbents with poor records of probity and competence, instead supporting those who offered the prospect of economic prosperity and political stability. Few candidates who appealed to sectarian or ethnic sentiment were successful and, at mid-2007, no candidate from the military had been able to secure election.

Preparations for the 10th legislative election since independence, to be held in April 2009, were surrounded by controversy and confusion. The new membership of the KPU, installed in 2008, was dominated by former bureaucrats and contained only one member with experience in managing elections; numerous NGO and academic candidates of high standing and expertise were rejected by the parliamentary committee charged with selecting the commission's members. The KPU's competence drew repeated criticism from parties and commentators who accused it of mismanaging the logistical preparations for the elections and of issuing confusing or unworkable guidelines. A number of the KPU's regulations relating to how votes were to be counted were later overruled by both the Constitutional Court and the Supreme Courts. The 2008 Election Law, which had taken more than two years of intense negotiation to finalize, provided for an open-list proportional representation system in which electors could either vote for a party and thereby allow votes to be distributed to candidates according to that party's list, or vote for an individual candidate. There were to be multi-member electorates, as before, but any votes 'left over' after filling the quotas for seats within electorates would be aggregated at the provincial level and distributed in order to fill the remaining vacant seats. The new law also allowed 'local' parties to present candidates for provincial and district level legislatures in Aceh, alongside 'national' parties. The local Aceh parties could contest only in that province. A total of 38 'national' parties met the validation requirements to compete in the election, as did six 'local' Aceh parties.

Despite the often chaotic preparations, the legislative election was held as scheduled on 9 April 2009 and proceeded relatively smoothly and peacefully; 71% of the 171m. registered electors cast their vote, a lower rate of participation than the 84% recorded at the 2004 election but nevertheless a comparatively high turn-out by global standards. Nine parties exceeded the 2.5% threshold needed to obtain seats in the DPR. President Yudhoyono's PD emerged as the strongest party, winning 20.85% of the votes cast, a percentage three times higher than in 2004, thus enabling it to take 148 of the 560 seats. Nearly all other major parties suffered declines. Support for both Golkar and the PDI—P decreased by about five percentage points to 14.45% and 14.03%, respectively, giving them 108 and 93 seats; votes for the PAN, which garnered 42 seats, declined to 6.01% of the total, the PPP to 5.32% and the PKB to 4.94%. The only established party to increase its vote was the PKS, which took 7.88% of the votes and 59 seats. Only two of the more than 20 newly established parties passed the 2.5% threshold: the Partai Gerakan Indonesia Raya (Great Indonesia Movement Party—Gerindra), which received 4.45% of the votes, and the Partai Hati Nurani Rakyat (People's Conscience Party—Hanura), with 3.77%. Both parties were formed by prominent retired generals: Gerindra was founded by Prabowo Subianto, and Wiranto was the Chairman of Hanura.

The results of the legislative election served to advance Yudhoyono's presidential re-election campaign. Most reliable survey organizations put his popularity and approval ratings at well above 50% throughout early 2009, and he was widely regarded as almost unbeatable. Few were surprised when the President recorded a comprehensive victory at the first round of the direct presidential election held on 9 July. He had chosen as his vice-presidential candidate the Governor of Bank Indonesia, Prof. Dr Boediono, a respected technocrat with no connections to any political party. The choice of Boediono angered some of Yudhoyono's coalition partners, who had been hoping that he would select one of their own cadres for the vice-presidency. Despite a somewhat lacklustre campaign by the incumbent President and Boediono, they secured 60.8% of the votes cast. The other two pairs of candidates—Megawati and Prabowo, and Kalla and Wiranto—won 26.8% and 12.4%, respectively.

The extent of President Yudhoyono's victory was generally attributed to various factors. First and foremost was his credibility as an economic manager. Public opinion surveys repeatedly showed that economic issues were paramount in the minds of voters, and Yudhoyono's Government was seen to have handled difficult economic conditions well. A particular source of approval was the Government's policy of giving direct payments to poorer households to offset the impact of higher fuel and energy prices. The President was also credited with conducting a successful campaign against corruption and as having managed security and social problems reasonably effectively. In October Yudhoyono was inaugurated for his second term of office, with Boediono as Vice-President. The new Cabinet incorporated 10 ministers who had served in the previous administration.

Yudhoyono's Second Term

The beginning of Yudhoyono's second term was overshadowed by a controversial government rescue programme for a failing financial institution, PT Bank Century Tbk. The bank had defaulted on loan repayments in late 2008 and was declared insolvent by a government committee chaired by the Minister of Finance, Dr Sri Mulyani Indrawati, and including Boediono (in his capacity as the then Governor of Bank Indonesia) among its members. Legislators, the media and the general public alike queried the probity of the rescue programme, particularly following the revelation in late 2009 that it had cost taxpayers about US $720m.—more than four times the amount originally agreed by the Government and the DPR; critics suggested that the size of the rescue programme far exceeded the amount that had actually been required to stabilize the bank. Opposition parliamentarians argued that Boediono and Indrawati had abused their respective positions to protect the interests of Bank Century without first securing the approval of the DPR, and speculation was rife that some of the funds transferred had been misappropriated to support the election campaign of Yudhoyono and Boediono. A special parliamentary committee was formed in late 2009 to investigate the circumstances surrounding 'Centurygate', as the scandal had become known. Boediono, Indrawati and other senior officials involved in the rescue programme were interrogated by the committee, with the proceedings often broadcast live on national television. Opponents of the government takeover, including members of several parties within the ruling coalition, demanded the resignation of Boediono and Indrawati, both of whom denied any wrongdoing. In March 2010 the committee published its final report, in which it stated that it had found no evidence of Bank Century money being used to support any political campaign; however, it did criticize the decision-making process, including the actions of Boediono and Indrawati, and urged the Government to pursue the possibility of prosecutions. Yudhoyono responded by defending the rescue programme as 'essential to saving the banking system' and stated that he saw no need for legal action against Boediono or Indrawati. The KPK and the Attorney-General's office continued to investigate the legality of the rescue programme, but few observers expected any prosecutions to be made.

The political impact of Centurygate was considerable. Most obviously, the scandal almost ruptured the governing coalition. Yudhoyono's PD vigorously defended the rescue programme and was supported by the PKB, the PAN and eventually the PPP; however, Golkar and the PKS were highly critical of the takeover, and their members repeatedly targeted Boediono and Indrawati during the parliamentary inquiry. PD members were especially irate with regard to the role of Golkar Chairman and business magnate Aburizal Bakrie, whom they accused of conducting a vendetta against Indrawati over her refusal to protect his business interests during the 2008/09 global financial crisis. In May 2010 Indrawati announced that she was to resign as Minister of Finance in order to take up a senior World Bank position in the USA. Subsequent media reports suggested that she was disappointed at the lack of support shown to her by Yudhoyono during the height of the Centurygate controversy. Indrawati's departure was a setback for the Government's reform agenda, as she had been the most vocal of those ministers striving for greater transparency and economic restructuring. Within a day of Indrawati's resignation, Yudhoyono announced the appointment of her bitter rival, Bakrie, as chairman of a newly appointed coalition secretariat, in an initiative that was widely interpreted as intended to reconcile the PD and Golkar and thereby to stabilize the Government. In late May a senior banking executive, Agus Martowardojo, was appointed Minister of Finance.

Indrawati's departure was one of several developments in 2009–10 that prompted observers to question whether Indonesia's democratization and reform programme had stalled. There appeared to be concerted efforts by the legislature, the police and the Attorney-General's office to undermine the standing and independence of the KPK. In October 2009 police detained two deputy chairmen of the KPK on suspicion of graft but released them in the following month after a public outcry following the submission to the authorities of covert recordings of conversations between several people widely accepted to have been senior members of the police force and the Attorney-General's office; the recordings revealed that the speakers, angered by the KPK's successful investigation of numerous officials, intended to destroy its reputation. In early 2010 the Government proposed the elimination of direct elections for provincial governors, and also for deputy district heads, suggesting that instead they be appointed by local legislatures from the ranks of the bureaucracy. These measures were driven by concerns about the cost of local elections and the seeming ineffectiveness of many regional administrations, but they were also at variance with the principles that had guided Indonesia's electoral reform: that voters be allowed to choose their political leaders at each of the three levels of government. A proposal to amend the Constitution, put forward by DP legislator Ruhut Sitompul in August 2010, in order to allow Yudhoyono to seek re-election for a third term as President elicited an angry response from many Indonesians, who contended that the proposal represented a serious affront to the principles of democracy. Ruhut, by contrast, argued that there were no suitable candidates to replace Yudhoyono at the 2014 election. Following considerable public criticism of the proposal, the President sought to distance himself from the comments, stating that he would not lend his support to any such attempts to amend the Constitution.

The issue of corruption continued to be a prevalent concern, and in January 2011 Minister of Home Affairs Gamawan Fauzi acknowledged the Government's awareness of the scale of the problem, noting that some 155 regional leaders, including 17 current or former governors, had been named as suspects in investigations since 2004. The Government suffered a further set-back in this regard when, in April 2011, Muhammad Nazaruddin, the Treasurer of the PD, was accused of demanding US $2.8m. in bribes from a construction company in exchange for a contract to build athletes' accommodation during the Southeast Asian Games, which Indonesia was due to host in November. Nazaruddin denied any wrongdoing, accusing other legislators and PD officials of being involved in the scandal, including Yudhoyono's son and PD Secretary-General Edhie 'Ibas' Baskoro Yudhoyono and PD Chairman Anas Urbaningrum. Other allegations against Nazaruddin soon emerged, including a claim that he had paid $120,000 for unspecified purposes to the Secretary-General of the Constitutional Court. The PD's leadership was divided over the question of how to respond to the allegations against Nazaruddin. Anas's supporters were reluctant to act against Nazaruddin as he had been a major fund-raiser for them, while Yudhoyono and his supporters, who were increasingly critical of Anas, wanted Nazaruddin to be held to account. Nazaruddin was eventually dismissed from his role as PD Treasurer but was allowed to retain his parliamentary seat pending an investigation by the KPK into the claims against him. In May he fled overseas, but in August he was arrested in Colombia when he attempted to leave the country using a forged passport, and was extradited to Indonesia. The episode, and particularly the question of how Nazaruddin had been able to flee the country despite the gravity of the claims against him, caused significant damage to both the PD and the Yudhoyono administration, further calling into question the latter's commitment to the combating of public corruption.

A major reorganization of the Cabinet was announced in mid-October 2011. Gita Wirjawan, hitherto Chairman of the Investment Co-ordinating Board, replaced Mari Pangestu as Minister of Trade; Pangestu was transferred to the post of Minister of Culture and Tourism. Dahlan Iskan, the head of the state electricity company, was allocated responsibility for state-owned enterprises, and Amir Syamsuddin became Minister of Justice and Human Rights. Jero Watchik was appointed as Minister of Energy and Mineral Resources

SECTARIAN CONFLICT

From the late 1990s there was a substantial increase in communal violence. In Maluku violent clashes between Muslims and Christians broke out in early 1999, with several hundred deaths reported; a number of those who died were killed by the military, who were drafted into the region in an attempt to restore order. Meanwhile, in West Kalimantan, indigenous Dayaks resumed their pursuit of Madurese settlers, this time with support from the majority Malay population; by late March, more than 165 Madurese were reported to have been killed, with numerous reports of the mutilation and cannibalization of the bodies of many of the victims. Many thousands of Madurese fled the province.

The rise of communal violence in Maluku, where Christians and Muslims were in approximately equal numbers, was the most serious problem confronting the Wahid Government upon its assumption of office in late 1999. Hostility between the two communities was based partly on traditional rivalries, exacerbated by a rise of religious orthodoxy on both sides. Migration into the province by Muslim traders during recent decades and the growing administrative dominance of Muslim officials had also served to accentuate the Christians' increasing sense of being beleaguered. However, the violence was precipitated principally by rivalry between Christian and Muslim gangs in Jakarta and in the provincial capital, Ambon, and then exacerbated by rumours of the massacre, rape and torture of members of each religious community and the desecration of places of worship. Sporadic violence following the fall of Suharto developed into a local civil war, with Christian and Muslim militias launching attacks on each other's villages and places of worship. By the end of 2001 more than 6,000 people were reported to have been killed, some 500,000 had been displaced, downtown Ambon had been destroyed, and the province was becoming increasingly partitioned into separate Christian and Muslim cantons. The formal separation of the predominantly Muslim northern districts of the region as the new province of North Maluku in late 1999 did nothing to resolve the tensions. Given the army's record of aggravating tensions in Aceh and Irian Jaya (now Papua), the President was reluctant to yield to military demands for the introduction of martial law in Maluku. In July 2000, however, Wahid also rejected suggestions that UN troops be sent to the province to quell the violence. Wahid placed Vice-President Megawati in charge of seeking a solution to the violence, but her limited activities had no apparent effect on the tensions, and her demonstrable lack of commitment to the project was widely criticized. In May 2000 local Muslims were joined by Laskar Jihad (Holy War Fighters), a paramilitary group predominantly drawn from Java, which eventually numbered an estimated 3,000 fighters. There was much speculation that the violence in the province was being encouraged by external forces, perhaps with a view to destabilizing the Wahid Government, or perhaps simply for local commercial reasons. By mid-2000 clear evidence had emerged that local army units were supporting the Muslims while the local police backed the Christians.

Levels of violence continued to increase considerably throughout the archipelago. In January 2000 Muslim demonstrators launched arson attacks on churches and Christian businesses in Lombok, and there were many reports of new militia groups training in Java. A series of co-ordinated bomb blasts across five provinces on Christmas Eve 2000 claimed 19 lives. Communal violence reportedly resulted in the deaths of 200 people in Sulawesi in June. Further clashes between indigenous Dayaks and immigrant Madurese in West Kalimantan claimed an estimated 500 lives in February 2001, and about 50,000 Madurese were displaced. The violence and general insecurity across the archipelago was estimated to have displaced perhaps 1m. people in 18 provinces.

In Central Sulawesi, where the violence had resulted in an estimated 2,000 deaths over a two-year period, representatives from the two sides agreed to meet in the southern town of Malino, where they reached a peace settlement in 2002. The success of this agreement encouraged the Government to schedule a similar meeting in Malino in February, bringing together the warring parties in Maluku. This meeting led to an agreement, known as 'Malino II', which included a provision that the Laskar Jihad forces should leave Maluku. Laskar Jihad itself rejected this provision and promised to stay in the region to undertake 'humanitarian' work. In April an unidentified gang attacked the Christian village of Soya, killing 12 people and setting fire to a 450-year-old church. Vice-President Hamzah Haz supported the Laskar Jihad decision to remain in Maluku, commenting that the province was not yet safe for

Muslims, but he visited Soya and made a donation to the cost of rebuilding the church. Bombs exploded in Christian areas of Ambon in July and September 2002, and in Poso there were fresh attacks on Christian communities, in which six people were killed and two churches burnt. In both cases suspicions were voiced that the security forces were responsible for the violence. The state of civil emergency was removed in North Maluku in May 2003, but remained in force in Maluku. In January 2003 two Christian separatist leaders from Maluku were sentenced to three-year prison terms for treason. They had not been present at their trial, which was held in Jakarta, while they remained in Maluku.

The violence between Muslims and Christians that had racked the provinces of Maluku, North Maluku and Central Sulawesi during the Wahid presidency largely abated as a result of peace agreements negotiated by national politicians, including Jusuf Kalla, and the state of civil emergency in Maluku was finally removed in September 2003. However, mutual suspicion between Christians and Muslims remained at a high level. A further clash took place in Poso in October 2003, and Ambon was once again affected by riots in April 2004, after a radical Christian group—the Maluku Sovereignty Front—staged a rally marking the 54th anniversary of the proclamation of the separatist South Maluku Republic. A total of 37 people died and more than 100 homes and churches were destroyed in the riots. In September 2004 the outgoing legislature created a new province of West Sulawesi, centred on Mamasa and the Mandar ethnic regions, but this initiative seemed unlikely to help resolve the conflict.

Following two bomb explosions in April 2005 in the predominantly Christian town of Tentena, which resulted in the deaths of 22 people, the town's only mosque was attacked by Christian demonstrators. In October three Christian teenage girls were beheaded on their way to school. Three alleged Islamist militants were subsequently found guilty of the brutal attack and sentenced to long prison terms. In September 2006 three Christian men were executed following their convictions on charges of inciting an attack on an Islamic school in Poso, in which approximately 200 people had been killed in May 2000. In early 2007, as police searched for Islamist suspects in the Poso area, a gun battle was reported to have left at least 12 dead, including 11 militants. Subsequent investigations confirmed that many of the militants had a connection to Jemaah Islamiah (JI—see Terrorism, below). Following this operation and the ensuing arrests, JI activities in Poso seemed largely to have ceased, although occasional incidents of sectarian violence continued to occur. In both the Ambon and Poso cases, a more professional enforcement of the law, combined with local community determination to prevent renewed conflict, had resulted in a dramatic reduction in the level of violence in these areas by 2008. When sectarian incidents did occur, both Muslim and Christian communities reacted quickly to ensure that there was no escalation.

Meanwhile, the status and security of the Ahmadiyah Muslim community emerged as a test of Indonesia's religious tolerance. In 2008 the Government partially banned the activities of Ahmadiyah, a sect long regarded by many members of the Islamic community as heretical because of its belief that its founder, Mirza Ghulam Ahmad, was a prophet. From the 1980s conservative Islamic groups urged the outlawing of Ahmadiyah, and the sect's property and members were subject to occasional attack by vigilantes. In June 2008 the Government issued a joint ministerial decree curtailing the activities of the sect. Civil libertarians condemned the decision as unwarranted state intervention into matters of faith, but a wide cross-section of Islamic groups supported it, including Indonesia's two largest Muslim organizations, the NU and Muhammadiyah, along with most mainstream political parties.

Attacks on members of Ahmadiyah intensified during 2011. In February a group of vigilantes attacked members and property of the sect in the village of Cikeusik, West Java, killing three Ahmadis and seriously assaulting several others. As in the case of many other anti-Ahmadiyah incidents, the police failed to arrest any of the perpetrators. Video footage of the entire attack, which had been recorded by a local Ahmadi, was subsequently broadcast on national television. Following the ensuing public outcry, the police arrested more than a dozen suspects, as well as several Ahmadis who were accused of provoking their attackers. Twelve vigilantes were subsequently convicted, but were sentenced to extremely brief prison terms of between three and six months. An Ahmadi also stood trial, during which he was subjected to hostile interrogation by several of the judges and was sentenced to six months' imprisonment. Far from prompting the authorities to increase protection of the Ahmadis, official responses to the situation were, for the most part, unsympathetic. The Minister of Religious Affairs, Drs Suryadharma Ali, blamed the Ahmadis themselves for 'inciting' the violence against them, and urged them to renounce their faith and 'return' to Islam. Numerous provincial and district administrations also 'banned' Ahmadiyah in their regions, although the legitimacy of such action remained moot given that religious affairs were solely the responsibility of the central Government.

The treatment of religious minorities in Indonesia became subject to increasing international scrutiny from 2008. In addition to the attacks against Ahmadiyah, some Christian and Buddhist communities experienced continued harassment and obstruction from the authorities of their efforts to build places of worship. The issue of 'unregistered' churches was a particular source of tension, particularly in West Java. Some local administrations refused to heed court rulings allowing the construction of churches, apparently without any intervention from the central Government. In early 2011 27 members of the US Congress wrote to the Indonesian Government expressing concern at the latter's failure to protect minority rights; a number of international rights organizations, including Freedom House, Human Rights Watch Asia and the International Crisis Group, as well as local human rights groups and activists, raised similar concerns.

TERRORISM

Indonesia has had a long history of Islamist militancy. Beginning with the DI movement in the late 1940s, small numbers of militant Muslims have been continually willing to engage in extreme violence in order to achieve their objectives. DI had special assassination squads (one of which nearly killed President Sukarno in an attack in 1957); mounted attacks on civilians in public places; and used terror as a weapon in its campaign to establish an Islamic state. Many thousands of people died in DI-related violence before the Indonesian military succeeded in suppressing the movement in the early 1960s. However, in the following decade DI activists quietly revived the organization, which continued to exist in the early 21st century, albeit in a fragmented and often fractious form. Many subsequent jihadist groups have links to DI or are inspired by its example.

The most important contemporary jihadist group is JI, which sees itself, in part, as a successor to DI and has retained that organization's determination to convert Indonesia into an Islamic state in which *Shari'a* law is comprehensively implemented. JI was founded in January 1993 by Abdullah Sungkar and Abu Bakar Bashir, two former DI leaders of Yemeni descent who were accused of having links to the al-Qa'ida international terrorist network of Osama bin Laden. The pair wanted JI to be more doctrinally strict and militarily competent than DI. Many of the early recruits to JI were Indonesian *mujahideen* who had been or were being trained in jihadist camps in Afghanistan or the Philippines. Initially, JI was based in Malaysia, where Sungkar and Bashir were in exile attempting to evade charges of sedition, but it relocated to Indonesia shortly after Suharto's resignation in 1998. JI's early targets were primarily Christian churches and clergy. A bomb attack on a church in Medan, North Sumatra, in May 2000 claimed one life, and was followed by an attack targeting the Philippines ambassador in Jakarta, which killed two bystanders. In December of that year JI executed its first large co-ordinated operation, bombing 35 churches across Indonesia, which resulted in 19 deaths.

JI's most deadly attack was carried out on 12 October 2002, when three suicide bombers detonated explosives on the island of Bali, including a massive car bomb outside a nightclub frequented by large numbers of Western tourists: 202 people, including 88 Australian tourists and 38 Indonesians, were killed in the attack. The perpetrators of the bombings later proclaimed that the attack was intended as retribution for Western-supported violence against Muslims and as a strategy to pressure foreign governments into desisting from 'anti-Islamic' policies. Following the bombings, a series of arrests was made, including that of Abu Bakar Bashir, JI's 'emir' since the death of Sungkar in 1999. Within a year, more than one-half of JI's leadership had either been arrested or put to flight. Several dozen people were eventually convicted of involvement in the Bali bombings, but public attention primarily focused on three men: Imam Samudra, Amrozi bin Nurhasyim and his brother Ali Ghufron bin Nurhasyim (alias Mukhlas). The three gained notoriety during their trials, which began in May 2003, for their angry outbursts against the Indonesian Government and Western states, and for their passionate defence of *jihad*. All three were given death sentences, and were executed by firing squad in November 2008. (Another brother of Amrozi, Ali Imron bin Nurhasyim, was sentenced to life imprisonment after expressing remorse for his actions.) Bashir's trial, which commenced in April 2003, also became the focus of intense media scrutiny. He denied all terrorism-related charges against him, including that of leading a terrorist organization, but in September was convicted of subversion and immigration offences and sentenced to four years' imprisonment; this was reduced to 18 months on appeal. However, he was released in April 2004, following which he was immediately rearrested and charged in connection with the bombing of the Marriott Hotel in Jakarta (see below). In September Bashir went on trial on charges of conspiring and inciting acts of terrorism, including the Bali and Marriott bombings, and in March 2005 he was convicted of conspiracy over the Bali attack and given a two-and-a-half-year prison sentence; however, he was acquitted of involvement in the Marriott bombing, and was released early, in June 2006, as part of measures to commemorate the 60th anniversary of Indonesia's accession to independence.

Meanwhile, in response to the Bali bombing, an emergency anti-terrorism decree was enacted. In March 2003 the DPR approved two bills specifically designating terrorism as a crime, and providing for detention without trial and for the use of intelligence reports in court cases; the legislation was also made retrospective in order to cover the Bali bombing. However, in July 2004 the Constitutional Court declared that the counter-terrorism legislation, which had been used to convict a number of those responsible for the Bali bombings, should not have been applied retrospectively. The Minister of Justice and Human Rights Affairs stated that the ruling did not rescind the convictions already secured but made it impossible to apply the law in future cases for crimes committed before its enactment.

A suicide car bombing at the Marriott Hotel in Jakarta in August 2003 claimed the lives of 12 people and injured about 150 others, and a similar attack outside the Australian embassy in the central business district of Kuningan in September 2004 killed nine people and injured more than 100 others. In October 2005 three suicide bombers attacked tourist spots in Denpasar, Bali, resulting in 23 deaths (including the assailants) and numerous injuries. Evidence suggested that all three attacks were undertaken by a network led by two Malaysians, Azahari Husin and Noordin Mohammad Top, using recruits from JI and other radical groups including DI. The emergence of Noordin's splinter group was evidence of a serious rift within JI between those favouring continued mass-casualty attacks and those who believed that such bombings were counter-productive to JI's aim of achieving an Islamic state. After the first Bali bombing, less militant elements in JI had reasserted their control over JI and made clear their disapproval of terrorist operations. This led Azahari and Noordin to set up their own network outside the remit of JI's command structure. Their model for struggle was that of Osama bin Laden, and on several occasions Noordin declared his organization to be the al-Qa'ida of South-East Asia. Following the 2003–05 attacks, the police made a large number of arrests, and in November 2005 Azahari was tracked down to a small town in East Java. In the ensuing gun battle, Azahari was shot dead before he could detonate a suicide bomb strapped to his body. Three others charged with involvement in the Australian embassy attack were convicted and given death sentences; in 2010 their final appeal was pending.

Bali continued to be seriously affected by terrorist activity. In January 2006 Noordin released a statement claiming responsibility for the 2005 Bali attacks. In his message, Noordin also claimed to have formed a new South-East Asian Islamist militant organization—Tanzim Qaedat al-Jihad (Organization for the Basis of Jihad).

On 17 July 2009 two suicide bombers detonated devices in the Marriott and Ritz-Carlton hotels in Jakarta, killing nine people and seriously injuring 55. The audacious nature of these attacks shocked the Indonesian Government and public alike. The two hotels were reputed to be among the most secure in Jakarta and were popular venues for senior foreign officials and businesspeople as well as members of the Indonesian élite. Posing as hotel guests, the bombers had checked into the Marriott two days before the attack and carefully assembled their bombs in a room using components that were seemingly smuggled into the hotel in small quantities over several days. Unlike other terrorist attacks since 2003, this bombing killed more foreigners (six in total) than Indonesians (three, including the two bombers). Noordin was widely believed to have been principally responsible for the attacks, although no formal claim of responsibility was made. As with previous bombings, police began arresting alleged members of Noordin's network who were suspected to have taken part in the operation. Noordin himself was shot dead in a police raid in Central Java in September 2009.

Police counter-terrorism efforts met with further success in early 2010, when they uncovered a cell engaged in training in Aceh. The cell was part of a new terrorist network led by Dulmatin, a former JI member and one of the main perpetrators of the 2002 Bali bombings. During a subsequent police operation in February 2010, three police officers were shot dead by cell members. Over the next few months, more than 100 people were arrested by police in connection with the cell and another 12 were shot dead, including Dulmatin in March, allegedly for resisting arrest. Leadership of the network was then reported to have passed to Abdullah Sonata, who was himself captured by police in mid-2010. Those arrested reportedly told the authorities that the cell had intended to assassinate President Yudhoyono and foreign ambassadors at celebrations to mark Independence Day on 17 August, to attack the headquarters of the Indonesian police force, and to launch co-ordinated attacks on five-star hotels in the capital, reminiscent of those perpetrated in the Indian city of Mumbai in November 2008 by members of Lashkar-e-Taiba, a Pakistan-based Islamist militant organization. The formation of this new network served as a disconcerting reminder of the rapid regenerative powers of Indonesian jihadists and their continued willingness to plan major attacks against senior Indonesian and foreign officials.The most controversial aspect of the Indonesian police operation in response to the newly emerged threat was the rearrest of Abu Bakar Bashir in August 2010 on suspicion of directly funding the Aceh cell and inciting others to commit terrorism. Following a four-month trial, he was convicted of funding the cell in June 2011 and was sentenced to 15 years' imprisonment.

In 2010–11 numerous new terrorist cells emerged, many of them containing young members who had not previously been associated with radical Islamist groups. Some of these cells had a 'mentor' who had experience in terrorist operations, but the cell members were thought to rely mainly on the internet for information about bomb-making and jihadist doctrine. A series of technically unsophisticated attacks, which included a suicide bombing of a mosque inside a police compound in Cirebon, West Java, in April 2011 and the sending of 'book bombs' to various public figures, suggested that terrorism would remain a major security problem in Indonesia for the foreseeable future. The cell-based structures of these new groups and their tenuous connections to established jihadist groups thus posed a severe challenge to counter-terrorism police, as such terrorist activity tended to be more difficult to detect. Furthermore, the police force was increasingly strained by its monitoring of more than 200 jihadists who had been released from prison since 2004.

Meanwhile, there had been a notable hardening of public attitudes towards terrorists. In the immediate aftermath of the first Bali bombing in 2002, surveys suggested that a majority of Indonesians believed that the attack had been either undertaken or co-ordinated by foreign powers. Even the leaders of major Islamic organizations, such as the NU and Muhammadiyah, publicly stated their belief that JI was not a product of Indonesia but of the US Central Intelligence Agency (CIA). Few Indonesian ministers at the time were prepared to speak candidly about the nature of the threat of terrorism, even though many understood the 'home-grown' origins of much of the JI and Noordin networks. However, this scepticism gradually abated, and the press and public largely came to accept that Indonesian terrorism was not the result of Western conspiracies. Extensive media coverage of terrorist trials helped considerably in this regard. Following the 2009 Marriott and Ritz-Carlton bombings, public disapproval of jihadists reached unprecedented heights, with numerous towns and villages refusing permission for deceased terrorists to be buried in their precincts.

SEPARATIST MOVEMENTS

Despite the archipelago's ethnic diversity, Indonesia experienced surprisingly few separatist movements during the first 50 years of independence. Regional movements generally sought only greater autonomy or aimed primarily to change the nature of the central Government rather than to achieve independence. During the 1970s, however, important separatist movements emerged in the provinces of Aceh and Irian Jaya (now Papua), and from 1975 Indonesia confronted persistent nationalist resistance in the occupied territory of East Timor. After the fall of President Suharto in 1998, all these movements gathered momentum, and in 1999 a referendum on independence was held in East Timor, leading to Indonesia's withdrawal from the territory in October of that year (see the chapter on Timor-Leste). Demands for independence were voiced for the first time in other regions, notably in the resource-rich provinces of Riau and East Kalimantan, but also in Bali and South Sulawesi. These new demands were intended principally to stake a claim for greater autonomy within Indonesia, rather than being envisaged as a serious contribution to the disintegration of the Republic. Since the decentralization process began in 2001, such fissiparous tendencies have declined.

Aceh

Aceh, the northernmost region of Sumatra, was an independent sultanate until the late 19th century, when it was conquered by the Dutch in a ferocious campaign. With a reputation as Indonesia's most staunchly Muslim region, Aceh was never fully subdued by the colonial power, and was one of the first areas where Indonesians took effective control from the Japanese after the declaration of independence in 1945. The Dutch never attempted to reoccupy the region, and Aceh ended the war of independence as a full province of the Indonesian Republic. After 1950 the Acehnese quickly became disillusioned with the Republic's leadership, which was generally perceived as corrupt, neglectful and 'un-Islamic'. Aceh's incorporation into the province of North Sumatra in 1950 was also resented. A rebellion erupted in September 1953 under Daud Beureu'eh, and the Aceh revolt formally joined the broader DI movement, which sought to make Indonesia an Islamic state. However, conciliatory policies by the central Government and a willingness to compromise on the part of the Acehnese ended the revolt in 1957. In 1959 Aceh became a special territory (Daerah Istimewa), with considerable autonomy in religious and educational affairs.

Dissent re-emerged in the mid-1970s, provoked by the central Government's exploitation of natural gas and coal fields in Aceh; many Acehnese felt that Aceh was receiving none of the benefits of these operations. Migration and transmigration of other Indonesians into the province, together with the growing power of the central Government, led to a feeling that the region's autonomy was being eroded. Hasan di Tiro formed the Gerakan Aceh Merdeka (GAM—Free Aceh Movement) in 1976 and declared independence in 1977. This small rebellion was quickly suppressed by the army, although Tiro later established a government-in-exile in Sweden.

Opposition to the central Government arose again in 1989, led by the National Liberation Front Acheh Sumatra. In 1990 Aceh was made a 'military operations zone', thus allowing the armed forces far greater freedom to counter the rebellion. The armed forces were accused of using excessive and indiscriminate force in their subsequent operations, and it was estimated that by mid-1991, when the rebellion had been largely suppressed, about 1,000 Acehnese had been killed. This figure continued to rise over subsequent years, and there were persistent reports of torture, kidnapping and sexual assault by the security forces. In July 1993 the human rights group Amnesty International produced a report accusing the Indonesian Government of protecting those members of the armed forces who were responsible for atrocities in Aceh and enabling them to act with impunity. Following the downfall of Suharto in May 1998, Aceh's status as a military operations zone was revoked in June, and in August 1,000 troops were withdrawn from the province. However, following rioting in September, the withdrawal of troops was suspended. Although President Habibie's decentralization measures were intended to defuse some of the resentment underlying the Aceh revolt by granting the province a greater share of oil and gas revenues, public opinion in Aceh became increasingly sympathetic towards the notion of independence. Violence continued to escalate in the province during the months following the accession of President Habibie. In January 1999 a total of 27 soldiers were court-martialled over the deaths in custody of four Acehnese earlier in the same month, but military violence in the countryside continued. Tension remained high in the province, and was exacerbated by the discovery of several mass graves of people killed by the army during security operations. Voter turn-out in the legislative elections of 7 June was low in many districts, and violence escalated still further following the poll as GAM guerrillas intensified their campaign for independence for the province. By late August a total of 2,000 Acehnese were reported to have been killed by the Indonesian armed forces since the instigation in June of a renewed military campaign in an attempt by the central Government to suppress the uprising.

On coming to power in October 1999, President Wahid envisaged a referendum on independence in the territory. In response, Acehnese nationalists belonging to the Aceh Referendum Information Centre (SIRA) organized a pro-referendum rally on 7–8 November in the provincial capital, Banda Aceh, which was attended by a reported 1m. people. However, the prospect of a referendum was rejected by the army. Whereas East Timor was, in some respects, accepted as having been a special case, independence for Aceh seemed likely to precipitate the disintegration of Indonesia. Sections of the armed forces also had extensive interests in Aceh's lucrative forestry and marijuana industries. Furthermore, GAM was seriously divided and lacked the international support that had helped the East Timorese independence movement to achieve its aim. Although there were signs of some material support from Acehnese living in Malaysia, the Malaysian Government emphatically declined to support independence for the province. By early 2000 President Wahid had retreated from the idea of a referendum on independence for Aceh, suggesting instead greater autonomy for the province, together with a larger share of revenue from natural resources and the limited introduction of Islamic law. However, this offer failed to satisfy the nationalists, and the violence in Aceh continued. By mid-2000 more than 300,000 people out of the province's total population of 4m. were reported to have been displaced by the violence, and GAM was said to control about half the villages in the province. At negotiations held in Geneva, Switzerland, in May the Indonesian Government and Acehnese rebel representatives agreed upon a three-month cease-fire ('humanitarian pause'), which took effect on 2 June. Also in May 24 junior soldiers and one civilian were sentenced to various terms of imprisonment for the murder in July 1999 of 58 Acehnese in Beutong Ateuh; the trial was criticized both by Acehnese community groups, who had demanded the death penalty for the accused, and by human rights lawyers, who urged a wider trial of crimes against humanity in the province. The cease-fire was later extended to January 2001, but appeared to have little influence on the level of violence. Pressure on the Government was increased by continued attacks on the major liquefied natural gas (LNG) plant in Aceh (see Economy). In April President Wahid signed an instruction for the police to assist the military in Aceh, effectively signalling a return to repressive strategies. An estimated 1,500 people were killed in 2001, mostly by the military, but some by GAM, the members of which increasingly targeted Javanese settlers.

Aside from maintaining military pressure on GAM, the central Government's main strategy for combating the insurgency was to prepare an enhanced autonomy plan for Aceh, giving the provincial government a greater share of gas revenue and imposing Islamic law within the province. The necessary legislation was drafted under Wahid's presidency but was signed into law by Megawati as one of her first acts in office. Although generous in the autonomy it granted to Aceh, the legislation was widely criticized by the Acehnese for failing to deal with the issue of the military presence within the province. Many Acehnese were sceptical about the implementation of Islamic law, suspecting that Jakarta was using religious sentiment to deflect attention away from more pressing political and economic issues. Thereafter, the Government sought to turn Islam into an instrument with which to counter GAM, with military commanders and senior officials claiming that the rebel movement was impious and that the Government was the real protector of Islamic values. GAM was, indeed, not Islamist in inclination. It had never proposed an Islamic state, and its relations with radical Muslim groups in Java were poor. Moreover, it had condemned the terrorist attacks on the USA of 11 September 2001 (see below) more strongly than the Indonesian Government.

The autonomy measures entered into force on 1 January 2002, when the province was renamed Nanggroë Aceh Darussalam (Islamic State of Aceh). The new regional Government was permitted to retain 70% of provincial revenues and began in March to implement its version of Islamic law by imposing a dress code. Aceh opened its first *Shari'a* court in March 2003, promising to implement Islamic law in a 'moderate' way. The Acehnese legislature subsequently approved a succession of *Shari'a*-inspired laws, which *inter alia* imposed strict dress and anti-fraternization codes, outlawed gambling and the public sale of alcoholic beverages, and required businesses to close for Friday prayers. A special *Shari'a* police force was also introduced, although it remained under the control of the civil police. The authority of *Shari'a* courts was greatly expanded, although all decisions could be referred to the national Supreme Court for appeal. One notable manifestation of the increasing implementation of *Shari'a* was the regular public caning, often attended by thousands of local people, of convicted gamblers. The physical punishment inflicted was minor (the number of 'lashes' was usually fewer than a dozen and the gambler's back was covered) but many of those subject to the caning resented the public humiliation and asked why those found guilty of much greater offences did not endure similar corporal measures.

Although President Megawati apologized to the Acehnese for past oppression in August 2001, she insisted that the province would not be permitted to leave Indonesia and that armed separatist movements would not be tolerated. She eventually obtained the release of five GAM negotiators who had been arrested in July during negotiations with the Government, but the time taken to achieve this release indicated the depth of resistance within the armed forces to any compromise with the rebels. From early 2002 military leaders adopted an increasingly stringent public policy towards separatism, and the military presence in Aceh rose to about 17,000. In January army units trapped and killed the GAM military leader, Abdullah Syafei, and in the same month the Iskandar Muda military command (Kodam) covering Aceh was restored. None the less, discussions between government and GAM representatives on the issue of restoring security took place in Geneva in May.

During 2002 the Government's tone hardened, and it insisted that GAM accept the autonomy proposals by 9 December or risk a resumption of military action. On 9 December the Indonesian Government and GAM signed a Cessation of Hostilities Agreement in Geneva, under the auspices of the Henri Dunant Centre and with the support of Japan, the USA and the European Union (EU). The agreement provided for a Joint Security Committee to monitor the cease-fire and for further discussions aimed at moving towards a peaceful permanent solution to the conflict. Levels of violence decreased dramatically after the agreement, but each side accused the other of using the cease-fire to consolidate its position, and the fundamental disagreement over Aceh's future remained unresolved. Gradually, the level of violence on both sides increased, and in April 2003 the army revealed that it planned a military operation to crush the rebels. The Government issued a deadline of 17 May for GAM to disarm and renounce its aim of independence. Peace talks resumed on that date in Tokyo, Japan, but neither side changed its position and on 19 May the Government declared martial law in Aceh. Widespread fighting broke out, some 200 schools were burnt down and hundreds of deaths were reported, although reliable information on the conflict was difficult to obtain owing to Indonesia's stringent control of external media. By early July the army claimed to be in full control of the province, but reports of fighting continued. In June a military court sentenced three soldiers to short prison terms for committing violent acts against Acehnese civilians.

Indonesia presented the operation in Aceh as an attack on Islamist terrorism and blamed GAM for several of the bomb attacks that had taken place in other parts of Indonesia in preceding months, but there was no clear evidence that GAM had undertaken any operations outside the province. Although the army claimed by the end of the year to have killed 800 rebels and captured another 1,700, reports from the province suggested that the GAM infrastructure had dispersed rather than disappeared. In November martial law was extended for a further six months and it was announced that the armed forces would use smaller-scale operations to attack the remnants of GAM and would co-operate more closely with civilians. The 30,000-strong Aceh expeditionary force was a major drain on army resources. Although martial law was removed in May 2004, the province remained under civilian emergency rule.

Resolving the Aceh conflict was a major priority for Yudhoyono upon assuming the presidency in October 2004, but he first disappointed observers by extending the state of civil emergency in the province for a further six months shortly after his inauguration. It was widely hoped that the December tsunami would work as a catalyst to bring the two sides back to the negotiating table, and this hope was fulfilled when representatives from both parties convened in Helsinki, Finland, for discussions under the mediation of the former Finnish President, Martti Ahtisaari. In a major breakthrough in February 2005, GAM agreed to abandon its claim for independence and to settle for 'self-rule'. After several rounds of negotiations, the two sides reached an agreement on 17 July, which included an agreement by GAM to disarm within three months in return for political amnesty and a phased withdrawal of Indonesian troops. In a concession that would require constitutional change, GAM was to be permitted to operate as a legal political party within Aceh (under existing laws, a political party was required to have its headquarters in Jakarta and to have branches in at least half of the country's 33 provinces). The EU and five members of the Association of Southeast Asian Nations (ASEAN), namely Brunei, Malaysia, the Philippines, Singapore and Thailand, were to monitor the situation. Vice-President Jusuf Kalla played a major role in ensuring the success of the Aceh negotiations. He gave close allies in the Cabinet—Minister of Justice and Human Rights Hamid Awaluddin and Minister of Information Sofyan Djalil—leading negotiating roles and defended them from criticism by nationalist groups, which claimed that the Government was making too many concessions to separatists. He also oversaw the offering of various inducements to GAM leaders to encourage them to cease hostilities and prepare for a return to civilian life.

Following the implementation of the peace agreement, Aceh was remarkably free of violence. Both GAM and the Indonesian military largely adhered to the terms of the agreement, and the rebels voluntarily surrendered most of their weapons and began reintegration into mainstream society. Local elections for provincial and district heads were held in December 2006.

GAM candidates unexpectedly won a large majority of positions. Two prominent GAM leaders, Irwandi Yusuf and Muhammad Nazar, were elected Governor and Vice-Governor, respectively, and many districts came under the control of former 'rebels'. Although Irwandi began impressively as provincial head, few of the former GAM leaders who took office at the district level had experience in government or management.

At the legislative election of April 2009, the GAM-dominated 'local party', Partai Aceh, won a large plurality, with 48% of the votes, giving sizeable majorities in both the provincial parliament and most of the district-level legislatures. Partai Aceh also strongly supported the incumbent Yudhoyono in the presidential election of July, resulting in the President's team receiving 93% of the votes cast in the province, a reflection of the approval for the President's efforts in pressing for peace in Aceh.

Papua

The western half of the island of New Guinea had been a part of the Netherlands East Indies before the Second World War, but it was scarcely integrated with the remainder of the colony and was inhabited by Melanesians who were ethnically different from the Malay peoples who dominated the rest of Indonesia. Partly on these grounds and partly to assuage the humiliation of defeat in the Indonesian war of independence, the Netherlands decided in 1949 to retain control of the region, envisaging its eventual self-determination. This decision, bitterly resented by Indonesians, led to more than a decade of diplomatic activity, which culminated in the transfer of the colony to Indonesia under UN auspices in 1962–63. Indonesia named the region Irian Barat (West Irian), but in 1972 changed it to Irian Jaya (Victorious Irian).

Under the UN agreement, the opinion of the indigenous population was to be heard in an 'Act of Free Choice' five years after integration, but this act was not internationally guaranteed or supervised and Indonesia carried it out in 1968 in a way that made acceptance of Indonesian rule mandatory. Resentment against Indonesian rule soon emerged. Indonesian authorities had little respect for traditional Papuan dress and custom, and attempted to impose Indonesian culture. The region became a major destination for internal migration and transmigration, and the less-educated local people often found themselves unable to compete with new inhabitants for bureaucratic, professional and other skilled jobs. Logging and copper-mining in the region, moreover, became major sources of export revenue for the Indonesian Government, while few of these funds seemed to reach the province.

A rebellion erupted in 1965, led by the Organisasi Papua Merdeka (OPM—Free Papua Movement) and unrest has continued in the province ever since. Seth Rumkorem declared a Republic of West Papua in 1971 and a major uprising took place in 1977. Despite grandiose claims, the movement controlled no significant territory by the early 1990s, although its forces were able to range widely in the difficult terrain and take sanctuary across the border in Papua New Guinea. In 1984 about 10,000 refugees crossed the border into Papua New Guinea (see also Foreign Relations, below).

Human rights organizations continued to report allegations of torture, killing, intimidation and cultural suppression in the province. Attention subsequently began to focus on Indonesia's largest source of gold and copper, the huge Grasberg mining complex near the province's southern coast, which was operated by US conglomerate Freeport. From mid-1994 the mine authorities were accused of complicity with Indonesian military forces in the deaths of dozens of local people who had protested against environmental degradation and what they saw as the privileged position of outsiders in the mining industry. In January 1996 the OPM launched a bid for greater international attention by kidnapping 26 people, including seven foreigners, in the south-east of the province. The OPM later released 15 of them but, during an operation launched by Indonesian special forces in May to free the remainder, the captors killed two Indonesian hostages. In August 1996 Indonesian forces freed several Indonesian forestry workers taken hostage by another OPM group.

In the months immediately after the downfall of President Suharto, Irian Jaya was relatively peaceful. In October 1998 the Indonesian Government revoked the status of Irian Jaya as a 'military operations zone' following the conclusion of a ceasefire agreement with the OPM in late September, but this action was not followed by any withdrawal of Indonesian troops from the province. However, the movement towards independence for East Timor (see below) encouraged the Irianese to begin pressing the case for independence for the region. In late February 1999 100 tribal leaders raised the issue of independence at a meeting with President Habibie, and pro-independence banners began to appear in the larger centres. However, Irian Jaya's immediate prospects for independence were weaker than those of East Timor, because 40% of the province's 2m. people were of non-Irianese descent, because its copper and gold mines were important to the national economy and because (unlike East Timor) it was formerly a part of the Netherlands East Indies.

In September 1999 President Habibie announced that the province of Irian Jaya would be divided into three. The initiative was widely perceived as a means of fracturing the region's independence movement. On coming to power in October, President Wahid revoked the partition, and in December he announced that the province's name would be changed from Irian Jaya to Papua. (However, the central authorities subsequently declined to ratify the change; nationalists, meanwhile, preferred the name of West Papua, Papua alone being widely used within the province itself but also being the traditional name for the southern part of Papua New Guinea.) The President, nevertheless, resisted any suggestion of independence for the territory, and the police and army continued to arrest Papuans for raising the nationalist flag; the flag was officially banned again on 1 December 2000. In February 2000 an unofficial Congress of the Papuan People met in Jayapura, formally repudiated the 1968 'Act of Free Choice' and began planning strategies for achieving independence for the province. Although, according to various reports, Indonesian military and intelligence operations had largely defeated or compromised the OPM as a resistance force, the example of East Timor had demonstrated to independence movements in other parts of the archipelago the critical importance of an international campaign and of a visible protest movement in the cities. The congress held in Jayapura was therefore dominated by urban NGOs rather than guerrillas. In response to the activities of the independence movement, the Indonesian military authorities apparently began to develop and support local pro-Indonesia militia groups similar to those used in East Timor. In 2001 these militia began receiving help from the Java-based radical Muslim group Laskar Jihad. In June a political congress held in the province, attended by about 3,000 Papuans, declared that the territory had never been legally integrated into Indonesia. The claim was immediately rebuffed by the Indonesian Government. In July, however, members of the Presidium Dewan Papua (PDP—Papua Presidium Council) held talks with President Wahid in Jakarta and renewed their demand for independence for the territory.

In October 2000 the Minister of Defence announced that firmer action was to be taken against separatism in the province. In November Theys Eluay, a moderate leader of the PDP, and four others were charged with sedition; shortly afterwards Eluay was assassinated after attending a dinner with the local army commander. An official investigation later concluded that members of the military were responsible for the murder. In April 2003 a court in Surabaya convicted four officers and three soldiers of responsibility for the death; they received sentences of between two and three-and-a-half years. However, legislation was also drafted to provide for special autonomy for the province, along lines broadly similar to those in Aceh, although without the implementation of Islamic law in the mainly Christian province. The progress of this law through the legislature was delayed by the long struggle in Jakarta to oust President Wahid, and by disagreement over the percentage of resource income that was to be retained by the provincial government. When the special autonomy bill was finally approved on 22 October 2001, it provided that 80% of revenue from forestry and fisheries and 70% from oil and gas would be retained by Papua. The bill confirmed the province's name as Papua and legalized the use of the Papuan flag. The legislation took effect on 1 January 2002.

In February 2003, however, the Government announced that it intended to implement the law, approved in 1999 but as yet unenforced, which was to divide the province of Papua into three. At the time of the law's conception in 1999, the proposal was presented by the Government as enabling the closer involvement of the people in the province's administration, but it was implemented without public consultation and against the wishes of virtually all Papuan leaders. The plan was also at variance with the 2001 special autonomy law, which specifically provided that no new provinces should be created without the approval of the Papuan consultative council, which awaited formation. Acting governors for the new provinces were appointed in May, in a measure generally seen as being intended to undermine Papuan separatism by promoting disunity.

Meanwhile, in late August 2002 two US teachers and an Indonesian teacher were killed and 11 others wounded in an attack on a vehicle convoy at the town of Timika, near the Freeport mine. The military attributed the attack to OPM separatists, but the organization denied any responsibility. Suspicion was raised by the police chief for Papua, I. Made Pastika, that the military had contrived the incident in order to incriminate the OPM. (Gun cartridges of a type used by the military were reported to have been found at the scene of the attack.) The Commander-in-Chief of the Armed Forces, Gen. Endriartono Sutarto, later threatened to sue the US newspaper the *Washington Post* for US $1,000m. for reporting the allegation as a fact. An initial investigation by the US Federal Bureau of Investigation (FBI) suggested that the attack had been carried out by soldiers angered by a reduction in the payments they received from the mining company, but later reports blamed Papuan rebels. In 2004 a US Federal Grand Jury indicted the alleged OPM commander, Antonius Wamang, in connection with the shootings; he and 11 followers were arrested by Indonesian police in early 2006 and charged with the shootings. Freeport's relationship with the Indonesian army also proved increasingly problematic. In 2003 the company admitted that it had paid $7m. to the army for 'security services' in the previous year, and it came under political and media pressure to desist from making any further payments. The Indonesian military subsequently announced that it would no longer provide special security for Freeport on the grounds that it was not a mercenary force. In mid-2006 the police formally took over the role of protecting the mine.

The creation of three provinces out of the former province of Papua was reported to have been effected in August 2003, prompting a three-day confrontation between supporters and opponents of the policy in Timika, the designated capital of Central Papua. Yudhoyono, at that time the Co-ordinating Minister for Political, Legal and Security Affairs, then declared that the division had been reversed and promised a review of the contradictory laws concerning the region. However, the creation of a province of West Irian Jaya (West Papua), based on Manokwari, did go ahead, despite the State Administrative Court rescinding a law appointing its governor. Uncertainty over the provincial status of Papua continued after Yudhoyono's election to the presidency. In November 2004 the Constitutional Court simultaneously overruled the law dividing the province into three and ratified the creation of the province of West Irian Jaya as an established fact. In early 2006 local elections were held in West Irian Jaya, despite strong protests from the recently formed Majelis Rakyat Papua (MRP—Papuan People's Council) that the province be abolished. The continued existence of the province continued to be a source of tension between the central Government and many sections of the Papuan élite. The Government changed the name of West Irian Jaya to West Papua in early 2007, in an attempt to appease its local critics, and issued a regulation in April 2008 affirming West Papua's existence under the law as a special autonomous region. In mid-2008 the DPR agreed to adopt legislation confirming the province's legal status.

Violence again broke out in Papua in mid-2009. In July three people, including an Australian employee of Freeport who was shot dead while travelling in a company vehicle, were killed near the mine. Police attributed the attacks to the OPM, but local NGOs claimed that members of the security forces, disgruntled at Freeport's reduction of payments for their services, might have been involved in the shooting incidents.

Criticism of and mobilization against special autonomy steadily increased in 2009–10. In June 2010 the MRP voted to reject West Papua's status as a special autonomous region, and in the following month several thousand Papuans gathered in Jayapura to appeal for the holding of a popular referendum on the issue of independence, claiming that the central Government was neglecting the province's interests. Papuan leaders expressed particular anger at continuing high levels of transmigration into the province from Java and Sulawesi, together with worsening poverty and HIV-infection levels, despite a sharp increase in local government revenues. Yudhoyono's Government was criticized for failing to understand Papuan grievances and for being slow to act, an argument that was lent weight when the President took several weeks to respond to the MRP motion in June.

Further evidence of worsening conditions and unrest in Papua emerged in mid-2011, when two dozen civilians and soldiers were killed in a number of violent incidents in highland areas, particularly in the Puncak Jaya region. Contributory factors in the unrest included severe poverty among highland tribes, unduly forceful operations by security officials, tribal rivalries and fragmentation within the OPM. A proposal initiated in 2010 by the Office of the Vice-President for a special government unit to address economic development and social problems in the province was still awaiting cabinet approval at mid-2011. The Papua Peace Conference was held in July, at which a framework for reform and policy action was proposed, but similarly this had yet to elicit a response from the central Government. Meanwhile, academics and NGOs, including the International Crisis Group, warned of deepening political unrest in Papua should the central Government fail to take effective action.

FOREIGN RELATIONS

Since independence Indonesia has prided itself on maintaining an 'active and independent' foreign policy. During the 1950s Indonesia was a founder-member of the Non-aligned Movement (NAM), and assumed the chairmanship of the organization in September 1992. However, Indonesia's dependent position in the international economy has never permitted it the freedom of action that it professes. During the period of 'Guided Democracy', Sukarno turned to the USSR and the People's Republic of China for support, and from 1965–66 'New Order' Indonesia solicited funds from Western donors.

The centre-piece of Indonesian foreign policy is its membership of ASEAN, which it founded with Malaysia, the Philippines, Singapore and Thailand in 1967. Indonesia also played a major role in establishing the Asia-Pacific Economic Cooperation (APEC) forum, and hosted the November 1994 APEC summit meeting in Bogor. ASEAN's original aims emphasized regional economic co-operation as a means of diminishing threats to internal security, but it has worked most effectively in defusing conflicts between its members and in creating a united diplomatic front on broader international issues. ASEAN support, for instance, helped to limit the damage to Indonesia's international reputation caused by its invasion and protracted pacification of East Timor and by its repeated disregard for UN resolutions on the colony.

Indonesian suspicion of China has been a major feature of foreign policy since 1965–66, when the military accused China of supporting the PKI and the attempted coup. Indonesia severed diplomatic relations with China in 1967. Poor relations were compounded by long-term doubts about the loyalty of Indonesia's ethnic Chinese minority and a belief that China might seek to take advantage of their support. To prevent such intervention, Indonesia banned the import of material written in Chinese characters. In May 1985, however, the two countries began to discuss the resumption of direct trade links, and in April 1988 Indonesia announced that it was willing to establish full diplomatic relations, provided China gave an assurance that it would not seek to interfere in Indonesia's internal affairs. Diplomatic relations were finally restored in August 1990, after Indonesia undertook to repay debts to

China incurred during the period of 'Guided Democracy'. Relations between Indonesia and China suffered a set-back in 1998 when, some six weeks after the perpetration of terrible violence against ethnic Chinese Indonesians around the time of the fall of Suharto in May, China issued a sharp diplomatic protest against the violence and gave prominent coverage in the state-controlled media to reports of the gruesome rapes, arson and murders. Following his accession to the presidency, President Habibie publicly expressed his sympathy for the plight of the ethnic Chinese victims of violence. Subsequently, in May 1999, as part of an ongoing programme of general reform, Habibie removed a ban that had existed on the use and teaching of the Mandarin Chinese language within Indonesia.

Indonesia aspired to be recognized as the major power in South-East Asia. It welcomed the withdrawal of the former USSR from its base in Cam Ranh Bay in Viet Nam and of the USA from Subic Bay in the Philippines. Indonesia has also been involved in diplomatic efforts to resolve long-standing regional conflicts. From June 1991 it hosted several informal meetings attended by representatives of Brunei, China, Malaysia, the Philippines, Taiwan and Viet Nam to discuss these countries' conflicting claims to all or parts of the Spratly Islands in the South China Sea, which are strategically important and show considerable potential for petroleum exploitation. The meetings resulted in a joint statement agreeing to resolve the dispute peacefully. Paradoxically, Indonesia's bilateral relations with Malaysia became strained in 1993 by a dispute over two islands, Sipadan and Ligitan, off the coast of Sabah. (The dispute was submitted to the International Court of Justice—ICJ—in The Hague, Netherlands, in June 2002, and in December the ICJ ruled in favour of Malaysia's claim.) A separate issue arose in March 2005, when Indonesia challenged Malaysia's claim to the small island of Ambalat, and its surrounding territorial waters in the Sulawesi Sea. Having lost its case over Sipadan and Ligitan, Indonesia was determined not to be thwarted again, and the issue was seen domestically as a major test of President Yudhoyono's willingness to stand up for Indonesia's international interests.

In April 1995 the Indonesian armed forces increased patrols in the South China Sea after China re-emphasized its claim to seas near the Natuna archipelago, which Indonesia has traditionally claimed. Indonesia also assumed an active diplomatic role in the protracted conflicts in Indo-China. Smoke from forest fires in Indonesia seriously disrupted commerce and communications and also damaged public health in Singapore and Malaysia during the second half of 1997. Although both countries attempted to disregard suggestions of tension with Indonesia, they were clearly irritated by Indonesia's failure to address the problem more promptly; President Suharto twice apologized publicly to the neighbouring countries for the haze. Indonesia's relations with Malaysia were also strained by the forced repatriation in early 1998 of thousands of Indonesian workers from Malaysia as a result of the impact of the regional economic crisis; many of those repatriated reported brutal treatment in detention centres prior to their removal. Under Malaysian regulations introduced in 2002, illegal immigrants risked up to five years in prison and six strokes of the cane. In mid-2003 some 22,000 illegal workers who had fled Malaysia were still living in refugee camps at Nunukan in East Kalimantan.

Indonesia's relations with the West have been periodically disrupted by disagreements over human rights and over East Timor (now Timor-Leste), the annexation of which by Indonesia remained widely unrecognized internationally in the late 1990s, prior to the referendum held in August 1999. In March 1992, after the Dutch Government linked the continuation of aid to an improvement in Indonesia's human rights performance, Indonesia rejected all Dutch aid and dissolved the donors' group, IGGI, which had been chaired by the Netherlands. A new international aid consortium, the Consultative Group on Indonesia (chaired by the World Bank and including 18 countries and 13 multilateral aid agencies, but excluding the Netherlands), met in Paris, France, in July 1992 to assume the functions of IGGI. In early 1994 the USA threatened to remove Indonesia's trade privileges unless it took steps to conform to International Labour Organization (ILO) standards for labour conditions. The events surrounding Megawati's expulsion from the PDI leadership led the USA to postpone the sale to Indonesia of nine F-16 fighter aircraft in September 1996. In June 1997, however, Indonesia cancelled the sale, on the grounds of unacceptable US criticism over the alleged abuse of human rights in the country. The British Government pledged to review the sale of 16 *Hawk* fighter aircraft to Indonesia, but allowed the sale to proceed after the Indonesian Government made it clear that it would simply buy from elsewhere. The continuing resistance in East Timor strengthened the international campaign to maintain pressure on Indonesia over its occupation of the territory.

Indonesia's relations with Australia, which had been increasingly close in the early 1990s, deteriorated when widespread public protests in Australia forced Indonesia to withdraw the nomination of Lt-Gen. Herman Mantiri as ambassador to Canberra. Mantiri had made remarks apparently defending the Dili massacre of November 1991, when between 100 and 180 East Timorese students were shot dead, and subsequent to which a further 100 witnesses to the massacre were executed, by Indonesian troops; the students had been protesting against Indonesian rule during the funeral procession of a fellow East Timorese student, himself killed by Indonesian troops in the previous month. The rift with Australia appeared to have been addressed when the two countries signed a security agreement in December 1995.

In March 1997 Indonesia and Australia signed a treaty concerning sea-bed and 'economic zone' boundaries. Following the downfall of President Suharto in May 1998, bilateral relations were significantly affected by the issue of East Timor. In January 1999 the Indonesian Government expressed its 'deep regret' at Australia's decision to change its policy on the territory and actively promote 'self-determination' in East Timor. In March the Indonesian Government announced that it was to permit the East Timorese people to vote on the issue of independence. In early May Indonesia and Portugal signed a UN-sponsored accord on East Timor, which allowed for total independence for the territory if the East Timorese people voted to reject autonomy proposals offered by Indonesia in the referendum scheduled to be held in August. On 28 December, following Indonesia's withdrawal from East Timor in October after the territory's population voted in favour of independence, diplomatic relations between Indonesia and Portugal (which had been severed in 1975) were restored. Meanwhile, however, Indonesia's relations with Australia deteriorated further, following the latter's involvement in peace-keeping operations in East Timor after the referendum. Furthermore, many members of the Indonesian élite deeply resented Australia's wider role in the detachment of East Timor from Indonesia, as well as the public claim made by the Australian Prime Minister, John Howard, that he had 'stood up' to Indonesia over the issue. There was also widespread suspicion in Indonesia that official Australian support for the territorial integrity of Indonesia might not endure increasing public pressure in favour of independence for the Indonesian province of Irian Jaya (now Papua—see above). Relations improved in June 2001, when Wahid finally made an official visit to Australia, the first by an Indonesian President for 26 years.

Relations between the incoming Megawati Government and Australia were strained almost immediately after the President's accession in mid-2001 by the issue of refugees, asylum-seekers and illegal immigrants, mainly from South Asia and the Middle East, who passed through Indonesia while attempting to reach Australia. The issue was one of great controversy in Australia but was of little direct importance to Indonesia, which objected to Australian claims that it should be doing more to prevent unauthorized migrants from passing through its territory.

At the end of January 2000 the UN Commission on Human Rights recommended that an international tribunal be established to try Indonesian military personnel and other individuals suspected of involvement in the violence in East Timor in August and September 1999. However, in late February 2000 UN Secretary-General Kofi Annan stated that the Indonesian legal process should be allowed to run its course before the establishment of any such tribunal. In January the EU removed an embargo on military assistance to Indonesia, which it had imposed in an attempt to force Indonesia to repatriate displaced East Timorese from West Timor and to bring to justice those responsible for the violence in the territory. However, a similar embargo imposed by the USA remained in place. During a visit to Indonesia in April, the US commander in the Pacific, Adm. Dennis Blair, publicly criticized the human rights record of the Indonesian military.

Indonesia's relations with Papua New Guinea were strained by the disputed border issue and by the question of the OPM. The Papua New Guinea Government scrupulously refrained from assisting the separatists: in May 1990 the OPM leader, Melkianus Salossa, was arrested in Papua New Guinea and deported to Indonesia, where he received a life sentence, and from October a new border agreement enabled the exchange of military intelligence and the conduct of joint border patrols. However, the insecure border and widespread sympathy for the OPM in Papua New Guinea meant that the rebels periodically obtained support and sanctuary across the border. Papua New Guinea was angered by regular incursions of Indonesian troops and aircraft into its territory. In March 2003 Papua New Guinea announced that it would return to Indonesia about 300 asylum-seekers who had crossed the border, claiming refugee status, in 2000.

The economic crisis of 1997 and the downfall of President Suharto in 1998 diverted Indonesian attention from international politics. ASEAN, in particular, was notably less effective during this period without the driving force of Indonesia behind it. Although Western countries generally welcomed President Habibie's reform programme, they expressed some doubts about the depth of Indonesia's commitment to fundamental change. The early months of President Wahid's leadership, in late 1999 and early 2000, were characterized by a hectic programme of foreign travel intended to strengthen his Government's credentials, to win international support for Wahid's own political position from within Indonesia itself and to restore business confidence in the country's future. In February 2000 President Wahid visited East Timor for the first time since the Timorese people's vote for independence, in an attempt to begin the process of Indonesia's reconciliation with the territory.

On 19 September 2001 a scheduled visit to Washington, DC, by President Megawati proceeded despite the terrorist attacks on New York and Washington only eight days previously. In her discussions with US President George W. Bush, Megawati offered support for the USA's campaign against terrorism, receiving in exchange promises of financial aid and improved access to defence equipment. However, the US response to the attacks added greatly to Megawati's difficulties. The US attack on Afghanistan was widely condemned in Muslim circles. There were protests against the US bombing in several Indonesian cities and demands for a boycott of US goods and firms. Radical Muslim groups began searching tourist areas in Jakarta, Central Java and Makassar to tell US citizens to leave the country, although there was little direct harassment of foreigners. None the less, with a widespread perception in Indonesia that the USA had over-reacted to the attacks, the Government was reluctant to be seen to be acting against Islam at the behest of the USA.

In early 2002 the USA and Indonesia agreed that the former would provide US $10m. to train Indonesian police in counter-terrorism techniques and to train bank officials in the tracing of terrorist financial transactions. Furthermore, in March 2006 the US State Department formally removed its ban on exports of military equipment to Indonesia. Australia also increased co-operation with Indonesia in police training and encouraged closer co-operation in police matters between Indonesia and its ASEAN neighbours. In July 2002 the US Senate Appropriations Committee voted to abandon conditions on providing US military training to the Indonesian armed forces, thus enabling the Indonesian military to participate in the US Department of Defense's International Military Education and Training programme (IMET). The Pentagon had argued that it needed Indonesia's co-operation in the global 'war on terror' and that this war should take precedence over human rights considerations. However, President Bush undertook to consult the US Congress before resuming formal co-operation, and the Congress authorization was withdrawn in 2003 when strong suspicions arose that the Indonesian military had been responsible for the murder of two US citizens at the Freeport mine in Papua (see above). These suspicions were allayed only in July 2004, when Antonius Wamang of the OPM was indicted over the incident.

The terrorist attacks on Bali in October 2002 were generally perceived to constitute a further reason for the strengthening of Indonesia's military links with the USA. Indonesia's relatively porous borders and the political difficulty of monitoring Islamist organizations made it an important element in terrorist networks in the view of the USA and Australia. Australia was also still concerned to prevent Indonesia from being used as a conduit for illegal immigrants from the Middle East and sought the help of the Indonesian authorities in preventing immigrant boats from leaving Indonesia. However, Australia's return of a boat-load of Kurdish refugees to Indonesia in November 2003 led to Indonesian complaints that it was being used by Australia as a 'dumping ground' for unwanted migrants.

Under President Yudhoyono, Indonesia's relations with Australia improved substantially, with the Indonesian leader developing an unexpected personal rapport with Australian Prime Minister John Howard. Yudhoyono visited Australia in April 2005, and the two countries agreed on closer co-operation in a range of security matters. Conversely, relations between the respective publics of the two countries were damaged by the case of Schapelle Corby, an Australian tourist to Bali who was detained when 4.1 kg of marijuana was found in her baggage. Her case was handled in a highly melodramatic way by the Australian press, and after she was convicted and sentenced to 20 years in prison in late May she was widely believed in Australia to be the innocent victim of corrupt customs officials and a prejudiced and incompetent Indonesian legal system. Another incident that generated international media interest, although less bilateral tension, was the case of the so-called 'Bali Nine'. In April 2005 nine Australians were arrested in Bali over the planned smuggling of 8.3 kg of heroin from the island into Australia. Unlike the Corby case, there was little doubt surrounding the guilt of the Bali Nine; members of the group had been video-taped with the heroin strapped to their bodies and most later confessed to and gave details of the operation. The two ringleaders were sentenced to death by firing squad and the remaining seven were sentenced to life imprisonment, three of which latter sentences were subsequently reduced to 20 years. However, following protests from the prosecutors about this perceived lenience, the Supreme Court decided in September 2006 to impose the death penalty on the three members of the group whose sentences had been reduced, together with a fourth man who had initially been given life imprisonment. These four death sentences were subsequently commuted to life imprisonment once again. In mid-2011, however, the final judicial appeals against the death sentence for the two ringleaders were rejected.

The most serious disruption to Australian-Indonesian relations during the Yudhoyono presidency thus far came in early 2006, when 43 Papuan refugees were granted asylum in Australia on the grounds that their safety would be threatened if they returned to Papua. The refugees had crossed the Arafura Sea in late 2005 seeking political asylum from alleged human rights abuses and had demanded Papuan independence. Yudhoyono had offered a personal assurance to Prime Minister Howard that the refugees were safe to return to Indonesia, but the Australian Government argued that international law required it to provide asylum. The decision prompted outrage in Jakarta, and many politicians accused Australia of undermining Indonesian sovereignty by accepting the claims of separatists. The Indonesian Government immediately recalled its ambassador, an unprecedented action in the bilateral relationship, and Yudhoyono strongly criticized Australia's actions.

President Yudhoyono pursued a more ambitious foreign policy than most of his immediate predecessors. He travelled frequently abroad and offered to mediate in disputes between North and South Korea, as well as between Israel and the Palestinian Authority. He also held, with US support, a summit meeting in Indonesia between Shi'a and Sunni leaders, primarily from Iran and Iraq, but no senior officials attended the conference, and most observers regarded the initiative as a failure. Yudhoyono had greater success with his diplomatic efforts regarding Israel's intervention in southern Lebanon in mid-2006. Together with Malaysian Prime Minister Abdullah Badawi, Yudhoyono featured prominently in a campaign by Muslim nations to press for Israel's withdrawal and for the deployment of peace-keeping forces. In November almost 1,000 Indonesian troops were sent to border regions in southern Lebanon. Indonesia also gained greater international stature in late 2006 when it was elected to a non-permanent seat on the UN Security Council, to be held for a period of two years. While many Indonesians welcomed their country's role in the Council, several of the Government's policies with regard to the UN led to widespread criticism, in particular the decision of Indonesia in March 2007 to support further sanctions against Iran in retaliation for the country's refusal to suspend its nuclear programme. Indonesia subsequently modified its stance on Iran's nuclear programme, abstaining from several Security Council votes on the issue. Yudhoyono also sought closer economic and diplomatic links with Iran, visiting Tehran in March 2008 and securing Iranian investment in Indonesia's natural resources sector.

The election of Barack Obama as President of the USA in late 2008 greatly altered the tone of relations between Indonesia and the USA. Whereas President Bush was held in low regard in Indonesia, Obama's installation was greeted with rapturous approval; this was due in no small part to the fact that the President had spent four of his childhood years in Jakarta and retained some ability to speak Indonesian. Moreover, the new US Administration signalled that it would seek much greater involvement with South-East Asia than had Bush, and that Indonesia would be a pivotal part of this revised policy. Following two postponements owing to pressing domestic issues, President Obama finally made his long-awaited state visit to Indonesia in November 2010, where he was enthusiastically received by the majority of the Indonesian population; however, some Islamic groups held protests against his visit, arguing that the US Government under Obama's presidency continued to oppress Muslims around the world. Like many other visiting Western leaders in recent years, Obama praised Indonesia for its progress in democratization, its Islamic moderation and its efforts to combat terrorism. The US President also reiterated statements that he had previously made in the Middle East about his determination to broker lasting peace in that region, and stressed his commitment to strengthening US-Indonesian co-operation, particularly within the fields of trade, politics and security.

A similar improvement in Indonesia's relations with Australia followed the election as Prime Minister of Kevin Rudd in December 2007. Rudd visited Indonesia twice in the first seven months of his tenure, and repeatedly stated that he wished to expand relations with Indonesia, particularly working through international forums such as the G20 (Group of 20 leading industrial nations), where he perceived Indonesia and Australia as sharing many middle-power policy concerns. His overtures were well received by President Yudhoyono, and both countries increased their co-operation on a range of diplomatic, environmental and economic issues.

Conversely, Indonesia's relations with Malaysia and Singapore grew increasingly tense during 2008–09. In the case of Malaysia, the chief irritant was the disputed sea zone of Ambalat. In October 2008, and again in early 2009, Indonesian and Malaysian naval vessels engaged in a confrontation, with the Indonesian ships several times threatening to open fire on Malaysian craft. In mid-2009 both sides agreed to intensify discussions over the zone and to avoid naval provocation. Another contentious issue was the treatment of Indonesian workers in Singapore and Malaysia. Malaysia had implemented a more stringent policy with regard to Indonesian workers, forcing many thousands to repatriate. A number of high-profile cases of abuse of Indonesians by their Singaporean and Malaysian employers similarly intensified Indonesian hostility towards both countries.

Relations with Malaysia reached a new nadir in August 2010, when the Malaysian navy detained three Indonesian fisheries officials, alleging that they were operating within Malaysian territory. The officials were released several days later following the decision by Indonesia to free a group of Malaysian fishermen arrested for fishing in Indonesian waters. Malaysia's actions drew a furious response from Indonesian politicians and nationalist groups. Some legislators urged the recall of Indonesia's ambassador in Kuala Lumpur and accused the Indonesian Minister of Foreign Affairs, Dr Raden (Marty) Mohammad Muliana Natalegawa, of being 'soft' in his response. Meanwhile, protesters gathered outside the Malaysian embassy in Jakarta threw faeces and burned Malaysian flags, in turn drawing strong criticism from the Malaysian Government. In late August Yudhoyono wrote to the Malaysian Prime Minister, Najib Tun Razak, appealing for calm to be restored in bilateral relations and promising senior-level negotiations on border issues.

Indonesia assumed the annually rotating chair of ASEAN in early 2011, declaring its intention to improve intra-ASEAN relations and also to encourage greater economic and strategic regional co-operation. Sporadic border clashes between Thailand and Cambodia (q.v.) became the focus of Indonesian diplomacy at the ASEAN summit meeting held in Jakarta in May, at which the neighbouring countries agreed to try to resolve the prolonged border dispute through dialogue. President Yudhoyono urged the creation of an ASEAN economic community by 2015, although many other member states remained cautious, declining to make any firm commitment to the concept.

Economy

SARWAR O. H. HOBOHM

Revised by the editorial staff

INTRODUCTION

Indonesia is the fourth most populous country in the world, with the census of May 2010 recording a total population of almost 237.6m. According to UN estimates, the population had risen to 242.3m. by mid-2011, giving a population density of 126.8 persons per sq km. With substantial deposits of petroleum, natural gas and other minerals, as well as the capacity to produce a wide range of agricultural commodities, Indonesia is richly endowed in terms of natural resources. Yet the country remains relatively poor, and achieved the status of a 'middle-income' country, by World Bank criteria, only in 1981, when its national income per caput first exceeded the threshold of US $500.

The Indonesian economy is characterized by a variety of distributional imbalances. The results of the 2010 population census showed that 59.1% of Indonesia's population lived on the three islands of Java (Jawa), Madura and Bali, which together comprised only 7.1% of the country's total land area. These islands also represent the most fertile regions of Indonesia, and are the most heavily urbanized and most developed areas, both industrially and infrastructurally. These advantages are, to a considerable extent, offset by the three islands' high population density, and they also contain areas of extreme poverty. This variation in income levels is emphasized by periodic surveys of consumption expenditure conducted by the Central Bureau of Statistics, as exemplified in 2007 when the poorest 40% of the population accounted for only

19.1% of total consumption expenditure, while the wealthiest 20% of the population accounted for 44.8% of the total.

After some brief set-backs in the mid-1980s the Indonesian economy recorded almost a decade of rapid economic growth, and by 1996 the country's gross domestic product (GDP) had risen to US $1,155 per head. However, the Asian financial crisis of 1997/98 led to a substantial regression. As demand contracted, the decline in the volume of Indonesia's output was exacerbated by a fall in its value in terms of US dollars; this was largely due to the significant depreciation of the rupiah, owing to speculative attacks on the Indonesian currency. The devaluation seriously threatened the international solvency of Indonesia's corporate and banking sector, which carried substantial volumes of unsecured short-term 'offshore' loans.

The serious deterioration of Indonesia's financial position led to the announcement of a US $23,000m. rescue programme by the IMF, the World Bank and the Asian Development Bank (ADB) in late 1997. In return, the Indonesian Government was required to introduce a wide range of reforms; however, these often conflicted with the interests of the politically influential business community and hence proved extremely difficult to implement. This further weakened the confidence of international financial markets in Indonesia's economy and its corporate sector. Furthermore, the regional crisis undermined the real economy, causing sharp increases in inflation and unemployment. Political and social tensions resulted in frequent riots and attacks on the economically powerful ethnic Chinese business community, developments that further eroded public confidence.

The sustainability of Indonesia's recovery from the repercussions of the Asian crisis was fraught with risks, foremost among which were the continued high levels of bad debt in the banking sector (estimated in some cases to account for as much as 75%–85% of total loans) and the extent of 'offshore' debt of the corporate sector (officially estimated at US $65,600m. in mid-1999). Unemployment remained high, with some 25% of the population reported to be living in absolute poverty in mid-1999. Progress was also impeded by the terrorist attacks on the island of Bali in October 2002, which led to a sharp decline not only in tourist arrivals but also in business confidence as a whole. The outbreak of the epidemic of Severe Acute Respiratory Syndrome (SARS) in Asia in 2003 also had a major impact. Nevertheless, as economic recovery continued, the Indonesian Government allowed the IMF-supported reform programme that had guided economic policy for most of the past six years to expire at the end of 2003. By 2005 GDP per caput had reached an estimated $1,190, moderately in excess of the pre-crisis figure recorded in 1996.

Indonesia's economic performance in 2006 remained robust, although the rate of GDP growth declined slightly, to 5.5% in real terms, in comparison with 5.7% in 2005. As in the previous year, growth in 2006 was driven by substantial increases in government recurrent expenditure. There was renewed public confidence in Indonesia, both in response to the restoration of political and macroeconomic stability by the new Government and in an appreciation of the revived economic potential of the country. The capital markets registered strong growth. These favourable trends continued in 2007, although the economy was somewhat constrained by external inflationary pressures, especially with regard to food and fuels. With increases in world market prices of several of Indonesia's staple food products, ranging from 20% (rice) to 50% (maize and crude palm oil) to 70% (soybeans) and more than 100% (wheat flour), the impact on several population groups was severe. The situation was exacerbated by the sharp rise in global oil prices. However, since most of this price increase appeared in the latter half of 2007, its overall effect on the year as a whole was limited. Indeed, the average rate of consumer price inflation decreased to the relatively low level of 6.6%, despite a depreciation of the rupiah. The rate of GDP growth accelerated to 6.3% in 2007. This growth was mainly due to increasing private consumption and higher gross fixed investment.

Although the performance of the Indonesian economy in 2008 was affected by the high fuel and food prices in the early part of the year, and by the subsequent onset of the global financial crisis in the latter months, the country withstood these unforeseen developments with a relatively high degree of resilience. The rate of economic growth eased only marginally to 6.0%, driven to a large extent by an increase in government consumption expenditure of 10.4%, in comparison with only 3.9% in the previous year, and to a lesser degree by an acceleration in the growth of private consumption expenditure to 5.3%, from 5.0% in 2007, and of gross fixed capital formation to 11.9% from 9.3%. This rise in domestic demand inevitably stimulated an increase in imports of goods and services, which exceeded the growth in exports and hence prompted the overall deceleration of the rate of economic growth. GDP per head reached US $2,150 in 2008. Meanwhile, the average annual rate of inflation rose to 9.8%, partly in response to the high fuel and food prices that prevailed early in the year and partly as a result of a significant weakening of the rupiah. The Indonesian currency depreciated significantly against the US dollar, from Rp. 9,419 to $1 at the end of 2007 to Rp. 10,950 to $1 by the end of 2008, with much of this decline occurring in October and November of the latter year. The capital markets suffered a similar weakening. In view of these developments, the Government announced a 10-point programme to stabilize the currency and capital markets in October 2008, and in November Bank Indonesia announced restrictions on purchases of foreign currency. These measures helped to arrest the depreciation of the rupiah and the decline in the stock exchange index.

Despite the global crisis, Indonesia's GDP expanded by 4.6% in 2009 as a whole. Government consumption expenditure increased by 15.7% in comparison with the previous year, while private consumption rose by 4.9%. Gross fixed capital formation expanded by 3.3%. Although the value of exports decreased (see below), the impact of this was mitigated by the capacity of the country's substantial domestic market and by its relatively low dependence on the export sector. The annual rate of inflation declined sharply in 2009, to 4.8%, and capital markets recorded a strong performance. As the global economy began to recover, Indonesia's GDP expanded by a robust 6.1% in 2010. Government consumption expenditure growth decelerated significantly, to just 0.3%, while private consumption growth slowed modestly, to 4.6%. However, growth in gross fixed capital formation accelerated to 8.5%. The rupiah appreciated against the US dollar from the latter half of 2009, reaching Rp. 9,400 to US $1 at the end of that year and Rp. 8,991 to $1 by the end of 2010. In comparison with the first six months of 2010, GDP was estimated to have increased by 6.5% in the first half of 2011; this was attributed primarily to robust growth in exports, private consumption and fixed investment.

AGRICULTURE

Until it was superseded by manufacturing in 1991, agriculture was the predominant sector of the Indonesian economy in terms of output, although it still accounted for almost 20% of GDP in that year. Its share of GDP stood at 15.3% in 2010, unchanged from the previous year but up from a low point of 13.0% in 2006. However, it remains the most important sector in terms of employment, engaging nearly 40% of the working population in 2010. The agricultural sector is divided into five subsectors—food crops, cash crops, animal husbandry, fishing and forestry—of which the food crop subdivision is the most important in terms of income and employment generation. The other subdivisions play a significant role as earners of non-oil and non-gas export revenues, and were estimated to account for approximately 30% of such earnings in 2008, in both unprocessed and processed forms.

Food Crops

The predominant food crops are rice and other 'secondary' (*palawija*) food staples such as maize, cassava, sweet potatoes and soybeans. Food crops form the most important component of the agricultural sector, accounting for approximately 49% of agricultural GDP in 2008. These crops have traditionally been cultivated on relatively small land-holdings (seldom exceeding 1 ha in size) and under highly complex traditional tenurial relationships, which have historically ensured an adequate level of subsistence for all members of the rural community.

Rice is by far the most important food crop, and is also the preferred staple of the vast majority of Indonesians. Several programmes were introduced in the 1960s–1980s to encourage farmers to apply productivity-enhancing cultivation techniques, higher-yielding seeds, and chemical fertilizers and pesticides, and substantial investments were made in the irrigation infrastructure, which permitted an expansion of cultivated area and increased multiple cropping. This resulted in significant increases in the production of dry husked paddy, known locally as *gabah*, and the long-cherished goal of self-sufficiency in rice was reached by 1984/85. From 1985, however, the growth of rice production became much more erratic, with substantial increases of output being recorded in some years and stagnation or contraction being recorded in others. This was due in part to unfavourable weather conditions and pest infestations, and in part to shifts in government policy, which aimed to match output growth with the growth in demand.

In 2002 fears over food security prompted the Government to propose a number of measures to provide domestic producers with financial incentives to raise output and enhance their capacity to compete with foreign suppliers, as well as an increase in the tariff on imported rice from Rp. 430 per kg to Rp. 753 per kg. These measures were reinforced in 2003 by the introduction of a new policy banning rice imports in the months of the main rice harvest, thereby supporting domestic prices during this period of glut. This ban continued to be extended, with the Government declaring in 2005 that imports would be resumed only if the domestic price of medium-quality rice were to rise above Rp. 3,500 per kg and the national stockpile were to fall below 1m. metric tons. Partly as a result of these measures, output rose to some 54m. tons per year in 2004–06. However, adverse weather conditions, related to a recurrence of the climatic phenomenon known as El Niño, caused some shortages in the latter half of 2006 and into 2007, prompting the Government to license exceptional rice imports in September and December 2006, and again in March 2007. Production recovered later in 2007, with the total harvest amounting to 57.2m. tons in the year as a whole, and increasing further to 60.3m. tons in 2008 and 64.4m. tons in 2009; according to official data, this was forecast to increase to 66.4m. in 2010.

In contrast to the emphasis placed on the intensification of rice production, relatively little effort was made to expand production of the secondary food staples. Consequently, output of crops such as maize, cassava, soybeans, groundnuts (peanuts) and sweet potatoes remained virtually stagnant during the 1970s, and the production increases that did occur were due to an expansion in planted area rather than to improved yields, which remained low by international standards. Although considerable production increases were achieved in the 1980s and early 1990s for most of these crops, the growth trends were erratic rather than steady. The output of most of these crops declined significantly in 1997 as a result of the droughts induced by El Niño, but subsequently recovered, with only a modest decline in 2001 prompted by a deterioration in climatic and economic conditions in that year. By 2008 production of cassava had risen to 21.6m. metric tons, and that of maize and soybeans to 16.3m. tons and 777,700 tons, respectively, while production of sweet potatoes had declined to below 1.88m. tons and that of groundnuts to just under 774,000 tons. In 2009 output of cassava, maize and soybeans increased to 22.0m. tons, 17.6m. tons and 974,500 tons, respectively; production of sweet potatoes recovered strongly to 2.06m. tons, while that of groundnuts increased to nearly 778,000 tons.

Cash Crops

Indonesia is an important producer of a wide range of cash crops, including rubber, palm oil, copra, coffee, tea, cocoa, sugar and tobacco. Most of these commodities are grown on commercial plantations as well as on smallholdings, and are destined primarily for export. Production of most major agricultural commodities expanded considerably during the 1980s and 1990s, when smallholders were provided with extension services and subsidized credit and inputs, and were encouraged to replant their fields with higher-yielding varieties and to employ yield-increasing cultivation techniques. The combined real value (in constant prices) of 'farm non-food crops' and 'estate crops' more than doubled between the late 1970s and the mid-1990s, and continued to rise thereafter. The rate of growth subsequently decelerated to a level similar to the growth rate of GDP as a whole, while the two components' contribution to total GDP remained broadly constant at about 8%–9% between 2004 and 2008. However, there has been considerable variation among crops, largely in response to market conditions and to the degree of government support granted to particular commodities. These factors have significantly affected the performance of the principal agricultural export commodities.

Efforts to rehabilitate the rubber industry resulted in rapid increases in production from the late 1970s. This growth trend was successfully sustained for much of the following 25 years with only a few exceptions; for example, in 2004 as a result of an earlier decision by Thailand, Indonesia and Malaysia, the three largest producers of natural rubber in the world, to limit production and exports of the commodity in an effort to boost international rubber prices. Indonesia's output of natural rubber totalled 1.85m. metric tons in 2004, with smallholders accounting for more than 1.4m. tons. Output continued to increase in subsequent years, reaching nearly 2.76m. tons in 2007, as newly planted trees became productive and as improving prices prompted the predominantly smallholder producers to tap their trees more intensively. This trend persisted in 2008, with total production increasing to an estimated 2.92m. tons in that year, although output declined to 2.79m. tons in 2009. Nevertheless, it was projected that Indonesia's output of natural rubber would exceed that of Thailand by 2015, making Indonesia the world's largest producer by that date.

The production of palm oil received considerable encouragement from the Government after 1970, and annual output increased from 216,500 metric tons in that year to 12.4m. tons in 2004. The continued development of large-scale plantations, especially on the island of Borneo, was estimated to have taken Indonesia's production to 15.5m. tons in 2006, and to 16.8m. tons in 2007, exceeding Malaysia's output (of 15.8m. tons) to become the leading global producer. Production of palm oil was estimated to have reached 18.9m. tons in 2008 and 20.55m. tons in 2009. It was expected that this resurgent growth would be sustained in the coming years in response to an increasing emphasis on biofuels as an alternative national and global source of energy. Since most of the existing production was destined for the edible oils industry, new plantations would need to be established to supply the biofuels industry, and in mid-2009 it was estimated that the area under oil palm cultivation would be increased from 5m. ha in 2006 to 10m. ha by 2020 for this purpose. However, the pace of these developments could be curbed to some extent by rising international concerns over the environmental damage that such a widespread conversion of virgin forest to oil palm plantations would cause. With projections issued by the Indonesian Palm Oil Board suggesting an increase in yields from the prevailing level of less than 3.0 tons per ha in 2009 to 4.5 tons per ha. by 2010, production was expected to increase significantly, even if the ambitious plans to increase the planted area were not realized.

Although palm oil has been produced primarily for export, shipments have occasionally been restricted in times of poor harvest in order to ensure adequate supplies of vegetable oil in the domestic market. Palm oil exports have increased steadily, reaching approximately 12.1m. metric tons in 2006 and an estimated 13.0m. tons in 2007. Largely owing to the global economic downturn, exports declined to 12.4m. tons in 2008 and further to 10.4m. tons in 2009; however, exports recovered strongly to reach 13.5m. tons in 2010, and were projected to continue increasing substantially in subsequent years in response to growing demand for both edible oils and biofuels. Meanwhile, in March 2006 Indonesia and Malaysia agreed to enter into a strategic alliance to produce, market and export palm oil, which strengthened their position in international markets since together they accounted for 84% of global palm oil production.

Similarly, efforts have been made to promote the growth of the coconut industry. Reflecting an expansion in planted area, production of coconuts increased substantially, from 12.1m. metric tons in 1990 to 15.2m. tons in 2000 and further to 21.6m. tons in 2009. Production of coconut oil increased from 605,000 tons in 1992 to a peak of 958,400 tons in 2007, but declined to 861,800 tons in 2008, before recovering to 908,400 tons in 2009.

Although Indonesia is the world's leading producer of coconut oil, with an estimated world market share of more than one-quarter, most of the coconut oil produced in Indonesia has traditionally been used to meet domestic demand for cooking oil; Indonesia's exports have therefore been erratic and have usually been surpassed by those of the Philippines. Since the cultivation of coconut palms is undertaken almost entirely by smallholders, who have traditionally accounted for well above 95% of the planted area, the productivity of the Indonesian trees is relatively low, at about 2.2 tons of coconuts per ha. Considerable scope therefore still exists for raising production levels, even if a further increase in planted area is prevented by the exhaustion of suitable land.

Indonesia is one of the world's largest producers of coffee, and output of its mainly robusta varieties increased steadily from the 1970s to reach more than 459,000 metric tons in 1996. Although output declined in 1997, the subsequent years witnessed a steady recovery, and production reached approximately 683,000 tons in 2008, increasing further to 700,000 tons in 2009, mainly as a result of significant growth in smallholder area planted to coffee. However, output was expected to have declined by around 15% in 2010, owing to unfavourable weather conditions. Following the suspension of quotas by the International Coffee Organization (ICO) in 1989, Indonesia's coffee exports initially increased, from 298,858 tons in 1988 to 421,627 tons in 1990, but declined to 269,176 in 1992; during 1993–2005 exports fluctuated sharply, from a low point of 230,066 tons in 1995 to a peak of 443,366 tons in 2005. Exports declined to 411,721 tons in 2006 and further to 320,600 tons in 2007, but recovered strongly in 2008 to reach 468,019 tons. Despite the strong performance of 2008, prospects for the Indonesian coffee industry were restrained by the fact that approximately one-third of the trees on Indonesia's large estates and smallholdings were more than 30 years old, and therefore past their prime producing age, leading to relatively low average yields of some 650 kg per ha. Furthermore, declining international coffee prices (with the price of robusta, for example, having decreased from US $2.20 per kg at October 2008 to just $1.10 by July 2009) and easing global demand was reported to have resulted in a decline in coffee exports, to 400,000 tons, in 2009, and a further decline, to 325,000 tons, was anticipated for 2010.

The production of cocoa, which was first planted on a large scale in the mid-1970s, has gained dramatically in importance in Indonesia, which has now become one of the world's largest producers. Output was estimated at 207,150 metric tons in 1992 and increased steadily to 374,000 tons in 1996, before declining to some 330,000 tons in 1997 as a result of El Niño and the Asian economic crisis. However, output growth was resumed in 1998, and production had reached almost 560,000 tons by 2002, when Indonesia overtook Ghana to become the world's second largest producer of cocoa after Côte d'Ivoire. Output levels continued to rise, to some 779,500 tons in 2006, but declined to 740,000 tons in 2007, before increasing to 793,000 tons in 2008, and was forecast to increase further to 800,000 tons in 2009. This growth in production was accompanied by a corresponding increase in exports, which rose from a mere 6,800 tons in 1981 to 365,650 tons in 2002. A substantial decrease, to 265,838 tons, in 2003, prompted by declining global prices, increased competition from Viet Nam, and a rise in domestic processing was followed by a modest increase, to 275,485 tons, in 2004 and by a full recovery during subsequent years to 490,778 tons in 2006. However, cocoa exports subsequently declined again, to 379,829 tons in 2007, before increasing only modestly, to 380,513 tons, in 2008.

Animal Husbandry and Fishing

Serious efforts were made in the late 1980s and early 1990s to promote the growth of the animal husbandry sector, *inter alia* through the import of large numbers of breeding animals, including dairy and beef cattle, pigs and poultry. All the main products of this sector have consequently recorded impressive growth since the early 1970s, with annual production of meat and eggs increasing from 430,184 metric tons to 2.64m. tons and from 75,600 tons to 1.31m. tons, respectively, between 1970 and 2009, and milk production rising from 173,800 tons to 1.28m. tons during the same period. Despite this growth, animal husbandry remains relatively underdeveloped in Indonesia, with its contribution to GDP never having risen above 2.0%. The sector was also seriously affected by the sharp depreciation of the rupiah in 1997–98, which raised the cost of imported animal feed and prompted the culling of substantial numbers of dairy animals and poultry. Extensive additional culling of poultry has also been necessitated from time to time since 2003 as a result of the epidemic of avian influenza ('bird flu'), which has remained endemic in Indonesia, having spread throughout the country to humans. Despite the Government's efforts to curb the individual ownership of 'backyard poultry', by March 2011 the number of confirmed human cases of 'bird flu' within Indonesia had reached 174, of which 144 had proved fatal.

International recognition of the concept of the archipelagic state in 1982 permitted Indonesia to declare the waters separating its many islands to be an exclusive economic zone (EEZ), thereby giving the country undisputed control over the vast marine fisheries resources of this sea area. These resources began to be developed in 1987, both through the issuing of licences to foreign fishing fleets, and the encouragement of private (including foreign) investment in the fishing industry, especially in shrimp and tuna fisheries. These developments notwithstanding, productivity in the sea-fishing industry has remained low, while overfishing in some areas is threatening to deplete fish stocks, especially in the western parts of the archipelago. Illegal fishing, by both foreign and domestic operators, also remains a serious problem, causing considerable environmental damage and substantial revenue losses to Indonesia. Meanwhile, efforts were also made to enhance the potential of Indonesia's freshwater fisheries, which provide the bulk of animal protein consumed in Indonesia, through the promotion of freshwater shrimp hatcheries and a nucleus fishpond scheme, similar to the expansion programme for cash crops. The shrimp hatcheries, which operated predominantly on a commercial basis, suffered serious set-backs as a result of the economic crisis of the late 1990s and consumer rejection in importing countries following reports of extensive use of antibiotics to prevent disease. According to FAO, the total fish catch increased to 6.83m. tons in 2009, from 6.69m. tons in 2008.

Forestry

With data indicating that 146.3m. ha, or approximately 76% of its land area, were covered by forest in 2005, Indonesia has some of the most extensive concentrations of tropical hardwoods in the world. These have been exploited at a rapid rate since the late 1960s, resulting in an extensive degree of deforestation over the subsequent three decades. Although no firm statistics are available, it has been variously estimated that between 840,000 and 3.8m. ha of forest cover is lost in Indonesia every year.

Having attracted a high level of foreign investment into its forestry industry during the 1970s, Indonesia's annual output of industrial logs increased from only 4m. cu m in 1963 to a range of 24m.–30m. cu m between the mid-1980s and mid-1990s, and a high point of 34.3 cu m by 1998. However, the industry suffered a serious set-back as a result of the economic crisis of 1997/98, which drove many producers out of business. After a brief recovery to 26.2m. cu m in 2003, production continued to decline gradually, to approximately 21.6m. cu m in 2007, before increasing to 26.9m. cu m in 2008; however, output declined to 22.4m. cu m in 2009, at which level it was estimated to have remained in 2010.

Following a government decision in 1980 to increase the content of domestic value added in its forestry exports, the export of raw logs was gradually reduced, and in 1985 it was prohibited altogether. Although this ban was replaced by a high export tax in 1992, it was reinstated in 2001 as a means of curbing the smuggling of illegally felled logs. The promotion of local processing resulted in a rapid increase in plywood production, which rose from 1.01m. cu m in 1980 to 10.10m. cu m in 1992. After remaining above 9m. cu m annually during 1993–97, output declined sharply following the economic crisis, and had fallen to 7.30m. cu m by 2001. Production increased slightly to 7.55m. cu m in 2002, but subsequently declined in each year during 2003–09, standing at just under 3.0m. cu m in 2009; output was estimated to be unchanged in 2010. The production of sawnwood expanded rapidly in the 1980s, reaching 10.4m. cu m in 1989, and thereafter fluctuated within the 6m.–8m. cu m range annually until 2004, in which year production stood at just 4.33m. cu m; production subsequently declined further to 4.17m. cu m in 2008, a level at which output was estimated to have remained in 2010. The remainder of the domestic wood-processing industry was devoted to the manufacture of veneers and to smaller quantities of furniture and wooden handicrafts.

The Government's efforts to protect the country's forestry resources, through the introduction of restrictions on logging and through reafforestation programmes, have been only partially successful, in part owing to widespread forest fires in Sumatra and Kalimantan that have become an almost regular phenomenon since the mid-1990s. Many of these fires, which generate huge clouds of smoke that are carried over much of South-East Asia, are started deliberately, both by subsistence farmers practising traditional 'slash-and-burn' methods of cultivation and by large-scale plantation owners seeking to clear the forest for new cash crop estates. Similarly, the growth of aquaculture facilities is also placing great strain on Indonesia's mangrove forests. In addition, illegal logging and the smuggling of timber remain serious problems, with some estimates having suggested that up to 68m. cu m may be cut illegally every year. In an effort to overcome these issues, the Government has supplemented its domestic enforcement efforts by signing international agreements with the European Union (EU), Malaysia, Japan and the People's Republic of China to ban the import of illegal logs from Indonesia.

In addition to tropical rain forests, Indonesia also has sizeable teak plantations. Other significant forestry products are rattan, resins and copal. In order to promote the domestic rattan-processing industry, the Government banned all exports of raw rattan with effect from January 1987, and of semi-processed rattan products from July 1988. This ban, which was temporarily replaced by an export tax in the early 1990s, was removed in September 2005.

MINING

Petroleum and Natural Gas

The petroleum and natural gas industries have played a crucial role in providing Indonesia with resources to fund its development programmes. Owing to the heavy dependence of the economy on these industries for both its foreign exchange and fiscal revenues, the country's prosperity has been closely linked to fluctuations in international petroleum markets. Even after extensive efforts to promote alternative sectors of the economy following the decline in international petroleum prices in 1986, the petroleum and natural gas industries have continued to make a disproportionately large contribution to public resources.

The state-owned oil company, Pertamina, was formed in 1968 by the merger of two existing companies. As a result of the technical and financial constraints confronting Pertamina, foreign oil companies were permitted to continue operating in Indonesia as contractors of state companies under several forms of agreement, the most common of which being the production-sharing contract. Pertamina's control over the hydrocarbons industry was significantly weakened following the promulgation of a new oil and gas law in October 2001. This law provided for a separation of the upstream and downstream activities formerly carried out by Pertamina, with the former (i.e. the regulatory functions and the management of the production-sharing contracts) being assigned to a new government agency known as BP Migas and the latter (i.e. the distribution and marketing of oil and fuel products) to another new agency, BPH Migas, both of which were established in 2002. In addition, Pertamina's monopoly over the downstream sector was ended, allowing other companies to compete in the retail market. This gave rise to considerable international interest, with Shell, the Anglo-Dutch oil company, opening Indonesia's first privately owned retail fuel station in a Jakarta suburb in November 2005. Petronas of Malaysia and Total of France subsequently entered the Indonesian retail market, as did the US-based company Chevron.

Foreign investment in the Indonesian petroleum industry has been actively encouraged since 1966, and some 375 production-sharing and other contracts had been signed by the end of 2006, of which 137 were still active. Particularly heavy investment took place in 1967–77, encouraged by the oil price rises of the 1970s. This resulted in a rapid increase in output, from 189m. barrels in 1967 to a record 615m. barrels in 1977. Thereafter, production levels declined gradually but steadily, albeit with some annual fluctuation, to reach an estimated 280m. barrels (including natural gas condensate) in 2009. This decrease was a result of the imposition of output restraints by the Organization of the Petroleum Exporting Countries (OPEC) in an effort to stabilize prices, and a decrease in investment interest by the international oil industry prompted by the declining attractiveness of the Indonesian regulatory and business environment. In March 2004 the volume of crude petroleum imports briefly exceeded that of exports for the first time in living memory, and this situation was repeated in several of the months of 2005. By 2006 Indonesia had become a net importer for the year as a whole, and, as output continued to decline, the Government announced in May 2008 that it did not intend to renew Indonesia's membership of OPEC. Consequently, the country suspended its membership of OPEC in January 2009. However, Indonesia was well placed to recover its position as a net exporter.

In February 2003 the Government adjusted the terms of the production-sharing contracts offered to foreign investors, raising the share offered to the contractors from 15% to between 20% and 25%. Subsequently, investor confidence was also boosted by the resolution in March 2006 of a protracted disagreement between Pertamina and ExxonMobil on the joint operation of the Cepu oilfield in East Java. Between 2003 and 2009 these developments helped to attract investors into 156 new production-sharing contracts, of which 18 were signed in 2006, 25 in 2007 (the highest annual number in 40 years), 36 in 2008 and a further 12 in May 2009.

As a result of these measures, the Government hoped to raise production levels. However, progress was slow, with the average output rising to only 1.00m. barrels per day (b/d) in 2008, before declining to less than 0.99m. b/d in 2010, mainly owing to disappointing exploratory efforts and to the fact that Indonesia's largest oilfields are mature, resulting in an inevitable decline in output from such sources. As international oil prices soared to unprecedented levels, Indonesia's own declining production led to a steady increase in import costs. A reduction in fuel subsidies, implemented in October 2005, precipitated a sharp increase in domestic fuel prices, following which domestic consumption of fuels was reported to have declined by between 15% and 20%. A further reduction in fuel oil subsidies in May 2008 followed the announcement in January that the Government was to promote the use of biofuels based on palm oil, jatropha, sugar and cassava to replace petroleum, especially as a transport fuel. According to this statement, biofuels were expected to account for some 10% of Indonesia's transport fuel consumption by 2010. Indonesia's proven reserves of petroleum totalled 4,200m. barrels at the end of 2010.

In addition to its petroleum resources, Indonesia had proven reserves of natural gas amounting to 3,100,000m. cu m at the end of 2010. More than one-half of these reserves were located off shore, notably near the Natuna Islands in the South China Sea and near the Bird's Head area of Papua. The commercial exploitation of these reserves began in 1977/78, when two major natural gas fields at Arun, in the province of Aceh in northern Sumatra, and Badak, in East Kalimantan, were brought into production, and facilities were established to permit the production of LNG. For the following three decades Indonesia remained the world's largest exporter of LNG, until it was overtaken by Qatar in 2006.

The initial development of the LNG industry was linked to the signing of several long-term export contracts with Japan in 1973 and 1981. These contracts were extended until 2010–11 in mid-1995, and again to 2015–16 in March 2008, albeit with reduced volumes in response to declining production and rising domestic demand. They were supplemented by a number of other sales agreements with Japanese, South Korean and Taiwanese utilities in the intervening period. This growing international demand for LNG and the increasing domestic use of natural gas to generate power and to fuel large manufacturing plants have resulted in a steady expansion of the natural gas production and liquefaction industries.

By 1997 Indonesia's production of natural gas and LNG had risen to 3,166,035m. cu ft (corresponding to about 542m. barrels) and 1,402,621,000m. British thermal units (20.6m. metric tons), respectively. The following years witnessed considerable fluctuations in output, with reductions being recorded in 1998 as a result of the economic crisis, and in 2000–01 owing to the political unrest in Aceh, which caused a brief shutdown on the Arun field in 2001. The production of LNG decreased by almost 7% in 2005, partly because of the declining productivity of the Arun field in particular, and partly because of the Government's policy of providing subsidized deliveries of natural gas to the country's fertilizer industry as feedstock. This formed part of a broader approach by the Government to channel a greater share of the country's gas production to the domestic market in order to diversify the domestic energy base, which was formalized in a presidential decree issued in March 2006. However, this policy caused some unease in the industry, since prices for most domestic uses continue to be set by the Government at levels below those prevailing in international markets. The Government was forced to issue a number of clarifications and amendments in January 2007 to ensure that it did not deter investments in the future expansion of gas production. LNG output was estimated at 85,700m. cu m in 2009.

With the Arun and Badak fields being gradually depleted, the need to develop new fields became increasingly urgent from the early 1990s. Following the signing in January 1995 of an agreement between Indonesia and Exxon for development of the West Natuna block, commercial production commenced in January 2001, with the inauguration of a 650-km undersea pipeline to Singapore with a capacity of 325m. cu ft/day under a 22-year contract. This was followed in August 2002 with the opening of a 96-km pipeline to Malaysia under a 20-year contract, through which Indonesia's sales were expected to rise from 100m. cu ft/day in 2002 to 250m. cu ft/day by 2007. However, the Natuna project was beset by frequent disagreements between the Government and Exxon over production levels and profit-sharing, which had not been resolved by mid-2008, when it was announced that Exxon's licence to manage the field had been transferred to Pertamina. In December 2010 Pertamina signed agreements with Exxon, Total and Petronas, providing for the joint development of the West Natuna block; work on the project was expected to take between five and 10 years to complete.

Major efforts have also been made to attract investment for the development of other new fields, with investors being offered a 30%–40% share of the output under a revised format of production-sharing contracts introduced in February 2003. Particular efforts have been made in recent years to develop the Tangguh field off Papua, and several long-term contracts to supply LNG from the field were signed in 2002–04 with the China National Offshore Oil Corporation (CNOOC), the US firm Sempra Energy, and the South Korean companies POSCO and K-Power. This was followed by the signing of a further agreement with the Japanese Tohoku Electric Power Company in May 2008. In mid-2009 the first shipments from the Tangguh field commenced.

In order to enhance the flexibility with which Indonesia's natural gas resources could be utilized, the state gas utility company, Perusahaan Gas Negara (PGN), planned the construction of a 4,200-km pipeline-based Integrated Gas Transportation System (IGTS) to link the islands of Sumatra, Java and Kalimantan. Financial support for the project was mobilized from the World Bank, the ADB and other institutions. One section of the pipeline in South Sumatra was completed and in August 2003 was extended to Singapore, in connection with a contract to supply Singapore with up to 350m. cu ft/day of natural gas over a 20-year period. Two further sections, linking South Sumatra with the industrial centres and power plants of West Java, and traversing the island of Java from west to east, were also completed subsequently. A further section, linking Central Java with East Kalimantan, was due to be completed in 2012. In 2002, meanwhile, regional energy ministers agreed to develop a region-wide pipeline-based natural gas grid by 2020. The pipelines linking the Natuna field with Singapore and Malaysia were to constitute a component of this grid, and proposals were being examined to build a third pipeline from Natuna to Thailand.

Indonesia has also sought to increase production and exports of liquefied petroleum gas (LPG), which until 1987 was produced almost entirely as a by-product of the refining of crude petroleum. A 1986 agreement to supply 2m. metric tons of LPG per year to Japan from 1988 led to the construction of specifically designed LPG facilities at the Arun and Badak natural gas-processing plants. Between 1981 and 1995 the production of LPG increased from 560,000 tons to 3.9m. tons, before decreasing gradually to approximately 1.2m. tons in 2006, in response to declining demand and increased external competition in export markets, as well as technical problems in some of the refineries producing LPG, such as the ones at Balikpapan in East Kalimantan and Cilacap in Central Java. Production recovered to 1.68m. tons in 2007, and increased further to 1.83m. tons in 2008 and to 2.32m. tons in 2009.

In 2007 the Indonesian Government introduced a programme to promote the replacement of kerosene by LPG as a domestic fuel, which was expected to lead to a significant increase in domestic demand. While this demand was to be met partially through an increase in domestic LPG refining capacity, which began with the inauguration in June 2009 of a refinery in Gresik to process natural gas from the Ujung Pangkah field off the city of Surabaya in East Java, it was also expected to lead to a dramatic increase in imports of LPG. In late 2008 Pertamina announced that it was to import 1m. metric tons of LPG per year for the next 10 years, prompting suggestions that Indonesia might soon become a net importer of LPG.

From mid-2007 the Government began to promote the extraction of coal-bed methane (CBM), a natural gas trapped in seams of coal, as an alternative energy source. Based on studies showing that the country had CBM resources of about 450,000,000m. cu ft, mostly located in South Sumatra, the Government offered production-sharing contracts with very favourable terms to private mining companies to develop these resources. By the end of 2008 seven such contracts had been signed.

Other Minerals

In addition to petroleum and natural gas, Indonesia has significant (but, in many cases, unquantified) reserves of a variety of other minerals, including coal, tin, bauxite, copper, nickel, iron sands, gold and silver. Most of these are localized, and are frequently situated in remote areas, so that their exploitation often involves high costs. Recognizing the need for the establishment of new framework conditions to reverse declines in investment and output in the industry, in early 2006 the Government submitted to the House of Representatives a new draft law on mining, which proposed a significant easing of the regulatory framework governing the mining industry, providing a variety of incentives for investment in the sector. However, its passage through the legislature was seriously delayed, and by the time it entered into force in January 2009 several restrictions had been added that gave rise to fears that it might, in fact, deter investment by large international corporations.

Although Indonesia's proven reserves of coal were modest (5,529m. metric tons at the end of 2010), total reserves—including proven, probable and possible reserves—were estimated to amount to as much as 36,000m. tons. In order to restrict the growth of domestic petroleum consumption (especially in the production of electricity), a major effort was made to expand the use of coal as a source of fuel, thereby increasing coal production from 304,000 tons in 1980 to some 188.7m. tons in 2008. This effort involved the expansion of the main existing coalfields at Bukit Asam, in South Sumatra, and Ombilin, in West Sumatra, the promotion of increased exploration and the development of new fields. The most significant of these was the opening of the Kaltim Prima open pit mine in East Kalimantan in 1992, which was subsequently expanded to become one of the world's largest coal mines. In 2004 the Government adopted a national coal policy specifically aimed at promoting coal production for domestic use and export, and in June 2008 it announced a production target of 261.6m. tons in the state budget for 2009, the first time that such a target had been set for coal production in the budget. According to the BP Statistical Review of World Energy 2011, actual output fell just short of this target, at 256.2m. tons in 2009, but increased to 305.9m. tons in 2010. Although the Government projected an increase in the contribution of coal to energy production from 23% in 2010 to 33% in 2025, in May 2011 the Minister of Energy and Mineral Resources, Dr Ir Darwin Zahedy Saleh, warned that the management of coal resources should be handled with caution since, at current rates of production, the country's reserves would be exhausted within 80 years.

Coal exports increased sharply from 2.5m. metric tons in 1989 to 291m. tons in 2010, making Indonesia the world's second largest exporter of coal after Australia. Despite this favourable performance, there was a strong divestment from the industry by Western companies—including Rio Tinto, BP and New Hope—owing to concerns about the security and legal environment, although their departure was being offset by increased investments by national and regional (including Chinese) companies. A government regulation issued in October 2005 levying a 5% export tax on coal was also widely criticized within the industry as reducing its international competitiveness.

Meanwhile, the Japanese firm Kobe Steel announced plans in July 2006 to launch a pilot project in South Kalimantan to convert the local deposits of low-grade coal with a high moisture content into higher-quality coal briquettes. This project to produce upgraded brown coal was regarded as potentially very important, since Indonesia was estimated to have almost 30,000m. metric tons of such low-grade coal, which had hitherto not been exploited commercially.

Indonesia is one of the world's leading producers of tin. This is mined primarily on the islands of Bangka and Belitung, off the eastern coast of Sumatra, by a state-owned company, PT Tambang Timah, a subsidiary of PT Timah Tbk, which was partially privatized in October 1995, and by PT Koba Tin, a joint venture between the Malaysia Smelting Corporation and PT Timah Tbk. Despite a number of adverse external factors—including the 1985–86 tin trading crisis, the subsequent imposition of supply controls by the Association of Tin Producing Countries (ATPC) from March 1987 to July 1996, and the Asian economic crisis of 1997/98—the industry managed to retain its competitiveness through stringent rationalization and cost reductions. Output increased sharply from an annual average of approximately 30,000 metric tons during the period of the ATPC supply controls to almost 55,175 metric tons in 1997. Following a decline to less than 54,000 tons in 1998 and 47,753 tons in 1999, as a result of the impact of the regional economic crisis, production recovered steadily to reach 88,142 tons in 2002. This recovery, which reflected improving international market conditions and an easing of domestic regulatory conditions, prompted a number of small independent producers to enter the industry, and approximately 20 small-scale smelters were established. The operations of these unlicensed producers, and their interplay with the major companies PT Tambang Timah and PT Koba Tin, contributed to significant fluctuations in officially reported output figures in subsequent years: production decreased to 70,338 metric tons in 2004, recovering to 78,404 tons in 2005 and to 80,933 tons in 2006, before declining again, to 66,137 tons, in 2007 and further to 53,228 tons in 2008, and then rising modestly, to around 55,000 tons, in 2009. However, as these statistics excluded the operations of the private operators, overall production was estimated to have averaged some 120,000 tons annually, with much of the tin being mined and exported by the unlicensed miners and smelters, avoiding royalty payments and other government levies.

In order to restore order to the industry, the Government introduced a new regulatory framework in October 2006, followed by the introduction of new export regulations in March 2007 aimed at reducing overall exports to a maximum of 90,000 tons by limiting exports to companies obtaining their tin from licensed sources that had paid a 3% royalty, and to tin with a purity of 99%. As anticipated, this led to a reduction in exports by more than 40,000 metric tons in 2007, from 121,100 tons in 2006 to 78,900 tons in 2007. The supply disruptions to the international market caused by these measures resulted in a strong increase in world prices from October 2006, with the cash price on the London Metal Exchange rising to a record level of almost US $14,700 per ton in mid-April 2007, before stabilizing temporarily at about $14,000–$14,500 per ton. Further price fluctuations in 2008 resulted in global tin prices rising to a record $25,500 per ton in May, before declining to below $10,000 in December, and recovering again to some $14,400 in early July 2009. The Government therefore began to reconsider the possibility of limiting Indonesia's tin production. Indonesia's external trade statistics indicated that the relatively high prices prevailing in 2008 had elicited a strong supply response, with the volume of exports rising to 112.9m. tons in that year.

West Borneo and the Riau archipelago are the main sources of Indonesia's bauxite, which is mined on the islands of Tembeling, Kelong, Dendang and Bintan by a state-owned company, PT Antam (Aneka Tambang). Output grew steadily from the mid-1990s, reaching approximately 1.3–1.5m. metric tons in 2005–06; however, production decreased to 1.25m. tons in 2007 and further to 1.15m. tons in 2008, before recovering only modestly, to 1.20m. in 2009. With the resources on Bintan gradually being depleted, PT Antam was planning to develop a bauxite deposit at Tayan on the Kapuas River in West Kalimantan. Other major hard minerals include nickel, which is mined at several locations in Celebes (Sulawesi), principally by the Canadian-owned Inco at Soroako and by PT Antam at Pomalaa, and copper, which is mined solely by a US company, PT Freeport Indonesia Inc, in a controversial large-scale mining operation in the province of Papua. Copper deposits have also been found in Sumatra, Borneo, Java and Celebes. While production of these metals has fluctuated according to changing market conditions, the long-term trend has been extremely positive, with output of nickel ore increasing from some 1.5m. tons in 1980 to almost 4.4m. tons in 2002, and output of copper ore concentrate increasing from approximately 186,200 tons to 3.8m. tons during the same period. More recently, however, output of these minerals has been erratic. Production of nickel ore decreased to approximately 3.7m. tons in 2005, before recovering to almost 4.4m. tons in 2006, rising to 7.1m. tons in 2007 and then declining to 6.6m. tons in 2008. Meanwhile, production of copper ore concentrate fluctuated between 2.8m. tons and 3.6m. tons between 2003 and 2007, before slipping to 2.3m. tons in 2008. This volatility was attributed mainly to the complexity of the operating conditions confronting the international mining companies engaged in these industries, as a result of legal and political uncertainties and security concerns.

Although the implementation of a programme to expand output of precious metals, and of gold in particular, from the late 1980s was hindered by a number of infrastructural constraints and the growing problem of illegal mining on concessions offered to private mining companies, output of gold increased substantially, to reach 166.1 metric tons, in 2001. More than one-half of this total amount was produced by PT Freeport Indonesia at its copper and gold mine in Papua. Nevertheless, the gold sector was not spared the subsequent general malaise that affected the mining industry, with output declining from 117,851 kg in 2007 to 64,390 kg in 2008, before increasing marginally, to 65,000 kg in 2009.

Operations at the Freeport mine in Papua were temporarily halted in July 2011 owing to an eight-day strike in which thousands of workers participated, demanding an increase in their wages, from the current hourly rate of between US $1.50 and $3 to between $30 and $200. Having adjusted their wage demands to between $17.50 and $43 per hour, the workers embarked on a second strike in mid-September, which was intended to last for a whole month. Although Freeport tried to downplay the negative impact of the industrial action on copper and gold production at the mine, most observers agreed that the disruption at the mine was contributing to rising global copper prices.

MANUFACTURING

High priority was given to industrial development from the late 1960s. While the Government played an active part in this process, through the establishment of numerous state-owned enterprises and through equity participation in large numbers of private enterprises, it also sought to encourage private investors, both domestic and foreign, to contribute to Indonesia's industrialization. This resulted in the rapid expansion of the country's manufacturing industry, so that by the mid-1990s Indonesia had the capacity to produce a wide variety of goods ranging from handicrafts to high-technology aerospace products. In 1991 the manufacturing sector superseded agriculture as the largest contributor to GDP, and by 1997 it had acquired a share of almost 27% of GDP.

Of Indonesia's main products, most consumer goods, such as processed foods and beverages, textiles and garments, motor vehicle components and assemblies, tobacco products and electrical appliances, are produced by the private manufacturing sector, often in joint ventures with foreign companies. In many of the capital and intermediate goods industries, such as chemicals, cement, glass, fertilizers, ceramics, machinery and basic metal products, the Government plays an important role, with the private sector excluded from some industries, such as those producing fertilizers. In addition to more 'formal' industries, the Government has also promoted the establishment of small-scale enterprises, often involving the production of handicrafts and organized on a co-operative basis, as a means of generating employment in rural areas.

One of the major objectives of Indonesia's industrialization policy has been to add value to domestically produced raw materials. Consequently, a variety of processing industries has been established, ranging from relatively small-scale units for the processing of agricultural commodities and forestry products (including food-processing enterprises, crumb rubber factories, processing plants for crude palm oil, plywood mills and sawmills and establishments for the manufacture of rattan products) to various large-scale petrochemical plants, as well as processing units for Indonesia's hard minerals, of which the aluminium smelter on the Asahan river in North Sumatra is the most significant.

A major new development in this policy approach was initiated in July 2006 when the Government announced an ambitious five-year programme for the expansion of Indonesia's manufacturing capacity for biofuels from palm oil, jatropha, cassava and sugar cane. The programme provided for an overall investment of approximately US $21,500m. over five years for the establishment of 6m. ha of new plantations for these crops and the associated processing plants and other infrastructure. The principal focus was on the production of biodiesel from palm oil and jatropha seeds, and bioethanol from cassava and sugar cane. In May 2006 the state oil company Pertamina began retailing biodiesel, under the brand name of 'Bio-Solar', at selected petrol stations in Jakarta.

While several of Indonesia's traditional export industries, such as shoes, textiles and garments, benefited from 'anti-dumping' measures imposed by importing countries on Chinese and Vietnamese exports of these goods (for example, it was reported that some 50 international footwear firms had relocated to Indonesia from these countries in 2006 and that the value of textile and garment exports had risen by 9.5% in that year), the eventual removal of these restrictions was expected to place Indonesia at a competitive disadvantage unless appropriate measures were taken. In addition, the manufacturing sector confronted a number of short-term adjustment challenges to various economic policy measures introduced by the Government, such as the elimination of fuel subsidies and the imposition of high interest rates. As a result, sectoral growth declined from 6.4% in 2004 to 4.6% in both 2005 and 2006, before increasing slightly to 4.7% in 2007; growth decreased to 3.7% in 2008 and further to 2.2% in 2009, but recovered to 4.5% in 2010. Manufacturing's share of GDP, meanwhile, decreased gradually to 27.0% in 2007, from a peak of 28.7% in 2002; following a modest recovery to 27.8% in 2008, the sector's contribution to GDP declined again, to 26.4% in 2009 and to 24.8% in 2010.

INFRASTRUCTURE

As a large country with a complex archipelagic structure, Indonesia confronts considerable difficulties in establishing the extensive infrastructure of transport, communications and public utilities that is an essential prerequisite for its economic and social development. The necessity of creating such an infrastructure has long been recognized by policy-makers in Indonesia, and considerable investments have been made in this field since the mid-1960s. However, financial constraints arising from the regional economic crisis of 1997/98 restricted such investments in subsequent years, both for new facilities and for repair and maintenance of existing structures, leaving a substantial backlog of infrastructure needs.

The Government of President Susilo Bambang Yudhoyono, which was inaugurated in October 2004, emphasized its commitment to addressing this backlog by holding an 'infrastructure summit' in Jakarta in January 2005, which was attended by business representatives from 22 countries and was aimed at attracting private investment in infrastructure projects worth US $145,000m. over the following five years. These included 91 priority projects with an estimated value of $22,500m., involving gas pipelines, electric power and water, telecommunications, road and rail construction, and airport and seaport development. Infrastructure development was thus a leading theme of the annual conference in June 2006 of the country's external donors, who designated this area as one of the priorities for their future assistance to Indonesia. It was raised again at an investment conference held in November, at which the Government proposed 111 projects costing $16,500m., including 10 'model projects' worth $4,400m. and comprising three water supply projects, a ferry terminal, a port project, two toll roads, a telecommunications project and two power generation projects.

The initial responses to these government initiatives were disappointing; this was largely due to delays in introducing the measures needed to create an attractive business environment for potential investors. Although a National Policy Committee for Accelerating Infrastructure Provision, chaired by the Co-ordinating Minister for Economic Affairs, Prof. Dr Boediono, was established in February 2006, a promise that more than 150 policy reform items would be addressed by the end of the year was left largely unfulfilled. However, the reform process subsequently accelerated, with a number of measures being introduced to improve investment conditions. These included the establishment of a simplified and more transparent regulatory framework, the provision of financial support for land acquisition, and the introduction of measures guaranteeing prices and sharing financial risk. This process culminated in March 2007 in the promulgation of a new investment law by the House of Representatives, which provided significant incentives to foreign investors.

In an attempt to address the increasingly serious shortcomings of the country's infrastructure, a private company, PT Indonesia Infrastructure Finance (IIF), was formally inaugurated in August 2010 with the objective of providing long-term financing for the development of facilities such as telecommunications, energy and transport networks. With initial capital of Rp. 1,600,000m., the IIF's shareholders were PT Sarana Multi Infrastruktur (the Indonesian infrastructure financing agency), the International Finance Corporation, the ADB and a subsidiary of Kreditanstalt für Wiederaufbau, a German state-owned company. Draft legislation on the acquisition of privately owned land for public interests, which supporters of the bill argued would result in a marked acceleration of infrastructure development, awaited parliamentary approval at mid-2011. However, critics of the draft law expressed concern about the potential for human rights violations and claimed that the bill was counter to the provisions of the Indonesian Constitution, which states that property rights must be respected and may not be seized arbitrarily.

Transport

In 2006 Indonesia had a total road length of 393,794 km, of which about 53% was asphalted. Some 60% of these roads were located in Sumatra, Java and Bali, where most cities are now connected by highways or secondary roads, and several major motorway projects have been completed. Indonesia's railway services are limited to the islands of Java (including Madura), where most major cities are connected, and Sumatra, where three separate networks, with a total track length of some 6,500 km, operate in the northern, western and southern parts of the island. Plans to establish a 15-km network to facilitate commuter travel between Jakarta and its suburbs, as well as an underground mass rapid transit system in central Jakarta, were delayed by the effects of the economic crisis of 2008/09. Considerable efforts have been made to expand and upgrade ports and shipping since the mid-1980s. Major investments were initiated in the Jakarta international container terminal to make it into one of the world's largest full-service international seaports.

Air transport in Indonesia is relatively well developed, with more than 60 recognized main airports, most of which are capable of handling aircraft of at least Fokker F-28 size. The largest airline is the state-owned Garuda Indonesia, which operated an all-jet fleet of 92 aircraft at mid-2011, having begun a significant expansion and modernization programme, with a further 199 aircraft on order. Some 50 other airlines, mostly privately owned, operate domestic and regional services. A proliferation of mostly small, low-cost airlines, offering 'no-frills' services on domestic and regional routes, followed the liberalization of the civil aviation sector in 2002. The largest of these budget carriers is Lion Air, which surpassed the state-owned domestic carrier, PT Merpati Nusantara Airlines, to become Indonesia's second largest airline in 2004 and had an all-jet fleet of 68 aircraft in mid-2011, with a further 128 aircraft on order. A spate of accidents in 2006–07 prompted the Government to initiate an audit of 20 passenger and cargo airlines in March 2007, which found that not a single one of these carriers was in full compliance with international safety standards and 13 met only minimal safety requirements. The poor safety record of the Indonesian aviation industry prompted the EU to issue a ban on Indonesian airlines in July 2007, which was subsequently extended, despite an agreement signed in the interim with the International Civil Aviation Organization whereby the Indonesian Government undertook to improve air safety. In July 2009 the EU removed Garuda Indonesia and three other Indonesian airlines—Airfast Indonesia, Mandala Airlines and Premiair—from its 'blacklist', citing a marked improvement in the airlines' safety standards.

Electric Power

Approximately two-thirds of Indonesia's electric power is generated by the state-owned firm PT PLN (Persero), formerly known as Perusahaan Listrik Negara (PLN), which expanded its power-generating capacity rapidly between 1966 and 2007, from approximately 650 MW to 24,719 MW. As late as 1980 some 95% of Indonesia's electricity was generated by oil- or gas-fuelled plants, but by 2000, as a result of a deliberate diversification policy, oil- and gas-fuelled plants (including combined-cycle plants) accounted for less than 50% of Indonesia's power-generating capacity, with the remainder being generated by coal-fired steam, hydropower and geothermal power plants. However, despite this substantial increase in installed capacity over the previous four decades, only about 60% of Indonesia's households were reported to have access to electric power in 2007.

Low investment by the public sector owing to resource constraints, and by the private sector owing to unfavourable investment conditions, have prompted growing concerns over impending power shortages, especially in the Java–Bali grid, where demand grew by about 11% annually from 2002 and where power failures became increasingly frequent from 2006. In response, the Government announced a '10,000 MW Acceleration Programme' to add 10,000 MW of new generating capacity by PLN, in partnership with private investors, by 2010. The new generating facilities were intended to include 30 plants, with a combined generating capacity of approximately 1,850 MW, in various locations outside Java and Bali, and at least 10 larger plants on Java. Several measures have been taken to enable PLN to proceed rapidly with this process, including the waiving of open bidding requirements for the award of contracts to private firms. By the end of 2006 contracts for the construction of two power plants at Suralaya in West Java and Paiton in East Java had already been awarded to the China National Import and Export Corporation and the Harbin Corporation, respectively. In January 2007 agreements were signed with various national private corporations for the construction of 10 of the smaller plants envisaged for outside Java and Bali. Despite some concerns that the target for the '10,000 MW Acceleration Programme' would not be reached, the Government began preparing a second phase of this programme in 2008; the second-phase target was to be met by 2014. Legislation introduced in 2009 permitted the generation, transmission and sale of electricity by private enterprises and local authorities independently of PLN.

Apart from the proposed expansion of its coal-fired power generation, the Government also announced plans in early 2007 to develop other sources of energy. These included a revival of the dormant 1,000-MW nuclear power plant project proposed for the Muria peninsula in Central Java, which had been postponed as a result of the financial crisis of 1997/98. Tenders for the project were to be issued in 2010, with power generation expected to commence in 2016. In addition, considerable efforts were made to promote geothermal power-generating capacity, which increased to 1,198 MW at mid-2011, from just 395 MW in 2006, and was officially projected to increase to 2,620 MW by 2014. Of the 10,000 MW expansion targeted by 2014, some 4,000 MW was to be provided by geothermal sources.

TRADE

Indonesia's merchandise trade has consistently recorded a surplus. A sharp increase in both export volumes and commodity prices raised the surplus to US $39,733m. in 2006, and this remained stable in 2007, when a surplus of $39,627m. was recorded; however, this declined to just $7,823m. in 2008, when export growth, at 20.1%, was vastly exceeded by import growth of some 73.5%. Merchandise exports decreased by 15.0% in 2009 as a whole; however, imports declined by 25.1%, thereby resulting in an increase in the trade surplus, to $19,681m.; the surplus increased further to $22,115m. in 2010.

However, the surplus on the merchandise account has usually been more than offset by a consistent deficit on invisible items, resulting from interest payments on Indonesia's external debt and the repatriation of profits by foreign investors, and also from Indonesia's heavy dependence on foreign transport services. Remittances from Indonesian workers abroad make a modest contribution. The substantial rise in the surplus on merchandise trade in 2006–07, combined with an increase in net transfers, had a strongly beneficial impact on the overall current account surplus, which reached US $10,859m. in 2006, declining only slightly, to $10,491m., in 2007. By contrast, as a result of the substantial erosion of the trade surplus, the current account surplus was reduced to a mere $126m. in 2008, before rising to $10,192m. in 2009; however, this declined to $6,295m. in 2010.

Despite their diminished importance since the 1980s, petroleum and natural gas remain the country's principal export products, with their contribution rising in tandem with strong energy prices and increases in production as new investments in the hydrocarbons sector yield results. The bulk of Indonesia's remaining exports consist of primary and semi-processed agricultural and mineral commodities. The most important of these have traditionally been rubber, coffee, tin, shrimps and palm oil. Exports of logs, which accounted for 7.6% of total exports in 1980, declined into virtual insignificance in subsequent years and were replaced by exports of processed wood (including plywood), which in 1994 contributed almost 13% of total export value. This share declined gradually but steadily in subsequent years, owing to marketing problems and increased foreign competition in Indonesia's main export markets, to less than 2.1% in 2008.

Among manufactured exports, textiles and garments accounted for 17.8% of total exports in 1999. From 2000, however, this trend began to be reversed, as the recovery in exports of other products gathered pace, while exports of garments and textiles were confronted by increasing competition from China and other producers. By 2006 this share had declined to 11.9%, despite an absolute increase in the value of exports from US $8,554m. in 2005 to $9,626m. in 2006, as Indonesia was able to take advantage of the restrictions placed on Chinese exports in the major import markets. While this absolute growth continued in 2007 and 2008, as the value of exports increased to $10,220m. in the latter year, it fell short of the growth of other exports, resulting in a continuing decline in the share of textile and garment exports in total exports to 7.5% in 2008.

Following efforts to promote non-oil and non-gas exports, a wide range of other manufactured goods also began to assume an increasingly important share of the country's exports in the early and mid-1990s, although this trend was interrupted during the late 1990s and early 2000s by the impact of the economic crisis of 1997. However, most categories of manufactured exports have experienced robust growth since 2002–03, with particularly strong expansion being recorded by processed rubber and palm oil as a result of the steady increase in the area planted to these crops and favourable commodity prices. Other manufactured exports, such as processed food, chemicals and electrical appliances, also exhibited strong growth. Electrical and electronic appliances emerged as a particularly important export, with revenue amounting to almost US $9,774m. and accounting for approximately 14.6% of total export earnings in 2005. The performance of these products was more measured in 2006–09, however, as stronger commodity prices led to a more rapid growth in commodity-based manufactures in the first half of the period and as the effects of the global economic downturn took hold in the latter half. However, revenue from the export of electrical and electronic appliances increased strongly to $10,432.5m. in 2010 (up from $8,148.1m. in 2009), although the share of these products in total export earnings stood at just 6.6%.

Indonesia's imports consisted largely of capital and intermediate goods between the mid-1980s and 2008, as the domestic expansion of rice production and import-substituting manufacturing caused imports of consumer goods to be sharply reduced. The country's trade was traditionally biased towards Japan, the USA and Singapore, which together accounted for approximately 77% of exports and 52% of imports during the 1980s. Despite a considerable diversification of Indonesia's trade relations in subsequent years, these countries remained major trading partners and together accounted for 34.1% of its exports and 34.4% of its imports in 2010. However, a significant shift has taken place in the rankings of these countries as sources of Indonesia's imports, with the value of imports from Singapore rising from US $2,525.9m. in 1999 to $10,034.5m. in 2006, before declining slightly, to $9,839.8m., in 2007 and surging to $21,790.1m. in 2008. This took Singapore from being the third largest source to being the most important, although to a large extent this growth is accounted for by transshipments of Indonesian imports from other countries and by Indonesia's growing imports of refined petroleum products from Singapore. In the early 1990s South Korea and China also emerged as increasingly important trading partners. China accounted for $20,424m. of the value of Indonesia's imports by 2010, thus relegating Singapore ($20,241m.) into second place, with Japan ($16,966m.) in third place. The opening of a natural gas pipeline linking the Natuna gasfield with Malaysia in 2002 boosted Indonesian exports to that country, which increased from $1,005m. in 2001 to $9,362.3m. in 2010.

TOURISM

The tourism industry in Indonesia developed rapidly from the 1980s, when the country emerged as an increasingly popular long-haul destination for tourists from Europe, the Americas and the Asia-Pacific region. This development was actively encouraged by the Government, which took a conscious decision in the early 1980s to promote the industry as a means of creating employment, generating foreign exchange and stimulating the economic and social development of some of the country's more remote, but touristically attractive, regions. In the following years various measures were taken to support the growth of the industry, including an easing of the previously highly restrictive visa requirements for foreign visitors in 1983, the encouragement of private sector investment in tourism-related facilities, the establishment of an increasing number of airports and seaports as 'gateways', the development of associated infrastructure and the progressive opening of regional airports to foreign carriers. Considerable efforts were also made to publicize Indonesia's tourism potential in the major overseas markets.

These measures had a dramatic impact, with the number of tourist arrivals exceeding 1m. for the first time in 1987, 2m. in 1990, 3m. in 1992, 4m. in 1994, and 5m. in 1996 and 1997 (in which years the value of receipts from tourism was recorded as US $6,308m. and $5,321m., respectively). This growth in tourist arrivals and spending was accompanied by a corresponding increase in tourist facilities, as exemplified by a rise in the number of star-rated hotel rooms from 34,300 in 1980 to almost 70,000 in 1996, and an increase in the number of travel agencies operating in Indonesia from 330 to 2,225 during the same period.

However, the tourism industry suffered a serious set-back as a result of political unrest and the Asian financial crisis, which in 1998 led to a sharp decline in the number of tourist arrivals to approximately 4.6m. A gradual recovery in the number of tourist arrivals in subsequent years, reaching 5.2m. in 2001, was undermined by the bomb attacks in the tourist resort of Kuta on the island of Bali in October 2002, which resulted in the deaths of 202 people (including many Australians) and which precipitated a substantial reduction in the number of tourist arrivals in the following months; the total for the year as a whole was only 5.0m. The reintroduction of visa requirements for nationals of most Western countries in April 2003 further affected the industry, with the number of tourist arrivals (through 13 main entry points) declining to 4.5m. in that year. As the political and economic situation in Indonesia subsequently stabilized, the industry experienced a significant recovery in 2004, with the number of arrivals increasing to more than 5.3m., but this positive trend was arrested by a second series of co-ordinated terrorist attacks on tourist facilities on Bali in October 2005 and by growing concern about the persistence of avian influenza, with led to a further decline in the number of tourist arrivals to 5.0m. in 2005 and 4.9m. in 2006. The restoration of social stability, combined with the hosting of the UN Climate Change Conference on Bali in December 2007, helped to reverse this downward trend; the number of tourist arrivals rose to 5.5m. in that year and increased further, to 6.2m., in 2008, when receipts reached US $7,375m. Arrivals rose modestly, to 6.3m., in 2009; however, receipts were provisionally estimated to have declined to $6,318m. As the global economy recovered, arrivals were estimated to have increased to around 7m. in 2010, with receipts estimated to total $7,636m. Thus encouraged, the Ministry of Culture and Tourism was projecting further robust growth in the number of arrivals, to 7.7m., in 2011.

ECONOMIC PLANNING

Following the restoration of political stability in the late 1960s, Indonesia's goal of rapid economic growth and development was initially pursued through a series of five-year Development Plans, known by the acronym Repelita, the first of which was initiated in 1969. These Plans, formulated by the National Development Planning Board (Bappenas), presented indicative guidelines for public sector investment projects, and also sought to encourage and guide private investment. Public expenditure targets under these Plans were generally quite ambitious, and their implementation required considerable quantities of external financial resources, although this dependence on foreign aid declined gradually. Five such Plans had been implemented in full by the end of the 1993/94 fiscal year. The sixth Plan was disrupted by the onset of the Asian financial crisis in 1997 and by the subsequent political upheaval that led in 1998 to the resignation of President Suharto, after 32 years in power.

With the conclusion of Repelita VI in March 1999, the new Government reviewed Indonesia's economic development strategy. This resulted in the formulation of a medium-term development programme, known by its Indonesian acronym of Propenas, for the period 2000–04. This programme established five broad objectives: to ensure national cohesion and social stability; to achieve good governance and the rule of law; to accelerate economic recovery and strengthen the foundations for sustained growth; to develop the social sectors and human welfare; and to strengthen the programmes for regional autonomy, rural and urban development and the reduction of structural poverty.

Following the expiry of the Propenas recovery programme, the Government reinstated a national planning mechanism in the form of a National Medium-Term Development Plan for 2004–09, known by its Indonesian name as RPJM Nasional. This plan was based on the fundamental objectives of enhancing peace and security, promoting justice and democracy, and improving the welfare of the people. It envisaged an average annual GDP growth rate of 6.6%, a halving of the incidence of poverty to about 8%, and a reduction of unemployment to 5%. Sectoral priorities included the development of physical and social infrastructure, rural development, and the improvement of public service delivery.

Indonesia's ambitious National Medium-Term Development Plan 2010–2014 envisaged average annual GDP growth of between 6.3% and 6.8% over the plan period. The provision of sufficient employment opportunities, particularly for new entrants to the job market, remained a major challenge, along with the reduction of the incidence of poverty. The Government hoped to reduce the rate of unemployment to between 5% and 6% of the labour force by 2014, with a focus on the development of small and medium enterprises. Investment conditions were to be enhanced. A substantial increase in development spending was projected. In particular, with support from IIF (see Infrastructure, above), priority was to be given to the upgrading of the country's infrastructure.

FOREIGN AID AND INVESTMENT

The ambitious development programmes introduced in Indonesia after the late 1960s necessitated enormous investments of capital. Since these capital needs were considerably in excess of Indonesia's own resources, a significant proportion of the country's investment requirements had to be met from abroad, in the form of commercial and concessional loans, as well as direct and portfolio foreign investments.

Aid

Indonesia has substantial foreign borrowings, which were estimated at US $146,247m. at the end of 2008, increasing to a record $157,517m. one year later. About $67,000m. of the debt in 2008 was held by the Government and state-owned enterprises, with the remainder being held by the private sector. The majority of Indonesia's public sector debt derives from loans that were disbursed through the Inter-Governmental Group for Indonesia (IGGI), which was established by Western creditors in the late 1960s and which co-ordinated the official financial assistance that donors provided to Indonesia until 1991, and its successor, the Consultative Group for Indonesia (CGI), which held its first meeting in France in July 1992. In a major departure from tradition, which highlighted the growing confidence of the international donor community in the Indonesian Government and a shift towards national ownership of the development process, Indonesia was invited to chair, and draft the agenda for, the 2005 pledging session of the CGI held in January, which resulted in a total sum of $5,100m. being committed. The 2006 pledging session, held in June of that year and again chaired by the Indonesian Government, resulted in a total commitment of $5,400m. In January 2007 the President announced that Indonesia would abolish the CGI and henceforth deal with its donors on a bilateral basis.

The liberalization of regulations governing foreign borrowing by Indonesian banks and firms from the late 1980s prompted a rapid rise in the private sector's foreign indebtedness. The corporate 'offshore' debt incurred by the Indonesian banking sector and many of the country's business conglomerates continued to grow and played a significant role in precipitating and exacerbating the financial and economic crisis of 1997/98. The Indonesian Government therefore sought to negotiate debt-rescheduling agreements with both its official and private creditors. The first such agreement was concluded with the 'Paris Club' of official creditors in 2000. In June 2002 it was announced that the 'London Club' of commercial creditors had similarly agreed, in principle, to extend the servicing of a number of loans taken out by the Indonesian Government in 1995–97. Although the Government's decision to terminate its financing programme with the IMF at the end of 2003 also ended its eligibility for further debt-restructuring agreements, it had by that time succeeded in rehabilitating itself in international capital markets. This was demonstrated in March 2004, when its first global sovereign bond issue since the late 1990s was eight times oversubscribed, and by the fact that subsequent bond offerings also attracted a high level of interest. The early repayment in mid-2006 of Indonesia's outstanding debt of some US $7,800m. to the IMF, which would otherwise have matured in December 2010, also helped to raise confidence, while releasing Indonesia from the conditions imposed by the IMF when the loans were extended.

In a significant development, the Government sought to enter into agreements with its official creditors to convert some of its debt into development resources. In July 2007 it achieved Indonesia's inclusion in a debt-for-nature swap arrangement initiated by the US Government, under which US $19.6m. of Indonesia's debt to the USA could be used to finance tropical forest conservation programmes within Indonesia. This was followed by the signing of a similar agreement with the USA, worth $30m., in June 2009. In June 2008 the Government concluded an innovative arrangement with the Government of Germany whereby it agreed to contribute €25m. to the Global Fund to Fight AIDS, Tuberculosis and Malaria to finance a programme against these diseases in return for relief of €50m. of Indonesia's debt to Germany. This brought the total value of debt relief granted by Germany to Indonesia to €143.6m.

Investment

The Foreign Investment Law of 1967 granted investors a high degree of protection and a wide range of privileges. Between 1967 and the end of 2008 foreign investment projects worth about US $370,000m. were approved by the national investment co-ordinating board, the Badan Koordinasi Penanaman Modal (BKPM), although this total excluded investments in the petroleum, natural gas and financial sectors, which were beyond the BKPM's jurisdiction. A particularly strong growth in foreign investment interest occurred between 1987 and 1997, following the introduction of a deregulation process by the Government aimed at relaxing the remaining restrictions on foreign investment. Investment levels fluctuated in subsequent years, but showed a sustained recovery from 2004. Foreign investment exceeded $40,100m. in 2007. However, this growth was arrested in 2008 by the effects of the global financial crisis, with the value of BKPM-approved projects decreasing to $17,000m. in that year. Moreover, the available data indicated that only a relatively small proportion (estimated at about 33%) of approved investment projects had actually been implemented by the end of 2008. As the Government continued to experience difficulties with regard to implementation, actual foreign direct investment (FDI)) was estimated by the ADB to have decreased from $9,318m. in 2008 to $5,300m. in 2009. As the global economy recovered in 2010, and reflecting improved domestic and foreign investment conditions, FDI increased to $12,700m.

The sectoral distribution of these investments has been heavily biased towards manufacturing, which had received about 70% of approved domestic and 65% of approved foreign capital investment by the end of 2006. Apart from the manufacturing sector, such investment has been channelled mainly into agriculture, tourism, infrastructure and financial services. A long-awaited measure to encourage increased private investment was the approval of a new investment law by the House of Representatives in March 2007. This provides a variety of enhanced incentives and guarantees relative to the previous legal framework, and was generally well received by the business community and international commentators. The sharp increase in investment approvals recorded in 2007 was widely regarded as a response to the introduction of this new law, which was also expected to stimulate a continued increase in private, and especially foreign, investment interest in subsequent years.

FINANCE

Between 1966 and the mid-1990s considerable efforts were made to stabilize the financial sector, but these efforts were undermined by the liberalization policies introduced after the mid-1980s and their abuse by an increasingly corrupt and politically well-connected business élite. The financial sector was consequently ill prepared to withstand the financial crisis of 1997/98 and its poor handling by the Government and multinational agencies such as the IMF.

Fiscal Policy

Following the onset of the Asian crisis in 1997, an agreement was reached with the IMF introducing more standard budgeting practices; it allowed a (domestically funded) budget deficit equivalent to 3.5% of GDP in the 1998/99 fiscal year to counteract the contraction caused by the ongoing economic crisis. Such deficits, albeit with a gradually declining magnitude, were permitted in subsequent years. The budgets for 2004–08 projected deficits of between 0.7% and 2.1% of GDP, with the Government initially setting the deficit for 2008 at 1.7% of projected GDP but later raising it to 2.1% in March 2008 in response to soaring fuel prices (which raised the cost of the government oil subsidy). When persistent high oil prices threatened to breach even this deficit target, the Government was forced to introduce a sharp reduction in the oil subsidy in May 2008, which resulted in the administered prices of various grades of fuel oil being raised by an average of 28.7%. The deficit for 2009 was originally set at 1.0% of GDP but was raised to 2.5% in March 2009 when the Government felt compelled to introduce an economic stimulus programme worth Rp. 73,300,000m., in order to offset the recessionary effects of the global economic crisis on the Indonesian economy. The plan incorporated tax incentives to the value of Rp. 56,300,000m., with Rp. 17,000,000m. being allocated to other government expenditure and subsidies. The programme aimed to maintain consumer spending and to create employment opportunities through the development of labour-intensive infrastructure projects. The amended draft budget for 2010 projected revenue of Rp. 974,820,000m. and expenditure of Rp. 1,104,640,000m. In view of the rise in global oil prices and the resultant need to increase its allocation to fuel subsidies, the Government revised its projected budget deficit from the equivalent of 1.6% to 2.1% of GDP; however, the actual deficit came in at just 0.62% of GDP, owing to lower-than-anticipated government expenditure. In July 2011 the Government upwardly revised its projected budget deficit for the year from the equivalent of 1.8% to 2.1% of GDP; this was partly due to a projected increase in its fuel subsidy bill, from Rp. 95,900,000m. to Rp. 120,800,000m. (owing to rising oil prices) and partly due to higher electricity costs; however, as in 2010, the actual deficit was widely expected to be lower than projected, owing to slow government spending and improved revenue collection. The draft budget for 2012, which proposed a reduction in the allocation to fuel and electricity subsidies, envisaged a budgetary deficit of 1.5% of GDP.

A number of other major fiscal policy reforms have also been introduced in the post-Suharto era. After a transitional nine-month budget period from 1 April to 31 December 2000, the fiscal year was adjusted to coincide with the calendar year from 2001. At the same time a wide-ranging decentralization of the budgetary process was introduced, with the generation of public revenues and expenditure being devolved to the provincial and district level to a large extent. This resulted in a dramatic reduction in the central Government's revenues, and threatened to increase the prosperity gap between the densely populated and resource-poor provinces of Java and the less heavily populated, resource-rich provinces in the outer islands. The devolution of many fiscal powers to the district level caused particularly serious problems, as it created considerable differences in local taxation levels and generated widespread uncertainty among personal and corporate taxpayers. Recognizing these weaknesses, the Government sought to rectify the situation, initially by shifting many of the powers held at district level to the provincial level, and later through the introduction of a new legal framework in October 2004 designed to strengthen the position of the central Government and to address regional inequalities arising from the existing revenue-sharing arrangements.

In 2001–03 the central Government's development expenditure amounted to some 15% of total government spending; this level was raised to 17.6% in the budget for 2004, before being gradually reduced to 10.6% in the 2007 budget. In the 2008 budget it was set at 11.9% and in 2009 at 10.0%.

Money and Banking

Indonesia's financial sector is headed by Bank Indonesia. For almost two decades, until the late 1980s, commercial banking was dominated by five large state-owned banks. In addition, there were 11 foreign branch banks (the activities of which, however, were confined to the Jakarta area) and some 70 private banks, of which 10 were licensed to deal in foreign exchange. The banking industry also comprised a state-owned national development bank, as well as provincial development banks in each of Indonesia's 27 provinces, and a state-owned savings bank. Fourteen 'non-bank financial institutions', performing a variety of merchant-banking functions, had also been established. By the end of 1988 there were also more than 80 leasing companies, 90 insurance companies, and a stock exchange, which had traded since 1977.

The Government initiated significant reforms in the banking sector from the mid-1980s, which culminated in the introduction of new banking legislation in 1992. The reforms were aimed at simplifying the structure of the banking system and facilitating an enhanced mobilization of resources available for investment, while simultaneously ensuring the efficient use of these resources in productive investments. The categories of recognized banking institutions were reduced to two—commercial banks and small-scale credit banks—and many of the remaining restraints on banking were withdrawn: foreign branch banks operating in Jakarta were given permission to open sub-branches in six regional capitals; domestic banks were allowed to form joint venture banks with international institutions that maintained representative offices in Jakarta; the upper limit on 'offshore' borrowing by Indonesian commercial banks was removed; privately owned banks were granted permission to compete with state-owned banks in attracting deposits from the parastatal enterprises; and licensing requirements for dealing in foreign exchange were relaxed.

The new reforms stimulated a dramatic expansion of the Indonesian financial sector. By the end of 1996 the number of commercial banks had risen to 239, while the number of secondary banks had risen to 9,276. In the capital markets the number of companies listed on the Jakarta Stock Exchange increased from 24 in 1988 to almost 290 by the end of 1996.

This unrestrained growth of the financial sector inevitably gave rise to fears about its viability, which were reinforced by a number of bank failures and several well-publicized scandals involving banks and securities firms. The Indonesian currency and capital markets came under severe speculative pressure in the second half of 1997, and precipitated a corresponding collapse of the rupiah's exchange rate and the prices of shares in companies listed on the Indonesian stock markets. The rationalization of the financial sector emerged as a major priority of the reform measures that the Indonesian Government agreed to undertake as part of the rescue programme negotiated with the IMF. The first measure was announced in November 1997, when the Government revealed plans to close 16 banks known to be burdened by a high level of bad debt. This was followed in January 1998 by the establishment of the Indonesian Bank Restructuring Agency (IBRA), which was assigned the task of rehabilitating the highly indebted financial and corporate sectors, and which acquired control of almost US $70,000m. in the form of both equity and debt from the banks that had failed during the financial crisis.

Although the financial sector rehabilitation programme generally lagged behind the somewhat ambitious targets set for it, IBRA had, for the most part, achieved its ultimate objectives by the time it was dissolved, on schedule, in February 2004. The major achievements of IBRA included the fact that it had met, or exceeded, the revenue collection targets set for it and that it had succeeded in restructuring and privatizing many of the banks and other commercial enterprises that it had acquired. The remaining assets, worth some

Rp. 40,000,000m., were transferred to a new, government-owned, holding company.

The consolidation of the banking system involved the closure of a total of 68 banks, with another 12 being taken under state control and 14 more being merged to form two larger entities. As a result, the total number of banks had been reduced to only 135 at the end of 2004, about half the number prevailing in 1997. The banks subsequently concentrated primarily on lending to the household sector and small businesses, thereby encouraging the growth in private consumption. By contrast, banks were more cautious about lending to the highly indebted corporate sector, which in turn resulted in the ratio of non-performing loans decreasing to 2.0% at the end of 2004, from 5.8% in 2000. Rising interest rates and the effects of the higher oil prices on corporate and domestic cash flows prompted a renewed increase in this ratio to 4.8% at the end of 2005, which continued until a high point of 5.6% was reached in mid-2006, before a gradual reduction to 3.6% by the end of the year. Meanwhile, in early 2007 the central bank introduced measures to encourage increased lending to small and medium-sized enterprises, and in March 2007 the year-long phasing-in of a deposit insurance scheme for the banking sector was finalized, with a newly established Deposit Insurance Agency providing cover for deposits up to a maximum of Rp. 100m. in the event of a bank failure.

With inflationary pressures easing, in March 2009 (for the fourth consecutive month) the central bank reduced its benchmark interest rate, to 7.75%. The rate was reduced further, to 6.50%, in August, but was increased to 6.75% in February 2011 in an attempt to combat food inflationary pressures; the interest rate remained unchanged as of September 2011. Meanwhile, however, commercial banks did not swiftly follow suit in reducing their interest rates, and the rate of growth of credit facilities decelerated in 2010.

The Jakarta Stock Exchange (subsequently renamed the Indonesia Stock Exchange) recorded one of the best performances of all Asian markets in 2006, and this trend continued in 2007. In 2008, however, the Composite Stock Exchange Index declined from 2,732 at the beginning of the year to a low point of 1,141 on 24 November. Various measures helped to arrest the decline in the stock exchange index, which ended the year at 1,355. The Indonesia Stock Exchange again registered one of the strongest performances in Asia in 2009, during the course of which its stock market index rose by nearly 86%. In the first week of January 2010, moreover, the index exceeded 2,600 points, rising further to reach an average of 3,038 for the month of August and reaching an historically high level of 4,193 in August 2011. However, this had decreased to 3,752 by mid-September, owing to a global market decline.

CONCLUSION

By 2008 the Indonesian economy had fully recovered from the profound effects of the Asian financial crisis of the late 1990s. The various reforms and the associated strengthening of economic governance structures, combined with the restoration of a high degree of political stability within a democratic framework, had generated renewed confidence in the country, both internally and abroad. The strong growth in private consumption remained a major factor in the Indonesian economy's robust performance. By early 2009, however, Indonesia was required to address the major challenges arising from the global financial crisis, which restricted credit markets, reduced demand in the economies of many of the country's principal trading partners and put severe pressure on the domestic productive and corporate sectors. Nevertheless, the reforms of the previous decade had significantly enhanced the economy's competitiveness and resilience, and the pro-active measures taken by policy-makers in response to external factors, including the adoption of fiscal stimulus measures, helped to ensure that the domestic impact of these external developments did not substantially undermine the country's economic stability.

Despite Indonesia's steady progress, long-term concerns were the inadequacy of the country's infrastructure and the shortage of formal employment opportunities. Although the rate of unemployment was reduced from 11.2% of the labour force in 2005 to 7.1% in 2010, and was projected by the draft budget for 2012 to decline further to 6.4%–6.6% in that year, underemployment (those working fewer than 35 hours a week—estimated by the ADB at almost 28% in early 2008) remained at a very high level. Low wages and job insecurity generally prevailed in the informal sector, in which the majority of workers were engaged. Moreover, income inequality was reported to be increasing. Under its medium-term plan, the Government hoped to reduce the incidence of poverty to 8%–10% by 2014; the draft budget for 2012 envisaged a reduction in the rate from 12.5% in 2011 to between 10.5% and 11.5% in 2012. As the global economy continued to recover in 2011 and as domestic demand continued to strengthen, economic growth was expected to be sustained; according to the ADB, GDP growth was forecast to increase from 6.1% in 2010 to 6.6% in 2011, and further to 6.8% in 2012. Meanwhile, the Master Plan for the Acceleration and Expansion of Economic Development 2011–2025, published by the Indonesian Government in May 2011, acknowledged the pressing need for, *inter alia*, greater economic diversification, a marked improvement in the quality of human resources, and sustained, accelerated infrastructural development.

Statistical Survey

Source (unless otherwise stated): Badan Pusat Statistik (Central Bureau of Statistics/Statistics Indonesia), Jalan Dr Sutomo 6–8, Jakarta 10710; tel. (21) 3507057; fax (21) 3857046; e-mail bpshq@bps.go.id; internet www.bps.go.id.

Note: Unless otherwise stated, figures for East Timor (now Timor-Leste, occupied by Indonesia between July 1976 and October 1999) are not included in the tables.

Area and Population

AREA, POPULATION AND DENSITY

Area (sq km)	1,910,931*
Population (census results)	
30 June 2000	206,264,595
31 May 2010	
Males	119,507,580
Females	118,048,783
Total	237,556,363
Population (UN estimate at mid-year)†	
2011	242,325,637
Density (per sq km) at mid-2011	126.8

* 737,814 sq miles.
† Source: UN, *World Population Prospects: The 2010 Revision*.

POPULATION BY AGE AND SEX
(UN estimates at mid-2011)

	Males	Females	Total
0–14	32,997,483	31,768,289	64,765,772
15–64	81,825,871	82,092,264	163,918,135
65 and over	5,995,608	7,646,122	13,641,730
Total	120,818,962	121,506,675	242,325,637

Source: UN, *World Population Prospects: The 2010 Revision*.

ISLANDS AND PROVINCES
(population at census of May 2010)*

	Area (sq km)	Population ('000)	Density (per sq km)
Jawa (Java) and Madura	129,438	136,563.1	1,055.0
DKI Jakarta†	664	9,588.2	14,440.1
Jawa Barat	35,378	43,021.8	1,216.1
Jawa Tengah	32,801	32,380.7	987.2
DI Yogyakarta†	3,133	3,452.4	1,101.9
Jawa Timur	47,800	37,476.0	784.0
Banten	9,663	10,644.0	1,101.5
Sumatera (Sumatra)	480,793	50,613.9	105.3
Nanggroe Aceh Darussalem†	57,956	4,486.6	77.4
Sumatera Utara	72,981	12,985.1	177.9
Sumatera Barat	42,013	4,846.0	115.3
Riau	87,024	5,543.0	63.7
Jambi	50,058	3,088.6	61.7
Sumatera Selatan	91,592	7,446.4	81.3
Bangkulu	19,919	1,713.4	86.0
Lumpung	34,624	7,596.1	219.4
Kepulauan Bangka-Belitung	16,424	1,223.0	74.5
Kepulauan Riau	8,202	1,685.7	205.5
Sulawesi (Celebes)	188,522	17,359.4	92.1
Sulawesi Utara	13,852	2,265.9	163.6
Sulawesi Tengah	61,841	2,633.4	42.6
Sulawesi Selatan	46,717	8,032.6	171.9
Sulawesi Tenggara	38,068	2,230.6	58.6
Gorontalo	11,257	1,038.6	92.3
Sulawesi Barat	16,787	1,158.3	69.0
—continued			
Kalimantan	544,150	13,772.5	25.3
Kalimantan Barat	147,307	4,393.2	29.8
Kalimantan Tengah	153,565	2,202.6	14.3
Kalimantan Selatan	38,744	3,626.1	93.6
Kalimantan Timur	204,534	3,550.6	17.4
Nusa Tenggara and Bali‡	73,070	13,067.6	178.8
Nusa Tenggara Barat	18,572	4,496.9	242.1
Nusa Tenggara Timur	48,718	4,679.3	96.0
Bali	5,780	3,891.4	673.3
Maluku (Moluccas) and Papua§	494,957	6,179.8	12.5
Maluku	46,914	1,531.4	32.6
Maluku Utara	31,983	1,035.6	32.4
Papua Barat†	97,024	760.9	7.8
Papua†	319,036	2,852.0	8.9
Total	1,910,931	237,556.4	124.3

* Figures refer to provincial divisions, organized according to geography, island or island groupings.
† Province with special status.
‡ The Nusa Tenggara provinces comprise most of the Lesser Sunda Islands, principally Flores, Lombok, Sumba, Sumbawa and part of Timor.
§ The Papua provinces were formerly known as Irian Jaya (West Papua).

PRINCIPAL TOWNS
(estimated population at 31 December 1996)

Jakarta (capital)	9,341,400	Malang	775,900
Surabaya	2,743,400	Padang	739,500
Bandung	2,429,000	Banjarmasin	544,700
Medan	1,942,000	Surakarta	518,600
Palembang	1,394,300	Pontianak	459,100
Semarang	1,366,500	Yogyakarta (Jogjakarta)	421,000
Ujung Pandang (Makassar)	1,121,300		

Mid-2010 (incl. suburbs, UN estimates): Jakarta 9,210,211; Surabaya 2,508,768; Bandung 2,412,271; Medan 2,131,060; Ujung Pandang 1,294,366; Palembang 1,244,144; Bogor 1,044,123 (Source: UN, *World Urbanization Prospects: The 2009 Revision*).

BIRTHS AND DEATHS
(annual averages, UN estimates)

	1995–2000	2000–05	2005–10
Birth rate (per 1,000)	21.9	21.0	19.1
Death rate (per 1,000)	7.6	7.4	7.2

Source: UN, *World Population Prospects: The 2010 Revision*.

Birth rate (per 1,000): 22.9 in 1997; 22.8 in 1998; 22.4 in 1999 (Source: UN, *Statistical Yearbook for Asia and the Pacific*).

Death rate (per 1,000): 7.5 in 1997; 7.7 in 1998; 7.5 in 1999 (Source: UN, *Statistical Yearbook for Asia and the Pacific*).

Life expectancy (years at birth, WHO estimates): 68 (males 66; females 71) in 2009 (Source: WHO, *World Health Statistics*).

ECONOMICALLY ACTIVE POPULATION
(persons aged 15 years and over, at February)

	2008	2009	2010
Agriculture, hunting, forestry and fishing	42,689,635	43,029,493	42,825,807
Mining and quarrying	1,062,309	1,139,495	1,188,634
Manufacturing	12,440,141	12,615,440	13,052,521
Electricity, gas and water	207,909	209,441	208,494
Construction	4,733,679	4,610,695	4,844,689
Trade, restaurants and hotels	20,684,041	21,836,768	22,212,885
Transport, storage and communications	6,013,947	5,947,673	5,817,680
Financing, insurance, real estate and business services	1,440,042	1,484,598	1,639,748
Public services	12,778,154	13,611,841	15,615,114
Total employed	102,049,857	104,485,444	107,405,572
Unemployed	9,427,590	9,258,964	8,592,490
Total labour force	111,477,447	113,744,408	115,998,062

Health and Welfare

KEY INDICATORS

Total fertility rate (children per woman, 2009)	2.1
Under-5 mortality rate (per 1,000 live births, 2009)	39
HIV/AIDS (% of persons aged 15–49, 2007)	0.2
Physicians (per 1,000 head, 2003)	0.10
Hospital beds (per 1,000 head, 1998)	0.60
Health expenditure (2008): US $ per head (PPP)	91
Health expenditure (2008): % of GDP	2.3
Health expenditure (2008): public (% of total)	54.4
Access to water (% of persons, 2008)	80
Access to sanitation (% of persons, 2008)	52
Total carbon dioxide emissions ('000 metric tons, 2007)	396,818.5
Carbon dioxide emissions per head (metric tons, 2007)	1.8
Human Development Index (2010): ranking	108
Human Development Index (2010): value	0.600

For sources and definitions, see explanatory note on p. vi.

Agriculture

PRINCIPAL CROPS
('000 metric tons, incl. East Timor)

	2007	2008	2009
Rice, paddy	57,157	60,251	64,399
Maize	13,288	16,324	17,630
Potatoes	1,004	1,045	1,175
Sweet potatoes	1,887	1,877	2,058
Cassava (Manioc)	19,988	21,593	22,039
Beans, dry*	320	325	330
Sugar cane	25,300†	26,000†	26,500*
Cashew nuts, with shell	146	157	145*
Soybeans (Soya beans)	593	777	975
Groundnuts, with shell	1,384	774	778
Coconuts	19,625†	19,500†	21,566*
Oil palm fruit*	78,000	85,000	86,000
Cabbages and other brassicas	1,289	1,324	1,335
Tomatoes	636	726	830
Pumpkins, squash and gourds	254	394	314
Cucumbers and gherkins	581	540	576
Aubergines (Eggplants)	391	427	450
Chillies and peppers, green	1,129	1,092	1,100*
Onions, dry	803	854	953
Beans, green	868	838	880
Carrots and turnips	351	367	353
Oranges	2,626	2,323	2,103
Avocados	202	225	258
Mangoes, mangosteens and guavas	1,819	2,013	2,150*
Pineapples	2,238	1,273	1,558
Bananas	5,454	5,741	6,273
Papayas	622	653	766
Coffee, green	677	683	700
Cocoa beans	740	793	800*
Tea	150	151	160*
Cinnamon*	60	64	67
Cloves	80	81	81*
Ginger	179	192	193*
Tobacco, unmanufactured	165	170	181*
Natural rubber	2,755	2,922	2,790*

* FAO estimate(s).
† Unofficial figure.

Aggregate production ('000 metric tons, may include official, semi-official or estimated data): Total cereals 70,444.9 in 2007, 76,575.0 in 2008, 82,028.6 in 2009; Total roots and tubers 23,332.9 in 2007, 24,874.5 in 2008, 25,636.7 in 2009; Total vegetables (incl. melons) 8,475.8 in 2007, 8,795.8 in 2008, 9,105.2 in 2009; Total fruits (excl. melons) 16,649.4 in 2007, 16,028.2 in 2008, 17,057.7 in 2009.

Source: FAO.

LIVESTOCK
('000 head)

	2007	2008	2009
Cattle	11,515	12,257	12,859
Sheep	9,860	9,605	10,200
Goats	14,470	15,147	15,769
Pigs	6,711	6,838	6,922
Horses	401	393	399
Buffaloes	2,086	1,931	1,925
Chickens	1,275,400	1,253,430	1,341,780
Ducks	35,867	39,840	42,367

Source: FAO.

LIVESTOCK PRODUCTS
('000 metric tons)

	2007	2008	2009
Cattle meat	339.5	392.5	408.1
Buffalo meat	41.8	39.0	34.8
Sheep meat	56.9	47.0	54.2
Goat meat	63.6	66.0	74.1
Pig meat*	596.8	636.8	636.8
Chicken meat	1,295.8	1,349.6	1,408.8
Cows' milk	568	647	882
Goats' milk*	238	264	276
Hen eggs	1,174.6	1,122.6	1,059.3
Other poultry eggs	207.5	201.0	247.1
Wool, greasy*	26.8	22.2	21.4

* FAO estimates.

Note: Figures for meat refer to inspected production only, i.e. from animals slaughtered under government supervision.

Source: FAO.

Forestry

ROUNDWOOD REMOVALS
('000 cubic metres, excl. bark, FAO estimates)

	2007	2008	2009
Sawlogs, veneer logs and logs for sleepers	21,602	26,855	22,405
Pulpwood	9,500	10,700	10,700
Other industrial wood	3,249	3,249	3,249
Fuel wood	67,825	65,034	62,341
Total	102,176	105,838	98,695

Source: FAO.

SAWNWOOD PRODUCTION
('000 cubic metres, incl. railway sleepers)

	2002	2003	2004
Total (all broadleaved)	6,230	7,620	4,330

2005–09: Production assumed to be unchanged from 2004 (FAO estimates).

Source: FAO.

Fishing

('000 metric tons, live weight)

	2007	2008	2009
Capture	5,050.3	5,002.3	5,099.4
Scads	305.5	327.4	330.7
Goldstripe sardinella	169.8	174.4	175.8
'Stolephorus' anchovies	175.5	199.7	207.5
Skipjack tuna	303.9	293.8	297.0
Indian mackerels	13.1	16.9	18.2
Aquaculture	1,392.9*	1,690.1*	1,733.4
Common carp	264.4	242.3	249.3
Milkfish	263.1	277.5	328.3
Total catch	6,443.2*	6,692.6*	6,832.8

* FAO estimate.

Note: Figures exclude aquatic plants ('000 metric tons): 1,733.1 (capture 4.6, aquaculture 1,728.5) in 2007; 2,148.0 (capture 2.9, aquaculture 2,145.1) in 2008; 2,965.9 (capture 2.3, aquaculture 2,963.6) in 2009. Also excluded are crocodiles, recorded by number rather than by weight. The number of crocodiles caught was: 17,910 in 2007; 16,306 in 2008; 12,251 in 2009.

Source: FAO.

Mining

('000 metric tons unless otherwise indicated)

	2007	2008	2009*
Crude petroleum (million barrels)†	305.0	311.0	280.0
Natural gas (million cubic metres)	79,410	81,842	85,000
Bauxite	1,251	1,152	1,200
Coal (bituminous)	178,791	188,717	190,000
Nickel‡	229.2	192.6	202.8
Copper‡	796.9	632.6	610.0
Tin ore (metric tons)‡	66,137	53,228	55,000
Gold (kg)§	117,851	64,390	65,000
Silver (kg)§	268,967	226,051	215,000

* Estimates.
† Including condensate.
‡ Figures refer to the metal content of ores and concentrates.
§ Including gold and silver in copper concentrate.

Source: US Geological Survey.

Industry

SELECTED PRODUCTS
('000 metric tons, unless otherwise indicated)

	2001	2002	2003
Raw sugar (centrifugal)[1]	2,025	1,902	1,780
Refined sugar[1,2]	2,023	1,750	2,431
Palm oil[1]	8,080[3]	9,350	10,530
Veneer sheets ('000 cubic metres)[1]	94	45[2]	289
Plywood ('000 cubic metres)[1]	7,300	7,550	6,111
Jackets (men's and boys', '000)	55,849	32,777	n.a.
Trousers (men's and boys', '000)	42,403	45,168	n.a.
Shirts (men's and boys', '000)	18,069	76,897	n.a.
Underwear (men's and boys', '000)	76,232	48,154	n.a.
Underwear (women's and girls', '000)	55,769	145,284	n.a.
Blouses (women's and girls', '000)	25,259	22,540	n.a.
Footwear ('000 pairs, excl. rubber)	325,169	306,761	n.a.
Newsprint	1,022	1,022	1,022
Other printing and writing paper[2]	5,394	5,394	5,394
Other paper and paperboard	3,620	3,612	3,612
Nitrogenous fertilizers[1,4]	2,549	n.a.	n.a.
Jet fuel	1,087	1,175	1,349
Motor spirit (petrol)	8,997	8,592	8,584
Naphthas	2,432	1,986	2,221
Kerosene	7,492	7,274	7,565
Gas-diesel oil	14,137	13,791	13,786
Residual fuel oils	12,009	11,951	11,755
Lubricating oils	382	318	404
Liquefied petroleum gas	1,684	1,833	2,316
Rubber tyres ('000)[5]	20,500[2]	n.a.	n.a.
Cement (hydraulic)[6]	n.a.	34,640	35,000
Aluminium (unwrought)[2,6,7]	209	160	200
Tin (unwrought, metric tons)[6,7]	53,470	67,455	65,000
Passenger motor cars ('000)[8]	74	n.a.	n.a.
Television receivers (colour, '000)	21,519	23,680	n.a.
Electric accumulators (for motor vehicles, '000)	49,496	22,510	n.a.
Batteries and cells (primary, millions)	14,059	14,800	n.a.
Electric energy (million kWh)	101,647	108,206	112,944
Gas from gasworks (terajoules)	30,400	30,000[2]	n.a.

Cigarettes (million): 254,276 in 1999.

2004 ('000 metric tons unless otherwise stated): Raw sugar 2,225; Palm oil 12,080[1,3]; Veneer sheets ('000 cubic metres) 155[1]; Plywood ('000 cubic metres) 4,514; Cement (hydraulic) 33,230[2,6]; Aluminium (unwrought) 241[6]; Tin (unwrought, metric tons) 49,872[6]; Gas-diesel oil 14,661; Residual fuel oils 10,995; Jet fuel 1,414; Motor spirit (petrol) 8,825; Naphthas 2,276; Lubricating oils 398; Kerosene 7,341; Electric energy (million kWh) 120,160.

2005 ('000 metric tons unless otherwise stated): Raw sugar 2,435; Palm oil 14,070[1,3]; Veneer sheets ('000 cubic metres) 101[1]; Plywood ('000 cubic metres) 4,534[1]; Cement (hydraulic) 33,917[6]; Aluminium (unwrought) 252[6]; Tin (unwrought, metric tons) 65,300[6]; Gas-diesel oil 13,889; Residual fuel oils 10,352; Jet fuel 1,418; Motor spirit (petrol) 8,325; Naphthas 2,554; Lubricating oils 399; Kerosene 7,131; Electric energy (million kWh) 127,369.

2006 ('000 metric tons unless otherwise stated): Raw sugar 2,510; Palm oil 16,050[1,3]; Veneer sheets ('000 cubic metres) 256[1]; Plywood ('000 cubic metres) 3,812[1]; Cement (hydraulic) 35,000[6]; Aluminium (unwrought) 250[6]; Tin (unwrought, metric tons) 65,357[6]; Gas-diesel oil 13,216; Residual fuel oils 10,127; Jet fuel 1,256; Motor spirit (petrol) 8,411; Naphthas 3,061; Lubricating oils 386; Kerosene 7,165; Electric energy (million kWh) 133,108.

2007 ('000 metric tons unless otherwise stated): Raw sugar 2,814; Palm oil 16,760[1,3]; Veneer sheets ('000 cubic metres) 299[1]; Plywood ('000 cubic metres) 3,454[1]; Cement (hydraulic) 36,000[6]; Aluminium (unwrought) 242[6]; Tin (unwrought, metric tons) 64,127[6]; Gas-diesel oil 11,368; Residual fuel oils 10,173; Jet fuel 1,087; Naphthas 3,017; Kerosene 6,894; Electric energy (million kWh) 142,236; Raw sugar 2,814; Gas-diesel oil 11,368; Residual fuel oils 10,173; Jet fuel 1,087; Naphthas 3,017; Kerosene 6,894.

2008 ('000 metric tons unless otherwise stated): Raw sugar 3,263; Palm oil 18,910[1,3]; Veneer sheets ('000 cubic metres) 427[1]; Plywood ('000 cubic metres) 3,353[1]; Cement (hydraulic) 37,000[6]; Aluminium (unwrought) 243[6]; Tin (unwrought, metric tons) 53,471[6]; Palm oil 18,910[1,3]; Raw sugar 3,263; Gas-diesel oil 12,766; Residual fuel oils 9,471; Jet fuel 1,445; Naphthas 2,663; Kerosene 6,182; Electric energy (million kWh) 149,437.

2009 ('000 metric tons unless otherwise stated): Palm oil 20,550[1,3]; Veneer sheets ('000 cubic metres) 685[1]; Plywood ('000 cubic metres) 2,996[1]; Cement (hydraulic) 38,000[6,2,6]; Aluminium (unwrought) 250[6,2,6]; Tin (unwrought, metric tons) 54,000[6,2,6]; Palm oil 20,550[1,3].

[1] Source: FAO.
[2] Provisional or estimated production.
[3] Unofficial figure.
[4] Production in terms of nitrogen.
[5] For road motor vehicles, excluding bicycles and motorcycles.
[6] Source: US Geological Survey.
[7] Primary metal production only.
[8] Vehicles assembled from imported parts.

Source (unless otherwise indicated): UN Industrial Commodity Statistics Database.

Finance

CURRENCY AND EXCHANGE RATES

Monetary Units

100 sen = 1 rupiah (Rp.).

Sterling, Dollar and Euro Equivalents (31 May 2011)

£1 sterling = 14,088.6 rupiah;
US $1 = 8,537.0 rupiah;
€1 = 12,280.47 rupiah;
100,000 rupiah = £7.10 = $11.71 = €8.14.

Average Exchange Rate (rupiah per US $)

2008	9,699.0
2009	10,389.9
2010	9,090.4

GOVERNMENT FINANCE

(central government operations, '000 million rupiah)

Summary of Balances

	2005	2006*	2007*
Revenue and grants	495,444	637,799	723,058
Less Expenditure and net lending	509,419	669,880	763,571
Overall balance	–13,975	–32,081	–40,513

Revenue and Grants

	2005	2006*	2007*
Tax revenue	346,834	409,020	509,462
Income tax	175,380	208,834	261,698
Value added tax (VAT) on goods and services, and tax on sales of luxury goods	16,184	20,684	21,267
Tax of rights in land and building	3,429	3,179	5,390
Excise duties	33,256	37,772	42,035
Import duties	14,921	12,142	14,417
Export taxes	318	1,094	453
Other taxes	2,051	2,287	3,158
Non-tax revenue	147,314	226,906	210,927
Grants	1,296	1,873	2,669
Total	495,444	637,799	723,058

Expenditure and Net Lending

	2005	2006*	2007*
Central government expenditure	358,903	443,509	504,776
Personnel expenditure	55,589	72,238	101,202
Material expenditure	33,060	46,944	72,186
Interest payments	57,651	78,910	85,087
Domestic interest	43,496	54,778	n.a.
External interest	14,155	24,132	n.a.
Subsidies	120,708	107,463	102,924
Oil subsidies	95,661	64,212	61,838
Non-oil subsidies	25,047	43,251	41,086
Social expenditure	24,247	43,254	51,409
Capital expenditure	36,854	59,605	73,130
Other expenditure	30,794	35,095	18,838
Regional expenditure	150,516	226,371	258,795
Balance funds	143,301	222,322	250,343
Specific autonomous fund	7,215	4,049	8,452
Total	509,419	669,880	763,571

* Preliminary figures.

2008 (central government operations, '000 million rupiah): Tax revenue 658,701; Non-tax revenue 320,604; Total 979,305. *Expenditure:* Personnel expenditure 112,830; Material expenditure 55,963; Interest payment 88,430; Subsidies 275,291; Social expenditure 57,741; Capital expenditure 72,773; Other expenditure 30,328; Total 693,356.

2009 (central government operations, '000 million rupiah): Tax revenue 619,922; Non-tax revenue 227,174; Total 847,096. *Expenditure:* Personnel expenditure 127,670; Material expenditure 80,668; Interest payment 93,782; Subsidies 138,082; Social expenditure 73,813; Capital expenditure 75,871; Other expenditure 38,926; Total 628,812.

2010 (central government operations, '000 million rupiah, preliminary figures): Tax revenue 743,326; Non-tax revenue 247,176; Total 990,502. *Expenditure:* Personnel expenditure 162,659; Material expenditure 112,594; Interest payment 105,650; Subsidies 201,263; Social expenditure 71,173; Capital expenditure 95,025; Other expenditure 32,927; Grant expenditures 243; Total 781,534.

2011 (central government operations, '000 million rupiah, budget proposals): Tax revenue 839,540; Non-tax revenue 243,090; Total 1,082,630. *Expenditure:* Personnel expenditure 180,624; Material expenditure 131,533; Interest payment 116,403; Subsidies 184,817; Social expenditure 61,526; Capital expenditure 121,659; Other expenditure 26,294; Grant expenditures 771; Total 823,627.

INTERNATIONAL RESERVES

(US $ million at 31 December)

	2008	2009	2010
Gold (market prices)	2,044	2,556	3,303
IMF special drawing rights	34	2,763	2,714
Reserve position in IMF	224	228	224
Foreign exchange	49,339	60,572	89,970
Total	51,641	66,119	96,211

Source: IMF, *International Financial Statistics*.

MONEY SUPPLY

('000 million rupiah at 31 December)

	2008	2009	2010
Currency outside depository corporations	209,747	226,006	260,227
Transferable deposits	359,890	414,211	484,312
Other deposits	1,322,922	1,497,663	1,717,592
Securities other than shares	3,279	3,504	9,075
Broad money	1,895,839	2,141,384	2,471,206

Source: IMF, *International Financial Statistics*.

COST OF LIVING

(Consumer Price Index; base: 2000 = 100)

	2008	2009	2010
Food	210.9	225.7	247.0
All items (incl. others)	207.2	216.1	227.2

Source: ILO.

NATIONAL ACCOUNTS

('000 million rupiah at current prices)

Expenditure on the Gross Domestic Product

	2007	2008	2009
Government final consumption expenditure	329,760	416,867	539,759
Private final consumption expenditure	2,510,504	2,999,957	3,290,843
Changes in inventories	−1,053	5,822	−5,492
Gross fixed capital formation	985,627	1,370,635	1,743,728
Total domestic expenditure	3,824,838	4,793,280	5,568,838
Exports of goods and services	1,162,974	1,475,119	1,354,221
Less Imports of goods and services	1,003,271	1,422,902	1,197,193
Statistical discrepancy	−33,647	105,859	−112,424
GDP in purchasers' values	3,950,893	4,951,357	5,613,442
GDP at constant 2000 prices	1,964,327	2,082,316	2,176,976

Gross Domestic Product by Economic Activity

	2007	2008	2009
Agriculture, forestry and fishing	541,932	716,065	858,252
Mining and quarrying	440,610	540,605	591,532
Manufacturing	1,068,654	1,380,713	1,480,905
Electricity, gas and water	34,724	40,846	46,823
Construction	304,997	419,642	554,982
Trade, hotels and restaurants	592,304	691,495	750,605
Transport, storage and communications	264,263	312,190	352,407
Finance, insurance, real estate and business services	305,214	368,130	404,116
Public administration	205,344	257,548	318,581
Other services	192,853	224,122	255,238
Total	3,950,893	4,951,357	5,613,442

Source: Asian Development Bank.

BALANCE OF PAYMENTS

(US $ million)

	2008	2009	2010
Exports of goods f.o.b.	139,606	119,646	158,201
Imports of goods f.o.b.	−116,690	−89,499	−127,108
Trade balance	22,916	30,147	31,093
Exports of services	15,247	13,155	16,789
Imports of services	−28,245	−22,831	−26,280
Balance on goods and services	9,918	20,471	21,602
Other income received	3,592	1,921	1,914
Other income paid	−18,747	−17,061	−22,172
Balance on goods, services and income	−5,238	5,331	1,344
Current transfers received	7,352	7,241	7,475
Current transfers paid	−1,989	−2,380	−2,524
Current balance	126	10,192	6,295
Capital account (net)	294	96	32
Direct investment abroad	−5,900	−2,249	−2,900
Direct investment from abroad	9,318	4,877	12,736
Portfolio investment assets	−1,294	−144	−492
Portfolio investment liabilities	3,059	10,480	15,697
Other investment assets	−10,755	−11,852	−2,118
Other investment liabilities	3,446	3,794	3,262
Net errors and omissions	−212	−2,689	−2,226
Overall balance	−1,918	12,506	30,284

Source: IMF, *International Financial Statistics*.

External Trade

PRINCIPAL COMMODITIES

(distribution by HS, US $ million)

Imports c.i.f.	2008	2009	2010
Mineral fuels, oils, distillation products, etc.	30,682.4	19,090.4	27,530.7
Crude petroleum oils	10,061.5	7,362.2	8,531.3
Non-crude petroleum oils	19,963.6	10,841.0	17,654.3
Organic chemicals	5,132.5	3,940.4	5,325.8
Plastics and articles thereof	3,949.7	3,216.1	4,827.0
Iron and steel	8,281.9	4,356.6	6,371.6
Machinery, nuclear reactors, boilers, etc.	18,305.0	14,724.0	20,506.1
Electrical and electronic equipment	14,188.4	11,087.8	15,089.5
Vehicles other than railway and tramway	6,655.7	3,886.6	7,377.2
Aircraft, spacecraft, and parts thereof	2,036.9	3,241.5	3,528.1
Helicopters, aeroplanes and satellites	1,852.5	3,125.5	3,140.8
Total (incl. others)	129,244.1	96,829.2	135,663.3

Exports f.o.b.	2008	2009	2010
Animal, vegetable fats and oils, cleavage products, etc.	15,624.0	12,219.5	16,312.2
Palm oil and its fraction	12,375.6	10,367.6	13,469.0
Ores, slag and ash	4,295.6	5,804.8	8,148.0
Copper ores and concentrates	3,344.6	5,101.3	6,882.2
Mineral fuels, oils, distillation products, etc.	39,782.5	32,952.3	46,765.3
Solid fuels manufactured from coal	10,488.9	13,799.1	18,169.7
Crude petroleum oils	12,418.7	7,820.3	10,402.9
Petroleum gases	13,160.5	8,935.7	13,669.5
Rubber and articles thereof	7,637.3	4,912.8	9,373.4
Natural rubber, balata, gutta-percha, etc.	6,058.2	3,244.0	7,329.1
Machinery, nuclear reactors, boilers, etc.	5,211.6	4,709.3	5,071.2
Electrical and electronic equipment	8,265.9	8,148.1	10,432.5
Total (incl. others)	137,020.4	116,510.0	157,779.1

Source: Trade Map-Trade Competitiveness Map, International Trade Centre, www.intracen.org/marketanalysis.

PRINCIPAL TRADING PARTNERS

(US $ million)*

Imports c.i.f.	2008	2009	2010
Australia	4,005.3	3,436.0	4,099.0
Brazil	1,375.7	1,087.0	1,717.5
Brunei	2,416.6	639.6	666.2
Canada	1,871.7	992.5	1,108.4
China, People's Republic	15,249.2	14,002.2	20,424.2
France (incl. Monaco)	1,692.5	1,634.2	1,340.9
Germany	3,069.0	2,373.4	3,006.7
Hong Kong	2,367.6	1,698.1	1,860.4
India	2,905.4	2,209.4	3,294.8
Japan	15,129.2	9,843.7	16,965.8
Korea, Republic	6,925.8	4,742.3	7,703.0
Kuwait	1,857.1	1,442.3	1,372.7
Malaysia	8,923.1	5,688.4	8,648.7
Russian Federation	1,325.2	458.8	1,076.2
Saudi Arabia	4,805.0	3,135.8	4,360.8
Singapore	21,790.1	15,550.4	20,240.8
Thailand	6,336.1	4,612.9	7,470.7
USA	7,898.0	7,094.4	9,416.0
Total (incl. others)	129,244.1	96,829.2	135,663.3

Exports f.o.b.	2008	2009	2010
Australia	4,111.0	3,264.2	4,244.4
China, People's Republic	11,636.5	11,499.3	15,692.6
Germany	2,465.2	2,326.7	2,984.7
Hong Kong	1,808.8	2,111.8	2,501.4
India	7,163.3	7,432.9	9,915.0
Italy	1,900.9	1,651.5	2,370.5
Japan	27,743.9	18,574.7	25,781.8
Korea, Republic	9,116.8	8,145.2	12,574.6
Malaysia	6,432.6	6,811.8	9,362.3
Netherlands	3,926.4	2,909.1	3,722.5
Philippines	2,053.6	2,405.9	3,180.7
Singapore	12,862.0	10,262.7	13,723.3
Spain	1,665.3	1,830.5	2,328.7
Thailand	3,661.3	3,233.8	4,566.6
United Arab Emirates	1,652.1	1,265.8	1,475.3
United Kingdom	1,546.9	1,459.4	1,693.2
USA	13,079.9	10,889.1	14,301.9
Viet Nam	1,672.9	1,454.2	1,946.2
Total (incl. others)	137,020.4	116,510.0	157,779.1

* Imports by country of production, exports by country of consumption; figures include trade in gold.

Source: Trade Map-Trade Competitiveness Map, International Trade Centre, www.intracen.org/marketanalysis.

Transport

RAILWAYS
(traffic)

	2006	2007	2008
Passengers embarked ('000)	159,419	150,407	194,076
Passenger-km (million)	15,579	15,872	n.a.
Freight loaded ('000 tons)	17,275	17,078	19,444
Total ton-km (million)	4,474	4,425	n.a.

2009: Passengers embarked ('000) 203,070; Freight loaded ('000 tons) 18,924.

2010: Passengers embarked ('000) 203,270; Freight loaded ('000 tons) 19,113.

ROAD TRAFFIC
(motor vehicles registered)

	2007	2008	2009
Passenger cars	8,864,961	9,859,926	10,364,125
Trucks	4,845,937	5,146,674	5,187,740
Buses	2,103,423	2,583,170	2,729,572
Motorcycles	41,955,128	47,683,681	52,433,132
Total	57,769,449	65,273,451	70,714,569

SHIPPING

Merchant Fleet
(registered at 31 December)

	2007	2008	2009
Number of vessels	4,469	4,464	5,205
Displacement ('000 grt)	5,669.8	5,810.2	8,093.1

Source: IHS Fairplay, *World Fleet Statistics*.

Sea-borne Freight Traffic
('000 metric tons)

	1999	2000	2001*
International:			
goods loaded	139,340	141,528	143,750
goods unloaded	43,477	45,040	46,659
Domestic:			
goods loaded	113,633	127,740	163,685
goods unloaded	122,368	137,512	138,667

* Preliminary figures.

CIVIL AVIATION
(traffic on scheduled services)

	2004	2005	2006
Kilometres flown (million)	263	266	287
Passengers carried ('000)	26,781	26,836	27,831
Passenger-km (million)	28,447	28,243	29,919
Total ton-km (million)	2,963	2,924	3,104

Source: UN, *Statistical Yearbook*.

2007: Passengers carried ('000) 41,446; Freight carried ('000 metric tons) 472.1.

2008: Passengers carried ('000) 43,442; Freight carried ('000 metric tons) 469.4.

2009: Passengers carried ('000) 49,707; Freight carried ('000 metric tons) 446.6.

Tourism

FOREIGN TOURIST ARRIVALS

Country of residence	2007	2008	2009
Australia	314,432	450,178	584,437
Germany	112,160	137,854	128,649
Japan	508,820	546,713	475,766
Korea, Republic	327,843	320,808	256,522
Malaysia	891,353	1,117,454	1,179,366
Netherlands	106,987	140,771	143,485
Singapore	1,352,412	1,397,056	1,272,862
Taiwan	227,586	224,194	203,239
United Kingdom	121,599	150,412	169,271
USA	155,652	174,331	170,231
Total (incl. others)	5,505,759	6,234,497	6,323,730

Receipts from tourism (US $ million, excl. passenger transport): 5,346 in 2007; 7,375 in 2008; 6,318 in 2009 (provisional) (Source: World Tourism Organization).

Communications Media

	2008	2009	2010
Telephones ('000 main lines in use)	30,378.1	33,957.9	37,959.6
Mobile cellular telephones ('000 subscribers)	140,578*	159,248	220,000
Internet subscribers ('000)	1,707.2	n.a.	n.a.
Broadband subscribers ('000)	981.6	1,700.0	1,900.3

* Subscription as at September.

Television receivers ('000 in use): 31,700 in 2000 (Source: UN, *Statistical Yearbook*).

Radio receivers ('000 in use): 31,500 in 1997 (Source: UN, *Statistical Yearbook*).

Daily newspapers: 225 (average circulation 4,782,000) in 1999; 863 in 2005 (Source: UN, *Statistical Yearbook*).

Non-daily newspapers: 433 (average circulation 7,838,000) in 1998; 349 (average circulation 5,617,000) in 2004 (Source: UN, *Statistical Yearbook*).

Book production: 6,000 titles in 2003.

Personal computers: 4,510,000 (20.3 per 1,000 persons) in 2006.

Source (unless otherwise indicated): mostly International Telecommunication Union.

Education

(2008/09 unless otherwise indicated)

	Institutions	Teachers	Pupils and Students
Kindergarten*	63,444	233,563	2,783,413
Primary schools	144,228	1,569,326	26,984,824
General junior secondary schools	28,777	629,036	8,992,619
General senior secondary schools	10,762	314,389	3,857,245
Vocational senior secondary schools	7,592	246,018	3,095,704
Tertiary institutions	2,975	228,781	4,281,695

* 2007/08 figure.

Source: Ministry of National Education.

Pupil-teacher ratio (primary education, UNESCO estimate): 16.6 in 2008/09 (Source: UNESCO Institute for Statistics).

Adult literacy rate (UNESCO estimates): 92.2% (males 95.4%; females 89.1%) in 2008 (Source: UNESCO Institute for Statistics).

Directory

The Constitution

Indonesia had three provisional Constitutions: in August 1945, February 1950 and August 1950. In July 1959 the Constitution of 1945 was re-enacted by presidential decree. The General Elections Law of 1969 supplemented the 1945 Constitution, which has been adopted permanently by the Majelis Permusyawaratan Rakyat (MPR—People's Consultative Assembly). Major amendments made to the Constitution in 2001 and 2002 took effect in 2004, when Indonesia held its next general election. The following is a summary of the Constitution's main provisions, with subsequent amendments:

GENERAL PRINCIPLES

The 1945 Constitution consists of 37 articles, four transitional clauses and two additional provisions, and is preceded by a preamble. The preamble contains an indictment of all forms of colonialism, an account of Indonesia's struggle for independence, the declaration of that independence and a statement of fundamental aims and principles. Indonesia's National Independence, according to the text of the preamble, has the state form of a Republic, with sovereignty residing in the People, and is based upon five fundamental principles, the *Pancasila*:

1. Belief in the One Supreme God.
2. Just and Civilized Humanity.
3. The Unity of Indonesia.
4. Democracy led by the wisdom of deliberations (*musyawarah*) and consensus among representatives.
5. Social Justice for all the people of Indonesia.

STATE ORGANS

Majelis Permusyawaratan Rakyat—MPR (People's Consultative Assembly)

Sovereignty is in the hands of the People and is exercised in full by the MPR as the embodiment of the whole Indonesian People. The MPR is the highest authority of the State, and is to be distinguished from the legislative body proper (Dewan Perwakilan Rakyat—DPR, see below), which is incorporated within the MPR. The bicameral MPR, with a total of 692 members (increased in 2009 from 678), is composed of the 560 members of the DPR and the 132 members of the Dewan Perwakilan Daerah—DPD (see below). Elections to the MPR are held every five years. The MPR sits at least once every five years, and its primary competence is to determine the Constitution and the broad lines of the policy of the State and the Government. It also inaugurates the President and Vice-President, who are responsible for implementing that policy. All decisions are taken unanimously in keeping with the traditions of *musyawarah*.

The President

The highest executive of the Government, the President, holds office for a term of five years and may be re-elected once. As Mandatory of the MPR he/she must execute the policy of the State according to the Decrees determined by the MPR during its Fourth General and Special Sessions. In conducting the administration of the State, authority and responsibility are concentrated in the President. The Ministers of the State are his/her assistants and are responsible only to him/her. The President and Vice-President are to be directly elected on a single ticket (until November 2001 the MPR had exercised the power to elect them). If no candidate succeeds in obtaining more than one-half of the votes cast in a presidential election, a second round of voting shall be held. The President and Vice-President may be dismissed by the MPR on the proposal of the DPR if it is proven that he/she has either violated the law or no longer meets the requirements of his/her office. The President may not suspend or dissolve the Dewan.

Dewan Perwakilan Rakyat—DPR (House of Representatives)

The legislative branch of the State, the Dewan Perwakilan Rakyat, sits at least once a year. Its members are all directly elected. Every statute requires the approval of the Dewan. Members of the Dewan have the right to submit draft bills, which require ratification by the President, who has the right of veto. In times of emergency the President may enact ordinances, which have the force of law, but such ordinances must be ratified by the Dewan during the following session or be revoked.

Dewan Perwakilan Daerah—DPD (House of Representatives of the Regions)

The Dewan Perwakilan Daerah is the second chamber of the MPR. Its members are directly elected from every province. Each province has an equal number of members and total membership of the DPD is no more than one-third of the total membership of the DPR. The DPD sits at least once a year. It may propose to the DPR bills relating to regional autonomy, the relationship between central and local government, the formation, expansion and merger of regions, the management of natural and other economic resources, and the financial balance between the centre and the localities. It may also participate in the discussion of such bills and oversee the implementation of regional laws, as well as the state budget, taxation, education and religion.

Dewan Pertimbangan Agung—DPA (Supreme Advisory Council)

The DPA is an advisory body assisting the President, who chooses its members from political parties, functional groups and groups of prominent persons.

Mahkamah Agung (Supreme Court)

The judicial branch of the State, the Supreme Court and the other courts of law (public courts, religious courts, military tribunals, administrative courts and a Constitutional Court) are independent of the Executive in exercising their judicial powers. There is an independent Judicial Commission, which is authorized to propose candidates for appointment as justices of the Supreme Court and to ensure the good behaviour of judges. Its members are appointed and dismissed by the President with the approval of the DPR.

Badan Pemeriksa Keuangan (Supreme Audit Board)

Controls the accountability of public finance, enjoys investigatory powers and is independent of the Executive. Its findings are presented to the Dewan.

The Government

HEAD OF STATE

President: Gen. (retd) SUSILO BAMBANG YUDHOYONO (elected 5 July 2004; re-elected 8 July 2009).

Vice-President: Prof. Dr BOEDIONO.

CABINET

(October 2011)

The Government includes members of the Partai Demokrat (PD), Golkar, Partai Amanat Nasional (PAN), Partai Damai Sejahtera (PDS), Partai Persatuan Pembangunan (PPP) and Partai Kebangkitan Bangsa (PKB), along with numerous unaffiliated members.

Co-ordinating Minister for Political, Legal and Security Affairs: Air Chief Marshal (retd) DJOKO SUYANTO.

Co-ordinating Minister for Economic Affairs: HATTA RAJASA.

Co-ordinating Minister for People's Welfare: Dr AGUNG LAKSONO.

Minister of Home Affairs: GAMAWAN FAUZI.

Minister of Foreign Affairs: Dr RADEN (MARTY) MOHAMMAD MULIANA NATALEGAWA.

Minister of Defence: Dr Ir PURNOMO YUSGIANTORO.

Minister of Justice and Human Rights: AMIR SYAMSUDDIN.

Minister of Finance: AGUS MARTOWARDOJO.

Minister of Energy and Mineral Resources: JERO WATJIK.

Minister of Industry: MOHAMAD S. HIDAYAT.

Minister of Trade: GITA WIRJAWAN.

Minister of Agriculture: Ir H. SUSWONO.

Minister of Forestry: ZULKIFLI HASAN.

Minister of Transportation: Vice-Adm. (retd) FREDDY NUMBERI.

Minister of Marine Affairs and Fisheries: SYARIF C. SUTARDJO.

Minister of Manpower and Transmigration: Drs MUHAIMIN ISKANDAR.

Minister of Public Works: DJOKO KIRMANTO.

Minister of Health: Dr ENDANG RAHAYU SEDYANINGSIH.

Minister of National Education: Dr Ir MUHAMMAD NUH.

Minister of Social Affairs: Dr SALIM SEGAF AL-JUFRIE.

Minister of Religious Affairs: Drs SURYADHARMA ALI.

Minister of Culture and Tourism: Dr MARI ELKA PANGESTU.

Minister of Communications and Information Technology: TIFATUL SEMBIRING.

Minister of State for Research and Technology: Dr Ir GUSTI MUHAMMAD HATTA.

Minister of State for Co-operatives and Small and Medium-Sized Businesses: Dr SYARIFUDDIN HASAN.

Minister of State for the Environment: BALTAZAR KAMBUAYA.

Minister of State for Women's Empowerment: LINDA AMALIA SARI.

Minister of State for Administrative Reform: AZWAR ABUBAKAR.

Minister of State for State Enterprises: DAHLAN ISKAN.

Minister of State for Development of Disadvantaged Regions: Ir AHMAD HELMI FAISAL ZAINI.

Minister of State for National Development Planning: ARMIDA ALISJAHBANA.

Minister of State for Public Housing: DJAN FARIDZ.

Minister of State for Youth and Sports Affairs: ANDI ALIFIAN MALLARANGENG.

Officials with the rank of Minister of State:

Attorney-General: BASRIEF ARIEF.

State Secretary: Lt-Gen. (retd) SUDI SILALAHI.

MINISTRIES

Office of the President: Istana Merdeka, 2nd Floor, Jakarta 10110; tel. (21) 3840946; internet www.presidenri.go.id.

Office of the Vice-President: Istana Wakil Presiden, Jalan Medan Merdeka Selatan 14, Jakarta 10110; tel. (21) 3844676; fax (21) 3446122; e-mail tirta_hidayat@yahoo.co.id; internet www.setwapres.go.id.

Office of the Attorney-General: Jalan Sultan Hasanuddin 1, Kebayoran Baru, Jakarta Selatan; tel. (21) 7221269; fax (21) 7392576; e-mail webmaster@kejaksaan.go.id; internet www.kejaksaan.go.id.

Office of the Cabinet Secretary: 4th Floor, Jalan Veteran 18, Jakarta Pusat 10110; tel. (21) 3846463; fax (21) 3866579; e-mail itcp@setkab.go.id; internet www.setkab.go.id.

Office of the Co-ordinating Minister for Economic Affairs: Jalan Lapangan Banteng Timur 2–4, Jakarta 10710; tel. (21) 3521974; fax (21) 3521985; e-mail humas@ekon.go.id; internet www.ekon.go.id.

Office of the Co-ordinating Minister for People's Welfare: Jalan Merdeka Barat 3, Jakarta Pusat; tel. (21) 3459444; fax (21) 3453289; internet www.menkokesra.go.id.

Office of the Co-ordinating Minister for Political, Legal and Security Affairs: Jalan Medan Merdeka Barat 15, Jakarta 10110; tel. (21) 3521121; fax (21) 3450918; e-mail dkpt@polkam.go.id; internet www.polkam.go.id.

Office of the State Secretary: Jalan Veteran 17–18, Jakarta 10110; tel. (21) 3849043; fax (21) 3452685; e-mail webmaster@setneg.go.id; internet www.setneg.go.id.

Ministry of Agriculture: Gedung D, 4th Floor, Jalan Harsono R. M. 3, Ragunan, Pasar Minggu, Jakarta Selatan 12550; tel. (21) 7822803; fax (21) 7816385; e-mail baran@deptan.go.id; internet www.deptan.go.id.

Ministry of Communication and Information Technology: Jalan Medan Merdeka Barat 9, Jakarta Pusat 10110; tel. (21) 3844227; fax (21) 3867600; e-mail info@depkominfo.go.id; internet www.depkominfo.go.id.

Ministry of Culture and Tourism: Gedung Sapta Pesona, Jalan Medan Merdeka Barat 17, Jakarta Pusat 10110; tel. (21) 3838167; fax (21) 3849715; e-mail pusdatin@budpar.go.id; internet www.budpar.go.id.

Ministry of Defence: Jalan Medan Merdeka Barat 13–14, Jakarta Pusat 10200; tel. (21) 3456184; fax (21) 3440023; e-mail postmaster@dephan.go.id; internet www.dephan.go.id.

Ministry of Energy and Mineral Resources: Jalan Medan Merdeka Selatan 18, Jakarta 10110; tel. and fax (21) 3519881; e-mail pusdatin@esdm.go.id; internet www.esdm.go.id.

Ministry of Finance and State Enterprises Development: Jalan Lapangan Banteng Timur 2–4, Jakarta 10710; tel. (21) 3841067; fax (21) 3808395; e-mail helpdesk@depkeu.go.id; internet www.depkeu.go.id.

Ministry of Foreign Affairs: 10th Floor, Jalan Taman Pejambon 6, Jakarta Pusat 10110; tel. (21) 3441508; fax (21) 3857316; e-mail infomed@deplu.go.id; internet www.deplu.go.id.

Ministry of Forestry: Gedung Manggala Wanabakti, Blok I, 3rd Floor, Jalan Jenderal Gatot Subroto, Senayan, Jakarta 10270; tel. (21) 5704501; fax (21) 5720216; e-mail pusdata@dephut.go.id; internet www.dephut.go.id.

Ministry of Health and Social Welfare: Blok X5, Jalan H. R. Rasuna Said, Kav. 4–9, Jakarta 12950; tel. (21) 5201590; fax (21) 5201591; e-mail webadmin@depkes.go.id; internet www.depkes.go.id.

Ministry of Home Affairs and Regional Autonomy: Gedung Utama, 4th Floor, Jalan Medan Merdeka Utara 7, Jakarta Pusat 10110; tel. (21) 3450038; fax (21) 3851193; e-mail pusdatinkomtel@depdagri.go.id; internet www.depdagri.go.id.

Ministry of Industry: Jalan Jenderal Gatot Subroto, Kav. 52–53, Jakarta Selatan 12950; tel. (21) 5252194; fax (21) 5261086; e-mail pusdatin@depperin.go.id; internet www.depperin.go.id.

Ministry of Justice and Human Rights: Jalan H. R. Rasuna Said, Kav. 6–7, Kuningan, Jakarta Selatan; tel. (21) 5253004; fax (21) 5253139; e-mail pullahta@depkumham.go.id; internet www.depkumham.go.id.

Ministry of Manpower and Transmigration: Jalan T. M. P Kalibata 17, Jakarta Selatan; tel. (21) 5255683; fax (21) 515669; e-mail redaksi_balitfo@nakertrans.go.id; internet www.nakertrans.go.id.

Ministry of Marine Affairs and Fisheries: Gedung Humpus, Jalan Medan Merdeka Timur 16, Jakarta 10110; tel. (21) 3500023; fax (21) 3519133; e-mail admin@dkp.go.id; internet www.dkp.go.id.

Ministry of National Education: Jalan Jenderal Sudirman, Senayan, Jakarta Pusat 12041; tel. (21) 57950226; fax (21) 5731177; e-mail pusdatin@depdiknas.go.id; internet www.depdiknas.go.id.

Ministry of Public Works: Jalan Pattimura 20, Kebayoran Baru, Jakarta Selatan 12110; tel. (21) 7392262; fax (21) 7200793; e-mail dkirmanto@pu.go.id; internet www.pu.go.id.

Ministry of Religious Affairs: Jalan Lapangan Banteng Barat 3–4, Jakarta Pusat 10710; tel. (21) 3843005; fax (21) 3812306; e-mail pinmas@depag.go.id; internet www.depag.go.id.

Ministry of Social Affairs: Jalan Salemba Raya 28, Jakarta 10430; tel. (21) 3103591; fax (21) 3103783; e-mail pusdatin@depsos.go.id; internet www.depsos.go.id.

Ministry of Trade: Blok I, 3rd Floor, Jalan Merdeka Ikhwan Ridwan Rais 5, Jakarta Pusat; tel. (21) 3840138; fax (21) 3846106; internet www.depdag.go.id.

Ministry of Transportation: Jalan Medan Merdeka Barat 8, Jakarta 10110; tel. (21) 3811308; fax (21) 3862371; e-mail pusdatin@dephub.go.id; internet www.dephub.go.id.

Office of the Minister of State for Co-operatives and Small and Medium-Sized Businesses: Jalan H. R. Rasuna Said, Kav. 3–5, POB 177, Jakarta Selatan 12940; tel. (21) 52992999; fax (21) 5204378; e-mail datin@depkop.go.id; internet www.depkop.go.id.

Office of the Minister of State for the Environment: Gedung A, 6th Floor, Jalan D. I. Panjaitan, Kav. 24, Kebon Nanas, Jakarta 13410; tel. and fax (21) 8517184; e-mail edukom@menlh.go.id; internet www.menlh.go.id.

Office of the Minister of State for Research and Technology: Gedung BPP Teknologi II, 5th–8th Floors, Jalan M. H. Thamrin 8, Jakarta Pusat 10340; tel. (21) 3169119; fax (21) 3101952; e-mail webmstr@ristek.go.id; internet www.ristek.go.id.

Office of the Minister of State for State Enterprises: Jalan Medan Merdeka Selatan 13, Jakarta 10110; e-mail sekretariat@bumn.go.id; internet www.bumn-ri.com.

Office of the Minister of State for Women's Empowerment: Jalan Medan Merdeka Barat 15, Jakarta 10110; tel. (21) 3805563; fax (21) 3805562; e-mail biroren@menegpp.go.id; internet www.menegpp.go.id.

Office of the Minister of State for Youth and Sports Affairs: Jalan Gerbang Pemuda Senayan, Jakarta 10270; internet www.kemenpora.go.id.

OTHER GOVERNMENT BODY

Badan Pemeriksa Keuangan (BPK) (Supreme Audit Board): Jalan Gatot Subroto 31, Jakarta 10210; tel. (21) 25549000; fax (21) 57854096; e-mail webmaster@bpk.go.id; internet www.bpk.go.id; Chair. Drs Hadi Poernomo; Vice-Chair. Dr Herman Widyananda.

President and Legislature

PRESIDENT

Presidential Election, 8 July 2009

Candidate	Votes	% of votes
Gen. (retd) Susilo Bambang Yudhoyono (PD)	73,874,562	60.80
Megawati Sukarnoputri (PDI—P)	32,548,105	26.79
Muhammad Jusuf Kalla (Golkar)	15,081,814	12.41
Total	121,504,481	100.00

LEGISLATURE

Majelis Permusyawaratan Rakyat (MPR)
(People's Consultative Assembly)

Jalan Jenderal Gatot Subroto 6, Jakarta 10270; tel. (21) 5715773; fax (21) 5734526; e-mail kotaksurat@mpr.go.id; internet www.mpr.go.id.

In late 2002 the Constitution was amended to provide for the direct election of all members of the Majelis Permusyawaratan Rakyat (MPR—People's Consultative Assembly) at the next general election, held in 2004. The MPR thus became a bicameral institution comprising the Dewan Perwakilan Daerah (DPD—House of Representatives of the Regions) and the Dewan Perwakilan Rakyat (DPR—House of Representatives). The MPR subsequently consisted of the 550 members of the DPR and 128 regional delegates, increasing to 560 and 132 respectively at the 2009 election.

Speaker: Taufik Kiemas.

	Seats
Members of the Dewan Perwakilan Rakyat	560
Regional representatives	132
Total	692

Dewan Perwakilan Rakyat (DPR)
(House of Representatives)

Jalan Gatot Subroto 16, Jakarta; tel. (21) 586833; e-mail humas@dpr.go.id; internet www.dpr.go.id.

Speaker: Marzuki Alie.

General Election, 9 April 2009

	Seats
Partai Demokrat (PD)	148
Partai Golongan Karya (Golkar)	108
Partai Demokrasi Indonesia Perjuangan (PDI—P)	93
Partai Keadilan Sejahtera (PKS)	59
Partai Amanat Nasional (PAN)	42
Partai Persatuan Pembangunan (PPP)	39
Partai Gerakan Indonesia Raya (Gerindra)	30
Partai Kebangkitan Bangsa (PKB)	26
Partai Hati Nurani Rakyat (Hanura)	15
Total	560

Election Commission

Komisi Pemilihan Umum (KPU): Jalan Imam Bonjol 29, Jakarta 10310; tel. (21) 31937223; fax (21) 3157759; e-mail redaktur@kpu.go.id; internet www.kpu.go.id; f. 1999; govt body; Chair. Abdul Hafiz Anshary.

Political Organizations

All parties must adhere to the state philosophy of *pancasila* and reject communism. A total of 38 national parties contested the legislative elections of April 2009.

Barisan Nasional (National Front): Jalan Gunawarman 32, Kebayoran Baru, Jakarta Selatan 12810; tel. (21) 7269588; fax (21) 7243081; f. 1998; committed to ensuring that Indonesia remains a secular state; merger with Gerindra announced in early 2011; Sec.-Gen. Rachmat Witoelar.

Koalisi Kebangsaan (Nationhood Coalition): Jakarta; f. 2004; coalition formed to contest the presidential election of 2004 in support of Megawati Sukarnoputri, comprising Golkar, PDI—P, PDS, PKB and PPP; PPP defected to Koalisi Kerakyatan following the election.

Koalisi Kerakyatan (People's Coalition): Jakarta; f. 2004; coalition formed in support of Gen. (retd) Susilo Bambang Yudhoyono to contest the presidential election of 2004, centred around PD, PAN and PKS; PPP joined after defecting from Koalisi Kebangsaan following the election.

Partai Amanat Nasional (PAN) (National Mandate Party): Rumah PAN, Jalan Raya Warung Buncit 17, Jakarta Selatan; tel. (21) 7975588; fax (21) 7975632; f. 1998; aims to achieve democracy, progress and social justice, to limit the length of the presidential term of office and to increase autonomy in the provinces; Chair. Hatta Rajasa; Sec.-Gen. Taufik Kurniawan.

Partai Bintang Reformasi (PBR) (Reform Star Party): Jalan K. H. Abdullah Syafei 2, Tebet, Jakarta Selatan; tel. (21) 8311715; f. 2002; est. by fmr PPP mems; Islamic party; merger with Gerindra announced in early 2011; Chair. Barusa Zarnubi; Sec.-Gen. Rusman Ali.

Partai Bulan Bintang (PBB) (Crescent Moon and Star Party): Jalan Raya Pasar Minggu 1B, Km 18, Jakarta Selatan; tel. (21) 79180734; fax (21) 79180765; f. 1998; Leader M. S. Kaban; Sec.-Gen. Sahar Hassan.

Partai Buruh (Labour Party): Jalan Kramat Raya 91A, Jakarta Pusat; tel. (21) 3154092; fax (21) 3909834; f. 2001; est. as Partai

Buruh Sosial Demokrat (PBSD—Socialist Democratic Labour Party); present name adopted 2005; merger with Gerindra announced in early 2011; Chair. MUCHTAR PAKPAHAN; Sec.-Gen. DIAH INDRIASTUTI.

Partai Damai Sejahtera (PDS) (Prosperous Peace Party): Jalan S. Parman G6, Bundaran Slipi, Jakarta Barat 11480; tel. (21) 5307488; fax (21) 5367039; e-mail pds_2014@yahoo.com; internet www.partaidamaisejahtera.com; f. 2001; merger with Gerindra announced in early 2011; Chair. RUYANDI MUSTIKA HUTASOIT; Sec.-Gen. FERRY B. REGAR.

Partai Demokrasi Indonesia Perjuangan (PDI—P) (Indonesian Democratic Struggle Party): Jalan Lenteng Agung 99, Jakarta Selatan; tel. (21) 7806028; fax (21) 7814472; est. by Megawati Sukarnoputri, fmr PDI leader, following her removal from PDI leadership by Govt in 1996; Chair. MEGAWATI SUKARNOPUTRI; Sec.-Gen. TJAHJO KUMOLO.

Partai Demokrat (PD): Jalan Pemuda 712A, Jakarta Timur 13220; tel. (21) 4755146; fax (21) 4757957; internet www.demokrat.or.id; f. 2001; Chair. of Advisory Bd Gen. (retd) SUSILO BAMBANG YUDHOYONO; Gen. Chair. ANAS URBANINGRUM; Sec.-Gen. EDHIE 'IBAS' BASKORO YUDHOYONO.

Partai Gerakan Indonesia Raya (Gerindra) (Great Indonesia Movement Party): Jalan Brawijaya IX 1, Kebayoran Baru, Jakarta Selatan 12160; tel. (21) 7279547; fax (21) 7395154; e-mail info@partaigerindra.or.id; internet www.partaigerindra.or.id; f. 2008; Chair. SUHARDI; Sec.-Gen. AHMAD MUZANI.

Partai Golongan Karya (Golkar) (Party of Functional Groups): Jalan Anggrek Nellimurni, Jakarta 11480; tel. (21) 5302222; fax (21) 5303380; e-mail info@golkar.or.id; internet www.golkar.or.id; f. 1964; reorg. 1971; Pres. and Chair. ABURIZAL BAKRIE; Sec.-Gen. IDRUS MARHAM.

Partai Hati Nurani Rakyat (Hanura) (People's Conscience Party): Jalan Diponegoro 1, Menteng, Jakarta; tel. (21) 31935334; fax (21) 3922054; e-mail info@hanura.or.id; internet www.hanura.com; f. 2006; Chair. WIRANTO; Sec.-Gen. YUS USMAN SUMANEGARA.

Partai Karya Peduli Bangsa (PKPB) (Concern for the Nation Functional Party): Jalan Cimandiri 30, Raden Saleh Cikini, Jakarta Pusat 13033; tel. (21) 31927421; fax (21) 31937417; internet www.pkpb.net; f. 2002; Chair. R. HARTONO; Sec.-Gen. H. ARY MARDJONO.

Partai Kasih Demokrasi Indonesia (PKDI) (The Indonesian Democratic Party of Devotion): Jalan Panglima Polim I 32, Jakarta Selatan; tel. and fax (21) 7230731; f. 2006; est. by merger of seven Christian parties.

Partai Keadilan dan Persatuan Indonesia (PKPI) (Justice and Unity Party): Jalan Raya Cilandak KKO 32, Pasar Minggu, Jakarta Selatan; tel. (21) 7807653; fax (21) 7807655; f. 2002; Chair. MEUTIA FARIDA HATTA; Sec.-Gen. HAYONO ISMAN.

Partai Keadilan Sejahtera (PKS) (Prosperous Justice Party): Jalan Mampang Prapatan Raya 98 D–F, Jakarta Selatan 12720; tel. (21) 7995425; fax (21) 7995433; e-mail partai@pks.or.id; internet www.pk-sejahtera.org; f. 2002; Islamic party; Chair. MUSTAFA KAMAL; Sec.-Gen. ANIS MATTA.

Partai Kebangkitan Bangsa (PKB) (National Awakening Party): Jalan Sukabumi 23, Jakarta Selatan 12740; tel. and fax (21) 3155138; e-mail dpp@dpp-pkb.or.id; internet www.dpp-pkb.or.id; nationalist Islamic party; f. 1998; Chair. MUHAIMIN ISKANDAR; Sec.-Gen. LUKMAN EDY.

Partai Kebangkitan Nasional Ulama (PKNU) (Scholars' National Awakening Party): Jalan Kramat VI 8, Jakarta Pusat 10430; tel. (21) 31923717; fax (21) 3905686; f. 2006; breakaway faction of PKB; Chair. CHOIRUL ANAM.

Partai Merdeka (Freedom Party): Jalan Mampang Prapatan XII 6, Jakarta Selatan 12790; tel. (21) 7991439; e-mail info@partaimerdeka.or.id; f. 2002; merger with Gerindra announced in early 2011; Chair. ADI SASONO; Sec.-Gen. DHARMA SETIAWAN.

Partai Nasional Benteng Kerakyatan (PNBK) (National Populist Fortress Party): Jalan Penjernihan I 50, Jakarta Utara; tel. (21) 5739550; fax (21) 5739519; f. 2002; est. as Partai Nasional Banteng Kemerdekaan; renamed as above prior to 2009 legislative election; Chair. EROS DJAROT; Sec.-Gen. SOEHARDI SOEDIRO.

Partai Nasional Indonesia Marhaenisme (PNI Marhaenisme): Jalan Gudang Peluru Raya B1 7B, Kebon Baru, Tebet, Jakarta Selatan; tel. and fax (21) 83795157; f. 2002; merger with Gerindra announced in early 2011; Chair. SUKMAWATI SUKARNOPUTRI; Sec.-Gen. ARDY MUHAMMAD.

Partai Patriot Pancasila (Pancasila Patriot Party): Jalan Manggis 12A, Ciganjur, Jakarta Selatan 12630; tel. (21) 7261522; f. 2001; Chair. YAPTO SULISTIO SOERJOSOEMARNO; Sec.-Gen. MAX BOBOY.

Partai Peduli Rakyat Nasional (PPRN) (National People's Concern Party): Jalan Pahlawan Revolusi 148, Pondok Bambu, Jakarta Timur 13140; tel. (21) 86600284; fax (21) 86614140; e-mail dpp.pprn@gmail.com; internet www.pprn.or.id; f. 2006; Chair. AMELIA ACHMAD YANI; Sec.-Gen. ALBERT SIMANJUNTAK.

Partai Pelopor (Pioneer Party): Jalan Pegangsaan Timur 17, Cikini, Jakarta Pusat; tel. and fax (21) 31903634; f. 2002; Chair. RACHMAWATI SUKARNOPUTRI; Sec.-Gen. EKO SURYO SANTJOJO.

Partai Penegak Demokrasi Indonesia (PPDI) (Indonesian Democratic Vanguard Party): Jalan Amil 26, RT-02/RW-05, Kalibata Pulo, Jakarta; tel. (21) 7992758; f. 2003; Chair. ENDUNG SUTRISNO; Sec.-Gen. V. JOES PRANANTO.

Partai Perhimpunan Indonesia Baru (PIB) (New Indonesia Alliance Party): Jalan Teuku Cik Ditiro 31, Menteng, Jakarta Pusat 10310; tel. (21) 3108057; e-mail partaipib@yahoo.com; f. 2002; Chair. Dr SYAHRIR; Sec.-Gen. AMIR KARAMOY.

Partai Persatuan Daerah (Regional United Party): Jalan Dr Satrio C-4 18, Jakarta Selatan 12940; tel. (21) 5273250; fax (21) 5273249; f. 2002; Chair. OESMAN SAPTA; Sec.-Gen. SYS NS.

Partai Persatuan Demokrasi Kebangsaan (PPDK) (National Democratic Unity Party): Jalan Ampera Raya 99, Jakarta Selatan 12560; tel. (21) 7807432; fax (21) 7817341; f. 2002; Chair. Dr RYAAS RASYID; Sec.-Gen. RIVAI PULUNGAN.

Partai Persatuan Nahdlatul Ummah Indonesia (PPNUI) (Indonesian Nahdlatul Community Party): Jalan K. H. Abdullah Syafi'i 5, RT-04/RW-06, Bukit Duri, Tebet, Jakarta Selatan; tel. (21) 70006444; f. 1998; est. as Partai Nahdlatul Ummah; present name adopted 2003; Islamic party; merger with Gerindra announced in early 2011; Chair. SYUKRON MA'MUN; Sec.-Gen. ACHMAD SJATARI.

Partai Persatuan Pembangunan (PPP) (United Development Party): Jalan Diponegoro 60, Jakarta Pusat 10310; tel. (21) 31936338; fax (21) 3142558; e-mail dpp@ppp.or.id; internet www.ppp.or.id; f. 1973; est. by merger of four Islamic parties; Leader SURYADHARMA ALI; Sec.-Gen. IRGAN CHAERUL MAHFIZ.

Partai Rakyat Demokratik (PRD) (People's Democratic Party): Jalan Tebet Barat Dalam VIII Nomor 4, Jakarta Selatan 12820; tel. and fax (21) 8296467; e-mail prd@centrin.net.id; internet www.prd.4-all.org; f. 1996; Chair. BUDIMAN SUDJATMIKO.

Partai Reformasi Tionghoa Indonesia (Chinese Indonesian Reform Party): Jakarta; e-mail parti_id@usa.net; f. 1998; Chinese.

Partai Sarikat Indonesia (PSI) (Indonesia Unity Party): Jalan Kemang Utara 6, Jakarta Selatan; tel. (21) 4199110; e-mail dpppsi@indosat.net.id; f. 2002; merger with Gerindra announced in early 2011; Chair. Drs H. MARDINSYAH; Sec.-Gen. NAZIR MUHAMMAD.

Partai Uni Demokrasi Indonesia (PUDI) (Democratic Union Party of Indonesia): Jalan Raya Tanjung Barat 81, Jakarta 12530; tel. (21) 7817565; fax (21) 7814765; e-mail pudi@pudi.or.id; f. 1996; Chair. Sri BINTANG PAMUNGKAS; Sec.-Gen. ESA HARUMAN.

Other groups with political influence include:

Ikatan Cendekiawan Muslim Indonesia (ICMI) (Association of Indonesian Muslim Intellectuals): Gedung BPPT, Jalan M. H. Thamrin 8, Jakarta; tel. (21) 3410382; internet www.icmi.or.id; f. 1990; est. with govt support; Chair. AZYUMARDI AZRA; Sec.-Gen. AGUS SALIM DASUKI.

Partai Syarikat Islam Indonesia 1905: Jalan Prof. Dr Latumenten, Brt 16, Jakarta; tel. (21) 5659790.

The following groups are, or have been, in conflict with the Government:

Gerakan Aceh Merdeka (GAM) (Free Aceh Movement): based in Aceh; e-mail info@asnlf.net; internet www.asnlf.net; f. 1976; signed a peace deal with the Indonesian Govt in July 2005, under the terms of which GAM agreed to relinquish its claims for independence and the Govt agreed to facilitate the establishment of Aceh-based political parties; Military Commdr MUZZAKIR MANAF.

Organisasi Papua Merdeka (OPM) (Free Papua Movement): based in Papua; e-mail opmpapua@yahoo.com; internet www.geocities.com/opm-irja; f. 1963; seeks unification with Papua New Guinea; Chair. MOZES WEROR; Military Commdr Gen. JECK KEMONG.

Presidium Dewan Papua (PDP) (Papua Presidium Council): based in Papua; e-mail pdp@westpapua.net; internet www.melanesianews.org/pdp/org; seeks independence from Indonesia; Chair. TOM BEANAL.

Diplomatic Representation

EMBASSIES IN INDONESIA

Afghanistan: Jalan Dr Kusuma Atmaja 15, Jakarta Pusat 10310; tel. (21) 3143169; fax (21) 31935390; e-mail afghanembassy_jkk@yahoo.com; Ambassador FAZLURRAHMAN FAZIL.

Algeria: Jalan H. R. Rasuna Said, Kav. 10-1, Kuningan, Jakarta 12950; tel. (21) 5254719; fax (21) 5254654; e-mail ambaljak@cbn.net.id; Ambassador ABDELKRIM BELARBI.

Argentina: Menara Thamrin, Suite 1602, 16th Floor, Jalan M. H. Thamrin, Kav. 3, Jakarta 10250; tel. (21) 2303061; fax (21) 2303962; e-mail embargen@cbn.net.id; Ambassador JAVIER A. SANZ DE URQUIZA.

Australia: Jalan H. R. Rasuna Said, Kav. C15–16, Kuningan, Jakarta 12940; tel. (21) 25505555; fax (21) 25505467; e-mail public-affairs-jakt@dfat.gov.au; internet www.indonesia.embassy .gov.au; Ambassador GREG MORIARTY.

Austria: Jalan Terusan Denpasar Raya 1, Kuningan, Jakarta 12950; tel. (21) 2593037; fax (21) 52920651; e-mail jakarta-ob@ bmeia.gv.at; internet www.austrian-embassy.or.id; Ambassador Dr KLAUS WOELFER.

Azerbaijan: Jalan Mas Putih D, Persil 29, Grogol Utara Kebayoran Lama, Jakarta Selatan 12430; tel. (21) 5491939; fax (21) 5491745; e-mail jakarta@mission.mfa.gov.az; internet www.azembassy.or.id; Chargé d'affaires FARID TALIBOV.

Bangladesh: Jalan Taman Ubud 1, 5 Kuningan Timur, Jakarta Selatan 12950; tel. (21) 52921271; fax (21) 5251143; e-mail bdootjak@ yahoo.com; internet sites.google.com/site/bangladesh embassy jakarta; Ambassador GOLAM MOHAMMED.

Belgium: Deutsche Bank Bldg, 16th Floor, Jalan Imam Bonjol 80, Jakarta 10310; tel. (21) 3162030; fax (21) 3162035; e-mail jakarta@ diplobel.fed.be; internet www.diplomatie.be/jakarta; Ambassador CHRISTIAAN TANGHE.

Bosnia and Herzegovina: Menara Imperium, 11th Floor, Suite D-2, Metropolitan Kuningan Super Blok, Kav. 1, Jalan H. R. Rasuna Said, Jakarta 12980; tel. (21) 83703022; fax (21) 83703029; Ambassador TARIK BUKVIC.

Brazil: Menara Mulia, Suite 1602, Jalan Jenderal Gatot Subroto, Kav. 9–11, Jakarta 12390; tel. (21) 5265656; fax (21) 5265659; e-mail embrasil@cbn.net.id; Ambassador MANUEL INNOCENCIO DE LACERDA SANTOS, Jr.

Brunei: Jalan Teuku Umar 9, Menteng, Jakarta Pusat 10350; tel. (21) 31906080; fax (21) 31905070; e-mail kbjindo@cbn.net.id; Ambassador Dato' Paduka MAHMUD Haji SAIDIN.

Bulgaria: Jalan Imam Bonjol 34–36, Menteng, Jakarta Pusat 10310; tel. (21) 3904048; fax (21) 3904049; e-mail bgemb.jkt@ centrin.net.id; internet www.mfa.bg/bg/33; Chargé d'affaires VENETA ZAIAKOVA.

Cambodia: Jalan T. B. Simatupang, Kav. 13, Jakarta Selatan 12520; tel. (21) 7812523; fax (21) 7812524; e-mail recjkt@indo.net .id; Ambassador KAN PHARITH.

Canada: World Trade Center, 6th Floor, Jalan Jenderal Sudirman, Kav. 29–31, POB 8324/JKS.MP, Jakarta 12920; tel. (21) 25507800; fax (21) 25507811; e-mail canadianembassy.jkrta@international.gc .ca; internet www.canadainternational.gc.ca/indonesia-indonesie; Ambassador MACKENZIE CLUGSTON.

Chile: Bina Mulia I, 7th Floor, Jalan H. R. Rasuna Said, Kav. 10, Kuningan, Jakarta 12950; tel. (21) 2525021; fax (21) 5201955; e-mail emchijak@indosat.net.id; internet chileabroad.gov.cl/indonesia; Ambassador EDUARDO RUIZ ASMUSSEN.

China, People's Republic: Jalan Mega Kuningan 2, Karet Kuningan, Jakarta 12950; tel. (21) 5761038; fax (21) 5761034; e-mail chinaemb_id@mfa.gov.cn; internet id.china-embassy.org/eng; Ambassador ZHANG QIYUE.

Croatia: Menara Mulia, Suite 2801, Jalan Gatot Subroto, Kav. 9–11, Jakarta 12930; tel. (21) 5257822; fax (21) 5204073; e-mail croemb@ rad.net.id; internet www.croatemb.or.id; Ambassador ŽELJKO ČIMBUR.

Cuba: Taman Puri, Jalan Opal, Blok K-1, Permata Hijau, Jakarta 12210; tel. (21) 5304293; fax (21) 53676906; e-mail cubaindo@cbn.net .id; internet embacuba.cubaminrex.cu/indonesia; Ambassador ENNA ESTHER VIANT VALDÉS.

Cyprus: c/o Jalan Purwakarta 8, Menteng, Jakarta Pusat; tel. (21) 3106367; fax (21) 3919256; e-mail nicpanayi@yahoo.com; Ambassador NICOS PANAYI.

Czech Republic: Jalan Gereja Theresia 20, Menteng, Jakarta Pusat 10350; tel. (21) 3904075; fax (21) 3904078; e-mail jakarta@ embassy.mzv.cz; internet www.mfa.cz/jakarta; Ambassador PAVEL ŘEZÁČ.

Denmark: Menara Rajawali, 25th Floor, Jalan Mega Kuningan, Lot 5.1, Jakarta 12950; tel. (21) 5761478; fax (21) 5761535; e-mail jktamb@um.dk; internet www.ambjakarta.um.dk; Ambassador BØRGE PETERSEN.

Ecuador: World Trade Center, 16th Floor, Jalan Jenderal Sudirman, Kav. 31, Jakarta 12920; tel. (21) 5211484; fax (21) 5226954; e-mail ecuadorinindonesia@gmail.com; Ambassador EDUARDO ALBERTO CALDERÓN LEDESMA.

Egypt: Jalan Teuku Umar 68, Menteng, Jakarta Pusat 10310; tel. (21) 3143440; fax (21) 3145073; e-mail egypt@indosat.net.id; internet www.mfa.gov.eg/Jakarta_Emb; Ambassador AHMED EL-KEWAISNY.

Fiji: Menara Topaz, 14th Floor, Jalan M. H. Thambrin, Kav. 9, Jakarta 10350; tel. (21) 3902543; fax (21) 3902544; Ambassador SEREMAIA TUI CAVUILATI.

Finland: Menara Rajawali, 9th Floor, Lot 5.1, Jalan Mega Kuningan, Kawasan Mega Kuningan, Jakarta 12950; tel. (21) 5761650; fax (21) 5761631; e-mail sanomat.jak@formin.fi; internet www.finland .or.id; Ambassador KAI SAUER.

France: Jalan M. H. Thamrin 20, Jakarta Pusat 10350; tel. (21) 23557600; fax (21) 23557601; e-mail ambassade@ambafrance-id.org; internet www.ambafrance-id.org; Ambassador PHILIPPE ZELLER.

Germany: Jalan M. H. Thamrin 1, Jakarta Pusat 10310; tel. (21) 39855000; fax (21) 3901757; e-mail kontakt-pr@jaka.diplo.de; internet www.jakarta.diplo.de; Ambassador Dr NORBERT BAAS.

Greece: Plaza 89, 12th Floor, Suite 1203, Jalan H. R. Rasuna Said, Kav. X-7 No. 6, Kuningan, Jakarta Selatan 12940; tel. (21) 5207776; fax (21) 5207753; e-mail grembas@cbn.net.id; internet www .greekembassy.or.id; Ambassador GEORGIOS VEIS.

Holy See: Jalan Merdeka Timur 18, POB 4227, Jakarta Pusat (Apostolic Nunciature); tel. (21) 3841142; fax (21) 3841143; e-mail vatjak@cbn.net.id; Apostolic Nuncio ANTONIO GUIDO FILIPAZZI (Titular Archbishop of Sutrium).

Hungary: Jalan H. R. Rasuna Said 36, Kav. X-3, Kuningan, Jakarta 12950; tel. (21) 5203459; fax (21) 5203461; e-mail mission.jkt@kum .hu; internet www.mfa.gov.hu/kulkepviselet/id; Ambassador SZILVESZTER BUS.

India: Jalan H. R. Rasuna Said, Kav. S-1, Kuningan, Jakarta 12950; tel. (21) 5204150; fax (21) 5204160; e-mail ambasador@net-zap.com; internet www.indianembassyjakarta.com; Ambassador BIREN NANDA.

Iran: Jalan Hos Cokroaminoto 110, Menteng, Jakarta Pusat 10310; tel. (21) 31931378; fax (21) 3107860; e-mail irembjkt@indo.net.id; internet www.iranembassy.or.id; Ambassador MAHMOUD FARAZANDER.

Iraq: Jalan Teuku Umar 38, Jakarta 10350; tel. (21) 3904067; fax (21) 3904066; e-mail iraqembi@rad.net.id; Ambassador ISMAEL SHAFIQ MUHSIN.

Italy: Jalan Diponegoro 45, Menteng, Jakarta Pusat 10310; tel. (21) 31937445; fax (21) 31937422; e-mail ambasciata.jakarta@esteri.it; internet www.ambjakarta.esteri.it; Ambassador ROBERTO PALMIERI.

Japan: Jalan M. H. Thamrin 24, Jakarta Pusat 10350; tel. (21) 31924308; fax (21) 31925460; internet www.id.emb-japan.go.jp; Ambassador YOSHINORI KATORI.

Jordan: Artha Graha Tower, 9th Floor, Sudirman Central Business District, Jalan Jenderal Sudirman, Kav. 52–53, Jakarta 12190; tel. (21) 5153483; fax (21) 5153482; e-mail jordanem@scbd.net.id; internet www.jordanembassy.or.id; Ambassador MOHAMMAD HASSAN DAWODIEH.

Korea, Democratic People's Republic: Jalan Teluk Betung 1–2, Jakarta Pusat 12050; tel. (21) 31908425; fax (21) 31908427; e-mail dprkorea@rad.net.id; Ambassador RI JONG RYUL .

Korea, Republic: Jalan Jenderal Gatot Subroto 57, Jakarta Selatan; tel. (21) 5201915; fax (21) 5254159; e-mail koremb_in@mofat.go .kr; internet idn.mofat.go.kr; Ambassador KIM YOUNG-SUN.

Kuwait: Jalan Mega Kuningan Barat III, Kav. 16–17, Jakarta; tel. (21) 5764159; fax (21) 5764561; e-mail jakarta@mofa.gov.kw; Ambassador NASER BAREH SHAHER EL-ENEZI.

Laos: Jalan Patra Kuningan XIV 1A, Kuningan, Jakarta 12950; tel. (21) 5229602; fax (21) 5229601; e-mail laoemjktof@hotmail.com; Ambassador PRASITH SAYASITH.

Lebanon: Jalan YBR V 82, Kuningan, Jakarta 12950; tel. (21) 5253074; fax (21) 5207121; e-mail lebanon_embassy_jkt@yahoo .com; Ambassador VICTOR ZMETER.

Libya: Jalan Kintamani Raya II, Blok C-17, Kav. 6–7, Kuningan Timur, Jakarta Selatan 12950; tel. (21) 52920033; fax (21) 52920036; e-mail gsplaj@cbn.net.id; Chargé d'affaires ABDUSSAMEE HARB.

Malaysia: Jalan H. R. Rasuna Said, Kav. X-6 Nos 1–3, Kuningan, Jakarta 12950; tel. (21) 5224947; fax (21) 5224974; e-mail maljakarta@kln.gov.my; internet www.kln.gov.my/web/ idn_jakarta; Ambassador Dato' SYED MUNSHE AFDZARUDDIN BIN SYED HASSAN.

Mexico: Menara Mulia, Suite 2306, Jalan Jenderal Gatot Subroto, Kav. 9–11, Jakarta Selatan 12930; tel. (21) 5203980; fax (21) 5203978; e-mail embmexic@rad.net.id; Ambassador MARY MELBA PRIA OLAVARRIETA.

Morocco: Jalan Denpasar Raya, Blok A-13, Kav. 1, Kuningan, Jakarta 12950; tel. (21) 5200773; fax (21) 5200586; e-mail sifamaind@gmail.com; Ambassador MOHAMED MAJDI.

Mozambique: Wisma GKBI, 37th Floor, Suite 3709, Jalan Jenderal Sudirman 28, Jakarta 10210; tel. (21) 5740901; fax (21) 5740907; e-mail embamoc@cbn.net.id; Ambassador CARLOS AGUSTINHO DO ROSÁRIO.

Myanmar: Jalan Haji Agus Salim 109, Menteng, Jakarta 10350; tel. (21) 327684; fax (21) 327204; e-mail myanmar@cbn.net.id; Ambassador NYAN LYNN.

Netherlands: Jalan H. R. Rasuna Said, Kav. S-3, Kuningan, Jakarta 12950; tel. (21) 5248200; fax (21) 5700734; e-mail jak@minbuza.nl; internet indonesia.nlembassy.org; Ambassador TJEERD DE ZWAAN.

New Zealand: Sentral Senayan 2, 10th Floor, Jalan Asia Afrika 8, Gelora Bung Karno, Jakarta Pusat 10270; tel. (21) 29955800; fax (21) 57974578; e-mail nzembjak@cbn.net.id; internet www.nzembassy.com/indonesia; Ambassador DAVID TAYLOR.

Nigeria: Jalan Taman Patra XIV 11, Kuningan Timur, POB 3649, Jakarta Selatan 12950; tel. (21) 5260922; fax (21) 5260924; e-mail embnig@centrin.net.id; Ambassador Alhaji IBRAHIM BABA MAI-SULE.

Norway: Menara Rajawali, 25th Floor, Kawasan Mega Kuningan, Jakarta 12950; tel. (21) 5761523; fax (21) 5761537; e-mail emb.jakarta@mfa.no; internet www.norway.or.id; Ambassador EIVIND HOMME.

Pakistan: Jalan Mega Kuningan, Blok E-3.9, Kav. 5–8, Kawasan Mega Kuningan, Jakarta Selatan 12950; tel. (21) 57851836; fax (21) 57851645; e-mail embassy@parepjakarta.com; internet www.mofa.gov.pk/indonesia; Ambassador SANAULLAH.

Panama: World Trade Center, 13th Floor, Jalan Jenderal Sudirman, Kav. 29–31, Jakarta 12920; tel. (21) 5711867; fax (21) 5711933; e-mail panaemb@net2cyber.web.id; Ambassador ROSEMARY SACETH DE LEÓN.

Papua New Guinea: Panin Bank Centre, 6th Floor, Jalan Jenderal Sudirman 1, Jakarta 10270; tel. (21) 7251218; fax (21) 7201012; e-mail kdujkt@cbn.net.id; Ambassador Cdre PETER ILAU (designate).

Peru: Menara Rajawali, 12th Floor, Jalan Mega Kuningan, Lot 5.1, Kawasan Mega Kuningan, Jakarta Selatan 12950; tel. (21) 5761820; fax (21) 5761825; e-mail embaperu@cbn.net.id; Ambassador JUAN JOSÉ ALVAREZ VITA.

Philippines: Jalan Imam Bonjol 6–8, Jakarta Pusat 10310; tel. (21) 3100334; fax (21) 3151167; e-mail phjkt@indo.net.id; Ambassador MARIA ROSARIO C. AGUINALDO.

Poland: Jalan H. R. Rasuna Said, Blok IV-3, Kav. X, Jakarta Selatan 12950; tel. (21) 2525938; fax (21) 2525958; e-mail poljkt@dnet.net.id; internet www.jakarta.polemb.net; Ambassador GRZEGORZ WIŚNIEWSKI.

Portugal: Jalan Indramayu 2A, Menteng, Jakarta 10310; tel. (21) 31908030; fax (21) 31908031; e-mail porembjak@cbn.net.id; internet www.embassyportugaljakarta.or.id; Ambassador CARLOS MANUEL LEITÃO FROTA.

Qatar: Jalan Mega Kuningan Barat I 7, Kawasan Mega Kuningan, Jakarta 12950; tel. (21) 2510751; fax (21) 2510754; e-mail qataremj@indosat.net.id; Ambassador AHMED ABDULLAH AL-MOHANNADI.

Romania: Jalan Teuku Cik Di Tiro 42A, Menteng, Jakarta Pusat; tel. (21) 3900489; fax (21) 3106241; e-mail romind@cbn.net.id; Ambassador GHEORGHE VÎLCU.

Russia: Jalan H. R. Rasuna Said, Kav. X-7 Nos 1–2, Jakarta 12940; tel. (21) 5222912; fax (21) 5222916; e-mail rusemb.indonesia@gmail.com; internet www.indonesia.mid.ru; Ambassador ALEKSANDR A. IVANOV.

Saudi Arabia: Jalan M. T. Haryono, Kav. 27, Cawang Atas, Jakarta 13630; tel. (21) 8011533; fax (21) 8011527; e-mail idemb@mofa.gov.sa; Ambassador ABDULLAH BIN ABDULRAHMAN A'ALIM AL-KHAYYAT.

Serbia: Jalan Hos Cokroaminoto 109, Jakarta Pusat 10310; tel. (21) 3143560; fax (21) 3143613; e-mail ambajaka@rad.net.id; Ambassador JOVAN JOVANOVIĆ.

Singapore: Jalan H. R. Rasuna Said, Blok X-4, Kav. 2, Kuningan, Jakarta 12950; tel. (21) 5201489; fax (21) 5201486; e-mail singemb_jkt@sgmfa.gov.sg; internet www.mfa.gov.sg/jkt; Ambassador ASHOK MIRPURI.

Slovakia: Jalan Prof. Mohammed Yamin 29, POB 1368, Menteng, Jakarta Pusat 10310; tel. (21) 3101068; fax (21) 3101180; e-mail emb.jakarta@mzv.sk; internet www.mzv.sk/jakarta; Ambassador ŠTEFAN ROZKOPÁL.

Somalia: Jalan Salak 5, Guntur, Jakarta Selatan 12980; tel. (21) 8311506; fax (21) 8352586; e-mail somalirep_jkt@yahoo.com; internet www.indonesia.somaligov.net; Ambassador MOHAMED OLOW BAROW.

South Africa: Wisma GKBI, Suite 705, Jalan Jenderal Sudirman 28, Jakarta 10210; tel. (21) 5740660; fax (21) 5740655; e-mail saembpol@centrin.net.id; internet www.southafricanembassy-jakarta.or.id; Ambassador NOEL NOA LEHOKO.

Spain: Jalan H. Agus Salim 61, Jakarta 10350; tel. (21) 3142355; fax (21) 31935134; e-mail emb.yakarta@mae.es; Ambassador RAFAEL CONDE DE SARO.

Sri Lanka: Jalan Diponegoro 70, Jakarta 10320; tel. (21) 3161886; fax (21) 3107962; e-mail lankaemb@rad.net.id; Ambassador Maj.-Gen. (retd) NANDA MALLAWAARACHCHI.

Sudan: Jalan Lembang 7, Menteng, Jakarta Pusat 10310; tel. (21) 3908234; fax (21) 3908235; e-mail sudanind@cbn.net.id; Ambassador IBRAHIM BUSHRA MOHAMED ALI.

Suriname: Jalan Padalarang 9, Menteng, Jakarta Pusat 10310; tel. (21) 3154437; fax (21) 3154556; e-mail suramjkt@cbn.net.id; Ambassador ANGELIC C. ALIHUSAIN-DEL CASTILHO.

Sweden: Menara Rajawali, 9th Floor, Jalan Mega Kuningan, Lot 5.1, Kawasan Mega Kuningan, Jakarta Selatan 12950; tel. (21) 55535900; fax (21) 5762691; e-mail ambassaden.jakarta@foreign.ministry.se; internet www.swedenabroad.com/jakarta; Ambassador EWA POLANO.

Switzerland: Jalan H. R. Rasuna Said, Blok X-3 No. 2, Kuningan, Jakarta Selatan 12950; tel. (21) 5256061; fax (21) 5202289; e-mail jak.vertretung@eda.admin.ch; internet www.eda.admin.ch/jakarta; Ambassador HEINZ WALKER-NEDERKOORN.

Syria: Jalan Karang Asem I 8, Jakarta 12950; tel. (21) 5255991; fax (21) 5202511; e-mail syrianemb@cbn.net.id; Chargé d'affaires BASSAM AL-KHATIB.

Thailand: Jalan Imam Bonjol 74, Jakarta Pusat 10310; tel. (21) 3904052; fax (21) 3107469; e-mail thaijkt@indo.net.id; internet www.thaiembassy.org/jakarta; Ambassador THANATIP UPATISING.

Timor-Leste: Gedung Surya, 11th Floor, Jalan M. H. Thamrin, Kav. 9, Jakarta Pusat 10350; tel. (21) 3902678; fax (21) 3902660; e-mail tljkt@yahoo.com; Ambassador MANUEL SERRANO.

Tunisia: Jalan Karang Asem Tengah, Blok C-5, Kav. 15, Kuningan, Jakarta Selatan 12950; tel. (21) 52892328; fax (21) 5255889; e-mail atjkt@uninet.net.id; Ambassador MOHAMED ANTAR.

Turkey: Jalan H. R. Rasuna Said, Kav. 1, Kuningan, Jakarta 12950; tel. (21) 5256250; fax (21) 5226056; e-mail cakartabe@telkom.net; internet cakarta.be.mfa.gov.tr; Ambassador MURAT ADALI.

Ukraine: World Trade Center, 8th Floor, Jalan Jenderal Sudirman, Kav. 29–31, Jakarta 12084; tel. (21) 5211700; fax (21) 5211710; e-mail emb_id@mfa.gov.ua; internet www.mfa.gov.ua/indonesia; Chargé d'affaires SERHIY TARHONIY.

United Arab Emirates: Jalan Prof. Dr Satrio, Blok C-4, Kav. 16–17, Jakarta 12950; tel. (21) 5206518; fax (21) 5206526; e-mail uaeemb@indo.net.id; Ambassador YOUSUF OMER AL-SHARHAN.

United Kingdom: Jalan M. H. Thamrin 75, Jakarta 10310; tel. (21) 23565200; fax (21) 23565351; e-mail commercial@dnet.net.id; internet ukinindonesia.fco.gov.uk; Ambassador MARTIN HATFULL.

USA: Jalan Medan Merdeka Selatan 4–5, Jakarta 10110; tel. (21) 34359000; fax (21) 34359922; e-mail jakconsul@state.gov; internet jakarta.usembassy.gov; Ambassador SCOT ALAN MARCIEL.

Uzbekistan: Menara Mulia, 19th Floor, Suite 1901, Jalan Jenderal Gatot Subroto, Kav. 9–11, Jakarta Selatan 12930; tel. (21) 5222581; fax (21) 5222582; e-mail registan@indo.net.id; Ambassador SHAVKAT DJAMOLOV.

Venezuela: Menara Mulia, 20th Floor, Suite 2005, Jalan Jenderal Gatot Subroto, Kav. 9–11, Jakarta Selatan 12930; tel. (21) 5227547; fax (21) 5227549; e-mail evenjakt@indo.net.id; Chargé d'affaires a.i. MARÍA VIRGINIA MENZONES LICCIONI.

Viet Nam: Jalan Teuku Umar 25, Jakarta Pusat 10350; tel. (21) 3100358; fax (21) 3149615; e-mail embvnam@uninet.net.id; internet www.vietnamembassy-indonesia.org; Ambassador NGUYEN XUAN THUY.

Yemen: Jalan Subang 18, Menteng, Jakarta Pusat 10310; tel. (21) 3108029; fax (21) 3904946; e-mail yemenemb@rad.net.id; Ambassador ALI AL-SOSWA.

Zimbabwe: Jalan Patra Kuningan VII 15, Jakarta Selatan 12950; tel. (21) 5221378; fax (21) 5250365; e-mail zimjakarta@yahoo.com; Ambassador ALICE MAGEZA.

Judicial System

There is one codified criminal law for the whole of Indonesia. In December 1989 the Islamic Judicature Bill, giving wider powers to *Shari'a* courts, was approved by the Dewan Perwakilan Rakyat (House of Representatives). The new law gave Muslim courts authority over civil matters, such as marriage. Muslims may still choose to appear before a secular court. Europeans are subject to the Code of Civil Law published in the State Gazette in 1847. Alien orientals (i.e. Arabs, Indians, etc.) and Chinese are subject to certain parts of the Code of Civil Law and the Code of Commerce. The work of codifying this law has started, but, in view of the great complexity and diversity of customary law, it may be expected to take a considerable time to achieve. In June 2005 a judicial commission was established; the seven-member body, appointed by the House of Representatives, was charged with reforming the judiciary and with nominating Supreme

Court justices, including the Chief Justice. In February 2006 the Judicial Commission announced that it was drafting a government regulation in lieu of law urging the re-evaluation of all justices as part of a wider process of judicial reform intended to address the issue of corruption within the legal system.

SUPREME COURT

The Supreme Court (Mahkamah Agung) is the final court of appeal. In February 2006 there were 49 Supreme Court justices.

Chief Justice: Dr HARIFIN A. TUMPA, Jalan Merdeka Utara 9–13, Jakarta 10110; tel. (21) 3843348; fax (21) 3811057; e-mail info@ma-ri.go.id; internet www.mahkamahagung.go.id.

Deputy Chief Justices: Drs AHMAD KAMIL, Dr ABDUL KADIR MAPPONG.

CONSTITUTIONAL COURT

The Constitutional Court was established in 2003 and is composed of nine justices, of whom three each are appointed by, respectively, the President, the Supreme Court and the House of Representatives. The Court adjudicates the following matters: constitutionality of a law; impeachment; dissolution of a political party; disputes between state agencies; and disputes concerning election results.

Chief Justice: MOHAMMAD MAHFUD, Jalan Medan Merdeka Barat 6, Jakarta 10110; tel. (21) 23529000; fax (21) 3520177; e-mail humas@mahkamahkonstitusi.go.id; internet www.mahkamahkonstitusi.go.id.

OTHER COURTS

High Courts in Jakarta Surabaya, Medan, Makassar, Banda Aceh, Padang, Palembang, Bandung, Semarang, Banjarmasin, Menado, Denpasar, Ambon and Jayapura deal with appeals from the District Courts. District Courts deal with marriage, divorce and reconciliation.

Religion

All citizens are required to state their religion. The Ministry of Religion accords official status to six religions—Islam, the Christian faiths of Protestantism and Catholicism, Hinduism, Buddhism and Confucianism. According to a survey in 2000, 88.2% of the population were Muslims, while 5.9% were Protestant, 3.1% were Roman Catholic, 1.8% were Hindus, 0.8% were Buddhists and 0.2% professed adherence to other religions, such as other Christian denominations and Judaism, which remains unrecognized.

National religious councils—representing the official religious traditions—were established to serve as liaison bodies between religious adherents and the Government and to advise the Government on the application of religious principles to various elements of national life.

ISLAM

Indonesia has the world's largest Muslim population.

Majelis Ulama Indonesia (MUI) (Indonesian Ulama Council): Jalan Proklamasi 51, Menteng, Jakarta Pusat; tel. (21) 31902666; fax (21) 31905266; e-mail mui-online@mui.or.id; internet www.mui.or.id; central Muslim org.; Chair. Dr SAHAL MAHFUDH; Sec.-Gen. ICHWAN SAM.

Muhammadiyah: Jalan Menteng Raya 62, Jakarta Pusat 10340; tel. (21) 3903021; fax (21) 3903024; e-mail pp_muhammadiyah@yahoo.com; internet www.muhammadiyah.or.id; f. 1912; 28m. mems; second largest Muslim org. in Indonesia; incorporates the Muhammadiyah Youth Asscn and 'Aisyiyah, a women's org.; religious, charitable and educational activities; has established more than 5,000 Islamic schools; Chair. Dr DIN SYAMSUDDIN; Sec.-Gen. Dr AGUNG DANARTO.

Nahdlatul Ulama (NU) (Council of Scholars): Jalan Kramat Raya 164, Jakarta 10430; tel. (21) 3914014; fax (21) 3914013; internet www.nu.or.id; f. 1926; 30m. mems; largest Muslim org. in Indonesia; promotes Islamic teachings, as well as culture, education and economic devt; directly involved in politics from the mid-1950s until 1984; Chair. Dr SAID AQIL SIRADJ; Sec.-Gen. Dr MARSUDI SYUHUD.

CHRISTIANITY

Persekutuan Gereja-Gereja di Indonesia (Communion of Churches in Indonesia): Jalan Salemba Raya 10, Jakarta Pusat 10430; tel. (21) 3150451; fax (21) 3150457; e-mail pgi@bit.net.id; internet www.pgi.or.id; f. 1950; 81 mem. churches; Chair. Rev. ROYKE OCTAVIAN RORING; Gen. Sec. GOMAR GULTOM.

The Roman Catholic Church

Indonesia comprises 10 archdioceses and 27 dioceses. At 31 December 2007 there were an estimated 6,537,062 adherents in Indonesia, representing 3.9% of the population.

Bishops' Conference: Konferensi Waligereja Indonesia (KWI), Jalan Cut Meutia 10, POB 3044, Jakarta 10340; tel. and fax (21) 31925757; e-mail dokpen@kawali.org; internet www.kawali.org; f. 1973; Pres. MARTINUS D. SITUMORANG.

Archbishop of Ende: Most Rev. VICENTIUS SENSI, Keuskupan Agung, POB 210, Jalan Katedral 5, Ndona-Ende 86312, Flores; tel. (381) 21176; fax (381) 21606; e-mail uskup@ende.parokinet.org.

Archbishop of Jakarta: Most Rev. IGNATIUS SUHARYO HARDJOATMODJO, Keuskupan Agung, Jalan Katedral 7, Jakarta 10710; tel. (21) 3813345; fax (21) 3855681.

Archbishop of Kupang: Most Rev. PETER TURANG, Keuskupan Agung Kupang, Jalan Thamrin, Oepoi, Kupang 85111, Timor NTT; tel. (380) 826199; fax (380) 833331.

Archbishop of Makassar: Most Rev. JOHANNES LIKU ADA', Keuskupan Agung, Jalan Thamrin 5–7, Makassar 90111, Sulawesi Selatan; tel. (411) 315744; fax (411) 326674; e-mail sekr_kams@yahoo.com.

Archbishop of Medan: Most Rev. BONGSU ANTONIUS SINAGA, Jalan Imam Bonjol 39, POB 1191, Medan 20152, Sumatra Utara; tel. (61) 4519768; fax (61) 4145745; e-mail sekrkam@hotmail.com.

Archbishop of Merauke: Most Rev. NICOLAUS ADI SEPTURA, Keuskupan Agung, Jalan Mandala 30, Merauke 99602, Papua; tel. (971) 321011; fax (971) 321311.

Archbishop of Palembang: Most Rev. ALOYSIUS SUDARSO, Keuskupan Agung, Jalan Tasik 18, Palembang 30135; tel. (711) 350417; fax (711) 314776; e-mail alva@mdp.net.id.

Archbishop of Pontianak: Most Rev. HIERONYMUS HERCULANUS BUMBUN, Keuskupan Agung, Jalan A. R. Hakin 92A, POB 1119, Pontianak 78011, Kalimantan Barat; tel. (561) 732382; fax (561) 738785; e-mail kap@pontianak.wasantara.net.id.

Archbishop of Samarinda: Most Rev. FLORENTINUS SULUI HAJANG HAU, Keuskupan Agung, POB 1062, Jalan Gunung Merbabu 41, Samarinda 75010; tel. (541) 741193; fax (541) 203120.

Archbishop of Semarang: Most Rev. JOHANNES MARIA TRILAKSYANTA PUJASUMARTA, Keuskupan Agung, Jalan Pandanaran 13, Semarang 50244; tel. (24) 8312276; fax (24) 8414741; e-mail uskup@semarang.parokinet.org.

Other Christian Churches

Protestant Church in Indonesia (Gereja Protestan di Indonesia): Jalan Medan Merdeka Timur 10, Jakarta 10110; tel. (21) 3519003; fax (21) 34830224; consists of 12 churches of Calvinistic tradition; 3,047,300 mems, 4,808 congregations; Chair. Rev. Dr SAMUEL B. HAKH.

Numerous other Protestant communities exist throughout Indonesia, mainly organized on a local basis.

BUDDHISM

All-Indonesia Buddhist Association: Jakarta.

Indonesian Buddhist Council: Jakarta.

HINDUISM

Hindu Dharma Council: Jakarta.

The Press

PRINCIPAL DAILIES

Bali

Harian Pagi Umum (Bali Post): Jalan Kepundung 67A, Denpasar 80232; tel. (61) 225764; fax (61) 249483; e-mail iklan@balipost.co.id; internet www.balipost.co.id; f. 1948; daily (Indonesian edn), weekly (English edn); Editor K. NADHA; circ. 25,000.

Java

Angkatan Bersenjata: Jalan Kramat Raya 94, Jakarta Pusat; tel. (21) 46071; fax (21) 366870; armed forces newspaper.

Bandung Post: Jalan Lodaya 38A, Bandung 40264; tel. (22) 305124; fax (22) 302882; f. 1979; Chief Editor AHMAD SAELAN; Dir AHMAD JUSACC.

Berita Buana: Jalan Tahah Abang Dua 33–35, Jakarta 10110; tel. (21) 5487175; fax (21) 5491555; f. 1970; relaunched 1990; Indonesian; circ. 150,000.

Bisnis Indonesia: Wisma Bisnis Indonesia, Jalan K. H. Mas Mansyur 12A, Karet, Jakarta 10220; tel. (21) 57901023; fax (21)

57901025; e-mail redaksi@bisnis.co.id; internet www.bisnis.com; f. 1985; available online; Indonesian; Editor SUKAMDANI S. GITOSARDJONO; circ. 60,000.

Harian Pelita: Jalan Minangkabau 35B-C Manggarai, Jakarta Selatan 12970; tel. (21) 83706765; fax (21) 83706771; e-mail redaksi@pelitaonline.com; internet www.harianpelita.com; f. 1974; Indonesian; Muslim; 6 a week; Chief Editor A. BASORI.

Harian Terbit: Jalan Pulogadung 15, Kawasan Industri Pulogadung, Jakarta 13920; tel. (21) 4603973; fax (21) 4603970; e-mail terbit@harianterbit.com; internet www.harianterbit.com; f. 1972; Indonesian; Editor-in-Chief TARMAN AZZAM; circ. 125,000.

Harian Umum AB: CTC Bldg, 2nd Floor, Kramat Raya 94, Jakarta Pusat; f. 1965; official armed forces journal; Dir GOENARSO; Editor-in-Chief N. SOEPANGAT; circ. 80,000.

Jakarta Post: Jalan Palmerah Barat 142–143, Jakarta 10270; tel. (21) 5300476; fax (21) 5350050; e-mail mds@thejakartapost.com; internet www.thejakartapost.com; f. 1983; English; Chief Editor MEIDYATAMA SURYODININGRAT; circ. 50,000.

Jawa Pos: Graha Pena Bldg, 4th Floor, Achmad Yani 88, Surabaya 60234; tel. (31) 8202216; fax (31) 8285555; e-mail editor@jawapos.co.id; internet www.jawapos.co.id; f. 1949; Indonesian; CEO DAHLAN ISKAN; Chief Editor LEAK KUSTIYA; circ. 400,000.

Kedaulatan Rakyat: Jalan P. Mangkubumi 40–44, Yogyakarta; tel. (274) 565685; fax (274) 563125; f. 1945; Indonesian; independent; Chief Editor OCTO LAMPITO; circ. 50,000.

Kompas: Gedung Kompas Gramedia, Unit II, Lantai 5, Jalan Palmerah Selatan 26–28, Jakarta 10270; tel. (21) 5350377; fax (21) 5360678; e-mail redaksikcm@kompas.co.id; internet www.kompas.com; f. 1965; Indonesian; Man. Editor M. SUPRIHADI; circ. 523,453.

Koran Tempo: Gedung Tempo, Jalan H. R. Rasuna Said, Kav. C-17, Kuningan, Jakarta 10270; tel. (21) 5201022; fax (21) 5200092; e-mail interaktif@tempo.co.id; internet www.korantempo.com; f. 2001; Indonesian; Editor-in-Chief BAMBANG HARYMURTI.

Media Indonesia Daily: Jalan Pilar Mas Raya, Kav. A–D, Kedoya Selatan, Kebon Jeruk, Jakarta 11520; tel. (21) 5812088; fax (21) 5812105; e-mail miol@mediaindonesia.co.id; internet www.mediaindo.co.id; f. 1989; fmrly Prioritas; Indonesian; Publr SURYA PALOH; Editor DJAFAR H. ASSEGAFF; circ. 2,000.

Pikiran Rakyat: Jalan Asia-Afrika 77, Bandung 40111; tel. (22) 51216; e-mail pdr@pikiran-rakyat.com; internet www.pikiran-rakyat.com; f. 1950; Indonesian; independent; Editor BRAM M. DARMAPRAWIRA; circ. 150,000.

Pos Kota: Yayasan Antar Kota, Jalan Gajah Mada 100, Jakarta 10130; tel. and fax (21) 5652603; e-mail redaksi@poskota.co.id; internet www.poskota.co.id; f. 1970; Indonesian; Editor-in-Chief H. JOHNNY LESTER; circ. 500,000.

Rakyat Merdeka: Graha Pena, 9th Floor, Jalan Raya Kebayoran Lama 12, Jakarta Selatan 12210; tel. (21) 5348460; fax (21) 53671716; e-mail redaksi@rakyatmerdeka.co.id; internet www.rakyatmerdeka.co.id; f. 1945; Indonesian; independent; Chief Editor TEGUH SANTOSA; circ. 130,000.

Republika: Jalan Warung Buncit Raya 37, Jakarta Selatan 12510; tel. (21) 7803747; fax (21) 7800649; e-mail sekretariat@republika.co.id; internet www.republika.co.id; f. 1993; organ of the Asscn of Indonesian Muslim Intellectuals (ICMI); Chief Editor NASIHIN MASHA.

Sin Chew Indonesia: Jalan Toko Tiga Seberang 21, POB 4755, Jakarta 11120; tel. (21) 6295948; fax (21) 6297830; internet www.sinchew-i.com/indonesia; f. 1966; Chinese; fmrly Harian Indonesia; Editor W. D. SUKISMAN; Dir HADI WIBOWO; circ. 42,000.

Solo Pos: Griya SOLOPOS, Jalan Adisucipto 190, Solo 57145; tel. (271) 724811; fax (271) 724833; internet www.solopos.co.id; Editor-in-Chief SUNYOTO YA.

Suara Karya: Jalan Bangka Raya 2, Kebayoran Baru, Jakarta Selatan 12720; tel. (21) 7192656; fax (21) 71790746; e-mail redaksi@suarakarya-online.com; f. 1971; Indonesian; Chief Editor RICKY RACHMADI; circ. 100,000.

Suara Merdeka: Jalan Pandanaran 30, Semarang 50241; tel. (24) 8412600; fax (24) 8411116; e-mail redaksi@suaramerdeka.info; internet www.suaramerdeka.com; f. 1950; Indonesian; Publr Ir H. TOMMY HETAMI; Editor-in-Chief HENDRO BASUKI; circ. 200,000.

Suara Pembaruan: The Aryaduta Suites Tower A, Lantai 1, Jalan Garnisun Dalam 8, Karet Semanggi, Jakarta 12930; tel. (21) 57851555; fax (21) 57851554; e-mail koransp@suarapembaruan.com; internet www.suarapembaruan.com; f. 1987; Chief Editor PRIMUS DORIMULU.

Surabaya Post: Ruko Rich Palace, Kav. 19–20, Jalan Mayjend Sungkono 149–150, Surabaya; tel. (31) 5667000; fax (31) 5635000; e-mail redaksi@surabayapost.co.id; internet www.surabayapost.co.id; f. 1953; independent; afternoon; Chief Editor and Dir BAMBANG HARIAWAN; Man. Editor AGUSTINA WIDYAWATI; circ. 115,000.

Surya: Jalan Rungkut Industri III, 68 & 70 SIER, Surabaya 60293; tel. (31) 8419000; fax (31) 8414024; e-mail redaksi@surya.co.id; internet www.surya.co.id; Editor-in-Chief RUSDI AMRAL.

Kalimantan

Banjarmasin Post: Gedung HJ Djok Mentaya, Jalan AS Musyaffa 16, Banjarmasin 70111; tel. (511) 3354370; fax (511) 4366123; e-mail redaksi@banjarmasinpost.co.id; internet www.banjarmasinpost.co.id; f. 1971; Indonesian; Editor-in-Chief YUSRAN PARE; circ. 50,000.

Harian Umum Akcaya: Pontianak Post Group, Jalan Gajah Mada 2–4, Pontianak 78121; tel. (561) 735071; fax (561) 736607; e-mail redaksi@pontianakpost.com; internet www.pontianakpost.com; Editor B. SALMAN.

Kaltim Post: Jalan Jenderal Sudirman RT XVI 82, Balikpapan 76144; tel. (542) 736459; fax (542) 730353; e-mail redaksi@kaltimpost.net; internet www.kaltimpost.co.id; f. 1988; fmrly *Manuntung* ; Editor-in-Chief Drs H. BAMBANG ISNOTO (acting).

Lampung Post: Jalan Pangkal Pinang, Lampung; e-mail webmaster@metrotvnews.com; internet www.lampungpost.com; Editor DJADJAT SUDRADJAT.

Maluku

Pos Maluku: Jalan Raya Pattimura 19, Ambon; tel. (911) 44614.

Suara Maluku: Komplex Perdagangan Mardikas, Blok D3/11A, Ternate; tel. (911) 44590.

Nusa Tenggara

Pos Kupang: Jalan Kenari 1, Kupang 85115; tel. (380) 833820; fax (380) 831801; e-mail poskpg@yahoo.com; internet kupang.tribunnews.com; Chief Editor DION D. B. PUTRA.

Papua

Cenderawasih Post: Jalan Cenderawasih 10, Kelapa II, Entrop, Jayapura 99013; tel. (967) 532417; fax (967) 532418; e-mail cepos_jpr@yahoo.com; internet www.cenderawasihpos.com; Editor-in-Chief DAUD SONY.

Teropong: Jalan Halmahera, Jayapura.

Riau

Batam Pos: Gedung Graha Pena, Lt. 2, Jalan Raya Batam Centre, Batam 29461; tel. (778) 460000; fax (778) 462162; e-mail redaksi@batampos.co.id; internet www.harianbatampos.com; Editor-in-Chief CANDRA IBRAHIM.

Riau Pos: Jalan H. R. Subrantas, Km 10.5, Pekanbaru, Riau 28294; tel. (761) 64633; fax (761) 64640; e-mail redaksi@riaupos.com; internet www.riaupos.co.id; Editor-in-Chief RAJA ISYAM AZWAR; circ. 40,000.

Sulawesi

Bulletin Sulut: Jalan Korengkeng 38, Lt. II, Manado 95114, Sulawesi Utara.

Cahaya Siang: Jalan Kembang II 2, Manado 95114, Sulawesi Utara; tel. (431) 61054; fax (431) 63393.

Fajar (Dawn): Gedung Graha Pena, Lantai 4, Jalan Urip Sumoharjo 21, Makassar 90231; tel. (411) 441441; fax (411) 441224; e-mail redaksi@fajar.co.id; internet www.fajar.co.id; Editor-in-Chief ALWI HAMU; circ. 35,000.

Manado Post: Manado Post Centre, Manado Town Sq., Blok B, Kav. 14–15, Manado; tel. (431) 855558; fax (431) 860398; e-mail editor@mdopost.com; internet www.mdopost.com; Editor-in-Chief SUHENDRO BOROMA.

Pedoman Rakyat: Jalan H. A. Mappanyukki 28, Makassar; f. 1947; independent; Editor M. BASIR; circ. 30,000.

Suluh Merdeka: Jalan R. W. Mongsidi 4/96, POB 1105, Manado 95110; tel. and fax (431) 866150.

Tegas: Jalan Mappanyukki 28, Makassar; tel. (411) 3960.

Sumatra

Harian Analisa: Jalan Balaikota 2, Medan 20111; tel. (61) 4154711; fax (61) 4151436; internet www.analisadaily.com; f. 1972; Indonesian; Editor H. ALI SOEKARDI; circ. 75,000.

Harian Berita Sore: Jalan Letjen Suprapto 1, Medan 20151; tel. (61) 4158787; fax (61) 4150383; e-mail redaksi@beritasore.com; internet www.beritasore.com; Indonesian; Publr SAID PRABUDI SAID; Editor-in-Chief H. TERUNA JASA SAID.

Harian Haluan: Jalan Damar 59 C/F, Padang; f. 1948; Editor-in-Chief Drs ASRIL KASOEMA; circ. 40,000.

Harian Umum Nasional Waspada: Jalan Brigjenderal 1 Katamso, Medan 20151; tel. (61) 4150858; fax (61) 4510025; e-mail redaksi

.online@waspada.co.id; internet www.waspada.co.id; f. 1947; Indonesian; Editor-in-Chief AVIAN E. TUMENGKOL.

Mimbar Umum: Merah, Medan; tel. (61) 517807; f. 1947; Indonesian; independent; Editor MOHD LUD LUBIS; circ. 55,000.

Padang Ekspres: Jalan Proklamasi 5D Tarandam, Padang, Sumatra Barat; tel. (751) 841300; fax (751) 841904; e-mail redaksi@padang-today.com; internet www.padang-today.com; Indonesian; Editor SHI MUSLIM.

Serambi Indonesia: Jalan Raya Lambaro, Km 4.5, Tanjung Permai, Manyang PA, Banda Aceh; tel. (651) 635544; fax (651) 637180; e-mail redaksi@serambinews.com; internet www.serambinews.com; Editor-in-Chief MAWARDI IBRAHIM.

Sinar Indonesia Baru: Jalan Brigjenderal Katamso 66, Medan 20151; tel. (61) 4512530; fax (61) 4538150; e-mail redaksi@hariansib.com; internet www.hariansib.com; f. 1970; Indonesian; Chief Editor G. M. PANGGABEAN; circ. 150,000.

Sriwijaya Post: Jalan Jenderal Basuki Rahmat 1608 B–D, Palembang; tel. (711) 310088; fax (711) 312888; e-mail redaksi@sripoku.com; internet palembang.tribunnews.com; f. 2002; Editor-in-Chief HADI PRAYOGO.

Suara Rakyat Semesta: Jalan K. H. Ashari 52, Palembang; Indonesian; Editor DJADIL ABDULLAH; circ. 10,000.

Waspada: Jalan Letjen Suprapto, cnr Jalan Brigjen Katamso 1, Medan 20151; tel. (61) 4150868; fax (61) 4510025; e-mail waspada@waspada.co.id; internet www.waspada.co.id; f. 1947; Indonesian; Chief Editors ANI IDRUS, PRABUDI SAID; circ. 60,000 (daily), 55,000 (Sun.).

PRINCIPAL PERIODICALS

Amanah: Jalan Garuda 69, Kemayoran, Jakarta; tel. (21) 410254; fortnightly; Muslim current affairs; Indonesian; Man. Dir MASKUN ISKANDAR; circ. 180,000.

Ayahbunda: Jalan H. R. Rasuna Said, Blok B, Kav. 32–33, Jakarta 12910; tel. (21) 5209370; fax (21) 5209366; e-mail langganan@feminagroup.com; internet www.ayahbunda.co.id; fortnightly; family magazine.

Berita Negara: Jalan Pertjetakan Negara 21, Kotakpos 2111, Jakarta; tel. and fax (21) 4207251; f. 1951; 2 a week; official gazette.

Bobo (PT Penerbitan Sarana Bobo): Gramedia Magazine Bldg, 2nd Floor, Jalan Panjang 8A, Kebon Jeruk, Jakarta 11530; tel. (21) 5330150; fax (21) 5320681; f. 1973; subsidiary of Gramedia Group; weekly; children's magazine; Editor KOES SABANDIYAH; circ. 206,000.

Bola: Tunas Bola, Jalan Palmerah Barat 33–37, Jakarta 10270; tel. (21) 53677835; fax (21) 5301952; e-mail redaksi@bolanews.com; internet www.bolanews.com; 2 a week; Tue. and Fri.; sports magazine; Indonesian; Chief Editor IAN SITUMORANG; circ. 715,000.

Buana Minggu: Jalan Tanah Abang Dua 33, Jakarta Pusat 10110; tel. (21) 364190; weekly; Sunday; Indonesian; Editor WINOTO PARARTHO; circ. 193,450.

Business News: Jalan H. Abdul Muis 70, Jakarta 10160; tel. (21) 3848207; fax (21) 3454280; f. 1956; 3 a week (Indonesian edn), 2 a week (English edn); Chief Editor SANJOTO SASTROMIHARDJO; circ. 15,000.

Cita Cinta: Jalan H. R. Rasuna Said, Blok B, Kav. 32–33, Jakarta 12910; tel. (21) 5254206; fax (21) 5262131; e-mail citacinta@feminagroup.com; internet www.citacinta.com; f. 2000; teenage lifestyle magazine.

Citra: Gramedia Bldg, Unit 11, 5th Floor, Jalan Palmerah Selatan 24–26, Jakarta 10270; tel. (21) 5483008; fax (21) 5494035; e-mail citra@gramedia-majalah.com; f. 1990; weekly; TV and film programmes, music trends and celebrity news; Chief Editor H. MAMAN SUHERMAN; circ. 239,000.

Depthnews Indonesia: Jalan Jatinegara Barat III/6, Jakarta 13310; tel. (21) 8194994; fax (21) 8195501; f. 1972; weekly; publ. by Press Foundation of Indonesia; Editor SUMONO MUSTOFFA.

Dunia Wanita: Jalan Brigjenderal 1 Katamso, Medan; tel. (61) 4150858; fax (61) 4510025; e-mail waspada@indosat.net.id; internet www.dunia-wanita.com; f. 1949; fortnightly; Indonesian; women's tabloid; Chief Editor Dr RAYATI SYAFRIN; circ. 10,000.

Economic Review: Bank BNI, Strategic Planning Division, Gedung Bank BNI, Jalan Jenderal Sudirman, Kav. 1, POB 2955, Jakarta 10220; tel. (21) 5728692; fax (21) 5728456; e-mail renkek01@bni.co.id; internet www.bni.co.id; f. 1946; 3 a year; English; economic and business research and analysis; Editor-in-Chief DARWIN SUZANDI.

Ekonomi Indonesia: Jalan Merdeka, Timur 11–12, Jakarta; tel. (21) 494458; monthly; English; economic journal; Editor Z. ACHMAD; circ. 20,000.

Eksekutif: Jalan R. S. Fatmawati 20, Jakarta 12430; tel. (21) 7659218; fax (21) 7504018; internet eksekutif.com.

Femina: Jalan H. R. Rasuna Said, Blok B, Kav. 32–33, Jakarta Selatan 12910; tel. (21) 5209370; fax (21) 5209366; e-mail redaksi@feminagroup.com; internet www.femina.co.id; f. 1972; weekly; women's magazine; Publr SVIDA ALISJAHBANA; Editor PETTY S. FATIMAH; circ. 160,000.

Gadis: Jalan H. R. Rasuna Said, Blok B, Kav. 32–33, Jakarta 12910; tel. (21) 5253816; fax (21) 5262131; e-mail palupi.ambardini@feminagroup.com; internet www.gadis.co.id; f. 1973; 3 a month; Indonesian; teenage lifestyle magazine; Editor-in-Chief PALUPI AMBARDINI; circ. 150,000.

Gatra: Gedung Gatra, Jalan Kalibata Timur IV/15, Jakarta 12740; tel. (21) 7973535; fax (21) 79196941; e-mail admin@gatra.com; internet www.gatra.com; est. by fmr employees of Tempo (banned 1994–98); Gen. Man. STEPHEN SIAHAYA; Editor-in-Chief BUDIONO KARTOHADIPRODJO.

Gugat (Accuse): Surabaya; politics, law and crime; weekly; circ. 250,000.

Hai: Jalan Panjang 8A, Kebon Jeruk, Jakarta Barat; tel. (21) 5330170; fax (21) 5220070; e-mail hai_magazine@gramedia-majalah.com; internet www.hai-online.com; f. 1973; weekly; youth magazine; Man. Editor JUNIOR EKA PUTRO; circ. 42,000.

Indonesia Business News: Wisma Bisnis Indonesia, 7th Floor, Jalan K. H. Mas Mansyur 12A, Karet, Jakarta 10220; tel. (21) 57901023; fax (21) 57901025; e-mail redaksi@bisnis.co.id; internet www.bisnis.co.id; Indonesian and English.

Indonesia Business Weekly: Wisma Bisnis Indonesia, Jalan Letjenderal S. Parman, Kav. 12, Slipi, Jakarta 11410; tel. (21) 5304016; fax (21) 5305868; English; Editor TAUFIK DARUSMAN.

Indonesia Magazine: Jalan Merdeka Barat 20, Jakarta; tel. (21) 352015; f. 1969; monthly; English; Chair. G. DWIPAYANA; Editor-in-Chief HADELY HASIBUAN; circ. 15,000.

Intisari (Digest): Gramedia Bldg, Unit II, 5th Floor, Jalan Palmerah Selatan 24–26, Jakarta 10270; tel. (21) 5483008; fax (21) 53696525; e-mail intisari@gramedia-majalah.com; internet www.intisari-online.com; f. 1963; monthly; Indonesian; popular science, health, technology, crime and general interest; Editors AL. HERU KUSTARA, IRAWATI; circ. 141,000.

Jakarta Jakarta: Gramedia Bldg, Unit II, 5th Floor, Jalan Palmerah Selatan 24–26, Jakarta 10270; tel. (21) 5483008; fax (21) 5494035; f. 1985; weekly; food, fun, fashion and celebrity news; circ. 70,000.

Jurnal Indonesia: Jalan Hos Cokroaminoto 49A, Jakarta 10350; tel. (21) 31901774; fax (21) 3916471; e-mail jurnal@cbn.net.id; monthly; political, economic and business analysis.

Keluarga: Jalan Sangaji 11, Jakarta; fortnightly; women's and family magazine; Editor S. DAHONO.

Kontan: Gedung Kontan, Jalan Kebayoran Lama 3119, Jakarta 12210; tel. (21) 5357636; fax (21) 5357633; e-mail red@kontan.co.id; internet www.kontan.co.id; weekly; Indonesian; business newspaper; Editor-in-Chief ARDIAN TAUFIK GESURI.

Majalah Ekonomis: POB 4195, Jakarta; monthly; English; business; Chief Editor S. ARIFIN HUTABARAT; circ. 20,000.

Majalah Kedokteran Indonesia (Journal of the Indonesian Medical Assen): Jalan Kesehatan 111/29, Jakarta 11/16; f. 1951; monthly; Indonesian, English.

Manglé: Jalan Lodaya 19–21, 40262 Bandung; tel. (22) 411438; f. 1957; weekly; Sundanese; Chief Editor Drs OEJANG DARAJATOEN; circ. 74,000.

Matra: Grafity Pers, Kompleks Buncit Raya Permai, Kav. 1, Jalan Warung, POB 3476, Jakarta; tel. (21) 515952; f. 1986; monthly; men's magazine; general interest and current affairs; Editor-in-Chief SRI RUSDY; circ. 100,000.

Mimbar Kabinet Pembangunan: Jalan Merdeka Barat 7, Jakarta; f. 1966; monthly; Indonesian; publ. by Dept of Information.

Mutiara: Jalan Dewi Sartika 136D, Cawang, Jakarta Timur; general interest; Publr H. G. RORIMPANDEY.

Nova: Gedung Kompas Gramedia, Lantai 3, Jalan Panjang 8A, Kebon Jeruk, Jakarta Barat 11530; tel. (21) 5330150; fax (21) 5321020; e-mail admin@tabloidnova.com; internet www.tabloidnova.com; weekly; Wed.; women's interest; Indonesian; Publr SAMINDRA UTAMA; circ. 618,267.

Oposisi: Jakarta; weekly; politics; circ. 400,000.

Otomotif: Gedung Kompas Gramedia, Lantai 7, Jalan Panjang 8A, Kebon Jeruk, Jakarta Barat 11530; tel. (21) 5330170; fax (21) 5330185; e-mail otomotifnet@gramedia-majalah.com; internet www.otomotifnet.com; f. 1990; weekly; automotive specialist tabloid; Editor-in-Chief SONI RIHARTO; circ. 215,763.

PC Magazine Indonesia: Jalan H. R. Rasuna Said, Blok B, Kav. 32–33, Jakarta 12910; tel. (21) 5209370; fax (21) 5209366; computers; Editor-in-Chief SVIDA ALISJAHBANA.

Peraba: Bintaran Kidul 5, Yogyakarta; weekly; Indonesian and Javanese; Roman Catholic; Editor W. KARTOSOEHARSONO.

Pertani PT: Jalan Pasar Minggu, Kalibata, POB 247/KBY, Jakarta Selatan; tel. (21) 793108; f. 1974; monthly; Indonesian; agricultural; Pres. Dir Ir RUSLI YAHYA.

Petisi: Surabaya; weekly; Editor CHOIRUL ANAM.

Rajawali: Jakarta; monthly; Indonesian; civil aviation and tourism; Dir R. A. J. LUMENTA; Man. Editor KARYONO ADHY.

Selecta: Kebon Kacang 29/4, Jakarta; fortnightly; illustrated; Editor SAMSUDIN LUBIS; circ. 80,000.

Swasembada: Jalan Taman Tanah Abang, III/23, Jakarta 10610; tel. (21) 3523839; fax (21) 3457338; internet www.swa.co.id; Editor-in-Chief KEMAL EFFENDI GANI.

Tempo: Gedung Temprint, Lantai 2, Jalan Palmerah Barat 8, Jakarta 12210; tel. (21) 5360409; fax (21) 5360412; e-mail interaktif@tempo.co.id; internet www.tempointeractive.com; f. 1971; weekly; Editor-in-Chief WAHYU MURYADI.

Tiara: Gramedia Bldg, Unit 11, 5th Floor, Jalan Palmerah Selatan 24–26, Jakarta 10270; tel. (21) 5483008; fax (21) 5494035; f. 1990; fortnightly; lifestyles, features and celebrity news; circ. 47,000.

Ummat: Jakarta; Islamic; sponsored by ICMI.

Wenang Post: Jalan R. W. Mongsidi 4/96, POB 1105, Manado 95115; tel. and fax (431) 866150; weekly.

NEWS AGENCIES

ANTARA (Indonesian News Agency): Wisma Antara, Lantai 19, 17 Jalan Medan Merdeka Selatan, POB 1257, Jakarta 10110; tel. (21) 3802383; fax (21) 3522178; e-mail newsroom@antaranews.com; internet www.antaranews.com; f. 1937; 33 brs in Indonesia, five overseas brs; 800 bulletins in Indonesian and in English; monitoring service of stock exchanges world-wide; photo service; CEO AHMAD MUKHLIS YUSUF; Chief Editor SAIFUL HADI.

Kantorberita Nasional Indonesia (KNI News Service): Jalan Jatinegara Barat III/6, Jakarta Timur 13310; tel. (21) 811003; fax (21) 8195501; f. 1966; independent national news agency; foreign and domestic news in Indonesian; Dir and Editor-in-Chief Drs SUMONO MUSTOFFA; Exec. Editor HARIM NURROCHADI.

PRESS ASSOCIATIONS

Aliansi Jurnalis Independen (AJI) (Alliance of Independent Journalists): Jalan Kembang Raya 6 Kwitang, Senen, Jakarta Pusat 10420; tel. (21) 3151214; fax (21) 3151261; e-mail ajioffice@aji-indonesia.or.id; f. 1994; unofficial; aims to promote freedom of the press; Pres. NEZAR PATRIA; Sec.-Gen. JAJANG JAMALUDIN.

Jakarta Foreign Correspondents' Club: Plaza Gani Djemat, Lantai 4, Jalan Imam Bonjol 76–78, Jakarta 10310; tel. (21) 3903628; fax (21) 3917453; e-mail office@jfcc.info; internet www.jfcc.info; more than 400 mems; Pres. JASON TEDJASUKMANA.

Persatuan Wartawan Indonesia (PWI) (Indonesian Journalists' Asscn): Gedung Dewan Pers, Lantai 4, Jalan Kebon Sirih 34, Jakarta 10110; tel. (21) 3453131; fax (21) 3453175; e-mail pwi@pwi.or.id; internet www.pwi.or.id; f. 1946; govt-controlled; 14,000 mems (Feb. 2009); Chair. MARGIONO; Gen. Sec. HENDRY BANGUN.

Serikat Penerbit Suratkabar (SPS) (Indonesian Newspaper Publishers' Asscn): Gedung Dewan Pers, 6th Floor, Jalan Kebon Sirih 34, Jakarta 10110; tel. (21) 3459671; fax (21) 3862373; e-mail spspusat@spsindonesia.or.id; f. 1946; mems: 451 publrs; Exec. Chair. DAHLAN IKSAN; Sec.-Gen. SUKARDI DARMAWAN.

Publishers

JAKARTA

Aries Lima/New Aqua Press PT: Jalan Rawagelan II/4, Jakarta Timur; tel. (21) 4897566; general and children's; Pres. TUTI SUNDARI AZMI.

Aya Media Pustaka PT: Wijaya Grand Centre C/2, Jalan Wijaya II, Jakarta 12160; tel. (21) 7206903; fax (21) 7201401; e-mail ayamedia@cbn.net.id; f. 1985; children's; Dir Drs ARIANTO TUGIYO.

PT Balai Pustaka Peraga: Jalan Gunung Sahari Raya 4, Gedung Balai Pustaka, 7th Floor, Jakarta 10710; tel. (21) 3451616; fax (21) 3855735; e-mail con_bpustaka@bumn-ri.com; f. 1917; children's, school textbooks, literary, scientific publs and periodicals; Dir R. SISWADI.

Bhratara Niaga Media PT: Jalan Cipinang Bali 17, Jakarta Timur 13420; tel. (21) 8520319; fax (21) 8191858; f. 1986; fmrly Bhratara Karya Aksara; university and educational textbooks; Man. Dir ROBINSON RUSDI.

Bina Rena Pariwara PT: Jalan Pejaten Raya 5E, Pasar Minggu, Jakarta 12510; tel. (21) 7901931; fax (21) 7901939; e-mail hasanbas@softhome.net; f. 1988; financial, social science, economic, Islamic, children's; Dir Drs HASAN BASRI.

Bulan Bintang PT: Jalan Kramat Kwitang I/8, Jakarta 10420; tel. (21) 3901651; fax (21) 3901652; e-mail bukubulanbintang@gmail.com; internet www.bulanbintang.co.id; f. 1954; Islamic, social science, natural and applied sciences, art; Man. Dir FAUZI AMELZ.

Bumi Aksara PT: Jalan Sawo Raya 18, Rawamanguu, Jakarta 13220; tel. (21) 4717049; fax (21) 4700989; e-mail info@bumiaksara.co.id; internet www.bumiaksara.co.id; f. 1990; university textbooks; Dir LUCYA ANDAM DEWI.

Cakrawala Cinta PT: Jalan Minyak I/12B, Duren Tiga, Jakarta 12760; tel. (21) 7990725; fax (21) 7974076; f. 1984; science; Dir Drs M. TORSINA.

Centre for Strategic and International Studies (CSIS): Jakarta Post Bldg, 3rd Floor, Jalan Palmerah Barat 142–143, Jakarta 10270; tel. (21) 53654601; fax (21) 53654607; e-mail csis@csis.or.id; internet www.csis.or.id; f. 1971; political and social sciences; Exec. Dir RIZAL SUKMA.

Cipta Adi Pustaka: Graha Compaka Mas Blok C 22, Jalan Cempaka Putih Raya, Jakarta Pusat; tel. (21) 4213821; fax (21) 4269315; f. 1986; encyclopedias; Dir BUDI SANTOSO.

Dian Rakyat PT: Jalan Rawagelas I/4, Kaw. Industri Pulo Gadung, Jakarta; tel. (21) 4604444; fax (21) 4609115; f. 1966; general; Dir MARIO ALISJAHBANA.

Djambatan PT: Jalan Paseban 29, Jakarta 10440; tel. (21) 7203199; fax (21) 7227989; e-mail djam@dnet.net.id; f. 1954; children's, textbooks, social sciences, fiction; Dir SJARIFUDIN SJAMSUDIN.

Dunia Pustaka Jaya: Jalan Kramat Raya 5K, Komp. Maya Indah, Jakarta 10450; tel. (21) 3909322; fax (21) 3909320; f. 1971; fiction, religion, essays, poetry, drama, criticism, art, philosophy and children's; Man. A. RIVAI.

EGC Medical Publishers: Jalan Agung Timur 4, No. 39 Blok 0–1, Jakarta 14350; tel. (21) 65306283; fax (21) 6518178; e-mail contact@egc-arcan.com; f. 1978; medical and public health, nursing, dentistry; Dir IMELDA DHARMA.

PT Elex Media Komputindo: Gramedia Bldg, 6th Floor, Jalan Palmerah Selatan 22, Jakarta 10270; tel. (21) 5483008; fax (21) 5326219; e-mail langganan@elexmedia.co.id; internet www.elexmedia.co.id; f. 1985; management, computing, software, children's, parenting, self-development and fiction; Dir AL. ADHI MARDHIYONO.

Erlangga PT: Kami Melayani II, Pengetahuan, Jalan H. Baping 100, Ciracas, Jakarta 13740; tel. (21) 8717006; fax (21) 87794609; internet www.erlangga.co.id; f. 1952; secondary school and university textbooks; Man. Dir GUNAWAN HUTAURUK.

Gaya Favorit Press: Jalan H. R. Rasuna Said. Kav. B 32–33, Jakarta 12910; tel. (21) 5209370; fax (21) 5209366; f. 1971; fiction, popular science, lifestyle and children's; Vice-Pres. MIRTA KARTOHADIPRODJO; Man. Dir WIDARTI GUNAWAN.

Gema Insani Press: Jalan Kalibata Utara II/84, Jakarta 12740; tel. (21) 7984391; fax (21) 7984388; e-mail penerbitan@gemainsani.co.id; internet www.gemainsani.co.id; f. 1986; Islamic; Dir UMAR BASYARAHIL.

Ghalia Indonesia: Jalan Pramuka Raya 4, Jakarta 13140; tel. (21) 8581814; fax (21) 8564784; f. 1972; children's and general science, textbooks; Man. Dir LUKMAN SAAD.

Gramedia Widyasarana Indonesia: Gramedia Bldg, 3rd Floor, Jalan Palmerah Barat 33–37, Jakarta 10270; tel. (21) 53650110; fax (21) 53698095; internet www.grasindo.co.id; f. 1973; university textbooks, general non-fiction, children's and magazines; Man. JAROT YUDHOPRATOMO.

Gunung Mulia PT: Jalan Kwitang 22–23, Jakarta 10420; tel. (21) 3901208; fax (21) 3901633; e-mail publishing@bpkgm.com; internet www.bpkgm.com; f. 1946; general, children's, Christian; Chair. IWAN ARKADY; Pres. Dir STEPHEN Z. SATYAHADI.

Hidakarya Agung PT: Jalan Percetakan Negara D51, Jakarta Pusat; tel. (21) 4219786; fax (21) 4247128; Dir MAHDIARTI MACHMUD.

Ichtiar: Jalan Majapahit 6, Jakarta Pusat; tel. (21) 3841226; f. 1957; textbooks, law, social sciences, economics; Dir JOHN SEMERU.

Indira PT: Jalan Borobudur 20, Jakarta 10320; tel. (21) 3148868; fax (21) 3921079; f. 1953; general science, general trade and children's; Dir BAMBANG P. WAHYUDI.

Kinta CV: Jalan Kemanggisan Ilir V/110, Pal Merah, Jakarta Barat; tel. (21) 5494751; f. 1950; textbooks, social science, general; Man. Drs MOHAMAD SALEH.

Midas Surya Grafindo PT: Jalan Kesehatan 54, Cijantung, Jakarta 13760; tel. (21) 8400414; fax (21) 8400270; f. 1984; children's; Dir Drs FRANS HENDRAWAN.

Mutiara Sumber Widya PT: Gedung Maya Indah, Jalan Kramat 55C, Jakarta 10450; tel. (21) 3909864; fax (21) 3160313; f. 1951;

textbooks, Islamic, social sciences, general and children's; Pres. FADJRAA OEMAR.

Penebar Swadya PT: Jalan Gunung Sahari III/7, Jakarta Pusat; tel. (21) 4204402; fax (21) 4214821; agriculture, animal husbandry, fisheries; Dir Drs ANTHONIUS RIYANTO.

Penerbit Universitas Indonesia: Jalan Salemba Raya 4, Jakarta; tel. (21) 335373; f. 1969; science; Man. S. E. LEGOWO.

Pradnya Paramita PT: Jalan Bunga 8–8A, Matraman, Jakarta 13140; tel. (21) 8504944; fax (21) 8583369; e-mail pradnya@centrin.net.id; f. 1973; children's, general, educational, technical and social science; Pres. Dir KONDAR SINAGA.

Pustaka Antara PT: Jalan Perdagangan 99, Bintaro, Jakarta 12330; tel. (21) 7361711; fax (21) 7351079; e-mail nacelod@indo.net.id; f. 1952; textbooks, political, Islamic, children's and general; Man. Dir AIDA JOESOEF AHMAD.

Pustaka Binaman Pressindo: Jalan Kembang Raya 8, Jakarta Pusat 10030; tel. (21) 2303157; fax (21) 2302051; e-mail pustaka@bit.net.id; f. 1981; management; Dir Ir MAKFUDIN WIRYA ATMAJA.

Pustaka LP3ES Indonesia: Jalan Letjen. S. Parman 81, Jakarta 11420; tel. (21) 5663527; fax (21) 56964691; e-mail puslp3es@indo.net.id; f. 1971; general; Dir M. D. MARUTO.

Pustaka Sinar Harapan PT: Jalan Dewi Sartika 136D, Jakarta 13630; tel. and fax (21) 8006982; internet penerbitsinarharapan.co.id; f. 1981; general science, fiction, comics, children's; Dir W. M. NAIDEN.

Pustaka Utma Grafiti PT: 25 Jalan Kramat VI, Jakarta Pusat 10250; tel. (21) 31903006; fax (21) 31906649; f. 1981; social sciences, humanities and children's books; Dir ZULKIFLY LUBIS.

Rajagrafindo Persada PT: Jalan Pelepah Hijau IV TN-1 14–15, Kelapa Gading Permai, Jakarta 14240; tel. (21) 4520951; fax (21) 4529409; f. 1980; general science and religion; Dir Drs ZUBAIDI.

Rineka Cipta PT: Kompang Perkantoran Mitra Matraman, 148 Jalan Matraman Raya B 1–2, Jakarta; tel. (21) 85918080; fax (21) 85918143; f. 1990; est. by merger of Aksara Baru (f. 1972) and Bina Aksara; general science and university texts; Dir Dr H. SUARDI.

Rosda Jayaputra PT: Jalan Kembang 4, Jakarta 10420; tel. (21) 3904984; fax (21) 3901703; f. 1981; general science; Dir H. ROZALI USMAN.

Sastra Hudaya: Jalan Kalasan 1, Jakarta Pusat; tel. (21) 882321; f. 1967; religious, textbooks, children's and general; Man. ADAM SALEH.

Tintamas Indonesia: Jalan Kramat Raya 60, Jakarta 10420; tel. and fax (21) 3911459; f. 1947; history, modern science and culture, especially Islamic; Man. MARHAMAH DJAMBEK.

Tira Pustaka: Jalan Cemara Raya 1, Kav. 10D, Jaka Permai, Jaka Sampurna, Bekasi 17145; tel. (21) 8841277; fax (21) 8842736; e-mail Tirapus@cbn.net.id; f. 1977; translations, children's; Dir ROBERT B. WIDJAJA.

Toko Buku Walisongo PT: Gedung Idayu, Jalan Kwitang 13, Jakarta 10420; tel. (21) 3154890; fax (21) 3154889; e-mail edp@tokowalisongo.com; f. 1986; fmrly Masagung Group; general, Islamic, textbooks, science; Pres. H. KETUT ABDURRAHMAN MASAGUNG.

Widjaya: Jalan Pecenongan 48C, Jakarta Pusat; tel. (21) 3813446; f. 1950; textbooks, children's, religious and general; Man. DIDI LUTHAN.

Yasaguna: Jalan Minangkabau 44, POB 422, Jakarta Selatan; tel. (21) 8290422; f. 1964; agricultural, children's, handicrafts; Dir HILMAN MADEWA.

BANDUNG

Alma'arif: Jalan Tamblong 48–50, Bandung; tel. (22) 4207177; fax (22) 4239194; e-mail almaarif@bdg.centrin.net.id; f. 1949; textbooks, religious and general; Man. H. M. BAHARTHAH.

Alumni PT: Jalan Bukit Pakar Timur II/109, Bandung 40197; tel. (22) 2501251; fax (22) 2503044; f. 1968; university and school textbooks; Dir EDDY DAMIAN.

Angkasa: Jalan Kiara Condong 437, Bandung; tel. (22) 7320383; fax (22) 7320373; e-mail akspst@centrin.net.id; Dir H. FACHRI SAID.

Armico: Jalan Madurasa Utara 10, Cigereleng, Bandung 40253; tel. (22) 5202234; fax (22) 5201972; f. 1980; school textbooks; Dir Ir ARSIL TANJUNG.

Citra Aditya Bakti PT: Jalan Geusanulun 17, Bandung 40115; tel. (22) 438251; fax (22) 438635; e-mail cab@citraaditya.com; internet www.citraaditya.com; f. 1985; general science; Dir Ir IWAN TANUATMADJA.

Diponegoro Publishing House: Jalan Mohammad Toha 44–46, Bandung 40252; tel. and fax (22) 5201215; fax (22) 5201815; e-mail dpnegoro@indosat.net.id; internet www.penerbitdiponegoro.com; f. 1963; Islamic, textbooks, fiction, non-fiction, general; Dir HADIDJAH DAHLAN.

Epsilon Group: Jalan Marga Asri 3, Margacinta, Bandung 40287; tel. (22) 7567826; f. 1985; school textbooks; Dir Drs BAHRUDIN.

Eresco PT: Jalan Megger Girang 98, Bandung 40254; tel. (22) 5205985; fax (22) 5205984; f. 1957; scientific and general; Man. Drs ARFAN ROZALI.

Ganeca Exact Bandung: Kawasan Industri MM 2100, Jalan Selayar Kav A5, Bekasi 17520; tel. (22) 89981946; fax (22) 89981947; e-mail presdir@ganeca-exact.com; internet www.ganeca-exact.com; f. 1982; school textbooks; Dir Ir KETUT SUARDHARA LINGGIH.

Mizan Pustaka PT: Jalan Cinambo 135, Bandung 40294; tel. (22) 7834310; fax (22) 7834311; e-mail info@mizan.com; internet www.mizan.com; f. 1983; Islamic and general books; Pres. Dir HAIDAR BAGIR.

Penerbit ITB: Jalan Ganesa 10, Bandung 40132; tel. and fax (22) 2504257; e-mail itbpress@bdg.centrin.net.id; f. 1971; academic books; Dir EMMY SUPARKA; Chief Editor SOFIA MANSOOR-NIKSOLIHIN.

Putra A. Bardin: 3 Jalan Kembar Timur II, Bandung 40254; tel. (22) 5208305; fax (22) 7300879; f. 1998; textbooks, scientific and general; Dir NAI A. BARDIN.

Remaja Rosdakarya PT: Jalan Ibu Inggit Garnasih 40, Bandung 40252; tel. (22) 5200287; fax (22) 5202529; e-mail rosda@indosat.net.id; textbooks and children's fiction; Pres. ROZALI USMAN.

Sarana Panca Karyam PT: Jalan Kopo 633, Km 13/4, Bandung 40014; f. 1986; general; Dir WIMPY S. IBRAHIM.

Tarsito PT: Jalan Guntur 20, Bandung 40262; tel. (22) 7304915; fax (22) 7314630; academic; Dir T. SITORUS.

FLORES

Nusa Indah: Jalan El Tari, Ende 86318, Nusa Tenggara Timur, Flores; tel. (381) 21502; fax (381) 23974; e-mail namkahu@yahoo.com; f. 1970; religious and general; Dir LUKAS BATMOMOLIN.

KUDUS

Menara Kudus: Jalan Menara 4, Kudus 59315; tel. (291) 437143; fax (291) 436474; f. 1958; Islamic; Man. CHILMAN NAJIB.

MEDAN

Hasmar: Jalan Letjenderal Haryono M. T. 1, POB 446, Medan 20231; tel. (61) 4144581; fax (22) 4533673; f. 1962; primary school textbooks; Dir FAUZI LUBIS; Man. AMRAN SAID RANGKUTI.

Impola: Jalan H. M. Joni 46, Medan 20217; tel. (61) 711415; f. 1984; school textbooks; Dir PAMILANG M. SITUMORANG.

Madju Medan Cipta PT: Jalan Amaliun 37, Medan 20215; tel. (61) 7361990; fax (61) 7367753; e-mail koboi@indosat.net; f. 1950; textbooks, children's and general; Pres. H. MOHAMED ARBIE; Man. Dir Drs DINO IRSAN ARBIE.

Masco: Jalan Sisingamangaraja 191, Medan 20218; tel. (61) 713375; f. 1992; school textbooks; Dir P. M. SITUMORANG.

Monora: Jalan Letjenderal Jamin Ginting 583, Medan 20156; tel. (61) 8212667; fax (61) 8212669; e-mail monora_cv@plasa.com; f. 1962; school textbooks; Dir CHAIRIL ANWAR.

SEMARANG

Aneka Ilmu: Jalan Raya Semarang Demak, Km 8.5, Sayung, Demak; tel. (24) 6580335; fax (24) 6582903; e-mail pemasaran@anekailmu.com; internet www.anekailmu.com; f. 1983; general and school textbooks; Dir H. SUWANTO.

Effhar COY PT: Jalan Dorang 7, Semarang 50173; tel. (24) 3511172; fax (24) 3551540; e-mail dahara@indosat.net.id; f. 1976; general books; Dir H. DARADJAT HARAHAP.

Intan Pariwara: Jalan Ki Hajar Dewantoro, Kotak Pos III, Kotif Klaten, Jawa-Tengah; tel. (272) 322441; fax (272) 322607; e-mail intan@intanpariwara.co.id; internet www.intanpariwara.co.id; school textbooks; Pres. CHRIS HARJANTO.

Mandira PT: Jalan Letjenderal M. T. Haryono 501, Semarang 50241; tel. (24) 8316150; fax (24) 8415092; f. 1962; Dir Ir A. HARIYANTO.

Mandira Jaya Abadi PT: Jalan Kartini 48, Semarang 50241; tel. (24) 3519547; fax (24) 3542189; e-mail mjabadi@indosat.net.id; f. 1981; Dir Ir A. HARIYANTO.

SOLO

Pabelan PT: Jalan Raya Solo, Kertasura, Km 8, Solo 57162; tel. (271) 743975; fax (271) 714775; f. 1983; school textbooks; Dir AGUNG SASONGKO.

Tiga Serangkai Pustaka Mandiri, PT: Jalan Dr Supomo 23, Solo 57141, Central Java; tel. (271) 714344; fax (271) 713607; internet www.tigaserangkai.com; e-mail tspm@tigaserangkai.co.id; f. 1959;

school textbooks, general textbooks; Pres. Commr ABDULLAH SITI AMINAH.

SURABAYA

Airlangga University Press: Kampus C, Jalan Mulyorejo, Surabaya 60115; tel. (31) 5992246; fax (31) 5992248; e-mail aupsby@rad.net.id; academic; Dir Dr ARIFAAN RAZAK.

Bina Ilmu PT: Jalan Tunjungan 53E, Surabaya 60275; tel. (31) 5323214; fax (31) 5315421; f. 1973; school textbooks, Islamic; Pres. ARIEFIN NOOR.

Bintang: Jalan Potroagung III/41C, Surabaya; tel. (31) 3770687; fax (31) 3715941; school textbooks; Dir AGUS WINARNO.

Grip PT: Jalan Rungkut Permai II/C11, Surabaya; tel. (31) 22564; f. 1958; textbooks and general; Man. SURIPTO.

Jaya Baya: Jalan Embong Malang 69H, POB 250, Surabaya 60001; tel. (31) 41169; f. 1945; religion, philosophy and ethics; Man. TADJIB ERMADI.

Sinar Wijaya: Jalan Raya Sawo VII/58, Bringin-Lakarsantri, Surabaya; tel. (31) 7406616; general; Dir DULRADJAK.

YOGYAKARTA

Andi Publishers: Jalan Beo 38–40, Yogyakarta 55281; tel. (274) 561881; fax (274) 588282; e-mail andi_pub@indo.net.id; f. 1980; Christian, computing, business, management and technical; Dir J.H. GONDOWIJOYO.

BPFE PT: Jalan Gambiran 37, Yogyakarta 55161; tel. (274) 373760; fax (274) 380819; f. 1984; university textbooks; Dir Drs INDRIYO GITOSUDARMO.

Centhini Yayasan: Gedung Bekisar UH V/716 E1, Yogyakarta 55161; tel. (274) 383148; f. 1984; Javanese culture; Chair. H. KARKONO KAMAJAYA.

Gadjah Mada University Press: Jalan Grafika 1, Kampus UGM, Bulaksumur, Yogyakarta 55281; tel. and fax (274) 561037; e-mail gmupress@ugm.ac.id; internet www.gmup.ugm.ac.id; f. 1971; university textbooks; Dir S. MUNANDAR.

Indonesia UP: Gedung Bekisar UH V/716 E1, Yogyakarta 55161; tel. (274) 383148; f. 1950; general science; Dir H. KARKONO KAMAJAYA.

Kanisius Printing and Publishing: Jalan Cempaka 9, Deresan, Yogyakarta 55281; tel. (274) 588783; fax (274) 563349; e-mail office@kanisiusmedia.com; internet www.kanisiusmedia.com; f. 1922; philosophy, children's, textbooks, Christian and general; Pres. Dir AUGUSTINUS SARWANTO.

Kedaulatan Rakyat PT: Jalan P. Mangkubumi 40–42, Yogyakarta; tel. (274) 2163; Dir DRONO HARDJUSUWONGSO.

Penerbit Tiara Wacana Yogya: Jalan Kaliurang, Km 7, 8 Kopen 16, Banteng, Yogyakarta 55581; tel. and fax (274) 880683; f. 1986; university textbooks and general science; Dir SITORESMI PRABUNINGRAT.

Government Publishing House

Balai Pustaka PT (Persero) (State Publishing and Printing House): 1 Jalan Pulokambing, Kav. 15, Kawasan Industri Pulogadung, Jakarta; tel. (21) 4613519; fax (21) 4613520; e-mail humas@balaipustaka.co.id; internet balaipustaka.co.id; history, anthropology, politics, philosophy, medical, arts and literature; Pres. Dir ZAIM UCHROWI.

PUBLISHERS' ASSOCIATION

Ikatan Penerbit Indonesia (IKAPI) (Asscn of Indonesian Book Publishers): Jalan Kalipasir 32, Jakarta Pusat 10330; tel. (21) 31902532; fax (21) 31926124; e-mail sekretariat@ikapi.org; internet www.ikapi.org; f. 1950; 1009 mems (July 2011); Pres. LUYA ANDAM DEWI; Gen. Sec. HUSNI SYAWIE.

Broadcasting and Communications

TELECOMMUNICATIONS

Directorate-General of Posts and Telecommunications (Postel): Gedung Sapta Pesona, Jalan Medan Merdeka Barat 17, Jakarta 10110; tel. (21) 3835955; fax (21) 3860754; e-mail admin@postel.go.id; internet www.postel.go.id; Dir-Gen. MUHAMMAD BUDI SETIAWAN.

PT Excelcomindo Pratama Tbk (Excelcom): Jalan Mega Kuningan Lot E4-7 1, Kawasan Mega Kuningan, Jakarta 12950; tel. (21) 5761881; fax (21) 57959036; e-mail corpcomm@xl.co.id; internet www.xl.co.id; f. 1996; fixed-line and cellular telephone network provider; Pres. Dir HASNUL SUHAIMI.

PT Hutchison CP Telecommunications (HCPT): Wisma Barito Pacific, Tower II, 2nd Floor, Jalan Letjenderal S. Parman, Kav. 62–63, Slipi, Jakarta 11410; tel. (21) 53650000; fax (21) 53660000; internet www.three.co.id; f. 2003; est. as PT Cyber Access Communications; present name adopted 2005; 60% owned by Hutchison Telecom Int. Ltd (Hong Kong), 40% owned by Charoen Pokphand Group (Thailand); cellular telephone network operator providing GSM 1800 and third-generation (3G) video services; CEO LAURENTIUS BULTERS.

PT Indonesian Satellite Corporation Tbk (INDOSAT): Jalan Medan Merdeka Barat 21, POB 2905, Jakarta 10110; tel. (21) 54388888; fax (21) 5449501; e-mail publicrelations@indosat.com; internet www.indosat.com; f. 1967; telecommunications; partially privatized in 1994; 41.94% stake sold to Singapore Technologies Telemedia in 2002; 40.81% share sold to QTEL in 2008; Pres. Dir HARRY SASONGKO TIRTOTJONDRO; Pres. Commr Sheikh ABDULLAH BIN MOHAMMED BIN SAUD AL-THANI.

PT Mobile-8 Telecom (Tbk): Menara Kebon Sirih, 18th Floor, Jalan Kebon Sirih, Kav. 17–19, Jakarta 10340; tel. (21) 3920218; fax (21) 3920129; e-mail recruitment@mobile-8.com; internet www.mobile-8.com; f. 2002; 2m. subscribers (2007); Pres. Dir MERZA FACHYS.

PT Natrindo Telepon Seluler (AXIS): Jalan Jenderal Gatot Subroto, Kav. 35–36, Jakarta Selatan 12950; tel. (21) 5200088; e-mail cs@axisworld.co.id; internet www.axisworld.co.id; f. 2001; cellular telephone network operator; provides GSM 1800 and 3G video services; Pres. Dir and CEO ERIK AAS.

PT Satelit Palapa Indonesia (SATELINDO): Jalan Daan Mogot Km 11, Jakarta 11710; tel. (21) 5455121; fax (21) 5418548; e-mail palapa-c@satelindo.co.id; internet satelindo.boleh.com; f. 1993; owned by INDOSAT; telecommunications and satellite services; Pres. Dir DJOKO PRAJITNO.

PT Telekomunikasi Indonesia Tbk (TELKOM): Corporate Office, Jalan Japati 1, Bandung 40133; tel. (22) 4527101; fax (22) 4240313; internet www.telkom.co.id; domestic telecommunications; 24.2% of share capital was transferred to the private sector in 1995; Pres. Commr TANRI ABENG; Pres. Dir RINALDI FIRMANSYAH.

PT Telekomunikasi Selular (TELKOMSEL): Wisma Mulia, 12th Floor, Jalan Jenderal Gatot Subroto, Kav. 42, Jakarta Selatan 12710; tel. (21) 5240811; fax (21) 52606112; e-mail investor@telkomsel.co.id; internet www.telkomsel.com; f. 1995; provides domestic cellular services with international roaming available through 356 network partners; jt venture between PT Telekomunikasi Indonesia Tbk (65%) and Singapore Telecommunications Ltd (35%); Pres. Commr RINALDI FIRMANSYAH; Pres. Dir SARWOTO ATMOSUTARNO.

BROADCASTING

Regulatory Authority

Komisi Penyiaran Indonesia—KPI (Indonesian Broadcasting Commission): Lantai 6, Jalan Gajah Mada 8, Jakarta 10120; tel. (21) 6340713; fax (21) 6340667; internet www.kpi.go.id; f. 2002; ind. broadcasting regulatory authority; Dir-Gen. DADANG RAHMAT HIDAYAT.

Radio

Radio Republik Indonesia (RRI): Jalan Medan Merdeka Barat 4–5, Jakarta 10110; tel. (21) 3846817; fax (21) 3457134; e-mail rri@rri-online.com; internet www.rri-online.com; f. 1945; 49 stations; Dir PARNI HADI.

Voice of Indonesia: Jalan Medan Merdeka Barat 4–5, POB 1157, Jakarta; tel. (21) 3456811; fax (21) 3500990; e-mail voi@rri-online.com; international service provided by Radio Republik Indonesia; daily broadcasts in Arabic, English, French, German, Bahasa Indonesia, Japanese, Bahasa Malaysia, Mandarin, Spanish and Thai.

Television

In March 1989 Indonesia's first private commercial television station began broadcasting to the Jakarta area. In 2008 there were 10 privately owned television stations in operation.

PT Cakrawala Andalas Televisi (ANTEVE): Gedung Sentra Mulia, 18th Floor, Jalan H. R. Rasuna Said, Kav. X-6 No. 8, Jakarta Selatan 12940; tel. (21) 30405555; fax (21) 57946140; e-mail humas@an.tv; internet www.an.tv; f. 1993; private channel; broadcasting to 10 cities; Pres. Commr PAUL FRANCIS AIELLO; Pres. Dir ANINDYA N. BAKRIE.

PT CIPTA TPI: Jalan Pintu II—Taman Mini Indonesia Indah, Pondok Gede, Jakarta Timur 13810; tel. (21) 8412473; fax (21) 8412470; e-mail info@tpi.tv; internet www.tpi.tv; f. 1991; private channel funded by commercial advertising; Pres. Commr DANDY NUGROHO RUKMANA; Pres. Dir SANG NYOMAN SUWISMA.

PT Rajawali Citra Televisi Indonesia (RCTI): Jalan Raya Pejuangan 3, Kebon Jeruk, Jakarta 11000; tel. (21) 5303540; fax (21) 5320906; e-mail webmaster@rcti.tv; internet www.rcti.tv;

f. 1989; first private channel; 20-year licence; Pres. Dir SUTANTO HARTONO; Vice-Pres. Commr BAMBANG RUDIJANTO TANOESOEDIBJO.

PT Surya Citra Televisi (SCTV): GRHA SCTV, 2nd Floor, Jalan Gatot Subroto, Kav. 21, Jakarta 12930; tel. (21) 5225555; fax (21) 5224777; e-mail pr@sctv.co.id; internet www.sctv.co.id; f. 1990; private channel broadcasting nationally; Pres. Dir FOFO SARIAATMADJA.

Televisi Republik Indonesia (TVRI): TVRI Senayan, Jalan Gerbang Pemuda, Senayan, Jakarta 10270; tel. (21) 5704720; fax (21) 5731973; e-mail support@tvri.co.id; internet www.tvri.co.id; f. 1962; fmrly state-controlled; became independent in 2003; Pres. Dir Maj.-Gen. (retd) I GDE NYOMAN ARSANA.

Finance

(cap. = capital; p.u. = paid up; res = reserves; dep. = deposits; m. = million; brs = branches; amounts in rupiah)

BANKING

Central Bank

Bank Indonesia (BI): Jalan M. H. Thamrin 2, Jakarta Pusat 10350; tel. (21) 2310108; fax (21) 3501867; e-mail humasbi@bi.go.id; internet www.bi.go.id; f. 1828; nationalized as central bank in 1953; cap. 7,610,885m., res 86,906,362m., dep. 503,825,034m. (Dec. 2009); Gov. DARMIN NASUTION; 42 brs.

State Banks

PT Bank Mandiri (Persero): Plaza Mandiri, Jalan Jenderal Gatot Subroto, Kav. 36–38, Jakarta 12190; tel. (21) 52997777; fax (21) 52997735; internet www.bankmandiri.co.id; f. 1998; est. following merger of four state-owned banks—PT Bank Bumi Daya, PT Bank Dagang Negara, PT Bank Ekspor Impor Indonesia and PT Bank Pembangunan Indonesia; cap. 10,485,058m., res 6,765,078m., dep. 331,268,432m. (Dec. 2009); Chair. EDWIN GERUNGAN; Pres. Dir ZULKIFLI ZAINI; 909 local brs; 6 overseas brs.

PT Bank Negara Indonesia (Persero) Tbk: Jalan Jenderal Sudirman, Kav. 1, Jakarta 10220; tel. (21) 2511946; fax (21) 2511214; e-mail hin@bni.co.id; internet www.bni.co.id; f. 1946; commercial bank; specializes in credits to the industrial sector; cap. 7,789,288m., res 6,691,845m., dep. 194,810,525m. (Dec. 2009); Pres. Commr ERY RIYANA HARDJAPAMEKAS; Pres. Dir GATOT MUDIANTORO SUWONDO; 919 local brs, 5 overseas brs.

PT Bank Rakyat Indonesia (Persero): Gedung BRI 1, Jalan Jenderal Sudirman, Kav. 44–46, POB 94, Jakarta 10210; tel. (21) 2510244; fax (21) 2500077; internet www.bri.co.id; f. 1895; present name since 1946; commercial and foreign exchange bank; specializes in agricultural smallholdings and rural devt; cap. 6,164,926m., res 3,257,761m., dep. 265,533,166m. (Dec. 2009); Pres. Commr BUNASOR SANIM; Pres. Dir SOFYAN BASIR; 326 brs.

PT Bank Tabungan Negara (Persero): Menara Bank BTN, 10th Floor, Jalan Gajah Mada 1, Jakarta 10130; tel. (21) 6336789; fax (21) 6336704; e-mail webadmin@btn.co.id; internet www.btn.co.id; f. 1964; commercial bank; state-owned; cap. 4,996,655m., res 104,182m., dep. 41,384,482m. (Dec. 2009); Pres. Commr ZAKI BARIDWAN; Pres. Dir IQBAL LATANRO; 44 brs.

PT BPD Jawa Timur (Bank Jatim): Jalan Basuki Rachmad 98–104, Surabaya; tel. (31) 5310090; fax (31) 5470159; e-mail humas@bankjatim.co.id; internet www.bankjatim.co.id; f. 1961; cap. 696,420m., res 846,115m., dep. 14,839,631m. (Dec. 2009); Chair. CHAIRUL DJAELANI; Pres. MULJANTO.

Indonesia Eximbank: Gedung Bursa Efek, Menara II, Lantai 8, Jalan Jenderal Sudirman, Kav. 52–53, Jakarta 12190; tel. (21) 5154638; fax (21) 5154639; e-mail intbank@indonesiaeximbank.go.id; internet www.indonesiaeximbank.go.id; cap. 4,321,586m., dep. 3,174,994m. (Dec. 2009), res 1,020,746m. (Dec. 2008); fmrly PT Bank Ekspor Indonesia (Persero); Chair. MADE GDE ERATA; Man. Dir ARIFIN INDRA SULISTYANTO.

Commercial Banks

PT ANZ Panin Bank: Panin Bank Centre, Ground Floor, Jalan Jenderal Sudirman (Senayan), Kav. 33A, Jakarta 10220; tel. (21) 5750300; fax (21) 5727447; e-mail products@anz.com; internet www.anz.com/indonesia; f. 1990; est. as Westpac Panin Bank; present name adopted 1993; 85% owned by Australia and New Zealand Banking Group Ltd; cap. 50,000m., res 10,000m., dep. 13,002,042m. (Dec. 2009); Pres. Dir JOSEPH ABRAHAM.

PT Bank Artha Graha Internasional Tbk: Bank Artha Graha Tower, 5th Floor, Jalan Jenderal Sudirman, Kav. 52–53, Jakarta 12190; tel. (21) 5152168; fax (21) 5153470; e-mail agraha@rad.net.id; internet www.arthagraha.com; f. 1967; est. as PT Bank Bandung; merged with PT Bank Arta Pratama in 1999 and with PT Bank Inter-Pacific in 2005; cap. 950,804.4m., res 418,462.2m., dep. 13,142,250.7m. (Dec. 2009); Pres. Dir ANDY KASIH; Pres. Commr KIKI SYAHNAKRI; 78 brs.

PT Bank Central Asia Tbk (BCA): Menara BCA, Grand Indonesia, Jalan M. H. Thamrin 1, Jakarta 10310; tel. (21) 23588000; fax (21) 23588300; e-mail halobca@bca.co.id; internet www.klikbca.com; f. 1957; 51% share sold to Farallon Capital Management (USA) in March 2002; cap. 1,540,938m., res 3,728,472m., dep. 248,469,919m. (Dec. 2009); Pres. Commr EUGENE KEITH GALBRAITH; Pres. Dir DJOHAN EMIR SETIJOSO; 760 local brs.

PT Bank Chinatrust Indonesia: Wisma Tamara, Lantai 15–17, Jalan Jenderal Sudirman, Kav. 24, Jakarta 12920; tel. (21) 5207878; fax (21) 5206767; e-mail ctcbjak@rad.net.id; internet www.chinatrust.co.id; f. 1995; cap. 150,000m., dep. 2,976,336m. (Dec. 2009); Pres. Dir PETER LIU; Chair. JEFFREY L. S. KOO.

PT Bank CIMB Niaga Tbk: Graha Niaga, Jalan Jenderal Sudirman, Kav. 58, Jakarta 12190; tel. (21) 2505252; fax (21) 2505205; e-mail 14041@bniaga.co.id; internet www.cimbniaga.com; f. 1955; cap. 1,552,420m., res 5,985,935m., dep. 88,029,672m. (Dec. 2009); Pres. Commr Dato' MOHD SHUKRI HUSSIN; Pres. Dir ARWIN RASYID; 227 brs.

PT Bank Danamon Indonesia Tbk: Menara Danamon, Jalan Prof. Dr Satrio 6, Kav. E-4, Mega Kuningan, Jakarta 12930; tel. (21) 34358888; fax (21) 34358800; e-mail danamon.access@danamon.co.id; internet www.danamon.co.id; f. 1956; placed under supervision of Indonesian Bank Restructuring Agency in April 1998; merged with PT Bank Tiara Asia, PT Tamara Bank, PT Bank Duta and PT Bank Nusa Nasional in 2000; 51% share sold to consortium led by Singapore's Temasek Holdings in May 2003; cap. 5,303,992m., res 2,760,125m., dep. 75,528,733m. (Dec. 2009); Pres. Commr NG KEE CHOE; Pres. Dir HENRY HO HON CHEONG; 483 brs.

PT Bank ICB Bumiputera Tbk: Menara ICB Bumiputera, Jalan Probolinggo 18, Menteng, Jakarta Pusat 10350; tel. (21) 3919898; fax (21) 3919797; e-mail bank@icbbumiputera.co.id; internet www.icbbumiputera.co.id; f. 1989; cap. 500,000m., res 3,469m., dep. 6,323,738m. (Dec. 2009); Pres. Commr Dato MAT AMIR BIN JAFFAR; Pres. Dir SRIDHAR NATARAJAN.

PT Bank Internasional Indonesia Tbk (BII): Plaza BII, Menara I, Lantai 8, Jalan M. H. Thamrin 51, Kav. 22, Jakarta 10350; tel. (21) 2300666; fax (21) 31934609; e-mail cs@bii.co.id; internet www.bii.co.id; cap. 3,226,706m., res 224,705m., dep. 51,190,708m. (Dec. 2009); Pres. Commr Tan Sri Dato' MEGAT ZAHARUDDIN BIN MEGAT MOHAMMAD NOR; Pres. Dir RIDHA WIRAKUSUMAH; 246 local brs; 3 overseas brs.

PT Bank KEB Indonesia: Wisma GKBI, Lantai 20, Suite 2002, Jalan Jenderal Sudirman, Kav. 28, Selatan, Jakarta; tel. (21) 5741030; fax (21) 5741031; e-mail contact.center@kebi.co.id; internet www.kebi.co.id; owned by KEB Seoul (99%) and PT Clemont Finance Indonesia (1%); f. 1990; fmrly PT Korea Exchange Bank Danamon; cap. 150,000m., dep. 2,519,337.1m. (Dec. 2009); Pres. Dir CHO YONG WOO; Chair. HO SUN YUN.

PT Bank Mayapada Internasional Tbk: Menara Mayapada, Jalan Jenderal Sudirman, Kav. 28, Jakarta 12920; tel. (21) 5212288; fax (21) 5211985; e-mail mayapada@bankmayapada.com; internet www.bankmayapada.com; f. 1989; cap. 412,956m., res 453,884m., dep. 6,571,318m. (Dec. 2009); Chair. Dr TAHIR; Pres. Dir HARIYONO TJAHJARIJADI; 41 brs.

PT Bank Mizuho Indonesia: Plaza B11, Lantai 24, Menara 2, Jalan M. H. Thamrin 51, Jakarta 10350; tel. (21) 3925222; fax (21) 3926354; f. 1989; fmrly PT Bank Fuji International Indonesia; name changed as above in 2001; cap. 323,574m., res 117,654m., dep. 8,244,996m. (Dec. 2009); Pres. Dir JIRO TOTSU.

PT Bank Muamalat Indonesia (BMI): Gedung Arthaloka, Jalan Jenderal Sudirman 2, Jakarta 10220; tel. (21) 2511414; fax (21) 2511453; internet www.muamalatbank.com; Indonesia's first Islamic bank; cap. 492.7m., res 132.4m., dep. 14,678.4m. (Dec. 2009); Pres. Dir Ir ARVIYAN ARIFIN; Pres. Commr WIDIGDO SUKARMAN.

PT Bank Mutiara Tbk: Gedung Sentral Senayan II, 22nd Floor, Jalan Asia Afrika 8, Jakarta 10270; tel. (21) 5724180; fax (21) 5724443; e-mail corsec@mutiarabank.co.id; internet www.mutiarabank.co.id; f. 2009; fmrly PT Bank Century Tbk; Pres. Commr PONTAS RIYANTO SIAHAAN; Pres. Dir MARYONO.

PT Bank OCBC NISP Tbk: Menara Bank OCBC NISP, Jalan Prof. Dr Satrio, Kav. 25, Jakarta 12940; tel. (21) 25533888; fax (21) 57944000; internet www.ocbcnisp.com; f. 1941; 81.9% owned by OCBC Bank, Singapore; cap. 726,822m., res 1,215,727m., dep. 30,875,568m. (Dec. 2009); Pres. Commr PRAMUKTI SURJAUDAJA; Pres. Dir PARWATI SURJAUDAJA; 168 brs.

PT Bank Permata Tbk: Menara PermataBank I, Lantai 17, Jalan Jenderal Sudirman, Kav. 27, Jakarta 12920; tel. (21) 5237899; fax (21) 5237253; e-mail isaptono@permatabank.co.id; internet www.permatabank.com; f. 1954; est. as Bank Persatuan Dagang Indonesia; became PT Bank Bali in 1971 and PT Bank Bali Tbk in 1990; name changed as above Sept. 2002 following merger with PT

Bank Prima Express, PT Bank Universal Tbk, PT Arthamedia Bank and PT Bank Patriot; cap. 7,127,512m., res 26m., dep. 46,394,206m. (Dec. 2009); Pres. Commr RAYMOND FERGUSON; Pres. Dir DAVID MARTIN FLETCHER; 288 brs.

PT Bank Rabobank International Indonesia: Plaza 89, Lantai 9, Jalan H. R. Rasuna Said, Kav. X-7 No. 6, Jakarta 12940; tel. (21) 2520876; fax (21) 2520875; e-mail indonesia@rabobank.com; internet www.rabobank.co.id; f. 1990; est. as PT Rabobank Duta Indonesia; name changed as above in 2001 when Rabobank Nederland secured sole ownership; cap. 715,000m., res 2,741m., dep. 8,910,657m. (Dec. 2009); Pres. Commr JAN ALEXANDER PRUIJS; Pres. Dir HENK MULDER.

PT Bank Sumitomo Mitsui Indonesia: Gedung Summitmas II, Lantai 10, Jalan Jenderal Sudirman, Kav. 61–62, Jakarta 12190; tel. (21) 5227011; fax (21) 5227022; f. 1989; fmrly PT Bank Sumitomo Indonesia; merged with PT Bank Sakura Swadharma in April 2001; cap. 1,502,441m., res -521,365m., dep. 7,906,763.5m. (Dec. 2009); Pres. Commr MASAYUKI SHIMURA; Pres. Dir SHUJI FUJIKAWA; 1 br.

PT Bank UOB Buana: UOB Plaza, Jalan M. H. Thamrin 10, Jakarta 10230; tel. (21) 23506000; fax (21) 29936632; e-mail cst.comm@uobbuana.com; internet www.uobbuana.com; f. 1956; fmrly PT Bank Buana Indonesia Tbk; cap. 1,663,339m., res 862,896m., dep. 17,285,563m. (Dec. 2009); Pres. Commr WEE CHO YAW; Pres. Dir ARMAND B. ARIEF; 32 brs.

PT Pan Indonesia Tbk (Panin Bank): Panin Bank Centre, Lantai 11, Jalan Jenderal Sudirman, Kav. 1, Senayan, Jakarta 10270; tel. (21) 2700545; fax (21) 2700340; e-mail panin@panin.co.id; internet www.panin.co.id; f. 1971; est. as a result of the merger of three private national banks; cap. 2,408,765m., res 3,570,446m., dep. 59,168,198m. (Dec. 2009); Pres. Commr JOHNNY N. WIRAATMADJA; Pres. Dir Drs H. ROSTIAN SJAMSUDIN; 250 local brs, 2 overseas brs.

PT Woori Bank Indonesia: Jakarta Stock Exchange Bldg, Lantai 16, Jalan Jenderal Sudirman, Kav. 52–53, Jakarta 12190; tel. (21) 5151919; fax (21) 5151477; e-mail indonesia@wooribank.com; internet id.wooribank.com; fmrly PT Hanvit Bank Indonesia; cap. 170,000m., dep. 2,395,013m. (Dec. 2008); Pres. CHEUL SU KIM.

Banking Association

The Association of Indonesian National Private Commercial Banks (Perhimpunan Bank-Bank Umum Nasional Swasta—PERBANAS): Griya Perbanas, Lantai 1, Jalan Perbanas, Karet Kuningan, Setiabudi, Jakarta 12940; tel. (21) 5223038; fax (21) 5223037; e-mail sekretariat@perbanas.org; internet www.perbanas.org; f. 1952; 78 mems; Chair. SIGIT PRAMONO; Sec.-Gen. FARID RAHMAN.

STOCK EXCHANGE

Indonesia Stock Exchange (IDX): Indonesia Stock Exchange Bldg, Menara 1, Jalan Jenderal Sudirman, Kav. 52–53, Jakarta 12190; tel. (21) 5150515; fax (21) 5150330; e-mail callcenter@idx.co.id; internet www.idx.co.id; fmrly Jakarta Stock Exchange; name changed as above upon merger with Surabaya Stock Exchange in 2007; 128 securities houses constitute the members and the shareholders of the exchange, each company owning one share; Pres. Dir ITO WARSITO.

Regulatory Authority

Badan Pengawas Pasar Modal (BAPEPAM) (Capital Market Supervisory Agency): Gedung Sumitro Djojohadikusumo, Jalan Lapangan Banteng Timur 1–4, Jakarta 10710; tel. (21) 3858001; fax (21) 3857917; e-mail bapepam@bapepam.go.id; internet www.bapepam.go.id; Chair. A. FAUD RAHMANY; Exec. Sec. NGALIM SAWEGA.

INSURANCE

In August 2006 there were 157 insurance companies, including 97 non-life companies, 51 life companies, four reinsurance companies and two social insurance companies.

Insurance Supervisory Authority of Indonesia: Directorate of Financial Institutions, Jalan Dr Wahidin, Jakarta 10710; tel. (21) 3451210; fax (21) 3849504; wing of the Ministry of Finance and State Enterprises Devt; Dir H. FIRDAUS DJAELANI.

Selected Life Insurance Companies

PT AIA Financial: Menara Matahari, Lantai 8, Jalan Bulevar Palem Raya 7, Lippo Karawaci 1200, Tangerang 15811; tel. (21) 54218777; fax (21) 5475409; e-mail id.customer@aia.com; internet www.aia-financial.co.id; f. 1983; CEO and Pres. Dir PETER J. CREWE.

PT Asuransi Allianz Life Indonesia: Gedung Summitmas II, Lantai 1, Jalan Jenderal Sudirman, Kav. 61–62, Jakarta 12190; tel. (21) 25989999; fax (21) 30003400; e-mail contactus@allianz.co.id; internet www.allianz.co.id; f. 1996; CEO JOACHIM WESSLING.

Asuransi Jiwa Bersama Bumiputera 1912: Wisma Bumiputera, Lantai 18–21, Jalan Jenderal Sudirman, Kav. 75, Jakarta 12910; tel. (21) 2512154; fax (21) 2512172; e-mail bp1912@bumiputera.com; internet www.bumiputera.com; Chair. Dr H. SUGIHARTO; Pres. Dir DIRMAN PARDOSI.

PT Asuransi Jiwa Central Asia Raya: Blue Dot Center, Blok A–C, Jalan Gelong Baru Utara 5–8, Jakarta Barat 11440; tel. (21) 56961929; fax (21) 56961939; e-mail lancar@car.co.id; internet www.car.co.id; Chair. SOEDONO SALIM.

PT Asuransi Jiwa 'Panin Putra': Jalan Pintu Besar Selatan 52A, Jakarta 11110; tel. (21) 672586; fax (21) 676354; f. 1974; Pres. Dir SUJONO SOEPENO; Chair. NUGROHO TJOKROWIRONO.

PT Asuransi Jiwasraya (Persero): Jalan H. Juanda 34, Jakarta 10120; tel. (21) 3444444; fax (21) 3862344; e-mail asuransi@jiwasraya.co.id; internet www.jiwasraya.co.id; f. 1959; Pres. Commr DJONNY WIGUNA; Pres. Dir HENDRISMAN RAHIM.

PT Asuransi Panin Life: Panin Life Center, Lantai 6, Jalan Letjenderal S. Parman, Kav. 91, Jakarta 11420; tel. (21) 25566888; fax (21) 25566711; e-mail customer@paninlife.co.id; internet www.paninlife.co.id; Pres. Dir HERU YUWONO.

Bumi Asih Jaya Life Insurance Co Ltd: Jalan Matraman Raya 165–167, Jakarta 13140; tel. (21) 2800700; fax (21) 8509669; e-mail baj@bajlife.com; internet www.bajlife.co.id; f. 1967; Chair. P. SITOMPUL; Pres. VIRGO HUTAGALUNG.

Selected Non-Life Insurance Companies

PT Asuransi Bina Dana Arta Tbk: Plaza ABDA, Lantai 27, Jalan Jenderal Sudirman, Kav. 59, Jakarta 122190; tel. (21) 51401688; fax (21) 51401698; e-mail contactus@abdainsurance.co.id; internet www.abdainsurance.co.id; Pres. Commr TJAN SOEN ENG; Pres. Dir CANDRA GUNAWAN.

PT Asuransi Bintang Tbk: Jalan R. S. Fatmawati 32, Jakarta Selatan 12430; tel. (21) 75902777; fax (21) 7656287; e-mail bintang@asuransibintang.com; internet www.asuransibintang.com; f. 1955; general insurance; Pres. Commr SHANTI POESPOSOETJIPTO; Pres. Dir ZAFAR DINESH IDHAM.

PT Asuransi Buana Independen: Jalan Pintu Besar Selatan 78, Jakarta 11110; tel. (21) 6266286; fax (21) 6263005; e-mail headoffice@buanaindependent.co.id; internet buanaindependent.co.id; Pres. Commr ISHAK SUMARNO; Pres. Dir MADE MARKA.

PT Asuransi Central Asia: Wisma Asia, Lantai 12–15, Jalan Letjenderal S. Parman, Kav. 79, Slipi, Jakarta Barat 11420; tel. (21) 56998288; fax (21) 5638029; e-mail info@aca.co.id; internet www.aca.co.id; Pres. Commr ANTHONY SALIM; Pres. Dir TEDDY HAILAMSAH.

PT Asuransi Dayin Mitra: Jalan Raden Saleh Raya, Kav. 1B–1D, Jakarta 10430; tel. (21) 3153577; fax (21) 3912902; e-mail nuning@dayinmitra.co.id; internet www.dayinmitra.co.id; f. 1982; general insurance; Man. Dir LARSOEN HAKER.

PT Asuransi Indrapura: Menara Chase Plaza, Lantai 4, Jalan Jenderal Sudirman, Kav. 21, Jakarta 12920; tel. (21) 5200338; fax (21) 5200175; e-mail insure@indrapura.co.id; internet www.indrapura.co.id; f. 1954; Pres. Commr A. WAHYUHADI; Pres. Dir MINTARTO HALIM.

PT Asuransi Jasa Indonesia: Jalan Letjenderal M. T. Haryono, Kav. 61, Jakarta 12041; tel. (21) 7994508; fax (21) 7995364; e-mail jasindo@jasindo.co.id; internet www.jasindo.co.id; Pres. Commr MOELYADI; Pres. Dir Drs EKO BUDIWIYONO.

PT Asuransi Jasa Tania: Wisma Jasa Tania, Jalan Teuku Cik Ditiro 14, Jakarta 10350; tel. (21) 3101850; fax (21) 31923089; e-mail ajstania@jasatania.co.id; internet www.jasatania.co.id; Pres. Dir BASRAN DAMANIK (acting).

PT Asuransi Maipark Indonesia: Gedung Setiabudi Atrium, Lantai 4, Suite 408, Jalan H. R. Rasuna Said, Kav. 62, Jakarta 12920; tel. (21) 5210803; fax (21) 5210738; e-mail maipark@maipark.com; internet www.maipark.com; fmrly PT Maskapai Asuransi Indonesia; Chair. and CEO KORNELIUS SIMANJUNTAK.

PT Asuransi Parolamas: Komplek Golden Plaza, Blok G 39–42, Jalan R. S. Farmawati 15, Jakarta 12420; tel. (21) 7508983; fax (21) 7506339; internet www.parolamas.co.id; Chief Commr TJUT ROEKMA RAFFLI; Pres. Dir Drs SYARIFUDDIN HARAHAP.

PT Asuransi Ramayana: Jalan Kebon Sirih 49, Jakarta 10340; tel. (21) 31937148; fax (21) 31934825; e-mail info@ramayanains.com; internet ramayanainsurance.com; f. 1965; Pres. Commr A. WINOTO DOERIAT; Pres. Dir SYAHRIL.

PT Asuransi Tri Pakarta: Jalan Paletehan I/18, Jakarta 12160; tel. (21) 711850; fax (21) 7394748; internet www.tripakarta.co.id; Chair. SAIFUDIEN HASAN; Pres. TEDDY PUSPITO.

PT Asuransi Wahana Tata: Jalan H. R. Rasuna Said, Kav. C-4, Jakarta 12920; tel. (21) 5203145; fax (21) 5203149; e-mail aswata@aswata.co.id; internet www.aswata.co.id; Chair. RUDY WANANDI; Pres. Dir ROBERT JEREMIA.

PT Berdikari Insurance: Jalan Merdeka Barat 1, Jakarta 10110; tel. (21) 3440266; fax (21) 3440586; e-mail ho@berdikariinsurance

.com; internet www.berdikariinsurance.com; Pres. ANGGIAT ISIDORUS SITOHANG.

PT Tugu Pratama Indonesia: Wisma Tugu I, Jalan H. R. Rasuna Said, Kav. C8–9, Kuningan, Jakarta Selatan 12920; tel. (21) 52961777; fax (21) 52961555; e-mail tpi@tugu.com; internet www.tugu.com; f. 1981; general insurance; Pres. Commr FEREDERICK SIAHAAN; Pres. Dir EVITA M. TAGOR.

Joint Ventures

PT Asuransi AIG Life: Matahari AIG Lippo Cyber Tower, 5th–7th Floors, Jalan Bulevar Palem Raya 7, Lippo Karawaci 1200, Tangerang 15811; tel. (21) 54218888; fax (21) 5475415; e-mail service@aig-life.co.id; internet www.aig-life.co.id; jt venture between American International Group, Inc, and PT Asuransi Lippo Life; life insurance; Dep. Pres. Dir S. BUDISUHARTO.

PT Asuransi Allianz Utama Indonesia: Gedung Summitmas II, 9th Floor, Jalan Jenderal Sudirman, Kav. 61–62, Jakarta Selatan 12190; tel. (21) 2522470; fax (21) 2523246; e-mail general@allianz.co.id; internet www.allianz.co.id; f. 1989; non-life insurance; Chair. EDI SUBEKTI; Pres. Dir VOLKER MISS.

PT Asuransi Jiwa Manulife Indonesia: Menara Selatan, Lantai 3, Jalan Jenderal Sudirman, Kav. 45, Jakarta 12930; tel. (21) 25557788; fax (21) 25557799; e-mail communication_id@manulife.com; internet www.manulife-indonesia.com; f. 1985; life insurance; Pres. Dir ALAN MERTEN.

PT Asuransi Jiwa Sinarmas: Wisma EKA Jiwa, Lantai 8, Jalan Mangga Dua Raya, Jakarta 10730; tel. (21) 6257808; fax (21) 6257837; e-mail cs@sinarmaslife.co.id; internet www.sinarmaslife.com; fmrly PT Asuransi Jiwa EKA Life; Pres. Commr INDRA WIDJAJA; Pres. Dir IVENA WIDJAJA.

PT Asuransi MSIG Indonesia: Gedung Summitmas II, Lantai 15, Jalan Jenderal Sudirman, Kav. 61–62, Jakarta 12190; tel. (21) 2523110; fax (21) 2524307; e-mail msig@id.msig-asia.com; internet www.msig.co.id; f. 1975; est. as PT Asuransi Mitsui Marine Indonesia; name changed to PT Asuransi Mitsui Sumitomo Indonesia in 2003, following merger with PT Asuransi Sumitomo Marine and Pool; present name adopted 2007; Chair. RUDY WANANDI; Pres. Dir TADASHI MAEKAWA.

PT Asuransi Tokio Marine Indonesia: Sentral Senayan I, Lantai 4, Jalan Asia Afrika 8, Jakarta 10270; tel. (21) 5725772; fax (21) 5724005; e-mail cp@tokiomarine.co.id; internet www.tokiomarine.co.id; jt venture between Tokio Marine Asia Pte Ltd and PT Asuransi Jasa Indonesia; Pres. Dir MITSUTAKA SATO.

PT Chartis Insurance Indonesia: The Indonesia Stock Exchange Bldg, Menara II, Lantai 3A, Jalan Jenderal Sudirman, Kav. 52–53, Jakarta 12190; tel. (21) 52914888; fax (21) 52914889; e-mail contact.us@chartisinsurance.com; internet www.chartisinsurance.co.id; f. 1970; fmrly PT Asuransi AIU Indonesia; Pres. Dir MICHAEL BLAKEWAY.

Insurance Associations

Asosiasi Asuransi Jiwa Indonesia (Indonesia Life Insurance Association): The Plaza Office Tower, Lantai 19, Jalan M. H. Thamrin, Kav. 28–30, Jakarta 10350; tel. (21) 29922929; fax (21) 29922828; e-mail aaji.info@aaji.or.id; internet www.aaji.or.id; f. 2002; 49 mems; Chair. EVELINA PEITRUSCKHA; Exec. Dir STEPHEN JUWONO.

Asosiasi Asuransi Umum Indonesia (General Insurance Association of Indonesia): Jalan Majapahit 34, Blok V-29, Jakarta 10160; tel. (21) 3454387; fax (21) 3454307; e-mail secretary@aaui.or.id; f. 1957; est. as Dewan Asuransi Indonesia (Insurance Council of Indonesia); present name adopted 2003; Chair. KORNELIUS SIMANJUNTAK; Exec. Dir FRANS WIYONO.

Trade and Industry

GOVERNMENT AGENCIES

Badan Pelaksana Kegiatan Usaha Hulu Minyak dan Gas Bumi (BP Migas): Gedung Wisma Mulia, Lantai 22, 42 Jalan Gatot Subroto, Jakarta 12710; tel. (21) 29241607; fax (21) 29249999; e-mail humas@bpmigas.go.id; internet www.bpmigas.go.id; f. 2002; regulates upstream petroleum and natural gas industry; Chair. R. PRIYONO.

Badan Pengatur Hilir Minyak dan Gas Bumi (BPH Migas): Gedung BPH Migas, Jalan Captain P. Tendean 28, Jakarta Selatan 12710; tel. (21) 5255500; fax (21) 5223210; e-mail humas@bphmigas.go.id; internet www.bphmigas.go.id; f. 2002; regulates downstream petroleum and gas industry; Chair. TUBAGUS HARYONO.

Badan Pengembangan Industri Strategis (BPIS) (Agency for Strategic Industries): Gedung Arthaloka, 3rd Floor, Jalan Jenderal Sudirman 2, Jakarta 10220; tel. (21) 5705335; fax (21) 3292516; f. 1989; co-ordinates production of capital goods.

Badan Pengkajian dan Penerapan Teknologi (BPPT) (Agency for the Assessment and Application of Technology): Jalan M. H. Thamrin 8, Jakarta 10340; tel. (21) 3168200; fax (21) 3904573; e-mail humas@bppt.go.id; internet www.bppt.go.id; Chair. Dr Ir MARZAN A. ISKANDAR.

Badan Tenaga Nuklir Nasional (BATAN) (National Nuclear Energy Agency): Jalan Kuningan Barat, Mampang Prapatan, Jakarta 12710; tel. (21) 5251109; fax (21) 5251110; e-mail humas@batan.go.id; internet www.batan.go.id; Chair. Dr SOEDYARTOMO.

Badan Urusan Logistik (BULOG) (National Logistics Agency): Jalan Jenderal Gatot Subroto, Kav. 49, Jakarta 12950; tel. and fax (21) 5256482; e-mail redaksiweb@bulog.co.id; internet www.bulog.co.id; Dir-Gen. SUTARTO ALIMOESO.

National Agency for Export Development (NAFED): Jalan M. I. Ridwan Rais 5, 3rd Floor, Jakarta 10110; tel. (21) 3858171; fax (21) 23528662; e-mail nafed@nafed.go.id; internet www.nafed.go.id; Chair. HESTI INDAH KRESNARINI.

National Economic Council: Jakarta; f. 1999; 13-mem. council formed to advise the President on economic policy; Chair. EMIL SALIM; Sec.-Gen. Sri MULYANI INDRAWATI.

DEVELOPMENT ORGANIZATIONS

Badan Koordinasi Penanaman Modal (BKPM) (Investment Co-ordinating Board): Jalan Jenderal Gatot Subroto 44, POB 3186, Jakarta 12190; tel. (21) 52921334; fax (21) 5264211; e-mail info@bkpm.go.id; internet www.bkpm.go.id; f. 1976; Chair. GITA IRAWAN WIRJAWAN.

Badan Perencanaan Pembangunan Nasional (Bappenas) (National Development Planning Board): Jalan Taman Suropati 2, Jakarta 10310; tel. (21) 3905650; fax (21) 3145374; e-mail admin@bappenas.go.id; internet www.bappenas.go.id; formulates Indonesia's economic devt plans; Chair. Dr ARMIDA ALISJAHBANA.

CHAMBER OF COMMERCE

Kamar Dagang dan Industri Indonesia (KADIN) (Indonesian Chamber of Commerce and Industry): Menara Kadin Indonesia, Lantai 29, Jalan H. R. Rasuna Said X5, Kav. 2–3, Jakarta 12950; tel. (21) 5274484; fax (21) 5274331; e-mail kadin@kadin-indonesia.or.id; internet www.kadin-indonesia.or.id; f. 1969; 33 provincial-level chambers and 442 district-level chambers; Chair. SURYO BAMBANG SULISTO; Exec. Dir Drs HARIADI SAPTADJI.

INDUSTRIAL AND TRADE ASSOCIATIONS

Association of Indonesian Automotive Industries (GAIKINDO): Jalan Hos Cokroaminoto 6, Jakarta Pusat 10350; tel. (21) 3157178; fax (21) 3142100; e-mail gaikindo@cbn.net.id; internet www.gaikindo.org; Chair. BAMBANG TRISULO.

Association of Indonesian Beverage Industries (ASRIM): 8/F, Wisma GKBI, Jalan Jenderal Sudirman 28, Jakarta 10210; tel. (21) 5723838; fax (21) 5740817; e-mail sekertariat.asrim@gmail.com; 22 mems; Chair. WILLY SIDHARTA; Sec.-Gen. SUROSO NATAKUSUMA.

Association of Indonesian Coffee Exporters (AIKE): Gedung AIKE, Lantai 3, Jalan R. P. Soeroso 20, Jakarta 10350; tel. (21) 3106765; fax (21) 3144115; e-mail bphaeki@yahoo.com; 800 mems; Chair. HASSAN WIDJAYA; Sec.-Gen. RACHIM KARTABRATA.

Association of State-Owned Companies: CTC Bldg, Jalan Kramat Raya 94–96, Jakarta; tel. (21) 346071; co-ordinates the activities of state-owned enterprises; Pres. ODANG.

BANI Arbitration Center (BANI): Wahana Graha, Lantai 2, Jalan Mampang Prapatan 2, Jakarta 12760; tel. (21) 7940542; fax (21) 7940543; e-mail bani-arb@indo.net.id; internet www.bani-arb.org; f. 1977; resolves business disputes; Chair. Prof. Dr H. PRIYATNA ABDURRASYID; Sec.-Gen. N. KRISNAWENDA.

Electric and Electronic Appliance Manufacturers' Association: Jalan Pangeran, Blok 20A-1D, Jakarta; tel. (21) 6480059.

Importers' Association of Indonesia (GINSI): Wisma Kosgoro Bldg, 8th Floor, Jalan M. H. Thamrin 53, Jakarta 10350; tel. (21) 39832510; fax (21) 39832540; f. 1956; 2,921 mems (1996); Chair. AMIRUDIN SAUD; Sec.-Gen. DEDDY BINTANG.

Indonesia National Shippers' Council (INSC): Jalan Cempaka Putih, Barat 6, Jakarta Pusat 10520; tel. (21) 4254677; fax (21) 4206303; e-mail depalindo@yahoo.com; Chair. SUARDI ZEN; Sec.-Gen. RACHIM KARTABRATA.

Indonesian Cement Association (ICA): Graha Irama Bldg, Lantai 11, Suite 11G, Jalan H. R. Rasuna Said, Blok X-1, Kav. 1–2, Jakarta Selatan 12950; tel. (21) 5261105; fax (21) 5261108; e-mail info@asi.or.id; internet www.asi.or.id; f. 1969; Chair. URIP TIMURYONO.

Indonesian Coal Mining Association (APBI-ICMA): Menara Kuningan, Lantai 1, Jalan H. R. Rasuna Said, Blok X-7, Kav. 5, Jakarta 12940; tel. (21) 30015935; fax (21) 30015936; e-mail apbi-icma@indo.net.id; internet www.apbi-icma.com; 84 mems; Chair. BOB KAMANDANU; Exec. Dir SUPRIATNA SUHALA.

Indonesian Cocoa Association (ASKINDO): Jalan Pungkur 115, Bandung 40262; tel. (22) 4262235; fax (22) 4214084; e-mail info@askindo.or.id; internet www.askindo.or.id; Chair. ZULHEFI SIKUMBANG.

Indonesian Exporters' Federation: Menara Sudirman, 8th Floor, Jalan Jenderal Sudirman, Kav. 60, Jakarta 12190; tel. (21) 5226522; fax (21) 5203303; Chair. HAMID IBRAHIM GANIE.

Indonesian Food and Beverages Association (GAPMMI): Kantor Pusat Departemen Pertanian, Ground Floor, Lot 2, Jalan Harsono, Rm 3, 224A Ragunan, Pasarminggu, Jakarta 12550; tel. (21) 70322627; fax (21) 7804347; e-mail gapmmi@cbn.net.id; internet www.gapmmi.or.id; f. 1976; 260 mems; Chair. ADHI SISWAJA LUKMAN.

Indonesian Footwear Association (APRISINDO): Gedung Adis Dimension Footwear, Jalan Tanah Abang III/18, Jakarta Pusat 10160; tel. (21) 3447575; fax (21) 3447572; e-mail aprisindo@vision.net.id; internet www.aprisindo.info; 95 mems; Chair. EDDY WIJANARKO; Sec.-Gen. YUDHI KOMARUDIN.

Indonesian Furniture Industry and Handicraft Association (ASMINDO): Jalan Pegambiran 5A, 3rd Floor, Rawamangun Jakarta 13220; tel. (21) 47864028; fax (21) 47864031; e-mail asmindo@indo.net.id; Chair. AMBAR TJAHYONO; Sec.-Gen. TANANGGA KARIM.

Indonesian Nutmeg Exporters' Association: c/o PT Berdirari (Persero) Trading Division, Jalan Yos Sudarso 1, Jakarta; tel. (21) 4301625; e-mail bnuina@indosat.net.id.

Indonesian Palm Oil Producers' Association (GAPKI): Sudirman Park Rukan, Blok B, Jalan K. H. Mas Mansyur 18, Kav. 35, Jakarta 10220; tel. (21) 57943871; fax (21) 57943872; internet www.gapki.or.id; Chair. JOEFLY J. BAHROENY.

Indonesian Precious Metals Association: Galva Bldg, 5th Floor, Jakarta Pusat, Jakarta 10120; tel. (21) 3451202; fax (21) 3812713.

Indonesian Pulp and Paper Association: Jalan Cimandiri 6, Flat I/2, Jakarta 10330; tel. (21) 326084; fax (21) 3140168; Chair. M. MANSUR.

Indonesian Tea Association (ATI): Jalan Polombangkeng 15, Kebayoran Baru, Jakarta; tel. (21) 7260772; fax (21) 7205810; e-mail insyaf@hotmail.com; internet www.indotea.org; Chair. SUGIAT; Gen. Sec. ATIK DHARMADI.

Indonesian Textile Association (API): Panin Bank Centre, 3rd Floor, Jalan Jenderal Sudirman 1, Jakarta Pusat 10270; tel. (21) 7396094; fax (21) 7396341; f. 1974; Sec.-Gen. DANANG D. JOEDONAGORO.

Indonesian Tobacco Association: Jalan H. Agus Salim 85, Jakarta 10350; tel. (21) 3140627; fax (21) 325181; Pres. H. A. ISMAIL.

Masyarakat Perhutanan Indonesia (MPI) (Indonesian Forestry Community): Gedung Manggala Wanabakti, 9th Floor, Wing B, Blok IV, Jalan Jenderal Gatot Subroto, Jakarta Pusat 10270; tel. (21) 5733010; fax (21) 5732564; f. 1974; nine mems; Pres. M. HASAN.

Rubber Association of Indonesia (Gapkindo): Jalan Cideng Barat 62A, Jakarta 10150; tel. (21) 3501510; fax (21) 3500368; e-mail karetind@indosat.net.id; internet www.gapkindo.org; 161 mems; Chair. Drs H. ASRIL SUTAN AMIR; Exec. Dir SUHARTO HONGGOKUSUMO.

UTILITIES

Electricity

PT Perusahaan Listrik Negara (Persero) (PLN): Jalan Trunojoyo, Blok M1/135, Kebayoran Baru, Jakarta Selatan 12160; tel. (21) 7251234; fax (21) 7204929; e-mail kontakkami@pln.co.id; internet www.pln.co.id; state-owned electricity co; Pres. (vacant).

Gas

PT Perusahaan Pertambangan Minyak dan Gas Bumi Negara (PERTAMINA): Jalan Medan Merdeka Timur 1A, Jakarta 10110; tel. (21) 3815111; fax (21) 3843882; e-mail wpurnama@pertamina.com; internet www.pertamina.com; f. 1968; state-owned petroleum and natural gas mining enterprise; Pres. Dir and CEO KAREN AUGUSTIAWAN.

Perusahaan Gas Negara (PGN) (Public Gas Corporation): Jalan K. H. Zainul Arifin 20, Jakarta 11140; tel. (21) 6334838; fax (21) 6333080; e-mail contact.center@pgn.co.id; internet www.pgn.co.id; monopoly of domestic gas distribution; Pres. Dir HENDI PRIO SANTOSO.

Water

PDAM DKI Jakarta (PAM JAYA): Jalan Penjernihan II, Pejompongan, Jakarta 10210; tel. (21) 5704250; fax (21) 5711796; internet www.pamjaya.co.id; f. 1977; responsible for the water supply systems of Jakarta; Pres. Dir HARYADI PRIYOHUTOMO.

PDAM Kodya Dati II Bandung: Jalan Badaksinga 10, Bandung 40132; tel. (22) 2509030; fax (22) 2508063; e-mail pdambdg@elga.net.id; f. 1974; responsible for the water supply and sewerage systems of Bandung; Pres. Dir Ir SOENITIYOSO HADI PRATIKTO.

PDAM Tirtanadi Medan: Jalan Sisingamangaraja 1, Medan 20212; tel. (61) 4571666; fax (61) 4572771; e-mail tirtanadi@pdamtirtanadi.co.id; internet www.pdamtirtanadi.co.id; f. 1979; manages the water supply of Medan and nearby towns and cities; Man. Dir Ir AZZAM RIZAL.

MAJOR COMPANIES

(cap. = capital; res = reserves; m. = million)

State Enterprises

PT Aneka Tambang Tbk: Gedung Aneka Tambang, Jalan Letjen T. B. Simatupang 1, Lingkar Selatan, Tanjung Barat, Jakarta 12530; tel. (21) 7891234; fax (21) 7891224; e-mail corsec@antam.com; internet www.antam.com; f. 1968; 65% state-owned; exploration, mining, processing and marketing of nickel ore, ferro-nickel, bauxite, iron, sand, gold and silver; sales Rp. 8,711,370m. (2009); Pres. Commr WISNU A. MARANTIKA; Pres. Dir ALWIN SYAH LOEBIS; 2,664 employees.

PT Barata Indonesia (Persero): Jalan Veteran 241, Gresik 61123; tel. (31) 3990555; fax (31) 3990666; e-mail info@barata.co.id; internet www.barata.co.id; f. 1971; state-owned; manufacture of heavy construction and industrial equipment; Pres. Dir IMAM KARTONO; 3,500 employees.

PT Boma Bisma Indra (BBI): Jalan K. H. Mas Mansyur 229, Surabaya 60162; tel. (31) 3530513; fax (31) 3531686; e-mail corporate@ptbbi.co.id; internet www.ptbbi.co.id; f. 1971; engineering services and the manufacture of industrial plant equipment; Pres. Dir Dr LALAK INDIYONO; 2,100 employees.

PT Dahana: Jalan Letkol Basir Surya, POB 117, Tasikmalaya 46196, Jawa Barat; tel. (265) 331853; fax (265) 332425; e-mail corporate@dahana.com; internet www.dahana.com; f. 1966; manufacture of dynamite and other industrial explosives and accessories; Pres. Dir TANTO DIRGANTORO.

PT Dirgantara Indonesia (IAe) (Indonesian Aerospace): Gedung GPM, Jalan Pajajaran 154, Bandung 40174; tel. (22) 6054168; fax (22) 6054185; e-mail pub-rel@indonesian-aerospace.com; internet www.indonesian-aerospace.com; f. 1976; fmrly PT Industri Pesawat Terbang Nusantara; name changed as above 2001; aircraft manufacture; Head Commr MARSHAL HERMAN PRAYITNO; Pres. Dir BUDI SANTOSO; 3,720 employees.

INKA: Jalan Yos Sudarso 71, Madiun 63122; tel. (351) 452271; fax (351) 452275; e-mail sekretariat@inka.web.id; internet www.inka.web.id; f. 1981; manufacture of railway rolling stock; cap. Rp. 220,280m., revenue Rp. 577,138.7m. (2009); Pres. Commr Ir SOEMINO EKO SAPUTRO; Pres. Dir Ir ROOS DIATMOKO.

PT Jasa Marga: Plaza Tol Taman Mini, Jalan Tol Jagorawi, Jakarta 13550; tel. (21) 8413630; fax (21) 8413540; e-mail jasmar@jasamarga.com; internet www.jasamarga.com; f. 1978; construction, maintenance and operation of toll roads and bridges; cap. and res Rp. 5,743,266m., sales Rp. 3,353,632m. (2009); Pres. Commr Drs GEMBONG PRIJONO; Pres. Dir Ir FRANS SATYAKI SUNITO; 5,443 employees.

PT Krakatau Steel: Gedung Krakatau Steel, 4th–8th Floors, 54 Jalan Gatot Subroto, Jakarta Selatan 12950; tel. (254) 5207595; fax (254) 5201610; e-mail info@krakatausteel.com; internet www.krakatausteel.com; f. 1971; mfr of metals and metal products; cap. and res Rp. 5,211,656m. (2005), sales Rp. 20,631,431m. (2009); Pres. Commr ZACKY ANWAR MAKARIM; Pres. Dir FAZWAR BUJANG; 7,000 employees.

LEN Industri: Jalan Sukarno Hatta 442, Bandung 40254; tel. (22) 5202682; fax (22) 5202695; e-mail marketing@len.co.id; internet www.len.co.id; f. 1965 as the National Electrotechnics Research Institute, became a state-owned company in 1991; manufactures electronic products and components; Pres. Dir WAHYUDDIN BAGENDA.

PT Mega Eltra: Jalan Menteng Raya 27, Jakarta 10340; tel. (21) 3909018; fax (21) 3102937; e-mail pr@megaeltra.com; internet www.megaeltra.com; f. 1960; building co and trader in cement, pharmaceuticals, chemicals and machinery; Pres. Commr SUDARSANA ERNAWAN; Pres. Dir JOHNY SUDHARMONO; 600 employees.

PT PAL Indonesia (Persero): POB 1134, Ujung, Surabaya 60155; tel. (31) 3292275; fax (31) 3292530; e-mail palsub@pal.co.id; internet www.pal.co.id; f. 1980; shipbuilding and general engineering; Pres. Dir Ir M. M. HARSUSANTO; 3,369 employees.

PT Perhutani (Persero) (State Forest Corporation): Gedung Manggala Wanabakti, Blok IV/Lantai 4, Jalan Gatot Subroto, Senayan, Jakarta Pusat 10270; tel. (21) 5721282; fax (21) 5733616; e-mail corporatesecretary@perumperhutani.com;

internet www.perumperhutani.com; f. 1973; revenue Rp. 2,305,988m. (2008); Pres. Dir Ir ROSALINA WASRIN.

PT Perusahaan Perniaagaan Indonesia (Indonesia Trading Company—ITC): Wisma ITC, Jalan Abdul Muis 8, Jakarta 10160; tel. (21) 3862141; fax (21) 3862143; internet www.tradingindonesia.com; f. 2003; formed by merger between PT Cipta Niaga, PT Pantja Niaga and PT Dharma Niaga in 2003; import, export, trade, distribution and construction of machinery and equipment, steel and metal products; net profit Rp. 38,000m. (2007); Pres. and CEO Dr Ir HEINRYCH NAPITUPULU; 4,000 employees.

PT Petrokimina Gresik: Jalan Jenderal Akhmad Yani, Gresik 61119, East Java; tel. (31) 3981811; fax (31) 3981722; e-mail pkg@petrokimia-gresik.com; internet www.petrokimia-gresik.com; f. 1972; produces fertilizers, ammonia and other related products; cap. and res Rp. 1,426,427m., revenue Rp. 14,372,937m. (2009); Pres. Commr Dr Ir ATO SUPRAPTO; Pres. Dir ARIFIN TASRIF; 3,286 employees.

PT Pindad (Persero): Jalan Jenderal Gatot Subroto 517, Bandung 40284; tel. (22) 7312073; fax (22) 7301222; e-mail info@pindad.com; internet www.pindad.com; manufacture of products for commercial and military markets; Pres. Dir ADI AVIANTO SUDARSONO.

PT Pos Indonesia (Persero): Jalan Anggrek 59, Bandung 40114; tel. (21) 4213640; fax (22) 4219012; e-mail mailopr@posindonesia.co.id; internet www.posindonesia.co.id; f. 1927; provides communication, logistic and financial services; Pres. Commr DADDY HARIADI; Pres. Dir KETUT MARDJANA; 27,000 employees.

PT Pupuk Iskandar Muda: Jalan Medan-Banda Aceh, POB 021, Lhok Seumawe, North Aceh; tel. (645) 56222; fax (645) 56095; e-mail info@pim.co.id; internet www.pim.co.id; f. 1982; produces ammonia and urea; Pres. Commr Ir BENNY WACHYUDI; Pres. Dir Dr MASHUDIANTO; 1,103 employees.

PT Pupuk Sriwwijaya (PT Pusri): Jalan Mayor Zen, Sungai Selayur, Palembang 30118; tel. (711) 712111; fax (711) 712100; e-mail info@pusri.co.id; internet www.pusri.co.id; f. 1959; produces ammonia and urea; sales Rp. 21,402,633m. (2008); Pres. Commr PARIKESIT SUPRAPTO; Pres. Dir Ir ARIFIN TASRIF; 6,000 employees.

PT Semen Gresik (Persero) Tbk: Gedung Utama Semen Gresik, Jalan Veteran, Gresik 61122; tel. (31) 3981732; fax (31) 3983209; e-mail ptsg@sg.sggrp.com; internet www.semengresik.com; f. 1969; cement plant; cap. Rp. 1,840,507m., revenue Rp. 6,767,276m. (2009); Pres. Commr DEDI ADITYA SUMANAGARA; Pres. Dir DWI SOETJIPTO.

PT Tambang Batubara Bukit Asam (Persero) Tbk (PTBA): Jalan Perigi 1, Tanjung Enim, 31716 Sumatra, Selatan; tel. (734) 451096; fax (734) 451095; e-mail ebudhiwijayanto@bukitasam.co.id; internet www.ptba.co.id; f. 1981; merged with Perum Tambang Batubara in 1990; coal-mining; Pres. Commr Dr SUPRIYADI; Pres. Dir Ir SUKRISNO.

PT Timah Tbk: Jalan Jenderal Sudirman 51, Pangkalpinang 33121, Bangka; tel. (717) 4258000; fax (717) 4258080; e-mail corsec@pttimah.co.id; internet www.timah.com; tin-mining; partially privatized in 1995; cap. Rp. 120,792m., revenue Rp. 7,709,856m. (2009); Pres. Commr INSMERDA LEBANG; Pres. Dir WACHID USMAN; 6,723 employees.

Management Board

General Management Board of the State Trading Corporations (BPU-PNN): CTC Bldg, 94 Jalan Kramat Raya, Jakarta; tel. (21) 3901578; fax (21) 3104287; f. 1961; Pres. Col SUHARDIMAN.

Private Companies

Agribusiness

PT Central Proteinaprima: Wisma GKBI, Lantai 19, Jalan Jenderal Sudirman, Jakarta 10210; tel. (21) 57851788; fax (21) 57851808; e-mail rizal.shahab@ccp.co.id; internet www.cpp.co.id; f. 1988; shrimp producer and processor; cap. Rp. 175,114m. (2007), sales Rp. 6,832,754m. (2009); Pres. Commr HARDIAN PURAWIMALA WIDJONARKO; Pres. Dir ERWIN SUTANTO; 6,000 employees.

PT Charoen Pokphand: Jalan Ancol VIII/I, Ancol Barat, Jakarta 14430; tel. (21) 6919999; fax (21) 6907324; e-mail cpi-jkt@cp.co.id; internet cp.co.id; f. 1972; mfr of livestock feeds, poultry farming; cap. Rp. 1,475,875m., sales Rp. 14,559,005m. (2009); Pres. Commr HADI GUNAWAN TJOE; Pres. Dir TJIU THOMAS EFFENDY; 4,186 employees.

PT Japfa Comfeed Indonesia: Graha Praba Samanta, Jalan Daan Mogot 9, Km 12, Jakarta 11730; tel. (21) 5448710; fax (21) 5448709; e-mail info@japfacomfeed.co.id; internet www.japfacomfeed.co.id; f. 1971; mfr of animal feeds, poultry and aquaculture farming; cap. Rp. 2,170,000m., sales Rp. 14,340,000m. (2009); Pres. Dir HANDOJO SANTOSA; Pres. Commr RADITYO HATARI; 10,500 employees.

Food Processing

PT Indofood Sukses Makmur Tbk: Sudirman Plaza, Indifood Tower, 27th Floor, Jalan Jenderal Sudirman, Kav. 76–78, Jakarta 12910; tel. (21) 57958822; fax (21) 57935960; e-mail elly.putranti@indofood.co.id; internet www.indofood.co.id; f. 1971; mfr of food, incl. noodles; cap. Rp. 2,375,776m., sales Rp. 37,140,830m. (2009); Pres. Dir and CEO ANTHONI SALIM; Pres. Commr MANUEL V. PANGILINAN; 66,400 employees.

PT Mayora Indah: Jalan Tomang Raya 21–23, Jakarta 11440; tel. (21) 5655315; fax (21) 5686570; e-mail export@mayora.co.id; internet www.mayora.com; f. 1977; mfr of processed food products; sales Rp. 2,828,400m. (2007); Chair. JOGI HENDRA ATMADJA; 7,000 employees.

PT Medan Tropical Canning and Frozen Industries: Jalan K. L. Yos Sudarso, Km 10.5, Kawasan Industri Medan, Medan 20242, North Sumatra; tel. (61) 6850038; fax (61) 6881973; e-mail sales@indonesiaseafood.com; internet www.indonesiaseafood.com; f. 1984; processing and packaging of seafood; Pres. Dir ABU DJAJA BUNJAMIN; Pres. Commr RUSLI ALI; 1,500 employees.

PT Multi Bintang Indonesia: Talavera Office Park, 20th Floor, Jalan Let. Jenderal, TB Simatupang, Kav. 22-26, Jakarta 12430; tel. (21) 75924611; fax (21) 75924617; e-mail info_mbi@multibintang.co.id; internet www.multibintang.co.id; producer and distributor of alcoholic and non-alcoholic beverages; cap. Rp. 22,872m., sales Rp. 1,616,264m. (2009); Pres. Commr COSMAS BATUBARA; Pres. Dir RICK LINCK; 850 employees.

PT SMART Corporation (Sinar Mas Agro Resources and Technology): BII Plaza, Tower 2, 30th Floor, Jalan M. H. Thamrin 51, Jakarta 10350; tel. (21) 3181288; fax (21) 3181389; e-mail investor@smart-tbk.com; internet www.smart-tbk.com; f. 1962; food and soft drinks mfr and plantation owner (tea, banana, coconut, rubber); subsidiary of Golden Agri-Resources Ltd (Singapore); cap. Rp. 1,597,000m., sales Rp. 14,201,000m. (2009); Pres. Commr MUKTAR WIDJAJA; Pres. Dir JO DAUD DHARSONO; 10,000 employees.

Heavy Equipment

PT Bakrie and Brothers Tbk: Wisma Bakrie 2, 16th–17th Floors, Jalan H. R. Rasuna Said, Kav. B-2, Jakarta 12920; tel. (21) 93633333; fax (21) 5200361; e-mail management@bakrie.co.id; internet www.bakrie-brothers.com; f. 1951; steel and pipe mfr, automotives construction, telecommunications, infrastructure support, etc.; cap. and res Rp. 4,195,120m. (2007), revenue Rp. 7,632,000m. (2009); Pres. Commr IRWAN SJARKAWI; Pres. Dir and CEO BOBBY GAFUR UMAR; 15,000 employees.

PT Komatsu Indonesia: Jalan Raya Cakung, Cilincing Km 4, Jakarta Utara 14140; tel. (21) 4400611; fax (21) 4400615; e-mail risdhianto@komi.co.id; internet www.komi.co.id; f. 1982; mfr of construction and mining equipment; cap. Rp. 192,780m. (Jan. 2006), sales Rp. 789,753m. (2003/04); Pres. Dir HARYANTO BAMBANG; Pres. Commr NOBUKI HASEGAWA; 840 employees.

PT United Tractors Tbk: Jalan Raya Bekasi, Km 22, Cakung, Jakarta 13910; tel. (21) 4605959; fax (21) 4600657; e-mail ir@unitedtractors.com; internet www.unitedtractors.com; f. 1972; 58% owned by Astra International, PT; distributor of heavy equipment; sales Rp. 29,240,000m. (2009); Pres. Commr PRIJONO SUGIARTO; Pres. Dir DJOKO PRANOTO; 8,000 employees.

Mining

PT Adaro Indonesia: Menara Karya, 22nd Floor, Blok X-5, Kav. 1–2, Jalan H. R. Rasuna Said, Jakarta 12950; tel. (21) 5211265; fax (21) 57944687; e-mail marketing@ptadaro.com; internet www.adaro.com; f. 1982; coal mining; cap. Rp. 7,840,833m., sales Rp. 26,938,020m. (2009); Pres. Commr EDWIN SOERYADJAYA; Pres. Dir GARIBALDI THOHIR; 6,000 employees.

PT Berau Coal: 40 Jalan Pemuda, Tanjung Redeb, Berau, East Kalimantan; tel. (554) 23400; fax (554) 23465; e-mail info@beraucoal.co.id; internet www.beraucoal.co.id; f. 1983; coal mining; jt venture between PT Armadian Tritunggal (51%), Rognar Holding B.V. of the Netherlands (39%) and Sojitz Corpn of Japan (10%); Pres. Dir DIDIK CAHYANTO.

PT Freeport Indonesia Co: Plaza 89, 5th Floor, Jalan H. R. Rasuna Said, Kav. X-7/6, Jakarta 12940; tel. (21) 2591818; fax (21) 2591945; internet www.ptfi.co.id; f. 1991; owned by Freeport-McMoRan Copper & Gold Inc (USA); copper, gold and silver mining; Chair. JAMES R. MOFFETT; 16,000 employees.

PT International Nickel Indonesia Tbk: Plaza Bapindo-Citibank Tower, 22nd Floor, Jalan Jenderal Sudirman, Kav. 54–55, Jakarta 12190; tel. (21) 5249000; fax (21) 5249020; e-mail sutedr@inco.com; internet pt-inco.co.id; f. 1968; nickel mining and processing; owned by CVRD Inco Ltd (60.8%), Sumitomo Metal Mining Co, Ltd (20.1%) and Masyarakat (17.9%); sales US $2,325.9m. (2007); Pres. Commr GERD PETER POPPINGA; Pres. Dir TONY WENAS; 3,495 employees.

PT Pamapersada Nusantara (PAMA): Jalan Rawagelam I 9, Jakarta Industrial Estate Pulogadung, Jakarta 13930; tel. (21) 4602015; fax (21) 4601916; e-mail busdev@pamapersada.com;

internet www.pamapersada.com; f. 1989; wholly owned subsidiary of PT United Tractors Tbk; mining contractor managing six coal mines and one gold mine; sales Rp. 3,800,000m. (2004); Pres. Commr DJOKO PRANOTO; Pres. Dir Ir SUDIARSO PRASETIO; 6,000 employees.

Motor Vehicle Assembly

ADR Group: Wisma ADR, Jalan Pluit Raya I, Jakarta 14440; tel. (21) 6690244; fax (21) 6696237; e-mail adr@adr-group.com; internet www.adr-group.com; f. 1973; mfr of motor vehicle parts; Pres. and CEO EDDY HARTONO.

PT Astra-Honda Motor: Jalan Laksda Yos Sudarso, Sunter I, Jakarta Utara 14350; tel. (21) 6518080; fax (21) 6503331; internet www.astra-honda.com; f. 2000; jt venture between PT Astra International Tbk (50%) and PT Honda Motor (50%); mfr of motorcycle parts; engine and body assemblage; cap. Rp. 185,000m. (2003); Gen. Man. DANDY SOELIP; 16,021 employees.

PT Astra International Tbk: Jalan Gaya Motor Raya 8, Sunter II, Jakarta Utara 14330; tel. (21) 6522555; fax (21) 6512058; e-mail purel@ai.astra.co.id; internet www.astra.co.id; f. 1957; car mfr, heavy industry, financial and non-financial services, agribusiness, information technology; cap. US $4,200m. (Dec. 2005), revenue Rp. 98,526,000m. (2009); Pres. Commr BUDI SETIADHARMA; Pres. Dir PRIJONO SUGIARTO; 154 subsidiaries with 126,700 employees.

PT Indomobil Suzuki International Tbk: Wisma Indomobil Lt. 6, Jalan M. T. Haryono, Kav. 8, Jakarta 13330; tel. (21) 8564530; fax (21) 8654833; internet www.indomobil.com; f. 1991; 51% owned by PT Indomobil, 49% owned by Suzuki Motor (Japan); cap. Rp. 635,079,069m., revenue Rp. 8,197,135m. (2008); Pres. Commr SOEBRONTO LARAS; Pres. Dir GUNADI SINDHUWINATA; 4,974 employees.

PT Yamaha Indonesia Motor: Jalan Raya Bekasi Km 23, Pulo Gadung, Jakarta 13920; tel. (21) 24575555; fax (21) 4616995; internet www.yamaha-motor.co.id; f. 1974.

Paper

PT Indah Kiat Pulp and Paper Corpn Tbk: BII Plaza, Menara II, 15th and 18th Floors, Jalan M. H Thamrin 51, Jakarta 10350; tel. (21) 3929266; fax (21) 3926104; e-mail Customer_talk@app.co.id; internet www.ikserang.com; f. 1976; sales Rp. 17,242,000m. (2007); Pres. Commr TEGUH GANDA WIDJAYA; Pres. Dir YUDI SETIAWAN LIN; 15,128 employees.

PT Pabrik Kertas Tjiwi Kimia: Jalan Raya Surabaya, Mojokerto Km 44, Sidoardjo, Jawa Timur; tel. (321) 361552; fax (321) 361615; internet www.tjiwi.co.id; f. 1972; mfr of writing and printing paper, stationery products and general office products; Pres. Dir YUDI SETIAWAN LIN; 13,114 employees.

PT Surabaya Agung Industri Pulp and Kertas: Jalan Kedungdoro 60, 8th–10th Floors, Surabaya 60251; tel. (31) 5482003; fax (31) 5482039; e-mail ird@suryakertas.com; internet www.suryakertas.com; f. 1973; producer of paper and packaging materials; cap. and res Rp. –2,378,231m., sales Rp. 412,976m. (2005); Pres. Commr YOGYO PRANOTO; Pres. Dir TIRTOMULYADI SULISTYO; 1,800 employees.

Petrochemicals

PT Cabot Indonesia: Jalan Salira Raya Desa Sumuranja, Kecamatan Pulo Ampel, Kabupaten Serang, Merak 42455; tel. (254) 5750093; fax (254) 5730310; internet www.cabot-corp.com; fmrly PT Continental Carbon Indonesia; acquired by Cabot in 1996; merged with PT Karbon Indonesia in 2001; production of carbon black; Gen. Man. XINSHENG ZHANG.

PT Eastern Polymer: Jalan Cilincing Raya, Tanjung Priok, North Jakarta; tel. (21) 4301167; fax (21) 496083; jt venture with Mitsubishi Corpn (50%) and PT Anugrah Daya Laksana (50%); production of PVC resin; Pres. Dir MOTONOBU TOKUDA.

PT Standard Toyo Polymer: Wisma Permata Plaza, 9th Floor, Jalan M. H. Thamrin 57, Jakarta 10350; tel. (21) 3903132; fax (21) 3903301; e-mail statomer@indo.net.id; jt venture between Tosoh Corpn (60%) and Mitsui Corpn (40%); production of PVC resin; Pres. KENICHI UDAGAWA.

PT Sulfindo Adiusaha: Panin Tower, 9th Floor, Senayan City, Jalan Asia Afrika, Lot 19, Jakarta 10270; tel. (21) 72781810; fax (21) 72781808; e-mail sulfindo@sulfindo.com; internet www.sulfindo.com; fmrly known as PT Indochlor Prakarsa, name changed as above in 1995; produces caustic soda, hydrochloric acid and liquid chlorine.

PT TITAN Petrokimia Nusantara: Gedung Setiabudi 2, 3rd Floor, Suite 306–307, Jalan H. R. Rasuna Said Kav. 62, Kuningan, Jakarta 12920; tel. (21) 52907008; fax (21) 52907281; e-mail cmlau@pttitan.com; internet www.pttitan.com; fmrly PT Petrokimia Nusantara Interindo; acquired by Indika Group in 2003; in 2006 bought by Titan Chemicals; production of polyethylene; Pres. Commr KEMAL STAMBOEL; Pres. Dir DAVID TSUNG-HUNG CHAO.

PT Tri Polyta Indonesia Tbk: Wisma Barito Pacific, Tower A, 6th Floor, Jalan Letjen S. Parman, Kav. 62–63, Jakarta 11410; tel. (21) 53660600; fax (21) 53660606; e-mail investor-relations@tripolyta.com; internet www.tripolyta.com; production of polypropylene, acrylic acid and acrylic ester; cap. Rp. 991,932m., sales Rp. 4,740,000m. (2009); Pres. Commr PRAJOGO PANGESTU; Pres. Dir IMAN SUCIPTO UMAR; 571 employees.

PT Unggul Indah Cahaya Tbk: Wisma UIC, 2nd Floor, Jalan Jenderal Gatot Subroto, Kav. 6–7, Jakarta 12930; tel. (21) 57905100; fax (21) 57905111; e-mail corp_sect@uic.co.id; internet www.uic.co.id; f. 1983; publicly listed; chemicals mfr and processor; sales US $343.5m. (2008); Pres. Commr ROMEO LLEDO; Pres. Dir YANI ALIFEN; 336 employees.

Pharmaceuticals

PT Darya-Varia Laboratoria Tbk: Talavera Office Park, 8th–10th Floor, Jalan Letjen T. B. Simatupang 22–26, Jakarta 12430; tel. (21) 75924500; fax (21) 75924501; e-mail info@darya-varia.com; internet www.darya-varia.com; f. 1976; mfr of pharmaceuticals and consumer healthcare products; sales Rp. 577,598m. (2008); Pres. Dir MANUEL P. ENGWA; 1,800 employees.

PT Enseval Putera Megatrading Tbk (EPM): Gedung Enseval, Jalan Puto Lentut 10, Kawasan Industri Pulogadung, Jakarta 13920; tel. (21) 46822422; fax (21) 4609039; e-mail investor.relations@enseval.com; internet www.enseval.com; f. 1988; distribution of pharmaceuticals, cosmetics, medical products, consumer products and raw materials; cap. Rp. 1,246,893m., sales Rp. 8,550,127m. (2009); Pres. Commr HERMAN WIDJAJA; Pres. Dir VIDJONGTIUS; 4,307 employees.

PT Kalbe Farma: Jalan M. H. Themrin Blok A3-I, Lippo-Cikarang, Bekasi 17550; tel. (21) 89907333; fax (21) 89907360; e-mail kalbeibd@pacific.net.id; internet www.kalbe.co.id; f. 1966; mfr of healthcare products, pharmaceuticals and veterinary products; sales Rp. 9,087,347m. (2009); Pres. Commr Drs JOHANNES SETIJONO; Pres. Dir BERNADETTE RUTH IRAWATI SETIADY; 10,506 employees.

Merck Indonesia Tbk: Jalan T. B. Simatupang 8, Pasar Rebo, Jakarta 13760; tel. (21) 28565600; fax (21) 28565601; e-mail contact@merck.co.id; internet www.merck.co.id; f. 1970; fmrly PT Merck Indonesia; mfr of pharmaceuticals and medicines; cap. Rp. 39,962m., sales Rp. 751,403m. (2009); Pres. Dir RALF ANNASENTZ; 802 employees.

PT Nellco Indopharma: Jalan Kebon Jeruk 18/6, Jakarta 11160; tel. (21) 6297562; fax (21) 6297753; f. 1963; production of pharmaceutical goods; Pres. Dir RUDY CHANDRA.

PT Surya Hidup Satwa: Jalan Angol Barat Blok A-5E/10, Jakarta 14430; tel. (21) 6909958; fax (21) 6909957; e-mail suryahidup@indoexchange.com; f. 1976; mfr and distribution of veterinary products and animal husbandry equipment; Pres. Dir SUMET JIARAVANON; 13,211 employees (2004).

PT Tempo Scan Pacific Tbk: Gedung Bina Mulia II, 5th Floor, Jalan H. R. Rasuna Said, Kav. 11, Jakarta 12950; tel. (21) 5201858; fax (21) 5201857; e-mail InvestorRelation@thetempogroup.net; f. 1970; part of Tempo Group; mfr of pharmaceutical, personal care and cosmetic products; cap. Rp. 349,457m., sales Rp. 4,497,931m. (2009); Pres. Commr DIAN PARAMITA TAMZIL; Pres. Dir HANDOJO SELAMET MULJADI; 4,600 employees.

PT Unilever Indonesia: Graha Unilever, Jalan Gatot Subroto, Kav. 15, Jakarta 12930; tel. (21) 5262112; fax (21) 5262046; e-mail unvr.indonesia@unilever.com; internet www.unilever.co.id; f. 1933; mfr of personal care and home care products; sales Rp. 18,247,000m. (2009); Pres. Commr JAN ZIJDERVELD; Pres. Dir MAURITS DANIEL RUDOLF LALISANG; 3,900 employees.

Plastics

PT Dinar Makmur Cikarang: Kawasan Jababeka Blok I-2, Cibitung, Bekasi 17530, Jawa Barat; fax (21) 5483412; specializes in styrofoam and air bubble film; Dir ICHWAN HARTONO; 169 employees.

PT Pioneer Plastic Ltd: Jalan Bandengan Utara 43, Jakarta Utara 14440; tel. (21) 6690908; fax (21) 6694431; f. 1954; mfr of plastic hardware products; Pres. PANDJI WISAKSANA; 200 employees.

PT Sinar Panah Industry Co: Jalan Padamulya IV, Gg. Karung 39, Jakarta 11330; tel. (21) 6317947; fax (21) 6318168; f. 1963; Man. HENDRA WIDJAJA.

Rubber

PT Bakrie Sumatera Plantations Tbk: Komplek Rasuna Epicentrum, Bakrie Tower, 18th–19th Floors, Jalan H. R. Rasuna Said, Jakarta 12960; tel. (21) 29941286; fax (21) 29941752; e-mail investor@bakriesumatera.com; internet www.bakriesumatera.com; f. 1911; owner and operator of rubber and oil palm plantations; cap. and res Rp. 2,669,843m., sales Rp. 2,325,282m. (2009); Pres. Commr SOEDJAI KARTASASMITA; Pres. Dir AMBONO JANURIANTO; 14,227 employees.

PT Gajah Tunggal Tbk: Wisma Hayam Wuruk, 10th Floor, Jalan Hayam Wuruk, Kav. 8, Jakarta 10120; tel. (21) 3459302; fax (21) 3804908; e-mail irc-marketing@gt-tires.com; internet www.gt-tires.com; f. 1951; produces automotive tyres; cap. and res Rp. 1,649,425m., sales Rp. 7,963,473m. (2008); Pres. Dir CHRISTOPHER CHAN SIEW CHOONG; 10,521 employees.

PT Goodyear Indonesia: Jalan Pemuda 27, Bogor 16161; tel. (251) 8322071; fax (251) 8328088; e-mail goodyear@indoexchange.com; internet www.goodyear-indonesia.com; f. 1935; mfr of tyres, inner tubes and other related rubber products; revenue Rp. 1,292,819m. (2009); Pres. Commr RICHARD FLEMING; Pres. Dir IRIAWAN IBARAT; 895 employees.

PT Hevea Latex and Rubber Works: Jalan Dr Setiabudhi 276A, Bandung 40143; tel. (22) 211149; fax (22) 212840; f. 1949; mfrs and exporters of sports and other shoes, rubber articles; Dir Ir SUGIRI.

PT Sepatu Bata: Jalan Taman Pahlawan Kalibata, Jakarta 12750; tel. (21) 7992008; fax (21) 7995679; e-mail jakarta@bataindonesia.com; internet www.bata.co.id; f. 1931; mfr of shoes and other footwear products; Chair. G. L. ZANACCO; 2,300 employees.

Textiles

PT Apac Citra Centertex Tbk: Gedung Graha BIP, 10th Floor, Jalan Jenderal Gatot Subroto, Kav. 23, Jakarta 12930; tel. (21) 5258118; fax (21) 5213255; e-mail jati@apac.co.id; f. 1987; mfr of textiles and textile products; Pres. Dir BENNY SOETRISNO; 15,732 employees.

PT Argo Pantes Tbk: Wisma Argo Manunggal, 2nd Floor, Jalan Gatot Subroto 95, Kav. 22, Jakarta 12930; tel. (21) 2521138; fax (21) 2525401; e-mail marketing@amt.co.id; f. 1977; textiles mfr; Pres. Commr SIDIK MURDIONO; Pres. Dir NICHOLAS THE; 4,887 employees.

PT Dan Liris: Kelurahan Banaran, Kecarnatan Grogol, Kabupaten Sukoharjo 57193, Central Java; tel. (271) 714400; fax (271) 717178; e-mail marketing-div@danliris.com; internet www.danliris.com; f. 1974; mfr of garments and integrated textile factory; Pres. Dir HANDIANTO TJOKROSAPUTRO; 18,000 employees.

PT Indorama Synthetics Tbk: Graha Irama, 17th Floor, Jalan H. R. Rasuna Said, Blok X-1, Kav. 1–2, Jakarta 12950; tel. (21) 5261555; fax (21) 5261501; e-mail info@indorama.com; internet www.indorama.com; f. 1974; mfr of polyester products and spun yarns; sales US $490m. (2009); Chair. S. P. LOHIA; 16,000 employees.

PT Panasia Indosyntec: Jalan Garuda 153/74, Bandung 40184; tel. (22) 6034123; fax (22) 6031643; e-mail panafil@panasiagroup.co.id; internet www.panasiagroup.co.id; f. 1973; producer of integrated textiles and selected clothing; Pres. Dir AWONG HIDJAJA; 8,000 employees.

Texmaco Jaya: Sentra Mulia 9th Floor, Suite 901, Jalan H. R. Rasuna Said, Kav. X-6 No. 8, Jakarta 12940; tel. (21) 2520656; fax (21) 2525069; e-mail contacts@texmaco.co.id; internet www.texmaco.com; fmrly Polysindo Eka Perkasa; mfr of raw materials for the textile industry; Pres. Commr ALEXANDER SHAIK; Pres. Dir VASUDEVAN RAVI SHANKAR; 3,464 employees.

Timber

Barito Pacific Tbk: Wisma Barito Pacific, Tower B, 8th Floor, Jalan Jenderal S. Parman, Kav. 62–63, Jakarta 11410; tel. (21) 5306711; fax (21) 5306680; e-mail corpsec@barito.co.id; internet barito-pacific.com; f. 1979; fmrly known as PT Bumi Raya Pura Mas Kalimantan; producer and processor of timber and wood; since 2007 also petrochemical industry and property; revenue Rp. 14,392,940m. (2009); Pres. Commr PRAJOGO PANGESTU; Pres. Dir LOEKI S. PUTERA; 1,686 employees.

PT Daya Sakti Unggul Corporation Tbk: Wisma BSG, 12th Floor, Jalan Abdul Muis 40, Jakarta 10160; tel. (21) 3859000; fax (21) 3505381; e-mail marketing@dsuc.co.id; internet www.dsuc.co.id; f. 1980; mfr of timber; cap. and res Rp. 80,000m., sales Rp. 521,000m. (2004); Pres. Dir BONIFASIUS; 1,806 employees.

PT Surya Dumai Industri Tbk: 7/F, Wisma 77, Jalan S. Parman, Kav. 77, Slipi, Palmerah, Jakarta 11410; tel. (21) 53670888; fax (21) 53671888; e-mail surdumind@indoexchange.com; producer of wood-based products and operator of forest and timber estate concessions; Chair. CITRA GUNAWAN.

PT Toba Pulp Lestari Tbk: Uniplaza East Tower, 7th Floor, Jalan Mt Haryono A-1, Medan 20231; tel. (61) 4532155; fax (61) 4573428; e-mail indorayon@indoexchange.com; internet www.tobapulp.com; f. 1983; fmrly known as PT Inti Indorayon Utama, name changed as above in 2002; mfr of processed wood products; Pres. Dir ROLI ARIFIN; 5,500 employees.

Tobacco

PT Bentoel Prima: Bapindo Plaza, Citibank Tower, 2nd Floor, Jalan Jenderal Sudirman Kav. 54–55, Jakarta 12190; tel. (21) 52919744; fax (21) 5268339; internet www.bentoel.co.id; f. 1930; fmrly known as PT Perusahaan Rokok Tjap Bentoel; mfr of clove cigarettes; sales Rp. 2,996,514m. (2006); Pres. Commr DJOKO MOELJONO; Pres. Dir JEREMY PIKE; 6,500 employees.

PT Gudang Garam Tbk (Perusahaan Rokok Tjap): Jalan Jenderal A. Yani 79, Jakarta 10510; tel. (21) 4202460; fax (21) 4243136; e-mail corporate_secretary@gudanggaramtbk.com; internet www.gudanggaramtbk.com; f. 1973; producer of clove cigarettes; cap. and res Rp. 12,185,883m. (2004), sales Rp. 34,000,000m. (2009); Pres. Commr JUNI SETIAWATI WONOWIDJONO; Pres. Dir SUSILO WONOWIDJONO; 41,000 employees.

PT Hanjaya Mandala Sampoerna Tbk: One Pacific Place, 18th Floor, Sudirman Central Business District, Jalan Jenderal Sudirman, Kav. 52–53, Jakarta; tel. (21) 5151234; fax (21) 5152234; e-mail contact@sampoerna.com; internet www.sampoerna.com; f. 1964; 97% owned by Philip Morris International Inc. (Switzerland); producer of clove cigarettes; cap. and res Rp. 10,462,000m., sales Rp. 38,972,000m. (2009); Pres. Commr MATTEO PELLEGRINI; Pres. Dir JOHN GLEDHILL; 30,000 employees.

Miscellaneous

PT AKR Corporindo Tbk: Wisma AKR, 7th–8th Floor, Jalan Panjang 5, Kebon Jeruk, Jakarta 11530; tel. (21) 5311110; fax (21) 5311388; e-mail suresh@akr.co.id; internet www.akr.co.id; f. 1960; mfr and distributor of industrial chemicals and petroleum products; cap. and res Rp. 1,039,093m., sales Rp. 3,970,323m. (2006); Pres. Commr SOEGIARTO ADIKOESOEMO; Pres. Dir HARYANTO ADIKOESOEMO; 2,000 employees.

PT Asahimas Flat Glass Co Ltd: Jalan Ancol IX/5, Ancol Barat, Jakarta 14430; tel. (21) 6904041; fax (21) 6918709; e-mail corporate-secretary@amfg.co.id; internet www.amfg.co.id; f. 1971; mfr of plate glass and other glass products; cap. and res Rp. 1,486,587m., sales Rp. 1,357,378m. (2007); Pres. Commr TAN PEI LING; Pres. Dir MASATO OE; 2,617 employees.

PT Bayu Buana: Jalan Ir H. Juanda III 2A, Jakarta 10120; tel. (21) 23509999; fax (21) 3517432; e-mail office@bayubuanatravel.com; internet www.bayubuanatravel.com; f. 1972; operator of travel agency, retail and leisure services; Pres. Dir TYRONE KASKAM AWAN; 403 employees.

PT Budi Acid Jaya: Wisma Budi, 8th–9th Floors, Jalan H. R. Rasuna Said, Kav. C-6, Jakarta 12940; tel. (21) 5213383; fax (21) 5213392; e-mail budiacid@centrin.net.id; internet www.budiacidjaya.co.id; f. 1979; mfr and marketer of tapioca starch, sulphuric acid, citric acid and polypropylene woven bags; cap. and res Rp. 626,000m., sales Rp. 1,350,300m. (2007); Pres. Commr WIDARTO; Pres. Dir SANTOSO WINATA; 3,856 employees.

PT Ciputra Development Tbk: Jalan Prof. Dr Satrio, Kav. 6, Karet Kuningan, Jakarta 12940; tel. (21) 5225858; fax (21) 5274125; e-mail investor@ciputra.com; internet www.ciputradevelopment.com; f. 1981; real estate and property development; cap. and res Rp. 1,577,435m., sales Rp. 891,189m. (2005); Pres. Commr Ir CIPUTRA; Pres. Dir CANDRA CIPUTRA; 3,865 employees.

PT Duta Pertiwi Tbk: ITC Mangga Dua, 7th and 8th Floors, Jalan Mangga Dua Raya, Jakarta 14430; tel. (21) 6019788; fax (21) 6017039; e-mail duti@simasred.com; internet www.simasred.com; f. 1972; subsidiary of Sinar Mas Developer and Real Estate (SIMASRED); property and real estate devt and investment; cap. and res Rp. 1,615,708m., sales Rp. 1,209,416m. (2003); Pres. Commr MUKTAR WIDJAJA; Pres. Dir HARRY BUDI HARTANTO; 3,415 employees.

PT Global Mediacom Tbk: Menara Kebon Sirih, 27th Floor, Jalan Kebon Sirih 17–19, Jakarta 10340; tel. (21) 3900310; fax (21) 3909207; e-mail investor.relations@bimantara.co.id; internet www.mediacom.co.id; f. 1981; fmrly PT Bimantara Citra Tbk; holding co with primary interests in advertising and mass media; cap. and res Rp. 2,890,274m., sales Rp. 2,276,788m. (2005); Pres. Commr ROSANO BARACK; Group Pres. and CEO BAMBANG HARY ISWANTO TANOESOEDIBJO; 9,750 employees.

PT Indocement Tunggal Prakarsa Tbk: Wisma Indocement, 8th Floor, Jalan Jenderal Sudirman, Kav. 70–71, Jakarta 12910; tel. (21) 2512121; fax (21) 2510066; e-mail corpsec@indocement.co.id; internet www.indocement.co.id; f. 1985; cement producer; cap. and res Rp. 5,629,000m. (2005), sales Rp. 7,324,000m. (2007); Pres. Commr ALBERT SCHEUER; Pres. Dir DANIEL LAVALLE; 5,858 employees.

PT Jababeka Tbk: Jababeka Centre, Plaza JB Jalan Niaga Raya Kav. 1–4, Kota Jababeka, Cikarang Baru, Bekasi 17550, Jawa Barat; tel. (21) 8934580; fax (21) 89833921; e-mail muljadi@jababeka.com; internet www.jababeka.com; f. 1989; industrial estate development; sales Rp. 375,000m. (2007); Pres. Commr BACELIUS RURU; Pres. Dir SETYONO DJUANDI DARMONO; 542 employees (2006).

PT Matahari Putra Prima Tbk: Menara Matahari, 20th Floor, Jalan Bulevard, Palem Raya 7, Lippo Karawari 12000, Tangerang 15811; tel. (21) 5469333; fax (21) 5475673; e-mail corporate.communication@matahari.co.id; internet www.matahari.co.id;

f. 1986; owner and operator of Indonesia's largest department store chain (81 stores); cap. and res Rp. 3,245,200m., sales Rp. 9,768,100m. (2007); Pres. Commr Dr CHENG CHENG WEN; Pres. Dir BENJAMIN J. MAILOOL; 17,658 employees (Sept. 2007).

PT Modern Internasional Tbk: Jalan Matraman Raya 12, Jakarta 13450; tel. (21) 2801000; fax (21) 8581620; e-mail publicrelation@moderninternasional.co.id; internet www.moderninternasional.co.id; f. 1971; mfr of photography products; fmrly Modern Photo Film Tbk, name changed as above in 2007; Pres. Commr ACHMAD FAUZI HASAN; Pres. Dir SUNGKONO HONORIS; 1,577 employees.

PT Mulialand Tbk: Wisma Mulia, 56th Floor, Jalan Jenderal Gatot Subroto 42, Jakarta 12710; tel. (21) 5200888; fax (21) 5200872; e-mail enquiry@mulialand.com; internet www.mulialand.com; f. 1987; property development and real estate investment, leasing of office blocks and residential apartments; Pres. Dir JOKO SOERGIARTO TJANDRA; 147 employees.

PT Ramayana Lestari Sentosa Tbk: Jalan K. H. Wahid Hasyim, Kav. 220A–B, Jakarta 10250; tel. (21) 3920480; fax (21) 3920484; e-mail corporate@ramayana.co.id; internet www.ramayana.co.id; f. 1983; operator of department stores and supermarkets; revenue Rp. 4,310,395m. (2009); Pres. Commr PAULUS TUMEWU; Pres. Dir AGUS MAKMUR; 17,867 employees.

PT Sinar Mas Multiartha: BII Plaza, Tower III, 7th Floor, Suite 702, Jalan M. H. Thamrin 51, Jakarta 10350; tel. (21) 3925660; fax (21) 3925788; e-mail multiartha@sinarmas.com; internet www.sinarmasmultiartha.com; provides financial services: banking, insurance, financing, capital markets, asset management, share admin., security, information technology; cap. and res Rp. 6,060,797m. (2006), revenue Rp. 8,021,136m. (2008); Pres. Commr INDRA WIDJAJA; Pres. Dir DODDY SUSANTO.

PT Supreme Cable Manufacturing Corporation Tbk: Jalan Daan Mogot km. 16, Jakarta 18265; tel. (21) 6190044; e-mail sales@sucaco.com; internet www.sucaco.com; f. 1970; mfr of cable, metal goods and alloys and plastic products and materials; Pres. Commr ERWIN SURYO RAHARJO; Pres. Dir ELLY SOEPONO; 846 employees.

PT Tigaraksa Satria Tbk: Gedung Tira, Jalan H. R. Rasuna Said, Kav. B3, Jakarta 12920; tel. (21) 5254208; fax (21) 5222422; e-mail tira@tigaraksa.co.id; internet www.tigaraksa.com; f. 1986; distributor of food products, personal care products, household products and garments; cap. and res Rp. 294,056m., sales Rp. 3,567,414m. (2007); Pres. Commr MEITY TJIPTOBIANTORO; Pres. Dir LIANNE WIDJAJA; 1,290 employees.

PT Warna Agung: Gedung Kompleks Delta, Blok C 3–6, Jalan Suryopranoto, Kav. 1–9, Jakarta 10160; tel. (21) 3808711; fax (21) 3809722; e-mail info@warna-agung.com; internet www.warna-agung.com; f. 1969; mfr of paints, emulsions and other related products; Chair. L. MOELJONO; Dir F. SUTADJI; 400 employees.

PT Wicaksana Overseas International Tbk: Jalan Ancol Barat VII, Blok A5D 2, Jakarta 14430; tel. (21) 6927293; fax (21) 6927768; e-mail wicaksana@indoexchange.com; f. 1973; distributor of consumer goods; revenue Rp. 512,321m. (2009); Pres. Dir EDDY SUWANDI; 2,800 employees.

TRADE UNIONS

Konfederasi Serikat Pekerja Seluruh Indonesia (KSPSI) (Confederation of All Indonesian Trades Unions): Jalan Raya Pasar Minggu 9, Km 17, Jakarta Selatan 12740; tel. (21) 7974359; fax (21) 7974361; f. 1973; renamed 2001; sole officially recognized Nat. Industrial Union; 5.1m. mems in June 2005; Gen. Chair. JACOB NUWA WEA; Gen. Sec. LATIEF NASUTION.

Konfederasi Serikat Buruh Sejahtera Indonesia (KSBSI) (Confederation of Indonesia Prosperity Trade Union): Jalan Cipinang Muara Raya 33, Jatinegara, Jakarta Timur 13420; tel. (21) 70984671; fax (21) 8577646; e-mail sbsi@pacific.net.id; internet www.ksbsi.or.id; f. 1998; application for official registration rejected in May 1998; 1,228,875 mems in 168 branches in 27 provinces throughout Indonesia; Pres. REKSON SILABAN; Sec.-Gen. IDIN ROSIDIN.

Transport

Directorate-General of Land Transport and Inland Waterways: Ministry of Transportation, Jalan Medan Merdeka Barat 8, Jakarta 10110; tel. (21) 3502971; fax (21) 3503013; e-mail info@hubdat.web.id; internet www.hubdat.web.id; Dir-Gen. ISKANDAR ABUBAKAR.

RAILWAYS

There are railways on Java, Madura and Sumatra. In 2006 the Japanese Government agreed to provide a US $741m. loan to finance a Mass Rapid Transport (MRT) rail system in Jakarta. Construction was due to commence in early 2011, with completion expected by 2016.

Directorate General of Railways: Ministry of Transportation, Jalan Medan Merdeka Barat 8, Jakarta 10110; tel. (21) 3800349; fax (21) 3860758; e-mail bagrenka_dephub@yahoo.com; internet perkeretaapian.dephub.go.id; Head Ir NUGROHO INDRIO.

PT Kereta Api Indonesia (Persero) (KAI): Jalan Perintis Kermedekaan 1, Bandung 40117; tel. (22) 4230031; fax (22) 4241370; e-mail kontak_pelanggan@kereta-api.co.id; internet www.kereta-api.co.id; six regional offices; transferred to the private sector in 1991; Chief Commr BUDHI MULYAWAN SUYITNO; Chief Dir IGNASIUS JONAN.

ROADS

There is an adequate road network on Java, Sumatra, Sulawesi, Kalimantan, Bali and Madura, but on many of the other islands traffic is by jungle track or river boat. In 2006 Indonesia had a total road length of 393,794 km, of which some 53% was asphalted.

SHIPPING

The four main ports are Tanjung Priok (near Jakarta), Tanjung Perak (near Surabaya), Belawan (near Medan) and Makassar (formerly Ujung Pandang, in South Sulawesi). More than 100 of Indonesia's ports and harbours are classified as capable of handling ocean-going shipping.

Directorate General of Sea Communications: Ministry of Transportation, Jalan Medan Merdeka Barat 8, Jakarta 10110; tel. (21) 3456332; internet www.dephub.go.id/ditlaut; Dir-Gen. SOENTORO.

Indonesian National Ship Owners' Association (INSA): Jalan Tanah Abang III, No. 10, Jakarta Pusat; tel. (21) 3850993; fax (21) 3849522; e-mail info@insa.or.id; internet insa.or.id; Chair. JOHNSON W. SUTJIPTO; Sec.-Gen. BUDHI HALIM.

Shipping Companies

PT Admiral Lines: POB 1476, Jakarta 10014; tel. (21) 4247908; fax (21) 4206267; e-mail admiral@uninet.net.id; f. 1966; fmrly PT Pelayaran Samudera Admiral Lines; Pres. Commr DAUHAN SYAMSURI; Pres. Dir MOCHAMAD SOEGIARTO.

PT Djakarta Lloyd: Jalan Senen Raya 44, Jakarta 10410; tel. (21) 3456208; fax (21) 3441401; internet www.djakartalloyd.co.id; f. 1950; services to USA, Europe, Japan, Australia and the Middle East; Pres. Dir Capt. ADRIAN MARTHIANUS.

PT Karana Line: Wisma Kalimanis, 12th and 13th Floors, Jalan M. T. Haryono, Kav. 33, Jakarta 12770; tel. (21) 7985914; fax (21) 7985913; internet www.karana.co.id; Pres. Dir BAMBANG EDIYANTO.

PT Pelayaran Bahtera Adhiguna (Persero): Jalan Kalibesar Timur 10–12, POB 4313, Jakarta 11110; tel. (21) 6912547; fax (21) 6901450; e-mail pelba@bahteradhiguna.co.id; internet www.bahteradhiguna.co.id; f. 1971; Pres. Commr HASUDUNGAN ARITONANG; Pres. Dir DJOKO TAHONO.

PT Pelayaran Nasional Indonesia (PELNI): Jalan Gajah Mada 14, Jakarta 10130; tel. (21) 6334342; fax (21) 63854130; e-mail humas@pelni.co.id; internet www.pelni.co.id; state-owned; national shipping co; Pres. Commr KALALO NUGROHO; Pres. Dir JUSSABELLA SAHEA.

PT Pertamina (Persero): Downstream Directorate for Shipping, Jalan Yos Sudarso 32–34, POB 14020, Tanjung Priok, Jakarta Utara 14320; tel. (21) 43930325; fax (21) 4370161; e-mail pcc@pertaminashipping.com; internet www.pertaminashipping.com; f. 1959; state-owned; maritime business services; Pres. Dir KAREN AGUSTIAWAN.

PT Perusahaan Pelayaran Gesuri Lloyd: Gesuri Lloyd Bldg, Jalan Tiang Bendera IV/45, Jakarta 11230; tel. (21) 6904000; fax (21) 6925987; e-mail operation_agency@gesuri.co.id; internet www.gesuri.co.id; f. 1963; Pres. Dir ANTONIUS NURIMBA.

PT Perusahaan Pelayaran Nusantara (PANURJWAN): Jalan Raya Pelabuhan Nusantara, POB 2062, Jakarta 10001; tel. (21) 494344; internet www.panurjwan.co.id; Pres. Dir A. J. SINGH.

PT Perusahaan Pelayaran Samudera 'Samudera Indonesia': Jalan Yos Sudarso 1, Blok A1-7, Tanjung Priok, Jakarta 14320; tel. (21) 4301150; fax (21) 43930116; internet www.samudera.com; Chair. SHANTI L. POESPOSOETJIPTO; Pres. Dir MASLI MULIA.

PT Perusahaan Pelayaran Samudera Trikora Lloyd: Graha Satria, 4th Floor, Jalan R. S. Fatmawati 5, Jakarta Selatan, Jakarta 12430; tel. (21) 75915381; fax (21) 75915385; internet www.boedihardjogroup.com/shipping/trikora_lloyd.htm; e-mail tkldir@cbn.net.id; f. 1964; Pres. Dir GANESHA SOEGIHARTO; Man. Dir P. R. S. VAN HEEREN.

CIVIL AVIATION

Sukarno-Hatta Airport, at Cengkareng, serves Jakarta. Other international airports include Ngurah Rai Airport at Denpasar (Bali), Polonia Airport in Medan (North Sumatra), Juanda Airport, near Surabaya (East Java), Sam Ratulangi Airport in Manado (North Sulawesi), Hasanuddin Airport, near Makassar (formerly Ujung Pandang, South Sulawesi) and Frans Kaisepo Airport, in Papua (formerly Irian Jaya). There are numerous other commercial airports. In 2000 the Government announced a policy of liberalization for the airline industry. By January 2005 there were 29 domestic airlines in operation, compared with only five in 2000.

Directorate-General of Civil Aviation: Jalan Medan Merdeka Barat 8, Jakarta Pusat 10110; tel. (21) 3505550; fax (21) 3505139; e-mail hubud@dephub.go.id; internet hubud.dephub.go.id; Dir-Gen. HERRY BAKTI.

PT Batavia Airlines: Jalan Ir H. Juanda 15, Jakarta Pusat 10120; tel. (21) 3864308; fax (21) 3864486; internet www.batavia-air.co.id; f. 2002; scheduled domestic and regional services; Pres. YUDIAWAN TANSARI.

Citilink: Juanda Business Centre, Jalan Juanda 1, Blok C2, Gedangan, Sidoarjo; tel. (31) 8549860; internet www.citilink.co.id; f. 2001; subsidiary of PT Garuda Indonesia; low-cost carrier providing shuttle services between 7 domestic destinations.

Deraya Air Taxi (DRY): Terminal Bldg, 1st Floor, Rm 150/HT, Halim Perdanakusuma Airport, Jakarta 13610; tel. (21) 8093627; fax (21) 8095770; e-mail admderaya@deraya.co.id; internet www.deraya.co.id; f. 1967; scheduled and charter passenger and cargo services to domestic and regional destinations; Pres. Dir SITI RAHAYU SUMADI.

Dirgantara Air Service (DAS): POB 6154, Terminal Bldg, Halim Perdanakusuma Airport, Rm 231, Jakarta 13610; tel. (21) 8093372; fax (21) 8094348; charter services from Jakarta, Barjarmas and Pontianak to destinations in West Kalimantan; Pres. MAKKI PERDANAKUSUMA.

PT Garuda Indonesia: Gedung Garuda Indonesia, Jalan Medan Merdeka Selatan 13, Jakarta 10110; tel. (21) 2311801; fax (21) 2311679; internet www.garuda-indonesia.com; f. 1949; state airline; operates scheduled domestic, regional and international services to destinations in Europe, the USA, the Middle East, Australasia and the Far East; Pres. and CEO EMIRSYAH SATAR; Chair. HADIYANTO.

Lion Air: Lion Air Tower, Jaland Gajah Mada 7, Jakarta Pusat; tel. (21) 63798000; fax (21) 6348744; e-mail info@lionair.co.id; internet www.lionair.co.id; f. 1999; budget carrier providing domestic and international services; Pres. Dir RUSDI KIRANA.

PT Mandala Airlines: Jalan Tomang Raya, Kav. 33–37, Jakarta 11440; tel. (21) 56997000; fax (21) 5663788; e-mail widya@mandalaair.com; internet www.mandalaair.com; f. 1969; privately owned; scheduled regional and domestic passenger and cargo services; Pres. Dir DIONO NURJADIN; CEO WARWICK BRADY.

PT Merpati Nusantara Airlines: Jalan Angkasa, Blok B-15, Kav. 2–3, Jakarta 10720; tel. (21) 6548888; fax (21) 6540620; e-mail marketing@merpati.co.id; internet www.merpati.co.id; f. 1962; subsidiary of PT Garuda Indonesia; domestic and regional services to Australia and Malaysia; Chair. GUNAWAN KOSWARA; Pres. Dir SARDJONO JHONY TJITROKUSUMO.

Pelita Air Service: Jalan Abdul Muis 52–56A, Jakarta 10160; tel. (21) 2312030; fax (21) 2312216; e-mail humas@pelita-air.com; internet www.pelita-air.com; f. 1970; subsidiary of state oil co Pertamina; domestic scheduled and charter passenger and cargo services; Pres. Dir ANDJAR WIBAWANUN.

Premiair: Halim Perdanakusuma Airport Terminal Bldg, Ground Floor, Jakarta 13610; tel. (21) 8091255; fax (21) 8002060; e-mail sales@flypremiair.com; internet www.flypremiair.com; f. 1989; domestic and international charter services; CEO Capt. ARI DARYATA SINGGIH.

Sriwijaya Air: No. 68, Blok C, 15–16, Jalan Pangeran Jayakarta, Jakarta; tel. (21) 6396006; internet www.sriwijayaair-online.com; f. 2003; domestic services; Dir CHANDRA LIE.

Wings Abadi Airlines (Wings Air): Lion Air Tower, Jalan Gajah Mada 7, Jakarta Pusat; tel. (21) 6326039; fax (21) 6348744; f. 2003; subsidiary co of Lion Air; budget carrier providing scheduled domestic passenger services.

Tourism

Indonesia's tourist industry is based mainly on the islands of Java, famous for its volcanic scenery and religious temples, and Bali, renowned for its scenery and Hindu/Buddhist temples and religious festivals. Lombok, Sumatra and Sulawesi are also increasingly popular. Domestic tourism within Indonesia has also increased significantly. Revenue from tourism (including passenger transport) was an estimated US $8,150m. in 2008. The average per caput expenditure rose from US $971.0 in 2007 to $1,178.5 in 2008. The number of tourist arrivals exceeded 6.3m. in 2009.

Indonesia Tourism Promotion Board: Wisma Nugra Santana, 9th Floor, Jalan Jenderal Sudirman 8, Jakarta 10220; tel. (21) 5704879; fax (21) 5704855; e-mail itpb@cbn.net.id; private body; promotes national and international tourism; Chair. PONTJO SUTOWO; CEO GATOT SOEMARTONO.

Defence

As assessed at November 2010, the total strength of the armed forces was an estimated 302,000: army 233,000, navy 45,000, and air force 24,000; paramilitary forces comprised some 280,000, including a police 'mobile brigade' of 14,000 and an estimated 40,000 trainees of KAMRA (People's Security). Reserve forces numbered 400,000. Military service, which is selective, lasts for two years. In support of international peace-keeping efforts, 1,324 Indonesian troops were stationed in Lebanon in November 2010 and 175 in the Democratic Republic of Congo.

Defence Expenditure: Estimated at Rp. 60,000,000m. for 2011.

Commander-in-Chief of the Armed Forces: Gen. AGUS SUHARTONO.

Chief of Staff of the Army: Gen. PRAMONO EDHIE WIBOWO.

Chief of Staff of the Navy: Adm. SOEPARNO.

Chief of Staff of the Air Force: Air Marshal IMAM SUFAAT.

Education

Education is administered mainly by the Ministry of National Education, but the Ministry of Religious Affairs also operates Islamic religious schools (*madrasahs*) at the primary level.

Primary education, beginning at seven years of age and lasting for six years, was made compulsory in 1987. In 1993 it was announced that compulsory education was to be expanded to nine years. Secondary education begins at 13 years of age and lasts for a further six years, comprising three years of junior secondary education and a further three years of senior secondary education. A further three years of academic level or five years of higher education may follow. In May 2010 the Government announced plans to implement compulsory 12-year education for all Indonesian children by 2014.

In 2008/09 there were 26,984,824 pupils enrolled at 144,228 primary schools, 8,992,619 pupils enrolled at 28,777 general junior secondary schools, and 3,857,245 pupils at 10,762 general senior secondary schools. Enrolment at primary level in 2007/08 included 96% of pupils in the relevant age group (males 97%; females 94%); enrolment at secondary level in the same year included 68% of children in the relevant age group (males 69%, females 68%). Vocational subjects have been introduced in the secondary schools. There were 3,095,704 pupils at 7,592 vocational senior secondary schools in 2008/09. In the same year there were 2,975 tertiary institutions, with enrolment totalling 4,281,695. In 2005/06 enrolment was equivalent to 17% of the relevant population. The Government's budget for 2009 allocated Rp. 244,440,000m., representing 20% of total expenditure, to education.

Bibliography

General

Bigalke, Terence W. *Tana Toraja: A Social History of an Indonesian People.* Singapore, Singapore University Press, 2005.

Cribb, Robert. *Historical Dictionary of Indonesia.* Metuchen, NJ, Scarecrow Press, 1992.

Historical Atlas of Indonesia. Richmond, Curzon Press, 2000.

Ford, Michele, and Parker, Lyn (Eds). *Women and Work in Indonesia.* London, Routledge, 2007.

Hazra, Kanai Lal. *Indonesia: Political History and Hindu and Buddhist Cultural Influences.* New Delhi, Decent Books, 2007.

O'Shaughnessy, Kate. *Gender, State and Social Power in Contemporary Indonesia: Divorce and Marriage Law.* Abingdon, Routledge, 2009.

Robinson, Kathryn. *Gender, Islam and Democracy in Indonesia.* London, Routledge, 2007.

Taylor, Jean Gelman. *Indonesia: Peoples and Histories.* New Haven, CT, Yale University Press, 2004.

History and Politics

Abdullah, Taufik. *Indonesia: Towards Democracy.* Singapore, Institute of Southeast Asian Studies, 2008.

Ananta, Aris. *The Indonesian Crisis: A Human Development Perspective.* Singapore, Institute of Southeast Asian Studies, 2002.

Ananta, Aris, Arifin, Evi Nurvidya, and Suryadinata, Leo. *Indonesian Electoral Behaviour: A Statistical Perspective.* Singapore, Institute of Southeast Asian Studies, 2004.

Emerging Democracy in Indonesia. Singapore, Institute of Southeast Asian Studies, 2005.

Ananta, Aris, and Lee Poh Onn (Eds). *Aceh: A New Dawn.* Singapore, Institute of Southeast Asian Studies, 2007.

Antlöv, Hans, and Cederroth, Sven. *Elections in Indonesia: The New Order and Beyond.* London and New York, RoutledgeCurzon, 2004.

Aspinall, Edward. *Opposing Suharto: Compromise, Resistance, and Regime Change in Indonesia.* Stanford, CA, Stanford University Press, 2005.

Islam and Nation: Separatist Rebellion in Aceh, Indonesia. Stanford, CA, Stanford University Press, 2009.

Aspinall, Edward, and Fealy, Greg (Eds). *Local Power and Politics in Indonesia: Decentralization and Democratization.* Singapore, Institute of Southeast Asian Studies, 2003.

Aspinall, Edward, and Mietzner, Marcus (Eds.) *Problems of Democratisation in Indonesia: Elections, Institutions and Society.* Singapore, Institute of Southeast Asian Studies, 2010.

Assyaukanie, Luthfi. *Islam and the Secular State in Indonesia.* Singapore, Institute of Southeast Asian Studies, 2009.

Banyu, Anak Agung. *Indonesia and the Modern World: Between Islam and Secularism in the Foreign Policy of Soeharto and Beyond.* Honolulu, HI, University of Hawaii Press, 2006.

Barton, Greg. *Abdurrahman Wahid: Muslim Democrat, Indonesian President.* Sydney, University of New South Wales Press, 2002.

Jemaah Islamiyah: Radical Islamism in Indonesia. Singapore, Singapore University Press, 2005.

Baüchler, Birgit. *Reconciling Indonesia: Grassroots Agency for Peace.* Abingdon, Routledge, 2009.

Bertrand, Jacques. *Nationalism and Ethnic Conflict in Indonesia.* New York, Cambridge University Press, 2004.

Beittinger-Lee, Verena. *(Un) Civil Society and Political Change in Indonesia: A Contested Arena.* Abingdon, Routledge, 2009.

Blackburn, Susan. *Women and the State in Modern Indonesia.* Cambridge, Cambridge University Press, 2004.

Blackburn, Susan, Smith, Bianca, and Syamsiyatun, Siti (Eds). *Indonesian Islam in a New Era: How Women Negotiate their Muslim Identities.* Singapore, Institute of Southeast Asian Studies, 2008.

Bourchier, David. *Illiberal Democracy in Indonesia.* Abingdon, Routledge, 2009.

Bowen, John R. *Islam, Law, and Equality in Indonesia.* Cambridge, Cambridge University Press, 2003.

Bräuchler, Birgit (Ed.). *Reconciling Indonesia: Grassroots Agency for Peace.* Abingdon, Routledge, 2011.

Bresnan, John. *Indonesia: The Great Transition.* Rowman & Littlefield, Lanham, MD, 2006.

Bünte, Marco, and Ufen, Andreas (Eds). *Democratization in Post-Suharto Indonesia.* Abingdon, Routledge, 2009.

Bush, Robin. *Islam and Civil Society in Indonesia: The Case of the Nahdlatul Ulama.* Singapore, Institute of Southeast Asian Studies, 2005.

Nahdlatul Ulama and the Struggle for Power Within Islam and Politics in Indonesia. Singapore, Institute of Southeast Asian Studies, 2009.

Butt, Simon. *Corruption and Law in Indonesia.* Abingdon, Routledge, 2011.

Cammack, Mark E., and Feener, R. Michael (Eds). *Islamic Law in Contemporary Indonesia: Ideas and Institutions.* Cambridge, MA, Harvard University Press, 2007.

Carnegie, Paul J. *The Road from Authoritarianism to Democratization in Indonesia.* Basingstoke, Palgrave Macmillan, 2010.

Chauvel, Richard. *Essays on West Papua.* Clayton, Vic, Monash Asia Institute, 2003.

Choi, Nankyung. *Local Politics in Indonesia: Pathways to Power.* Abingdon, Routledge, 2011.

Coppel, Charles A. (Ed.) *Violent Conflicts in Indonesia: Analysis, Representation, Resolution.* Abingdon, Routledge, 2011.

Cribb, Robert, and Brown, Colin. *Modern Indonesia: A History Since 1945.* London, Longman, 1995.

Crouch, Harold. *Political Reform in Indonesia after Soeharto.* Singapore, Institute of Southeast Asian Studies, 2010.

Davidson, Jamie S., and Henley, David (Eds). *The Revival of Tradition in Indonesian Politics: The Deployment of Adat from Colonialism to Indigenism.* Abingdon, Routledge, 2007.

Davies, Matt. *Indonesia's War over Aceh.* Abingdon, Routledge, 2006.

Eklöf, Stefan. *Indonesian Politics in Crisis: The Long Fall of Suharto 1996–98.* Copenhagen, Nordic Institute of Asian Studies, 1999.

Power and Political Culture in Suharto's Indonesia: The Indonesian Democratic Party and Decline of the New Order (1986–98). Copenhagen, Nordic Institute of Asian Studies, 2003.

Eliraz, Giora. *Islam in Indonesia: Modernism, Radicalism and the Middle East Dimension.* Brighton, Sussex Academic Press, 2004.

Elson, R. E. *Suharto: A Political Biography.* Cambridge, Cambridge University Press, 2008.

The Idea of Indonesia: A History. Cambridge, Cambridge University Press, 2008.

Fealy, Greg, and White, Sally (Eds). *Expressing Islam: Religious Life and Politics in Indonesia.* Singapore, Institute of Southeast Asian Studies, 2008.

Federspiel, Howard M. *Indonesian Muslim Intellectuals of the Twentieth Century.* Singapore, Institute of Southeast Asian Studies, 2006.

Graf, Arndt, Schröter, Susanne, and Wieringa, Edwin (Eds). *Aceh—History, Politics and Culture.* Singapore, Institute of Southeast Asian Studies, 2010.

Hadiwinata, Bob S. *The Politics of NGOs in Indonesia: Developing Democracy and Managing a Movement.* London, RoutledgeCurzon, 2002.

Hadiz, Vedi. *Localizing Power in Post-Authoritarian Indonesia: A Southeast Asia Perspective.* Stanford, CA, Stanford University Press, 2010.

Hadiz, Vedi, and Dhakidae, Daniel (Eds). *Social Science and Power in Indonesia.* Singapore, Institute of Southeast Asian Studies, 2005.

Hedman, Eva-Lotta E. *Conflict, Violence, and Displacement in Indonesia.* Ithaca, NY, Cornell University Press, 2008.

Herring, Bob. *Soekarno: Founding Father of Indonesia, 1901–1945.* Leiden, KITLV Press, 2002.

Heryanto, Ariel. *State Terrorism and Political Identity in Indonesia.* Abingdon, Routledge, 2008.

Hidayat, Syarif, and Carunia, Mulya Firdausy. *Beyond Regional Autonomy: Local State-Elites' Perspectives on the Concept and Practice of Decentralisation in Contemporary Indonesia.* Pustaka Quantum, Jakarta, Indonesia, 2003.

Hill, David T., and Sen, Krishna (Eds). *Politics and the Media in Twenty-First Century Indonesia: Decade of Democracy.* Abingdon, Routledge, 2010.

Hilmy, Masdar. *Islamism and Democracy in Indonesia: Piety and Pragmatism.* Singapore, Institute of Southeast Asian Studies, 2010.

Holtzappel, Coen J. G., and Ramstedt, Martin (Eds). *Decentralization and Regional Autonomy in Indonesia: Implementation and Challenges.* Singapore, Institute of Southeast Asian Studies, 2010.

Honna, Jun. *Military and Democracy in Indonesia.* London, RoutledgeCurzon, 2002.

Hosen, Nadirsyah. *Shari'a and Constitutional Reform in Indonesia.* Singapore, Institute of Southeast Asian Studies, 2007.

Hull, Terence H. *People, Population, and Policy in Indonesia.* Singapore, Institute of Southeast Asian Studies, 2005.

Hunter, Helen-Louise. *Sukarno and the Indonesian Coup: The Untold Story.* Westport, Praeger Security International, 2007.

Huxley, Tim. *Disintegrating Indonesia?: Implications for Regional Security.* Abingdon, Routledge, 2005.

Kingsbury, Damien. *Peace in Aceh: A Personal Account of the Helsinki Peace Process.* Jakarta, Equinox Publishing, 2006.

Kingsbury, Damien (Ed.). *The Presidency of Abdurrahman Wahid: An Assessment After the First Year.* Clayton, Vic, Monash Asia Institute, 2001.

Power Politics and the Indonesian Military. London, RoutledgeCurzon, 2003.

Kingsbury, Damien, and Aveling, Harry (Eds). *Autonomy and Disintegration in Indonesia.* London, RoutledgeCurzon, 2002.

Kivimaki, Timo. *US-Indonesian Hegemonic Bargaining: Strength or Weakness?* Aldershot, Ashgate, 2003.

Laffan, Michael F. *Islamic Nationhood and Colonial Indonesia: The Umma Below the Winds.* London, RoutledgeCurzon, 2003.

Lane, Max. *Catastrophe in Indonesia.* London, Seagull Books, 2010.

Latif, Yudi. *Indonesian Muslim Intelligentsia and Power.* Singapore, Institute of Southeast Asian Studies, 2008.

Lukens-Bull, Ronald. *A Peaceful Jihad: Negotiating Identity and Modernity in Muslim Java.* Basingstoke, Palgrave Macmillan, 2005.

McIntyre, Angus. *Indonesian Presidency: The Shift From Personal Toward Constitutional Rule.* Lanham, MD, Rowman and Littlefield Publishers, 2005.

McLeod, Ross, and MacIntyre, Andrew (Eds) *Indonesia: Democracy and the Promise of Good Governance.* Singapore, Institute of Southeast Asian Studies, 2007.

Mietzner, Marcus. *Military Politics, Islam, and the State in Indonesia: From Turbulent Transition to Democratic Consolidation.* Singapore, Institute of Southeast Asian Studies, 2009.

Missbach, Antje. *Separatist Conflict in Indonesia: The Long-Distance Politics of the Acehnese Diaspora.* Abingdon, Routledge, 2011.

Monfries, John (Ed.). *Different Societies, Shared Futures: Australia, Indonesia and the Region.* Singapore, Institute of Southeast Asian Studies, 2006.

Nguyen, Thang D. (Ed.). *The Indonesian Journey: A Nation's Quest for Democracy, Stability and Prosperity.* Hauppauge, NY, Nova Science Publishers, 2010.

O'Rourke, Kevin. *Reformasi: The Struggle for Power in Post-Soeharto Indonesia.* Crow's Nest, NSW, Allen and Unwin, 2002.

Perwita, Anak Agung Banyu. *Indonesia and the Muslim World: Between Islam and Secularism in the Foreign Policy of Soeharto and Beyond.* Copenhagen, Nordic Institute of Asian Studies, 2007.

Picard, Michel, and Madinier, Rémy (Eds). *The Politics of Religion in Indonesia: Syncretism, Orthodoxy, and Religious Contention in Java and Bali.* Abingdon, Routledge, 2011.

Platzdasch, Bernhard. *Islamism in Indonesia: Politics in the Emerging Democracy.* Singapore, Institute of Southeast Asian Studies, 2009.

Priyono, A. E., et al. *Making Democracy Meaningful—Problems and Options in Indonesia.* Singapore, Institute of Southeast Asian Studies, 2007.

Reid, Anthony J. S. *An Indonesian Frontier: Acehnese and other Histories of Sumatra.* Honolulu, HI, University of Hawaii Press, 2006.

To Nation by Revolution: Indonesia in the 20th Century. Singapore, Singapore University Press, 2011.

Reid, Anthony J. S. (Ed.). *Verandah of Violence: The Background to the Aceh Problem.* Singapore, Singapore University Press, 2006.

Ricklefs, M. C. *A History of Modern Indonesia since c. 1200.* Basingstoke, Hampshire, Palgrave Macmillan, 4th Edn, 2008.

Rinakit, Sukardi. *The Indonesian Military After the New Order.* Singapore, Institute of Southeast Asian Studies, 2005.

Robinson, Kathryn, and Bessell, Sharon (Eds). *Women in Indonesia: Gender, Equity and Development.* Singapore, Institute of Southeast Asian Studies, 2002.

Robison, Richard, and Hadiz, Vedi (Eds). *Reorganising Power in Indonesia: The Politics of Oligarchy in an Age of Markets.* London, RoutledgeCurzon, 2004.

Rosser, Andrew. *The Politics of Liberalization in Indonesia: State, Market and Power.* Richmond, Curzon Press, 2001.

Salim, Arskal, and Azra, Azyumardi (Eds). *Shari'a and Politics in Modern Indonesia.* Singapore, Institute of Southeast Asian Studies, 2002.

Saltford, John. *The United Nations and the Indonesian Takeover of West Papua, 1962–1969: The Anatomy of a Betrayal.* Richmond, Curzon Press, 2002.

Schwarz, Adam. *A Nation in Waiting: Indonesia in the 1990s.* St Leonards, NSW, Allen and Unwin, 1994.

Indonesia: The 2004 Election and Beyond. Singapore, Institute of Southeast Asian Studies, 2004.

Sebastian, Leonard. *Realpolitik Ideology: Indonesia's Use of Military Force.* Singapore, Institute of Southeast Asian Studies, 2005.

Sen, Krishna, and Hill, David T. *Internet and Democracy in Indonesia.* London, RoutledgeCurzon, 2003.

Sidel, John T. *Riots, Pogroms, Jihad: Religious Violence in Indonesia.* Ithaca, NY, Cornell University Press, 2006.

Singh, Bilveer. *Papua: Geopolitics and the Quest for Nationhood.* Piscataway, NJ, Transaction Publishers, 2008.

Steele, Janet. *Wars Within: The Story of Tempo, an Independent Magazine in Soeharto's Indonesia.* Singapore, Institute of Southeast Asian Studies, 2005.

Sulistiyanto, Priyambudi. *Reconciliation in Post-Suharto Indonesia.* Abingdon, Routledge, 2009.

Suryadinata, Leo. *Elections and Politics in Indonesia.* Singapore, Institute of Southeast Asian Studies, 2001.

Indonesia's Foreign Policy Under Suharto: Aspiring to International Leadership. New York, Marshall Cavendish Academic, 2005.

Interpreting Indonesian Politics. New York, Marshall Cavendish Academic, 2005.

Suryadinata, Leo, et al (Eds). *Indonesia's Population: Ethnicity and Religion in a Changing Political Landscape.* Singapore, Institute of Southeast Asian Studies, 2003.

Tamara, Nasir. *Indonesia Rising: Islam, Democracy and the Rise of Indonesia as a Major Power.* Singapore, Select Publishing, 2009.

Tomsa, Dirk. *Party Politics and Democratization in Indonesia: Golkar in the Post-Suharto Era.* Abingdon, Routledge, 2007.

van Klinken, Geert Arend. *Communal Violence and Democratization in Indonesia: Small Town Wars.* New York, NY, Routledge, 2007.

van Klinken, Geert Arend, and Nordholt, Henk Schulte (Eds). *Renegotiating Boundaries: Local Politics in Post-Suharto Indonesia.* Leiden, KITLV Press, 2007.

van Klinken, Gerry. *Communal Violence and Democratization in Indonesia—Small Town Wars.* Abingdon, Routledge, 2009.

Vickers, Adrian. *A History of Modern Indonesia.* Cambridge, Cambridge University Press, 2005.

Wadley, Reed L. (Ed.). *Histories of the Borneo Environment: Economic, Political and Social Dimensions of Change and Continuity.* Singapore, Institute of Southeast Asian Studies, 2006.

Widjojo, Muridan S. (Ed.) *Papua Road Map: Negotiating the Past, Improving the Present and Securing the Future.* Singapore, Institute of Southeast Asian Studies, 2010.

Yudhoyono, Susilo Bambang. *Indonesia: The Challenge of Change.* Singapore, Institute of Southeast Asian Studies, 2005.

Ziegenhain, Patrick. *The Indonesian Parliament and Democratization.* Singapore, Institute of Southeast Asian Studies, 2008.

Economy

Alishahbana, Armida S., and Brodjonegoro, Bambang B. S. (Eds). *Regional Development in the Era of Decentralization: Growth, Poverty, and the Environment.* University of Padjadjaran (UNPAD) Press, Bandung, Indonesia, 2004.

Ananta, Aris, Soekarni, Muljana, and Arifin, Sjamsul (Eds). *The Indonesian Economy: Entering a New Era.* Singapore, Institute of Southeast Asian Studies, 2011.

Basri, M. Chatib, and Van Der Eng, Pierre (Eds). *Business in Indonesia: New Challenges, Old Problems.* Singapore, Institute of Southeast Asian Studies, 2004.

Bird, Kelly, Cuthbertson, Sandy, and Hill, Hal. *Making Trade Policy in a New Democracy After a Deep Crisis: Indonesia.* Canberra, Australian National University, Research School of Pacific and Asian Studies, 2007.

Chandra, Alexander C. *Indonesia and the ASEAN Free Trade Agreement: Nationalists and Regional Integration Strategy.* Lanham, MD, Lexington Books, 2008.

Chua, Christian. *Chinese Big Business in Indonesia: The State of Capital.* Abingdon, Routledge, 2009.

Collins, Elizabeth Fuller. *Indonesia Betrayed: How Development Fails.* Honolulu, HI, University of Hawaii Press, 2007.

Dick, Howard, et al. *The Emergence of a National Economy: An Economic History of Indonesia, 1800–2000.* Honolulu, University of Hawaii Press, 2002.

Djiwandono, J. Soedradjad. *Bank Indonesia and the Crisis: An Insider's View.* Singapore, Institute of Southeast Asian Studies, 2005.

Glassburner, Bruce (Ed.). *The Economy of Indonesia: Selected Readings.* Jakarta, Equinox Publishing, 2007.

Hill, Hal. *The Indonesian Economy.* Cambridge, Cambridge University Press, 2000.

Leinbach, Thomas (Ed.). *The Indonesian Rural Economy: Mobility, Work and Enterprise.* Singapore, Institute of Southeast Asian Studies, 2003.

Manning, Chris, and Sumarto, Sudarno (Eds). *Employment, Living Standards and Poverty in Contemporary Indonesia.* Singapore, Institute of Southeast Asian Studies, 2011.

Matsumoto, Yasuyuki. *Financial Fragility and Instability in Indonesia.* Abingdon, Routledge, 2007.

Pepinsky, Thomas B. *Economic Crises and the Breakdown of Authoritarian Regimes: Indonesia and Malaysia in Comparative Perspective.* New York, Cambridge University Press, 2009.

Ramstetter, Eric D., and Sjöholm, Frederik. *Multinational Corporations in Indonesia and Thailand.* Basingstoke, Palgrave Macmillan, 2006.

Resosudarmo, Budy P. (Ed.). *The Politics and Economics of Indonesia's Natural Resources.* Baltimore, MD, Johns Hopkins University Press, 2008.

Resosudarmo, Budy P., and Jotzo, Frank (Eds). *Working with Nature against Poverty: Development, Resources and the Environment in Eastern Indonesia.* Singapore, Institute of Southeast Asian Studies, 2009.

Strauss, John, et al. *Indonesian Living Standards: Before and After the Financial Crisis.* Singapore, Institute of Southeast Asian Studies, 2004.

Thee Kian Wie (Ed.). *Recollections: The Indonesian Economy, 1950s–1990s.* Singapore, Institute of Southeast Asian Studies, 2003.

Titus, Milan J., and Burgers, Paul P. M. (Eds). *Rural Livelihoods, Resources and Coping with Crisis in Indonesia: A Comparative Study.* Singapore, Institute of Southeast Asian Studies, 2009.

Turner, Mark, et al. *Decentralization in Indonesia: Redesigning the State.* Canberra, Australian National University, 2003.

JAPAN

Physical and Social Geography

JOHN SARGENT

The archipelago comprising Japan, or Nihon Koku (Land of the Rising Sun), lies to the east of the Asian mainland in an arc stretching from latitude 45° N to latitude 24° N, covering a land area of 377,944 sq km (145,925 sq miles). The Tsushima Strait, which separates Japan from Korea, is about 190 km wide, while 800 km of open sea lie between Japan and the nearest point on the coast of the Chinese mainland. Four large and closely grouped islands—Hokkaido, Honshu, Shikoku and Kyushu—constitute 98% of the territory of Japan, the remainder being made up by numerous smaller islands.

PHYSICAL FEATURES

The Japanese islands belong to a belt of recent mountain-building, which extends around the rim of the Pacific Ocean and which is characterized by frequent volcanic activity and crustal movement. Around the fringes of the western Pacific, this belt takes the form of a complex series of island arcs, stretching southwards from the Aleutians and including Japan. In the Japanese islands, the Kurile, Kamchatka, Bonin, Ryukyu and Korean arcs converge. Where two or more of these major arcs meet, as in Hokkaido and in central Honshu, conspicuous knots of highland occur. In the latter area, the Japan Alps, which rise to more than 3,000 m above sea-level, form the highest terrain in the country, although the highest single peak, Mt Fuji (3,776 m), is an extinct volcano unrelated to the fold mountains of the Alps.

Three major zones of active volcanoes and hot springs occur: in Hokkaido, in northern and central Honshu, and in southern Kyushu. Further evidence of crustal instability is provided by the occurrence, each year, of more than 1,000 earth tremors. Earthquakes strong enough to cause damage to buildings are less frequent. In 1995 the Great Hanshin earthquake, commonly referred to as the Kobe earthquake, caused the loss of 6,433 lives. Measuring 7.2 on the scale of magnitude, this was the most serious earthquake to strike the country since the Great Kanto earthquake of 1923, in which approximately 140,000 people died. In March 2011 Japan was struck by what was thought to be the worst earthquake in its history, measured at 9.0. With its epicentre in the Pacific Ocean off the north-east coast of Honshu, the Great East Japan earthquake, as it became known, gave rise to a devastating tsunami; more than 23,000 Japanese were killed or listed as missing following the disaster.

While the major arcs determine the basic alignment of the main mountain ranges, complex folding and faulting has resulted in an intricate mosaic of landform types, in which rugged, forested mountains alternate with small pockets of intensively cultivated lowland.

In the mountains, short, fast-flowing torrents, fed by melt-water in the spring and by heavy rains in the summer, have shaped a landscape that is characterized by steep and sharply angled slopes. Narrow, severely eroded ridges predominate and rounded surfaces are rare. Although the mountain torrents provide many opportunities for the generation of hydroelectric power, marked seasonal changes in precipitation cause wide fluctuations in the rate of flow, and consequently hinder the efficient operation of hydroelectric plant throughout the year.

The extreme scarcity of level land is one of the salient features of the geography of Japan. Only about 12% of the total land area was cultivated in 2005. Thus, the small areas of lowland, which contain not only most of the cultivated land but also all the major concentrations of population and industry, are of vital importance.

Most Japanese lowlands consist of small coastal plains which have been formed through the regular deposition of river-borne alluvium. On encountering the low-lying land of the coastal plain, the typical torrent becomes a slow river, which meanders across the gently sloping surface of the plain, to terminate in a shallow estuary. The river bed is usually raised above the surface of the surrounding plain, and the braided channel is contained by levees, both man-made and natural. Most alluvial plains are bounded inland by rugged upland, and many are flanked by discontinuous benches of old and poorly consolidated alluvial material. None of the alluvial plains of Japan is extensive: the Kanto, which is the largest, has an area of only 12,800 sq km. Many plains are merely small areas of nearly level land, closely surrounded by the sea and the steeply sloping mountains.

The coastline of Japan is long and intricate. On the Pacific coast, where major faults cut across the prevailing grain of the land, large bays, flanked by relatively extensive alluvial plains, are conspicuous features. Three of these bay-head plains—the Kanto, the Nobi and the Kansai—contain more than one-third of the population of the country, and more than one-half of its industrial output. Further west along the Pacific coast, two narrow channels lead into the sheltered waters of the Inland Sea, which occupies a zone of subsidence between Shikoku and western Honshu. By contrast with the Pacific coasts, the Japan Sea coastline is fairly smooth. The overall insularity of Japan may be indicated by reference to the fact that very few parts of the country are more than 100 km from the sea.

CLIMATE

Climatic conditions are generally favourable. Japanese summers are of sufficient warmth and humidity to allow the widespread cultivation of paddy rice; yet cold, dry winters clearly differentiate Japan from those countries of subtropical and tropical Asia. The climate of Japan is characterized by a marked seasonal alternation in the direction of the prevailing winds. In winter, in association with the establishment of a centre of high atmospheric pressure over Siberia, cold, dry air masses flow outwards from the continent. During their passage over the Sea of Japan (or the East Sea as it is known on the Korean Peninsula), these air masses are warmed in their lower layers, and pick up moisture, which, when the air masses rise on contact with the Japanese coast, is precipitated in the form of snow. Thus, winter weather along the Sea of Japan coastlands is dull, cloudy and characterized by heavy falls of snow. By contrast, the Pacific side of the country experiences cold, dry weather, with low amounts of cloud. Near the Pacific coast, winter temperatures are ameliorated by the influence of the warm Kuro Shio sea current.

Besides this contrast between the two sides of the country, a latitudinal variation in temperature, similar to that of the Atlantic seaboard of the USA, is also apparent. Thus, north of latitude 38° N, average January temperatures fall below 0°C, and reach −10°C in Hokkaido. In this northern zone, winter weather conditions prohibit the double cropping that is elsewhere characteristic of Japanese agriculture. South of latitude 38° N, January temperatures gradually rise, reaching 4°C at Tokyo, and 6°C at Kagoshima in southern Kyushu.

After mid-March the winter pattern of atmospheric circulation begins to change, with high pressure developing over the Aleutians, and low pressure over Siberia. In association with these unstable conditions, the first of the two annual rainfall maxima occurs, with the onset of the Baiu rains in June. By July, however, the high pressure centre to the east of Japan has fully developed, and, with low pressure prevailing over the continent, a south-easterly flow of warm, moist air covers the entire country. On the Pacific coast, August temperatures rise to over 26°C, and the weather becomes unpleasantly hot and humid. August temperatures to the north are lower, reaching only 18°C in Hokkaido.

In late August and early September the Pacific high pressure centre begins to weaken, and the second rainfall maximum occurs, with the arrival of typhoons, or tropical cyclones, which travel northwards to Japan from the equatorial regions of the Pacific Ocean. These severe storms, which frequently coincide with the rice harvest, cause widespread damage. By October high pressure has again developed over Siberia, and the north-westerly winter monsoon is consequently re-established.

Annual precipitation in Japan varies from 850 mm in eastern Hokkaido to more than 3,000 mm in the mountains of central Honshu, and in those parts of the Pacific coast that are fully exposed to the force of the late summer typhoons.

RESOURCES

Although about two-thirds of the total area of Japan is forested, not all of the forest cover is commercially valuable, and large areas of woodland must be preserved to prevent soil erosion. As many houses are still built of wood, the demand for timber is high, and the domestic output is supplemented by imports.

In terms of value, and also of volume, the Japanese fish catch is one of the world's largest. Seafood provides a large proportion of the protein content of the average Japanese diet, and demand is therefore high. Rich fishing grounds occur in both the Sea of Japan and the Pacific Ocean to the east of Japan.

Japan has few mineral resources, and industry is heavily dependent upon imported raw materials and fuels. Japan's coal is of poor to medium quality, and seams are thin and badly faulted. The two main coalfields are located towards the extremities of the country, in Hokkaido and in northern Kyushu. Japanese coal deposits are particularly weak in coking coal, much of which is imported, mainly from the USA and Australia. The small Japanese oilfields, which are located in north-east Honshu, supply a minimal percentage of domestic fuel demand. Japan is heavily dependent on foreign iron ores, imported mainly from Australia, Brazil and India. Many other minerals are mined, but none exists in large quantities. Japan is self-sufficient only in limestone and sulphur.

POPULATION

In 1867, on the eve of modernization, the population of Japan was already approximately 30m., a level at which it had remained, with little fluctuation, for the preceding 150 years. With industrialization, the population increased rapidly and by 1930 had reached 65m. After the Second World War, the population policy initiated by the Japanese Government succeeded in drastically lowering the rate of population increase, and during the second half of the 20th century the growth rate closely corresponded to the rates prevailing in Western Europe. In the early 21st century, however, Japan's demographic situation was becoming an increasing cause for concern. The country's fertility rate continued to decline steadily, and in 2005, when the number of deaths exceeded that of births, the population experienced its first natural decrease since records began in 1899. Moreover, as a result of Japan's exceptionally high life expectancy the population was also progressively ageing, thus raising the question of the ability of the declining labour force to support the increasing number of elderly dependants.

According to census results, the population of Japan was 126,925,843 on 1 October 2000, reaching an estimated 128,056,026 on 1 October 2010. By 1 July 2011, according to official estimates, the population had declined to 127,920,000, this figure giving an average density of 338.5 persons per sq km. None the less, the country's population was the 10th largest in the world in 2010. Three conspicuous urban-industrial concentrations are centred upon Tokyo, Osaka and Nagoya. Tokyo, the capital of Japan and one of the largest cities in the world, had an estimated annual average population of 8,847,000 in 2010.

Apart from the very small number of Ainu (a people who exhibit certain Caucasian characteristics), the Japanese population has been, since early times, ethnically and linguistically uniform. The racial origins of the Japanese remain conjectural, but both Mongol and southern Pacific strains are apparent in the present-day population.

History up to 1952

RICHARD STORRY

ANTIQUITY AND THE MIDDLE AGES

It is generally agreed that the ancestors of the Japanese must have been immigrants from the mainland of Asia. It is also claimed that there was probably some migration to Japan from the islands of South-East Asia, but the subject has remained one of pure conjecture. What does seem undeniable is that the forebears of the small and dwindling Ainu communities of Hokkaido once occupied the whole country and were in fact the original inhabitants. Be that as it may, an elaborate mythology surrounds the origins of Japan and the Japanese. This declares, for example, that the country itself was created by the gods, and that the first Emperor, Jimmu (c. 660 BC), was a direct descendant, in the fifth generation, of the sun goddess.

Yamato Period

It seems probable that the invading immigrants from Asia, who no doubt crossed over from Korea, gradually forced their way eastwards from Kyushu along the shores of the Inland Sea, until, around the beginning of the Christian era, they found themselves in the fertile Kansai plain (the modern Kyoto-Osaka region). Here, in the Yamato district, they established an ordered society under chieftains who became priest-kings, dedicated to the cult of the Sun.

This early Japanese society was profoundly influenced by the civilizations of Korea and China. The Chinese ideographic script is only one important and very striking example of many such cultural influences. Of even greater significance was the introduction of Buddhism in the sixth century AD. It was at this stage that the existing body of religious practices, associated with sun worship and animism, became known as Shinto, or 'The Way of the Gods'. Neither the theology of Buddhism, nor the ethics of Confucianism (also imported from the continent) made Shinto superfluous. Traditional beliefs existed side by side with the new; and over the course of time Chinese ideas of religion, morality, artistic excellence, good governance and sound agriculture were adapted to Japanese conditions, undergoing a degree of change in the process.

Nara and Heian Periods

At the beginning of the eighth century Nara became the capital, being built on the contemporary Chinese model. The early Buddhist sects flourished. The temples surviving at Nara are the best remaining examples anywhere of Chinese architecture of the Tang period. Nara was intended to be a permanent capital. This was, in fact, Heian-kyo, later to be known as Kyoto, founded in 794 and constructed, like Nara, on the model of the Chinese capital. It was to be the home of the Japanese imperial family until 1868. The establishment of this city marks the opening of the Heian age (794–1185), a period remarkable for the artistic sophistication of the court and metropolitan aristocracy.

By the middle of the 12th century effective power in Kyoto was held by a warrior household, the Taira. Their great rivals were another family, the Minamoto. At first the Taira carried all before them; and Kiyomori, the head of the family, ruled Japan in the Emperor's name for a generation. However, after his death in 1181 the situation was reversed; and in a final battle in 1185 the Minamoto annihilated their enemies. Thereafter the leader of the Minamoto, Yoritomo, established a new system of government, known as the *bakufu* (literally 'camp office'), at Kamakura in the east of the country, far from the imperial capital. The Emperor gave Yoritomo the title *Sei-i Tai Shogun*, or 'Barbarian-subduing Generalissimo'—usually abbreviated, in Western use, as 'Shogun'.

Kamakura Period

The original purpose of Yoritomo's *bakufu* was the control and administration of the Japanese warrior class, which was now a distinct entity, and one that was rapidly becoming all-powerful in society. The Japanese fighting man was already a member of an élite class by the 12th century. The true rulers of the country from that time until the late 19th century would tend nearly always to belong to the warrior class. This class did not seek to overthrow the imperial dynasty; indeed the idea was unthinkable, since the Emperor's line was descended from the sun goddess. Ceremonious respect was always paid to the Kyoto court; but it was exceptional, and usually a sign of uncharacteristic weakness, for any warrior administration to allow real power to revert to the imperial household. Every Shogun governed in the Emperor's name and received his appointment from the Emperor.

The Kamakura *bakufu* lasted until well into the 14th century. Yoritomo was a man of exceptional energy, organizing ability and ruthlessness, and he did not hesitate to pursue a vendetta against his younger half-brother Yoshitsune, who as a military commander had been mainly responsible for the ultimate defeat of the Taira. Yoritomo died in 1199. His successors in the office of Shogun were leaders of inferior calibre, and the *bakufu* was administered by the house of Hojo, related to the Minamoto by marriage. It was the Hojo who rallied the country in resistance to the Mongol invasions of 1274 and 1281. Japanese martial courage was a vital element in the discomfiture of the invaders; but the decisive factor, both in 1274 and 1281, seems to have been the storms that wrecked the Mongol ships lying off the coast. With some justice the Japanese described the great typhoon of 1281 as a *kami-kaze*, or 'divine wind'.

Some 50 years later both the Hojo family and the Kamakura *bakufu* were overthrown in the course of a civil war. The climax occurred in 1331 when, with their enemies overrunning Kamakura, the Hojo and their supporters—more than 800 in all—committed *seppuku*, the formal term for the act of *hara-kiri*, the warrior's suicide by self-disembowelling.

Muromachi Period

Over the next 250 years and beyond there was great disorder, including much fierce fighting in and near Kyoto. A new *bakufu* was established, this time in the Muromachi district of the capital, with members of the Ashikaga house (of the Minamoto line) holding office as Shogun. From the fall of Kamakura to the latter half of the 16th century political events, so often influenced by domestic warfare, were extremely complicated. This period was marked not only by civil war but also by economic growth and artistic achievement. The disintegration of central government gave at least some provincial lords the freedom and incentive to embark on foreign trade on their own account, especially with China. One consequence of this commerce was a substantial import in the 15th century of copper cash from China, which promoted the growth of money instead of rice as a medium for exchange. At the same time painting, classical drama, architecture, landscape gardening, ceramics, the tea ceremony and flower arrangement—much of this recognized today as Japan's magnificent cultural heritage—blossomed in these turbulent years. Zen Buddhism, in all its manifestations, played a central part. Japan presented a paradoxical scene of savagery and civilization, of barbarism and beauty, intertwined.

TOKUGAWA RULE

Effective central government and internal peace were not finally secured until the early years of the 17th century, after Ieyasu founded the Tokugawa *bakufu* in Edo (the modern Tokyo), giving the whole country a domestic order that would endure until the coming of US and European men-of-war in the 1850s. Tokugawa Ieyasu consolidated the achievements of two notable captains, Oda Nobunaga (1534–82) and Toyotomi Hideyoshi (1536–98). The former contrived, before his death, to unify about one-half of the provinces of Japan. Hideyoshi, the son of a foot-soldier, was one of Nobunaga's commanders. Within 10 years of Nobunaga's death he made himself master of the whole country, with the help of a wise and cautious ally, Tokugawa Ieyasu.

The 'Closed Country'

After Hideyoshi's death Ieyasu lost little time in making his own position supreme. He defeated his most formidable rivals in battle in 1600, and three years later he was appointed Shogun by the Emperor. The Shogun's government business was best conducted, like Yoritomo's regime, well away from Kyoto, and he made Edo Castle the headquarters of his administration.

Ieyasu and his immediate descendants adopted a number of important measures to strengthen the dominant position of the Tokugawa house (a branch of the seemingly indestructible Minamoto line). Careful watch at all times was kept on those lords considered to be unreliable. Yet a more effective way of controlling all feudatories was the rule, strictly enforced, that they spend part of every year in the Shogun's capital at Edo. It was also decreed that when a lord returned to his own province he must leave his wife and family behind him, in Edo.

Moreover, the Tokugawa *bakufu* adopted a policy of strict national isolation. From 1628 only the Chinese and Dutch were allowed in, as traders, and their commerce was confined to the port of Nagasaki, where the limited number of Dutch merchants was restricted to the tiny island of Deshima. No other foreigners were granted access. No Japanese was permitted to go abroad. Vessels above a certain tonnage could not be built. The modest foreign trade at Nagasaki was a Tokugawa monopoly, controlled by officials appointed by Edo.

This situation, known as *sakoku* or the 'closed country', did not change until 1853 and 1854, when Cdre Matthew Perry's squadron of US warships visited Edo (now Tokyo) Bay. On his second visit Perry secured *bakufu* consent to the opening of two ports and the acceptance, at a future date, of a resident US consul. Other powers rapidly followed the example of the USA, and a decade after Perry's expedition a community of foreign diplomats and traders had settled on Japanese soil.

While none of Japan's leaders really welcomed this intrusion by the West, some were implacable in their hostility, insisting that the 'barbarians' be expelled. Others perceived the weakness of their country and argued that it must come to terms with the situation, learning the techniques of modern Western civilization. Only then would Japan attain the necessary power to hold its own. At the cost of much humiliation, the second, more realistic, course was adopted as the national policy.

THE RISE OF IMPERIAL JAPAN

Modernization followed the domestic transformation known as the Meiji Restoration. The Tokugawa Shogunate had lost face from the moment the first concessions were made to Perry and other intruders. Eventually, in 1868, the much weakened *bakufu* was overthrown by provincial lords from the south-west, acting in concert and impelled by a coalition of their own most vigorous, far-sighted, warrior retainers. The Emperor, still in his teens, was persuaded to leave Kyoto for Edo, which was renamed Tokyo and became the new capital. Nominally, full governing powers were 'restored' to the ancient monarchy, but the young Emperor, Meiji, reigned rather than governed. Real power was exercised by an oligarchy composed almost entirely of the provincial warriors (all of them young or still in the prime of life) who had brought about the downfall of the Shogunate. These men, the Meiji modernizers, dominated Japanese politics, actively or from their retirement, for the best part of 50 years. The pace of modernization, with the abolition of so many cherished customs and privileges, inevitably gave acute offence to many conservatives. There was more than one unsuccessful armed rising against the Government in the decade following the Restoration of 1868.

The heritage of Confucian ethics, with their strong emphasis on loyalty to seniors and superiors, fortified the traditions of Shinto, with its veneration of the imperial house, in sustaining a spirit of harmony and hard work, deeply influencing the great majority of the people. Educational indoctrination played a significant part here. The Meiji Government founded an impressive structure of schools, colleges and universities. In 1890 the Emperor issued his famous Rescript on Education, an exhortation commending the nation's fundamental ethical code to all young people. The Rescript, stressing the patriotic virtues of obedience and self-sacrifice, was read aloud in all schools on days of national festival and commemoration.

A Constitution promulgated in 1889, establishing a bicameral legislature, represented a concession by the oligarchy to the growing demand for some form of national legislative assembly. However, the powers of the Diet (as the new legislature was known) were modest. Nevertheless, the party leaders in the Diet soon became a serious irritant to the Government.

Wars with China and Russia

Domestic political disputes were put aside as a result of a crisis with China over Korea in 1894; this led to a war in which Japan won spectacular victories on land and at sea. Under the Treaty of Shimonoseki of 1895, China surrendered to Japan the island of Taiwan (Formosa) and the Liaodong peninsula in South Manzhou (Manchuria), including Lushun (Port Arthur). Within a few days Japan was forced by Russia, Germany and France to waive its claim to Manzhou. A few years later Russia established its control of Lushun and its hinterland. Revenge was taken in the Russo-Japanese War of 1904–05, which was a much more costly affair for Japan in terms of men and material resources than the Sino-Japanese War, waged 10 years previously. However, Japan's victories, including the destruction of the Tsar's Baltic fleet in the Tsushima Strait in May 1905, were dramatic.

THE TAISHO ERA

The death of Emperor Meiji in 1912 was a decisive point, the end of a not inglorious chapter. The new Emperor proved to be mentally unstable, and in 1921 his eldest son, Crown Prince Hirohito, became regent, succeeding to the throne at the end of 1926.

The period 1912–26 is known as the Taisho era, after the title chosen for the reign of Meiji's successor. It is noteworthy for three important developments and one major natural disaster. First, owing to the First World War of 1914–18, the nation's economic power began to expand in a dynamic way, as Japanese shipyards, factories and foundries were overwhelmed with orders from the Allied countries. Second, as the United Kingdom's ally, Japan invaded and occupied Shandong (Shantung), Germany's leased territory in China, bringing Japan firmly into China's affairs. The temptation to dictate to China could not be resisted, with the result that Chinese dislike and distrust of Japan increased dramatically, setting the tone of relations between the two countries for years to come. Third, Lenin's triumph in Russia gave some impetus to protest movements created by the contrast in the standards of living between those who had been enriched by the war and the poorer sections of the urban working class. Left-wing groups began to obtain a measure of representation in the Diet; democracy appeared to be coming into vogue. Then, in September 1923, more than one-half of the city of Tokyo and the whole of Yokohama were destroyed in a series of earth tremors and subsequent fires. In recorded history there have been few comparable natural disasters so calamitous in loss of life and destruction of property.

THE PRE-WAR SHOWA PERIOD

After Emperor Taisho's death in 1926 his successor chose as the title for the new reign two Chinese characters, Sho Wa, which can be translated as 'Bright Harmony'. However, the years that followed belied the promise implicit in these words. In 1930 the Prime Minister, Osachi Hamaguchi, was shot and wounded by a nationalist fanatic and died some months later from his injuries. In 1932 another Prime Minister, Tsuyohsi Inukai, was assassinated; and in 1936 two former premiers, Makoto Saito and Korekiyo Takahashi, were shot dead in their homes by parties of mutinous troops. These and other instances of civil bloodshed and violence were representative of irrational nationalist hysteria, prompted partly by events on the continent of Asia and in part by the economic consequences for Japan of the world depression, which had badly affected the country in the early 1930s. Diet politicians, wealthy capitalists and liberal-minded men at the palace and in other influential positions drew much criticism. Public opinion came to regard such figures as weak, corrupt and incompetent. In 1931 Japanese forces in South Manzhou carried out a coup against the Chinese in Shenyang (Mukden), and this soon developed into the forcible seizure of all Manzhou.

Military Expansion in Asia

Condemned by the League of Nations for aggression in Manzhou, Japan left that body in 1933. Manzhou became a vassal state (Manchukuo), an apanage of the Empire, dominated by the army and only in name more independent than Taiwan, or Korea, which had been annexed in 1910. Domination of Manzhou led to involvement in northern China, and out of this came undeclared war in mid-1937. By the end of that year Japan and China were engaged in a combat that did not end until 1945. As the war continued, Japan's relations with other powers underwent a change. It drew closer to Nazi Germany and Fascist Italy, eventually joining them in full alliance in September 1940. Increasingly, both the United Kingdom and the USA, powers that supported the Chinese Government in Chongqing, were regarded as potential enemies.

In July 1941 Vichy France agreed to the Japanese occupation of bases in the Saigon area; bases in northern French Indo-China had been occupied by Japan in the previous year. The move southward seemed a clear threat to both Malaya and the Netherlands East Indies. It indicated, too, that for the time being Japan was not going to join its ally Germany in the assault on the USSR. There was an immediate response by the British Commonwealth, the USA and the Netherlands, in the form of a virtual embargo on all trade with Japan. This was serious, for it meant that petroleum imports into that country ceased. US-Japanese talks were inconclusive. Inexorably, Japan drifted towards armed confrontation with the Western powers.

The Sino-Japanese War of 1894–95 and the Russo-Japanese War of 1904–05 had started with surprise attacks by the Japanese navy. On 7 December 1941 Japan followed the same strategy, attacking the US fleet at Pearl Harbor in Hawaii. Later that month Japanese forces invaded Hong Kong, Malaya, Singapore and the Netherlands East Indies.

THE PACIFIC WAR

For the first six months the Japanese advance was virtually unhindered. Hong Kong, Malaya, Singapore, Java and the Indies, the Philippines, Burma and the Andaman Islands, New Britain and the Solomons all fell to Japanese forces. However, there had been a grave miscalculation of the spirit and resources of the nation's principal enemies. Allied submarines, US island-hopping strategy and superior fire-power led to a reversal of Japan's position. From mid-1944 the situation turned against Japan, and by mid-1945 military collapse was imminent. US air raids had inflicted terrible destruction. The Japanese merchant fleet, like the battle fleet, had practically ceased to exist. Germany was out of the war. The USSR was an unknown but threatening factor, returning no answer to pleas that it should act as a mediator.

The Potsdam proclamation at the end of July 1945 seemed to leave the Government unmoved, although in reality the Premier, the aged Baron Suzuki, was seeking ways and means of ending the war short of abject capitulation. On 6 August the first atomic bomb laid waste Hiroshima. On 9 August the second descended on the suburbs of Nagasaki. Between those dates the Soviet army overran Manchukuo. In this unprecedented crisis the nation's leaders were divided between those who favoured surrender (with the proviso that the monarchy be maintained) and those who were ready to fight on. Invited to give an unprecedented decision of his own, the Emperor declared that the Potsdam terms must be accepted.

THE OCCUPATION

US Gen. Douglas MacArthur represented all the Allies in Japan, but the occupation was nevertheless an almost exclusively US undertaking; to a very great extent MacArthur took his own decisions, without direct reference to the US Government. He rejected the view that the Japanese would be better off without the traditional institution of the monarchy. He felt that the Emperor was a stabilizing factor in a society traumatized by the capitulation. However, popular regard for the Emperor no longer rested on the belief that he partook of divinity because of his descent from the sun goddess. When, at the beginning of 1946, the Emperor formally renounced his 'divinity', it created little interest among the majority of Japanese.

In his administration of Japan, MacArthur acted through the Japanese Government, a procedure that worked smoothly in nearly every instance. Between conquerors and conquered there was indeed an unforeseen harmony. However, the Japanese could be intensely pragmatic. The events of 1945 seemed to demonstrate that their own way of conducting affairs was inefficient and harmful to themselves. When the US occupying forces arrived, and once it was clear that their general behaviour was by no means vengeful and oppressive, the Japanese were ready to learn from them in all manner of activities.

Political, Economic and Social Reforms

The guiding theme of the occupation, in the early days especially, was disarmament and democratization. A new Constitution, promulgated in 1946, reflected both these aims. One clause declared that the Japanese people renounced war; and it went on to state that 'land, sea, and air forces, as well as other war potential, will never be maintained'. A further clause laid down that the Prime Minister and his cabinet colleagues should be civilians. The other articles of the Constitution reflected the authentic spirit of North American democracy, with full emphasis on the rights of the individual. Sovereignty of the people was declared. The Emperor was made 'the symbol of the State and of the unity of the people', and it was affirmed that he derived his position 'from the will of the people'. Although undeniably US-inspired, the post-war Constitution captured the imagination of the Japanese.

Another measure of profound social and political importance, instigated by MacArthur's headquarters, was the land reform programme. Thousands of tenant farmers were able to obtain ownership of the land they cultivated. Up to the war a depressed class, the farmers of Japan, thanks to the land reform, became firm, if not always satisfied, upholders of the political status quo. Left-wing parties found the farming vote difficult to entice. The average farmer, freed from the burden of rent and assured of sales for his crop at guaranteed prices, was not impressed by advocates of collectivization and other projects of agrarian socialism.

The educational system was comprehensively reformed. In terms of organization and syllabus, it was restructured to resemble that of the USA. The Rescript on Education was discarded, and there was a thorough revision of school-books concerned with history, political science and ethics.

These manifold and generally liberating changes were not far short of revolutionary in character. Political freedom gave the parties of the Left an opportunity to exploit these changes and to make them even more far-reaching. However, except for the period between May 1947 and March 1948, when a coalition Government under Tetsu Katayama of the Socialist Party was in office, electoral success always attended the conservative parties. Until the end of 1954 the political scene was dominated by Shigeru Yoshida; and, even after his retirement, the elderly politician was influential, as adviser to successive Governments, until his death in 1967.

Consolidation of Relations with the West

As the international situation developed into the protracted period of mutual hostility known as the Cold War, the attitude of MacArthur's headquarters underwent a subtle but definite change. The emphasis shifted from reform to rehabilitation. In particular, as the armies of Mao Zedong began to gain ground in China, and as it became clear that US influence on the Chinese mainland might soon be eliminated, the importance of Japan's future role in the non-communist world was perceived with growing clarity. After the Korean War broke out in June 1950 it seemed all the more desirable, and in fact urgent, to encourage the revival of Japan. Indeed, Japan was now regarded not as a recent enemy but rather as a new, albeit junior, ally. In these circumstances the disarmament clause of the Constitution appeared as an embarrassment. In practice, however, it was to be disregarded.

The US military occupation lasted until 1952. This was much longer than had been planned. Soon after his basic reforms had been introduced, MacArthur had decided that the situation required a treaty of peace. When he was dismissed by President Harry Truman in 1951 the Japanese feared that progress towards a peace treaty would be impeded. However, on 8 September, in the US city of San Francisco, the treaty was concluded between Japan and 48 nations (but not the USSR). It was a magnanimous settlement, free from punitive clauses, although Japan's territorial losses were confirmed. On the same day a bilateral security pact was signed by Japan and the USA. In this, Japan requested the USA to retain its forces in and around the Japanese islands as a defence against external attack. When all the signatories of the San Francisco Treaty had ratified the document, it duly entered into force; on 28 April 1952 Japan became, once again, formally an independent state.

Recent History

LESLEY CONNORS

Based on an earlier article by AKIRA YAMAZAKI

THE POST-WAR POLITICAL ORDER

The reforms introduced during the US military occupation created the institutional framework within which Japan was to conduct its social and political life. The conservative political forces, under the guidance of Shigeru Yoshida (Prime Minister in 1946–47 and 1948–54), and bolstered by the return to the Kokkai (Diet) of pre-war political leaders who had been removed, were divided between two main parties, the Liberals and the Democrats. They were united in their desire to change the institutional framework and to reverse many of the democratic reforms. The conservatives were confronted by a vigorous opposition, dominated by the Japan Socialist Party (JSP), which regarded any attempt to tamper with the reforms and, above all, with the Constitution (particularly Article 9, the 'peace clause', whereby Japan renounces the use of war) as a potential threat to return Japan to the militarism of the 1930s and 1940s.

The contest between these groups was resolved in 1955, at which time the foundations of the post-war political order were established. At a general election for the House of Representatives (the lower house of the Diet) in February, the JSP received 29.2% of the total votes and won 156 of the 467 seats in the chamber. The JSP thus controlled the minimum number of seats (one-third of the total) necessary to obstruct any proposed revision of the post-war Constitution. However, the radical policies (and even more radical rhetoric) of the JSP alarmed business interests, who were organized in the Japan Federation of Economic Organizations (Keidanren). Business leaders urged the Liberals and the Democrats (who had together won 63.2% of the votes and 297 seats at the election) to merge into a single party, which they did in November 1955. The new party, the Liberal-Democratic Party (LDP), which was to govern Japan for several decades from 1955, led the country during a period of remarkable economic expansion.

The advantages that the LDP enjoyed were overwhelming: as the incumbent governing party, it obtained the political benefits of the 'economic miracle', while Japan's electoral arrangements provided an additional asset for the LDP. At the national level, the opposition parties were unable to achieve as much support, even temporarily, as they had locally. A high degree of ideological fragmentation precluded any serious possibility that the opposition might replace the LDP in government in the foreseeable future. Some of the opposition parties, notably Komeito ('Clean Government Party'), the Democratic Socialist Party (DSP) and the New Liberal Club (NLC), were more inclined to co-operate with the LDP than with the increasingly isolated Japanese Communist Party (JCP).

Furthermore, the opposition parties were hampered by the uneven distribution of parliamentary constituencies. For many years successive LDP Governments steadfastly refused to allow any revision of electoral boundaries, to take account of population movements, with the result that the rural areas, where support for the LDP was strong, were substantially over-represented in the Diet. In April 1976 the Supreme Court ruled that the allocation of seats in the House of Representatives was unconstitutional, owing to 'mal-apportionment', which denied equal rights to urban voters (as guaranteed by the Japanese Constitution). In 1990 the LDP leadership announced its commitment to the implementation of comprehensive changes to the procedure for the allocation of seats to the lower house (see below).

Finance was another factor in the success of the LDP. Politics in Japan, and particularly elections, had become extremely costly: the officially reported income of the political parties in 1990 (not an unusually expensive year) was US $700m., which was probably little more than one-quarter of their actual income. To win elections, a political party must be able to raise enormous funds. The LDP traditionally enjoyed a close relationship with the business community; thus the party was well placed to obtain large-scale financial support. One estimate suggested that Japanese business interests transferred more than 45,000m. yen per year to the LDP.

LIBERAL-DEMOCRATIC GOVERNMENTS

Nobusuke Kishi became Prime Minister in February 1957, and held office until July 1960, when he was succeeded by Hayato Ikeda. In November 1964 Ikeda resigned, owing to ill health, and was replaced by Eisaku Sato. Japan enjoyed strong economic growth under Ikeda and Sato. The latter remained in office until July 1972, when he was succeeded by Kakuei Tanaka, hitherto the Minister of International Trade and Industry.

Meanwhile, many of Japan's outer islands, surrendered to the USA at the time of the 1945 armistice, were restored to Japanese sovereignty. The Tokara Archipelago and the Amami Islands (parts of the Ryukyu group) had been restored to Japan in December 1951 and December 1953, respectively. The Bonin Islands and the remainder of the Ryukyu Islands (including Okinawa) reverted to Japan in June 1968 and May 1972, respectively.

Developments in 1972–82

Tanaka's period of tenure as Prime Minister was characterized primarily by scandals, illustrating the problem of widespread corporate involvement in Japanese politics, although initially more noteworthy was Japan's recognition of the People's Republic of China in September 1972. During his premiership, Tanaka allegedly accepted bribes totalling 500m. yen from the Marubeni Corporation, a representative in Japan of the Lockheed Aircraft Corporation (a leading US aerospace company). Following a severe reduction in the LDP's majority in the House of Councillors (upper house of the Diet) at elections held in July 1974, Tanaka's hold on the premiership became tenuous. In December he resigned in favour of Takeo Miki, a former Deputy Prime Minister. Tanaka was subsequently arrested, in July 1976, on charges of accepting bribes, and resigned from the LDP. Largely as a result of voters' disapproval of the LDP's alleged involvement in corruption, the party lost its majority in the House of Representatives in December. Miki was forced to resign, and was succeeded by Takeo Fukuda, who had resigned in November as Deputy Prime Minister.

At the elections held in July 1977 for the House of Councillors Fukuda was unable to reverse the LDP's decline. He was defeated in the LDP presidential election by Masayoshi Ohira, the party's Secretary-General, who became Prime Minister in December 1978. Although Ohira managed to retain his position as Prime Minister following the election of October 1979 for the House of Representatives (when the LDP once again failed to obtain a majority and there were significant gains by the JCP), the Government was defeated on a motion of no confidence in the House of Representatives in May 1980. The lower house was thus dissolved, and at elections held in June the LDP received 47.9% of the total votes and won 284 of the 511 seats. A compromise candidate, Zenko Suzuki, was elected President of the LDP in July, and was subsequently appointed Prime Minister. Suzuki's Government was beset by serious economic problems and growing factionalism within the LDP. As the economic crisis worsened, Suzuki was forced to resign as Prime Minister and President of the LDP in October 1982.

The Nakasone Administration

Suzuki's successor was Yasuhiro Nakasone, who was supported by the Suzuki and Tanaka factions of the LDP. At elections in June 1983 the LDP increased its strength in the upper house from 134 to 137 members in the 252-seat chamber. This result was seen as an endorsement of Nakasone's policies of increased spending on defence, closer links with the USA and greater Japanese involvement in international affairs.

In October 1983, after judicial proceedings lasting seven years, a Tokyo court found Tanaka, the former Prime Minister, guilty of accepting bribes. He immediately began appeal proceedings against the conviction and the sentence, and refused to relinquish his legislative seat, which led to a boycott of the Diet by the opposition. This forced Nakasone to dissolve the House of Representatives in preparation for a premature general election in December. The LDP suffered its worst reverse to date, losing 36 seats (and its majority) in the lower house. Nakasone was placed second (behind Fukuda) in his district, whereas Tanaka was returned with an overwhelming majority. Komeito, the DSP and the JSP gained seats, while the JCP and the NLC lost seats. A coalition was formed between the LDP, the NLC (which had split from the LDP over the Tanaka affair in 1976) and several independents, and Nakasone remained as President of the LDP, promising to reduce Tanaka's influence. However, six members of Tanaka's faction held posts in Nakasone's new Cabinet.

Nakasone's domestic policy was based on the 'three reforms': administrative reforms, particularly of government-controlled enterprises; fiscal reforms, to enable the Government to balance its budget after many years of deficit; and educational reforms, to liberalize the rigid examination-dominated system. In November 1984 Nakasone was re-elected as President of the LDP, guaranteeing him a further two years in office as Prime Minister, the first to serve a second term since Eisaku Sato (1964–72). Nakasone was committed to raising Japan's international status by fostering good relations with other world leaders. He made successful tours to the USA, Australia and South-East Asia in 1984, and to Europe in 1985. However, there was continued concern in the European Community (EC, now European Union—EU) over trade protectionism in Japan, and in the USA over the imbalance of bilateral trade.

In May 1986 an agreement was reached on a redistribution of seats in the House of Representatives between urban and rural constituencies, reducing the maximum ratio of discrepancy in constituency size to less than 3:1, the limit that the Supreme Court had stipulated as permissible. The lower house was dissolved in June, enabling the holding of a general election to coincide with the triennial election for one-half of the seats in the House of Councillors. Polling for both houses of the Diet took place in July and produced decisive victories for the LDP. In the election for the House of Representatives, the LDP received 49.4% of the votes, its highest level of electoral support since 1963, and won a record 304 of the 512 seats. The LDP, therefore, was able to dispense with its coalition partner, the NLC (which disbanded in August 1986 and rejoined the LDP).

Nakasone's second term as President of the LDP (a position that had to be held in order to be Prime Minister) ended in October 1986, and party rules prohibited a third term. However, the leaders of the five main LDP factions agreed to change the party's rules to permit a one-year extension of a President's term, with the approval of two-thirds of the LDP members of the Diet. Nakasone was confirmed as party President in September.

In September 1983, meanwhile, Masashi Ishibashi became Chairman of the JSP and initiated a shift from the party's traditional left-wing policies towards a position closer to the centre of the political spectrum. The JSP's moderation resulted in a slight increase in support at the election, and a policy of further moderation was implemented, which brought about the end of the domination of the Marxist-orientated Shakaishugi Kyokai (Socialist Association) within the party. However, at the 1986 election the JSP's less extreme image failed to attract voters, and the party lost 26 of the 112 seats won in 1983. This disastrous result brought about Ishibashi's resignation and the appointment, in September 1986, of Takako Doi, the first woman to lead a major Japanese political party.

Following the 1986 elections, Nakasone's priorities were to oversee an untroubled transfer to private sector control of the Japanese National Railways (JNR), to alleviate economic tensions with the USA, and to reform both the education and tax systems. The JNR was successfully reorganized in April 1987, but Nakasone failed to make significant progress in other areas. Educational reforms remained under discussion by a specially established council, while proposed reforms to the tax system were withdrawn after the LDP suffered a serious defeat in the unified local elections. In spite of Nakasone's efforts, economic tensions with the USA continued.

Meanwhile, Tanaka's illness led to the disintegration of his faction. In July 1987 Noboru Takeshita (who had been appointed Secretary-General of the LDP after the 1986 election) formed a new grouping within the LDP, the Takeshita faction. He gained the support of 113 other members of the Tanaka faction, while around 20 Tanaka faction members remained with Susumu Nikaido, a former Vice-President of the LDP and the second most powerful man in the Tanaka faction. In October Nakasone nominated Takeshita as his successor.

The Takeshita Administration

On 6 November 1987 the Diet was convened and Takeshita was formally elected as Prime Minister. In the new Cabinet, Takeshita carefully maintained a balance among the five major factions of the LDP. He claimed that he would work to continue Nakasone's policies, with particular emphasis on correcting the external trade imbalance, further liberalizing the financial market, reforming the tax system, land policy and the education system.

In contrast to its failure to curb the rapid rise in land prices, the Takeshita administration initially achieved steady progress in easing friction with overseas trading partners. The restrictions on imports in the agricultural sector were abolished, while US companies were permitted greater access to the Japanese domestic construction market. However, trade tensions worsened during the course of Takeshita's tenure of office. The primary cause of concern was the continuing trade imbalance between Japan and the USA (the US trade deficit with Japan still accounted for about one-third of the USA's total world trade deficit). In May 1989 the situation deteriorated when the USA named Japan, together with India and Brazil, as unfair trading partners.

The implementation of a programme of tax reform, which Nakasone had failed to achieve, was one of the most important issues confronting Takeshita's Government. In June 1988 the LDP's tax deliberation council proposed the introduction of a new indirect tax (a general consumption tax or a form of value-added tax), which was to be levied at a 3% rate. However, this proposal encountered widespread disapproval.

Takeshita and the LDP suffered a serious political reversal in June 1988, when several leading figures in the party, including Nakasone, Shintaro Abe, Kiichi Miyazawa and Takeshita himself, were alleged to have been indirectly involved in share-trading irregularities with the Recruit Cosmos Company. Although these politicians strenuously denied any knowledge of, or involvement in, such transactions, the Prime Minister expressed his concern that these allegations would alienate public opinion from the proposals for tax reform and hinder their progress towards approval by the Diet. As the situation regarding the Recruit affair became increasingly serious, the opposition demanded the resignation of the alleged participants and the commissioning of a full parliamentary investigation into the alleged share transactions. In November, in exchange for the establishment of a committee to investigate the affair, the House of Representatives approved the tax reform measures (which constituted the most wide-ranging revision of the tax system for 40 years); they were approved by the House of Councillors in the following month.

In late 1988 and early 1989 three ministers, including the Deputy Prime Minister and Minister of Finance, Kiichi Miyazawa, were forced to resign from their posts, owing to their alleged involvement in the Recruit affair. Hiromasa Ezoe, who founded the Recruit group, was said to have given large amounts of shares and money, totalling some 1,300m. yen, to many leading politicians and bureaucrats, in an attempt to buy influence and to help to expand his business empire.

In late April 1989 Takeshita suddenly resigned from his post. There were several factors leading to his decision: Takeshita, personally, was found to have received political contributions worth more than 150m. yen from the Recruit group in the form of pre-listed shares and money; the Takeshita Cabinet's public approval rating had declined to less than 10%; and, finally, there was a growing consensus among LDP officials that Takeshita's continued leadership would adversely affect the party's prospects in the elections to the House of Councillors at the end of July. Hard-pressed to find a candidate who was not only willing to accept the position but also suitable (three of the leading contenders, Michio Watanabe, Kiichi Miyazawa and Shintaro Abe, were, temporarily at least, out of the question, as they had all received pre-listed Recruit shares), Takeshita finally nominated Sosuke Uno, the incumbent Minister for Foreign Affairs. Uno was elected Prime Minister at a Diet session on 2 June, becoming the first Japanese Prime Minister since the LDP was founded in 1955 not to command his own political faction.

At the end of May 1989, following an eight-month investigation, public prosecutors indicted 13 people (eight on charges of offering bribes, and five for allegedly accepting them). Two of those indicted were politicians: Takao Fujinami, an LDP member belonging to the Nakasone faction, and Katsuya Ikeda, a former Deputy Secretary-General of Komeito. At the same time Nakasone resigned from his faction and from the LDP, assuming complete moral responsibility for the Recruit affair, since it had occurred during his administration, but announced that he would continue to undertake his political activities and that he would not resign from his seat in the Diet.

The Showa era came to an end when, after a long illness, Emperor Hirohito, who had reigned since 1926 (and who was, thus, the longest-reigning monarch in Japan's history), died in January 1989. He was succeeded by his son, Akihito, and the Government announced that the new era was to be known as the Heisei ('achievement of universal peace') era.

The Uno Administration

Within days of Uno's appointment in June 1989, the LDP was confronted with further scandal, when a Japanese magazine published allegations that Uno had paid a geisha girl for a five-month sexual affair in 1985–86. In response to these allegations (on which Uno refused to comment), there were demands from outraged women's groups and from various members of the opposition for the immediate resignation of the new Prime Minister. The LDP's fears of waning support appeared to be confirmed in July 1989, when the ruling party lost its majority in the House of Councillors for the first time in history. At elections for one-half of the seats in the upper house, the LDP obtained only 27% of the total votes, while the JSP received 35%. The leader of the JSP, Takako Doi, attracted widespread support during the election campaign. Women voters, expressing disgust at the corruption in male-dominated politics, were attracted by the image of an intellectual female political leader. Consequently, Uno offered to resign as soon as the LDP had decided on a suitable successor, assuming total responsibility for his party's defeat. On 8 August the LDP chose the relatively unknown Toshiki Kaifu, a former Minister of Education and a member of the small faction led by Toshio Komoto, to replace Uno as the party's President and as the new Prime Minister. Although the House of Councillors' ballot rejected Kaifu as the new Prime Minister in favour of Takako Doi, the decision of the lower house was adopted (in accordance with constitutional procedures). This was the first time in 41 years that the two houses of the Diet had disagreed over the choice of Prime Minister.

The Kaifu Administration

At the end of August 1989 the LDP suffered another reversal when the Chief Cabinet Secretary was forced to resign, owing to a sex scandal. Nevertheless, Kaifu swiftly gained the approval of the electorate, owing to his untainted political record and his promise to revise the unpopular consumption tax introduced in April. In October Kaifu was re-elected unopposed as President of the LDP for a two-year term.

Meanwhile, in August 1989 the JSP, in an apparent effort to broaden its base of support, unanimously approved a change of policy that would commit it to retaining the bilateral security treaty with the USA (see below) and a free market economy in the event of the establishment of a coalition government.

At the election for the House of Representatives held in February 1990 the LDP was returned to power with 46.1% of the votes cast and 275 of the 512 seats in the lower house. The JSP made substantial gains, winning 136 seats. The election results were significant in demonstrating not only the willingness of the electorate to forgive past indiscretions (many major politicians who had been implicated in recent scandals were returned to the lower house, including former Prime Ministers Nakasone and Uno) but also the possibility of a future polarization of voters, with the role of the smaller parties becoming increasingly insignificant.

In May 1990 Prime Minister Kaifu announced his commitment to the implementation of the electoral reforms that had been proposed in April. The proposals, for the House of Representatives, included a plan to replace the present multi-seat constituencies with a combination of single seats and proportional representation (PR). Although the proposals were presented as an attempt to counter electoral corruption, LDP members expressed fears that the changes would invest more power in party committees responsible for nominating candidates, and would therefore increase the scope for bribery.

Kaifu's domestic and international standing altered significantly following Iraq's invasion of Kuwait in August 1990, and the subsequent outbreak of hostilities in the Persian (Arabian) Gulf region. In September Japan announced a US $4,000m. contribution to the international effort to force an unconditional Iraqi withdrawal from Kuwait. Controversial legislation providing for the dispatch to the Gulf region of some 2,000 non-combatant personnel encountered severe opposition and provoked widespread discussion on the constitutional legitimacy of the deployment of Japanese personnel (in any capacity) in such a conflict. The proposals were withdrawn in November. In January 1991, following repeated demands by the USA for a greater financial commitment (and a swifter disbursement of funds already pledged), the Kaifu Government announced plans to increase its contribution by $9,000m. and to provide aircraft for the transport of refugees in the Gulf region. Opposition to the proposal within Japan was again vociferous.

Meanwhile, a developing power struggle within the LDP had also weakened Kaifu's political authority. Former Prime Minister Takeshita took advantage of diplomatic and political errors committed by Shin Kanemaru, the leader of the LDP faction that supported Kaifu, to ease his way back into a position of prominence in the LDP. In order to bolster his preparations for a return to the political forum, Takeshita also promoted Nakasone's return to the party, together with that of Kiichi Miyazawa. In June 1991 Kaifu broached the controversial issue of political reform by requesting that the LDP endorse a series of electoral reform bills. This initiative was viewed as an attempt not only to regain public confidence but also to obstruct the efforts of tainted party leaders to return to office when Kaifu's LDP presidential term expired in October. Later that month, however, the Diet rejected Kaifu's proposals, leaving the way open for Kiichi Miyazawa.

Having successfully prevented the Government from dispatching Self-Defence Force (SDF) personnel overseas during the Gulf War, the JSP was unable to sustain popular support for its strict pacifist stance. Although the party, in a bid to attract wider support, had changed the English rendering of its name to the Social Democratic Party of Japan (SDPJ) in February 1991, it suffered defeat on an unprecedented scale in the unified local elections in April. The set-back forced the party to discard the abolition of the consumption tax, and to approve the LDP's proposal to revise the tax in the following month. In July Makoto Tanabe was appointed as the new SDPJ leader, following the resignation earlier in the month of Takako Doi.

The Miyazawa Administration

At the election for the presidency of the LDP in October 1991 Miyazawa (with the support of Shin Kanemaru, a former Deputy Prime Minister) defeated Michio Watanabe and Hiroshi Mitsuzuka. Miyazawa attempted to win control of the ruling party by strengthening his long-established links with Takeshita, Watanabe and Mitsuzuka on the one hand, and by establishing new links with Kanemaru on the other. Watanabe was appointed to the posts of Deputy Prime Minister and Minister for Foreign Affairs. However, a bitter feud developed between Kanemaru and Takeshita over the allocation of posts within the party executive and the Cabinet. The new Cabinet comprised the same proportion of the LDP's four major factions as its predecessor, but with the Takeshita faction obtaining more of the senior portfolios than it had previously held.

The new Prime Minister attempted to enact controversial legislation to allow SDF troops to serve abroad on UN peace-keeping missions. Realizing the need to gain Kanemaru's full support, Miyazawa repeatedly requested that he assume the post of LDP Vice-President. In January 1992 Kanemaru at last accepted the offer, together with Miyazawa's pledge of loyalty. Subsequently, the peace-keeping legislation was approved, with the support of Komeito and the DSP, on the condition that SDF personnel join only non-military operations. The legislation was enacted in June, despite SDPJ opposition.

In July 1992 the LDP recovered from a period of apparent unpopularity to achieve unexpected gains in elections to the upper house of the Diet, although it failed to recapture the majority that it had lost in 1989. However, the dominant Takeshita faction of the LDP was beset by crisis when it emerged that the former president of the Sagawa Kyubin transport company, Hiroyasu Watanabe, had made an unreported 500m.-yen donation to Kanemaru in February 1990. In late August 1992 Kanemaru was forced to resign as LDP Vice-President, offering also to resign as head of the Takeshita faction, since he had been charged with violating the Political Funds Control Law. However, he avoided trial by admitting the charge in a written statement to the authorities. The Tokyo Summary Court responded with a fine of 200,000 yen, prompting a public outcry over the failure to prosecute this case more resolutely. Kanemaru returned to his duties as head of the Takeshita faction for two weeks, only to yield to mounting pressure and resign from the Diet in mid-October. Two days prior to the opening of an extraordinary Diet session in late October, Ichiro Ozawa, a protégé of Kanemaru, announced the split of his group of 36 lower house members from the Takeshita faction, following his failure to obtain the chairmanship. Further changes in the political map occurred with the formation in November of the Sirius Group of 27 reform-minded Diet members belonging to the SDPJ, Social Democratic Federation and RENGO, the trade union organization. Other such party and cross-party groups increased in prominence and number, reflecting the growing demand for political and electoral reform. As the trials connected to the Sagawa Kyubin scandal continued, seven leading LDP politicians, including Kanemaru, were accused of dealings with an extreme rightist group and with an organized crime gang in 1987, during

Takeshita's ascent to the leadership of the party. In a bid to restore confidence in the embattled Government, Miyazawa reorganized the Cabinet in December 1992. Seiroku Kajiyama, Ozawa's rival, became the LDP's Secretary-General.

With the arrest of Kanemaru and his secretary, Masahisa Haibara, in March 1993, on suspicion of evading the payment of 1,040m. yen in tax, groups seeking political reform within the Diet gained fresh momentum. Each of the established parties, apart from the Communists, assembled proposals for changes to the electoral system. While the LDP's preference was for a single-member constituency system, the opposition parties produced a variety of suggestions, which incorporated elements of PR. Within the ruling party itself, differences between younger Diet members and their seniors emerged, as the former, led by Ozawa and his ally, Tsutomu Hata, encouraged an agreement with the opposition parties. A cross-party consensus was needed for any legislation to pass through the upper house, where the LDP was in the minority.

In June 1993 the LDP confirmed that it would not compromise its proposal in order to meet the demands of the opposition, thus effectively abandoning the reforms. The lower house adopted a no-confidence motion against the Miyazawa Government by 255 to 220 votes; 39 LDP members voted against their party, while 16 other LDP politicians did not vote. The Hata-Ozawa group, consisting of 44 members of the LDP, immediately formed a new party, Shinseito (Japan Renewal Party—JRP). Another group of 10 LDP Diet members also broke away to form the New Party (Shinto/Sakigake).

The election for the House of Representatives was held on 18 July 1993. Apart from the record low turn-out of 67%, voting patterns changed surprisingly little. The LDP won 223 of the 511 seats, slightly more than it had held immediately prior to the election, but still well short of an overall majority. The SDPJ fared particularly badly, its number of seats being almost halved to 70. Of the parties formed by ex-LDP members, Shinseito and New Party Sakigake won 55 and 13 seats, respectively, most of which had been previously occupied by LDP members. The performance of the other recently established party, the Japan New Party (JNP), was impressive; led by Morihiro Hosokawa, the party presented no incumbent candidates, its 35 seats being secured mainly in urban constituencies and in the same marginal seats where new political parties had enjoyed success in the past. The remaining parties managed to maintain their strength in the lower house: Komeito took 51 seats, the JCP 15, the DSP 15 and the Social Democratic Federation/United Social Democratic Party (USDP) four, while candidates with no party affiliations won 30 seats. Nevertheless, the LDP remained a potent electoral force.

COALITION GOVERNMENT

The election of July 1993 thus marked the end of uninterrupted LDP rule. Prime Minister Miyazawa resigned, since there was no prospect of his party regaining its majority in the lower house. Amid widespread expectations that the LDP would remain in power, either as a minority government, or as part of a coalition government, the other non-communist parties formed an alliance to oust the LDP. Thus, Morihiro Hosokawa, possessor of an illustrious aristocratic lineage and leader of the JNP, became Japan's first non-LDP Prime Minister for 38 years, defeating the new LDP President, Yohei Kono, by 262 votes to 224. Hosokawa formed a coalition Government, which included representatives of all the coalition partners. However, there was some dissatisfaction within the SDPJ concerning the distribution of principal government posts. In spite of being the largest coalition partner, the SDPJ secured relatively few important positions, although its Chairman, Sadao Yamahana, was appointed Minister Responsible for Political Reform. Tsutomu Hata, one of Shinseito's leaders, became Deputy Prime Minister and Minister for Foreign Affairs, while his party also took responsibility for the crucial Ministries of Finance, and of International Trade and Industry. The sense of irritation within the SDPJ was exacerbated by its failure to obtain the position of Chief Cabinet Secretary, or even one of the two Deputy Chief Cabinet Secretary posts, leaving the party with no influence over the direction and co-ordination of policy. The former SDPJ Chairman, Takako Doi, who might have articulated such disaffection, was silenced by her reluctant acceptance of the post of Speaker of the lower house. Yamahana was replaced as Chairman of the SDPJ by Tomiichi Murayama in September 1993.

One of the Hosokawa Government's outstanding achievements was the approval of legislation on political reform, which was surrounded by much controversy until its final passage through the Diet in January 1994. Under the new electoral system, Japan's 511 medium-sized, multi-member constituencies in the House of Representatives were to be replaced by 500 seats, 300 of which were to be filled from single-member constituencies in a 'first-past-the-post' contest, and the remaining 200 in 11 regional blocks by PR. New funding rules allowed politicians to receive a maximum of 500,000 yen per year from each company wishing to donate, for the next five years, after which time payments to individual politicians from businesses would be illegal. Under the reforms, a 40% increase in state funding for political parties was also promised. The legislation was approved despite strong opposition from within the coalition, owing to a late agreement between Hosokawa and the LDP President. Their compromise thus met LDP demands for an increased number of single-member constituencies, for 11 regional PR lists rather than one national list, and for no immediate termination of corporate donations to individual politicians.

Encouraged by record public approval ratings, Hosokawa promised further, wide-ranging reform. Economic strategy was revised by the Economic Reform Research Council, under the chairmanship of Gaishi Hiraiwa. The co-operation of Hiraiwa, who was Chairman of Japan's leading business association, Keidanren, reinforced the impression of change in the relationship between business and politics. This had already been suggested by Keidanren's decision in mid-1993 to abandon its role as a conduit for funds to the LDP. These developments reflected trends in trade unions, which were disengaging themselves from exclusive relationships with their former political partners.

Although the Socialists were recognized as a potential source of instability within the coalition, the breakdown of the relationship between Hosokawa and his close ally, Masayoshi Takemura, leader of New Party Sakigake, was unexpected. The apparent cause of the rift was the sudden announcement by the Prime Minister in February 1994 of his intention to introduce a 6,000,000m.-yen reduction in income and residential taxes, while planning to establish a national welfare tax of 7% in 1997. The rise in indirect taxation, from its current level of 3%, was strongly opposed not only by the SDPJ, which threatened to leave the coalition, but also by Chief Cabinet Secretary Takemura. Hosokawa was forced to withdraw the proposed tax increases.

The 1994/95 budget was agreed by the Cabinet in February 1994. However, the opposition prevented its being approved by directing political discussion to details of a 100m.-yen loan received by Hosokawa, during his time as Governor of Kumamoto, from the scandal-tainted Sagawa Kyubin distribution company. This, together with speculation surrounding the Prime Minister's former share dealings, fuelled intense discussion in the Diet. In June Hosokawa was forced to give sworn testimony in the Diet concerning his financial activities.

With the coalition becoming increasingly fragile, Hosokawa resigned on 8 April 1994 amid controversy over his financial dealings. During the subsequent negotiations between the coalition partners regarding the succession to the premiership, the differences between the SDPJ and Shinseito over tax policy and the North Korean nuclear issue (see below) became apparent. Tsutomu Hata of Shinseito and Michio Watanabe were both potential candidates for the premiership. However, Watanabe eventually decided against leaving the LDP along with some of his supporters, and on 25 April Tsutomu Hata was chosen as Prime Minister. The SDPJ was offended by the creation in the lower house of a parliamentary organization, Kaishin (Reform), comprising Shinseito, the JNP, the DSP and two smaller political groupings (subsequently joined by Komeito), which had facilitated Hata's appointment. Hata was therefore obliged to form a minority Government, without the SDPJ and New Party Sakigake, which pledged support only until the passage of all budget legislation through the Diet in mid-June.

This political realignment encouraged Satsuki Eda in May 1994 to dissolve the USDP and merge the party with the JNP. Within weeks, however, the future of the JNP itself was uncertain. Keigo Ouchi was replaced as leader of the DSP by Takashi Yonezawa in early June. Largely paralysed by the Government's minority status, Hata resigned as Prime Minister on 25 June. In an unexpected development, the SDPJ united with the LDP and New Party Sakigake to secure the election of Tomiichi Murayama, the SDPJ Chairman, as Prime Minister on 29 June, the first Socialist Prime Minister for 47 years. In the House of Representatives' ballot, Murayama defeated Toshiki Kaifu, the former LDP Prime Minister, who had left the LDP to join Ozawa, by 261 to 214 votes. Many LDP members opposed Murayama's election, and even within the SDPJ there was disapproval, especially following Murayama's statement that the unarmed neutrality policy of the SDPJ was outdated and that he no longer considered the SDF to be unconstitutional.

In August 1994 leaders of the major Japanese opposition parties, at the instigation of former Prime Ministers Hata, Hosokawa and Kaifu, agreed to establish a consultative body, as a first step towards founding a joint party to counter the LDP-New Party Sakigake-SDPJ coalition Government. In the same month Murayama appointed Sohei Miyashita, the former Director-General of the Defence Agency, as the Director-General of the Environment Agency in place of Shin Sakurai, who had angered China and the Republic of Korea (South Korea) by denying Japan's 'war of aggression' in the Pacific during the Second World War. Sakurai was the second Cabinet member to resign within three months over controversial remarks about Japan's war record; Shigeto Nagano, the Minister of Justice, had been forced to resign in May after describing the 1937 Nanjing massacre (in which more than 300,000 Chinese citizens were killed by Japanese soldiers) as a 'fabrication'.

The longer the SDPJ remained in government, the more difficult it became for it to appeal to traditional supporters. In September 1994 Murayama announced an increase in the consumption tax, from 3% to 5%, to take effect in April 1997. Although, in mitigation, a two-tiered reduction in income and residential taxes of some 5,500,000m. yen was to be introduced, it seemed ironic that a Socialist Prime Minister should announce this increase in tax, the introduction of which his party had so long opposed. In October Murayama was forced to question another of his party's former policy commitments, when he suggested that the construction of further nuclear power plants might be unavoidable. On the following day, to Murayama's apparent consternation, the Secretary-General of the SDPJ, Wataru Kubo, expressed his support for the dissolution of the party and the formation of a new grouping of social democrats and liberals. Kubo planned to co-operate with Sadao Yamahana, who was poised to lead his own faction out of the SDPJ.

Meanwhile, among the opposition parties, although Shinseito, Komeito, DSP, JNP and LDP splinter groups had largely agreed by September 1994 that they should merge, misgivings remained among some of the smaller partners that Shinseito and Komeito would dominate a new opposition party. In October significant differences on foreign policy emerged between Komeito and Shinseito. Ozawa urged Japan to become an 'ordinary country', whereas Komeito reaffirmed its position that Japan should not become involved in peace-keeping operations or any collective security system that required the use of force.

However, driven by electoral realities, Komeito opted to divide into two groups at the party's extraordinary congress in early December 1994. The first comprised all 52 Komeito lower house members and a majority (24) of its upper house members. This group was to participate in the anticipated merger of the opposition parties. The second group, which included those not standing for election to the House of Councillors in 1995 and all Komeito local politicians (approximately 3,000), retained the party's apparatus, including its newspaper and its headquarters, and adopted the name Komei. Later in December 1994 the New Frontier Party (Shinshinto), comprising all the major opposition parties with the exception of the JCP, held its inaugural congress, during which the former LDP Prime Minister, Toshiki Kaifu, was elected leader, defeating Hata and Yonezawa. Ozawa was elected unopposed as the new party's Secretary-General.

In January 1995 Yamahana began negotiations in preparation for the creation of a new party, claiming the support of as many as 30 SDPJ Diet members. The SDPJ leadership sought a delay and promised to introduce measures to form a new party at a party congress scheduled to be held in February. However, Yamahana made it clear that a split in the party was imminent.

On 18 January 1995 the country suffered its worst disaster since the Second World War when a massive earthquake struck the Kobe region, killing more than 6,000 people. The scale of this calamity effectively postponed the dissolution of the SDPJ, as public and media attention focused on the efforts to bring relief to the disaster area. The Government was severely criticized (and subsequently acknowledged responsibility) for the poor co-ordination of the relief operation.

In March 1995 12 people died and more than 5,000 were injured, when a poisonous gas, sarin, was released into the Tokyo underground railway system. The religious sect Aum Shinrikyo, which was believed to be responsible for a similar incident in Matsumoto in 1994, was widely suspected of launching the attack, although the sect's leader, Shoko Asahara, initially denied that Aum Shinrikyo had been involved. Following a further gas attack in Yokohama in April 1995, a number of sect members were detained by the authorities, and in June Asahara was indicted on a charge of murder. The sect was declared bankrupt in March 1996 and the trial of Asahara opened in the following month. In September Asahara and two other members of the sect were instructed to pay some US $7.3m. in compensation to victims of the Tokyo incident. Attempts by the Ministry of Justice to outlaw the sect, on the grounds that it had engaged in subversive activities, were unsuccessful; however, the sect was denied legal status as a religious organization.

The gas attack in Tokyo, and the sensation generated in the media by the sporadic acts of terrorism that followed, kept party politics at a low ebb. This was reflected in the unified local elections held in April 1995. Despite the election of independent candidates, Yukio Aoshima and Nokku Yokoyama (both former comedians), in the Tokyo and Osaka gubernatorial elections, it was hard to detect anything but apathy in the record low turn-out registered in the vote for members of Japan's local assemblies and local chief executives. In accordance with his campaign pledges, Aoshima took a controversial decision in May to halt the Tokyo Exposition, despite the 98,200m.-yen loss that was expected to ensue. In the same month the SDPJ established a working group to study policy in preparation for the creation of a new party. Yamahana had resigned from the SDPJ earlier in the month.

Following considerable disagreement in the Diet, during which New Party Sakigake threatened to withdraw from the coalition if an apology for Japanese actions in the war were not adopted, a resolution was approved in June 1995 to commemorate the 50th anniversary of the end of the Second World War. The New Frontier Party (Shinshinto) boycotted the vote, while the resolution was openly criticized by a group of 160 LDP Diet members, led by Seisuke Okuno, who objected to the labelling of Japan as an aggressor, preferring to characterize the war as one of liberation for the peoples of Asia. The resolution was also widely criticized as insufficiently explicit by nations whose citizens had been prisoners of the Japanese army during the Second World War.

In late June 1995 a total of some 29,900m. yen was allocated to political organizations in the country's first distribution of subsidies to political parties. In elections to the House of Councillors, held in July, the coalition parties suffered as the electorate registered a post-war record low turn-out of 44.5%. With one-half of the 252 seats being contested, the LDP won 49 seats, the SDPJ 16 and New Party Sakigake three. The New Frontier Party (Shinshinto), benefiting from the strong organizational support of the Soka Gakkai religious organization, was able to win some 40 seats. In August Murayama undertook a major reorganization of the Cabinet. Yohei Kono announced that he would not seek re-election in September to the presidency of the LDP, and was succeeded by Ryutaro Hashimoto, the Minister of International Trade and Industry.

In October 1995 the Minister of Justice was obliged to resign, following allegations that he had accepted an unreported loan of 200m. yen from a Buddhist group. The Director-General of the Management and Co-ordination Agency resigned in November, owing to controversy arising from his suggestion that Japanese colonial rule over Korea had been of some benefit.

Murayama announced his resignation as Prime Minister on 5 January 1996. The three-party coalition continued to govern under the premiership of the LDP President, Ryutaro Hashimoto, whose experience as Minister of Finance and of International Trade and Industry was well respected by Japanese business leaders and US officials. Hashimoto's first task as Prime Minister was to gain Diet approval for the 1996 draft budget, which included expenditure of 685,000m. yen for the liquidation of seven insolvent housing loan companies (*jusen*). The use of public funds for the settlement of the *jusen* issue aroused considerable opposition, particularly from the New Frontier Party (Shinshinto). The budget proposals were eventually approved in May with little revision; however, the liquidation of the *jusen* was postponed, pending the introduction of a tighter financial regulatory system.

The New Frontier Party (Shinshinto) elected Ichiro Ozawa as President in December 1995. However, the contest for the party leadership aggravated the internal division between the Ozawa group and the Hata-Hosokawa group. Other parties also experienced internal problems. Some local organizations opposed the transformation of the SDPJ, under Murayama's chairmanship, into a moderate liberal party, and an independent New Socialist Party was formed by left-wing members of the SDPJ. In September 1996, as the end of her term as Speaker of the House of Representatives approached, Takako Doi agreed to resume the leadership of the SDPJ, replacing Murayama. In August Masayoshi Takemura resigned as leader of New Party Sakigake, the smallest coalition partner, and the Secretary-General of the party, Yukio Hatoyama, also resigned. With Naoto Kan, the Sakigake Minister of Health and Social Welfare, and several members of the SDPJ, Hatoyama formed a new party in September, the Democratic Party of Japan (DPJ); he felt that New Party Sakigake's electoral prospects had been damaged by the poor performance of its leader, Takemura, during the latter's tenure as Minister of Finance. In late August Shoichi Ide and Hiroyuki Sonoda became leader and Secretary-General, respectively, of New Party Sakigake.

The Election of October 1996

Such developments indicated that the parties and individual politicians were preparing for a general election, which Hashimoto duly declared would take place on 20 October 1996. The election was to be the first for the lower house to be held under the new electoral system of 300 single-seat constituencies and 200 PR seats. In an effort to strengthen the electoral bases in new single-member districts, the parties promoted co-operation even with formerly rival organizations. The LDP, for example, approached labour unions, and the New Frontier Party (Shinshinto) received some support from local labour union organizations that refused to support the new SDPJ. At the election the LDP won 239 of the 500 seats in the House of Representatives. The New Frontier Party (Shinshinto) secured 156 seats, the DPJ 52 seats, the JCP 26 seats and the SDPJ 15 seats. New Party Sakigake won only two seats. The low turn-out (59%) was regarded as an indication of widespread electoral disillusionment with all the political parties.

At an extraordinary session of the Diet, convened on 7 November 1996, Ryutaro Hashimoto was re-elected Prime Minister, winning a majority in the first ballot in both houses, with the support of not only his own LDP but also members of the SDPJ and New Party Sakigake. Both the SDPJ and New Party Sakigake entered into a policy agreement with the LDP, but decided to remain outside the Government. Thus, the new Cabinet consisted entirely of LDP members for the first time since August 1993. The LDP also secured the co-operation of both the New Frontier Party (Shinshinto) and the DPJ, while maintaining the basic framework of the LDP-SDPJ-New Party Sakigake policy accord, which highlighted administrative reform as a priority.

The incoming Government was almost immediately beset by corruption scandals, including allegations that some 10 LDP members, among them the Ministers of Finance and of Health and Welfare, had received political donations from Junichi Izui, the owner of an oil company, who had been detained on charges of tax evasion. Although not illegal in themselves, the payments should have been disclosed, following the introduction of new legislation concerning political funds.

ADMINISTRATIVE AND ECONOMIC REFORM

A programme of comprehensive administrative and economic reforms was inaugurated by the new administration, with the establishment of special commissions, chaired by the Prime Minister, to examine a reorganization of ministries and to investigate ways of reducing government expenditure. These commissions proposed a reduction in the number of central ministries, an increase in the powers of the Prime Minister, the establishment of an effective crisis management system to be headed by the Prime Minister, and a review of the structure of public investment. In February 1997 the Government released details of a series of financial deregulation measures: among other reforms, government control over the financial sector was to be reduced and a new financial supervisory agency was to be established, to assume responsibility for some of the Ministry of Finance's regulatory duties. Social welfare reforms were also introduced, with revisions to the national health insurance system and the introduction of a nursing assistance insurance scheme. The Government's management of the nuclear programme was comprehensively reviewed, following two accidents, in December 1995 and March 1997, at plants managed by the Power Reactor and Nuclear Fuel Development Corporation, a public organization supervised by the Science and Technology Agency. Allegations that the corporation had failed to report a further 11 radiation leaks over the previous three years served to heighten public disquiet over Japan's nuclear research and development programme.

In elections to the Tokyo Metropolitan Assembly, held in June 1997, the LDP performed well; moreover, with the defection to the party of several New Frontier Party (Shinshinto) members, the LDP increased its number of seats in the House of Representatives to 247. The New Frontier Party (Shinshinto) had experienced serious internal difficulties since its dismal performance in the 1996 general election. In January 1997 Tsutomu Hata had left the New Frontier Party (Shinshinto) to form a new party, the Sun Party (Taiyoto), and in June Hosokawa also relinquished his membership. The New Frontier Party (Shinshinto) sustained a defeat in the elections to the Tokyo Metropolitan Assembly, failing to win a single seat. In July, as a result of the apparent decline in the party's influence, several New Frontier Party (Shinshinto) members formed a parliamentary faction with members of the DPJ and the Sun Party. The JCP continued to attract voters who were frustrated with the major parties, and became the second largest party in the Tokyo Metropolitan Assembly.

In September 1997 Hashimoto was re-elected unopposed to the presidency of the LDP. A wide-ranging cabinet reorganization was effected, but the appointment of Koko Sato, who had been convicted on charges of bribery, as Director-General of the Management and Co-ordination Agency caused widespread anger, and he was forced to resign shortly afterwards. Meanwhile, the LDP regained its majority in the House of Representatives, following a series of defections by members of the New Frontier Party (Shinshinto). The New Frontier Party (Shinshinto) was dissolved in December; several new opposition parties were established by former party members, including the Liberal Party (LP), led by Ichiro Ozawa. A subsequent realignment of six political parties, including the DPJ, in January 1998, resulted in the formation of a new opposition grouping, Minyuren. In March the members of Minyuren announced their integration into the DPJ, to form a single party, led by Naoto Kan. The new DPJ was formally established in April, and became the second largest party in the

House of Representatives; Naoto Kan and Tsutomu Hata were elected as President and Secretary-General, respectively, of the party.

Meanwhile, in late 1997 a series of corruption scandals, involving substantial payments to corporate racketeers by leading financial institutions, had a severe impact on the Japanese economy. The crisis was exacerbated by an increase in the rate of the unpopular consumption tax, in April, from 3% to 5%, and a decrease in public expenditure (as part of the Government's fiscal reforms), which resulted in a significant weakening in consumer demand. The collapse of several prominent financial institutions in November deepened the economic crisis. The Government announced a series of measures designed to encourage economic growth, including a reduction in taxes and, in a major reversal of policy, proposed the use of public money to support the banking system. However, the credibility of the Ministry of Finance was weakened in late January 1998, when two senior officials were arrested on suspicion of accepting bribes from banks. The Minister of Finance, Hiroshi Mitsuzuka, resigned, accepting full moral responsibility for the affair. He was replaced by Hikaru Matsunaga. The repercussions of the bribery scandal widened in early 1998, as other banks were implicated in the affair. The Bank of Japan, the central bank, subsequently began an internal investigation into its own practices, and in March the Governor resigned, as a result of further bribery allegations made against a senior bank official. He was replaced by Masaru Hayami.

Attempts to stimulate the Japanese economy continued. Legislation for the reorganization of government ministries was approved by the Diet in June 1998: from 2001 the number of central ministries and agencies was to be reduced from 22 to 13. However, restricted by his commitment to achieve a balanced budget, Hashimoto was unable to introduce significant tax reductions, the measure that many analysts considered necessary for economic revival. As the economy continued to stagnate during 1998, Hashimoto was increasingly criticized for his lack of decisive action, and in June the SDPJ and New Party Sakigake left the governing coalition.

In the election for one-half of the seats in the House of Councillors, held on 12 July 1998, the LDP performed poorly, losing 17 of its 61 seats contested. The DPJ, by contrast, won 27 seats, bringing its total to 47, and the JCP more than doubled its representation, taking 15 seats. Electoral turn-out was low, at some 58%. Hashimoto resigned as President of the LDP, and was replaced by Keizo Obuchi, formerly Minister for Foreign Affairs, and leader of the largest faction in the LDP. Despite the party's preference for a consensus candidate, the election for LDP President was unusually open, and two other candidates, Seiroku Kajiyama and Junichiro Koizumi also contested the ballot of party members in the Diet. However, all three candidates were unanimous in emphasizing the need for permanent tax reductions and reform of the tax system. Obuchi was subsequently elected Prime Minister, on 30 July, at an extraordinary session of the Diet, despite the election by the House of Councillors of Naoto Kan as their choice for Prime Minister. The decision of the lower house, nevertheless, prevailed.

Obuchi's Government, designated an 'economic reform' cabinet, comprised a large number of 'hereditary' politicians (whose relatives had previously held office). However, the appointment of Kiichi Miyazawa, a former Prime Minister, as Minister of Finance, was welcomed by some observers, owing to his financial expertise. Doubts nevertheless remained about the new Government's commitment to economic reform, and Obuchi's administration failed to attract the support of the electorate, achieving extremely low approval ratings. In his inaugural policy address to the legislature, Obuchi announced that attempts to achieve a balanced budget were to be postponed, and proposed additional tax decreases, to the value of 7,000,000m. yen. However, his reluctance to commit the Government to the closure of failing banks and to a fundamental restructuring of the banking sector led to a further weakening of confidence in the Japanese economy. In October 1998 the Diet approved banking legislation that included provisions for the nationalization of failing banks, as demanded by the opposition. In November the Government presented a 24,000,000m.-yen programme aimed at revitalizing the country's economy, but ruled out a reduction in the consumption tax.

In November 1998 Komei merged with Shinto Heiwa (New Peace Party, founded in 1997) to form New Komeito, which thus became the second largest opposition party. In the same month Fukushiro Nukaga, the Director-General of the Defence Agency, resigned from the Government to assume responsibility for a procurement scandal involving his agency. In mid-November the LDP and the LP reached a basic accord on the formation of a coalition, which would still remain short of a majority in the upper house. In January 1999 agreement was reached on coalition policies. Ozawa appeared to have won concessions on a number of proposals that the LP wanted to be submitted for consideration by the Diet in forthcoming sessions, including a reduction in the number of seats determined by PR in the House of Representatives from 200 to 150 and provision for an expansion of Japan's participation in UN peace-keeping operations. The Cabinet was reorganized to include the LP, with the number of ministers reduced from 20 to 18 (excluding the Prime Minister). Takeshi Noda of the LP, the only new member of the Cabinet, was appointed as Minister of Home Affairs. At the end of January the Government adopted an administrative reform plan, which aimed to reduce further the number of cabinet ministers and public servants and to establish an economic and fiscal policy committee. Draft legislation on the implementation of the plan was introduced to the Diet in April. In March Shozaburo Nakamura resigned as Minister of Justice following allegations of repeated abuse of power.

Local elections in April 1999 were largely unremarkable; 11 of the 12 governorships contested were won by the incumbents, all standing as independents. The 19-candidate gubernatorial election for Tokyo created by far the most interest. The convincing victory of Shintaro Ishihara, a nationalist writer and a former Minister of Transport under the LDP (although now unaffiliated), was regarded as an embarrassment for the ruling party, which had supported Yasushi Akashi, a former senior UN official. Ishihara immediately provoked controversy, making a series of inflammatory comments about the 1937 Nanjing massacre and criticizing the Chinese Government, which responded angrily, prompting the Japanese Government to distance itself publicly from the new Governor's remarks.

In July 1999 New Komeito agreed to join the ruling LDP-LP coalition, giving the Government a new majority in the upper house and expanding its control in the lower house to more than 70% of the seats. However, negotiations on policy initiatives proved difficult, owing to differences over a number of contentious issues such as constitutional revision and New Komeito's opposition to a reduction in the number of seats in the lower house, as favoured by the LP. Obuchi was re-elected to the presidency of the LDP in September, defeating Koichi Kato, a former Secretary-General of the party, and Taku Yamasaki, a former policy chief. However, Naoto Kan failed to retain the presidency of the DPJ, and was replaced by Yukio Hatoyama.

A new Cabinet was appointed in October 1999. The Minister of Finance, Kiichi Miyazawa, and the Director-General of the Economic Planning Agency retained their portfolios, while Michio Ochi was appointed Chairman of the Financial Reconstruction Commission. The LP and New Komeito each received one cabinet post. A basic accord on coalition policy included an agreement to seek a reduction in the number of seats in the House of Representatives, initially by 20 and subsequently by a further 30.

Trials continued in 1997–99 of members of Aum Shinrikyo, the cult believed to be responsible for the sarin gas attack on the Tokyo underground railway system in 1995. In September 1999 Masato Yokoyama, a leading member of the cult, became the first of those accused to receive the death sentence; at least five other cult members had been sentenced to death by mid-2000. In late 1999 the Diet enacted legislation aimed at curbing the activities of Aum Shinrikyo and, in an attempt to prevent any such restriction, the cult's leaders announced a suspension of all external activities, and acknowledged culpability for a number of crimes, including the gas attack. In January 2000 the cult announced that its name was to change to Aleph, and that it no longer considered Shoko Asahara, on trial for his part in the gas attack, to be its leader.

At the end of 1999 the very fabric of Japan seemed to be fragmenting, as the economy regressed, juvenile involvement in serious crimes rose, various police scandals were uncovered, rocket launches by Japan's Space Agency failed, railway tunnels collapsed and nuclear power workers ladled radioactive material with buckets. There was persistent scepticism regarding the fate of the administrative reforms that had been adopted in July and about the Government's commitment to fiscal discipline. The new coalition, which was regularly threatened with withdrawal by Ozawa and the LP, did not inspire confidence in rational decision-making, and the promise made to Ozawa that priority would be given during the forthcoming Diet session to the bill to reduce the number of seats in the House of Representatives indicated difficulties to come.

Unpopular as the three-party alliance was, its significance became apparent as Obuchi was forced, in the interests of keeping his coalition together, to honour his promise to Ozawa of electoral reform. The coalition between the LP and the LDP had been underpinned by Obuchi's agreement to reduce by 50 the number of seats determined by PR. New Komeito, a party that was heavily dependent on these seats and passionately opposed to the proposed legislation, was, in turn, promised a lesser reduction in PR seats, of only 20, to be followed by a reduction of 30 single-member seats at a later date. The nature of the divisions between the alliance parties meant that no compromise was possible with the principal opposition party, the DPJ, which, as the potential second party in a two-party system, was strongly in favour of a reduction in the number of PR seats from 200 to 150. However, the size of the coalition rendered a compromise unnecessary. In February 2000, without committee debate, and despite a boycott of the Diet by opposition parties, legislation was approved to reduce the number of seats determined by PR in the House of Representatives from 500 to 480.

Meanwhile, in January 2000 multi-party commissions had been established in both houses to review the Constitution over a five-year period. Their range of discussion was broad and included both the structure of the bicameral legislature itself and Article 9. The inauguration of the commissions was a significant development, which marked a new openness and a wide agreement on the need for debate.

The first ordinary session of the Diet in 2000 was different, owing not only to the boycott and the 'alternative Diet' established by the opposition, but also to the implementation of changes to Diet procedure, which ended the system of responses being given by bureaucrats on behalf of ministers. The end of the 100-year-old practice was expected to enliven Diet debate, and was regarded as a means of educating a new style of politician and facilitating the shift to a more politician-led pattern of policy-making. To that end, the cabinet reorganization in October 1999 had brought the appointment of parliamentary vice-ministers with particular expertise in the areas covered by their ministries. Vice-ministerial appointments thus included senior people who might previously have been appointed to a cabinet position. Among these was Nishimura Shingo, of the LP, who was forced to resign from the Defence Agency after arguing that the Diet should debate the possibility of Japan acquiring nuclear weapons. The goal of politician-led governance was also behind the inauguration of a Prime Minister's question time. However, the new Diet standing committee, which became the forum for the 40-minute weekly debate between the Prime Minister and the leaders of the opposition parties, failed to win critical acclaim. In February 2000 the Chairman of the Financial Reconstruction Commission, Michio Ochi, was forced to resign after he remarked that he would endeavour to ensure that bank inspections were lenient.

In February 2000 Japan's first female governor took office in Osaka, having won a by-election necessitated by the resignation of the previous incumbent after his indictment in December 1999 for sexually harassing a female member of his staff. In April 2000 a second female governor was voted into office in southern Japan. Japan's governors, and local government, played an increasingly prominent role, drawing attention to their desire for greater autonomy. Growing opposition to a number of government projects became evident in 2000; a project to construct a nuclear power plant in Mie Prefecture was stopped, and in a referendum held in Tokushima, on Shikoku island, in January 90% of the electorate voted against a proposed dam across the Yoshino River (although senior ministers announced that the project would proceed, as local referendums were not legally binding). In February Governor Ishihara of Tokyo proposed that a tax be levied on major banks based on the size of their business rather than their profits; he was criticized by the central Government, which had previously been the only body able to introduce taxes. Ishihara attracted criticism from the foreign residents of Tokyo, and from neighbouring countries, in April, when, in an address to members of the SDF, he blamed foreign residents for a number of serious crimes and referred to them as *sangokujin*, a derogatory wartime term for people from Taiwan and Korea.

Friction within the ruling coalition continued throughout the early months of 2000, as the LP pressed for the consideration of elements of its policy programme, such as the upgrading of the Defence Agency to a ministry and the revision of education legislation, policies that were opposed by New Komeito. As elections to the House of Representatives drew inexorably closer, tension mounted over which coalition candidates would be endorsed. Finally, on 1 April Ozawa told Obuchi that he intended to withdraw the LP from the coalition. On the following day Obuchi suffered a stroke and went into a coma from which he never regained consciousness.

There was criticism of the secrecy initially surrounding Obuchi's collapse; the manner of the subsequent selection by a few politicians of Secretary-General Yoshiro Mori, head of the third largest faction in the LDP, as leader of the LDP and consequently as Prime Minister, led many to believe that nothing had changed in the conception of the nature of leadership since the end of the 1955 system. The events in the first days following Obuchi's stroke exposed the lack of adequate legislation to prevent a political vacuum in such circumstances. (The Government subsequently clarified the law, designating a ranking of five ministers to assume the premiership, starting with the Chief Cabinet Secretary.)

Mori immediately announced his commitment to the economic and political reform initiatives of his predecessor, and in early April 2000 formed a coalition with New Komeito and a new party, Hoshuto (New Conservative Party, formed by 26 members of the LP on 3 April). All ministers from the Obuchi administration were reappointed to their posts.

Obuchi's death was just one element of a dramatic change in the cast of leading political characters. During April 2000 both Seiroku Kajiyama, a former Chief Cabinet Secretary, and former Prime Minister Noboru Takeshita, hospitalized since April 1999 but still involved in behind-the-scenes manoeuvring, announced their retirement from politics and from the LDP; both men died shortly afterwards. Former Prime Minister Ryutaro Hashimoto was appointed head of the Takeshita faction of the LDP, which had been led by Obuchi prior to his stroke. The physical decline of the old guard, combined with party realignments and a need for expertise that the older politicians lacked, at a time when the demand for greater political input into, and accountability for, policy-making was growing, resulted in greater prominence for the younger generation of politicians. By 2000 the 'policy-making new generation', *seisaku shinjinrui*, was appearing in live television debates, drafting private members' bills, demanding structural change within the parties and rejecting factional discipline.

Following his appointment as Prime Minister, Mori made a number of controversial public statements, expressing imperialist views. He was heavily criticized by the opposition and the media and was forced to issue apologies, although he did not retract his remarks.

The election held on 25 June 2000 was the first that the LDP had contested as part of a coalition and the first in which it did not present candidates for every seat. The LDP won the most seats (233), although its representation was reduced (from 239 at the 1996 election), and many of the leading politicians, including current and former cabinet ministers, lost their seats, particularly in metropolitan areas. The DPJ increased its representation to 127 seats. New Komeito won 31 seats, the LP 22, Hoshuto 20 and the SDPJ 19. Only the JCP among the opposition parties suffered a loss of seats. Down six seats, from 26 to 20, the JCP was left without the minimum number of members required to propose legislation to the lower house. The party subsequently demonstrated a greater inclination to co-operate with the other opposition parties. The LDP benefited from the electoral system, which gives rural areas (where the LDP maintained strong support) disproportionately high representation. Tradition and family connections remained important, with two candidates (the brother of Noboru Takeshita and the daughter of Keizo Obuchi) winning seats despite their lack of political credentials and experience. Only 62.5% of those eligible participated in the election.

Following the June 2000 election, questions were immediately raised about how long the new Mori administration could survive in the light of the difficulties confronting it: further bribery scandals, a reduced mandate, Mori's own poor ratings in public opinion surveys, LDP factionalism and rivalries, and the need to balance the coalition both in the Cabinet and in terms of policy-making. Within the LDP itself there were growing demands for Mori's resignation by a cross-factional group of younger Diet members.

The Diet reconvened in September 2000. In the new session electoral reform again became a source of conflict between the Government and opposition parties. In October an amendment to the existing electoral system for the upper house, whereby voters cast their ballots for parties, to one in which electors could choose to vote either for a party or for an individual candidate, was proposed by the governing coalition. The issue was again the subject of dispute within the coalition, and, as they had done in January, the opposition parties, which argued that the proposed changes would make campaigning in elections more costly, commenced a boycott of Diet proceedings in protest against the Government forcing the bill through the upper house. The boycott, which lasted 18 days, ended following an agreement between the governing coalition and the opposition to debate the bill in the House of Representatives. The legislation, which was enacted in late October, also reduced the number of seats in the upper house, from 252 to 247.

Throughout September and October 2000 there was considerable public demand for the suspension of outdated, meaningless public works projects. In November the coalition parties approved the cancellation of 255 such projects, at an estimated saving of 2,500,000m. yen. Popular alienation from the major parties continued, and trust was undermined by ongoing revelations of misconduct. A leading LDP politician, the Chief Cabinet Secretary, Hidenao Nakagawa, resigned in October after it was alleged, *inter alia*, that he had links to a right-wing activist and had conducted an extramarital affair. Once again, the scandal provoked demands for Mori's resignation and criticism of the Prime Minister by senior officials within his own party.

In November 2000 the leaders of two LDP factions, Koichi Kato and Taku Yamasaki, joined the campaign to force Mori to resign and threatened to abstain if the opposition parties were to propose a vote of no confidence. With a total of 72 members in the House of Representatives, abstention by the Kato and Yamasaki factions was not sufficient to result in the approval of such a motion. Opposition from Miyazawa (Kato's former faction leader and political mentor), a lack of public support for the initiative, together with splits within the factions over the wisdom of leaving the relative safety of the LDP prior to elections to the upper house, which were scheduled for July 2001, brought the rebellion to a muted end. Mori survived the no-confidence vote, and in December he reorganized his Cabinet to include former Prime Minister Hashimoto in the post of Minister of State for the Development of Okinawa and the Settlement of the Northern Territories, areas of particular involvement for Hashimoto during his own premiership.

The new Diet session opened at the end of January 2001, with apologies for the most recent scandal (the misuse of funds by officials of the Ministry of Foreign Affairs). The new Diet was declared by Mori to be a 'Reform Diet', which would bring about the rebirth of the country. Mori particularly emphasized the role of information technology and education reform in this process. When the Diet reconvened, the restructuring of central government ministries and agencies was largely complete. A new Cabinet Office had been created, under the control of the Prime Minister, which was ranked higher than other ministries and charged with inter-ministry policy co-ordination. Within the Cabinet Office, a new Council on Economic and Fiscal Policy (CEFP), led by the Prime Minister, had been established to address budgetary, financial and economic issues. The Cabinet Secretariat had been strengthened and expanded, and 22 other ministries had been consolidated down to 12. New political posts were established in each of the ministries and agencies to increase political input into the policy-making process. The administrative reforms had a number of objectives, including increased transparency and streamlining, but the major aim was to enable greater political leadership to be assumed by the Prime Minister and the Cabinet.

Despite the enhanced powers afforded to the Prime Minister by the administrative reforms (the ability to propose policy, majority voting in the Cabinet, greater control over appointments, etc.), Mori became increasingly ineffectual during the early months of 2001, suffering one scandal after another. The coalition parties were made even less sanguine about their prospects in the forthcoming elections when the DPJ, the LP and the SDPJ agreed, at the end of March, to put forward joint opposition candidates in 13 of 27 single-seat constituencies.

At the beginning of April 2001 another reform came into effect, requiring the disclosure of administrative documents on request, although there were suggestions that many documents had been disposed of in the January restructuring. These institutional changes were important, but so too were the people who were to implement them. In the same month four candidates contested the presidency of the LDP, a first since the election of Yasuhiro Nakasone as President in 1982. The four were Ryutaro Hashimoto, Junichiro Koizumi, Taro Aso and Shizuka Kamei. The principal contender was former Prime Minister Hashimoto, the leader of the largest faction of the LDP, with more than 100 members. Koizumi, who had just resigned as Chairman of the Mori faction, had high public ratings, but had alienated significant sections of the LDP with his plans for the privatization of the postal services. At a time when other traditional sources of LDP support, such as the construction industry and agricultural unions, were losing their ability to gather votes, this was regarded as important and worried Koizumi's supporters, who included Koichi Kato and Taku Yamasaki. Kamei and Aso were regarded as outsiders. The system used by the LDP to elect its President has varied over time. On this occasion, the election took place in two stages: a prefectural membership vote, which accounted for 30% of the total, followed by a vote by LDP Diet members. The nature of the election process proved crucial. Although there was much political manoeuvring between the LDP factions, and within the factions between the generations, the overwhelming support of the local branches of the party for Koizumi, whose slogan was 'Change the LDP, Change Japan', was decisive, and the LDP Diet members also backed him. Overall, Koizumi received 298 of the 478 presidency votes, while Hashimoto won 155. With the support of the coalition, Koizumi was confirmed as Prime Minister by the Diet.

The Koizumi Administration

Junichiro Koizumi, perceived as eccentric, a reformist and a nationalist, rapidly became a political phenomenon, with unparalleled popularity ratings. Although seven ministers were retained from the previous administration, the new Cabinet contained an unprecedented five women, including Makiko Tanaka as Minister for Foreign Affairs. It also included three non-Diet members, most notably Heizo Takenaka, a pro-reformist economics professor at Keio University and adviser to two previous Cabinets, as Minister of State in charge of Economic and Fiscal Policy and Information Technology Policy, and Nobuteru Ishihara, the son of the controversial Governor of Tokyo, and one of the LDP 'Young Turks', as Minister of State in charge of Administrative Reform and Regulatory Reform.

Koizumi's depiction in the foreign press as a nationalist was further encouraged by his announcement that he would visit the Yasukuni Shrine (a memorial constructed in 1869 and dedicated to Japanese men, women and children who died in the name of their country, including those convicted of war crimes) on 15 August 2001, the 56th anniversary of the end of the Second World War. The ensuing controversy was exacerbated by his support for constitutional revision, beginning with the public election of the Prime Minister, but also embracing changes that would allow Japan to exercise the right of collective security. Koizumi's political philosophy and policies were close to those of former Prime Minister Nakasone, who strongly supported Koizumi, comparing the new Prime Minister's reforms with his own 'final settlement of post-war politics'.

The Koizumi reform plan, drafted by the CEFP, was published in June 2001. The overall short-term objectives of the plan were to eradicate bad loans and to implement reforms in seven areas, including privatization, deregulation, the encouragement of entrepreneurial activity and fiscal reform. The longer-term aim was for private sector demand to become the driving force of the economy. The proposals reiterated the promise to reduce the issuance of new government bonds in the 2002/03 budget, and to that end, to decrease public works, reform special public corporations and reduce central government grants to local administrations.

At elections to the Tokyo Metropolitan Assembly in early July 2001, the LDP secured five additional seats; the result was attributed to 'Koizumi fever' and indicated what the LDP might expect in the elections to the House of Councillors scheduled for later in the month. The new electoral system for the upper house, which allowed votes for individuals as well as parties, led, predictably, to a large number of celebrity candidates. The results of the elections, which were held on 29 July, were even better than anticipated for the LDP, which regained Tokyo and Osaka (lost in 1998), and took 25 of the 27 contested single-seat constituencies. Overall, the coalition won 79 of the 121 contested seats, giving the Government a useful majority of 140 seats in the 247-member chamber. Although Koizumi hailed the results as a mandate for reform, the stock market fell on the following day to a 16-year low point, driven by two conflicting fears: first, that Koizumi would fail to carry out reform owing to LDP opposition; and second, that his reforms would lead rapidly to short-term bankruptcies and loss of corporate earnings. However, Koizumi's public support, the absence of a viable challenger within the LDP and the lack of concerted opposition from outside placed him in a strong position.

Koizumi's attempts to give budgetary priority to seven specific areas (environment, the ageing society, local revitalization, urban redevelopment, science, education and information technology) were undermined by equivocation between ministries and by a failure to persuade the new so-called 'super ministries' to make any changes to the budgetary share of their constituent ministries and agencies. The Prime Minister's non-consensual and decisive leadership style and his reliance on private advisory bodies created opposition within the LDP policy committees and within the LDP leadership itself. His criticism of the faction system in general, and of the *Keiseikai* (a faction of the LDP) in particular, left him isolated within the party and caused the pace of reform to decelerate. Although Koizumi retained his exceptionally high popularity ratings throughout late 2001, the media began to focus on his failure to deliver reform. The restructuring of the public corporations, one of Koizumi's central aims and one of his more popular reforms, showed signs of failing under concerted opposition both from the ministries, which provided more than half the corporations' directors, and the LDP policy committees (*zoku*), to which the corporations provided funding in return for political favours. An outbreak of bovine spongiform encephalopathy (BSE, or so-called mad cow disease), the first outside Europe, was confirmed in September. The Ministry of Agriculture, Forestry and Fisheries stood accused of failing to heed World Health Organization warnings on the use of meat and bone meal feed, and of failing to provide adequate crisis management. The failures were attributed to the lack of cohesion within the ministry, despite previous efforts to restructure it. The ministry's structural problems were exacerbated by the strength of LDP Diet members' links with agricultural interests and their influence on civil servants.

Media evaluations of the workings of the new government structure, one year after its inception, reported rigidity in bureaucratic structures, and continued bureaucratic dominance, despite increased formal powers for the Prime Minister's Office, the creation of the Financial Services Agency and the CEFP, and the introduction of senior vice-ministers and parliamentary secretaries. The media viewed the redeployment of a number of these vice-ministers and parliamentary secretaries in January 2002 as a retreat by Koizumi on faction-based appointments and a victory for Hashimoto. In July a review of the functions of the CEFP was ordered in response to suggestions that it was not fulfilling its original purpose of transferring responsibility for economic and fiscal policy from the bureaucracy to the Prime Minister and Cabinet.

Koizumi's dismissal of Makiko Tanaka in January 2002 after weeks of pressure from the LDP, despite his pledge not to reallocate cabinet portfolios during his term of office, appeared to precipitate a sharp decline in the Prime Minister's popularity. Predictions of a return to factional politics and an end to the prospects for reform caused falls in the stock market, in government bonds and in the value of the yen. Tanaka claimed that the Prime Minister had broken his pledges on reform and was allowing his Cabinet to be influenced by former Prime Minister Mori. The DPJ began to conduct itself more in the manner of an opposition party and criticized Koizumi's handling of the economy, rising unemployment and the growing number of scandals involving senior members of the LDP. For the first time Koizumi was no longer able to use the promise of an approach to the DPJ as a credible threat to control the LDP.

In March 2002 one of Koizumi's two closest allies, Koichi Kato, resigned following the arrest of the former head of his Tokyo office on charges of tax evasion and accepting bribes for facilitating the allocation of public works. Kato's resignation from the LDP followed that of the former Director-General of the Hokkaido and Okinawa Development Agency, Suzuki Muneo, on charges of malpractice. The scandals focused attention on the urgent need to address the issues of the relationship of LDP Diet members and the bureaucracy with regard to policy-making.

Almost simultaneously with the resignations, a draft report was produced by the LDP National Vision Project Headquarters under Koizumi, and submitted to the Prime Minister without prior consideration by the General Council. The report, which proposed a study of measures to create a cabinet-led system and deny influence to politicians with vested interests, drew an angry response from the LDP, both for its content and the manner of its introduction. The proposals included cabinet drafting of all bills and policies, restrictions on contact between back-bench politicians and bureaucrats, and an end to approval of bills by party committees before submission to the Diet. The report, and its rejection by the LDP, was best viewed in the context of Koizumi's attempt to open up the postal delivery service to private competition, which, under the LDP operating methods, might be diverted by one dissenting LDP vote.

Restructuring of the postal services remained the basis of Koizumi's reform programme because of the implications for controlling vested-interest politics. It was opposed by many in the LDP for the same reasons. In an unusual procedure, the four postal bills were submitted to the Diet without the support of the LDP, and the passage of the legislation was secured only after some modification of the content and the promise of a cabinet reorganization. The compromises resulted in requirements for entering the mail delivery sector being set at a level that would exclude most private companies. The extended Diet session ended on 31 July 2002.

In September 2002, as a direct result of the Prime Minister's North Korean initiative on relations with the Democratic People's Republic of Korea (DPRK—North Korea: see Foreign Reations, below), his popularity rose dramatically. In a cabinet reorganization in late September, changes included the removal of Hakuo Yanagisawa, Minister of State responsible for the Financial Services Agency and widely regarded as an opponent of reform, and his replacement by Heizo Takenaka; (an unelected official with few allies within the LDP) who also continued as Minister of State for Economic and Fiscal Policy. The reorganization, which included six new cabinet appointments, was generally perceived as having been carried out without consultation or regard for factional considerations and as a reaffirmation of Koizumi's commitment to reform. Koizumi's adherence to Takenaka's firm policy on the disposal of bad loans was given further support by five LDP by-election victories at the end of October, although this did not put an end to criticism of Koizumi's reform policies by senior LDP Diet members.

The closing months of 2002 were even less satisfactory for the DPJ and its leader. In September the party re-elected Yukio Hatoyama as leader in a close contest with Naoto Kan. The four candidates in the election all favoured electoral co-operation with the LP and SDPJ but, like a microcosm of the DPJ itself, differed on economic policy and constitutional revision. Barely three months later losses in the by-elections, compounded by a failed attempt to merge with the LP to form a new opposition party, led to Hatoyama's resignation and the election of Kan in December. Kan commanded greater support among the public, many of whom regarded him as a potential prime minister, but support for the DPJ remained static. In late December four defectors from the DPJ and nine members of the New Conservative Party (NCP), formed a new NCP, which aligned itself with the governing coalition. This minor change represented only the latest development in 10 years of unfulfilled hopes for proper party realignment that would deliver an alternating system of government.

Figures released in the latter part of 2002 showed that in 2001 donations to all political parties had declined for the fifth consecutive year. However, the purchase of tickets by individual companies to party fund-raising events had increased to exceed all other forms of corporate donations combined, provoking fears of a decline in transparency. State subsidies to political parties, as revised in the Hosokawa reforms of 1994 and having increased to account for more than 28% of total funds raised, were a factor in the timing and nature of party realignment. Koizumi's proposals in March 2002 further to restrict donations from companies involved in public works had made no progress because of LDP antagonism and mixed sentiments among the opposition parties. In early 2003 the LDP was embarrassed by scandals connected with political funding, including the arrest of a sitting Diet member belonging to Koizumi's own faction for concealing political donations; and the resignation of the Minister of Agriculture, Forestry and Fisheries over the misuse of funds by a former aide. Senior members of the LDP, including Koizumi, therefore welcomed a decision in May by the Japan Business Federation (JBF—the former Keidanren, the influence of which on government policy-making had weakened since its suspension of fund-raising for political parties in 1993) to return to brokering political contributions in 2004. The avowed aim of the JBF was to use donations to encourage tax and social security reforms. To this end, LDP members drafted guidelines for evaluating party policy. The anticipated shift from party ticket sales, which depended on the strength of individuals and factions, to corporate grants direct to the parties was expected to bolster the power of central party officials. The decline in the ability of factions to provide either funding or position was matched by a loss of factional loyalty, especially among younger party members, and even within the biggest LDP faction led by former Prime Minister Hashimoto.

The debate on constitutional revision was revived in November 2002 by the release, against the wishes of the JCP and SDPJ, of an interim report by the Research Commission on the Constitution, which had been established in the House of Representatives in January 2000. The report set out the arguments for and against amending Article 9 of the Constitution (on the renunciation of war), without reaching a conclusion; it also discussed the popular election of the Prime Minister, changes to the bicameral legislature and the introduction into the Constitution of new human rights. The relevance of the debate on Article 9 was brought into focus in April 2003 by the conflict in Iraq and developments in North Korea. Former Prime Ministers Nakasone and Miyazawa found themselves, unusually, agreeing that under certain circumstances, collective self-defence was allowed under the present Constitution.

The extraordinary Diet session convened in October 2002 and ended in December, having failed for a second time to approve government bills on defence and privacy. A combination of the international situation, divisions in the DPJ and concessions by the Government resulted in the privacy bill not being enacted into law until May, followed by the defence bills in June. The ordinary legislative session was extended by the governing coalition by 40 days to 28 July to enable the passage of a bill that would permit the dispatch of SDF personnel to assist reconstruction in Iraq, but only after a week of opposition boycotting of the Diet. The last few days of this extended session were enlivened by the announcement of a planned merger of the DPJ and Ichiro Ozawa's LP (which, upon its conclusion in September, brought the total representation of the two parties to 136 in the lower and 66 in the upper house). The DPJ was eager to persuade the SDPJ, which was beset by a funding scandal, to join them. The Government's announcement of plans for an extraordinary Diet session from mid-September to amend the Anti-terrorism Law before its expiry on 1 November, and a planned visit by US President George W. Bush, provoked rumours of a forthcoming dissolution of the Diet and demands for detailed manifestos from the various parties. Koizumi promised that if he were re-elected as President of the LDP, his policy pledges would become the party platform. In late September Koizumi was re-elected leader of the LDP, winning 399 of the 657 votes cast—260 more than Shizuka Kamei, the nearest of his three rivals. Koizumi then effected a major reorganization of the Cabinet without consulting the LDP factions. The new appointments brought a more youthful image to the Cabinet. This promotion of reform-minded politicians was part of a broader attempt to produce a generation shift, which included the appointment of 49-year-old Shinzo Abe as LDP Secretary-General and the introduction of a mandatory retirement age of 73 for LDP Diet members elected from constituencies determined by means of PR. Former Prime Minister Miyazawa (aged 84) accepted the proposal, but former Prime Minister Nakasone (85), who in 1996 had been promised a position at the head of the PR list for the rest of his life and whose ambition was to see reform of the Constitution during his political career, deplored his enforced retirement.

In October 2003 the legislation to extend the Anti-terrorism Law by two years was approved by both Houses, and the Prime Minister announced the dissolution of the House of Representatives in advance of a general election, scheduled for 9 November. One of the last acts of the Diet before its dissolution was to amend the Public Offices Election Law to permit the distribution by candidates of their party manifesto during the election campaign from designated places, although not from within newspapers. In addition to clarifying the differences between the parties and countering public apathy, the introduction of manifestos was expected to limit the influence of the LDP *zoku* and the bureaucracy over policy-making. The election itself was seen as a potential watershed in post-war Japanese politics—partly because the DPJ, having recently merged with Ozawa's LP, was presenting 277 candidates (267 in single-seat constituencies, of whom 246 were in direct conflict with the LDP), and partly because Koizumi had promised not to remain in power if the ruling coalition did not maintain a majority.

Despite the availability of party manifestos and the attendant publicity, the turn-out at the election on 9 November 2003 decreased to just under 60% of the electorate. With the LDP benefiting in a significant number of single-seat constituencies from the backing of its coalition partner, New Komeito, and its supporting group, the Soka Gakkai, the distribution of seats among the main political parties in the House of Representatives after the election was: LDP 237 seats (compared with 247 before the election); DPJ 177 (previously 137); New Komeito 34 (31); JCP nine (20); SDPJ six (18); and NCP four (10). The NCP, one of the governing coalition parties in partnership with New Komeito and the LDP, disbanded and merged with the LDP after Hiroshi Kumagai and other party leaders lost their seats. The merger thus gave the LDP a simple majority in the lower house where it now held a total of 241 of the 480 seats. In addition, four independent members of the House of Representatives joined the LDP after the election. With 279 seats, the new LDP-New Komeito coalition still had an absolutely stable majority, giving it control of all committee chairmanships and a majority in all standing committees. Major individual losses in the election included LDP Vice-President Taku Yamasaki and SDPJ leader Takako Doi, who nevertheless was returned to a PR seat in the legislature. The big gains made by the DPJ, and the fact that it even outperformed the LDP in PR voting, suggested that a genuine two-party system might indeed be emerging. In the event, 84% of the seats in the election were won by the two major parties.

Policy debate during the election, sharpened somewhat by the manifestos though still lacking in specific proposals, focused on the issues of retirement pensions and tax reform, the privatization of the postal system and of road-building corporations, and the dispatch of the SDF to Iraq. These questions continued to dominate Japanese domestic politics in 2004. On the subject of the revision of the Constitution, the manifestos of both the LDP and the DPJ favoured an expansion of the debate. This was facilitated by the substantial losses of seats suffered by the SDPJ and JCP. The issue was placed firmly on the agenda in January 2004 when Koizumi promised that the LDP would draft a revised constitution by 2005, the 50th anniversary of the founding of the party. The DPJ announced its own intention to produce a draft constitution by 2006. Revision would require the approval of a two-thirds' majority in both houses, followed by a referendum. Legislation for establishing the legal procedures for constitutional amendment would be the first stage. Some of the central issues were the right to collective defence, the introduction of a constitutional court, changes to the requirements for constitutional revision and the shift to a unicameral legislature.

Following his re-election as party President and the return of the LDP to government at the lower house election of November 2003, Koizumi was generally regarded as having a brief opportunity for reform, which would last until the upper house election in July 2004; beyond that date there would be no further need for his rivals in the party to support him. Even during this period, however, the contest for power within the party remained intense. During his three years in office Koizumi had undermined the LDP factions by disregarding their recommendations for cabinet and party appointments, and had made particular efforts to weaken the largest grouping, the Hashimoto faction. The elections for LDP President in September 2003 divided the Hashimoto faction into those led by Mikio Aoki, who supported Koizumi, and those led by Hiromu Nonaka, who did not favour the incumbent leader. Those who had supported Koizumi were rewarded with cabinet positions. The November election further directed the factional balance in the lower house away from the Hashimoto faction, which lost eight seats to leave it with 51 in the new legislature, and towards Koizumi's former faction, the Mori faction, which gained 12 seats to give it a total of 52. When the Hashimoto faction lost 11 members in the upper house elections in July 2004, Hashimoto announced his resignation as faction leader and his intention not to seek re-election in a single-seat constituency in the next election. Hashimoto, whose faction was directly descended from the scandal-ridden Tanaka and Takeshita factions, was at the time under investigation for allegedly receiving undisclosed political contributions of 100m. yen from the Japan Dental Association.

The DPJ entered the campaign for the upper house election, due to be held on 11 July 2004, under the leadership of Katsuya Okada, after first Naoto Kan and then Ichiro Ozawa resigned because of their failure to pay pension contributions. The election campaign focused on only two main issues—pension reform and SDF participation in Iraq; a discussion of postal reform was eschewed by both major parties. A revision of the Public Offices Election Law reduced the number of upper house seats by five, to 242, leaving 121 seats to be contested (one-half of the members being elected every three years for a six-year term, with the chamber not being subject to dissolution).

The outcome of the election, in which the DPJ for the second time won more votes than the LDP, was regarded as another milestone on the road to a two-party system. The DPJ secured 50 seats and the LDP, which had lost its majority in the upper house in 1989, failed not only to win the 56 that it had needed to regain it, but even to achieve the 'safe' 51-seat target that it had set for itself. (However, the ruling coalition as a whole, including New Komeito, did continue to hold a majority in the House of Councillors.) The results were seen as a serious set-back to Koizumi's leadership, not least within his own party, and represented a major threat to his reform programme, particularly to his plans for privatization of public financial services supplied by post offices. A major cabinet reorganization was implemented in September 2004.

The issue of postal privatization dominated and defined all aspects of domestic politics, at the expense of other matters, throughout 2005, until the rejection of the reform proposals by the House of Councillors in August precipitated a dissolution of the Diet by Prime Minister Koizumi and the scheduling of a general election for 11 September. The failure to build a consensus for postal reform within the LDP began with Koizumi's refusal to consult senior party members on cabinet and party appointments and his installation of two notably uncompromising candidates, Tsutomu Takebe and Kaoru Yosano, in the respective posts of LDP Secretary-General and Chairman of the Policy Affairs Research Council. The initial favourable public response to the reorganization gave Koizumi some short-term protection from the opponents within his own party, but did nothing to bridge the gap between the limited postal reform policy of the LDP General Council and the more radical and extensive privatization plans of the Government. The Prime Minister's commitment to dividing Japan Post into four separate units—responsible for savings, life insurance, mail delivery and the post office network—was intended not only to achieve fiscal reform and reform of government finances but also to reduce waste in public spending by diverting funds from the public to the private sector, to reduce the size of government and to promote fundamental changes in the conduct of politics.

Hostility to the bills from both the opposition and government parties resulted in an unexpectedly small majority of five in favour of the reforms in a vote by the House of Representatives on 5 July 2005. Both the Hashimoto faction and the Kamei faction were divided over the reforms. Altogether, 37 LDP members voted against the bills in the lower house and 14 abstained. When the House of Councillors rejected the bills on 8 August by 125 votes to 108 (22 LDP members voted against, 14 abstained), Koizumi ignored intense pressure from inside his own party and defiance from within the Cabinet and, to the surprise of many, immediately dissolved the lower house. The dissolution of the House of Representatives in response to the rejection of a bill by the upper house, and the dismissal of a cabinet minister who refused to sign the dissolution order, were both unprecedented events in Japanese politics. Koizumi announced that the election would represent a referendum on postal privatization and instructed the party to de-select the rebels and to present official LDP candidates in all rebel-held constituencies. The party slogans for the September election bore testament to the pervasiveness of the privatization issue: for the LDP, 'Don't thwart reform'; for New Komeito, 'Power to reform'; and for the DPJ, 'There are more important things (than postal reform)'. Both Koizumi and the leader of the DPJ, Katsuya Okada, promised to resign if they failed to win the election.

The general election on 11 September 2005 resulted in a decisive victory for Koizumi and the LDP, which secured 296 of the 480 seats in the House of Representatives, increasing its share by 84. The LDP's ally, New Komeito, took 31 seats, thus giving the ruling coalition a two-thirds' majority in the house. The DPJ, meanwhile, won 113 seats, 64 fewer than it had held in the previous assembly. Participation in the election was 67.5%. Okada subsequently fulfilled his promise to resign, and one week later DPJ members of the Diet elected 'shadow' cabinet member Seiji Maehara as his successor. In October the Diet approved legislation providing for the privatization of Japan Post, thus permitting Koizumi's reform programme finally to proceed.

In a statement celebrating the 50th anniversary, in 2005, of the founding of the LDP, the party reaffirmed its original six conservative goals, which included national morality, national independence, peaceful diplomacy, economic self-reliance, a welfare-orientated society and educational, political and administrative reform. In accordance with this agenda, the LDP set about the tortuous and divisive task of producing its own draft for a revised constitution, for publication in November. In April the Constitution Research Commissions, established in both houses of the Diet in January 2000, produced study reports that identified the need for revision, but were inconclusive about the nature of the changes required. There was majority agreement in both Commissions on the need for new human rights provisions relating to privacy and the environment, and a majority in the lower house (but not the upper house) panel were in favour of a change to the preamble to include: a reference to Japan's history, tradition and culture; recognition of the SDF (which had celebrated its own 50th anniversary in 2004); a definition of 'military emergency'; the establishment of a constitutional court; a reference to the legality of government subsidies to private schools; and the introduction of larger regional administrative blocks. Neither panel was eager to allow collective self-defence or to relax the conditions for revising the Constitution. Both panels were in agreement that the status of the Emperor should remain as 'symbol of the state', and not be redefined as 'head of state' as proposed by former Prime Minister Nakasone. The next requirement was for the passage of a national procedural referendum bill. Although no agreement on the necessary changes had yet been reached, 58 years after its passage the taboo on revision of the post-war peace Constitution had finally been ended.

The 12 months following the LDP electoral victory of September 2005 represented a test for candidates hoping to become the next Prime Minister, upon the expiry of Koizumi's term of office scheduled for September 2006. The contest began with Koizumi's appointment of Shinzo Abe as Chief Cabinet Secretary, Taro Aso as Minister for Foreign Affairs and Sadakazu Tanigaki as Minister of Finance in the October reallocation of cabinet portfolios that followed the passage of the post office legislation. Former Chief Cabinet Secretary Yasuo Fukuda's popularity, which remained strong until he withdrew from the contest in late July, was closely related to his policy on diplomatic and security matters, not least his opposition to prime ministerial visits to the Yasukuni Shrine. Fukuda's stance was taken up by Tanigaki, who then declared his candidacy. By contrast, the forthright Abe, who had taken a consistently firm stand against China and North Korea, strongly supported Koizumi's visits to the controversial memorial to the war dead and had made regular visits himself. These two questions—the succession to Koizumi and the appropriateness of visits to Yasukuni by the Prime Minister—had thus become the central issues of domestic politics and, furthermore, had also begun to have a negative impact on Japan's regional relations (see below).

Koizumi's visits to the Yasukuni Shrine were judged by the Osaka High Court in September 2005 to violate the constitutional separation of state and religion, but the renewed ruling did not prevent the Prime Minister from making further visits. The Prime Minister's visits became an inter-party as well as an intra-party issue when the new DPJ President, Ichiro Ozawa, visited the Chinese capital, Beijing, and met with President Hu Jintao, who had boycotted meetings with Koizumi since the visit to the Yasukuni Shrine in October. The criticism from China and South Korea that followed the visit was intensified by what appeared to be a request from Taro Aso for a visit to Yasukuni by the Emperor. It later became clear from a memorandum written by a former imperial official that the Showa Emperor had stopped visiting Yasukuni as a result of the decision to enshrine there 14 Class-A war criminals (those convicted at the most serious level of crimes against peace) in 1978. Koizumi made his final gesture on Yasukuni with a visit on 15 August 2006, the anniversary of the ending of the Second World War and a date that he had previously avoided.

The delayed postal reform bill secured passage through the upper house in October 2005. The legislation ensured that by October 2007 Japan Post would be split into four divisions: deliveries, post office branches, savings and life insurance services, which would be overseen by a holding company. Other structural reforms—which would reduce the size of government, reform the government-affiliated financial institutions, reduce the number of central government employees and associated costs, and implement fiscal decentralization—encountered mixed results. An administrative reform law regarded as the centre-piece of the legislative programme and crucial to further post-Koizumi reform was approved in May 2006. The law provided, *inter alia*, for a 5% decrease in the number of government employees, including SDF members, to achieve a reduction of 16,600 personnel, and plans exceeding this target were agreed in June.

A decision by Koizumi not to extend the Diet session beyond its deadline of June 2006 meant that other important but politically controversial legislation was carried forward for consideration by an extraordinary Diet session after the LDP presidential election. The postponed items of draft legislation included a twice-rejected Conspiracy Bill, which would make the plotting of a crime a criminal offence. They also included revisions to the Fundamental Law on Education, where the obstacle was finding an acceptable way of fostering patriotism.

Although the Conspiracy Bill was delayed, the Japanese administration, like many Western governments, had implemented a number of measures to improve its homeland security. These included revisions to the Immigration Control and Refugee Recognition Law, which provided for the fingerprinting and photographing of foreign visitors, the deportation of those designated as terrorists and the prior submission of crew and passenger lists by incoming vessels. In May 2006 the Government also approved threat contingency plans for all prefectures, as part of the 2004 war contingency legislation against armed attack by a foreign country or terrorist groups. Meanwhile, other longer-term domestic concerns persisted, including the steady decline in the population and the birth rate, which continued to provoke demands for financial assistance for child care and education and a reappraisal of immigration policy.

During his five-year tenure Koizumi (the third longest-serving post-war Prime Minister) had achieved a great deal, not least the shift of the locus of policy-making from the bureaucracy to the Prime Minister's Office, through the creation of the CEFP, and the erosion of factions and structural changes to the LDP. He also achieved a significant reduction in both bad debt and expenditure on public works, although his reforms arguably contributed to the growth in economic disparities.

The Abe Administration

The Koizumi administration ended on 26 September 2006, when Shinzo Abe, who had been elected President of the LDP in the previous week, was appointed Prime Minister. The grandson of former Prime Minister Nobusuke Kishi and son of Shintaro Abe, the former Minister for Foreign Affairs, Shinzo Abe had established a reputation as an uncompromising, conservative politician. At the age of 52, Abe was Japan's youngest post-war Prime Minister. He immediately named a new Cabinet, replacing all the incumbent ministers with the exception of Taro Aso as Minister for Foreign Affairs. In his first policy speech to the lower house, Abe stated that he wanted to emphasize patriotism and hard work at home, while repairing relations with South Korea and China. He revealed that he wanted to move quickly towards the revision of Japan's Constitution and specifically to reconsider the matter of collective defence. He also promised structural reforms to raise economic growth, while launching a 'rechallenge initiative' aimed at helping the unemployed and failed entrepreneurs.

Abe's first month in office brought him two victories in by-elections to the House of Representatives and positive press coverage of his diplomatic overtures to China and South Korea, with visits to both countries within days of his appointment; his attempts to reduce bureaucratic input into policy-making were also favourably received. The LDP continued to rely on its coalition partner, New Komeito (from September 2006 led by Akihiro Ota), to advance its policies and maintain political stability. One such piece of legislation was the bill to extend by a further year the special anti-terrorism legislation to enable the Marine Self-Defence Force (MSDF) to continue refuelling ships in the Indian Ocean, as support for the US-led forces in Afghanistan, which was enacted in October despite opposition from the DPJ. Other controversial legislation introduced during the first session included bills to upgrade the Defence

Agency to a full ministry and to include international peacekeeping duties as part of regular SDF activities, and a bill to define the necessary procedure for a referendum on changes to the Constitution. A controversial bill on basic education, which passed into law in December despite an opposition motion of no confidence in the Government, urged the development of 'an attitude that respects tradition and culture and loves the nation and homeland that have fostered them'. In addition to promoting patriotism, the revised Fundamental Law on Education extended central government involvement in education. In November, with a view to the July 2007 upper house elections and to the political subsidies dependent on numbers of party Diet members, Abe had initiated procedures to readmit to the LDP a number of the so-called 'postal rebels' (members who had defected in protest at postal reforms in 2005—see above) subject to certain conditions. The initiative, seen as a shift away from Koizumi's reforms, was opposed by many and was followed by a decrease in the Cabinet's approval ratings. Abe ended his first 85-day extraordinary parliamentary session having made a decisive start on introducing his promised 'post-war regime', but beset by political funding scandals involving Genichiro Sata, the Minister responsible for the administrative reform portfolio, and Masaaki Honma, Chairman of the Tax Commission.

Allegations of offences under the Political Fund Control Law by ministers continued into early 2007, when the Diet reconvened for the 150-day regular session that would be followed closely by elections to the upper house. The Prime Minister's policy speech at the start of the session promised restructuring to promote a new national identity; further education reform, including the eradication of bullying and the removal of underperforming teachers; tax reform and new strategies for economic growth; pro-active diplomacy, including a reinforcement of the US-Japanese alliance and greater engagement with North Korea; and a review of collective self-defence. However, Abe did not address an issue that had gained prominence during 2006: that of widespread social disparities and the growth of an underclass in what had previously been characterized as an egalitarian, middle-class society.

Government plans to establish a constitutional revision process made steady progress. In April 2007 the lower house's Special Committee for Research on the Constitution approved the Government's bill on national referendums on constitutional amendments, and the Government established an expert panel to review the constitutional ban on collective defence. The bill to establish referendum procedures, which was approved by the upper house in May, was scheduled to enter into force in 2010, the earliest date at which drafts of a new constitution could be presented to the Diet. The law allowed for participation by Japanese citizens aged 18 years or more (contrasting with the current voting age of 20 and therefore necessitating further legislative changes) and imposed no minimum requirements with regard to the level of participation. A two-thirds' majority in both houses in favour of any revision would be necessary for a national referendum to be called; as expected, therefore, constitutional revision became a major issue in the upper house elections of July, prior to which the governing coalition was 29 seats short of the two-thirds' threshold. Divisions within, as well as among, the parties meant that the issue had the potential to cause major political realignment; nevertheless, it appeared that voters' attention remained firmly focused on the issues of pensions and social welfare. Article 9 lost one of its staunchest defenders when former Prime Minister Kiichi Miyazawa died in June.

As the upper house election approached, Abe struggled with the crisis caused by the Social Insurance Agency's loss of 50m. pension files. In a 12-day extension to the parliamentary session that resulted in the upper house election being postponed by one week to 29 July 2007, the Government forced through three vital pieces of legislation: a revised Political Funds Control bill; revisions to the National Civil Service Law aimed at controlling the controversial practice of *amakudari* (whereby senior civil servants retired to well-paid positions, often with organizations linked to the government ministry or agency in which they were formerly employed); and pensions-related bills to extend the five-year statute of limitations on claims and to disband the failing Social Insurance Agency and disperse its functions. The pension reform bills drew criticism from the financial press for their lack of detail. Although arguably a bureaucratic failure, the pension crisis caused further damage to an LDP beset by continuing financial scandals, which included the suicide of the Minister of Agriculture, Forestry and Fisheries, Toshikatsu Matsuoka, in May. In the same month legislation providing for a new criminal trial system, under which lay judges (six Japanese citizens aged 20 or above) would sit alongside the existing panels of three judges and be involved in deciding sentences, was approved by the Diet.

By June 2007 popular support for Abe had declined considerably, and the LDP's electoral prospects were further set back by the controversy surrounding the Minister of Defence, Fumio Kyuma. Kyuma resigned after making contentious remarks suggesting that the US nuclear attacks on Japan during the Second World War had been unavoidable, but his departure did little to help the popularity of Abe, who had lent him public support. Yuriko Koike became the first female Minister of Defence when she was appointed to replace Kyuma. Campaigning for the 121 seats (73 prefectural district, 48 PR) to be contested in the upper house election began on 12 July, with the coalition needing to win 64 seats to maintain its all-important majority. Electioneering was interrupted briefly and an emergency task force was established in the Prime Minister's Office when a major earthquake wreaked havoc in Niigata and Nagano prefectures, causing a fire at a nuclear power plant and a leak of water contaminated with radioactive materials. A relaxation of regulations, which resulted in more than 10m. absentee ballots being cast, may have contributed to a 2% increase in the level of voter participation to almost 59%. The LDP suffered an historic defeat at the election, winning a total of 37 seats (23 prefectural district, 14 PR), with its biggest losses in the rural, agricultural districts. New Komeito won nine seats (two prefectural, seven PR), leaving the coalition with 103 seats overall, the DPJ with 109, and the combined opposition parties with 127 seats and an overall majority for the first time since the LDP was formed in 1955. Abe acknowledged public anger over pensions, political funding and ministerial gaffes, but rejected the idea that the results were a repudiation of his reform agenda and refused to resign or to reorganize his Cabinet.

In late August 2007 Abe effected a cabinet reorganization in an effort to bolster public confidence in his Government, appointing Nobutaka Machimura as Minister for Foreign Affairs (a position that he had filled in a previous Koizumi administration), to replace Taro Aso, who had become Secretary-General of the LDP. In early September, however, the new Minister of Agriculture, Forestry and Fisheries, Takehiko Endo, resigned amid a corruption scandal. Abe himself announced his resignation in the following week, citing a general lack of public support, as well as political conflict over the extension of Japan's co-operation with the US mission in Afghanistan. Former Chief Cabinet Secretary Yasuo Fukuda, son of former Prime Minister Takeo Fukuda, was elected President of the LDP in late September and appointed Prime Minister shortly afterwards.

The Fukuda Administration

Fukuda's reorganized Cabinet included numerous ministers from the Abe era. The LDP's loss of control of the upper house resulted in a divided, or so-called 'twisted', Diet (*nejire kokkai*) and legislative deadlock that was to dominate domestic politics and to trouble the new Fukuda administration throughout the three parliamentary sessions to mid-2008. In November 2007 the prospect of the DPJ obstructing the passage of an urgent bill to authorize the resumption of MSDF refuelling operations in the Indian Ocean, which had been discontinued at the beginning of the month, brought an offer of a 'grand coalition' from Fukuda to the DPJ's leader, Ozawa. This offer, which was rejected by senior DPJ officials, created suspicion on all sides and led to problems for both party leaders, with Ozawa tendering his resignation as President of the DPJ to take responsibility for the political confusion. Ozawa withdrew his resignation following two days of talks with party members, rejecting the possibility of any future power-sharing arrangements, but leaving many in the DPJ perplexed and angry, and the party itself less popular in public opinion polls. The House of Representatives voted to extend the extraordinary Diet session to mid-December and then, in an unusual action, again to mid-January 2008 to enable the approval of the special bill on anti-terrorism measures; however, the political uncertainty continued. Suggestions that the Government might avail itself of the constitutional provision allowing the House of Representatives to adopt a bill sent back by the House of Councillors, with a majority of two-thirds, provoked threats of a censure motion by the upper house, which, if carried out, was expected to lead to an early dissolution of the lower house and a general election. However, this provision did not apply to nominations to government bodies, and the dispute between the two houses continued in mid-November 2007 with the House of Councillors' rejection, for the first time in 56 years, of three former bureaucrat nominees endorsed by the House of Representatives, on the grounds that they would be unable to withstand pressure from their previous ministries.

Scandals continued to damage the popularity of the Fukuda Government, with the issue of lost pension records and misdemeanours in the Ministry of Defence contributing to a perception of a 'lack of leadership'. As the Government struggled to secure the passage of its legislation, the major opposition party in the upper house began to put forward its own competing legislative agenda and tax proposals, including, most notably, the annulment of the special measures law under which Japan continued to provide support for reconstruction in Iraq, a reduction in fuel taxes to the levels at which they stood in the mid-1970s before they were 'temporarily' doubled, and the abolition of the hypothecation of fuel and other taxes for the purposes of road construction. Some opposition bills that differed in only minor ways from government proposals were adopted with the support of the Government, and where government legislation was approved concessions were generally made on both sides.

On 11 January 2008, for the first time since 1951, the LDP-led coalition invoked the lower house's constitutional primacy under Article 59 (2), using its more than two-thirds' majority to secure the passage of the Government's anti-terrorism bill first approved in that chamber in November 2007 and subsequently rejected by the upper house on 10 January 2008. The legislation, which allowed only the supply of oil and water for counter-terrorism operations related to Afghanistan and which was valid for just one year, led to the resumption of refuelling operations in February. On the last day of February, despite the opposition parties' boycott of the vote at both committee and plenary sessions and the threat of further boycotts in the upper house (which subsequently paralysed Diet proceedings for more than a week), the lower house approved the 2008 budget and a bill to extend the existing tax rate on fuel for 10 years. In March two deadlines approached: the final day in post of the Governor of the Bank of Japan (19 March) and the last day for adoption of the tax bill (31 March), after which fuel taxes would revert to their mid-1970s levels. Much attention was devoted to the Government's unsuccessful efforts to appoint its nominee, former Vice-Minister of Finance Toshiro Muto, as central bank Governor and the three-week vacancy that was created as the opposition parties, enraged by the ruling coalition's decision to force the budget through the lower house, manipulated this issue against that of the tax reform bill. A last-minute agreement between the Speakers of the two houses of the Diet provided for an interim bill that allowed the extension of provisional tax measures on a range of non-road-related categories but still resulted in a temporary decrease in fuel prices. However, this was overruled by a second vote in the House of Representatives at the end of April, 60 days after the bill had first been approved by the lower house, in accordance with Article 59 (4) of the Constitution, again invoked for the first time in 56 years. When the upper house voted against the 2008 budget at the end of March the Fukuda Government again used a constitutional provision, Article 60 (2), to declare the budget law. The Cabinet's approval rating declined to a low point of around 21% in April, following the introduction of a new health insurance programme for pensioners aged 75 and over, and the reintroduction of the road tax measures.

Despite five months of threats from the DPJ, the repeated invocation of the constitutional precedence of the House of Representatives failed to precipitate a motion of censure by the House of Councillors until mid-June 2008 in response to the Government's failure to approve an opposition bill to abolish the new health care programme for the elderly. The non-binding motion, another unprecedented constitutional development, precipitated a rare vote of confidence in the Prime Minister in the lower house and was symbolic of the division of the Diet.

A reorganization of the largely inherited Cabinet was regarded as a means of giving the Fukuda administration a distinct image, a sense of direction and some much-needed popularity prior to the next general election, which was required to be held by September 2009 at the latest. Both the Government and the LDP executive were therefore reorganized at the beginning of August 2008, precipitating a rise in the Cabinet's approval rating, largely, it appeared, owing to the appointment of the popular Taro Aso as LDP Secretary-General, which was generally interpreted as an attempt to unify the party and a further shift away from Koizumi's structural reform policy. This departure from the Koizumi approach was emphasized by the appointment of two 'postal rebels' to ministerial posts. At the beleaguered Ministry of Defence, Shigeru Ishiba was replaced by upper house member Yoshimasa Hayashi, a first-time cabinet appointee (one of five) and the fourth Minister of Defence in 12 months. Fukuda announced his new Cabinet, promising to address price rises, while a stated commitment to participate in the 'war on terror' was expected to lead to a repetition of the struggle to extend the special anti-terrorism law, with implications for the stability of the LDP-New Komeito coalition. At the beginning of September, after less than one year in the post, Fukuda announced his resignation as Prime Minister, owing to the lack of support.

The Aso Administration and the End of LDP Rule

As widely anticipated, Taro Aso was chosen as President of the LDP in an election contested by five candidates. He was duly confirmed as Prime Minister at the end of September 2008, having secured the majority of votes in the House of Representatives, although the House of Councillors signalled its preference for DPJ leader Ichiro Ozawa. The election and composition of the new Cabinet were notable for the minimal role played by the LDP factions. Appointments included that of Hirofumi Nakasone as Minister for Foreign Affairs and Shoichi Nakagawa as Minister of Finance and Minister of State for Financial Affairs. Ozawa was subsequently re-elected unopposed as leader of the DPJ.

It was generally expected that Aso, the third Prime Minister in succession to come to office without a mandate from the public, and with a very modest national support rate of 53%, would dissolve the House of Representatives either before, or immediately after, the approval of an early supplementary budget, thereby bringing about a general election in late 2008. However, the ruling coalition failed to present the planned second supplementary budget to the autumn session of the Diet. In the latter part of 2008, as the global financial crisis developed and as the Japanese economy deteriorated, public opinion surveys showed general support for economic stimulus plans. Aso's proposals for individual cash payments to all citizens, with the intention of stimulating consumer spending, were opposed by the DPJ. The proposals became the subject of an extended debate by the 20-member joint committee of both houses (called into action in the event of conflicting votes in the upper and lower houses) and emphasized the continuing difficulties presented by a divided Diet.

In February 2009 the public disagreement between Koizumi and Aso over the cash payments to citizens and the future of postal privatization provided a boost to the electoral hopes of the DPJ, as did the resignation of Shoichi Nakagawa from the finance portfolio following allegations of drunkenness during his appearance at a Group of Seven (G7) industrialized nations news conference in Italy. In early March, however, the momentum of the DPJ appeared to be curbed by the revelation that illegal contributions had allegedly been made to a senior aide to Ozawa. At the centre of the scandal was the failure of the Political Funds Control Law properly to manage corporate donations (which amounted to 41% of LDP and 29% of DPJ income). The potential for the LDP to capitalize on the allegations was restricted by the fact that Nishimatsu, the construction company implicated in the scandal, had also made donations to senior LDP members. Ozawa's determination to remain as President of the DPJ, even after the indictment of his aide and the consequent impact on DPJ support levels, nevertheless gave Aso some much-needed respite from the incessant demands for the dissolution of the Diet, and the fillip of a recovery in support levels. Meanwhile, political commentaries increasingly used expressions such as a 'leadership vacuum' and 'political paralysis'. Yielding to the decline in his popularity, Ozawa finally announced his resignation as leader of the DPJ in May after three years in the post. The presidency of the party, contested by Secretary-General Yukio Hatoyama (seen as the pro-Ozawa candidate) and Vice-President Katsuya Okada, was secured by Hatoyama, with 124 votes to 95.

Hatoyama presented his agenda for the forthcoming election: an end to government waste and *amakudari*; reform of the bureaucracy; a reduction in bureaucratic influence on policy-making, including the setting of the budget; and less foreign policy emphasis on Japan's relations with the USA and more on 'fraternal' relations with neighbouring countries regardless of their ideologies. Rising support for Hatoyama was evident in public opinion polls in June 2009 and was confirmed by DPJ victories in four mayoral elections. In July, at the Tokyo Metropolitan Assembly election (long seen as a reliable indicator of general election results), the DPJ won a majority for the first time, with increased voter turn-out and a strong showing among unaffiliated voters. The DPJ reinforced its victory with the tabling of a no-confidence motion in the upper house against the Cabinet. As demands from within the LDP for a leadership election grew, Aso responded by setting the date of the lower house election for 30 August. The House of Representatives was dissolved on 21 July, becoming the first Diet to go to full term since 1976. The DPJ election manifesto covered five main issues and elaborated on the party's plans for political reform and on its spending proposals: child allowances; support for farmers; an end to road tolls and the fuel surcharge; and free high schools. However, except with regard to the plans to reduce government waste through reform, the manifesto was less clear about how the proposals would be funded. The DPJ political reform project to deliver a system of 'new politics' was reminiscent of earlier attempts by Prime Ministers Nakasone, Hashimoto and Koizumi. Proposals centred on enhancing the role of the Prime Minister and Cabinet at the expense of the ruling party and bureaucracy, and this stood out as a defining difference between the two major parties. The LDP campaign, meanwhile, focused on promises to stimulate economic growth and recovery and to retreat on the market reforms promoted by Koizumi that had led to 'social distortions'. On non-economic issues, both parties pledged to tackle the issue of hereditary politicians (the DPJ sooner than the LDP, which boasted hereditary politicians comprising 11 of the 17 cabinet members and 40% of its total Diet membership) and to reduce the number of Diet seats (the DPJ proposed to reduce the number of seats determined by proportional representation from 180 to 100; the LDP to reduce the overall number of seats by 30% in 10 years' time). Both parties undertook to redress the balance between local and central politics: the DPJ by increasing the revenues and authority of local municipalities; the LDP by the introduction of a new regional system to replace the prefectural system. The LDP claimed to be maintaining an active approach to constitutional revision, while the DPJ, for which the debate presented more of an internal threat, promised revision if and where necessary.

Although the victory of the DPJ in the general election held on 30 August 2009 surprised few people, the scale of the LDP's defeat and the potential implications for the nature of Japan's democratic political system were of historic proportions. After 54 years of almost unbroken dominance over government, the LDP was reduced from 300 seats in the House of Representatives to 119 (64 in single-member districts and 55 in PR districts), in the process losing many senior leaders. These included former Prime Minister Toshiki Kaifu and faction leaders Nobutaka Machimura and Bunmei Ibuki, as well as almost all the so-called Koizumi children (LDP members who had been elected for the first time in 2005). Prime Minister Aso and former Prime Ministers Abe, Fukuda and Mori retained their seats. The DPJ took many former LDP districts, finishing with 308 seats, up from 115 (221 single-member districts, 87 PR). In its worst performance since 1967, New Komeito, the LDP's coalition partner, was defeated in every single-member district that it contested and lost 10 seats, including those of its President and its Secretary-General, finishing with 21 seats (all in PR districts). The JCP and the SDPJ retained nine and seven seats, respectively. Voter turn-out rose to 69%.

THE HATOYAMA AND KAN ADMINISTRATIONS

The election of the new DPJ Government was widely regarded as the beginning of a true Westminster-style two-party system of alternating government in Japan. Holding 308 of the 480 seats in the lower house, and without a single-party majority in the upper house, the DPJ had majorities on all the standing committees but not the two-thirds' majority needed to overrule a decision of the House of Councillors. With the next upper house election not due until July 2010, Hatoyama sought to address this potential difficulty by forming a coalition with the SDPJ and the People's New Party (PNP). The promise of a new policy-making body, the National Strategy Bureau, a combination of Diet members, bureaucrats and advisers, was expected to establish a new administrative framework that would change the balance of power within government, reduce the power of the *zoku* and facilitate 'top-down' leadership. Hatoyama assumed the office of Prime Minister on 16 September 2009, whereupon he committed his administration to a programme of welfare reform and an independent foreign policy. Former DPJ President Naoto Kan was appointed Deputy Prime Minister and allocated the newly created portfolio of national strategy, with responsibility for implementing the DPJ-led coalition policy commitments and managing its relationship with the bureaucracy. (Kan's role was expanded further when he was appointed Minister of Finance, following the resignation of Hirohisa Fujii in January 2010.) Hirofumi Hirano was appointed Chief Cabinet Secretary, while another former DPJ President, Ichiro Ozawa, a long-standing proponent of structural reform of the government, was appointed DPJ Secretary-General, with far-ranging responsibilities for the 2010 election strategy, DPJ Diet tactics and committee appointments. The potential for Ozawa to use his extensive powers and personal support in the Diet covertly to influence appointments and to direct policy was explored regularly in the media, and his central prominence was emphasized in December 2009 when he put forward a list of budget priorities that formed the basis of the Government's rationalization of its various manifesto promises.

Acclaimed initially as 'the third revolution' in Japanese history, the Hatoyama Government ultimately proved to be a considerable disappointment. From an early approval rating of 75%, second only to the support enjoyed by the Koizumi administration in its early days, public opinion surveys showed a steady decline to just 24% by April 2010. Early support, which was generated by the Cabinet's efforts both to reduce waste in government spending and to limit the power of the bureaucracy, was undermined by a loss of faith in Hatoyama's leadership abilities and a growing perception that the coalition Cabinet lacked unity and was unable to develop a coherent economic strategy. The administration was damaged further by indecisiveness with regard to national security and diplomatic strategy, as well as by allegations of contraventions of the Political Funds Control Law involving aides of DPJ Secretary-General Ozawa and Prime Minister Hatoyama himself. Other issues that further heightened the Government's unpopularity included its handling of the relocation of the US Futenma air base (see National Security, Defence and Rearmament, below) and a controversial new highway toll system. As Hatoyama's self-imposed deadline, of 30 May, for a decision on the relocation of the Futenma base approached, the issue threatened further to disrupt the cohesion of the DPJ and placed the coalition under additional pressure, at a time when it should have been focusing on the forthcoming upper house elections, due to be held in July. Hatoyama's eventual decision, announced in late May, to revert to the previous LDP Government's plan to relocate the base within the Okinawa Prefecture, thereby breaking one of the central pledges of his election campaign, led to the SDPJ's withdrawal from the coalition at the end of the month. The Government was thus deprived of its two-thirds' majority in the lower house, and its unpopularity further increased.

Under pressure from his own upper house members to relinquish the premiership, Hatoyama announced his resignation on 2 June 2010, and Ozawa agreed to step down as DPJ Secretary-General soon after. The *Nikkei* newspaper summed up the public sense of anti-climax and frustration: 'For all its boasting about the biggest revolution Japan had seen since the 19th century Meiji Restoration ending the feudal era, the government produced nothing except more disappointment and distrust in politics.' Standing as an anti-Ozawa candidate, Naoto Kan was elected President of the DPJ for the third time, and was inaugurated as Prime Minister, to great public acclaim, on 8 June. His appointments to cabinet and party positions, including that of Yoshito Sengoku as Chief Cabinet Secretary and Yukio Edano as DPJ Secretary-General, were designed to restrict, but not to eliminate, the influence of Ozawa. One of Kan's first decisions as premier was to reinstate the DPJ policy research committee abolished by Ozawa, as a means of re-engaging back-bench politicians in the policy-making process. Another was to withdraw criticism of the bureaucratic input into policy-making, which was judged to have been a contributory factor in the failure of the Hatoyama administration.

The DPJ's prospects in the upper house election were much improved by the change of leadership and the distancing from Ozawa, and its increasing popular support came primarily at the expense of the various small parties that had grown in number during the Hatoyama administration. Kan's decision to proceed with the upper house election as scheduled on 11 July 2010, and not to extend the Diet session to enable the passage of the postal reform bills championed by the DPJ's surviving coalition partner, the PNP, led to the resignation of the PNP's Shizuka Kamei from the Cabinet, although the party remained a loyal coalition member. In the event, the results of the election were devastating for the DPJ, which won only 44 of the 121 contested seats in the House of Councillors, 10 fewer than Kan's target and 16 short of a single-party majority. The loss by the PNP of all three of its contested seats left the coalition Government 12 seats short of a majority and recreated the *nejire kokkai* ('twisted' Diet) of old, and one that was arguably more divided than the chamber that had confronted the Abe administration three years earlier. Kan ascribed the DPJ losses to his 'sudden' and poorly explained proposal for a doubling of the rate of consumption tax to 10%.

Following a challenge to his leadership of the DPJ, in mid-September 2010 Kan, helped by public disapproval of Ozawa's 'old-style' approach to politics, and with a narrow margin of support from DPJ members of the Diet, defeated Ozawa to retain the party presidency. The Prime Minister's subsequent reorganization of the Cabinet excluded the Ozawa group. The group's influence was further undermined by the decision of an independent judicial panel to demand the indictment of Ozawa for his alleged role in a funding scandal. According to public opinion surveys, approval of Kan declined by 31% in October (from 71% in the previous month), the result, in part, of his response to the collision of a Chinese trawler with a Japan Coast Guard vessel off the disputed Senkaku Islands (see Foreign Relations, below) and, in part, of his failure to enforce Ozawa's co-operation with the Diet inquiry into the funding scandal. In November the Government's popularity declined further following the resignation of the Minister of Justice, Minoru Yanagida, whose remarks were perceived as having shown contempt for the Diet, and the censure of two further cabinet members, Chief Cabinet Secretary Yoshito Sengoku and the Minister of Land and Transport, Sumio Mabuchi, by the opposition-controlled upper house. By the time the Diet session ended in early December, the DPJ had failed to implement a number of its manifesto promises, including the reform of party funding and of public works. The number of government-sponsored bills approved was only 14 out of 37, or 37.8%, the lowest for a decade; the Prime Minister's popularity ratings had declined by a further 10% and the LDP's approval ratings had drawn level with those of the DPJ at 30%. It was therefore no surprise when Kan began to discuss co-operation with his former coalition partner, the SDP, and to suggest the possibility of a grand coalition including the LDP, a suggestion that was well received by the chairman of the LDP's Policy Research Council on the understanding that the Ozawa group would be excluded. The idea of a grand coalition found widespread support among the public as measured by a *Nikkei* survey.

In early 2011 Ozawa continued to refuse to testify to the lower house ethics committee, and the Ozawa group continued to pose a threat to party unity. Kan struggled unsuccessfully to retain Sengoku and Mabuchi in the Cabinet despite opposition threats to boycott budget deliberations, and both men were removed from office in January in a cabinet reorganization that included the appointment of the former LDP Minister of Finance, Kaoru Yosano, as Minister for Economic and Fiscal Policy, in charge of reforming the tax and social security system. The eventual indictment by a citizens' panel of the influential and resilient Ozawa, in late January, on charges of submitting false financial statements, was widely regarded as the end of an era. Ozawa had entered the lower house aged 27, under the patronage of the LDP faction leader Kakuei Tanaka, and over the course of four decades had strategically shifted both faction and party. In the course of so doing he had succeeded in dividing the LDP and creating the DPJ, and had emphatically brought to an end the long period of one-party dominance. The problem of formulating an appropriate response to Ozawa's indictment exacerbated the Government's difficulties in controlling the lower house; any chance that Kan could gain the two-thirds majority that would allow the Government to secure the adoption of budget-related legislation, including authorization to issue deficit-covering bonds, that might be rejected by the opposition-dominated upper house, would require not only a rapprochement with the SDP, but also with the Ozawa group within the DPJ, a number of whom threatened to oppose the budget-related bills. Requests for Kan to resign, in exchange for the passage of the bills, were expressed within the DPJ; the Cabinet's approval rating in public opinion surveys declined to 22%, and demands increased for a dissolution of the lower house and an election. The 2011 budget was adopted by the lower house at the beginning of March, in time for enactment on 1 April, even though it was not expected to survive upper house deliberations. At the same time, the passage of related bills to fund the budget remained problematic. Kan encountered a further difficulty when the man most widely regarded as his successor, the Minister for Foreign Affairs, Seiji Maehara, resigned after it emerged that he had received an illegal donation from a foreign national.

On 11 March 2011 there occurred the most severe earthquake in Japan's history, a wide, shallow, tremor of magnitude 9, with its epicentre 130 km off the coast of Miyagi prefecture. It caused widespread devastation and was followed by a massive and hugely destructive tsunami that struck the coastal areas of north-east Japan with unprecedented consequences. Loss of auxiliary power to the Tokyo Electric Power company's Fukushima nuclear power station as a result of damage caused by the tsunami, and the threat of radiation leakage, precipitated a government declaration of a nuclear emergency and an evolving series of measures to assess and contain the nuclear threat, alongside more conventional recovery efforts to restore water and electricity, secure infrastructure and distribute essential supplies. In the weeks following the disaster aftershocks continued; workers struggled with limited success to bring the Fukushima reactors under control; the evacuation area around the power station was increased; vegetables and beef from affected areas were withdrawn from the market; children were kept indoors; and the official total of those who were dead or missing rose to more than 23,000.

Various political repercussions followed the natural disaster and its social and economic consequences. First, Kan's Government gained a reprieve from demands for it to resign. Since the 1995 Kobe earthquake and the sarin gas attacks in Tokyo in the same year, considerable improvements had been made to Japan's crisis management institutions, but the sheer scale of the disaster threatened to overwhelm them. Almost immediately, the opposition parties declared a political truce and stated their intention to co-operate with the Government in developing supplementary budgets to fund relief efforts. The DPJ indicated its willingness to reallocate to relief and reconstruction some of the funding previously reserved, in accordance with the party's manifesto promises, for child allowances, toll-free highways, free high-school tuition and agricultural income support, and attempted, unsuccessfully, to recruit the leader of the LDP, Sadakazu Tanigaki, to the Cabinet as vice-premier. Proposals for a grand coalition continued to attract support, including that of former Prime Ministers Nakasone and Abe, and more broadly within the LDP.

However, as the weeks passed,there was increasing criticism, both at home and abroad, of a perceived breakdown of crisis management on the part of the Government. This breakdown was attributed to the Government's failure to share information, Kan's failure to delegate, disunity in the DPJ, and an unsatisfactory relationship between the DPJ and the civil servants from whom they had promised to wrest political power. A *Nikkei* survey of prefectural governors indicated that about 60% were dissatisfied with Kan's response to the earthquake and nuclear crisis. The Governor of Fukushima prefecture was especially critical of the Government's failure to explain and justify its evacuation warnings, and to clarify how radioactive substances generated by the reactor were likely to spread. Less than five weeks after the earthquake struck, the LDP was again urging Kan to 'fall on his sword', and the idea of a grand coalition was no longer regarded as feasible. Within the DPJ dissatisfaction with Kan was at a high level, and was exacerbated by poor results for DPJ-supported candidates in two rounds of local elections in April 2011. None the less, a supplementary budget to provide funding to the areas devastated by the earthquake was approved unanimously at the beginning of May. In early June the LDP, New Komeito and the Sunrise Party of Japan submitted a motion of no confidence against the Prime Minister. The motion was rejected only because disaffected groups within the DPJ were dissuaded from voting for it by a promise from Kan to resign 'when the current emergency response stage is over'. When, after the motion was rejected, Kan made clear his intention to remain in office for several months at least, the DPJ was thrown into disarray, and the opposition parties declared their intention to prevent the adoption of a bill that provided 40% of funding for the 2011 budget. Once again the idea of a grand LDP-DPJ coalition was proposed by DPJ leaders and rejected by the LDP, its offer of co-operation on funding bills being conditional upon the Prime Minister's resignation. The *Nikkei* summed up the situation: 'Kan's clinging to power has brought about political paralysis'. As the DPJ unilaterally extended the Diet session by 70 days, the 'paralysis' appeared likely to continue.

Following the earthquake in March 2011 energy security, the balance of energy generation, nuclear-generated energy and its regulation and safety were much debated. The committee that was established to investigate the disaster at the Fukushima plant was also charged with a broader investigation into the Nuclear and Industrial Safety Agency and its alleged lack of independence, since the administrative reforms of 2001, from the Ministry of Economy, Trade and Industry. Generation at the nuclear plant at Hamaoka was suspended on the order of the Prime Minister, because of its proximity to Tokyo, and reactors that had been closed for their regular 13-monthly inspections seemed likely to be kept under closure by local authorities. When Kan decided, in July 2011, to make stress-testing of these reactors mandatory, the threat to the power supply became even more urgent. By the end of July the Prime Minister was promising to reduce Japan's reliance on nuclear power. The implications of all this for short-term energy supply were great, and energy-saving measures, supported by penalties, were imposed. Before the March earthquake nearly 30% of Japan's electricity had been nuclear-generated, and the Government had previously undertaken to raise this proportion to over 50% by 2030; it had also agreed (in accordance with the Kyoto Protocol to the UN Framework Convention on Climate Change) to make a reduction of 6% in greenhouse gas emissions from 1990 levels by 2012, and to increase such reductions to 25% of 1990 levels by 2020, a pledge that had been expected to necessitate the building of nine new nuclear plants. The implications of Kan's promise for energy policy in the longer term were therefore huge. In June 2011 Kan unexpectedly declared that his resignation would be conditional upon the successful passage of a renewable energy bill and legislation to allow the Government to issue deficit-covering bonds, as well as the adoption of a second supplementary budget. In July Kan was further isolated by his unilateral naming of an LDP member as a parliamentary secretary, and by his appointment of Ryu Matsumoto to the new post of Minister for Reconstruction, only for the latter to resign nine days later after a disastrous visit to the devastated areas. At this point, a national opinion poll concluded that around 65% of the public wanted Kan to resign in August, and both the DPJ and the LDP seemed determined to support the Prime Minister's three bills in order to secure his resignation. The second supplementary budget, amounting to 2,000,000m. yen, was adopted at the end of July, providing local authorities with funds for combating radiation contamination and building new homes.

On 26 August 2011, following the approval of the remaining two bills by the legislature, Kan announced his resignation. Four days later Yoshihiko Noda, hitherto the Minister of Finance, was elected to the presidency of the ruling DPJ and duly confirmed in the post of Prime Minister. The new Cabinet included Koichiro Genba as Minister for Foreign Affairs and Jun Azumi as Minister of Finance.

FOREIGN RELATIONS

In the 20 years following the Second World War, successive Japanese Governments sought to shelter the country behind its alliance with the USA, and to avoid independent commitments in foreign policy. When Japan signed the San Francisco Treaty in 1951, it also signed a bilateral security treaty with the USA, whereby the Japanese Government granted the use of military bases in Japan exclusively to the USA in return for a US commitment to provide military support to Japan in the event of external aggression. Japan has since then functioned as a major base for US forces in eastern Asia, its sole military obligation being to defend its own territory. Thus, Japan will not go to the defence of its ally if the USA is attacked elsewhere. The insistence of the USA that Japan rearm was a significant factor in the reawakening of Japanese foreign policy.

Prime Minister Hosokawa expended every effort to promote Japan's international status, embarking in September 1993 upon a visit to New York, where he met President Clinton and also addressed the General Assembly of the UN. Although a long-standing US demand to liberalize the Japanese rice market was met in December, it was significant that the agricultural trade accord was drafted by the Secretariat of the General Agreement on Tariffs and Trade (GATT), and accepted by Japan in the context of the successful attempt to complete the 'Uruguay Round' of negotiations. The agreement gave foreign rice producers access to Japanese domestic markets, beginning with 4% of the market and rising to 8% over six years, after which rice would be subject to a tariff system.

In its relations with the USA, Japan was unable to demonstrate any shift in policy, resisting efforts by the Clinton Administration to introduce numerical targets as 'objective criteria' in the trade negotiations at the Washington Summit in July 1994. The failure of these talks, with Hosokawa's rejection of US demands, was heralded in Japan as an indication of a new maturity in the bilateral relationship. Japan's policy towards the USA subsequently began to follow two different directions. On the one hand, in negotiations on the automobile trade, an uncompromising position was maintained, despite US demands for concessions. On the other hand, however, Japan was prepared to meet US expectations in areas such as Japanese involvement in UN activities, and security links with the USA (for the latter see below).

After 10 months of trade negotiations at the sub-cabinet level, the USA expressed strong dissatisfaction with the proportion of Japanese government contracts awarded to non-Japanese firms. A 60-day consultation period was established, following the expiry of which the USA promised that retaliatory sanctions would be imposed against Japan. While agreement was reached by early October 1994 in three of the four main areas under discussion, the two sides had yet to resolve their dispute over the automobile trade. Following the failure of the trade negotiations in early May 1995, the USA threatened to impose severe sanctions on a number of luxury car models. Japan responded by lodging a complaint with the World Trade Organization (WTO), the successor to GATT, on the grounds that the USA's actions violated the WTO Agreement and other international accords. The USA retaliated by filing a complaint of its own and added the threat of further sanctions on Japanese air cargo after access to flights was not granted to a US carrier. In late June, immediately prior to the introduction of US sanctions, an agreement was reached, whereby Japan promised to allow an increase in the proportion of US-manufactured parts bought by Japanese car makers in North America, and to guarantee that Japanese manufacturers would not contravene their 1994 purchase plans. An agreement on the air cargo dispute was also reached in July 1995, although discussions continued on perceived obstacles to foreign competition in the Japanese photographic film market.

Trade negotiations with the USA in 1996 continued to focus on the opening of the Japanese market. Specific areas of contention included photographic film and insurance, and discussions began on the renegotiation of two previous agreements on semiconductors and airline routes, which were due to expire in that year. Agreement on the issue of semiconductors was reached in August, whereby two new bodies were to be established to regulate the market. However, following the events in Okinawa (see below), Prime Minister Hashimoto and President Clinton were more concerned with reinforcing the bilateral security relationship than trade disputes in late 1996 and early 1997. At a meeting in April 1997 they discussed co-operation in regional affairs, focusing on the issue of stability in the Korean peninsula. As Japan's trade surplus with the USA increased in early 1997, with notably, a growth in the export of automobiles, it was feared that the friction over trade issues might intensify. The USA continued to put pressure on Japan to open its market further and to transform its export-orientated economy to one based on the domestic market. In September the USA imposed large fines on three Japanese shipping companies, following complaints about restrictive harbour practices in Japan; however, an agreement to reform Japanese port operations was concluded shortly thereafter. Negotiations on increased access to airline routes for Japanese and US carriers were also successfully concluded in January 1998.

During 1998 the USA became increasingly concerned about the deceleration of the Japanese economy and its impact on other Asian economies, already severely depressed by the regional currency crisis. Discussion of Japan's economic and financial problems was the focus of the G7 summit meeting in April. During a two-day visit to Japan in November, President Clinton urged the Government to implement measures rapidly to encourage domestic demand, reform the banking sector and liberalize the country's markets, reinforcing earlier warnings that it risked provoking protectionist measures. The USA was also critical of Japan's refusal to lower tariffs on rice and forestry and fisheries products, or to curb low-priced steel exports to the USA. Japan's trade surplus with the USA continued to increase, growing by some 33% in 1998, to reach its highest level since 1987. In May 1999, during a six-day visit by Prime Minister Obuchi to the USA (the first such official state visit in 12 years), Clinton praised Obuchi's efforts to stimulate economic recovery and welcomed Japanese plans for further deregulation in several sectors, including telecommunications, energy, housing and financial services. Meanwhile, the dispute over Japanese steel exports had escalated. A ruling, in April, by the US Department of Commerce that Japan had 'dumped' hot-rolled steel into the US market was endorsed, in June, by the US International Trade Commission, and punitive duties were subsequently imposed. In November Japan brought a complaint before the WTO against the US ruling.

Stability in the Asia-Pacific region is a vital consideration in Japanese foreign policy, since Japan depends on regional markets for a substantial proportion of its foreign trade, as well as for its imports of vital raw materials. In January 1993, on a tour of member countries of the Association of Southeast Asian Nations (ASEAN), Prime Minister Miyazawa outlined his policy for the area, which included regional co-operation, a commitment to economic openness in the Asia-Pacific area, and a fuller political and security dialogue among ASEAN countries. In August the incoming Prime Minister, Hosokawa, promised to initiate a new era in Japan's relations with its neighbours by making a full apology for Japan's war record in his first policy speech. However, political pressure forced him to moderate his language and to state that Japan would not pay compensation to victims of Japanese aggression. On a tour of the Philippines, Viet Nam, Malaysia and Singapore in August 1994, Prime Minister Murayama emphasized Japan's responsibility and remorse for its actions in the Second World War, and its desire for reconciliation. Shortly afterwards, Murayama announced the 'Peace, Friendship and Exchange Initiative', a 100,000m.-yen programme to promote historical studies and exchanges among Asian nations. Murayama chaired the Asia-Pacific Economic Cooperation (APEC) meeting in Osaka in November 1995, as part of Japan's commitment to regional co-operation. Although Japan's close security co-operation with the USA sometimes caused concern among its Asia-Pacific neighbours, Japan's relations with these countries remained stable in the late 1990s. Murayama's successor, Hashimoto, visited ASEAN countries in January 1997, and the Japanese Minister for Foreign Affairs participated in the meeting of ASEAN and other foreign ministers in July. However, the Asian economic crisis that began in late 1997 threatened to disrupt Japan's trading relations with its neighbours. At the annual IMF-World Bank conference, held in September in Hong Kong, Japan proposed the establishment of an Asian Monetary Fund, a regional organization in which only Asian countries would participate. Strong objections were voiced by the USA and European countries, which advocated a more international response to the crisis. Japan responded by co-operating with the USA and international financial institutions in providing aid for, among other countries, Thailand and Indonesia. However, Asian Governments remained dissatisfied with Japan's response to the crisis, fearing that the weakness of the Japanese currency would prevent regional economic recovery by inhibiting a growth in exports. In response to increasing international pressure, in October 1998 the Japanese Government announced a US $30,000m. aid 'package' for Asian countries, and in November the USA and Japan presented a joint initiative for growth and economic recovery in the region. In addition, at an ASEAN summit meeting, held in Hanoi, Viet Nam, in December, Japan pledged further assistance, in the form of loans worth some $5,000m., to be disbursed over a three-year period.

In May 1990 Japan's relations with the South Korea, which had been strained since the Second World War, were greatly improved following a visit by President Roh Tae-Woo, during which Prime Minister Kaifu offered an unequivocal apology for Japanese colonial aggressions on the Korean peninsula in the past, and promised to improve legislation protecting the basic rights of those Koreans and their descendants resident in Japan, by 1993. In February 1995 Prime Minister Murayama publicly acknowledged that Japan had been responsible, in part, for the post-war division of the Korean peninsula. However, he was forced to retract the statement, following bitter controversy in the Diet. In June the Diet issued a resolution expressing deep regret for the atrocities committed by Japanese troops during the Second World War. However, the resolution, which was timed to coincide with the 50th anniversary of the end of the war, was widely criticized by former prisoners of war of the Japanese, as insufficiently explicit and for being a personal statement by the Prime Minister, rather than a representation of the views of the Government as a whole. In August Murayama formally reiterated the statement of remorse, expressing 'a heartfelt apology' and admitting that Japanese national policy during the Second World War had been 'mistaken'. However, he discounted the possibility of individual compensation payments by the Government to Asian (mostly Korean) women, used by Japanese troops for sexual purposes during the war ('comfort women').

In February 1996 a report issued by the UN criticized Japan's treatment of the 'comfort women' and urged it to accept full responsibility for its actions. The first payments from a private fund, created to provide compensation to the victims, were disbursed in August, together with a letter of apology from Hashimoto, to four Philippine women. Further payments were made in January 1997 to several South Korean victims, but the majority of groups representing the women refused to accept payment from the fund, demanding that compensation be forthcoming from official, rather than private, sources. In April 1998, however, in the first such ruling, a Japanese district court ordered the Government to compensate three former 'comfort women' from South Korea. Meanwhile, in June 1996 Hashimoto met the South Korean President, Kim Young-Sam, to discuss bilateral co-operation in economic and security affairs. Japan's relations with South Korea were strained in late 1996 over a territorial dispute concerning a group of islands, called Takeshima in Japanese (or Dokdo in Korean), to which both countries laid claim.

Relations with South Korea deteriorated in early 1998, when Japan unilaterally terminated a bilateral fisheries agreement, following the failure of negotiations concerning the renewal of the accord. Discussions were held at intervals during 1998 to attempt to renegotiate the terms of the agreement. The Japanese Government contributed financial aid to South Korea as part of the international effort to stimulate its economic recovery. Japan's relations with South Korea improved considerably in October, during a four-day visit to Tokyo by President Kim Dae-Jung. A joint declaration was signed by the South Korean President and Prime Minister Obuchi, in which Japan apologized for its conduct towards Korea during the period of Japanese colonial rule. Emperor Akihito also expressed deep sorrow for the suffering inflicted on the Korean people. In addition, South Korea agreed to revoke a ban on the import of various Japanese goods, while Japan promised US $3,000m. in aid to South Korea in support of its efforts to stimulate economic recovery. In November the two countries concluded negotiations on the renewal of their bilateral fisheries agreement, which came into effect in January 1999. An agreement to modify some of the terms of the accord was reached in March, following a series of differences over its implementation. Increased co-operation was emphasized during a visit by Obuchi to South Korea later that month, when both countries agreed to strengthen bilateral economic relations, and Japan pledged further aid to South Korea. At the end of May 2000 Prime Minister Mori visited Seoul and held a meeting with President Kim Dae-Jung, in which he affirmed Japan's support for the forthcoming inter-Korean summit and advocated close co-operation between Japan and South Korea with a view to establishing peace and stability on the Korean peninsula.

Japan's attempts to establish full diplomatic relations with the DPRK in early 1991 were hindered by the latter's insistence that Japan make financial reparations for losses sustained during and following Japan's colonial rule of Korea in 1910–45. The refusal of North Korea to allow inspection of its nuclear facilities featured prominently on Japan's national and international agenda. Japan stressed the need to find a diplomatic solution and any substantial support for military intervention was ruled out. In March 1995 a delegation comprising members of all three parties in the Japanese Government visited North Korea to prepare for negotiations on the establishment of normal relations between the two countries. Japan provided emergency aid to North Korea in 1995/96, when a serious food shortage appeared to threaten the stability of the Korean peninsula. The Japanese Government supported a US initiative of dialogue involving North Korea, China and the USA, aimed at negotiating a formal peace treaty between the two Korean states. Concerns that North Korea had developed a missile capable of reaching Japanese territory resulted in the suspension of food aid in early 1997, but later in that year agreement was reached concerning visits to relatives in Japan by Japanese nationals resident in North Korea. The first such visits took place in November. It was announced in August that the two countries were to conduct negotiations aimed at restoring full diplomatic relations. It was subsequently reported that the Japanese Government had pledged some US $27m. in food aid to North Korea. However, food aid and negotiations on the resumption of full diplomatic relations, which had commenced following the visit to North Korea by an LDP delegation, were suspended in mid-1998, following the testing by North Korea of a suspected missile in the sea near Japan. Tensions were exacerbated in March 1999, when two suspected North Korean spy ships, which had infiltrated Japanese waters, were pursued and fired on by Japanese naval forces, in the first such operation since the establishment of the Japanese SDF. In September the Japanese Government welcomed North Korea's agreement with the USA to suspend its reported plans to test a new long-range missile, but remained cautious regarding any easing of sanctions against Pyongyang. In October unofficial talks were held in Singapore between Japanese and North Korean government officials, and Japan subsequently removed a ban on charter flights to North Korea. Following a visit to North Korea by a multi-party delegation of Diet members in December, the Japanese Government announced that it would resume the provision of food aid. Later that month intergovernmental preparatory talks on re-establishing diplomatic relations were held in China, following an agreement between Japanese and North Korean Red Cross officials on humanitarian issues, most notably the commitment by the Red Cross organization of North Korea to urge its Government to co-operate in an investigation into the fate of some 10 missing Japanese nationals, believed by Japan to have been abducted by North Korean agents in the 1970s and 1980s. Three sessions of official talks on the normalization of diplomatic relations held during 2000 were inconclusive.

In 1978 a treaty of peace and friendship was signed with the People's Republic of China. During an official visit to China in August 1988, Prime Minister Takeshita announced that Japan would advance 810,000m. yen in loans to China between 1990 and 1995. These loans were withheld following the massacre by Chinese troops in Tiananmen Square, Beijing, in June 1989, but were released in mid-1990 following the Chinese Government's declaration, in January, that a state of martial law no longer existed. There was further dissatisfaction with the Chinese Government in early 1992, when Chinese sovereignty was declared over the Ryukyu island group, which was claimed by Japan. Nevertheless, good relations between the two countries were bolstered by visits to China by Emperor Akihito in October 1992 and by Prime Minister Hosokawa in March 1994. Having protested strongly against the resumption of French nuclear testing in the Pacific, in August Japan announced that it would suspend economic aid to China, following renewed nuclear testing by the Chinese Government. The provision of economic aid was resumed in early 1997, following a moratorium on Chinese nuclear testing.

In mid-1996 Japan's relations with both China and Taiwan were strained when a group of nationalists, the Japan Youth Federation, built a lighthouse and war memorial on the Senkaku Islands (or Diaoyu Islands in Chinese), a group of uninhabited islets situated in the East China Sea, to which all three countries laid claim. The situation was further aggravated in September by the drowning of a Hong Kong citizen during a protest against Japan's claim to the islands. In October a flotilla of small boats, operated by 300 activists from Taiwan, Hong Kong and Macao evaded Japanese patrol vessels and raised the flags of China and Taiwan on the disputed islands. However, Japan sought to defuse tensions with China and Taiwan by withholding official recognition of the lighthouse.

In September 1997 Prime Minister Hashimoto visited China to celebrate the 25th anniversary of the normalization of relations between the two countries. China expressed concern at the revised US-Japanese security arrangements, following a statement by a senior Japanese minister that the area around Taiwan might be covered under the new guidelines. Procedures for the removal of chemical weapons, deployed in China by Japanese forces during the Second World War, were also discussed. Japan's economic policy was criticized by the Chinese Government in 1998, which feared that the weakening yen would force a devaluation of the Chinese currency. In November, during a six-day state visit by the Chinese head of state, Prime Minister Obuchi and President Jiang Zemin issued (but declined to sign) a joint declaration on friendship and co-operation, in which Japan expressed deep remorse for past aggression against China. However, China was reported to be displeased by the lack of a written apology, and remained concerned by the implications of US-Japanese defence arrangements regarding Taiwan. A subsequent US-Japanese agreement to initiate joint technical research on the development of a theatre missile defence system, followed by the Japanese Diet's approval, in May 1999, of legislation on the implementation of the revised US-Japanese defence guidelines provoked severe criticism from China, despite Japan's insistence that military co-operation with the USA was purely defensive. In July a meeting in Beijing between Obuchi and the Chinese Premier, Zhu Rongji, resulted in the formalization of a bilateral agreement on China's entry to the WTO, following several months of intense negotiations on the liberalization of trade in services.

Japan and the USSR were, historically and geopolitically, rivals for supremacy in north-eastern Asia, over which they disputed control in large- and small-scale wars. Mutual mistrust was maintained from the end of the Second World War until the mid-1980s. Japan's treaty of peace and friendship, signed with the People's Republic of China in 1978, signified an end to Japan's policy of maintaining equal distance from both China and the USSR. Japan's relations with the USSR were further strained by the Soviet military intervention in Afghanistan, in December 1979, and by the concomitant reinforcement of Soviet territory to the north of Japan. In January 1986 the Soviet Minister of Foreign Affairs, Eduard Shevardnadze, visited Japan (the first such visit by a Soviet Minister of Foreign Affairs for 10 years). The two countries agreed to improve economic and trade relations and to resume regular ministerial consultations.

The major obstacle to any substantial improvement in Soviet-Japanese relations was the seemingly intractable dispute over the Northern Territories. Japan has a strong claim to two islands, Habomai and Shikotan, which were formerly administered as part of Hokkaido. In addition, Japan claims Etorofu (Iturup) and Kunashiri (Kunashir), which, together with the rest of the Chishima (Kurile) chain and the southern part of Karafuto (Sakhalin), were captured by Soviet forces during the closing stages of the Second World War. Following a visit to Tokyo by the Soviet Minister of Foreign Affairs in December 1988, Japan and the USSR agreed to establish a senior-level joint working group to negotiate the future of the disputed territory and the conclusion of a peace treaty. After the dissolution of the Soviet Union at the end of 1991, the President of Russia, Boris Yeltsin, reconfirmed the existence of this territorial dilemma.

The G7 summit meeting held in Tokyo in July 1993 provided the opportunity for Yeltsin to visit Japan, two proposed trips having been cancelled in the previous 12 months. However, despite this and a repeat visit in October, no solution was found to the dispute over the Northern Territories. The US $500m. in bilateral aid promised to Yeltsin at the summit fell far short of the $4,000m. that President Clinton had initially suggested as a privatization fund. Despite US pressure, Japan's continuing reservations towards the provision of aid for Russia reflected both its frustration that the resolution of its territorial claims was still distant, as well as the development of more assertive diplomacy.

Bilateral negotiations over the status of the disputed territory opened in March 1995. Relations between the two countries steadily improved, and a commitment was made to resume negotiations on the signing of a peace treaty to bring a formal conclusion to the Second World War. In November 1996 Japan indicated that it was prepared to resume the disbursement of US $500m. in aid, withheld since 1991, and in May 1997 the Japanese Government abandoned its opposition to Russia's proposed membership of the G7. Russian plans for joint development of the mineral and fishing resources of the disputed territory were followed, in July, by an outline agreement on the jurisdiction of the islands. A meeting between Hashimoto and Yeltsin later in that month resulted in the forging of a new diplomatic policy, based on 'trust, mutual benefit and long-term prospects'. At an informal summit meeting, held between Yeltsin and Hashimoto in Krasnoyarsk, Russia, in November, the two parties agreed to work towards the conclusion of a formal peace treaty by the year 2000. A series of measures aimed at encouraging Japanese assistance in the revival of the Russian economy were also discussed. Bilateral negotiations resulted in the conclusion of a framework fisheries agreement in December 1997. Yeltsin visited Japan in April 1998, and the Japanese Government's commitment to an improvement in bilateral relations was confirmed by its offer of financial aid, in the form of loans, and an expansion in economic co-operation. The Japanese Government also indicated its support for Russia's application for membership of the WTO and APEC. At the beginning of September 1999 Japan agreed to resume lending to Russia, which had been suspended since the Russian Government had effectively devalued the rouble and defaulted on some of its debts in mid-1998. At the same time an accord was concluded on improved access to the disputed islands for former Japanese inhabitants.

Negotiations on the territorial dispute achieved little progress during 2000, a major obstacle being the issue of how many of the islands should be returned. Despite Russian President Vladimir Putin's repudiation of Japan's claim to any of the islands during his first official visit to Tokyo in September, Russia subsequently offered to abide by a 1956 declaration that it would relinquish two of the islands after the signature of a peace treaty, but Japan initially rejected this partial solution. Talks held in March 2001 on the interpretation of the 1956 declaration proved inconclusive, although Prime Minister Mori and President Putin reaffirmed that the declaration would ultimately form the basis for a peace treaty. Meanwhile, in November 2000 a former Japanese naval officer on trial in Tokyo admitted spying for Russia.

The sharp increase in world petroleum prices in 1973–74 illustrated the vulnerability of the Japanese economy to developments in the international arena. Japan's increasingly pragmatic approach in foreign affairs was demonstrated by its support for the Arab countries in its pronouncements on Middle East issues, thus ensuring a continuing supply of petroleum. Moreover, its growing involvement in world affairs was signalled by the financial aid granted to the international effort to force the Iraqi withdrawal from Kuwait in 1991. In September 1995 Prime Minister Murayama visited the Middle East. During meetings with the Syrian President, Hafiz al-Assad, the Israeli Prime Minister, Itzhak Rabin, and the Palestinian leader, Yasser Arafat, Murayama pledged economic aid to the Middle East, the promotion of trade with the region and Japan's involvement in the UN Disengagement Observer Force (UNDOF) operation in the Golan Heights.

With the possibility that Japan might be given a permanent seat on the UN Security Council having receded, during the late 1990s the Japanese Government campaigned for a greater proportion of senior-level positions within the UN to be allocated to Japanese personnel, as a reflection of its contribution to the UN budget. From January 1997 until January 1999 Japan held a non-permanent seat on the UN Security Council, while continuing to seek permanent membership. Prime Minister Mori addressed the UN General Assembly on this issue in October 2000 and also advocated Japan's membership to a gathering of Asian and African nations. Japan had the strong backing of the United Kingdom and guarded support from Russia and China, but controversy over the whole idea of permanent membership meant that no new developments were expected in the near future, despite the fact that Japan was the second largest contributor to the UN in 2000, being responsible for more than 20% of the total budget.

Japan's foreign relations generally failed to flourish under the leadership of the Mori Cabinet, which seemed to lack a coherent national vision or strategy. Mori's propensity to make inappropriate remarks and his mishandling of various issues drew constant criticism in the domestic media, which was taken up by the foreign press. The summit meeting of G8 nations held in Okinawa in July 2000 contributed little of value to Japan's international standing. Revelations of scandals involving misuse of funds within the Ministry of Foreign Affairs and the subsequent dismissal of top officials, including the ambassadors to the USA and the United Kingdom, left the ministry weakened. Disputes between senior officials and the new Minister for Foreign Affairs in the Koizumi Cabinet, Makiko Tanaka, also made the Ministry less effective.

Economic issues were also a source of friction between Japan and its allies in 2001, with Japan subjected to conflicting demands for economic reform and deregulation and for disposal of its bad debts and adoption of import targets. Measures taken by Japan in April against the import of three agricultural products—leeks, shiitake mushrooms and *tatami* reeds—from China led to broad tariff increases by the Chinese against a number of Japanese industrial products, including automobiles. Trade difficulties with China were symptomatic of attempts to deal with the shifting power balance in the region, as Japan formulated its strategy to position itself advantageously with regard to China's economic and military strength. The Ministry of Economy, Trade and Industry's policy document on international trade, which was published in May, warned of heightening competition with China for economic leadership within the region, as China experienced outstanding levels of growth, and predicted that Japanese industry would relocate to China. The Japanese Government welcomed the new Administration of President George W. Bush in the USA and its shift from a policy of 'strategic partnership' with China to one of 'engagement'. A number of regional conferences in 2001 took as their theme the need for a new regional framework and for efforts to balance the emergent strength of China. Sub-regional economic co-operation and bilateral free trade, as well as the creation of an East Asia free trade area, were all under discussion. Diplomatic and security questions were identified as possible areas of difficulty for Prime Minister Koizumi. Disputes over the contents of Japanese textbooks continued to strain relations with both China and South Korea under the Koizumi Cabinet, which, in early June, refused to make any of a number of requested revisions to a textbook produced by the Japanese Society for History Textbook Reform, which seeks to teach historical pride in the nation. Tensions were exacerbated by the perception of Koizumi as a dangerous nationalist by those countries.

The repercussions of the suicide attacks on the USA in September 2001, three days after the 50th anniversary of the signing of the San Francisco Peace Treaty and the US-Japan Security Treaty, dominated many of Japan's subsequent international relations. The US-Japanese relationship improved to a level not seen since the days of the 'Ron-Yasu' relationship enjoyed by US President Ronald Reagan and Yasuhiro Nakasone in the 1980s. Koizumi's own aggressive image meant that his normalization of Japan's foreign policy necessitated skilful diplomacy if it were not to be perceived as a threat to the stability of the region. As a consequence, at the same time as Japan was drawn into a more active global role, for example in its contributions to peace-keeping operations and in its initiatives for a UN-sponsored World Summit on the reconstruction of Afghanistan, it also become more closely involved in regional activity on both a bilateral and multilateral level. Koizumi's regional offensive encompassed a meeting with Chinese President Jiang Zemin in October 2001, visits to five ASEAN nations in January 2002, the signing of a New-Age Economic Partnership with Singapore and participation in the first annual Boao Economic Forum for Asia in the Chinese province of Hainan in April when he argued in favour of an Asian free trade zone. These initiatives were also driven by concern over China's rapid economic and military growth and by that country's proposals for a China-ASEAN free trade agreement; demands were made in Japan for drastic reductions in ODA to China. In May tensions were exacerbated when the Chinese authorities seized North Korean nationals seeking refuge in the Japanese consulate in Shenyang.

An unexpected official visit to the Yasukuni Shrine by Koizumi in April 2002 resulted in the cancellation of a visit to Japan by the South Korean Minister of National Defence and led 800 South Koreans to join a pending legal action against the Prime Minister for unconstitutional behaviour. The joint hosting of the 2002 football World Cup in June brought an increase in co-operation and cultural exchange between Japan and South Korea. This, along with the initiation of a joint history study group, contributed to a steady improvement in relations between the two countries. Economic relations were strengthened by an investment alliance and by progress in talks for a broader free trade agreement. Although Japan did not agree with the Bush Administration's description of North Korea, Iraq and Iran as an 'axis of evil', North Korea continued to be a source of growing concern, with a worsening situation on the Korean peninsula and incursions into Japanese waters by North Korean spy ships. The relationship took a dramatic turn in mid-September when Koizumi returned from an unprecedented visit to Pyongyang with an apology for the abduction of 12 Japanese nationals by North Korea during the 1970s and 1980s, and the news that eight of the abductees had died. Apparent progress was made in the other major area of concern, ballistic missiles and nuclear weapons, with the signing of the Pyongyang Declaration whereby the North Korean Government promised to continue its moratorium on missile test launches, to respect international agreements on nuclear weapons inspections and to halt operations on spy ships in Japanese waters. For its part, Japan expressed remorse and apologies for its colonial past, and a readiness to pursue negotiations on the restoration of normal relations and resumption of economic assistance.

The continuing impact of the 'war on terror' provoked by the attacks of 11 September 2001 on the USA made the distinction between international relations and national security debatable. Nowhere was this truer than in the case of Japan where, as the extensive coverage in the Japanese print media attested, North Korea continued to dominate the debate on Japan's foreign relations and national security in subsequent months. The situation in Iraq was also much debated in Japan. The two issues were clearly related and the underlying common concern, the potential for damage to Japan's relationship with the USA (the 'cornerstone of Japanese diplomacy'), was critical in determining Japan's responses to relations with both countries. In April 2003 North Korea's admission of its possession of nuclear weapons and its offer, during three-way talks with the USA and China, to end nuclear weapons development and the export of missiles after the establishment of normal relations with the USA and Japan, further complicated the issue for Japanese officials. In late June Japan unexpectedly took the initiative with proposals for wider negotiations encompassing also Japan and South Korea. In July with a proposal for a resumption of bilateral negotiations alongside the multilateral talks.

In June 2003 discussions were held in Tokyo with South Korean President Roh Moo-Hyun. The talks stressed a 'forward-looking' approach to bilateral relations and shared concerns over North Korea. A visit to Japan was scheduled for August for the Chinese Minister of Foreign Affairs, Li Zhaoxing, to discuss the options on North Korea and an exchange of visits by Koizumi and Chinese Premier Wen Jiabao was proposed for later in the year. Wen's previous planned visit had been cancelled following disputes over the leasing by Japan of the Senkaku/Diaoyu Islands and a visit by Koizumi to the Yasukuni Shrine earlier in the year. The 25th anniversary of the signing of the Peace and Friendship Treaty with China appeared likely to be marked by a more positive note, as negotiations on the waiving of visas for Japanese visitors approached completion. As was acknowledged by a prime ministerial task force on foreign policy in November 2002, China remained 'the most important theme' for Japan's diplomacy in the 21st century.

Tension in relations with North Korea increased in late October 2003 with the firing of two *Silkworm* missiles into the Sea of Japan (or the East Sea as it is known on the Korean peninsula), but bilateral efforts to resolve the remaining issues related to the Japanese nationals abducted by North Korea continued, with Japanese diplomats making visits to Pyongyang in January and February 2004 prior to the six-party talks on North Korea's nuclear programme held in Beijing at the end of February, involving North and South Korea, Japan, China, Russia and the USA. Throughout the six-party talks and the associated bilateral discussions, progress on the abduction issue and the dismantling of North Korea's nuclear arms and missile programme remained obstacles to Japanese participation in any provision of aid or agreement to normalization of relations, and the talks ended without any decisions being reached. Diplomatic discussions continued, alongside a hardening of the Japanese position that included the introduction of legislation to allow the imposition of economic sanctions on North Korea, as well as, subsequently, legislation to ban port visits from foreign ships deemed a threat to public security. In May, to a mixed domestic reaction, Koizumi made a second trip to Pyongyang and returned to Tokyo with five children of abductees who had themselves been repatriated in 2002. There was no further clarification of the fate of the remaining 10 missing Japanese. None the less, Japan promised food and financial aid in return for the release of the abductees' children. In June 2004 Koizumi stated his goal as the normalization of diplomatic relations within one to two years, and in August his Cabinet gave authorization for dispatch, via UN agencies, of the first batch of the 250,000 tons of food and US $10m. worth of medical supplies he had promised. Diplomatic negotiation continued, and a fourth round of six-party talks was scheduled for the end of September (a third round having taken place in June, without reaching any significant conclusion).

Relations with North Korea worsened towards the end of 2004 as a direct result of the failure to provide a proper account of the fate of the remaining 10 and possibly as many as 70 abductees. Public ire was particularly aroused when DNA testing of what purported to be the repatriated remains of one young abductee, Megumi Yokota, showed them to be inauthentic. A popular outcry led to demands in the Diet for economic sanctions that went beyond the termination of current food aid; demands that were resisted by the Koizumi Government as it pursued its goal of six-party talks and the normalization of relations with a denuclearized North Korea. Koizumi's reluctance to perform what North Korea had claimed would amount to an act of war was bolstered by the need to retain the support of China and South Korea and the knowledge that Japanese sanctions would have little effect as long as North Korea continued to receive the assistance of South Korea and China. The situation deteriorated further in February 2005 with the confirmation by North Korea that it possessed nuclear weapons, and again in April when US intelligence suggested that Pyongyang had launched a short-range missile into the Sea of Japan. In March steps were taken to apply indirect sanctions by the implementation of a law requiring marine insurance not normally held by North Korean ships. The six-party talks on North Korea's nuclear programme finally resumed in July after a break of 13 months. It was indicative of the difficult path followed by Japan that Tokyo drew criticism from South Korea, China and Russia for raising the bilateral abduction issue at these multilateral talks and for being too passive in its efforts to end the crisis over the North's nuclear weapons. The talks were temporarily suspended without result in August as the USA refused to sanction North Korea's demand to be allowed to pursue peaceful nuclear activities for civilian purposes and at the same time to be rewarded with light-water reactors as provided for in the 1994 Agreement.

Meanwhile, relations with China suffered several set-backs from October 2003, although there were some positive developments. The Japanese Government undertook to send more experts to China to facilitate the ongoing removal of chemical weapons left behind during the Second World War; the yearly tripartite summit meeting with South Korea begun under Prime Minister Obuchi committed itself to greater closeness on security and economic issues, and visa restrictions for Chinese visitors were loosened. Nevertheless, Japan continued to be concerned about the potential for trouble between China and Taiwan following the re-election of President Chen Shuibian in March 2004. There were also heightened tensions over the disputed territories of the Senkaku/Diaoyu islands. Japan arrested and then immediately deported without prosecution seven Chinese activists who had landed on one of the islands. The US Government, possibly in gratitude for Japan's support in Iraq, made clear that the islands were included in the scope of the US-Japan Security Treaty. In response, China cancelled or postponed various ceremonies, visits and conferences including one on incursions by its ocean survey ships into the waters of the Japanese exclusive economic zone (EEZ). There was also concern within Japan that China was accessing natural gas in Japan's EEZ from installations close by in the South China Sea. A dispute over the boundary between the EEZs claimed by the two countries seemed possible in July when Japanese ships surveying in the area were prevented from carrying out their activities by the Chinese navy. There was a new development on the continuing issue of official visits to the Yasukuni Shrine when in April 2004 a Japanese District Court ruled Prime Minister Koizumi's August 2001 visit to have been unconstitutional. Both China and Korea welcomed the ruling that the visit violated the separation of state and religion.

In 2005 relations with China were fraught with difficulties, ranging from the incursion by a Chinese nuclear submarine into Japanese waters and violent attacks on Japanese property across China, to a joint US-Japanese statement on Taiwan and the announcement that all yen loans to China would be ended by 2008. Underlying these matters of contention were the growing strength of China, the attempts by Japan to secure a permanent seat on the UN Security Council, and the ever-present legacy of history in the form of nationalistic textbooks and visits by senior politicians to the Yasukuni Shrine. The wave of anti-Japanese demonstrations in April 2005 consisted of electronically organized protests that lacked prior official authorization, carried out predominantly by young men. The Chinese Government refused to apologize formally for the riots or to give official compensation. In May, immediately after the violence, Chinese Deputy Premier Wu Yi cancelled a meeting with Koizumi and returned to China in protest both at Koizumi's Yasukuni visit and at other shifts in Japanese policy that were regarded as provocative. Disputes continued meanwhile at government level over Chinese development of gas-fields near the disputed demarcation line between the two countries' economic waters and the granting of test drilling rights by the Japanese Government to Teikoku Oil, a Japanese company, near the same area. The rapid decline in this bilateral relationship had implications not only for the six-party talks but also for Japan's attempt to win permanent membership of the UN Security Council. The state of Japan's relations with Asia became an election issue when the DPJ leader, Katsuya Okada, criticized Koizumi's foreign policy for placing too much emphasis on relations with the USA, and promised to prioritize instead good relations with China and Korea.

The strained relations with China and South Korea were widely regarded as the greatest negative legacy of Koizumi's five years in office. The long-standing frictions between China and Japan over disputed territory, the historical legacy and annual visits by the Prime Minister to the Yasukuni Shrine were exacerbated by rising nationalism, increased defence spending, an expansion of pro-active involvement in the international arena and growing interdependency. The two issues of Koizumi's visit in October 2005 to Yasukuni and China's expanded extraction of gas in disputed areas of the East China Sea led to an escalation of existing tensions during the remainder of Koizumi's tenure. Chinese leaders had cancelled the visits of senior officials to and from Japan in 2001, but now declined to hold similar discussions on the sidelines of international meetings in third countries and warned that economic relations might be affected, as might China's position on Japan's application for a permanent seat on the UN Security Council. In late 2005 the Koizumi Government temporarily suspended the concessionary yen loans to China, which continued to form the majority of Japan's ODA. Japan's outgoing ambassador from Beijing made it known that the deterioration in popular sentiment between the two countries should be the greatest cause for concern.

Relations with South Korea during Koizumi's final year in office began on a promising note, with close co-operation on the North Korean nuclear issue, identified by Koizumi as their most important common agenda. However, relations deteriorated rapidly following the Yasukuni visit in October 2005, when South Korea ended bilateral and trilateral summit talks with Koizumi, and again in April 2006 when the Japanese Maritime Agency announced a plan to conduct a marine survey near Takeshima/Dokdo, a development that President Roh Moo-Hyun described as equivalent to 'justifying its history of crimes committed during the war of aggression'. Subsequent discussions in June on EEZ demarcation—the first in six years—failed to reach an agreement, and in July South Korea carried out its own survey within the EEZ claimed by Japan. Koizumi's long-promised visit to the Yasukuni Shrine on 15 August, the first by an incumbent premier on the anniversary of Japan's surrender in the Second World War since Nakasone's visit in 1985, drew the expected condemnation from South Korea and China, but also an acknowledgement that the imminent change of administration held the potential for an improvement in relations. All the contenders to succeed Koizumi stressed the need to improve relations with these two neighbours.

However, it was North Korea that provoked Japan into its most pro-active diplomatic efforts to date. This occurred when, after weeks of rumours of a forthcoming Korean missile launch, throughout which Japan promised a united response with the USA and threatened retaliatory measures ranging from economic sanctions to bringing the matter to the UN Security Council, North Korea launched six missiles on 5 July 2006 (4 July and Independence Day in the USA). Japan took the initiative in drafting a proposal, supported by the USA, for unofficial sanctions, including sanctions against the transfer of money or technology to North Korea that could be used to develop weapons of mass destruction. Japan subsequently rejected a Russo-Chinese proposal of a non-binding presidential statement and initiated discussions on the need for Japan to build the capability to attack foreign bases. After long negotiations, the Security Council unanimously adopted a resolution against North Korea. Japan subsequently intensified its own efforts to enforce new and more rigorous sanctions, including plans for legislation to ban financial institutions from dealing with those suspected of money-laundering for that country.

The USA, meanwhile, remained supportive of Japan's growing regional and international role. Koizumi's final visit to the USA as Prime Minister in June 2006 provided the opportunity for a joint statement to reiterate the US-Japanese alliance more broadly than hitherto, and to define the areas of co-operation beyond simple security to include the propagation of shared values and interests, the promotion of clean energy development and responses to natural and man-made disasters. The intermittent embargo on US beef imports, begun in December 2001 following an outbreak of BSE, was finally removed in time for Koizumi's US visit, and imports resumed in August 2006. In mid-2006 Japan's ongoing efforts to raise its diplomatic profile were furthered in Koizumi's final parliamentary summer recess by the dispatch of almost all of the cabinet ministers and ministers of state to countries of strategic importance to Japan and to those countries that had not previously received an official visitor. New sections were also created in the Ministry of Foreign Affairs to improve capacity in ODA planning. With every UN member country having one vote irrespective of size, these efforts were calculated to promote Japan's hitherto unsuccessful bid for a permanent seat on the UN Security Council. Japan's ODA programme had steadily declined as successive governments attempted to address the country's massive public debt, until by 2007 Japan had declined to the third largest provider of aid. The restructuring of aid policy within the Cabinet under the direct control of the Prime Minister was an attempt strategically to focus its decreasing aid budget.

In late September 2006 Shinzo Abe, as the new Prime Minister, promised to pursue a policy of more assertive diplomacy, to co-exist symbiotically with the rest of Asia and to increase trust between Japan and neighbouring countries. In his efforts to improve the relationship with China, with which trade had now exceeded that between the USA and Japan, Abe made his first overseas visit as Prime Minister to Beijing to meet with President Hu Jintao and Premier Wen Jiabao. This summit meeting, the first since October 2001, and the subsequent meeting with President Roh Moo-Hyun of South Korea, took place during Abe's first weeks in office, despite his refusal to clarify whether he intended to pay his respects at the Yasukuni Shrine during his premiership. Japan's relationship with China, which had suffered in recent years from the rise of Chinese nationalism and anti-Japanese sentiment, as well as from Koizumi's diplomatic failures, was recognized inside and outside Japan as crucial to regional stability. Significantly, the joint summit statement confirmed that 'strategic' bilateral relations, including exchanges at the most senior levels and between defence officials, would be moved to a higher level in recognition of their importance to both countries and to Asia. Chinese leaders accepted an invitation to visit Japan (Wen Jiabao visited Japan in April 2007 and delivered a speech to the Diet), and agreement was reached on advancing the six-party talks, pursuing reform of the UN Security Council, strengthening regional co-operation frameworks and finding a solution to East China Sea territorial issues. Academic history panels were established to discuss differences in interpretations of history. Abe's efforts yielded results domestically with growing popular support for strengthening relations with China.

Differences between China and Japan on the North Korean issue quickly became clear during the course of the APEC summit meeting held in Hanoi in November 2006, Abe's first attendance at such a meeting. While China, South Korea and Russia favoured dialogue and a negotiated end to the sanctions imposed following North Korea's nuclear test in October, Japan and the USA stressed the need for a sustained application of pressure on North Korea. The fifth round of the six-party talks resumed in Beijing in December but made no progress on the issue of nuclear disarmament; North Korea insisted that this be linked to the removal of financial sanctions, which in Japan's case had reduced trade with the communist regime by 95% compared with a year previously. Abe used his trip to Europe in January 2007 to urge support for Japanese efforts to secure the return from North Korea of Japanese abductees and the abandoning of its nuclear programme, and backing for Japan's attempts to secure a permanent seat on the UN Security Council. In February the delegates to the six-way talks agreed on energy, economic and humanitarian aid to North Korea. Bilateral discussions between North Korea and the USA, and between North Korea and Japan, were aimed at the restoration of normal relations. North Korea, for its part, was to shut down and seal its nuclear facilities in Yongbyon and allow IAEA inspections. Despite the agreement and suggestions that it might find itself on the periphery of the talks, Japan continued to refuse to offer aid to North Korea while the abduction issue remained open. The IAEA confirmed the closure of all five North Korean nuclear facilities in July, and the first bilateral meeting between Japan and North Korea since the conclusion of the six-party talks began shortly after.

In November 2006 a government panel had been established to develop plans for a Japanese National Security Council (NSC) that would lead on foreign policy and national security and, unlike the existing Security Council of Japan, could make policy without the need for cabinet approval. The panel, which reported in February 2007, recommended that the NSC should consist of the Prime Minister, Minister for Foreign Affairs, Minister of Defence and the Chief Cabinet Secretary, and that the council should set basic diplomatic and security policy for the country, make policy decisions in those areas that concerned more than one ministry or agency and respond to national emergencies. Meanwhile, the Ministry of Foreign Affairs defined the new pillar of Japan's diplomacy as the policy of 'Creating an Arc of Freedom and Prosperity' based on universal values stretching from the Baltic through the Middle East and South-East Asia to North-East Asia. Regionally this meant confidence-building with other countries; a multi-layered approach to common issues and an acknowledgement of the historical damage that Japan had inflicted on the region. US-Japanese relations, which had thrived under Koizumi, were to continue as 'a cornerstone of Japanese diplomacy' under Abe, who finally visited President Bush in April.

Abe's successor as Prime Minister, Yasuo Fukuda, made his first overseas visit to the USA in November 2007, but was unable to deliver an extension to the legislation that allowed Japan to provide logistical support, in the form of refuelling ships in the Indian Ocean, to the US-led coalition engaged in the 'war on terror' in and around Afghanistan. By contrast, Fukuda's December visit to China was notably cordial (Chinese Premier Wen Jiabao later described the bilateral relationship as having seen the 'arrival of spring') and included an unprecedented joint press conference with Wen and a live speech on Chinese television. Issues discussed during the visit ranged from the dispute over gas exploration rights in the East China Sea, on which no progress was made; wartime militarism, which Fukuda described as 'an unfortunate period'; the mutual distrust caused by military build-up; Japan's position on the anticipated Taiwanese referendum on an application for UN membership under the name of Taiwan, in relation to which Fukuda reiterated Japan's support for a 'one China' policy and its opposition to any action that would lead to unilateral change; and plans for a visit to Japan by President Hu Jintao.

Fukuda continued to consolidate Abe's efforts to promote better regional relations with a visit to South Korea in February 2008, on the occasion of the inauguration of Lee Myung-Bak as Roh's successor as President. Envisaging a new era in Japanese relations with South Korea, but avoiding contentious issues such as the enduring territorial disputes over Takeshima/Dokdo, the two leaders agreed to resume reciprocal visits, restart free trade talks and co-operate on North Korean nuclear and abduction issues. Following a further meeting of the two leaders in Tokyo in April, a joint press release announced a 'new Japan-South Korea era', co-operation on denuclearization of the Korean peninsula and a promise of further 'shuttle diplomacy'. Also in April Fukuda visited the Russian capital, Moscow, endeavouring to 'raise bilateral relations to a higher dimension'. Chinese President Hu's planned visit to Tokyo to mark the 30th anniversary of the Japan-China Peace and Friendship Treaty was delayed by disagreements over the source of the contamination of dumplings exported to Japan, but finally took place in early May. In June, following ongoing discussions, a commitment was made to hold a trilateral summit meeting of the leaders of Japan, China and South Korea separate from and independent of the usual regional conferences. In the same month an agreement was reached on the future of gas exploration in the East China Sea, although doubts remained about the possibility of real joint exploration.

Despite Japanese lobbying, in late June 2008 the USA began the process of removing North Korea from its list of state sponsors of terrorism, following that country's submission of a declaration of its nuclear programme. The action revitalized the moribund six-party talks, but deprived Tokyo of useful leverage in its efforts to resolve the abduction issue. However, in what was regarded as a diplomatic triumph for Japan, the G8 leaders, meeting in Hokkaido in July, took the opportunity to urge North Korea to resolve the abduction issue and co-operate fully with verification of the declaration. None the less, this was not enough to persuade Japan to remove remaining economic sanctions against North Korea. Relations with South Korea also suffered in July when the Ministry of Education, Culture, Sports, Science and Technology issued non-binding teaching guidelines that claimed the disputed territory of Takeshima/Dokdo as unequivocally Japanese territory. Foreign policy during the year of the Fukuda administration was denied the expected fillip from the introduction of an NSC similar to that in the USA when the plan was abandoned owing to the problems of the divided Diet (see above).

The impact of the global financial crisis provided the setting for the foreign policy endeavours of Fukuda's successor, Taro Aso. In October 2008 Prime Minister Aso travelled to Beijing to meet for the first time with Premier Wen Jiabao of China and President Lee Myung-Bak of South Korea. Aso pledged to work closely with those countries to address the global financial crisis. The first independent summit meeting of China, South Korea and Japan, was held in Kyushu in December, when it was agreed to hold further trilateral summits in China and South Korea in 2009 and 2010. (By the time of his resignation, Aso had met the leaders of both countries eight times.) During 2008 China become Japan's largest trading partner, and there were concerns in Japan that the incoming Administration of newly elected US President Barack Obama might result in a strengthening of Chinese relations with the USA, at the expense of Japan, and an acknowledgement that Japan might come under pressure to be more flexible in its approach to North Korea, to its contributions to the 'war on terror' and to the long-standing issue of the funding and positioning of US military bases in Japan. At the same time, the USA remained a major palliative to Japanese fears about an ascendant China that might soon overtake Japan to become the world's second largest economy.

Prime Minister Aso chose to highlight two particular areas of Japan's diplomacy in a speech to the Japan Institute of International Affairs at the end of June 2009. One area was strategic international co-operation, a recent example of which was the so-called 'Corridor for Peace and Prosperity' initiative in the Palestinian territories, which, by promoting the co-operative development of agriculture through technology, aimed to facilitate the peace process in the Middle East. The second was the promotion of 'soft power', which envisaged the fostering of cultural and ethical values through the export of literature and language. ODA, once a powerful instrument of Japanese foreign policy, had suffered from a decline in budget, to the extent that Japan had slipped from the top of the rankings to become the fifth largest provider of assistance (behind the USA, Germany, the United Kingdom and France).

In his campaign for the legislative election of August 2009, Aso was critical of the DPJ's foreign policy manifesto, in particular of the impact that a change of government would have on Japanese relations with the USA. For its part, the DPJ maintained that the relationship would remain the 'cornerstone' of Japan's foreign policy and that there would not be a change in direction but rather a greater assertiveness, independence and transparency. One major difference that the DPJ promised in its electoral campaign was to bring foreign policy under the control of the Prime Minister, who would be advised by a national strategy panel comprising private sector officials.

The Hatoyama administration, formed in September 2009, was expected to pursue greater equality in US-Japanese relations and a strengthening of Japan's links with China and South Korea. Addressing the UN General Assembly during his first few days in office, the new Prime Minister announced his desire to form an East Asian Community that would work together to resolve regional economic and security concerns; to secure a permanent seat for Japan on the UN Security Council; and for Japan to serve as a bridge between East and West, rich and poor, and nuclear and non-nuclear nations. At the 2009 UN Summit on Climate Change held in the same month, Hatoyama had committed Japan to a 25% reduction in greenhouse gas emissions from 1990 levels by 2020, predicated on a pledged commitment to similarly ambitious targets by other developed countries.

Hatoyama's undertaking not to visit the Yasukuni Shrine and to consider giving municipal voting rights to Korean nationals resident in Japan were warmly welcomed by South Korea, as was the Prime Minister's proposal for an East Asian Community. In May 2010 Hatoyama gave details of his vision for such a Community, which, he proposed, would include not only economic partnership agreements but also cultural and artistic exchanges, together with a shared cross-border framework for a co-operative emergency response to environmental and natural disasters, health, piracy, and maritime search and rescue incidents.

The resignations in early June 2010 of Hatoyama and DPJ Secretary-General Ozawa (who had led a 140-member DPJ delegation to China in December 2009) were received with disappointment in China. Premier Wen Jiabao had paid a visit to Japan in late May 2010 when progress had been made with regard to a resolution on joint development of gasfields in the East China Sea and measures to defuse tension that had arisen over various naval incidents, including the sighting in April of a group of Chinese warships near Okinawa (the Chinese authorities had denied any wrongdoing, stating that the ships had been engaged in a routine training exercise and had violated no international laws). Wen's visit to Japan had followed a trilateral summit, held in mid-May, between the Chinese Premier, South Korean President Lee and Hatoyama, at which the three leaders had reached agreement on proposals for greater economic integration and joint research into the Vision 2020 initiative. Following his inauguration as Prime Minister in June 2010, Naoto Kan accepted an invitation to China from Premier Wen. Kan's ambassadorial appointments, including that of Uichiro Niwa, an adviser to the trading company Itochu Corporation, as the new envoy to China, showed a marked increase in those drawn from the private sector.

Since the start of deregulation in qualifications for tourist visas for Chinese visitors in 2008 there had been a steady rise in the number of Chinese tourists visiting Japan, with projections for 2012 of over 2m. visitors. The majority of these visitors were under 30 years of age, university graduates and wealthy. However, one unwilling visitor to Japan was the captain of a Chinese fishing boat, arrested in September 2010 after deliberately colliding with a Japan Coast Guard vessel near the disputed Senkaku Islands. China's response to the detention was to demand the release of its national, to suspend cabinet-level contact with Japan, to withdraw from the bilateral discussions with Japan on joint development of the disputed gasfields, to arrest four Japanese for allegedly entering a military zone and to suspend exports of rare-earth minerals to Japan. Alarmed by its heavy dependency on China for its supply of rare earths (90% of total supplies), the Japanese Government began efforts to diversify supply, with approaches to the USA, Australia, Kazakhstan and Viet Nam, and encouraged research into new technologies. The decision to release the captain later in September seemed, as opposition politicians predicted, to encourage China to take advantage of Japan's apparent weakness and to promote further strengthening of China's presence in the East China Sea. For Japan, which undoubtedly responded to urgings from Washington in releasing the captain, one advantageous result of the incident was the confirmation by the USA that the US-Japan Security Alliance applied to the Senkaku Islands. Speculation about why China had adopted such a belligerent stance focused on the damage to US-Japan relations caused by the Hatoyama administration, and a general perception that Japanese weakness in times of crisis management had been made worse by the attempts of the DPJ Government to reduce the role of the bureaucracy in policy-making. The confirmation of China's replacement of Japan as the world's second largest economy (after the USA) in February 2011 added to altered perceptions of the balance of power between the two countries.

The hardening of China's attitude to Japan, following the deterioration in the US-Japanese relationship over the previous year, was duplicated in Russia, which for the first time sent its President, Dmitrii Medvedev, to visit Kunashiri in the disputed Northern Territories in November 2010. This was followed by further ministerial visits, by the development of joint ventures on the islands by Russia with China and South Korea, and by a build-up in the Russian military presence in the area. At the same time Russia appeared ready to pursue a diplomatic initiative with Japan for a peace treaty and a joint economic programme. China's dispatch in June 2011, without prior notice, of naval vessels to an area that included territory claimed as an exclusive economic zone by Japan; an increase in Chinese naval activity off Okinawa, and official visits by South Korea to the disputed territory of Takeshima, all took advantage of the paralysis that affected the Japanese Government as Kan struggled to retain power (see above). The weak status of the Kan Government also meant that a visit to Beijing by Takeaki Matsumoto, the Minister for Foreign Affairs, in July failed to produce any progress on issues such as the joint development of gasfields, or disputes over patents for technologies used in the new Beijing–Shanghai high-speed railway.

In contrast, the Kan Government's relationship with South Korea began well. In August 2010, prior to the 100th anniversary of Japan's annexation of Korea in 1910, Kan apologized to South Korea for the suffering endured under colonial rule and promised the transfer of various Korean cultural artefacts. The administration also announced that ministers would 'voluntarily refrain' from visiting the Yasukuni Shrine. Fears in South Korea about the deterioration in US-Japanese relations were also allayed. After the concern caused in Washington by Hatoyama's advocacy of an East Asian Council to counterbalance US influence in Asia, and Hatoyama's failure to resolve the Futenma issue, Kan's acknowledgement of the importance of the alliance with the USA was greeted favourably. President Obama's meeting with Kan in November 2010 resulted in an agreement to press ahead with strengthening the alliance. The value of the US-Japanese alliance to the two countries and to the wider region had been the subject of debate for many years, but the rise of China and the volatility of North Korea were perceived as providing strong arguments in the alliance's favour. During 2010 the sinking of a South Korean naval vessel, the *Cheonan*, and the shelling of the South Korean island of Yeonpyeong by North Korean forces provided a serious reminder of the need to reinforce the bilateral relationship.

When a devastating earthquake and tsunami struck northern Japan on 11 March 2011, there was an immediate and massive response in the form of goods and personnel from around the world, especially from the USA. US military relief efforts in the disaster area, a joint operation with the SDF, code-named Operation Tomodachi ('Friend'), were expected to reinvigorate ties that had recently weakened, and to reinforce Japan's position in the area against any further growth in China's influence in the aftermath of the disaster. China, in its turn concerned about the deepening of US-Japanese relations, sent Premier Wen Jiabao on a visit to the affected area. There was, moreover, not simply an outpouring of sympathy, but a notable sense of respect and admiration at the conduct of those affected by the disaster. Gradually, however, the international evaluation of the Japanese Government's response to the crisis became critical. As fears of radioactive contamination increased, exacerbated by the failure of the administration properly to provide the public with accurate data, trading partners began to restrict imports of goods from Japan, especially of foodstuffs. By the end of April 34 countries, along with the EU and other regions, had banned a variety of imports. There was criticism in the foreign press of the handling of the nuclear crisis and of the relationship between the Government and the nuclear industry. The release of water contaminated by low-level radioactivity, without warning or explanation, into the Pacific Ocean caused particular anger among Japan's immediate neighbours, South Korea, China and Russia. The loss of supplies from Japan to its Asian customers in particular had an ongoing impact on production in those countries and was a reminder of their interdependence. A further cause of concern for the states that rely on nuclear power was what appeared to be a shift in Japan's energy policy away from nuclear production and the potential loss of Japan as a leading supplier of components for nuclear facilities.

NATIONAL SECURITY, DEFENCE AND REARMAMENT

The initial basis for Japan's bilateral security arrangements with the USA was concluded by treaty in 1951. This granted the use of military bases in Japan to the USA, in return for a US commitment to provide military support to Japan in the event of external aggression. The Treaty of Mutual Co-operation and Security between Japan and the USA was signed in 1960. Serious consideration of rearmament, in order to make Japan both an economic and a military power, would have been welcomed by the USA in the 1970s, but there were many fundamental obstacles. Constitutional revision was one prerequisite, since Article 9 of Japan's post-war Constitution is usually interpreted to mean that Japan's armed forces are for defence only, must remain relatively small in number and cannot be equipped with inter-continental ballistic missiles. However, any attempt to revise the Constitution would cause a major domestic political crisis. Moreover, rearmament would be bitterly contested in South-East Asia, where anti-Japanese sentiment remains very strong. Attention, therefore, was turned to alternative solutions, which included, in 1979, Prime Minister Ohira's plan for 'comprehensive security'. Briefly, this proposal envisaged a commitment by Japan to promote the integrity of the geopolitical structures within which it conducted its economic relations. Prime Minister Nakasone favoured the creation of a strong defence force and a broader role for Japan in regional affairs.

Nakasone's decision to permit the transfer to the USA of new technologies with military applications indicated a change of policy, which was welcomed in the USA. In January 1987 the Japanese Government announced that it was to abandon its self-imposed limit on defence expenditure of 1% of the gross national product (GNP), which had operated since 1976. Defence spending equivalent to 1.004% of the forecast GNP was proposed for 1987/88; it was also announced that defence expenditure would be maintained at about this level until 1991. This decision was welcomed by the USA but harshly criticized by the USSR and the People's Republic of China.

After failing to win the approval of the Diet for proposals to send SDF personnel overseas in November 1990, the LDP agreed with Komeito and the DSP that the Government would establish a new body to participate in UN peace-keeping operations. Although Komeito initially insisted that SDF personnel be excluded from the new body, the proposal was finally approved on the condition that SDF personnel be confined to non-combat duties. In July 1991 the three political parties dispatched a mission to Cambodia and other Asian countries to assess the possibility of Japanese involvement in a UN-sponsored peace plan for Cambodia. In September 1992 683 Japanese personnel, including some civilian police officers, were sent to Cambodia to participate in the UN Transitional Authority in Cambodia (UNTAC) mission. The death of two Japanese personnel in Cambodia, in early 1993, heightened domestic opposition to Japan's involvement in UN peace-keeping operations. In September 1995 it was announced that SDF personnel would participate in a UN observer force in Israel from February 1996. In November 1999 the ruling parties agreed to postpone the consideration of a proposal to expand Japan's participation in UN peace-keeping operations.

The report of the Advisory Group on Defence Issues, commissioned by Hosokawa's Government, was published in August 1994. The report urged a reduction in SDF personnel from some 274,000 to 240,000, recognizing the difficulties of the SDF ground forces in achieving full recruitment. The proposals were largely adopted in early January 1995 in a draft document on new defence policy guidelines. The report also envisaged reductions in aircraft and ships, the modernization of Japan's defence capability, and improvements in command, communications and intelligence. A case was also made for co-operation with the USA on the development of weapons systems such as anti-ballistic missile defences.

In September 1995 a 12-year-old girl was raped by three US servicemen in Okinawa. The incident led to nation-wide demonstrations against the three men (who were found guilty and sentenced to prison terms in March 1996) and against the Government's policy on Japanese-US security arrangements. Public support for the 35-year-old mutual security treaty declined sharply. In view of such public discontent, Governor Masahide Ota of Okinawa refused to approve the continued use of land by US military forces when the Defence Agency requested an extension of the leases, demanding a review of the Japanese-US security arrangements in general, and of the Status of Forces Agreement in particular. A referendum, held in Okinawa in September 1996, revealed that the majority of residents favoured a reduction in the number of US bases. Nevertheless, later in that month Ota reversed his decision and agreed to sign the documents renewing the leases. In December it was announced that the USA was to return some 20% of the land used for military bases and to build a floating offshore helicopter base. However, there was to be no significant reduction in the number of troops stationed in Okinawa. In order to reduce the financial and other obligations borne by Okinawa, some US military exercises were relocated to other prefectures, and the Government also began to negotiate special measures to promote economic development in the region.

In December 1997, in a non-binding referendum held in Nago, Okinawa, to assess public opinion concerning the construction of the offshore helicopter base, the majority of voters rejected the proposal. The Mayor of Nago, who advocated the construction of the base in return for measures to stimulate the region's economy, tendered his resignation. Governor Ota stated his opposition to the proposed base. The new Mayor, elected in February 1998, initially approved of the helicopter base, but subsequently announced that he would support Ota in opposing the construction. In November Keiichi Inamine defeated Ota in the Okinawa gubernatorial election. Inamine, who had been supported by the LDP, presented an alternative solution, in an attempt to gain government support for the local economy, proposing that a military-commercial airport be built in northern Okinawa and leased to the USA for a period of 15 years. In December a US military site was officially returned to the Japanese Government, the first of the 11 bases to be returned under the 1996 agreement. In December 1999 Inamine's proposal for the relocation of the US air base to northern Okinawa was approved by both the local authorities and the Japanese Government, with the Henoko district of Nago chosen as the site for the new airport; at the same time funding was allocated for a 10-year development plan for the area. Negotiations with the USA, which opposed any time limit on its use of the airport, subsequently took place; although it had been hoped that negotiations would be concluded by July 2000, when the summit meeting of G8 nations was held in Nago, no agreement was reached by that time. In March, during a visit by the US Secretary of Defense, William Cohen, some agreements were concluded, giving Japan control of the US Kadena air base and resolving an air pollution problem in Kanagawa prefecture, but the central issues of a time limit on US use of the new airport and of the level of Japan's payments to the USA as a host nation to its military forces remained unresolved.

Following the signing of a US-Japan Joint Declaration on Security in April 1996 by President Clinton and Prime Minister Hashimoto, the review of the Guidelines for Japan-US Defense Co-operation (compiled in November 1978) continued in 1997, and culminated in the issuing of a joint statement detailing the new Guidelines in mid-September. China expressed concern at the provisions of the new agreement, which envisaged enhanced co-operation between the USA and Japan, not only on Japanese territory, but also in situations in unspecified areas around Japan. Despite opposition from its coalition partners, in April 1998 the LDP Government approved legislation to define the operations of the SDF under the revised Guidelines. The legislation was enacted in May 1999, prompting criticism from China and Russia. Its approval was ensured by an agreement between the LDP, its new coalition partner, the LP, and New Komeito to exclude a clause that would have allowed the inspection of unidentified foreign ships by the SDF, with the aim of enforcing economic sanctions; separate legislation on this issue was expected to be proposed later in the year. In August the Japanese Government formally approved a memorandum of understanding with the USA stipulating details of joint technical research on the development of a theatre missile defence system, which aims to detect and shoot down incoming ballistic missiles within a 3,000-km radius. The Defence Agency estimated that Japan would have to allocate up to 30,000m. yen to the controversial research project over a period of five years.

Instability on the Korean peninsula was a cause of concern for the Japanese Government in 1998, particularly following the testing of a suspected missile by North Korea (see above). Officials from the ministries of foreign affairs and defence of South Korea and Japan agreed to convene regular bilateral security meetings. The incursion into Japanese waters of two suspected North Korean spy ships in March 1999 prompted the first-ever invocation of legislation allowing naval forces to engage in maritime policing operations (see above). The incident also provided the first opportunity for the South Korean and Japanese armed forces to operate a new 'emergency liaison system', which had been established as a result of a recent bilateral security agreement. The Japanese Government criticized India and Pakistan for conducting nuclear tests in mid-1998, and suspended grants of non-humanitarian aid and loans to India in response to the tests. A series of missile tests carried out by India and Pakistan in April 1999 again provoked criticism from Japan. Relations had improved by the end of 1999; in late 1999 and early 2000 the Indian Ministers of External Affairs and of Defence paid official visits to Tokyo, and in February 2000 former Prime Minister Ryutaro Hashimoto visited India as a special envoy. During his visit he urged India to sign the UN's Comprehensive Test Ban Treaty, although he also indicated that Japan had no desire for bilateral relations to be determined by India's response to the Treaty. In late August Yoshiro Mori visited India as part of a tour of South Asia, in his first overseas trip as Prime Minister.

As part of efforts to combat increasing piracy in South-East Asia, Japan advocated the creation of a regional patrol for these waters. Although constitutionally unable to provide members of its navy for this task, Japan proposed the involvement of its coastguard, a non-military organization, in a regional force. In May 2000 Japan hosted a conference of coastguard officials from 15 Asian nations, at which the problem of piracy, and possible solutions, were discussed.

A new five-year mid-term defence programme was adopted in December 2000, in response to the changing nature of security threats in the post-Cold War world and to demands for a greater international contribution to peace by Japan. The new defence programme was to develop readiness to deal with nuclear, biological and chemical threats and terrorist attacks and was intended to bring Japan's defence capability to the levels prescribed in the national defence programme outline.

Under the Mori Cabinet, the long-standing issues that bedevilled the US-Japanese relationship continued. Military bases in Okinawa contributed to anti-US sentiment as a result of rising crime in the area. US demands for a greater contribution to the maintenance of regional security from Japan grew under the new Bush Administration. The sinking of the fisheries training ship, the *Ehime-Maru*, by a US nuclear submarine in February 2001 exacerbated this growing anti-US nationalism.

Japan maintained its official position of 'understanding' the missile defence initiative and its support for joint US-Japanese technical studies, while steadfastly avoiding any decision on whether it would enter into joint development of the Theater Missile Defense system. After his appointment as Prime Minister in April 2001, Junichiro Koizumi emphasized the need to avoid the sort of international isolation that had led to the last war, the importance of the US-Japanese security alliance, and the value of changing the Constitution over time to recognize the right to existence of the SDF and to take part in collective self-defence. The terrorist attacks on the mainland USA in September and President Bush's insistence on co-operation from the rest of the world in the so-called 'war on terror' revived unpleasant memories in Japan of the tensions created by the character and timing of Japan's contributions to the Gulf War in the early 1990s. Such memories clearly contributed to the speed and strength of the Government's response. Despite the USA's later omission of Japan from the list of countries contributing to the 'war on terror', the Prime Minister's response was rapid and positive, going further than ever before towards normalizing Japan's international role, although without leading to any change in the Government's interpretation of its ability to exercise the right to collective defence. The Government's seven-point response plan included legislation to allow deployment of the SDF as theatre support, the dispatch of information-gathering warships as far as the Indian Ocean and the resumption of aid to India and Pakistan.

Anti-terrorism legislation was implemented in early November 2001, effective for two years but with the possibility of subsequent renewal. The legislation allowed for the dispatch of the SDF to non-combat zones in areas of conflict, subject to consent by the host government and to approval by the Diet within 20 days of troops being dispatched, or at the start of a new session. Such troops were given expanded powers to use weapons to protect refugees and injured foreign servicemen. In mid-November two destroyers and a supply ship sailed for the Indian Ocean in the first of several SDF contributions.

The other major legislation introduced in the 2002 ordinary Diet session consisted of three defence bills, one setting out the response to a direct foreign military attack or expected attack, and the others revising the Self Defence Forces Law and the Law on the Establishment of the Security Council. Efforts to create a new framework to deal with national emergencies had begun in the mid-1970s, one reason perhaps why the proposed legislation did not include responses to terrorism or incursions into Japan's territorial waters, despite the urgings of Koizumi. The new legislation provided for an emergency headquarters in the Cabinet Office, headed by the Prime Minister, established that the government would make plans to deal with military emergencies on the basis of UN Security Council recommendations, granted the Prime Minister extended powers to direct the operations of local government and reduced restrictions on the domestic activities of the SDF. Flaws in the drafting, a scandal involving the Defence Agency, and LDP internal disputes meant that debate on the bills was initially postponed until the October 2002 session of the Diet, but the proposed legislation was still pending in early 2003 at the height of the conflict in Iraq and the confrontation with North Korea. A bipartisan agreement was finally reached in May, following the inclusion of opposition provisions on protection of human rights, and the bills became law with the support of more than 80% of the Diet in early June. The passage of the military emergency bills was indicative of the dramatic changes in both party politics and public opinion over the previous 10 years. Such, indeed, were the changes that Prime Minister Koizumi felt able to suggest that Japan could attack foreign missile bases if it perceived there to be an imminent threat and to argue that the Constitution should be revised to acknowledge the SDF to be a military force. Following its launch of the first two of four spy satellites in March 2003, Japan's capacity to monitor any threatening activity on the part of North Korea was greatly enhanced.

The establishment of guidelines for responding to foreign attack was not the only difficult issue to be tackled. The controversial decision in December 2002 to dispatch to the Indian Ocean a destroyer capable of sharing military data with the US fleet was perceived by many opponents as an erosion of the constitutional prohibition against collective self-defence. Similar criticisms were made of the Government's decision in June 2003 to move to the development and deployment stage of the missile defence initiative with the USA. The decision, which raised a number of legal and constitutional issues, was facilitated by evidence of nuclear and missile development on the part of North Korea. Joint exercises with the USA on missile interception were scheduled to begin in the 2004 fiscal year, and a decision on moving to the final stage was to be made immediately afterwards. The Defence Agency announced that the Constitution would allow Japan to intercept missiles aimed at a third country but overflying Japan. The deployment of a missile defence system was likely to be part of a US 'military transformation', which would include a significant reduction in the 37,000 US forces stationed in South Korea but not in the number of troops deployed in Japan itself.

There was little support for Koizumi's strong, early backing of the US decision to oust the regime of Saddam Hussain in Iraq, either among the Japanese public, 49% of whom were against the operation, or in the Diet, where 68% opposed any action without a UN Security Council resolution. In defence of his position, Koizumi cited both the importance of the US-Japanese alliance and the North Korean nuclear and missile crisis. The same combination of factors stood behind Japan's contributions to post-war reconstruction work in Iraq. The controversial legislation needed to authorize the sending of SDF personnel to help in the rebuilding of Iraq raised issues about the use of weapons, conditions for dispatch and parliamentary approval.

The Prime Minister continued to jeopardize his position as a consequence of his efforts to convince the USA that Japan was a 'trustworthy ally'. The overwhelming importance of Japan's security relationship with the USA was evident in the Government's downplaying of the need for international co-operation through the UN and in the high political risks taken by Koizumi in his decision to send troops to Iraq. Deployment of the Air Self-Defence Force (ASDF) to provide reconstruction and humanitarian assistance to Iraq was delayed by domestic opposition that grew as the situation in Iraq deteriorated, with the killing in November 2003 of two Japanese diplomats, the first Japanese casualties since the start of the conflict. Parliamentary debate on the deployment began during the legislature's recess at the end of 2003. In accordance with the special law approved in the previous July, the deployment of all SDF personnel was given *ex post facto* approval in a forced vote in the House of Representatives in January 2004. This led to a short opposition boycott of the House of Councillors. The dispatch of the SDF was seen as a further step in the 'normalization' of Japan's foreign and security policies, a step that Koizumi insisted did not violate the constitution. Ground Self-Defence Force (GSDF) units totalling 550 men arrived in southern Iraq in February and March. The taking of Japanese hostages in April, widely seen as a crisis that could bring down the Government, ended without incident and without the withdrawal of Japanese forces. At a meeting with President Bush prior to a UN Security Council resolution in June, Koizumi announced that the SDF would, for the first time, participate in a multinational force following the return of sovereignty to Iraq. The conditions set out by Koizumi were that there would be no use of force and no activities outside non-combat zones, and that the Japanese forces would act within the existing special law and remain under Japanese command.

In December 2003, meanwhile, commitment to the missile defence initiative was taken a stage further when the Government made a formal decision to introduce the system and authorized the signing of contracts. The Defence Agency made known its intention to propose legislation that would give the Prime Minister the power to mobilize the missile defence system without the authorization of the Cabinet or the Security Council of Japan in case of emergency. A new defence plan proposed by the Defence Agency provided for further shifts away from the defence posture of the 1995 outline towards missile defence and anti-terrorism measures more fitting to the international situation following the events of 11 September 2001 and to the heightened threat from a nuclear-capable North Korea. The Government's new defence guidelines were to be finalized in the latter part of 2004 and adopted in December. It was also announced that restrictions on the export of weapons were to be revised and that the Acquisition and Cross-Servicing Agreement (ACSA), regulating relations between the SDF and US forces, was to be extended. Special anti-terrorist units were created by the Defence Agency, and the 2004 budget made extra funds available to the police to expand internal security measures. The war contingency law approved in June 2003 was expanded with further legislation in June 2004 that set down detailed rules on responses by US forces in Japan and by the MSDF in the event of a foreign attack on Japan. The legislation was supported by both the ruling coalition and the DPJ. A defence 'white paper' published in July set out the strategic background to all these changes. In addition to these substantial developments in Japan's defence posture, there were various proposals on issues including the upgrading of the Defence Agency to a ministry, SDF units dedicated to international operations, a comprehensive, permanent law on the dispatch abroad of the SDF and the revision of Article 9 of the Constitution to allow collective defence.

Japan announced its bid for a permanent seat on the UN Security Council at a meeting of the UN General Assembly in September 2004. The country's pacifist Constitution was seen by some as a potential obstacle to the achievement of this aim, but not by Prime Minister Koizumi, who claimed that Japan could play its role in the international community under the terms of the current Constitution. The major obstacles to permanent membership for Japan were: the USA, which, although it supported Japan's efforts, was implacably opposed to strengthening and enlarging the Security Council; China, which cited Japan's lack of historical consciousness; and fellow Group of Four (G4) alliance members Germany, Brazil and India, whose own bids for membership were creating opposition from Mexico, Italy and Pakistan. The G4 proposal presented in July 2005 to the General Assembly called for the creation of six new permanent members alongside four new non-permanent members, with a decision on the right of veto to be postponed for 15 years. The USA's counter-proposal was for two new permanent members, one of which was to be Japan, and two or three new non-permanent members. An attempt by the G4 to win support for a joint proposal from the 53-member African Union failed, and the vote on the resolution was abandoned.

The beheading in October 2004 of a Japanese national held hostage in Iraq brought demands from all the opposition parties for a withdrawal of SDF troops, with no extension of the December deadline. Public opinion polls showed growing support for this sentiment, which was driven by the deteriorating circumstances in Iraq, not least by a rocket attack on the SDF camp at Samawah, which suggested that Japanese troops were not operating in a 'non-combat zone'. Those who did support an extension of the deadline did so overwhelmingly on humanitarian grounds (65%), compared with 32% who saw it as necessary to the alliance with the USA. Despite opposition from inside and outside the LDP, and the increased danger that Japanese troops might be drawn into military action for the first time in the post-1945 period, the Cabinet endorsed a one-year extension to the deployment of the 600 GSDF troops and eight ASDF aircraft, and, in response to the Iraqi Transitional Government's request for the multinational forces to remain beyond the end of 2005, Koizumi indicated the possibility of further extensions. Prior to the poll of September, the main opposition party, the DPJ, made the withdrawal of the SDF from Iraq by December an election pledge, along with a relaxation of SDF rules of engagement.

The steady growth in Japan's pro-active approach to security was given greater structure in the new 2005/06 National Defence Program Outline (NDPO) and the accompanying mid-term defence plan for 2005–09, which ventured into new territory by defining international peace-keeping and counter-terrorism as integral to Japan's security and identifying China and North Korea as specific threats. The 2005 NDPO also noted the need for reductions in personnel along with the centralization of the SDF command structure, and a strengthening of the US-Japanese alliance, including enhanced intelligence-sharing and joint development of missile defence. A separate statement issued by the Government indicated that there would also be a relaxation of the ban on weapons exports to facilitate the sale of missile defence components to the USA, and consideration of arms exports for other purposes on a case-by-case basis. A Japan-US Statement on Common Strategic Objectives was released by the two Governments in February. These objectives included co-operation on global terrorism and weapons of mass destruction; the peaceful reunification of the Korean peninsula; the peaceful resolution of the Taiwan Straits problem; the reform of the Security Council and the elevation of Japan to permanent membership; continued consultation on roles, duties and capabilities of the SDF and US Forces; realignment of US Forces in Japan and the implementation of the final report of the joint Special Action Committee on Okinawa (established in November 1995 following a deterioration in relations—see above) on reduction of US military facilities in Okinawa. The reference to the Taiwan Straits, which was not included in the 1996 joint statement (see above), remained central to considerations of US military realignment. Missile defence co-operation took a further step forward in June when both houses of the Diet approved a bill revising the Self Defence Forces Law to permit the head of the Defence Agency to order the interception of ballistic missiles without the prior approval of the Prime Minister and Cabinet.

Koizumi's final year in office consolidated the expansion of Japan's international security role, the strengthening of the US-Japanese security alliance and the proposals for constitutional revision outlined in his first press conference in 2001. In October 2005 the special anti-terrorism legislation under which the SDF had provided refuelling facilities for the 'war on terror' was extended for one more year, and in December the deployment of the SDF in Iraq was extended to December 2006, with the expectation that the GSDF would be withdrawn at the same time as British and Australian troops. In the event, the troops were withdrawn in July when Iraqi forces assumed responsibility for security from coalition troops. In April 2006 the GSDF, MSDF and ASDF operations were integrated and a newly created SDF Joint Chief of Staff was appointed as chief aide to the Director-General of the Defence Agency. In May an agreement was reached on a 'roadmap' for the realignment of US troops in Japan by 2014 in order to restructure, relocate and streamline the US military presence. The 'roadmap', which formed part of a global US military redeployment plan, would involve the relocation of the US Marine Corps Futenma Air Station to a less densely populated area at Camp Schwab, and the transfer of 8,000 US marines and 9,000 dependants from Okinawa to the Pacific island of Guam, with Japan bearing 59% of the estimated costs of US $10,270m. It was also agreed that the SDF would share command centres with US forces in order better to unify chains of command in case of emergency. A subsequent defence 'white paper' for the first time devoted an entire chapter to the US-Japanese alliance, in which the importance of fulfilling the various initiatives was elucidated. The document also explained the bill to upgrade the Defence Agency to the status of an independent ministry headed by a minister of defence with the authority to submit budgets and make proposals to cabinet meetings, while the Prime Minister would retain the position of Supreme Commander. The proposed legislation would also redefine the SDF's primary duties to include UN-led peace-keeping operations, international emergency relief and logistical support in areas surrounding Japan.

Meanwhile, the gradual erosion of the self-definition of Japan as a country without a military continued, and for the first time the LDP produced a full draft constitution that retained the first part of Article 9, forever renouncing war, but gave overt recognition to the existence of a Japanese military headed by the Prime Minister as Commander-in-Chief. As budget requests were submitted at the end of August 2006, in the final days of Koizumi's premiership in August 2006, the Defence Agency announced its rejection of the Ministry of Finance's demands for reductions and its intention to request a 1.5% increase in view of the enhanced threat from North Korea. In response to the North Korean ballistic missile tests in July, the Defence Agency also requested a 56% increase in funding for the Ballistic Missile Defence (BMD) system.

The appointment of the uncompromising Shinzo Abe as Prime Minister was widely expected to provide further impetus to the changes to Japan's defence position. The new Government's response to North Korea's nuclear tests in October 2006 was the immediate introduction of sanctions against the regime, including the barring of all North Korean ships from Japanese ports, and the banning of imports and the entry of North Korean nationals. A unanimous UN vote in favour of economic sanctions that included provisions for inspection of cargo entering or leaving the communist nation increased the urgency of Diet clarification of what constituted 'an emergency in nearby areas that could pose a clear and present danger to the country's peace and security', the legal basis for government action. The nuclear tests underlined the need for the planned deployment of the BMD system, and at their first meeting in Hanoi in November Prime Minister Abe and President Bush agreed to accelerate co-operation on BMD issues. Deployment of Japan's first ballistic missile interceptors began at the Iruma Air Base in Saitama in March 2007. International fears that the tests would lead to a nuclear 'arms race' in East Asia were exacerbated first by the Chairman of the LDP Policy Research Council, Shoichi Nakagawa—who acknowledged growing domestic sentiment in favour of the initiative and recommended active debate on the issue of whether arming Japan with nuclear weapons would diminish the likelihood of an attack—and subsequently by Minister for Foreign Affairs Taro Aso, who defended Nakagawa's remarks. The issue of the nuclear option had been raised in a report published in September 2006 by an independent research institute chaired by former Prime Minister Nakasone. While the report urged Japan to consider the nuclear option but at the same time to maintain its non-nuclear stance and promote non-proliferation, it was suggestive of a growing readiness to discuss hitherto unmentionable topics. Abe, in the mean time, restated Japan's continuing adherence to the three non-nuclear principles (not to possess, produce or allow the admission of nuclear weapons into Japan), but argued that public discussion of the issue must not be suppressed. The integrity of the three non-nuclear principles suffered another reverse when the Director of the Defence Agency, Fumio Kyuma, told the Diet Security Committee that Japan would allow the passage of nuclear arms in the event of an emergency.

The government bill extending the Anti-Terrorism Law was approved by the Diet in late October 2006. On the same day parliamentary debate began on two defence-related bills, the first to upgrade the Defence Agency, which operated under the Cabinet Office, to a ministry able to propose legislation and make budget requests on its own initiative, and the second to revise SDF laws to include international peace-keeping duties as part of SDF core functions. These bills were approved by both houses before the end of the first session, and the new Ministry of Defence began operation in January 2007. The Prime Minister retained supreme command of the armed forces, ensuring that the SDF remained under civilian control, albeit potentially less so than before. The fact that the new Ministry of Defence, unlike the old Agency, was able to convene a cabinet meeting to authorize immediate responses in the event of a threat to national security was expected to facilitate a rapid, more flexible response to emergencies. The Ministry was also to assume new responsibilities for formulating national security policy, including the reorganization of US troops in Japan. The proposed NSC would also have an impact on the locus of responsibility for national security policy, shifting it into the ambit of the Prime Minister and away from the bureaucracy in a pattern similar to that established in relation to the economy by the Council on Economic and Fiscal Policy. In May a government national security advisory panel began a review of the interpretation of the Constitution, which denied Japan the right to engage in collective self-defence. Japan continued the slow process of responding to the threat of terrorism with the introduction of a 3,200-strong GSDF quick-response division under the direct control of the Minister of Defence.

The coalition Government's loss of its majority in the upper house in July 2007, the resignation of Abe as Prime Minister, citing the fact that he had become an 'obstacle' to the renewal of the anti-terrorism law, and the failure of the subsequent Fukuda Cabinet to extend the temporary legislation authorizing the dispatch of the MSDF to the Indian Ocean had implications for Japan's security alliance with the USA and, by extension, for the security situation in Asia. These developments gave momentum to the idea of new permanent legislation allowing the overseas deployment of troops without the need for case-by-case special measures, thus enabling Japan to play a more active role in peace-building, and thereby enhancing its international reputation, which had been affected by the growing strength of China and Russia. However, the adoption of such legislation was made more difficult by the divisions within the Diet (see above), and was further complicated by the scandals surrounding the new Ministry of Defence, which included accusations of promoting disinformation about the amount and destination of oil that the MSDF had provided to the USA during a refuelling mission in 2003, and inappropriate links between Vice-Minister of Defence Takemasa Moriya and former Defence Agency Directors-General Fumio Kyuma and Fukushiro Nukaga and executives of the military equipment trader Yamada Corporation. The Ministry of Defence suffered a further set-back in April 2008 when the Nagoya High Court ruled that the ASDF's airlifts of armed troops from the multinational forces in Iraq were unconstitutional since they were tantamount to 'acts integral' to the use of force by others in a war zone. Plans to gain some much-needed kudos by using SDF rather than civilian aircraft to supply emergency aid to China's Sichuan Province, in response to a devastating earthquake in May, were abandoned when they were opposed by the Chinese public. However, the ASDF did fly Prime Minister Fukuda to the Olympic Games in Beijing in August. Meanwhile, in December 2007 an MSDF destroyer showed the extent of the progress made in the development of BMD when it successfully intercepted a ballistic missile in a space test off Hawaii. Changes to emergency response guidelines against a missile attack were also being studied. Missile launchers were scheduled to be in place on four *Aegis* destroyers and at 10 ASDF bases around Japan by 2010. One piece of government legislation that did pass smoothly through the divided Diet, receiving approval from both houses in May 2008, was the bill to allow the use of space for defence purposes such as the deployment of early warning and spy satellites.

In September 2008 the increasingly ineffective Fukuda Government announced that the ASDF reconstruction mission to Iraq would be withdrawn by the end of the year when the UN Security Council resolution authorizing the presence of the multinational forces expired and six months before the expiry of the law that had enabled the dispatch. The withdrawal of the ASDF would bring to an end Japan's SDF participation in Iraq. Later in that month Fukuda's successor, Taro Aso, stated to the UN General Assembly that his Government would continue to contribute to the 'war on terror' in Afghanistan by extending legislation permitting the refuelling of ships in the Indian Ocean. Aso told assembled reporters that the provision of such logistical support did not violate the terms of the Japanese Constitution, but that the Constitution should be interpreted to allow collective defence. Japan's participation in the 'war on terror' was further emphasized in October by the signing with India of a joint security declaration, similar to those that Japan had concluded with the USA and Australia, and by its pledge in April 2009 of US $1,000m. in aid to Pakistan. This was just a part of Japan's ODA allocated in 2009 to fighting terrorism, as became evident when the Government, for the first time, revealed its aid objectives. Other spending in this category included Palestinian aid, Iraqi restructuring funds and loans to the oil-producing Gulf states.

In December 2008, as the threat to Japanese ships of piracy off the coast of Somalia had became increasingly troubling, the Government struggled to respond within the limits of the Japanese Constitution. Despite a UN Security Council resolution in favour of force and the dispatch of troops from countries including China, it was not until March 2009 that the Japanese Cabinet took the decision to dispatch the SDF, under the SDF Law, to operate off Somalia and in the Gulf of Aden. Two naval destroyers were charged with the task of protecting both Japanese and foreign vessels until such time as anti-piracy legislation could be enacted. The operations included officers of both the Japan Coast Guard and the MSDF. Legislation rendering acts of piracy illegal under Japanese law was finally enacted in mid-June. Unlike previous legislation, the Anti-Piracy Law, which was not opposed or dismissed as a form of collective defence by the DPJ, was not bound by time limits. The prospect of further legislative changes was mooted in August when a report prepared for the Government suggested a revision of Japan's ban on the export of weapons, together with the implementation of permanent legislation governing the overseas deployment of the SDF, as a means of 'contributing to international efforts to counter terrorism'.

North Korea (which had been removed from the US list of state sponsors of terrorism in October 2008) continued to develop its nuclear programme in 2009, with rocket launches over Japan in April and an underground nuclear test in May, which provoked angry responses from the Japanese Government and population and support for the extension of sanctions and UN Security Council resolutions of condemnation. Prior to the missile launch, the Japanese Government had made extensive provisions to monitor the flight and to keep residents informed; in addition, missile interceptors were deployed and *Aegis* destroyers equipped with BMD had been dispatched to the Sea of Japan. North Korea's response to the first UN resolution imposing sanctions was to demand an apology and to threaten to boycott any resumption of the six-party talks that had stalled in December 2008 (see above) and restart its programme of reprocessing, testing and launches. Its response to the second resolution was to threaten to recommence uranium enrichment and the 'weaponization' of all newly extracted plutonium. The activities of North Korea prompted discussions within Japan concerning the need for a debate about strike-first capability and even a nuclear option. It subsequently emerged, in July, that since 1960 a secret agreement had existed between Japan and the USA whereby the deployment of nuclear weapons in Japanese territory under certain conditions was permitted. The Japanese Minister for Foreign Affairs, Hirofumi Nakasone, followed US President Obama's global nuclear disarmament initiative, announced in April 2009, with his own 11-point plan that stressed the need for transparency, the regulation of ballistic missiles and a freeze on nuclear development, urging the North Korean Government to abide by the denuclearization demands of the six-party talks and UN Security Council resolutions. The Chinese Government took issue with Prime Minister Aso's suggestions that its own nuclear programme lacked transparency and that China and North Korea were negative influences on regional security. In June Yukio Hatoyama, who had replaced Ozawa as President of the DPJ (and subsequently became Prime Minister), made his first official overseas trip to discuss with South Korean President Lee Myung-Bak the need to persuade China to support a strong UN resolution (including financial sanctions) against North Korea's nuclear tests. Opposition from China resulted in the final resolution failing to include a ban on dealings with North Korean banks, the mandatory inspection of North Korean ships or the issue of the abductees still pursued by Japan. The North Korean Government persisted in its refusal to restart six-party talks, but did not dismiss the idea of 'a specific and reserved form of dialogue' (bilateral talks with the USA). In early August an unexpected visit to North Korea by former US President Bill Clinton was dismissed by the USA as a 'solely private mission' to secure the release of two detained US journalists.

In May 2009 legislation was revised to open up the policy-making structure of the Ministry of Defence to non-government personnel, in an effort to address scandals that had undermined the Ministry and the SDF in previous months. The bill gained the support of the DPJ in the upper house and (unlike the Anti-Piracy Law, which was enacted only after a second vote in the lower house) passed into law without difficulty. In July the Ministry of Defence published a 'white paper' entitled 'Defence of Japan 2009', which identified the expansion of Chinese military capabilities and scope and North Korea's ongoing development of its nuclear programme, against a background of domestic instability, as being of particular concern. As the August general election approached, the DPJ seemed to soften its rhetoric on a number of foreign policy and security-related issues and to stress its commitment to closer relations with the USA. Although Hatoyama confirmed his intention to terminate MSDF involvement in refuelling operations in the Indian Ocean, he stressed that this would take time and would require the adoption of other measures in order to maintain stability.

A new National Defense Program Guidelines report was originally planned for late 2009. However, the DPJ-led coalition Government that assumed office in September announced its decision to postpone the compilation of the report until late 2010. The agreement between the DPJ and junior coalition partners pledged to 'propose the revision of the Japan-US Status of Forces Agreement and move in the direction of re-examining the realignment of the US military forces in Japan and the role of US military bases in Japan so as to reduce the burden on Okinawa Prefecture residents'. While this seemed to suggest that the administration of incoming Prime Minister Hatoyama was reconsidering the 2006 agreement with the US Administration whereby the Futenma heliport functions were to be transferred to nearby Nago (i.e. within the Okinawa Prefecture), the issue was not among those discussed at a bilateral meeting between Japan and the USA at the sidelines of the UN General Assembly in mid-September 2009. Another potentially disruptive issue, that of Hatoyama's intention to terminate MSDF involvement in the refuelling of US warships in the Indian Ocean, was also absent from the talks. A visit to Japan by President Obama in November similarly failed to result in any progress being made on either issue.

The Futenma debate was the single largest source of contention between the USA and Japan in early 2010, and the resultant loss of trust between the two Governments became a cause for particular concern in May, when, following the international condemnation of the sinking in March of a South Korean naval vessel, reportedly by a North Korean torpedo, the situation on the Korean peninsula became extremely precarious. International criticism of the incident ranged from 'unforgiveable' (Japan) and 'an act of aggression' (USA) to 'unfortunate' (China), and efforts to resume the six-party talks stalled. Crucially, the failure of Japan and the USA to reach consensus on the issue of Futemna was undermining the countries' ability effectively to co-operate in addressing the crisis on the Korean peninsula, and, succumbing to mounting pressure, Hatoyama agreed at the end of May to abide by the long-standing agreement to relocate the base to Nago. This was one of the main factors in Hatoyama's decision in early June to resign from the premiership, and led to a manifesto promise by the DPJ under its new leader, Naoto Kan, to deepen the alliance with the USA. Nevertheless, following its loss of a coalition majority in the upper house elections held in July, the Kan administration reopened the Futenma debate. US congressional reductions in the budgetary allocation for the relocation of marines from Okinawa to Guam, together with US requests that Japan assume responsibility for a greater proportion of the costs, resulted in the issue continuing to be keenly debated in the following months.

During 2010, the year of the 50th anniversary of the US-Japanese Treaty of Mutual Co-operation and Security, discussions on nuclear deterrence between Japan and the USA commenced. The anniversary brought more intense scrutiny of the bilateral alliance, including an investigation by the Japanese Ministry of Foreign Affairs into the long-denied secret bilateral pact that had allowed the USA to bring ships carrying nuclear weapons into Japanese ports without prior consultation—an agreement that violated Japan's non-nuclear principles. A further secret pact had authorized the USA to use its military bases in Japan without prior consultation in the event of a emergency on the Korean peninsula. In the USA, plans were drafted for a review in 2010 of the East Asia Strategy Report that would focus on the alliance with Japan, together with the issues of Chinese military expansion and North Korea's nuclear programme. The US Administration sought to persuade Japan of the need for greater co-operation to meet what it regarded as a growing threat from China's military build-up. While Hatoyama remained unconvinced of the need for concern, the Japanese Ministry of Defence made its 2010 report on China's security strategy its first priority. In view of North Korea's nuclear tests and missile launches during 2009, Japan welcomed the decision by South Korea and the USA in July 2010 to postpone for three years the implementation of planned changes to the military command structure in East Asia whereby wartime operational control would have been transferred from Washington to Seoul by 2012. In late July 2010 the Japanese Government announced the postponement until September of its annual defence report, which was originally to have been released in early August. The decision to delay the release of the publication, which was reported to contain a controversial reference to two South Korean-controlled islets and a number of reefs as being an integral part of Japanese territory, was widely interpreted as an attempt to avoid a bilateral dispute prior to the 100th anniversary, on 29 August, of Japan's annexation of the Korean peninsula.

Towards the end of 2010 there were two major national security concerns for the Kan administration, Japan's regional allies and the USA: the growing assertiveness of China in the South China Sea and the threat that this posed to trade routes; and developments on the Korean Peninsula, most notably the bombardment by North Korea of the South Korean island of Yeonpyeong in November. Bilateral US-Japanese meetings in July had explored responses to likely events in the peninsula in view of China's military build-up, and developments in Japan's defence strategies in the following months reflected these concerns. In December Japan and the USA conducted large-scale military exercises, which included SDF *Aegis* destroyers, capable of countering guided missiles, deployed off eastern Okinawa in a display of strength against North Korea, and practice drills for defending and recapturing small islands such as those disputed with China. Japan's new National Defense Program guidelines, published in December, recognized the need to respond to the two-fold threat by moving away from the old strategic concept of a basic defence force, with uniform deployment of SDF units across the country, and towards a flexible, mobile, 'dynamic defence capability' with improved intelligence-gathering facilities which would enable a shift of focus from the north of the country to the south-western islands. Planned changes to military equipment and deployment included an increase in the number of *Aegis* destroyers from four to six, all equipped to counter North Korean ballistic missiles, with further support from PAC-3 anti-ballistic missiles around the country; an increase in the number of submarines from 16 to 22 to counteract the expansion of China's ocean-going fleet, and the transfer of GSDF personnel to engage in monitoring activities on the westernmost shores of Japan. While reductions in other areas meant that Japan's defence spending would not increase, China's military budget for 2011 was set to rise by almost 13% compared with the previous year. Continued public controversy meant that the new guidelines reiterated the commitment to an exclusively defence-orientated policy and the three non-nuclear principles. The guidelines also recognized the primacy of the US-Japanese alliance, in particular in the area of 'cyberspace', and the need to deepen and expand co-operation.

For the first time Japan's annual defence 'white paper', published in August 2011, devoted an entire section to China's activities in the South China Sea and the threat that these were perceived as posing to the 'peace and stability of the region and international society'. The document identified China as a particular target for observation in connection with 'cyberspace' attacks. It also warned of developments in North Korea's nuclear plans and delivery systems, and of that country's increased recourse to military provocation. The paper stressed the DPJ's view of the USA as an ally against the threats posed by China and North Korea, and noted that more than 80% of Japanese politicians across the ideological spectrum were of the same opinion. A decision reached jointly with the US Government in June, to extend the 2014 deadline for the repositioning of the US Futenma base within Okinawa, defused for the time being a controversy that had threatened the alliance for several years and which had increased in importance along with China's growing military power.

Economy

MICHAEL SMITKA

INTRODUCTION

Japan appeared to be recovering from the recent global economic downturn when on 11 March 2011 a major earthquake occurred off the north-east coast of the main island of Honshu, principally affecting the Tohoku region. Despite its horrendous scale (magnitude 9.0), the earthquake itself caused surprisingly little damage. As a testament to strict construction standards, there were no scenes of collapsed buildings in Sendai (population 1.0m.), the only metropolitan area near the epicentre. The tsunami that followed was a different matter, washing away portions of several cities and accounting for most of the dead and missing in the disaster, who numbered well over 20,000. The reverberations of the earthquake will be felt for years to come, literally in the form of aftershocks (550 exceeding magnitude 5.0 during March–July alone) and figuratively in a ravaged regional economy.

Many local businesses will never reopen; some coastal tourist sites have simply vanished. Rice-fields along the coast are now laden with salt and silt. The docks and warehouses of regional fishing harbours have disappeared (although the ships themselves survived). All of this was along a swathe of coast that would in the USA extend from Cape Hatteras in North Carolina to Cape Cod in Massachusetts, or in Europe be the entire Atlantic coast of Iberia. However, Japan has a modern, robust economy. Output is primarily of services; thus, although schools started late and in temporary quarters, they did not cease to function. The same was true for retailing and hospitals; roads were likewise quickly reopened, even if sometimes requiring detours. Japan's economy is also large. While the cost of the damage perhaps totalled 25,000,000m. yen (US $324,000m.), with 120,000 homes and other buildings having been completely destroyed, this represented only 2% of Japan's stock of fixed assets. Those who died were but 0.015% of the population; it was a human tragedy but not an economic disaster.

Furthermore, developed economies are highly competitive: most markets have multiple suppliers and customers, and so the loss of a few firms is at most a temporary disruption. The vehicle manufacturer Toyota, for example, relied upon output from 659 different factories and repair shops in the Tohoku region, and itself had factories making engines and assembling Lexus vehicles. Toyota could often turn to the rivals of its Tohoku suppliers. In addition, the company could make use of resources from the rest of the country, dispatching 50,000 different individuals at one point or another to help bring plants back into production. By July 2011 the last of the region's semiconductor plants were back in operation, and most other production difficulties had been resolved. Toyota's output revived from 50% of normal in May to 84% of normal in June. Furthermore, consumers could buy the vehicles of other manufacturers: Nissan and Mitsubishi Motors were less affected. The losses incurred by individual firms thus overstate the loss of output for the economy as a whole.

Data to be published in late 2011 were likely to indicate that the economy grew strongly in June–August. However, the effects of the earthquake were expected to remain in evidence: 30% of Japan's electricity supply depends on nuclear power, and the initial response to the radiation leaks from reactors in Fukushima prefecture, damaged by the tsunami, was to shut down all nuclear plants. Ultimately, many may be allowed to resume operations, as most are of a more modern and intrinsically safer design; for example, a plant in Onagawa, Miyagi prefecture, was both closer to the earthquake's epicentre and struck by a higher tsunami, but suffered only minor external damage and had no cooling problems. If not, then Japan is likely to experience disruptions to the electricity supply during the summer months for several years, which would be an ongoing hindrance to the economy. However, immediate reconstruction expenditures will boost the economy and should support robust growth throughout 2012 and into early 2013.

Long-term challenges remain. Japan still suffers from the ongoing effects of the bursting of a purely domestic real-estate and stock-market 'bubble' that reached its height in 1991. In particular, Japan has suffered mild deflation since 1994, the first developed economy to experience an extended period of declining prices since the 1930s. Nominal gross domestic product (GDP) stood at 500,000,000m. yen per annum in the fourth quarter of 2010, before the impact of the earthquake, or the same level as in 1990. Japan also has a declining population, because fertility has been below replacement levels since 1967; owing to the cumulative impact of the low birth-rate, the labour force is declining at 1% per annum. With the 'baby boomers' (those born in the years following the conclusion of the Second World War) beginning to retire, 23% of Japan's population are over the age of 65, the highest percentage of any country. With declining inputs, potential aggregate output growth is weak, at about 1.5% per annum in real terms, and Japan has failed to achieve even that. The high retirement rate is increasing state expenditure, while revenues have been impaired by deflation and low growth. After 20 years of large deficits, Japan has gross debt of 216% of GDP, the highest in the developed world. While this is less of a problem than the figures suggest, it adds to the challenges that are described below.

Not all Japan's prospects are negative. The country has benefited from proximity to the People's Republic of China, which has become Japan's largest trading partner for both exports and imports. For consumers, this means that a wide array of goods for daily consumption are now available in '100 yen' stores. Similarly, grocery stores offer a wider array of fruits and vegetables, housing is now on average larger, and car ownership is pervasive. For retirees, a national system provides home health care. This is not only cost-effective, but is welcomed by recipients, who prefer to live at home. Other transformations are less welcome, including the rise of contingent labour (part-time and contract jobs) that typically also provides lower pay. This has enhanced flexibility and facilitated an expansion of the proportion of women in the labour force, but means that many have yet to obtain a 'regular' job and the status that comes with it: they are instead likely to be still living with their parents, unmarried. In short, there are many areas of change, if not full dynamism—but change generates losers as well as winners.

These and other facets of the economy are described below. The first section provides historical background, concluding with an overview of the main trends and other basic information helpful for putting Japan in international perspective. This is followed by sections tracing the structure of output and production (agriculture, manufacturing and services), the structure of final demand (consumption, investment, government services and trade), input markets—labour and finance—and concludes by returning to macroeconomic and other policy issues.

UNITS AND GEOGRAPHY

With a population of just over 128.0m. at the census of October 2010, Japan had a nominal GDP of almost exactly 500,000,000m.yen in the October–December quarter of 2010. For the Government and most companies the fiscal year begins on 1 April, which is also the start of the school year and the first day of work for new employees at large firms; the financial year 2011 thus ended on 31 March 2011. When practical, data are given on a calendar year basis. The bulk of the population lives on the largest island, Honshu; far fewer live on the other three large islands of Hokkaido in the north, Shikoku to the south and Kyushu to the south-west. Most of Japan is temperate, although the winter in Hokkaido lasts into March, while Okinawa, to the extreme south, has a fully tropical climate. The economy is dominated by the Tokyo (or Kanto) region, a metropolitan area of about 30m. people that includes the adjacent cities of Kawasaki, Yokohama and portions of Chiba, Saitama and Gunma Prefectures. The second largest centre is the Kansai region, of about 12m. people, that includes the major cities of Osaka, Kyoto and Kobe. The third is Nagoya, with 4m. inhabitants. About one-half of Japan's population and economic activity is thus concentrated in a 300-mile (500-km) stretch on the eastern side of the main island.

Data are quoted in the domestic currency, the yen. However, Japan has a freely floating exchange rate and the nominal value of the yen was volatile during 2006–11. The real effective exchange rates calculated by the Bank for International Settlements (BIS) are more meaningful, as they are a trade-weighted average of currencies, adjusted for inflation or deflation. Even the BIS estimates show a large 38% variation between June 2006 and June 2011, subdued because prices in Japan declined while mild inflation persisted in the rest of the world, and because the currency of China, a major trading partner, appreciated relative to the dollar (hence the yen rose only modestly against the Chinese yuan). Using market rates is thus misleading for making international comparisons, as the size of Japan's economy was little changed. A more useful comparison is provided by purchasing power parity (PPP) exchange rates, which are less volatile and which also take account of the significant role of housing, health care and other non-traded items. PPP comparisons by the World Bank give Japanese GDP as US $32,600 per person for 2010, below the USA ($46,400) or Australia ($38,900), but comparable with the level of the United Kingdom ($34,600) or Germany ($34,200), and well ahead of the Republic of Korea (South Korea—$28,000) or China ($6,600). In terms of GDP in 2010, using PPP comparisons, Japan ($4,300,000m.) ranked fourth after the USA ($14,600,000m.), the euro area ($11,400,000m.) and China ($10,100,000m.); as an individual country it ranked third, ahead of Germany ($3,100,000m.), the largest single constituent economy of the European Union (EU). For reference, in 2009 the Organisation for Economic Co-operation and Development (OECD) estimated PPP for private consumption at 122 yen per US dollar and for GDP at 111 yen.

HISTORY OF ECONOMIC DEVELOPMENT

Japan before 1945

By 1720 Japan already had a modern economy, with farmers in the more developed region outside Osaka growing cotton as a cash crop and buying food. Urban residents worked for wages in a monetized economy that in some regions used paper currency; rice futures were traded on a formal commodity exchange, while shippers could buy marine insurance. The flexibility that came from this market structure, together with high levels of literacy and familiarity with metal-working and simple machines, helped Japan quickly to adopt new technologies and government structures. Export revenues enabled Japan to build up a modern military force; rather than being colonized, it was able to build its own empire, defeating China in 1895 and Russia in 1905.

As was the case with other non-combatants, Japan's economy boomed during the First World War (1914–18), with farmers' children flocking into cities. In the 1920s, however, there was less robust growth, as during much of the period the Government followed an austerity policy aimed at returning to the gold standard at the pre-war parity, while encouraging rice imports from Taiwan and Korea to provide for the rising urban population. During the 1920s the country was electrified, while urban transport developed—the Kanto earthquake of 1923, which destroyed Tokyo and killed some 140,000 people, if anything led to faster growth.

With unfortunate timing, Japan returned to the gold standard in January 1930, in the process causing the yen to appreciate just as export markets collapsed. After a change in governments in 1931, Japan promptly left the gold standard and allowed its currency to depreciate, while boosting domestic public works and other expenditures. Within a year, the economy was growing strongly; indeed, the Minister of Finance, Takahashi Korekiyo, felt it necessary to begin reining in growth in 1936 to prevent increasing inflation. That effort included a reduction in the budget for the army; a group of young officers objected, and assassinated him. The Government fell, to be replaced by one dominated by the military rather than by elected politicians. By the next year Japan had begun to conduct a war in northern China, expanding the conflict in December 1941 with a concerted push into south-east Asia. Little thought was given to the domestic implications; there was no economic planning to support extended hostilities. Rationing was haphazard and ineffective, and once submarine warfare had obstructed the movement of shipping, shortages of materials caused production to decline. When US occupation forces took charge in late 1945, the population was starving, cities were in ashes, factories had ceased operations, transport had collapsed, and soon the economy was gripped by hyperinflation.

1945–75: Occupation, Recovery and High Growth

The end of the Second World War in August 1945 led to the forced repatriation of more than 2m. soldiers and citizens who had emigrated across Asia during Japan's half-century as a colonial power. They returned to a country lacking in food, housing or jobs. The payment of salary arrears to soldiers and displaced factory workers quickly led to hyperinflation, which peaked at 200% in 1947; inflation remained above 10% until the end of 1949. The initial policy of the Allied occupation—to keep Japan poor—changed, first owing to humanitarian concerns in 1945 and 1946, and then from 1947 because of the growing rivalry of the Cold War (the protracted period of mutual hostility between the USA and the USSR). The result was an inflow of food aid and other necessities. The real priority of the occupation was democratization. Thorough land reform in the countryside and the dissolution of the zaibatsu corporate groups in the cities targeted the presumed power bases of the military. Workers were the other concern; within two years an estimated 60% of the industrial labour force was unionized. In contrast, the government administrative structure was left intact, and most bureaucrats remained in place, while most politicians were removed. By default, civil servants became the centre of power, drafting legislation and administrative guidelines with relative autonomy.

The occupying authority's concern over fiscal imprudence and high inflation led to the imposition of the Dodge Plan (conceived by US banker Joseph Dodge) in April 1949. Deficit financing was prohibited; the Reconstruction Finance Corporation, the loans of which were effectively cash subsidies, was disbanded; and measures were introduced to encourage trade, with the exchange rate fixed at 360 yen per US dollar. Within a year inflation had been brought under control, while US military expenditure in Japan, linked to the outbreak of the Korean War in June 1950, reduced the impact of austerity measures. When the occupation formally ended in April 1952, inflation was at an acceptable level and the economy was growing; by 1955, when the political system stabilized under the coalition of conservative groups that formed the Liberal-Democratic Party (LDP), output had returned to its previous peak of 1940.

During the following 18 years Japan's economy grew at an historically unprecedented rate, with real GDP increasing by an average of 9.3% per annum in 1955–73, and rising more than five-fold overall. In 1955 Japan had a work-force that was highly literate and rich in technical skills, a legacy of government investment in schooling that had resulted in near-universal primary education by 1910. The reconstruction of cities provided demand for workers, as did export markets in textiles and other light manufactures. For almost 15 years firms had been isolated from technical advances in the rest of the world; anyone who could import new machinery found it easy to be more productive and profitable. In the late 1950s and into the 1960s Japan was also the largest borrower from the World Bank, funds from which proved particularly helpful in revitalizing the steel industry. By 1968 Japan had surpassed the German economy in size, and in the 1970s a comfortable middle class emerged, while there were very low levels of unemployment and poverty. In fact, excess growth created difficulties, as inflation averaged more than 5% throughout the 1960s. Growth led to strong demand for imports, and a series of balance of payments crises prompted the Government to seek assistance from the IMF. A 'boom-and-bust' cycle resulted, with the downward phase brought about by the Bank of Japan (BOJ) through interest rate increases and restrictions on credit growth, enabled by the strict regulatory framework left in place after the war. Economic growth rates were volatile, declining for example by 8.2 percentage points from a peak of 13% in the first quarter of 1964 to 5% in the second quarter of 1965, before increasing rapidly to 11% in 1966. Balance of payments problems, inflation, and volatility in growth, of course, are not unusual for a developing country, as Japan still was at that time.

By the early 1970s growth was clearly decelerating. The initial technological 'catch-up' period was over, while educational standards had risen and the 'baby-boomers', with their higher levels of education, had entered the labour force. Similarly, the rural-to-urban transition and accompanying high demand for housing, infrastructure and consumer durables had drawn to a close; the migration from the countryside had been completed. Investment, therefore, also declined. Psychologically, the high-growth era closed with the first oil crisis of 1973–74. The fixed exchange rate system broke down in 1971, and the yen was revalued from 360 yen per US dollar to 300 yen. Fearing declining exports and a consequent recession, the BOJ maintained a loose monetary policy. However, exports remained buoyant, while Prime Minister Kakuei Tanaka's proposal to 'rebuild the archipelago' boosted expenditure on infrastructure. Inflation had already reached double-digit levels by May 1973, before the Organization of the Petroleum Exporting Countries (OPEC) quadrupled petroleum prices; inflation increased to 25%, and remained above 20% throughout 1974. Austerity measures led to four quarters of outright recession in 1974, the first period of negative growth since 1949. Since 1973 growth has never been above 5% on a sustained basis; however, inflation has also been held in check, with fiscal and monetary stringency restraining price increases in the late 1970s, in sharp contrast to the experience of the USA.

The 1980s–2000s: The 'Bubble' and its Aftermath

As a result of the shift in fundamentals (slower expansion of the labour force and lower investment) and despite expectations, growth subsequently never approached the levels of the 1960s. Nevertheless, real growth averaged 4.1% during 1975–93, the highest among the OECD member countries, while inflation was the lowest. Japan was the success story of the global economy. While its experience of repeated balance of payments crises influenced perceptions, Japan's level of exports first reached 6% of GDP only in 1970, and surpassed 10% only in 1981. Growth was not export-led. However, from the perspective of the rest of the world the shift in exports was large, occurring as it did against the rising denominator of GDP. Furthermore, it was highly visible, heightened by the success of specific industries—in the 1980s, passenger cars, consumer electronics, machine tools and semiconductors. According to some observers, Japan was poised to overtake the USA as the leading industrial power. Tokyo, at least, was booming.

In fact, with hindsight part of this growth was due to the development of a major 'bubble' during the late 1980s, when stock and real estate prices increased four-fold. The stock market reached its highest point on 31 December 1989; real estate prices continued rising throughout 1991. The collapse was dramatic and instigated a long period of stagnation, with three recessions and minimal growth during the subsequent decade. Unlike the more recent real estate 'bubble' in the USA and parts of Europe, in this case the corporate sector had played the principal part, and bore the brunt of the direct losses. Businesses reduced investment sharply, in an attempt to repay debt; a dozen 'on-again, off-again' government stimulus programmes that boosted the size of the construction sector were too timid to offset this. Monetary policy also proved impotent. While ultimately the BOJ reduced interest rates to 0% and bank lending rates declined to under 2%, deflation meant that it was still costly to borrow. Real growth averaged only 0.8% during the decade between the third quarter of 1992 and the third quarter of 2002.

From the third quarter of 2002 the economy began to grow on a sustained basis, and there followed 23 consecutive quarters of growth, until the first quarter of 2008. Unemployment declined to 3.6% by July 2007, from an historic peak of 5.6% in 2003, despite a rise in labour market participation. However, despite more than six years of continuous economic growth, the composition of jobs was shifting towards contract and part-time work. Other after-effects of the 'bubble' remain. Despite a pause in 2006–08 in the three major metropolitan areas, real estate prices continued to decline. In 2010 residential land in major cities was worth 35% of its 1991 peak price, while commercial real estate was worth a mere 15% of its peak. The Nikkei 225 stock market index, standing at 9,000 on 10 August 2011, was at one-quarter of its 1989 peak of 38,916. Asset prices did not simply decline but have failed to recover, despite the passage of more than 20 years. In addition, consumer prices began decreasing in 1994 and, except for modest increases during 1997–98 and 2008, the economy has continued to experience mild deflation. In 2011 prices in major cities were above the level of 1990, but below their 2000 peak; the prices of corporate services and corporate goods have moved similarly. This is the first such extended period of deflation in a major economy since the Great Depression of the 1930s. Unlike during the 1930s, it has shown no tendency to accelerate, but it has complicated policy-making.

Not all of this diminution of growth was due to the 'bubble'. Fertility has been below replacement levels since the 1970s, as a result of which the working-age population began declining in 1996 and was expected to decline at a rate of 0.6%–0.8% annually over the decade from 2010. In 2005 official population data showed a slight overall decline, making Japan the first society to witness a population decrease as a result of fewer births, rather than a rise in mortality. The large generation of 'baby boomers' were due to start retiring in large numbers from 2012 (when those born in 1947 reach the age of 65). These demographic shifts will inevitably depress growth to a sustainable level of only 1.0%–1.5%; the question of how a declining labour force can provide for the needs of a rapidly expanding population of elderly people remains the central long-term policy issue in Japan.

Low growth was nevertheless accompanied by significant change, with a decline in the size of the construction and manufacturing sectors, restructuring in the retail and financial sectors, and wide-ranging, if modest, reforms of the tax system, of the government administrative structure and public corporations, including plans gradually to privatize the postal savings and life insurance systems, and of higher education. The retirement of the 'baby boomers' will drive further changes, as there will be a shortage of skilled health care workers and pressures to encourage immigration to fill the gap. Meanwhile, the slow growth during the 1990s led to greater inequality and the existence of a cohort of youth who had yet to hold a full-time job. Further change depends on political developments. The victory of the Democratic Party of Japan (DPJ) in the legislative elections at the end of August 2009 (see Recent History) brought to an end the long-standing rule of the LDP, but political instability continued. Yukio Hatoyama, the DPJ's initial Prime Minister, remained in office for less than nine months and his successor, Naoto Kan, following electoral losses in July 2010, promised to resign once reconstruction measures for the region devastated by the March 2011 earthquake were in place; he did so in August. Meanwhile, the country has large budget deficits, and an already high level of debt, while pension and health care expenditures will automatically rise as the 'baby boomers' retire. While leaders of both the DPJ and the LDP acknowledge that tax increases will be necessary to guarantee fiscal stability, neither party wanted to adopt such changes in the period preceding an election. It is unclear how that dilemma will be resolved.

STRUCTURE OF OUTPUT AND EMPLOYMENT

Agriculture

In 1945, at the end of the Second World War, more than one-half of Japan's population lived on farms, but subsequent outward migration meant that the population was overwhelmingly urban by the 21st century, with almost one-quarter of all Japanese living in the Greater Tokyo area. Together with forestry and fisheries, output in 2009 was 1.4% of GDP, while in 2010 only 360,000 households considered themselves to be primarily farmers; for another 1.27m. households, farming was a sideline activity—the threshold to be classified as a 'commercial farmer' is a mere 0.3 ha under cultivation or 500,000 yen in annual sales. Reflecting this sideline status, there were 25% more women than men among the 2.5m. individuals still working in agriculture and forestry; indeed, women over the age of 60 years outnumber all farm workers aged 15–59. The sector was highly inefficient and, quite literally, dying out; as of 2005, the primary farmer on 60% of farms was over the age of 65. This was reflected in the composition of the Japanese diet: from being self-sufficient in the 1950s, Japan now depended upon imports for 40% of calorific intake, including one-half of its meat, fish and fruit consumption, three-quarters of its grain and almost all soybeans. Silk and cotton, the two most important commercial non-grain crops in the 19th century, were no longer produced domestically.

Land reform, implemented in 1947–49, during the US occupation, succeeded in eliminating landlords. The process gave strong rights to the actual tiller. However, with landholdings highly fragmented, it remains difficult to consolidate land into contiguous fields, either directly via purchase or indirectly via renting or sharecropping. Farms thus remain extremely small; excluding Hokkaido, 85% are less than 2.0 ha in area. Similarly, the land/labour ratio is slanted: in 2008 there were 35 farmers in Japan per 100 ha under cultivation, compared with 17 in Brazil and 1.6 in the USA, but this will surely change as the current generation of farmers dies out. In 2010 some 34% of farm households rented land to add to their own, a significant increase from the previous decade, with the average amount rented rising from 0.57 ha in 1990 to 1.35 ha in 2010. In the interim, however, the amount of farmland left fallow rose from 217,000 ha to 396,000 ha.

Political factors impeded change. As in other representative political systems, the combination of geographic concentration and common interests gave farmers disproportionate power at the polls. Given the small farm size and consequent limits on output per head, disproportionately large price supports were required to maintain farm incomes; rice prices in Japan were seven times world levels (more for high-end varieties). Agriculture remained extremely capital-intensive and focused unduly on irrigated rice, at the expense of vegetables and other dry-field crops. To reduce subsidies, the Government encouraged farmers to withdraw land from cultivation, with some success: by 2010 the area devoted to rice had declined by 22% since 1990, total cultivated land was reduced by 12%, and the rice harvest had contracted by 20%, while the total value of agricultural output had decreased by 44%. The cost of price supports remains high, at over 3% of the national budget and close to 10% of public works, in addition to the implicit subsidy received through very high consumer prices. Of course, similar pressures exist in other advanced economies; at one point in the early 2000s total agricultural subsidies exceeded total farm income in the USA, while the cost of the Common Agricultural Policy dominates the budget of the EU.

Membership of the World Trade Organization (WTO) forced Japan to eliminate direct prohibition of rice imports, but allowed tariffs to be set at very high levels, achieving the same purpose. Agricultural issues were probably the single greatest barrier to moving ahead with the WTO's 'Doha Round' of trade talks, as Japan was steadfast in its devotion to protecting the small number of farmers who remain, farmers whose agriculture-related revenue represented only one-third of their total income. Yet it is useful to bear in mind that, among the major developed economies, Japan was the most dependent upon imported foodstuffs and had totally abandoned the domestic production of many crops, including cotton and soybeans. From that perspective, Japan is an example of how a developed country could shift out of crops in which it had no comparative advantage and over time reduce the agricultural sector despite underlying political barriers. As agriculture's political influence wanes, Japan may be able to play a more constructive role in future trade talks, such as the proposed Trans-Pacific Partnership (TPP).

Manufacturing

By the beginning of the 21st century manufacturing was also a declining sector in Japan, although certain individual industries remained strong. It remained a major portion of the economy, down from 28% of the economy in 1980 but still accounting for 18% of value added in 2009 and a third of the value of listed firms. In addition, because Japan's exports were dominated by manufactured goods, firms in this sector were some of the best-known overseas. According to the 2009 Census of Manufactures, total employment at firms with four or more workers contracted from 11.8m. in 1990 and 9.2m. in 2000 to 8.2m., decreasing in every year except 2005 and 2006. In 2009 there were 370,000 textile and apparel workers, 22% of the sector's 1970 level of 1.68m. workers, and down by 44% even since 2000. This decline was acompanied by a rapid increase in imports, particularly from China. However, in comparison with agriculture Japan had managed its departure from declining areas of manufacturing relatively well, without resort to either subsidies or more than episodic protectionism.

The Japanese manufacturing sector exhibited several distinctive features. One was the very high share accounted for by small firms, a factor in common with other sectors of the economy, with 69% of all employment in firms with 300 or fewer workers in 2008 and 27% in firms with fewer than 30 employees. A second was the widespread presence of a vertical network of subsidiaries and affiliates linked by shareholdings, sometimes as a deliberate strategy to maintain the tax and regulatory advantages that accrue to small-firm status, but in large part to maintain functional specialization at the company level. A third feature was that, in view of the small size of individual firms, extensive networks of suppliers were needed; many small firms also rely on wholesalers for marketing and distribution. In the automobile industry, for example, in the 1980s assemblers in Japan historically bought 70% or more of the parts they required, compared with the 50% of parts purchased externally by the 'Detroit Three' US vehicle manufacturers, General Motors (GM), Ford and Chrysler. These primary suppliers, in turn, purchased inputs from an array of second-tier suppliers, many of them small firms, in a vertical structure. For example, Toyota itself directly employed 320,590 workers world-wide in March 2010, of whom only 52,000 were at the parent company rather than its 530 domestic and overseas subsidiaries. The inclusion of a few of its largest close affiliates—firms in which it had a substantial shareholding but that stopped short of being subsidiaries—raised this to 679,000, and many additional workers were employed in independent suppliers for which Toyota was the primary customer. In general, in the Japanese automobile industry there were three workers in suppliers for every one worker in a final assembler such as Toyota or Nissan. Other industries, such as machine tools, tend towards a horizontal structure, with firms, for example, making a single type of lathe rather than a broad product range, while buying most of the components that they use. Throughout industry, then, learning to work with outside suppliers was critical in Japan, including joint development and engineering initiatives. The close co-operation that this entailed made it difficult for Japanese firms to turn to new suppliers, and this was reflected in a tendency for suppliers to follow their customers when major Japanese companies established manufacturing operations abroad. For example, Toyota's suppliers in Japan were also its suppliers in the USA. The same tendency to replicate supplier networks was visible in the direct foreign investment patterns of Japanese electronics manufacturers in Asia.

Another claim made by observers of Japan's manufacturing sector relates to an important role for horizontal groups of firms, commonly referred to as keiretsu (more accurately, corporate groups), such as the many Mitsubishi, Sumitomo and Mitsui firms, linked to a bank and a trading company. The relevance of such claims was difficult to gauge; the presumption of the researchers who compiled such lists in the early 1960s was that every major firm belonged to one or another such group. As a result, using such lists guaranteed that keiretsu would be found to be of importance, whatever the underlying reality. The compilation process resulted in occasional absurdities, such as companies being included in more than one group, or Toyota, renowned for its independence, being included as a Mitsui firm. Cross-shareholdings are widespread, but can be dated to anti-takeover measures adopted during the initial period of capital market liberalization in the early 1960s. By the 2000s the merger of several large banks that were presumed to be the core organizers of rival keiretsu, as well as the 'unwinding' of bank shareholdings, called into further question the continued relevance of such labels. The term is thus more misleading than helpful.

The structure of manufacturing shifted significantly during the last decades of the 20th century; detailed data from the 2008 Census of Manufactures (released in April 2009) help to trace this. (The 2008 Census changed methodology, making longitudinal comparisons difficult, but there was little qualitative change in trends.) The short-term impact of the global financial crisis makes 2009 data unrepresentative; automotive employment, for example, was down by 161,000 at the time of the 2009 Census relative to 2008, but had rebounded by 2010. In the initial consumption boom that followed the end of the Second World War, electric fans, rice cookers and vacuum cleaners were highly successful products. For the export sector, textiles, steel and shipbuilding were important, while the single most export-intensive industry was ceramics. By the early 21st century virtually all such light consumer goods were imported, textiles and shipbuilding were minor industries in the economy as a whole, while steel had been in gradual decline until the recent global boom stimulated by the rapid growth of demand from China and other developing countries. This shift away from light manufactures continued; during 2003–07 the largest employment declines were seen in garments, leather, wood products and textiles. Given the world-wide consumption boom that was evident by 2007, other industries that had been shedding jobs owing to the transfer to offshore assembly, such as information technology (IT) goods, began creating new employment. This was most visible in the transport equipment sector, which added 200,000 jobs between 2001 and 2007, but was also apparent in iron and steel, electronic components and general machinery, which also reversed earlier employment losses. The rapid growth in trade provided a respite for shipbuilding, the US market helped the automotive industry, and China's construction and automotive booms supported the Japanese steel industry. In 2005 Tokyo Electric Steel even began building a new plant, the first in Japan in 15 years, and the major steel mills were all busy adding new galvanizing lines in 2006 and 2007.

However, the largest sector of manufacturing was not one of the export-orientated sectors, but instead was food-processing, which employed 1.2m. workers (13% of the total) in 2008, a segment that included a large number of small, inefficient firms that survived because of highly fragmented local markets. The growing importance of national distribution and retailing networks meant that the number of such firms was likely to decline quickly with the ageing of the current generation of owners (see Retailing and Wholesaling, below). The next largest sectors were transport equipment, comprising mainly light motor vehicle assembly and automotive parts production, and metal products, which employed 1.0m. workers (12% of the total) and 0.7m. workers (8%), respectively. Finally, electrical equipment accounted for 520,000 workers (6%). When combined with electronic parts (525,000, or 6%) and IT goods (240,000, or 3%), electronics was the single most important overall area, engaging 1.3m. workers, or 15% of all manufacturing employees. This was hardly surprising, given that by 2009 more than 99% of Japanese households owned colour television sets (62% of which were flat-screen televisions), 98% had a microwave oven, 61% had DVD (digital versatile disc) players, 81% digital cameras, 76% computers, 87% washing machines, 88% room air-conditioners and 63% heated toilet seats, and some 93% of the Japanese population possessed a mobile (cellular) telephone. So while sales of new products such as flat-screen televisions, DVD recorders and digital cameras remained strong, overall Japan was a mature market for consumer goods. Slow growth had intensified competition, both domestically and from external trade. Furthermore, light industry had almost disappeared; the leading sectors of the 1960s—textiles and garments—had contracted by one-half in the 1990s and lost 182,000 (approximately one-third of remaining workers) during 2001–08.

Individual sectors and firms performed very well both domestically and internationally. During the late 1990s and early 2000s the automobile sector was restructured. From a peak production level of 13.5m. units in 1992 (and a capacity to produce 15m. units), domestic output plummeted to under 10m. units. However, output rose to 10.8m. vehicles in 2005 and to 11.6m. units in 2006–08. This was despite poor domestic sales, which, with 83% of households already owning a vehicle and given the ageing of the population, peaked in 2004 at 5.8m. units, declining to 5.3m. units by 2007, before the onset of the global recession. In the 12 months to June 2009 domestic sales reached only 4.5m. units, 39% of peak, although sales recovered to 5.0m. units in 2010 and output to 9.6m. units, 21% more than in 2009. The industry thus relied upon strong export markets to absorb 60% of output, leaving it extremely vulnerable to the recent shifts in overseas demand and in 2011 to the appreciation of the yen; the fact that a large proportion of production was taking place inside Japan probably also magnified the short-term impact of parts shortages following the March 2011 earthquake.

Reflecting more than a decade of output well below its early 1990s peak, the industry was restructured, with the majority of domestic assemblers losing their independence. Toyota acquired Daihatsu (mini-cars) and in October 2005 agreed to purchase from GM a major stake in Fuji Heavy Industries (Subaru). DaimlerChrysler sold its controlling stake in Mitsubishi Motors to a consortium of domestic non-auto firms (and later sold Chrysler), but retained the truck operations of the latter (renamed Fuso). Renault of France controlled Nissan, while Ford controlled Mazda, although it reduced its shareholding in 2009 from 33.4% to 13.4%, and in November 2010 to 3%, while in 2010 Volkswagen purchased a non-controlling 19.9% stake in Suzuki. Honda has been unique in avoiding inter-firm alliances. Consolidation in the truck and bus segment was part of a global shift. As noted above, Daimler, the world's largest truck producer, retained Fuso when it sold its stake in Mitsubishi. Toyota, which already owned the truck producer Hino, bought Isuzu in 2006. The Swedish firm Volvo, the world's second largest truck and bus manufacturer, bought control of Nissan Diesel in 2006. Hino likewise confirmed an agreement in mid-2006 with Scania, the third largest producer (also based in Sweden). These developments helped the Japanese vehicle industry to reduce the 30% excess capacity with which it was burdened following the collapse of the 'bubble' economy.

Nevertheless, the collapse of sales in the USA and other countries led the industry to lose money; in the first half of 2009 Toyota actually lost more than GM, although Toyota's cash reserves meant that there was no danger of bankruptcy. While the industry returned to profitability in mid-2010, domestic production continued to be affected by the strength of the yen. The production of small cars was particularly problematic. Toyota was to start new Corolla assembly operations in the USA in 2010 and was also to launch production of the hybrid Prius in Thailand; Nissan was likewise to produce its sub-compact 'March' model in Thailand. At 11.8m. units in 2007, overseas production had outpaced domestic output for several years; the strong yen would accelerate that. However, sharp variations in output and changing alliances during the global financial crisis meant that Volkswagen assumed the leading global position in 2010, while in 2011 GM recovered the lead as the largest global producer, helped by its success in China, where Toyota and other Japanese firms had a late start. In the first half of 2011 Toyota was in third place.

Various automotive parts firms were similarly prominent; Denso was the second largest global parts producer, following Bosch of Germany but ahead of Magna of Canada. Similarly, a few individual parts firms dominated their sectors; one example was Yazaki Corporation in wire harnesses, which employed about 20,000 workers inside Japan and 160,000 overseas in 2010. However, as with assemblers, there was consolidation among domestic parts firms, with Bosch, for example, purchasing several electrical suppliers. In addition, as production overseas displaced exports—with a modest increase in imports—there was a gradual contraction of production within Japan.

A similar pattern can be observed in many other sectors of manufacturing. While Japanese firms played a major or even dominant role in certain sectors of semiconductor equipment, digital cameras and flat-screen televisions, in the five years to 2005 restructuring took place at individual firms. Sony, for example, made a loss in 2004–09 before returning to profit in June 2010, with a non-Japanese manager (Sir Howard Stringer) having been appointed as chief executive officer in 2005. Japanese firms were now minor protagonists in the personal computer market and in mobile phones; the largest, Toshiba, was ranked fifth, retaining only 4% of the global market, compared with the 50% held by the leading four companies. Likewise, South Korea's Samsung held second position in semiconductor manufacturing, after Intel. Renaissance Technologies (Renesas Technology Corporation), formed by the merger and restructuring of the operations of NEC, Hitachi and Mitsubishi Electric, ranked third; Toshiba ranked fourth. Other leading firms in the electrical and electronics sectors included Matsushita (now renamed Panasonic), Fujitsu and Sharp. Most of these underwent difficult restructurings of their consumer goods operations, particularly in white goods, as a mature domestic market, greater imports and reforms in retailing that lessened their control over distribution all combined to eliminate profits. Illustrative of the problem is Sanyo, once one of the leading firms but which has been effectively liquidated, with its operations either closed or sold to rivals. These include Panasonic, which will eliminate 'Sanyo' as a brand name on televisions and other consumer products, and for its washing machines and similar 'white goods' the Chinese firm Haier. Problems have extended to high-technology segments; Sanyo sold its semiconductor business in 2007, and Elpida—formed by the merger of the dynamic random access memory (DRAM) chip operations of Hitachi, NEC and Mitsubishi—arranged for a capital infusion from the government-owned Development Bank of Japan in mid-2009. Similar examples abound in hard disk manufacturing and other areas. At the same time, these firms' technological resources mean that while they may not dominate broad segments, individual companies may be global leaders in more specialized product lines. Sharp, for example, became the global leader in small-sized liquid crystal displays, while Renesas took 40% of the automotive microcontroller market.

Overall, the restructuring among 'basic' industries was impressive. The aluminium refining industry all but disappeared, with production at just 1% of its peak. Mergers between former rivals reshaped steel, cement, petrochemicals. Another example is the paper industry, which had many small firms. In August 2006 a hostile takeover bid by Oji Paper for Hokuetsu Paper failed, in part because Hokuetsu strengthened production sharing with a different Japanese firm and a South Korean firm. While Hokuetsu's management kept their jobs, the end result was a shifting set of alliances and further consolidation of the industry. More dramatic was the halting takeover of Pentax by Hoya, finally implemented in the latter part of 2007. After the Pentax board of directors dismissed a new president, who had favoured the deal, they were unable to formulate a convincing restructuring plan and were overruled by shareholders; the takeover went through under terms less favourable to Pentax than the original offer, and all of Pentax's directors lost their jobs. 'Spin-offs', mergers and acquisitions were not limited to manufacturing, although it was difficult to keep track of change with about 2,700 deals each year during 2005–07 (of which about 2,100 were purely domestic), a further 2,400 deals in 2008 (of which 1,800 were purely domestic), 1,900 transactions in 2009, and 1,707 in 2010. This shift was indicative of increased flexibility in the economy, belying the rigid keiretsu paradigm that was present in many descriptions of Japan's corporate world.

For all the strengths of the country's manufacturing industry, in some important global sectors Japanese firms were virtually absent. The structure of the domestic health care system and the ability of firms to rely upon licensing a small number of foreign drugs left the pharmaceuticals industry highly fragmented. While recent mergers may change the situation, the only Japanese pharmaceutical company with a noteworthy reputation outside Japan was Takeda, but it remained well behind the leading 10 global firms in terms of size. Outside the area of computer games—a visible and profitable exception—no Japanese firm was a major force in computer software. (In 2004, for example, Japan imported software to the value of 364,583m. yen, but exported items worth only 14,466m. yen.) This contributed to the weakness of Japanese firms in a number of other sectors. Similarly, in shoes, clothing, fashion items (particularly the luxury goods segment), beverages and a number of other globally important industries, Japanese firms were not major forces; indeed, in many of these segments, such as Coca-Cola for soft drinks, foreign brands dominated the domestic market. The lack of petroleum resources likewise meant that there was only a weak Japanese presence in petrochemicals and related industries. Most Japanese manufacturers remained small and domestic in their focus. Sectors such as food-processing were manifestly inefficient, and on-going restructuring appeared likely. At the same time the need for additional workers to provide for retirees can be met only if manufacturing continues to contract. Over the medium term 'hollowing out', as imports replace domestic manufacturing, has been and will continue to be necessary for the economy, however difficult the process might be for those linked to declining sectors. Despite political discourse that views its revival as crucial to Japan's economic recovery, in fact the manufacturing sector remains too big.

For the segments that remain, research and development (R & D) will be increasingly vital. During the aftermath of the 'bubble' R & D levels decreased. By 2003, however, such expenditure had rebounded by one-third from the 1994 low point, to reach 2% of GDP, while about 1.2% of workers were in R & D. That percentage was similar to that of the USA, although variations in classifying which expenditure constituted R & D rendered precise cross-national comparisons impossible. However, almost all Japanese R & D was conducted in the corporate sector; therefore, in relation to that in the USA and other economies with large shares of R & D accounted for by government and university laboratories, it probably made a greater contribution to increasing productivity. At the same time it was concentrated in export-related sectors, such as automobiles and electronics. In many other sectors, it seemed likely that productivity would improve more through the departure of the least efficient firms, rather than through gains made by all companies. The strength of the manufacturing sector was thus linked to reforms that would make the overall economy more flexible and to the improvement of the education system, particularly higher education, for the better training of the workers of the future.

Services

Overview

As in all other high-income countries, the services sector was the largest component of the Japanese economy in the early 21st century, whether measured as a share of GDP (76% in 2009, including construction) or of employment (79%), belying the 'industrialized country' image which implied that manufacturing was the engine of growth. Major components, as measured by employment, included retail and wholesale, miscellaneous services, health care, transport, restaurants and lodging, education and government bureaucracy. It was also an area in which much change was occurring. There are four long-standing factors in this evolution. The first was the transition of Japan from extreme privation in 1946 to middle-income status by the mid-1960s, then to European levels of income by the 1970s. Accompanying this was a marketization of services formerly provided within the household—typified by the growth of restaurants and pre-packaged and processed foods—and greater concern with dentistry, hair styling and so on. Demand for education, transport, financial and government services was part of this. The second factor was the urbanization of the population, with about one-half of Japan's population living in the three largest urban agglomerations, and with it the increased number of nuclear families physically remote from close relatives. Production by households for their own consumption decreased. The third was the demographic transition and the rapid ageing of the population, which in turn was leading to a growth in the demand for health care. This includes kaigo (home health) nursing services for the elderly, as a substitute for care homes or care by relatives; after all, the children of today's 90-year-olds were themselves approaching the age of 70 and, even if living locally, were often themselves in need of care. Fourth, and varying across sectors, technical change expanded the range of services available, while lowering their cost.

Access to telecommunications was no longer reserved only for better-off households; mobile phones were omnipresent, while broadband internet access was widespread and, by international comparisons, inexpensive. The same was true, of course, for the whole spectrum of entertainment services. Among other changes, the growth of automobile culture was important; in 2010 there were 112 cars registered per 100 households, ranging from 54 cars per 100 households in Tokyo to 150 or more in rural prefectures. With most of the population living outside city centres, cars were central to shopping and, in rural areas, for commuting to work. All of these combined factors produced a revolution in the type of services consumed and the manner in which they were provided. Select examples are provided below.

Retailing and Wholesaling

Until the 1980s the streets leading away from train stations were lined with small retail and service operations, formally supported at the local level through shoten-gai (shopping district) associations. In general, refrigerators were small and storage space sparse; housewives would shop on a daily basis and commuters would pick up items as they proceeded home on foot or by bicycle. The high population densities facilitated the proliferation of numerous small, specialized stores, typically operated on a family basis, with a residence over the ground-floor retail space. Such shopping districts are rapidly declining, and have totally disappeared in many rural areas, replaced by modern shopping malls and large stores located along major roads that, compared with the small, family stores they replaced, offer a far greater selection of goods and longer hours of service combined with lower prices.

The Establishment Survey, carried out once every three years, provides an insight into the magnitude of changes; it will henceforth be replaced by the Economic Census, the first of which was undertaken in 2009, but only preliminary results were available at mid-2011. (Note that an 'establishment' is defined as a discrete place of business; a firm can, and often does, operate multiple establishments.) The June 2007 survey found 1.47m. retail and wholesale establishments, employing a total of 11.1m. workers; the 2009 Census found 1.56m. establishments and 12.7m. workers, although because of the change in methodology it is unclear how comparable these data are. The discussion below thus uses only the older survey. The 2007 survey found that, compared with 2004, the number of wholesale and retail establishments had contracted by 20% and employment by 3%. Most of this change occurred among very small (one- to four-person) establishments, which contracted by 11% (and 24% compared with 1999). The only growth in the wholesale and retail sector was of the largest establishments (300-plus employees), where total numbers increased by 4% (but employment by only 1%).

Two retail groups, Aeon (5,100,000m. yen in sales in the 12 months to February 2011) and Seven & I (at 5,120,000m. yen), were by far the largest in Japan. Exact comparisons are difficult because each maintains a web of shareholdings that may give control without requiring consolidation. For example, Aeon has a 19.8% stake in Daiei, with 912,000m. yen in sales, which it does not consolidate. Daiei is a good example of other trends. During the 'bubble' Daiei had been by far the largest retailer, but it overexpanded during the 'bubble' and succumbed to excess debt. It had been taken over temporarily by the Industrial Revitalization Corporation of Japan, a special government entity created to handle large bankruptcies. The initial restructuring was completed in August 2006, with shares transferred to Marubeni Trading and other private investors. In a bidding contest, the Aeon group defeated the USA's Wal-Mart to take over Daiei in March 2007: Aeon was now the largest shareholder, with a 19.85% stake, and the trading company Marubeni had an 18.41% stake. Aeon obtained the Daiei-affiliated Maruetsu food supermarket and was to share some of its brands and provide IT services to Daiei. Aeon began as a food supermarket, and that sector remained the core of its operations, but it expanded with the Jusco hypermarket chain, Ministop convenience stores and speciality retail chains in sporting goods, clothing and other areas. Much of its recent expansion in the 2000s came through mergers and acquisitions; it was relatively successful at integrating regional food supermarkets into its operations, and at reviving bankrupt hypermarkets such as Maikaru. Like stores in the USA and the EU, it had moved 'upstream' to develop its own warehouses and to work with manufacturers to build its own private brand merchandise. It remained to be seen whether it could turn around the much larger Daiei in the same manner as the smaller operations that it had acquired.

Seven & I, by contrast, began by developing the Yokado hypermarkets, and in 1973 launched two new ventures with US partners. One was Dennys Japan, which was the first successful family restaurant chain in Japan, emphasizing locations with parking facilities. The other was the 7-Eleven convenience store chain. By the mid-2000s Dennys had 580 stores, while the network of 24-hour, 365-day franchised convenience stores proved immensely successful, subsequently operating 14,000 stores (with 12,753 domestic outlets in February 2010) and becoming Japan's most profitable retail operation while providing the majority of the profits of the parent group. One of the initial strengths of 7-Eleven operations was that most of the franchisees ran local liquor stores, and when reconfigured as convenience stores they could continue to sell alcoholic beverages. (After 2005 almost any food retailer could obtain a licence to sell alcoholic beverages, removing that advantage.) Another innovation was the introduction of sophisticated point-of-sales data analysis linked to their own distribution centres; this helped 7-Eleven to restock stores more than three times per day, including different take-away foods for the breakfast, lunch, dinner and late-night time slots. This was vital to profits: such sophisticated management tools, together with the operating efficiencies of the franchise system, helped 7-Eleven limit 'dead' inventory and increase sales several-fold. Seven & I also developed a variety of speciality retailers and, as with the Aeon group, expanded in part by acquiring a number of troubled firms such as the Seibu department store chain and the bankrupt Sogo department store chain. Ironically, a firm that helped to undermine traditional department stores became a major owner of them.

Similar changes were taking place in other retail segments. Appliances and electronic goods were previously sold through small neighbourhood shops, going back to the distribution networks established in the 1930s–50s by Matsushita and other early makers of such items to sell lighting, electric fans and other goods for which no retail outlets then existed; there were similar networks of camera shops and small stores selling men's and women's clothing, often tied to a single manufacturer through a layer of wholesalers. During the 1990s, however, large-floor-space discount stores achieved sufficient volume to let them circumvent traditional wholesalers and deal directly with manufacturers; small-scale speciality retailers lost their competitiveness. The new retailers handled all brands, and the market shifted from one controlled by manufacturers to one that was increasingly led by retailers. In electronics, Yamada Denki was by far the most successful, relying exclusively on suburban locations alongside major roads. With 2,020,000m. yen in sales in the year ending February 2010, it was more than double the size of Yodobashi Camera (701,000m. yen in sales), which was far better known among foreign visitors because of its focus on locations next to major train stations. In clothing, Uniqlo stores and other outlets of the Fast Retailing group projected sales of 834,000m. yen in the year to August 2010; Shimamura, which specialized in women's clothing (431,000m. yen in sales to February 2010), and Aoyama, in men's clothing (195,000m. yen in sales to March 2010), were the leaders in their sectors. These clothing firms developed their own fashions and contracted directly with factories in China, gaining control of branding, price and logistics. This corresponded with the shift in power over the value chain from manufacturers and wholesalers noted above for other retail segments.

One final sector was that of discount stores. By far the largest chain was Don Quixote, with 488,000m. yen in parent company sales (June 2010), from 150 suburban stores. It gained initial fame for its distinctive and ever-changing products and for staying open until late at night; in 2007 it also gained control of the bankrupt chain of small department stores, Nagasakiya. A second variety of discount stores was the innovative '100 yen shops', which, as their name implies, sold goods that with few exceptions cost exactly 100 yen (or 105 yen with sales tax). Clean and well-lit, with long hours and a remarkable variety of goods, their retail concept was easy to grasp. This concept also had a dominant firm, Daiso Sangyo, with 2,570 domestic and 550 overseas stores and 341,000m. yen in sales in the year to March 2010, selling a product line of 90,000 items, many made to its own designs. It stimulated entry by many rivals, including a chain of Yen 99 Stores (subsequently merged into Lawsons as Lawsons Store 100), which focused on food items, including vegetables and fruits in small units, ideal portions for young singles and elderly people living alone. Both Daiso and Don Quixote were expanding outside Japan, as were other innovative retailers, including the convenience store chains (Lawsons, 7-Eleven, Ministop), and Uniqlo and Muji in clothes.

By contrast, department stores reached their zenith in 1990 when their sales totalled 12,085,000m. yen, or 8.3% of retail sales in that year. With the brief exception of 1997–98, their revenue has declined in every subsequent year, as shoppers have shifted their purchases from city-centre stores, adjacent to major train stations, to suburban shopping malls and specialized discounters reached by car. In 2009 sales declined to 7,172,000m. yen or 59% of their peak. Several chains that took on debt to expand during the 'bubble' went bankrupt. Remaining chains are busy consolidating. As noted above, Seven & I absorbed the failed Sogo and Seibu chains with effect from August 2009. Mitsukoshi (the origins of which go back to the 17th century) and Isetan, both based in Tokyo, merged with several regional chains in April 2008; Daimaru and Matsuzakaya merged in September 2007; and in the Osaka region Hankyu and Hanshin chains merged to form H2O in October 2007. In addition, by 2008 about 10% of stores had physically closed. This, of course, was hardly surprising, given the similar eclipse of downtown retailing in the USA.

At the opposite end is the rise of online sales and television shopping networks. Here the leaders are Rakuten, Yahoo! Japan (a joint venture of the Japanese firm SoftBank and US-based Yahoo!), and (with an emphasis on books) Amazon. While difficult to measure, in 2009 revenue was estimated to total 6,700,000m. yen or about 5% of retail sales. A 2009 survey found that 19% of total transactions were done from a mobile (cell) phone, representing about 1,000,000m. yen—many retailers have websites tailored to suit smaller screens. In addition, about 378,000m. yen of content was downloaded with payment made via mobile phones, which now embed e-money chips that can be used to make purchases from vending machines and convenience stores as well as serving as a rail pass. This is the fastest-growing area of retail. Overall, therefore, the retail world was evolving rapidly. A tremendous number of small stores remained in existence, at least on paper, but casual observation suggested that many were seldom open or had no customers; such businesses were so numerous as to have earned a nickname, 'shataa gai' (shuttered shopping streets). As the entrepreneurs who had started these shops 30 and 40 years previously began to retire, they appeared certain to close permanently. The cessation of operations among poorly managed large stores was also slow. The Japanese Government helped to arrange a rescue programme for Daiei, one of several retail groups that had many medium-sized stores around smaller train stations, which were neither accessible to cars nor readily expandable. While Daiei's debt was drastically reduced, years after its demise the bulk of its stores remained open and continued to lose sales; at the time of its sale to the Aeon group one-third were highly unprofitable. Bank forbearance, and the difficulty in selling or leasing out the associated real estate, meant that there was no apparent advantage in closing such chains.

As the 'baby boom' generation of small store proprietors retire and close their shops, and as larger stores gradually continue to disappear, the sales of the remaining, better-managed and better-located retail groups should improve, bringing greater profits to their owners and lower prices to consumers. However, such changes will occasion the disappearance of the sense of community that accrued through the many local shopping districts, and the personal relationships and high levels of attention they provided. This shift generated public anxiety among politicians and community groups. Although consumers bemoaned such changes, in practice they wanted the greater variety and convenience offered by the new type of retailers, and they were unwilling to pay the higher prices needed to maintain low-volume, labour-intensive 'traditional' (although largely post-1945) neighbourhood retailers.

Restaurants

Similar changes were occurring in the restaurant sector by the early 21st century, with new concepts and shifts in the types of food that were popular. Most eating establishments remained relatively small in scale: this was allowed in part by the growth of franchising. McDonald's was important, both for helping to demonstrate the potential of the franchise restaurant approach and for making hamburgers popular; with 3,750 outlets and 362,000m. yen in sales in 2009, the US company was six times the size of the next largest hamburger chain and was the largest of the many chains of fast food. Other successful ventures were Mr Donuts, with 181,000m. yen in sales and 1,300 outlets, and Kentucky Fried Chicken, with 84,900m. yen in sales and 1,500 outlets. As with McDonald's, both served foods that were, until recently, new to the market. Family restaurants also expanded, although the leader was no longer Dennys, but Skylark, with 3,500 outlets and 385,000m. yen in sales. That may change. In 2006 Skylark became a private company in Japan's largest ever management buy-out, although profitability decreased rather than rose, with the firm losing more than US $100m. in 2006 and again in 2007. In August 2008 investors forced out the 70-year-old doyen of the founding family, replacing him with a 56-year-old who had been operating a successful buffet-style subsidiary; by 2011 it was not yet clear whether sales had improved as a result.

A purely domestic Japanese example was that of gyudon restaurants, which served sukiyaki-style beef over rice. Yoshinoya, the pioneer, had 1,584 outlets and 180,000m. yen in annual sales in the year ending February 2010, while newcomer Sukiya, with 3,934 outlets, had surpassed it with sales totalling 334,000m. yen. Other domestic concepts included chains of izakaya (which began as local, pub-like drinking establishments, serving grilled fish and other light dishes to accompany sake and beer), conveyor-belt kaiten sushi restaurants, coffee shops (with the once-pervasive independent small corner shop replaced by one or another chain, of which Detours and Starbucks were the largest), and bento shops, which provided ready-made and made-to-order boxed lunches. Finally, two early post-war concepts were ramen ('Chinese' noodle) shops and Japanese curry restaurants; these independent operations were also gradually being displaced by outlets of franchise chains.

The restaurant sector remained highly fragmented but dynamic. The range of foods available was large, and ethnic foods were widely available (Chinese, Italian, Korean, French and even Indian food), as were tempura, soba, tonkatsu and other more specifically Japanese formats. Supermarkets and malls in train stations continued to offer a wide array of ready-to-cook or ready-to-consume dishes, and bakeries abounded. There was a constant inflow of new concepts, and of course there remained many unique family-run restaurants. The sector was an interesting example of the ability of entrepreneurs to respond to higher incomes, and of the shift, from the mid-1990s, to locations away from train stations as Japan moved towards a more car-based culture. With franchising and constant mergers, acquisitions and 'spin-offs', an ever-shifting landscape was provided, as new concepts, domestic and international, were able to spread quickly across the country. The Skylark management change noted above reflected that spirit.

Health Care and Related Services

With the ageing of the population, the demand for health care services is rapidly expanding. In 2001 the sector employed 4.5m. workers. According to the monthly Labour Force Survey, by the last quarter of 2010 that number had expanded by one-third to engage 6.7m., adding 400,000 workers over the previous 12 months and making it the fastest-growing component of the service sector. While still smaller than the numbers employed in manufacturing (10.5m. workers) and wholesaling and retailing/wholesaling (10.5m. workers), the number of nurses, for example, now exceeds the number of workers in the automobile industry. Like all of the developed world (with the exception of the USA), Japan had a national health care insurance system that, since 1961, had covered virtually the entire population. In addition to medical and dental care, it provided home health care for the elderly (kaigo hoken), disability insurance, care for the disabled and a variety of other services. This was part of a wider array of social insurance; virtually all Japanese, for example, were also covered by a national pensions system (although administrative problems here, involving the loss of 50m. records, became one of the issues that brought about Prime Minister Shinzo Abe's resignation in 2007).

In the fiscal year 2009 budget government-funded health care expenditure was set at 31,000,000m. yen, including home health care, medical training and related expenses. In the aggregate, such expenditure represented about 8.2% of GDP, one of the lowest levels within OECD; adding the 4.4% for health care and insurance that are part of consumer expenditure raises the total to 12.6%. Health care normally entailed a co-payment for regular care and for medicines, with relatively low limits on the maximum additional expenditure. More important, the fees and prices were regulated by the Government. This kept costs to the consumer low, while maintaining reasonable access. None the less, regulations were subjected to some degree of manipulation, with doctors managing small hospitals with long patient stays and scheduling frequent follow-up visits to help augment their income. However, tighter regulation forced most of these very small hospitals (some of them with only a few beds) to close. What is striking was that in 2004/05 only 4% of the expenditure of the average household was on health care; despite their greater utilization of the facilities, elderly households spent more, but still only 5%.

With the decrease in rural populations, some remote areas now had no full-time doctor. That was particularly true in the case of obstetricians and paediatricians; with the decline in the birth rate and the shift in population structure, those aged 0–14 years incurred only 6% of health care costs, and few young people were left in regions that depended on farming and seasonal tourism. The structure of the system was evolving as well. In 1980 strokes were the major cause of death, with heart attacks third; by 2006 the two combined accounted for fewer deaths than cancer. Today's 65-year-old man could expect to reach the age of 83, while a woman of a corresponding age could expect to reach the age of 88. The demands on health care of the extreme elderly are increasing. Although those who were quite sick were still admitted to hospital, the role of specialized elderly care facilities was now far greater; by October 2009 there were 11,000 residential care facilities.

The kaigo system was noteworthy. Started in 1996 with the current structure dating from 2000, the system assisted families who did not want to place relatives in hospitals or residential facilities. This system combined in-home care provided by licensed workers with day-care and other outpatient facilities. By April 2007 some 27m. individuals aged 65 and above had joined the system (including 12.3m. over the age of 75); as of 2010 4.85m. qualified for care, more than double the number in 2000. Such services ranged from providing meals and helping people to bathe to physical rehabilitation and day care for individuals with dementia or other disabilities. In the financial year 2009 some 1.1m. individuals received preventive services, 2.8m. individuals received at-home assistance (e.g. help with bathing) or outpatient care (e.g. rehabilitation), while 1.1m. received in-patient care. Eliminating double-counting, 4.7m. individuals were provided with services. The two systems combined employed over 1.3m. workers.

However, attracting and training additional personnel to health care was difficult; with a decline in the college-aged population it was very hard to expand the number of medical and nursing students, even if teachers and facilities could be created instantly. During 1994–2004 the number of doctors rose by 17%, to 268,000, while the number of nurses increased by 54% and pharmacists by 42%. This apparent success belies the difficulty of filling positions. Nursing was until recently one of the few well-paid professions open to women. However, almost all hospitals mandated rotating between day, evening and night shifts, and changing technology and the greater number of seriously ill patients were increasing the workload. Meanwhile, a wider range of jobs became available for women; reinforced by demographics, fewer women were interested in nursing careers, and more left the profession after only a few years of work. In 2005–06 shortages became widespread, with some major hospitals able to recruit only 70% of the numbers they needed. That led to more extensive recourse to overtime, exacerbating the pressures that drive nurses away from hospitals within five years. Rigid staffing practices (originating in civil service norms, as most major hospitals were government-affiliated) and pay scales tied to national health insurance reimbursement rules provided hospitals with little ability to respond. The public policy response was limited; one of the few initiatives was a system of licensing foreign medical professionals, including nurses from the Philippines and Indonesia, but the initial implementation permitted only a very small number to enter Japan. Meanwhile, senior members of the Japan Nurses Association were actually advocating imposing additional educational requirements, making it more difficult to become a nurse. The shortage of nursing and medical personnel might well become a significant policy issue in the near future.

Finally, it is interesting to note the growth of day-care centres. One reason for the decrease in the birth rate was that more women were working longer and delaying marriage; once married, they were not having children. This was a trend common to all developed countries, partly reflecting the opportunity cost of forgone income as wages rose. A contributory factor was a lack of child care. In 2000 there were only 22,200 day-care centres nation-wide; with a limited budget, only about 100 new ones per year are being set up. As a result, for many women the nearest centre was located too far away. More importantly, only 60% were open after 18:00, making it impossible to hold a job that involved commuting, much less to perform overtime. In addition, a barrier for professionals and the large number of women working in retailing, health care and similar industries, only 798 facilities were open at weekends and during holidays. The Government's goal was to increase extended hours facilities to 16,200 by 2009 and to increase the number of day-care centres open on holidays to 2,200. Those goals hardly seemed ambitious. A small but growing number of employers (such as Toyota and several major universities) began to offer on-site day care, which lessens commuting issues; such efforts garnered much publicity. Similarly, the number of after-school programmes was expanding. However, child care remained one of the major concerns of women; of those with jobs, one-third relied upon their children's grandparents for care.

Business and Other Services

From the 1980s the growth of entirely new services was witnessed. Until the 1980s computer services were trivial in scale, and information-providers were virtually non-existent, but this industry has expanded to become a significant source of employment in Japan. Accounting reforms increased demand, spurred by the bankruptcy of the supposedly highly profitable internet company Livedoor, the 'solvent' Murakami investment fund and the 'healthy' Resona Bank. (These events in turn led to the collapse in 2006 of Chuo Aoyama, one of Japan's 'Big Four' accounting firms.) Vehicle ownership is pervasive; the 75m. registered cars, trucks and buses need periodic servicing. Mobile phones are almost universal; stores are everywhere, trying to encourage new customers with the latest design. Moreover, as discretionary or leisure time has increased, recreational facilities have expanded: sports clubs (more than 4m. Japanese swim regularly); bowling alleys; and—despite competition from DVD rentals—even cinemas. There are also around 50m. fans of karaoke. With more retirees, leisure travel has increased in importance and, alongside tourism, more Japanese listed driving as a hobby than any other activity.

Transport

In 1965 only 25% of Japan's freight traffic was moved by truck, while 31% went by rail and 43% by ship. By 2004 the rail component was of minimal importance (4% of the total) while trucks accounted for 58% and ships 38%. Similarly, in 1965 some 67% of passenger-kilometres travelled were accounted for by rail, and 32% by bus. By 2004, despite greater urbanization and the huge commuting systems of the major metropolitan areas, only 27% of passenger travel was by rail. Instead, 61% was by car and only 6% by bus, while air travel rose three-fold between 1980 and the mid-2000s. Rail and bus services had been reduced throughout rural Japan; by 2004 bus utilization was only 27% of that in 1980. In contrast, after 1980 car traffic rose almost eight-fold, reflected in a doubling of car ownership. As noted above, this had a major effect on the structure of retailing and an intangible, but significant, impact on the rhythm of daily life.

While most areas of transport were at best not growing, parcel delivery was a major exception. At one time the post office was the only way to send small packages, but it was expensive, lacked an express service and would deliver only during normal working hours, when people were not at home. In the mid-1970s Yamato Transport entered the market to serve this latent demand, and by 2006 had progressed from being a freight hauler with an unpromising future to a company with annual sales in its fiscal year ending March 2009 of 1,250,000m. yen, employing 170,000 people and making more than 1,230m. deliveries annually. Its success attracted other entrants to the market, including Sagawa Kyubin and Japan Transport, although the latter remained primarily a household relocation and freight transport company. In response, the Japan Post also restructured its package delivery servicer. Competition drove down prices and profits, but it remained a profitable and innovative segment. As with many services, this had indirect benefits, as it enabled the expansion of catalogue and internet purchases by consumers, inventory control by retailers and the delivery of repair parts and special orders for industry and wholesalers.

Telecommunications

Japan's telecommunications sector was long dominated by two monopolies, Nippon Telegraph and Telephone Corporation (NTT) for fixed lines and KDDI for international services. Several large electronics companies grew up around manufacturing telephones and telephone switching equipment, including NEC. However, throughout much of the era of rapid growth the wait for a telephone was lengthy, as the installation of new lines did not keep pace with demand. Telephone utilities had no orientation towards customer service; those who wanted to have a phone installed, for example, had to buy a special 50,000-yen NTT bond, and calls remained expensive. At the same time the diffusion of personal computers was very slow, in part because the initial corporate market was served by mainframe makers that supplied incompatible systems. That changed rapidly after 1991, when Microsoft introduced a Windows version adapted for the Japanese language, and accelerated with the entry of Dell Computers, which brought down prices. The rapid decrease in the price of mobile telephone services in the late 1990s began to change the nature of telecommunications and, from the early 21st century, that process accelerated with the spread of internet services. Traditional telephone lines are now in decline, as a result of rapid technical change; broadband internet service over fibre optic lines is now widespread, and in 2010 this was both faster and less expensive than in the USA or the EU. Between mobile telephones and computers, by March 2010 there were 32m.

broadband subscribers and an additional 95.5m. mobile telephones with internet service. Overall, 94m. Japanese had internet service, representing well over 90% of all households.

In March 2010 there were 112m. mobile telephone subscribers, of which 109m. were 3G (third generation) telephones with numerous features, from the omnipresent text messaging to maps based on the Global Positioning System (GPS), a megapixel camera, a 2D barcode reader for online ordering and internet access for e-mail, news, train reservations and even television. Some of these features were unique to Japan—which therefore limited the size of the market for telephone manufacturers—but in any case there appeared to be little room for further diffusion and the rate of uptake of these new features was slowing. Already the changes were reflected in a restructuring of the retailing of telephones and telephone services, and of providers themselves. In March 2006 Vodafone, the third largest company, with about one-sixth of the market, sold its business to the Japanese company SoftBank. The second largest firm, KDDI, commands about one-third of the market, while NTT DoCoMo, a subsidiary of the national fixed-line telephone monopoly, holds just over one-half of the market and accounted for one-half of all sales and three-quarters of the profits of the consolidated NTT operation. Profits from basic telephone services were no longer growing, and from November 2006 government regulation mandated 'number portability', allowing customers to maintain their telephone numbers if they switched providers. KDDI and SoftBank promoted this capability with aggressive pricing, encroaching upon the market share and profits of NTT DoCoMo. The market is continuing to evolve: from 2011 companies were obliged to start selling telephones with switchable chips, so that address books and ringtones can be swapped among telephones. This will further lessen the ability of either hardware or connection providers to 'lock in' customers.

There was intense competition to provide content and to capture advertising revenues. Television still dominated corporate advertising budgets, with 30% of the market, and it had maintained its share. Newspapers were also a major outlet: at 545 per 1,000 head of population, circulation was far higher than in any other major economy, double that of Germany and three times that of the USA. The most popular newspaper, Yomiuri Shimbun, had a daily circulation in late 2008 of 10.0m. Where advertising revenue was concerned, the contrast between the financial years 2000 and 2009 was great, with traditional media advertising down 32%. In the background were new media: while internet and satellite television advertising were still modest (about 12% of the market in 2008) they had been virtually nil in 2000. Traditional content providers were failing to capture new markets, and circulation was being affected by the younger generation's preference for surfing the web and renting DVDs, rather than reading or watching television. After 2008 the recession induced an even steeper decline in newspaper advertising. Asahi Shimbun, despite a circulation of 8.0m., showed its first-ever operating loss at the end of 2008.

Recreation

The largest travel agent, JTB, had 1,660,000m. yen in sales in 2008/09. While domestic travel increased by 20% over 2000–07, international travel rose by only 4% and overall was volatile. However, both travel sectors were affected by the impact of the recession, with domestic travel decreasing by 16% during 2007–09 and international travel by 27%. Hotel expenditure, for example, was no higher than in 2000, and hotel occupancy rates had not improved. The tourism industry had high hopes of recovery, with the improvement in the economy and the retirement of the 'baby boom' generation, which began in 2007, and the prospect of an increase in Chinese tourism. Instead, the global economic crisis and (following the earthquake of March 2011) the fear of radiation exposure have badly affected the industry. Japan Air Lines (JAL), the country's 'flagship' carrier, filed for bankruptcy in January 2010 (emerging in March 2011), reducing the number of its workers by one-third, while also curtailing its routes. Resorts throughout Japan were expected to have difficulty in surviving the precipitous decline in tourism.

Attendance levels at baseball, the largest sports segment, produced around 55,000m. yen in annual revenue, but remained virtually unchanged over the financial years 2003–09. The same was true of resorts, by far the largest of which was Tokyo Disneyland, with 26m. visitors and revenues of 371,000m. yen in the financial year 2009. Its facilities were heavily damaged by the March 2011 earthquake, and visitor numbers subsequently remained at a fraction of their previous level; in that fiscal year it was expected to lose money for the first time since opening. Universal Studios Japan, located outside Osaka, was the second largest facility, with 8m. visitors in 2008. While there were a wide variety of other theme parks and zoos, those two facilities accounted for 70% of the entire industry. Cinema attendance declined by 22% between 2003 and 2009; even in 2005 it generated far less revenue (198,000m. yen annually) than DVD rentals (338,000m. yen). Gaming/karaoke centres and pachinko parlours were omnipresent, but were also in decline, with karaoke decreasing by 18% during 2000–07, pachinko by 30% and game centres by 8%. Finally, many golf courses have closed, while membership fees have declined, and newly retired people have not taken up the sport.

FINAL DEMAND

On a GDP basis, final expenditure consists of personal consumption expenditure (C), gross private investment (I), government purchases of goods and services (G), and net trade of goods and services (X-M). During the first quarter of 2011, in real seasonally adjusted terms, these accounted, respectively, for 60% (C), 16% (I), 20% (G) and 0% (X-M), the last reflecting curtailed exports and emergency imports following the earthquake. On the national income side, for which details are published only in retrospect, in the financial year 2008 household wage and bonus income comprised 75% (including 11% deducted for social insurance contributions) and capital income a mere 5%, while corporate income was 22%. Companies thus retained a very high share of income, using it for investment as well as (beginning in 1998 and continuing in 2010) to reduce debt.

Because of the distorting impact of the short but severe recession in 2009, a result of the economic problems in the USA and Europe, statistics for 2008 are used below; comprehensive GDP data for 2010 were not to be released until late 2011 or early 2012. Provisional data for the second quarter of 2011 were expected to reflect the short-term distortions (and data collection problems) caused by the Tohoku earthquake. Given the expected transitory impact, data released by the final quarter of 2011 were likely to be more representative. As the underlying structure of the economy has been changing only very slowly, the following account uses older data, which should be similar to what will be observed by the end of 2011.

Consumption

As with most economies, consumption forms the largest portion of domestic demand, at 58% of GDP in 2008. Japan's System of National Accounts provides only 16 categories. Within consumption, services represented 57% of the total, non-durable goods, such as food, 26%, durable goods (such as automobiles) 9.1% and semi-durables (for example, clothing) 7.3%. GDP data highlight the high share of food and beverages, at 18% of consumption. This has shifted significantly in recent decades; given lower incomes and higher food prices in 1980, some 26% of consumption was on food, and that level was much higher during the 1950s. By contrast, as incomes rose Japanese spent more on housing, which rose to 25% from 19% in 1980. Spending on eating out, recreation and communications rose from 16% to 22%. At the same time household savings declined from 12% or more of disposable income during 1980–93, to 1.9% in 2008. This reflects the larger share of retirees in the population as well as the impact of slow growth on household budgets. (While health care expenditure is significant, most costs are paid directly by the Government and so are not shown in the GDP personal consumption expenditures.)

Using the Household Consumption and Expenditure Survey allows much greater detail, covering over 500 categories on a monthly basis. In 1970 the average household bought 277 kg of rice, but in 2009 only 85 kg. Reflecting high prices and the diversification of the diet, by 2009 expenditure on bread surpassed that on rice, and for urban dwellers under the age of 40 spending was also lower than that on noodles and pasta. By contrast, in 2009 the average household consumed 393 kg of meat, an increase of one-third from the level of 294 kg recorded in 1970. With the presence of national health care, direct expenditure on health care was small, at 4.4% including casualty insurance. Automobile ownership also increased, from 22% of households in 1970 to 57% in 1980 and 83% in 2009. However, the market has matured not only in ownership terms; with the population ageing, the number of licensed drivers is declining. In 2008, before the full impact of the recession, sales were 5.1m. units, 35% below the 1990 peak of 7.8m. It is possible to look to these data for many other patterns; it will be interesting to see how consumption patterns shift as the population ages.

Investment

Japan has an unusually high level of investment; in the financial year 2008, before the impact of the recession, it stood at 23.2% of GDP, including 4.0% public investment in roads and other infrastructure. However, this was a decrease of 32.4% in comparison with 1990, at the height of the 'bubble' economy. Most of the 18.8% in private investment was by the corporate sector; residential construction by households was only 3.3% of GDP. The largest shift was in the share of public investment, as public works construction was pared back, by 51% from its 1996 peak.

Private investment is volatile and in Japan has historically been the proximate cause of booms and recessions. That remained the case in the most recent recession: residential construction declined to 2.3% of GDP in the first quarter of 2010, while business investment decreased from 16.1% of GDP in the first quarter of 2008 to 13.0% of GDP in the first quarter of 2010. The high level of investment relative to consumption adds to this instability, which is partly due to the high share of income that accrues to the corporate sector relative to the household sector.

Government and Public Finance

Japan has a small government sector by OECD standards, accounting for 22.1% of GDP in the first quarter of 2010. Unlike in some countries, the post office, toll roads, utilities and the railway system are either privately owned or operated as independent entities. Japan does have large social security programmes, primarily the national health care system and the national pension system, as well as smaller unemployment and welfare programmes. In the financial year 2008 these accounted for 19.3% of GDP. Given the recession and the increased number of retirees, all components grew in the financial year 2009 (April–March).

Japan has a unified government framework, rather than a federal system. While prefectural and local governments have a measure of autonomy and taxing authority, the overall framework is specified in Tokyo. However, budgets are not consolidated, although many of the revenue sources of local government come from the centre. The budget for the fiscal year beginning 1 April 2010 envisioned that about 33% of general government expenditure would be allocated to local and prefectural governments and 51% to health care, retirement and other transfers. However, analysis is complicated. The Diet (national legislature) generally adopts two budgets per year for the central Government: a regular budget that covers most expenditure and a supplementary budget that contains allocations for public works and other special items. (Owing to the earthquake, three supplemental budgets were to be adopted in 2011: the initial pre-earthquake supplemental budget, a second one comprising emergency measures, and a third supporting an initial reconstruction plan.) Combined with disparities in the time-scale for actual expenditure, the gap between actual outlays and budgeted amounts varies widely; it was 8% or more in the financial years 1989, 1998 and 1999, but less than 1% in 2003. Finally, the postal savings system was used historically to fund a variety of government banks and bond-issuing authorities through the Fiscal Investment and Loan Programme (FILP), and thus indirectly funded local government activities as well as construction projects and small business lending. FILP activities were not reflected in either the regular or the supplementary budgets. Ongoing reforms, including the privatization of the postal savings system that began in October 2007, may eventually make the budgeting process more transparent, but that was not yet the case in 2011.

One approach is to use national accounts data, which aim to give a comprehensive assessment. GDP data for the financial year 2008 showed the general government sector accounting for 18.9% of GDP. Of this, 37.9% represented direct government purchases of household consumption goods (health care). Of the remaining amount of direct government purchases, 67.5% was made by prefectural and local government for roads, teachers' salaries and other purposes. Some 3.0% of government expenditure was for investment; again, 72% of this was carried out by prefectural and local government to construct schools, roads and other infrastructure. (Additional amounts were provided by local airport, bridge, road and water corporations, in principle to be paid for by tolls and fees.) Such a division was to be expected; as with most modern economies, the provision of education and other locally administered activities dominate those of the centre. On a sectoral approach, in the financial year 2008 insurance programmes (including health care) were the largest single component, at 38.2% of government consumption, an increase from 28.3% in 1980; the next largest portion was for education, at 17.7%, down from 25.0% in 1980. Other large sectors included environmental protection (6.5% of the total), fire services, police and safety (6.1%) and national defence (4.4%), along with general administrative (7.8%) and regulatory functions (14.4%).

Social insurance includes several parallel pension programmes, including separate schemes for central government employees, local government employees, the self-employed and regular employees. Health care, likewise, includes a separate scheme for government employees, a programme for the very old, and a home health care programme, alongside the standard national health care system through which almost all Japanese are covered. In the financial year 2008 pension payments totalled 52,600,000m. yen, or 10.6% of GDP. Next came health insurance, with the two main medical insurance programmes spending 14,600,000m. yen, and and health and other care for the very old totalling 11,100,000m. yen; the various health care-orientated programmes in total were 31,700,000m. yen, or 6.4% of GDP. However, these amounts reflected only direct expenditure; additional funds, such as social security payroll taxes, amounting to approximately 14% of GDP, flowed directly through the pension system to recipients, so that total social security and health care costs were about 24% of GDP in 2005. Japan operated with massive budget deficits from the early 1990s, owing first and foremost to the impact of slow growth on tax receipts, second to increasing health care and pension costs, and third to active fiscal policy to offset periodic recessions. On a general budget basis (central plus local government), these amounted to 7.5% of GDP in the calendar year 2000, by far the highest level among OECD members; subsequent fiscal restraint reduced deficits to a projected 6.4% in 2005 and, with buoyant income tax receipts, to less than 2% in 2006. The budget is unusually sensitive to variations in corporate profits, and so with the slowdown associated with the global economic crisis, deficits again increased. The budget for the year beginning 1 April 2010 anticipated tax receipts of 37,400,000m. yen and expenditure of 92,300,000m. yen, a deficit of 51,900,000m. yen, or about 10% of GDP. The Government projected a deficit of 9.1% for 2010—about the level that OECD projected for France, but smaller than the projections for the USA and the United Kingdom. Even though the eventual resumption of growth would boost tax receipts, under the current tax and expenditure structure large deficits would remain; fiscal reform remains a topic of intense political debate.

Measures have been taken in this regard. The 'Trinity Reforms' agreed upon by the Cabinet in November 2004 reduced various subsidies to local government, with changes in the funding for compulsory education and the conversion of public works subsidies into fixed grants over which local government would have greater control. A second component was to transfer a larger part of tax revenues directly to local governments, giving them control of inhabitants' taxes while reducing allocations out of national income taxes. The third

Trinity component was the incorporation into the general budget of a larger part of local allocation taxes; since these moneys would be lost if not spent, local governments tended to engage in infrastructure projects whether or not they had value. Other expenditure reforms included streamlining a variety of long-term health care programmes and continued reductions in public works, as well as abolishing direct loans by the Government Housing Loan Corporation, many of which in the past went awry. In the short term, this was at variance with the political pressure to stimulate growth through fiscal policy: despite continued reductions in public works, the overall budget for 2010 was increased by 3.4%.

At the local level, greater flexibility was of little help while the local economy remained depressed, as was the case in much of rural Japan throughout the 2000s. In particular, local governments were unable to use their newly obtained taxing authority to generate revenues. In mid-2006 Yubari City, a former coal-mining town in Hokkaido, defaulted on its debt, and subsequent investigations revealed 'illegal' borrowing to cover budget deficits within five other local governments. Some 70 local governments were operating with deficits, eight of them of 20% or more, too big to finance under the new system. The bureaucracy began proposing legislation to address what was by then recognized as a widespread problem, in view of the greater transparency in local government finances. However, as of 2010 localities were experiencing reduced services, in contrast to the largesse that they received in the 1990s. The initial policy response to the Tohoku earthquake in March 2011 reflects the potential of greater local autonomy, just as the Yubari case highlighted its dangers. Local government officials and politicians in the most severely affected towns ended up in emergency shelters, like everyone else. They quickly organized living arrangements and established systems for dispensing water and other items in short supply, while engaging in the search for survivors. The Governor of Miyagi prefecture reacted speedily. In contrast, in Tokyo the bureaucrats quickly became involved in disputes over which ministry should supervise what area, proposing to establish committees for every aspect of the response to the emergency. What emerges will thus reflect a balance along the lines of the administrative structure rather than local priorities. The earthquake may ultimately serve to force the political and administrative structure to delegate more power to adapt national rules and regulations.

The FILP is the third component of central government activities. Its source of funds was the postal savings and life insurance systems. The FILP borrowed those moneys to lend to a large set of government financial institutions, to buy bonds issued to finance public works and local government deficits, and to purchase general government bonds. Under the reform programme of Prime Minister Junichiro Koizumi (2001–06), Japan Post was no longer obligated to place all of its funds with the FILP; the creation in 2007 of Japan Postal Bank (JPB) as a separate entity strengthened its ability to resist funding the FILP. The outstanding balance of loans declined by just over 50% from its peak in the financial year 2000 of 417,800,000m. yen, to a projected 202,700,000m. yen in 2010. The programme nevertheless remained large, at 41% of GDP and with plans for new investments of 18,800,000m. yen in 2010. Programmes and institutions that were budgeted to receive large FILP allocations included the Japan Finance Corporation (64% of the total, the JFC having been founded in 2008 by a merger of specialized government financial institutions for trade and small business and agricultural co-operatives), local government and the Japan Highway Public Corporation.

The system historically had very loose controls; many public works projects, although funded by bonds purchased by FILP, in fact generated no revenue. As a result, such projects were in fact government expenditure, as at some point the central Government would have to reimburse bondholders, which in most cases meant the postal savings system. Estimates of such bad debts were around 15% of GDP. The Koizumi Government reformed a number of the recipients, with the Government Housing Loan Corporation, in particular, obtaining virtually no new funds. Alongside the FILP were 31 special accounts, to which various types of allocated revenue accrued. These included pension and health care accounts and national debt accounts, which were relatively innocuous, but through which a huge 225,000,000m. yen flowed. However, other accounts were for items such as road construction (drawing upon petrol taxes), agricultural insurance and other activities that concealed an array of subsidies and 'pork barrel' public works spending; they also included the accounts that were used to transfer funds to local governments. As with the FILP, such accounts often lacked transparency, as they fell outside the regular budget process. By 2010 one-half of these were to be abolished, although the proposals then languished in the Diet.

Japan's tax system has numerous elements, at both the central and local level (accounting for 13% and 10%, respectively, of national income). The largest single component is a graduated personal income tax, which the 2009 budget expected to total 33% of central government receipts. The second largest budgeted component was corporate income tax, at 22%, followed by 21% derived from consumption (sales) tax. A wide variety of levies, including those on inheritance, alcohol, gasoline, tobacco and car taxes, comprised the remaining 24%. Local government shared in some of these and had additional taxes, including those on real estate, local residences and automobiles. Given the size of the deficit and the political realities that only incremental reductions can be made on the expenditure side (with the exception, perhaps, of raising the retirement age), restoring budgetary balance solely through taxes would require that, on average, they be raised by 50%. A doubling of the consumption tax to 10% was discussed by Prime Minister Kan in mid-2010, but while the public expressed some support for that in principle, the prevalent levels of unemployment made it highly unpopular and contributed to the DPJ's loss of its majority in the upper house at the July elections.

An additional component that Kan proposed was the introduction of a national tax identification number. This would make the system for tracking pensions (where 50m. records were lost in 2007) and many other administrative tasks easier, and it would also impede tax evasion. A large proportion of employment is in small businesses, which handle most of their transactions in cash; payments to farmers are likewise often in cash. By keeping multiple bank accounts, evasion is easy—unlike in the case of employees whose income is taxed at source. Indicative of the problem is that 70% of small firms have seemingly never managed to make a profit, while farmers were in principle not audited. Again, while tax administration improved during the 2000s, many Japanese perceived the system as unfair. Owing to that, the Government will almost certainly focus on adjusting the consumption tax, which is easier to collect and is viewed by the public as less subject to evasion. That is reflected by recent proposals, including a detailed study from the IMF, which suggest a target tax rate of 15%, to be reached by increasing the level by two percentage points a year for five years.

Trade and International Flows

Despite images to the contrary, trade is responsible for a modest share of the Japanese economy; exports and imports accounted for a combined 29% of GDP in the first quarter of 2010, and (distorted by the earthquake) 32% in the first quarter of 2011. This level is similar to that of the USA but well below those of the contiguous member nations of the EU. Exports are focused on high value-added goods, particularly differentiated consumer durables such as passenger cars and electronic and precision components, but also high-quality steel and other materials. Imports consist of energy, other raw materials and food, labour-intensive manufactures, and differentiated industrial and consumer goods. Japan is, for example, both a major importer and exporter of semiconductors.

In the first six months of 2009, on a balance of payments basis, Japan's exports of goods decreased by 44% compared with the first half of 2008, the sharpest decline on record. Trade recovered during 2010, with exports for the year as a whole increasing by 25% over 2009 to 63,900,000m. yen. Meanwhile, imports, which had declined by 40% in the first half of 2009, also rose in 2010, by 19%, to 55,900,000m. yen. In the first half of 2009 the trade surplus decreased by 82%; in 2010 it almost doubled to 8,000,000m. yen. The deterioration in early 2009 was dominated by the collapse of the export of durable goods and particularly passenger cars, leading to what could be termed the 'Toyota recession'. This company and other exporters of consumer durables quickly adjusted inventory levels in the USA and other major markets, and in the first half of 2010 exports increased by 38%. This still left the volume of trade in 2010 some 20% below that of 2008, but helped to revive the production of consumer durables and end the recession of 2009. In contrast to its surplus in goods, Japan has long been a net importer of services, with imports of 13,800,000m. yen and exports of 12,300,000m. yen in 2010, giving a net deficit of 1,480,000m. yen, slightly smaller than in 2009. The overall balance of trade in goods and services was thus a surplus of 6,500,000m. yen, triple that of 2009 but still well below peak levels of 2007 and earlier.

The composition of trade has shifted markedly over time. In 1960 textiles accounted for 30% of exports, and ships and steel for another 10%; automobiles only barely surpassed 1%, whereas transistor radios alone accounted for over 3% of exports. By 2010 exports of textiles and radios were both insignificant, while ships and steel together accounted for just under 9%. In contrast, automobiles and their parts comprised 18% of all exports, while integrated circuits accounted for 4% and other electronics 4.5%. Imports likewise were quite different: in 1960 raw cotton, wool, steel and scrap steel were major imports, as was wheat; petroleum was about 12% of the total. By 2010 cotton and wool imports were insignificant, and while imports of wheat had increased it was not among the dozen principal commodities. In contrast, energy formed a huge category of imports, with petroleum, petroleum products, natural gas and coal accounting for 29% of all imports. A wide variety of machinery in the aggregate accounted for 21%, the largest single category being integrated circuits, also a major export. Then came clothing at 4%, while a glance at store shelves showed that many types of consumer electronics were imported, including televisions, once a major export. This represented a remarkable shift from a half-century earlier when this category formed the dominant export, reflecting the evolution of Japan's comparative advantage from labour-intensive to capital- and knowledge-intensive goods.

The direction of trade likewise changed. In 1960 some 27% of exports were to the USA, and it was the source of 34% of imports. Asia was next at 36% of exports and 30% of imports; China accounted for well under 1%. In 2010, however, Asia dominated, with 60% of exports and 62% of imports, and China was Japan's largest trading partner, the purchaser of 19% of Japan's exports and the source of 22% of its imports. The USA was a distinct second, at 15% of exports and 10% of imports; Europe's share was relatively constant, at 10%–13% throughout for both imports and exports.

The current account also includes net profits on overseas investment. Years of cumulative trade surpluses have been recycled into investments in the USA, the EU and more recently Asia, with net foreign reserves totalling US $1,010,000m. at the end of 2010, and total net foreign assets, including private investment, of $2,865,000m. (see Foreign Exchange, below.) This generates sizeable income flows, amounting to $133,000m. in 2010. This was in fact one-third larger than the trade balance of $91,000m., despite a decline in returns since the onset of the global financial crisis. Such profits formed the largest component of the current account surplus during the years 2000–10, and despite the strength of the yen, net foreign income in the first quarter of 2011 was the highest since the same period in 2008. Japan's current account surplus was expected to recover strongly in 2011, although the initial increase in imports and the reduction of exports owing to supply interruptions following the Tohoku earthquake led to the first trade deficit in many years in April and May, and a small deficit in June. Over time, however, the ageing of the population will lead to a continued decline in household savings, so that there will be less pressure to accumulate assets abroad and a corresponding increase in consumption. Corporate restructuring is largely complete, and balance sheets are again sound; this will increase corporate investment relative to savings. As those two trends evolve, the trade balance should decline or even become negative. However, while the accumulation of foreign assets may decelerate, it will take a very large change to offset likely levels of investment income (discussed below under Foreign Exchange). The 'hollowing out' of manufacturing and the ageing of the population will not lead to balance of payments problems, while the yen will appreciate as the demand for new foreign assets diminishes.

FACTOR MARKETS

Labour

Japan's population was estimated at 128m. in the October 2010 census. Those aged 15–64 years numbered 81.4m., down 6% since 2001. By contrast, the number of Japanese aged 65 and above rose by 30%. The single largest cohort in the population was the 'baby boom' generation, those aged 60–64 years and poised for retirement, at 10.5m. By contrast, in the 35–39 age group, representing their children, there were only 9.7m.; and in the 10–14 age bracket, the peak group for the grandchildren of the 'baby boomers', there were only 5.95m. The total population was now declining and would continue to do so in the foreseeable future. It is very difficult to foresee what implications this will have for the demand for workers, but what is certain is that today's youth will have a very different work experience from that of their parents and, especially, their grandparents, who remember the poverty and grinding labour of the early post-war era.

Of the working-age population, 65.7m. were in the labour force in October–December 2010; 62.6m. were employed, while 3.2m. or 4.8% were unemployed. The official rate of unemployment in June 2011 was 4.6%, essentially unchanged over the first half of the year. However, this excludes the three prefectures worst affected by the March earthquake, where 100,000 people remained in emergency shelters at the beginning of August and many businesses had yet to resume full operations. Collecting data using the standard methodology was not yet possible; rough estimates suggested that unemployment in these prefectures was over 20%. Male labour force participation rates in 2010 were 97% for those aged between 30 and 59, declining to 76% for those aged 60–64, some 50% for those aged 65 and above, and 20% for those age 70 and above (all very high by European standards). Nevertheless, this represents a large shift towards greater periods of retirement, since in 1968 some 82% of men aged 60–64 were still in the labour force, declining to 68% for men aged 65–69 and 39% of men aged 70 and above. This decline reflects a combination of reduced opportunities for formal employment and the decline of farming and other forms of self-employment, an increase in wealth and the near-universal availability of pensions. Some 90% of employers impose mandatory retirement; of those, 90% specify retirement at the age of 60, before the starting age of 63 for access to most pensions. Finding a post-initial-retirement job—including short-term contracts at lower pay with the same employer—is thus important. In conditions of slow growth, these are less desirable (taxi drivers, for example, are on average 58 years old) and, upon re-employment, men typically suffer a sharp decline in income (of 30%–50%). By contrast, with the increase in high school and subsequently college education, the labour force participation rate for young people aged 15–19 years decreased from 36% in 1965 to 16% in 2008, while that for the 20–24 age group declined over the same period from 86% to 69%.

Female participation in the labour force followed a very different pattern, averaging only 63% for the 15–64 age bracket in 2009. In addition, it exhibits a distinct 'M' shape, with participation peaking at 78% in the 25–29 age bracket, then declining to 66% at 35–39 years, as women marry and have children, before rising to 76% at 45–49, once their children are in middle school. Such a pattern was once observed in most other developed countries, but disappeared in the USA and northern Europe (but not Italy) as women pursued education, as child care became more widely available and as social mores changed. Japan is not unaffected by these forces: over time the 'M' has become less pronounced. In 1975 only 43% of women in the 25–29 age bracket were in the labour force. From the early 1990s female educational attainment came to equal that of men, while the age of women at first marriage rose from 24.0 in 1970 to 28.5 in 2008; women also tended to work until their first child was born, rather than relinquishing their jobs upon marriage. However, in many areas of Japan child care is still problematic, and the tax system penalizes women who earn above 1.5m. yen annually. A very high 53% of women choose part-time work, often at 35 hours per week, as that is the threshold at which employers are mandated to provide a variety of benefits and which results in an income below 1.5m. yen. Reforms in the tax system and labour regulations could potentially boost women's participation in the labour force and partially offset the decline in the working-age population.

At present most full-time employees have a five-day working week and an eight-hour day, a reduction of 25% from the 1960s, when a six-day week and a longer working day prevailed. However, at 1,836 hours in 2008, the average working year remains similar to that in the USA, but far above the 1,600-hour working year of Germany and France. (The average declined to 1,733 hours in 2009, but this reflects the recession, as 2.9m. workers were working reduced hours, a rise of 0.8m. from 2008.) At the other end of the spectrum, a distinct trend since the mid-1980s has been the rise of part-time workers, who do not qualify for benefits. In 1985 such employees totalled 11.1% of the labour force, and were mainly women and older workers; in June 2010 they represented 27.4% of all workers. In terms of gender, in 2009 on average 83% of men were 'regular' employees with permanent, full-time status, but only 49% of women were employed on that basis. Some 7.9% of men were part-time workers, in contrast with 39% of all women.

This shift is distinct enough to have generated the specific term 'freeters', young women and now increasingly men who live with their parents—the 'free' element—while holding part-time or temporary jobs, and changing employers with some frequency (after all, many of the jobs are temporary). This is partly a function of the decade-long period of slow growth that was ushered in with the 1992 recession. When possible, firms preferred to rely on attrition to reduce their work-force, depressing the demand for new employees. Large firms vigorously recruited among college seniors due to graduate in March 2008. Even at third-tier universities most of those seeking work had already found jobs by the autumn (third quarter) of 2007. However, that shifted with the recession, and unemployment in the new school-leaver age bracket was 10.7% in June 2010, more than double the average.

The above issue is an important one, as there remains a distinct pattern of 'lifetime' employment in large firms, which hire primarily recent school-leavers as 'regular' workers, and therefore promote from within, while providing an annual increase in pay in accordance with age (with little variation across workers of the same age) and maintaining an implicit policy of no redundancies. In practice, this applies to perhaps 20% of the labour force, including teachers and public sector workers. About 70% of all workers are in small and medium-sized enterprises (firms with 300 employees or fewer), which are unable to offer such guarantees and cannot offer a systematic change for career progression. In addition, comparatively few women in large firms are accorded 'regular' status. This also tends to coincide with union membership, which stands at about 18.5% of all employees, or 10.1m. workers in 2009. Not all unions are aggressive; at the same time firms with 300 or more employees must, by law, have a consultative council, some of which function as de facto unions. In any case, workers in most large firms are unionized, including banks; teachers and local government civil servants are also unionized. From the early 1990s, however, many large companies encountered management difficulties and encouraged 'voluntary' resignations and early retirement, including Nissan in the automobile industry and Sony and Matsushita in consumer electronics. The bitter and even violent strikes of the 1950s had become a distant memory, but large firms still go to great lengths to avoid dismissing workers, instead relying whenever possible on attrition. While the model of 'lifetime employment' was still how workers and employer framed discussion of the employment relationship, it applied to an ever-smaller proportion of the labour force. The expectations of young workers now reflected the greater unease that comes from uncertainty over how they would fare in a more varied, less stable work environment. Turnover among young workers rose even in traditionally 'lifetime' jobs, as they seemed less willing to remain with employers they disliked in return for job security, a situation that used to be normal.

Japan has not been free of business cycles: the economy of the 1960s was relatively volatile; in the decade 1992–2002 alone there were three recessions, and the 'Lehman Shock' (as it is termed in Japan, referring to the consequences of the bankruptcy of the US investment bank Lehman Brothers in 2008) led to another recession from mid-2008. Despite this, unemployment remained low in comparison with other OECD members. Three practices in the labour market helped to provide the flexibility required for firms to maintain employment stability. One was that non-regular workers (especially women) had a high turnover and, as non-union members, could be more readily dismissed. A second was that, in periods of strong growth, firms made heavy use of mandatory overtime and thus avoided increasing the size of their work-forces. In 1970, for example, manufacturing workers averaged 19.0 hours per month of overtime; in 1975, in the recession following the first global oil crisis, overtime decreased to 9.1 hours per month. During the 'bubble' period overtime working again rose, to 19.7 hours per month in 1990 (albeit with a shorter average working week). Work hours among salaried staff also vary, but are more difficult to measure. However, since they find it hard to claim overtime, fearing that it will damage promotion opportunities, actual hours worked are surely greater.

A final means of flexibility lay in the bonus system, under which workers received large lump-sum payments in August and again (slightly larger) in December. For government employees these are relatively standardized, at about 3.5 months per year of their basic pay (salary before a variety of routine monthly adjustments). Including such adjustments, bonuses averaged closer to three months' regular pay, or 20% of annual compensation. For larger, unionized firms these amounts were negotiated on an annual basis, co-ordinated within industries by the highly public 'spring offensive' in which annual contracts were re-negotiated. In the peak years of the 1980s profitable firms in prosperous industries could pay bonuses equivalent to as much as 11 months' pay. With the passage of time, base pay gradually rose, but the system of bonuses helped employers to restrain the increases in basic pay that would be incorporated into future wage levels. Curbing these bonuses also provided a firm with considerable ability to reduce its wage bill without dismissing workers. During 1998–2004 the average summer bonus decreased in five of those seven years and the winter payment in six. Indeed, total compensation declined during 1998–2004 and changed little in 2007. However, in 2009 the August bonus was reduced by 17%, to an average of 363,000 yen (and 710,000 yen at large firms), while the December bonus decreased by 15% to an average of 380,000 yen (and 727,000 yen at large firms). In 2010 and 2011 summer bonuses were very slightly above the (low) level of August 2009.

During the early 21st century the media publicized the implementation of job-based pay, performance-based pay and other revisions to this 'lifetime employment system' model of linking compensation to age and education. Empirical work to date has found only slight differences in compensation systems from an aggregate standpoint. Similarly, there was always considerable variation across firms relative to the 'lifetime employment' model, so case studies are at best indicative. The conclusion is that such systems are not yet pervasive, and appear to have been implemented so as not to cause disruption; the principles may be new, but practice has yet to follow. That may begin to change during the coming years; certainly there is a widening of differentials in bonuses and promotion rates amid a levelling of pay scales. During the high-growth era of the 1960s every 'lifetime' employee could expect to reach middle management. Older workers are 'grandfathered' in their lifetime employment pay trajectory, but for workers under 40 years there is a greater distinction between 'staff' and 'line' positions, both in terms of pay and promotion opportunities. However, with the number of such posts no longer expanding, that is not now possible. Today's young workers can expect future career paths very different from those of their parents, even if the economy resumes steady growth.

Education

Japan has a highly educated, literate labour force. The underlying system of education (in terms of batches of years) is '6-3-3-4', nine years of which are compulsory; in addition, 50% of three-to-five-year-olds attended pre-school programmes, most of which are privately administered. Attendance in elementary and middle schools and, increasingly, high schools was based on residence, while admission to private and élite public high schools was by examination, as was admission to university. However, with the decline in the population of 18-year-olds, from 2006 there were more university places than there were applicants and any student who desired to proceed to tertiary education could gain admission somewhere. Indeed, about 40% of students were admitted without needing to take an entrance exam, or only a perfunctory one that all passed. Overall, 58% of men and 54% of women continued their education at a two- or four-year college after high school graduation in 2009; another 22% took courses at a technical or trade school, although often on a part-time basis.

Changes in education were rapid. In 1960 only 58% of young people continued on to high school or other upper secondary programmes; by 1975 92% were doing so, and in 2006 more than 96% continued beyond middle school, almost all to regular high schools. Higher education enrolments likewise increased sharply, with slightly greater numbers of women than men obtaining education beyond high school. In 2001 only 30% of the men aged 45–54 years had completed some higher education, while 42% of younger men had done so; among women, the proportion rose from 22% of older women to 49% of younger women. More recently, interest in professional careers has risen, particularly among women, while some professions such as pharmacy now require a master's degree. In addition, with so many holding a four-year degree, there is of course a general incentive to acquire more distinctive credentials. As a result, in 2008 some 67,000 graduates (12% of the total) entered graduate school immediately after completing their college education.

The largest part of the higher education system is composed of four-year colleges; two-year colleges were in rapid decline, with a 68% reduction in enrolments between 1995 and 2009. This reflected both a decrease in the college-age population and a rapid shift in enrolment among women from two-year to four-year institutions. At a peak in 1994, 25% of women graduating from high school went on to two-year colleges, compared with 21% to four-year colleges. By 2009 those proportions had changed to 11% and 44%, respectively. About one-third of junior colleges had closed their doors by 2009.

Japan's education system comprises a mixture of public (state) and private (independent) schools. More than 99% of elementary schools were public, but the proportion of private education increased with level; 29% of high schools were private institutions in 2003 and 75% of colleges (similar figures applied in terms of the number of students). In addition, there was a wide array of 'crammer' schools directed at preparation for entrance examinations, of speciality schools and, increasingly, of continuing education programmes aimed at adults.

Various reforms were under way, driven in part by demographic changes and in part by government reorganization. The decline in births initially affected the lower end of the education system. Some 1,850 (about 8% of the total) elementary schools closed between 2000 and 2009, and the pace was accelerating. Many remote rural schools in particular now had only a very small number of children. About 4% of middle schools had also closed, and the decline in population was likewise affecting high schools. At the opposite end of the spectrum, in April 2004 the 100 former national universities were converted into non-profit educational corporations; as a result, university professors lost their civil service status. In the past the budgetary and administrative system of the Ministry of Education, Culture, Sports, Science and Technology resulted in uniformity across both private and public universities. However, government subsidies to universities were being reduced each year by 1% of their initial level; with no ability to expand enrolments, even the (former) national universities would experience intense budgetary pressures. In the short term, reform has changed little, although in principle, as newly private institutions, they will have the ability to restructure their curricula and otherwise differentiate themselves.

Alongside similar changes at the 76 universities administered by prefectures or cities, and with 595 private universities, this should lead to a wider array of choices, to match shifts in the structure of careers and changes in the economy. Hitherto, it was the less prestigious among the private universities that had difficulties maintaining enrolments, and it was the élite private universities, which had more resources and pride in their independence, that had experimented with classes conducted in English, graduate programmes aimed at those wanting to change careers and courses targeted at retirees and other non-traditional students. Such experiments will surely be extended, as institutions attempt to differentiate themselves in the contracting educational market.

However, time is running out for many universities. In 2008 new enrolments at Japan's 565 private universities declined by 1.4%, to 478,000 students, although enrolments were at a similar level in 2010. The divergence across institutions was increasing. While élite universities such as Keio and Waseda were faring better, 266 (or 47% of) private universities were unable to meet their enrolment targets, with 29 achieving less than one-half of their authorized enrolment. Since tuition fees are the major source for covering operating budgets, and government subsidies are linked to enrolments, many universities appeared fated to close their doors within a few years. Particularly affected were institutions located outside the three main metropolitan regions, but even in the major urban areas the smaller universities were finding recruiting difficult. Universities everywhere have vigorously pursued shakai-jin (adults) and foreign students, and many new graduate programmes have been introduced. Although the best-known universities have had some success thereby, these strategies have proven insufficient to offset the decline in the college-age population, and have not worked at lesser-ranked institutions.

CAPITAL MARKETS

Financial Markets

As a large, diversified economy, Japan is replete with a full range of financial institutions. There are nevertheless various distinctive features in Japanese capital markets. In common with practices in the USA and elsewhere (but unlike pre-1940 Japanese practice), financial markets were segmented; different types of banks, securities firms and insurance companies were prevented from entering each other's businesses, and were in some cases also restricted geographically. While equity markets were important in the 1950s, firms gradually developed cross-shareholdings as an anti-takeover mechanism, making the stock market less useful; after a crisis in 1963, when the largest brokerage house had to be rescued, the stock market ceased to be important. Thereafter banks dominated, both as a source of funds for business investment and as the place where households deposited their savings.

Bond markets were likewise repressed, to protect other financial institutions from competition, to make it easier for the Government to place the bonds it issued and to help the BOJ to control interest rates. During the late 1970s, however, the Japanese Government ran large budget deficits, flooding the market with bonds. By 1979 banks were no longer willing to accept them all; the Government had to deregulate the market in order to finance its deficit. As Japanese firms became better known overseas, they were also able to raise money outside Japan, while domestic growth also slowed in the 1970s; both factors lessened the demand for bank loans. Similar trends affected other organizations, and domestic financial institutions began to lobby for deregulation. A series of measures followed, ranging from the elimination of foreign-exchange controls in 1980 to the deregulation measures of 1997 known as the 'big bang', which removed limitations on bank mergers and holding companies, and otherwise made it easier to enter new lines of business. The insurance and securities industries were likewise affected.

By 2000 Japanese financial markets were market-driven, with only modest residual restrictions on their activities. They had also undergone radical change, with various new entries, mergers and exits having resulted in new participants. This change took place partly as an adjustment to the new competitive environment. In part, however, it was driven by the need to revitalize institutions damaged by the collapse of the asset 'bubble' of 1987–91, during which equity and real estate prices quadrupled after 1981 and then fell back sharply to their previous levels. Stock prices rose to a peak in December 1989, with the Nikkei 225 index at 38,915 points, and reached their nadir at 7,300 in April 2003, when they stood at just under 20% of their peak level. With the economy growing during 2002–08, prices then rose to just above the 18,000 level in June 2006. With the impact of the 'Lehman Shock' the market plummeted to below 7,600 before recovering to 11,200, by March 2010; in August the Nikkei 225 index had retreated to 9,600, and under the impact of the Tohoku earthquake and uncertainties in the USA and the EU it was at 9,000 in August 2011. Similarly, real estate prices peaked in 1991, but in the second half of 2005, for the first time in 15 years, the real estate price index for the six largest urban areas rose, as well as that for commercial and residential sub-indices. While prices increased by double-digits in some prime urban locations, the overall market remained moribund, with prices up only 0.4% in the period to June 2007. With the 'Lehman Shock', prices again declined. However, the price of land zoned for industrial use continued to decline from 1991 to June 2010, as did prices in virtually all smaller cities and rural areas (see Real Estate Markets, below). The financial sector was badly affected by the repercussions of those declines, with several major banks and securities firms failing (see Banking, below).

After 2000 major restructuring took place and, overall, this had a positive effect on the financial sector. After declining for eight consecutive years, total loans expanded in 2006, and profitability improved. (Again, that process was reversed, although only in November 2009.) Yet, from an international perspective, most Japanese financial institutions remain low in profitability; with excess capacity in many sectors and continued corporate emphasis on improving profits, the need for external finance remained modest. In the aggregate, it was thus natural that the Japanese economy as a whole operated with a large current account surplus on the balance of payments, as domestic savers sought higher returns in overseas markets.

Banking

Until the 1990s the banking system was highly segmented. At the top were 13 money-centre 'city' banks that focused on large commercial loans, with branches in major cities. There were also three long-term credit banks, seven trust banks, an array of about 180 regional banks, approximately 450 local credit unions of different types, and nearly 4,000 agricultural co-operatives. Finally, there were 24,000 post office branches, which accepted deposits but did not make loans. The 'city' banks were not allowed to expand their branch networks, and there were other restrictions to limit competition among these institutions, including a ceiling on interest rates. Banks were prohibited from engaging in non-banking businesses and generated very little fee income; their profits depended on the gross margin of their loan portfolio, almost all of which consisted of corporate borrowers. However, as a long-term investment, banks were allowed to hold equity in their customers, 40% of the unrealized capital gains of which they could count as capital.

Beginning in 1980, financial deregulation led to disintermediation, as large borrowers issued stocks, bonds and commercial paper, taking advantage of their growing reputation in international capital markets. Commercial banks, therefore, pursued new customers, particularly small businesses and consumers. The collapse of the 'bubble' left the banking system with a high level of non-performing loans (NPLs). With hindsight, it is clear that banks became heavily involved in lending to firms that used the money to speculate in property and the stock market; other customers, such as several department store chains, used the easy access to loans and bond issues to invest in new capacity that proved unprofitable. The collapse of share prices also decimated the capital of banks; unrealized capital gains turned into capital losses. This led to the failure of several major banks, including the Hokkaido Takushoku Bank and the Long-Term Credit Bank (LTCB), in a crisis in 1997, and of Resona Bank in 2003.

The bank failures of 1997 were totally unexpected by the Ministry of Finance, the main regulator, while a recession arising from inept timing of tax increases and a series of internal scandals rendered the ministry politically vulnerable. The BOJ had been indirectly controlled by the Ministry of Finance, but a June 1997 revision of its enabling legislation gave it formal independence. At the same time legislation was approved removing financial supervision responsibilities from the Ministry of Finance and giving them to a newly created Financial Supervisory Agency (FSA, now the Financial Services Agency); the FSA was also given the power to close down banks that were insolvent or had insufficient capital. The FSA promptly began a series of new bank inspections, which exposed a far higher level of NPLs than that revealed under the supervision of the Ministry of Finance, leading to the closures in 1998 of the LTCB (see below) and of The Nippon Credit Bank. As a result, the FSA issued new accounting guidelines, and began to place pressure on banks to improve the situation with regard to their bad loans. Failed banks were either nationalized or merged with other institutions, with an infusion of government funding. To strengthen the capital base of the former 'city' banks, the Government purchased subordinate debt and allowed the banks to count deferred tax credits as capital. The latter, in fact, precipitated the failure of Resona, as the bank's accountants refused to accept the profit projections used to claim such tax credits. Overall, the combination of debt purchases and tax credits meant that the Government was initially the de facto holder of the majority of the capital in several of the weaker banks.

By 2007 the initial restructuring was over, with the merger of two of the five largest banking groups in October 2005. Of the original 13 'city' banks, seven trust banks and three special debenture-issuing banks, only five institutions remained. Similar changes took place in the securities industry, as under the 'big bang' reforms financial holding companies could now include stockbrokers and related firms. The most spectacular reversal of fortune was that of the failed LTCB, which was purchased out of government receivership by Ripplewood, a US investment fund, in 2000. The bank was renamed Shinsei, and the new management team rapidly dealt with the remaining bad loans, reorganized its retail operations, replaced its outdated mainframe-based IT system and otherwise improved operations. By the mid-2000s it had become the most profitable bank in Japan in terms of return on assets, and the original investment group in 2004 was able to sell a 35% stake for 250,000m. yen, a tremendous return in relation to their initial investment of about 100,000m. yen. As a small bank with a weak domestic customer base, it was one of the Japanese banks most heavily affected by the 2008/09 global financial crisis. One other small institution, the Nippon Credit Bank, was also bought by private investors, to be re-launched as Aozora Bank (changing its name in January 2001), in a successful, but less spectacular, reversal of fortunes. It, too, suffered after 2008, and Shinsei sought a merger with Aozora, unsuccessfully as of August 2011.

The remaining three banking groups are far larger (with Resona a distant fourth in size and profitability). Management devoted attention to the task of absorbing formerly rival institutions, discharging NPLs that were much larger in sheer number—hence harder to handle in a bureaucratic operation—and trying to incorporate new sorts of businesses into a coherent structure. The largest of these, the Bank of Tokyo-Mitsubishi, absorbed the failing UFJ banking group in January 2006, to become Mitsubishi UFJ Financial Group (MUFG). With 206,000,000m. yen in assets in March 2011 (equivalent to 38% of Japan's GDP), it became the world's largest financial group. To give a perspective of the extent of mergers, Mitsubishi Bank began by absorbing the Bank of Tokyo in 2005. UFJ, in turn, was the product of a 2001 merger of Sanwa Bank, Tokai Bank and Toyo Trust. MUFG eventually acquired Mitsubishi Trust, Japan Trust, Tokyo Trust, and Tokai Trust; securities firms and stockbrokers consolidated as Mitsubishi UFJ Securities and Kabu Dot Com Securities; the credit card companies UFJ Card, NICOS and DC Card; Acom, a consumer finance company with 1,800,000m. yen in assets; and leasing and other financial subsidiaries. In October 2008 it also purchased 21% of Morgan Stanley for US $9,000m., absorbing the latter's stock-broking and fund management activities in Japan. While less dramatic, the other two 'megabanks', Mizuho Financial Group (161,000,000m. yen in assets) and Mitsu Sumitomo Financial Group (138,000,000m. in assets) also grew through mergers. In the background was the JPB, with 193,000,000m. yen in assets.

Alongside these are 105 regional banks; an array of new internet and other specialized banks that permit retailers such as Aeon and Seven & I to issue credit cards and participate in e-money; 271 Shinkin credit associations for local small businesses; 158 credit unions; agricultural co-operatives that are under the supervision of the Norinchukin Bank; and a small number of similar labour and fisheries co-operatives with their associated semi-governmental banks. There has been substantial restructuring in this sector. For example, there were about 380 credit unions in 1990, but subsequently there were 188 bankruptcies and 93 mergers, including institutions that failed and then merged. Similarly there have been mergers among regional banks, both by institutions that failed and were merged into other banks, and by strong regional banks that used mergers proactively to strengthen their position. At least six of these are in fact sizeable operations, a rank below the former 'city' banks; Yokohama Bank, for example, had 10,500,000m. yen in assets at the end of 2010. These large regional banks are well-capitalized, profitable, and operate internationally and not just domestically. They have a strong position, lending to smaller firms, and enjoy better lending margins. Indeed, the regional banks are gaining share in the lending market, while total lending by the 'megabanks' was declining in 2011. Even five that had been experiencing difficulties succeeded in repaying government emergency loans, while two that had been delisted from the Tokyo Stock Exchange were able to relist. About one-half of the regional banks continued to have problems in 2011; two mergers were under way but not yet completed, and a dozen more were rumoured to be under consideration. In the aggregate, NPLs declined from 9% at the end of the 1990s to 3.2% in September 2010 and were continuing to decrease. Regional banks in the Tohoku region were expected to encounter problems because many of their borrowers were affected directly by the earthquake in March 2011, or indirectly by declines in their businesses; government policy concerning those institutions was still being formulated later in the year.

Change will continue as Japan remains 'over-banked' and as borrowers become more diverse and more sophisticated in their financing needs. It is likely that the market for traditional bank loans will decline, not increase; indeed, personal loans (including home mortgages) were the only consistent area of growth during 2007–10. While individual institutions may fare better than average, the banking system as a whole must be reduced in size by perhaps one-third. Complicating this was the privatization of Japan's postal savings system, the world's largest financial institution in terms of deposits, and also the largest seller of life insurance. Launched in October 2007, with 182,746,000m. yen in deposits (one-sixth of all household financial assets) the JPB initially surpassed even Japan's three 'megabanks'. The JPB had a branch in every post office, all of which opened for longer hours than banks; it also had the largest network of automatic teller machines and no tax obligations. It had long provided 'unfair' competition to commercial financial institutions by offering terms to depositors that could not be matched. However, historically it was prohibited from making standard bank loans. Instead, its funds were invested through the FILP or used to buy government bonds; the JPB received greater freedom in allocating its assets as an institutional investor, but was still prevented from offering loans.

Whether it would prove competent in areas where it had no experience was open to doubt; the new management appeared to share those fears and was proceeding cautiously. One of its first ventures was an alliance with the regional Suruga Bank, known for its skills in mortgage lending; the alliance provided an instant nation-wide expansion for Suruga and a new competitor in Japan's 100,000,000m.-yen mortgage market. The privatization itself reflected banks' tarnished reputation, for they opposed it politically, as had leading members of the DPJ, which at that time was in opposition to the LDP Prime Minister Koizumi, who championed privatization. Indeed, the goal was not to provide the banks with a new competitor, but to lessen the role of the post office in politics, as most branches were operated on a contract basis, a potent source of patronage. Privatization would also make it harder for the Government to finance public works projects without scrutiny.

Other components of the banking sector underwent various degrees of restructuring. This included the reduction of operations of an array of specialized government banks, such as the effective closure of the Export-Import Bank of Japan and the merger in 2008 of several government small-business financial institutions into the Japan Finance Corporation, and restrictions on the operations for the Housing Loan Finance Corporation. At the same time a boom in mergers and acquisitions created a need for investment bankers and other specialists for which in the past there had been little or no market. Similarly, there were new entries into trust banking, as foreign securities firms expanded their operations from Japan. In the other direction, increased competition from banks (including through their role as credit card issuers) in personal loans, combined with tighter restrictions on lending practices, eroded the market for personal finance companies: these factors, together with a ruling that required them to refund excessive interest charges, meant that such companies began to incur heavy losses. As a result, the industry effectively collapsed, with firms bought up by one or another bank.

Insurance

Insurers in Japan were also segmented, into life insurance, casualty insurance and special insurance. From the 1960s life insurers in particular were an important source of long-term funds to business, partially compensating for the underdeveloped bond market; they were also able to offer 'whole' life insurance policies to individuals with higher after-tax interest rates than banks were allowed to give. As a result, the sector was unusually large, accounting for 216,100,000m. yen (having decreased by 6% since 2006) or 26.8% of household financial assets as of June 2009, although by various criteria insurance peaked in 1995. In addition, consumers held 181,400,000m. yen (up by 8% since 2006) or 22.6% of their assets with insurance companies in the form of annuities and trust funds. As long-term lenders and borrowers, life insurers also suffered from the effects of the 'bubble': having promised high returns to policy-purchasers, they were then caught by the decrease in the value of their shareholdings and by the very low interest rates that followed stimulative monetary policy (see Recent Macroeconomic Issues, below), and also had non-performing loans. In addition, there was competition from the now-privatized postal life insurance system. While some small insurers failed, the larger life insurers were able to resort to a previously unused legislative provision that permitted them unilaterally to lower the contracted rate of return. In effect, policy-holders were being forced to absorb the losses incurred by life insurers. Meanwhile, insurers reduced their writing of new policies—and, with lower interest rates, consumers curbed their purchases—so that the total value of policies outstanding decreased by 28% during 2000–08. In addition, the largest life insurers had been mutuals, owned by policyholders; they have been converting into regular companies and listing their shares on the Tokyo Stock Exchange, which has made it much easier for them to raise capital. The claims resulting from the Tohoku earthquake were not expected to impair their operations to a significant extent. Casualty insurers are generally sound, with profits coming in particular from car insurance. They will be required to meet some claims resulting from the earthquake, but many policies excluded earthquake and flood damage, while the Government was to provide general assistance to help cover losses in the Tohoku region. Neither they nor global reinsurers appear likely to suffer major problems affecting their businesses.

Equities

The Tokyo Stock Exchange (TSE) was founded in 1878. The largest futures exchange is in Osaka, near the site of the futures market that had operated from 1720. Securities trading thus has a long history, but the colourful floor exchange disappeared in 1997 when an electronic trading system took over the matching of buyers and sellers. As of December 2010, some 1,670 firms were listed on the TSE First Section, 450 on the Second Section and 185 on the related 'Mothers' over-the-counter market for smaller firms, all, except a few dozen, domestic ones. In addition, there were smaller Jasdaq and Hercules markets, aimed at small, high-growth companies, which merged in October 2010 to form the New Jasdaq exchange, with about 1,400 companies listed. Alongside stocks, the TSE trades real estate investment trusts (REITS) and a variety of other products, including a range of options, futures and bonds. While the TSE promotes its own 'TOPIX' index, the most widely followed measure is the Nikkei 225 Average. Reflecting the 'bubble' and Japan's economic problems during the 1990s, a long-term investor who had put money in the market in August 1983 would have only just turned a profit in August 2011, almost three decades later. In the shorter term, investors who had bought shares in early 2003 or early 2009 would have made money; the post-'bubble' market nadir was 7,831, in April 2003. The TSE is smaller than other major markets, with a total value of domestic shares of 288,800,000m. yen at the end of June 2010. Trading was moderate, with an average daily turnover of 1,538,000m. yen in the financial year 2009; in August 2011 trading volume was similar, at 1,600,000m. yen.

Given the decline in valuations, in 2011 the market was much smaller than at its peak in 1989; correspondingly, the shareholdings of Japanese households declined from 14% of the total in 1990 to 6% in 2003 and 7.9% in March 2009. Another 6.6% was in investment trusts and hence indirectly in the market; this was also a sharp decrease, from 14% at the height of the 'bubble'. This, of course, badly affected the brokerage sector. Yamaichi Securities, the dominant firm from the 1920s until the early 1960s, failed in 1997; despite scandals, the leading company, Nomura Securities, survived the collapse of the market (and avoided major losses during 2008/09). Overall, the leading three domestic firms had lost market share; they accounted for some 26% of the Tokyo market in 2005, down from 50% in 1990, while bank-related, internet and foreign brokers gained. Foreign firms performed particularly well in bond trading and derivatives as well as in mergers and acquisitions, an area where the restructuring of many industries had created new businesses; they were also experienced in selling to non-residents, who were now major investors in the Tokyo market, accounting for one-third of the value of trading in 2009. Furthermore, with an average yield of 2.0% in June 2010, Japanese stocks are unusually attractive, given the low yield of Japanese government bonds (under 1%) and many foreign bonds. However, problems of the parent companies of foreign firms have already led to the sale of the Japan operations of Citigroup and Morgan Stanley to Japanese firms, which in the process acquired critical human capital. An even bigger change was at Nomura Securities, which purchased the overseas assets of Lehman Brothers in October 2008, immediately gaining a place as one of the major global trading houses.

Another major change came with the evolution of pension funds and foreign investors. Since the mid-1990s firms had shifted from making lump-sum retirement payments to providing pensions. The operation of such funds became a major new business, and one that continues to grow. Foreign firms again possess expertise in this area, contributing to their inroads into the Tokyo market; two of the principal five book-makers were foreign-owned, as were three of the leading five mergers and acquisitions advisers. In the 1980s banks and life insurers were the largest shareholders in the Tokyo market; in 1988 foreigners held only 5% of shares, households 20% and financial institutions 45%. This frequently took the form of cross-shareholdings, where the bank that was the largest lender to a company would own the biggest block of its shares, and that company would, in turn, hold a block of the bank's stock. Together with cross-shareholdings by non-financial companies, some 40% of all shares had thus effectively been kept off the market. During the first decade of the 21st century the level of bank shareholdings declined sharply, as banks sold equities to improve their balance sheets; as of March 2011 the percentage held by financial institutions had decreased to below 30%, and the number of frozen shares had declined to under 20%.

As yet no hostile takeovers had succeeded, but several attempts were made, and the threat was changing the behaviour of at least some managers. In the Oji Paper case of August 2006 (with, it should be noted, a Japanese investment bank as adviser) the target firm readily accepted the terms offered. Similarly, in the Pentax/Hoya case, the willingness of shareholders to take account of the views of outside investors led to a 'friendly' takeover tinged with hostility (see Manufacturing, above). While pension funds remained a smaller share of the market than in the USA or the United Kingdom, they represented a growth of outside investors that was causing managers to pay more attention to shareholders.

Real Estate Markets

Property markets, like stocks, were central to the 1987–91 'bubble'. During the period leading up to 1991 real estate prices had never declined, bolstered by strong economic growth and the process of urbanization. Like those of stocks, urban land prices roughly quadrupled during the 'bubble' period, affecting almost all major cities. However, in contrast to the stock market, prices in most of the country continued to decline long after the 'bubble' burst. Across the country as a whole prices at the end of 2009 were 41.5% of their 1991 peak. Prices for land in the three major urban areas rose much more during the 'bubble', before reaching a nadir of 24% of their peak in 2005. They then rose during 2006–08, and even with a 9.6% decline in 2009 were still 12% above the lowest point at that time. The 'bubble' did not just affect prices, it also led to the construction of many new office buildings and of studio flats or 'one-room mansions' (condominiums), as well as numerous golf courses and other resorts. This burdened the market with excess capacity, while (in the case of bankrupt golf courses) later providing select opportunities for entrepreneurs to build new housing developments. Local governments likewise sponsored all kinds of projects, often quite grandiose, from amusement parks in remote Kyushu to bay-side roads, bridges and commercial space in Tokyo and Yokohama.

More positive was a series of major urban redevelopments in the 2000s, such as Roppongi Hills, Shiodome in Tokyo, office towers over Nagoya station, and new projects in central Osaka. These were based either on former railway goods yards, sold with the privatization of the national railway network, or as the culmination of redevelopment projects that over the course of the 1970s and 1980s had accumulated blocks of older housing and office buildings that could be razed to make way for modern buildings. Rents in such convenient locations began rising in 2004, offering some hope that the decline in real estate prices would moderate, and in 2006 average prices in Osaka and Tokyo began to rise; that movement spread to suburban areas in the two biggest metropolitan regions, and to the Nagoya region and the central or downtown areas in a number of other major cities. This was enough to raise average prices for the country as a whole, albeit by a mere 0.4%. However, with the population contracting and with slim prospects for vigorous economic growth, new household formation or further urbanization, it is hard to envisage prices rising much, or stopping their decline in rural areas. Indeed, by 2010 residential vacancy rates were at 13% (7.6m. units); in rural areas many houses seem to have been simply abandoned.

Yet renovation remains an ongoing opportunity, and was emphasized in the 2010 Economic White Paper. There are also modest shifts in residential patterns. In the early 21st century about one-half of the metropolitan Tokyo population lived in housing that was more than 25 years old, but both the size and quality of construction had improved in the interim, and most older housing did not meet the building code renovations introduced following the Kobe earthquake in 1995. At the same time, the average dwelling size had risen to 120.9 sq m (1,300 sq feet), 19% above the average of 1978, while in the interim the size of the average household also contracted. Similarly, the shift to car-based shopping in suburban and rural areas contributed to a revolution in retailing, again leading to new construction, while new regulations permitted the construction of residential skyscrapers; as of late 2008 some 572,000 households lived in buildings with 15 or more floors, with few constructed before the 2000s. As a consequence, there was a small increase in population in and around urban centres, with people moving back in, and a construction boom in condominiums in nearby suburbs, aimed at couples in their thirties, as the closing of older factories and warehouses made tracts of land available within relatively easy commuting distance. As the population ages, such shifts in residential choice, combined with the growth of suburban shopping malls and roadside restaurants, and the continued decline in rural areas and manufacturing and agriculture, will gradually change Japan's economic geography.

Foreign Exchange

In the background to the trading aspect of Japan's economy were foreign-exchange markets and trade policy. From 1980 Japan had a freely floating exchange rate, with a full array of the futures, options and swaps that kept markets deep and liquid. In April 2010, according to the triennial survey of the BIS, 19% of the US $4,000,000m. daily turnover in foreign-exchange markets involved the Japanese yen. In such trading it ranked third, after the US dollar and the euro, but ahead of the United Kingdom's pound sterling. However, the Tokyo market itself accounted for only 6% of foreign-exchange trading and an even smaller share of derivatives; London, the capital and financial centre of the United Kingdom, dominated these markets.

Japanese foreign-exchange rates were volatile over time. From April 1949 until the collapse of the Bretton Woods system in August 1971 the rate was fixed at 360 yen per US dollar. It was at the 240 yen level in the first half of the 1980s, before appreciating steadily until it reached 80 yen per dollar in April 1995. It then depreciated to 146 yen in June 1998, oscillating between 100 and 120 yen for most of 1999–2007. From April 2007 it then appreciated steadily to peak at 76 yen per dollar in July 2011. Following a major multilateral intervention in foreign exchanges markets on 4 August, the first intervention since 2004, the yen briefly depreciated to 80.2 yen per dollar, but by the next day was back at 78.4 and two days later was at 76.5, near its record high level.

However, this description exaggerates the changes, because Japan trades with countries that use many currencies that move independently of the dollar. In addition, domestic deflation can lower costs and make it easier to export, effectively causing the yen to depreciate. So, as discussed in the introductory section above, the BIS trade-weighted, inflation-adjusted real effective exchange rate index provides a better approximation of the impact on the overall economy. Setting the index at its average 2005 value at 100, the yen appreciated by 56% between 1990 and 1995, before falling back to 100 in mid-1998. By the end of 1999 the currency had depreciated again, by 35%, to reach 148, then appreciated to a high point of 84 in July 2007. In June 2011 it was back at 101. Overall, the real value of the yen was thus about the same as in the mid-2000s, and near its average over the past 25 years, despite large variations in the nominal yen-dollar rate.

Over the short term such movements in exchange rates were dominated by changing trends in capital flows. Given low nominal interest rates (and typically low real returns) inside Japan, relative to those in the USA and elsewhere, purchases of foreign assets by Japanese residents dominated. During 2007 gross monthly Japanese purchases of foreign assets reached as high as 10,030,000m. yen (and a net flow, given purchases of Japanese assets, of 7,450,000m. yen), primarily of bonds. However, the financial crisis led to the repatriation of investments, while non-residents sought the comparative safety of Japan, with net inflows after July 2008 rising to 2,380,000m. yen in December. This shift in net outflows, from 37,240,000m. yen in 2007 to 9,960,000m. yen in 2009, lay behind the appreciation of the yen. While there will be some volatility in flows in the aftermath of the earthquake of March, the comparative loss of confidence in the euro and the US dollar in 2011, owing to fiscal problems, increases the attractiveness of yen assets, and may keep the yen from depreciating.

Consistent with this and the large trade surpluses over the previous two decades, Japan had accumulated a huge amount of foreign assets: as of June 2010 official reserves stood at US $1,050,000m. or approximately 90,000,000m. yen. The foreign financial assets of banks and other financial institutions are hard to estimate, but it appears that at the end of 2008 Japanese investors had a gross position of 519,200,000m. yen. (107% of GDP); net of liabilities and foreign holdings of Japanese assets, a position of 185,300,000m. yen (37% of GDP) was recorded.

While the bulk of these assets was in bonds, and was invested in the markets in the USA and the EU, foreign direct investment (FDI) was an important sub-category. Annual direct investment through the establishment or purchase of overseas operations averaged 3,760,000m. yen during 2000–04, but then rose to an average 5,400,000m. yen in 2005–06, increasing to 13,200,000m. yen in 2008, before declining by one-half in 2009. As with portfolio investment, North America and the EU were the primary destinations, but by 2006 Japanese firms had invested 3,600,000m. yen in China, 1,800,000m. yen in Thailand and 1,300,000m. yen in South Korea. While they lagged behind US and EU firms for a long time in expanding into China, there are now more Japanese FDI ventures there than in any other single country. Between the late 1990s and 2006 Japanese firms invested 2,600,000m. yen in electrical equipment operations in China, 1,800,000m. yen in the automotive industry and 1,200,000m. yen in financial institutions. However, such activity was visible in almost every country, and the value of investments in developed countries remained larger than that in the developing world. In the USA, for example, in 2010 several Japanese automobile companies were building or had just completed new assembly plants (Toyota had 16 major North American factories and extensive design and research facilities), while Mitsubishi UFJ Financial Group acquired Union Bank of California in August 2008. Unusually, FDI into Japan has been lower, in part a legacy of past restrictions, and more recently owing to the poor performance of the economy. Foreign firms were nevertheless also active in Japan; Coca-Cola, McDonalds and IBM were all leaders in their segments, while in 2007 there were 309 foreign merger and acquisition transactions in Japan (an increase of more than 50% over the previous peak), their value totalling 3,000,000m. yen.

FDI of this type is highly visible, and probably brings far greater benefits to the host country than financial investment, both through the transfer of technology and by increasing local competition. In the 1960s and 1970s Japan's FDI was concentrated in natural resource development; during the 'bubble' FDI extended to 'trophy' real estate holdings such as the Rockefeller Center in New York City and the Pebble Beach Golf Club in California—both of which were later sold at a loss. However, since then one-half of Japanese FDI has been in manufacturing, and much of the remainder in services. Collecting data is difficult, but a regular survey by the Ministry of Economy, Trade and Industry that offers comparability across time shows the number of foreign operating subsidiaries increasing from 3,600 in 1977 to 13,200 in 1997 and 16,400 in 2006, representing a 24% increase in the preceding decade. Sales rose even faster, up 55% in the 10 years to 2006, with the majority of the increase in manufacturing. These operations employed an estimated 4.6m. workers outside Japan, with total sales of US $1,600,000m. The transport equipment sector alone accounted for 1.1m., while 300,000 worked in wholesale trades, and 137,000 in the rapidly expanding retail sector. About 17% of production by Japanese manufacturers took place outside Japan; for Honda, that ratio was more than 50%.

One issue is that while the aggregate amount of investment and income are both large, the return on investment remains low in comparison to that earned by US and European investors. Portfolio investment has concentrated on bonds, which generate lower returns. On FDI Japan earns a return of about 8% on average, up from 4% in 2000 but still well below the 12%–14% earned by US multinationals. In China, Japanese companies reported a return of about 5% on investment in 2007; US firms reported a 21% return. This could be partly attributed to the fact that many major Japanese projects had only recently been completed, while US ones were already in operation. Nevertheless, a lower rate of return has been characteristic of Japanese investment for at least two decades, both at home and abroad.

RECENT MACROECONOMIC ISSUES

As of mid-2010, Japan was just emerging from what might be termed the 'Toyota Recession'. Unlike in the USA and the EU, no Japanese financial institutions had failed, and domestic capital markets otherwise remained calm. Instead, the proximate cause was the inventory cycle, exacerbated by a decline in residential and commercial investment. Japan's domestic economy expanded during the overseas 'bubble' owing to robust exports; firms, particularly manufacturers of consumer durables and related investment goods, increased production and investment. However, consumer durables and production equipment, directly or indirectly the core of Japan's exports, are quite sensitive to business conditions. In this case, reflecting production and logistics lead times, and undue optimism about the depth of the recessions overseas, firms continued shipping goods even after sales started decreasing in the USA. Customers—for Toyota, its dealership networks in the USA and the EU—thus ended up with extra inventory as sales declined, and stopped ordering. Exports plummeted and firms were forced to curtail or stop production in Japan; Toyota closed most of its factories for 11 days in early 2009. Then, once overseas customers had pared their inventory levels—and in addition when sales increased—they began ordering again. That led to a sharp recovery in output to restore inventories, which then weakened in 2010 because overseas demand failed fully to return to previous levels. The result was a classic V-shaped recession.

In the background lies macroeconomic policy. Modest budget increases, the elimination of high school tuition fees and cash rebates to taxpayers provided a boost. However, the Government was ambiguous in its response: the trend towards paring public works continued, while talk of doubling consumption tax from 5% to 10% undermined confidence. Monetary policy was similarly restrained, or rather constrained: entering the recession interest rates were already at 0.5%, and while the BOJ decreased its 'call rate' to 0.1%, there was little room for further reduction; indeed, because deflation also increased, real interest rates actually rose. Over time the decline in the working-age population should combine with modest growth to bring down unemployment and then boost wages and consumption. Eventually, therefore, there were no obvious sources to provide for growth of more than 1.5% in 2011.

Monetary Policy

The BOJ is in charge of monetary policy, with decisions made by the nine-member Monetary Policy Board; its decisions are highly transparent, with meetings every four weeks and English-language minutes released five weeks later. Until about 1980 the BOJ operated by setting short-term interest rates supported by the direct lending of reserves and unofficial 'window guidance' to the 13 'city' (national) banks; these reserves were then traded in the overnight call market with regional banks, credit associations and credit unions. Since 1980 it has operated as do the other central banks in the OECD countries, through open market operations, buying and selling short-term government bonds.

In response to the second oil price crisis, in 1980 the BOJ raised interest rates to 9%, but slow growth and low inflation in the mid-1980s led it to reduce rates to 5% in October 1983, and to begin lowering rates again from early 1986 to a then post-war record low level of 2.5% by early 1987. The BOJ did not raise rates again until 1989, at which point the 'bubble' was well under way, and continued to raise them, to 6% in mid-1990. While it began reducing rates from July 1991, it did so only gradually, to 0.5% in September 1995, despite recession, declining asset prices and the onset of deflation. Finally, it implemented its zero interest rate policy (ZIRP) during 1999–2000 and then again from 2001. The BOJ also engaged in 'quantitative easing' in 2001–06, which expanded base money from 15% to 85% of GDP. Under normal circumstances this would have been presumed to lead to high inflation; instead, it had no visible impact. At the time many prominent monetary economists outside Japan (including Ben Bernanke, Chairman of the US Federal Reserve System) derided the BOJ as incompetent for its failure to halt the economy's slide into deflation; when their turn came, with the 2008–09 financial crisis, other central banks were more aggressive, but equally ineffective. With impaired balance sheets and dismal job prospects, firms were simply unwilling to borrow; instead, they focused on repaying debt, and were still running surpluses net of investment of 6% of GDP in 2010, offsetting the decline in aggregate household savings induced by population ageing.

Consumer prices rose in 2006, and other price indices also moderated or turned to increases. The BOJ voted in July to raise the target call rate from 0% to 0.25% per year, and the discount rate that it charged on its own loans from 0.25% to 0.4%. The central bank made a second small increase in February 2007, to 0.50% for the call rate, and to 0.75% for the discount rate. This therefore seemed to be the end of the zero interest rate policy. With hindsight, the BOJ's assumption that deflation had ended was premature, as by April 2009 the economy had slipped back into deflation. Japan has now returned to its zero interest rate policy, and has pledged to keep rates at zero until deflation has ended. Of course, with deflation cash gains value, lessening the attractiveness of purchasing real estate or corporate securities. Even with bank corporate lending rates at 1.0%–1.5% in August 2011, the decline in the prices that companies can charge for their products means that money is not sufficiently cheap to encourage investment that might boost growth. With households understandably cautious (particularly retirees with limited savings and modest pensions), and trade intermittent, the Government has been left to deal with the situation—or not.

Fiscal Policy

Unlike monetary policy, there is no single measure for the stance of fiscal policy. Standardized budget deficits, such as the primary balance metric used by OECD, correct for the impact of one-off factors to isolate the impact of policy changes. Tax revenues also decline when growth is low. (Japan's welfare and unemployment systems are not generous, so expenditures do not automatically rise, unlike in most of the OECD countries.) However, there are also rising expenditures on retirement pensions and health care that could be predicted a decade in advance, but which the Government has deliberately not offset by increasing revenue, even during the period of rising expenditure. In practice all three factors have played a role in Japan: weak growth has led to reduced revenues, population ageing has boosted expenditures, while policy changes (tax reductions and particularly public works projects) have been used to boost the economy.

By those criteria, fiscal policy has been expansive. According to OECD, for example, the primary balance, which ignores various one-off factors, declined from a surplus in 1992 to deficits of 7% of GDP by 2000. Deficits were reduced during the extended period of growth in 2005–08, but then rose sharply to 8% of GDP in 2009 and 8.5% in 2010, and were estimated by the IMF at 9% in 2011, before supplemental budgets. Expenditures on infrastructure projects increased sharply from just under 6% of GDP in 1991 to 9% of GDP in 1997. Despite continued slow growth, concerns about the size of the deficit and corruption tied to public works led to restraint, with expenditures declining steadily to below 4% in 2006 and to nearly 3% in 2008. Public works and other expenditures were included in 12 supplementary stimulus 'packages' during the decade after 1991. These included many accounting devices that disguised the fact that the actual size of the stimulus measures was much smaller than proclaimed, reducing the credibility of these policies. Nevertheless, econometric studies suggest that such expenditures were effective; they were simply too small to make much difference. In late 2011 and 2012, however supplementary budgets for reconstruction and the evacuation costs for residents near the Fukushima nuclear plant (damaged by the earthquake and tsunami of March 2011) were expected to double public investment and cause measured deficits to exceed 10% of GDP. Those amounts will be large enough to boost growth from perhaps a decline of 1% over the entirety of 2011 to a 3% increase in 2012.

Complicating the response to the earthquake has been the shift in attitudes across the developed world towards deficits. (Politically, fiscal constraint also enhances the power of the Ministry of Finance over the rest of the bureaucracy, as it is this ministry that draws up budgets.) First, all serious plans for stabilizing the budget through tax increases have been deferred; while leaders of both parties continued to debate the matter privately, the July 2010 electoral losses following Prime Minister Kan's inexplicable decision to discuss tax increases just prior to voting will make politicians loath to discuss the subject until there is strong growth. Instead, deficits were expected to rise as corporate income tax receipts decline owing to the impact of the earthquake on production, perhaps by 2% of GDP. Meanwhile the 'baby boomers' are retiring, increasing pension and health care expenditures, boosted further by an increase in the government share of national pension premiums. A series of stimulus measures have added to that, including in April 2009 a programme worth about 0.6% of GDP, transfers to local governments of 0.5% of GDP, employment support of 0.4% of GDP and other measures that were expected to raise total expenditures in 2009/10 by about 2.6% of GDP (and in 2010/11 by 2.2% of GDP) above their pre-recession 2007/08 levels. Recent additions included a lowering or elimination of highway tolls, the elimination of high-school tuition fees, child benefits and, following the earthquake of March 2011, reconstruction expenditures, although the first supplementary budget of 4,000,000m. yen in April, net of reductions in other expenditures, was under 1% of GDP, while the second supplementary budget, including provisions to cover debts of companies put out of business by the earthquake, was an even more modest 1,000,000m. yen (0.2% of GDP).

The primary constraint on fiscal policy is the accumulation of government debt. As noted above, Japan's debt is the highest in OECD, and in the aftermath of the Greek debt crisis of early 2010 it was natural to ask whether Japan might be next. That did not prove to be the case, and in the short term there is no need for fiscal constraint. The best evidence for that is provided by the interest rates on 10-year Japanese government bonds, which in August 2010 had a yield of under 1%, and were still at that level one year later, while short-term interest rates remained below 0.1%. Financial markets want more government bonds, not fewer. There are several reasons for this. First, in the short term banks and pension funds have nowhere else to go. None of Japan's debt is denominated in a foreign currency, and only 5% is held by non-residents. There is no channel through which problems in European or US financial markets can directly affect Japan. Second, there is no immediate risk of a 'meltdown'. With short-term interest rates near 0%, debt imposes very low budgetary costs; indeed, in the 2010 budget interest expenses were expected to be below the level of the early 2000s despite the expansion of debt by the equivalent of an additional 30% of GDP. Third, domestic savings continue to outstrip domestic investment; Japan does not need to turn to international capital markets to sell its bonds. While that could change with an eventual increase in interest rates, at present the average maturity is about 5.8 years, so that a shift in borrowing costs would only gradually affect budgets. Indeed, while rates are low the Government is shifting towards issuing more long-term bonds. Fourth, debt holders have few other assets to which they could switch. In view of the low demand for loans, banks therefore hold bonds. Finally, the Government itself holds one-half of all debt. While indirectly portions are owed to the general public, such as depositors of the JPB, in practical terms those bonds are not subject to sale. At mid-2011 debt net of government holdings was 11% of GDP, using IMF data, not 216%.

Nevertheless, while there is no special threshold, debt cannot increase faster than GDP indefinitely; because the accumulation of debt makes eventual adjustment more difficult, it is also better to begin sooner rather than later. However, with underlying growth dynamics low, the budgetary adjustments also ought to be phased in over the better part of a decade. The Government, for example, discussed doubling the consumption tax, from 5% to 10% in one increase; the IMF and outside estimates suggest the eventual level needs to be at least 15%, or a 10% boost. It would be better instead to raise it by 1.0 points every six months for five years, until the later target is reached.

The arithmetic of that target is as follows. Given net debt of 100% of GDP, an increase in interest rates by 1% would eventually require adding 1% of GDP to the budget to cover payments; as noted above, because only about one-fifth of the debt becomes due each year, the impact would not be immediate. Stabilizing debt levels will thus require running a budget surplus adequate to pay interest without borrowing additional money. If the economy grows in nominal terms at 3% while interest rates are at 4%, then that net interest burden is 1%. Even using the 200% gross debt level, paying that 1% adds up to only 2% of GDP, clearly within the realm of feasible tax increases. However, since the starting point is one of deficit, about another 4%–5% of GDP in revenues is needed (with 4% disappearing as tax revenues rise with economic recovery: regular tax receipts, for example, were down by about 10% in 2010 compared with 2005). Additional revenues to cover the expenses of an ageing population (optimistically) require another 2%; if these increases are added together, the total is 10%. More realistically, retirement costs will add 8%, even with an extension of the retirement age used for pension calculations that would reflect the longevity of Japan's population. That will mean a consumption tax level of near 20%, in line with the various national sales and value-added taxes of Canada and Europe. The politics are difficult, but it is clearly a level that is tractable from an economic perspective if implemented gradually; and since there is no likelihood of crisis, there is no need for sudden increases.

PROSPECTS FOR FUTURE GROWTH

Data released in August 2011 show that Japan's population declined by 827,000 in the year ending 31 March 2011, despite net immigration of 23,000 (lower than in recent years owing to the earthquake). The population aged 24–65 was expected to decline by about 1% per annum in the years to 2015 as the 'baby boomers' retire, which would reduce the number of workers per retiree from the current level of 3:1 to 1.5:1 by 2050. Even if the Government undertook policies that might succeed in boosting fertility and increasing immigration, such yet-to-be-born youth would not start entering the labour force until 2030 at the earliest. There were already 600,000 Chinese, 300,000 Brazilians and 200,000 Filipinos in Japan by the end of 2007, and it is no longer unusual to find that a waitress or supermarket check-out operator speaks with a foreign accent. Yet such immigrants tend to be lower in productivity than native-born workers, and have dependants. With a working-age population that will decline by 600,000 per year, the requisite number of immigrants would be very large. Greater participation by women in the labour force will help, but because the number of women in the labour market is already large (and the increases are among younger women, who are fewer in number), that can only partially offset population decline.

Japan's labour force was thus likely to continue to contract in the indefinite future. As a result, without a productivity revolution, the economy will grow at an annual rate of 1% or less through the middle of the century. Fiscal adjustments, if mishandled, would depress growth to an even lower level; failing to make fiscal adjustment would eventually be even more disruptive. However, with a declining labour force, even slow growth through modest productivity increases and additions to the capital stock would be sufficient to boost workers' wages.

However, no modern economy has undergone this sort of population decline. Manufacturers will encounter smaller markets, and retailers will find it harder to justify upgrading their physical facilities. To give one example, with fewer young people, the number of skiers is decreasing. While several ski resorts have closed, there is on average lower capacity utilization and lower productivity. As noted above, new retail formats have higher productivity, but their positive impact is subdued by the slow exit of old and less efficient retailers. Without growth, higher-productivity firms can expand only if other enterprises contract, and firms are reluctant to leave the market; simply outgrowing rivals will not be enough. Yet, despite such challenges, as noted in the section on retailing above, there remain areas of dynamism. Ultimately, Japan will continue to be a large and overall prosperous economy—but not an economy that is growing significantly.

Short-term prospects are more positive. Manufacturing output increased sharply in June 2011, as automotive firms added shifts to try to rebuild inventories. The poor performance of the US and European economies, and slower growth in China, were expected to restrain the increase later in the year, but in the mean time exports increased as firms attempted to improve on levels of shipments that had been lower in the period March–June. Reconstruction spending was increasing in the second half of the year, and consumers who had held back in March and April were now more willing to spend. Both will keep the economy growing as the contribution of exports diminishes. These dynamics may not persist until the end of 2013, but together they should maintain growth throughout the whole of 2012.

Statistical Survey

Source (unless otherwise stated): Statistics Bureau and Statistics Center, 2-1-2, Kasumigaseki, Chiyoda-ku, Tokyo 100-8926; tel. (3) 5253-5111; fax (3) 3504-0265; e-mail webmaster@stat.go.jp; internet www.stat.go.jp.

Area and Population

AREA, POPULATION AND DENSITY

Area (sq km)	377,944*
Hokkaido district	83,457
Honshu district	231,112
Shikoku district	18,792
Kyushu district	42,190
Okinawa district	2,276
Population (census results)†	
1 October 2005	
Males	62,348,977
Females	65,419,017
Total	127,767,994
1 October 2010 (preliminary)	128,056,026
Population (official estimate at 1 July) 2011‡	127,920,000
Density (per sq km) at 1 July 2011	338.5

* 145,925 sq miles; total includes 118 sq km (45.6 sq miles) within Honshu and Shikoku districts yet to be demarcated fully.

† Excluding foreign military and diplomatic personnel and their dependants.

‡ Provisional.

POPULATION BY AGE AND SEX

('000 persons, official provisional estimates at 1 July 2011)

	Males	Females	Total
0–14	8,670	8,230	16,900
15–64	40,940	40,420	81,350
65 and over	12,670	17,010	29,680
Total	62,270	65,650	127,920

Note: Totals may not be equal to the sum of components, owing to rounding.

PREFECTURES

(population at 2010 census, preliminary)

Prefecture	Area (sq km)	Population ('000)	Density (per sq km)
Aichi	5,165	7,408	1,434.3
Akita	11,612	1,086	93.5
Aomori	9,607	1,373	142.9
Chiba	5,157	6,217	1,205.5
Ehime	5,678	1,431	252.0
Fukui	4,190	806	192.4
Fukuoka	4,977	5,073	1,019.3
Fukushima	13,783	2,029	147.2
Gifu	10,621	2,081	195.9
Gumma	6,363	2,008	315.6
Hiroshima	8,479	2,861	337.4
Hokkaido	83,457	5,507	66.0
Hyogo	8,396	5,589	665.7
Ibaraki	6,096	2,969	487.0
Ishikawa	4,186	1,170	279.5
Iwate	15,279	1,331	87.1
Kagawa	1,877	996	530.6
Kagoshima	9,189	1,706	185.7
Kanagawa	2,416	9,050	3,745.9
Kochi	7,105	765	107.7
Kumamoto	7,406	1,817	245.3
Kyoto	4,613	2,637	571.6
Mie	5,777	1,855	321.1
Miyagi	7,286	2,348	322.3
Miyazaki	7,735	1,135	146.7
Nagano	13,562	2,153	158.8
Nagasaki	4,104	1,427	347.7
Nara	3,691	1,400	379.3
Niigata	12,583	2,375	188.7
Oita	6,340	1,196	188.6
Okayama	7,113	1,945	273.4
Okinawa	2,276	1,393	612.0
Osaka	1,898	8,863	4,669.7
Saga	2,440	850	348.4
Saitama	3,797	7,195	1,894.9
Shiga	4,017	1,410	351.0
Shimane	6,708	716	106.7
Shizuoka	7,780	3,765	483.9
Tochigi	6,408	2,007	313.2
Tokushima	4,147	786	189.5
Tokyo-to	2,188	13,162	6,015.5
Tottori	3,507	588	167.7
Toyama	4,248	1,093	257.3
Wakayama	4,726	1,001	211.8
Yamagata	9,323	1,169	125.4
Yamaguchi	6,114	1,451	237.3
Yamanashi	4,465	863	193.3
Total	377,944*	128,056	338.8

* Total includes 59 sq km of area straddling more than one prefecture or not fully demarcated.

PRINCIPAL CITIES

(census results at 1 October 2005)*

Tokyo (capital)†	8,489,653	Oita	462,317
Yokohama	3,579,628	Utsunomiya	457,673
Osaka	2,628,811	Kanazawa	454,607
Nagoya	2,215,062	Nagasaki	442,699
Sapporo	1,880,863	Yokosuka	426,178
Kobe	1,525,393	Toyama	421,239
Kyoto	1,474,811	Fukuyama	418,509
Fukuoka	1,401,279	Toyota	412,141
Kawasaki	1,327,011	Machida	405,534
Saitama	1,176,314	Hirakata	404,044
Hiroshima	1,154,391	Gifu	399,931
Sendai	1,025,098	Fujisawa	396,014
Kitakyushu‡	993,525	Toyonaka	386,623
Chiba	924,319	Kashiwa	380,963
Sakai	830,966	Nagano	378,512
Hamamatsu	804,032	Wakayama	375,591
Niigata	785,134	Toyohashi	372,479
Shizuoka	700,886	Nara	370,102
Okayama	674,746	Asahikawa	355,004
Kumamoto	669,603	Okazaki	354,704
Sagamihara	628,698	Iwaki	354,492
Kagoshima	604,367	Suita	353,885
Funabashi	569,835	Takatsuki	351,826

Hachioji	560,012	Koriyama	338,834
Matsuyama	514,937	Takamatsu	337,902
Higashiosaka	513,821	Tokorozawa	336,100
Himeji	482,304	Kawagoe	333,795
Kawaguchi	480,079	Kochi	333,484
Matsudo	472,579	Akita	333,109
Kurashiki	469,377	Maebashi	318,584
Ichikawa	466,608	Koshigaya	315,792
Nishinomiyai	465,337	Naha	312,393
Amagasaki	462,647	Aomori	311,508

* With the exception of Tokyo, the data for each city refer to an urban county (*shi*), an administrative division that may include some scattered or rural population as well as an urban centre.

† The figure refers to the 23 wards (*ku*) of the old city. The population of Tokyo-to (Tokyo Prefecture) was 12,577,000 at the census of 1 October 2005.

‡ Including Kokura, Moji, Tobata, Wakamatsu and Yahata (Yawata).

2006 ('000 persons, annual averages, official estimates): Chiba 930; Fukuoka 1,414; Hiroshima 1,158; Kawasaki 1,342; Kitakyushu 991; Kobe 1,529; Kyoto 1,473; Nagoya 2,223; Osaka 2,635; Saitama 1,192; Sakai 832; Sapporo 1,889; Sendai 1,027; Shizuoka 712; Tokyo 8,568.

2007 ('000 persons, annual averages, official estimates): Chiba 937; Fukuoka 1,427; Hamamatsu 811; Hiroshima 1,162; Kawasaki 1,369; Kitakyushu 987; Kobe 1,530; Kyoto 1,469; Nagoya 2,237; Niigata 813; Osaka 2,644; Saitama 1,200; Sakai 835; Sapporo 1,894; Sendai 1,029; Shizuoka 711; Tokyo 8,653.

2008 ('000 persons, annual averages, official estimates): Chiba 947; Fukuoka 1,438; Hamamatsu 813; Hiroshima 1,167; Kawasaki 1,390; Kitakyushu 985; Kobe 1,533; Kyoto 1,467; Nagoya 2,248; Niigata 812; Osaka 2,652; Saitama 1,210; Sakai 836; Sapporo 1,898; Sendai 1,031; Shizuoka 710; Tokyo 8,736.

2009 ('000 persons, annual averages, official estimates): Chiba 955; Fukuoka 1,451; Hamamatsu 811; Hiroshima 1,171; Kawasaki 1,410; Kitakyushu 983; Kobe 1,537; Kyoto 1,466; Nagoya 2,258; Niigata 812; Osaka 2,662; Saitama 1,222; Sakai 838; Sapporo 1,904; Sendai 1,034; Shizuoka 717; Tokyo 8,802.

2010 ('000 persons, annual averages, official estimate): Tokyo 8,847.

BIRTHS, MARRIAGES AND DEATHS*

	Registered live births		Registered marriages†		Registered deaths	
	Number	Rate (per 1,000)	Number	Rate (per 1,000)	Number	Rate (per 1,000)
2002	1,153,855	9.2	757,331	6.0	982,379	7.8
2003	1,123,610	8.9	740,191	5.9	1,014,951	8.0
2004	1,110,721	8.8	720,417	5.7	1,028,602	8.2
2005	1,062,530	8.4	714,265	5.7	1,083,796	8.6
2006	1,092,674	8.7	730,971	5.8	1,084,450	8.6
2007	1,089,818	8.6	719,822	5.7	1,108,334	8.8
2008	1,091,156	8.7	726,106	5.8	1,142,407	9.1
2009	1,070,035	8.5	707,734	5.6	1,141,865	9.1

* Figures relate only to Japanese nationals in Japan.

† Data are tabulated by year of registration rather than by year of occurrence.

Source: Ministry of Health, Labour and Welfare, Tokyo.

Life expectancy (years at birth, WHO estimates): 83 (males 80; females 86) in 2009 (Source: WHO, *World Health Statistics*).

ECONOMICALLY ACTIVE POPULATION*
(annual averages, '000 persons aged 15 years and over)

	2008	2009	2010
Agriculture and forestry	2,450	2,420	2,340
Fishing and aquaculture	230	200	180
Mining and quarrying	30	30	30
Manufacturing	11,440	10,730	10,490
Electricity, gas and water	320	340	340
Construction	5,370	5,170	4,980
Wholesale and retail trade	11,050	10,550	10,570
Restaurants and hotels	3,340	3,800	3,870
Transport, information and communications	5,290	5,410	5,460
Financing, insurance, real estate and business services	2,470	2,750	2,730
Health and welfare	5,980	6,210	6,530

—continued	2008	2009	2010
Education	2,880	2,870	2,880
Government	2,230	2,220	2,200
Other services and activities not elsewhere classified	10,010	9,510	9,360
Sub-total	63,090	62,210	61,960
Activities not adequately defined	760	610	610
Total employed	63,850	62,820	62,570
Unemployed	2,650	3,360	3,340
Total labour force	66,500	66,180	65,900
Males	38,880	38,470	38,220
Females	27,620	27,710	27,680

* Figures are rounded to the nearest 10,000 persons, and totals may not be equal to the sum of components as a result.

Health and Welfare

KEY INDICATORS

Total fertility rate (children per woman, 2009)	1.3
Under-5 mortality rate (per 1,000 live births, 2009)	3
HIV/AIDS (% of persons aged 15–49, 2005)	<0.1
Physicians (per 1,000 head, 2004)	2.1
Hospital beds (per 1,000 head, 2005)	14.1
Health expenditure (2008): US $ per head (PPP)	2,817
Health expenditure (2008): % of GDP	8.3
Health expenditure (2008): public (% of total)	80.5
Total carbon dioxide emissions ('000 metric tons, 2007)	1,253,516.7
Carbon dioxide emissions per head (metric tons, 2007)	9.8
Human Development Index (2010): ranking	11
Human Development Index (2010): value	0.884

For sources and definitions, see explanatory note on p. vi.

Agriculture

PRINCIPAL CROPS
('000 metric tons)

	2007	2008	2009
Wheat	910.1	881.2	674.2
Rice, paddy	10,893.0	11,028.8	10,592.5*
Barley	194.6	217.2	179.2
Potatoes	2,873.0	2,743.0	2,398.0
Sweet potatoes	968.4	1,011.0	1,026.0
Taro (Cocoyam)	173.2	179.7	182.0
Yams	190.4	181.2	190.0†
Sugar cane	1,500.0	1,598.0	1,515.0
Sugar beets	4,297.0	4,248.0	3,649.0
Beans, dry	87.5	93.8	68.7
Soybeans (Soya beans)	226.7	261.7	229.9
Cabbages and other brassicas	1,359.0	1,389.0	1,300.0†
Lettuce and chicory	543.7	544.3	535.0†
Spinach	298.2	292.7	288.0†
Tomatoes	750.3	732.8	716.9
Cauliflowers and broccoli	150.4	161.4	158.0†
Pumpkins, squash and gourds	228.0	242.8	235.0†
Cucumbers and gherkins	641.0	627.4	620.2
Aubergines (Eggplants)	371.8	365.9	349.2
Chillies and peppers, green	149.6	150.3	142.7
Onions and shallots, green	558.7	575.5	570.0†
Onions, dry	1,265.0	1,271.0	1,154.0
Carrots and turnips	665.9	656.8	620.0†
Maize, green	256.7	266.0	258.0†
Mushrooms and truffles†	67.0	67.5	64.1
Watermelons	421.6	402.0	389.9
Cantaloupes and other melons	221.3	208.5	200.0†
Grapes	209.1	201.0	210.0†

—continued	2007	2008	2009
Apples	840.1	910.7	845.6
Pears	322.4	361.7	351.5
Peaches and nectarines	150.2	157.3	150.7
Plums and sloes	21.9	26.0	20.9
Oranges†	65.0	63.0	62.0
Tangerines, mandarins, clementines and satsumas	1,066.0	906.1	1,018.0
Persimmons	244.8	266.6	258.0
Strawberries	191.4	190.7	184.7
Tea	94.1	96.5	86.0
Tobacco, unmanufactured	37.8	38.5	36.6

* Unofficial figure.
† FAO estimate(s).

Aggregate production ('000 metric tons, may include official, semi-official or estimated data): Total cereals 12,024.9 in 2007, 12,151.2 in 2008, 11,461.9 in 2009; Total roots and tubers 4,263.2 in 2007, 4,178.2 in 2008, 3,861.0 in 2009; Total vegetables (incl. melons) 10,970.3 in 2007, 10,982.9 in 2008, 10,475.8 in 2009; Total fruits (excl. melons) 3,438.9 in 2007, 3,416.1 in 2008, 3,415.2 in 2009.

Source: FAO.

LIVESTOCK
('000 head at 30 September)

	2007	2008	2009
Horses*	18	18	18
Cattle	4,398	4,423	4,423
Pigs	9,759	9,745	9,899
Sheep*	11	13	14
Goats*	15	15	15
Chickens	288,531	284,651	285,349

* FAO estimates.

Source: FAO.

LIVESTOCK PRODUCTS
('000 metric tons)

	2007	2008	2009
Cattle meat	503.9	519.9	517.0
Pig meat	1,250.5	1,248.8	1,309.8
Chicken meat	1,366.1	1,369.3	1,394.5
Cows' milk	8,007.4	7,982.0	7,909.5
Hen eggs	2,583.0	2,554.0	2,505.0

Source: FAO.

Forestry

ROUNDWOOD REMOVALS
('000 cubic metres, excl. bark)

	2007	2008	2009
Sawlogs, veneer logs and logs for sleepers	13,613	13,247	12,222
Pulpwood	4,037	4,462	4,397
Fuel wood*	101	96	92
Total*	17,751	17,805	16,711

* FAO estimates.

Source: FAO.

SAWNWOOD PRODUCTION
('000 cubic metres, incl. railway sleepers)

	2007	2008	2009
Coniferous (softwood)	11,411	10,688	9,134
Broadleaved (hardwood)	221	196	157
Total	11,632	10,884	9,291

Source: FAO.

Fishing

('000 metric tons, live weight)

	2007	2008	2009
Capture	4,277.7	4,323.6	3,847.0*
Chum salmon (Keta or Dog salmon)	221.0	174.2	214.3
Alaska (Walleye) pollock	216.6	211.0	223.7
Pacific saury (Skipper)	296.5	354.7	311.9*
Japanese jack mackerel	170.4	172.3	165.7*
Japanese anchovy	362.5	345.0	344.8*
Skipjack tuna (Oceanic skipjack)	301.4	311.5	263.9
Chub mackerel	456.6	520.3	470.9
Yesso scallop	258.3	310.2	319.6*
Japanese flying squid	253.5	217.5	216.6
Aquaculture	771.4	730.0	786.9
Japanese amberjack	159.7	155.1	154.9
Pacific cupped oyster	204.5	190.3	210.2
Yesso scallop	247.5	225.6	256.7
Total catch	5,049.1	5,053.6	4,633.9*

* FAO estimate.

Note: Figures exclude aquatic plants ('000 metric tons): 617.6 (capture 103.6, aquaculture 514.0) in 2007; 561.0 (capture 104.7, aquaculture 456.3) in 2008; 560.6 (capture 104.2, aquaculture 456.4) in 2009 (FAO estimates). Also excluded are aquatic mammals (generally recorded by number rather than by weight), pearls, corals and sponges. The number of whales caught was: 1,435 in 2007; 1,258 in 2008; 1,478 in 2009. The number of dolphins and porpoises caught was: 12,741 in 2007; 8,903 in 2008; 10,846 in 2009. The catch of other aquatic mammals ('000 metric tons) was: 1.6 in 2007; 1.2 in 2008; 1.4 in 2009. For the remaining categories, catches (in metric tons) were: pearls 27.4 in 2007; 24.0 in 2008; n.a. in 2009; and corals 4.0 in 2007; 4.0 in 2008; 5.0 in 2009.

Source: FAO.

Mining

('000 metric tons unless otherwise indicated)

	2007	2008	2009
Hard coal*	1,340	1,300	1,100
Quartzite stone	12,258	10,682	9,189
Limestone	165,982	156,813	132,350
Gold ore (kg)†	8,869	6,868	7,708
Crude petroleum ('000 barrels)	6,041	6,200	5,795
Natural gas (million cu m)‡	3,708	3,735	3,539

* Estimates.
† Figures refer to the metal content of ores.
‡ Includes output from gas wells and coal mines.

Source: US Geological Survey.

Industry

SELECTED PRODUCTS
('000 metric tons unless otherwise indicated)

	2006	2007	2008
Cotton yarn—pure and mixed*	79	72	66
Woven cotton fabrics—pure and mixed (million sq m)	400	368	327
Flax yarn	1	1	1
Woven silk fabrics—pure and mixed (million sq m)	19	15	14
Wool yarn—pure and mixed	15	13	11
Woven woollen fabrics—pure and mixed (million sq m)	71	68	61
Woven fabrics of cellulosic fibres—pure and mixed (million sq m)†	160	149	n.a.
Woven fabrics of non-cellulosic fibres (million sq m)	1,083	1,096	1,008

—continued	2006	2007	2008
Leather footwear ('000 pairs)	25,094	24,836	22,298
Newsprint	3,771	3,802	3,680
Other printing and writing paper	11,567	11,666	11,501
Paperboard	12,042	12,074	11,800
Rubber products	1,641	1,660	1,638
Road motor vehicle tyres	1,336	1,344	1,330
Sulphuric acid—100%	6,843	7,098	7,227
Caustic soda—Sodium hydroxide	4,453	4,482	4,373
Ammonia	1,328	1,355	1,244
Liquefied petroleum gas‡	4,644	4,409	4,096
Naphthas‡	15,938	16,699	15,104
Motor spirit—gasoline‡	42,437	42,801	41,882
Kerosene‡	20,120	18,783	16,562
Jet fuel‡	10,433	11,633	12,416
Distillate fuel oil‡	54,711	55,299	54,565
Lubricating oil‡	2,378	2,325	n.a.
Petroleum bitumen—Asphalt‡	5,435	4,974	4,694
Coke-oven coke‡	44,710	45,400	42,338
Cement	69,942	67,685	62,810
Pig-iron	84,270	86,771	86,171
Ferro-alloys§	834	858	828
Crude steel	116,226	120,203	118,739
Aluminium—unwrought‖	1,424	1,438	1,308
Refined copper—unwrought	1,532	1,577	1,540
Electrolytic, distilled and rectified zinc—unwrought	614	598	616
Air-conditioning machines ('000)	24,706	24,155	22,772
Calculating machines ('000)	31	19	8
Video cameras ('000)	12,524	10,228	7,928
Digital cameras ('000)	37,150	31,991	36,273
DVD players ('000)	2,046	1,486	2,366
Cellular telephones ('000)	48,034	45,891	35,326
Personal computers ('000)	8,534	8,328	7,608
Passenger motor cars ('000)	9,755	9,945	9,916
Lorries and trucks ('000)	1,641	1,538	1,508
Motorcycles, scooters and mopeds ('000)	1,771	1,676	1,227
Bicycles ('000)	1,335	1,136	1,095
Watches	474,925	428,828	n.a.
Construction: new dwellings started ('000)	1,290	1,061	1,093
Electric energy (million kWh)‡	1,161,110	1,192,771	1,146,269

* Including condenser cotton yarn.
† Fabrics of continuous and discontinuous rayon and acetate fibres, including pile and chenille fabrics at loom stage.
‡ Source: UN Industrial Commodity Statistics Database.
§ Including silico-chromium.
‖ Including alloys.

2009 ('000 metric tons unless otherwise indicated): Cotton yarn—pure and mixed 47; Woven cotton fabrics—pure and mixed (million sq m) 221; Wool yarn—pure and mixed 8; Woven fabrics of non-cellulosic fibres (million sq m) 699; Leather footwear ('000 pairs) 17,941; Newsprint 3,455; Other printing and writing paper 9,120; Paperboard 10,436; Rubber products 1,186; Sulphuric acid (100%) 6,396; Caustic soda—Sodium hydroxide 3,895; Ammonia 1,021; Cement 54,800; Pig-iron 66,943; Crude steel 87,534; Video cameras ('000) 4,155; Digital cameras ('000) 24,696; DVD players ('000) 2,115; Motorcycles, scooters and mopeds ('000) 645; Construction: new dwellings started ('000) 788.

2010 ('000 metric tons unless otherwise indicated): Cotton yarn—pure and mixed 45; Woven cotton fabrics—pure and mixed (million sq m) 124; Wool yarn—pure and mixed 9; Woven fabrics of non-cellulosic fibres (million sq m) 730; Leather footwear ('000 pairs) 17,366; Newsprint 3,349; Other printing and writing paper 9,547; Paperboard 10,977; Rubber products 1,429; Sulphuric acid (100%) 7,037; Caustic soda—Sodium hydroxide 4,217; Ammonia 1178; Cement 51,526; Pig-iron 82,283; Crude steel 109,599; Video cameras ('000) 3,856; Digital cameras ('000) 24,253; DVD players ('000) 1,843; Motorcycles, scooters and mopeds ('000) 663.

Finance

CURRENCY AND EXCHANGE RATES

Monetary Units
100 sen = 1 yen.

Sterling, Dollar and Euro Equivalents (31 May 2011)
£1 sterling = 133.427 yen;
US $1 = 80.850 yen;
€1 = 116.303 yen;
1,000 yen = £7.49 = $12.37 = €8.60.

Average Exchange Rate (yen per US $)
2008 103.359
2009 93.570
2010 87.780

BUDGET
('000 million yen, year ending 31 March)*

Revenue	2009/10	2010/11†	2011/12‡
Tax and stamp revenues	36,861	37,396	40,927
Government bond issues	53,455	44,303	44,298
Total (incl. others)	102,558	92,299	92,412

Expenditure	2009/10	2010/11†	2011/12‡
Defence	4,820	4,790	4,775
Social security	28,807	27,269	28,708
Public works	8,787	5,773	4,974
Servicing of national debt§	19,251	20,649	21,549
Transfer of local allocation tax to local governments	16,573	17,477	16,785
Total (incl. others)	102,558	92,299	92,412

* Figures refer only to the operations of the General Account budget. Data exclude transactions of other accounts controlled by the central Government: two mutual aid associations and four special accounts (including other social security funds).
† Initial forecasts.
‡ Budget figures.
§ Including the repayment of debt principal and administrative costs.

Source: Ministry of Finance, Tokyo.

INTERNATIONAL RESERVES
(US $ million at 31 December)

	2008	2009	2010
Gold (national valuation)	1,326	1,350	1,326
IMF special drawing rights	3,032	20,968	20,626
Reserve position in IMF	2,658	4,313	4,608
Foreign exchange	1,003,674	996,955	1,036,256
Total	1,010,690	1,023,586	1,062,816

Source: IMF, *International Financial Statistics*.

MONEY SUPPLY
('000 million yen at 31 December)

	2008	2009	2010
Currency outside depository corporations	76,600	76,724	78,399
Transferable deposits	415,302	421,515	435,513
Other deposits	558,191	573,111	578,772
Broad money	1,050,094	1,071,349	1,092,684

Source: IMF, *International Financial Statistics*.

COST OF LIVING

(Consumer Price Index; average of monthly figures; base: 2005 = 100)

	2008	2009	2010
Food (incl. beverages)	103.4	103.6	103.3
Housing	100.0	99.8	99.4
Rent	99.8	99.5	99.1
Fuel, light and water charges	110.7	106.1	105.9
Clothing and footwear	101.9	101.0	99.8
Miscellaneous	102.1	101.7	103.0
All items	101.7	100.3	99.6

NATIONAL ACCOUNTS

('000 million yen at current prices, year ending 31 December)

National Income and Product

	2007	2008	2009
Compensation of employees	262,013.2	262,508.7	251,354.9
Operating surplus and mixed income	99,652.4	86,492.0	71,998.3
Domestic primary incomes	361,665.6	349,000.7	323,353.2
Consumption of fixed capital	107,128.3	108,041.4	103,938.1
Statistical discrepancy	6,346.7	7,526.3	8,511.4
Gross domestic product (GDP) at factor cost	475,140.6	464,568.4	435,802.7
Indirect taxes	43,407.1	42,698.3	38,755.8
Less Subsidies	3,027.3	2,889.2	3,621.8
GDP in purchasers' values	515,520.4	504,377.6	470,936.7
Primary incomes received from abroad	26,360.5	24,783.3	18,612.6
Less Primary incomes paid abroad	9,122.1	8,035.3	5,693.5
Gross national income (GNI)	532,758.8	521,125.4	483,855.8

Expenditure on the Gross Domestic Product

	2007	2008	2009
Government final consumption expenditure	92,217.6	93,242.7	94,477.3
Private final consumption expenditure	292,523.2	291,595.6	279,909.6
Changes in stocks	3,910.5	2,328.5	–4,512.3
Gross fixed capital formation	118,236.7	116,475.2	99,625.6
Total domestic expenditure	506,888.0	503,642.0	469,500.2
Exports of goods and services	90,830.4	88,493.7	59,524.0
Less Imports of goods and services	82,198.0	87,758.1	58,087.5
GDP in purchasers' values	515,520.4	504,377.6	470,936.7

Gross Domestic Product by Economic Activity

	2007	2008	2009
Agriculture, hunting, forestry and fishing	7,325.8	7,192.1	6,659.2
Mining and quarrying	348.0	311.2	300.3
Manufacturing	109,089.6	102,981.8	84,731.9
Electricity, gas and water	10,280.0	9,000.1	10,890.4
Construction	31,443.6	29,997.5	29,230.1
Wholesale and retail trade	69,905.9	69,326.2	59,014.7
Transport, storage and communications	34,129.6	34,115.0	31,999.2
Finance and insurance	34,317.2	29,852.1	27,356.9
Real estate*	61,292.0	61,806.2	62,304.6
Public administration	29,269.3	29,628.0	29,374.6
Other government services	18,482.6	18,420.0	17,658.4
Other business, community, social and personal services	113,821.7	113,630.4	110,677.5
Private non-profit services to households	10,697.0	10,834.3	10,727.4
Sub-total	530,402.0	517,094.7	480,925.2
Import duties	5,711.7	5,945.2	4,368.1
Less Imputed bank service charge	23,260.0	22,601.5	20,264.8
Less Consumption taxes for gross capital formation	3,680.1	3,587.0	2,603.2
Statistical discrepancy	6,346.7	7,526.3	8,511.4
GDP in purchasers' values	515,520.4	504,377.6	470,936.7

* Including imputed rents of owner-occupied dwellings.

Source: Economic and Social Research Institute, Tokyo.

BALANCE OF PAYMENTS

(US $ million)*

	2008	2009	2010
Exports of goods f.o.b.	746,470	545,280	730,080
Imports of goods f.o.b.	–708,340	–501,650	–639,100
Trade balance	38,130	43,630	90,970
Exports of services	148,750	128,340	141,460
Imports of services	–169,540	–148,720	–157,570
Balance on goods and services	17,340	23,250	74,860
Other income received	212,100	175,220	173,680
Other income paid	–59,760	–43,880	–40,390
Balance on goods, services and income	169,680	154,590	208,150
Current transfers received	9,100	9,520	10,090
Current transfers paid	–22,150	–21,910	–22,480
Current balance	156,630	142,190	195,750
Capital account (net)	–5,470	–4,990	–4,960
Direct investment abroad	–130,820	–74,620	–57,220
Direct investment from abroad	24,550	11,830	–1,360
Portfolio investment assets	–189,640	–160,250	–262,640
Portfolio investment liabilities	–102,960	–56,260	111,640
Financial derivatives assets	271,950	333,850	403,460
Financial derivatives liabilities	–247,160	–323,300	–391,510
Other investment assets	139,460	202,750	–130,140
Other investment liabilities	61,990	–64,150	197,300
Net errors and omissions	52,340	19,870	–16,460
Overall balance	30,880	26,920	43,850

* Figures are rounded to the nearest US $10m., and totals may not, therefore, be equal to the sum of components.

Source: IMF, *International Financial Statistics*.

JAPANESE DEVELOPMENT ASSISTANCE

(net disbursement basis, US $ million)

	2006	2007	2008
Official flows	13,574	7,890	7,593
Bilateral assistance	7,262	5,778	6,823
Grants	7,160	5,983	7,764
Grant assistance	5,047	3,414	4,777
Technical assistance	2,603	2,569	2,987
Loans	–389	–205	–940
Contributions to multilateral institutions	3,874	1,901	2,756
Other official flows	2,438	211	–1,986
Export credits	–1,305	–772	–629
Direct investment finance, etc.	4,038	543	–1,952
Transfers to multilateral institutions	–294	441	594
Private flows	12,290	21,979	23,738
Export credits	275	2,586	–4,878
Direct investment and others	14,144	18,037	25,710
Bilateral investment in securities, etc.	–1,201	3,251	3,952
Transfers to multilateral institutions	–928	–1,896	–1,046
Grants from private voluntary agencies	315	446	452
Total	26,179	30,315	31,783

External Trade

PRINCIPAL COMMODITIES

('000 million yen)

Imports c.i.f.	2008	2009	2010
Food and live animals	6,212	4,999	5,199
Fish and fish preparations*	1,453	1,208	1,260
Crude materials (inedible) except fuels	5,538	3,395	4,766
Mineral fuels, lubricants, etc.	27,658	14,202	17,398
Crude and partly refined petroleum	16,262	7,564	9,406
Liquefied natural gas	4,652	2,827	3,472
Chemicals	5,737	4,583	5,379
Manufactured goods	7,336	4,345	5,379
Non-electrical machinery	6,074	4,225	4,826
Electrical machinery	8,628	6,509	8,101
Transport equipment	2,316	1,501	1,681
Other	9,454	7,742	8,036
Clothing and clothing accessories	2,643	2,358	2,328
Total (incl. others)†	78,955	51,499	60,765

Exports f.o.b.	2008	2009	2010
Chemicals	7,269	5,780	6,925
Manufactured goods	10,177	7,017	8,785
Iron and steel	4,574	2,906	3,675
Machinery and transport equipment	51,364	32,290	41,225
Non-electrical machinery	15,928	9,669	13,317
Power-generating machinery	2,509	1,839	2,327
Electrical machinery, apparatus, etc.	15,368	10,771	12,650
Thermionic valves, tubes, etc.	4,625	3,419	4,153
Transport equipment	20,068	11,850	15,258
Road motor vehicles	13,736	6,693	9,174
Road motor vehicle parts	3,065	2,309	2,893
Other	8,883	6,944	8,007
Scientific instruments and optical equipment	2,024	1,578	2,014
Total (incl. others)‡	81,018	54,171	67,400

* Including crustacea and molluscs.
† Including re-imports not classified according to kind.
‡ Including re-exports not classified according to kind.

PRINCIPAL TRADING PARTNERS

('000 million yen)*

Imports c.i.f.	2008	2009	2010
Australia	4,922	3,242	3,948
Brazil	943	593	859
Canada	1,323	858	958
Chile	820	495	678
China, People's Republic	14,830	11,436	13,413
France	1,100	854	901
Germany	2,159	1,563	1,689
Indonesia	3,378	2,038	2,476
Iran	1,897	867	980
Italy	824	595	595
Korea, Republic	3,052	2,051	2,504
Kuwait	1,584	836	901
Malaysia	2,398	1,558	1,987
Philippines	872	598	695
Qatar	2,752	1,483	1,904
Russia	1,389	826	1,412
Saudi Arabia	5,293	2,720	3,149
Singapore	817	570	715
South Africa	930	465	636
Switzerland	665	586	596
Taiwan	2,258	1,711	2,025
Thailand	2,152	1,495	1,840
United Arab Emirates	4,872	2,115	2,569
United Kingdom	774	531	559
USA	8,040	5,512	5,911
Viet Nam	942	649	716
Total (incl. others)	78,955	51,499	60,765

Exports f.o.b.	2008	2009	2010
Australia	1,793	1,135	1,392
Belgium	879	498	586
Canada	1,116	723	817
China, People's Republic	12,950	10,236	13,086
France	931	577	585
Germany	2,484	1,553	1,777
Hong Kong	4,178	2,975	3,705
India	819	591	792
Indonesia	1,304	870	1,394
Italy	706	448	490
Korea, Republic	6,168	4,410	5,460
Malaysia	1,705	1,200	1,545
Mexico	1,032	637	838
Netherlands	2,185	1,260	1,431
Panama	1,132	1,197	1,359
Philippines	1,034	767	969
Russia	1,714	307	703
Saudi Arabia	814	502	568
Singapore	2,758	1,933	2,209
Taiwan	4,782	3,399	4,594
Thailand	3,051	2,070	2,994
United Arab Emirates	1,124	605	643
United Kingdom	1,707	1,102	1,241
USA	14,214	8,733	10,374
Total (incl. others)	81,018	54,171	67,400

* Imports by country of production; exports by country of last consignment.

Transport

RAILWAYS

(traffic, year ending 31 March)

	2008	2009	2010
Japan Railways Group:			
Passengers (million)	8,984	8,841	8,818
Passenger-km (million)	253,556	244,247	244,593
Freight ('000 tons)	32,850	30,849	30,790
Freight ton-km (million)	22,081	20,404	20,228
Other private railways:			
Passengers (million)	13,992	13,884	13,851
Passenger-km (million)	151,030	149,657	148,805
Freight ('000 tons)	13,376	12,401	12,854
Freight ton-km (million)	175	157	171
Total:			
Passengers (million)	22,976	22,725	22,669
Passenger-km (million)	404586	393,904	393,398
Freight ('000 tons)	46,226	43,250	43,644
Freight ton-km (million)	22,256	20,561	20,399

ROAD TRAFFIC

('000 motor vehicles owned, year ending 31 March)

	2007	2008	2009
Passenger cars	41,469	40,799	40,419
Buses and coaches	231	230	228
Trucks, incl. trailers	6,884	6,568	6,362
Special use vehicles	1,578	1,528	1,512
Light two-wheeled vehicles	1,479	1,505	1,524
Light motor vehicles	27,440	28,171	28,648
Total	79,081	78,801	78,693

SHIPPING

Merchant Fleet
(registered at 31 December)

	2007	2008	2009
Number of vessels	6,519	6,316	6,221
Total displacement ('000 grt)	12,788	13,536	14,725

Source: IHS Fairplay, *World Fleet Statistics*.

International Sea-borne Traffic
('000 metric tons)

	2006	2007	2008
Exports	54,697	56,702	47,781
Imports	503,152	527,467	547,888
Cross transport	245,203	249,048	270,784
Total	803,051	833,217	866,453

CIVIL AVIATION

(traffic on scheduled services)

	2006	2007	2008
Kilometres flown (million)	1,007	1,023	1,027
Passengers carried (million)	113,727	113,295	109,313
Passenger-km (million)	165,454	163,493	155,675
Total ton-km (million)	8,996	9,554	8,467

2009 (traffic on scheduled services): Passengers carried (million) 99,300; Passenger-km (million) 142,537; Total ton-km (million) 7,432.

2010 (traffic on scheduled services): Passengers carried (million) 95,942; Passenger-km (million) 133,659; Total ton-km (million) 7,340.

Tourism

FOREIGN VISITOR ARRIVALS

(excl. Japanese nationals resident abroad)

Country of nationality	2008	2009	2010
Australia	242,031	211,659	225,751
Canada	168,307	152,756	153,303
China, People's Republic	1,000,416	1,006,085	1,412,875
Germany	126,207	110,692	124,360
Hong Kong	550,192	449,568	508,691
Korea, Republic	2,382,397	1,586,772	2,439,816
Philippines	82,177	71,485	77,377
Singapore	167,894	145,224	180,960
Taiwan	1,390,228	1,024,292	1,268,278
Thailand	191,881	177,541	214,881
United Kingdom	206,564	181,460	184,045
USA	768,345	699,919	727,234
Total (incl. others)	8,350,835	6,789,658	8,611,175

Source: mainly Japan National Tourist Organization.

Receipts from tourism (US $ million, excl. passenger transport): 9,334 in 2007; 10,821 in 2008; 10,305 in 2009 (provisional) (Source: World Tourism Organization).

Communications Media

	2008	2009	2010
Telephones ('000 main lines in use)	48,427	44,364	40,419
Mobile telephones ('000 subscribers)	110,395	114,917	120,709
Internet users ('000)*	95,979	116,295	n.a.
Broadband subscribers ('000)	30,117	31,655	34,055
Book production:			
titles	76,322	78,555	74,714
copies (million)	751	718	702
Daily newspapers:			
number	121	121	120
circulation ('000 copies)	51,491	50,352	49,322

* Estimates.

Television receivers ('000 in use): 92,000 in 2000.

Radio receivers ('000 in use): 120,500 in 1997.

Personal computers: 69,200,000 (542 per 1,000 persons) in 2005.

Sources: The Japan Newspaper Publishers and Editors Association; Foreign Press Center, *Facts and Figures of Japan*; UNESCO, *Statistical Yearbook*; UN, *Statistical Yearbook*; International Telecommunication Union.

Education

(2009)

	Institutions	Teachers*	Students
Kindergartens	13,516	110,692	1,630,000
Elementary schools	22,258	419,518	7,064,000
Lower secondary schools	10,864	250,771	3,600,000
Upper secondary schools	5,183	239,342	3,347,000
Schools for special needs	1,030	74,141	117,035
Colleges of technology	64	4,400	59,386
Junior colleges	406	10,128	161,000
Universities	773	172,039	2,846,000
Special training schools	3,348	40,922	625,000
Miscellaneous vocational schools	1,533	9,655	135,000

* Figures refer to full-time teachers only.

Pupil-teacher ratio (primary education, UNESCO estimate): 18.3 in 2007/08 (Source: UNESCO Institute for Statistics).

Directory

The Constitution

The Constitution of Japan was promulgated on 3 November 1946 and came into force on 3 May 1947. The following is a summary of its major provisions, with subsequent amendments:

THE EMPEROR

Articles 1–8. The Emperor derives his position from the will of the people. In the performance of any state act as defined in the Constitution, he must seek the advice and approval of the Cabinet, though he may delegate the exercise of his functions, which include: (i) the appointment of the Prime Minister and the Chief Justice of the Supreme Court; (ii) promulgation of laws, cabinet orders, treaties and constitutional amendments; (iii) the convocation of the Diet, dissolution of the House of Representatives and proclamation of elections to the Diet; (iv) the appointment and dismissal of Ministers of State, the granting of amnesties, reprieves and pardons, and the ratification of treaties, conventions or protocols; (v) the awarding of honours and performance of ceremonial functions.

RENUNCIATION OF WAR

Article 9. Japan renounces for ever the use of war as a means of settling international disputes.

Articles 10–40 refer to the legal and human rights of individuals guaranteed by the Constitution.

THE DIET

Articles 41–64. The Diet is convened once a year, is the highest organ of state power and has exclusive legislative authority. It comprises the House of Representatives (480 seats—300 single-seat constituencies and 180 determined by proportional representation) and the House of Councillors (242 seats). The members of the former are elected for four years whilst those of the latter are elected for six years and election for approximately one-half of the members takes place every three years. If the House of Representatives is dissolved, a general election must take place within 40 days and the Diet must be convoked within 30 days of the date of the election. Extraordinary sessions of the Diet may be convened by the Cabinet when one-quarter or more of the members of either House request it. Emergency sessions of the House of Councillors may also be held. A quorum of at least one-third of the Diet members is needed to carry out parliamentary business. Any decision arising therefrom must be passed by a majority vote of those present. A bill becomes law having passed both Houses, except as provided by the Constitution. If the House of Councillors either vetoes or fails to take action within 60 days upon a bill already passed by the House of Representatives, the bill becomes law when passed a second time by the House of Representatives, by at least a two-thirds' majority of those members present.

The Budget must first be submitted to the House of Representatives. If, when it is approved by the House of Representatives, the House of Councillors votes against it or fails to take action on it within 30 days, or failing agreement being reached by a joint committee of both Houses, a decision of the House of Representatives shall be the decision of the Diet. The above procedure also applies in respect of the conclusion of treaties.

THE EXECUTIVE

Articles 65–75. Executive power is vested in the Cabinet, consisting of a Prime Minister and such other Ministers as may be appointed. The Cabinet is collectively responsible to the Diet. The Prime Minister is designated from among members of the Diet by a resolution thereof.

If the House of Representatives and the House of Councillors disagree on the designation of the Prime Minister, and if no agreement can be reached even through a joint committee of both Houses, provided for by law, or if the House of Councillors fails to make designation within 10 days, exclusive of the period of recess, after the House of Representatives has made designation, the decision of the House of Representatives shall be the decision of the Diet.

The Prime Minister appoints and may remove other Ministers, a majority of whom must be from the Diet. If the House of Representatives passes a no-confidence motion or rejects a confidence motion, the whole Cabinet resigns, unless the House of Representatives is dissolved within 10 days. When there is a vacancy in the post of Prime Minister, or upon the first convocation of the Diet after a general election of members of the House of Representatives, the whole Cabinet resigns.

The Prime Minister submits bills, reports on national affairs and foreign relations to the Diet. He exercises control and supervision over various administrative branches of the Government. The Cabinet's primary functions (in addition to administrative ones) are to: (a) administer the law faithfully; (b) conduct State affairs; (c) conclude treaties subject to prior (or subsequent) Diet approval; (d) administer the civil service in accordance with law; (e) prepare and present the budget to the Diet; (f) enact Cabinet orders in order to make effective legal and constitutional provisions; (g) decide on amnesties, reprieves or pardons. All laws and Cabinet orders are signed by the competent Minister of State and countersigned by the Prime Minister. The Ministers of State, during their tenure of office, are not subject to legal action without the consent of the Prime Minister. However, the right to take that action is not impaired.

Articles 76–95. Relate to the Judiciary, Finance and Local Government.

AMENDMENTS

Article 96. Amendments to the Constitution are initiated by the Diet, through a concurring vote of two-thirds or more of all the members of each House, and are submitted to the people for ratification, which requires the affirmative vote of a majority of all votes cast at a special referendum or at such election as the Diet may specify.

Amendments when so ratified must immediately be promulgated by the Emperor in the name of the people, as an integral part of the Constitution.

Articles 97–99 outline the Supreme Law, while Articles 100–103 consist of Supplementary Provisions.

The Government

HEAD OF STATE

His Imperial Majesty AKIHITO, Emperor of Japan (succeeded to the throne 7 January 1989).

THE CABINET

(October 2011)

A coalition of the Democratic Party of Japan (DPJ) and the People's New Party (PNP).

Prime Minister: YOSHIHIKO NODA (DPJ).

Minister for Internal Affairs and Communications and for Regional Revitalization, Minister of State for Okinawa and Northern Territories' Affairs and for Promotion of Local Sovereignty: TATSUO KAWABATA (DPJ).

Minister of Justice: HIDEO HIRAOKA (DPJ).

Minister for Foreign Affairs: KOICHIRO GEMBA (DPJ).

Minister of Finance: JUN AZUMI (DPJ).

Minister of Education, Culture, Sports, Science and Technology: MASAHARU NAKAGAWA (DPJ).

Minister of Health, Labour and Welfare: YOKO KOMIYAMA (DPJ).

Minister of Agriculture, Forestry and Fisheries: MICHIHIKO KANO (DPJ).

Minister of Economy, Trade and Industry and for Nuclear Incident Economic Countermeasures, Minister of State for the Corporation in Support of Compensation for Nuclear Damage: YUKIO EDANO (DPJ).

Minister of Land, Infrastructure, Transport and Tourism, and for Ocean Policy: TAKESHI MAEDA (DPJ).

Minister of Environment and for the Restoration from and Prevention of Nuclear Accident, Minister of State for the Nuclear Power Policy and Administration: GOSHI HOSONO (DPJ).

Minister of Defence: YASUO ICHIKAWA (DPJ).

Chief Cabinet Secretary: OSAMU FUJIMURA (DPJ).

Chairman of the National Public Safety Commission, Minister for the Abduction Issue and Minister of State for Consumer Affairs and Food Safety: KENJI YAMAOKA (DPJ).

Minister for Postal Reform and Minister of State for Financial Services: SHOZABURO JIMI (PNP).

Minister for Total Reform of Social Security and Tax, for National Policy and for Space Policy, Minister of State for Economic and Fiscal Policy and for Science and Technology Policy: MOTOHISA FURUKAWA (DPJ).

Minister for Civil Service Reform, Minister of State for the New Public Commons, for Government Revitalization and for Measures for Declining Birthrate and Gender Equality: RENHO (DPJ).

Minister for Reconstruction Measures from the Great East Japan Earthquake and Minister of State for Disaster Management: TATSUO HIRANO (DPJ).

MINISTRIES

Imperial Household Agency: 1-1, Chiyoda, Chiyoda-ku, Tokyo 100-8111; tel. (3) 3213-1111; fax (3) 3282-1407; e-mail information@kunaicho.go.jp; internet www.kunaicho.go.jp.

Prime Minister's Office: 1-6-1, Nagata-cho, Chiyoda-ku, Tokyo 100-8968; tel. (3) 3581-2361; fax (3) 3581-1910; internet www.kantei.go.jp.

Cabinet Office: 1-6-1, Nagata-cho, Chiyoda-ku, Tokyo 100-8968; tel. (3) 5253-2111; internet www.cao.go.jp.

Ministry of Agriculture, Forestry and Fisheries: 1-2-1, Kasumigaseki, Chiyoda-ku, Tokyo 100-8950; tel. (3) 3502-5517; fax (3) 3592-7697; internet www.maff.go.jp.

Ministry of Defence: 5-1, Ichigaya, Honmura-cho, Shinjuku-ku, Tokyo 162-8801; tel. and fax (3) 3268-3111; e-mail infomod@mod.go.jp; internet www.mod.go.jp.

Ministry of Economy, Trade and Industry: 1-3-1, Kasumigaseki, Chiyoda-ku, Tokyo 100-8901; tel. (3) 3501-1511; fax (3) 3501-6942; e-mail webmail@meti.go.jp; internet www.meti.go.jp.

Ministry of Education, Culture, Sports, Science and Technology: 3-2-2, Kasumigaseki, Chiyoda-ku, Tokyo 100-8959; tel. (3) 5253-4111; fax (3) 3595-2017; internet www.mext.go.jp.

Ministry of the Environment: 5 Godochosha, 1-2-2, Kasumigaseki, Chiyoda-ku, Tokyo 100-8975; tel. (3) 3581-3351; fax (3) 3502-0308; internet www.env.go.jp.

Ministry of Finance: 3-1-1, Kasumigaseki, Chiyoda-ku, Tokyo 100-8940; tel. (3) 3581-4111; fax (3) 5251-2667; e-mail info@mof.go.jp; internet www.mof.go.jp.

Ministry of Foreign Affairs: 2-2-1, Kasumigaseki, Chiyoda-ku, Tokyo 100-8919; tel. (3) 3580-3311; fax (3) 3581-2667; e-mail webmaster@mofa.go.jp; internet www.mofa.go.jp.

Ministry of Health, Labour and Welfare: 1-2-2, Kasumigaseki, Chiyoda-ku, Tokyo 100-8916; tel. (3) 5253-1111; fax (3) 3501-2532; e-mail www-admin@mhlw.go.jp; internet www.mhlw.go.jp.

Ministry of Internal Affairs and Communications: 2-1-2, Kasumigaseki, Chiyoda-ku, Tokyo 100-8926; tel. (3) 5253-5111; fax (3) 3504-0265; internet www.soumu.go.jp.

Ministry of Justice: 1-1-1, Kasumigaseki, Chiyoda-ku, Tokyo 100-8977; tel. (3) 3580-4111; fax (3) 3592-7011; e-mail webmaster@moj.go.jp; internet www.moj.go.jp.

Ministry of Land, Infrastructure, Transport and Tourism: 2-1-3, Kasumigaseki, Chiyoda-ku, Tokyo 100-8918; tel. (3) 5253-8111; fax (3) 3580-7982; e-mail webmaster@mlit.go.jp; internet www.mlit.go.jp.

Financial Services Agency: 3-2-1, Kasumigaseki, Chiyoda-ku, Tokyo 100-8967; tel. (3) 3506-6000; internet www.fsa.go.jp.

National Public Safety Commission: 2-1-2, Kasumigaseki, Chiyoda-ku, Tokyo 100-8974; tel. (3) 3581-0141; internet www.npsc.go.jp.

National Strategy Bureau: Tokyo.

Legislature

KOKKAI

(Diet)

The Diet consists of two Chambers: the House of Councillors (upper house) and the House of Representatives (lower house). The members of the House of Representatives are elected for a period of four years (subject to dissolution). The House of Representatives has 480 members: 300 single-seat constituencies and 180 seats determined by proportional representation. The 242 members of the House of Councillors serve a six-year term of office, with elections for one-half of the members (including 48 chosen by proportional representation) being held every three years.

House of Councillors

Speaker: TAKEO NISHIOKA.

Party	Seats after elections*	
	29 July 2007	11 July 2010
Democratic Party of Japan	109	106
Liberal-Democratic Party	83	84
New Komeito	20	19
Your Party	—	11
Japanese Communist Party	7	6
Social Democratic Party of Japan	5	4
People's New Party	4	3
Sunrise Party of Japan	—	3
New Renaissance Party	—	2
New Party Nippon	1	1
Independents and others	13	3
Total	242	242

* One-half of the seats are renewable every three years.

House of Representatives

Speaker: TAKAHIRO YOKOMICHI.

General Election, 30 August 2009

Party	Seats
Democratic Party of Japan	308
Liberal-Democratic Party	119
New Komeito	21
Japanese Communist Party	9
Social Democratic Party of Japan	7
Your Party	5
People's New Party	3
New Party Nippon	1
New Party Daichi	1
Independents	6
Total	480

Election Commission

Central Election Management Council: 2nd Bldg of Central Common Government Office, 2-1-2, Kasumigaseki, Chiyoda-ku, Tokyo 100-8926; tel. (3) 5253-5111; fax (3) 5253-5575; mems nominated by Diet and approved by Cabinet; regulates proportional representation electoral elements for both legislative chambers; single-constituency elections for both chambers are supervised by an Election Control Cttee est. by each prefectural govt; Chair. AKIRA ISHIHARA.

Political Organizations

The Political Funds Regulation Law provides that any organization wishing to support a candidate for an elective public office must be registered as a political party. There are more than 10,000 registered parties in the country, mostly of local or regional significance.

Democratic Party of Japan (DPJ): 1-11-1, Nagata-cho, Chiyoda-ku, Tokyo 100-0014; tel. (3) 3595-9988; fax (3) 3595-9961; e-mail dpjenews@dpj.or.jp; internet www.dpj.or.jp; f. 1998; est. by the integration into the original DPJ (f. 1996) of the Democratic Reform League, Minseito and Shinto Yuai; advocates a cabinet formed and controlled by the people; absorbed Party Sakigake in 2001; absorbed Liberal Party in 2003; Pres. YOSHIHIKO NODA; Sec.-Gen. AZUMA KOSHIISHI.

Japanese Communist Party (JCP): 4-26-7, Sendagaya, Shibuya-ku, Tokyo 151-8586; tel. (3) 3403-6111; fax (3) 5474-8358; e-mail info@jcp.or.jp; internet www.jcp.or.jp; f. 1922; 400,000 mems (2007); Chair. of Exec. Cttee KAZUO SHII; Sec.-Gen. TADAYOSHI ICHIDA.

Liberal-Democratic Party (LDP) (Jiyu-Minshuto): 1-11-23, Nagata-cho, Chiyoda-ku, Tokyo 100-8910; tel. (3) 3581-6211; fax (3) 5511-8855; e-mail koho@ldp.jimin.or.jp; internet www.jimin.jp; f. 1955; advocates establishment of a welfare state, promotion of industrial devt, improvement of educational and cultural facilities, and constitutional reform as needed; absorbed New Conservative Party in 2003; 2,369,252 mems (2001); Pres. SADAKAZU TANIGAKI; Sec.-Gen. TADAMORI OSHIMA.

New Komeito: 17, Minami-Motomachi, Shinjuku-ku, Tokyo 160-0012; tel. (3) 3353-0111; fax (3) 3225-0207; internet www.komei.or.jp; f. 1964; est. as Komeito; renamed Komei in 1994 following defection of some mems to the New Frontier Party (Shinshinto, dissolved in 1997); absorbed Reimei Club in 1998; renamed as above in 1998 following merger of Komei and Shinto Heiwa; advocates political moderation, humanism and globalism; 400,000 mems (2003); Pres. NATSUO YAMAGUCHI; Sec.-Gen. YOSHIHISA INOUE.

New Party Daichi (Shinto Daichi): 1-5, Minami, Chuo-ku, Sapporo 060-0061; tel. (11) 251-5351; fax (11) 251-5357; internet www.muneo.gr.jp; f. 2005; regional grouping based in Hokkaido; Leader MUNEO SUZUKI.

New Party Nippon (Shinto Nippon): 1-7-11, Hirakawa-cho, Chiyoda-ku, Tokyo 102-0093; tel. (3) 5213-0333; fax (3) 5213-0888; internet www.love-nippon.com; f. 2005; founding mems included LDP rebels opposed to postal reform proposals of Prime Minister Koizumi; Leader YASUO TANAKA.

New Renaissance Party (Shinto Kaikaku): 2-16-5, Hirakawa-cho, Chiyoda-ku, Tokyo; internet shintokaikaku.jp; f. 2010; conservative grouping; Pres. YOICHI MASUZOE; Sec.-Gen. HIROYUKI ARAI.

New Socialist Party: Miyako Sakura Kosan Bldg, 3/F, 7-9, Nihonbashi Tomizawa-cho, Chuo-ku, Tokyo; tel. (3) 5643-6002; fax (3) 3639-0150; e-mail honbu@sinsyakai.or.jp; internet www.sinsyakai.or.jp; f. 1996; est. by left-wing defectors from SDPJ; opposed to US military bases on Okinawa and introduction in 1996 of new electoral system; seeks to establish an ecological socio-economic system; Chair. KIMIKO KURIHARA; Sec.-Gen. MATSUE YOSHIHIRO.

People's New Party (PNP) (Kokumin Shinto): Kohase Bldg, 3/F, 2-14-7, Hirakawa-cho, Chiyoda-ku, Tokyo 102-0093; tel. (3) 5275-2671; fax (3) 5275-2675; e-mail info@kokumin.or.jp; internet www.kokumin.or.jp; f. 2005; est. by rebels from LDP opposed to postal reform proposals of Prime Minister Koizumi; Leader SHIZUKA KAMEI; Sec.-Gen. SHOZABURO JIMI.

Social Democratic Party of Japan (SDPJ) (Shakai Minshuto): 1-8-1, Nagata-cho, Chiyoda-ku, Tokyo 100-8909; tel. (3) 3580-1171; fax (3) 3580-0691; e-mail kokusai@sdp.or.jp; internet www.sdp.or.jp; f. 1945; est. as Japan Socialist Party (JSP); adopted present name in 1996; seeks the establishment of collective non-aggression and a mutual security system incl. Japan, the USA, the People's Republic of China and the Commonwealth of Independent States; Chair. MIZUHO FUKUSHIMA; Sec.-Gen. YASUMASA SHIGENO.

Sunrise Party of Japan (Tachiagare Nippon): c/o House of Councillors, Tokyo; internet www.tachiagare.jp; f. 2010; est. by fmr mems of LDP; nationalist conservative grouping; Leader TAKEO HIRANUMA.

Your Party (Minna No To): Towa Hanzomon Corp. Bldg, Rm 606, 2-12, Hayabusa-cho, Chiyoda-ku, Tokyo 102-0092; tel. (3) 5216-3710; fax (3) 5216-3711; internet www.your-party.jp; f. 2009; est. by fmr mems of LDP and DPJ; advocates reform of bureaucracy; President YOSHIMI WATANABE; Sec.-Gen. KENJI EDA.

Diplomatic Representation

EMBASSIES IN JAPAN

Afghanistan: 2-2-1, Azabudai, Minato-ku, Tokyo 106-0041; tel. (3) 5574-7611; fax (3) 5574-0195; e-mail info@afghanembassyjp.org; internet www.afghanembassyjp.org; Ambassador MOHAMMAD AMIN FATIMIE.

Albania: Hokkoku Shimbun Bldg, 4/F, 6-4-8, Tsukiji, Chuo-ku, Tokyo 104-0045; tel. (3) 3543-6861; fax (3) 3543-6862; e-mail embassy.tokyo@mfa.gov.al; internet emb-al.jp; Ambassador BUJAR DIDA.

Algeria: 2-10-67, Mita, Meguro-ku, Tokyo 153-0062; tel. (3) 3711-2661; fax (3) 3710-6534; Ambassador SID ALI KETRANDJI.

Angola: 2-10-24, Daizawa, Setagaya-ku, Tokyo 155-0032; tel. (3) 5430-7879; fax (3) 5712-7481; e-mail angolaembassy@angola.or.jp; internet www.angola.or.jp; Chargé d'affaires a.i. MIGUEL BOMBARDA F. COELHO DA CRUZ.

Argentina: 2-14-14, Moto-Azabu, Minato-ku, Tokyo 106-0046; tel. (3) 5420-7101; fax (3) 5420-7109; e-mail ejapo@mb.rosenet.ne.jp; internet www.embargentina.or.jp; Ambassador RAÚL GUILLERMO DEJEAN RODRÍGUEZ.

Australia: 2-1-14, Mita, Minato-ku, Tokyo 108-8361; tel. (3) 5232-4111; fax (3) 5232-4149; internet www.australia.or.jp; Ambassador BRUCE MILLER.

Austria: 1-1-20, Moto-Azabu, Minato-ku, Tokyo 106-0046; tel. (3) 3451-8281; fax (3) 3451-8283; e-mail tokio-ob@bmeia.gv.at; internet www.bmeia.gv.at/tokio; Ambassador Dr JUTTA STEFAN-BASTL.

Azerbaijan: 1-19-15, Higashi-Gaoka, Meguro-ku, Tokyo 152-0021; tel. (3) 5486-4744; fax (3) 5486-7374; e-mail info@azeembassy.jp; internet www.azembassy.jp; Chargé d'affaires a.i. ROVSHAN KAZIMOV.

Bahrain: Residence Viscountess 720 & 520, 1-11-36, Akasaka, Minato-ku, Tokyo 107-0052; tel. (3) 3584-8001; e-mail info@bahrain-embassy.or.jp; internet www.bahrain-embassy.or.jp; Ambassador Dr KHALIL HASSAN.

Bangladesh: 4-15-15, Meguro, Meguro-ku, Tokyo 153-0063; tel. (3) 5704-0216; fax (3) 5704-1696; e-mail bdembjp@yahoo.com; internet www.bdembjp.com; Ambassador A. K. M. MAJIBUR RAHMAN BHUIYAN.

Belarus: Shirogane K House, 4-14-12, Shirogane, Minato-ku, Tokyo 108-0072; tel. (3) 3448-1623; fax (3) 3448-1624; e-mail japan@belembassy.org; internet www.japan.belembassy.org; Chargé d'affaires a.i. VYACHESLAV BESKOSTY.

Belgium: 5-4, Niban-cho, Chiyoda-ku, Tokyo 102-0084; tel. (3) 3262-0191; fax (3) 3262-0651; e-mail tokyo@diplobel.fed.be; internet www.diplomatie.be/tokyo; Ambassador LUC LIEBAUT.

Benin: Asahi Bldg, 4/F, 1-2-2, Hirakawa-cho, Chiyoda-ku, Tokyo 102-0093; tel. (3) 3556-2562; fax (3) 3556-2563; e-mail abenintyo@mist.ocn.ne.jp; Ambassador ALLASSANE YASSO.

Bolivia: No. 38 Kowa Bldg, Rm 804, 4-12-24, Nishi-Azabu, Minato-ku, Tokyo 106-0031; tel. (3) 3499-5441; fax (3) 3499-5443; e-mail emboltk1@ad.il24.net; Ambassador LUIS MASAHARU HIGA TOMITA.

Bosnia and Herzegovina: 2–3/F, 5-3-29, Minami-Azabu, Minato-ku, Tokyo 106-0047; tel. (3) 5422-8231; fax (3) 5422-8232; e-mail bih8emb@gol.com; Ambassador PERO MATIC.

Botswana: Kearny Place, 6/F, 4-5-10, Shiba, Minato-ku, Tokyo 108-0014; tel. (3) 5440-5676; fax (3) 5765-7581; e-mail botjap@sepia.ocn.ne.jp; internet www.botswanaembassy.or.jp; Ambassador PULAENTLE KENOSI.

Brazil: 2-11-12, Kita-Aoyama, Minato-ku, Tokyo 107-8633; tel. (3) 3404-5211; fax (3) 3405-5846; e-mail brasemb@brasemb.or.jp; internet www.brasemb.or.jp; Ambassador MARCOS BEZERRA ABBOTT GALVÃO.

Brunei: 6-5-2, Kita-Shinagawa, Shinagawa-ku, Tokyo 141-0001; tel. (3) 3447-7997; fax (3) 3447-9260; e-mail contact@bruemb.jp; internet www.bruemb.jp; Ambassador MUHAMMAD ALIAS BIN SERBINI.

Bulgaria: 5-36-3, Yoyogi, Shibuya-ku, Tokyo 151-0053; tel. (3) 3465-1021; fax (3) 3465-1031; e-mail bulemb@gol.com; internet www.mfa.bg/en/76; Ambassador Dr LUBOMIR TODOROV.

Burkina Faso: Apt 301, Hiroo Glisten Hills, 3-1-17, Hiroo, Shibuya-ku, Tokyo 150-0012; tel. (3) 3400-7919; fax (3) 3400-6945; e-mail faso-amb@khaki.plala.or.jp; internet www.embassy-avenue.jp/burkina; Chargé d'affaires a.i. LAMBERT ALEXANDRE OUEDRAOGO.

Cambodia: 8-6-9, Akasaka, Minato-ku, Tokyo 107-0052; tel. (3) 5412-8521; fax (3) 5412-8526; e-mail camembassyjp@gmail.com; internet www.cambodianembassy.jp; Ambassador HOR MONIRATH.

Cameroon: 3-27-16, Nozawa, Setagaya-ku, Tokyo 154-0003; tel. (3) 5430-4985; fax (3) 5430-6489; e-mail ambacamtokyo@gol.com; Ambassador Dr PIERRE NDZENGUE.

Canada: 7-3-38, Akasaka, Minato-ku, Tokyo 107-8503; tel. (3) 5412-6200; fax (3) 5412-6249; e-mail tokyo-cs@international.gc.ca; internet www.canadainternational.gc.ca/japan-japon; Ambassador JONATHAN FRIED.

Chile: Nihon Seimei Akabanebashi Bldg, 8/F, 3-1-14, Shiba, Minato-ku, Tokyo 105-0014; tel. (3) 3452-7561; fax (3) 3452-4457; e-mail embajada@chile.or.jp; internet chileabroad.gov.cl/japon; Ambassador PATRICIO TORRES.

China, People's Republic: 3-4-33, Moto-Azabu, Minato-ku, Tokyo 106-0046; tel. (3) 3403-3380; fax (3) 3403-3345; e-mail lsb@china-embassy.or.jp; internet www.china-embassy.or.jp; Ambassador CHENG YONGHUA.

Colombia: 3-10-53, Kami Osaki, Shinagawa-ku, Tokyo 141-0021; tel. (3) 3440-6451; fax (3) 3440-6724; e-mail embajada@emcoltokyo.or.jp; internet www.colombiaembassy.org; Ambassador PATRICIA CÁRDENAS.

Congo, Democratic Republic: 1–2/F, 5-8-5, Asakusabashi, Taito-ku, Tokyo 111-0053; tel. (3) 5820-1580; fax (3) 3423-3984; Ambassador MARCEL MULUMBA TSHIDIMBA.

Costa Rica: No. 38 Kowa Bldg, Rm 901, 4-12-24, Nishi-Azabu, Minato-ku, Tokyo 106-0031; tel. (3) 3486-1812; fax (3) 3486-1813; e-mail mfdzsilva@yahoo.com; Ambassador MARIO FERNÁNDEZ SILVA.

Côte d'Ivoire: 2-19-12, Uehara, Shibuya-ku, Tokyo 151-0064; tel. (3) 5454-1401; fax (3) 5454-1405; e-mail ambacijn@yahoo.fr; internet www.ahibo.com/ambaci-jp; Ambassador LILIANE MARIE LAURE BOA.

Croatia: 3-3-10, Hiroo, Shibuya-ku, Tokyo 150-0012; tel. (3) 5469-3014; fax (3) 5469-3015; e-mail croemb.tokyo@mvpei.hr; internet jp.mfa.hr; Ambassador MIRA MARTINEC.

Cuba: 1-28-4, Higashi-Azabu, Minato-ku, Tokyo 106-0044; tel. (3) 5570-3182; fax (3) 5570-8566; e-mail embajada@ecujapon.jp; internet embacuba.cubaminrex.cu/japon; Ambassador JOSÉ FERNÁNDEZ DE COSSIO.

Czech Republic: 2-16-14, Hiroo, Shibuya-ku, Tokyo 150-0012; tel. (3) 3400-8122; fax (3) 3400-8124; e-mail tokyo@embassy.mzv.cz; internet www.mzv.cz/tokyo; Ambassador KATEŘINA FIALKOVÁ.

Denmark: 29-6, Sarugaku-cho, Shibuya-ku, Tokyo 150-0033; tel. (3) 3496-3001; fax (3) 3496-3440; e-mail tyoamb@um.dk; internet www.ambtokyo.um.dk; Ambassador FRANZ-MICHAEL SKJOLD MELLBIN.

Djibouti: 5-18-10, Shimo Meguro, Meguro-ku, Tokyo 153-0064; tel. (3) 5704-0682; fax (3) 5725-8305; e-mail djibouti@fine.ocn.jp; internet www.djiboutiembassy.jp; Ambassador AHMED ARAITA ALI.

Dominican Republic: No. 38 Kowa Bldg, Rm 904, 4-12-24, Nishi-Azabu, Minato-ku, Tokyo 106-0031; tel. (3) 3499-6020; fax (3) 3499-2627; Ambassador PEDRO VERGÉS.

Ecuador: No. 38 Kowa Bldg, Rm 806, 4-12-24, Nishi-Azabu, Minato-ku, Tokyo 106-0031; tel. (3) 3499-2800; fax (3) 3499-4400; e-mail info@ecuador-embassy.or.jp; internet www.ecuador-embassy.or.jp; Ambassador JAVIER PONCE.

Egypt: 1-5-4, Aobadai, Meguro-ku, Tokyo 153-0042; tel. (3) 3770-8022; fax (3) 3770-8021; e-mail egyptemb@leaf.ocn.ne.jp; internet www.mfa.gov.eg/Tokyo_Emb; Ambassador WALID ABDELNASSER.

El Salvador: No. 38 Kowa Bldg, 8/F, 4-12-24, Nishi-Azabu, Minato-ku, Tokyo 106-0031; tel. (3) 3499-4461; fax (3) 3486-7022; e-mail embesaltokio@gol.com; Chargé d'affaires a.i. MARTHA LIDIA ZELAYANDÍA.

Eritrea: Shirokanedai ST Bldg, Rm 401, 4-7-4, Shirokanedai, Minato-ku, Tokyo, 108-0071; tel. (3) 5791-1815; fax (3) 5791-1816; e-mail info@eritreaembassy-japan.org; internet www.eritreaembassy-japan.org; Ambassador ESTIFANOS AFEWORKI.

Estonia: 2-6-15, Jingu-mae, Shibuya-ku 150-0001; tel. (3) 5412-7281; fax (3) 5412-7282; e-mail embassy.tokyo@mfa.ee; internet www.estemb.or.jp; Ambassador TOIVO TASA.

Ethiopia: Takanawa Kaisei Bldg, 2/F, 3-4-1, Takanawa, Minato-ku, Tokyo 108-0074; tel. (3) 5420-6860; fax (3) 5420-6866; e-mail info@ethiopia-emb.or.jp; internet www.ethiopia-emb.or.jp; Ambassador MARKOS TEKLE RIKE.

Fiji: Noa Bldg, 14/F, 2-3-5, Azabudai, Minato-ku, Tokyo 106-0041; tel. (3) 3587-2038; fax (3) 3587-2563; e-mail info@fijiembassy.jp; internet www.fijiembassy.jp; Ambassador ISIKELI MATAITOGA.

Finland: 3-5-39, Minami-Azabu, Minato-ku, Tokyo 106-8561; tel. (3) 5447-6000; fax (3) 5447-6042; e-mail sanomat.tok@formin.fi; internet www.finland.or.jp; Ambassador JARI GUSTAFSSON.

France: 4-11-44, Minami-Azabu, Minato-ku, Tokyo 106-8514; tel. (3) 5798-6330; fax (3) 5798-6328; e-mail ambafrance.tokyo@

diplomatie.fr; internet www.ambafrance-jp.org; Ambassador PHILIPPE FAURE.

Gabon: 1-34-11, Higashi-Gaoka, Meguro-ku, Tokyo 152-0021; tel. (3) 5430-9171; fax (3) 5430-9175; e-mail info@gabonembassy-tokyo.org; internet www.geocities.jp/gabontky; Ambassador JEAN-CHRISTIAN OBAME.

Georgia: Residence Viscountess 220, 1-11-36, Akasaka, Minato-ku, Tokyo 107-0052; tel. (3) 5575-6091; fax (3) 5575-9133; e-mail tokio.emb@mfa.gov.ge; internet japan.mfa.gov.ge; Ambassador REVAZ BESHIDZE.

Germany: 4-5-10, Minami-Azabu, Minato-ku, Tokyo 106-0047; tel. (3) 5791-7700; fax (3) 5791-7773; e-mail info@tokyo.diplo.de; internet www.tokyo.diplo.de; Ambassador Dr VOLKER STANZEL.

Ghana: 1-5-21, Nishi-Azabu, Minato-ku, Tokyo 106-0031; tel. (3) 5410-8631; fax (3) 5410-8635; e-mail mission@ghanaembassy.or.jp; internet www.ghanaembassy.or.jp; Ambassador WILLIAM BRANDFUL.

Greece: 3-16-30, Nishi-Azabu, Minato-ku, Tokyo 106-0031; tel. (3) 3403-0871; fax (3) 3402-4642; e-mail gremb.tok@mfa.gr; Ambassador NIKOLAOS TSAMADOS.

Guatemala: No. 38 Kowa Bldg, Rm 905, 4-12-24, Nishi-Azabu, Minato-ku, Tokyo 106-0031; tel. (3) 3400-1830; fax (3) 3400-1820; e-mail embguate@vega.ocn.ne.jp; internet www.embassy-avenue.jp/guatemala; Ambassador BYRON RENE ESCOBEDO MENÉNDEZ.

Guinea: 12-9, Hachiyama-cho, Shibuya-ku, Tokyo 150-0035; tel. (3) 3770-4640; fax (3) 3770-4643; e-mail ambagui-tokyo@gol.com; Ambassador MOHAMED LAMINE TOURE.

Haiti: No. 38 Kowa Bldg, Rm 906, 4-12-24, Nishi-Azabu, Minato-ku, Tokyo 106-0031; tel. (3) 3486-7096; fax (3) 3486-7070; e-mail ambhaiti@cuber.ocn.ne.jp; Chargé d'affaires a.i. JEAN-CLAUDE BORDES.

Holy See: Apostolic Nunciature, 9-2, Sanban-cho, Chiyoda-ku, Tokyo 102-0075; tel. (3) 3263-6851; fax (3) 3263-6060; Apostolic Nuncio Most Rev. JOSEPH CHENNOTH (Titular Archbishop of Milevum).

Honduras: No. 38 Kowa Bldg, Rm 802, 4-12-24, Nishi-Azabu, Minato-ku, Tokyo 106-0031; tel. (3) 3409-1150; fax (3) 3409-0305; e-mail honduras@interlink.or.jp; Ambassador MARLENE VILLELA.

Hungary: 2-17-14, Mita, Minato-ku, Tokyo 108-0073; tel. (3) 3798-8801; fax (3) 3798-8812; e-mail mission.tio@kum.hu; internet www.mfa.gov.hu/kulkepviselet/JP/HU; Chargé d'affaires a.i. JÁNOS ALBERT.

Iceland: 4-18-26, Takanawa, Minato-ku, Tokyo 108-0074; tel. (3) 3447-1944; fax (3) 3447-1945; e-mail icemb.tokyo@utn.stjr.is; internet www.iceland.org/jp; Ambassador STEFAN LARUS STEFANSSON.

India: 2-2-11, Kudan-Minami, Chiyoda-ku, Tokyo 102-0074; tel. (3) 3262-2391; fax (3) 3234-4866; e-mail embassy@indembjp.org; internet www.embassyofindiajapan.org; Ambassador ALOK PRASAD.

Indonesia: 5-2-9, Higashi-Gotanda, Shinagawa-ku, Tokyo 141-0022; tel. (3) 3441-4201; fax (3) 3447-1697; e-mail info@indonesianembassy.jp; internet www2.indonesianembassy.jp; Ambassador MUHAMMAD LUTFI.

Iran: 3-13-9, Minami-Azabu, Minato-ku, Tokyo 106-0047; tel. (3) 3446-8011; fax (3) 3446-9002; e-mail info@iranembassyjp.org; internet www.iranembassyjp.org; Ambassador SEYYED ABBAS ARAGHCHI.

Iraq: 2-16-11, Takanawa, Minato-ku, Tokyo 108-0074; tel. (3) 5449-3231; fax (3) 5449-7718; e-mail embassy@iraqi-japan.com; internet www.iraqi-japan.com; Ambassador LUQMAN ABD AL-RAHEEM AL-FAILI.

Ireland: Ireland House, 2-10-7, Kojimachi, Chiyoda-ku, Tokyo 102-0083; tel. (3) 3263-0695; fax (3) 3265-2275; e-mail tokyoembassy@dfa.ie; internet www.irishembassy.jp; Ambassador JOHN NEARY.

Israel: 3, Niban-cho, Chiyoda-ku, Tokyo 102-0084; tel. (3) 3264-0911; fax (3) 3264-0791; e-mail consular@tokyo.mfa.gov.il; internet tokyo.mfa.gov.il; Ambassador NISSIM BEN-SHITRIT.

Italy: 2-5-4, Mita, Minato-ku, Tokyo 108-8302; tel. (3) 3453-5291; fax (3) 3456-2319; e-mail ambasciata.tokyo@esteri.it; internet www.ambtokyo.esteri.it/ambasciata_tokyo; Ambassador VINCENZO PETRONE.

Jamaica: Toranomon Yatsuka Bldg, 2/F, 1-1-11, Atago, Minato-ku, Tokyo 105-0002; tel. (3) 3435-1861; fax (3) 3435-1864; e-mail mail@jamaicaemb.jp; internet www.jamaicaemb.jp; Ambassador CLAUDIA CECILE BARNES.

Jordan: 39-8, Kamiyama-cho, Shibuya-ku, Tokyo 100-0014; tel. (3) 5478-7177; fax (3) 5478-0032; e-mail jor-emb@bird.ocn.ne.jp; internet www18.ocn.ne.jp/~jor-emb; Ambassador DEMIYE HADDAD.

Kazakhstan: 5-9-8, Himonya, Meguro-ku, Tokyo 152-0003; tel. (3) 3791-5273; fax (3) 3791-5279; e-mail japan_tokyo@mfa.kz; internet www.embkazjp.org; Ambassador AKYLBEK KAMALDINOV.

Kenya: 3-24-3, Yakumo, Meguro-ku, Tokyo 152-0023; tel. (3) 3723-4006; fax (3) 3723-4488; e-mail general@kenyarep-jp.com; internet www.kenyarep-jp.com; Ambassador BENSON H. O. OGUTU.

Korea, Republic: 1-2-5, Minami-Azabu, Minato-ku, Tokyo 106-0047; tel. (3) 3452-7611; fax (3) 5232-6911; e-mail information_jp@mofat.go.kr; internet jpn-tokyo.mofat.go.kr; Ambassador SHIN KAK-SOO.

Kosovo: 3-13-7, Nishi-Shinbashi, Minato-ku, Tokyo 105-0003; tel. (3) 6809-2577; fax (3) 6809-2579; e-mail embassy.japan@ks-gov.net; Ambassador SAMI UKELLI.

Kuwait: 4-13-12, Mita, Minato-ku, Tokyo 108-0073; tel. (3) 3455-0361; fax (3) 3456-6290; e-mail consular@kuwait-embassy.or.jp; internet kuwait-embassy.or.jp; Ambassador Sheikh ABDUL RAHMAN AL-OTAIBI.

Kyrgyzstan: 5-6-16, Shimomeguro, Meguro-ku, Tokyo 153-0064; tel. (3) 3719-0828; fax (3) 3719-0868; e-mail chancery@kyrgyzemb.jp; Ambassador MOLDOGAZIEV RYSBEK TURGANBAEVICH.

Laos: 3-3-22, Nishi-Azabu, Minato-ku, Tokyo 106-0031; tel. (3) 5411-2291; fax (3) 5411-2293; Ambassador SITHONG CHITNHOTHINH.

Latvia: 37-11, Kamiyama-cho, Shibuya-ku, Tokyo 150-0047; tel. (3) 3467-6888; fax (3) 3467-6897; e-mail embassy.japan@mfa.gov.lv; Ambassador PĒTERIS VAIVARS.

Lebanon: Residence Viscountess 410, 1-11-36, Akasaka, Minato-ku, Tokyo 107-0052; tel. (3) 5114-9950; fax (3) 5114-9952; e-mail ambaliba@cropos.ocp.ne.jp; Ambassador MOHAMMED EL-HARAKE.

Lesotho: U & M Akasaka Bldg, 3/F, 7-5-47, Akasaka, Minato-ku, Tokyo 107-0052; tel. (3) 3584-7455; fax (3) 3584-7456; e-mail bochabela@lesothotokyo.org; internet www.lesothotokyo.org; Ambassador RICHARD RAMOELETSI.

Liberia: 4-11-7, Hukazawa, Setagaya-ku, Tokyo 158-0081; tel. (3) 3703-6926; fax (3) 3726-5712; Ambassador YOUNGOR SEVELEE TELEWODA.

Libya: 10-14, Daikanyama-cho, Shibuya-ku, Tokyo 150-0034; tel. (3) 3477-0701; fax (3) 3464-0420; Chargé d'affaires a.i. GIUMA S. G. OUN.

Lithuania: 3-7-18, Moto-Azabu, Minato-ku, Tokyo 106-0046; tel. (3) 3408-5091; fax (3) 3408-5092; e-mail amb.jp@urm.lt; internet jp.mfa.lt; Chargé d'affaires a.i. JOLANTA VITKAUSKAITĖ.

Luxembourg: Luxembourg House, 1/F, 8–9, Yonban-cho, Chiyoda-ku, 102-0081; tel. (3) 3265-9621; fax (3) 3265-9624; e-mail infotokyo.amb@mae.etat.lu; internet tokyo.mae.lu/jp; Ambassador PAUL STEINMETZ.

Madagascar: 2-3-23, Moto-Azabu, Minato-ku, Tokyo 106-0046; tel. (3) 3446-7252; fax (3) 3446-7078; e-mail ambtyo@r5.dion.ne.jp; internet www.madagascar-embassy.jp; Ambassador JIMMY RAMIANDRISOA.

Malawi: Takanawa-Kaisei Bldg, 7/F, 3-4-1, Takanawa, Minato-ku, Tokyo 108-0074; tel. (3) 3449-3010; fax (3) 3449-3220; e-mail malawi@luck.ocn.ne.jp; internet www.malawiembassy.org; Ambassador RUEBEN NGWENYA.

Malaysia: 20-16, Nanpeidai-cho, Shibuya-ku, Tokyo 150-0036; tel. (3) 3476-3840; fax (3) 3476-4971; e-mail maltokyo@kln.gov.my; internet www.kln.gov.my/web/jpn_tokyo; Ambassador Dato' SHAHARUDDIN BIN MOHAMMED SOM.

Maldives: Iikura MINT Bldg, 8/F, 1-9-10, Azabudai, Minato-ku, Tokyo 106-0041; tel. (3) 6234-4315; fax (3) 6234-4316; e-mail info@maldivesembassy.jp; internet www.maldivesembassy.jp; Ambassador AHMED KHALEEL.

Mali: 3-12-9, Kami-Osaki, Shinagawa-ku, Tokyo 141-0021; tel. (3) 5447-6881; fax (3) 5447-6882; e-mail info@ambamali-jp.org; internet www.ambamali-jp.org; Chargé d'affaires a.i. TAOULE KEITA.

Marshall Islands: Meiji Park Heights, 1/F, Rm 101, 9-9, Minami-Motomachi, Shinjuku-ku, Tokyo 106-0012; tel. (3) 5379-1701; fax (3) 5379-1810; e-mail alfred@rmiembassyjp.org; Ambassador JIBA KABUA.

Mauritania: 5-17-5, Kita-Shinagawa, Shinagawa-ku, Tokyo 141-0001; tel. (3) 3449-3810; fax (3) 3449-3822; e-mail ambarim@seagreen.ocn.ne.jp; internet www.amba-mauritania.jp; Ambassador YAHYA NGAM.

Mexico: 2-15-1, Nagata-cho, Chiyoda-ku, Tokyo 100-0014; tel. (3) 3581-1131; fax (3) 3581-4058; e-mail embajadamexicojapon@sre.gob.mx; internet www.sre.gob.mx/japon; Ambassador MIGUEL RUIZ-CABAÑAS IZQUIERDO.

Micronesia, Federated States: Reinanzaka Bldg, 2/F, 1-14-2, Akasaka, Minato-ku, Tokyo 107-0052; tel. (3) 3585-5456; fax (3) 3585-5348; e-mail fsmemb@fsmemb.or.jp; Ambassador JOHN FRITZ.

Mongolia: Pine Crest Mansion, 21-4, Kamiyama-cho, Shibuya-ku, Tokyo 150-0047; tel. (3) 3469-2088; fax (3) 3469-2216; e-mail embmong@gol.com; Ambassador RENTSENDOOGIIN JIGJID.

Morocco: 5-4-30, Minami-Aoyama, Minato-ku, Tokyo 107-0062; tel. (3) 5485-7171; fax (3) 5485-7173; e-mail sifamato@circus.ocn.ne.jp; internet www.morocco-emba.jp; Ambassador Dr SAMIR ARROUR.

Mozambique: Shiba Amerex Bldg, 6/F, 3-12-17 Mita, Minato-ku, Tokyo 108-0073; tel. (3) 5419-0973; fax (3) 5442-0556; e-mail mozambiq@tkk.att.ne.jp; internet www.embamoc.jp; Ambassador Belmiro José Malate.

Myanmar: 4-8-26, Kita-Shinagawa, Shinagawa-ku, Tokyo 140-0001; tel. (3) 3441-9291; fax (3) 3447-7394; e-mail contact@myanmar-embassy-tokyo.net; internet www.myanmar-embassy-tokyo.net; Ambassador Khin Maung Ting.

Nepal: 7-14-9, Todoroki, Setagaya-ku, Tokyo 158-0082; tel. (3) 3705-5558; fax (3) 3705-8264; e-mail nepembjp@big.or.jp; internet www.nepal-embassy.org; Ambassador Ganesh Yonzan Tamang.

Netherlands: 3-6-3, Shiba Koen, Minato-ku, Tokyo 105-0011; tel. (3) 5776-5400; fax (3) 5776-5535; e-mail tok@minbuza.nl; internet japan.nlambassade.org; Ambassador Philip de Heer.

New Zealand: 20-40, Kamiyama-cho, Shibuya-ku, Tokyo 150-0047; tel. (3) 3467-2271; fax (3) 3467-2278; e-mail nzemb.tky@mfat.govt.nz; internet www.nzembassy.com/japan; Ambassador Ian Kennedy.

Nicaragua: No. 38 Kowa Bldg, Rm 903, 4-12-24, Nishi-Azabu, Minato-ku, Tokyo 106-0031; tel. (3) 3499-0400; fax (3) 3710-2028; e-mail nicjapan@gol.com; Ambassador Saúl Arana Castellón.

Nigeria: 3-6-1 Toranomon, Minato-ku, Tokyo 105-0001; tel. (3) 5425-8014; fax (3) 5425-8021; e-mail info@nigeriaembassy.jp; internet www.nigeriaembassy.jp; Ambassador Godwin Nsude Agbo.

Norway: 5-12-2, Minami-Azabu, Minato-ku, Tokyo 106-0047; tel. (3) 3440-2611; fax (3) 3440-2620; e-mail emb.tokyo@mfa.no; internet www.norway.or.jp; Ambassador Arne Walther.

Oman: 4-2-17, Hiroo, Shibuya-ku, Tokyo 150-0012; tel. (3) 5468-1088; e-mail omanemb@gol.com; Ambassador Khalid bin Hashil bin Mohammed al-Muslahi.

Pakistan: 4-6-17, Minami-Azabu, Minato-ku, Tokyo 106-0047; tel. (3) 5421-7741; fax (3) 5421-3610; e-mail info@pakistanembassyjapan.com; internet www.pakistanembassyjapan.com; Ambassador Noor Muhammad Jadmani.

Palau: Rm 201, 1-1, Katamachi, Shinjuku-ku, Tokyo 160-0001; tel. (3) 3354-5500; Ambassador Dr Minoru Ueki.

Panama: No. 38 Kowa Bldg, Rm 902, 4-12-24, Nishi-Azabu, Minato-ku, Tokyo 106-0031; tel. (3) 3499-3741; fax (3) 5485-3548; e-mail panaemb@gol.com; internet www.embassyofpanamainjapan.org; Ambassador Jorge Demetrio Kosmas Sifaki.

Papua New Guinea: Mita Kokusai Bldg, 3/F, Rm 313, 1-4-28, Mita, Minato-ku, Tokyo 108-0073; tel. (3) 3454-7801; fax (3) 3454-7275; e-mail png-tyo@nifty.ne.jp; Ambassador Gabriel Dusava.

Paraguay: Ichibancho TG Bldg 2, 7/F, 2-2, Ichiban-cho, Chiyoda-ku, Tokyo 102-0082; tel. (3) 3265-5271; fax (3) 3265-5273; e-mail embajada-consulado@embapar.jp; internet www.embapar.jp; Ambassador Naoyuki Toyotoshi.

Peru: 4-4-27, Higashi, Shibuya-ku, Tokyo 150-0011; tel. (3) 3406-4243; fax (3) 3409-7589; e-mail embperutokyo@embperujapan.org; internet www.embajadadelperuenjapon.org; Ambassador Juan Carlos Capuñay Chávez.

Philippines: 5-15-5, Roppongi, Minato-ku, Tokyo 106-8537; tel. (3) 5562-1600; fax (3) 5562-1603; e-mail info@philembassy.net; internet tokyo.philembassy.net; Ambassador Manuel Lopez.

Poland: 2-13-5, Mita, Meguro-ku, Tokyo 153-0062; tel. (3) 5794-7020; fax (3) 5794-7024; e-mail tokio.amb.sekretariat@msz.gov.pl; internet www.tokio.polemb.net; Ambassador Jadwiga Maria Rodowicz.

Portugal: Kamiura-Kojimachi Bldg, 5/F, 3-10-3, Kojimachi, Chiyoda-ku, Tokyo 102-0083; tel. (3) 5212-7322; fax (3) 5226-0616; e-mail embportj@zb4.so-net.ne.jp; internet www.embaixadadeportugal.jp; Ambassador José Ferraz.

Qatar: 2-3-28, Moto-Azabu, Minato-ku, Tokyo 106-0046; tel. (3) 5475-0611; fax (3) 5475-0617; e-mail tokyo@mofa.gov.qa; Ambassador Yousuf Mohamed Bilal.

Romania: 3-16-19, Nishi-Azabu, Minato-ku, Tokyo 106-0031; tel. (3) 3479-0311; fax (3) 3479-0312; e-mail office@ambrom.jp; internet tokyo.mae.ro; Chargé d'affaires a.i. Petre Stoian.

Russia: 2-1-1, Azabudai, Minato-ku, Tokyo 106-0041; tel. (3) 3583-4224; fax (3) 3505-0593; e-mail rosconsl@ma.kcom.ne.jp; internet www.russia-emb.jp; Ambassador Mikhail M. Bely.

Rwanda: Annex Fukazawa, 1-17-17, Fukazawa, Setagaya-ku, Tokyo 158-0081; tel. (3) 5752-4255; fax (3) 3703-0342; internet www.rwandaembassy-japan.org; Chargé d'affaires a.i. Benedicto Nshimyimana.

Samoa: Seiko Bldg, 3/F, 2-7-4, Irifune, Chuo-ku, Tokyo 104-0042; Ambassador Leiataua Tuitolova'a Dr Kilifoti Eteuati.

San Marino: 3-5-1, Moto-Azabu, Minato-ku, Tokyo 106-0046; tel. (3) 5414-7745; fax (3) 3405-6789; e-mail sanmarinoemb@tiscali.it; Ambassador Manlio Cadelo.

Saudi Arabia: 1-8-4, Roppongi, Minato-ku, Tokyo 106-0032; tel. (3) 3589-5241; fax (3) 3589-5200; e-mail info@saudiembassy.or.jp; internet www.saudiembassy.or.jp; Ambassador Abdulaziz Turkistani.

Senegal: 1-3-4, Aobadai, Meguro-ku, Tokyo 153-0042; tel. (3) 3464-8451; fax (3) 3464-8452; e-mail senegal@senegal.jp; Ambassador Bouna Sémou Diouf.

Serbia: 4-7-24, Kita-Shinagawa, Shinagawa-ku, Tokyo 140-0001; tel. (3) 3447-3571; fax (3) 3447-3573; e-mail embassy@serbianembassy.jp; internet www.serbianembassy.jp; Chargé d'affaires a.i. Miroslava Malić-Kljaković.

Singapore: 5-12-3, Roppongi, Minato-ku, Tokyo 106-0032; tel. (3) 3586-9111; fax (3) 3582-1085; e-mail singemb_tyo@sgmfa.gov.sg; internet www.mfa.gov.sg/tokyo; Ambassador Tan Chin Tiong.

Slovakia: 2-11-33, Moto-Azabu, Minato-ku, Tokyo 106-0046; tel. (3) 3451-2200; fax (3) 3451-2244; e-mail emb.tokyo@mzv.sk; internet www.tokyo.mfa.sk; Ambassador Drahomír Štos.

Slovenia: 7-14-12, Minami-Aoyama, Minato-ku, Tokyo 107-0062; tel. (3) 5468-6275; fax (3) 5468-1182; e-mail vto@gov.si; internet tokyo.embassy.si; Ambassador Helena Drnovšek Zorko.

South Africa: Oriken Hirakawa Bldg, 3–4/F, 2-1-1, Hirakawa-cho, Chiyoda-ku, Tokyo 102-0093; tel. (3) 3265-3366; fax (3) 3265-3573; e-mail cronjet@dfa.gov.za; internet www.sajapan.org; Ambassador Dr Gert Johannes Grobler.

Spain: 1-3-29, Roppongi, Minato-ku, Tokyo 106-0032; tel. (3) 3583-8531; fax (3) 3582-8627; e-mail emb.tokio@maec.es; internet www.maec.es/subwebs/Embajadas/Tokio/es; Ambassador Miguel Ángel Navarro Portera.

Sri Lanka: 2-1-54, Takanawa, Minato-ku, Tokyo 108-0074; tel. (3) 3440-6911; fax (3) 3440-6914; e-mail tokyojp@lankaembassy.jp; internet www.lankaembassy.jp; Ambassador Wasantha Karannagoda.

Sudan: 4-7-1, Yakumo, Meguro-ku, Tokyo 152-0023; tel. (3) 5729-6170; fax (3) 5729-6171; e-mail info@sudanembassy.jp; internet www.sudanembassy.jp; Ambassador Abdon Terkoc Matuet.

Sweden: 1-10-3-100, Roppongi, Minato-ku, Tokyo 106-0032; tel. (3) 5562-5050; fax (3) 5562-9095; e-mail ambassaden.tokyo@foreign.ministry.se; internet www.sweden.or.jp; Ambassador Stefan Noreén.

Switzerland: 5-9-12, Minami-Azabu, Minato-ku, Tokyo 106-8589; tel. (3) 5449-8400; fax (3) 3473-6090; e-mail tok.vertretung@eda.admin.ch; internet www.eda.admin.ch/tokyo; Ambassador Urs Bucher.

Syria: Homat Jade, 6-19-45, Akasaka, Minato-ku, Tokyo 107-0052; tel. (3) 3586-8977; fax (3) 3586-8979; internet syrian-embassy.jp; Ambassador Mohamed Ghassan al-Habash.

Tajikistan: NK Bldg, Nishi Azabu, 1-4-43, Minato-ku, Tokyo; tel. (3) 6804-3661; fax (3) 5410-3677; e-mail tajembjapan@yahoo.com; internet www.tajikistan.jp; Ambassador Bobozoda Gulomjon Jura.

Tanzania: 4-21-9, Kami Yoga, Setagaya-ku, Tokyo 158-0098; tel. (3) 3425-4531; fax (3) 3425-7844; e-mail tzrepjp@tanzaniaembassy.or.jp; internet www.tanzaniaembassy.or.jp; Ambassador Salome T. Sijaona.

Thailand: 3-14-6, Kami Osaki, Shinagawa-ku, Tokyo 141-0021; tel. (3) 3447-2247; fax (3) 3442-6750; e-mail infosect@thaiembassy.jp; internet www.thaiembassy.jp; Ambassador Virasakdi Futrakul.

Timor-Leste: Rokuban-cho House, 1/F, 3-4, Rokuban-cho, Chiyoda-ku, Tokyo 102-0085; tel. (3) 3238-0210; Ambassador Isilio Antonio da Silva.

Tunisia: 3-6-6, Kudan-Minami, Chiyoda-ku, Tokyo 102-0074; tel. (3) 3511-6622; fax (3) 3511-6699; e-mail mailbox@tunisia.or.jp; internet www.tunisia.or.jp; Ambassador Ilyes El Kosri.

Turkey: 2-33-6, Jingumae, Shibuya-ku, Tokyo 150-0001; tel. (3) 6439-5700; fax (3) 3470-5136; e-mail embassy.tokyo@mfa.gov.tr; internet tokyo.be.mfa.gov.tr; Ambassador Abdurrahman Bilgiç.

Uganda: 9-23, Hachiyama-cho, Shibuya-ku, Tokyo 150-0035; tel. (3) 3462-7107; fax (3) 3462-7108; e-mail ugabassy@hpo.net; internet www.uganda-embassy.jp; Ambassador Wasswa Biriggwa.

Ukraine: 3-15-31, Nishi-Azabu, Minato-ku, Tokyo 106-0031; tel. (3) 5474-9770; fax (3) 5474-9772; e-mail ukrcn@rose.ocn.ne.jp; internet www.mfa.gov.ua/japan; Ambassador Mykola Kulinich.

United Arab Emirates: 9-10, Nanpeidai-cho, Shibuya-ku, Tokyo 150-0036; tel. (3) 5489-0804; fax (3) 5489-0813; Ambassador Saeed Ali al-Nowais.

United Kingdom: 1, Ichiban-cho, Chiyoda-ku, Tokyo 102-8381; tel. (3) 5211-1100; fax (3) 5275-3164; e-mail consular.tokyo@fco.gov.uk; internet ukinjapan.fco.gov.uk; Ambassador David Warren.

USA: 1-10-5, Akasaka, Minato-ku, Tokyo 107-8420; tel. (3) 3224-5000; fax (3) 3505-1862; internet tokyo.usembassy.gov; Ambassador John V. Roos.

Uruguay: No. 38 Kowa Bldg, Rm 908, 4-12-24, Nishi-Azabu, Minato-ku, Tokyo 106-0031; tel. (3) 3486-1888; fax (3) 3486-9872; e-mail urujap@luck.ocn.ne.jp; Ambassador Ana María Estévez Mercader.

Uzbekistan: 5-11-8, Shimo-Meguro, Meguro-ku, Tokyo 153-0064; tel. (3) 3760-5625; fax (3) 3760-5950; Ambassador KARAMATOV KHAMIDULLA SADULLAEVICH.

Venezuela: No. 38 Kowa Bldg, Rm 703, 4-12-24, Nishi-Azabu, Minato-ku, Tokyo 106-0031; tel. (3) 3409-1501; fax (3) 3409-1505; e-mail embavene@interlink.or.jp; Ambassador SEIKO LUIS ISHIKAWA KOBAYASHI.

Viet Nam: 50-11, Moto-Yoyogi-cho, Shibuya-ku, Tokyo 151-0062; tel. (3) 3466-3313; fax (3) 3466-3391; e-mail vnembasy@blue.ocn.ne.jp; internet www.vietnamembassy-japan.org; Ambassador NGUYEN PHU BINH.

Yemen: No. 38 Kowa Bldg, Rm 807, 4-12-24, Nishi-Azabu, Minato-ku, Tokyo 106-0031; tel. (3) 3499-7151; fax (3) 3499-4577; e-mail info@yemen.jp; internet www.yemen.jp; Chargé d'affaires a.i. TAREQ ABDULLATIF ABDULLA MOTAHAR.

Zambia: 1-10-2, Ebara, Shinagawa-ku, Tokyo 142-0063; tel. (3) 3491-0121; fax (3) 3491-0123; e-mail infoemb@zambia.or.jp; internet www.zambia.or.jp; Ambassador MBIKUSITA WAMUNDILA LEWANIKA.

Zimbabwe: 5-9-10, Shiroganedai, Minato-ku, Tokyo 108-0071; tel. (3) 3280-0331; fax (3) 3280-0466; e-mail zimtokyo@chive.ocn.ne.jp; Ambassador STUART H. COMBERBACH.

Judicial System

The basic principles of the legal system are set forth in the Constitution, which lays down that judicial power is vested in the Supreme Court and in such inferior courts as are established by law, and enunciates the principle that no organ or agency of the Executive shall be given final judicial power. Judges are to be independent in the exercise of their conscience, and may not be removed except by public impeachment, unless judicially declared mentally or physically incompetent to perform official duties. The justices of the Supreme Court are appointed by the Cabinet, the sole exception being the Chief Justice, who is appointed by the Emperor after designation by the Cabinet.

The Court Organization Law, which came into force on 3 May 1947, decreed the constitution of the Supreme Court and the establishment of four types of lower court—High, District, Family (established 1 January 1949) and Summary Courts. The system of trial by jury, suspended since 1943, was reinstated in 2009. Jurors are selected at random from the electoral register.

SUPREME COURT

This court is the highest legal authority in the land, and consists of a Chief Justice and 14 associate justices. It has jurisdiction over Jokoku (Jokoku appeals) and Kokoku (Kokoku appeals), prescribed in codes of procedure. It conducts its hearings and renders decisions through a Grand Bench or three Petty Benches. Both are collegiate bodies, the former consisting of all justices of the Court, and the latter of five justices. A Supreme Court Rule prescribes which cases are to be handled by the respective Benches. It is, however, laid down by law that the Petty Bench cannot make decisions as to the constitutionality of a statute, ordinance, regulation, or disposition, or as to cases in which an opinion concerning the interpretation and application of the Constitution, or of any laws or ordinances, is at variance with a previous decision of the Supreme Court.

Chief Justice: HIRONOBU TAKESAKI, 4-2, Hayabusa-cho, Chiyoda-ku, Tokyo 102-8651; tel. (3) 3264-8111; fax (3) 3221-8975; internet www.courts.go.jp.

Secretary-General: TOSHIMITSU YAMASAKI.

LOWER COURTS

High Court

A High Court conducts its hearings and renders decisions through a collegiate body, consisting of three judges, though for cases of insurrection the number of judges must be five. The Court has jurisdiction over the following matters:

Koso appeals from judgments in the first instance rendered by District Courts, from judgments rendered by Family Courts, and from judgments concerning criminal cases rendered by Summary Courts.

Kokoku appeals against rulings and orders rendered by District Courts and Family Courts, and against rulings and orders concerning criminal cases rendered by Summary Courts, except those coming within the jurisdiction of the Supreme Court.

Jokoku appeals from judgments in the second instance rendered by District Courts and from judgments rendered by Summary Courts, except those concerning criminal cases.

Actions in the first instance relating to cases of insurrection.

Presidents: TOKUJI IZUMI (Tokyo), YOSHIO OKADA (Osaka), REISUKE SHIMADA (Nagoya), TOYOZO UEDA (Hiroshima), TOSHIMARO KOJO (Fukuoka), FUMIYA SATO (Sendai), KAZUO KATO (Sapporo), FUMIO ARAI (Takamatsu).

District Court

A District Court is generally the court of first instance, except for matters specifically coming under the exclusive original jurisdiction of other types of court. It also has appellate jurisdiction over appeals in civil cases lodged against judgments of summary courts. The Court conducts hearings and renders decisions through a single judge or, for certain types of cases, through a collegiate body of three judges. Japan has 50 district courts, with 203 branches.

Family Court

A Family Court handles cases through a single judge in case of rendering judgments or decisions. However, in accordance with the provisions of other statutes, it conducts its hearings and renders decisions through a collegiate body of three judges. A conciliation is effected through a collegiate body consisting of a judge and two or more members of the conciliation committee selected from among citizens.

It has jurisdiction over the following matters:

Judgment and conciliation with regard to cases relating to family as provided for by the Law for Adjudgment of Domestic Relations.

Judgment with regard to the matters of protection of juveniles as provided for by the Juvenile Law.

Actions in the first instance relating to adult criminal cases of violation of the Labour Standard Law, the Law for Prohibiting Liquors to Minors, or other laws especially enacted for protection of juveniles.

Summary Court

A Summary Court handles cases through a single judge, and has jurisdiction in the first instance over the following matters:

Claims where the value of the subject matter does not exceed 1.4m. yen.

Criminal cases of offences liable to a fine or lesser penalty, offences liable to a fine as an optional penalty, and certain specified offences such as theft and embezzlement.

A Summary Court cannot impose imprisonment or a graver penalty. When it deems proper the imposition of a sentence of imprisonment or a graver penalty, it must transfer such cases to a District Court, but it can impose imprisonment with labour not exceeding three years for certain specified offences.

Religion

The traditional religions of Japan are Shintoism and Buddhism. Neither is exclusive, and many Japanese subscribe at least nominally to both.

SHINTOISM

Shintoism is an indigenous religious system embracing the worship of ancestors and of nature. It is divided into two cults: national Shintoism, which is represented by the shrines; and sectarian Shintoism, which developed during the second half of the 19th century. In 1868 Shinto was designated a national religion and all Shinto shrines acquired the privileged status of a national institution. Complete freedom of religion was introduced in 1947.

BUDDHISM

World Buddhist Fellowship: Hozenji Buddhist Temple, 3-24-2, Akabane-dai, Kita-ku, Tokyo; Head Rev. FUJI NAKAYAMA.

CHRISTIANITY

National Christian Council in Japan: Japan Christian Center, 2-3-18-24, Nishi-Waseda, Shinjuku-ku, Tokyo 169-0051; tel. (3) 3203-0372; fax (3) 3204-9495; e-mail general@ncc-j.org; internet ncc-j.org; f. 1923; 14 mems (churches and other bodies), 18 assoc. mems; Chair. ISAMU KOSHIISHI; Gen. Sec. HIROKO UEDA (acting).

The Anglican Communion

Anglican Church in Japan (Nippon Sei Ko Kai): 65, Yarai-cho, Shinjuku-ku, Tokyo 162-0805; tel. (3) 5228-3171; fax (3) 5228-3175; e-mail general-sec.po@nskk.org; internet www.nskk.org; f. 1887; 11 dioceses; Primate of Japan Most Rev. NATHANIEL MAKOTO UEMATSU (Bishop of Hokkaido); Gen. Sec. JOHN MAKITO AIZAWA; 54,898 mems (2007).

The Orthodox Church

Japanese Orthodox Church (Nippon Haristosu Seikyoukai): Holy Resurrection Cathedral (Nicolai-Do), 4-1-3, Kanda Surugadai, Chiyoda-ku, Tokyo 101; tel. (3) 3291-1885; fax (3) 3291-1886;

e-mail info@orthodoxjapan.jp; internet www.orthodoxjapan.jp; three dioceses; Archbishop of Tokyo, Primate and Metropolitan of All Japan Most Rev. DANIEL NUSHIRO; 24,821 mems.

Protestant Church

United Church of Christ in Japan (Nihon Kirisuto Kyodan): 2-3-18, Nishi-Shinjuku, Shinjuku-ku, Tokyo 169-0051; tel. (3) 3202-0541; fax (3) 3207-3918; e-mail ecumeni-c@uccj.org; internet www.uccj.or.jp; f. 1941; union of 34 Congregational, Methodist, Presbyterian, Reformed and other Protestant denominations; Moderator Rev. HIDEO ISHIBASHI; Gen. Sec. Rev. AOBORA TAEMAE; 196,044 mems (2007).

The Roman Catholic Church

Japan comprises three archdioceses and 13 dioceses. There were an estimated 554,447 adherents at 31 December 2007.

Catholic Bishops' Conference of Japan (Chuo Kyogikai): 2-10-10, Shiomi, Koto-ku, Tokyo 135-8585; tel. (3) 5632-4411; fax (3) 5632-4453; e-mail info@cbcj.catholic.jp; internet www.cbcj.catholic.jp; Pres. Most Rev. LEO JUN IKENAGA (Bishop of Osaka).

Archbishop of Nagasaki: Most Rev. JOSEPH MITSUAKI TAKAMI, Catholic Centre, 10-34, Uenomachi, Nagasaki-shi 852-8113; tel. (95) 846-4246; fax (95) 848-8310; internet www.nagasaki.catholic.jp.

Archbishop of Osaka: Most Rev. LEO JUN IKENAGA, Archbishop's House, 2-24-22, Tamatsukuri, Chuo-ku, Osaka 540-0004; tel. (6) 6941-9700; fax (6) 6946-1345; internet www.osaka.catholic.jp.

Archbishop of Tokyo: Most Rev. PETER TAKEO OKADA, Archbishop's House, 3-16-15, Sekiguchi, Bunkyo-ku, Tokyo 112-0014; tel. (3) 3943-2301; fax (3) 3944-8511; e-mail diocese@tokyo.catholic.jp; internet www.tokyo.catholic.jp.

Other Christian Churches

Japan Baptist Convention: 1-2-4, Minami-Urawa, Minami-ku, Saitama-shi, Saitama 336-0017; tel. (48) 883-1091; fax (48) 883-1092; internet www.bapren.jp; f. 1947; Gen. Sec. Rev. MAKOTO KATO; 33,734 mems (March 2003).

Japan Baptist Union: 2-3-18, Nishi-Waseda, Shinjuku-ku, Tokyo 169-0051; tel. (3) 3202-0053; fax (3) 3202-0054; e-mail gs@jbu.or.jp; internet www.jbu.or.jp; f. 1958; Moderator YOSHIHISA SAWANO; Gen. Sec. MAKOTO TANNO; 4,600 mems.

Japan Evangelical Lutheran Church: 1-1, Sadohara-cho, Ichigaya-shi, Shinjuku-ku, Tokyo 162-0842; tel. (3) 3260-8631; fax (3) 3260-8641; e-mail contact@jelc.or.jp; internet www.jelc.or.jp; f. 1893; Pres. Rev. SUMIYUKI WATANABE; Exec. Dir Rev. YASUHIRO TATENO; 21,990 mems (2010).

Korean Christian Church in Japan: Japan Christian Center, Rm 52, 2-3-18, Nishi-Waseda, Shinjuku-ku, Tokyo 169-0051; tel. (3) 3202-5398; fax (3) 3202-4977; e-mail info@kccj.jp; internet kccj.jp; f. 1909; Moderator CHOI YOUNG-SHIN; Gen. Sec. HONG SONG-WAN; 6,319 mems (2010).

West Japan Evangelical Lutheran Church: 2-2-11 Nakajimadori, Chuo-Ku, Kobe 651-0052; tel. (78) 242-0887; fax (78) 242-4166; e-mail office@wjelc.or.jp; internet www.wjelc.or.jp; 3,887 mems (2010).

Among other denominations active in Japan are the Christian Catholic Church, the German Evangelical Church and the Tokyo Union Church.

OTHER COMMUNITIES

Bahá'í Faith

The National Spiritual Assembly of the Bahá'ís of Japan: 7-2-13, Shinjuku, Shinjuku-ku, Tokyo 160-0022; tel. (3) 3209-7521; fax (3) 3204-0773; e-mail info@bahaijp.org; internet www.bahaijp.org; f. 1955; Mem. DARYOUSH YAZDANI.

Judaism

Jewish Community of Japan: 3-8-8, Hiroo, Shibuya-ku, Tokyo 150-0012; tel. (3) 3400-2559; fax (3) 3400-1827; e-mail office@jccjapan.or.jp; internet www.jccjapan.or.jp; f. 1953; Pres. JEROME ROSENBERG; Leader Rabbi ANTONIO DI GESÙ.

Islam

Islam has been active in Japan since the late 19th century. There is a small Muslim community, maintaining several mosques, including those at Kobe, Nagoya, Chiba and Isesaki, the Arabic Islamic Institute and the Islamic Center in Tokyo. The construction of Tokyo Central Mosque was completed in 2000.

Islamic Center, Japan: 1-16-11, Ohara, Setagaya-ku, Tokyo 156-0041; tel. (3) 3460-6169; fax (3) 3460-6105; e-mail info@islamcenter.or.jp; internet www.islamcenter.or.jp; f. 1965; Chair. Dr SALIH AL-SAMARRAI.

The New Religions

Many new religions (Shinko Shukyo) emerged in Japan after 1945, based on a fusion of Shinto, Buddhist, Daoist, Confucian and Christian beliefs. Among the most important of these are Tenrikyo, Omotokyo, Soka Gakkai, Rissho Kosei-kai, Kofuku-no-Kagaku and Agonshu.

Kofuku-no-Kagaku (Institute for Research in Human Happiness): 1-6-7, Shinagawa-ku, Tokyo 142-0041; tel. (3) 6384-3777; fax (3) 6384-3778; e-mail info@irhpress.co.jp; internet www.irhpress.co.jp; f. 1986; believes its founder to be reincarnation of Buddha; 8.25m. mems; Leader RYUHO OKAWA.

Rissho Kosei-kai: 5/F, Fumon Hall, 2-6-1, Wada, Suginami-ku, Tokyo 166-8537; tel. and fax (3) 5341-1124; e-mail info@rk-world.org; internet www.kosei-kai.or.jp; internet www.rk-world.org; f. 1938; Buddhist lay org. based on the teaching of the Lotus Sutra, active inter-faith co-operation towards peace; Pres. Rev. Dr NICHIKO NIWANO; 2.05m. mem. households with 245 brs world-wide (2009).

Soka Gakkai: 32, Shinano-machi, Shinjuku-ku, Tokyo 160-8583; tel. (3) 5360-9830; fax (3) 5360-9885; e-mail contact@sgi.org; internet www.sgi.org; f. 1930; society of lay practitioners of the Buddhism of Nichiren; membership of 8.27m. households (2005); group promotes activities in education, international cultural exchange and consensus-building towards peace, based on the humanist world view of Buddhism; Hon. Pres. DAISAKU IKEDA; Pres. MINORU HARADA.

The Press

In 2009 there were 121 daily newspapers in Japan. Their average circulation was among the highest in the world. The large number of weekly news journals is a notable feature of the Japanese press.

NATIONAL DAILIES

Asahi Shimbun: 5-3-2, Tsukiji, Chuo-ku, Tokyo 104-8011; tel. (3) 3545-0131; fax (3) 3545-0358; internet www.asahi.com; f. 1879; also publ. by Osaka, Seibu and Nagoya head offices and Hokkaido branch office; Pres. KOTARO AKIYAMA; Editor-in-Chief YOICHI FUNABASHI; circ. morning 8.1m., evening 3.7m.

Mainichi Shimbun: 1-1-1, Hitotsubashi, Chiyoda-ku, Tokyo 100-8051; tel. (3) 3212-0321; fax (3) 3211-3598; internet www.mainichi.co.jp; f. 1882; also publ. by Osaka, Seibu and Chubu head offices, and Hokkaido branch office; Pres. MASATO KITAMURA; Editor-in-Chief TOSHIFUMI KAWANO; circ. morning 4.0m., evening 2.0m.

Nihon Keizai Shimbun: 1-3-7, Otemachi, Chiyoda-ku, Tokyo 1008066; tel. (3) 3270-0251; fax (3) 5255-2661; e-mail ecntct@nikkei.co.jp; internet www.nikkei.co.jp; f. 1876; also publ. by Osaka head office and Sapporo, Nagoya and Seibu branch offices; Pres. TSUNEO KITA; Editor-in-Chief YUICHI TAKAHASHI; circ. morning 3.0m., evening 1.6m.

Sankei Shimbun: 1-7-2, Otemachi, Chiyoda-ku, Tokyo 100-8077; tel. (3) 3231-7111; internet sankei.jp; f. 1933; also publ. by Osaka head office; Pres. and CEO NAGAYOSHI SUMIDA; Editor-in-Chief MASAFUMI KATAYAMA; circ. morning 2.0m., evening 636,649.

Yomiuri Shimbun: 1-7-1, Otemachi, Chiyoda-ku, Tokyo 100-8055; tel. (3) 3242-1111; e-mail webmaster@yomiuri.co.jp; internet www.yomiuri.co.jp; f. 1874; also publ. by Osaka, Seibu and Chubu head offices, and Hokkaido and Hokuriku branch offices; Chair. and Editor-in-Chief TSUNEO WATANABE; circ. morning 10.0m., evening 4.0m.

PRINCIPAL LOCAL DAILIES

Tokyo

Daily Sports: 2-14-8, Kiba, Koto-ku, Tokyo 135-8566; tel. (3) 5434-1752; e-mail dsmaster@daily.co.jp; internet www.daily.co.jp; f. 1948; morning; Pres. TAKASHI KAORI; circ. 400,254.

The Daily Yomiuri: 1-7-1, Otemachi, Chiyoda-ku, Tokyo 100-8055; tel. (3) 3242-1111; internet www.yomiuri.co.jp; f. 1955; morning; English; Man. Editor SHIGEYUKI OKADA; circ. 33,743 (2009).

Dempa Shimbun: 1-11-15, Higashi-Gotanda, Shinagawa-ku, Tokyo 141-8790; tel. (3) 3445-6111; fax (3) 3444-7515; e-mail multim@dempa.co.jp; internet www.dempa.co.jp; f. 1950; morning; Pres. TETSUO HIRAYAMA; Man. Editor TOSHIO KASUYA; circ. 298,000.

The Japan Times: 4-5-4, Shibaura, Minato-ku, Tokyo 108-8071; tel. (3) 3453-5312; internet www.japantimes.co.jp; f. 1897; morning; English; Chair. and Pres. TOSHIAKI OGASAWARA; Dir and Editor-in-Chief YUTAKA MATAEBARA; circ. 61,929.

The Mainichi Daily News: 1-1-1, Hitotsubashi, Chiyoda-ku, Tokyo 100-8051; tel. (3) 3212-0321; internet mdn.mainichi.jp; f. 1922; morning; English; also publ. from Osaka; Man. Editor TETSUO TOKIZAWA; combined circ. 49,200.

Naigai Times: 1-3-2, Tsukishima, Chuo-ku, Tokyo 104-0052; tel. (3) 6204-4121; e-mail koukoku@naigai-times.net; internet www.npn.co.jp; f. 1949; evening; Pres. MITSUGU ONDA; Vice-Pres. and Editor-in-Chief KENICHIRO KURIHARA; circ. 410,000.

Nihon Kaiji Shimbun (Japan Maritime Daily): Mori Bldg, 5-19-2, Shimbashi, Minato-ku, Tokyo 105-0004; tel. (3) 3436-3221; fax (3) 3436-3247; e-mail webmaster@jmd.co.jp; internet www.jmd.co.jp; f. 1942; morning; Man. Editor OSAMI ENDO; circ. 55,000.

Nihon Nogyo Shimbun (Agriculture): 2-3, Akihabara, Taito-ku, Tokyo 110-8722; tel. (3) 5295-7411; fax (3) 3253-0980; internet www.agrinews.co.jp; f. 1928; morning; Man. Editor YASUNORI INOUE; circ. 423,840.

Nihon Sen-i Shimbun (Textile and Fashion): 1-6-5, Nihonbashi Kobuna-cho, Chuo-ku, Tokyo 103-0012; tel. (3) 5649-8711; fax (3) 5469-8717; internet www.nissenmedia.com; f. 1943; morning; Man. Editor KIYOSHIGE SEIRYU; circ. 116,000.

Nikkan Kogyo Shimbun (Industrial Daily News): 14-1, Nihonbashi Koami-cho, Chuo-ku, Tokyo 103-8548; tel. (3) 5644-7000; fax (3) 5644-7100; internet www.nikkan.co.jp; f. 1915; morning; Man. Editor HIDEO WATANABE; circ. 533,145.

Nikkan Sports News: 3-5-10, Tsukiji, Chuo-ku, Tokyo 104-8055; tel. (3) 5550-8888; fax (3) 5550-8901; e-mail webmast@nikkansports.co.jp; internet www.nikkansports.com; f. 1946; morning; Man. Editor MOTOHIRO MIURA; circ. 993,240.

Sankei Sports: 1-7-2, Otemachi, Chiyoda-ku, Tokyo 100-8077; tel. (3) 3231-7111; internet www.sanspo.com; f. 1963; morning; Man. Editor YUKIO INADA; circ. 809,245.

Shipping and Trade News: Tokyo News Service Ltd, 1-1-2, Uchisaiwai-cho, Chiyoda-ku, Tokyo 100-0011; tel. (3) 5510-8961; fax (3) 3504-6039; e-mail editorial.a@tokyonews.co.jp; internet www.tokyonews.co.jp/marine; f. 1949; English; Man. Editor TAKASHI TAKEDA; circ. 15,000.

Sports Hochi: 4-6-49, Kohnan, Minato-ku, Tokyo 108-8485; tel. (3) 5479-1111; e-mail webmaster@hochi.yomiuri.co.jp; internet hochi.yomiuri.co.jp; f. 1872; fmrly *Hochi Shimbun*; morning; Pres. HIROTO KISHI; Man. Editor TATSUE AOKI; circ. 755,670.

Sports Nippon: 2-1-30, Etchujima, Koto-ku, Tokyo 135-8735; tel. (3) 3820-0700; e-mail customer@sponichi.co.jp; internet www.sponichi.co.jp; f. 1949; morning; Man. Editor SUSUMU KOMURO; Pres. MORITO YUKIO; circ. 929,421.

Suisan Keizai Shimbun (Fisheries): 6-8-19, Roppongi, Minato-ku, Tokyo 106-0032; tel. (3) 3404-6531; fax (3) 3404-0863; internet www.suikei.co.jp; f. 1948; morning; Man. Editor KOSHI TORINOUMI; circ. 61,000.

Tokyo Chunichi Sports: 1-4, Uchisaiwai-cho, Chiyoda-ku, Tokyo 100-8505; tel. (3) 6910-2211; internet www.chunichi.co.jp/chuspo; f. 1956; evening; Pres. OOSHIMA TORAO; circ. 330,431.

Tokyo Shimbun: 1-4, Uchisaiwai-cho, Chiyoda-ku, Tokyo 100-8505; tel. (3) 6910-2211; internet www.chunichi.co.jp; f. 1942; Pres. OOSHIMA TORAO; circ. morning 655,970, evening 354,191.

Tokyo Sports: 2-1-30, Etchujima, Koto-ku, Tokyo 135-8721; tel. (3) 3820-0801; internet www.tokyo-sports.co.jp; f. 1959; evening; Man. Editor YOSHINOBU EBATA; circ. 1,321,250.

Yukan Fuji: 1-7-2, Otemachi, Chiyoda-ku, Tokyo 100-8077; tel. (3) 3231-7111; fax (3) 3246-0377; e-mail desk@zakzak.co.jp; internet www.zakzak.co.jp; f. 1969; evening; Man. Editor MASAMI KATO; circ. 268,984.

Osaka District

Daily Sports: 1-18-11, Edobori, Nishi-ku, Osaka 550-0002; tel. (6) 6443-0421; f. 1948; morning; Man. Editor TOSHIAKI MITANI; circ. 562,715.

The Mainichi Daily News: 3-4-5, Umeda, Kita-ku, Osaka 530-8251; tel. (6) 6345-1551; internet www.mainichi.co.jp; f. 1922; morning; English; Man. Editor KATSUYA FUKUNAGA.

Nikkan Sports: 3-14-24, Hanshin, Fukushima Ward, Osaka; tel. (6) 7632-7700; internet www.nikkansports.com; f. 1950; morning; Man. Editor KATSUO FURUKAWA; circ. 513,498.

Sankei Kansai: 2-1-57, Minato-cho, Naniwa-ku, Osaka 556-8660; tel. (6) 6633-1221; fax (6) 6633-9738; e-mail osaka-soukyoku@sankei.co.jp; internet www.sankei-kansai.com; f. 1922; evening; fmrly Osaka Shimbun, name changed as above 2004; Pres. SUMIDA NAGAYOSHI; circ. 88,887.

Sankei Sports: 2-1-57, Minato-cho, Naniwa-ku, Osaka 556-8660; tel. (6) 6343-1221; fax (6) 6633-9738; f. 1955; morning; Pres. SUMIDA NAGAYOSHI; circ. 552,519.

Sports Nippon: 3-4-5, Umeda, Kita-ku, Osaka 530-8278; tel. (6) 6346-8500; f. 1949; morning; Man. Editor HIDETOSHI ISHIHARA; circ. 477,300.

Kanto District

Chiba Nippo (Chiba Daily News): 4-14-10, Chuo, Chuo-ku, Chiba 260-0013; tel. (43) 222-9211; internet www.chibanippo.co.jp; f. 1957; morning; Man. Editor NOBORU HAYASHI; circ. 190,187.

Ibaraki Shimbun: 2-15, Kitami-cho, Mito 310-8686; tel. (29) 248-5500; fax (29) 248-7745; e-mail i-net@ibaraki-np.co.jp; internet www.ibaraki-np.co.jp; f. 1891; morning; Pres. TAKASHI KOTABE; circ. 117,240.

Jomo Shimbun: 1-50-21, Furuichi-machi, Maebashi 371-8666; tel. (27) 254-9911; internet www.raijin.com; f. 1887; morning; Man. Dir KOUZOU TAKAHASHI; circ. 311,534.

Joyo Shimbun: 2-7-6, Manabe, Tsuchiura 300-0051; tel. (298) 21-1780; e-mail info-02@joyo-net.com; internet www.joyo-net.com; f. 1948; morning; Pres. MINEO IWANAMI; Man. Editor AKIRA SAITO; circ. 88,700.

Kanagawa Shimbun: 2-23, Ota-cho, Kanagawa, Naka-ku, Yokohama 231-8445; tel. (45) 227-1111; e-mail soumu@kanagawa-np.co.jp; internet www.kanagawa-shimbun.jp; f. 1890; morning; Pres. KENJI HOTTA; circ. 238,203.

Saitama Shimbun: 2-282-3, Yoshino, Kita-ku, Saitama; tel. (48) 795-9930; fax (48) 653-9020; e-mail desk@saitama-np.co.jp; internet www.saitama-np.co.jp; f. 1944; morning; Man. Editor EIICHI ISHINO; circ. 162,071.

Shimotsuke Shimbun: 1-8-11, Showa, Utsunomiya 320-8686; tel. (286) 25-1111; internet www.shimotsuke.co.jp; f. 1884; morning; Man. Dir and Editor-in-Chief EISUKE TODA; circ. 306,072.

Tohoku District
(North-east Honshu)

Akita Sakigake Shimpo: 1-1, San-no-rinkai-machi, Akita 010-8601; tel. (18) 888-1800; fax (18) 866-9285; internet www.sakigake.co.jp; f. 1874; Man. Editor SHIGEAKI MAEKAWA; circ. 263,246.

Daily Tohoku: 1-3-12, Shiroshita, Hachinohe 031-8601; tel. (178) 44-5111; internet www.daily-tohoku.co.jp; f. 1945; morning; Man. Editor TOKOJU YOSHIDA; circ. 104,935.

Fukushima Mimpo: 13-17, Ota-machi, Fukushima 960-8602; tel. (24) 531-4111; fax (24) 531-4022; internet www.minpo.jp; f. 1892; Pres. and Editor-in-Chief TSUTOMU HANADA; circ. morning 308,353, evening 9,489.

Fukushima Minyu: 4-29, Yanagi-machi, Fukushima 960-8648; tel. (24) 523-1191; fax (24) 523-2605; internet www.minyu-net.com; f. 1895; Man. Editor KENJI KANNO; circ. morning 201,414, evening 6,066.

Hokuu Shimpo: 3-2, Nishi-Dori-machi, Noshiro 016-0891; tel. (185) 54-3150; internet www.hokuu.co.jp; f. 1895; morning; Chair. KOICHI YAMAKI; circ. 31,490.

Ishinomaki Shimbun: 2-1-28, Sumiyoshi-machi, Ishinomaki 986; tel. (225) 22-3201; f. 1946; evening; Man. Editor MASATOSHI SATO; circ. 13,050.

Iwate Nichi-nichi Shimbun: 60, Minami-Shinmachi, Ichinoseki 021-8686; tel. (191) 26-5114; e-mail iwanichi@iwanichi.co.jp; internet www.iwanichi.co.jp; f. 1923; morning; Pres. TAKESHI YAMAGISHI; Man. Editor SEIICHI WATANABE; circ. 59,850.

Iwate Nippo: 3-7, Uchimaru, Morioka 020-8622; tel. (19) 653-4111; fax (19) 626-1882; e-mail center@iwate-np.co.jp; internet www.iwate-np.co.jp; f. 1876; Man. Editor TOKUO MIYAZAWA; circ. morning 230,073, evening 229,815.

Kahoku Shimpo: 1-2-28, Itsutsubashi, Aoba-ku, Sendai 980-8660; tel. (22) 211-1127; fax (22) 211-1448; e-mail houdou@po.kahoku.co.jp; internet www.kahoku.co.jp; f. 1897; Exec. Dir and Man. Editor MASAHIKO ICHIRIKI; circ. morning 503,318, evening 133,855.

Mutsu Shimpo: 2-1, Shimo-shirogane-cho, Hirosaki 036-8356; tel. (172) 34-3111; fax (172) 32-3138; e-mail box@mutusinpou.co.jp; internet www.mutusinpou.co.jp; f. 1946; morning; Man. Editor YUJI SATO; circ. 53,500.

Shonai Nippo: 8-29, Baba-cho, Tsuruoka 997-8691; tel. (235) 22-1480; fax (235) 22-1427; internet www.shonai-nippo.co.jp; f. 1946; morning; Pres. and CEO MASAYUKI HASHIMOTO; circ. 19,100.

To-o Nippo: 3-1-89, Dainitonya-machi, Aomori 030-0180; tel. (17) 739-1111; internet www.toonippo.co.jp; f. 1888; Exec. Dir YOSHIO WAJIMA; Man. Editor TAKAO SHIOKOSHI; circ. morning 262,532, evening 258,590.

Yamagata Shimbun: 2-5-12, Hatagomachi, Yamagata 990-8550; tel. (23) 622-5271; e-mail info@yamagata-np.jp; internet yamagata-np.jp; f. 1876; Man. Editor TOSHINOBU SHIONO; circ. morning 213,057, evening 213,008.

Yonezawa Shimbun: 3-3-7, Monto-cho, Yonezawa 992-0039; tel. (238) 22-4411; fax (238) 24-5554; e-mail info@www.yoneshin.com; internet www.yoneshin.com; f. 1879; morning; Man. Dir and Editor-in-Chief MAKOTO SATO; circ. 13,750.

Chubu District
(Central Honshu)

Chubu Keizai Shimbun: 4-4-38, Meieki, Nakamura-ku, Nagoya 450-8561; tel. (52) 561-5215; fax (52) 561-5229; internet www.chukei-news.co.jp; f. 1946; morning; Man. Editor NORIMITSU INAGAKI; circ. 91,000.

Chukyo Sports: Chunichi Kosoku Offset Insatsu Bldg, 4-3-9, Kinjo, Naka-ku, Nagoya 460-0847; tel. (52) 982-1911; f. 1968; evening; Head Officer OSAMU SUETSUGU; circ. 289,430.

Chunichi Shimbun: 1-6-1, San-no-maru, Naka-ku, Nagoya 460-8511; tel. (52) 201-8811; internet www.chunichi.co.jp; f. 1942; Pres. OOSHIMA TARAO; circ. morning 2.7m., evening 748,635.

Chunichi Sports: 1-6-1, San-no-maru, Naka-ku, Nagoya 460-8511; tel. (52) 201-8811; internet www.chunichi.co.jp/chuspo; f. 1954; evening; Pres. OOSHIMA TARAO; circ. 631,429.

Gifu Shimbun: 10, Imako-machi, Gifu 500-8577; tel. (58) 264-1151; internet www.gifu-np.co.jp; f. 1881; Exec. Dir and Man. Editor TADASHI TANAKA; circ. morning 170,176, evening 31,775.

Higashi-Aichi Shimbun: 62, Torinawate, Shinsakae-machi, Toyohashi 441-8666; tel. (532) 32-3111; fax (532) 32-3737; e-mail hensyu@higashiaichi.co.jp; internet www.higashiaichi.co.jp; f. 1957; morning; Man. Editor YOSHIYUKI SUZUKI; circ. 52,300.

Nagano Nippo: 3-1323-1, Takashima, Suwa 392-8611; tel. (266) 52-2000; fax (266) 58-8895; e-mail info@nagano-np.co.jp; internet www.nagano-np.co.jp; f. 1901; morning; Man. Editor ETSUO KOIZUMI; circ. 73,000.

Nagoya Times: 1-3-10, Marunouchi, Naka-ku, Nagoya 460-8530; tel. (52) 231-1331; internet www.meitai.net; f. 1946; evening; Man. Editor NAOKI KITO; circ. 146,137.

Shinano Mainichi Shimbun: 657, Minami-Agatamachi, Nagano 380-8546; tel. (26) 236-3000; fax (26) 236-3197; internet www.shinmai.co.jp; f. 1873; Man. Editor SEIICHI INOMATA; circ. morning 469,801, evening 55,625.

Shizuoka Shimbun: 3-1-1, Toro, Suruga-ku, Shizuoka 422-8670; tel. (54) 284-8900; fax (54) 284-8994; e-mail webmaster@shizuokaonline.com; internet www.shizuokaonline.com; f. 1941; Man. Editor HISAO ISHIHARA; circ. morning 730,746, evening 730,782.

Yamanashi Nichi-Nichi Shimbun: 2-6-10, Kita-Guchi, Kofu 400-8515; tel. (552) 31-3000; internet www.sannichi.co.jp; f. 1872; morning; Man. Editor HIROSHI FUJIHARA; circ. 210,373.

Hokuriku District
(North Coastal Honshu)

Fukui Shimbun: 56, Owada-cho, Fukui 910-8552; tel. (776) 57-5111; internet www.fukuishimbun.co.jp; f. 1899; morning; Man. Editor KAZUO UCHIDA; circ. 201,121 (2009).

Hokkoku Shimbun: 2-5-1, Korinbo, Kanazawa 920-8588; tel. (762) 63-2111; e-mail admin@hokkoku.co.jp; internet www.hokkoku.co.jp; f. 1893; Man. Editor WATARU INAGAKI; circ. morning 335,826, evening 93,021.

Hokuriku Chunichi Shimbun: 2-12-30, Korinbo, Kanazawa 920-8573; tel. (76) 261-3111; internet www.chunichi.co.jp/hokuriku; f. 1960; Pres. OOSHIMA TORAO; circ. morning 107,652, evening 11,373.

Kita-Nippon Shimbun: 2-14, Azumi-cho, Toyama 930-8680; tel. (764) 45-3300; internet www.kitanippon.co.jp; f. 1884; Dir and Man. Editor HITOSHI ITAKURA; circ. morning 246,001.

Niigata Nippo: 772-2, Nishi-ku, Niigata 950-1189; tel. (25) 378-9111; internet www.niigata-nippo.co.jp; f. 1942; Dir and Man. Editor MICHIEI TAKAHASHI; circ. morning 499,545, evening 63,790.

Toyama Shimbun: 5-1, Ote-machi, Toyama 930-8520; tel. (766) 23-2131; e-mail koho@hokkoku.co.jp; internet www.toyama.hokkoku.co.jp; f. 1923; morning; Man. Editor SACHIO MIYAMOTO; circ. 42,988.

Kinki District
(West Central Honshu)

Daily Sports: 1-5-7, Higashi-Kawasaki-cho, Chuo-ku, Kobe 650-8571; tel. (78) 362-7100; e-mail dsmaster@daily.co.jp; internet www.daily.co.jp; morning; Man. Editor TAKASHI HIRAI; circ. 584,448.

Ise Shimbun: 34-6, Honmachi, Tsu 514-0831; tel. (59) 224-0003; fax (59) 226-3554; internet www.isenp.co.jp; f. 1878; morning; Man. Editor FUJIO YAMAMOTO; circ. 108,630.

Kii Minpo: 100, Akizu-cho, Tanabe 646-8660; tel. (739) 22-7171; fax (739) 26-0077; internet www.agara.co.jp; f. 1911; evening; Man. Editor KAZUSADA TANIGAMI; circ. 37,904 (2009).

Kobe Shimbun: 1-5-7, Higashi-Kawasaki-cho, Chuo-ku, Kobe 650-8571; tel. (78) 362-7100; internet www.kobe-np.co.jp; f. 1898; Pres. TAKASHI KAORI; circ. morning 563,717, evening 239,604 (2009).

Kyoto Shimbun: 239, Shoshoi-machi, Ebisugawa-agaru, Karasuma-dori, Nakagyo-ku, Kyoto 604-8577; tel. (75) 241-5430; e-mail kpdesk@mb.kyoto-np.co.jp; internet www.kyoto-np.co.jp; f. 1879; Man. Editor KIYOSHI; circ. morning 504,304, evening 319,015.

Nara Shimbun: 2-4, Sanjo-machi, Nara 630-8686; tel. (742) 32-1000; fax (742) 32-2770; e-mail info@nara-np.co.jp; internet www.nara-np.co.jp; f. 1946; morning; Dir and Man. Editor HISAMI SAKAMOTO; circ. 126,324.

Chugoku District
(Western Honshu)

Chugoku Shimbun: 7-1, Dobashi-cho, Naka-ku, Hiroshima 730-8677; tel. (82) 236-2111; fax (82) 236-2321; e-mail denshi@hiroshima-cdas.or.jp; internet www.chugoku-np.co.jp; f. 1892; Man. Editor NOBUYUKI AOKI; circ. morning 723,981, evening 75,248.

Nihonkai Shimbun: 2-137, Tomiyasu, Tottori 680-8688; tel. (857) 21-2888; fax (857) 21-2891; e-mail info@nnn.co.jp; internet www.nnn.co.jp; f. 1976; morning; Man. Editor KOTARO TAMURA; circ. 171,120.

Okayama Nichi-Nichi Shimbun: 3-30, Hon-cho, Kita-ku, Okayama 700-8678; tel. (86) 231-4211; fax (86) 231-4282; internet www.okanichi.co.jp; f. 1946; evening; Man. Dir and Man. Editor TAKASHI ANDO; circ. 20,000.

San-In Chuo Shimpo: 383, Tono-machi, Matsue 690-8668; tel. (852) 32-3440; e-mail sanin@sanin-chuo.co.jp; internet www.sanin-chuo.co.jp; f. 1882; morning; Man. Editor MASAMI MOCHIDA; circ. 15,310,018 (Jan. 2011).

Sanyo Shimbun: 2-1-1, Yanagi-machi, Okayama 700-8634; tel. (86) 803-8008; internet www.sanyo.oni.co.jp; f. 1879; Man. Dir and Man. Editor MATSUDA YUKI; circ. morning 461,876, evening 71,911.

Ube Jiho: 3-6-1, Kotobuki-cho, Ube 755-8557; tel. (836) 31-1511; internet www.ubenippo.co.jp; f. 1912; evening; Exec. Dir and Man. Editor KAZUYA WAKI; circ. 52,300.

Yamaguchi Shimbun: 1-1-7, Higashi-Yamato-cho, Shimonoseki 750-8506; tel. (83) 266-3211; fax (83) 266-5344; e-mail info@minato-yamaguchi.co.jp; internet www.minato-yamaguchi.co.jp; f. 1946; morning; Pres. MASAAKI INOUE; circ. 89,060.

Shikoku Island

Ehime Shimbun: 1-12-1, Otemachi, Matsuyama 790-8511; tel. (89) 935-2111; fax (89) 941-8108; e-mail webmaster@ehime-np.co.jp; internet www.ehime-np.co.jp; f. 1876; morning; Man. Editor RYOJI YANO; circ. 49,810,029 (Jan. 2011).

Kochi Shimbun: 3-2-15, Honmachi, Kochi 780-8572; tel. (88) 822-2111; e-mail master@kochinews.co.jp; internet www.kochinews.co.jp; f. 1904; Dir and Man. Editor KENGO FUJITO; circ. morning 129,749, evening 207,059 (2010).

Shikoku Shimbun: 15-1, Nakano-cho, Takamatsu 760-8572; tel. (87) 833-1111; internet www.shikoku-np.co.jp; f. 1889; morning; Man. Editor JUNJI YAMASHITA; circ. 204,999.

Tokushima Shimbun: 2-5-2, Naka-Tokushima-cho, Tokushima 770-8572; tel. (88) 655-7373; fax (86) 654-0165; e-mail jouhou@topics.or.jp; internet www.topics.or.jp; f. 1944; Dir and Man. Editor HIROSHI MATSUMURA; circ. morning 251,741, evening 52,593 (2010).

Hokkaido Island

Doshin Sports: 3-6, Nishi-Odori, Chuo-ku, Sapporo 060-8711; tel. (11) 210-5573; fax (11) 210-5575; e-mail koe@hokkaido-np.co.jp; internet www.hokkaido-np.co.jp; f. 1982; morning; Pres. MURATA MASATOSHI; circ. 150,988 (Feb. 2011).

Hokkaido Shimbun: 3-6, Nishi-Odori, Chuo-ku, Sapporo 060-8711; tel. (11) 210-5573; fax (11) 210-5575; internet www.hokkaido-np.co.jp; f. 1942; Man. Editor RYOZO ODAGIRI; circ. morning 1.2m., evening 701,934.

Kushiro Shimbun: 7-3, Kurogane-cho, Kushiro 085-8650; tel. (154) 22-1111; fax (154) 22-0050; internet www.news-kushiro.jp; f. 1946; morning; Man. Editor YUTAKA ITO; circ. 62,600.

Muroran Mimpo: 1-3-16, Hon-cho, Muroran 051-8550; tel. (143) 22-5121; fax (143) 24-1337; e-mail honsya@muromin.mnw.jp; internet www.muromin.mnw.jp; f. 1945; Man. Editor TSUTOMO KUDO; circ. morning 60,300, evening 52,630.

Nikkan Sports: 3-1-30, Higashi, Kita-3 jo, Chuo-ku, Sapporo 060-8521; tel. (11) 242-3900; fax (11) 231-5470; internet www.nikkansports.com; f. 1962; morning; Pres. YOSHITAKA SUZUKI; circ. 138,966 (Feb. 2011).

Tokachi Mainichi Shimbun: 8-2, Minami, Higashi-Ichijo, Obihiro 080-8688; tel. (155) 22-2121; fax (155) 25-2700; e-mail info@kachimai.co.jp; internet www.tokachi.co.jp; f. 1919; evening; Editor-in-Chief MITSUSHIGE HAYASHI; circ. 88,220 (Oct. 2010).

Tomakomai Mimpo: 3-1-8, Wakakusa-cho, Tomakomai 053-8611; tel. (144) 32-5311; fax (144) 32-6386; e-mail henshu@tomamin.co.jp; internet www.tomamin.co.jp; f. 1950; evening; Dir and Man. Editor RYUICHI KUDO; circ. 60,676.

Yomiuri Shimbun: 4-1, Nishi, Kita-4 jo, Chuo-ku, Sapporo 060-8656; tel. (11) 242-3111; internet www.yomiuri.co.jp; f. 1959; Head Officer TSUTOMO IKEDA; circ. morning 261,747, evening 81,283.

Kyushu Island

Kumamoto Nichi-Nichi Shimbun: 172, Yoyasu-machi, Kumamoto 860-8506; tel. (96) 361-3082; internet www.kumanichi.com; f. 1942; Man. Editor MAKOTO MATSUSHITA; circ. morning 385,784, evening 99,049.

Kyushu Sports: Fukuoka Tenjin Center Bldg, 2-14-8, Tenjin-cho, Chuo-ku, Fukuoka 810-0001; tel. (92) 781-7401; f. 1966; morning; Head Officer HIROSHI MITOMI; circ. 449,850.

Minami-Nippon Shimbun: 1-9-33, Yojirou, Kagoshima 890-8603; tel. (99) 813-5001; fax (99) 813-5016; e-mail webmaster@373news.com; internet www.373news.com; f. 1881; Man. Editor YASUSHI MOMIKI; circ. morning 405,795.

Miyazaki Nichi-Nichi Shimbun: 1-1-33, Takachihodori, Miyazaki 880-8570; tel. (985) 26-9315; fax (985) 20-7254; e-mail info@the-miyanichi.co.jp; internet www.the-miyanichi.co.jp; f. 1940; morning; Man. Editor MASAAKI MINAMIMURA; circ. 235,759.

Nagasaki Shimbun: 3-1, Mori-machi, Nagasaki 852-8601; tel. (95) 844-2111; e-mail houdou@nagasaki-np.co.jp; internet www.nagasaki-np.co.jp; f. 1889; Dir and Man. Editor SADAKATSU HONDA; circ. morning 196,016.

Nankai Nichi-Nichi Shimbun: 10-3, Nagahama-cho, Naze 894-8601; tel. (997) 53-2121; fax (997) 52-2354; e-mail nankainn@po.synapse.ne.jp; internet www.nankainn.com; f. 1946; morning; Man. Editor TERUMI MATSUI; circ. 23,615.

Nishi-Nippon Shimbun: 1-4-1, Tenjin, Chuo-ku, Fukuoka 810-8721; tel. (92) 711-5555; internet www.nishinippon.co.jp; f. 1877; Exec. Dir and Man. Editor AKIRA KOJIMA; circ. morning 840,110, evening 148,750.

Nishi-Nippon Sports: 1-4-1, Tenjin, Chuo-ku, Fukuoka 810-8721; tel. (92) 711-5555; f. 1954; Man. Editor KENJI ISHIZAKI; circ. 198,207.

Oita Godo Shimbun: 3-9-15, Funai-machi, Oita 870-8605; tel. (975) 36-2121; internet www.oita-press.co.jp; f. 1886; Dir and Man. Editor MASAKATSU TANABE; circ. morning 250,300, evening 250,264.

Okinawa Times: 1-3-31, Omoro-machi, Naha 900-8678; tel. (98) 860-3000; fax (98) 860-3664; internet www.okinawatimes.co.jp; f. 1948; Dir and Man. Editor MASAO KISHIMOTO; circ. morning 205,624.

Ryukyu Shimpo: 905, Naha 900-8525; tel. (98) 865-5111; fax (98) 861-0100; internet www.ryukyushimpo.co.jp; f. 1893; Man. Editor TOMOKAZU TAKAMINE; circ. 203,470.

Saga Shimbun: 3-2-23, Tenjin, Saga 840-8585; tel. (952) 28-2111; fax (952) 29-4829; internet www.saga-s.co.jp; f. 1884; morning; Man. Editor TERUHIKO WASHIZAKI; circ. 136,399.

Yaeyama Mainichi Shimbun: 614, Tonoshiro, Ishigaki 907-0004; tel. (9808) 2-2121; internet www.y-mainichi.co.jp; f. 1950; morning; Exec. Dir and Man. Editor YOSHIO UECHI; circ. 14,761.

WEEKLIES

An-An: Magazine House, 3-13-10, Ginza, Chuo-ku, Tokyo 104-8003; tel. (3) 3545-7050; fax (3) 3546-0034; internet magazineworld.jp/anan; f. 1970; fashion; Editor MIYOKO YODOGAWA; circ. 650,000.

Diamond Weekly: Diamond Bldg, 6-12-17, Jingumae, Shibuya-ku, Tokyo 150-8409; tel. (3) 5778-7200; e-mail info@diamond.co.jp; internet www.diamond.co.jp; f. 1913; economics; Editor YUTAKA IWASA; circ. 78,000.

Focus: Shincho-Sha, 71, Yarai-cho, Shinjuku-ku, Tokyo 162; tel. (3) 3266-5271; fax (3) 3266-5390; politics, economics, sport; Editor KAZUMASA TAJIMA; circ. 850,000.

Friday: Kodan-Sha Co Ltd, 2-12-21, Otowa, Bunkyo-ku, Tokyo 112; tel. (3) 5395-3440; fax (3) 3943-8582; current affairs; Editor-in-Chief TETSU SUZUKI; circ. 1m.

Hanako: Magazine House, 3-13-10, Ginza, Chuo-ku, Tokyo 104-8003; tel. (3) 3545-7070; fax (3) 3545-7281; internet magazineworld.jp/hanako; f. 1988; consumer guide; Editor AYAKO OTA; circ. 350,000.

Nikkei Business: Nikkei Business Publications Inc, 1-17-3, Shirokane, Minato-ku, Tokyo 108-8646; tel. (3) 6811-8101; fax (3) 5421-9117; internet www.nikkeibp.co.jp; f. 1969; Pres. TAIRA HIROSHI NAGATA; circ. 330,000.

Shukan Asahi: Asahi Shimbun Publishing Dept, 5-3-2, Tsukiji, Chuo-ku, Tokyo 104-8011; tel. (3) 3545-0131; f. 1922; general interest; Editor-in-Chief KAZUOMI YAMAGUCHI; circ. 482,000.

Shukan Bunshun: Bungei-Shunju Ltd, 3-23, Kioi-cho, Chiyoda-ku, Tokyo 102-8008; tel. (3) 3288-6123; fax (3) 3234-3964; e-mail kawabe@bunshun.co.jp; internet www.bunshun.co.jp; f. 1959; general interest; Editor MAKOTO SHIMADA; circ. 800,000.

Shukan Gendai: Kodan-Sha Co Ltd, 2-12-21, Otowa, Bunkyo-ku, Tokyo 112; tel. (3) 5395-3438; fax (3) 3943-7815; f. 1959; general; Editor-in-Chief TETSU SUZUKI; circ. 930,000.

Shukan Josei: Shufu-To-Seikatsu Sha Ltd, 3-5-7, Kyobashi, Chuo-ku, Tokyo 104; tel. (3) 3563-5130; fax (3) 3563-2073; f. 1957; women's interest; Editor HIDEO KIKUCHI; circ. 638,000.

Shukan Post: Shogakukan Publishing Co Ltd, 2-3-1, Hitotsubashi, Chiyoda-ku, Tokyo 101-01; tel. (3) 3230-5951; internet www.weeklypost.com; f. 1969; general; Editor NORIMICHI OKANARI; circ. 696,000.

Shukan SPA: Fuso-Sha Co, 1-15-1, Kaigan, Minato-ku, Tokyo 105; tel. (3) 5403-8875; f. 1952; general interest; Editor-in-Chief TOSHIHIKO SATO; circ. 400,000.

Shukan ST: Japan Times Ltd, 4-5-4, Shibaura, Minato-ku, Tokyo 108-8071; tel. (3) 3452-4077; fax (3) 3452-3303; e-mail shukanst@japantimes.co.jp; internet www.japantimes.co.jp/shukan-st; f. 1951; English and Japanese; Editor MITSURU TANAKA; circ. 150,000.

Shukan Yomiuri: Yomiuri Shimbun Publication Dept, 1-2-1, Kiyosumi, Koto-ku, Tokyo 135; tel. (3) 5245-7001; e-mail yw@yomiuri.com; internet www.yomiuri.co.jp; f. 1938; general interest; Editor SHINI KAGEYAMA; circ. 453,000.

Sunday Mainichi: Mainichi Newspapers Publishing Dept, 1-1-1, Hitotsubashi, Chiyoda-ku, Tokyo 100-51; tel. (3) 3212-0321; fax (3) 3212-0769; f. 1922; general interest; Editor KENJI MIKI; circ. 237,000.

Tenji Mainichi: Mainichi Newspapers Publishing Dept, 3-4-5, Umeda, Osaka; tel. (6) 6346-8386; fax (6) 6346-8385; f. 1922; in Japanese braille; Editor TADAMITSU MORIOKA; circ. 12,000.

Weekly Economist: Mainichi Newspapers Publishing Dept, 1-1-1, Hitotsubashi, Chiyoda-ku, Tokyo 100-51; tel. (3) 3212-0321; f. 1923; Editorial Chief NOBUHIRO SHUDO; circ. 120,000.

Weekly Toyo Keizai: Toyo Keizai Inc, 1-2-1, Hongoku-cho, Nihonbashi, Chuo-ku, Tokyo 103-8345; tel. (3) 3246-5481; fax (3) 3270-0159; e-mail sub@toyokeizai.co.jp; internet www.toyokeizai.net; f. 1895; business, economics, finance, and corporate information; Editor SHUNICHI OTAKI; circ. 80,000.

PERIODICALS

All Yomimono: Bungei-Shunju Ltd, 3-23, Kioicho, Chiyoda-ku, Tokyo 102; tel. (3) 3265-1211; fax (3) 3239-5481; f. 1930; monthly; popular fiction; Editor KOICHI SASAMOTO; circ. 95,796.

Any: 1-3-14, Hirakawa-cho, Chiyoda-ku, Tokyo 102; tel. (3) 5276-2200; fax (3) 5276-2209; f. 1989; every 2 weeks; women's interest; Editor YUKIO MIWA; circ. 380,000.

Asahi Camera: Asahi Shimbun Publishing Dept, 5-3-2, Tsukiji, Chuo-ku, Tokyo 104-8011; tel. (3) 3545-0131; fax (3) 5565-3286; f. 1926; monthly; photography; Editor HIROSHI HIROSE; circ. 90,000.

Balloon: Shufunotomo Co Ltd, 2-9, Kanda Surugadai, Chiyoda-ku, Tokyo 101; tel. (3) 3294-1132; fax (3) 3291-5093; f. 1986; monthly; expectant mothers; Dir MARIKO HOSODA; circ. 250,000.

Brutus: Magazine House, 3-13-10, Ginza, Chuo-ku, Tokyo 104-8003; tel. (3) 3545-7000; fax (3) 3546-0034; internet magazineworld.jp/brutus; f. 1980; every 2 weeks; men's interest; Pres. ISHIZAKI TAKESHI; circ. 250,000.

Bungei-Shunju: Bungei-Shunju Ltd, 3-23, Kioi-cho, Chiyoda-ku, Tokyo 102-8008; tel. (3) 3265-1211; fax (3) 3221-6623; internet www.bunshun.co.jp; f. 1923; monthly; general; Pres. HIROSHI TAKASHI; Editor KIYONDO MATSUI; circ. 656,000.

Business Tokyo: Keizaikai Bldg, 2-13-18, Minami-Aoyama, Minato-ku, Tokyo 105; tel. (3) 3423-8500; fax (3) 3423-8505; f. 1987; monthly; Dir TAKUO IDA; Editor ANTHONY PAUL; circ. 125,000.

Chuokoron: Chuokoron-Shinsha Inc, 2-8-7, Kyobashi, Chuo-ku, Tokyo 104-8320; tel. (3) 3563-1261; fax (3) 3561-5929; e-mail hanbai@chuko.co.jp; internet www.chuko.co.jp; f. 1887; monthly; general interest; Chief Editor JUN MAYIMA; circ. 90,000.

Croissant: Magazine House, 3-13-10, Ginza, Chuo-ku, Tokyo 104-03; tel. (3) 3545-7111; fax (3) 3546-0034; f. 1977; every 2 weeks; home; Editor MASAAKI TAKEUCHI; circ. 600,000.

Fujinkoron: Chuokoron-Sha Inc, 2-8-7, Kyobashi, Chuo-ku, Tokyo 104; tel. (3) 3563-1866; fax (3) 3561-5920; f. 1916; monthly; women's literature; Editor YUKIKO YUKAWA; circ. 185,341.

Geijutsu Shincho: Shincho-Sha, 71, Yarai-cho, Shinjuku-ku, Tokyo 162-8711; tel. (3) 3266-5381; fax (3) 3266-5387; e-mail geishin@shinchosha.co.jp; f. 1950; monthly; fine arts, music, architecture, films, drama and design; Editor-in-Chief MASASHI MATSUIE; circ. 50,000.

Gendai: Kodan-Sha Ltd, 2-12-21, Otowa, Bunkyo-ku, Tokyo 112; tel. (3) 5395-3517; fax (3) 3945-9128; f. 1966; monthly; cultural and political; Editor SHUNKICHI YABUKI; circ. 250,000.

Ginza: Magazine House, 3-13-10, Ginza, Chuo-ku, Tokyo 104-8003; tel. (3) 3545-7080; fax (3) 3542-6375; internet magazineworld.jp/

ginza; f. 1997; monthly; women's interest; Editor MIYOKO YODOGAWA; circ. 250,000.

Hot-Dog Press: Kodan-Sha Ltd, 2-12-21, Otowa, Bunkyo-ku, Tokyo 112-01; tel. (3) 5395-3473; fax (3) 3945-9128; every 2 weeks; men's interest; Editor ATSUHIDE KOKUBO; circ. 650,000.

Ie-no-Hikari (Light of Home): Ie-no-Hikari Asscn, 11, Ichigaya Funagawaramachi, Shinjuku-ku, Tokyo 162-8448; tel. (3) 3266-9000; fax (3) 3266-9048; e-mail hikari@mxd.meshnet.or.jp; internet www.ienohikari.net; f. 1925; monthly; rural and general interest; Pres. SHUZO SUZUKI; Editor KAZUO NAKANO; circ. 928,000.

Japan Company Handbook: Toyo Keizai Inc, 1-2-1, Nihonbashi Hongoku-cho, Chuo-ku, Tokyo 103-8345; tel. (3) 3246-5551; fax (3) 3279-0332; e-mail info@toyokeizai.co.jp; internet www.toyokeizai.co.jp; f. 1974; quarterly; English; Editor MASAKI HARA; total circ. 100,000.

Junon: Shufu-To-Seikatsu Sha Ltd, 3-5-7, Kyobashi, Chuo-ku, Tokyo 104-8357; tel. (3) 3563-5120; fax (3) 5250-7081; e-mail webmaster@mb.shufu.co.jp; internet www.shufu.co.jp/junon; f. 1973; monthly; television and entertainment; circ. 560,000.

Kagaku (Science): Iwanami Shoten Publishers, 2-5-5, Hitotsubashi, Chiyoda-ku, Tokyo 102; tel. (3) 5210-4070; fax (3) 5210-4073; f. 1931; Editor NOBUAKI MIYABE; circ. 29,000.

Kagaku Asahi: Asahi Shimbun Publishing Dept, 5-3-2, Tsukiji, Chuo-ku, Tokyo 104-8011; tel. (3) 5540-7810; fax (3) 3546-2404; f. 1941; monthly; scientific; Editor TOSHIHIRO SASAKI; circ. 105,000.

Keizaijin: Kansai Economic Federation, Nakanoshima Center Bldg, 6-2-27, Nakanoshima, Kita-ku, Osaka 530-6691; tel. (6) 6441-0104; fax (6) 6443-0443; e-mail kef_60_eng@kankeiren.or.jp; internet www.kankeiren.or.jp; f. 1947; monthly; economics; Editor M. YASUTAKE; circ. 2,600.

Lettuce Club: Toranomon Corpn, 2-2-5, Minatu-ku, Tokyo 105-8455; tel. (3) 3560-8700; e-mail info@sscom.co.jp; internet www.lettuceclub.net; f. 1987; every 2 weeks; cookery; Editor MITSURU NAKAYA; circ. 800,000.

Money Japan: Toranomon Corpn, 2-2-5, Minato-ku, Tokyo 105-8455; tel. (3) 3560-8700; e-mail info@sscom.co.jp; internet www.moneyjapan-web.com; f. 1985; monthly; finance; Editor TOSHIO KOBAYASHI; circ. 500,000.

Popeye: Magazine House, 3-13-10, Ginza, Chuo-ku, Tokyo 104-8003; tel. (3) 3545-7160; fax (3) 3545-9026; internet magazineworld.jp/popeye; f. 1976; every 2 weeks; fashion, youth interest; Editor KATSUMI NAMAIZAWA; circ. 320,000.

President: President Inc, Hirakawacho Mori Tower, 13/F, 2-16-1, Hirakawa-cho, Chiyoda-ku, Tokyo 102-8641; tel. (3) 3237-3711; fax (3) 3237-3748; internet www.president.co.jp; f. 1963; monthly; business; Editor KAYOKO ABE; circ. 263,308.

Ray: Shufunotomo Co Ltd, 2-9, Kanda Surugadai, Chiyoda-ku, Tokyo 101; tel. (3) 3294-1163; fax (3) 3291-5093; f. 1988; monthly; women's interest; Editor TATSURO NAKANISHI; circ. 450,000.

Ryoko Yomiuri: Yomiuri Travel Publishing Co Inc, 18-3, Nihonbashi, Chuo-ku, Tokyo 103-8545; tel. (3) 5847-8271; fax (3) 5847-8270; e-mail ryokoyomiuri@ryokoyomiuri.co.jp; internet www.ryokoyomiuri.co.jp; f. 1966; monthly; travel; Pres. MIZHUSHIMA TOSHIO; circ. 470,000.

Sekai: Iwanami Shoten Publishers, 2-5-5, Hitotsubashi, Chiyoda-ku, Tokyo 101-8002; tel. (3) 5210-4141; fax (3) 5210-4144; e-mail sekai@iwanami.co.jp; internet www.iwanami.co.jp/sekai; f. 1946; monthly; review of world and domestic affairs; Editor ATSUSHI OKAMOTO; circ. 120,000.

Shinkenchiku: Shinkenchiku-Sha Co Ltd, 2-31-2, Yushima, Bunkyo-ku, Tokyo 113-8501; tel. (3) 3811-7101; fax (3) 3812-8229; internet www.shinkenchiku.net; f. 1925; monthly; architecture; Editor NOBUYUKI YOSHIDA; circ. 87,000.

Shiso (Thought): Iwanami Shoten Publishers, 2-5-5, Hitotsubashi, Chiyoda-ku, Tokyo 101-8002; tel. (3) 5210-4055; fax (3) 5210-4037; e-mail shiso@iwanami.co.jp; internet www.iwanami.co.jp/shiso; f. 1921; monthly; philosophy, social sciences and humanities; Editor KIYOSHI KOJIMA; circ. 20,000.

Shosetsu Shincho: Shincho-Sha, 71, Yarai-cho, Shinjuku-ku, Tokyo 162-8711; tel. (3) 3266-5241; fax (3) 3266-5412; f. 1947; monthly; literature; Editor-in-Chief TSUYOSHI MENJO; circ. 80,000.

Shufunotomo: Shufunotomo Co Ltd, 2-9, Kanda Surugadai, Chiyoda-ku, Tokyo 101; tel. (3) 5280-7531; fax (3) 5280-7431; e-mail international-info@shufunotomo.co.jp; internet www.shufunotomo.co.jp; f. 1917; monthly; home and lifestyle; Editor KYOKO FURUTO; circ. 450,000.

So-en: Bunka Publishing Bureau, c/o Bunka Fashion College, 3-22-7, Yoyogi, Shibuya-ku, Tokyo 151-8524; tel. (3) 3299-2531; fax (3) 3370-3712; e-mail info-bpb@bunka.ac.jp; internet books.bunka.ac.jp; f. 1936; monthly; fashion; Editor KEIKO SASAKI; circ. 270,000.

NEWS AGENCIES

Jiji Tsushin (Jiji Press Ltd): 5-15-8, Ginza, Chuo-ku, Tokyo 104-8178; tel. (3) 6800-1111; e-mail info@jiji.co.jp; internet www.jiji.com; f. 1945; Pres. MASAHIRO NAKATA; Man. Dir and Man. Editor HIROYUKI YAMAKI.

Kyodo Tsushin (Kyodo News): Shiodome Media Tower, 1-7-1, Higashi-Shimbashi, Minato-ku, Tokyo 105-7201; tel. (3) 6252-8301; e-mail kokusai@kyodonews.jp; internet www.kyodonews.jp; f. 1945; Pres. SATOSHI ISHIKAWA; Man. Editor TOSHIEI KOKUBU.

Radiopress Inc: R-Bldg Shinjuku, 5F, 33-8, Wakamatsu-cho, Shinjuku-ku, Tokyo 162-0056; tel. (3) 5273-2171; fax (3) 5273-2180; e-mail rptokyo@oak.ocn.ne.jp; f. 1945; provides news from China, the former USSR, Democratic People's Repub. of Korea, Viet Nam and elsewhere to the press and govt offices; Pres. AKIO IJUIN.

Sun Telephoto: Palaceside Bldg, 1-1-1, Hitotsubashi, Chiyoda-ku, Tokyo 100-0003; tel. (3) 3213-6771; e-mail photo@suntelephoto.com; internet www.suntelephoto.com; f. 1952; Pres. KOZO TAKINO; Man. Editor GORO SHIMAZAKI.

PRESS ASSOCIATIONS

Foreign Correspondents' Club of Japan: Yaruku-cho Denki Kita Bldg, 20/F, 1-7-1, Yuraku-cho, Chiyoda-ku, Tokyo 100-0006; tel. (3) 3211-3161; fax (3) 3211-3168; e-mail nakamura@fccj.or.jp; internet www.fccj.or.jp; f. 1945; 193 cos; Pres. GEORGES BAUMGARTNER; Gen. Man. AKIRA NAKAMURA (acting).

Foreign Press Center: Nippon Press Center Bldg, 6/F, 2-2-1, Uchisaiwai-cho, Chiyoda-ku, Tokyo 100-0011; tel. (3) 3501-3401; fax (3) 3501-3622; e-mail rr@fpcjpn.or.jp; internet www.fpcj.jp; f. 1976; est. by the Japan Newspaper Publrs' and Editors' Asscn and the Japan Fed. of Economic Orgs; provides services to the foreign press; Pres. TERUSUKE TERADA.

Nihon Shinbun Kyokai (The Japan Newspaper Publishers and Editors Asscn): Nippon Press Center Bldg, 2-2-1, Uchisaiwai-cho, Chiyoda-ku, Tokyo 100-8543; tel. (3) 3591-4401; fax (3) 3591-6149; e-mail nsk_intl@pressnet.or.jp; internet www.pressnet.or.jp; f. 1946; mems include 133 cos (106 daily newspapers, 4 news agencies and 23 radio and TV cos); Pres. HITOSHI UCHIYAMA; Man. Dir MOTOYOSHI TORII.

Nihon Zasshi Kyokai (Japan Magazine Publishers Asscn): 1-7, Kanda Surugadai, Chiyoda-ku, Tokyo 101-0062; tel. (3) 3291-0775; fax (3) 3293-6239; f. 1956; 85 mems; Pres. HARUHIKO ISHIKAWA; Sec. GENYA INUI.

Publishers

Akane Shobo Co Ltd: 3-2-1, Nishi-Kanda, Chiyoda-ku, Tokyo 101-0065; tel. (3) 3263-0641; fax (3) 3263-5440; e-mail info@akaneshobo.co.jp; internet www.akaneshobo.co.jp; f. 1949; juvenile; Pres. MASAHARU OKAMOTO.

Akita Publishing Co Ltd: 2-10-8, Iidabashi, Chiyoda-ku, Tokyo 102-8101; tel. (3) 3264-7011; fax (3) 3265-5906; internet www.akitashoten.co.jp; f. 1948; social sciences, history, juvenile; Chair. SADAO AKITA; Pres. SADAMI AKITA.

ALC Press Inc: 2-54-12, Eifuku, Suginami-ku, Tokyo 168-8611; tel. (3) 3323-1101; fax (3) 3327-1022; e-mail info@alc.co.jp; internet www.alc.co.jp; f. 1969; linguistics, educational materials, dictionaries, juvenile; Pres. TERUMARO HIRAMOTO.

Asahi Shimbun Publications Division: 5-3-2, Tsukiji, Chuo-ku, Tokyo 104-8011; tel. (3) 5541-8757; fax (3) 3545-0311; e-mail doors@asahi.com; internet publications.asahi.com; f. 1879; general; Pres. KAZUMOTO URUMA.

Asakura Publishing Co Ltd: 6-29, Shin Ogawa-machi, Shinjuku-ku, Tokyo 162-8707; tel. (3) 3260-0141; fax (3) 3260-0180; e-mail edit@asakura.co.jp; internet www.asakura.co.jp; f. 1929; natural science, medicine, social sciences; Pres. KUNIZO ASAKURA.

Asuka Publishing Inc: 2-11-5, Suido, Bunkyo-ku, Tokyo 112-0005; tel. (3) 5395-7650; fax (3) 5395-7654; e-mail askaweb@asuka-g.co.jp; internet www.asuka-g.co.jp; f. 1973; sociology, law, economics, languages; Pres. EIICHI ISHINO.

Baifukan Co Ltd: 4-3-12, Kudan-Minami, Chiyoda-ku, Tokyo 102-0074; tel. (3) 3262-5256; fax (3) 3262-5276; e-mail bfkeigyo@mx7.mesh.ne.jp; internet www.baifukan.co.jp; f. 1924; engineering, natural and social sciences, psychology; Pres. ITARU YAMAMOTO.

Baseball Magazine-Sha: 3-10-10, Misaki-cho, Chiyoda-ku, Tokyo 101-8381; tel. (3) 3238-0081; fax (3) 3238-0106; internet www.bbm-japan.com; f. 1946; sports, physical education, recreation, travel; Pres. TETSUO IKEDA.

Bensey Publishing Inc: 2-20-6, Kanda Jimbo-cho, Chiyoda-ku, Tokyo 101-0051; tel. (3) 5215-9021; fax (3) 5215-9025; e-mail bensey@

bensey.co.jp; internet www.bensey.co.jp; f. 1967; philosophy, religion, history, art, languages, literature; Pres. YOJI IKEJIMA.

Bijutsu Shuppan-Sha Ltd: Inaoka Kudan Bldg, 6/F, 2-38, Kanda Jimbo-cho, Chiyoda-ku, Tokyo 101-8417; tel. (3) 3234-2151; fax (3) 3234-9451; e-mail artmedia@bijutsu.co.jp; internet www.bijutsu.co.jp; f. 1905; fine arts, graphic design; Pres. KENTARO OSHITA.

Bonjinsha Co Ltd: 1-3-13, Hirakawa-cho, Chiyoda-ku, Tokyo 102-0093; tel. (3) 3263-3959; fax (3) 3263-3116; e-mail info@bonjinsha.com; internet www.bonjinsha.com; f. 1973; Japanese language teaching materials; Pres. HISAMITSU TANAKA.

Bun-eido Publishing Co Inc: 28, Kamitoba, Daimotsu-cho, Minami-ku, Kyoto 601-8691; tel. (75) 671-3161; fax (75) 671-3165; e-mail fujita@bun-eido.co.jp; internet www.bun-eido.co.jp; f. 1921; reference books, dictionaries, textbooks, juvenile, history; Pres. HIDEOHIRO MASUI.

Bungei Shunju Ltd: 3-23, Kioi-cho, Chiyoda-ku, Tokyo 102-8008; tel. (3) 3265-1211; fax (3) 3265-1363; internet www.bunshun.co.jp; f. 1923; fiction, general literature, recreation, economics, sociology; Dir TAKAHIRO HIRAO.

Bunri Co Ltd: 1-1-5, Sekiguchi, Bunkyo-ku, Tokyo 112-0014; tel. (3) 3268-4110; fax (3) 3268-1462; e-mail tezukatak@bnet.bunri.co.jp; internet www.bunri.co.jp; f. 1950; Pres. SHIRO HATA.

Chikuma Shobo: Chikumashobo Bldg, 2-5-3, Kuramae, Taito-ku, Tokyo 111-8755; tel. (3) 5687-2671; fax (3) 5687-1585; e-mail henshuinfo@chikumashobo.co.jp; internet www.chikumashobo.co.jp; f. 1940; general literature, fiction, history, juvenile, fine arts; Pres. AKIO KIKUCHI.

Child-Honsha Co Ltd: 5-24-21, Koishikawa, Bunkyo-ku, Tokyo 112-8512; tel. (3) 3813-3781; fax (3) 3813-3778; e-mail ehon@childbook.co.jp; internet www.childbook.co.jp; f. 1930; juvenile; Pres. SHUNJI ASAKA.

Chuo Hoki Publishing Co Ltd: 2-27-4, Yoyogi, Shibuya-ku, Tokyo 151-0053; tel. (3) 3379-3784; fax (3) 5351-7855; e-mail info@chuohoki.co.jp; internet www.chuohoki.co.jp; f. 1947; law, social sciences; Pres. AKIHIKO SHOMURA.

Chuo University Press: 742-1, Higashi-Nakano, Hachioji-shi, Tokyo 192-0393; tel. (426) 74-2351; fax (426) 74-2354; f. 1948; law, history, sociology, economics, science, literature; Pres. TAKEHIKO TAMATSUKURI.

Chuokoron-Shinsha Inc: 2-8-7, Kyobashi, Chuo-ku, Tokyo 104-8320; tel. (3) 3563-1261; fax (3) 3561-5920; internet www.chuko.co.jp; f. 1886; philosophy, history, sociology, general literature; Pres. TAMOTSU ASAMI.

Corona Publishing Co Ltd: 4-46-10, Sengoku, Bunkyo-ku, Tokyo 112-0011; tel. (3) 3941-3131; fax (3) 3941-3137; e-mail info@coronasha.co.jp; internet www.coronasha.co.jp; f. 1927; electronics, medical books, mechanical engineering, computer science; Pres. MASAYA GORAI.

Dempa Publications Inc: 1-11-15, Higashi-Gotanda, Shinagawa-ku, Tokyo 141-8715; tel. (3) 3445-6111; fax (3) 3444-7515; f. 1950; electronics, personal computer software, juvenile, trade newspapers, English and Japanese language publications; Pres. TETSUO HIRAYAMA.

Diamond Inc: 6-12-17, Jingumae, Shibuya-ku, Tokyo 150-8409; tel. (3) 5778-7233; fax (3) 5778-6618; e-mail info@diamond.co.jp; internet www.diamond.co.jp; f. 1913; business, management, economics, financial; Pres. FUMIAKI SHIKATANI.

Dohosha Ltd: TAS Bldg, 2-5-2, Nishi-Kanda, Chiyoda-ku, Tokyo 101-0065; tel. (3) 5276-0831; fax (3) 5276-0840; e-mail intl@dohosha.co.jp; f. 1997; general works, architecture, art, Buddhism, business, children's education, cooking, flower-arranging, gardening, medicine.

East Press Co Ltd: 1-19, Kanda Jimbo-cho, Chiyoda-ku, Tokyo 101-0051; tel. (3) 5259-7707; fax (3) 5259-7708; e-mail webmaster@eastpress.co.jp; internet www.eastpress.co.jp; f. 2005; literature, comics, business, self-help, parenting, health, sports, music; Chair. SHINGERU KOBAYASHI; Pres. OSAMU ASOSHINA.

Froebel-Kan Co Ltd: 6-14-9, Honkomagome, Bunkyo-ku, Tokyo 113-8611; tel. (3) 5395-6600; fax (3) 5395-6621; e-mail info-e@froebel-kan.co.jp; internet www.froebel-kan.co.jp; f. 1907; juvenile, educational; Pres. HIDEO MUTO.

Fukuinkan Shoten Publishers Inc: 6-6-3, Honkomagome, Bunkyo-ku, Tokyo 113-8686; tel. (3) 3942-2151; fax (3) 3942-1401; internet www.fukuinkan.co.jp; f. 1952; juvenile; Pres. NOBORU OGURA; Chair. KATSUMI SATO.

Fusosha Publishing Inc: 1-15-1, Kaigan, Minato-ku, Tokyo 105-8070; tel. (3) 5403-8851; fax (3) 3578-3078; e-mail gshoseki@fusosha.co.jp; internet www.fusosha.co.jp; f. 1984; social science, business, mystery, magazines, textbooks; Pres. EIICHI KUBOTA.

Futabasha Publishers Ltd: 3-28, Higashi-Goken-cho, Shinjuku-ku, Tokyo 162-8540; tel. (3) 5261-4832; fax (3) 5261-3480; e-mail general@futabasha.co.jp; internet www.futabasha.co.jp; f. 1948; fiction, non-fiction, comics, guide books; Pres. HIROSHI MOROZUMI.

Gakken Co Ltd: 4-40-5, Kamiikedai, Ota-ku, Tokyo 145-8502; tel. (3) 3726-8111; fax (3) 3493-3338; e-mail personnel@gakken.co.jp; internet www.gakken.co.jp; f. 1946; juvenile, educational, art, encyclopaedias, dictionaries; Pres. YOCHIRO ENDO.

Graphic-sha Publishing Co Ltd: 1-14-17 Kudan-Kita, Chiyoda-ku, Tokyo 102-0073; tel. (3) 3263-4318; fax (3) 3263-5297; e-mail info@graphicsha.co.jp; internet www.graphicsha.co.jp; f. 1962; art, design, architecture, manga techniques, hobbies; Pres. KUZE TOSHIRO.

Gyosei Corpn: 1-18-11, Shinkiba, Koto-ku, Tokyo 136-8575; tel. (3) 6892-6666; fax (3) 6892-6925; e-mail eigyo1@gyosei.co.jp; internet www.gyosei.co.jp; f. 1893; law, education, science, politics, business, art, language, literature, juvenile; Pres. YUJIRO SAWADA.

Hakusui-Sha Co Ltd: 3-24, Kanda Ogawa-machi, Chiyoda-ku, Tokyo 101-0052; tel. (3) 3291-7821; fax (3) 3291-7810; e-mail hpmaster@hakusuisha.co.jp; internet www.hakusuisha.co.jp; f. 1915; general literature, science and languages; Pres. NAOSHI OIKAWA.

Hayakawa Publishing Inc: 2-2, Kanda-Tacho, Chiyoda-ku, Tokyo 101-0046; tel. (3) 3252-3111; fax (3) 3258-0250; internet www.hayakawa-online.co.jp; f. 1945; wine books, children's books, coffee-table books, drama, comic books, monthly magazines; Pres. HIROSHI HAYAKAWA.

Heibonsha Ltd: 2-29-4 Hakusan, Bunkyo-ku, Tokyo 112-0001; tel. (3) 3818-0873; fax (3) 3818-0857; e-mail shop@heibonsha.co.jp; internet www.heibonsha.co.jp; f. 1914; encyclopaedias, art, history, geography, literature, science; Pres. NAOTO SHIMONAKA.

Hirokawa Publishing Co: 3-27-14, Hongo, Bunkyo-ku, Tokyo 113-0033; tel. (3) 3815-3651; fax (3) 5684-7030; f. 1925; natural sciences, medicine, pharmacy, nursing, chemistry; Pres. SETSUO HIROKAWA.

Hoikusha Publishing Co: 18-24, Hiroshi-bacho, Suita-shi, Osaka 564-0052; tel. (6) 6330-5680; fax (6) 6330-5681; e-mail matsui@hoikusha.co.jp; internet www.hoikusha.co.jp; f. 1947; natural science, juvenile, fine arts, geography; Pres. TAKAHIKO MATSUI.

Hokkaido University Press: Kita-9, Nishi-8, Kita-ku, Sapporo 060-0809; tel. (11) 747-2308; fax (11) 736-8605; e-mail hupress_2@hup.gr.jp; internet www.hup.gr.jp; f. 1970; social science, natural science, technology, humanities; Pres. KATSUMI YOSHIDA.

Hokuryukan Co Ltd: 3-8-14, Takanawa, Minato-ku, Tokyo 108-0074; tel. (3) 5449-4591; fax (3) 5449-4950; e-mail hk-ns@hokuryukan-ns.co.jp; internet www.hokuryukan-ns.co.jp; f. 1891; natural science, medical science, juvenile, dictionaries; Pres. HISAKO FUKUDA.

The Hokuseido Press: Hayashi Bldg, 1-21-9, Sugamo, Toshima-ku, Tokyo 170-0002; tel. (3) 5940-0511; fax (3) 5940-0512; e-mail info@hokuseido.com; f. 1914; regional non-fiction, dictionaries, textbooks; Pres. KEISUKE YAMAMOTO.

Horitsubunka-sha: 71, Iwagakakiuchi-cho, Kamigamo, Kita-ku, Kyoto 603-8053; tel. (75) 791-7131; fax (75) 721-8400; e-mail henshu@hou-bun.co.jp; internet www.hou-bun.co.jp; f. 1947; law, politics, economics, sociology, philosophy; Pres. YASUSHI AKIYAMA.

Hosei University Press: 3-2-7, Kudan-Kita, Chiyoda-ku, Tokyo 102-0073; tel. (3) 5214-5540; fax (3) 5214-5542; e-mail mail@h-up.com; internet www.h-up.com; f. 1948; philosophy, history, economics, sociology, natural science, literature; Pres. TOSHIO MASUDA.

Ie-No-Hikari Association: 11, Funagawara-cho, Ichigaya, Shinjuku-ku, Tokyo 162-8448; tel. (3) 3266-9000; fax (3) 3266-9048; e-mail hikari@mxd.mesh.ne.jp; internet www.ienohikari.net; f. 1925; social science, agriculture, cooking; Pres. TOSHIHIRO SONODA.

Igaku-Shoin Ltd: 1-28-23, Hongo, Bunkyo-ku, Tokyo 113-8719; tel. (3) 3817-5610; fax (3) 3815-4114; e-mail info@igaku-shoin.co.jp; internet www.igaku-shoin.co.jp; f. 1944; medicine, nursing; Pres. YU KANEHARA.

Ikubundo Publishing Co Ltd: 5-30-21, Hongo, Bunkyo-ku, Tokyo 113-0033; tel. (3) 3814-5571; fax (3) 3814-5576; e-mail webmaster@ikubundo.com; internet www.ikubundo.com; f. 1899; languages, dictionaries; Pres. TOSHIYUKI OI.

Institute for Financial Affairs Inc (KINZAI): 19, Minami-Moto-machi, Shinjuku-ku, Tokyo 160-8519; tel. (3) 3358-1161; fax (3) 3359-7947; e-mail JDI04072@nifty.ne.jp; internet www.kinzai.or.jp; f. 1950; finance and economics, banking laws and regulations, accounting; Pres. MASATERU YOSHIDA.

Ishiyaku Publishers Inc: 1-7-10, Honkomagome, Bunkyo-ku, Tokyo 113-8612; tel. (3) 5395-7600; fax (3) 5395-7606; e-mail webmaster@ishiyaku.co.jp; internet www.ishiyaku.co.jp; f. 1921; medicine, dentistry, rehabilitation, nursing, nutrition and pharmaceutics; Pres. HIDEHO OHATA.

Iwanami Shoten, Publishers: 2-5-5, Hitotsubashi, Chiyoda-ku, Tokyo 101-8002; tel. (3) 5210-4000; fax (3) 5210-4039; e-mail rights@iwanami.co.jp; internet www.iwanami.co.jp; f. 1913; natural and social sciences, humanities, literature, fine arts, juvenile, dictionaries; Pres. Akio Yamaguchi.

Iwasaki Publishing Co Ltd: 1-9-2, Suido, Bunkyo-ku, Tokyo 112-0005; tel. (3) 3812-0151; fax (3) 3812-1381; e-mail ask@iwasakishoten.co.jp; internet www.iwasakishoten.co.jp; f. 1934; juvenile; Pres. Hiroaki Iwasaki.

Japan Broadcast Publishing Co Ltd: 41-1, Udagawa-cho, Shibuya-ku, Tokyo 150-8081; tel. (3) 3464-7311; fax (3) 3780-3394; e-mail kikaka@nhk-book.co.jp; internet www.nhk-book.co.jp; f. 1931; foreign language textbooks, gardening, home economics, sociology, education, art, juvenile; Pres. Akihide Mizoguchi.

Japan External Trade Organization (JETRO): Ark Mori Bldg, 6/F, 1-12-32, Akasaka, Minato-ku, Tokyo 107-6006; tel. (3) 3582-5511; fax (3) 3587-2485; internet www.jetro.go.jp; f. 1958; trade, economics, investment; Chair. Yasuo Hayashi.

Japan Publications Trading Co Ltd: 1-2-1, Sarugaku-cho, Chiyoda-ku, Tokyo 101-0064; tel. (3) 3292-3751; fax (3) 3292-0410; e-mail jpt@jptco.co.jp; internet www.jptco.co.jp; f. 1942; general works, art, health, sports; Pres. Hirobumi Annoshita.

The Japan Times Ltd: 4-5-4, Shibaura, Minato-ku, Tokyo 108-8071; tel. (3) 3453-2013; fax (3) 3453-8023; e-mail jt-books@kt.rim.or.jp; internet bookclub.japantimes.co.jp; f. 1897; linguistics, culture, business; Pres. Toshiaki Ogasawara.

Jikkyo Shuppan Co Ltd: 5, Goban-cho, Chiyoda-ku, Tokyo 102-8377; tel. (3) 3238-7700; fax (3) 3238-7719; internet www.jikkyo.co.jp; f. 1941; textbooks; Pres. Yoji Totsuka.

Jimbun Shoin: 9, Nishi-Uchihata-cho, Takeda, Fushimi-ku, Kyoto 612-8447; tel. (75) 603-1344; fax (75) 603-1814; e-mail jmsb@jimbunshoin.co.jp; internet www.jimbunshoin.co.jp; f. 1927; general literature, philosophy, fiction, social science, religion, fine arts; Pres. Hiroshi Watanabe.

Jitsugyo No Nihonsha Ltd: 1-3-9, Ginza, Chuo-ku, Tokyo 104-8233; tel. (3) 3562-1021; fax (3) 3562-2662; e-mail soumu@j-n.co.jp; internet www.j-n.co.jp; f. 1897; general, social sciences, juvenile, travel, business, comics; Pres. Yoshikazu Masuda.

JTB Publishing (Japan Travel Bureau): Urban-net Ichigaya Bldg, 25-5, Haraikatamachi, Shinjuku-ku, Tokyo 162-8446; tel. (3) 6888-7811; fax (3) 6888-7809; e-mail jtbpublishing@rurubu.ne.jp; internet www.jtbpublishing.com; f. 2004; travel, geography, history, fine arts, languages; Pres. Yuzuru Takenami.

Kadokawa Group Publishing Inc: 2-13-3, Fujimi, Chiyoda-ku, Tokyo 102-8177; tel. (3) 3238-8715; fax (3) 3262-7734; e-mail k-master@kadokawa.co.jp; internet www.kadokawa.co.jp; f. 1945; literature, history, dictionaries, religion, fine arts, books on tape, compact discs, CD-ROMs, comics, animation, video cassettes, computer games; Pres. Koichi Sekiya.

Kaibundo Publishing Co Ltd: 2-5-4, Suido, Bunkyo-ku, Tokyo 112-0005; tel. (3) 5684-6289; fax (3) 3815-3953; e-mail okadayo@kaibundo.jp; internet www.kaibundo.jp; f. 1914; marine affairs, natural science, engineering, industry; Pres. Setsuo Okada.

Kaiseisha Publishing Co Ltd: 3-5, Ichigaya Sadohara-cho, Shinjuku-ku, Tokyo 162-8450; tel. (3) 3260-3229; fax (3) 3260-3540; e-mail foreign@kaiseisha.co.jp; internet www.kaiseisha.net; f. 1936; juvenile; Pres. Masaki Imamura.

Kanehara & Co Ltd: 2-31-14, Yushima, Bunkyo-ku, Tokyo 113-8687; tel. (3) 3811-7185; fax (3) 3813-0288; e-mail kanehara@abox5.so-net.ne.jp; internet www.kanehara-shuppan.co.jp; f. 1875; medical, agricultural, engineering and scientific; Pres. Hiromitsu Kawai.

Keiso Shobo Publishing Co Ltd: 2-1-1, Suido, Bunkyo-ku, Tokyo 112-0005; tel. (3) 3814-6861; fax (3) 3814-6968; e-mail h-imura@keisoshobo.co.jp; internet www.keisoshobo.co.jp; f. 1948; law, economics, politics, literature, psychology, philosophy, sociology; Pres. Hisato Imura.

Kenkyusha Ltd: 2-11-3, Fujimi, Chiyoda-ku, Tokyo 102-8152; tel. (3) 3288-7777; fax (3) 3288-7799; e-mail hanbai@kenkyusha.co.jp; internet www.kenkyusha.co.jp; f. 1907; bilingual dictionaries, books on languages; Pres. Yusuke Kosakai.

Kinokuniya Co Ltd: 3-7-10, Shimomeguro, Meguro-ku, Tokyo 153-8504; tel. (3) 6910-0508; fax (3) 6420-1354; e-mail publish@kinokuniya.co.jp; internet www.kinokuniya.co.jp; f. 1927; humanities, social science, natural science; Chair. and CEO Osamu Matsubara; Pres. Masashi Takia.

KK Best Sellers Co Ltd: 2-29-7, Minami-Otsuka, Toshima-ku, Tokyo 170-8457; tel. (3) 5976-9121; fax (3) 5976-9237; e-mail muramatsu@bestsellers.co.jp; internet www.kk-bestsellers.com; f. 1967; non-fiction, general literature; Pres. Mikio Kurihara.

Kodansha Ltd: 2-12-21, Otowa, Bunkyo-ku, Tokyo 112-8001; tel. (3) 3946-6201; fax (3) 3944-9915; e-mail n-okazaki@kodansha.co.jp; internet www.kodansha.co.jp; f. 1909; fine arts, fiction, literature, juvenile, comics, dictionaries; Pres. Yoshinobu Noma.

Kosei Publishing Co Ltd: 2-7-1, Wada, Suginami-ku, Tokyo 166-8535; tel. (3) 5385-2319; fax (3) 5385-2331; e-mail kspub@kosei-shuppan.co.jp; internet www.kosei-shuppan.co.jp; f. 1966; general works, philosophy, religion, history, pedagogy, social science, art, juvenile; Pres. Moriyasu Okabe.

Kumon Publishing Co Ltd: Gobancho Grand Bldg, 3-1, Gobancho, Chiyoda-ku, Tokyo 102-8180; tel. (3) 3234-4004; fax (3) 3234-4483; e-mail international@kumonshuppan.com; internet www.kumonshuppan.com; f. 1988; juvenile, dictionaries, education; Pres. Shoichi Dokai.

Kwansei Gakuin University Press: 1-155, Uegahara Ichiban-cho, Nishi-Nomiya-shi, Hyogo 662-0891; tel. (798) 53-7002; fax (798) 53-9592; internet www.kwansei.ac.jp/press; f. 1997; natural science, social science, philosophy, literature; Pres. Kojiro Miyahara.

Kyoritsu Shuppan Co Ltd: 4-6-19, Kohinata, Bunkyo-ku, Tokyo 112-8700; tel. (3) 3947-2511; fax (3) 3947-2539; e-mail general@kyoritsu-pub.co.jp; internet www.kyoritsu-pub.co.jp; f. 1926; scientific and technical; Pres. Mitsuaki Nanjo.

Kyoto University Press: Kyodai-Yoshida-Minami, 69, Yoshidakonoe-cho, Sakyo-ku, Kyoto 606-8305; tel. (75) 761-6182; fax (75) 761-6190; e-mail sales@kyoto-up.or.jp; internet www.kyoto-up.or.jp; f. 1989; history, literature, philology, anthropology, sociology, economics, area studies, ecology, architecture, psychology, philosophy, space physics, earth and planetary science; Rep. Prof. Tamejiro Hiyama.

Kyushu University Press: 7-1-146, Hakozaki, Higashi-ku, Fukuoka 812-0053; tel. (92) 641-0515; fax (92) 641-0172; e-mail kup@mocha.ocn.ne.jp; internet www1.ocn.ne.jp/~kup; f. 1975; history, political science, law, economics, technology, linguistics, literature, psychology, medicine, agriculture; Chief Dir Naoyuki Isogawa.

Maruzen Co Ltd: Shinagawa Bldg, 4-13-14, Higashi-Shinagawa, Shinagawa-ku, Tokyo 140-0002; tel. (3) 3272-0521; fax (3) 3272-0527; e-mail sitepub@maruzen.co.jp; internet pub.maruzen.co.jp; f. 1869; general works; Dir Takehiko Ogi.

Meisei University Press: 2-1-1, Hodokubo, Hino-shi, Tokyo 191-8506; tel. (42) 591-9979; fax (42) 593-0192; f. 1975; humanities, education, social science, natural science; Pres. Tetsuo Ogawa.

Minerva Shobo: 1, Tsutsumidani-cho, Hinooka, Yamashina-ku, Kyoto 607-8494; tel. (75) 581-5191; fax (75) 581-8379; e-mail info@minervashobo.co.jp; internet www.minervashobo.co.jp; f. 1948; general non-fiction and reference; Pres. Keizo Sugita.

Misuzu Shobo Ltd: 5-32-21, Hongo, Bunkyo-ku, Tokyo 113-0033; tel. (3) 3815-9181; fax (3) 3818-8497; e-mail info@msz.co.jp; internet www.msz.co.jp; f. 1947; general, philosophy, history, psychiatry, literature, science, art; Pres. Hisao Mochitani.

Morikita Shuppan Co Ltd: 1-4-11, Fujimi, Chiyoda-ku, Tokyo 102-0071; tel. (3) 3265-8341; fax (3) 3261-1349; e-mail hiro@morikita.co.jp; internet www.morikita.co.jp; f. 1950; natural science, engineering; Pres. Hiroshi Morikita.

Nagaoka Shoten Co Ltd: 1-7-14, Toyotama-Kami, Nerima-ku, Tokyo 176-8518; tel. (3) 3992-5155; fax (3) 3948-9161; e-mail info@nagaokashoten.co.jp; internet www.nagaokashoten.co.jp; f. 1963; dictionaries, home economics, sports, recreation, law; Pres. Shuichi Nagaoka.

Nakayama-Shoten Co Ltd: 1-25-14, Hakusan, Bunkyo-ku, Tokyo 113-8666; tel. (3) 3813-1100; fax (3) 3816-1015; e-mail kojima@nakayamashoten.co.jp; internet www.nakayamashoten.co.jp; f. 1948; medicine, biology, zoology; Pres. Tadashi Hirata.

Nanzando Co Ltd: 4-1-11, Yushima, Bunkyo-ku, Tokyo; tel. (3) 5689-7868; fax (3) 5689-7869; e-mail nanzando-soumubu@nanzando.com; internet www.nanzando.com; f. 1901; medical reference, paperbacks; Pres. Hajime Suzuki.

Nigensha Publishing Co Ltd: 6-2-1, Honkomagome, Bunkyo-gu, Tokyo, 113-0021; tel. (3) 5395-2041; fax (3) 5395-2045; e-mail info@nigensha.jp; internet www.nigensha.co.jp; f. 1955; calligraphy, fine arts, art reproductions, cars, watches; Pres. Yukiko Kurosu.

Nihon Vogue Co Ltd: 3-23, Ichigaya Honmura-cho, Shinjuku-ku, Tokyo 162-8705; tel. (3) 5261-5139; fax (3) 3269-8726; e-mail asai@tezukuritown.com; internet www.tezukuritown.com; f. 1954; quilting, needlecraft, handicrafts, knitting, decorative painting, pressed flowers; Pres. Nobuaki Seto.

Nihonbungeisha Co Ltd: 1-7, Kanda Jimbo-cho, Chiyoda-ku, Tokyo 101-0051; tel. (3) 3294-7771; fax (3) 3294-7780; e-mail mmac@nihonbungeisha.co.jp; internet www.nihonbungeisha.co.jp; f. 1959; home economics, sociology, fiction, technical books; Pres. Souji Nishizawa.

Nikkei Publishing Inc: Mitsubishi-Soken Bldg, 2-3-6, Otemachi, Chiyoda-ku, Tokyo 100-0004; tel. (3) 5255-2836; fax (3) 5255-2864; internet www.nikkeibook.com; f. 1876; economics, business, politics, fine arts, video cassettes, CD-ROMs; Pres. Tsutomu Hado.

Nippon Hyoronsha: 3-12-4, Minami-Otsuka, Toshima-ku, Tokyo 170-8474; tel. (3) 3987-8611; fax (3) 3987-8593; e-mail inform@nippyo.co.jp; internet www.nippyo.co.jp; f. 1918; jurisprudence, economics, science, mathematics, medicine, psychology, business; Pres. TOSHIMASA KURODA.

Nippon Jitsugyo Publishing Co Ltd: 3-2-12, Hongo, Bunkyo-ku, Tokyo 113-0033; tel. (3) 3814-5651; fax (3) 3818-2723; e-mail int@njg.co.jp; internet www.njg.co.jp; f. 1950; business, management, finance and accounting, sales and marketing; Chair. and CEO YOICHIRO NAKAMURA.

Nosan Gyoson Bunka Kyokai (Rural Culture Association): 7-6-1, Akasaka, Minato-ku, Tokyo 107-8668; tel. (3) 3585-1141; fax (3) 3589-1387; e-mail rural@mail.ruralnet.or.jp; internet www.ruralnet.or.jp; f. 1940; agriculture, food and health, education, economics, philosophy; Pres. YOSHIHIRO HAMAGUCHI.

NTT Publishing Co Ltd: JR Tokyu Meguro Bldg, 7/F, 3-1-1, Kami-Osaki, Shinagawa-ku, Tokyo 141-8654; tel. (3) 5434-1011; fax (3) 5434-1008; internet www.nttpub.co.jp; f. 1987; essays, biography, philosophy, sociology, history, management, economics, technology, telecommunications, picture books, computer game guides; Pres. SHINJI JIKUYA.

Obunsha Co Ltd: 55, Yokodera-cho, Shinjuku-ku, Tokyo 162-8680; tel. (3) 3266-6429; fax (3) 3266-6412; internet www.obunsha.co.jp; f. 1931; textbooks, reference, general science and fiction, magazines, encyclopaedias, dictionaries; software; audio-visual aids; CEO FUMIO AKAO.

Ohmsha Ltd: 3-1, Kanda Nishiki-cho, Chiyoda-ku, Tokyo 101-8460; tel. (3) 3233-0641; fax (3) 3233-2426; e-mail kaigaika@ohmsha.co.jp; internet www.ohmsha.co.jp; f. 1914; engineering, technical and scientific; Pres. SEIJI SATO.

Ongaku No Tomo Sha Corpn (ONT): 6-30, Kagurazaka, Shinjuku-ku, Tokyo 162-8716; tel. (3) 3235-2111; fax (3) 3235-2110; e-mail home_ontomo@ongakunotomo.co.jp; internet www.ongakunotomo.co.jp; f. 1941; compact discs, videograms, music magazines, music books, music data, music textbooks; Pres. KUMIO HORIUCHI.

Osaka University of Economics and Law: 6-10, Gakuonji, Yao-shi, Osaka 581-8511; tel. (729) 41-8211; fax (729) 41-9979; e-mail kondo-t@keiho-u.ac.jp; internet www.keiho-u.ac.jp/research/syuppan/index.html; f. 1987; economics, law, philosophy, history, natural science, languages, politics; Pres. SHUNKUO KANAZAWA.

Osaka University Press: 2-7, Yamadaoka, Suita-shi, Osaka 565-0871; tel. and fax (6) 6877-1614; e-mail info@osaka-up.or.jp; internet www.osaka-up.or.jp; f. 1993; economics, history, literature, medicine, philosophy, politics, science, sociology, technology; Pres. KIYOKAZU WASHIDA.

PHP Institute Inc: 11, Kita-Nouchi-cho, Nishi-Kujo, Minami-ku, Kyoto 601-8411; tel. (75) 681-3268; fax (75) 681-4560; internet www.php.co.jp; f. 1946; social science; Pres. MASAYUKI MATSUSHITA.

Poplar Publishing Co Ltd: 22-1, Daikyo-cho, Shinjuku-ku, Tokyo 160-8565; tel. (3) 3357-2216; fax (3) 3351-0736; e-mail info@poplar.co.jp; internet www.poplar.co.jp; f. 1947; general, children's, comics; CEO HIROYUKI SAKAI.

Sanrio Co Ltd: 1-6-1, Osaki, Shinagawa-ku, Tokyo 141-8603; tel. (3) 3779-8101; fax (3) 3779-8702; internet www.sanrio.co.jp; f. 1960; juvenile; Pres. SHINTARO TSUJI.

Sanseido Co Ltd: 2-22-14, Misaki-cho, Chiyoda-ku, Tokyo 101-8371; tel. (3) 3230-9411; fax (3) 3230-9547; e-mail ssd-s@sanseido-publ.co.jp; internet www.sanseido.co.jp; f. 1881; dictionaries, educational, languages, social and natural science; Pres. KATSUHIKO KITAGUCHI.

Sanshusha Publishing Co Ltd: Aoyama Kumano Jinja Bldg, 2-2-22, Jingu-mae, Shibuya-ku, Tokyo 150-0001; tel. (3) 3405-4511; fax (3) 3405-4522; e-mail webmaster@sanshusha.co.jp; internet www.sanshusha.co.jp; f. 1938; languages, dictionaries, philosophy, sociology, electronic publishing (CD-ROM); Pres. TOSHIHIDE MAEDA.

Seibido Shuppan Co Ltd: 1-7, Shinogawamachi, Shinjuku-ku, Tokyo 162-8445; tel. (3) 5206-8151; fax (3) 5206-8159; internet www.seibidoshuppan.co.jp; f. 1969; sports, recreation, travel guides, music, motor sports, cooking, novels, computer, child care, picture books; Pres. ETSUJI FUKAMI.

Seibundo-Shinkosha Co Ltd: 3-3-11, Hongo, Bunkyo-ku, Tokyo 113-0033; tel. (3) 5800-5775; fax (3) 5800-5773; internet www.seibundo-shinkosha.net; f. 1912; scientific, gardening, electronics, graphic design; Pres. YUICHI OGAWA.

Seishun Publishing Co Ltd: 12-1, Wakamatsu-cho, Shinjuku-ku, Tokyo 162-0056; tel. (3) 3203-5121; fax (3) 3207-0982; e-mail info@seishun.co.jp; internet www.seishun.co.jp; f. 1955; science, education, history, sociology, philosophy, economics, literature; Pres. GENTARO OZAWA.

Seitoku University Press: 550, Iwase, Matsudo-shi, Chiba 271-8755; tel. (47) 365-1111; fax (47) 363-1401; e-mail shuppan@seitoku.ac.jp; f. 2002; human science, medicine, art; Pres. HIROAKI KAWAKAMI.

Seizando Shoten Publishing Co Ltd: 4-51, Minami-Motomachi, Shinjuku-ku, Tokyo 160-0012; tel. (3) 3357-5861; fax (3) 3357-5867; e-mail publisher@seizando.co.jp; internet www.seizando.co.jp; f. 1954; maritime affairs, aviation, engineering; Pres. NORIKO OGAWA.

Sekai Bunka Publishing Inc: 4-2-29, Kudan-Kita, Chiyoda-ku, Tokyo 102-8187; tel. (3) 3262-5111; fax (3) 3262-5750; e-mail y-muta@sekaibunka.co.jp; internet www.sekaibunka.com; f. 1946; history, natural science, geography, education, art, literature, juvenile; Pres. MINAKO SUZUKI.

Shincho-Sha Co Ltd: 71, Yarai-cho, Shinjuku-ku, Tokyo 162-8711; tel. (3) 3266-5250; fax (3) 3266-5432; e-mail shuppans@shinchosha.co.jp; internet www.shinchosha.co.jp; f. 1896; general literature, fiction, non-fiction, fine arts, philosophy; Pres. TAKANOBU SATO.

Shinkenchiku-Sha Co Ltd: 2-31-2, Yushima, Bunkyo-ku, Tokyo 113-8501; tel. (3) 3811-7101; fax (3) 3812-8229; e-mail ja-business@japan-architect.co.jp; internet www.japan-architect.co.jp; f. 1925; architecture; Pres. AKIHIKO OMORI.

Shinsei Publishing Co Ltd: 4-7-6, Taito, Taito-ku, Tokyo 110-0016; tel. (3) 3831-0743; fax (3) 3831-0758; internet www.shin-sei.co.jp; f. 1944; guidebooks, state examinations, personal computers; Pres. YASUHIRO TOMINAGA.

Shogakukan Inc: 2-3-1, Hitotsubashi, Chiyoda-ku, Tokyo 101-8001; tel. (3) 3230-5658; fax (3) 3230-9750; internet www.shogakukan.co.jp; f. 1922; juvenile, education, geography, history, encyclopaedias, dictionaries; Pres. MASAHIRO OHGA.

Shokabo Publishing Co Ltd: 8-1, Yomban-cho, Chiyoda-ku, Tokyo 102-0081; tel. (3) 3262-9166; fax (3) 3262-7257; e-mail info@shokabo.co.jp; internet www.shokabo.co.jp; f. 1716; natural science, engineering; Pres. KAZUHIRO YOSHINO.

Shokokusha Publishing Co Ltd: 25, Saka-machi, Shinjuku-ku, Tokyo 160-0002; tel. (3) 3359-3231; fax (3) 3357-3961; e-mail eigyo@shokokusha.co.jp; internet www.shokokusha.co.jp; f. 1932; architectural, technical and fine arts; Pres. TAKESHI GOTO.

Shueisha Inc: 2-5-10, Hitotsubashi, Chiyoda-ku, Tokyo 101-8050; tel. (3) 3230-6111; fax (3) 3262-1309; e-mail yoshizumi@shueisha.co.jp; internet www.shueisha.co.jp; f. 1925; literature, fine arts, language, juvenile, comics; Pres. and CEO HIDEKI YAMASHITA.

Shufunotomo Co Ltd: 2-9, Kanda Surugadai, Chiyoda-ku, Tokyo 101-8911; tel. (3) 5280-7567; fax (3) 5280-7568; e-mail international@shufunotomo.co.jp; internet www.shufunotomo.co.jp; f. 1916; domestic science, fine arts, gardening, handicraft, cookery and magazines; Pres. YOSHIYUKI OGINO.

Shufu-To-Seikatsusha Ltd: 3-5-7, Kyobashi, Chuo-ku, Tokyo 104-8357; tel. (3) 3563-5120; fax (3) 3563-2073; internet www.shufu.co.jp; f. 1935; home economics, recreation, fiction, medicine, comics, cooking, interiors, handicraft, fishing, fashion; Pres. KATSUHISA TAKANOU.

Shunju-Sha: 2-18-6, Soto-Kanda, Chiyoda-ku, Tokyo 101-0021; tel. (3) 3255-9611; fax (3) 3253-1384; e-mail main@shunjusha.co.jp; internet www.shunjusha.co.jp; f. 1918; philosophy, religion, literature, economics, music; Pres. AKIRA KANDA.

Sony Magazines Inc: Banchokaikan, 12-1, Goban-cho, Chiyoda-ku, Tokyo 102-8679; tel. (3) 3234-5811; fax (3) 3234-5842; internet www.sonymagazines.jp; f. 1979; music books, general literature; Pres. SHIGERU MURATA.

Taishukan Publishing Co Ltd: 2-1-1, Yushima, Bunkyo-ku, Tokyo 113-8541; tel. (3) 3868-2651; fax (3) 3868-2640; e-mail kimura@taishukan.co.jp; internet www.taishukan.co.jp; f. 1918; reference, Japanese and foreign languages, sports, dictionaries, audio-visual aids; Pres. KAZUYUKI SUZUKI.

Takahashi Shoten Co Ltd: 1-26-1, Otowa, Bunkyo-ku, Tokyo 112-0013; tel. (3) 3943-4525; fax (3) 3943-4288; e-mail ta_contact@takahashishoten.co.jp; internet www.takahashishoten.co.jp; f. 1952; business, food and drink, sport, dictionaries, education, juvenile; Pres. HIDEO TAKAHASHI.

Tamagawa University Press: 6-1-1, Tamagawa-Gakuen, Machida-shi, Tokyo 194-8610; tel. (42) 739-8933; fax (42) 739-8940; e-mail tup@tamagawa.ac.jp; internet www.tamagawa.jp/introduction/press; f. 1929; education, philosophy, religion, arts, juvenile, area studies; Pres. YOSHIAKI OBARA.

Tankosha Publishing Co Ltd: 19-1, Miyanishi-cho Murasakino, Kita-ku, Kyoto 603-8691; tel. (75) 432-5151; fax (75) 432-5152; e-mail info@tankosha.co.jp; internet www.tankosha.co.jp; f. 1949; tea ceremony, fine arts, history; Pres. YOSHITO NAYA.

Teikoku-Shoin Co Ltd: 3-29, Kanda Jimbo-cho, Chiyoda-ku, Tokyo 101-0051; tel. (3) 3262-0834; fax (3) 3262-7770; e-mail kenkyu@teikokushoin.co.jp; internet www.teikokushoin.co.jp; f. 1926; geography, atlases, maps, textbooks, history, civil studies; Pres. MASAYOSHI SAITO.

Tohoku University Press, Sendai: 2-1-1, Katahira, Aoba-ku, Sendai 980-8577; tel. (22) 214-2777; fax (22) 214-2778; e-mail info@tups.jp; internet www.tups.jp; f. 1996; natural science, social science, humanities, history, literature, psychology, philosophy, art, language; Chair. SHIGERU HISAMICHI.

Tokai University Press: 3-10-35, Minami-Yana, Hadano-shi, Kanagawa 257-0003; tel. (463) 79-3921; fax (463) 69-5087; e-mail webmaster@press.tokai.ac.jp; internet www.press.tokai.ac.jp; f. 1962; social science, cultural science, natural science, engineering, art; Pres. TATSURO MATSUMAE.

Tokuma Shoten Publishing Co Ltd: 2-2-1, Shiba-Daimon, Minato-ku, Tokyo 105-8055; tel. (3) 5403-4300; fax (3) 5403-4375; e-mail takeuti@shoten.tokuma.com; internet www.tokuma.jp; f. 1954; Japanese classics, history, fiction, juvenile; Pres. TORU IWABUCHI.

Tokyo News Service Ltd: Hamarikyu Park Side Place Bldg, 7-16-3, Tsukiji, Chuo-ku, Tokyo 104-8415; tel. (3) 6367-8000; fax (3) 3545-3628; internet www.tokyonews.co.jp; f. 1947; shipping, trade and television guides; Pres. T. OKUYAMA.

Tokyo Shoseki Co Ltd: 2-17-1, Horifune, Kita-ku, Tokyo 114-8524; tel. (3) 5390-7513; fax (3) 5390-7409; e-mail shoseki@tokyo-shoseki.co.jp; internet www.tokyo-shoseki.co.jp; f. 1909; textbooks, reference books, cultural and educational books; Pres. YASUNORI KAWABATA.

Tokyo Sogen-Sha Co Ltd: 1-5, Shin-Ogawa-machi, Shinjuku-ku, Tokyo 162-0814; tel. (3) 3268-8201; fax (3) 3268-8230; internet www.tsogen.co.jp; f. 1954; mystery and detective stories, science fiction, literature; Pres. SHINICHI HASEGAWA.

Toyo Keizai Inc: 1-2-1, Nihonbashi Hongoku-cho, Chuoku, Tokyo 103-8345; tel. (3) 3246-5661; fax (3) 3231-0906; e-mail info@toyokeizai.co.jp; internet www.toyokeizai.net; f. 1895; periodicals, economics, business, finance, corporation information; Pres. SEISHI SHIBOHTA.

Tuttle Publishing Co Inc: Yaekari Bldg, 3/F, 5-4-12, Osaki Shinagawa-ku, Tokyo; tel. (3) 5437-0171; fax (3) 5437-0755; e-mail customer@tuttle.co.jp; internet www.tuttle.co.jp; f. 1948; Japanese and Asian religion, history, social science, arts, languages, literature, juvenile, cookery; Pres. ERIC OEY.

United Nations University Press: 5-53-70, Jingumae, Shibuya-ku, Tokyo 150-8925; tel. (3) 5467-1212; fax (3) 3499-2828; e-mail sales@hq.unu.edu; internet www.unu.edu; f. 1975; social sciences, humanities, pure and applied natural sciences; Head KONRAD OSTERWALDER.

University of Nagoya Press: 1, Furocho, Chikusa-ku, Nagoya 464-0814; tel. (52) 781-5027; fax (52) 781-0697; e-mail sogo@unp.nagoya-u.ac.jp; internet www.unp.or.jp; f. 1982; social science, humanities, natural science, medicine; Chair. MITSUKI ISHII.

University of Tokyo Press: 7-3-1, Hongo, Bunkyo-ku, Tokyo 113-8654; tel. (3) 3811-0964; fax (3) 3815-1426; e-mail info@utp.or.jp; internet www.utp.or.jp; f. 1951; natural and social sciences, humanities; Japanese and English; Chair. HIROSHI WATANABE.

Waseda University Press: 1-9-12-402, Shinjuku-ku, Tokyo 169-0071; tel. (3) 3203-1551; fax (3) 3207-0406; e-mail shuppanbu@list.waseda.jp; internet www.waseda-up.co.jp; f. 1886; politics, economics, law, sociology, philosophy, literature; Pres. KENJI HORIGUCHI.

Yama-Kei Publishers Co Ltd: Tokyo; tel. (3) 6744-1900; fax (3) 6234-1628; e-mail info@yamakei.co.jp; internet www.yamakei.co.jp; f. 1930; natural science, geography, mountaineering, outdoor activity; Pres. SEKIMOTO CHANGDA.

Yoshikawa Kobunkan: 7-2-8, Hongo, Bunkyo-ku, Tokyo 113-0033; tel. (3) 3813-9151; fax (3) 3812-3544; e-mail hongo@yoshikawa-k.co.jp; internet www.yoshikawa-k.co.jp; f. 1857; history, biography, art, languages, religion; Pres. MOTOYASU MAEDA.

Yuhikaku Publishing Co Ltd: 2-17, Kanda Jimbo-cho, Chiyoda-ku, Tokyo 101-0051; tel. (3) 3264-1312; fax (3) 3264-5030; e-mail shinsuke-ito@yuhikaku.co.jp; internet www.yuhikaku.co.jp; f. 1877; social sciences, law, economics; Pres. SADAHARU EGUSA.

Yuki Shobo: 3-7-9, Kudan-Minami, Chiyoda-ku, Tokyo 102-0074; tel. (3) 5275-8008; fax (3) 5275-8099; e-mail takeshi.nanri@yukishobo.co.jp; internet www.yukishobo.co.jp; f. 1957; home economics, juvenile, recreation, sociology, sports; Pres. MASAO OKAJIMA.

Yuzankaku Shuppan: 2-6-9, Fujimi, Chiyoda-ku, Tokyo 102-0071; tel. (3) 3262-3231; fax (3) 3262-6938; e-mail info@yuzankaku.co.jp; internet www.yuzankaku.co.jp; f. 1916; history, fine arts, religion, archaeology; Pres. TETSUO MIYATA.

Zen-on Music Co Ltd: 2-13-3, Kami-Ochiai, Shinjuku-ku, Tokyo 161-0034; tel. (3) 3227-6270; fax (3) 3227-6276; e-mail akira@zen-on.co.jp; internet www.zen-on.co.jp; f. 1931; classics, pop, books on music; Pres. NORIYUKI HONMA.

Zoshindo Juken Kenkyusha Co Ltd: 2-19-15, Shinmachi, Nishi-ku, Osaka 550-0013; tel. (6) 6532-1581; fax (6) 6532-1588; e-mail jzoshindo@ybb.ne.jp; internet www.zoshindo.co.jp; f. 1890; educational, juvenile; Pres. AKITAKA OKAMATO.

GOVERNMENT PUBLISHING HOUSE

Government Publications' Service Centre: 1-2-1, Kasumigaseki, Chiyoda-ku, Tokyo 100-0013; tel. (3) 3504-3885; fax (3) 3504-3889.

PUBLISHERS' ASSOCIATIONS

Japan Book Publishers Association: 6, Fukuro-machi, Shinjuku-ku, Tokyo 162-0828; tel. (3) 3268-1302; fax (3) 3268-1196; e-mail rd@jbpa.or.jp; internet www.jbpa.or.jp; f. 1957; 459 mems (2010); Pres. MASAHIRO OGA; Exec. Dir TADASHI YAMASHITA.

Publishers' Association for Cultural Exchange, Japan: 1-2-1, Sarugaku-cho, Chiyoda-ku, Tokyo 101-0064; tel. (3) 3291-5685; fax (3) 3233-3645; e-mail culturalexchange@pace.or.jp; internet www.pace.or.jp; f. 1953; 75 mems (2010); Pres. TADATAKA EGUSA; Man. Dir HARUHIKO ISHIKAWA.

Broadcasting and Communications

TELECOMMUNICATIONS

EMOBILE Ltd: Shin-Nikko Bldg, 2-10-1, Toranomon, Minato-ku, Tokyo; tel. (3) 3588-7682; fax (3) 3588-7201; internet www.emobile.jp; f. 2005; owned by eAccess Ltd; mobile voice and data services; Pres. ERIC GAN.

KDDI Corpn: Garden Air Tower, 3-10-10, Iidabashi, Chiyoda-ku, Tokyo 102-8460; tel. (3) 3347-0077; fax (3) 6678-0305; internet www.kddi.com; f. 1984; est. by merger of DDI Corpn, Kokusai Denshin Denwa Corpn (KDD) and Nippon Idou Tsuhin Corpn (IDO); major international telecommunications carrier; Pres. TADASHI ONODERA.

Livedoor Co Ltd: Roppongi Hills Mori Tower, 38/F, 6-10-1, Roppongi, Minato-ku, Tokyo; tel. (3) 5766-7211; fax (3) 5766-7221; e-mail info@livedoor.jp; internet www.livedoor.com; f. 1996; acquired by NHN Japan in 2010; internet portal; network operations and maintenance; Pres. TAKESHI IDEZAWA.

Nippon Telegraph and Telephone Corpn (NTT): 2-3-1, Otemachi, Chiyoda-ku, Tokyo 100-8116; tel. (3) 5205-5111; internet www.ntt.co.jp; f. 1985; operates local, long-distance and international services; largest telecommunications co in Japan; holding co for NTT East, NTT West, NTT Communications, NTT Data Corpn and NTT DoCoMo; Pres. and CEO SATOSHI MIURA.

NTT DoCoMo: 2-11-1, Nagatacho, Chiyoda-ku, Tokyo 100-6150; tel. (3) 5156-1111; fax (3) 5156-0271; e-mail ir@nttdocomo.co.jp; internet www.nttdocomo.co.jp; f. 1991; operates mobile phone network; Pres. and CEO RYUJI YAMADA.

SoftBank Telecom Corpn: 1-9-1, Higashi-Shimbashi, Minato-ku, Tokyo 105-7316; tel. 0088-41; e-mail tcsc@tm.softbank.co.jp; internet www.softbanktelecom.co.jp; fmrly Japan Telecom; fixed-line business acquired by Ripplewood Holdings in 2003; acquired by SoftBank Corpn in 2004; merged with International Digital Communications (IDC) in 2005; name changed as above in 2006; Chair. and CEO MASAYOSHI SON.

Digital Phone and Digital TU-KA also operate mobile telecommunication services in Japan.

BROADCASTING

NHK (Japan Broadcasting Corporation): 2-2-1, Jinnan, Shibuya-ku, Tokyo 150-8001; tel. (3) 3465-1111; fax (3) 3469-8110; e-mail webmaster@www.nhk.or.jp; internet www.nhk.or.jp; f. 1925; fmrly Nippon Hoso Kyokai (NHK—Japan Broadcasting Corpn); Japan's sole public broadcaster; operates five TV channels (incl. two terrestrial services—general TV and educational TV, and three satellite services—BS-1, BS-2 and digital Hi-Vision—HDTV), three radio channels, Radio 1, Radio 2, and FM Radio, and three worldwide services, NHK World TV, NHK World Premium and NHK World Radio Japan; headquarters in Tokyo, regional headquarters in Osaka, Nagoya, Hiroshima, Fukuoka, Sendai, Sapporo and Matsuyama; Pres. MASAYUKI MATSUMOTO; Exec. Dir-Gen. of Broadcasting HIDEMI HYUGA.

National Association of Commercial Broadcasters in Japan (NAB-J): 3-23, Kioi-cho, Chiyoda-ku, Tokyo 102-8577; tel. (3) 5213-7711; fax (3) 5213-7730; internet www.nab.or.jp; f. 1951; includes 133 TV cos and 110 radio cos, of which 42 operate both radio and TV, with 664 radio stations and 8,315 TV stations (incl. relay stations); Pres. MICHISADA HIROSE; Exec. Dir TOSHIO TAMAGAWA.

In June 2000 there were a total of 99 commercial radio broadcasting companies and 127 commercial television companies operating in Japan.

Some of the most important companies are:

Asahi Hoso—Asahi Broadcasting Corpn: 1-1-30, Fukushima, Fukushima-ku, Osaka 553-8503; tel. (6) 6458-5321; internet www.asahi.co.jp; f. 1951; Pres. KATSUNOBU WATANABE.

Bunka Hoso—Nippon Cultural Broadcasting, Inc: 1-31, Hamamatsu-cho, Minato-ku, Tokyo 105-8002; tel. (3) 5403-1111; internet www.joqr.co.jp; f. 1952; Pres. MIKI AKIHIRO.

Chubu-Nippon Broadcasting Co Ltd: 1-2-8, Shinsakae, Naka-ku, Nagoya 460-8405; tel. (052) 241-8111; internet hicbc.com; f. 1950; Pres. YOICHI OISHI.

Fuji Television Network, Inc: 2-4-8, Daiba, Minato-ku, Tokyo 137-8088; tel. (3) 5500-8888; fax (3) 5500-8027; internet www.fujitv.co.jp; f. 1959; owns Nippon Broadcasting System, Inc; 12.75% stake in internet provider Livedoor; Chair. and CEO HISASHI HIEDA; Pres. KOU TOYODA.

Kansai TV Hoso (KTV)—Kansai Telecasting Corpn: 2-1-7, Ogimachi, Kita-ku, Osaka 530-8408; tel. (6) 6314-8888; internet www.ktv.co.jp; f. 1958; Pres. SUMIO FUKUI.

Mainichi Hoso (MBS)—Mainichi Broadcasting System, Inc: 17-1, Chayamachi, Kita-ku, Osaka 530-8304; tel. (6) 6375-7504; fax (6) 6359-3503; internet www.mbs.jp; f. 1950; Pres. MASAHIRO YAMAMOTO.

Nippon Hoso—Nippon Broadcasting System, Inc: 2-4-8, Daiba, Minato-ku, Tokyo 137-8686; tel. (3) 5500-1234; fax (3) 5500-3902; internet www.jolf.co.jp; f. 1954; 49.8% controlling stake acquired by Livedoor Co Ltd in 2005, but subsequently purchased by Fuji TV Network, Inc; Pres. AKINOBU KAMEBUCHI.

Nippon TV Hoso-MO (NTV)—Nippon Television Network Corpn: 1-6-1, Higashi-Shimbashi, Minato-ku, Tokyo 105-7444; tel. (3) 6215-1111; fax (3) 6215-3157; internet www.ntv.co.jp; f. 1953; Chair. SEIICHIRO UJIIE; Pres. SHINTARO KUBO.

Okinawa TV Hoso (OTV)—Okinawa Television Broadcasting Co Ltd: 1-2-20, Kumoji, Naha 900-8588; tel. (988) 63-2111; fax (988) 61-0193; internet www.otv.co.jp; f. 1959; Pres. BUNKI TOMA.

Radio Tampa—Nihon Short-Wave Broadcasting Co: 1-9-15, Akasaka, Minato-ku, Tokyo 107-8373; tel. (3) 3583-8151; fax (3) 3583-7441; f. 1954; Pres. TAMIO IKEDA.

Ryukyu Hoso (RBC)—Ryukyu Broadcasting Co: 2-3-1, Kumoji, Naha 900-8711; tel. (98) 867-2151; fax (98) 864-5732; e-mail info@rbc.co.jp; internet www.rbc-ryukyu.co.jp; f. 1954.

Tokyo Hoso (TBS)—Tokyo Broadcasting System Holdings Inc: 5-3-6, Akasaka, Minato-ku, Tokyo 107-8006; tel. (3) 3746-1111; fax (3) 3588-6378; internet www.tbs.co.jp; f. 1951; Chair. HIROSHI INOUE; Pres. TOSHICHIKA ISHIHARA.

TV Asahi Corpn: 6-9-1, Roppongi, Minato-ku, Tokyo 106-8001; tel. (3) 6406-1111; fax (3) 3405-3714; internet www.tv-asahi.co.jp; f. 1957; Pres. HIROSHI HAYAKAWA.

TV Osaka (TVO)—Television Osaka, Inc: 1-2-18, Otemae, Chuo-ku, Osaka 540-8519; tel. (6) 6947-0019; fax (6) 6946-9796; internet www.tv-osaka.co.jp; f. 1982; Pres. MAKOTO FUKAGAWA.

TV Tokyo Corpn: 4-3-12, Toranomon, Minato-ku, Tokyo 105-8012; tel. (3) 5470-7777; fax (3) 5473-6393; internet www.tv-tokyo.co.jp; f. 1964; Chair. and Co-CEO SADAHIKO SUGAYA; Pres. and Co-CEO MASAYUKI SHIMADA.

Yomiuri TV Hoso (YTV)—Yomiuri Telecasting Corporation: 2-2-33, Shiromi, Chuo-ku, Osaka 540-8510; tel. (6) 6947-2111; internet www.ytv.co.jp; f. 1958; 20 hrs broadcasting daily; Pres. KOJI TAKADA.

Satellite, Cable and Digital Television

In addition to the two broadcast satellite services that NHK introduced in 1989, a number of commercial satellite stations are in operation. Cable television is available in urban areas. Satellite digital television services, which first became available in 1996, are provided by Japan Digital Broadcasting Services (f. 1998 by the merger of PerfecTV and JSkyB—now Sky Perfect Communications Inc) and DirecTV. Terrestrial digital broadcasting was launched in Japan in December 2003.

Finance

(cap. = capital; p.u. = paid up; res = reserves; dep. = deposits; m. = million; brs = branches; amounts in yen)

BANKING

Japan's central bank and bank of issue is the Bank of Japan. At August 2005 more than one-half of the credit business of the country was handled by 152 private commercial banks, 47 trust banks and three long-term credit banks, collectively designated 'All Banks'.

An important financial role is played by co-operatives and by the many small enterprise institutions. There are also two types of private financial institutions for small business. At August 2005 there were 175 Credit Co-operatives and 297 Shinkin Banks (credit associations), which lend only to members. The latter also receive deposits.

The most popular form of savings is through the post office network. In October 2005 legislation was approved to permit the privatization of Japan Post. Following its initial transfer to a holding company, Japan Post was divided into four units (savings, insurance and postal services, along with personnel and property management). The first disposals took place in 2007. Having been established in September 2006, the Japan Post Bank (JPB) commenced operations on 1 October 2007. The JPB thus became the world's largest financial institution in terms of deposits; it is also the largest provider of life insurance.

Central Bank

Nippon Ginko (Bank of Japan): 2-1-1, Motoishi-cho, Nihonbashi, Chuo-ku, Tokyo 103-0021; tel. (3) 3279-1111; fax (3) 5200-2256; e-mail prd@info.boj.or.jp; internet www.boj.or.jp; f. 1882; cap. 100m., res 2,660,006m., dep. 38,168,703m. (March 2010); Gov. MASAAKI SHIRAKAWA; Dep. Govs HIROHIDE YAMAGUCHI, KIYOHIKO NISHIMURA; 32 brs.

Principal Commercial Banks

The Asahi Shinkin Bank: 2-1-2, Higashi-Kanda, Chiyoda-ku, Tokyo 101-0031; tel. (3) 3862-0321; fax (3) 5687-6867; internet www.asahi-shinkin.co.jp; f. 1923; est. as Shinyo Kumiai Tomin Kinko; name changed as above after merger in 2002; cap. 22,608m., res 26,231m., dep. 1,609,416m. (March 2010); Chair. KUNITAKE MORIWAKI; Pres. KAZUO KOBAYASHI; 69 brs.

Ashikaga Bank Ltd: 4-1-25, Sakura, Utsunomiya, Tochigi 320-8610; tel. (28) 622-0111; e-mail ashigin@ssctnet.or.jp; internet www.ashikagabank.co.jp; f. 1895; nationalized Nov. 2003 owing to insolvency; cap. 135,000m., res 14,448m., dep. 4,651,651m. (March 2010); CEO SATOSHI FUJISAWA; 149 brs.

Bank of Fukuoka Ltd: 2-13-1, Tenjin, Chuo-ku, Fukuoka 810-8727; tel. (92) 723-2442; fax (92) 711-1371; internet www.fukuokabank.co.jp; f. 1945; cap. 82,329m., res 127,904m., dep. 7,933,053m. (March 2010); Chair. RYOJI TSUKUDA; Pres. MASAAKI TANI; 167 brs.

Bank of Tokyo-Mitsubishi UFJ Ltd: 2-7-1, Marunouchi, Chiyoda-ku, Tokyo 100-8388; tel. (3) 3240-1111; fax (3) 3240-4197; internet www.bk.mufg.jp; f. 2006; est. through merger of Bank of Tokyo-Mitsubishi Ltd and UFJ Bank Ltd; specializes in international banking and financial business; subsidiary of Mitsubishi UFJ Financial Group (f. 2005 through merger of Mitsubishi Tokyo Financial Group and UFJ Holdings); cap. 1,711,958m., res 4,468,751m., dep. 136,213,699m. (March 2010); Pres. KATSUNORI NAGAYASU; 848 brs (772 domestic, 76 overseas).

Bank of Yokohama Ltd: 3-1-1, Minatomirai, Nishi-ku, Yokohama, Kanagawa 220-8611; tel. (45) 225-1111; fax (45) 225-1160; e-mail iroffice@hamagin.co.jp; internet www.boy.co.jp; f. 1920; cap. 215,628m., res 270,524m., dep. 10,721,975m. (March 2010); Chair. SADAAKI HIRASAWA; Pres. TADASHI OGAWA; 201 brs.

Chiba Bank Ltd: 1-2, Chiba-minato, Chuo-ku, Chiba 260-8720; tel. (43) 245-1111; e-mail int@chibabank.co.jp; internet www.chibabank.co.jp; f. 1943; cap. 145,069m., res 182,850m., dep. 9,462,726m. (March 2010); Pres. HIDETOSHI SAKUMA; Chair. TOSHIAKI ISHII; 167 domestic brs, 3 overseas brs.

The Chiba Kogyo Bank Ltd: 2-1-2, Saiwa-cho, Mihama-ku, Chiba; tel. (43) 243-2111; fax (43) 244-9203; internet www.chibakogyo-bank.co.jp; f. 1952; cap. 57,941m., res 36,315m., dep. 2,022,811m. (March 2010); Pres. and CEO TOSHIKAZU AOYAGI; 71 brs.

Hachijuni Bank: 178-8, Okada, Nagano-shi, Nagano 380-8682; tel. (26) 227-1182; fax (26) 226-5077; internet www.82bank.co.jp; f. 1931; cap. 52,243m., res 94,087m., dep. 5,529,324m. (March 2010); Chair. KAZUYUKI NARUSAWA; Pres. YOSHIYUKI YAMAURA.

Hokkaido Bank Ltd: 4-1, Nishi-Odori, Chuo-ku, Sapporo 060-8678, Hokkaido; tel. (11) 233-1093; fax (11) 231-3133; internet www.hokkaidobank.co.jp; f. 1951; cap. 93,524m., res 22,836m., dep. 3,951,850m. (March 2010); Pres. YOSHIHIRO SEKIHACHI; 129 brs.

Hokkoku Bank Ltd: 1 Shimotsutsumi-cho, Kanazawa 920-8670, Ishikawa; tel. (76) 263-1111; fax (76) 223-3362; internet www.hokkokubank.co.jp; f. 1943; cap. 26,673m., res 32,079m., dep. 2,919,655m. (March 2010); Pres. TATEKI ATAKA; 130 brs.

Hokuetsu Bank Ltd: 2-2-14, Otedori, Nagaoka 940-8650, Niigata; tel. (258) 353-111; fax (258) 375-113; internet www.hokuetsubank.co.jp; f. 1942; cap. 24,538m., res 29,080m., dep. 2,111,419m. (March 2010); Pres. KUSUMI TAKASHI; 89 brs.

Hokuriku Bank Ltd: 1-2-26, Tsutsumichodori, Toyama 930-8637; tel. (76) 423-7111; fax (76) 491-5908; e-mail info@hokuhoku-fg.co.jp; internet www.hokugin.co.jp; f. 1877; cap. 140,409m., res 31,376m., dep. 5,477,385m. (March 2010); Pres. SHIGEO TAKAGI; 176 brs.

Hokuto Bank Ltd: 3-1-41, Nakadori, Akita 010-0001; tel. (18) 833-4211; fax (18) 832-1942; e-mail hokutobank@hokutobank.co.jp; internet www.hokutobank.co.jp; f. 1895; est. as Masuda Bank Ltd, name changed as above after merger with Akita Akebono Bank in 1993; cap. 11,000m., res 23,953m., dep. 1,066,070m. (March 2010); Pres. EIKICHI SAITO; 84 brs.

Japan Net Bank: 2-1-1, Nishi-Shinjuku, Shinjuku-ku, Tokyo 163-0406; tel. (3) 6739-5000; internet www.japannetbank.co.jp; f. 2000; Japan's first internet-only bank; cap. 372m. (2010); Pres. NAOTO MURAMATSU.

Joyo Bank Ltd: 2-5-5, Minami-Machi, Mito-shi, Ibaraki 310-0021; tel. (29) 231-2151; fax (29) 255-6522; e-mail joyointl@po.net-ibaraki.ne.jp; internet www.joyobank.co.jp; f. 1935; cap. 85,113m., res 79,617m., dep. 6,846,502m. (March 2010); Chair. ISAO SHIBUYA; Pres. KUNIO ONIZAWA; 172 brs.

Juroku Bank Ltd: 8-26, Kandamachi, Gifu 500-8516; tel. (582) 652-111; fax (582) 661-698; internet www.juroku.co.jp; f. 1877; cap. 36,839m., res 57,694m., dep. 4,035,793m. (March 2010); Pres. NOBUO KOJIMA; 147 brs.

Kansai Urban Banking Corpn: 1-2-4, Nishi-Shinbashi, Chuo-ku, Osaka; tel. (6) 6834-4581; internet www.kansaiurban.co.jp; f. 1922; cap. 470,039m., res 63,352m., dep. 4,069,491m. (March 2010); Chair. AKIYOSHI KITAMURA; 147 brs.

Kumamoto Family Bank Ltd: 6-29-20, Suizenji, Kumamoto 862-8601; tel. (96) 385-1111; fax (96) 385-4272; internet www.kf-bank.jp; f. 1992; cap. 26,347m., res 27,858m., dep. 1,073,486m. (March 2010); Pres. KENJI HAYASHI.

Miyazaki Bank Ltd: 4-3-5, Tachibanadori-Higashi, Miyazaki 880-0805; tel. (985) 273-131; fax (985) 225-952; e-mail kokusai@miyagin.co.jp; internet www.miyagin.co.jp; f. 1932; cap. 14,697m., res 16,184m., dep. 1,833,901m. (March 2010); Pres. ISAO SATO; 97 brs.

Mizuho Bank Ltd: 1-1-5, Uchisaiwai-cho, Chiyodu-ku, Tokyo 100-0011; tel. (3) 3596-1111; fax (3) 3596-2179; internet www.mizuhobank.co.jp; f. 1971 as Dai-Ichi Kangyo Bank; merged with Fuji Bank and Industrial Bank of Japan to form above in 2002; cap. 700,000m., res 800,674m., dep. 65,592,993m. (March 2010); Pres. and CEO SATORU NISHIBORI; 334 domestic brs, 17 overseas brs.

North Pacific Bank (Hokuyo Bank): 3-7, Nishi-Odori, Chuo-ku, Sapporo 060-8661; tel. (11) 261-1416; fax (11) 232-6921; internet www.hokuyobank.co.jp; f. 1917; est. as Hokuyo Sogo Bank Ltd; adopted present name 1989; cap. 121,101m., res 137,422m., dep. 6,882,771m. (March 2010); Chair. IWAO TAKAMUKI; Pres. RYUZO YOKOUCHI.

Resona Bank Ltd: 2-2-1, Bingo-machi, Chuo-ku, Osaka 540-8610; tel. (6) 6271-1221; internet www.resona-gr.co.jp; f. 1918; merged with Asahi Bank in 2002 and changed name as above; cap. 279,928m., res 92,885m., dep. 22,786,624m. (March 2010); Chair. EIJI HOSOYA; Pres. SEIJI HIGAKI; 334 brs.

Saitama Resona Bank Ltd: 7-4-1, Tokiwa, Urawa-ku, Saitama 330-9088; tel. (48) 824-2411; internet www.resona-gr.co.jp/saitamaresona; f. 2002; cap. 70,000m., res 124,193m., dep. 10,100,154m. (March 2010); Pres. KENJI KAWADA.

San-in Godo Bank Ltd: 10, Uomachi, Matsue, Shimane 690-0062; tel. (852) 551-000; fax (852) 273-398; e-mail soki@gogin.co.jp; internet www.gogin.co.jp; f. 1941; cap. 20,705m., res 42,509m., dep. 3,525,963m. (March 2010); Pres. MAKOTO FURUSE; Chair. HIROYUKI WAKASA; 148 brs.

The Senshu Ikeda Bank Ltd: 18-14, Kita-ku, Osaka Chayamachi; tel. (6) 6375-1005; internet www.sihd-bk.jp; cap. 507,000m. (2010); Chair. NORIMASA YOSHIDA; Pres. MORITAKA HATTORI.

Shiga Bank Ltd: 1-38, Hamamachi, Otsu 520-8686, Shiga; tel. (77) 521-2360; fax (77) 521-2892; e-mail sigajpjt@gold.ocn.ne.jp; internet www.shigagin.com; f. 1933; cap. 33,076m., res 77,963m., dep. 3,590,958m. (March 2010); Chair. KOICHI TAKATA; Pres. YOSHIO DAIDO; 134 brs.

Shikoku Bank Ltd: 1–1–1, Minami-Harimaya-cho, Kochi 780-8605; tel. (88) 823-2111; fax (88) 873-0322; internet www.shikokubank.co.jp; f. 1873; cap. 25,000m., res 25,890m., dep. 2,394,236m. (March 2010); Chair. AKIHIRO AOKI; Pres. TADASHI NOMURA; 121 brs.

Shimizu Bank: 2-1, Fujimi-cho, Shimizu-ku, Shozuoka-shi, Shizuoka 424-8715; tel. (543) 535-151; fax (543) 535-333; internet www.shimizubank.co.jp; f. 1928; cap. 8,670m., res 6,957m., dep. 1,271,683m. (March 2010); Chair. KOICHI SUGIYAMA; Pres. NORIJI YAMADA; 78 brs.

Shizuoka Bank Ltd: 1-10, Gofuku-cho, Aoi-ku, Shizuoka 420-8761; tel. (54) 345-5700; fax (54) 349-5501; internet www.shizuokabank.co.jp; f. 1943; cap. 90,845m., res 128,366m., dep. 7,993,870m. (March 2010); Chair. TORU SAKURAI; Pres. and CEO KATSUNORI NAKANISHI; 168 domestic brs, 3 overseas brs.

Sumitomo Mitsui Banking Corpn: 1-2, Marunouchi, Chiyoda-ku, Tokyo 100-0005; tel. (3) 3230-8811; fax (3) 3239-4170; internet www.smbc.co.jp; f. 1895; present name adopted following merger with Sakura Bank Ltd in 2001; wholly owned subsidiary of Sumitomo Mitsui Financial Group (SMFG—f. 2002); cap. 1,770,996m., res 2,984,119m., dep. 106,451,620m. (March 2010); Chair. TEISUKE KITAYAMA; Pres. MASAYUKI OKU; 436 domestic brs, 15 overseas brs.

Toho Bank Ltd: 3-25, Ohmachi, Fukushima 960-8633; tel. (24) 523-3131; fax (24) 524-1583; internet www.tohobank.co.jp; f. 1941; cap. 23,519m., res 19,476m., dep. 2,984,708m. (March 2010); Chair. TOSHIO SEYA; Pres. SEISHI KITAMURA; 113 brs.

Tokyo Star Bank: 1-6-16 Akasaka, Minato-ku, Tokyo; tel. (3) 3586-3111; fax (3) 3586-5137; internet www.tokyostarbank.co.jp; f. 2001; est. as Nippon Finance Investment Ltd, name changed as above in May 2001; cap. 21,000m., res 21,463m., dep. 1,904,286m. (March 2010); Chair. TODD BUDGE; Pres. ROBERT BERARDY; 36 brs.

Tokyo Tomin Bank Ltd: 2-3-11, Roppongi, Minato-ku, Tokyo 106-8525; tel. (3) 3582-8251; fax (3) 3582-1979; e-mail jdu02670@nifty.ne.jp; internet www.tominbank.co.jp; f. 1951; cap. 48,120m., res 12,748m., dep. 2,332,001m. (March 2010); Chair. TETSUYA SHIINA; Pres. ISAO KOBAYASHI; 72 brs.

Tomato Bank Ltd: 2-3-4, Bancho, Okayama 700-0811, Ehime; tel. (86) 221-1010; fax (86) 221-1040; internet www.tomatobank.co.jp; f. 1931; est. as Sanyo Sogo Bank; became a commercial bank in 1989, when present name was assumed; cap. 14,310m., res 13,688m., dep. 816,155m. (March 2010); Pres. TAKANOBU NAKAGAWA.

Tsukuba Bank Ltd: 2-11-7, Chuo-ku, Tsuchiura, Ibaraki 305-0032; tel. (29) 859-8111; internet www.tsukubabank.co.jp; f. 1952; cap. 31,368m., res 14,762m., dep. 1,979,098m. (March 2010); Pres. KOZO KIMURA; 147 brs.

Principal Trust Banks

Chuo Mitsui Trust and Banking Co Ltd: 3-33-1, Shiba, Minato-ku, Chuo-ku, Tokyo 105-8574; tel. (3) 5445-3500; fax (3) 5232-8879; internet www.chuomitsui.co.jp; f. 1962; est. as Chuo Trust and Banking Co Ltd, name changed as above in 2000, following merger with Mitsui Trust and Banking Co Ltd; cap. 399,697m., res 155,132m., dep. 12,329,375m. (March 2010); Pres. KAZUO TANABE; 66 brs.

Mitsubishi UFJ Trust and Banking Corporation: 1-4-5, Marunouchi, Chiyoda-ku, Tokyo 100-8212; tel. (3) 3212-1211; fax (3) 3514-6660; internet www.tr.mufg.jp; f. 2005; est. upon merger of Mitsubishi Tokyo Financial Group and UFJ Holdings to form Mitsubishi UFJ Financial Group, of which it is a subsidiary; cap. 324,279m., res 462,526m., dep. 17,744,376m. (March 2010); Chair. HARUYA UEHARA; Pres. KINYA OKAUCHI; 68 domestic brs, 7 overseas brs.

Mizuho Trust and Banking Co Ltd: 1-2-1, Yaesu, Chuo-ku, Tokyo 103-8670; tel. (3) 3278-8111; fax (3) 3281-6947; internet www.mizuho-tb.co.jp; f. 1925; fmrly Yasuda Trust and Banking Co Ltd; cap. 247,260m., res 49,047m., dep. 4,451,546m. (March 2010); Pres. and CEO TAKASHI NONAKA; 38 brs.

Sumitomo Trust and Banking Co Ltd: 4-5-33, Kitahama, Chuo-ku, Osaka 540-8639; tel. (6) 6220-2121; fax (6) 6220-2043; e-mail ipda@sumitomotrust.co.jp; internet www.sumitomotrust.co.jp; f. 1925; cap. 342,037m., res 358,829m., dep. 16,408,565m. (March 2010); Chair. ATSUSHI TAKAHASHI; Pres. and CEO HITOSHI TSUNEKAGE; 63 domestic brs, 8 overseas brs.

Long-Term Credit Banks

Aozora Bank: 1-3-1, Kudan-Minami, Chiyoda-ku, Tokyo 102-8660; tel. (3) 3263-1111; fax (3) 3265-7024; e-mail sora@aozora.co.jp; internet www.aozorabank.co.jp; f. 1957; nationalized Dec. 1998, sold to consortium led by Softbank Corpn in Aug. 2000; fmrly The Nippon Credit Bank, name changed as above 2001; 62% owned by Cerberus Group; cap. 419,780m., res 15,437m., dep. 4,324,674m. (March 2010); Pres. and CEO BRIAN PRINCE; Chair. YUJI SHIRAKAWA; 20 brs.

Mizuho Corporate Bank Ltd (The Industrial Bank of Japan Ltd): 1-3-3, Marunouchi, Chiyoda-ku, Tokyo 100-8210; tel. (3) 3214-1111; fax (3) 3201-7643; internet www.mizuhocbk.co.jp; f. 1902; renamed as above in 2002 following merger of the Dai-Ichi Kangyo Bank, the Fuji Bank and the Industrial Bank of Japan; medium- and long-term financing; cap. 1,404,065m., res 947,050m., dep. 55,720,550m. (March 2010); Pres. and CEO SATO YASUHIRO; 277 domestic brs, 21 overseas brs.

Shinsei Bank Ltd: 2-4-3, Nihonbashi-muromachi, Chuo-ku, Tokyo; tel. (3) 6680-7000; internet www.shinseibank.com; f. 1952; est. as The Long-Term Credit Bank of Japan; nationalized Oct. 1998, sold to Ripplewood Holdings (USA), renamed as above June 2000; cap. 476,296m., res –16,124m., dep. 8,698,559m. (March 2010); Pres. and CEO SHIGEKI TOMA; 30 domestic brs, 1 overseas br.

Co-operative Bank

Shinkin Central Bank: 1-3-7, Yaesu, Chuo-ku, Tokyo 103-0028; tel. (3) 5202-7700; fax (3) 3278-7031; e-mail s1000551@facetoface.ne.jp; internet www.shinkin-central-bank.jp; f. 1950; cap. and res 1,002,570m., dep. 26,903,428m. (March 2010); Chair. KOJI OMAE; Pres. and CEO MITSUO TANABE; 14 domestic brs, 4 overseas brs.

Principal Government Institutions

Development Bank of Japan: 1-9-1, Otemachi, Chiyoda-ku, Tokyo 100-0004; tel. (3) 3270-3211; fax (3) 3245-1938; e-mail safukas@dbj.go.jp; internet www.dbj.jp; f. 1951; est. as Japan Devt Bank; renamed Oct. 1999 following consolidation with Hokkaido and Tohoku Devt Finance Public Corpn; provides long-term loans; subscribes for corporate bonds; guarantees corporate obligations; invests in specific projects; borrows funds from Govt and abroad; issues external bonds and notes; provides market information and consulting services for prospective entrants to Japanese market; legislation providing for the bank's privatization (by 2015) approved in 2008; cap. 1,181,194m., res 1,078,540m., dep. 12,978,852m. (March 2010); Pres. and CEO MINORU MUROFUSHI; 10 domestic brs, 6 overseas brs.

Japan Finance Corporation (JFC): 1-9-3, Otemachi, Chiyoda-ku, Tokyo 100-0004; internet www.jfc.go.jp; f. 2008; govt financial institution formed from merger of National Life Finance Corpn (NLFC), Agriculture, Forestry and Fisheries Finance Corpn (AFC), Japan Finance Corpn for Small and Medium Enterprise (JASME) and International Finance Operations (IFOs) of Japan Bank for International Cooperation (JBIC); cap. 3,251,700m., res 2,405,100m. (March 2010); Gov. and CEO SHOSAKU YASUI; 152 brs.

Japan Bank for International Cooperation (JBIC): 1-4-1, Otemachi, Chiyoda-ku, Tokyo 100-8144; tel. (3) 5218-3304; fax (3) 5218-3960; e-mail ir@jbic.go.jp; internet www.jbic.go.jp; f. 1999; est. by merger of The Export-Import Bank of Japan (f. 1950) and The Overseas Economic Co-operation Fund (f. 1961); governmental financial institution, responsible for Japan's external economic policy and co-operation activities; cap. 1,055,500m. (March 2010); Pres. and CEO HIROSHI WATANABE.

Japan Post Bank Co Ltd (JPB): 1-3-2, Kasumigaseki, Chiyoda-ku, Tokyo 100-8798; tel. (3) 3504-4411; internet www.jp-bank.japanpost.jp; f. 2006; wholly owned by Japan Post Holdings Co Ltd; cap. 3,500,000m., dep. 182,736,000m. (2007); Chair. SHIGEO KAWA; Pres. YOSHIYUKI IZAWA.

Norinchukin Bank (Central Co-operative Bank for Agriculture, Forestry and Fisheries): 1-13-2, Yuraku-cho, Chiyoda-ku, Tokyo 100; tel. (3) 3279-0111; fax (3) 3218-5177; internet www.nochubank.or.jp; f. 1923; main banker to agricultural, forestry and fisheries co-operatives; receives deposits from individual co-operatives, federations and agricultural enterprises; extends loans to these and to local govt authorities and public corpns; adjusts excess and shortage of funds within co-operative system; issues debentures, invests funds and engages in other regular banking business; cap. 3,425,909m., res –312,733m., dep. 56,137,011m. (March 2010); Chair MAMORU MOTEKI; Pres. and CEO YOSHIO KONO; 34 domestic brs, 5 overseas brs.

Shoko Chukin Bank (Central Co-operative Bank for Commerce and Industry): 2-10-17, Yaesu, Chuo-ku, Tokyo 104-0028; tel. (3) 3272-6111; fax (3) 3272-6169; e-mail JDK06560@nifty.ne.jp; internet www.shokochukin.co.jp; f. 1936; provides general banking services to facilitate finance for smaller enterprise co-operatives and other organizations formed mainly by small and medium-sized enterprises; issues debentures; began process of privatization in 2008; cap. 218,653m., res 554,819m., dep. 10,877,658m. (March 2010); Pres. TETSUO SEKI; 99 domestic brs, 3 overseas brs.

Other government financial institutions include the Japan Finance Corpn for Municipal Enterprises, the Small Business Credit Insurance Corpn and the Okinawa Development Finance Corpn.

Foreign Banks

In 2004 there were 84 foreign banks operating in Japan.

Bankers' Associations

Japanese Bankers Association: 1-3-1, Marunouchi, Chiyoda-ku, Tokyo 100-8216; tel. (3) 3216-3761; fax (3) 3201-5608; internet www.zenginkyo.or.jp; f. 1945; fmrly Fed. of Bankers Asscns of Japan; 123 full mems, 61 assoc. mems, 62 special mems, 3 bank holding co mems; Chair. SATORU NISHIBORI.

Tokyo Bankers Association, Inc: 1-3-1, Marunouchi, Chiyoda-ku, Tokyo 100-8216; tel. (3) 3216-3761; fax (3) 3201-5608; f. 1945; 105 mem. banks; conducts the Japanese Bankers Asscn's administrative business; Chair. MASAYUKI OKU.

National Association of Labour Banks: 2-5-15, Kanda Surugadai, Chiyoda-ku, Tokyo 101-0062; tel. (3) 3295-6735; fax (3) 3295-6751; e-mail kikaku@ho.rokinbank.or.jp; internet all.rokin.or.jp; f. 1951; Pres. YASUHIKO OKADA.

Regional Banks Association of Japan: 3-1-2, Uchikanda, Chiyoda-ku, Tokyo 101-8509; tel. (3) 3252-5171; fax (3) 3254-8664; internet www.chiginkyo.or.jp; f. 1936; 64 mem. banks; Chair. TADASHI OGAWA.

Second Association of Regional Banks: 5, Sanban-cho, Chiyoda-ku, Tokyo 102-0075; tel. (3) 3262-2181; fax (3) 3262-2339; e-mail hp-master@dainichiginkyo.or.jp; internet www.dainichiginkyo.or.jp; f. 1989; fmrly Nat. Asscn of Sogo Banks; 42 commercial banks; Chair. NOBUO KOJIMA.

STOCK EXCHANGES

Nagoya Stock Exchange: 3-8-20, Sakae, Naka-ku, Nagoya 460-0008; tel. (52) 262-3172; fax (52) 241-1527; e-mail kikaku@nse.or.jp; internet www.nse.or.jp; f. 1949; Pres. NOBORU KUROYANAGI; Exec. Vice-Pres. MASAKI TAKEDA.

Osaka Securities Exchange (OSE): 1-8-16, Kitahama, Chuo-ku, Osaka 541-0041; tel. (6) 4706-0875; fax (6) 6231-2639; e-mail koho@ose.or.jp; internet www.ose.or.jp; f. 1949; 83 regular transaction partners, 5 transaction partners in futures and options trading, 2 IPO transaction partners; Pres. and CEO MICHIO YONEDA.

Jasdaq: 1-5-8, Nihonbashi Kayaba-cho, Chuo-ku, Tokyo 103-0025; tel. (3) 3669-5410; internet www.ose.or.jp/e/jasdaq; f. 1963; became wholly-owned subsidiary of Osaka Securities Exchange 2009; resumed operations following merger of smaller markets, Jasdaq, Hercules and NEO in 2010; over 1400 listed cos.

Sapporo Securities Exchange: 5-14-1, Nishi, Minami 1-jo, Chuo-ku, Sapporo 060-0061; tel. (11) 241-6171; fax (11) 251-0840; e-mail info@sse.or.jp; internet www.sse.or.jp; 75 listed cos; Pres. YOSHIRO ITOH.

Tokyo Stock Exchange, Inc: 2-1, Nihonbashi Kabuto-cho, Chuo-ku, Tokyo 103-8224; tel. (3) 3665-1881; fax (3) 3662-0547; internet www.tse.or.jp; f. 1949; 97 general trading participants, 56 bond futures trading participants, 2 stock index futures trading participants; cap. 11,500m., issued shares 2,300,000 (June 2010); Chair. TAIZO NISHIMURO; Pres. and CEO ATSUSHI SAITO.

Supervisory Body

The Securities and Exchange Surveillance Commission: 3-2-1, Kasumigaseki, Chiyoda-ku, Tokyo 100-8922; tel. (3) 3581-7868; fax (3) 5251-2151; internet www.fsa.go.jp/sesc; f. 1992; est. for the surveillance of securities and financial futures transactions; Chair. KENICHI SADO.

INSURANCE

Principal Life Companies

AIG Edison Life Insurance Co: Olinas Tower, 4-1-3, Sumida-ku, Tokyo 130-8625; tel. (3) 6658-6000; internet www.aigedison.co.jp; fmrly GE Edison Life Insurance Co, itself fmrly Toho Mutual Life Insurance Co; became subsidiary of Gibraltar Life Insurance in Feb. 2011; Pres. TORU MATSUZAWA.

AIG Star Life Insurance Co Ltd: 4-1-3, Sumida-ku, Tokyo 130-8625; internet www.aigstar-life.co.jp; fmrly Chiyoda Mutual Life Insurance Co, acquired by American International Group, Inc (AIG) in 2001; became subsidiary of Gibraltar Life Insurance in Feb. 2011; Pres. NORIO TOMONO.

Aioi Life Insurance Co Ltd: 3-1-6, Nihonbashi, Chuo-ku, Tokyo 103-0027; tel. (3) 3273-0101; internet www.ioi-life.co.jp; Pres. YOSHIHISA ISHII.

American Family Life Assurance Co of Columbus AFLAC Japan: Shinjuku Mitsui Bldg, 12/F, 2-1-1, Nishi-Shinjuku, Shinjuku-ku, Tokyo 163-0456; tel. (3) 3344-2701; fax (3) 0424-3001; internet www.aflac.co.jp; f. 1974; Chair. YOSHIKI OTAKE; Pres. HIDEFUMI MATSUI.

American Life Insurance Co (Japan): 4-1-3, Sumida-ku, Tokyo; tel. (3) 3284-4111; fax (3) 3284-3874; internet www.alico.co.jp; f. 1972; Pres. KAZUYUKI TAKAHASHI.

Asahi Mutual Life Insurance Co: 1-23, Tsurumaki, Tama-shi, Tokyo 206-8611; tel. (42) 338-3111; internet www.asahi-life.co.jp; f. 1888; Pres. MIKI SATO.

AXA Japan Holding Co Ltd: NBF Platinum Tower, 1-17-3, Minato-ku, Tokyo 150-8020; tel. (3) 3407-6210; internet www.axa.co.jp; Pres. and CEO JEAN-LOUIS LAURENT JOSI.

Cardif Assurance Vie: Infoss Tower, 9/F, 20-1, Sakuragaoka-cho, Shibuya-ku, Tokyo 150-0031; tel. (3) 6415-8275; internet www.cardif.co.jp/vie; f. 2000; Pres. ATSUSHI SAKAUCHI.

Dai-ichi Mutual Life Insurance Co: 1-13-1, Yuraku-cho, Chiyoda-ku, Tokyo 100-8411; tel. (3) 3216-1211; fax (3) 5221-8139; internet www.dai-ichi-life.co.jp; f. 1902; Chair. TOMIJIRO MORITA; Pres. KOICHIRO WATANABE.

Fuji Life Insurance Co Ltd: 1-18-17, Minami-Senba, Chuo-ku, Osaka-shi 542-0081; tel. (6) 6261-0284; fax (6) 6261-0113; internet www.fujiseimei.co.jp; f. 1996; Pres. YOSHIAKI YONEMURA.

Fukoku Mutual Life Insurance Co: 2-2-2, Uchisaiwai-cho, Chiyoda-ku, Tokyo 100-0011; tel. (3) 3508-1101; fax (3) 3591-6446; internet www.fukoku-life.co.jp; f. 1923; Chair. TOMOFUMI AKIYAMA; Pres. YOSHITERU YONEYAMA.

Gibraltar Life Insurance Co Ltd: 2-13-10, Tamati Hisashi, Tokyo 100-8953; tel. (3) 5501-6001; internet www.gib-life.co.jp; f. 1947; fmrly Kyoei Life Insurance Co Ltd, declared bankrupt Oct. 2000; resumed operations in 2001 as mem. of Prudential Financial, USA; Pres. MITSUO KURASHIGE.

Hartford Life Insurance K. K.: Shiodome Bldg, 15/F, 1-2-20, Kaigan, Minato-ku, Tokyo 105-0022; tel. (3) 6219-3784; internet www.hartfordlife.co.jp; f. 2000; Pres. AIDAN KIDNEY.

ING Life Insurance Co Ltd: New Otani Garden Court, 26/F, 4-1, Kioi-cho, Chiyoda-ku, Tokyo 102-0094; tel. (3) 5210-0300; fax (3) 5210-0430; internet www.ing-life.co.jp; f. 1985; Pres. EDDIE BERMAN.

Japan Post Insurance: 1-3-2, Kasumigaseki, Chiyoda-ku, Tokyo 100-8798; tel. (3) 3504-4411; internet www.jp-life.japanpost.jp; f. 2006; wholly owned by Japan Post Holdings Co Ltd; Chair. and CEO JOSUKE SHINDO; Pres. IZUMI YAMASHITA.

Kyoei Kasai Shinrai Life Insurance Co Ltd: 1-18-6, Shimbashi, Minato-ku, Tokyo 105-8604; tel. (3) 3504-0131; fax (3) 5372-7701; internet www.kyoeikasai.co.jp; f. 1996; Pres. KENZI SUGIYAMA.

Manulife Life Insurance Co: 4-34-1, Kokuryo-cho, Chofu-shi, Tokyo 182-8621; tel. (3) 2442-7120; fax (3) 2442-7977; e-mail craig_bromley@manulife.com; internet www.manulife.co.jp; f. 1999; fmrly Manulife Century Life Insurance Co; absorbed bankrupt Daihyaku Mutual Life Insurance Co in 2001; Pres. and CEO CRAIG BROMLEY.

MassMutual Life Insurance Co: 1-5-7, Ariake, Koto-ku, Tokyo 135-0063; internet www.massmutual.co.jp; Pres. MASANORI MIZOGUCHI.

Meiji Yasuda Life Insurance Co: 2-1-1, Marunouchi, Chiyoda-ku, Tokyo 100-0005; tel. (3) 3283-8111; fax (3) 3215-5219; internet www.meijiyasuda.co.jp; f. 2004; est. by merger of Meiji Life Insurance Co (f. 1881) and Yasuda Mutual Life Insurance Co (f. 1880); Chair. NORIKAJU SEKIGUTI; Pres. KENJI MATSUO.

Mitsui Life Insurance Co Ltd: 2-1-1, Otemachi, Chiyoda-ku, Tokyo 100-8123; tel. (3) 6831-8000; internet www.mitsui-seimei.co.jp; f. 1927; Chair. HIROSUMI TSUSUE; Pres. YUKITERU YAMAMOTO.

Nippon Life Insurance Co (Nissay): 3-5-12, Imabashi, Chuo-ku, Osaka 541-8501; tel. (6) 6209-5525; e-mail hosokawa15560@nissay.co.jp; internet www.nissay.co.jp; f. 1889; Chair. IKUO UNO; Pres. KUNIE OKAMOTO.

Nipponkoa Life Insurance Co Ltd: 4-2, Tsukiji, Chuo-ku, Tokyo 104-8407; tel. (3) 5565-8080; fax (3) 5565-8365; internet www.nipponkoa.co.jp/life; f. 1996; formed by merger of Nippon Fire and Marine Insurance and Koa Fire and Marine Insurance; Pres. KAZUO HASHIMOTO.

ORIX Life Insurance Corpn: Mita NN Bldg, 4-1-23, Shiba, Minato-ku, Tokyo 108-0014; tel. (3) 5419-5102; fax (3) 5419-5901; e-mail koho@orix.co.jp; internet www.orix.co.jp; f. 1991; Chair. and CEO YOSHIHIKO MIYAUCHI; Pres. MAKOTO INOUE.

Prudential Life Insurance Co Ltd: Prudential Tower, 2-13-10, Nagata-cho, Chiyoda-ku, Tokyo 100-0014; tel. (3) 5501-5500; fax (3) 3221-2305; internet www.prudential.co.jp; f. 1987; Chair. and CEO JOHN STRANGFELD; Pres. MITSUO KURASHIGE.

Sompo Japan DIY Life Insurance Co Ltd: 6-10-1, Shinjuku-Nishi, Shinjuku-ku, Tokyo 160-0023; tel. (3) 5345-7603; fax (3) 5345-7608; internet www.diy.co.jp; f. 1999; Pres. TATSUO SHIBUYA.

Sompo Japan Himawari Life Insurance Co Ltd: Shinjuku Mitsui Bldg, 35/F, 1-2-1, Nishi-Shinjuku, Shinjuku-ku, Tokyo; internet www.himawari-life.com; f. 2002; Pres. TOSHIO MATSUZAKI.

Sony Life Insurance Co Ltd: Shin-Aoyama Bldg, 3/F, 1-1-1, Minami-Aoyama, Minato-ku, Tokyo 107-8585; tel. (3) 3475-8811; fax (3) 3475-8914; internet www.sonylife.co.jp; Chair. KUNIKITA ANDO; Pres. TARO OKUDA.

Sumitomo Life Insurance Co: 7-18-24, Tsukiji, Chuo-ku, Tokyo 104-8430; tel. (3) 5550-1100; fax (3) 5550-1160; internet www.sumitomolife.co.jp; f. 1907; Pres. YOSHIO SATO.

T & D Holdings Inc: Shiodome Shiba-Rikyu Bldg, 1-2-3, Kaigan, Minato-ku, Tokyo 105-0022; tel. (3) 3434-9111; fax (3) 3434-9055; internet www.td-holdings.co.jp; f. 1895; fmrly Tokyo Mutual Life Insurance Co; T & D Financial Life Insurance Co Holdings company formed in April 2004 through merger of T & D Financial Life Insurance Co, Taiyo Mutual Life Insurance Co and Daido Life Insurance Co; Pres. NAOTERU MIYATO.

Tokio Marine & Nichido Life Insurance Co Ltd: 5-3-16, Ginza, Chuo-ku, Tokyo 106-0041; tel. (3) 5223-2111; fax (3) 5223-2165; internet www.tmn-anshin.co.jp; Pres. SUKEAKI OHTA.

Yamato Mutual Life Insurance Co: 1-1-7, Uchisaiwai-cho, Chiyoda-ku, Tokyo 100-0011; tel. (3) 3508-3111; fax (3) 3508-3118; internet www.yamato-life.co.jp; f. 1911; Pres. TAKEO NAKAZONO.

Zurich Life Insurance Co Ltd: Shinanomachi Rengakan, 35, Shinanomachi, Shinjuku-ku, Tokyo 160-0016; tel. (3) 5361-2700; fax (3) 5361-2705; internet www.zurichlife.co.jp; f. 1996; Pres. NAGANO TOSHIYUKI.

Principal Non-Life Companies

ACE Insurance: Arco Tower, 1-8-1, Shimomeguro, Meguro-ku, Tokyo 153-0064; tel. (3) 5740-0600; fax (3) 5740-0608; internet www.ace-insurance.co.jp; f. 1999; Chair. SHINIJI NOMOTO; Pres. TAKASHI IMAI.

Aioi Nissay Dowa Insurance Co Ltd: 1-28-1, Ebisu, Shibuya-ku, Tokyo 150-8488; tel. (3) 5424-0101; internet www.aioinissaydowa.co.jp; est. by merger of Aioi Insurance Co Ltd and Nissay Dowa General Insurance Co Ltd in 2010; Pres. KUNI SUZUKI.

Allianz Fire and Marine Insurance Japan Ltd: Anzen Bldg, 1-6-6, Moto-Akasaka, Minato-ku, Tokyo 107-0051; tel. (3) 4558-7500; e-mail netadmin@allianz.co.jp; internet www.allianz.co.jp; f. 1990; Chair. AXEL THEIS; Pres. MICHAEL MAICHER.

The Asahi Fire and Marine Insurance Co Ltd: 2-6-2, Kaji-cho, Chiyoda-ku, Tokyo 101-8655; tel. (3) 3294-2211; fax (3) 3254-2296; e-mail asahifmi@blue.ocn.ne.jp; internet www.asahikasai.co.jp; f. 1951; Pres. KAZUHO OYA.

AXA Japan Holding Co Ltd: NBF Platinum Tower, 1-17-3, Minato-ku, Tokyo 150-8020; tel. (3) 3407-6210; internet www.axa.co.jp; f. 1998; Pres. JEAN-LOUIS LAURENT JOSI.

The Daido Fire and Marine Insurance Co Ltd: 1-12-1, Kumoji, Naha-shi, Okinawa 900-8586; tel. (98) 867-1161; fax (98) 862-8362; internet www.daidokasai.co.jp; f. 1971; Pres. NAOTO MIRAYA.

The Fuji Fire and Marine Insurance Co Ltd: 1-18-11, Minami-Senba, Chuo-ku, Osaka 542-8567; tel. (6) 6271-2741; fax (6) 6266-7115; internet www.fujikasai.co.jp; f. 1918; Pres. and CEO AKIRA KONDOH.

The Japan Earthquake Reinsurance Co Ltd: Fuji Plaza, 4/F, 8-1, Nihonbashi Kobuna-cho, Chuo-ku, Tokyo 103-0024; tel. (3) 3664-6074; fax (3) 3664-6169; e-mail kanri@nihonjishin.co.jp; internet www.nihonjishin.co.jp; f. 1966; Chair. SHOZO WAKABAYASHI; Pres. HIDEO SUZUKI.

JI Accident & Fire Insurance Co Ltd: A1 Bldg, 20-5, Ichiban-cho, Chiyoda-ku, Tokyo 102-0082; tel. (3) 3237-2045; fax (3) 3237-2250; internet www.jihoken.co.jp; f. 1989; Pres. MITSUHITO MINAMISAWA.

The Kyoei Mutual Fire and Marine Insurance Co: 1-18-6, Shimbashi, Minato-ku, Tokyo 105-8604; tel. (3) 3504-0131; fax (3) 3508-7680; e-mail reins.intl@kyoeikasai.co.jp; internet www.kyoeikasai.co.jp; f. 1942; Pres. KENJI SUGIYAMA.

Meiji Yasuda General Insurance Co Ltd: 2-11-1, Kanda Tsukasa-cho, Chiyoda-ku, Tokyo 101-0048; tel. (3) 3257-3111; fax (3) 3257-3295; internet www.meijiyasuda-sonpo.co.jp; f. 1996; Pres. SEIJI NISHI.

Mitsui Direct General Insurance Co Ltd: 1-5-3, Koraku, Bunkyou-ku, Tokyo 112-0004; tel. (3) 5804-7711; internet www.mitsui-direct.co.jp; f. 1996; Pres. TOSHIO KITAMURA.

Mitsui Sumitomo Insurance Co Ltd: 27-2-2, Shinkawa, Chuo-ku, Tokyo 104-8252; tel. (3) 3297-1111; internet www.ms-ins.com; f. 2001; formed by merger of Mitsui Marine and Fire Insurance and Sumitomo Marine and Fire Insurance; Chair. TOSHIAKI EGASHIRA; Pres. YASUYOSHI KARASAWA.

The Nipponkoa Insurance Co Ltd: 3-7-3, Kasumigaseki, Chiyoda-ku, Tokyo 100-8965; tel. (3) 3593-3111; fax (3) 3593-5388; internet www.nipponkoa.co.jp; f. 1892; fmrly The Nippon Fire and Marine Insurance Co Ltd before merging with The Koa Fire and Marine Insurance Co Ltd; acquired Taiyo Fire and Marine Insurance Co Ltd in 2002; Pres. and CEO MAKOTO HYODO.

The Nisshin Fire and Marine Insurance Co Ltd: 2-3, Kanda Surugadai, Chiyoda-ku, Tokyo 100-8329; tel. (3) 5282-5534; fax (3) 5282-5582; e-mail nisshin@mb.infoweb.ne.jp; internet www.nisshinfire.co.jp; f. 1908; Pres. HIROSHI MIYAJIMA.

Saison Automobile and Fire Insurance Co Ltd: Sunshine 60 Bldg, 3-1-1, Higashi-Ikebukuro, Toshima-ku, Tokyo 170-6068; tel. (3) 3988-2572; fax (3) 3980-7367; internet www.ins-saison.co.jp; f. 1982; Pres. KOSHIN MATUZAWA.

Secom General Insurance Co Ltd: 2-6-2, Hirakawa-cho, Chiyoda-ku, Tokyo 102-8645; tel. (3) 5216-6129; fax (3) 5216-6149; internet www.secom-sonpo.co.jp; Pres. ITIRO OJEKI.

Sompo Japan Insurance Inc: 26-1-1, Nishi-Shinjuku, Shinjuku-ku, Tokyo 160-8338; tel. (3) 3349-3111; fax (3) 3349-4697; internet www.sompo-japan.co.jp; f. 2002; est. by merger of Yasuda Fire and Marine Insurance (f. 1888) and Nissan Fire and Marine Insurance (f. 1911); Pres. MATATOSHI SATO.

Sonpo 24 Insurance Co Ltd: Sunshine 60 Bldg, 44/F, 3-1-1, Higashi-Ikebukuro, Toshima-ku, Tokyo 170-6044; tel. (3) 5957-0111; internet www.sonpo24.co.jp; Pres. ATSUSHI KUMANOMIDO.

Sony Assurance Inc: Aroma Sq., 11/F, 5-37-1, Kamata, Ota-ku, Tokyo 144-8721; tel. (3) 5744-0300; fax (3) 5744-0480; internet www.sonysonpo.co.jp; f. 1999; Pres. SHINICHI YAMAMOTO.

The Toa Reinsurance Co Ltd: 3-6, Kanda Surugadai, Chiyoda-ku, Tokyo 101-8703; tel. (3) 3253-3171; fax (3) 3253-1208; internet www

.toare.co.jp; f. 1940; Chair. TERUHIKO OHTANI; Pres. HIROSHI FUKUSHIMA.

Tokio Marine & Nichido Fire Insurance Co Ltd: 1-2-1, Marunouchi, Chiyoda-ku, Tokyo 100-8050; tel. (3) 3212-6211; internet www.tokiomarine-nichido.co.jp; f. 2004; Pres. SHUZO SUMI.

Insurance Associations

The General Insurance Association of Japan, Inc (Nihon Songai Hoken Kyokai): Non-Life Insurance Bldg, 2-9, Kanda Awaji-cho, Chiyoda-ku, Tokyo 101-8335; tel. (3) 3255-1439; fax (3) 3255-1234; e-mail kokusai@sonpo.or.jp; internet www.sonpo.or.jp; f. 1946; 26 mems (March 2011); Chair. MASATOSHI SATO; Exec. Dir KATSUO HANDA.

The Life Insurance Association of Japan (Seimei Hoken Kyokai): Shin-Kokusai Bldg, 3/F, 3-4-1, Marunouchi, Chiyoda-ku, Tokyo 100-0005; tel. (3) 3286-2652; fax (3) 3286-2630; e-mail kokusai@seiho.or.jp; internet www.seiho.or.jp; f. 1908; 47 mem. cos (Sept. 2010); Chair. KOICHIRO WATANABE.

Nippon Export and Investment Insurance: Chiyoda First Bldg, East Wing, 3/F, 3-8-1, Kanda Nishi, Chiyoda-ku, Tokyo; internet www.nexi.go.jp; f. 2001; Chair. and CEO TAKASHI SUZUKI.

Non-Life Insurance Rating Organization of Japan: 1-9, Kanda Nishiki-cho, Chiyoda-ku, Tokyo 101-0054; tel. (3) 3233-4762; fax (3) 3295-9301; e-mail service@nliro.or.jp; internet www.nliro.or.jp; f. 2002; 37 mems (Jan. 2011); Chair. AKIO MORISHIMA; Sr Exec. Dir YASUYUKI TAYAMA.

Trade and Industry

CHAMBERS OF COMMERCE AND INDUSTRY

The Japan Chamber of Commerce and Industry (Nippon Shoko Kaigi-sho): 3-2-2, Marunouchi, Chiyoda-ku, Tokyo 100-0005; tel. (3) 3283-7824; fax (3) 3211-4859; e-mail info@jcci.or.jp; internet www.jcci.or.jp; f. 1922; the central org. of all chambers of commerce and industry in Japan; mems: 517 local chambers of commerce and industry; Chair. TADASHI OKAMURA; Pres. TOSHIO NAKAMURA.

Principal chambers include:

Kobe Chamber of Commerce and Industry: 6-1, Minatojima-nakamachi, Chuo-ku, Kobe 650-8543; tel. (78) 303-5806; fax (78) 306-2348; e-mail info@kobe-cci.or.jp; internet kobe-cci.weebly.com; f. 1878; 12,000 mems; Chair. OHASHI TADAHARU; Pres. YASUO MURATA.

Kyoto Chamber of Commerce and Industry: 240, Shoshoi-cho, Ebisugawa-agaru, Karasumadori, Nakakyo-ku, Kyoto 604-0862; tel. (75) 212-6420; fax (75) 251-0743; e-mail kokusai@kyo.or.jp; internet www.kyo.or.jp/kyoto; f. 1882; 11,500 mems; Chair. YOSHIO TATEISI; Pres. TUNEOKI OKUHARA.

Nagoya Chamber of Commerce and Industry: 2-10-19, Sakae, Naka-ku, Nagoya, Aichi 460-8422; tel. (52) 223-5722; fax (52) 232-5751; e-mail info@nagoya-cci.or.jp; internet www.nagoya-cci.or.jp; f. 1881; 17,000 mems; Chair. JIRO TAKAHASHI.

Naha Chamber of Commerce and Industry: 2-2-10, Kume Naha, Okinawa; tel. (98) 868-3758; fax (98) 866-9834; e-mail cci-naha@nahacci.or.jp; internet www.nahacci.or.jp; f. 1927; 4,874 mems; Chair. AKIRA SAKIMA; Pres. KOSEI YONEMURA.

Osaka Chamber of Commerce and Industry: 2-8, Hommachi-bashi, Chuo-ku, Osaka 540-0029; tel. (6) 6944-6400; fax (6) 6944-6293; e-mail intl@osaka.cci.or.jp; internet www.osaka.cci.or.jp; f. 1878; 28,500 mems; Chair. SHIGETAKA SATO; Pres. DOI MICHIO.

Tokyo Chamber of Commerce and Industry: 3-2-2, Marunouchi, Chiyoda-ku, Tokyo 100-0005; tel. (3) 3283-7523; fax (3) 3216-6497; e-mail kokusai@tokyo-cci.or.jp; internet www.tokyo-cci.or.jp; f. 1878; 77,247 mems (April 2010); Chair. TADASHI OKAMURA; Pres. TOSHIO NAKAMURA.

Yokohama Chamber of Commerce and Industry: Sangyo Boueki Center Bldg, 8/F, Yamashita-cho, Naka-ku, Yokohama 231-8524; tel. (45) 671-7400; fax (45) 671-7410; e-mail soumu@yokohama-cci.or.jp; internet www.yokohama-cci.or.jp; f. 1880; 14,965 mems; Chair. KENJI SASAKI; Pres. NAMIO OBA.

INDUSTRIAL AND TRADE ASSOCIATIONS

General

The Association for the Promotion of International Trade, Japan (JAPIT): 1-9-13, Chiyoda-ku, Tokyo 101-0047; tel. (3) 6740-8261; fax (3) 6740-6160; internet www.japitcn.com; f. 1954 to promote trade with the People's Repub. of China; 700 mems; Chair. YOHEI KONO.

Industry Club of Japan: 1-4-6, Marunouchi, Chiyoda-ku, Tokyo; tel. (3) 3281-1711; fax (3) 3281-1797; e-mail soumu@kogyoclub.or.jp; internet www.kogyoclub.or.jp; f. 1917; est. to develop closer relations between industrialists at home and abroad and promote expansion of Japanese business activities; c. 1,600 mems; Pres. IMAI TAKASHI; Exec. Dir KOUICHIROU SHINNO.

Japan Commercial Arbitration Association: Hirose Bldg, 3/F, 3-17, Kanda Nishiki-cho, Chiyoda-ku, Tokyo 101-0054; tel. (3) 5280-5200; fax (3) 5280-5170; e-mail arbitration@jcaa.or.jp; internet www.jcaa.or.jp; f. 1950; 700 mems; provides facilities for mediation, conciliation and arbitration in international trade disputes; Pres. TADASHI OKAMURA.

Japan External Trade Organization (JETRO): Ark Mori Bldg, 6/F, 1-12-32, Akasaka-cho, Minato-ku, Tokyo 107-6006; tel. (3) 3582-5511; fax (3) 3582-5662; e-mail seh@jetro.go.jp; internet www.jetro.go.jp; f. 1958; information on international trade, investment, import promotion, exhibitions of foreign products; Chair. and CEO YASUO HAYASHI; Pres. TADASHI IZAWA.

Japan Federation of Smaller Enterprise Organizations (JFSEO) (Nippon Chusokigyo Dantai Renmei): 2-8-4, Nihonbashi, Kayaba-cho, Chuo-ku, Tokyo 103-0025; tel. (3) 3669-6862; f. 1948; 18 mems and c. 1,000 co-operative socs; Pres. MASATAKA TOYODA; Chair. of Int. Affairs SEIICHI ONO.

Japan General Merchandise Exporters' Association: 2-4-1, Hamamatsu-cho, Minato-ku, Tokyo; tel. (3) 3435-3471; fax (3) 3434-6739; f. 1953; 40 mems; Pres. TADAYOSHI NAKAZAWA.

Japan Productivity Center (JPC): 3-1-1, Shibuya, Shibuya-ku, Tokyo 150-8307; tel. (3) 3409-1112; fax (3) 3409-1986; internet www.jpc-net.jp; f. 1994; est. by merger between Japan Productivity Center and Social Economic Congress of Japan; fmrly Japan Productivity Center for Socio-Economic Development, renamed as above 2009; 10,000 mems; concerned with management problems and research into productivity; Chair. JIRO USHIO; Pres. TSUNEAKI TANIGUCHI.

Keizai Doyukai (Japan Association of Corporate Executives): 1-4-6, Marunouchi, Chiyoda-ku, Tokyo 100-0005; tel. (3) 3211-1271; fax (3) 3213-2946; e-mail kdcontact205@doyukai.or.jp; internet www.doyukai.or.jp; f. 1946; c.1,400 mems; corporate executives concerned with national and international economic and social policies; Chair. MASAMITSU SAKURAI.

Nihon Boeki-Kai (Japan Foreign Trade Council, Inc): World Trade Center Bldg, 6/F, 2-4-1, Hamamatsu-cho, Minato-ku, Tokyo 105-6106; tel. (3) 3435-5959; fax (3) 3435-5979; e-mail mail@jftc.or.jp; internet www.jftc.or.jp; f. 1947; 192 mems; Chair. SHOEI UTSUDA; Exec. Man. Dir MASAYOSHI AMANO.

Chemicals

Japan Chemical Industry Association: Sumitomo Fudosan Rokko Bldg, 1-4-1, Shinkawa, Chuo-ku, Tokyo 104-0033; tel. (3) 3297-2550; fax (3) 3297-2610; e-mail chemical@jcia-net.or.jp; internet www.nikkakyo.org; f. 1948; 266 mems; Chair. HIROMASA YONEKURA.

Japan Cosmetic Industry Association: 45 MT Bldg, 6/F, 5-1-5, Toranomon, Minato-ku, Tokyo 105-0001; tel. (3) 5472-2530; fax (3) 5472-2536; e-mail info@jcia.org; internet www.jcia.org; f. 1959; 687 mem. cos; Chair. REIJIRO KOBAYASHI.

Japan Perfumery and Flavouring Association: Saeki No. 3 Bldg, 3/F, 37, Kandakonya-cho, Chiyoda-ku, Tokyo 101-0035; tel. and fax (3) 3526-7855; f. 1947; Chair. YONEJIRO KORAYASHI.

Japan Pharmaceutical Manufacturers' Association: Torii Nihonbashi Bldg, 3-4-1, Nihonbashi Hon-cho, Chuo-ku, Tokyo 103-0023; tel. (3) 3241-0326; fax (3) 3242-1767; internet www.jpma.or.jp; 67 mems; Pres. YASUCHIKA HASEGAWA.

Photo-Sensitized Materials Manufacturers' Association: JCII Bldg, 25, Ichiban-cho, Chiyoda-ku, Tokyo 102-0082; tel. (3) 5276-3561; fax (3) 5276-3563; internet pmma.a.la9.jp; f. 1948; Pres. SHIGETAKA KOMORI.

Fishing and Pearl Cultivation

Japan Fisheries Association (Dainippon Suisankai): Sankaido Bldg, 1-9-13, Akasaka, Minato-ku, Tokyo 107-0052; tel. (3) 3585-6681; fax (3) 3582-2337; e-mail japan@suisankai.or.jp; internet www.suisankai.or.jp; Pres. TOSHIRO SHIRASU.

Japan Pearl Export and Processing Co-operative Association: 3-6-15, Kyobashi, Chuo-ko, Tokyo 104-0031; tel. (3) 3562-5011; f. 1951; 130 mems.

Japan Pearl Exporters' Association: 122, Higashi-Machi, Chuo-ku, Kobe 650-0031; tel. (78) 331-4031; fax (78) 331-4345; e-mail jpeakobe@lime.ocn.ne.jp; internet www.japan-pearl.com; f. 1954; 56 mems; Pres. YOSHIHIRO SHIMIZU.

Machinery and Precision Equipment

Camera and Imaging Products Association (CIPA) (Camera Eizo Kiki Kogyo-kai): JCII Bldg, 25, Ichiban-cho, Chiyoda-ku, Tokyo 102-0082; tel. (3) 5276-3891; fax (3) 5276-3893; internet www.cipa.jp;

f. 1954; fmrly Japan Camera Industry Asscn, renamed as above 2002; 54 mems; Pres. TSUYOSHI KIKUKAWA.

Japan Clock and Watch Association: Kudan Sky Bldg, 1-12-11, Kudan-Kita, Chiyoda-ku, Tokyo 102-0073; tel. (3) 5276-3411; fax (3) 5276-3414; internet www.jcwa.or.jp; Chair. SHINJI HATTORI.

Japan Electric Association: Denki Bldg, 4/F, 1-7-1, Yuraku-cho, Chiyoda-ku, Tokyo 100-0006; tel. (3) 3216-0551; fax (3) 3214-6005; internet www.denki.or.jp; f. 1921; 4,610 mems; Pres. TATSUO KAWAI.

Japan Electric Measuring Instruments Manufacturers' Association (JEMIMA): Keisoku Kaikan Bldg, 2-15-12, Nihonbashi-Kakigara-cho, Chuo-ku, Tokyo 103-0014; tel. (3) 3662-8181; fax (3) 3662-8180; e-mail admi.@jemima.or.jp; internet www.jemima.or.jp; 79 mems; Chair. SEIJI ONOKI.

Japan Electrical Manufacturers' Association: 17-4, Ichiban-cho, Chiyoda-ku, Tokyo 102-0082; tel. (3) 3556-5881; fax (3) 3556-5889; internet www.jema-net.or.jp; f. 1948; 262 mems; Chair. MICHIHIRO KITAZAWA; Pres. TOSHIMI HAYANO.

Japan Electronics and Information Technology Industries Association (JEITA): Ote Center Bldg, 1-1-3, Otemachi, Chiyoda-ku, Tokyo 100-0004; tel. (3) 5218-1050; fax (3) 5218-1070; internet www.jeita.or.jp; promotes manufacturing, international trade and consumption of electronics products and components; Chair. SETSUHIRO SHIMOMURA; Pres. TSUTOMU HANDA.

Japan Energy Association: Kawate Bldg, 1-5-8, Nishi-Shimbashi, Minato-ku, Tokyo 105-0003; tel. (3) 3502-1261; fax (3) 3502-2760; e-mail info@jea-wec.or.jp; internet www.jea-wec.or.jp; f. 1950; 133 mems; Chair. TERUAKI MASUMOTO; Exec. Dir HAJIME MURATA.

Japan Machine Tool Builders' Association: Kikai Shinko Bldg, 3-5-8, Shiba Koen, Minato-ku, Tokyo 105-0011; tel. (3) 3434-3961; fax (3) 3434-3763; e-mail intl@jmtba.or.jp; internet www.jmtba.or.jp; f. 1951; 112 mems; Chair. KENICHI NAKAMURA; Pres. TOSHIONI SHONO.

Japan Machine Tools Importers' Association: Toranomon Kogyo Bldg, 1-2-18, Toranomon, Minato-ku, Tokyo 105-0001; tel. (3) 3501-5030; fax (3) 3501-5040; e-mail info@jmtia.gr.jp; internet www.jmtia.gr.jp; f. 1955; 50 mems; Chair. YUZO CHIBA.

Japan Machinery Center for Trade and Investment (JMC): Kikai Shinko Bldg, 4/F, 3-5-8, Shiba Koen, Minato-ku, Tokyo 105-0011; tel. (3) 3431-9507; fax (3) 3436-6455; e-mail info@jmcti.or.jp; internet www.jmcti.org; f. 1952; 290 mem. cos; Pres. KENJI MIYAHARA.

The Japan Machinery Federation: Kikai Shinko Bldg, 3-5-8, Shiba Koen, Minato-ku, Tokyo 105-0011; tel. (3) 3434-5381; fax (3) 3434-2666; e-mail koho@jmf.or.jp; internet www.jmf.or.jp; f. 1952; Pres. MOTOTSUGU ITO; Exec. Dir KYOSHI ISHIZAKA.

Japan Microscope Manufacturers' Association: Kikai Shinko Bldg, 5-8-3, Shibakoen, Minato-ku, Tokyo 105-0011; tel. (3) 3432-5100; fax (3) 3432-5611; e-mail jmma@olympus.co.jp; f. 1954; 26 mems; Chair. T. KIKUKAWA.

Japan Motion Picture Equipment Industrial Association: Kikai Shinko Bldg, 3-5-8, Shiba Koen, Minato-ku, Tokyo 105-0011; tel. (3) 3434-3911; fax (3) 3434-3912; Pres. MASAO SHIKATA; Gen. Sec. TERUHIRO KATO.

Japan Optical Industry Association: Kikai Shinko Bldg, 3-5-8, Shiba Koen, Minato-ku, Tokyo 105-0011; tel. (3) 3431-7073; f. 1946; 7 mems; Chair. MICHIO KARIYA; Exec. Sec. SHIRO IWAHASHI.

The Japan Society of Industrial Machinery Manufacturers: Kikai Shinko Bldg, 3-5-8, Shiba Koen, Minato-ku, Tokyo 105-0011; tel. (3) 3434-6821; fax (3) 3434-4767; e-mail obd@jsim.or.jp; internet www.jsim.or.jp; f. 1948; 170 mems; Pres. YOSHIO HINOU.

Japan Textile Machinery Association: Kikai Shinko Bldg, Rm 101, 5-22, Shiba Koen, Minato-ku, Tokyo 105-0011; tel. (3) 3434-3821; fax (3) 3434-3043; e-mail am-jtma@jtma.or.jp; internet www.jtma.or.jp; f. 1951; Pres. JUNICHI MURATA.

Metals

Japan Aluminium Association (JAA): Tsukamoto-Sozan Bldg, 4-2-15, Ginza, Chuo-ku, Tokyo 104-0061; tel. (3) 3538-0221; fax (3) 3538-0233; internet www.aluminum.or.jp; f. 1999; est. by merger of Japan Aluminium Federation and Japan Light Metal Association; 146 mems; Chair. ISHIYAMA TAKASHI.

Japan Copper and Brass Association: Usagiya Bldg, 5/F, 1-10-10, Ueno, Taito-ku, Tokyo 110-0005; tel. (3) 3836-8801; fax (3) 3836-8808; e-mail jbmajwcc@copper-brass.gr.jp; internet www.copper-brass.gr.jp; f. 1948; 62 mems; Chair. TAKAO HASHIDA; Sec.-Gen. TOSHINOBU HIDAKA.

The Japan Iron and Steel Federation: Tekko Kaikan Bldg, 3-2-10, Nihonbashi Kayaba-cho, Chuo-ku, Tokyo 103-0025; tel. (3) 3669-4811; fax (3) 3664-1457; internet www.jisf.or.jp; f. 1948; mems: 61 mfrs, 61 dealers, six orgs; Chair. EIJI HAYASHIDA.

Japan Stainless Steel Association: TMM Bldg, 3/F, 1-10-5, Iwamoto-cho, Chiyoda-ku, Tokyo; tel. (3) 5687-7831; fax (3) 5687-8551; e-mail yabe@jssa.gr.jp; internet www.jssa.gr.jp; f. 1959; 80 mems; Chair. HIROSHI KINOSHITA.

Steel Castings and Forgings Association of Japan (JSCFA): Shikoku Bldg Bekkan, 8/F, 1-14-4, Uchikannda, Chiyoda-ku, Tokyo 101-0047; tel. (3) 5283-1611; fax (3) 5283-1613; e-mail cf@jscfa.gr.jp; internet www.jscfa.gr.jp; f. 1972; mems: 48 cos, 44 plants; Pres. YAMAGUCHI IKUHIRO.

Mining and Petroleum

Japan Coal Energy Center (JCOAL): Meiji Yasuda Seimei Mita Bldg, 9/F, 3-14-10, Mita, Minato-ku, Tokyo 108-0073; tel. (3) 6400-5191; fax (3) 6400-5206; e-mail jcoal-qa@jcoal.or.jp; internet www.jcoal.or.jp; f. 1997; est. by merger of Japan Coal Asscn, Coal Mining Research Centre, and the Japan Technical Cooperation Center for Coal Resources Devt; 111 mems; Pres. YOSHIHIKO NAGASAKI.

Japan Mining Industry Association: c/o Eiha Bldg, 17-11-3, Kanda Nishiki-cho, Chiyoda-ku, Tokyo 101-0054; tel. (3) 5280-2321; fax (3) 5280-7128; internet www.kogyo-kyokai.gr.jp; f. 1948; 52 mem. cos; Chair. SADAO SENDA; Pres. SHINICHI OZEKI.

Japan Petrochemical Industry Association: 1-4-1, Shinkawa, Chuo-ku, Tokyo 104-0033; tel. (3) 3297-2011; fax (3) 3297-2017; e-mail inquiries_hp@jpca.or.jp; internet www.jpca.or.jp; Chair. KYOHEI TAKAHASHI.

Japan Petroleum Development Association: Keidanren Bldg, 17/F, 1-3-2, Otemachi, Chiyoda-ku, Tokyo 100-0004; tel. (3) 3214-1701; fax (3) 3214-1703; e-mail jpda-sekkoren@sekkoren.jp; internet www.sekkoren.jp; f. 1961; Chair. YUJI TANAHASHI.

Paper and Printing

Japan Federation of Printing Industries: 1-16-8, Shintomi, Chuo-ku, Tokyo 104-0041; tel. (3) 3553-6051; fax (3) 3553-6079; internet www.jfpi.or.jp; f. 1985; 10 mems; Chair. SATOSHI SAWATARI.

Japan Paper Association: Kami Parupu Bldg, 3-9-11, Ginza, Chuo-ku, Tokyo 104-8139; tel. (3) 3248-4801; fax (3) 3248-4826; internet www.jpa.gr.jp; f. 1946; 54 mems; Chair. KAZUHISA SHINODA; Pres. MASATAKA HAYAMA.

Japan Paper Exporters' Association: Kami Parupu Bldg, 3-9-11, Ginza, Chuo-ku, Tokyo 104-8139; tel. (3) 3248-4831; fax (3) 3248-4834; e-mail info@jpeta.or.jp; internet www.jpeta.or.jp; f. 1952; 32 mems; Chair. YUTAKA SEKIGUCHI.

Japan Paper Importers' Association: Kami Parupu Bldg, 3-9-11, Ginza, Chuo-ku, Tokyo 104-8139; tel. (3) 3248-4831; fax (3) 3248-4834; e-mail info@jpeta.or.jp; internet jpeta.or.jp; f. 1981; 21 mems; Chair. TOSHINORI UMEZAWA; Man. KENJI IMAMURA.

Japan Paper Products Manufacturers' Association: 4-2-6, Kotobuki, Taito-ku, Tokyo; tel. (3) 3543-2411; f. 1949; Exec. Dir KIYOSHI SATOH.

Textiles

Central Raw Silk Association of Japan: 1-9-4, Yuraku-cho, Chiyoda-ku, Tokyo; tel. (3) 3214-5777; fax (3) 3214-5778.

Japan Chemical Fibers Association: Seni Kaikan, 7/F, 3-1-11, Nihonbashi-Honcho, Chuo-ku, Tokyo 103-0023; tel. (3) 3241-2311; fax (3) 3246-0823; internet www.jcfa.gr.jp; f. 1948; 17 mems, 1 assoc. mem, 20 supporting mems; Pres. AKIHIRO NIKKAKU; Dir-Gen. TSUNEHIRO OGARA.

Japan Cotton and Staple Fibre Weavers' Association: 1-8-7, Nishi-Azabu, Minato-ku, Tokyo; tel. (3) 3403-9671; internet www.jcwa-net.jp; 28 mems; Pres. OSAMU MAKOTO.

Japan Silk Spinners' Association: f. 1948; 95 mem. cos; Chair. ICHIJI OHTANI.

Japan Spinners' Association: Mengyo Kaikan Bldg, 6/F, 2-5-8, Bingomachi, Chuo-ku, Osaka 541-0051; tel. (6) 6231-8431; fax (6) 6229-1590; e-mail spinas@cotton.or.jp; internet www.jsa-jp.org; f. 1948; 16 mems; Head KOJIRO ABE.

Transport Machinery

Japan Association of Rolling Stock Industries: Awajicho Suny Bldg, 7/F, 1-2, Kanda Suda-cho, Chiyoda-ku, Tokyo 101-0041; tel. (3) 3257-1901; e-mail info@tetsushako.or.jp; internet www.tetsushako.or.jp; Chair. HIRAI MASAHARU.

Japan Auto Parts Industries Association: Jidosha Buhin Bldg, 5/F, 1-16-15, Takanawa, Minato-ku, Tokyo 108-0074; tel. (3) 3445-4211; fax (3) 3447-5372; e-mail info@japia.or.jp; internet www.japia.or.jp; f. 1948; 530 mem. cos; Chair. HISATAKA NOBUMOTO; Exec. Dir K. SHIBASAKI.

Japan Automobile Manufacturers Association, Inc (JAMA): Jidosha Kaikan, 1-1-30, Shiba Daimon, Minato-ku, Tokyo 105-0012; tel. (3) 5405-6126; fax (3) 5405-6136; e-mail kaigai_tky@mta.jama.or.jp; internet www.jama.or.jp; f. 1967; 14 mem. cos; Chair. TOSHIYUKI SHIGA; Pres. YOSHIYASU NAO.

Japan Bicycle Manufacturers' Association: 1-9-3, Akasaka, Minato-ku, Tokyo 107; tel. (3) 3583-3123; fax (3) 3589-3125; f. 1955.

Japan Ship Exporters' Association: Toranomon 30 Mori Bldg, 5/F, 3-2-2, Toranomon, Minato-ku, Tokyo 105-0001; tel. (3) 5425-9671; fax (3) 5425-9674; e-mail postmaster@jsea.or.jp; internet www.jsea.or.jp; 32 mems; Pres. MASAMOTO TAZAKI.

Japanese Marine Equipment Association: Kaiyo Senpaku Bldg, 15-16, Toranomon, Minato-ku, Tokyo 105-0001; tel. (3) 3502-2041; fax (3) 3591-2206; e-mail info@jsmea.or.jp; internet www.jsmea.or.jp; f. 1956; 219 mems; Chair. ZENSHICHI ASASAKA.

Japanese Shipowners' Association: Kaiun Bldg, 2-6-4, Hirakawa-cho, Chiyoda-ku, Tokyo 102-8603; tel. (3) 3264-7171; fax (3) 3262-4760; internet www.jsanet.or.jp; Pres. KOJI MIYAHARA.

Shipbuilders' Association of Japan: 30 Mori Bldg, 5/F, 3-2-2, Toranomon, Minato-ku, Tokyo 105-0001; tel. (3) 5425-9527; fax (3) 5425-9533; internet www.sajn.or.jp; f. 1947; 21 mems; Chair. TAKAO MOTOYAMA.

Society of Japanese Aerospace Companies (SJAC): Toshin-Tameike Bldg, 2/F, 1-1-14, Akasaka, Minato-ku, Tokyo 107-0052; tel. (3) 3585-0511; fax (3) 3585-0541; e-mail itahara-hiroharu@sjac.or.jp; internet www.sjac.or.jp; f. 1952; reorg. 1974; 117 mems, 41 assoc. mems; Chair. KAZUO TSUKUDA; Pres. KOSUKE IMASHIMIZU.

Miscellaneous

Communications Industry Association of Japan (CIA-J): Shuwa Dai-ichi Hamamatsucho Bldg, 3/F, 2-2-12, Hamamatsu-cho, Minato-ku, Tokyo 105-0013; tel. (3) 5403-9363; fax (3) 5463-9360; e-mail admin@ciaj.or.jp; internet www.ciaj.or.jp; f. 1948; non-profit org. of telecommunications equipment mfrs; 236 mems; Chair. KAWAMURA TAKASHI; Pres. YOSHIYUKI SUKEMUNE.

Japan Canners' Association: Tokyo; tel. (3) 5256-4801; fax (3) 5256-4805; internet www.jca-can.or.jp; Pres. KEINOSUKE HISAI.

Japan Cement Association: Daiwa Nihonbashi-Honcho Bldg, 7/F, 1-9-4, Chuo-ku, Tokyo 103-0023; tel. (3) 5200-5057; fax (3) 5200-5062; e-mail international@jcassoc.or.jp; internet www.jcassoc.or.jp; f. 1948; 18 mem. cos; Chair. KEIJI TOKUUE.

Japan Lumber Importers' Association: Yushi Kogyo Bldg, 3-13-11, Nihonbashi, Chuo-ku, Tokyo 103-0027; tel. (3) 3271-0926; fax (3) 3271-0928; f. 1950; 130 mems; Pres. TAMBA TOSIKHITO.

Japan Plastics Industry Federation: Kaseihin-Kaikan, 5-18-17, Roppongi, Minato-ku, Tokyo 106-0032; tel. (3) 3586-9761; fax (3) 3586-9760; e-mail info@jpif.gr.jp; internet www.jpif.gr.jp; f. 1950; 93 mems; Exec. Dir TSUGUO KATSUURA.

Japan Plywood Manufacturers' Association: Meisan Bldg, 1-18-17, Nishi-Shimbashi, Minato-ku, Tokyo 105; tel. (3) 3591-9246; fax (3) 3591-9240; f. 1965; 92 mems; Pres. KOICHI MATAGA.

Japan Pottery Manufacturers' Federation: Toto Bldg, 1-1-28, Toranomon, Minato-ku, Tokyo; tel. (3) 3503-6761.

The Japan Rubber Manufacturers' Association: Tobu Bldg, 2/F, 1-5-26, Moto-Akasaka, Minato-ku, Tokyo 107-0051; tel. (3) 3408-7101; fax (3) 3408-7106; e-mail s-shioya@jrma.gr.jp; internet www.jrma.gr.jp; f. 1950; 129 mems; Pres. MITSUAKI ASAI.

Japan Spirits and Liquors Makers' Association: Koura Dai-ichi Bldg, 7/F, 1-1-6, Nihonbashi-Kayaba-cho, Chuo-ku, Tokyo 103; tel. (3) 3668-4621.

Japan Sugar Refiners' Association: 5-7, Sanban-cho, Chiyoda-ku, Tokyo 102; tel. (3) 3288-1151; fax (3) 3288-3399; internet www.sugar.or.jp; f. 1949; 17 mems; Senior Man. Dir KATSUYUKI SUZUKI.

Japan Tea Exporters' Association: 17, Kitaban-cho, Shizuoka, Shizuoka Prefecture 420-0005; tel. (54) 271-3428; fax (54) 271-2177; e-mail japantea1953@yahoo.co.jp; 66 mems; Pres. SHOICHI KOBAYASHI.

Japan Toy Association: 4-22-4, Higashi-Komagata, Sumida-ku, Tokyo 130; tel. (3) 3829-2513; fax (3) 3829-2510; e-mail otoiawase2009@toys.or.jp; internet www.toys.or.jp; 228 mems; Chair. TAKEO TAKASU.

Motion Picture Producers' Association of Japan, Inc: Nihonbashi Bldg, 2/F, 1-17-12, Nihonbashi, Chuo-ku, Tokyo 103-0027; tel. (3) 3243-9100; fax (3) 3243-9101; e-mail info@eiren.org; internet www.eiren.org; f. 1945; Pres. NOBUYOSHI OTANI.

EMPLOYERS' ORGANIZATION

Japan Business Federation (JBF) (Nippon Keidanren): Keidanren Kaikan, 1-3-2, Otemachi, Chiyoda-ku, Tokyo 100-8188; tel. (3) 6741-0171; fax (3) 6741-0301; e-mail webmaster@keidanren.or.jp; internet www.keidanren.or.jp; f. 2002; est. by merger of Keidanren (f. 1946) and Nikkeiren (f. 1948); 1,601 mems (June 2010); Chair. HIROMASA YONEKURA; Dir-Gen. YOSHIO NAKAMURA.

UTILITIES

Electricity

Chubu Electric Power Co Inc: 1, Higashi-Shin-cho, Higashi-ku, Nagoya 461-8680; tel. (52) 951-8211; fax (52) 962-4624; internet www.chuden.co.jp; f. 1951; Chair. TOSHIO MITA; Pres. AKIRA HISASHI.

Chugoku Electric Power Co Inc: 4-33, Komachi, Naka-ku, Hiroshima 730-8701; tel. (82) 241-0211; fax (82) 523-6185; e-mail angel@inet.energia.co.jp; internet www.energia.co.jp; f. 1951; Chair. TADASHI FUKUDA; Pres. TAKASHI YAMASHITA.

Electric Power Development Co Ltd (J-Power): 6-15-1, Ginza, Chuo-ku, Tokyo 104-8165; tel. (3) 3546-2211; e-mail webmaster@jpower.co.jp; tel. www.jpower.co.jp; f. 1952; Pres. MASAYOSHI KITAMURA.

Hokkaido Electric Power Co Inc: 1-2, Higashi-Odori, Chuo-ku, Sapporo, Hokkaido 060-8677; tel. (11) 251-1111; internet www.hepco.co.jp; f. 1951; Chair. TATSUO KONDO; Pres. YOSHITAKA SATO.

Hokuriku Electric Power Co Inc: 15-1, Ushijima-cho, Toyama-shi, Toyama 930-8686; e-mail pub-mast@rikuden.co.jp; internet www.rikuden.co.jp; f. 1951; Chair. ISAO NAGAHARA; Pres. SUSUMU KYUWA.

Kansai Electric Power Co Inc: 3-6-16, Nakanoshima, Kita-ku, Osaka 530-8270; tel. (6) 6441-8821; fax (6) 6441-8598; e-mail postmaster@kepco.co.jp; internet www.kepco.co.jp; Pres. MAKOTO YAGI.

Kyushu Electric Power Co Inc: 2-1-82, Watanabe-dori, Chuo-ku, Fukuoka 810-8726; tel. (92) 761-3031; fax (92) 731-8719; internet www.kyuden.co.jp; Chair. SHINGO MATSUO; Pres. TOSHIO MANABE.

Okinawa Electric Power Co Inc: 5-2-1, Makiminato, Urasoe, Okinawa 901-2602; tel. (98) 877-2341; fax (98) 877-6017; e-mail ir@okiden.co.jp; internet www.okiden.co.jp; f. 1972; Chair. TSUGIYOSHI TOMA; Pres. DENICHIRO ISHIMINE.

Shikoku Electric Power Co Inc: 2-5, Marunouchi, Takamatsu 760-8573; tel. (878) 21-5061; fax (878) 26-1250; e-mail postmaster@yonden.co.jp; internet www.yonden.co.jp; f. 1951; Chair. MOMOKI TOKIWA; Pres. AKIRA CHIBA.

Tohoku Electric Power Co Inc: 1-7-1, Hon-cho, Aoba-ku, Sendai 980-8550; tel. (22) 225-2111; fax (22) 225-2550; e-mail webmaster@tohoku-epco.co.jp; internet www.tohoku-epco.co.jp; Chair. HIROAKI TAKAHASHI; Pres. MAKOTO KAIWA.

Tokyo Electric Power Co Inc: 1-1-3, Uchisaiwai-cho, Chiyoda-ku, Tokyo 100-8560; tel. (3) 6373-1111; fax (3) 3596-8508; internet www.tepco.co.jp; Chair. TSUNEHISA KATSUMATA; Pres. TOSHIO NISHIZAWA.

Federation

Federation of Electric Power Companies of Japan (FEPC JAPAN): 1-3-2, Keidanren Kaikan, Ohte-machi, Chiyoda-ku, Tokyo 100-8118; tel. (3) 5221-1440; fax (3) 6361-9024; e-mail webadmin2@fepc.or.jp; internet www.fepc.or.jp; f. 1952; Chair. MASATAKA SHIMIZU; Dir and Sec.-Gen. YUZURU HIROE.

Gas

Hokkaido Gas Co Ltd: 7-3-1, Nishi-Odori, Chuo-ku, Sapporo; tel. (11) 231-9511; internet www.hokkaido-gas.co.jp; Chair. SHIGERO KUSANO; Pres. HIROSHI OHTSUKI.

Keiyo Gas Co Ltd: 2-8-8, Ichikawa-Minami, Ichikawa, Chiba 272-8580; tel. (47) 361-0211; fax (47) 325-1049; internet www.keiyogas.co.jp; f. 1927; Chair. TOMO KIKUCHI; Pres. NOBUO SAKUMA.

Osaka Gas Co Ltd: 4-1-2, Hiranomachi, Chuo-ku, Osaka 541-0046; tel. (6) 6205-4503; fax (6) 6222-5831; e-mail keiri@osakagas.co.jp; internet www.osakagas.co.jp; f. 1905; Chair. AKIO NOMURA; Pres. HIROSHI OZAKI.

Saibu Gas Co: 1-17-1, Chiyo, Hakata-ku, Fukuoka; tel. (92) 633-2345; internet www.saibugas.co.jp; f. 1930; Chair. HIROKI OGAWA; Pres. YUUJI TANAKA.

Toho Gas Co Ltd: 19-18, Sakurada-cho, Atsuta-ko, Nagoya 456-8511; tel. (52) 871-3511; internet www.tohogas.co.jp; f. 1922; Chair. TOSHITAKA HAYAKAWA; Pres. TAKASHI SEIKI.

Tokyo Gas Co Inc: 1-5-20, Kaigan, Minato-ku, Tokyo 105; tel. (3) 3433-2111; fax (3) 5472-5385; internet www.tokyo-gas.co.jp; f. 1885; Chair. MITSUNORI TERIHARA; Pres. OKAMOTO TAKASHI.

Association

Japan Gas Association: 1-1-3, Nishi-Shinbashi, Minato-ku, Tokyo 105-0003; tel. (3) 3502-0116; fax (3) 3502-3676; internet www.gas.or.jp; f. 1947; comprises 211 city gas utilities and 270 assoc. mems; Chair. MITSUNORI TORIHARA.

Water

Nagoya City Waterworks & Sewerage Bureau: 3-1-1, Sannomaru, Naka-ku, Nagoya 460-8508; tel. (52) 972-3608; fax (52) 972-

3710; e-mail mail@water.city.nagoya.jp; internet www.water.city.nagoya.jp.

Osaka City Waterworks Bureau: 1-14-16, Nanko-Kita, Suminoe-ku, Osaka 530-8201; tel. (6) 6458-1132; fax (6) 6458-2100.

Sapporo City Waterworks Bureau: 2-11, Higashi-Odori, Chuo-ku, Sapporo 060-8611; tel. (11) 211-7007; fax (11) 232-1740; e-mail su.somu@suido.city.sapporo.jp; internet www.city.sapporo.jp/suido.

Tokyo Bureau of Waterworks: 2-8-1, Nishi-Shinjuku, Shinjuku-ku, Tokyo 163-8001; tel. (3) 5326-1100; internet www.waterworks.metro.tokyo.jp.

Yokohama Waterworks Bureau: 1-1, Minato-cho, Naka-ku, Yokohama; tel. (45) 671-3055; fax (45) 664-6774; e-mail su-somu@city.yokohama.jp; internet www.city.yokohama.jp/suidou.

Association

Japan Water Works Association (JWWA): 4-8-9, Kudan-Minami, Chiyoda-ku, Tokyo 102-0074; tel. (3) 3264-2281; fax (3) 3262-2244; e-mail kokusai@jwwa.or.jp; internet www.jwwa.or.jp; f. 1932; Exec. Dir YOSHIHIKO MISONO.

MAJOR COMPANIES

(cap. = capital; res = reserves; m. = million; amounts in yen, unless otherwise indicated)

Aeon Co Ltd: 1-5-1, Nakase, Mihama-ku, Chiba 261-8515; tel. (43) 212-6042; fax (43) 212-6849; internet www.aeon.info; f. 1758; est. as a co selling kimonos and fabrics; changed name to Jusco in 1926; est. as Aeon in 1989; revenue 5,054,000m. (2009/10); supermarkets, drug stores, financial services; Chair. AKIHIKO HARADA; Pres. MOTOYA OKADA; 54,161 employees.

Aisin Seiki Co Ltd: 2-1, Asahi-machi, Kariya, Aichi 448-8650; tel. (566) 24-8441; internet www.aisin.com; f. 1949; revenue 2,054,474m. (2009/10); automotive parts; Chair. KANSHIRO TOYODA; Pres. FUMIO FUJIMORI; 74,495 employees.

Ajinomoto Co Inc: 1-15-1, Kyobashi, Chuo-ku, Tokyo 104-8315; tel. (3) 5250-8111; fax (3) 5250-8293; e-mail g-webmaster@ajinomoto.com; internet www.ajinomoto.com; f. 1907; est. as Suzuki Pharmaceutical Co, assumed present name in 1946; sales 1,170,876m. (2008/09); mfrs and distributors of seasonings, edible oils, processed foods, beverages, dairy products, pharmaceuticals, amino acids, speciality chemicals; Pres. and CEO MASATOSHI ITO; 27,882 employees (group).

Asahi Breweries Ltd: 1-23-1, Azumabashi, Sumida-ku, Tokyo 130-8602; fax (3) 5608-5152; internet www.asahibeer.co.jp; f. 1949; sales 1,472,468m. (2009); alcoholic beverages; Chair. and CEO HITOSHI OGITA; Pres. NAOKI IZUMIYA; 17,134 employees.

Asahi Glass Co Ltd: 1-12-1, Yuraku-cho, Chiyoda-ku, Tokyo 100-8405; tel. (3) 3218-5555; fax (3) 3201-5390; internet www.agc.co.jp; f. 1907; sales 1,148,198m. (2009); manufacture and sale of flat glass, TV bulbs, alkali and other chemicals, refractories and electronics; associated cos and subsidiaries in Belgium, India, Indonesia, Singapore, Thailand and the USA; Pres. KAZUHIKO ISHIMURA; 6,330 employees.

Asahi Kasei Corpn: 1-105, Kanda Jimbo-cho, Chiyoda-ku, Tokyo 100-8101; tel. (3) 3296-3000; fax (3) 3296-3161; e-mail csr@om.asahi-kasei.co.jp; internet www.asahi-kasei.co.jp; f. 1931; sales 1,433,595m. (2009/10); holding co for operations in chemicals and fibre, homes and construction materials, electronics, health care, etc.; Chair. ICHIRO ITOH; Pres. TAKETSUGU FUJIWARA; 25,016 employees.

Astellas Pharma Inc: 2-3-11, Nihonbashi, Chuo-ku, Tokyo 103-8411; tel. (3) 3244-3271; internet www.astellas.com; f. 1923; est. from merger of Yamanouchi Pharmaceutical Co Ltd and Fujisama Pharmaceutical Co Ltd; sales 974,877m. (2009/10); mfrs, importers and exporters of pharmaceuticals; Chair. MASAFUMI NOGIMORI; Pres. and CEO YOSHIHIKO HATANAKA; 16,105 employees.

Bridgestone Corpn: 1-10-1, Kyobashi, Chuo-ku, Tokyo 104-8340; tel. (3) 3567-0111; fax (3) 3567-4615; internet www.bridgestone.co.jp; f. 1931; sales 2,597,002m. (2009); mfrs of rubber tyres and tubes, shock absorbers, conveyor belts, hoses, foam rubber, polyurethane foam, golf balls; Chair. SHOSHI ARAKAWA; 138,218 employees.

Canon Inc: 3-30-2, Shimomaruko, Ohta-ku, Tokyo 146-8501; tel. (3) 3758-2111; fax (3) 5482-5130; internet www.canon.com; f. 1937; revenue 3,209,201m. (2009); mfrs of cameras, business machines, etc.; Chair. and CEO FUJIO MITARAI; Pres. TSUNEJI UCHIDA; 25,683 employees.

Casio Computer Co Ltd: 1-6-2, Hon-machi, Shibuya-ku, Tokyo 151-8543; tel. (3) 5334-4803; fax (3) 5334-4669; e-mail webmaster@casio.co.jp; internet casio.jp; f. 1957; sales 427,925m. (2009/10); manufacture and sale of electronic calculators, digital watches, electronic musical instruments, liquid crystal televisions, Japanese language word processors; Pres. and CEO KAZUO KASHIO; 12,247 employees.

Chiyoda Corpn: 2-12-1, Tsurumi-cho, Tsurumi-ku, Yokohama 230-8601; tel. (45) 506-7105; fax (45) 503-0200; e-mail chyod@ykh.chiyoda.co.jp; internet www.chiyoda-corp.com; f. 1948; revenue 312,985m. (2009/10); engineering contractor, mainly to the hydrocarbon and chemical industries; Pres. and CEO TAKASHI KUBOTA; 3,710 employees.

Citizen Holdings Co Ltd: 6-1-12, Tanashi-cho, Nishi-Tokyo City, Tokyo 188-8511; tel. (3) 2466-1231; fax (3) 2466-1280; e-mail info@citizen.co.jp; internet www.citizen.co.jp; f. 1930; sales 252,502m. (2009/10); manufacture and sale of wristwatches and parts, machine tools and tools, jewellery and eyeglasses, information and electronic equipment, precision machine and precision measuring instruments; Pres. and CEO MITSUYUKI KANAMORI; 19,226 employees.

Cosmo Oil Co Ltd: 1-1-1, Shibaura, Minato-ku, Tokyo 105-8528; tel. (3) 3798-3211; fax (3) 3798-3411; internet www.cosmo-oil.co.jp; f. 1986; sales 2,612,141m. (2009/10); importing of petroleum, refining, sales and distribution of petroleum products and related activities; Chair. KEIICHIRO OKABE; Pres. YAICHI KIMURA; 2,180 employees.

Dai Nippon Printing Co Ltd: 1-1-1, Ichigaya Kaga-cho, Shinjuku-ku, Tokyo 162-8001; tel. (3) 3266-2111; fax (3) 5225-8239; e-mail info@mail.dnp.co.jp; internet www.dnp.co.jp; f. 1876; sales 1,583,382m. (2009/10); printing, packaging, paper products, plastics, precision electronic products; Chair. and Pres. YOSHITOSHI KITAJIMA; 39,643 employees.

Daido Steel Co Ltd: Urbannet Nagoya Bldg, 1-10-1, Higashi-Sakura, Higashi-ku, Nagoya 461-8581; tel. (52) 963-7501; fax (52) 963-4386; internet www.daido.co.jp; f. 1916; sales 362,507m. (2009/10); metal refining, steel, etc.; Chair. MASATOSHI OZAWA; Pres. TADASHI SHIMAO; 3,338 employees.

Daihatsu Motor Co Ltd: 1-1, Daihatsu-cho, Ikeda, Osaka 563-8651; tel. (727) 54-3062; fax (727) 53-6880; internet www.daihatsu.co.jp; f. 1907; subsidiary of Toyota Motor Corpn; sales 1,574,727m. (2009/10); Chair. KATSUHIKO OKUMURA; Pres. KOICHI INA; 12,572 employees (April 2007).

Daiichi Sankyo Co Ltd: 3-5-1, Nihonbashi-honcho, Chuo-ku, Tokyo 103-8426; tel. (3) 6225-1017; internet www.daiichisankyo.co.jp; f. 2005; est. through the merger of Sankyo Co Ltd and Daiichi Pharmaceutical Co Ltd; sales 952,105m. (2009/10); pharmaceutical mfrs; Chair. TAKASHI SHODA; Pres. JOJI NAKAYAMA; 29,272 employees.

Dainippon Ink & Chemicals Inc: DIC Bldg, 3-7-20, Nihonbashi, Chuo-ku-ku, Tokyo 103-8233; tel. (3) 3272-4511; fax (3) 3278-8558; e-mail webmaster@dic.co.jp; internet www.dic.co.jp; f. 1908; sales 757,849m. (2009/10); manufacture and sale of printing inks, printing supplies, machinery, chemicals, etc.; Chair. KOJI OE; Pres. and CEO KAZUO SUGIE; 22,583 employees.

Denso Corpn: 1-1, Showa-cho, Kariya-shi, Aichi 448-8661; tel. (566) 25-5850; fax (566) 25-4537; e-mail admin@web.denso.co.jp; internet www.denso.co.jp; f. 1949; sales 2,976,709m. (2009/10); car electrical equipment, air conditioners, automobile parts; Chair. KOICHI FUKAYA; Pres. and CEO NOBUAKI KATOH; 121,914 employees.

Elpida Memory Inc: Sumitomo Seimei Yaesu Bldg, 2-2-1, Yaesu, Chuo-ku, Tokyo 104-0028; tel. (3) 3281-1500; fax (3) 3281-1571; e-mail press@elpida.com; internet www.elpida.com; f. 1999 as NEC Hitachi Memory Inc; cap. 158,665m., sales 466,953m. (2009/10); devt operations for dynamic random access memory (DRAM) products; name changed as above in 2000, incorporating DRAM chip operations of Mitsubishi Electric Corpn; Pres. and CEO YUKIO SAKAMOTO; 5,863 employees.

Fast Retailing Co Ltd: 717-1, Sayama, Yamaguchi City, Yamaguchi 754-0894; internet www.fastretailing.com; f. 1963; sales 685,043m. (2009/10); apparel retailing; Chair., Pres. and CEO TADASHI YANAI; 11,245 employees.

Fuji Electric Co Ltd: Gate City Ohsaki, East Tower, 1-11-2, Ohsaki, Shinagawa-ku, Tokyo 141-0032; tel. (3) 5435-7111; fax (3) 5435-7493; e-mail info@fujielectric.co.jp; internet www.fujielectric.co.jp; f. 1923; cap. and res 2,632,000m. (2008/09), sales 691,223m. (2009/10); manufacture of electrical machinery; Pres. and CEO MICHIHIRO KITAZAWA; 25,634 employees.

Fuji Heavy Industries Co Ltd: 1-7-2, Nishi-Shinjuku, Shinjuku-ku, Tokyo 160-8316; tel. (3) 3347-2111; fax (3) 3347-2295; internet www.fhi.co.jp; f. 1953; sales 1,428,690m. (2009/10); motor vehicles and industrial products; Chair. IKUO MORI; 12,483 employees.

Fujifilm Holdings Corpn: Midtown West, 9-7-3, Akasaka, Minato-ku, Tokyo 107-0052; tel. (3) 6271-1111; fax (3) 3406-2193; internet www.fujifilmholdings.com; f. 1934; est. as Fuji Photo Film Co Ltd; cap. and res 1,875,829m., sales 2,181,693m. (2009/10); films and photographic materials, magnetic tapes, carbonless copying paper; Pres. and CEO SHIGETAKA KOMORI; 74,216 employees.

Fujitsu Ltd: Shiodome City Center, 1-5-2, Higashi-Shimbashi, Minato-ku, Tokyo 105-7123; tel. (3) 6252-2220; fax (3) 3216-9365; e-mail pr@fujitsu.com; internet www.fujitsu.com; f. 1935; sales 4,679,519m. (2009/10); manufacture and sale of electronic computers, data-processing equipment, tel. equipment, etc.; Chair. MICHIYOSHI MAZUKA; Pres. MASAMI YAMAMOTO; 172,438 employees.

Furukawa Electric Co Ltd: Marunouchi Nakadori Bldg, 2-2-3, Marunouchi, Chiyoda-ku, Tokyo 100-8322; tel. (3) 3286-3518; fax (3) 3286-3747; e-mail pub@ho.furukawa.co.jp; internet www.furukawa.co.jp; f. 1884; cap. 69,395m., sales 809,693m. (2009/10); manufacture and sale of electric, telephone and optic-fibre wires, cables and non-ferrous metal products; Pres. MASAO YOSHIDA; Chair. HIROSHI ISHIHARA; 4,326 employees.

Hino Motors Ltd: 3-1-1, Hinodai, Hino-shi, Tokyo 191-8660; tel. (42) 586-5011; fax (3) 5419-9363; internet www.hino.co.jp; f. 1910; cap. 72,717m., sales 746,876m. (2009/10); diesel trucks and buses; Chair. KAZUO OKAMOTO; Pres. YOSHIO SHIRAI; 10,867 employees.

Hitachi Ltd: 1-6-6, Marunouchi, Chiyoda-ku, Tokyo 100-8280; tel. (3) 3258-1111; fax (3) 3258-5480; e-mail webmaster@hitachi.co.jp; internet www.hitachi.co.jp; f. 1910; sales 8,968,546m. (2009/10); manufacture and sale of power systems, information and communication systems, electronic devices, industrial machinery, metals, chemicals, wire, cable and other products; Chair., Pres. and CEO TAKASHI KAWAMURA; 359,746 employees.

Hitachi Maxell Ltd: 1-1-88, Ushitora, Ibaraki-shi, Osaka 567-8567; tel. (3) 3515-8283; fax (3) 5467-9328; internet www.maxell.co.jp; f. 1960; cap. 12,203m., sales 172,652m. (2008/09); information storage media, batteries, small electrical appliances; Chair. TAKASHI KAWAMURA; Pres. and CEO YOSHIHIRO SENZAI; 4,584 employees.

Hitachi Zosen Corpn: 1-7-89, Nanko-Kita, Suminoe-ku, Osaka 559-8559; tel. (6) 6569-0001; fax (6) 6569-0002; e-mail webadmin@hitachizosen.co.jp; internet www.hitachizosen.co.jp; f. 1881; cap. 45,442m., sales 273,526m. (2008/09); ship-building, ship repairing, conversion, manufacture of diesel engines, offshore equipment, marine auxiliary machinery and fittings; mfrs of industrial machinery and plant for chemicals, paper, petroleum, sugar, cement and iron, steel bridges and steel structures, environmental equipment; Chair. and Pres. MINORU FURUKAWA; 8,004 employees.

Honda Motor Co Ltd: 2-1-1, Minami-Aoyama, Minato-ku, Tokyo 107-8556; tel. (3) 3423-1111; fax (3) 5412-1515; internet www.honda.co.jp; f. 1948; cap. 86,000m., sales 8,579,174m. (2009/10); mfrs of automobiles, motorcycles, power tillers, general purpose engines, outboard motors, lawn mowers and portable generators; 24 foreign subsidiaries; Chair. SATOSHI AOKI; Pres. and CEO TAKANOBU ITO; 176,933 employees.

Hoya Corpn: 2-7-5, Naka-Ochiai, Shinjuku-ku, Tokyo 161-8525; tel. (3) 3952-1151; fax (3) 3952-1314; internet www.hoya.co.jp; f. 1941; cap. 6,264m., sales 413,500m. (2009/10); mfrs of medical and ophthalmic equipment; Pres. and CEO HIROSHI SUZUKI; 4,911 employees.

Idemitsu Kosan Co Ltd: 3-1-1, Marunouchi, Chiyoda-ku, Tokyo 100; tel. (3) 3213-3115; internet www.idemitsu.com; f. 1911; cap. 108,606m. sales 3,112,300m. (2008/09); manufacture and sale of petroleum products and petrochemicals, and related enterprises; Chair. AKIHIKO TEMBO; Pres. KAZUHISA NAKANO; 8,330 employees.

IHI Corpn: Toyosu IHI Bldg, 3-1-1, Toyosu, Koto-ku, Tokyo 135-8710; tel. (3) 6204-7800; fax (3) 6204-8800; internet www.ihi.co.jp; f. 1853; fmrly Ishikawajima-Harima Heavy Industries Co Ltd; cap. 95,700m. (Feb. 2010), sales 1,242,000m. (2009/10); rocket and satellite propulsion systems, jet engines, gas turbine power generation systems, nuclear power equipment, solid waste treatment systems, industrial machinery, semiconductor and LCD panel equipment, infrastructure, etc.; Pres. and CEO KAZUAKI KAMA; 7,723 employees.

Inpex Corpn: 5-3-1, Akasaka, Minato-ku, Tokyo 107-6332; tel. (3) 5572-0200; internet www.inpex.co.jp; f. 1966; merged with Teikoku Oil Co in 2006 through formation of jt holding co, Inpex Holdings Inc; cap. 30,000m., sales 840,427m. (2009/10); devt of petroleum and natural gas resources; Chair. NAOKI KURODA; Pres. TOSHIAKI KITAMURA.

Isuzu Motors Ltd: 6-26-1, Minami-Oi, Shinagawa-ku, Tokyo 140-8722; tel. (3) 5471-1141; fax (3) 5471-1042; e-mail pr@notes.isuzu.co.jp; internet www.isuzu.co.jp; f. 1916; cap. 40,600m., sales 1,080,900m. (2009/10); manufacture and sale of trucks, buses, sports utility vehicles, components and engines; Chair. YOSHINORI IDA; Pres. SUSUMU HOSOI; 24,440 employees.

Japan Tobacco Inc (JT): 2-2-1, Toranomon, Minato-ku, Tokyo 105-8422; tel. (3) 3582-3111; fax (3) 5572-1441; internet www.jti.co.jp; f. 1985; cap. 100,000m., sales 6,134,695m. (2009/10); tobacco, pharmaceuticals, food, agribusiness, real estate, engineering; Chair. YOJI WAKUI; Pres. and CEO HIROSHI KIMURA; 49,665 employees.

JFE Steel Corpn: 2-2-3, Uchisaiwai-cho, Chiyoda-ku, Tokyo; tel. (3) 3597-3111; internet www.jfe-steel.co.jp; f. 2003; mem. of JFE Group; est. by consolidation of NKK and Kawasaki Steel; manufacture and sale of pig iron, steel ingots, tubes, plates, sheets, bars, special steels and ferro-alloys, coal-derived chemicals, refractories and slag wool; engineering and construction of pipelines, steel plants, steel structures, water treatment plants, waste incineration plants, ships; Pres. and CEO EIJI HAYASHIDA.

JS Group Corpn: 2-1-1, Ojima, Koto-ku, Tokyo 136-8535; tel. (3) 3638-8115; fax (3) 3638-8343; internet www.jsgc.co.jp; f. 1949 as Nihon Tategu Kogyo Co Ltd; current name adopted in 2004; cap. 68,100m., sales 982,600m. (2009/10); housing and building materials, fabricated home products; Chair. YOICHIRO USHIODA; Pres. and CEO YOSHIAKI FUJIMORI; 35,976 employees.

JX Nippon Oil and Energy Corpn: 2-6-3, Otemachi, Chiyoda-ku, Tokyo 100-8162; tel. (3) 6275-5046; internet www.noe.jx-group.co.jp; f. 2010; est. following merger of Japan Energy Corpn and Nippon Oil Corpn; refining and selling of petrochemical products; generating and selling electricity; cap. 139,400m. (2010); Pres. YASUSHI KIMURA.

Kao Corpn: 1-14-10, Nihonbashi Kayaba-cho, Chuo-ku, Tokyo 103-8210; tel. (3) 3660-7111; fax (3) 3660-7103; internet www.kao.co.jp; f. 1887; cap. 85,400m., sales 1,184,384m. (2009/10); health and household items; Chair. TAKUYA GOTO; Pres. and CEO MOTOKI OZAKI; 34,913 employees.

Kawasaki Heavy Industries Ltd: Kobe Crystal Tower 1-1-3, Higashi-Kawasaki-cho, Chuo-ku, Kobe 650-8680; tel. (78) 371-9530; fax (78) 371-9568; e-mail webadmin@khi.co.jp; internet www.khi.co.jp; f. 1896; cap. 104,328m., sales 1,173,473m. (2009/10); manufacture and sale of ships, rolling stock, aircraft, machinery, engines and motorcycles, plant engineering; Chair. TADAHARU OHASHI; Pres. SATOSHI HASEGAWA; 32,297 employees.

Kawasaki Microelectronics Inc: 1-3, Nakase, Mihama-ku, Chiba 261-8501; tel. (43) 296-7414; fax (43) 296-3285; internet www.k-micro.com; f. 2001; mem. of JFE Group; cap. 5,000m. (2005); silicon wafers, gases, opto-electronic products, consumer durables and chemical products, sale of super-microcomputers, provision of construction, information, computer software, data communications and engineering services; Pres. and CEO YUKIO YAMAUCHI; 5,000 employees.

Kirin Brewery Co Ltd: 2-10-1, Shinkawa, Chuo-ku, Tokyo 104-8288; tel. (3) 5540-3411; fax (3) 5540-3547; internet www.kirin.co.jp; f. 1907; sales 1,801,164m. (2007); production and sale of beer, soft drinks, dairy foods, pharmaceuticals, engineering and information systems; Chair. and CEO KOICHIRO ARAMAKI; Pres. KOICHI MATSUZAWA; 3,435 employees.

Kobe Steel Ltd (Kobelco): 5-9-12, Kita-Shinagawa, Shinagawa-ku, Tokyo 141-8688; tel. (3) 5739-6000; fax (3) 5739-6903; e-mail admin@kobelco.co.jp; internet www.kobelco.co.jp; f. 1905; cap. 233,300m., sales 1,671,000m. (2009/10); iron and steel, wholesale power supply, aluminium and copper, machinery, construction machinery, real estate, electronic materials and other businesses; Pres. and CEO HIROSHI SATO; 33,629 employees.

Komatsu Ltd: 2-3-6, Akasaka, Minato-ku, Tokyo 107-8414; tel. (3) 5561-2616; fax (3) 3505-9662; e-mail info@komatsu.co.jp; internet www.komatsu.co.jp; f. 1921; sales 1,431,564m. (2009/10); mfrs of construction equipment and industrial machinery incl. bulldozers, motor graders, wheel loaders, dump trucks, hydraulic excavators, presses, machine tools, arc welding robots and diesel engines; Chair. MASAHIRO SAKANE; Pres. and CEO KUNIO NOJI; 38,518 employees.

Konica Minolta Holdings, Inc: Marunouchi Center Bldg, 1-6-1, Marunouchi, Chiyoda-ku, Tokyo; internet www.konicaminolta.com; f. 1936; cap. 37,519m., sales 804,465m. (2009/10); cameras, scanners, printers and other imaging equipment; Chair. YOSHIKATSU OTA; Pres. and CEO MASATOSHI MATSUZAKI; 36,000 employees.

Kracie Holdings Ltd: 3-20-20, Kaigan, Minato-ku, Tokyo 108-8080; tel. (3) 5446-3002; fax (3) 5446-3027; internet www.kracie.co.jp; f. 1887; fmrly Kanebo Ltd; cap. 9,905m. (2009), sales 528,816m. (2001/02); mfr of toiletries, cosmetics, pharmaceuticals and foodstuffs; cosmetics subsidiary purchased by Kao Corpn in Dec. 2005; Chair. AKIYOSHI NAKAJIMA; Pres. YASUYA ISHIBASHI; 2,860 employees.

Kubota Corpn: 1-2-47, Shikitsu-Higashi, Naniwa-ku, Osaka 556-8601; tel. (6) 6648-2111; fax (6) 6648-3862; internet www.kubota.co.jp; f. 1890; cap. 840,070m., sales 643,090m. (2008/09); manufacture and sale of ductile iron pipes, pumps, valves, spiral-welded steel pipes, polyvinyl chloride pipes, tractors, combines, engines, mini-excavators, general farming equipment, cement roofing materials, fire-resistant sidings, sale and installation of environmental control plant and other steel structures, building materials; Pres. and CEO YASUO MASUMOTO; 24,140 employees.

Kyocera Corpn: 6, Takeda Tobadono-cho, Fushimi-ku, Kyoto 612-8501; tel. (75) 604-3500; fax (75) 604-3501; e-mail webmaster@kyocera.co.jp; internet global.kyocera.com; f. 1959; cap. 115,703m., sales 1,073,805m. (2009/10); manufacture of fine ceramic parts, semiconductor parts, electronic components and equipment, solar panels, cutting tools, optical instruments and consumer-related products; Chair. MAKOTO KAWAMURA; Pres. TETSUO KUBA; 63,876 employees.

Marubeni Corpn: 1-4-2, Ohtemachi, Chiyoda-ku, Tokyo 100-8088; tel. (3) 3282-2111; internet www.marubeni.com; f. 1858; cap.

262,686m., sales 3,807,480m. (2008/09); textiles, agri-marine products, chemicals, energy, power projects, metal and mineral resources, construction, forest products and general merchandise; Chair. NOBUO KATSUMATA; Pres. and CEO TERUO ASADA; 3,951 employees.

Maruha Nichiro Holdings Inc: 1-1-2, Otemachi, Chiyoda-ku, Tokyo 100-0004; tel. (3) 3216-0226; fax (3) 3216-0870; internet www.maruha-nichiro.co.jp; f. 1880; fmrly Maruha Corpn; name changed as above in 2007; cap. 310,000m., sales 828,715m. (2009/10); fishing, processing and sale of agricultural marine and meat products; canned and frozen salmon, crab, etc.; food processing, marine transport, export and import; refrigeration, ice production and cold storage; manufacture and sale of pharmaceuticals, organic fertilizers and sugar; Chair. YUJI IGARASHI; Pres. TOSHIO KOSHIRO; 1,084 employees.

Mazda Motor Corpn: 3-1, Shinchi, Fuchu-cho, Aki-gun, Hiroshima 730-8670; tel. (82) 282-1111; fax (82) 287-5190; internet www.mazda.co.jp; f. 1920; fmrly Toyo Kogyo Co Ltd; 33% owned by Ford Motor Co (USA); cap. 186,499m., sales 21,639,000m. (2009/10); manufacture and sale of 'Mazda' passenger cars and commercial vehicles; 121 sales cos overseas; Chair., Pres. and CEO TAKASHI YAMANOUCHI; 38,987 employees.

Meg Snow Brand Co Ltd: 13, Honshio-cho, Shinjuku-ku, Tokyo 160-8575; tel. (3) 3226-2111; fax (3) 3226-2150; internet www.megmilk-snowbrand.co.jp; f. 1950; fmrly Snow Brand Milk Products Co Ltd; name changed as above after merger with Nippon Milk Co in 2009; cap. 14,800m., sales 291,059m. (2009/10); mfrs of liquid milk, condensed and powdered milk, butter, cheese, ice-cream, infant foods, instant foods, margarine, fruit juices, frozen foods; also imported wine distribution; Pres. YOSHIHARU NAKANO; 1,316 employees.

Mitsubishi Chemical Corpn: 4-14-1, Shiba, Minato-ku, Tokyo 108-0014; tel. (3) 6414-3730; fax (3) 3283-6287; internet www.m-kagaku.co.jp; f. 1994 by merger of Mitsubishi Kasei Corpn and Mitsubishi Petrochemical Co Ltd; cap. 50,000m., sales 1,874,776m. (2009/10); Japan's largest integrated chemical co; manufacture and sale of coke and coal-tar derivatives, dyestuffs and intermediates, caustic soda, organic solvents and chemicals, reagents, ammonia derivatives, inorganic chemicals, pesticides and herbicides, fertilizers, food additives and pharmaceutical intermediates; Pres. and CEO YOSHIMITSU KOBAYASHI; 24,705 employees (March 2009).

Mitsubishi Electric Corpn: Tokyo Bldg, 2-7-3, Marunouchi, Chiyoda-ku, Tokyo 100-8310; tel. (3) 3218-2111; fax (3) 3218-2431; e-mail prd.prdesk@hq.melco.co.jp; internet www.mitsubishielectric.co.jp; internet global.mitsubishielectric.com; f. 1921; cap. 175,820m., sales 3,353,298m. (2009/10); manufacture and sale of electrical machinery and equipment (for power plant, mining, ships, locomotives and other rolling stock, aircraft), electronic products and systems, domestic electric appliances, radio communication equipment, radio and television sets, meters and relaying equipment, fluorescent lamps, lighting, fixtures, refrigerators, lifts, electric tools, sewing machines; Chair. SETSUHIRO SHIMOMURA; Pres. and CEO KENICHIRO YAMANISHI; 109,565 employees.

Mitsubishi Heavy Industries Ltd: 2-16-5, Konan, Minato-ku, Tokyo 108-8215; tel. (3) 6716-3111; fax (3) 6716-5800; internet www.mhi.co.jp; f. 1884; cap. and res 1,264,721m., sales 2,940,887m. (2009/10); shipbuilding, ship repairing, power systems, chemical plant and machinery, industrial machinery, heavy machinery, rolling stock, precision machinery, steel structures, construction machinery, refrigerating and air-conditioning machinery, engines, aircraft, special purpose vehicles, space systems; major subsidiaries in Japan, Brazil and other countries; Pres. HIDEAKI OMIYA; 34,139 employees.

Mitsubishi Materials Corpn: 1-3-2, Otemachi, Chiyoda-ku, Tokyo 100-8117; tel. (3) 5252-5201; fax (3) 5252-5272; e-mail adm@mmc.co.jp; internet www.mmc.co.jp; f. 1950; cap. 119,400m., sales 1,119,400m. (2009/10); metal and metal forming; Chair. AKIHIKO IDE; Pres. HIROSHI YAO; 21,641 employees.

Mitsubishi Motors Corpn: 5-33-8, Shiba, Minato-ku, Tokyo 108-8410; tel. (3) 3456-1111; fax (3) 5232-7747; internet www.mitsubishi-motors.co.jp; cap. 657,355m., sales 14,456,000m. (2009/10); f. 1970; mfrs of motor vehicles; Chair. TAKASHI NISHIOKA; Pres. OSAMU MASUKO; 31,003 employees.

Mitsui Chemicals, Inc: Shiodome City Center, 1-5-2, Higashi-Shimbashi, Minato-ku, Tokyo 105-7117; tel. (3) 6253-2100; fax (3) 6253-4245; internet www.mitsui-chem.co.jp; f. 1997; est. by merger of Mitsui Petrochemical Industries Ltd and Mitsui Toatsu Chemicals; cap. 125,053m., sales 1,207,735m. (2009/10); industrial chemicals, fertilizers, dyestuffs, fine chemicals, agricultural and pharmaceuticals, adhesives, electric materials and resins, etc.; Chair. KENJI FUJIYOSHI; Pres. TOSHIKAZU TANAKA; 12,814 employees (Sept. 2008).

Mitsui Engineering & Shipbuilding Co Ltd: 1-3-16, Nihonbashi, Chuo-ku, Tokyo 103-0027; tel. (3) 5202-3147; fax (3) 5202-3064; e-mail prdept@mes.co.jp; internet www.mes.co.jp; f. 1917; cap. 44,385m., sales 765,989m. (2009/10); ship-building and industrial machinery; Pres. YASUHIKO KATOH; 10,563 employees.

NEC Corpn: 5-7-1, Shiba, Minato-ku, Tokyo 108-8001; tel. (3) 3454-1111; fax (3) 3798-1510; internet www.nec.com; f. 1899; cap. 397,200m., sales 3,583,100m. (2009/10); integrating computers and communications, manufacture and sale of telephone switching systems, carrier transmission and terminals, digital radio and satellite communications, broadcasting electronic data processing and industrial electronic systems, electronic devices and consumer electronic products; Chair. KAORU YANO; Pres. NOBUHIRO ENDO; 142,358 employees.

Nidec Corpn: 338, Tonoshiro-cho, Kuze, Minami-ku, Kyoto 601-8205; tel. (75) 935-6140; e-mail ir@jp.nidec.com; internet www.nidec.co.jp; f. 1973; cap. 66,551m., sales 587,459m. (2009/10); mfr of precision motors, medium-sized motors and machinery; acquired the automotive business of French motor mfr Valeo SA in 2006; Pres. and CEO SHIGENOBU NAGAMORI; 96,482 employees.

Nintendo Co Ltd: 11-1, Kamitoba Hokotate-cho, Minami-ku, Kyoto 601-8501; tel. (75) 662-9600; fax (75) 662-9615; internet www.nintendo.co.jp; f. 1947 as Marufuku Co Ltd, mfr of playing cards; mfr of electronic video games systems; cap. 10,065m., sales 1,434,365m. (2009/10); Pres. SATORU IWATA; 4,603 employees.

Nippon Meat Packers Inc: 3-6-14, Itou Bldg, Minami-Honmachi, Chuo-ku, Osaka 541-0054; tel. (6) 6282-3031; fax (6) 6282-1056; internet www.nipponham.co.jp; f. 1949; cap. 24,166m., sales 953,616m. (2009/10); Pres. HIROSHI KOBAYASHI; 27,950 employees.

Nippon Paper Industries Co Ltd: 1-2-2, Hitotsubashi, Chiyoda-ku, Tokyo 100-0003; tel. (3) 6665-1111; fax (3) 3217-3001; internet www.np-g.com; f. 1949; est. by merger between Jujo Paper and Sanyo-Kokusaku Pulp Co Ltd; mem. of Nippon Paper Group Inc; paper, pulp, chemical, wood products; cap. 104,873m., sales 1,095,233m. (2009/10); Pres. YOSHIO HAGA; 4,196 employees.

Nippon Steel Corpn: Marunouchi Park Bldg, 2-6-1, Chiyoda-ku, Tokyo 100-8071; tel. (3) 6867-4111; fax (3) 6867-5607; e-mail info@nsc.co.jp; internet www.nsc.co.jp; f. 1970 by merger of Yawata Iron & Steel Co Ltd and Fuji Iron & Steel Co Ltd; cap. 419,524m., sales 4,769,821m. (2008/09); Chair. AKIO MIMURA; Pres. SHOJI MUNEOKA; 15,503 employees.

Nippon Suisan Kaisha Ltd: 2-6-2, Otemachi, Chiyoda-ku, Tokyo 100-8686; tel. (3) 3244-7000; fax (3) 3244-7085; e-mail ir@nissui.co.jp; internet www.nissui.co.jp; f. 1911; cap. 23,729m., sales 481,574m. (2009/10); marine fisheries and fish products; food processing; cargo and tanker services; Pres. and CEO NAOYA KAKIZOE; 8,803 employees.

Nissan Motor Co Ltd: 1-1-1, Takashima, Nishi-ku, Yokohama, Kanagawa 220-8623; tel. (45) 523-5523; internet www.nissan.co.jp; f. 1933; cap. 605,813m. (Aug. 2009), sales 8,437,000m. (2008/09); manufacture and sale of automobiles, rockets, textile machinery, other machines and appliances and parts; Pres. and CEO CARLOS GHOSN; COO TOSHIYUKI SHIGA; 175,766 employees.

Nissan Shatai Co Ltd: 10-1, Amanuma, Hiratsuka-shi, Kanagawa-ken 254-8610; tel. (463) 21-8001; fax (463) 21-8155; internet www.nissan-shatai.co.jp; f. 1949; cap. 7,904m., sales 424,497m. (2009/10); auto-bodies for passenger cars and small trucks; Pres. YOSHIAKI WATANABE; 4,981 employees.

Nisshin Steel Co Ltd: Shinkokusai Bldg, 3-4-1, Marunouchi, Chiyoda-ku, Tokyo 100-8366; tel. (3) 3216-5566; fax (3) 3214-1895; internet www.nisshin-steel.co.jp; f. 1928; cap. and res 361,463m., sales 441,486m. (2009/10); mfrs of coated steel, stainless steel, special steel and various secondary products; Chair. HIDEO SUZUKI; Pres. and CEO TOSHINORI MIKI; 5,040 employees.

Oji Paper Co Ltd: 4-7-5, Ginza, Chuo-ku, Tokyo 104-0061; tel. (3) 3563-1111; fax (3) 3563-1135; e-mail info@ojipaper.co.jp; internet www.ojipaper.co.jp; f. 1873; name changed 1996; cap. 103,880m. (2009), sales 1,147,300m. (2009/10); newsprint, packing paper and printing paper; Chair. SHOICHIRO SUZUKI; Pres. and CEO KAZUHISA SHINODA; 4,289 employees (March 2009).

Oki Electric Industry Co Ltd: 3-16-11 Nishi-Shimbashi, Minato-ku, Tokyo 105-8460; tel. (3) 5403-2111; fax (3) 3581-5522; e-mail admin@oki.co.jp; internet www.oki.co.jp; f. 1949; cap. 76,940m., sales 443,949m. (2009/10); mfr of products, technologies and software for telecommunications and information systems; Pres. and CEO HIDEICHI KAWASAKI; 18,111 employees.

Omron Corpn: Shiokoji Horikawa, Shimogyo-ku, Kyoto 600-8530; tel. (75) 344-7000; fax (75) 344-7001; internet www.omron.co.jp; f. 1933; cap. 64,100m., sales 2,213,670m. (2009/10); mfr of advanced computer, communications and control technologies; Chair. HISAO SAKUTA; Pres. and CEO YOSHIHITO YAMADA; 5,133 employees.

Panasonic Electric Works Co Ltd: 1-5-1, Higashi Shimbashi, Minato-ku, Tokyo 105-8301; tel. (3) 6218-1131; internet panasonic-electric-works.net; f. 1918; fmrly Matsushita Electric Industrial Co Ltd; name changed as above in 2008; cap. 148,500m., sales 1,457,486m. (2009/10); manufacture of electrical and electronic home appliances; manufacturing and sales cos in 47 countries under global brand name Panasonic; Pres. and Dir SHUSAKU NAGAE; 56,103 employees.

Pioneer Corpn: 1-1, Shin-ogura, Saiwai-ku, Kawasaki, Kanagawa 212-0031; tel. (44) 580-3211; fax (44) 580-4014; e-mail pioneer_ir@post.pioneer.co.jp; internet pioneer.jp; f. 1938; cap. 87,257m., sales 438,998m. (2009/10); electronics; Pres. SUSUMU KOTANI; 29,046 employees.

Renesas Electronics Corpn: Nippon Bldg, 2-6-2, Ote-machi, Chiyoda-ku, Tokyo 100-0004; tel. (3) 5201-5111; fax (3) 3207-5003; internet www.renesas.com; f. 2003; est. as Renesas Technology Corpn; name changed as above following its merger with NEC Electronics in 2010; cap. 153,200m. (2009/10); manufacture and sale of electronic devices, products and systems; Chair. and CEO JUNSHI YAMAGUCHI; Pres. YASUSHI AKAO; 47,000 employees.

Ricoh Co Ltd: Ricoh Bldg, 8-13-1, Ginza, Chuo-ku, Tokyo 104-8222; tel. (3) 3479-3111; fax (3) 3403-1578; internet www.ricoh.co.jp; f. 1936; cap. 135,300m., sales 2,016,300m. (2009/10); electronics; Chair. MASAMITSU SAKURAI; Pres. and CEO SHIRO KONDO; 108,500 employees.

Sanyo Electric Co Ltd: 2-5-5, Keihan Hondori, Moriguchi City, Osaka 570-8677; tel. (6) 6991-1181; fax (6) 6991-5411; internet jp.sanyo.com; f. 1947; cap. 322,242m., sales 1,594,640m. (2009/10); manufacture and sale of electrical and electronic machinery and appliances—refrigerators, washing machines, electric fans, television and radio sets, bicycle dynamos, personal computers, commercial air conditioning systems, etc.; Pres. SEIICHIRO SANO; 104,882 employees.

Sega Sammy Holdings Inc: Shiodome Sumitomo Bldg, 21/F, 1-9-2, Higashi-Shimbashi, Minato-ku, Tokyo; internet www.segasammy.co.jp; f. 1940; est. in Honolulu, Hawaii, as Standard Games; registered in 1952 as Service Games of Japan (SEGA); merged with Sammy Corpn in 2004; cap. 29,900m., sales 384,679m. (2009/10); manufacture of electronic video games and games systems; Chair. and CEO HAJIME SATOMI.

Seiko Epson Corpn: 3-3-5, Owa, Suwa, Nagano 392-8502; tel. (266) 52-3131; internet www.epson.jp; f. 1942 as Daiwa Kogyo Ltd; cap. 53,204m., sales 985,363m. (2009/10); development, manufacturing, sales, marketing and servicing of information-related equipment; Chair. and CEO SEIJI HANAOKA; Pres. MINORU USUI; 77,936 employees.

Sekisui Chemical Co Ltd: 2-4-4, Nishi-Tenma, Kita-ku, Osaka 5308565; tel. (6) 6365-4122; fax (6) 6365-4370; internet www.sekisui.co.jp; f. 1947; cap. 100,000m., sales 858,514m. (2009/10); chemicals, building materials, etc.; Pres. NAOFUMI NEGISHI; 19,761 employees.

Sharp Corpn: 22-22, Nagaike-cho, Abeno-ku, Osaka 545-8522; tel. (6) 6621-1221; fax (6) 6628-1653; internet www.sharp.co.jp; f. 1912; cap. 204,675m., sales 2,147,682m. (2009/10); manufacture and sale of consumer electronic products, information systems and electronic components; Chair. KATSUHIKO MACHIDA; Pres. MIKIO KATAYAMA; 22,500 employees.

Shin-Etsu Chemical Co Ltd: 2-6-1, Otemachi, Chiyoda-ku, Tokyo 100-0004; tel. (3) 3246-5011; fax (3) 3246-5350; e-mail sec-pr@shinetsu.co.jp; internet www.shinetsu.co.jp; f. 1926; cap. 119,419m., sales 916,837m. (2009/10); chemicals, electronics materials, etc.; Chair. CHIHIRO KANAGAWA; Pres. SHUNZO MORI; 16,955 employees.

Shiseido Co Ltd: 7-5-5, Ginza, Chuo-ku, Tokyo 104-8010; tel. (3) 3572-5111; fax (3) 3572-6973; internet www.shiseido.co.jp; f. 1872; cap. 64,506m., sales 2,445m. (2009/10); manufacture and export of cosmetics and toiletries; Chair. SHINZO MAEDA; Pres. and CEO HISAYUKI SUEKAWA; 3,573 employees.

Showa Denko KK: 1-13-9, Shiba Daimon, Minato-ku, Tokyo 105-8518; tel. (3) 5470-3235; fax (3) 3431-6215; e-mail pr_office@hq.sdk.co.jp; internet www.sdk.co.jp; f. 1939; cap. 140,564m., sales 678,200m. (2009); manufacture and sale of bulk and speciality chemicals, plastics, ferro-alloys, electronics materials, electrodes and abrasives; Chair. KYOHEI TAKAHASHI; Pres. HIDEO ICHIKAWA; 11,564 employees.

Showa Shell Sekiyu KK: 2-3-2, Daiba, Minato-ku, Tokyo 135-8074; tel. (3) 5531-5601; fax (3) 5531-5609; internet www.showa-shell.co.jp; f. 1985 by merger of Showa Oil Co Ltd and Shell Sekiyu KK; cap. 34,197m., sales 2,022,520m. (2009); petroleum; Chair. SHIGEYA KATO; Pres. JUN ARAI; 939 employees.

Sojitz Corpn: 6-1-20, Akasata, Minato-ku, Tokyo 107-8655; tel. (3) 5520-5000; fax (3) 5520-2390; internet www.sojitz.com; f. 2003; est. through merger of Nichimen Corpn and Nissho Iwai Corpn; cap. 160,399m., sales 3,844,418m. (2009/10); machinery, aerospace, energy and mineral resources, chemicals and plastics, real estate; Chair. AKIO DOBASHI; Pres. and CEO YUTAKA KASE; 16,812 employees.

Sony Corpn: 1-7-1, Konan, Minato-ku, Tokyo 108-0075; tel. (3) 5448-2111; fax (3) 5448-2244; internet www.sony.net; f. 1946; cap. and res 3,370,704m. (2007/08), sales 7,213,998m. (2008/09); manufacture and sale of electronic appliances, incl. professional and consumer audio and video equipment; production and distribution of music, motion pictures and television programmes; Chair. of Bd YOTARO KOBAYASHI; Chair., Pres. and CEO Sir HOWARD STRINGER; 171,900 employees.

Sumitomo Chemical Co Ltd: 2-27-1, Shinkawa, Chuo-ku, Tokyo 104-8260; tel. (3) 5543-5102; fax (3) 5543-5901; internet www.sumitomo-chem.co.jp; f. 1913; sales 1,620,900m. (2009/10); manufacture and sale of chemical fertilizers, dyestuffs, agricultural chemicals, intermediates, organic and inorganic industrial chemicals, synthetic resins, finishing resins, synthetic rubber and rubber chemicals; many subsidiaries; Chair. HIROMASA YONEKURA; Pres. MASAKAZU TOKURA; 27,828 employees.

Sumitomo Electric Industries Ltd: 4-5-33, Kitahama, Chuo-ku, Osaka 541-0041; tel. (6) 6220-4141; fax (6) 6222-3380; e-mail www@prs.sei.co.jp; internet www.sei.co.jp; f. 1911; cap. 99,737m., sales 1,836,352m. (2009/10); mfrs of electric wires and optical-fibre cables, high carbon steel wires; sintered alloy products; rubber and plastic products; disc brakes; radio-frequency products; Chair. NORIYO OKAYAMA; Pres. and CEO MASAYOSHI MATSUMOTO; 157,203 employees.

Sumitomo Heavy Industries Ltd: ThinkPark Tower, 2-1-1, Osaki, Shinagawa-ku, Tokyo 141-6025; tel. (3) 6737-2000; fax (3) 5488-8057; e-mail webadmin@shi.co.jp; internet www.shi.co.jp; f. 1934; cap. 30,871m., revenue 516,165m. (2009/10); industrial machinery and shipbuilding; Chair. YOSHIO HINO; Pres. and CEO YOSHINOBO NAKAMURA; 15,463 employees.

Sumitomo Metal Industries Ltd: 4-5-33, Kitahama, Chuo-ku, Osaka 541-0041; tel. (6) 6220-5111; fax (6) 6223-0305; internet www.sumitomometals.co.jp; f. 1897; cap. 262,000m., sales 1,285,800m. (2009/10); manufacture and sale of pig iron, steel ingots, steel bars, shapes, wire rods, tubes, pipes, castings, forgings, rolling stock parts, engineering; 100 subsidiaries in Japan; 8 offices abroad; Chair. HIROSHI SHIMOZUMA; Pres. HIROSHI TOMONO; 23,674 employees.

Sumitomo Metal Mining Co Ltd: 5-11-3, Shimbashi, Minato-ku, Tokyo 105-8716; tel. (3) 3436-7701; fax (3) 3434-2215; internet www.smm.co.jp; f. 1590; cap. 93,200m., sales 725,800m. (2009/10); Pres. NOBUMASA KEMORI; 9,309 employees.

Suzuki Motor Corpn: 300, Takatsuka, Hamamatsu, Shizuoka 432-8611; tel. (53) 440-2030; fax (53) 440-2776; internet www.suzuki.co.jp; f. 1920; cap. 120,210m. (2008/09), sales 4,691,000m. (2009/10); motor vehicles, outboard motors, motorized wheelchairs, industrial equipment; Pres., Chair. and CEO OSAMU SUZUKI; 14,504 employees.

Taiheiyo Cement Corpn: Daiba Garden City Bldg, 2-3-5, Daiba, Minato-ku, Tokyo 135-8578; tel. (3) 5214-1520; fax (3) 5214-1707; e-mail webmaster@taiheiyo-cement.co.jp; internet www.taiheiyo-cement.co.jp; fmrly Chichibu Onoda Cement Corpn; cap. 69,499m., sales 728,500m. (2009/10); building materials; Pres. KEIJI TOKUUE; 2,173 employees.

Taisei Corpn: 1-25-1, Nishi-Shinjuku, Shinjuku-ku, Tokyo 163-0606; tel. (3) 3348-1111; fax (3) 3345-0481; internet www.taisei.co.jp; f. 1873; cap. 112,448m., sales 1,441,975m. (2009/10); engineering, construction; Chair., Pres. and CEO TAKASHI YAMAUCHI; 8,243 employees.

Takeda Pharmaceutical Co Ltd: 4-1-1, Doshomachi, Chuo-ku, Osaka 540-8645; tel. (6) 6204-2111; fax (6) 6204-2880; internet www.takeda.co.jp; f. 1781; cap. 63,500m., sales 1,466,000m. (2009/10); mfrs and distributors of pharmaceuticals, industrial chemicals, OTC drugs, food additives; enriched foods and drinks, agricultural chemicals, fertilizers; Pres. and CEO YASUCHIKA HASEGAWA; 19,654 employees.

TDK Corpn: 1-13-1, Nihonbashi, Chuo-ku, Tokyo 103-8272; tel. (3) 5201-7100; fax (3) 5201-7110; internet www.tdk.co.jp; f. 1935; cap. 32,641m., sales 8,089,000m. (2009/10); mfrs of recording media and electronic materials and components; Chair. HAJIME SAWABE; Pres. and CEO TAKEHIRO KAMIGAMA; 80,590 employees.

Teijin Ltd: 1-6-7, Minami-Honmachi, Chuo-ku, Osaka 541-8587; tel. (6) 6268-2132; fax (6) 6268-3205; internet www.teijin.co.jp; f. 1918; cap. 70,816m., sales 765,800m. (2009/10); mfrs of fibres, yarns and fabrics from polyester, fibres (Teijin Tetoron), nylon, polyvinyl chloride fibre (Teijin Teviron), acetate, acrylic fibre (Teijin Beslon), polycarbonate resin (Panlite), acetate resin (Tenex), petrochemicals, pharmaceuticals; 156 subsidiaries; Chair. TORU NAGASHIMA; Pres. and CEO SHIGEO OHYAGI; 18,778 employees.

Toppan Printing Co Ltd: 1, Kanda Izumi-cho, Chiyoda-ku, Tokyo 101-0024; tel. (3) 3835-5111; fax (3) 3835-0674; e-mail info.e@toppan.co.jp; internet www.toppan.co.jp; f. 1900; cap. 104,986m., sales 1,506,750m. (2009/10); Chair. NAOKI ADACHI; Pres. and CEO SHINGO KANEKO; 8,769 employees.

Toray Industries Inc: Toray Bldg, 2-1-1, Nihonbashi-Muromachi, Chuo-ku, Tokyo 103-8666; tel. (3) 3245-5111; fax (3) 3245-5555; internet www.toray.co.jp; f. 1926; cap. 147,873m., sales

1,359,600m. (2009/10); mfrs of nylon, Toray Tetoron (polyester fibre), Toraylon (acrylic fibre), Torayca (carbon fibre), pharmaceuticals and medical equipment, plastics and chemicals; Chair. SADAYUKI SAKAKIBARA; Pres. and CEO AKIHIRO NIKKAKU; 37,936 employees.

Toshiba Corpn: 1-1-1, Shibaura, Minato-ku, Tokyo 105-8001; tel. (3) 3457-4511; fax (3) 3456-1631; internet www.toshiba.co.jp; f. 1875; cap. 439,901m., toal assets 6,381,599m. (2009/10); manufacture, sale and export of electric appliances, apparatus and instruments; heavy electric machinery; overseas offices in 24 countries; Chair. ATSUTOSHI NISHIDA; Pres. and CEO NORIO SASAKI; 204,000 employees.

Toyo Seikan Kaisha Ltd: 1-3-1, Uchisaiwai-cho, Chiyoda-ku, Tokyo 100-8522; tel. (3) 3508-2112; fax (3) 3592-9471; internet www.toyo-seikan.co.jp; f. 1917; cap. 11,094.6m., sales 733,746m. (2008/09); metal products; Chair. HIROFUMI MIKI; Pres. SHUNJI KANEKO; 4,817 employees.

Toyobo Co Ltd: 2-2-8, Dojima Hama, Kita-ku, Osaka 530-8230; tel. (6) 6348-3137; fax (6) 6348-3149; internet www.toyobo.co.jp; f. 1882; cap. 43,341m., sales 318,773m. (2009/10); mfrs of films and functional polymers, industrial materials and textiles; Chair. JUNJI TSUMURA; Pres. RYUZOU SAKAMOTO; 10,398 employees.

Toyota Auto Body Co Ltd: 100, Kanayama, Ichiriyama-cho, Kariya, Aichi 448-8666; tel. (566) 36-2121; fax (566) 36-9113; internet www.toyota-body.co.jp; f. 1945; cap. 10,370m., sales 1,498,400m. (2009/10); Chair. TOSHIO MIZUSHIMA; Pres. TAKUJI AMIOKA; 16,794 employees.

Toyota Industries Corpn: 2-1, Toyoda-cho Kariya-shi, Aichi 448-8671; tel. (566) 22-2511; fax (566) 27-5650; internet www.toyota-industries.com; f. 1926; cap. 80,400m., sales 1,377,700m. (2009/10); transport manufacture, industrial equipment, textile machinery; Chair. AKIRA IMURA; Pres. TETSURO TOYODA; 39,903 employees.

Toyota Motor Corpn: 1, Toyota-cho, Toyota, Aichi 471-8571; tel. (565) 28-2121; fax (565) 23-5800; internet www.toyota.co.jp; f. 1937; cap. 397,050m., sales 18,950,900m. (2009/10); manufacture and sale of passenger cars, trucks, forklifts and parts; Chair. FUJIO CHO; Pres. AKIO TOYODA; 320,590 employees.

Toyota Tsusho Corpn: 4-9-8, Meieki, Nakamura-ku, Nagoya 450-8575; tel. (52) 584-5000; fax (52) 584-5636; internet www.toyota-tsusho.com; f. 1920; cap. 64,936m., sales 5,102,261m. (2009/10); f. 1948; distributors of natural resources and manufactured goods; Chair. MITSUO KINOSHITA; Pres. JUN KARUBE; 29,832 employees.

UBE Industries Ltd: 1978-96, Kogushi, Ube City, Yamaguchi 775-8633; tel. (8) 3631-1111; fax (8) 5419-6230; internet www.ube-ind.co.jp; f. 1897; cap. 58,400m., sales 549,500m. (2009/10); production, processing and sale of coal, limestone, chemical fertilizers, sulphuric acid, nitric acid, oxalic acid, ammonium nitrate, ammonia, pharmaceuticals, cement, caprolactam, high pressure polyethylene, industrial machinery and equipment, cast steel products, synthetic rubbers; Chair. HIROAKI TAMURA; Pres. MICHIO TAKESHITA; 11,108 employees.

Yamaha Corpn: 10-1, Nakazawa-cho, Hamamatsu, Shizuoka 430-8650; tel. (3) 5488-6602; fax (3) 5488-5060; e-mail ngc-y@post.yamaha.co.jp; internet www.yamaha.co.jp; cap. 28,534m., sales 414,811m. (2009/10); musical instruments, electronic devices; Pres. MITSURU UMEMURA; 25,658 employees.

Yamaha Motor Co Ltd: 2500, Shingai Iwata-shi, Shizuokaken 438-8501; tel. (538) 32-1117; fax (538) 32-1131; internet www.yamaha-motor.co.jp; f. 1955; cap. 85,666m. (June 2010), sales 1,153,642m. (2009); mfrs of motorcycles, outboard motors, boats, snowmobiles; Pres. HIROYUKI YANAGI; 49,994 employees.

TRADE UNIONS

A feature of Japan's trade union movement is that the unions are usually based on single enterprises, embracing workers of different occupations in that enterprise. In June 2006 there were 27,507 unions; union membership stood at 10.0m. workers in that year.

Japanese Trade Union Confederation (JTUC–RENGO): 3-2-11, Kanda Surugadai, Chiyoda-ku, Tokyo 101-0062; tel. (3) 5295-0526; fax (3) 5295-0548; e-mail jtuc-kokusai@sv.rengo-net.or.jp; internet www.jtuc-rengo.org; f. 1989; est. by merger of SOHYO and RENGO; 6.8m. mems; Pres. NOBUAKI KOGA.

Principal Unions

Ceramics Rengo (All-Japan Federation of Ceramics Industry Workers): 3-11, Heigocho, Mizuho-ku, Nagoya-shi, Aichi 467; tel. (52) 882-4562; fax (52) 882-9960; e-mail info@jcw-u.or.jp; internet www.jcw-u.or.jp; 30,083 mems; Pres. TSUNEYOSHI HAYAKAWA.

Denki Rengo (Japanese Electrical, Electronic & Information Union): Denkirengo Bldg, 1-10-3, Mita, Minato-ku, Tokyo 108-8326; tel. (3) 3455-6911; fax (3) 3452-5406; e-mail denki-rengo@jeiu.or.jp; internet www.jeiu.or.jp; f. 1953; 688,436 mems; Pres. NOBUAKI KOGA.

Denryoku Soren (Federation of Electric Power Related Industry Workers' Unions of Japan): TDS Mita, 3/F, 7-13-2, Mita, Minato-ku, Tokyo 108-0073; tel. (3) 3454-0231; fax (3) 3798-1470; e-mail info@denryokusoren.or.jp; internet www.denryokusoren.or.jp; 223,000 mems; Pres. HIROYUKI NAGUMO.

Dokiro (Hokkaido Seasonal Workers' Union): Hokuro Bldg, Kita-4, Nishi-12, Chuo-ku, Sapporo, Hokkaido 060; tel. (11) 261-5775; fax (11) 272-2255; 19,063 mems; Pres. YOSHIZO ODAWARA.

Food Rengo (Federation of All Japan Foods and Tobacco Workers' Unions): Hiroo Office Bldg, 8/F, 1-3-18, Hiroo, Shibuya-ku, Tokyo; tel. (3) 3446-2082; fax (3) 3446-6779; internet www.jfu.or.jp; f. 2000; est. as Shokuhin Renmei, following merger of Shokuhin Rengo and Shokuhin Rokyo; present name adopted 2002; 111,599 mems.

Gomu Rengo (Japanese Rubber Workers' Union Confederation): 2-3-3, Mejiro, Toshima-ku, Tokyo 171; tel. (3) 3984-3343; fax (3) 3984-5862; 60,070 mems; Pres. YASUO FURUKAWA.

Health Care Rokyo (Japanese Health Care Workers' Union): 2-17-20, Shiba, Minato-ku, Tokyo 105-0014; tel. (3) 3451-6025; fax (3) 3451-6040.

Insatsu Roren (Federation of Printing Information Media Workers' Unions): Yuai Kaikan, 7/F, 2-20-12, Shiba, Minato-ku, Tokyo 105-0014; tel. (3) 5442-0191; fax (3) 5442-0219; 22,303 mems; Pres. HIROFUMI NAKABAYASHI.

JA Rengo (All-Japan Agriculture Co-operative Staff Members' Union): 218, Nishi-Nomachi, Sanzaemon-bori, Himeji-shi, Hyogo 670-0940; tel. and fax (792) 85-3618; 2,772 mems; Pres. YUTAKA OKADA.

JAM (Japanese Association of Metal, Machinery and Manufacturing Workers' Unions): Yuai Kaikan, 2-20-12, Shiba, Minato-ku, Tokyo 105-0014; tel. (3) 3265-2171; fax (3) 3230-0172; e-mail mail@jam-union.or.jp; internet www.jam-union.or.jp; f. 1999; est. through merger of Kinzoku Kikai (National Metal and Machinery Workers' Union of Japan) and Zenkin Rengo (Japanese Federation of Metal Industry Unions).

Japan Federation of Service and Distributive Workers' Unions: 2-23-1, Yoyogi, Shibuya-ku, Tokyo 151-0053; tel. (3) 3370-4121; fax (3) 3370-1640; e-mail international@jsd-union.org; internet www.jsd-union.org; f. 2001; 210,000 mems; Pres. SHOICHI HACHINO.

Japan Postal Group Union (JPGU): 5-2-2, Higashi-Ueno, Taito-ku, Tokyo 110-0015; tel. (3) 5830-2655; fax (3) 5830-2484; internet www.jprouso.or.jp; f. 2007; est. by merger of Japan Postal Workers' Union and All-Japan Postal Labour Union.

JEC Rengo (Japanese Federation of Energy and Chemistry Workers' Unions): Senbai Bldg, 5-26-30, Shiba, Minato-ku, Tokyo 108-8389; tel. (3) 3452-5591; fax (3) 3454-7464; internet www.jec-u.com; formed by merger of Goka Roren and Zenkoku Kagaku; 104,000 mems; Pres. KATUTOSHI KATO.

Jichi Roren (National Federation of Prefectural and Municipal Workers' Unions): 1-15-22, Oji-honcho, Kita-ku, Tokyo 114; tel. and fax (3) 3907-1584; 5,728 mems; Pres. NOBUO UENO.

Jichiro (All-Japan Prefectural and Municipal Workers' Union): Jichiro Bldg, 1, Rokuban-cho, Chiyoda-ku, Tokyo 102-0085; tel. (3) 3263-0263; fax (3) 5210-7422; e-mail info@jichiro.gr.jp; internet www.jichiro.gr.jp; f. 1954; 903,139 mems; Pres. KENJI OKABE.

Jidosha Soren (Confederation of Japan Automobile Workers' Unions): U-Life Center, 1-4-26, Kaigan, Minato-ku, Tokyo 105-8523; tel. (3) 3434-7641; fax (3) 3434-7428; internet www.jaw.or.jp; f. 1972; 757,000 mems; Pres. KOICHIRO NISHIHARA.

Jiunro (Japan Automobile Drivers' Union): 2-3-12, Nakameguro, Meguro-ku, Tokyo 153; tel. (3) 3711-9387; fax (3) 3719-2624; 1,958 mems; Pres. SADAO KANEZUKA.

Joho Roren (Japan Federation of Telecommunications, Electronic Information and Allied Workers): Zendentsu-rodo Bldg, 3-6, Kanda Surugadai, Chiyoda-ku, Tokyo 101-0062; tel. (3) 3219-2231; fax (3) 3253-3268; e-mail info@joho.or.jp; internet www.joho.or.jp; 265,132 mems; Pres. KAZUO SASAMORI.

JR-Rengo (Japan Railway Trade Unions Confederation): TOKO Bldg, 9/F, 1-8-10, Nihonbashi Muromachi, Chuo-ku, Tokyo 103; tel. (3) 3270-4590; fax (3) 3270-4429; internet homepage1.nifty.com/JR-RENGO; 78,418 mems; Pres. KAZUAKI KUZUNO.

JR Soren (Japan Confederation of Railway Workers' Unions): Meguro Satsuki Bldg, 3-2-13, Nishi-Gotanda, Shinagawa-ku, Tokyo 141-0031; tel. (3) 3491-7191; fax (3) 3491-7192; internet www.jru7.net; 62,300 mems; Pres. YUJI ODA.

Kaiin Kumiai (All-Japan Seamen's Union): 7-15-26, Roppongi, Minato-ku, Tokyo 106-0032; tel. (3) 5410-8330; fax (3) 5410-8336; e-mail iss@jsu.or.jp; internet www.jsu.or.jp; 35,000 mems; Pres. YOUJI FUJISAWA.

Kamipa Rengo (Japanese Federation of Pulp and Paper Workers' Unions): 2-12-4, Kita-Aoyama, Minato-ku, Tokyo 107-0061; tel. (3)

3402-7656; fax (3) 3402-7659; e-mail kamipa-rengo@jpw.jtuc-rengo.jp; internet www.jpw.or.jp; 50,858 mems; Pres. TUNEO MUKAI.

Kensetsu Rengo (Japan Construction Trade Union Confederation): Yuai Bldg, 7/F, 2-20-12, Shiba, Minato-ku, Tokyo 105; tel. (3) 3454-0951; fax (3) 3453-0582; e-mail vg-sec@krw.jtuc-rengo.jp; internet www.jtuc-rengo.jp/kensetu; 13,199 mems; Pres. MASAYASU TERASAWA.

Kikan Roren (Japan Federation of Basic Industry Workers' Unions—JBU): I & S Riverside Bldg, 4/F, 1-23-4, Shinkawa, Chuo-ku, Tokyo 104-0033; tel. (3) 3555-0401; fax (3) 3555-0407; internet www.kikan-roren.or.jp; f. 2003; est. by merger of Tekko Roren (Japan Fed. of Steel Workers' Unions), Zosen Juki Roren (Japan Confed. of Ship-building and Engineering Workers' Unions) and Hitetsu Rengo (Japanese Metal Mine Workers' Union); 243,000 mems; Pres. JUNRO NAITO.

Kokko Rengo (Japan Public Sector Union): Hosaka Bldg, 1-10-3, Kanda Ogawamachi, Chiyoda-ku, Tokyo 101-0052; tel. (3) 5209-6205; fax (3) 5209-6209.

Kokko Soren (Japan General Federation of National Public Service Employees' Unions): Hosaka Bldg, Kanda Ogawamachi, 1-10-3, Chiyoda-ku, Tokyo 101-0052; tel. (3) 5209-6207; fax (3) 5209-6206; e-mail kokko-soren@kokko-soren.jp; internet www.kokko-soren.jp; 33,350 mems; Pres. SEIICHI FUKUDA.

Koku Rengo (Japan Federation of Aviation Industry Unions): 6-5, Haneda-kuko, Ota-ku, Tokyo 144-0041; tel. (3) 5708-7161; fax (3) 5708-7163; e-mail avinet03@jfaiu.gr.jp; internet www.jfaiu.gr.jp.

Kokuzei Roso (Japanese Confederation of National Tax Unions): Okurasho Bldg, Rm 154, 3-1-1, Kasumigaseki, Chiyoda-ku, Tokyo 100; tel. (3) 3581-2573; fax (3) 3581-3843; 40,128 mems; Pres. TATSUO SASAKI.

Kotsu Roren (Japan Federation of Transport Workers' Unions): Yuai Bldg, 3/F, 2-20-12, Shiba, Minato-ku 105-0014; tel. (3) 3451-7243; fax (3) 3454-7393; 97,239 mems; Pres. SHIGEO MAKI.

Koun-Domei (Japanese Confederation of Port and Transport Workers' Unions): 5-10-2, Kamata, Ota-ku, Tokyo 144-0052; tel. (3) 3733-5285; fax (3) 3733-5280; f. 1987; 1,638 mems; Pres. SAKAE IDEMOTO.

NHK Roren (Federation of All-NHK Labour Unions): NHK, 2-2-1, Jinnan, Shibuya-ku, Tokyo 150; tel. (3) 3485-6007; fax (3) 3469-9271; 12,526 mems; Pres. YASUZO SUDO.

Nichirinro (National Forest Workers' Union of Japan): 1-2-1, Kasumigaseki, Chiyoda-ku, Tokyo 100; tel. (3) 3580-8891; fax (3) 3580-1596; Pres. KOH IKEGAMI.

Nikkenkyo (Council of Japan Construction Industry Employees Unions): Moriyama Bldg, 1-31-16, Takadano-baba, Shinjuku-ku, Tokyo 169-0075; tel. (3) 5285-3870; fax (3) 5285-3879.

Nikkokyo (Japan Senior High School Teachers and Staff Union): 2-11, Kanda Ta-cho, Chiyoda-ku, Tokyo 101-0046; tel. (3) 3230-0284; fax (3) 3230-1659; internet www.nikkokyo.org.

Nikkyoso (Japan Teachers' Union): Japan Education Hall, 2-6-2, Hitotsubashi, Chiyoda-ku, Tokyo 101-0003; tel. (3) 3265-2171; fax (3) 3230-0172; internet www.jtu-net.or.jp; f. 1947; 300,000 mems; Pres. YUZURU NAKAMURA.

Rosai Roren (National Federation of Zenrosai Workers' Unions): 2-12-10, Yoyogi, Shibuya-ku, Tokyo 151; tel. (3) 3299-0161; fax (3) 3299-0126; internet rosai.roren.jp; 2,091 mems; Pres. TADASHI TAKACHI.

Seiho Roren (National Federation of Life Insurance Workers' Unions): Tanaka Bldg, 3-19-5, Yushima, Bunkyo-ku, Tokyo 113-0034; tel. (3) 3837-2031; fax (3) 3837-2037; internet www.liu.or.jp; 414,021 mems; Pres. YOHTARU KOHNO.

Seiroren (Labour Federation of Government-Related Organizations): Hasaka Bldg, 4–6/F, 1-10-3, Kanda Ogawa-cho, Chiyoda-ku, Tokyo 101; tel. (3) 5295-6360; fax (3) 5295-6362; e-mail info@lafgo.gr.jp; internet www.lafgo.gr.jp; 27,500 mems; Chair. MITSURU WATANABE.

Shin Unten (F10-Drivers' Craft Union): 4/F, 3-25-6, Negishi, Taito-ku, Tokyo 110; tel. (3) 5603-1015; fax (3) 5603-5351; 4,435 mems; Pres. SHOHEI SHINOZAKI.

Shinrin Roren (Japanese Federation of Forest and Wood Workers' Unions): 3-28-7, Otsuka, Bunkyo-ku, Tokyo 112; tel. (3) 3945-6385; fax (3) 3945-6477; 13,928 mems; Pres. ISAO SASAKI.

Shitetsu Soren (General Federation of Private Railway Workers' Unions): 4-3-5, Takanawa, Minato-ku, Tokyo 108-0074; tel. (3) 3473-0166; fax (3) 3447-3927; f. 1947; 160,000 mems; Pres. RYOICHI IKEMURA.

Sonpo Roren (Federation of Non-Life Insurance Workers' Unions of Japan): Kanda MS Bldg, 4/F, 27, Kanda Higashi-Matsushita-cho, Chiyoda-ku, Tokyo 101; tel. (3) 5295-0071; fax (3) 5295-0073; internet www.fniu.or.jp; Pres. KUNIO MATSUMOTO.

Toshiko (The All-Japan Municipal Transport Workers' Union): 3-1-35, Shibaura, Minato-ku, Tokyo 108; tel. (3) 3451-5221; fax (3) 3452-2977; internet www.toshiko.or.jp; 43,612 mems; Pres. SHUNICHI SUZUKI.

Ui Zensen Domei (Japanese Federation of Textile, Chemical, Food, Commercial, Service and General Workers' Unions): 4-8-16, Kudan-Minami, Chiyoda-ku, Tokyo 102-0074; tel. (3) 3288-3723; fax (3) 3288-3728; e-mail kokusai@uizensen.or.jp; internet www.uizensen.or.jp; f. 2002; est. by merger of CSG Rengo, Zensen Domei and Sen'i Seikatsu Roren; 1,986 affiliates; 790,289 mems (Jan. 2003); Pres. TSUYOSHI TAKAGI.

Unyu Roren (All-Japan Federation of Transport Workers' Union): Zennittsu Kasumigaseki Bldg, 5/F, 3-3-3, Kasumigaseki, Chiyoda-ku, Tokyo 100-0013; tel. (3) 3503-2171; fax (3) 3503-2176; internet www.unyuroren.or.jp; f. 1968; 143,084 mems; Pres. KAZUMARO SUZUKI.

Zeikan Roren (Federation of Japanese Customs Personnel Labour Unions): 3-1-1, Kasumigaseki, Chiyoda-ku, Tokyo 100; tel. and fax (3) 3593-1788; Pres. RIKIO SUDO.

Zen Insatsu (All-Printing Agency Workers' Union): 3-59-12, Nishi-Gahara, Kita-ku, Tokyo 114; tel. (3) 3910-7131; fax (3) 3910-7155; 5,431 mems; Chair. TOSHIO KATAKURA.

Zenchuro (All-Japan Garrison Forces Labour Union): 3-41-8, Shiba, Minato-ku, Tokyo 105; tel. (3) 3455-5971; fax (3) 3455-5973; Pres. EIBUN MEDORUMA.

Zendensen (All-Japan Electric Wire Labour Union): 1-11-6, Hatanodai, Shinagawa-ku, Tokyo 142; tel. (3) 3785-2991; fax (3) 3785-2995; e-mail info@densen.or.jp; internet www.densen.or.jp; Pres. NAOKI TOKUNAGA.

Zen-eien (National Cinema and Theatre Workers' Union): Hibiya Park Bldg, 1-8-1, Yuraku-cho, Chiyoda-ku, Tokyo 100; tel. (3) 3201-4476; fax (3) 3214-0597; Pres. SADAHIRO MATSUURA.

Zengin Rengo (All-Japan Federative Council of Bank Labour Unions): 1-14-12, Higashi-Kanda, Chiyoda-ku, Tokyo 101-0031; tel. (3) 5687-5155; fax (3) 5687-5156; e-mail zengin@ceres.ocn.ne.jp; internet www.zengin.jp; 16,474 mems; Pres. YOSHIHIRO KONO.

Zenjiko Roren (National Federation of Automobile Transport Workers' Unions): 3-7-9, Sendagaya, Shibuya-ku, Tokyo 151; tel. (3) 3408-0875; fax (3) 3497-0107; internet www.zenjiko.or.jp; Pres. OSAMU MIMASHI.

Zenkoku Gas (Federation of Gas Workers' Unions of Japan): 5-11-1, Omori-Nishi, Ota-ku, Tokyo 143; tel. (3) 5493-8381; fax (3) 5493-8216; internet ws1.jtuc-rengo.or.jp/zenkokugas/index/index.htm; 31,499 mems; Pres. AKIO HAMAUZU.

Zenkoku Keiba Rengo (National Federation of Horse-racing Workers): 2500, Mikoma, Miho-mura, Inashiki-gun, Ibaragi 300-04; tel. (298) 85-0402; fax (298) 85-0416; Pres. TOYOHIKO OKUMURA.

Zenkoku Nodanro (National Federation of Agricultural, Forestry and Fishery Corporations' Workers' Unions): 1-5-8, Hamamatsu-cho, Minato-ku, Tokyo 105; tel. (3) 3437-0931; fax (3) 3437-0681; internet www.nodanro.or.jp; 26,010 mems; Pres. SHIN-ICHIRO OKADA.

Zenkoku Semento (National Federation of Cement Workers' Unions of Japan): 5-29-2, Shimbashi, Minato-ku, Tokyo 105; tel. (3) 3436-3666; fax (3) 3436-3668; Pres. KIYONORI URAKAWA.

Zenkoku Union (Japan Community Workers Union Federation): 7-22-18, Nishi-Shinjuku, Shinjuku-ku, Tokyo 160-0023; tel. (3) 5338-2627; fax (3) 5338-1267.

Zenkoku-Ippan (National Union of General Workers): Zosen Bldg, 5/F, 3-5-6, Misaki-cho, Chiyoda-ku, Tokyo 101-0061; tel. (3) 3230-4071; fax (3) 3230-4360; internet www.zenkoku-ippan.or.jp; 54,708 mems; Pres. YASUHIKO MATSUI.

Zenkyoro (National Race Workers' Union): Nihon Kyoiku Kaikan, 7/F, 2-6-2, Hitotsubashi, Chiyoda-ku, Tokyo 101-0003; e-mail zenkoro-honbu@nifty.com; internet homepage2.nifty.com/zenkyoro; tel. (3) 5210-5156; fax (3) 5210-5157; 24,720 mems; Pres. TAKESHI KAWASHIMA.

Zenrokin (Federation of Labour Bank Workers' Unions of Japan): Nakano Bldg, 3/F, 1-11, Kanda Awaji-cho, Chiyoda-ku, Tokyo 101; tel. (3) 3256-1015; fax (3) 3256-1045; internet zenrokin.or.jp; Pres. EIICHI KAKU.

Zenshin Roren (All Japan Community Bank Labour Union Association): 2-6-10, Higashi-Shimbashi, Minato-ku, Tokyo 105-0021; tel. (3) 3437-6017; fax (3) 3437-1204.

Zentanko (National Union of Coal Mine Workers): 1162, Ikeshima, Sotome-cho, Nishi-Sonogi-gun, Nagasaki 857-0071; tel. (9) 5926-0004; fax (9) 5926-1000; Pres. NOBORU TAGAWA.

Zenzohei (All-Mint Labour Union): 1-1-79, Temma, Kita-ku, Osaka-shi, Osaka 530; tel. and fax (6) 6354-2389; Pres. CHIKASHI HIGUCHI.

Zenzosen-kikai (All-Japan Ship-building and Engineering Union): Zosen Bldg, 6th Floor, 3-5-6, Misakicho, Chiyoda-ku, Tokyo 101; tel. (3) 3265-1921; fax (3) 3265-1870; Pres. YOSHIMI FUNATSU.

Transport

RAILWAYS

Japan Railways (JR) Group: 1-6-5, Marunouchi, Chiyoda-ku, Tokyo 100-0005; tel. (3) 3215-9649; fax (3) 3213-5291; internet www.japanrail.com; fmrly the state-controlled Japanese National Railways (JNR); reorg. and transferred to private sector in 1987; high-speed Shinkansen rail network consists of Tokaido line (Tokyo to Shin-Osaka, 552.6 km), Sanyo line (Shin-Osaka to Hakata, 623.3 km), Tohoku line (Tokyo to Morioka, 535.3 km) and Joetsu line (Omiya to Niigata, 303.6 km); Yamagata Shinkansen (Fukushima to Yamagata, 87 km) converted in 1992 from a conventional railway line and is operated as a branch of the Tohoku Shinkansen with through trains from Tokyo; total railway route length was about 19,955 km in 2008.

Central Japan Railway Co: JR Central Shinagawa Bldg, A Wing, 2-1-85, Konan, Minato-ku, Tokyo 108-8204; tel. (3) 3274-9727; fax (3) 5255-6780; internet www.jr-central.co.jp; f. 1987; also operates travel agency services, etc.; Chair. YOSHIYUKI KASAI; Pres. YOSHIOMI YAMADA.

East Japan Railway Co: 2-2-2, Yoyogi, Shibuya-ku, Tokyo 151-8578; tel. (3) 5334-1151; fax (3) 5334-1110; internet www.jreast.co.jp; privatized in 1987; Chair. MUTSUTAKE OTSUKA; Pres. and CEO SATOSHI SEINO.

Hokkaido Railway Co: 15-1-1, Kita-11-jo, Chuo-ku, Sapporo 060-8644; tel. (11) 700-5717; fax (11) 700-5719; e-mail keieki@jrhokkaido.co.jp; internet www.jrhokkaido.co.jp; Chair. YOSHIHIRO OHMORI; Pres. (vacant).

Japan Freight Railway Co: 3-13-1, Iidabashi, Chiyoda-ku, Tokyo; internet www.jrfreight.co.jp; f. 1987; Pres. MASAAKI KOYABASHI.

Kyushu Railway Co: 3-25-21, Hakataekimae, Hakata-ku, Fukuoka 812-8566; tel. (92) 474-2501; fax (92) 474-9745; internet www.jrkyushu.co.jp; f. 1987; Chair. KOJI KARAIKE; Pres. SUSUMU ISHIHARA.

Shikoku Railway Co: 8-33, Hamano-cho, Takamatsu, Kagawa 760-8580; tel. (87) 825-1626; fax (87) 825-1623; internet www.jr-shikoku.co.jp; Chair. MATSUDA KIYOSHI; Pres. IZUMI MASAHUMI.

West Japan Railway Co: 2-4-24, Shibata, Kita-ku, Osaka 530-8341; tel. (6) 6375-8981; fax (6) 6375-8919; e-mail wjr01020@mxy.meshnet.or.jp; internet www.westjr.co.jp; fully privatized in 2004; Chair. NORITAKA KARAUCHI; Pres. TAKAYUKI SASAKI.

Other Principal Private Companies

Hankyu Hanshin Holdings Inc: 1-16-1, Shibata, Kita-ku, Osaka 530-0012; tel. (6) 6373-5001; fax (6) 6373-5042; e-mail web-info@hankyu-hanshin.co.jp; internet www.hankyu-hanshin.co.jp; f. 1907; links Osaka, Kyoto, Kobe and Takarazuka; Chair. HIROSHI OJIMA; Pres. KAZUO SUMI.

Keihan Electric Railway Co Ltd: 1-7-31, Otemae, Chuo-ku, Osaka; tel. (6) 6944-2521; fax (6) 6944-2501; internet www.keihan.co.jp; f. 1906; Chair. SHIGETAKA SATO; Pres. SEINOSUKE UEDA.

Keihin Express Electric Railway Co Ltd (Keikyu): 2-20-20, Takanawa, Minato-ku, Tokyo 108-8625; tel. (3) 3280-9120; fax (3) 3280-9199; internet www.keikyu.co.jp; f. 1899; Chair. MASARU KOTANI; Pres. TSUNEO ISHIWATA.

Keio Electric Railway Co Ltd: 1-9-1, Sekido, Tama City, Tokyo 206-8052; tel. (42) 337-3106; fax (42) 374-9322; internet www.keio.co.jp; f. 1913; Chair. KAN KATO; Pres. TADASHI NAGATA.

Keisei Electric Railway Co Ltd: 1-10-3, Oshiage, Sumida-ku, Tokyo 131; tel. (3) 3621-2242; fax (3) 3621-2233; internet www.keisei.co.jp; f. 1909; Chair. HIROSHI OHTSUKA; Pres. TSUTOMU HANADA.

Kinki Nippon Railway Co Ltd (Kintetsu): 6-1-55, Uehommachi, Tennoji-ku, Osaka 543-8585; tel. (6) 6775-3444; fax (6) 6775-3468; internet www.kintetsu.co.jp; f. 1910; Chair. MASANORI YAMAGUCHI; Pres. TETSUYA KOBAYASHI.

Nagoya Railroad Co Ltd: 1-2-4, Meieki, Nakamura-ku, Nagoya-shi 450-8501; tel. (52) 588-0813; fax (52) 588-0815; e-mail info@meitetsu.co.jp; internet www.meitetsu.co.jp; Chair. EIICHIRO KINOSHITA; Pres. ADO YAMAMOTO.

Nankai Electric Railway Co Ltd: 5-1-60, Namba, Chuo-ku, Osaka 542; tel. (6) 6644-7121; internet www.nankai.co.jp; f. 1925; Chair. MAKOTO YAMANAKA; Pres. SHINJI WATARI.

Nishi-Nippon Railroad Co Ltd: 1-11-17, Tenjin-cho, Chuo-ku, Fukuoka 810; tel. (92) 761-6631; fax (92) 722-1405; e-mail www-admin@nnr.co.jp; internet www.nnr.co.jp; serves northern Kyushu; Chair. TSUGUO NAGAO; Pres. KAZAYUKI TAKESHIMA.

Odakyu Electric Railway Co Ltd: 1-8-3, Nishi-Shinjuku, Shinjuku-ku, Tokyo 160-8309; tel. (3) 3349-2526; fax (3) 3346-1899; e-mail ir@odakyu-dentetsu.co.jp; internet www.odakyu.jp; f. 1948; Chair. TATSUZO TOSHIMITSU; Exec. Pres. YORIHIKO OSUGA.

Sanyo Electric Railway Co Ltd: 3-1-1, Oyashiki-dori, Nagata-ku, Kobe 653; tel. (78) 653-0843; internet www.sanyo-railway.co.jp; Pres. FUMIHIRO AMANO.

Seibu Railway Co Ltd: 1-11-1, Kasunokidai, Tokorozawa-shi, Saitama 359; tel. (429) 26-2035; fax (429) 26-2237; internet www.seibu-group.co.jp/railways; f. 1894; Chair. TAKASHI GOTOH; Pres. and CEO SUSUMU SHIRAYAMA.

Tobu Railway Co Ltd: 1-1-2, Oshiage, Sumida-ku, Tokyo 131-8522; tel. (3) 3621-5057; internet www.tobu.co.jp; f. 1897; Chair. KAICHIRO NEZU; Pres. YOSHIZUMI NEZU.

Tokyo Express Electric Railway (Tokyu) Co Ltd: 5-6, Nanpeidai-cho, Shibuya-ku, Tokyo 150-8511; tel. (3) 3477-0109; fax (3) 3477-6109; e-mail public@tokyu.co.jp; internet www.tokyu.co.jp; f. 1922; Pres. TOSHIAKI KOSHIMURA.

Principal Subways, Monorails and Tunnels

Subway services operate in Tokyo, Osaka, Kobe, Nagoya, Sapporo, Yokohama, Kyoto, Sendai and Fukuoka. A subway was being planned for Kawasaki in 2010. Most subway lines operate reciprocal through-services with existing private railway lines which connect the cities with suburban areas.

The first commercial monorail system was introduced in 1964 with straddle-type cars between central Tokyo and Tokyo International Airport, a distance of 13 km. Monorails also operate in other cities, including Chiba, Hiroshima, Kitakyushu and Osaka.

In 1985 the 54-km Seikan Tunnel (the world's longest undersea tunnel), linking the islands of Honshu and Hokkaido, was completed. Electric rail services through the tunnel began operating in March 1988.

Fukuoka City Subway: Fukuoka Municipal Transportation Bureau, 2-5-31, Daimyo, Chuo-ku, Fukuoka 810-0041; tel. (92) 732-4107; fax (92) 721-0754; internet subway.city.fukuoka.jp; 2 lines of 17.8 km open; Dir KENNICHIROU NISHI.

Kobe Rapid Transit Railway Co Ltd: 3-3-9 Tamondoori, Chuo-ku, Kobe; tel. (78) 351-0881; fax (78) 351-1607; internet www.kobe-kousoku.jp; 22.7 km open; Dir YASUO MAENO.

Nagoya Subway: Transportation Bureau City of Nagoya, Nagoya City Hall, 3-1-1, Sannomaru, Naka-ku, Nagoya 460-8508; tel. (52) 972-3824; fax (52) 972-3938; e-mail goiken@tbcn.city.nagoya.lg.jp; internet www.kotsu.city.nagoya.jp; 87 km open; Dir-Gen. NOBUO YOSHII.

Osaka Monorail: 1-1-5, Higashi-Machi, Shin-Senri, Toyonakashi, Osaka 560-0082; tel. (6) 6871-8280; fax (6) 6871-8284; internet www.osaka-monorail.co.jp; 113.5 km open; Pres. HIRONOBU IANA.

Osaka Underground Railway: Osaka Municipal Transportation Bureau, 1-12-62, Kujo-Minami, Nishi-ku, Osaka 550-8552; tel. (6) 6585-6137; fax (6) 6585-6154; internet www.kotsu.city.osaka.jp; f. 1933; 129.9 km; the 7.9 km computer-controlled 'New Tram' service began between Suminoekoen and Nakafuto in 1981; seventh line between Kyobashi and Tsurumi-ryokuchi opened in 1990; eighth line between Itakano and Imazato opened in 2006; Gen. Man. YOSHIHIDE KUSUMOTO.

Sapporo Transportation Bureau: 2-4-1, Oyachi-Higashi, Atsubetsu-ku, Sapporo 004-8555; tel. (11) 896-2708; fax (11) 896-2790; internet www.city.sapporo.jp/st; f. 1971; 3 lines of 48 km; Dir T. IKEGAMI.

Sendai City Subway: Sendai City Transportation Bureau, 1-4-15, Kimachidori, Aoba-ku, Sendai-shi, Miyagi-ken 980-0801; tel. (22) 224-5111; fax (22) 224-6839; internet www.kotsu.city.sendai.jp; 15.4 km open; Dir T. IWAMA.

Tokyo Metro Co Ltd: 3-19-6, Higashi-Ueno, Taito-ku, Tokyo 110-8614; tel. (3) 3837-7046; fax (3) 3837-7219; internet www.tokyometro.jp; f. 2004; operates eight lines; 195.1 km open (2010); Pres. HISASHI UMEZAKI.

Tokyo Metropolitan Government (TOEI) Underground Railway: Bureau of Transportation, Tokyo Metropolitan Government, 2-8-1, Nishi-Shinjuku, Tokyo 163-8001; tel. (3) 5320-6026; internet www.kotsu.metro.tokyo.jp; operates four underground lines, totalling 105 km.

Yokohama Municipal Subway: Municipal Transportation Bureau, 1-1, Minato-cho, Naka-ku, Yokohama 231-0017; tel. (45) 664-2525; fax (45) 664-2828; internet www.city.yokohama.jp/me/koutuu; 40.4 km open; Dir-Gen. MICHINORI KISHIDA.

ROADS

In 2006 Japan's road network extended to an estimated 1,196,999 km, including 7,383 km of motorways and 54,347 km of highways. In May 1999 work was completed on a 29-year project to construct three routes, consisting of a total of 19 bridges, between the islands of Honshu and Shikoku across the Seto inland sea, at a cost of some US $25,000m. There is a national omnibus service, 60 publicly operated services and 298 privately operated services.

In October 2005 the major state-owned road authorities were transferred to the private sector. The Japan Highway Public Corpn was privatized and divided into three separate regional expressway companies, servicing central, eastern and western zones. The others were Metropolitan Expressway Public Corpn, Hanshin Expressway Public Corpn and Honshu-Shikoku Bridge Authority.

Central Nippon Expressway Co Ltd: Nagoya Sumimoto Bldg, 8/F, 2-18-19, Nishiki Naka-ku, Nagoya 460-0003; tel. (52) 222-1620; internet www.c-nexco.co.jp; f. 2005; Chair. KANEKO TAKESHI.

East Nippon Expressway Co Ltd: Kasumigaseki Bldg, 15/F, 3-2 Kasumigaseki, Chiyoda-ku, Tokyo 100-8979; tel. (3) 3506-0111; internet www.e-nexco.co.jp; f. 2005; Chair. TATSUO SATO.

West Nippon Expressway Co Ltd: 1-6-20, Dojima, Kita-ku, Osaka; tel. (6) 6344-4000; internet corp.w-nexco.co.jp; f. 2005; Chair. HIDETOSHI NISHIMURA.

SHIPPING

At 31 December 2009 the Japanese merchant fleet comprised 6,221 vessels, with a total displacement of 14,725,189 grt. The main ports are Tokyo, Yokohama, Nagoya and Osaka.

Principal Companies

Daiichi Chuo Kisen Kaisha: 2-14-4, Shintomi-cho, Chuo-ku, Tokyo 104-8544; tel. (3) 5540-1997; fax (3) 3523-8987; internet www.firstship.co.jp; f. 1960; liner and tramp services; Pres. SABURO KOIDE.

Iino Kaiun Kaisha Ltd: Shiba-Daimon Front Bldg, 1-7-13, Shiba-koen, Minato-ku, Tokyo 105-0011; tel. (3) 5408-0356; e-mail ikk_soumu2@ex.iino.co.jp; internet www.iino.co.jp; f. 1899; cargo and tanker services; Chair. TOMOYUKI SEKINE; CEO YOSHIHIKO NAKAGAMI.

Kansai Kisen KK: Osaka Bldg, 3-6-32, Nakanoshima, Kita-ku, Osaka 552; tel. (6) 6574-9131; fax (6) 6574-9149; internet www.kanki.co.jp; f. 1942; domestic passenger services; Pres. MAKOTO KUROISHI.

Kawasaki Kisen Kaisha Ltd (K Line): 1-2-9, Nishi-Shimbashi, Minato-ku, Tokyo 105-8421; tel. (3) 3595-5000; fax (3) 3595-5001; e-mail otaki@email.kline.co.jp; internet www.kline.co.jp; f. 1919; containers, cars, LNG, LPG and oil tankers, bulk carriers; Chair. of Bd HIROYUKI MAEKAWA; Pres. KURODANI KENICHI.

Mitsui OSK Lines Ltd: Shosen Mitsui Bldg, 2-1-1, Toranomon, Minato-ku, Tokyo 105-8688; tel. (3) 3587-7092; fax (3) 3587-7734; internet www.mol.co.jp; f. 1942; merged with Navix Line Ltd in 1999; world-wide container, liner, tramp, and specialized carrier and tanker services; Chair. AKIMITSU ASHIDA; Pres. KOICHI MUTO.

Nippon Yusen Kaisha (NYK) Line: 2-3-2, Marunouchi, Chiyoda-ku, Tokyo 100-0005; tel. (3) 3284-5151; fax (3) 3284-6361; internet www.nyk.com; f. 1885; merged with Showa Line Ltd in 1998; world-wide container, cargo, pure car and truck carriers, tanker and bulk carrying services; Chair. KOJI MIYAHARA; Pres. YASUMI KUDO.

Nissho Shipping Co Ltd: Mori Bldg, 7/F, Rm 33, 3-8-21, Toranomon, Minato-ku, Tokyo 105-0001; tel. (3) 3438-3511; fax (3) 3438-3566; internet www.nissho-shipping.co.jp; f. 1943; Pres. KENICHI YAMAGUCHI.

Ryukyu Kaiun KK: 1-24-11, Nishi-Machi, Naha, Okinawa 900-0036; tel. (98) 868-8161; fax (98) 868-8561; internet www.rkkline.co.jp; f. 1950; cargo and passenger services on domestic routes; Pres. YAMASHIRO HIROMI.

Taiheiyo Kaiun Co Ltd: Mitakokusai Bldg, 23/F, 1-4-28, Minato-ku, Tokyo 108-0073; tel. (3) 5445-5800; fax (3) 5445-5801; internet www.taiheiyokk.co.jp; f. 1951; cargo and tanker services; Pres. TAKESHI MATSUNAGA.

CIVIL AVIATION

Three international airports serve Tokyo: Narita, located in Chiba prefecture; Haneda; and Ibaraki, which opened in March 2010. A second runway was opened at Narita in 2002. A fourth runway at Haneda, along with a third terminal for international flights, opened in October 2010. In 1994 the world's first offshore international airport (Kansai International Airport) was opened in Osaka Bay, and a second runway was completed in 2007. Nearly 100 other airports handle regional and some international flights.

Air Central: c/o Central Japan International Airport, 1-1, Centrair, Tokoname, Aichi 479-0881; tel. (569) 389-300; fax (569) 389-305; internet www.air-central.co.jp; f. 1988; fmrly Nakanihon Airlines, name changed as above Feb. 2005; regional and domestic services; Pres. JUNICHI MIDORO.

Air Do (Hokkaido International Airlines Co Ltd): 1-2-9, Kita Sanjo Nishi, Chuo-ku, Sapporo; tel. (11) 252-5533; fax (11) 252-5580; e-mail postbear@airdo.co.jp; internet www.airdo.co.jp; f. 1996; domestic service between Tokyo and Sapporo; Pres. SAITO SADAO.

Air Nippon Co Ltd (Air Nippon Koku—ANK): Shiodome City Centre, 1-5-2, Higashi-Shinbashi, Minato-ku, Tokyo 105–7137; internet www.air-nippon.co.jp; f. 1974; fmrly Nihon Kinkyori Airways; wholly owned subsidiary of All Nippon Airways; domestic passenger services, international service to Taiwan; Pres. and CEO HIDEO YAGUCHI.

All Nippon Airways (ANA): Shiodome City Center, 1-5-2, Higashi-Shimbashi, Minato-ku, Tokyo 105-7133; tel. (3) 6735-1000; fax (3) 6735-1005; internet www.ana.co.jp; f. 1952; operates domestic passenger and freight services; scheduled international services to the Far East, the USA and Europe; charter services world-wide; Chair. YOJI OHASHI; Pres. and CEO SHINCHIRO ITO.

Hokkaido Air System: New Chitose Airport, Bibi Chitose City, Hokkaido 066-0055; tel. (123) 46-5533; fax (123) 46-5534; internet www.hac-air.co.jp; f. 1997; domestic services on Hokkaido; Pres. NISHIMURA KIMITOSHI.

Ibex Airlines: 1-2-3, Shinsuna, Koto-ku, Tokyo 136-8640; internet www.ibexair.co.jp; f. 1999; operates domestic flights from Osaka and Narita International Airports; Chair. TAKAO ASAI; Pres. HATTORI HIROYUKI.

JALways Co Ltd: Japan Airlines Narita Operation Center, 3/F, Narita International Airport, Narita, Chiba 282-8610; tel. (476) 34-3360; fax (476) 34-3366; e-mail jazbz.jaz@jal.com; internet www.jalways.co.jp; f. 1990; subsidiary of JAL; domestic and international scheduled and charter services; Pres. and CEO HIROSHI IKEDA.

Japan Air Commuter: 787-4, Mizobe Humototyou, Kirishima, Kagoshima Prefecture; tel. (995) 582-151; fax (995) 582-673; e-mail info@jac.co.jp; internet www.jac.co.jp; f. 1983; subsidiary of JAL; domestic services; Chair. YOSHITOMI ONO; Pres. ARATA YASUJIMA.

Japan Airlines (JAL): 2-4-11, Higashi-Shinagawa, Shinagawa-ku, Tokyo 140-8605; tel. (3) 5769-6476; internet www.jal.com; f. 2002; Chair. KAZUO INAMORI; Pres. MASARU ONISHI.

Japan Transocean Air: 3-24, Yamashita-cho, Naha-shi, Okinawa 900-0027; tel. (98) 857-2112; fax (98) 857-9396; internet www.jal.co.jp/jta; f. 1967; adopted present name 1993; subsidiary of JAL; domestic passenger services; 8 brs; Pres. AOKI MAKOTO.

Skymark Airlines: 1-5-5, Haneda Airport, Ota-ku, Tokyo 144-0041; tel. (3) 5402-6767; fax (3) 5402-6770; e-mail info@skymark.co.jp; internet www.skymark.co.jp; f. 1997; domestic services; Pres. and CEO SHINICHI NISHIKUBO.

Tourism

The ancient capital of Kyoto, pagodas and temples, forests and mountains, traditional festivals and the classical Kabuki theatre are some of the many tourist attractions of Japan. Receipts from tourism (excluding passenger transport) in 2009 totalled an estimated US $10,305m. International arrivals rose by an estimated 26.8% in 2010 to total 8.6m. The Republic of Korea, China and Taiwan are leading sources of visitors.

Department of Tourism: 2-1-3, Kasumigaseki, Chiyoda-ku, Tokyo 100; tel. (3) 3580-4488; fax (3) 3580-7901; f. 1946; Dir-Gen. KIMITAKA FUJINO.

Japan National Tourist Organization (JNTO): Tokyo Kotsu Kaikan Bldg, 2-10-1, Yuraku-cho, Chiyoda-ku, Tokyo 100-0006; tel. (3) 3216-1901; fax (3) 3216-1846; internet www.jnto.go.jp; Pres. MINORU NAKAMURA.

Japan Tourism Agency (JTA): General Affairs Division, National and Regional Planning Bureau, 2-1-3, Kasumigaseki, Chiyoda-ku, Tokyo 100-8918; tel. (3) 5253-8111; fax (3) 3580-7982; e-mail webmaster@mlit.go.jp; internet www.mlit.go.jp/kankocho; f. 2008; aims to promote Japan as a tourist destination and, in conjunction with JNTO, to achieve govt objectives; Commr HIROSHI MIZOHATA.

Defence

As assessed at November 2010, the total strength of the Japanese Self-Defence Forces was some 247,746: ground self-defence 151,641, maritime self-defence 45,518, air self-defence 47,123 and central staff 3,464. Paramilitary forces numbered 12,636, and reserve forces comprised an additional 56,379 personnel. Military service is voluntary. At November 2010 US forces stationed in Japan comprised 2,677 army, 12,380 air force and 3,539 navy personnel, together with 17,002 members of the US Marine Corps.

Defence Expenditure: Estimated at 5,030,000m. yen for 2011.

Chief of the Joint Staff Council: Gen. RYOICHI ORIKI.

Chief of Staff of Ground Self-Defence Force: Gen. YOSHIFUMI HIBAKO.

Chief of Staff of Maritime Self-Defence Force: Adm. MASAHIKO SUGIMOTO.

Chief of Staff of Air Self-Defence Force: SHIGERU IWASAKI.

Education

Education is compulsory between the ages of six and 15. A kindergarten (*yochien*) system provides education for children aged between three and five years of age, although the majority of kindergartens are privately controlled. In 2009 there were 13,516 kindergartens, which were attended by 1.6m. children. All children between six and 15 are required to attend six-year elementary schools (*shogakko*) and three-year lower secondary schools (or middle schools—*chugakko*). In 2007/08 enrolment at pre-primary school included 89% of pupils in the relevant age group, while enrolment at primary level included 100% of pupils in the relevant age group. Enrolment at secondary level included 98% of students in the relevant age group in the same year. In 2009 there were 22,258 elementary schools, at which nearly 7.1m. pupils were enrolled, and 10,864 lower secondary schools, at which 3.6m. pupils were enrolled. Upper secondary schools (or high schools— *kotogakko*) provide a three-year course in general topics, or a vocational course in subjects such as agriculture, commerce, fine art and technical studies. In 2009 there were 5,183 upper secondary schools, at which 3.3m. pupils were enrolled.

There are four types of institution for higher education. Universities (*daigaku*) offer degree and postgraduate courses. In 2009 there were 773 universities and graduate schools, at which 2.8m. students were enrolled. Junior colleges (*tanki-daigaku*) provide less specialized two- to three-year courses, credits for which can count towards a first degree. In 2009 there were 406 junior colleges in Japan. Both universities and junior colleges offer facilities for teacher-training. Colleges of technology (*koto-senmon-gakko*), of which there were 64 in 2009, offer a five-year specialized training. Since 1991 colleges of technology have been able to offer short-term advanced courses. A combined total of 220,386 students were enrolled at junior colleges and colleges of technology in 2009. Special training colleges (*senshu-gakko*) offer advanced courses in technical and vocational subjects, lasting for at least one year. In 2009 there were 3,348 special training colleges in Japan. Central government expenditure on culture, education and science was projected at 5,312,200m. yen for the 2008/09 financial year.

Bibliography

General

Bowring, Richard, and Kornicki, Peter (Eds). *The Cambridge Encyclopedia of Japan.* Cambridge, Cambridge University Press, 1993.

Carpenter, Susan. *Japan's Nuclear Crisis: The Routes to Responsibility.* Basingstoke, Palgrave Macmillan, 2011.

Cooney, Kevin J. *Japan's Foreign Policy Since 1945.* London, M. E. Sharpe, 2007.

Coulmas, Florian. *Population Decline and Ageing in Japan—The Social Consequences.* Abingdon, Routledge, 2008.

Ellwood, Robert. *Introducing Japanese Religion.* Abingdon, Routledge, 2007.

Ertl, John, Grayburn, Nelson, and Tierney, R. Kenji (Eds). *Multiculturalism in the New Japan: Crossing the Boundaries Within.* New York, Berghahn Books, 2007.

Furukawa, Kojun. *Social Welfare in Japan: Principles and Applications.* Melbourne, Trans Pacific Press, 2008.

Hendry, Joy (Ed.). *Understanding Japanese Society.* London, RoutledgeCurzon, 2003.

Holroyd, Carin, and Coates, Ken (Eds). *Japan in the Age of Globalization.* Abingdon, Routledge, 2011.

Inouye, Charles Shiro. *Evanescence and Etiquette: The Search for Meaning and Identity in Japanese Culture.* Basingstoke, Palgrave Macmillan, 2007.

Martinez, J. P. *Modern Japanese Culture and Society.* London, Routledge, 2007.

Narramore, Terry. *Rethinking Modern Japan: Politics, Economics, Identity.* Abingdon, Routledge, 2006.

Nathan, John. *Japan Unbound: A Volatile Nation's Quest for Pride and Purpose.* Boston, MA, Houghton Mifflin, 2004.

Osawa, Mari. *Social Security in Contemporary Japan.* Abingdon, Routledge, 2011.

Rebik, Marcus, and Takenaka, Ayumi (Eds). *The Changing Japanese Family.* Abingdon, Routledge, 2006.

Sato, Yoichiro, and Limaye, Satu (Eds). *Japan in a Dynamic Asia.* Lanham, MD, Rowman and Littlefield, 2006.

Schwartz, Frank J., and Pharr, Susan J. (Eds). *The State of Civil Society in Japan.* Cambridge, Cambridge University Press, 2003.

Segers, Rien T. (Ed.). *A New Japan for the Twenty-First Century: An Inside Overview of Current Fundamental Changes and Problems.* Abingdon, Routledge, 2008.

Starr, Don. *Japan: A Historical and Cultural Dictionary.* Richmond, Curzon Press, 2001.

Sugimoto, Yoshio. *An Introduction to Japanese Society.* Cambridge, Cambridge University Press, 3rd Edn, 2010.

Vij, Ritu. *Japanese Modernity and Welfare: State, Civil Society and Self in Contemporary Japan.* Basingstoke, Palgrave Macmillan, 2007.

Willis, David Blake, and Murphy-Shigematsu, Stephen. *Transcultural Japan: At the Borderlands of Race, Gender and Identity.* Abingdon, Routledge, 2008.

History

Allinson, Gary D. *Japan's Postwar History.* Ithaca, NY, Cornell University Press, 2nd Edn, 2004.

Best, Anthony (Ed.). *Imperial Japan and the World, 1931–1945.* Abingdon, Routledge, 2010.

Buruma, Ian. *Inventing Japan: From Empire to Economic Miracle 1853–1964.* London, Weidenfeld and Nicolson, 2003.

Coaldrake, William H. (Ed.). *Japan from War to Peace: The Coaldrake Records 1939–1956.* London, RoutledgeCurzon, 2003.

Doak, Kevin Michael. *A History of Nationalism in Modern Japan: Placing the People.* Boston, MA, Brill, 2007.

Duus, Peter (Ed.). *The Cambridge History of Japan, Volume 6: The Twentieth Century.* New York, Cambridge University Press, 1989.

Hata, Ikuhiko. *Hirohito: The Showa Emperor in War and Peace.* Folkestone, Global Oriental, 2007.

Hotta, Eri. *Pan-Asianism and Japan's War 1931–1945.* New York, Palgrave Macmillan, 2008.

Huffman, James L. *Modern Japan: A History in Documents.* New York, Oxford University Press, 2010.

Iokibe, Makoto (Ed.). *The Diplomatic History of Postwar Japan.* Abingdon, Routledge, 2010.

Jansen, Marius B. *The Making of Modern Japan.* Harvard, MA, Harvard University Press, 2001.

Large, Stephen S. (Ed.). *Showa Japan—Political, Economic and Social History 1926–1989.* London, Routledge, 1998.

Maddox, Robert J. (Ed.). *Hiroshima in History: The Myths of Revisionism.* Columbia, MO, University of Missouri Press, 2007.

Reimann, Kim D. *The Rise of Japanese NGOs: Activism from Above.* Abingdon, Routledge, 2009.

Ruoff, Kenneth J. *The People's Emperor: Democracy and the Japanese Monarchy, 1945–1995.* Harvard, MA, Harvard University Press, 2002.

Saito, Hisho (trans. by Elizabeth Lee). *A History of Japan.* Abingdon, Routledge, 2010.

Steele, M. William. *Alternative Narratives in Modern Japanese History.* London, RoutledgeCurzon, 2003.

Storry, Richard. *A History of Modern Japan.* London, Penguin Books, 1990.

Japan and the Decline of the West in Asia 1894–1943. London, Macmillan Press, 1979.

Takao, Yasuo. *Reinventing Japan: from Merchant Nation to Civic Nation.* New York, Palgrave Macmillan, 2008.

Tipton, Elise K. *Modern Japan: A Social and Political History.* Abingdon, Routledge, 2008.

Totman, Conrad. *Japan Before Perry: A Short History.* Berkeley, CA, University of California Press, 2008.

Williams, David. *Defending Japan's Pacific War.* London, RoutledgeCurzon, 2004.

Winters, Francis X. *Remembering Hiroshima: Was it Just?* Aldershot, Ashgate, 2009.

Yamazuki, Jane. *Japanese Apologies for World War II: A Rhetorical Study.* Abingdon, Routledge, 2005.

Yoshiaki Yoshimi. *Comfort Women: Sexual Slavery in the Japanese Military During World War II.* New York, Columbia University Press, 2001.

Politics

Akaha, Tsuneo, and Arase, David. *The US-Japan Alliance: Balancing Soft and Hard Power in East Asia*. Abingdon, Routledge, 2009.

Anderson, Mark. *Japan and the Specter of Imperialism*. New York, Palgrave Macmillan, 2009.

Calder, Kent E. *Pacific Islands: Reviving US-Japan Relations*. New Haven, CT, Yale University Press, 2009.

Chan, Jennifer. *Another Japan is Possible: New Social Movements and Global Citizenship Education*. Stanford, CA, Stanford University Press, 2008.

DiFilippo, Anthony. *Japan's Nuclear Disarmament and the U. S. Security Umbrella*. Basingstoke, Palgrave Macmillan, 2006.

US-Japan-North Korea Security Relations: Irrepressible Interests. Abingdon, Routledge, 2011.

Eldridge, Robert D., and Midford, Paul. *Japanese Public Opinion and the War on Terrorism*. New York, Palgrave Macmillan, 2008.

Ferguson, Joseph P. *Japanese-Russian Relations: 1907–2007*. Abingdon, Routledge, 2008.

Gaunder, Alisa. *Political Reform in Japan: Leadership Looming Large*. Abingdon, Routledge, 2007.

Green, Michael. *Japan's Reluctant Realism: Foreign Policy Challenges in an Era of Uncertain Power*. London, Palgrave Macmillan, 2003.

Hagström, Linus. *Japan's China Policy: A Relational Power Analysis*. Abingdon, Routledge, 2005.

Hamayaka, Shintaro. *Asian Regionalism and Japan: The Politics of Membership in Regional Diplomatic, Financial and Trade Groups*. Abingdon, Routledge, 2011.

Hood, Christopher (Ed.). *Politics of Modern Japan*. Abingdon, Routledge, 2008.

Hook, Glenn D. *Japan and the Emerging Pacific Order*. Abingdon, RoutledgeCurzon, 2008.

Hook, Glenn D., et al. *Japan's International Relations—Politics, Economics and Security*. Abingdon, Routledge, 3rd Edn, 2011.

Hook, Glenn D. (Ed.). *Contested Governance in Japan*. London, RoutledgeCurzon, 2005.

Decoding Boundaries in Contemporary Japan: The Koizumi Administration and Beyond. Abingdon, Routledge, 2010.

Hori, Harumi. *The Changing Japanese Political System*. Abingdon, Routledge, 2005.

Hughes, Christopher W. *Japan's Economic Power and Security—Japan and North Korea*. London, Routledge, 1999.

Japan's Security Policy and Ballistic Missile Defence System. London, RoutledgeCurzon, 2004.

Japan's Remilitarisation. Abingdon, Routledge, 2009.

Hyde, Sarah. *The Transformation of the Japanese Left—From Old Socialists to New Democrats*. Abingdon, Routledge, 2009.

Jain, Purnendra. *Japan's Subnational Governments in International Affairs*. Abingdon, Routledge, 2005.

Jones, Christopher. *The Political Philosophy of Japan*. London, RoutledgeCurzon, 2004.

Kabashima, Ikuo, and Steel, Gill. *Changing Politics in Japan*. Ithaca, NY, Cornell University Press, 2010.

Katzenstein, Peter. J. *Rethinking Japanese Security: Internal and External Dimensions*. Abingdon, Routledge, 2008.

Kawabata, Eiji. *Contemporary Government Reform in Japan: The Dual State in Flux*. London, Palgrave Macmillan, 2006.

Kawashima, Yutaka. *Japanese Foreign Policy at the Crossroads: Challenges and Options for the Twenty-First Century*. Washington DC, Brookings Institution Press, 2003.

Kersten, Rikki, and Williams, David. *The Left in Japanese Politics*. London, RoutledgeCurzon, 2004.

Krauss, Ellis S., and Pekkanen, Robert J. *The Rise and Fall of Japan's LDP: Political Party Organizations as Historical Institutions*. Ithaca, NY, Cornell University Press, 2010.

Lam, Peng Er. *Japan's Peace Building Diplomacy in Asia*. Abingdon, Routledge, 2009.

Japan's Peace-Building Diplomacy in Asia: Seeking a More Active Political Role. Abingdon, Routledge, 2010.

Lam, Peng Er (Ed.). *Japan's Relations With China: Facing a Rising Power*. Abingdon, Routledge, 2006.

Lucken, Michael, Bayard-Sakai, Anne, and Lozer, Emmanuel (Eds), trans. by J. A. A. Stockwin. *Japan's Postwar*. Abingdon, Routledge, 2011.

Martin, Sherry. *Popular Democracy in Japan: How Gender and Community Are Changing Modern Electoral Politics*. Ithaca, NY, Cornell University Press, 2011.

Nakasone, Yasuhiro. *Japan—A State Strategy for the Twenty-First Century*. London, RoutledgeCurzon, 2002.

Ogawa, Akihiro. *The Failure of Civil Society? The Third Sector and the State in Contemporary Japan*. Albany, NY, State University of New York Press, 2009.

Oka, Takashi. *Policy Entrepreneurship and Elections in Japan: A Political Biogaphy of Ozawa Ichiro*. Abingdon, Routledge, 2011.

Pooley. A. *Japan's Foreign Policies*. Abingdon, Routledge, 2010.

Pyle, Kenneth B. *Japan Rising: The Resurgence of Japanese Power and Purpose*. New York, Public Affairs, 2007.

Reed, Steven R. *Political Change in Japan: Electoral Behavior, Party Realignment and the Koizumi Reforms*. Stanford, CA, Stanford University Press, 2008.

Reed, Steven (Ed.). *Japanese Electoral Politics: Creating a New Party System*. London, RoutledgeCurzon, 2003.

Rose, Caroline. *Sino-Japanese Relations: Towards a Future-Oriented Diplomacy*. London, RoutledgeCurzon, 2004.

Shimazu, Naoko (Ed.). *Nationalisms in Japan*. Abingdon, Routledge, 2006.

Söderberg, Marie. *Changing Power Relations in Northeast Asia: Implications for Relations between Japan and South Korea*. Abingdon, Routledge, 2010.

Söderberg, Marie, and Nelson, Patricia. *Japan's Politics and Economy: Perspectives on Change*. Abingdon, Routledge, 2011.

Starrs, Roy (Ed.). *Politics and Religion in Modern Japan: Red Sun, White Lotus*. Basingstoke, Palgrave Macmillan, 2011.

Stockwin, J. A. A. *Governing Japan: Divided Politics in a Major Economy*. Oxford, Blackwell, 1999.

Dictionary of the Modern Politics of Japan. London, Routledge, 2003.

Williams, Brad. *Resolving the Russo-Japanese Territorial Dispute: Hokkaido-Sakhalin Relations*. Abingdon, Routledge, 2007.

Yamamoto, Mari. *Pacifism and Revolt in Post-War Japan*. London, RoutledgeCurzon, 2004.

Winkler, Christian G. *The Quest for Japan's New Constitution: An Analysis of Visions and Constitutional Reform Proposals 1980–2009*. Abingdon, Routledge, 2010.

Yuzawa, Takeshi. *Japan's Security Policy and the ASEAN Regional Forum: The Search for Multilateral Security in the Asia-Pacific*. Abingdon, Routledge, 2010.

Economy

Adams, F. Gerard, et al. *Accelerating Japan's Economic Growth: Resolving Japan's Growth Controversy*. New York, Routledge, 2007.

Alexander, Arthur. *The Arc of Japan's Economic Development*. Abingdon, Routledge, 2007.

Allen, G. C. *Short Economic History of Modern Japan*. Abingdon, Routledge, 2010.

Amyx, Jennifer. *Japan's Financial Crisis: Institutional Rigidity & Reluctant Change*. Princeton, NJ, Princeton University Press, 2006.

Amyx, Jennifer, and Drysdale, Peter (Eds). *Japanese Governance: Beyond Japan Inc*. London, RoutledgeCurzon, 2002.

Aoki, Masahiko, Jackson, Gregory, and Miyajima, Hideaki. *Corporate Governance in Japan: Institutional Change and Organizational Diversity*. Oxford, Oxford University Press, 2007.

Bailey, David, Coffey, Dan, and Tomlinson, Phil (Eds). *Crisis or Recovery in Japan: State and Industrial Economy*. Cheltenham, Edward Elgar Publishing, 2007.

Blomström, Magnus, and La Croix, Sumner (Eds). *Institutional Change in Japan*. Abingdon, Routledge, 2006.

Carlson, Matthew. *Money Politics in Japan: New Rules, Old Practices*. Boulder, CO, Lynne Rienner Publishers, 2007.

Colignon, Richard A., and Usui, Chikako. *Amakudari: The Hidden Fabric of Japan's Economy*. Ithaca, NY, Cornell University Press, 2003.

Coulmas, Florian, Conrad, Harald, Schad-Seifert, Annette, and Vogt, Gabriele (Eds). *The Demographic Challenge: A Handbook About Japan*. Leiden and Boston, MA, Brill, 2008.

Debroux, Philippe, and Jackson, Keith. *Innovation in Japan: Emerging Patterns, Enduring Myths*. Abingdon, Routledge, 2009.

Estevez-Abe, Margarita. *Welfare and Capitalism in Postwar Japan*. New York, Cambridge University Press, 2008.

Flath, David. *The Japanese Economy*. Oxford, Oxford University Press, 2000.

Francks, Penelope. *Japanese Economic Development: Theory and Practice*. London, Routledge, 2nd Edn, 1999.

Rural Economic Development in Japan: From the Nineteenth Century to the Pacific War. Abingdon, Routledge, 2005.

Fuller, Mark B., and Beck, John C. *Japan's Business Renaissance: How the World's Greatest Economy Revived, Renewed and Reinvented Itself.* New York, McGraw-Hill, 2005.

Gotemba, Goro, and Iwamoto, Yoshiyuki. *Japan on the Upswing: Why the Bubble Burst and Japan's Economic Renewal.* New York, Algora Publishing, 2006.

Graham, Fiona. *Japanese Company in Crisis.* London, Routledge, 2006.

Hamada, Koichi, and Kasuya, Munehisa. *Financial Crises in Japan: Past, Present and Future.* Cheltenham, Edward Elgar Publishing, 2003.

Hamada, Koichi, and Kuroda, Hirami. *Ageing and the Labor Market in Japan.* Cheltenham, Edward Elgar Publishing, 2007.

Hamada, Koichi, et al. *Miraculous Growth and Stagnation in Post-War Japan.* Abingdon, Routledge, 2011.

Hara, Taguji, Kambayashi, Norio, and Matsushima, Noboru. *Industrial Innovation in Japan.* Abingdon, Routledge, 2008.

Hunter, Janet (Ed.). *Japanese Economic History, 1930–1960.* London, Routledge, 2000.

Inagami, T., and Whittaker, D. Hugh. *The New Community Firm: Employment, Governance and Management Reform in Japan.* Cambridge, Cambridge University Press, 2011.

Ito, Takatoshi, Patrick, Hugh, and Weinstein, David E. *Reviving Japan's Economy: Problems and Prescriptions.* Cambridge, MA, MIT Press, 2005.

Katz, Richard. *Japan: The System that Soured—The Rise and Fall of the Japanese Economic Miracle.* Armonk, NY, M. E. Sharpe, 1998.

Japanese Phoenix: The Long Road to Economic Recovery. Armonk, NY, M. E. Sharpe, 2003.

Kohama, Hirohisa. *Industrial Development in Postwar Japan.* Abingdon, Routledge, 2007.

Kojima, Kyoshi. *Japan and a New World Economic Order.* Abingdon, Routledge, 2010.

Leheny, David, and Warren, Kay. *Japanese Aid and the Construction of Global Development: Inescapable Solutions.* Abingdon, Routledge, 2009.

Matanle, Peter. *Japanese Capitalism and Modernity in a Global Era.* London, RoutledgeCurzon, 2003.

Mosk, Carl. *Japanese Economic Development: Markets, Norms, Structures.* Abingdon, Routledge, 2007.

Mouer, Ross, and Kawanishi, Hirosuke. *A Sociology of Work in Japan.* New York, Cambridge University Press, 2005.

Nakamura, Takafusa, and Odaka, Konosuke (Eds). *The Economic History of Japan 1600–1990.* New York, Oxford University Press, 2003.

O'Bryan, Scott. *The Growth Idea: Purpose and Prosperity in Post-War Japan.* Honolulu, HI, University of Hawaii Press, 2009.

Okazaki, Tetsuji (Ed.). *Production Organizations in Japanese Economic Development.* New York, Routledge, 2007.

Paprzycki, Ralph, and Fukao, Kyoji. *Foreign Direct Investment in Japan: Multinationals' Role in Growth and Globalization.* Abingdon, Routledge, 2007.

Rebick, Marcus E. *The Japanese Employment System: Adapting to a New Economic Environment.* New York, Oxford University Press, 2005.

Rix, Alan. *Japan's Economic Aid: Policy Making and Politics.* Abingdon, Routledge, 2010.

Rosenbluth, Frances McCall, and Thies, Michael F. *Japan Transformed: Political Change and Economic Restructuring.* Princeton, NJ, Princeton University Press, 2010.

Rosenbluth, Frances McCall (Ed.). *The Political Economy of Japan's Low Fertility.* Stanford, CA, Stanford University Press, 2007.

Sako, Mari. *Shifting Boundaries of the Firm: Japanese Company–Japanese Labor.* Oxford, Oxford University Press, 2006.

Schoppa, Leonard J. *Race for the Exits: The Unraveling of Japan's System of Social Protection.* Ithaca, NY, Cornell University Press, 2006.

Sorensen, André. *The Making of Urban Japan: Cities and Planning from Edo to the 21st Century.* Abingdon, Routledge, 2008.

Stern, Robert M. (Ed.). *Japan's Economic Recovery: Commercial Policy, Monetary Policy and Corporate Governance.* Cheltenham, Edward Elgar Publishing, 2003.

Tandon, Rameshwar. *The Japanese Economy and the Way Forward.* Basingstoke, Palgrave Macmillan, 2005.

Tolliday, Steven. *The Economic Development of Modern Japan, 1868–1945—From the Meiji Restoration to the Second World War.* Cheltenham, Edward Elgar Publishing, 2001.

The Economic Development of Modern Japan, 1945–1995. Cheltenham, Edward Elgar Publishing, 2001.

Toya, Tetsuro. *Political Economy of the Japanese Financial Big Bang: Institutional Change in Finance and Public Policymaking.* Oxford, Oxford University Press, 2006.

Vestel, James. *Planning for Change: Industrial Policy and Japanese Economic Development 1945–1990.* Oxford, Oxford University Press, 1994.

Vogel, Steven. *Japan Remodeled: How Government and Industry are Reforming Japanese Capitalism.* Ithaca, NY, Cornell University Press, 2006.

Witt, Michael A. *Changing Japanese Capitalism: Societal Coordination and Institutional Adjustment.* Cambridge, Cambridge University Press, 2011.

Yoda, Tomiko, and Harootunian, Harry (Eds). *Japan After Japan: Social and Cultural Life from the Recessionary 1990s to the Present.* Durham, NC, Duke University Press, 2006.

Yoshikawa, Hiroshi. *Japan's Lost Decade.* Tokyo, International House of Japan, 2002.

KOREA

Physical and Social Geography

JOHN SARGENT

The total area of Korea is 223,670 sq km (86,360 sq miles), comprising the Democratic People's Republic of Korea (North Korea), the Republic of Korea (South Korea) and the demilitarized zone (DMZ) between them. North Korea has an area of 122,762 sq km (47,399 sq miles) and South Korea an area of 99,646 sq km (38,474 sq miles). The DMZ covers 1,262 sq km (487 sq miles). The Korean peninsula is bordered to the north by the People's Republic of China, and has a very short frontier with Russia in the north-east.

PHYSICAL FEATURES

Korea is predominantly an area of ancient folding, although in the south-east, where a relatively small zone of recent rocks occurs, a close geological similarity with Japan may be detected. Unlike Japan, the peninsula contains no active volcanoes and earthquakes are rare.

Although, outside the extreme north, few mountains rise to more than 1,650 m, rugged upland, typically blanketed in either pine forest or scrub, predominates throughout the peninsula. Cultivated lowland forms only 20% of the combined area of North and South Korea.

Two broad masses of highland determine the basic relief pattern of the peninsula. In the north the Changpai Shan and Tumen ranges form an extensive area of mountain terrain, aligned from south-west to north-east, and separating the peninsula proper from the uplands of eastern Manzhou (Manchuria) in the People's Republic of China. A second mountain chain runs for almost the entire length of the peninsula, close to, and parallel with, the eastern coast. Thus, in the peninsula proper, the main lowland areas, which are also the areas of maximum population density, are found in the west and south.

The rivers of Korea, which are short and fast-flowing, drain mainly westwards into the Yellow Sea (also known as the West Sea). Of the two countries, North Korea, with its many mountain torrents, is especially well endowed with opportunities for hydroelectric generation. However, wide seasonal variations in the rate of flow tend to hamper the efficient operation of hydroelectric plants.

In contrast with the east coast of the peninsula, which is smooth and precipitous, the intricate western and southern coasts are well endowed with good natural harbours, an asset which, however, is partly offset by an unusually wide tidal range.

CLIMATE

In its main elements, the climate of Korea is more continental than marine, and is thus characterized by a wide seasonal range in temperature. In winter, with the establishment of a high pressure centre over Siberia and Mongolia, winds are predominantly from the north and north-west. North Korea in winter is extremely cold, with January temperatures falling, in the mountains, to below −13°C. Owing to the warming influence of the surrounding seas, winter temperatures gradually rise towards the south of the peninsula, but only in the extreme southern coastlands do January temperatures rise above freezing point. Winter precipitation is light, and falls mainly in the form of snow, which, in the north, lies for long periods.

In the southern and western lowlands summers are hot and humid, with July temperatures rising to 26°C. In mid-summer violent cloudbursts occur, often causing severe soil erosion and landslides. In the extreme north-east summers are cooler, and July temperatures rarely rise above 17°C.

Annual precipitation, of which more than one-half falls in the summer months, varies from about 600 mm in the north-east to more than 1,500 mm in the south.

NATURAL RESOURCES

Although 70% of the total area of Korea is forested, high-quality timber is virtually limited to the mountains of North Korea, where extensive areas of larch, pine and fir provide a valuable resource. Elsewhere, excessive felling has caused the forest cover to degenerate into poor scrub.

Korea is relatively rich in mineral resources, but most deposits are concentrated in the north, where large-scale mining operations were begun by the Japanese before the Second World War. In North Korea the main iron-mining areas are located south of Pyongyang, and in the vicinity of Chongjin in the extreme north-east. North Korea also has substantial reserves of coal, limestone and magnesite. Other mineral deposits include gold, copper, fluorspar, lead, limestone, magnesite, graphite, zinc, tungsten, mica and fluorite. There is evidence of uranium deposits in North Korea, and there have also been unconfirmed reports of reserves of petroleum and gas.

POPULATION

At mid-2010 the estimated population of North Korea was 23,990,703, while that of South Korea was 48,874,539, giving a combined total of nearly 72.9m. The population of the Korean peninsula has thus more than doubled since 1954, when the combined total was 30m.

Population density is much higher in South Korea (483.9 per sq km at the time of the 2010 census) than in North Korea (an estimated 199.2 per sq km in mid-2011). However, these mean density figures conceal the concentration of population on the limited area of agricultural land, which is a salient characteristic of the geography of South Korea.

According to UN estimates for mid-2010, Seoul, the capital of South Korea, had a population of 9,772,717, while Busan, with 3,425,291 inhabitants, was the second largest city, followed by Incheon (2,582,967) and Daegu (2,458,372).

According to the 2008 census results, the population of Pyongyang, the capital of North Korea, was 2,581,076. Apart from Pyongyang's port of Nampo (population of 310,531), the other two principal cities are Hamhung (703,610) and Chongjin, the leading port of the north-east coast (614,892).

History up to the Korean War

ANDREW C. NAHM

With revisions by JAMES E. HOARE

HISTORICAL BACKGROUND

Political History

Archaeological studies conducted since the Korean War of 1950–53 have steadily moved back the dates for the earliest occupation of the Korean peninsula. Palaeolithic people were present 40,000–50,000 years ago, while late palaeolithic sites date back 30,000 years. However, it is not known if these early peoples were the ancestors of modern Koreans, or whether they were replaced entirely by later arrivals. The ancestors of modern Koreans seem to have been Tungusic people who migrated into what is now north-east China (Manzhou in Chinese, known as Manchuria in the West) and the Korean peninsula in about 3000 BC. They brought with them their Ural-Altaic tongue, shamanistic religion and a Neolithic culture. In this period a mythological figure called Dan'gun, half-divine and half-human, is said to have consolidated tribal units into a 'kingdom' named Joseon in the northern part of Korea in 2333 BC. According to legend, ancient Joseon of the Dan'gun, the Kija and the Wiman dynasties lasted some 2,225 years, until overthrown by the Chinese in 108 BC. The Chinese established four military colonies, known as the commanderies, in the north-western region of Korea, which lasted until the fourth century AD. These commanderies contested with local tribal groupings for control of the peninsula.

Around 37 BC one of these tribes emerged as the kingdom of Goguryeo, which began in the southern region of Manzhou, along the Yalu River, and later extended into the Korean peninsula. Goguryeo combined Chinese and proto-Korean elements to make a new synthesis. Chinese domination over the peninsula ended, and the new kingdom successfully defended its territory against Chinese aggression in the late sixth and early seventh centuries. Meanwhile, other tribal federations existing in the central and southern regions of the peninsula consolidated into the kingdoms of Baekje and Silla in 18 BC and 57 BC respectively, ushering in the 'Three Kingdom' period in Korean history.

Silla destroyed Baekje in 663 AD and Goguryeo in 668, in collaboration with China, so unifying Korea. There followed a period of intense cultural development, but the kingdom of Goryeo, which rose in the central region in 918, brought about the demise of Silla in 935. Korea (Corea in Latin languages) is the Western version of Goryeo. During the Goryeo period, all the peninsula, except for the far north-eastern area, came under one ruler, the political system similar to that of China. In the 13th century, however, China's Yuan (Mongol) dynasty conquered Korea, which remained under Mongol domination until the fall of the Yuan dynasty in 1368.

In 1392 Gen. Yi Song Gye overthrew the Goryeo dynasty, establishing the Yi dynasty and renaming the kingdom Joseon, thus emphasizing links with the earliest Korean kingdom. Soon afterwards he transferred the capital from Kaesong to Seoul, a more central defensible position. The Yi dynasty brought the entire Korean peninsula and the island of Jeju (Cheju) under its rule. Yi Song Gye and his successors governed the kingdom with a bureaucracy manned by an élite class of scholar-officials, although the scholars were drawn from only one class in society. Korea became increasingly Confucianized with close political, social and economic links to Ming China, but at the same time retaining both domestic and international autonomy. However, the early successes of the Yi dynasty were not maintained, and power struggles among scholar-officials and between the monarchy and bureaucracy weakened the foundation of the nation. Korea suffered much from Japanese invasions in the late 16th century and Manzhou invasions in the early 17th century, as the latter struggled to take control of the Chinese Empire. While formally acknowledging the Manzhou Qing dynasty after 1644, many Koreans remained loyal to the memory of the Ming, feeling that Korea was now more true to Confucian principles than the usurper court in Beijing. However, outwardly, the formal links remained the same and were to cause confusion among the Western powers that began to press for the opening of Korea in the mid-19th century.

Japan was the first country to impose a Western-style treaty on a reluctant Korea in 1876, and was soon followed by Western countries, led by the USA, which concluded a treaty in 1882. Thereafter, an international power struggle developed in Korea, initially between China and Japan, and then between Russia and Japan. The Japanese victories in the Sino-Japanese War of 1894–95 and the Russo-Japanese War of 1904–05 virtually sealed the fate of Korea, although nationalistic reformists made valiant efforts to save the declining nation.

Despite the repeated invasions, Korea had maintained its independence and preserved its national territory for 1,000 years. However, in 1905 Korea became a Japanese protectorate, and in 1910 was annexed by Japan, ending the rule of the Yi dynasty as well as Korea's independence. Although the Japanese colonial authorities introduced modern educational and economic ideas, the whole thrust of these changes was to Japan's advantage, and any benefits for the Koreans were incidental. Japanese colonial rule in Korea was highly repressive and exploitative. Freedom of speech and press was severely limited, human rights were heavily curtailed, farm lands were confiscated under various pretexts, economic and educational opportunities were extremely limited, and Korean workers and peasants alike were exploited under the repressive rule of the Japanese.

The Koreans retaliated in various ways. In the early stages of Japanese colonialism there was some Korean military opposition, although this could hardly prevail against the power of the Japanese military forces, and many guerrilla fighters moved into Russian or Chinese territory. There were also peaceful demonstrations against the Japanese. Developments during the First World War prompted new Korean demands for independence. On 1 March 1919 a 'Korean Declaration of Independence' was read out in Pagoda Park in Seoul. The signatories, drawn from all the main religious groups in the country, were arrested, but some 2m. Koreans demonstrated peacefully throughout the peninsula, expressing their desire to be free from Japanese colonialism and for a return to national independence under the principle of self-determination and the concept of 'one people, one nation'. These protests were brutally suppressed. A provisional government of Korea in exile (established in Shanghai in April 1919), together with various non-violent as well as militant organizations of overseas Koreans, sustained hopes for the eventual restoration of the Korean nation.

Economic and Social Development

An agricultural life developed during the bronze and iron ages (c. 2000 BC–200 AD), and a fully-fledged agricultural economy grew during the 'Three Kingdom' period, when land was monopolized by the aristocrats and cultivated by peasants who constituted the majority of the population. Domestic commerce did not develop until after the 10th century, but foreign trade with China and Japan had flourished during the 'Three Kingdom' and the unified periods.

The anti-commercialism of Confucianism did not encourage the development of a commercial economy. However, as cities and towns expanded during the Yi period, government-approved commercial enterprises, as well as rural markets and fairs, increased in number, and cottage industries developed rapidly. Land continued to be owned by the gentry class (*yangban*), and cultivated by peasants and slaves.

Social evolution brought about the stratification of the people into the landed gentry and the toiling masses. The toiling masses were classified into 'good people' or 'common people', who were engaged in agriculture, and 'the low-born', who were engaged in trade, manufacturing of goods and other lesser occupations. The *yangban* formed the educated and land-owning class of the Yi period, and provided all high-ranking government officials. The 'middle people' class provided the middle- and lower-ranking officials. Only those who passed the civil service examinations were qualified to be government officials during the Yi period.

Modern commerce and industry developed during the Japanese colonial period. Food production was accelerated to feed the ever-growing number of Japanese as an increasing amount of Korean rice was exported to Japan. Rapid industrial growth came after the Japanese invasions of Manzhou and China proper in the 1930s. With this, the number of industrial workers increased rapidly as the influence of the gentry class diminished.

Cultural History

During and after the period of Chinese domination of the north-western region of Korea, the sinification of Korean culture occurred. Buddhism, which migrated from China to Korea during the third century AD, reached its zenith following the unification of Korea by Silla. Many historic and renowned Buddhist temples, pagodas, statues of Buddha and Buddhist writings were produced by the Koreans during the 'Three Kingdom' and the unified Silla periods.

Buddhism became the state religion of Goryeo. With the growing influence of Buddhism, advanced and sophisticated book-printing techniques developed. *Tripitaka Koreana*, a Buddhist text of over 81,000 pages, and other Buddhist works were printed in Korea with movable type (wooden and metal blocks) in the 13th and 14th centuries.

Confucianism spread slowly but, after the establishment of the Tang dynasty in China in the early seventh century, Confucian influence was strengthened in Korea. The increasing influence of Chinese culture had led to the development of native songs, called *hyangga*, as well as the creation of a system of writing Korean words in Chinese, called *idu*, during the unified Silla period. During the Goryeo and Yi periods, scholarship grew rapidly as Confucian scholars published books on early Korean history, geography, and many other subjects. All scholarly books were written in the Chinese language.

The adoption of neo-Confucianism as the state creed and the rapid Confucianization of political and social patterns and institutions during the Yi period brought about a decline of Buddhism. It ceased to be the court religion, being replaced by neo-Confucianism. Buddhism never disappeared, but increasingly temples and other Buddhist centres moved from the cities to the countryside. Shamanism too, while officially disapproved, continued to exist among the common people, and even among the ladies of the court. At the same time, the growing number of public and private schools of Confucian and Chinese learning, and the introduction of the Chinese civil service examination system, resulted in the rise of an educated élite.

The adoption and promulgation of a new Korean script, commonly called *han'geul* ('Korean Letters'), by King Sejong in 1446 represented an important development in the cultural history of Korea. With this, the Korean form of poetry, called *sijo*, flourished, as it enabled more Koreans to become literate.

From the 17th century the *Sirhak* ('Practical Learning') school of reformist Confucian scholars not only stimulated the development of a new interpretation of Confucianism, but also Korean studies, including historical and geographical studies. Genre and folk painters, together with folk musicians, dancers and players, contributed greatly to the preservation, and also to the growth, of a distinctive Korean folk culture during the Yi period, as novels and travelogues written in *han'geul* appeared.

The arrival and growth of Roman Catholicism and 'Western Learning' in the late 18th century, and the establishment of contacts with the West after 1882, led to the modernization of Korea. The creation of a modern educational system and the introduction of Western culture during the late Yi and Japanese colonial periods brought about a rapid expansion of an educated population, and the growth of modern culture. Many Koreans became Christians as the result of the efforts of missionaries, mainly from the USA. A number of modern Korean schools, universities and medical centres trace their origins to early missionary establishments.

As the Japanese moved increasingly onto a war footing in the 1930s, their attempts to impose Japanese culture on Korea increased. Koreans were forced to adopt Shintoism and the cult of the Emperor, and to change their names to read like Japanese names. These efforts to destroy the language and the racial and cultural identity of the Koreans were to no avail.

Liberation and Partition

On 15 August 1945 the Japanese surrendered to the Allies. The Cairo Declaration of December 1943, issued by the British and US leaders and Chiang Kai-shek of China, had stated that 'in due course Korea shall become free and independent'. The USSR accepted the Cairo agreement, but proposals made by the USA in 1945 led to the division of Korea into two military zones to effect the Japanese surrender: the area south of the 38th parallel line (latitude 38°N) under US occupation and the northern area under Soviet control.

The Japanese Governor-General in Korea had persuaded Yo Un-Hyong, a prominent left-wing nationalist (socialist), to form a political body to maintain law and order at the end of the Japanese colonial rule. The Committee for the Preparation of the National Construction of Korea was thus organized. After Japan's surrender, Korean political prisoners were freed and the committee began to function as a government. Provincial, district and local committees were organized to maintain law and order. On 6 September 1945, two days before the arrival of US occupation forces, the committee called a 'National Assembly' and established a 'People's Republic of Korea', claiming jurisdiction over the whole country. Meanwhile, Soviet troops, which had entered Korea in early August, quickly moved southwards as they crushed Japanese resistance, and within a month the entire northern half of Korea had come under Soviet occupation.

The US occupation authority accepted the surrender of Korea from the Japanese Governor-General, but, unlike the Soviet authorities in the North, refused to recognize the legitimacy of either the 'People's Republic' or the provisional Government of Korea, based in China. The United States Army Military Government in Korea (USAMGIK) was established and operated until the proclamation of South Korea's independence in August 1948.

Exiled political leaders returned to Korea toward the end of 1945: Dr Syngman Rhee from the USA; Kim Ku and Dr Kim Kyu-Sik from China; and Kim Il Sung and other communists from the USSR and China. Pak Hon Yong, a communist who had been released from Japanese imprisonment, quickly formed the communist South Korean Workers' Party in the US-occupied zone. Freedom of political activity permitted by USAMGIK resulted in a proliferation of political parties and social organizations of all political orientations, each vying for prominence. USAMGIK attempted in vain to bring about a coalition of moderate nationalists and the non-communist left wing.

In December 1945 representatives of the United Kingdom, the USA and the USSR entered into the Moscow agreement, providing for a five-year trusteeship for Korea under a four-power regime (China was the fourth power), with a view to establishing an independent and united nation of Korea. Despite violent anti-trusteeship demonstrations throughout the peninsula, the Allied occupation authorities resolved to implement the Moscow plan. Then, abruptly, at Soviet prompting, the communists throughout Korea changed their attitude in favour of the Moscow plan, splitting the Korean people into two opposing camps. In the US-occupied zone left-wing organizations created serious political and economic problems. Communist-directed labour strikes became widespread, and both right- and left-wing organizations engaged in terrorism.

A joint US-Soviet commission was formed to establish a national government of Korea in consultation with Korean political and social organizations. The first session of the joint commission was held in Seoul, the capital of the South, in March–May 1946. The Soviet delegate insisted that only 'democratic' organizations should participate and that only organizations which supported the Moscow agreement were 'democratic'. It became clear that the USSR sought to establish a national government of Korea dominated by the communists. In May 1947 the second session of the joint commission, held in the northern capital, Pyongyang, similarly failed to achieve any agreement and in June the commission's business was suspended indefinitely.

Realizing that the establishment of Korean unity and of a national government was a remote possibility, USAMGIK adopted new plans for South Korea. The Soviet occupation authority likewise proceeded to establish a client regime under Kim Il Sung. All anti-Soviet and anti-communist organizations were either dissolved or placed under communist leadership. A centralized, communist state began to emerge in the North, as Kim Il Sung formed his own party in defiance of Pak Hon Yong, head of the South Korean Workers' Party, whose headquarters were in Seoul.

The USA established a South Korean interim Legislative Assembly in late 1946, and in May 1947 an interim Government was created, both under moderate nationalists. These actions were bitterly criticized by right-wing leaders such as Dr Rhee and Kim Ku. The relationship between the USA and the right-wing nationalists worsened, while terrorist activities created an extremely uneasy situation. Several prominent politicians were assassinated. Neither the interim Legislative Assembly nor the interim Government was effective, for conservative nationalists regarded them as US protégés attempting to prolong the US military occupation of Korea.

In September 1947 the US Government discarded the Moscow plan and placed the Korean question before the UN. The UN General Assembly formed the UN Temporary Commission on Korea (UNTOCK) in November and authorized it to conduct a national election in Korea to create a national government for the whole country.

The UN decision was welcomed by the USA and by most people in South Korea. However, the Soviet occupation authority and the Korean communists in the North rejected the UN plan, and did not allow the UNTOCK to visit North Korea. It soon became apparent that the UN plan would not work in the whole of Korea, and the Commission adopted an alternative plan to hold elections in those areas where it was possible, namely in South Korea only. It was assumed by the Commission that UN-sponsored and supervised elections would be held in the North in the near future, that a National Assembly created by the first democratic elections in Korea would represent the entire country, that the government to be established would be that of all Korea, and that the people in the North would elect their representatives to the National Assembly at a later date.

Whereas the right-wing nationalists welcomed such an alternative plan, the moderate and progressive nationalists, such as Kim Kyu-Sik, the head of the Democratic Independence Party, as well as Kim Ku, an extreme right-wing nationalist, vehemently opposed it, fearing that it would turn the temporary division of Korea into a permanent political partition. They visited North Korea and talked with Kim Il Sung and other communists, but failed to achieve their objective.

The Soviet authorities in the North had already begun to transfer power to the Supreme People's Assembly and the Central People's Committee, both established in early 1947. Dr Rhee's organization, the National Society for the Acceleration of Korean Independence, advocated the immediate independence of South Korea. The UN-sponsored elections held in the South in May 1948 created a National Assembly heavily dominated by the right wing. About 7.5m. people, or 75% of the electorate, elected 198 of 210 representatives from the South, while 100 unfilled seats in the 310-member Assembly were reserved for North Korean representatives. The National Assembly drew up a democratic Constitution for the Republic of Korea. Dr Rhee was elected the first President of the Republic of Korea, whose legitimacy was immediately recognized by the UN. On 15 August 1948 the Republic of Korea was inaugurated, and the US occupation came to an end.

In August 1948 the communists in the North held an election and established the new 527-member Supreme People's Assembly of the Democratic People's Republic of Korea (DPRK), which was proclaimed on 9 September.

THE KOREAN WAR, 1950–53

Soviet forces left North Korea soon after the establishment of the Democratic People's Republic in September 1948, leaving a group of military advisers. US forces were withdrawn from the Republic of Korea in June 1949, also leaving a small military mission. However, the two new states were by no means equal in military terms. Much Soviet effort had gone into creating a modern North Korean army, equipped with some 240 tanks and other heavy equipment, and numbering about 165,000 troops. In addition, the North Korean air force possessed more than 200 aircraft, although most were obsolete. In South Korea, by contrast, the USA had not created anything comparable. South Korean forces were much smaller and weaker than those of the North, without any tanks and only a small number of training aircraft.

After the emergence of separate states in 1948, both North and South Korea claimed jurisdiction over the whole peninsula and both demanded the reunification of the country, by force if necessary. Each side conducted intelligence forays and cross-border raids, sometimes leading to heavy fighting. North Korea seems to have pressed for Soviet agreement to an attack, but the Soviet leader, Stalin (Iosif Dzhugashvili), was reluctant to begin a conflict that might lead to a war with the USA. The communist victory in the Chinese civil war, followed by the proclamation of the People's Republic of China in October 1949, prompted Kim Il Sung to reopen the issue in early 1950. Apparent US disinterest in the Korean peninsula may have been one factor, following the US Secretary of State's exclusion in January 1950 of Korea from a list of areas where the USA would be prepared to act. The Chinese leader, Mao Zedong, also seemed to be less in awe of the USA than Stalin and more ready to contemplate a war. The end of the conflict in China freed up many experienced Korean soldiers who had been fighting with the communist forces, and who were now available to expand the numbers of the North Korean army. In March or April 1950 Stalin and Mao endorsed Kim Il Sung's plans for reunification by force. The results of the May 1950 South Korean elections, which indicated a distinct lack of confidence in Syngman Rhee's Government, were seen by Kim as an indication that there would be support in the South for a reunification attempt.

In the early hours of 25 June 1950, a Sunday morning when many South Korean troops were on leave from their posts for the weekend, North Korea began a major bombardment along the 38th parallel. A North Korean force of more than 60,000 troops, supported by Soviet-built tanks, then crossed the parallel and swept all before them. Four days later the North Koreans captured Seoul; the South Korean Government abandoned the capital and retreated, first to Daejeon, then later to Daegu and finally, in August, to Busan in the far south-east of the country. The Government remained there until 1954.

South Korea appealed for international assistance. The USA responded immediately, and the first US forces arrived on 30 June 1950. However, they were lightly armed, and had come from garrison duty in Japan. Whatever the reason, they proved no match for the North Korean army. Meanwhile, the USA had put the issue to the UN. On 27 June the UN Security Council, in the absence of the Soviet delegate, condemned North Korea as an aggressor and urged member states to aid South Korea. A total of 16 member states responded with armed forces, operating under a Unified Command, to which South Korean forces were also assigned. The Supreme Commander of the Allied Forces in Japan, General Douglas MacArthur, was appointed as its head.

The North Koreans continued their drive southwards, advancing so rapidly that they soon occupied most of the south of the peninsula, leaving South Korean and newly arriving UN troops confined to the south-east corner of Korea. This area became known as the Busan perimeter. In the occupied areas, the North Koreans carried out radical removals of alleged 'rightists' and began to introduce similar social and economic policies to those in place in the North.

The North Korean occupation was destined to be brief. The UN forces quickly established air command over most of the peninsula, and MacArthur planned a dual policy to regain the initiative. As well as a break-out from the Busan perimeter, he organized a sea-borne landing by UN forces at Incheon, the port of Seoul, in September 1950. This was highly successful, and the invaders were driven back. Despite earlier statements that any UN advance would stop at the 38th parallel, and despite indications from China that if UN forces were to cross the parallel it would intervene, UN troops pressed on into North Korea, capturing Pyongyang in October and reaching the Chinese frontier on the Yalu River in November. The North Korean army had effectively disintegrated along large areas of the front, and MacArthur, assuming that the war was over and ignoring intelligence that pointed to a major military build-up by the Chinese, boasted that the UN troops would be 'home by Christmas'.

This assertion proved to be over-optimistic. In mid-October 1950 some 250,000 Chinese troops began clandestinely crossing the Yalu River into North Korea. Although the Chinese forces were drawn from regular People's Liberation Army units, they were designated as the 'Chinese People's Volunteers' while in Korea, perhaps in an attempt to forestall any direct UN attack on China. Although not acknowledged at the time, Soviet pilots flew against UN deployments, and Soviet military officers were also present in Korea as advisers to the North Korean forces. Weakened by determined Chinese attacks, the UN forces began to retreat, despite their superior equipment and command of the air. Although some units fought well, many did not, and in some areas the retreat became a rout, known as 'The Big Bug-Out', in which large amounts of equipment and stores were jettisoned or destroyed. The Chinese advanced into South Korea, capturing Seoul on 4 January 1951, but were unable to consolidate their attack. The UN line stabilized at Wonju, about 160 km south of Seoul. Chinese lines were now very extended, and they could not maintain their advantage. UN forces drove them back, with Seoul retaken in March. The Chinese made a further attempt to capture the capital, but were driven back, with heavy casualties, by a UN counter-attack in April. Effectively, the line of battle now stabilized roughly where it had begun, with the two forces straddling the 38th parallel. Also in April 1951 Gen. Matthew Ridgway replaced MacArthur as head of the Unified Command after the latter had indicated publicly that he disagreed with the US Government's policies on the conduct of the war.

After a proposal from the Soviet Union, now once again present on the Security Council, peace negotiations began in July 1951 at Kaesong, a South Korean city that had fallen to the North Koreans at the very beginning of the conflict. The communist side suspended negotiations in August, and when they were resumed in October they were transferred to a new venue at the village of Panmunjom. Hostilities continued as each side sought to improve its position on the ground, but the fighting now resembled the trench warfare of the First World War (1914–18) rather than the war of movement that had marked the first year of fighting. Chinese forces also helped rebuild the North Korean army during this period, while UN forces performed similar rehabilitation work with the South Koreans. The truce talks made little progress as the two sides argued over questions such as the repatriation of prisoners of war. The UN's position was complicated by South Korean President Rhee's vehement opposition to anything short of a complete victory over the communists.

Despite Rhee's objections, and apparent willingness to sabotage the negotiations, an armistice agreement was concluded on 27 July 1953. Gen. Ridgway signed for the UN, Kim Il Sung for North Korea and Peng Dehuai for the 'Chinese People's Volunteers'; no South Korean representative signed the document. The agreement provided for the end of hostilities, repatriation of prisoners, and the establishment of a Demilitarized Zone (DMZ) on either side of the Demarcation Line between the two sides. The Demarcation Line followed the line of actual control at the cessation of the fighting, and roughly corresponded to the original 1945 division along the 38th parallel. This has remained the boundary between North and South Korea.

To supervise the armistice, a Neutral Nations Supervisory Commission was established, made up of representatives from Sweden, Switzerland, Poland and Czechoslovakia. This commission has remained in existence, although North Korea has refused to co-operate with it since the early 1990s. The armistice also recommended that a Political Conference should be held to discuss the future of the Korean peninsula and the question of reunification. This convened in the Swiss city of Geneva in 1954, and also considered Indo-China. However, it failed to reach agreement on the Korean issues, and therefore the 1953 armistice agreement remained in force in the early 21st century.

The war resulted in enormous losses for both North and South Korea. Each side committed atrocities, some of which were revealed only decades later. Exact figures may never be known, but it is estimated that of the South Korean armed forces some 226,000 were killed and another 717,000 wounded. Civilian deaths totalled 374,000, while 226,000 were wounded and 388,000 went missing. Many were killed by occupation forces and others were taken to the North. There were huge numbers of orphans and widows. On the North Korean side, some 294,000 members of the armed forces were killed and 230,000 wounded, with another 91,000 missing. Civilian casualties were also high in the North, which was heavily bombed during the war; 407,000 were reported killed, 1.5m. wounded and 680,000 missing. A further 1.5m. fled south during the war. There was widespread disruption to housing and infrastructure, disease was rampant and families were divided not just by the DMZ but also because of the disruption caused by the war. When family reunion programmes began in South Korea in the 1980s, many husbands and wives found that former partners were still alive, and in many cases had created second families.

Other groups that fought in Korea also suffered heavy losses. Some 34,000 US personnel were killed, while a further 106,000 were wounded and several hundred were missing. Of the other UN forces, about 2,000 were killed and 10,000 wounded. Chinese losses were estimated at 900,000, including Mao Zedong's son, Mao Anying.

The war did not achieve any solution. Korea remained more bitterly divided than before, and both sides concentrated on consolidating their own power bases rather than trying to resolve the division. Debates have continued about whether the war was a civil war or a proxy war between the two superpowers. In reality, it seems to have been both, brought about by the initial decision to divide the peninsula, which all Koreans resented, and the growing antagonism between the USA and the USSR, which prevented any real progress towards reunification.

THE DEMOCRATIC PEOPLE'S REPUBLIC OF KOREA

History

AIDAN FOSTER-CARTER

Based on an earlier article by ANDREW C. NAHM

With revisions by JAMES E. HOARE

INTRODUCTION

Strong nationalist leadership, with potentially large popular support, was available in North Korea at the end of the Second World War. It consisted mainly of democratically inclined individuals. Educated by Western missionaries, the most prominent leader among the reformists was Cho Man Shik. In August 1945, as Japan admitted defeat, the Japanese Governor in Pyongyang relinquished control to Cho and a newly formed Provincial People's Committee. When Soviet troops reached Pyongyang after the Japanese surrender, they accepted the legitimacy of the committee, and approved Cho as Chairman of the Five Provinces Administrative Bureau, formed to act as the indigenous government organ for North Korea.

In September 1945 Kim Il Sung, a young communist who in the 1930s had led a guerrilla group of Korean communists in Korea and in south-eastern Manzhou (Manchuria), and who later moved to the USSR, returned to Korea with Soviet troops. However, Kim had to cope with the 'domestic' communists who challenged his 'Kapsan' or 'partisan' faction. Two further groups of communists returned to North Korea following its liberation from the Japanese: one was associated with the Soviet Army and known as the 'Soviet faction', the other came from the Chinese Communist Party (CCP)'s headquarters at Yanan, China, and was under the leadership of Kim Tu Bong of the Korean Independence League. In the early power struggle among the communists, Hyon Chun Hyok, the leader of the 'domestic' faction, was assassinated in September 1945. In the following month Kim Il Sung formed the North Korean Central Bureau of the Korean Communist Party (KCP) in order to consolidate his political position. In this he received covert support from the USSR.

Cho Man Shik organized the Korean Democratic Party (KDP), which received the support of the majority of the people, but his uncompromising stand against the Soviet plan for a five-year trusteeship of the Allied powers led to his downfall in January 1946. He was promptly placed under house arrest, and many members of the KDP fled to South Korea.

After the departure of the nationalists, a North Korean Provisional People's Committee was established in February 1946, with Kim Il Sung as Chairman and Kim Tu Bong as Vice-Chairman. The USSR accorded government status to the Committee. Kim Tu Bong formed the New People's Party (NPP) in March, to expand his power base, and managed to increase his party's membership. In July the North Korean Central Bureau of the KCP and the NPP merged to form the North Korean Workers' Party, with Kim Tu Bong as its Chairman and Kim Il Sung as Vice-Chairman. However, real power rested with the latter.

In early 1947 the Supreme People's Assembly (SPA) was established as the highest legislative body in North Korea, and the Assembly, in turn, established a Central People's Committee to exercise executive authority. The Committee's first major act was to direct land reforms. No real attempts were made to establish collective farms, and the land distributed to landless peasants became the private property of the cultivators. It was not until the end of the Korean War, in 1953, that the agricultural 'co-operativization' programme was inaugurated. Land reform was followed by the nationalization of industry, transport, communications and financial institutions. Since most of these areas had been under Japanese control, their transfer caused few problems.

In early 1948 Pak Hon Yong, with other leaders of the communist South Korean Workers' Party, fled from the South when the party was outlawed by the US occupation authority. Pak, who enjoyed strong support from the 'domestic' faction, felt that he, instead of Kim Il Sung, should lead the movement in Korea. However, he was unable to achieve his objectives, and he grudgingly accepted a position subordinate to that of Kim.

THE ESTABLISHMENT OF THE DEMOCRATIC PEOPLE'S REPUBLIC

After refusing to allow the United Nations Temporary Commission on Korea to visit North Korea and to conduct elections there, Kim Il Sung established a separate, pro-USSR state. In August 1948, elections were held in the North for a new SPA. The newly created Assembly drafted a Constitution, ratified it on 8 September, and proclaimed the Democratic People's Republic of Korea (DPRK) on the following day. Kim Il Sung was named Premier, while Pak Hon Yong was made Vice-Premier and Minister for Foreign Affairs. The establishment of two distinct regimes on the peninsula converted what had been a temporary military division of Korea into a permanent political partition. The USSR announced the withdrawal of its troops from North Korea, completing the process in December 1949. However, a large number of Soviet advisers in various fields, including the military, remained. In June 1949 the merger of the North Korean Workers' Party and the South Korean Workers' Party led to the establishment of a unified communist party, the Korean Workers' Party (KWP), with Kim as its Chairman and Pak as its Vice-Chairman.

During 1950 North Korea substantially increased the size and strength of its armed forces with the help of Soviet supplies. In June the North Korean invasion of the South precipitated the Korean War, resulting in great damage to both sides. (See History up to the Korean War for details of the conflict of 1950–53.) During and after the unsuccessful attempt to reunify the peninsula, Kim Il Sung removed many of his enemies, including Pak Hon Yong. However, conflict among the surviving communist leaders did not end, and Kim Tu Bong remained a formidable figure. Kim Il Sung's economic reconstruction programme, which emphasized the development of heavy industry and which contributed to a devastating famine in 1955–56, encountered strong opposition. The debate lasted until 1956, when Kim Tu Bong fell from power. Meanwhile, in the aftermath of 'de-Stalinization' in the USSR, the 'Yanan' faction condemned the growing personality cult of Kim Il Sung; he counter-attacked, forcing some 'Yanan' communists to flee to China. The USSR and China effected a temporary reconciliation, but leaders of the 'Yanan' faction were systematically relegated to less important posts or eased entirely out of power. By 1958 it had ceased to pose any further threat, and Kim Il Sung continued to consolidate his position of unassailability during the following decade. One side-effect of this struggle was a growing xenophobia in many aspects of life in North Korea, especially in the arts, since many of the more cosmopolitan members of the North Korean élite had come from China.

DEVELOPMENTS DURING THE 1970S

During the 1960s the two Korean states, while urging reunification, had no contacts, and North Korea attempted to destabilize the South on several occasions. However, following growing Soviet-US rapprochement and the beginning of China-US contacts, the two sides established links that led to the announcement in 1972 of a joint North-South agreement to open dialogue for the peaceful unification of the peninsula. To strengthen its position in these negotiations, the KWP proposed amendments to the Constitution. General elections to the fifth SPA were held in December. The newly elected representatives adopted a socialist Constitution, and elected Kim Il Sung and Kim Il as President and Premier, respectively. For the first time, the North Korean Constitution named Pyongyang, not Seoul, as the capital. It also elevated the Central People's Committee, headed by the President, to become the highest organ of state, while an Administration Council, headed by the Premier, was established as the DPRK's cabinet.

In the late 1950s North Korea began to pursue a more active foreign policy, in particular, in competition with South Korea, by attempting to develop relations with the newly independent former colonial states. At the same time it emphasized North Korea's independence, following the withdrawal of the last foreign troops in 1958. By 1973 these policies had begun to produce results, with North Korea gaining observer status at the UN. More importantly, the UN overruled the Korean War-era Commission for the Reunification and Rehabilitation of Korea (UNCURK). UNCURK had assumed that the Government of South Korea was the only lawful government on the Korean peninsula, and this had been used to justify non-recognition of the DPRK by most Western countries. With UNCURK's repeal, a number of Western countries recognized the DPRK, and some established resident diplomatic missions. Both Koreas were invited to the UN General Assembly in November 1973 for a debate on the Korean question. North Korea was also granted membership of the UN Conference on Trade and Development in May of that year.

In February 1974 the Central Committee of the KWP launched the 'Three Great Revolutions': ideological, technical and cultural. It emphasized the promotion of a self-orientated, self-reliant and independent (*Juche*) ideology. The KWP also reorganized the structure of the Administration Council and reorganized its membership twice in 1974. Kim Yong Ju, younger brother of Kim Il Sung, who had been regarded as heir apparent, was demoted in the party hierarchy, while Kim Il Sung's son, Kim Jong Il, rose in rank as a possible successor to his father. Significantly, a military leader, Gen. O Jin U, also rose in rank within the KWP. However, Kim Jong Il's new status was not formally made public; for some years to come, he was not mentioned by name and was referred to only as 'The Party Centre'.

One of North Korea's major objectives in the mid-1970s was the intensification of diplomatic activity to strengthen links with non-aligned countries. The ministerial conference of the non-aligned nations in Lima, Peru, in August 1975 voted to accept North Korea's application for participation.

Economic problems increasingly troubled the Pyongyang regime. Critical shortages of food and commodities were reported in the mid-1970s. Attempts to improve North Korea's industry by importing high-quality machinery from the West foundered following the 1973 oil crisis and the subsequent decline in commodity prices, which affected the North's export trade. Unable to meet its debts, North Korea became the first communist country to default. In 1977 North Korea signed a new trade pact with the People's Republic of China and also an economic and technical co-operation agreement with the USSR. The latter agreement reportedly led to large shipments of Soviet military goods and the deployment of technical advisers to North Korea.

During 1978 an important ideological-political campaign was undertaken to strengthen *Juche* thought. A renewed campaign to promote 'Three Revolutions' in ideology, technology and culture was reportedly led by Kim Jong Il. In April a new socialist labour law was promulgated, which envisaged a change in the way of life for workers—eight hours of work, eight hours of rest, and eight hours of study of Kim Il Sung's *Juche* thought.

The visits to Pyongyang by China's then Premier, Hua Guofeng, and his Vice-Premier, Deng Xiaoping, in 1978, and the trade agreement between North Korea and China, seemed to improve Sino-North Korean relations. China reportedly promised to supply more petroleum and greater economic assistance. Pyongyang proceeded cautiously with regard to the new Sino-US relationship and, while criticizing the Vietnamese invasion of Kampuchea (now Cambodia), eschewed any comments on China's punitive war against Viet Nam.

Nevertheless, the North Korean leadership did not neglect the other major communist power. At the end of the 1970s a new trade agreement with the USSR was reached. Vice-President Pak Song Chol's visit to the Soviet capital in January 1979, and increasing contacts between Soviet and North Korean military leaders, appeared to indicate a growing solidarity between the two countries. North Korea provided special privileges to the USSR in the port of Rajin on the north-eastern coast, making it a Soviet 'leased' territory and a Soviet naval base.

THE EMERGENCE OF KIM JONG IL

After conducting intense campaigns to select reliable and loyal supporters of Kim Il Sung's son, Kim Jong Il, as delegates, the Sixth Congress of the KWP met in early October 1980, the first such congress since 1970. Many significant structural and personnel changes in the party hierarchy were made. Although Kim Jong Il was not officially designated as successor to his father, he became an important member of several crucial committees in the party. A new five-member Standing Committee of the Political Committee (Politburo) of the Central Committee of the KWP was established, with Kim Il Sung as its Chairman, thus strengthening the concentration of power in the hands of a few. Many new members of the Central Committee and its subcommittees were supporters of Kim Jong Il, and it was reported that those who opposed his succession to power were removed from other important positions in the party, Government and military.

In April 1981 elections were held for members of provincial, city and county people's assemblies in the usual manner: one candidate named by the KWP for each position and a 100% turn-out of voters. In February 1982 elections were held to the SPA, and the Seventh Assembly emerged in early April. It approved the reappointment of the President, three Vice-Presidents, the Premier and 13 Vice-Premiers, but failed to name Kim Jong Il as a Vice-President.

Shortly before the convening of the SPA, the Central Committee of the KWP met, followed by a joint conference in mid-April 1982 of the Central Committee and the SPA. Both meetings failed to resolve the question of succession. Meanwhile, the power struggle intensified between the respective supporters of Kim Jong Il and his half-brother, Kim Pyong Il, son of Kim Il Sung's second wife. While the political turmoil surrounding the issue of succession increased instability in North Korea, several armed clashes between the military and workers occurred in Chongjin, in the north-east, in September 1981, followed in June 1982 by civil disturbances in Nampo, near Pyongyang, involving Koreans who had come to North Korea from Japan. Some 500 workers were reported to have been killed in the clashes in the north-eastern regions, while many fled into Soviet territory. For undisclosed reasons, an emergency meeting of the Central Committee of the KWP was convened in April 1982, and it was reported that some 12 generals and a large number of party leaders were removed in July. Furthermore, Choe Hyon, an experienced politician and important member of the Central Committee of the ruling KWP, died in April; there were rumours that he had been murdered. However, Gen. O Jin U, a staunch supporter of Kim Jong Il, was retained as Minister of the People's Armed Forces.

THE 1980s: SURVIVAL OF THE REGIME

Elections were held in March 1983 to choose members for the local people's committees. The second session of the Seventh SPA met in April and elected Rim Chun Chu as Vice-President, succeeding Kang Ryang Uk. At the same time, it elected Yang

Hyong Sop as Chairman of the SPA. Both were believed to be trusted supporters of Kim Jong Il.

The defection of a North Korean airman, with his fighter aircraft, to South Korea in February 1983, a labour uprising in Yanggang (North Hamgyong Province) and mass riots among workers in Wonsan (Kangwon Province) in April indicated serious domestic problems. It was reported that some 500 air force officers had been removed, on charges of disloyalty. As a result of the Rangoon (Yangon) bombing incident of October 1983 (see North-South Relations, below), which was allegedly planned by North Korean agents, the intra-party struggle between moderates and radicals intensified.

In January 1984 Ri Jong Ok was dismissed from the premiership, a post he had held since 1977, and replaced by Kang Song San. Ri became a Vice-President. In early March 1984 Vice-President Kim Il, who had been critical of the junior Kim, died after a long illness. His death effectively marked the conclusion of the period of dominance by the 'old guard' of political leaders who had been associates of Kim Il Sung before he came to power.

In August 1984 North Korea's official radio station confirmed, for the first time in a public broadcast, that Kim Jong Il would succeed his father as President, claiming that the transfer of power had been 'internationally acknowledged'. When the Central Committee met in early December, Kim Il Sung resumed direct control over economic and international affairs, including policy toward South Korea, which had been under the direction of Kim Jong Il. It was reported that there was conflict between the uncompromising, pro-Soviet faction of the junior Kim, and the moderates who had been pro-China.

Frequent changes of personnel in the KWP Politburo and the Administration Council, effected during 1985 and 1986, were interpreted as an indication of North Korea's complex economic problems. In the elections to the Eighth SPA, held in November 1986, (when its 655 members were elected unopposed), Kim Il Sung was re-elected President, and a new Administration Council was formed. Ri Kun Mo, a member of the Central People's Committee, became Premier, replacing Kang Song San.

In February 1988 Gen. Choe Kwang replaced Gen. O Kuk Ryol as Chief of General Staff of the Korean People's Army (KPA). Gen. O was regarded as a close ally of Kim Jong Il. His replacement by Gen. Choe, a veteran associate of Kim Il Sung, led to speculation among foreign observers that the President had strengthened his position to the detriment of his son, possibly owing to a series of economic failures for which the latter was allegedly responsible.

In December 1988 Ri Kun Mo resigned as Premier, reportedly because of ill health, and was replaced by Yon Hyong Muk, a former Vice-Premier and a member of the KWP Politburo. In late 1988 suspicions increased that Kim Il Sung was reclaiming much of Kim Jong Il's power in favour of Kim Pyong Il. However, in April 1989, when the then General Secretary of the CCP, Zhao Ziyang, visited Pyongyang, Kim Jong Il played a conspicuous diplomatic role.

In July 1989 North Korea hosted the 13th World Festival of Youth and Students, both in an attempt to enhance the country's international image, and as a rival event to the Olympic Games held in Seoul in 1988. Earlier demands that North Korea be allowed to share the hosting of Olympic events had come to nothing. More than 15,000 delegates from 165 countries (including one student from South Korea) participated in the festival, which was the largest international event ever staged in North Korea.

The announcement in February 1990 that elections to the SPA would be held on 22 April, six months ahead of schedule, led to renewed speculation that Kim Il Sung was preparing to transfer presidential power to Kim Jong Il. However, in the event Kim Il Sung was re-elected President, although the junior Kim did acquire his first state (as distinct from party) post: in late May he was elected First Vice-Chairman of the National Defence Commission (NDC), a body responsible to the Central People's Committee.

Following the elections to the SPA, the number of seats in the Assembly was increased from 655 to 687. On this occasion the electoral turn-out was put at only 99.78%, rather than the usual 100%, excluding those abroad or at sea. All 100% of those who did vote were claimed to have supported the single approved list of candidates.

CRACKS IN THE MONOLITH

Compared with the momentous developments in inter-Korean and foreign relations (see below), North Korean domestic politics showed few overt signs of change in the early 1990s. Speculation that Kim Jong Il would formally take over from Kim Il Sung intensified in early 1992, when father and son celebrated, respectively, their 80th and 50th birthdays, but once again proved premature. However, the younger Kim's role did become more emphasized, and there was a noticeable intensification of 'loyalty campaigns' for the promotion of his personality cult. In December 1991 Kim Jong Il was appointed Supreme Commander of the KPA, a post hitherto constitutionally reserved for the President. One month later, a major policy statement issued in the junior Kim's name declared North Korea's unwavering allegiance to socialism, including an explicit rebuttal of any market-orientated economic reforms.

Such public continuity and defiance scarcely concealed the pressures for change in a country increasingly isolated and impoverished. Defectors (including the first diplomat ever to do so) revealed that even major enterprises were often inoperative owing to shortages of power and raw materials, and that senior officials were now openly critical of party economic policy. Rumours of unrest also continued. Japanese press reports that young Soviet-trained army officers had, in February 1991, attempted a coup against Kim Jong Il were denied in Pyongyang. Better attested were demonstrations in the north-western border town of Sinuiju in August by 7,000 people, protesting against food shortages and working conditions.

Meanwhile, evidence from the Korean War period appeared to confirm that North Korea had established several concentration camps for political dissidents and 'undesirables' in north-east Korea as early as 1947. By the early 1980s there were reports that more than 100,000 persons, including 23,000 Koreans who had emigrated from Japan to North Korea, were among the internees. Numbers grew during the political manoeuvring that marked the emergence of Kim Jong Il, and in January 1992 a report by the US Department of State estimated that there was a total of 12 concentration camps in North Korea, holding between 105,000 and 150,000 political prisoners.

During 1992 several measures, seemingly designed to quell internal discontent, were adopted by the Government. In February, immediately before Kim Jong Il's customarily lavish birthday celebrations, it was announced that wages were to be increased by an average of 43.4%. Two months later, the SPA approved the budget for 1992, which included an increase of 11.6% in expenditure on social welfare (compared with an increase of only 3.5% in the 1991 budget). Efforts to placate the armed forces were also apparent. In April 1992 the celebrations of Armed Forces Day were given an unusually high profile, and included the first military parade in seven years and promotions for several hundred senior officers. In the same month Kim Il Sung was given the title of Grand Marshal, while his former rank of Marshal was conferred on Kim Jong Il and on O Jin U, Minister of the People's Armed Forces and hitherto Vice-Marshal.

There was a minor reorganization of the Administration Council in December 1992, which included the replacement of Yon Hyong Muk as Premier by Kang Song San, an economist who had previously held the post in 1984–86. His appointment was interpreted by foreign observers as an attempt to provide fresh stimulus for economic reform. However, the fact that Kang was neither seen in public nor mentioned in official news reports for several months subsequently led to speculation that his reputed reformist tendencies had fallen foul of close confidants of Kim Jong Il.

Two further promotions at the same time raised hopes of a liberalization in Pyongyang. Both Vice-Premier Kim Tal Hyon and Kim Yong Sun attained candidate (alternate) membership of the Politburo. Moreover, the former, who had impressed his hosts during a business-orientated visit to South Korea in July 1992, relinquished responsibility for external economic affairs to become Chairman of the State Planning Commission. In April 1993 Kim Yong Sun, who (as the KWP's international secretary) had also impressed foreign opinion, replaced Choe Thae Bok as the party's secretary for reunification. However, initial hopes for a new openness proved unfounded, as from late 1992 North Korea reverted to the adoption of a more uncompromising stance.

In October 1992 the SPA adopted three new laws on foreign investment and joint ventures. However, the overall commitment to centrally planned socialism remained unchanged, and indeed was constantly reaffirmed. Meanwhile, certain constitutional amendments had been made in April 1992, although they were not published (except several months later in South Korea). Principal among the changes were the deletion of the last remaining references to Marxism-Leninism, and the upgrading of the NDC (now chaired by Kim Jong Il, and the highest military organ of state power) to become the most senior executive body below the President.

The first party youth congress for 12 years was held in February 1993, amid fulsome pledges of loyalty to both the 'Great Leader' (Kim Il Sung) and the 'Dear Leader' (Kim Jong Il). Both Kim Il Sung's birthday and that of his son were much less lavishly celebrated in 1993 than in the previous year. Kim Jong Il was not seen in public between late April and late July, when he re-emerged for the 40th anniversary of what North Korea proclaims as its 'victory' in the Korean War. There were reports that he had been treated for a heart condition (related to his alleged unhealthy lifestyle). An intriguing alternative version was that he had suffered a nervous breakdown after an upbraiding by his father on account of various policy errors, above all North Korea's threatened withdrawal from the Treaty on the Non-Proliferation of Nuclear Weapons (see Foreign Relations, below).

Important economic and political changes took place at the end of 1993. In what may have been the first admission ever of failure by North Korea, the KWP Central Committee announced, in early December, that the Seven-Year Plan (1987–93) had not been fulfilled. It was to be followed by a three-year 'adjustment period', giving priority to agriculture, light industry and foreign trade. As scapegoat for these economic failures, Kim Tal Hyon was removed from his post of Chairman of the State Planning Commission and reportedly allocated the even more onerous task of directing the Sunchon Vinalon Works—a perennially underperforming favourite project of Kim Il Sung. His replacement was the previously unknown Hong Sok Hyong, who formerly managed the Kimchaek Iron and Steel Complex (the largest in the country).

What attracted most attention was the return to political life of Kim Il Sung's younger brother, Kim Yong Ju, after a 17-year absence, as both a full member of the Politburo and one of four state Vice-Presidents. Kim Yong Ju's reappearance now was interpreted less as the emergence of a rival to Kim Jong Il than as evidence of a continuing need to bolster the 'Dear Leader' as successor, with the overt backing of such a senior figure. Also appointed as Vice-President was Kim Pyong Shik, a returnee from Japan, who earlier in 1993 had assumed the chairmanship of the 'puppet' Korean Social Democratic Party.

The hardships of ordinary North Koreans, meanwhile, intensified, and in 1994 the small number of defectors increased both in quantity and 'quality', the latter including two sons-in-law of government ministers. All gave a grim account of deteriorating economic conditions and strict political control. The former was confirmed by the 1994 budget, which for the second successive year anticipated only modest increases in expenditure. However, it was revealed that actual spending on social services in 1993 had needed to be greater than that originally budgeted for.

THE DEATH OF KIM IL SUNG AND BEYOND

Questions as to how long the world's last remaining Stalinist regime could endure unchanged acquired a sharp new focus in mid-1994. On 8 July, after almost 46 years in power, Kim Il Sung died, reportedly of a heart attack. Amid extraordinary scenes of mass mourning, Kim Jong Il was named as head of the funeral committee and, as in the past, he was generally referred to as the inheritor of his father's work. North Korea's first year without its founding 'Great Leader' presented a mixture of continuity and ambiguity. Continuity was evident in the style of the regime, where internally the cult of Kim Il Sung continued unabated, culminating in his embalmed body being placed on display in his former palace, now referred to as the 'holy land of *Juche*'. There was continuity, too, in personnel, with few major new appointments among the ruling élite. The second most powerful member of the regime, Marshal O Jin U, died in February 1995; his successor as Minister of the People's Armed Forces, Marshal Choe Kwang, was announced only in October. North Korea's stance toward the wider world also displayed elements of continuity, with characteristic militancy of rhetoric shown toward South Korea, Japan and the USA.

However, there was also growing ambiguity in North Korean political life. More than a year after the death of Kim Il Sung, his son and heir-presumptive, Kim Jong Il, had still not been officially appointed to any of the three leading posts: General Secretary of the KWP, state President, and Chairman of the party's Central Military Commission. This was not the only failure of due process. Elections to the SPA (due to have been held by April 1995) did not take place, and the Assembly (still operational, albeit technically unconstitutional) failed to hold its annual meeting to consider the state budget. Amid increasingly unconvincing excuses of the need to observe a period of national mourning, the official media continued to treat Kim Jong Il as de facto leader, particularly in 1995, referring to him as the 'Great Leader'. Kim remained as reclusive as ever. His appearances were confined mainly to army units and military occasions, which suggested that Kim's acceptance by the armed forces was not yet complete. The rise to prominence in early 1995 of several Vice-Marshals of the KPA, who were believed to be sympathetic to Kim, was interpreted as a further attempt by Kim to enhance his prestige among the military. Meanwhile, speculation continued that Kim was in poor health. There were renewed rumours of coup attempts and popular unrest.

Nevertheless, there were signs of attempts to change. These included an international sports festival, held in Pyongyang in April 1995, which was attended by several thousand foreign visitors. More substantially, the nuclear agreement with the USA, signed in October 1994 (see below), gradually began to be implemented in the ensuing months, despite many difficulties. North Korea also expanded efforts to attract foreign (including South Korean) firms to invest in its only free economic and trade zone, at Rajin-Sonbong (renamed Rason following an administrative reorganization in 2004), in the north-east of the country. However, hopes for a more general turn toward economic reform, as in China and Viet Nam, remained unfulfilled. Rather, works by Kim Jong Il continued to inveigh against private ownership, pluralism and any effort to 'pollute' pure socialism.

Kim Jong Il continued to be treated by the media as de facto leader, and to appear periodically, both at major state occasions and local 'guidance' visits. There were several indications that the military was in the ascendant. In October 1995 the 50th anniversary of the KWP was celebrated more as an army than a party affair. At official events, senior Vice-Marshals were given higher precedence than party and state representatives. One of these, Kim Kwang Jin, made two extremely bellicose speeches in March and July 1996, warning that it was only a matter of time before an inter-Korean war broke out, and threatening that North Korea would be the first to attack. However, in other respects, such as the nuclear issue (see below), North Korea was pragmatic and co-operative.

There was little overt sign of the problems attendant upon any political succession. Two senior leaders, Vice-President Kim Yong Ju and Premier Kang Song San, hardly appeared in public in the first half of 1996; yet in July both were cited as still in office, with their membership of the Politburo intact. Kim Jong Il was said to favour some Vice-Ministers, such as the First Deputy Minister of Foreign Affairs, Kang Sok Ju, who seemed to be acting as Minister—for example, with regard to nuclear negotiations—while his nominal superior, Kim Yong Nam, appeared on ceremonial occasions.

The uncertainties over the situation in North Korea were not confined to the higher echelons of society. Ordinary citizens saw their already spartan living standards further eroded as the economy, still unreformed, contracted throughout the 1990s. Furthermore, the main farming areas in the west of the country were badly damaged in August 1995 by the worst floods of the century, forcing the 'hermit kingdom' to appeal for help from the international community. Foreign aid workers were given unprecedented access to the country, and were impressed by the degree of organization of the Government and the stoicism of the people, despite ever-worsening living conditions. Further flooding in mid-1996 threatened to exacerbate an already critical situation.

Despite earlier indications, the third anniversary of Kim Il Sung's death passed in July 1997 without the formal inauguration of Kim Jong Il. However, the mourning period was officially declared to be over, prompting renewed speculation that the junior Kim would soon succeed his father officially, although some analysts regarded it as too risky to essay the pomp and circumstance of a 'coronation' while the country suffered serious famine. Nevertheless, in April Kim Jong Il presided over a typical parade in Pyongyang, taking the salute (in front of Western television cameras, for the first time) from soldiers of the KPA.

The long-delayed reorganization seemed to be under way in February 1997, when the defection of a senior party official, Hwang Jang Yop (see North-South Relations, below), was followed by the death of the Minister of the People's Armed Forces, Marshal Choe Kwang, and that of his deputy, Kim Kwang Jin, a few days later. The latter was replaced by the head of the navy, Vice-Marshal Kim Il Chol, who by late 1998 had also assumed the responsibilities of Choe Kwang. The most powerful man in the military was evidently Vice-Marshal Jo Myong Rok, head of the KPA Political Bureau and Kim Jong Il's constant companion.

Meanwhile, North Korea's condolences on the death of the Chinese leader, Deng Xiaoping, in February 1997 were sent by Hong Song Nam as acting Premier, implying that Kang Song San had been dismissed. The impression that other changes had taken place was strengthened by the composition of Choe Kwang's funeral committee, from which several senior pro-reform officials were absent. Besides Kang, these included the former Premier, Yon Hyong Muk, and the Minister of the Metal Industry, Choe Yong Rim. However, all these absentees subsequently reappeared (if briefly) at major ceremonies in April and July. To mark the third anniversary of the passing of the 'Great Leader', North Korea introduced a new *Juche* calendar, starting from 1912, his year of birth.

From late 1997 there were some signs of the development of political normalization, at least by North Korea's own standards. The official rationale was that, following the end of the three years of official mourning for Kim Il Sung, normal life could now resume. Thus, on 8 October, Kim Jong Il at last assumed one of his late father's two vacant posts, becoming General Secretary of the KWP. However, the manner of his elevation was unorthodox, being by acclamation at a series of provincial party conferences, rather than through election by the Central Committee, as laid down in the KWP's rules. There was still no sign that the Central Committee had actually met since Kim Il Sung's death. However, elections for the SPA, which should have been held in 1995, finally took place on 26 July 1998. The electorate was presented with a single list of candidates, which it reportedly endorsed unanimously: some 99.85% of electors voted (that is, all North Koreans except those who were abroad or at sea), and fully 100% of voters were declared to have supported the candidates.

The 10th SPA was duly convened in September 1998, the 50th anniversary of the foundation of the DPRK, but the expected and long-awaited appointment of Kim Jong Il as President did not take place. In an unexpected development, the Constitution was amended to elevate Kim Il Sung posthumously to the rank of 'Eternal President' and thus perpetual Head of State. The chairmanship of the NDC (the highest military office, to which Kim Jong Il had been re-elected, having stood for election in a military constituency) was defined as the most senior position in the state hierarchy. Kim Jong Il consequently assumed the role of de facto Head of State, while remaining overshadowed by the legacy of his father. The 10th SPA, like the Ninth, had 687 members. Usually the number increases at each election, so there was speculation that famine had taken its toll on population growth. Of the 687 members, as many as 443 (or 64%) were new, indicating that Kim Jong Il was at last able to promote his own generation and supporters. Military predominance was striking, with some 50 younger generals included among the new deputies. The composition of the assembly was also a guide to the ongoing power struggles in Pyongyang. Absentees included Kim Song Ae, Kim Il Sung's widow (and Kim Jong Il's stepmother); Kang Song San, at last officially replaced as Premier by Hong Song Nam (as part of the extensive government reorganization of September); and several officials who in the past had handled relations with South Korea, including Kim Tal Hyon (who had been regarded as a possible candidate for the premiership). On the other hand, Vice-President Kim Yong Ju, Kim Jong Il's uncle and once his rival for the succession, retained an SPA seat despite having maintained a low profile since the death of his brother, Kim Il Sung.

Several reports claimed that So Kwan Hi, the long-serving party secretary for agriculture, had been executed during late 1997, presumably having been held responsible for the ongoing food crisis. The head of the youth league, Choe Ryong Hae (a friend of Kim Jong Il since childhood), was removed in January 1998 after reports that several youth league officials had been executed for spying for South Korea. It was reported in October that Kim Jong U, formerly the reformist Chairman of the DPRK Committee for the Promotion of External Economic Co-operation, had been executed.

In April 1999 the SPA resumed the annual sessions to consider the budget, which had lapsed since the death of Kim Il Sung in 1994. Unusually, some 50 of the newly elected members were absent, prompting speculation that further dismissals had occurred. The budget itself gave only broad assessments, but these revealed that both revenue and expenditure had declined by one-half in the five years since figures were last published: a fact that passed almost without comment. The SPA approved a new economic planning law during the same session. Several other economic laws were also announced during 1999, covering specific areas such as agriculture, forestry, and even fish-breeding. Most of this legislation appeared to codify rather than alter existing arrangements, and gave the impression of a 'rearguard action' by the centre, to try to exert control over an economy which had become increasingly anarchic, as the long-standing system of the planned economy had disintegrated. The revised Constitution of September 1998 gave slightly more scope to private enterprise and market forces, but the amendments failed to keep pace with the actual situation, even though in theory the DPRK remained bonded to communism and hostile to any explicit market reforms. In June 1999 a major policy statement proclaimed a 'military-first' policy, giving defence absolute priority.

Kim Jong Il himself remained elusive, although his 'on the spot guidance' broadened from visits to military bases to include more economic sites (many of them run by the military). He continued to delegate the task of meeting foreigners to Kim Yong Nam, the former Minister of Foreign Affairs, in his new capacity as President of the SPA Presidium. From mid-2000, however, Kim Jong Il adopted a less reclusive attitude and a startling change of image, if only for the purposes of external display. Within two months he met the heads of state of China, South Korea and Russia, while his polite but affable manner at the North-South summit meeting, which took place in mid-June, impressed television viewers in South Korea.

In early 2001 Kim Jong Il undertook a business-orientated visit to Shanghai, China (see below); this was followed by his publication of maxims emphasizing the need to adapt to new times. However, by late 2001 none of this had been implemented. In fact, the year was largely devoid of overt domestic political activity of any kind. In April the SPA met for just one day, instead of the usual three. As well as approving a budget, the few figures of which suggested that the economy might have stabilized, the SPA ratified laws on copyright and the processing trade, although no details of these were given. This failure to change suggested fierce internal debate. Seoul press sources reported that Kim Yong Sun, the party secretary in charge of dialogue with South Korea, had spent a week under arrest in March before Kim Jong Il ordered his release. The implication was that the initial hostility of the new US Administration under President George W. Bush undermined North Korea's more reform-minded officials and strengthened the position of its 'hard-liners': this interpretation was supported by the suspension of talks with South Korea (see below). Meanwhile, the world had its first glimpse of Kim Jong Nam, son of the 'Dear Leader' and reputed heir: in a bizarre incident in May the young Kim and his family were detained on entering Japan at Narita airport, having been found to be travelling under false names and on fake Dominican Republic passports. They admitted their identity, stated that they hoped to visit the Disneyland theme park, and were swiftly deported to Beijing.

In March 2002 the Kim Il Sung Socialist Youth League met for the first time in six years. Amid much emphasis on the need to inherit revolutionary traditions, no details were announced. In April it became known that Shin Il Nam, hitherto a Vice-Minister of People's Security, had been appointed as Vice-Premier and Chairman of the Commission for Capital Construction. In August Japanese sources reported that another of Kim Jong Il's sons, Kim Hyon (also known as Kim Hyon Nam), had been appointed head of the KWP's propaganda and agitation department.

The year 2002 also witnessed two major anniversaries: Kim Jong Il's 60th birthday—in Korea an important event, called *hwan'gap*— in February, and the 90th anniversary of his late father's birth, in April. Both were celebrated with the usual lavish displays. This ceremonial mode continued with North Korea's largest ever mass arts and gymnastics festival, *Arirang*, held from May to August. Despite denials, this appeared as if it was intended to counter the football World Cup in South Korea; yet poor marketing meant that few foreign visitors attended. Substantive politics was harder to discern. As previously, the SPA convened for just a single day, in March. Besides approving the budget, it discussed an (unrevealed) 'organizational matter', and approved a law on land management, thought to be aimed at curbing illicit private use of land and resources, a practice that had spread since the famine of the late 1990s.

The latter part of 2002, however, brought radical changes in economic management. No formal announcements had been made; officials, when pressed, spoke of 'perfecting socialism'. Thus, the full scope of the innovations was unclear. Their core consisted of drastic increases in prices, broadly to match those in the 'black market', and concomitant—but lesser, and uneven—wage increases. Some subsidies remained in place, but in general people and firms alike were thenceforth required to pay, and firms allowed to charge, the real cost of goods and services.

In 2003 domestic politics was overshadowed by the growing nuclear crisis (see Foreign Relations). The year began in militant style, with a joint editorial of the three main daily newspapers hailing the 'Great Banner of Army-Based Policy' and warning soldiers to 'combat illusion about the enemy and peace'. State television reported in mid-January that of Kim Jong Il's 207 'on-the-spot guidance' visits in the previous year, more than half (120) were to military units. In brief mention of the economy, the New Year joint editorial envisioned 'the largest profitability while firmly adhering to socialist principles'. As nuclear tensions grew, Kim Jong Il disappeared from public view for seven weeks between February and April. He thus missed the celebrations for his 61st birthday on 16 February, and, unusually, the annual SPA spring session in late March. As had become the norm, the SPA met for just one day, which sufficed to approve both that year's budget and the report by the Minister of Finance on the previous year's budget. Mun Il Bong provided information only in percentages terms, presumably because of problems in reconciling data before and after the massive devaluation of July 2002. For 2003, a planned rise in spending of 14.4% was to be financed by North Korea's first bond issue in half a century. This was unlikely to be voluntary, suggesting yet another effort by the regime to gain access to private household savings. The SPA also adopted five items of legislation previously approved by its Presidium (which continued to meet when the SPA was not in session): on military service, city planning, accounting, rivers, and 'structures'. Conditions of military service were said to have been eased, but with action against draft evaders.

In February 2003 South Korean sources claimed that a campaign was under way to promote another of Kim Jong Il's sons, Kim Jong Chul (born in 1981) as his heir. A KPA study document in August 2002 praised an unnamed 'respected mother' who 'assists the comrade supreme commander closest to his body'. This was interpreted as a reference to Kim Jong Il's partner, Ko Yong Hui, a returnee from Japan, former dancer and Kim Jong Chul's mother. Little was known of Kim Jong Chul, except that he had studied in Switzerland and was said to hold an important post in the KWP's agitation and propaganda department. Kim Jong Il's marital history appeared complex, with reports of at least two other sons by different partners.

In early August 2003 elections for the SPA, as well as provincial and local councils, were held. Unlike the last SPA election in 1998, which was three years late, this reverted to the five-yearly intervals stipulated in the Constitution. Typically, a 99.9% turnout was proclaimed—only those abroad or 'working on the far-off seas' could not participate—and 100% reportedly voted for the single list of candidates. Kim Jong Il cast his ballot at Kim Il Sung Military University, whose candidate was a KPA officer. The 'Dear Leader' himself was elected by another military constituency; he apologized to voters elsewhere that the rules forbade him to accept the nominations which all 686 other constituencies had unanimously bestowed upon him. As in 1998, at least half the deputies were reported to be new members. Separately, in July 2003 the elderly Minister of People's Security, Paek Hak Rim, had been replaced by Choe Ryong Su, whose background was unknown. Other posts rotated in 2003 included the Ministry of Education, where Kim Yong Jin replaced Pyon Yong Rip, and the heads of the Sinuiju and Kaesong special economic zones and of Nampo, the port for Pyongyang. It was believed that this last trio of appointments might lead to more economic opening. In an important development, in June, the role of markets had for the first time been officially acknowledged; the official Korean Central News Agency (KCNA) carried a photograph of a large covered market under construction in Pyongyang.

When the 11th SPA convened a month after its election, on 3 September 2003, it endorsed a partial cabinet reorganization, mainly of economic portfolios. Pak Pong Ju, hitherto Minister of Chemical Industry, replaced Hong Song Nam as Premier. In his former post Pak had visited South Korea in 2002 in an economic delegation, impressing his hosts. Also on that trip were Pak Nam Gi, who moved from managing the State Planning Commission (SPC) to chairing the SPA budget committee; and Kim Kwang Rin, promoted from SPC Vice-Chairman to replace him. Two new Vice-Premiers were appointed: the little-known Ro Tu Chol and Jon Sung Hun, who was previously Minister of Metal and Machine-Building Industries; he was replaced by his Vice-Minister, Kim Sung Hyon.

There were changes, too, on the NDC (which outranked the Cabinet). Three aged generals left the body. They were replaced by the new Minister of People's Security, Choe Ryong Su, and by a hitherto unknown official, Paek Se Bong. Yon Hyong Muk, a former Premier and rare civilian on the NDC, became a Vice-Chairman; he replaced the Minister of the People's Armed Forces, Vice-Marshal Kim Il Chol, who remained an ordinary member of the Commission.

As the full SPA met for only a few days each year, if that, most legislative business continued to be conducted by its Presidium. The latter's officials were unchanged, but four of the 11 ordinary members were new. Most notable was a return by Hong Sok Hyong, a former chief planner and alternate Politburo member, appointed party secretary in North Hamgyong in the north-east, the province worst affected by famine and the source of most migrants to China. Other new members were Kim Kyong Ho, secretary of the youth league, which underwent a major reorganization; Pak Sun Hui, who chaired the women's union; and Pyon Yong Rip, the former Minister of Education who had moved earlier in the year to head the Academy of Sciences. Of the four Presidium members ousted, only one was known to have transferred to a new post: Ri Kil Song, formerly party secretary in South Pyongan province, was appointed as Procurator-General.

Soon after the SPA meeting, Kim Jong Il again disappeared from public view. After the DPRK 55th anniversary ceremonies on 9 September 2003, he was not seen again until 21 October, having missed, unusually, the KWP's 58th anniversary, on 10 October. Once more rumours abounded: that his consort Ko Yong Hui was ill with cancer, and that a power struggle was taking place for the succession between Kim Jong Chul and another hitherto unknown son, Kim Jong Un, aged only 20. According to a book by Kim Jong Il's former sushi chef, Kenji Fujimoto, the 'Dear Leader' favoured the latter. Questions were also raised by the death of one of Kim Jong Il's closest aides, the urbane and able Kim Yong Sun, in October 2003. A party secretary and long-serving senior diplomat, Kim had latterly been in charge of North-South links. He had been in a coma since a road accident in June

In April 2004 Japanese reports claimed that Kim Jong Il's brother-in-law Jang Song Thaek, hitherto a close confidant, had been demoted following a disagreement with the Premier. Jang had reportedly criticized recent reforms as inviting 'unhealthy ideas from outside'. Jang was not part of Kim Jong Il's entourage when he visited Beijing in April. Ambivalence over reform was evident at the SPA's usual spring meeting to review the budget, in March, when not a single meaningful figure was given, but only a few percentages. Premier Pak Pong Ju emphasized the importance of profitability—alongside socialism and 'the fighting trait and working method created by the People's Army', with priority going to the defence industry.

In April 2004 a serious railway explosion occurred at Ryongchon, near the Chinese border, just hours after Kim Jong Il had passed through on his way back from Beijing by train. Initial reports claimed 3,000 casualties, but the eventual official toll was 161 dead and more than 1,300 injured. This might have been lower, had the Government accepted international aid immediately. Nevertheless, for a state where news of accidents was routinely suppressed, the fact that North Korea allowed access to foreign aid workers two days after the accident represented some progress. The official account stated that this had been a shunting accident: a short circuit had ignited flammable cargoes of fuel and fertilizer. However, rumours of foul play were rife. A ban in May on mobile telephones (the use of which had been permitted only 18 months previously) was interpreted by some as reflecting suspicions that such a device had been used to trigger the explosion. A less conspiratorial view was that Kim Jong Il's special train had disrupted the usual timetables, thus contributing to the accident. Given the dire condition of North Korea's rail network and other infrastructure, the catastrophe was not unexpected. Yet the dismissal in July of the Minister of People's Security, Choe Ryong Su, after just a year in office suggested that concerns remained in this area. His successor was an army general, Ju Sang Song.

THE RISE OF KIM JONG UN AND OTHER DEVELOPMENTS

In the latter half of 2004 there were rumours of tensions in Pyongyang, especially in relation to the eventual succession to Kim Jong Il. In September there were reports that the 'Dear Leader's main consort, Ko Yong Hui, had died aged 51, probably in July and from cancer. In November claims that Kim Jong Il's portrait was no longer to be seen in Pyongyang prompted speculation of a power struggle. Amid (unusually) conflicting comments in official media, the truth seemed to be that some portraits had been removed in sites frequented by foreigners, but elsewhere his visage remained ubiquitous.

Subsequently, reports from Austria claimed that in November 2004 a plot had been foiled there to assassinate Kim Jong Il's eldest son, Kim Jong Nam. Rarely seen since his unmasking in Japan in 2001, in December 2004 the latter (or someone purporting to be him) made e-mail contact with Japanese journalists who had previously encountered him at Beijing airport and given him their business cards. Admitting that he was based mainly abroad, he denied being in exile but would not divulge what work he did. Regarding the succession, he said that no decision had been made but that his father's word would be final. These communications stopped abruptly after four days. There was speculation about rivalries between Kim Jong Nam and his younger half-brothers Kim Jong Chul and Kim Jong Un, sons of the late Ko Yong Hui. A further contender was thought to be Kim Hyon Nam, a natural son of the late Kim Il Sung by a nurse, later adopted by Kim Jong Il's brother-in-law, Jang Song Thaek. The latter's demotion in 2004 might therefore, it was thought, have been connected to the issue of succession as well as policy differences. Other reports suggested that Kim Sol Song, daughter of the 'Dear Leader' by his official wife, Kim Yong Suk, was also a potential successor. A trained economist, she was observed to accompany her father in 'on-the-spot guidance' visits and to provide him with advice.

There were signs of unrest in 2005 among the traditionally quiescent populace, as well as among the élite. In January a South Korean non-governmental organization (NGO) released what it claimed were the first videotaped images of dissent in the North, including anti-regime posters and an interview with an alleged dissident. Some in Seoul questioned the tape's authenticity. Separately, the Japanese television channel NTT acquired a film apparently showing grim scenes (but no dissent) in the north-eastern city of Chongjin, including alcoholism among street children and public trials for rape, prostitution and robbery. Yet another video, broadcast in Japan in March, appeared to show two public executions of men who had tried to organize defections from North Korea. Official politics, meanwhile, remained largely ceremonial. There were the customary celebrations for Kim Jong Il's birthday in February and for Kim Il Sung's in April. For unexplained reasons, the SPA's regular spring session, scheduled for 9 March, was postponed at short notice; it was eventually held on 11 April. Kim Jong Il attended, having been absent in 2004. The 'Dear Leader' apart, the only dignitaries named as attending were Kim Yong Nam, Jo Myong Rok and Pak Pong Ju. For the third consecutive year, neither the Premier's economic report nor the budget speech contained a single solid statistic, suggesting that any reforms had been limited.

In the latter half of 2005 the 60th anniversaries of two major events were celebrated: the liberation of the Korean peninsula from Japanese occupation (on 15 August) and the foundation of the KWP (on 10 October). To mark the former, the *Arirang* mass gymnastics festival, held in 2002 to commemorate Kim Jong Il's 60th birthday and the 90th anniversary of the birth of his father Kim Il Sung (see above), was revived and enlarged. In July 2005 the KWP's Central Committee and Central Military Commission issued some 185 new slogans. The overall tenor of these slogans was old-fashioned, triumphalist and militarist, disappointing those who hoped that North Korea's political system might be in the process of change. By contrast, foreign tourists—including categories usually banned such as journalists and US citizens—were allowed entry in unprecedented numbers to see *Arirang*.

Yon Hyong Muk, Vice-Chairman of the NDC and a former premier, died of cancer in October 2005. Regarded as a reformer, he was the senior civilian on the NDC. No replacement was announced. Typically for North Korea, other personnel changes were largely unsignalled, instead emerging incidentally in news reports. Thus at some point in 2005 Kang Min Chol replaced Ri Kwang Nam as Minister of Extractive Industries, while Jo Pyong Ju became Minister for Machine Building; perhaps at the end of May, when this portfolio was separated from the metals industry.

Other senior officials may have been removed. Party secretary Jong Ha Chol, the hitherto prominent director of the KWP's agitation and propaganda department, was last cited in reports in October 2005. Paek Se Bong, unknown when he suddenly joined the NDC in 2003 and largely unheard of since, appeared to have been accorded an inferior position on Yon Hyong Muk's funeral committee, suggesting a demotion. The Minister of Finance, Mun Il Bong, had last been heard of in September 2005, visiting Mongolia. In April 2006 he failed to present the customary budget report at the SPA. That task fell instead to Vice-Premier Ro Tu Chol, an increasingly important official who had also led a delegation to China in December 2005, signing a US $500m. agreement on the joint exploitation of undersea petroleum.

The most significant change was the return of Jang Song Thaek, Kim Jong Il's brother-in-law and former 'right-hand man'. Removed in late 2003, Jang reappeared in January 2006 in a slightly less senior Party post than before. The North Korean media did not report that in March Jang led a delegation to China, which retraced Kim's own recent itinerary there. It was unclear if this rehabilitation meant that Jang was now politically subordinate to Kim or whether he was too powerful to be marginalized.

In November 2006 Kye Ung Thae, a full Politburo member who as party secretary for national security had been one of the most powerful members of the regime, died; he had not been seen since April 2004. In January 2007 the Minister of Foreign Affairs, Paek Nam Sun, also died. In that post since 1998, his role was mainly ceremonial, but not wholly: a week-long visit to China in May–June 2006 had looked substantive. (Paek had also briefly met the US Secretary of State, Colin Powell, at the Association of Southeast Asian Nations (ASEAN) Regional Forum (ARF) in Brunei in August 2002, the first North Korean Minister of Foreign Affairs ever to do so. Earlier, Paek had been active in the first inter-Korean talks, which began in the 1970s; he was then known as Paek Nam Jun.) However, two of Paek's nominal deputies assumed responsibility for serious matters: Kang Sok Ju, who negotiated the 1994 Agreed Framework with the USA, and Kim Kye Gwan, the chief delegate to the six-party talks on nuclear issues (see below). In that sense Paek's death was not as untimely as might have been feared, removed as he was from policy-making at the highest level, whereas both Kang and Kim were said to report directly to Kim Jong Il. Paek's replacement, who was not named until mid-May 2007, was the elderly Pak Ui Chun, who from 1998 to 2006 had served as ambassador in Moscow, where he had been authorized to speak freely on current issues.

In April 2007 the SPA met as usual for a single day and approved another opaque budget. Premier Pak Pong Ju was unexpectedly replaced by Kim Yong Il, Minister of Land and Marine Transport since 1994. It was speculated that Pak had been dismissed for being too outspoken about his pro-reform or pro-China stance, or corrupt. His little-known successor seemed a curious choice, the transport sector having been an area that had attracted regular criticism. The SPA also appointed Vice-Marshal Kim Yong Chun, the KPA Chief of General Staff, as a Vice-Chairman of the NDC, a belated replacement for Yon Hyong Muk. Kim's successor as Chief of General Staff was a relatively unknown General, Kim Kyok Sik. The fact that the position of Vice-Chairman of the NDC had become a full-time post implied an upgrading of the body: hitherto a committee (albeit powerful) of persons whose main function lay elsewhere, the NDC was now acquiring its own staff. Thus, at a Russian embassy reception in Pyongyang in August 2007, it was Kim Yong Chun—evidently outranking Minister of Foreign Affairs Pak Ui Chun, despite the latter's many years' experience in Moscow—who gave a speech. The party also included Jon Hui Jong, described as director of the NDC's foreign affairs department (it was not previously known to have one) and listed above a Vice-Minister of Foreign Affairs, Kung Sok Ung. Jon was a former ambassador to Egypt, and his transfer from the Ministry of Foreign Affairs to the NDC appeared to confirm the latter's rise as a bureaucracy in its own right. Two other important officials were Gen. Hyon Chol Hae, former vice-director of the KPA General Political Bureau, who moved to the post of NDC vice-director in 2003; and Gen. Ri Myong Su, the KPA's former operations director, who had recently been appointed to the NDC.

Although the 'Dear Leader' reportedly banned all discussion of the succession issue, strong rumours that he had a heart operation in May 2007 (a German medical team visiting Pyongyang) appeared to be confirmed by subsequent photographs that showed him looking distinctly more gaunt. However, he seemingly made a good recovery, and the number and frequency of his 'on-the-spot guidance' visits increased during the first half of 2008. On 9 April the SPA met for the customary one day. This sufficed to hear an economic report and to approve a budget that as ever contained no precise figures. Kim Jong Il was absent from the proceedings, as was, for the third consecutive year, the Minister of Finance, Mun Il Bong, seemingly having been removed but not replaced. Vice-Premier Ro Tu Chol delivered the budget speech.

The next election to the SPA was due to take place in August 2008. However, amid much speculation the event was postponed. It was subsequently reported that in that month Kim Jong Il had suffered another medical emergency, rumoured to have been a stroke. Kim's absence from the official parade for the 60th anniversary of the founding of the DPRK on 9 September prompted further conjecture, and in subsequent photographs he appeared visibly frail. Despite official reports that Kim's 'on-the-spot guidance' visits in the first half of 2009 were more numerous than ever, speculation persisted that he was unwell. None the less, he received former US President Bill Clinton in August, by which time he appeared to be in command both of his faculties and of the State.

Kim Jong Il's illness had two main political effects. The first was a more bellicose foreign policy stance (see below). The reasons for this were unclear, although some postulated that it might reflect the ascendancy of belligerent military personnel, or be an attempt to deflect attention at a time of great vulnerability for the regime were Kim to die with no successor in place. The second effect, not before time, was to accelerate the process of choosing a political heir. As with Kim's illness, there was no official word from Pyongyang, but by mid-2009 most sources agreed that leadership would be conferred upon Kim's youngest and least-known son, Kim Jong Un, who was just 26 years old. This was confirmed by his half-brother Kim Jong Nam, who in recent years had lived mainly in Macao and who, as the eldest son of the 'Dear Leader', had previously been considered the most likely successor. However, in a series of increasingly unorthodox (but never overtly critical) interviews with Japanese and other media, Kim Jong Nam explicitly ruled himself out as a potential successor to his father.

In early 2009 there was a partial return to some degree of political normality in Pyongyang, as well as some significant changes. In January it was announced that the overdue election for the SPA was to be held on 8 March. In February Vice-Marshal Kim Yong Chun was appointed as Minister of the People's Armed Forces in place of Kim Il Chol, who was demoted to the position of First Vice-Minister at the country's equivalent of a ministry of defence. Gen. Ri Yong Ho replaced Gen. Kim Kyok Sik, who had been in office for less than two years, as Chief of General Staff of the KPA. Also in February O Kuk Ryol was appointed as Vice-Chairman of the NDC. Vice-Marshal O Kuk Ryol, the KPA's most senior general and ranked second only to Kim Jong Il on the KWP's Central Military Commission, had been out of public view for more than a decade, although he had retained an important post as strategy chief of the KWP Central Committee. A former air force commander, O Kuk Ryol as Chief of Staff 30 years previously had played a vital role in consolidating Kim Jong Il's position in relation to the KPA, which had been suspicious of his lack of military experience. O Kuk Ryol's return to a prominent position suggested that his skills were once again needed to effect an even more difficult succession on behalf of the young and hitherto untested Kim Jong Un. Unusually, details of these KPA changes were announced publicly.

The SPA election was duly held on 8 March 2009, following which it was announced that 99.98% of the electorate had voted, apparently every registered voter except those 'staying abroad or working in oceans'; and that 100% of voters had cast their ballot in favour of the single candidate in each constituency. That North Korea could still carry off such a procedure, despite the uncertainty surrounding the country's leadership and despite the privation of the populace, was testament to the regime's control of power. Kim Jong Il was again elected by a military constituency, having issued his standard apology for having had to decline offers from all 686 other constituencies to nominate him. Despite speculation, none of his sons was elected, unless under a pseudonym (which was possible). Of those elected, 43.5% were newcomers to the SPA, which remained an important channel through which to draw fresh members into the system, while the ruling élite aged and while party institutions like the Central Committee no longer appeared to function.

The newly elected 12th SPA convened on 9 April 2009, for its customary one-day session. Kim Jong Il attended, and in a television broadcast of the event he appeared haggard. The session was revealing in several ways. Unusually, a list of the full Cabinet was published; this showed that 14 out of the 37 ministers had changed at some point during the past year, mostly unannounced at the time. The three most notable shifts involved positions related to the economy. Kim Wan Su, hitherto President of the Central Bank of the DPRK, became Minister of Finance in place of Mun Il Bong, last seen publicly in 2005. Ro Tu Chol, who had delivered the budget speeches during 2006–08, was appointed as Chairman of the SPC while retaining the position of Vice-Premier. O Su Yong, previously Minister of the Electronics Industry, was named as a new Vice-Premier. Other portfolios with new incumbents were those of electric power, oil, the metal industry, railways, agriculture, forestry, fishing, urban management, commerce, and procurement and food administration. However, the new openness with names did not extend to statistics. Kim Wan Su's first budget speech, like those of his predecessors since 2003, contained no definitive figures.

The NDC, which continued to outrank the Cabinet, was enlarged from eight to 13 members. Not only were all of these members named but, in an unprecedented development, photographs of each appeared the next day in the two main daily newspapers, *Rodong Sinmun* (an organ of the KWP) and *Minju Choson* (a government organ). The NDC's enhanced prominence implicitly signalled that there would be no power vacuum in any eventuality. The few civilians in the new NDC now included Jang Song Thaek, Kim Jong Il's brother-in-law, an appointment that confirmed his growing importance, which had been in ascendancy since late 2008. It was speculated that Jang might have acted as de facto leader during Kim's illness; he accompanied him everywhere, and it was rumoured that he might serve as a transitional caretaker leader until Kim Jong Un was deemed capable of ruling alone. However, it remained unclear when or how this succession might be formally promulgated, and whether Kim Jong Un would be accepted by either the élite or the public. Kim Jong Un's succession was expected to be far harder to accomplish than that of Kim Jong Il (itself not without difficulties, despite 20 years of prior planning) in 1994, with both the domestic economy and foreign relations in a parlous state.

In April 2009 the SPA adopted the text of a revised Constitution (although this was not published until the end of September): for the first time, this gave official recognition to the Chairman of the NDC (the post held by Kim Jong Il) as the 'supreme leader' of the nation, and added a reference to *Songun* (the 'military first' ideology favoured by Kim Jong Il) alongside *Juche* as guiding principles.

Meanwhile, the ranks of the gerontocracy continued to be depleted. Pak Song Chol, once a very senior official and still nominally a Politburo member, died at the age of 95 in October 2008. One of the last of Kim Il Sung's guerrilla comrades, born in present-day South Korea, Pak had served as Minister of Foreign Affairs, Premier and Vice-President at various stages of his political career. Another war veteran, Vice-Marshal Kim Il Hyon, died in January 2009, aged 87. Hong Song Nam, a senior technocrat and alternate member of the Politburo who had served three times as Chairman of the SPC and was Premier during 1998–2003, but was thereafter demoted to the position of chief party secretary for South Hamgyong province, died at the age of 79 in March 2009.

In an unexpected development, KCNA announced in late June 2010 that the KWP was to convene in early September in order to elect 'its highest leading body'. At the last such meeting of party delegates, held in 1966, Kim Il Sung's younger brother, Kim Yong Ju, had been chosen as his successor (although he was later outmanoeuvred by Kim Jong Il). KCNA's announcement therefore prompted speculation that at the September 2010 meeting Kim Jong Un might finally emerge in public, if not yet formally appointed as successor to his father. It was speculated that formal succession might take place in 2012, the centenary of Kim Il Sung's birth, which the regime set as a deadline to achieve a 'strong and prosperous nation'.

Meanwhile, in early June 2010 the SPA held a rare second session devoted wholly to personnel matters; it was unclear why these had not been dealt with at the SPA's customary one-day session in April. Kim Jong Il attended, as he had not in April, and proposed Jang Song Thaek as Vice-Chairman of the NDC, thus consolidating his brother-in-law's position of influence. Choe Yong Rim, a veteran loyalist, formerly Secretary-General of the SPA Presidium, was appointed Premier, replacing Kim Yong Il. A further reorganization of the Cabinet reflected economic problems. Three Vice-Premiers—Kwak Pom Gi, O Su Yong and Pak Myong Son—were dismissed, and four new (albeit elderly) ones were appointed: Kang Nung Su, Kim Rak Hui, Ri Tae Nam and Jon Ha Chol. No reason was offered for the dismissals, Pak having been appointed only in September 2009. By contrast, Kwak was an experienced economist, in post since 1998, who had only recently given the keynote speech at a national meeting on light industry; his removal just a week later thus appeared related to the concomitant dismissals of the Minister of Light Industry, Ri Ju O, and the Minister of the Foodstuff and Daily Necessities Industry, Jong Yon Gwa, who were replaced by An Jong Su and Jo Yong Chol, respectively. Two other Ministers, Jo Pyong Ju (of Machine-Building Industries) and Han Kwang Bok (of the Electronics Industry), were concurrently appointed Vice-Premiers.

In May 2010 it was announced that Senior Vice-Minister of the People's Armed Forces Kim Il Chol had been removed. The NDC also relieved him of his position on the Commission, citing 'his advanced age of 80'. However, given the high number of octogenarians still occupying senior positions, and Kim Il Chol's apparent good health during recent public appearances, this explanation left many unconvinced and prompted conjecture that Kim's sudden 'retirement' might have been in response to dissent following his demotion in February 2009. Another theory was that his dismissal was in some way connected to the sinking in March 2010 of a South Korean naval vessel, the *Cheonan* (see Part One, The Korean Peninsula: Conflict and Dialogue).

The sudden death of another senior official, KWP vice-director Ri Je Gang, who was reported to have been killed in a car crash in June 2010, raised further questions. Ri was said to have been an important sponsor and tutor of Kim Jong Un, and thus a rival to Jang Song Thaek for influence over the putative dauphin. As a result, rumours emerged that Ri's death had prepared the way for Jang's promotion to the NDC vice-chairmanship, announced at the SPA's special session less than one week later.

There were also unconfirmed reports of several senior officials having been executed because of policy failures. The director of the KWP's department for planning and finance, Pak Nam Gi, was reported to have been dismissed in February 2010; he was rumoured to have been executed in March owing to his alleged culpability for a disastrous currency revaluation in December 2009, which had resulted in a sharp increase in inflationary pressures, disruption to the distribution of goods and food shortages (see Economy), and provoked popular protests. By some accounts the then Premier, Kim Yong Il, had issued an unprecedented apology to local activists for the mishandling of this matter. Other prominent officials reported to have been executed included former Minister of Railways Kim Yong Sam, following the revelation that 100 trains kept in storage in preparation for the outbreak of war (a striking fact in itself) had been sold off as scrap metal by railway workers; and Kwon Ho Ung, who had been North Korea's chief delegate for inter-Korean talks during 2004–07. Meanwhile, Kim Jong Nam dismissed the notion that he had sought asylum in Europe as a result of two alleged government plots to kill him, following a raid in 2009 on a residence in Pyongyang where his supporters had allegedly held secret meetings.

With the urgency of the succession depending on Kim Jong Il's state of health, reports in July 2010 that Kim's mental faculties were failing caused renewed concern. Physical ailments attributed to the 'Dear Leader' ranged from diabetes to pancreatic cancer. However, none of this was confirmed, and Kim's apparent brisk schedule of guidance visits gave an altogether different impression, as was doubtless intended.

A rare meeting of KWP delegates was convened towards the end of September 2010. However, rather than serving as a forum for a discussion of policy directions, the gathering was primarily an occasion for Kim Jong Un finally to appear in public. On the eve of this meeting, and without mention of the relationship, the appointment of Kim Jong Il's third son as a four-star general within the KPA was announced, despite still being only in his twenties and lacking any known military experience. Kim Jong Il's sister, Kim Kyong Hui, a civilian economist and wife of Jang Song Thaek, was promoted to the same rank, appearing to indicate a closing of ranks in the upper echelons of the KPA within Kim Jong Il's immediate family.

A full roster of Politburo and Central Committee members was named at the meeting, thus at last regularizing the KWP's upper ranks, which since Kim Jong Il's inheritance of power in 1994 had atrophied, while military influence grew. Kim Jong Un was appointed as a member of the KWP Central Committee, although not of the new Politburo. He was also appointed joint Vice-Chairman of the KWP Central Military Commission (CMC), along with newly promoted Vice-Marshal Ri Yong Ho, Chief of General Staff of the KPA, who was concurrently appointed to the Politburo. Although little was known of him, Ri had risen to become the most powerful figure within the KPA, his prominence being reflected in his positioning between the 'Dear Leader' and Kim Jong Un in the first official photograph of the latter, released shortly after the convention.

Kang Sok Ju, hitherto First Vice-Minister of Foreign Affairs, was appointed Vice-Premier on the eve of the KWP meeting, at which he was also appointed to the Politburo; he was replaced as First Vice-Minister of Foreign Affairs by Kim Kye Gwan, dispelling rumours that the latter had fallen out of favour. Kim was replaced as chief delegate to the six-party talks on nuclear issues (see below) by Ri Yong Ho (not to be confused with the Vice-Marshal of the same name—see above), a former ambassador to the United Kingdom; Ri was also appointed as a Vice-Minister of Foreign Affairs.

Kim Jong Un's debut aside, the filling of the upper ranks of the KWP did not result in any real sense of renewal or generational change; there were few newcomers and the average age of the members of the new Central Committee was 78. The Committee's youngest member, at 64, was Kim Kyong Hui, who thus outranked her influential husband, as Jang Song Thaek became merely an alternate member of the Politburo. The effects of this preference for gerontocracy were predictable. In early November 2010, barely one month after being appointed to the Central Committee's five-member Presidium despite a long illness, Vice-Marshal Jo Myong Rok, once the KPA's most powerful figure, died at the age of 82; the vacancy remained unfilled at mid-2011.

In October 2010 the North Korean public, as well as members of the international media, who were unexpectedly granted last-minute visas, were afforded their first glimpse of the apparent heir presumptive, at a military parade held to commemorate the 65th anniversary of the KWP's foundation. To excited cheers from the assembled multitudes, Kim Jong Un stood near his father, who appeared to be in poor physical health. Nevertheless, Kim Jong Il continued to maintain a brisk pace of reported guidance visits into 2011, now often accompanied by his son.

In a rare interview broadcast on Japanese television in mid-October 2010, Kim Jong Nam, who remained in quasi-exile in China, declared that he was opposed to the dynastic succession whereby Kim Jong Un would inherit power from their father. However, he also stated that he was 'prepared to help his younger brother whenever necessary', while remaining abroad, and hoped that Kim Jong Un would strive to improve the lives of the North Korean people upon assuming power.

In January 2011 KCNA reported that the Cabinet had adopted a 10-year State Strategy Plan for Economic Development, which was to be implemented by the newly established State General Bureau for Economic Development, in conjunction with the Korea Taepung International Investment Group (KTIIG—a joint venture chaired by Chinese-Korean businessman Pak Chol Su). The Bureau and KTIIG were also involved in the State Development Bank (SDB), which was founded in March 2010 but which had gone unmentioned since. Similarly, beyond its initial adoption, no further information about the new economic strategic plan was forthcoming. With no detail or transparency, it was difficult to gauge the real significance of such measures.

Neither Kim Jong Il nor Kim Jong Un, both of whom were reported to be giving 'on-the-spot guidance' in the northern border province of Jagang, attended the one-day session of the SPA in April 2011, thus highlighting the legislature's irrelevance. Ri Myong Su, a general and an important aide to Kim Jong Il, was appointed Minister of People's Security. He replaced another general, Ju Sang Song, who had held the post since 2004 but, in an unusual announcement by state media in March 2011, was reported to have been dismissed by the NDC owing to illness. However, no mention of illness had been made when Ju had received his visiting Chinese counterpart in February, prompting speculation that he might have been dismissed for other reasons. Jon Pyong Ho, Secretary of the Military Industry within the KWP Central Committee until being replaced in September 2010 by Pak To Chun, formerly chief party secretary of Jagang Province was dismissed from the NDC, and was also replaced in that capacity by Pak To Chun.

On 24 July 2011 North Korea held 'elections' for provincial (municipal), city (district) and county people's assemblies. It was claimed that 99.97% of voters (all except those abroad or at sea) took part, and that all voted in favour of the candidates selected by the KWP. With 28,116 workers, farmers, intellectuals and officials thus endorsed, KCNA hailed the polls as marking 'an important occasion in consolidating the people's power of the DPRK by building new local power bodies with able officials'.

RELATIONS WITH SOUTH KOREA

A full account of North-South relations is given in Part One, The Korean Peninsula: Conflict and Dialogue (see p. 10).

FOREIGN RELATIONS

Despite (or perhaps because of) North Korea's roots in Soviet military government, it has been the regime's consistent goal to emphasize and maximize what its own slogans call *chaju, chalip, chawi*: independence in politics, economics and defence. In practice, this has largely meant a refusal to be beholden to—let alone a satellite of—either of its giant neighbours and erstwhile sponsors, the USSR and China, while simultaneously exhibiting unremitting hostility towards the USA, Japan and, of course, South Korea. Although the Sino-Soviet dispute enabled Kim Il Sung for many years to position himself between the USSR and China, thus receiving aid from both, the end of the protracted period of mutual hostility between the USSR and the USA known as the Cold War, and the subsequent collapse of the USSR, exposed North Korea's vaunted self-reliance as ultimately self-defeating isolation.

North Korean foreign policy underwent several phases over the years. During the 1950s North Korea emphasized its adherence to the communist bloc, receiving both military aid during the Korean War (1950–53) and assistance for reconstruction thereafter from the USSR, China and Eastern Europe. Yet already there were disputes with the USSR over how best to use Soviet aid, with North Korea preferring to develop its own heavy industry rather than join the Council for Mutual Economic Assistance. Meanwhile, although Japan had relations with neither Korean government at this stage, more than 75,000 pro-communist Koreans in Japan (mainly of southern origin) emigrated to the new socialist fatherland in the late 1950s.

Following the public Sino-Soviet split in the early 1960s, North Korea demonstrated broad sympathy with China's more revolutionary position, which led to the temporary suspension of Soviet aid. North Korea's own bellicosity peaked in 1968, with its seizure of the *USS Pueblo* and its dispatch of a commando unit to attack the presidential mansion in Seoul.

By contrast, the 1970s were an era of broadening contacts. Suspicious of China's amenability to US 'ping-pong diplomacy', North Korea not only repaired relations with the USSR but sought new allies, particularly in the developing countries and within the Non-aligned Movement (which it joined in 1975). Other initiatives were less successful. North Korea's progress in establishing diplomatic relations with the four Nordic countries (its first such links in the West) was marred shortly thereafter when, in 1976, all four of its ambassadors were expelled, their staff accused of systematic smuggling (a practice in which North Korean diplomats were subsequently alleged to be widely engaged). Similarly, what seemed a useful development of economic relations with Japan and Western

European countries came to an abrupt halt when it became clear that North Korea had no overt intention of paying for several hundred million dollars' worth of capital equipment imported in the early 1970s.

By the early 1980s North Korea's relations with many of its communist allies showed signs of deterioration. Neither the USSR nor China approved at first of the official designation of Kim Jong Il as his father's successor, although China at length relented and, in 1983, invited the 'Dear Leader' on his first known visit there.

This did not prevent a distinct inclination towards the USSR in the mid-1980s, inspired perhaps by suspicion of Deng Xiaoping's reforms, yet continuing into the era of the new Soviet leader, Mikhail Gorbachev. In 1984 Kim Il Sung visited Moscow for the first time in 23 years, and also spent several weeks touring Eastern Europe. He returned to meet Gorbachev in 1986, in which year joint Soviet-North Korean naval exercises were undertaken. In addition, the North Korean Government granted port facilities and overflying rights to the Soviet fleet and air force, reportedly in return for the supply of Soviet MiG-23 fighters and surface-to-air missiles. North Korea's trade with the USSR grew rapidly in the late 1980s.

However, within a period of less than five years, a series of set-backs comprehensively undermined North Korea's foreign policy orientations of the previous four decades. It was inevitable that the attraction of South Korea's far greater economic prospects (coupled with the skilful diplomacy of Seoul's 'nordpolitik') would eventually lead pragmatists such as Deng and Gorbachev to qualify their inherited Cold War loyalties towards a Pyongyang that they increasingly considered to be a political and economic liability. Although China acted first to begin trading with South Korea, it was the USSR under Gorbachev's leadership that dealt both the diplomatic and financial *coup de grâce*: first by establishing full diplomatic relations with South Korea in September 1990, and then by stipulating that, from January 1991, its trade with North Korea would be conducted in convertible currencies at world market prices. This caused North Korea's total trade volume to decline by more than US $1,100m. (almost one-quarter) in 1991. Although the demise of the USSR itself afforded a certain grim satisfaction, Russia's President Boris Yeltsin had no vestige of comradeship with the Pyongyang regime.

The deterioration in relations with Moscow left China as North Korea's only major ally, although even this relationship was qualified by increasing impatience in Beijing, as much over Kim Il Sung's failure to embrace economic reform as for his suspected nuclear ambitions (see below). With reformers once again dominant in the Chinese leadership, economic links with South Korea rapidly increased and, in August 1992, full diplomatic relations were established between China and South Korea, much to the consternation of North Korea. Sino-North Korean relations subsequently deteriorated significantly. Although China opposed UN action against North Korea over the nuclear issue, its support was tenuous at best.

In view of these shifts of allegiance, North Korea had no option but to try to repair relations with its traditional enemies. In late 1990 significant progress with Japan seemed likely, after a highly successful visit to Pyongyang by Shin Kanemaru, the senior mediator of the ruling Liberal-Democratic Party. However, eight rounds of talks, held in 1991–92 with a view to the possible restoration of normal relations between North Korea and Japan, made no progress, owing to intransigent demands from both sides. None the less, regular charter flights between the two countries led to an increase in unofficial contacts and visits, although not yet to the aid and investment which North Korea desperately needed. Relations with Japan were severely strained in May 1993, following North Korea's successful testing of the *Rodong-1* medium-range missile in the Sea of Japan. According to US intelligence reports, the missile would be capable of reaching most of Japan's major cities (and possibly of carrying either a conventional or a nuclear warhead).

Contacts with the USA also increased considerably in the early 1990s, although by mid-2010 diplomatic relations had yet to be established. North Korea on four occasions returned the remains of US soldiers listed as 'missing in action' (MIA) during the Korean War, and several senior-level US delegations, including retired political and military leaders (and even the evangelist Rev. Billy Graham), visited Pyongyang. In January 1992 the KWP's international secretary, Kim Yong Sun, visited New York for discussions with the US Under-Secretary of State (although one year later he was refused a visa to attend ceremonies marking the inauguration of President Clinton). US-North Korean discussions on the nuclear issue resumed in mid-1993.

For both the USA and Japan, a major obstacle to better relations with Pyongyang was and remained their suspicion that North Korea was seeking to develop nuclear weapons. In July 1991, after several years of prevarication, North Korea finally agreed a draft Nuclear Safeguards Agreement (NSA) with the International Atomic Energy Agency (IAEA), permitting the outside inspection of North Korean nuclear facilities. Following the announcement by President George Bush, Sr of proposals to withdraw all US tactical nuclear weapons worldwide, and President Roh Tae-Woo's confirmation that none remained in South Korea, North Korea signed the NSA in January 1992. Moreover, Pyongyang subsequently submitted an unexpectedly detailed report on its nuclear facilities, almost one month ahead of schedule. The IAEA Director-General visited North Korea in May 1992 and formal IAEA inspections began later in that month.

Yet, despite this unprecedented progress, suspicions were not allayed. Indeed, one large building at the Yongbyon installation, north of Pyongyang, was believed by some outside observers to be a nuclear-reprocessing plant. Likewise, North Korea's apparent attempts to obstruct the separate inter-Korean mutual nuclear inspections (see above) aroused widespread mistrust. Finally, although not part of the nuclear issue as such, the fact that North Korea sold improved *Scud* missiles to Iran and Syria in exchange for petroleum did nothing to enhance relations with the West.

These issues combined to produce a crisis in 1993. In January North Korea refused to allow special inspections (as demanded by the IAEA) of two sites at Yongbyon, which were thought likely to reveal that more plutonium had been extracted than Pyongyang had admitted. Then, in an unprecedented development, in March North Korea announced that it was to withdraw from the Treaty on the Non-Proliferation of Nuclear Weapons (the Non-Proliferation Treaty—NPT), which it had signed with the IAEA in 1985. This led to protracted diplomatic activity between Washington, Seoul and Tokyo, as well as muted criticism by the UN Security Council (in part because China would not support decisive action at this stage). However, the main channel for defusing the crisis was the holding of two rounds of direct talks between North Korea and the USA in mid-1993, which resulted in North Korea suspending implementation of its withdrawal from the NPT.

Despite this hopeful sign, the nuclear crisis continued for a further year. In May 1993 international concern about North Korea's weapons programme was heightened following the successful testing of an intermediate-range missile, the *Rodong-1* (see above). Negotiations between North Korea and the USA, and separate inter-Korean talks, continued during the latter part of the year, but with no tangible results. Although some IAEA monitoring and intermittent inspection activities at Yongbyon were permitted, it remained uncertain whether North Korea had already succeeded in producing a nuclear weapon. Alarm was aroused again in May 1994, when North Korea began replacing spent fuel rods without effective supervision, prompting the IAEA to suggest the imposition of international sanctions. The situation deteriorated further on 13 June, when North Korea retaliated by announcing its complete withdrawal from the IAEA (and not merely the NPT), although in fact inspectors subsequently remained at Yongbyon. Meanwhile, the USA began to lobby the UN Security Council to impose sanctions on North Korea, despite objections by China and Russia and an unenthusiastic response from Japan.

The rising sense of crisis was defused in June 1994, when former US President Jimmy Carter visited Pyongyang. After 10 hours of talks with Kim Il Sung, he returned with two offers: a summit meeting with South Korea (see above), and a pledge to suspend North Korea's nuclear programme. While the latter was vague, it sufficed for the USA to resume senior-level talks.

However, when the third round commenced in Geneva, Switzerland, in July, Kim Il Sung was already dead, and the discussions were duly postponed. None the less, following several subsequent rounds, a 'framework agreement' between North Korea and the USA was signed in Geneva in October. In essence, North Korea agreed to close down its nuclear site at Yongbyon in exchange for substantial compensation, principally in the form of new light-water reactors (LWRs) worth some US $4,500m., as well as up to 500,000 metric tons of heavy fuel oil annually during the estimated 10 years' construction period of the LWRs.

Although not written into the agreement, it was understood that South Korea would play an important part, both as supplier and main financier of the LWRs, and as a core member, with the USA and Japan, of the Korean Peninsula Energy Development Organization (KEDO), the consortium that was to supervise the entire project. North Korea initially protested against South Korea's involvement, and for several months it seemed as if the Geneva accord might collapse. By August 1995, however, North Korea had tacitly abandoned its opposition to the South's de facto participation.

The Geneva nuclear accord perhaps set the pattern for a new development in North Korean foreign policy, which might be termed 'militant mendicancy'. Thus, in May 1995, a North Korean delegation visiting Japan made an unprecedented request for rice as aid. Not only was this granted, but South Korea insisted that the North should also, and first, accept free rice from fellow Koreans. This produced the remarkable spectacle of the North Korean regime being in effect sustained by its three oldest foes—which it continued to denounce—without any proviso requiring Pyongyang to reform or mend its ways.

North Korea continued to undermine the existing armistice agreements. In March 1995 it expelled the Polish observers of the Neutral Nations Supervisory Commission at Panmunjom, following which it closed its side of the Joint Security Area to all visitors from the South. The North's professed aim was a bilateral peace treaty with the USA, excluding the South. North Korea continued to pursue this quixotic quest in 1996, declaring in April that it would no longer observe protocol in the demilitarized zone (DMZ), and raising tension with a few symbolic incursions into the South Korean half of the zone. This prompted the USA and South Korea to propose four-way talks with North Korea and China.

In any case, the Pyongyang regime had de facto achieved the direct line of communication to Washington that it had long sought. While there were no formal relations, and talks on an exchange of liaison offices stalled, there were now regular contacts between the US Department of State and the North Korean UN mission in New York. Discussions on missile control were held in Berlin, Germany, in April 1996, albeit without result. Progress was also made on MIA issues: the USA paid US $2m. (in cash, at Panmunjom) for remains that had already been returned, and US investigators were, for the first time, allowed to search directly inside North Korea. In early 1996 there were also many visits to the USA, including separate delegations led by two leading reformists, Kim Jong U and Ri Jong Hyok.

However, all this was regarded as appeasement in some quarters, both in Seoul and in the Republican Party in the USA. In June 1996 Congress granted barely one-half of the modest US $25m. sought by the President as the US contribution to KEDO's oil shipments. This was regrettable, since KEDO had achieved the remarkable feat of turning what had been the peninsula's worst risk into its best hope. Not only had North Korea abandoned its initial hostility to the South's leading role in the project, but for much of 1995–96 its delegates were in New York taking constructive part in negotiations over the text of the agreement. South Korean engineers were now travelling routinely to the LWR site at Shinpo, albeit via Beijing, and in August 1997 construction work began.

North Korea also made overtures to Japan about resuming negotiations towards establishing diplomatic relations. Japan cautiously insisted that North Korea must first accept the four-way talks with South Korea and the USA. None the less, regular contacts continued. In July 1996 Kim Jong U toured several Japanese cities to try to encourage investment in the Rajin-Sonbong free zone, but had little success. (Kim Jong U subsequently fell from favour, and in 1998 was reported to have been executed; other reports denied this.)

With its long-standing (and former) allies, too, North Korea experienced mixed fortunes. China's avowed support for inter-Korean dialogue annoyed the North, but China, for its part, was equally irritated at Kim Jong Il's refusal of economic reform, not least because the Chinese Government had been continually obliged to offer the country vital assistance. In July 1996 the 35th anniversary of the Sino-North Korean friendship treaty was marked by the exchange of middle-ranking delegations, as well as by a rare visit to Nampo by a Chinese naval flotilla.

Meanwhile, Moscow, which had created North Korea and sustained it until the beginning of the collapse of the USSR in 1990, occupied a much less significant position in North Korea's foreign relations. In April 1996 a Deputy Chairman of the Russian Government, Vitalii Ignatenko, led the first major delegation from the new Russia to Pyongyang. There was talk of resuming economic co-operation: most major North Korean industrial installations were originally Soviet aid projects; but since both countries were in economic difficulties, not to mention North Korea's huge debts to the USSR, prospects for co-operation were not bright. They did not improve in 1997, when North Korea criticized Russia for supplying ultra-modern armaments (including tanks) to South Korea, in payment of debts.

North Korea's foreign relations neither changed nor advanced greatly during 1996–97. With no Head of State yet inaugurated, there were few high-ranking visitors either to or from Pyongyang, which appeared more isolated than ever. Only with China were there regular exchanges of delegations, and most of these were not senior-level. Still, as seen in the defection of Hwang Jang Yop (see above), China remained concerned for North Korea's sensitivities, even as its economic and other links with South Korea continued to progress smoothly. China was also the biggest provider of food aid to North Korea. This was so, despite China's displeasure at the somewhat unexpected improvement of relations between North Korea and Taiwan: far apart ideologically, yet perhaps united in their pariah status. In January 1997 an agreement was signed whereby North Korea would dispose of low-grade nuclear waste from Taiwan, in a contract believed to be worth more than US $100m. South Korea protested vociferously, and this project seemed to have been abandoned.

Elsewhere, Japan began to adopt a more rigid policy towards North Korea than previously. The seizure in April 1997 of amphetamines worth US $90m. on a North Korean ship in a Japanese port did not improve relations. Unlike the USA, or even South Korea, Japan declined to respond to the UN's increasingly desperate appeals for food aid for North Korea. (It had supplied 500,000 metric tons of rice in 1995 and received scant gratitude.) Japan insisted that improved relations, including aid, would depend on North Korea making concessions, including the disclosure of details of the alleged kidnappings of Japanese citizens in the 1970s. In late August, however, agreement was reached between the two countries, whereby some now-elderly Japanese wives of Koreans who had settled in North Korea in the 1950s and 1960s were to be allowed to visit their native land for the first time. Only with the USA, ironically, did North Korea succeed in improving relations. The USA was swift to respond to UN appeals for food aid, and bilateral contacts continued in areas ranging from further joint excavation for MIA remains to talks about North Korea's missile development and sales. Several senior US politicians visited North Korea, usually by military aircraft, which would have been unthinkable in the past. The USA's main aim was to persuade North Korea to agree to attend the four-way talks first proposed in April 1996. After much prevarication by North Korea, preliminary discussions were held in New York in August 1997. China, the fourth party (which was also initially hesitant), became much more positive about the proposal during 1997.

Full four-way talks finally commenced in Geneva in December 1997, and were followed by more substantial discussions in March 1998. However, these were unsuccessful, owing to wide differences over the agenda, with North Korea demanding that this should include the withdrawal of US troops from the peninsula. Further four-way talks took place in October, when agreement was reached on the establishment of two subcommittees, with a view to instituting a permanent peace mechanism. Otherwise, North Korea's foreign relations remained fairly constant during 1998. Of the four major powers, Russia continued to count the least, in stark contrast to its predominance in the Soviet era. Efforts to revise the 1961 friendship treaty, not least in order to strike out its commitment to mutual military assistance, stalled for several years, until 1999 (see below). China, by contrast, continued to support North Korea with aid, even as its relations with South Korea become ever closer. Senior-level dialogue with the North went into abeyance for a decade, whereas Chinese and South Korean leaders exchanged regular bilateral visits as well as meeting in multilateral forums such as Asia-Pacific Economic Cooperation (APEC) and Asia-Europe Meeting (ASEM). China's long-term aim was to displace the USA as the broker of choice between the two Koreas.

Relations with Japan continued to follow an uneven course. The first ever home visits of two groups of elderly Japanese-born wives of North Koreans were finally realized in late 1997 and early 1998. Thereafter, however, the kidnapping issue (in particular, anger in Japan at what was seen as a perfunctory 'investigation' of the matter by North Korea) once again prevented the resumption of talks towards restoring diplomatic relations. At the end of August 1998 relations deteriorated, when Japan accused North Korea of test-firing an unarmed *Taepo Dong* medium-range missile over its territory. The North Korean regime subsequently claimed that the object launched had, in fact, been a satellite intended to broadcast patriotic music. That rocket launch, whatever its purpose, had a lasting effect on North Korea's relations with its main foes. Japanese opinion and policy hardened, both towards Pyongyang and on defence issues more generally; all the more so after a further provocation in March 1999, when the Japanese navy pursued and fired on two intruding boats, which were later traced to the North Korean port of Chongjin. Unlike South Korea and the USA, Japan still gave no food aid to the DPRK, and considered further sanctions such as banning remittances sent by pro-North Koreans living in Japan. The possibility, widely canvassed in mid-1999, that North Korea might test another missile carried a real risk that Japan would withdraw from KEDO; this in turn threatened to reopen the North Korean nuclear issue and reactivate the tensions of mid-1994.

The USA shared Japan's alarm at North Korea's missile activities, albeit more with regard to proliferation: purchasers included Libya, Syria, Iran and Pakistan. In the past Pyongyang had hinted that it might be 'bought off', as with its nuclear programme, but this seemed less likely after the NATO bombing of Yugoslavia in early 1999. Missiles were only one cause of US concern during 1998–99, the other being a large construction site at Kumchang-ri, near the disused nuclear site at Yongbyon, which was feared to be a covert continuation of nuclear activity. Kumchang-ri dominated US-North Korean relations for many months, until in May 1999 a US inspection team pronounced it 'clean'. While denying any link, the USA simultaneously announced a further 400,000 metric tons of grain in aid. The USA continued to be the mainstay of the UN World Food Programme's (WFP's) aid to North Korea, this operation being its largest ever, prior to Afghanistan in 2001–02. Meanwhile, under pressure from Republican critics in the US Congress, in November 1998 the Clinton Administration appointed William Perry, a former Secretary of Defense, to carry out a full review of US policy towards North Korea. Perry visited Pyongyang in May 1999, and his report was published in September of that year. It offered substantial incentives, in exchange for a definitive and verifiable end to North Korea's nuclear and missile ambitions. During talks in Berlin in mid-September the USA removed sanctions on trade and travel in return for a promise by North Korea that it would refrain from testing long-range missiles until 2003. As for allies (past or present), in March 1999 a new treaty with Russia was at last agreed, to replace that of 1961 with the former USSR. This was assumed to exclude the military support provided for in the old version. The treaty was signed during a visit to Pyongyang by the Russian Minister of Foreign Affairs, Igor Ivanov, in February 2000; it was ratified by North Korea in April of that year. With China effectively remaining North Korea's sole ally and source of finance, a senior-level delegation visited Beijing in June 1999 for the first time in eight years. Led by Kim Yong Nam, the delegates included the Premier and the ministers responsible for defence and foreign affairs—but no economic cadres, to China's reported annoyance. Multilaterally, the quadripartite talks involving the two Koreas, China and the USA continued to be held in Geneva, the sixth round taking place in August 1999, but with no obvious progress.

From the latter part of 1999 onwards, North Korea's diplomacy took a striking new turn, with conscious efforts made both to restore old relationships and to foster new alliances. The first sign was a wide range of meetings held at the UN in September 1999 by the North Korean Minister of Foreign Affairs, Paek Nam Sun. In January 2000 Italy became the first of the Group of Seven (G7) industrialized nations to establish full diplomatic relations with the DPRK. Later in the year Kuwait, the Philippines and Australia followed suit, with Australia resuming links first forged in 1975 but abruptly severed by North Korea soon after. In October 2000 the United Kingdom announced that it planned to restore normal relations with North Korea, and duly established diplomatic relations with the DPRK in December. Meanwhile, in July Paek travelled to Bangkok, Thailand, for North Korea's admission as the 23rd member of the ARF; at this regional forum Canada and New Zealand also announced plans to establish relations. Paek also held unprecedented meetings with his South Korean, US and Japanese counterparts.

Progress continued in the development of relations with the USA. In October 2000 Vice-Marshal Jo Myong Rok, North Korea's most powerful military leader, visited Washington as a special envoy of Kim Jong Il. This led in the same month to a visit to Pyongyang by the US Secretary of State, Madeleine Albright. President Clinton was ready to follow to sign an agreement on missiles, but this foundered on verification difficulties. Agreement also eluded senior-level bilateral talks with Japan, in abeyance since 1992, of which three rounds were held in 2000. Despite a show of cordiality, the two sides' agendas remained far apart. North Korea demanded compensation of up to US $10,000m. for Japanese colonial rule prior to 1945, whereas Japan continued to prioritize its missile and abduction concerns. There was no obvious way to overcome this impasse. However, in 2000 Japan gave 100,000 metric tons of food aid to North Korea for the first time in several years, and was permitted to monitor its distribution. A third visit home by Japanese wives of North Koreans, the first since 1998, took place in September 2000.

The most important development was a new effort to improve relations with North Korea's original major allies. In May 2000 Kim Jong Il made an unofficial, and initially secret, visit to China, his first overseas trip since 1983. As well as meeting President Jiang Zemin and other leaders, he toured a computer factory and was quoted—for the first time—explicitly praising China's reform programme. This visit prepared Kim Jong Il for hosting Kim Dae-Jung a fortnight afterwards. One month later the 'Dear Leader' welcomed the President of Russia, Vladimir Putin, as the first ever Russian or Soviet leader to visit the DPRK. By this simple gesture, in a trip lasting less than 24 hours, Putin reversed a decade of hostility which had begun when the then Soviet leader, Mikhail Gorbachev, hastily forged links with South Korea in 1990; further, the Russian President reconfirmed his country's importance with regard to the possible reunification of Korea, later presenting the G8 (the G7 plus Russia) with an offer by Kim Jong Il to abandon his missile programme in return for access to satellite-launching facilities.

Relations with the USA suffered a set-back in 2001 when the new Republican Administration under President George W. Bush expressed mistrust towards North Korea, prompting the latter to suspend inter-Korean dialogue as well. No further talks were held with Japan, which Pyongyang denounced (as did South Korea) for a new schools' history textbook that minimized the significance of pre-1945 atrocities, and for Prime Minister Junichiro Koizumi's visit to the Yasukuni Shrine commemorating (among others) convicted war criminals. However, with other Western countries, there was more progress. By June 2001 13 of the 15 member states of the

European Union (EU), and the organization as such, had restored full diplomatic relations with the DPRK; the exceptions were France, which cited human rights concerns, and Ireland. In May a senior-level EU delegation led by the Swedish Prime Minister, Göran Persson, had visited Pyongyang and met Kim Jong Il, in what was interpreted as a prompt to President Bush to resume dialogue. It was reported that North Korea's leader had pledged to maintain his country's moratorium on missile-testing until 2003.

In January 2001 Kim Jong Il paid his second visit to China in nine months. Again nominally secret, this trip was mainly to Shanghai and clearly business-related: the week-long itinerary incorporated several joint-venture factories and even the Stock Exchange, raising hopes that North Korea might at last adopt market reforms. In September President Jiang Zemin reciprocated, with the first visit to Pyongyang by a senior Chinese leader in over a decade. Behind the formal warmth, Jiang would have pressed the case for reform (not least to save China the cost of supporting the North Korean economy, and coping with an outflow of refugees) and openly urged his hosts to resume dialogue with South Korea, which they promptly did.

Relations with Russia also deepened. A scheduled visit by Kim Jong Il in April 2001 did not materialize, but his defence minister returned from Moscow with reported pledges of unspecified new military co-operation. The 'Dear Leader' finally made the journey to Russia in August: by special train, taking over three weeks and causing many complaints as stations along the route were cleared of normal traffic as he passed. A joint statement with President Putin referred to Russian 'understanding' of North Korea's demand for US troops to leave South Korea. Reports also suggested that a deal had been concluded to repay North Korea's Soviet-era debts, mainly by sending contract labour, whose working conditions the *Moscow Times* likened to serfdom. As this implied, not all Russians endorsed their Government's efforts for renewed friendship with this relic of Stalinism.

Following the events of 11 September 2001, North Korea remained on the US Department of State's list of nations alleged to sponsor terrorism, if mainly for sheltering a number of Japanese hijackers since 1970, rather than for any recent transgressions. No links to the Islamist militant group al-Qa'ida were seriously alleged, and North Korea swiftly condemned the suicide attacks on the mainland USA, but went on to criticize the US war in Afghanistan. For its part, the USA for the first time cited North Korea's suspected biological weapons programme as a major threat, in addition to its nuclear and missile concerns. Besides such weapons of mass destruction, the Bush Administration also gave notice that North Korea's conventional force posture was unacceptably threatening. In January 2002 President Bush notoriously grouped North Korea with Iraq and Iran in what he termed an 'axis of evil'. None the less, MIA co-operation and US food aid continued. In December 2001 the pursuit and sinking by the Japanese navy of a suspected North Korean spy ship, later salvaged and put on public display, did nothing for either North Korea's relations with Japan or its wider reputation.

North Korea's image also suffered from a growing diplomatic problem. North Korean fugitives in China (numbering up to 300,000, none of whom the Chinese authorities acknowledged as refugees) became more militant in 2002; aided by foreign NGOs, several sought asylum in foreign embassies. Chinese police intrusions to seize them caused disputes with both South Korea and Japan; yet ultimately all, including those arrested, were allowed to travel to Seoul via third countries. Many more migrants were arrested and deported to an uncertain fate in North Korea. It was doubtful if signs of reform in North Korea, or repression there and in China, could stem this tide from swelling over time, to destabilizing effect. The number of North Korean defectors reaching South Korea remained negligible compared with most refugee situations elsewhere, but was nearly doubling each year. From 148 in 1999, the total rose to 312 in 2000, 583 in 2001 and 1,141 in 2002.

In early 2002 North Korea's diplomacy temporarily turned away from the major powers, and seemed mainly to be motivated by economic needs. The Minister of Foreign Trade toured Western Europe, while Kim Yong Nam, President of the SPA Presidium, went to Thailand and Malaysia, securing rice and palm oil on generous terms. In Pyongyang Kim Jong Il hosted Indonesia's President, Megawati Sukarnoputri (their late fathers had been close associates), who then travelled on to Seoul. The 'Dear Leader' also visited the Russian embassy in Pyongyang three times in as many months. In July Russia's Minister of Foreign Affairs, after visiting both Koreas, declared Kim Jong Il ready for dialogue 'without preconditions'. In July, therefore, Paek Nam Sun returned to the ARF, in Brunei, having been absent in 2001. An informal meeting with the US Secretary of State, Colin Powell, was the first senior-level contact with the Bush Administration. A month later a less senior envoy, Jack Pritchard, represented the USA at KEDO's LWR ground-breaking ceremony in Shinpo; he urged North Korea to submit to full IAEA inspections.

With Japan there was faster movement. In Brunei Paek signed a joint statement with his Japanese counterpart, Yoriko Kawaguchi. Within a month, bilateral Red Cross and diplomatic talks were held in Pyongyang, cordially, but with no visible progress. However, Junichiro Koizumi made a historic visit to Pyongyang in September 2002, becoming the first Japanese Prime Minister ever to do so. This was a considerable risk, in view of the outstanding disputes between the two countries. The most significant outcome of Koizumi's summit meeting with Kim Jong Il was the latter's admission that North Korean agents had indeed kidnapped 11 or 12 Japanese nationals in the 1970s and 1980s, and of these, only five were still alive. North Korea's long denial of this had been an obstacle to the restoration of diplomatic relations, and the revelation shocked the Japanese public. Kim apologized for the kidnappings, blaming rogue military elements, and agreed to return the surviving Japanese; Koizumi apologized for Japan's colonization of the Korean peninsula. Kim also told Koizumi that he would allow international inspections of North Korea's nuclear facilities, and would maintain the moratorium on missile-testing beyond 2003. Amid the emerging nuclear crisis, Japanese public anger at North Korea's failure to divulge the facts of the deaths of most of the abductees, and its refusal to let the survivors' children join them in Japan, returned relations to their prior state of hostility.

Meeting in Vladivostok in August 2002, for the third time in as many years, Russian President Putin pressed Kim Jong Il for inter-Korean rail links, in the hope of creating an 'iron silk road'—a freight route from South Korea to Europe via Siberia, which Putin hoped would encourage economic development in Russia's depressed Far East. For his part, Kim Jong Il reportedly sought modern weapons, and visited factories in the region as well as a Russian Orthodox church. (Although not officially acknowledged, Kim was born in the Russian city of Khabarovsk in 1942, where his father was in exile.)

From October 2002, however, the growing nuclear crisis dominated North Korea's foreign relations. In mid-October the USA revealed that, two weeks earlier, the Bush Administration's first senior envoy to Pyongyang, the Assistant Secretary of State for East Asian and Pacific Affairs, James Kelly, had confronted his hosts with evidence that they were pursuing a second covert nuclear weapons programme, this time based on highly enriched uranium, in violation of the 1994 Agreed Framework (AF) and that North Korea had, against expectations, admitted this. In November 2002 KEDO's executive board, at US urging, voted to suspend heavy fuel oil shipments due under the AF until North Korea returned to full compliance. In December Spanish and US forces detained a North Korean vessel carrying *Scud* missiles off the Horn of Africa; however, they later let it proceed to its destination, Yemen, since no laws had been broken (neither buyer nor seller being a signatory to the Missile Technology Control Regime). Thereafter the crisis escalated rapidly. North Korea stated that it would reopen its nuclear site at Yongbyon, suspended under the AF, and asked the IAEA to remove seals and monitoring cameras. Later that month it expelled the IAEA's inspectors, and in January 2003 announced its immediate withdrawal from the NPT: the first signatory state ever to do so. In February and March North Korea test-fired two short-range missiles, and one of its jets briefly entered South Korean airspace. More seriously, in early March four North Korean jet fighters harassed a US spy plane west of the peninsula, in an apparent effort to force it to land in Pyongyang. Such provocations dissipated with the start of hostilities in Iraq.

These developments aroused widespread concern, but initially elicited no unified policy response. The Bush Administration, preoccupied with Iraq, stated that it sought a peaceful solution, but it seemed in no hurry to negotiate. A further problem was North Korea's demand for bilateral talks with the USA, which insisted on a wider multilateral forum. Not until April 2003 did discussions take place, in Beijing, involving the USA, North Korea and China, which under its new leader, Hu Jintao, had become an active mediator. China of late had become vexed by its old ally's maverick behaviour, and not only on the nuclear issue. In September 2002, meanwhile, North Korea declared the establishment of a free economic zone at Sinuiju on its north-western border with China, and appointed a wealthy Sino-Dutch orchid dealer, Yang Bin, to manage it. Furious at not being consulted about either the zone or the appointment of its head, China promptly arrested Yang; in July 2003 he was imprisoned for 18 years on fraud and corruption charges. On the nuclear issue, North Korea's statements remained ambiguous. Before the Beijing meeting, it seemed to claim to have finished reprocessing spent fuel rods from Yongbyon to produce plutonium. At the talks, its chief delegate unofficially told the USA that North Korea had nuclear weapons and reserved the right to sell them. In the absence of hard intelligence data (but with the release of much politically motivated information) on how far advanced either of North Korea's two nuclear programmes might be, it was unclear to what extent such brinkmanship was bluff. In its public statements North Korea asserted a right to nuclear defence, abandoning its earlier claim that Yongbyon's purpose was to generate electricity.

From May 2003 US policy, in so far as there was one, shifted more towards interdicting North Korean shipments regarded as suspicious, with a new Proliferation Security Initiative (PSI). The 11 nations supporting the PSI included Australia, which in April seized a North Korean freighter suspected of landing heroin worth US $125m., and Japan, which tightened port inspections of North Korean ships, hitherto laxly supervised despite suspicions of smuggling methamphetamines to Japan, as well as missile parts and other strategic materials into North Korea. South Korea did not join the PSI, but fears of a breach with the USA were allayed after its new President, Roh Moo-Hyun, adopted a more aggressive stance on his first visit to Washington in May. Yet with younger South Koreans inclined to blame the USA for exacerbating tensions on the peninsula, acute awareness of the closeness of greater Seoul's 20m. people to the front line (Seoul being within range of KPA heavy artillery, the arsenal of which was believed to include chemical shells) led to much anxiety. Despite this, inter-Korean contacts continued as normal throughout the crisis.

After much diplomatic activity, it was agreed that six-party talks, involving the two Koreas, China, the USA, Japan and Russia, would be held in Beijing in August 2003. While, by any measure, this was a full complement of concerned parties, and despite relief at this prospect, the chances for substantive progress were unclear. Kim Jong Il confronted a difficult decision: whether to exchange nuclear programmes, or other activities, such as missile exports, for aid and security guarantees, or keep them as a deterrent against sharing the fate of the regime of Saddam Hussain in Iraq. For his interlocutors, the many dilemmas included: how to prioritize an agenda, with so many concerns; how any nuclear agreement could realistically be verified; and what combination of incentives and punishments to apply. Six-party talks were held in August as scheduled, but ended without resolution. The USA appeared isolated in insisting that North Korea not be compensated for nuclear disarmament. Divisions in the Bush Administration, between those willing to engage Kim Jong Il and 'hard-liners' who sought regime change, seemed likely to culminate in difficulties. On the eve of the six-party talks, Jack Pritchard, who had since the Clinton era been considered the US 'point man' on North Korea (meeting regularly in New York with North Korean diplomats at the UN) resigned, apparently having failed to persuade the USA to recommit to serious and sustained engagement with North Korea.

Once launched, the six-party process continued, albeit at a desultory pace and with scant substantive progress. Despite much shuttle diplomacy (especially by China, which as host had invested heavily in this initiative), hopes of holding a second meeting before the end of 2003 were not fulfilled. In November KEDO's executive board voted to suspend the consortium's LWR project for a year. While South Korea hoped this would resume in due course, the USA—which had pushed for formal suspension—made clear that it saw no future for the LWRs. In January 2004 a senior private US delegation visited Pyongyang and the Yongbyon nuclear site, which was once more operational. One US scientist was allowed to handle a lump of what appeared to be plutonium: a signal that North Korea's nuclear intentions were in earnest. A second round of six-party talks was eventually held in Beijing in February, but again made little progress. This time, China and even South Korea were dismayed that the USA merely repeated its demand of CVID—complete, verified, irreversible dismantling of nuclear facilities—and refused to entertain North Korea's step-by-step offer, starting with a 'freeze'. However, it was agreed to meet again by the end of June, with prior working groups to discuss details. The latter met briefly in April, and again just before the third round of full talks in June.

At the third round of talks the USA modified its position to offer a phased process, including interim incentives. Details were not published, but this seemed to be a hopeful sign. By now, however, the US electoral cycle had become a factor. A fourth round, due by September 2004, did not take place, since Kim Jong Il was thought to expect a better deal if the Democratic candidate, Senator John Kerry, defeated George W. Bush at the presidential election. Other US incentives, such as a donation of 50,000 metric tons of grain in July, failed to mollify North Korea, which instead reacted angrily to US urgings to emulate Libya and definitively surrender all of its weapons of mass destruction.

Meanwhile, in April 2004 Kim Jong Il visited Beijing for the third time in four years. As ever, he travelled by train, his journey being shrouded in secrecy: his brief trip (of just two nights) was confirmed only after it was over. All was publicly cordial, as usual. This was Kim's first encounter with China's new leadership under Hu Jintao; the main aim of the People's Republic was to ensure North Korea's commitment to the six-party talks, and its amenability more generally. This all came at a price: China admitted offering aid, but details were not given. By contrast to the China visit, in neither 2003 nor 2004, unlike the two previous years, did Kim's train roll north for summits with Vladimir Putin. However, Russia continued to foster good relations with North Korea, and to take a moderate line within the six-party talks. In July 2004 Sergei Lavrov, Russia's Minister of Foreign Affairs, returned home by way of Seoul and Pyongyang from the ARF held in Jakarta.

Japan, meanwhile, displayed its own combination of persuasion and incentives. The Koizumi Government approved laws restricting transfers to hostile nations (although North Korea was not named, nor was the legislation implemented), and intensified inspections of North Korean vessels in Japanese ports. Yet this did not stop Koizumi making a second day-trip to Pyongyang in May 2004. This time he brought back five children of two abductee couples returned in 2002—the apparent price being 250,000 metric tons of rice. In a more complex case, the US husband of another ex-abductee, a former sergeant who had apparently deserted across the DMZ in 1965, and their two daughters, were brought to Jakarta for the family to be reunited. They all then travelled to Japan, despite the possibility of the husband, Charles Jenkins, facing a US court martial. Jenkins received only token punishment and a dishonourable discharge. In August 2004 Japan and North Korea resumed bilateral talks; however, despite Koizumi predicting diplomatic relations to be feasible within a year or two, the abduction, nuclear and missile issues all prevented any progress from being made. From December relations deteriorated further after Japan claimed that the supposed cremated remains of one abductee returned by North Korea were in fact not hers. This caused outrage in Tokyo, despite suggestions that the DNA test might not be conclusive.

In December 2003 North Korea and Ireland established full diplomatic relations, leaving France as the sole EU member still resisting this. France's ground remained the issue of human rights abuses: also a major concern for the EU majority, which had now recognized the Democratic People's Republic. In 2003, and again in 2004 and 2005, European nations successfully introduced resolutions condemning such abuses at the UN Commission on Human Rights in Geneva. China opposed on both occasions, while South Korea absented itself in 2003 and abstained thereafter. The latter resolution provided for the appointment of a special rapporteur, ensuring that the issue would remain on the agenda. In a similar vein, in 2004 both houses of the US Congress unanimously approved a North Korea Human Rights Act (NKHRA), signed into law in October, which committed the US Government to raise this matter.

Foreign relations in 2005 remained dominated by the nuclear crisis, now in its third year. The year began promisingly when two US congressional delegations (one led by a sponsor of the NKHRA, Tom Lantos, a veteran member of the US House of Representatives who had also played an important role in Libya's rapprochement with the USA) visited Pyongyang in early January. A statement released in the same month by KCNA envisaged treating the USA 'as a friend', provided the USA reciprocated. However, this apparent upturn in relations was jeopardized when in February North Korea not only stated that it would indefinitely suspend participation in the six-party talks, but also made its boldest claim yet that it possessed a nuclear deterrent and intended to keep it. The reaction of the USA was calm, but a concerned China dispatched a senior envoy, Wang Jiarui, to meet Kim Jong Il; the latter reaffirmed his commitment to denuclearization and the six-party talks, provided conditions were 'mature'.

Relations between the USA and North Korea were not improved by vague US charges that the latter had aided Libya's former nuclear programme, nor by the description of North Korea as an 'outpost of tyranny' in January 2005 by the newly appointed US Secretary of State, Condoleezza Rice. In April South Korean intelligence confirmed that the Yongbyon reactor had been shut down, prompting fears that spent fuel was being reprocessed to create further plutonium. At the beginning of May North Korea fired a short-range missile off its east coast. Following acrimonious bilateral exchanges, the contract of Charles Kartman, a career US diplomat and supporter of engagement who had been appointed at the time of the Clinton presidency as head of the KEDO consortium, was not renewed. The US Secretary of Defense, Donald Rumsfeld, summarily suspended joint US searches with the KPA for MIA remains, a programme that had been ongoing since 1996 (see above), with several visits planned for 2005.

In June 2005, however, the USA donated 50,000 metric tons of grain to North Korea via WFP. A senior North Korean diplomat, Ri Gun, met US officials at a seminar in New York. It was announced that a fourth round of six-party talks would be held in late July. This announcement followed a secret dinner in Beijing between the head of the North Korean delegation, Vice-Minister of Foreign Affairs and Trade Kim Kye Gwan, and his new US counterpart, Christopher Hill, Assistant Secretary of State for East Asian and Pacific Affairs. That meeting in itself suggested a fresh US stance; this was subsequently confirmed when the six-party talks duly recommenced, with Hill clearly having more authority to be flexible (including eight one-on-one meetings with Kim Kye Gwan) than James Kelly, his predecessor. In another innovation, this round of talks continued for almost two weeks before going into recess. Further discussions resulted in September in North Korea's apparent renunciation of its nuclear activities and the country's commitment to rejoin the NPT, in return for aid, with the six nations agreeing to resume their talks in November. On the following day, however, the accord was undermined when North Korea unexpectedly reiterated its right to conduct peaceful nuclear activities and declared that it would not abandon its nuclear programme unless it was given a light-water reactor for the purposes of electricity generation. As this suggested, the issues remained intractable, particularly with regard to the refusal of the USA to countenance North Korea's retention of a civil nuclear capability.

A short fifth round of six-party talks in November 2005 made no progress. Thereafter North Korea refused to return to the negotiating table, citing a hostile US attitude in general and financial sanctions in particular. In September the US Department of the Treasury accused a bank in Macao, Banco Delta Asia (BDA), of facilitating North Korean financial crimes for more than 20 years, including money laundering and counterfeiting US currency. This prompted a 'run' on the assets of BDA, which required intervention by the Macao authorities. Under this pressure, the bank suspended some 40 North Korean accounts worth approximately US $23m. They remained inaccessible for well over a year, to fury in Pyongyang as well as complaints by foreign joint ventures operating there that this peremptory measure had affected innocent parties. Ill-concealed glee in Washington raised the question of US policy coherence, since these measures, however justified, gave North Korea a fresh pretext not to return to the six-party nuclear talks, which it exploited to the full.

This US action appeared to be one factor in Kim Jong Il's unexpected decision in January 2006 to make his fourth visit to China in five years, just weeks after meeting Hu Jintao in late October on the latter's first visit to Pyongyang in his capacity as China's President. His nine-day trip, as on previous occasions unannounced until after the event, focused on economic sites in China's rapidly expanding areas in the south-east, Guangzhou, Zhuhai, and Shenzhen, while also encompassing Beijing and the Three Gorges Dam project. Kim's entourage, unusually, included no generals. Kim spoke more fulsomely than ever before of China's 'new line'. His generous reception, involving most of China's senior leaders, hardly suggested that he was in disfavour over either nuclear or financial issues, despite the latter affecting Chinese territory in Macao. In October, however, the Chinese Government swiftly condemned the nuclear tests as 'brazen.'

In April 2006 all parties to the six-way talks convened in Tokyo for a 'track two' dialogue. Amid many bilateral encounters, Christopher Hill refused to meet Kim Kye Gwan. These negotiations began two months after Japan and North Korea had held their first fully official bilateral talks since 2002 (the 13th since 1991) in Beijing. Despite adopting a new format in the hope that the abduction issue would not obstruct all progress, there was no movement in any area. Relations thereafter worsened in 2006, as Japan imposed more stringent trade controls, and legislation to permit economic sanctions was approved.

Japan's many concerns included drug-trafficking, an issue that also arose in Australia, where in March 2006 a jury acquitted the captain and senior crew members of a North Korean freighter, the *Pong Su*, seized in 2003 after landing 125 kg of heroin. Although the jury believed the crew's claim to have been unaware of the contents of the ship's freight, the Australian Government's view of this verdict was made clear when bomber aircraft were dispatched to sink the forfeited vessel soon afterwards.

In late 2005 North Korea had given notice that from 2006 it would no longer need humanitarian aid but would accept development assistance. While doubting this assessment, aid agencies had little power to dispute it. Most resident NGOs were obliged to leave, or regrouped under EU auspices. By mid-2006 WFP had negotiated a much-reduced role.

On 5 July 2006 North Korea attracted international attention by firing seven missiles; one being the first-ever test of a long-range *Taepo Dong-2*, which apparently failed soon after launch. Unlike its 1998 precursor, this was not unexpected: the *Taepo Dong* missile had been visible on its gantry since mid-May 2006, prompting much concern and appeals to North Korea not to fire it. By late June it seemed that, as in 1999, this was a feint. The actual launch, on 4 July 2006, coinciding with Independence Day in the USA, was thus a calculated rebuff to all. The most militant reaction came from Tokyo, where discussion by senior officials of a right to pre-emption seemed to antagonize South Korea more than the actual missile tests. Japan also filed a firm resolution in the UN Security Council, which in mid-July unanimously approved a weaker version, condemning the tests and imposing limited sanctions, supported by Russia and China; the latter had warned it would veto any reference to Chapter VII of the UN Charter, which allows for the use of force.

Over subsequent months several attempts were made to persuade North Korea to return to the six-way talks, but without success. In early October 2006 news reports from North Korea indicated that it was about to conduct a nuclear test. China urged North Korea to 'exercise necessary calm and restraint', while the USA and Japan issued similar warnings. The North Korean media reported that an underground test had been conducted in Gilju, in the north-eastern Hamgyong Province. This was later confirmed by US intelligence sources, although experts suggested that the magnitude of the explosion—less than one kiloton—indicated that it might not have been as successful as had been claimed. The declared test prompted immediate international criticism, and in mid-October the members of the UN Security Council unanimously adopted Resolution No. 1718, imposing sanctions on North Korea. The sanctions, which Russia and China agreed to with reservations, included the inspection of cargo being transported to and from the North, travel bans on certain North Korean officials and measures to restrict the supply of luxury goods to the country. However, implementation of the sanctions was another matter: while Japan, for example, implemented further measures to ban all imports, vessels and (for a time) visitors from North Korea, it was unclear how effective all this would be against a state with which trade exchanges were already minimal and largely covert.

Nevertheless, following a disappointing first resumption in mid-December, which recessed after a week of no progress, in early 2007 the six-party talks were not only revived but also achieved their first substantial results. The main factor here was a drastic shift in policy by the USA, where forces favouring engagement had finally won President Bush's support. In January Kim Kye Gwan and Christopher Hill met in Berlin, opening the way for a further six-party round held in Beijing in mid-February, when agreement was reached on a remarkably clear programme, albeit only of 'initial actions', rather than a detailed 'roadmap' towards full denuclearization. Within 60 days North Korea was to 'shut down and seal for the purpose of eventual abandonment' its Yongbyon nuclear site, an act to be verified by the IAEA; the North Korean Government would also list all of the nuclear activities that were eventually to be discontinued. In return, North Korea would receive aid equivalent to 50,000 metric tons of heavy fuel oil. A further 950,000 tons, worth some US $300m., would follow once it furnished 'a complete declaration of all nuclear programmes and disablement of all existing nuclear facilities.' Addressing wider issues alongside this, the USA and Japan would each begin bilateral talks with North Korea; the USA moved to end its long-standing sanctions under the Trading with the Enemy Act, as well as its designation of North Korea as a state sponsor of terrorism; Japan hoped to establish an agenda for 'the settlement of unfortunate past' (sic), an indirect reference to past abductions of Japanese. These talks occupied two of five new working groups; the others, each chaired by a different participant nation, covered economic and energy co-operation, denuclearization of the Korean peninsula, and the establishment of a North-East Asia peace and security mechanism. Ranging more broadly still, another clause stated that 'the directly related parties will negotiate a permanent peace regime on the Korean peninsula', thus addressing North Korea's long-standing demand for a treaty formally to end the 1950–53 Korean War.

What this accord did not explicitly mention was the BDA obstacle. After separate negotiations, the US Department of the Treasury, under pressure from the Department of State, yielded, agreeing not only to return all North Korean funds frozen in Macao, suspect or not, but to do so by wire transfer to signify that North Korea was an acceptable partner. Embarrassingly, the transfer of funds proved technically difficult inasmuch as BDA remained sanctioned, so the 14 April deadline passed with the Yongbyon plant remaining open; no party seemed unduly alarmed. Not until late June 2007 did North Korea declare the BDA issue settled, after the funds had been transferred via a complex route to a private Russian bank. IAEA inspectors then arrived, and Yongbyon was finally shut down in mid-July.

Meanwhile, Christopher Hill's 'shuttle diplomacy' for the first time incorporated Pyongyang for an unannounced visit in June 2007. Despite this, the next round of six-party talks, held in Beijing in July, seemed to mark time: no new timetable was laid down, although it was agreed that working groups would meet again, and several duly did in the following month. Challenges ahead included how and when Yongbyon's closure would develop into permanent disablement and dismantlement, and whether North Korea's required declaration of all nuclear facilities would admit its suspected covert highly enriched uranium activities—the catalyst of the second ongoing nuclear crisis since the USA applied pressure on this in 2002 (although some in Washington had subsequently expressed uncertainty over the actual extent of the programme's progress). Renewed demands by North Korea for light water reactors posed another problem. Overall, in mid-2007 Kim Jong Il appeared to have gained the advantage, with no opponent (except a now-isolated Japan) minded to take an uncompromising approach. It suited Kim's other interlocutors, including a weakened Bush Administration, to point to the six-party process as constituting progress, even though it was far from clear how the following stages would develop, or when North Korea would in fact be required to give up its nuclear weapons; indeed, whether it would ever do so. With typical defiance, North Korea test-fired three new missiles during May and June.

Relations with Japan deteriorated further after a Tokyo court ruled in June 2007 that a state credit agency could seize the headquarters of the pro-Pyongyang General Association of Korean Residents in Japan (Chongryon in Korean, Chongsoren in Japanese), in order to cover unpaid debts of credit unions affiliated to Chongryon. Regarded as North Korea's potential embassy in Tokyo if normal relations were ever to be established, Chongryon was said to perform numerous diplomatic functions; the building was seized in early August. North Korea threatened unspecified retribution.

Elsewhere, in April 2007 Myanmar announced the resumption of diplomatic relations with North Korea, and in September the two countries were reported to be engaged in senior-level talks. North Korea and Myanmar had been allies until the Rangoon (Yangon) bombing in 1983 (see above), after which Myanmar (then known as Burma) broke off relations. In May 2007, Nicaragua followed suit with the return to power of Daniel Ortega, whose Sandinista guerrillas North Korea had helped to train in the 1970s. In August 2007 North Korea and Iran agreed to increase energy co-operation, including the exchange of crude petroleum from the latter for refined oil from the former. During July and August Kim Yong Nam, the titular Head of State, visited Mongolia, Algeria, Egypt, Ethiopia and Singapore, in an apparent effort to improve relations. In September diplomatic relations were opened with four new countries: the United Arab Emirates, Swaziland, the Dominican Republic and Guatemala.

North Korea's foreign relations continued to revolve around the nuclear issue, with the usual fluctuations. The six-party talks reconvened at the end of September 2007, this time to better purpose. In a detailed accord, North Korea agreed not only to disable its already closed Yongbyon site under US supervision but also to declare all of its other nuclear activities, in both cases by 31 December. In return, it would receive a further 900,000 metric tons of heavy fuel oil, or equivalent aid. In the event, this deadline was not met, amid discord over the scope of the nuclear declaration. Besides the ongoing issue of highly enriched uranium, a new factor was that of suspected nuclear proliferation; with rumours that a mysterious facility being built in Syria's eastern desert, destroyed in early September by Israeli bombing, was a replica of the Yongbyon installation.

After a long silence on the part of the USA, in late April 2008 members of the US Congress were shown video evidence of a North Korean presence at this site, in what some saw as a rearguard action by opponents of engagement within the Bush Administration. Similarly, in mid-January Jay Lefkowitz, the US special envoy on North Korean human rights, broke ranks, stating that North Korea was 'not serious about disarming in a timely manner'. For this he was firmly rebuked by the US Secretary of State, Condoleezza Rice.

In late February 2008 the New York Philharmonic became the first major Western, much less US, classical orchestra ever to perform in North Korea. The audience included William Perry, US President Bill Clinton's first Secretary of Defense in 1994 when war was a real risk; Perry had since advocated pre-emptive strikes on North Korea's long-range missiles. Both the US and North Korean flags adorned the stage. The concert was broadcast live across North Korea, and around the world, thanks to technical aid from a South Korean broadcasting corporation, which drove an 18-vehicle convoy of equipment to Pyongyang via the DMZ. The concert was widely and well covered by the foreign media, with 80 Western reporters forming part of the orchestra's 300-strong entourage. Most comment was rather positive, albeit with few illusions about the real nature of the situation in North Korea.

Abandoning all pretence of the multilateralism on which President Bush had insisted for many years (hence the six-party talks), Christopher Hill met thrice with Kim Kye Gwan: first in Beijing in February 2008, then in Geneva in March and again in Singapore in April. It appeared that both the issues of enriched uranium and of Syria would be handled elsewhere, in accordance with a secret bilateral memorandum whereby the USA would state its concerns and North Korea would not deny them, outside the formal six-party process as such.

On this somewhat tenuous basis, progress resumed. In May 2008 Sung Kim, the US Department of State's senior Korea specialist, returned from Pyongyang (crossing into South Korea via the DMZ, a rare privilege) with 19,000 pages of documents: apparently the complete logbooks from Yongbyon. In late June, six months later than scheduled, North Korea delivered its nuclear declaration. Foreign media were invited to film the demolition of Yongbyon's main cooling tower, as proof that this site would never again reopen. President Bush responded swiftly by removing the application to North Korea of the Trading with the Enemy Act, which had banned most bilateral trade for more than half-a-century since the Korean War. However, the separate sanctions imposed by the UN Security Council after North Korea's missile and nuclear tests in 2006 remained in force.

Simultaneously, Bush gave Congress the statutory 45 days' notice of taking North Korea off the Department of State's list of countries regarded as sponsoring terrorism. It had been so listed for 20 years, mandating the USA to oppose any attempt by North Korea to join bodies such as the World Bank or the IMF. While this would make delisting possible by 11 August 2008, the USA later clarified that this would not be done unless formal talks towards the next phase—that of nuclear verification—had first begun. Verification was the main theme of a further round of six-party talks, held in July. In another sign of amity, at the ARF convened in Singapore in the same month Condoleezza Rice shook hands with her North Korean counterpart, Minister of Foreign Affairs Pak Ui Chun. In fact, in the order of protocol peculiar to Pyongyang, Pak carried less weight than his nominal deputies: the First Deputy Minister of Foreign Affairs, Kang Sok Ju, and Kim Kye Gwan. It remained to be seen how fast North Korea would move on the issue of verification, the intrusiveness of which would be uncongenial; and also how soon it would be required to reveal, much less surrender, its nuclear weapons, a further striking lacuna in the six-party process thus far.

Meanwhile, Japan remained focused on the abductions issue and was reluctant to see Kim Jong Il exonerated of state terrorism while its particular concern remained unresolved. In June 2008 North Korea agreed to reopen its investigations, but a month later Japan stated that it perceived no progress and would continue to withhold aid, the only participant in the six-party talks to do so. Conversely, the USA in May had already rewarded North Korea's resumed nuclear co-operativeness, while implausibly denying any such linkage, by giving a much-needed 500,000 metric tons of grain: its largest donation since 1999 and the first since 2005. South Korea had usually sent the same amount of grain in recent years, but not this time.

Relations with an impatient, but still supportive, China were consolidated in June 2008 when Xi Jinping, the new Chinese Vice-President, and a likely successor to President Hu Jintao, chose Pyongyang as his first foreign destination for an official visit. However, a report published in January by two US 'think tanks' had shown that Chinese analysts shared the same concerns about North Korea as observers elsewhere, including the fear of regime collapse. This also revealed that China had contingency plans for military intervention in North Korea, as did South Korea and the USA.

From late 2008 North Korea's foreign policy adopted a markedly harder stance. The last positive development (although not perceived as such by all, with Japan expressing deep dismay) was its delisting as a state sponsor of terrorism by President Bush in October, two months later than originally expected. This followed a visit to Pyongyang by Christopher Hill in early October, when disputes over the delay in delisting and on nuclear verification were threatening to undermine progress; in late September the North Korea Government had told IAEA inspectors to leave Yongbyon. Despite Hill's apparent success, and a later bilateral meeting with Kim Kye Gwan in Singapore in early December on the eve of the next round of six-party talks, it was clear when these discussions reconvened in Beijing that disagreements on the question of verification had not in fact been resolved. It appeared that Kim Kye Gwan, and perhaps also Hill, had offered more than their respective leaders were ready to endorse.

In any case, North Korea had scant reason to reward a US President whom it still deeply mistrusted, when his successor might soon bring a new approach or offer better terms. More enigmatic was the decision to greet incoming US President Barack Obama, known to be ready to talk to 'enemies' of the USA, with a display of rhetorical militancy. Early in 2009 four separate senior US delegations visited Pyongyang; these were nominally private delegations, but included Stephen Bosworth, who was soon after named as the new US special envoy to North Korea, replacing Hill (who had been appointed as US ambassador to Iraq). All four delegations were denied access to their usual interlocutors, and reportedly found their hosts in no mood, much less hurry, for better relations with the USA or for progress in any other area.

In January 2009 a senior CCP official, Wang Jiarui, became the first foreign visitor to meet Kim Jong Il since his suspected stroke in August 2008. However, rather than a return to normal business, this was followed by the detection by spy satellites of apparent preparations for a long-range missile test. On 16 February (Kim Jong Il's birthday) KCNA criticized 'vicious' rumours of a missile test. A week later the Korean Committee of Space Technology announced a forthcoming satellite launch. In March the International Maritime Organization and the International Civil Aviation Organization were notified of the date and range co-ordinates of the launch, which finally took place on 5 April. As in its first long-range missile test (the *Taepo Dong* missile fired without warning over Japan in August 1998—see above), North Korea claimed to have put a satellite into orbit. However, as in 1998, no signals were detected by external parties, suggesting that the real motive for the launch was a military purpose, the rocket itself being dual-use. Unlike the previous unsuccessful testing of the *Taepo Dong-2* in July 2006 (see above), this time the missile travelled as far as 3,800 km, a record for a North Korean rocket.

Western powers were adamant that this rocket breached UN Security Council Resolution No. 1718, approved unanimously in October 2006 after North Korea's first nuclear test, which forbade any ballistic missile activity. However, China and Russia urged moderation. Not until 13 April 2009 was compromise reached on a unanimous Security Council Presidential Statement (weaker than a Resolution). Drafted by China, this relatively mild reproach elicited a furious response from North Korea. The Ministry of Foreign Affairs denounced the Presidential Statement as 'brigandish. . . an intolerable mockery of the Korean people and a thrice-cursed crime'. Having warned in advance that UN censure of its 'satellite' 'would deprive the six-party talks of any ground to exist or meaning', it now declared that 'the DPRK will never participate in such six-party talks nor will it be bound any longer to any agreement of the talks'. Moreover, it would 'boost its nuclear deterrent for self-defence in every way', including reopening facilities that had been disabled as agreed at the six-party talks. On 15 April (Kim Il Sung's birthday—celebrated as 'Sun's Day') IAEA inspectors at the Yongbyon site removed seals and switched off surveillance cameras, at North Korea's behest; they left the country on the following day.

Hopes that these threats were merely rhetorical were ended on 25 May 2009 when, with no warning, North Korea carried out its second nuclear test, and launched five short-range missiles on 25–26 May and another on 29 May. It also reacted to South Korea's decision, itself a swift riposte to the nuclear test, finally to join the US-led PSI by threatening a military strike if any South Korean vessel were to intercept a Northern one. Further raising tensions, on 27 May it declared itself no longer bound by the 1953 Armistice and stated that it could no longer guarantee safety for South Korean or US vessels (military or civilian) in the West (Yellow) Sea border area.

The UN response to the nuclear test was more robust than that to the missile launch. Security Council Resolution No. 1874, unanimously approved on 12 June 2009, banned almost all arms exports and imports from or to North Korea, and authorized the searching of suspect ships. Soon after a vessel thought to be carrying weapons to Myanmar, where military, and perhaps nuclear, co-operation with North Korea had prompted growing regional concern, came under close scrutiny until the ship turned round and headed back to Nampo, thus avoiding a potential confrontation. The USA set about deploying financial pressure on North Korea as it had in the BDA case during 2005–07 (see above), while Japan banned all trade with the country. On 2–4 July North Korea launched two more sets of mainly small missiles (11 in total), and was duly censured for a third time by the UN Security Council, although only in an oral statement, the mildest form of rebuke and not entered into the record.

Further complicating matters, in June 2009 North Korea sentenced two female US journalists, arrested in mid-March on its border with China for illegal entry, to 12 years' hard labour with no appeal. Former US Vice-President Al Gore, who had founded the company for whom the pair worked, was widely expected to visit North Korea to intercede on their behalf. However, in the event it was the former US President Bill Clinton who flew to Pyongyang in early August. During a meeting with Kim Jong Il, Clinton successfully negotiated the release of both journalists, who returned to the USA on the following day. Meanwhile, North Korean officials became embroiled in an acrimonious exchange with US Secretary of State Hillary Clinton. Amid relief in the USA that the journalists were safe, intense debate followed Bill Clinton's action, which was reminiscent of former President Jimmy Carter's trip to Pyongyang in 1994 (during Bill Clinton's own presidency), again raising the question of whether efforts to isolate North Korea had been undermined. Others argued that such a senior-level visit could only be helpful, both in re-establishing communications and in moving closer to answering what remained the two major questions: what was really going on in North Korea, and what Kim Jong Il truly wanted. During a visit to Pyongyang in December 2009 US special envoy Bosworth delivered a letter to Kim Jong Il from President Obama, but his visit made no progress in terms of providing any answers to these questions.

In late December 2009 a US Christian activist, Robert Park, crossed into North Korea from neighbouring China, preaching the Christian Gospel and urging Kim Jong Il to repent for the human rights atrocities allegedly carried out under the regime. (North Korea's human rights record had once again been condemned by the UN in November, and was the subject of a UN Periodic Review in Geneva in early December; North Korean diplomats denied most charges as 'recycled hearsay', but did admit that public executions occurred in the country.) Duly arrested, Park was released in February 2010 in a seemingly fragile state of mind. Meanwhile, in January another US Christian activist, Aijalon Mahli Gomes, also entered North Korean territory from China, protesting against North Korea's human rights record. However, Gomes was less fortunate than Park, being sentenced in April to eight years' hard labour, having been convicted of entering the country illegally; reports in July claimed that the activist had attempted suicide. However, Gomes was allowed to return to the USA following successful negotiations with North Korean authorities during a two-day diplomatic visit to Pyongyang by former US President Jimmy Carter in August. Unlike Bill Clinton on his similar rescue mission in the previous year, Carter was not granted a meeting with Kim Jong Il, who chose this moment to depart for China (see below).

Meanwhile, in December 2009 Thai authorities seized a Georgian-registered cargo plane that had stopped in Bangkok to refuel. It was found to be carrying 35 metric tons of North Korean weaponry, including rocket launchers, explosives, rocket-propelled grenades and components for surface-to-air-missiles, collectively worth some US $18m. and in direct contravention of UN Security Council Resolution No. 1874. The Kazakh flight crew members were later deported. While the intended final destination of the weaponry remained unclear, with Iran and Lebanon being cited among the various possibilities, the main concern raised by the incident was the question of how many consignments of North Korean weapons had successfully arrived at their intended destinations undetected.

Chinese influence in, if not necessarily on, North Korea increased following several senior-level exchanges. In October 2009 Chinese Premier Wen Jiabao arrived in Pyongyang in commemoration of the 60th anniversary of the establishment of diplomatic relations between the two countries, amid reports of increased Chinese aid. Kim Jong Il met and embraced Wen at the airport, a rare public honour. In early February 2010 the director of the International Department of the Central Committee of the Chinese Communist Party, Wang Jiarui, visited Pyongyang, and later in that month his counterpart Kim Yong Il (as distinct from Premier Kim Yong Il) made a reciprocal visit to Beijing, whereupon he had direct talks with President Hu Jintao; issues discussed were reported to include bilateral aid, the nuclear issue and the sinking of the *Cheonan* in March.

In early May 2010 Kim Jong Il made a long-anticipated visit to China. As in the past, the visit was unofficial and theoretically secret, but a special armoured train and 40-car motorcade were hard to conceal. Kim visited a range of economic sites in Dalian and Tianjin before meeting President Hu in Beijing. He was believed to have returned to Pyongyang one day earlier than planned, amid reports that China's offers of financial aid had been less generous than hoped.

Whatever was said in private between the two leaders with regard to the sinking of the *Cheonan*, publicly China continued to profess scepticism as to North Korea's culpability, to the fury of the South Korean Government. With Russia taking a similar view, when the UN Security Council finally pronounced on the issue in July 2010 it stopped short of issuing a full resolution, releasing only an ambivalently worded presidential statement and imposing no new sanctions. North Korea claimed a diplomatic victory. South Korean efforts to convince regional and other leaders gathered at the ARF held in the Vietnamese capital, Hanoi, to condemn North Korea over the incident were similarly frustrated. However, during a visit to Seoul, also in July, US Secretary of State Clinton announced the imposition of new sanctions against North Korea and reiterated US demands that the North admit responsibility for the attack. While South Korea's Western allies offered strong support, much of the wider world seemed to regard the *Cheonan* incident as an inter-Korean altercation rather than a violation of international law.

At the ARF in July 2010 US Secretary of State Clinton had expressed concerns with regard to the apparent nuclear ambitions of Myanmar. A cordial visit to the country's administrative capital of Nay Pyi Taw a few days later by the North Korean Minister of Foreign Affairs, Pak Ui Chun, would have done little to allay these concerns.

The latter half of 2010 brought unambiguous evidence of North Korea's drawing closer to China. In August Kim Jong Il unexpectedly travelled by train to north-eastern China, where he visited revolutionary sites associated with his father as well as factories. His itinerary included Jilin, Harbin and Changchun, where President Hu Jintao hosted a banquet for him. Kim Jong Un, although not officially named as being part of Kim Jong Il's entourage, was thought to be with him. It was speculated that the aim of the visit was to secure China's assent to, and perhaps even financing of, his succession.

Evidently such support was obtained. In October 2010 a senior member of China's Politburo, Zhou Yongkang, stood with Kim Jong Il and Kim Jong Un on the podium in Pyongyang at the military parade to commemorate the 65th anniversary of the KWP's foundation. Zhou was accompanied by senior officials from the Chinese provinces adjacent to North Korea, namely Jilin, Liaoning and Heilongjiang. A bilateral economic accord was signed on the previous day, but no details were released. Soon after, all North Korea's provincial party secretaries visited north-eastern China and Beijing, where they were hosted by Zhou. Later in October the North Korean ambassador in Beijing, Choe Pyong Gwan, was replaced, after only six months in the post, by the more senior and better-connected Ji Jae Ryong, in a further sign of the deepening and upgrading of bilateral relations.

Similarly, on 19 October 2010 the 60th anniversary of China's entry into the Korean War—which ultimately had saved the emerging DPRK from destruction—was marked with rare pomp and public expressions of gratitude. A week later the entire senior North Korean leadership assembled at the Chinese People's Volunteers' cemetery, east of Pyongyang, where Kim Jong Il laid a wreath on the grave of Mao Zedong's son, Mao Anying, who had been killed in the conflict.

Such assiduous courtship paid diplomatic dividends. On 23 November 2010 when North Korean forces fired in excess of 150 artillery shells and rockets at South Korea's Yeonpyeong island, resulting in four fatalities, China did not condemn the act, its state media merely reiterating the North Korean version of events: that this was a response to South Korean provocation. However, in contrast to the Chinese response to the sinking of the *Cheonan*, this time China did not strongly oppose the USA reacting by holding joint naval manoeuvres with South Korea in the Yellow Sea, in which the aircraft carrier *USS George Washington* participated. The dispatch of the US super-carrier was widely interpreted as being intended both to deter further attacks by North Korea and also to warn China against allowing its ally to act in such a bellicose manner.

On the day prior to the attack on Yeonpyeong, a leading US nuclear scientist, Dr Siegfried Hecker of Stanford University, had reported that, during a visit to Yongbyon earlier in the month, he and his party had been hurried through a new and hitherto unsuspected uranium enrichment plant, containing an estimated 2,000 centrifuges. Although their hosts insisted that the plant's purpose was purely civilian, clearly North Korea had progressed much further than had previously been thought along this second potential route to making nuclear weapons. By contrast, many of Yongbyon's original facilities, which involved the extraction of plutonium, were in apparent desuetude. President Obama at once dispatched his Special Representative for North Korea, Stephen Bosworth, to Seoul, Tokyo and Beijing, but no further visible action followed.

In February 2011 it was reported that North Korean embassies world-wide had been instructed to appeal for food aid. The USA and the United Kingdom both confirmed that they had been approached to this end. This prompted fresh debate on the question of whether or not to assist North Korea. South Korea remained staunchly of the view that no assistance would be granted; at mid-2011 an ever-more vacillating USA had yet to decide, but the EU announced €10m. in food aid for North Korea in July. During a visit to Pyongyang in late April (see Part One, The Korean Peninsula: Conflict and Dialogue), Jimmy Carter angered some in Seoul by describing the refusal by South Korea and the USA to give food aid to those in need in the North as a human rights violation. The USA denied that it was deliberately withholding food aid, insisting that North Korea had suspended US aid in mid-2009 amid rising bilateral tensions and that aid agencies had been ordered to leave the country.

In May 2011 Kim Jong Il made an unprecedented third trip to China in little over a year, during which he visited, among other places, Beijing and the south-eastern city of Yangzhou, where Kim Il Sung had held a meeting with China's then leader Jiang Zemin 20 years previously. It was rumoured that it was Kim Jong Un, rather than his father, who had been intended to make the visit but that China had vetoed the plan on the grounds that it would be inappropriate for Chinese senior cadres to have to treat the young general as their counterpart.

Soon after Kim Jong Il's visit, two new bilateral economic zones were announced on consecutive days in early June 2011: one on the undeveloped Hwanggumphyong and Wihwa islands, at the estuary of the Yalu river near the cities of Dandong in China and Sinuiju in North Korea; and the other in Rason, which was to incorporate the existing free zone in the north-eastern town, which had hitherto failed to attract any significant investment since its inception in the 1990s. In both zones, China was to finance and carry out the development work, a role that it was reportedly happier to take on in Rason—an ice-free port convenient for its own landlocked north-eastern regions. By contrast, China was thought to have been opposed to the Hwanggumphyong and Wihwa zone, deeming it pointless, which was rumoured to have caused friction and to have delayed the opening ceremonies of both zones, originally scheduled to have taken place in late May.

There were other signs that China might be losing its patience with its ally. At a trilateral Chinese-Japanese-South Korean summit meeting held in Japan in May 2011, Chinese Premier Wen Jiabao declared that the purpose of Kim's visit was to learn from China's development. In June at the Shangri-La Dialogue, an annual regional security summit meeting hosted by Singapore, China's Minister of National Defence, Liang Guanglie, claimed that Chinese engagement with North Korea comprised 'much more than what the outside world may expect', with China 'trying to persuade them not to take risks'.

Perhaps fearing to entrust all to China, from mid-2011 North Korea appeared keen to improve relations with other, more hostile interlocutors. In mid-July the South Korean and North Korean nuclear envoys unexpectedly met on the Indonesian island of Bali, following which they agreed to make joint efforts to resume the six-party talks as soon as possible (see Part One, The Korean Peninsula: Conflict and Dialogue, see p. 10). In the following week Kim Kye Gwan held talks with US Special Representative for North Korea Stephen Bosworth in New York, the first 'face-to-face' meeting between high-level representatives of the two countries since 2009; no results were announced, but both sides described the talks as 'constructive'. It was even strongly rumoured that Japan, with which relations had seemingly been mired in an irreparable nadir over the abductions issue (see above), had held secret bilateral talks in Changchun in late July, although officially this was denied.

In sum, at mid-2011 a mood for renewed dialogue with the North Korean regime appeared to be building within the international community. As well as a growing sense that the many concerns generated by North Korea would only worsen if left unaddressed, other regional and international powers were beginning to fear, not before time, that their own inaction might serve further to strengthen the close bond between China and North Korea.

Economy

ROBERT F. ASH

Following the formal establishment of the Democratic People's Republic of Korea (DPRK) on 9 September 1948, the national economy was rapidly transformed into a Soviet-style, highly centralized and planned system. To this day, many of the essential attributes of this system remain in place. Indeed, since the implementation of market-orientated reform in the People's Republic of China, the former USSR and other previously socialist countries, North Korea has become perhaps the most isolated, monocratic and autarchic economic regime in the world. Such isolation, emphasized by a lack of clear official policy statements and an absence of reliable published statistics, makes it enormously difficult to assess economic developments. Economic reports from North Korea contain few 'real' statistics, and virtually all authoritative comment on the quantitative dimensions of the country's economic performance derive from outside sources, especially from South Korea.

Even allowing for impressive rates of economic growth that have sometimes been achieved, central planning systems throughout the world have generated severe problems of waste and inefficiency. In North Korea the Government's rigid adherence to central planning has undoubtedly inhibited economic growth and constrained its long-term economic performance. Until the early 1960s economic expansion was admittedly rapid, but this owed more to recovery from a war-ravaged economy than to net growth. Until the late 1960s economic growth in North Korea (averaging around 12% annually) exceeded that of the South, and not until the mid-1970s did South Korea's gross national product (GNP) surpass that of its Northern neighbour. In per caput terms, the South's pre-eminence emerged even later. However, the overwhelmingly heavy industry bias of the North meant that rises in per caput GNP were not matched by commensurate improvements in material consumption.

Economic growth in all communist regimes was driven by the physical accumulation of resources (especially capital), rather than by productivity improvements. In this respect, North Korea has been no exception. Over time, infrastructural shortcomings have also become increasingly serious, further highlighting the need to enhance efficiency through more effective resource use and the adoption of more advanced technology in order to maintain the growth momentum. Throughout its existence, North Korea's development strategy has been guided by the ideology of *Juche*, or 'self-reliance'. The notion of *Juche* for economic development', which has come to acquire almost mythical overtones, was first articulated by the country's then leader, Kim Il Sung, in December 1956. It dominated the formulation and implementation of development policies until well after Kim's death in 1994, most clearly manifesting itself in a continuing emphasis on the need to generate an independent, self-reliant economy. Thus, following the death of his father, Kim Il Sung, North Korea's new paramount leader, Kim Jong Il (the 'Dear Leader'), continued to defend socialist ownership and the consolidation and development of a socialist economic system embodying the *Juche* ideology, while emphatically rejecting the introduction of capitalist methods. Despite a more recent willingness to embrace qualified and modest market-orientated policies, *Juche* has remained a dominant influence on economic policy in North Korea.

The flexibility with which *Juche* can be interpreted does not necessarily make it incompatible with economic liberalization. It is, for example, significant that a constitutional amendment introduced in 1998 made explicit reference to privatization, material incentives and profitability, while continuing to endorse North Korea's pursuit of a planned, socialist and self-reliant economy. In the same year the North Korean Government sought advice from the World Bank on the establishment of a market economy. Yet even now it remains premature to speculate about the outcome of such initiatives. On the one hand, the North Korean Government has shown itself eager to expand foreign trade, encourage foreign investment and embrace modern technology; nor is there much doubt that some within the North Korean leadership are strongly in favour of more comprehensive reforms, similar to those pursued by China since the 1980s. On the other hand, there is an influential 'hardline' faction that is opposed to market-orientated reforms for fear of jeopardizing central control over important national assets and undermining socialization, not to mention damaging the political control of the Korean Workers' Party (KWP). In testimony to the US Senate in April 2006, Marcus Noland, a senior fellow of the International Institute for Economics in Washington, DC, described North Korea's response to market reforms as having been 'reactive and ambivalent', a statement that succinctly captures the Government's hesitancy on the issue. For the time being, uncertainties surrounding the political succession to Kim Jong Il strongly favour maintenance of the economic status quo and make it unlikely that any radical changes to economic policy will be forthcoming in the near future. In short, the tension between the pragmatic benefits of Chinese-style economic reform and the political demands of maintaining the ideological orthodoxies of planning and *Juche* remains very real.

Among the obstacles to Chinese-style reforms are the economically distorting effects of North Korea's *Songun* ('military first') strategy. The *Songun* ethos is reflected in the country's possession of the fourth largest armed forces in the world (estimated at 1.19m. members at November 2010, around one-fifth of all men of military age) and military spending that is thought to absorb about one-quarter of gross domestic product (GDP). The overwhelming emphasis on military construction not only distorts economic growth, but also seriously constrains the potential for welfare improvements among the population.

North Korea retains the structural features of a poor economy. For many years it has suffered persistent shortages of skilled labour, modern equipment and technology. Capacity under-utilization, reflecting congestion in the energy, transport and mining sectors, and inadequate infrastructural investment have further impeded development. With agriculture still accounting for more than one-fifth of GDP, the performance of the farm sector is crucial to overall economic performance. The central role of agriculture is reflected not only in its impact on the economy, but also on the living standards and welfare of the population, of which it is a prime determinant. Yet arable land constraints, along with economic and technical obstacles, have undermined agricultural production, giving rise to continued food shortages, widespread malnutrition and starvation through to the present day. In the mid-1990s the shortcomings of the state distribution system were sufficiently severe to prompt the spontaneous emergence in many parts of North Korea (especially urban areas) of a private economy in order to provide supplementary supplies of food and other basic necessities.

Overall, it is clear that North Korea continues to confront severe problems inherited from the past. The chronic lack of resources, both financial and material, and reliance on obsolete equipment and technology have become increasingly serious problems. North Korea's poor recent economic record also reflects the implementation of the inward-looking policies of the past, which, as in other former socialist countries, placed undue emphasis on heavy industry at the expense of welfare-enhancing consumer goods and services. Its 'closed door' stance has also effectively downgraded the role of foreign trade and inhibited the productivity-enhancing effects of technology transfer. The outcome of such structural imbalances has been to offer protection to domestic industries behind artificial barriers, and thereby to prevent the emergence of internationally competitive industries. This, in turn, has not only led to a serious shortage of foreign exchange, but has also exacerbated North Korea's long-standing and growing foreign indebtedness. It remains to be seen how, and indeed whether, the Government can fulfil its stated aspiration to develop and strengthen economic links with other countries while maintaining its official adherence to the traditional orthodoxy of self-reliance.

Many would argue that North Korea's economic salvation lies in the direction of gradual, if not radical, economic reform, embracing Chinese-style market-orientated policies and comprehensively opening the economy to the outside world. As a long-term goal, this is a process that may be facilitated by Korean unification, although the short-term economic and social costs of integration are likely to be considerable. Meanwhile, important initiatives have been taken to encourage foreign investment in North Korea. One of these was the establishment, in 1991, of the 746-sq-km Rajin-Sonbong Free Economic and Trade Zone (FETZ), designed in imitation of the Chinese model to facilitate inflows of foreign direct investment (FDI). Another was the creation of the Kaesong Industrial Complex just north of the demilitarized zone (DMZ), which has become an important conduit for the transfer of advanced technology from South Korea into the DPRK. It is still too soon to speculate whether the current, or indeed any future, North Korean Government will be capable of following China's example in using reform to propel its economy onto a sustained path of renewed growth.

ECONOMIC GROWTH AND STRUCTURAL CHANGE

Throughout its existence, North Korea's economic development has been characterized by pursuit of an unbalanced industrial strategy, geared towards maximizing heavy industrial growth. This, in turn, has been reflected in significant economic structural change. At the time of partition, agriculture (including fishing and forestry) generated almost two-thirds of GDP, compared with an industrial contribution of less than 20%. According to estimates by the Bank of Korea (BOK—the South Korean central bank), agriculture's share had decreased to 20.9% by 2009, although mining added a further 12.7% to GDP, so that the primary sector's contribution overall was about one-third. Despite the industrial thrust of North Korea's development strategy, the contribution of secondary sector activities—34.2%—was only marginally greater than that of the primary sector. This figure comprised manufacturing (only 22.1%), construction (8.0%, its share having decreased from 9.6% in 2005) and electricity, gas and water (4.1%); services, meanwhile, accounted for an estimated 32.1% of GDP, of which 22.8% reflected government activities. Even allowing for a significant margin of error (see below), such figures reveal that the agricultural contribution to overall economic activity is significantly higher than that of most low-income countries, while the shares of industry and non-government services are lower.

Industrial growth (excluding mining and construction) during 2005–09 averaged less than 2% annually, a figure that concealed much higher heavy industrial growth than that of light industry, as well as low levels of efficiency and productivity. Industrial plants, most of which have remained under strict state ownership and control, reportedly operated at an average of 30% below capacity for many years prior to Kim Il Sung's death in 1994, and by the late 1990s were believed to be functioning at about 20% of capacity. In view of the persistent shortages of energy and spare parts, it is likely that conditions have since deteriorated even further. Owing to the disproportionately high allocation of resources to heavy industry and military expenditure, industrial growth in North Korea has not been translated into significant improvements in material consumption and living standards.

The high level of secrecy in North Korea has resulted in a paucity of published economic data. The questionable reliability and ambiguities of the limited available official statistics pose further formidable problems in measuring its economic performance. Despite these and other, more familiar, difficulties associated with estimating the national output of a communist country on a US dollar basis, there is substantial agreement on the quantitative dimensions of North Korea's recent economic performance. The picture that emerges is one of long-term positive growth during the early decades of the regime (for example, average national income growth was probably around 9% annually during 1960–89), followed by a serious contraction during most of the 1990s, after economic links with the USSR and Eastern bloc countries disintegrated. This contraction was exacerbated by problems of energy shortages, poor maintenance of existing industrial and infrastructural facilities, technological backwardness and inadequate investment. (Some suggest that by the second half of the 1990s investment had fallen below replacement level, generating negative net capital growth.) During 1990–98 GDP contracted at an average annual rate of 3.8%, as a result of which aggregate GDP contracted by just over one-third. This trend was eventually reversed in 1999, owing mainly to higher farm production and—more significantly from the perspective of longer-term development—to much-needed inflows of foreign aid (estimated at US $650m.). Thus, GDP rose by an estimated 6.2% in 1999, and maintained a positive momentum until and including 2005. The improved economic performance reflected efforts by the North Korean Government to stabilize production in traditional core heavy industries, while seeking to expand the output of consumer goods and promote the development of information and communications activities. A major initiative in 2002 was the introduction of a policy 'package', designed to encourage limited marketization (see below). In 2006, however, seven consecutive years of positive GDP growth gave way to a negative trend, which intensified in 2007 and, despite being temporarily reversed in 2008, reasserted itself in 2009. According to the Economist Intelligence Unit (EIU—a research and analysis organization based in London, the United Kingdom), GDP expanded by 2.1% in 2010.

The most authoritative estimates of recent and current GDP and sectoral growth in North Korea are those published by the BOK. These show that North Korea's GDP contracted by 0.9% in 2009. On the basis of estimated aggregate nominal gross national income (GNI) of 28,634,600m. won, the BOK postulated average per caput GNI of 1,125,000 won, 4.2% below the figure for 2008, and a mere 5.6% of the corresponding figure for South Korea. However, using exchange rates in order to convert this figure to a US-dollar equivalent is fraught with difficulty, given the huge discrepancy between the official exchange rate (145 won = US $1 in 2009) and the market rate (3,500 won = $1).

Concealed within the BOK estimates is the finding that the downturn in North Korea's economic performance in 2009 reflected a fall in agricultural production caused by adverse cold weather conditions, as well as declines in mining and manufacturing output resulting from raw material and power shortages. Following two years of decline (by 2.6% in 2006 and 9.4% in 2007), in 2008 good weather conditions had facilitated an 8.2% increase in farm output; by contrast, in 2009 agricultural production (including forestry and fisheries) decreased by 1.0% in real terms. The growth performance of the secondary sector was even worse, with real GDP declining by 2.3%, within which there was a 0.9% decline in mining output and a 2.3% contraction in that of manufacturing. The only sector to record positive growth was that of services, output of which rose by a marginal 0.1% (a performance that was carried entirely by a 0.5% rate of increase in government services, other services recording a 0.8% decline). Construction GDP increased by 0.8%. Meanwhile, following two years of buoyant growth (4.8% and 6.0% in 2007 and 2008, respectively), in 2009 the production of electricity, gas and water remained unchanged, with zero growth.

At the end of November 2009 the North Korean Government unexpectedly launched a currency reform programme that was apparently intended to revive socialism and combat what it regarded as the unfavourable side-effects of the recent expansion of private markets. Currency redenominations have traditionally been used to address severe inflationary pressures, and senior North Korean officials argued that this was the principal rationale of the 2009 adjustments. According to Marcus Noland, however, the main driver of the currency reform was the Government's wish to 'reassert state control over the economy'. In the event, the announcement, made without prior warning, that the former currency would be recalibrated at a ratio of one new won per 100 old won precipitated chaos. Two factors were responsible for the panic that followed the announcement: first, the population was informed that it would be given just one week in which to convert its holdings of old currency; second, a strict limit of

100,000 won per household was imposed on the amount that residents would be allowed to exchange; this amount was barely sufficient to buy a 50-kg bag of rice at existing retail prices. The outcome was predictable: citizens sought to offload the old currency by engaging in panic-buying of foreign exchange or goods that were likely to hold their value. In turn, the 'black market' value of the North Korean won collapsed, leading the Government to introduce further new regulations in an attempt to prevent the use of foreign currency, set new official prices for the exchange of goods, and limit both the number of products that could be legally traded and also the times when market exchanges of such goods could be transacted. The consequences were catastrophic. As Noland put it, the net result was 'a literal disintegration of the market, as traders, intimidated by the changing rules of the game, withheld supply, reportedly forcing some citizens to resort to barter'.

If, as some sources suggest, the original reform initiative was devised by Kim Jong Un (Kim Jong Il's third son and apparent successor), in an attempt to mark his emergence as a major political figure, it was a clear failure. Indeed, on any rational calculation, the currency redenomination proved disastrous, effectively eliminating many people's cash savings. Meanwhile, government efforts to obviate the impact of the initiative, in the form of compensatory wage increases, gave rise to serious inflationary pressures. The impact of the currency reform on food prices was demonstrated by the fact that between December 2009 and March 2010 the price of a kilogram of rice rose from 20 to 1,500 won. Notwithstanding the ubiquitous rigid controls on freedom of speech and action in North Korea, social protests ensued; reports by the Daily NK, a Seoul-based online news publication devoted to North Korean issues, suggested that some people had even resorted to burning piles of money in order to highlight the old currency's worthlessness. According to the International Crisis Group, a non-governmental organization endeavouring to prevent and resolve conflict globally, soaring food prices forced the Government to release emergency food supplies, although even this was insufficient to prevent the occurrence of deaths from starvation.

By February 2010 government officials, including Premier Kim Yong Il, reportedly expressed regret for the mishandling of the currency reform, appearing to mark the beginning of a policy retreat. Unconfirmed reports in March suggested that the director of the KWP Planning and Finance Department, Pak Nam Gi, had been executed by firing squad. Although Yonhap, the South Korean News Agency, quoted a North Korean source to the effect that Pak had been convicted of treason for 'ruining the national economy as the son of a big landlord who (had) infiltrated the ranks of revolutionaries', the more likely explanation was that he had been made a scapegoat for the mishandling of the currency initiative.

The economic report of April 2010, delivered by Premier Kim Yong Il, was even more opaque than usual, a reflection perhaps of worsening economic conditions. Such comment as had emerged was stronger for its rhetorical content than for the substance of its policy insights. Thus, it was difficult, if not impossible, to assess the meaning, let alone the significance, of the Premier's statement, during which he announced a new five-year national science and technology development plan.

As in previous years, the annual one-day meeting of the Supreme People's Assembly (SPA) held in April 2011 offered no precise economic data beyond a few figures contained in the budgetary report (see Finance, below). Choe Yong Rim, who had replaced Kim Yong Il as Premier in June 2010, gave a speech focusing on the importance of agriculture and light industry in order to raise living standards, but also emphasizing the need to enhance energy supplies and expand foreign trade (in the latter case, through implementation of projects that 'effectively incorporate economic and technological co-operation').

With its goal of achieving self-sufficiency and its pursuit of an inward-looking developmental policy that has rejected integration into the international economic order, North Korea's strategy has most closely resembled that of China during the rule of Mao Zedong (who led the country until his death in 1976). North Korea is also one of the world's most highly defence-constrained economies, and among the obstacles to Chinese-style reforms have been the economically distorting effects of North Korea's *Songun* strategy. As noted above, the *Songun* ethos is reflected in the country's possession of the fourth largest armed forces in the world and military spending that absorbs a significant share of GDP. The overwhelming emphasis on military construction not only distorts economic growth, but also seriously constrains the potential for welfare improvements among the population. Official estimates suggest that the share of spending on defence has declined steadily, from a high point of 32% in 1968 to about 17% in 2004. However, defence expenditure is notoriously difficult to assess, and some Western sources suggest that as much as 25%–30% of GDP may still be allocated to the North Korean military sector. In 2006 the then Premier, Pak Pong Ju, reaffirmed that North Korea's budgetary priority was to increase the country's military capabilities through the provision of even greater funding support to the defence industry. Whatever the true level of military spending, what is certain is that maintaining such high levels of budgetary allocations to defence has been a major constraint on an economy that experienced three years of negative growth during 2006–09 and was unable sufficiently to ensure material welfare for the general population.

PLANNING

Even today, the legacy of central planning is very apparent in North Korea, where an estimated 90% of economic activity remains under state control in the guise of collectivized agriculture and state-controlled industrial and service activities. During the interim post-war Soviet occupation of North Korea (1945–48), the North Korean Provisional People's Committee introduced a series of radical economic reforms (including land reform and the nationalization of major industries), which signalled a strong orientation towards the socialization of economic activities and the introduction of a centralized planning system on the Soviet model. Following the formal establishment of the DPRK on 9 September 1948, the new Government launched its first Two-Year Plan (1949–50), through which it sought to consolidate the foundations of a self-reliant national economy. However, this process was interrupted by the Korean War.

From the end of the Korean War, in 1953, until 1984 North Korea's economic policy was conducted within the framework of five development plans. As a result of revisions, early fulfilment and delays, the dates of these plans are somewhat confusing and discontinuous: a Three-Year (Post-war Reconstruction) Plan (1954–56); a Five-Year Plan (which was actually implemented over four years between 1957 and 1960); the first Seven-Year Plan (in fact, 1961–70); a Six-Year Plan (1971–76); and, with the designation of 1977 as a year of readjustment, the second Seven-Year Plan (1978–84). Following a second period of adjustment, the third Seven-Year Plan was intended to run from 1987 until 1993. During the 1990s the process of orderly planning was seriously disrupted by the emergence of severe economic problems. The dominance of planning has also been weakened, but not yet challenged, by recent market-orientated initiatives.

The division of Korea after Japan's defeat in 1945 left North Korea in possession of about two-thirds of the peninsula's heavy industrial facilities and infrastructure. With post-war economic rehabilitation completed during the 1954–56 Plan, the country made substantial progress under the 1957–60 Plan towards establishing a firm foundation for industrialization. During this period the 'socialization' process was completed, and the *chollima* movement (which took its name from a legendary flying horse, symbolizing rapid progress) was introduced. However, not until the 1960s did the process of industrialization begin in earnest. Because of the emergence of economic and infrastructural constraints, as well as to meet military needs, the Government was compelled to extend the first Seven-Year Plan and to adjust some of its policies. As a result, some of the planned targets for 1961–70 remained unfulfilled.

In the subsequent 1971–76 Plan, core objectives remained unchanged, although additional priorities also emerged. These included the need for technological upgrading, the attainment

of self-sufficiency in industrial raw materials, expansion of energy industries, raising product quality and the attainment of a more balanced economic structure. This strategy was also notable for its attempt to revise North Korea's policy of self-reliance in favour of seeking greater access to foreign capital and technology. Pre-fulfilment of some major economic targets suggested that the new strategy was effective. However, the expansion of capital and technology imports generated increasing foreign debts, and eventually gave rise to problems of debt repayment. As a result, North Korea became the first communist country to default on its debt, preventing further purchases of advanced Western technology and forcing it to return to the previous strategy of self-reliance.

Consequently, the subsequent 1978–84 Plan once more stressed the imperative of self-reliance, while also seeking to reduce North Korean dependence on Soviet economic aid. In an attempt to upgrade production and management techniques, it also placed a high premium on modernization and 'scientization'. Available evidence suggests that, despite major targets being set no higher than in the previous Plan, the results of the new Plan were disappointing. The seriousness of continuing economic problems was reflected in the admission by North Korean officials that the targeted growth of net material product (NMP) and several major commodities had not been fulfilled. The lapse of three years before the implementation of the next economic plan highlighted the severity of North Korea's economic difficulties in the mid-1980s.

The less ambitious targets of the third Seven-Year Plan (1987–93) reflected persistent economic shortcomings, but also pointed to the adoption of a more realistic approach by economic planners. Modernization and 'scientization' were again central to the Plan, which envisaged a 70% increase in NMP and average annual industrial growth of 10% (both below the respective targets of the previous Plan). In December 1993, however, official sources conceded that many targets had, once again, not been fulfilled. The disappointing outcome was attributed to difficulties associated with the demise of the USSR and other former socialist bloc countries. For example, gross industrial output was reported to have risen by only 50% during the seven-year period (implying an average annual growth rate of 5.6%), and even this figure was questioned by Western sources. Output targets for power, coal, non-ferrous metal ores, steel and chemical fertilizers were all unfulfilled.

Such was the scale of North Korea's economic problems at this point that the Government found it difficult to formulate a new long-term economic programme. In the second half of the 1990s formal economic planning gave way to greater emphasis on rhetoric, urging the work-force to 'rally under the Red Banner, continue on their arduous march and demonstrate their revolutionary zeal'. Simultaneously, market initiatives now began to play a small, but significant, supplementary role to that of planning. The years between 1994 and 1997 were designated a 'period of adjustment in socialist economic construction'. It would be hard to adjudge the transitional programme a success, given that economic decline continued into the second half of the 1990s. Nevertheless, there were some significant positive developments, which indicated official recognition of the need for a reconsideration of strategic priorities. These included the enactment of constitutional amendments (in September 1998), providing for a greater role for private enterprise and market reform, and, early in the following year, the adoption of a new economic planning law, which sought to codify the principles and mechanisms of the centralized economy. The imperative of state control was reiterated in a revised version of the economic planning law, which was enacted in 2010. Some sources have speculated that the explicit endorsement of the dominant role of central planning may presage an attempt to reassert greater control over informal market activities in North Korea, although there is no evidence of such markets having yet been affected.

North Korea's most recent planning initiative was announced in January 2011 in the form of a new 10-Year State Strategy Plan for Economic Development (2011–20), intended to promote North Korea to the ranks of the world's 'advanced countries' by 2020. Predictably enough, details of how this ambitious goal is to be achieved have not been made public, although a new body, the State General Bureau for Economic Development, was to be established in order to oversee the implementation of the 10-Year Plan. An EIU report suggests that the Plan's priorities will include infrastructural construction, intensified agricultural development and the expansion of basic industries (especially power generation, coal and oil production and metallurgy). The ambitious nature of the macroeconomic goals contained in the Plan implies the allocation of investment on a huge scale, and it is likely that one of the purposes of Kim Jong Il's visit to China in May 2011 (see History) was to seek Chinese assistance for the funding of the project.

It is a salutary reminder of the unreformed nature of the North Korean economy that the Government still sets all wages, prices and production levels, and industrial production is still overwhelmingly dominated by state-owned enterprises (SOEs). Meanwhile, virtually all property is owned by the state, and merchandise trade remains under the monopoly control of the Government. In short, in interpreting the significance of recent reform initiatives, it is important to keep in mind that, outside of a small number of state-approved market places and special economic zones (SEZs), free enterprise is still not officially sanctioned.

ECONOMIC REFORM AND KOREAN REUNIFICATION

China's experience since the 1980s highlights the formidable challenge of reforming a socialist economic system. In North Korea's case, a continuing strong commitment to central planning has rendered economic liberalization and market-orientated reform much more difficult. An unambiguous commitment to thorough-going reform has yet to be demonstrated by North Korea, and the Government has often preferred to take advantage of the desire of other countries to bring peace and stability to the Korean peninsula and use diplomatic pressure in order to secure much-needed foreign exchange and other resources.

Nevertheless, although their long-term impact remains in some doubt, the 'economic improvement measures' announced by the North Korean Government on 1 July 2002 undoubtedly marked an important departure in official economic thinking and macroeconomic policy formulation unmatched since 1945. Central to the 2002 initiative were incentive- and efficiency-enhancing reforms, such as the withdrawal of subsidies to state enterprises, the payment of factory wages on a piece-rate basis, and the legalization and extension of markets for agricultural and industrial products. In short, the initiative implied a withdrawal of state control in favour of a degree of decentralized decision-making and greater autonomy for producers. There was also an external dimension, captured in the establishment of administrative and industrial zones, designed to encourage foreign investment inflows.

Also effective from July 2002, prices and wages were simultaneously increased in an effort to enhance economic management and improve living standards. Alongside major rises in prices of basic goods, including staple foods (the price of rice rose from 0.08 to 44 won per kg), transport (bus fares up from 0.1 to 2 won), accommodation and energy (electricity rates up from 0.035 to 1.8 won per kWh), workers' basic wages were also raised almost 20-fold. The underlying rationale of the price increases was to eliminate the serious drain on fiscal resources resulting from the use of state subsidies and to encourage prices to reflect more closely the true cost of production.

Essentially pragmatic factors—above all, food shortages—have also encouraged spontaneous marketization. As one observer commented in the aftermath of the famine conditions of the 1990s, 'those who could not trade are long dead'. Even today, when the average monthly wage is sufficient to buy only a few kilograms of rice, private economic activity of an informal kind offers the only means of survival for increasing numbers of people (including, it would seem, even local officials). Nor have attempts to counter so-called 'subversive, anti-socialist activities' and to restrict market activities been successful. An instructive example in this regard was the failure of government efforts in 2005 to revive the former rationing system.

Even though Kim Jong Il is on record as stressing the importance of formulating an economic model that reflects

the country's unique economic conditions, China is probably the most obvious reformist model for North Korea to follow. Certainly, the Chinese example has been influential in helping to shape the North Korean Government's future economic policies. Kim's various visits to China since 2000 seem to have been at least partly motivated by the desire to familiarize himself with Chinese reformist strategies. His trip to China in 2006 included visits to two major urban centres of reform (Guangzhou and Wuhan), as well as to Shenzhen and Zhuhai SEZs, bordering Hong Kong and Macao, respectively. Kim was reported to have spoken enthusiastically of the role of the SEZs and their contribution to building a 'socialist market economic system' in China. Commentators interpreted such remarks as evidence of the likely acceleration of North Korea's own market reform efforts and other outward-orientated initiatives. The content of some of the reports subsequently made to the SPA appeared to lend credence to this interpretation. However, the political obstacles that confront the North Korean Government in pursuing economic reform are much greater than those that have challenged the Chinese authorities, while North Korea's base economic conditions are less favourable than those enjoyed by China at the end of the 1980s.

The economic implications for North Korea of reunification with the South have attracted much speculation. So opaque are North Korea's operations that it is extremely difficult to interpret the country's motives with regard to diplomatic initiatives of recent years. The most important of these include normalization of relations with various countries, the June 2000 Pyongyang Summit meeting between the two Korean leaders (Kim Jong Il and Kim Dae-Jung), subsequent ministerial-level talks and the meeting between North Korea's titular Head of State, Kim Yong Nam, and the South Korean Prime Minister, Lee Hae-Chan, in the Indonesian capital of Jakarta (where both were attending the Asian-African Summit) in April 2005. A second summit meeting, in this case between the then South Korean President, Roh Moo-Hyun, and Kim Jong Il, which was scheduled for August 2007, was postponed because of flooding in the North, but took place in October. Since the election of President Lee Myung-Bak in December 2007, bilateral relations have deteriorated significantly (see History).

After the first contacts between North and South Korea, the establishment of discussions by working-level groups facilitated discussion of a number of issues such as payments settlements, mutual investment protection, the avoidance of double taxation and the arbitration of disputes. However, by 2006, six years after the first Pyongyang summit meeting and despite well over 50 meetings on economic issues, there was still little evidence of deepening bilateral economic co-operation through trade liberalization, let alone through the establishment of a free trade area or some other form of economic union. The agreement of the two Governments to resume contacts, following the visit to Pyongyang, in April 2002, by the South Korean presidential envoy, Lim Dong-Won, seemed at the time a promising development. However, within a month of the election in February 2003 of President Roh Moo-Hyun, North Korea unilaterally cancelled the next scheduled round of economic talks. Discussions in Jakarta between Kim Yong Nam and Lee Hae-Chan in April 2005 (see above) offered hope of the resumption of a more substantive inter-Korean economic dialogue. Meetings of the North-South Committee for the Promotion of Economic Co-operation, which continued to take place until April 2007, also failed to generate any significant progress. For the time being, substantive inter-Korean economic co-operation remains a distant goal. Indeed, the heightened tensions that have characterized bilateral relations since the election of Lee Myung-Bak suggest, in the words of an EIU report, published in May 2008, that previous plans for expanded North-South co-operation 'are now on hold'.

The massive economic, developmental and welfare disparities between North and South Korea promise to make the process of economic integration no less difficult than the reunification of Germany. The income disparities between North and South Korea (about 18 : 1 in per caput terms) are, for example, much greater than those that formerly existed between West and East Germany (just over 2 : 1), and the costs of reunification are likely to be much higher. At the beginning of the 1990s the Korea Development Institute estimated that the total cost of reunification would be US $240,000m. More recently, it has been calculated that unification could require the expenditure of the equivalent of 5% of South Korea's GNP for a decade—a total of some $350,000m. The World Bank's figure, of between $2,000,000m. and $3,000,000m., is much higher still, and such estimates highlight the immensity of the challenge confronting North and South Korea in pursuit of reunification.

A watershed in cross-border economic relations was reached in 1998 in the form of an agreement with the South Korean conglomerate Hyundai to promote the tourism potential of Mount Kumgang and, potentially far more important, to develop a new industrial park in North Korea, at Kaesong. However, progress towards fulfilling the goals of these co-operative ventures has been halting. For example, road access to Mount Kumgang, which was initiated in 2005, was for several years confined to tour buses; only in March 2008 were South Korean tourists for the first time permitted to drive across the DMZ in their own cars. However, the impact of this initiative was nullified by an incident in July, when a South Korean visitor to the Mount Kumgang resort was killed by a North Korean soldier. North Korea's failure to respond to the South Korean Government's demand for a joint investigation into the shooting of the woman resulted in the South's suspension of tourist visits to the region, causing the loss of an estimated US $165m. in revenue. The resort remained closed at mid-2011. Meanwhile, with no prospect of the South Korean authorities authorizing the resumption of tourist visits, in April 2010 North Korea seized South Korean infrastructural assets worth $300m. at the resort and shortly afterwards ordered the expulsion of almost all of the South Korean employees still based there. In June 2011 North Korean sources indicated that the seized assets would be disposed of in accordance with new regulations governing Mount Kumgang; however, representatives of the two sides remained engaged in talks in the hope of rescuing the situation.

Construction work on the Kaesong Industrial Complex (KIC), located on the western border between North and South Korea, has been similarly halting. At mid-2011 there was a significant presence of some 120 South Korean companies at the KIC, employing more than 46,000 North Korean workers, most of whom were engaged in export-orientated manufacturing activities. The KIC is an important source of hard currency for the North: in 2005 it accounted for almost one-fifth of all inter-Korean trade. However, political factors have frequently intervened to impede faster progress in developing Kaesong's economic potential, and at various times both the North and South Korean Governments have delayed plans to expand the Complex. Indeed, in view of continuing difficulties, there are signs that some South Korean investors may even decide to withdraw their operations. The USA too has refused to accept Chinese and South Korean exports produced in Kaesong on the grounds that their provenance makes them North Korean goods. China and South Korea apart, the only foreign company with a presence in KIC is the German Prettl Group, which manufactures car parts.

Expressions of co-operation between North Korea and the rest of the outside world have been few. In 1991 the Rajin-Sonbong (Rason) FETZ was established to fulfil a three-fold role as a centre of transit trade, an export-processing centre, and a focus for tourist and financial services. It offered rail access to Russia and road access to China, but was only accessible to the rest of North Korea by helicopter. In February 2008 Russian and North Korea signed an agreement to facilitate infrastructural improvements in the FETZ, including the modernization of the 54-km railway connecting the Russian border town of Khasan with Rajin, North Korea's most north-easterly port. A more ambitious plan to make Rajin a trans-shipment centre serving Busan (in South Korea) and Europe (via the Trans-Siberian Railway) had yet to be realized at mid-2011.

POPULATION, LABOUR AND WAGES

Serious demographic losses (estimated at around 1.5m. persons) during the Korean War (1950–53) and migration to the

South, as well as a relatively low population density, have exacerbated labour scarcities in North Korea. As in pre-reform China, an effective household registration system has enabled official authorities to keep accurate records of demographic change (including migration). The annual rate of total population growth rose from 2.7% in 1960 to a peak of 3.6% in 1970, but thereafter it declined markedly, reaching 1.9% only five years later. This deceleration reflected a sharp decrease in the fertility rate, the average number of children born to women declining from 6.5 in 1966 to 2.5 in 1988. According to the Population Reference Bureau (PRB), North Korea's total population as of mid-2010 was 22,800,000, less than one-half that of South Korea, and growing at an average annual rate of 0.5% (birth rate 15 per 1,000; death rate 10 per 1,000).

North Korea's rate of natural population increase is below the world average, although in recent years this is likely to have reflected the impact of food shortages more than that of family-control policies. Data made available by the US Central Intelligence Agency (CIA) indicate a dependency ratio of 31.4% at mid-2011. This figure conceals a remarkably low, albeit slowly rising, age-dependency ratio, with only 9.1% of the population aged 65 years and above. The fact that this category included so many more women than men—1.483m., compared with 0.734m.—highlights a wide gap in average life expectancy for men (61 years) and women (66). Children (those aged 14 years and under) accounted for 22.4% of the total population. In 2010 the infant mortality rate was estimated by the PRB to be 53 per 1,000 live births, while the total fertility rate was 2. Projections suggest that North Korea's population will stabilize at 34m. persons in 2045, after which it will gradually decline (South Korea's population is expected to peak at 52.6m. in 2023).

PRB estimates suggest that only 22% of the North Korean population live in the urban sector. Migration is strictly controlled, both within and across the country's borders. Reports suggest that large numbers of urban residents have sometimes been dispatched to the countryside to help support agricultural, especially food, production. As for cross-border movements, between the end of the Korean War in 1953 and 2000 a mere 5,000 North Koreans successfully entered South Korea. However, the numbers have since increased dramatically, with hundreds of thousands of North Koreans fleeing to South Korea, China and other nearby countries since the turn of the century, in the hope of securing refugee status. Many of these illegal migrants have subsequently been returned to North Korea, where they have faced severe punishment. The risks taken by would-be refugees are suggested by reports that in February 2008 13 women and two men were executed for illegal entry into China in search of food, and for assisting others to do the same.

The constraint on manpower resulting from the maintenance of large armed forces has been offset by the ability of a strong central state to mobilize military personnel for civilian economic purposes. According to CIA estimates, at mid-2011 68.6% of the population—more than 16.5m. men and women—were of working age (15–64 years). Estimating employment levels in North Korea is fraught with difficulties, although there is less disputing the high proportion of the labour force that is still engaged in farming (about 35% in 2009, according to the CIA). Estimates of unemployment are not available, although (as in pre-reform China) the likelihood is that the organizational framework of the economy conceals large numbers of people who are de facto unemployed. In recent years factory closures have resulted in the compulsory redundancy of large numbers of workers, who have been forced to meet their own and their families' subsistence needs from whatever sources they can find. One consequence of this has been the emergence of informal labour market networks. A significant event in 2006 was the convening of a national labour planning conference—the first such meeting to take place for many years—as the Government sought, not wholly successfully, to reassert its control over labour allocation. The experience of other reforming socialist countries suggests that even more important than the maintenance of central control over employment is likely to be the delegation of labour planning responsibilities to enterprises in order to raise industrial productivity and efficiency.

Information on wages is scarce. However, reports revealed that in 2002–03 there were dramatic wage increases, especially among some privileged groups such as KWP officials, military personnel and scientists. Industrial workers' wages rose by almost 2,000%, while those of soldiers and government officials increased by an extraordinary 6,000%. By contrast, miners were awarded a wage rise of 1,500%, while the corresponding figure for agricultural workers was 900%. Such increases need to be viewed in the context of sharp rises in prices, especially of consumer staples (see below). In general, higher industrial wages have probably not compensated for rises in the overall cost of living. Meanwhile, one sign of greater rationality in wage policy has been the gradual withdrawal of subsidies to SOEs and their replacement by productivity-related bonus payments.

AGRICULTURE, FORESTRY AND FISHING

North Korea occupies about 55% of the total area of the Korean peninsula, although less than one-fifth of this is suitable for crop cultivation. Estimates by FAO indicate a total arable area of about 1.9m. ha. Of this, 0.4m. ha comprise high-quality, permanently-irrigated land; 0.7m. ha comprise medium-quality, semi-irrigated land capable of supporting rice production; and 0.8m. ha is low-quality land suitable for cultivating other cereal crops. Harsh climatic conditions restrict the output of arable farming to one crop per year, although a relatively high irrigation ratio helps to offset the high concentration of rainfall during summer, as well as combating the effects of frequent spring droughts.

The Land Reform Act of March 1946 abolished tenancy and significantly increased the possession of land ownership rights among farmers, albeit at the expense of temporarily further reducing the average size of already small farms. Private farming persisted until the end of the Korean War, but as collectivization subsequently intensified, it contracted and was eventually eliminated. From August 1958, except on tiny private plots allocated to households, farming was conducted within the framework of large-scale co-operative farms (collectives), or state farms. Agricultural collectivization was accompanied by the institution of production plans (including the imposition of compulsory output quotas) and monopoly state procurement and distribution of grain. By the 1980s there were about 3,800 co-operative farms in North Korea, responsible for the management of more than 90% of the total arable area (the rest fell under the remit of some 180 state farms). In the mid-1990s, however, the Government began gradually to transfer collective farms to state ownership, which was considered to be more ideologically sound. Despite tentative market-orientated reforms in recent years, for the time being there is no prospect of agricultural privatization reasserting itself.

Attempts to extend North Korea's land base through reclamation have been only partially successful, leaving the pursuit of output growth much more dependent on the extension of irrigation and the application of modern farm inputs. By the early 1990s the water requirements of about 70% of arable land were said to be met by an extensive water conservation and irrigation infrastructure, comprising artificial lakes, reservoirs, pumping stations, groundwater facilities and flumes. Be this as it may, the subsequent combined impact of flooding, insufficient investment and lack of fuel and repair facilities seems to have taken its toll on the irrigation infrastructure. According to FAO, for example, between 1994 and 2000 soil erosion and sedimentation from floods and droughts caused serious loss of farm output. In 1995 and 1996 alone 16% of arable land was damaged by floods, which also destroyed irrigation and transport infrastructure. Serious flooding in mid-2007 also had a major impact on the harvest. In recent years, one response to declining production has been to cut down trees in an attempt to convert steep, previously forested slopes into agricultural land. However, the outcome was not only to denude about one-quarter of hilly and mountainous non-farm land, but also to exacerbate the problem of soil erosion. A more integrated approach to watershed management was reportedly being pursued from 2005 in order to alleviate such problems.

Another important element in North Korea's farm strategy has been the Government's attempt to raise farm yields through an expansion of mechanization, deep ploughing, close planting and the intensive use of fertilizers. In view of declining food production, there have also been attempts to introduce double-cropping, although its success has been constrained by the increased labour and working capital requirements, as well as climatic factors. The number of tractors increased more than three-fold between 1970 and the late 1990s, and had reached well over 70,000 by the early 2000s. However, their impact on farming has been constrained by shortages of diesel fuel and shortages of spare parts.

Chemical fertilizer applications rose quite strongly during the 1970s and 1980s to reach about one metric ton per hectare. However, under the impact of North Korea's increasing economic difficulties, in the 1990s there was a sharp contraction in supplies, which appears to have continued to the present day. The farm sector requires about 700,000 tons of fertilizers a year (460,000 tons for food production alone). In the past, North Korea was capable of producing up to 800,000 metric tons annually, but since 1995 domestic output has declined to less than 100,000 tons. Despite benefiting from fertilizer aid in some recent years, shortages have persisted. In 2006, for example, a report by the Korea Rural Economic Institute in Seoul indicated that North Korean fertilizer consumption was still 60% below what was required. Such figures highlight the critical importance of fertilizer imports, as well as of the threat to farm production posed by occasional interruptions in such supplies (as in 2008, when North Korea declined to seek fertilizer aid from the new South Korean Government of Lee Myung-Bak). In the absence of a sustained increase in supplies of chemical fertilizers, it will be difficult to generate sufficient growth to return grain yields to their previous peak levels, attained as long ago as the 1980s. In particular, North Korea needs to put in place a comprehensive programme to generate increased domestic production of high-quality fertilizers, alongside expanded provision of organic products, in order to secure more rapid, stable output growth. Amid raw material and energy shortages, fulfilling this goal will not be easy. Meanwhile, other agricultural chemicals also remain in short supply.

Agriculture in North Korea is dominated by grain farming. In terms of both production and consumption, paddy rice and maize are the two most important crops, followed by potatoes. (Wheat, barley, millet, sorghum, oats and rye are less important as sources of energy.) Potatoes have high energy (calorific) yields, which, against the background of developing food shortages, explains why their cultivation has undergone a significant expansion in recent years.

Rice was an important export item until the mid-1980s, although from the late 1990s North Korea began to purchase rice, as well as some wheat, abroad (from Thailand, South Korea and other countries). According to FAO estimates, between 1997 and 1998 the value of rice imports rose from US $104m. to $112m., although that of wheat imports fell sharply from $80.5m. to $48.0m. However, in 2000 North Korea imported an estimated 200,000 metric tons of grain on a commercial basis, while a further 500,000 tons were made available on concessionary terms by China and South Korea.

Reliable production data are scarce, but it is clear that from the mid-1990s, under the impact of policy failures and natural disasters, declining output resulted in widespread hunger and starvation. FAO data show, for example, that while annual food production growth (2.1%) between 1979–81 and 1990–92 exceeded that of total population (1.5%), the relationship was subsequently reversed. Thus, between 1990–92 and 1995–97 food output increased by a mere 0.3% annually, compared with population growth of 1.3%; between 1995–97 and 2001–03 the corresponding figures were 0.6% and 0.7%. The severity of the situation in the 1990s is further highlighted in FAO statistics showing that annual total cereal production decreased from 9.14m. metric tons in 1993 to 2.6m. tons in 1996, a decline of by more than 70%; maize and rice output decreased from 8.72m. tons to 2.54m. tons during the same period. The initial response of the North Korean Government to emerging food shortages in the 1990s was to urge the population to follow a 'two-meals-a-day' campaign; however, it was subsequently forced to seek external food aid (see below).

As early as 1992–93, grain imports probably accounted for almost one-third of food requirements. As the food crisis deepened, North Korean policy-makers accorded higher priority to agriculture, allocating additional fertilizer, farm machinery and manpower to the farm sector, including sending urban workers and members of the armed forces to supplement farm labour. However, such measures offered only temporary relief. In the second half of the 1990s cereal output was once more in serious decline, causing widespread hunger and malnutrition (see below). According to Hwang Jang Yop, a senior diplomat who defected from North Korea in 1997, some 2.5m. people died as a result of famine in 1995–98—about 10% of the North Korean population before the 1990s food crisis. More conservative estimates suggest a loss of between 600,000 and 1m. lives (3%–5% of the pre-crisis population).

Between 2000 and 2005 grain production increased year-on-year to reach 4.54m. metric tons in 2005 (of which rice accounted for 1.8m. tons—a rise of 26.8%). However, despite this encouraging performance, the 2005 grain harvest was still almost one-quarter below North Korea's estimated grain requirements. Moreover, in the next two years serious flooding caused farm conditions once more to deteriorate, and by 2007 output was reported to have declined to between 3m. and 4m. tons. Despite the worsening situation, North Korea requested that the World Food Programme (WFP—already a major source of food aid) should implement future food shipments as development, rather than humanitarian, aid. In 2006 a new agreement was signed by North Korea and WFP, which the latter described as being 'developmental, with humanitarian features'. It provided for the distribution of 150,000 tons of food to 1.5m. people, especially the most vulnerable, small children, pregnant women, nursing mothers, the elderly and the unemployed.

Against this background, it is not surprising that authoritative sources warned of serious famine conditions once more emerging in North Korea. In May 2008 the Peterson Institute for International Economics, based in Washington, DC, reported evidence of severe malnutrition and suggested that 'hunger-related deaths are nearly inevitable'. Elsewhere, it was reported that more and more families had to subsist on just one meal a day. FAO predicted that North Korea's food deficit in 2008 would reach 1.7m. metric tons, almost double that of 2007 and higher than in any year since 2001. Even North Korean officials acknowledged that the official Public Distribution System (PDS) had come under strain, forcing the Government in 2005 to reduce urban rations from 300 to 250 grams per person per day (i.e. to a mere 40% of the internationally recommended minimum calorie intake). Meanwhile, conditions were further exacerbated by rising international food prices and the imposition of export controls by some food-exporting countries, including China. The combined impact of the poor 2009 harvest and the mishandled currency reform significantly exacerbated chronic food shortages. FAO projections suggested that North Korea would need to import some 1.1m. tons of cereals in 2009–10, or about one-quarter of its total requirements. However, the same source was doubtful that such requirements could be met, necessitating the implementation of various 'survival strategies', such as reducing the number of meals per day, eating inferior and wild foods, and reducing the size of meal portions. A report issued in May 2011 by the Institute for Far Eastern Studies in Seoul noted that about 20% of the North Korean population still had access to only two meals a day, comprising corn noodles or porridge.

The events of recent years are merely the latest episodes in a series of crop failures that since the mid-1990s have caused widespread malnutrition, starvation and famine-related diseases. Food aid notwithstanding, malnutrition rates in North Korea have been among the highest in the world since the early 1990s. One consequence of the physical weakening of the population has been a resurgence in epidemics and the return of diseases and illnesses, such as tuberculosis, measles and scarlet fever, which were thought previously to have been brought under control or even eliminated. Food shortages have also given rise to large-scale emigration, with estimates suggesting that by 1998 between 100,000 and 400,000 refugees had tried, mainly unsuccessfully, to flee across the Tumen River into China. Although the severity of conditions in the second half of the 1990s has not been repeated (not least, thanks to overseas relief efforts and mass mobilization of labour in support of agriculture), the existence of a surplus above even subsistence food requirements has not yet been re-established. The sale of grain (rice and maize) in informal markets has increasingly filled the vacuum left by the ineffectiveness of PDS rationing. According to an unconfirmed report, in March 2008 up to 10,000 women had demonstrated in markets and at government offices in Chongjin (a city in the north-east of the country), demanding the right to trade. Elsewhere, nine women were said to have been arrested (one of whom was alleged to have been tortured subsequently), following altercations between women seeking to engage in trade.

A report published by WFP in March 2005 suggested that in 2004 37% of young children were chronically malnourished (7% suffering from acute malnutrition); almost one-quarter of them were underweight. One in five children suffered from diarrhoea, and one in eight was susceptible to acute respiratory infection. Almost one-third of women were found to be anaemic and malnourished.

Without the existence of large-scale food aid, such figures would be even worse. WFP has been working in North Korea since 1995 and has access to 161 out of its 203 counties. Between 1995 and the end of 2005 it supplied more than 4m. metric tons of food, valued at US $1,700m. It has also extended support through the implementation of food-for-work projects. Other international bodies associated with the activities of WFP in North Korea include the UN Children's Fund (UNICEF), the UN Development Programme, the Adventist Development and Relief Agency, and the International Fund for Agricultural Development. Bilateral assistance has also been important, the most important donors having been China, the USA, South Korea and Japan. At times, however, political tensions have affected food shipments via these sources. For example, US food aid decreased sharply following the election of George W. Bush as US President in late 2000, although in June 2008 the US Department of State revealed that the USA had once more begun to provide food assistance through WFP and US non-governmental organizations (NGOs), and would extend funding support to these NGOs in order to help combat the increased incidence of infectious diseases caused by the 2007 floods. However, food aid from US agencies was reported to have been suspended in March 2009, amid rising bilateral tensions.

Although climatic factors have played a part in causing food deficits in recent years, systemic policy defects have probably been an even more important contributory factor. Until such problems are successfully addressed, dependence on food aid is likely to continue into the foreseeable future. The continuing severity of grain shortages has also been exacerbated by shortages of fresh vegetables and fruit. With minimal access to fat, protein and micronutrients, most North Koreans suffer from critical dietary deficiencies, while the cost of food has increased substantially. The price of food available through the official rationing system has remained relatively stable, but such supplies are insufficient to meet even basic requirements, forcing consumers to resort to private food markets, where prices have increased dramatically. Between 2003 and 2004 rice and maize prices in private markets rose by 400% and almost 300%, respectively, so that a kilogram of rice cost the equivalent of 30% of a typical monthly wage. Following the floods of 2006 and 2007, sharp upward pressure on food prices was once again evident, with staple food prices reported to have doubled in Pyongyang between mid-2007 and mid-2008. In the aftermath of the 2009 currency reforms, food prices also rose very sharply: according to one authoritative source, for example, between December 2009 and March 2010 the price of rice rose by an extraordinary 7,500%.

MINING

With 80%–90% of the entire peninsula's important mineral deposits concentrated within its borders, North Korea is relatively well endowed in natural resources. Its reserves of coal, iron ore, limestone and magnesite are of global significance; also important are copper, fluorspar, lead, graphite, zinc, tungsten, mica, fluorite and precious metals. There is also evidence of uranium mines being worked in North Korea. The mining sector is a major driver of both the domestic economy and foreign trade. The upgrading in December 2010 of the State Guidance Bureau of Resource Development under the Ministry of Mining Industry to full ministerial status under a new name, the Ministry of State Resource Development, appears to indicate renewed emphasis on the mining sector.

Mining experienced substantial negative growth during most of the 1990s and into the early 2000s. Since 2002, however, a more buoyant and mostly positive growth trajectory has been re-established, owing to improvement in labour morale resulting from a major wage increase, as well as the favourable outcome of surveys and increased investment in coal mines. In 2009 the mining sector's contribution to GDP was almost 13%, according to BOK data.

However, the challenge confronting the mining sector is a major one: energy shortages and the increasing obsolescence of equipment remain formidable problems, and most mines and mineral processing plants operate well below their capacity. Perhaps the best hope for renewed expansion lies in the possibility of foreign investment in the exploitation of North Korea's mineral deposits. Most important in this respect has been the massive increase in FDI in North Korea from China in recent years, most of which is thought to have been within the mining sector. In 2005 a Chinese consortium comprising the Sinosteel Corporation (subsequently replaced in the venture by China Minmetals Corporation), Tonghua Iron and Steel Group and Yanbian Tianchi Stock Holding Co secured 50 years' mining rights at the Musan Iron Ore Mine Complex, close to the Chinese border, in a contract valued at 7,000m. yuan. In the following year China's Liuzhou Iron and Steel bought a majority (51%) stake, giving it mining rights for 15 years, in the largest copper mine in the North Korean city of Hyesan. Meanwhile, in 2005 the Korea Resources Corporation (KORES) of South Korea announced the establishment of a liaison office in Pyongyang in order to promote consortium-based mineral resource development in the North, focusing on copper, iron ore, magnesite and zinc (see also below)

Iron ore has also been a major source of foreign exchange. According to Western estimates, by the end of the 1980s output had reached 8m. metric tons, reflecting large-scale state investment in mines at Tokson and Sohaeri. However, despite the commissioning in 1991 of the Chongpyong mine in South Hamgyong Province, production declined thereafter, to a mere 2.89m. tons in 1998. Output partially recovered to reach about 5m. tons in 2005 (of which about one-fifth was exported to China), and 5.3m. tons in 2009, according to the US Geological Survey (USGS). Reserves at Musan are estimated at between 3,000m. and 7,000m. tons. However, Chinese involvement notwithstanding, authoritative sources indicate that Musan has produced no more than about 3m. tons per annum in recent years.

North Korea is especially rich in magnesite. Reserves, which are mainly concentrated in the Tanchon District in the north-east, are estimated at 6.5m. metric tons (the largest in the world and worth an estimated US $6,100,000m., according to South Korean sources). After China, it is the second largest producer of magnesia products in the world. Mining of magnesite and production of its derivative, clinker, are important both for supporting the domestic refractory industry and for the export market. An agreement signed by North Korea and the USA in 1994 providing for the removal of restrictions on bilateral trade offered an important new market for clinker, and facilitated a large-scale expansion of North Korea's magnesite production capacity. In June 1995 the first North Korean trade mission to visit the USA concluded an agreement to export 100,000 tons of magnesite to a US company. In August 2000 a US mining company announced the formation of a joint venture with the Korea Magnesia Clinker Industry group to mine, process and export magnesia products from North Korea. The first phase of the project envisaged the export of 200,000 tons of magnesia products to the USA and Asia. In 2006 KORES signed a contract with the North Korean Government for the development of a magnesite mine at Taehung, with estimated ore reserves of 3,600m. tons; the mine was expected to begin commercial operations in 2009 and ultimately to generate annual production of 3m. tons. The ambitious scale of such targets is captured in the reality that in 2009 North Korea's output of crude magnesite totalled just 150,000 tons; although this was well above the 55,000 tons produced the previous year, it was still some 20% below the level of 2003. KORES is also a partner in a $5.1m. graphite mining project in Hwanghae South Province. USGS estimated graphite production at 30,000 tons in 2009.

Other minerals produced in large quantities by North Korea are lead (13,000 metric tons in 2009—Pb content), zinc (70,000 tons, compared with 67,000 tons in 2005), copper (12,000 tons—Cu content—unchanged since before 2005), tungsten (350 tons—W content—40% above the level of 2007, but 60% below that of 2006), phosphates (300,000 tons, unchanged since 2004), salt (500,000 tons, unchanged since 2004), gold (2,000 kg—Au content—unchanged since 2004), silver (20 tons—Ag content—unchanged since 2004), fluorspar (12,500 tons, unchanged since 2005) and sulphur (42,000 tons, unchanged since 2004). Both zinc and lead ore are smelted domestically (at Tanchon, Nampo, Komdok and Haeju), and zinc and lead ingots are major exports. At the end of the 1980s North Korea ranked third in the world in terms of zinc production. In 1994 it produced an estimated 200,000 tons of high-grade electrolytic zinc and 80,000 tons of lead. A joint venture project to redevelop the Unsan gold mine began operation in April 1987, and the first shipment of gold to Japan (totalling some 100 kg) was reported three months later. Unsan is potentially one of the world's major gold mines, with deposits estimated at more than 1,000 tons. North Korea's non-ferrous metals production in 2009 was estimated by the BOK to be 91,000 tons (just over 3% below that of 2008).

In 2009 almost 60% of North Korean export earnings came from the sale of minerals and mining products. China was by far the most important trading partner, with the value of bilateral mineral trade totalling US $2,670m., while South Korea accounted for a further $1,680m.

The USGS predicts that for the foreseeable future North Korea's mining industry will continue to be dominated by coal (see Energy, below), iron ore, limestone and magnesite. According to the same source, China's investment in the Musan iron ore mine complex and the Yongtung coal mine is likely to give a significant boost to coal and iron ore mining, although the inexorable demand for minerals associated with China's rapid economic growth is likely also to extend its activities into other mining activities, such as copper, gold, molybdenum and nickel.

MANUFACTURING AND CONSTRUCTION

In line with its Soviet-style planning system, North Korea has consistently prioritized the development of heavy industry. However, the share of heavy industry in total industrial output has decreased significantly in recent years, from 80% in 1990 to about 69% in 2009. As the basis of a comprehensive development strategy, the emphasis on heavy industry has been a failure. Even when rapid heavy industrial growth has taken place, it has concealed major qualitative deficiencies. In particular, excessive emphasis on machine-building (critical for armaments production) has generated a highly distorted industrial structure. As in pre-reform China, inherent weaknesses of material balance planning and the inwardly orientated nature of North Korea's industrial economy generated major inefficiencies and minimal factor productivity growth. It has yet to be seen whether or not the Government's stated willingness to embrace a greater role for prices, markets and other 'orthodox' economic criteria, such as profitability, will be translated into major improvements in manufacturing production efficiency. Meanwhile, in 2009 the share of manufacturing in GDP was just over 22%.

Notwithstanding North Korean claims to have fulfilled the second Seven-Year Plan (1978–84) target of increasing industrial gross value output by 120%, it is unlikely that the implied average annual growth of 12.2% was really achieved. In the third Seven-Year Plan (1987–93), official claims that industrial growth rose by 5.6% annually were also contested by Western sources, which suggested that industrial output had in fact declined. The years from 1994 to 1997 were designated a period of 'adjustment in socialist economic construction', during which emphasis shifted from mining, power and metallurgical industries towards agriculture, light industry and trade—an adjustment that reflected the severity of North Korea's agricultural crisis and the urgent need to restore food supplies. According to BOK statistics, manufacturing output decreased cumulatively by almost 36% (or an average annual rate of 5.4%) between 1990 and 1998. By the early 2000s manufacturing GDP was still about one-fifth below the 1990 level, although recovery was subsequently reflected in average annual growth of about 3% between 2003 and 2008. This quite buoyant performance was followed by a contraction of 3% in 2009.

The downturn in manufacturing production was reflected in the construction sector, which contracted by 37% during 1990–98. The 1990 level of construction activity was reattained in 2001, since when construction growth has been quite volatile, with years of expansion alternating with years of contraction.

Machine-building and Metallurgy

Through its provision of machinery for domestic industry and agriculture, the machine-building industry is central to any strategy designed to achieve industrial self-sufficiency. In North Korea it has also made available an extensive range of military equipment, including rifles, mortars, machine-guns, multiple rocket launchers, artillery, anti-aircraft weapons, tanks, personnel carriers, patrol craft and frigates, missile-equipped fast attack craft and amphibious vessels, submarines, medium-range *Scud*-type surface-to-surface missiles, and long-range *Taepo Dong* missiles. Between 1946 and the early 1980s the industry's share of total industrial value-output rose from just over 5% to about one-third. In more recent years declines in production have reflected those in other branches of heavy industry.

The machine-building industry is capable of producing a wide range of large-scale construction, power, mining, agricultural and transport equipment. However, the quality of such products is poor, reflecting technological levels that, despite efforts to introduce more advanced production techniques, remain well below international standards. Accelerated economic reform and the extension of joint ventures would appear to offer the most effective way of achieving much-needed technological upgrading in North Korea's machine-building industry.

Outdated technology, shortages of coking coal and the low purity of domestic iron ore have imposed serious constraints on the growth of the metallurgical industry. In the past, in addition to new construction and extension of existing facilities, mass mobilization campaigns to collect scrap iron have been instituted to alleviate steel shortages. Such efforts are no more than palliatives, and, as Kim Jong Il himself has pointed out, the more fundamental requirement is to implement the wholesale technological modernization of the industry (including using foreign investment). The USGS suggests that North Korea's crude steel capacity in 2009 was 5.62m. metric tons. The same source estimates that domestic crude steel output rose from 1.07m. tons to 1.3m. tons between 2005 and 2009, an average annual rate of growth of about 5%. Since 2002 ferro-alloy and pig iron production has remained unchanged (at 10,000 tons and 900,000 tons, respectively)

With an annual production capacity of 10m. metric tons of steel and a work-force of 20,000–30,000, the Kimchaek iron and steel works complex, located in Chongjin (in Hamgyong North Province) close to the Musan iron ore mine, has replaced the Hwanghae iron works (in Songrim) as the largest North Korean centre for the production of iron and steel. According to the USGS, Kimchaek's annual production capacity in 2009 was 2.4m. tons, and it is currently thought to produce more than 40% of national steel output (Hwanghae iron works generates a further quarter). In 1996 Kimchaek installed equipment to produce low-carbon steel, although subsequent reports indicated that coke shortages and other problems left the plant operating well below capacity (as recently as 2006 it was reported that Kimchaek had been forced to suspend operations as a result of energy shortages and equipment breakdowns).

Other major steel mills exist at Chongjin (established in 1938 by the Mitsubishi Corporation of Japan, and expanded in the 1950s and 1960s as part of Kim Il Sung's heavy industrialization strategy) and Taean.

Chemicals

Important integrated chemical plants include the Chongyun Works (located in the Anju District, north of Pyongyang), the construction of which began, with French assistance, during the Six-Year Plan (1971–76). This was the country's first petrochemical complex, designed to produce ethylene, polyethylene, acrylo-nitrite and urea, using crude petroleum supplied by the nearby refinery at Sonbong (formerly Unggi). North Korea's output capacity of ammonium nitrate and nitric acid is thought to be around 200,000 metric tons, three-quarters of which is produced at the Hungnam fertilizer complex. It also possesses a small-scale production capability for refined chemicals (especially organophosphates). In general, energy shortages and capital obsolescence have made chemical production an under-performing sector. Nevertheless, the ability to produce dual-use chemicals, such as ammonium, chloride, fluoride, phosphate and sulphur compounds, is the basis of a chemical weapons production infrastructure (a South Korean source has estimated that North Korea has a peace-time chemical weapons production capacity of 4,500 tons).

Because of its importance to agriculture, the chemical fertilizer industry has been the beneficiary of large-scale investment. A study published in 2000 noted that North Korea had three major fertilizer plants (the largest of which is located at Hungnam, with others at Aoji and Namhung), with a combined production capacity of 400,000 metric tons of nitrogen nutrient. It is estimated that total domestic production rose from 300,000 tons to 460,000 tons between 1970 and 1975 (an average rate of growth of almost 9% annually); in the following 15 years output continued to rise, reaching 850,000 tons in 1990. Thereafter, authoritative sources (including FAO and the World Bank) indicate a decline in production; according to the BOK, fertilizer production in 2009 stood at 466,000 tons. Industrial collapse in the 1990s had serious implications for fertilizer supplies, with oil and raw material shortages having a major negative impact on the production of urea and ammonium sulphate (the main fertilizers used in North Korea). Increasing plant obsolescence and poor maintenance of facilities have further exacerbated the situation. Imports and, in particular, the provision of fertilizer aid have helped partially to offset domestic shortages. FAO data show, for example, that in 1999–2000 almost 77% of nutrient availability derived from humanitarian assistance. In the past, South Korea has been a major supplier of fertilizer to the North. Since 2008, however, such shipments have been interrupted, and South Korean reports in December 2010 suggested that, confronted by acute shortages of fertilizers, some North Korean shops had begun to sell human excrement to farmers.

Textiles

Central to North Korea's textile industry is the Pyongyang integrated textile mill, built with Soviet assistance in the late 1950s. Its production derives mainly from locally produced synthetics, such as vinalon and petrochemically-based fibres, as well as cotton and silk. Although Pyongyang remains the centre of the national textile industry, plants in Sinuiju and Sariwon have become increasingly important. Having reportedly expanded quite rapidly during the 1980s, North Korea's textile output subsequently declined to 1,000m. metres by the end of the following decade. Indeed, South Korean sources indicate that between 1999 and 2004 there was no production growth at all. The performance of synthetic fibres has been even more disappointing: except for 2000, output declined consistently on an annual basis between 1995 and 2004 (from 56,000 to 25,000 metric tons), registering a cumulative decline of 55%. Although a degree of recovery subsequently took place, total production in 2009 was just 30,000 tons—54% of the 1995 level (and barely 2% of the corresponding South Korean figure).

Despite such difficulties, textiles remain the most important branch of light industry and are a significant source of foreign exchange. In the second half of the 1990s stagnation in trade with Japan and difficulties in maintaining North Korea's industrial competitiveness were reflected in a relatively sharp contraction in trade. Subsequently, however, although exports to Japan continued to decline, those to China and India rose significantly. An important recent development has been the transfer of operations by South Korean textile producers to Kaesong in order to take advantage of cheap, but efficient, North Korean labour. According to statistics published by the EIU in February 2011, in 2006 the textile industry was the third most important source of foreign exchange after electronic goods, earning US $214m.

SERVICES

Until 1984 all outlets for the provision of services and the distribution of goods, including retail shops, were either state-owned or run as co-operatives. However, following the introduction in 1984 of the so-called '3 August Consumer Goods Movement', local governments were permitted to establish direct sales outlets in their districts for the distribution of consumer locally produced goods. By the early 1990s the total number of shops, service establishments and 'food-processing and storage bases' was estimated to be 130,000. Outside special economic zones, markets (in which farmers were allowed to sell surplus farm products, products raised on private plots and a range of non-farm products at free-market prices reflecting scarcity values) were the only official exception to monopoly powers exercised by the state. However, as economic reforms have continued (albeit tentatively), the number of market outlets—both formal and informal—has increased.

Between 1990 and 1998 tertiary activities grew rapidly—by an average of 9.8% annually—as a result of which their contribution to GDP doubled (from 18.0% to 35.6%). However, this momentum was not subsequently maintained: during 1998–2003 average annual growth slowed to 2.8%, and it has since declined below 2% per annum. In 2007 services were the second fastest growing area of economic activity, increasing by 1.7%—a performance mostly attributable to the buoyant restaurant and hotels sector serving foreign tourists, but also reflecting an upturn in transport, posts and telecommunication activities. In 2008 growth slowed to just 0.7%, but in 2009 the tertiary sector was the only major production sector that did not record negative growth, rising by a marginal 0.1%. At just over 32%, the service sector's contribution to GDP in 2009 remained below the peak level attained in the late 1990s. The extent to which distribution in North Korea is still state-controlled is suggested by the finding that the Government's share in the output of services increased from 61% in 1990 to 71% in 2009.

INFRASTRUCTURE

Transport

By the 1970s shortcomings in the transport sector were being blamed for the failure to fulfil major targets under the Six-Year Plan (1971–76). In particular, difficulties in delivering raw materials (especially coal) and semi-finished goods constrained mining and manufacturing growth, as well as adversely affecting energy supplies and impeding foreign trade. The Government responded by the modernization and extension of railway, road and marine transport facilities, especially for freight purposes. It also made available large-scale investment for the expansion and renovation of port facilities in order to alleviate problems in the handling of shipping cargo. Notwithstanding these efforts, transport problems persisted, and North Korea's transport infrastructure has remained severely deficient, probably on a par with that of South Korea in the mid-1970s. In 2009 the length of North Korea's road network was only one-quarter that of South Korea's. As in so many other areas of economic activity, the future enhancement of North Korea's transport facilities is likely to depend significantly on overseas involvement.

With a total route length of 5,242 km in 2009, about one-half of which was constructed during the Japanese colonial period, the railway system has remained North Korea's principal means of transport, handling about 90% of the country's freight, and 60%–70% of its passenger traffic. Consignments of coal, minerals, construction materials, metals, timber, grain and chemical fertilizers account for about three-quarters of rail freight. Passenger rail traffic is subject to frequent and long delays, as well as severe overcrowding (according to some reports, travel from Pyongyang to distant areas of the country can take up to two weeks or more). Railway services are also severely constrained by energy shortages. About 95% of the rail system comprises only single track, although about two-thirds of this is electrified. In recent years, the main thrust of investment efforts has been to improve rail access to remote regions, and to areas near the Chinese border.

Following the inaugural North-South summit meeting, held in June 2000, at which the two Koreas agreed, *inter alia*, to promote bilateral economic co-operation, construction work—partly funded by the South Korean Government—began to reconnect the 486-km inter-Korean Kyongui railway line, which, prior to the division of the Korean peninsula, ran from Sinuiju in the North through Pyongyang to Seoul in the South. Associated with the 2000 initiative was a parallel project (also based, in part, on South Korean investment) to build a highway running alongside the railway. Once opened, the railway was expected not only to facilitate inter-Korean travel, but also to enhance rail links with Russia, China and Japan. However, despite the official opening of the Kyongui line in June 2003 and eventual trial runs in May 2007, the introduction of a full service has been delayed, owing mainly to the vagaries of North Korea's foreign relations.

Fuel constraints and the near-absence of private automobiles have minimized the importance of road transport. Roads tend to be used mainly for short-distance transport and for the provision of access to railway stations and remote areas. BOK estimates show that in 2009 the length of North Korea's road network was a mere 25,854 km, although only a small proportion (less than 3% in 2006, according to CIA estimates) of this was properly surfaced and paved. There also exists a network of multi-lane highways (724 km in 2006), including an expressway connecting Pyongyang and Kaesong (a distance of 170 km), which was completed in April 1992. Other expressways link Pyongyang and Nampo (53 km), Pyongyang–Wonsan on the east coast (189 km), Pyongyang–Sunan (15 km), Pyongyang–Huichon (120 km), Wonsan–Mount Kumgang (114 km) and Sariwon–Sinchon (30 km). A 135-km highway, known as the Tourist Expressway, connecting Pyongyang and Hyangsan, via Anju, was completed in October 1995. Local transport between villages is provided by rural bus services, while bus and tram services operate in towns and cities. Inter-city bus transport scarcely exists. Roads account for a mere 10% of freight transport, but for 30%–40% of passenger traffic.

Water transport plays a minor but growing role in freight and passenger traffic. The total length of inland waterways is about 2,250 km, most of which is navigable only by small craft (exceptions are the Yalu and Taedong rivers). In November 1995 the creation of a marine transport system in the port of Rajin-Sonbong FETZ was announced, as part of the Tumen Delta development project. This initiative, jointly implemented by North Korea and China's Yanbian Sea Transport Corporation, is part of North Korea's economic reform efforts, designed to connect Rajin with Yanji City (China) and Busan (South Korea) and thereby to save shipping time and transport costs in the interests of enhancing inter-Korean trade. Plans to construct a joint venture container terminal at Rajin and an agreement signed with the Chinese border city of Hunchun are expected to be significant port developments. No less important as a sign of the modest opening of the North Korean economy, and perhaps a portent for the future, has been the opening of container operations between Incheon in South Korea and Nampo in the North. According to the CIA, as of 2010 North Korea's merchant fleet comprised 158 ships (1,000 grt or over), including 132 cargo vessels (of which three were refrigerated vessels), 11 oil tankers, eight bulk carriers, three container ships, two roll on-roll-off vessels, one carrier vessel and one passenger/cargo ship. (This list excludes an additional 19 foreign-owned ships, and five vessels registered outside North Korea.) In 2009 shipping tonnage totalled 840,000 grt, and the total harbour loading and unloading capacity was 37m. metric tons. Principal ports include Chongjin, Haeju, Hungnam (Hamhung), Kimchaek, Kosong, Rajin, Nampo, Sinuiju, Songnim, Sonbong (formerly Unggi) and Ungsang.

In 2010 there were 79 airports, of which only 37 possessed paved runways; there were also 22 heliports. North Korea's international air connections remain largely undeveloped. Regular flights connect Pyongyang to Vladivostok (Russia), Beijing and Shenzhen (China), Nagoya (Japan) and Bangkok (Thailand), as well as a few other destinations. In addition, there are irregular flights between Pyongyang and Eastern European, Middle Eastern and African destinations. Internal flights are very restricted, serving mainly to connect Pyongyang with the port cities of Hungnam and Chongjin. Two significant developments were the signing in Bangkok (October 1997) of an agreement with South Korea, allowing foreign commercial flights through North Korean airspace; and, in order to facilitate the North-South summit meeting in June 2000, the opening of a direct air route between Seoul and Pyongyang (albeit one that has remained little used). Meanwhile, regular direct flights to and from China have been inaugurated: since June 2004, between Shenyang and Pyongyang; since March 2008, between Beijing and Pyongyang; and, since 2010, between Shanghai and Pyongyang. In March 2001 DHL Korea instituted services to corporations authorized to do business with North Korea for delivery of parcels, but not letters or cash, to selected destinations including Pyongyang, Rajin-Sonbong, Hamhung and Nampo.

Energy

North Korea's importance as a source of fuel and energy dates from pre-partition years, when the North, through the Japanese-built Supung hydroelectric plant, supplied more than 90% of the electricity needs of the entire peninsula. Hydroelectric plants continued to provide for energy requirements until the 1970s, when North Korea began increasingly to move towards greater reliance on coal. This shift in energy policy was a response to the perceived disadvantages of hydroelectric plants, such as high initial costs, long construction periods and instability engendered by prolonged drought. However, benefits of the new strategy, such as being able to site coal-based power plants close to industrial and heavily populated areas, were offset by the poor quality and inaccessibility of coal deposits.

The International Energy Agency (IEA) showed North Korea's total energy supply in 2008 to have been 20.260m. metric tons of oil equivalent (TOE) on a net calorific basis. Of this total, coal (and some peat) provided 84.6%, hydropower 6.0% and oil (crude and refined products—all imported) 4.3%, the balance being supplied by combustible renewables and waste. In 2007 North Korea was a net exporter of energy: its overseas sales of coal exceeded its purchases of oil and oil products. The main claimant on energy was the industrial sector, which absorbed 68% of total consumption, while transport accounted for a further 2.3% (data for other sectors are not available).

According to the Statistical Review of World Energy published by the London-based oil and gas company BP, at the end of 2010 North Korea's proven reserves of coal stood at 600m. metric tons. Statistics published by the US Energy Information Agency show that total coal output in 2009 was 41.345m. short tons (16% more than in 2008), which, after deduction of exports—overwhelmingly shipped to China—generated total consumption of 38.353m. short tons. IEA data for 2008 indicate that more than three-quarters of final coal consumption was allocated to the industrial sector. North Korea's two main coal mines are the Anju and Sunchon complexes in Pyongannam Province (annual capacity of 9.5m. tons) and the Saebyol complex in Hamgyongbuk Province (6m. tons).

Following a steady increase in national coal production in the 1980s, output stagnated. In general, the expansion of coal production has lagged behind the industrial sector's energy needs, creating a persistent energy shortage and constraining economic growth. In the 1990s declining imports, caused by shortages of foreign exchange, exacerbated the situation. Ageing mining equipment, inefficiencies associated with the need to mine deeper seams, the low level of mechanization and the lack of advanced equipment have contributed to the poor performance of the coal industry.

In 1980 North Korea had one of the largest electricity networks in Asia. During the following decade, widespread construction of small and medium-scale hydroelectric plants got under way: by the end of 1994 some 1,300 such plants were reported to be operational; and in 2000 it was reported that a further 250 power plants, with a generating capacity of 50,000 kWh, had been constructed in previous recent years, facilitating attainment of electricity self-sufficiency in Jagang Province. According to IEA statistics, North Korea's electricity production in 2008 totalled 23,206 GWh (more than 60% of it powered by hydroelectric plants). After allowance for allocations to the energy sector itself and distribution losses of 3,668 GWh (mainly attributable to reliance on an antiquated transmission grid) total final consumption was 16,080 GWh. Industry accounted for about one-half of total electricity consumption.

Problems in the coal industry have seriously impinged on the provision of electricity. Fuel shortages have caused significant underutilization of generating capacity, and current electricity consumption remains significantly lower than at the beginning of the 1990s. The outcome has been a persistent problem of power cuts lasting for extended periods of time, as well inadequate provision of heating facilities. In order to save energy, the Government has also reduced the voltage, thereby reducing the intensity of lighting in towns and cities. Although per caput electricity consumption is still above the average for Asia, it is only about one-third of the corresponding global figure. The possible use of South Korean facilities to help resolve North Korea's electricity shortages was discussed at the June 2000 summit meeting, and in March 2005 electricity was made available to the KIC from Southern sources, the first time since Korea's division in 1948 that South Korean electricity had been supplied to the North.

According to IEA statistics, in 2008 oil accounted for less than 3% of North Korea's total primary energy consumption, all of it being used for transport purposes. Petroleum exploration in North Korea began as long ago as 1965 and, despite high drilling costs, continues to the present day. The most likely locations of crude petroleum deposits are the West Sea Bay (a geological extension of China's Bohai Bay) and Anju Basin. Despite the disappointing results of exploration efforts undertaken by Swedish, British and Australian oil companies off the west and east coasts of North Korea, in June 2006 it was announced that North Korea and China would undertake joint oil exploration in the West Sea (otherwise known as the Yellow Sea). However, in general, exploration has thus far generated negligible output, and North Korea remains wholly reliant on imports for its oil supplies. During the last two decades, Russia, China and the Middle East oil have all, at different times, been significant sources of oil imports. According to the IEA, in 2008 North Korea imported 450,000 metric tons of crude petroleum, as well as more than 400,000 tons of petrol, diesel and other fuel oils. Most of this was purchased from China. Such heavy import dependence on a single source carries obvious risks, as was highlighted by the reported reduction, in August 2006, of oil supplies from China, allegedly in retaliation for North Korea's missile tests (see History).

A Soviet-designed nuclear research reactor, with a generating capacity of about 3 MW, was reportedly installed in Pyongyang as early as 1959, although a North Korean-Soviet agreement signed in 1985, whereby the USSR would construct a 1,760-MW nuclear power plant in North Korea, is thought never to have been fulfilled. In October 1994 North Korea and the USA signed a 'framework agreement' whereby Pyongyang agreed to suspend the development of nuclear weapons in exchange for the construction of two light-water reactors (LWRs) worth US $4,500m., in addition to receiving up to 500,000 metric tons of oil annually for the duration of the construction period (forecast at 10 years). The construction project was to be managed by the Korean Peninsula Energy Development Organization (KEDO), and South Korea's state-run Korea Electric Power Corporation was to be its prime contractor. Initial construction work commenced in August 1997, with some 5,000 South Korean engineers expected to work on the project. However, progress towards its completion has been beset by political disagreements. In 2003 KEDO stated that North Korea had failed to meet the conditions necessary for construction to continue and the project was suspended. In January 2006 the remaining South Korean personnel working at the site were finally withdrawn, despite South Korea's investment of $1,100m. in the project.

Such problems, which continue to the present day, highlight the peculiar obstacles that impede progress towards enhancing energy supplies in North Korea. Even allowing for the positive impact of continuing domestic construction of small- and medium-scale facilities, increased investment in the power industry and higher imports, improvements in the provision of energy are likely to be slow. Large-scale infrastructural construction will also be necessary, which, in turn, almost certainly will require funding from overseas. In short, energy constraints will continue to impede North Korean economic growth into the foreseeable future.

Telecommunications

Telecommunications remain seriously underdeveloped in North Korea. In 1997 only 1.1m. main telephone lines were estimated to be in use; according to the CIA, the corresponding figure in 2008 was 1.18m. The use of mobile telephones is still in its infancy: Yonhap reported that at the end of June 2010 subscriptions to the sole mobile service (Koryolink, operated by Egypt's Orascom—thought by the EIU to be the largest foreign investor in North Korea—in partnership with the North Korean Government) had reached almost 185,000, these being overwhelmingly concentrated in Pyongyang. International telephone connections are mainly made through Beijing and Moscow, although in the second half of the 1990s a direct telephone line was established with South Korea. A national internet and e-mail network has existed since 2001, although users can log on only from within North Korea and can access only filtered internet content.

No recent data appear to be available, but it is estimated that in 1997 there were about 3.36m. radios and 1.2m. television sets available to the North Korean population. Only about 10% of radios and 30% of television sets are privately owned, although most urban households have access to both. Domestic media censorship is strictly enforced, and radios and TV sets are all pre-tuned to government stations (listening to foreign media broadcasts, except by senior party cadres, is strictly forbidden). There are 17 AM, 14 FM and 11 shortwave radio stations, and four TV stations.

FISCAL POLICY

There exist in North Korea a central government budget and local government budget, which are consolidated into the national (state) budget. The central government budget is largely financed from the central Government's net income, transfers from local governments and other revenue sources. Revenue for the local government budget derives from local industrial and other sources, as well as from central government subsidies. Traditionally, the principal sources of revenue under the state budget have been turnover (sales) taxes and state enterprise profits (which were projected to account for almost 80% of anticipated revenue in 2011).

In early 2009 Kim Wan Su was appointed to the post of Minister of Finance, but less than six months later, in September, was replaced—for reasons not explained—by Pak Su Gil. At a meeting of the SPA in April 2011, Pak announced his second budget, which was characteristically lacking in precise facts and data (with published statistics comprising only percentage changes over base figures that remain unknown). State revenue was projected to rise by 7.5% in 2011, while expenditure was to increase by 8.9%. Agriculture and light industry were to be the main beneficiaries of increased spending, with allocations up by 9% and 12.9%, respectively. Pak also spoke of the urgent need to upgrade technological levels through the economy, and to this end he pledged a 10.1% increase in expenditure on scientific and technological development. National defence was to receive 15.8% of total budgeted expenditure.

As in previous years, interpreting the latest budgetary estimates is extremely difficult, and not all the figures can be taken at face value. In particular, there is a strong presumption that the projected increase in defence spending is understated, some sources suggesting that North Korea allocates one-quarter or more of its GDP to the military (the highest defence allocation, as a percentage of GDP, in the world). A reduction in political tensions on the Korean Peninsula, let alone peaceful reunification, would permit a significant reduction in military expenditure and thereby allow a major reallocation of resources to more productive economic ends. Apart from fiscal benefits, demobilization, by rendering more labour available, would also facilitate the accelerated expansion of labour-intensive light industrial manufactures, perhaps in line with the pattern of development shown by China's township and village enterprises. Integration into the international economic community would similarly improve North Korea's fiscal health and financial viability, but its pariah status seems certain to prevent it from joining any major international financial institutions. In 2000, for example, strong US and Japanese opposition was instrumental in blocking a North Korean application to join the Asian Development Bank.

FOREIGN TRADE AND FOREIGN INVESTMENT

North Korea's emphasis on self-reliance has, at least until recently, minimized the role of foreign trade. As a result, the Government has pursued an essentially conservative and passive trade policy in support of its programme of heavy industrialization, rather than a more overtly export-orientated strategy. This passive approach has been reflected in a level of foreign trade that is much smaller than might be expected of a country of North Korea's size and structure. In 2009 the value of North Korea's merchandise trade was a mere 0.5% of the corresponding South Korean figure.

In addition, even allowing for an expansion in North Korea's trade with capitalist countries, there was a significant contraction in foreign trade in the 1990s as a result of the country's growing economic difficulties. Having expanded at an average annual rate of 9.4% during 1960–90 to reach US $4,800m. in 1990, the combined value of exports and imports subsequently declined sharply. According to the Korea Trade-Investment Promotion Agency (KOTRA) in Seoul, between 1990 and 1998 the value of North Korea's merchandise trade (excluding trade with South Korea) declined from $4,170m. to $559m., a cumulative decrease of 86.6% (an average of 22.2% per annum). Sharp recovery took place in 2000, when the combined value of exports and imports (excluding inter-Korean trade) rose by one-third to $1,969m., and by 2008 the figure had reached $3,820m. (30% more than in 2007, but still below the level of a decade earlier). Although North Korea's total merchandise trade declined by almost 11% to $3,410m. in 2009, data issued by KOTRA suggest that the previous buoyant growth trend was re-established in 2010, with trade increasing significantly to reach $4,170m. (9.2% above the 2008 level). It is noteworthy that North Korea has consistently suffered a deficit on its merchandise trade account. BOK estimates indicate that its deficit in 2009 was $1,630m. Current account transactions have contributed most to this deficit. North Korea's current account deficit and foreign debt difficulties have been alleviated by inflows of convertible currency, estimated at $600m.–$1,000m. per annum, from pro-Pyongyang Koreans living in Japan.

In support of its economic modernization programme, in the early 1970s North Korea sought to use massive imports of advanced machinery and equipment from Western Europe and Japan. During the first half of the 1970s its trade balance steadily worsened, and, unable to repay loans incurred as a result of such imports, in January 1976 it attracted world-wide notoriety when it became the first communist country to default on its foreign debt. North Korea's growing trade deficit and debt problem were attributable to a variety of factors, including falling prices for its principal exports, rising import costs associated with the 1973 oil price rise, domestic transport difficulties and the onset of global recession. The default resulted in a severe curtailment of Western credits to North Korea. Thereafter, its position continued to worsen, its debt rising to US $5,200m. in 1988, and further to $11,900m. in 1997. After the decision, in early 1999, by Dutch investment bank ING Barings to cease operations in North Korea, the Government was forced to conduct international banking transactions through a limited number of banks in Japan and Macao. The current level of North Korea's external debt is not known.

Ideological and economic imperatives dictated that until the 1990s North Korea's principal trading partners were other communist countries. The most important of these was the former Soviet Union, which in 1990 still accounted for 57% of North Korea's total foreign trade. The subsequent disintegration of the USSR had a major impact on trade patterns, and by 1991 the former USSR's share had fallen to a mere 17.3%. By 1995 Russia was the source of only 5% of North Korea's imports, and the destination for a mere 1% of its exports. Some recovery has since taken place, and in 2005 trade with Russia accounted for 7.7% of the total, although this recent expansion conceals a precipitate decline in North Korean exports to Russia. The declining importance of Russia as a trading partner has been offset by the increasingly important role, at various times, of countries such as India, Thailand and Brazil.

Well before the collapse of North Korean-Soviet trade, in the 1970s North Korea began to purchase much-needed capital goods from capitalist countries (especially Japan). Between 1965 and 1975 bilateral trade with Japan rose by 23% annually (North Korean imports increasing by 27% per annum), and during the next decade by a further 6% per year. More recently, however, political tensions between the two countries have been accompanied by a major contraction in bilateral trade. The most dramatic interruption of trade took place towards the end of 2006, when Japanese purchases of North Korean goods were suspended in retaliation for Pyongyang's decision to conduct a nuclear test in October of that year. According to the Bloomberg news service, bilateral trade in 2008 totalled 793m. Japanese yen—some 97% below the corresponding figure of three years earlier. This collapse had serious foreign exchange consequences for North Korea. More recently still, in the aftermath of the sinking of a South Korean naval vessel in May 2010 (see Part One, The Korean Peninsula: Conflict and Dialogue), later in the month the Japanese Government lowered the limit on cash transfers to North Korea from 10m. yen to 3m. yen.

Between 1965 and 1985 bilateral trade between North Korea and China rose by more than 5% annually, reaching US $2,100m. in 1985, in which year it accounted for almost 15% of North Korea's foreign trade. Thereafter, China's importance as a trading partner declined, and by 1999 the value of bilateral trade was just $370m. However, following the dramatic contraction in trade with the former USSR, China swiftly emerged as North Korea's largest trading partner. Between 1999 and 2007, according to the South Korean Ministry of Unification, the value of bilateral merchandise trade increased at an average annual rate of growth in excess of 23% to reach almost $2,000m. By 2010 the corresponding figure had reached $3,500m., accounting for some 83% of North Korea's total trade.

In November 1988, for the first time since the Korean War, limited indirect trade with South Korea was resumed, and just two years later direct inter-Korean trade also resumed, its value rising to US $210m. in 1992. By the end of the decade (and notwithstanding the temporary negative impact of the 1997/98 Asian financial crisis) inter-Korean trade had reached a record level of $333.4m. (including some $200m. in tour fees associated with the Mount Kumgang project), making South Korea the North's third largest trading partner. In 2000 bilateral trade increased further, to $425m., raising South Korea to second place after China, a ranking that it has subsequently retained. From a base of $425.2m. in 2000, bilateral trade had risen to $1,822.4m. by 2008, generating a small bilateral surplus for North Korea of $44.2m. Mainly as a result of declining imports from South Korea, in the following year there was a contraction of almost 8% in two-way trade, as a result of which North Korea's trade surplus increased more than four-fold to $189.5m. Inter-Korean trade recovered in 2010 to a record-high $1,910m., according to KOTRA.

North Korea's trade with the USA has been of minor importance and has been almost wholly one-way, reflecting shipments from the USA. In the 1990s there were two years (1995 and 1999) in which the value of US shipments to North Korea exceeded US $11m. US exports to North Korea peaked at

$52.2m. in 2008, before declining to a mere $0.9m. in 2009. In 2010 the USA shipped goods worth $1.9m. to North Korea; as of April 2011 the corresponding figure was $1.8m.

The fall of communist regimes in Eastern Europe and the dissolution of the USSR, the insistence by both Russia and China of abandoning barter trading systems in favour of charging international prices for oil and other products, and the rapid expansion of inter-Korean trade all help to explain the significant realignment of North Korea's economic relations that has taken place during the last two decades. At the same time, inefficiencies and infrastructural constraints (for example, low product quality and lack of variety, poor packaging, failure to meet delivery dates, and limited transport and harbour facilities) have continued to impede North Korean efforts to expand exports and increase much-needed foreign exchange earnings.

According to the EIU, North Korea's principal exports in 2006 included electronic goods (worth US $386m.), minerals and metals ($284m.), textiles ($214m.), and machinery ($188m.). In the same year the main imports were mineral fuels and oil ($975m.), machinery and electronic products ($430m.), cereals and meats ($334m.) and fertilizers ($156m.). According to the same source, the value of the North Korean currency increased from 141.3 won per US dollar in 2006 to 139 won per $1 in 2009, before declining to 145 won per $1 in 2010.

The introduction, in 1984, of joint venture legislation (revised in 1994) signalled North Korea's willingness to adopt radical measures in order to acquire Western capital and technology. To date, such aspirations are far from having been realized, joint venture projects having been dominated by partnerships with South Korean and Chinese companies, especially in the KIC, and, to a lesser extent, the Rajin-Sonbong FETZ (see above). Slow progress notwithstanding, it is likely that North Korea will maintain its efforts to encourage greater foreign involvement in its economic development. The greatest challenge will be to persuade foreign investors to invest in a country that has such a discouraging economic record.

Statistical Survey

Area and Population

AREA, POPULATION AND DENSITY*

Area (sq km)	122,762†
Population (census results)	
31 December 1993	21,213,378
1 October 2008‡	
Males	11,722,403
Females	12,328,815
Total	24,051,218
Population (UN estimates at mid-year)§	
2009	24,238,184
2010	24,346,229
2011	24,451,282
Density (per sq km) at mid-2011	199.2

* Excluding the demilitarized zone between North and South Korea, with an area of 1,262 sq km (487 sq miles).

† 47,399 sq miles.

‡ Provisional figures.

§ Source: UN, *World Population Prospects: The 2010 Revision*.

POPULATION BY AGE AND SEX
(UN estimates at mid-2011)

	Males	Females	Total
0–14	2,809,563	2,675,265	5,484,828
15–64	8,357,142	8,238,200	16,595,342
65 and over	831,949	1,539,163	2,371,112
Total	11,998,654	12,452,628	24,451,282

Source: UN, *World Population Prospects: The 2010 Revision*.

ADMINISTRATIVE DIVISIONS
(population at 2008 census)

	Area (sq km)	Population ('000)	Density (per sq km)
Chagang Province	16,968	1,299,830	76.6
Hamgyong North Province*	17,570	2,327,362	132.5
Hamgyong South Province	18,970	3,066,013	161.6
Hwanghae North Province	9,262	2,113,672	228.2
Hwanghae South Province	8,002	2,310,485	288.7
Kangwon Province	11,152	1,477,582	132.5
Pyongan North Province	12,191	2,728,662	223.8
Pyongan South Province	12,330	4,051,696	328.6
Yanggang (Ryanggang) Province	14,317	719,269	50.2
Pyongyang City	2,000	3,255,288	1,627.6
Total	122,762	24,051,218†	195.9

* Includes Najin-Sonbong, which enjoys the administrative status of Special City.

† Total includes population living in military camps.

Source: partly Thomas Brinkhoff, *City Population* (www.citypopulation.de).

PRINCIPAL TOWNS
(population at 2008 census)*

Pyongyang (capital)	2,581,076	Sariwon	271,434
Hamhung	703,610	Kaechon	262,389
Chongjin	614,892	Kanggye	251,971
Sinuiju	334,031	Sunchon	250,738
Wonsan	328,467	Haeju	241,599
Nampo	310,531	Tanchon	240,873

* Population for urban areas of cities, as enumerated at census.

BIRTHS AND DEATHS
(annual averages, UN estimates)

	1995–2000	2000–05	2005–10
Birth rate (per 1,000)	19.8	16.3	14.6
Death rate (per 1,000)	9.8	9.0	9.6

Source: UN, *World Population Prospects: The 2010 Revision*.

2008 census (12 months ending 1 October 2008): Live births 345,630; deaths 216,616.

Life expectancy (years at birth, WHO estimates): 70 (males 67; females 72) in 2009 (Source: WHO, *World Health Statistics*).

EMPLOYMENT

(persons aged 16 years and over at 2008 census)

	Males	Females	Total
Agriculture, forestry and fishing	2,082,297	2,304,598	4,386,895
Mining and quarrying	458,484	259,711	718,195
Manufacturing	1,507,014	1,375,968	2,882,982
Electricity, gas and water	161,098	55,184	216,282
Construction	285,941	81,709	367,650
Wholesale and retail trade; repair of motor vehicles	173,962	383,393	557,355
Transport, storage and communications	337,983	144,175	482,158
Hotels and restaurants	26,591	114,614	141,205
Finance and insurance activities	12,374	13,854	26,228
Professional, scientific and technical activities	80,574	37,558	118,132
Administrative and support service activities	287,951	163,385	451,336
Public administration and defence; compulsory social security	439,586	284,592	724,178
Education	263,635	284,497	548,132
Health and social welfare	134,306	196,396	330,702
Arts, entertainment and recreation	72,290	58,292	130,582
Other services	35,852	66,856	102,708
Total employed	6,359,938	5,824,782	12,184,720

Note: Of the remaining total population aged 16 years and over, 940,886 were studying, 155,093 were disabled, 3,147,553 were retired, 921,191 were engaged in housework and 17,326 were described as 'other'.

Health and Welfare

KEY INDICATORS

Total fertility rate (children per woman, 2009)	1.9
Under-5 mortality rate (per 1,000 live births, 2009)	33
HIV/AIDS (% of persons aged 15–49, 1994)	<0.01
Physicians (per 1,000 head, 2003)	3.3
Health expenditure (2006): US $ per head (PPP)	1
Health expenditure (2006): % of GDP	3.5
Health expenditure (2006): public (% of total)	85.6
Access to sanitation (% of persons, 2004)	59
Total carbon dioxide emissions ('000 metric tons, 2007)	70,652.9
Carbon dioxide emissions per head (metric tons, 2007)	3.0

For sources and definitions, see explanatory note on p. vi.

Agriculture

PRINCIPAL CROPS

('000 metric tons)

	2007	2008	2009
Wheat*	195	175	169
Rice, paddy	1,870	2,862*	2,336
Barley*	75	65	63
Maize	1,587*	1,411	1,705
Rye	60*	73†	69†
Oats	15*	18†	17†
Millet	61*	61†	61†
Sorghum	30*	36†	34†
Potatoes	1,900†	1,520	1,560
Sweet potatoes	370†	380	390
Beans, dry†	225	250	216
Soybeans (Soya beans)*	345	345	350
Cabbages and other brassicas†	700	768	751
Tomatoes†	65	61	69
Pumpkins, squash and gourds†	80	82	78
Cucumbers and gherkins†	66	68	72
Aubergines (Eggplants)†	46	45	49
Chillies and peppers, green†	60	57	53
Onions and shallots, green†	98	101	116
Onions, dry†	84	79	70
Garlic†	95	104	101
Apples†	635	681	720
Pears†	125	131	138
Peaches and nectarines†	132	139	147
Watermelons†	95	96	99
Cantaloupes and other melons†	110	93	95
Tobacco, unmanufactured†	63	74	80

* Unofficial figure(s).

† FAO estimate(s).

Aggregate production ('000 metric tons, may include official, semi-official or estimated data): Total cereals 3,893 in 2007, 4,702 in 2008, 4,454 in 2009; Total roots and tubers 2,270 in 2007, 1,900 in 2008, 1,950 in 2009; Total vegetables (incl. melons) 3,756 in 2007, 3,929 in 2008, 4,627 in 2009; Total fruits (excl. melons) 1,390 in 2007, 1,439 in 2008, 1,527 in 2009.

Source: FAO.

LIVESTOCK

('000 head)

	2007*	2008	2009
Horses*	47	48	48
Cattle	576	576	576
Pigs	2,500	2,178	2,150
Sheep	168	167	165
Goats	3,260	3,441	3,570
Chickens	15,000	14,071	13,859
Ducks	6,000	5,878	5,900

* FAO estimate(s).

Source: FAO.

LIVESTOCK PRODUCTS

('000 metric tons, FAO estimates)

	2007	2008	2009
Cattle meat	21.8	21.8	21.8
Goat meat	13.4	14.1	14.6
Pig meat	130.0	110.0	110.0
Chicken meat	33.6	31.9	31.9
Cows' milk	96.0	96.0	95.2
Hen eggs	147.9	156.5	158.2

Source: FAO.

Forestry

ROUNDWOOD REMOVALS

('000 cubic metres, excl. bark, FAO estimates)

	2007	2008	2009
Sawlogs, veneer logs and logs for sleepers	1,000	1,000	1,000
Other industrial wood	500	500	500
Fuel wood	5,873	5,911	5,949
Total	7,373	7,411	7,449

Sawnwood production ('000 cubic metres, incl. railway sleepers): 280 (coniferous 185, broadleaved 95) per year in 1970–2009 (FAO estimates).

Source: FAO.

Fishing

('000 metric tons, live weight, FAO estimates)

	2007	2008	2009
Capture	205.0	205.0	205.0
Freshwater fishes	5.0	5.0	5.0
Alaska pollock	60.0	60.0	60.0
Other marine fishes	107.6	107.6	107.6
Marine crustaceans	16.0	16.0	16.0
Squids	9.5	9.5	9.5
Aquaculture	63.9	64.0	64.1
Molluscs	63.0	60.0	60.0
Total catch	268.9	269.0	269.1

Note: Figures exclude aquatic plants (FAO estimates, '000 metric tons, aquaculture only): 444.3 in 2007–09.

Source: FAO.

Mining

('000 metric tons, unless otherwise indicated, estimates)

	2007	2008	2009
Hard coal	24,100	25,060	25,000
Iron ore: gross weight	5,130	5,316	5,300
Iron ore: metal content	1,400	1,488	1,500
Copper ore*	12	12	12
Lead ore*	13	13	13
Zinc ore*	70	70	70
Tungsten concentrates (metric tons)*	250	350	350
Silver (metric tons)*	20	20	20
Gold (kg)*	2,000	2,000	2,000
Magnesite (crude)	55,000	150,000	150,000
Phosphate rock†	300	300	300
Fluorspar‡	13	13	13
Salt (unrefined)	500	500	500
Graphite (natural)	30	30	30
Talc, soapstone and pyrophyllite	50	50	50

* Figures refer to the metal content of ores and concentrates.
† Figures refer to gross weight.
‡ Metallurgical grade.

Note: No recent data were available for the production of molybdenum ore and asbestos.

Source: US Geological Survey.

Industry

SELECTED PRODUCTS
('000 metric tons unless otherwise indicated)

	2006	2007	2008
Motor spirit (petrol)	122	146	151
Kerosene	24	29	30
Gas-diesel (distillate fuel) oils	131	157	161
Residual fuel oils	75	90	92
Cement*	6,160	6,415	6,415
Pig-iron*	900	900	900
Crude steel*	1,180	1,230	1,279
Refined copper (primary and secondary metal)*	15	15	15
Refined lead (primary and secondary metal)*	9	9	9
Zinc (primary and secondary metal)	72	75	75
Electric energy (million kWh)	22,436	21,523	23,206

* US Geological Survey estimates.

Source: mostly UN Industrial Commodity Statistics Database.

2009 ('000 metric tons, estimates): Cement 6,400; Pig-iron 900; Crude steel 1,300; Refined copper (primary and secondary metal) 15; Refined lead (primary and secondary metal) 9; Refined zinc (primary and secondary metal) 75 (Source: US Geological Survey).

Finance

CURRENCY AND EXCHANGE RATES

Monetary Units
100 chon (jun) = 1 won.

Sterling, Dollar and Euro Equivalents (31 May 2011)
£1 sterling = 157.769 won;
US $1 = 95.600 won;
€1 = 137.521 won;
1,000 won = £6.34 = $10.46 = €7.27.

Note: In August 2002 it was reported that a currency reform had been introduced, whereby the exchange rate was adjusted from US $1 = 2.15 won to $1 = 150 won: a devaluation of 98.6%. In November 2009 reports of further currency reform emerged; a 'currency exchange' was believed to have been implemented in December, whereby denominations of the former currency were exchanged for new currency at a rate of 100 old won for 1 new won. In January 2010 it was reported that an exchange rate of US $1 = 96.9 won had been established by some financial institutions.

BUDGET
(million won, projected)

	1992	1993	1994
Revenue	39,500.9	40,449.9	41,525.2
Expenditure	39,500.9	40,449.9	41,525.2
Economic development	26,675.1	27,423.8	28,164.0
Socio-cultural sector	7,730.6	7,751.5	8,218.3
Defence	4,582.1	4,692.2	4,816.9
Administration and management	513.1	582.4	326.0

1998 (million won, estimates): Total revenue 19,790.8; Total expenditure 20,015.2.

1999 (million won, estimates): Total revenue 19,801.0; Total expenditure 20,018.2.

2000 (million won, estimates): Total revenue 20,955.0; Total expenditure 20,903.0.

2001 (million won, projected): Total revenue 21,571.0; Total expenditure 21,571.0.

2002 (million won, projected): Total revenue 22,174.0; Total expenditure 22,174.0.

2003: Exact figures not made available following price reforms of August 2002.

2004 (million won, reported): Total revenue 337,546; Total expenditure 348,807.

2005 (million won, reported): Total expenditure 419,700.

2006 (million won, reported): Total expenditure 388,950.

2007 (million won, reported, estimate): Total expenditure 440,200 (Defence 69,200).

2008 (million won, reported): Total expenditure 451,500 (Defence 71,300).

2009 (million won, reported): Total expenditure 482,600 (Defence 76,300).

NATIONAL ACCOUNTS
(million won, UN estimates)

Expenditure on the Gross Domestic Product

	2007	2008	2009
Total domestic expenditure	2,102,142.4	1,951,407.1	1,761,724.5
Exports of goods and services	118,806.2	108,924.2	97,858.0
Less Imports of goods and services	221,791.3	206,516.3	186,696.3
GDP in purchasers' values	1,999,157.4	1,853,815.0	1,672,886.2
GDP in constant 2005 prices	1,761,880.2	1,816,468.5	1,799,957.3

Gross Domestic Product by Economic Activity

	2007	2008	2009
Agriculture, hunting, forestry and fishing	423,821.4	400,424.0	349,633.2
Mining, manufacturing and utilities	719,696.7	704,449.7	650,752.7
Manufacturing	399,831.5	417,108.4	369,707.8
Construction	175,925.8	153,866.6	133,830.9
Services	681,712.7	596,928.4	536,996.5
Sub-total	2,001,156.5	1,855,668.8	1,671,213.3
Indirect taxes (net)*	–1,999.1	–1,853.8	1,672.9
GDP in purchasers' values	1,999,157.4	1,853,815.0	1,672,886.2

* Figures obtained as a residual.

Source: UN National Accounts Main Aggregates Database.

External Trade

PRINCIPAL COMMODITIES
(US $ million)*

Imports	2000	2001	2002
Live animals and animal products	20.3	73.9	103.4
Vegetable products	159.0	221.0	118.4
Animal or vegetable fats and oils; prepared edible fats; animal or vegetable waxes; Prepared foodstuffs; beverages, spirits and vinegar; tobacco and manufactured substitutes	89.1	89.9	72.3
Mineral products	171.2	231.1	235.9
Products of chemical or allied industries	108.4	123.4	122.1
Plastics, rubber and articles thereof	67.5	66.0	66.0
Textiles and textile articles	171.9	203.9	158.5
Base metals and articles thereof	85.2	100.4	88.2
Machinery and mechanical appliances; electrical equipment; sound and television apparatus	205.1	243.8	234.7
Vehicles, aircraft, vessels and associated transport equipment	146.2	88.4	76.1
Total (incl. others)	1,406.5	1,620.3	1,525.4

Exports	2000	2001	2002
Live animals and animal products	97.9	158.4	261.1
Vegetable products	30.3	42.0	27.5
Mineral products	43.2	50.5	69.8
Products of chemical or allied industries; Plastics, rubber and articles thereof	44.9	44.6	42.4
Wood, cork and articles thereof; wood charcoal; manufactures of straw, esparto, etc.	10.9	5.6	10.2
Textiles and textile articles	140.0	140.5	123.1
Natural or cultured pearls, precious or semi-precious stones, precious metals and articles thereof; imitation jewellery; coin	9.8	14.1	14.6
Base metals and articles thereof	43.9	60.2	57.4
Machinery and mechanical appliances; electrical equipment, sound and television apparatus	105.2	97.9	85.6
Total (incl. others)	565.8	650.2	735.0

* Excluding trade with the Republic of Korea (US $ million): *Imports:* 272.8 in 2000; 226.8 in 2001; 370.2 in 2002. *Exports:* 152.4 in 2000; 176.2 in 2001; 271.6 in 2002.

Source: Korea Trade-Investment Promotion Agency (KOTRA), Republic of Korea.

2005 (US $ million, unofficial estimates): *Excluding Republic of Korea:* Total imports 200; Total exports 100. *Republic of Korea only:* Total imports 715.5; Total exports 340.3 (Source: Bank of Korea, Republic of Korea).

2006 (US $ million, unofficial estimates): *Excluding Republic of Korea:* Total imports 205; Total exports 95. *Republic of Korea only:* Total imports 830.2; Total exports 519.5 (Source: Bank of Korea, Republic of Korea).

2007 (US $ million, unofficial estimates): *Excluding Republic of Korea:* Total imports 202; Total exports 92. *Republic of Korea only:* Total imports 1,032.6; Total exports 765.3 (Source: Bank of Korea, Republic of Korea).

2008 (US $ million, unofficial estimates): *Excluding Republic of Korea:* Total imports 269; Total exports 113. *Republic of Korea only:* Total imports 888.1; Total exports 932.3 (Source: Bank of Korea, Republic of Korea).

PRINCIPAL TRADING PARTNERS
(US $ million)*

Imports	2001	2002	2003
China, People's Republic	570.7	467.3	627.6
Germany	82.1	140.4	n.a.
Hong Kong	42.6	29.2	n.a.
India	154.8	186.6	157.9
Japan	249.1	135.1	91.5
Netherlands	9.1	27.6	n.a.
Russia	63.8	77.0	115.6
Singapore	112.3	83.0	n.a.
Spain	31.6	n.a.	n.a.
Thailand	106.0	172.0	203.6
United Kingdom	40.7	n.a.	n.a.
Total (incl. others)	1,620.3	1,525.4	1,614.4

Exports	2001	2002	2003
Bangladesh	38.0	32.3	n.a.
China, People's Republic	166.8	270.9	395.3
Germany	22.8	27.8	n.a.
Hong Kong	38.0	21.9	n.a.
India	3.1	4.8	1.6
Japan	225.6	234.4	173.8
Netherlands	10.4	6.4	n.a.
Russia	4.5	3.6	2.8
Spain	12.6	n.a.	n.a.
Thailand	24.9	44.6	50.7
Total (incl. others)	650.2	735.0	777.0

* Excluding trade with the Republic of Korea (US $ million): *Imports:* 226.8 in 2001; 370.2 in 2002; 435.0 in 2003. *Exports:* 176.2 in 2001; 271.6 in 2002; 289.3 in 2003.

Source: Korea Trade-Investment Promotion Agency (KOTRA).

2004 (US $ million): *Imports:* China, People's Republic 800; Japan 89; Korea, Republic 439; Total (incl. others) 2,280. *Exports:* China, People's Republic 586; Japan 163; Korea, Republic 258; Total (incl. others) 1,280 (Source: Ministry of Unification, Republic of Korea).

Trade with Republic of Korea (US $ million, unofficial estimates): *Total imports:* 715.5 in 2005; 830.2 in 2006; 1,032.6 in 2007; 888.1 in 2008. *Total exports:* 340.3 in 2005; 519.5 in 2006; 765.3 in 2007; 932.3 in 2008 (Source: Bank of Korea, Republic of Korea).

Transport

SHIPPING

Merchant Fleet
(registered at 31 December)

	2007	2008	2009
Number of vessels	301	296	252
Total displacement ('000 grt)	985.6	982.8	870.8

Source: IHS Fairplay, *World Fleet Statistics*.

International Sea-borne Freight Traffic
(estimates, '000 metric tons)

	1988	1989	1990
Goods loaded	630	640	635
Goods unloaded	5,386	5,500	5,520

Source: UN, *Monthly Bulletin of Statistics*.

CIVIL AVIATION
(traffic on scheduled services)

	2004	2005	2006
Kilometres flown (million)	1	1	1
Passengers carried ('000)	94	101	105
Passenger-km (million)	39	42	43
Total ton-km (million)	6	6	6

Source: UN, *Statistical Yearbook*.

Tourism

	1996	1997	1998
Tourist arrivals ('000)	127	128	130

Source: World Tourism Organization.

Communications Media

	1994	1995	1996
Radio receivers ('000 in use)	2,950	3,000	3,300
Television receivers ('000 in use)	1,000	1,050	1,090
Telefax stations (number in use)	3,000*	n.a.	n.a.
Daily newspapers:			
number	11	11*	3
average circulation ('000 copies)*	5,000	5,000	4,500

* Estimate(s).

1997 ('000 in use): Radio receivers 3,360; Television receivers 1,200.

Daily newspapers (number of titles): 15 in 2004.

Main telephones lines ('000 in use): 1,000 in 2006; 1,180 in 2007–10.

Mobile cellular telephones ('000 subscribers): 69.3 in 2009; 431.9 in 2010.

Sources: UNESCO, *Statistical Yearbook*; UN, *Statistical Yearbook*; International Telecommunication Union.

Education

(2000)

	Institutions	Students
Kindergartens	14,167	748,416
Primary	4,886	1,609,865
Senior middle schools	4,772	2,181,524

Source: mainly Government of the Democratic People's Republic of Korea, *UNESCO Education for All Assessment Report 2000*.

Universities and Colleges: The *UNESCO Education for All Assessment Report 2000* identified more than 300 universities and colleges with 1.89m. students and academics.

Teachers (1987/88, UNESCO estimates): Pre-primary 35,000, Primary 59,000, Secondary 111,000, Universities and colleges 23,000, Other tertiary 4,000 (Source: UNESCO, *Statistical Yearbook*).

Directory

The Constitution

A new Constitution was adopted on 27 December 1972. Several amendments were reportedly made in April 1992, including the deletion of references to Marxism-Leninism, the extension of the term of the Supreme People's Assembly from four to five years, and the promotion of limited 'economic openness'. Extensive amendments to the Constitution were approved in September 1998. Further amendments were reported to have been enacted in April 2009. These incorporated a reference to the Chairman of the National Defence Commission, a position held by Kim Jong Il since 1993, as the 'supreme leader', the first official acknowledgement of this in the Constitution. The main provisions of the revised Constitution are summarized below:

The Democratic People's Republic of Korea is an independent socialist state; the revolutionary traditions of the State are stressed (its ideological basis being the *Juche* (self-reliance) idea of the Korean Workers' Party), as is the desire to achieve national reunification by peaceful means on the basis of national independence. The Late President Kim Il Sung is the Eternal President of the Republic.

National sovereignty rests with the working people, who exercise power through the Supreme People's Assembly and Local People's Assemblies at lower levels, which are elected by universal, equal and direct suffrage by secret ballot.

The foundation of an independent national economy, based on socialist and *Juche* principles, is stressed. The means of production are owned solely by the State and socialist co-operative organizations.

Culture and education provide the working people with knowledge to advance a socialist way of life. Education is free, universal and compulsory for 11 years.

Defence is emphasized, as well as the rights of overseas nationals, the principles of friendly relations between nations based on equality, mutual respect and non-interference, proletarian internationalism, support for national liberation struggles and due observance of law.

The basic rights and duties of citizens are laid down and guaranteed. These include the right to vote and to be elected (for citizens who are more than 17 years of age), to work (the working day being eight hours), to free medical care and material assistance for the old, infirm or disabled, and to political asylum. National defence is the supreme duty of citizens.

THE STRUCTURE OF STATE

The Supreme People's Assembly

The Supreme People's Assembly is the highest organ of state power, exercises legislative power and is elected by direct, equal, universal and secret ballot for a term of five years. Its chief functions are: (i) to adopt, amend or supplement legal or constitutional enactments; (ii) to determine state policy; (iii) to elect the Chairman of the National Defence Commission; (iv) to elect the Vice-Chairmen and other members of the National Defence Commission (on the recommendation of the Chairman of the National Defence Commission); (v) to elect the President and other members of the Presidium of the Supreme People's Assembly, the Premier of the Cabinet, the President of the Central Court and other legal officials; (vi) to appoint the Vice-Premiers and other members of the Cabinet (on the recommendation of the Premier of the Cabinet); (vii) to approve the State Plan and Budget; (viii) to receive a report on the work of the Cabinet and adopt measures, if necessary; (ix) to decide on the ratification or abrogation of treaties. It holds regular and extraordinary sessions, the former being once or twice a year, the latter as necessary at the request of at least one-third of the deputies. Legislative enactments are adopted when approved by more than one-half of those deputies present. The Constitution is amended and supplemented when approved by more than two-thirds of the total number of deputies.

The National Defence Commission

The National Defence Commission, which consists of a Chairman, first Vice-Chairman, other Vice-Chairmen and members, is the highest military organ of state power, and is accountable to the Supreme People's Assembly. The National Defence Commission directs and commands the armed forces and guides defence affairs. The Chairman of the National Defence Commission is the Supreme Leader.

The Presidium of the Supreme People's Assembly

The Presidium of the Supreme People's Assembly, which consists of a President, Vice-Presidents, secretaries and members, is the highest organ of power in the intervals between sessions of the Supreme People's Assembly, to which it is accountable. It exercises the following chief functions: (i) to convene sessions of the Supreme People's Assembly; (ii) to examine and approve new legislation, the State Plan and the State Budget, when the Supreme People's Assembly is in recess; (iii) to interpret the Constitution and legislative enactments; (iv) to supervise the observance of laws of State organs; (v) to organize elections to the Supreme People's Assembly and Local People's Assemblies; (vi) to form or abolish ministries or commissions of the Cabinet; (vii) to appoint or remove Vice-Premiers and other cabinet or ministry members, on the recommendation of the Premier, when the Supreme People's Assembly is not in session; (viii) to elect or transfer judges of the Central Court; (ix) to ratify or abrogate treaties concluded with other countries; (x) to appoint or recall diplomatic envoys; (xi) to confer decorations, medals, honorary titles and diplomatic ranks; (xii) to grant general amnesties or special pardons. The President of the Presidium represents the State and receives credentials and letters of recall of diplomatic representatives accredited by a foreign state.

The Cabinet

The Cabinet is the administrative and executive body of the Supreme People's Assembly and a general state management organ. It serves a five-year term and comprises the Premier, Vice-Premiers, Chairmen of Commissions and other necessary members. Its major functions are the following: (i) to adopt measures to execute state policy; (ii) to guide the work of ministries and other organs responsible to it; (iii) to establish and remove direct organs of the Cabinet and main administrative economic organizations; (iv) to draft the State Plan and adopt measures to make it effective; (v) to compile the State Budget and to implement its provisions; (vi) to organize and execute the work of all sectors of the economy, as well as education, science, culture, health and environmental protection; (vii) to adopt measures to strengthen the monetary and banking system; (viii) to adopt measures to maintain social order, protect State interests and guarantee citizens' rights; (ix) to conclude treaties; (x) to abolish decisions and directives of economic administrative organs which run counter to those of the Cabinet. The Cabinet is accountable to the Supreme People's Assembly.

Local People's Assemblies

The Local People's Assemblies and Committees of the province (or municipality directly under central authority), city (or district) and county are local organs of power. The Local People's Assemblies consist of deputies elected by direct, equal, universal and secret ballot. The Local People's Committees consist of a Chairman, Vice-Chairmen, secretaries and members. The Local People's Assemblies and Committees serve a four-year term and exercise local budgetary functions, elect local administrative and judicial personnel and carry out the decisions at local level of higher executive and administrative organs.

THE JUDICIARY

Justice is administered by the Central Court (the highest judicial organ of the State), local courts and the Special Court. Judges and other legal officials are elected by the Supreme People's Assembly. The Central Court protects state property and constitutional rights, guarantees that all state bodies and citizens observe state laws, and executes judgments. Justice is administered by the court comprising one judge and two people's assessors. The court is independent and judicially impartial. Judicial affairs are conducted by the Central Procurator's Office, which exposes and institutes criminal proceedings against accused persons. The Office of the Central Procurator is responsible to the Chairman of the National Defence Commission, the Supreme People's Assembly and the Central People's Committee.

The Government

HEAD OF STATE

President: President KIM IL SUNG died on 8 July 1994 and was declared 'Eternal President' in September 1998.

Chairman of the National Defence Commission: Marshal KIM JONG IL.

Titular Head of State: KIM YONG NAM.

CABINET

(October 2011)

The Government is formed by the Korean Workers' Party (KWP).

Premier: CHOE YONG RIM.

Vice-Premiers: KANG NUNG SU, KIM RAK HUI, JON HA CHOL, KANG SOK JU.

Vice-Premier and Chairman of the State Planning Commission: RO TU CHOL.

Vice-Premier and Minister of Finance: PAK SU GIL.

Vice-Premier and Minister of the Electronics Industry: HAN KWANG BOK.

Vice-Premier and Minister of Machine-Building Industries: JO PYONG JU.

Vice-Premier and Minister of Chemical Industry: RI MU YONG.

Minister of Foreign Affairs: PAK UI CHUN.

Minister of People's Security: RI MYONG SU.

Minister of Electric Power Industry: HO TAEK.

Minister of the Coal Industry: KIM HYONG SIK.

Minister of the Mining Industry: KANG MIN CHOL.

Minister of the Oil Industry: KIM HUI YONG.

Minister of the Metal Industry: KIM THAE BONG.

Minister of Construction and Building Materials Industries: TONG JONG HO.

Minister of Railways: JON KIL SU.

Minister of Land and Marine Transport: RA TONG HUI.

Minister of Agriculture: YI KYONG SIK.

Minister of Light Industry: AN JONG SU.

Minister of Foreign Trade: RI RYONG NAM.

Minister of Forestry: KIM KWANG YONG.

Minister of Fisheries: PAK THAE WON.

Minister of Urban Management: HWANG HAK WON.

Minister of Land and Environmental Protection: KIM CHANG RYONG.

Minister of Land Development and Construction Affairs: KIM SOK JUN.

Minister of Commerce: KIM PONG CHOL.

Minister of Food Procurement and Administration: MUN UNG JO.

Minister of Education: KIM YONG JIN.

Minister of Higher Education: SONG JA RIP.

Minister of Post and Telecommunications: RYU YONG SOP.

Minister of Culture: AN TONG CHUN.

Minister of Labour: JONG YONG SU.

Minister of Public Health: CHOE CHANG SIK.

Minister of State Inspection: KIM UI SUN.

Minister of Capital City Construction: KIM UNG GWAN.

Minister of the Foodstuff and Daily Necessities Industry: JO YONG CHOL.

Minister of Physical Culture and Sports: PAK MYONG CHOL.

President of the National Academy of Sciences: PYON YONG RIP.

President of the Central Bank: PAEK RYONG CHON.

Director of the Central Statistical Board: KIM CHANG SU.

Director of the Secretariat of the Cabinet: KIM YONG HO.

Note: the Minister of People's Armed Forces is not a member of the Cabinet (see under Defence).

MINISTRIES

All Ministries and Commissions are in Pyongyang.

Legislature

CHOE KO IN MIN HOE UI
(Supreme People's Assembly)

The 687 members of the 12th Supreme People's Assembly (SPA) were elected unopposed for a five-year term on 8 March 2009. The SPA's permanent body is the Presidium.

Chairman: CHOE TAE BOK.

President of the Presidium: KIM YONG NAM.

Vice-Presidents of the Presidium: YANG HYONG SOP, KIM YONG DAE.

Political Organizations

Democratic Front for the Reunification of the Fatherland: Pyongyang; f. 1946; vanguard org. comprising political parties and mass working people's orgs seeking the unification of North and South Korea; Dir KIM YANG GON.

The component parties are:

Chondoist Chongu Party: Pyongyang; tel. (2) 334241; f. 1946; follows the guiding principle of *Innaechon* (the realization of 'heaven on earth'); satellite party of the KWP; Chair. RYU MI YONG.

Korean Social Democratic Party (KSDP) (Joson Sahoeminju-dang): Pyongyang; tel. (2) 5591323; fax (2) 3814410; f. 1945; advocates national independence and a democratic socialist society; satellite party of the KWP; Chair. KIM YONG DAE; First Vice-Chair. SIN PYONG CHOL.

Korean Workers' Party (KWP): Pyongyang; f. 1945; merged with South Korean Workers' Party in 1949; follows the guiding principle of *Juche*, based on the concept that man is the master and arbiter of all things; most significant political entity in the DPRK; Central Cttee of 124 full mems and 105 alternate mems; 3m. mems; Gen. Sec. Marshal KIM JONG IL.

SEVENTH CENTRAL COMMITTEE OF THE KWP

General Secretary: Marshal KIM JONG IL.

POLITICAL BUREAU (POLITBURO) OF THE KWP

Presidium: Marshal KIM JONG IL, KIM YONG NAM, CHOE YONG RIM, VICE-MARSHAL RI YONG HO.

Full Members: Marshal KIM JONG IL, KIM YONG NAM , CHOE YONG RIM, VICE-MARSHAL RI YONG HO, KIM YONG CHUN, JON PYONG HO, KIM KUK THAE, KIM KI NAM, CHOE THAE BOK, YANG HYONG SOP, KANG SOK JU, PYON YONG RIP, RI YONG MU, JU SANG SONG, HONG SOK HYONG, KIM KYONG HUI.

Alternate Members: KIM YANG GON, KIM YONG IL, PAK TO CHUN, CHOE RYONG HAE, JANG SONG THAEK, JU KYU CHANG, RI TAE NAM, KIM RAK HUI, THAE JONG SU, KIM PHYONG HAE, U TONG CHUK, KIM JONG GAK, KIM CHANG SOP, MUN KYONG DOK.

Secretariat: Marshal KIM JONG IL, KYE UNG TAE, JON PYONG HO, HAN SONG RYONG, CHOE TAE BOK, KIM KI NAM, KIM KUK TAE, JONG HA CHOL.

The component mass working people's organizations (see under Trade Unions) are:

General Federation of Trade Unions of Korea (GFTUK).

Kim Il Sung Socialist Youth League.

Korean Democratic Women's Union (KDWU).

Union of Agricultural Working People of Korea.

Diplomatic Representation

EMBASSIES IN THE DEMOCRATIC PEOPLE'S REPUBLIC OF KOREA

Cambodia: Munsudong, Taedongkang District, Pyongyang; tel. (2) 3817283; fax (2) 3817625; e-mail recpyongyang@gmail.com; Ambassador CHHORN HAY.

China, People's Republic: Kinmauldong, Moranbong District, Pyongyang; tel. (2) 3823316; fax (2) 3813425; e-mail chinaemb_kp@mfa.gov.cn; internet kp.china-embassy.org; Ambassador LIU HONGCAI.

Cuba: Munsudong, Taedongkang District, POB 5, Pyongyang; tel. (2) 3817370; fax (2) 3817703; e-mail embacuba@rpdc.embacuba.cn; Ambassador GERMÁN HERMÍN FERRAS ALVAREZ.

Czech Republic: Taedongkang Guyok 38, Taehakgori, Puksudong, Pyongyang; tel. (2) 3817021; fax (2) 3817022; e-mail pyongyang@embassy.mzv.cz; internet www.mzv.cz/pyongyang; Ambassador DUŠAN STRAUCH.

Egypt: 39 Munsudong, Taedongkang District, Pyongyang; tel. (2) 3817414; fax (2) 3817410; e-mail embassy.pyongyang@mfa.gov.eg; Ambassador ISMAIL ABDELRAHMAN GHONEIM HUSSEIN.

Ethiopia: Munsudong, Taedongkang District, POB 55, Pyongyang; tel. (2) 3827554; fax (2) 3827550; Chargé d'affaires FEKADE S. G. MESKEL.

Germany: Munsudong, Pyongyang; tel. (2) 3817385; fax (2) 3817397; e-mail info@pjoe.diplo.de; Ambassador GERHARD THIEDEMANN.

India: 6 Taehak St, Munsudong, Taedongkang District, Pyongyang; tel. (2) 3817274; fax (2) 3817619; e-mail amb.pyongyang@mea.gov.in; Ambassador PRATAP SINGH.

Indonesia: 5 Foreigners' Bldg, Munsudong, Taedongkang District, Pyongyang; tel. (2) 3827439; fax (2) 3817620; e-mail kompyg2@public2.bta.net.cn; Ambassador NASRI GUSTAMAN.

Iran: Munhungdong, Monsu St, Taedongkang District, Pyongyang; tel. (2) 3817214; fax (2) 3817612; e-mail embpyong@mfa.gov.ir; Ambassador MORTEZA MORADIAN.

Laos: Munhungdong, Taedongkang District, Pyongyang; tel. (2) 3827363; fax (2) 3817722; Ambassador CHALEUNE WARINTHRASAK.

Libya: Munsudong, Taedongkang District, Pyongyang; tel. (2) 3827544; fax (2) 3817267; Secretary of People's Bureau BASHIR RAMADAN KHALIFA ABU JANAH.

Malaysia: Munhungdong Diplomatic Enclave, Pyongyang; tel. (2) 3817125; fax (2) 3817845; e-mail malpygyang@kln.gov.my; Ambassador RAHIMI BIN HARUN.

Mali: Pyongyang; Ambassador NAKOUNTE DIAKITÉ.

Mongolia: 17 Taehak St, Munsudong, Taedongkang District, Pyongyang; tel. (2) 3827322; fax (2) 3817616; e-mail mon-emb@kcckp.net; Ambassador SODOVJAMTSYN KHÜRELBAATAR.

Nigeria: Munsudong, Taedongkang District, POB 535, Pyongyang; tel. (2) 3827558; fax (2) 3817293; e-mail empngrdprk@yahoo.com; Ambassador MACLEAN IGONIKON OMUSO.

Pakistan: 23, Blk 66, Munsudong, Taedongkang District, Pyongyang; tel. (2) 3827479; fax 3817622; e-mail parep.pyongyang@kcckp.net; internet www.mofa.gov.pk/northkorea; Ambassador ARIF MAHMOOD.

Poland: Munsudong, Taedongkang District, Pyongyang; tel. (2) 3817325; fax (2) 3817634; e-mail phenian.amb.sekretariat@msz.gov.pl; internet www.phenian.polemb.net; Ambassador EDWARD PIETRZYK.

Romania: Munhungdong, Taedongkang District, Pyongyang; tel. (2) 3827336; fax (2) 3817336; e-mail ambrophe@gmail.com; Chargé d'affaires a.i. IANCU RIVIU OVIDIU.

Russia: Sinyangdong, Central District, Pyongyang; tel. (2) 3813101; fax (2) 3813427; e-mail rusembdprk@yahoo.com; internet www.dprk.mid.ru; Ambassador VALERII SUKHININ.

Sweden: Munsudong, Taedongkang District, Pyongyang; tel. (2) 3817485; fax (2) 3817663; e-mail ambassaden.pyongyang@foreign.ministry.se; Ambassador BARBRO ELM.

Syria: Munsudong, Taedongkang District, Pyongyang; tel. (2) 3827473; fax (2) 3817635; Chargé d'affaires a.i. HAISSAM SAAD.

United Kingdom: Munsudong Diplomatic Compound, Pyongyang; tel. (2) 3817980; fax (2) 3817985; e-mail postmaster.PYONX@fco.gov.uk; Ambassador KAREN WOLSTENHOLME.

Viet Nam: 7 Munsudong, Taedongkang District, Pyongyang; tel. (2) 3817358; fax (2) 3817649; e-mail vnembassydprk@mofa.gov.vn; internet www.vietnamembassy-pyongyang.org; Ambassador LE QUANG BA.

Judicial System

The judicial organs include the Central (Supreme) Court—the highest judicial organ, which supervises the work of all courts—the Court of the Province (or city under central authority) and the People's Court. Each court is composed of judges and people's assessors.

The Central Procurator's Office, headed by the Procurator-General, supervises the work of procurator's offices in provinces, counties and cities. Procurators supervise the ordinances and regulations of all ministries and the decisions and directives of local organs of state power to ensure that they conform to the Constitution, laws and decrees, as well as to the decisions and other measures of the Cabinet. Procurators bring suits against criminals in the name of the State, and participate in civil cases to protect the interests of the State and citizens.

President of the Central Court: KIM PYONG RYUL.

First Vice-President of the Central Court: KANG SOK JU.

Procurator-General: RI KIL SONG.

Religion

The religions that are officially reported to be practised in the DPRK are Buddhism, Christianity and Chundo Kyo, a religion peculiar to Korea combining elements of Buddhism and Christianity. Religious co-ordinating bodies are believed to be under strict state control. The exact number of religious believers is unknown.

Korean Religious Believers Council: Pyongyang; f. 1989; brings together members of religious organizations in North Korea; Chair. JANG JAE ON.

BUDDHISM

In 2002 it was reported that there were an estimated 300 Buddhist temples in the DPRK; the number of believers was estimated at about 10,000 in 2003.

Korean Buddhists Federation: POB 77, Pyongyang; tel. (2) 43698; fax (2) 3812100; f. 1945; Chair. Cen. Cttee SHIM SANG JIN; Sec. JONG SO JONG.

CHRISTIANITY

In 2003 it was reported that there were approximately 13,000 Protestants and 3,000 Catholics in the country, many of whom worshipped in house churches (of which there were said to be about 500 in 2002). The construction of North Korea's first Russian Orthodox church was completed in August 2006.

Korean Christians Federation: Pyongyang; f. 1946; Chair. Cen. Cttee KANG YONG SOP; Sec. O KYONG U.

The Roman Catholic Church

For ecclesiastical purposes, North and South Korea are nominally under a unified jurisdiction. North Korea contains two dioceses (Hamhung and Pyongyang), both suffragan to the archdiocese of Seoul (in South Korea), and the territorial abbacy of Tokwon (Tokugen), directly responsible to the Holy See.

Diocese of Hamhung: Catholic Mission, Hamhung; 134-1 Waekwan-dong Kwan Eub, Chil kok kun, Gyeongbuk 718-800, Republic of Korea; tel. (545) 970-2000; Bishop (vacant); Apostolic Administrator of Hamhung and of the Abbacy of Tokwon Fr PLACIDUS DONG-HO RI.

Diocese of Pyongyang: Catholic Mission, Pyongyang; Bishop Rt Rev. FRANCIS HONG YONG HO (absent); Apostolic Administrator Most Rev. NICHOLAS CHEONG JIN-SUK (Archbishop of Seoul, South Korea).

Korean Catholics Association: Changchung 1-dong, Songyo District, Pyongyang; tel. (2) 23492; f. 1988; Chair. Cen. Cttee JANG JAE ON; Vice-Chair. MUN CHANG HAK.

CHUNDO KYO

According to officials quoted in 2002, there were approximately 40,000 practitioners of Chundo Kyo in the DPRK.

Korean Chundoists Association: Pyongyang; tel. (2) 334241; f. 1946; Chair. of Central Guidance Cttee RYU MI YONG.

The Press

PRINCIPAL NEWSPAPERS

Choldo Sinmun: Pyongyang; f. 1947; every two days.

Joson Inmingun (Korean People's Army Daily): Pyongyang; f. 1948; daily; Editor-in-Chief RI TAE BONG.

Kyowon Sinmun: Pyongyang; f. 1948; publ. by the Education Commission; weekly.

Minju Choson (Democratic Korea): Pyongyang; f. 1946; govt organ; 6 a week; Editor-in-Chief KIM JONG SUK; circ. 200,000.

Nongup Kunroja: Pyongyang; publ. of Cen. Cttee of the Union of Agricultural Working People of Korea.

Pyongyang Sinmun: Pyongyang; f. 1957; general news; 6 a week; Editor-in-Chief SONG RAK GYUN.

Rodong Chongnyon (Working Youth): Pyongyang; f. 1946; organ of the Cen. Cttee of the Kim Il Sung Socialist Youth League; 6 a week; Editor-in-Chief RI JONG GI.

Rodong Sinmun (Labour Daily): Pyongyang; internet www.kcna.co.jp/today-rodong/rodong.htm; f. 1946; organ of the Cen. Cttee of the Korean Workers' Party; daily; Editor-in-Chief KIM KI RYONG; circ. 1.5m.

Rodongja Sinmun (Workers' Newspaper): Pyongyang; f. 1945; organ of the Gen. Fed. of Trade Unions of Korea; Editor-in-Chief RI SONG JU.

Saenal (New Day): Pyongyang; f. 1971; publ. by the Kim Il Sung Socialist Youth League; 2 a week; Deputy Editor CHOE SANG IN.

Sonyon Sinmun: Pyongyang; f. 1946; publ. by the Kim Il Sung Socialist Youth League; 2 a week; circ. 120,000.

Tongil Sinbo: Kangan 1-dong, Youth Ave, Songyo District, Pyongyang; f. 1972; non-affiliated; weekly; Chief Editor PAK JIN SIK; circ. 300,000.

PRINCIPAL PERIODICALS

Chollima: Pyongyang; popular magazine; monthly.

Choson (Korea): Pyongyang; social, economic, political and cultural; bi-monthly.

Choson Minju Juuiinmin Gonghwaguk Palmyonggongbo (Official Report of Inventions in the DPRK): Pyongyang; 6 a year.

Choson Munhak (Korean Literature): Pyongyang; organ of the Cen. Cttee of the Korean Writers' Union; monthly.

Choson Yesul (Korean Arts): Pyongyang; organ of the Cen. Cttee of the Gen. Fed. of Unions of Literature and Arts of Korea; monthly.

Economics: POB 73, Pyongyang; fax (2) 3814410; quarterly.

History: POB 73, Pyongyang; fax (2) 3814410; quarterly.

Hwahakgwa Hwahakgoneop: Pyongyang; organ of the Hamhung br. of the Korean Acad. of Sciences; chemistry and chemical engineering; 6 a year.

Jokook Tongil: Kangan 1-dong, Youth Ave, Songyo District, Pyongyang; organ of the Cttee for the Peaceful Unification of Korea; f. 1961; monthly; Chief Editor LI MYONG GYU; circ. 70,000.

Korean Medicine: POB 73, Pyongyang; fax (2) 3814410; quarterly.

Kunroja (Workers): 1 Munshindong, Tongdaewon, Pyongyang; f. 1946; organ of the Cen. Cttee of the Korean Workers' Party; monthly; Editor-in-Chief RYANG KYONG BOK; circ. 300,000.

Kwahakwon Tongbo (Bulletins of the Academy of Science): POB 73, Pyongyang; fax (2) 3814410; organ of the Standing Cttee of the Korean Acad. of Sciences; 6 a year.

Mulri (Physics): POB 73, Pyongyang; fax (2) 3814410; quarterly.

Munhwao Haksup (Study of Korean Language): POB 73, Pyongyang; fax (2) 3814410; publ. by the Publishing House of the Acad. of Social Sciences; quarterly.

Philosophy: POB 73, Pyongyang; fax (2) 3814410; quarterly.

Punsok Hwahak (Analysis): POB 73, Pyongyang; fax (2) 3814410; organ of the Cen. Analytical Inst. of the Korean Acad. of Sciences; quarterly.

Ryoksagwahak (Historical Science): Pyongyang; publ. by the Acad. of Social Sciences; quarterly.

Saengmulhak (Biology): Pyongyang; fax (2) 3814410; publ. by the Korea Science and Encyclopedia Publishing House; quarterly.

Sahoekwahak (Social Science): Pyongyang; publ. by the Acad. of Social Sciences; 6 a year.

Suhakkwa Mulli: Pyongyang; organ of the Physics and Mathematics Cttee of the Korean Acad. of Sciences; quarterly.

FOREIGN LANGUAGE PUBLICATIONS

The Democratic People's Republic of Korea: Korea Pictorial, Pyongyang; f. 1956; illustrated news; Korean, Russian, Chinese, English, French, Arabic and Spanish edns; monthly; Editor-in-Chief HAN POM CHIK.

Foreign Trade of the DPRK: Foreign Trade Publishing House, Potonggang District, Pyongyang; economic developments and export promotion; English, French, Japanese, Russian and Spanish edns; monthly.

Korea: Pyongyang; f. 1956; illustrated; Korean, Arabic, Chinese, English, French, Spanish and Russian edns; monthly.

Korea Today: Foreign Languages Publishing House, Pyongyang; current affairs; Chinese, English, French, Russian and Spanish edns; monthly; Vice-Dir and Editor-in-Chief HAN PONG CHAN.

Korean Women: Pyongyang; English and French edns; quarterly.

Korean Youth and Students: Pyongyang; English and French edns; monthly.

The Pyongyang Times: Sochondong, Sosong District, Pyongyang; tel. (2) 51951; English, Spanish and French edns; weekly.

NEWS AGENCY

Korean Central News Agency (KCNA): Potonggangdong 1, Potonggang District, Pyongyang; e-mail eng-info@kcna.co.jp; internet www.kcna.co.jp; f. 1946; sole distributing agency for news in the DPRK; publs daily bulletins in English, Russian, French and Spanish; Dir-Gen. KIM PYONG HO.

PRESS ASSOCIATION

Korean Journalists Union: Pyongyang; tel. (2) 36897; f. 1946; assists in the ideological work of the Korean Workers' Party; Chair. Cen. Cttee KIM SONG GUK.

Publishers

Academy of Sciences Publishing House: Nammundong, Central District, Pyongyang; tel. (2) 51956; f. 1953.

Academy of Social Sciences Publishing House: Pyongyang; Dir CHOE KWAN SHIK.

Agricultural Press: Pyongyang; labour, industrial relations; Pres. HO KYONG PIL.

Central Science and Technology Information Agency: Pyongyang; f. 1963; Dir JU SONG RYONG.

Education Publishing House: Pyongyang; f. 1945; Pres. KIM CHANG SON.

Foreign Language Press Group: Sochondong, Sosong District, Pyongyang; tel. (2) 841342; fax (2) 812100; f. 1949; Dir CHOE KYONG GUK.

Foreign Language Publishing House: Oesong District, Pyongyang; Dir KIM YONG MU.

Higher Educational Books Publishing House: Pyongyang; f. 1960; Pres. PAK KUN SONG.

Kim Il Sung University Publishing House: Pyongyang; f. 1965.

Korea Science and Encyclopedia Publishing House: POB 73, Pyongyang; tel. (2) 18111; fax (2) 3814410; publishes numerous periodicals and monographs; f. 1952; Dir-Gen. KIM JUNG HYOP; Dir of International Co-operation JEAN BAHNG.

Korean People's Army Publishing House: Pyongyang; Pres. YUN MYONG DO.

Korean Social Democratic Party Publishing House: Pyongyang; tel. (2) 5591709; fax (2) 3814410; f. 1946; publishes quarterly journal *Joson Sahoemingjudang* (in Korean) and *KSDP Says* (in English); Dir RI KANG SIK.

Korean Workers' Party Publishing House: Pyongyang; f. 1945; fiction, politics; Dir RYANG KYONG BOK.

Kumsong Youth Publishing House: Pyongyang; f. 1946; Dir HAN JONG SOP.

Literature and Art Publishing House: Pyongyang; f. by merger of Mass Culture Publishing House and Publishing House of the Gen. Fed. of Literary and Art Unions; Dir-Gen. RI PHYO U.

Transportation Publishing House: Namgyodong, Hyongjaesan District, Pyongyang; f. 1952; travel; Editor PAEK JONG HAN.

Working People's Organizations Publishing House: Pyongyang; f. 1946; fiction, government, political science; Dir MIN SANG HYON.

WRITERS' UNION

Korean Writers' Union: Pyongyang; Chair. Cen. Cttee KIM PYONG HUN.

Broadcasting and Communications

In October 2001 North Korea launched its first e-mail service provider in co-operation with China-based company Silibank.com, which was used for business and trade purposes. However, access to the internet remained severely limited, with information flow within North Korea still being conducted mainly via a closed intranet system (the Kwangmyong, meaning 'light', system). Although a mobile telephone network was established in 2002, the use of mobile telephones was banned in 2004, and it was reported that handsets had been confiscated by the authorities. However, the ban was subsequently removed, and Orascom Telecom Holding, a provider based in Egypt, was permitted to establish an operation in North Korea. In January 2008 Cheo Technology, a subsidiary of Orascom, was granted a licence to provide a mobile telephone service, and by March 2011 the number of subscribers to Koryolink was reported to have reached 535,000.

TELECOMMUNICATIONS

Korea Post and Telecommunications Co: Pyongyang; Dir KIM HYON JONG.

BROADCASTING

Regulatory Authorities

DPRK Radio and Television Broadcasting Committee: see Radio, below.

Pyongyang Municipal Broadcasting Committee: Pyongyang; Chair. KANG CHUN SHIK.

Radio

There are 17 AM radio stations, 14 FM stations and 11 shortwave stations.

DPRK Radio and Television Broadcasting Committee: Jonsungdong, Moranbong District, Pyongyang; tel. (2) 3816035; fax (2) 3812100; programmes relayed nationally with local programmes supplied by local radio cttees; loudspeakers are installed in factories and in open spaces in all towns; home broadcasting 22 hours daily; foreign broadcasts in Russian, Chinese, English, French, German, Japanese, Spanish and Arabic; Chair. (vacant).

Television

There are four television stations in operation.

General Bureau of Television: Gen. Dir CHA SUNG SU.

DPRK Radio and Television Broadcasting Committee: see Radio.

Kaesong Television: Kaesong; broadcasts five hours on weekdays, 11 hours at weekends.

Korean Central Television Station: Ministry of Post and Telecommunications, Pyongyang; broadcasts five hours daily; satellite broadcasts commenced Oct. 1999.

Mansudae Television Station: Mansudae, Pyongyang; f. 1983; broadcasts nine hours of cultural programmes, music and dance, foreign films and news reports at weekends.

Finance

(cap. = capital; res = reserves; dep. = deposits; m. = million; br(s) = branch(es); amounts in won)

BANKING

A total of 18 banks were reported to be in operation in mid-2011.

Central Bank

Central Bank of the DPRK: Munsudong, Seungri St 58-1, Central District, Pyongyang; tel. (2) 3338196; fax (2) 3814624; e-mail kcb_idkb@co.chesin.com; f. 1946; bank of issue; supervisory and control bank; Pres. PAEK RYONG CHON; 13 brs.

State Banks

Credit Bank of Korea: Chongryu 1-dong, Munsu St, Otandong, Central District, Pyongyang; tel. (2) 3818285; fax (2) 3817806; f. 1986; est. as International Credit Bank, name changed 1989; Pres. LI SUN BOK; Vice-Pres. SON YONG SUN.

Foreign Trade Bank of the DPRK: FTB Bldg, Jungsongdong, Seungri St, Central District, Pyongyang; tel. (2) 3815270; fax (2) 3814467; e-mail ftb@co.chesin.com; f. 1959; deals in international settlements and all banking business; Pres. and Chair. O KWANG CHOL; 12 brs.

International Industrial Development Bank: Jongpyong-dong, Pyongchon District, Pyongyang; tel. (2) 3818610; fax (2) 3814427; f. 2001; Pres. SHIN DOK SONG.

Korea Daesong Bank: Segoridong, Gyongheung St, Potonggang District, Pyongyang; tel. (2) 3818221; fax (2) 3814576; f. 1978; cap. 158,205.8m., res 25,917.6m., dep. 1,990,582.5m. (Dec. 2006); Pres. RI GYONG HA.

Koryo Bank: Ponghwadong, Potonggang District, Pyongyang; tel. (2) 18333; fax (2) 3814410; e-mail krbankpy@co.chesin.com; f. 1989; est. as Koryo Finance Joint Venture Co, name changed 1994; co-operative, devt, regional, savings and universal bank; Pres. PAK YONG CHIL.

Kumgang Bank: Jungsongdong, Central District, Pyongyang; tel. (2) 3818532; fax (2) 3814467; f. 1979; Chair. KIM JANG HO.

State Development Bank: Pyongyang; f. 2010; Dir-Gen. JEON IL CHUN.

Private Banks

Bank of East Land: BEL Bldg, Jonseung-dong, Moranbong District, POB 32, Pyongyang; tel. (2) 3818923; fax (2) 3814410; f. 2001; commercial, investment, merchant, private and retail banking; Pres. PAK HYONG GIL.

Tanchon Commercial Bank: Saemaeul 1-dong, Pyongchon District, Pyongyang; tel. (2) 18111999; fax (2) 3814793; e-mail cbktm828@co.chesin.com; f. 1983; fmrly Changgwang Credit Bank, merged with Samchon-ri Bank and named as above Nov. 2003; cap. 50,043.9m., res 93,817.9m., dep. 875,021.9m. (Dec. 2003); Chair. KIM CHOL HWAN; Pres. KYE CHANG HO.

Joint-Venture Banks

Korea Joint Bank (KJB): Ryugyongdong, Potonggang District, Pyongyang; tel. (2) 3818151; fax (2) 3814410; f. 1989; est. with co-operation of Fed. of Korean Traders and Industrialists in Japan; 50% owned by Korea Int. General Jt Venture Co, 50% owned by Gen. Asscn of Koreans in Japan; Gen. Man. O HO RYOL; 6 domestic brs, 1 br. in Tokyo.

Korea Joint Financial Co: f. 1988; jt venture with Koreans resident in the USA.

Korea Nagwon Joint Financial Co: f. 1987; est. by Nagwon Trade Co and a Japanese co.

Korea Rakwon Joint Banking Co: Pyongyang; Man. Dir HO POK DOK.

Korea United Development Bank: Central District, Pyongyang; tel. (2) 3814165; fax (2) 3814483; e-mail kudb888@yahoo.com; f. 1991; 51% owned by Zhongce Investment Corpn (Hong Kong), 49% owned by Osandok Gen. Bureau; Pres. KIM SE HO.

Koryo Commercial Bank: tel. (2) 3812060; fax (2) 3814441; f. 1988; jt venture with Koreans resident in the USA.

Foreign Investment Banks

Daedong Credit Bank: Potonggang Hotel, 401 Ansan-dong, Pyongchon District, Pyongyang; tel. (2) 3814866; fax (2) 3814723; internet www.daedongcreditbank.com; f. 1996; est. as Peregrine-Daesong Devt Bank; jt venture between Oriental Commercial Holdings Ltd (Hong Kong) and Korea Daesong Bank; Gen. Man. and CEO NIGEL COWIE.

Golden Triangle Bank: Rajin-Sonbong Free Economic and Trade Zone; f. 1995.

INSURANCE

State Insurance Bureau: Central District, Pyongyang; tel. (2) 38196; handles all life, fire, accident, marine, hull insurance and reinsurance.

Korea Foreign Insurance Co (Chosunbohom): Central District, Pyongyang; tel. (2) 3818024; fax (2) 3814464; f. 1974; conducts marine, motor, aviation and fire insurance, reinsurance of all classes, and all foreign insurance; brs in Chongjin, Hungnam and Nampo, and agencies in foreign ports; overseas representative offices in Chile, France, Germany, Pakistan, Singapore; Pres. RI JANG SU.

Korea International Insurance Co: Pyongyang; Dir PAEK MYONG RON.

Korea Mannyon Insurance Co: Pyongyang; Pres. PAK IL HYONG.

Trade and Industry

GOVERNMENT AGENCIES

DPRK Committee for the Promotion of External Economic Co-operation: Jungsongdong, Central District, Pyongyang; tel. (2) 333974; fax (2) 3814498; Chair. PAEK HONG BONG.

DPRK Committee for the Promotion of International Trade: Central District, Pyongyang; Pres. RI SONG ROK; Chair. KIM YONG JAE.

Economic Co-operation Management Bureau: Ministry of Foreign Trade, Pyongyang; f. 1998; Dir KIM YONG SUL.

Korea International Joint Venture Promotion Committee: Pyongyang; Chair. CHAE HUI JONG.

Korean Association for the Promotion of Asian Trade: Pyongyang; Pres. RI SONG ROK.

Korean International General Joint Venture Co: Pyongyang; f. 1986; promotes jt economic ventures with foreign countries; Man. Dir RO TU CHOL.

CHAMBER OF COMMERCE

DPRK Chamber of Commerce: Jungsongdong, Central District, POB 89, Pyongyang; tel. (2) 3815926; fax (2) 3815827; e-mail micom@co.chesin.com.

INDUSTRIAL AND TRADE ASSOCIATIONS

Korea Building Materials Trading Co: Tongdaewon District, Pyongyang; tel. (2) 18111-3818085; fax (2) 3814555; chemical building materials, woods, timbers, cement, sheet glass, etc.; Dir SHIN TONG BOM.

Korea Cereals Export and Import Corpn: Jungsongdong, Central District, Pyongyang; tel. (2) 18111-3818278; fax (2) 3813451; high-quality vegetable starches, etc.

Korea Chemicals Export and Import Corpn: Central District, Pyongyang; petroleum and petroleum products, raw materials for the chemical industry, rubber and rubber products, fertilizers, etc.

Korea Daesong General Trading Corpn: Pulgungori 1-dong, Potonggang District, Pyongyang; tel. (2) 18111; fax (2) 3814432; e-mail Daesong@silibank.com; Gen. Dir CHOE JONG SON.

Korea Daesong Jei Trading Corpn: Pulgungori 1-dong, Potonggang District, Pyongyang; tel. (2) 18111-3818213; fax (2) 3814431; machinery and equipment, chemical products, textiles, agricultural products, etc.

Korea Daesong Jesam Trading Corpn: Pulgungori 1-dong, Potonggang District, Pyongyang; tel. (2) 18111-3818562; fax (2) 3814431; remedies for diabetes, tonics, etc.

Korea Ferrous Metals Export and Import Corpn: Potonggang 2-dong, Potonggang District, Pyongyang; tel. (2) 18111-3818078; fax (2) 3814581; steel products.

Korea Film Export and Import Corpn: Taedongmundong, Central District, POB 113, Pyongyang; tel. (2) 180008034; fax (2) 3814410; f. 1956; feature films, cartoons, scientific and documentary films; Dir-Gen. CHOE HYOK U.

Korea First Equipment Export and Import Co: Central District, Pyongyang; tel. (2) 334825; f. 1960; export and import of ferrous and non-ferrous metallurgical plant, geological exploration and mining equipment, communication equipment, machine-building plant, etc.; construction of public facilities such as airports, hotels, tourist facilities, etc.; jt-venture business in similar projects; Pres. CHAE WON CHOL.

Korea Foodstuffs Export and Import Corpn: Kangan 2-dong, Songyo District, Pyongyang; tel. (2) 18111-3818289; fax (2) 3814417; cereals, wines, meat, canned foods, fruits, cigarettes, etc.

Korea Fruit and Vegetables Export Corpn: Central District, Pyongyang; tel. (2) 35117; vegetables, fruit and their products.

Korea General Corpn for External Construction (GENCO): Sungri St 25, Jungsongdong, Central District, Pyongyang; tel. (2) 18111-3818090; fax (2) 3814611; e-mail gen122@co.chesin.com; f. 1961; construction of dwelling houses, public establishments, factories, hydroelectric and thermal power stations, irrigation systems, ports, bridges, transport services, technical services; Gen. Dir CHOE BONG SU.

Korea General Machine Co: Tongsin 3-dong, Tongdaewon, Pyongyang; tel. (2) 18555-3818102; fax (2) 3814495; Dir RA IN GYUN.

Korea Hyopdong Trading Corpn: Othan-dong, Kangan St, Central District, Pyongyang; tel. (2) 18111-3818011; fax (2) 3814454; fabrics, glass products, ceramics, chemical goods, building materials, foodstuffs, machinery, etc.

Korea Industrial Technology Co: Jungsongdong, Central District, Pyongyang; tel. (2) 18111-3818025; fax (2) 3814537; Pres. KWON YONG SON.

Korea International Chemical Joint Venture Co: Pyongyang; Chair. RYO SONG GUN.

Korea Jangsu Trading Co: Kyogudong, Central District, Pyongyang; tel. (2) 18111-3818834; fax (2) 3814410; medicinal products and clinical equipment.

Korea Jeil Equipment Export and Import Corpn: Jungsongdong, Central District, Pyongyang; tel. (2) 334825; f. 1960; ferrous and non-ferrous metallurgical plant, geological exploration and mining equipment, power plant, communications and broadcasting equipment, machine-building equipment, railway equipment, construction of public facilities; Pres. CHO JANG DOK.

Korea Koryo Trading Corpn: Jongpyongdong, Pyongchon District, Pyongyang; tel. (2) 18111-3818104; fax (2) 3814646; Dir KIM HUI DUK.

Korea Kwangmyong Trading Corpn: Jungsongdong, Central District, Pyongyang; tel. (2) 18111-3818111; fax (2) 3814410; dried herbs, dried and pickled vegetables; Dir CHOE JONG HUN.

Korea Light Industry Import-Export Co: Juchetab St, Tongdaewon District, Pyongyang; tel. (2) 37661; exports silk, cigarettes, canned goods, drinking glasses, ceramics, handbags, pens, plastic flowers, musical instruments, etc.; imports chemicals, dyestuffs, machinery, etc.; Dir CHOE PYONG HYON.

Korea Machine Tool Trading Corpn: Tongdaewon District, Pyongyang; tel. (2) 18555-381810; fax (2) 3814495; Dir KIM KWANG RYOP.

Korea Machinery and Equipment Export and Import Corpn: Potonggang District, Pyongyang; tel. (2) 333449; f. 1948; metallurgical machinery and equipment, electric machines, building machinery, farm machinery, diesel engines, etc.

Korea Mansu Trading Corpn: Chollima St, Central District, POB 250, Pyongyang; tel. (2) 43075; fax (2) 812100; f. 1974; antibiotics, pharmaceuticals, vitamin compounds, drugs, medicinal herbs; Dir KIM JANG HUN.

Korea Marine Products Export and Import Corpn: Central District, Pyongyang; canned, frozen, dried, salted and smoked fish, fishing equipment and supplies.

Korea Minerals Export and Import Corpn: Central District, Pyongyang; minerals, solid fuel, graphite, precious stones, etc.

Korea Namheung Trading Co: Sinri-dong, Tongdaewon District, Pyongyang; tel. (2) 18111-3818974; fax (2) 3814623; high-purity reagents, synthetic resins, vinyl films, essential oils, menthol and peppermint oil.

Korea Non-ferrous Metals Export and Import Corpn: Potonggang 2-dong, Potonggang District, Pyongyang; tel. (2) 18111-3818247; fax (2) 3814569.

Korea Okyru Trading Corpn: Kansongdong, Pyongchon District, Pyongyang; tel. (2) 18111-3818110; fax (2) 3814618; agricultural and marine products, household goods, clothing, chemical and light industrial products.

Korea Ponghwa Contractual Joint Venture Co: Pyongyang; Dir MUN YONG OK.

Korea Ponghwa General Trading Corpn: Jungsongdong, Central District, Pyongyang; tel. (2) 18111-3818023; fax (2) 3814444; machinery, metal products, minerals and chemicals.

Korea Publications Export and Import Corpn: Yokjondong, Yonggwang St, Central District, Pyongyang; tel. (2) 3818536; fax (2) 3814404; f. 1948; export of books, periodicals, postcards, paintings, cassettes, videos, CDs, CD-ROMs, postage stamps and records; import of books; Pres. RI YONG.

Korea Rungra Co: Sinwondong, Potonggang District, Pyongyang; tel. (2) 18111-3818112; fax (2) 3814608; Dir CHOE HENG UNG.

Korea Rungrado Trading Corpn: Segori-dong, Potonggang District, Pyongyang; tel. (2) 18111-3818022; fax (2) 3814507; food and animal products; Gen. Dir PAK KYU HONG.

Korea Ryongaksan General Trading Corpn: Pyongyang; Gen. Dir HAN YU RO.

Korea Samcholli General Corpn: Pyongyang; Dir JONG UN OP.

Korea Technology Corpn: Jungsongdong, Central District, Pyongyang; tel. (2) 18111-3818090; fax (2) 3814410; scientific and technical co-operation.

Korea Unha Trading Corpn: Rungra 1-dong, Taedongkang District, Pyongyang; tel. (2) 18111-3818236; fax (2) 3814506; clothing and fibres.

Korea Yonghung Trading Co: Tongan-dong, Central District, Pyongyang; tel. (2) 18111-3818223; fax (2) 3814527; e-mail greenlam@co.chesin.com; f. 1979; export of freight cars, vehicle parts, marine products, electronic goods; import of steel, chemical products; Pres. CHOE YONG DOK.

Pyongsu JV Co Ltd: Pyongyang; f. 2004; pharmaceutical mfr, medical products incl. analgesics; jt venture with Interpacific/Zuellig Pharma (Switzerland).

TRADE UNIONS

General Federation of Trade Unions of Korea (GFTUK): Dongmun-dong, Taedongkang District, POB 333, Pyongyang; fax (2) 3814427; f. 1945; 1.6m. mems (2003); seven affiliated unions (2003); Pres. RYOM SUN GIL.

Trade Union of Construction and Forestry Workers of Korea: Pyongyang; f. 1945; 160,000 mems (2003); Pres. WON HYONG GUK.

Trade Union of Educational and Cultural Workers: Dongmun-dong, Taedongkang District, POB 333, Pyongyang; fax (2) 3814427; f. 1946; 89,800 mems (2003); Pres. KIM YONG DO.

Trade Union of Light and Chemical Industries of Korea: Pyongyang; f. 1945; 372,500 mems (2003); Pres. RI JIN HAK.

Trade Union of Metal and Engineering Industries of Korea: Pyongyang; f. 1945; 332,800 mems (2003); Pres. CHOE GWANG HYON.

Trade Union of Mining and Power Industries of Korea: Pyongyang; f. 1945; 221,000 mems (2003); Pres. SON YONG JUN.

Trade Union of Public Employees and Service Workers of Korea: Pyongyang; f. 1945; 305,900 mems (2003); Pres. KIM GANG HO.

Trade Union of Transport and Fisheries Workers of Korea: Pyongyang; f. 1945; 119,800 mems (2003); Pres. CHOE RYONG SU.

General Federation of Agricultural and Forestry Technique of Korea: Chung Kuyuck Nammundong, Pyongyang; f. 1946; 523,000 mems.

General Federation of Unions of Literature and Arts of Korea: Pyongyang; f. 1946; seven br. unions; Chair. Cen. Cttee CHANG CHOL.

Kim Il Sung Socialist Youth League: Pyongyang; fmrly League of Socialist Working Youth of Korea; First Sec. KIM GYONG HO.

Korean Architects' Union: Pyongyang; f. 1954; 500 mems; Chair. Cen. Cttee PAE TAL JUN.

Korean Democratic Lawyers' Association: Ryonhwa 1, Central District, Pyongyang; fax (2) 3814644; f. 1954; Chair. HAM HAK SONG.

Korean Democratic Scientists' Association: Pyongyang; f. 1956.

Korean Democratic Women's Union: Jungsongdong, Central District, Pyongyang; fax (2) 3814416; f. 1945; Chief Officer RO SONG SIL.

Korean General Federation of Science and Technology: Jungsongdong, Seungri St, Central District, Pyongyang; tel. (2) 3224389; fax (2) 3814410; f. 1946; 550,000 mems; Chair. Cen. Cttee CHOE HUI JONG.

Korean Medical Association: Pyongyang; f. 1970; Chair. CHOE CHANG SHIK.

Union of Agricultural Working People of Korea: Pyongyang; f. 1965; est. to replace fmr Korean Peasants' Union; 2.4m. mems; Chair. Cen. Cttee RI MYONG GIL.

Transport

RAILWAYS

In 2009 the total length of track was estimated at 5,242 km, of which at least 70% was electrified. There are international train services to Moscow (Russia) and Beijing (People's Republic of China). Construction work on the reconnection of the Kyongui (West Coast, Sinuiju to Seoul, in South Korea) and East Coast Line (Wonsan–Seoul) began in September 2002. The two lines were officially opened in June 2003, but were not yet open to traffic, as construction work on the Northern side remained to be completed. The lines were reportedly completed in 2005, and in May 2007 the first cross-border trial runs were conducted. In the long term, the two were to be linked to the Trans-China and Trans-Siberian railways, respectively, greatly enhancing the region's transport links.

There is an underground railway system in Pyongyang, with two public lines serving 17 stations. Unspecified plans to expand the system were announced in February 2002.

ROADS

In 2009 the road network was estimated at 25,854 km, of which most were unpaved. Road links between the DPRK and the Republic of Korea were reported to have opened in late 2005. As part of the Government's 10-year plan, an additional 3,000 km of expressways were to be constructed by 2020.

INLAND WATERWAYS

In 2005 the total length of inland waterways was estimated at 2,253 km, most of which was navigable only by small craft. The Yalu (Amnok-gang), Taedong, Tumen and Ryesong are the most important commercial rivers. Regular passenger and freight services: Nampo–Chosan–Supung; Chungsu–Sinuiju–Dasado; Nampo–Jeudo; Pyongyang–Nampo.

SHIPPING

The principal ports are Nampo, Wonsan, Chongjin, Rajin, Hungnam, Songnim and Haeju. At 31 December 2009 North Korea's merchant fleet comprised 252 vessels, with a combined displacement of 870,800 grt.

Bochon Shipping Co: Pyongchon District, Pyongyang.

Chon Song Shipping Co Ltd: Sochang-dong, Potonggang District, Pyongyang.

Korea Ansan Shipping Co: Nampo.

Korea Chartering Corpn: Central District, Pyongyang; arranges cargo transport and chartering.

Korea Daehung Shipping Co: Ansan 1-dong, Pyongchon District, Pyongyang; tel. (2) 18111, ext. 8695; fax (2) 3814508; f. 1994; owns 6 reefers, 3 oil tankers, 1 cargo ship.

Korea East Sea Shipping Co: Pyongyang; Dir RI TUK HYON.

Korea Foreign Transportation Corpn: Central District, Pyongyang; arranges transport of cargoes for export and import (transit goods and charters).

Korea Myohyang Shipping Co: Ryonhwadong Changgoan St, Chung District, Pyongyang; tel. (3) 8160590; fax (3) 8146420.

Korea Myongsang Shipping Co: Chongpyong-dong, Pyongchon District, Pyongyang; tel. (2) 3815842; fax (2) 3815942.

Korea Tonghae Shipping Co: Changgwang St, Central District, POB 120, Pyongyang; tel. (2) 345805; fax (2) 3814583; arranges transport by Korean vessels.

Korea Undok Shipping Co Ltd: Nampo.

Korean-Polish Shipping Co Ltd: Moranbong District, Pyongyang; tel. (2) 3814384; fax (2) 3814607; f. 1967; maritime trade mainly with Polish and Far East ports.

Ocean Maritime Management Co Ltd: Tonghungdong, Central District, Pyongyang.

Ocean Shipping Agency of the DPRK: Moranbong District, POB 21, Pyongyang; tel. (2) 3818100; fax (2) 3814531; Pres. O Jong Ho.

CIVIL AVIATION

In 2010 there were 79 airports, 42 of which possessed paved runways. The international airport is at Sunan, 22 km north-west of the centre of Pyongyang. The airport has two runways, and a new terminal building opened in mid-2011.

Chosonminhang/General Civil Aviation Bureau of the DPRK: Sunan Airport, Sunan District, Pyongyang; tel. (2) 37917; fax (2) 3814625; f. 1954; internal services and external flights by Air Koryo to Beijing and Shenyang (People's Republic of China), Bangkok (Thailand), Macao, Nagoya (Japan), Kuala Lumpur (Malaysia), Moscow, Khabarovsk and Vladivostok (Russia), Sofia (Bulgaria) and Berlin (Germany); charter services are operated to Asia, Africa and Europe; Pres. Kim Yo Ung.

Tourism

Tourism is permitted only in officially accompanied parties. In 1999 there were more than 60 international hotels (including nine in Pyongyang) with 7,500 beds. Mount Kumgang has been developed as a tourist attraction, as part of a joint venture between North Korea and Hyundai, the South Korean conglomerate. Mount Paekdu, Korea's highest mountain, is another tourist attraction. In 2003 it was estimated that around 1,500 Western tourists visited North Korea annually. It was estimated that more than 101,700 South Koreans visited the North in 2006 (of whom about 88,000 were business travellers to Kaesong), excluding visitors to Mount Kumgang.

Korea International Tourist Bureau: Pyongyang; Pres. Han Pyong Un.

Korean International Youth Tourist Co: Mankyongdae District, Pyongyang; tel. (2) 73406; f. 1985; Dir Hwang Chun Yong.

Kumgangsan International Tourist Co: Central District, Pyongyang; tel. (2) 31562; fax (2) 3812100; f. 1988.

Ryohaengsa (Korea International Travel Company): Central District, Pyongyang; tel. (2) 3817201; fax (2) 3817607; f. 1953; has relations with more than 200 tourist companies throughout the world; Pres. Cho Song Hun.

State General Bureau of Tourism: Jungsongdong, Central District, Pyongyang; Pres. Kim Do Jun.

Defence

The estimated total strength of the armed forces as assessed at November 2010 was 1,190,000: army 1,020,000, air force 110,000, and navy 60,000. Security and border troops numbered 189,000, and there was a workers' and peasants' militia ('Red Guards') numbering about 5.7m. Military service is selective: army for five to 12 years; navy for five to 10 years; and air force for three to four years. Reserve forces were estimated to total 6m. in 2010.

Defence Expenditure: total expenditure was estimated at 76,300m. won in 2009.

Supreme Commander of the Korean People's Army and Chairman of the National Defence Commission: Marshal Kim Jong Il.

First Vice-Chairman of the National Defence Commission: (vacant).

Vice-Chairman of the National Defence Commission and Minister of People's Armed Forces: Vice-Marshal Kim Yong Chun.

Vice-Chairmen of the National Defence Commission: Vice-Marshal Ri Yong Mu, Vice-Marshal O Kuk Ryol, Jang Song Thaek.

Other members of the National Defence Commission: Paek Se Bong, U Tong Chuk, Ju Kyu Chang, Kim Jong Gak, Ju Sang Song, Pak To Chun .

Chief of General Staff of the Korean People's Army: Vice-Marshal Ri Yong Ho.

Commander of the Air Force: Col-Gen. Ri Pyong Chol.

Commander of the Navy: Gen. Kim Yun Shim.

Education

Universal, compulsory primary and secondary education were introduced in 1956 and 1958, respectively, and are provided at state expense. Free and compulsory 11-year education in state schools was introduced in 1975. Children enter kindergarten at five years of age, and primary school at the age of six. After four years, they advance to senior middle school for six years. English is compulsory as a second language from the age of 14. A report submitted to UNESCO by the North Korean Government in 2000 stated that there were 27,017 nurseries for 1,575,000 pupils, 14,167 kindergartens for 748,416 pupils, 4,886 primary schools for 1,609,865 pupils, 4,772 senior middle schools for 2,181,524 pupils, and more than 300 universities and colleges with 1.89m. students and academics. The adult literacy rate was reported by UNESCO in 2003 to be 98%. In 2001 the Ministry of Education announced plans for the establishment of a university of information science and technology in Pyongyang, in co-operation with a South Korean education foundation: the Pyongyang University of Science and Technology (PUST) was expected to open in 2010. In June 2010 it was reported that the Ministry of Education was to be reorganized as the Education Commission, comprising the Ministry of Higher Education and the Ministry of Common Education.

Bibliography

A Bibliography of the Democratic People's Republic of Korea and the Republic of Korea is to be found at the end of the chapter on the Republic of Korea (see p. 637).

THE REPUBLIC OF KOREA

History

AIDAN FOSTER-CARTER

Based on an earlier article by ANDREW C. NAHM

With revisions by JAMES E. HOARE

THE FIRST REPUBLIC, 1948–60

The foundation of the Republic was hardly settled when a communist-inspired military rebellion broke out in October 1948. The rebellion was suppressed, but this demoralized the nation and increased the repressive character of the Government. The democratic aspirations and trends of the pre-Korean War period diminished as the Government became more autocratic during and after the war. Political and social conditions became chaotic as economic hardships multiplied. (See History up to the Korean War for details of the conflict of 1950–53.)

Confronted by a series of crises, President Syngman Rhee and his Liberal Party (LP), established in 1952, acted in an autocratic manner towards their opponents, and various constitutional amendments were forced through the National Assembly. In July 1952 the National Assembly adopted an amendment to elect the President by popular vote; conducted under martial law, the election was won by Dr Rhee. In 1954 the National Assembly adopted another series of amendments, including the exemption of the incumbent President from the constitutional limitation of two terms of office, and the abolition of the post of Prime Minister.

In the 1956 presidential election, a new opposition Democratic Party (DP), founded in 1955, nominated candidates for the offices of President and Vice-President. The sudden death of the opposition's presidential candidate assured victory for the 81-year-old Dr Rhee, but the DP candidate, Chang Myon, defeated the LP candidate for the vice-presidency.

Increased corruption among government officials and LP members, as well as repression by the police, led to a widespread desire for change, particularly among urban voters. At the National Assembly election in 1958, the DP substantially increased its number of seats. Aware of the danger of losing absolute control, the LP-dominated National Assembly repealed local autonomy laws and approved a new national security law.

The death of the DP presidential candidate, Dr Cho Pyong-Ok, some weeks before the fourth presidential election, contributed to the re-election of Dr Rhee in March 1960, following a campaign characterized by violence and intimidation of opposition candidates and supporters. Popular reaction against the administration's corrupt and fraudulent practices increased, and student riots began throughout the country. The student uprising of 19 April forced President Rhee and his Government to resign one week later. An interim Government was established under Ho Chong, and in mid-June the National Assembly adopted a constitutional amendment instituting a strong parliamentary system, reducing the presidency to a ceremonial office, and reviving the office of Prime Minister. In August the National Assembly elected Yun Po-Son as President and Chang Myon as Prime Minister, marking the emergence of the Second Republic.

With the exception of the Land Reform Law of 1949, the First Republic achieved little success in the economic field. In the post-Korean War period a degree of recovery was achieved with aid from UN agencies and the USA, but South Korea remained economically undeveloped, suffering shortages of power, fuel, food and consumer goods.

THE SECOND REPUBLIC, 1960–61

The Second Republic was hampered from the start: it had no mandate from the people, and both President Yun and Prime Minister Chang lacked fortitude and practical ability. The Chang administration was indecisive in dealing with former leaders of the Rhee regime and proved unable effectively to address ideological and social differences between political and sectional groups, while gaining neither new support nor the loyalty of the people. Divisions emerged within the DP, and no solutions to economic and social problems appeared imminent. With the exception of the (totally ineffective) Five-Year Plan, the Chang administration failed to adopt measures for solving the country's serious economic problems. Meanwhile, there were renewed demonstrations, as communist influence spread among students. Agitation by students for direct negotiations with their North Korean counterparts towards reunification of the country, which was compounded by shortages of food and jobs, increased the perceived threat to national security.

MILITARY RULE, 1961–63

On 16 May 1961 a military junta, led by a small group of young army officers headed by Maj.-Gen. Park Chung-Hee, overthrew the Chang administration. The junta dissolved the National Assembly, banned all political activity and declared martial law, prohibiting student demonstrations and censoring the press. Lt-Gen. Chang Do-Yong, the army chief of staff, became Chairman of a Supreme Council for National Reconstruction. President Yun remained in office, but power remained with the military. The Supreme Council issued pledges to resist communism and adhere to UN principles, envisaging a strengthening of links with the USA and the Western bloc, and promising a wide-ranging programme of economic and political reform, as well as the eventual restoration of civilian rule.

The Supreme Council acted as a legislative body, and a 'national reconstruction extraordinary measures law' replaced the Constitution. In July 1961, when Gen. Chang was arrested for an alleged anti-revolutionary conspiracy, Gen. Park assumed the chairmanship of the Supreme Council. In August Gen. Park announced that political activity would be permitted in early 1963, as a prelude to the restoration of a civilian government. A constitutional amendment was endorsed by national referendum in December 1962, restoring a strong presidential system while limiting presidential office to two four-year terms. When President Yun resigned in March 1962, Gen. Park was appointed acting President.

In January 1963 the military junta formed the Democratic Republican Party (DRP), which nominated Gen. Park as its presidential candidate. In mid-March a plot to overthrow the military Government was allegedly uncovered and the acting President announced that a plebiscite would be held on a four-year extension of military rule. The reaction was strongly negative, and in July civilian government was promised within a year. In August Gen. Park retired from the army and became an active presidential candidate of the DRP. Freedom of political activity was restored for those not charged with past political crimes. The opposition forces were divided, but Yun Po-Son eventually emerged as the candidate of the Civil Rule Party. The election in October resulted in victory by a narrow margin for Gen. Park. At the National Assembly election held in November the DRP won an overwhelming majority of the

votes. Civilian constitutional rule was restored on 17 December 1963, with the inauguration of President Park and the convening of the Assembly.

THE THIRD REPUBLIC, 1963–72

Despite the establishment of a supposed civilian government, all important positions in the administration were occupied by ex-military men, and the National Assembly was fully controlled by the DRP, headed by President Park. Although considerable economic development was achieved under the two Five-Year Plans (1962–66 and 1967–71), the Third Republic confronted many domestic difficulties. In March 1964 large-scale student demonstrations broke out in Seoul, in protest at negotiations being conducted with Japan to restore normal relations between the two countries. Despite demonstrations in opposition, the Government dispatched troops to South Viet Nam in co-operation with the USA, declared martial law in June 1965 in the Seoul area, and concluded a treaty to restore normal relations with Japan.

In order to promote a parliamentary democracy, if not to weaken the power of the ruling party, minor parties formed a coalition grouping, the New Democratic Party (NDP), in January 1967. However, in the presidential election in May, the incumbent President defeated Yun Po-Son, nominee of the NDP, again by a large margin, and the ruling party won a substantial majority of seats in the National Assembly. Following the disclosure of electoral irregularities involving the ruling party, the NDP demanded the nullification of the results and the holding of a fresh election.

Prompted by the growing popularity of the NDP in urban areas, the increase in threats from North Korea and the realization that President Park's aims of 'national regeneration' were not being realized, the ruling party proposed a constitutional amendment in order to allow the incumbent President to serve a third term of office. This was adopted in September 1969 at a session of the National Assembly (boycotted by the NDP). A national referendum, held in October, endorsed the amendment. In the seventh presidential election, held in April 1971, President Park defeated Kim Dae-Jung, nominee of the NDP, by a narrow margin.

On 4 July 1972 the North and South Korean Governments simultaneously issued a statement announcing the opening of dialogue to achieve national unification by peaceful means without outside intervention. A North-South Co-ordinating Committee was duly established for the purpose.

THE FOURTH REPUBLIC, 1972–79

The two Five-Year Plans, spanning the period 1962–71, had established a sound foundation, and the economic future of the nation seemed more promising. Sudden changes in the international situation, resulting from the Sino-US détente and new developments in North-South relations from 1972, provided the ruling party with pretexts to perpetuate President Park's rule. The Government proclaimed martial law in October 1972, dissolved the National Assembly and suspended the 1962 Constitution, in order to prepare the way for Park's continuation in office. A new Constitution was proposed by the Extraordinary State Council and approved in a referendum in November.

The new Constitution, known as the *Yusin* ('Revitalizing Reform') Constitution, gave the President greatly expanded powers, authorizing him to issue emergency decrees and establish the National Conference for Unification (NCU) as an electoral college. In December 1972 the NCU, with 2,359 members, was created, and it elected Park to serve a new six-year term. Thus, the Fourth Republic emerged.

At the legislative election of February 1973, the DRP won 71 of the 146 directly elective seats in the National Assembly. Meanwhile, a new political movement, named *Yujonghoe* ('Political Fraternity for the Revitalizing Reform'), was established as a companion organization to the DRP, and 73 of its members were elected by the NCU, on the President's recommendation, to serve a three-year term in the National Assembly. Thus, President Park was assured an absolute majority.

South Korea witnessed tremendous economic growth during the period of the third Five-Year Plan (1972–76) and the fourth Five-Year Plan (which began in 1977), accompanied by rapid industrialization and an increase in per caput income. This, in turn, brought about remarkable educational and cultural development. However, the increasingly autocratic and bureaucratic nature of the administration, combined with corruption, adversely affected the democratic movement, as freedom of speech and the press, and other civil rights, were suppressed or violated; the number of political dissidents increased.

The kidnapping in 1973 of Kim Dae-Jung (who had been campaigning against President Park in the USA and Japan) from Tokyo to South Korea by agents of the Korean Central Intelligence Agency (KCIA) created serious problems for South Korea's relations with the US and Japanese Governments. Domestically, anti-Government agitation and demands for the abolition of the 1972 *Yusin* Constitution continued to cause political instability. To address the unrest, the Government temporarily banned all anti-Government activities and agitation for constitutional reform. As tensions mounted, Park's wife was killed in August 1974 in an assassination attempt against the President. The opposition NDP and others relentlessly pressed for constitutional reform and for the release of political prisoners. After the death of his wife, Park became increasingly reclusive.

The Presidential Emergency Measure for Safeguarding National Security, which was proclaimed in May 1975 (ostensibly to strengthen national security against a mounting threat of aggression from North Korea, following the fall of South Viet Nam), only antagonized the dissidents further. The new measure imposed further prohibitions on opponents of the 1972 Constitution and banned student demonstrations (with limited success). In March 1978 the three most prominent dissident leaders issued a joint statement, demanding the abolition of the 1972 Constitution and the complete restoration of human rights. The re-election in May 1978 of President Park to serve a further six-year term exacerbated the situation, as student unrest, supported by the opposition party, caused greater political turmoil.

At the election for the National Assembly in December 1978, the DRP received only 31.7% of the votes cast, while the NDP won 32.9%; however, the election of 22 independent candidates was a clear display of the voters' displeasure with both parties. President Park carried out a major ministerial reorganization in that month; he also released 1,004 prisoners, including Kim Dae-Jung.

In July 1979 the NDP elected Kim Young-Sam as its new President. However, Kim's anti-Government speeches and press interviews led to the suspension of his presidency, and then to his expulsion from the National Assembly. In October all the NDP legislators tendered their resignations in protest. A power struggle within the NDP ensued, although the resignation notices were returned. Some conciliatory measures taken by President Park, such as the release of more political and 'model' prisoners in mid-1979, did not satisfy the dissidents and students. The resulting protests led to a serious uprising in Busan and other southern cities in October, while students in Seoul prepared for a large-scale protest towards the end of that month. In the midst of the crisis, Kim Chae-Kyu, director of the KCIA, who had disagreed with the Government's policies, shot and killed President Park in a restaurant at KCIA headquarters on 26 October. The Prime Minister, Choi Kyu-Ha, was named acting President, as martial law was proclaimed. Kim Jong-Pil assumed the presidency of the DRP. The cancellation of the Emergency Measure of May 1975 was announced in December 1979, and the termination of the *Yusin* rule was effected. A further 1,640 prisoners were pardoned in December.

THE INTERIM PERIOD, 1979–81

The NCU elected Choi Kyu-Ha as the new President of the Republic on 6 December 1979, and a new State Council (cabinet), headed by Shin Hyun-Hwack, emerged. Park's assassin, Kim Chae-Kyu, and his accomplices were executed in May 1980. Meanwhile, power struggles developed within the DRP and within the military leadership. In December 1979 Lt-Gen. Chun Doo-Hwan, Commander of the Defence Security Com-

mand, led a coup within the armed forces, removing the martial law commander.

In April 1980 there was more violent anti-Government agitation by students and the NDP (the presidency of which had been resumed by Kim Young-Sam). The appointment of Gen. Chun Doo-Hwan as acting director of the KCIA in April only exacerbated the situation further. More campus rallies followed in May, demanding the immediate end of martial law, the adoption of a new constitution without delay and the resignation of Gen. Chun. Troops were mobilized, and in mid-May martial law was extended throughout the country. Some 30 political leaders, including Kim Jong-Pil and Kim Dae-Jung, were arrested and interrogated. Kim Young-Sam was placed under house arrest and the National Assembly was closed, as were colleges, while all political activities, assemblies and public demonstrations were banned. In spite of these restrictions, protesters took control of the city of Gwangju on 19 May, after several days of clashes with paratroopers and police. This uprising, which became known as the 'Gwangju Incident', was violently suppressed by the army, with the loss of nearly 200 lives; some estimates put the figure much higher.

On 20 May 1980 all members of the State Council tendered their resignation, and a new State Council (headed by the acting Prime Minister, Park Choong-Hoon) emerged. Meanwhile, as riots spread to other cities, the martial law command brought charges against Kim Dae-Jung for alleged seditious activities, including a plot to overthrow the Government by force, and for instigating student uprisings and the Gwangju rebellion, even though he had been in prison at the time. A Special Committee for National Security Measures (SCNSM) was formed on 31 May. President Choi became its Chairman but real power rested with Gen. Chun and 15 other army generals, appointed by him to the SCNSM. With the establishment of the SCNSM, Gen. Chun resigned as acting director of the KCIA; however, as Chairman of the Standing Committee of the SCNSM, he continued to exercise absolute power.

President Choi resigned unexpectedly in August 1980. The electoral college chose Gen. Chun to be the next President, and he was inaugurated in early September. An all-civilian State Council, headed by Nam Duck-Woo, took office. President Chun made it known that he intended to offer himself as a candidate for the presidency under the new Constitution. Kim Dae-Jung was sentenced to death, but the sentence was subsequently commuted to life-imprisonment following vigorous international protests. The National Assembly, which had been in recess since May, dissolved itself in late September. In October a national referendum was held to approve a new Constitution. Meanwhile, the Legislative Council for National Security (LCNS) was created to replace the SCNSM. All members of the LCNS were appointed by President Chun. The Government carried out intensive investigations and removed from office some 835 politicians in November. Political leaders of both parties, such as Kim Jong-Pil and Kim Young-Sam, were not only deprived of rights to participate in the political process, but were imprisoned during the investigation period. Although later released, they were placed under house arrest. Journalists too found themselves at variance with the new regime, which forcibly effected a series of media amalgamations designed to reduce opposition.

THE FIFTH REPUBLIC, 1981–88

The partial removal of martial law was announced in January 1981. New political parties, all government-funded, were organized, and a new electoral college of 5,278 members was created by popular election in February. On 25 February this electoral college elected the incumbent President as the 12th President of the Republic, to serve a single seven-year term under the new Constitution, which banned re-election. On 3 March President Chun was inaugurated, thus beginning the Fifth Republic. A new State Council was formed, with Nam Duck-Woo remaining as Prime Minister. Later in the month an election for the new 276-member National Assembly was held. The Democratic Justice Party (DJP), headed by President Chun, won 151 seats and became the majority party, while the newly formed Democratic Korea Party (DKP) secured 81 seats. With the establishment of the new National Assembly, the LCNS was dissolved. The KCIA was renamed the Agency for National Security Planning (ANSP) in April, but its functions did not change.

In January 1982 Yoo Chang-Soon, a former politician, replaced Nam Duck-Woo as Prime Minister and four other ministers were replaced. Some concessions to the wishes of the students and others were made by the Government, and Chun pledged that he would retire at the end of his term in 1988, thus becoming South Korea's first Head of State to transfer power constitutionally. In January 1982 the midnight curfew, in force since September 1945, was removed, except in the area near the demilitarized zone (DMZ) and along the coasts. In March 1982 some 2,860 prisoners were granted amnesty, which included the reduction of the life sentence for Kim Dae-Jung to a 20-year term.

A financial scandal, involving relatives of the wife of President Chun, precipitated another crisis in May 1982. As a result, there was a large-scale reorganization of the State Council, in which 11 ministers were replaced. Meanwhile, Kim Young-Sam, former leader of the now defunct NDP, was put under house arrest. In late June Chun appointed Kim Sang-Hyop, a respected academic, as the new Prime Minister. In December Kim Dae-Jung was released from prison and allowed to visit the USA for medical treatment.

South Korea's political climate was relatively calm for most of 1983, despite some campus disturbances in the latter part of the year. There was widespread shock and dismay in September at the shooting-down by the USSR of a Korean Air Lines passenger jet (which had apparently strayed into Soviet airspace), with the loss of 269 lives. In October President Chun embarked upon an overseas tour of several Asian and Australasian countries. However, his trip was cut short by an assassination attempt against him in Rangoon, Burma (now Yangon, Myanmar), allegedly perpetrated by North Korean agents. A bomb exploded at the Aung Sun Mausoleum only minutes before the arrival of President Chun, killing 17 South Korean officials, among whom were the Deputy Prime Minister, three other ministers, three vice-ministers and two members of the President's personal staff. Following the Rangoon incident, the surviving ministers tendered their resignations *en bloc*. Chin Iee-Chong, hitherto Chairman of the DJP, was appointed Prime Minister.

In February 1984 President Chun restored the political rights of 202 of the politicians who had been removed from office in 1981. However, 99 remained on the political 'blacklist', including Kim Jong-Pil, Kim Dae-Jung and Kim Young-Sam. In November 1984 Chun restored political rights to a further 84 persons. A campaign initiated by a group of former politicians who had regained their political rights brought about the formation of the New Korea Democratic Party (NKDP) in January 1985. Shortly after this, and just before the legislative election of February, Kim Dae-Jung returned to Seoul from the USA, ending his self-imposed exile. He was promptly placed under house arrest on his arrival.

In the next election to the National Assembly, held in mid-February 1985, the ruling DJP retained its majority, with 148 seats in the 276-member Assembly. Significantly, the NKDP (taking 67 seats) won the majority of urban votes. President Chun reorganized the State Council, appointing Lho Shin-Yong, a former Minister of Foreign Affairs and later director of the ANSP, as Prime Minister, and 12 other new ministers.

In April 1985 the Government restored political rights to the remaining 14 persons, including Kim Jong-Pil, Kim Dae-Jung and Kim Young-Sam, who had been on the political 'blacklist' since 1980. Mass defections from the DKP and some defections from the Korea National Party increased the NKDP representation in the Assembly to 102 seats. Kim Young-Sam officially joined the NKDP in March 1986, and became adviser to the party President, Lee Min-Woo.

In March and April 1986 mass rallies demanded constitutional reform and the resignation of President Chun. In June Chun finally agreed to the formation of a special parliamentary committee to discuss constitutional reform, which was to include members of the opposition parties; in the same month a special session of the National Assembly was convened to consider the findings of the committee, and negotiations continued for the remainder of the year. The NKDP proposed a new system of government, based on a direct presidential election. However, the DJP favoured a system centred on a powerful Prime Minister, elected by the National Assembly, with greater responsibility to be accorded to the State Council, while the role of the President would be mainly ceremonial. The negotiations made little progress, despite a major concession by the NKDP when Kim Dae-Jung announced in November that he would not stand as a presidential candidate if the DJP accepted the NKDP's proposals.

In January 1987 the death of a university student, following torture in police custody, led to further anti-Government rallies and to the dismissal by President Chun of the Minister of Home Affairs and of the Chief of Police. Meanwhile, internal divisions were developing within the NKDP. In December 1986 the NKDP President, Lee Min-Woo, indicated his willingness to consider the Government's reform programme. While Lee's conditional endorsement of DJP proposals was supported by some members of the NKDP leadership, Kim Dae-Jung and Kim Young-Sam, together with 74 of the party's 90 National Assembly members, left the NKDP and formed the Reunification Democratic Party (RDP). In April 1987 President Chun unexpectedly announced the suspension of the reform process until the conclusion of the Olympic Games in Seoul in 1988.

At its inaugural meeting in May 1987, the RDP elected Kim Young-Sam to the chairmanship and issued a strong denunciation of Chun's suspension of the reform process. The DJP responded by refusing to recognize the RDP as the main opposition party; in mid-May it reallocated committee chairmanships in the National Assembly, electing new chairmen without the participation of RDP members. In late May, following new disclosures about the circumstances of the death in January of the student under detention by the Seoul police, new riots began. In an attempt to curb the continued unrest, a reorganization of the State Council was effected, which included the appointment of a new Prime Minister, Lee Han-Key. The nomination in early June of Roh Tae-Woo, the Chairman of the DJP, as the ruling party's presidential candidate further exacerbated anti-Government sentiment.

The RDP organized mass rallies in support of its demands for immediate constitutional reform; violent confrontations between demonstrators and riot police became a daily occurrence. In late June 1987, after having conferred with former Presidents Yun and Choi, as well as with Cardinal Stephen Sou-Hwan Kim (the Roman Catholic Archbishop of Seoul) and other religious leaders, President Chun met Kim Young-Sam in an unsuccessful attempt to resolve the country's political crisis. However, Chun refused to offer any major concessions. The RDP responded by mobilizing mass support for a 'great peace march', with tens of thousands taking to the streets of Seoul. Kim Young-Sam and other opposition leaders were arrested, and Kim Dae-Jung was returned to house arrest. Roh Tae-Woo informed President Chun that he would relinquish both the DJP chairmanship and his presidential candidature if the main demands of the RDP for electoral reform were not met. Chun acceded, and negotiations for a new constitutional framework were announced.

In July 1987 the Government granted amnesty and the restoration of their civil rights to about 2,335 political prisoners, including Kim Dae-Jung. President Chun relinquished the presidency of the DJP (to which Roh Tae-Woo was elected in early August) and reorganized the State Council, appointing Kim Chung-Yul (a former air force chief of staff and Minister of Defence) as Prime Minister, and reorganizing eight other portfolios. In late August the DJP and the RDP agreed on the basic draft of a new Constitution, which was to be submitted to a public referendum in October; a direct presidential election was to be conducted in December. Nevertheless, students continued to hold anti-Government demonstrations, and more than 500 industrial disputes arose, mainly in the motor vehicle, mining and shipbuilding industries. By mid-October, however, nearly all the disputes had been settled, the Government having conceded a hasty revision of labour laws, guaranteeing workers' rights to form trade unions and to conduct collective bargaining.

In October 1987 the National Assembly approved a constitutional amendment providing for direct presidential elections, and the new Constitution (to take effect in February 1988) was submitted to a national referendum. About 20m., or 78.2%, of the eligible voters cast their ballots, 93.3% of whom were in favour of the new Constitution.

Negotiations between Kim Dae-Jung and Kim Young-Sam failed to achieve agreement on a single RDP presidential candidate. Kim Young-Sam declared his candidacy, and in early November 1987 Kim Dae-Jung, together with 27 of the RDP's National Assembly members, formed the Peace and Democracy Party (PDP), which selected Kim Dae-Jung as its presidential candidate. The formation of the PDP resulted in the virtual dissolution of the Korea National Party and the NKDP. Meanwhile, Kim Jong-Pil revived Park Chung-Hee's DRP, renaming it the New Democratic Republican Party (NDRP), and was chosen as its candidate.

The first direct presidential election for 16 years took place in December 1987. Some 23m. voters, representing 89.2% of the eligible electorate, cast their ballots; Roh Tae-Woo was elected President for a non-renewable five-year term of office, receiving 36.6% of the total votes cast. Kim Dae-Jung and Kim Young-Sam each received about 27% of the votes cast; they both alleged electoral fraud.

THE SIXTH REPUBLIC, 1988–

On 25 February 1988 Roh Tae-Woo was inaugurated as President. In his inaugural address, he proclaimed that the era of 'ordinary people' had arrived, and that 'the day when freedom and human rights could be relegated in the name of economic growth and national security has ended'. Shortly before his inauguration, Roh had appointed a new State Council, with Lee Hyun-Jae (a former President of Seoul University) as Prime Minister.

At the legislative election held in late April 1988 under the newly adopted electoral law, four major parties (the DJP, the PDP, the RDP and the NDRP) competed for 299 seats. Of 26m. eligible voters, 75.8% turned out to elect 224 district representatives. The DJP secured the most seats but failed to win a majority in the National Assembly, while the PDP, led by Kim Dae-Jung, became the main opposition party.

The Sixth Republic granted an increased measure of autonomy to national and private universities, and permitted the organization of student associations, thus expanding the initiatives taken during the period of the Fifth Republic. It also liberalized the press law, revoking the ban on the works of artists and writers who had defected to the North and allowing the circulation of certain North Korean publications. Restrictions on foreign travel were eased considerably. A campaign to bring to justice those who had been involved in political corruption resulted in the indictment of Chun Kyung-Hwan, a brother of former President Chun, and two of his brothers-in-law, who, as leading officials of the New Community Movement, were alleged to have embezzled US $9.7m. In April 1988, in response to this scandal, former President Chun resigned from all of the public offices that he held.

In late May 1988 thousands of students in Seoul and Gwangju took part in anti-Government and anti-US demonstrations, in commemoration of the uprising of May 1980. Demonstrations continued throughout June, July and August 1988, often leading to violent confrontations between students and riot police. Despite fears that civil unrest would disrupt the Olympic Games in Seoul in September–October, the event was concluded successfully. A panel of the National Assembly began public hearings on alleged official corruption and violations of human rights during the Fifth Republic. As the opposition increased pressure for the punishment of former President Chun and his aides, the anti-Government National Council of Student Representatives (Chondaehyop) intensified its activities.

In November 1988 Chun apologized to the nation for the misdeeds of the Fifth Republic in an address televised nationwide; he subsequently returned his property to the State and retreated with his wife to a Buddhist monastery. Meanwhile, 47 former advisers and officials of the Chun administration were arrested and put on trial. Roh reorganized the State Council in early December, replacing 21 of its 25 members and appointing Dr Kang Young-Hoon (a former general) as Prime Minister.

In January 1989 about 200 anti-Government groups formed the Pan-National Coalition of the Democratic Movement (Chonminyon) and, in conjunction with Chondaehyop, increased strike activities. As these events, together with the clandestine visit to North Korea in March by a Presbyterian minister and three others, created a new political crisis, the Minister of Government Administration, Kim Yong-Kap, resigned, warning against the growing threat of 'leftist tendencies'. Confronted by this new crisis, in March Roh announced the indefinite postponement of a referendum to provide an interim appraisal of his first year in office, causing fresh protests. The citizens of Gwangju held a peaceful week-long rally to commemorate the ninth anniversary of the events of 1980. However, further demonstrations resulted in injuries to a large number of students and police officers.

In January 1990 it was announced that the RDP and the NDRP were to merge with the ruling DJP to form a new party, the Democratic Liberal Party. While this decision secured for the Democratic Liberal Party control of more than two-thirds of the seats in the National Assembly (the DJP having lacked a majority), the broader aim of creating Japanese-style consensus politics was not attained in the months that followed. Outside the new ruling bloc, the PDP, which was effectively isolated as the sole opposition party in the National Assembly, complained of a virtual coup, while the public responded by rejecting one Democratic Liberal Party candidate and nearly ousting another at by-elections for the National Assembly in April. As the Democratic Liberal Party's popularity declined sharply, a new opposition party, the Democratic Party (DP), was formed, largely comprising those members of the RDP opposed to the merger.

In March 1990 President Roh announced a major reorganization of the State Council, in which 15 of its 27 members, including all the economic ministers, were replaced. In late April there was renewed industrial unrest, followed by student demonstrations. In late July some 200,000 people participated in a rally in Seoul to protest at the approval by the National Assembly of several items of controversial legislation, which included proposals to restructure the military leadership and to reorganize the broadcasting media. All the opposition members of the National Assembly tendered their resignations in protest at the contentious legislation. They also demanded the dissolution of the National Assembly and the holding of an early legislative election. However, the Democratic Liberal Party claimed that the resignations were illegal and would not be accepted. The PDP deputies returned to the National Assembly only in mid-November, following an agreement with the Democratic Liberal Party that local council elections would be held, as demanded by the PDP, in the first half of 1991, to be followed by gubernatorial and mayoral elections in 1992. The Democratic Liberal Party also agreed to abandon plans for constitutional amendments, whereby executive power, currently vested in the President, would be transferred to the State Council. In late December 1990 there was an extensive government reorganization, in which Kang Young-Hoon was replaced as Prime Minister by Ro Jai-Bong, hitherto chief presidential secretary.

The revelation of two new scandals dominated domestic politics in early 1991. The first involved the acceptance of bribes by senior officials and prompted Roh to effect a minor government reorganization in February. The second was the beating to death by police of a student protester in an anti-Government rally in April, which prompted weeks of widespread demonstrations. In response, Roh appointed a new Minister of Home Affairs in late April, and in the following month legislation was introduced to increase control over the police and to relax the National Security Law. However, these concessions were undermined by the hasty manner in which both measures secured passage through the National Assembly, to the outrage of many opposition members who wished to debate more comprehensive reforms.

During May 1991 public unrest escalated to a level unprecedented during President Roh's tenure of office, as demonstrations by students and workers occurred throughout the country. The 11th anniversary of the 'Gwangju Incident' again occasioned widespread unrest, and in Gwangju itself more than 100,000 people were estimated to have participated in anti-Government activity. In late May the second government reorganization of the year took place, and included the replacement of Ro Jai-Bong as Prime Minister by Chung Won-Shik, a former Minister of Education. Following the reorganization, an amnesty for more than 250 political detainees was announced.

Meanwhile, the Government drew some encouragement from its results in the first local elections to be held in South Korea for 30 years. The Democratic Liberal Party won 65% of the seats in the elections to provincial and large city councils in June 1991, securing control of 11 out of 15 assemblies (in fact, all except the opposition's south-western strongholds of the two Jeolla provinces and the city of Gwangju, and Jeju island, where independents gained a narrow majority). Opposition parties secured almost as many votes as the Democratic Liberal Party, but were disadvantaged by the 'first past the post' electoral system. The smaller opposition DP suffered particularly: its 14% of the votes cast secured it only 2.4% of the seats. Nevertheless, its seats were at least distributed across the country, whereas the 19% of the seats and 22% of the votes cast obtained by the newly established New Democratic Party (NDP, created in April by a merger of the PDP with the smaller, dissident Party for New Democratic Alliance) remained overwhelmingly confined to the south-west, excluding some successes in Seoul. In September Kim Dae-Jung and Lee Ki-Taek agreed to a merger of their respective parties, the NDP and the DP, to form a stronger opposition front. The new party retained the latter's name: the Democratic Party (DP).

The main political development in the latter part of 1991 was a serious altercation between the Government and the Hyundai *chaebol* (conglomerate), in particular its founder and honorary Chairman, Chung Ju-Yung. What was widely regarded as a politically motivated investigation into Hyundai share dealings resulted in claims for 136,000m. won (almost US $170m.) in unpaid taxes being brought against Chung and members of his family. In January 1992 Chung severed formal links with Hyundai and formed a new political party, the Unification National Party (UNP), which attracted a mixed membership, including former dissidents, malcontents and media personalities. The UNP performed well, as did the DP, in the election for the National Assembly, held in late March. The Democratic Liberal Party suffered a humiliating set-back, securing only 38.5% of the votes cast, compared with the 73% which its then separate pre-merger component parties had received in the 1988 legislative election. The Democratic Liberal Party thus emerged with 149 seats, one short of an absolute majority in the 299-member Assembly (although enough independents had been won over by the time the Assembly opened in July 1992 to ensure a working majority). The opposition DP obtained 97 seats (having won 29.2% of the votes cast), including 25 of the 44 seats in Seoul; as expected, it also won a clear majority of the seats in Kim Dae-Jung's heartland in the south-west, although it won few seats elsewhere. By contrast, the UNP's 31 seats and 17.4% of the votes cast were more evenly distributed nation-wide.

The emergence of the UNP (which subsequently changed its name to the United People's Party—UPP) added a new dimension to the presidential election due to be held in December 1992. In May the Democratic Liberal Party chose the former opposition leader, Kim Young-Sam, as its candidate, by a majority of two to one over his rival, Lee Jong-Chan. In late August Kim replaced Roh as Democratic Liberal Party President. The Government succeeded in postponing a third round of elections (mayoral and gubernatorial), on the grounds that three elections in one year would be prohibitively expensive. Both student and labour activism were more muted than in previous years, except for a brief outbreak of pro-North Korean demonstrations in some universities in early 1992. In June and October President Roh effected the second and third partial government reorganizations of the year. The latter was presented as the formation of a politically neutral State Council to guarantee a fair presidential election, and included the unusual occurrence of the entire Government, as well as the President, resigning from the ruling party.

The Presidency of Kim Young-Sam

The presidential election, on 18 December 1992, gave a convincing victory to Kim Young-Sam, who received some 42% of the votes cast. Kim thus became the first South Korean President since 1960 not to have a military background. Of the six other candidates, his nearest rivals were Kim Dae-Jung, with 34% of the votes cast, and Chung Ju-Yung, with 16%. Kim Dae-Jung, after his third presidential defeat, announced his retirement from politics. Chung Ju-Yung resigned as President of the UPP in early 1993, following allegations that he had embezzled money from Hyundai to fund his election campaign. Subsequent defections from the UPP caused the party to lose its status as a parliamentary negotiating group, and in 1994 the UPP merged with a smaller opposition party.

The opposition was further weakened by the new President's unexpected emergence as a radical reformer. In a campaign against corruption, which won him widespread approval, Kim publicly declared his own assets and forced the entire political élite to follow his example. This was an astute political move, since it exposed many of the ex-DJP old guard in the Democratic Liberal Party as possessing undue wealth. At first it seemed as if this campaign might go awry, when three newly appointed ministers and several presidential aides were forced to resign on various charges of corruption. By mid-1993 the scandal appeared to be widening. The military were also targeted, and a number of senior officers were removed, charged either with corruption or with association with the military coup of December 1979. The popularity of this anti-corruption campaign accounted for the Democratic Liberal Party winning five out of six by-elections held in April and June 1993, including seats in Seoul that the opposition had been expected to take.

In the first half of 1993 the customary May student riots were firmly quelled, as was unrest in July at the Hyundai motor works in Ulsan—itself an exception to a generally quiescent labour situation. Elsewhere, a number of dissidents expressed support for President Kim, whose overall position appeared strong. The same mixture of radicalism and conservatism continued during the latter part of 1993. In August, as the President's efforts to address corruption continued, a ban was announced on bank accounts held under false names. This was an issue that previous administrations had not dared to address, and in the event the severity of the initial decree was mitigated by various concessions.

Another bold initiative was President Kim's announcement in December 1993 that his Government would ratify the recently concluded Uruguay Round of the General Agreement on Tariffs and Trade (GATT), even though this contravened his campaign pledge never to permit the opening of South Korea's rice market to foreign competition. The violent public demonstrations that followed this policy change prompted Kim to effect a major government reorganization in mid-December. The lacklustre Hwang In-Sung was replaced as Prime Minister by Lee Hoi-Chang, who, as Chairman of the Board of Audit and Inspection, had played a major role in the President's campaign against corruption. However, the new Prime Minister's tenure lasted barely four months. He resigned in April 1994, after a dispute over his exclusion from a new committee established to co-ordinate policy towards North Korea. Lee Yung-Duk succeeded him as Prime Minister, while the veteran Lee Hong-Koo resumed the unification portfolio (in which capacity he had earlier served under Roh Tae-Woo).

Two scandals that emerged in early 1994 implicated Kim Young-Sam in financial malpractices, but the President managed to evade prosecution. In June strike action by railway workers culminated in mass arrests. The Government's popularity then began to decline markedly. One reason for this was a series of disasters, the most perturbing of which was the collapse in June 1995 of the luxury Sampoong department store in Seoul, with the loss of 458 lives. In the resultant public outcry, the Government was blamed for inadequate safety regulations and was accused of lack of co-ordination in its responses to such disasters when they occurred. Moreover, officials were alleged to have accepted bribes to overlook sub-standard work and malpractice in the construction industry.

A major restructuring of the State Council in December 1994, only one year after the last reorganization, prompted criticism that when in opposition Kim Young-Sam had condemned such frequent reallocations of portfolios. Lee Hong-Koo was promoted to the post of Prime Minister, while other appointments were regarded as conciliatory gestures to the increasingly restive ex-DJP old guard in the ruling party.

Further ministerial changes were effected in 1995, including the dismissal of Lee Hyung-Koo, the Minister of Labour, who was accused of corruption, amid harsh government action against worker protest. In early June, in an act unprecedented under past military regimes or even Japanese colonial rule, riot police stormed the Catholic Myeongdong Cathedral and a leading Buddhist temple in Seoul to seize 13 trade union leaders from the state telecommunications agency, Korea Telecom, who had sought sanctuary there.

In August 1995 one of the President's closest confidants, Seo Seok-Jai, the Minister of Government Administration, provoked an outcry by an unguarded comment to journalists that a former President was in possession of a huge political 'slush fund', which had allegedly been deposited under false and borrowed names in various accounts. Seo's prompt resignation and partial retraction did not quell rumours. For a while there had been no great public support for opposition attempts to have Chun Doo-Hwan and Roh Tae-Woo prosecuted for their role in the 1979 coup and the Gwangju massacre of 1980. (In October 1994 a tribunal investigating the 1979 coup had found that Chun and Roh had participated in a 'premeditated military rebellion' but it had decided not to prosecute the former Presidents; likewise, in July 1995, during an official investigation into the Gwangju events, Chun and Roh were cleared of having committed 'homicide aimed at achieving insurrection'.) The scandal deepened in late October 1995, when Roh Tae-Woo, in an emotional televised address, admitted to having amassed 500,000m. won (some US $650m.) in illicit political funds during his term of office. In early November Roh appeared before the Chief Justice's office for cross-examination. After a second interrogation in mid-November, Roh was arrested on charges of corruption.

Meanwhile, in South Korea's first full local elections for 34 years, held in June 1995, the Democratic Liberal Party won only five of the 15 major gubernatorial and mayoral posts, followed by the DP, which took four (including the mayorship of Seoul). Four posts were also won by the United Liberal Democrats (ULD), a grouping established in March by defectors from the Democratic Liberal Party; the new party's President was Kim Jong-Pil, who had resigned as Democratic Liberal Party Chairman in January.

The DP also performed well in major city and provincial council elections, winning 355 of the total of 875 seats, followed by the Democratic Liberal Party (286), independents (151) and the ULD (83). In July 1995, however, Kim Dae-Jung, the DP's former leader and continuing *éminence grise*, announced that he was returning to politics and was to found his own party. This, the National Congress for New Politics (NCNP), was formally constituted in early September, severely undermining the DP, as 54 of its 96 deputies defected to the new party.

However, party politics and local government were subsequently eclipsed by the public disgrace of those formerly in power. The charges against Roh Tae-Woo were widened to include the coup of December 1979 and the Gwangju massacre of May 1980; in December 1995 another former President, Chun Doo-Hwan, was also arrested on these charges, and his trial began in February 1996. He was subsequently arraigned for accumulating illicit funds even greater than those of Roh. The prosecutors requested that Chun receive the death penalty and Roh life imprisonment, and in late August they were sentenced accordingly; however, these sentences were subsequently commuted to life and 17 years, respectively.

Despite the many uncertainties surrounding the source of funds for Kim Young-Sam's 1992 election campaign, the reputation of the President, an adroit politician, remained untarnished. In December 1995 Kim renamed the ruling Democratic Liberal Party the New Korea Party (NKP) and Lee Soo-Sung, the president of Seoul National University, replaced Lee Hong-Koo as Prime Minister. Further government changes took place in an attempt to reassure the business community. In the election for the National Assembly, held on 11 April 1996, the NKP obtained 139 of the 299 seats, including most of the seats in Seoul (the first time that a ruling party had achieved this). The NCNP took 79, fewer than it had hoped, mostly in the south-west. Kim Dae-Jung failed to win a seat. The ULD increased their tally of members from 32 to 50, while the DP was reduced to 15 seats.

Although the ruling party was thus 11 votes short of a working majority, it had acquired the necessary majority by the time the Assembly convened in June 1996, having persuaded 12 DP and independent members to join. This provoked protests from the NCNP and the ULD, who worked together to delay the Assembly's normal business until July. This unlikely co-operation (Kim Jong-Pil, the ULD's President, had founded the fearsome KCIA, which had tried to assassinate Kim Dae-Jung in 1973) proved surprisingly durable.

In August 1996 the annual pro-unification rallies by radical students were violently suppressed. The students were besieged for several days in Yonsei University, Seoul, before an assault was launched by police, which destroyed the building. One riot policeman was killed and more than 5,000 students were taken into custody, the largest number ever arrested. The latter half of 1996 also witnessed a remarkable rate of attrition among ministers, with many dismissals and resignations taking place in the months prior to Kim Young-Sam's customary cabinet reorganization in mid-December, when a further nine ministers were relieved of their posts. In late December 1996, having spent much of that year failing to persuade both sides of industry to agree on labour law reform, the Government approved legislation that gave employers enhanced powers of engagement and dismissal, but which failed to legalize the powerful Korean Confederation of Trade Unions (KCTU). The legislation was approved at a swift dawn session of the National Assembly, of which the opposition was not informed. The KCTU then attracted wide support for strikes. However, in March 1997 legislation incorporating a compromise was approved, which recognized the KCTU, while postponing the introduction of greater flexibility for employers.

In mid-January 1997 the Hanbo group, a major *chaebol*, was declared bankrupt with debts of some US $6,000m. For a President whose image had already been tarnished by accusations that his election campaign might have drawn on the illicit funds of his predecessor, the procession of senior aides, ministers, bank chairmen and others who were implicated in 'Hanbogate', as the scandal soon became known, was a severe set-back. Yet more serious were separate charges of influence-peddling against his own son, Kim Hyun-Chul; in October Kim junior was found guilty of receiving bribes and of tax evasion.

In early March 1997 Goh Kun became Kim Young-Sam's sixth Prime Minister in four years. The entire economics team was replaced, and an experienced former Minister of Finance, Kang Kyung-Shik, was appointed Deputy Prime Minister in charge of the economy. Efforts to promote financial reform, the urgency of which had been illustrated by the near or total collapse of several further conglomerates after Hanbo, none the less experienced difficulties, partly owing to the reluctance of politicians to address unpopular issues in an election year.

In mid-July 1997 an NKP convention approved Lee Hoi-Chang, the former Prime Minister, as its candidate for the presidential election. In September the increasingly unpopular Kim resigned as President of the NKP and was replaced by Lee. However, allegations that Lee's sons had evaded military service proved damaging. Factional disunity in the NKP was highlighted by the decision of Rhee In-Je (who had challenged Lee Hoi-Chang for the party's nomination) to resign from the party and announce his intention to stand in the election. In the event Rhee's act was decisive, as it divided the ruling bloc.

The Presidency of Kim Dae-Jung

The outcome of the presidential election, held on 18 December 1997, was a triumph at last for Kim Dae-Jung, some 26 years after his first bid for the presidency. The election represented a new stage in South Korean democracy, with the first ever transfer of power to the opposition. On a turn-out of 80% of the electorate, Kim won 40.3% of the votes cast, only just ahead of Lee (38.7%), while Rhee was placed third (19.2%). Kim Jong-Pil of the ULD had withdrawn his candidacy in favour of Kim Dae-Jung (representing the NCNP) in exchange for promises of the premiership and of constitutional change, to be effected by 2000, with a view to giving the Prime Minister more power. Similarly, Lee had been aided by the decision of Cho Soon, a former governor of the Bank of Korea (and one-time political protégé of Kim Dae-Jung) who was representing the ailing DP, to merge that party with the NKP, thus forming the Grand National Party (GNP) and presenting a more effective challenge to the new NCNP-ULD alliance. Regional loyalties were once again much in evidence. As ever, the Jeolla provinces in the south-west voted *en masse* for their favourite politician, Kim Dae-Jung, and Kim Jong-Pil's heartland, the usually conservative Chungcheong provinces in the centre-west, also duly delivered a majority to Kim Dae-Jung. Conversely, in the south-eastern Gyeongsang provinces, which had furnished all previous Presidents since 1961, the votes were split between Lee and Rhee. The unprecedented opposition victory also reflected popular anger at the administration's handling of the economy. This had reached crisis point in November 1997, when South Korea was forced to seek emergency rescue loans from the IMF. Kim Dae-Jung initially announced that he would renegotiate with the IMF. However, once elected he rapidly took a leading role in calming markets, and emerged as a champion of deregulation and liberalization. Such intervention, while not strictly constitutional (as Kim did not take office formally until 25 February 1998), averted disaster during what would otherwise have been a dangerous power vacuum at a crucial time. After his inauguration various radical reforms were introduced, including new legislation to allow labour flexibility.

President Kim Dae-Jung confronted major obstacles. In the formal political arena, the GNP held a majority in the National Assembly. It refused to confirm Kim Jong-Pil as Prime Minister until August 1998, prior to which he was designated as 'acting' premier. As such, he was not permitted to form a cabinet, although, fortunately, the outgoing Prime Minister, Goh Kun, agreed to do this, appointing a State Council in March (see below). Goh later joined the NCNP, for which, in June, he was elected Mayor of Seoul in local elections that boosted support for the new ruling coalition. Parliamentary discord rendered the National Assembly largely inactive from May to August, provoking widespread popular disgust. The NCNP-ULD strategy was to break the GNP's hold on the legislative body by encouraging defections to the ruling camp, and this looked likely eventually to produce a working majority for the Government.

The new Government instituted several changes in early 1998. The two posts of Deputy Prime Minister, which formerly accompanied the economy and unification portfolios, were abolished. Responsibility for foreign trade and foreign affairs was combined under the new Ministry of Foreign Affairs and Trade, while the Ministry of Commerce, Industry and Economy replaced the former Ministry of Trade, Industry and Economy. The Ministries of Home Affairs and Government were merged. Two new bodies were created: the Financial Supervisory Commission, which replaced three old regulatory bodies for banks, insurance and the stock market, and the Planning and Budget Commission, within the Office of the President; those institutions that lost powers were resentful, notably the Ministry of Finance and the Economy and the Bank of Korea, resulting in rivalry and arguments over policy. Compromise was evident in Kim Dae-Jung's first State Council, announced in March 1998, which allocated seven ministerial posts to the NCNP and five to the ULD. Non-party appointees included the Minister of Finance and the Economy, Lee Kyu-Song, who had held the same post a decade previously. Fears that he would clash with the Presidential Secretary for Economics, Kim Tae-Dong, a professor famously critical of the *chaebol*, were eased when the latter was quickly transferred to another post. Other interesting appointments included that of the Minister of Unification, Kang In-Duk, whose uncompromising reputation and KCIA background did not prevent his implementation of Kim Dae-Jung's conciliatory 'sunshine' policy with regard to relations with North Korea (see the chapter on the Democratic People's Republic of Korea). Another former KCIA official, Lee Jong-Chan, returned to head the Agency for National Security Planning (NSP); it was subsequently further renamed, as the National Intelligence Service (NIS), in a bid to distance itself from an insalubrious past, which had included efforts at every election to tarnish

Kim Dae-Jung as pro-communist, culminating in 1997 in alleged co-operation with its equivalent in Pyongyang to forge the required documents.

More generally, Kim Dae-Jung's desire for reconciliation was seen in the release from prison, four days after his election victory, of ex-Presidents Chun Doo-Hwan and Roh Tae-Woo. He resisted demands for Kim Young-Sam to be called to account for the 1997 financial crisis, although hearings on this were promised. He also offered amnesty to political prisoners who undertook to obey the law, a modification of the previous insistence that they renounce their leftist beliefs. However, many refused this offer, leaving South Korea still holding some of the world's longest-serving prisoners of conscience; nevertheless, most were subsequently released.

A much faster economic recovery than expected helped to ease the difficulties of transition. A further reorganization of government was effected in 1999, mainly in connection with Kim Dae-Jung's first major reallocation of portfolios in late May. The Planning and Budget Commission became a full ministry, with the reformer Jin Nyum retaining the portfolio. With another reformist, Kang Bong-Kyun, appointed at its head, the normally conservative Ministry of Finance and the Economy was expected to vie with the new Financial Supervisory Commission for control of restructuring. Other cabinet changes affected a further 10 portfolios, including defence, unification, commerce and industry. Two months earlier the ministers responsible for science and maritime affairs had also been replaced. Although in March it had taken two seats from the GNP, in June the ruling coalition lost two by-elections. Following the involvement of his wife in a scandal related to gifts from the wife of a tycoon being tried for corruption, the new Minister of Justice, Kim Tae-Joung, was later dismissed over another matter: during his tenure of the post of Prosecutor-General, a drunken underling had boasted of fomenting a strike at the national mint as a pretext to take action against trade union militants. The new Minister of the Environment, Son Sook, an actress, resigned after only one month for accepting gifts of US $20,000 from businessmen during a performance in the Russian capital, Moscow, when already appointed to the post. The National Assembly remained idle for long periods, owing to disputes between government and opposition. The ruling coalition too became strained, with the ULD frustrated at their leader Kim Jong-Pil's agreement not to press for constitutional changes which would have given him, as Prime Minister, greater power. In January 2000 Kim Jong-Pil resigned as premier. He was replaced by another ULD member, Park Tae-Joon, the founder of the Pohang Iron and Steel Co (POSCO), the world's largest steel-maker, which remained partly state-owned. A wider reorganization of the administration followed, with Lee Hun-Jai, the dynamic reformer heading the Financial Supervisory Commission, taking over as Minister of Finance and the Economy. Various other portfolios, including that of foreign affairs and trade, were also reallocated. Earlier, a new Minister of Unification and head of national intelligence had been appointed.

With the legislative election approaching, the ULD ended their coalition with Kim Dae-Jung's party, the NCNP, itself relaunched as the Millennium Democratic Party (MDP) in a bid to widen its appeal. The MDP had hoped to absorb the ULD, but Kim Jong-Pil objected to the MDP's support for the posting on the internet (use of which had spread rapidly in South Korea) by civic groups of 'blacklists' of politicians deemed unfit for office, whether as corrupt, opportunists, idle or involved with past military regimes. Kim Jong-Pil himself was thus named, as were many other ULD representatives. Confusingly, Park Tae-Joon and other ULD ministers remained in government positions, while the ULD declared themselves to be an opposition party and presented their own candidates against the MDP. The result was the decimation of the ULD at the election for the National Assembly on 13 April 2000, held under controversially revised rules that reduced the number of seats from 299 to 273: of these, 227 were directly elective on a 'first-past-the-post' basis, and 46 were chosen from party lists based on the share of the overall vote. ULD representation declined from 50 to 17 seats, with the party losing ground even in its regional heartland of Chungcheong, south of Seoul. Three days prior to the election it was announced that a summit meeting was to take place in June between Kim Dae-Jung and the North Korean leader, Kim Jong Il. (Kim Dae-Jung was awarded the Nobel Peace Prize in October in recognition of his progress towards reconciliation with North Korea.) However, the MDP's tally only rose from 98 seats to 115, well short of the majority for which it had hoped. The GNP remained the largest party, gaining 11 seats to reach 133, four short of overall control. A small new party, the Democratic People's Party (DPP), took two seats, and there were six independents (most pro-MDP). Regional loyalties persisted in some areas, to the GNP in the Gyeongsang provinces and to the MDP in Jeolla.

Kim Dae-Jung chose to rebuild his alliance with the remaining members of the ULD, who furnished a third Prime Minister, Lee Han-Dong, in May 2000, when Park Tae-Joon had to resign over a tax scandal. The new Assembly, like its predecessor, remained largely paralysed by boycotts and disputes. A cabinet reorganization followed in August 2000. The security team—comprising foreign affairs, defence, unification and national intelligence—was retained, but economics ministers were removed. After only seven months, Lee Hun-Jai was replaced at the Ministry of Finance and the Economy by Jin Nyum, hitherto Minister of Planning and Budget, who was succeeded by Jeon Yun-Churl, previously head of the Fair Trade Commission (FTC), the main anti-trust body. The Ministers of Education, Labour, Health and Welfare, Agriculture, and Commerce, Industry and Energy were also replaced, as well as the heads of several cabinet-level agencies. With both the Ministry of Finance and the Economy and the Ministry of Commerce, Industry and Energy now allocated to their fourth minister in 30 months, Furthermore, the new Minister of Education resigned after just three weeks, on suspicion of involvement in a scandal. This was followed by the resignation of the Minister of Culture and Tourism, Park Jie-Won, a leading official in the secret talks that had led to the recent North-South summit meeting. Despite the summit's success, in domestic affairs the Government appeared to lose some control. An ill-conceived reform of health care brought doctors and pharmacists out on strike in mid-2000. The parties continued to disagree, delaying the next session of the National Assembly for a month.

In January 2001 the MDP 'loaned' four deputies to the ULD, to give the latter the numbers needed to become a recognized parliamentary floor group. In the same month two posts of Deputy Prime Minister were reinstated: one, as was the case previously, was allocated to the Minister of Finance and the Economy; the other was a new post of Education and Human Resources Development—with yet another new education minister. At the same time, the Presidential Commission on Women's Affairs, which was created under Kim Dae-Jung, was upgraded to become the Ministry of Gender Equality.

Another cabinet reorganization was effected in March 2001, as the MDP formalized its coalition with the ULD and the minor DPP to gain a narrow majority in the National Assembly. Nine ministers, three other officials of cabinet rank and two senior presidential secretaries were replaced. The DPP's Han Seung-Soo, a former ambassador to the USA, became the Minister of Foreign Affairs and Trade, bespeaking a need for better relations with the new US Administration under President George W. Bush (see below). Various other replacements included those of the Ministers of National Defence and of Unification. The Government's economic team was retained, despite recent criticisms. Other commentators condemned the President for appointing nine professional politicians, including three ULD appointees, and six from his home region of Jeolla in the south-west of the country. The frequent turnover of personnel continued: in May an incoming Minister of Justice served for just 43 hours after the 'leak' of a letter in which he pledged fealty to President Kim Dae-Jung in feudal tones.

A resurgence of violent strikes and demonstrations included action at Daewoo Motor, where some workers (but not a majority) opposed its proposed sale to General Motors. A tax audit of leading newspapers, most of them critical of the Government, led to substantial fines, amid accusations of threats to press freedom. The *chaebol*, the reckless overexpansion of which and their refusal to reform had been regarded by many as responsible for the nation's financial plight in the late 1990s, successfully demanded an easing of deadlines for restructuring. Dissension grew over the 'sunshine' policy, as North Korea broke off talks, provoked the South with naval incursions and manipulated a visiting South Korean delegation. As a result, in September 2001 the conservative ULD voted with the GNP to approve a proposal to dismiss the Minister of Unification, Lim Dong-Won. Although this vote had no binding force, Lim resigned (he was promptly made a special adviser to the President), as did the entire State Council. ULD ministers were dismissed, while the ULD in turn expelled Lee Han-Dong for agreeing to stay on as Prime Minister. For separate reasons, South Korea had four different transport ministers in the space of six weeks during August and September. In October the MDP lost three by-elections to the GNP. Soon after, Kim Dae-Jung symbolically resigned from the party presidency.

During 2002 Kim Dae-Jung had to witness the imprisonment of two sons for alleged corruption, in a series of scandals that demonstrated the limits of the reform process, involving as it did close associates, as well as kin, of a leader who had claimed moral superiority. Institutions too, notably the tax and intelligence services and the prosecution office, were shown to be involved in corrupt practices. In January another reallocation of cabinet portfolios drew general criticism except for the appointment of a woman, Park Sun-Sook, as presidential spokesperson. Lee Sang-Joo became the administration's seventh Minister of Education, while the Minister of Unification, Hong Soon-Young, was removed as a result of the failure of inter-Korean talks. An unfortunate loss was the experienced Minister of Foreign Affairs and Trade, Han Seung-Soo, ostensibly in the interests of creating a politically neutral cabinet (although the DPP, as such, was of no consequence), just as he was arranging a diplomatically sensitive visit by US President George W. Bush. The new ministers responsible for unification and foreign affairs, Jeong Se-Hyun and Choi Sung-Hong, were both formerly vice-ministers for their respective portfolios.

As the presidential election approached, the MDP won some plaudits for introducing Korea's first ever primary elections, which in March 2002 produced unexpected support (dubbed the 'Roh wind') for an unlikely candidate: Roh Moo-Hyun, a populist lawyer and outsider from a poor farming background, without a university degree and with a left-wing image. An early bid by Park Geun-Hye (daughter of the late President Park Chung-Hee), who in February left the GNP to form her own Korean Coalition for the Future, made little impact. Instead, the leading contender appeared to be Chung Mong-Joon, an independent legislator, scion of the Hyundai business conglomerate and, most significantly, organizer of South Korea's co-hosting of the association football World Cup 2002. Lee Hoi-Chang again became a candidate, representing the GNP.

Two tests of public opinion were the local elections held in June and by-elections in August 2002. The GNP achieved a decisive victory in both, with a margin of 3.9m. votes in the former, the widest in Korean electoral history. Winning 11 of the 13 by-elections brought control of the National Assembly, which the party then used to veto two successive presidential nominations for the post of Prime Minister after yet another government reorganization in July. In early October Kim Suk-Soo, a career judge and former Head of the National Election Commission (formerly Central Election Management Committee), was appointed Prime Minister, his nomination having been confirmed by the National Assembly.

President Kim's final ministerial reorganization brought no respite. The outgoing Minister of Justice indicated that he had been removed for failing to protect the President's sons, while the dismissed Minister of Health and Welfare blamed foreign pharmaceutical companies. Also replaced were the Ministers of Information and Communication, and National Defence, the latter as a consequence of an incident in which North Korean warships had fired on and sunk a South Korean patrol boat in the Yellow Sea (see the chapter on the Democratic People's Republic of Korea). Lee Jun was a former general and also a previous head of Korea Telecom, as was the new Minister of Information and Communication, Lee Sang-Chul.

In November 2002 Roh Moo-Hyun and Chung Mong-Joon agreed to join forces. They debated on television, leaving it to opinion polls to judge who performed the better. That proved to be Roh, who hitherto had been faring so badly that the MDP had begun to split, with up to 40 of its deputies abandoning the party and being expected to support Chung. The 'Roh wind' then rose again, aided by public anger at the acquittal in November by courts martial of the US Forces of Korea (USFK) of two soldiers whose vehicle had killed two teenage girls in June.

Against all predictions, Roh narrowly won the presidential election held on 19 December 2002, even though Chung withdrew his support shortly before the poll over an alleged anti-US remark. Out of almost 35m. eligible voters, ballots were cast by fewer than 25m. (70%), a record low turn-out. Having received 48.9% of the total votes cast, compared with Lee Hoi-Chang's 46.6%, Roh's margin was wider than that of Kim Dae-Jung in 1997. Kwon Young-Gil of the leftist Democratic Labour Party (DLP) more than doubled his 1997 result, but came a distant third, with 3.9%, fewer than 1m. votes. Three other candidates together received just 0.6% of the votes. Youth and technology were credited with this upset, the internet and mobile telephones having been used to urge normally apolitical young electors to vote. (South Korea had rapidly become one of the world's most 'wired' societies.). Jeolla in the south-west voted overwhelmingly for Roh, but he also attracted 20%–30% of the vote in his native south-east, the GNP heartland. Chungcheong in the centre-west, whither Roh had promised to transfer the capital, favoured him more narrowly; as did greater Seoul, which contained 40% of the electorate.

The Presidency of Roh Moo-Hyun

In the context of the emerging North Korean nuclear crisis (see the chapter on the Democratic People's Republic of Korea), the outcome of the presidential election caused unease. The disquiet was not allayed by the composition of Roh's 25-strong transition team, dominated by left-leaning provincial academics and including no politicians. His inauguration on 25 February 2003 was overshadowed by a North Korean missile test, and the ceremony was also scaled down in response to a recent subway disaster in Daegu, South Korea's third city, in which some 200 people lost their lives. For two days the new President had no cabinet, as the opposition-controlled National Assembly refused to endorse his chosen Prime Minister, Goh Kun, a former premier, until legislation was approved to appoint a special counsel to investigate the 'cash for peace' scandal; this had arisen from revelations that the previous administration of Kim Dae-Jung had in 2000 secretly sent some US $100m. to North Korea via the Hyundai group, which itself had remitted a further $400m. Roh's first cabinet was less radical than his transition team. Kim Jin-Pyo, Deputy Premier for Finance and the Economy, was an experienced career bureaucrat, as were the Ministers of Commerce, Industry and Energy, Yoon Jin-Shik, and of Planning and Budget, Park Bong-Heum. The only radical member was Lee Joung-Woo, the head of policy planning in the Office of the President. The Minister of Foreign Affairs and Trade, Yoon Young-Kwan, was an academic with no diplomatic experience. Ra Jong-Yil, lately ambassador to the United Kingdom, took the new ministerial-level post of presidential national security adviser. The Minister of Unification, Jeong Se-Hyun, was the sole incumbent to be retained from the previous administration. Apart from the President, only two cabinet ministers were members of the MDP, while four were women. The Minister of Justice, Kang Kum-Sil, was a radical lawyer whose appointment was not well received within her ministry.

Within two months Roh Moo-Hyun himself, beset by challenges, declared himself overwhelmed by the job: a view widely shared. On the recurrent issue of corporate reform, highlighted anew when a US $1,200m. accounting fraud was revealed at SK, the country's third largest *chaebol*, he seemed to retreat from his earlier radicalism. In June 2003 riot police broke up an illegal strike against privatization by railway workers, but other strikers—truck drivers who in May blockaded the main ports and bank workers who shut down computers to resist a merger—achieved most of their demands. This encouraged militancy elsewhere, including a seven-week strike at Hyundai Motor, a major exporter, which won a five-day working week. Furthermore, the new administration was rapidly embroiled in scandal. In August Roh Moo-Hyun sued four leading Seoul dailies over allegations of real estate deals involving him and his brother. Separately, the MDP Chairman, Chyung Dai-Chul, admitted taking money from a businessman charged with embezzlement, and embarrassingly claimed that the MDP's election campaign had received 20,000m. won ($16.9m.) from business interests, much of it apparently undeclared. Also in August, Hyundai Chairman Chung Mong-Hun, who had been charged in June in connection with the 'cash for peace' scandal, committed suicide.

In July 2003 five legislators left the GNP after it elected a new leader, Choe Byung-Yul, a former editor, mayor of Seoul and cabinet minister, who was of conservative bent. (Lee Hoi-Chang had resigned after losing the 2002 presidential election.) The nominally ruling MDP was by now barely functioning, divided between supporters of Roh Moo-Hyun, who openly planned to found a new party, and an old guard loyal to Kim Dae-Jung. In September the MDP formally split, when 36 of its parliamentary members broke away and joined five from the GNP to form a new party, eventually named Uri (meaning 'We'). Roh declared that he would leave the MDP, which accused him of betrayal, and joined the GNP in opposition. However, Roh did not immediately join Uri, professing to remain above the fray. Meanwhile, the GNP had used its majority to force the removal of the Minister of Government Administration and Home Affairs, Kim Doo-Kwan, a Roh ally, for not preventing an incursion by radical students into a US military base near Seoul in August. He was succeeded by the Minister of Maritime Affairs and Fisheries, Huh Sung-Kwan, whose deputy, Choi Lark-Jung, replaced him. The latter's ministerial career lasted less than a fortnight: he was dismissed after a series of gaffes. His successor was Chang Seung-Woo, a former Minister of Planning and Budget.

In October 2003 the beleaguered Roh Moo-Hyun caused consternation by declaring that he would seek a public verdict on his stewardship and resign if this went against him. In early 2004 investigations revealed that both main parties had accepted illicit funds from most major *chaebol* during the 2002 presidential election campaign. However, with the GNP having received the larger share, Roh was able to deflect public opprobrium onto the opposition and onto the tycoons and firms that had given the funds. The GNP used its control of the legislature to appoint a special counsel to investigate finances in the President's camp, thus implying that the public prosecution service could not be trusted. In late November 2003 Roh Moo-Hyun vetoed this, but the National Assembly overruled the President's veto in early December: the first time that this had happened since 1961.

Although the President had pledged to end the practice of frequent ministerial changes, by the end of 2003 eight of Roh's original cabinet had been replaced within 10 months. In December Yoon Jin-Shik resigned as Minister of Commerce, Industry and Energy, taking responsibility for an ongoing dispute over a proposed nuclear waste dump that had led to violent protests. His replacement was Lee Hee-Beom, hitherto president of Seoul National University of Technology and a former vice-minister. Five days later the Deputy Prime Minister for Education and Human Resources Development, Yoon Deok-Hong, resigned over the issue of management of personal information on students. He was succeeded by Ahn Byung-Young, a professor and former Minister of Education. In a cabinet reorganization in late December 2003 Kim Byung-Il was named Minister of Planning and Budget in place of Park Bong-Heum, who was appointed chief policy planner at the Blue House (Office of the President).

In January 2004 Roh Moo-Hyun dismissed the Minister of Foreign Affairs and Trade, Yoon Young-Kwan, followed by his defence and national security advisers, after a dispute in which a number of foreign ministry officials, alarmed at growing anti-US tendencies, had allegedly criticized the President. The new Minister of Foreign Affairs and Trade, Ban Ki-Moon, was a seasoned diplomat whose appointment was intended to assuage any US concerns. In February Lee Hun-Jai, who had led Kim Dae-Jung's reform drive as founding head of the Financial Supervisory Commission (FSC) before serving briefly as Deputy Prime Minister for Finance and the Economy, returned to the latter post after Kim Jin-Pyo resigned in order to stand as a parliamentary candidate (cabinet ministers not normally being members of the National Assembly). For the same reason Kim Dae-Hwan, an academic, replaced Kwon Ki-Hong as Minister of Labour, followed a week later by the Minister of the Environment, Han Myun-Sook, who was replaced by her Vice-Minister, Kwak Kyul-Ho.

Answering a question at a press conference in March 2004, President Roh Moo-Hyun expressed support for Uri. Although his views were hardly a secret, it was illegal under strict laws, drafted after years of abuse by dictators, for a government official, even a President elected on a party political platform, to be partisan. The National Election Commission reprimanded Roh but did not take any further action, seeing this as a minor infraction. However, the MDP seized the opportunity and, with the GNP, drew up a motion of impeachment, adding charges of corruption and economic mismanagement. An apology from Roh would have deflected the crisis, but none was immediately forthcoming. Uri parliamentary members slept around the Speaker's podium to try to prevent a vote, but they were forced out by the GNP's and MDP's larger numbers, in fierce scuffles shown live on television. The impeachment motion, the first ever in the Republic's history, was then carried by 193 votes to two (Uri members having walked out), easily surpassing the requisite two-thirds of the (then) 273-member assembly.

South Korean politics thus entered an unprecedented situation. Roh Moo-Hyun took a quasi-sabbatical period of leave, remaining in the Blue House, on full pay and with no official duties. The Prime Minister, Goh Kun, who had served the past six Presidents as a 'safe pair of hands', assumed the role of acting President while the Constitutional Court deliberated whether to endorse or reject Roh's impeachment. The GNP chose a new leader: Park Geun-Hye. The daughter of the late President was popular in her native south-east, the GNP heartland, and, as a woman, projected a new image for a conservative party. The MDP too, amid much internecine turmoil, appointed a female leader, Chu Mi-Ae.

At the election for the National Assembly, now restored to 299 seats, on 15 April 2004 the new Uri Party won 152 seats, more than tripling its representation, to wrest control from the GNP, which took 121 seats, compared with its previous 137. The MDP was decimated, its 59 seats being reduced to nine, while the ULD, which under Kim Dae-Jung had held the balance of power, appeared moribund, its representation declining from 10 seats to four. The socialist DLP won 10 seats, its first ever, receiving 13% support nation-wide. Turnout, at just under 60% of the 35.6m. electors, was 2% higher than in 2000. The GNP won 60 of 68 seats in the south-east (Gyeongsang), but none in Jeolla and just one in Chungcheong. Of the new members of the National Assembly, 39 were women, twice as many as previously. Only 95 former legislators retained their seats, and 135 of the 204 newcomers were wholly new to party politics.

In May 2004 the Constitutional Court overruled President Roh Moo-Hyun's impeachment, dismissing charges of economic mismanagement and corruption. It found that he had broken election law, if inadvertently, by expressing support for the Uri Party; and had also violated the Constitution with his unsuccessful request in late 2003 for the holding of a referendum; however, these transgressions were not considered grave enough to warrant his dismissal. Despite apologizing belatedly for this episode, once restored to office Roh continued much as before. He at once argued with Prime Minister Goh Kun, who refused to endorse a minor cabinet reorganization and then resigned. For a month South Korea had no Prime Minister, as Roh was determined to appoint Kim Hyuck-Kyu, a former provincial governor who had left the GNP, which therefore vowed to oppose him. Roh only relented after local by-elections in early June rebuffed Uri as firmly as the legislative election of April had endorsed it, albeit on a low turn-out of 28.5%. The GNP took three of four mayoralties and governorships being contested, in Busan, Jeju and South Gyeongsang, while the MDP won in South Jeolla, its former heartland.

The President chose as Prime Minister Lee Hae-Chan, a former education minister and a close ally. His appointment was confirmed by the National Assembly at the end of June 2004 by 200 votes to 84; the GNP allowed a free vote. This cleared the way for Roh to bring three senior Uri members into the State Council. Chung Dong-Young, the former Uri Chairman who had managed the party's election campaign, became Minister of Unification; while Kim Geun-Tae, Uri's former parliamentary leader, took the health and welfare portfolio. Chung Dong-Chae, a former journalist who was Roh Moo-Hyun's chief of staff before his election, replaced Lee Chang-Dong as Minister of Culture and Tourism.

The summer strikes of mid-2004 had a new focus: the introduction of a five-day working week, for which militant unions demanded no loss of pay. Sectors affected included the usual car manufacturers, hospitals and subways, along with some new areas, notably a 19-day strike (the longest ever in the financial sector) at KorAm Bank against its new owners, Citigroup, and a walk-out at LG-Caltex, which refined 30% of the nation's petroleum. These last two actions were illegal, and in August the Government arrested leaders of both.

The Minister of National Defence, Cho Young-Kil, resigned in July 2004 after a complex episode in which the South Korean navy initially denied, but then allowed it to be known, that it had had prior radio contact with the North before firing warning shots at an intruding North Korean patrol boat. The President's defence adviser, Yoon Kwang-Ung, a retired admiral, took over as Minister of National Defence. In an unexpected development, Kim Seung-Kyu, a lawyer, became Minister of Justice, replacing the controversial Kang Kum-Sil, who had resigned, reportedly as a result of fatigue, after her efforts to reform the prosecution service were continually blocked.

Meanwhile, President Roh was determined to fulfil an election pledge to transfer the capital from Seoul, in the interests of balanced national development. In July 2004 a presidential committee selected a site at Yeongi-Gongju, in South Chungcheong province, 140 km south of Seoul, as the location for a new administrative capital to be completed by 2014. The legal basis for this had been enacted in the previous December, and had been supported at the time by the GNP, for fear (as the party later admitted) of losing Chungcheong votes in the forthcoming legislative election. Seoul opposed the plan, and the city's GNP mayor, Lee Myung-Bak, was especially outspoken. In October 2004 the Constitutional Court ruled that the transfer of the capital would violate the Constitution. Undeterred, Roh proposed a less radical new 'administrative city', even though the GNP seemed likely to abandon this plan if it were to win the next presidential election, scheduled for late 2007. In March 2005 GNP junior members forced the resignation of the party's parliamentary leader, Kim Deog-Ryong, after he agreed to this modified version.

With the dispute over the capital intensifying, President Roh used his Liberation Day speech on 15 August 2004 to open another controversy by urging the need to 'set . . . historic distortions right'. Specifying two periods (collaboration with Japanese colonialism before 1945 and the era of military dictatorship in 1961–87) the President urged the establishment of a parliamentary committee to clarify these episodes comprehensively. It was not only the GNP that suspected that the real aim of this initiative was to discredit its leader Park Geun-Hye, whose father, Park Chung-Hee, had ruled as a dictator in 1961–79 and in his youth had been an officer in the Japanese Imperial Army. (However, the initiative unexpectedly resulted in the resignation of the Chairman of Uri, Shin Ki-Nam, after revelations that his father had worked for the Japanese military police.)

Following the drafting of a controversial bill to abolish the long-established National Security Law in the latter part of 2004, Uri attracted further adverse publicity when it proposed legislation to curb market freedom for newspapers. Education was yet another area of contention, owing to Uri's drafting of legislation prohibiting universities from setting their own entrance examinations and allowing teachers to choose one-third of the directors of private schools. With the National Assembly's normal business being paralysed for long periods, South Korea almost entered 2005 with no budget having been approved and without a renewed mandate for its troops in Iraq. A last-minute deal appeared to be a victory for the GNP: of the various contentious pieces of legislation, only that on the media was approved, with the others postponed for further discussion. Uri back-benchers, furious at this compromise, forced their parliamentary leader, Chun Jung-Bae, to resign on 1 January, which was followed two days later by the departure of the party Chairman, Lee Bu-Young. Uri chose a moderate, experienced legislator, Lim Chae-Jung, as interim Chairman pending the party's national convention in April.

Also in January 2005, reaction to Roh Moo-Hyun unexpected replacement of six cabinet ministers was overwhelmingly negative. The core portfolios of foreign affairs, security and economic teams remained intact, but several of the ministries affected—education, agriculture, home affairs, gender equality, maritime affairs and legislation—were regarded as politically sensitive. Roh freely admitted that the Ministers of Education and of Agriculture had been made scapegoats for public discontent in these fields, rather than having been removed because of any shortcomings on their part. Widespread dismay greeted the appointment of the new Minister of Education, a post that also carried the rank of deputy premier. Lee Ki-Jun, a former head of Seoul National University, had resigned in 2002 when he was found to have outside business interests; following further charges of undeclared real estate holdings, he resigned after just three days in the post. Far from refreshing Roh's image in mid-term, these developments increased doubts about the President's consistency and competence. In late January the education portfolio was allocated to Kim Jin-Pyo, who until a year previously had been Deputy Prime Minister for Finance and the Economy. His successor in that post, Lee Hun-Jai, resigned barely a month later in early March, over allegations (albeit denied) of illicit real estate dealings by his wife. Lee's replacement was Han Duck-Soo, an experienced former Minister of Trade.

As the GNP continued to resist Uri's reform bills, in April 2005 Uri elected a new leadership with pragmatists defeating radicals for the most important posts. The electorate was unimpressed: at the end of April the ruling party lost six by-elections, and thus its narrow majority in the National Assembly. This left Uri with 146 seats in the 299-member Assembly; the GNP held 125, the DLP 10, the MDP nine and the ULD three, with six independents including the Speaker. (Uri also fared badly in local by-elections; the GNP won five posts of mayor or governor, plus eight seats on local councils, while the MDP and independents won one of each.)

Henceforth, approval of legislation would need co-operation from the DLP or MDP. (In May 2005 the latter renamed itself as simply the Democratic Party—DP.) At the end of June the DLP helped Uri block an opposition motion to oust the Minister of National Defence, Yoon Kwang-Ung, after an incident at the DMZ earlier in the month when a young conscript had used guns and grenades to kill eight fellow soldiers; he complained of bullying. Amid fresh debate about the state of the military, Yoon offered to resign, but President Roh regarded him as indispensable to the pursuit of military reform. Also in late June the Minister of Justice, Kim Seung-Kyu, was appointed head of the NIS by President Roh. The previous NIS head, Ko Young-Koo, had resigned on health grounds; as a radical lawyer, he had been mistrusted by conservatives, who preferred his successor, a career prosecutor. After only 16 months in the post, the Minister of the Environment was also replaced.

Meanwhile, political scandal remained another ongoing issue. The resignation in May 2005 of two presidential aides over their role in a resort project off the south-west coast and an affair involving Korean National Railroad (Korail—the state-owned rail operator), which had lost US $3.5m. in an unsuccessful oil investment in the Russian island of Sakhalin, were rapidly eclipsed by the return to Seoul in mid-June of Kim Woo-Choong. The founder and former Chairman of Daewoo, once the country's second largest *chaebol*, had been a fugitive since its collapse in 1999; no concerted efforts to locate him had been made. Now in poor health, Kim was indicted at the beginning of July, charged with ordering Daewoo executives to inflate group assets during 1997–98 and using this fraud to borrow 9,800,000m. won illegally from local banks. He reportedly admitted the accounting fraud, but denied further charges of illicitly channelling money abroad and of maintaining political 'slush funds'.

In July 2005 a fresh scandal broke when MBC, a leading broadcasting network, revealed that it had in its possession a tape of a telephone conversation made illegally by the NIS in 1997. A senior official of the Samsung Group and the head of a prominent daily newspaper with links to Samsung, the *Joong Ang Ilbo*, were allegedly heard to discuss the transfer of 10,000m. won (US $9.8m.) in illicit funds to Lee Hoi-Chang, the unsuccessful conservative contender in the presidential election of 1997. The then press magnate Hong Seok-Hyun had since become South Korea's ambassador to the USA; he swiftly resigned, after just five months in the post. In late July 2005 the Samsung Group, now by far the largest *chaebol*, issued a guarded apology, which was widely criticized as inadequate. Furthermore, prosecutors seized 274 tapes from the home of Kong Un-Yong, who had been responsible for the NIS operation and had attempted suicide. With demands for full publication being countered by privacy concerns, the parties were divided: the GNP favoured an independent counsel, while Uri wanted a special civilian committee. In early August the NIS admitted it had continued illegal wire-tapping until 2002, well into the administration of President Kim Dae-Jung. These developments strengthened already widespread disgust with traditional power élites—politicians, the press, major businesses and bureaucrats—seen as united in the practice of corruption.

In October 2005 the GNP won four by-elections, holding one seat and gaining three: two from Uri and one from the DLP in Ulsan, its industrial heartland. Coming after an earlier loss of five seats in by-elections in April, this consolidated Uri's loss of overall control of the National Assembly; to secure the passage of legislation Uri would now need the support of minor parties; Uri's leaders promptly resigned.

Despite President Roh's offer in July 2005 to relinquish half his power to a GNP-led coalition government, party politics remained bitterly contested. In December a scuffle in the National Assembly failed to prevent the passage of a controversial law increasing the regulation of private schools. In response, the GNP began a boycott of the legislature, which continued into 2006. However, polls showed that the new law had public support. At the end of December 2005, at the third attempt, Uri managed to secure the approval of the 2006 budget and other vital pieces of legislation, such as the renewal of the mandate for South Korea's (now reduced) force in Iraq, with the help of smaller parties.

A reallocation of cabinet portfolios at the beginning of 2006 was widely criticized. The main aim was to allow Uri's two rivals for the next presidential nomination—Minister of Unification Chung Dong-Young, a centrist, and the more left-wing Kim Geun-Tae, Minister of Health and Welfare—to return to the party after barely 18 months in the Government, the convention being that serving ministers were above the fray while in their posts. Their successors, and three other unexpected ministerial changes, proved contentious. Lee Jong-Seok, the new Minister of Unification, had long guided policy on North Korea as deputy director of the National Security Council (NSC) and was one of President Roh's closest confidants. Conservatives viewed him as being opposed to the USA and too flexible with regard to North Korea. Lee Sang-Soo, the incoming Minister of Labour, was a long-standing associate of the President, and had been imprisoned in 2004 for receiving illicit funds in 2002 while managing Roh's election campaign. Although swiftly amnestied (a common practice in South Korea), his early return to office was regarded as unseemly. Kim Woo-Sik, a former academic and presidential chief of staff who became a Deputy Prime Minister and Minister of Science and Technology, was obliged to contain the repercussions of the disgracing of the supposed cloning pioneer Hwang Woo-Suk, whose now-discredited scientific research had enjoyed strong official support. Two other appointments also resulted in the President angering his own party. He rendered Uri effectively leaderless, until its national convention in February, by selecting its acting Chairman, Chung Sye-Kyun, to be Minister of Commerce, Industry and Energy. By contrast, the new Minister of Health and Welfare, Rhyu Si-Min, was an abrasive Roh loyalist.

Lee Hae-Chan held more power than previous incumbents, since President Roh had, de facto, devolved responsibility for domestic affairs to him. In March 2006, however, the Prime Minister lost his position as the result of a gaffe involving a game of golf, which coincided not only with a rail strike but also with a solemn holiday commemorating an anti-Japanese rising in 1919. Most seriously, his golfing party included a businessman fined the next day by the FTC for price-fixing, provoking suspicions of lobbying. The Prime Minister's action provoked a furore that forced him to resign. President Roh's choice of successor was confirmed by the National Assembly on 19 April, after a hearing of rare smoothness: Han Myeong-Sook, a former dissident and Minister of Gender Equality and the Environment, thus became South Korea's first female Prime Minister. However, although widely respected, she lacked her predecessor's influence.

In February 2006 the Secretary-General of the GNP, Choi Yeon-Hee, resigned after an incident involving an inappropriate advance to a female journalist. He resigned from the party whip, but resisted all demands, including a rare formal but non-binding vote of the National Assembly, to give up his seat. In April the GNP filed an unprecedented suit against two of its own senior legislators for allegedly taking bribes from potential candidates in the forthcoming local elections.

Nevertheless, the GNP triumphed at the local elections held at the end of May 2006, when it received 54.5% of the votes cast nation-wide; Uri took 21.2%. Turn-out was 51.3% of the electorate, up by 2.4% in comparison with 2002. Of the 16 provincial governor and city mayor positions, the GNP secured 12, while Uri won only one; the DP took two, and in Jeju an independent governor narrowly defeated the GNP. All three Uri and DP victories were in the south-western Jeolla provinces, reflecting traditional regional loyalties; similarly, the GNP continued to dominate the more populous Gyeongsang region in the south-east. This regional loyalty meant that the votes cast in Greater Seoul, where 40% of voters resided, were decisive. In Seoul's mayoral contest Oh Se-Hoon of the GNP won a clear victory over Uri's Kang Kum-Sil, receiving 61% of the votes, compared with 27% for Kang. Both parties had chosen relatively youthful outsider candidates, believed to have a wider appeal than professional politicians. Kang was a feminist and a former Minister of Justice, while Oh was a former legislator who had previously abandoned politics in disgust. The GNP won all 25 district headships in the capital, nine out of 10 in its port of Incheon and 67% of all such posts nationally (155 out of 230). It also took 75% of the 3,621 council posts nation-wide, including again all 96 city councillor positions in Seoul. (This partly reflected the 'first-past-the-post' electoral system.) Uri won only 19 district headships, fewer than the DP's 20. The newly founded regional People First Party (PFP) secured seven such positions in the Chungcheong provinces, south of Seoul.

The GNP attracted widespread sympathy after Park Geun-Hye was badly injured in the face by an ex-convict, only to defy medical advice and return to the campaign trail. The electoral set-back to Uri was severe. At the beginning of June 2006 its Chairman, Chung Dong-Young, hitherto a leading contender for the nomination to succeed President Roh, resigned, taking responsibility for the defeat. A week later an emergency committee chose his rival Kim Geun-Tae, whom Chung had defeated in a party election in February, as Uri's ninth leader in just 30 months. Kim swiftly warned against undue haste to conclude a free trade agreement (FTA) with the USA, the achievement of which Roh had set as a strategic goal before the end of his term.

Another government reorganization was effected in early July 2006, when President Roh replaced the Deputy Prime Ministers responsible for the economy and for education, as well as the Minister of Planning and Budget. The new Minister of Finance and the Economy, Kwon O-Kyu, had served hitherto as chief presidential secretary for national policy, while Kim Byong-Joon, who had held that post until May, became Minister of Education and Human Resources Development. Kwon was replaced in the Blue House by the former Minister of Planning and Budget, Byeon Yang-kyoon, who in turn was succeeded by his deputy, Chang Byung-Wan. The outgoing Minister of Education, Kim Jin-Pyo, had been widely criticized following a mass outbreak of food poisoning in Seoul schools. Han Duck-Soo had resigned as Minister of Finance and Economy in order to give Roh greater flexibility for the rest of his term; Han was a doughty defender of foreign business, a community that was relieved that his successor held similar views, Kwon O-Kyu being the main force behind Roh's commitment to negotiate an FTA with the USA. Kim Byong-Joon, by contrast, was a contentious choice as the unrepentant creator of unpopular new real-estate taxes, intended to curb speculation but widely blamed for Uri's heavy losses in the local elections. He immediately encountered difficulties over allegations (which he admitted) that as a professor he had twice published identical papers in two separate journals. He finally submitted his letter of resignation to Roh in early August. Yet another new appointee in July was Jun Gun-Pyo, deputy head of the National Tax Service (NTS), as the new NTS commissioner, succeeding Lee Ju-Sung, who had resigned abruptly for undisclosed reasons. In the following month Kim Sung-Ho, deputy head of the presidential Korea Independent Commission Against Corruption, was named as the new Minister of Justice, replacing Chun Jung-Bae, who had returned to Uri in the previous month.

As labour unrest and violent protest continued, legislation to improve conditions for non-regular workers passed its committee stage in February 2006 against physical opposition by the DLP, but had yet to become law several months later. Unions opposed it as not being radical enough, while employers complained that it would restrict flexibility. In early March an illicit strike by rail workers on this and other issues was firmly and promptly suppressed. By contrast, in July construction workers occupied the headquarters in Pohang of the steelmaker POSCO, which was not even their direct employer, and stayed there for nine days, causing financial losses of US $210m. as well as serious damage to the building. Police reluctance to intervene at POSCO was due partly to the fact that in 2005 the Chief of Police had been forced to resign when two farmers died following demonstrations against the policies of the World Trade Organization. However, that protest appeared relatively insignificant in comparison with the losses of $1,400m. suffered by Hyundai Motor in July as a result of the now-annual strike by some of South Korea's most highly paid workers. Subsequent anti-FTA and other demonstrations were also violent.

Political activity intensified with the approach of the presidential election, scheduled for 19 December 2007, and the legislative election, due in April 2008. Within the ruling party long-standing tensions between President Roh, now widely regarded as ineffectual, and a Uri party that increasingly saw him as a liability re-emerged in December 2006. Uri Chairman Kim Geun-Tae belatedly criticized Roh for his proposal for the establishment of a coalition with the GNP. Roh riposted with an open letter; while blaming the GNP's intransigence, he criticized those in Uri who wanted to co-operate with the DP for arousing regionalism; none the less, Roh declared his intention to remain in the party. This emboldened the President's supporters in Uri to demand that Kim Geun-Tae resign. By early 2007 Uri was openly divided.

In January 2007 Goh Kun, the centrist former Prime Minister who despite having no party base had led opinion polls as the public's preferred choice to become the country's next head of state, withdrew from the presidential contest. It had appeared increasingly unlikely either that Uri's own prospective candidates would stand aside for Goh on a united centre-left platform, or that he would be able to defeat the GNP, even if they did decide not to participate. Goh's campaign was also damaged by negative comments from Roh, who expressed regret at ever having appointed him as Prime Minister.

Meanwhile, the practice of frequent ministerial reorganizations continued. At the beginning of November 2006 President Roh nominated a new foreign affairs and security team, including the appointment of the third Minister of Unification of the year. Ban Ki-Moon's election as UN Secretary-General meant that a new Minister of Foreign Affairs was required. In a clear signal of Roh's determination to adhere to the 'sunshine' policy, the members of the new team were even more willing to compromise than their predecessors, outraging the GNP, which obstructed some confirmations until mid-December. Thus, the new Minister of Foreign Affairs, Song Min-Soon, was a career diplomat who, as Vice-Minister of Foreign Affairs, had recently negotiated an agreement on principles at the six-party talks on the North Korean nuclear issue (see below) before they faltered; Roh had subsequently appointed him as presidential security adviser. After less than a year in his position, Lee Jong-Seok was replaced as Minister of Unification by the accommodating Lee Jae-Joung, an Anglican priest, who had been head of a Seoul seminary before entering politics. Imprisoned, but subsequently pardoned, for raising illegal funds for Roh's presidential election campaign in 2002, he had latterly chaired a unification advisory body. With no prior experience of office, his appointment was an unexpected choice. The new Minister of National Defence was drawn once again from the upper echelons of the military: Kim Jang-Soo, hitherto army chief of staff, succeeded Yoon Kwang-Woong, a former admiral who since 2004 had led Roh's efforts to reform a military often wary of the 'sunshine' policy.

The NIS also acquired a new director: Kim Man-Bok, hitherto deputy director, was the first internal appointee in the agency's history. The NIS was usually seen as conservative, like the Ministry of National Defence, but Kim supported the 'sunshine' policy. The outgoing Kim Seung-Kyu indirectly criticized his successor, and he did not deny claims by the press and GNP that he had been forced to resign on account of his pursuit of South Korea's first espionage case for several years, in which five persons, including a vice-secretary of the DLP, had been accused of spying for North Korea. Conservatives claimed that the NIS had been restrained in this area, for fear of damaging détente with the North.

Further minor reorganizations of the Government followed on an almost monthly basis. Amid mounting criticism of ever-changing but ineffectual policies to try to control property prices in Seoul, the Minister of Construction and Transportation, Choo Byung-Jik, resigned in mid-November 2006. He was subsequently replaced by Lee Yong-Sup, hitherto Minister of Government Administration and Home Affairs, and Park Myung-Jae, the former head of a training institute, assumed responsibility for the latter portfolios. In January 2007 President Roh appointed Kim Young-Joo, the head of the Office for Government Policy Coordination, as Minister of Commerce, Industry and Energy, to succeed Chung Sye-Kyun, who returned to Uri in the hope of restoring unity. Kim in turn was replaced by Im Sang-Gyu, the Vice-Minister of Science and Technology.

In March 2007 the Prime Minister, Han Myeong-Sook, resigned after only a year in office, with a view to pursuing her presidential ambitions. Her successor, confirmed in early April, was Han Duck-Soo, an experienced technocrat who had previously served as acting Prime Minister and Minister of Finance. A further government reorganization followed in mid-April: Kim Jong-Min, hitherto head of the Korea National Tourism Organization, replaced Kim Myong-Gon as Minister of Culture and Tourism, while Kang Moo-Hyun was appointed Minister of Maritime Affairs and Fisheries for a second time. A daily newspaper calculated that, in his four years in office thus far, Roh had appointed 75 persons to 20 cabinet posts, including that of Prime Minister; making an average of 3.7 incumbents per portfolio, each serving for just 14 months.

In early August 2007 further cabinet changes were implemented. As Minister of Justice, Kim Sung-Ho had clashed with President Roh, rebuking him for criticizing constitutional provisions forbidding the President to intervene in electoral matters; Roh was censured twice by the National Election Commission for commenting on the forthcoming elections. Kim's successor, Chung Soung-Jin, who had chaired the Korean Independent Commission Against Corruption, thus became the Republic of Korea's 59th Minister of Justice in as many years, since the foundation of the Republic in 1948. Other appointments included Im Sang-Gyu, hitherto head of the Office for Government Policy Co-ordination, as Minister of Agriculture and Forestry; Im's successor was Yoon Dae-Hee, formerly the senior presidential secretary for economic policy. Yoo Young-Hwan, Vice-Minister of Information and Communication, was promoted to Minister. Kim Jong-Hoon, South Korea's chief negotiator for the FTA with the USA, became the Minister for Trade at the Ministry of Foreign Affairs and Trade, replacing Kim Hyun-Chong, who was appointed the country's ambassador to the UN.

As the volatility of party politics increase, in a remarkable succession of events, the Uri party suffered a series of ruptures, only to reunite in effect under a new name in August 2007. In January and February two bloc defections reduced the party's representation in the legislature to 108 seats. Delegates to the party convention in mid-February, despite opposition from a minority loyal to President Roh, voted to relax membership rules and seek mergers with other parties to form a new political grouping. The former Minister of Commerce, Chung Sye-Kyun, was re-elected as party leader. In late February Roh left the party that had been created to support him, but his departure was ultimately relatively amicable.

Despite Uri's travails, the results of by-elections in April 2007 warned the GNP against complacency. The latter party won only one of the three National Assembly seats contested; in the other two, regional loyalties triumphed. Despite having served time in prison for bribery, Kim Dae-Jung's son, Kim Hong-Up, won a seat for the DP in the party's south-western heartland, South Jeolla. The PFP, based in the Chungcheong provinces south of Seoul, won in Daejeon, the region's main city. Uri had stood aside for the DP and PFP, with which it hoped to form alliances. The level of voter participation was a poor 28%, decreasing from 34% in the previous year's by-elections. Furthermore, the GNP won only one of six mayoral and gubernatorial posts, for which elections were held concurrently. The party suffered from the intense rivalry between Lee Myung-Bak and Park Geun-Hye, with the latter's camp joining Uri in denouncing the former, accusing him of past financial and other improprieties. In an extraordinary live television programme in mid-July, senior GNP officials questioned Lee and Park separately, each on charges ranging from corruption and tax evasion to being the parent of a clandestine illegitimate child. By mid-August Lee appeared to have withstood the crisis after he admitted registering false addresses, his stated purpose being to secure places in good schools for his children, rather than real estate speculation. The GNP chose Lee as its presidential candidate; Park had more intra-party support, but a clear lead among non-party voters (eligible for the first time) gave Lee the nomination by a margin of 1.5%. Owing to a change in electoral law, the loser would be banned from standing for another party or as an independent candidate (as Rhee In-Je had done in 1997, thus dividing the right and resulting in Kim Dae-Jung's election to the presidency).

With an interplay of factions divided less by ideology than by personalities and tactics, Uri continued to disintegrate. An additional 16 members of the legislature left the party in mid-June 2007, a further 16 a week later and 15 more in the latter part of July. Prior to that, in late June an earlier group of Uri defectors joined forces with most of the DP to form the Centrist United Democratic Party (CUDP). In August, however, the United New Democratic Party (UNDP) was established by 85 legislators, most of them former members of the Uri Party. The UNDP at once declared that it would merge with the remainder of Uri, in effect reconstituting the latter under a new name. This duly occurred in mid-August, rendering the 'new' UNDP the largest party in the National Assembly, holding 143 seats in comparison with the GNP's 129. Nevertheless, factional divisions persisted, amid competition to become the party's presidential candidate. The strongest of the party's three main contenders was Chung Dong-Young, a former television news presenter and Minister of Unification. More popular with the public was Sohn Hak-Kyu, an ex-dissident and former governor of Gyeonggi province (greater Seoul) for the GNP, who had crossed the floor earlier in the year. Lee Hae-Chan, the former Prime Minister, was favoured by a now largely ineffectual President Roh, but by few others. In September this trio embarked upon a month-long primary election process, the innovations of which included, for the first time in the world (but possibly unconstitutionally), voting by mobile phone. The National Election Commission refused to supervise the UNDP's poll, which was marred by very low rates of participation (16%–20%) and by charges that Chung's camp had manipulated the ballot. Sohn and Lee temporarily boycotted the campaign in protest, but both accepted the eventual result in mid-October: a convincing victory for Chung, who received 44% of the total eligible votes cast; Sohn took 34% and Lee 22%.

Meanwhile, corporate governance issues remained a concern, and leading businesses continued to be beset by scandal. In February 2006 Lee Kun-Hee, the Chairman of the Samsung group, returned from five months of quasi-exile in the USA and offered 800,000m. won of his personal fortune to 'society' in implicit atonement for various scandals, albeit without admitting liability. Attention then shifted to Hyundai Motor, of which the Chairman, Chung Mong-Koo, was charged in April with embezzlement of 79,700m. won and breach of trust in raising secret 'slush funds' worth some 103,000m. won. Chung spent two months in prison before being bailed in late June. He was convicted in February 2007 and sentenced to three years in prison, but his sentence was suspended in September. Meanwhile, in May 2006 the founder of Daewoo, Kim Woo-Choong, received a 10-year prison sentence and fines totalling 22,400,000m. won for accounting fraud; he was acquitted of bribery. In view of his ill health and continuing support in some circles, it was not unexpected when he was pardoned in Roh Moo-Hyun's final New Year amnesty in January 2008; his term of imprisonment had already been reduced. In late April Kim Seung-Youn, the Chairman of Hanwha (a major *chaebol*) and one of the country's richest men, surrendered to police in Seoul for questioning. Following charges that in March his bodyguards and hired gangsters had kidnapped and assaulted several men with whom his son had been involved in a brawl in a bar, Kim was found guilty in July and sentenced to 18 months in prison; he served a few weeks before being released on grounds of ill health. These two in turn would be pardoned in the first amnesty of the new presidency, in August 2008; critics protested that tycoons appeared to be above the law.

The presidential election was held on 19 December 2007 and resulted in a decisive victory for Lee Myung-Bak. At 62.9%, the turn-out was low, the level of participation having declined steadily at each election since the record 89.2% witnessed in 1987. Lee took almost one-half (48.7%) of all votes cast, thus attracting more support than the next two candidates combined. The runner-up, Chung Dong-Young of the UNDP, received 26.1%, faring better than forecast. In third place was Lee Hoi-Chang: the GNP's losing candidate in 1997 and 2002, this time a late entrant as an independent conservative (having deemed the other Lee too moderate), who received 15.1%. Three other centre-left candidates were unable to muster 10% among them. Moon Kook-Hyun, a former CEO of Yuhan-Kimberly who formed his own Creative Korea Party (CKP), polled a respectable 5.8%. Kwon Young-Gil, standing for the third time for the uncompromising left-wing DLP, took 3.0%. Rhee In-Je this time represented the DP (having inherited from Kim Dae-Jung the leadership of the party that had ruled during 1997–2002), but received just 0.7% of the votes cast.

Lee Myung-Bak's margin of victory was unprecedented. He won in 13 out of 16 provinces and cities, including all 25 districts in Seoul, the capital's vote usually being more varied. The exceptions—North and South Jeolla, and Gwangju city—were all in the south-west of the country, reflecting that region's continuing suspicion of the GNP's origins in former military dictatorships. Regionalism apart, if the two Lees' votes were aggregated, conservatives took almost two-thirds (63.8%) of votes cast. So resounding a rebuff of a decade of centre-left rule belied claims made in 2002 that Roh Moo-Hyun's victory marked a permanent generational shift in the political landscape. Rather, and besides Roh's personal failings, Lee Myung-Bak's appeal derived from his business background; he emphasized pragmatism and competence, rather than ideology, and he intended to prioritize economic growth. He also pledged to improve relations with the USA and to demand more reciprocity from North Korea.

Voters had thus dismissed new allegations concerning Lee Myung-Bak's past business dealings. In early December 2007 prosecutors had cleared him of any involvement in the so-called BBK case in which Lee's former business partner, Kim Kyung-Joon, extradited from the USA in November and charged with a US $42m. fraud, had implicated him. Lee denied any role in BBK; but in mid-December a videotape from 2002 emerged in which he claimed to have co-founded the business advisory firm. This prompted the National Assembly, after scuffles in the chamber and a GNP boycott, to appoint an independent counsel to investigate not only BBK but also other allegations against Lee. After a somewhat perfunctory investigation, this exonerated the President-elect on 21 February 2008, just four days before his inauguration.

The Presidency of Lee Myung-Bak

Lee had already been acting on a quasi-presidential basis in the two-month interim period between election and inauguration, appointing a transition team that issued a plethora of initiatives. One such plan was to reduce government operations by merging 17 ministries into 12. Resistance by the still opposition-controlled National Assembly spared two: the Ministries of Unification and of Gender Equality. Several ministries underwent changes of name, sometimes more than once. The post of Deputy Prime Minister was abolished. President Lee Myung-Bak's first cabinet was criticized as dull and unduly wealthy: three of the 15 nominees (including the only two women) withdrew when questioned in relation to the source of their wealth. For the position of Prime Minister President Lee chose the experienced Han Seung-Soo; a former president of the UN General Assembly, he had served as Minister of Foreign Affairs and had also held the finance and trade portfolios. There was more scepticism regarding the new Minister of Strategy and Finance, Kang Man-Soo, who a decade previously had resigned as Vice-Minister of Finance as being responsible for the country's near-default in 1997.

Under the four-yearly voting cycle, within weeks of starting his five-year presidential term an early challenge for Lee Myung-Bak was the forthcoming legislative election. On 9 April 2008 the GNP won control, albeit narrowly, of the National Assembly. Like the presidential election, the result was another rout for the centre-left. The United Democratic Party (UDP, a merger of the UNDP and DP) received 4.3m. votes (barely one-half of the 8.2m. won by its predecessor Uri in 2004) and took 81 of the 299 seats (compared with its previous representation of 143). The DLP lost one-half of its 10 seats, while the newly founded CKP took three seats. This time right-wing support was split four ways. The GNP secured 6.4m. votes (37.4%), thus attracting 5m. fewer than Lee Myung-Bak's tally of 11.5m. at the presidential election of December 2007 and giving the party 153 Assembly seats. Lee Hoi-Chang's new Liberty Forward Party (LFP) won 18 seats, nearly all in the Chungcheong region. Reflecting continued discord in the GNP, a Pro-Park Coalition (PPC) of legislators loyal to Park Geun-Hye but deselected by the GNP, won 2.3m. votes and 14 seats. With most of the 25 independents elected also being supporters of Park, she commanded some 54 legislators in the new Assembly; this left the GNP little choice but to readmit in July those it had lately expelled, raising its representation to at least 172 seats.

By mid-2008 the new Government was in difficulty. From early May protests against a decision to allow imports of US beef, largely banned for almost five years since a case of 'mad cow disease', escalated by late June into what became almost nightly and sometimes violent confrontations, which paralysed downtown Seoul. Voters were apparently finding Lee's 'CEO style'—viewed as a virtue only months previously—autocratic, as shown in his grandiose plan to build a nationwide canal network, criticized by most experts as impracticable for so mountainous a land. These protests placed Lee on the defensive; his poll ratings declined to below 20%, and neither two televised apologies in May and June, nor the dismissal of the ministers responsible for agriculture, health and education in early July (most of his Blue House secretariat also resigned), assuaged public opinion. Critics felt that Kang Man-Soo, the Minister of Strategy and Finance, should also have been replaced for his vain attempts to maintain the weakness of the won in order to help exporters and boost growth, the effect of which was to exacerbate inflation as import costs rose; however, in the event a vice-minister took responsibility for the policy failure. The UDP, re-emerging yet again as the Democratic Party (DP), took advantage of the issue of beef imports; the new Assembly, elected in April, did not begin normal working until 19 August, when the parties finally agreed on apportioning committee chairmanships.

On 15 August 2008, the 60th anniversary of the Republic, Lee Myung-Bak sought to revitalize his presidency, promising a 'green and unified' Korea. This represented a new emphasis; hitherto he had focused on economic growth, rashly promising to raise this to 7% annually despite rapidly worsening external conditions. On the issue of unification, relations with North Korea had markedly worsened in recent months. Meanwhile, a strike by truck drivers in June caused trade losses of more than US $6,000m., raising fears that other militant unions might seek to take advantage of the Government's unpopularity. Buddhists (still a nominal majority in South Korea) also demonstrated, complaining that the new Government was pro-Christian (Lee being a devout Presbyterian) and anti-Buddhist.

Furthermore, corporate governance concerns finally overwhelmed South Korea's largest business group. After a series of forcible searches of Samsung offices, the group's Chairman, Lee Kun-Hee, and others were charged with various financial offences; Lee resigned in April 2008. In July he was fined US $109m. and given a suspended three-year prison sentence for tax evasion, but acquitted of other charges. Despite having stated at the time that he took full responsibility, Lee appealed against his sentence, as did the prosecution, who wanted a heavier sentence. (In August 2009, Lee received another three-year suspended sentence and a fine of $89m. in a separate protracted case, for an illicit transfer of bonds at below market price to his son Lee Jae-Yong in 1999; despite these two convictions and his notional retirement, Lee was still considered to hold ultimate power in South Korea's biggest business, and to be preparing Jae-Yong to take charge of Samsung in due course.)

Relations between the parties remained poor: by the end of November 2008, of 2,787 bills submitted to the new National Assembly, just nine had been approved. Those still languishing included government plans to reduce real estate, income, corporate and inheritance taxes, as well as to expand the provision of basic social security and penalize the posting of malicious gossip online. (The last was a major local issue, blamed for recent suicides.)

Not for the first time, the annual budget missed its constitutional deadline of 2 December. On 11 December 2008 the DLP physically prevented the Assembly's Legislative Committee from deliberating the budget. A week later DP lawmakers used sledgehammers to force their way into a barricaded committee room; the GNP responded with fire extinguishers. A further scuffle in early January 2009 left 100 with minor injuries. With the usual end-of-year haste to ensure legality and avoid complete gridlock, on the last day of the parliamentary session in mid-January, the National Assembly approved 66 laws; it had thus voted on 910 out of 3,505 bills.

On 19 January 2009 President Lee Myung-Bak carried out his first cabinet reorganization after less than a year in office. Kang Man-Soo was replaced as Minister of Strategy and Finance by Yoon Jeung-Hyun, a former head of the Financial Supervisory Commission (FSC, which had become the Financial Services Commission, with a slightly altered remit). The new FSC Chairman, Chin Dong-Soo, was a former Vice-Minister of Finance with World Bank experience. Yoon Jin-Shik, the new Presidential Secretary for Economic Affairs, had served as Minister of Commerce, Industry and Energy (subsequently renamed Knowledge Economy) in 2002–03 under Roh Moo-Hyun; he went on to be a campaign adviser to Lee Myung-Bak.

These appointments were generally welcomed; others were regarded as more contentious. Officials in the North Korean capital of Pyongyang, and in some quarters of Seoul, deplored the replacement as Minister of Unification of career diplomat Kim Ha-Joong by Hyun In-Taek, an uncompromising academic who had devised President Lee Myung-Bak's firmer policy towards the North. Amid a more extensive reorganization at vice-ministerial level, with 15 changes, dismay greeted the return of two men who had resigned in disgrace as presidential secretaries only months earlier. Lee Joo-Ho became Vice-Minister of Education, Science and Technology, the same portfolio that he had held at the Blue House, while Park Young-Joon was made Vice-Chief of Staff in the Office of the Prime Minister. This led to accusations of patronage, as did the choice of Won Sei-Hoon, another long-standing aide to President Lee, to head the NIS.

In January 2009, two days after his nomination for the post of national police commissioner, the Chief of Police in Seoul, Kim Seok-Ki, authorized the removal of tenants who had seized a building in Yeongsan to protest against being evicted. The military-style assault led to a fire and six fatalities, including one police officer. Compulsory purchase in South Korea had come to be widely regarded as corrupt, with scant redress for those evicted (often from perfectly good buildings, by menacing thugs) to make way for profitable new construction. In February, amid a public outcry, Kim Seok-Ki withdrew his nomination. A protracted dispute over responsibility for the bodies of those who had died in the January fire followed.

Also regarded as over-zealous by many was the arrest in early January 2009 of a financial blogger known only as Minerva, who had attracted a huge online readership with gloomy, but often accurate, predictions. Assumed to be an industry insider, Park Dae-Sung was revealed to be a young unemployed graduate of a minor provincial college with no formal education in economics, financial experience or stockholdings. Charged with spreading false information, he was found not guilty by a Seoul court in April.

In March 2009 'leaked' e-mails from late 2008 showed Shin Young-Chul, then head of the Seoul Central District Court, exerting pressure on subordinates to convict those charged over the protests against beef imports earlier in the year. Shin had since been promoted to the Supreme Court, whose ethics committee censured him in April 2009. This was unprecedented; many felt that he should resign, but he did not do so. Meanwhile, after a television documentary was accused of encouraging the beef protests by distorting scientific information, its producer was arrested on charges of defaming government officials, leading to fears that press freedom was being threatened.

On 29 April 2009 voters in five by-elections rebuffed both main parties. The GNP won no seats, the DP only one: in Incheon, on a turn-out of 29.6%. The socialist New Progressive Party (NPP), which in 2008 had split from the DLP, deeming it too forbearing on the issue of North Korea, gained its first seat in the National Assembly in the industrial city of Ulsan, the location of Hyundai's car-manufacturing and ship-building operations. Elsewhere, independent candidates, of a sort, triumphed. Chung Dong-Young, the unsuccessful centre-left presidential candidate in 2007, was denied the DP nomination in his home town of Jeonju by factional disputes. He therefore stood as an independent candidate and won 72% of the votes cast. His ally Shin Kun, a former head of the NIS, also won a seat in Jeonju; both stated that they would seek to rejoin the DP. The GNP fared similarly in Gyeongju: losing to a former general, Chung Soo-Sung, who was close to Park Geun-Hye. This result highlighted again Lee Myung-Bak's failure to reach an accommodation with his powerful rival.

North Korea's nuclear test on 25 May 2009 (see the chapter on the Democratic People's Republic of Korea) overshadowed the suicide two days previously of former President Roh Moo-Hyun. Roh's image as a scourge of corruption had been tarnished by his admission in early April that, for the purpose of settling a debt, his wife had accepted money from Park Yeon-Cha, a businessman and formerly his main financial supporter, who was now indicted for bribery. At the end of April Roh had been questioned by prosecutors, amid press reports that he had received US $6m. from Park, some of it in cash at the Blue House. With indictment thought to be imminent, Roh jumped from a cliff near his rural home. His death jolted society, reinforcing political antagonisms: opinion polls showed that a majority of the public believed that the investigation into Roh's affairs was politically motivated. The Prosecutor-General, Lim Chae-Jin, resigned in early June, conceding that his office was subject to 'outside pressure'.

The man first nominated to succeed Lim, Chun Sung-Gwan, withdrew in July 2009 after denying links to a businessman who, it emerged, had funded his golfing and shopping trips abroad. The next nominee, Kim Joon-Gyu, admitted to having registered false addresses in the past in order that his children could attend élite schools in Seoul. Despite further pleading guilty to tax evasion and to having registered a lower price for a house sale than the sum he actually received, Kim was approved by the National Assembly's Legislation and Judiciary Committee. He began work in August, enjoined by President Lee to show no tolerance of corruption among public servants. In June 2010 Kim apologized to the nation after a special investigating committee concluded that allegations made by an imprisoned construction company owner named Jeong were true. Jeong had claimed in April 2010 that for 25 years Kim had bribed prosecutors in his native south-east, offering entertainment including the services of prostitutes, as well as money.

In July 2009 the GNP unilaterally forced through the National Assembly the passage of three bills allowing print media to own broadcasters, amid further scuffles. The Government defended the legislation as an overdue restructuring; the opposition claimed that it would produce conservative monopolies.

As a recovery in the economy assuaged fears of another summer of protest, in May 2009 a major fracas in the city of Daejeon, where a demonstration by 7,000 striking truckers had led to 457 arrests, 154 injuries and damage to 99 police buses, was not in the event a harbinger of wider or prolonged unrest. A truckers' strike called in June had scant support and was swiftly settled. In August, however, police stormed Ssangyong Motor's factory in Pyeongtaek, ending a two-month occupation by dismissed workers. This followed pitched battles with strikers, who set vehicles alight while police helicopters dropped tear gas on the plant. A settlement was agreed and production resumed. Police arrested 64 of the occupiers, the largest number arraigned on public security charges for 12 years. Despite fears that this episode, which caused losses of US $250m., would prove the *coup de grâce* for the ailing carmaker (which has been transferred to creditors, after its Chinese owner gave up on South Korean intransigence), a year later its sale attracted six bidders; in August 2010 the Indian firm Mahindra was named as preferred buyer.

In the second such loss within three months, former President Kim Dae-Jung died of pneumonia in August 2009. Most Koreans now credited him for his long fight for democracy and skilful restructuring after the 1997/98 financial crisis. However, his 'sunshine' policy towards North Korea remained controversial: appeasement to some, to others a bold opening and more forward-looking than the subsequent more rigid stance.

In a major reorganization of the State Council in September 2009, President Lee Myung-Bak announced the nomination of Professor Chung Un-Chan, a progressive economist and former president of Seoul National University, as Prime Minister. This was a surprising choice: in 2007 Chung had been courted by the DP's predecesssor as a potential presidential candidate of the centre-left. Other nominees included Gen. Kim Tae-Young, hitherto Chairman of the Joint Chiefs of Staff, as Minister of National Defence; Lee Kwi-Nam as Minister of Justice; Choi Kyung-Hwan as Minister of Knowledge Economy; Yim Tae-Hee, as Minister of Labour; and Paik Hee-Young as Minister of Gender Equality. Joo Ho-Young was nominated for the post of Minister for Special Affairs, a new portfolio that was to carry responsibility for improving co-operation among political parties. All took office on 29 September, duly confirmed by the National Assembly. Among the new cabinet members, Yim was a long-time aide of Lee, while Choi was close to his rival Park Geun-Hye; his appointment was thus seen as a gesture to placate her.

In late October 2009 five by-elections were held concurrently, all the vacancies having arisen because sitting members had been debarred after being convicted for electoral violations. In contrast to the April elections, the two-party pattern reasserted itself: the DP won three seats and the GNP took two. The ruling party won in the north-east (Gangwon province) and south-east (Gyeongsang), both areas of traditionally strong support, while the DP took two seats in Gyeonggi and one in Chungcheong in the centre of the country. Lacking fixed allegiances, Gyeonggi and Chungcheong (like Seoul) often provided good indications of the public mood; therefore, this result appeared to rebuff President Lee.

In September 2009 Hyundai Motor's famously combative trade union narrowly elected its first moderate leader in 15 years. However, prior to this the Korean Government Employees' Union (KGEU), a newly merged entity with 110,000 members, voted to join the radical KCTU. By law civil servants were not permitted to engage in politics; KGEU's co-chairman Sohn Young-Tae was arrested in October. This uncompromising stance alienated KCTU's moderate rival, the Federation of Korean Trade Unions (FKTU), which had initially supported

Lee Myung-Bak. Meanwhile, the FKTU 'declared war' on the Government, accusing it of intransigence on several vexed issues, including firms paying union officials' salaries (a practice that was shortly to be banned) and multiple unions in a workplace (soon to be allowed). However, talk of a general strike came to nothing, except for an eight-day walk-out by railway workers (their longest ever), in protest at reductions in jobs and wages as part of a restructuring programme. From late November this reduced freight traffic to one-third of its normal level, especially when truckers joined the protest. Passenger services were also disrupted, rendering the strikers unpopular. Estimating its total losses at 20,000m. won (US $17m.), Korail stated that it would discipline the strike leaders and seek compensation. Kim Ki-Tae, head of the Korean Rail Workers' Union, was taken into custody in mid-December, accused of leading an illegal strike.

The National Assembly approved the 2010 budget on 31 December 2009, just hours before the start of the new fiscal year. This was the seventh consecutive year that the official deadline of 2 December had been missed. Like several other bills, the budget legislation was unilaterally forced through the legislature by the GNP. Having staged a sit-in since mid-December, DP members tried to barricade the Speaker's podium. Such tactics were not only regarded as unseemly, but also prevented serious scrutiny and debate of plans to spend in excess of US $250,000m. of public funds.

Moreover, the obstructors were not themselves united. In mid-January 2010 about 4,000 supporters of the late Roh Moo-Hyun met in Seoul to create the People's Participation Party (PPP). Lee Jae-Joung, a former Minister of Unification, was elected as its leader. Rhyu Si-Min, an outspoken former Minister of Health and Welfare under Roh, was another leading figure. The DP deplored the formation of the new group, which it denounced as an 'exact duplicate' of itself that would divide liberal forces. However, the parliamentary DP maintained its unity, and none of its elected legislators joined the PPP.

Major controversy arose from Roh's plan to build what was originally intended to be a new capital, later scaled down to an administrative city, at Yeongi-Gongju, 150 km south of Seoul. In January 2010 Prime Minister Chung, himself from this region, announced that, rather than transferring one-half of government functions to the new site of Sejong City, which was already under construction at a cost of US $15,000m., this site would now be 'an economic hub for science and education'. This change of role, which many observers found sensible, was vociferously opposed not only by the DP and the LFP (the latter largely based in the Chungcheong region, the location of Sejong) but also by Park Geun-Hye's faction of the GNP; thus, the GNP lacked a majority to secure parliamentary approval for the revised legislation.

Controversy continued over politics and the judiciary. In January 2010 three separate verdicts acquitted opponents of the Government: the DLP's Kang Ki-Kab, who had overturned items of furniture in the National Assembly; four left-wing teachers who had led anti-Government protests; and five television producers, found not guilty of defaming officials in a programme blamed for inciting protests against US beef imports in 2008. This triple set-back incensed prosecutors, the Korean Bar Association and the GNP, which criticized the Chief Justice, Lee Yong-Hoon, for tolerating left-leaning judges. Members of far-right groups, who had been picketing Lee's home, pelted his car with eggs as he left for work. To his credit, Prime Minister Chung criticized the GNP's campaign as excessive and a violation of the principle of the separation of powers.

In an unexpected reverse, in March 2010 the Catholic Bishops' Conference of Korea criticized the Four Major Rivers Restoration Project (FMRRP), citing serious environmental concerns. Costing US $19,000m., the FMRRP represented South Korea's largest-ever land development initiative and the Lee administration's biggest project: 3,200 km of the Han, Nakdong, Yeongsan and Geum rivers were to be dredged, dammed and given new banks. The professed aims include flood control, better water quality and recreational access. Despite denials, the FMRRP was seen as a revision of Lee Myung-Bak's controversial earlier plan to build a nation-wide canal network, which he had been forced to abandon. The financial crisis of late 2008, however, rendered major public works defensible as stimulus measures. Critics charged that the project had been inappropriately implemented, with undue haste and without proper consultation or studies of its environmental impact. Also in March 2010 a separate dispute (not the first) arose with Buddhists, when a leading monk and critic of the Government, Ven. Myeongjin, claimed that a government plot had led to his removal as head monk at Bongeun temple in the affluent Gangnam district of southern Seoul.

In April 2010 a Seoul court acquitted former Prime Minister Han Myeong-Sook of a charge of taking a US $50,000 bribe. From the outset this charge against an upright Christian lady had seemed implausible. The chief prosecution witness, Kwak Young-Wook, a convicted former CEO of Korea Express (a logistics company), twice changed his evidence, thus jeopardizing the case. Undeterred, in July prosecutors again indicted Han on a separate bribery charge, this time in relation to a sum of more than $800,000. As before, she refused a summons to be questioned, claiming that the charge was politically motivated.

The sinking of the corvette *Cheonan* on 26 March 2010 (see Part One, The Korean Peninsula: Conflict and Dialogue) subsequently dominated domestic politics. South Korea's initial position of restraint changed sharply in late May, after an international team of experts implicated North Korea in the incident. A report by the Board of Audit and Inspection found grave flaws in the armed forces' initial reaction and recommended reprimands and courts martial. In mid-June the Chairman of the Joint Chiefs of Staff, Lee Sang-Eui, tendered his resignation.

The net effect was to weaken President Lee, as demonstrated by the results of the four-yearly local elections held on 2 June 2010. Contrary to predictions that a 'North wind' would sway voters towards the right (as in the past) the GNP lost six of the 12 important gubernatorial and mayoral posts that it had won at the last elections in 2006, retaining six. The DP won seven, the LFP one and independents two. As ever, regional loyalties were evident. The DP easily retained its south-western strongholds, North and South Jeolla provinces and Gwangju city, while the GNP held most, but not all, of its equivalent heartland in the south-east: North Gyeongsang province and the cities of Busan, Daegu and Ulsan. The minor right-wing LFP won Daejeon, the main city in the central Chungcheong region. The island of Jeju re-elected a former governor on an independent platform.

Other results were unexpected. The DP defeated the locally based LFP to win both North and South Chungcheong, seen as a 'swing' area and indicative of national trends. It also won for the first time the normally conservative Gangwon province in the north-east (a rural and mountainous area bordering North Korea). The DP gained Incheon city, the port for Seoul, and very nearly took the capital too. The GNP held Gyeonggi province, but in a major upset it lost South Gyeongsang in the south-east to Kim Doo-Kwan, a close ally of the late President Roh Moo-Hyun. Although Kim stood as an independent candidiate, he was expected to support the DP on most matters.

In Seoul Oh Se-Hoon, a dynamic mayor with presidential ambitions, who had expected to win an easy victory, won by only a narrow margin against the DP's recently acquitted Han Myeong-Sook, who campaigned as the peace candidate; they polled 47.4% and 46.8% of the vote, respectively. At other levels the capital's voters changed sides, giving control of Seoul city council to the DP, which took 79 of the capital's 106 seats. In contrast to 2006, when the GNP had secured all Seoul's district headships, this time 21 of the 25 went to the DP. Nation-wide the outcome was more even than that witnessed in Seoul, but the change was none the less striking. The DP won 92 out of 228 district headships, and the GNP 82. Independents took 36, the LFP 13 and the DLP three; two minor opposition parties secured one each.

Furthermore, Seoul and the surrounding Gyeonggi province, despite each re-electing a GNP mayor or governor, at the same time voted for 'progressive' education superintendents, who immediately attempted to thwart central government policy across a wide range of issues: they opposed tests for students and teachers, the establishment of autonomous high schools (seen as unfairly benefiting the rich), the punishment of teachers for taking part in political activity, and (most radically) corporal punishment; they also advocated the extension of the provision of free school meals to all. In a further setback to the Government, in mid-June 2010 a Seoul court sentenced the capital's first-ever elected education chief to four years' imprisonment for taking bribes. The elderly Kong Jeong-Taek had been a close ally of President Lee. Moreover, while in office Kong had been accused of exerting pressure on schools to reject left-wing textbooks, which was yet another area of conflict.

The GNP's poor showing in Chungcheong forced Lee to concede a free vote on the issue of the development of Sejong City. At the end of June 2010 GNP legislators who supported Park Geun-Hye joined the opposition to defeat the revised plan, by 164 votes to 105, thus confirming the city's original designation as an administrative city, despite doubts as to the wisdom of splitting government between two sites and civil servants' willingness to relocate there.

The electoral rebuff also prompted personnel changes. The GNP's leadership resigned, and at its convention in mid-July 2010 the party chose as its new Chairman Ahn Sang-Soo, a former parliamentary floor leader who was close to Lee Myung-Bak. Lee's allies won four out of five positions on the party's Supreme Council, with only one post going to a supporter of Park Geun-Hye. Eight legislators from the Future Hope Alliance (formerly the PPC, comprising supporters of Park) rejoined the GNP. Meanwhile, President Lee reorganized his secretariat, bringing his close ally Yim Tae-Hee from the Ministry of Labour into the Blue House as Chief of Staff. A week later Lee appointed new senior presidential secretaries for political affairs, public affairs and social integration, as well as creating a new post of senior secretary for policy co-ordination.

Two troubling matters arose in July 2010. First, five police officers in Seoul were indicted for torturing suspects allegedly to obtain confessions. The press suggested that this was common practice. Separately, in an unprecedented operation prosecutors searched the Office of the Prime Minister in connection with allegations that its public ethics division (the remit of which encompassed civil servants) had illegally pursued a private citizen who had uploaded onto the internet a video mocking the President. The alleged victim, Kim Jong-Ik, claimed that he had lost his job as a result of surveillance and harassment. Lee In-Kyu, the official in the Office of the Prime Minister accused of directing this action, belonged to the Yeongpo Club: a clique of public servants from the same part of the south-east as President Lee, whom they supported. In what was swiftly dubbed 'Yeongpogate', even the conservative daily *JoongAng Ilbo* charged that the ethics division of the Office of the Prime Minister was being 'ridiculed as the personal police of the presidential office', deeming the affair 'a shameful reminder' of past abuses by authoritarian regimes. A GNP legislator then alleged that his wife had also been similarly mistreated by the Office of the Prime Minister. Lee In-Kyu was subsequently arrested and was indicted in August.

Having rejected the ruling party in June 2010, the electorate re-embraced it in eight by-elections on 27 July. On a low turnout (34%, compared with more than 54% in June) the GNP won five seats, having held only one prior to the polls. The DP took three: one in the south-west and two in Gangwon in the north-east. Two of the GNP victories were in Chungcheong, suggesting that this region had forgiven Lee Myung-Bak. While it was hard to interpret two such contrasting electoral outcomes in successive months, the net result was that the GNP occupied 181 of the National Assembly's 299 seats: more than twice as many as the DP's 87. The LFP held 16 seats, the DLP and another left-wing party six, with nine independents and various others.

A cabinet reorganization followed on 7 August 2010. Defeated over the Sejong City project, Prime Minister Chung Un-Chan had tendered his resignation in June, but it was not immediately accepted. His nominated successor was Kim Tae-Ho, a former governor of South Gyeongsang and regarded as a potential contender for the presidency in 2012. Park Geun-Hye's supporters saw this as a bid to thwart her, and were unassuaged by the choice of one of them, Yoo Jeong-Bok, as the new Minister of Agriculture. Elsewhere three vice-ministers—Lee Ju-Ho, Shin Jae-Min and Lee Jae-Hoon—were promoted as Ministers of Education, Science and Technology, of Culture, Sports and Tourism, and of Knowledge Economy, respectively. Chin Soo-Hee, of the GNP, was named Minister of Health, Welfare and Family Affairs. The President's closest aide, Lee Jae-Oh, was appointed Minister for Special Affairs (Minister without Portfolio) just days after being returned to the National Assembly in a by-election. On 29 August 2010, however, following rigorous questioning during his confirmation hearing, Prime Minister-designate Kim relinquished his nomination, owing to suggestions of financial impropriety in his relationship with a convicted businessman (see above). Two other cabinet nominees, Lee Jae-Hoon and Shin Jae-Min also withdrew after allegations of unethical conduct emerged. Their predecessors ultimately remained in post. President Lee's next nominee for the post of Prime Minister was a native of South Jeolla, Kim Hwang-Sik, head of the Board of Audit and Inspection and a former justice of the Supreme Court, who was approved by the National Assembly on 1 October.

However, prior to Kim's confirmation as premier, yet another senior cabinet member was forced to leave office. On 4 September 2010 the Minister of Foreign Affairs and Trade, Yu Myung-Hwan, resigned when it transpired that he had secured a senior post in his ministry for his daughter. Embarrassing at any time, this was all the worse coming just two months before South Korea was due to host the summit meeting of the Group of 20 (G20) leading industrialized and developing nations in mid-November; Yu had played a leading role in the preparations. Over a month passed before he was replaced by Kim Sung-Hwan, a career diplomat and latterly senior presidential secretary for security and foreign affairs. Kim was not spared a parliamentary cross-examination, which focused, *inter alia*, on how, like many élite figures, he had managed to avoid conscription for national service: in his case on account of a jaw condition.

In early October 2010 the DP chose a new leader. In a close election, Sohn Hak-Kyu defeated Chung Dong-Young, the centre-left's unsuccessful presidential candidate in 2007, and the outgoing party Chairman, Chung Sye-Kyun, who had been expected to retain the post. A former dissident persecuted in the era of dictatorship, then a professor of politics, Sohn surprised many by initially joining the GNP. As governor of Gyeonggi during 2002–06, he successfully attracted foreign investment. Crossing the floor in 2007, he remained a moderate centrist moderate; his presidential ambitions were well known.

North Korea's second attack of 2010, its shelling of Yeonpyeong island on 23 November (see Part One, The Korean Peninsula: Conflict and Dialogue) inevitably had domestic political repercussions in the South. As with the sinking of the *Cheonan* in March, Lee Myung-Bak's prudent failure to retaliate militarily left him looking weak. The Minister of National Defence, Kim Tae-Young, who had offered his resignation in May, found it summarily accepted on 25 November. There was some confusion as to his successor. Initial media reports named Lee Hee-Won, the President's security adviser, but the eventual choice was Kim Kwan-Jin, a former Chairman of the Joint Chiefs of Staff from the south-western Jeolla region; it was suggested that this origin counted in his favour, as President Lee was often accused of favouring his own region, the south-east. Swiftly confirmed in office, Kim warned in very strong terms that the South would 'surely' retaliate, using aircraft, if the North were to attack a third time. That chimed with the public mood, which had turned significantly against North Korea after this second act of aggression, there being no ambiguity or doubt whatsoever, unlike the *Cheonan* incident.

With the election still two years away, the next presidential race in effect began on 27 December 2010, when Park Geun-Hye launched her own 'think tank', the National Future Institute, with 78 experts to advise her in 15 fields. Although consistently far ahead in opinion polls, Park had never held office.

Four days later her nemesis, President Lee, belatedly finished the ill-conceived government reorganization begun in August. His new nominee as Minister of Knowledge Economy, Choi Joong-Kyung, was severely questioned about his business affairs and professional competence by a parliamentary committee, chaired by the DP, which refused formally to confirm him; but its role was only advisory and President Lee appointed him regardless. In contrast, the new Minister of Culture, Sports and Tourism, Choung Byoung-Gug—a GNP legislator who had led recent changes in media ownership rules—received more lenient treatment from the same parliamentary committee, which he had hitherto chaired. Further cabinet-level appointees included Kim Seok-Dong, a former vice-Minister of Finance, as Chairman of the FSC, while Kim Dong-Soo, head of the state-owned Export-Import Bank of Korea, became Chairman of the FTC. Kim Young-Ran, the first-ever female Supreme Court justice, was appointed to head the Anti-Corruption and Civil Rights Commission. President Lee also named no fewer than 10 new senior Blue House staff. Ahn Kwang-Chan, a former general, filled a newly created post of senior presidential secretary for national crisis management, tasked with responding to future emergencies. Two new senior presidential secretaries were, as often, academics: Kim Young-Ho (on North Korea), and Lee Jong-Hwa (international economic policy). Two former aides returned, with Park Heong-Joon, formerly senior secretary for political affairs, becoming special adviser for social affairs, and Lee Dong-Kwan, once senior secretary for public affairs, named as special adviser for media policy. Accusing the President of cronyism, the DP described Lee Dong-Kwan as 'dregs not worth recycling'.

Kim Hwang-Sik's elevation to the premiership had left the chairmanship of the Board of Audit and Inspection vacant since September 2010. Here, the President's unerring instinct for unfortunate choices struck again. The Board must be rigorously independent, its job being to scrutinize the rest of government. To nominate Chung Tong-Ki was thus crass. A former prosecutor, Chung was a known ally of Lee Myung-Bak, serving both in his transition team and as a senior presidential secretary. The DP immediately launched a tirade of criticism of Chung, with a raft of accusations, and in a rare display of insubordination the ruling party followed suit; on 10 January 2011 the GNP Chairman, Ahn Sang-Soo, deemed him unfit to lead the Board of Audit and Inspection. Chung withdrew two days later, bitterly denouncing 'false claims' against him. The Blue House was furious too, but this incipient rift between party and a weakening President was likely to widen as the year progressed.

Meanwhile, at the end of December 2010 four leading daily newspapers— *Chosun Ilbo*, *Dong-A Ilbo*, *JoongAng Ilbo* and *Maeil Business News*—as well as the semi-official Yonhap News Agency, were allowed to commence cable television services. This ended a long-standing policy of maintaining barriers between the ownership of print and broadcast media, but did not end fierce debate about the motives or merits of the change. Proponents saw such mergers as both functionally and financially necessary in a modern multi-media age, while critics—mainly on the left, but now also including rival bidders who had failed to win licences—claimed that this was a plot by Lee Myung-Bak to render the media more right-wing and pliant. The print press in Seoul tended towards conservatism, whereas broadcasters were, or at least had been, more liberal.

In parliamentary politics, on 18 February 2011 the two main parties finally agreed to open an extraordinary session of the National Assembly, after a two-month impasse. They then made up for lost time, adopting 37 pending bills and electing a new chairman of the parliamentary committee for culture, sports and tourism, as well as a new member of the Human Rights Commission, itself rent by political feuding. They also established five special committees, each covering a different topic, including inter-Korean relations, political reform and domestic social issues.

In mid-February 2011 the quality of the President's judgement, and of his circle, was yet again thrown in question when his close ally, Chang Soo-Man, resigned as head of the Defense Acquisition Program Administration. A former Vice-Minister of National Defence and career financial official, Chang had been tasked with modernizing military procurement systems. His sudden departure was related to two separate scandals. The first—which had also led to the arrest in late January of a former national Chief of Police, Kang Hee-Rak, on suspicion of taking some US $170,000 in bribes—involved franchises for canteens on construction sites. In the second, Chang was questioned by prosecutors over whether he had received gift certificates from Daewoo Engineering and Construction. In 2010 the company had won a $43m. contract to relocate the Special Warfare Command and an airborne unit; Chang was Vice-Minister of National Defence at the time.

The President also came under criticism from an unexpected quarter. Conservative Protestants, his core supporters, opposed a bill—intended to attract Middle Eastern investors—that would have given the same tax benefits to Islamic bonds (*sukuk*) as those afforded to other types of bond. Hostility by some GNP legislators, who claimed that this measure could be used to finance terrorism, forced the ruling party to suspend the bill until after by-elections due in April 2011. David Yonggi Cho, founder of Yoido Full Gospel Church, the world's largest single congregation, warned the Minister of Strategy and Finance, Yoon Jeung-Hyun, in February to expect 'a life-or-death fight'. A bid to appease such sentiments rebounded adversely. In early March President Lee, a Presbyterian, was pictured kneeling at a Protestant prayer breakfast: a gesture widely criticized as both inappropriate and partisan.

Meanwhile, former premier Chung Un-Chan was also in trouble. Now chairing the Commission on Shared Growth for Large and Small Companies (a presidential initiative), in February 2011 he suggested that large firms should share profits with their small sub-contractors. That prompted a rare outburst in March from Korea's richest and most powerful tycoon, Lee Kun-Hee of Samsung, who described it as a communist idea. Chung offered to resign, but the Blue House defended him. Later in the year Samsung and other *chaebol* did offer to assist small and medium-sized enterprises. Aside from economic advantages or disadvantages, the political thrust here was to try to counter the widespread view that Lee and the GNP stood for big business but were indifferent to the plight of smaller firms and and the ordinary citizen.

Four by-elections held on 27 April 2011 went badly for the ruling party, although all but one of the results were close. Suncheon, in South Jeolla province, was an opposition stronghold; the GNP did not even present a candidate. The three left-of-centre parties had made a pact not to stand against each other in these by-elections. In Suncheon, 36% of the vote sufficed for Kim Sun-Dong of the hard-left DLP easily to defeat six independents, five of whom had recently abandoned the DP and were supported by some DP legislators, thus demonstrating the difficulty of forging unity on the left.

The crucial result was in Bundang, just south of Seoul, hitherto always conservative. A high turn-out resulted in a narrow victory for the DP's leader, Sohn Hak-Kyu, over a former head of the GNP, Kang Jae-Sup, thus boosting the moderate Sohn's bid for his fractious party's presidential nomination in 2012. A further vacancy was not for the National Assembly but to administer Gangwon province in the north-east, replacing a DP governor who had been dismissed for electoral violations. Here, the two main parties each nominated former heads of the broadcaster MBC. In an unseemly contest, the DP's Choi Moon-Soon narrowly defeated his successor at MBC, Ohm Ki-Young. Gangwon included Pyeongchang, which in July 2011 was chosen, at its third attempt, to host the 2018 Winter Olympic Games.

The ruling party's sole consolation came in Gimhae-B, in South Gyeongsang, its regional heartland in the south-east, where the province's former governor, Kim Tae-Ho, defeated Lee Bong-Soo of the PPP, again by a very close margin. Demonstrating the salience of personal as well as regional ties, the PPP was a breakaway group of supporters of late President Roh Moo-Hyun, who hailed from Gimhae. Kim's return to politics did not, notably, involve addressing the issues and doubts that had forced his withdrawal as a prime ministerial nominee in 2010. It sufficed, apparently, to maintain a low profile for a few months in China, and then re-emerge triumphantly as if nothing were amiss.

The GNP fared better in local council by-elections also held on 27 April 2011, winning 14 of 28 contests in comparison with the DP's seven. The LFP took three seats, the DLP two, and independent candidates also two. Voter turn-out (including that for local seats) was 39.4%, higher than the average of 32.8% recorded in by-elections since 2000. In all four national contests the turn-out exceeded 40%, reaching 49.1% in Bundang.to

In routine penance, the GNP's leaders resigned *en masse* to take responsibility for the electoral defeat, and on 6 May 2011 President Lee reorganized his cabinet. The main casualty was Yoon Jeung-Hyun, the Minister of Strategy and Finance, highly regarded by most observers. He was replaced by Bahk Jae-Wan, previously Minister of Employment and Labour and an associate of the President. Bahk, in turn, was replaced by Lee Chae-Pil, hitherto Vice-Minister of Employment and Labour and, like the other new appointees, a long-serving technocrat rather than a politician. Also promoted from vice-minister to minister were Kwon Do-Yup at the Ministry of Land, Transport and Maritime Affairs and Suh Kyu-Yong at the Ministry of Food, Agriculture, Forestry and Fisheries, the latter having retired as vice-minister in 2010, after 30 years of service in that ministry. The new Minister of Environment was Yoo Young-Sook, a senior researcher at Korea Institute of Science and Technology and only the third woman in the cabinet. All the nominees survived their non-binding confirmation hearings at the National Assembly, and were formally in office by the end of May. Contrary to most predictions, the uncompromising Minister of Unification, Hyun In-Taek, retained his post, despite inter-Korean relations being at their worst for many years. An editorial writer at the centre-right *JoongAng Ilbo* subsequently claimed credit for this. Kim Jin wrote that he and other 'conservative North Korea experts' had dined with presidential advisers a few days before the reorganization, at which point Hyun was expected to be replaced by Yu Woo-Ik, South Korea's ambassador to China. However, Kim and his colleagues argued against this, lest it be interpreted by North Korea as a sign that Lee Myung-Bak was softening his stance.

Also on 6 May 2011, after the DP's ratings overtook those of the GNP for the first time in two years in an opinion poll, the ruling party's legislators confounded expectations and the GNP élite by electing two outsiders, Hwang Woo-Yea and Lee Ju-Young, as parliamentary floor leader and chief policy maker, respectively. So confident was the GNP old guard, itself factionalized, of maintaining control of the party that it had fielded two sets of candidates, loyal, respectively, to the President's elder brother, Lee Sang-Deuk, and his right-hand man, Minister for Special Affairs Lee Jae-Oh. The faction loyal to President Lee's main rival, Park Geun-Hye, put forward no candidates, but was pleased by the backbenchers' triumph, which was regarded as a set-back to Lee and a clarion call for new policies, lest voters reject the GNP as favouring the wealthy and being unmindful of their concerns. Hwang immediately began to criticize existing policies that he regarded as vote-losers, such as tax reductions for the rich, while advocating more welfare spending: an important factor in the DP's appeal. This caused some irritation in the Blue House, but electoral self-interest was liable to result in the GNP moving further in a centrist, or even populist, direction as the elections drew nearer.

Meanwhile, a new corruption scandal emerged. At the beginning of May 2011 the Chairman, CEO and other officials of Busan Savings Bank (BSB)—the largest of several regional savings banks that had been rescued from feared insolvency earlier in the year—were indicted for financial crimes amounting to US $7,000m., including illicit loans of $4,000m. It was alleged that owners and managers had borrowed with impunity from BSB, mis-stated accounts, colluded with financial regulators to avoid exposure and warned some clients to withdraw their funds before the bank was suspended in mid-February. Regulators at the Financial Supervisory Service (FSS) not only failed to prevent irregularities at the Bank, but some were suborned. Yoo Byung-Tae, a former FSS official, was sentenced in July to 18 months' imprisonment for receiving bribes totalling 210m. won. In late May Eun Jin-Soo—a commissioner at the Board of Audit and Inspection until his resignation days earlier and an associate of President Lee, whose elevation to the Board had been criticized as being political—was charged with accepting bribes of 170m. in the case. Several other élite figures were also implicated. Politically, the BSB affair boded ill for the GNP in its south-eastern heartland. Typically, it was the less well-off who had accounts in regional savings banks, often investing all their money. If they lost everything, while the rich were forewarned, this would reinforce an impression of the GNP as being the party of the privileged.

At the beginning of June 2011, after five months of talks, 12 left-wing groups agreed to form a new party by September to 'meet the desires of labourers, farmers, the working class and civic society'. Those involved included the militant KCTU, the allied DLP and the NPP, a breakaway from the DLP. The DLP currently had six legislators and the NPP just one. As in the original DLP–NPP split, North Korea was the main issue of contention; the NPP deemed the DLP and KCTU too uncritical, especially of the North's succession. If the new merger was sustained, it might attract votes from the DP in the 2012 elections, as would the PPP, if it remained separate.

The GNP convened to elect a new Chairman and council members one month later, in early July 2011. Heavy rain was blamed for a low turn-out (25.9%) among the 210,000-strong electoral college. In the same rebellious spirit observed in May, of the seven candidates for the chairmanship, the winner was an outsider: Hong Joon-Pyo, a former prosecutor and four-term legislator with a maverick reputation. Popular with the public for his outspokenness, Hong did not change his style. Later that month he described President Lee as being 'good at everything, including diplomacy, but bad at politics ... [As] a former CEO, he is running the country as if he is running a company . . .it is hard to lead the country high-handedly.' The Blue House's response was notably muted, reflecting Lee's growing weakness, both structural and personal. With just 21 months left to serve and legislative elections barely eight months away, the President was, in a familiar pattern, beginning to be perceived as a liability and a 'lame duck', even by his own party members, who increasingly felt that to distance themselves from him would improve their own electoral prospects..

In June 2011, meanwhile, the GNP (rather than the Government) announced that college tuition fees would be reduced by 30% by 2014. The first phase alone, a 15% decrease in 2012, would cost 2,000,000m. won. This hasty move followed student protests—an annual ritual, but this time extending to the streets in large rallies—against these fees, and a pledge by the DP to halve their level. Average tuition fees had doubled in a decade to US $8,000, the third highest among members of the Organisation for Economic Co-operation and Development (OECD), but scholarships were few. The wider problem was that 80% of school leavers went on to attend colleges, 80% of which were private (some third-rate) and relied on fee income. Many studied the 'wrong' subjects: graduate unemployment was at least 10%. With the young a diminishing cohort, what was needed was a co-ordinated policy to reduce numbers, tailor courses more to economic need and close weak institutions, as well as improve financial support. However, the forthcoming elections raised the risk that instead parties would compete with populist gestures.

South Korea's reputation for labour militancy, often cited as a deterrent to potential investors, was reinforced in late June 2011 by industrial action at Standard Chartered First Bank Korea, the country's sixth largest bank. Unionized employees, constituting about one-half of the total work-force of 6,500, went on indefinite strike against management efforts to introduce performance-related pay. Some large Korean firms had adopted performance-related pay, but in the financial sector pay and promotion were based on seniority. At mid-August the strike was still ongoing, making it the longest ever at a Korean bank. In an even lengthier protest, at the shipbuilder Hanjin, in Busan, a female activist, Kim Jin-Suk, had been occupying a crane since January to protest against redundancies. A 'Bus of Hope' campaign organized in her support brought thousands of demonstrators to Busan, but the third such protest in late July was small, and momentum seemed to be dwindling. Korean car manufacturers, where unions were especially combative, appeared set to avoid strike action in 2011, as in 2010, but only by agreeing to concede large pay increases and bonuses.

The National Assembly reconvened in August 2011 for what was described as an 'undramatic' session. The main parties agreed to vote at the end of the month on less contentious bills already approved in standing committee. They were also due to discuss college tuition fees, BSB and the Hanjin crisis. The FTA with the USA did not feature on the agenda. With regard to BSB, in early August senior prosecutors ignored subpoenas to testify before the National Assembly, claiming that the latter's summons was *ultra vires*. Separately, a long-standing dispute between prosecutors and police over their respective powers of investigation was supposedly resolved in June. However, the former claimed that judicial reform legislation adopted a week later reneged on the agreement by unduly curbing their powers and those of the Minister of Justice. Several senior prosecutors promptly resigned, including the Prosecutor-General, Kim Joon-Kyu, whose term was due to expire in barely a month; his decision was much criticized. He was succeeded by Han Sang-Dae, whom President Lee confirmed in office in mid-August, despite his admission of having used a false address to secure his daughters' enrolment in a better school. Lee also confirmed as the new Minister of Justice, Kwon Jae-Jin, formerly his senior secretary for civil affairs, amid criticism even within the GNP that Kwon was too close to the President to be able to undertake the further judicial reforms widely regarded as necessary.

Overall, as the second half of 2011 progressed, Lee Myung-Bak encountered the familiar predicament of a South Korean President whose term was drawing towards its close. Compounding this structural issue, which was not his fault, with problems of his own making (especially his personnel policy and general style), Lee would struggle to remain relevant, as attention increasingly shifted to the contest to succeed him. In that regard, he confronted a particular dilemma: whether to endorse his foe, Park Geun-Hye, as the GNP's candidate for the next presidential election, due in December 2012; or to risk splitting the party, and thus jeopardizing its electoral prospects, by supporting a rival contender (whose identity was far from clear). More broadly, preparing for the 2012 elections was likely to distract and detract from sound policy, with signs already of a populist 'race to the bottom', as both main parties offered ever more generous welfare pledges with little regard for fiscal implications. Despite this, the GNP might well lose its overall majority in legislative elections of April 2012, although it would probably remain the largest party in the National Assembly. Given the volatility of the electorate, the outcome of the separate presidential election, to be held eight months later, was impossible to predict as of mid-2011.

RELATIONS WITH NORTH KOREA

A full account of North-South relations is given in Part One, The Korean Peninsula: Conflict and Dialogue (see p. 10).

FOREIGN RELATIONS

Following the proclamation of the Republic of Korea in 1948, South Korean foreign policy was influenced by the circumstances of the partition of Korea and by the Cold War (as the protracted period of mutual hostility between the USA and the USSR became known). As the successor to three years of US military government, the Republic of Korea consistently inclined towards the USA to an extent unique in Asia. In the early 21st century this continued to be symbolized by the presence (with nuclear weapons until 1991) of 37,000 US personnel (USFK). South Korea's commitment of troops to the US war effort in Viet Nam in the late 1960s was substantial. The relationship with the USA was strengthened by regular senior-level visits, including a trip to Seoul by President George Bush in January 1992 and a similarly positive visit by his successor, President Bill Clinton, in July 1993. However, this had disadvantages, notably North Korea's propaganda victory in the 1970s, when it achieved its aim of excluding South Korea from the Non-aligned Movement as an alleged 'lackey' of the USA.

Much more significant in the longer term were the effects of successful 'nordpolitik' (see below) and the ending of the Cold War, both of which reflected a reassertion of geopolitics over ideology and led to better relations with South Korea's close neighbours, Russia and the People's Republic of China. However, South Korea's good relations with the USA remained vital, as testified from the 1990s by their close co-operation on the issue of North Korea's suspected nuclear programme.

By contrast, South Korea's other major strategic relationship, that with Japan, was more problematic. Koreans' deep resentment of Japan's harsh colonial rule in the first half of the 20th century was regularly reinforced by allegations of, for example, continued discrimination against the Korean minority in Japan and attempts by the Japanese Government to 'whitewash' the imperialist period. One such issue concerned the so-called 'comfort women': as many as 200,000 mostly Korean young women and girls who were forcibly recruited in the late 1930s and early 1940s for the sexual use of Japanese troops. The problem lay in the Japanese Government's persistent efforts to deny the overwhelming evidence of official complicity, to rule out any question of compensation, and to avoid a full and frank apology. These issues surrounded the visit by the Japanese Prime Minister, Kiichi Miyazawa, to Seoul in January 1992. However, in August 1993 the Japanese Government admitted for the first time that Korean and other Asian women had been forced to serve in Japanese military brothels, and offered full official apologies.

A notable feature of South Korea's foreign policy was its so-called 'nordpolitik', namely the replacement of unqualified anti-communism by a more subtle pursuit of improved relations with China and the USSR. This was highly successful in both its direct and indirect aims: to forge better relations with those powerful neighbours and thereby to exert pressure on their ally, North Korea, to adopt a more accommodating attitude. The crucial turning-point of 'nordpolitik' was the holding of the 1988 Olympic Games in Seoul. Of North Korea's communist allies, only Cuba, Ethiopia and Albania heeded its demand for a boycott, while China, the USSR and the remaining Eastern European countries all participated in the sporting events. In 1989 Hungary, Poland and Yugoslavia established diplomatic relations with the Republic of Korea (prompting strong denunciations by the North Korean Government), a process that became more general with the collapse of communist rule in Eastern Europe in the early 1990s.

The decisive stage was the USSR's full recognition of the Republic of Korea in September 1990, accompanied by close personal relations between Presidents Mikhail Gorbachev and Roh (who met three times within a 10-month period during 1990-91). With the subsequent demise of the USSR, these relations were continued not only with Russia but also with other republics of the Commonwealth of Independent States (CIS). President Boris Yeltsin visited Seoul in November 1992, and gave assurances that Russia no longer supported the North Korean regime. The Presidents of Kazakhstan and Uzbekistan (where both populations include Korean ethnic minorities, deported by Stalin to Central Asia from the Soviet Far East during the 1930s) had already visited South Korea.

With China, the rapprochement was more protracted. Trade developed intermittently from the early 1980s, and a large Chinese team attended the Asian Games, held in Seoul in 1986. From the late 1980s Sino-South Korean trade increased rapidly, and trade offices were opened in Seoul and Beijing in 1991. In the following year there was a further strengthening of links, culminating in the establishment of full diplomatic relations in August (and the consequent severance of relations by Taiwan).

Apart from these fundamental relationships with the above-mentioned four powers, South Korean foreign policy was mainly dictated by two factors: growing economic success (until the economic decline of the late 1990s) and rivalry with North Korea. Sometimes these went in tandem, for instance in ensuring good relations with Western European nations (although there had been some friction on trade issues with the European Union—EU). Elsewhere, they diverged, as in Africa, where the contest for influence led both Koreas to open embassies wherever they could, at considerable expense. As North Korea began to draw back, South Korea extended its network, as former supporters of the North, such as Algeria, Angola and Tanzania, finally granted recognition to South Korea as well.

In December 1992 South Korea restored relations with Viet Nam, severed in 1975. As with China, trade links preceded diplomatic relations, and Hanoi seemingly bore no grudge for the South Korean involvement on the Saigon side during the Viet Nam War. The other Indo-Chinese states appeared less susceptible to South Korean advances, especially Cambodia: Prince Sihanouk was an old friend of Kim Il Sung, who had a palace built for him in Pyongyang.

While President Kim Young-Sam's initial priorities were domestic—like those of Bill Clinton who also took office in early 1993—he subsequently visited all four major powers involved in Korea. Starting with the USA in November 1993, he then travelled to Japan and China in March 1994. He completed his tour of the quartet with a visit to Russia (and also Uzbekistan) in June.

In general, this 'quadrangular diplomacy' (as it was officially called) inevitably revolved around the North Korean nuclear issue in 1993–95. South Korea pursued close policy co-ordination with the USA and Japan on the matter, while with Russia and China it became a question of strengthening what were still very new links. The relationship with China, in particular, expanded rapidly, underpinned by increasing trade.

With regard to Japan, President Kim Young-Sam set himself the task of overcoming the legacy of bitterness dating back to Japan's colonial rule in Korea. Kim developed very cordial relations with Morihiro Hosokawa, whose resignation as Japan's Prime Minister in April 1994 was regretted in Seoul. The visit to South Korea in July of the new Japanese Prime Minister, Tomiichi Murayama, was significant in that his Social Democratic Party had traditionally maintained cordial relations with North Korea, while not recognizing the Republic. In August 1995 South Korea acknowledged a statement made by Murayama on the occasion of the 50th anniversary of the end of the Second World War, in which the Japanese Prime Minister expressed 'deep reflection and sincere apologies' for Japan's colonial aggression.

The crucial relationship with the USA was consolidated by two visits to that country by President Kim Young-Sam in 1995: first in July for the dedication of the (long overdue) Korean War memorial in Washington, and then in October for the UN's 50th anniversary celebrations. Kim also made his first official visit to Europe in March, travelling to six countries: the United Kingdom, France, Germany, Belgium, Denmark and the Czech Republic. The meetings of the Asia-Pacific Economic Cooperation (APEC) forum in November 1994 provided an occasion for Kim to visit Australia and the Philippines, as well as the host nation, Indonesia.

In November 1994 Chinese Premier Li Peng became the most senior leader yet to travel from Beijing to Seoul; a year later this new relationship was confirmed by a state visit by Chinese President Jiang Zemin. Scarcely less significant was the arrival in May 1995 of Gen. Pavel Grachev, the Russian Minister of Defence, accompanied by many of Moscow's élite. Various agreements were concluded, including one concerning the exchange of military intelligence, which was sure to antagonize North Korea.

Relations with Japan were tested in 1996. In addition to South Korean dissatisfaction at Japan's failure to be properly contrite for its past aggression, two more immediate issues dominated. A dispute arose over a group of islets, called Dokdo (in Korean) or Takeshima (in Japanese), long claimed by both countries but newly salient with their adoption of 200-nautical-mile exclusive economic zones; there was also rivalry over staging the football World Cup in 2002, which became so hostile that in June 1996 FIFA, the international football federation, took the unprecedented action of offering it to them both to co-host.

To a lesser extent, relations with the USA were tested too. In May 1996 students demonstrated against the presence of US forces in the country, demanding that the USA accept some responsibility for the Gwangju massacre of 1980 (see above). Further demonstrations followed in August 1996 at Yonsei University, Seoul, in which students were barricaded in the university, demanding reunification with North Korea and the withdrawal of US troops. Following a nine-day siege, riot police stormed the building and 5,715 students were detained. South Korea remained wary of the Clinton Administration's overtures to North Korea. As far as the security of the country was concerned, South Korea chafed alike at US procrastination in revising the Status of Forces Agreement (SOFA) in order to give Korean courts more jurisdiction over errant soldiers, and at restrictions on its own right to develop missiles to counter the threat from North Korea. There was some resentment at pressure from the USA for easier access to the Korean market, the more so since South Korea had accumulated a large trade deficit with the USA. Yet underlying relations remained sound, and were strengthened by Clinton's visit to Seoul in April 1996.

South Korea also extended its foreign policy interests beyond the peninsula and the four major powers. Kim Young-Sam attended the first Asia-Europe Meeting (ASEM) in February 1996 in Bangkok, Thailand, and took the opportunity to visit India and Singapore, where, as in the whole Asian region, South Korea had substantial and expanding business interests. South Korea became the 29th member of OECD in December. Meanwhile, South Korea remained a dutiful supplier of personnel and funds to UN peace-keeping operations around the world.

The once extensive, but now dwindling, list of countries refusing to recognize South Korea decreased further in 1996. The involvement of the North Korean embassy in a forged currency scandal gave the Cambodian Government its chance to overrule King Sihanouk's objections to the recognition of South Korea. Hun Sen, one of Cambodia's then Co-Prime Ministers, visited Seoul in July, and it was agreed to exchange missions. South Korea already had flourishing relations with Viet Nam (despite having fought for the former South Viet Nam) and with Laos.

In September 1996 President Kim Young-Sam visited Central and South America. In Guatemala he held meetings with leaders of the five other Central American countries, who requested increased South Korean investment in their economies. Kim then visited Chile, Argentina, Brazil and Peru, with all of which South Korea maintained good political relations and rapidly expanding commercial links. He omitted to visit Mexico, possibly because Roh Tae-Woo had been there in 1991, but paid a separate visit in June 1997. The Colombian President had earlier visited Seoul.

However, for the most part South Korea's foreign links centred on the quartet of major powers interested in maintaining stability on the peninsula. Relations with the USA remained broadly good, despite differences over how to deal with the North Korean leadership, and the occasional trade dispute. Several senior US officials visited Seoul in early 1997: Vice-President Al Gore and the Speaker of the House of Representatives, Newt Gingrich, as well as the newly appointed Secretaries of State and of Defense, Madeleine Albright and William Cohen. In June Kim Young-Sam briefly met President Clinton, while attending the UN summit meeting on the environment in New York. Relations with Japan were also mostly positive, and included close co-operation over policy towards North Korea. In June and July 1997, however, there was anger in Seoul when Japan detained five South Korean boats for allegedly fishing in Japanese waters.

Among South Korea's newer allies, relations with China were undamaged after the defection of Hwang Jang Yop (see the chapter on the Democratic People's Republic of Korea). Sino-South Korean amity was regularly reinforced when the two Presidents met at APEC sessions, or when their respective Ministers of Foreign Affairs conducted meetings at the Association of Southeast Asian Nations (ASEAN) Regional Forum, whereas North Korea no longer had such ready access to the Chinese leadership. As far as Russia was concerned, the Minister of Foreign Affairs, Yevgenii Primakov, was the most senior of several Russian visitors to South Korea in mid-1997. He announced that a direct line of communication was to be established between the respective leaderships; the post-communist Russia had no such channel to the North Korean administration.

The election of President Kim Dae-Jung in December 1997 signalled no major changes in South Korean external policy, with the important exception of North Korea. The fact that Kim had lived as a political exile in the USA and Japan, and was thus well connected in both Washington and Tokyo, was expected to promote better relations with these two major allies. Thus, in June 1998 President Kim undertook a trip to the USA, where he was fêted as a rare Asian leader wholly in favour of both democracy and free markets. Unlike his prede-

cessor, Kim also shared the Clinton Administration's preference for engagement with North Korea.

President Kim Dae-Jung inherited a slightly more complex relationship with Japan, owing to long-standing animosity over such issues as 'comfort women', fishing rights and the Dokdo/Takeshima islets. In addition, South Koreans shared the rest of Asia's concern at Japan's economic stagnation, while the Asian financial crisis pitted South Korean exports against Japanese. On the other hand, Kim Dae-Jung's connections with Japan, as well as the fact that Prime Minister Kim Jong-Pil was the very man who, in 1965, had negotiated the first post-war formal relations between the two countries, were positive factors. In any case, a visit by Kim Dae-Jung to Tokyo in October 1998 proved a huge success, resulting in greatly improved relations between the two countries and mutual pledges to co-operate fully henceforth in strengthening bilateral economic, security and cultural relations. The Japanese Prime Minister, Keizo Obuchi, publicly apologized for Japan's conduct towards South Korea during its occupation of the peninsula between 1910 and 1945. In the economic arena South Korea agreed to remove a number of restrictions on Japanese imports, while Japan announced that it would commit US $3,000m. in addition to existing financial assistance to its neighbour. A year of vigorous and successful presidential diplomacy ended with a visit to China in November 1998, followed by two regional summits—APEC in Kuala Lumpur, Malaysia, and ASEAN in Hanoi, Viet Nam—and a visit to Seoul by US President Clinton. Kim Dae-Jung's stay in China was as cordial as that in Japan.

In March 1999 Kim Dae-Jung welcomed the Japanese Prime Minister, Keizo Obuchi, to Seoul. His own first journey of the year was in May, to Russia and Mongolia. Relations with Russia had been damaged in mid-1998 by the expulsion of a South Korean diplomat for spying, an affair that eventually led to the resignation of South Korea's Minister of Foreign Affairs. A more protracted issue was that of Russia's debt of US $1,700m., dating from loans extended by Roh Tae-Woo in 1990 as a reward for diplomatic relations. South Korea was reluctant to accept Russia's offer to repay its debt in military equipment, preferably submarines. More widely, Russia resented being excluded from multilateral fora on the peninsula, be it the four-party talks or the Korean Peninsula Energy Development Organization (see the chapter on the Democratic People's Republic of Korea). In July 1999 Kim Dae-Jung made a second visit as President to the USA (and a first to Canada). This was not quite as successful as that of the year before; his hosts were disconcerted when Kim requested that South Korea be allowed to develop missiles with a range of 500 km, rather than the 300 km recently agreed in principle. The improving links with Beijing were strengthened further in August, when for the first time a South Korean Minister of Defence visited China. Any military co-operation between these former Cold War adversaries was expected to proceed tentatively, for fear of antagonizing North Korea, and perhaps also the USA. The Russian Minister of Defence visited Seoul in September. Relations with the USA were reaffirmed in September by a three-way summit with Keizo Obuchi in Auckland, New Zealand, to show a common stance against any new missile launch by North Korea. This took place just before the APEC meeting, which Kim Dae-Jung combined with bilateral visits to Australia and New Zealand. In November he visited the Philippine capital, Manila, for meetings of the ASEAN + 3 (the Association's member countries, plus South Korea, China and Japan). Kim met the Chinese and Japanese Prime Ministers in the first summit for that particular troika, and one of several signs of Kim's Asianist—but not anti-Western—proclivities. All this consolidated his reputation as South Korea's most internationally minded leader to date.

During 2000 Kim extended his focus to Europe, with visits in March to France, Germany, Italy and the Vatican (as a devout Catholic). He had visited the United Kingdom in 1998 for the ASEM, which Seoul hosted in October 2000. In a speech in Berlin (Germany), he offered aid to rebuild North Korean infrastructure, an offer that led to inter-Korean summit talks being announced a month later. Relations with Japan continued to improve, despite the death of Keizo Obuchi, whose funeral in June gave Kim Dae-Jung the chance to meet his successor, Yoshiro Mori, as well as Bill Clinton.

New challenges in relations with the USA arose in 2000. Allegations emerged that US troops had massacred civilian refugees early in the Korean War at a village called Nogun-ri; both Governments established official inquiries into this. It subsequently transpired that two US soldiers who had testified to being present at the massacre were in fact elsewhere at the time of the killings. Anti-US sentiment was also heightened by an accident at a bombing range at Maehyang-ri, south-west of Seoul, which provoked a protest campaign, as well as by revelations of a toxic leak into the Han river from a US base in Seoul. The North-South summit meeting implicitly raised the question of an eventual withdrawal of the 37,000 US troops stationed in South Korea, although Kim Dae-Jung insisted that Kim Jong Il had accepted his argument that they should stay to perform a regional peace-keeping role. A fresh agreement governing US troops in Korea was concluded in December, after five years of negotiation.

South Korea's relations with China remained good, despite protests in January 2000 when the Chinese authorities repatriated seven young North Korean refugees (previously expelled from Russia). There was criticism of the Government's weakness towards China on the refugee issue and other matters, such as its refusal to grant a visa to the Dalai Lama (the spiritual leader of Tibet), or to congratulate the new President of Taiwan, Chen Shui-bian. Kim Dae-Jung publicly welcomed Vladimir Putin's election as Russian President in March, although the latter's prompt visit to Pyongyang concerned some in Seoul. Multilaterally, the third ASEM, which South Korea hosted in October, was the largest event ever held in South Korea's diplomatic history, with more than 20 heads of state or government attending. The United Kingdom and Germany used the occasion to announce their intention to open relations with North Korea, as a boost for the 'sunshine' policy. In November Kim Dae-Jung took a prominent role as usual in two regional summit meetings, APEC in Brunei and the ASEAN + 3 in Singapore, with state visits there and to Indonesia. The President concluded a remarkable year with visits to Sweden and Norway, where he received his Nobel Peace Prize.

Fears that the new US Administration would harm détente with North Korea proved correct in March 2001, when Kim Dae-Jung became the first Asian leader to visit President George W. Bush, who publicly voiced mistrust of North Korea. By contrast, the US Secretary of State, Colin Powell, expressed readiness to continue engagement. Prior to Kim's visit a joint statement with Russian President Putin, who visited Seoul in February, strongly supported the 1972 Anti-Ballistic Missile Treaty, which Bush's missile defence proposals were set to breach. Relations improved as a result of the devastating terrorist attacks perpetrated against US targets in September 2001, which brought strong sympathy from South Korea and a reaffirmation of security relations with the USA.

Meanwhile, President Kim Dae-Jung's efforts to forge better relations with Japan encountered a set-back. A new history textbook to be used in Japanese schools, which concealed that country's pre-1945 aggression, caused strong repercussions in both Koreas and China: these were compounded by Japanese Prime Minister Junichiro Koizumi's visit to the Yasukuni Shrine, a controversial war memorial, in August 2001. By contrast, relations with China remained good despite the latter's persecution of North Korean refugees, and a growing perception of China as an economic competitor. Senior visitors to Seoul included Premier Li Peng. Later in 2001 Kim Dae-Jung made his customary forays to the APEC and ASEAN + 3 meetings. Ever at ease in Europe, his politics being essentially 'Christian Democrat' in nature, in December 2001 Kim visited the United Kingdom, Norway and Hungary; he became the first Asian leader to address the European Parliament in the French city of Strasbourg.

President George W. Bush's identification in January 2002 of North Korea, together with Iran and Iraq, as forming an 'axis of evil' was difficult to reconcile with the 'sunshine' policy. In the circumstances, Bush's visit to Seoul in February proceeded better than many had feared. However, there was dismay at a decision to buy South Korea's next-generation combat aircraft

from the USA. The choice of the latter's F-15K *Eagle* fighter was widely seen as a political decision, considering the technical superiority of a French alternative. Other trade disputes were less fraught. A nationalist rebuff that prevented a US firm, Micron, from buying the chip-maker Hynix was balanced by General Motors' agreement to take over Daewoo Motor.

Relations with Japan were improved in 2002 by the two nations' co-hosting, albeit with largely separate organization, of the football World Cup. This afforded opportunities for mutual visits by Koizumi for the opening and Kim for the closing matches, as well as the first visit to post-war Korea by a member of the Japanese royal family (but not yet the Emperor or Crown Prince). Kim was also glad of Koizumi's unexpected decision to visit North Korea, as an indication of support for the 'sunshine' approach. It was surprising, therefore, that South Korea persisted in an international campaign to have the waters between the two countries, the Sea of Japan, renamed as the East Sea.

Relations with Russia were not especially close in 2002, despite agreement to settle a long-standing debt in part by South Korean weapons purchases. The Russian Minister of Foreign Affairs, Igor Ivanov, visited both Koreas in July. Kim Dae-Jung endorsed President Putin's decision to prioritize the improvement of relations with North Korea. One shared interest was in an 'iron silk road', a proposed rail freight route linking South Korea to Europe via Siberia. Yet this depended not only on Kim Jong Il's consent, but on the investment of US $3,000m. to upgrade North Korea's decrepit network. Russia hoped that South Korea would finance this.

Also in 2002 some overdue realism entered South Korea's hitherto rather ingenuous view of China. Trade disputes enhanced the image of a robust economic competitor, while the sight of Chinese police in Beijing beating South Korean diplomats who were protecting North Korean refugees, was salutary also. Even so, not only was the Dalai Lama again refused a visa, but Asiana Airlines declined even to carry him from India to Mongolia via Seoul. South Korea's priority with China remained a perceived need to maintain Beijing's engagement, especially in exerting pressure on North Korea to make peace and introduce reforms.

From late 2002 four developments threatened South Korea's alliance with the USA. The acquittal in November by USFK courts martial of two US soldiers, whose vehicle had in June killed two Korean girls in a road accident, provoked major demonstrations. The unexpected election of Roh Moo-Hyun as President in February 2003 gave the US Department of Defense an opportunity to press for a redeployment of US forces, back from their 'tripwire' position near the DMZ to a line south of Seoul. This led to renewed concern in South Korea, not least over fears that such a redeployment would make it easier for the USA to contemplate an air strike on North Korea if its own troops were no longer in the firing line. Once in office, Roh Moo-Hyun acted to improve relations with the USA, including an unpopular decision to send non-combat forces to Iraq in April. His first visit to the USA in May, which was carefully prepared, went well, although here again Roh alienated supporters by the issue of a joint statement with President George W. Bush, warning North Korea of 'further steps' if its nuclear defiance persisted. While in the USA, Roh visited high-technology sites in 'Silicon Valley' and the New York stock exchange, lobbying for investment; Samsung took the opportunity to announce a US $500m. addition to its chip plant in Austin, Texas. South Korea reluctantly accepted the USFK redeployment, to be phased over several years.

The little-travelled President Roh Moo-Hyun, whose provincial background contrasted with the international experience and renown of his predecessor Kim Dae-Jung, followed his US trip with visits to South Korea's neighbouring powers: Japan in June 2003, and then China in July. Both were successful, although with poor timing the Japanese Diet on the day of his arrival ratified three new wartime contingency laws, which had caused the usual friction in some quarters in Seoul over alleged Japanese militarism. North Korea remained a major item on the agenda in both Tokyo and Beijing. Trade relations with China were more dynamic, although South Korea's bilateral surplus was as much a concern in Beijing as Japan's persistent surplus was to Koreans. The China visit, which included a tour of a Hyundai car plant, had more of a business focus. Despite fears of competition in almost every field of industry, South Korea had a level of ease with China that was lacking with Japan. As trading links continued to grow, the question of how far politics and security might follow suit was current. If China continued to present itself as a peace-maker on the peninsula, while the Bush Administration was widely perceived as raising tensions, the long-term consequences for the strategic orientations of a more assertive South Korea (or of an eventual united Korea) could be profound.

Six-party talks on North Korea's nuclear weapons programme, held in Beijing in August 2003, brought together the two Koreas with the four powers of the USA, China, Japan and Russia for the first time in half a century. A degree of unity among the five seeking to curb North Korea's nuclear and other threats belied both tactical differences over how to accomplish this and longer-term divergences of strategy and goals, and the talks ended without resolution. A second session in Beijing in February 2004 again achieved little. South Korea reportedly shared the frustration of China and Russia at the US refusal to compromise with North Korea. At a third round of six-party talks in June, the USA for the first time offered a detailed proposal (said to be based on a South Korean draft) for phased nuclear disarmament, including incentives of immediate energy aid. North Korea did not reject this outright, pending further discussion.

Bringing together the five states most central to South Korean foreign policy, the six-party process, despite its lack of results, allowed for a wide range of other consultations. Elsewhere, in October 2003 President Roh Moo-Hyun attended the ASEAN + 3 meetings on the Indonesian island of Bali and the APEC summit meeting in Bangkok, also making a state visit to Singapore. In early 2004 his impeachment curtailed diplomacy: a planned visit to Russia was postponed.

However, the two main foci of South Korean foreign policy (North Korea apart) continued to be the USA and China. If, superficially, relations with the USA remained better than many had feared, underlying tensions persisted. Although South Korea welcomed the Bush Administration's belated softer approach towards North Korea, it was still anxious about the USA's plans to move its forces back from the DMZ to south of Seoul. In addition, in May 2004 it was revealed that 3,600 USKF troops would soon be redeployed to Iraq, and at the beginning of June it was announced that one-third of the total USFK strength of 37,000 (12,500, including the 3,600) were to depart permanently by the end of 2005. If in one sense, ironically, this forced the more independent defence posture that Roh Moo-Hyun had long advocated, South Korea felt a lack of consultation, while also being concerned that the new US doctrine of mobile forces might lead to the use of USFK in the Taiwan Straits, to the detriment of South Korea's relations with China. At the end of July 2004 it was announced that 13 US bases would revert to South Korea by 2006, far sooner than expected; while the main Yongsan garrison in Seoul, long a focus of complaint, was to close by 2008.

China displaced the USA as South Korea's main export market in 2003, and became its largest trade partner overall in 2001. In August 2003, however, a major dispute arose over China's revisionist claim that the Goguryeo (Koguryo) kingdom (37 BC–AD 668), covering much of modern North Korea and Manchuria, was Chinese rather than Korean. This seemed to be part of a wider Chinese effort to secure its frontiers by claiming all its present borderlands as primordially Chinese in all aspects, thereby pre-empting any conceivable irredentist claims.

Similarly with Japan, Koreans had long had issues over history. In July 2004 President Roh Moo-Hyun and Prime Minister Junichiro Koizumi held an informal one-day summit meeting on the South Korean resort island of Jeju. Roh was criticized by South Koreans for stating that he would not raise contentious issues of the past, such as Koizumi's visits to the Yasukuni Shrine, revisionist Japanese school textbooks and so-called 'comfort women'.

From the latter part of 2004 President Roh embarked upon various overseas visits. In September he completed his tour of the four major powers with a trip to Russia, taking in Kazakh-

stan en route. In both cases, energy agreements were a major focus. Barely a week later, he departed for a nine-day visit to India and Viet Nam, including the ASEM summit meeting in Hanoi. In November he attended the APEC meeting in Chile, preceded by visits to Argentina and Brazil—all somewhat eclipsed by President Hu Jintao of China, on a similar itinerary and with more to offer. Roh's next destination was Laos, for the ASEAN + 3 summit meeting, whence he flew directly to London for the first state visit to the United Kingdom by a South Korean President; he went on to Poland and France. In December he visited Japan for another informal summit meeting with Prime Minister Koizumi.

In early 2005 long-standing disagreements with Japan re-emerged, over the disputed Dokdo/Takeshima islets and over school textbooks. When the Japanese prefecture of Shimane provocatively declared a 'Takeshima day', rather than disregarding a symbolic act by a local assembly as inconsequential South Koreans went into a frenzy of protest, which no politician dared try to quell. South Korea scrambled fighter aircraft to pursue a small plane used by a Japanese television station and also warned off two Japanese reconnaissance planes, flying 70 km away from the islets. In March the South Korean Minister of Maritime Affairs and Fisheries cautioned that the country might resort to military force. In April the approval by the Japanese Ministry of Education of a new edition of a revisionist high-school history textbook, which was regarded as concealing pre-1945 aggression, only exacerbated the situation, even though just 18 of Japan's 11,102 junior high schools in fact used the book in question. The issue also caused serious protests in China, the scale of which rapidly eclipsed the dispute between South Korea and Japan. Nevertheless, the latter altercation was a sad reverse for relations between the two neighbouring countries, both long-standing allies of the USA, in a year that had been intended to celebrate the 40th anniversary of the re-establishment of post-war diplomatic relations in 1965. President Roh Moo-Hyun entered the fray, demanding that Japan apologize and compensate for the colonial past, although there had been several such apologies and officially the matter was closed. An unwelcoming atmosphere prevailed when Prime Minister Koizumi visited Seoul in June 2005, when almost all discussion was devoted to these negative factors.

With the USA, meanwhile, formal cordiality did not conceal fundamental differences. In April 2005 it emerged that South Korea's NSC had vetoed a plan for US forces to take the lead in reacting to any collapse of North Korea, considering this to be an infringement of South Korean sovereignty. While South Korea retained peacetime control of its own forces, in wartime, under current rules, combined forces would come under US control. The issue, therefore, was whether a North Korean collapse would be defined as a war situation; the USA's concern was that the resulting power vacuum might allow nuclear weapons to fall into terrorist hands. Concerns were also raised in April when President Roh described South Korean conservatives as being 'more like Americans than Americans'.

None the less, the two allies agreed on pressing North Korea to return to the six-party nuclear talks. In an unusual summit meeting in June 2005, President Roh Moo-Hyun flew to Washington for a single three-hour meeting with US President George W. Bush. It seemed feasible that, during the meeting, Roh might have persuaded Bush both to moderate his Administration's hostility to Kim Jong Il, and to let the South offer its own programme of incentives. Later in that month the Minister of Unification, Chung Dong-Young, made a visit to the USA, during which he reported on his recent meeting with Kim Jong Il even to US Vice-President Cheney, renowned for his scepticism.

There were brief hopes of progress in the six-party talks in September 2005 when, after a protracted session that had begun in July, a joint statement was agreed. However, the statement appeared to comprise only general principles, and it was immediately presented by both the USA and North Korea in ways that signalled that they remained far apart. A fifth round of talks in November resulted in no progress. This was oddly timed, being perforce brief since all except North Korea promptly decamped to Busan for the APEC summit meeting. North Korea, not a member of APEC and hence not invited (the USA having rejected the possibility of observer status), did not even report the occasion.

The main foreign policy development in early 2006 was negative: a fresh dispute with Japan in April over the Dokdo/Takeshima islets. Japan's plan to send two oceanographic ships to the area antagonized South Korea, which placed 20 patrol boats on high alert. Emergency talks in Seoul temporarily defused the crisis, although a trenchant speech by President Roh Moo-Hyun did nothing to calm matters. This continuing dispute affected weightier issues; in July patrol boats were pursuing each other round the rocks when North Korea fired seven test missiles. President Roh was quicker to criticize Japan's stern reaction to that provocation than the missile launch itself. The Government also continued to criticize the controversial visits by Japanese Prime Minister Koizumi to the Yasukuni Shrine. Visits by Koizumi to the shrine early in the year had prompted the South Korean Minister of Foreign Affairs and Trade to refuse to visit Japan. In August, however, he embarked on his first tour of the nation for 10 months.

With China, the main trend was a growing rivalry for influence in North Korea. While South Korea and China (like Russia) formed an alliance against US and Japanese efforts to press North Korea, each was also concerned lest Kim Jong Il should fall wholly into the other's sphere of influence. This began to resemble the Sino-Soviet rivalry that Kim Il Sung had exploited so effectively in an earlier period.

Relations with North Korea deteriorated in July 2006 when the North fired seven test missiles into the Japan Sea. South Korea reacted by suspending food aid and by postponing the planned expansion of a joint industrial park in the border town of Kaesong. Tensions escalated in October, when North Korea announced that it had conducted its first nuclear test. While the South expressed reservations about the sanctions imposed by the UN Security Council in mid-October in response to the test, Lee Jong-Seok, the Minister of Unification, conceded that the South would have to make 'certain changes' to its policy of engagement with the North.

In the wider arena, President Roh's travels in 2006 were driven mainly by a growing realization that South Korea was not only acutely dependent on imported energy and other raw materials, but that it had been tardier than regional rivals such as China and Japan in securing sources of supply in an ever more ruthless global market. In March Roh conducted state visits to Egypt, Nigeria and Algeria, followed in May by Mongolia, Azerbaijan and the United Arab Emirates. He was accompanied by leading business representatives, including some from Korea's major petroleum refiners (SK Corp, GS Caltex and Hyundai Oil Bank), and new agreements on resources were signed.

In September 2006 President Roh undertook state visits to Greece, Romania and Finland, where he attended a summit of the ASEM. Returning via the USA, he conferred with President Bush. In October he hosted a working summit meeting with the new Japanese Prime Minister, Shinzo Abe, in Seoul, before flying to Beijing for a similar exercise with the Chinese President, Hu Jintao. In November Roh attended the APEC summit in Viet Nam and paid a state visit to Cambodia. Concluding the year with state visits to Indonesia, Australia and New Zealand in December, he began 2007 with the postponed ASEAN + 3 summit in the Philippines in January, followed by a state visit to Spain and visits to Italy and the Vatican in February. In March the theme of energy was reprised with visits to Saudi Arabia, Qatar and Kuwait.

In 2007 South Korea's conduct of foreign affairs largely revolved around the revival of the six-party talks and a related improvement in relations with North Korea, notably with the announcement that in August President Roh would visit Pyongyang for a summit meeting with Kim Jong Il—only the second of its kind ever. (However, in the event this was postponed owing to severe flooding in North Korea.) Although apparently running in parallel, below the surface there was tension between these multilateral and bilateral approaches. From the perspective of Seoul, in the six-party talks the USA and China wielded the most influence with North Korea.

Having long caused some consternation in Washington with vague references to a more independent security posture,

President Roh somewhat unexpectedly gave strong support to a bilateral FTA with the USA. After several sessions of difficult negotiations and fierce demonstrations in South Korea an agreement was signed in April 2007.

A crisis arose in July 2007 when Taliban insurgents seized a group of 23 South Korean Protestants who had defied official warnings not to travel to Afghanistan, where they claimed to be engaged in aid work rather than missionary activity. Two of the hostages were killed in that month. Negotiations between the Taliban and the South Korean Government began in August, following which two hostages were released. There were fears that South Korea would pay a ransom or press the US and Afghan Governments to free Taliban prisoners, and that any unfortunate dénouement would increase anti-US sentiment in South Korea. At the end of August the remaining 19 hostages were freed. The full terms of the agreement between the South Korean Government and the Taliban were not immediately revealed, leading to speculation that a ransom had indeed been paid.

In 2008 South Korean foreign policy changed direction sharply, with the election of Lee Myung-Bak as President. In April the strongly pro-US Lee became the first South Korean leader ever to be invited to Camp David, the US presidential retreat. The bonhomie with George W. Bush was short-lived; as domestic protests grew against the unbanning of US beef (see above), Lee lost credibility in Washington too by pleading to renegotiate this agreement. A compromise was found, but this episode made it all the more unlikely that either country's legislature would ratify the bilateral FTA signed in 2007. In August 2008 Bush briefly visited Seoul en route to Beijing for the Olympic Games, prompting both pro- and anti-US demonstrations; at 30,000 versus 20,000 protesters, respectively, the former outnumbered the latter.

Lee's pro-US leaning and his uncompromising policy on North Korea inevitably led to a worsening of relations with Pyongyang, a development ironically unwelcome to the Bush Administration, which was keen to conclude a nuclear deal. Elsewhere, a laudable pledge to improve relations with Japan (where Lee was born) proved brief. Despite two early meetings with Japanese Prime Minister Yasuo Fukuda, who attended Lee's inauguration, the Dokdo/Takeshima issue re-emerged in July 2008 in two spheres: a new Japanese teachers' manual suggested telling middle-school children that the islets' status was contested; and the US Bureau of Geographical Names changed their designation from 'Korean' to 'disputed', thus prompting a fresh outbreak of indignation in Seoul. Hence, at an ASEAN Regional Forum meeting convened in July in Singapore, while US Secretary of State Condoleezza Rice shook hands with North Korea's Minister of Foreign Affairs, Pak Ui Chun, the latter shunned his South Korean counterpart, Yu Myung-Hwan, who in turn rebuffed Japan's Masahiko Koumura. None of this appeared to serve South Korea's real diplomatic interests.

In Beijing, President Lee's pro-US stance risked being construed as anti-Chinese. South Korean opinion, hitherto rather pro-China, turned in late April 2008 when Chinese students in Seoul, cheering on the Olympic torch, attacked a small group of protesters against China's repatriation of North Korean refugees. None the less, Lee strove to counter any hostile impression with two visits in short order to Beijing; first in late May, and then to the Olympic opening ceremonies in August. Chinese President Hu Jintao visited Seoul in late August; Lee asked him not to send back fugitives from North Korea. They agreed to expand military exchanges and to initiate strategic discussions between senior diplomats.

In August 2008 the Olympic Games afforded some respite, as South Koreans rejoiced at unexpected success, winning a total of 31 medals, with North Korea taking six. Once again the two Koreas competed separately and, unlike in 2000 or 2004, the two teams did not march as one in the opening ceremony. President Lee shook hands with Kim Yong Nam, North Korea's titular Head of State, but they had no meaningful exchange. In Beijing Lee also met the leaders of Algeria, Kazakhstan, Turkmenistan and Uzbekistan, these meetings being indicative of his concern, and South Korea's need, to secure energy and other resources. In early July, meanwhile, as President of one of the major economies invited to attend the G8 (Group of Eight industrialized nations) summit meeting in Japan, Lee met briefly with the leaders of Brazil, India, Indonesia and Mexico, as well as those of the USA and Russia.

Energy was also a focus of President Lee's visit to Moscow in late September 2008. Among several business agreements signed with his Russian counterpart, Dmitrii Medvedev, the most striking was a memorandum of understanding for Kogas, the world's largest gas importer, to buy gas worth US $90,000m. from Gazprom over a period of 30 years, starting in 2015. A pipeline was mooted; this would have to cross North Korea, which did not appear to have been consulted.

In late October 2008 President Lee attended the ASEM in Beijing. He held official talks with his counterparts from Japan, France, Viet Nam, Denmark and Poland, and unofficially met with the leaders of Italy and Bulgaria, as well as with the British Secretary of State for Foreign and Commonwealth Affairs. A brief meeting with French President Nicolas Sarkozy and José Manuel Barroso, President of the European Commission, did not resolve obstacles to a proposed FTA with the EU. In November President Lee attended the APEC summit meeting in Lima, Peru, holding talks with the leaders of the host country, Chile and Colombia; earlier, he also visited Brazil.

In mid-December 2008 the South Korean President joined the Prime Ministers of China and Japan in the Japanese city of Fukuoka for the first ever summit meeting of North-East Asia's three major powers. President Lee and Japanese Prime Minister Taro Aso met again, in Seoul, in January 2009. In February, on her first overseas tour as US Secretary of State, Hillary Clinton visited East Asia, her itinerary including Seoul. Fears that the new Administration of President Barack Obama would prove too conciliatory on the issue of North Korea (already receding after the six-party talks were deadlocked in December—see the chapter on the Democratic People's Republic of Korea) eased when Clinton offered robust reassurance of US support for South Korea. In March Lee visited New Zealand, Australia and Indonesia, and in April he travelled to the United Kingdom for the G20 summit meeting of leading industrial nations in London, where he also met bilaterally with the leaders of China, Japan, the United Kingdom, Australia (again) and the USA (his first meeting with President Obama).

Later in April 2009 President Lee travelled to Thailand for the ASEAN + 3 summit meeting, which was curtailed by demonstrations. A significant development in South Korean diplomacy was the hosting of a summit meeting on the resort island of Jeju at the beginning of June, attended by representatives of every ASEAN member state. Lee held bilateral meetings with the leaders of Brunei, Indonesia, Laos, the Philippines, Thailand and Viet Nam. In mid-May he visited Kazakhstan and Uzbekistan, where energy matters dominated the agenda. In mid-June, in Washington, DC, Lee became the first foreign leader to share a press conference with President Obama in the White House Rose Garden. They found more accord on North Korea than on the 'KORUS' FTA, still unratified by the US Congress. In July Lee travelled to Italy for the expanded G8 summit meeting, also visiting Poland, Sweden and the Vatican. In the Swedish capital of Stockholm he announced a final agreement on an FTA with the EU; this was initialled in October, signed a year later and entered into force in July 2011 (see below). In August 2009 a Comprehensive Economic Partnership Agreement, similar to an FTA, was signed with India. In September Lee attended the third G20 summit in the US city of Pittsburgh, and in late October he returned to Thailand for the reconvened ASEAN and related summit meetings—Korea-ASEAN, ASEAN + 3, and a troika with China and Japan—while also attending some bilateral talks. He also visited Cambodia and Viet Nam, where South Korea had become a leading investor. In mid-November he attended the APEC summit meeting in Singapore, and then hosted US President Obama during his brief stopover in Seoul.

During 2010 South Korea chaired the G20, yet the contrast sharpened between President Lee's vigorous global diplomacy and worsening relations with North Korea. In January Lee visited India, touring a Hyundai car plant in Chennai before meeting Prime Minister Manmohan Singh. He travelled on to Switzerland to attend the World Economic Forum in Davos, where in an interview with the British Broadcasting Corporation he expressed his willingness to hold a summit meeting with Kim Jong Il. He also met the leaders of Canada, Spain, Switzerland and Jordan, as well as Microsoft's Bill Gates and John Chambers, the CEO of Cisco Systems, which announced plans to invest in South Korea.

In February 2010 President Lee hosted the Presidents of Germany, the Palestinian National Authority and Uzbekistan. For the last, Islam Karimov, this was his sixth visit, courted for his country's natural resources, with no mention of the human rights concerns that troubled others. Lee's next guest was the Japanese Minister for Foreign Affaris, Katsuya Okada, who apologized for his country's misdeeds during its rule of Korea in 1910–45, the first such official comment by the recently installed Government led by the Democratic Party of Japan. Also in February 2010, in a little-reported development, South Korea for the first time joined the 29th annual US-led Cobra Gold military exercises, held in Thailand; other participants were Indonesia, Japan and Singapore.

In April 2010 the Japanese Diet approved the country's annual report on foreign policy, which this year restated Tokyo's claim to the disputed Dokdo-Takeshima islets. The Japanese Government had recently authorized school textbooks that included the same claim. The inevitable protests duly issued from Seoul. President Lee then travelled to Washington, DC, to attend the first Nuclear Security Summit (NSS). South Korea was chosen as the venue for the next NSS in 2012. Publicly cordial with his host, in private he reportedly exerted pressure for US ratification of the 'KORUS' FTA. Lee returned home to welcome the President of Kazakhstan, Nursultan Nazarbayev, on his fourth visit to Seoul.

From May 2010, when an international group of investigators concluded that North Korea was responsible, the sinking of the *Cheonan* in March came to dominate South Korean foreign policy. The main impact of the incident was to worsen relations with China, which welcomed Kim Jong Il in early May while officially professing scepticism with regard to North Korea's culpability for the sinking. President Lee Myung-Bak failed to make progress with Chinese President Hu Jintao, whom he met at the end of April at the opening of the Shanghai Expo. A month later China's Premier, Wen Jiabao, undertook a difficult visit to South Korea for bilateral talks and the now-annual trilateral summit meeting with Japan; Yukio Hatoyama, the Japanese Prime Minister, joined in pressing him over the *Cheonan* issue. More positively, the three leaders agreed to create a permanent Trilateral Cooperation Secretariat in 2011, to be based in Seoul.

President Lee fared better in Canada at the G8 and G20 summits in late June 2010. The G8's final communiqué included a strong condemnation of the sinking of the *Cheonan* and of North Korea, although (presumably at Russian insistence) this stopped short of a direct accusation. US President Barack Obama had what he described as 'blunt talks' with his Chinese counterpart, Hu Jintao, on the same topic. Bilaterally, on the sidelines of the G20 meeting, the USA agreed to postpone the transfer of wartime operational control of joint forces (OpCon) by three-and-a-half years, from 17 April 2012 to 1 December 2015. South Korean satisfaction at this was tempered by what appeared to be a *quid pro quo*: a US demand to reopen aspects of the 'KORUS' FTA, so that Obama could send it to Congress for ratification soon after the next G20 summit meeting, scheduled to be convened in Seoul in November 2010. While the final ratification of the FTA would represent a significant achievement for Lee, any hint of yielding to US pressure risked weakening his position.

In July 2010, meanwhile, the UN Security Council issued a presidential statement (not a full resolution) on the *Cheonan* incident. Its complex wording did not directly attribute the vessel's sinking to North Korea; indeed the North Korean ambassador to the UN, Sin Son Ho, hailed the statement as 'a diplomatic victory'. Similar ambivalence emerged later in July in Viet Nam, at the ASEAN Regional Forum convened in Hanoi, where some seemed to regard the *Cheonan* incident as simply a local skirmish. By contrast, the USA showed strong support for the South Korean case. Later in July both the US Secretaries of Defense and of State visited Seoul for a rare '2 + 2' meeting with their South Korean counterparts. This was followed by a large joint naval exercise, 'Operation Invincible Spirit', which involved 8,000 troops, 200 aircraft and 20 ships, including the nuclear-powered aircraft carrier *USS George Washington*. In the light of Chinese warnings against others 'snoring beside our beds', these manoeuvres were held in waters east of the peninsula rather than as originally planned in the Yellow Sea, where the *Cheonan* had sunk. Soon afterwards South Korea held its own anti-submarine drill in the Yellow Sea, while its annual joint exercise with the USA, now known as 'Ulchi Freedom Guardian', followed in August. North Korea denounced all these displays of strength as plans to invade, vowing retaliation in the strongest terms.

Robert Einhorn, US co-ordinator for sanctions against Iran and North Korea, visited Seoul in early August 2010, hoping to persuade South Korea to reinforce sanctions against Iran. Bank Mellat, Iran's second largest bank, which was subject to US sanctions, had four overseas branches: three in Turkey and one (hitherto operating freely) in Seoul. Iran's ambassador warned that 150,000 South Koreans would lose their jobs if bilateral economic relations were severed. Iran was the fourth largest supplier of crude petroleum to South Korea, and more than 2,000 Korean firms conducted trade worth US $10,000m. annually with Iran. In the end, South Korea restricted Bank Mellat's activities, but did not shut it down. The South Korean press openly discussed how new sanctions might be circumvented; for instance, by routing payments via a third country, such as Dubai.

In August 2010, in a statement approved by his Cabinet, Japan's Prime Minister, Naoto Kan, again apologized for the 'enormous damage and suffering caused by colonization' of Korea by Japan in 1910–45, expressing 'deep remorse'. This was fairly well received in Seoul, the more so as Kan pledged to return items seized from the Korean court during the colonial era: the first such restitution since 1965. There was also sympathy for Japan following a devastating earthquake and tsunami in that country in March 2011. Unfortunately, this was soon eroded by a fresh disagreement, of extreme pettiness, over the Dokdo/Takeshima islets. In mid-June Korean Air gratuitously flew its first new Airbus A380 aircraft over the disputed islets. In reprisal, Japan's Ministry of Foreign Affairs forbade its diplomats to use the airline for a month. South Korea, in return, refused entry to a group of right-wing Japanese legislators, who had planned to travel to Seoul to protest. On 14 August, the eve of Liberation Day, the Chairman of the ruling GNP suggested that Dokdo should be garrisoned by marines rather than coastguards as was currently the case. Given the real threat from North Korea, such behaviour on all sides was dismaying.

Meanwhile, in early October 2010 President Lee attended the eighth ASEM in Brussels, Belgium. More importantly, on the day after the meeting the EU-Korean FTA was signed. Following ratification by the European Parliament in February 2011 and by the South Korean National Assembly in May, it entered into force on 1 July 2011, six months later than planned, after late objections by Italy (apparently made at the behest of car manufacturer Fiat), which found scant support among other EU member states. With the 'KORUS' FTA signed in 2007 still unratified, this was important both substantively and symbolically. The President of the European Commission, José Manuel Barroso, described it as 'by far the most important trade deal ever concluded by the European Union with one country'. It provided for the immediate removal of duties totalling €1,600m. annually on EU exports, while Korean car parts and information technology companies also expected to gain. Over a three-year period 99% of EU tariffs and 96% of Korea's would be eliminated on mutual trade.

Seoul hosted its most important international gathering to date in mid-November 2010: the summit of the G20, which South Korea chaired in that year. However, what President Lee had hoped would be his finest hour and confirm South Korea's emergence as a global power proved to be a a disappointment, since disarray among major powers over currencies and other issues meant that little of substance was achieved. The meeting was untroubled by either demonstrations (owing to massive security) or North Korean provocations. The latter came later that month, with the shelling of Yeonpyeong island. As with the *Cheonan* sinking, this prompted a show of force in response. The USA dispatched a battle group, including the aircraft carrier *USS George Washington*, for joint exercises in the Yellow Sea. Supposedly long-planned, these manoeuvres sent a clear signal to both North Korea and China, which had again infuriated South Korea by not criticizing the North for its attack, although it did not object this time to the counter-exercises being held in the Yellow Sea.

President Lee attended the Bali Democracy Forum in Indonesia in December 2010, subsequently visiting Malaysia to mark 50 years of diplomatic relations. The crisis with North Korea shortened the trip; for two of his three nights away Lee slept on the presidential jet. Both visits were described as sales diplomacy, with talk of a bilateral FTA with Malaysia, in addition to the one in force between South Korea and ASEAN since 2007, and closer defence co-operation (including sales of weapons) with Indonesia. Prospects for the latter were not enhanced by a bizarre incident in Seoul in mid-February 2011. Three people fled when disturbed while copying data from a laptop computer in the hotel room of a delegation of visiting Indonesian officials, who South Korea had hoped would be the first foreign buyers of its T-50 *Golden Eagle* supersonic trainer jet. The intruders were thought to be agents of the NIS, which did not deny this; the police refused to investigate. Demands, even within the ruling party, for the resignation of the head of the NIS, Won Sei-Hoon, an associate of President Lee, went unheeded, and Indonesia made surprisingly little fuss.

National pride, damaged by North Korea's two attacks, received a fillip in January 2011, when South Korean special forces stormed and recaptured the *Samho Jewelry*, a chemical cargo vessel seized a week earlier by Somali pirates. Eight pirates were killed and five captured. All of the 21 crew were rescued; the captain suffered a serious gunshot wound, and three South Korean soldiers were injured. Three days before, with the destroyer *Choi Young* already following the hijacked ship, a South Korean helicopter had killed several pirates who broke away in an attempt to seize a Mongolian freighter as well. This daring rescue came just weeks after the owners of *Samho Jewelry* had paid a reported US $9m. ransom to free the supertanker *Samho Dream*, seized in April 2010 and held for seven months. Its success boosted the popularity of President Lee, who had ordered the mission. The semi-official Yonhap News Agency reported Lee as asserting, 'in a resolute tone', that 'we will not tolerate any act threatening the life and safety of our people'. No doubt this message was also intended to be heard in Pyongyang. In May the five captured pirates were sentenced in Seoul to long prison terms.

With unfortunate timing, in mid-March 2011 President Lee flew to the United Arab Emirates (UAE) for a ground-breaking ceremony for the first of four nuclear power stations that South Korea was supplying. Aides had reportedly urged him to cancel the trip, in response to the earthquake and ensuing nuclear disaster in Japan, but Lee's signing of a separate agreement with the UAE, potentially worth up to US $98,000m., to develop oilfields containing at least 1,000m. barrels of oil, was an indication of how much else was at stake. The meltdown at Japan's Fukushima nuclear plant diminished hopes that the UAE nuclear export agreement would be the first of many.

In May 2011 President Lee spent a week visiting Germany, Denmark and France. In Berlin, a major topic of discussion was reunification, which infuriated North Korea. In the Danish capital, Copenhagen, a joint Green Growth Alliance was announced. Finally, in Paris, the agenda included the G20, France having succeeded South Korea as chair of the group. Barely a week later, Lee was in Tokyo for the now-regular trilateral summit meeting with Japan and China. The three countries agreed to establish a formal Trilateral Cooperation Secretariat, based in Seoul, which opened in September. Such progress, despite various tensions, was encouraging. South Korea was pleased to host this office; comparisons were drawn with the role of Brussels as the site of the main EU institutions.

President Lee travelled to sub-Saharan Africa in early July 2011. He spent a day in the Democratic Republic of the Congo, discussing resources, and two days in Ethiopia, where the agenda focused on development aid. Before that he devoted four days to South Africa, where he successfully lobbied for Pyeongchang to host the 2018 Winter Olympic Games, the Korean resort being chosen over its French and German rivals by a convincing 63 votes out of 95. This was Pyeongchang's third bid for the Games. South Korea continued to set great store by hosting such events. In late August Daegu staged the International Association of Athletics Federations' World Championships in Athletics, while from May to August 2012 the obscure south-western port of Yeosu would address the daunting challenge of following Shanghai in hosting the next World Expo. Curbing the mood of national self-congratulation, the day after Pyeongchang's triumph prosecutors indicted 46 football players and 11 others on charges of match-fixing. This scandal prompted further claims that corruption and other abuses, such as violence by coaches, were rife in South Korean sports milieux.

Progress on FTAs remained uneven. In June 2011 the National Assembly ratified an FTA with Peru that had been signed in March. A tax on Peruvian coffee ended at once, while Korean cars would be cheaper in Peru within five years. The far more important accord with the EU took effect in July. By contrast, the 'KORUS' FTA remained stalled. In renegotiations in December 2010 South Korea, having initially refused to revise the accord, yielded a little on car tariffs, in return for US concessions on its pork exports. This retreat was widely criticized at home. In 2011 efforts by both Governments to secure ratification of the accord fell victim to the play of politics. With elections due in both countries in 2012, there were no votes to be gained in supporting this.

Economy

ROBERT F. ASH

Based on an earlier article by JOSEPH S. CHUNG

INTRODUCTION

Until the end of the 1980s, the Republic of Korea (South Korea) operated a mixed economic system. On the one hand, it adhered to the basic tenets of private enterprise and a market economy; on the other hand, it simultaneously followed a highly visible policy of government intervention. Through planning, direct or indirect ownership and control of enterprises and financial institutions, regulation of foreign exchange, and the implementation of appropriate monetary and fiscal policies, the Government played a crucial role in making market adjustments and maximizing incentives in order to fulfil its economic, social and political goals. However, economic success, the increasing complexity of economic management, the emergence of a more democratic and pluralistic society (including greater participation in decision-making by various interest groups), and increasing international competitiveness were major factors in reducing, from the late 1980s, the Government's economic role. Accordingly, the 1990s witnessed a retreat from 'command capitalism' and significant progress towards privatization. The reformist thrust of government economic policy was meanwhile driven by the need for greater efficiency, improved labour productivity and enhanced competitiveness in order to meet the demands of globalization. The admission of South Korea, in December 1996, to membership of the Organisation for Economic Co-operation and Development (OECD) was another important development, which heightened the importance of economic reform. So too, but from a negative perspective, was the impact in the late 1990s of the Asian financial crisis, which not only temporarily halted South Korea's growth momentum but also, by highlighting long-standing structural weaknesses in the economy, threatened to undermine and negate its previous economic achievements. However, the subsequent implementation of an IMF rescue programme and the successful negotiation of foreign debt restructuring with creditor banks facilitated swift recovery, and growth was quickly resumed. In 2008 and 2009, however, the global financial crisis had serious implications for the South Korean economy. Annual growth was more than halved in 2008, declining to its lowest level since the 1997 crisis; in 2009 there was barely any growth at all (see below). In both years the most resilient sector was agriculture, which registered 1.6% growth, compared with growth of 1.0% in services and a decline of 1.6% in the manufacturing sector. In 2010 the economy recorded a much more buoyant performance, owing to strong consumption and investment demand, as well as a significant recovery in exports. As a result, the growth rate of gross domestic product (GDP) rose sharply, to 6.2%, its highest level since 2002. Forecasts published by the Economist Intelligence Unit (EIU—a research and analysis organization based in the United Kingdom) in its *Country Report* on South Korea in April 2011 predicted a slowing of growth to 4.7% in 2011 (virtually the same as the projected OECD estimate) and to 3.9% in 2012.

Recent difficulties notwithstanding, a wide variety of indicators highlighted South Korea's continuing international economic importance. In 2004 its GDP for the first time exceeded US $1,000,000m. According to data made available by the US Central Intelligence Agency (CIA), in 2010 South Korea had the 12th largest GDP in the world, excluding the European Union (EU), measured in terms of purchasing-power parity (PPP). The same source showed it to have been the seventh biggest exporter—ahead of Hong Kong, Singapore and Taiwan, but below the People's Republic of China and Japan among Asian countries; it was the ninth largest importer, one place behind Hong Kong. In terms of average per caput GDP in PPP terms, at $30,000 South Korea ranked 45th, behind Singapore ($62,100), Hong Kong ($45,900) and Taiwan ($35,700). South Korea's strong outward economic orientation is captured in its high degree of trade dependency: in 2008 its trade-to-GDP ratio was 53.5%, compared, for example, with an average of 28.9% for all OECD member countries. As of December 2010 it ranked sixth in the world in terms of its reserves of foreign exchange and gold. In East Asia it is the third largest economy, after China and Japan, although its GDP is also significantly smaller than that of India (whether measured in PPP terms or on the basis of official exchange rates). After surpassing Japan in 2002, South Korea became the largest shipbuilder in the world, a rank it retained until 2010 when it was overtaken by China. It has overtaken France and Spain to become the fifth largest car producer (after China, Japan, the USA and Germany), and in 2008 Hyundai-Kia Automotive Group emerged as the world's fifth largest automobile firm. It is also a global competitor in electronics and semiconductor manufacturing. In 2009 (the most recent year for which data are available) South Korea ranked 29th in terms of the World Bank's 'Knowledge Economy Index'—well above China, but below Hong Kong, Japan, Singapore and Taiwan. As yet, however, the Government's aspiration to take South Korea into the G10 group of developed countries has not been fulfilled.

In common with other first-echelon Asian newly industrializing countries, South Korea's modern economic transformation was driven by strong GDP growth sustained over a long period. From the beginning of the 1960s until the early 1990s, apart from one year of contraction in 1980 caused by sharply rising oil prices, the pace of economic growth remained consistently robust—for much of that period, according to data provided by the Bank of Korea (BOK—the central bank of South Korea), averaging more than 9% annually. From this perspective, a major factor was the onset of the Asian financial crisis, which abruptly halted the rate of economic expansion and caused GDP to contract by 6.6% in 1998, compared with positive growth of 5.0% in 1997. Renewed GDP growth, averaging around 9% in 1999 and 2000 (in 2000 prices), apparently signalled rapid recovery from this crisis. In fact, the true significance of the events of 1997–98 lay in the serious systemic and structural problems of the industrial and financial sectors that they revealed. Such difficulties, as well as others associated with the vagaries of South Korea's domestic politics, were reflected in fluctuating growth after 2000. Having fallen back from 8.5% to 3.8% between 2000 and 2001, in 2002 real GDP growth accelerated to 7.2%. However, this surge was not maintained, and recessionary conditions in the first half of 2003 restricted annual growth to 2.8%. Recovery raised the corresponding figure to 4.6% in 2004 and, after a slight decrease to 4.0% in 2005, in 2006 the rate of growth reached 5.2%, its highest level since 2002. This momentum was almost maintained through 2007, when annual growth was 5.1%. However, in 2008 and 2009 South Korea was badly affected by the global economic crisis, causing GDP growth to fall back to 2.3% and 0.3%, respectively, before recovering sharply to 6.2% in 2010. Preliminary estimates by the BOK suggested that GDP expanded by 4.2% on a year-on-year basis in the first quarter of 2011, and by 3.4% in the second quarter.

An IMF report published in October 2006 acknowledged the remarkable economic record of South Korea since 1970. On the basis of average 7% annual growth during this period, per caput income in South Korea had risen seven-fold from a mere 20% of the OECD average to 70% of that figure. Whereas before the 1997 crisis annual growth was around 8%, in the intervening years the deceleration of investment and productivity growth had reduced that figure to about 4.5%. Looking beyond the short term, the IMF speculated that annual GDP growth might decline to as low as 2.5% by 2030.

THE PHYSICAL AND HUMAN RESOURCE BASE

South Korea contains quite rich concentrations of iron ore in the north-east of the country, although no more than 20% of these deposits are thought to be high-grade. It also has significant reserves of limestone, the basis of the cement industry and therefore critically important for construction purposes, as well as minor deposits of gold, silver and copper. Its energy resources, which are located mainly in the north-east, are limited to anthracite coal, firewood and hydroelectric power. The US Energy Information Administration has estimated, for example, that South Korea has just 88m. short tons of recoverable coal reserves. Thus, almost all its energy requirements are met by imports.

South Korea occupies only about 45% of the total area of the Korean peninsula, although its total population (numbering 48.22m. at the 2010 census) is more than double that of North Korea. Its total area is some 99,646 sq km, but little more than 20% of this is cultivable land (the remainder being shared between forest, which represents 65%–70% of total surface area, and land allocated to urban and transport uses). Such statistics highlight the high density of population—around 484 persons per sq km—a figure that is exceeded throughout the world, small islands and city states apart, only by Bangladesh and Taiwan.

As in the North, the main demographic impact of the Korean War was on mortality, which rose sharply between 1950 and 1953. Total military and civilian casualties attributable to the war were probably around 2m., of which a conservative estimate points to deaths of some 600,000. However, subsequent years witnessed a remarkable transformation. Between 1955 and 1975 the death rate declined sharply (from 33 per 1,000 to 15 per 1,000), although a rapidly decelerating birth rate resulted in a decline in the annual rate of natural increase to below 2%. The deceleration in population growth has continued to the present day: between 2000 and 2011, for example, the average rate of natural increase declined from 9.3 to 2.3 per 1,000. Concealed within the 2011 figure are crude birth and crude death rates of 8.55 and 6.26 per 1,000. Projections made by the National Statistical Office (NSO, which was renamed Statistics Korea in 2009) indicate that South Korea's total population will reach a peak of 49.96m. in 2020, thereafter falling back to the level of the end of the 1980s by mid-century. Although South Korea ranks 109th in the world in terms of land area, it has the 26th largest population.

From a peak of 0.89 in 1966 South Korea's dependency ratio had declined to the remarkably low level of 0.37 by mid-2011. In the same year 72.9% of the total population were between the ages of 15 and 64 years, compared with only 53% in 1966. The total fertility rate was 1.23. Children below the age of 15 constituted 15.7% of the population, while the share of the elderly (those aged 65 and above) was 11.4%. However, the population is ageing rapidly, and OECD estimates suggest that within two decades (marginally faster than in Japan, and much faster than in Germany, the United Kingdom, the USA and France) South Korea will, on the basis of UN criteria, have become an 'aged' society, with 14% of its population at or above the age of 65 years. NSO projections suggest that by 2030 there will be almost 12m. people, or 24.1% of the population, of 65 or more years of age, implying an age dependency ratio of 37.3%. CIA estimates indicated an average life expectancy at birth of 79.05 years (82.49 for women, 75.84 for men) in 2011.

Rapid urbanization has been a notable characteristic of demographic change in South Korea. In 1955 the urban share of total population was less than 25%. By 1975 the corresponding figure was already over 50%, and by the end of the 1980s it had reached 70%. In 2010 the rate of urbanization was 83%, a figure that was expected to rise to 84.4% by 2015. The most important urban centres have long been Seoul and Busan, which by 1990 already contained well over one-half of the urban population and 33% of the total population. (However, their share has since decreased to just over one-quarter.) Indeed, in the mid-1990s UN data showed Seoul to be the most populous city in the world, just ahead of the Brazilian city of São Paulo. With almost one-half of the total population living in 'Greater Seoul', infrastructural pressures and security concerns have intensified. Despite plans to relocate the functions of the national capital to a greenfield site in the middle of the country, it seemed unlikely that Seoul would lose its status as the industrial and financial centre of the country. From this perspective, even if the plan is fulfilled, hopes that a more balanced regional distribution of economic development can be attained are unlikely to be realized. Other major South Korean cities include Daegu, Incheon, Gwangju and Daecheon.

In 2011 there were just over 35.5m. people of working age (15–64 years) in South Korea. Estimates published by the Ministry of Employment and Labour show that the economically active population in 2010 numbered 24.75m., of whom 23.83m. were employed. The employment rate (employed persons aged 15 years and above as a proportion of the population in the same age-group) was 58.7%. The rate of unemployment rose from 2.0% to 4.4% between 1995 and 2000, before falling back to 3.2% in 2008. In 2009, however, under the impact of global recessionary conditions, unemployment rose quite sharply to 3.6% (from 770,000 to 888,000 persons). In January 2010 unemployment reached a peak of 1.22m. (5.0%), but thereafter declined. For the entire year, the unemployment rate was 3.7%, a figure that the EIU expected to rise to 3.9% in 2012. It is noteworthy that, although it remained relatively high by the standard of pre-1997 years, among OECD member countries South Korea's average overall unemployment rate in 2010 was bettered only by that of Norway.

As for the structure of employment, in 2010 a mere 6.6% of the employed labour force were engaged in agriculture (crop farming, forestry and fishing), while, at 17.0%, industry also accounted for a relatively low share of total employment. In short, it is a mark of the advanced level of development reached by South Korea that more than 75% of all employment now takes place outside farming and manufacturing. Business, personal and public services account for about one-half of all tertiary sector employment, while a further one-third takes place in wholesale trade, retail trade, hotels and catering.

As in Taiwan, the pressure to relocate manufacturing activities to cheaper foreign locations, especially mainland China, has in recent years exacerbated the employment situation in South Korea. Despite a fairly buoyant labour market, the targeted reduction in unemployment to around 2.5% by the end of 2007 was not fulfilled. Moreover, even before the onset of the global financial crisis in the latter part of 2008, employment growth was, if anything, slowing: as of August 2008, it had increased year-on-year by only 0.7%. Nevertheless, an encouraging sign was that an increasing number of new jobs were full-time, rather than part-time or temporary. For example, it was significant that alongside increasing lay-offs in 2009, the number of 'regular' workers among wage earners continued to rise (the increase in unemployed being accommodated by a decline in the number of temporary workers). For the time being, the most contentious employment issues are those affecting young people seeking jobs. Data from the Ministry of Employment and Labour for May 2011 showed, for example, that alongside the national unemployment rate of 3.2%, the corresponding figure for young people (between 15 and 29 years) was 7.3%, higher than in any other OECD member state. A cause for additional concern is that, in terms of educational attainment, unemployment is highest among college and university graduates.

Prices, Wages and Labour Relations

In the second half of the 1980s the rate of increase in the urban consumer price index (CPI) averaged 4.1% per year, a figure that accelerated to 6% annually between 1990 and 1995. Rising prices during this period reflected the award of large wage rises, associated with emerging shortages of labour, growing unionization and a higher incidence of labour disputes. Thus, by 1995 the average monthly manufacturing wage had reached 1,123,895 won (about US $1,500).

The effect of the Asian financial crisis was quickly to exacerbate inflationary pressures. From an annual CPI increase of 4.4% in 1997, by February 1998 the index had risen to 9.5%, although the rate of increase subsequently slowed: for the whole of 1998 the CPI rose by 7.5%. In 1999 consumer price rises declined sharply (to 0.8%), but thereafter again rose to reach 4.1% in 2001. Between 2002 and 2005 rises in the CPI remained in a band between 2.8% and 3.6%. Under the impact of rising international oil prices and domestic food prices, consumer price inflation accelerated in the first half of 2006, and in August the BOK sought to counter price pressures by raising its benchmark interest rate to 4.5%, its highest level for five years. In the event, expectations that the rate of CPI increase in 2006 would be around 3% proved to be unfounded, the eventual figure being 2.2%, which was significantly below the BOK's medium-term target band of between 2.5% and 3.5%. Inflationary pressures remained modest in the first nine months of 2007, and despite a relatively sharp increase in price rises in the final quarter, the annual rate of CPI inflation was only slightly above that of the previous year at 2.5%. However, rising international prices of food, energy and industrial commodities were the source of a sharp increase in inflationary pressure in 2008: between January and June the year-on-year monthly rise of core consumer prices rose from 3.9% to 5.9%, although by the end of the year the corresponding figure had fallen back to 4.1%. Thus, the average rate of increase in the CPI for the whole of 2008 was 4.1%, a rate higher than in any year since 1998. Such high rates of price inflation were a major constraint on the BOK's ability to reduce interest rates in support of more rapid GDP growth. However, weakening domestic demand and downward pressure on international commodity prices offset the effects of a weakening currency to bring about a significant decline in annual consumer price inflation in 2009 to 2.8%. In 2010 this decline gave way to a modest increase in inflationary pressures, with the CPI registering a year-on-year increase of 3.5% (but an average of 2.9% for the year as a whole). EIU projections, published in April 2011, forecast an annual rise in the CPI of 4.5% for 2011, declining to 3.4% in 2012.

Increasing labour unionization and the award of higher 'fringe' benefits have combined to undermine South Korea's export competitiveness in relation to a number of low-wage industrializing countries. Total union membership more than doubled in the 1970s, and in the next decade almost doubled again, to reach a peak of 1.93m. in 1989. In the 1990s the number of union members declined, although it subsequently recovered to reach 1.54m. Between the end of the 1980s and 2004 the unionization rate almost halved, declining from 19.8% to 10.6%, a figure that has since remained almost unchanged. About 60% of all trade unions are company-based, although since the end of the 1990s there has been a shift towards the integration of such organizations into industrial and sectoral unions. About three-quarters of all trade union members are male. Since 1987 a minimum wage system has been in place in South Korea. Between the end of 2006 and 2010 the minimum hourly wage rose from 3,100 to 4,110 won (around US $3.2, or the equivalent of about 40% of average GDP per head). The 2.75% rise in the minimum wage in 2010, despite being the lowest rate of increase for more than a decade, benefited some 2.2m. workers. In 2011 the minimum wage increased by 5.1%, to 4,320 won per hour, to the benefit of a further 3.8m. workers. OECD estimates indicated that having reached a peak in 2007, average annual wages (expressed in constant 2009 prices) declined in 2008 and 2009, but once more rose to a new record level in 2010.

In 1999 and 2000 there was a resurgence of strike activity, reflecting growing confidence by the trade unions in their ability to press claims for wage increases and enhanced job security on behalf of their members, as the economy achieved rapid recovery from the regional financial crisis of 1997. In 2000 almost 178,000 workers were involved in 250 union disputes, causing the loss of almost 1.9m. working days. Although even more strikes and lock-outs occurred in subsequent years, in terms of loss of working days and numbers of those involved, the figures have not reached 2000 levels. Between 2004 and 2008 the average number of daily labour disputes decreased from 462 to 108, as a result of which the number of working days lost through strikes also declined, from 1,198,779 to 809,042 (although the last figure was more than 50% higher than in 2007). In 2009, however, the average number of daily disputes rose to 121, causing the loss of 626,921 working days. In 2010 the corresponding figures were 86 and 511,307. For individual companies, strikes have continued to pose a serious threat: between May and August 2009, for example, production at Ssangyong Motor was at a standstill, owing to a strike by its workers in protest against the company's decision to shed about 1,000 jobs.

Following his assumption of office in February 2003, President Roh Moo-Hyun declared his determination to address outstanding labour issues, but serious tensions between employers and trade unions persisted. It was telling, for example, that the announcement of a minimal (2.75%) rise in the minimum hourly wage, implemented in 2010 (see above), was made against the background of demands by management that the rate be reduced by almost 16%, and parallel demands by workers that it be increased by 29%. As temporary job opportunities in the informal sector have come increasingly to dominate employment markets (according to one source, irregular workers have come to account for well over one-half of the South Korean work-force—far more than the 40% cited by the Government), the existence of wide differentials in earnings between those working on long-term contracts and those on temporary contracts became a major issue. Despite quite significant wage rises (see below), strikes and other forms of union agitation in support of greater job security have continued. Overseas labour organizations have been strongly critical of South Korean labour law and practice, especially with regard to prohibitions on strike activity, state intervention in union activities and the absence of trade union representation among public servants. Conflict, at times accompanied by violence, characterized labour relations in 2005 and 2006. The extent to which poor labour relations will cause major companies, such as Hyundai, to relocate production activities to countries where union activity is less vigorous, remains to be seen. In July 2010 a significant development was the introduction of new regulations, designed to reduce significantly the number of fully paid full-time union officials to no more than 24 such employees, depending on the size of the work-force in a given company and the size of the relevant trade union. The new norms elicited resistance from within unions, although some observers argued that in the longer term the regulations would help to mitigate what was widely perceived to be the excessive politicization of union activity.

Between 1987 and 1997 wages increased five-fold, although such rapid growth was ended by the onset of the Asian financial crisis in the latter year. According to data published by the International Labour Organization, between 1999 and 2008 monthly earnings in manufacturing almost doubled (rising from 1.44m. to 2.76m. won). According to survey data published by the Ministry of Employment and Labour, in the final quarter of 2010 the average real wage for all workers was 2.40m. won, 0.6% higher than at the same point in 2009.

ECONOMIC GROWTH AND STRUCTURAL CHANGE

The social and economic legacy of the Korean War of 1950–53 was devastating. In addition to casualties, some 1.5m. refugees from the North had to be accommodated in the South. The cost of physical damage to property is estimated to have equalled South Korea's entire gross national product (GNP) for 1953, or more than 10 times the then annual rate of fixed capital investment. In 1953 levels of production in all sectors were well below the previous peak levels of the early 1940s, and output was heavily skewed towards agriculture, with manufacturing production accounting for less than 9% of GNP. Such conditions dictated that, following the war, rehabilitation, reconstruction and stabilization assumed the highest economic priority. In part owing to large-scale US aid, these goals were fulfilled fairly quickly, and by 1957 war damage had been repaired and prices stabilized. However, the pace of South Korea's economic expansion then slowed considerably, until the military coup of May 1961 brought Park Chung-Hee to power.

The implementation of the First Five-Year Plan (1962–66) marked an important stage in South Korea's post-war development, not only because it directed the economy towards a new, more buoyant growth path, but also because it marked the start of a distinctly new policy approach, symbolized by a fundamental shift from inward-looking import-substitution to an outward-looking growth strategy of export promotion. The speed of transformation after the 1962 'take-off' was remarkable. By 1970 South Korea had already acquired the status of a newly industrializing economy; by 1986 it had reached the stage of self-sustaining growth, with domestic savings more than able to finance investment and with the balance of payments having shifted from chronic deficit into surplus (thereby obviating the need for aid or overseas borrowing). Although the momentum of growth slowed in and after the 1990s, South Korea's development record remains unmatched in post-1945 experience, except perhaps among the other first-echelon newly industrializing economies of Asia.

In the aftermath of the Korean War, massive inflows of aid facilitated rapid economic reconstruction, although recovery was accompanied by severe inflationary pressures. By the end of the 1950s South Korea's productive facilities had been restored and the economy was poised for renewed growth. Thereafter, between the First (1962–66) and Sixth (1987–91) Five-Year Plans, and driven by a rapid and sustained expansion of exports, South Korea's GDP grew, on average, by more than 9% per year. Although this average estimate conceals significant year-to-year fluctuations, the rapid and mutually reinforcing expansion of output, income and exports during these years was accompanied by increasing shares of savings, investment and foreign trade in national income. Much slower economic expansion in the 1990s (GNP increased, on average, by 5.7% annually during 1990–99) reflected decelerating growth in the early 1990s, but mostly the impact of the Asian financial crisis during 1997–98. By 2000 South Korea's aggregate GDP had reached US $457,219m., a figure exceeded by only 11 other countries throughout the world, although that of India was almost identical. The fact that aggregate GDP in that year was 44% higher than in 1998 was a sign of how far and how fast the Korean economy had recovered, in purely quantitative terms, from the worst point of the Asian financial crisis.

The momentum of rapid and sustained growth over almost three decades from the early 1960s reflected the deliberate choice of a strategy designed to maximize growth through the pursuit of outward-orientated policies. During this period the imperative of export-led growth dominated South Korea's development plans and replaced the previous emphasis on indigenous import-substitution. Other complementary measures were adopted, and the mutually reinforcing impact of a variety of factors—the existence of an abundant supply of highly skilled, highly educated, disciplined and (at least initially) cheap labour, a readiness to use advanced foreign capital and technology, the growth of an indigenous managerial class, and a growing research and development capacity—contributed to the success of the new strategy. From a demand perspective, rising real wages that benefited a wide cross-section of the population, especially in the urban sector, also facilitated the emergence of a sizeable middle class that commanded considerable purchasing power.

Under the impact of rapid and sustained growth over several decades, the structure of the South Korean economy has undergone dramatic change. Predictably, the role of agriculture as a source of GDP has given way to that of industry (construction, mining and manufacturing) and, latterly, services. In the mid-1960s the farm sector still accounted for about 40% of GDP, compared with a contribution of some 16% from industry (including mining and construction) and 44% from services. By 2010 the agricultural share had declined to a mere 2.6%, while industry accounted for a further 39.3% (with a little more than one-quarter being derived from manufacturing alone). The contribution of services to GDP had meanwhile risen to 58.2%. Projections suggest that the relative contributions of the three major sectors to GDP are unlikely to change significantly in the foreseeable future. Contained within the changing structure is the finding that, like its neighbouring 'dragon' economies (Hong Kong and Taiwan), South Korea has since the 1960s not only industrialized, but also subsequently transformed itself into a mature, services-dominated economy.

A characteristic institutional feature of South Korea's economy has been the dominant role played by *chaebol*, or conglomerates—a Korean variant of the Japanese *zaibatsu*. The concentration of industrial production in such a small number of conglomerates is probably greater than in any other comparable country. Their sheer size is remarkable. For example, by the mid-1990s the Samsung Group had a global work-force of almost 85,000 employees, who generated significant shares of South Korean exports and government revenue. Until the 1997 crisis the Government adopted a policy of inducements backed up by sanctions, which enabled it to use the *chaebol* as an instrument of its economic policies. That the relationship between government and *chaebol* facilitated rapid industrial growth is beyond doubt, although it also had a negative effect through encouraging and facilitating the emergence of 'crony capitalism'.

In 1995 the leading 30 *chaebol* accounted for 16% of GDP, 41% of manufacturing value-added and 50% of export value; the domination of these large-scale entities thus inhibited the growth of small and medium-scale enterprises (SMEs) of the kind that played such a vital role in Taiwan's post-1945 economic growth. Following almost 14,000 SME bankruptcies in South Korea in 1995, a Small and Medium Business Administration, intended to promote more sustained SME growth, was established in 1996, but its potential role was overtaken by the onset of the financial crisis; by the end of 1998 the failure of 22,828 SMEs had been recorded. However, much more serious in terms of its economic consequences was a series of corporate bankruptcies, affecting even major *chaebol* (for example, Hanbo, Kia and Yuwon). In the case of Samsung, such was the impact of the 1997/98 Asian recession that it was forced to restructure its operations, as a result of which its work-force was reduced by about one-third to some 55,000. Indeed, the collapse of Daewoo was the most serious corporate bankruptcy in the country's history. Precipitated by the 1997 financial crisis, the demise of major enterprises had severe repercussions for the country's financial system, dramatically increasing the scale of outstanding non-performing loans (NPLs) and underlining the need for radical and far-reaching corporate and financial restructuring, not least in order to loosen the complex web of ownership and cross-subsidies among *chaebol* and simultaneously to weaken their clientelist relationship with government.

Significant progress towards improving the state of the *chaebol* sector was achieved under the Kim Dae-Jung administration (1997–2003), and Kim's successor as President, Roh Moo-Hyun (2003–08), maintained this policy thrust in his promise to make the conglomerates more open and accountable. In 2003 accounting frauds were uncovered within the SK Corporation—the fourth largest business group in South Korea—which led to a three-year prison sentence for SK's Chairman, Chey Tae-Won. Further scandals, which appeared to highlight continuing corrupt practices by leading *chaebol*, subsequently emerged. Chung Mong-Koo, Chairman of Hyundai Motor, and Lee Kun-Hee, Chairman of Samsung, were two senior business leaders who were investigated for alleged misdemeanours. Indeed, in February 2007 Chung, the second richest man in South Korea, was given a three-year prison sentence for the embezzlement of 100,000m. won, of which almost 70,000m. won had been used for the purposes of illegal political donations. (The sentence was subsequently suspended subject to an undertaking by Chung to donate 1,000,000m. won—or around US $1,000m.—to charity.) By contrast, in April 2008 the investigations into allegations of corruption against Lee Kun-Hee and Samsung were dismissed, although Lee himself subsequently resigned both as Chairman of the company and as a member of the Board of Directors of Samsung Electronics (SEC). Lee paid $140m. in overdue taxes; he was also given a three-year suspended prison sentence and fined $80m. However, the view of most observers was that neither Lee's resignation nor the announcement of the closure of Samsung's strategic planning office was likely to have a major impact in the near term on group organization and management.

Overall, the ramifications of such scandals highlight both the urgency of the challenge of corporate sector restructuring in South Korea and the difficulties of improving corporate governance. However, for the time being, post-1997 reforms notwithstanding, the dominance of the *chaebol* remains very much a central part of South Korean economic reality. It was also felt that the advent in 2008 of the new pro-business Government under President Lee Myung-Bak might signal a slowing of efforts to increase regulatory controls over 'big business'. For example, an EIU report of May 2008 suggested that the previous emphasis of Korea's Fair Trade Commission on seeking to limit excessive *chaebol* expansion had been abandoned in favour of encouraging those same companies to 'go on an investment spree'. In the event, such fears appear not to have been realized. The Government of President Lee reaffirmed its commitment to upholding free market principles. Meanwhile, in June 2009 the announcement by Kumho Asiana (the eighth largest *chaebol*) that it was to sell its one-third stake in Daewoo Engineering and Construction offered further evidence that the momentum of corporate restructuring was being maintained.

The consequences of such a shift in emphasis are likely to be significant. In the early 21st century, even allowing for significant recovery from the low point that followed the Asian financial crisis, there remained major challenges. Nor were such challenges limited to the need for intensified corporate and financial restructuring, even if these have once more come to the fore as a result of pressures brought about by the global financial crisis of 2008 and the subsequent recession. (In 2009 Doosan Group—hitherto a major success among South Korea's second-tier *chaebol*—was forced to embrace a radical programme of corporate restructuring in response to a deterioration in its finances occasioned by the effects of the global downturn.) Looking further ahead, other priority tasks include the implementation of measures, such as the further deregulation of services, to accelerate employment creation; and the formulation of effective ways of accommodating the growth of protective sentiments in the USA, Japan and EU member states—precisely the countries that, in the past, have absorbed a high share of Korean exports. The nature of future political and economic development in China and North Korea will also be critically important determinants of South Korea's own development trajectory.

A major initiative was the endorsement by the South Korean and US Governments, in April 2007, of a free trade agreement (FTA). This agreement, which was easily the most significant of its kind ever reached by South Korea, envisaged an increase in the value of annual bilateral trade by as much as US $20,000m., and it was expected to give South Korea a competitive advantage over China and Japan with regard to trading with the USA. The FTA was expected also to act as a counter-weight to Seoul's rapidly expanding links with China, to the advantage of the USA. The two sectors expected to gain most in South Korea were steel- and car-manufacturing (including automotive parts). The terms of the agreement provided for the elimination of all tariffs within three years.

Overall, the potential gains for both sides are considerable, although it was expected that some aspects of the FTA would encounter considerable opposition in the US Congress and the South Korean National Assembly. One obstacle was the insistence by US negotiators that goods produced by South Korean companies operating in the Kaesong industrial zone across the border with North Korea should be excluded from the agreement. In spite of such obstacles, the two sides duly signed the FTA in June 2007. As of mid-2011, despite US President Barack Obama's support for the agreement, the FTA still awaited ratification by both the US and South Korean legislatures..

Meanwhile, in May 2007 negotiations with a view to establishing an FTA between South Korea and the EU commenced, and in October 2009, in the Belgian capital of Brussels, officials from the two sides initialled an agreement. A year later the FTA was formally signed, and in February 2011 it received the overwhelming approval of members of the European Parliament. The FTA—the EU's largest ever and its first with an Asian country—took effect on 1 July 2011. Under the terms of the agreement, 98.7% of duties in trade value would be eliminated within five years. The FTA's potential economic impact was suggested in a study, which argued that it would facilitate a 100% increase in trade between the EU and South Korea within a 20-year period.

PLANNING

From 1962 the Government used formal economic planning as a framework through which to influence the behaviour of the private sector and to guide economic development. Although the Government's use of 'indicative' planning did not directly compel enterprises to adhere strictly to specific targets, it did bring indirect pressure to bear through the market mechanism and other means. Thus, enterprises were expected to conform to the basic objectives of plans, while the Government resorted to fiscal, monetary and other measures in order to fulfil planned targets. The existence of a private sector and the absence of compulsion highlights the peculiarly 'managerial approach' inherent in the Korean economy—a major contrast with the planned system of the former Soviet bloc, which sought to integrate all major economic inputs and outputs in accordance with preconceived objectives and priorities through a vertical hierarchy in which orders were passed down from higher to lower administrative levels. In short, the Korean experience was one of planning pursued within a market-based economic system. Although vestiges of this approach remain, structural reforms in the financial, corporate, public and labour sectors, under way since the 1997 economic crisis, highlight the continuing retreat by the Government from its previous interventionist role in economic activities and its commitment to a more 'orthodox' free market economy.

Except for the Fourth Five-Year Plan (1977–81), during which South Korea experienced a serious recession, GDP growth consistently over-fulfilled targeted rates. A common theme in all the national plans was a strong emphasis on the outward orientation of national economic development—in particular, the need for export expansion. However, policy thrusts of successive plans differed. For example, under the First Five-Year Plan (1962–66), a major priority was the expansion of infrastructural capital in electric power, railways, ports and communications, in order to obviate resource and other physical obstacles to development. In the Second Plan (1967–71), special attention was directed to the growth of electronic and petrochemical industries, as well as to raising farm incomes by maintaining high prices for rice (the staple crop). Priority development of heavy and chemical industries—especially steel, petrochemicals and shipbuilding—was strongly in evidence in the Third Plan (1972–76) and defined a major new policy thrust in South Korea's development strategy. In the Fourth Plan, initiatives focused on industrial development based on the intensive use of technology and skilled labour. The same Plan, for the first time, also stressed the importance of social development, based on higher government welfare spending as a means of promoting a more equal and equitable distribution of income.

Under the Fifth (1982–86) and Sixth (1987–91) Plans, the strategy of export-led growth was strongly reaffirmed alongside unprecedented efforts to liberalize domestic markets, intended to dismantle regulations that had previously constrained the South Korean economy in its attempt to adjust to changing internal and external environments. In the simultaneous search for welfare and efficiency improvements, the Plans also articulated the need for more balanced sectoral and regional development.

In 1993 a revised Five-Year Plan was introduced. Within the framework of a targeted growth rate of 6.9%, the new Plan sought to elevate South Korea into the ranks of advanced economies and to lay the economic foundation for eventual reunification with the North. In line with the requirements of OECD membership, measures were introduced in an effort to combat official corruption and to initiate structural reforms within the economy. To these ends, three separate sub-plans were formulated, embracing deregulation, financial liberalization, and the management of foreign exchange and capital flows.

THE CRISIS OF 1997, THE GLOBAL DOWNTURN OF 2008/09 AND ITS AFTERMATH

With the benefit of hindsight, it is clear that, despite its record of several decades of high growth and rising living standards, as of the mid-1990s the South Korean economy suffered deeply rooted structural problems. In particular, two structural features made it highly vulnerable to external 'shocks'. The first was the influence of the corporate financial structure; the second was the disproportionate share, alongside an external debt-to-GDP ratio of around 25%, of short-term debt (which had reached almost 60% of the total by the end of 1996). Such problems were the major contributory factors that precipitated the severe financial dislocation and economic collapse that affected South Korea, as well as other Asian countries, during 1997–98. Even before the onset of the Asian financial crisis, bankruptcy proceedings against a major *chaebol*, namely the Hanbo group, had served notice of the scale of difficulties confronting the Government in Seoul. In early 1997 six of Korea's 30 largest *chaebol* (Hanbo, Sammi, Jinro, Kia, Haitai and New Core) petitioned for court protection in bankruptcy proceedings. In July of the same year the Kia Group defaulted on its loans. Efforts to rescue the situation were unsuccessful and the crisis deepened, leading to severe pressure on the national currency and stock market. The banking sector was particularly affected by the conglomerate bankruptcies, and the incidence of NPLs, which was eventually to reach some 20% of GDP, increased sharply in the second half of 1997. Against this background, fears began to grow that the Government might find itself with insufficient foreign-currency reserves to service its foreign debt.

Central to understanding this rapid economic and financial deterioration are the close links that had evolved over many years between the Government, banks and *chaebol*. These links had concealed serious underlying economic weaknesses and had created an economic 'bubble', characterized by excessive investment in productive capacity and the overvaluation of the domestic currency. In the absence of adequate regulatory and supervisory controls, the financial system lacked transparency. With tacit acceptance by the Government, industrial projects had been duplicated, generating excess capacity. Meanwhile, many *chaebol* had invested aggressively, frequently in disregard of normal risk criteria, on the basis of profligate loans from domestic financial institutions, while also funding long-term investments by recourse to short-term foreign capital markets. In July 1997, immediately prior to the onset of the Asian crisis, the average debt-to-equity ratio of Korea's 30 largest *chaebol* was in excess of 400%, a figure that had increased to 500% by the end of the year.

By the end of 1997 capital flight had become a serious problem, as foreign investors withdrew capital and many Koreans moved their savings overseas. Between October and December of that year capital outflows totalled some US $9,800m. Local firms sought to avoid hard-currency exposure, and export revenue declined. Such developments brought further pressure to bear on stock prices and on land values, which both decreased sharply. Despite intervention by the central bank, the won continued to slide, and by the end of the year it had lost more than one-half of its value against the US dollar.

After protracted negotiations, IMF officials approved a rescue programme involving a US $57,000m. loan arrangement for South Korea on 3 December 1997—a day that some Korean newspapers described as the 'second day of national disgrace' in the country's history (the first having been the start of Japanese occupation in 1905). Of the total, $10,000m. was to be made available as 'accelerated aid', most of it to be provided by the World Bank and the IMF. This rescue programme, the largest ever undertaken by the Fund, was designed to facilitate a solution to South Korea's serious foreign-exchange difficulties and help reverse the precipitate decline in its international credit status. In return, the Government in Seoul committed itself to the introduction of more rigorous fiscal and monetary policies (including the maintenance of high interest rates), the strengthening of regulatory control mechanisms, the institution of financial and corporate restructuring, consolidation of labour market reform, and the enhancement of financial transparency in both public and private sectors. Central to the success of these reforms was the implementation of a policy 'package' embracing economic and institutional measures. These sought to fulfil the following goals: to lower the level of corporate debt and institute a system of corporate governance in order to improve competitiveness by facilitating greater transparency in management; to reduce and eliminate NPLs through financial restructuring (including bank purchases, mergers and acquisitions); to institute budgetary reforms in the interests of improved public sector efficiency; and to liberalize employment mechanisms in order to make the labour market more flexible.

As a result of the financial crisis, severe economic and associated social strains were in evidence throughout 1998. Annual GDP contracted by 6.9%, while the unemployment rate rose from 2.6% to 7.0% (and increased further to 8.7% in March 1999—higher than at any point in the previous three decades). Labour unrest and social demoralization were exacerbated by a rapid salary depreciation (real wages decreased by 21%), mounting personal bankruptcies, and sharp increases in the prices of foreign consumer goods and energy imports. More than 17,000 firms—most of them SMEs—declared bankruptcy, and in the first half of 1998 losses suffered by listed Korean companies totalled some 14,000,000m. won. In July deepening recessionary conditions led the IMF to relax the fiscal and monetary conditions of its loan 'package'. However, with the currency successfully stabilized, in the second half of 1998 the Government, now headed by President Kim Dae-Jung, introduced measures designed to stimulate domestic demand. Interest rates were lowered, spending on unemployment relief was increased, and efforts to promote financial and corporate restructuring were intensified.

As indicated above, a major issue in *chaebol* restructuring plans was the reduction of their extremely high level of indebtedness, which was thought to be one of the principal reasons for the severity of South Korea's financial crisis. For manufacturing industry as a whole, between 1997 and 2002 the debt ratio decreased from 396.3% to 130.0%—well below the targeted 200% level set by the Government in 1999. By 2004 the debt-to-equity ratio of listed companies in the Korean Stock Exchanges had declined to 118%. However, a significant part of this decline was attributable to equity issues, asset revaluations and selective debt exclusion, rather than to genuine debt reduction. In addition, the record of the largest *chaebol* was more disappointing: in 2002, for example, the debt-to-equity ratio of the 19 largest *chaebol* averaged 171.7%, and in the case of Hyundai the ratio was still an extraordinary 977.6%. Nevertheless, despite declining profitability, such was the progress in addressing the debt issue that in 2006 the BOK was able to claim that the corporate sector had achieved what it described as a 'comparatively healthy overall debt-servicing capacity, with sound financial status and ample liquidity'.

Initially, burdened with NPLs of 160,000,000m. won—far in excess of the 64,000,000m. won allocated by the Government to buy back bad loans and recapitalize the banking system—and preoccupied with mere survival, the banks themselves were in a weak position to assist in corporate restructuring. An important institutional initiative was the reorganization, in November 1997, of the Korea Asset Management Corporation (KAMCO), which subsequently played a central role in addressing Korea's NPL problem. Between 1997 and 2007 KAMCO purchased 38,700,000m. won of NPLs. In 2000, despite the closure of five large commercial banks and 16 smaller merchant banks, as well as the provision of further large-scale government funding (the Government made available some 102,000,000m. won in rescue programmes), it was clear that further reform and consolidation, including the disposal of government holdings in banking institutions, were needed. Subsequent rationalization of the banking sector indicated that such needs were being met, and in 2004 South Korea's 19 banks reported record profits of 8,800,000m. won. In 2005 such profits increased by a further remarkable 52.4% to reach a new peak of 13,400,000m. won. In 2006 the banking sector continued to show strong profitability, supported by increased profits from loans and the disposal of shares acquired in debt-for-equity swaps. Between 2003 and 2005 the banks' average capital-adequacy ratio rose from 11.2% to 13.0%, before falling back marginally to 12.8% in 2006 (this average concealing individual bank ratios ranging from a low of 10.9% to a high point of 14.2%) and 12% at the end of 2007. At the same time, low and declining rates of return on deposits encouraged banks increasingly to turn to borrowing overseas in order to finance domestic loans, although owing to South Korea's massive foreign-exchange reserves, rising short-term foreign debt seemed unlikely to pose a significant risk. It is a measure of the scale of the recovery from the 1997 crisis that by the end of 2006 the banking sector's NPL ratio had declined to 0.85%, the lowest level since 1999. The intervention of the financial crisis of 2008 and its aftermath raised the possibility that the NPL ratio might rise once more, as a result of an increasing incidence of corporate and household loan defaults. In a *Country Report* published in August 2009, IMF analysts noted that South Korea's NPL ratio had risen to 1.6% and predicted that corporate defaults would raise it further to 3.2%.

Following the crisis conditions of 1997–98, South Korea's economic performance improved markedly in 1999, the contraction in GDP of the previous year (by 6.9%) being transformed into positive growth of 9.5%. An easing of fiscal and monetary policy kept interest rates low and helped stabilize the currency, with the won reaching a two-year high. Meanwhile, private consumption spending and business investment rose sharply in 1999 and 2000 (by 10.1% and 46.8%, respectively). As annual manufacturing growth accelerated to 21%, the rate of unemployment began to decline (from 6.8% in 1998 to 6.3% in 1999). Overseas demand for South Korean goods meanwhile strengthened, and by the end of 1999 the current account surplus was US $24,479m., compared with a deficit of $8,183m. two years previously. Foreign-currency reserves also continued their recovery from the low point of 1997, when they were just $19,710m., to reach almost $74,000m. in 1999. Compared with foreign direct investment (FDI) inflows of $5,400m. in 1998, in the following year FDI inflows were restored to $9,300m. (rising from 1.7% to 2.3% of GDP). It was against this background that President Kim Dae-Jung claimed that his Government had 'completely overcome' the financial crisis and, moreover, had done so without full recourse to the IMF rescue 'package'.

Owing to a sharp slowdown in private consumption in the final quarter, GDP growth in 2000 decreased to 9.3%—slightly lower than the 9.5% growth that had been predicted. The failure to maintain the momentum of rapid economic expansion in the first half of 2000 through the rest of the year was partly attributable to stagnation in traditional manufacturing industries (for example, textiles and car production). However, the main contributory factor was the decline in domestic demand. A similar but less pronounced pattern was apparent in the external sector, where export growth of 23.5% during January–September slowed to around 18% in the final quarter. As a result, by the end of 2000 the current account surplus had been reduced from US $24,479m. at the end of 1999 to $14,803m. In the following two years the surplus declined further, to $8,428m. and $7,542m. (in 2001 and 2002, respectively), before recovering sharply to reach $15,584m. in 2003. In

2004 the current account surplus more than doubled to reach $32,312m. (the 11th largest in the world). A forecast by the Korea Development Institute (KDI—a government-sponsored 'think tank') suggested that, as a result of currency appreciation, rising oil prices and widening deficits on service, income and transfer balances, the current account surplus would contract to around $14,000m. in 2005. Although KDI's prediction proved overly pessimistic, the 2005 surplus ($18,607m.) was 42% below that of the previous year, and by the end of the following year South Korea's current account balance had decreased to $14,083m. Although there was a small improvement in 2007, to $21,770m., in 2008 the effect of the global economic downturn was to reduce the current account surplus by 85%, to $3,197m. However, owing to a significant improvement in the merchandise trade balance, in 2009 the overall current account surplus recovered to $32,791m. (3.9% of GDP). The current account surplus declined to $28,214m. (2.8% of GDP) in 2010, although the EIU predicted a modest recovery to $30,200m. in 2012.

If South Korea's recovery from the economic crisis of 1997–98 was striking, doubts about the long-term sustainability of the high rates of GDP growth attained in 1999 and 2000 were reinforced by the volatility of domestic politics and perceptions of government policy confusion. The future growth trajectory was expected to be determined by a combination of familiar internal and external forces. The former include the pattern of domestic consumer and investment demand. One effect of depressed conditions in 1998 was to reduce private consumption by 13.5%. Although in the following year private consumption demand recovered (rising by 11.5%), in the second half of 2000 it decreased substantially. The trend of 2001 and the first half of 2002 was one of recovery and renewed growth in private consumption. However, in mid-2002 consumer expectations once more declined sharply, and not until the final quarter of 2004 did they improve (in 2004 the annual rate of increase in private consumption was only 0.3%). In March 2005 the NSO's consumer expectation index was at its highest level since September 2003, and renewed private consumption growth was maintained throughout the year and into 2006 and 2007 (up by 4.7% and 5.1%, respectively). However, as early as the first quarter of 2008 there was a significant slowing of domestic demand, with private consumption increasing by a mere 0.6% quarter-on-quarter, and for the year as a whole the corresponding annual figure was just 1.3%. Under the impact of rising unemployment and declining real incomes occasioned by the deteriorating economic environment, private consumption growth in 2009 fell back sharply, although a positive, albeit minimal, rate of increase (0.2%) was maintained. Significant recovery took place in 2010, with annual private consumption rising by 4.1%. However, as consumer sentiment weakened, EIU projections suggested that this rate of improvement would not be maintained and that consumption growth would slow to 3% in 2011. The potential seriousness of the declining trend is captured in the finding that private consumption has been a major driving force of South Korea's economic growth (in 2008, for example, it accounted for 53% of GDP, compared with only 14.4% from government spending). Unlike its private counterpart, government consumption maintained buoyant growth in 2009, although it slowed significantly in 2010.

Between 1996 and 1997 the rate of gross domestic capital formation fixed investment, measured in constant 2000 prices, declined sharply, from 8.4% to –2.3%. However, the full impact of the crisis only became apparent in 1998, when the rate of decrease reached 22.9%, a figure that concealed a 42.3% contraction in the demand for machinery and equipment. During 1999 and 2000, despite the continuing decline in construction demand, gross domestic capital formation rose, cumulatively, by over 20%. Between 2001 and 2007 the real annual growth rate of gross capital formation remained positive, but varied considerably from a high point of 5.9% (2001) to 1.9% (2005). However, under the impact of the unfolding global economic crisis, in 2008 and 2009 the rate of increase became negative (contracting by 1.9% and 0.2%, respectively, according to BOK data). In particular, the shift to negative investment growth in 2008 reflected declining corporate profitability, the postponement of investment plans and a rapid deterioration in the domestic housing market. Recovery was, however, swift: in 2010 gross fixed capital formation rose by 7%. EIU projections suggested that annual investment growth in 2011 and 2012 would maintain quite buoyant expansion, rising by 4.9% and 3.0%, respectively. In 2010 the share of fixed investment in GDP was 26.6%.

South Korea's strong outward economic orientation means that external forces have a major bearing on its overall performance. In the aftermath of the financial crisis, the value of exports rose, in terms of Korea's domestic currency, by 12.7% (15.9% for merchandise exports) in 1998, while the value of imports declined by 21.8% (a contraction of 24.8% for foreign merchandise purchases). The effect of these changes was to transform a merchandise trade deficit of 30,000m. won in 1997 into a surplus of 25,300m. won in 1998. However, because of the sharp decline in the value of the domestic currency, in US dollar terms the effect was to change a deficit of US $3,861m. to a surplus of $43,237m., a level that had not previously and has not subsequently been (re)attained. Between 2006 and 2007 the surplus increased from $31,433m. to $37,129m. However, with imports growing significantly faster than exports, in 2008 South Korea's trade surplus decreased by 86%, to $5,170m. Under the increasingly serious impact of the global economic recession, there was a sharp decline in both exports and imports in 2009, although the more severe contraction in imports facilitated a major increase in the merchandise trade balance to $37,866m. In 2010, despite imports rising slightly faster than exports, the surplus increased to $41,904m.

One of the effects of the 1997/98 Asian crisis was to bring about the demise of what had come to be known as 'Korea Inc'—the nexus of state-business relations, whereby industrial activities were subject to serious political interference and characterized by widespread corruption. Nevertheless, the legacy of such practices remains, and central to South Korea's future economic trajectory is the Government's ability to address the need for further corporate restructuring by enhancing competition in order to regulate the power of the *chaebol*, the activities of which will continue to dominate industry and exports. In 2002 the need for greater self-regulation by the corporate sector was demonstrated by several developments: the bankruptcy of Daewoo and the purchase of Daewoo Motor by General Motors, the separation of Hyundai into smaller constituent elements, and official endorsement of the purchase of South Korea's third largest life insurance company (Korea Life Insurance) by Hanhwa, a *chaebol* with a reputation for financial misconduct. Following the accession to the country's presidency of Lee Myung-Bak in February 2008, the pace of corporate restructuring did not seem to slowed, and it was possible that declining corporate profitability under the impact of recessionary conditions would forcibly accelerate the process (see the example of the Doosan Group, above).

In general, the moral of recent developments seems clear: in the absence of the strict implementation of rigorous control mechanisms, problems of costly mismanagement and misconduct within the corporate business sector have remained a real threat, especially if privatization offers new opportunities for corporate expansion. Meanwhile, if South Korea is to retain, let alone improve, its place in the global economy, it is incumbent on the Government, as privatization leads it to downsize its interventionist economic role, to strengthen structural reforms (including banking reforms) and to put in place an effective legal and regulatory framework that will facilitate increased competitiveness by autonomous decision-making enterprises. At the same time, research and development and educational investment must be increased in order to make the South Korean economy a truly knowledge-based economy that can compete effectively in the global environment. The global financial crisis of 2008/09 merely served to reinforce the importance of such object lessons.

As the foregoing analysis has suggested, the impact on the South Korean economy of the global financial crisis and subsequent recession has been serious. Between 2007 and 2008 annual GDP growth decreased from 5.1% to 2.3%, its lowest level since the Asian financial crisis of 1997/98. In 2009 growth declined further, to just 0.3%. Concealed within this aggregate figure is the finding that the agricultural sector has demonstrated the best growth performance (rising from 4.0% to 5.6%

between 2007 and 2008, before weakening to 3.2% in 2009). By contrast, the industrial growth rate declined from 7.1% in 2007 to a negative performance of –1.5% in 2009, while service sector growth was almost halved from 5.1% to 2.8% during 2007–08, and decreased further to 1.2% in 2009. Construction growth in South Korea turned negative in 2008 (declining from 2.6% to –2.5%, according to the BOK) but, owing to the impact of the stimulus programme, recovered to 1.8% in 2009. As noted above, the annual rate of increase of fixed asset investment was also negative in both 2008 and 2009.

The Government's immediate response to the developing global crisis was, in November 2008, to announce the introduction of a stimulus programme, envisaging expenditure of 14,000,000m. won (US $11,000m.). It pledged that two-thirds of the funds would be spent within the first half of 2009. Of the total committed to the programme, 11,000,000m. won would represent new spending: thus, 4,600,000m. would be allocated to infrastructural projects, 3,400,000m. to help support SMEs, and 1,000,000m. to assist low-income households. A further 1,100,000m. won would be allocated to local government spending. The remaining 3,000,000m. won would be raised through tax cuts.

In March 2009 the South Korean National Assembly approved a supplementary budget of 28,400,000m. won (US $21,100m.), designed to lend further support to efforts to facilitate economic recovery. The perceived scale of the challenge for the Government was suggested by the fact that the supplementary budget was more than twice as large as the extra budgetary allocation made available in 1998 in response to the Asian financial crisis. Of the total budget, 11,200,000m. won would be used to offset anticipated shortfalls in tax revenue; the remaining 17,200,000m. won (slightly less than the 17,700,000m. the Government had sought to raise) would be allocated to stabilize employment and provide further support for low-income families.

Growth recovered sharply in 2010, with GDP rising by 6.2%. This performance owed much to a major reversal in the fortunes of manufacturing, which expanded by 14.8%. At mid-2011 there was reason to believe that South Korea's economy had stabilized and that the Government's concerns would revert to addressing the serious structural and systemic problems inherited from the past. Even so, authoritive sources (including the EIU) warned against expectations that stimulus measures would be quickly reversed, not least in view of increasing competition from China for both domestic and export markets.

AGRICULTURE

South Korea is a mountainous country. Only 20% of the surface area (1.9m. ha) is arable, 65% being designated as forest land. The Taebaek range, which runs from north to south along the east coast, is the watershed of the Korean peninsula and the source of the country's principal rivers (the Han, Nakdong and Kum). South Korea's farming is concentrated mainly in these river basins and in the surrounding plains in the west and south. Owing to its more favourable climate and longer growing seasons (between 170 and 226 days), South Korea is more suited to farming than the North, especially in the cultivation of rice. This is still the main crop, with paddy fields accounting for about 60% of the total cultivated area. In general, pressures of industrialization and urbanization have led to the abandonment of the production of grain and economic crops, such as wheat, millet, sorghum and cotton. For example, a noteworthy development from the beginning of the 1980s was a sharp decline in the sown area of barley, as a result of which the overall arable area contracted from 2.2m. ha in 1980 to 1.9m. ha in 2000. The change reflected the reduction in the double-cropping of barley alongside rice.

In the 1950s Korea remained a typical pre-industrial country, in which almost one-half of GDP was derived from agriculture and an even larger proportion of its work-force was engaged in farming. However, thereafter vigorous industrialization and export promotion transformed the agrarian character of the economy: between 1960 and the early 1980s the share of agriculture in GDP decreased to about 15%, while the countryside's share of total population declined from 58% to less than 25%. In 2010 crop farming, forestry and fisheries accounted for 2.6% of GDP and 6.6% of total employment. In terms of its share of value added generated throughout the economy, the contribution of the farm sector declined from 8.5% to 3.3% between 1990 and 2005, while that of industry remained largely unchanged (in fact, it declined from 38.8% to 38.0%) and the tertiary sector's share rose from 52% to 58.7%. Such figures highlight the low productivity of farming relative to that of other sectors, although viewed from an international perspective South Korea's long-term record of agricultural growth since the early 1960s has exceeded the world average, as well as that of many Asian countries.

Agricultural production contracted steeply (by 6.4%) in the immediate aftermath of the 1997 financial crisis, but by 2000 it had fully recovered. Since then, agriculture has demonstrated quite wide variations in annual growth. Expressed in constant 2005 prices, in 2002 and 2003 agricultural GDP growth was negative (–2.2% and –5.4%). However, production recovered sharply in 2004, rising by 9.1%. Thereafter, following two years (2005 and 2006) of growth averaging no more than 1.5%, in 2007 and 2008 performance was much more buoyant: farm output rose by 4.0% and 5.6%, respectively, although the rate of expansion slowed to 3.2% in 2009 and was negative in 2010 (decreasing by 4.3%). The output of principal food grains has steadily declined, not least because of a reduction in government price support as required by World Trade Organization (WTO) regulations. According to the FAO 2009 *Statistical Yearbook*, between 1999 and 2001 (average) and 2007 total cereal production decreased from 7.6m. metric tons to 6.3m. tons, a cumulative decline of 17%. Underlying this decrease was a small reduction in average yield and a much larger contraction (by just over 12%) in total sown area, although from a longer historical perspective it was noteworthy that in 2007 cereal yields were some 4% above those of 1990, while sown area had contracted by almost 30%. In any case, in 2008 and 2009 the previous downward trend in cereal production was reversed: in 2009, owing to average yields rising sufficiently to offset the continuing decline in sown area, total output recovered to 7.4m. tons. In general, as a result of the contraction in domestic output, South Korea has become increasingly dependent on imports to meet its consumption requirements, both for direct and indirect purposes. The pressure on feed sources for animals is illustrated by the fact that in recent years imports of maize have exceeded 8m. tons annually (between 2000 and 2008 the cost of maize imports more than tripled, from US $933m. to $2,820m., although the corresponding figure in 2009 was $1,638m.). A further consequence of the negative trend in crop production has been pressure on food prices, increases in which have been a major element contributing to consumer price inflation in recent years.

South Korea has used protectionist and farm support mechanisms in search of food self-sufficiency as a basis on which to ensure food security. In particular, rice is central to the country's agricultural policy, and South Korea is the world's 15th largest rice producer (both in terms of quantity and value). As recently as 2001, rice accounted for about 40% of agricultural households' average farm income; and through its purchase of traditionally around one-quarter of domestic output, the Government exerted a significant control over prices and the incomes of rice producers. Between 2001 and 2007 total output of milled rice declined by more than one-quarter, from 5.52m. metric tons to 4.10m. tons; recovery subsequently took place, but in 2009 production (at 4.92m. tons) was still almost 2% lower than in 2004. The use of implicit subsidies entailed a high budgetary and fiscal cost, although the burden has been eased since South Korea's accession to the WTO. Membership of the WTO compelled the Government to adjust its farm policies, but it succeeded in maintaining import restrictions under special domestic regulations and negotiated a deal whereby its rice imports were restricted to a minimum of 4% of consumption up to 2004. From 2005 rice import quotas were set to rise by more than 20,000 tons annually until 2014, with the ultimate goal of fully opening Korea's rice market in 2015. However, recent reports have suggested that, against the background of high global grain prices and in anticipation of only minor increases in rice imports, the Government might open its market ahead of schedule. Between 2000 and 2009, for example, imports of rice increased from a mere 312 tons to more than 243,000 tons.

The Land Reform Acts of 1947 and 1948 abolished tenancy and defined the legal framework in which small owner-operated farms emerged. The rural population, which remained almost static at slightly more than 15m. until 1969, thereafter steadily declined. As industrialization attracted increasing numbers of people to urban areas, farm production underwent increased mechanization. However, the rate of arable land contraction failed to match the decline in the size of the farm population, as a result of which the average size of a farm actually increased slightly. The average availability of arable land per head of farm population is currently around 0.5 ha (1.45 ha per farm household), compared with 0.41 ha in 1995. The tiny scale of farming in South Korea is highlighted in the finding that in 2002 one-third of all farmers had plots that were smaller than 0.5 ha in size, while only 14% of farmers had plots that were greater than 2 ha. Meanwhile, agricultural operations have come to depend not only on a wide variety of modern farm machines, but also on other kinds of modern inputs. For example, reliance on increasingly sophisticated chemical fertilizers is high, although in purely physical terms chemical fertilizer use reached its highest point in 1996. Since then consumption and production (which accounts for about one-half of total supplies) have steadily contracted. Official figures reveal that in 2008 returns from agricultural work accounted for only 31.6% of farm household income, the balance being made up from non-farm income (37.2%), 'irregular' income (13.8%) and transfer income (17.3%). In general, the main thrust of agricultural developments in recent years is captured in a shift towards the cultivation of high-profit crops on a larger-scale commercialized basis, using advanced farm technology.

Despite the use of price subsidies, government farm purchases and import restrictions, the economic role of agriculture has steadily weakened. In particular, deficiencies associated with the labour-intensive (and often still small-scale) operation of farming, an ageing farm population and inefficiencies in the farm marketing system have left improvements in agricultural productivity lagging substantially behind those in the industrial sector. The rise in food imports that followed South Korea's accession to the WTO was such that by the early 1990s the value of such sales exceeded US $7,150m., making South Korea the sixth largest importer of farm products in the world. Between 1990 and 1995 the cost of all agricultural imports rose by 80%. According to the US Department of Agriculture, in 2010 South Korea imported agricultural, fishery and forestry products worth almost $20,000m. (about one-third more than in 2009 and the highest figure on record), which accounted for 4.7% of all its imports; the value of farm exports was $3,100m., or about 25% above the 2009 level. As a result, the deficit on its agricultural trade account was some $16,900m. in 2010, compared with $12,504m. in the previous year. The USA has long been the most important source of agricultural imports, accounting for around one-quarter of total imports, at a cost of $5,300m., in 2010. China has also become an important supplier of agricultural products (especially maize for feed). Other important sources include Canada, the EU, Australia and New Zealand. In 2009 South Korea was the sixth largest market for agricultural exports from the USA.

Since the 1980s increasing affluence has accompanied major changes in the pattern of food consumption, reflected in improved access to a more varied diet by the South Korean population. Statistics published by the Ministry of Agriculture in Seoul showed that between 1980 and 2003 average annual per caput consumption of food crops declined from 195.1 kg to 142.1 kg (about 60% of this from rice alone), while consumption of non-grain products all rose significantly: livestock products from 28 kg to 95.7 kg; vegetables from 120.3 kg to 145.6 kg; and fruit from 22.3 kg to 55.8 kg. Overall, average calorific intake is now over 3,000 per day; meat consumption is comparable with that of Japan, although it remains well below that of the USA and other Western countries.

Net imports of live animals and meat have played an increasingly important role in meeting domestic consumption requirements. Indeed, the domestic output of most important animal categories has been in decline, most notably in the rearing of beef cattle, numbers of which more than halved between 1997 and 2002. The value of net imports of food and live animals rose from US $5,926m. in 1995 to $6,496m. in 2000, and reached $9,956m. in 2005. Meanwhile, between 2000 and 2007 pork imports more than doubled, rising from 136,000 metric tons to almost 336,000 tons (during the same period the value of such imports increased from $250m. to $863m., although it subsequently declined to $672m. in 2009). From time to time outbreaks of foot-and-mouth disease have disrupted South Korea's livestock industry. The most serious outbreak occurred in the winter of 2010/11, when some 3.5m. cattle and pigs were culled at an estimated cost of $2,800m.

Fisheries

South Korea has a long coastline, and fishing remains important for its contribution to national diet, livelihood and exports. Although accounting for only 0.5% of the labour force, South Korea's aquatic activities are profitable and make a significant contribution to export earnings. Until the second half of the 1990s aquatic production exceeded 3m. metric tons annually, although, under the dual impact of the imposition of exclusive fishing zones by countries such as Russia and the USA and the introduction of stricter fishery regulations for resource management, since reaching a peak in 1996 it has been in decline. In 2005 gross imports of aquatic products were valued at US $2,500m.

Forest Products

Although two-thirds of South Korea's surface area is forest land, and the country's moist climate is conducive to forest development, indiscriminate felling before 1945 depleted most of the original tree cover. However, nation-wide afforestation and soil conservation campaigns have successfully reversed the trend: since the early 1990s, for example, the forested area has remained quite stable (in 2003 it was 6.406m. ha, compared with 6.476m. ha in 1990). During the same period the growing stock of trees rose from 248.4m. cu m to 468.2m. cu m, and timber production from 0.84m. cu m to 1.10m. cu m, (although output reached a peak in 2000). Major tree species include red pine, Korean white pine, larch and oak. Lumbering, mainly of coniferous trees, is limited to the mountains of Gangwon and Gyeongsang Provinces and contributes only a fraction of domestic timber needs.

MINING

In the absence of any known reserves of petroleum and possessing only 10%–20% of the Korean peninsula's mineral deposits, South Korea is poorly endowed with natural resources. Indeed, mining and quarrying—most of it owned and operated by private companies—constitutes the smallest sector in the national economy, employing around 11,000 workers (more than one-half of whom were coal miners), whose contribution to GDP is negligible (about 0.2% in 2008). In recent years the growth performance of the mining and quarrying sector has been quite volatile: between 2001 and 2008 the annual rate of increase in output ranged from 2.4% (2001) to 9.9% (2004). Between 2007 and 2008 growth slowed sharply, and in 2009, expressed in constant 2005 prices, the value of mineral production declined by 9.2%. According to the Korea Resources Corporation (KORES), around 70% of total mineral output derives from the industrial minerals (non-metal) sector.

Although more than 50 different minerals (including graphite, fluorite, gold, silver and tungsten) have been found, for supplies of bituminous coal, iron, copper, lead and zinc ores, as well as fluorite, gypsum, magnesite and phosphate, South Korea remains almost entirely dependent on imports. However, there are exceptions to this general image of scarcity. For example, South Korea is the world's sixth largest steel producer (behind China, Japan, the USA, Russia and India, but ahead of Germany), with total output of 58.4m. metric tons in 2010. Of this, Pohang Iron and Steel Company (POSCO) produced 34.7m. tons, making it the fourth largest steel-making company in the world, after ArcelorMittal, Nippon Steel and Baosteel. Despite its status as a global producer, South Korea is a major importer of steel: indeed, in both 2009 and 2010 the cost of its overseas purchases of steel was marginally greater than the value of its exports. South Korea is also the largest global producer of cadmium and the third largest of slate zinc. Within the Asia-Pacific region, South Korea is a major regional producer of cement, refined copper, pyrophyllite, talc and zeolite. In absolute terms, the value of mining production reached its peak level in 1987, although since the early 1980s the mining sector's share in GDP has never exceeded 1.5%. As a result of ever-increasing domestic industrial requirements, the value of South Korea's imports of minerals (especially iron, zinc, copper and aluminium ores) has far exceeded that of exports (talc, agalmatolite, tungsten and graphite). In an attempt to enhance the provision of minerals, South Korean enterprises have in the past used joint ventures in order to participate in mineral extraction projects in resource-rich countries, such as Australia, Canada, Indonesia and the USA. KORES reported its involvement, as of late 2006, in 26 'mine categories' in 33 countries; cumulative investment in associated projects totalled US $2,315.05m. The same source announced that the South Korean Government planned to invest $340m. by 2010 in mines overseas (including operations in the Philippines, Indonesia, Mongolia and Peru) in order to meet rising domestic demand for coal, copper and other raw materials. KORES also planned to invest $200m. in developing a copper mine in Bolivia, the corporation being the sole beneficiary of production there. The importance of South Korea's participation in overseas mining development is highlighted in targets set for 2010 by KORES, showing the planned shares of total imports forthcoming from overseas investments wholly or partly owned by KORES, namely coal 30%; copper and zinc 20% each; iron ore and uranium 10% each; and rare earths 5%.

In October 2005, following a meeting in Gyeongju, ministers from 18 member countries of Asia-Pacific Economic Cooperation (APEC) adopted a joint statement whereby they undertook to co-operate in facilitating mineral exploration, development and trade. In recent years South Korean delegations have visited a number of African countries, including South Africa and Zimbabwe, where they have shown considerable interest in the possibilities of mining investment. In 2005 South Korea reached an agreement to invest in an iron mine and steel mill in Orissa, India (see Metallurgy, below). Co-operation with North Korea is also likely to give South Korea access to rich mineral resources, including gold, iron ore, magnesite and silver.

Coal

Coal, mostly anthracite, was formerly one of South Korea's leading mineral resources, with estimated deposits of 276m. metric tons. However, its production has decreased sharply in recent years. Output of anthracite reached a peak of 24.3m. tons in 1988, after which the depletion of reserves, high production costs and the closure of small-scale, uneconomic mines caused a sharp decline—to 5.0m. tons in 1995, 2.83m. tons in 2005 and 2.52m. tons in 2009. Rising domestic demand and declining production have necessitated imports of anthracite, mainly for domestic heating and cooking, as well as much greater quantities of bituminous coal for use in power plants, industrial boilers, and the iron and steel industry. By 2009 South Korea imported 103m. tons of coal, or 3% more than in 2008. (See Energy, below.)

Metallic Minerals

Although it is the largest producer of cadmium in the world, in general, South Korea lacks sufficient deposits of non-fuel minerals to service its industrial needs, the average import ratio of such minerals being about 70%. Ore reserves of lead, zinc, copper and tungsten, in terms of metal content, have been estimated at 492m., 738m., 105m. and 100m. metric tons, respectively. Production of lead and especially zinc ore has declined markedly since the early 1980s. Other ores mined in South Korea include copper, gold, silver, molybdenum and tungsten. The molybdenum-tungsten mine at Sangdong was at one time the second largest of its kind in the world, but in 1992 it was forced to close as a result of depressed metal prices. In October 2006 it was purchased by a Canadian company, Oriental Minerals Inc, which began hole drilling in the following month. Sangdong is thought to have reserves of 85,730 tons of tungsten trioxide and 63,550 tons of molybdenum. It has been reported that the acquisition agreement for Sangdong also included several other mineral properties, including the Chongyang molybdenum-tungsten mine (closed in 1977), the Muguk gold and silver mine, and the gold and silver resources located on Gasado island.

Around 98% of South Korea's metallic mineral requirements, including aluminium, copper, iron ore, nickel and zinc, must be supplied from abroad, and only 10 out of 45 Korean metallic minerals satisfy more than 90% of domestic demand. Despite, for example, a doubling in domestic production (both in terms of gross weight and iron content), about 99% of the country's iron ore requirements are met from imports (mainly from Australia, Brazil, India and South Africa). A significant recent development was the signing of a sales agreement between POSCO and the Brazilian Companhia Vale do Rio Doce (the world's leading ore producer) to supply more than 100m. metric tons of iron ore over a 10-year period (2005–15). Against the background of negligible domestic production, in 2009, for the fourth consecutive year, imports of primary aluminium decreased, by 0.6%, to 1.078m. tons (0.866m. tons of primary aluminium ingot, the rest being alloys), of which 42% came from Australia, 28% from Russia, 11% from Canada, and 9% each from China and Bahrain. In the same year South Korea imported some 1.6m. tons of copper ore and concentrates (8% more than in 2007), as well as 0.5m. tons of refined copper (up by about 23%). With domestic production having risen by 250% (albeit to a still insignificant level), South Korea's consumption of refined copper increased by about 12% in 2009, on the basis of which it generated an output of 390,000 tons of blister and anode copper and 573,000 tons of refined output. Concealed within these figures was the finding that South Korea was the third largest producer of refined copper in the Asia-Pacific region and the second largest consumer. Finally, virtually all the raw material needs for the nickel and zinc-refining industries were imported, the single most important supplier being Australia. In general, the value of non-ferrous metals imports, which showed no growth between 2000 and 2002, has since risen rapidly.

Non-metallic Minerals

With estimated deposits of 30m. metric tons of amorphous graphite and 2.6m. tons of crystalline graphite, South Korea is an important global source of natural graphite. Production of a number of industrial minerals—for example, feldspar, graphite and mica—reached a high point in 2004, before subsequently declining. In the most extreme case, that of graphite, total output in 2006 was more than 70% below that of two years previously, and in 2007 it declined by a further 23.5% to 52,000 tons; only in 2008 did production recover to 73,000 tons. An important initiative, made possible by a joint venture between KORES and a North Korean firm, was the opening in April 2006 of the Jeongchon graphite mine in North Korea. According to the US Geological Survey, the mine contains 6.25m. tons of graphite and has an annual production capacity of 3,000 tons, of which almost two-thirds were to be exported to South Korea in the period to 2021. Limestone is abundant in South Korea, with reserves estimated at 1,500m. tons, and output rose steadily from the early 1980s to reach 88m. tons (at 50% purity) by the mid-1990s. Following the 1997 Asian financial crisis, production decreased to 69.9m. tons in 1998, after which it recovered and reached a new record level of more than 90m. tons in 2003. Output subsequently contracted again, to 79.4m. tons in 2006 (a decrease of 12% in just three years), but recovered to between 82m. and 83m. tons in 2007 and 2008, before falling back to 77.9m. tons in 2009. Limestone deposits are the basis of the cement industry, and, in turn, of construction activities, which from the 1960s underwent rapid expansion in support of accelerated national economic growth. In 2008, with a total output capacity of just over 70m. tons (almost 60% of which was accounted for by just three companies—Ssangyong, Sung Shin and Tong Yang), and a work-force of 6,640, South Korea was the world's fifth largest cement producer, after China, India, the USA and Japan. Cement exports have been an important source of foreign-exchange earnings. In 1997, at the time of the onset of the financial crisis, cement production totalled 60.3m. tons, but this decreased sharply to 46.8m. tons in the following year. Recovery subsequently took place, and by 2006 output had reached almost 54m. tons. Subsequently, however, it once more declined and in 2009 was barely 50m. tons. South Korea has been a major global producer of kaolin, although in recent years there has been quite a sharp decrease in output.

MANUFACTURING

In the early stages of its industrialization and economic modernization, South Korea's labour-intensive consumer goods industry was quite successful in meeting the demands of expanding domestic and foreign markets. In the early 1970s, however, the previous bias towards light manufacturing industry shifted towards more capital-intensive activities, such as machine-building, engineering, shipbuilding, whole plant construction, and the production of electronic goods, transport equipment and petrochemicals. Defence-related heavy industries were also, and have remained, a high priority. In the 1980s another important stage was passed, as increasing emphasis was given to the development of high-technology and knowledge-intensive industries, including telecommunications and information technology (IT) activities, which have become core export-orientated industries in South Korea. Implicit in these strategic structural shifts has been a recognition of South Korea's changing comparative advantage, based on a scarcity of natural resources and ready access to a skilled and increasingly highly educated labour force.

As a stimulus to rapid and sustained national industrial and economic growth, the expansion of exports has played a critically important role. The penetration of global markets has required South Korean manufacturing enterprises to become efficient and internationally competitive. This was achieved through the provision of incentives that facilitated a reduction in costs, the attainment of optimal scales of production and the introduction of productivity-enhancing innovations. In addition, the forces of international competition gave impetus to specialized production in those areas in which the country maximized its comparative advantage. South Korea has thus been able to create world-class industries in car-manufacturing, shipbuilding, nuclear energy, and the production of semiconductors, telecommunications and IT equipment.

Between 1965 and 1980 the average annual rate of growth of manufacturing output was a remarkable 16.4%, a figure that decreased to a still-impressive 12% during 1980–90. In the 1990s manufacturing growth continued to decline, although by international standards it remained impressive, averaging 8.6% annually between 1990 and 1995. After 1995 growth decelerated sharply, especially in the aftermath of the financial crisis, according to the BOK contracting by 7.9% in 1998. Subsequent recovery was driven by shipbuilding, semiconductors and car production, and in 1999 and 2000 manufacturing output expanded by 21.8% and 17%, respectively. However, such growth was not wholly translated into sales, as revealed by an almost six-fold increase in industrial inventories in 2000. Between 2001 and 2008 manufacturing output experienced steady growth, averaging 6.2% annually, while manufacturing capacity increased by more than one-fifth. However, by the second half of 2008 weaker export demand associated with the global economic downturn had taken its toll: in contrast to the second quarter, when industrial production had risen by 9.9%, in the third quarter the rate of growth slowed to 4.4% and in the final quarter became negative (–11.6%). The lowest point was reached in the first three months of 2009, when a contraction of 16.2% was recorded, after which recovery began to take place. For the year as a whole manufacturing GDP (in constant 2005 prices) decreased by 1.5%. However, strong recovery followed and in 2010 preliminary estimates indicated growth of 14.8%. The manufacturing sector's share of GDP has remained largely unchanged since 2000, at around 28%.

Textiles

South Korea has the sixth largest textile industry in the world (behind China, the EU, Turkey, India and the USA), and during the early phase of modernization the textile industry made a major contribution to domestic employment, exports and economic growth. Textiles' contribution to total exports reached a peak in 1971, when they accounted for 42% of exports. However, their pre-eminence—in terms of employment as well as production and exports—subsequently declined steadily, and by the late 1980s textiles had been replaced by electronics as South Korea's largest single export item. In 1997, prior to the Asian financial crisis, the value of textile exports was US $18,500m. and accounted for 13.6% of total export value. As a result of the financial crisis, in 1998 textile exports decreased to $16,700m. (12.6% of total export value), but by 2000 they had recovered and reached a new peak of $18,900m. They subsequently weakened: between 2000 and 2005, for example, the value of textile exports decreased from $15,076.8m. to $9,709.9m., a decline of more than one-third. Recovery subsequently took place, and in 2008 the overseas sales of textiles reached $13,317m. (with a global market share of 2%). In 2009, however, there was a 12.6% decline in the value of textile exports to $11,634m., or 3.2% of total exports. This decline was reversed in 2010, when the value of overseas sales rose by 13.9% (to $13,920m.), and projections suggested that the value of exports would rise to $15,900m. in 2011—the highest figure since 2000. The decline of the textile industry after 2000 mainly reflected the loss of competitiveness in relation to China and other low-cost producers. Such trends have in recent years encouraged major textile enterprises to diversify into other fields, embodying high technology and biotechnology, although whether domestic producers will succeed in establishing high value-added brands to replace cheap products in which they have lost their competitiveness remains to be seen. The eventual ratification of the FTA with the USA (see above) was also expected to revitalize textile production by facilitating access to the largest export market in the world. Even allowing for recent contractionary trends, the textile industry remains a significant force in the South Korean economy: in 2008, for example, it provided more than 250,000 jobs, accounted for 8.7% of manufacturing GDP, generated 3.2% of all exports and earned a surplus on its trading account of $5,400m.

Shipbuilding and Car Industries

Construction of new plants during the late 1960s laid the basis for a shift of emphasis in the 1970s, from production of light machinery products and simple metal-working machinery to the manufacture of transport and communications equipment, industrial machinery, precision machinery, textile machinery, and electric and electronic appliances.

The shipbuilding industry was badly affected by the Asian crisis of 1997, in the immediate aftermath of which there was a sharp reduction in South Korea's export sales. Yet recovery was swift, and by 2000 the value of shipping exports had reached a record US $8,230m. Not least, the financial crisis served to highlight the weak financial position of many shipbuilding companies, which had for many years benefited from subsidies that took no account of commercial realities. For example, the competitiveness of Daewoo Shipbuilding and Marine Engineering, since 1995 the largest shipbuilding company in the world, was enhanced following the crisis by an extensive programme of restructuring, which enabled it to return to profitability in 2002. Nevertheless, subsidies have remained an issue. In 2003, for example, the European Commission delivered a formal protest on behalf of European shipbuilders, which alleged that official subsidies were enabling their South Korean competitors to produce at between 15% and 40% below cost price, thereby undercutting competition from European shipyards.

In 2004 South Korea overtook Japan to become the biggest shipbuilder in the world, a position it retained until the end of 2009 when, some years earlier than had been anticipated, it was in turn surpassed by China. South Korea has seven of the world's 10 largest shipyards, which have the capacity to deliver super-container vessels, liquefied natural gas (LNG) carriers and offshore oil production facilities. While South Korea cannot compete with China's lower labour costs, it has sought to maintain its competitive advantage by developing and introducing new technologies and advanced production methods. In the first half of 2010 South Korean companies secured 38% of global shipbuilding orders, compared with 41% for China. China's rise to pre-eminence in recent years is captured in the finding that in 2005 South Korean shipyards had taken

71.3% of all new orders for LNG carriers (the most lucrative branch of shipbuilding), 64.3% for large container vessels and 42.4% for large tankers. However, despite China's increased shipbuilding activities, demand for Korean ships associated with China's own economic expansion has generated significant excess demand in the industry. For example, according to a report by British shipbroker Clarkson PLC, in October 2008 Korean shipyards had backlogs of orders worth US $212,400m., almost 40% of the global total, which promised to be sufficient to enable the industry to sustain its strong position for the foreseeable future. In 2008 the value of South Korea's shipping exports was $43,200m. Unlike most export categories, overseas sales continued to rise in 2009, albeit by a much smaller margin than in the previous year, and by 2010 had reached $49,100m. Despite increasing competition from China, as well as the pressures of global recession, South Korea's large shipbuilding companies (for example, Hyundai, Daewoo and Samsung) are likely to maintain quite buoyant growth; however, the prospects for some SMEs may be less secure, even to the extent of necessitating major restructuring.

The origins of the South Korean automobile industry lie in developments that took place in the 1960s (Hyundai Motor was founded in 1967). The sustained growth of the motor industry reflects the successful exploration of both domestic and overseas markets. Until the 1980s the main orientation of the industry was towards exports; however, during that recession-affected decade and into the 1990s greater emphasis was placed on meeting the needs of an increasingly affluent domestic market. The success of this strategy is illustrated by the fact that in 2004 the Korean company brands of Hyundai and Kia, and foreign-invested GM-Daewoo and Ssangyong (the last-named acquired by China's Shanghai Automotive Industry Corporation) accounted for a remarkable 95% of domestic passenger car sales. In 2004 the total number of licensed drivers in South Korea was 24.48m. and by the end of 2006 there were around 16m. car vehicle registrations. New car registrations rose from 914,000 to 1.17m. between 2005 and 2009, and EIU estimates suggest that this figure rose further to 1.4m. in 2010 and will exceed 1.7m. by 2014. Notwithstanding impressive growth since the 1990s, car ownership remains significantly below the levels of the USA, Japan and many Western European countries.

During 1988–91 South Korean car output grew, on average, by 11.4% annually; in 1993 total production exceeded 2m. units for the first time; and in 1995 South Korea became the world's fifth largest car producer (after the USA, Japan, Germany and France). Although its global ranking fell back under the impact of the Asian financial crisis, and despite having been overtaken in 2002 by China, in 2003 it regained fifth place (after the USA, Japan, Germany and China). Hyundai is also the world's fifth largest car manufacturer. Between 1995 and 2007, with the exception of 1998, car output rose steadily to reach 3.72m. units. However, the onset of the global economic downturn presaged a reversal of what had been quite buoyant growth, and in both 2008 and 2009 car production declined. In 2009 total output of passenger cars decreased to 3.16m. units—15% below the peak of 2007 and only a single percentage point above the production level of 2004. As in other sectors, recovery in 2010 was swift, and by the end of the year car output had risen to 3.87m. units (more than 22% above the level of the previous year). Concealed in the production figures are parallel trends in domestic and overseas sales. Thus, according to the authoritative Korea Automobile Manufacturers Association (KAMA), domestic car sales increased from 858,000 to 986,400 between 2004 and 2007; in 2008 the upward trend was temporarily reversed, but by 2010 sales exceeded 1.2m. A further increase (of 3.5% year-on-year) was recorded in the first seven months of 2011. Meanwhile, exports rose steadily from 1.72m. to a peak of 2.72m. between 2003 and 2007, recording an average annual rate of increase of more than 12%. By 2009, however, the corresponding figure had decreased to barely 2m. (a decline of more than one-quarter in just two years), the lowest level since 2003. Only in 2010 did recovery take place, with 2.61m. cars being sold overseas (just 4% below the 2007 level). Exports rose by 13.3% during the first seven months of 2011. Projections made by KAMA indicated a 3.3% increase in total car output (to 3.99m. units) in 2011, with domestic sales forecast to rise by 2.6% to 1.25m. and a 4.6% increase in exports (to 2.73m. units).

It is clear that, against the background of slowing domestic demand (except in 2009), the principal boost to increased production has come from overseas markets, especially in the USA and the EU. In 2010, for example, the respective shares of domestic and foreign markets in total sales were 32% and 68%. In view of the Government's commitment to strengthen legislation on environmental protection and climate change, one of the major challenges for South Korean car manufacturers in the future will be to increase research and development spending to accommodate new carbon dioxide emission and related environmental regulations.

The South Korean car industry's aspiration is to become a major global force and a regional market leader. In pursuit of this goal, producers have already begun, with some success, to target emerging country markets, such as India and China. South Korea began to export motor vehicles to Canada in 1983, and had begun to penetrate the European market by 1985. The country's automobile producers reached another important stage when, in the mid-1980s, they entered the US market (in 1986 Hyundai's 'Excel' model proved to be the most successful new foreign car ever to enter the US automobile market). The value of exported passenger cars rose from US $209.5m. in 1983 to a record $3,594.2m. in 1988. In the following two years export proceeds declined by almost two-thirds. Thereafter, however, recovery was swift, and, except for a modest decline in 1998, steady growth has continued. Between 2000 and 2005 car exports rose by almost 20% annually to reach $26,925m., according to data from KAMA. By 2007 revenue from overseas car sales had reached $33,841m., a further 26% higher than in 2005 and around 10.0% of the value of all exports. However, such was the impact of the global economic crisis that in 2010 the value of car exports was still marginally below that of 2007, despite increasing by 46%; a further 30% rise followed in January–July 2011 (to $24,471m.).

The overseas reputation of Korean cars, particularly Hyundai, for reliability has improved markedly in recent years, although the recall of more than 1m. Toyota cars in 2010 was a major set-back. A significant initiative was the opening in the USA, in May 2005, of a US $1,100m. Hyundai plant in Montgomery, Alabama, which was to produce 300,000 cars annually. In April 2007 two further plants were opened by Hyundai in Slovakia and the Czech Republic. It remained to be seen to what extent the overseas plants would affect domestic industry and exports in the longer term. However, domestic producers were hopeful that, when recovery from the global recession took place, the ratification of the FTA with the USA would give a boost to the automobile sector through the elimination of tariffs on imported passenger cars and commercial vehicles.

Electronics

The origins of the electronics industry lie in the assembly, in the early 1960s, of vacuum tube radios from imported parts. Subsequently, South Korea's electronics industry expanded rapidly, and in 1969 it received full-scale government support through the enactment of the Electronics Industry Promotion Law, which designated electronics as a priority industry and recognized its strategic export potential. The implementation of a comprehensive eight-year development programme was accompanied by major inflows of foreign capital and technology, which played a crucial role in generating 'foreign-led' electronics exports. In the early 1970s the manufacture of electronic components (such as transistors, diodes, integrated circuits, radio receivers and parts for monochrome television receivers) dominated the industry. After 1974 colour television receivers were produced, fuelling a rapid expansion in consumer electronics. By the end of the 1970s South Korean-made products included electronic calculators and watches, and in 1979 the country had become one of the most important global producers of video-cassette recorders (VCRs). The production and export of computers and peripheral equipment also expanded rapidly, as computer manufacturers began to pursue a policy of import substitution.

With a total output and export value of US $23,531m. and $15,200m., respectively, by 1988 the electrical and electronics industry already accounted for 13.4% of GNP and 25.0% of total exports. In that year South Korea was the sixth largest exporter of electronic goods in the world and electronics had surpassed textiles as the country's principal export item. In 1992 South Korea became one of the five largest electronics-producing countries in the world, with overseas sales accounting for 25.9% of total exports. By 1997 exports of the electrical and electronics sector had reached $36,744.9m. They declined by 6.7% in 1998, but quickly recovered and until 2005 the trend was strongly upwards, except during 2001–02. Export growth was then rapid, and in 2007 overseas sales reached $126,914.3m. (23% higher than in 2005). By the end of 2009, however, the impact of the global economic downturn had become evident in the industry (in November alone, exports decreased by some 27%), and BOK data showed that the value of overseas sales during January–November rose by less than 4% to $120,863.1m. South Korea's IT sector experienced a 4.2% decline in exports in 2009, but recovery was swift, and in 2010 exports rose by 26%. Even before the onset of the 2008 global crisis, the depressed market for wireless communications equipment and computers had serious implications for South Korean producers, causing a decline in overseas sales as a result of downward pressure on retail prices, as well as the continued strength of the Korean won. Also significant was the impact of increasing competition from China in the production of low-end electronic goods and telecommunications equipment.

The growth of semiconductor production is considered essential if a country is to secure an internationally competitive position in high-technology areas, especially in the production of automatic data-processing equipment. Thus, as in Taiwan, semiconductors have played a major role in the development of South Korea's electronics industry. Indeed, by the mid-1990s it had become one of the foremost international producers of semiconductors, South Korean companies having established global brand name recognition for their products. Helped by strong growth in the global market for semiconductor chips, SEC garnered 10.8% of the world's memory chip market in 1993, thereby becoming the seventh largest semiconductor chip producer in the world. In the same year South Korea's share in the global semiconductor market was 17.9%, and in the dynamic random access memory (DRAM) chip market its share was 23.6%. Such was the pace of subsequent expansion that by the first quarter of 2009 its share of the global DRAM market had reached 34.3% (with another South Korean company, Hynix, ranked second with a market share of 21.6%). However, manufacturers have remained dependent on Japan for the supply of many of the components that they use, although in 1993 a number of Japanese electronics and machinery manufacturers began themselves to purchase electronic parts and components from South Korean companies. The experience of the USA and other countries highlighted the critical need to allocate increasing investment to research and development in order to enhance international competitiveness, and in the early 1990s the three leading electronics manufacturers—SEC, Daewoo and LG (formerly Lucky Goldstar)—substantially increased their research and development expenditure. Meanwhile, by the mid-1990s South Korea ranked second in the world in terms of production capacity of VCRs, microwave ovens, fax machines and videocassette tapes, and third for colour television receivers and telephones. In March 1996 SEC initiated a DRAM plant in Texas—its first semiconductor facility to be located in the USA, attesting to the globalization of the country's electronics industry. Since the 1990s SEC has also undertaken major investment in China, where it now has large-scale production facilities to manufacture semiconductors, digital appliances and IT products. Such initiatives are a sign of South Korean companies' expanding horizons in China, although SEC has experienced difficulties in recent years with regard to its governance (see above). Between 2004 and 2006 South Korea's exports of semiconductors increased from US $27,039.7m. to $37,359.9m. (a rise of 38.0%), suggesting a strong performance in the country's semiconductor industry. However, there was a significant slowing of overseas demand in 2007, reflected in an increase of only 4.5% in exports (to $39,045.6m.). The deceleration was even more evident in 2008 and 2009 (in the latter year exports declined by 2.7%), although a strong recovery took place in 2010, with semiconductor exports recording a 61.2% increase in that year.

Chemicals

The construction, in 1959, of the Chungju Fertilizer Plant marked the beginning of South Korea's development of an indigenous chemical industry. Prior to this, all chemical fertilizer requirements were imported. By 1968, however, chemical fertilizer self-sufficiency had been secured, and in 1976 South Korea became a net exporter of fertilizers. The peak level of output (4.3m. metric tons, or 1.8m. tons in terms of primary nutrients) was reached in 1994. Since then, although annual variations have sometimes been significant, the production trend has been downward, reaching 3.6m. tons in 2004, almost half of which was exported. Complex fertilizers now account for about 70% of total consumption.

Diversification of the chemical industry has been under way since the 1960s. Major products include sulphuric acid, ammonia, compressed oxygen, dye, insecticides, polyethylene, polypropylene, polyvinyl chloride, polyester fibres and acrylic fibres. As a result of rapid development in recent years, South Korea is now one of the world's leading chemical-producing countries. Between 2005 and 2007 output increased by more than 9.0% and growth averaged about 4.6% per annum, while export growth averaged more than 16% annually to reach US $37,544.7m. In 2007 chemicals ranked third as a source of export earnings, marginally ahead of machinery and precision equipment, and accounted for about 10% of the value of all South Korean exports. Despite a sharp decline in overseas sales in the final quarter, exports of chemicals for the entire year increased by almost 14% to reach $42,709.9m., but decreased in 2009 to $37,414.7m. (almost identical to the total for 2007), before recovering strongly in 2010, to $48,951.5m. South Korea has also been a major importer of chemical products: between 2005 and 2008 the value of overseas purchases rose from $24,502.4m. to $36,658.2m.; following a contraction to $31,504.9m. in 2009, imports rose to $41,147.7m. in 2010.

Metallurgy

The construction, in 1973, of POSCO—South Korea's first integrated steel plant—was an important stage in the development of a national steel industry. By 1996, with an annual production capacity of some 40m. metric tons, South Korea had become the world's fifth largest producer of steel after China, Japan, the USA and Russia. It retained this position until India overtook it, relegating it to sixth place (excluding the EU), thus becoming the third, and then fourth, largest producer in Asia. According to statistics published by the International Steel Statistics Bureau (ISSB), in 2010 South Korea generated an estimated 4% of global crude steel output and 6.5% of production in Asia (China's shares were 44% and an astonishing 70%, respectively). Owing to the pre-eminent role of the car industry, shipbuilding and electronics manufacturing in the economy, South Korea's per caput consumption of steel is the highest in the world (1,077 kg in 2010), ahead of Taiwan (772 kg), Japan (503 kg) and China (427 kg). The country's total steel consumption in 2007 was 48m. metric tons, but, under the impact of the global recession, declined to little more than 42m. tons in 2009, before recovering to 52m. tons in 2010 (making it the fifth largest consumer in the world after China, the USA, Japan and India).

The steel sector was seriously affected by the 1997 Asian crisis, which caused domestic demand for steel to decline, precipitating the bankruptcy of three of the country's largest producers. Having reached 42.55m. metric tons in 1997, output fell back in the following year. However, recovery was swift, and a new high point of 43.11m. tons was attained in 2000. Thereafter production of crude steel increased at an average annual rate of 2.7% per year to reach 53.32m. tons in 2008. Despite South Korea's accelerated expansion in 2007, taking total output to 51.00m. tons, India's even faster growth resulted in South Korea's ranking as a global steel producer slipping to sixth place (albeit well ahead of the seventh ranking country, Ukraine). Despite the global economic downturn in the final quarter of the year, in 2008 steel production recorded a further increase of 4.5%, to 53.32m. tons, although data published by the Korea Iron and Steel Association showed that in 2009 there was a sharp year-on-year decline of almost 9% to 48.57m. tons (almost identical to total output in 2006). It is noteworthy that the decline in national output in 2009 was less pronounced than in the rest of Asia, including or excluding China. In any case, in 2010 there was a sharp rise in production to 58.4m. tons, and in the first seventh months of 2011 there was a further increase of almost 19%. A significant feature of the steel industry's performance in 1999–2000 was that it was achieved against the background of a decrease in the price of steel and consequent pressure on exports, and the value of exports of iron and steel products declined in 2000–02. However, subsequent recovery and growth were strong, and by 2008 the value of exports of such products had risen to US $38,100m. The ISSB's data showed that physical exports of steel in 2008 totalled 19.7m. tons, and declined by only 0.5% to 19.6m. tons in 2009. In 2010 exports increased by 22% to reach 22.9m. tons. South Korea is also a major importer of steel. Statistics show its steel imports to have exceeded exports in recent years, at least until 2009, when physical shipments overseas exceeded in-shipments by 0.3m. tons (this figure increasing further to 0.4m. tons in 2010). Rising imports in recent years are likely mainly to have been the result of increasing demand for low-priced steel (especially from China, imports from this source having risen rapidly).

POSCO was at one time the largest steel producer in the world, although by 2010 the process of global consolidation had relegated it to fourth place. The annual production capacity of its Pohang Works is 13m. metric tons of crude steel and stainless steel, while its Gwangyang Works has an annual capacity of 15m. tons of crude steel. In 2009 POSCO produced 31.11m. tons of crude steel (almost two-thirds of the national total), and it also produces around 3m. tons of stainless steel annually. In 2005 POSCO signed an agreement to invest US $12,000m. to establish a steel plant in the Indian state of Orissa—the biggest single FDI project ever undertaken by South Korea, with a planned annual output of 12m. tons. It also has major production facilities in Viet Nam and Mexico.

INFRASTRUCTURE

Transport

Until quite recently, the principal means of freight and passenger traffic in South Korea was railway transport. With the rapid expansion of the motorway network, improvements in its quality, and extended motor vehicle ownership, roads have now assumed the position previously occupied by railways. Since 1990 the road network has expanded from less than 57,000 km to more than 100,000 km (including about 14,000 km of national highways and almost 3,500 km of expressways). Between 1995 and 2007 freight carried on roads increased from 408m. metric tons to 550m. tons (that is, from 69% to 77% of total freight traffic). By contrast, the railway network's share of freight decreased from 9.7% to little more than 6% (the percentages carried by water and air also having contracted). Data published by the International Transport Forum showed that in 2009 South Korea's railways carried 9,273m. ton-km, 19.8% less than in 2008 (although passenger traffic was almost unchanged). Recent trends in passenger traffic display a different pattern: although roads still carry far more passengers than any other form of transport, the percentage of passengers on roads has declined, while that of the rail network (including subways) has increased. The contraction in road passengers is most dramatically highlighted by the fact that passenger traffic on roads reached its highest level as long ago as 1991. The increasing popularity of railways is partly attributable to the expansion of subway systems that are linked to the national overground rail network. Mass transit rail systems in the largest cities have been accorded special priority in recent years, as exemplified by the construction of underground railway systems in Seoul, Busan, Daegu, Daejeon, Gwangju and Incheon. In 2007 subways carried 2,090m. passengers and accounted for 16.6% of total passenger traffic. In 2008 the total length of rail track in South Korea was 3,381 km, of which more than one-half (1,843 km) was electrified.

Air transport capacity, both internal and external, has expanded markedly. Until the end of 1988 Korean Air was the only airline company to operate in and from South Korea. In December of that year, however, Asiana Airlines began operations on domestic routes, and in 1995 these were extended to include international destinations (in Japan, China, South-East Asia and the USA). A major development was the opening of a new international airport at Incheon in 2001, by which time the number of air passengers using South Korean airports was around 40m. (shared roughly equally between those on domestic and on international routes). In 2010 South Korea possessed 72 airports, four of which had runways in excess of 3,047 m. In more than a decade after 1995 international air passenger traffic expanded by more than 7% annually, taking the total number of international passengers (including those in transit) in and out of South Korea to a record 36.86m. in 2007; the corresponding number of domestic passengers was only 16.85m. (numbers having declined steadily during the previous decade from 25.64m. in 1997). Total air freight (domestic and international) was just 3.45m. metric tons in 2007.

The capacity of South Korea's ports, including newly constructed facilities at Bukbyong on the east coast, has also expanded rapidly. The cargo handling capacity of all ports was 469.6m. metric tons in 2001, rising to 727.2m. tons by 2007. In line with this expansion, the national merchant fleet has greatly increased and now totals more than 800 vessels (as of 2008, the 14th largest merchant marine in the world), including 212 bulk carriers, 226 cargo ships, 133 chemical and 61 oil tankers, 80 container vessels and 33 LNG carriers. With a cargo-handling capacity of about 165m. tons, the southern city of Busan is the 10th largest port in the world. It handles about 45% of South Korea's exports and 95% of total container throughput. A new port (Busan New Port) is currently under construction and is scheduled for completion by 2015.

The vagaries of inter-Korean relations are reflected in the halting progress that has so far been made towards restoring and developing transport links between North and South Korea. Nevertheless, there has been limited progress, as in the agreement of both governments to reconnect North–South road and rail links. Trial runs on a North–South rail link, on which work began in 2000, were scheduled to take place in May 2006, but were cancelled at short notice by North Korea. Finally, in May 2007 test runs were made by two trains—one from the South, the other from the North—in an historic event that marked the first cross-border rail journey to have taken place in 56 years. Following a summit meeting between the then President of South Korea, Roh Moo-Hyun, and the North Korean leader, Kim Jong Il, in December 2007 a cross-border rail service was finally officially inaugurated. The service was designed to facilitate freight transport to a joint industrial complex in Kaesong (some 20 km inside North Korea). The intention is that two roads (a western and an eastern corridor) will also be permanently opened to facilitate passenger and freight traffic across the border. Other goals include the rebuilding of the Seoul–Sinuiju (North Korea) Railway Line and the construction of a four-lane highway linking Seoul and the North Korean capital, Pyongyang. Much more ambitious (and, from the present perspective, remote) are plans to build a gas pipeline from Siberia to both Koreas. The idea has even been mooted of constructing a freight route, sometimes referred to as the 'iron silk road', from Europe to South Korea via Siberia and North Korea.

Telecommunications

Owing to the vigorous government-sponsored promotion of the industry, South Korea has emerged as a global leader in telecommunications. Investment in the industry in 2002 exceeded US $1,000m. for the first time, and with more than 90% of all households having access to an outside line, fixed-line telephone penetration has reached a very high level (in 2010 there were 60 lines per 100 inhabitants—a sharp contrast to the situation in the early 1970s, when 250,000 lines had to serve a population of more than 40m.). However, the most dramatic development has been the extraordinarily rapid take-up, starting in the second half of the 1990s, of mobile cellular telephone subscriptions. The total number of mobile subscribers exceeded that of wire telephone subscribers for the first time in September 1999. According to statistics published by the International Telecommunication Union (ITU), between 2002 and 2010 the mobile cellular subscription rate rose from 68.4% to 105.4%—among the highest penetration rates in the Asia-Pacific region. In 2010 the subscriber base numbered 50.77m., many of whom had access to third generation (3G) technology. The mobile telecommunications industry in South Korea is dominated by three companies—SK Telecom, KT Freetel and LG Telecom.

In 2002 60% of all households already owned a personal computer (PC). ITU data showed that in 2007 80% of households owned a computer, placing South Korea second only to Japan in the Asia-Pacific region. Associated with the increasing popularity of PC ownership has been extraordinarily rapid growth in access to the internet. Between 2000 and 2010 there was a spectacular rise in the number of internet users, with the penetration rate increasing from 45% to 84% of the total population (the highest figure in Asia). During the same period the number of households subscribing to high-speed broadband services increased from 3.9m. to 17.7m., reaching a national penetration rate of 36.6%. Such data confirm that South Korea has become one of the most 'wired' countries in the world. Looking ahead, consolidation is likely to be one consequence of the highly competitive environment of the internet industry, although there will also be growing emphasis on the development of new generation mobile communications, as well as major efforts to increase access to new services (for example, entertainment, telematics and home network services). In January 2003 Hanaro Telecom, South Korea's second largest broadband provider, acquired a controlling share in its smaller rival, Thrunet. The deal gave Hanaro a 42% market share, bringing it close to the 47% share of its rival and South Korea's largest company in the industry, KT (Korea Telecom) Corporation.

Energy

Total consumption of primary energy increased almost fourfold between 1964 and 1980, from 11.5m. metric tons of oil equivalent (TOE) to 43.9m. TOE. By 2008, according to the International Energy Agency (IEA—based in France), the corresponding figure had risen to 226.95m. TOE. Such rapid long-term growth reflected the demands of a generally buoyant economy and an increasingly prosperous society (not least in terms of car ownership). On a per caput basis, at about 5 TOE in 2009, South Korea's energy consumption is more than twice as high as the world average. Oil is the most important source of energy, accounting for 40% of total primary energy supplies in 2008. The other major energy sources, in descending order of importance, were: coal (28%), nuclear fuel (17%) and gas (14%). Hydropower, renewables, firewood and miscellaneous other minor sources provided the remainder.

Since 1990 the average annual rate of increase of domestic energy production has been less than one-half that of consumption, thus placing an increasing burden on imports, which have grown (in gross terms) by well in excess of 10% annually to reach over 85% of total primary energy supplies. South Korea's dependence on overseas energy supplies is reflected in its global status as the fifth largest net importer of crude oil in 2009 (behind the USA, Japan, China and India, but ahead of Germany) and the ninth largest importer of natural gas. The absence of domestic reserves of sufficiently high quality means that South Korea also imports virtually all the coal that it needs (in 2009 it was the third largest coal importer in the world, after Japan and China). The fact that energy consumption growth has overtaken the rate of GDP and industrial expansion by a significant margin highlights considerable inefficiency in energy use. Data available in the OECD *Factbook* show that since 1990 consumption of energy per unit of GDP in South Korea has consistently been higher than the OECD average (in 2008 it was 0.17 TOE per US $1,000 of GDP (in constant 2000 prices, based on PPP calculations). South Korea ranks ninth in the world in terms of its reliance on fossil fuels. It was against this background that the Government set a target of reducing energy intensity by 11.3% by 2012 (on a 2007 basis) and by 46% by 2030. The heavy burden of imports is revealed in the finding that in 2007 energy imports cost South Korea $94,626.2m. (more than one-quarter of its total import bill), of which crude petroleum purchases accounted for 64% ($60,323.5m.). Government efforts to reduce the country's vulnerability to petroleum price rises and interruptions in supply, as well as public demands for cleaner, high-grade energy, have met with some success; between 1995 and 2006, for example, dependence on oil as a source of primary energy decreased from 62.5% to 56.0%.

South Korea lacks domestic petroleum reserves and relies entirely on imports. It has the sixth largest distillation capacity in the world after the USA, Russia, China, Japan and India. SK Corporation's Ulsan plant is the second largest in the world. However, oil imports exceed consumption, since around one-quarter of gross imports are re-exported as refined petroleum products, mainly to neighbouring countries (such re-exports totalled 30m. metric tons in 2008). Despite the contraction in oil as a share of total primary energy supplies, crude petroleum imports grew by 11.2% annually between 1990 and 2000. IEA data show that in 2009 net imports of crude petroleum totalled 116m. tons. Such overwhelming reliance on foreign supplies of oil has left South Korea exposed to the consequences of the volatility of changes in international prices. For example, even allowing for the effect of the global downturn in the final quarter of 2008, rising oil prices led to a significant increase in the annual cost of South Korea's imports (to US $85,900m.). In 2009, however, the cost of overseas purchases of crude petroleum decreased to $50,800m., and in 2010, at $68,700m., was still 30% below the 2008 level. Despite efforts by the Government to diversify import sources, between 1996 and 2006 the share of oil imports from Persian Gulf countries rose from 64% to 75% (the single most important supplier being Saudi Arabia, which in 2006 provided 29% of the total, or 860,000 barrels per day). In order to obviate shortages resulting from the interruption of imports, the Government has developed a strategic oil reserve, managed by the state-owned Korea National Oil Corporation (KNOC), which seeks to guarantee stocks sufficient to meet needs over a 90-day period. In addition, in an effort to minimize energy dependence, KNOC is developing its own petroleum and gas fields. In 2006 it was involved in 32 exploration and production projects in 15 countries, including four fields already in production in Yemen, Argentina, Peru and the North Sea. The Government sought to increase KNOC's equity share of net oil imports to 10% by 2010, to which end it allocated $7,000m. in June 2006 to facilitate further exploration and production activities.

LNG production has been promoted as part of a strategy to diversify South Korea's sources of energy for both domestic and industrial consumption. The first LNG terminal, in Pyeongtaek, was completed in April 1987 and has an annual processing capacity of 1m. metric tons. The Korea Gas Corpn (KGC), which operates the terminal, signed a 20-year agreement with Indonesia, providing for the import of 2m. tons of LNG annually from 1986 until 2006. A second terminal has since been established at Incheon, and construction of a third facility at Kwangyang—a joint venture by Japan's Mitsubishi Corporation and POSCO—was completed in 2005. In 1987 KGC began to supply LNG to the Seoul metropolitan area, making South Korea the seventh nation in the world to use LNG. It subsequently became the second largest importer of LNG in the world. In 2008 LNG supplied about 14% of primary energy consumption, compared with 6.1% in 1995. Net LNG imports in 2009 were 33m. tons, most of which came from Qatar, Indonesia, Malaysia and Oman. Since November 2003 South Korea has produced a tiny amount of natural gas from its own Donghae-1 facility: about 19,000m. cu ft in 2010, which was sufficient to meet a mere 1.3% of total demand.

Coal accounts for just one-quarter of total energy consumption. IEA data indicate that in 2008 total coal consumption was 112.84m. short tons, or almost 15% more than in 2007. More than 95% of coal requirements are imported (mainly from Australia, China and Indonesia), and South Korea is, after Japan and China, the third largest coal importer in the world. In 2009 it purchased 103m. tons, most of which was bituminous coal needed to generate power (almost all the rest was used for steel production). As a result of rising coal import costs, in 2005 working-level talks took place in the North Korean border town of Kaesong between officials from Seoul and Pyongyang about the possibility of joint mining of North Korean coal reserves, in return for which the South would secure mineral rights in the North.

The importance of nuclear energy is revealed in the finding that South Korea's 20 nuclear power plants, the first of which began operations in 1978 and the most recent in 2005, contribute a little more than one-third of domestic electricity supply. South Korea is able to manufacture nuclear plants independently, and it ranks as one of the leading nations in terms of nuclear power production and consumption. In 2008 it was the fifth largest producer of nuclear energy in the world, accounting for about 5.5% of global output, and it also had the sixth largest production capacity (some 18 GW), quite close to that of Germany (20 GW) and Russia (23 GW), but well behind that of the USA, France and Japan. South Korea ranked fourth, after France, Sweden and Ukraine, in terms of the share of total electricity generation derived from nuclear sources. The Government views the construction of nuclear power plants as one way in which to reduce carbon emissions. There are plans to construct up to a dozen more nuclear power stations by 2015, six of which were scheduled to be in operation by 2011, thus significantly raising nuclear contribution to energy supplies. In 2008 electric power generation (from thermal and hydroelectric, as well as nuclear sources) totalled 412,680m. kWh (8.7% above the level of 2007). A report issued by the Ministry of Knowledge Economy in 2010 noted that eight more nuclear units were already under construction, with an aggregate capacity of 9.6 GW, and that four more (with additional 5.6 GW capacity) were planned for completion by 2020. By 2030 further construction projects would bring the number of reactors to 38 or 39, sufficient to meet almost 60% of South Korea's electricity needs.

INTERNATIONAL TRADE

Although South Korea lacks natural resources and is constrained by its small domestic market, it enjoys the benefits of a committed and highly educated labour force, which has helped facilitate the expansion of exports that has sustained high economic growth rate over several decades. In every year between 1953 and 1985 imports exceeded exports, although accelerating export growth facilitated a marked contraction in the trade deficit as a share of exports—from 772.2% in 1953 to 137.5% in 1970, and to a mere 2.8% in 1985. In 1986 South Korea recorded a trade surplus of US $3,413m.—the first to be achieved since the end of the Korean War—and by 1988 the corresponding figure had reached $11,172m. This surplus was virtually eliminated in 1989, after which, until 1998, the trade balance moved back into deficit, with the exception of a small surplus in 1993. Among the factors responsible for the rapid rise in import costs during this period were the enormous increase in oil prices following the Iraqi invasion of Kuwait in August 1990, the rising value of the Japanese yen, and the expansion of domestic demand in South Korea itself. Between 1996 and 1997 South Korea's merchandise trade deficit narrowed from $15,462m. to $3,861m. In the following year, as South Korea's demand for imports declined sharply during the recession, a sizeable surplus of $43,237m. emerged. Trade remained in surplus in subsequent years—although the absolute level declined from $27,893m. in 1999 to $13,029m. in 2001. This sharp contraction reflected a combination of factors, including adverse global economic conditions, reduced international demand for telecommunications and IT products, and the effects of the 11 September terrorist attacks in the USA. South Korea's trade balance in 2001 would have been even more adversely affected, had not imports also decreased as a result of slowing global economic growth and declining international crude petroleum prices. In the next two years the merchandise trade surplus expanded once again, and by 2004 it had reached $39,661m. However, it contracted again thereafter, declining to $31,433m. by 2006, before rising to $37,129m. in 2007. In 2008 rising import costs were responsible for a major contraction in South Korea's merchandise trade surplus, to $5,170m. In 2009, owing to a much larger decline in imports compared with exports, the trade surplus increased to $37,866m. In 2010 both exports and imports increased sharply, generating an even larger merchandise surplus of $41,904m.

Exports

Rapid export growth commenced in the 1960s, following a deliberate decision vigorously to promote exports in pursuit of rapid and sustained economic growth. Between 1965 and 1980 exports grew, on average, by a remarkable 27.2% per year, a record unmatched anywhere in the world. In the 1980s the export sector encountered difficulties and was subject to wide annual fluctuations (e.g. a nominal rate of increase of 36.2% in 1987 compared with one of just 2.8% in 1989), while also recording a sharp downturn in average annual growth (to 15.3%).

The 1990s too were a decade of varying fortunes. Between 1990 and 2000 average annual export growth was a very creditable 10.5%. However, there were large annual fluctuations within this figure, ranging from 30.3% in 1994 to –2.8% in 1998, the former reflecting widening international demand for Korean electronic goods (especially semiconductors), cars and ships; the latter figure was not simply a familiar reflection of the impact of the financial crisis but was also the result of declining international prices for Korean goods and of the weakness of the Japanese yen. Following this small contraction in 1998, renewed expansion took place, with exports rising, on average, by 11.6% annually between 1998 and 2005. However, this buoyancy was interrupted in 2001, when exports declined by 12.7% (see above). In 2006 the value of exports was US $336,494.4m., 16.1% more than in the previous year (compared with annual rises of 31.0% and 12.0% in 2004 and 2005, respectively). The corresponding figure for 2007 was $389,568.5m., or 15.8% above the level of the previous year. In the first half of 2008, owing to rising demand for Korean goods in emerging markets, export growth accelerated, showing an increase, year-on-year, of almost 17%. However, in the third quarter exports showed virtually no growth, and in the final quarter of the year, owing to the global economic crisis, they decreased by 8.9%—the biggest quarterly decline since the first oil crisis in 1974. The outcome, as reported in the BOK's *Annual Report*, was that between 2007 and 2008 the rate of growth of exports contracted, in real terms, from 12.6% to 5.7% ($434,651.5m.). Between the final quarter of 2008 and the first three months of 2009 there was a further decline (from $93,070.6m. to $74,564.6m.), and the annual value of exports in 2009 decreased by 17.6%, to $358,189.7m. However, such was the force of recovery in 2010 that by the end of the year exports had risen by 29.6%, to total $464,286.9m.

In recent years South Korean producers have confronted formidable challenges from a variety of sources. One is fierce competition from low-wage economies, such as China and countries in South-East Asia. Another external pressure has been the impact of protectionist measures introduced by advanced countries. In the most recent past the impact of the global economic recession has also been severe, and at home labour unrest and upward pressure on wages have taken their toll too. Nevertheless, South Korean products have competed favourably with goods produced in developed countries, and in some cases (for example, cars, microwave ovens, television receivers, VCRs and PCs) their brand names have gained ever-wider international customer recognition. It was noteworthy that the negative growth during 2006 of wireless communication equipment was reversed in 2007, with exports of such products rising by 12.7%. Even more impressively, in the first half of 2008 the corresponding year-on-year rate of expansion was about 30%, although it proved impossible to sustain this through the rest of the year.

As recently as 1995 light industrial goods generated almost 25% of the total value of exports, with 8.4% coming from textiles and apparel; by 2005, under the impact of the forces of structural readjustment, the corresponding figures were 9.3% and 2.9%. Competition from China has been a major factor in the loss of foreign markets for Korean labour-intensive light industrial goods. Meanwhile, in the period 1995–2005 average annual export growth for major heavy industries was as follows: iron and steel products 8.5%; machinery and precision equipment 13.9%; electrical goods and electronics

9.7%; automobiles 15.3%; and ships 12%. However, a distortion was associated with the downturn in overseas demand for electronics and IT goods in 2001. Thus, if growth is calculated between 1995 and 2000, electrical goods and electronics emerge as an export leader, alongside passenger cars, having grown by 12.1% annually (see also above). In particular, China has been a strong source of overseas demand for such goods (as it has for South Korean steel). Nevertheless, overall, heavy industry continues to dominate export proceeds, accounting for more than 90% of the total. In value terms, important individual sources of export earnings in 2010 were (in order of importance): semiconductors (US $50,680m.), shipping vessels ($49,750m.), general machinery ($36,220m.), petrochemicals ($35,700m.), automobiles ($35,400m., excluding parts—worth $19,040m.), petroleum products ($31,490m.), LCD (liquid crystal display) devices ($29,950m.), steel products ($28,890m.) and wireless communication devices ($27,410m.).

Export destinations are dominated by Asia, followed by North America and Europe. In terms of individual countries, in 2003, for the first time ever, China overtook the USA as South Korea's most important export destination, these two countries being followed by Japan, Hong Kong and Taiwan. The most significant purchasers of South Korea's exports in 2010 were China (25.1%), EU member states (11.5%), countries of the Association of Southeast Asian Nations (ASEAN) (11.4%), the USA (10.7%) and Japan (6.0%). Latin America (dominated by Brazil) and the Middle East (led by the United Arab Emirates) accounted for 7.8% and 6.1% of the total, respectively. In 2010 exports to China, Latin America, the USA and ASEAN all increased by 30% or more.

Imports

Annual import growth between 1965 and 1980 was 15.2%, declining to 10.8% per year during the 1980s. Between 1990 and 1996 the momentum of rapid growth was maintained, with imports expanding, on average, by almost 12% annually. Thereafter the collapse of domestic demand in the aftermath of the Asian financial crisis had a dramatic effect, and imports contracted by 3.8% in 1997, and, much more dramatically, by 35.5% in 1998. However, recovery from the downturn was swift. As demand for industrial raw materials, machinery and high-price petroleum recovered, so imports rose again—by 28.4% in 1999 and by a further 34% in 2000 (by which time the value of imports was almost 7% above the previous 1996 peak level). Another sharp decline—by 12%—in 2001 was subsequently followed by consistent recovery and annual growth, as a result of which the value of imports in 2005 reached a new peak of US $257,016.0m. (16.6% more than in 2004), of which 59% were for domestic consumption, the remaining 41% being used for export purposes. In 2006 imports surged by 18.7% to reach $305,061.0m., and in 2007 a further increase, of 15.5%, took them to $352,439.4m. The import growth momentum remained strong during January–September 2008, but between the third and final quarters of the year the value of imports decreased sharply from $122,901m. to $91,528m. Factoring out the effect of price rises, BOK data showed the real rate of increase of imports to have declined from 11.7% to just 3.0% between 2007 and 2008. Between 2008 and 2009 imports declined by more than one-quarter to $320,323.7m., although 2010 saw a sharp recovery, with imports rising by 31.9%, to $422,383.1m. Raw materials and fuel accounted for almost 59% of all imports in 2010, compared with 31.4% for capital goods and just under 10% for consumer products. The three most important categories of imports have been electrical goods and electronic machinery, crude petroleum (accounting for $68,700m., or just over 16% of the total, in 2010), and machinery and precision equipment. Other significant import categories include semiconductors, and chemicals and chemical compounds.

Japan and the USA were traditionally the two most important sources of South Korean imports, and import dependence on Japan for machinery and electronic goods has become increasingly strong in recent years. However, South Korea has also become an increasingly important customer for Chinese products. Between 1991 and 1995 the value of Chinese imports rose from US $3,400m. to $7,402m., an average increase of almost 17% per year. During 1999–2004 the corresponding figure was 15.8%, taking the value of imports from China to $27,722m. In 2004 China surpassed the USA to become the second largest import source, and in 2007 it usurped first place from Japan. By 2010 imports from China had reached $71,574m.: this represented an annual increase of 31.9% above the level of 2009, although it remained almost 7% below the peak 2008 level. The balance of bilateral trade has favoured South Korea, which in 2010 recorded a merchandise surplus of $45,264m. (the total value of bilateral trade was $188,411m.).

In response to the mounting trade deficit with South Korea in the late 1980s, the US Government began to exert strong pressure for greater US access to South Korean markets. Anxious to avoid economic sanctions similar to those that the USA had already imposed on certain Japanese electronic products, South Korea introduced measures designed to liberalize its import trade, while also encouraging voluntary export restraints on selected products. In order to appease US protectionist sentiment, and to counter the effects of the appreciation of the Japanese yen, it began to import from the USA some 100 products that had previously come from Japan. The South Korean Government also sought to placate its US critics by allowing the exchange value of the won to appreciate, thereby enhancing the competitiveness of US imports. Between 1998 and 2005 the value of the won in relation to the US dollar declined from 1,401.4 to 1,012.0, and by the end of 2007 it had declined further to 936.1. However, at the end of 2008 it had once more risen to 1,365.5. In 2010 South Korean exports to the USA totalled $49,816m., compared with imports of $40,403m. The outcome was a trade surplus for South Korea of $9,413m.

Throughout the 1980s and 1990s South Korea consistently recorded a trade deficit with Japan (rising from US $3,000m. to $15,400m. between 1985 and 1996). Its bilateral deficit position has persisted and indeed the level of the deficit has increased quite significantly, rising from $24,400m. in 2005 to $36,120m. in 2010. In 2010 South Korea's leading sources of imports were China (16.8%), Japan (15.1%) and the USA (9.5%). The EU share was just over 9%, but that of ASEAN (10.4%) exceeded that of the USA. However, in broad regional terms, owing to the high proportion of oil in total imports, the biggest source of South Korean imports was the Middle East, accounting for 19% of the total.

Like other countries in the region—not least China—South Korea has shown an active interest in pursuing bilateral trade agreements. In February 2003, in spite of considerable opposition (especially in the farming and fisheries sectors), South Korea signed its first FTA, with Chile. At the end of 2003 discussions with Japanese officials got under way, with the aim of establishing a bilateral FTA. If successful, an FTA with Japan would lead to the creation of one of the biggest trading zones in the world. However, there are significant difficulties to be overcome, not least problems arising out of Japan's wartime legacy, the persistence of the South Korean trade deficit with Japan, and differences between the two sides over agriculture (especially Japan's reluctance to lower rice tariffs) and the automobile sector. Such political and economic obstacles were responsible for the suspension of bilateral FTA talks in late 2004, and thereafter negotiations remained stalled until April 2008, when working-level meetings resumed following the Korea-Japan Summit. Despite business leaders of both sides urging government officials to seek an early FTA settlement, progress has remained halting, although in September 2010 free trade talks at the level of director-general were resumed.

In February 2006 South Korea entered discussions with US officials on the possibility of establishing an FTA. On the South Korean side, progress was hampered by strong criticism of the proposal from trade unions and other parties fearful that any agreement would undermine workers' welfare. The Government responded defensively: on the one hand, it insisted that no deal would be signed if it threatened its agricultural and service sector interests; on the other hand, it committed itself to the establishment of a fund designed to provide financial support to those adversely affected by any agreement with the USA (or by any other FTA). Ultimately, all such obstacles were overcome, and in June 2007 the FTA was duly signed, although it remained to be officially ratified by the two countries' legislatures (see also above).

In addition to its accord with Chile, South Korea has already signed FTAs with India, Peru, Singapore and the EU. It has also negotiated a Comprehensive Economic Cooperation Agreement with ASEAN and is party to the Asia-Pacific Trade Agreement. In addition, a number of other FTA negotiations are ongoing: with Australia, Colombia, Canada, the Gulf States, Mexico, Turkey and New Zealand. In October 2009 the leaders of South Korea, China and Japan declared their commitment to the objective of establishing a trilateral FTA. Various other potential FTAs are at the consultative and preparatory study stage.

Invisible Trade

With the single exception of 1975, during the period from the conclusion of the Korean War in 1953 to the end of the 1970s South Korea consistently enjoyed a surplus in its invisible trade, at times sufficiently large to offset its merchandise trade deficit and move its current account into surplus. However, between 1980 and 1985 this position was reversed, as construction contracts with Middle Eastern countries declined and interest payments on outstanding foreign debt increased. Since 1986 the current account has moved between periods of surplus and deficit. In 1996 a record deficit of US $22,953m. was reached, although in 1997 this figure contracted sharply and from 1998 it moved back into surplus. Since 1998 the current account has remained in surplus, although the size of the surplus has fluctuated considerably. Following the Asian financial crisis, it declined from $42,644m. in 1998 to just $7,542m. in 2002, before recovering to $15,584m. in 2003. In 2007 South Korea's current account surplus reached a new peak of $21,770m., but in 2008 it contracted sharply to $3,197m., only to rise once more to $32,791m. in 2009. Owing mainly to a deterioration in the services trade balance, in 2010 the current account surplus contracted by 14% to $28,214m. (equivalent to 2.8% of GDP). In April 2011 the EIU predicted that the corresponding figure for 2012 would be $30,200m. (an estimated 2.7% of GDP).

Inflows of foreign investment capital into South Korea began in the 1970s, but only reached significant levels towards the end of the 1980s. In particular, the second half of the 1990s represented a high point in terms of investment capital inflows: between 1995 and 1999 annual contractual FDI inflows rose from US $1,776m. to $9,333m., and the cumulative value of utilized inward FDI is estimated to have exceeded the corresponding figure for the previous 30 years. However, OECD data show that having reached record levels of more than $9,000m. in 1999 and 2000, contractual inflows declined by almost two-thirds, to $3,528m., in 2001, and by a further 32% to $2,392m. in the following year. Strong recovery (to $9,246m.) took place in 2004, although a downward trend once more reasserted itself thereafter, and by 2007 annual inward FDI had declined to $1,784m., the lowest level since 1995. Although a degree of recovery took place in 2008, it was not sustained, and preliminary OECD estimates showed the annual figure for 2010 to have decreased by $150m. Some observers interpreted the decline as a sign that foreign investors, especially in Japan and the USA, were finding more attractive destinations for their investment activities, not least in view of the rising value of the won. The surge in inward FDI in the late 1990s no doubt reflected the exigencies of the financial crisis and urgent need for financial support for ailing industries. However, more positively, it also reflected the Government's recognition of the need to accommodate the demands of economic globalization. Since 2000 services have replaced manufacturing as the most important functional destination of inward investment. In 2004 the USA was the most important investor in South Korea, accounting for 40% of total inflows. However, its position has since been usurped by Europe (which accounted for 46.1% of inward FDI in 2009), followed by Japan (16.8%), the US share in that year having declined to 12.9%. In 2010 the cumulative stock of inward FDI stood at $127,050m.

South Korea is also an important source of outward investment. Outflows first exceeded US $1,000m. in 1991. Between 1990 and 2000 annual outflows rose from $1,052m. to $4,482m. Although there was a sharp decline to $2,196m. in 2001, recovery was swift, and by 2004 a new peak of $5,651m. had been reached. During the next four years outward FDI grew, on average, by almost 38% per annum to reach $20,251m. in 2008. Annual outflows fell back to $17,197m. in 2009, but had risen to $19,233m. by the end of 2010. In the same year the cumulative stock of outward FDI was $1138,980m. In 2008 one-half of all outward investment went to Asia, compared with 23.5% to the Middle East, 14.0% to North America and 7.5% to Europe. Within Asia, China has become the single most important destination, and South Korea has become the third largest source of FDI to China, after Hong Kong and Taiwan. Official Chinese sources indicated that in 2009 South Korea accounted for 3% ($2,700,070m.—almost 14% less than in 2008) of all utilized FDI inflows into China, although (excluding the Virgin Islands, through which a lot of Taiwanese investment passes en route to China) it was still the fourth largest single investor in China, after Hong Kong, Japan and Singapore.

FINANCE

Fiscal Policy

The South Korean Government has used tax reforms in order to influence resource allocation and guide the direction and pattern of national economic development. Early (pre-1960) measures were primarily designed to limit consumption and promote capital accumulation. By contrast, more comprehensive reforms introduced in the 1960s sought to put in place a more indigenously financed growth strategy, by replacing economic aid with increased domestic savings. Thus, between 1965 and 1975 the savings rate rose sharply (from 7.4% to 19.1% of GDP). By 1986 it had reached 30%, for the first time making it possible to finance investment wholly from domestic sources. Since that time, South Korea's domestic savings rate has exceeded the investment rate, facilitating net exports of capital.

General government revenues as a share of GDP have risen steadily since the mid-1990s: from 23.6% (1995) to 33.3% (2008) (data from OECD *Factbook*, 2010). Between 1995 and 2003 the share of government spending in GDP increased from 19.8% to 28.9%, but then declined, before reaching a new peak of 30.0% in 2008. As a result, the general government balance varied between 5.4% of GDP in 2000 and 0.5% in 2003 (in 2008 the corresponding figure was 3.3%). From a long-term perspective, the tax burden has risen fairly consistently since the early 1970s. Fiscal policy was relaxed in mid-1998, as South Korea's economic recession deepened, in order to facilitate increased expenditure on social security benefits, job creation and financial restructuring. The central government budget, having been in surplus in 1993, during 1997–99 reverted to deficit (reaching a peak of 18,800m. won in 1998, or 4.3% of GNP). In 2000, however, as a result of more stringent fiscal and monetary policies, it moved back into surplus, where it subsequently remained until the onset of the 2008/09 global economic recession. It was inevitable that the stimulus programme and special supplementary budget announced by the Government in an attempt to address the effects of the global economic downturn would put significant pressure on public finances, as personal tax cuts and company tax exemptions were announced. Thus, EIU data, which differ somewhat from those published by OECD, showed the general government balance moving from surplus into deficit between 2008 and 2009, but returning to a surplus position in 2010. According to data published in the KDI's *Monthly Economic Bulletin*, in 2010 public sector revenue totalled 270,920,000m. won (23.1% of GDP), while expenditure was 254,231,000m. won (21.7%). As the economy continues to recover from the recent crisis, the Ministry of Strategy and Finance will be anxious to reduce government spending. Hence its emphasis on 'selection and stabilization' in 2011—a slogan that highlights the need to focus efforts on technology-intensive projects that promise the greatest returns in terms of growth and employment. In 2010 central government debt was equivalent to 31.9% of GDP.

Foreign Debt

Between 1985 and 1990 South Korea's total outstanding debt was reduced from US $47,100m. to $35,000m. However, financial liberalization subsequently encouraged increasingly large inflows of foreign capital. As a result, total debt rose sharply until, by 1997, it had reached $139,100m. (an average annual growth of 18.8% since 1990). Meanwhile, many enterprises continued to finance their industrial expansion by borrowing large amounts of capital from abroad. The seriousness of the situation was highlighted in the finding that by 1996 (shortly before the financial crisis) some 57% of outstanding debt was in the form of short-term debt. This was a dangerously high figure: in 1996, for example, interest on short-term debt was $3,900m., compared with only $2,800m. on long-term; and by 1998 the cost of debt-servicing equated with 12.9% of revenue from exports of goods and services. The deterioration in its external debt situation was the background against which, during 1997–99, South Korea had recourse to IMF credit, cumulatively totalling over $34,000m.

Between 1995 and 2000 South Korea's gross external debt (short-term and long-term) rose from US $119,799m. to $148,119m. According to estimates published by the EIU, in 2005 the external debt stock had reached $180,744m., and by 2008 the corresponding figure had increased further to $381,121m. In the following year there was a contraction of almost 3%, to $370,780m., but the external debt stock rose again to $380,617m. in 2010, and was expected to increase further to $415,007m. in 2011. Compared with conditions in the mid-1990s, in recent years there has been a major improvement in the structure of South Korea's external debt: by 2004, for example, two-thirds was long-term debt (compared with 54% 10 years previously) and only one-third was short-term.

Boosted by a strong performance on the capital account, in 2000 national foreign-exchange reserves reached a record level of US $96,130m. (30% above the level of the previous end-year and 85% above that of 1998). They subsequently rose steadily, and by the end of 2007 had reached $262,224m., a figure exceeded only by China, Japan, Russia and Taiwan. However, such was the impact of the volatile conditions of 2008 that by the end of the year South Korea's foreign-exchange reserves (excluding gold) had decreased by almost one-quarter to $201,220m. Significant recovery followed, and EIU data indicated that by the end of 2010 the corresponding figure had risen to a new peak of $315,231m.

Monetary Policy and Banking

Through the operations of the central bank and by means of direct ownership—or control through equity participation—of most financial institutions, until the 1980s the Government maintained very tight control over interest rate determination, the underwriting of private loans from abroad, and the allocation of financial resources to the private sector and other enterprises. In 1964 a government-sponsored foreign-exchange rate initiative involving a major currency devaluation (of about 50%) and the introduction of a unified floating rate system greatly facilitated export expansion. In view of subsequent economic growth, the case in favour of financial liberalization became increasingly pressing, and in the 1980s significant monetary reforms took place. Among these were denationalization of the commercial banking sector; the first progress towards the freeing of interest rates from government control; and the abolition of credit 'ceilings' and quotas governing bank lending. By such means, banks were given unprecedented discretion in managing loanable funds in pursuit of profit maximization. More recent evidence of increasing reliance on indirect control is afforded by the BOK's involvement in limited open-market operations.

By 1991 interest rate deregulation had embraced most money market instruments, large certificates of deposits and repurchase agreements. By the end of 1993 lending rates at banks and non-banks had also been freed, while interest rates on policy loans and special credit facilities were scheduled for decontrol during 1994–97. As interest rate liberalization took place, the BOK began to shift from using direct monetary controls, involving the imposition of 'ceiling rates' on bank loans, to reliance on indirect policy instruments and open market operations. Meanwhile, starting in October 1993, the range of permissible daily interbank foreign exchange rate fluctuations was widened. December 1994 witnessed the introduction of the Foreign Exchange Reform Plan, designed to be implemented in three stages between 1995 and 1999, focusing, in turn, on economic globalization-related issues, the liberalization of cross-border transactions, and improvements in the foreign-exchange system.

A major reform, introduced in August 1993, was the implementation of a 'real-name' system of financial transactions to replace the previous system, which had allowed financial accounts and property to be recorded under false, assumed or borrowed names. The desired effect was to curb corruption and enhance incentives, as well as to facilitate the emergence of a more equitable tax regime. Following the publication of the findings of a presidential commission on financial reform in mid-1997, the Government also undertook to seek to curb the influence of the powerful Ministry of Finance and the Economy through the creation of a Financial Supervisory Commission. The principal purpose of the new body, which would be directly responsible to the Prime Minister, was to strengthen supervision over the financial sector. Measures to increase the independence of the BOK were also proposed.

During 1986–89 a by-product of an appreciating won was a significant narrowing of the gap between official and 'black-market' rates for foreign currencies. From 1990 until 1994 the value of the won registered a declining trend, although after mid-1994 its value began to rise again. This trend, combined with the depreciation of the Japanese yen in mid-1995, did not bode well for South Korean exports. Following the rapid depreciation of the won in late 1997, the Government adopted tight monetary policies in order to stabilize the currency. This having been achieved, from mid-1998 monetary policy was eased, with interest rates lowered substantially in a bid to stimulate domestic demand. Subsequently, concerns about flat private consumption growth and the low level of US interest rates constrained upward adjustments of domestic interest rates. The average deposit rate declined from 5.0% to 4.1% between the first quarter of 2002 and the third quarter of 2003; by the end of 2004 it had decreased further, to 3.6%, where it remained until the third quarter of the following year, before once more starting to rise.

The period of relative stability was interrupted by the events of late 2008. Between January and July of that year the BOK kept its base rate at 5.0%, before making an upward adjustment to 5.25% in August, in anticipation of increasing inflationary pressures. However, such pressures subsequently weakened and were overtaken by the onset of the financial crisis in the USA. In an attempt to address the effects of slowing domestic growth, between October 2008 and July 2009 the BOK made six reductions in base rate to 2.0%; this record low rate remained unchanged until July 2010, when a small increase was announced. Further rises followed as the BOK tightened monetary policy in response to growing inflationary pressures, although in August 2011 the IMF argued that interest rates were still too low.

South Korea's banking system was severely tested in 1997, with the collapse of the Hanbo Group. Following revelations that, notwithstanding the lack of adequate collateral, several of the country's largest banks had lent money to Hanbo under government pressure, an investigation was launched in an attempt to discover how such loose credit creation could have taken place. Emergency funds were released into the banking system by the Ministry of Finance and the Economy in order to prevent further corporate bankruptcies.

In 1998 financial institutions and industrial corporations were radically restructured in accordance with the IMF programme. By mid-2000 the Government had closed 440 failing financial institutions, including five large commercial banks, as a result of which more than one-third of workers in the financial sector lost their jobs. In addition, the Government recapitalized 15 of the 17 remaining commercial banks to internationally required standards, and introduced regulatory reforms in an effort to improve the transparency of banking operations. Such measures notwithstanding, in 1999 the banking sector recorded losses of 5,000,000m. won, principally as a result of huge liabilities resulting from the collapse of the Daewoo Group. In September agreement was reached to sell Korea First Bank—one of five banks (the others were Hanvit Bank, Cho Hung Bank, Korea Exchange Bank and Seoulbank) that had been nationalized in 1998—to Newbridge Capital, a US investment fund.

Between late 1997 and early 2000 the Korean Government spent some 102,000,000m. won in an attempt to prevent the collapse of the banking sector. In May 2000, as severe difficulties continued, plans to spend a further 30,000,000m. won were announced. A consensus view was that significant progress had been made towards improving the state of South Korea's banking sector, even though the position of some individual institutions remained far from good. It is an essential condition of future sustained economic growth that the benefits of banking reforms in recent years should not be jeopardized. Measures are needed to address the high level of NPLs in the non-bank financial sector (especially investment trust companies). However, most important of all is the need to intensify the programme of bank privatization in order to enhance efficiency and transparency within the industry. A serious recent problem for the financial market has been growing delinquency rates associated with the excessive issue of credit cards and made worse by slowing economic growth. Between the end of 2002 and November 2003 the average delinquency rate among eight credit card firms was reported to have more than doubled (from 6.6% to 13.5%). Indeed, in November 2003 lack of funds forced the largest credit card company, LG Card, to suspend cash advances, and bankruptcy was only averted by massive cash infusions. However, between 2003 and 2004 collective losses of the six largest credit card firms were reduced from 6,000,000m. won to 1,300,000m. won, a decrease of almost 80%, and by the end of 2005 it seemed clear that the credit card 'bubble' had finally burst.

The opening, in 1967, of a branch of the Chase Manhattan Bank was a signal for other foreign banks to establish branches in South Korea. By the end of 1993 some 74 foreign banks had established offices throughout the country. Arising from the programme of recovery from the 1997 financial crisis was a willingness to open up domestic banks to foreign involvement, a process that was strengthened by government recognition of the need to embrace globalization in a more active manner. The extent to which such involvement took place was revealed in BOK statistics, showing that in 2003 foreign ownership of South Korea's banks was 38.6%, a level much higher than in Japan (7%), the Philippines (15%) and Malaysia (19%). Against this background, the BOK urged the Government to restrain a further expansion of foreign ownership. At mid-2011 there were 37 foreign banks operating in South Korea.

In the 1990s measures were also introduced to provide foreign access to the domestic securities market, and from January 1992 direct investments by foreigners in South Korea's stock market were permitted, albeit initially with an upper limit of 10% of total shares. In May 1996 it was announced that most restrictions on the entry of foreign firms into the stock market would be removed by 2000. Meanwhile, in July 1993 the limit for foreign equity investment had already been eliminated for companies with a 50% or greater foreign ownership, but in December 1997 the IMF insisted, as a condition of its rescue programme, that the limit for foreign equity investment should be abandoned entirely; this was in the hope that foreign investors would purchase stakes in the ailing *chaebol*.

The onset of the regional financial crisis of 1997 led to a dramatic decline in the main index of the South Korean stock market at the end of that year but, following a sharp rise, by the end of 1999 the stock price index was 173% higher than two years previously. In 2000, however, it lost 50% of its value—not least because of struggling investment trust companies' divestment of their portfolios in order to finance their debts. Substantial, but limited, recovery took place in 2001 (during which the index rose by more than 37% to outperform the stock market of every country in the world except Russia) and during January–September 2002. Thereafter, however, there was a substantial decline until, in the second half of 2003, renewed and accelerating recovery took place. Even so, in the last quarter of 2003 the Korea Composite Stock Price Index (KOSPI), at 810.7 (4 January 1980 = 100), was still almost 10% below the level prevailing at the beginning of 2002. A weakening in the index was observed during the second and third quarters of 2004, but a strong recovery during October–December took it to 895.9, and in the first quarter of 2005 to 965.7. A record was reached in February 2005, when KOSPI exceeded 1,000 for the first time. Strong growth in the second half of 2005 took the index to 1,379.4 at the end of the year. With strong demand from overseas investors, it rose to 1,434.5 in December 2006; although it moved little in the first quarter of 2007, it reached a high point of 1,946 in the third quarter of the year, before ending at 1,897 in the final quarter. In the first half of 2008 there was little significant movement in KOSPI, but in the second half of the year it declined sharply to reach a low point of 1,076 in November. A slight improvement followed, but by February 2009 the index had declined to 1,063. Signs that the South Korean economy might be entering recovery thereafter generated greater optimism, and by the final quarter of 2010 KOSPI had risen to 2,051 (25.7% higher than in the same period of 2009). By May 2011 the index had reached more than 2,200, but by the third week of August it had fallen back to barely 1,700.

Statistical Survey

Source (unless otherwise stated): Statistics Korea, Bldg III, Government Complex-Daejeon 920, Dunsan-dong, Seo-gu, Daejeon 302-701; tel. (42) 481-2120; fax (42) 481-2460; internet kostat.go.kr.

Area and Population

AREA, POPULATION AND DENSITY*

Area (sq km)	99,646†
Population (census results)	
1 November 2005	47,041,434
1 November 2010‡	
Males	24,045,000
Females	24,174,000
Total	48,219,000
Density (per sq km) at 2010 census	483.9

* Excluding the demilitarized zone between North and South Korea, with an area of 1,262 sq km (487 sq miles).

† 38,474 sq miles. The figure indicates territory under the jurisdiction of the Republic of Korea, surveyed on the basis of land register in 2005.

‡ Preliminary results, rounded figures.

POPULATION BY AGE AND SEX
(official estimates at mid-2011)

	Males	Females	Total
0–14	3,978,912	3,664,502	7,643,414
15–64	18,337,401	17,470,946	35,808,347
65 and over	2,276,143	3,260,929	5,537,072
Total	24,592,456	24,396,377	48,988,833

Note: Data not adjusted to take account of results of 2010 census.

ADMINISTRATIVE DIVISIONS
(population at census of 1 November 2010)

Province	Area (sq km)	Population ('000)*	Density (per sq km)
Seoul	605.4	9,708	16,035.7
Busan	764.4	3,403	4,451.9
Daegu	884.5	2,444	2,763.1
Incheon	994.1	2,638	2,653.7
Gwangju	501.4	1,469	2,929.8
Daejeon	539.8	1,495	2,769.5
Ulsan	1,057.1	1,082	1,023.6
Gyeonggi-do	10,130.9	11,270	1,112.4
Gangwon-do	16,613.5	1,456	87.6
Chungcheongbuk-do	7,431.4	1,504	202.4
Chungcheongnam-do	8,600.5	2,010	233.7
Jeollabuk-do	8,054.6	1,755	217.9
Jeollanam-do	12,073.5	1,719	142.4
Gyeongsangbuk-do	19,026.0	2,583	135.8
Gyeongsangnam-do	10,520.8	3,154	299.8
Jeju-do	1,848.3	528	285.7
Total	99,646.2	48,219	483.9

* Preliminary figures.

PRINCIPAL TOWNS
(population at 1995 census)

Seoul (capital)	10,231,217	Jeonju (Chonju)	563,153
Busan (Pusan)	3,814,325	Jeongju (Chongju)	531,376
Daegu (Taegu)	2,449,420	Masan	441,242
Incheon (Inchon)	2,308,188	Jinju (Chinju)	329,886
Daejeon (Taejon)	1,272,121	Kunsan	266,559
Gwangju (Kwangju)	1,257,636	Jeju (Cheju)	258,511
Ulsan	967,429	Mokpo	247,452
Seongnam (Songnam)	869,094	Chuncheon (Chunchon)	234,528
Suwon	755,550		

2000 census: Seoul 9,853,972; Busan 3,655,437; Daegu 2,473,990; Incheon 2,466,338; Daejeon 1,365,961; Gwangju 1,350,948; Ulsan 1,012,110.

Mid-2010 (incl. suburbs, UN estimates): Seoul 9,772,717; Busan 3,425,291; Incheon 2,582,967; Daegu 2,458,372; Daejeon 1,509.201; Gwangju 1,475,655; Suwon 1,131,704; Ulsan 1,081,119; Goyang 960,983; Seongnam 954,787 (Source: UN, *World Urbanization Prospects: The 2009 Revision*).

BIRTHS, MARRIAGES AND DEATHS*

	Registered live births		Registered marriages		Registered deaths	
	Number	Rate (per 1,000)	Number	Rate (per 1,000)	Number	Rate (per 1,000)
2003	490,543	10.2	302,503	6.3	244,506	5.1
2004	472,761	9.8	308,598	6.4	244,217	5.0
2005	435,031	8.9	314,304	6.5	243,883	5.0
2006	448,153	9.2	330,634	6.8	242,266	5.0
2007	493,189	10.0	343,559	7.0	244,874	5.0
2008	465,892	9.4	327,715	6.6	246,113	5.0
2009	444,849	9.0	309,759	6.2	246,942	5.0
2010	469,900	9.4	326,104	6.5	255,100	5.1

* Owing to late registration, figures are subject to continuous revision.

Life expectancy (years at birth, WHO estimates): 80 (males 77; females 83) in 2009 (Source: WHO, *World Health Statistics*).

ECONOMICALLY ACTIVE POPULATION*
(labour force survey, '000 persons aged 15 years and over)

	2006	2007	2008
Agriculture, forestry and fishing	1,785	1,779	1,686
Mining and quarrying	18	18	23
Manufacturing	4,167	4,014	3,963
Electricity, gas and water	76	86	90
Construction	1,835	1,849	1,812
Wholesale and retail trade, repair of motor vehicles and personal and household goods	3,713	3,673	3,631
Restaurants and hotels	2,049	2,049	2,044
Transport, storage and communications	1,470	1,498	1,875
Financial intermediation	786	806	821
Real estate, renting and business activities	2,168	2,350	2,219
Public administration and defence; compulsory social security	801	797	840
Education	1,658	1,740	1,784
Health and social work	686	740	842
Other community, social and personal service activities	1,781	1,845	1,782
Households with employed persons	138	161	150
Extra-territorial organizations and bodies	20	15	16
Statistical discrepancy	—	13	—
Total employed	23,151	23,433	23,577
Unemployed	827	783	769
Total labour force	23,978	24,216	23,346
Males	13,978	14,124	14,208
Females	10,000	10,092	10,139

* Excluding armed forces.

Source: ILO.

2009 ('000 persons aged 15 years and over): Agriculture, forestry and fishing 1,648; Industry 3,859 (Manufacturing 3,836); Services 17,998; *Total employed* 23,506; Unemployed 889; *Total labour force* 24,395.

2010 ('000 persons aged 15 years and over): Agriculture, forestry and fishing 1,566; Industry 4,048 (Manufacturing 4,028); Services 18,214; *Total employed* 23,829; Unemployed 920; *Total labour force* 24,749.

Health and Welfare

KEY INDICATORS

Total fertility rate (children per woman, 2009)	1.2
Under-5 mortality rate (per 1,000 live births, 2009)	5
HIV/AIDS (% of persons aged 15–49, 2007)	<0.1
Physicians (per 1,000 head, 2003)	1.6
Hospital beds (per 1,000 head, 2006)	8.6
Health expenditure (2008): US $ per head (PPP)	1,806
Health expenditure (2008): % of GDP	6.5
Health expenditure (2008): public (% of total)	53.9
Access to water (% of persons, 2008)	98
Total carbon dioxide emissions ('000 metric tons, 2007)	502,909.6
Carbon dioxide emissions per head (metric tons, 2007)	10.4
Human Development Index (2010): ranking	12
Human Development Index (2010): value	0.877

For sources and definitions, see explanatory note on p. vi.

Agriculture

PRINCIPAL CROPS
('000 metric tons)

	2007	2008	2009
Rice, paddy	6,038.0	6,919.2	7,023.0*
Barley	168.9	170.1	260.0*
Maize	83.5	92.8	77.0*
Potatoes	574.4	604.6	640.0†
Sweet potatoes	352.3	329.4	310.0†
Beans, dry	7.6	7.6	8.0†
Chestnuts	77.5	75.2	73.0†
Soybeans (Soya beans)	114.2	132.7	139.0*
Sesame seed	17.5	19.5	20.0†
Cabbages and other brassicas	2,537.6	2,901.9	3,100.0†
Lettuce and chicory	154.8	160.0†	167.0†
Spinach	81.5	93.4	104.0†
Tomatoes	479.9	408.2	400.0†
Pumpkins, squash and gourds	330.0	327.5	330.0†
Cucumbers and gherkins	330.2	383.9	400.0†
Chillies and peppers, green	414.1	385.8	415.0†
Onions and shallots, green	488.0	505.1	540.0†
Onions, dry	1,213.4	1,035.1	1,200.0†
Garlic	347.5	375.5	380.0†
Carrots and turnips	76.7	99.6	130.0†
Mushrooms	28.7	28.4	28.0†
Watermelons	741.9	856.8	900.0†
Cantaloupes and other melons	205.4	220.4	221.0†
Tangerines, mandarins, clementines and satsumas	777.5	636.4	620.0†
Apples	435.7	470.9	480.0†
Pears	467.4	470.7	470.0†
Peaches and nectarines	184.5	189.1	190.0†
Plums and sloes	64.8	66.7	65.0†
Strawberries	203.2	204.0†	205.0†
Grapes	328.7	333.6	340.0
Persimmons	395.6	430.5	450.0†
Tobacco, unmanufactured*	33.0	39.0	42.1

* Unofficial figure(s).
† FAO estimate.

Aggregate production ('000 metric tons, may include official, semi-official or estimated data): Total cereals 6,312 in 2007, 7,203 in 2008, 7,381 in 2009; Total vegetables (incl. melons) 10,718 in 2007, 11,290 in 2008, 11,959 in 2009; Total fruits (excl. melons) 2,967 in 2007, 2,915 in 2008, 2,937 in 2009.

Source: FAO.

LIVESTOCK
('000 head)

	2007	2008	2009
Cattle	2,654	2,876	3,079
Pigs	9,606	9,087	9,585
Goats	372	266	260
Chickens	119,365	119,784	138,768

Source: FAO.

LIVESTOCK PRODUCTS
('000 metric tons)

	2007	2008	2009
Cattle meat	219.0	246.0	283.0
Pig meat*	1,043.0	1,056.0	1,000.0
Chicken meat*	513.0	488.0	498.0
Duck meat*	57.0	54.0	55.0
Cows' milk	2,188.0	2,200.0	2,200.0
Goats' milk†	5.2	4.2	4.1
Hen eggs	543.8	566.1	566.0†
Other poultry eggs†	29.6	30.8	31.2
Honey	26.5	26.0†	26.0†

* Unofficial figures.
† FAO estimate(s).

Source: FAO.

Forestry

ROUNDWOOD REMOVALS
('000 cubic metres, excl. bark)

	2007	2008	2009
Sawlogs, veneer logs and logs for sleepers	440	456	451
Pulpwood	1,643	1,757	1,919
Other industrial wood	597	489	806
Fuel wood*	2,472	2,475	2,477
Total	5,152	5,177	5,653

* FAO estimates.

Source: FAO.

SAWNWOOD PRODUCTION
('000 cubic metres, incl. sleepers)

	2002	2003	2004
Coniferous (softwood)	4,209	4,200	4,200*
Broadleaved (hardwood)	201	180	166†
Total	4,410	4,380	4,366*

* FAO estimate.
† Unofficial figure.

2005–09: Figures assumed to be unchanged from 2004 (FAO estimates).

Source: FAO.

Fishing

('000 metric tons, live weight)

	2007	2008	2009
Capture	1,869.8	1,949.8	1,856.6
Croakers and drums	44.0	39.6	35.6
Japanese anchovy	221.1	261.5	203.7
Skipjack tuna	214.9	187.3	257.5
Chub mackerel	145.0	188.2	119.0
Largehead hairtail	66.0	72.9	85.5
Argentine shortfin squid	193.7	157.8	57.6
Japanese flying squid	174.5	186.2	189.2
Aquaculture	606.1	473.8	473.1
Pacific cupped oyster	321.3	250.0	240.9
Total catch	2,476.0	2,423.6	2,329.7

Note: Figures exclude aquatic plants ('000 metric tons): 811.2 (capture 18.2, aquaculture 793.0) in 2007; 934.9 (capture 13.9, aquaculture 921.0) in 2008; 869.5 (capture 10.8, aquaculture 858.7) in 2009. Also excluded are aquatic mammals, recorded by number rather than by weight; the number of dolphins and whales caught was: 610 in 2007; 728 in 2008; 556 in 2009.

Source: FAO.

Mining

('000 metric tons unless otherwise indicated)

	2007	2008	2009
Hard coal (Anthracite)	2,886	2,773	2,519
Iron ore: gross weight	291	366	455
Iron ore: metal content	163	205*	200*
Lead ore (metric tons)†	12	449	2,064
Zinc ore (metric tons)†	4,067	3,672	—
Kaolin	688	955	695
Feldspar	398.5	344.3	622.7
Salt (unrefined)	249.5	384.3	382.3
Mica (metric tons)	42,385	49,474	27,078
Talc (metric tons)	9,557	6,438	5,996
Pyrophyllite	798.1	892.6	617.4

* Estimate.

† Figures refer to the metal content of ores.

Source: US Geological Survey.

Industry

SELECTED PRODUCTS

('000 metric tons unless otherwise indicated)

	2006	2007	2008
Wheat flour	1,850	1,760	1,681
Refined sugar	1,317	n.a.	n.a.
Beer (million litres)	17,400	18,200	19,073
Cigarettes (million)	119,966	124,570	129,543
Cotton yarn—pure and mixed	217	216	206
Plywood ('000 cu m)	736	716	682
Newsprint	1,654	1,666	1,600
Rubber tyres ('000)*	65,231	68,771	n.a.
Caustic soda	1,477	1,578	1,590
Liquefied petroleum gas	3,098	2,927	2,977
Naphtha	21,537	23,147	20,441
Kerosene	5,410	3,827	4,116
Gas-diesel (distillate fuel oil)	32,392	34,314	35,860
Residual fuel oil	30,793	27,363	22,370
Cement	55,021	58,188	51,653
Pig-iron	27,559	29,437	31,043
Crude steel	48,259	51,003	53,322
Passenger cars—produced ('000 units)	3,489	n.a.	n.a.
Electric energy (million kWh)	404,021	427,316	446,428
Carbon black†	484.3	497.2	484.0‡
Products of petroleum refineries ('000 barrels)†	717,493	770,523	747,827‡

* Tyres for passenger cars and commercial vehicles.

† Source: US Geological Survey.

‡ Estimate.

Shipbuilding (merchant ships launched, '000 grt): 8,977 in 1999; 11,211 in 2000; 8,385 in 2001.

Source: mostly UN, *Industrial Commodity Statistics Yearbook*.

2009 ('000 metric tons unless otherwise indicated): Cement 50,127; Crude steel 48,572; Pig-iron 27,475; Carbon black 500.0 (estimate); Products of petroleum refineries ('000 barrels) 750,000 (estimate) (Source: US Geological Survey).

Finance

CURRENCY AND EXCHANGE RATES

Monetary Units
100 chun (jeon) = 10 hwan = 1 won.

Sterling, Dollar and Euro Equivalents (31 May 2011)
£1 sterling = 1,783.31 won;
US $1 = 1,080.60 won;
€1 = 1,554.44 won;
10,000 won = £5.61 = $9.25 = €6.43.

Average Exchange Rate (won per US $)
2008 1,102.05
2009 1,276.93
2010 1,156.19

BUDGET

('000 million won)

Revenue	2004	2005	2006
Current revenue	177,432	190,165	208,091
Tax revenue	140,643	152,371	165,359
Non-tax revenue	36,788	37,794	42,733
Capital revenue	1,329	1,281	1,482
Total	178,760	191,447	209,573

Expenditure	2004	2005	2006
Current expenditure	145,148	160,274	173,688
General public services	11,909	14,743	17,208
Defence	19,995	21,976	23,428
Education	22,113	27,467	28,457
Social security and welfare	15,125	16,716	18,536
Economic services	30,753	28,250	30,115
Transport and communications	14,458	14,041	13,903
Capital expenditure	26,992	24,648	26,493
Net lending	1,398	3,024	5,746
Total	173,538	187,946	205,928

2007: Total revenue 243,633 (Current 241,693, Capital 1,940); Total expenditure and net lending 209,810 (Current 169,658, Capital 33,045, Net lending 7,107).

2008: Total revenue 250,713 (Current 248,809, Capital 1,904); Total expenditure and net lending 238,834 (Current 196,879, Capital 36,475, Net lending 5,480).

2009: Total revenue 255,252 (Current 252,720, Capital 2,532); Total expenditure and net lending 272,873 (Current 209,689, Capital 45,134, Net lending 18,049).

2010: Total revenue 270,923 (Current 268,540, Capital 2,383); Total expenditure and net lending 254,231 (Current 216,937, Capital 34,209, Net lending 3,084).

Source: partly Bank of Korea, Seoul.

INTERNATIONAL RESERVES

(US $ million at 31 December)

	2008	2009	2010
Gold (national valuation)	75.7	79.0	79.6
IMF special drawing rights	85.6	3,745.5	3,540.0
Reserve position in IMF	579.8	985.2	1,024.8
Foreign exchange	200,479.1	265,202.3	286,926.4
Total	201,220.2	270,012.0	291,570.7

Source: IMF, *International Financial Statistics*.

MONEY SUPPLY

('000 million won at 31 December)

	2008	2009	2010
Currency outside banks	25,323	31,209	36,983
Demand deposits at deposit money banks	63,203	72,953	77,028
Total money (incl. others)	92,143	105,398	114,214

Source: IMF, *International Financial Statistics*.

COST OF LIVING
(Consumer Price Index; base: 2005 = 100)

	2008	2009	2010
Food and non-alcoholic beverages	108.2	116.3	123.8
Alcoholic beverages and cigarettes	100.8	101.9	102.3
Housing, water and fuels	109.7	110.9	113.6
Furnishings and household goods	111.2	116.3	117.3
Clothing and footwear	108.1	113.6	116.9
Health	105.8	108.1	110.2
Education	117.2	120.1	122.8
Communication	95.3	95.2	94.3
Transport	117.9	113.7	119.3
All items (incl. others)	109.7	112.8	116.1

NATIONAL ACCOUNTS
('000 million won at current prices)

National Income and Product

	2008	2009	2010
Compensation of employees	474,953.8	493,685.7	527,568.9
Operating surplus	295,368.0	310,604.0	361,408.2
Domestic factor incomes	770,321.8	804,289.7	888,977.1
Consumption of fixed capital	135,876.4	142,094.1	154,328.8
Gross domestic product (GDP) at factor cost	906,198.2	946,383.8	1,043,305.9
Indirect taxes, *less* subsidies	120,253.6	118,653.1	129,497.5
GDP in purchasers' values	1,026,451.8	1,065,036.8	1,172,803.4
Net factor income from abroad	7,663.6	4,746.2	320.0
Gross national income	1,034,115.4	1,069,783.1	1,173,123.4
Less Consumption of fixed capital	135,876.4	142,094.1	154,328.8
National income in market prices	898,239.0	927,689	1,018,794.6

Expenditure on the Gross Domestic Product

	2008	2009	2010
Final consumption expenditure	718,571.6	746,294.9	795,460.7
Households (incl. non-profit institutions serving households)	561,627.5	575,970.2	615,406.9
General government	156,944.1	170,324.7	180,053.8
Gross capital formation	320,368.8	279,858.0	341,902.9
Gross fixed capital formation	300,794.1	309,714.0	335,889.5
Changes in inventories	19,574.7	–29,856.0	6,013.4
Total domestic expenditure	1,038,940.4	1,026,152.9	1,137,363.6
Exports of goods and services	544,110.7	529,645.1	614,451.0
Less Imports of goods and services	556,197.9	490,188.3	581,735.8
Statistical discrepancy	–401.4	–573.0	2,724.6
GDP in market prices	1,026,451.8	1,065,036.8	1,172,803.4

Gross Domestic Product by Economic Activity

	2007	2008	2009
Agriculture, forestry and fishing	25,208.8	24,686.0	26,615.0
Mining and quarrying	2,001.2	2,336.0	2,220.5
Manufacturing	238,610.9	256,209.4	266,578.2
Electricity, gas and water	19,155.3	12,298.6	17,258.2
Construction	64,979.0	64,612.2	66,576.6
Wholesale and retail trade, restaurants and hotels	93,405.5	100,419.3	103,994.8
Transport, storage and communications	79,268.6	81,279.9	81,387.5
Financial intermediation	61,114.0	65,132.2	65,035.5
Real estate, renting and business activities	114,491.7	121,791.9	125,363.0
Public administration and defence, compulsory social security	55,515.9	59,396.8	63,706.6
Education	55,554.4	60,940.1	63,448.7
Health and social work	35,451.6	38,452.1	43,092.1
Other service activities	30,025.2	32,133.5	33,559.3
Gross value added at basic prices	874,782.0	919,688.0	958,836.0
Taxes, less subsidies, on products	100,231.0	106,763.8	106,200.8
Total	975,013.0	1,026,451.8	1,065,036.8

Source: Bank of Korea.

BALANCE OF PAYMENTS
(US $ million)

	2008	2009	2010
Exports of goods f.o.b.	434,699	358,217	464,301
Imports of goods f.o.b.	–429,525	–320,355	–422,425
Trade balance	5,174	37,862	41,876
Exports of services	90,587	73,553	82,706
Imports of services	–9,6326	–80,190	–93,907
Balance on goods and services	–565	31,226	30,675
Other income received	21,653	14,514	15,879
Other income paid	–17,218	–12,238	–15,111
Balance on goods, services and income	3,871	33,502	31,443
Current transfers received	14,070	12,700	13,396
Current transfers paid	–14,744	–13,412	–16,626
Current balance	3,197	32,791	28,214
Capital account (net)	109	290	–174
Direct investment abroad	–20,251	–17,197	–19,230
Direct investment from abroad	3,311	2,249	–150
Portfolio investment assets	23,484	1,436	–3,542
Portfolio investment liabilities	–25,890	48,292	42,094
Financial derivatives assets	54,978	74,846	49,550
Financial derivatives liabilities	–69,748	–77,939	–49,557
Other investment assets	–13,742	1,688	–12,258
Other investment liabilities	–9851	394	–4,971
Net errors and omissions	–2043	1,804	–2,805
Overall balance	–56,447	68,652	27,172

Source: IMF, *International Financial Statistics*.

External Trade

PRINCIPAL COMMODITIES
(distribution by SITC, US $ million)*

Imports c.i.f.	2008	2009	2010
Food and live animals	16,405.5	13,438.4	16,335.1
Crude materials (inedible) except fuels	28,272.1	20,310.1	30,632.2
Mineral fuels, lubricants, etc.	145,514.8	91,669.2	122,596.2
Petroleum, petroleum products, etc.	104,812.6	64,527.6	87,676.7
Gas (natural and manufactured)	24,892.6	17,146.7	21,788.7
Chemicals and related products	36,658.2	31,504.9	41,147.7
Organic chemicals	10,978.5	8,907.4	12,136.9
Basic manufactures	64,983.5	43,250.4	56,142.6
Iron and steel	33,554.9	17,430.2	22,726.5
Machinery and transport equipment	114,541.8	96,881.6	123,316.7
Machinery specialized for particular industries	13,336.8	9,634.3	18,148.8
General industrial machinery, equipment and parts	13,193.4	12,367.7	13,779.1
Office machines and automatic data-processing machines	7,526.5	6,443.6	8,855.1
Telecommunications and sound equipment	10,560.6	8,631.0	10,486.6
Other electrical machinery, apparatus, etc.	48,655.5	41,913.0	48,856.3
Thermionic valves and tubes, microprocessors, transistors, etc.	29,781.1	25,261.4	28,637.0
Miscellaneous manufactured articles	28,644.1	23,292.6	31,597.6
Total (incl. others)	435,274.7	323,084.5	425,212.2

Exports f.o.b.	2008	2009	2010
Mineral fuels, lubricants, etc.	38,454.7	23,786.0	32,579.7
Petroleum, petroleum products, etc.	38,311.3	23,663.4	32,375.2
Chemicals and related products	42,709.9	37,414.7	48,951.5
Organic chemicals	15,560.5	12,847.5	16,531.1
Plastics in primary forms	15,524.3	13,874.9	17,817.3
Basic manufactures	59,559.9	48,114.5	60,430.1
Textile yarn, fabrics, etc.	10,370.9	9,155.4	10,967.7
Iron and steel	25,037.8	17,468.0	24,432.9
Machinery and transport equipment	233,688.1	206,334.1	263,902.6
Office machines and automatic data-processing machines	10,688.0	8,991.8	12,889.8
Automatic data-processing machines and units, etc.	2,791.9	2,377.2	2,987.5
Parts and accessories for office machines and automatic data-processing equipment	6,161.1	5,074.9	8,266.8
Telecommunications and sound equipment	49,192.8	41,226.4	40,403.0
Other electrical machinery, apparatus, etc.	49,180.2	47,500.1	70,194.3
Thermionic valves and tubes, microprocessors, transistors, etc.	28,189.2	26,957.9	43,291.1
Road vehicles	48,099.2	36,294.6	53,209.0
Motor cars and other motor vehicles	31,287.5	22,399.1	31,781.7
Other transport equipment	42,170.4	43,592.6	48,617.7
Ships, boats and floating structures	40,967.6	42,483.4	46,735.3
Miscellaneous manufactured articles	37,223.3	36,906.7	46,860.0
Total (incl. others)	422,007.3	363,533.6	466,383.8

* Excluding trade with the Democratic People's Republic of Korea.

Source: Korea International Trade Association.

PRINCIPAL TRADING PARTNERS
(US $ million)*

Imports c.i.f.	2008	2009	2010
Australia	18,000.3	14,756.1	20,456.2
Brazil	4,380.5	3,743.5	4,712.1
Canada	4,403.5	3,535.3	4,350.9
China, People's Republic	76,930.3	54,246.1	71,573.6
France	4,877.4	4,006.1	4,283.5
Germany	14,769.1	12,298.5	14,304.9
Hong Kong	2,222.7	1,487.2	1,945.9
India	6,581.2	4,141.6	5,674.4
Indonesia	11,320.3	9,264.1	13,985.8
Iran	8,223.1	5,745.7	6,940.2
Iraq	4,227.6	3,812.2	4,427.7
Italy	4,151.4	3,512.9	3,723.3
Japan	60,956.4	49,427.5	64,296.1
Kuwait	12,128.8	7,991.5	10,850.1
Malaysia	9,909.1	7,574.1	9,531.0
Oman	5,694.7	4,124.5	4,095.9
Philippines	3,099.5	2,651.6	3,488.1
Qatar	14,374.6	8,386.5	11,915.5
Russia	8,340.1	5,788.7	9,899.5
Saudi Arabia	33,781.5	19,736.8	26,820.0
Singapore	8,361.8	7,871.8	7,849.5
Taiwan	10,642.9	9,851.4	13,647.1
Thailand	4,281.7	3,238.6	4,168.8
United Arab Emirates	19,248.5	9,310.0	12,170.1
United Kingdom	3,637.1	2,895.8	3,265.5
USA	38,364.8	29,039.5	40,402.7
Total (incl. others)	435,274.7	323,084.5	425,212.2

Exports f.o.b.	2008	2009	2010
Australia	5,171.3	5,243.1	6,641.6
Brazil	5,925.9	5,311.2	7,752.6
Canada	4,057.2	3,439.6	4,101.9
China, People's Republic	91,388.9	86,703.2	116,837.8
France	3,495.5	2,910.6	3,004.3
Germany	10,522.7	8,820.9	10,702.2
Hong Kong	19,771.9	19,661.1	25,294.3
India	8,977.1	8,013.3	14,830.6
Indonesia	7,933.6	5,999.9	8,897.3
Iran	4,342.6	3,991.9	4,596.7
Italy	3,545.6	2,797.3	3,569.1
Japan	28,252.5	21,770.8	28,176.3
Liberia	2,801.5	4,884.6	5,401.7
Malaysia	5,794.5	4,324.8	6,114.8
Mexico	9,089.9	7,132.8	8,845.5
Netherlands	6,405.6	4,527.5	5,306.2
Philippines	5,016.3	4,567.3	5,838.0
Russia	9,478.0	4,194.1	7,759.8
Singapore	16,293.0	13,617.0	15,244.2
Spain	3,192.5	1,737.1	1,858.0
Taiwan	11,462.0	9,501.1	14,830.5
Thailand	5,779.1	4,528.2	6,459.8
Turkey	3,772.6	2,660.7	3,752.9
United Arab Emirates	5,748.5	4,977.8	5,487.0
United Kingdom	5,936.2	3,796.6	5,555.1
USA	46,376.6	37,649.9	49,816.1
Viet Nam	7,804.8	7,149.5	9,652.1
Total (incl. others)	422,007.3	363,533.6	466,383.8

* Excluding trade with the Democratic People's Republic of Korea.

Source: Korea International Trade Association.

Trade with the Democratic People's Republic of Korea (US $ million, unofficial estimates): *Total imports:*519.5 in 2006; 765.3 in 2007; 932.3 in 2008. *Total exports:* 830.2 in 2006; 1,032.6 in 2007; 888.1 in 2008 (Source: Bank of Korea, Republic of Korea).

Transport

RAILWAYS
(traffic)

	2003	2004	2005
Passengers carried ('000)	894,620	921,223	950,995
Passenger-km (million)	27,228	28,459	31,004
Freight ('000 metric tons)	47,110	44,512	41,669
Freight ton-km (million)	11,057	10,641	10,108

ROAD TRAFFIC
(motor vehicles in use at 31 December)

	2002	2003
Passenger cars	9,737,428	10,278,923
Goods vehicles	2,894,412	3,016,407
Buses and coaches	1,275,319	1,246,629
Motorcycles and mopeds	1,708,457	1,730,193

2006 (motor vehicles in use at 31 December): Passenger cars 11,606,971; Goods vehicles 3,182,627; Buses and coaches 1,105,636; Motorcycles and mopeds 1,747,925 (Source: IRF, *World Road Statistics*).

2007 (motor vehicles in use at 31 December): Passenger cars 12,020,730; Goods vehicles 4,189,042; Buses and coaches 182,132; Motorcycles and mopeds 1,821,323 (Source: IRF, *World Road Statistics*).

SHIPPING

Merchant Fleet
(registered at 31 December)

	2007	2008	2009
Number of vessels	2,946	3,001	3,009
Total displacement ('000 grt)	13,102.0	14,144.7	12,892.5

Source: IHS Fairplay, *World Fleet Statistics*.

Sea-borne Freight Traffic
('000 metric tons)*

	2002	2003	2004
Goods loaded	319,570	340,527	317,799
Goods unloaded	615,555	616,326	593,361

* Including coastwise traffic loaded and unloaded.

CIVIL AVIATION*

	2003	2004	2005
Passengers ('000)	42,839	45,824	46,841
Passenger-km (million)	82,231	96,583	101,664
Freight ('000 metric tons)	2,632	2,978	2,989
Freight ton-km (million)	11,696	13,810	13,597

* Domestic and international flights.

Tourism

FOREIGN VISITOR ARRIVALS*

Country of residence	2006	2007	2008
China, People's Republic	896,969	1,068,925	1,167,891
Hong Kong	142,786	140,138	160,325
Japan	2,338,921	2,235,963	2,378,102
Philippines	248,262	263,799	276,710
Russia	144,611	140,426	136,342
Taiwan	338,162	335,224	320,244
Thailand	128,555	146,792	160,687
USA	555,704	587,324	610,083
Total (incl. others)	6,155,046	6,448,240	6,890,841

* Including same-day visitors (excursionists) and crew members from ships; also including Korean nationals resident abroad.

Total foreign visitor arrivals ('000): 7,818 in 2009 (provisional).

Receipts from tourism (US $ million, incl. passenger transport, unless otherwise indicated): 8,508 in 2006; 8,947 in 2007; 12,783 in 2008; 9,442 in 2009 (provisional, excl. passenger transport).

Source: World Tourism Organization.

Communications Media

	2008	2009	2010
Telephones ('000 main lines in use)	23,390.3	25,949.4	28,543.2
Mobile cellular telephones ('000 subscribers)	46,516.2	48,671.2	50,767.2
Internet subscribers ('000)*	15,474.1	16,347.7	n.a.
Broadband subscribers ('000)	15,921.5	16,804.1	17,649.5

* Estimates based on percentage.

Radio receivers ('000 in use): 47,500 in 1997.

Television receivers ('000 in use): 17,229 in 2000.

Book production: 27,527 titles (82,097,000 copies) in 2004.

Personal computers: 27,886,536 (575.5 per 1,000 persons) in 2007.

Sources: mainly UNESCO, *Statistical Yearbook*; UN, *Statistical Yearbook*; International Telecommunication Union; and Korean Association of Newspapers.

Education

(2007)

	Institutions	Teachers	Pupils
Kindergarten	8,294	33,504	541,550
Primary schools	5,756	167,182	3,829,998
Middle schools	3,032	107,986	2,063,159
General high schools	1,457	83,662	1,347,363
Vocational high schools	702	36,549	494,011
Junior colleges	148	11,685	795,519
Teachers' colleges	11	855	25,834
Universities and colleges	175	52,763	1,919,504
Graduate schools	1,042	2,895	296,576

Pupil-teacher ratio (primary education, UNESCO estimate): 24.1 in 2007/08 (Source: UNESCO Institute for Statistics).

Adult literacy rate (UNESCO estimates): 97.9% (males 99.2%; females 96.6%) in 2001 (Source: UN Development Programme, *Human Development Report*).

Directory

The Constitution

The Constitution of the Sixth Republic (Ninth Amendment) was approved by national referendum on 29 October 1987. It came into effect on 25 February 1988. The main provisions are summarized below:

THE EXECUTIVE

The President

The President shall be elected by universal, equal, direct and secret ballot of the people for one term of five years. Re-election of the President is prohibited. In times of national emergency and under certain conditions the President may issue emergency orders and take emergency action with regard to budgetary and economic matters. The President shall notify the National Assembly of these measures and obtain its concurrence, or they shall lose effect. He may, in times of war, armed conflict or similar national emergency, declare martial law in accordance with the provisions of law. He shall lift the emergency measures and martial law when the National Assembly so requests with the concurrence of a majority of the members. The President may not dissolve the National Assembly. He is authorized to take directly to the people important issues through national referendums. The President shall appoint the Prime Minister (with the consent of the National Assembly) and other public officials.

The State Council

The State Council shall be composed of the President, the Prime Minister and no more than 30 and no fewer than 15 others appointed by the President (on the recommendation of the Prime Minister), and shall deliberate on policies that fall within the power of the executive. No member of the armed forces shall be a member of the Council, unless retired from active duty.

The Board of Audit and Inspection

The Board of Audit and Inspection shall be established under the President to inspect the closing of accounts of revenue and expenditures, the accounts of the State and other organizations as prescribed by law, and to inspect the administrative functions of the executive agencies and public officials. It shall be composed of no fewer than five and no more than 11 members, including the Chairman. The Chairman shall be appointed by the President with the consent of the National Assembly, and the members by the President on the recommendation of the Chairman. Appointments shall be for four years and members may be reappointed only once.

THE NATIONAL ASSEMBLY

Legislative power shall be vested in the National Assembly. The Assembly shall be composed of not fewer than 200 members, a number determined by law, elected for four years by universal, equal, direct and secret ballot. The constituencies of members of the Assembly, proportional representation and other matters pertaining to the Assembly elections shall be determined by law. A regular session shall be held once a year and extraordinary sessions shall be convened upon requests of the President or one-quarter of the Assembly's members. The period of regular sessions shall not exceed 100 days and of extraordinary sessions 30 days. The Assembly has the power to recommend to the President the removal of the Prime Minister or any other Minister. The Assembly shall have the authority to pass a motion for the impeachment of the President or any other public official, and may inspect or investigate state affairs, under procedures to be established by law.

THE CONSTITUTIONAL COURT

The Constitutional Court shall be composed of nine members appointed by the President, three of whom shall be appointed from persons selected by the National Assembly and three from persons nominated by the Chief Justice. The term of office shall be six years. It shall pass judgment upon the constitutionality of laws upon the request of the courts, matters of impeachment and the dissolution of political parties. In these judgments the concurrence of six members or more shall be required.

THE JUDICIARY

The courts shall be composed of the Supreme Court, which is the highest court of the State, and other courts at specified levels (for further details, see section on Judicial System). The Chief Justice and justices of the Supreme Court are appointed by the President, subject to the consent of the National Assembly. When the constitutionality of a law is a prerequisite to a trial, the Court shall request a decision of the Constitutional Court. The Supreme Court shall have the power to pass judgment upon the constitutionality or legality of administrative decrees, and shall have final appellate jurisdiction over military tribunals. No judge shall be removed from office except following impeachment or a sentence of imprisonment.

ELECTION MANAGEMENT

Election Commissions shall be established for the purpose of fair management of elections and national referendums. The National Election Commission shall be composed of three members appointed by the President, three appointed by the National Assembly and three appointed by the Chief Justice of the Supreme Court. Their term of office is six years, and they may not be expelled from office except following impeachment or a sentence of imprisonment.

POLITICAL PARTIES

The establishment of political parties shall be free and the plural party system guaranteed. However, a political party whose aims or activities are contrary to the basic democratic order may be dissolved by the Constitutional Court.

AMENDMENTS

A motion to amend the Constitution shall be proposed by the President or by a majority of the total number of members of the National Assembly. Amendments extending the President's term of office or permitting the re-election of the President shall not be effective for the President in office at the time of the proposal. Proposed amendments to the Constitution shall be put before the public by the President for 20 days or more. Within 60 days of the public announcement, the National Assembly shall decide upon the proposed amendments, which require a two-thirds' majority of the National Assembly. They shall then be submitted to a national referendum not later than 30 days after passage by the National Assembly and shall be determined by more than one-half of votes cast by more than one-half of voters eligible to vote in elections for members of the National Assembly. If these conditions are fulfilled, the proposed amendments shall be finalized and the President shall promulgate them without delay.

FUNDAMENTAL RIGHTS

Under the Constitution all citizens are equal before the law. The right of habeas corpus is guaranteed. Freedom of speech, press, assembly and association are guaranteed, as are freedom of choice of residence and occupation. No state religion is to be recognized and freedom of conscience and religion is guaranteed. Citizens are protected against retrospective legislation, and may not be punished without due process of law.

Rights and freedoms may be restricted by law when this is deemed necessary for the maintenance of national security, order or public welfare. When such restrictions are imposed, no essential aspect of the right or freedom in question may be violated.

GENERAL PROVISIONS

Peaceful unification of the Korean peninsula, on the principles of liberal democracy, is the prime national aspiration. The Constitution mandates the State to establish and implement a policy of unification. The Constitution expressly stipulates that the armed forces must maintain political neutrality at all times.

The Government

HEAD OF STATE

President: LEE MYUNG-BAK (took office 25 February 2008).

STATE COUNCIL
(October 2011)

The Government is formed by the Grand National Party (GNP).

Prime Minister: KIM HWANG-SIK.

Minister of Strategy and Finance: BAHK JAE-WAN.

Minister of Unification: YU WOO-IK.

Minister of Foreign Affairs and Trade: KIM SUNG-HWAN .

Minister of Justice: KWON JAE-JIN.

Minister of National Defence: KIM KWAN-JIN.

Minister of Public Administration and Security: MAENG HYUNG-KYU.

Minister of Education, Science and Technology: LEE JU-HO.

Minister of Culture, Sports and Tourism: CHOE KWANG-SIK.

Minister of Food, Agriculture, Forestry and Fisheries: SUH KYU-YONG.

Minister of Knowledge Economy: CHOI JOONG-KYUNG.

Minister of Health and Welfare: RIM CHE-MIN.

Minister of Environment: YOO YOUNG-SOOK.

Minister of Employment and Labour: LEE CHAE-PIL.

Minister of Gender Equality and Family: KIM KUM-LAE.

Minister of Land, Transport and Maritime Affairs: KWON DO-YUP.

Minister for Special Affairs: LEE JAE-OH.

MINISTRIES

Office of the President: Chong Wa Dae (The Blue House), 1, Sejong-no, Jongno-gu, Seoul; tel. (2) 730-5800; e-mail foreign@president.go.kr; internet www.bluehouse.go.kr.

Office of the Prime Minister: 55, Sejong-no, Jongno-gu, Seoul 110-760; tel. (2) 2100-2114; fax (2) 739-5830; e-mail webmaster@pmo.go.kr; internet www.pmo.go.kr.

Office of the Minister for Special Affairs: c/o Office of the Prime Minister, 55, Sejong-no, Jongno-gu, Seoul 110-760.

Ministry of Culture, Sports and Tourism: 42, Sejong-no, Jongno-gu, Seoul 110-703; tel. (2) 3704-9114; fax (2) 3704-9119; e-mail webadmin@www.mct.go.kr; internet www.mcst.go.kr.

Ministry of Education, Science and Technology: 77-6, Sejong-no, Jongno-gu, Seoul 110-760; tel. (2) 6222-6060; fax (2) 2100-6133; e-mail webmaster@mest.go.kr; internet www.mest.go.kr.

Ministry of Employment and Labour: Govt Complex, 1, Jungang-dong, Gwacheon City, Gyeonggi Prov. 427-718; tel. (2) 2110-7497; fax (2) 503-6623; internet www.molab.go.kr.

Ministry of Environment: 88, Gwanmunro, Gwacheon City, Gyeonggi Prov. 427-729; tel. (2) 2110-6546; e-mail webmaster@me.go.kr; internet www.me.go.kr.

Ministry of Food, Agriculture, Forestry and Fisheries: Govt Complex, 1, Jungang-dong, Gwacheon City, Gyeonggi Prov.; tel. (2) 503-7200; fax (2) 503-7249; e-mail wmaster@maf.go.kr; internet www.mifaff.go.kr.

Ministry of Foreign Affairs and Trade: 37, Sejong-no, Seoul 110-787; tel. (2) 2100-2114; fax (2) 2100-7999; e-mail web@mofat.go.kr; internet www.mofat.go.kr.

Ministry of Gender Equality and Family: Premiere Place Bldg, 96, Mugyo-dong, Jung-gu, Seoul 100-777; tel. (2) 2075-4500; fax (2) 2075-4780; e-mail webadmin@moge.go.kr; internet www.moge.go.kr.

Ministry for Health and Welfare: 75, Yulgong-ro, Jongno-gu, Seoul 110-793; internet www.mohw.go.kr.

Ministry of Justice: 88, Gwanmunro, Gwacheon City, Gyeonggi Prov. 427-720; tel. (2) 2110-3009; fax (2) 503-7113; e-mail webmaster@moj.go.kr; internet www.moj.go.kr.

Ministry of Knowledge Economy: 88, Gwanmunro, Gwacheon City, Gyeonggi Prov. 427-723; tel. (2) 1577-0900; e-mail webmke@mke.go.kr; internet www.mke.go.kr.

Ministry of Land, Transport and Maritime Affairs: 1, Jungang-dong, Gwacheon City, Gyeonggi Prov. 427-712; tel. (2) 1599-0001; fax (2) 2150-1000; e-mail webmaster@mltm.go.kr; internet www.mltm.go.kr.

Ministry of National Defence: 1, 3-ga, Yeongsan-dong, Yeongsan-gu, Seoul 140-701; tel. (2) 795-0071; fax (2) 703-3109; e-mail cyber@mnd.go.kr; internet www.mnd.go.kr.

Ministry of Public Administration and Security: Govt Complex, 77-6, Sejong-no, 1-ga, Jongno-gu, Seoul 110-760; tel. (2) 2100-3399; e-mail unah88@mopas.go.kr; internet www.mopas.go.kr.

Ministry of Strategy and Finance: Govt Complex II, 88, Gwanmunro, Gwacheon City, Gyeonggi Prov. 427-725; tel. (2) 2150-2450; fax (2) 503-9070; e-mail fppr@mosf.go.kr; internet www.mosf.go.kr.

Ministry of Unification: Govt Complex, 77-6, Sejong-no, Jongno-gu, Seoul 110-760; tel. (2) 2100-5747; fax (2) 2100-5727; e-mail hanabyun@unikorea.go.kr; internet www.unikorea.go.kr.

President and Legislature

PRESIDENT

Election, 19 December 2007

Candidate	Votes	% of total
Lee Myung-Bak (Grand National Party)	11,492,389	48.7
Chung Dong-Young (United New Democratic Party)*	6,174,681	26.1
Lee Hoi-Chang (Independent)	3,559,963	15.1
Moon Kook-Hyun (Creative Korea Party)	1,375,498	5.8
Kwon Young-Gil (Democratic Labour Party)	712,121	3.0
Rhee In-Je (Democratic Party)*	160,708	0.7
Huh Kyung-Young (Economic Republican Party)	96,756	0.4
Geum Min (Korea Socialist Party)	18,223	0.1
Chung Kun-Mo (True Owner Coalition)	15,380	0.1
Chun Kwan (Chamsaram Society Full True Act)	7,161	0.0
Total (incl. others)	23,732,854	100.0

* In 2008 the United New Democratic Party merged with the Democratic Party to form the United Democratic Party, subsequently known as the Democratic Party.

LEGISLATURE

Kuk Hoe
(National Assembly)

1 Yeouido-dong, Yeongdeungpo-gu, Seoul 150-701; tel. (2) 788-2001; fax (2) 788-3375; e-mail webmaster@assembly.go.kr; internet www.assembly.go.kr.

Speaker: KIM HYONG-O.

General Election, 9 April 2008

	Representatives		
Party	Elected	Proportional	Total
Grand National Party	131	22	153
United Democratic Party*	66	15	81
Liberty Forward Party	14	4	18
Pro-Park Coalition†	6	8	14
Democratic Labour Party	2	3	5
Creative Korea Party	1	2	3
Independents	25	—	25
Total	245	54	299

* Later renamed the Democratic Party.
† Comprising supporters of Park Geun-Hye, former Chairwoman of the GNP.

Election Commission

National Election Commission: 2-3 Junggang-dong, Gwacheon-si, Gyeonggi-do 427-727; tel. (2) 503-1114; e-mail e_nec@nec.go.kr; internet www.nec.go.kr; Chair. YANG SUNG-TAE.

Political Organizations

Centrist Reformists Democratic Party: 25-4, Yeouido-dong, Yeongdeungpo-gu, Seoul; tel. (2) 784-7007; fax (2) 780-4074; internet minjoo.org.kr; f. 2005; fmrly Millennium Democratic Party; Pres. RHEE IN-JE.

Creative Korea Party (CKP): Unit 601, 484-74, Bulgwang-dong, Eunpyeong-gu, Seoul 122-860; tel. (2) 784-4701; fax (2) 784-4705; e-mail master@ckp.kr; internet www.ckp.kr; f. 2007; Pres. SONG YOUNG-OH.

Democratic Labour Party (DLP): Jongdo Bldg, 1st and 2nd Floors, 25-1, Moonrae-dong, Yeongdeungpo-gu, Seoul 150-092; tel. (2) 2139-7777; fax (2) 2139-7890; e-mail kdlpinter@hotmail.com; internet www.kdlp.org; f. 2000; Pres. KANG KI-GAP.

Democratic Party (DP): 13-17, Yeouido-dong, Yeongdeungpo-gu, Seoul 150-701; tel. (2) 1577-7667; fax (2) 2630-0145; e-mail help@undp.kr; internet minjoo.kr; est. as United New Democratic Party in 2007 by defectors and mems of the Uri Party and the Democratic Party; name changed to United Democratic Party following merger with Democratic Party in Feb. 2008; name changed as above in mid-2008; Chair. SOHN HAK-KYU.

Grand National Party (GNP) (Hannara Party): 14-31, Yeouido-dong, Yeongdeungpo-gu, Seoul 156-768; tel. (2) 3786-3000; fax (2) 3786-3610; internet www.hannara.or.kr; f. 1997; est. by merger of the original Democratic Party (f. 1990) and New Korea Party; Chair. HONG JOON-PYO; Sec.-Gen. KIM JUNG-KWON.

Korea Socialist Party: Nagyeong Bldg, 11th Floor, 115-62, Gongdeok-dong, Mapo-gu, Seoul 121-801; tel. (2) 711-4592; fax (2) 706-4118; internet sp.or.kr; f. 1998; Pres. GEUM MIN.

Liberty Forward Party (LFP): Yeongsan Bldg, 3rd Floor, 14-14, Yeouido-dong, Yeoungdeungpo-gu, Seoul; tel. (2) 780-3988; fax (2) 780-3983; e-mail webmaster@jayou.or.kr; internet www.jayou.or.kr; conservative; merger with People First Union announced Aug. 2011; Leader LEE HOI-CHANG.

New Progressive Party (NPP): Daeha Bldg, Unit 801, 14-11, Yeouido-dong, Yeoungdeungpo-gu, Seoul; tel. (2) 6004-2000; fax (2) 6004-2001; e-mail newjinbo@gmail.com; internet www.newjinbo.org; f. 2008; left-wing; est. by splinter group of DLP; Pres. ROH HOE-CHAN ; Sec.-Gen. LEE SUNG-HWA.

People's Participation Party: Dongbok Bldg, 4th Floor, 5-5, Changjeon-dong, Mapo-gu, Seoul 121-880; tel. (2) 1670-2010; fax (2) 784-2091; e-mail admin@handypia.org; internet www.handypia.org; f. 2010; est. by fmr members of Uri Party; Chair. RHYU SI-MIN.

Other parties that presented candidates for the 2007 presidential election were the Economic Republican Party, the True Owner Coalition and the Chamsaram Society Full True Act.

Civic groups play an increasingly significant role in South Korean politics. These include: the People's Solidarity for Participatory Democracy (Dir JANG HASUNG); the Citizens' Coalition for Economic Justice (Sec.-Gen. PARK BYEONG-OK); and the Citizens' Alliance for Political Reform (Leader KIM SOK-SU).

Diplomatic Representation

EMBASSIES IN THE REPUBLIC OF KOREA

Afghanistan: 27-2, Hannam-dong, Yeongsan-gu, Seoul 140-210; tel. (2) 793-3535; fax (2) 795-2662; e-mail info@afghanistanembassy.or.kr; internet www.afghanistanembassy.or.kr; Ambassador MOHAMMAD KARIM RAHIMI.

Algeria: 2-6, Itaewon 2-dong, Yeongsan-gu, Seoul 140-857; tel. (2) 794-5034; fax (2) 794-5040; e-mail sifdja01@kornet.net; internet www.algerianemb.or.kr; Ambassador HOCINE SAHRAOUI.

Angola: 737-11, Hannam 2-dong, Yeongsan-gu, Seoul 140-212; tel. (2) 792-8463; fax (2) 792-8467; e-mail embassy@angolaembassy.or.kr; internet www.angolaembassy.or.kr; Ambassador ALBINO MALUNGO.

Argentina: Chun Woo Bldg, 5th Floor, 534, Itaewon-dong, Yeongsan-gu, Seoul 140-861; tel. (2) 793-4062; fax (2) 792-5820; e-mail info@argentina.or.kr; internet www.argentina.or.kr; Ambassador CARLOS ALBERTO ARGAÑARAZ.

Australia: Kyobo Bldg, 19th Floor, 1, Jongno 1-ga, Jongno-gu, Seoul 110-714; tel. (2) 2003-0100; fax (2) 2003-0196; e-mail seoul-inform@dfat.gov.au; internet www.southkorea.embassy.gov.au; Ambassador SAM GEROVICH.

Austria: Kyobo Bldg, 21st Floor, 1-1, Jongno 1-ga, Jongno-gu, Seoul 110-714; tel. (2) 732-9071; fax (2) 732-9486; e-mail seoul-ob@bmeia.gv.at; internet www.bmeia.gv.at/seoul; Ambassador Dr JOSEF MÜLLNER.

Azerbaijan: Hannam Tower, Annex Bldg, 3rd Floor, 730, Hannam-dong, Yeongsan-gu, Seoul 140-893; tel. (2) 797-1765; fax (2) 797-1767; e-mail info@azembassy.co.kr; internet www.azembassy.co.kr; Ambassador ROVSHAN JAMSHIDOV.

Bangladesh: 310-22, Dongbinggo-dong, Yeongsan-gu, Seoul; tel. (2) 796-4056; fax (2) 790-5313; e-mail bdootseoul@kornet.net; internet www.bdembseoul.org; Ambassador MOHAMMAD SHAHIDUL ISLAM.

Belarus: 432-1636, Sindang 2-dong, Jung-gu, Seoul 100-835; tel. (2) 2237-8171; fax (2) 2237-8174; e-mail korea@belembassy.org; internet www.korea.belembassy.org; Ambassador NATALLIA ZHYLEVICH (designate).

Belgium: 737-10, Hannam-dong, Yeongsan-gu, Seoul 140-893; tel. (2) 749-0381; fax (2) 797-1688; e-mail seoul@diplobel.fed.be; internet www.belgium.or.kr; Ambassador PIERRE CLÉMENT DUBUISSON.

Brazil: Ihn Gallery Bldg, 4th and 5th Floors, 141, Palpan-dong, Jongno-gu, Seoul; tel. (2) 738-4970; fax (2) 738-4974; e-mail braseul@kornet.net; internet seul.itamaraty.gov.br; Ambassador EDMUNDO SUSSUMU FUJITA.

Brunei: 39-1, Cheongun-dong, Jongno-gu, Seoul 110-030; tel. (2) 790-1078; fax (2) 790-1084; e-mail kbnbd_seoul@yahoo.com; Ambassador Dato' Paduka Haji HARUN BIN Haji ISMAIL.

Bulgaria: 723-42, Hannam 2-dong, Yeongsan-gu, Seoul 140-894; tel. (2) 794-8626; fax (2) 794-8627; e-mail seoul_bg@yahoo.co.uk; internet www.mfa.bg/bg/44; Ambassador KOSSIO KITIPOV.

Cambodia: 653-110, Hannam-dong, Yeongsan-gu, Seoul 140-887; tel. (2) 3785-1041; fax (2) 3785-1040; e-mail camemb.jpn@mfa.gov.kh; Ambassador KY SIM CHAN.

Canada: 16-1, Jeong-dong, Jung-gu, CPOB 6299, Seoul 100-662; tel. (2) 3783-6000; fax (2) 3783-6239; e-mail seoul@international.gc.ca; internet www.canadainternational.gc.ca/korea-coree; Ambassador DAVID CHATTERSON.

Chile: Coryo Daeyungak Tower, Unit 1801, 25-5, Chungmoro 1-ga, Jung-gu, Seoul 100-706; tel. (2) 779-2610; fax (2) 779-2615; e-mail echilekr@yahoo.co.kr; internet www.coreachile.org; Ambassador HERNÁN BRANTES.

China, People's Republic: 54, Hyoja-dong, Jongno-gu, Seoul 110-033; tel. (2) 738-1038; fax (2) 738-1046; e-mail chinaemb_kr@mfa.gov.cn; internet www.chinaemb.or.kr; Ambassador ZHANG XINSEN.

Colombia: Korea Tourism Org. Bldg, 7th Floor, 40, Cheonggyecheon-no, Jung-gu, Seoul 100-180; tel. (2) 720-1369; fax (2) 725-6959; e-mail eseul@cancilleria.gov.co; internet www.cancilleria.gov.co/wps/portal/embajada_corea; Ambassador JAIME ALBERTO CABAL SANCLEMENTE.

Congo, Democratic Republic: Daewoo Complex Bldg, Unit 702, 167, Naesu-dong, Jongno-gu, Seoul 110-070; tel. (2) 722-7958; fax (2) 722-7998; e-mail congokoreaembassy@yahoo.com; Ambassador N. CHRISTOPHE NGWEY.

Costa Rica: Iljin Bldg, Unit 8, 50-1, Dohwa-dong, Mapo-gu, Seoul 121-040; tel. (2) 707-9249; fax (2) 707-9255; e-mail embajadacr@ecostarica.or.kr; internet www.ecostarica.or.kr; Ambassador FERNANDO BORBÓN ARIAS.

Côte d'Ivoire: Chungam Bldg, 2nd Floor, 794-4, Hannam-dong, Yeongsan-gu, Seoul 140-894; tel. (2) 3785-0561; fax (2) 3785-0564; e-mail acisel1@hanafos.com; internet cotedivoireembassy.or.kr; Ambassador KOUASSI FLORENT EKRA.

Czech Republic: 1-121, Sinmun-no 2-ga, Jongno-gu, Seoul 110-062; tel. (2) 725-6765; fax (2) 734-6452; e-mail seoul@embassy.mzv.cz; internet www.mzv.cz/seoul; Ambassador JAROSLAV OLŠA, Jr.

Denmark: Namsong Bldg, 5th Floor, 260-199, Itaewon-dong, Yeongsan-gu, Seoul 140-200; tel. (2) 795-4187; fax (2) 796-0986; e-mail selamb@um.dk; internet www.ambseoul.um.dk; Ambassador PETER L. HANSEN.

Dominican Republic: Taepyeong-no Bldg, 19th Floor, 310, Taepyeong-no 2-ga, Jung-gu, Seoul; tel. (2) 756-3513; fax (2) 756-3514; e-mail embadom@kornet.net; Chargé d'affaires a.i. ERNESTO TORRES PEREYRA.

Ecuador: SC First Bank Bldg, 19th Floor, 100, Gongpyeong-dong, Jongno-gu, Seoul 110-702; tel. (2) 739-2401; fax (2) 739-2355; e-mail eecucorea@mmrree.gob.ec; Ambassador NICOLÁS TRUJILLO NEWLIN.

Egypt: 46-1, Hannam-dong, Yeongsan-gu, Seoul 140-210; tel. (2) 749-0787; fax (2) 795-2588; e-mail embassyegyptkorea@yahoo.com; internet www.mfa.gov.eg/Missions/southkorea/seoul/embassy/en-GB/default.htm; Ambassador MOHAMED ABDEL RAHIM EL-ZORKANY.

El Salvador: Samsung Life Insurance Bldg, 20th Floor, 150, Taepyeong-no 2-ga, Jung-gu, Seoul 100-716; tel. (2) 753-3432; fax (2) 753-3456; e-mail koresal@kornet.net; Ambassador HÉCTOR ROBERTO GONZÁLEZ URRUTIA.

Finland: Kyobo Bldg, 18th Floor, 1, Jongno 1-ga, Jongno-gu, Seoul 110-714; tel. (2) 732-6737; fax (2) 723-4969; e-mail sanomat.seo@formin.fi; internet www.finland.or.kr; Ambassador PEKKA WUORISTO.

France: 30, Hap-dong, Seodaemun-gu, Seoul 120-030; tel. (2) 3149-4300; fax (2) 3149-4310; e-mail ambafrance@hanafos.com; internet www.ambafrance-kr.org; Ambassador ELISABETH LAURIN.

Gabon: Yoosung Bldg, 4th Floor, 738-20, Hannam-dong, Yeongsan-gu, Seoul; tel. (2) 793-9575; fax (2) 793-9574; e-mail amgabsel@unitel.co.kr; Ambassador JEAN-PIERRE SOLE-EMANE.

Germany: 308-5, Dongbinggo-dong, Yeongsan-gu, Seoul 140-816; tel. (2) 748-4114; fax (2) 748-4161; e-mail info@seoul.diplo.de; internet www.seoul.diplo.de; Ambassador Dr HANS-ULRICH SEIDT.

Ghana: 5-4, Hannam-dong, Yeongsan-gu, CPOB 3887, Seoul 140-884; tel. (2) 3785-1427; fax (2) 3785-1428; e-mail ghana3@kornet.net; internet www.ghanaembassy.or.kr; Ambassador MARGARET CLARKE-KWESIE.

Greece: Hanwha Bldg, 27th Floor, 1, Janggyo-dong, Jung-gu, Seoul 100-797; tel. (2) 729-1401; fax (2) 729-1402; e-mail greekemb@kornet.net; Ambassador PETROS AVIERINOS.

Guatemala: 614, Lotte Hotel, 1, Sogong-dong, Jung-gu, Seoul 100-635; tel. (2) 771-7582; fax (2) 771-7584; e-mail embcorea@minex.gob.gt; Ambassador RAFAEL A. SALAZAR.

Holy See: 2, Gungjeong-dong, Jongno-gu, Seoul 110-031 (Apostolic Nunciature); tel. (2) 736-5725; fax (2) 739-5738; e-mail apnunkr@yahoo.com; Apostolic Nuncio Most Rev. OSVALDO PADILLA (Titular Archbishop of Voli).

Honduras: Jongno Tower Bldg, 22nd Floor, 6, Jongno 2-ga, Jongno-gu, Seoul 110-160; tel. (2) 738-8402; fax (2) 738-8403; e-mail hondseul@kornet.net; Ambassador MICHEL IDIAQUEZ BARADAT.

Hungary: 1-103, Dongbinggo-dong, Yeongsan-gu, Seoul 140-230; tel. (2) 792-2105; fax (2) 792-2109; e-mail mission.sel@kum.gov.hu; internet www.mfa.gov.hu/emb/seoul; Ambassador MIKLÓS LENGYEL.

India: 37-3, Hannam-dong, Yeongsan-gu, CPOB 3466, Seoul 140-210; tel. (2) 798-4257; fax (2) 796-9534; e-mail eoiseoul@sinbiro.com; internet www.indembassy.or.kr; Ambassador SKAND R. TAYAL.

Indonesia: 55, Yeouido-dong, Yeongdeungpo-gu, Seoul 150-010; tel. (2) 783-5675; fax (2) 780-4280; e-mail kbriseoul@kornet.net; internet www.kemlu.go.id/seoul; Ambassador NICHOLAS TANDI DAMMEN.

Iran: 1-93, Dongbinggo-dong, Yeongsan-gu, Seoul 140-809; tel. (2) 793-7751; fax (2) 792-7052; e-mail iranssy@chol.com; internet www.iranembassy.or.kr; Ambassador AHMAD MASOUMIFAR.

Iraq: 1-94, Dongbinggo-dong, Yeongsan-gu, Seoul 140-811; tel. (2) 790-4202; fax (2) 790-4206; e-mail sulemb@iraqmfamail.com; internet www.mofamission.gov.iq/kor; Ambassador KHALIL AL-MOSAWI.

Ireland: Leema Bldg, 13th Floor, 146-1, Susong-dong, Jongno-gu, Seoul 110-755; tel. (2) 774-6455; fax (2) 774-6458; e-mail seoulembassy@dfa.ie; internet www.embassyofireland.or.kr; Ambassador EAMONN MCKEE.

Israel: Cheonggye 11 Bldg, 18th Floor, 149, Seorin-dong, Jongno-gu, Seoul 110-726; tel. (2) 3210-8500; fax (2) 3210-8555; e-mail info@seoul.mfa.gov.il; internet seoul.mfa.gov.il; Ambassador TUVIA ISRAELI.

Italy: Ilshin Bldg, 3rd Floor, 714, Hannam-dong, Yongsan-gu, Seoul 140-894; tel. (2) 796-0491; fax (2) 797-5560; e-mail embassy.seoul@esteri.it; internet www.ambseoul.esteri.it; Ambassador SERGIO MERCURI.

Japan: 18-11, Junghak-dong, Jongno-gu, Seoul 110-150; tel. (2) 2170-5200; fax (2) 734-4528; e-mail info@japanem.or.kr; internet www.kr.emb-japan.go.jp; Ambassador MASATOSHI MUTO.

Jordan: 6th Floor, Twin-Tree Tower, Bldg B, 14 Joonghak-dong, Jongno-gu, Seoul 110-792; tel. (2) 318-2897; fax (2) 318-3644; e-mail jdembassy@gmail.com; Ambassador OMAR AL-NAHAR.

Kazakhstan: 271-5, Hannam-dong, Yeongsan-gu, Seoul 140-885; tel. (2) 379-9714; fax (2) 395-9719; e-mail kazkor@chollian.net; internet www.kazembassy.org; Ambassador DARKHAN BERDALIYEV.

Kenya: 243-36, Itaewon-dong, Yeongsan-gu, Seoul 140-200; tel. (2) 3785-2903; fax (2) 3785-2905; e-mail info@kenya-embassy.or.kr; internet www.kenya-embassy.or.kr; Ambassador NGOVI KITAU.

Kuwait: 309-15, Dongbinggo-dong, Yeongsan-gu, Seoul; tel. (2) 749-3688; fax (2) 749-3687; e-mail kuwaitembassykorea@hotmail.com; Ambassador MUTEB AL-MUTOTEH.

Kyrgyzstan: Namsong Bldg, Unit 403, 260-199, Itaewon-dong, Yeongsan-gu, Seoul 140-200; tel. (2) 379-0951; fax (2) 379-0953; e-mail seoulembassykg@gmail.com; Chargé d'affaires a.i. CHYNGYZ ESHIMBEKOV.

Laos: 657-9, Hannam-dong, Yeongsan-gu, Seoul 140-887; tel. (2) 796-1713; fax (2) 796-1771; e-mail laoseoul@korea.com; Ambassador SOUKTHAVONE KEOLA.

Lebanon: 310-49, Dongbinggo-dong, Yeongsan-gu, Seoul 140-230; tel. (2) 794-6482; fax (2) 794-6485; e-mail emleb@lebanonembassy.net; internet www.lebanonembassy.net; Ambassador ISSAM MUSTAPHA.

Malaysia: 4-1, Hannam-dong, Yeongsan-gu, Seoul 140-884; tel. (2) 2077-8600; fax (2) 794-5480; e-mail malseoul@kln.gov.my; internet www.malaysia.or.kr; Ambassador Dato' RAMLAN BIN IBRAHIM.

Mexico: 33-6, Hannam 1-dong, Yeongsan-gu, Seoul 140-885; tel. (2) 798-1694; fax (2) 790-0939; e-mail embajada@embamexcor.org; internet portal.sre.gob.mx/corea; Ambassador MARTHA ORTIZ DE ROSAS GÓMEZ.

Mongolia: 33-5, Hannam-dong, Yeongsan-gu, Seoul 140-885; tel. (2) 794-1350; fax (2) 794-7605; e-mail mongol6@kornet.net; internet www.mongolembassy.com; Ambassador DORJPALAMYN GEREL.

Morocco: Hannam Tower, Annex Bldg, 4th Floor, 730, Hannam-dong, Yeongsan-gu, Seoul; tel. (2) 793-6249; fax (2) 792-8178; e-mail sifamase@kornet.net; Ambassador MOHAMED CHRAÏBI.

Myanmar: 724-1, Hannam-dong, Yeongsan-gu, Seoul 140-210; tel. (2) 790-3814; fax (2) 790-3817; e-mail myanmar@kotis.net; Ambassador NYO WIN.

Nepal: 244-143, Huam-dong, Yeongsan-gu, Seoul; tel. (2) 3789-9770; fax (2) 736-8848; e-mail info@nepembseoul.gov.np; internet www.nepembseoul.gov.np; Ambassador KAMAL KOIRALA.

Netherlands: KPOB 509, Seoul 110-605; tel. (2) 737-9514; fax (2) 735-1321; e-mail seo@minbuza.nl; internet southkorea.nlembassy.org; Ambassador PAUL MENKVELD.

New Zealand: Kyobo Bldg, 15th Floor, 1, Jongno 1-ga, Jongno-gu, KPOB 2258, Seoul 110-110; tel. (2) 3701-7700; fax (2) 3701-7701; e-mail nzembsel@kornet.net; internet www.nzembassy.com/korea; Ambassador RICHARD MANN.

Nigeria: 310-19, Dongbinggo-dong, Yeongsan-gu, CPOB 3754, Seoul 140-230; tel. (2) 797-2370; fax (2) 796-1848; e-mail chancery@nigerianembassy.or.kr; internet www.nigerianembassy.or.kr; Ambassador DESMOND AKAWOR.

Norway: 13th Floor, Jeong-dong Bldg, 15-5 Jeong-dong, Jung-gu, Seoul 100-784; tel. (2) 727-7100; fax (2) 727-7199; e-mail emb.seoul@mfa.no; internet www.norway.or.kr; Ambassador DIDRIK TØNSETH.

Oman: 309-3, Dongbinggo-dong, Yeongsan-gu, Seoul; tel. (2) 790-2431; fax (2) 790-2430; e-mail omanembs@kornet.net; Ambassador MOHAMED SALIM AL-HARTHY.

Pakistan: 124-13, Itaewon-dong, Yeongsan-gu, Seoul 140-200; tel. (2) 796-8252; fax (2) 796-0313; e-mail consular@pkembassy.or.kr; internet www.pkembassy.or.kr; Ambassador SHAUKAT ALI MUKADAM.

Panama: Gwanghwamun Platinum Bldg, Unit 709, 7th Floor, 156, Jeokseon-dong, Jongno-gu, Seoul; tel. (2) 734-8610; fax (2) 734-8613; e-mail panaemba@kornet.net; Ambassador JAIME LASSO DEL CASTILLO.

Papua New Guinea: Doosan We've Pavilion Bldg, Unit 210, 58, Soosong-dong, Jongno-gu, Seoul 110-858; tel. (2) 2198-5771; fax (2) 2198-5779; e-mail ambassador@kunduseoul.kr; Ambassador BILL VERI.

Paraguay: Hannam Tower, Annex Bldg, 3rd Floor, 730, Hannam-dong, Yeongsan-gu, Seoul; tel. (2) 792-8335; fax (2) 792-8334; e-mail pyemc2@kornet.net; internet www.embaparcorea.org; Ambassador CEFERINO ADRIAN VALDEZ PERALTA.

Peru: Daeyungak Bldg, Unit 2002, 25-5, Jungmu-no 1-ga, Jung-gu, Seoul 100-706; tel. (2) 757-1735; fax (2) 757-1738; e-mail lpruseul@uriel.net; internet www.embassyperu.or.kr; Ambassador MARCELA LÓPEZ BRAVO.

Philippines: 5-1, Itaewon 2-dong, Yeongsan-gu, Seoul; tel. (2) 796-7387; fax (2) 796-0827; e-mail seoulpe@philembassy-seoul.com; internet www.philembassy-seoul.com; Ambassador LUIS TEODORO CRUZ.

Poland: 70, Sagan-dong, Jongno-gu, Seoul; tel. (2) 723-9681; fax (2) 723-9680; e-mail embassy@polandseoul.org; internet www.seul.polemb.net; Ambassador KRZYSZTOF MAJKA.

Portugal: Wonseo Bldg, 2nd Floor, 171, Wonseo-dong, Jongno-gu, Seoul 110-280; tel. (2) 3675-2251; fax (2) 3675-2250; e-mail portcoreia@hotmail.com; internet www.portugalseoul.com; Ambassador HENRIQUE SILVEIRA BORGES.

Qatar: 309-5, Dongbinggo-dong, Yeongsan-gu, Seoul 140-817; tel. (2) 798-2444; fax (2) 790-1027; e-mail qatarembassy@koreamail.com; Ambassador ALI HAMAD MUBARAK AL-MARRI.

Romania: 1-104, Dongbinggo-dong, Yongsan-gu, Seoul 140-809; tel. (2) 797-4924; fax (2) 794-3114; e-mail ambseul@uriel.net; Chargé d'affaires a.i. SEVER COTU.

Russia: 34-16, Jeong-dong, Jung-gu, Seoul 100-120; tel. (2) 318-2116; fax (2) 754-0417; e-mail rusemb@uriel.net; internet www.russian-embassy.org; Ambassador KONSTANTIN VNUKOV.

Rwanda: Sooyong Bldg, Unit 503, 64-1, Hannam-dong, Yeongsan-gu, Seoul 140-889; tel. (2) 798-1052; fax (2) 798-1054; e-mail info@rwanda-embassy.or.kr; internet rwanda-embassy.or.kr; Ambassador EUGENE S. KAYIHURA.

Saudi Arabia: 36-37, Itaewon 1-dong, Yeongsan-gu, Seoul 140-201; tel. (2) 739-0631; fax (2) 739-0041; e-mail embassysaudi@yahoo.co.kr; Ambassador AHMED BIN YUNUS AL-BARRAK.

Senegal: Coryo Daeyungak Tower, 13th Floor, Unit 1302, 25-5, Chungmuro 1-ga, Jung-gu, Seoul 100-706; tel. (2) 745-5554; fax (2) 745-5524; e-mail ambassenseoul@hotmail.com; Ambassador AMADOU DABO.

Serbia: 730, Hannam-dong, Yeongsan-gu, Seoul; tel. (2) 797-5109; fax (2) 790-6109; e-mail emserbseul@yahoo.com; internet www.embserb.or.kr; Ambassador SLOBODAN MARINKOVIĆ.

Singapore: Seoul Finance Bldg, 28th Floor, 84, Taepyeong-no 1-ga, Jung-gu, Seoul 100-101; tel. (2) 774-2464; fax (2) 773-2463; e-mail singemb_seo@sgmfa.gov.sg; internet www.mfa.gov.sg/seoul; Ambassador PETER TAN HAI CHUAN.

Slovakia: 389-1, Hannam-dong, Yeongsan-gu, Seoul 140-210; tel. (2) 794-3981; fax (2) 794-3982; e-mail emb.seoul@mzv.sk; internet www.mzv.sk/seoul; Ambassador DUSAN BELLA.

South Africa: 1-37, Hannam-dong, Yeongsan-gu, Seoul 140-885; tel. (2) 792-4855; fax (2) 792-4856; e-mail general@southafrica-embassy.or.kr; internet www.southafrica-embassy.or.kr; Ambassador HILTON ANTHONY DENNIS.

Spain: 726-52, Hannam-dong, Yeongsan-gu, Seoul 140-894; tel. (2) 794-3581; fax (2) 796-8207; e-mail emb.seul@maec.es; internet www.maec.es/subwebs/Embajadas/Seul; Ambassador LUIS ARIAS ROMERO.

Sri Lanka: 229-18, Itaewon-dong, Yeongsan-gu, Seoul 140-202; tel. (2) 735-2966; fax (2) 737-9577; e-mail lankaemb@kornet.net; Ambassador W. W. T. WIJERATNE.

Sudan: Vivien Bldg, 3rd Floor, 4-52, Seobinggo-dong, Yeongsan-gu, Seoul 140-240; tel. (2) 793-8692; fax (2) 793-8693; e-mail sudanseoul@yahoo.com; internet www.sudanembassy.co.kr; Ambassador TAGELDIN EL-HADI.

Sweden: Danam Bldg, 8th Floor, 120, Namdaemunro 5-ga, Jung-gu, CPOB 3577, Seoul 100-635; tel. (2) 3703-3700; fax (2) 3703-3701; e-mail embassy@swedemb.or.kr; internet www.swedenabroad.com/seoul; Ambassador LARS VARGÖ.

Switzerland: 32-10, Songwol-dong, Jongno-gu, CPOB 2900, Seoul 110-101; tel. (2) 739-9511; fax (2) 737-9392; e-mail seo.vertretung@eda.admin.ch; internet www.eda.admin.ch/seoul; Ambassador THOMAS KUPFER.

Thailand: 653-7, Hannam-dong, Yeongsan-gu, Seoul 140-210; tel. (2) 795-3098; fax (2) 798-3448; e-mail rteseoul@kornet.net; internet www.thaiembassy.or.kr; Ambassador Dr CHAIYONG SATJIPANON.

Timor-Leste: Hannam Tower Bldg II, Unit 405, 725-23, Hannam-dong, Yeongsan-gu, Seoul 140-894; tel. (2) 797-6151; fax (2) 797-6152; e-mail tlembseoul@gmail.com; Ambassador JOÃO VIEGAS CARRASCALÃO.

Tunisia: 1-17, Dongbinggo-dong, Yeongsan-gu, Seoul 140-809; tel. (2) 790-4334; fax (2) 790-4333; e-mail ambtnkor@kornet.net; Ambassador AMMAR AMMARI.

Turkey: Vivien Corpn Bldg, 4th Floor, 4-52, Seobinggo-dong, Yeongsan-gu, Seoul 140-240; tel. (2) 794-0255; fax (2) 797-8546; e-mail turkemb.seoul@hotmail.com; internet www.seul.be.mfa.gov.tr; Ambassador NACI SARIBAŞ.

Ukraine: 1-97, Dongbinggo-dong, Yeongsan-gu, Seoul; tel. (2) 790-5696; fax (2) 790-5697; e-mail emb_kr@mfa.gov.ua; internet www.mfa.gov.ua/korea; Ambassador BELASHOV VOLODYMYR.

United Arab Emirates: 5-5, Hannam-dong, Yeongsan-gu, Seoul 140-884; tel. (2) 790-3235; fax (2) 790-3238; e-mail uaeemb@kornet.net; Ambassador ABDULLAH MUHAMMAD AL-MAAINAH.

United Kingdom: Taepyeong-no 40, 4, Jeong-dong, Jung-gu, Seoul 100-120; tel. (2) 3210-5500; fax (2) 725-1738; e-mail postmaster.seoul@fco.gov.uk; internet www.ukinkorea.fco.gov.uk; Ambassador SCOTT WIGHTMAN (designate).

USA: 32, Sejong-no, Jongno-gu, Seoul 110-710; tel. (2) 397-4114; fax (2) 397-4080; e-mail embassyseoulpa@state.gov; internet seoul.usembassy.gov; Ambassador KATHLEEN STEPHENS.

Uruguay: LIG Kangnam Bldg, 14th Floor, 708-6, Yeoksam-dong, Gangnam-gu, Seoul 135-919; tel. (2) 6245-3179; fax (2) 6245-3181; e-mail uruseul@embrou.or.kr; internet www.embrou.or.kr; Ambassador ALBA ROSA FLORIO LEGNANI.

Uzbekistan: Diplomatic Center, Unit 701, 1376-1, Seocho 2-dong, Seocho-gu, Seoul; tel. (2) 574-6554; fax (2) 578-0576; e-mail uzbek001@yahoo.co.kr; internet www.uzbekistan.or.kr; Ambassador VITALI V. FEN.

Venezuela: SC First Bank Bldg, 16th Floor, 100, Gongpyeong-dong, Jongno-gu, CPOB 10043, Seoul 110-702; tel. (2) 732-1546; fax (2) 732-1548; e-mail emvesel@soback.kornet.net; internet www.venezuelaemb.or.kr; Chargé d'affaires a.i. WOLFGANG GONZÁLEZ.

Viet Nam: 28-58, Samcheong-dong, Jongno-gu, Seoul 140-210; tel. (2) 738-2318; fax (2) 739-2064; e-mail vndsq@yahoo.com; internet www.vietnamembassy-seoul.org; Ambassador TRAN TRONG TOAN.

Judicial System

SUPREME COURT

The Supreme Court is the highest court, consisting of 14 Justices, including the Chief Justice. The Chief Justice is appointed by the President, with the consent of the National Assembly, for a term of six years. Other Justices of the Supreme Court are appointed for six years by the President on the recommendation of the Chief Justice. The appointment of the Justices of the Supreme Court also requires the consent of the National Assembly. The Chief Justice may not be reappointed. The Supreme Court is empowered to receive and decide on appeals against decisions of the High Courts, the Patent Court, and the appellate panels of the District Courts or the Family Court in civil, criminal, administrative, patent and domestic relations cases. It is also authorized to act as the final tribunal to review decisions of courts-martial and to consider cases arising from presidential and parliamentary elections.

Chief Justice: YANG SUNG-TAE, 219, Seocho-dong, Seocho-gu, Seoul; tel. (2) 533-2824; fax (2) 533-1911; e-mail webmaster@scourt.go.kr; internet www.scourt.go.kr.

Justices: CHA HAN-SUNG, LEE HONG-HOON, YANG CHANG-SOO, PARK SI-HWAN, KIM JI-HYUNG, PARK ILL-HOAN, KIM NUNG-HWAN, JEON SOO-AHN, AHN DAI-HEE, SHIN YOUNG-CHUL, MIN IL-YOUNG, LEE IN-BOK, LEE SANG-HOON.

CONSTITUTIONAL COURT

The Constitutional Court is composed of nine adjudicators appointed by the President, of whom three are chosen from among persons selected by the National Assembly and three from persons nominated by the Chief Justice. The Court adjudicates the following matters: constitutionality of a law (when requested by the other courts); impeachment; dissolution of a political party; disputes between state agencies, or between state agencies and local governments; and petitions relating to the Constitution.

President: LEE KANG-KUK, 15 Gahoero, Jongno-gu, Seoul 110-250; tel. (2) 708-3460; e-mail interdiv@ccourt.go.kr; fax (2) 708-3566; internet www.ccourt.go.kr.

HIGH COURTS

There are five courts, situated in Seoul, Daegu, Busan, Gwangju and Daejeon, with five chief, 78 presiding and 145 other judges. The courts have appellate jurisdiction in civil and criminal cases and can also pass judgment on administrative litigation against government decisions.

PATENT COURT

The Patent Court opened in Daejeon in March 1998, to deal with cases in which the decisions of the Intellectual Property Tribunal are challenged. The examination of the case is conducted by a judge, with the assistance of technical examiners.

DISTRICT COURTS

District Courts are established in 13 major cities; there are 13 chief, 241 presiding and 966 other judges. They exercise jurisdiction over all civil and criminal cases in the first instance.

MUNICIPAL COURTS

There are 103 Municipal Courts within the District Court system, dealing with small claims, minor criminal offences, and settlement cases.

FAMILY COURT

There is one Family Court, in Seoul, with a chief judge, four presiding judges and 16 other judges. The court has jurisdiction in domestic matters and cases of juvenile delinquency.

ADMINISTRATIVE COURT

An Administrative Court opened in Seoul in March 1998, to deal with cases that are specified in the Administrative Litigation Act. The Court has jurisdiction over cities and counties adjacent to Seoul, and deals with administrative matters, including taxes, expropriations of land, labour and other general administrative matters.

COURTS-MARTIAL

These exercise jurisdiction over all offences committed by armed forces personnel and civilian employees. They are also authorized to try civilians accused of military espionage or interference with the execution of military duties.

Religion

BUDDHISM

Korean Mahayana Buddhism has about 80 denominations. The Chogye-jong is the largest Buddhist order in Korea, having been introduced from China in AD 372. The Chogye Order accounts for almost two-thirds of all Korean Buddhists. Won Buddhism combines elements of Buddhism and Confucianism.

Korean United Buddhist Association (KUBA): 46-19, Soosong-dong, Jongno-gu, Seoul 110-140; tel. (2) 732-4885; 28 mem. Buddhist orders; Pres. SONG WOL-JOO.

CHRISTIANITY

National Council of Churches in Korea: Christian Bldg, Rm 706, 136-46, Yeonchi-dong, Jongno-gu, Seoul 110-736; tel. (2) 744-8981; fax (2) 744-6189; e-mail kncc@kncc.or.kr; internet www.kncc.or.kr; f. 1924; est. as National Christian Council; present name adopted 1946; eight mem. churches; Pres. Rev. LEE YOUNG-HOON; Gen. Sec. Rev. KIM YOUNG-JU.

The Anglican Communion

South Korea has three Anglican dioceses, collectively forming the Anglican Church of Korea (founded as a separate province in April 1993), under its own Primate, the Bishop of Seoul.

Bishop of Pusan (Busan): Rt Rev. SOLOMON JONG-MO YOON, 18, 2-ga, Daechung-dong, Jung-gu, Busan 600-600; tel. (51) 463-5742; fax (51) 463-5957; e-mail adpusan@hanmail.net; internet skhpusan .onmam.com.

Bishop of Seoul: Rt Rev. PAUL KIM KEUN-SANG, 3, Jeong-dong, Jung-gu, Seoul 100-120; tel. (2) 738-6597; fax (2) 738-3982; e-mail skhseoul@skhseoul.or.kr; internet www.skhseoul.or.kr.

Bishop of Taejon (Daejeon): Rt Rev. MICHAEL KWON HI-YEON, POB 22, Daejeon 300-600; tel. (42) 256-9988; fax (42) 255-8918; e-mail djdio@djdio.or.kr; internet www.djdio.or.kr.

The Roman Catholic Church

For ecclesiastical purposes, North and South Korea are nominally under a unified jurisdiction. South Korea comprises three archdioceses, 12 dioceses and one military ordinate. At 31 December 2007 some 4,821,020 people were adherents of the Roman Catholic Church.

Bishops' Conference

Catholic Bishops' Conference of Korea, 643-1, Junggok-dong, Gwangjin-gu, Seoul 143-912; tel. (2) 460-7500; fax (2) 460-7505; e-mail cbck@cbck.or.kr; internet www.cbck.or.kr.

f. 1857; Pres. Most Rev. PETER KANG (Bishop of Cheju—Jeju).

Archbishop of Kwangju (Gwangju): Most Rev. HYGINUS KIM HEE-JONG, Archdiocesan Office, 997-1, Sangmu 2-dong, Gwangju 502-855; tel. (62) 380-2801; fax (62) 380-2806; e-mail biseo1@kjcatholic.or .kr; internet www.kjcatholic.or.kr.

Archbishop of Seoul: Cardinal NICHOLAS CHEONG JIN-SUK, Archdiocesan Office, 1, 2-ga, Myeong-dong, Jung-gu, Seoul 100-022; tel. (2) 727-2114; fax (2) 773-1947; e-mail ao@seoul.catholic.or.kr; internet www.catholic.or.kr.

Archbishop of Daegu (Taegu): THADDEUS CHO HWAN-KIL, Archdiocesan Office, 225-1, Namsan 3-dong, Jung-gu, Daegu 700-804; tel. (53) 253-7011; fax (53) 253-9441; e-mail taegu@tgcatholic.or.kr; internet www.tgcatholic.or.kr.

Protestant Churches

Korean Methodist Church: 64-8, 1-ga, Taepyeong-no, Jung-gu, Seoul 100-101; KPO Box 285, Seoul 110-602; tel. (2) 399-4300; fax (2) 399-4307; e-mail bishop@kmcweb.or.kr; internet www.kmcweb.or .kr; f. 1885; 1,534,504 mems (2007); Bishop KANG HEUNG-BOK.

Presbyterian Church in the Republic of Korea (PROK): Academy House, San 76, Suyu 6-dong, Kangbuk-ku, Seoul 142-714; tel. (2) 3499-7600; fax (2) 3499-7630; e-mail prok3000@chol.com; internet www.prok.org; f. 1953; 337,570 mems (2007); Gen. Sec. Rev. BAE TAE-JIN.

Presbyterian Church of Korea (PCK): The Korean Church Centennial Memorial Bldg, 135, Yunji-dong, Jongno-gu, Seoul 110-470; tel. (2) 741-4350; fax (2) 766-2427; e-mail thepck@pck.or .kr; internet www.pck.or.kr; 2,395,323 mems (Dec. 2003); Moderator Rev. JUNG SUH-KIM; Gen. Sec. Rev. SEONGI CHO.

There are some 160 other Protestant denominations in the country, including the Korea Baptist Convention and the Korea Evangelical Church.

OTHER RELIGIONS

Chundo Kyo, a religion indigenous and unique to Korea, combines elements of Shaman, Buddhist, and Christian doctrines. Confucianism also has a significant number of followers. Taejong Gyo is Korea's oldest religion, dating back 4,000 years, and comprising beliefs in the national foundation myth, and the triune god, Hanul. By the 15th century the religion had largely disappeared, but a revival began in the late 19th century.

The Press

NATIONAL DAILIES

(In Korean, unless otherwise indicated)

Chosun Ilbo: 61, 1-ga, Taepyeong-no, Jung-gu, Seoul 100-756; tel. (2) 724-5114; fax (2) 724-5059; e-mail englishnews@chosun.com; internet www.chosun.com; f. 1920; morning, weekly and children's edns; independent; Korean, English, Chinese and Japanese; Exec. Editor BYUN YONG-SHIK; circ. 2,470,000.

Daily Sports Seoul: 25, 1-ga, Taepyeong-no, Jung-gu, Seoul; tel. (2) 721-5114; fax (2) 721-5396; internet www.seoul.co.kr; f. 1985; morning; sports and leisure; Pres. LEE HAN-SOO; Man. Editor SON CHU-WHAN.

Dong-A Ilbo: 139-1, 3-ga, Sejong-no, Jongno-gu, Seoul 100-715; tel. (2) 2020-0114; fax (2) 2020-1239; e-mail newsroom@donga.com; internet www.donga.com; f. 1920; morning; independent; Publr and CEO KIM JAE-HO; Editor-in-Chief LEE HYUN-NAK; circ. 2,150,000.

Han-Joong Daily News: 91-1, 2-ga, Myeong-dong, Jung-gu, Seoul; tel. (2) 776-2801; fax (2) 778-2803; Chinese.

Hankook Ilbo: 14, Junghak-dong, Jongno-gu, Seoul; tel. (2) 724-2114; fax (2) 724-2244; internet www.hankooki.com; f. 1954; morning; independent; Pres. CHANG CHAE-KEUN; Editor-in-Chief YOON KOOK-BYUNG; circ. 2,000,000.

Hankuk Kyungje Shinmun (Korea Economic Daily): 441, Junglim-dong, Jung-gu, Seoul 100-791; tel. (2) 360-4114; fax (2) 779-4447; e-mail hkinfo@hankyung.com; internet www.hankyung.com; f. 1964; morning; Pres. and CEO KIM KI-WOONG; Man. Dir and Editor-in-Chief CHOI KYU-YOUNG.

Hankyoreh Shinmun (One Nation): 116-25, Gongdeok-dong, Mapo-gu, Seoul 121-020; tel. (2) 710-0114; fax (2) 710-0210; internet www.hani.co.kr; f. 1988; centre-left; Korean, English; CEO and Publr CHUNG TAE-KI; Editor-in-Chief SUNG HAN-PYO; circ. 500,000.

Ilgan Sports (The Daily Sports): 14, Junghak-dong, Jongno-gu, Seoul 110-792; tel. (2) 724-2114; fax (2) 724-2299; internet www.dailysports.co.kr; morning; f. 1969; Pres. CHANG CHAE-KEUN; Editor KIM JIN-DONG; circ. 600,000.

Jeil Economic Daily: 146, Ssangrin-dong, Jung-gu, Seoul; tel. (2) 6325-3114; e-mail ysk@jed.co.kr; internet www.jed.co.kr; f. 1988; morning; Pres. PARK JUNG-GU; Editor-in-Chief JANG CHANG-YONG.

JoongAng Ilbo (JoongAng Daily News): 7, Soonhwa-dong, Jung-gu, 100-759 Seoul; tel. (2) 751-9215; fax (2) 751-9219; e-mail iht@joongang.co.kr; internet joongangdaily.joins.com; f. 1965; morning; Korean and English; Publr LHO CHOL-SOO; Exec. Dir KIM DONG-KYUN; circ. 2,300,000.

Kookmin Ilbo: Kookmin Ilbo Bldg, 5/F, 12, Yeouido-dong, Yeongdeungpo-gu, Seoul; tel. (2) 781-9114; fax (2) 781-9781; e-mail kimyh@kmib.co.kr; internet www.kukminilbo.co.kr; Pres. RO SEUNG-SOOK; Editorial Dir KIM Y. H.

Korea Daily News: 25, 1-ga, Taepyeong-no, Jung-gu, Seoul; tel. (2) 2000-9000; fax (2) 2000-9659; e-mail webmaster@seoul.co.kr; internet www.kdaily.com; f. 1945; morning; independent; Publr and Pres. SON CHU-HWAN; Man. Editor LEE DONG-HWA; circ. 700,000.

The Korea Herald: 1-17, Jeong-dong, Jung-gu, Seoul; tel. (2) 727-0205; fax (2) 727-0670; e-mail editor@heraldm.com; internet www.koreaherald.co.kr; f. 1953; morning; English; independent; Pres. WOOK HONG-JUNG; Man. Editor CHON SHI-YONG; circ. 150,000.

The Korea Times: 43, Chungmuro 3-ga, Chung-gu, Seoul 100-013; tel. (2) 724-2859; fax (2) 723-1623; e-mail webmaster@koreatimes.co.kr; internet www.koreatimes.co.kr; f. 1950; morning; English; independent; Pres. PARK MOO-JONG; Man. Editor SAH DONG-SEOK; circ. 100,000.

Kyung-hyang Shinmun: 22, Jeong-dong, Jung-gu, Seoul; tel. (2) 3701-1114; fax (2) 737-6362; internet www.khan.co.kr; f. 1946; evening; independent; Pres. HONG SUNG-MAN; Exec. Editor KIM JI-YOUNG; circ. 350,000.

Maeil Business Newspaper: 30-1, 1-ga, Bil-dong, Jung-gu, Seoul 100-728; tel. (2) 2000-2114; fax (2) 2269-6200; internet www.mk.co.kr; f. 1966; evening; economics and business; Korean, English; Pres. CHANG DAE-WHAN; Chief Editor JANG YONG-SUNG; circ. 235,000.

Munhwa Ilbo: 68, 1-ga, Chungjeong-no, Jung-gu, Seoul 110-170; tel. (2) 3701-5114; fax (2) 3701-5566; internet www.munhwa.co.kr; f. 1991; evening; Pres. and Publr LEE BYUN-KYU; Editor-in-Chief KANG SIN-KU.

Naeway Economic Daily: 1-12, 3-ga, Hoehyon-dong, Jung-gu, Seoul 100; tel. (2) 727-0114; fax (2) 727-0661; f. 1973; morning; Pres. KIM CHIN-OUK; Man. Editor HAN DONG-HEE; circ. 300,000.

Segye Times: 550-15, Gasan-dong, Seoul; tel. (2) 2000-1160; fax (2) 2000-1349; e-mail webmaster@segye.com; internet www.segyetimes.co.kr; f. 1989; morning; Pres. SA KWANG-KEE; Editor MOK JUNG-GYUM.

Seoul Kyungje Shinmun (Seoul Economic Daily): 14, Junghak-dong, Jongno-gu, Seoul; tel. (2) 724-2114; fax (2) 732-2140; e-mail webmaster@hanooki.com; internet economy.hankooki.com; f. 1960; morning; Pres. LIM KONG-JON; Man. Editor LEE JONG-WHAN; circ. 500,000.

Sports Chosun: 61, 1-ga, Taepyeong-no, Jung-gu, Seoul; tel. (2) 3219-8114; fax (2) 724-6979; e-mail readers@sportschosun.com; internet www.sportschosun.com; f. 1964; Publr BANG SANG-HOON; circ. 400,000.

LOCAL DAILIES

Chungcheong Daily News: 304, Sachang-dong, Hungduk-gu, Cheongju, N. Chungcheong Prov.; tel. (43) 279-5000; fax (43) 279-5050; e-mail webmaster@ccilbo.com; internet www.ccilbo.com; f. 1946; morning; Pres. SEO JEONG-OK; Editor IM BAIK-SOO.

Daegu Ilbo: 177-10, Sincheon 2-dong, Dong-gu, Daegu; tel. (53) 757-5700; fax (53) 757-5757; internet www.idaegu.com; f. 1953; morning; Pres. LEE TAE-YEUL; Editor KIM KYUNG-PAL.

Daejon Ilbo: 1-135, Munhwa 1-dong, Jung-gu, Daejeon; tel. (42) 251-3311; fax (42) 253-3320; f. 1950; evening; Pres. CHO JOON-HO; Editor KWAK DAE-YEON.

Halla Ilbo: 568-1, Samdo 1-dong, Jeju; tel. (64) 750-2114; fax (64) 750-2520; e-mail webmaster@ihalla.com; internet www.ihalla.com; f. 1989; evening; Chair. KANG YONG-SOK; Man. Editor HONG SONG-MOK.

Incheon Ilbo: 18-1, 4-ga, Hang-dong, Jung-gu, Incheon; tel. (32) 763-8811; fax (32) 763-7711; e-mail webmaster@itimes.co.kr; internet www.itimes.co.kr; f. 1988; evening; Chair. MUN PYONG-HA; Man. Editor LEE JAE-HO.

Jeju Daily News: 2324-6, Yeon-dong, Jeju; tel. (64) 740-6114; fax (64) 740-6500; e-mail webmaster@jejunews.com; internet www.jejunews.com; f. 1945; evening; Pres. KIM DAE-SUNG; Man. Editor KANG BYUNG-HEE.

Jeonbuk Domin Ilbo: 417-62, 2-ga, Deokjin-dong, Deokjin-gu, Jeonju, N. Jeolla Prov.; tel. (63) 251-7113; fax (63) 251-7127; internet www.domin.co.kr; f. 1988; morning; Pres. LIM BYOUNG-CHAN; Man. Editor YANG CHAE-SUK.

Jeonbuk Ilbo: 710-5, Kumam-dong, Deokjin-gu, Jeonju, N. Jeolla Prov.; tel. (63) 250-5500; fax (63) 250-5550; f. 1950; evening; Chair. SUH CHANG-HOON; Man. Editor LEE KON-WOONG.

Jeonju Ilbo: 568-132, Sonosong-dong, Deokjin-gu, Jeonju, N. Jeolla Prov.; tel. (63) 285-0114; fax (63) 285-2060; f. 1991; morning; Chair. KANG DAE-SOON; Man. Editor SO CHAE-CHOL.

Jeonnam Ilbo: 700-5, Jungheung-dong, Buk-gu, Gwangju 500-758; tel. (62) 527-0015; fax (62) 510-0436; f. 1989; morning; Pres. PARK KEE-JUNG; Editor-in-Chief KIM YONG-OK.

Joongdo Ilbo: 274-7, Galma-dong, Seo-gu, Daejeon; tel. (42) 530-4114; fax (42) 535-5334; f. 1951; morning; CEO KIM WOK-SIK; Man. Editor SONG HYOUNG-SOP.

Kangwon Ilbo: 23, Jungang-no, Chuncheon, Gangwon Prov.; tel. (33) 258-1000; fax (33) 258-1114; internet www.kwnews.co.kr; f. 1945; evening; Pres. CHOI SEUNG-IK; Editor-in-Chief KIM SUNG-KEE.

Kookje Daily News: 76-2, Goje-dong, Yeonje-gu, Busan 611-702; tel. (51) 500-5114; fax (51) 500-4274; e-mail jahwang@ms.kookje.co.kr; internet www.kookje.co.kr; f. 1947; morning; Pres. ROH KI-TAE; Editor-in-Chief JEONG WON-YOUNG.

Kwangju Ilbo: 20-2, Geumnam-no, Dong-gu, Gwangju; tel. (62) 222-8111; fax (62) 227-9500; e-mail kwangju@kwangju.co.kr; internet www.kwangju.co.kr; f. 1952; evening; Chair. KIM CHONG-TAE; Man. Editor CHO DONG-SU.

Kyeonggi Ilbo: 452-1, Songjuk-dong, Changan-gu, Suwon, Gyeonggi Prov.; tel. (31) 250-3333; fax (31) 250-3306; e-mail webmaster@ekgib.co.kr; internet www.kgib.co.kr; f. 1988; evening; Pres. SHIN CHANG-GI; Man. Editor LEE CHIN-YONG.

Kyeongin Ilbo: 1276, Maetan-dong, Yeongtong-gu, Suwon, Gyeonggi-do; tel. (31) 231-5114; fax (31) 232-1231; e-mail webmaster@kyeongin.com; internet www.kyeongin.com; f. 1960; evening; Pres. WOO JE-CHAN; Man. Editor KIM HWA-YANG.

Kyungnam Shinmun: 100-5, Sinwol-dong, Changwon, S. Gyeongsang Prov.; tel. (55) 283-2211; fax (55) 210-6048; internet www.knnews.co.kr; f. 1946; evening; Pres. KIM DONG-KYU; Editor PARK SUNG-KWAN.

Maeil Shinmun: 71, 2-ga, Gyesan-dong, Jung-gu, Daegu; tel. (53) 255-5001; fax (53) 255-8902; e-mail imaeil@msnet.co.kr; internet www.imaeil.com; f. 1946; evening; Pres. CHO HWAN-KIL; Editor LEE YONG-KEUN; circ. 300,000.

Pusan Daily News: 1-10, Sujeong-dong, Dong-gu, Busan 601-738; tel. (51) 461-4114; fax (51) 463-8880; internet www.pusanilbo.co.kr; f. 1946; Pres. JEONG HAN-SANG; Man. Editor AHN KI-HO; circ. 427,000.

Yeongnam Ilbo: 111, Sincheon-dong, Dong-gu, Daegu; tel. (53) 756-8001; fax (53) 756-9011; internet www.yeongnam.co.kr; f. 1945; morning; Chair. PARK CHANG-HO; Man. Editor KIM SANG-TAE.

SELECTED PERIODICALS

Academy News: 50, Unjung-dong, Bundang-gu, Seongnam, Gyeonggi Prov. 463-791; tel. (31) 709-8111; fax (31) 709-9945; organ of the Acad. of Korean Studies; Pres. HAN SANG-JIN.

Eumak Dong-A: 139, Sejong-no, Jongno-gu, Seoul 110-715; tel. (2) 781-0640; fax (2) 705-4547; f. 1984; monthly; music; Publr KIM BYUNG-KWAN; Editor KWON O-KIE; circ. 85,000.

Han Kuk No Chong (FKTU News): 35, Yeouido-dong, Yeongdeungpo-gu, Seoul 150-885; tel. (2) 6277-0026; fax (2) 6277-0068; internet www.fktu.or.kr; f. 1961; labour news; circ. 20,000.

Hyundae Munhak: Seoul; tel. (2) 516-3770; fax (2) 516-5433; e-mail webmaster@hdmh.co.kr; internet www.hdmh.co.kr; f. 1955; literature; Publr KIM SUNG-SIK; circ. 200,000.

Korea Business World: Yeouido, POB 720, Seoul 150-607; tel. (2) 532-1364; fax (2) 594-7663; f. 1985; monthly; English; Publr and Pres. LEE KIE-HONG; circ. 40,200.

Korea Buyers Guide: Rm 2301, Korea World Trade Center, 159, Samseong-dong, Gangnam-gu, Seoul; tel. (2) 551-2376; fax (2) 551-2377; e-mail info@buyersguide.co.kr; internet www.buykorea21.com; f. 1973; monthly, consumer goods; quarterly, hardware; Pres. YOU YOUNG-PYO; circ. 30,000.

Korea Journal: Korean National Commission for UNESCO, CPOB 64, Seoul 100-600; tel. (2) 695-84112; fax (2) 6958-4252; e-mail kj@unesco.or.kr; internet www.ekoreajournal.net; f. 1961; quarterly; organ of the Korean National Commission for UNESCO; focus on Korean Studies; Editor KIM MIN-A; Publr CHUN TAEK-SOO.

Korea Newsreview: 1-12, 3-ga, Hoehyeon-dong, Jung-gu, Seoul 100-771; tel. (2) 756-7711; weekly; English; Publr and Editor PARK CHUNG-WOONG.

Korea and World Affairs: Rm 1723, Daewoo Center Bldg, 5-541, Namdaemun-no, Jung-gu, Seoul 100-714; tel. (2) 777-2628; fax (2) 319-9591; organ of the Research Center for Peace and Unification of Korea; Pres. CHANG DONG-HOON.

Korean Business Review: FKI Bldg, 28-1, Yeouido-dong, Yeongdeungpo-gu, Seoul 150-756; tel. (2) 3771-0114; fax (2) 3771-0138; monthly; publ. by Fed. of Korean Industries; Publr KIM KAK-CHOONG; Editor SOHN BYUNG-DOO.

Literature and Thought: Seoul; tel. (2) 738-0542; fax (2) 738-2997; f. 1972; monthly; Pres. LIM HONG-BIN; circ. 10,000.

Monthly Travel: Cross Bldg, 2nd Floor, 46-6, 2-ga, Namsan-dong, Jung-gu, Seoul 100-042; tel. (2) 757-6161; fax (2) 757-6089; e-mail kotfa@unitel.co.kr; Pres. SHIN JOONG-MOK; circ. 50,000.

News Maker: 22, Jung-dong, Jung-gu, Seoul 110-702; tel. (2) 3701-1114; fax (2) 739-6190; e-mail hudy@kyunghyang.com; internet www.kyunghyang.com/newsmaker; f. 1992; Pres. JANG JUN-BONG; Editor PARK MYUNG-HUN.

Reader's Digest: 295-15, Deoksan 1-dong, Geumcheon-gu, Seoul 153-011; tel. (2) 3670-5497; fax (2) 3670-5001; internet www.readersdigest.co.kr; f. 1978; monthly; general; Pres. YANG SUNG-MO; Editor PARK SOON-HWANG; circ. 115,000.

Shin Dong-A (New East Asia): 139, Chungjeong-no, Seodaemun-gu, Seoul 120-715; tel. (2) 361-0974; fax (2) 361-0988; e-mail hans@donga.com; internet shindonga.donga.com; f. 1931; monthly; general; Publr KIM JAE-HO; Editor LEE HYUNG-SAM; circ. 150,000.

Taekwondo: Joyang Bldg 113, 4/F, Samseong-dong, Gangnam-gu, Seoul; tel. (2) 566-2505; fax (2) 553-4728; e-mail wtf@wtf.org; internet www.wtf.org; f. 1973; annual; organ of the World Taekwondo Federation; Pres. Dr CHOUE CHUNG-WON.

Vantage Point: 85-1, Susong-dong, Jongno-gu, Seoul, 110-140; tel. (2) 398-3114; fax (2) 398-3539; e-mail master@yna.co.kr; internet www.yonhapnews.co.kr; f. 1978; monthly; developments in North Korea; Editor KWAK SEUNG-JI.

Weekly Chosun: 61, Taepyeong-no 1, Jung-gu, Seoul; tel. (2) 724-5114; fax (2) 724-6199; weekly; Publr BANG SANG-HOON; Editor CHOI JOON-MYONG; circ. 350,000.

The Weekly Hankook: 14, Junghak-dong, Jongno-gu, Seoul; tel. (2) 732-4151; fax (2) 724-2444; f. 1964; Publr CHANG CHAE-KUK; circ. 400,000.

Wolgan Mot: 139, Sejong-no, Jongno-gu, Seoul 110-715; tel. (2) 733-5221; f. 1984; monthly; fashion; Publr KIM SEUNG-YUL; Editor KWON O-KIE; circ. 120,000.

Women's Weekly: 14, Junghak-dong, Jongno-gu, Seoul; tel. (2) 735-9216; fax (2) 732-4125.

Yosong Dong-A (Women's Far East): 139, Sejong-no, Jongno-gu, Seoul 110-715; tel. (2) 721-7621; fax (2) 721-7676; f. 1933; monthly; women's magazine; Publr KIM BYUNG-KWAN; Editor KWON O-KIE; circ. 237,000.

NEWS AGENCY

Yonhap News Agency: 85-1, Susong-dong, Jongno-gu, Seoul; tel. (2) 398-3114; fax (2) 398-3567; e-mail ldm@yna.co.kr; internet www.yonhapnews.co.kr; f. 1980; Pres. KIM KUN.

PRESS ASSOCIATIONS

Journalists Association of Korea (JAK): Korea Press Center Bldg, 25 1-ga, Taepyeong-no, Jung-gu, Seoul; tel. (2) 737-2483; fax (2) 738-1003; e-mail jakmaster@journalist.or.kr; internet www.journalist.or.kr; Pres. JANG KYUNG-WOO.

Korean Association of Newspapers: Korea Press Center, 13th Floor, 25, 1-ga, Taepyeong-no, Jung-gu, Seoul 100-745; tel. (2) 733-2251; fax (2) 720-3291; e-mail iwelcome@presskorea.or.kr; internet www.presskorea.or.kr; f. 1962; 48 mems; Pres. JAE-HO; Sec.-Gen. MOON HAN-KWON.

Korean Newspaper Editors' Association: Korea Press Center, 13th Floor, 25, 1-ga, Taepyeong-no, Jung-gu, Seoul; tel. (2) 732-1726; fax (2) 739-1985; f. 1957; 416 mems; Pres. SEONG BYONG-WUK.

Seoul Foreign Correspondents' Club: Korea Press Center, 18/F, 1-ga, Taepyeong-no, Jung-gu, Seoul; tel. (2) 734-3272; fax (2) 734-7712; e-mail master@sfcc.or.kr; internet www.sfcc.or.kr; f. 1956; Pres. RYOJI ITO.

Publishers

Ahn Graphics Ltd: 260-288, Seongbuk-dong, Seongbuk-gu, Seoul 136-823; tel. (2) 743-8065; fax (2) 744-3251; e-mail ask@ag.co.kr; internet www.ag.co.kr; f. 1985; art, literature, computer graphics; Pres. KIM OK-CHUL.

BIR Publishing Co Ltd: 4/F, Gangnam Publishing Culture Center, 506 Sinsa-dong, Gangnam-Gu, Seoul 135-887; tel. (2) 515-2000; fax (2) 3442-4661; e-mail bir@bir.co.kr; internet www.bir.co.kr; children's books; Pres. PARK SANG-HEE.

Bobmun Sa Publishing Co: 526-3, Munbal-ri, Gyoha-eup, Paju-si, Gyeonggi-do 413-756; tel. (31) 955-6500; fax (31) 955-6525; internet www.bobmunsa.co.kr; f. 1954; law, politics, philosophy, history; Pres. BAE HYO-SEON.

Bookhouse Publishing Co Ltd: 6/F, Dongsomun Bldg, Seoul 136-034; tel. (2) 3144-3123; e-mail editor@bookhouse.co.kr; internet www.bookhouse.co.kr; business, foreign novels, health; CEO KIM JEONG-SUN.

Bumwoo Publishing Co: 525-2, Paju Book City, Munbal-ri, Gyoha-eup, Paju-si, Gyeonggi-do; tel. (31) 955-6900; fax (31) 955-6905; e-mail bumwoosa@chol.com; internet www.bumwoosa.co.kr; f. 1966; philosophy, religion, social science, technology, art, literature, history; Pres. YOON HYUNG-DOO.

Chaeksesang Publishing Co (Book World): 68-7, Sinsu-dong, Mapu-gu, Seoul 121-854; tel. (2) 704-1251; fax (2) 719-1258; e-mail webmaster@bkworld.co.kr; internet www.bkworld.co.kr; f. 1975; art, literature, religion, science and technology; Pres. KIM JIK-SEUNG.

Changhae Publishing: 336-10, Ahyun 2-dong, Seoul 121-012; tel. (2) 313-3200; fax (2) 313-3204.

Cheong Moon Gak Publishing Co Ltd: 486-9, Kirum 3-dong, Seongbuk-gu, Seoul 136-800; tel. (2) 985-1451; fax (2) 988-1456; e-mail cmgbook@cmgbook.co.kr; internet www.cmgbook.co.kr; f. 1974; science, technology, business; subsidiaries HanSeung Publishers, Lux Media; Pres. KIM HONG-SEOK; Man. Dir HANS KIM.

Crayon House Co Ltd: 5/F, Crayon House Bldg, Seoul; tel. (2) 3436-1711; fax (2) 3436-1410; e-mail crayong@korea.com; internet www.crayonhouse.co.kr; f. 1996; children's books.

Dai Won Publishing Co: 40-456, Hangangno 3-ga, Yeongsan-gu, Seoul 140-880; tel. (2) 2071-2000; fax (2) 793-8994; e-mail webmaster@dwci.co.kr; internet www.dwci.co.kr; f. 1990; comics.

Design House Publishing Co: Taekwang Bldg, 162-1, Jangchung-dong, 2-ga, Jung-gu, Seoul 100-855; tel. (2) 2275-6151; fax (2) 2267-6158; e-mail yhlee@design.co.kr; internet www.design.co.kr; f. 1987; social science, art, literature, languages, children's periodicals; Pres. LEE YOUNG-HEE.

Dong-Hwa Publishing Co Ltd: 509-3, Munbal-ri, Gyoha-eup, Paju-si, Gyeonggi-do 413-756; tel. (31) 955-4961; fax (31) 955-4960; f. 1968; art, children's books, literature; Pres. LIM IN-KYU.

Dongmoonsun Publishing Co: 21 Insa-dong-gil, Jongno-gu, Seoul 110-300; tel. (2) 737-2795; fax (2) 723-4518; e-mail dmspub@hanmail.net; humanities; Pres. SIN SUNG-DAE.

Doosan Corporation Publishing BG: 14-34, Yeouido-dong, Yeongdeungpo-gu, Seoul; tel. (2) 2167-0601; fax (2) 2167-0668; e-mail dudvkf@doosan.com; internet www.bookdonga.com; f. 1951; general works, school reference, social science, periodicals; Pres. CHOI TAE-KYUNG.

E*Public Co: 923-11, Mok 1-dong, Yangcheon-gu, Seoul 158-051; tel. (2) 2653-5131; fax (2) 2653-2454; e-mail webmaster@epublic.co.kr; internet www.epublic.co.kr; f. 1955; social science, pure science, technology, medicine, linguistics; Pres. and CEO LIU SUNG-KWON.

Eulyoo Publishing Co Ltd: 46-1, Susong-dong, Jongno-gu, Seoul 110-603; tel. (2) 733-8151; fax (2) 732-9154; e-mail eulyoo1945@gmail.com; internet www.eulyoo.co.kr; f. 1945; linguistics, literature, social science, history, philosophy; Pres. CHUNG JEE-YOUNG.

Gilbut Publishing Co Ltd: 467-9, Seogyo-dong, Mapo-gu, Seoul 121-842; tel. (2) 332-0931; fax (2) 323-0586; e-mail gilbut@gilbut.co.kr; internet www.gilbut.co.kr; f. 1991.

Gimm-Young Publishers Inc: 515-1, Munbal-ri, Gyoha-eup, Paju-si, Gyeonggi-do 413-756; tel. (31) 955-3100; fax (31) 955-3111; e-mail marketing@gimmyoung.com; internet www.gimmyoung.com; f. 1979; current affairs, humanities, history, religion, children's books; Pres. PARK EUN-JU.

Hainaim Publishing Co Ltd: 5/F, Hainaim Bldg, 368-4, Seogyo-dong, Mapo-gu, Seoul; tel. (2) 326-1600; fax (2) 326-1624; e-mail jwlee@hainaim.com; internet www.hainaim.com; f. 1983; philosophy, literature, children's; Pres. SONG YOUNG-SUK.

Haksan Publishing Co: Haksan Bldg, 777-1, Sangdo-dong, Dongjak-gu, Seoul 156-830; tel. (2) 828-8988; fax (2) 828-8890; internet www.haksanpub.co.kr; f. 1995; children's books, comics, magazines.

Hakwon Publishing Co Ltd: Seocho Plaza, 4th Floor, 1573-1, Seocho-dong, Seocho-gu, Seoul; tel. (2) 587-2396; fax (2) 584-9306; f. 1945; general, languages, literature, periodicals; Pres. KIM YOUNG-SU.

Hangilsa Corpn: 520-11, Paju Book City, Munbal-ri, Gyoha-eup, Paju-si, Gyeonggi-do; tel. (31) 955-2000; fax (31) 955-2005; e-mail hangilsaone@hangilsa.co.kr; internet www.hangilsa.co.kr; f. 1976; social science, history, literature; Pres. KIM EOUN-HO.

Hanul Publishing Company: 3/F Seoul Bldg, 105-90 Gongdeok-dong, Mapo-gu, Seoul 121-801; tel. (2) 336-6183; fax (2) 333-7543; e-mail hanul@hanulbooks.co.kr; internet www.hanulbooks.co.kr; f. 1980; general, philosophy, university books, periodicals; Pres. KIM CHONG-SU.

Hollym Corporation: 13-13, Gwancheol-dong, Jongno-gu, Seoul 110-111; tel. (2) 735-7551; fax (2) 730-5149; e-mail info@hollym.co.kr; internet www.hollym.co.kr; f. 1963; academic and general books on Korea in English; Pres. HAM KI-MAN.

Hyang Mun Sa Publishing Co: 3/F, Burim Bldg, 1668-14, Seocho 1-dong, Seocho-gu, Seoul 137-881; tel. (2) 584-5671; fax (2) 584-5673; f. 1950; science, agriculture, history, engineering, home economics; Pres. NAH JOONG-RYOL.

Hyeonam Publishing Co Ltd: 481-12, Seogyo-dong, Mapo-gu, Seoul 121-841; tel. (2) 365-5051; fax (2) 365-2729; e-mail ks@hyeonamsa.com; internet www.hyeonamsa.com; f. 1951; general, children's, literature, periodicals; Pres. CHO KEUN-TAE.

Hyungseul Publishing Co: 7-33, Tongeui-dong, Jongno-gu, Seoul; tel. (2) 738-6052; fax (2) 736-7134; e-mail hs@hyungseul.co.kr; internet www.hyungseul.co.kr; social science, university books.

Il Jin Sa Publishing Co: 5-104, Hyochang-dong, Yeongsan-gu, Seoul; tel. (2) 704-1616; fax (2) 715-3536; e-mail webmaster@iljinsa.com; internet www.iljinsa.com; f. 1956; literature, social sciences, juvenile, fine arts, philosophy, linguistics, history; Pres. KIM SUNG-JAE.

Ilchokak Publishing Co Ltd: 1-335, Sinmunno 2-ga, Jongno-gu, Seoul 110-062; tel. (2) 733-5430; fax (2) 738-5857; e-mail ilchokak@hanmail.net; internet www.ilchokak.co.kr; f. 1953; history, literature, sociology, linguistics, medicine, law, engineering; Pres. KIM SI-YEON.

Jigyungsa Publishers Ltd: 790-14, Yeoksam-dong, Gangnam-gu, Seoul 135-080; tel. (2) 557-6351; fax (2) 557-6352; e-mail jigyung@uriel.net; internet www.jigyung.co.kr; f. 1979; children's, periodicals; Pres. KIM BYUNG-JOON.

Jihak Publishing Co Ltd: 180-20, Dongkyo-dong, Mapo-gu, Seoul 121-200; tel. (2) 330-5200; fax (2) 325-4488; e-mail webmaster@jihak.co.kr; internet www.jihak.co.kr; f. 1965; philosophy, language, literature; Pres. KWON BYONG-IL.

Jimoondang: 95, Waryon-dong, Jongno-gu, Seoul 110-360; tel. (2) 743-0227; fax (2) 742-4657; e-mail plan@jipmoon.co.kr; internet www.jimoon.co.kr; f. 1970; scholarly books on Korean history, society, language, literature, religion, art, folklore, politics and economy; Pres. LIM SAM-KYU.

Jisik Sanup Publications Co Ltd: 35-18, Dongui-dong, Jongno-gu, Seoul 110-040; tel. (2) 734-1978; fax (2) 720-7900; e-mail jsp@jisik.co.kr; internet www.jisik.co.kr; f. 1969; religion, social science, art, literature, history, children's; Pres. KIM KYUNG-HEE.

Kemongsa Publishing Co Ltd: 772, Yeoksam-dong, Gangnam-gu, Seoul 135-080; tel. (2) 531-5335; fax (2) 531-5520; internet www.kemongsa.co.kr; f. 1946; picture books, juvenile, encyclopaedias, history, fiction; Pres. RHU SEUNG-HEE.

Kookminbooks Co Ltd: 514-4, Paju Book City, Munbal-ri, Gyoha-eup, Paju-si, Gyeonggi-do; tel. (31) 955-7851; fax (31) 955-7855; internet www.kmbooks.com; f. 1961; children's books.

Korea Britannica Corpn: 117, 1-ga, Jungchung-dong, Seoul 100-391; tel. (2) 272-2151; fax (2) 278-9983; e-mail webmaster@britannica.co.kr; internet www.britannica.co.kr; f. 1968; encyclopaedias, dictionaries; Pres JANG HO-SANG, SUJAN ELEN TAPANI.

Korea University Press: 1-2, Anam-dong, 5-ga, Seongbuk-gu, Seoul 136-701; tel. (2) 3290-4232; fax (2) 923-6311; e-mail kupress@korea.ac.kr; internet www.kupress.com; f. 1956; philosophy, history, language, literature, Korean studies, education, psychology, social science, natural science, engineering, agriculture, medicine; Pres. LEE KI-SU.

Kum Sung Publishing Co: 242-63, Gongdeok-dong, Mapo-gu, Seoul 121-022; tel. (2) 713-9651; fax (2) 701-9345; e-mail webmaster@kumsungpub.co.kr; internet www.kumsung.co.kr; f. 1965; literature, juvenile, social sciences, history, fine arts; Pres. KIM NAK-JOON.

Kyohak-sa Publishing Co Ltd: 105-67, Gongdeok-dong, Mapo-gu, Seoul 121-020; tel. (2) 707-5110; fax (2) 707-5160; internet www.kyohak.co.kr; f. 1952; dictionaries, educational, children's; Pres. YANG CHEOL-WOO.

Kyung Hee University Press: 1, Hoeki-dong, Dongdaemun-gu, Seoul 130-701; tel. (2) 961-0106; fax (2) 962-8840; f. 1960; general, social science, technology, language, literature; Pres. CHOE YOUNG-SEEK.

Kyungnam University Press: 28-7, Samchung-dong, Jongno-gu, Seoul 110-230; tel. and fax (2) 3700-0700; e-mail ifes@kyungnam.ac.kr; internet ifes.kyungnam.ac.kr; Pres. PARK JAE-KYU.

Minumsa Publishing Co Ltd: 5/F Kangnam Publishing Culture Centre, 506, Sinsa-dong, Gangnam-gu, Seoul 135-120; tel. (2) 515-2000; fax (2) 514-3249; e-mail webmaster@minumsa.com; internet www.minumsa.com; f. 1966; literature, philosophy, linguistics, pure science; Pres. PARK MAENG-HO.

Munhakdongne Publishing Co Ltd: 513-8, Paju Book City, Munbal-ri, Gyoha-eup, Paju-si, Gyeonggi-do 413-756; tel. (31) 955-8888; fax (31) 955-8855; e-mail editor@munhak.com; internet www.munhak.com; f. 1993; art, literature, science, philosophy, non-fiction, children's, periodicals; Pres. KANG BYUNG-SUN.

Sakyejul Publishing Ltd: 513-3, Paju Book City, Munbal-ri, Gyoha-eup, Paju-si, Gyeonggi-do; tel. (31) 955-8558; fax (31) 955-8596; e-mail skj@sakyejul.co.kr; internet www.sakyejul.co.kr; f. 1982; social sciences, art, literature, history, children's; Pres. KANG MAR-XILL.

Sam Joong Dang Publishing Co: 261-23, Soke-dong, Yeongsan-gu, Seoul 140-140; tel. (2) 704-6816; fax (2) 704-6819; f. 1931; literature, history, philosophy, social sciences, dictionaries; Pres. LEE MIN-CHUL.

Sam Seong Dang Publishing Co: 101-14, Non Hyun-dong, Gangnam-gu, Seoul 135-010; tel. (2) 3442-6767; fax (2) 3442-6768; e-mail kyk@ssdp.co.kr; f. 1968; literature, fine arts, history, philosophy; Pres. KANG MYUNG-CHAE.

Samseongdang Publishing Co Ltd: 9/F, Samsungdang Bldg, 101-14, Nonhyeon-dong, Gangnam-gu, Seoul 135-820; tel. (2) 3443-2681; fax (2) 3443-2683; internet www.ssdp.co.kr; children's; Pres. KANG JEAN-KYUN.

Samsung Publishing Co Ltd: Samsung Publishing Bldg, 1516-2, Seocho 3-dong, Seocho-gu 137-871; tel. (2) 3470-6800; fax (2) 525-5057; e-mail jykim@samsungbooks.com; internet www.samsungbooks.com; children's books, comics, cooking, parenting, health, travel; f. 1951; Pres. KIM JIN-YONG.

Segyesa Publishing Co Ltd: 529-2, Munbal-ri, Gyoha-eup, Paju-si, Gyeonggi-do 413-756; tel. (31) 955-8080; fax (31) 955-8070; e-mail info@segyesa.co.kr; internet www.segyesa.co.kr; f. 1988; general, philosophy, literature, periodicals; Pres. CHOI SUN-HO.

Se-Kwang Music Publishing Co: 232-32, Seogye-dong, Yeongsan-gu, Seoul 140-140; tel. (2) 719-2652; fax (2) 719-2191; e-mail sekwang@sekwang.co.kr; internet www.sekwang.co.kr; f. 1953; music, art; Pres. PARK SEI-WON; Chair. PARK SHIN-JOON.

Seong An Dang Publishing Co: 4579, Singil-6-dong, Yeongdeungpo-gu, Seoul 150-056; tel. (2) 3142-4151; fax (2) 323-5324;

f. 1972; technology, text books, university books, periodicals; Pres. LEE JONG-CHOON.

Seoul National University Press: 599, Gwanak-ro, Gwanak-gu, Seoul 151-742; tel. (2) 889-0785; fax (2) 888-4148; e-mail snubook@snu.ac.kr; internet www.snupress.com; f. 1961; philosophy, engineering, social science, art, literature; Pres. LEE KI-JUN.

Si-sa-young-o-sa, Inc: 55-1, 2-ga, Jongno, Jongno-gu, Seoul 110-122; tel. (2) 274-0509; fax (2) 271-3980; internet www.ybmsisa.co.kr; f. 1959; language, literature; Pres. CHUNG YOUNG-SAM.

Sogang University Press: 1, Sinsu-dong, Mapo-gu, Seoul 121-742; tel. (2) 705-8114; fax (2) 705-8612; e-mail acafice@sogang.ac.kr; internet www.sogang.ac.kr; f. 1978; philosophy, religion, science, art, history; Pres. LEE JONG-WOOK.

Sookmyung Women's University Press: 53-12, 2-ga, Jongpa-dong, Yeongsan-gu, Seoul 140-742; tel. (2) 710-9162; fax (2) 710-9090; f. 1968; general; Pres. LEE KYUNG-SOOK.

Sungkyunkwan University Press: 53, Myeongnyun-dong 3-ga, Jongno-gu, Seoul; tel. (2) 760-1252; fax (2) 762-7452; internet www.skku.edu.

Sungshin Women's University Press: 249-1, Dongsun-dong 3-ga, Seongbuk-gu, Seoul; tel. (2) 920-7327; fax (2) 920-7326; internet www.sungshin.ac.kr/press.

Tam Gu Dang Publishing Co: 158, 1-ga, Hanggangno, Yeongsan-gu, Seoul 140-011; tel. (2) 3785-2211; fax (2) 3785-2272; e-mail tamgudang@tamgudang.co.kr; internet www.tamgudang.co.kr; f. 1950; linguistics, literature, social sciences, history, fine arts; Pres. HONG YOUNG-SOO.

Woongjin Think Big Co Ltd: 24/F, Kukdong Bldg, Chungmuro 3-ga, Jung-gu, Seoul; tel. (2) 3670-1832; fax (2) 766-2722; e-mail webmaster@wjholdings.co.kr; internet www.woongjin.com; children's; Pres. YOON SEOK-KEUM.

Yearimdang Publishing Co Ltd: Yearim Bldg, 153-3, Samseong-dong, Gangnam-gu, Seoul 135-090; tel. (2) 566-1004; fax (2) 567-9660; e-mail yearim@yearim.co.kr; internet www.yearim.kr; f. 1973; children's; Pres. NA CHOON-HO.

Yonsei University Press: 134, Sincheon-dong, Seodaemun-gu, Seoul 120-749; tel. (2) 2123-3380; fax (2) 2123-6673; e-mail dykim@yonsei.ac.kr; internet www.yonsei.ac.kr/press; f. 1955; philosophy, religion, literature, history, art, social science, pure science; Pres. KIM BYUNG-SOO.

Youl Hwa Dang: Paju Book City, 520-10, Munbal-ri, Gyoha-eup, Paju-si, Gyeonggi-do 413-832; tel. (31) 955-7000; fax (31) 955-7010; e-mail yhdp@youlhwadang.co.kr; internet www.youlhwadang.co.kr; f. 1971; art; Pres. YI KI-UNG.

Younglim Cardinal Inc: Hyecheon Bldg, 831, Yeoksam-dong, Gangnam-gu, Seoul 135-792; tel. (2) 553-8516; fax (2) 552-0436; e-mail edit@ylc21.co.kr; internet www.ylc21.co.kr; f. 1987.

PUBLISHERS' ASSOCIATION

Korean Publishers' Association: 105-2, Sagan-dong, Jongno-gu, Seoul 110-190; tel. (2) 735-2702; fax (2) 738-5414; e-mail kpa@kpa21.or.kr; internet www.kpa21.or.kr; f. 1947; Pres. BAEK SOK-GHEE; Sec.-Gen. KO HUNG-SIK.

Broadcasting and Communications

TELECOMMUNICATIONS

Korea Telecom: 206 Jungja-dong, Bundang-gu, Seongnam-si, Gyeonggi Prov. 463-711; tel. (2) 727-0114; fax (2) 750-3994; internet www.kt.co.kr; domestic and international telecommunications services and broadband internet services; privatized in June 2002; CEO JOONG SOO-NAM.

Korea Telecom (KT) Freetel: Seoul; internet www.ktf.co.kr; subsidiary of Korea Telecom; 10m. subscribers (2002); CEO JOONG SOO-NAM.

LG Dacom Corpn: Dacom Bldg, 706-1, Yeoksam-dong, Gangnam-gu, Seoul 135-610; tel. (2) 6220-0220; fax (2) 6220-0702; internet www.lgdacom.net; f. 1982; domestic and international long-distance telecommunications services and broadband internet services; CEO PARK JONG-WOOK.

LG Telecom: LG Gangnam Tower, 19th Floor, 679 Yeoksam-dong, Gangnam-gu, Seoul 135-985; tel. (2) 2005-7114; fax (2) 2005-7505; e-mail englishweb@lgtel.co.kr; internet www.lgtelecom.com; subsidiary of LG Corpn; mobile telecommunications and wireless internet services; commenced commercial CDMA2000 1x service in May 2001; 4m. subscribers (2002); CEO JUNG IL-JAE.

Onse Telecom: 192-2, Gumi-dong, Bundang-gu, Seongnam-si, Gyeonggi Prov. 463-500; tel. and fax (31) 738-6000; internet www.onse.net; domestic and international telecommunications services; Pres. and CEO HWANG KYU-BYUNG.

SK Telecom Co Ltd: 11, Euljiro, 2-ga, Jung-gu, Seoul 100-999; tel. (2) 6100-2114; fax (2) 2121-3999; e-mail webmaster@sktelecom.com; internet www.sktelecom.com; cellular mobile telecommunications and wireless internet services; merged with Shinsegi Telecom in Jan. 2002; 16m. subscribers (2002); Pres. and CEO SHIN BAE-KIM.

BROADCASTING

Regulatory Authority

Broadcasting and Communications Commission: KBS Bldg, 923-5, Mok-dong, Yangcheon-gu, Seoul 158-715; tel. (2) 3219-5117; fax (2) 3219-5371; e-mail admin@kbc.go.kr; internet www.kbc.go.kr; Chair. CHOI SI-JUNG.

Radio

Korean Broadcasting System (KBS): 18, Yeouido-dong, Yeongdeungpo-gu, Seoul 150-790; tel. (2) 781-1000; fax (2) 781-4179; internet www.kbs.co.kr; f. 1926; publicly owned corpn with 26 local broadcasting and 855 relay stations; overseas service in Korean, English, German, Indonesian, Chinese, Japanese, French, Spanish, Russian and Arabic; Pres. LEE BYUNG-SOON.

Buddhist Broadcasting System (BBS): 140, Mapo-dong, Mapo-gu, Seoul 121-050; tel. (2) 705-5114; fax (2) 705-5229; e-mail webmaster@bbsfm.co.kr; internet www.bbsfm.co.kr; f. 1990; Pres. CHO HAE-HYONG.

Christian Broadcasting System (CBS): 917-1, Mok-dong, Yangcheon-gu, Seoul 158-701; tel. (2) 650-0500; fax (2) 654-0505; e-mail changsoo@cbs.co.kr; internet www.cbs.co.kr; f. 1954; independent religious network with 14 network stations, incl. Seoul, Daegu, Busan and Gwangju; also satellite, cable and digital media broadcasting; programmes in Korean; Pres. LEE JEONG-SIK.

Educational Broadcasting System (EBS): 92-6, Umyeon-dong, Seocho-gu, Seoul 137-791; tel. (2) 526-2000; fax (2) 526-2179; e-mail hotline@ebs.co.kr; internet www.ebs.co.kr; f. 1990; Pres. Dr PARK HEUNG-SOO.

Far East Broadcasting Co (FEBC): 89, Sangsu-dong, Mapo-gu, Seoul 121-707; tel. (2) 320-0114; fax (2) 320-0229; e-mail febcadm@febc.net; internet www.febc.net; Christian programmes; nine local stations; Pres. KIM EUN-GI.

Radio Station HLAZ: MPO Box 88, Seoul 121-707; tel. (2) 320-0114; fax (2) 320-0129; e-mail febcadm@febc.net; internet www.febc.net; f. 1973; religious, educational service operated by Far East Broadcasting Co; programmes in Korean, Chinese, Russian and Japanese; Pres. Dr BILLY KIM.

Radio Station HLKX: MPO Box 88, Seoul 121-707; tel. (2) 320-0114; fax (2) 320-0129; e-mail febcadm@febc.net; internet www.febc.net; f. 1956; religious, educational service operated by Far East Broadcasting Co; programmes in Korean, Chinese and English; Pres. Dr BILLY KIM.

Munhwa Broadcasting Corpn (MBC): 31, Yeouido-dong, Yeongdeungpo-gu, Seoul 150-728; tel. (2) 784-2000; fax (2) 784-0880; e-mail mbcir@imbc.com; internet www.imbc.com; f. 1961; public; Pres. and CEO OHM KI-YOUNG.

Pyong Hwa Broadcasting Corpn (PBC): 2-3, 1-ga, Jeo-dong, Jung-gu, Seoul 100-031; tel. (2) 270-2114; fax (2) 270-2210; internet www.pbc.co.kr; f. 1990; religious and educational programmes; Pres. Rev. PARK SHIN-EON.

Seoul Broadcasting System (SBS): 10-2, Yeouido-dong, Yeongdeungpo-gu, Seoul 150-010; tel. (2) 786-0792; fax (2) 780-2530; internet www.sbs.co.kr; f. 1991; Pres. HA KUM-LOUL.

US Forces Network Korea (AFN Korea): Seoul; tel. (2) 7914-6495; fax (2) 7914-5870; e-mail info@afnkorea.net; internet afnkorea.com; f. 1950; six originating stations and 19 relay stations; 24 hours a day.

Television

Educational Broadcasting System (EBS): see Radio.

Jeonju Television Corpn (JTV): 656-3, Sonosong-dong, Deokjin-gu, Jeonju, N. Jeolla Prov.; tel. (63) 250-5231; fax (63) 250-5249; e-mail jtv@jtv.co.kr; f. 1997.

Korean Broadcasting System (KBS): 18, Yeouido-dong, Yeongdeungpo-gu, Seoul 150-790; tel. (2) 781-1000; fax (2) 781-4179; internet www.kbs.co.kr; f. 1961; publicly owned corpn with 25 local broadcasting and 770 relay stations; Pres. JUNG YUN-JOO.

Munhwa Broadcasting Corpn (MBC-R/TV): 31, Yeouido-dong, Yeongdeungpo-gu, Seoul 150-728; tel. (2) 789-2851; fax (2) 782-3094; e-mail song@mbc.co.kr; internet www.imbc.com; f. 1961; public; owned by the Foundation for Broadcast Culture (70%) and the Chung-Soo Scholarship Foundation (30%); includes terrestrial, cable and satellite TV stations, regional stations and radio stations; Pres. and CEO CHOI MOON-SOON.

Seoul Broadcasting System (SBS): see Radio.

US Forces Network Korea (AFN Korea): Seoul; tel. (2) 7914-2711; fax (2) 7914-5870; f. 1950; main transmitting station in Seoul; 19 rebroadcast transmitters and translators; 168 hours weekly.

Finance

(cap. = capital; res = reserves; dep. = deposits; m. = million; brs = branches; amounts in won, unless otherwise indicated)

REGULATORY AUTHORITIES

Financial Services Commission: 97, Yeouido-dong, Yeongdeungpo-gu, Seoul 150-743; tel. (2) 2156-8000; internet www.fsc.go.kr; f. 1998; deliberates on and resolves financial supervision issues; oversees Financial Supervisory Service; Chair. KIM SEOK-DONG.

Financial Supervisory Service: 97, Yeouido-dong, Yeongdeungpo-gu, Seoul 150-743; tel. (2) 3145-5114; fax (2) 785-3475; e-mail fssintl@fss.or.kr; internet www.fss.or.kr; f. 1999; examines and supervises financial institutions; Gov. KWON HYOUK-SE.

BANKING

In 2003 there were 59 commercial banks in South Korea, comprising eight nation-wide banks, six regional commercial banks, five specialized banks and 40 branches of foreign banks. In mid-2006 there were 32 foreign banks operating in South Korea. The Financial Supervisory Service oversees the operations of commercial banks and the financial services sector.

Central Bank

Bank of Korea: 110, 3-ga, Namdaemun-no, Jung-gu, Seoul 100-794; tel. (2) 759-4114; fax (2) 759-4060; e-mail bokdplp@bok.or.kr; internet www.bok.or.kr; f. 1950; bank of issue; res 3,342m., dep. 283,785m. (Dec. 2009); Gov. KIM CHOONG-SOO; Sr Dep. Gov. LEE JU-YEOL; 16 domestic brs, 6 overseas offices.

Commercial Banks

Citibank Korea Inc: 39, Da-dong, Jung-gu, Seoul 100-180; tel. (2) 3455-2114; fax (2) 3455-2966; internet www.citibank.co.kr; f. 1983; fmrly KorAm Bank, name changed as above 2004; acquired by Citigroup in 2004; cap. 1,518,322m., res 1,187,253m., dep. 34,637,975m. (Dec. 2009); CEO and Chair. HA YUNG-KU; 222 brs.

Hana Bank: 101-1, 1-ga, Ulchi-no, Jung-gu, Seoul 100-191; tel. (2) 2002-1111; fax (2) 775-7472; e-mail webmaster@hanabank.co.kr; internet www.hanabank.co.kr; f. 1991; merged with Boram Bank in Jan. 1999; merged with Seoulbank in Dec. 2002; cap. 1,147,404m., res 7,790,795m., dep. 89,884,425m. (Dec. 2009); Chair. and CEO KIM JUNG-TAE; 604 brs.

Kookmin Bank: 9-1, 2-ga, Namdaemun-no, Jung-gu, CPOB 815, Seoul 100-703; tel. (2) 2073-7114; fax (2) 2073-3296; e-mail corres@kookminbank.com; internet www.kookminbank.com; f. 1963; est. as Citizen's National Bank, renamed 1995; re-est. Jan. 1999, following merger with Korea Long Term Credit Bank; merged with H & CB in Nov. 2001; cap. 2,481,896m., res 7,810,968m., dep. 170,385,878m. (Dec. 2009); Chair. EUH YOON-DAE; Pres. and CEO MIN BYUNG-DUK; 1,122 domestic brs, 6 overseas brs.

Korea Exchange Bank: 181, 2-ga, Ulchi-no, Jung-gu, Seoul 100-793; tel. (2) 729-0114; fax (2) 775-2565; internet www.keb.co.kr; f. 1967; merged with Korea International Merchant Bank in Jan. 1999; cap. 3,224,534m., res 1,234,496m., dep. 56,951,887m. (Dec. 2009); Chair. and CEO LARRY A. KLANE; 345 domestic brs, 19 overseas brs.

Shinhan Bank: 120, 2-ga, Taepyeong-no, Jung-gu, Seoul 100-102; tel. (2) 756-0505; fax (2) 774-7013; e-mail corres@shinhan.com; internet www.shinhan.com; f. 1982; merged with Chohung Bank in April 2006; cap. 7,928,078m., res 1,502,360m., dep. 159,041,712m. (Dec. 2009); Pres. and CEO EUNG CHAN RA; 957 domestic brs, 12 overseas brs.

Standard Chartered First Bank Korea Limited: 100, Gongpyeong-dong, Jongno-gu, Seoul 110702; tel. (2) 3702-3114; fax (2) 3702-4934; e-mail webmaster@scfirstbank.com; internet www.scfirstbank.com; f. 1929; acquired by Standard Chartered Bank in Jan. 2005, name changed from Korea First Bank to above in Sept. 2005; cap. 1,313,043m., res 978,767m., dep. 46,300,583m. (Dec. 2009); Chair. ROBERT T. BARNUM; Pres. and CEO RICHARD HILL; 367 domestic brs, 2 overseas brs.

Woori Bank: 203, 1-ga, Hoehyeon-dong, Jung-gu, Seoul; tel. (2) 2002-3000; fax (2) 2002-5687; internet www.wooribank.com; f. 2002; est. by merger of Hanvit Bank and Peace Bank of Korea; 78% govt-owned; privatization plans deferred in 2008; cap. 3,829,783m., res 1,948,126m., dep. 147,541,287m. (Dec. 2009); CEO LEE SOON-WOO; 712 domestic brs.

Development Banks

Export-Import Bank of Korea: 16-1, Yeouido-dong, Yeongdeungpo-gu, Seoul 150-996; tel. (2) 3779-6114; fax (2) 3779-6750; e-mail iro@koreaexim.go.kr; internet www.koreaexim.go.kr; f. 1976; cap. 5,008,755m., res 350,392m. (Dec. 2009); Chair. and Pres. KIM YONG-HWAN; 11 brs.

Korea Development Bank: 16-3, Yeouido-dong, Yeongdeungpo-gu, Seoul 150-973; tel. (2) 787-6934; fax (2) 787-6991; e-mail KDBir@kdb.co.kr; internet www.kdb.co.kr; f. 1954; cap. 9,241,861m., res 797,919m., dep. 15,582,933m. (Dec. 2009); Chair. KANG MAN-SOO; 40 domestic brs, 6 overseas brs.

Specialized Banks

Industrial Bank of Korea: 50, 2-ga, Ulchi-no, Jung-gu, Seoul 100-758; tel. (2) 729-6114; fax (2) 729-6402; e-mail ifd@ibk.co.kr; internet www.ibk.co.kr; f. 1961; est. as the Small and Medium Industry Bank; 85.5% govt-owned; cap. 3,207,944m., res 5,297,187m., dep. 50,711,514m. (Dec. 2009); Chair. and CEO YOON YONG-RO; 417 domestic brs, 5 overseas brs.

Meritz Investment Bank: Seoul Financial Center, 5th Floor, 84, Taepyeong-no 1-ga, Jung-gu, Seoul 100-768; tel. (2) 777-7711; fax (2) 318-7060; internet home.imeritz.com; f. 1977; fmrly Korean-French Banking Corpn (SogeKo).

Provincial Banks

Daegu Bank Ltd: 118, 2-ga, Susong-dong, Susong-gu, Daegu 706-712; tel. (53) 756-2001; fax (53) 756-2095; internet www.daegubank.co.kr; f. 1967; cap. 660,625m., res 19,795m., dep. 17,641,673m. (Dec. 2009); Chair. and CEO HA CHUN-SOO; 209 brs.

Jeju Bank: 1349, Ido-1-dong, Jeju 690-021, Jeju Prov.; tel. (64) 720-0200; fax (64) 753-4132; internet www.e-jejubank.com; f. 1969; cap. 55,500m., res. 30,700m., dep. 1,044,100m. (2002); merged with Central Banking Co in 2000, joined the Shinhan Financial Group in 2002; Chair. and Pres. KANG JOON-HONG; 29 brs.

Jeonbuk Bank Ltd: 669-2, Geumam-dong, Deokjin-gu, Jeonju 561-711, N. Jeolla Prov.; tel. (63) 250-7114; fax (63) 250-7078; internet www.jbbank.co.kr; f. 1969; cap. 266,797m., res 14,310m., dep. 5,251,565m. (2009); Chair. and Pres. HONG SUNG-JOO; 74 brs.

Kwangju Bank Ltd: 7-12, Daein-dong, Dong-gu, Gwangju 501-719; tel. (62) 239-5000; fax (62) 239-5199; e-mail kbjint1@nuri.net; internet www.kjbank.com; f. 1968; cap. 247,069m., res 95,825m., dep. 12,314,239m. (Dec. 2009); Chair. JEONG TAE-SEOK; 124 brs.

Kyongnam Bank: 246-1, Sokjeon-dong, Hoewon-gu, Masan 630-010, Gyeongsang Prov.; tel. (551) 290-8000; fax (551) 294-9426; internet www.knbank.co.kr; f. 1970; est. as Gyeongnam Bank Ltd, name changed 1987; cap. 290,250m., res 120,728m., dep. 15,302,799m. (Dec. 2009); Pres. and CEO MOON DONG-SUNG; 110 brs.

Banking Association

Korea Federation of Banks: 4-1, 1-ga, Myeong-dong, Jung-gu, Seoul 100-021; tel. (2) 3705-5000; fax (2) 3705-5337; internet www.kfb.or.kr; f. 1928; Chair. SHIN DONG-KYU; Vice-Chair. KIM KONG-JIN.

STOCK EXCHANGE

Korea Exchange (KRX): Nulwon Bldg, 825-3, Beomil-dong, Dong-gu, Busan 601-720; tel. (51) 662-2000; fax (51) 662-2478; internet www.krx.co.kr; f. 2005; formed by merger of Korea Stock Exchange, Korea Futures Exchange, Kosdaq Stock Market, Korea Securities Dealers Association; Chair. and CEO KIM BONG-SOO.

INSURANCE

Principal Life Companies

Allianz Life Insurance Co Ltd: Allianz Tower, 45-21 Yeouido-dong, Yeongdeungpo-gu, Seoul 150-978; tel. (2) 3787-7000; e-mail webadmin@allianzlife.co.kr; internet www.allianzlife.co.kr; fmrly Allianz Jeil Life Insurance; formed in 2000 following acquisition of Jeil (First Life) by Allianz Group; renamed as above in 2002; Pres. and CEO MANUEL BAUER.

American International Assurance Korea: Shinil Bldg, 5/F, 64-5, 2-ga, Chungmu-ro, Jung-gu, Seoul; tel. (2) 3707-4800; fax (67) 725-0783; e-mail kr.webmaster@aia.com; internet www.aia.co.kr; f. 1977; CEO SANG LEE.

Dongbu Life Insurance Co Ltd: Dongbu Bldg, 7th Floor, 891-10, Daechi-dong, Gangnam-gu, Seoul 135-820; tel. (2) 1588-3131; fax (2) 3011-4100; internet www.dongbulife.co.kr; f. 1989; cap. 85,200m. (2003); CEO CHO JAE-HONG.

Green Cross Life Insurance Co Ltd: 395-68, Shindaebang-dong, Dongjak-gu, Seoul; tel. (2) 3284-7000; fax (2) 3284-7455; internet www.healthcare.co.kr; CEO LEE JUNG-SANG.

Hana HSBC Life Insurance Ltd: Hana Bank HQ Bldg, 17/F, 101-1 Ulchiro-1ga, Jung-gu, Seoul 100-191; tel. (2) 3709-7300; fax (2) 755-

0668; internet www.hanahsbclife.co.kr; jt venture between HSBC Insurance (Asia-Pacific) Holdings Ltd and Hana Financial Group; CEO DAVID YOON.

Hungkuk Life Insurance Co Ltd: 226, Sinmun-no 1-ga, Jongno-gu, Seoul 100-061; tel. (2) 2002-7000; fax (2) 2002-7804; e-mail webmaster@hungkuk.co.kr; internet www.hungkuk.co.kr; f. 1958; CEO JIN HUN-JIN.

ING Life Insurance Co Korea Ltd: ING Center, 53 Sunhwa-dong, Jung-gu, Seoul 100-130; tel. (2) 3703-9500; fax (2) 734-3309; e-mail webmaster@inglife.co.kr; internet www.inglife.co.kr; f. 1991; cap. 64,820m. (2002); Pres. and CEO JOHN WYLIE.

KB Life Insurance Co Ltd: 2–5/F, 16-49, Hangangro-3 ga, Yong-san-gu, Seoul; tel. (2) 398-6800; fax (2) 398-6843; e-mail webmaster@kbli.co.kr; internet www.kbli.co.kr.

Korea Life Insurance Co Ltd: 60, Yeouido-dong, Yeongdeungpo-gu, Seoul 150-603; tel. (2) 789-5114; fax (2) 789-8173; internet www.korealife.com; f. 1946; cap. 3,550,000m. (2002); CEO SHIN EUN-CHUL.

Korean Reinsurance Company: 80, Susong-dong, Jongno-gu, Seoul 110-733; tel. (2) 3702-6000; fax (2) 739-3754; internet www.koreanre.co.kr; f. 1963; cap. 57,000m. (2010); Pres. PARK JONG-WON.

Kumho Life Insurance Co Ltd: 57, 1-ga, Sinmun-no, Jongno-gu, Seoul 110-061; tel. (2) 1588-4040; fax (2) 771-7561; internet www.kumholife.co.kr; f. 1988; acquired Dong-Ah Life Insurance in 2000; cap. 211,249m. (2002); Pres. CHOI BYEONG-GIL.

Kyobo Life Insurance Co Ltd: 1, 1-ga, Jongno, Jongno-gu, Seoul 110-714; tel. (2) 721-2121; fax (2) 737-9970; internet www.kyobo.co.kr; f. 1958; cap. 92,500m.; Chair. and CEO SHIN CHANG-JAE; 84 main brs.

Life Insurance Association of North America: Seoul City Tower, 14/F, 581, Namdaemunro-5-ga, Jung-gu, Seoul; tel. (2) 3781-1000; fax (2) 792-6063; internet www.lina.co.kr; f. 1987; CEO BENJAMIN HONG.

MetLife Insurance Co of Korea Ltd: Sungwon Bldg, 8/F, 141, Samseong-dong, Gangnam-gu, Seoul 135-716; tel. (2) 3469-9600; fax (2) 3469-9700; internet www.metlifekorea.co.kr; f. 1989; cap. 97,700m. (2002); Pres. STUART B. SOLOMON.

Mirae Asset Life Insurance: Times Sq. Bldg A, 442, 4-ga, Yeong-deungpo-dong, Seoul 150-034; tel. (2) 3271-4114; fax (2) 3271-4400; e-mail msp@miraeasset.com; internet www.miraeassetlife.com; f. 2005; CEO PARK HYEON-JOO.

New York Life Insurance Ltd: 10/F, Shinyoung Bldg, 68-5, Chung Dam-dong, Gangnam-gu, Seoul; tel. (2) 2107-4600; fax (2) 2107-4700; f. 1990.

PCA Life Insurance Co Ltd: PCA Life Tower, 706, Yeoksam-dong, Gangnam-gu, Seoul; tel. (2) 6960-1700; fax (2) 6960-1606; internet www.pcakorea.co.kr; f. 1990; cap. 52,100m. (2002); Pres. MIKE BISHOP.

Prudential Life Insurance Co of Korea Ltd: Prudential Bldg, Yeoksam-dong, Gangnam-gu, Seoul; tel. (2) 2144-2000; fax (2) 2144-2100; internet www.prudential.co.kr; f. 1989; cap. 26,400m.; Pres. HWANG OU-JIN.

Samsung Life Insurance Co Ltd: 150, 2-ga, Taepyeong-no, Jung-gu, Seoul 100-716; tel. (2) 751-8000; fax (2) 751-8100; e-mail samsunglife.ir@samsung.com; internet www.samsunglife.com; f. 1957; cap. 100,000m. (2002); Pres. LEE SOO-CHANG; 1,300 brs.

Shinhan Life Insurance Co Ltd: 120, 2-ga, Taepyeong-no, Jung-gu, Seoul 100-102; tel. (2) 3455-4000; fax (2) 775-3286; internet www.shinhanlife.co.kr; f. 1990; CEO GWEON JEUM-JOO.

Tong Yang Life Insurance Co Ltd: 185, Ulchi-no 2-ga, Jung-gu, Seoul 100-192; tel. (2) 728-9114; fax (2) 728-9563; internet www.myangel.co.kr; f. 1989; cap. 340,325m. (2002); Pres. KU JA-HONG.

Woori Aviva Life Insurance Co Ltd: Woori Aviva Life Insurance Bldg, Sujung 3-dong, Dong-gu, Busan 601-716; tel. (2) 2087-9337; fax (2) 2087-93258; internet www.wooriaviva.com; f. 1988; fmrly LIG Life Insurance Co Ltd; name changed as above after joint acquisition by Woori Finance Holdings Co Ltd and Aviva Life Insurance Co; Pres. SEON HWAN-KYU.

Non-Life Companies

American Home Insurance Co: Seoul Central Bldg, 15–18/F, 136 Seorin-dong, Jongno-gu, Seoul; tel. (2) 2260-6800; fax (2) 2260-6707; e-mail ask.chartis@chartisinsurance.com; internet www.chartisinsurance.com; f. 1947; operates under the brand name Chartis; Pres. BRAD BENNETT.

Dongbu Insurance Co Ltd: Dongbu Financial Center, 12/F, 891-10, Daechi-dong, Gangnam-gu, Seoul 135-840; tel. (2) 2262-3450; fax (2) 3001-3159; e-mail dongbu@dongbuinsurance.co.kr; internet www.idongbu.com; f. 1962; cap. 30,000m.; Pres. KIM JING-NAM.

First Fire and Marine Insurance Co Ltd: 12-1, Seosomun-dong, Jung-gu, CPOB 530, Seoul 100-110; tel. (2) 316-8114; fax (2) 771-7319; f. 1949; cap. 17,200m.; Pres. KIM WOO-HOANG.

Green Non-Life Insurance Co Ltd: Green Non-Life Insurance Co Bldg, 705-19, Yeoksam-dong, Gangnam-gu, Seoul; tel. (2) 3788-2000; fax (2) 774-8368; internet www.greenfire.co.kr; Pres. LEE YOUNG-DOO.

Heungkuk Fire and Marine Insurance Co Ltd: 226, Sinmun-no, 1-ga, Jongno-gu, Seoul; tel. (2) 724-9000; fax (2) 774-8368; e-mail sfmi@ssy.insurance.co.kr; internet www.insurance.co.kr; f. 1948; fmrly Ssangyong Fire and Marine Insurance Co; cap. 27,400m.; Pres. KIM YONG-GWON.

Hyundai Marine and Fire Insurance Co Ltd: 178, Sejongno, Jongno-gu, Seoul 110-731; tel. (2) 732-1212; fax (2) 732-5687; e-mail webpd@hdinsurance.co.kr; internet www.hi.co.kr; f. 1955; cap. 30,000m.; Pres. and CEO SEO TAI-CHANG.

Korean Reinsurance Co: 80, Susong-dong, Jongno-gu, Seoul 100-733; tel. (2) 3702-6000; fax (2) 739-3754; e-mail service@koreanre.co.kr; internet www.koreanre.co.kr; f. 1963; cap. 57,000m.; Pres. PARK JONG-WON.

Kyobo AXA General Insurance Co Ltd: 395-70, Sindaebang-dong, Dongjak-gu, Seoul; tel. (2) 3479-4900; fax (2) 3479-4800; internet www.kyobodirect.com; fmrly Kyobo Auto Insurance Co Ltd, name changed as above in 2007; Pres. GUY MARCILLAT.

LIG Insurance Co Ltd: 649-11, Yeoksam-dong, Gangnam-gu, Seoul; tel. (2) 310-2391; fax (2) 753-1002; e-mail webmaster@lginsure.com; internet www.lig.co.kr; f. 1959; fmrly LG Insurance Co; Pres. JANG NAM-SIK.

Lotte Insurance Co Ltd: 51-1, Namchang-dong, Jung-gu, Seoul 100-778; tel. (2) 1588-3344; fax (2) 754-5220; internet www.lotteins.co.kr; f. 1946; cap. 19,500m.; fmrly Daehan Fire and Marine Insurance Co Ltd, name changed as above in 2008; Pres. and CEO KIM CHANG-JAE.

Meritz Fire and Marine Insurance Co Ltd: 825-2, Yeoksam-dong, Gangnam-gu, Seoul 135-080; tel. (2) 3786-1910; fax (2) 3786-1940; e-mail ir@meritzfire.com; internet www.meritzfire.com; f. 1922; Vice-Chair. and CEO WOHN MYUNG-SOO.

Samsung Fire and Marine Insurance Co Ltd: Samsung Insurance Bldg, 87, 1-ga, Ulchi-no, Jung-gu, Seoul 100-191; tel. (2) 758-7948; fax (2) 758-7831; internet www.samsungfire.com; f. 1952; cap. 6,566m.; Pres. LEE SOO-CHANG.

Seoul Guarantee Insurance Co: 136-74, Yeonchi-dong, Jongno-gu, Seoul 110-470; tel. (2) 3671-7459; fax (2) 3671-7480; internet www.sgic.co.kr; f. 1969; CEO BAANG YOUNG-MIN.

Shindongah Fire and Marine Insurance Co Ltd: 43, 2-ga, Taepyeong-no, Jung-gu, Seoul; tel. (2) 6366-7000; fax (2) 755-8006; internet www.sdafire.com; f. 1946; cap. 60,220m.; CEO KWON CHU-SIN.

Insurance Associations

General Insurance Association of Korea: KRIC Bldg, 6th Floor, 80, Susong-dong, Jongno-gu, Seoul; tel. (2) 3702-8539; fax (2) 3702-8549; e-mail jhero@knia.or.kr; internet www.knia.or.kr; f. 1946; 16 corporate mems; fmrly Korea Non-Life Insurance Asscn; Chair. MOON JAE-WOO.

Korea Life Insurance Association: Kukdong Bldg, 16th Floor, 60-1, 3-ga, Jungmu-no, Jung-gu, Seoul 100-705; tel. (2) 2262-6600; fax (2) 2262-6580; e-mail info@klia.or.kr; internet www.klia.or.kr; f. 1950; Chair. LEE WOO-CHEOL.

Trade and Industry

GOVERNMENT AGENCIES

Fair Trade Commission: 217, Banpo-dong, Seocho-gu, Seoul; tel. (2) 2023-4248; fax (2) 2023-4241; e-mail kftc@korea.kr; internet www.ftc.go.kr; Chair. KIM DONG-SOO; Sec.-Gen. LEE DONG-KYU.

Federation of Korean Industries: FKI Bldg, 14/F, 28-2, Yeouido-dong, Yeongdeungpo-gu, Seoul 150-756; tel. (2) 3771-0354; fax (2) 3771-0110; e-mail webmaster@fki.or.kr; internet www.fki.or.kr; f. 1961; conducts research and survey work on domestic and overseas economic conditions and trends; advises the Govt and other interested parties on economic matters; exchanges economic and trade missions with other countries; sponsors business conferences; 366 corporate mems and 63 business asscns; Chair. HUH CHANG-SOO.

Korea Appraisal Board: 171-2, Samseong-dong, Gangnam-gu, Seoul; tel. (2) 2189-8000; fax (2) 561-6133; internet www.kab.co.kr; Chair. KWAN JIN-BONG.

Korea Asset Management Corpn (KAMCO): 450, Gangnam-daero, Gangnam-gu, Seoul; tel. (2) 3420-5000; fax (2) 3420-5030; e-mail irkamco@kamco.or.kr; internet www.kamco.or.kr; f. 1963;

collection and foreclosure agency; appointed following Asian financial crisis as sole institution to manage and dispose of non-performing loans for financial institutions; Chair. and CEO CHANG YONG-CHUL.

Korea Export Industrial Corpn: 33, Seorin-dong, Jongno-gu, Seoul; tel. (2) 853-5573; f. 1964; encourages industrial exports, provides assistance and operating capital, conducts market surveys; Pres. KIM KI-BAE.

Korea Industrial Research Institutes: FKI Bldg, 28-1, Yeouido-dong, Yeongdeungpo-gu, Seoul; tel. (2) 780-7601; fax (2) 785-5771; f. 1979; analyses industrial and technological information from abroad; Pres. KIM CHAE-KYUM.

Korea Institute for Industrial Economics and Trade (KIET): 66 Hoegi-ro, Dongdaemun-gu, Seoul; tel. (2) 3299-3114; fax (2) 963-8540; e-mail webmaster@kiet.re.kr; internet www.kiet.re.kr; f. 1976; economic and industrial research; Pres. SONG BYOUNG-JUN.

Korea Land and Housing Corpn: 217, Jeongja-dong, Seongnam-shi, Gyeonggi-do; tel. (31) 738-7114; fax (31) 717-5431; internet www.lh.or.kr; f. 1975; land development; est. by merging Korea Land Corpn and Korea National Housing Corpn; CEO LEE JI-SONG.

Korea Resources Corpn (KORES): 606, Siheung-daero, Dongjak-gu, Seoul; tel. (2) 840-5600; e-mail csmaster@kores.or.kr; internet www.kores.or.kr; f. 1967; provides technical and financial support for the national mining industry; Pres. KIM SHIN-JONG.

Korea Trade Insurance Corpn: Seoul Central Bldg, 2/F, 136, Seorin-dong, Jongno-gu, Seoul 110-729; tel. (2) 399-6800; fax (2) 399-7439; internet www.ksure.or.kr; f. 1992; financial support services for traders; fmrly Korea Export Insurance Corpn; Chair. and Pres. RYU CHANG-MOO.

Korea Trade-Investment Promotion Agency (KOTRA): 300-9, Yeomgok-dong, Seocho-gu, Seoul; tel. (2) 3460-7114; fax (2) 3460-7777; e-mail digitalkotra@kotra.or.kr; internet www.kotra.or.kr; f. 1962; various trade promotion activities, market research, cross-border investment promotion, etc.; 102 overseas brs; Pres. CHO HWAN-EIK.

Korean Intellectual Property Office: Government Complex-Daejeon Bldg 4, 189, Cheongsa-ro, Seo-gu, Daejeon; tel. (42) 481-5071; fax (42) 472-9314; e-mail kipoicd@kipo.go.kr; internet www.kipo.go.kr; Commissioner LEE SOO-WON.

CHAMBER OF COMMERCE

Korea Chamber of Commerce and Industry: 45, 4-ga, Namdaemun-no, Jung-gu, Seoul 100-743; tel. (2) 6050-3114; fax (2) 6050-3400; e-mail webmaster@korcham.net; internet www.korcham.net; f. 1884; over 47,000 mems; 70 local chambers; promotes development of the economy and of international economic co-operation; Chair. SOHN KYUNG-SHIK.

INDUSTRIAL AND TRADE ASSOCIATIONS

Construction Association of Korea: Construction Bldg, 8th Floor, 71-2, Nonhyon-dong, Gangnam-gu, Seoul 135-701; tel. (2) 3485-0200; fax (2) 542-6264; internet www.cak.or.kr; f. 1947; national licensed contractors' asscn; 6,823 mem. firms (2006); Pres. KWON HONG-SA.

Korea Agro-Fisheries Trade Corpn (aT): aT Center, 232 Yangjae-dong, Seocho-gu, Seoul; tel. (2) 6300-1114; fax (2) 6300-1600; internet www.at.or.kr; f. 1967; fmrly Agricultural and Fishery Marketing Corpn; integrated devt for secondary processing and marketing distribution for agricultural products and fisheries products; Pres. JANG BAE-YOO; Exec. Vice-Pres. KIM JIN-KYU.

Korea Automobile Manufacturers Association (KAMA): 1461-15, Seocho 3-dong, Seocho-gu, Seoul 137-720; tel. (2) 3660-1854; fax (2) 3660-1900; e-mail webmaster@kama.or.kr; internet www.kama.or.kr/index.jsp; f. 1988; Chair. YOUN YEO-CHUL.

Korea Electronics Association: Digital Innovation Center, 11–12/F, 1599, Sangnam-dong, Mapo-gu, Seoul; tel. (2) 6388-6000; fax (2) 6388-6009; e-mail webmaster@gokea.org; internet www.gokea.org; f. 1976; 328 mems; Chair. YUN JONG-YONG.

Korea Federation of Textile Industries: Textile Center, 16/F, 944-31, Daechi 3-dong, Gangnam-gu, Seoul 135-713; tel. (2) 528-4052; fax (2) 528-4069; e-mail kofoti@kofoti.or.kr; internet www.kofoti.or.kr; f. 1980; 50 corporate mems; Chair. CHAN RO-HEE.

Korea Foods Industry Association: 1002-6, Bangbae-dong, Seocho-gu, Seoul; tel. (2) 3470-8100; fax (2) 3471-3492; internet www.kfia.or.kr; f. 1969; 104 corporate mems; Pres. CHUN MYUNG-KE.

Korea Importers Association (KOIMA): 218, Hangang-no, 2-ga, Yeongsan-gu, Seoul 140-875; tel. (2) 792-1581; fax (2) 785-4373; e-mail koima@koima.or.kr; internet www.koima.or.kr; f. 1970; 6,804 mems; Chair. Dr LEE JU-TAE.

Korea International Trade Association: 159-1, Samseong-dong, Gangnam-gu, Seoul; tel. (2) 6000-5114; fax (2) 6000-5115; e-mail kitainfo@kita.net; internet www.kita.org; f. 1946; private, non-profitmaking business org. representing all licensed traders in South Korea; provides foreign businesses with information, contacts and advice; 80,000 corporate mems; Chair. and CEO IL SAKONG.

Korea Iron and Steel Association: 19/F, Posteel Tower, 735-3, Yeoksam-dong, Gangnam-gu, Seoul; tel. (2) 559-3500; fax (2) 559-3508; internet www.kosa.or.kr; f. 1975; 39 corporate mems; Chair. YOO SANG-BOO.

Korea Oil Association: 28-1, Yeouido-dong, Yeongdeungpo-gu, Seoul; tel. (2) 555-8322; fax (2) 555-7825; e-mail oilassn@yahoo.co.kr; internet www.koreaoil.or.kr; f. 1980; Pres. CHOI DOO-HWAN.

Korea Productivity Center: 122-1, Jeokseon-dong, Jongno-gu, Seoul 110-751; tel. (2) 724-1114; fax (2) 736-0322; internet www.kpc.or.kr; f. 1957; services to increase productivity of industries, consulting services, education and training of specialized personnel; Chair. and CEO CHOI DONG-KYU.

Korea Sericultural Association: 17-9, Yeouido-dong, Yeongdeungpo-gu, Seoul; tel. (2) 783-6072; fax (2) 780-0706; e-mail jamsa@silktopia.or.kr; internet ksa.silktopia.or.kr; f. 1946; improvement and promotion of silk production; 50,227 corporate mems; Pres. PARK DONGCHUI.

Korea Shipbuilders' Association: Landmark Tower, 18/F, 837-36, Yeoksam-dong, Gangnam-gu, Seoul 135-937; tel. (2) 2112-8181; fax (2) 2112-8182; internet www.koshipa.or.kr; f. 1977; 9 mems; Chair. NAM SANG-TAE.

Korea Textiles Trade Association: Textile Center, 16/F, 944-31, Daechi 3-dong, Gangnam-gu, Seoul 135-713; tel. (2) 528-5158; fax (2) 528-5188; e-mail keat@kotis.net; internet www.textra.or.kr; f. 1981; 947 corporate mems; Pres. KANG TAE-SEUNG.

Korean Apparel Industry Association: Textile Center, 16/F, 944-31, Daechi 3-dong, Gangnam-gu, Seoul 135-713; tel. (2) 528-0114; fax (2) 528-0120; internet www.kaia.or.kr; f. 1993; 741 corporate mems; Chair. LEE IN-SUNG.

Mining Association of Korea: 35-24, Dongui-dong, Jongno-gu, Seoul 110; tel. (2) 737-7748; fax (2) 720-5592; f. 1918; 128 corporate mems; Pres. KIM SANG-BONG.

Spinners and Weavers Association of Korea: 43-8, Gwancheol-dong, Jongno-gu, Seoul 110; tel. (2) 735-5741; fax (2) 735-5749; internet www.swak.org; f. 1947; 20 corporate mems; Chair. KIM HYONG-SANG.

EMPLOYERS' ORGANIZATION

Korea Employers' Federation: KEF Bldg, 276-1, Daeheung-dong, Mapo-gu, Seoul 121-726; tel. (2) 3270-7310; fax (2) 3270-7431; e-mail admin@kef.or.kr; internet www.kef.or.kr; f. 1970; advocates employers' interests with regard to labour and social affairs; 13 regional employers' asscns, 20 economic and trade asscns, and 4,000 major enterprises; Chair. LEE HEE-BEOM.

UTILITIES

Electricity

Korea Electric Power Corpn (KEPCO): 167, Samseong-dong, Gangnam-gu, Seoul; tel. (2) 3456-3114; fax (2) 3456-3699; internet www.kepco.co.kr; f. 1961; transmission and distribution of electric power, and development of electric power sources; six power generation subsidiaries formed in 2001; CEO KIM SSANG-SOO.

Oil and Gas

Daegu City Gas Co Ltd: 2268-1, Namsan 4-dong, Jung-gu, Daegu; tel. (53) 606-1000; fax (53) 606-1004; e-mail kej@taegugas.co.kr; internet www.taegugas.co.kr; f. 1983; Pres. and CEO LEE CHONG-MOO.

Daehan City Gas: 27-1, Daechi-dong, Kangnam-gu, Seoul; tel. (2) 3410-8000; internet www.daehancitygas.com; f. 1978; supplies liquefied natural gas (LNG) to customers in Seoul and Gyeonggi Province; Co-CEOs NAH SEONG-HWA, KIM BOK-HWAN.

GS Caltex: GS Tower, 679 Yeoksam-dong, Gangnam-gu, Seoul; tel. (2) 2005-1114; internet www.gscaltex.com; subsidiary of GS Holdings Corpn; fmrly LG Caltex Oil, renamed as above March 2005; Chair. and CEO HUR DONG-SOO.

Hanjin City Gas: 711, Sanggye 6-dong, Nowon-gu, Seoul; tel. (2) 950-5000; fax (2) 950-5001; e-mail webmaster@hjcgas.com; internet www.hjcgas.com; f. 1985; supplies natural gas to Seoul and Gyeonggi; CEO LEE SEUNG-CHIL.

Incheon City Gas Corpn: 178-24, Gajoa-dong, Seo-gu, Incheon; tel. (32) 1600-0002; fax (32) 576-2710; internet www.icgas.co.kr; f. 1983; CEO PARK DAE-YONG.

Jungbu City Gas Co Ltd: Jungbu; fax (41) 533-6748; e-mail webmaster@jbcitygas.com; internet www.cbcitygas.co.kr; f. 1992.

Korea Gas Corpn: 215, Jeongja-dong, Bundang-gu, Seongnam, Gyeonggi-do; tel. (31) 710-0114; fax (31) 710-0117; e-mail kogasmaster@kogas.or.kr; internet www.kogas.or.kr; f. 1983; state-owned; privatization pending; Pres. and CEO CHOO KANG-SOO.

Korea National Oil Corpn (KNOC): tel. 380-2114; fax 387-9321; e-mail webmaster@knoc.co.kr; internet www.knoc.co.kr; CEO KANG YOUNG-WON.

KyungDong City Gas Co: 939, Jinjang-dong, Book-gu, Ulsan; tel. (52) 219-5300; internet www.kdgas.co.kr; distributes liquefied natural gas (LNG) to residential, commercial and industrial customers in Ulsan and Yangsan; CEO SONG JAE-HO.

Kyungnam Energy Co Ltd: 55-5, Ungnam-dong, Changwon, Gyeongsangnam-do 641-290; tel. (55) 260-4432; fax (55) 285-9861; e-mail admin@knenegy.co.kr; internet www.knenergy.co.kr; f. 1972; supplies natural gas to Changwon and the surrounding area; Pres. and CEO CHUNG YEUN-WOOK.

Samchully Co Ltd: 35-6, Yeouido-dong, Yeongdeungpo-gu, Seoul; tel. (2) 368-3300; fax (2) 783-1206; e-mail webmaster@samchully.co.kr; internet www.samchully.co.kr; f. 1966; gas supply co for Seoul metropolitan area and Gyeonggi Prov; Pres. and CEO CHUNG SOON-WON.

Seoul City Gas Co: 281, Yeomchang-dong, Gangseo-gu, Seoul 157-864; tel. (2) 810-8000; fax (2) 828-6740; internet www.seoulgas.co.kr; f. 1983; distributes gas in Seoul and Gyeonggi Province; Chair. and CEO KIM YOUNG-MIN.

SK E & S: 99, Seorin-dong, Jongno-gu, Seoul; tel. (2) 2121-3114; fax (2) 2121-3198; internet www.skens.net; f. 1999; jt venture between SK Corpn and Enron Corpn (USA); supplies natural gas through various cos, incl.: Chongju City Gas, Chonnam City Gas, Chungnam City Gas, Iksan City Gas, Iksan Energy, Kangwon City Gas, Kumi City Gas and Pusan City Gas; Pres. and CEO MOON DUK-KYU.

Yesco Co Ltd: 249-8, Yongdap-dong, Sungdong-gu, Seoul; tel. (2) 1644-0303; fax (2) 3390-3117; e-mail webmaster@lsyesco.com; internet www.gaspia.com; f. 1981; fmrly Kukdong City Gas Co; part of the LS Group; supplies liquefied natural gas (LNG) to the Seoul metropolitan area; CEO and Pres. CHOI KYUNG-HOON.

Water

Korea Water Resources Corpn: 6-2, Yeonchuk-dong, Daedeok-gu, Daejeon; tel. (42) 629-3114; fax (42) 623-0963; e-mail mwshi@kwater.or.kr; internet www.kowaco.or.kr; CEO KIM KUEN-HO.

Office of Waterworks, Seoul Metropolitan Govt: 27-1 Hap-dong, Seodaemun-gu, Seoul; tel. (2) 390-7332; fax (2) 362-3653; internet arisu.seoul.go.kr; f. 1908; responsible for water supply in Seoul; Head SON JANG-HO.

Ulsan City Water and Sewerage Board: 646-4, Sin-Jung 1-dong, Nam-gu, Ulsan; tel. (52) 743-020; fax (52) 746-928; f. 1979; responsible for water supply and sewerage in Ulsan; Dir HO KUN-SONG.

CO-OPERATIVES

Korea Auto Industries Co-operative Association: 1638-3, Seocho-dong, Seocho-gu, Seoul 137-070; tel. (2) 587-0014; fax (2) 583-7340; e-mail kaica@kaica.or.kr; internet www.kaica.or.kr; f. 1962; Chair. SHIN DAL-CHUK.

Korea Computers Co-operative: 14-8, Yeouido-dong, Yeongdeungpo-gu, Seoul; tel. (2) 780-0511; fax (2) 780-7509; f. 1981; Pres. MIN KYUNG-HYUN.

Korea Federation of Knitting Industry Co-operatives: 586-1, Sinsa-dong, Gangnam-gu, Seoul; tel. (2) 548-2131; fax (2) 3444-9929; e-mail kts01@korea.com; internet www.knit.or.kr; f. 1962; Chair. JOUNG MAN-SUB.

Korea Federation of Non-ferrous Metal Industry Co-operatives: Backsang Bldg, Rm 715, 35-2, Yeouido-dong, Yeongdeungpo-gu, Seoul; tel. (2) 780-8551; fax (2) 784-9473; f. 1962; Chair. PARK WON-SIK.

Korea Federation of Plastic Industry Co-operatives: 146-2, Ssangrim-dong, Jung-gu, Seoul; tel. (2) 2280-8200; fax (2) 2277-3915; internet www.koreaplastic.or.kr; f. 1973.

Korea Federation of Small and Medium Business (Kbiz): 16-2, Yeouido-dong, Yeongdeungpo-gu, Seoul 150-740; tel. (2) 2124-3114; fax (2) 3775-1981; e-mail webmaster@kbiz.or.kr; internet www.kbiz.or.kr; f. 1962; Chair. KIM KI-MUN.

Korea Federation of Weaving Industry Co-operatives: tel. (2) 752-8097; fax (2) 755-6994; e-mail weaving3@hanmail.net; internet www.weaving.or.kr; f. 1964.

Korea Information and Communication Industry Co-operative: tel. (2) 711-2266; fax (2) 7111-2272; e-mail webmaster@kicic.or.kr; internet www.kicic.or.kr; f. 1962; CEO JOO DAE-CHULL.

Korea Metal Industry Co-operative: tel. (2) 780-4411; fax (2) 785-5067; e-mail master@koreametal.or.kr; internet www.koreametal.or.kr; f. 1962.

Korea Mining Industry Co-operative: 35-24, Dongui-dong, Jongno-gu, Seoul; tel. (2) 735-3490; fax (2) 735-4658; f. 1966; Chair. JEON HYANG-SIK.

Korea Steel Industry Co-operative: 915-14, Bangbae-dong, Seocho-gu, Seoul; tel. (2) 587-3121; fax (2) 588-3671; internet www.kosic.or.kr; f. 1962; Pres. KIM DUK-NAM.

National Agricultural Co-operative Federation (NACF): Saemunangil 91, Jung-gu, Seoul; tel. (2) 2080-5114; fax (2) 1544-2100; internet www.nonghyup.com; f. 1961; international banking, marketing, co-operative trade, utilization and processing, supply, co-operative insurance, banking and credit services, education and research; Chair. CHOI WUN-BYUNG.

National Federation of Fisheries Co-operatives: 11-6, Sincheon-dong, Songpa-gu, Seoul; tel. (2) 2240-2114; fax (2) 2240-3024; e-mail webmaster@suhyup.co.kr; internet www.suhyup.co.kr; f. 1962; CEO LEE JONG-KOO.

MAJOR COMPANIES

The following are some of South Korea's major industrial groups and companies, arranged by sector (cap. = capital; res = reserves; m. = million; amounts in won, unless otherwise indicated):

Major Industrial Groups (Chaebol)

Daelim Group: 146-12 Susong-dong, Jongno-gu, Seoul; tel. (2) 2011-7114; fax (2) 2011-8000; internet www.daelim.co.kr; cap. and res 2,537,000m. (2006), sales 6,275,000m. (2009); mfrs of construction materials, light industrial goods; Chair. and CEO YONG KOO-LEE.

Daewoo International Corpn: 84-11, 5-ga, Namdaemun-no, Jung-gu, Seoul 100-753; tel. (2) 759-2114; fax (2) 753-9489; internet www.daewoo.com; f. 1967; cap. and res 1,389,731m., sales 11,147,952m. (2008/09); steel, machinery, automotive components, electronics, textiles, chemicals, light industry, etc.; CEO LEE DONG HEE; 2,621 employees.

Dongbu Group: 21-9, Jeo-dong, Jung-gu, Seoul; tel. (2) 2279-9426; fax (2) 278-3615; internet www.dongbu.co.kr; f. 1969; mfrs of chemicals, semiconductors, steel and steel products; civil engineering and construction; insurance and asset management; sales US $157,004m. (2009); Chair. KIM JUN-KI.

Doosan Group: Doosan Tower, 18-12, 6-ga, Euljiro, Jung-gu, Seoul; tel. (2) 3398-0114; fax (2) 3398-1135; internet www.doosan.co.kr; cap. and res 18,156,000m., sales 11,616,000m. (2009); industrial machinery, construction, electro-materials, glass; Chair. Y. H. PARK; CEO YONGMAAN PARK.

GS Group (GS Holdings Corpn): GS Tower, 23rd Floor, 679 Yeoksam-dong, Gangnam-gu, Seoul; tel. (2) 2005-1114; fax (2) 2005-8181; internet www.gsholdings.com; f. 2004; est. after demerger of LG Corpn and GS in July 2004; cap. and res 4,082,060m., operating revenue 533,563.8m. (2009); Chair. HUH CHANG-SOO.

Hanjin Group: 51, Sogong-dong, Jung-gu, Seoul; tel. (2) 756-7739; fax (2) 757-7478; e-mail webmaster@hanjin.net; internet www.hanjin.net; f. 1945; transport, shipping, heavy industries; sales 185,228,000m. (2009); Chair. YANG HO-CHO; 25,666 employees.

Hanwha Group: 1, Janggyo-dong, Jung-gu, Seoul; tel. (2) 729-2700; fax (2) 729-3000; e-mail webmaster@hanwha.co.kr; internet www.hanwha.co.kr; f. 1952; chemicals; manufacturing and construction; finance; total assets US $70,693m., sales US $22,836m. (2009); Chair. KIM SEUNG-YOUN.

Hyosung Group: Gongdeok Bldg, 450 Gongdeok-dong, Mapo-gu, Seoul 121-020; tel. (822) 707-6228; fax (822) 707-6226; internet www.hyosung.co.kr; f. 1957; steel and metals, electronics, industrial equipment, chemicals, fabrics, leather goods; cap. and res 2,451,958m., sales 6,925,725m. (2008); Chair. CHO SOOK-RAE; Pres. CHO HYUN-JOON; 25,000 employees.

Hyundai Group: 140-2, Kye-dong, Jongno-gu, Seoul 110-793; tel. (2) 390-1114; e-mail jcyoon@hyundaicorp.com; internet www.hyundaicorp.com; f. 1953; electronics, construction, heavy industry, petrochemicals, automobile manufacture, finance and securities, etc.; cap. 146,692m., sales 2,577,549m. (2009); Chair. CHUNG MONG-HYUCK; Pres. and CEO KIM YOUNG-NAM; 180,000 employees.

Hyundai Asan: 12/F Hyundai Bldg, 140-2 Kye-dong, Jongno-gu, Seoul 110-790; tel. (2) 3669-3000; fax (2) 3669-3690; internet www.hyundai-asan.com; also offices in Kaesong and Mount Kumgang; f. 1999; subsidiary of Hyundai Group; est. as the group's inter-Korean business arm; organizes tours to Mount Kumgang in North Korea; manages the Kaesong Industrial Park; involved in construction work in North Korea, mainly in infrastructure projects; cap. and res 133,464m., sales 228,809m. (2008); Pres. and CEO CHANG KYUNG-CHAK.

Kolon Group: Kolon Tower, 1-23, Byulyang-dong, Kwacheon-city, Kyunggi-do; tel. (2) 311-8114; fax (2) 754-5314; internet www.ikolon.com; f. 1957; chemicals, construction, electric machinery; Jt Pres and CEO BAE YOUNG-HO, BAIK DUK-HYUN.

Kumho Asiana Group: Kumho Asiana Main Tower, 1-ga, Shinmun-no, Jongno-gu, Seoul; tel. (2) 6303-0114; fax (2) 6303-1679; e-mail webmaster@kumhoasiana.com; internet www.kumho.net;

construction, engineering, chemicals, textiles, finance and transport; revenue 20,775,400m. (2007); Chair. PARK SAM-KOO.

LG Corpn: 20, Yeouido-dong, Yeongdeungpo-gu, Seoul 100; tel. (2) 787-1114; fax (2) 785-7762; e-mail ir@lg.com; internet www.lg.co.kr; f. 1947; fmrly Lucky-Goldstar Group, renamed LG Group in 1995; est. after demerger of LG Group and Goldstar (GS Corpn) in July 2004; chemicals and energy, electronics and telecommunications, financial services, etc.; cap. and res 7,399,500m., sales 100,668,069m. (2009); 147 subsidiary cos; Chair. and CEO KOO BON-MOO; 186,000 employees.

Lotte Group: 23, 4-ga, Yangpyeong-dong, Yeongdeungpo-gu, Seoul; tel. (2) 670-6114; fax (2) 6672-6600; internet www.lotte.co.kr; f. 1967; cap. 8,183,553m., sales 9,768,132m. (2007); foods and beverages, distribution, tourism and leisure, chemicals, construction and machinery; Chair. and CEO SHIN DONG-BIN.

Samsung Group: Samsung Electronics Bldg, 1320-10, Seocho 2-dong, Seocho-gu, Seoul 137-857; tel. (2) 2255-0114; internet www.samsung.com/sec; f. 1945; electronics, service industries, financial services, etc.; sales 136,300,000m. (2009); Chair. LEE YOON-WOO; CEO CHOI GEE-SUNG; 263,000 employees.

SK Group: 99 Seorin-dong, Jongno-gu, Seoul 110-110; tel. (2) 2121-5114; fax (2) 2121-7004; e-mail info@sk.com; internet www.sk.co.kr; f. 1956; cap. and res 7,135,589m., sales 766,714m. (2009); engineering, electronics, petroleum and gas, industry; Chair. and CEO CHEY TAE-WON; Pres. and CEO KIM YOUNG-TAE; 25,000 employees.

Ssangyong Group: 24-1, 2-ga, Jeo-dong, Jung-gu, Seoul; tel. (2) 2270-5114; fax (2) 2275-7040; e-mail webadm@www.ssy.co.kr; internet www.ssangyong.co.kr; f. 1954; cap. and res 1,090,152m., sales 1,083,603m. (2009); cement, construction materials, iron and steel, electronic goods, machinery, chemicals, automobiles, garments, textiles, etc.; Chair. HONG SA-SEUNG; Pres. and CEO KIM YONG-SIK.

Cement

Asia Cement Manufacturing Co Ltd: 726, Yoksam-dong, Gangnam-gu, CPOB 5278, Seoul; tel. (2) 527-6400; fax (2) 527-6532; e-mail webmaster@asiacement.co.kr; internet www.asiacement.co.kr; f. 1957; manufactures and exports Portland cement, sulphate resistant cement, concrete; cap. and res 775,267m., sales 322,607m. (2009); Chair. LEE BYUNG-MOO; Pres. GOH GYU-HWAN; 480 employees.

Hanil Cement Co Ltd: 832-2, Yeoksam-dong, Gangnam-gu, Seoul; tel. (2) 531-7000; fax (2) 531-7115; internet www.hanilcement.co.kr; f. 1961; cap. and res 1,023,679m. (2007), sales 594,027m. (2008); Chair. HU JUNG-SUP; Pres. GI HO-HUH; 666 employees.

Hyundai Cement Co Ltd: 1424-2, Seocho-dong, Seocho-gu, Seoul; tel. (2) 520-2114; fax (2) 520-2118; internet www.hdcement.co.kr; f. 1970; cap. and res 304,685.7m., sales 595,740.1m. (2008); mfrs of Portland cement and various building materials; Pres. KIM KWANG-YONG; 918 employees.

Ssangyong Cement Industrial Co Ltd: 24-1, 2-ga, Jeo-dong, Jung-gu, Seoul 100-748; tel. (2) 2270-5114; fax (2) 2278-4205; e-mail youngmin0419@ssyc.co.kr; internet www.ssangyongcement.co.kr; f. 1962; cap. and res 2,161,727m., sales 1,083,603m. (2009); cement mfrs; mine excavating, exporting and importing, civil engineering; Chair. HONG SA-SEUNG; Pres. and CEO KIM YONG-SIK; 1,321 employees.

Tong Yang Cement Corpn: Alpha Bldg, 70, Seorin-dong, Jongno-gu, Seoul 110-110; tel. (2) 3770-3000; fax (2) 3770-3305; e-mail pr@tycement.co.kr; internet www.tycement.co.kr; f. 1957; mfrs of Portland cement and ready-mixed concrete; Chair. HYUN JAE-HYUN; Pres. JEON SANG-YIL; 1,040 employees.

Chemicals

Hanwha Chemical Corpn: Hanwha Bldg, 1, Changgyo-dong, Jung-gu, Seoul 100-797; tel. (2) 729-2700; fax (2) 729-2997; e-mail webhcc@hanwha.co.kr; internet hcc.hanwha.co.kr; f. 1974; fmrly Hanyang Chemical Corpn; now part of Hanwha Group; mfrs of dynamite and other industrial explosives, safety fuses, electric detonators, ammunition, precision machinery and chemicals; cap. and res 26,686,000m., sales 30,337,000m. (2009); CEO HONG KI-JOON; 2,033 employees.

Korea Kumho Petrochemical Co Ltd: Kumho Asiana Main Tower, 21st–24th Floors, 1157, 1-ga, Jongno-gu, Seoul 110-857; tel. (2) 399-7560; fax (2) 399-9248; e-mail webmaster@kkpc.com; internet www.kkpc.co.kr; f. 1976; cap. and res 535,110m., sales 2,801,662m. (2009); Chair. PARK CHAN-KOO; Pres LEE SUH-HYUNG, KIM SEONG-CHAE; 750 employees.

LG Chemical Ltd: LG Twin Towers, 20, Yeouido-dong, Yeongdeungpo-gu, Seoul 150-721; tel. (2) 3773-7223; fax (2) 3773-7899; e-mail chparkb@mail.lgchem.lg.co.kr; internet www.lgchem.co.kr; f. 1947; cap. and res 5,484,335m., sales 13,694,515m. (2009); subsidiary of LG Corpn; petrochemical products; Vice-Chair. and CEO PETER BAHNSUK KIM; 8,183 employees.

OCI Co Ltd: 50, Sogong-dong, Jung-gu, Seoul 100-718; tel. (2) 727-9500; fax (2) 756-9565; internet www.oci.co.kr; f. 1959; fmrly DC Chemical Co Ltd; renamed as above in 2009; production of basic chemicals, agrochemicals and fine chemicals; alsopolysilicon production and insulation business; cap. 1,672,000m., sales 2,728,000m. (2009); Chair. LEE SOO-YOUNG; Pres. and CEO BAIK WOO-SUNG; 2,487 employees.

Construction

Daewoo Engineering and Construction Co Ltd: Daewoo Center Bldg, 541, Namdaemun-no 5-ga, Jung-gu, Seoul 100-714; tel. (2) 2288-3114; fax (2) 2288-3113; e-mail webmaster@mail.dwconst.co.kr; internet www.dwconst.co.kr; f. 1973; construction projects; Pres. and CEO SEO JONG-UK; 3,050 employees.

Dong Ah Construction Industrial Co Ltd: Prime Center, 34th–36th Floors, Gu-ui-dong, Gwangjin-gu, Seoul; tel. (2) 3709-2114; fax (2) 3709-3801; e-mail webmaster@dongah.co.kr; internet www.dongah.co.kr; contracting, construction; cap. and res 522,470m., sales 216,739m. (2009); Pres. and CEO PARK SIK-YOUNG; 4,956 employees.

GS Engineering and Construction Corpn: GS Yeokjeon Tower, 537, 5-ga, Namdaemun-ro, Joong-gu, Seoul; tel. (2) 2005-1114; fax (2) 774-6610; e-mail ir@gsconst.co.kr; internet www.gsconst.co.kr; f. 1969; subsidiary of GS Holding Corpn; contracting, construction; fmrly LG Engineering and Construction Co Ltd, name changed as above in 2005, following demerger of LG Corpn and GS Corpn in 2004; sales 7,377,000m. (2009); Pres. and CEO HUH MYUNG-SOO.

Hanjin Heavy Industries and Construction Co Ltd: 168-23, Samsung-dong, Kangnam-gu, Seoul 135-090; tel. (2) 2006-7114; fax (2) 2006-7055; e-mail webmaster@hanjinsc.com; internet www.hanjinsc.com; f. 1967; cap. and res 2,104,845m., sales 3,848,033m. (2008); construction, electrical work, mining, gas and petroleum transport; Chair. N. H. CHO; 5,295 employees.

Hyundai Engineering & Construction Co Ltd: 140-2, Kye-dong, Chongro-ku, Seoul; tel. (2) 746-1114; fax (2) 743-8963; internet www.hdec.co.kr; f. 1947; merged with LG Semicon in 1999; cap. and res 3,025,699m., revenue 9,278,579m. (2009); engineering, manufacture and supply of civil, architectural and industrial plants and electrical works; Pres. JUNG SOO-HYUN; 4,500 employees.

Samsung C&T Engineering and Construction Group: 1321-20 Samsung Corporation Bldg, 21st Floor, Seocho 2-dong, Seocho-Gu, Seoul 137-857; tel. (2) 2145-6338; fax (2) 2145-6343; e-mail kd78.park@samsung.com; internet www.secc.co.kr; f. 1938; total assets 11,274,200m., sales 11,811,600m. (2008); construction projects; Chair. and CEO JUNG YEON-JOO; 5,600 employees.

Electrical and Electronics

Anam Electronics Co Ltd: 645 Seonggok-dong, Danwon-gu, Ansan-si, Gyeonggi-do, Korea; tel. (2) 490-2000; fax (2) 460-5393; e-mail mdc_sales@aname.co.kr; internet www.aname.co.kr; f. 1973; cap. and res 45,073m., sales 118,152m. (2009); electronics; CEO CHOI SUNG YEO; 1,714 employees.

Daewoo Electronics Co Ltd: 541, Daewoo Center Bldg, Namdaemun-no 5-ga, Jung-gu, Seoul; tel. (2) 360-7114; fax (2) 360-7700; internet www.dwe.co.kr; f. 1972; mfrs of computers, TV, hi-fi, microwave ovens, refrigerators and other consumer electronic components; Pres. and CEO LEE SUNG; 8,700 employees.

Hynix Semiconductor Inc: San 136-1, Ami-ri, Pubal-up, Ichon-shi, Gyeonggi; tel. (336) 630-4114; fax (336) 630-4103; internet www.hynix.com; f. 1949; fmrly Hyundai Electronics Industrial Co Ltd, merged with LG Semiconductor in 1999; cap. and res. 5,919,278m, sales 7,906,350m. (2009); mfr of electronic equipment for industries; Chair. and CEO KIM JONG-KAP; Pres. KWAN OH-CHUL; 14,000 employees.

LG Electronics Inc: LG Twin Towers, 20, Yeouido-dong, Yeongdeungpo-gu, Seoul 150-721; tel. (2) 3777-1114; fax (2) 3777-3428; internet www.lge.co.kr; f. 1958; mfrs and exporters of electric and electronic products, incl. computers and communications equipment; merged with LG Information and Communications in 2000, subsidiary of LG Corpn; CEO KOO BON-JOON; 66,614 employees.

Samsung Electro-Mechanics Co Ltd: Samsung Seocho Tower, 21st Floor, 1320-10, Seocho 2-dong, Seocho-ku, Seoul; tel. (31) 210-5114; fax (31) 210-6363; internet www.sem.samsung.co.kr; f. 1973; cap. and res 3,880,000m., sales 26,904,000m. (2007); mfr of electronic components; Pres. and CEO PARK JONG-WOO; 8,500 employees.

Samsung Electronics Co Ltd: 11/F Samsung Main Bldg, 250, Taepyeong-no 2-ga, Jung-gu, Seoul; tel. (2) 727-7114; fax (2) 727-7892; internet www.samsungelectronics.com; f. 1969; sales US $105,206.4m. (2007); world's largest producer of dynamic random access memory (DRAM) semiconductor chips; mfrs of wide range of electronic goods, incl. TVs, washing machines, hi-fi, refrigerators and industrial electronic equipment; Chair. LEE KUN-HEE; CEO LEE YOON-WOO; 254,000 employees.

Samsung SDI Co Ltd: 428-5, Gongse-dong, Giheung-gu, Yongin, Gyeonggi-do; tel. (31) 8006-3100; fax (31) 210-7887; internet www .samsungsdi.co.kr; mfr of colour television tubes; cap. and res 5,270,800m., sales 4,950,400m. (2009); Chair. LEE KUN-HEE; Pres. and CEO PARK SANG-JIN; 8,207 employees.

Samsung Techwin Co Ltd: 701 Sampyeong-dong, Bundang-gu, Seongnam-si, Gyeonggi-do 463-400; tel. (70) 7147-6315; fax (70) 740-3737; e-mail webmaster@samsungtechwin.co.kr; internet www .samsung-smt.com; fmrly Samsung Aerospace Industries; mfrs of aerospace parts, semiconductors, industrial robots, optical and defence-related products; Pres. and CEO KIM CHEOL-GYO.

Engineering

Doosan Heavy Industries and Construction: 1303-22 Seocho-dong, Seocho-gu, Seoul 137-920; tel. (2) 513-6114; fax (2) 513-6200; internet www.doosanheavy.com; f. 1962; cap. and res 3,319,500m., sales 6,279,500m. (2009); merged with Daewoo Heavy Industries & Machinery (DHIM) in 2005; builds nuclear, thermal, combined cycle and hydro power plants; Chair. Y. S. PARK; Pres. and CEO PARK GEE-WON.

Hyundai Heavy Industries Co Ltd: 1, Jeonha-dong, Dong-gu, Ulsan-shi, Gyeonsang nam-do; tel. (52) 202-2114; fax (52) 202-3470; e-mail ir@hhi.co.kr; internet www.hhi.co.kr; f. 1973; cap. and res 9,808,401m., sales 21,142,197m. (2009); industrial and offshore construction and engineering, shipbuilding; Chair. and CEO MIN KEH-SIK; Pres. and CEO LEE JAI-SEONG; 24,180 employees.

Hyundai Mobis Co Ltd: 135-977 ING Tower, 679-4, Yeoksam-1-dong, Gangnam-gu, Seoul; tel. (2) 2018-5114; fax (2) 741-4244; internet www.mobis.co.kr; f. 1977; cap. and res 7,850,128m., sales 10,633,020m. (2009); largest container producer in the world; also manufactures heavy machinery, rolling stock, machine tools; Vice-Chair. and CEO CHUNG SUK-SOO; 6,129 employees.

Samsung Heavy Industries Co Ltd: Samsung Life Insurance Seocho Tower, 1321-15, Seocho-dong, Seocho-gu, Seoul; tel. (2) 3458-7000; fax (2) 3458-6501; e-mail isnam@samsung.co.kr; internet www .shi.samsung.co.kr; f. 1974; sales 13,094,944m. (2009); shipbuilding, industrial and construction equipment; Pres. and CEO ROH IN-SIK; 12,760 employees.

Iron and Steel

Dongkuk Steel Mill Co Ltd: Union Steel Bldg, 412 Teherallo, Gangnam-gu, Seoul; tel. (2) 317-1114; fax (2) 317-1391; internet www .dongkuk.co.kr; f. 1954; cap. and res 2,802,917m., sales 4,565,157m. (2009); iron and steel mfrs; Pres. and CEO KIM YOUNG-CHUL; 1,599 employees.

Hyundai Steel Co Ltd: 231, Yangjae-dong, Seocho-gu, Seoul; tel. (2) 3464-6114; fax (2) 3464-6090; internet www.hyundai-steel.com; f. 1953; fmrly INI Steel and previously Inchon Iron and Steel Co Ltd; cap. and res 6,606,464m., sales 7,966,444m. (2009); mfrs of iron and steel products; CEO PARK SEUNG-HA; 4,499 employees.

Pohang Iron & Steel Co (POSCO) Ltd: 1, Goedong-dong, Pohang-shi, Gyeongbuk; tel. (562) 220-0114; fax (562) 220-6000; internet www.posco.co.kr; f. 1968; state-owned; proposed transfer to private-sector ownership announced in July 1998; cap. and res 30,951,291m., sales 26,953,945m. (2008); mfr of steel and steel products; Chair. CHUNG JOON-YANG; Pres. LEE DONG-HEE; 19,012 employees.

Sammi Steel Co Ltd: 5F, Ildong Bldg, 968-5 Daechi 3-dong, Gangnam-gu, Seoul; tel. (2) 2222-4114; fax (2) 538-3806; e-mail webmaster@sammi.co.kr; internet www.sammi.co.kr; f. 1966; mfr of steel products; Chair. and CEO PARK WON-YANG; Pres. KIM YOUNG-HUN; 3,321 employees.

Motor Vehicles

GM Daewoo Motor Co Ltd: 426-1 Chongchon-dong, Bupyeong-gu, Incheon; tel. (32) 510-4114; fax (32) 520-4606; e-mail webmaster@dm .co.kr; internet www.dm.co.kr; f. 1972; absorbed by General Motors (USA) in April 2002; mfr of buses, passenger cars, heavy-duty trucks; sales 2,685,608m. (2009); Pres. and CEO LEE DONG-HO; 13,555 employees.

Hyundai Motor Co Ltd: 231, Yangjae-dong, Seocho-gu, Seoul; tel. (2) 3464-1114; fax (2) 3464-3453; internet worldwide.hyundai.com; f. 1967; cap. and res 22,029,023m., sales 31,859,327m. (2009); mfrs and assemblers of passenger cars, trucks, buses, etc.; Chair. CHUNG MONG-KOO; Pres. SEUNG SUK-YANG; 48,831 employees.

Renault Samsung Motors: 25, 1-ga, Bongrae-dong, Jung-gu, Seoul; tel. (2) 3707-5000; fax (2) 3707-5369; internet www .renaultsamsungm.com; f. 2000; mfr of passenger cars; CEO FRANCOIS PROVOST; 5,548 employees.

Ssangyong Motor Co Ltd: 150-3, Chilgoe-dong, Pyeongtaek-shi, Gyeonggi-do; tel. (31) 610-1114; fax (31) 610-3700; internet www .smotor.com; f. 1954; mfrs of passenger cars, minibuses and special-purpose vehicles; cap. and res 257,869.9m., sales 2,495,216m. (2008); 48.9% stake acquired by Shanghai Automotive in Oct. 2004; CEO CHOI HYUNG-TAK; 6,126 employees.

Textiles, Silk and Synthetic Fibres

Cheil Industries Inc: 290, Kandan-dong, Gumi-shi, Gyeongbuk; tel. (54) 468-2811; fax (54) 468-2821; e-mail ciidesk@samsung.co.kr; internet www.cii.samsung.com; f. 1954; owned by Samsung Corpn; mfrs of clothing, textiles and petrochemical products; cap. and res 19,695,000m., sales 42,611,000m. (2009); Pres. and CEO HWANG BAEK; 1,800 employees.

Hanil Synthetic Fiber Co Ltd: Hans Tower, 5th Floor, 46-5, Guro-dong, Guro-gu, Seoul; tel. (2) 791-1114; fax (2) 791-1200; e-mail webmaster@hanisf.com; internet www.hanilsf.co.kr; f. 1964; mfrs and exporters of synthetic fibre; part of Tong Yang Group; Pres. SON BYUNG-SUK; 1,000 employees.

Ilshin Spinning Co Ltd: 15-15, Yeouido-dong, Yeongdeungpo-gu, Seoul; tel. (2) 3774-0114; fax (2) 786-5893; internet www.ilshin.co.kr; f. 1951; cap. and res 408,539.7m., sales 362,778.8m. (2008); cotton spinning and production of yarn and fabrics; one subsidiary with dyeing and finishing factories; import and export; Chair. KIM YOUNG-HO; 1,120 employees.

Taekwang Industries: 162-1, Jangchung-dong, Jung-gu, Seoul; tel. (2) 3406-0300; fax (2) 2273-9160; internet www.taekwang.co.kr; f. 1954; miscellaneous household goods and textiles; cap. and res 1,680,623m., sales 1,963,651m. (2009); Pres. OH YONG-IL; 6,499 employees.

Miscellaneous

Daelim Industrial Co Ltd: 146-12 Susong-dong, Jongno-gu, Seoul; tel. (2) 2011-7114; fax (2) 2011-8000; internet www.daelim.co.kr; f. 1939; cap. and res 3,794,079m., sales 6,275,000m. (2009); general contractor for all construction fields, engineering and petrochemical producer; Chair. LEE YONG-KU; 2,500 employees.

Hankuk Glass Industry Co Ltd: Youngpoong Bldg, 15th Floor, 33 Seorin-dong, Jongno-gu, Seoul 110-752; tel. (2) 3706-9114; fax (2) 778-4678; e-mail ehjang@hanglas.co.kr; internet www.hanglas.co .kr; f. 1957; cap. and res 561,156m., sales 292,656m. (2008); mfrs of flat glass, figured glass and tube glass; one subsidiary; Pres. KIM SUNG-MAN; 830 employees.

Korea Coal Corpn: CRC Bldg, 501-1 Uijeongbu 2-dong, Uijeongbu-si, Gyeonggi-do, Seoul 480-848; tel. (31) 826-0600; fax (31) 871-0548; e-mail webmaster@kocoal.or.kr; internet www.kocoal.or.kr; f. 1950; operation and development of coal mines, and related research, sales, import, export, etc.; Pres. LEE KANG-HOO; 2,007 employees.

Korea Land and Housing Corpn: 94 Dolmaro, 217 Jungja-dong, Bundang-gu, Seongnam-shi, Gyeonggi-do 463-755; tel. (31) 738-7114; internet www.lh.or.kr; f. 1962; housing business; fmrly Korea National Housing Corpn; merged with Korea Land Corpn and renamed as above in 2009; cap. and res 20,828,171.7m., revenue 6,662,588.7m. (2009); CEO LEE JI-SONG; 5,600 employees.

Korea Tobacco and Ginseng Corpn: 100 Pyong chon-dong, Daedeog-gu, Daejeon; tel. (2) 3404-4522; fax (2) 3404-4515; e-mail paulkim@ktng.com; internet www.ktng.com/eng; cap. and res 3,852,900m., sales 2,776,400m. (2009); mfr of cigarettes, tobacco, and ginseng products; Pres. and CEO MIN YOUNG-JIN; 4,430 employees.

Shinsegae Co Ltd: 52-5, 1-ga, Jungmu-no, Jung-gu, Seoul 100-747; tel. (2) 727-1234; fax (2) 727-1880; internet www.shinsegae.com; retailing and department stores; cap. and res 3,853,085.2m. (2008), sales 10,415,933m. (2009); Chair. and CEO LEE MYEONG-HUI; 12,893 employees.

SK Energy: 99 Seorin-dong, Jongno-gu, Seoul 110-110; tel. (2) 2121-5114; fax (2) 2121-7001; internet www.skcorp.com; f. 1962; fmrly Yukong Ltd; holding co; production and marketing of petroleum, petrochemical and lubricating oil products; cap. and res 7,745,000m., sales 35,828,000m. (2009); Chair. and CEO CHEY TAE-WON; 4,541 employees.

SK Networks Co Ltd: 199-15, Euljiro-2 Ga, Jung-gu, Seoul 100-192; tel. (70) 7800-0393; fax (2) 754-9414; e-mail webmaster@ sknetworks.co.kr; internet www.sknetworks.com; f. 1953; fmrly Sunkyong Ltd and previously SK Global; cap. and res 3,071,275m., sales 21,190,407m. (2009); provision of services to various sectors, incl. energy, chemicals, telecommunications, engineering and construction; CEO LEE CHANG-KYU; 2,485 employees.

S-Oil Corpn: Yeouido POB 758, 63, Yeouido-dong, Yeongdeungpo-gu, Seoul 150-607; tel. (2) 3772-5151; fax (2) 786-4031; internet www .s-oil.com; oil refining and production of petrochemicals and lubricants; cap. and res 3,919,000m., sales 17,424,000m. (2009); CEO AHMED A. SUBAEY.

Whashin Industrial Co Ltd: 360-1, Magok-dong, Gangseo-gu, Seoul 157-210; tel. (2) 3661-5331; fax (2) 3661-5347; e-mail whashin@whashin.com; internet www.whashin.com; f. 1962; exporters, importers, domestic sales of stationery, textiles, electrical consumer products, commercial air-conditioning equipment and other merchandise; 8 subsidiaries; Pres. and CEO AHN TAE-RANG; 2,000 employees.

TRADE UNIONS

Federation of Korean Trade Unions (FKTU): 35, Yeouido-dong, Yeongdeungpo-gu, Seoul 150-885; tel. (2) 6277-0026; fax (2) 6277-0068; e-mail fktu@fktu.or.kr; internet www.fktu.or.kr; f. 1941; Pres. LEE YONG-DEUK; affiliated to ITUC; 26 union federations are affiliated, including:.

Federation of Korean Chemical Workers' Unions: FKTU Bldg 802, 35, Yeouido-dong, Yeongdeungpo-gu, Seoul 150-980; tel. (2) 6277-1234; fax (2) 6277-1235; e-mail fkcu@chollian.net; internet www.fkcu.or.kr; f. 1959; Pres. HAN KWANG-HO; 116,286 mems.

Federation of Korean Metal Workers Trade Unions: 208 Samsung IT Valley, 197-5, Guro-dong, Guro-gu, Seoul; tel. (2) 2028-1260; fax (2) 2028-1273; e-mail dykim@metall.or.kr; internet www.metall.or.kr; f. 1961; Pres. JANG SOEK-CHUN; 130,000 mems.

Federation of Korean Seafarers' Unions: 544, Donhwa-dong, Mapo-gu, Seoul; tel. (2) 716-2764; fax (2) 702-2271; e-mail zzoinn@naver.com; internet www.fksu.or.kr; f. 1961; Pres. BANG DONG-SIK; 60,037 mems.

Federation of Korean State-invested Corporation Unions: Sunwoo Bldg, 501, 350-8, Yangjae-dong, Seocho-gu, Seoul; tel. (2) 529-2268; fax (2) 529-2270; internet public.inochong.org; f. 1998; Pres. JANG DAE-IK; 19,375 mems.

Federation of Korean Taxi & Transport Workers' Unions: 415-7, Janan 1-dong, Dongdaemun-gu, Seoul; tel. (3) 633-0099; fax (3) 638-0090; internet www.ktaxi.or.kr; f. 1988; Pres. KWAN OH-MAN; 105,118 mems.

Korea Automobile & Transport Workers' Federation: 4-2, Yangjae 1-dong, Seocho-gu, Seoul 137-886; tel. (2) 554-0890; f. 1963; Pres. KANG SUNG-CHUN; 84,343 mems.

Korea Federation of Communication Trade Unions: 10th Floor, 106-6, Guro 5-dong, Guro-gu, Seoul; tel. (2) 864-0055; fax (2) 864-5519; f. 1961; Pres. OH DONG-IN; 18,810 mems.

Korea Federation of Food Industry Workers' Unions: 7-57, Yeongdeungpo-dong, Yeongdeungpo-gu, Seoul; tel. (2) 2679-6441; fax (2) 2679-6444; e-mail hpunion@hanmir.com; internet food.inochong.org; f. 2000; Pres. BAEK YOUNG-GIL; 19,146 mems.

Korea Federation of Port & Transport Workers' Unions: 19th Floor, Pyouk-San Bldg, 12-5 Dongja-dong, Yeongsan-gu, Seoul; tel. (2) 727-4741; fax (2) 727-4749; e-mail kfptwu@chollian.net; f. 1980; Pres. CHOI BONG-HONG; 33,347 mems.

Korea National Electrical Workers' Union: 167, Samseong-dong, Gangnam-gu, Seoul; tel. (2) 3456-6017; fax (2) 3456-6004; internet www.knewu.or.kr; f. 1961; Pres. KIM JU-YOUNG; 16,741 mems.

Korea Tobacco & Ginseng Workers' Unions: 100, Pyeong-chon-dong, Daedeok-gu, Daejeon; tel. (42) 939-6884; fax (42) 939-6891; e-mail ktgson35@ktng.com; internet tobac.inochong.org; f. 1960; Pres. KANG TAE-HEUNG; 6,008 mems.

Korea Union of Teaching and Education Workers: tel. (2) 720-5334; fax (2) 720-5336; e-mail leemo@korea.com; internet www.kute.or.kr; f. 1999; 18,337 mems.

Korean Financial Industry Union: Dong-A Bldg, 9/F, 88, Da-dong, Chung-gu, Seoul; tel. (2) 2095-0000; fax (2) 2095-0018; e-mail accuchung@hanmail.net; internet www.kfiu.org; f. 1960; Pres. KIM MOON-HO.

Korean Government Employees' Union (KGEU): Rm 202, Hyundai Plaza Bldg, 49-1, 5-ga, Yeongdeungpo-gu, Seoul 150-986; tel. (70) 7728-4728; fax (2) 2631-1949; e-mail kgeu.inter@gmail.com; internet inter.kgeu.org; f. 2009; est. following merger of Fed. of Govt Employees' Union, United Municipal Education Civil Servants' Union and Fed. of Local Govt Employees' Union; Pres. YANG SUNG-YUN.

Korean Postal Workers' Union: 154-1, Seorin-dong, Jongno-gu, Seoul 110-110; tel. (2) 2195-1773; fax (2) 2195-1761; e-mail cheshin@chol.com; internet www.kpwu.or.kr; f. 1958; Pres. JUNG HYUN-YOUNG; 23,500 mems.

Korean Railway Workers' Union (KRWU): 40-504, 3-ga, Hangang-no, Yeongsan-gu, Seoul; tel. (2) 797-1126; fax (2) 790-2598; internet www.krwu.or.kr; f. 1947; Pres. KIM KI-TAE; 31,041 mems.

Korean Tourist Industry Workers' Federation: 749, 5-ga, Namdaemun-no, Jung-gu, Seoul 100-095; tel. (2) 779-1297; fax (2) 779-1298; f. 1970; Pres. JEONG YOUNG-KI; 27,273 mems.

Korean Confederation of Trade Unions: 5th Daeyoung Bldg, 139, 2-ga, Yeouido-dong, Yeongdeungpo-gu, Seoul 150-032; tel. (2) 2670-9234; fax (2) 2635-1134; internet www.kctu.org; f. 1995; legalized 1999; Chair. KIM YOUNG-HOON; 600,000 mems.

Transport

RAILWAYS

In 2008 there were 3,381 km of railways in operation. The first phase of construction of a new high-speed rail system connecting Seoul to Busan (412 km) via Cheonan, Daejeon, Daegu, and Gyungju, was completed in early 2004. The second phase, Daejeon–Busan, became operational in November 2010.

Korean National Railroad (Korail): 293-74 Soje-dong, Dong-gu, Daejeon 300-720; tel. (42) 472-3014; fax (42) 259-2197; e-mail admin@korail.com; internet www.korail.com; f. 1963; operates all railways under the supervision of the Ministry of Land, Transport and Maritime Affairs; Pres. and CEO HUH JOON-YOUNG.

City Underground Railways

Busan Subway: Gyotonggongsa 1-ro, Busanjin-gu, Busan 614-722; tel. (51) 640-7186; fax (51) 640-7010; e-mail ipsubway@buta.or.kr; internet www.subway.busan.kr; f. 1988; length of 71.6 km (2 lines, with a further line under construction); Pres. AN JUN-TAE.

Daegu Metropolitan Transit Corpn: 1500, Sangin 1-dong, Dal-seo-gu, Daegu 704-808; tel. (53) 643-2114; fax (53) 640-2189; e-mail webmaster@daegusubway.co.kr; internet www.dtro.or.kr; length of 28.3 km (one line, with a further five routes totalling 125.4 km planned or under construction); CEO BAE SANG-MIN.

Daejeon Metropolitan Express Transit Corpn: tel. (42) 539-3114; fax (42) 539-3119; e-mail qnsdlqkr@hanmail.net; internet www.djet.co.kr; f. 2006; operates one line, with a further four lines planned.

Gwangju Metropolitan Rapid Transit Corpn: 529, Sangmu-no, Seo-gu, Gwangju 502-750; tel. (62) 604-8000; fax (62) 604-8069; internet www.gwangjusubway.co.kr; f. 2004; one line, with a further line planned; Pres. OH HAENG-WON.

Incheon Rapid Transit Corpn: 67-2, Gansok-dong, Namdong-gu, Incheon 405-233; tel. (32) 451-2290; fax (32) 451-2160; e-mail sehong4450@gmail.com; internet www.irtc.co.kr; length of 31.1 km (29 stations, 1 line), with two further lines planned; Pres. LEE KWANG-YUONG.

Seoul Metropolitan Rapid Transit Corporation: 133-783, Seongdong-gu, Yongdap-dong 223-3, Seoul; tel. (2) 6311-2200; e-mail eumsj@smrt.co.kr; internet www.smrt.co.kr; operates lines 5–8; Pres. EUM SEONG-JIK.

Seoul Metropolitan Subway Corpn: 447-7, Bangbae-dong, Seo-cho-gu, Seoul; tel. (2) 520-5020; fax (2) 520-5039; internet www.seoulsubway.co.kr; f. 1981; length of 134.9 km (115 stations, lines 1–4); Pres. KIM YOUNG-KEOL.

ROADS

At the end of 2006 there were 102,062 km of roads. A network of motorways (3,103 km) links all the principal towns, the most important being the 428-km Seoul–Busan motorway. Improvements in relations with North Korea resulted in the commencement of work on a four-lane highway to link Seoul and the North Korean capital, Pyongyang, in September 2000. In February 2003 a road link between the two countries was reportedly opened.

Korea Expressway Corpn: 293-1, Kumto-dong, Sujong-gu, Seong-nam, Gyeonggi-do 461-703; tel. (822) 2230-4114; fax (822) 2230-4308; internet www.freeway.co.kr; f. 1969; responsible for construction, maintenance and management of toll roads; Pres. LIEU CHULLHO.

SHIPPING

In December 2009 South Korea's merchant fleet (3,009 vessels) had a total displacement of 12.8m. grt. Major ports include Busan, Incheon, Donghae, Masan, Yeosu, Gunsan, Mokpo, Pohang, Ulsan, Jeju and Gwangyang.

Busan Port Authority: 79-9, Jungangdong 4-ga, Junggu, Busan 600-817; tel. (2) 999-3000; fax (2) 988-8878; e-mail bpmaster@busanpa.com; internet www.busanpa.com; f. 2004; Pres. KI TAE-ROH.

Korea Shipowners' Association: Sejong Bldg, 10th Floor, 100, Dangju-dong, Jongro-gu, Seoul 110-071; tel. (2) 739-1551; fax (2) 739-1558; e-mail korea@shipowners.or.kr; internet www.shipowners.or.kr; f. 1960; 181 shipping co mems (March 2011); Chair. LEE JONG-CHUL.

Korea Shipping Association: 660-10, Dungchon 3-dong, Gangseo-gu, Seoul 157-033; tel. (2) 6096-2000; fax (2) 6096-2059; e-mail kimny@haewoon.co.kr; internet www.haewoon.co.kr; f. 1962; management consulting and investigation, mutual insurance; 1,189 mems; Chair. PARK HONG-JIN; CEO JUNG YOU-SUB.

Principal Companies

DooYang Line Co Ltd: 170-8, Samseong-dong, Gangnam-gu, Seoul 135-091; tel. (2) 569-7722; fax (2) 550-1777; internet www.dooyang.co.kr; f. 1984; world-wide tramping and conventional liner trade; Pres. CHO DONG-HYUN.

Hanjin Shipping Ltd: 25-11, Yeouido-dong, Yeongdeungpo-gu, Seoul; tel. (2) 3770-6114; fax (2) 3770-6748; e-mail micaela@hanjin.com; internet www.hanjin.com; f. 1977; marine transport, harbour service, warehousing, shipping and repair, vessel sales, harbour department and cargo service; Chair. and CEO CHOI EUN-YOUNG.

Hyundai Merchant Marine Co Ltd: 1-7, Yeonje-dong, Jongno-gu, Seoul 110-052; tel. (2) 3706-5114; fax (2) 778-4341; internet www.hmm.co.kr; f. 1976; Pres. and CEO KIM SEONG-MAN.

Korea Line Corpn: 135-878 KLC Bldg, 145-9, Samseong-dong, Gangnam-gu, Seoul; tel. (2) 3701-0114; fax (2) 733-1610; internet www.korealines.co.kr; f. 1968; world-wide transport service and shipping agency service; Pres. KIM CHANG-SHIK.

STX Pan Ocean Co Ltd: STX Namsan Tower, 631 Namdaemunno 5-ga, Jung-nu, Seoul; tel. (2) 316-5114; fax (2) 316-5296; e-mail panocean@stxpanocean.com; internet www.stxpanocean.co.kr; f. 1966; transport of passenger cars and trucks, chemical and petroleum products, dry bulk cargo; STX Shipbuilding Co Ltd became the majority shareholder in 2004; Chair. KANG DUK-SOO.

CIVIL AVIATION

There are international airports at Incheon (Seoul), Gimpo (Seoul), Busan, Jeongju, Daegu, Gwangju, Jeju and Yangyang. The main gateway into Seoul is Incheon International Airport, located 52 km from Seoul, which opened for service in 2001. The second phase of construction was completed in mid-2008.

Asiana Airlines Inc: 47, Osae-dong, Gangseo-gu, Seoul; tel. (2) 2669-8000; fax (2) 2669-8180; internet flyasiana.com; f. 1988; serves 12 domestic cities and 67 destinations in 20 countries; fmrly Seoul Air International; CEO YOON YOUNG-DOO.

Hansung Airlines: Jeongju; tel. (43) 1599-1090; fax (43) 210-0520; internet www.gohansung.com; f. 2004; operates low-cost flights between Jeongju and Jeju City; CEO HAN WOO-BONG.

Jeju Air: tel. (64) 746-7003; fax (64) 746-7011; internet www.jejuair.net; f. 2005; 25% owned by Jeju provincial govt, 75% by the Aekyung Group; operates low-cost flights between Jeju and the mainland; CEO KIM JONG-CHUL.

Jin Air Co Ltd: 653-25 Deungchon-dong, Gangseo-gu, Seoul; internet www.jinair.com; f. 2008; low-cost subsidiary of Korean Air; CEO KIM JAE-KUN.

Korean Air: 1370, Gonghang-dong, Gangseo-gu, Seoul 157-712; tel. (2) 2656-7857; fax (2) 656-7289; internet www.koreanair.com; f. 1962; est. by the Govt, privately owned since 1969; fmrly Korean Air Lines (KAL); operates domestic and regional services and routes to the Americas, Europe, the Far East and the Middle East, serving 116 cities in 39 countries; Chair. and CEO CHO YANG-HO.

Tourism

South Korea's mountain scenery and historic sites are the principal attractions for tourists. Jeju Island, located some 100 km off the southern coast, is a popular resort. In comparison with the previous year, the number of visitor arrivals reportedly increased by 12.5% in 2010, to reach nearly 8.8m. Japan and the People's Republic of China are the leading sources of visitors. Receipts from tourism in 2008 amounted to US $12,783m.

Korea Tourism Organization: KTO Bldg, 40, Cheonggyecheon-ro, Jung-gu, Seoul 100-180; tel. (2) 729-9600; fax (2) 757-5997; e-mail webmaster@mail.knto.or.kr; internet kto.visitkorea.or.kr; f. 1962; est. as International Tourism Corpn; name changed to Korea National Tourism Corpn in 1982 and to Korea National Tourism Organization in 1996, before present name was adopted; Chair. and CEO LEE CHARM.

Korea Tourism Association: KTO Bldg, 8th Floor, 40, Cheonggyecheon-ro, Jung-gu, Seoul 100-180; tel. (2) 757-7485; fax (2) 757-7489; internet www.koreatravel.or.kr; f. 1963; Chair. SHIN JOONG-MOK.

Defence

As assessed at November 2010, the strength of the active armed forces was 655,000 (including an estimated 140,000 conscripts): army 522,000, navy 68,000, air force 65,000. Paramilitary forces included a 3m.-strong civilian defence corps. Military service is compulsory and lasts for 26 months. In November 2010 US forces stationed in South Korea comprised 17,130 army personnel, 254 navy, 7,857 air force and 133 marines.

Defence Expenditure: Budgeted at 25,600,000m. won for 2011.

Chairman of the Joint Chiefs of Staff: Gen. HAN MIN-KOO.

Chief of Staff (Army): Gen. KIM SANG-KI.

Chief of Staff (Air Force): Gen. PARK JONG-HEON.

Chief of Naval Operations: Adm. KIM SUNG-CHAN.

Education

Education, available free of charge, is compulsory for nine years between the ages of six and 15 years. Primary education begins at six years of age and lasts for six years. In 2007/08 enrolment at primary schools included 99% of children in the appropriate age-group. Secondary education begins at 12 years of age and lasts for up to six years, comprising two cycles of three years each. Enrolment at secondary schools in 2007/08 included 95% of children in the relevant age group. In 2006 school pupils were granted two Saturdays off school every month; previously, they had attended school six days every week. The Government was reportedly planning the introduction of a five-day school week in 2007. In 2007 there were 175 colleges and universities, with a student enrolment of 1,919,504. There were 1,042 graduate schools in that year. In 2001, according to UNESCO estimates, the rate of adult literacy averaged 97.9% (males 99.2%, females 96.6%). Expenditure on education by the central Government in 2007 was projected at 30,395,000m. won, representing 19.7% of total projected spending.

Bibliography of the Democratic People's Republic of Korea and the Republic of Korea

(See also The Korean Peninsula in Part One)

General

Ahn Byong-Man. *Elites and Political Power in South Korea.* Cheltenham, Edward Elgar Publishing, 2003.

Akaha, Tsuneo (Ed.). *The Future of North Korea.* London, Routledge, 2002.

Armstrong, Charles K. *Korean Society: Civil Society, Democracy, and the State.* London, Routledge, 2002.

Becker, Jasper. *Rogue Regime: Kim Jong Il and the Looming Threat of North Korea.* New York, Oxford University Press, 2005.

Bermudez, Joseph S., Jr. *The Armed Forces of North Korea.* London and New York, I. B. Tauris, 2001.

Bluth, Christoph. *Crisis on the Korean Peninsula.* Dulles, VA, Potomac Books Inc, 2011.

Breen, Michael. *The Koreans: Who They Are, What They Want, Where Their Future Lies.* London, Orion, Revised Edn, 2004.

Kim Jong-Il: North Korea's Dear Leader. Hoboken, NJ, John Wiley & Sons, 2004.

Cha, Victor, and Kang, David. *Nuclear North Korea—A Debate on Engagement Strategies.* Irvington, NY, Columbia University Press, 2003.

Approaching Korean Unification: What We Learn from Other Cases. Washington, DC, Center for Strategic and International Studies (CSIS), 2010.

Chamberlain, Paul F., and Kim, Kihwan. *Korea 2010: The Challenges of the New Millennium.* Washington, DC, Center for Strategic and International Studies, 2001.

Chang, Gordon G. *Nuclear Showdown: North Korea Takes on the World.* Random House, 2006.

Chang, Kyung-Sup. *South Korea under Compressed Modernity: Familial Political Economy in Transition.* Abingdon, Routledge, 2011.

Chang, Yun-shik, and Lee, Steven Hugh (Eds). *Transformations in Twentieth Century Korea.* Abingdon, Routledge, 2006.

Chang Yun-Shik, Seok Hyun-Ho, and Baker, Donald L. (Eds). *Korea Confronts Globalization.* New York, Routledge, 2008.

Chinoy, Mike. *Meltdown: the Inside Story of the North Korean Nuclear Crisis.* New York, St Martin's Press, 2008.

Cornell, Erik. *North Korea under Communism: Report of an Envoy to Paradise.* London, RoutledgeCurzon, 2002.

Cumings, Bruce. *North Korea: Another Country.* New York, New Press, 2003.

DiFilippo, Anthony. *US-Japan-North Korea Security Relations: Irrepressible Interests.* Abingdon, Routledge, 2011.

Eberstadt, Nicholas. *Policy and Economic Performance in Divided Korea during the Cold War Era: 1945–91.* Washington, DC, American Enterprise Institute Press, 2010.

Eberstadt, Nicholas, and Ellings, Richard J. (Eds). *Korea's Future and the Great Powers.* Seattle and London, University of Washington Press, 2001.

Feffer, John (Ed). *The Future of US-Korean Relations: The Imbalance of Power.* Abingdon, Routledge, 2006.

Fitzpatrick, Mark. *North Korean Security Challenges: A Net Assessment.* London, International Institute for Strategic Studies, 2011.

Foley, James. *Korea's Divided Families—Fifty Years of Separation.* Abingdon, Routledge, 2009.

Ford, Glyn, and Kwon, Soyoung. *North Korea on the Brink: Struggle for Survival.* London, Pluto Press, 2008.

Gateward, Frances K. *Seoul Searching: Culture and Identity in Contemporary Korean Cinema.* Albany, State University of New York Press, 2007.

Haggard, Stephan, and Noland, Marcus. *Witness to Transformation: Refugee Insights into North Korea.* Washington, DC, Peterson Institute for International Economics, 2011.

Engaging North Korea: The Role of Economic Statecraft. Hawaii, HI, East-West Center, 2011.

Hagström, Linus, and Söderberg, Marie (Eds). *North Korea Policy: Japan and the Great Powers.* Abingdon, Routledge, 2006.

Harrison, Selig S. *Korean Endgame: A Strategy for Reunification and US Disengagement.* Princeton, NJ, Princeton University Press, 2002.

Hart, Joyce. *Kim Jong Il: Leader of North Korea.* New York, Rosen Publishing Group, 2008.

Hassig, Ralph C., and Oh, Kongdan. *The Hidden People of North Korea: Everyday Life in the Hermit Kingdom.* Lanham, MD, Rowman and Littlefield, 2009.

Hoare, James E., and Pares, Susan. *Conflict in Korea: An Encyclopedia.* Santa Barbara, CA, ABC-Clio, 1999.

North Korea in the 21st Century: An Interpretive Guide. Folkestone, Global Oriental, 2005.

Hundt, David. *Korea's Developmental Alliance: State, Capital and the Politics of Rapid Development.* Abingdon, Routledge, 2008.

Hyun, In-Taek, Lee, Shin-Wa, and Rozman, Gilbert. *South Korean Strategic Thought Toward Asia.* New York, Palgrave Macmillan, 2008.

Jae Cheon-Lim. *Kim Jong Il's Leadership of North Korea.* Abingdon, Routledge, 2009.

Jeffries, Ian. *Contemporary North Korea: A Guide to Economic and Political Developments.* Revised Edn, Abingdon, Routledge, 2009.

Jongryn, R. Mo, and Brady, David W. *The Rule of Law in South Korea.* Stanford, CA, Hoover Institution Press, 2008.

Kak Twae-Han and Joo Seung-Ho. *North Korea's Foreign Policy under Kim Jong-Il: New Perspectives.* Burlington, VT, Ashgate Publishing, 2009.

Kang, David C., and Kim Sung Chull. *Engagement with North Korea: a Viable Alternative.* Albany, NY, State University of New York Press, 2009.

Kim Kyong Ju. *The Development of Modern South Korea: State Formation, Capitalist Development and National Identity.* Abingdon, Routledge, 2006.

Kim, Mike. *Escaping North Korea: Defiance and Hope in the World's Most Repressive Country.* Lanham, MD, Rowman and Littlefield, 2008.

Kim, Samuel S. (Ed.). *The North Korean System in the Post-Cold War Era.* New York, Palgrave Macmillan, 2001.

Inter-Korean Relations: Problems and Prospects. New York, Palgrave Macmillan, 2004.

Two Koreas and the Great Powers. Cambridge, Cambridge University Press, 2006.

Kim Suk Hi, Seliger, Bernhard, and Roehrig, Terence (Eds). *The Survival of North Korea: Essays on Strategy, Economics and International Relations.* Jefferson, NC, McFarland & Co, 2011.

Kim, Sun Joo (Ed). *The Northern Region of Korea: History, Identity, and Culture.* Seattle, WA, University of Washington Press, 2010.

Kim, Sung Chull. *North Korea under Kim Jong Il: From Consolidation to Systemic Dissonance.* New York, State University of New York Press, 2006.

Kim Yongho. *North Korean Foreign Policy: Security Dilemma and Succession.* Lanham, MD, Rowman & Littlefield, 2010.

Kim, Youngmi. *The Politics of Coalition in Korea: Between Institutions and Culture.* Abingdon, Routledge, 2011.

Kirk, Donald. *Korea Betrayed: Kim Dae Jung and Sunshine.* New York, Palgrave Macmillan, 2010.

Kwak, Tae-Hwan (Ed.). *North Korea's Foreign Policy under Kim Jong Il.* Aldershot, Ashgate Publishing, 2009.

LaRoche, Christopher D. *Negotiating with the Hermit Kingdom: Approaches and Interests in the Korean Nuclear Dilemma.* Halifax, Dalhousie University, 2008.

Lee, Chae-Jin. *Troubled Peace: U.S. Policy and the Two Koreas.* Baltimore, MD, Johns Hopkins University Press, 2006.

Lee Myung-Bak. *Making Hyundai, Remaking Seoul: From CEO to South Korea's President: The Autobiography of Lee Myung-Bak.* Lanham, MD, Rowman & Littlefield, 2010.

Lewis, James B., and Sesay, Amadu (Eds). *Korea and Globalization: Politics, Economics, and Culture.* London, RoutledgeCurzon, 2002.

Lintner, Bertil. *Great Leader, Dear Leader: Demystifying North Korea under the Kim Clan.* Chiang Mai, Silkworm Books, 2005.

McEachern, Patrick. *Inside the Red Box: North Korea's Post-Totalitarian Politics.* New York, Columbia University Press, 2010.

Michishita, Narushige. *North Korea's Military-Diplomatic Campaigns, 1966–2008.* Abingdon, Routledge, 2009.

Moltz, James Clay, and Mansourov, Alexandre Y. (Eds). *The North Korean Nuclear Program: Security, Strategy, and New Perspectives from Russia.* New York and London, Routledge, 2000.

Noland, Marcus. *Korea After Kim Jong Il.* Washington, DC, Institute for International Economics, 2003.

Oh, Kongdan, and Hassig, Ralph C. (Eds). *North Korea Through the Looking Glass.* Washington, DC, Brookings Institution, 2000.

Korea Briefing 2000–01: First Steps Toward Reconciliation and Reunification. Armonk, NY, M. E. Sharpe, 2002.

Park, Han S. *North Korea: The Politics of Unconventional Wisdom.* Boulder, CO, Lynne Rienner, 2002.

Park Kyung-Ae (Ed.). *Korean Security Dynamics in Transition.* New York, Palgrave Macmillan, 2001.

New Challenges of North Korean Foreign Policy. New York, Palgrave Macmillan, 2010.

Park, Phillip H. *The Dynamics of Change in North Korea: An Institutionalist Perspective.* Boulder, CO, Lynne Rienner Publishers, 2009.

Park Soon-Wan, Shin Gi-Wook, and Yang Daqing (Eds). *Rethinking Injustice and Reconciliation in Northeast Asia: The Korean Experience.* Abingdon, Routledge, 2006.

Portal, Jane. *Art under Control in North Korea.* London, Reaktion, 2005.

Reese, David. *The Prospects for North Korea's Survival.* Abingdon, Routledge, 2005.

Ringen, Stein, et al. *The Korean State and Social Policy: How South Korea Lifted Itself from Poverty and Dictatorship to Affluence and Democracy.* New York, Oxford University Press, 2011.

Rudiger, Frank, Hoare, James E., and Pares, Susan. *Korea 2010: Politics, Economy and Society.* Leiden, Brill, 2010.

Ryang, Sonja (Ed.). *Korea: Toward a Better Understanding.* Lanham, MD, Lexington Books, 2009.

Shin Dong-Myeon. *Social and Economic Policies in Korea.* London, RoutledgeCurzon, 2003.

Shin, Gi-Wook. *Ethnic Nationalism in Korea: Genealogy, Politics, and Legacy.* Stanford, CA, Stanford University Press, 2006.

Söderberg, Marie. *Changing Power Relations in Northeast Asia: Implications for Relations between Japan and South Korea.* Abingdon, Routledge, 2010.

Son Key-Young. *South Korean Engagement Policies and North Korea: Identities, Norms and the Sunshine Policy.* Abingdon, Routledge, 2006.

Song, Jesook (Ed.). *New Millennium South Korea: Neoliberal Capitalism and Transnational Movements.* Abingdon, Routledge, 2010.

Steinberg, David I. (Ed.). *Korean Attitudes toward the United States: Changing Dynamics.* Armonk, NY, M. E. Sharpe, 2004.

Korea's Changing Role in Southeast Asia: Expanding Influence and Relations. Singapore, Institute of Southeast Asian Studies, 2010.

Suh, Doowon. *Political Protest and Labour Movements in Korea: Solidarity Among Korean White-Collar Workers.* Abingdon, Routledge, 2008.

Yang Sung-Chul. *The North and South Korean Political Systems: A Comparative Analysis.* Elizabeth, NJ, Hollym, 2001 (Revised Edn).

Yoon Dae-Kyu. *Law and Democracy in South Korea: Democratic Development Since 1987.* Boulder, CO, Lynne Rienner Publishers, 2010.

History

Bateman, Robert. *No Gun Ri: A Military History of the Korean War Incident.* Mechanicsburg, PA, Stackpole, 2002.

Buzo, Adrian. *The Guerrilla Dynasty: Politics and Leadership in North Korea.* Boulder, CO, Westview Press, 1999.

The Making of Modern Korea: A History. New York, Routledge, 2nd Edn, 2007.

Catchpole, Brian. *The Korean War 1950–1953.* London, Robinson, 2001.

Chung, Chin O. *Pyongyang Between Peking and Moscow: North Korea's Involvement in the Sino-Soviet Dispute 1958–75.* University of Alabama Press, 1978.

Clay, Blair (Jr). *The Forgotten War: America in Korea 1950–53.* Annapolis, MD, United States Naval Institute, 2003.

Cumings, Bruce. *Korea's Place in the Sun: A Modern History.* New York, W. W. Norton & Co, 1997.

The Korean War: A History. New York, Modern Library, 2010.

Dudden, Alexis. *Troubled Apologies Among Japan, Korea and the United States.* New York, Columbia University Press, 2008.

Grayson, James H. *Korea: A Religious History.* London, RoutledgeCurzon, 2002.

Hanley, Charles J., Choe Sang-Hun, and Mendoza, Martha. *The Bridge at No Gun Ri.* New York, Henry Holt & Co, 2001.

Katsiaficas, Georgy, and Na Kahn-che (Eds). *South Korean Democracy: Legacy of the Gwangju Uprising.* Abingdon, Routledge, 2006.

Kim Byung Kook and Vogel, Ezra F. (Eds) et al. *The Park Chung Hee Era: The Transformation of South Korea.* Cambridge, MA, Harvard University Press, 2011.

Kim, C. I. Eugene, and Ki Han-Kyo. *Korea and the Politics of Imperialism, 1876–1910.* Berkeley, CA, University of California Press, 1970.

Kim, C. I. Eugene, and Mortimore, D. E. (Eds). *Korea's Response to Japan: The Colonial Period 1910–45.* Kalamazoo, MI, The Center for Korean Studies, Western Michigan University, 1977.

Kim, Hyuk-Rae and Bok Song (Eds). *Modern Korean Society: Its Development and Prospect.* Berkeley, CA, Center for Korean Studies, Institute of East Asian Studies, University of California, 2007.

Kim Joong-Seop. *The Korean Paekjong under Japanese Rule: The Quest for Equality and Human Rights.* London, RoutledgeCurzon, 2003.

Larsen, Kirk W. *Tradition, Treaties and Trade: Qing Imperialism and Choson Korea, 1850-1910.* Cambridge, MA, Harvard University Press, 2008.

Lee Jong-Sup and Heo Uk. *The US-South Korean Alliance, 1961–88: Free-riding or Bargaining?* New York, Edwin Mellen Press, 2002.

Lee, Jongso James. *The Partition of Korea after World War II: A Global History.* London, Palgrave Macmillan, 2006.

Lee, Namhee. *The Making of Minjung: Democracy and the Politics of Representation in South Korea.* Ithaca, NY, Cornell University Press, 2009.

Lewis, James B. *Frontier Contact between Choson Korea and Tokugawa Japan.* London, RoutledgeCurzon, 2003.

Lewis, Linda Sue. *Laying Claim to the Memory of May: A Look Back at the 1980 Kwangju Uprising.* Honolulu, University of Hawaii Press, 2002.

Malkasian, Carter. *The Korean War 1950–53.* London, Fitzroy Dearborn, 2001.

McCormack, Gavan. *Target North Korea: Pushing North Korea to the Brink of Nuclear Catastrophe.* New York, Nation Books, 2004.

Michishita, Narushige. *North Korea's Military-Diplomatic Campaigns, 1966–2008.* Abingdon, Routledge, 2011.

Myers, Ramon H., and Peattie, Mark R. (Eds). *The Japanese Colonial Empire, 1895–1914.* Princeton, NJ, Princeton University Press, 1984.

Nahm, Andrew C. (Ed.). *Korea Under Japanese Colonial Rule.* Kalamazoo, MI, The Center for Korean Studies, Western Michigan University, 1973.

The United States and Korea—American-Korean Relations 1866–1976. Kalamazoo, MI, The Center for Korean Studies, Western Michigan University, 1979.

A Panorama of 5,000 Years: Korean History. Seoul and Elizabeth, NJ, Hollym International Corpn, 1983.

Oberdorfer, Don. *The Two Koreas: A Contemporary History.* New York, Basic Books, 2002 (2nd Edn).

Oh, Bonnie B. C. *Korea Under the American Military Government, 1945–48.* Westport, CT, Praeger, 2002.

Pollack, Jonathan D. *No Exit: North Korea, Nuclear Weapons, and International Security.* Abingdon, Routledge, 2011.

Pratt, Keith. *Everlasting Flower: A History of Korea.* London, Reaktion, 2006.

Salmon, Andrew. *Scorched Earth, Black Snow: Britain and Australia in the Korean War, 1950.* Aurum Press, 2011.

Seth, Michael J. *A History of Korea: From Antiquity to the Present.* Lanham, MD, Rowman and Littlefield, 2010.

Summers, Harry G. *Korean War Almanac.* Bridgewater, NJ, Replica Books, 2001.

Szalontai, Balazs. *Khrushchev Versus Kim Il-Sung: Soviet-DPRK Relations and the Roots of North Korean Despotism, 1953-1964.* Stanford, CA, Stanford University Press, 2006.

Economy

Becker, Alan K. (Ed.). *South Korea: International Relations, Trade and Policies.* Hauppage, NY, Nova Science Publishers, 2011.

Carlin, Robert, and Wit, Joel. *North Korean Economic Reform: Politics, Economics and Security.* Abingdon, Routledge, 2006.

Chang, Dae-Oup. *Capitalist Development in Korea: Labour, Capital and the Myth of the Developmental State.* Abingdon, Routledge, 2008.

Cherry, Judith. *Foreign Direct Investment in Post-Crisis Korea: European Investors and 'Mismatched Globalization'.* Abingdon, Routledge, 2007.

Choi, E. Kwan, Merrill, Yesook, and Kim, E. Han (Eds). *North Korea in the World Economy.* London, RoutledgeCurzon, 2003.

Chung Duck-Koo and Eichengreen, Barry (Eds). *The Korean Economy Beyond the Crisis.* Cheltenham, Edward Elgar Publishing, 2004.

Chung, Young-Iob. *South Korea in the Fast Lane: Economic Development and Capital Formation.* New York, Oxford University Press, 2007.

Cyhn, Jin W. *Technology Transfer and International Production: The Development of the Electronics Industry in Korea.* Cheltenham, Edward Elgar Publishing, 2002.

Elwood, Paul H., and Albertus, Jeremy B. (Eds). *Korea: Economic, Political and Social Issues.* Haupaugge, NY, Nova Science Publishers, 2008.

Gray, Kevin. *Korean Workers and Neoliberal Globalization.* Abingdon, Routledge, 2007.

Hart-Landsberg, Martin, Jeong, Seongjin, and Westra, Richard (Eds). *Marxist Perspectives on South Korea in the Global Economy.* Burlington, VT, Ashgate Publishing, 2007.

Harvie, Charles, Lee Hyun-Hoon and Oh Junggun (Eds). *The Korean Economy—Post-Crisis Policies, Issues and Prospects.* Cheltenham, Edward Elgar Publishing, 2004.

Jwa Sung-Hee. *The Evolution of Large Corporations in Korea.* Cheltenham, Edward Elgar Publishing, 2002.

Jwa Sung-Hee and Lee In-Kwon (Eds). *Competition and Corporate Governance in Korea—Reforming and Restructuring the Chaebol.* Cheltenham, Edward Elgar Publishing, 2004.

Kwon O Yul. *The Korean Economy in Transition: An Institutional Perspective* Cheltenham, Edward Elgar Publishing, 2010.

Kwon O Yul, Jwa Sung-Hee and Lee Kyung Tae (Eds). *Korea's New Economic Strategy in the Globalization Era.* Cheltenham, Edward Elgar Publishing, 2003.

Kwon Seung-Ho and O'Donnell, Michael. *The Chaebol and Labour in Korea.* London, Routledge, 2001.

Lansbury, Russell D., Suh Chung-Sok and Kwon Seung-Ho. *The Global Korean Motor Industry: The Hyundai Motor Company's Global Strategy.* Abingdon, Routledge, 2007.

Lee Kyu-Sung. *The Korean Financial Crisis of 1997: Onset, Turnaround, and Thereafter.* World Bank Publications, 2011.

Mahlich, Jörg, and Pascha, Werner (Eds). *Innovation and Technology in Korea: Challenges of a Newly Advanced Economy*. Heidelberg, Physica Verlag, 2010.

Moonjoong Tcha and Suh Chung-Sok. *The Korean Economy at the Crossroads: Triumphs, Difficulties and Triumphs Again*. London, RoutledgeCurzon, 2003.

Moore, Phoebe. *Globalisation and Labour Struggle in Asia: A Neo-Gramscian Critique of South Korea's Political Economy*. London, Tauris Academic Studies, 2007.

Nicolas, Françoise (Ed.). *Korea in the New Asia: East Asian Integration and the China Factor*. Abingdon, Routledge, 2007.

Noland, Marcus. *Avoiding the Apocalypse: The Future of the Two Koreas*. Washington, DC, Institute for International Economics, 2000.

Noland, Marcus (Ed.) *Economic Integration of the Korean Peninsula*. Washington, DC, Institute for International Economics, 1998.

Pirie, Ian. *The Korean Developmental State: From Dirigisme to Neo-Liberalism*. Abingdon, Routledge, 2007.

Roh, Han-Kyun. *Shareholder Activism: Corporate Governance Reforms in Korea*. Basingstoke, Palgrave Macmillan, 2007.

Shim T. Joun-Ja (Ed.). *Korean Entrepreneurship: The Foundation of the Korean Economy*. Basingstoke, Palgrave Macmillan, 2010.

Shin Jang-Sup and Chang Ha-Joon. *Restructuring 'Korea Inc'*. London, RoutledgeCurzon, 2003.

Song Byung-Nak. *The Rise of the Korean Economy*. Oxford, Oxford University Press, 2001 (3rd Edn).

United States Congress Senate Committee. *Corruption in North Korea's Economy*. BiblioGov, 2010.

LAOS

Physical and Social Geography

HARVEY DEMAINE

The Lao People's Democratic Republic is a land-locked state in South-East Asia, bordered by the People's Republic of China to the north, by Viet Nam to the east, by Cambodia to the south, by Thailand to the west and by Myanmar (formerly Burma) to the north-west. Covering an area of 236,800 sq km (91,400 sq miles), Laos consists almost entirely of rugged upland, except for the narrow floors of the river valleys. Of these rivers, by far the most important is the Mekong, which forms the western frontier of the country for much of its 1,898-km length.

In the northern half of Laos, the deeply dissected plateau surface is more than 1,500 m above sea-level over wide areas. The average altitude of the Annamite chain, which occupies most of the southern half of the country, is somewhat lower, but its rugged and more densely forested surface makes it equally inhospitable. Temperatures on the plateau and in the Annamite chain are mitigated by altitude, but the more habitable lowlands experience tropical conditions throughout the year, and receive a total annual rainfall of about 1,250 mm, most of which falls between May and September. In Vientiane, the capital, temperatures range between 23°C and 38°C in April, the hottest month, and from 14°C to 28°C in January, the coolest month.

Although deforestation in Laos has given rise to concern, in 2010 it was estimated by FAO that more than 66% of the country was covered by forest. Laos has considerable mineral resources: iron ore, copper, coal, tin, gold, gemstones and gypsum are among the minerals that are exploited. Other mineral deposits include zinc, nickel, silver, lead, potash, limestone and bauxite. The Mekong River offers substantial potential for fisheries, irrigation and hydroelectricity. The Nam Ngum dam and power complex, built on the Mekong 80 km north of Vientiane, began operations in 1971. In 1991 a second major hydroelectric project, the Xeset dam in southern Laos, was completed. In 2002 the Government granted a concession to the Nam Theun 2 Power Company, permitting it to assume control of the construction of a major new hydroelectric dam. Commercial operations at Nam Theun 2 commenced in early 2010.

The population of Laos was enumerated at 4,581,258 at the census of 1 March 1995 and at 5,621,982 at the census of 1 March 2005. According to UN estimates, the population of Laos totalled 6,288,039 at mid-2011, with an average density of 26.6 per sq km. About 60% of the population are ethnic Lao, residing mainly in the western valleys. A further 35% belong to various hill tribes, although the important Hmong group has been affected by conflict. The remainder are either Vietnamese or Chinese. The urban population is an estimated 20% of the total; Vientiane, the capital, is the only large town. Its population was 176,637 in 1973; at the census of 1995 the total population of the Vientiane metropolitan area had increased to 528,109. According to UN estimates, the population of Vientiane totalled 831,472 at mid-2010.

History

MARTIN STUART-FOX

Revised for this edition by VOLKER GRABOWKSY

EARLY HISTORY: THE KINGDOM OF LAN XANG

More than 60 different ethnic groups inhabit present-day Laos. They can be divided into three broad categories on the basis of settlement patterns, culture and language. The earliest inhabitants were those minorities now known as 'Lao of the mountain slopes' (Lao Thoeng), who spoke Austro-Asiatic languages akin to Khmer and farmed using swidden ('slash-and-burn') methods. From perhaps the 10th century they began to be displaced by speakers of Tai languages who entered Laos from the north-east. These included the now politically dominant lowland (or ethnic) Lao, along with other Tai groups, which together comprised the 'Lao of the plains' (Lao Lum). All practised wet-rice cultivation and most became Theravada Buddhists. The 'Lao of the mountain tops' (Lao Sung) were the last to arrive, from southern China, in the 19th century. They spoke either Hmong-Mien or Tibeto-Burman languages, followed their own various religions, and often cultivated opium as a cash crop. Fewer than two-thirds of the country's 6.3m. inhabitants at mid-2011 were lowland Lao or members of other Tai-speaking groups. As a result of the delineation of borders by colonial powers in the late 19th and early 20th centuries, the vast majority (15m.–20m.) of Lao speakers today live in modern-day Thailand.

Very early human remains have been discovered in northern Laos, but the first culture to have been archaeologically investigated was centred on the Plain of Jars, and was an iron-age megalithic culture which built both underground burial chambers and massive stone mortuary urns to hold the ashes of the dead. Some of these 'jars' (after which the plain was named) were more than 2 m high and weighed at least 10 metric tons. However, who these people were, and what became of them, has remained a mystery.

By the eighth or ninth century north-eastern Thailand and Laos had begun to be influenced by the early Indianized kingdoms in mainland South-East Asia. Laos was situated at an important crossroads of trade routes along which travelled not only merchants, but also Buddhist monks. In the areas of Thakhek in central Laos, Vientiane (or Viang Chan) and Luang Prabang small principalities were formed, which at first owed allegiance to more powerful states. By the late 12th century the Cambodian Angkorian empire had begun to expand north to include not only southern Laos, but most of the Mekong basin, perhaps as far north as Luang Prabang. However, Khmer power was brief: as the Khmer empire contracted, Tai-speaking peoples established their own kingdoms in northern Laos and northern and central Thailand. By the late 13th century it is known that there was an established Lao principality in the region of Luang Prabang, and others in the central Mekong basin. In the mid-14th century an enterprising ruler, King Fa Ngum, took advantage of Khmer support to incorporate the Lao principalities into a powerful kingdom known as Lan Xang Hom Khao ('A Million Elephants and the White Parasol'), a title indicating both military might and royal kingship. Many of the symbols of the modern Laotian state originate in the Kingdom of Lan Xang. For two centuries Luang Prabang (then known as Xiang Dong Xiang Thong) served as the capital of the kingdom. Lan Xang was loosely organized as a tributary state comprising several *mueang* (semi-feudal principalities of variable extent), each of which not only paid an annual tribute of gold and other valuable products, but was also expected to raise an army in time of conflict.

The kings of Lan Xang were ardent Buddhists and, as in the other Tai states and Burma (now Myanmar) and Cambodia, Theravada Buddhism served to legitimize their rule. In return for his patronage of the *Sangha* (the monastic order), monks taught that the King ruled because he possessed superior *karma* (moral merit accumulated during previous lifetimes). The image of Buddha known as the *Phra Bang* became the much revered palladium of the kingdom. Cultural and dynastic relations with the neighbouring Tai Yuan kingdom of Lan Na (now northern Thailand) were particularly close from the late 15th century, and in the mid-16th century both kingdoms were politically united, albeit only for a few years. By the early 16th century the kingdom of Lan Xang was the equal of other states in mainland South-East Asia, and defeated and expelled invaders from Viet Nam and Burma. Lao settlers advanced south down the Mekong valley as far as Champasak and beyond, and on to the Khorat plateau (now north-eastern Thailand). As they did so, the centre of the Lao population shifted south. The north–south movement of the Lao people and the gradual assimilation of the autochthonous Mon-Khmer speaking populations continued well into the 19th century. When Burmese armies threatened Luang Prabang in the mid-16th century, King Xetthathirat decided to re-establish the capital at the more strategically situated and less vulnerable site of Vientiane.

Lan Xang was at its apogee in the 17th century during the long reign of King Surinyavongsa (1637–94). It was then that the first European merchants and missionaries arrived in Vientiane. Their descriptions of the wealth of the city and the brilliance of its court were the first independent accounts, and portray a centre of art, culture and religion attracting scholars and artists from throughout the region. Surinyavongsa's death was followed by one of the periodic successional disputes that served to weaken the kingdom. Within two decades the kingdom had split into three parts, centred on Luang Prabang in the north, Vientiane in the centre with control over much of the Khorat plateau, and Champasak in the south. Xiangkhouang, on the Plain of Jars, reluctantly acknowledged the suzerainty of Vientiane, but took every opportunity to assert its autonomy. The weakened Lao kingdoms could no longer match their powerful neighbours. Even before the disintegration of Lan Xang, the maritime states of mainland South-East Asia had been much better placed than the inland states to benefit from increased sea-borne trade, with the recently arrived Europeans and with China. Their greater wealth enabled them to purchase new weapons and to equip larger armies; thus, well before all three Lao kingdoms were reduced to tributaries of Siam in the late 18th century, the balance of power had begun shifting against the Lao.

In 1827 Chao Anouvong, the last King of Vientiane, made a desperate bid to free himself and his kingdom from Siamese hegemony. The war that followed was a disaster: Vientiane was captured and sacked, its people were forcibly resettled, and the king was removed to Bangkok, where he subsequently died. Appeals by local Lao rulers to the Vietnamese were unsuccessful, except in Xiangkhouang, where Viet Nam had an historic interest. Whereas Vientiane and Champasak were fully integrated into the Siamese kingdom, Luang Prabang—which had refused to join the Vientiane uprising—retained its status as an autonomous vassal state. In the 1870s the Laotian territories were ravaged by marauding bands of Chinese and, despite appeals for assistance, the Siamese—themselves hard-pressed by encroaching European powers—were slow to respond. The court in Bangkok was nevertheless determined to assert Siamese suzerainty, even over the remote Tai highlands in what is now north-western Viet Nam. It was there in the late 1880s that it encountered the French.

LAOS UNDER FRENCH RULE

French interest in Laos derived initially from a belief that the Mekong River would provide a 'river road' to southern China. When the Mekong expedition of 1867–68 proved that the river was unnavigable, interest waned. However, French commercial interests in Saigon still hoped to tap the wealth of the Mekong basin and, with the annexation of central and northern Viet Nam as a French protectorate in 1884, French interest in Laos was revived. French control of the Mekong was deemed essential to the strategic defence and economic prosperity of the new possession; at a minimum, the Laotian territories east of the Mekong had to be annexed to 'round out' French Indo-China.

Attempts to assert Vietnamese claims to these Laotian lands were hardly convincing, and were contested by Siam. However, the creation of a French presence through exploration and commerce was more successful. Eventually, the determined efforts of Auguste Pavie, the French consul appointed to Luang Prabang, and 'gunboat diplomacy' in Bangkok, forced the Siamese in 1893 to cede all territories east of the Mekong to France. Subsequent treaties in 1904 and 1907 established the present borders that both Cambodia and Laos share with Thailand.

For half a century Laos was ruled as a French colony, although the former kingdom of Luang Prabang nominally enjoyed the status of a protectorate. The French rebuilt Vientiane as the administrative capital of French Laos, and extended a minimal presence throughout the rest of the country. Their first priority in Laos was to cover the cost of administration. However, the depleted population that had escaped Siamese resettlement provided an insufficient tax base. Although taxes were high and all had to perform unpaid *corvée* labour, Laos was always dependent on a subsidy from the federal budget for Indo-China. The French devised various schemes designed to 'open up' Laos to economic exploitation, including construction of a railway from the Vietnamese coast to the Mekong, and mass immigration of Vietnamese to provide an adequate work-force. From the beginning, the middle ranks of the civil service in Laos were largely filled by Vietnamese, but the Great Depression of the 1930s prevented construction of the railway, and relatively few Vietnamese migrated. However, by the late 1930s the Vietnamese constituted the majority population in Vientiane and all the major provincial towns, with the exception of Luang Prabang; had the Second World War (1939–45) not intervened, the French might well have succeeded in their intention to reduce the Lao to a minority in their own country.

In 1939 Siam was renamed Thailand as part of a policy designed to appeal to all Tai-speaking peoples, including notably the Lao. To counter this appeal, after 1940 the French administration began to encourage a weak Laotian nationalism among the small and educated élite. Thai seizure of Laotian territories west of the Mekong provoked Lao anger against both the Thai and the French for failing to protect the borders.

Under an agreement between the Japanese Government and Vichy France, administration of French Indo-China remained the responsibility of the French, while the Japanese had the right to move and station troops throughout the region. Not until 9 March 1945 did the Japanese forces stage a lightning pre-emptive attack to neutralize and intern all French military and civilian personnel. Only in Laos did a few French officers and men escape the Japanese net, their survival in jungle hideouts being due to the support they received from loyal Laotians.

As in other parts of South-East Asia, the élite in Laos was divided between opposition to the Japanese and opposition to colonialism. While some fought for the Allies, others collaborated. In Laos King Sisavang Vong, though pro-French, was forced on 8 April 1945 to declare the independence of his country, while, less reluctantly, his distant cousin, Prince Phetsarath, served as Prime Minister under the Japanese. The surrender of Japan in August left a political vacuum throughout Indo-China, which nationalists in all three countries moved to exploit: in Viet Nam the communist Viet Minh seized power; in Laos the nationalist Lao Itsara, or Free Laos movement. On 1 September Prince Phetsarath in Vientiane reaffirmed the independence of Laos, even though the King in Luang Prabang had welcomed the return of the French. When the King repudiated Phetsarath's actions, the Prince declared the reunification of the protectorate of Luang Prabang with the rest of the country. In October the King dismissed Phetsarath as Prime Minister but, in response, a newly constituted Lao

Itsara Government deposed the King shortly after, thereby initiating a struggle for power.

Under the terms of the Potsdam Agreement between the Allies, the Japanese surrender in Indo-China was accepted by the Chinese Nationalists north of the 16th parallel and by the British to the south. While the British facilitated the return of the French to southern Laos, the Chinese favoured the Lao Itsara. Not until the Chongqing Agreement had been concluded between France and China did the Chinese withdraw, thus allowing French forces to reoccupy central and northern Laos. In March 1946 French forces and their Laotian allies moved north. Lao Itsara volunteers, supported by local Vietnamese, attempted to hold the French advance at Thakhek, but were defeated. French troops successfully reoccupied Vientiane on 24 April and Luang Prabang on 13 May. Some 2,000 Lao Itsara supporters and several thousand Vietnamese crossed the Mekong to Thailand, where Phetsarath established a government-in-exile in Bangkok. The French, meanwhile, set about reasserting their control. Prince Bunum of Champasak, who had aided the French reconquest, renounced his claim to a separate southern kingdom, and Laos was unified under the royal house of Luang Prabang. The nominally independent Kingdom of Laos was incorporated into the French Union, but was still closely tied (in terms of, *inter alia*, defence, currency and customs regulations) to Viet Nam and Cambodia.

By early 1947 the new Kingdom of Laos had begun to take shape. The territories west of the Mekong seized by Thailand in early 1941 had been returned, elections for a Constituent Assembly had been held, and in May 1947 a new Constitution was proclaimed. The Government, which was both conservative and pro-French, was acutely aware of its nationalist opponents in Bangkok. Its members, drawn from the powerful families of the élite that had benefited most from the French presence, reflected a judicious balance from northern, central and southern Laos. While some attempt was made, with French support, to improve woefully neglected services such as education, health and agricultural extension, much of the politicking was between influential leaders who sought to obtain regional or family advantage. However, perhaps the most serious shortcoming of the new Government was its failure to generate any real sense of national unity or purpose. The country remained deeply divided, with regional and family loyalties counting for more than national allegiance. The only unifying symbol might have been the monarchy, as in Thailand or Cambodia, but the King remained in Luang Prabang, and the political opportunity to unify the royal and administrative capitals and overcome regionalism by moving the royal court to Vientiane was lost.

The outbreak of the First Indo-China War in December 1946 between the Viet Minh and their allies and the French, and the activities of the Lao Itsara, both served to complicate the establishment of governmental authority. The radical anti-French nationalism of the Viet Minh provided an example for the like-minded elements of the Lao Itsara, led by Phetsarath's younger half-brother, Prince Souphanouvong. Lao Itsara guerrilla raids targeting the French in Laos were co-ordinated by and carried out with the Viet Minh. However, the proximity of the alliance between Souphanouvong and the Viet Minh caused divisions within the Lao Itsara. Criticism of Souphanouvong eventually led him to resign from the organization in March 1949, and two months later the moderate majority responded by formally relieving him of all his ministerial functions.

In July 1949 a Franco-Lao Convention was signed, giving the Laotian Government much greater powers and sufficient independence to meet the demands of the moderates in the Lao Itsara. In October, led by Phetsarath's younger brother, Souvanna Phouma, the Lao Itsara was dissolved, and most of its still-exiled members returned to Laos. Only Phetsarath himself remained in Bangkok. Souphanouvong went to Viet Nam, where he made contact with the Viet Minh. While the moderate Lao Itsara joined the new Royal Lao Government (RLG) in August 1950, Souphanouvong established his own government of the 'Land of the Lao' (Pathet Lao, the name by which the communist movement in Laos became known). Over the next four years, as communist Chinese military support flowed to the Viet Minh and the USA supported France, the First Indo-China War engulfed the region. Twice Laos was subjected to major Viet Minh invasions, during which a large area in the north-east of the country was seized and turned over to the Pathet Lao. The French responded by granting Laos formal independence in October 1953. The defeat of French forces at Dien Bien Phu, located in a mountain valley close to the border with Laos, represented the end of French military involvement in Viet Nam. Meetings were already under way in Geneva, Switzerland, to seek an end to the conflict, and with respect to Laos, the Geneva Conference agreed in July 1954 to an armistice and a regrouping of opposing forces, prior to elections within two years. The Pathet Lao was allotted the two north-eastern provinces of Phongsali and Xam Nua, while the RLG administered the rest of the country. By the end of that year Lao independence was reinforced by the abrogation of all agreements linking Laos with the other states of Indo-China.

THE QUEST FOR UNITY AND NEUTRALITY

For the RLG in Vientiane, the first priority was to regain administrative control of the two Pathet Lao provinces so that elections could be held in accordance with the Geneva Agreement. However, as a *quid pro quo*, the Pathet Lao insisted on changes to the electoral law and on freedom for its front organization—the Lao Patriotic Front (behind which stood the secret Lao People's Party)—to operate as a political party. Negotiations continued throughout 1955, but failed to bring results. In December the Government proceeded with elections in the provinces that it controlled. These resulted in the formation of a Government once again under the leadership of Souvanna Phouma, who immediately entered into new negotiations with his half-brother, Souphanouvong.

By early 1956 the USA had replaced France as the dominant Western power in Indo-China. As of early 1955 a US Operations Mission (USOM) was functioning in Vientiane and the USA was financing not only much of the Laotian budget, but also meeting the entire cost of the Lao National Army (LNA). Under the terms of the Geneva Agreement, a French Military Mission continued to train the LNA, but growing numbers of US military personnel in civilian guise were attached to the US embassy. Both the US Information Service and the Central Intelligence Agency (CIA) were also active. From 1955 to 1962 US aid to Laos, the overwhelming majority of it military, was, in per caput terms, the highest for any country in South-East Asia, including South Viet Nam. In the context of the Cold War, the USA aimed to prevent Laos from becoming communist and thus was strongly opposed to the inclusion of communists in the Government. Souvanna Phouma's agreement with the Pathet Lao to include two of its members in a coalition government as the price for reintegration of the two provinces under its control met strenuous opposition from the USA. However, Souvanna Phouma pressed ahead in the belief that national unity and a policy of neutrality were essential for the preservation of the Laotian state. An agreement was signed with the Pathet Lao in November 1957. Supplementary elections held in the following May gave leftist candidates 21 seats in the National Assembly, much to the alarm of the USA.

With the active support of the US embassy and the CIA, right-wing politicians and army officers formed the Committee for the Defence of National Interests (CDNI). When US aid was withheld in July 1958, Souvanna Phouma's first coalition collapsed, and was replaced by a right-wing Government led by Phuy Sananikon. In January 1959, on the basis of alarmist reports of an imminent North Vietnamese invasion, Phuy received emergency powers to govern for a year without reference to the National Assembly. Gen. Phoumi Nosavan, a powerful military figure who enjoyed US support, was appointed Vice-Minister of Defence in the new Government. The Pathet Lao watched these events with mounting concern. Negotiations to integrate two Pathet Lao battalions into the LNA stalled, and in May one battalion absconded to Xam Nua. As insurgent activity resumed, the Government responded by imprisoning Pathet Lao members of the National Assembly in Vientiane. However, the Government was internally divided by personal and political differences, and in December Gen. Phoumi, with the support of the CDNI, mounted a coup.

Although Gen. Phoumi failed to gain the premiership, the coup resulted in the formation of a new Government dominated by the military. New elections were held in April 1960 and, owing to malpractice, all left-wing candidates lost their seats, much to US satisfaction. However, as the country moved towards civil war, even elements of the military became concerned at the turn of events. In August a young army captain, Kong Le, unexpectedly seized control of Vientiane under the banner of neutrality and an end to 'Lao killing Lao'. Souvanna Phouma was again invited to form a Government, which Gen. Phoumi refused to join. With the support of the CIA, acting in defiance of the US embassy, Phoumi built up his forces in central Laos. In mid-December, after his efforts to prevent a civil war had failed, Souvanna flew to Phnom-Penh, Cambodia, and Gen. Phoumi seized control of Vientiane. Kong Le's neutralist force staged an orderly withdrawal to the Plain of Jars, where they were welcomed by the Pathet Lao. As Gen. Phoumi failed to follow up his victory, large areas of the country fell to the combined neutralist and Pathet Lao forces.

Following the undermining and collapse of Souvanna's first coalition Government in 1957, the communists made impressive gains, and achieved a major propaganda victory in May 1960, when Prince Souphanouvong and the other detained Pathet Lao leaders escaped from the tightly controlled Phon Kheng prison with the tacit support of government security guards. In March 1961, as a renewed neutralist and Pathet Lao offensive got under way, President John F. Kennedy declared US support for a political settlement involving the neutralization of Laos. The communist response was conciliatory and a cease-fire came into effect in early May, followed by the convening of a second conference of interested powers at Geneva. Nevertheless, it took more than a year for the feuding Laotian factions to reach agreement on the formation of a second coalition Government of National Union, and then only after renewed fighting had resulted in a decisive defeat for the LNA at the battle of Luang Namtha in north-western Laos. The new Government, including two full ministers and two vice-ministers from the Pathet Lao, eventually signed the final document in Geneva, proclaiming the neutralization of Laos on 21 July 1962.

However, the second coalition failed to achieve either of its two objectives: to reunify the country and, through neutralization, to insulate Laos from the gathering war in Viet Nam. Of the three factions comprising the coalition, the neutralists were the weakest and under the greatest political pressure. While the Pathet Lao and the right-wing elements enjoyed military and economic assistance from their principal supporters, North Viet Nam and the USA respectively, the neutralists enjoyed only diplomatic backing, principally from France. Neutralist armed forces were dependent for supplies on either the Pathet Lao or the LNA. As both the left and right wings attempted to absorb the neutralist centre, divisions developed between the neutralists themselves. Only a façade of coalition government and neutrality remained, as Laos was drawn increasingly into the Second Indo-China War. The Government lasted less than a year and, after the assassination in April 1963 of the neutralist Minister of Foreign Affairs, Kinim Phonsena, Pathet Lao ministers left Vientiane, fearing their own assassination or arrest. Thereafter, both the USA and North Viet Nam subverted Laotian neutrality for their own purposes in pursuing the war in Viet Nam. The North Vietnamese had two strategic aims in Laos: to prevent northern Laos, particularly the Plain of Jars, from being used by the USA to threaten North Viet Nam, and to control the Ho Chi Minh trail in the mountainous east of Laos down which combatants and weapons flowed to communist forces in South Viet Nam. US policy sought to challenge communist control of both areas: on the Plain of Jars by building up a clandestine army recruited mainly from the Hmong ethnic minority and commanded by the popular Hmong General, Vang Pao; and on the Ho Chi Minh trail through the (initially secret) massive use of air power. For a decade, until the cease-fire of February 1973 brought fighting to an end, the country was caught up in the Viet Nam War. The war in Laos was of much greater strategic significance to both sides than the war in Cambodia, and in the north the Hmong suffered considerable casualties against North Vietnamese regular forces and had to be reinforced by Thai 'volunteers'. A great number of North Vietnamese and their Pathet Lao allies were killed in the US bombing in both northern and southern Laos (200,000 killed and more than 400,000 wounded is a conservative estimate); by 1973 2m. metric tons of bombs had been dropped, making Laos the most heavily bombed country per caput in the history of warfare. One-quarter of the entire population of the country was displaced by the war.

The Lao people themselves were unable to prevent the use of their territory by opposing forces. While the North Vietnamese were nominally 'aiding' the Pathet Lao, the US embassy was directing bombing 'in defence of Laotian neutrality'. Souvanna Phouma attempted to preserve a minimum freedom of action, but retained office despite attempted right-wing coups only with the support of foreign ambassadors. Not until peace talks got under way did the Laotians regain some influence over their own affairs. Negotiations lasting over a year eventually led to the formation in April 1974 of a third coalition Government, the composition of which reflected the gains made by the Pathet Lao during a decade of war: one-half of the ministerial portfolios went to communists or left-leaning 'neutralists' and the remainder to right-wing figures. The only real neutralist left was Souvanna Phouma, who once again presided as Prime Minister. Souphanouvong headed the National Political Consultative Council (NPCC), a policy-making body that met in the royal capital of Luang Prabang.

The NPCC agreed upon a relatively moderate 18-point programme, and it seemed initially that Laos might gradually work towards its own form of mild socialism, preserving both the monarchy and traditional Buddhist values. However, events in other parts of Indo-China had repercussions for Laos. In April 1975 first Phnom-Penh, then Saigon, fell to Cambodian and Vietnamese communist forces. In Laos, Pathet Lao forces advanced towards Vientiane. As towns in southern Laos were progressively 'liberated', demonstrations were mounted in Vientiane against both the continuing US presence (in the form of the US Agency for International Development—USAID) and right-wing political and military figures. Five ministers and several generals fled the country, but even as power shifted to the Pathet Lao the façade of the third coalition was retained. On 23 August Vientiane was symbolically 'liberated' by the arrival of a contingent of 50 women soldiers of the Pathet Lao. Fearing Pathet Lao reprisals, some families fled to Thailand at this time, but many more elected to stay and to serve the new regime. Thousands of civil servants and military officers went willingly to re-education 'seminars' in the remote north-east of the country, which they were assured would last only a few weeks. However, the Pathet Lao took advantage of the absence of its opponents to press ahead with the final stage of its assumption of power. On 2 December a National Congress of People's Representatives accepted the abdication of King Savang Vatthana and proclaimed the Lao People's Democratic Republic (LPDR). While Souphanouvong was named President, real power lay with the little-known Secretary-General of the (renamed) Lao People's Revolutionary Party (LPRP) and Chairman of the Council of Ministers (Prime Minister), Kaysone Phomvihane.

THE LAO PEOPLE'S DEMOCRATIC REPUBLIC

The leaders of communist Laos saw their task as building and defending socialism by means of 'bypassing' the capitalist stage of development through three simultaneous revolutions: in production, through nationalizing industry and collectivizing agriculture; in science and technology, through their application to the economy; and in ideology and culture, in order to create new Lao 'socialist men and women' devoted to the regime. Laos was seen by its new leaders as the vanguard of socialism in South-East Asia, and as such they believed the country was a prime target for destabilization by its principal opponents, the USA and Thailand. Support for both building and defending socialism in Laos came from the communist bloc countries, notably the USSR, Viet Nam and the People's Republic of China, but also from East European states and even Mongolia and Cuba, all of which established embassies in Vientiane.

The steady progress towards modernization expected by the new regime encountered difficulties almost immediately, largely owing to unimaginative and dogmatic policies. The end of US aid and Thailand's closure of its border with Laos, which curtailed the supply of consumer goods, both contributed to the collapse of the urban economy; new government restrictions also limited internal trade. Shops closed as their owners fled to Thailand and factories, deprived of imported inputs, had to cease production. An unpopular tax on agricultural production, introduced when much of the country was suffering from drought and poor harvests, further reduced the availability of food supplies as farmers withheld produce from markets. The new Government's policies, which sought to reduce religious expenditure and placed restrictions on freedom of movement because of security fears, further lost it support. However, the principal concern of the educated middle class, which had been prepared to co-operate with the new Government, was the latter's refusal to allow the return of those undergoing political re-education. Terms of imprisonment (in 're-education' camps), frequently extending into years, deprived many families of their principal income-earner and forced them to sell their possessions in order to survive. Many crossed the Mekong River into Thailand. Most of those eventually released also fled the country at the first opportunity. In a decade Laos lost 10% of its population, comprising an estimated 90% of its educated class, a loss that probably set the country back a generation in its development.

Increasing domestic disillusionment and the growing numbers of refugees in camps in Thailand created ideal conditions for the recruitment of opponents of the regime; a 'Lao National Revolutionary Front' was consequently established in Thailand to send anti-Government propaganda and sabotage teams into Laos. When in March 1977 rebel remnants of the Hmong 'secret army' in northern Laos briefly captured a village not far from Luang Prabang, the regime feared that the former King might instigate a revolt. The royal family was arrested and banished to a remote region of Xam Nua, where the elderly King and Queen subsequently both died, as did the Crown Prince, reportedly of malaria. Vietnamese forces assisted in putting down the Hmong revolt, and in July Laos and Viet Nam signed a 25-year Treaty of Friendship and Co-operation to formalize Vietnamese political, economic and military assistance, including the stationing of 30,000–40,000 Vietnamese troops in Laos over the next decade. Relations with Viet Nam and the USSR were close over these years, but those with China and Cambodia became increasingly difficult. As hundreds of Soviet technicians and Vietnamese advisers drew Laos firmly into the Soviet sphere of influence, Chinese aid was limited to projects in the north of the country, in an area where Chinese influence had always been strong. Though the Government tried hard to maintain good relations with both sides in the Sino-Soviet dispute, the Vietnamese invasion of Cambodia in December 1978 and China's response in invading the northern border provinces of Viet Nam eventually forced Laos to take sides. China was requested to terminate its aid projects and reduce the size of its embassy staff. Subsequent Chinese warnings to the Laotian regime, and the acceptance of several thousand Lao refugees from Thailand for settlement in China, led to charges by Laos of a Chinese-supported insurgency. Not many LPRP members dared to question the anti-Chinese policy of their leadership, and by the end of 1981 only a few senior Party leaders had sought asylum in China. Not until the mid-1980s did Laotian-Chinese relations begin to improve.

As relations with China became more strained, those with Thailand improved. Both sides agreed to suppress insurgent activity aimed at the other and to encourage bilateral trade. However, relations with Thailand were variable, and it was not long before the Government in Vientiane was accusing Thailand of collusion with China in attempts to destabilize the regime. Security concerns were an important reason for the decision in July 1979 to suspend further co-operativization of agriculture. This unpopular programme had been pursued over two years, leading to the rapid formation, on paper at least, of some 2,500 co-operatives. In fact, most were inadequately organized and the benefits promised did not materialize, not least because the Government had so few economic resources. Moreover, peasants objected to pooling their land and working for 'work points' rather than wages. Some peasants, mostly in the south, slaughtered their livestock and left for Thailand, while others joined the anti-Government resistance. By 1979 both the Soviet and Vietnamese Governments were advising that the programme be halted.

The external and internal threats by then confronting the regime forced a reappraisal of government policy. By the end of 1979 the decision had been taken to reform the currency (a new National Bank kip replaced the former 'liberation kip') and to adopt a less rigid form of socialism. The change in direction was justified by reference to Lenin's 'new economic policy' of the early 1920s, but the regime could barely disguise the fact that earlier policies had been a failure. The economy of Laos was recognized as comprising a mix of modes of production, including subsistence farming and a capitalist sector, all of which were to be officially encouraged. Profit was introduced as a criterion of efficiency, economic decision-making was decentralized, and controls on the circulation and marketing of goods and produce were eliminated, preparing for the successful return of a market economy. On these new economic foundations the LPDR launched its first five-year economic development plan (1981–85), to coincide with those of other Soviet bloc countries. However, the plan's targets were over-ambitious and, partly owing to a shortage of trained personnel and to structural inadequacies, virtually none was met. Both party and governmental organization was weak, and cadres lacked training and commitment. At the Third Party Congress held in April 1982, the first since the formation of the LPDR, there was considerable criticism of the reforms. While the same seven-member Political Bureau (Politburo) was re-elected, the Central Committee was more than doubled in size to include new members from the provinces, the military and the Government. Provinces were given the right to trade directly with foreign countries and to determine their own development strategies in conformity with central government planning, a measure that considerably strengthened the political power of the Party's provincial secretaries. Party reform extended to the expulsion of members on the basis of ideological shortcomings or for corruption.

Early in 1984 relations with Thailand deteriorated following the outbreak of fighting in the vicinity of three villages on the border of Sayabouri Province claimed by both Laos and Thailand. In June a full-scale attack by 1,500 Thai troops failed to take the disputed area. A cease-fire was agreed upon, but subsequent negotiations failed to resolve the problem, and border demarcation remained a matter of dispute, which four years later again erupted in border fighting. However, relations with both China and the USA improved. Border trade resumed with China, and an agreement in February 1985 with the USA led to the first excavation at the crash site of a US aircraft to determine the fate of US servicemen missing in action during the Viet Nam War.

In March 1985 the LPRP celebrated 30 years of 'correct and creative' leadership of the revolution, and in December the regime celebrated both its first decade in power and the completion of the first Five-Year Plan, but the country remained desperately poor, and as dependent as ever on foreign aid. The per caput income of the country's 3.5m. people was estimated at just over US $100 a year, making Laos one of the poorest countries in the world. However, the country was more or less self-sufficient in rice—given favourable weather conditions—although only a tiny fraction of paddy land was irrigated. Industrial production stood at little more than 5% of gross domestic product (GDP), a figure low even for the least developed countries. Most state-owned enterprises continued to make losses. Claims of 100% literacy were manifestly false, and both educational and health standards had actually declined through loss of trained personnel. Moreover, according to the human rights organization Amnesty International, some 6,000 political prisoners still remained in detention in remote internment camps. The feeling grew within the Party that a change of direction was necessary—especially given a likely reduction in aid from the USSR and Viet Nam.

For some time the LPRP Secretary-General, Kaysone Phomvihane, had been warning of a 'two-line struggle' being waged, although between which factions and in pursuit of which policies remained unclear at the time. Only subsequently

was it revealed that the struggle was between those who wanted to introduce more radical economic reforms, led by Kaysone himself, and those who resisted them in the name of socialist orthodoxy, led by Kaysone's deputy in charge of the economy, Nouhak Phoumsavanh. Kaysone eventually succeeded in securing his policy orientation, but only after intense debate within the Party had led to the postponement of the Fourth Party Congress and of the introduction of the second Five-Year Plan until November 1986. When it eventually met, the Congress endorsed what was called the 'New Economic Mechanism', which introduced elements of a market economy. State-owned enterprises were granted greater autonomy and expected to make a profit, food subsidies were progressively eliminated and the civil service was reduced in size.

Economic difficulties in 1987, brought on by drought and decreased electricity exports to Thailand, served to strengthen the position of the reformers. As the currency continued to depreciate and revenue consistently failed to cover expenditure, so dependency on foreign aid increased. Pressure for further reform came from the IMF, from foreign aid donors, and even from the USSR and Viet Nam, which were then undertaking their own programmes of reform. Measures were subsequently taken to dismantle the remaining elements of the centralized socialist economy. Over the next two years, as communism began to collapse in Eastern Europe and the USSR, and as Viet Nam withdrew its forces from both Laos and Cambodia, the LPDR strengthened links with Thailand (following border fighting early in 1988) and with friendly capitalist states, notably Japan, Sweden and Australia. At the same time, the Government approved a liberal foreign investment law, and began to lay the necessary legal foundations to attract foreign capital.

In April 1988 the first local elections since 1975 took place, followed in November by district, municipal and provincial elections. In March 1989 national elections were held to replace the Supreme People's Assembly appointed in 1975. The LPRP was the only political party, though a few carefully vetted independents were permitted to stand for office. The new 79-member Assembly met in June and elected Nouhak Phoumsavanh as Chairman. Its first task was to appoint a Constitution Drafting Committee to draw up the long-delayed Constitution. Even though all candidates were members or supporters of the LPRP, these elections did provide some popular legitimacy for the regime at a time when, in response to the collapse of communism in Eastern Europe and events in Cambodia, anti-communist opposition to the regime had increased. Bolstered by the possibility of international support, both Hmong and right-wing Lao guerrillas operating from Thailand intensified their activities, though never sufficiently to threaten the Party's hold on power.

The broadening of diplomatic and economic relations that followed the Government's 'open-door' approach reflected both increased confidence on the part of the regime and a series of important political initiatives. By 1991 the LPRP had sufficiently recovered from the impact of events in the former USSR to hold its own Fifth Congress. During the previous year the Party had orchestrated debate on the new Constitution, which subsequently underwent three separate drafts. It had also indicated that it would permit no challenge to its monopoly hold on political power when it arrested and subsequently imprisoned three prominent critics—including the Vice-Minister of Science and Technology, Thongsouk Sayasankghi—whom it accused of 'activities aimed at overthrowing the regime'. The three were members of a group of some 40 intellectuals who advocated greater democracy. (Thongsouk died in detention; the other two were released only in 2004.) The Fifth Congress not only endorsed the draft Constitution but also introduced major changes in Party structure and in relations between the Party and government. The Party Secretariat was abolished, and Kaysone was named Party President. Three members of the Politburo retired, and changes were also made to the membership of the Central Committee, with a number of younger members gaining election, several of whom were closely related to, or protégés of, senior members of the Party. Equally important, the Party endorsed the direction of economic reform in accordance with free-market principles, symbolically replacing the communist red star in the national crest by an outline of the That Luang stupa (the pre-eminent Laotian monument) and simultaneously eliminating the word 'socialism' from the national motto.

On 14 August 1991, more than 15 years after the formation of the LPDR, the Supreme People's Assembly finally adopted a Constitution that referred to the 'Party' only once (as the 'leading nucleus' of the political system), and formally established Laos as a 'people's democracy' in the Marxist sense. The Constitution also guaranteed basic freedoms and the right to private ownership of property. The Supreme People's Assembly was renamed the National Assembly, the title used by the former RLG, and its powers were enunciated. The executive powers of the President of the State were greatly enhanced, and provision was made for the appointment of a Vice-President, though none was named. Kaysone was appointed President of the LPDR, while the former Minister of National Defence, Khamtay Siphandone, took Kaysone's place as Prime Minister, so entitled in preference to Chairman of the Council of Ministers.

The internal cohesion of the Party and the strength of the new institutions were tested in November 1992 by the death of Kaysone. He had led the Lao communist movement since the formation of the Lao People's Party in 1955, and his power as President of both the State and Party had been unchallenged. On his death, power was divided between the President of the National Assembly, Nouhak Phoumsavanh, who became State President, and Khamtay Siphandone, who added the presidency of the Party to his post as Prime Minister. The transition had clearly been worked out in advance and was remarkably smooth, thereby ensuring continued political stability. Within a month scheduled elections for the National Assembly went ahead as planned. The 85 seats were contested by 154 candidates, all endorsed by the Party-controlled Lao Front for National Construction (LFNC). At its initial sitting in February 1993, the new Assembly confirmed the appointments of Nouhak and Khamtay, elected Saman Vignaket as its President in place of Nouhak, and endorsed a new ministry based on an extensively reorganized structure of government.

The new Government undertook to continue the economic reform programme, to extend the rule of law, to limit the worst excesses resulting from earlier decentralization of power, and to curb corruption. Reforms to the tax system sought to increase revenue collection, and further to liberalize conditions for foreign investment. Thailand continued to be the largest source of investment (inflows having reached US $1,940m. by the end of 1995), followed by the USA, with Australia, France and China also being prominent. Inflation and the chronic underlying trade deficit continued to cause concern, although it was hoped that the future completion of major hydro-electricity and mining projects would improve the balance of payments situation.

In March 1996 the LPRP's Sixth Congress revealed the concern felt by senior party members over the pace and implications of economic change. Secret political discussions prior to the Congress led to an outcome that was unexpected by most observers: the ruling Politburo was reduced from 11 to nine members, six of whom were former or serving army officers; Khamtay Siphandone remained President of the Party, but Deputy Prime Minister Khamphoui Keoboualapha, widely identified as a leading proponent of economic reform, was excluded from both the Politburo and the Central Committee (itself reduced from 55 to 49 members), while Sisavat Keobounphan (a close associate of Khamtay) not only regained his membership of the Politburo, but was also named as the country's first Vice-President. As expected, Nouhak Phoumsavanh stepped down from the Politburo, leaving the Party firmly under the control of the army.

In December 1997 elections were held for the 99-seat National Assembly. Seventeen of the candidates elected were army officers, while only one was not a member of the ruling Party. At the first session of the Assembly in February 1998, Khamtay Siphandone was named President of the country, as well as President of the LPRP, while Vice-President Sisavat replaced Khamtay as Prime Minister. Political developments since the Sixth Party Congress confirmed both the dominance of the army and its desire to exercise closer, and

more conservative, control over the economy, although political appointments still reflected family and clan influence, regionalism and the country's ethnic diversity. The military was determined to gain a substantial share of the benefits to be derived from resource exploration and development projects. Three military-controlled companies divided the country among them to develop commercial agriculture, logging, mining and tourism; contracts for construction projects constituted another profitable source of income. However, along with other state-owned companies, these military enterprises failed to repay substantial bank loans. Another form of corruption was the use of political influence to gain lucrative appointments for family members or clients, a development that the Prime Minister's Anti-Corruption Commission seemed unwilling or unable to prevent.

By 1999 the repercussions of the Asian economic crisis had become evident in Laos, with reduced investment, a slowing of economic activity and rapid inflation. In August the crisis claimed its first victims with the replacement of two leading finance officials, following allegations of mismanagement of fiscal and banking policy. However, economic conditions were subsequently slow to improve, and popular dissatisfaction continued to increase. In October students staged a rare anti-Government protest in Vientiane. A number of the demonstrators were promptly arrested, while others suspected of involvement in the protest fled across the border to Thailand. The Laotian Government refused even to acknowledge that either the incident or the arrests had ever taken place, but Amnesty International claimed that some of the leaders of the demonstration were still in detention a decade later.

In June 1999 Hmong insurgent groups in north-eastern Laos renewed their anti-Government activities. It was speculated that the unrest had been fomented from abroad by Hmong activists linked to former Gen. Vang Pao. In March 2000 a bomb exploded in a restaurant in Vientiane, injuring a number of people, several of them foreigners. This attack was followed by a series of further explosions over subsequent months. Although no organization claimed responsibility, a government spokesperson attributed the explosions to Hmong insurgents and other 'bad elements'. However, the Hmong denied responsibility, and the incidents appeared instead to have been organized by Lao dissidents operating from abroad, with the aim of discrediting the Government by showing it to be incapable of maintaining security.

A more serious attack took place in July 2000, when about 50 suspected royalist insurgents seized customs and immigration offices on the Laotian–Thai border, near the southern Laotian town of Paksé. At least six of the dissidents were subsequently killed by government troops, some were captured, while a further 28 were arrested by the Thai authorities. The Laotian Government immediately demanded the extradition of those captured who were Lao nationals. A long legal dispute followed, during the course of which Laos and Thailand signed their first extradition treaty. Finally, in July 2004 16 Lao were transferred to the Laotian authorities, despite a ruling by the Thai courts rejecting their extradition on the grounds that the enabling legislation could not be applied retrospectively. All were tried and given prison sentences of between three and 12 years.

Laos entered the new millennium with some trepidation. Short-term economic prospects were unfavourable. Security remained a concern, and both the Government and the Party feared continuing popular dissatisfaction, precipitated by growing social and regional disparities and endemic corruption. Nevertheless, the Seventh Congress of the LPRP was held according to schedule, in March 2001. The outcome was as expected, with the military retaining control of the Politburo. All eight surviving members of the previous Politburo were re-elected, together with three new members. Of these 11 members, eight were either retired or serving military officers; of the other three, two were senior Party officials in charge of mass mobilization and Party organization, while the third was the new first Deputy Prime Minister, Thongloun Sisolit. The only unexpected omission from the new Politburo was that of the second Deputy Prime Minister and Minister of Foreign Affairs, Somsavat Lengsavat. Twelve new members were appointed to the Central Committee, increasing total membership to 53, including all 16 provincial governors. Party membership was reported to have increased by one-third since 1996, to 105,000.

This LPRP leadership proved to be both cautious and conservative with respect to political liberalization and economic reform. The Party Congress reiterated its opposition to multi-party democracy, and proclaimed ambitious targets for economic growth. The Congress endorsed a reduction in tariffs in accordance with its commitment to the Association of South-east Asian Nations (ASEAN—see Foreign Relations, below), in particular the ASEAN Free Trade Area (AFTA). The Congress also restated its aim to join the World Trade Organization (WTO), although the target date of 2010 was not to be met. However, the success of the new five-year plan endorsed by the LPRP was threatened by the Government's failure to improve tax collection. Any improvement in living standards was therefore dependent on funds promised to Laos under the IMF Poverty Reduction and Growth Facility.

Following the Congress in March 2001, the National Assembly convened to endorse a change of government. Boungnang Volachit, hitherto Deputy Prime Minister and Minister of Finance, replaced the elderly Sisavat Keobounphan as Prime Minister, with Thongloun Sisolit as the new first Deputy Prime Minister and President of the State Planning Committee. Lt-Gen. Choummaly Sayasone, hitherto the Minister of National Defence, was elected the country's Vice-President (following the death of Oudom Khattigna in December 1999). Nevertheless, most government ministers retained their portfolios, thereby reinforcing the conservative continuity demonstrated by the LPRP Congress. However, if the Party's intention was to perpetuate existing policies, significant popular discontent remained, largely resulting from poor economic performance and increasing levels of corruption and crime (especially in Vientiane).

In an apparent attempt to reinforce its legitimacy, the Government advanced the date of elections to the National Assembly to 24 February 2002, several months ahead of schedule. The Assembly was enlarged from 99 to 109 members, elected from provincial lists numbering 166 candidates, all of whom were pre-endorsed by the LFNC. Of those elected, again only one was not a member of the LPRP. A total of 25 were women, while 39 were members of minority ethnic groups (including six from upland Tai minorities). The remaining 70 were ethnic Lao. Overall, the members of the new [illegible]bly were younger (with an average age of 51) and better [illegible]ated (63% had received some tertiary education) than th[illegible]edecessors.

By the end of 2002 the Government could claim sub[illegible]tial political and economic achievements. The Seventh Party Congress and the National Assembly elections had both been well managed, the regime had withstood the Asian economic crisis and accompanying unrest, and there was no overt political opposition. However, with the collapse of its Marxist ideology, the legitimacy of the LPRP was more than ever dependent on its ability to manage the economy and to improve the performance of its own cadres. This perhaps explained an apparent increase in official support for Buddhist ceremonies and celebrations in the new millennium, and for a new emphasis on Lao nationalism. In January 2003 an elaborate pageant took place, during which a statue of King Fa Ngum was erected, to commemorate the 650th anniversary of the founding of the Lao kingdom of Lan Xang in 1353.

In response to the changing requirements of the times, in 2002 the Ministry of the Interior was renamed the Ministry of Security. Its mandate was soon challenged by two fatal attacks on buses on the highway linking Vientiane with Luang Prabang in February and April 2003. In total, 23 people were killed, including two Swiss cyclists accidentally caught up in the first attack, with dozens more injured. The Government blamed Hmong 'bandits' for both attacks, but downplayed any suggestion that the ongoing Hmong insurgency, which had been active intermittently since 1975, had entered a new phase. A further bus attack took place in August 2003 in northern Laos, killing five people, while two other attacks were reported in the south of the country. At a time of global concern about terrorism, these incidents were sufficient to attract the attention of the world press. For the first time, two foreign journalists managed to contact Hmong insurgents in the mountainous Phou Bia region, 120 km north-east of Vientiane, revealing an insurgency at the point of exhaustion and desperate for assistance. This was confirmed after two more journalists and their US-Hmong interpreter also made contact with Hmong insurgents, only to be arrested by the Laotian authorities and sentenced to 15 years' imprisonment each. Following widespread international condemnation of the severity of the sentences, all three were released and expelled from the country. Such international attention was not welcomed by the Laotian Government, which feared the effect that it might have on foreign investment and tourism. In fact, independent reports on the desperate state of the insurgents served to confirm the Government's claim that the Hmong insurgency had been reduced to only a few hundred scattered guerrillas.

In February and March 2004 some 1,000 Hmong, mostly women, children and the elderly, surrendered to the Laotian authorities in Xiangkhouang and Luang Prabang Provinces. As many as 8,000 others fled to Thailand. While this did not necessarily signify the end of the Hmong insurgency, it did indicate that, after years of skirmishing, government forces had gained the advantage in the conflict. Nevertheless, the Hmong issue remained unresolved. In September Amnesty International accused the Laotian Government of 'war crimes' on the basis of a video supposedly smuggled out of the country, which purported to show the execution of Hmong teenagers. The Government denied these accusations and denounced the video as a 'fabrication'. Security in other areas of Laos did not appear to be a cause for major concern, despite a spate of attacks involving five small, home-made bombs that exploded in Vientiane between October 2003 and June 2004. These resulted in the death of one bomber, owing to the premature explosion of his device, but no other casualties. Two other minor bomb attacks were reported to have taken place in southern Laos, leaving one person dead and six injured. A covert organization that called itself the Free Democratic People's Government of Laos (FDPGL) claimed responsibility for all the explosions that had occurred since 2000, and threatened to carry out further attacks unless the Government reduced its dependence on Viet Nam and instituted democratic reforms.

The Events of 2006 and Subsequent Developments

Three significant political events occurred in the first half of 2006: the Eighth Congress of the ruling LPRP was held in March, followed in April by elections for the National Assembly, which endorsed a new State President, Vice-President, Prime Minister and cabinet at its first session in June. As expected, Gen. Khamtay Siphandone relinquished the post of Party President and was replaced by Lt-Gen. Choummaly Sayasone (who was elected the country's President in June), but other ageing members remained in place. The only two new additions were the long-serving Minister of Foreign Affairs, Somsavat Lengsavat, and the first woman ever appointed, Pany Yathotou, an ethnic Hmong. Thus, six out of 11 positions (including five of the six most senior roles) continued to be occupied by conservative former military officers. Any radical reformist shift in policy therefore seemed unlikely. Nevertheless, 22 new members were elected to the Central Committee, and it was hoped that they might generate an infusion of youth and new ideas. Two other significant outcomes of the Congress were the revival of a seven-member Secretariat, now known as the Executive Committee of the Party, and the appointment of Gen. Asang Laoli as the head of the Party Inspectorate, which was expected to monitor more closely the activities of Party members and thus perhaps limit corruption.

Elections for the National Assembly on 30 April 2006 were held several months earlier than anticipated. Of the 115 members elected (out of 175 candidates), two were reported to be independents, while more than 60% were new members. Politburo member Thongsing Thammavong was named President of the National Assembly, and Pany Yathotou and Dr Xaysomphone Phomvihane, son of the late President Kaysone, were both appointed to the position of Vice-President. The legislature's first task was to endorse the Government presented by the new Prime Minister, Bouasone Bouphavanh (Boungnang Volachit having been appointed Vice-President). Fifteen of the incoming 28 members of the Council of Ministers were new appointees, including two women. However, perhaps the most significant ministerial change was the transfer of the foreign affairs portfolio from Somsavat Lengsavat to Thongloun Sisolit, one of four Deputy Prime Ministers—all of whom were members of the LPRP Politburo. Indeed, 19 out of the 28 ministers were members of the LPRP Central Committee. The only structural changes were the fusion of the Ministries of Commerce and of Industry, and the creation of a new Ministry of Energy and Mining, the latter innovation reflecting the growing importance of the energy and mining sectors to the Laotian economy.

All three political institutions—the LPRP Central Committee, the National Assembly and the Government—had thus witnessed a substantial influx of new members, several of them close relatives of powerful LPRP officials. However, while the long-standing conservative military leadership remained in place, it seemed unlikely, at least in the short term, that this new generation would embark upon the implementation of new policies. Certainly, Prime Minister Bouasone began by keeping a low profile. Although he had the support of outgoing President Khamtay and of the new President, Choummaly Sayasone, Bouasone required time to establish his authority within the Government and Party. He announced his first cabinet changes in June 2007, when Minister of Finance Chansy Phosikham was appointed Governor of Vientiane Province, and the finance portfolio was awarded to Chansy's deputy, Somdy Douangdy. In addition, there were three new appointees to the Prime Minister's Office, including former Asian Development Bank (ADB) Vice-President Khempheng Pholsena, who assumed responsibility for water and the environment.

Bouasone confronted some serious difficulties, a major problem being corruption. Anti-corruption legislation approved in 2005 had done little to address the issue. Unlike China and Viet Nam, where examples were made of senior party officials, in Laos only minor culprits were charged. Yet in Laos, Party officials at all levels were reportedly enriching themselves at the expense of the State, through abetting smuggling (of goods in and resources out), exacting payment for services (such as providing employment and scholarships, influencing court cases, and awarding government contracts), and through illegally expropriating land for plantation agriculture. Bouasone had demanded firm action against corruption, and the matter was debated in the National Assembly. According to National Assembly Vice-President Dr Xaysomphone Phomvihane, corruption had become the country's principal social vice, followed by crime and drug abuse.

Three new laws relating to corruption were approved by the Assembly in July 2007, concerning public security (to create a 'principled and modern' police force), state auditing (to curb the plunder of state funds), and state inspection (to investigate and deal with corruption). The State Inspection Authority was accorded new legal powers to investigate administrative decisions. It was even suggested that the press might be given limited freedom to investigate corruption, although in the event this did not materialize. In 2009 Laos ratified the UN Convention Against Corruption, but this had little discernible effect, and widespread embezzlement of state revenues continued unabated. In 2010 irate members of the National Assembly appealed for a wealth register for LPRP members and for improved law enforcement. However, the political culture of the LPRP condones patronage, nepotism and other forms of corruption, while intermarriage and other connections between the leading families of the political-economic élite make it difficult to prosecute corrupt officials.

Meanwhile, security improved following the series of relatively minor bomb attacks of previous years, but attention continued to focus on the Hmong. Several hundred Hmong, mainly women and children, surrendered to the authorities in December 2006, while others made their way to Thailand, where almost 8,000 congregated in Phetchabun Province. An agreement between the Thai and Laotian Governments to repatriate these Hmong to Laos provoked international criticism and offers of resettlement in third countries. None the less, the Thai authorities proceeded with the repatriation of the

Hmong, claiming to have received assurances from the Laotian authorities that the Hmong would be treated well upon their return to Laos. The final 4,000 or so Hmong, who were described by the Thai Government as economic migrants, were deported from Ban Huay Nam Khao camp in Phetchabun in December 2009. According to the authorities, the deportation was accomplished peacefully; however, up to 5,000 security personnel were deployed in the operation. A visit to a resettlement village by an international delegation was organized by the Laotian authorities in 2010 in an attempt to appease critics.

Just as the Hmong insurgency seemed at an end in Laos, Hmong in the USA devised a last desperate plot to overthrow the Laotian Government. Dubbed 'Operation Popcorn' (Political Opposition Party's Coup Operation to Rescue the Nation), it planned to raise US $28m. to purchase weapons for an attack on Vientiane by a force of 1,000 men, in the hope that large numbers of Lao would rise up and overthrow the ruling Party. The plot was thwarted when 11 ringleaders (10 Hmong led by Gen. Vang Pao, plus a retired lieutenant-colonel from the California National Guard) were arrested by the US authorities in June 2007 and charged under the Neutrality Act, prohibiting US citizens from plotting to overthrow foreign governments. In September 2009 a US federal court withdrew all charges against Gen. Vang Pao. However, a revised indictment was issued in respect of the remaining 10 defendants, as well as two further suspects; all were liable to receive long prison terms if convicted. Gen. Vang Pao died in January 2011.

Another concern for the Laotian Government was the emergence of avian influenza ('bird flu'), with the deaths in 2007, in a rural area of Vientiane Province, of the first two victims of the H5N1 deadly strain of the disease. Another outbreak occurred in northern Laos in 2008. In both cases poultry were culled, but the Laotian authorities were ill-equipped to control a major outbreak. Two other serious health concerns were HIV/AIDS and the prevalence of counterfeit drugs from China, which had a fatal effect when used, for example, to treat malaria. In part, these health concerns reflected the consequences of greater sub-regional integration, with more bridges and border crossing-points open, and better roads to facilitate the movement of people and goods. Tourist arrivals had been steadily increasing, with Laos becoming a major destination for adventure and eco-tourism, and the Government even opened up the wartime Pathet Lao headquarters in the caves of Viang Xai to visitors. However, the problem of unexploded ordnance remained; unexploded bombs left over from the Viet Nam War still needed to be cleared in remote areas—a task due to be completed by 2020. These issues, along with an influx of resident foreigners, from prospectors for minerals and hydrocarbons to plantation managers, business people and tourist operators, appeared to be placing additional strains on Laotian society in both urban and rural areas. As corruption continued to diminish government revenues, the UN World Food Programme reported that up to one-half of rural children were malnourished, while public services such as education and health care remained chronically underfunded.

The global financial crisis of 2008/09 further depleted government revenues. The Government acted to stimulate foreign investment by easing restrictive regulations and by abolishing visa requirements for those under the age of 15 years or over the age of 65. In the longer term, prospects were more encouraging. Significant investment was procured from Thai interests to finance the Theun-Hinboun dam and the Hongsa lignite power plant, and around one dozen other hydropower projects were under construction in 2011. Initial operations at the 615-MW Nam Ngum 2 hydropower plant commenced at the end of 2010, with the project reported to be 90% complete at September 2011, and with official electricity sales due to commence at the end of that year. It was hoped that these projects would make a significant contribution to government revenue.

Meanwhile, heavy rains in northern Laos caused the country's worst floods in living memory in August 2008, when the Mekong River rose rapidly and flooded parts of Vientiane; the resultant landslides killed four people. In the same month Samantha Orobator, a Nigerian-born citizen of the United Kingdom, was arrested for possession of heroin.Upon her conviction in June 2009, she was sentenced to life imprisonment, avoiding the death penalty by having intentionally become pregnant. As a result of the recently concluded prisoner exchange agreement between Laos and the United Kingdom, Orobator was transferred to a British prison in August. In January 2010 the High Court in the United Kingdom rejected Orobator's claim that she was being unlawfully detained, but affirmed that she had been 'treated unjustly' while in Laos; her life sentence was commuted to a minimum of 18 months' imprisonment.

Following the Eighth Party Congress in 2006, Prime Minister Bouasone quietly consolidated his position and power with the support of his principal cabinet colleagues. At the Ninth Congress of the ruling LPRP, due to be held in 2011, several ageing generals now in the Politburo were expected to retire, leaving the way open for a new generation to assume senior positions within the Party. Upon his appointment as premier, Bouasone had vowed to reduce poverty, increase per caput income and address the problem of burgeoning corruption, much of which was associated with senior party members. For these policies, he reportedly had the support of both Viet Nam and China, but by the end of 2010 his success with regard to these issues had been limited. Nevertheless, Bouasone's resignation from the premiership on 23 December was unexpected, with the outgoing Prime Minister having been widely expected to be re-elected at the forthcoming Ninth Party Congress. Although Bouasane stated publicly that he could no longer perform his duties because of 'family problems', some observers suggested that he had fallen victim to a power struggle between pro-Chinese and pro-Vietnamese elements within the LPRP leadership. Thongsing Thammavong was subsequently elected unanimously as the new Prime Minister by the National Assembly.

The Ninth Party Congress, which was held in mid-March 2011, produced fewer surprises. Choummaly Sayasone was re-elected as Secretary-General of the LPRP, while a new 61-member Central Committee and an 11-member Politburo were also chosen. Three new members, all of whom were cadres from northern provinces, were elected to the Politburo; with two of the three outgoing members hailing from the south, the previous southern dominance in the Politburo thus gave way to a more balanced regional representation. As all three new members had a non-military background, there was a net gain for civilian party 'apparatchiks'. However, the Lao People's Army remained influential, as four members of the Politburo were retired senior military officers.

On 30 April 2011 more than 3.2m. Lao went to the polls to elect a new National Assembly. Of the 132 members elected, 33 were women; this fell slightly short of the official target of achieving 30% female representation in the legislature. An indirect presidential poll was conducted on 15 June, when Choummaly Sayasone was re-elected by the members of the National Assembly for a further five-year term. Thongsing Thammavong was similarly confirmed as Prime Minister, and a new cabinet was formally approved by the National Assembly. The incoming Council of Ministers comprised a significant number of ministers who were bound by family ties. The main challenge for the new Government would be to maintain the robust rate of economic growth of recent years (GDP having expanded by an average of almost 8% annually during 2006–10) with the aim of raising Laos's status from that of a least developed country, according to UN criteria, to that of a developing country by 2020.

The Government spent much of 2010 preparing to celebrate the 450th anniversary of the establishment of Vientiane as the Laotian capital. A number of Lao-language books on the history of Laos, and of Vientiane in particular, were published during the year. New roads were built and temples renovated, but the majority of activity was reserved for the Mekong River, where new embankments and a river-side park—to be named after Chao Anouvong, the 19th-century King of Vientiane—were constructed. A statue of the King looking out over the former Lao territories lost to Thailand was unveiled at the opening of the park on 6 November, the 93rd anniversary of the October Revolution in Russia; some observers interpreted the timing of this as an indication that the LPRP leadership was seeking to dissipate fears of an ideological shift from communism to nationalism in the LPDR.

Environmental and Social Issues

In addition to concerns about the threat that rapid regional integration (see below) poses to Lao culture, there exists a growing awareness of the importance of environmental issues such as the impact of dam construction, the rate of timber extraction and threats to the country's natural biodiversity. The huge Nam Theun 2 project, located on the Nam Theun River in central Laos and completed in 2009, covered a large portion of the bio-diverse Nakai Plateau. Commercial exports of electricity to Thailand commenced in March 2010, and revenue from the project was to be directed to the country's ambitious poverty reduction programme.

However, non-governmental organizations concerned with environmental protection have been critical of the impact of the Nam Theun 2 dam. The Laotian authorities have a poor record for resettlement of villagers displaced by the dam, which has had a significant impact on wildlife on the Nakai Plateau, and on fisheries downstream from the dam. In May 2000, meanwhile, the Government imposed a ban on all timber exports, in an attempt to reduce the endemic over-exploitation and smuggling of the country's dwindling timber reserves. However, by then, the entire area of the Nam Theun 2 dam had been clear felled by timber interests allied to the Laotian military. Most was sold to Viet Nam to supply its booming furniture industry. Even after the ban, illegal logging continued along the length of the Laotian–Vietnamese border, reportedly under the protection of corrupt authorities and the military. While Laotian officials enriched themselves with bribes, the ethnic minorities who depended on the forest were being steadily deprived of their livelihood.

The Government has attributed the environmental degradation to the 'slash-and-burn' farming of ethnic minorities, and has vowed to curtail it by relocating villages at lower altitudes where they can farm on a permanent basis and be provided with government services. This programme has been inefficiently carried out and has been beset by corruption. Services have not been provided, and poverty has increased. Meanwhile, tribal lands have been stripped of valuable timber or given over in long-term concessions to foreign companies for plantation agriculture. In other areas, reafforestation has proved only partially successful. In 1993, in an initiative to preserve unique Laotian flora and fauna, the Government set aside 17 'national biodiversity conservation areas', which collectively constituted just over 10% of Laos's total land area. These have been renamed 'national protected areas', but they are not national parks; they are inhabited, and some timber extraction is permitted. Illicit trade in exotic wildlife, mainly for Chinese consumption, remains a serious problem in Laos. Increasing tourism is also likely to have an impact on the Laotian environment (although 'adventure' tourism and 'eco-tourism' are being encouraged). The fragile beauty of the city of Luang Prabang, approved by UNESCO in December 1995 as a World Heritage site, is likely to come under severe pressure in the coming years, as a result of the sheer numbers of tourists expected to visit the city, which attracts up to one-third of the total number of tourists who travel to Laos every year. A World Heritage site listing for the Wat Phu temple complex in southern Laos (approved in December 2001) and for the Plain of Jars (for which an application was submitted in 2004) may have a similar effect. However, tourism is viewed by the Government as an expandable source of national income.

In addition to the issue of corruption (see above), other social concerns relate to the impact on Laos of consumerism, drugs, HIV/AIDS and prostitution, as the country's boundaries become more porous. Despite the imposition of relatively strict controls by the Government, prostitution has reappeared. Laos has not been unaffected by the growing rates of HIV/AIDS in the region, and HIV/AIDS awareness campaigns are now part of the national public health programme. Of equal concern in the spread of the disease is intravenous drug use. Despite a ban on opium cultivation in Laos, imposed in 1997 as a result of pressure from foreign governments, and, notwithstanding the Laotian authorities' stated goal to eradicate opium production by 2008, the drug subsequently remained readily available. The area under opium poppy cultivation rose by some 58% year-on-year in 2010 to reach 3,000 ha. While Laos produces only a small fraction of the quantity of opium produced in Afghanistan, there was a worrying rise in production to 18 metric tons in 2010, from 11 tons in 2009, an increase of some 63.6%. Moreover, heroin and amphetamines also enter the country from neighbouring Myanmar, attracting Western 'drug tourists' and an increasing number of young Lao. (As many as 15% of Lao students aged between 15 and 20 years old are reported to be addicted.) In 2001 the Government introduced the death penalty for drugs-trafficking and launched an intensive anti-drugs campaign aimed at the country's youth. As an indication of the Government's mounting concern, a Central Committee for Drug Control—chaired by the Prime Minister—was established in 2001, and Laos has entered into drug control agreements with neighbouring states.

FOREIGN RELATIONS

Traditionally, there have been two distinct tendencies in Laotian foreign policy: to seek a close relationship with a single powerful ally or neighbour; and to preserve a degree of neutrality by entering into cordial relations with opposing powers. During the Viet Nam War the Pathet Lao developed close relations with North Viet Nam, while the political right wing in Laos developed equally close relations with the USA and Thailand. Both represented the first tendency. Souvanna Phouma, in his hopeless pursuit of neutrality, represented the second. The Pathet Lao victory of 1975 marked the end of Laotian neutrality. The LPDR proclaimed a 'special relationship' with Viet Nam, an alliance formalized by the 25-year Treaty of Friendship and Co-operation signed by the two countries in 1977.

The basis for this special relationship originated in the support given by the Viet Minh to the Pathet Lao during the First Indo-China War. Not only did Vietnamese and Lao fight the French together, but the latter were entirely dependent on the former for all weapons, training and advice. During this time close personal relations developed between the leaders of both revolutionary movements, but it was the long struggle under intense US bombardment during the Viet Nam War that consolidated their relationship. Throughout the war the Pathet Lao depended on Vietnamese military support, and the sacrifice of Vietnamese forces fighting in Laos. After 1975 the LPDR had insufficient numbers of educated cadres to administer the country, and so continued to be dependent on Viet Nam. The relationship that developed was multi-faceted, but Laotian leaders knew that they could always rely on Viet Nam. The relationship between the military establishments of both countries was particularly close.

When the Third Indo-China War broke out with the Vietnamese invasion of Cambodia at the end of 1978, followed by China's attack on Viet Nam a couple of months later, Laos, somewhat reluctantly, aligned itself with Viet Nam. This immediately provoked the Chinese Government's anger, and for a while it seemed that China might support an insurgency in Laos aimed at overthrowing the Government. Kong Le, leader of the neutralist coup of 1960, and several dissident Lao communists organized small-scale guerrilla activities in Luang Namtha. As the movement failed to attract sufficient support from the local population, the insurgency collapsed and Kong Le returned to France in 1983. In the following years Laotian-Chinese relations gradually improved. With the collapse of communism in the USSR and Eastern Europe at the end of the 1980s, Viet Nam was deprived of its principal source of military and financial support, and the cost of its continued occupation of Cambodia in view of Chinese antagonism became too great. Viet Nam withdrew its forces from both Cambodia and Laos in an attempt to improve relations with China. Laos followed suit, to the point where in May 1988 Laos and China re-established full diplomatic relations. In the following October Kaysone Phomvihane, leader of the LPRP, headed a high-ranking Laotian delegation to Beijing to reinforce the much-improved relations with China, a visit reciprocated in December 1990 when the Chinese Premier, Li Peng, arrived in Vientiane.

Relations between Laos and Thailand were even more difficult as Laotian and Thai troops fought two serious border skirmishes in 1984 and 1988, but they rapidly improved after the Thai Prime Minister, Gen. Chatichai Choonhavan, took advantage of moves towards solving the Cambodian problem to declare that his vision was to convert mainland South-East Asia from a war zone to a market-place. Chatichai exchanged visits with Kaysone in November 1988 and February 1989, as Thai business executives took advantage of the new investment climate in Laos. The principal cause of friction between the two countries came from the activities of insurgents across their common border. In June 1991 an agreement was concluded between Laos and Thailand to address the fundamental causes of the problem. In conjunction with the UN High Commissioner for Refugees (UNHCR), most of the 60,000 Laotian refugees, the majority of them Hmong, remaining in Thai camps were resettled in third countries. Although the programme advanced more slowly than envisaged, owing partly to Hmong resistance, the closure of several camps proceeded, with a corresponding reduction in support for insurgents operating against the Laotian Government. Laos had, meanwhile, ended all support for the Communist Party of Thailand. A system was put in place allowing Laotian and Thai Governors of provinces along the common border to meet regularly to discuss frontier issues.

By the early 1990s, therefore, Laos had succeeded in developing good relations with all its neighbours. Laos continued to maintain its special relationship with Viet Nam, but no longer to the exclusion of China and Thailand. In effect, Laos reverted to its more traditional policy of developing friendly relations with neighbouring states. An important aspect of these improved relations was the delineation of common borders. The first to be negotiated was the Laotian–Vietnamese frontier (although the last of the border markers were not expected to be in place until 2014), followed by border agreements with China and Myanmar. Border demarcation with Cambodia was due for completion by the end of 2010. Although this target was not met, progress continued to be made, and as of mid-2011 the Cambodian authorities claimed to have planted 121 of the requisite 148 border posts along the border with Laos. In June Laos, Cambodia and Viet Nam signed an agreement to accelerate border demarcation in order to create a 'peaceful and co-operative triangle economic zone'. Only the long Laotian–Thai border remained a matter of dispute; slow progress was made, and as of mid-2011 some difficult points of contention remained unresolved.

Although the USA never broke off diplomatic relations with Laos, it did withdraw its ambassador, and relations were strained for the first decade of the regime of the LPDR. Co-operation began over the search for missing US servicemen, and resulted in 1992 in the re-establishment of full ambassadorial relations. The two sides also co-operated on drug control measures. The resumption of US aid to Laos followed three years later, when an exception was made to the restrictions imposed by the US Administration on granting aid to communist states. It was not until mid-1998 that the USA agreed to extend financial and logistical support for the ongoing programme to clear unexploded ordnance from the Viet Nam War. However, overall, US aid to Laos remained limited, at a fraction of that provided by Japan, and also less than that of Sweden, France or Australia.

Australia and Sweden were the first two Western countries to establish foreign aid programmes in Laos. Sweden was particularly active in assisting the Laotian forestry industry, while Australia provided most of the English-language instruction and scholarships for Lao to study abroad. Diplomatic relations between Laos and France were severed for five years from 1978 to 1983, and were fragile thereafter until the problem of Laos's outstanding debt to France was resolved. The issue of debt also complicated relations with Russia after the collapse of the USSR, until an agreement was reached on reduction in accordance with exchange rates and rescheduling. In the 1990s other European countries provided aid to Laos: notably Germany, but also Norway and Belgium. Japan funded a variety of programmes, from infrastructure to irrigation, including a bridge across the Mekong and a new international airport terminal for Vientiane.

In July 1997 Laos formally joined ASEAN; membership entailed costs as well as benefits for Laos, not the least of which was the financial burden of participating in the organization's many regional forums. Relations with neighbouring states continued to be cordial in the 1990s; Laos developed amicable links with Myanmar and Cambodia, both of which shared a degree of suspicion of Thai ambitions in the region. Relations with China also remained good: delegations were frequently exchanged, and China provided not only economic and technical assistance to Laos, but also some military aid. China was particularly helpful during the Asian economic crisis of the late 1990s, providing a reported US $1,700m. to stabilize the Laotian currency. However, the Laotian Government was careful to balance its foreign relations. Owing to historically close political relations, Viet Nam continued to wield considerable influence in Laos: links between Vietnamese and Laotian parties and military establishments remained strong, and several memorials were erected recognizing the sacrifice of Vietnamese troops who had died in Laos during the Second Indo-China War. Japan, meanwhile, remained the largest foreign aid donor, followed by Germany, Sweden, France and Australia. Cordial relations with the USA were maintained through continued co-operation over the issues of drugs and of US servicemen missing in action since the Viet Nam War. However, initiatives to restore Normal Trading Relations (NTR) encountered resistance, and the USA remained critical of Laos's human rights record. Nevertheless, full diplomatic relations were established with the Republic of Korea (South Korea) and with several Central Asian republics that were formerly part of the USSR. Laos also maintained its strong links with India.

In response to the risk posed to national security by the attacks of 2000 and to the ongoing economic crisis, the Laotian Government sought a consolidation of relations with its communist neighbours. Both Viet Nam and China offered to increase economic assistance to Laos. Cross-border trade was stimulated in order to reduce Laotian dependency on Thai imports and the country's substantial negative trade balance with Thailand, while Chinese and Vietnamese investment both increased. China agreed to provide Laos with technical assistance and emergency loans, partly for the purchase of military equipment, while the Vietnamese provided security advice.

The rising power of China, and its Government's obvious intention to increase its influence in South-East Asia, led to improved relations with Laos. In July 2000 President Khamtay made an official visit to China, and in November President Jiang Zemin became the first Chinese head of state to visit Laos. In 2001 the National Cultural Palace, a huge building showcasing traditional Lao architecture, was inaugurated in the centre of Vientiane; constructed with Chinese financial support, this grandiose building subsequently hosted a wide range of cultural activities and political events.

However, in the conduct of its foreign relations, Laos maintained an even balance between Viet Nam and China. Senior Laotian and Vietnamese officials frequently exchanged visits, and, following his appointment as Prime Minister in 2001, Boungnang Volachit visited first the Vietnamese capital of Hanoi and then Beijing in 2002, as did the new Minister of National Defence, Lt-Gen. Douangchai Phichit. On each occasion new bilateral agreements were signed, including an accord reinforcing security links with Viet Nam. The month of July 2002 marked both the 40th anniversary of the establishment of diplomatic relations between Laos and Viet Nam, and the 25th anniversary (and expiry) of the Treaty of Friendship and Co-operation signed by the two countries in 1977. President Khamtay paid an official four-day visit to Hanoi in May 2002, during which both sides agreed to hold joint celebrations and to protect and develop their 'traditional relations'. No mention was made of an extension of the Treaty, which seemed unnecessary as both states had by then acceded to ASEAN membership, but the 30th anniversary of its signing, coinciding with the 45th anniversary of the formal establishment of diplomatic relations between the two countries, was celebrated in 2007.

Relations with Cambodia were never as close as with Viet Nam. One-third of the population of Stung Treng in north-western Cambodia, once part of Champasak, are still lowland Lao. Once consensus was reached on the issue of border demarcation, plans were announced for a new development zone in the border area shared by Laos, Cambodia and Viet

Nam—the so-called 'Emerald Triangle'. Although demarcation of the border between Laos and Thailand also progressed, relations with Thailand continued to be uneasy, even after the visit to Vientiane of Thai Prime Minister Thaksin Shinawatra in June 2001. Tensions centred upon river works being undertaken by both countries, Thai naval patrols, drugs- and people-trafficking, the activities of Lao anti-Government insurgents in Thailand, and even a Thai film that the Lao considered insulting to the 19th-century King of Vientiane, Chao Anouvong. While production of the film was halted, other matters proved more intractable.

Relations with Viet Nam, particularly with regard to the military, continued to be close. A bilateral agreement was concluded to promote co-operation between the general staffs of the Laotian and Vietnamese armed forces. Laos also maintained cordial relations with significant donor countries, although some frustration was caused by delays in the granting of NTR status by the USA. These delays were largely attributable to lobbying by Lao-Americans and US concerns over the lack of democracy and religious freedom in Laos. NTR status was eventually granted in December 2004, thereby placing Lao-US relations on a new basis, but a later US offer of military co-operation in the form of army medical teams and civil engineers was rejected as premature. US aid to Laos remained minimal. Meanwhile, the European Union opened a representative office in Vientiane and increased its aid to the country.

The Laotian Government benefited from its heightened international profile in 2004–05 as the host of both the 10th ASEAN summit meeting at the end of November 2004 and the 38th ASEAN Ministerial Meeting in July 2005. These were the largest official events ever to be held in Laos, each involving thousands of delegates and officials, as well as hundreds of journalists. Despite initial concerns over security, both events passed without incident, much to the relief of the Laotian authorities.

For Laos the most significant of the 30 or so documents signed at the ASEAN summit meeting was the Vientiane Action Programme (VAP), designed to reduce the development gap between the wealthier nations of ASEAN 6 (Brunei, Indonesia, Malaysia, the Philippines, Singapore and Thailand) and the less-developed members of the Association (Cambodia, Laos, Myanmar and Viet Nam). To this end an ASEAN Development Fund was established to promote various projects in the poorer countries during the period 2005–10. The Fund was to seek contributions from ASEAN dialogue partners represented at both meetings (particularly the so-called ASEAN + 3 group, encompassing the Association's members along with Japan, China and South Korea). Laos was less likely to benefit from moves by the ASEAN + 3 group and India towards the conclusion of free trade agreements with ASEAN.

In 2006 the first official visits undertaken by the new Laotian leaders, President Choummaly and Prime Minister Bouasone, were to Viet Nam and China, respectively. This had become customary, but it highlighted the direction in which Laos, as one of the world's few remaining Marxist states, turned for international support. Cordial relations with Japan were strengthened by the agreement of land-locked Laos to join the International Whaling Commission in 2007, at Japan's invitation.

In March 2008 Laos hosted the third summit meeting of heads of state of the countries that constitute the Greater Mekong Subregion. Premier Wen Jiabao represented China. The leaders agreed to make the integration of transport and energy the priority for the period 2008–12, supported by an improved institutional framework and increased co-operation. The completion in April of Route 3 from the Chinese border to Ban Houayxay on the Mekong, where a new bridge was to link Laos to Thailand, would ultimately allow road traffic to cover the distance between Bangkok and Kunming, in Yunnan Province, China, in little over a day.

As major Chinese projects in the mining, hydropower and rubber sectors came to fruition, China overtook Thailand to become the leading investor in Laos in the 2006/07 fiscal year. China also became the principal provider of low-interest loans, displacing Japan. However, the increasing Chinese presence in Laos was a source of some consternation. The appropriation of land for plantations provoked popular resentment, while lack of transparency in granting mining concessions attracted criticism. Of particular concern was an agreement between the Laotian Government and a Chinese company in 2008 to construct a new national stadium (which was completed in time for Laos successfully to host the 2009 South-East Asian Games in December of that year) in return for a concession to construct a 1,600-ha housing development in Vientiane. The Government was forced to deny rumours that the development would be reserved for 50,000 Chinese migrants. The influx of Chinese settlers into the sparsely populated border zones of northern Laos has remained a matter of concern. However, one positive side-effect of this has been that the growing Chinese presence in these once-impoverished areas has allowed the Laotian Government to extend its electricity grid to remote villages.

In early 2008 the Swedish Government announced that, after 34 years, it was to phase out Sweden's aid programme to Laos, at that time amounting to US $20m.–$25m. per annum. Projects affected included resource management and road construction.

The greatest foreign policy concern for the Laotian Government during 2008/09 was the global financial crisis. Following an official visit to China in December 2008, President Choummaly travelled to Viet Nam in April 2009 and to Thailand in May. Thai Prime Minister Somchai Wongsawat made a state visit to Vientiane in November 2008, as did his successor, Abhisit Vejjajiva, in January 2009. This series of official visits produced little in the way of substantive results for Laos, apart from commitments to continue to promote investment, trade and tourism, all of which had been affected by the global downturn. Relations with China were slightly tempered by Laos's refusal to grant the Chinese company building the new stadium its preferred site for its housing development in Vientiane. Privately, the Laotian authorities were also concerned about the transfer of ownership of the Sepon mining venture from Australia's OZ Minerals to China's Minmetals group.

Relations with Viet Nam remained cordial. However, relations with Thailand continued to be troubled by persistent problems: these included the issue of Lao Hmong refugees in Thailand (see above), illegal Lao immigrants working in Thailand, the trafficking of people and drugs, the theft and sale in Thailand of Buddha statues from southern Laos, and the ongoing failure to complete demarcation of the Laotian–Thai frontier. In a more positive development, Thai companies agreed to buy Laotian electricity and to build the Theun-Hinboun hydropower project in central Laos, while the first rail link between the two countries (from Nong Khai to Tha Naleng, near Vientiane) commenced operations in March 2009.

A brief visit to Laos by Ban Ki-Moon in April 2009 was the first for several decades by a UN Secretary-General. Ban praised the Laotian Government for its reduction of poverty over the previous decade from 46% to 33% of the population. He committed the UN and its agencies, which were administering several important aid programmes in Laos, to supporting the country's goal of eliminating poverty by 2020.

Laos continued to pursue its policy of promoting friendly relations with those states prepared to provide aid and/or investment, both of which lagged behind targets set in the Seventh Five-Year Plan. President Choummaly paid a state visit to Japan in March 2010 and welcomed Japan's Prince Akishino, son of Emperor Akihito, to Laos later in the same month. This was followed by an official visit to Japan by Prime Minister Bouasone in May, during which Japan pledged continued aid for poverty reduction in Laos. Meanwhile, delegations arrived in Vientiane from India, South Korea and Malaysia, all of which have increased their levels of investment in Laos. Thai investment also increased, particularly in the hydropower sector.

Perhaps the most significant diplomatic exchange in 2010 was the meeting in Washington, DC, in July between Deputy Prime Minister and Minister of Foreign Affairs Thongloun Sisolit and US Secretary of State Hillary Clinton, the first official visit to the USA by a Laotian minister responsible for foreign affairs since the establishment of the LPDR in 1975. An air travel co-operation agreement was signed with a view to enhancing tourism; other areas of discussion included bilateral trade, US aid and military co-operation.

However, any improvement in relations with the USA was counterbalanced by continuing close relations with Viet Nam and China. An official visit to Laos in April 2010 by Nong Duc Manh, General Secretary of the Communist Party of Viet Nam (CPV), was followed by the arrival in June of a high-level Chinese delegation; during the latter visit Laos and China signed 18 co-operation agreements pertaining to a wide range of fields, including bilateral trade and development. Furthermore, Deputy Prime Minister and Minister of National Defence Lt-Gen. Douangchai Phichit made a visit to Beijing in July, during which he signed a military co-operation agreement with his Chinese counterpart. In mid-September Prime Minister Bouasone, accompanied by a senior-level ministerial delegation, embarked on an official visit to Viet Nam. In June 2011 Nguyen Phu Trong, the General Secretary of the CPV Central Committee, visited Vientiane. During his stay, both countries stressed the strategic significance of the Laotian-Vietnamese relationship and designated 2012 as the 'Year of Viet Nam-Laos friendship and solidarity'; the two countries also pledged to organize joint celebrations to commemorate the 35th anniversary of the signing of the (now defunct) Treaty of Friendship and Co-operation.

Owing to its geographical position, Laos has remained a strategic state in the economic integration of mainland South-East Asia. The first bridge across the Mekong River, the Lao-Thai Friendship Bridge, some 30 km downstream from Vientiane, was opened in 1994, the first in a series of infrastructure projects (see Economy) destined eventually to link Thailand, Viet Nam and southern China via Laos. Construction of a fourth bridge over the Mekong, between the Laotian province of Khammouane and the Thai province of Nakhon Pathom, was reported to be 97% complete in September 2011 and was scheduled to be officially inaugurated in November of that year. A fifth bridge over the Mekong, to be financed jointly by Thailand and China, was to link the Laotian province of Bokeo and the northernmost Thai province, Chiang Rai; however, the project encountered numerous delays and construction was reported to be less than 10% complete at early 2011, with completion not expected until mid-2012. Attention has also been given to the development of the road network as part of a programme supported by the ADB to promote integration in the so-called Greater Mekong Subregion (comprising Cambodia, China's Yunnan Province, Laos, Myanmar, Thailand and Viet Nam). Much of the trade between Thailand and Viet Nam now passes through Laos. Construction of Laos's first railway, a 3.5-km line linking Nong Khai in Thailand across the Friendship Bridge to Tha Naleng, near Vientiane, was completed in April 2008, and the first passenger train service commenced in March 2009. In April 2010 China signed a memorandum of understanding (MOU) agreeing to co-operate with Laos in developing a railway from the Laos–China border to Vientiane, from where it would ultimately link up with the rail network in Viet Nam, via Nong Khai and Thakhek. Few details were provided in the MOU, but a long-term Chinese government loan was expected to fund the project, the total cost of which was estimated at US $4,000m.

Meanwhile, as Lao citizens became increasingly concerned by the rapid pace of regional integration and the threats to their society and environment, the impact of a series of dams that China had constructed on the upper reaches of the Mekong River was among a number of issues discussed at the first summit meeting of the Mekong River Commission—hosted by Thailand in April 2010, and attended by the respective heads of government of Thailand, Laos, Cambodia and Viet Nam—which was convened in order to examine the long-term sustainability of the entire system. As a result of the Chinese dams, at mid-2010 the water level in the river was reported to be at its lowest in some 50 years, a level too shallow for the safe operation of river boats. (Conversely, heavy rainfall in mid-2011 led to a rapid increase in the water level in the Mekong River, prompting concerns about widespread flooding.) Moreover, as elsewhere, increasing pressure on shared water resources owing to population growth was beginning to affect Laos's relations with neighbouring states.

During 2011 Laos intensified preparations for its hosting of the ninth summit of the Asia-Europe Meeting (ASEM), which was due to be held in Vientiane in November 2012. Laotian and Chinese companies signed an agreement in April 2011 pertaining to a 25-ha urban development project in Vientiane. The US $180m. project was to be divided into three phrases, and upon completion would incorporate residential housing, offices and hotels, as well as shopping, entertainment, education and medical centres. The first phase of construction, which was expected to be finished shortly prior to the ASEM summit in 2012, was to include 50 villas and conference buildings.

Economy

NICK FREEMAN

The establishment of the Lao People's Democratic Republic (LPDR) in December 1975 marked the end of a lengthy civil war in Laos. Caught within the vortex of Cold War rivalry and the intensive conflict being waged in neighbouring Viet Nam, the civil war in Laos was primarily fought between pro-communist Pathet Lao forces and the anti-communist Royal Lao Government (RLG) military. The chaos and division caused by the civil war had excluded the possibility of any significant economic development occurring in Laos following the end of French colonial rule in 1953. The preceding 70 years of French administration had resulted in very little economic development in the country. Having been regarded as little more than a colonial backwater within the French empire, Laos had been governed by France on a low budget. Compared with the relatively significant investment made in Viet Nam, French entrepreneurs identified few commercial projects in Laos, other than a limited number of businesses principally relating to mining, agriculture and some basic trading. Rather, land-locked Laos's role was deemed to be primarily a strategic one, with the country acting as a buffer between France's more lucrative occupation of Viet Nam, and British interests in colonial Burma (now Myanmar) and the independent Kingdom of Siam (now Thailand).

Following the Pathet Lao victory in 1975, senior members of the political leadership, the Lao People's Revolutionary Party (LPRP), descended from their headquarters in the remote north-east of the country and took power in the capital, Vientiane. In addition to the social, political and security challenges confronting the new Government, the LPRP rapidly had to contend with an economy that would now have to function without the massive levels of US assistance that had financially supported the RLG regime, and grossly distorted Laos's economy for much of the previous decade. The immense damage inflicted on the country during the Viet Nam War, most notably as a result of US 'carpet bombing' of areas along Laos's eastern border with Viet Nam, also needed to be addressed, in order that refugees could be resettled and agricultural activity could recommence. Furthermore, areas of upland Laos that had previously been under LPRP control now had to be integrated with the newly liberated lowland parts of the country. With Soviet-inspired central planning techniques, and under the guidance of fraternal sponsors, the LPRP leadership set about addressing these challenges with the kind of zeal perhaps to be expected of those still flushed with military victory. The Government's aim was to create a centrally planned economy in Laos, based on the notion of collective ownership. Most private companies in the nascent industry and service sectors were nationalized, as was the entire banking sector, the latter being consolidated into a single mono-bank structure. It is estimated that up to 80% of Laos's small industrial sector was placed under direct state ownership during this period, and market forces were replaced by fixed output targets set by the new and inexperienced State Planning Committee.

A state marketing board to which peasants were obliged to sell their surplus agricultural goods was established in 1976, setting prices for staple goods, including rice. The marketing board issued coupons in payment for agricultural products, which people could then use to buy goods in state-run stores. Adverse weather conditions during 1976–78, compounded by ill-conceived policies, resulted in a marked decline in agricultural output. Mass collectivization of agriculture was also attempted by the LPRP, albeit relatively briefly. Initially at least, the number of agricultural collectives was low, but by 1978 the total exceeded 1,000. Although mandatory directives on collectivization were abandoned as early as 1979, the subsequent introduction of various inducements—such as privileged access to cheap credit and lower tax rates—resulted in an increase in the number of collectives to almost 4,000 by 1986. However, some of these collectives were little more than quasi-formal groups of peasants providing mutual assistance, content to be classified as collectives in order to qualify for the privileges granted by the Government. Not surprisingly, collectivization was particularly strong in areas that had previously been under the control of the LPRP prior to 1975, or where the provincial Government's socialist vigour was most ardent, and weakest in areas where swidden (shifting) cultivation was practised. For example, over 80% of the cultivated area of Champasak Province was under collectivization in 1984, compared with 8.5% in Vientiane and less than 6% in the former royal capital of Luang Prabang. State-owned trading companies enjoyed a monopoly on both external and even inter-provincial trading activity. In addition, a broad policy of import-substitution was introduced by Laos's policy-makers, despite the blatant limitations of the country's domestic industrial sector.

The scale of the challenge confronting the relatively inexperienced leadership, together with the inappropriate use of economic planning methods and the lack of sensitivity shown to those who had previously lived in areas controlled by the RLG, cumulatively served to create an economic crisis. The exodus of those Lao who had been directly associated with the RLG, its regular armed forces or irregular ethnic minority forces, was soon followed by the departure of those entrepreneurs and professionals who did not relish the prospect of living under a communist regime, where property rights were no longer respected and where business assets were arbitrarily seized by LPRP fiat. Within a few years, Laos lost a substantial proportion of its already small educated middle and entrepreneurial classes, and a paucity of skilled human resources has been a significant factor in the slow pace of economic development ever since.

Prior to 1975 Laos had been heavily dependent upon trade with neighbouring Thailand for a wide range of goods. However, tension between Vientiane and Bangkok (particularly over the fate of the Laotian royal family after 1975) led to a disruption of border trade in the late 1970s. High inflation soon developed, exacerbated by an expansive monetary and fiscal policy implemented by the new leadership. The scale and vehemence of popular resistance to the leadership's attempt at the collectivization of lowland agriculture, as well as opposition to its efforts to halt swidden upland agriculture, along with various other elements of the country's 'socialist transformation', appear to have surprised the LPRP leadership. Far from showing early signs of a vigorous new economy, and deriving the anticipated benefits of the peace dividend and central planning methods, the first years of the LPDR were characterized by declining output, lower living standards for the urban Lao (no longer supported by US aid) and stubborn rural resistance to the policies of the new leadership. Quite clearly, the attempt to create a centrally planned economy was not generating the required results. Consequently, in 1979 the LPRP was obliged to adopt a less vigorous approach to the socialist transformation of the Laotian economy, following a similar decision taken in neighbouring Viet Nam earlier that year. The concept of obligatory collectivization was abandoned, and a limited role for the private sector was reluctantly recognized. State enterprises were slowly granted a greater degree of independence over day-to-day decision-making. At the Third Congress of the LPRP, held in 1982, the leadership affirmed that Laos's transition to a socialist system could not be conducted according to the rapid pace envisaged after the party's military victory in 1975. Instead, it was decided that a more gradual and incremental approach would be pursued, although the ultimate goal of a socialist transformation of the economy remained. While these partial reforms helped dissipate the economic crisis confronting Laos in the late 1970s, they were insufficient to effect a sustained economic revival, and by the mid-1980s it had become clear that a more substantive programme of economic liberalization measures would be needed.

A more radical and comprehensive programme of economic reforms, often referred to as the New Economic Mechanism (NEM), was endorsed by the Fourth Party Congress in November 1986. The NEM involved a transition of the economy towards a more market-orientated system, albeit with many socialist elements remaining in place, and from an economy striving towards collective ownership to one tentatively based on private ownership. The NEM principally entailed the long-awaited introduction of a Constitution and a legal regime; the recognition of property rights; the privatization of most state enterprises; price reform; the creation of factor markets and the end of state distribution systems; financial sector reforms; and the opening of the economy to foreign trade and investment. As the period of central planning in Laos had endured for less than a decade, it was possible to dismantle much of the socialist economic system within the first five years of the reform programme. The collapse of the socialist bloc in the late 1980s also influenced Laos's economic reforms, as relatively significant quantities of aid from fraternal allies contracted sharply. The country was thus obliged to seek alternative sources of external assistance and, in order to attract funding from the international donor community, the Laotian leadership had little choice but to make changes to its economic management methods. In 1987 the state marketing board was closed, allowing the prices and distribution of items like rice to be dictated by the market. The policy of import-substitution was also abandoned, in favour of greater external trade, and state-owned trading enterprises slowly began to lose their monopoly privileges on import and export activities. One year later the tax and credit privileges granted to agricultural collectives were halted. The local currency was again devalued in 1987, and the fixed exchange rate system was abandoned in the following year. Subsequently, the official exchange rate was adjusted to correspond to the unofficial market rate, ultimately allowing for a managed 'float' of the kip to be formally adopted in 1995.

The first, and long overdue, Constitution of the LPDR was promulgated in August 1991, a full 16 years after the LPRP took power, and heralded the leadership's belated recognition that genuine and sustained economic development could not proceed without the rule of law (as opposed to arbitrary Party fiat) and some respect for property rights. Foreign investors in particular, who were perceived as an important source of both financial and non-financial contributions to the economic development of the country, were unwilling to commit substantial sums of investment capital in Laos without some recognition of property rights and a legal process, however vague and untested they might be. A property law (albeit based more on user rights than on private ownership per se), contract law and inheritance law were all approved in 1990. A number of other reforms were enacted in 1990–91, including the reintroduction of central government control over regional bank branches and state enterprises, responsibility for which had previously rested with the relevant provincial authorities. The provincial authorities also lost control over the collection of tax revenues and the allocation of state expenditure. A second foreign investment law was approved in 1994, along with a basic business law and customs law, and remaining restrictions on internal movement were removed. A domestic investment law and a tax law were approved one year later, with the latter undergoing slight revision in 1998. A Law on Promotion of Foreign Investment was promulgated in 2004, and a significantly revised Enterprise Law (replacing the 1994 Business Law) was adopted by the National Assembly in late 2005. A new investment promotion law, encompassing both domestic and foreign investors, and intended to liberalize arrangements for approving investment projects, was adopted by the National Assembly in July 2009 and promulgated in March 2010. Under the law, additional incentives were offered to those investing in hospitals, schools and public utilities, while foreigners providing investment of at least US $500,000 would be entitled to purchase residential land use rights in certain areas.

The Laotian economy is small, with a gross domestic product (GDP) of an estimated US $6,461m. in 2010, according to the IMF. The average per caput gross national income (GNI) in Laos remains low, at around $880 in 2009, albeit a marked improvement upon the 2001 level of $310. However, about one-third of the population lives below the poverty line, with income of less than $1 per day—statistics more typical of sub-Saharan Africa than of the dynamic region of South-East Asian. In 2010, according to the Asian Development Bank (ADB), the GDP of Laos expanded by 7.3% in 2009 and by 7.5% in 2010. The World Health Organization estimated that in 2008 average life expectancy at birth in Laos was just 62 years (up from 40 years in 1960), which compared poorly with 73 years in neighbouring Viet Nam. The country had an adult literacy rate of 73.2% in 2007, according to UNESCO estimates. In 2008 only 31% of the population lived in urban areas. The annual rate of population growth was estimated at 1.7% in 2000–08. Laos has a youthful demographic profile. The distribution of the population in Laos is far from uniform, with 52% of the country's population living in just four of its 18 provinces (Vientiane, Savannakhet, Champasak and Luang Prabang) in 2009; 20% of the population resided within Vientiane Province alone. Population density in Laos as a whole is very low, at 27.7 people per sq km in mid-2011. The total work-force in Laos was estimated by FAO at around 3.4m. at mid-2011. However, only about 10%–15% were believed to be salaried, while 74.7% were involved in agriculture, the majority of whom were engaged in subsistence rather than commercial farming. An estimated 200,000 Lao were working in Thailand, earning as much as $100m. per year in inward remittances (equivalent to about 5% of the country's GDP).

The latter part of the 1990s witnessed a marked deceleration in the momentum of economic reform. This was attributable in part to the adverse impact of the regional economic crisis, which engendered indecision within the Laotian leadership over whether further economic liberalization was the correct way to proceed. This indecision was exacerbated by changes in the profile of the senior leadership, and the development of much greater military representation in the senior ranks of the LPRP: by 2000 all but one of the eight members of the Political Bureau (Politburo) were serving or retired military men. The sharp economic deterioration in neighbouring Thailand in 1997 undoubtedly had an adverse impact on Laos, most notably through a very sharp downturn in the value of the kip against both the US dollar and the Thai baht. Relative to the US dollar, the kip lost 80% of its value in the two years following the onset of the regional economic crisis in July 1997. However, not all of the depreciation in the value of the kip could be attributed directly to contagion from Thailand: a relatively large spending programme was implemented by the Laotian Government at that time in an attempt to augment substantially the production of dry-season paddy through a mass acquisition of water pumps. Under this programme, funding from the central bank was directed both to state enterprises, to enable them to import the pumps, and as credit to farmers for the purchase of the imported pumps. Thus, at a time when fiscal restraint might have been most appropriate in order to restore confidence in the Laotian currency and economy, the Government embarked upon an expansionary monetary programme to fund this (off-budget) dry-season irrigation programme. This, together with a vigorous campaign against unlicensed foreign exchange dealers (which prompted some Lao to fear an impending revaluation of the currency), served further to erode popular confidence in the local currency. Consequently, many Lao citizens and companies alike sought to convert into foreign currency or gold.

The damage done to the value of the kip in 1998–99 was even greater than that inflicted on the Indonesian rupiah, and the Laotian currency depreciated from around 1,500 kips to more than 7,500 kips to the US dollar within just a few years. This decline in the value of the currency resulted in triple-digit inflation in 1998–99, as the price of imported goods rose sharply. Consequently, the spending power of the urban populace decreased considerably, forcing the Government to reduce the length of the working week for civil servants in order that they might devote more time to the pursuit of secondary incomes. The value of the kip against the US dollar depreciated further during 2000–05, to an average of 10,655 kips to the dollar in 2005, but appreciated marginally over the following four years, reaching an average of 8,516 kips to the dollar in 2009. At mid-2011 the Laotian kip stood at roughly 8,000 kips to the dollar, at around 260 kips to the Thai baht. The rate of inflation in Laos declined markedly, from 128.4% in 1999 to 7.7% in 2001. Such a commendable contraction in the inflation rate allowed the Government to embark upon upward price adjustments for heavily subsidized water (by 100%), electricity and domestic aviation tariffs. Following an increase to 7.5% in 2008, the rate of inflation was only 0.1% in 2009, as international food and oil prices decreased substantially. An increase in the inflation rate to about 5.5% in 2010 was attributed to higher food and oil prices, as well as pressure resulting from a significant expansion in the availability of credit and reductions in interest rates during 2009.

AGRICULTURE AND FORESTRY

Agriculture remains the primary source of income and employment in Laos, although much agricultural activity continues to be conducted on a subsistence basis, and overall productivity levels are relatively low. While the economy as a whole achieved relatively high average annual rates of growth during much of the 1990s and the following decade, the agricultural sector recorded more modest growth rates. The GDP of the sector (including forestry and fishing) grew by 3.0% in both 2009 and 2010, according to figures from the ADB. Despite the relatively rapid growth of the industrial and service sectors under the economic reform programme, the agricultural sector continues to dominate the Laotian economy, accounting for 32.8% of the country's total GDP in 2009 and more than 70% of all employment. Rice production accounts for about 75% of total land under cultivation, although the Government has been encouraging farmers to diversify their crop production and, also, to pursue animal husbandry. Adverse weather conditions have the potential to cause a marked impact on the country's overall economic performance, as witnessed during the drought of 1987–88 and the floods of 1995–96, 2000, 2002 and 2008. This is particularly true in the upland areas of Laos, where subsistence farming dominates, most households are poor, there is a lack of capital for the upgrading of technology, environmental degradation has been accelerating, and transport to the limited number of markets remains inadequate. Conversely, the lowland areas began to show signs of greater vitality in the 1990s, with households able to sell a proportion of their increased output, as the revival of market forces began to generate benefits. Lowland farmers are now able to invest in new technology and to buy pesticides and fertilizer, and have better access to markets where they can sell surplus output, thereby benefiting from a conducive spiral of improved income and living standards. The change is particularly evident in the lowland 'Mekong corridor', where the creation of all-weather roads and the development of increased border trade have been identified as the main catalysts behind the achievement of improved productivity and income levels. This divergence between the two agro-economic zones—the uplands and the lowlands—warrants some concern, as all indicators suggest that the disparity between the two areas has continued to widen since the early 1990s.

In 2009 crop production and livestock activities in Laos accounted for an estimated 78.0% of total agricultural GDP, followed by fishing (11.3%) and forestry (10.7%). The dominant crop by far is rice, in which Laos is broadly self-sufficient, with approximately 3.14m. metric tons of paddy harvested in 2009 (compared with just 1.49m. tons in 1990). Vientiane municipality has tended to be the most productive province for growing paddy, followed by Bokeo, Xiangkhouang, Saravan and Champasak Provinces; Sekong, Phongsali and Luang Prabang Provinces, by contrast, have tended to be the least productive. Factors influencing the level of productivity in each province include the quality of transport available, the level of foreign assistance provided, and the presence of unexploded ordnance. In the past Laos tended to have just one main rice harvest per year, during the wet season, yielding only a much smaller harvest during the dry season. Although the Lao population continued to increase during the 1990s, rice output remained broadly static, resulting in a fairly substantial deficit that had to be offset through imports of the commodity from elsewhere. In subsequent years, however, the Government sought to increase substantially the size of the dry-season rice crop in a bid to make the country self-sufficient in rice. In 1997–98 the Government took a risk when it spent a considerable proportion of its foreign exchange reserves on the purchase of a substantial number of diesel-powered water pumps to help farmers irrigate the dry-season paddy fields in lowland areas. The initiative constituted part of a wider 'strategic vision' for the agricultural sector, announced by the Ministry of Agriculture and Forestry in late 1999. This vision included the extension of policies and initiatives that had previously worked well in the lowland areas (including transport upgrading, access to micro-financing for farmers and guidance on diversifying crop production) to the upland areas. However, aid donors noted the omission of some important aspects from the 'strategic vision', with little attention being paid to the fishery sub-sector (despite fish being an important source of protein in Laos, with about 104,925 tons caught in 2008) and livestock (with production of cattle, buffalo, pig and chicken meat estimated by FAO at 102,230 tons in 2009).

Other crops grown in Laos include maize, sugar cane, cassava, sweet potatoes, watermelons, peanuts, soybeans, coffee, tea and tobacco. Total coffee production remains relatively small, despite increasing markedly since the mid-1990s. According to FAO, a record 46,035 metric tons were harvested in 2009 (compared with just 8,576 tons in 1995, and a peak of around 5,000 tons during the French colonial period), across an area of about 52,430 ha. The main coffee-growing area is the high-altitude Bolaven Plateau, in Champasak Province. Around 80% of total production is in the form of robusta, and the rest arabica. Laos has significant potential in this field, and it is conceivable that coffee might become a more prominent source of foreign exchange earnings in the future, particularly once the international price of coffee has stabilized. The development of a dry-season harvest of cash crops should also result in an increase in the output of other agricultural products, providing a useful addition to farmers' incomes and increasing the foreign exchange earnings of the country as a whole.

Swidden cultivation persists in some upland provinces, notwithstanding the Government's concerted attempt to halt this form of activity. In 2006 it was estimated that the number of families involved in swidden cultivation had declined to around 32,000, covering an area of 22,400 ha, compared with more than 155,000 households in 1998 and around 280,000 in the mid-1990s. Many practitioners of swidden cultivation tend to be from ethnic minorities that have sought to resist what they perceive as lowland Lao interference. However, under the Government's 'strategic vision' for the agricultural sector, a renewed attempt to convert swidden farmers to more sedentary forms of cultivation is being made through the implementation of measures including the introduction of feeder roads to allow better market access, improved rural savings mobilization and credit techniques, support for crop diversification, and the development of land entitlement and land use zoning practices.

The Government has set a number of targets in the agricultural sector, to be achieved by 2015. These include: aiming to raise annual rice production to 4m. metric tons, by expanding average yields to 3.9 tons per ha; to increase meat production to 32kg and fish production to 22kg per person annually; to boost annual production of maize and fish to 40,000 tons and 553,000 tons, respectively; to rehabilitate 3.9m. ha of poor forest and reforest a further 200,000 ha; and to increase the amount of irrigated land able to support dry-season food production to 500,000 ha, including 300,000 ha for rice.

With assistance from the UN Development Programme (UNDP), the Laotian Government has sought to clear substantial areas of southern and eastern Laos of unexploded ordnance, most of which was dropped by the US military during the Viet Nam War. Approximately one-half of Laos remains contaminated by over 0.5m. metric tons of unexploded ordnance, resulting in about 120 casualties per year, and effectively rendering parts of 14 provinces unsafe for habitation or cultivation. This unexploded ordnance—and small anti-personnel devices known as 'bombies', in particular—has also hindered the expansion of agriculture in certain areas. UNDP's 'UXO' land clearance project is staffed by almost 1,000 people, making it one of the largest employers in Laos.

According to the UN Office on Drugs and Crime (UNODC), Laos was the third largest opium producer in the world during the 1990s, after Afghanistan and neighbouring Myanmar. The Laotian Government has sought aggressively to eradicate the cultivation of opium in remote upland areas of the country since 2001. In that year the Government boldly pledged to eradicate opium production by the end of 2005, and all other drugs by 2015. It thus received US $80m., principally from the USA and the European Union (EU), in early 2002 to fund a three-year programme to rid Laos of opium. Most opium cultivated in Laos was produced by small-scale subsistence farmers, for medicinal purposes and as a cash crop, as well as for use in traditional festivities. Previously cultivated across 11 northern provinces of Laos, particularly Phongsali and Houaphanh Provinces, opium was subsequently believed to have been confined to just five of Laos's six most northern provinces. The harvest area for the opium poppy steadily declined from a peak of 26,800 ha in 1998 to 12,000 ha in 2002. The area under cultivation was then reported by UNODC to have decreased to just 1,500 ha in 2007, before expanding to 1,600 ha in 2008 and to 1,900 ha in 2009. Calculated by UNODC on the basis of the area under cultivation, the country's potential production of dry opium decreased from an estimated 20.0 metric tons in 2006 to 9.0 tons in 2007 (when it was concluded that Laos had 'virtually eliminated' opium production), before rising to 9.6 tons in 2008 and to 11.4 tons in 2009. The number of new opium addicts, according to UNODC, decreased to just 4,906 in 2008, compared with 7,700 in 2007, although the 2008 figure did not take into account the possible relapse of recently treated addicts. The total number of opium addicts in the northern provinces of Laos was estimated at 12,000–15,000 in 2009. Most opium addicts live in remote upland areas, making it difficult for detoxification programmes to reach them. Although the Government's ambitious eradication programme initially appeared to have been successful, some concern was expressed regarding the strident methods used, including the forced relocation of some hill tribes to lowland locations in which they were ill-suited to settle. This has resulted in markedly higher rates of disease and mortality, according to some reports. It has also removed the primary source of income for some former opium farmers, with insufficient emphasis placed on creating new sources of income in the Government's programme. An additional concern is that the substantial reduction in the production of opium might prompt some addicts to resort to synthetic amphetamines, such as 'yaaba', imported from neighbouring Thailand and Myanmar. In 2011 UNODC reported that the number of amphetamine addicts in Laos totalled around 40,000.

About 42% of Laos (or 9.7m. ha) is covered in natural forestland, a marked reduction from about 50% in 1985 and 70% in 1940. In 2009 forestry accounted for an estimated 3.5% of GDP; timber remained an important source of foreign exchange, providing an estimated 8.0% of export earnings in 2008 (compared with 27.2% in 2003, prior to the growth of copper exports). Additional government revenue is derived from the payment of forest royalties. A small number of companies connected to the Laotian military dominate the logging industry in Laos, and have been particularly active in those areas identified for eventual flooding under proposed hydropower projects. Companies affiliated with the Vietnamese army have also been implicated in illegal logging in Laos, principally to supply the furniture industry in Viet Nam, according to a report published in July 2011 by the British-based non-governmental organization Environmental Investigation Agency. An estimated 596,000 cu m of logs were produced in 2008. An Environment Protection Law was approved in 1999, although Laos's legal institutions lack sufficient institutional capacity to enforce this law properly, particularly with regard to powerful vested interests. The Government aims to have regained forest cover of 65% by 2015 and 70% by 2020, although these targets will be difficult to achieve.

INDUSTRY

The industrial sector (comprising manufacturing, mining, construction and utilities) has recorded a faster rate of growth since the enactment of the NEM reforms than either the agricultural or service sectors. During the early 1990s the rate of growth for the industrial sector was in double figures, although this subsequently declined to single digits in the latter part of that decade. Industrial GDP increased by 16.6% in 2009 and by 17.7% in 2010, according to figures from the ADB, these strong growth rates being driven by substantial activity in the mining and construction sectors. Foreign investment participation—most notably in the energy, mining, beverage, cement and garment sub-sectors—has played a vital role in the industrial sector's relatively impressive performance. Yet, despite commendable growth since the late 1990s, the industrial sector still accounted for only 25.2% of GDP in 2009.

The manufacturing sector accounted for 41.9% of industrial GDP in 2009, and includes a relatively substantial export-orientated garment sector, which recorded improved performance following the reinstatement by the EU of its Generalized System of Preferences (GSP) for Laos in late 1997. The expiry of the Multi-Fibre Arrangement (MFA) on 1 January 2005 has had some impact on Laos's garment sector, obliging producers to find specialist niches where they can compete more effectively with their larger rivals in the neighbouring People's Republic of China and Viet Nam, as well as Cambodia. In addition to garments, the principal products of the manufacturing sector include beer and soft drinks, wood products, plastic products, tobacco and cigarettes. Heavy industry is virtually non-existent in Laos, with the exception of cement production. The industrial sector is also unevenly distributed within Laos, with more than 60% of all enterprises located in Vientiane, Savannakhet, Champasak and Luang Prabang Provinces. Indeed, two-thirds of all Laos's large-scale manufacturing companies are to be found within Vientiane Province alone. Similarly, the vast majority of Laos's garment, footwear and textiles companies are located within municipal Vientiane.

Despite having been granted partial managerial autonomy in the late 1970s, state enterprises continued to perform poorly during much of the 1980s. The Government responded by introducing a programme of privatization for all non-strategic state firms, commencing in 1989. The privatization programme comprised a number of different forms of divestment, including leasing arrangements, management buy-outs, transfer of ownership to provincial authorities, outright sales to local or foreign enterprises, partial equity sales into joint venture companies with foreign investors, and several liquidations. However, the programme encountered a number of difficulties and criticisms relating to: the methods used to value state assets; the opacity of sales procedures; and the rather vague terms of fixed-term leasing arrangements. Nevertheless, by the late 1990s most state enterprises (including the state telecommunications company) had been partially or fully divested, with the exception of those strategic state organizations that the Government did not wish to transfer to the private sector. By 2003 only 158 state-owned companies remained from among the 800 or so that had existed a decade earlier, prompting the IMF to describe the country's privatization programme as 'one of the most successful parts of Laos's structural reforms thus far'. Of the companies that remained, approximately 40 were strategic enterprises that were to continue to be state-owned, while the remainder were non-strategic companies that had proven impossible to divest and it was presumed would ultimately risk liquidation. Since the late 1990s the strategic state enterprises—such as Electricité du Laos, Postes du Laos, the National Tourism Administration, Nam Papa Lao (Lao Water Supply Authority) and the Banque pour le Commerce Extérieur Lao—have been undergoing a process of 'commercialization', primarily entailing financial and managerial restructuring, in order that they might be better able to compete with their private sector equivalents. Moves by the Government to allow strategic state enterprises to charge viable rates for most of their products and services, such as water and electricity, have also helped to put them on a more sustainable commercial footing.

ENERGY

The utilities sector, dominated by electricity generation, accounted for 11.6% of industrial GDP in 2009. The vast majority of Laos's energy supplies are derived from hydroelectric generators, with a relatively small amount of electricity also being sourced from diesel-powered installations. Laos's hydroelectricity generation totalled 3,428m. kWh in 2009 (compared with 1,044m. kWh in 1995), with installed capacity of 1,826 MW. About 80% of the electricity generated by Laos is exported to neighbouring Thailand, providing significant foreign exchange earnings. Despite the presence of a growing number of major power installations in Laos, the country does not yet have a national power grid, although the Government signed an agreement on the construction of one with China Southern Power Grid in June 2010. Three regional transmission sub-systems serve Vientiane and Luang Prabang, Savannakhet and Thakek, and Champasak and Saravan. Significant progress has been made in improving the provision of electricity to the Lao population in recent years: by mid-2011 roughly 72% of households had access to electricity, compared with just 15% in 1995, and the Government aims to increase this percentage to 90% by 2020. Domestic electricity prices were subsidized in the past, but the Government has gradually increased tariffs to cost-recovery levels since 2002.

Laos's potential power-generating capabilities are considerable, with the country's exploitable hydropower potential alone being estimated at approximately 23,000 MW, and the Government aspires for Laos to become the 'battery of Asia'. Plans for the construction of a substantial number of hydropower plants on rivers feeding into the Mekong progressed slowly in the late 1990s and early years of the following decade, partly owing to a lack of finance, although approvals of foreign investment in the electricity generation sector increased substantially in 2005–08, amounting to US $640m. (52.7% of total foreign investment approvals) in 2008. At mid-2011 no fewer than 73 projects, with an estimated installed capacity of over 23,000 MW, were in various stages of development. Of these, 37 were still undergoing feasibility studies, and five were under construction at mid-2011: Nam Ngum 5 and Nam Xong projects in Vientiane Province; the Theun Hiboun expansion project in Khammouane Province; Nam Hone in Luang Namtha Province; and Xekhaman 3 in Sekong Province.

The mighty 1,088-MW Nam Theun 2 project, located 250 km east of Vientiane, which was the single biggest investment project ever undertaken in Laos, at a cost of around US $1,450m., was financed in large part (around $1,000m.) through commercial loans. Construction of Nam Theun 2 was originally scheduled to commence in 1996 and to be completed by 2000, but extended delays occurred in attaining World Bank approval to provide partial risk cover for the build-own-operate-transfer (BOOT) project, deemed essential for the developers to raise sufficient financing for the venture. This emanated in large part from the World Bank's desire to evaluate the potential environmental, social and other costs entailed in the construction of the dam and the 450-sq km reservoir it was to create, which would necessitate the relocation of 17 village communities. The World Bank made a decision to support the project in 2005, and the power plant commenced commercial operations in early 2010; as a result, electricity exports were forecast to reach $300m. in that year, compared with an estimated $118m. in 2008. A final power-purchasing agreement between the Nam Theun 2 Power Company (NTPC) and the Electricity Generating Authority of Thailand was approved by the Thai Government in 2003. Under this agreement, Thailand was committed to buy 995 MW of electricity from the NTPC over the course of 25 years, at an agreed price of an estimated $5,000m.; the additional foreign exchange revenue attracted by the project would serve as a major fillip for Laos's current account balance.

Having been commissioned in 1971, the ageing Nam Ngum hydropower plant, located 80 km north of Vientiane, was for many years the primary source of electricity generation in Laos, with an installed capacity of just 150 MW. A 45-MW plant located at Xeset was completed in 1991, and generates power solely for export purposes. In April 1998 the 187-MW Theun-Hinboun hydropower project became operational, also raising export earnings through the sale of the electricity generated to Thailand. The 126-MW power project at Huay Ho and the 60-MW Nam Leuk power plant in north-western Laos were both commissioned in 2000, and the 40-MW Nam Mang hydropower plant entered into service in 2005. In 2006 construction began on a 250-MW hydropower plant in Sekong Province. Structured as a build-operate-transfer (BOT) project, it was being developed by a Vietnamese company, and was reported to be the single largest foreign investment project enacted by Viet Nam. Following the entry into service of Nam Theun 2 in early 2010, a further major boost to installed generating capacity was anticipated by 2011, with the commissioning of Nam Ngum 2 (615 MW). In early 2011 Viet Nam was successful in pressuring the Laotian Government to suspend construction of a US $3,500m. hydropower dam at Sayabouri, which the Vietnamese Government feared would have a marked impact on the downstream flow of the Mekong River.

MINING

Laos is rich in mineral resources, and the mining sector accounted for 28.8% of industrial sector GDP in 2009 (compared with only 1.4% in 2002). Substantial deposits of such natural resources as gold, copper, lignite, tin, gypsum, potash, iron ore, coal, silver, manganese, zinc and lead are believed to be present, along with some precious stones. (Proven gold and copper reserves are estimated at 72 metric tons and 1.7m. tons, respectively, while total reserves may be as high as 600 tons for gold and 10m. tons for copper.) However, a lack of sufficient physical and legal infrastructure, together with the remote location of many of the mineral deposits, has until recently rendered mining a challenging proposition for foreign investors. During the period of French colonial rule tin-mining was the largest single area of industry in Laos, accounting for about 40% of total export earnings in the years prior to the Second World War. In 1986 Laos's tin reserves were estimated at 70,000 tons, although some reports suggest that this may be a conservative figure. In 2008 Laos produced an estimated 700 tons of tin. Gypsum production is centred on mines in Savannakhet Province, and totalled an estimated 775,000 tons in 2008. Potentially viable coal seams have been identified in Saravan Province and north of Vientiane, while high-quality iron ore reserves are located on the Plain of Jars, 170 km north-east of the capital. The British-Australian mining company Rio Tinto began exploration in 1992 at a wholly owned copper and gold mine at Sepon, east of Savannakhet, under a 36-year exploration and production agreement with the Government. The mine is believed to contain 1m. tons of high-grade copper, more than 3.5m. oz of gold, and some silver, all of which can be extracted using open-pit mining techniques. In 2000 Rio Tinto sold an 80% stake in this mine, for US $22m., to Oxiana Resources of Australia, which conducted exploratory work and feasibility studies during 2001, prior to investing $150m. in the mine. Construction of the mine began in late 2001, and gold production commenced in 2003; in 2008 the mine produced 93,072 oz of gold and 55,942 oz of silver. Assisted by a $140m. loan to finance the further development of the mine, copper extraction began in 2005; more than 60,000 tons were produced annually in 2006–08. The success of the mine elevated Oxiana to being the second largest Australian gold producer. In late 2004 Oxiana bought Rio Tinto's remaining 20% stake, and also signed an exploration agreement with AngloGold Ashanti, the world's second largest gold-mining company, with an exploration mandate that encompassed the whole of Laos. Any future mines emanating from the exploration agreement were to be jointly owned by Oxiana and AngloGold Ashanti on an equal parity basis. In 2008 Oxiana was merged with another Australian mining company, and in 2009 an attempt was made by China Minmetals Corpn to acquire the merged entity, OZ Minerals, but this was subsequently blocked by the Australian Government.

Other ongoing mining projects in Laos include: a granite and limestone mine in Bolikhamsai Province (awarded to a Laotian-Taiwanese joint venture); a tin mine in Khammouane Province (awarded to a Laotian-South Korean joint venture); a gypsum mine, also in Khammouane Province (awarded to a Thai company); and several copper and gold mines at various locations across the country. In 2006 Pan Australian Resources announced that it was to embark on a new US $230m. copper and gold mine, at Phu Kam in northern Laos. Production at the Phu Kam mine commenced in April 2008, and amounted to more than 54,000 metric tons of copper, 56,759 oz of gold and 440,306 oz of silver in 2009, the first full year of operations. Also in 2006 Rox Resources, another Australian company, reported that it had possibly found commercial deposits of zinc and lead in Laos, and was seeking to develop them in conjunction with a local firm, First Pacific; however, in November 2009 Rox Resources announced its withdrawal from the project, noting the difficulties that it had encountered in obtaining a foreign investment licence in Laos. At mid-2011 Sino Australian Resources (Laos) Co Ltd, a joint venture between Ord River Resources of Australia and China Nonferrous Metal Industry's Foreign Engineering and Construction Co Ltd, was conducting a feasibility study into a large bauxite deposit in the Bolaven Plateau. Padaeng Industry of Thailand had also commenced exploration for zinc deposits around Vientiane.

Three production-sharing contracts for the exploration and production of petroleum have been signed between the Laotian Government and a number of foreign energy companies, relating to substantial concessions in the southern panhandle of the country and Vientiane Province. The first of these contracts was signed in the late 1980s between the Laotian Government and a consortium led by Enterprise Oil of the United Kingdom, and related to a 20,000-sq km area in the Savannakhet basin. The project was halted after initial surveying work was completed, but recommenced in 2007 by Salamander Energy. In December 2009 Origin Energy of Australia acquired a 30% interest in the Savannakhet concession; retaining a 30% stake itself, Salamander Energy remained the operator of the project, in which Petrovietnam also held a 25% share. A concession to explore a 41,140-sq-km area in Champasak and Saravan Provinces was also jointly held by Petrovietnam (80%) and Salamander Energy (20%). However, survey work in the southern provinces was hampered by the considerable quantities of unexploded ordnance that remained scattered over large parts of the country, necessitating intensive land clearance in advance of any exploration activity. Despite fairly extensive surveys and limited exploratory drilling, no commercial reserves of petroleum or gas have yet been identified in Laos.

In 2006 a new government ministry for energy and mining was created, separating responsibilities previously included in the portfolio of the Ministry of Industry and Handicrafts. One of the initial tasks charged to the new Ministry of Energy and Mining was to review the existing mining law and foreign investment regulations pertaining to mining activities, as well as prepare for an economy that will be radically altered by a small number of mining and power projects. A new minerals law was adopted by the National Assembly in December 2008, and entered into force in March 2009, although it was not made public until later that year. The IMF has cautioned that Laos needs to be careful in managing the windfall income emanating from successful mining and power projects. There are few linkages between the natural resources sector and the rest of the economy, but markedly increased electricity, copper and gold production could fuel inflationary pressures and foreign exchange appreciation. The IMF estimated that the net present value of mineral exports for the period 2007–20 could be equivalent to 110% of projected GDP for 2007, with a similar figure anticipated for electricity exports. The mining sector recorded strong GDP growth, of 46.1%, in 2009, as total production of copper and gold increased by some 40% and 39%, respectively, and international prices for copper recovered steadily throughout the year, after declining substantially in the second half of 2008.

TRANSPORT, COMMUNICATIONS AND TOURISM

In 2009 transport, storage and communications accounted for only 5.2% of total GDP. In the late 1990s about 40% of the Government's capital expenditure budget was allocated to transport and communications, compared with just 9% for education and 5% for public health. Despite this, the road and communications networks remained inadequate. The national highway system comprised 39,568 km of roads in 2009, according to the Ministry of Communications, Transport, Post and Construction, although a large proportion of these are in poor condition, and some can be used only during the dry season. It is estimated that about one-third of all villages in Laos, and 22% of the population, are located in areas that are not accessible by vehicles. About 5,412 km of roads have a concrete, asphalt or tarred surface, while a further 13,864 km have a gravel surface. Around 20,293 km of roads are simply made of earth. The country's river network constitutes an important element of the transport system, with a total of about 4,600 km of navigable waterways available along stretches of the Mekong and its tributaries. A number of river dock facilities were constructed or upgraded during the 1980s and 1990s, and improvements were also made to some river routes through the dynamiting of rapids, most notably on parts of the upper Mekong that link Laos with southern China.

Only one of Laos's 18 provinces does not have a border with a neighbouring country and, for some of the more outlying towns, transport and trading links with the neighbouring country are better than those with the capital of Vientiane. The poor transport infrastructure continues to keep most transaction costs high, thereby preventing the establishment of a more integrated national economy, and hinders regions in their attempts at the development of specialized inputs. In 1994 the Friendship Bridge (also referred to as the Mitraphab Bridge)—the first bridge to span the Mekong River—was completed. This road bridge, the construction of which was funded by the Australian Government, connects Nong Khai in northern Thailand with Tha Naleng (a relatively short distance east of Vientiane) in Laos. Another Mekong road bridge (a 1.4-km suspension bridge, costing US $50m. and funded largely by Japan), linking Paksé in Laos with Thailand's Phongthong district, was opened in August 2000. A second Friendship Bridge across the Mekong, extending 2 km and linking Savannakhet with Mukdahan in Thailand (costing $45m. and largely funded by the Japan Bank for International Cooperation), was completed in December 2006. The construction of a third Friendship Bridge, linking Khammouane Province with the Thai province of Nakhon Pathom, commenced in May 2009; work was reported to be approaching completion in mid-2011, with the bridge expected to be inaugurated in November. The erection of a fourth Friendship Bridge, between Ban Houayxay in Bokeo Province and Chiang Khong in Thailand's Chiang Rai Province, was to be co-funded by China and Thailand, with completion anticipated for 2014.

The ADB envisages the second Friendship Bridge forming part of an east–west arterial corridor, along what is commonly referred to as Route 9, which will run from the coastal port of Da Nang in Viet Nam, heading due west across Laos's southern panhandle and the Annamite cordillera into north-eastern Thailand. The main purpose of the road is to enable companies in both north-eastern Thailand and land-locked Laos to use the seaport facilities at Da Nang as a conduit for exports, with the aid of more favourable customs agreements at the various border crossing-points. At present, Lao exporters rely heavily on transporting goods by truck through Thailand, at prohibitive cost, owing to the heavily regulated system imposed by the Thai Government. None the less, most Lao exporters prefer to transport their goods through Thailand, despite the cost, because of the elaborate customs and other bureaucratic procedures involved when exporting via Viet Nam. In 2002 the Governments of Laos, Thailand and China agreed to construct a transnational highway linking Kunming, in Yunnan Province, south-western China, with Bangkok.

After five years of negotiations, Laos signed a pact on the navigation of the Mekong River with China, Myanmar and Thailand in May 2000. The pact, which took effect in 2001, allowed for the cross-border commercial navigation of an 886-km stretch of the upper Mekong, from Simao in China's Yunnan Province to Luang Prabang in Laos. Of the 14 river ports designated under the pact, six were in Laos. Authorized vessels using this stretch of the river were no longer obliged to pay transit fees, and it was therefore anticipated that the use of the river for both goods and passenger traffic would increase substantially. It has been proposed to widen the course of this stretch of the Mekong River, which at present can take vessels of only 50 metric tons during the wet season (and vessels of just 15 tons during the dry season).

In 1997 the Laotian Government announced bold plans to develop a comprehensive railway network in the country. Although a contract was subsequently awarded to a Thai company, no timetable for the implementation of the scheme was announced. A short, narrow-gauge railway line near the Khone waterfalls, in the southern panhandle, was built and operated during the colonial period, as a means to transport goods around an unnavigable part of the Mekong River, but has not been in operation for more than 50 years. More recently, the Friendship Bridge was designed to take a single railway track across its span, in addition to a two-lane road on either side. A railway track from the Thai rail terminus at Nong Khai to the centre of the Friendship Bridge was laid in 1996. In February 2004 the Thai and French Governments agreed to provide concessionary loans and grants to fund a 12.5-km railway line across the Friendship Bridge to the outskirts of Vientiane. The first 3.5-km section, linking Nong Khai to Tha Naleng, was formally inaugurated in March 2009, with Thai Princess Maha Chakri Sirindhorn travelling on the first train to cross the Mekong River; it was envisaged that two trains per day would make the 30-minute journey. The Laotian Government has an ambitious plan to extend the railway line 1,000 km further north, via Luang Prabang and up to the border with China. In April 2010 the Chinese Government agreed to assist Laos in the construction of a railway line from the Laotian–Chinese border checkpoint at Boten, Luang Namtha Province, to Vientiane, but this was postponed indefinitely in 2011, after the arrest of China's Minister of Railways on corruption charges.

Given the challenging terrain and poor road system, there is an important role for a domestic airline service in Laos. With the assistance of various bilateral donors, the country's main airports were steadily upgraded during the 1990s. Domestic flights provided by Lao Airlines (formerly Lao Aviation) currently link Vientiane with Houeisay, Luang Namtha, Luang Prabang, Oudomxay, Paksé, Savannakhet, Sayabouri and Xiangkhouang. International flights provided by Lao Airlines link Vientiane with Bangkok and Chiang Mai in Thailand, with Kunming in China, with Hanoi and Ho Chi Minh City in Viet Nam, and with Phnom-Penh and Siem Reap (Siem Reab) in Cambodia. There are also international flights to several of these destinations from Luang Prabang, Paksé and Savannakhet. At mid-2011 Lao Airlines operated a fleet of just eight turboprop aircraft. A private company, Lao Air, also operates a scheduled service to a few domestic destinations not served by the flag carrier, as well as a charter service for mining and energy companies, using helicopters and small fixed-wing aircraft. A small number of foreign airlines also fly to Vientiane, including China Eastern Airlines, Thai Airways International and Viet Nam Airlines. In 2007 AirAsia, a Malaysian budget airline, commenced a service between Kuala Lumpur and Vientiane. With some 70 foreign airlines transiting Lao airspace, there are a considerable number of flights over Laotian territory each day, generating additional revenue for the Government in the form of overflight fees.

Having previously been very cautious in the development of its tourism industry, Laos began to place greater emphasis on generating tourism receipts from the late 1990s. The number of tourist arrivals totalled 2.0m. in 2009, an increase of 15.6% compared with 2008, as a 42.9% rise in visitors from Thailand more than compensated for a reduction in those travelling from Europe, the USA and Canada; arrivals from neighbouring countries were notably boosted by Vientiane's hosting of the Southeast Asian Games in December 2009. Estimated receipts in 2008 amounted to US $275.5m., representing around 5.1% of GDP. Approximately 32,000 Lao people are reported to work directly in the tourism industry, with a further 400,000 deriving indirect income from tourists. Chief attractions are the former royal capital of Luang Prabang (a UNESCO world heritage site), the Plain of Jars and Vang Vieng in the centre, Wat Phu and Kong Island in the southern panhandle, and the capital of Vientiane. Approximately 40% of foreign tourist arrivals come through the three international airports of Vientiane, Luang Prabang and Paksé, with the remainder entering through one of 15 land border-crossings. Laos's attempts to attract more tourists have been hindered by the sporadic bomb attacks carried out in Vientiane since 2000 (see History) and by ongoing concerns about the safety record of Lao Airlines (in 2000 two of its aircraft crashed, in Xam Nua and Xiangkhouang). Tourists have been cautioned against travelling on roads traversing areas affected by intermittent acts of banditry, including parts of Xiangkhouang, Xaysomboun and Bolikhamsai Provinces, and Route 13, which links Vientiane and Luang Prabang. Tourist numbers in Laos have also traditionally been constrained by a shortage of adequate hotel accommodation, although the number of hotels in the country has increased in recent years, from 165 in 2005 to 357 in 2009, with the improvement in capacity particularly notable in Vientiane, where the number of hotels rose from 58 in 2005 to 175 in 2009. The Government hoped by 2015 to attract 2.8m. visitors to the country annually, generating yearly tourism receipts of $350m.

In the mid-1990s the Laotian Government urged the involvement of foreign investors in the country's relatively primitive telephone network. In 1995 Vientiane licensed a joint venture agreement between Entreprises des Postes et Télécommunications de Laos (a state-owned enterprise) and Shin Satellite of Thailand, the joint venture being known as Lao Télécommunications (LTC). The company was granted an exclusive five-year concession to operate all telecommunications services in Laos, including pagers, mobile telephones and internet services. In 2006 Shin Satellite sold some of its stake in the company to Asia Mobile Holdings. The number of fixed-line telephones per 1,000 people increased from 15.8 in 2005 to 16.6 in 2010, while the total number of fixed lines rose from 90,800 to 103,100 during the same period. The number of mobile telephone users reached 4,003,400 in 2010, a significant increase from 657,500 in 2005, and a mere 12,000 in 2000. In 2003 Millicom International began to provide a national GSM wireless network in Laos, in collaboration with the Government, known locally as 'Tango'. As with electricity tariffs, the Government has been gradually increasing domestic telephone charges in recent years, in order to bring pricing more into line with underlying operational costs. Conversely, the prices of international calls—which are among the highest in Asia—are being reduced, in order to comply with international benchmarks. Laos's three internet service providers—GlobeNet, LaoTel (which dominates) and PlaNet Online—reportedly had a combined client base of 300,000 internet users in 2009.

BANKING

Laos's small banking sector has experienced a number of transformations since economic reforms commenced in the late 1980s, yet it remains underdeveloped. Prior to 1988 the two principal banks in Laos were the Banque d'Etat de la RDP Lao and its subsidiary, the Banque pour le Commerce Extérieur Lao (BCEL). The former was responsible for all domestic banking, including local currency issuance and public sector accounts, and subsidized lending to state enterprises. The latter's remit extended to all foreign trade financing, foreign exchange reserves, foreign loans and debt. This standard format for banking in command economies was revised in 1988, in order to conform with reforms being implemented in other areas of the economy. The Banque d'Etat de la RDP Lao lost its monopoly status and became a more conventional central bank, subsequently renamed the Banque de la RDP Lao. BCEL became one of several state-owned commercial banks, losing its monopoly over all international currency transactions, but continued to be the principal participant in the area of trade financing, and remained the largest of Laos's commercial banks. Between 1988 and 1991 a further six state-run commercial banks came into operation (two in Vientiane, and one each in Luang Prabang, Savannakhet, Champasak and Xiangkhouang), formed from various branches of the former central bank. These banks were joined by an eighth state-run commercial bank in 1993, the Agriculture Promotion Bank, which is principally designed to provide low-cost loans to farmers and to administer micro-financing credit schemes (funded by external donors) through its substantial branch network. In 1999 six of the eight state-run commercial banks were merged back into just two entities. It was subsequently decided in 2001 that these two banks should be further merged into a single entity, leaving just three state-owned commercial banks (which accounted for about 60% of total bank assets in 2009).

Several foreign joint venture banks exist in Laos. One of these (Joint Development Bank) has Thai investor participation, having commenced operations as early as 1989. Another joint venture bank, Vientiane Commercial Bank Ltd, was established in 1993 by Taiwanese, Thai and Australian equity partners; in 2007 Australia and New Zealand Banking Group Ltd (ANZ) acquired a majority (60%) stake in the bank, which was renamed ANZ Vientiane Commercial Bank Ltd. Lao-Viet Bank, a US $10m. joint venture between BCEL and the Bank for Investment and Development of Vietnam—one of Viet Nam's four state-run commercial banks—was established in 1999. Based in Vientiane, this bank's primary aim is to help finance burgeoning trade flows between Laos and Viet Nam, and it has subsequently opened branch offices in Champasak, Ho Chi Minh City and Hanoi. Standard Chartered Bank has operated a small representative office in Vientiane since 1996. A number of new private banks have opened in recent years, encouraged by the adoption, in December 2006, of a banking law permitting them to open branches in all provinces of Laos (the operations of private banks having previously been limited to Vientiane). The establishment of locally owned Phongsavanh Bank in 2007 was followed by that of Acleda Bank (of Cambodia) and International Commercial Bank (of Switzerland) in 2008, Indochina Bank (a Laotian-South Korean joint venture) in 2009 and Banque Franco-Lao (a Laotian-French joint venture) in 2010. In addition, state-owned Nayoby Bank was established in 2007, to provide low-interest loans to farmers. Following its business model in Cambodia, Acleda Bank was aiming to expand its Laotian network to 34 branches within just a few years. Most other foreign banks have restricted their presence within Laos to just a few branches, concentrated on the main Mekong River towns.

Laos's banking sector remains weak, despite the repeated efforts of both the ADB and the World Bank to recapitalize the country's state-run commercial banks since 1994. Non-performing loans at these banks have been reduced significantly, however, from some 70% of total loans in 2004 to less than 10% by 2007. None the less, in 2009 the IMF urged the Laotian authorities to strengthen the financial position of the state-owned commercial banks further, warning that a recent expansion in the availability of credit posed a threat to the banking sector. Credit growth in Laos was unsustainably high at 85%, 90% and 43% in 2008, 2009 and 2010, respectively, according to the IMF. Many Laotian citizens do not have bank accounts, preferring instead to keep their savings in gold, foreign currency, or even livestock in rural areas. Indeed, the Laotian economy is highly 'dollarized': at March 2009 some 50% of broad money (compared with some 70% in 2003) was in the form of foreign currency deposits (mostly US dollars and Thai baht), much of which was held outside the formal banking sector. Urban Lao remain generally reluctant to use bank savings accounts, owing in part to fluctuations in the value of the local currency, the fragility of the banks themselves and the fact that interest rates have not always kept pace with inflation. The Government hoped that by 2015 total deposits in the banking sector would be equivalent to 30% of GDP, and that total loans would be equivalent to 20%–30% of GDP; if such targets are to be met, it will necessitate expanding both deposits and loans by 20% each year.

Laos has experimented with kip-denominated bond issues in a bid to improve the mobilization of domestic savings, raise funds for bank recapitalizations and absorb any excess liquidity. The country's first stock exchange, the Lao Securities Exchange, commenced operations in January 2011 as a joint venture owned by the Laotian Government (51%) and the South Korean stock exchange (49%). At mid-2011 just two companies were listed on the exchange: Banque pour le Commerce Extérieur Lao and Electricité du Laos—both large, state-run firms. All shares were denominated in Lao kip, although foreign investors were eligible to buy listed stocks, and at mid-2011 there were two licensed brokerage companies operating in the country, one of which was a joint venture with Sacombank of Viet Nam.

FOREIGN TRADE AND INVESTMENT

Laos has consistently recorded a trade deficit, which totalled an estimated US $1,365m. in 2010, according to the IMF; in that year a current account deficit of an estimated $1,173m. was registered. In 2010 Laotian exports increased to an estimated $2,217m., a year-on-year increae of some 45.8%, while imports increased by 23.8% to an estimated $3,582m. Copper became the country's principal export in 2006, when earnings grew almost four-fold, and accounted for an estimated 37.9% of total export revenue in 2008. The other main export items are garments, timber, gold and electricity. However, most data pertaining to Laos's external trade tend to be rather inaccurate given the relatively substantial amount of smuggling and informal trading activity that is conducted across the country's five porous land borders, as well as inadequacies in the formal data-gathering and analysis process itself.

Laos commenced garment exports in the late 1980s, and this sector of export activity developed into an important source of foreign exchange earnings—as well as a major source of urban employment—in the 1990s, offsetting in part the decline in the export of wood-related items. Under the GSP, a large proportion of garment exports are directed to EU countries. Laos's GSP status was briefly revoked in the mid-1990s, after an EU delegation found that the country was not complying with the minimum 60% local content required for goods exported under the GSP programme; however, Laos subsequently regained its GSP privileges. Thailand has traditionally been the destination for about one-quarter of Laos's total exports, ahead of all other countries in the Asia-Pacific region and beyond, although since the mid-1990s Viet Nam has also become a leading recipient of Laos's exports, reflecting the development of closer economic relations between the two countries since the onset of the Asian crisis in the late 1990s. Major import items include consumption goods, fuels, materials for the garment industry, construction and electrical equipment, and motorcycle parts. Thailand tends to provide more than one-half of Laos's total imports (although it should be borne in mind that figures may include transit goods), followed by China and Viet Nam. Capital goods represent the largest proportion of official imports, followed by petroleum.

Having participated as an observer at meetings of the Association of Southeast Asian Nations (ASEAN) since 1992, Laos applied for full membership of the Association in 1993 and was inducted into the grouping in mid-1997. In July 2004 Laos assumed the rotating chairmanship of ASEAN, and hosted the organization's summit meeting in November—the biggest event of its kind ever to be staged in the Laotian capital. As part of its commitments to ASEAN, Laos must comply with a wide range of tariff reductions under the ASEAN Free Trade Area (AFTA) agreement; these include reducing tariff rates for most products imported from other ASEAN member countries to below 5%. The reduction of tariff rates has had some impact on government funds, as around 20% of Laos's total budgetary revenues had been derived from import duties. However, Laos's tariff rates have tended not to be particularly high (with the exception of cars and luxury items), and any revenue shortfall should be more than mitigated by additional income from the resources sector. After signing a second bilateral trade accord with the USA in September 2003 (the first having been signed, but not ratified, in 1997), Laos then sought normal trading relations (NTR) status—formerly known as most favoured nation (MFN) status—with the USA. However, concerns in the USA regarding Laos's record on human rights, particularly towards the ethnic Hmong, as well as the perception of insufficient respect for religious and political freedoms, became an obstacle in this regard. None the less, US President George W. Bush formally granted Laos NTR status in December 2004, following Senate approval one month earlier. NTR status permits Laos to have a markedly lower tariff rate for goods exported to the USA, reduced from an average of 45% to around 2.5%. Under NTR, US tariffs on Lao imports have been decreased from 40% to 7% for cotton garments; from 60% to zero for handicrafts; from 42% to zero for wooden furniture; from 90% to less than 1% for Lao silk textiles; and from 10% to zero for coffee and tea. The Laotian Government was also seeking accession to the World Trade Organization (WTO). In September 2010 the Government announced that it had finalized bilateral goods and services agreements with both China and Japan; by June 2011 this had been extended to include Australia, Canada, the Republic of Korea and Taiwan. Similar agreements with the EU, the USA and Ukraine were reported to be at various stages of development at mid-2011, with the EU deal expected to be the next to be concluded.

Since the onset of the regional economic crisis of the late 1990s, Laos's heavy reliance on Thailand as a source of investment and trade has been diminished by a reorientation towards the country's other immediate neighbours, particularly Viet Nam and China. While Vientiane's close links with Hanoi and Beijing are most apparent in the political realm, they are also evident in the economic sphere, as demonstrated by burgeoning cross-border investment and trading activity, and various other business-related initiatives. Trade and investment relations between Laos and Yunnan Province in China developed rapidly in the late 1990s, as exemplified by the construction of a number of new cement plants by Yunnan companies. Investors from Viet Nam have also been active across a spectrum of projects, with hydropower plants, rubber plantations, copper cable manufacturing and pharmaceutical plants all being announced in recent years.

The Laotian and Thai Governments have been working on an economic co-operation agreement (similar to those Thailand already has with Cambodia and Myanmar), focusing on the areas of electricity, agriculture, telecommunications and transport, and investment, since 1997. However, trade relations between Laos and Thailand have not always been straightforward, partly as a result of various differences of opinion between the two Governments on non-trade issues (such as border demarcation), but also because of a perception in Vientiane that Thailand has taken unfair advantage of Laos's land-locked state to exact onerous transshipment costs on the country's exports. Such concerns have been partly allayed, if not wholly removed, by an agreement to liberalize the transshipment business, thereby ending the oligopoly that six Thai transport companies had previously held.

Foreign direct investment (FDI) activity in Laos is regulated under the 2009 Law on Investment Promotion, which replaced the Law on the Promotion of Foreign Investment and the Law on the Promotion of Domestic Investment. The foreign investment regime is relatively liberal, at least in theory, with wholly foreign-owned projects permitted. The law harmonizes incentives for domestic and foreign investors and permits foreigners investing at least US $500,000 to purchase residential land use rights in certain areas. Expatriates also pay an attractive 10% flat rate for personal income tax, and foreign investors enjoy a corporate income tax rate of 20%, which is markedly below the 35% set for local companies, although it was reported in mid-2010 that the Government intended to revise the tax law to equalize the rates paid by local and foreign-owned companies. The Investment Promotion Department (IPD), under the Committee for Planning and Investment, is the government agency that approves, monitors and promotes all FDI activity in Laos and reports directly to the Prime Minister's office. Between 2001 and 2009 Laos approved 1,387 foreign investment projects, with an aggregate registered value of around $12,226m., according to the IPD. However, it is likely that many licensed projects will never be implemented. In terms of actual FDI inflows, a peak inflow of around $1,300m. was recorded in 1996, prior to the Asian financial crisis of 1997–98, which precipitated a significant decline in FDI. Inflows gradually recovered from 2000, reaching $930m. in 2008, according to the ADB, but declined to $769m. in 2009, largely owing to a contraction in global economic activity, and decreasing further to $394 in 2010. Perhaps unsurprisingly, the largest single investor in Laos has been neighbouring Thailand (accounting for 21.7% of the value of foreign investment projects approved between 2001 and 2009), followed by China, Viet Nam, France, South Korea, Japan, India, Australia, Malaysia and Singapore. In recent years a large proportion of foreign investment activity has been focused on the energy and mining sectors, with Australian firms notably apparent in the latter. Outside of the mining and energy sectors, one of the largest foreign investment projects announced in 2005 was a $25m. joint venture brewery, formed by Asia Pacific Breweries of Singapore and the Laotian Government.

In terms of sectoral distribution, the energy sector has witnessed the largest proportion of total FDI inflows by far, as a spectrum of foreign companies have sought to develop power generation (primarily hydropower) projects in Laos. About 34% of total foreign investment in Laos approved during 2001–09 pertained to electricity generation, followed by mining (26%), services, agriculture, and industry and handicrafts. Agriculture-related FDI activity has risen in recent years, particularly as food security issues have come to the fore, and there have been some media reports that sovereign wealth funds have been seeking to long-term leases on land in Laos.

INTERNATIONAL AID AND DEBT

The economy is heavily dependent on external assistance and aid, both from multilateral agencies and bilateral donors. The largest bilateral donors in Laos in recent years have been Japan, France, Sweden, Germany and Australia, while multilateral agencies active in Laos include the ADB and World Bank. International donations account for around 18%–20% of the country's total GDP. In particular, external grants help fund both the current account deficit and the budget deficit, with budget revenues rarely exceeding more than 70% of government expenditure. In 2009, according to the IMF, Laos's overall budget deficit amounted to 7.2% of GDP, owing to a sharp increase in extra-budgetary spending. According to the ADB, of the total tax revenues forecast to be collected by the Government in 2008/09, 22.7% were to come from profits tax (principally from the mining sector), 22.6% from excise duties, 21.3% from turnover tax, 13.2% from import duties, 5.7% from income tax, 4.9% from natural resources tax (i.e. mining royalties), 1.6% from timber royalties and 1.0% from hydropower royalties. Timber royalties have been declining since 2002, when the Government banned the export of unprocessed timber. Other sources of revenue include overflight fees (collected from airlines using Laotian airspace) and dividend payments from state-owned firms. Although tax revenues have previously been weakened by the inadequacy of tax administration, government receipts increased from 4,176,700m. kips in 2005/06 to 7,030,400m. kips in 2008/09, according to the ADB. The Government introduced a value-added tax, at a rate of 10%, at the beginning of 2010. Total revenues equivalent to 18%–19% of GDP, and public expenditure equivalent to 20%–22% of GDP, resulting in a budgetary deficit of between 3% and 5% of GDP, were projected by 2015.

At the end of 2010, according to the ADB, Laos's external debt totalled an estimated US $3,270m.; in 2009 the cost of debt-servicing was equivalent to 6.5% of revenue from exports of goods and services, compared with 4.6% in 2008 and 8.9% in 2004. In 2003 the Russian Government agreed to cancel 70% of Laos's $1,300m. debt and to permit Laos to clear the remaining $378m. over the following 33 years at preferential interest rates. Laos is eligible to participate in the Heavily Indebted Poor Countries (HIPC) initiative—a scheme launched in 1996 by the IMF and the World Bank 'to reduce to sustainable levels' the external debt burdens of the most heavily indebted poor nations—but has so far chosen not to do so. At the end of 2010 foreign exchange reserves (excluding gold) were estimated by the IMF at $717.5m.

The ADB's Greater Mekong Subregion (GMS) programme has contributed to Laos's economic development plans since its commencement in 1992. The GMS programme—which also encompasses Cambodia, Myanmar, Thailand, Viet Nam and Yunnan Province in China—has sought to bring private sector participants together with external assistance agencies to conduct a series of economic and business initiatives in the participant countries. Meanwhile, in addition to supporting the unexploded ordnance clearing programme in Laos, the USA has contributed to attempts to eradicate the production and trafficking of opium in the country. The USA has continued to assist in the establishment of counter-narcotics enforcement units in each of the relevant provinces, as well as crop control and development projects in Houaphanh and Phongsali Provinces. According to the IMF, in 2008 an estimated US $88m. was provided in aid donations, of which 55% came from multilateral agencies and 45% came from bilateral donors. The value of loans disbursed in the same year was estimated at $173m., of which, again, some 55% emanated from multilateral agencies, and the remainder from bilateral donors.

PROBLEMS AND PROSPECTS

By 2020 Laos aims to graduate from its current status as a less-developed country to that of a developing country. The Seventh National Socio-economic Development Plan, for the 2011–15 period, was announced by the Government in early 2011. Among the goals of the plan were annual GDP growth of at least 8% and per caput GDP of at least US $1,700 by 2015. It also projected the fulfilment of all MDGs by the global deadline of 2015, by which year the working-age population of Laos was expected to have increased to 4.1m. By 2015 it was hoped that the maternal mortality ratio would be lower than 260 per 100,000 live births, the infant mortality rate would be no more than 45 per 1,000 live births, the under-five child mortality rate would be lower than 70 per 1,000 live births, and that at least 80% of households would have access to potable water.

The economic challenges confronting Laos in attaining these targets are those commonly experienced by less-developed countries in Asia and beyond: namely, the identification of policy prescriptions to address the problem of economic under-achievement; the coherent and competent execution of those policies by state agencies with sufficient institutional capacities; the tackling of excessive bureaucracy and burdensome corruption; and a fairly radical improvement in the human development level of the country. The US Department of State notes that corruption continues to hamper economic development in Laos, with neither a 1999 anti-corruption decree nor the adoption of an anti-corruption law in 2005 seeming to have made significant progress. In its 2010 Corruption Perceptions Index, the non-governmental organization Transparency International ranked Laos 154th out of 178 countries, equal to Cambodia and perceived to be less corrupt than only Myanmar within the Asia-Pacific region. The revenues emanating from increased production in the natural resources sector also pose challenges in terms of corruption, as well as more general macroeconomic risks. Laos will need to avoid the threat of so-called 'Dutch disease' (whereby rapid growth in exports of newly exploited natural resources causes a country's currency to appreciate, adversely affecting other sectors of its economy), and seek to ensure that the windfall benefits from the resources sector are utilized sustainably. The non-resources sector (i.e. the economy beyond mining and energy) must not be allowed to decline, additional tax revenues need to be spent wisely, the local currency must not appreciate excessively, and rent-seeking activities need to be thwarted.

Widening disparities in income between rural and urban Lao—and even between those living in rural upland and rural lowland areas—need to be addressed, particularly where they are congruent with ethnic divisions. The better integration into the national economy of the activities of subsistence farmers, the diversification of crops, the creation of specialized markets and a general improvement in agricultural output levels are also required if the living standards of the Lao populace as a whole are to be improved. To date, the benefits of the economic reform process in Laos have mostly been experienced in the urban areas of the country, and largely through advances made in the services and industrial sectors. However, there is a need to ensure that the effects of future development initiatives are extended to the rural areas, both upland and lowland, through parallel advances in the agricultural sector. Furthermore, economic development will also require a strengthening of the capacities of numerous state institutions, strident moves towards good governance, improved macroeconomic management and the effective enforcement of the legislative regime. With about one-quarter of the population illiterate, the need to improve the education and skills levels of the country's populace remains a particularly critical issue in relation to the sustained economic development of Laos. The Government appears to recognize this pressing need, as demonstrated by recent public sector spending increases on health and education. None the less, education-related spending has accounted for only 10% of total budget spending, or around 2% of GDP, in recent years, and health-related spending comprised just 5% of total budget spending, or 1% of GDP.

Looking ahead, economic reform in Laos seems likely to continue at a cautious pace, as the Government remains mindful of the potential social and political risks of instituting more rapid reforms. Most external observers would concur that this pace is too slow, and reflects a degree of ambivalence by policy-makers towards meaningful economic reform, as well as the political influence held by entrenched lobbies. None the less, the Government has gradually introduced trade- and investment-related reforms in order to achieve its aim of accession to the WTO by 2015. Such developments suggest that the need for business liberalization is grudgingly recognized by the Government, and that the impact of a number of high-profile investment projects—such as the Sepon and Phu Kam gold and copper mines and the Nam Theun 2 power project—has not wholly distracted policy-makers from the long-term economic reform agenda. The continued growth of the mining sector is also anticipated, supported by buoyant prices for copper and record-breaking prices for gold.

Finally, on the issue of climate change, Laos's 'carbon footprint' is minimal, as one would expect of a small and less-developed economy. According to figures from the World Bank, Laos's total carbon dioxide emissions in 2007 were the equivalent of a mere 1.5m. metric tons, compared with 111.3m. tons for neighbouring Viet Nam. On a per caput basis, Laos's carbon dioxide emissions were equivalent to just 0.3 tons, compared with 1.3 tons in Viet Nam. However, this does not mean that Laos will be immune to the impact of climate change. Growing variations in river water levels and weather patterns could reduce the country's GDP by 1.1% each year, according to the Laotian Government's own estimate. Given their dependence on agriculture, any marked changes in climatic conditions could be particularly troubling for poor farmers and low-income households.

Statistical Survey

Source (unless otherwise stated): National Statistics Centre, rue Luang Prabang, Vientiane; tel. (21) 214740; fax (21) 219129; e-mail nscp@laotel.com; internet www.nsc.gov.la.

Area and Population

AREA, POPULATION AND DENSITY

Area (sq km)	236,800*
Population (census results)	
1 March 1995	4,581,258
1 March 2005	
Males	2,800,551
Females	2,821,431
Total	5,621,982
Population (UN estimates at mid-year)†	
2009	6,112,145
2010	6,200,894
2011	6,288,039
Density (per sq km) at mid-2011	26.6

* 91,400 sq miles.

† Source: UN, *World Population Prospects: The 2010 Revision*.

POPULATION BY AGE AND SEX
(UN estimates at mid-2011)

	Males	Females	Total
0–14	1,079,754	1,037,127	2,116,881
15–64	1,950,929	1,974,828	3,925,757
65 and over	108,168	137,233	245,401
Total	3,138,851	3,149,188	6,288,039

Source: UN, *World Population Prospects: The 2010 Revision*.

PROVINCES
(population at mid-2005, official estimates)

	Area (sq km)	Population ('000)	Density (per sq km)
Vientiane (municipality)	3,920	698	178.1
Phongsali	16,270	166	10.2
Luang Namtha	9,325	145	15.5
Oudomxay	15,370	265	17.2
Bokeo	6,196	145	23.4
Luang Prabang	16,875	407	24.1
Houaphanh	16,500	281	17.0
Sayabouri	16,389	339	20.7
Xiangkhouang	15,880	230	14.5
Vientiane	18,526	389	21.0
Bolikhamsai	14,863	225	15.1
Khammouane	16,315	337	20.7
Savannakhet	21,774	826	37.9
Saravan	10,691	324	30.3
Sekong	7,665	85	11.1
Champasak	15,415	607	39.4
Attopu	10,320	112	10.9
Xaysomboun SR	4,506	39	8.7
Total	236,800	5,622	23.7

Note: In January 2006 the Xaysomboun special region was dissolved, and its administrative responsibilities were transferred to Vientiane and Xiangkhouang provinces.

PRINCIPAL TOWNS
(population at 1995 census)

Viangchan (Vientiane—capital)	160,000	Xam Nua (Sam Neua)	33,500
Savannakhet (Khanthaboury)	58,500	Luang Prabang	25,500
Pakxe (Paksé)	47,000	Thakhek (Khammouane)	22,500

Source: Stefan Helders, *World Gazetteer* (internet www.world-gazetteer.com).

Mid-2010 (incl. suburbs, UN estimate): Vientiane 831,472 (Source: UN, *World Urbanization Prospects: The 2009 Revision*).

BIRTHS AND DEATHS
(annual averages, UN estimates)

	1995–2000	2000–05	2005–10
Birth rate (per 1,000)	33.6	27.8	24.1
Death rate (per 1,000)	9.4	7.9	6.6

Source: UN, *World Population Prospects: The 2010 Revision*.

Life expectancy (years at birth, WHO estimates): 63 (males 62; females 64) in 2009 (Source: WHO, *World Health Statistics*).

ECONOMICALLY ACTIVE POPULATION
('000 persons in 2003)

	Total
Agriculture, etc.	2,085
Industry	235
Services	217
Total employed	2,537
Unemployed	136
Total labour force	2,673

2005 ('000 persons): Agriculture 2,091; Total employed 2,664; Unemployed 38; Total labour force 2,701.

Source: Asian Development Bank.

Mid-2011 (estimates in '000): Agriculture, etc. 2,424; Total labour force 3,244 (Source: FAO).

Health and Welfare

KEY INDICATORS

Total fertility rate (children per woman, 2009)	3.4
Under-5 mortality rate (per 1,000 live births, 2009)	59
HIV/AIDS (% of persons aged 15–49, 2007)	0.2
Physicians (per 1,000 head, 2004)	0.4
Hospital beds (per 1,000 head, 2005)	1.2
Health expenditure (2008): US $ per head (PPP)	84
Health expenditure (2008): % of GDP	4.0
Health expenditure (2008): public (% of total)	17.6
Access to adequate water (% of persons, 2008)	57
Access to adequate sanitation (% of persons, 2008)	53
Total carbon dioxide emissions ('000 metric tons, 2007)	1,535.2
Carbon dioxide emissions per head (metric tons, 2007)	0.3
Human Development Index (2010): ranking	122
Human Development Index (2010): value	0.497

For sources and definitions, see explanatory note on p. vi.

Agriculture

PRINCIPAL CROPS
('000 metric tons)

	2007	2008	2009
Rice, paddy	2,710	2,927	3,145
Maize	621	948	849
Potatoes*	37	38	42
Sweet potatoes	126	126*	128*
Cassava (Manioc)	233	262	153
Sugar cane	324	417	434
Watermelons	91	100	115
Cantaloupes and other melons*	38	42	48
Bananas*	54	58	61
Oranges*	48	42	38
Tangerines, mandarins, clementines and satsumas*	31	28	25
Pineapples	31	33	46
Coffee, green	33	39	46
Tobacco, unmanufactured	23	33	26

* FAO estimate(s).

Aggregate production ('000 metric tons, may include official, semi-official or estimated data): Total cereals 3,331 in 2007, 3,874 in 2008, 3,994 in 2009; Total vegetables (incl. melons) 877 in 2007, 906 in 2008, 104 in 2009; Total fruits (excl. melons) 253 in 2007, 248 in 2008, 259 in 2009.

Source: FAO.

LIVESTOCK
('000 head, year ending September)

	2007	2008	2009
Horses*	31	31	31
Cattle	1,353	1,449	1,426
Buffaloes	1,123	1,155	1,178
Pigs	2,186	2,548	2,947
Goats	268	289	367
Chickens	20,453	21,983	22,521
Ducks*	3,200	3,200	3,200

* FAO estimates.

Source: FAO.

LIVESTOCK PRODUCTS
('000 metric tons, FAO estimates)

	2007	2008	2009
Cattle meat	23.8	26.0	27.6
Buffalo meat	18.5	19.0	19.0
Pig meat	46.0	54.0	65.0
Chicken meat	16.0	17.2	17.2
Cows' milk	6.8	7.5	7.6
Hen eggs	13.4	14.5	14.8

Source: FAO.

Forestry

ROUNDWOOD REMOVALS
('000 cubic metres, excl. bark, FAO estimates)

	2007	2008	2009
Sawlogs, veneer logs and logs for sleepers	62	91	86
Other industrial wood	132	132	132
Fuel wood	5,944	5,945	5,946
Total	6,138	6,168	6,164

Source: FAO.

SAWNWOOD PRODUCTION
('000 cubic metres, incl. railway sleepers)

	2003	2004	2005
Total (all broadleaved)	125	125	130

2006–09: Production assumed to be unchanged from 2005 (FAO estimate).

Source: FAO.

Fishing

('000 metric tons, live weight, FAO estimates)

	2007	2008	2009
Capture	28.4	29.2	30.0
Cyprinids	4.3	4.4	4.5
Other freshwater fishes	24.1	24.8	25.5
Aquaculture	63.3	64.3	75.0
Common carp	4.7	4.8	5.6
Roho labeo	4.3	4.4	5.1
Mrigal carp	3.8	3.9	4.5
Bighead carp	5.3	5.4	6.3
Silver carp	6.4	6.6	7.6
Nile tilapia	15.9	16.1	18.8
Total catch	91.7	93.5	105.0

Source: FAO.

Mining

('000 metric tons unless otherwise indicated)

	2007	2008	2009
Coal (all grades)*	620.0	600.0	600.0
Gemstones, sapphire ('000 carats)*	1,200.0	1,200.0	1,200.0
Gold (kg)	5,137	4,333	5,033
Gypsum*	775.0	775.0	775.0
Salt*	35.0	35.0	35.0
Copper (metric tons)†	62,541	64,075	67,561
Tin (metric tons)*†	570	690	350

* Estimates.

† Figures refer to metal content.

Source: US Geological Survey.

Industry

SELECTED PRODUCTS

	2007	2008	2009
Beer ('000 hectolitres)	1,029	1,363	1,391
Soft drinks ('000 hectolitres)	257	270	273
Cigarettes (million packs)	124	136	137
Garments (million pieces)	47	53	51
Plastic products (metric tons)	7,383	7,625	7,750
Detergent (metric tons)	1,255	1,613	1,713
Agricultural tools ('000 metric tons)	n.a.	46,500	52,750
Nails (metric tons)	2,168	2,225	2,313
Bricks (million)	244	266	269
Hydroelectric energy (million kWh)	3,474	3,705	3,428
Tobacco (metric tons)	3,991	4,738	5,063
Plywood (million sheets)	952	996	1,009

Source: Ministry of Industry and Commerce, Vientiane.

Finance

CURRENCY AND EXCHANGE RATES

Monetary Units
100 at (cents) = 1 new kip.

Sterling, Dollar and Euro Equivalents (28 February 2011)
£1 sterling = 13,072.6 new kips;
US $1 = 8,052.6 new kips;
€1 = 11,140.0 new kips;
100,000 new kips = £7.65 = $12.42 = €8.98.

Average Exchange Rate (new kips per US $)
2008 8,744.2
2009 8,516.1
2010 8,258.8

Note: In September 1995 a policy of 'floating' exchange rates was adopted, with commercial banks permitted to set their rates.

GENERAL BUDGET
('000 million new kips, year ending 30 September)*

Revenue†	2006/07	2007/08	2008/09‡
Tax revenue	4,711	5,624	6,338
Profits tax	1,170	1,655	1,804
Income tax	252	333	364
Turnover tax	1,046	1,229	1,347
Excise tax	999	1,191	1,432
Import duties	573	674	834
Timber royalties	212	110	100
Non-tax revenue	749	811	975
Payment for depreciation or dividend transfers	157	293	482
Overflight	231	235	225
Other revenue	361	283	268
Total	5,460	6,436	7,313

Expenditure	2006/07	2007/08	2008/09‡
Current expenditure	3,445	4,621	5,702
Wages and salaries	1,534	2,057	2,793
Compensation and allowances, subsidies and transfers	806	1,013	1,327
Interest	277	361	388
Other recurrent expenditure	828	1,191	1,195
Capital expenditure and net lending	3,089	3,155	3,569
Domestically financed	833	984	1,485
Foreign-financed and net onlending	2,328	2,171	2,084
Debt repayment and contingency expenses	586	427	512
Total	7,120	8,202	9,783

* Since 1992 there has been a unified budget covering the operations of the central Government, provincial administrations and state enterprises.

† Excluding grants received ('000 million new kips): 674 in 2006/07; 599 in 2007/08; 752 in 2008/09 (budget).

‡ Budget forecasts.

Source: IMF, *Lao People's Democratic Republic: Statistical Appendix* (September 2009).

2008/09 ('000 million new kips, year ending 30 September): *Revenue:* Tax revenue 6,208 (Income taxes 425, Profit taxes 1,303, Value added tax 1,401, Excise duties 1,432, Import duties 726, Royalties 297, Other taxes 623); Non-tax revenue 823; Total 7,031 (excl. grants 1,068). *Expenditure:* Current expenditure 6,070 (Compensation of employees 2,772, Transfers 1,369, Interest payments 264, Other recurrent expenditure 1,666); Net acquisition of non-financial assets 5,305 (Domestically financed 3,220, Externally financed 2,085); Total 11,375 (Source: IMF, *Lao People's Democratic Republic—Staff Report; Staff Supplement; Public Information Notice on the Executive Board Discussion; and Statement by the Executive Director for Lao P.D.R.* (August 2011)).

2009/10 ('000 million new kips, year ending 30 September, budget figures): *Revenue:* Tax revenue 6,989 (Income taxes 494, Profit taxes 993, Value added tax 1,697, Excise duties 1,799, Import duties 746, Royalties 377, Other taxes 884); Non-tax revenue 836; Total 7,825 (excl. grants 1,081). *Expenditure:* Current expenditure 6,565 (Compensation of employees 2,830, Transfers 1,391, Interest payments 502, Other recurrent expenditure 1,842); Net acquisition of non-financial assets 3,508 (Domestically financed 1,104, Externally financed 2,404); Total 10,073 (Source: IMF, *Lao People's Democratic Republic—Staff Report; Staff Supplement; Public Information Notice on the Executive Board Discussion; and Statement by the Executive Director for Lao P.D.R.* (August 2011)).

2010/11 ('000 million new kips, year ending 30 September, budget figures): *Revenue:* Tax revenue 8,170 (Income taxes 486, Profit taxes 1,474, Value added tax 1,911, Excise duties 1,832, Import duties 1,010, Royalties 607, Other taxes 849); Non-tax revenue 1,042; Total 9,212 (excl. grants 1,171). *Expenditure:* Current expenditure 7,159 (Compensation of employees 3,138, Transfers 1,462, Interest payments 498, Other recurrent expenditure 2,061); Net acquisition of non-financial assets 4,437 (Domestically financed 1,587, Externally financed 2,850); Total 11,596 (Source: IMF, *Lao People's Democratic Republic—Staff Report; Staff Supplement; Public Information Notice on the Executive Board Discussion; and Statement by the Executive Director for Lao P.D.R.* (August 2011)).

INTERNATIONAL RESERVES

(US $ million at 31 December)

	2008	2009	2010
Gold (national valuation)	9.99	9.99	9.99
IMF special drawing rights	15.10	80.06	78.65
Foreign exchange	613.64	622.73	717.46
Total	638.73	712.78	806.10

Source: IMF, *International Financial Statistics*.

MONEY SUPPLY

(million new kips at 31 December*)

	2006	2007	2008
Currency outside banks	1,230,590	1,837,920	2,223,230
Demand deposits at commercial banks	767,660	1,226,740	1,491,680
Total (incl. others)	1,998,320	3,064,720	3,715,330

* Figures rounded to the nearest ten million.

Source: IMF, *International Financial Statistics*.

COST OF LIVING

(Consumer Price Index; base: December 1999 = 100)

	2007	2008	2009
Food	208.6	231.9	237.3
Others	187.9	196.2	191.9
All items	197.3	212.1	212.4

Source: Asian Development Bank.

NATIONAL ACCOUNTS

Gross Domestic Product by Economic Activity

('000 million new kips at current prices)

	2007	2008	2009
Agriculture, hunting, forestry and fishing	12,621.4	13,889.3	14,549.5
Mining and quarrying	4,245.3	4,595.0	3,220.4
Manufacturing	3,399.4	3,998.8	4,683.7
Electricity, gas and water	1,048.3	1,172.9	1,299.9
Construction	2,030.7	2,187.3	1,969.1
Wholesale and retail trade	7,517.9	8,741.8	9,324.1
Transport, storage and communications	1,723.6	2,120.0	2,317.8
Finance	1,126.4	1,483.5	1,820.3
Government services	1,609.9	2,123.7	2,171.9
Other services	2,509.0	2,812.7	2,963.8
Sub-total	37,831.9	43,125.0	44,320.5
Taxes on imports	2,635.2	3,089.7	3,246.1
GDP in purchasers' values	40,467.1	46,214.7	47,566.6

Source: Asian Development Bank.

BALANCE OF PAYMENTS

(US $ million)

	2007	2008	2009
Exports of goods f.o.b.	922.7	1,091.9	1,005.3
Imports of goods c.i.f.	−1,064.7	−1,403.2	−1,413.5
Trade balance	−142.0	−311.3	−408.2
Services and other income (net)	115.9	261.6	143.2
Balance on goods, services and income	−26.1	−49.7	−265.0
Current transfers (net)	102.3	140.9	132.9
Current balance	76.2	91.2	−132.2
Direct investment (net)	323.5	227.8	318.6
Other investments (net)	76.4	191.8	297.8
Net errors and omissions	−283.0	−410.3	−488.0
Overall balance	193.2	100.5	−3.7

Source: Asian Development Bank.

External Trade

PRINCIPAL COMMODITIES
(US $ million)

Imports c.i.f.	2006	2007	2008*
Petroleum	208.7	311.0	421.8
Capital goods	728.1	1,084.8	1,171.8
Materials for garments industry	98.7	80.3	143.7
Electricity	28.0	37.4	43.3
Total (incl. others)	1,589.3	2,156.1	2,816.1

Exports f.o.b.	2006	2007	2008*
Timber	195.6	179.0	131.4
Coffee	9.8	28.9	18.5
Garments	151.2	152.8	189.7
Electricity	122.6	114.1	118.3
Copper	409.3	446.0	620.3
Gold (incl. re-exports)	117.9	93.2	118.9
Total (incl. others)	1,132.6	1,320.7	1,638.6

* Estimates.

Source: IMF, *Lao People's Democratic Republic: Statistical Appendix* (September 2009).

PRINCIPAL TRADING PARTNERS
(US $ million)

Imports	2007	2008	2009
Australia	24.1	15.5	9.6
China, People's Republic	195.2	295.0	312.5
France	12.6	20.1	62.7
Germany	34.8	25.1	17.9
Hong Kong	14.7	23.4	18.5
Japan	41.7	69.1	83.5
Korea, Republic	61.2	58.5	51.7
Singapore	43.0	28.1	40.4
Thailand*	1,442.8	1,932.6	1,800.5
Viet Nam	120.7	164.8	145.5
Total (incl. others)	2,107.9	2,829.5	2,722.8

Exports	2007	2008	2009
Belgium	11.2	17.9	14.7
China, People's Republic	77.3	135.9	219.2
France	27.2	23.0	12.8
Germany	43.0	42.0	48.2
Korea, Republic	63.9	48.2	42.5
Malaysia	32.4	2.7	0.2
Thailand*	431.5	568.7	423.7
United Kingdom	42.3	54.5	62.3
USA	19.1	40.4	41.7
Viet Nam	192.1	248.3	219.3
Total (incl. others)	1,324.5	1,604.9	1,459.2

* Trade with Thailand may be overestimated, as it may include goods in transit to and from other countries.

Note: Data reflect the IMF's direction of trade methodology and, as a result, the totals may not be equal to those presented for trade in commodities.

Source: Asian Development Bank.

Transport

ROAD TRAFFIC
(motor vehicles in use at 31 December, estimates)

	1994	1995	1996
Passenger cars	18,240	17,280	16,320
Motorcycles and mopeds	169,000	200,000	231,000

2007: Passenger cars 12,822; Buses and coaches 6,411; Lorries and vans 108,984; Motorcycles and mopeds 506,454.

Source: IRF, *World Road Statistics*.

SHIPPING

Inland Waterways
(traffic)

	2007	2008	2009
Freight ('000 metric tons)	767.0	883.0	961.0
Freight ton-kilometres (million)	60.9	67.6	69.5
Passengers ('000)	1,953.0	1,811.0	1,810.0
Passenger-kilometres (million)	50.5	48.9	48.7

Source: Ministry of Communications, Transport, Post and Construction, Vientiane.

Merchant Fleet
(registered at 31 December)

	2007	2008	2009
Number of vessels	2	1	1
Displacement ('000 grt)	2.9	0.5	0.5

Source: IHS Fairplay, *World Fleet Statistics*.

CIVIL AVIATION
(traffic on scheduled services)

	2004	2005	2006
Kilometres flown (million)	3	3	4
Passengers carried ('000)	272	293	327
Passenger-kilometres (million)	113	124	141
Total ton-kilometres (million)	12	13	14

Source: UN, *Statistical Yearbook*.

2007 ('000): Passengers carried 328 (Source: World Bank, World Development Indicators database).

2008 ('000): Passengers carried 323 (Source: World Bank, World Development Indicators database).

Tourism

FOREIGN VISITOR ARRIVALS
(incl. excursionists)

Country of nationality	2006	2007	2008
China, People's Republic	50,317	54,920	105,852
France	32,453	34,584	39,077
Japan	23,147	29,770	31,569
Thailand	675,845	949,452	891,448
United Kingdom	31,684	31,352	36,038
USA	46,829	45,691	54,717
Viet Nam	190,442	290,584	351,384
Total (incl. others)	1,215,107	1,623,943	1,736,787

2009 (provisional): Total visitor arrivals 1,239,000.

Tourism receipts (US $ million, excl. passenger transport): 173 in 2006; 233 in 2007; 276 in 2008; 268 in 2009 (provisional).

Source: World Tourism Organization.

Communications Media

	2008	2009	2010
Telephones ('000 main lines in use)	127.8	100.2	103.1
Mobile cellular telephones ('000 subscribers)	2,022.1	3,234.6	4,003.4
Internet subscribers ('000)	13.4	15.6	n.a.
Broadband subscribers ('000)	6.1	8.4	12.0

Personal computers: 100,000 (17.0 per 1,000 persons) in 2005.

Radio receivers ('000 in use): 730 in 1997.

Television receivers ('000 in use): 280 in 2001.

Book production (1995): Titles 88; copies ('000) 995.

Daily newspapers (2004): 6 (average circulation 14,558).

Non-daily newspapers (1988, estimates): 18 (average circulation 34,550).

Sources (unless otherwise specified): International Telecommunication Union; UNESCO, *Statistical Yearbook*.

Education

(2009/10, unless otherwise indicated)

	Institutions	Teachers	Students
Pre-primary	1,123	3,920	85,357
Primary	8,871	29,100	908,900
Secondary:			
lower	722	17,600	264,600
upper	35	6,000†	157,300
vocational	51	1,000	16,000
University level	4	3,000	54,000
Other higher	96	2,000	59,000

* 2008/09 figure.

Source: Ministry of Education, Vientiane.

Pupil-teacher ratio (primary education, UNESCO estimate): 30.5 in 2007/08 (Source: UNESCO Institute for Statistics).

Adult literacy rate (UNESCO estimates): 73.2% (males 80.0%; females 66.6%) in 2007 (Source: UNESCO Institute for Statistics).

Directory

The Constitution

The new Constitution was unanimously endorsed by the Supreme People's Assembly on 14 August 1991. Its main provisions are summarized below:

POLITICAL SYSTEM

The Lao People's Democratic Republic (Lao PDR) is an independent, sovereign and united country and is indivisible.

The Lao PDR is a people's democratic state. The people's rights are exercised and ensured through the functioning of the political system, with the Lao People's Revolutionary Party as its leading organ. The people exercise power through the National Assembly, which functions in accordance with the principle of democratic centralism.

The State respects and protects all lawful activities of Buddhism and the followers of other religious faiths.

The Lao PDR pursues a foreign policy of peace, independence, friendship and co-operation. It adheres to the principles of peaceful co-existence with other countries, based on mutual respect for independence, sovereignty and territorial integrity.

SOCIO-ECONOMIC SYSTEM

The economy is market-orientated, with intervention by the State. The State encourages all economic sectors to compete and co-operate in the expansion of production and trade.

Private ownership of property and rights of inheritance are protected by the State.

The State authorizes the operation of private schools and medical services, while promoting the expansion of public education and health services.

FUNDAMENTAL RIGHTS AND OBLIGATIONS OF CITIZENS

Lao citizens, irrespective of their sex, social status, education, faith and ethnic group, are equal before the law.

Lao citizens aged 18 years and above have the right to vote, and those over 21 years to be candidates, in elections.

Lao citizens have freedom of religion, speech, press and assembly, and freedom to establish associations and to participate in demonstrations which do not contradict the law.

THE NATIONAL ASSEMBLY

The National Assembly is the legislative organ, which also oversees the activities of the administration and the judiciary. Members of the National Assembly are elected for a period of five years by universal adult suffrage. The National Assembly elects its own Standing Committee, which consists of the Chairman and Vice-Chairman of the National Assembly (and thus also of the National Assembly Standing Committee) and a number of other members. The National Assembly convenes its ordinary session twice annually. The National Assembly Standing Committee may convene an extraordinary session of the National Assembly if it deems this necessary. The National Assembly is empowered to amend the Constitution; to endorse, amend or abrogate laws; to elect or remove the President of State and Vice-Presidents of State, as proposed by the Standing Committee of the National Assembly; to adopt motions expressing no confidence in the Government; to elect or remove the President of the People's Supreme Court, on the recommendation of the National Assembly Standing Committee.

THE PRESIDENT OF STATE

The President of State, who is also Head of the Armed Forces, is elected by the National Assembly for a five-year tenure. Laws adopted by the National Assembly must be promulgated by the President of State not later than 30 days after their enactment. The President is empowered to appoint or dismiss the Prime Minister and members of the Government, with the approval of the National Assembly; to appoint government officials at provincial and municipal levels; and to promote military personnel, on the recommendation of the Prime Minister.

THE GOVERNMENT

The Government is the administrative organ of the State. It is composed of the Prime Minister, Deputy Prime Ministers and Ministers or Chairmen of Committees (which are equivalent to Ministries), who are appointed by the President, with the approval of the National Assembly, for a term of five years. The Government implements the Constitution, laws and resolutions adopted by the National Assembly and state decrees and acts of the President of State. The Prime Minister is empowered to appoint Deputy Ministers and Vice-Chairmen of Committees, and junior-level government officials.

LOCAL ADMINISTRATION

The Lao PDR is divided into provinces, municipalities, districts and villages. Provincial governors and mayors of municipalities are appointed by the President of State. Deputy provincial governors, deputy mayors and district chiefs are appointed by the Prime Minister. Administration at village level is conducted by village heads.

THE JUDICIARY

The people's courts comprise the People's Supreme Court, the people's provincial and municipal courts, the people's district courts and military courts. The President of the People's Supreme Court and the Public Prosecutor-General are elected by the National Assembly, on the recommendation of the National Assembly Standing Committee. The Vice-President of the People's Supreme Court and the judges of the people's courts at all levels are appointed by the National Assembly Standing Committee.

The Government

HEAD OF STATE

President of State: Lt-Gen. CHOUMMALY SAYASONE (elected 8 June 2006; re-elected 15 June 2011).

Vice-President: BOUNGNANG VOLACHIT.

COUNCIL OF MINISTERS
(October 2011)

The Council of Ministers comprises members of the Phak Pasason Pativat Lao (Lao People's Revolutionary Party—LPRP).

Prime Minister: THONGSING THAMMAVONG.

Deputy Prime Minister and Minister of Foreign Affairs: THONGLOUN SISOLIT.

Deputy Prime Minister and Minister of National Defence: Lt-Gen. DOUANGCHAI PHICHIT.

Deputy Prime Ministers: Maj.-Gen. ASANG LAOLI, SOMSAVAT LENGSAVAT.

Minister of Finance: PHOUPHET KHAMPHOUNVONG.

Minister of Public Security: THONGBANH SENGAPHONE.

Minister of Justice: CHALEUN YIAPAOHEU.

Minister of Agriculture and Forestry: VILAYVANH PHOMKHE.

Minister of Post, Telecommunication and Communication: HIEM PHOMMACHANH.

Minister of Industry and Commerce: Dr NAM VIYAKET.

Minister of Information, Culture and Tourism: Dr BOSENGKHAM VONGDARA.

Minister of Labour and Social Welfare: ONECHANH THAMMAVONG.

Minister of Education and Sports: PHANKHAM VIPHAVANH.

Minister of Public Health: Dr EKSAVANG VONGVICHIT.

Minister of Energy and Mining: SOULIVONG DALAVONG.

Minister of Planning and Investment: SOMDY DOUANGDY.

Minister of Interior: KHAMPANE PHILAVONG.

Minister of Natural Resources and Environment: NOULIN SINBANDITH.

Minister of Public Works and Transport: SOMMAD PHOLSENA.

Minister of Science and Technology: Dr BOVIENGKHAM VONGDARA.

Minister to the Office of the President: PHONGSAVATH BOUPHA.

Ministers to the Office of the Prime Minister: SINLAVONG KHOUPHAYTHOUNE, Dr BOUNTIEM PHITSAMAY, BOUNPHENG MOUNPHOSAY, KHEMPHENG PHOLSENA, Dr DOUANGSAVAT SOUPHANAOUVONG, BOUNHEUANG DUANGPHACHANH.

Governor of the Central Bank: SOMPAO PHAYSITH.

MINISTRIES

Office of the President: rue Lane Xang, Vientiane; tel. (21) 214200; fax (21) 214208.

Office of the Prime Minister: Ban Sisavat, Vientiane; tel. (21) 213653; fax (21) 213560.

Ministry of Agriculture and Forestry: Ban Phonxay, Vientiane; tel. (21) 412359; fax (21) 412344; internet www.maf.gov.la.

Ministry of Education and Sports: 1 rue Lane Xang, BP 67, Vientiane; tel. (21) 216013; fax (21) 216006; e-mail esitc@moe.gov.la; internet www.moe.gov.la.

Ministry of Energy and Mining: rue Nongbone, Ban Hatsady, BP 4708, Vientiane.

Ministry of Finance: 23 rue Singha, BP 24, Ban Phonxay, Vientiane; tel. and fax (21) 900798; e-mail ict@mof.gov.la; internet www.mof.gov.la.

Ministry of Foreign Affairs: 23 rue Singha, Ban Phonxay, Vientiane; tel. (21) 413148; fax (21) 414009; e-mail cabinet@mofa.gov.la; internet www.mofa.gov.la.

Ministry of Industry and Commerce: rue Phonxay, BP 4107, Vientiane; tel. (21) 412009; fax (21) 412434; e-mail citd@moic.gov.la; internet www.moic.gov.la.

Ministry of Information, Culture and Tourism: rue Setthathirath, Ban Xiengnyeun, Chanthaboury, BP 122, Vientiane; tel. (21) 212406; fax (21) 212408; e-mail email@mic.gov.la.

Ministry of Interior: Vientiane.

Ministry of Justice: Ban Phonxay, Vientiane; tel. (21) 414105.

Ministry of Labour and Social Welfare: rue Pangkham, Ban Sisaket, Vientiane; tel. (21) 213003.

Ministry of National Defence: rue Kaysone Phomvihane, Ban Phone Kheng, Vientiane; tel. (21) 911550; fax (21) 911118; e-mail kongthap@yahoo.com; internet www.kongthap.gov.la.

Ministry of Natural Resources and Environment: Vientiane.

Ministry of Planning and Investment: rue Luang Prabang, Vientiane 01001; tel. (21) 218377; fax (21) 215491; internet www.investlaos.gov.la.

Ministry of Post, Telecommunication and Communication: ave Lane Xang, Vientiane; tel. (21) 412251; fax (21) 414123.

Ministry of Public Health: rue Samsenthai, Ban That Khao, Sisattanak, Vientiane; tel. (21) 214000; fax (21) 214003; e-mail contact@moh.gov.la.

Ministry of Public Security: rue Nongbone, Ban Hatsady, Vientiane; tel. (21) 212500.

Ministry of Public Works and Transport: ave Lane Xang, Vientiane; tel. (21) 452167; fax (21) 451826.

Ministry of Science and Technology: Vientiane.

Legislature

The National Assembly was expanded from 115 to 132 members in 2011. At the election held on 30 April 128 candidates of the Lao People's Revolutionary Party (LPRP) and four independents were elected to the legislature.

President of the National Assembly: PANY YATHOTOU.

Vice-Presidents: Dr XAYSOMPHONE PHOMVIHANE, SOMPHANH PHENGKHAMMY.

Political Organizations

COMMUNIST PARTY

Phak Pasason Pativat Lao (Lao People's Revolutionary Party—LPRP): Vientiane; f. 1955; est. as People's Party of Laos; reorg. under present name in 1972; 191,700 mems (2011); Cen. Cttee of 61 full mems elected at Ninth Party Congress in March 2011; Sec.-Gen. Lt-Gen. CHOUMMALY SAYASONE.

Political Bureau (Politburo)

Full members: Lt-Gen. CHOUMMALY SAYASONE, THONGSING THAMMAVONG, BOUNGNANG VOLACHIT, Maj.-Gen. ASANG LAOLI, THONGLOUN SISOLIT, Lt-Gen. DOUANGCHAI PHICHIT, SOMSAVAT LENGSAVAT, PANY YATHOTOU, Dr BOUNTHONG CHITMANY, Dr BOUNPONE BOUTTANAVONG, Dr PHANKHAM VIPHAVANH.

OTHER POLITICAL ORGANIZATIONS

Lao Front for National Construction (LFNC): Thanon Khouvieng, Ban Sisakhet, Chanthaboury, Vientiane; tel. and fax (21) 213752; f. 1979; est. to replace Lao Liberal Front and Lao Patriotic Front; comprises representatives of various political and social groups, of which the LPRP is the dominant force; fosters national solidarity; 165-mem. cttee elected in July 2011; Chair. PHANDOUANGCHIT VONGSA.

Numerous factions are in armed opposition to the Government. The principal groups are:

Democratic Chao Fa Party of Laos: led by PA KAO HER until his death in Oct. 2002; Pres. SOUA HER; Vice-Pres. TENG TANG.

Free Democratic Lao National Salvation Force: based in Thailand.

United Front for the Liberation of Laos: Leader PHOUNGPHET PHANARETH.

United Front for the National Liberation of the Lao People: f. 1980; led by Gen. PHOUMI NOSAVAN until his death in 1985.

United Lao National Liberation Front: Sayabouri Province; comprises an est. 8,000 mems, mostly Hmong (Meo) tribesmen; Sec.-Gen. VANG SHUR.

Diplomatic Representation

EMBASSIES IN LAOS

Australia: rue Thadeua, Ban Wat Nak, Km 4, Sisattanak, Vientiane; tel. (21) 353800; fax (21) 353801; e-mail austemb.laos@dfat.gov.au; internet www.laos.embassy.gov.au; Ambassador LYNDA WORTHAISONG.

Brunei: Unit 12, 30 Lao-Thai Friendship Rd, Ban Thoungkang, Sisattanak, Vientiane; tel. (21) 352294; fax (21) 352291; e-mail laosfeedbk@mfa.gov.bn; Ambassador Pengiran KASMIRHAN Pengiran Haji TAHIR.

Cambodia: rue Thadeua, Km 2, BP 34, Vientiane; tel. (21) 314952; fax (21) 314951; e-mail recamlao@laotel.com; Ambassador DAN YI.

China, People's Republic: rue Wat Nak, Sisattanak, BP 898, Vientiane; tel. (21) 315100; fax (21) 315104; e-mail chinaemb_la@mfa.gov.cn; Ambassador BU JIANGUO.

Cuba: Ban Saphanthong Neua 128, BP 1017, Vientiane; tel. (21) 314902; fax (21) 314901; e-mail embacuba@etllao.com; Ambassador WALDO REYES SARDINAS.

France: rue Setthathirath, BP 06, Vientiane; tel. (21) 267400; fax (21) 267439; e-mail contact@ambafrance-laos.org; internet www.ambafrance-laos.org; Ambassador FRANÇOIS SÉNÉMAUD.

Germany: rue Sok Paluang 26, Sisattanak, BP 314, Vientiane; tel. (21) 312110; fax (21) 351152; e-mail info@vientiane.diplo.de; internet www.vientiane.diplo.de; Ambassador PETER WIENAND.

India: 2 Ban Wat Nak, rue Thadeua, Km 3, Sisattanak, BP 225, Vientiane; tel. (21) 352301; fax (21) 352300; e-mail indiaemb@laotel.com; internet indemblao.nic.in; Ambassador Dr JITENDRA NATH MISRA.

Indonesia: ave Phone Keng, BP 277, Vientiane; tel. (21) 413909; fax (21) 214828; e-mail kbrivte@laotel.com; internet www.vientiane.deplu.go.id; Ambassador KRIA FAHMI PASARIBU.

Japan: rue Sisangvone, Vientiane; tel. (21) 414401; fax (21) 414406; internet www.la.emb-japan.go.jp; Ambassador JUNKO YOKOTA.

Korea, Democratic People's Republic: quartier Wat Nak, Vientiane; tel. (21) 315261; fax (21) 315260; Ambassador HAN PONG HO.

Korea, Republic: Lao-Thai Friendship Rd, Ban Wat Nak, Sisattanak, BP 7567, Vientiane; tel. (21) 352031; fax (21) 352035; e-mail laorok@etl.com; internet lao.mofat.go.kr; Ambassador LEE GUN-TAE.

Malaysia: 23 rue Singha, Ban Phonxay, BP 789, Vientiane; tel. (21) 414205; fax (21) 414201; e-mail mwvntian@laopdr.com; internet www.kln.gov.my/web/lao_vientiane; Ambassador Dato' THAN TAI HING.

Mongolia: Ban Wat Nak, Km 3, BP 370, Vientiane; tel. (21) 315220; fax (21) 315221; e-mail embmong@laotel.com; Ambassador TOGTOKHBAYARYN BATBAATAR.

Myanmar: Lao-Thai Friendship Rd, Ban Wat Nak, Sisattanak, BP 11, Vientiane; tel. (21) 314910; fax (21) 314913; e-mail mevlao@laotel.com; Ambassador NYUNT HLAING.

Philippines: Ban Saphanthong Kang, Sisattanak, BP 2415, Vientiane; tel. (21) 452490; fax (21) 452493; e-mail pelaopdr@laotel.com; Ambassador MARILYN J. ALARILLA.

Russia: rue Thadeua, Ban Thaphalanxay, Km 4, BP 490, Vientiane; tel. (21) 312222; fax (21) 312210; e-mail embrus_lao@mail.ru; internet www.laos.mid.ru; Ambassador OLEG V. K. KABANOV.

Singapore: Unit 4, rue Thadeua, Ban Wat Nak, Km 3, Sisattanak, Vientiane; tel. (21) 353939; fax (21) 353938; e-mail singemb_vte@sgmfa.gov.sg; internet www.mfa.gov.sg/vientiane; Ambassador DILEEP NAIR.

Thailand: ave Kaysone Phomvihane, Xaysettha, Vientiane; tel. (21) 214581; fax (21) 214580; e-mail thaivte@mfa.go.th; internet www.thaiembassy.org/vientiane; Ambassador VITAVAS SRIVIHOK.

USA: 19 rue Bartholonie, BP 114, That Dam, Vientiane; tel. (21) 267000; fax (21) 267190; e-mail conslao@state.gov; internet laos.usembassy.gov; Ambassador KAREN BREVARD STEWART.

Viet Nam: Unit 85, 23 rue Singha, Ban Phonxay, Xaysettha, Vientiane; tel. (21) 990986; fax (21) 416720; e-mail vnemba.la@mofa.gov.vn; internet www.mofa.gov.vn/vnemb.la; Ambassador TA MINH CHAU.

Judicial System

President of the People's Supreme Court: KHAMPHANH SITTHIDAMPHA.

Vice-President: PASEUTH SAUKHASEUM.

People's Supreme Court Judges: NOUANTHONG VONGSA, NHOTSENG LITTHIDETH, PHOUKHONG CHANTHALATH, SENGSOUVANH CHANTHALOUNNAVONG, KESON PHANLACK, KONGCHI YANGCHY, KHAMPON PHASAIGNAVONG.

Public Prosecutor-General: KHAMSAN SOUVONG.

Religion

The 1991 Constitution guarantees freedom of religious belief. The principal religion of Laos is Buddhism.

BUDDHISM

Lao Unified Buddhists' Association: Maha Kudy, Wat That Luang, Vientiane; f. 1964; Pres. (vacant); Sec.-Gen. Rev. SIHO SIHAVONG.

CHRISTIANITY

The Roman Catholic Church

For ecclesiastical purposes, Laos comprises four Apostolic Vicariates. At 31 December 2007 an estimated 0.6% of the population were adherents.

Episcopal Conference of Laos and Cambodia

c/o 787 Preah Monivong Blvd, Boeung Trabek, Chamkarmon, Phnom-Penh.

f. 1971; Pres. Rev. LOUIS-MARIE LING MANGKHANEKHOUN (Vicar of Paksé).

Vicar Apostolic of Luang Prabang: (vacant), Evêché, BP 74, Luang Prabang.

Vicar Apostolic of Paksé: Mgr LOUIS-MARIE LING MANGKHANEKHOUN (Titular Bishop of Proconsulari), Centre Catholique, BP 77, Paksé, Champasak; tel. (31) 212879; fax (31) 251439.

Vicar Apostolic of Savannakhet: Fr JEAN MARIE PRIDA INTHIRATH (Titular Bishop of Lemfocta), Centre Catholique, BP 12, Thakhek, Khammouane; tel. (51) 212184; fax (51) 213070.

Vicar Apostolic of Vientiane: Mgr JEAN KHAMSÉ VITHAVONG (Titular Bishop of Moglaena), Centre Catholique, BP 113, Vientiane; tel. (21) 216593; fax (21) 215085.

The Anglican Communion

Laos is within the jurisdiction of the Anglican Bishop of Singapore.

The Protestant Church

Lao Evangelical Church: BP 4200, Vientiane; tel. (21) 169136; Exec. Pres. Rev. KHAMPHONE KOUTHAPANYA.

BAHÁ'Í FAITH

National Spiritual Assembly: BP 189, Vientiane; tel. and fax (21) 216996; e-mail usme@laotel.com; f. 1956; Sec. SUSADA SENCHANTHISAY.

The Press

Aloun Mai (New Dawn): rue That Luang, Ban Nongbone, Xaysettha, Vientiane; tel. (21) 413029; fax (21) 413037; f. 1985; quarterly; theoretical and political organ of the LPRP; Editor-in-Chief SISOUK PHILAVONG.

Finance: rue That Luang, Ban Phonxay, Vientiane; tel. (21) 412401; fax (21) 412415; organ of Ministry of Finance.

Heng Ngan: 87 ave Lane Xang, BP 780, Vientiane; tel. (21) 212756; fax (21) 219750; fortnightly; organ of the Federation of Lao Trade Unions; Editor CHANSING KOKKEOBOUNMA.

Khao Tourakit (Business News): rue Sihom, Ban Sihom, Chanthaboury, Vientiane; tel. (21) 219244; fax (21) 219223; e-mail bsnews@laotel.com; f. 1999; fortnightly; organ of the Lao National Chamber of Commerce and Industry; Editor-in-Chief SOMCHIT THIPTHIENGTHAM.

Khaokila (Sports Daily News): Ban Mixay, Chanthaboury, Vientiane; tel. (21) 252908; fax (21) 252909; e-mail khaokila@hotmail.com; f. 1999; Editor-in-Chief SUKSAKHONE SIPRASEUTH.

Lao Dong (Labour): 87 ave Lane Xang, Vientiane; f. 1986; fortnightly; organ of the Federation of Lao Trade Unions; circ. 46,000.

Laos: 80 rue Setthathirath, BP 3770, Vientiane; tel. (21) 21447; fax (21) 21445; quarterly; published in Lao and English; illustrated; Editor V. PHOMCHANHEUANG; English Editor O. PHRAKHAMSAY.

Meying Lao: rue Manthatoarath, BP 59, Vientiane; e-mail chansoda@hotmail.com; f. 1980; monthly; women's magazine; organ of the Lao Women's Union; Editor-in-Chief VATSADY KHUTNGOTHA; Editor CHANSODA PHONETHIP; circ. 7,000.

Noum Lao (Lao Youth): rue Phonthan, Ban Phonthan Neua, Xaysettha, Vientiane; tel. (21) 951067; fax (21) 416727; f. 1979; fortnightly; organ of the Lao People's Revolutionary Youth Union; Editor KHANKAB BUDARAT; circ. 1,500.

Pasason Van Athit: rue Pangkham, Ban Xiengyeun Thong, Chanthaboury, Vientiane; tel. (21) 212471; fax (21) 212470; weekly; Editor THONGLITH LIEMXAYYACHAK; circ. 2,000.

Pasaxon (The People): 80 rue Setthathirath, BP 110, Vientiane; tel. (21) 212466; fax (21) 212470; e-mail infonews@pasaxon.org.la; internet www.pasaxon.org.la; f. 1940; daily; Lao; organ of the Cen. Cttee of the LPRP; Editor-in-Chief BOUALAPHANH THANPHILOM; circ. 28,000.

Pathet Lao: 80 rue Setthathirath, Vientiane; tel. (21) 212447; f. 2001; daily; Lao and English; organ of the Lao News Agency, Khao San Pathet Lao (KPL); Editor KHEMTHONG SANOUBAN.

Sciences and Technics: Science, Technology and the Environment Agency (STEA), BP 2279, Vientiane; f. 1991; est. as Technical Science Magazine; quarterly; organ of the Dept of Science and Technology; scientific research and development.

Siang Khong Gnaovason Song Thanva (Voice of the 2nd December Youths): Vientiane; monthly; youth journal.

Sieng Khene Lao: Vientiane; monthly; organ of the Lao Writers' Association.

Suksa Mai: Vientiane; monthly; organ of the Ministry of Education.

Valasan Khosana (Propaganda Journal): Vientiane; f. 1987; organ of the Cen. Cttee of the LPRP.

Vannasinh: Vientiane; monthly; literature magazine.

Vientiane Mai (New Vientiane): 36 rue Setthathirath, BP 989, Vientiane; tel. (21) 212623; fax (21) 215989; e-mail admin@vientianemai.net; internet www.vientianemai.net; f. 1975; morning daily; organ of the LPRP Cttee of Vientiane province and city; Editor SOMPHET INTHISARATH; circ. 2,500.

Vientiane Times: rue Pangkham, BP 5723, Vientiane; tel. (21) 216364; fax (21) 216365; e-mail info@vientianetimes.gov.la; internet www.vientianetimes.org.la; f. 1994; daily; English; Editor-in-Chief SAVANKHONE RAZMOUNTRY; circ. 3,000.

Vientiane Tourakit Sangkhom (Vientiane Business-Social): 36 rue Setthathirath, Vientiane; tel. (21) 2623; fax (21) 6365; weekly; publ. in conjunction with Vientiane Mai; Editor SOMPHET INTHISARATH; circ. 2,000.

There is also a newspaper published by the Lao People's Army, and several provinces have their own newsletters.

NEWS AGENCY

Khao San Pathet Lao (Lao News Agency—KPL): 80 rue Setthathirath, BP 3770, Vientiane; tel. (21) 215402; fax (210 212446; e-mail kplnews@yahoo.com; internet www.kplnet.net; f. 1968; dept of the Ministry of Information and Culture; news service for press, radio and television broadcasting; daily bulletins in Lao, English and French; Gen. Dir KHAMSENE PHONGSA; English Editor BOUNLERT LOUANEDOUANGCHANH.

PRESS ASSOCIATION

Lao Journalists' Association (LJA): BP 122, Vientiane; tel. (21) 212420; fax (21) 212408; Pres. Dr BOSENGKHAM VONGDARA; Sec.-Gen. KHAM KHONG KONGVONGSA.

Publishers

Khoualuang Kanphim: 2–6 Khoualuang Market, Vientiane.

Lao-phanit: Ministry of Education, Bureau des Manuels Scolaires, rue Lane Xang, Ban Sisavat, Vientiane; educational, cookery, art, music, fiction.

Pakpassak Kanphin: 9–11 quai Fa-Hguun, Vientiane.

Department of Publishing, Printing, Distribution and Libraries: Ministry of Information and Culture, BP 122, Vientiane; tel. (21) 212421; fax (21) 212408; oversees the State Publishing and Book Distribution House and the State Printing Enterprise; Dir NOUPHAY KOUNLAVONG.

Broadcasting and Communications

TELECOMMUNICATIONS

Entreprise de Télécommunications de Laos (ETL): rue Saylom, Ban Saylom, Chanthaboury, Vientiane; tel. (21) 215767; fax (21) 212779; e-mail csd@etllao.com; internet www.etllao.com; state enterprise, telephone, mobile and voice over internet protocol (VOIP) services; Dir-Gen. KHAMMOUANE XOMSIHAPANYA.

Lao Télécommunications Co Ltd: ave Lane Xang, BP 5607, 01000 Vientiane; tel. (21) 244212; fax (21) 241638; e-mail marketin@laotel.com; internet laotel.com; f. 1996; jt venture between a subsidiary of Shinawatra Group of Thailand and Entreprises des Postes et Télécommunications de Laos; awarded 25-year contract by Govt in 1996 to undertake all telecommunications projects in Laos; Dir-Gen. THANSAMAY KOMMASITH.

BROADCASTING

Radio

In mid-2010 there were 44 radio stations broadcasting throughout Laos.

Lao National Radio: rue Phangkham, Km 6, BP 310, Vientiane; tel. (21) 212468; fax (21) 212430; e-mail laonradio@lnr.org.la; internet www.lnr.org.la; f. 1960; state-owned; programmes in Lao, French, English, Thai, Khmer and Vietnamese; domestic and international services; Dir-Gen. SIPHA NONGLATH.

Television

A domestic television service began in December 1983.

Lao National Television (TVNL): rue Sivilay, BP 5635, Vientiane; tel. (21) 710067; fax (21) 710182; e-mail tnlinfo@tnl.gov.la; internet www.tnl.gov.la; f. 1983; colour television service; Dir-Gen. BOUMCHOM VONGPHET.

Laos Television 3: BP 860, Vientiane; tel. (21) 315449; fax (21) 215628; f. 1994; est. as IBC Channel 3; 30% govt-owned, 70% owned by Int. Broadcasting Corpn Co Ltd (Thailand); operated by latter; programmes in Lao.

Finance

(cap. = capital; dep. = deposits; br.(s) = branch(es); m. = million)

BANKING

The banking system was reorganized in 1988–89, ending the state monopoly of banking. Some commercial banking functions were transferred from the central bank and the state commercial bank to a new network of autonomous banks. The establishment of joint ventures with foreign financial institutions was permitted.

Central Bank

Banque de la RDP Lao: rue Yonnet, BP 19, Vientiane; tel. (21) 213109; fax (21) 213108; e-mail bol@bol.gov.la; internet www.bol.gov.la; f. 1959 as the bank of issue; became Banque Pathetlao 1968; took over the operations of Banque Nationale du Laos 1975; known as Banque d'Etat de la RDP Lao from 1982 until adoption of present name; dep. 394,017m. kips, total assets US $361m. (Dec. 2002); Gov. SOMPAO PHAYSITH.

Commercial Banks

Acleda Bank Lao: 372 cnr rues Dongpalane and Dongpaina, Unit 21, Ponesavanh, Sisattanak, Vientiane; tel. (21) 264994; fax (21) 264995; e-mail acledabank@acledabank.com.la; internet www.acledabank.com.la; f. 2008; cap. 100,000m. kips, dep. 122,152m. kips (Dec. 2009); Chair. CHEA SOK; Pres. and CEO PHON NARIN.

Agriculture Promotion Bank: 58 rue Hengboun, Ban Haysok, BP 5456, Vientiane; tel. (21) 241394; fax (21) 223714; e-mail apblao@laotel.com; internet www.apblaos.com; Dir BOUANGEUN PHONGSAVATH.

ANZ Vientiane Commercial Bank Ltd: 33 ave Lane Xang, Ban Hatsady, Chanthaboury, Vientiane; tel. (21) 222700; fax (21) 213513; e-mail vccbank@laotel.com; internet www.anz.com/laos; f. 1993; renamed as above in 2007; private jt venture owned by Laotian, Thai, Taiwanese and Australian investors; Man. Dir KERROD THOMAS.

Banque pour le Commerce Extérieur Lao (BCEL): 1 rue Pangkham, Ban Xiengnheun, Chanthaboury, Vientiane; tel. (21) 213200; fax (21) 213202; e-mail bcelhqv@bcel.com.la; internet www.bcel.com.la; f. 1975; 100% state-owned; cap. 329,201m. kips, res 109,427m. kips, dep. 6,059,189m. kips (Dec. 2009); Chair. VIENGTHONG SYPHANDONE; Man. Dir SONEXAY SITPHAXAY.

Banque Franco-Lao: ave Lane Xang, Ban Hatsady, Chanthaboury, Vientiane; tel. (21) 285111; fax (21) 285222; e-mail contact@bfl.la; internet www.banquefrancolao.com; f. 2010; Laotian-French jt venture; Man. Dir GUILLAUME PERDON.

Indochina Bank: 116 Capital Tower, 23 rue Singha, POB 6029, Vientiane; tel. (21) 455000; fax (21) 455111; e-mail info@indochinabank.com; internet www.indochinabank.com; f. 2009; Laotian-South Korean jt venture; Man. Dir TAY HONG HENG.

International Commercial Bank: 127/07, rue Hatsady, Hatsady Tai, Chanthaboury, Vientiane; tel. (21) 250388; fax (21) 250479; e-mail enquiry@icb-lao.com; internet www.icb-lao.com; f. 2008; Man. Dir ZHUKIBLI KUAN.

Joint Development Bank: 82 ave Lane Xang, BP 3187, Vientiane; tel. (21) 213531; fax (21) 213530; e-mail jdb@jdbbank.com; internet www.jdbbank.com; f. 1989; the first jt venture bank between Laos and a foreign partner; 30% owned by Banque de la RDP Lao, 70% owned by Phrom Suwan Silo and Drying Co Ltd of Thailand; cap. US $4m.; Dir SAROGE SINGSOMBOON.

Lao Development Bank (LDB): BP 2700, Ban Sihome, Chanthaboury, Vientiane; tel. (21) 213300; fax (21) 213304; e-mail ldbhovte@ldblao.com; internet www.ldb.org.la; f. 1999; est. as Lao May Bank upon consolidation by the Govt of ParkTai Bank, Lao May Bank and Nakornluang Bank; merged with Lane Xang Bank Ltd in 2001; name changed as above in 2003; 100% govt-owned; lends mainly to SMEs; Man. Dir BOUNTA DALAVY; 18 brs.

Lao-Viet Bank (LVB): 44 ave Lane Xang, Ban Hatsady, Chanthaboury, Vientiane; tel. (21) 216316; fax (21) 212197; e-mail lvbho@laotel.com; f. 1999; jt venture between BCEL and Bank for Investment and Devt of Vietnam; cap. US $15m.; Chair. PHANSANA KHOUNNOUVONG; Man. Dir NGUYEN KIM DIEU; 3 brs.

Nayobay Bank: rue Kaisorn Phomvihane, Ban Phonphanao, Saysettha, Vientiane; tel. (21) 264407; fax (21) 264408; f. 2007; 100% state-owned; Man. Dir BOUALONG XAYAVONG.

Phongsavanh Bank: Unit 1, rue Kaisorn Phomvihane, Ban Phakhao, Xaythany, Vientiane; tel. (21) 215666; e-mail info@phongsavanhbank.com; internet www.phongsavanhbank.com; f. 2007; Man. Dir OD PHONGSAVANH; cap. US $10m. (2007).

STOCK EXCHANGE

Lao Securities Exchange (LSX): Ban Phonethan Neue, rue T4, Saysettha, Vientiane; internet www.lsx.com.la; f. 2010; establishment funded by Bank of Laos (51% of capital) and Republic of Korea (49%); Chair. and CEO DETHPHOUVANG MOULARAT.

INSURANCE

Assurances Générales du Laos (AGL): Vientiane Commercial Bank Bldg, 33 ave Lane Xang, BP 4223, Vientiane; tel. (21) 215903; fax (21) 215904; e-mail agl@agl-allianz.com; internet www.agl-allianz.com; f. 1990; jt venture between Laotian Govt (49%) and Assurances Générales de France (51%); Group Chair. Dr MICHAEL DIEKMANN; Man. Dir GUY APOVY.

Lane Xang Assurance Co (LAP): Vientiane; f. 2010; equal jt venture between Lao Development Bank and Post and Telecommunication Joint Venture Insurance Corpn; life and general.

Trade and Industry

GOVERNMENT AGENCY

National Economic Research Institute (NERI): ave Kaysone Phomvihan, Ban Sivilay, Xaythany, Vientiane; tel. and fax (21) 711181; e-mail nerilaos@yahoo.com; govt policy development unit; Dir SOUPHAN KEOMISAY.

DEVELOPMENT ORGANIZATIONS

Department of Domestic and Foreign Investment (DDFI): rue Luang Prabang, 01001 Vientiane; tel. (21) 222690; fax (21) 215491; e-mail fimc@laotel.com; internet invest.laopdr.org; fmrly Foreign Investment Management Committee (FIMC); provides information and assistance to existing and potential investors.

Department of Livestock and Fisheries: Ministry of Agriculture and Forestry, Ban Phonxay, BP 811, Vientiane; tel. (21) 416932; fax (21) 415674; e-mail eulaodlf@laotel.com; public enterprise; imports and markets agricultural commodities; produces and distributes feed and animals; Dir-Gen. BOUAPHAN KONEDAVONG.

National Agriculture and Forestry Research Institute (NAFRI): Nongviengkham, BP 7170, Vientiane; tel. (21) 770084; fax (21) 770047; e-mail bounthong@nafri.org.la; internet www.nafri.org.la; f. 1999; supports sectoral devt and formulation of strategies and programmes in accordance with govt policy; Dir-Gen. Dr BOUNTHONG BOUAHOM.

State Committee for State Planning: Office of the Prime Minister, Ban Sisavat, Vientiane; tel. (21) 213653; fax (21) 213560.

CHAMBER OF COMMERCE

Lao National Chamber of Commerce and Industry (LNCCI): ave Kaysone Phomvihane, Ban Phonphanao, Xaysettha, BP 4596, Vientiane; tel. (21) 452579; fax (21) 452580; e-mail lncci@laopdr.com; internet www.lncci.laotel.com; f. 1989; 800 mems; Pres. KISSANA VONGSAY; Sec.-Gen. KHAMPANH SENGTHONGKHAM.

TRADE ASSOCIATION

Société Lao Import-Export (SOLIMPEX): 43–47 ave Lane Xang, BP 2789, Vientiane; tel. (21) 213818; fax (21) 217054; Dir KANHKEO SAYCOCIE; Dep. Dir PHONGSAMOUTH VONGKOT.

UTILITIES

Electricity

Electricité du Laos (EDL): rue Nongbone, BP 309, Vientiane; tel. (21) 451519; fax (21) 416381; e-mail edlgmo@laotel.com; internet www.edl-laos.com; f. 1959; state-owned corpn; responsible for production and distribution of electricity; shares in subsidiary Electricité du Laos Generation Co offered in 2011; Chair. KHAMMONE PHONEKEO; Man. Dir KHAMMANY INTHIRATH.

Lao National Grid Co: Vientiane; responsible for Mekong hydroelectricity exports.

Water

Nam Papa Vientiane (Vientiane Water Supply Authority): rue Phone Kheng, Ban That Luang Neue, Xaysettha, Vientiane; tel. (21) 412880; fax (21) 414378; e-mail daophet@laotel.com; f. 1962; fmrly Nam Papa Lao; responsible for the water supply of Vientiane; Gen. Man. DAOPHET BOUAPHA.

Water Supply Authority (WASA): Dept of Housing and Urban Planning, Ministry of Public Works and Transport, ave Lane Xang, Vientiane; tel. and fax (21) 452167; fax (21) 451826; e-mail nvirabouth@yahoo.com; internet www.wasa.gov.la; f. 1998; Dir NOUPHEUAK VIRABOUTH.

STATE ENTERPRISES

Agricultural Forestry Development Import-Export and General Service Co: trading co of the armed forces.

Bolisat Phatthana Khet Phoudoi Import-Export Co: rue Khoun Boulom, Vientiane; tel. (21) 216234; fax (21) 215046; f. 1984; trading co of the armed forces.

Dao-Heuang Import-Export Co: 242-7 Route 13 South, Ban Thaluang, Paksé, Champasak Province; tel. (31) 212250; fax (31) 212438; e-mail daoheuangcafe@laopdr.com; internet www.daoheuangcoffee.com; f. 1990; imports and distributes whisky, beer, mineral water, coffee and foodstuffs; Pres. LEUANG LITDANG.

Lao Commodities Export Co Ltd (Lacomex): Ban Wattuang, Paksé, Champasak Province; tel. (31) 212552; fax (31) 212553; e-mail sisanouk@laotel.com; f. 1994; exports coffee under the Paksong Cafe Lao brand; Man. Dir SISANOUK SISOMBAT.

Lao Houng Heuang Export-Import Co: rue Nongbone, Vientiane; tel. (21) 217344; fax (21) 212107.

Lao State Material Import-Export Co (Lasmac): 59 Ban Hatsady Tai, Chanthaboury, Vientiane; tel. (21) 216578; fax (21) 217149; e-mail lasmac@laotel.com; internet www.lasmac.laopdr.com; f. 1983; mfr of wood products and woven plastic; exports agricultural and wood products; imports construction materials.

Luen Fat Hong Lao Plywood Industry Co: BP 83, Vientiane; tel. (21) 314990; fax (21) 314992; e-mail lfhsdsj@laotel.com; internet www.luenfathongyada.laopdr.com; devt and management of forests, logging and timber production.

CO-OPERATIVES

Central Leading Committee to Guide Agricultural Co-operatives: Vientiane; f. 1978; helps to organize and plan regulations and policies for co-operatives; by the end of 1986 there were some 4,000 co-operatives, employing about 74% of the agricultural labour force; Chair. (vacant).

TRADE UNION ORGANIZATION

Federation of Lao Trade Unions: 87 ave Lane Xang, BP 780, Vientiane; tel. (21) 212754; e-mail kammabanlao@pan-laos.net.la; f. 1956; 21-mem. Cen. Cttee and five-mem. Control Cttee; Pres. KHAMLA LORLONESY; 70,000 mems.

Transport

RAILWAYS

In 2003 the Thai Government agreed to finance a 3.5-km rail link from Tha Naleng (near Vientiane) to Nong Khai, in north-eastern Thailand; construction was completed in April 2008, and the first passenger train service commenced in March 2009. Proposals to extend the track, to link Tha Naleng with Vientiane and to extend southwards and eastwards to Vinh in Viet Nam via Thakhek in central Laos, were also announced.

ROADS

The Asian Development Bank has supported an extensive development programme for the road network in Laos. In 2009 there were an estimated 39,568 km of roads. The main routes link Vientiane and Luang Prabang with Ho Chi Minh City in southern Viet Nam and with northern Viet Nam and the Cambodian border, Vientiane with Savannakhet, Phongsali to the Chinese border, Vientiane with Luang Prabang and the port of Ha Tinh (northern Viet Nam), and Savannakhet with the port of Da Nang (Viet Nam). Laos, Thailand and China are linked by the Kunming–Bangkok Highway, 250 km of which traverse Laos. In February 2004 construction of a 245-km national road (Route 9) was completed, linking Laos with Thailand and Viet Nam.

A number of bridges across the Mekong River link Laos to Thailand. A bridge linking Khammouane in Laos with the Thai province of Nakhon Pathom was scheduled for completion in November 2011. Construction of a fifth bridge, between the Laotian province of Bokeo and the northernmost Thai province of Chiang Rai, was expected to be completed by 2014.

INLAND WATERWAYS

The Mekong River, which forms the western frontier of Laos for much of its length, is the country's greatest transport artery. However, the size of river vessels is limited by rapids, and traffic is seasonal. There are about 4,600 km of navigable waterways.

CIVIL AVIATION

Wattay airport, Vientiane, is the principal international airport. In 1998 Luang Prabang airport also gained formal approval to receive international flights. Construction of a new airport in Oudomxay Province was completed in the late 1990s. Savannakhet Airport was to be developed into an international facility, as part of plans for the east–west economic corridor project, a proposed transport network linking Laos with Myanmar, Thailand and Viet Nam.

Lao Civil Aviation Department: BP 119, Vientiane; tel. (21) 512163; fax (21) 520236; e-mail laodca@laotel.com; internet www.dca.mpwt.gov.la; Dir-Gen. YAKUA LOPANGKAO.

Lao Airlines: National Air Transport Co, 2 rue Pangkham, BP 6441, Vientiane; tel. (21) 212057; fax (21) 212065; e-mail laoairlines@laoairlines.com; internet www.laoairlines.com; f. 1975; state airline, fmrly Lao Aviation; operates internal and international passenger and cargo transport services within South-East Asia; CEO SOMPHONE DOUANGDARA.

Tourism

Laos has spectacular scenery and ancient pagodas. Luang Prabang was approved by UNESCO as a World Heritage site in 1995, as was the Wat Phu temple complex in southern Laos in 2001. Foreign visitor arrivals were reported to have increased by 24.5% in 2010 to exceed 2.5m. Receipts were estimated at US $360m. in 2010.

National Tourism Administration of Lao PDR: ave Lane Xang, BP 3556, Hatsady, Chanthaboury, Vientiane; tel. (21) 212251; fax (21) 212769; e-mail tmpd_lnta@yahoo.com; internet www.tourismlaos.org; parastatal org.;promotes Laos as a tourist destination and regulates the tourism industry; 17 provincial offices; Chair. SOMPHONG MONGKHONVILAY.

Defence

As assessed at November 2010, the total strength of the armed forces was an estimated 29,100: army 25,600 (including an army marine section of an estimated 600); air force 3,500. Conscription lasts a minimum of 18 months. Paramilitary forces comprise militia self-defence forces numbering about 100,000 men.

Defence Expenditure: Budgeted for 2009: 119,000m. kips.

Supreme Commander of the Lao People's Army (Commander-in-Chief): Lt-Gen. CHOUMMALY SAYASONE.

Chief of the General Staff: Lt-Gen. SANYAHAK PHOMVIHANE.

Education

A comprehensive educational system is in force, and Lao is the medium of instruction.

In 2007/08 enrolment in pre-primary education included 14% of pupils in the relevant age-group (males 13%; females 14%). In the same year enrolment in primary education, which begins at six years of age and lasts for five years, included 82% of children in the relevant age-group (males 84%; females 81%). Secondary education, beginning at the age of 11, lasts for six years, comprising two three-year cycles. In 2006/07 enrolment in secondary education included 36% of pupils in the relevant age-group (males 39%; females 33%).

In the 2009/10 academic year there were 1,123 pre-primary institutions, which were attended by 85,357 children, and 8,871 primary schools, attended by 908.900 pupils. The 722 secondary schools provided education for a total of 437,900 students (including 51 vocational schools at which 16,000 students were enrolled). There were 100 tertiary institutions, including four universities at which 54,000 students were enrolled, while 59,000 were studying at other institutions of higher education. There are several regional technical colleges. The National University of Laos was founded in 1995. Enrolment in tertiary education in 2006 was equivalent to 9% of the relevant age-group (males 11%; females 7%). Government spending on education in 2006 reached an estimated 15.8% of total budgetary expenditure.

Bibliography

(See also Cambodia and Viet Nam)

Anderson, Kym. *Lao Economic Reform and WTO Accession: Implications for Agriculture and Rural Development.* Singapore, Institute of Southeast Asian Studies, 1999.

Askew, Marc, Long, Colin, and Logan, William. *Vientiane: Transformations of a Lao Landscape.* Abingdon, Routledge, 2006.

Bourdet, Yves. *The Economics of Transition in Laos: From Socialism to ASEAN Integration.* Cheltenham, Edward Elgar Publishing, 2000.

Brown, M., and Zasloff, J. *Apprentice Revolutionaries: The Communist Movement in Laos, 1930–1985.* Stanford, CA, Hoover Institution Press, 1986.

Castle, Timothy N. *A War in the Shadow of Vietnam.* New York, Columbia University Press, 1995.

Chazee, Laurent (Ed.). *The People of Laos.* Bangkok, White Lotus, 2001.

Coleman, Brett, and Wynne-Williams, John. *Rural Finance in the Lao People's Democratic Republic: Demand, Supply, and Sustainability: Results of Household and Supplier Surveys.* Manila, Asian Development Bank, 2006.

Conroy, Paul. *10 Months in Laos: A Vast Web of Intrigue, Missing Millions and Murder.* Melbourne, Crown Content, 2002.

Cooper, R., Tapp, N., Yia Lee, G., and Schwoer-Kohl, G. *The Hmong.* Bangkok, Artasia Press, 1992.

Deuve, J. *Le Royaume de Laos, 1949–1965.* Paris, 1984.

Dommen, A. J. *Conflict in Laos: The Politics of Neutralization.* London, Pall Mall Press, 2nd Edn, 1971.

Epprecht, Michael. *The Geography of Poverty and Inequality in Lao PDR.* Bern, International Food Policy Research Institute, 2008.

Evans, Grant. *Lao Peasants Under Socialism.* New Haven, CT, Yale University Press, 1991.

The Politics of Ritual and Remembrance: Laos since 1975. Chiang Mai, Silkworm Books, 1998.

A Short History of Laos: The Land in Between. St Leonards, Allen and Unwin, 2003.

Evans, Grant (Ed.). *Laos: Culture and Society.* Chiang Mai, Silkworm Books, 1999.

The Last Century of Lao Royalty: a Documentary History. Chiang Mai, Silkworm Books, 2009.

Evans, G., and Rowley, K. *Red Brotherhood at War.* London, Verso, Revised Edn, 1990.

Freeman, Nick J. 'Laos: No Safe Haven from the Regional Tumult' in *Southeast Asian Affairs, 1998.* Singapore, Institute of Southeast Asian Studies, 1998.

Goscha, Christopher, and Ivarsson, Soren (Eds). *Contesting Visions of the Lao Past: Lao Historiography at the Crossroads.* London, Routledge, 2004.

Goudineau, Yves, and Lorrillard, Michel (Eds). *New Research on Laos / Recherches nouvelle sur le Laos.* Bilingual Edn, Chiang Mai, Silkworm Books, 2009.

Gunn, Geoffrey C. *Rebellion in Laos.* Bangkok, White Lotus, 2003.

Political Struggles in Laos (1930–1954). Bangkok, White Lotus, 2007.

Hamilton-Merritt, Jane. *Tragic Mountains: The Hmong, the Americans, and the Secret Wars for Laos, 1942–1992.* Bloomington, IN, Indiana University Press, 1993.

Ireson-Doolittle, Carol, and Moreno-Black, Geraldine. *The Lao: Gender, Power and Livelihood.* Boulder, CO, Westview Press, 2003.

Ivarsson, Soren. *The Making of a Lao Space Between Indochina and Siam, 1860–1945.* Copenhagen, Nordic Institute of Asian Studies Press, 2008.

Kremmer, Christopher. *Stalking the Elephant Kings.* St Leonards, Allen and Unwin, 1998.

Lancaster, D. *The Emancipation of French Indo-China.* London, Oxford University Press, 1961.

Langer, P. F., and Zasloff, J. J. *North Vietnam and the Pathet Lao.* Cambridge, MA, Harvard University Press, 1970.

Mansfield, Stephen. *Lao Hill Tribes: Traditions and Patterns of Existence.* Kuala Lumpur, Oxford University Press, 2001.

Menon, Jayant. *Laos in the ASEAN Free Trade Area: Trade, Revenue and Investment Implications.* Pacific Economic Papers, No. 276, Canberra, Australia-Japan Research Centre, 1998.

Ngaosrivathana, Mayoury, and Breazeale, K. (Eds). *Breaking New Ground in Lao History.* Seattle, WA, University of Washington Press, 2002.

Ngaosrivathana, Mayoury, and Ngaosrivathana, Pheuiphanh. *Kith and Kin Politics: The Relationship Between Laos and Thailand.* Manila, Journal of Contemporary Asia Publishers, 1994.

Oakes Whittington, Jerome. *The Simulation of Politics: Developmental Natures in Lao Hydropower.* Charleston, SC, BiblioLabs, 2011.

Pham, Chi Do (Ed.). *Economic Development in Lao P.D.R.: Horizon 2000.* Vientiane, 1994.

Pholsena, Vatthana. *Post-War Laos: The Politics of Culture, History, and Memory.* Singapore, Institute of Southeast Asian Studies, 2005.

Pholsena, Vatthana, and Banomyong, Ruth. *Laos: From Buffer State to Crossroads?* Chiang Mai, Mekong Press, 2007.

Phraxayavong, Viliam. *History of Aid to Laos.* Chiang Mai, Silkworm Books, 2009.

Program for South-East Asian Studies. *New Laos, New Challenges.* Tempe, Arizona State University Press, 1998.

Quincy, Keith. *Harvesting Pa Chay's Wheat: The Hmong and America's Secret War in Laos.* Washington, DC, University of Washington Press, 2000.

Rantala, Judy Austin. *Laos: Caught in the Web—The Vietnam War Years.* Bangkok, Orchid Press, 2004.

Rehbein, Boike. *Globalization, Culture, and Society in Laos.* Abingdon, Routledge, 2007.

Rigg, Jonathan. *Living With Transition in Laos: Market Integration in Southeast Asia.* London, RoutledgeCurzon, 2005.

Sagar, D. J. *Major Political Events in Indochina 1945–1990.* Oxford, Facts on File, 1991.

Simms, Peter and Sanda. *The Kingdoms of Laos: Six Hundred Years of History.* Richmond, Surrey, Curzon Press, 1998.

Sisouphanthong, Bounthavy, and Taillard, Christian. *Atlas of Laos.* Copenhagen, Nordic Institute of Asian Studies, 2000.

Stuart-Fox, Martin. *Laos: Politics, Economics and Society.* London, Frances Pinter, 1986.

'Laos: Towards Subregional Integration' in *Southeast Asian Affairs, 1995.* Singapore, Institute of Southeast Asian Studies, 1995.

Buddhist Kingdom, Marxist State: The Making of Modern Laos. Bangkok, White Lotus, 1995.

A History of Laos. Cambridge, Cambridge University Press, 1997.

The Lao Kingdom of Lan Xang: Rise and Decline. Bangkok, White Lotus, 1998.

Historical Dictionary of Laos. Metuchen, NJ, Scarecrow Press, 3rd Edn, 2007.

Stuart-Fox, Martin (Ed.). *Contemporary Laos.* St Lucia, University of Queensland Press, 1982.

Taillard, Christian. *Le Laos, stratégie d'un Etat-tampon.* Montpellier, Reclus, 1989.

Tapp, Nicholas. *Sovereignty and Rebellion: The White Hmong of Northern Thailand.* Bangkok, White Lotus, 2005.

Than, Mya, and Tan, Joseph L. H. (Eds). *Laos' Dilemmas and Options: The Challenge of Economic Transition in the 1990s.* Singapore, Institute of Southeast Asian Studies, 1996.

Toye, Hugh. *Laos: Buffer State or Battleground.* London, Oxford University Press, 1971.

Van Staaveren, Jacob. *Interdiction in Southern Laos, 1960–1968.* Honolulu, HI, University Press of the Pacific, 2005.

Warner, Roger. *Back Fire: The CIA's Secret War in Laos.* New York, Simon & Schuster, 1995.

Zasloff, J. J., and Unger, L. (Eds). *Laos: Beyond the Revolution.* Basingstoke, Macmillan, 1991.

MALAYSIA

Physical and Social Geography

HARVEY DEMAINE

Malaysia covers a total area of 330,803 sq km (127,724 sq miles), comprising the 11 states of Peninsular Malaysia, with an area of 132,631 sq km (51,209 sq miles), together with the two states of Sarawak and Sabah (with the Federal Territory of Labuan), in northern Borneo, with areas of, respectively, 124,450 sq km (48,051 sq miles) and 73,722 sq km (28,464 sq miles). Peninsular Malaysia includes a number of islands, the largest being Langkawi and Pulau Pinang (Penang).

While Peninsular Malaysia, Sabah and Sarawak lie in almost identical latitudes between 1° N and 7° N of the Equator, and have characteristic equatorial climates with uniformly high temperatures and rain in all seasons, there is nevertheless a fundamental difference in their geographical position. Peninsular Malaysia forms the southern tip of the Asian mainland, bordered by Thailand to the north and by the island of Singapore at its southernmost point. On its western side, facing the sheltered and calm waters of the Straits of Melaka (Malacca), Peninsular Malaysia flanks one of the oldest and most frequented maritime highways of the world, whereas Sabah and Sarawak lie off the main shipping routes, along the northern fringe of the remote island of Borneo, bordered by Indonesia and, in north-eastern Sarawak, by Brunei.

PHYSICAL FEATURES

Structurally, both parts of Malaysia form part of the old stable massif of Sundaland, although whereas the dominant folding in the Malay peninsula is of Mesozoic age, that along the northern edge of Borneo dates from Tertiary times. In Peninsular Malaysia the mountain ranges, whose summit levels reach 1,200 m–2,100 m, run roughly north to south and their granitic cores have been widely exposed by erosion. The most continuous is the Main Range, which, over most of the peninsula, marks the divide between the relatively narrow western coastal plain draining to the Straits of Melaka, and the much larger area of mountainous interior and coastal lowland which drains to the South China Sea.

Because of the much greater accessibility of the western lowlands to the main sea-routes, and also of the existence of extensive areas of alluvial tin in the gravels deposited at the break of slope in the western foothills of the Main Range, the strip of country lying between the latter and the western coast of Peninsular Malaysia has been much more intensively developed than the remaining four-fifths of the country. The planting of rubber became concentrated in the vicinity of roads, railways and other facilities originally developed in connection with the tin industry. In contrast to the placid waters of the west coast, the east coast is open to the full force of the north-east monsoon during the period from October to March.

In many respects Sabah and Sarawak display similar basic geographical characteristics to eastern Peninsular Malaysia, but in a more extreme form. Thus, the lowlands are mostly wider, the rivers longer and even more liable to severe flooding, the coastline exposed to the north-east monsoon and avoided by shipping, and the equatorial forest cover even denser and more continuous than that of the peninsula. Moreover, while in general the mountains of Sabah and Sarawak are of comparable height to those in Peninsular Malaysia, there is one striking exception in Mt Kinabalu, a single isolated horst, which towers above the Croker Range of Sabah, its peak at an altitude of 4,101 m.

Throughout Malaysia, average daily temperatures range from about 21°C to 32°C, although in higher areas temperatures are lower and vary more widely. Rainfall averages about 2,540 mm throughout the year, although this is subject to regional variation.

NATURAL RESOURCES

The mineral resources of Malaysia include bauxite, iron ore, coal (which is mined mainly in Sarawak) and gold. The importance of tin has declined substantially, and the mining of copper ceased in 1999.

East Malaysia's principal wealth remains the coastal and offshore deposits of hydrocarbons. Petroleum production from the original Miri field, in onshore Sarawak, has ceased, but discoveries off shore, made in the 1960s, have maintained production. At the end of 2010, according to oil industry figures, Malaysia's proven petroleum reserves totalled 5,800m. barrels, and natural gas reserves 2,400,000m. cu m. Malaysia's production of crude petroleum was estimated at 32.1m. metric tons in 2008, with production averaging 716,000 barrels per day.

Until the rise of petroleum, Malaysia's main economic resource was the agricultural potential of the peninsula. This derived not so much from the inherent superiority of its soils (indeed, those of Sarawak and Sabah are similar) but rather from its accessibility for commercial enterprise. Rubber and, subsequently, oil palm flourished in this environment, although in the early 21st century the relative significance of rubber continued to decline. Sabah and Sarawak have relied heavily upon their vast wealth in tropical timbers. However, the rate of extraction of timber was so rapid from the late 1970s that serious efforts were subsequently made to conserve resources, particularly on the peninsula.

POPULATION AND ETHNIC GROUPS

The total population of Malaysia, according to the preliminary results of the census of July 2010, was 27,565,821 (compared with the August 1991 census total of 18,379,655), thus giving an average density was 83.3 per sq km. The majority of the population resides in Peninsular Malaysia, the most urbanized part of the country. The indigenous population, apart from some aboriginal minorities, consists mainly of Muslim Malays, who accounted for about 51% of the population in 2009. There is a large Chinese element, constituting 23% of the total population in 2009, and a significant minority of Indians (an ethnic term generally applied to those of Indian, Pakistani or Bangladeshi origin), who accounted for nearly 7%. In Sabah and Sarawak Malays and other Muslim peoples have been confined mainly to the coastal zone, while various other ethnic groups occupy the interior.

History

ROBERT CRIBB

Based on an earlier article by IAN BROWN

Revised by WILLIAM F. CASE

The founding of the Melaka (Malacca) sultanate in c. AD 1400 conventionally marks the beginning of the modern history of the territory that constitutes present-day Malaysia. Until its capture by the Portuguese in 1511, Melaka was not only the dominant trading centre in the region, and arguably the greatest emporium in the Asia of that period, but also a vigorous centre of Malay culture, influential in shaping the political institutions and traditional culture of the Malays through the succeeding centuries.

The Portuguese were unable to maintain Melaka's dominance in regional trade and in 1641 they lost control of the city to the Dutch. However, the Dutch were principally interested in Java, and during the 17th and 18th centuries local and outside influences vied for power in the Malay peninsula. Johor (Johore) inherited some of the prestige of Melaka, but it was rivalled in influence by the Dutch, the Aceh and Siak in Sumatra, and the Siamese. Refugees and explorers from southern Sulawesi (in what is now Indonesia) took control of some regions, including Johor, and Minangkabau migrants from Sumatra became a strong presence in Negeri Sembilan (Negri Sembilan). By the mid-18th century the peninsula was divided into a number of small Malay states, which had various links with outside powers.

The United Kingdom began its territorial advance in the late 18th century, aiming to expand its commercial activities east of India, and, in particular, to secure the trade route to China through the Straits of Melaka. Pinang (Penang) was acquired in 1786; a trading settlement was founded on the island of Singapore in 1819; and Melaka was ceded to the United Kingdom through an agreement with the Netherlands in 1824, which established the Straits as the boundary of their respective spheres of influence. In 1826 Pinang, Melaka and Singapore became a single administrative unit, the Straits Settlements, which remained under the authority of British India until 1867, when administrative responsibility was transferred to the Colonial Office in London, United Kingdom. The Anglo-Dutch treaty of 1824 contained no reference to Borneo, but in 1841 an English adventurer, James Brooke, was installed by the Sultan of Brunei as Raja of Sarawak, thus founding a dynasty of 'white rajas' that was to rule the territory for over a century (see History of Brunei). In 1847 Brunei ceded the small island of Labuan to the United Kingdom as a coaling station. In the north-east corner of Borneo concessions granted by the Sultans of Brunei and Sulu were eventually acquired by the British North Borneo Co, formed in 1881 as a chartered company under the British crown. Brunei itself was reduced to two small enclaves under British protection.

Through the middle decades of the 19th century, British policy (formulated in Calcutta—now Kolkata—in India, and in London) sought to avoid involvement in the Malay states, but important economic developments in the west coast states of the peninsula gradually drew the Straits Settlements into a closer commercial, and then political, relationship with its hinterland.

The discovery of major tin deposits in Larut, in Perak, in the 1840s led to a substantial expansion of mining activity on the west coast, financed in large part by mercantile interests in the Straits, and dependent on a very considerable influx of Chinese immigrant labour. Rival Chinese secret societies, frequently in alliance with factions within the Malay ruling houses, fought for control of this important new source of wealth. By the late 1860s Perak and Selangor, in particular, were approaching anarchy, and the British administration in the Straits Settlements was urged by local merchants, Chinese as well as European, to intervene to restore order.

Eventually, in 1873, the British Government itself agreed to intervene, possibly because it feared that a rival European power, imperial Germany, might take advantage of the disorder in the peninsula to establish a base that would threaten the British strategic domination of the Straits, but more fundamentally in order to secure wider British commercial interests in the east. With the Pangkor Treaty of January 1874, British administration was accepted in Perak; it was then rapidly extended to Selangor, Negeri Sembilan and, in 1888, to Pahang. In 1896 these four states were brought together as the Federated Malay States (FMS), with the federal capital at Kuala Lumpur. In 1909 the four northern states of Kedah, Perlis, Kelantan and Terengganu (Trengganu), long within the influence of Siam, were transferred to British authority and accepted British advisers; the northern Malay states, including Pattani and Singgora (Songkhla), remained under Siamese hegemony. In 1914 a permanent adviser was appointed to Johor, the one remaining independent Malay state. However, these five states did not enter the centralized administration of the FMS, but became collectively known as the Unfederated Malay States (UMS). Thus, by 1914 British authority had been extended throughout the Malay Peninsula, except for the Siamese north, but with considerable variation in both constitutional form and administrative practice.

BRITISH RULE IN THE MALAY STATES

The basis of British administration in the Malay states, until the Japanese invasion in 1941, was a short phrase in the Pangkor Treaty that required the Sultan to accept a British Resident whose advice 'must be asked and acted upon on all questions other than those touching Malay religion and custom'. Consequently, as the residential system evolved in the FMS, government was in the name of the Sultan, but executive authority lay very firmly with the Resident. Although there was a brief Malay uprising in Perak in 1875, resulting in the assassination in November of that year of the state's Resident, J. W. W. Birch, in general the Malay ruling families found little difficulty in reconciling themselves to their loss of political powers. Acceptance was eased by the fact that the British administration, eager to sustain the fiction of Malay rule with British advice, not only maintained the full splendour of Malay court ceremonial, but also treated the Malay rulers in public with the deference due to royalty. In the UMS, particularly in Johor and Kedah, the appointed British official, here called the Adviser, in general carried significantly less executive authority than his counterpart, the Resident, in the FMS. The more assertive Sultans here could exercise some power independently of British advice.

Malaya emerged as a major world producer of tin and, from the early 20th century, of rubber. Both the tin industry and the plantation rubber interests were heavily dependent on immigrant labour, from the southern coastal provinces of China in the case of the former, and from southern India in the case of the latter. By 1931 Chinese constituted 39% of the population of British Malaya, compared with 45% Malays. Moreover, Chinese clearly outnumbered Malays in the states of the west coast, and in the main urban centres: it was only in the four northern unfederated states that the Malays maintained their numerical superiority. Chinese (and Indians) were dominant in the production of tin and rubber for the world market, in internal trade and in money-lending. The Malays mostly remained subsistence rice farmers and fishermen, although they did develop considerable rubber smallholding production, despite strong opposition from a colonial administration that sought to reinforce the self-sufficiency of their *kampung* economy and to encourage their cultivation of food crops for the immigrant labouring populations.

In the inter-war period Malay nationalism began to develop, fostered principally by a vocal generation of village teachers trained at the Malay-medium Sultan Idris Training College, founded in 1922 by English-educated Malay civil servants and by religious figures who drew on the Islamic reformist ideas then emanating from the Middle East. The political concerns of the Chinese and Indians in this period lay primarily outside Malaya. From the 1920s the Kuomintang Government in China sought political support and financial contributions from among the Malayan Chinese, and, as China itself fell victim to Japanese aggression in the following decade, there was an upsurge of patriotism among the community in Malaya, which manifested itself most clearly in a series of boycotts of Japanese trade. Similarly, the Indians in Malaya focused their attention on the gathering independence struggle in the sub-continent. With the important exception of the Communist Party of Malaya (CPM), formally organized in 1930, no radical party emerged to secure significant support among the Malayan peoples. The colonial order, founded on accommodation with both the Malay aristocracy and the wealthy Chinese mercantile class, appeared invincible.

OCCUPATION AND INDEPENDENCE

The Japanese invasion and occupation of Malaya rapidly removed that order and made its full restoration impossible. The rapid collapse of British power in Malaya and Singapore in the early weeks of 1942 did much to destroy the myth of white superiority that had sustained colonial rule in Malaya, as elsewhere, while the three years of Japanese administration that followed the British surrender greatly heightened the political sensibilities and racial antagonisms of the diverse elements in the Malayan population. The Malay rulers, who had refused to evacuate with the retreating British administration, largely collaborated with the Japanese, but did not receive the deference that they had enjoyed under the pre-war colonial order. Moreover, through the organization of mass demonstrations, pan-Malayan conferences and paramilitary youth groups, the Japanese sought to weaken the established allegiance of the Malays to their individual state and sultan, and to encourage loyalty to a peninsula-wide entity. In August 1943, however, Japan transferred the four northern states, which were predominantly Malay, to Thailand, giving the immigrant communities overwhelming numerical dominance in the remaining states. The Indian community fared less well. Many Indian estate workers were forcibly conscripted for Japanese projects, including work on the Siam–Burma railway, and never returned. However, substantial enlistment into the Indian National Army, which was supported by Japan, helped to protect the community from the harshest treatment. The Chinese offered the only serious resistance to Japanese rule, for the anti-Japanese patriotism of the community had been strongly encouraged by the aggression of the 1930s, and they suffered most brutally during the occupation. Chinese comprised by far the largest component in the Malayan People's Anti-Japanese Army, the main resistance force, which was dominated by the CPM. When the Japanese administration suddenly collapsed in mid-August 1945, the CPM was left as the only effective political-military organization in the peninsula in advance of the returning British.

During the Japanese occupation, British officials in London, isolated from Malayan reality, drew up proposals for major post-war constitutional reforms. Previous attempts to simplify the peninsula's complex constitutional and administrative structures had been largely unsuccessful, but the perceived need to promote rapid economic recovery in the post-war years gave greater urgency to centralized direction. The British proposed, then, to incorporate the FMS, the UMS, Pinang and Melaka into a unified administrative unit, the Malayan Union, while making Singapore a separate crown colony. It was also proposed that citizenship of the Malayan Union be extended to all, irrespective of ethnicity or origin, and that all citizens would have equal rights. Sovereignty was to be transferred from the Malay rulers to the British crown. The opening of liberal citizenship provisions for Chinese and Indians reflected, in part, an awareness that both populations had now taken on the character of a predominantly settled community, and, in part, a recognition that they had, in general, remained loyal to the United Kingdom during the occupation. However, it seriously challenged the long-established privileged position and rights of the Malays, who considered themselves to be the indigenous people of the country, despite the long history of migration from other parts of South-East Asia.

When this proposal for a Malayan Union was announced by the restored colonial administration in January 1946, and formally introduced in April, the usually quiescent Malay community was angered, not only by the actual provisions, but also by the overbearing manner in which the new constitutional form had been introduced. Malay opposition was brought together in a new political force, the United Malays National Organization (UMNO), inaugurated in May. The provisions of the Union could not be brought into effect owing to determined Malay opposition. The British then began negotiations with the Malay rulers and UMNO for a new constitutional arrangement. This, the Federation of Malaya, was inaugurated in February 1948. The Federation maintained the Malayan Union concept of a unified administrative unit (embracing the FMS, the UMS, Pinang and Melaka), but it also reaffirmed the sovereignty of the Sultans, preserved the special privileges of the Malays, and introduced citizenship provisions, which, for Chinese and Indians, were markedly more restrictive than those contained in the abortive Malayan Union.

Many Chinese saw in the Federation a betrayal of the loyalty that they had shown towards the colonial power during the Japanese invasion and occupation, and in this sense its introduction undoubtedly strengthened the position of those within the CPM who sought an armed confrontation with the British. For the three years from the re-establishment of British administration in 1945, the CPM had pursued an 'open and legal' struggle, which had principally involved organizing and radicalizing the labour movement in Malaya. In the immediate post-war years a high level of labour unrest prevailed, notably on the rubber-growing estates and in the public services. In late 1947 the Government introduced stringent controls over the organization and structure of trade unions. With its legal position thus threatened, in early 1948 the CPM moved towards armed struggle. A spate of murders of European planters signalled to the authorities the change in CPM strategy, and on 18 June 1948 the Government proclaimed a state of emergency throughout Malaya.

The communist insurrection posed a severe military challenge to the colonial Government. The guerrilla forces attacked many European plantation and mining personnel, and in October 1951 they assassinated the British High Commissioner, Sir Henry Gurney. The CPM received only limited support from the Malayan population at large, for its overwhelmingly Chinese membership denied it access to the Malay community, while its ideology found little acceptance among wealthy Chinese. Moreover, from the early 1950s the colonial Government undertook a resettlement of the Chinese squatter communities, which had sustained the CPM with food, information and recruits, relocating them into secured, military-protected 'new villages'. By the mid-1950s the communist insurrection had collapsed, although the state of emergency officially remained in force until 1960. The CPM finally abandoned its armed struggle in December 1989, when the long-term leader, Chin Peng, signed agreements with the Malaysian and Thai Governments.

The CPM's strength in the mid-1950s was also undermined by a British announcement that Malaya would move quickly to political independence. From the late 1940s the colonial administration had sought to encourage a non-communal Malayan leadership, and in this context placed its faith largely in Dato' Onn Ja'afar, President of UMNO. However, Onn's inability to persuade his party to open its membership to all races, and the subsequent electoral failure of his non-communal, but élite, Independence of Malaya Party, ended that possibility. An alternative approach to securing a viable political leadership for an independent Malaya emerged from within the Malayan communities themselves. In the Kuala Lumpur municipal elections of February 1952, the local branches of UMNO and the Malayan Chinese Association (MCA) successfully contested seats as a united front. From this grew a national alliance (into which the Malayan Indian Congress—MIC—was incorporated in 1954), in which each party retained its separate identity and policies, while the Alliance acted as a single organization in selecting the candidates and party to contest each particular seat. In the 1955 federal elections the UMNO-MCA-MIC Alliance secured 51 of the 52 contested seats and 81% of the vote.

As Malaya now approached self-government, a new constitution was prepared, providing for a single nationality, with citizenship open to all those in Malaya who qualified either by birth or by fulfilling requirements of residence and language. In order to address Malay unease that these provisions were too liberal, the Constitution also provided for an unusual elective monarchy. The Yang di-Pertuan Agong (paramount ruler) was to be selected for a five-year term by, and from among, the nine ruling Sultans of the Malay states. He held a special responsibility for safeguarding the privileged position of the Malays, who were designated *bumiputra* ('sons of the soil'). Islam was made the official religion, but the degree to which Islamic law might be implemented remained under the control of the states. Independence (*merdeka*) was proclaimed on 31 August 1957, with Tunku Abdul Rahman, President of UMNO, becoming the first Prime Minister.

FORMATION OF MALAYSIA

Singapore, kept separate from the unified Malaya created in 1948, followed a different course to political independence. Internal self-government was secured in 1959, with the prospect of full independence being achieved in 1963. However, this prospect caused considerable concern in independent Malaya, for it was feared that Singapore, the politics of which had been notably radical in the 1950s, might soon be in a position to encourage and aid the remnants of Chinese left-wing elements in the peninsula. It was therefore proposed from 1961, notably by Tunku Abdul Rahman, that an independent Singapore be incorporated into a federation with Malaya: this would not only enable the latter to restrain the more volatile political forces in Singapore, but would also reinforce the natural economic relationship between the island entrepôt and its peninsular hinterland. However, federation with overwhelmingly Chinese Singapore threatened the numerical superiority of the Malays, and it was therefore further proposed that the United Kingdom's northern Borneo territories also be brought within the new alignment. Sarawak and North Borneo both had significant Chinese communities, but the Muslim Malays and the often Christian indigenous peoples (principally Iban in Sarawak and Kadazan in North Borneo) together outnumbered the immigrant communities in Malaysia.

Since 1946 both Sarawak and North Borneo had been crown colonies, following the respective terminations of Brooke rule and the administration of the British North Borneo Co, while Brunei remained a British protectorate; however, in none of these territories had the United Kingdom made significant preparations for self-government, and there were strong local doubts regarding the prospect of being ruled from distant Kuala Lumpur. The Sultan of Brunei considered himself senior to the Sultans of the peninsula and, in view of Brunei's petroleum resources, the federation had few economic attractions for the protectorate. A basic nationalist movement thus emerged, with the aim of establishing an independent northern Borneo. However, the United Kingdom exploited disunity within the movement, as well as the concern that neighbouring Indonesia might seek to annex any small independent state that was formed. Accordingly, the United Kingdom proceeded with its amalgamating proposal, although the Sultan of Brunei finally decided not to participate. In September 1963 both Sarawak and North Borneo (now renamed Sabah) joined Singapore and the Federation of Malaya to form the independent Federation of Malaysia. Within this Federation, Sarawak and Sabah retained a higher degree of autonomy than the peninsular states, including the right to control immigration from the peninsula.

Indonesia, for reasons that derived primarily from its own internal political tensions, sought from the first to break up the Federation. In addition, the Philippines pursued a claim to the territory of Sabah. In September 1963 Indonesia and the Philippines broke off diplomatic relations with Malaysia. Indonesia subsequently launched a series of military raids into Sarawak and Sabah from its own Borneo territory (Kalimantan), an action it depicted as 'confrontation'. A few paratroops were also dropped into Peninsular Malaysia. However, this military challenge was successfully contained by Malaysian and Commonwealth forces and, following the fall from power of President Sukarno, a rapprochement between the two countries was achieved in August 1966.

An internal challenge to Malaysia also arose from the determination of the People's Action Party (under Lee Kuan Yew), the governing party in Singapore, to campaign for the Chinese vote in peninsular elections, and so, in effect, oppose the MCA. This strategy threatened to undermine the Alliance consensus, and Malaysian leaders accused Singapore of provoking intercommunal animosity. In August 1965 Singapore was effectively expelled from Malaysia, despite protests from the island's leaders.

RESHAPING THE POLITICAL ORDER

The 1957 Constitution envisaged a multi-ethnic Malaysia in which the political and administrative dominance of the Malays would be balanced by the continuing economic pre-eminence of the Chinese and, to a lesser extent, the Indians. Within the parliamentary system, it was assumed, the interests of these groups would be represented by their respective élites, UMNO, the MCA and the MIC, who would negotiate policies aimed primarily at preserving the status quo and then at gradually achieving a convergence in the social standing of the three communities. Thus, it was expected that the Malays would gain a steadily greater role in the economy, while the Chinese and Indians would gradually obtain more political influence; however, there was no model for the kind of society this process might eventually produce and there was no prospect of any kind of ethnic or cultural fusion. The expulsion of Singapore from the Federation appeared to ensure that Malays would take part in this system from a position of numerical dominance, and would thus enjoy perpetual political pre-eminence, as long as they remained disciplined in their support of UMNO. However, the planners of the 1950s had not allowed for the rapidity of social change in the new country. Among Malays, the impact of modernization contributed to a growing responsiveness to Islam and to political support for the Parti Islam se Malaysia (PAS—Islamic Party of Malaysia). This party initially found support among rural Islamic teachers and scholars, who were generally unsympathetic to the Malay aristocracy dominating UMNO, but later also gained influence among the gradually expanding urban Malay middle class. The Chinese, in turn, grew increasingly dissatisfied with their political subordination, and in the federal election of May 1969 the MCA lost considerable ground among the Chinese voters to opposition parties, notably Gerakan Rakyat Malaysia (GERAKAN—Malaysian People's Movement) and the Democratic Action Party (DAP), which had demanded a more rapid end to Malay political predominance. Subsequent communal violence in the federal capital left many hundreds dead. To restore order, the Constitution was suspended and a national emergency declared.

The May 1969 riots forced a major readjustment both in the terms upon which communal interests and aspirations were accommodated, and in the manner in which the details of that accommodation were negotiated between the principal communities. Thus, the UMNO-led Government swiftly introduced the New Economic Policy (NEP), to be implemented over the 20 years to 1990. Its primary objectives were to eradicate poverty (irrespective of race) and the identification of race with economic function. The latter objective implied securing for the Malays not only a far greater share in the wealth of the country, but also a much wider range of educational and employment opportunities. It was intended that by 1990 30% of commercial and industrial share capital would be under *bumiputra* ownership. In addition, new legislation removed from public discussion such sensitive issues as the powers and status of the Sultans, Malay special rights, the status of Islam as the official religion and citizenship rights. At the same time the structure of coalition politics changed. The tripartite UMNO-MCA-MIC alliance was replaced by a broader coalition, registered in 1974 and called the Barisan Nasional (BN—National Front), which aimed to draw as many parties as possible into the Government under the leadership of UMNO. This strategy had the aim not only of giving the Government a broader electoral base, but also of muting criticism by involving potential opposition parties in government policy. The BN continued to govern Malaysia in the 21st century, and all significant parties except the DAP and Semangat '46 (see below, dissolved in October 1996) have joined it in government, at least for a time.

A major complicating factor in Malaysian politics is the position of the state Governments. The states vary greatly in their ethnic composition, their socio-economic structure and even their constitutional relationship to the federal Government. Politics, for instance, has a very different character in Pinang (urbanized, mainly Chinese), Kelantan (rural, predominantly Malay and ruled by a Sultan) and Sabah (indigenous Christians, indigenous Muslims and Chinese in roughly equal proportions). The nine peninsular states with reigning Sultans have greater political influence in the Conference of Rulers than the four states that do not (Pinang, Melaka, Sabah and Sarawak), but the two Borneo states have maintained the distinct status that allows them to control immigration from the peninsula as well as to exercise greater economic and cultural autonomy than any peninsular state. Most of Malaysia's politicians, therefore, work from a power base within just one state, and build their national political careers by means of alliances with politicians from other regions. Movement between the state and federal legislatures and governments is also quite common. Although the political role of the Sultans is constitutionally limited, individual Sultans have had considerable influence within their own states from time to time.

Under the rule of the BN, the idiom of politics changed from one of national coalition between ethnic groups to one of Malay dominance as *bumiputra*. The term *bumiputra* has always been problematic: not only does the Malay community include the descendants of 17th and 18th century immigrants to the peninsula from Sumatra and Sulawesi, in what is now Indonesia, but more recent migrants from Indonesia and the Philippines, and even Muslim Cham refugees from Cambodia, have sometimes found it possible to acquire 'indigenous' status, even though their links to the country are much more recent than those of some Chinese communities. Whereas on the peninsula *bumiputra* status, moreover, was closely linked to Islam, the indigenous peoples of the Borneo states are mostly animist or Christian. However, because of the sedition laws governing discussion of the rights of Malays and the position of Islam, such issues seldom received more than tangential mention in Malaysian political discourse. Nevertheless, the growing influence of the Malays was unmistakable. Bahasa Malaysia was adopted as the language of education and administration at all levels, racial quotas gave advantages to Malays, especially in the education system, and the cultural heritages of Chinese and Indian Malaysians were given clearly subordinate standing. UMNO patronage became increasingly important in the allocation of government posts, while Chinese and Indians appeared to be losing ground in the administration. Malays also began to make rapid gains in the economy, both through private firms receiving significant support from the Government and through state-owned enterprises. A steady flow of educated Chinese and Indian Malaysians to Singapore and other destinations contributed to Malay dominance. In 1995 official policy on the use of Bahasa Malaysia was partially reversed, with a decision to reintroduce English as a language of instruction at tertiary level for the sake of international business and technological connections. In July 2002 the Government announced that, from primary level, all schools would shift from the use of Bahasa Malaysia to English as the language of instruction, despite strong resistance from leaders of the Chinese community, who perceived the decision as being an incursion against Chinese culture. The Government later announced that the use of English would initially be limited to education in science and mathematics.

THE MAHATHIR YEARS, 1981–2003

Within UMNO itself, important changes were also under way. Malaysia's first Prime Minister, Tunku Abdul Rahman (1963–70), was a royal prince, and his successors, Tun Abdul Razak (1970–76) and Dato' Hussein bin Onn (1976–81), were both Malay aristocrats. In 1981, however, Hussein Onn was succeeded by Dr Mahathir Mohamad, a medical doctor and a commoner, widely seen as representing a new generation of modern Malays who were in thrall neither to the traditional aristocratic élite nor to the Islamic teachers of the countryside. Mahathir, who had earlier written a controversial defence of Malay interests (*The Malay Dilemma*, 1970), also represented a generation determined to consolidate the dominant position of the Malays in Malaysia. Mahathir's rule was characterized by a determined modernizing campaign, based on both industrialization and the exploitation of raw materials (especially petroleum). At the beginning of Mahathir's tenure the Government was commended for its forceful insistence on efficiency and honesty, but by the mid-1980s accusations of corruption and of abuse of power for economic advantage had become increasingly common. Business leaders linked with UMNO appear to have prospered greatly from their connections, although legal restrictions have hampered detailed investigation of these allegations. In June 1991 the New Development Policy (NDP) was launched to succeed the NEP. The NDP shifted the emphasis from the NEP's ethnic restructuring to general economic prosperity. Racial quotas were retained, but no specific date was set for achieving the NEP's target of 30% *bumiputra* control of the country's corporate assets. An important part of this programme was the so-called 'Vision 2020', which Mahathir outlined in February 1991, embodying an ambition to turn Malaysia into a 'fully developed' country by the year 2020. Under this vision, Malaysia was not only to enjoy the material benefits of being fully developed (health care, public transport, education and general infrastructure), but was also to be self-confident, harmonious, just, dynamic and democratic. Inevitably, however, progress towards the material signs of development was easier to achieve than the less tangible goals.

The UMNO leadership confronted two main challenges to its dominance over the Malays. Its main base being in rural Kelantan and Terengganu, PAS also increased its support among urban Malays who continued to resent Chinese economic influence and who wished to see Malaysia become more Islamic. The traditional Malay élite also resented Mahathir's pressure for the development of a more meritocratic society (at least among the Malays), and were shocked in 1983 by his proposals to restrict the power of the hereditary rulers by effectively removing the rulers' right to withhold assent from legislation. The Government and Sultans later reached a compromise on the proposals, but the conflict persisted in a growing rift between Mahathir and his Minister of Trade and Industry, Tengku Razaleigh Hamzah, an aristocrat from Kelantan. Razaleigh narrowly failed in a challenge to Mahathir's party leadership in April 1987. Mahathir then removed Razaleigh supporters from strategic positions in both the Government and the party, but was given an unexpected opportunity to consolidate his dominance in February 1988 when the High Court ruled that, because of irregularities in the UMNO elections of 1987, the party was in breach of the Societies Act and was technically illegal. To regularize the party's position, Mahathir created a new party, UMNO Baru (New UMNO), in February, which inherited the property of the 'old' UMNO. However, all members of the former party were required to apply anew for registration. In this way, Razaleigh and other opponents were excluded without recourse to expulsion proceedings. A number of dissidents subsequently accepted Mahathir's dominance and joined UMNO Baru (henceforth referred to as UMNO), but in October 1989 Razaleigh announced the creation of a new movement called Semangat '46 (Spirit of 1946, the year of founding of the original UMNO).

Although the ideas and social groups represented by Razaleigh still had considerable support among Malays, the electoral prospects of the new party (which was registered in May 1990) were hampered by its lack of access to government patronage and by its need to seek allies among the forces outside the BN. Semangat '46 then entered into an alliance with PAS (although PAS and the Razaleigh group had been bitter rivals in Kelantan state politics and Razaleigh himself had engineered the expulsion of PAS from the BN in 1978), under the name Angkatan Perpaduan Ummah (APU—Muslim Unity Movement). However, as the 1990 elections approached, Semangat '46 also developed an alliance, called the Gagasan Rakyat (People's Concept), with the overwhelmingly Chinese DAP. Although PAS and the DAP each shared interests and concerns with Semangat '46, they had virtually nothing in common with each other, and the coalition looked implausible as an alternative government. The elections of October 1990 thus returned the Mahathir Government. The BN won slightly fewer seats (127 of the 180 seats in the extended House of Representatives), but retained the two-thirds' majority required to amend the Constitution. The opposition did well in the DAP stronghold of Pinang and won overwhelmingly in Kelantan, but for the most part performed poorly elsewhere. Semangat '46 in fact won only six of the 61 seats it contested.

This victory gave Mahathir a platform from which to resume his campaign to limit the Sultans' authority. In July 1992 he oversaw the introduction of a code of conduct for the rulers, which restricted their ability to intervene in the political process. In January 1993 Parliament approved legislation removing the Sultans' personal legal immunity. When the rulers withheld assent from the bill, the Government co-ordinated a campaign of public revelations of excesses and abuses of position on the part of various Sultans until the Sultans capitulated. The Government also rescinded the traditional privileged treatment that the rulers had enjoyed from government officials and which some of them had used to develop significant business interests. In May 1994 the House of Representatives approved a constitutional amendment definitively removing the rulers' power to block legislation by withholding assent. In September 1997 Mahathir again restructured state power, convening a conference to centralize the administration of Islamic law, previously a state matter. However, his target in this case was not so much state politicians as state religious authorities whose conservative *fatwa* (edicts), he adjudged, were impeding national development. At the UMNO assembly in September, he accused many Muslims of being more concerned with form (beards, clothing, etc.) than with the substance of Islamic teaching.

During the late 1980s the Mahathir Government came into increasing conflict with the judiciary after a number of cases in which government decisions were overruled. In May 1987, just before one of the crucial court hearings over the legal status of UMNO, the Yang di-Pertuan Agong suspended the Lord President of the Supreme Court, Tun Salleh Abbas, from his post. A tribunal of judges then concluded that he was guilty of 'misbehaviour' in the form of bias against the Government and he was dismissed in August. Five of the remaining Supreme Court judges were also suspended at this time, and two were dismissed, in connection with the legal proceedings surrounding the dismissal of Salleh Abbas. These measures were followed in March 1988 by constitutional amendments limiting the power of the judiciary to interpret laws. In 1994 the Government restyled the Supreme Court as the Federal Court and the Lord President as the Chief Justice, as well as introducing a mandatory code of ethics for judges.

The Government was also willing to use its extensive security powers against opposition groups. In October 1987 several politicians, journalists, lawyers and leaders of pressure groups were imprisoned, including Lim Kit Siang, the Secretary-General of the DAP. (All were released by the following April.) Three newspapers were closed by government order and political rallies were banned. As the BN extended its dominance over the media, legislation was introduced imposing stringent penalties on editors and publishers if they produced what the Government regarded as 'false' news, and empowering the Minister of Information to monitor all radio and television broadcasts, and to revoke the licence of any private broadcasting company not conforming with 'Malaysian values'. In June 1988 the Government introduced legislation removing the right of persons being detained under the Internal Security Act (ISA) to have recourse to the courts. At the end of December 1991 the High Court upheld a ruling by the Ministry of Home Affairs to ban the public sale of party newspapers. This was widely interpreted as an attempt to undermine further the potential effectiveness of the opposition parties, because it mainly affected opposition journals, including *The Rocket* (DAP), *Harakah* (PAS) and *Berita Rakyat* (Parti Rakyat Malaysia), all of which were henceforth allowed to be distributed only to party members.

As the general election of April 1995 approached, few observers believed that the opposition had any chance of victory. Malaysia's rapid economic growth had led to a widespread perception that the administration was performing well. The uneasy alliance between Semangat '46, the DAP and PAS, moreover, had been strained further by an announcement from the PAS state Government in Kelantan in 1992 that it intended to introduce the Islamic criminal code (*hudud*) in the state. Unlike the laws on Islamic religious practice that the state already applied to Muslims in Kelantan, this would have subjected non-Muslims to Islamic law. It also prescribed the death sentence for apostasy. The legislation was adopted in 1993, despite claims that it contravened the Constitution's guarantee of freedom of religion. This and related issues led to such discord in opposition ranks that the DAP withdrew from the Gagasan Rakyat in January 1995. The opposition also had to function without media coverage and the limiting of the official campaign period by the Government to just nine days. In fact, the only issues that seemed likely to detract significantly from the Government's electoral support were the persistent allegations of corruption that emerged against senior officials. In September 1994 the Chief Minister of Melaka and leader of the powerful UMNO youth wing, Tan Sri Datuk Rahim Thamby Chik, was forced to resign following allegations that he had had sexual relations with a minor, an offence constituting statutory rape. The charges were later abandoned. The DAP youth leader, Lim Guan Eng, was subsequently tried for sedition for remarks that he had made suggesting that the authorities had not acted impartially in the case, and in April 1997 he was convicted and fined RM 15,000 (Lim was released in August 1999 following the failure of an appeal against his conviction—the judgment automatically disqualified him from holding a parliamentary seat).

The election results of April 1995 were a triumph for Mahathir. The BN's share of the popular vote rose from 53% in 1990 to 64%, and the coalition won 162 of the 192 seats in the extended House of Representatives, as well as all the seats in the State Legislative Assemblies in Perlis and Johor, and a majority in every other state except Kelantan. The PAS-Semangat '46 coalition retained power in Kelantan and lost only two seats nationally, but the DAP lost 11 of its 20 seats in the House of Representatives and all but one of its 14 state seats in Pinang. The set-back suffered by the opposition led to a crisis of confidence in Semangat '46. The party's coalition with PAS in Kelantan began to break down, and in October 1996 the party was formally dissolved, with its 200,000 members rejoining UMNO.

At the UMNO party congress in late 1993 there had been considerable speculation over likely successors to Mahathir, who was born in 1925. Attention focused then on the Minister of Finance and former UMNO youth leader, Dato' Seri Anwar Ibrahim, who was elected Deputy President of the party (normally a stepping stone to the leadership) and whose self-styled 'Vision Team' won all three vice-presidential positions. The 1995 election results briefly ended such speculation, but by the end of the year it had re-emerged as signs of vying for power grew at all levels of the UMNO organization. Dato' Sri Najib Tun Razak was moved from the defence to the education portfolio, a significant post because the last three Malaysian Prime Ministers had all served in that department before acceding to power. Najib had been one of Anwar's leading 'Vision Team' members, but was now seen as having shifted to the Mahathir camp. In November 1995 the annual UMNO assembly decided not to allow any challenge to Mahathir or Anwar at the triennial party congress scheduled for October 1996. However, the succession contest continued by proxy over the several junior leadership positions that were at stake, although in July 1996 the party's Supreme Council banned open campaigning by or for any candidate. The return of

Semangat '46 members to UMNO took place too late to affect the outcome of the congress, but most observers believed that their presence strengthened the position of Mahathir, whose relations with Razaleigh were surprisingly cordial. The vice-presidential elections resulted in the return to office of Najib and of Mohammad Taib, associated at this point with Anwar, and the election of a Mahathir supporter, the Minister of Foreign Affairs, Abdullah Ahmad Badawi. On the other hand, two Mahathir allies who had been damaged by corruption accusations, Rafidah Aziz (head of the UMNO women's wing) and Rahim Thamby Chik, were defeated by Anwar supporters, Dr Siti Zaharah Sulaiman and Ahmad Zahid Hamidi. Both were thus victims, in part, of Mahathir's increasing outspokenness against what was commonly called 'money politics', which he described in October 1995 as the only factor that could destroy UMNO. Taib fell victim to the same affliction in December 1996, when he was arrested at the airport in Brisbane, Australia, carrying the equivalent of more than RM 2.3m., thus contravening an Australian law requiring the declaration of amounts greater than about RM 10,000 being taken into or out of the country. Taib subsequently resigned as Chief Minister of Selangor, and in May 1997 he was forced to resign as Vice-President of UMNO; however, he was later acquitted of all charges. New Chief Ministers in Selangor and Melaka announced strict standards of probity for politicians and senior officials within their states, but appeared to find it difficult to distinguish clearly between legitimate business interests and corrupt behaviour. Throughout 1996–98 many lesser figures were charged or otherwise disciplined for alleged financial irregularities, but public opinion did not interpret these moves as a genuine attempt to eliminate corrupt practices. However, the weakening of Anwar's position that Taib's disgrace implied was counterbalanced by a period of two months from mid-May 1997, during which Mahathir took leave to travel, write and promote Malaysia abroad, leaving Anwar as acting Prime Minister in his place.

Mahathir returned in time to confront a growing political challenge arising from the Asian financial crisis. In mid-July 1997 the ringgit began to depreciate sharply, placing sudden pressure on the many firms and investors who had borrowed in foreign currency. The Malaysian crisis was precipitated by events in Thailand, but the markets swiftly focused on what were seen as structural problems in the Malaysian system. Mahathir's public response was to portray the crisis as an assault on Malaysia's economic achievements by a small group of foreign speculators and Western media, possibly in league with unfriendly governments. As the regional financial crisis worsened, Mahathir took the view that Malaysia's salvation lay in protection and continued economic expansion, whereas Anwar supported the introduction of austerity measures. Malaysia declined to accept IMF intervention, which would almost certainly have required the abandonment of most of the major infrastructure projects favoured by Mahathir. Nevertheless, Minister of Finance Anwar was able to persuade Mahathir to abandon several large projects. In December 1997 all federal and state ministers accepted a 10% reduction in salary and smaller decreases were imposed on parliamentarians and senior bureaucrats. Most observers agreed that Anwar's standing had been strengthened by his measured response to the crisis.

In November 1997 Anwar moved a parliamentary motion of confidence in Mahathir in order to dispel the growing speculation about a possible change of leadership. Internal elections for divisional committee members in UMNO in March 1998 left most of Mahathir's supporters in place and Anwar with no clear power base from which to launch a challenge. Attention then began to focus on the business activities of Mahathir's three sons. The Prime Minister's eldest son, Mirzan Mahathir, received government assistance to save his businesses from bankruptcy under circumstances that some Malaysians regarded as favouritism.

Anwar spoke out publicly against corruption and political restriction in a way that clearly set out a case for a change of leadership, and at the UMNO annual conference in June 1998 one of Anwar's supporters strongly criticized the party leadership over the same issues. Mahathir's supporters responded with a brochure entitled *Fifty Reasons Why Anwar Ibrahim Cannot Become Prime Minister*, in which Anwar was accused of conspiracy and of sexual offences. Information on Anwar associates who appeared to have benefited from 'cronyism' was also released. During the following weeks Mahathir systematically dismantled Anwar's power base, appointing Dato' Paduka Daim Zainuddin to oversee the economy, dismissing newspaper editors close to Anwar, and ordering the arrest of a close associate of Anwar on firearms charges that carried the death penalty. Increasingly lurid accounts of Anwar's alleged sexual misdemeanours began to circulate, and Mahathir reportedly pressed his deputy to resign or to accept dismissal and criminal charges. Anwar declined to resign and was dismissed as Minister of Finance in September. The UMNO Supreme Council voted unanimously in favour of Anwar's expulsion from the party.

Anwar responded to his dismissal by denying all rumours of sexual misconduct, alleging that there was a political conspiracy against him. Although government officials were quick to accuse Anwar of hypocrisy in criticizing the system of which, until recently, he had himself been a part, the authorities in turn had difficulty in explaining why a minister so central to the Mahathir administration should suddenly be so ferociously vilified. As well as arousing his own considerable following, Anwar's dismissal reinforced broader resentment of the autocratic methods of the Mahathir Government. As demonstrations in support of Anwar gathered momentum, in September Anwar and 16 supporters were detained by riot police under the ISA. Anwar's wife, Dr Wan Azizah Wan Ismail, was summoned for questioning by police. A restriction order was issued, banning her from holding rallies at her house, which had become a focus for the *reformasi* (reform) movement. In court Anwar was charged with five counts of corruption and five of unnatural sexual acts. He appeared badly bruised and claimed to have been assaulted while in custody. Anwar's allegations provoked expressions of extreme concern from foreign governments—in particular from the Presidents of the Philippines and Indonesia—and prompted the UN Secretary-General, Kofi Annan, to urge the Malaysian Government to ensure humane treatment for Anwar. Although the Malaysian Government initially dismissed Anwar's claims of assault, it was subsequently announced that a special investigation was to be established. In December the Inspector-General of the Malaysian police force, Tan Sri Abdul Rahim Noor, resigned after an initial inquiry blamed the police for the injuries that Anwar had sustained. Malaysia's Attorney-General publicly admitted in January 1999 that Anwar had been assaulted while in police custody, and an official inquiry completed in March found Tan Sri Rahim Noor to be personally responsible for the beating. He was later sentenced to two months' imprisonment and a fine of RM 2,000.

Meanwhile, popular demonstrations demanding Mahathir's resignation, Anwar's release and the abolition of the ISA continued to take place, but gained no coverage in the local media. In October 1998, however, the influential Malaysian Bar unanimously adopted resolutions condemning detention without trial, while demanding that independent inquiries be held into allegations of police brutality. It was subsequently announced that Anwar was no longer to be detained under the ISA, but would be transferred to a regular prison. The trial of Anwar on four charges of corruption (which referred to efforts allegedly made by Anwar in 1997 to use his position to suppress an investigation of his alleged sexual misconduct) began in November 1998. During the trial the credibility of the prosecution was undermined by a number of factors, and in January 1999 the charges against Anwar were unexpectedly amended, with the emphasis being shifted from sexual misconduct to abuse of power; the amendment meant that the prosecution would no longer have to prove that Anwar had committed sexual offences, but only that he had attempted to use his position to influence the police to quash the investigation into the allegations, effectively making it easier for a conviction to be obtained. The judge subsequently ruled that further testimony relating to the earlier allegations of sexual misconduct was irrelevant, leading the defence to claim that it had been denied the opportunity to refute the accusations. (The ruling also meant that the defence would no longer be able to carry out its planned cross-examination of Mahathir and Daim

Zainuddin on the issue of whether the allegations of sexual misconduct in particular were part of a political conspiracy against Anwar.) The proceedings, the longest criminal trial in Malaysia's history, were ended abruptly in late March, and the verdict was delivered in mid-April: Anwar was found guilty on each of the four charges of corruption and was sentenced to six years' imprisonment. (Under Malaysian law, a sentence of this length was automatically followed by a five-year period of disqualification from political office.)

Meanwhile, Mahathir sought to confirm his dominance by appointing a new Deputy Prime Minister, Abdullah Badawi, in a major reorganization of the Cabinet effected in January 1999. He relinquished the home affairs portfolio to Abdullah and the finance portfolio to Daim Zainuddin, thus restoring a 'normal' distribution of portfolios in the Cabinet. The former's background as Minister of Foreign Affairs rendered him a useful foil to the continuing allegations of UMNO corruption, while his subdued political style meant that he was unlikely to become a political threat to Mahathir. Within UMNO, many known Anwar supporters were removed. With Mahathir preparing for UMNO's campaign in the forthcoming general election (which was to be held by June 2000), Anwar's supporters countered by founding a new political party, the Parti Keadilan Nasional (PKN—National Justice Party), in April 1999 under the leadership of Wan Azizah. The new party aimed to establish itself as a multi-ethnic and multi-religious party (although its initial membership appeared to be predominantly Muslim), and declared that, should it come to power, it would seek a royal pardon for Anwar. PAS membership reportedly grew by 25%, to 600,000, between September 1998 and mid-1999, while the PKN claimed to have 150,000 members. PAS also sought to broaden its appeal by opening a dialogue with non-Muslims, attempting to attract local businessmen and opening social welfare centres, which provided legal and medical assistance to those Malaysians suffering the effects of the regional financial crisis. In June 1999 PAS, the PKN, the DAP and the Parti Rakyat Malaysia (PRM—Malaysian People's Party) formed a coalition, the Barisan Alternatif (BA—Alternative Front), to contest the elections, prompting Mahathir to accuse them of being supported by foreigners who wished to undermine the Malaysian economy. The BA was a disparate group united mainly by hostility to Mahathir. The coalition subsequently selected Anwar as its prime ministerial candidate, but disagreed over electoral strategy and long-term aims. The Government responded to this dissent by accusing its opponents of deliberately inciting chaos and by issuing numerous civil lawsuits in which ruling politicians sued journalists and opposition leaders for defamation. The Attorney-General warned that those who alleged selective prosecution would themselves be prosecuted for contempt of court.

In April 1999 Anwar was further charged with one count of illegal homosexual activity, to which he pleaded not guilty; it was announced that four other similar charges and one additional corruption charge against him had been 'suspended'. The second trial of Anwar opened in June. The prosecution amended the wording of its charge, changing the month and year in which the alleged crimes were supposedly committed. Meanwhile, at the UMNO General Assembly in May, Mahathir made it clear that there was no prospect of any reconciliation with Anwar. Anwar responded from prison with accusations that Mahathir and his colleagues were guilty of corruption and nepotism, and claimed that he had been removed from the Government because of his commitment to ending such practices. (In October the Government countered with accusations that Anwar himself had accumulated RM 780m. in illicit funds.) On 29 April the Court of Appeal upheld Anwar's original conviction on charges of abuse of power, and the former Deputy Prime Minister and Minister of Finance was finally convicted of sexual misconduct in August, receiving a sentence of nine years' imprisonment to commence after the expiry of his earlier sentence, meaning that he could remain imprisoned until 2014. In May 2001 the prosecution abandoned the five remaining charges against Anwar. In July 2002 Anwar's appeal against his corruption conviction was finally rejected by the High Court; his appeal against the sodomy conviction suffered the same fate in April 2003, and he was also refused bail to travel to Germany for medical treatment.

Following the Government's unexpected announcement that a general election was to be held and with only a brief campaign period, the poll on 29 November 1999 returned the BN to government: the coalition won 148 of the 193 seats in the House of Representatives. Although the BN retained the two-thirds' majority required to allow the Government to amend the Constitution, the coalition's share of the national vote declined from 64.1% (at the previous general election) to 56.5%, while UMNO's representation in the legislature decreased to 72 members. There was a substantial vote against UMNO in the states of Kedah and Pahang, and even Mahathir's winning margin in his own constituency declined from 17,000 to 10,000 votes. PAS, by contrast, increased its number of seats from seven to 27 and the PAS leader, Fadzil Nor, was officially appointed parliamentary leader of the opposition. The party also retained power in the state of Kelantan and took office in Terengganu. However, PAS's partners in the BA performed poorly. The DAP won 10 seats, but its Secretary-General, Lim Kit Siang, lost his seat, as did the party's Deputy Chairman, Karpal Singh (who was also Anwar's legal representative). Wan Azizah retained Anwar's former seat for the PKN, but the party won only four other seats, all of them in regions that otherwise would probably have returned a PAS candidate. The distribution of votes suggested that 70% of Chinese voters and 90% of Indians had voted for the BN, whereas only about 50% of Malays had done so. For the first time in a federal election, there were widespread allegations of malpractice.

Mahathir made few changes to his Cabinet after the election, although the former Minister of Education, Najib Tun Razak, who only narrowly retained his seat in the House of Representatives, was demoted from the education portfolio to that of defence, which he had held before the 1995 election. However, there was much interest in the policies of the new PAS state legislature in Terengganu. The new Chief Minister, Abdul Hadi Awang, had pledged to ban gambling, restrict alcohol sales and make Friday a public holiday, and had also suggested the introduction of both strict Islamic criminal law and a religious income tax, *kharaj*, on non-Muslims. Once in office, Awang banned *karaoke* entertainment and gambling, but postponed more radical proposals and concentrated on winning business confidence and establishing for himself a reputation for efficiency and honesty. Expensive prestige projects were cancelled, and a new openness was introduced into the allocation of government tenders and licences. In early September 2000 the federal Government, alarmed by Terengganu's successes, announced that it would no longer pay Terengganu a royalty percentage on petroleum production in the state, but would instead channel the revenue into a federally controlled development fund.

In January 2000 the authorities arrested five prominent opposition leaders, including Karpal Singh and the editor and publisher of the popular PAS newspaper, *Harakah*, most of them on charges of sedition. *Harakah* itself was threatened with closure, as a result of the newspaper's illegal sale to the public. In March the Ministry of Home Affairs announced that it would permit *Harakah* to be published only twice a month, rather than twice a week, but later emphasized Mahathir's insistence that Malaysian internet websites, including opposition news websites, such as that of *Harakah* itself, would not be censored. In April and May 2001 16 opposition activists, most of them members of the PKN, were arrested under the ISA. Both courts and the Malaysian Human Rights Commission criticized the Government for using legislation that was intended to combat communist insurrection as a means of suppressing its political opponents. With increasing restrictions on the print media, an internet newspaper, *Malaysiakini*, established in mid-2000, became an increasingly important alternative source of information for the Malaysian public.

Contrary to many expectations, the BA did not disintegrate after the election, but continued to function as a coalition in opposition, creating a form of 'shadow cabinet' in March 2000, maintaining pressure on the BN in parliamentary debates and continuing to minimize the fundamental policy differences between its members on the issue of the place of Islam in Malaysian politics and society. As PAS broadened its appeal to Muslim professionals and younger, urban voters, the party's Islamic character became steadily less intimidating to non-

Malay groups. The PAS Government in Terengganu further sought the favour of non-Muslims by allowing a Chinese cultural festival to take place, and issuing permits for non-Muslim places of worship, which had been repeatedly refused by the BN Government. The PKN, by contrast, became divided over whether to promote public demonstrations against the Government. In June, however, the party achieved increased support in a by-election, although failing to win the seat, and it received a further boost when the PRM agreed in principle to merge with it. In November 2000 the BA defeated the BN in a by-election for the Lunas seat in Kedah, which had been won by the BN one year previously. The victory was significant, since Kedah was Mahathir's home state and the result deprived the BN of its symbolic former two-thirds' majority in the state legislature. The UMNO leadership was also concerned by internal resistance to a proposal to hold party elections every five years, rather than every three.

Moreover, the MCA became mired in corruption scandals. UMNO responded by striving to improve its Islamic credentials. In March 2000 the BN state Government of Perlis introduced legislation prescribing detention at a Faith Rehabilitation Centre for those found guilty of 'deviationism' and apostasy, while Johor activated 1997 legislation, whereby lesbianism, pre-marital sex, prostitution and incest would be punishable by whipping and terms of imprisonment. The federal Government envisaged legislation to make misuse of religion a criminal offence. In May 2000 the Government introduced a requirement for all Muslim civil servants to attend religious classes twice weekly. The Government also continued to emphasize long-term reforms, such as the introduction of Islamic banking and insurance. In September the Government charged 29 members of the al-Ma'unah cult with treason, following a robbery of weapons in Perak in July, in which two hostages were killed. Government attempts to attribute the incident to PAS were received with much scepticism. In December 2001 19 of those charged were found guilty of treason, three being sentenced to death and the remainder to life imprisonment, while 10 others pleaded guilty to lesser charges and were given 10-year prison terms.

Controversy continued over the random destruction of Chinese cultural heritage in Malaysia. In 2000 the federal Government announced a new 10-year plan, the National Vision Policy, which replaced the NDP. Although the new plan maintained affirmative action policies for Malays, speculation that the extent of these policies would be reduced prompted Malay demonstrations against Chinese organizations and fierce condemnation of alleged Chinese extremism. Chinese and Indian communities, in turn, criticized government plans for multi-ethnic so-called 'Vision Schools'.

As the result of a decision of the UMNO Supreme Council, the post of President, held by Mahathir, was not contested at the UMNO General Assembly in May 2000, and Abdullah Badawi stood as the sole candidate for the post of Deputy President, vacant since Anwar's dismissal. However, there was strong competition for the three positions of Vice-President. Minister of Defence Najib, an incumbent Vice-President, was re-elected, along with the former Chief Minister of Selangor, Mohammad Taib, and the Minister of Domestic Trade and Consumer Affairs, Tan Sri Dato' Haji Muhyiddin Yassin. Although all three had been members of Anwar's 'Vision Team' in 1993, they were nominated by Mahathir's own Kubang Pasu faction in UMNO. Hints from the Prime Minister that he was not happy with the outcome of the ballot seemed to be disingenuous, as none of the defeated candidates, including three state Chief Ministers, had Mahathir's favour. At the conclusion of the Assembly, Mahathir announced that he had not decided when to retire but that he intended to relinquish greater responsibility to Abdullah Badawi in preparation for the eventual transfer of power.

During 2001 Mahathir continued his public condemnation of corruption within UMNO, urging party officials to declare their assets. Six division-level UMNO leaders were dismissed for having resorted to bribery to win party elections in April, and the Minister of Information and UMNO Secretary-General, Khalil Yacoob, was charged with misuse of public funds. However, many observers considered the Minister of Finance, Daim Zainuddin, who was one of Malaysia's wealthiest men, to be Mahathir's main focus. Daim took two months' leave of absence from his post from 19 April, and formally resigned in June. Mahathir assumed the finance portfolio, in addition to his duties as Prime Minister. Daim had been widely criticized for using public funds to assist Malay business associates.

In September 2000 Datuk Haji Nik Abdul Aziz Nik Mat, spiritual leader of PAS, aroused controversy when he declared, *inter alia*, that the revealing clothes worn by some women encouraged rape; in October he urged women to be banned from competitions in the reading of the Koran because their voices might seduce men. In July 2001 a senior Islamic leader, Hashim Yahya, ruled that a man might divorce his wife by sending her a text message from a mobile cellular telephone. Women's groups urged the Government to reject the finding and to insist that divorce cases continue to be heard in the courts. Fadzil Nor assured PAS's partners in the BA that his party would not seek to impose an Islamic state without fully discussing the topic with other groups; however, he was unable to dissuade the DAP from leaving the BA over the issue in September of that year. In contrast, the continuation of serious tensions within the MCA, which had publicly divided into two factions, 'Team A' and 'Team B', did not seem to affect the BN. The BA's Islamic character was reinforced when the uncompromising Chief Minister of Terengganu, Abdul Hadi Awang, became leader of PAS after Fadzil Nor's death in June 2002. Abdul Hadi Awang's pronounced hostility towards the US-led campaign to oust the regime of Saddam Hussain in Iraq in early 2003 garnered further public support for his party.

The Government responded to the developments of October 2000 by suspending proposed legislation that would have authorized punishment for Muslims who abandoned their faith. Addressing a conference on Islamic law, Mahathir condemned Islamic intolerance, urging flexibility and tolerance in the observance of Islam. The Government tightened its control over Islamic groups in August 2001, detaining Nik Adli Nik Abdul Aziz, son of Nik Abdul Aziz Nik Mat, and 16 others on charges of planning to overthrow the Government. They were ordered to be detained for two years without trial under the ISA. In the same month the Government banned public political meetings and adopted legislation formally outlawing discrimination against women and making it possible for women to sue in cases where they had suffered discrimination. In September measures were also announced against religious leaders who raised political themes in sermons. Mahathir declared that Malaysia was in fact already an Islamic state, apparently implying that further Islamization, as proposed by PAS, was unnecessary (although this declaration caused consternation in non-Muslim circles). Meanwhile, under a new Chief Justice, Tan Sri Dato' Mohamed Dziaddin bin Haji Abdullah, the High Court had significantly recovered its reputation for independence, and had opposed the Government in prominent cases in which contempt proceedings and defamation charges had been used against opposition activists.

The terrorist attacks of 11 September 2001 on the USA gave the Government a further opportunity to suppress Islamist extremism. In October six people were arrested under the ISA on suspicion of membership of the Kumpulan Mujahidin Malaysia (KMM), which was suspected of having connections with the al-Qa'ida international terrorist network. During 2002 a further 65 people were arrested, and in late 2002 the Government announced plans to tighten the ISA still further by removing all recourse to the courts for those arrested under its provisions. The Government implied openly that the KMM and the related Jemaah Islamiah (JI) regional terrorist group were connected with PAS. Nik Abdul Aziz Nik Mat encouraged these perceptions by demanding a *jihad* ('holy war') against the USA and urging Malaysians to support the Taliban regime of Afghanistan. During campaigning for a by-election in January 2002, propaganda produced by the Government explicitly linked PAS with the Taliban, drawing particular attention to the subordinate position of women under Taliban rule. In February 2001 UMNO had established Puteri UMNO, an organization aimed at women under the age of 35. This group was generally perceived to hold more modern views and to be opposed to radical Islamic practices. In late 2002 the head of Puteri UMNO, Azalina Othman Said, was publicly accused of lesbianism, but the case was dismissed. Increasingly, the BN

Government was concerned by what it perceived to be the propagation of radical Islamic ideas in private schools for Muslim children, which comprised 80% of all schools in Kelantan. In October 2002 the Government announced that funding for these schools would be reduced and that it would introduce 'after-hours' religious education in government-controlled schools, with the aim of promoting a less radical view of Islam.

In June 2002 Mahathir cast Malaysian politics into confusion by abruptly announcing his resignation during a speech to the annual congress of UMNO. Within an hour, however, party officials announced that the Prime Minister had been persuaded to withdraw his resignation. At the congress Minister of Home Affairs Abdullah Badawi, Mahatir's likely successor, had already sought to strengthen his position by adopting as a theme the cleansing of UMNO of corruption. During the approach to the congress, six senior party officials had been dismissed on corruption charges. Abdullah Badawi's credentials as an Islamic scholar were widely seen to be an advantage in UMNO's political contest with PAS. A transfer of power within the faction-ridden MCA in June 2003, from the rival leaders of 'Team A' and 'Team B' to younger members, was generally perceived to constitute the first stage in a wider process of generational renewal in Malaysia. In September 2002 Mahathir announced that he would not contest the general election due in 2004, and later scheduled his retirement for October 2003.

The credibility of Malaysia's security forces was undermined in July 2003, when police identified an unregistered paramilitary movement, Pasukan Khas Persekutuan Malaysia (PKPM—Federal Special Forces of Malaysia), headed by a self-styled lieutenant-general, Nor Azami Ahmad Ghazali, who had formerly been a technician in the Draining and Irrigation Department. The PKPM allegedly planned to overthrow the Government and claimed a membership of 8,000, including civil servants and former army personnel. However, its funds appeared to come from the sale to its members of ranks and uniforms resembling those of the federal police. PKPM members held 'authority cards', supposedly issued by the Prime Minister's Office, authorizing them to arrest political leaders and ministers. The organization also raided shops selling pirated video compact discs. The existence of the PKPM highlighted dissatisfaction with the performance of the police itself, which was increasingly believed to be involved in corruption and abuse of power.

When Mahathir promised in June 2002 to relinquish his post in the following year, he designated his deputy, Abdullah Badawi, as his successor. However, owing to Mahathir's dominant position, and the fate of his previous deputies and presumed successors, especially Anwar Ibrahim and Datuk Musa Hitam (who had resigned as Deputy Prime Minister in February 1986, citing 'irreconcilable differences' with Mahathir), an air of uncertainty surrounded the succession issue until the final stages. In May 2003, as Minister of Home Affairs, Abdullah ordered the release of three senior PKN officials who had been detained under the ISA, on the grounds that the PKN no longer presented a security threat. In August the PKN merged with the smaller PRM, forming the Parti Keadilan Rakyat (PKR, People's Justice Party).

THE GOVERNMENT OF ABDULLAH BADAWI

Mahathir resigned as Prime Minister on 31 October 2003, and Abdullah Badawi was sworn in on the following day. Mahathir's farewell speech included a condemnation of factionalism and 'money politics' and a desire for the emergence of 'New Malays' who would be better able to compete with other communities. Preparations immediately began for the 2004 general election, which would be Abdullah Badawi's first test of public approval. The number of parliamentary seats to be filled was increased from 193 to 219, and the deposit required from candidates was also raised. As UMNO local branches were based on electorates, the increase in seats provided the UMNO leadership with an opportunity to reorganize local branches and to tighten central control.

Three days before Mahathir's resignation, the PAS Government in Terengganu followed Kelantan in introducing new state regulations conforming to *Shari'a* (Islamic) law, including the *hudud* code of punishments, while women's groups were incensed that the new laws required the testimony of four male witnesses to 'prove' that rape had occurred. With criminal law remaining the responsibility of the federal Government, the implementation of the new regulations seemed impossible. However, PAS's action did enable Abdullah Badawi to signal his intentions, and the federal Attorney-General immediately instigated a court case to have the law rescinded.

Abdullah delayed appointing a Deputy Prime Minister until January 2004, and then chose Minister of Defence Najib, who had been publicly favoured for the post by Mahathir. Furthermore, Abdullah's first Cabinet largely retained appointees of the Mahathir era. A Royal Commission of Inquiry into the police force was established in December 2003, but its terms of reference excluded corruption and the abuse of power. By contrast, Abdullah cancelled a number of Mahathir's so-called 'megaprojects', and spoke many times in public about the need to develop Malaysia's democratic culture and to respect the independence of the judiciary. The new Prime Minister also promised to expand the use of parliamentary committees to examine draft legislation, and instigated a high-profile campaign against corruption. In February 2004 police arrested a number of senior and middle-ranking officials, including the Minister of Land and Co-operative Development, Kasitah Gaddam, on corruption charges.

Abdullah's new approach produced a dramatic improvement in the BN's performance at national elections held on 21 March 2004, when the ruling alliance won 198 of the 219 seats in the House of Representatives. The elections proceeded peacefully, although fears of violence had led the authorities to reduce the campaigning period to a mere seven days. There was some evidence of irregularities and malpractice, but overall the result seemed to reflect widespread approval for the new Prime Minister. PAS performed poorly, its parliamentary representation declining from the 27 seats won in the 1999 election to seven. The Islamic party also lost control of the state Government in Terengganu and retained Kelantan only by a narrow margin. Middle-class voters who had previously voted against the BN in protest at the treatment of Anwar were believed to account for much of the trend towards the party. Abdullah's promises to reduce poverty and combat corruption were also popular, whereas the implementation of Islamic law by PAS state governments had irked many urbanized Muslims. Coming from a family of Muslim scholars and holding a degree in Islamic studies, Abdullah had argued that Islam was a religion not of social restriction but rather of development, encouraging hard work and a desire for science, technology and knowledge. The PKR lost four of the five seats previously held by the PKN, with only Anwar Ibrahim's wife, Wan Azizah, retaining her seat. Meanwhile, the DAP increased its number of seats from 10 to 12.

Abdullah sought to consolidate his position prior to the UMNO General Assembly, convened in late September 2004. After party members were 'advised' not to challenge him or Najib for the respective posts of UMNO President and Deputy President, only a few nominations were made in support of the sole competitor, Tengku Razaleigh Hamzah, who had previously challenged Mahathir unsuccessfully in 1987. Although Abdullah's own position was thus secure, one of the newly elected Vice-Presidents was Isa Abdul Samad, who, as former UMNO leader in Negeri Sembilan, had clashed previously with Abdullah. The other Vice-Presidents, Mohamad Ali Rustam, Chief Minister of Melaka, and Minister of Agriculture and Agro-Based Industry Muhyiddin Yassin, were not considered a threat to Abdullah. However, there was a general perception that Abdullah's supporters had not performed strongly.

Thus, in meeting significant resistance within his party, Abdullah's progress in addressing corruption and power abuses following the party election remained limited. Indeed, in preparing for the UMNO General Assembly in September 2004, he had urged party members to avoid 'money politics'. In addition, the Government launched the National Integrity Plan, which emphasized the development of civic and environmental consciousness. However, when the chairman of the Royal Commission of Inquiry into the national police force, former Chief Justice Mohamed Dzaiddin Abdullah, presented

Abdullah with a report on police corruption and brutality in August, the Prime Minister sought to keep the details secret and failed to specify reforms to address the problems that had been identified.

Even so, Abdullah's promises of a more independent judiciary appeared to be substantiated when in September 2004 a federal court overruled Anwar Ibrahim's conviction for sexual misconduct. Since Anwar had already served his sentence for corruption while detained in custody, he was released from prison. However, under Malaysian law, he would remain ineligible to stand for office for a further five years because of his corruption conviction. None the less, Anwar indicated that he planned to resume political activity, and there was widespread speculation over whether he would seek at this point to return to UMNO or to remain in opposition, notably with the PKR, which had been formed to protest against his treatment. UMNO youth leaders publicly referred to Anwar as a 'traitor', suggesting that any return to UMNO was likely to be fraught with conflict. Thus, he soon set his sights on reviving the BA, although at first he had little success in narrowing the gap between the DAP and PAS.

Meanwhile, the debate over the role of Islam within Malaysian society continued. Although PAS moderated its commitment to creating an Islamic state, particularly after its research suggested that Islamist policies had contributed to its loss of Terengganu in March 2004, the party refused to abandon its goal altogether. In March 2005 the PAS state Government in Kelantan announced that it would extend to women of all religions the dress code that it had previously applied only to Muslim women. In August two followers of the religious movement Sky Kingdom argued in court in Terengganu that they had not broken a *fatwa* banning Muslims from links with the group because they had repudiated their former affiliation with Islam. However, state government officials responded by demolishing the sect's headquarters.

Up to this point in Abdullah's premiership, the country had mostly avoided the kinds of political and economic upheavals that had so regularly punctuated the tenure of his predecessor. Nevertheless, as Abdullah proceeded cautiously, navigating between pressures to reduce corruption on one side and a need to provide patronage to party supporters on the other, while keeping Islamist pressures at bay, a popular perception arose that the country's political and business spheres lacked the dynamism associated with the Mahathir years. In March 2006 Abdullah's Government introduced the Ninth Malaysia Plan, which envisaged greater private investment in industrial parks, with the southern state of Johor to be established as a particular focus of growth. However, state-led efforts would mostly be dedicated to agricultural pursuits, especially palm oil and rubber production. This apparent shift prompted Mahathir to criticize the shortfall in technology investment, which, in his view, was producing mediocre levels of economic development.

However, Abdullah remained sufficiently popular at this point to be able to deflect Mahathir's criticisms, contain challenges within UMNO and implement policies that weakened the appeal of opposition parties and non-governmental organizations (NGOs). Thus, after Isa Samad had been suspended from UMNO for six years on vote-buying charges in May 2005, Abdullah relaxed his anti-corruption campaign. Indeed, suspicions began to mount over the business dealings of Abdullah's own family, with a subsidiary of Scomi Group—operated by the Prime Minister's son, Kamaluddin—securing a major state contract for reconditioning the country's railway carriages through a restricted tender. Abdullah also refused to act vigorously on the recommendation by the Royal Commission of Inquiry that an Independent Police Misconduct and Complaints Commission (IPMCC) be formed. Despite the parliamentary opposition leader, Lim Kit Siang, raising the issue repeatedly in the House of Representatives, Abdullah generally remained silent, evidently yielding to threats by the police force, circulated on an internal web page, that it would support PAS in the next general election if any independent commission were established.

By mid-2007 only two corruption cases involving senior officials were in progress: one involving Kasitah Gaddam (see above), and a second involving Eric Chia, the former head of Malaysia's national steel company, Perwaja Steel. Chia had been accused of making an unauthorized and unnecessary payment of RM 76.4m. through a non-existent company to the NKK Corporation of Japan. However, the prosecution neglected even to call material witnesses in the trial, as a result of which the sessions court judge acquitted Chia in June 2007. With the proposals to create the IPMCC remaining dormant, therefore, many analysts concluded that Abdullah's anti-corruption campaign had come to an end.

Yet, even if corrupt practices persisted, Abdullah remained sufficiently concerned about budgetary deficits to ensure that efforts continued to rationalize government-linked corporations. In this context, the head of Proton, Malaysia's heavily subsidized, yet struggling national automobile industry, was replaced. Negotiations were then undertaken with various foreign companies, including Citroën and Volkswagen, to secure a new partner. Proton's motorcycle division, MV Augusta, was also sold off for a nominal sum. Mahathir, having strongly supported Proton since its formation during the early 1980s and, notwithstanding his retirement, still serving at this time as a principal company adviser, began to vent grievances. He had become particularly critical in mid-2005 of the Government's policy of providing 'approved permits' (APs), entitling individuals chosen by the Ministry of International Trade and Industry to import cars duty-free. Although introduced initially as a means by which to assist indigenous businesspeople in entering automobile retail sectors, the system had long been distorted by favouritism. However, the former Prime Minister mainly focused his criticism on the adverse impact of APs on Proton's domestic sales, already under pressure from tariff reductions. Thus, Mahathir openly criticized the Minister of International Trade and Industry, Rafidah Aziz, an erstwhile ally, leading to robust exchanges conducted through the media and parliamentary proceedings.

In April 2006 the Government also cancelled a troubled project to build a new bridge to replace the causeway linking Malaysia's southern state of Johor with Singapore, further enraging Mahathir. The project was perceived as costly and frivolous, with construction of the bridge, had it been allowed to continue, unable to extend beyond the causeway's mid-point, owing to the Singaporean Government's refusal to participate. Mahathir harshly criticized Abdullah as having yielded to pressure from Singapore, consequently reneging on assurances that the bridge and other projects, including a monorail linking Kuala Lumpur with the administrative capital, Putrajaya, would be continued. In an extraordinary interview, Mahathir claimed that he had favoured Deputy Prime Minister Najib over Abdullah as his successor. Cabinet ministers, most of whom had originally been appointed by Mahathir, reacted angrily and declared their loyalty to Abdullah.

Throughout 2006 Mahathir became increasingly confrontational. In September he even attempted to return to active politics, contesting the UMNO division-level election in his previous stronghold of Kubang Pasu. However, Abdullah's local allies apparently intervened to thwart this bid, a serious set-back for Mahathir, who in November suffered a heart attack, further frustrating his efforts. In addition, the standing of Deputy Prime Minister and Minister of Defence Najib, a possible challenger for the premiership, appeared to be weakened by the trial of his close associate and security adviser, Abdul Razak Baginda. Abdul Razak was charged with ordering the murder of Altantuya Shaariibuu, a Mongolian translator who was reported to have been involved in a relationship with Abdul Razak, whom she had allegedly been blackmailing prior to her death in 2006; Najib denied repeated allegations of his own involvement in the murder. (Abdul Razak was subsequently acquitted of Shaariibuu's murder, of which two members of a special police unit were convicted in April 2009; both were sentenced to death.)

Meanwhile, although tensions persisted within UMNO, and citizens grew disillusioned over the Government's campaign against corruption, the economy continued to be sufficiently robust to ensure that opposition parties remained unable to attract support. PAS held a general assembly election in June 2005, with so-called young professionals wresting some leadership positions from uncompromising *ulama* (scholars). Most importantly, Nasaruddin Mat Isa, a relatively young academic who had trained as an *ulama*, but was widely perceived to be reformist, secured the party's deputy presidency. The 'professionals' then confirmed their standing when the next party election was held in mid-2007. Nevertheless, PAS remained bitterly divided between pragmatic and Islamist elements, a schism that weakened its appeal for broader constituencies. As it began to prepare for the next general election, PAS viewed its one-seat majority in Kelantan's state assembly with some apprehension; it was widely expected that PAS would remain so preoccupied with its base in Kelantan that it would forgo campaigning effectiveness at the national level.

The PKR also made little progress during this period, even as Anwar assumed a more prominent role. Indeed, after spending much of his time overseas since his release from prison, holding university fellowships or conducting speaking tours, during 2007 Anwar began to exercise greater leadership over PKR affairs. In April he campaigned fervently on behalf of a PKR candidate in a by-election for a state assembly seat in the semi-rural Selangor constituency of Ijok, a strategy that was interpreted as a bid for a return to politics. However, although Anwar drew large crowds, the BN candidate finally won the election with an increased majority for the Government. Furthermore, as Anwar grew more assertive within the PKR, he alienated other party leaders to such an extent that some of them resigned from their positions.

The DAP had reclaimed enough of its earlier standing through the 2004 election to ensure that its central policy and strategic planning commissioner, Lim Kit Siang, was reappointed as opposition leader in Parliament. However, this seemed only to shift societal divisions, with recent rifts over Islamic religiosity within the Malay community giving way to more traditional confrontation between Malays and ethnic Chinese. In this regard, long-standing controversies over the breakdown of ethnic ownership of equity stakes, heavily restructured under the NEP, re-emerged during this period. Accordingly, the DAP seemed unable to extend its appeal beyond the Chinese community's declining population.

While the opposition parties languished, the Government responded with nuanced strategies. On the one hand, parliamentary debate was permitted to become livelier and more meaningful, while print media and internet news-reporting were afforded a greater level of freedom. Thus, even the *New Straits Times*, a major English-language daily newspaper closely associated with UMNO, began to provide more objective critical commentary. The Government also set up a text message 'hotline' through which citizens might respond via their mobile telephones to new policy measures. None the less, this new tolerance on the part of the Government did not appear to extend to public protests. When demonstrators gathered in March 2006 in front of the iconic Petronas twin towers in Kuala Lumpur to denounce the Government's reductions in fuel subsidies, they were forcibly dispersed by riot police. The Government also appeared to avoid taking any action when, in mid-2006, mobs closed down meetings organized by a coalition called Article 11; the group had gathered in order to advocate the protection of minority rights, guaranteed under the Constitution, as new so-called Islamizing policies were imposed. Following the protests, Abdullah ordered the group to cease its planned public activities. Similarly, at the UMNO General Assembly in late 2006, the Minister of Education and UMNO youth chief, Hishammuddin Tun Hussein, denounced proposals to form an inter-faith commission. The Cabinet also rejected a demand by the Malaysian Bar Council that the judicial upheavals of 1988, involving the removal of the Lord President and several other judges, be reviewed. Thus, by averting challenges from Mahathir, resuming patronage flows to supporters within UMNO, allowing greater debate in Parliament, yet taking action against civil society organizations, Abdullah appeared to strengthen his position. He was helped also by reasonable levels of economic growth and rivalries among the opposition parties.

However, while Abdullah grew complacent, corruption in his Government appeared to increase. In late 2006 development funds totalling RM 600m. were released to *bumiputra* contractors for small-scale road-building and renovation projects. The loyalties of many mid-ranking UMNO officials were thereby perpetuated, with the contracting firms with which they were associated prioritized for development spending. Abdullah also revived some of the 'megaprojects' that had previously been suspended. A project to construct a hydroelectric dam at Bakun, in Sarawak, continued, despite its reliance on untested cabling technologies for energy transfers, while two more dams were proposed in the state's Rejang basin. Approval was also given for a second bridge linking Peninsular Malaysia and the island of Pinang. Furthermore, government contracts were awarded without tender to little-known companies to construct a new palace for the Yang di-Pertuan Agong.

In early 2007 a public advocacy group revealed that a former colleague of the Director-General of the Anti-Corruption Agency (ACA), Zulkipli Mat Noor, had earlier alleged that, while serving in the state of Sabah, Zulkipli had acquired properties far in excess of what he had recorded in his asset declaration. Evidence also emerged of Zulkipli's apparent ownership of additional properties in Johor, but in July the Attorney-General's Chambers announced that, after conducting investigations, the complaints against Zulkipli had been found to be baseless. Allegations were also made that the Deputy Minister of Internal Security, Mohd Johari Baharum, had been bribed to arrange the release from prison of three men suspected of being involved in organized crime, generating a scandal of 'freedom for sale'. The Inspector-General of Police, Musa Hassan, assisted the ACA's investigations into Johari. However, as with Zulkipli, the Attorney-General again ordered that proceedings be halted. Johari retaliated none the less, filing a report with the ACA against Musa, whom he alleged had himself been bribed to free gangsters, but Musa was also exonerated by the ACA.

These troubles in the police force shed light on the wealth that many senior officers seemed to accumulate. However, soon afterwards yet another scandal emerged, diverting attention to the judiciary. In September 2007 an extraordinary video was circulated in which a senior lawyer, V. K. Lingam, was recorded holding a telephone conversation with the Chief Justice of the Federal Court, Ahmad Fairuz. Together, they appeared to be negotiating judicial promotions and court rulings. Amid the uproar that followed, including a protest march by hundreds of lawyers upon the Palace of Justice in the administrative capital, Putrajaya, demands were made that a royal investigative commission be formed. Abdullah prevaricated, consenting only to the establishment of a panel to examine the authenticity of the video.

As revelations of corrupt practices mounted, public scrutiny focused anew on Abdullah's family. Attention turned from Abdullah's son, Kamaluddin, who had gained lucrative government contracts (see above), to Abdullah's son-in-law, Khairy Jamaluddin. While serving as deputy leader of UMNO's youth wing, Khairy had become involved in several investment companies linked to the Government, including Khazanah Holdings and Avenue Capital Resources.

At the same time, with public anger rising over the issue of corrupt practices, Abdullah, by acquiescing in attempts by UMNO politicians to revitalize their ethnic Malay followings, deepened the alienation of Chinese and Indians. Specifically, at UMNO General Assemblies, whereas Mahathir had discouraged delegates from making declarations of Malay dominance during debates and addresses, Abdullah, probably more from laxity than conviction, gave them greater freedom. Indeed, at the UMNO Assemblies in 2006 and 2007, the Minister of Education and leader of the party's youth wing, Hishammuddin Hussein, raised a ceremonial Malay dagger, the mystical *keris*, high over his head. Taking the cue, other speakers declared the inviolability of Malay special rights, embodied in the NEP and its successor programmes. The frenzy to which delegates in attendance were then driven was duly broadcast on state-owned television and reported extensively through the party-allied print media. Much anecdotal evidence suggested that even if loyalties among the wider Malay community were revived to some degree, grievances among the ethnic Chinese and Indians were exacerbated during these episodes.

In addition, during late 2007 and early 2008 Malaysia's economic performance began to falter, in tandem with that of most of the world. The 'growth corridor' that had been announced in Johor, along with several more in the north and on the east coast, showed little progress. Moreover, food and fuel prices began to soar. In this context, with Malaysia having developed to the point where car ownership and extensive commuting had become entrenched in the country's economy and culture, citizens were angered by the Government's pledge to rescind subsidies on fuel in June 2008.

Thus, as public resentment mounted, Anwar Ibrahim, serving as the de facto leader of the PKR, campaigned intensively on the party's behalf. Although he remained barred from standing as a candidate until April 2008, he began his bid to return to politics by leading rallies around the country as by-elections took place. He displayed much charisma at his appearances, unlike the reticent Abdullah, and analysts quickly took note of the return of the 'Anwar factor' to Malaysia's political life.

As the general election approached, the Government gave less attention to strengthening reforms than to curbing Anwar's advance. Most signally, it imposed new controls on communication, especially internet weblogs. In July 2007 the PKR's webmaster (website administrator), Nathaniel Tan, was arrested under the Official Secrets Act after copying onto his weblog the allegations that had been made against the Deputy Minister of Internal Security, Johari. At the same time, the Government attempted to suppress demonstrations, which were increasing rapidly in frequency and size, especially in Kuala Lumpur and its environs, but also in Terengganu. Converging on Kuala Lumpur, agricultural labourers protested over distributive unfairness within their community, in particular the concentration of NEP benefits among senior UMNO politicians and their corporate allies, prompting the swift intervention of the riot police. Ethnic Indian NGOs, collaborating through the Hindu Rights Action Force (HINDRAF), also protested in late 2007 against their community's economic marginalization, as well as against the steady destruction of Hindu temples and Tamil-language schools as rubber plantations gave way to urbanization and development projects. Large-scale marches conducted by Indians were also met by the police, and several HINDRAF leaders were detained under the ISA. Demonstrators from all ethnic communities united to protest against the rising cost of living and deepening unemployment. An umbrella organization known as Gabungan Pilihanraya Bersih dan Adil (Bersih—the Coalition for Clean and Fair Elections), while mobilizing societal discontent over a range of issues, focused on government corruption and the electoral manipulation that activists anticipated in the forthcoming polls.

The general election was held on 8 March 2008. Although the BN was returned to power, it sustained such heavy losses that in the aftermath of the election its standing continued to weaken. Speculation thus mounted over whether a democratic transition had been set in train and, if so, whether it would provoke an authoritarian reversal. The BN's share of the popular vote declined to 52% nation-wide from the 60%–65% of the total that it had generally secured at previous polls, with slightly less than a majority being achieved on the peninsula. Thus, notwithstanding the cumulative effects of the plurality system, with 140 seats, the BN claimed no more than 63% of the 222 seats in the enlarged House of Representatives, leaving it short of a two-thirds' majority for the first time since 1969. As in 1969, when the Government suffered a similar set-back, it regained its standing by absorbing most opposition parties into its coalition, then subordinating its partners. However, in 2008 the opposition was so invigorated that instead anticipation grew that it would instigate the necessary parliamentary realignments to replace the Government. Among the opposition forces, PAS and the DAP together boosted their total number of seats from 19 to 51. Yet, rising precipitously between these parties was Anwar's PKR, appealing mostly to Malays, although remaining avowedly multi-ethnic and moderately Muslim, while attempting to attract middle-class voters. The PKR thus increased its representation from a single seat to 31, qualifying it to head the opposition in Parliament. Moreover, these three parties together formed governments in five states, including two of the country's most industrialized, Pinang and Selangor.

The results of the election were equated to a 'political tsunami', astonishing UMNO politicians and citizens. Indeed, Mahathir demanded that Abdullah resign from the position of Prime Minister. Disgusted by Abdullah's refusal to stand down, Mahathir resigned from UMNO in May 2008, urging other members to do likewise. Although it had been anticipated that the BN would lose some support among the Chinese and Indian communities, their long-standing ethnic grievances had been exacerbated by the behaviour of UMNO politicians at recent party general assemblies. However, the extent to which these concerns would drive non-Malay voters to support the opposition and, furthermore, would come to be shared by some Malays too had not been foretold in any serious analysis. In fact, Malays, in moving by an estimated 5% against the Government, had given their votes not only to PAS and the PKR, but even, in some districts, to the DAP.

Following their electoral success, in April 2008 the opposition parties coalesced more closely as the People's Alliance (Pakatan Rakyat), with the multi-ethnic PKR mediating between PAS and the DAP. Furthermore, in exploring new models of policy effectiveness, they contemplated replacing the NEP-era quotas with 'decommunalized' forms of welfare distribution in the states that they controlled. They also began boldly to propose the formation of a new People's Alliance government at the federal level, with Anwar stating repeatedly that the alliance he now led had enticed enough defectors from the BN to enable a transfer of power soon to take place. Indeed, he named 16 September as the date when the BN would fall. Meanwhile, a member of the BN coalition, the Sabah Progressive Party (SAPP), threatened to file a parliamentary motion of no confidence against Abdullah. Local analysts thus anticipated that communally ordered single-party dominance might soon be replaced by two-party competitiveness, therein amounting to a transition to a much fuller democracy.

The Government at first responded by renewing its commitment to reform. Seeking to placate citizens, UMNO politicians canvassed liberalizing changes, in particular removing the print media's annual licensing requirements, allowing students to participate in political activities and abolishing the ISA. More profoundly, they proposed judicial reforms, while bringing new corruption charges against several bureaucrats.

Thus, as UMNO politicians underwent deep introspection, the People's Alliance pressed ahead in attempting to attract BN defectors in the hope of replacing the Government. Anwar's wife, Wan Azizah, resigned from the parliamentary seat that she held in Pinang, thus forcing a by-election in August 2008, which (his five-year ban having expired) Anwar contested and won, enabling him finally to assume his place as parliamentary opposition leader.

However, UMNO then began to resort to coercive strategies. Liberalizing reforms were quietly abandoned or modified; demonstrations were suppressed; and, in order to curb Anwar's advance, further charges of sexual misconduct and sodomy were filed against him. Anwar was thus drawn into lengthy and debilitating court proceedings, likely to be followed by his imprisonment. Meanwhile, UMNO used state- and party-controlled. media outlets to raise tensions between component parties of the People's Alliance, highlighting their apparent contradictions and doubtful competencies. In September 2008 prominent DAP parliamentarian Teresa Kok, well-known dissident blogger Raja Petra Kamaruddin and several other activists were arrested in renewed use of the ISA.

Despite efforts to curb the opposition, candidates from the People's Alliance defeated the BN in several more parliamentary and state-level by-elections. However, the Government retaliated yet more vigorously, undermining the state governments that had been formed by the opposition. Deputy Prime Minister Najib took the post of Perak chairman of the BN and also that of state chairman of the UMNO liaison committee in late January 2009. The defection of a number of PKR state legislators in early February was sufficient to cause the People's Alliance, led by Mohammad Nizar Jamaluddin of PAS, to lose its majority in Perak. The PKR defectors were reported to have been threatened with corruption investigations. The Sultan of Perak then dismissed the sitting Government so that UMNO might lead in forming a new administration, with Datuk Seri Zambry Abdul Kadir of

UMNO as Chief Minister of Perak. However, the Sultan refused to dissolve the State Legislative Assembly so that a new election could be held, thereby precipitating a constitutional crisis, an occupation of the assembly, mass demonstrations and numerous arrests. In an apparent display of independence, the Kuala Lumpur High Court ruled in May, one month after Najib had ascended to the premiership (see below), that the removal of Nizar Jamaluddin from office had been illegal, hence restoring the People's Alliance to power; however, the Court of Appeal then reinstated Zambry as Chief Minister, pending an appeal.

In Kedah a PKR state legislator was expelled from the local assembly as a result of the Sultan's machinations, undermining the narrow majority of the People's Alliance and necessitating yet another by-election. The Chief Minister of Selangor, Tan Sri Abdul Khalid Ibrahim of the PKR, was threatened with the instigation of corruption charges by the Malaysian Anti-Corruption Commission (MACC, formerly the ACA—see below), indicating that, despite the body's reconfiguration, it would not shrink from its steeply partisan mission. Meanwhile, various parliamentary suspensions were imposed and sedition charges were brought against other legislators and state assembly members who belonged to the People's Alliance. Thus, at the end of 2008, with perceptions of the Government's legitimacy having been eroded but support for the opposition still fragmented, Malaysia appeared to be entering a period of protracted and damaging deadlock.

THE LEADERSHIP OF NAJIB TUN RAZAK

By mid-2008, as UMNO politicians began to recover from their electoral set-back, Prime Minister Abdullah became increasingly beleaguered. He thus pledged in July to cede power to Najib Tun Razak at the next UMNO General Assembly. During his remaining time in office, although even Abdullah had come to regard his premiership as a 'wasted opportunity', he tried to prepare his legacy. During the final parliamentary session in December, the Government tabled three pieces of legislation, restructuring the ACA as the MACC, and creating the Judicial Appointments Commission (JAC) and the Special Complaints Commission (SCC). However, these measures were widely considered to be insufficient and tardy. The MACC was not empowered to bring charges; a decision to prosecute could be made only by the Attorney-General's Office, a notoriously partisan body. Indeed, over the next six months, although some new cases were brought against mid-level government officials, many senior members of the PKR and the DAP soon found themselves under investigation. Furthermore, in June 2009 the MACC's harsh methods were highlighted by the death in the commission's Selangor facility of Teoh Beng Hock, the political secretary of a DAP state executive councillor, after many hours of interrogation. The MACC avowed that the young secretary had committed suicide, but many Malaysian citizens remained sceptical. The Government acceded to increasing demands for a Royal Commission of Inquiry into the incident; however, the inquiry's scope was limited to an examination of the MACC's interrogation methods and precluded an investigation into the controversial death. (Following the recording in January 2011 of an open verdict by the coroner, who declared that there was insufficient evidence to determine how Teoh had died, but ruled out suicide as a possible cause of death while also noting the absence of 'evidence of third-party involvement', Najib agreed to extend the scope of the Royal Commission of Inquiry to include the specific circumstances surrounding Teoh's death.) The new JAC was also perceived to lack independence, with its judicial appointments still requiring approval by the Prime Minister, while the SCC was ridiculed as an ineffective version of the IPMCC that had been proposed years earlier. Thus, although this proliferation of new legislation in Abdullah's final parliamentary session attracted much attention, it ultimately did little to enhance his standing as a reformer.

The UMNO General Assembly was held in March 2009, having been rescheduled from December 2008. As Abdullah's designated successor, Najib was challenged for the party presidency by only one other candidate, Tengku Razaleigh Hamzah; however, with Najib having won an overwhelming number of divisional nominations beforehand, his election was unstoppable. The Minister of International Trade and Industry, Muhyiddin Yassin, a former Chief Minister of the UMNO-controlled state of Johor and a staunch critic of Abdullah, was elected Deputy President. However, many other candidates who were regarded as enjoying Najib's favour were defeated in their bids for the party vice-presidencies and posts in the UMNO Supreme Council. At the same time, Abdullah gave a stirring address, displaying a verve that had been lacking since the early days of his tenure, while his son-in-law, Khairy Jamaluddin, defeated Mahathir's son, Mukhriz, in the contest for the most senior position in the powerful UMNO youth wing, seemingly qualifying him for an important ministerial post. However, after ascending to the premiership in April, Najib reorganized the Cabinet in such a way as to promote his allies and consolidate his own power. Thus, he overlooked Khairy, instead promoting Mukhriz as Deputy Minister of International Trade and Industry. Factional bitterness resurged within the party over the manner in which Abdullah's supporters had been treated, although by 2010 these sentiments appeared to have subsided.

Just as Mahathir had done upon coming to office, Najib tried initially to strike a conciliatory note, seeking to broaden his popular appeal. Pledging greater respect for civil liberties, one of his first major decisions was to order the release of 13 detainees held under the ISA, among them leaders of HINDRAF. He also permitted several newspapers that had previously been banned to resume publication. As his administration evolved, Najib initiated a new programme—'1Malaysia'—by which to promote greater national unity among Malaysia's increasingly polarized ethnic communities. Deputy Prime Minister Muhyiddin adopted a staunchly pro-Malay line, while the Minister of Home Affairs, Hishammuddin Hussein, was accused in some quarters of condoning aggressive Malay actions, while at the same time vowing to suppress anti-Government demonstrations. After a group of Muslim activists paraded the severed head of a cow through the streets of Shah Alam, Selangor, in August 2009 in protest at proposals to erect a Hindu temple in the vicinity, before tossing it defiantly at a local government office, Hishammuddin appealed to the public to understand their deep frustrations, to the fury of the ethnic Indian population. In July 2010 12 Muslim men were fined RM 1,000 each for their role in the incident after pleading guilty to a charge of illegal assembly. Two of the 12 men, purported to be the ringleaders of the group, also pleaded guilty to a separate charge of sedition for 'inciting racial tension' after carrying and stamping on the cow's head; both were fined an additional RM 3,000 and one of the pair was sentenced to a week's imprisonment. (A further four of the 12 men had initially been charged with sedition, but these charges were subsequently dismissed.) While the sentences went some way towards appeasing the Hindu population, the Government's tempered response in the immediate aftermath of the incident led to a significant increase in ethnic tensions.

A series of *Shari'a* court rulings and police actions further exacerbated communal rivalries. In December 2009 the High Court of Malaysia ruled that *The Herald*, a weekly Catholic magazine, was permitted to use the word 'Allah', rescinding an existing government ban on the use of the word by non-Muslims on the grounds that it was 'unconstitutional'. The High Court ruling outraged some within the Muslim community, leading to a series of attacks on Christian places of worship, in which eight churches were set on fire; a number of mosques were targeted in retaliatory attacks.

Meanwhile, under the 1Malaysia programme, Najib was able during his first year in office to enact some meaningful economic reforms and political compromises. Many Malaysian citizens were initially sceptical of Najib's leadership abilities, recalling rumours relating to his alleged involvement in dubious defence procurements, Abdul Razak's lurid trial proceedings and suggestions of misadventures in his personal life. However, as he reached out to foreign investors, to Malay oppositionists, and to alienated Chinese and Indian communities, his popularity began to increase. In his role as Minister of Finance, Najib responded to a critical World Bank report by taking measures to liberalize the economy, including the identification of nearly 30 important service sub-sectors, among them tourism, health and transport, in which foreign investors would henceforth be exempt from 30% quotas on equity for *bumiputra* beneficiaries. Najib also introduced the Government Transformation Programme (GTP), delineated through six National Key Results Areas: enhancing the quality of education; reducing crime; tackling corruption; raising the living standards of low-income households; advancing public transport; and improving rural development. University scholarships that would be awarded strictly according to merit were announced. While declaring these measures, Najib repeatedly emphasized his Government's steadfast commitment to the policies of affirmative action that addressed Malay grievances. To this end, the establishment of a new fund, National Equity Bhd (Ekuinas), was announced, through which it was hoped that the global competitiveness of *bumiputra* entrepreneurs would be enhanced. Nevertheless, Najib's liberalizing initiatives were welcomed by foreign investors and non-Malay citizens.

At the same time, Najib sought to revitalize the non-Malay parties in the BN coalition, which were still suffering from the electoral set-back of 2008. However, beyond issuing advice and warnings, there was little that the Prime Minister could do to unify the MCA, with the party still bitterly divided. Mired in scandals relating to campaign financing and the involvement of several party officials in a high-profile corruption case concerning escalating costs at Port Klang Free Trade Zone (a major commercial and industrial project adjacent to Malaysia's principal port), the MCA was beset by repeated internal disagreements over prominent committee positions and party resources. It seemed unlikely, therefore, that the party would soon be able to revitalize its Chinese constituencies.

Najib also sought to stabilize the MIC, which arguably had been even more damaged by the 2008 election than the MCA. At the MIC's urging, Najib introduced new social programmes that sought specifically to benefit its Indian constituencies. However, as this seemed sooner to restore the control of MIC stalwarts—most notably, party President Dato' Seri S. Samy Vellu—than to reinvigorate the loyalties of the broader community, Najib began also to patronize a second ethnic Indian grouping that had earlier organized anti-Government protests, the Malaysia People's Power Party (Partai Makkal Sakti Malaysia—founded in early 2009 by R. S. Thanenthiran).

While UMNO's coalition parties were undoubtedly beset with challenges, their counterparts in the People's Alliance confronted their own difficulties. The coalition's gains in the 2008 general election, and its victory in eight of nine by-elections held in 2009 had inspired new hopes for wider democratization, a competitive two-party system and greater social justice in Malaysia. Having thus raised expectations, the coalition's performance in the five states that it governed inevitably fell short. Tensions thus set in within and among the People's Alliance's three constituent parties. In Selangor, the coalition's Chief Minister and most of its executive councillors were investigated in connection with allegations of corruption. In Perak, the Alliance suffered numerous defections, as a result of which it lost its majority, enabling the BN to return to office. Defections also eroded the Alliance's majority in Kedah. The DAP-led Government in Penang came under significant pressure from the state's Malay and Indian communities over planning failures and redistributive policies, while in Kelantan senior PAS leaders were divided over the extent to which the party should remain loyal to the People's Alliance or seek accommodation with UMNO, creating suspicions that reverberated throughout the coalition. Such tensions were partly responsible for a series of by-election defeats experienced by the People's Alliance during 2010.

However, the disappointing performance of the People's Alliance was not entirely of its own doing. Although Prime Minister Najib had promised political reforms, and had initially made some progress in terms of market liberalization, little of this spirit survived. During 2009–10 the federal Government withheld development funds from state governments administered by the People's Alliance; directed the MACC against senior Alliance officials in Selangor; used the courts to seal the fate of the Alliance's government in Perak; and reimposed bans on opposition publications, including the PKR's *Suara-Keadilan*, PAS's *Harakah*, and the DAP's *The Rocket*. Most egregiously, the protracted trial of Anwar Ibrahim on a second charge of sodomy, which commenced in February 2010 and was regularly interrupted by judicial manoeuvrings and subsidiary scandals, continued during 2011 but appeared to be leading inexorably to Anwar's conviction and subsequent return to prison, and to a renewed fragmentation of the opposition. In December 2010 Anwar was also suspended from Parliament for six months, having been found to have 'misled' its members, following claims by Anwar that the '1Malaysia' programme had been inspired by the 'One Israel' electoral campaign of Israeli Prime Minister Ehud Barak in 1999. (Muslim-majority Malaysia had no diplomatic relations with Israel and was a staunch proponent of an independent Palestinian state.) However, with the economy displaying signs of recovery and the People's Alliance having revealed serious shortcomings, the Malaysian population seemed to be increasingly resigned to the status quo. At mid-2010 the approval ratings of Najib remained high, and opinion surveys indicated that many citizens had come to doubt the viability of the People's Alliance as a prospective government.

During the first half of 2010 Najib attempted to give more a programmatic structure to his socio-economic initiatives. He introduced the first stage of the New Economic Model (NEM) in March, followed by the Economic Transformation Programme (ETP) in September, which asserted that state-led industrialization and affirmative action had come to hinder Malaysia's continuing advancement. Thus, while declaring that pro-Malay measures would necessarily continue, the NEM also stressed the importance of adopting more merit-based strategies for improving governance and expanding the economy. In order to support low-income citizens, the NEM, which envisaged a doubling of average per caput income by 2020, advocated welfare distributions based on need rather than ethnic affiliation—an approach that, even if continuing disproportionately to benefit the poorer Malay community, was welcomed by non-Malays.

However, as had been the case with Abdullah, Najib's efforts to liberalize the economy and reach out to the non-Malay community soon encountered criticism from Malay constituents. In particular, a *bumiputra* economic congress was organized in May 2010 by the Malay Consultative Council—an association comprising many dozens of Malay NGOs—and was attended by Najib. At the congress, the Council openly criticized the NEM, demanding that Najib remain attuned to the Malay community's special rights and its distributive quotas. Ibrahim Ali, the head of Pertubuhan Pribumi Perkasa Malaysia (a nativist organization dedicated to the empowerment of Malaysia's *bumiputra*), delivered a memorandum to Najib, reminding him of the deprivation that Malays continued to suffer and their entitlement to sustained government assistance. Speaking in response, Najib appeared to yield, inviting the Malay Consultative Council to participate in formulating the NEM.

In June 2010 the Government introduced the 10th Malaysia Plan, the country's most important medium-term planning document. Its provisions revealed the extent to which Najib had retreated from his initial liberalizing and unifying aims. In a 428-page document, the Plan lauded the NEP for 'overcoming past obstacles and driving the national forward economically and socially'. The GTP and the NEM were mentioned only fleetingly. The document declared that the Government would 'continue to support Malaysian companies to emerge as regional champions', appearing to highlight the centrality that the state would retain in driving economic growth. Moreover, although blurring the notion of stark quotas that had been imposed by earlier affirmative action programmes, the Plan also pledged that, in advancing the 'Bumiputera agenda', attention would now be given to promoting the 'new Bumiputera middle class'. Nevertheless, although the record and underlying principles of the NEP remained sacrosanct, the 10th Malaysia Plan did note the need for 'fresh approaches' and 'market friendly mechanisms'. The document also noted the Government's commitment to helping the poorest 40% of the population, irrespective of ethnicity.

However, the budget for 2011, announced in October 2010, defied liberalizing aims by specifying vast new spending commitments. The reforms contained in the ETP were ignored, with new public works projects now emphasized as the primary means of driving economic expansion. In view of the lavish spending, some observers interpreted the budget as a harbinger of early elections. Furthermore, the final instalment of the NEM, which was released at the end of 2010, abruptly restored to prominence the 30% quota on *bumiputra* equity ownership, a mainstay of the NEP in an apparent attempt to re-energize Malay support in advance of a possible early election; however, it also revived non-Malay resentment. The President of the MCA, Datuk Seri Dr Chua Soi Lek, complained openly of Malay 'supremacy', while demanding more genuine power-sharing in Barisan.

Perhaps most striking was the reactivation in mid-2011 of Bersih (see above), relaunched as 'Bersih 2.0', in advance of a major rally, described by Bersih as the 'Walk for Democracy'. The resumption of activity from Bersih, which was now chaired by Ambiga Sreenevasan, a former President of the Malaysian Bar Council and recipient of an International Women of Courage Award from the US Department of State, was in part motivated by the holding of state elections in Sarawak in April, Bersih being prohibited from monitoring the polls. However, despite doubts over the propriety with which the election in Sarawak had been conducted, the BN state government, led for three decades by Chief Minister Taib Mahmud, suffered a set-back in the contest, with its representation in the state assembly declining from 63 of the 71 seats to 55. Pledging effectively to address rural poverty issues, Anwar Ibrahim's PKR led the People's Alliance to win 15 seats—the best result achieved by an opposition party in Sarawak since the 1980s.

Asserting that the Election Commission had failed to address the many shortcomings in electoral procedures that had initially been identified in 2007, Bersih demanded the improvement of the electoral roll, an extension of the campaign period to a minimum of 21 days, reform of the postal voting system and mandatory use of indelible ink at polling stations. After meeting with the Yang di-Pertuan Agong and negotiating with the police, Bersih leaders believed that they had obtained permission to hold the rally in Kuala Lumpur's Stadium Merdeka, thereby reducing the risk of street protests and violence. However, the police subsequently withdrew this permission, and Bersih came under severe criticism from various Malay nationalist groups, including the youth division of UMNO and Perkasa. Perkasa leader Ibrahim Ali was reported to have stated: 'There will be a clash. If that happens, so much the better.' Najib and Minister of Home Affairs Hishammuddin Hussein also warned that the rally was illegal and would result in chaos. The police arrested some 150 Bersih supporters in late June and early July 2011 prior to the rally. Despite the police action, designated 'Operation Erase Bersih', the protest took place as planned on 9 July, attended by an estimated 10,000–20,000 people. The police reacted with ferocity, making extensive use of tear gas and water cannon. Nearly 1,700 demonstrators were arrested, among whom were Bersih's leaders, including Ambiga and PAS President Abdul Hadi Awang. Anwar Ibrahim was reported to have suffered minor injuries when attempting to flee. Najib dismissed the rally as representing only a minority of Malaysians, while Hishammuddin Hussein commended the police for their 'restraint'. Nevertheless, in view of the outcome of the Sarawak state election and the intensity of the Bersih 2.0 rally, at mid-2011 it appeared unlikely that the Government would risk calling an early general election in late 2011 or early 2012.

FOREIGN RELATIONS

Malaysia effected a major realignment of its external alliances after it achieved independence in 1957. Whereas the country formerly enjoyed a strong relationship with the Western powers, notably the United Kingdom, it began, in the years following independence, to show a greater commitment towards its neighbours in South-East Asia and to develop closer links with the emerging powers of eastern Asia.

In the early and middle years of the 1960s the newly formed Federation confronted major challenges from Indonesia and the Philippines: in surmounting those challenges, Malaysia was assisted by Commonwealth military forces, composed mainly of British troops. Malaysia's pro-Western orientation was illustrated by its support of US involvement in Viet Nam, and by the absence of formal diplomatic relations with any communist countries, including the USSR and the People's Republic of China. The shift in Malaysia's foreign policy commenced in 1970, following the British Government's decision to withdraw British military forces 'east of Suez', including those in the Malaysia-Singapore area, and the reduction, and subsequent complete withdrawal, of US land forces from Viet Nam. The Western withdrawal was accompanied in the early 1970s by the emergence of China and Japan as major political and economic influences in South-East Asia. Diplomatic relations between Malaysia and the People's Republic of China were established in 1974, when the latter undertook not to interfere in Malaysia's internal affairs.

The most important development in this period was the formation of a regional grouping in South-East Asia in 1967, the Association of Southeast Asian Nations (ASEAN), the founding members of which were Malaysia, Indonesia, the Philippines, Thailand and Singapore; Brunei joined in January 1984. ASEAN was primarily concerned with economic development, although co-operation in foreign policy issues increased rapidly. The organization represented its members' political solidarity in opposing the Vietnamese occupation of Cambodia (then Kampuchea), and played a significant role in negotiations prior to the Vietnamese withdrawal from Cambodia, effected in 1989. Following the admission of Viet Nam to ASEAN in 1995, there was a general expectation that Laos, Cambodia and Myanmar (formerly Burma) would follow in due course. Initially, Malaysia preferred to make admission dependent on stable and reasonably democratic conditions in the candidate countries, but by mid-1996 it had come to favour rapid and unconditional admission, partly because Malaysian firms had become major investors in Myanmar. This policy led to verbal clashes with the USA and other Western countries, which wished to see Myanmar excluded until its observance of human rights improved. In the event, Myanmar and Laos were admitted to ASEAN in July 1997. Malaysia then pressed to have Myanmar accepted as a participant at the 1998 Asia-Europe Meeting (ASEM) in London, threatening to boycott the meeting if Myanmar were excluded, as the British Government announced would be the case. However, by the time the summit took place, the Asian financial crisis had intervened and the issue of Myanmar's participation was postponed. Cambodia joined ASEAN in 1999. In July 2002 Malaysia offered to host a permanent secretariat for ASEAN + 3, the informal grouping linking ASEAN with China, Japan and the Republic of Korea. However, at a meeting of ASEAN ministers of foreign affairs in Brunei, the proposal was rejected on the grounds that it might weaken ASEAN as an institution.

In January 1992, at the fourth ASEAN summit, the member states agreed to establish an ASEAN Free Trade Area (AFTA) within 15 years. (AFTA was formally established on 1 January 2002.) In July 1994 the first ASEAN Regional Forum (ARF) was convened in Bangkok, Thailand; the ARF was expected to provide a platform for the discussion of political and security issues. Malaysia's and Mahathir's role within ASEAN and within groupings of developing nations over trade and security issues continued to expand. Mahathir's articulation of his proposal to establish an East Asia Economic Caucus (EAEC), a trade group that was to exclude the USA, Australia and New Zealand, angered both the US Government (which was anxious to continue to promote the US-inspired Asia-Pacific Economic Cooperation—APEC) and other nations. In July 1993, at the ASEAN ministerial meeting, a consensus was reached on the EAEC. It was agreed, despite the continuing reluctance of Japan to participate, that the EAEC should operate as an East Asian interest group within APEC. The EAEC formally came into existence at an ASEAN informal summit in November 2000. Its economic significance was limited by the aftermath of the Asian economic crisis, but it provided an opportunity for Malaysia's proposal for the establishment of a trans-Asian railway, which would promote economic integration in the region.

In the early 1990s international attention focused on the issues surrounding the logging of the rainforest and its effect on the lives and land of indigenous communities. Prior to the

UN Conference on Environment and Development in Rio de Janeiro, Brazil, in June 1992, this issue received much attention both within Malaysia and internationally. Mahathir became the effective international spokesperson for the developing countries against those of the industrialized North. In April 1992 he chaired a meeting on the environment attended by the developing nations, in Kuala Lumpur, in which he led demands for a withdrawal of international criticism on such issues as logging in developing nations, and appealed to the countries of the North to stop their 'imperialist agendas' and to adjust their own consumption and production patterns to avoid environmental pollution. This message, in the form of the Kuala Lumpur Declaration, which also included a rejection of the linking of development aid with human rights improvements, was taken to the Rio Conference. Prior to the 1995 election, Mahathir also offered sharp criticism of what he termed the continuing racism, hedonism and immorality of Western countries. However, Malaysia also hosted an annual 'International Dialogue' between heads of state of developing countries and senior international business executives, which acted as a forum for seeking practical solutions to the problems of globalization. During 2000 Mahathir argued that the next meeting of the World Trade Organization (WTO) should be postponed until problems arising from existing agreements had been solved. He strongly condemned the West over what he depicted as its abandonment of the Muslims in Bosnia and Herzegovina and sought, without conspicuous success, to co-ordinate a more vigorous response by the international Muslim community to the crisis. Although Mahathir formally wrote to the Indonesian President, Suharto, to protest against the smoke that disrupted commerce and daily life in much of Malaysia in September 1997, Malaysia's public criticism of Indonesia was muted, perhaps because its own environmental record was vulnerable to criticism.

From the mid-1990s relations with Singapore underwent some strain, in part owing to several incidents in which Singaporean officials were openly critical of Malaysia. For example, in mid-1996 Singapore's former Prime Minister, Lee Kuan Yew, stated that a reunification of Singapore and Malaysia might be possible and desirable if Malaysia abandoned its policy of preference for *bumiputra*. The first volume of Lee's memoirs, published in September 1998, also contained criticisms of Malaysian leaders of the 1950s and 1960s, provoking a further deterioration in relations. Relations were further strained in 1998 when Singapore unilaterally transferred its immigration officials from Tanjong Pagar railway station in Singapore to a modern facility near the Malaysian border. Other bilateral problems included Malaysia's failure to provide a formal agreement on water supply to Singapore and Singapore's refusal to allow Peninsular Malaysians to withdraw mandatory savings until the age of 55 even if they left Singapore, a rule that did not apply to other foreign workers. Most of these issues were resolved in a treaty signed on 4 September 2001. However, during 2002 the two sides clashed again over allegations that land reclamation work being carried out by Singapore was impeding access to Malaysian ports, and over rival plans for replacing the causeway linking the two countries with one or more bridges. In 2003 Malaysia referred the issue to the International Tribunal on the Law of the Sea, but in 2005, after the accession of Abdullah Badawi (who had a pre-existing cordial relationship with his Singaporean counterpart, Lee Hsien Loong), Malaysia withdrew its claim and the two nations settled the dispute bilaterally. However, contention relating to the bridge project re-emerged in January 2006 when the Malaysian Government announced that construction of the Malaysian side of the bridge was to commence, without Singaporean approval. Construction began in March, but was halted by Abdullah Badawi in the following month, raising hopes of a future resolution to the dispute between the neighbouring states.

In May 1997 the Malaysian and Indonesian Governments agreed to refer to the International Court of Justice (ICJ) their conflicting claims to the sovereignty of two small islands off the coast of Borneo, Sipadan and Ligitan. The ICJ's judgment, handed down in December 2002, awarded the islands to Malaysia on the basis of occupation and use before the dispute had arisen. Further disagreement with Indonesia arose in 2004 when Malaysia awarded an oil concession to Royal Dutch Shell covering disputed waters near the island of Ambalat, off the coast of Sabah. In March 2005 Indonesia sent four F-16 fighter planes and seven warships to the area while Malaysia deployed two warships. Another territorial claim pursued through the ICJ was the dispute with Singapore over the island of Batu Puteh (Pedra Branca). The two countries had originally agreed to refer the dispute to the ICJ in September 1994, but the formal agreement was signed only in February 2003. In May 2008 the ICJ ruled that Batu Puteh belonged to Singapore, while Malaysia had sovereignty over some rock formations known as Middle Rocks. Negotiations were to be held between the two countries over another outcrop, South Ledge, sovereignty over which remained unresolved. In March 1998 Malaysia began to construct a building on Investigator Shoal, a part of the disputed Spratly Islands to which Malaysia, the Philippines and China maintained overlapping claims; Malaysia's move was probably prompted by China's construction of substantial facilities on Mischief Reef further to the north. The discovery of new oil reserves off the northern Borneo coast in 2002 gave immediacy to an unresolved maritime boundary dispute with Brunei.

During the early 1990s, as economic growth increased the demand for labour, Malaysia became an increasingly attractive destination for illegal immigrants from nearby countries, especially the Philippines, Indonesia and Bangladesh. About 1m. illegal immigrants were believed to be living in Malaysia in the mid-1990s. By 1995 both the number of illegal immigrants and their treatment (by employers and, if they were apprehended, by the Government) had become an issue of increasing public concern. In June 1996 the Malaysian and Indonesian authorities agreed on joint measures to limit the flow of illegal workers into Malaysia. Malaysia repatriated the remaining Vietnamese refugees from its territory by the UN-imposed deadline of June 1996; some had been held in camps since 1975. The financial crisis led Malaysia to prepare plans for the large-scale repatriation of both illegal and now unemployed legal immigrant workers. By March 1998 17,000 Indonesians had been arrested as part of 'Operation Nyah (Go Away)' and naval patrols of the coastline were increased.

The restriction of illegal immigration to Malaysia became more stringent during 2001, and an estimated 120,000 illegal immigrants were expelled from the country. In early 2002 the Government ended the legal recruitment of labourers from Indonesia and began a campaign of bulldozing squatter settlements; sea patrols to interdict people-smugglers also increased in number. The Malaysian authorities routinely expelled illegal immigrants from Myanmar across its northern border into Thailand, despite compelling evidence that some were being captured by criminal gangs and held for ransom, sold into slavery or smuggled back into Malaysia. In April the Government announced that it would take yet firmer action against illegal immigrants, who were estimated to number between 300,000 and 1m. The move was prompted by several factors. Malaysia's economic difficulties (see Economy) had led to increased rates of unemployment and public pressure for a 'Malaysians First' policy. Members of the public also perceived the illegal workers as being responsible for rising crime levels; the perception of the immigrants as being unruly was reinforced when clashes occurred between police and Indonesian illegal immigrants in a detention centre in December 2001, and in a textile factory in January 2002. Moreover, especially after the 11 September 2001 terrorist attacks on the USA, the Government feared that the immigrants might include political and religious militants. Under new legislation that entered into force from 1 August 2002, illegal immigrants risked punishments of fines, whipping or prison terms, although an amnesty was granted to those with confirmed tickets to leave the country by the end of the month. For the first time the employers of illegal immigrants were subject to the imposition of heavy penalties.

Many of the immigrants came from Indonesia and the Philippines, and both countries sent ships to assist in the repatriation of their citizens. Bangladeshis and Muslim Rohingyas from Myanmar were also affected. There was much controversy over the conditions in which illegal immigrants were held in Malaysian detention centres, and both Indonesia and the Philippines formally complained to Malaysia concerning the treatment of their nationals. Government officials estimated that about 300,000 people, mainly Indonesians, had left the country prior to the implementation of the new legislation. On the eve of the deadline imposed for departure, hundreds of illegal immigrants, mainly Acehnese from Indonesia and Rohingyas, sought certification of refugee status from the office of the UN High Commissioner for Refugees (UNHCR) in Kuala Lumpur, claiming that they would suffer discrimination if they returned to their own countries. However, Malaysia was not a signatory of the 1951 UN Convention on Refugees, and seemed unlikely to accept any immigrants on these grounds. An estimated 1.7m. foreign workers remained legally in Malaysia, but by 2003 the departure of illegal workers had begun to cause labour shortages in some sectors, leading Malaysia to negotiate agreements with Indonesia and the Philippines to allow illegal immigrants to continue working under some circumstances. In 2004 Malaysia offered an 'amnesty' to illegal residents, promising that they would not be fined or otherwise punished if they left the country before 31 December 2004 (subsequently extended to 1 March 2005). An estimated 400,000 people left the country during this amnesty period. The expulsions resumed in March 2005, and within two weeks 2,696 people were reported to have been detained; 45 were later sentenced to one or two strokes of the cane. Both the Indonesian authorities and Malaysian human rights groups protested that caning was a degrading colonial legacy that should be abolished. Indonesia also protested that Malaysian employers were exploiting the illegal status of workers to refuse them wages that were due to them. At mid-2005 it was estimated that about 500,000 illegal immigrants remained in the country.

Relations with Thailand were strained in early 1996 by Malaysia's construction of a wall along its border with Thailand to stem the arrival of illegal immigrants. Thailand accused Malaysia of arbitrarily expelling illegal immigrants to Thai territory and of making insufficient efforts to prevent Muslim separatists in southern Thailand from using Malaysian territory as a sanctuary. However, in January 1998 three Thai Muslim separatists were arrested by the Malaysian authorities and deported to Thailand, and in April an agreement was signed jointly to develop a huge offshore gas and oilfield in a disputed area of the Gulf of Thailand. The arrest of the former Deputy Prime Minister and Minister of Finance, Anwar Ibrahim, in September 1998 prompted critical reactions from President B. J. Habibie of Indonesia and President Joseph Estrada of the Philippines, both of whom had enjoyed good relations with Anwar; for the most part, however, Malaysia was able to invoke the ASEAN custom that implicitly prohibited interference in the internal affairs of fellow member countries. The Malaysian Government reacted indignantly in November when the US Vice-President, Al Gore, expressed support for the *reformasi* movement while attending an APEC summit meeting in Malaysia. Relations with the Philippines were further strained in 2000 after Muslim separatists from the southern Philippines kidnapped 21 tourists, 12 of them foreigners, from the island of Sipadan, off Sabah, in April. Malaysia complained that lack of security in the Philippines had damaged its interests. Meanwhile, Malaysia's relations with China became closer during May 1999, when the two countries signed a 12-point co-operation agreement. Mahathir and the Chinese Prime Minister, Zhu Rongji, exchanged state visits later in the year. The rapprochement partly reflected the countries' shared suspicion of economic liberalization. However, criticism from Western countries over the conviction of Anwar on sodomy charges in August 2000 left Malaysia temporarily somewhat isolated in world affairs.

The attacks on the US cities of New York and Washington, DC, on 11 September 2001 initially prompted speculation that the USA would identify Malaysia as a country that harboured terrorists, especially after Mahathir described the attacks as a retaliation for Israel's 'state terrorism'. Evidence was also discovered revealing that two of those who had perpetrated the September attacks had stayed in the home of a former Malaysian army captain in 2000. Malaysia criticized the USA for killing innocent people during its attacks on the Taliban regime in Afghanistan. In the event, however, the Malaysian Government's swift suppression of the KMM allowed it to be perceived as clearly opposing Islamist extremism. Malaysia also promised to co-operate with the USA in tracing al-Qa'ida funds in Malaysia. In May 2002 Mahathir visited the USA to reinforce the improved bilateral relationship and to sign a formal agreement to co-operate in combating terrorism, but he warned the West against becoming 'impatient' with Malaysia over democratization and human rights issues, stating that a transition to democracy was, invariably, a gradual process. The two sides later announced plans for the establishment of a joint anti-terrorism training centre in Malaysia to serve the ASEAN countries. The Malaysian Government also initiated a major expansion of the country's military capacity, purchasing both submarines and F/A-18 fighter jets. Malaysia also signed an anti-terrorism agreement with Australia in August 2002, but relations were strained by official warnings against travel to Malaysia issued by the Australian Department of Foreign Affairs and Trade, which Malaysia considered to be unwarranted. In December the Malaysian Government also agreed to work closely with that of Indonesia. Mahathir was strongly critical of US policies on Iraq both before and after the US-led invasion in early 2003 had taken place, and the UMNO youth wing collected 2.5m. signatures for a petition against the offensive. However, Mahathir retained surprisingly good relations with the USA, owing to his determination to prevent Malaysia from becoming a haven for groups identified as posing a terrorist threat.

Mahathir's last months in office were marked by several verbal clashes with neighbouring countries and world powers. In a speech at the summit meeting of the Organization of the Islamic Conference (OIC), held in Malaysia just before his retirement, in October 2003, the Prime Minister accused Jews of ruling the world by proxy and of using others to fight and die for them. He was consequently condemned by the US Congress, while the US Senate voted to reduce military aid to Malaysia. In a speech at the APEC summit meeting in Bangkok shortly afterwards, he criticized globalization, the WTO and free trade, calling instead for fair trade. Meanwhile, in August of that year Mahathir signed a contract to replace the Malaysian half of the causeway to Singapore with a bridge that would enable shipping to pass through the strait separating the two countries (see above). He also accused Singapore of profiteering in the complex arrangements by which Malaysia supplies untreated water to Singapore and receives some treated water in exchange. Malaysia's relations with Singapore were further strained by that country's programme of land reclamation, which produced changes in the median-line maritime boundary between the two countries. Malaysia came under international pressure, on the other hand, over its failure to recognize as refugees Acehnese who were fleeing the Indonesian military operations in Aceh province.

Mahathir's successor as Prime Minister, Abdullah Badawi, soon adopted a less dogmatic approach to international relations, seeking a rapprochement with both Singapore and Australia. Progress was made in resolving the protracted dispute with Singapore over water supplies, while negotiations began with Australia concerning a possible bilateral free trade agreement. As Chairman of the OIC, Abdullah Badawi sought to stress the commitment of Muslim states to suppressing Islamist terrorism, while insisting that Islam itself was not a religion of extremism or violence. His concept of *Islam Hadhari* ('Civilizational Islam'), emphasizing cultural and scientific achievement over strategies of violence, was thus adopted by the OIC as part of a reform process. In August 2004 Abdullah became the first Muslim Prime Minister to address the World Council of Churches, which was meeting in Kuala Lumpur. He urged moderation and resistance to extremism, hatred and violence, and he broke down with emotion during his speech. Relations with Thailand were strained when Thai troops reportedly killed 112 Islamist militants in southern Thailand in April 2004, and Malaysia offered sanctuary to Muslim Thais seeking refuge. Thailand accused Malaysia of harbouring Islamist militants. In response, Malaysia agreed to closer co-operation with Thailand in its operations against Islamists in southern Thailand. The situation was exacerbated in October when seven Muslim protesters died during clashes with the Thai security forces outside a police station in Tak Bai,

Narathiwat province (which borders on Malaysia), and 78 detainees suffocated or were crushed to death during the course of their transfer to an army barracks in overcrowded vehicles. In January 2005 Thai Prime Minister Thaksin demanded that Malaysia relinquish to Thailand the Islamist militant, Abdul Rahman Ahmad, also known as Deramae Koteh, who was accused of being the mastermind behind Muslim unrest in southern Thailand. Ahmad had been arrested in Malaysia in early January and was being held under the ISA. At a meeting conducted by UNHCR in September, Thaksin confronted Abdullah Badawi and criticized UNHCR for its handling of a dispute that arose between Malaysia and Thailand concerning 131 Thai Muslim asylum-seekers who had fled to Malaysia to escape the ongoing violence in Thailand's southernmost regions (see History of Thailand). Malaysia's relations with Thailand seemed to improve slightly when Thaksin was ousted by the Thai military in September 2006.

Meanwhile, relations with Indonesia, troubled by reports of poor treatment of Indonesian domestic workers in Malaysia, were eased by Deputy Prime Minister and Minister of Defence Najib Tun Razak's agreement to new protection measures. In November 2003 Abdullah Badawi had dismissed the editor of the *New Straits Times* over an article that accused the Government of Saudi Arabia of hypocrisy, profligacy and of encouraging Islamist extremism. The Saudi Government had strongly criticized Malaysia and had sharply reduced Malaysia's quota for the *Hajj* (pilgrimage to Mecca). In April 2004 Najib reacted sharply to a suggestion from the US naval commander in the Pacific, Adm. Thomas Fargo, that US warships might patrol the Straits of Melaka to guard against terrorist attacks. Subsequently, however, he agreed to closer collaboration with the USA against terrorist groups and permitted the USA to station customs officials at two Malaysian posts to inspect US-bound cargoes. Negotiations between Malaysia and the USA over a free trade agreement made little progress in 2007, an outcome that was welcomed by some Malaysian NGOs, including the Consumers Association of Penang.

On a multilateral level, while Malaysia chaired the OIC in 2005, Prime Minister Abdullah Badawi extolled the merits of *Islam Hadhari* to the membership of that organization. Malaysia also chaired the Non-aligned Movement (NAM) in 2003–06 and proposed the creation of a Centre on Gender and Development. In December 2005 Kuala Lumpur hosted the 11th ASEAN summit meeting, followed by the inaugural East Asia Summit, essentially extending the ASEAN + 3 approach to Australia and other countries, thereby presaging what had been canvassed as an East Asian Community.

Malaysia intensified its criticisms of Myanmar's Government during 2007–08 over the latter's refusal to release opposition leader Aung San Suu Kyi from house arrest or, more generally, to liberalize political life. Relations with Indonesia also became strained during this period, with Malaysia accused of having treated illegal migrant workers from Indonesia with extreme callousness. The Malaysian Government was also slow to act in cases of alleged abuse of Indonesian domestic staff by their Malaysian employers. Indonesia thus complained regularly of Malaysia's 'arrogance' in their dealings. However, relations with Thailand improved during this period, as tensions over the fate of Muslims in Thailand's southern provinces subsided.

Malaysia's relations with China continued to strengthen during 2007–08, with trade between them growing by about 20% per year. However, while Malaysia's petroleum exports to China expanded, exports of manufactured goods declined, leaving it with a widening bilateral trade deficit. There was a similar imbalance in investment patterns, with Malaysian businesses investing far more capital in China than China had invested in Malaysia.

With competing claims to sovereignty over the Spratly Islands in the South China Sea, Malaysia continued discreetly to support a sustained US naval presence in the region. However, deliberations with the USA, initiated in 2006, over a proposed free trade agreement remained tenuous. A ninth round of negotiations, scheduled for November 2008, was postponed by the US authorities and, following the election of Barack Obama as the new US President and the formation of a new US Administration in early 2009, the prospects for the agreement remained uncertain.

Malaysia's most important bilateral relationship has remained that with Singapore, owing to their mutual dealings in investment and employment. Yet relations have often been strained, not least by territorial disputes. In May 2008 the ICJ determined sovereignty over Batu Puteh and Middle Rocks (see above). Malaysia's Government publicly professed satisfaction with the outcome, but was reported to have been severely disappointed. Meanwhile, South Ledge appeared to be the next rocky outcrop over which possession would be negotiated. In August 2009 the Malaysian Minister of Foreign Affairs, Datuk Anifah bin Haji Aman, revealed that a government committee had twice met with Singapore officials in order to advance discussions over territorial waters and economic exclusive zones.

Further afield, in February 2009 Rais Yatim, the then Minister of Foreign Affairs, met with his Australian counterpart, Stephen Smith, in Canberra, where Rais declared that the strains that had marred bilateral relations over the past several decades had passed. It was widely suggested in the media that the refusal of Australia's Prime Minister, Kevin Rudd, during the previous year to meet with Anwar Ibrahim had done much to mollify Malaysia's leadership. Rais and Smith discussed restarting negotiations on a free trade agreement that had remained in abeyance since 2006, and the holding of regular meetings between the two countries' respective Ministers of Foreign Affairs.

In January 2009 Prime Minister Abdullah Badawi joined the international condemnation of Israel's invasion of Gaza. Moreover, in protesting against US support for Israel, Muhyiddin Yassin, Malaysian Minister of International Trade and Industry, announced that the Government was to suspend negotiations with the USA on the proposed bilateral free trade agreement. The troubled negotiations had in any event been halted by the USA as it prepared for the transfer of power to the incoming Administration of President Obama. In March, however, the US ambassador to Malaysia stated that the Obama Administration welcomed Malaysia's participation in the Middle East peace process, drawing particular attention to Malaysia's active role in the OIC.

In April 2009, shortly after becoming Prime Minister, Najib declared that Malaysia's foreign policy would conform with the '1Malaysia' concept. What this might mean in practice was not immediately apparent. Although often referred to as a Mahathir's 'protégé', Najib mostly remained reactive within the international arena, in contrast to the foreign policy innovations of Mahathir. Indeed, recognizing the importance of China's rise in the region, one of Najib's first foreign policy decisions was to lead an official mission there. Indeed, his visit signalled the extent to which the bilateral relationship had evolved. Najib's father, Tun Abdul Razak, Malaysia's Prime Minister during the 1970s, had established diplomatic relations with the People's Republic in 1974. During Najib's visit to China in 2009, he hailed the rise of China as a global economic power, and negotiated the partial abolition of visa requirements for holders of diplomatic and official passports. Elsewhere in East Asia, Malaysia's Government joined others in May in urging the Democratic People's Republic of Korea (North Korea) to discontinue its nuclear-testing programme. One month later, however, during a visit to South Korea, Najib declared Malaysia's wish to emulate that country by building a small nuclear reactor for power generation.

Najib also declared Malaysia's willingness to help Iran to regularize its relations with the international community, relations that had been severely strained by the issue of Iran's nuclear programme. In November 2009 Malaysia, along with Cuba and Venezuela, voted against an International Atomic Energy Agency (IAEA) resolution censuring Iran for the covert construction of a uranium enrichment plant; the motion was endorsed by a margin of 25 votes to three. However, the Government subsequently recalled its UN envoy, stating that the vote that he had cast was not in accord with its own position. Malaysia also denied that it was in any way involved with the development of Iran's nuclear technologies.

Under the administration of Najib, the influence of Islam on Malaysia's foreign policy became much less pronounced than under Mahathir and Abdullah. Malaysia thus retreated from its leadership role in the OIC, and began to give more focused attention to secular issues of trade and investment, and to security concerns. In July 2010 Malaysia hosted a joint command US-Malaysian military exercise in Kuantan. Code-named 'KERIS Strike 2010', the exercise indicated a further strengthening of security links between the two countries, reflecting a marked change of policy and a deepening of relations with the USA in the years since Mahathir's departure from office.

In June 2010, after a dispute lasting for decades, the Governments of Malaysia and Singapore reached agreement on an issue regarding land owned by Malayan Railways in Singapore. Malaysia agreed to transfer its station from Tanjong Pagar in central Singapore to a location closer to the causeway linking the two countries across the Strait of Tebrau. A company owned jointly by both countries' respective Governments was scheduled to develop the railway properties. This new co-operation, the terms for which were finalized in mid-2011, and which was hailed as a reflection of significantly improved bilateral relations, boded well for efforts to resolve other contentious issues, most notably the price that Malaysia charged Singapore for water supplies.

However, while the Najib administration improved relations with the USA and Singapore, several domestic developments drew criticism from foreign media and NGOs, with the attacks on churches from January 2010 eliciting particularly strong criticism from Christian groups around the world. However, a source of far greater disquiet among Western governments and legal groups was the ongoing court proceedings against former Deputy Prime Minister Anwar Ibrahim, who, both they and Anwar himself maintained, was the victim of a politically motivated campaign to eliminate the threat that he posed to the UMNO-led ruling coalition. Tensions in relations with Indonesia also emerged over the ongoing issue of the abuse apparently suffered by many Indonesian migrant workers, especially domestic helpers, in Malaysia. An Indonesian NGO organized protests outside the Malaysian embassy and the ambassador's residence in the Indonesian capital, Jakarta, and the Indonesian Government imposed a temporary ban on its nationals from migrating to Malaysia to work. However, Najib responded by reminding Malasyians of the economic and cultural importance of the country's links with Indonesia. He also sought to improve relations with Thailand, following bilateral tension over the latter's strategies in its southernmost Malay-speaking provinces. Such efforts to strengthen Malaysia's relations with its neighbours reflected the increasingly pragmatic, secular and reactive nature of Malaysia's foreign policy—in keeping with the tenor of the '1Malaysia' concept—under the administration of Najib.

Economy

ROKIAH ALAVI

Based on an earlier article by CHRIS EDWARDS

INTRODUCTION

From the mid-1970s Malaysia had one of the most dynamic and fastest-growing economies in Asia, and between 1985 and 1995 it was the eighth fastest-growing economy in the world. In the 25 years following the adoption of the New Economic Policy (NEP) in 1971, Malaysia's gross domestic product (GDP) grew at an average annual rate of about 7%. Between 1985 and 1995 GDP growth averaged more than 8% per annum, which, with the population expanding at a little over 2.5% annually, gave an average annual growth in per caput income of 5.7%. During the 1980s real GDP growth averaged 5% annually, but the growth rate was uneven. The year-by-year GDP growth rate was particularly spectacular until the mid-1990s. However, Malaysia's economy decelerated drastically in 1997 as a result of the regional economic crisis that started in July of that year. The impact of the crisis became more evident in 1998, in which year GDP contracted by 7.4%. However, various government policies helped the economy to recover, and GDP grew by more than 6.0% in both 1999 and 2000. The rate of growth remained steady in subsequent years, with GDP per caput increasing annually by 4%–6% between 2001 and 2007. Despite the adverse economic circumstances that resulted from the global financial crisis from the second half of 2008, the Malaysian economy registered a growth rate of 4.6% in that year. The impact of the crisis became evident in 2009, when the economy contracted by 1.7%. However, the economy recovered in 2010, recording an impressive growth rate of 7.2%, supported by strong domestic demand.

The Sectoral Growth Pattern

Malaysia experienced a substantial change in the sectoral growth pattern following independence, moving from an economy based on agriculture to one based on industry. The change clearly demonstrates the shifts in the emphasis of the country's development strategy.

The agricultural sector, which traditionally provided the impetus for growth in the economy, experienced a continued deceleration in growth rates and hence a reduction in its importance to the economy. The sector's contribution to GDP declined substantially, from 29% in 1970 to 9.3% in 2009, and stood at 10.4% in 2010, according to the Asian Development Bank (ADB). According to official data, the sector grew at an average rate of 5% annually in the 1970s, but the rate of growth declined to 3.8% in the 1980s, 2.0% during 1990–95, 2.2% in 1996 and 3.5% in 1997. The lowest growth recorded was during the crisis period; the sector experienced a contraction of 2.8% in 1998, before recording growth of about 0.5% in 1999. The agricultural sector recovered strongly in 2000, expanding by 6.1%, before contracting by 0.6% in 2001, owing to slower growth in the production of crude palm oil. In 2002 the sector recorded a moderate growth rate of 2.6%, subsequently expanding at rates of between 3% and 6% in 2003–06, before growth slowed to 2.2% in 2007. In 2008 the agricultural sector expanded by 3.8%, primarily owing to a 12.2% increase in palm oil production. The sector grew by just 0.4% in 2009, following a reduction in the output of industrial crops, but recovered partially in 2010, when growth of 1.7% was recorded, aided by high commodity prices.

The manufacturing sector's share of GDP increased significantly from 16.9% in 1975 to 34.4% in 1998, indicating the sector's considerable importance in the context of the economy as a whole. The manufacturing sector continued to contribute between one-quarter and one-third of annual GDP during 1999–2009 and stood at 25.5% in 2010, according to the ADB. According to official data, the manufacturing sector registered the highest rate of output growth during 1971–90, expanding by an average of 10.3% per annum. In 1990–95 the sector grew even faster, recording an average annual growth rate of 13.3%. Sectoral growth declined slightly, to 12.2% in 1996 and 12.5% in 1997. In 1998 the sector contracted by 13.4%, the first decline since 1985; this was due mainly to the economic slowdown in the Asia-Pacific region as a whole. However, the sector recorded strong positive growth of 11.7% and 18.3% in 1999 and 2000, respectively, as a result of a significant increase in external demand as well as sustained strong domestic requirements. The average annual growth rate of the sector subsequently slowed to 4.1% during 2001–05. The growth rate of the manufacturing sector recovered in 2006, to 7.1%, before slowing again in 2007, to 3.1%. The sector registered a lower growth rate of 1.3% in 2008, mainly as a result of a decline in the electrical and electronic sub-sector, and contracted by 9.4% in 2009, owing to the global economic downturn and a significant decline in manufacturing exports from the end of 2008. In 2010 the sector registered robust growth of 11.4%, predominantly owing to expansion in electrical and electronics export-orientated industries and domestic consumption activities.

The services sector has gained in importance over time, with its overall contribution to GDP increasing from 38.3% in 1970 to 46.8% in 1990, and amounting to 46.0% in 2010, according to the ADB. The services sector also expanded rapidly, growing at an average annual rate of 7.6% during 1971–90, 9.3% between 1990 and 1995, and 9.7% and 8.7% in 1996 and 1997, respectively, according to official data; however, as a result of the economic problems of 1997–98, this sector contracted by 0.4% in 1998. In accordance with the strong expansion of the economy as a whole, the services sector grew at a faster rate of 4.5% in 1999 and at an annual rate of between 6% and 7% in 2001–06. In 2007 the sector grew at a faster rate of 9.7%, but growth decelerated to 7.3% in 2008, before slowing further, to 2.6%, in 2009. Strong external and domestic demand contributed to an acceleration of sectoral growth, to 6.8%, in 2010.

The construction sector had a lower average annual growth rate during 1971–90 (6.4%), but this accelerated to 13.3% during 1990–95, and growth was recorded at 14.2% and 9.5% in 1996 and 1997, respectively. In 1998 the sector experienced a contraction in output of 24.5%, mainly as a result of lower aggregate demand. In 1999, however, the sector strengthened owing to various policy measures introduced by the Government, recording a rate of contraction of only 4.4%, and the sector recorded a positive growth rate of 0.6% in 2000. The sector grew at an average annual rate of just 0.5% during 2001–05. In 2006 the sector contracted by 0.5%. The completion of several large infrastructure projects and a substantial reduction in government spending on new and existing projects were significant contributory factors in the weak performance of the sector. However, the expansion of civil engineering activity and the implementation of several projects under the Ninth Malaysia Plan (2006–10, see below) led to a recovery in the sector in 2007, when growth of 4.6% was registered. In 2008 the sector registered slower growth of 2.1%, which was mainly attributable to reduced growth in the civil engineering sub-sector. Fiscal stimulus measures and further implementation of projects under the Ninth Malaysia Plan accelerated sectoral growth to 5.7% in 2009. The construction sector's growth decelerated slightly, to 5.2%, in 2010.

Regional and Rural–Urban Divisions

Regional development strategies implemented since independence have resulted in improved living standards and a higher quality of life for the inhabitants of all states, as well as the reduction of regional disparities. The total population of Malaysia in 2007 was approximately 27.2m.; an estimated 43% of the population resided in the less developed states, with Sabah and Sarawak populated by more than 5m. people. According to the preliminary results of the census conducted in July 2010, the total population had increased to 27.6m. Based on the composite index of development in 2005, the states of Johor (Johore), Perak, Pulau Pinang (Penang), Melaka (Malacca), Negeri Sembilan (Negri Sembilan), Selangor and the Federal Territory of Kuala Lumpur were categorized as more developed states, while Kedah, Kelantan, Pahang, Perlis, Sabah, Sarawak and Terengganu (Trengganu) were categorized as less developed states. The average per caput income of those living in the more developed states was RM 17,410 in 2000, compared with RM 10,893 for the inhabitants of the less developed states. In 2010 the national average per caput income was US $8,140. The overall incidence of poverty has declined significantly from 49.3% in 1970 to 8.7% in 1995, and further to 3.8% in 2009. In that year the mean monthly income of households in the poorest 40% of the population was RM 1,440 ($450).

Malaysia is a rapidly urbanizing society. In 1980 just over one-third of the Malaysian population lived in urban areas, but this had increased to 51% by 1991 and further, to 65%, by 2007. During 1999–2005 the urban population increased at an average annual rate of 3%, much faster than the 2% increase in the population as a whole. Between 1999 and 2004 the average incomes of urban households grew faster (at 27.5% per annum) than those of rural households (at 9.1%). However, since 2004 the rural–urban income gap has narrowed considerably, with higher income growth in rural areas (6.8% between 2004 and 2007) than urban areas (3.3%).

Employment and Income Distribution

The economically active population accounted for 67.0% of the total population of working age in 2007. The Labour Force Survey indicated that 67.4% of the labour force was concentrated in urban areas. The creation of new jobs took place mainly in the services sector, although a substantial number were also created in the manufacturing, agricultural and construction sectors.

Malaysia began to experience persistent labour shortage problems from the second half of the 1990s. The number of registered foreign workers in the labour force had tripled, from 650,000 in 1995 to 2.2m. in 2008 (constituting just under one-fifth of the total work-force), but these figures were widely thought to be underestimates. Foreign workers were predominantly engaged in the manufacturing sector (36%), agricultural (25%) and construction (14%) sectors, while many female employees worked as maids (15%). In 2007 75.6% originated from Indonesia, while those from Nepal and India constituted 14.5% and 9.1%, respectively. Other expatriate workers originated mainly from Bangladesh, Myanmar and Viet Nam. In 2007 35,052 expatriates were hired as professionals, specialists and skilled workers, 48% of whom were engaged in the services sector and 35% in manufacturing. India accounted for the largest number of approved skilled workers (48%), followed by Japan and the People's Republic of China. In terms of occupational groups, directors accounted for the largest number, followed by managers and engineers. The Government has formulated various measures to reduce dependency on foreign workers and aims to reduce the number of foreign workers to 1.5m. by 2015.

In 2010 unemployment in Malaysia averaged 3.2% of the labour force, compared with a rate of 8.7% in 1987; at June 2011 the rate of unemployment stood at 3.2%. The average rate conceals quite considerable disparities among states: for example, Terengganu and Kelantan, in the east of the peninsula, and Sabah and Sarawak all had unemployment rates of 4.5% or more in 2007, whereas the federal capital, Selangor and Pulau Pinang (Penang) had rates of 1.1% or below.

The avowed aim of the NEP was to bring about (over a 20-year period from 1971 to 1990) a redistribution of income and wealth, particularly in favour of the *bumiputra* (indigenous population, mostly Malays), since in 1971 Malays were disproportionately poor. In 1995 about 58% of the total population possessed *bumiputra* status. In terms of reducing absolute poverty, the NEP was successful since, whereas in 1970 almost one-half of the households in Peninsular Malaysia were classified as poor, by 1990 less than one-sixth of Malaysian households were so classified, and by 1995 this had declined further to less than 9%. In 1997 the overall incidence of poverty declined to 6.1%; however, the regional economic crisis led to an increase in this index to 8.5% in 1998. Subsequent favourable economic growth and successful poverty eradication programmes eventually reduced the poverty incidence to 3.6% in 2007. The Ninth Malaysia Plan reported the poverty rate in rural areas to be five times higher than in urban areas. The average monthly income of households living in rural areas (RM 2,283 in 2007) is considerably less than that of urban households (RM 4,356). However, between 1995 and 2007 the incidence of rural poverty decreased from 14.9% to 7.1%, while urban poverty declined from 3.6% to 2.0%. The proportion of households living in 'hardcore' poverty (defined as having less than one-half of the poverty line income) has also declined in recent years, from 3.9% in 1990 to 0.7% in 2007. Between 1995 and 2007 the incidence of rural 'hardcore' poverty declined from 3.6% to 1.4%, while in urban areas it decreased from 0.9% to 0.3%.

In terms of reducing relative poverty, the NEP was less successful. Between 1970 and 2004 income distribution in

Malaysia generally remained unequal, with the 'Gini coefficient' (a measure of economic disparity within a society, whereby zero represents total equality and one equals total inequality) worsening from 0.446 in 1990 to 0.462 in 2004. The gap between the two major ethnic groups, i.e. Chinese and *bumiputra*, is high, although it has narrowed since 1970. The average monthly income of *bumiputra* households was the lowest in 2004, at RM 2,711, compared with an average for Chinese and Indian households of RM 4,437 and RM 3,456, respectively. In the 10th Malaysia Plan (2011–15) the Government stated that the income disparity ratio between *bumiputra* and Chinese households had declined from 1:2.29 in 1970 to 1:1.38 in 2009, while the comparable ratio between *bumiputra* and Indian households had declined from 1:1.77 to 1:1.10 during the same period.

Meanwhile, in 1991 the NEP was replaced by the National Development Policy (NDP), which was in turn replaced by the National Vision Policy (NVP) in 2000. Under both the NDP and the NVP, there was less rhetorical emphasis on *bumiputra* preferences, but both provided for a continuation of the NEP's strategy of encouraging the emergence of a sizeable core of Malay entrepreneurs. (One of the original objectives of the NEP had been to achieve 30% *bumiputra* equity ownership—see Development and Planning, below.) Furthermore, there was a widespread belief that the beneficiaries of preferences consisted disproportionately of prominent politicians and their close associates. The NVP was abandoned, and the NEP reinstated, in 2006. However, the Government announced in June 2009 that certain aspects of the NEP were to be abandoned, as a result of which nearly 30 important service subsectors, including tourism, health and transport, would no longer be required to reserve 30% of their shares for *bumiputra* beneficiaries.

AGRICULTURE, FORESTRY AND FISHING

In 1995 it was officially reported that a little under 19m. ha of land in Malaysia was under forest, compared with about 20.5m. ha in 1980. This 19m. ha represented just under 60% of Malaysia's total land area (of 33m. ha). The strength of agricultural production in Malaysia lies in the large plantations of commercial crops such as rubber, oil palm, cocoa and pineapple. These crops occupy most of the arable land. The area used for cultivation of agricultural commodities in 2000 was 6m. ha or about 18% of the total land area, of which 8% was under oil palm cultivation, 5% rubber, 2% paddy and 1% each under cocoa, coconuts and fruit. The land usage for agriculture increased substantially to 6.6m. ha in 2007, mainly owing to the expansion in plantations of oil palm, coconuts, vegetables and fruits.

The contribution of agriculture, forestry and fishing to total export earnings has declined rapidly, from 53% in 1973 to 7.5% in 2008. The traditional dominance of rubber, which provided almost one-half of Malaysia's export earnings in 1961, continues to be eroded. In 2010 rubber accounted for only 1.4% of total exports and 13.2% of total agricultural exports. The most significant export-earner of all agricultural commodities is palm oil, constituting 65.2% of agricultural exports, and 7.1% of total exports, in 2010.

Rubber

Rubber, a principal export of Malaysia since colonial times, has experienced a relative decline in recent decades. Since the 1960s there has been considerable replanting of rubber land with other crops, especially oil palm. As a result, the area under rubber declined from 2m. ha in 1980 to 1.66m. ha in 1997, and decreased further, to 1.03m. ha, in 2010. About 77% of the land under rubber is in Peninsular Malaysia and only 23% in East Malaysia. The contribution of rubber production to national GDP has declined substantially, from 5% in the early 1980s to 0.4% in 2005. However, rubber remains important in a socio-economic context, especially in terms of providing job opportunities. In 2010 about 94% of total rubber output was produced by smallholdings, with the remainder produced by estates. The sector also has strong linkages to domestic, downstream, rubber-based industries such as those manufacturing rubber gloves, tyres and tubes, as well as rubber footwear. Malaysia's most significant rubber export product is rubber gloves; the country is believed to control around two-thirds of the global rubber glove market, with key manufacturers including Top Glove Corporation Bhd, Supermax, Kossan, Hartalega, Latex Partners and Adventure. Local producers of tyres and related products include Sime Darby Bhd and Silverstone Bhd. In 2010 Malaysia's rubber exports totalled RM 9,210m. Malaysia is the third largest producer of natural rubber in the world, after Thailand and Indonesia, with a 9.4% share of world output in 2010. China is the main importer of Malaysian rubber and rubber products, purchasing 38.4% of the total exports from this sector in 2010. Other major buyers are the European Union (EU), the Republic of Korea (South Korea), the USA, Iran and Brazil, with market shares of 26.0%, 5.4%, 4.4%, 4.3% and 3.0%, respectively.

Palm Oil

Since the early 1960s, when the Government and the private sector began to diversify agriculture away from rubber, palm oil output has increased substantially, with an average annual growth rate in production of 19.6% between 1970 and 1980. As a result, Malaysia has become the largest producer and exporter of palm oil, accounting for 40% of world production in 2010, and for 46% of world exports of palm oil.

Most crude palm oil comes from Peninsular Malaysia, which accounted for an estimated 55.0% of the country's production (or 8.2m. metric tons) in 2005. Sarawak produced 1.4m. tons, or 9.4% of the total, in that year, while Sabah produced 5.3m. tons, or 35.6% of the total. The total area planted with oil palm in 2010 was estimated at almost 4.8m. ha, of which 4.2m. ha were matured holdings. In terms of ownership, the industry is dominated by private estates, which constituted 60% of the total planted in 2009. Until 2007 there were four large oil palm corporations in Malaysia—Kumpulan Guthrie Bhd, Golden Hope Plantations Bhd, IOI Corporation Bhd and Sime Darby Bhd; the equity of plantation companies was largely under Malaysian ownership and they were primarily owned by Perbadanan Nasional Bhd and the Employee Provident Fund. In 2007 Sime Darby, Kumpulan Guthrie and Golden Hope were merged under the ownership of a private entity, Sime Darby Bhd, to create the world's largest listed palm oil producer, accounting for 8% of global production. Other palm oil producers are mainly smallholders organized under the Federal Land Development Authority, the Federal Land Consolidation and Rehabilitation Authority and the Rubber Industry Smallholders Development Authority; various state land schemes accounted for 27.4% of the total area planted with oil palm in 2009, with independent smallholders and state agencies owning 12.6%.

After 1975 the Government attempted to change the emphasis of the industry from planting and exporting crude palm oil to producing, refining, manufacturing and selling oil-based products. Consequently, by the early 1990s there were 264 operational palm oil mills, 54 palm oil refineries and a growing oleochemical industry. By 1996 there were 290 mills in the country. Labour shortages were becoming a serious problem as workers moved to urban areas in pursuit of higher wages; on some estates migrant foreign labour accounted for up to 70% of the work-force. However, Malaysian plantation workers were paid more than three times the amount earned by their Indonesian counterparts in 1993, and Indonesian labour remained a cheaper option despite a government levy payable for every foreign worker employed. Another way in which Malaysian companies were able to take advantage of cheaper Indonesian labour was by investing in projects in Indonesia. Malaysian and Indonesian firms co-signed 27 joint venture agreements and memoranda of understanding to develop 1.5m. ha of oil palm, but in early 1997 the Indonesian Government imposed a 'freeze' on Malaysian investment in the oil palm sector, stating that it had reached an unacceptably high level. Other such joint ventures are in India, the Philippines, Papua New Guinea, Latin America and Africa.

In May 2000 the Malaysian Palm Oil Board (MPOB) was established, following the merger of the Palm Oil Registration and Licensing Authority and the Palm Oil Research Institute of Malaysia. The objective of establishing the MPOB was to strengthen the role of agricultural agencies; the Board was expected to undertake research and development, licensing and enforcement of regulations for the industry, and to disseminate information related to palm oil. By 2007 the MPOB had introduced 405 new technologies with a commercialization rate of 32%. In August 2005 the Government announced the National Biofuel Policy. The Government standardized the B5 biodiesel mixture (5% processed palm oil and 95% diesel) for domestic usage, and a pilot project to utilize the B5 biofuel was implemented by selected government agencies. By 2007 the Government had issued 90 licences to companies for the production of biodiesel. However, only seven plants had commenced operations, most of them below capacity. Envo Diesel, a locally made biodiesel, was launched in March 2006, but by mid-2010 it had yet to enter into general use, largely because the high price of crude palm oil had made the production of biodiesel commercially unviable. The Government has agreed to set aside up to 40% of Malaysia's total palm oil production for biodiesel.

In 1980 exports of palm oil totalled RM 2,500m., but they had risen to RM 4,300m. by 1990 and to RM 45,571m. by 2010. Palm oil exports are the largest contributor to total agriculture export earnings, accounting for 65.2% in 2010. Major buyers in 2010 were China (21.9%), Pakistan (12.6%), the Middle East (10.9%), the EU (10.6%) and India (6.7%). In 2008 the Government increased the windfall taxes on oil palm companies from the crude palm oil threshold price of RM 2,000 per metric ton to RM 2,500 per ton for planters in Peninsular Malaysia and to RM 3,000 for those in Sabah and Sarawak. Under the new tax framework, palm oil companies in Peninsular Malaysia were to be charged a 15% tax, while planters in Sabah and Sarawak were to be charged 7.5%. The justification given by the authorities for this disparity was that in Sabah and Sarawak additional sales taxes were imposed on companies by the respective state governments.

Forestry

The production of timber is an important sector of the Malaysian economy. Total sawlog production in 1994 was 36m. cu m, but this declined to 22.1m. cu m in 2007. Output then decreased further to 20.1m. cu m and 16.7m. cu m in the first 11 months of 2008 and 2009, respectively. The central bank, Bank Negara Malaysia (BNM), reported that the decline was principally a result of weaker demand from traditional buyers (mainly from within the Asia-Pacific region). As well as adverse weather conditions, overall production in the late 1990s was also affected by the Government's conservation policy and commitment to the achievement of sustainable forest management by the year 2000, in compliance with the requirements of the International Tropical Timber Organization.

In 2006 Sarawak remained the principal producer of sawlogs, accounting for 62% of total production, with Sabah accounting for 12% and Peninsular Malaysia 26%. The principal markets for Malaysian logs in 2005 were China (which purchased 28.3% of the total), India (25.1%), Japan (19.1%), Taiwan (12.9%) and South Korea (2.0%). To ensure sustainable forest management, the Government initiated a National Forestry Policy in 1978, aimed at encouraging sustainable development of Malaysia's timber resources through forest conservation, the promotion of under-utilized species and the reduction of waste. Successive five-year plans reduced logging targets from 223,000 ha per year for the Fourth Plan (1981–86) to 152,140 ha per year for the 1986–90 period. The annual permissible logging area in permanent forests was reduced to 46,000 ha in Peninsular Malaysia, 60,000 ha in Sabah and 170,000 ha in Sarawak during the Seventh Malaysia Plan period (1996–2000). In addition, logging companies in Sarawak were required to allocate 50% of their output to local processors. This was to increase the domestic value-added of the sector. Further evidence of the government policy of encouraging downstream activity in the forestry sector was apparent in 1993, when the Government introduced for the first time export levies on selected species of timber and veneer. From January 1994 the export of rubberwood was banned, in order to encourage local furniture and panel manufacturing activities.

As a result of these measures, the production of sawlogs declined by 5.6% annually, from 31.8m. cu m in 1995 to 18.4m. cu m in 2009. Accordingly, the production of sawn timber decreased from 7.5m. cu m in 1995 to 3.8m. cu m in 2009. However, rubberwood became a major source of raw material in the furniture and other wood-based industries, with total exports increasing from RM 1,900m. in 1995 to RM 7,620m. in 2009. By 2009 rubberwood furniture accounted for 80% of exports of wooden furniture. In that year Malaysia was the 10th largest exporter of furniture in the world, and second in Asia behind only China.

Although the Government has promoted conservation, Malaysia has attracted international and domestic criticism from anti-tropical-hardwood campaigners for its forestry policies. In response to this, the Malaysian timber industry has established its own certification scheme, operated by the Malaysian Timber Certification Council (MTCC). BNM reported that by the end of 2005 eight states had been awarded the certificate for forest management, and 83 timber companies had been given permission to use the MTCC logo. The objective of certification was to assure buyers of Malaysian timber and timber products that they were derived from sustainable and legal sources. This effort proved successful, and in 2003 Denmark endorsed the certification scheme as one of the accepted schemes in its Environmental Guidelines for Purchasing Tropical Timber. It also received acceptance from the United Kingdom and the Netherlands. One of the most significant challenges to the timber industry was related to trade in ramin timber. In February 2004 the United Kingdom's Environmental Investigation Agency and an Indonesian-based non-governmental organization, Telapak, released a report claiming that Malaysian traders and officials were involved in the smuggling of Indonesian ramin, marketed as being of Malaysian origin, into Malaysia, in direct contravention of a ban on the import of Indonesian logs, which had been introduced in June 2002. The Malaysian Government stressed that it would not condone such activities, and consequently implemented various measures to prevent the entry of illegal logs and timber into the country in future. Aided by these stricter enforcement measures, in 2003 Malaysian officials successfully intercepted 120 cases containing illegal imports, of which 16 cases (417 cu m) were found to contain ramin. Malaysia also supported the EU's Action Plan on Forest Law Enforcement, Governance and Trade. In 2005 the Government announced a RM 200m. grant to establish a forest plantation programme as part of its strategy on implementing sustainable forest management. The forest plantation schemes were to be undertaken by the private sector. About 50% of the area was to be planted with rubberwood; the remainder was to be planted with acacia, teak and sentang.

Subsistence and Other Agriculture

The principal subsistence crop in Malaysia is rice. Malaysia was about 71% self-sufficient in rice in 2009, compared with about 80% self-sufficiency in 1990. The Government aimed to achieve 86% and 100% self-sufficiency by the end of 2010 and 2015, respectively; however, the 2010 target did not appear to have been met, with self-sufficiency levels of just 71.4% reported. In its efforts to facilitate the fulfilment of these targets, the Government had provided incentives worth RM 1,000m. to 220,000 rice planters under the 2009 budget. Furthermore, government subsidies for the rice sector totalled RM 1,472m. in 2008, up from RM 800m. in 2006 and RM 900m. in 2007 (with the latter figure representing 2.2% of total government subsidies in that year). In addition, efforts have been made to upgrade the drainage and irrigation system, new high-yielding varieties of rice have been introduced in an attempt to boost productivity. Poverty is high in the paddy-producing areas, and there is little prospect of overcoming this through paddy production itself. The trend of youths leaving the paddy-producing areas is likely to continue, exacerbating the existing labour shortages in these areas. Nevertheless, unmilled rice production increased from 2.14m. metric tons in 2000 to 2.38m. tons in 2007, before declining slightly to 2.35m. tons in 2008; however, output increased to 2.51m. tons in 2009 and was expected to increase further in 2010. Malaysia remains a net importer of rice and imported about 660,000 tons of rice in 2008, mainly from Thailand (which usually accounts for about 60%), Viet Nam, India and Pakistan. Rice is a controlled item in Malaysia, and the sole importer of rice is

Padiberas Nasional Bhd (BERNAS). Despite demands for the ending of its monopoly, especially in view of the forthcoming liberalization of the rice trade by the Association of Southeast Asian Nations (ASEAN), in accordance with the establishment of the ASEAN Free Trade Area (AFTA) in 2002, BERNAS's import licence was extended for a further 10-year period, with effect from January 2011.

Cocoa production expanded rapidly during the late 1980s to become Malaysia's fourth most important agricultural sub-sector after oil palm, timber and rubber. Production increased from 88,000 metric tons in 1984 to 235,000 tons in 1991, when it accounted for around 7% of total global production, thus making Malaysia the world's fourth largest producer of cocoa in that year (after Côte d'Ivoire, Brazil and Ghana), a position that Malaysia was subsequently unable to maintain. Nevertheless, Malaysia has remained a major cocoa producer and the largest grinding and processing hub in Asia. In 1991 the Malaysian Cocoa Board introduced compulsory grading to control the quality of exports. However, low cocoa prices, the conversion of cocoa-cultivated land to other crops, increasing labour costs and the rising cost of agricultural inputs together resulted in a decrease in Malaysian cocoa production and exports throughout the 1990s. In 2007 cocoa production totalled 35,180 tons (compared with 57,700 tons in 2001). This output was able to meet only about 10% of demand from local industries, with the remaining 90% being imported. In order to promote the production of cocoa and involvement of the smallholders in the sector, the Malaysian Cocoa Board implemented the Cocoa Smallholders' Development Programme. As a result, the number of smallholders involved in the production of cocoa increased to 4,680. In addition, the Government provided the cocoa smallholders with a 100% replanting grant and gave assistance in the form of high-yielding varieties, disease-resistant planting materials and technological support. Under the Ninth Malaysia Plan, the Government offered an incentive of RM 6,500 per ha to those planting new cocoa crops or rehabilitating idle land for cocoa cultivation. According to FAO, output declined to 27,955 tons in 2008 and to 18,152 tons in 2009. In 2010, however, Malaysia was reported to be the largest cocoa processor in Asia and the fifth largest producer in the world.

Pepper production rapidly increased in the late 1980s to reach 31,000 metric tons in 1990. However, production declined by more than 50% to about 15,000 tons in 1995. The decline in output was partly a result of substantial hectarage being replanted to replace old and diseased pepper plants, and also reflected a marginal decrease in the area under cultivation. Malaysia was the fifth largest producer and exporter in the world in 2010, when the country's production and exports totalled about 24,000 and 14,400 tons, respectively. Malaysia produces mainly black pepper, which constitutes 85% of total production. In 2010 Sarawak was by far the largest source of pepper production within Malaysia, accounting for some 95% of total output.

Fruit production has expanded in Malaysia and has more than kept pace with consumption. As a result, in 2010 Malaysia was 138% self-sufficient in fruits (compared with 94% in 2000) and 108% self-sufficient in vegetables (95% in 2000); however, it is a net importer of both fruits and vegetables. The value of fruit and vegetable exports in 2005 was RM 963.5m., while the value of imports was RM 2,315.1m. Vegetables are grown on a small scale largely for domestic consumption, with most cultivation based in Johor, Pahang, Kelantan and Perak; Singapore is the main destination for vegetable exports. A total of 15 different types of fruit were promoted for commercial cultivation, including banana and durian—the principal local fruits, which together account for over two-thirds of fruit output—as well as papaya, pineapple, watermelon, starfruit, mango, rambutan, guava and citrus fruits. Fruit production registered an average annual increase of 6.2% in 1995–2000, rising from 1m. metric tons to 1.4m. tons, while vegetable production recorded a growth rate of 7.2% per annum during the same period. In 2002 production of vegetables and fruits expanded by 19.9% and 4.2%, respectively, owing largely to an expansion in the areas under cultivation, including Permanent Food Production Parks (PFPP). By 2008 more than 7,000 ha of land had been allocated for the development of 45 PFPPs, which involved 764 agro-entrepreneurs. Under the Ninth Malaysia Plan, the production of fruits and vegetables was projected to reach 2.56m. tons and 1.13m. tons, respectively, in 2010. The Government allocated RM 4,000m. to achieving these targets.

In 1990 Malaysia was more than self-sufficient in poultry, pork and egg production, and remained a net exporter in 1995, with the principal market being Singapore. The self-sufficiency level for pork increased from 104% in 1995 to 132% in 2010. In beef and mutton production, in 2010 Malaysia was 28% self-sufficient (compared with 19.2% in 1995) and 10% (compared with 6% in 1995), respectively.

In 2010 Malaysia was about 104% self-sufficient in fishery products (compared with 90% in 1990). Malaysia is a net importer of fisheries products in terms of volume and a net exporter in terms of value. In 2007 the country's total fish production amounted to 1.56m. metric tons. About 80% of the value of fisheries production comes from the sea. Under the Third National Agricultural Policy, aquaculture production was envisaged to increase four-fold, to reach 600,000 tons, in 2010. Since 2000 the Government has been encouraging aquaculture production and, as a result, the share of aquaculture in total fisheries production rose from 13% in 2000 to 19% in 2001 and further to 20% in 2007; the Government hoped to increase the aquaculture industry's contribution to 25% in 2010.

MINING

Mineral output accounts for over 40% of Malaysia's industrial production and accounted for 7.2% of total GDP in 2010, with about 80% of this being accounted for by petroleum. The mining sector's contribution to GDP remained consistent, at approximately 14% during 2005–07, before increasing to 17% in 2008.

Tin

Tin production was traditionally one of Malaysia's leading industries, but between 1980 and 2006 the annual output of tin-in-concentrates declined substantially, from 61,000 metric tons to less than 2,400 tons, decreasing further in 2007. In 1980 Malaysia was the largest tin producer in the world, accounting for 31% of global output. By contrast, in 2006 Malaysia was only the fourth largest global producer, providing only an estimated 0.7% of total output. Indonesia and China were the two largest producers of tin in that year, accounting for 74% of world production.

The decline in Malaysian production reflected a fall in the tin price. In 1980 the price was RM 35.7 per kg, but it had decreased sharply to RM 15.5 by 1986. Prices (and Malaysian production) experienced a mild recovery until 1989, as the Supply Rationalization Scheme of the Association of Tin Producing Countries managed to limit the supply of tin through the imposition of export controls on member countries. However, the international recession, the political turmoil in Eastern Europe and the unpredictable release of tin stocks by the US Defence Logistics Agency caused a further decline in tin prices, from RM 23.1 per kg in 1989 to less than RM 15 in late 1996. In 2007 only 13 mines were in production, compared with 847 in 1980. In 2007 employment in the sector had decreased to 861 workers, compared with almost 50,000 in 1970 and 39,000 in 1980. These mines were operating near the end of leasing periods and the quality of tin extracted was of a lower grade. The cost of production was also high, as the tin could only be obtained from a greater depth.

The Malaysia Smelting Corporation, the world's fourth largest tin company in 2006, is the only tin smelter in Malaysia, following the closure of the Escoy smelter in March 1998. It processed 95% of the tin produced in Malaysia in 2006. As domestic production of tin-in-concentrates declined, Malaysia was obliged to import supplies in order to keep its smelters working at near capacity. In 2009 imports of tin-in-concentrates totalled 22,928 metric tons, representing a significant increase from 7,661 tons in 2003. In 2010 Malaysia exported 33,700 tons of processed tin, mainly to Singapore, South Korea, Japan and Taiwan.

Petroleum and Gas

Malaysian petroleum production is not significant in international terms: in 1997 Malaysia's production of crude petroleum accounted for just 1.0% of world output. However, Malaysia is more than self-sufficient in primary commercial energy, and the surplus over self-sufficiency increased from 176 petajoules in 1990 to 511 petajoules in 1995.

The bulk of output is from Peninsular Malaysia, which contributes about 55% of the country's crude petroleum production. At the end of 1998 there were 37 oilfields in production, including two new oilfields in Peninsular Malaysia and one in Sabah: of these 37 oilfields, 16 were in Peninsular Malaysia, while 13 were in Sabah and eight were in Sarawak. By 2000 the number of oilfields in production had declined to 33; however, by 2010 this number had increased to 68. Average production in the 2009/10 financial year (ending 31 March 2010) was 657,200 barrels per day. New oil production projects included the Kikeh block, the country's first deep-water oil and natural gas discovery, which was operated by Murphy Oil, and the Sabah oil and gas terminal, which was operated by Petroliam Nasional Bhd (PETRONAS). Other projects included Shell-operated Gumusut/Kakap and the Malikai deep-water fields, which were scheduled to begin production in 2012 and 2014, delayed from initial estimates of 2010 and 2012, respectively. A new oilfield (Anjung Kecil) was discovered in offshore Sarawak in 2010. Domestic crude petroleum in Malaysia, which has a low sulphur content and is therefore considered to be of premium quality, was largely exported. Total exports of crude petroleum reached RM 43,040m. in 2008 bolstered by record international energy prices in the first half of the year, but decreased to just RM 25,360m. in 2009, owing to a marked decline in prices amid deteriorating global economic conditions; exports recovered partially, to RM 30,765m., in 2010. The principal export markets in 2010 were Australia (which purchased 33.4%), India (14.0%), Thailand (13.8%), China (8.5%), Singapore (5.8%) and South Korea (5.7%).

Petroleum and gas production is the responsibility of PETRONAS, which operates mainly through production-sharing contracts. In 1995 PETRONAS was partially privatized by the Government. By the end of 1991 a total of 29 production-sharing contracts (PSCs) had been signed under the revised terms introduced in 1985. Four new domestic PSCs and 17 PSCs with foreign companies were signed during the course of 2009; these new contracts brought the total number of PETRONAS's international upstream ventures to 73 in 23 countries. PETRONAS has also ventured into upstream activities abroad by securing the rights to several exploration areas in Algeria, Angola, Chad, Gabon, Indonesia, Iran, Libya, Myanmar, Pakistan, Sudan, Syria, Tunisia, Turkmenistan and Viet Nam. The national oil company is one of the major contributors to the government revenue: between 1974 and 2008 it paid a total of RM 403,300m. to the Government, with RM 67,700m. disbursed in 2008 alone; however, this declined in 2009 to RM 57,600m., owing to lower revenues primarily as a result of lower world petroleum prices.

Malaysia had the 23rd largest reserves of crude petroleum in the world in 2009, when the country's total reserves were estimated at 5,520m. barrels; at the beginning of 2010 reserves were estimated to have increased to 5,800m. barrels. At the 2010 rate of production, Malaysia's petroleum reserves were projected to last for a further 24 years. In 1980 the Government implemented the National Depletion Policy, in order to slow exploitation rates and hence conserve the country's reserves. During the recession of the early 1980s the Government became increasingly dependent on revenue from petroleum exports, and the policy was reportedly abandoned. However, production since the early 1990s has been in accordance with the policy's guidelines.

The liquefied natural gas (LNG) complex in Bintulu, Sarawak, is the world's single largest gasfield. After Qatar, Malaysia is the world's second largest exporter of LNG. The export value of Malaysian LNG was RM 38,099m. in 2010. Major importers of LNG are Japan (which accounted for 60.2%), South Korea (21.1%) and Taiwan (12.3%). Malaysia imports 23% of its LNG needs from Viet Nam and the Malaysia-Thailand Joint Development Authority. Gas reserves in Malaysia at the beginning of 2010 were estimated at 14,760m. barrels of oil equivalent (boe), up marginally from 14,660m. boe in 2009; at the 2010 rate of production, reserves were expected to last for another 38 years. In the 2011 budget, announced in October 2010, RM 146m. was allocated to the oil, gas and energy industry.

To ensure the sustainable development of gas resources, a long-term utilization limit of 2,000m. cu ft of processed gas was adopted for Peninsular Malaysia in 1993. Of this, 1,300m. cu ft were reserved for electricity generation, with most of the remainder set aside for use as a feedstock by the petrochemical industries. Under the Ninth Malaysia Plan efforts were being made to diversify sources of fuel through greater utilization of renewable energy. Among the efforts was the National Biofuel Policy (see Palm Oil, above), which aimed to encourage private sector involvement in the production of biodiesel. In the 2011 budget, the Government reaffirmed its commitment to the development of green technology, primarily as a means of supporting sustainable development initiatives. Several policy measures to support the industry were announced, including: the extension until the end of 2015 of pioneer status, investment tax allowance for energy generation from renewable resources and energy efficiency activities; the extension until the end of 2011 on exemptions on import and excise duties on hybrid cars; and the extension until 2012 of tax exemptions on income from the trading of Certified Emission Reductions certificates. In June 2011 B5 composite oil (comprising 5% biodiesel and 95% petroleum diesel) was introduced commercially, following successful trials (in operation since mid-2009) on vehicles used by various government agencies and the armed forces. Initially the biodiesel was made available at just six petrol stations in Putrajaya, but this was to be expanded gradually.

Other Minerals

The production of other minerals in Malaysia generally declined in the 1990s. In 2005 production of bauxite was an estimated 4,735 metric tons, compared with 376,418 tons in 1991, although output increased to 91,806 tons in 2006 and to an estimated 157,000 tons in 2007, according to the US Geological Survey. All bauxite output is exported to countries in South-East Asia as Malaysia does not have an aluminium refinery or smelter. In 2007 Cahya Mata Sarawak Bhd (CMS) and Rio Tinto Alcan, a United Kingdom-based company, established a joint venture—Sarawak Aluminium Company (SALCO)—which was to develop a RM 7,000m. aluminium smelter in Similajau, Sarawak. The proposed smelter was to have an annual production capacity of 550,000 tons during its initial phase, which ultimately would be expanded to 1.5m. tons. Production was scheduled to commence by the end of 2010; however, in early 2009 the project was reported to be significantly behind schedule, with initial production not expected until 2011 at the earliest. In 2008 Malaysia imported approximately 182,000 tons of primary aluminium.

Production of iron ore in 1996 increased by an estimated 60.7% compared with the previous year, but was still below production in 1991, which had totalled 375,869 metric tons. Iron ore production subsequently increased further, to reach 950,000 tons in 2005 and an estimated 667,000 tons in 2006. Malaysia imports iron ore from Bahrain and Brazil, mainly to fulfil the needs of its two major metal producers, Lion Group and Perwaja Steel. In 2006 total imports of iron ore amounted to 2,145m. tons. Malaysia is a net exporter of coal, iron ore, copper concentrate, rare earths, zircon concentrate and smelted tin. There were reports that Vale International SA, the world's second largest diversified metals and mining company, based in Brazil, was to open an iron ore centre in Manjung Perak by 2013. The centre was expected to be the leading production and distribution centre for iron ore in Asia.

INDUSTRY AND INDUSTRIAL POLICY

Manufacturing

Following independence in 1957, Malaysia, like many developing countries, had only a rudimentary manufacturing sector, with the majority of national income coming from the exploitation of its primary resources. However, successive five-year plans focused on developing Malaysia's industrial base, producing a rapid expansion in manufacturing output, which culminated in manufacturing superseding agriculture as the largest contributor to GDP in 1987, providing 22.3%, compared with 8.7% in 1960. Since the Second Malaysia Plan (1971–75), an additional aim of the industrialization policy has been to increase the participation by indigenous Malays in non-agricultural activities. During the 1960s industrialization proceeded through an import substitution strategy, which focused on increasing domestic processing of natural products and on producing basic consumer goods for domestic consumption. However, during the 1970s the emphasis shifted to export-orientated, labour-intensive industries such as textiles and electronics, which were predominantly financed by foreign investment. During the first half of the 1980s there was a second phase of import substitution focusing on heavy industries, such as steel and car production, and led by the public sector, particularly the Heavy Industries Corporation of Malaysia. This was the period when the national car project (Perusahaan Otomobil Nasional—Proton) was launched.

The manufacturing sector has played an important role in the economic growth of Malaysia. The sector's share of GDP grew from less than 9% in 1960 to nearly 15% in 1970 and to 21%, in 1988; by 2010 the sector accounted for 27.7% of GDP. The contribution of manufactured exports to overall export earnings increased significantly from 12% in 1970 to 22% in 1980 and, more sharply, to 59% in 1990 and further to 76.1% in 2010.

Manufactured exports have been concentrated mainly in the electrical and electronics industrial sub-sector since the mid-1970s. Its share of total manufactured exports increased rapidly from 9% in 1970 to 48% in 1980, and subsequently rose further, to 57%, 66% and 70% in 1990, 1997 and 2002, respectively; the sub-sector accounted for 42.4% of manufactured exports in 2010. Of the total electrical and electronics industry work-force, 73.7% were employed in the sub-sector of semiconductor devices. The major export destinations for electrical and electronics products were the USA, Singapore, China, Japan and Hong Kong.

The majority of Malaysian manufacturing operations comprise small and medium-sized enterprises (SMEs). The Third Industrial Master Plan reported that 96.6% of 39,219 active manufacturing enterprises were categorized as SMEs. Most of the SMEs are textile and apparel businesses and resource-based industries. The textile and apparel industry accounted for 23.2% of SMEs, followed by food and beverages (15.0%), metals and metal products (12.4%) and paper, printing and publishing (9.2%). In the information and communication technology sector, 73.7% of the total number of companies approved by the Multimedia Super Corridor (see below) were SMEs in 2005; these firms are largely in the software application development and software engineering sub-sectors.

Foreign Direct Investment

Since independence in 1957 the Malaysian Government has striven to attract foreign direct investment (FDI) into the manufacturing sector. It was estimated that in 1970 foreign investors owned around 60% of the manufacturing sector. The statistics on ownership in Malaysia are very basic, but it is clear that the flow of FDI into Malaysia has been exceptionally high. Between 1967 and 1986 FDI inflows into Malaysia amounted to just under 5% of GDP—not as high as the flow into Singapore (7% of GDP), but well above the flows into Indonesia and South Korea over the same period (less than 1%). Between 1989 and 1994 inflows of FDI into Malaysia totalled US $22,500m., equivalent to 5% of GDP; the comparable figures for Singapore and Thailand were $26,300m. (7% of GDP) and $10,700m. (1%), respectively. In 2007 inflows of FDI reached RM 46,100m., largely through the acquisition of local companies by foreign corporations, and Malaysia was the third largest FDI recipient within ASEAN, after Singapore and Thailand. FDI inflows moderated to RM 36,100m. in 2009 as a result of the deterioration in global financial and economic conditions. The subsequent global economic recovery contributed to higher FDI inflows of RM 89,200m. in 2010.

There has been a notable development in the nature of FDI inflows, which have become more broadly based with greater shares of new inflows being directed towards the services sector. In 2010 this sector received 30% of total FDI (up from 28% in 2009), while the manufacturing and gas sectors attracted 60% (47% in 2009) and 9% (25% in 2009), respectively. This trend appears to be similar to that witnessed in the 1990s, when the manufacturing sector accounted for about 65% of total FDI inflows; the oil and gas sector received 18%, services only 10% and the property sector 7%. Prior to the regional financial crisis of the late 1990s the major investing countries were Japan, Singapore, the USA, Taiwan and the United Kingdom. In the aftermath of the crisis some significant changes in terms of major investing countries took place: countries that provided a large share of investment in Malaysia in 2010 included the USA, Japan and the Netherlands

Malaysia has continued to attempt to attract FDI on an ever-increasing scale, by improving investment conditions and by creating a more attractive destination for the relocation of overseas firms. Prior to 1994 companies that had been granted pioneer status were given tax exemption on 70% of statutory income for a period of five years. After that date companies granted the Income Tax Allowance (ITA) enjoyed a concession of 60% of qualifying capital expenditure, with the amount to be given exemption for any year of assessment not to exceed 70% of statutory income. These percentages were subsequently raised to 80% and 85%, respectively. As a result, during the Sixth Plan period (1991–95) a substantial inflow of FDI continued. In this period approved private investment in the manufacturing sector totalled RM 116,000m., of which FDI accounted for 53%. Foreign investment was particularly important in petroleum products, textiles and electronic products. To encourage greater domestic investment, in 1993 the Government instigated the Domestic Investment Initiative, and in that year approved domestic investment exceeded the approvals for foreign investment for the first time since 1987. The Government had implemented measures to promote high technology, and knowledge-based and capital-intensive industries, and foreign investment in these areas was highly encouraged. Among various initiatives undertaken by the Government was the establishment in 1996 of the Multimedia Super Corridor (MSC) project, in accordance with which companies with approved MSC status enjoyed attractive benefits under a 10-point guarantee plan. At January 2007 there were 1,733 MSC-status companies, of which 74% were locally owned and 92 were multinational corporations. For comparison, the number of companies that were granted MSC status in 1997 was 94. By 2009 the number of MSC-status companies had increased to 2,520. The cumulative number of jobs created by MSC-status companies in 2010 was 51,494, having increased from 33,853 in 2005.

Overseas investment by Malaysian-owned companies had risen rapidly in the 1990s. Net overseas investment increased from RM 8,100m. in 1998 to RM 42,600m. in 2010. Direct investment abroad in 2010 was mainly channelled into the services (67%), oil and gas (19%), and manufacturing sectors (11%). Major overseas investments have been made by the state-controlled hydrocarbon company, PETRONAS (with investments in Algeria, Iran and Sudan), and by the private sector. Both private and public corporations have invested particularly heavily in South Africa since 1994, and in early 1996 Proton, the national car-maker, acquired a prestigious British car company, Lotus. In 2005 ASEAN countries received more than 50% of Malaysia's total investment abroad. Other significant recipients in that year were China, the USA and Hong Kong. In 2009 PETRONAS invested in a gas-processing plant in Turkmenistan and in an LNG project in Australia. Meanwhile, investment outflows in the area of agriculture were directed mainly to the oil palm plantations of Indonesia. In the construction sector, the focus has been on infrastructure projects, residential housing and highways in the Middle East and South Asia, while investment abroad in the services sector was made in gaming and resort businesses, shipping and the telecommunications sector in South-East Asia.

TOURISM

Tourism was not identified as a potential area for growth until 1986. In 1987 the Ministry of Tourism was formed and in 1990 the Government sponsored 'Visit Malaysia Year 1990', which comprised an international promotion and advertising campaign. The approach was so successful that a similar campaign was conducted in 1994, which led to an increase of 12% in tourist arrivals compared with the previous year. The number of tourist arrivals subsequently increased further, from 5.6m. in 1998 to 24.6m. in 2010. Several tourist destinations in the island resorts of Langkawi, Pangkor and Redang and in the highland resorts also recorded a hotel occupancy rate of more than 80% (the average occupancy rate in 2007 was 70%). The number of hotels rose from 1,492 in 2000 to 2,373 in 2009, an increase of 59.0%. In 2010 75.8% of tourists came from ASEAN countries, 4.6% from China, 2.8% from India, 2.3% from Australia, and 1.7% from both Japan and the United Kingdom. The most rapid increase in the number of tourist arrivals in recent years has been from emerging markets such as India and China, with average annual growth rates of 32.4% and 17.6%, respectively, in 1998–2007. The large inflows of West Asians into Malaysia, predominantly during the summer months, were mainly as a result of successful campaigning by the Malaysian Tourism Board, combined with the repercussions of the terrorist attacks on the USA in 2001.

Domestic tourism expanded significantly in the late 1990s as a result of aggressive promotional activities such as 'Cuti-cuti Malaysia' (an internet information and reservation service), 'Visit Perak Year', 'Visit Selangor Year' and other similar campaigns. In addition, the declaration of holidays for those employed in public services on the first Saturday of the month, effective from January 1999, and also the third Saturday of the month, effective from February 2000, had a positive effect on domestic tourism. The introduction of budget airlines, particularly AirAsia Sdn Bhd, was another contributory factor. The number of domestic tourist excursions increased by 89.9% in 1999, to 15.8m. trips, compared with 8.3m. trips between August 1997 and July 1998. Domestic tourism subsequently continued to increase, and this sector expanded by 30.1% between 2000 and 2005. Health tourism has grown notably in the country in recent years. In 2008 a total of 35 private hospitals participated in this programme. In 2008 some 370,000 foreign patients sought medical treatment in Malaysia, of whom 75% were from ASEAN states, 3% were from both Japan and Europe, and 2% were from India. Foreign patients seeking treatment in Malaysia increased to 392,956 in 2010. Home-stay and eco-tourism are new niche areas being promoted by the Malaysian Government in order to enhance the tourism industry. By end of 2010 there were 2,998 trained and licensed home-stay operators in Malaysia; in the first half of that year the sector attracted a total of 88,666 visitors.

In 2010 the Government announced several measures intended to boost the tourism sector, including the abolition of import duties on 300 goods preferred by tourists and locals in an attempt to promote Malaysia as a regional shopping hub; the allocation of RM 85m. to develop infrastructural facilities to support the construction of hotels and resorts in remote areas with the potential to attract additional tourists; and the allocation of a further RM 3m. to develop world's first integrated eco-nature resort in Karambunai in Sabah.

INFRASTRUCTURE

Energy

The development of the energy sector in Malaysia essentially focused on ensuring a cost-effective and reliable supply of energy as well as achieving an efficient utilization of energy resources. Petroleum products constituted the main source of energy consumed in the country (54% of the total in 2008), followed by electricity (18%) and natural gas (24%). The Ninth Malaysia Plan reported that the transport sector was the largest consumer of energy, accounting for 40.5% of the total final commercial energy demand in 2005. By 2008 the industrial sector had become the largest energy consumer (accounting for 43% of the total), followed by the transport sector (36%), the residential and commercial sector (14%), non-energy use (needed for the process of production—6%) and agriculture (1%).

In 2005 urban areas had 100% access to the electricity supply, compared with 98.6% of rural areas in Peninsular Malaysia. By contrast, only 72.8% and 80.8% of Sabah and Sarawak, respectively, had access. Tenaga Nasional Bhd (TNB), a partially state-owned company, contributes about 60% of total electricity generation in the country, with the remainder being supplied by the independent power producers (IPPs). The IPPs entered the market only in the early 1990s when there was a serious shortage of electricity in Malaysia. Five IPPs were licensed to build and operate electricity-generating plants. By 1996 the power shortage had been transformed into a significant surplus, as the IPPs established more than 4,000 MW of capacity. In March 1997, in this context of over-supply, TNB submitted proposals to the Government for the restructuring of its operations. It proposed a separation of its generating and distribution facilities, a diversification of investments into other sectors and a revised consumer tariff formula. By the end of 1996 a wholly owned subsidiary had been established, with responsibility for managing the 7,621 MW of installed capacity. The revised tariff formula proposed that more of the burden of buying high-priced electricity from the five IPPs be passed on to consumers. Between 1995 and 2000 the other two major utilities—Sabah Electricity Board and Sarawak Electricity Supply Corporation—were also restructured.

In 2008 the average electricity tariff for domestic consumers in Peninsular Malaysia increased from 23.5 sen per kWh (last revised in 1997) to 28.90 sen per kWh for usage between 201 kWh and 1,000 kWh and 31.20 sen per kWh for usage above 1,000 kWH (the rate for usage below 200 kWh remained unchanged). Sabah maintained its tariff at 24.4 sen per kWh, while that in Sarawak was reduced from 28.5 sen per kWh to 27.1 sen per kWh. In June 2011 electricity tariffs in Peninsular Malaysia increased by an average of 2.23 sen per kWh (or 7.12%) to 33.54 sen per kWh (the tariff remained unchanged for domestic consumers consuming 300 kWh or less). Effective from 15 July, the average electricity tariff in Sabah and on the island of Labuan increased by 3.75 sen per kWh (or 15%) to 29.25 sen per kWh.

In view of increasing costs, TNB was seeking a lower price for gas feedstock purchased from PETRONAS, and the IPPs began to bear some of the cost of subsidizing supplies to rural areas. Meanwhile, in December 2000 a contract was signed between a local Malaysian IPP, GB3 (75% owned by Malakoff Corporation Bhd—MCB), and the French company ALSTOM for an additional 650-MW generation unit to be built at the site of the Lumut power plant. In the same month the German company Siemens AG was contracted to construct two 710-MW power plants, one at Teluk Gong for the IPP Powertek Sdn Bhd, and one in Sepang for the Malaysian Resources Corporation Bhd. In December 2009 MCB opened a 2,100-MW coal-fired power plant at Tanjung Bin in Johor. At that time MCB controlled six power stations with a total generating capacity of 5,020 MW. No more IPPs were expected to be licensed in the near future.

In the longer term some 2,400 MW of additional capacity were to be provided upon the completion of the controversial Bakun hydroelectric dam in Sarawak. The six shareholders in the company that was to manage the plant formally committed themselves to the project in April 1997. The main shareholder (with a 32% holding) was the private company Ekran. Five government institutions held a further 43% of the shares. The huge project, which was expected to cost RM 13,600m. to complete, was largely unsuccessful in attracting foreign investors and was deferred in December 1997, owing to the regional economic crisis. At the end of the 1990s, however, the project resumed; Sarawak Hidro Sdn Bhd, a company operating under the control of the Ministry of Finance, was appointed to act as the project's implementing agency. The Government subsequently awarded the project to Sime Darby Group in 2002. On account of these developments, the scheduled completion date for the project was deferred until 2010, four years behind the initial schedule. In June 2009 Sime Darby withdrew from the project, citing escalating costs. The Government subsequently awarded the project to TNB and Sarawak Energy Bhd. Construction work was completed in late 2010, and the project commenced operations in August 2011; full production capacity was expected to be achieved in 2012.

Meanwhile, in 2005 the concept of an undersea transmission line was abandoned, and the Malaysian Government began exploring the possibility of sales of electricity to Brunei and Indonesia. However, in 2007 there appeared to be a revival of the project to construct two undersea high-voltage direct current (HVDC) cables (each 700 km long) under the South China Sea to transport electricity from Sarawak to Peninsular Malaysia. The first cable was due for completion in 2013 and the second in 2015, the transmission points being from the Bakun plant to Tanjung Leman, in the state of Johor. Upon completion, the submarine cable would be the longest in the world.

The Malaysian Government has introduced various initiatives concerning the production and utilization of sustainable and renewable energy resources and the achievement of energy efficiency. One of the most important of these was the recognition of renewable energy as the country's fifth fuel in the Eighth Malaysia Plan (2001–05). In line with this, the Government introduced a Fuel Diversification Policy in 2001 that envisaged renewable energies such as biomass, biogas, solar and mini-hydro providing a significant contribution to the country's electricity supply. Various policy measures and institutional mechanisms were introduced to support the policy. For example, the Small Renewable Energy Programme was to allow small power plants, utilizing renewable energy, to sell electricity to TNB. In addition, fiscal incentives such as 'pioneer status', investment tax allowance and import duty and sales tax exemption were granted to companies using energy-conserving equipment. The Government also announced the National Biofuel Policy in 2005 to encourage the production and utilization of biofuel based on palm oil as an alternative energy resource (see above). Wind power and nuclear energy were other alternatives being considered by the Government. The Government was considering the establishment of Malaysia's first, 1,000-MW nuclear power plant in 2021, and aimed for 10%–12% of the country's electricity supply to be nuclear powered by 2030.

Telecommunications

The telecommunications sector continues to develop, following its partial liberalization in mid-1994, which allowed for the establishment of several new operators. However, Telekom Malaysia (in which the Government holds a controlling interest) maintained a dominant share of the market, precisely because the liberalization remained partial, with the Government deciding to defer equal access for other operators to Telekom's network from July 1996 to January 1999. Competition has been keener in the more liberalized, and rapidly expanding, mobile telephone market. In 1996 this market grew by 49%, to reach 1.5m. subscribers, with foreign investors gaining sizeable stakes (of between 20% and 30%) in three domestic companies. The Government decided to raise the permitted ceiling on foreign ownership of telecommunications companies from 30% to 49% in February 1998, and increased it further, to 61%, in April. However, foreign companies were required to reduce their stake to 49% again within five years.

The number of cellular telephone subscribers increased significantly, from 7.4m. in 2001 to 31.5m. in 2010. New cellular network services were introduced, such as third-generation (3G) cellular phone services, short messaging services (SMS), voice mail and calling line identification, as well as wireless application protocol (WAP) internet access. The three main service providers are Maxis Communications Bhd, which controls about 40% of the market, Celcom (Malaysia) Sdn Bhd (31%) and DiGi Telecommunications Sdn Bhd (24%); other service providers include U Mobile Sdn Bhd. The mobile phone penetration rate in Malaysia was 108.8% in mid-2010. Internet service was introduced in Malaysia in 1987 by MIMOS Bhd, a government-controlled research institute. In 1996 a new internet service provider licence was issued to Telekom Malaysia Bhd. In 2008 the Government granted a high-speed broadband (HSBB) licence to Telekom Malaysia. The service was launched in March 2010, with Telekom Malaysia offering bandwidth at access speeds of 10Mb/s under the Streamyx brand. Nation-wide coverage was expected within 10 years. Some 96% of 'last-mile' connections (i.e. the final leg of delivering connectivity from a communications provider to a customer) in Malaysia is owned by Telekom Malaysia, affording it an effective monopoly on internet services in the country. Other internet service providers are Time dotcom Bhd, Maxis Communications Bhd and Jaring. Subscription to internet services has increased substantially, from 2.6m. subscribers in 2002 to 16.9m. at mid-2010. At the end of 2010 the broadband penetration rate was estimated at 55.6%, surpassing the Government's target of 50%. The 2011 budget introduced measures intended to support the industry, including: a two-year extension, until 2012, to import duty and sales tax exemption on broadband equipment; the introduction of sales tax exemption on all types of mobile phone; and the allocation of RM 119m. for a Multimedia Development Corridor scheme to create an innovative digital economy.

Transport

In general, road, rail and port communications are well developed in Malaysia, and are more highly developed in Peninsular than in East Malaysia. The total network of main roads in 2004 was an estimated 98,721 km, of which about 81% were paved. During the Sixth Plan period (1991–95) road development was based on a three-point strategy, to improve inter-urban links, to alleviate capacity constraints and to open new growth areas. As well as the 848-km North–South Highway down the western corridor of the peninsula (which opened in September 1994), three major projects were undertaken along the east–west corridor. In addition, various projects were initiated along the Klang Valley between Kuala Lumpur and Port Klang, the main seaport. However, congestion in the major urban areas grew rapidly in the Sixth Plan period. It was particularly bad in Johor Bahru, George Town and Kuala Lumpur. Traffic entering the capital city increased by 17% annually, and it was clear that new road improvements would do little to alleviate congestion. As a result, the Government embarked on the construction of an integrated public transport system, in which a major part was to be played by the Light Rail Transit (LRT) system. LRT System I (LRT STAR) began its commercial operations in December 1996, followed by LRT System II (LRT PUTRA) in September 1998. By June 1999 the LRT System in the Klang Valley encompassed a total route length of 56 km. Use of the LRT STAR increased from an initial average of 46,853 passengers per day in 1997 to an average of 125,208 passengers per day by the end of 2005. The LRT PUTRA also experienced a high growth rate, with the number of passengers increasing from an average of 12,532 per day to 165,695 per day over the same period. Owing to the substantial rises in fuel prices in the latter months of the year, which discouraged the use of private motor vehicles, the LRT service experienced a sharp increase in passenger numbers, to an average of 326,095 passengers per day, in 2008. As of March 2011 Kelana Jaya and Ampang LRT lines averaged 210,000 and 161,000 passengers per day, respectively, on weekdays.

The main problem with the LRT service is shortage of rolling stock, which has caused overcrowding on commuter trains. In fact, Malaysia has a low rate of public transport usage (about 20% of journeys) owing to the unsatisfactory nature of services. In an attempt to improve public bus services, the eight existing Kuala Lumpur-based bus companies were amalgamated into two consortia in 1994. The KL Monorail and the Express Rail Link to Kuala Lumpur International Airport (KLIA, see below) from Kuala Lumpur Sentral, a privatized intra-city light rail network of 8.6 km in length, have been in operation since April 2001. In 2008 Syarikat Prasarana Negara Bhd, the asset operator for the LRT STAR and LRT PUTRA, announced plans to procure an additional 32 trains to increase daily passenger capacity to about 500,000; the new trains were to be introduced in stages, with full delivery due to be completed by the end of 2011. In November 2010 the Government announced proposals to expand the Kelana Jaya LRT line, linking Lembah Subang and Kelana Jaya Business Centre. Another initiative announced by the Government in order to provide a comprehensive and efficient public transport system was the construction of a high-capacity mass rapid transit (MRT) system, which was to cover a 20-km radius from Kuala Lumpur city centre. Three lines have been proposed: the first line was to connect Sungai Buloh with Kajang, via Kota Damansara, Kuala Lumpur and Cheras; a second line was to connect Sungai Buloh, Kepong, Kuala Lumpur and Serdang; and the final line would form a loop around Kuala Lumpur's central business district, providing a link between the monorail and LRT services. Malaysian company Syarikat Prasarana Negara Bhd, which also operates the KL Monorail system, bus operations in Penang and cable car services in Langkawi, was expected to be named as the MRT operator. Gamuda Bhd and MMC Corporation Bhd were chosen as project developers. The construction of the MRT system was scheduled to commence in January 2012 and to be completed in 2016.

The railway development programme was aimed at increasing haulage capacity, enhancing operational safety and improving commuter train services. Major projects undertaken during the Eighth Malaysia Plan period were a 180-km inter-city electrified double-track railway linking Rawang and Ipoh; a 32-km rail link from Kempas to the Port of Tanjung Pelepas; a 14-km rail link to Port Klang; a 3-km rail link to the North Butterworth Container Terminal; and a rail link to the Segamat Inland Port. In 2008 the Government had allocated RM 200m. to procure 10 sets of Electric Multiple Units (EMU) to meet the increasing demand of KTM *Komuter* services in Klang Valley (operated by Keretapi Tanah Melayu Bhd since 1995) and an additional five sets of EMU to facilitate the KL Sentral–Ipoh fast train services, which entered into service in August 2010. Meanwhile, KTM *Komuter* services were extended to Tanjung Malim from June 2009. A KTM electrified double-track project connecting Sentul and the popular tourist destination Batu Caves was launched in July 2010.

Malaysia's two main seaports handled 8.8m. 20-ft equivalent units (TEUs) in January–July 2010, of which Port Klang, to the west of Kuala Lumpur, handled almost one-half of the total, while Port of Tanjung Pelepas in Johor, which commenced operations in 2000, handled more than one-third of the total. Port Klang is now one of the world's leading container terminals, having risen from 57th to 14th in the rankings between 1980 and 2010. As a result of the increase in the volume of cargo handled by the major ports in Malaysia, various expansion plans were being undertaken by the Government to enhance port facilities and services. BNM reported that at West Port in Pulau Indah, for example, work had begun on the construction of a new 600-m terminal that would increase the capacity of the port to 1.8m. TEUs annually. The construction of 12 new berths at the Kuantan Port Consortium was expected to raise the port's capacity by 9m. metric tons. In the south, PTP recorded notable success, attaining a capacity of 3.7m. TEUs during January–July 2010. This was attributable mainly to the relocation of the operations of Maersk Sealand and Evergreen, two of the world's largest shipping companies, from Singapore to the port. Another port in the south, the Segamat Inland Port, which began operations in October 1998, was expected to attract shippers located mainly in southern Melaka and northern Johor. Other projects included a container terminal and oil jetty in Seangar Bay, Sabah, and the Second Inner Harbour Basin of Bintulu Port in Sarawak. During the Seventh Malaysia Plan, more than 90% of Malaysia's international trade was conducted through seaports.

As part of the expansion of infrastructural facilities, in 1991 the Government announced plans for a new airport at Sepang, 70 km south of Kuala Lumpur, to ease congestion at the existing main airport at Subang (renamed the Sultan Abdul Aziz Shah Airport in 1996). The first phase of the new KLIA, costing RM 9,000m., began operations in June 1998. The airport, consisting of two 4-km runways and a four-winged satellite building with monorail, was able to handle 25m. passengers a year initially, and ultimately 45m., compared with the previous airport's capacity of 14m. passengers. In 2010 passenger traffic at KLIA reached 34.1m. passengers.

The main airline is Malaysia Airlines (formerly the Malaysian Airline System—MAS), which operates an extensive domestic and international service. The number of international destinations to which it operated services increased from 66 in 1995 to more than 100 at mid-2011, while the number of domestic destinations was reduced. In 1994 AirAsia was launched as a second national carrier to operate both domestic and regional flights. Passengers carried by budget airlines, which tapped into a growing customer base in the Indonesia-Malaysia-Thailand Growth Triangle area (a sub-regional economic co-operation zone, established in 1993, that encompasses 32 provinces and states in the named countries), totalled 1.1m. in 2004, increased to 2.4m. in 2007 and rose further in 2008, to reach about 3m. passengers by September of that year; this increase was largely attributable to the introduction of new routes by AirAsia. In 2009 AirAsia and MAS flew 15.2m. and 13.9m. passengers, respectively.

Megaprojects and the Construction Industry

Megaprojects that were undertaken in the 1990s included the hydroelectric dam at Bakun in Sarawak (at an estimated cost of RM 13,600m.), the world's tallest twin towers in Kuala Lumpur (RM 2,000m.), the new airport (RM 9,000m.) and the new administrative capital at Putrajaya (RM 20,000m.), south of Kuala Lumpur. In 1997 several of the projects were deferred, in an attempt to reduce the trade deficit and restore confidence in the financial markets, following the significant decline in the value of the ringgit and concomitant turmoil in the stock exchange.

In 2000 growth in the construction industry emanated largely from four privatized road projects (the Kajang Ring Road, Ipoh–Lumut Highway, the Shah Alam–Kuang Expressway (Guthrie Corridor) and the Butterworth Outer Ring Road) and one independent power plant (the Technology Tenaga in Perlis). In 2002 major ongoing public projects included the electrified double tracking of the railway track between Ipoh and Rawang. In 2006 the Government announced the second Penang Bridge project. Construction of the bridge, linking the town of Batu Maung on the island and Batu Kawan on the mainland, commenced in late 2008 and was expected to be completed in mid-2012, at a projected cost of RM 3,000m. In addition, 880 new construction projects, costing a total of RM 15,000m., were announced under the Ninth Malaysia Plan in July 2006. The Duta–Ulu Kelang Expressway and the Kajang–Seremban Expressway were completed in 2009. Other ongoing projects included the East Coast Expressway Phase 2, which upon completion (scheduled for late 2011) would connect Jabur with Kuala Terengganu, and an electrified double-track railway project linking Seremban and Gemas, due for completion in 2012.

The Government has initiated five economic development corridors since 2006: Iskandar Malaysia in southern Johor (in 2006), the Northern Corridor Economic Region (NCER, 2007), the East Coast Economic Region (ECER, 2007), Sabah Development Corridor (SDC, 2008) and Sarawak Corridor of Renewable Energy (SCORE, 2008). Iskandar Malaysia, which was formerly known as the Iskandar Development Region and the South Johor Economic Region, was established in July 2006 and named after Sultan Iskandar of Johor. In 2008 Airport City (Aeropolis), a RM 1,000m. project covering 1,133 ha of land, was launched near Senai International Airport in Iskandar Malaysia. The project was to comprise three main components—residential, commercial and hospitality amenities; an air cargo logistic centre; and a hi-tech park. The NCER, covering Perlis, Kedah, Pulau Pinang and the north of Perak, was intended to accelerate economic growth and elevate income levels in the northern region of Peninsular Malaysia until its completion in 2025. Agriculture, manufacturing and services were identified as the most important economic sectors to be developed under the NCER, involving projects costing some RM 177,000m., of which two-thirds were to be undertaken by private sector concerns.

The ECER, which was to run until 2019, comprised four states in eastern Peninsular Malaysia, Kelantan, Terengganu, Pahang and the north of the Mersing district of Johor. PETRONAS was to lead the ECER initiatives focusing on the oil and gas industry. The ECER's other focal points were tourism; oil, gas and petrochemicals; manufacturing; agriculture; and education. It was reported that, of the 105 planned ECER projects, 77 were ongoing and were expected to commence in mid-2009, and the Government has allocated a total of RM 2,600m., which was approved during the mid-term review of the Ninth Malaysia Plan. The Government announced in 2008 that it was to allocate 7,400 ha in Pahang under the ECER project to create a Pekan-Rompin pineapple integrated development project, a programme to help Malaysia regain its dominance as one of the world's leading three pineapple producers. The areas identified were Permatang Bedon (2,000 ha) in Pekan, and Kampung Jemari (5,000 ha) and Kampung Tebu

Hitam (400 ha) in Rompin. Another project launched in 2008 under the ECER was the Kertih Plastic Park, the only specialized industrial park in the country focusing on the plastics industry. The park is located near to the resin production plants in Kertih, Terengganu, and Kuantan, Pahang. As of mid-2009 more than 95% of the plastics-manufacturing companies were located outside the East Coast. In August Prime Minister Dato' Sri Najib Tun Razak announced that the country's first Special Economic Zone (SEZ) was to be established in Pekan. The SEZ was to form part of the ECER and was to serve as an integrated development zone with special incentives to attract investments and boost economic activities. The SEZ extends from Kertih, Chukai, Kuantan Port City, Kuantan and Gambang to Pekan. Some of the projects include: Kuantan Port City; Kertih Integrated Petrochemical Complex; Kertih Polymer Industrial Park; Kemaman Heavy Industries Park; Gambang Science and Halal Park; Pekan Automotive Industrial Park; and Tanjong Agas Maritime Industrial Hub. The implementation of free zones was planned for Kemaman Port, Kuantan Port, Kuantan Airport and Tanjong Agas, as well as tourism zones in Kemasik-Kijal, Cherating, Pantai Sepat and Kuala Pahang.

The SDC was launched in February 2008 and was expected to take 18 years to complete, with a projected annual budget of RM 5,830m. The west coast of Sabah was to be the location of an industrial sub-corridor and an agro-food zone for SMEs, while the establishment of industrial, marine tourism, integrated agro-food, agro-biotechnology and palm oil industry zones was planned for the eastern region of the state, with the central region designated for the development of tourism, highland agriculture and agro-forestry zones. SCORE, which was also initiated in February, focused on the development of energy resources in the central region of Sarawak, particularly renewable energy, taking advantage of the abundance of hydropower, natural gas and coal in the state. Three growth centres were identified, Tanjung Manis, Similajau and Mukah. Proposed SCORE projects included energy supply agreements worth RM 12,500m., the RM 22,000m. Bakun dam and undersea transmission cables, the construction of steel cluster complexes costing RM 15,000m., the development of pulp and paper mills, aquaculture projects, fisheries projects, shipyards, zinc electro-refinery plants and aluminium smelters.

The construction sector experienced a downward trend following the 1997 regional financial crisis. Many major construction and infrastructure projects were cancelled or abandoned. The growth of the construction sector between 1996 and 2002 was the lowest recorded since 1980. Several measures were introduced in 1998 and 1999 to support the construction industry. Emphasis was placed upon the construction of low- and medium-cost houses, for which demand remained strong. The Real Property Gains Tax was reduced to 5%. The implementation of the Foreign Investment Committee (FIC) guidelines, effective from April 2001, resulted in a substantial increase in the foreign purchase of residential properties in Malaysia. The Government introduced further changes to the rules on foreign ownership of property in 2006, permitting foreigners to purchase residential properties valued above RM 250,000 without the FIC's approval. The construction sector has registered positive growth since 2007, facilitated by generous government stimulus packages, improved consumer confidence and stabilized labour market conditions. The sector expanded by 5.2% in 2010. Meanwhile, conditions in the non-residential sub-sector improved, and by mid-2010 the average occupancy rates for office space and retail complexes were 84.2% and 81.2%, respectively.

In 2008 the Malaysian Government liberalized the pricing structure of steel and cement owing to a sharp increase in the global prices of building materials. The 'ceiling' price on steel bars, billets and cement was abolished. Import duty on certain steel bars was abolished, while import duty on steel bars and billets from non-ASEAN countries was reduced from 50% to 10%. In addition, the 10% import duty on cement was abolished, as was the duty on various types of long steel products. Consequently, building material prices increased, further constraining growth in the construction sector.

The 2011 budget outlined plans for another major construction project, Warisan Merdeka, which upon completion (scheduled for 2015, at a projected cost of RM 5,000m.) would become the tallest building in Malaysia, incorporating a 100-storey tower. Other megaprojects to which the budget allocated development funding included: the construction of infrastructure projects to accelerate corridor and regional development (to which RM 850m. was allocated); a development project including the construction of affordable housing in Sungai Buloh (RM 10,000m.); Iskandar Malaysia (RM 339m.); the Northern Corridor Economic Region (RM 133m.); the East Coast Economic Region (RM 178m.) and the Sarawak Corridor of Renewable Energy (RM 93m.). The Government also introduced a scheme for first-time house buyers, which would provide a guarantee on a 10% deposit on residential property below the RM 220,000 threshold. In addition, first-time house buyers were also eligible for stamp duty exemption of 50% on instruments of transfer on properties worth RM 350,000 or less.

PRIVATIZATION

In 1991 the Privatization Master Plan (PMP) was introduced, and during the Sixth Malaysia Plan period a total of 204 projects were privatized. It is in the area of transport and infrastructure that the main thrust of privatization has taken place in Malaysia. Principal projects included the LRT system in Kuala Lumpur, the National Sports Complex, Proton, the ports of Klang and Johor, the Second Causeway Link to Singapore, and TNB, the electricity supply company.

During the Seventh Malaysia Plan period (1996–2000) 98 projects were privatized, of which 47 were existing projects and 51 new projects. Of the total number of new projects, 49 were in the construction, transport, and electricity and gas sectors. Five of the projects were completed—the Damansara–Puchong Highway, the upgrading of the Sungei Besi Road, and the three IPPs in Sandakan, Karambunai and Batu Sapi in Sabah—while 25 were in various stages of implementation and the remainder in the planning stage. During the Eighth Malaysia Plan period (2001–05) the Government assumed responsibility for the operations and management of privatized light rail services, i.e. LRT STAR and LRT PUTRA, to ensure uninterrupted transportation services. In April 2006 the Government announced its decision to abort the Johor Strait 'crooked' bridge project, which had been estimated to cost RM 620m., after nearly a decade of negotiations.

Malaysia's water and health care services have also undergone privatization. The transfer to the private sector of national water utilities began in the 1990s, when deals were designed by states under guidelines determined by the federal Government. More than 20 local companies provide water supply-related services in Malaysia, with three or four foreign enterprises also involved in the sector. Privatization of health care services also started in the early 1990s. In 1992 the Ministry of Health announced that haemodialysis clinics in 16 hospitals would be contracted to private companies. In the same year the Institut Jantung Negara (IJN—National Heart Institute) was separated from the Kuala Lumpur General Hospital and was corporatized as a fully government-owned referral heart centre. (In 2008 the privatization of IJN was proposed; however, as this would have involved a take-over by Sime Darby, owing to strong public opposition the authorities decided against such a scheme.) In 1994 Malaysia's drug distribution system, which was previously administered by the Government's General Medical Store, was privatized. All state hospitals were required to procure their supplies from a new company, Southern Tasek Sdn Bhd, a subsidiary of Renong. In view of various problems and a generally poor performance, the Government awarded a 15-year renewable concession to another company, Remedi Pharmaceuticals, a subsidiary of United Engineers (Malaysia) Bhd, in 1994. Food supplies for hospitals were privatized in 1996. Meanwhile, under the Seventh Malaysia Plan, it was indicated that many health facilities, including hospitals and specialist units, would eventually be privatized. In 2004 the Government announced that it would commence privatization of state hospital dispensaries during the course of 2005.

Under the 10th Malaysia Plan, the Government announced a new wave of privatization in order to increase the flow of private investment into the economy, improve efficiency in the delivery of public services and relieve the Government's financial burden, to be achieved through private funding initiatives and public-private partnership (PPP) programmes. Under the Plan, 52 high-impact projects, collectively worth some RM 62,700m., were to be constructed by public-private partnerships. The projects included were seven highway projects—among them the West Coast Expressway, the Guthrie–Damansara Expressway, the Sungai Juru Expressway and the Paroi–Senawang–KLIA Expressway—to be constructed at a combined estimated cost of RM 15,000m; two coal-fired electricity generation plants at a combined estimated cost of RM 10,000m; and development of the Malaysian Rubber Board's land in Sungai Buloh, Selangor, covering an area of 3,300 acres, at an estimated cost of RM 10,000m. Several PPP projects identified in the 10th Malaysia Plan were highlighted in the 2011 budget and were to be implemented through private investment of RM 12,500m. These projects included, *inter alia*, construction of highways such as the Ampang–Cheras–Pandan elevated highway; construction of a 300-MW combined-cycle gas power plant in Kimanis, Sabah; development of a teaching hospital at the International Islamic University Malaysia in Kuantan, construction of the MRT system (see above); and development of land owned by the Malaysian Rubber Board in Sungai Buloh, Selangor.

TRADE, BALANCE OF PAYMENTS AND EXCHANGE RATE

Malaysia is an extremely open economy in the sense that exports of goods and non-factor services are slightly greater than GDP. The merchandise account has always remained in surplus. The average annual growth of exports of goods and services has remained high, recording impressive rates of 9.2% during 1971–90, 18.4% during 1990–95 and 13.3% in 1997. Growth in exports was sustained at double-digit rates, for example of 17.0% in 2000 and 10.3% in 2006. Export growth moderated to 2.7% in 2007, before recovering to 9.6% in 2008. Meanwhile, imports increased by an average of 10.0% per year during 1971–90, by 19.7% during 1990–95 and by 9.9% in 1999. The expansion in imports was mainly attributable to capital goods, followed by consumer goods and intermediate goods. In 2010 this trend was still much in evidence, with the import of intermediate goods accounting for some 70.0% of gross imports. The trade surplus has traditionally been predominantly a result of strong primary commodity exports, which have a low import content (in 2007 the contribution of primary commodities to the trade surplus was 73%). Primary commodities continued to be the major contributor to export growth in 2008. In the first half of that year commodity exports recorded impressive growth of 50.2%, largely driven by significantly higher prices for palm oil, rubber, crude petroleum and LNG; export earnings from palm oil, for example, surged by 90.9% in that year, while exports of minerals experienced 43.2% growth. However, in 2009 commodity exports contracted by 27.6%, largely owing to lower commodity prices, while manufacturing exports contracted by 12.8%. This, combined with weak global demand as a result of the economic downturn, contributed to a 16.6% contraction in total exports in 2009. However, helped by the global economy recovery, gross exports expanded by 15.6% in 2010, boosted by robust primary commodity growth of 26.9%; manufacturing exports grew by 13.0%.

The services account has traditionally been in deficit since the late 1970s, and the deficit increased in the 1980s, largely because of high outflows of investment income, freight and insurance and other services. It was this rapid growth in the services deficit that caused the deficits registered in the current account from 1990. In the second half of the 1990s, however, the services account deficit narrowed; this improvement was supported by the significant increase in tourism receipts and, to a lesser extent, by higher foreign-exchange earnings on airport and port-related services. BNM reported that, in terms of gross national income (GNI), the services account deficit declined to 2.9% in the period 1996–2002, from 4.6% in 1991–95. In 2006 the services account remained in deficit, at RM 7,400m. However, in 2007 the services account recorded a surplus of RM 1,000m., further improving in 2008 to register a RM 1,700m. surplus. The surplus was attributable to an improvement in the travel services balance, which recorded a surplus of RM 28,200m. in 2008, and to a lower deficit in transport services owing to increased earnings from passenger, cargo and charter operations—the transport services deficit declined from RM 19,600m. in 2006 to RM 14,600m. in 2008. The services account surplus increased further in 2009, to RM 3,200m., before declining to RM 863m. in 2010 (the transport services deficit increased further to RM 23,034m.). Aided by growth in tourist arrivals, the travel services balance registered a surplus of RM 32,037m.

At the end of the 1980s the current account of the balance of payments was in surplus, but by the early 1990s it had moved sharply into deficit. According to the 1997 BNM Annual Report, prior to 1980 Malaysia had not experienced prolonged periods of deficit on the current account of the balance of payments. The first period of sustained current account deficit occurred in 1980–86, when the deficits averaged 6.5% of GNI. However, following voluntary structural adjustment policies undertaken by the Government, surpluses were recorded in the period 1987–89. The current account deficit re-emerged during the period 1990–97, averaging 6.2% of GNI. However, there was a significant improvement in the current account position in 1998, when the first surplus on the current account of the balance of payments since 1989 was recorded. In terms of GNI, the surplus increased to 13.7% of GNI in 1998 from 5.4% in 1997, surpassing the previous high of 8.9% achieved in 1987 after the previous recession. The current account improved further in 1999, recording an increased surplus of RM 47,381m., or 16.9% of GNI (compared with a surplus of RM 36,800m. in 1998). The surplus expanded significantly to reach RM 129,400m. in 2008, but declined marginally, to RM 112,700m., in 2009, and further to RM 90,511m. in 2010 owing to stronger demand for imports and larger net income outflows.

Large inflows of long-term capital into Malaysia were more than sufficient to finance the current account deficit. Net inflows of long-term capital were moderate in the 1960s and 1970s. In the late 1970s and early 1980s the Government relied on external loans to sustain public sector investments, leading to higher net inflows in the long-term official capital account (reaching a peak of RM 6,300m. in 1983). The net long-term official capital account was in deficit during 1987–92, indicating repayment for the large external debt incurred in the early 1980s. However, increasing net long-term private capital inflows from 1988 onwards caused an overall surplus on the balance of payments. This was due to new incentives introduced in 1986, combined with the buoyant domestic economy and the lower exchange rate of the ringgit. This led to large inflows of FDI, mainly into the manufacturing and petroleum sectors, with smaller amounts accruing to the agricultural and property sectors. It increased from RM 1,100m. in 1987 to total more than RM 10,000m. annually throughout the 1990s. In 1997 the net inflow of long-term capital increased by 27.7% in real terms to RM 18,800m. (compared with RM 13,600m. in 1996). This consisted of RM 13,200m. (RM 12,800m. in 1996) of net long-term private investment and RM 5,600m. (RM 800m. in 1996) of net official long-term capital. Thus, a surplus of RM 5,700m. was recorded on the capital account in 1997, compared with a surplus of RM 1,300m. in 1996.

In 1998 the surplus on the current account was higher than the surplus on the capital account, and from 1999 the current account surplus began to offset the deficit on the capital account. In 1998 the surplus on the current account was RM 37,394m., while that on the long-term capital account declined to RM 10,900m. as a result of the weakened global economy and of a risk-averse attitude among investors. Since the first quarter of 2001 Malaysia's balance of payment accounts have been estimated in accordance with the guidelines prescribed by the fifth edition of the *Balance-of-Payments Manual*. In this new format, the capital account has become known as the 'financial account', recording direct, portfolio and other investments. Using this format, the current account surplus for 2000 was RM 31,959m., and that for 2001 was RM 25,070m., while the financial account displayed deficits of RM 23,848m. and RM 17,948m. in 2000 and 2001, respectively. In 2002 and 2003 the financial account recorded an improvement, registering a lower net outflow of about RM 12,000m. in both years. In 2004 the account recorded a surplus of RM 15,083m., before showing large deficits of RM 41,952m. and RM 39,900m. in 2005 and 2006, respectively, as a result of substantial outflows of short-term portfolio investment from the country. In 2007 the deficit narrowed to RM 37,000m., as the net outflows of direct investment and other investments were partially offset by the net surplus in portfolio investment. In 2008 the financial account recorded a larger net outflow of RM 118,500m., largely as a result of a reversal of portfolio funds (see below), but the deficit narrowed to RM 82,900m. in 2009 and further to RM 22,103m. in 2010. Meanwhile, net direct investment abroad by Malaysian companies increased from RM 38,200m. in 2007 to RM 47,100m. in 2008, but declined to RM 27,900m. in 2009, before increasing to RM 42,632m. in 2010, as Malaysian companies continued to expand and invest within existing operations. Direct investment abroad is concentrated in the finance and insurance, communication, and electricity, gas and water sub-sectors.

Movement of private short-term capital only became significant in 1989. Net short-term capital inflows increased from RM 1,600m. in 1989 to RM 13,000m. in 1993, owing to an increase in the net external liabilities of the commercial banks and large inflows of portfolio funds into the booming stock market. In 1994 Malaysia experienced a high net outflow, totalling RM 7,900m., for speculative reasons. In 1995 the net inflow of short-term capital improved, and there was a small surplus of RM 734m., which increased rapidly to RM 11,200m. in 1996. However, the short-term capital account recorded a large outflow of RM 14,000m. and RM 21,700m. in 1997 and 1998, respectively, in the aftermath of the currency turmoil in the region. The short-term capital account recorded a further substantial net outflow of RM 36,000m. in 1999. The bulk of the net outflow of funds in 1997 was due to the liquidation of portfolio investment as well as intervention to support the ringgit exchange rate. This resulted in a huge deficit in the overall balance of the balance of payments. In 1998 the overall balance of payments reverted to a surplus. In 1999 larger outflows of short-term capital, together with exchange revaluation losses, led to a decline in the overall balance of payments surplus. The level of external reserves increased steadily, from RM 113,541m. in 2000 to RM 335,700m. in 2007. In 2008 Malaysia experienced a large outflow of portfolio investment, totalling some RM 92,400m.; this was mainly attributable to a reversal of portfolio funds in the second and third quarters of the year, as foreign institutions responded to the worsening global economic recession. However, in 2009 there was a modest net inflow of portfolio investment, of RM 800m., as a result of the normalization in financial international markets and stronger growth prospects in the Asia-Pacific region. Net portfolio investment inflows in 2010 amounted RM 44,949m., which was mainly channelled into equity and debt securities markets. According to BNM, Malaysia has the policy capacity to manage large portfolio investment inflows and is therefore able to circumvent any economic and financial imbalances associated with short-term capital inflows. Overall net international reserves increased to RM 331,300m. in 2009, from RM 317,400m. in 2008, but declined slightly, to RM 328,649m., in 2010.

It was argued that deficits in the 1990s were largely driven by the private sector, unlike the deficits in the 1980s, which were led by the government sector. Large-scale investment projects undertaken by the private sector in the 1990s resulted in deficits in the resource balance. Prior to the 1980s there had been no serious deficit in the savings-investment position. However, in the first half of the 1980s the savings–investment gap widened to 8.8%, mainly owing to large-scale investment by the Government. Following the voluntary adjustment programme undertaken by the Government, in the latter half of the 1980s savings were higher than investment. However, the national resource position reverted to a deficit in 1990. For the first half of the 1990s the deficit increased further, as investment growth continued to accelerate. The deficit in the resource balance in the 1990s was mainly due to a significant growth in private sector investment activities, despite the high rate of domestic savings in the country by international standards. In terms of GNI, the share of gross national savings was 38.5% and 40.0% in 1996 and 1997, respectively. Meanwhile, gross domestic capital formation as a share of GNI was 45.1% in 1997, compared with 43.6% in 1996. This led to a deficit in the savings-investment position of RM 14,200m. in 1997 (compared with RM 12,300m. in 1996). However, the situation was reversed in 1998, in which year gross national savings increased by 5.1% in spite of the ongoing regional financial crisis, and thereby increased its share of GNI to 41.2%. This increase, combined with a decline in gross capital formation of 38.4%, resulted in a surplus in the savings-investment position of RM 36,100m., or 13.7% of GNI. The country's resource balance position recorded an increased surplus of RM 47,900m., or 17.1% of GNI, in 1999. A smaller total resource surplus of RM 31,200m., accounting for 10% of GNI, was recorded for 2000. In 2002 the stronger economic performance resulted in a slightly lower resource surplus of RM 27,400m., or 8.1% of GNI (compared with a surplus of RM 27,700m., or 9% of GNI, in 2001).

BNM reported that total medium- and long-term external debt at the end of 1998 had increased by 3% on the previous year to RM 131,300m. In US dollar terms, the debt increased by 5.5%, to US $34,500m. in 1998 from $32,700m. in 1997. However, owing to prudent management and an efficient debt-monitoring system, total external debt outstanding declined by 1.4% to RM 159,000m. in 1999. Short-term debt, comprising mainly the external borrowings of commercial banks and the non-bank private sector, had declined by 34% to RM 28,500m. at the end of 1998, and further by 29% to RM 22,800m. at the end of 1999. In 1999 the private sector recorded a net repayment of external loans of RM 1,800m., the highest level since 1989. However, this was offset by higher net borrowing by the federal Government and non-financial public enterprises (NFPEs) totalling RM 6,800m. in 1999. The federal Government's external debt, which accounted for 9.3% of total external debt in 1998, had increased by 15.2% to RM 14,900m. at the end of 1998 from RM 12,900m. in 1997. This debt had increased further, by 23%, to RM 18,400m. at the end of 1999, accounting for an increased share of 12.0% of total external debt. Meanwhile, the outstanding debt of the NFPEs increased by 10.2% to RM 58,600m. in the same year. Private sector external debt declined by 37.4% to RM 9,600m. in 1998 from RM 15,400m. in 1997, mainly because of the slowdown of the economy resulting from the financial crisis. In 2007 the private sector external debt totalled RM 8,600m. Total outstanding external debt declined by 3% to RM 157,000m. at the end of 2000, principally reflecting the reduction in short-term debt and, to a lesser extent, the revaluation gains resulting from the stronger ringgit. In 2001 the total debt was RM 169,800m. and the ratio of external debt to GNI was 55.4% (the ratio had been 64% in 1997 following the regional financial crisis). The new loans were mainly drawn by the public sector (RM 7,200m.), with new external borrowing totalling RM 2,800m. The total external debt increased to RM 186,640m. and RM 200,586m. in 2003 and 2004, respectively. BNM reported that the total external debt declined to RM 197,700m. in 2005 and further, to RM 187,400m., in 2007 (33.6% of GNI), before increasing to RM 235,600m. in 2008 (32.9% of GNI). Malaysia's total external debt declined modestly in 2009, to an estimated RM 233,917m. (35.3% of GNI), in 2009, and declined further in 2010, to RM 226,297m. (30.2% of GNI).

From September 1998 Malaysia maintained the fixed exchange rate regime of US $1 to RM 3.80. During this period the exchange value of the ringgit was influenced solely by fluctuations in the US dollar. However, in July 2005 the Government decided to float the ringgit against a basket of currencies of major trading partners and regional countries, as a consequence of changes in the importance of regional countries as trading partners. At the end of 2007 the exchange rate between the ringgit and the US dollar was 3.065, but by the end of 2008 the ringgit had weakened against the dollar, with the exchange rate standing at 3.464. The exchange rate remained relatively stable during 2009, ending the year at 3.425, appearing to lend weight to BNM's claims that the current system had accorded a level of stability against the currencies of Malaysia's major trading partners. In 2010 the ringgit appreciated by 11.1% against the US dollar, with an average exchange rate of 3.0835 in that year.

FINANCE AND BANKING

Monetary policy has emerged as an important aspect of economic management in Malaysia, with the rapid expansion in the external reserves held by the central bank and the commercial banks, and with the growth in the money and capital markets. Since the inflationary problems experienced in the early 1980s, BNM has attempted to exercise strict control over commercial and merchant banks, in order to control the growth in the money supply. However, following an apparently successful period of low inflation and high growth in the mid- to late 1980s, the inflation rate (up to 4.4% in 1991 and 4.8% in 1992, compared with less than 1% during 1985–87) and the growth in the money supply (11% in 1991, compared with 3.6% in 1987) increased during the early 1990s. The renewed inflationary pressures were a consequence of the strong domestic demand for credit and the sharp increase in liquidity caused by inflows of foreign capital, which were related to Malaysia's rapid economic growth. In August 1991 BNM introduced a strict monetary policy to curb inflation and restrict the growth in the money supply. During 1992 high interest rates and restrictions on credit resulted in a slowing of consumer spending. However, these high interest rates attracted funds from abroad, accelerating the appreciation of the ringgit. In December 1992 the dollar notation was abandoned, and the official currency denomination became ringgit Malaysia (RM).

In the mid-1990s BNM increasingly resorted to direct action to control the monetary sector, attempting to stabilize liquidity by changing reserve requirements, and imposing limits on the composition of lending. In early 1998 monetary policy was tightened in order to contain inflation and restore stability in the foreign-exchange market. Through a combination of monetary and fiscal policy, together with a rapidly expanding economy, the Government was also quite successful in controlling inflation. In April 2004 Malaysia adopted a new interest framework. Under this new system, the overnight policy rate (OPR) replaced the three-month intervention rate. The OPR was set at the prevailing average inter-bank overnight rate of 2.70%. This meant that the banking institutions were to set their best lending rates based on their respective cost structures and business strategies. As a result of intense competition among banks, lending rates were near historically low levels, at about 5%, throughout 2008. As a policy response to the economic slowdown, BNM reduced the OPR by 150 basis points between November 2008 and March 2009 to 2.0%, and lowered the statutory reserve requirement by 300 basis points over the same period to 1.0%, with the objective of reducing the cost of intermediation, including monthly loan repayments. During 2010 huge portfolio inflows and geopolitical tensions on the Korean peninsula, combined with the sovereign debt and banking system crisis in Europe, raised concerns about possible economic and financial imbalances in the region as well as in the country. Concerned that such imbalances would undermine the economic recovery, BNM responded by increasing interest rates. The OPR was raised by 25 basis points on three separate occasions in 2010, in March, May and July; consequently, the overnight interbank rate increased from 2.00% in March to 2.75% in July, at which level it remained at mid-2011.

In the late 1990s a comprehensive plan to restructure the banking sector included a merger programme and the creation of an asset management company, Pengurusan Danaharta Nasional Bhd. The merger programme for the domestic banking sector was completed with the merger of Arab-Malaysian Finance Bhd with MBf Finance Bhd in June 2002, and the acquisition of Bank Utama (Malaysia) Bhd by RHB Bank Bhd at the end of 2002. With the completion of these mergers, the previously highly fragmented domestic banking system has been transformed, with the 71 institutions prior to the 1997 regional crisis being consolidated into 30 banking institutions under 10 domestic banking groups.

In 1990 the Government declared the island of Labuan an international 'offshore' financial centre, as part of an attempt to stimulate Malaysia's financial sector. By 1993, however, only 13 banks were licensed to establish 'offshore' units in Labuan. Its failure to attract significant investment was largely due to a lack of basic infrastructure and telecommunications systems. In mid-1993 Malaysia banned Singapore-based 'offshore' banks from financing Malaysian business ventures in an attempt to promote Labuan. By September 1998 Labuan had issued 64 licences. In April 1996 it was announced that foreign state-owned banks would be permitted to establish offices in Malaysia, but a ban on new privately owned foreign banks (except in the 'offshore' centre of Labuan) was to remain in place to protect the financial markets. In the late 1990s the domestic financial system moved towards greater liberalization, as evidenced by the significant foreign presence in the Malaysian financial sector by 2000.

In March 2005 BNM announced the framework for the creation of investment banks under which an investment bank could be formed through mergers of merchant banks and stock-broking companies within the banking group. The deadline for the rationalization exercise was 30 June 2006. To facilitate the establishment of investment banks, and for regulatory purposes, the Guidelines on Investment Banking were issued jointly by BNM and the Securities Commission.

Other developments since the mid-1980s have included the establishment of Islamic banking, the formation of a secondary mortgage market, the establishment of property unit trusts and, in 1991, of the country's first credit rating company, the Rating Agency of Malaysia. The first full Islamic bank, Bank Islam Malaysia Bhd, was established in 1983 under the Islamic Banking Act. In the second phase of the development of Islamic banking, conventional banking institutions were allowed to offer Islamic banking services on a window basis (allocating a designated area for the facility). The third phase was enacted in 2004 with the introduction of a new framework known as Islamic subsidiary (IS). BNM approved the applications of five domestic banking groups to establish an IS under their commercial banking wing, and in 2005 the Islamic banking system was represented by 30 Islamic banking institutions—four Islamic banks and 26 conventional banking institutions (eight commercial banks, four foreign banks, four merchant banks, three finance companies and seven discount houses). The Islamic banking sector has flourished over the years, and from 2000 its assets grew at an average rate of 18% per annum. At the end of 2005 the total assets of the Islamic banking industry were valued at RM 111,800m.; in terms of market share, the largest portion of the assets (53.4%) remained with the commercial banks in the Islamic Banking Scheme. The financial liberalization of the Islamic banking sector was brought forward from the original scheduled date of 2007 to 2004. In line with this new development, the BNM issued new Islamic banking licences to three foreign Islamic financial institutions from the Middle East—Kuwait Finance House; Al-Rajhi Banking and Investment Corporation; and RUSD Investment Bank Inc and Global Investment House, a consortium represented by Qatar Islamic Bank. In April 2009 the BNM issued RM 2,000m. worth of Bon Simpanan Merdeka bonds as an additional savings instrument for Malaysian citizens aged 56 and above. In addition, the Government announced the issuance of Syariah (*Shari'a*)-compliant savings bonds, worth a total of RM 5,000m., for citizens above the age of 21. With a nominal return of 5.0% per annum, the real return on both these bonds was expected to average in excess of 3.0% in 2009.

The Islamic banking and finance system remained resilient throughout 2010, largely as a result of high capitalization and improvement in asset quality. A government initiative to continue to liberalize the sector and the issuance of new licences to predominantly foreign-led operators, in order to make Malaysia a regional Islamic finance hub, further supported sectoral growth. BNM reported that Islamic banking assets increased by 16% in 2010, reaching RM 350,800m., and accounted for 21% of total banking assets. Syariah -compliant lending rose by 19% to reach RM 222,300 m. in 2010, which represented 23% of total loans in the country. Syariah-compliant bonds sold in Malaysia reached US $94,000m. in 2010. *Takaful* (Syariah-compliant) insurance assets rose by 18% in 2010 to a record-high RM 14,700m. The Government approved four licences for foreign Islamic life insurance operators in 2010, including a 70:30 joint venture between American International Assurance Co Ltd and Alliance Bank Malaysia Bhd.

In April 1994 the Government announced the establishment of Khazanah Nasional to manage government assets. Khazanah, which was based on the highly successful state-operated investment agency in Singapore, Temasek Holdings, unified all government corporate holdings, and was able to invest in industries considered important for the country's economic development. To enhance the capacity of the domestic banking sector, the Government introduced an integrated commercial bank and finance company (BAFIN) framework, which came into force in January 2004 and whereby domestic banks were afforded the option of conducting commercial banking and finance company business through a single entity. In 2004 five out of 10 finance companies successfully merged with their respective banks, namely Alliance Bank Malaysia Bhd, EON Bank Bhd, Hong Leong Bank Bhd, Malayan Banking Bhd and Public Bank Bhd. In April 2009 BNM announced measures to liberalize the financial sector, including the issuance of up to seven new banking licences and two insurance licences, and an increase in foreign ownership limits from 49% to 70% for investment banks, Islamic banks, conventional insurance companies and *takaful* (Syariah-compliant) operators. As a result, in June 2010 Malaysia issued commercial banking licences to five foreign banks (BNP Paribas of France, Indonesia's PT Bank Mandiri (Persero), the United Arab Emirates' National Bank of Abu Dhabi, and Japan's Mizuho Corporate Bank Ltd and Sumitomo Mitsui Banking Corpn).

From the early 1980s the Government focused on decreasing its budget deficit, primarily through a reduction in public expenditure and the privatization of publicly owned companies. However, the severe deflationary impact of the regional financial crisis of the late 1990s on the domestic economy resulted in a revision of policy. Additional budgetary funds were allocated from mid-1998, mainly for infrastructure development, and this contributed to a fiscal deficit equivalent to 3.7% of GDP in 1998. According to the IMF, the budget deficit amounted to US $9,488m. in 1999 (equivalent to 3.2% of GDP). The budget deficits for 2000 and 2001 were estimated at 4.0% and 5.5% of GDP, respectively. The Government's budgetary operations remained expansionary in 2002, resulting in a deficit of approximately RM 20,300m., or 5.6% of GDP. In 2003 and 2004, however, the fiscal deficit narrowed, to 5.3% and 4.3% of GDP, respectively. In 2007 the deficit was 3.2% of GDP. The reduction of this deficit reflected the Government's strong commitment to consolidation of fiscal policy.

To mitigate the impact of the global slowdown, the Malaysian Government introduced two economic stimulus programmes in 2008, providing for a total allocation of RM 67,000m., equivalent to almost 10% of GDP. As a result, the budget deficit increased to 4.8% of GDP in 2008. The first range of measures, worth RM 7,000m., was announced on 4 November 2008, and was intended to offset the shortfall in private sector demand and to stimulate private spending. On 10 March 2009 the second stimulus programme, worth RM 60,000m., was announced, with the aim of supporting domestic economic activities and strengthening future growth capacity. Of the total, RM 15,000m. was to be in the form of fiscal stimulus, RM 25,000m. for guarantee funds, RM 10,000m. for equity investments, RM 7,000m. for private finance initiatives and RM 3,000m. in the form of tax incentives. The budget deficit in 2009 therefore increased to 7.0%. In 2010 the Government announced a series of reform measures to reduce the budget deficit. A reduction in fuel and sugar subsidies was expected to reduce government expenditure by more than RM 750m. In July the Government announced that fuel prices were to rise by 5 sen, with 1 litre of petrol costing RM 1.85 and 1 litre of diesel RM 1.75, while higher-grade petrol would no longer be subsidized and would be determined by a market float. The price of liquefied petroleum gas increased by 10 sen, to RM 1.85 per kg, while sugar rose by 25 sen, to RM 1.90 per kg. Nevertheless, the Government was still projected to spend RM 7,820m. on fuel and sugar subsidies alone in 2010. The budget deficit in that year was estimated at 5.6% of GDP; this was forecast to decrease slightly to 5.4% of GDP in 2010. A series of policy measures was implemented to reduce government expenditure and to increase government revenue. In December the price of higher-grade petrol was increased to RM 2.30 per litre, with additional increases of 10 sen and 30 sen, respectively, in January and April 2011. As a measure to generate additional revenue for its national development programme, the Government announced an increase in the service tax rate from 5% to 6%, effective from 1 January 2011, and widened the service tax base by introducing the tax on monthly subscription fees for premium television broadcasting services. In addition, it was hoped that the revenue collection system would be strengthened by increased auditing and enforcement.

The Kuala Lumpur Stock Exchange (KLSE) was established in 1973, but assumed an independent existence only after the traditional links with the Stock Exchange of Singapore were severed in December 1989. Confidence in the Exchange was eroded in the first half of 1990, leading the Government to introduce higher capital requirements for licensed brokerage firms from June of that year, which caused many companies to merge. As a result of the Government's privatization policy, the KLSE's market capitalization was higher than that of its regional competitors in Singapore and Bangkok, Thailand. In 1995 the Government announced a series of measures that aimed to liberalize the capital market, including permission for the full foreign ownership of fund-management companies, in anticipation of a future role as a major regional capital market. In May 1996 the Government granted an operating licence for the country's second financial futures exchange, the Commodity and Monetary Exchange of Malaysia. An additional exchange, the Malaysian Exchange of Securities Dealing and Automated Quotation (MESDAQ), which was aimed at technology companies, began operating at the end of 1998. (In March 2002, however, MESDAQ merged with the KLSE and ceased to operate as a stock exchange.) The KLSE was demutualized in January 2004 and was converted into an exchange holding company known as Kuala Lumpur Stock Exchange Bhd (KLSE). Consequently, it transferred its stock exchange business to its wholly owned subsidiary, Malaysia Securities Exchange Bhd. In April 2004 the KLSE adopted a new corporate identity and name, Bursa Malaysia Bhd. Its wholly owned subsidiary, Malaysia Securities Exchange Bhd, then became known as Bursa Malaysia Securities Sdn Bhd. Between 2001 and 2005 funds raised by the capital market totalled RM 416,100m., an increase of 89% compared with the period 1996–2000. In 2007 net funds raised in the capital market amounted to RM 45,478m. Of the total funds raised, the private sector and public sector accounted for 44.6% and 55.4%, respectively. The first exchange-traded fund, the ASEAN Bond Fund, was listed on Bursa Malaysia in July 2005.

In February 2000 multilateral trade negotiations concerning the services sector commenced, under the auspices of the World Trade Organization (WTO). By 2005 Malaysia had undertaken, under the General Agreement on Trade in Services (GATS), to allow an aggregate maximum foreign equity limit in the domestic banking institutions of 30%. A commitment was also made to allow existing, original, foreign shareholders to own up to 51% of companies within the insurance sector. The ASEAN Framework Agreement on Services (AFAS) was signed in 1995, with the intention of liberalizing financial services in ASEAN. The ASEAN countries' finance ministers agreed that the commitment offer under the AFAS was preferable to existing commitments under the GATS. Foreign ownership in the financial sector is quite substantial, with about one-half of the commercial banks being wholly foreign-owned. Of the total of 63 insurance companies, 25 were completely under foreign ownership.

DEVELOPMENT AND PLANNING

Malaysia has undertaken 11 national development plans since independence: the First Malaya Plan (1956–60), the Second Malaya Plan (1961–65) and the nine five-year Malaysia Plans covering the period 1966–2010.

In the 1950s a basic feature of the Malaysian economy was the concentration of Malays and other indigenous people in the 'traditional', subsistence agriculture sector of the economy with other races, notably the Chinese, having the major role in the modern rural and urban sectors. In order to redress the balance, the Second Malaysia Plan and, to some extent, the Third Plan were based on the NEP, which was inaugurated in 1970 in the aftermath of the 1969 racial riots. The two main aims of the NEP (and of the Second Malaysia Plan) were to reduce, and eventually eradicate, poverty by increasing income levels and employment opportunities for all Malaysians, irrespective of race; and to accelerate the process of restructuring Malaysian society in order to correct economic and geographical imbalances, thereby reducing, and eventually eliminating, the identification of race with economic function. The period 1971–80 represented the first decade of the Outline Perspective Plan (OPP) 1971–90, within which the objectives of the NEP were to be realized.

Over the period covered by the NEP, the controversial target of 30% *bumiputra* equity ownership was not achieved. However, the *bumiputras'* share of the corporate sector increased from 2.4% to 20.3% between 1970 and 1990. Chinese and Indian equity ownership increased from 32% to 46% over the same period, while that of foreigners was reduced from 63% to 25%. The proportion not accounted for was held by nominee companies that were not classified by race, promoting conflicting claims about the accuracy of the declared share of *bumiputra* ownership. However, the transfer of state assets to *bumiputra* ownership resulted in the creation of a wealthy élite within the Malay community, where income disparity was now greater than in other ethnic groups.

In June 1991 the NDP, the successor to the NEP, was announced. This formed the basis of the Prime Minister's 'Vision 2020', the date by which he intended Malaysia to become an industrialized country. The focus of the NDP differed slightly from that of the NEP; racially based economic and social engineering was relaxed in favour of national unity. The 30% target for *bumiputra* corporate ownership was retained, but there was no deadline set for its achievement. The emphasis was placed on the development of skills to promote the consolidation of *bumiputra* wealth. In the early 1990s there were too few Malays with relevant managerial qualifications; this shortage of suitable personnel hindered government efforts to broaden *bumiputra* participation at a high level. The NDP's macroeconomic and social targets were contained in the OPP for 1991–2000. Real GDP was projected to grow at an average rate of 7% per year, while development expenditure was to total RM 224,000m. Manufacturing's share of exports was projected to increase to more than 80%, while average annual growth in imports was to be restrained to 11.8%, compared with the average 15.7% increase that had occurred under the NEP. The level of unemployment was to be reduced from 6% of the labour force in 1991 to 4% by 2000, and the poverty rate was to decrease from 17% to 7%.

In May 1996 the Seventh Malaysia Plan (1996–2000) was introduced. Under this, the average annual GDP growth target was set at 8.6%, with the manufacturing sector expected to grow at an average annual rate of just under 11%. Exports of manufactures were expected to increase by an average of 17% annually. The major focus of the Seventh Malaysia Plan was to upgrade the economy and to achieve a strategic shift from low-skill, low value-added output to high-skill, high value-added output. A major aspect of this was an emphasis on improved vocational training, which was to be stimulated by the Human Resources Development Council, and the provision of greater opportunities within tertiary education under a commercialized and partly privatized university system.

However, one of the major obstacles to this restructuring, which the Seventh Plan did not address in detail, was the increasing reliance of the Malaysian economy on imported unskilled labour. There was also a growing caucus that was concerned about the increasing pollution and congestion problems, which were seen to be related to the rapid rate of growth that Malaysia achieved in the late 1980s and early 1990s and which was projected to continue under the Seventh Malaysia Plan. However, these concerns were superseded by the economic crisis of 1997–98, which transformed the economic situation and delayed by at least 10 years the attainment of industrialized status.

In early 2001 the Malaysian Government introduced the Third OPP, a 10-year development programme for 2001–10, which focused on creating a resilient and competitive economy. In addition, the Eighth Malaysia Plan (2001–05) was announced in April 2001. The main aims of the Plan were: to shift the growth strategy from one that was input-driven to one that was knowledge-driven; to accelerate structural transformation within the manufacturing and services sectors; and to strengthen socio-economic stability through the equitable distribution of income and wealth. The Plan laid emphasis on nine principal strategies: maintaining macroeconomic stability; eradicating poverty and restructuring society; enhancing productivity-driven growth; increasing competitiveness in strategic sectors; expanding usage of information and communications technology; enhancing human resource development; achieving sustainable development; ensuring quality of life; and strengthening moral and ethical values. Under the Plan, the Government aimed to achieve economic growth averaging 7.5% per year, with low inflation and sustainable budgetary and external accounts. It was envisaged that the manufacturing and services sectors would continue to provide the greatest contribution to the economic growth of Malaysia.

The Ninth Malaysia Plan, encompassing the period 2006–10, was announced in March 2006. The main emphasis of the Plan was to enhance the nation's capability to compete globally by developing human capital, providing a business-friendly environment and accelerating economic activities. The Plan aimed to address the five aims envisaged in the National Mission, a new policy framework formulated to reinforce the country's efforts towards achieving Vision 2020. The first objective of the Mission was to move the economy up the value chain. The Plan outlined several efforts to achieve this: enhancing value added in manufacturing, services and agriculture; generating new sources of wealth through information communication technology and biotechnology; enhancing job creation; emphasizing the private sector as the main engine of economic development; and expanding the market for Malaysian products and services. The second objective of the National Mission was to raise the country's capacity for knowledge, creativity and innovation and nurture a 'first class mentality'. Strategies outlined to achieve this objective were: improving the access to and quality of the education system at all levels; making national schools the 'school of choice'; producing tertiary institutions of international standing; promoting high-quality research and development, scientific and innovation capability; empowering women and youth; and fostering a society with strong values. The third objective was to address persistent socio-economic inequalities. To attain this, the Ninth Malaysia Plan aimed to eradicate poverty, reduce income, regional and employment disparities, reduce asset and wealth disparity, develop competitive *bumiputra* entrepreneurs, bridge the digital divide and review past programmes for effectiveness. The fourth objective was to improve the standard and sustainability of quality of life. Here, the Government focused on housing needs, urban services, health care services, transport services, energy and water supply, environmental protection and the role of culture, arts and heritage in society, as well as on sporting activities, in achieving this objective. The fifth objective was to strengthen institutional and implementation capacity through the promotion of good governance, enhancement of public services and the development of international co-operation.

The Third Industrial Master Plan (2006–20) was launched in August 2006 to direct the development of the industrial and services sectors for the next 15 years and to facilitate government efforts to realize the objectives and emphases of the Ninth Malaysia Plan and of Vision 2020. The emphasis of the plan was to sustain growth in the manufacturing sector and to facilitate the expansion of the services sector. The principal aim was to render the country an attractive, cost-effective and business-friendly base for trade and investment.

Under the premiership of Najib Tun Razak, the Government pledged in 2009 to reduce dirigiste interventions through state-owned enterprises, raise new revenue through a goods and services tax, and lower subsidies on staples. Such liberalizing measures were welcomed by foreign investors.

In March 2010 Malaysia announced the New Economic Model (NEM), which was intended to facilitate the country's progression from a middle-income country to developed nation status by 2020, envisaging per caput GDP of US $15,000, and to promote inclusiveness and increase the income of 40% of households. To this end the NEM proposed the implementation of eight strategic research initiatives: re-energizing the private sector; developing a high-quality work-force; forging a competitive domestic economy; strengthening the public sector; providing for transparent and market-friendly affirmative action; building knowledge-based infrastructure; enhancing sources of growth; and ensuring the sustainability of growth. Strategic direction and reform initiatives in the NEM were to be followed under the 10th Malaysia Plan.

The 10th Malaysia Plan, encompassing the period 2011–15, was announced in June 2010. The main objectives of the Plan included: charting development for a high-income nation; creating a private sector-led economy; stimulating innovation-led growth; achieving full employment; and restructuring subsidies. Per caput GNI was targeted to increase to RM 38,850 (US $12,140) by 2015, which would require real GDP growth of 6.5% per annum. The Plan allocated RM 230,000m. to development expenditure, of which 55% was to be disbursed to the financial sector, 30% to the social sector, 10% to defence and security, and 5% to general administration. Emphasis was to be accorded to efforts to develop non-physical infrastructure, including human capital development such as the development of skills and innovation capabilities. The funding allocated to non-physical infrastructure was to be increased to 40%, compared with 21.8% in the Ninth Malaysia Plan. The 10th Malaysia Plan was to focus on 12 key economic areas identified as having the potential to generate high income: oil and gas; palm oil and related products; financial services; wholesale and retail; tourism; information and communications technology; education services; electrical and electronics; business services; private health care; agriculture; and greater Kuala Lumpur. The Government also intended to promote environmentally friendly housing via the introduction of an environmental rating system and guidelines.

Statistical Survey

Sources (unless otherwise stated): Department of Statistics, Blok C6, Parcel C, Pusat Pentadbiran Kerajaan Persekutuan, 62514 Putrajaya; tel. (3) 88857000; fax (3) 88889248; e-mail jpbpo@stats.gov.my; internet www.statistics.gov.my; Bank Negara Malaysia (Central Bank of Malaysia), Jalan Dato' Onn, POB 10922, 50929 Kuala Lumpur; tel. (3) 26988044; fax (3) 26912990; e-mail info@bnm.gov.my; internet www.bnm.gov.my; Departments of Statistics, Kuching and Kota Kinabalu.

Note: Unless otherwise indicated, statistics refer to all states of Malaysia

Area and Population

AREA, POPULATION AND DENSITY

Area (sq km)	
Peninsular Malaysia	132,631
Sabah (incl. Labuan)	73,722
Sarawak	124,450
Total	330,803*
Population (census results)	
5–20 July 2000†	23,274,690
6 July 2010 (preliminary)	
Males	14,112,667
Females	13,453,154
Total	27,565,821
Density (per sq km) at July 2010 census	83.3

* 127,724 sq miles.

† Including adjustment of 4.6% for underenumeration, enumerated total was 22,198,276.

POPULATION BY AGE AND SEX

('000, official estimates at mid-2009)

	Males	Females	Total
0–14	4,647.0	4,367.7	9,014.7
15–64	9,157.6	8,848.4	18,005.8
65 and over	602.7	683.5	1,286.2
Total	14,407.2	13,899.4	28,306.7

Note: Estimates not adjusted to take account of preliminary results of 2010 census; totals may not be equal to the sum of components, owing to rounding.

PRINCIPAL ETHNIC GROUPS

(at census of August 1991)*

	Peninsular Malaysia	Sabah†	Sarawak	Total
Malays and other indigenous groups	8,433,826	1,003,540	1,209,118	10,646,484
Chinese	4,250,969	218,233	475,752	4,944,954
Indians	1,380,048	9,310	4,608	1,393,966
Others	410,544	167,790	10,541	588,875
Non-Malaysians	322,229	464,786	18,361	805,376
Total	14,797,616	1,863,659	1,718,380	18,379,655

* Including adjustment for underenumeration.

† Including the Federal Territory of Labuan.

Mid-2009 ('000 persons): Malays 14,409.9; Other indigenous groups 3,128.4; Chinese 6,437.7; Indian 1,939.2; Others 340.5; Non-Malaysians 2,051.0; Total 28,306.7.

ADMINISTRATIVE DIVISIONS

(population at 2010 census, preliminary results)

	Area (sq km)	Population ('000)	Density (per sq km)	Capital
States				
Johor (Johore)	19,210	3,233.4	168	Johor Bahru
Kedah	9,500	1,890.1	199	Alor Star
Kelantan	15,099	1,460.0	97	Kota Bharu
Melaka (Malacca)	1,664	788.7	474	Melaka
Negeri Sembilan (Negri Sembilan)	6,686	997.1	149	Seremban
Pahang	36,137	1,443.4	40	Kuantan
Perak	21,035	2,258.4	107	Ipoh
Perlis	821	227.0	277	Kangar
Pulau Pinang (Penang)	1,048	1,520.1	1,451	George Town
Sabah	73,631	3,120.0	42	Kota Kinabalu
Sarawak	124,450	2,420.0	19	Kuching
Selangor	8,104	5,411.3	668	Shah Alam
Terengganu (Trengganu)	13,035	1,015.8	78	Kuala Terengganu
Federal Territories				
Kuala Lumpur	243	1,627.2	6,696	—
Labuan	91	85.3	937	—
Putrajaya	49	68.0	1,387	—
Total	330,803	27,565.8	83	

PRINCIPAL TOWNS

(population at 2000 census)

Kuala Lumpur (capital)	1,305,792	Sabang Jaya	447,183
Johor Bahru	642,944	Shah Alam	314,440
Kelang (Klang)	626,699	Kota Kinabalu	306,920
Ipoh	536,832	Seremban	290,709
Petaling Jaya	432,619	Kuantan	288,727
Kuching	422,240	Sandakan	276,791

2010 census (preliminary): Kuala Lumpur 1,627,172.

BIRTHS AND DEATHS*

	Registered live births		Registered deaths	
	Number	Rate (per 1,000)	Number	Rate (per 1,000)
2004	477,800	19.1	112,700	4.5
2005	469,200	18.5	113,700	4.5
2006	465,100	18.1	115,100	4.5
2007	472,000	18.1	118,200	4.5
2008	487,300	18.4	124,900	4.7
2009†	481,700	17.9	129,000	4.8

* Numbers are rounded to nearest 100.
† Preliminary estimates.

Life expectancy (years at birth, official estimates, 2010): Males 71.7; females 76.6.

ECONOMICALLY ACTIVE POPULATION*
(sample surveys, ISIC major divisions, '000 persons aged 15 to 64 years)

	2008	2009	2010
Agriculture, hunting, forestry and fishing	1,487.7	1,471.1	1,475.1
Mining and quarrying	54.5	62.7	55.3
Manufacturing	1,944.7	1,807.1	1,879.7
Electricity, gas and water	60.5	58.1	113.7
Construction	998.0	1,015.9	1,019.0
Wholesale and retail trade; repair of motor vehicles, motorcycles and personal and household goods	1,729.4	1,831.8	1,806.5
Hotels and restaurants	783.6	800.5	810.7
Transport, storage and communications	583.4	592.0	693.0
Financial intermediation	276.0	271.5	305.2
Real estate, renting and business activities	553.2	601.9	650.1
Public administration and defence; compulsory social security	751.1	813.9	772.1
Education	656.5	731.4	771.7
Health and social work	252.6	271.7	276.2
Other community, social and personal service activities	274.2	303.3	262.4
Private households with employed persons	253.0	262.5	236.6
Extra-territorial organizations and bodies	1.1	1.7	2.3
Total employed	10,659.6	10,897.3	11,129.4
Unemployed	368.5	418.0	387.9
Total labour force	11,028.1	11,315.3	11,517.2
Males	7,074.6	7,218.1	7,351.8
Females	3,953.5	4,097.2	4,165.4

* Excluding members of the armed forces.

Health and Welfare

KEY INDICATORS

Total fertility rate (children per woman, 2009)	2.5
Under-5 mortality rate (per 1,000 live births, 2009)	6
HIV/AIDS (% of persons aged 15–49, 2007)	0.5
Physicians (per 1,000 head, 2002)	0.7
Hospital beds (per 1,000 head, 2006)	1.9
Health expenditure (2008): US $ per head (PPP)	621
Health expenditure (2008): % of GDP	4.3
Health expenditure (2008): public (% of total)	44.1
Access to sanitation (% of persons, 2008)	96
Total carbon dioxide emissions ('000 metric tons, 2007)	194,316.6
Carbon dioxide emissions per head (metric tons, 2007)	7.3
Human Development Index (2010): ranking	57
Human Development Index (2010): value	0.744

For sources and definitions, see explanatory note on p. vi.

Agriculture

PRINCIPAL CROPS
('000 metric tons)

	2007	2008	2009
Rice, paddy	2,375	2,353	2,510
Maize	32	33	35
Sweet potatoes	30	18	19
Cassava (Manioc)*	448	435	440
Sugar cane	560	694	700*
Coconuts	503	455	460
Oil palm fruit*	79,100	83,000	84,842
Cabbages	66	73	77*
Tomatoes	73	76	80*
Cucumbers and gherkins	56	58	55
Watermelons	154	220	229
Bananas*	530	600	625
Pineapples	316	385	400
Papayas*	81	55	72
Coffee, green	31	29	30*
Cocoa beans	35	28	18
Pepper	20	25	23
Natural rubber	1,200	1,072	857

* FAO estimate(s).

Aggregate production ('000 metric tons, may include official, semi-official or estimated data): Total cereals 2,407 in 2007, 2,386 in 2008, 2,545 in 2009; Total oilcrops 17,819 in 2007, 19,949 in 2008, 19,746 in 2009; Total vegetables (incl. melons) 678 in 2007, 739 in 2008, 759 in 2009; Total fruits (excl. melons) 1,452 in 2007, 1,428 in 2008, 1,486 in 2009.

Source: FAO.

LIVESTOCK
('000 head, year ending September)

	2007	2008	2009*
Cattle	785	797	800
Buffaloes	130	128	128
Goats	335	336	336
Sheep	113	110	116
Pigs	2,024	2,028	2,050
Chickens*	190,000	195,000	205,000
Ducks*	47,000	47,500	48,000

* FAO estimates.

Source: FAO.

LIVESTOCK PRODUCTS
('000 metric tons)

	2007	2008	2009
Cattle meat*	22.3	22.7	23.2
Buffalo meat*	4.2	3.8	4.0
Pig meat	200.1	195.1	199.1
Chicken meat	931.0†	931.0*	952.0*
Duck meat*	106.6	107.1	107.9
Cows' milk*	39.3	39.6	40.9
Buffaloes' milk*	8.4	9.0	10.7
Hen eggs*	476.0	505.5	540.0
Other poultry eggs*	11.7	11.3	13.9

* FAO estimate(s).
† Unofficial figure.

Source: FAO.

Forestry

ROUNDWOOD REMOVALS
('000 cubic metres, excl. bark)

	2007	2008	2009
Sawlogs, veneer logs and logs for sleepers	23,522	21,244	18,713
Pulpwood	703	703	703
Other industrial roundwood	769	798	710
Fuel wood	2,959	2,908	2,858
Total	27,953	25,653	22,984

Source: FAO.

SAWNWOOD PRODUCTION
('000 cubic metres, incl. railway sleepers)

	2007	2008	2009
Total (all broadleaved)	5,084	4,486	3,875

Source: FAO.

Fishing

('000 metric tons, live weight)

	2007	2008	2009
Capture	1,385.7	1,398.9	1,395.6
Indian scad	90.0	96.9	92.0
Kawakawa	24.0	30.0	21.0
Indian mackerels	156.7	170.3	185.5
Squids	59.7	56.4	56.2
Aquaculture	178.2	243.1*	333.4
Blood cockle	49.6	61.1	64.9
Total catch	1,563.9	1,642.0*	1,729.0

* FAO estimate.

Note: Figures exclude crocodiles, recorded by number rather than by weight. The number of estuarine crocodiles caught was: 540 in 2007; 1,043 in 2008; 587 in 2009. Also excluded are shells and corals. Catches of turban shells (metric tons, FAO estimates) were: 80 in 2007–09. Catches of hard corals (metric tons, FAO estimates) were: 4,000 in 2007–09.

Source: FAO.

Mining

PRODUCTION
(metric tons unless otherwise indicated)

	2008	2009	2010
Tin-in-concentrates	3,007	2,412	2,642*
Bauxite	275,069	263,432	124,474*
Iron ore†	981,932	1,470,186	3,465,895*
Kaolin	419,157	463,736	n.a.
Gold (kg)	2,490	2,794	3,766
Hard coal	1,151,024	2,122,651	2,399,699*
Ilmenite†‡	36,779	15,983	16,947*
Crude petroleum ('000 barrels)	251,811	240,479	232,965
Natural gas (net production, million cu ft)	2,154,853	2,119,356	2,159,533
Zirconium†§	984	1,145	n.a.

* Preliminary figure.
† Figures refer to the gross weight of ores and concentrates.
‡ Concentrate from amang retreatment plants.
§ Source: US Geological Survey.

Industry

SELECTED PRODUCTS
('000 metric tons unless otherwise indicated)

	2008	2009	2010
Canned fish, frozen shrimps/prawns	45.8	47.7	41.8
Palm oil (crude)	17,734	n.a.	n.a.
Refined sugar	1,519.0	1,488.8	1,661.7
Soft drinks ('000 litres)	2,069.4	1,667.0	2,980.7
Cigarettes (metric tons)	23,004	20,892	20,935
Woven cotton fabrics (million metres)	200.7	166.3	172.7
Veneer sheets ('000 cu metres)	948.1	753.5	1,016.6
Plywood ('000 cu metres)	4,557.8	3,655.2	4,094.6
Kerosene and jet fuel	3,940.4	3,402.8	3,350.4
Liquefied petroleum gas	3,625.6	3,265.3	3,054.6
Inner tubes and tyres ('000)	35,532	27,647	30,105
Rubber gloves (million pairs)	22,585.6	23,132.7	26,257.3
Earthen brick and cement roofing tiles (million)	1,129.7	311.6	528.4
Cement	19,629	19,457	19,762
Iron and steel bars and rods	2,368.3	1,890.7	2,217.0
Television receivers ('000)	5,732.4	6,361.8	13,163.3
Radio receivers ('000)	61,539	58,410	57,350
Semiconductors (million)	20,520	14,885	17,997
Electronic transistors (million)	31,346	29,271	34,184
Integrated circuits (million)	30,752	23,279	38,007
Passenger motor cars ('000)*	419.6	409.4	474.7
Commercial vehicles ('000)*	85.2	67.6	72.6
Motorcycles and scooters ('000)	550.3	514.5	634.9
Electric energy (million kWh)†	106,357	106,943	n.a.

* Vehicles assembled from imported parts.
† Source: Asian Development Bank.

Tin (smelter production of primary metal, metric tons): 25,471 in 2007; 31,691 in 2008; 36,407 in 2009 (Source: US Geological Survey).

Finance

CURRENCY AND EXCHANGE RATES

Monetary Units
100 sen = 1 ringgit Malaysia (RM—also formerly Malaysian dollar).

Sterling, US Dollar and Euro Equivalents (31 May 2011)
£1 sterling = RM 4.9699;
US $1 = RM 3.0115;
€1 = RM 4.3320;
RM 100 = £20.12 = US $33.21 = €23.08.

Average Exchange Rate (ringgit Malaysia per US $)
2008 3.336
2009 3.525
2010 3.221

FEDERAL BUDGET
(RM million)

Revenue	2008	2009	2010
Tax revenue	112,897	106,504	109,515
Taxes on income and profits	82,138	78,375	79,009
Companies (excl. petroleum)	37,741	30,199	27,234
Individuals	14,966	15,590	29,252
Petroleum	24,191	27,231	16,797
Export duties	2,779	1,152	1,810
Import duties	2,635	2,114	1,966
Excises on goods	10,682	10,068	11,770
Sales tax	8,374	8,603	8,171
Service tax	3,345	3,344	3,926
Others	2,944	2,847	2,863
Other revenue	46,896	52,135	50,138
Total	159,793	158,639	159,653

Expenditure	2008	2009	2010
Emoluments	41,011	42,778	46,663
Pensions and gratuities	10,022	10,146	11,515
Debt service charges	12,797	14,222	15,621
Domestic	11,642	13,312	14,963
External	1,155	909	658
Supplies and services	25,197	26,372	23,841
Subsidies	35,166	20,345	23,106
Asset acquisition	2,835	2,582	1,869
Other grants and transfers	25,623	39,937	27,862
Other expenditure	849	685	1,155
Total	153,499	157,067	151,633

FEDERAL DEVELOPMENT EXPENDITURE
(RM million)

	2007	2008	2009
Defence and security	5,702	5,779	3,956
Social services	12,893	13,717	17,388
Education	6,271	7,892	10,827
Health	1,496	1,652	2,575
Housing	2,947	1,780	1,395
Economic services	20,116	21,353	26,440
Agriculture and rural development	3,842	4,184	5,508
Public utilities	2,358	2,795	2,899
Trade and industry	4,904	4,581	4,916
Transport	8,500	9,212	9,450
General administration	1,853	1,998	1,731
Sub-total	40,564	42,847	49,515
Less Loan recoveries	3,105	959	519
Total	37,460	41,889	48,997

INTERNATIONAL RESERVES
(US $ million at 31 December)

	2008	2009	2010
Gold (national valuation)	379	1,281	1,641
IMF special drawing rights	226	2,124	2,088
Reserve position in IMF	317	442	471
Foreign exchange	90,605	92,865	102,325
Total	91,527	96,712	106,525

Source: IMF, *International Financial Statistics*.

MONEY SUPPLY
(RM million at 31 December)

	2008	2009	2010
Currency outside depository corporations	40,431	43,438	47,685
Transferable deposits	150,840	170,431	192,266
Other deposits	681,907	749,555	800,434
Securities other than shares	47,606	28,628	27,424
Broad money	920,784	992,052	1,067,808

Source: IMF, *International Financial Statistics*.

COST OF LIVING
(Consumer Price Index; base 2005 = 100)

	2008	2009	2010
Food and non-alcoholic beverages	115.9	120.7	123.6
Alcoholic beverages and tobacco	123.6	131.2	136.3
Clothing and footwear	96.8	95.9	94.6
Rent and other housing costs, heating and lighting	104.4	105.9	107.1
Furniture, domestic appliances, tools and maintenance	105.3	108.4	109.2
Medical care	106.0	108.4	110.1
Transport	123.6	112.0	113.8
Communications	96.8	96.3	96.1
Education	105.8	108.3	110.1
All items (incl. others)	111.4	112.1	114.0

NATIONAL ACCOUNTS
(RM million at current prices)

Expenditure on the Gross Domestic Product

	2008	2009	2010
Government final consumption expenditure	91,855	95,918	97,513
Private final consumption expenditure	335,213	339,395	367,991
Changes in inventories	–1,948	–39,288	8,443
Gross fixed capital formation	145,414	137,504	155,594
Total domestic expenditure	570,534	533,529	629,541
Exports of goods and services	766,096	655,336	745,311
Less Imports of goods and services	594,160	508,927	608,886
GDP in purchasers' values	742,470	679,938	765,965
GDP at constant 2000 prices	530,683	522,001	559,554

Gross Domestic Product by Economic Activity

	2008	2009	2010
Agriculture, forestry and fishing	75,611	64,724	81,400
Mining and quarrying	123,978	84,102	96,131
Manufacturing	194,324	173,558	200,028
Electricity, gas and water	16,950	17,803	19,213
Construction	20,605	22,436	24,773
Trade	84,871	83,592	92,957
Restaurants and hotels	16,055	16,926	18,080
Transport and storage	24,821	23,923	25,801
Communications	21,384	22,725	25,001
Finance and insurance	59,463	61,983	65,988
Real estate and business services	30,007	31,472	34,766
Government services	53,237	55,096	58,488
Other services	33,223	35,367	37,421
Sub-total	754,529	693,707	780,047
Import duties	7,531	6,964	7,669
Less Financial intermediation services indirectly measured	19,589	20,733	21,751
GDP in purchasers' values	742,470	679,938	765,965

BALANCE OF PAYMENTS
(US $ million)

	2007	2008	2009
Exports of goods f.o.b.	176,220	199,733	157,655
Imports of goods f.o.b.	–138,493	–148,472	–117,402
Trade balance	37,727	51,261	40,253
Exports of services	29,462	30,321	28,769
Imports of services	–28,668	–30,270	–27,472
Balance on goods and services	38,520	51,313	41,551
Other income received	11,380	12,081	11,213
Other income paid	–15,462	–19,218	–15,382
Balance on goods, services and income	34,438	44,176	37,381
Current transfers received	391	419	1,077
Current transfers paid	–5,059	–5,681	–6,657
Current balance	29,770	38,914	31,801
Capital account (net)	–54	187	–45
Direct investment abroad	–11,334	–15,203	–8,014
Direct investment from abroad	8,590	7,376	1,387
Portfolio investment assets	–3,932	–2,878	–6,339
Portfolio investment liabilities	9,320	–21,083	6,048
Financial derivatives assets	198	–1,165	32
Financial derivatives liabilities	–246	506	651
Other investment assets	–17,400	3,826	–17,667
Other investment liabilities	3,427	–5,352	1,263
Net errors and omissions	–5,195	–8,578	–5,199
Overall balance	13,144	–3,450	3,918

Source: IMF, *International Financial Statistics*.

External Trade

PRINCIPAL COMMODITIES
(RM million)

Imports c.i.f.	2008	2009	2010
Capital goods*	69,913	65,769	76,435
Intermediate goods	379,136	297,340	363,154
Miscellaneous industrial supplies, processed	120,230	94,001	116,312
Parts and accessories of capital goods (excl. transportation equipment)	164,120	132,962	158,993
Consumption goods	32,304	31,427	34,591
Total (incl. others)†	519,804	434,670	529,195

Exports f.o.b.	2008	2009	2010
Palm oil	45,951	36,329	45,449
Crude petroleum and condensates	43,582	25,360	30,765
Liquefied natural gas	41,475	29,018	38,099
Semi-conductors	89,938	93,057	97,857
Electronic components	106,086	87,686	96,587
Consumer electrical products	19,874	18,793	25,807
Industrial and commercial electrical products	32,807	24,606	22,513
Electrical industrial machinery and equipment	24,729	21,641	24,942
Chemicals and chemical products	40,723	34,079	41,674
Metal manufactures	29,066	22,645	26,199
Total (incl. others)	663,014	552,518	639,428

* Figures net of re-exports.
† Including re-exports.

PRINCIPAL TRADING PARTNERS
(RM million)

Imports c.i.f.	2008	2009	2010
Australia	11,720	9,480	10,188
China, People's Republic	66,854	61,026	66,430
France	7,550	7,058	6,255
Germany	22,454	18,411	21,332
Hong Kong	13,530	10,811	12,681
India	10,278	7,872	7,978
Indonesia	24,177	23,019	29,390
Japan	64,878	54,316	66,535
Korea, Republic	24,226	20,132	28,687
Philippines	6,943	4,006	11,308
Singapore	57,056	49,359	60,278
Taiwan	25,094	18,469	23,829
Thailand	29,152	26,299	32,972
United Kingdom	7,624	5,997	5,826
USA	56,135	48,834	56,259
Total (incl. others)	519,804	434,670	529,195

Exports f.o.b.	2008	2009	2010
Australia	24,364	20,190	24,016
China, People's Republic	63,435	67,359	80,105
France	6,360	5,448	7,109
Germany	15,347	14,854	17,346
Hong Kong	28,209	29,113	32,408
India	24,728	17,306	20,934
Indonesia	20,703	17,235	18,090
Japan	71,688	53,345	66,763
Korea, Republic	26,956	20,318	24,330
Netherlands	23,439	18,525	20,216
Philippines	9,712	6,956	9,968
Singapore	97,019	77,009	85,253
Taiwan	16,867	14,520	20,209
Thailand	31,625	29,808	34,136
United Kingdom	9,455	7,082	7,195
USA	82,700	60,811	60,951
Total (incl. others)	663,014	552,518	639,428

Transport

RAILWAYS
(traffic, Peninsular Malaysia only)

	2002	2003	2004
Passenger-km (million)	1,138	1,031	1,152
Freight ton-km (million)	1,073	887	1,017

Source: UN, *Statistical Yearbook*.

ROAD TRAFFIC
(registered motor vehicles at 31 December)

	2001	2002	2003
Passenger cars	4,624,557	5,069,412	5,499,707
Buses and coaches	49,771	51,158	52,846
Lorries and vans	689,668	713,148	1,101,737
Road tractors	329,198	345,604	n.a.
Motorcycles and mopeds	5,609,351	5,842,617	6,164,958

2006: Passenger cars 7,024,043; Buses and coaches 59,991; Lorries and vans 836,579; Motorcycles and mopeds 7,458,128.

2008: Passenger cars 8,056,999; Buses and coaches 64,050; Lorries and vans 909,243; Motorcycles and mopeds 8,487,451.

Source: IRF, *World Road Statistics*.

SHIPPING

Merchant Fleet
(registered at 31 December)

	2007	2008	2009
Number of vessels	1,151	1,238	1,344
Total displacement ('000 grt)	6,974.6	7,078.2	7,717.8

Source: IHS Fairplay, *World Fleet Statistics*.

Sea-borne Freight Traffic*
(Peninsular Malaysia, international and coastwise, '000 metric tons)

	2008	2009	2010
Goods loaded	103,669	101,664	112,404
Goods unloaded	125,885	110,892	136,824

* Including transshipments.

Source: UN, *Monthly Bulletin of Statistics*.

CIVIL AVIATION
(traffic on scheduled services)

	2004	2005	2006
Kilometres flown (million)	278	291	291
Passengers carried ('000)	19,227	20,369	21,009
Passenger-km (million)	44,642	49,578	47,442
Total ton-km (million)	6,672	7,103	6,971

Source: UN, *Statistical Yearbook*.

2007: Passengers carried ('000) 21,325.8 (Source: World Bank, World Development Indicators database).

2008: Passengers carried ('000) 22,420.9 (Source: World Bank, World Development Indicators database).

Tourism

TOURIST ARRIVALS BY COUNTRY OF RESIDENCE*

	2008	2009	2010
Brunei	1,085,115	1,061,357	1,124,406
China, People's Republic (incl. Hong Kong and Macao)	949,864	1,019,756	1,130,261
Indonesia	2,428,605	2,405,360	2,506,509
Japan	433,462	395,746	415,881
Singapore	11,003,492	12,733,082	13,042,004
Thailand	1,493,789	1,449,262	1,458,678
Total (incl. others)	22,052,488	23,646,191	24,577,196

* Including Singapore residents crossing the frontier by road through the Johore Causeway.

Source: Malaysia Tourism Promotion Board.

Tourism receipts (US $ million, excl. passenger transport): 14,044 in 2007; 15,277 in 2008; 15,772 in 2009 (provisional) (Source: World Tourism Organization).

Communications Media

	2008	2009	2010
Telephones ('000 main lines in use)	4,514	4,524	4,573
Mobile cellular telephones ('000 subscribers)	27,713	30,144	34,456
Internet subscribers ('000)	5,221.6	5,591.8	n.a.
Broadband subscribers ('000)	1,318.5	1,671.8	2,078.5

Personal computers: 6,040,000 (231.5 per 1,000 persons) in 2006.

Radio receivers ('000 in use, 1997): 9,100.

Television receivers ('000 in use, 2001): 4,773.

Book production (incl. pamphlets, 1999): 5,084 titles (29,040,000 copies in 1996).

Daily newspapers (2004): 35 (average circulation 2,753,000 copies).

Non-daily newspapers (1997): 3 (average circulation 312,000 copies).

Periodicals (1992): 25 titles (average circulation 996,000 copies).

Sources: International Telecommunication Union; UNESCO, *Statistical Yearbook*; UN, *Statistical Yearbook*.

Education

(at 30 June 2008, unless otherwise indicated)

	Institutions	Teachers	Students
Primary	7,644	210,912	3,154,090
Secondary	2,181	159,019	2,310,660
Regular	1,845	139,740	2,126,146
Fully residential	54	3,368	33,289
Technical	90	7,713	69,006
Religious	55	3,306	38,865
Special	4	190	773
Special Model	11	879	10,437*
Sports	2	174	912†
Tertiary‡	48	14,960	210,724
Universities	9	7,823	97,103
Teacher training	31	3,220	46,019
MARA Institute of Technology	1	2,574	42,174

* 2004 figure.

† 2003 figure.

‡ 1995 figures.

Source: Ministry of Education, Putrajaya.

Teachers (2006/07): Pre-primary 27,389; Primary 205,772; Secondary 166,940; Tertiary 42,355 (Source: UNESCO Institute for Statistics).

Students (2006/07): Pre-primary 654,150; Primary 3,103,579; Secondary 2,499,165; Tertiary 805,136 (Source: UNESCO Institute for Statistics).

Pupil-teacher ratio (primary education, UNESCO estimate): 14.6 in 2007/08 (Source: UNESCO Institute for Statistics).

Adult literacy rate (UNESCO estimates): 92.5% (males 94.6%; females 90.3%) in 2009 (Source: UNESCO Institute for Statistics).

Directory

The Constitution

The Constitution of the Federation of Malaya became effective at independence on 31 August 1957. As subsequently amended, it is now the Constitution of Malaysia. The main provisions are summarized below.

SUPREME HEAD OF STATE

The Yang di-Pertuan Agong (King or Supreme Sovereign) is the Supreme Head of Malaysia.

Every act of government is derived from his authority, although he acts on the advice of Parliament and the Cabinet. The appointment of a Prime Minister lies within his discretion, and he has the right to refuse to dissolve Parliament even against the advice of the Prime Minister. He appoints the Judges of the Federal Court and the High Courts on the advice of the Prime Minister. He is the Supreme Commander of the Armed Forces. The Yang di-Pertuan Agong is elected by the Conference of Rulers, and to qualify for election he must be one of the nine hereditary Rulers. He holds office for five years or until his earlier resignation or death. Election is by secret ballot on each Ruler in turn, starting with the Ruler next in precedence after the late or former Yang di-Pertuan Agong. The first Ruler to obtain not fewer than five votes is declared elected. The Deputy Supreme Head of State (the Timbalan Yang di-Pertuan Agong) is elected by a similar process. On election the Yang di-Pertuan Agong relinquishes, for his tenure of office, all his functions as Ruler of his own state and may appoint a Regent. The Timbalan Yang di-Pertuan Agong exercises no powers in the ordinary course, but is immediately available to fill the post of Yang di-Pertuan Agong and carry out his functions in the latter's absence or disability. In the event of the Yang di-Pertuan Agong's death or resignation he takes over the exercise of sovereignty until the Conference of Rulers has elected a successor.

CONFERENCE OF RULERS

The Conference of Rulers consists of the Rulers and the heads of the other states. Its prime duty is the election by the Rulers only of the Yang di-Pertuan Agong and his deputy. The Conference must be consulted in the appointment of judges, the Auditor-General, the Election Commission and the Services Commissions. It must also be consulted and concur in the alteration of state boundaries, the extension to the federation as a whole, of Islamic religious acts and observances, and in any bill to amend the Constitution. Consultation is mandatory in matters affecting public policy or the special position of the Malays and natives of Sabah and Sarawak. The Conference also considers matters affecting the rights, prerogatives and privileges of the Rulers themselves.

FEDERAL PARLIAMENT

Parliament has two Houses—the Dewan Negara (Senate) and the Dewan Rakyat (House of Representatives). The Senate has a membership of 70, comprising 26 elected and 44 appointed members. Each state legislature, acting as an electoral college, elects two Senators; these may be members of the State Legislative Assembly or otherwise. The Yang di-Pertuan Agong appoints the other 44 members of the Senate; these include four Senators representing the three Federal Territories—Kuala Lumpur, Labuan and Putrajaya. Members of the Senate must be at least 30 years old. The Senate elects its President and Deputy President from among its members. It may initiate legislation, but all proposed legislation for the granting of funds must be introduced in the first instance in the House of Representatives. All legislative measures require approval by both Houses of Parliament before being presented to the Yang di-Pertuan Agong for the Royal Assent in order to become law. A bill originating in the Senate cannot receive Royal Assent until it has been approved by the House of Representatives, but the Senate has delaying powers only over a bill originating from and approved by the House of Representatives. Senators serve for a period of three years, but the Senate is not subject to dissolution. Parliament can, by statute, increase the number of Senators elected from each state to three. The House of Representatives consists of 219 elected members (see Amendments). Of these, 165 are from Peninsular Malaysia (including 11 from Kuala Lumpur and one from Putrajaya), 28 from Sarawak and 26 from Sabah (including one from Labuan). Members are returned from single-member constituencies on the basis of universal adult franchise. The term of the House of Representatives is limited to five years, after which time a fresh general election must be held. The Yang di-Pertuan Agong may dissolve Parliament before then if the Prime Minister so advises.

THE CABINET

To advise him in the exercise of his functions, the Yang di-Pertuan Agong appoints the Cabinet, consisting of the Prime Minister and an unspecified number of Ministers (who must all be Members of Parliament). The Prime Minister must be a citizen born in Malaysia and a member of the House of Representatives who, in the opinion of the Yang di-Pertuan Agong, commands the confidence of that House. Ministers are appointed on the advice of the Prime Minister. A number of Deputy Ministers (who are not members of the Cabinet) are also appointed from among Members of Parliament. The Cabinet meets regularly under the chairmanship of the Prime Minister to formulate policy.

PUBLIC SERVICES

The Public Services, civilian and military, are non-political and owe their loyalty not to the party in power but to the Yang di-Pertuan Agong and the Rulers. They serve whichever government may be in power, irrespective of the latter's political affiliation. To ensure the impartiality of the service, and its protection from political interference, the Constitution provides for a number of Services Commissions to select and appoint officers, to place them on the pensionable establishment, to determine promotion and to maintain discipline.

THE STATES

The heads of nine of the 13 states are hereditary Rulers. The Ruler of Perlis has the title of Raja, and the Ruler of Negeri Sembilan that of Yang di-Pertuan Besar. The rest of the Rulers are Sultans. The heads of the States of Melaka (Malacca), Pulau Pinang (Penang), Sabah and Sarawak are each designated Yang di-Pertua Negeri and do not participate in the election of the Yang di-Pertuan Agong. Each of the 13 states has its own written Constitution and a single Legislative Assembly. Every state legislature has powers to legislate on matters not reserved for the Federal Parliament. Each State Legislative Assembly has the right to order its own procedure, and the members enjoy parliamentary privilege. All members of the Legislative Assemblies are directly elected from single-member constituencies. The head of the state acts on the advice of the State Government. This advice is tendered by the State Executive Council or Cabinet in precisely the same manner in which the Federal Cabinet tenders advice to the Yang di-Pertuan Agong.

The legislative authority of the state is vested in the head of the state in the State Legislative Assembly. The executive authority of the state is vested in the head of the state, but executive functions may be conferred on other persons by law. Every state has its own Executive Council or Cabinet to advise the head of the state, headed by its Chief Minister (Ketua Menteri in Melaka, Pulau Pinang, Sabah and Sarawak and Menteri Besar in other states), and collectively responsible to the state legislature. Each state in Peninsular Malaysia is divided into administrative districts, each with its District Officer. Sabah is divided into five divisions: West Coast, Interior, Sandakan, Tawau and Kudat. Sarawak is divided into 11 Divisions, each in the charge of a Resident: Betong, Bintulu, Kapit, Kota Samarahan, Kuching, Limbang, Miri, Mukah, Sarikei, Sibu and Sri Aman.

AMENDMENTS

From 1 February 1974, the city of Kuala Lumpur, formerly the seat of the Federal Government and capital of Selangor State, is designated the Federal Territory of Kuala Lumpur. It is administered directly by the Federal Government and returns five members to the House of Representatives.

In April 1981 the legislature approved an amendment empowering the Yang di-Pertuan Agong to declare a state of emergency on the grounds of imminent danger of a breakdown in law and order or a threat to national security.

In August 1983 the legislature approved an amendment empowering the Prime Minister, instead of the Yang di-Pertuan Agong, to declare a state of emergency.

The island of Labuan, formerly part of Sabah State, was designated a Federal Territory as from 16 April 1984.

The legislature approved an amendment increasing the number of parliamentary constituencies in Sarawak from 24 to 27. The amendment took effect at the general election of 20–21 October 1990. The total number of seats in the House of Representatives, which had increased to 177 following an amendment in August 1983, was thus expanded to 180.

In March 1988 the legislature approved two amendments relating to the judiciary (see Judicial System).

In October 1992 the legislature adopted an amendment increasing the number of parliamentary constituencies from 180 to 192. The Kuala Lumpur Federal Territory and Selangor each gained three seats, Johor two, and Perlis, Kedah, Kelantan and Pahang one. The amendment took effect at the next general election (in April 1995).

In March 1993 an amendment was approved that removed the immunity from prosecution of the hereditary Rulers.

In May 1994 the House of Representatives approved an amendment that ended the right of the Yang di-Pertuan Agong to delay legislation by withholding his assent from legislation and returning it to Parliament for further consideration. Under the amendment, the Yang di-Pertuan Agong was obliged to give his assent to a bill within 30 days; if he failed to do so, the bill would, none the less, become law. An amendment was simultaneously approved restructuring the judiciary and introducing a mandatory code of ethics for judges, to be drawn up by the Government.

In 1996 an amendment was approved, increasing the number of parliamentary constituencies from 192 to 193.

In July 2001 an amendment was approved banning all discrimination on grounds of gender.

From 1 February 2001 the city of Putrajaya, formerly part of Selangor State, was designated a Federal Territory.

In 2003 the legislature approved an amendment increasing the number of parliamentary constituencies from 193 to 219. The amendments took effect at the next general election, held in March 2004.

In 2005 an amendment was approved increasing the number of parliamentary constituencies from 219 to 222, following the delineation of additional constituencies in Sarawak. The changes were implemented at the general election of March 2008.

The Government

SUPREME HEAD OF STATE

HM Yang di-Pertuan Agong: HRH Sultan Tuanku MIZAN ZAINAL ABIDIN IBNI AL-MARHUM Sultan MAHMUD (Sultan of Terengganu) (took office 13 December 2006).

Deputy Supreme Head of State

Timbalan Yang di-Pertuan Agong: HRH Tuanku Haji ABDUL HALIM MU'ADZAM SHAH IBNI AL-MARHUM Sultan BADLISHAH (Sultan of Kedah).

CABINET

(October 2011)

The Government is formed by the Barisan Nasional (National Front), led by the United Malays National Organization (UMNO).

Prime Minister and Minister of Finance: Dato' Sri MOHD NAJIB BIN Tun Haji ABDUL RAZAK.

Deputy Prime Minister and Minister of Education: Tan Sri Dato' Haji MUHYIDDIN BIN MOHD YASSIN.

Minister of Foreign Affairs: Dato' Sri ANIFAH BIN Haji AMAN.

Minister of Home Affairs: Dato' Seri HISHAMMUDDIN BIN Tun HUSSEIN.

Minister of Defence: Dato' Seri Dr AHMAD ZAHID BIN HAMIDI.

Minister of International Trade and Industry: Dato' Sri MUSTAPA BIN MOHAMED.

Minister of Domestic Trade, Co-operatives and Consumerism: Dato' Sri ISMAIL SABRI BIN YAAKOB.

Minister of Transport: Dato' Seri KONG CHO HA.

Minister of Energy, Green Technology and Water: Dato' Sri PETER CHIN FAH KUI.

Minister of Works: Dato' SHAZIMAN BIN ABU MANSOR.

Minister of Higher Education: Dato' Seri MOHAMED KHALED BIN NORDIN.

Minister of Information, Communications and Culture: Datuk Seri Dr RAIS YATIM.

Minister of Human Resources: Datuk Dr S. SUBRAMANIAM.

Minister of Natural Resources and the Environment: Dato' Sri DOUGLAS UGGAH EMBAS.

Minister of Plantation Industries and Commodities: Tan Sri BERNARD GILUK DOMPOK.

Minister of Tourism: Dato' Sri Dr NG YEN YEN.

Minister of Science, Technology and Innovation: Datuk Seri Dr MAXIMUS JOHNITY ONGKILI.

Minister of Health: Dato' Sri LIOW TIONG LAI.

Minister of Agriculture and Agro-Based Industry: Datuk Seri Haji NOH BIN OMAR.

Minister of Rural and Regional Development: Dato' Seri Haji MOHD SHAFIE BIN Haji APDAL.

Minister of Federal Territories and Urban Well-being: Dato' Raja NONG CHIK BIN Dato' Raja ZAINAL ABIDIN.

Minister of Women, Family and Community Development: Dato' Seri SHAHRIZAT ABDUL JALIL.

Minister of Finance II: Dato' Seri Haji AHMAD HUSNI BIN MOHAMAD HANADZLAH.

Minister of Housing and Local Government: Dato' CHOR CHEE HEUNG.

Minister of Youth and Sports: Dato' Sri AHMAD SHABERY CHEEK.

Ministers in the Prime Minister's Department: Tan Sri Dr KOH TSU KOON, Dato' Seri MOHAMED NAZRI BIN ABDUL AZIZ, Maj.-Gen. Dato' Seri JAMIL KHIR BIN BAHARUM, Tan Sri NOR MOHAMED BIN YAKCOP, Dato' Sri IDRIS JALA, Dato' G. PALANIVEL.

MINISTRIES

Prime Minister's Office (Jabatan Perdana Menteri): Federal Government Administration Center, Bangunan Perdana Putra, 62502 Putrajaya; tel. (3) 88888000; fax (3) 88883444; e-mail fuad@pmo.gov.my; internet www.pmo.gov.my.

Ministry of Agriculture and Agro-Based Industry: Wisma Tani, 28 Persiaran Perdana, Presint 4, Pusat Pentadbiran Kerajaan Persekutuan, 62624 Putrajaya; tel. (3) 88701000; fax (3) 88886020; e-mail pro@moa.gov.my; internet www.moa.gov.my.

Ministry of Defence (Kementerian Pertahanan): Wisma Pertahanan, Jalan Padang Tembak, 50634 Kuala Lumpur; tel. (3) 26921333; fax (3) 26914163; e-mail szy.ppm@mod.gov.my; internet www.mod.gov.my.

Ministry of Domestic Trade, Co-operatives and Consumerism (Kementerian Perdagangan Dalam Negeri, Koperasi Dan Kepenggunaan): 13 Persianan Perdana, Presint 2, Pusat Pentadbiran Kerajaan Persekutuan, 62623 Putrajaya; tel. (3) 88825500; fax (3) 88825762; e-mail aduan@kpdnkk.gov.my; internet www.kpdnkk.gov.my.

Ministry of Education (Kementerian Pendidikan): Blok E8, Parcel E, Pusat Pentadbiran Kerajaan Persekutuan, 62604 Putrajaya; tel. (3) 88846000; fax (3) 88895235; e-mail kpkpm@moe.gov.my; internet www.moe.gov.my.

Ministry of Energy, Green Technology and Water (Kementerian Tenaga, Teknologi Hijau dan Air): Blok E4–5, Parcel E, Pusat Pentadbiran Kerajaan Persekutuan, 62668 Putrajaya; tel. (3) 88836000; fax (3) 88893712; e-mail webmaster@kettha.gov.my; internet www.kettha.gov.my.

Ministry of Federal Territories and Urban Well-being (Kementerian Wilayah Persekutuan Dan Kesejahteraan Bandar): Aras G-4, Blok 2, Menara PJH, Presint 2, 62100 Putrajaya; tel. (3) 88897888; fax (3) 88880375; e-mail zainor@kwp.gov.my; internet www.kwp.gov.my.

Ministry of Finance (Kementerian Kewangan): Kompleks Kementerian Kewangan, 5 Persiaran Perdana, Presint 2, Pusat Pentadbiran Kerajaan Persekutuan, 62592 Putrajaya; tel. (3) 88823000; fax (3) 88823893; e-mail shafei@treasury.gov.my; internet www.treasury.gov.my.

Ministry of Foreign Affairs (Kementerian Luar Negeri): Wisma Putra, 1 Jalan Wisma Putra, Presint 2, 62602 Putrajaya; tel. (3) 88874000; fax (3) 88891717; e-mail webmaster@kln.gov.my; internet www.kln.gov.my.

Ministry of Health (Kementerian Kesihatan): Blok E1, E6–7 & E10, Parcel E, Pusat Pentadbiran Kerajaan Persekutuan, 62590 Putrajaya; tel. (3) 88833888; fax (3) 26985964; e-mail kkm@moh.gov.my; internet www.moh.gov.my.

Ministry of Higher Education (Kementerian Pengajian Tinggi): Blok E3, Parcel E, Pusat Perbadanan Kerajaan Persekutuan, 62505 Putrajaya; tel. (3) 88835000; fax (3) 88893921; e-mail minister@mohe.gov.my; internet www.portal.mohe.gov.my.

Ministry of Home Affairs (Kementerian Hal Ehwal Dalam Negeri): Blok D1–2, Parcel D, Pusat Pentadbiran Kerajaan Persekutuan, 62546 Putrajaya; tel. (3) 88868000; fax (3) 88891613; e-mail menteri@moha.gov.my; internet www.moha.gov.my.

Ministry of Housing and Local Government (Kementerian Perumahan dan Kerajaan Tempatan): Aras 1–7, Blok K, Pusat Bandar Damansara, 50782 Kuala Lumpur; tel. (3) 20947033; fax (3) 20949720; e-mail pro@kpkt.gov.my; internet www.kpkt.gov.my.

Ministry of Human Resources (Kementerian Sumber Manusia): Tingkat 6–9, Blok D3, Parcel D, Pusat Pentadbiran Kerajaan Persekutuan, 62530 Putrajaya; tel. (3) 88865000; fax (3) 88892381; e-mail ksm1@mohr.gov.my; internet www.mohr.gov.my.

Ministry of Information, Communications and Culture (Kementerian Penerangan Komunikasi Dan Kebudayaan): Tingkat 5, Wisma TV, Angkasapuri, Bukit Putra, 50610 Kuala Lumpur; tel. (3) 22825333; fax (3) 22848115; e-mail azmi@kpkk.gov.my; internet www.kpkk.gov.my.

Ministry of International Trade and Industry (Kementerian Perdagangan Antarabangsa dan Industri): Blok 10, Kompleks Pejabat Kerajaan, Jalan Duta, 50622 Kuala Lumpur; tel. (3) 62033022; fax (3) 62012337; e-mail webmiti@miti.gov.my; internet www.miti.gov.my.

Ministry of Natural Resources and the Environment (Kementerian Sumber Asli dan Alam Sekitar): Wisma Sumber Asli, 25 Persiaran Perdana, Presint 4, Pusat Pentadbiran Kerajaan Persekutuan, 62574 Putrajaya; tel. (3) 88861111; fax (3) 88892672; e-mail james@nre.gov.my; internet www.nre.gov.my.

Ministry of Plantation Industries and Commodities (Kementerian Perusahaan Perladangan dan Komoditi): Aras 6–13, 15 Persiaran Perdana, Presint 2, Pusat Pentadbiran Kerajaan Persekutuan, 62654 Putrajaya; tel. (3) 88803300; fax (3) 88803441; e-mail aduan@kppk.gov.my; internet www.kppk.gov.my.

Ministry of Rural and Regional Development (Kementerian Kemajuan Luar Bandar dan Wilayah): Aras 4–9, Blok D9, Parcel D, Pusat Pentadbiran Kerajaan Persekutuan, 62606 Putrajaya; tel. (3) 88863500; fax (3) 88892104; e-mail sitisarah@rurallink.gov.my; internet www.rurallink.gov.my.

Ministry of Science, Technology and Innovation: Aras 1–7, Blok C4–5, Parcel C, Pusat Pentadbiran Kerajaan Persekutuan, 62662 Putrajaya; tel. (3) 88858000; fax (3) 88889070; e-mail info@mosti.gov.my; internet www.mosti.gov.my.

Ministry of Tourism (Kementerian Pelancongan): Tingkat 17, Menara Dato' Onn, Pusat Dagangan Dunia Putra, 45 Jalan Tun Ismail, 50695 Kuala Lumpur; tel. (3) 26937111; fax (3) 26941146; e-mail info@motour.gov.my; internet www.motour.gov.my.

Ministry of Transport (Kementerian Pengangkutan): Aras 4–7, Blok D5, Parcel D, Pusat Pentadbiran Kerajaan Persekutuan, 62616 Putrajaya; tel. (3) 88866000; fax (3) 88891569; e-mail woon@mot.gov.my; internet www.mot.gov.my.

Ministry of Women, Family and Community Development (Kementerian Pembangunan Wanita, Keluarga dan Masyarakat): Aras 1–6, Blok E, Kompleks Petabat Kerajaan Bukit Perdana, Jalan Dato' Onn, 50515 Kuala Lumpur; tel. (3) 26930095; fax (3) 26934982; e-mail info@kpwkm.gov.my; internet www.kpwkm.gov.my.

Ministry of Works (Kementerian Kerja Raya): Tingkat 6, Blok B, Kompleks Kerja Raya, Jalan Sultan Salahuddin, 50580 Kuala Lumpur; tel. (3) 27111100; fax (3) 27111590; e-mail pro@kkr.gov.my; internet www.kkr.gov.my.

Ministry of Youth and Sports (Kementerian Belia dan Sukan): Aras 17, Menara KBS, 27 Persiaran Perdana, Presint 4, Pusat Pentadbiran Kerajaan Persekutuan, 62570 Putrajaya; tel. (3) 88713333; fax (3) 88888770; e-mail hanizan@kbs.gov.my; internet www.kbs.gov.my.

Legislature

PARLIAMENT

Dewan Negara
(Senate)

The Senate has 70 members, of whom 26 are elected. Each State Legislative Assembly elects two members. The Supreme Head of State appoints the remaining 44 members, including four from the three Federal Territories.

President: Dato' WONG FOON MENG.

Dewan Rakyat
(House of Representatives)

The House of Representatives has a total of 222 members: 165 from Peninsular Malaysia (including 11 from Kuala Lumpur and one from the Federal Territory of Putrajaya), 31 from Sarawak and 26 from Sabah (including one from the Federal Territory of Labuan).

Speaker: Tan Sri PANDIKAR AMIN MULIA.

Deputy Speakers: Datuk RONALD KIANDEE, Datuk Dr WAN JUNAIDI TUANKU JAAFAR.

General Election, 8 March 2008

Party	Seats
Barisan Nasional (National Front)	140
United Malays National Organization	79
Malaysian Chinese Association	15
Parti Pesaka Bumiputera Bersatu	14
Parti Rakyat Sarawak	6
Sarawak United People's Party	6
Sabah Progressive Democratic Party	4
United Kadazan People's Organization	3
Sarawak Progressive Party	3
Malaysian Indian Congress	3
Parti Bersatu Sabah	3
Parti Gerakan Rakyat Malaysia	2
Parti Bersatu Rakyat Sabah	1
Liberal Democratic Party	1
Parti Keadilan Rakyat	31
Democratic Action Party	28
Parti Islam se Malaysia	23
Total	222

The States

JOHOR
(Capital: Johor Bahru)

Sultan: HRH Tuanku IBRAHIM ISMAIL IBNI AL-MARHUM Sultan ISKANDER.

Menteri Besar: Datuk Haji ABDUL GHANI OTHMAN.

State Legislative Assembly: internet www.johor.gov.my; 56 seats: Barisan Nasional 50; Democratic Action Party 4; Parti Islam se Malaysia 2; elected March 2008.

KEDAH
(Capital: Alor Star)

Sultan: HRH Tuanku Haji ABDUL HALIM MU'ADZAM SHAH IBNI AL-MARHUM Sultan BADLISHAH.

Menteri Besar: AZIZAN ABDUL RAZAK.

State Legislative Assembly: internet www.kedah.gov.my; 36 seats: Parti Islam se Malaysia 16; Barisan Nasional 14; Parti Keadilan Rakyat 4; Democratic Action Party 1; Independent 1; elected March 2008.

KELANTAN
(Capital: Kota Bharu)

Sultan: HRH Sultan MUHAMMAD V PETRA.

Menteri Besar: Tuan Guru Haji Nik ABDUL AZIZ BIN Nik MAT.

State Legislative Assembly: internet www.kelantan.gov.my; 45 seats: Parti Islam se Malaysia 38; Barisan Nasional 6; Parti Keadilan Rakyat 1; elected March 2008.

MELAKA (MALACCA)
(Capital: Melaka)

Yang di-Pertua Negeri: Tan Sri KHALIL YAAKOB.

Ketua Menteri: Datuk WIRA MOHAMED ALI RUSTAM.

State Legislative Assembly: internet www.melaka.gov.my; 28 seats: Barisan Nasional 23; Democratic Action Party 5; elected March 2008.

NEGERI SEMBILAN
(Capital: Seremban)

Yang di-Pertuan Besar: Tuanku MUKHRIZ IBNI AL-MARHUM Tuanku MUNAWIR.

Menteri Besar: Datuk MOHAMAD HASAN.

State Legislative Assembly: 36 seats: Barisan Nasional 21; Democratic Action Party 10; Parti Keadilan Rakyat 4; Parti Islam se Malaysia 1; elected March 2008.

PAHANG
(Capital: Kuantan)

Sultan: HRH Haji AHMAD SHAH AL-MUSTA'IN BILLAH IBNI AL-MARHUM Sultan ABU BAKAR RI'AYATUDDIN AL-MU'ADZAM SHAH.

Menteri Besar: Dato' ADNAN BIN YAAKOB.

State Legislative Assembly: Unit Pengurusan Teknologi Maklumat, Pejabat Setiausaha Kerajaan, Negeri Pahang, Tingkat 6, Wisma Sri Pahang, 25503 Kuantan, Pahang Darul Makmur; tel. (9) 5129425; fax (9) 5163490; internet www.pahang.gov.my; 42 seats: Barisan Nasional 37; Democratic Action Party 2; Parti Islam se Malaysia 2; Independent 1; elected March 2008.

PERAK
(Capital: Ipoh)

Note: the federal Government took direct control of the state legislature in May 2009, and the ruling coalition installed its own Speaker in the Perak legislature (see Contemporary Political Affairs).

Sultan: HRH Sultan Tuanku AZLAN MUHIBUDDIN SHAH IBNI AL-MARHUM Sultan YUSUF IZUDDIN GHAFARULLAH SHAH.

Menteri Besar: Datuk ZAMBRY ABDUL KADIR.

State Legislative Assembly: Pejabat Setiausaha Kerajaan Negeri Perak, Bangunan Perak Darul Ridzuan, Bahagian Majlis, Jalan Panglima Bukit Gantang Wahab, 30000 Ipoh; tel. (5) 2531957; fax (5) 2414869; e-mail prosuk@perak.gov.my; internet www.perak.gov.my; 59 seats: Barisan Nasional 28; Democratic Action Party 18; Parti Keadilan Rakyat 7; Parti Islam se Malaysia 6; elected March 2008.

PERLIS
(Capital: Kangar)

Raja: HM Tuanku SYED SIRAJUDDIN IBNI AL-MARHUM SYED PUTRA JAMALULLAIL.

Menteri Besar: Datuk Dr MOHAMMAD ISA SABU.

State Legislative Assembly: e-mail sukpls@perlis.gov.my; internet www.perlis.gov.my/webperlis/welcome.html; 15 seats: Barisan Nasional 14; Parti Islam se Malaysia 1; elected March 2008.

PULAU PINANG (PENANG)
(Capital: George Town)

Yang di-Pertua Negeri: HE Datuk ABDUL RAHMAN Haji ABBAS.

Ketua Menteri: LIM GUAN ENG.

State Legislative Assembly: 40 seats: Democratic Action Party 19; Barisan Nasional 11; Parti Keadilan Rakyat 9; Parti Islam se Malaysia 1; elected March 2008.

SABAH
(Capital: Kota Kinabalu)

Yang di-Pertua Negeri: HE Datuk JUHAR MAHIRUDDIN.

Ketua Menteri: Datuk Seri MUSA AMAN.

State Legislative Assembly: Dewan Undangan Negeri Sabah, Aras 4, Bangunan Dewan Undangan Negeri Sabah, Peti Surat 11247, 88813 Kota Kinabalu; tel. (88) 427533; fax (88) 427333; e-mail pejduns@sabah.gov.my; internet www.sabah.gov.my; 60 seats: Barisan Nasional 59; Democratic Action Party 1; elected March 2008.

SARAWAK
(Capital: Kuching)

Yang di-Pertua Negeri: HE Tun Datuk Patinggi Abang Haji MUHAMMED SALAHUDDIN.

Ketua Menteri: Datuk Patinggi Tan Sri Haji ABDUL TAIB BIN MAHMUD.

State Legislative Assembly: Bangunan Dewan Undangan Negeri, Petra Jaya, 93502 Kuching, Sarawak; tel. (82) 441955; fax (82) 440628; e-mail abangof@sarawaknet.gov.my; internet www.dun.sarawak.gov.my; f. 1867; 71 seats: Barisan Nasional 55; Democratic Action Party 12; Parti Keadilan Rakyat 3; Independent 1; elected April 2011.

SELANGOR
(Capital: Shah Alam)

Sultan: Tuanku IDRIS SHARAFUDDIN ALHAJ SHAH.

Menteri Besar: Tan Sri Dato' ABDUL KHALID BIN IBRAHIM.

State Legislative Assembly: internet www.selangor.gov.my; 56 seats: Barisan Nasional 20; Parti Keadilan Rakyat 15; Democratic Action Party 13; Parti Islam se Malaysia 8; elected March 2008.

TERENGGANU
(Capital: Kuala Terengganu)

Yang Di-Pertuan Muda (Regent): Tuanku MUHAMMAD ISMAIL Sultan MIZAN ZAINAL ABIDIN.

Menteri Besar: Datuk AHMAD SAID.

State Legislative Assembly: internet www.terengganu.gov.my; 32 seats: Barisan Nasional 24; Parti Islam se Malaysia 8; elected March 2008.

Election Commission

Suruhanjaya Pilihan Raya (SPR): Aras 4–5, Blok C7, Parcel C, Pusat Pentadbiran Kerajaan Persekutuan, 62690 Putrajaya; tel. (3) 88856500; fax (3) 88889117; e-mail spr@spr.gov.my; internet www.spr.gov.my; f. 1957; Chair. Tan Sri Dato' Seri ABD AL-AZIZ BIN MUHAMMAD YUSOF.

Political Organizations

Barisan Nasional (BN) (National Front): Suites 1–2, Tingkat 8, Menara Dato' Onn, Pusat Dagangan Dunia Putra, Jalan Tun Ismail, 50480 Kuala Lumpur; tel. (3) 26920384; fax (3) 26934743; e-mail info@bn.org.my; f. 1973; the governing multiracial coalition of 14 parties; Chair. Dato' Sri MOHD NAJIB BIN Tun Haji ABDUL RAZAK; Sec.-Gen. Datuk Sri Tengku ADNAN Tengku MANSOR; comprises:

Liberal Democratic Party: Tingkat 1, Unit 33, Karamunsing Warehouse, POB 16033, 88868 Kota Kinabalu, Sabah; tel. (88) 218587; fax (88) 240598; e-mail ldpkk@tm.net.my; internet ldp.org.my; f. 1989; Chinese-dominated; Pres. Datuk LIEW VUI KEONG; Sec.-Gen. TEO CHEE KANG.

Malaysian Chinese Association (MCA): Wisma MCA, Tingkat 8, 163 Jalan Ampang, POB 10626, 50450 Kuala Lumpur; tel. (3) 21618044; fax (3) 21619772; e-mail info@mca.org.my; internet www.mca.org.my; f. 1949; 900,000 mems; Pres. Datuk Seri Dr CHUA SOI LEK; Sec.-Gen. Dato' Seri KONG CHO HA.

Malaysian Indian Congress (MIC): Menara Manickavasagam, 6th Floor, 1 Jalan Rahmat, 50350 Kuala Lumpur; tel. (3) 40424377; fax (3) 40427236; e-mail michq@mic.org.my; internet www.mic.org.my; f. 1946; 401,000 mems (1992); Pres. Datuk G. PALANIVEL; Sec.-Gen. Dr S. MURUGESAN.

Parti Bersatu Rakyat Sabah (PBRS) (United Sabah People's Party): POB 20148, Luyang, Kota Kinabalu, 88761 Sabah; tel. and fax (88) 269282; f. 1994; breakaway faction of the PBS; mostly Christian Kadazans; Leader Datuk JOSEPH KURUP.

Parti Bersatu Sabah (PBS) (Sabah United Party): Blok M, Lot 4, Tingkat 2–3, Donggongon New Township, 89500 Penampang, Sabah; tel. (88) 702111; fax (88) 718067; e-mail pbshq@pbs-sabah.org; internet www.pbs-sabah.org; f. 1985; left the BN in 1990; rejoined in Jan. 2002; multiracial party; Pres. Datuk Seri JOSEPH PAIRIN KITINGAN; Sec.-Gen. HENRYNUS AMIN.

Parti Gerakan Rakyat Malaysia (GERAKAN) (Malaysian People's Movement): Tingkat 5, Menara PGRM, 8 Jalan Pudu Ulu, Cheras, 56100 Kuala Lumpur; tel. (3) 92876868; fax (3) 92878866; e-mail gerakan@gerakan.org.my; internet www.gerakan.org.my; f. 1968; 300,000 mems; Pres. Tan Sri KOH TSU KOON; Sec.-Gen. TENG CHANG YEOW.

Parti Pesaka Bumiputera Bersatu (PBB) (United Traditional Bumiputra Party): Lot 401, Jalan Bako, POB 1053, 93722 Kuching, Sarawak; tel. (82) 448299; fax (82) 448294; e-mail pbb1@bumiputerasarawak.org.my; internet www.bumiputerasarawak.org.my; f. 1983; Pres. Tan Sri Datuk Patinggi Amar Haji ABDUL TAIB MAHMUD; Dep. Pres. Datuk ALFRED JABU AK NUMPANG.

Parti Progresif Penduduk Malaysia (PPP) (People's Progressive Party): 74 Jalan Rotan, Kampung Attap, 50460 Kuala Lumpur; tel. (3) 22738199; fax (3) 22736199; e-mail ppporg@ppp.org.my; internet www.ppp.org.my; f. 1953; est. as Perak Progressive Party; joined the BN in 1972; Pres. Datuk M. KAYVEAS.

Parti Rakyat Sarawak (PRS) (Sarawak People's Party): Sarawak; f. 2003; reported to be considering merger with the SPDP; Pres. Datuk Sri Dr JAMES MASING; Sec.-Gen. Datuk WILFRED NISSOM.

Sabah Progressive Party (SAPP) (Parti Maju Sabah): Lot 23, 2nd Floor, Bornion Centre, 88300 Kota Kinabalu, Sabah; tel. (88) 242107; fax (88) 249188; e-mail sappkk@streamyx.com; internet www.sapp.org.my; f. 1994; non-racial; Pres. Datuk YONG TECK LEE; Sec.-Gen. Datuk RICHARD YONG WE KONG.

Sarawak Progressive Democratic Party (SPDP): Lot 4319–4320, Jalan Stapok, Sungai Maong, 93250 Kuching, Sarawak; tel. (82) 311180; fax (82) 311190; f. 2003; est. by breakaway faction of Sarawak Nat. Party; reported to be considering merger with the PRS; Pres. Datuk WILLIAM MAWAN ANAK IKOM; Sec.-Gen. NELSON BALANG RINING.

Sarawak United People's Party (SUPP): 7 Jalan Tan Sri Ong Kee Hui, POB 454, 93710 Kuching, Sarawak; tel. (82) 246999; fax (82) 256510; e-mail supphq@gmail.com; internet www.supp.org.my; f. 1959; Sarawak Chinese minority party; Pres. Tan Sri Dr CHEN KANG NAM; Sec.-Gen. SHEN YOSHITERU.

United Kadazan People's Organization (UPKO) (United Pasokmomogun Kadazandusun Murut Organization): Penampang Lot 9 & 10, New World Commercial Centre, Tingkat 2–3, Peti Surat 420, 89507 Penampang, Sabah; tel. (88) 718182; fax (88) 718180; e-mail upkohq@gmail.com; internet www.upko.org.my; f. 1994; est. as Parti Demokratik Sabah (PDS—Sabah Democratic Party) after collapse of PBS Govt by fmr PBS leaders; represents mostly Kadazandusun, Rungus and Murut communities; Pres. Tan Sri BERNARD GILUK DOMPOK; Sec.-Gen. Datuk WILFRED M. TANGAU.

United Malays National Organization (Pertubuhan Kebangsaan Melayu Bersatu—UMNO Baru) (New UMNO): Menara Dato' Onn, 38th Floor, Jalan Tun Ismail, 50480 Kuala Lumpur; tel. (3) 40429511; fax (3) 40412358; e-mail email@umno.net.my; internet www.umno-online.com; f. 1988; replaced the original UMNO (f. 1946), which had been declared an illegal org., owing to the participation of unregistered brs in party elections in April 1987; Supreme Council of 45 mems; 2.5m. mems; Pres. Dato' Sri MOHD NAJIB BIN Tun Haji ABDUL RAZAK; Sec.-Gen. Datuk Seri Tengku ADNAN Tengku MANSOR.

Barisan Alternatif (Alternative Front): Kuala Lumpur; f. 1999; est. to contest 1999 general election; opposition electoral alliance originally comprising the PAS, the DAP, the PKN and the PRM; the DAP left in 2001; the PKN and the PRM merged in 2003 to form the PKR.

Barisan Jama'ah Islamiah Sa-Malaysia (Berjasa) (Pan-Malaysian Islamic Front): Kelantan; f. 1977; pro-Islamic; 50,000 mems; Pres. Dato' Haji WAN HASHIM BIN Haji WAN ACHMED; Sec.-Gen. MAHMUD ZUHDI BIN Haji ABDUL MAJID.

Bersatu Rakyat Jelata Sabah (Berjaya) (Sabah People's Union): Natikar Bldg, 1st Floor, POB 2130, Kota Kinabalu, Sabah; f. 1975; 400,000 mems; Pres. Haji MOHAMMED NOOR MANSOOR.

Democratic Action Party (DAP): 24 Jalan 20/9, 46300 Petaling Jaya, Selangor; tel. (3) 79578022; fax (3) 79575718; e-mail dap@dapmalaysia.org; internet www.dapmalaysia.org; f. 1966; main opposition party; advocates multiracial society based on democratic socialism; 12,000 mems; Chair. KARPAL SINGH; Sec.-Gen. LIM GUAN ENG.

Human Rights Party (HRP): 6 Jalan Abdullah, off Jalan Bangsar, 59000 Kuala Lumpur; tel. (3) 22825241; fax (3) 22825245; e-mail info@humanrightspartymalaysia.com; internet www.humanrightspartymalaysia.com; f. 2009; Sec.-Gen. P. UTHAYAKUMAR.

Kongres Indian Muslim Malaysia (KIMMA): Kuala Lumpur; tel. (3) 2324759; f. 1977; aims to unite Malaysian Indian Muslims politically; 25,000 mems; Pres. SAMMY VELLU; Sec.-Gen. MOHAMMED ALI BIN Haji NAINA MOHAMMED.

Malaysia Makkal Sakti Party (MMSP): Shah Alam, Selangor; f. 2009; est. by fmr mems of the Hindu Rights Action Force; represents ethnic Indians in Malaysia; Founder R. S. THANENTHIRAN; Pres. KANNAN RAMASAMY.

Pakatan Rakyat (People's Alliance): f. 2008; est. following the legislative election; opposition alliance of the PKR, the DAP and PAS.

Parti Hisbul Muslimin Malaysia (Hamim) (Islamic Front of Malaysia): Kota Bharu, Kelantan; f. 1983; est. as an alternative party to PAS; Pres. Datuk ASRI MUDA.

Parti Ikatan Masyarakat Islam (Islamic Alliance Party): Terengganu.

Parti Islam se Malaysia (PAS) (Islamic Party of Malaysia): 318A Jalan Raja Laut, 50350 Kuala Lumpur; tel. (3) 26925000; fax (3) 26938399; e-mail editor@parti-pas.org; internet www.pas.org.my; f. 1951; seeks to establish an Islamic state; 700,000 mems; Pres. Dato' Seri ABDUL HADI AWANG; Sec.-Gen. Dato' Haji MUSTAFA ALI.

Parti Keadilan Rakyat (PKR) (People's Justice Party): A1-09, 1 Merchant Sq., 1 Jalan Tropicana Selatan, 47410 Petaling Jaya; tel. (3) 78850530; fax (3) 78850531; e-mail contact@partikeadilanrakyat.org; internet www.keadilanrakyat.org; f. 2003; est. following merger of Parti Keadilan Nasional and Parti Rakyat Malaysia; comprises supporters of Anwar Ibrahim; Pres. Datin Seri Dr WAN AZIZAH WAN ISMAIL; Sec.-Gen. SAIFUDDIN NASUTION ISMAIL.

Parti Kesejahteraan Insan Tanah Air (KITA) (Malaysian People's Welfare Party): B-2-19, Merchant Sq., Jalan Tropicana Selatan 1, PJU 3, 47410 Petaling Jaya, Selangor; tel. (3) 78850023; fax (3) 78850027; e-mail info@partikita.com; internet www.partikita.com; f. 1995; fmrly Angkatan Keadilan Insan Malaysia (AKIM); relaunched as above in 2010; Pres. Datuk ZAID IBRAHIM.

Persatuan Rakyat Malaysia Sarawak (PERMAS) (Malaysian Sarawak Party): Kuching, Sarawak; f. 1987; est. by fmr mems of PBB; Leader Haji BUJANG ULIS.

Sabah Chinese Consolidated Party (SCCP): POB 704, Kota Kinabalu, Sabah; f. 1964; 14,000 mems; Pres. JOHNNY SOON; Sec.-Gen. CHAN TET ON.

Sabah Chinese Party (PCS): Kota Kinabalu, Sabah; f. 1986; Pres. FRANCIS LEONG.

Sarawak National Party (SNAP): 304–305 Bangunan Mei Jun, 1 Jalan Rubber, POB 2960, 93758 Kuching, Sarawak; tel. (82) 254244; fax (82) 253562; internet sarawak-national-party.blogspot.com; f. 1961; deregistered Nov. 2002, but deregistration deferred indefinitely in April 2003 following appeal; Pres. EDWIN DUNDANG BUGAK; Sec.-Gen. STANLEY JUGOL.

Setia (Sabah People's United Democratic Party): Sabah; f. 1994.

Diplomatic Representation

EMBASSIES AND HIGH COMMISSIONS IN MALAYSIA

Afghanistan: 2nd Floor, Wisma Chinese Chamber, 258 Jalan Ampang, 50450 Kuala Lumpur; tel. (3) 42569400; fax (3) 42566400; e-mail consular@afghanembassykl.org; Ambassador ABDUL SAMAD.

Albania: UBN Tower 10, 31st Floor, Jalan P. Ramlee, 50250 Kuala Lumpur; tel. (3) 20788690; fax (3) 20702285; e-mail embassy.kualalumpur@mfa.gov.al; Chargé d'affaires a.i. DILAVER QESJA.

Algeria: 5 Jalan Mesra, off Jalan Damai, 55000 Kuala Lumpur; tel. (3) 21488159; fax (3) 21488154; e-mail dz@algerianembassy.org.my; internet www.algerianembassy.org.my; Ambassador ABDELMALEK BOUHEDDOU.

Argentina: Suite 16-03, 16th Floor, Menara Keck Seng, 203 Jalan Bukit Bintang, 55100 Kuala Lumpur; tel. (3) 21441451; fax (3) 21441428; e-mail emsia@pd.jaring.my; Ambassador MARÍA ISABEL RENDON.

Australia: 6 Jalan Yap Kwan Seng, 50450 Kuala Lumpur; tel. (3) 21465555; fax (3) 21415773; e-mail public-affairs-klpr@dfat.gov.au; internet www.australia.org.my; High Commissioner MILES KUPA.

Austria: Suite 10.01–02, Tingkat 10, Wisma Goldhill 67, Jalan Raja Chulan, 50200 Kuala Lumpur; tel. (3) 20570020; fax (3) 23817168; e-mail kuala-lumpur-ob@bmeia.gv.at; internet www.bmeia.gv.at/kualalumpur; Ambassador ANDREA WICKE.

Azerbaijan: 2nd Floor, Wisma Chinese Chamber, 258 Jalan Ampang, 50450 Kuala Lumpur; tel. (3) 42526800; fax (3) 42571800; e-mail kualalumpur@mission.mfa.gov.az; internet www.azembassy.com.my; Ambassador TAHIR KARIMOV.

Bangladesh: Blok 1, Lorong Damai 7, Jalan Damai, 55000 Kuala Lumpur; tel. (3) 21487940; fax (3) 21413381; e-mail bddoot@streamyx.com; internet www.bangladesh-highcomkl.com; High Commissioner ATIQUR RAHMAN.

Belgium: Suite 10-02, 10th Floor, Menara Tan & Tan, 207 Jalan Tun Razak, 50400 Kuala Lumpur; tel. (3) 21620025; fax (3) 21620023; e-mail kualalumpur@diplobel.fed.be; internet www.diplomatie.be/kualalumpur; Ambassador MARC MULLIE.

Bosnia and Herzegovina: JKR 854, Jalan Bellamy, 50460 Kuala Lumpur; tel. (3) 21440353; fax (3) 21426025; e-mail embbhkl@tm.net.my; Ambassador ENSAR EMINOVIĆ.

Brazil: Suite 20-01, 20th Floor, Menara Tan & Tan, 207 Jalan Tun Razak, 50400 Kuala Lumpur; tel. (3) 21711420; fax (3) 21711427; e-mail embassy@brazilembassy.org.my; internet kualalumpur.itamaraty.gov.br; Ambassador SÉRGIO DE SOUZA ARRUDA.

Brunei: Suite 19-01, 19th Floor, Menara Tan & Tan, 207 Jalan Tun Razak, 50400 Kuala Lumpur; tel. (3) 21612800; fax (3) 21631302; e-mail bhckl@brucomkul.com.my; High Commissioner Dato' Paduka Haji ISHAAQ BIN Haji ABDULLAH.

Cambodia: 46 Jalan U Thant, 55000 Kuala Lumpur; tel. (3) 42571150; fax (3) 42571157; e-mail reckl@tm.net.my; Ambassador HRH Samdech Preah ANOCH NORODOM ARUNRASMY.

Canada: 17th Floor, Menara Tan & Tan, 207 Jalan Tun Razak, 50400 Kuala Lumpur; tel. (3) 27183333; fax (3) 27183399; e-mail klmpr@international.gc.ca; internet www.canadainternational.gc.ca/malaysia-malaisie; High Commissioner RANDOLPH MANK.

Chile: 8th Floor, West Block, Wisma Selangor Dredging, 142C Jalan Ampang, Peti Surat 27, 50450 Kuala Lumpur; tel. (3) 21616203; fax (3) 21622219; e-mail eochile@embassyofchile.org.my; internet chileabroad.gov.cl/malasia; Ambassador JOSÉ MANUEL OVALLE BRAVO.

China, People's Republic: 229 Jalan Ampang, 50450 Kuala Lumpur; tel. (3) 21428495; fax (3) 21414552; e-mail cn@tm.net.my; internet my.china-embassy.org/eng; Ambassador CHAI XI.

Colombia: UOA Centre, Tingkat 28, 19 Jalan Pinang, 50450 Kuala Lumpur; tel. (3) 21645488; fax (3) 21645487; e-mail ekualalumpur@cancilleria.gov.co; internet www.ecolombia.com.my; Chargé d'affaires a.i. LUIS GERARDO GUZMÁN VALENCIA.

Croatia: 3 Jalan Menkuang, off Jalan Ru Ampang, 55000 Kuala Lumpur; tel. (3) 42535340; fax (3) 42535217; e-mail croemb.kuala-lumpur@mvpei.hr; Ambassador ZELJKO BOSNJAK.

Cuba: No. 18, 2 Jalan Kent, off Jalan Maktab, 54000 Kuala Lumpur; tel. (3) 26911066; fax (3) 26911141; e-mail admin@cubemb.com.my; internet www.cubaemb.com.my; Ambassador CARLOS A. AMORES.

Czech Republic: 32 Jalan Mesra, off Jalan Damai, 55000 Kuala Lumpur; tel. (3) 21427185; fax (3) 21412727; e-mail kualalumpur@embassy.mzv.cz; internet www.mzv.cz/kualalumpur; Ambassador JAN FÜRY.

Denmark: Wisma Denmark, 22nd Floor, 86 Jalan Ampang, 50450 Kuala Lumpur; tel. (3) 20322001; fax (3) 20322012; e-mail kulamb@um.dk; internet www.ambkualalumpur.um.dk; Ambassador SVEND WAEVER.

Ecuador: 10th Floor, West Block, Wisma Selangor Dredging, 142C Jalan Ampang, 50450 Kuala Lumpur; tel. (3) 21635078; fax (3) 21635096; e-mail embecua@po.jaring.my; Ambassador LOURDES PUMA PUMA.

Egypt: 12 Jalan Rhu, off Jalan Ampang, 55000 Kuala Lumpur; tel. (3) 42568184; fax (3) 42573515; e-mail egyembkl@tm.net.my; Ambassador MOHAMED SAAD IBRAHIM EBEID.

Fiji: Menara Chan, Tingkat 2, 138 Jalan Ampang, 50450 Kuala Lumpur; tel. (3) 27323335; fax (3) 27327555; e-mail fhckl@pd.jaring.my; internet www.fijibulamaleya.org.my; High Commissioner SULIASI LUTUBULA.

Finland: Wisma Chinese Chamber, 5th Floor, 258 Jalan Ampang, 50450 Kuala Lumpur; tel. (3) 42577746; fax (3) 42577793; e-mail sanomat.kul@formin.fi; internet www.finland.org.my; Ambassador TAPIO SAARELA.

France: 192–196 Jalan Ampang, 50450 Kuala Lumpur; tel. (3) 20535500; fax (3) 20535501; e-mail ambassade.kuala-lumpur-amba@diplomatie.gouv.fr; internet www.ambafrance-my.org; Ambassador MARC BARÉTY.

Germany: 26th Floor, Menara Tan & Tan, 207 Jalan Tun Razak, 50400 Kuala Lumpur; tel. (3) 21709666; fax (3) 21619800; e-mail info@kuala-lumpur.diplo.de; internet www.kuala-lumpur.diplo.de; Ambassador GÜNTER GRUBER.

Ghana: 14 Ampang Hilir, off Jalan Ampang, 55000 Kuala Lumpur; tel. (3) 42526995; fax (3) 42578698; e-mail ghcomkl@tm.net.my; High Commissioner DANIEL K. ABODAKPI.

Guinea: 5 Jalan Kedondong, off Jalan Ampang Hilir, 55000 Kuala Lumpur; tel. (3) 42576500; fax (3) 42511500; e-mail mwcnakry@sotelgui.net.gn; Ambassador MOHAMED SAMPIL.

Hungary: Menara Tan & Tan, 10th Floor, Suite 10-04, Jalan Tun Razak, 50400 Kuala Lumpur; tel. (3) 21637914; fax (3) 21637918; e-mail mission.kul@kum.hu; Ambassador SZILVESZTER BUS.

India: 2 Jalan Taman Duta, off Jalan Duta, 50480 Kuala Lumpur; tel. (3) 20933510; fax (3) 20933507; e-mail cons@indianhighcommission.com.my; internet www.indianhighcommission.com.my; High Commissioner VIJAY K. GOKHALE.

Indonesia: 233 Jalan Tun Razak, POB 10889, 50400 Kuala Lumpur; tel. (3) 21164000; fax (3) 21423878; e-mail info@kbrikualalumpur.org; internet www.kbrikualalumpur.org; Ambassador DA'I BACHTIAR.

Iran: 1 Lorong U Thant Satu, off Jalan U Thant, 55000 Kuala Lumpur; tel. (3) 42514824; fax (3) 42521563; e-mail ir_emb@tm.net.my; internet www.iranembassy.com.my; Ambassador MOHAMMAD MEHDI ZAHEDI.

Iraq: 2 Jalan Langgak Golf, off Jalan Tun Razak, 55000 Kuala Lumpur; tel. (3) 21480555; fax (3) 21414331; e-mail quaemb@iraqmofamail.net; Ambassador AMAL MUSSA HUSSAIN ALI AL-RUBAYE.

Ireland: Ireland House, The Amp Walk, 218 Jalan Ampang, POB 10372, 50450 Kuala Lumpur; tel. (3) 21612963; fax (3) 21613427; e-mail info@ireland-embassy.com.my; internet www.ireland-embassy.com.my; Ambassador DECLAN KELLY.

Italy: 99 Jalan U Thant, 55000 Kuala Lumpur; tel. (3) 42565122; fax (3) 42573199; e-mail ambasciata.kualalumpur@esteri.it; internet www.ambkualalumpur.esteri.it; Ambassador FOLCO DE LUCA GABRIELLI.

Japan: 11 Pesiaran Stonor, off Jalan Tun Razak, 50450 Kuala Lumpur; tel. (3) 21772600; fax (3) 21672314; internet www.my.emb-japan.go.jp; Ambassador SHIGERU NAKAMURA.

Jordan: 2 Jalan Kedondong, off Jalan Ampang Hilir, 55000 Kuala Lumpur; tel. (3) 42521268; fax (3) 42528610; e-mail general@jordanembassy.org.my; internet www.jordanembassy.org.my; Ambassador MAHER LUKASHA.

Kazakhstan: 115 Jalan Ampang Hilir, 55000 Kuala Lumpur; tel. (3) 42522999; fax (3) 42523999; e-mail kuala-lumpur@kazembassy.org .my; internet www.kazembassy.org.my; Ambassador BEIBUT ATAMKULOV.

Kenya: 8 Jalan Taman U Thant, 55000 Kuala Lumpur; tel. (3) 21461163; fax (3) 21451087; e-mail admin@kenyahighcom.org.my; internet www.kenyahighcom.org.my; High Commissioner SAMORI AN'GWA OKWIYA.

Korea, Democratic People's Republic: 4 Jalan Persiaran Madge, off Jalan U Thant, 55000 Kuala Lumpur; tel. (3) 42569913; fax (3) 42569933; e-mail dprkorea@streamyx.com; Ambassador JANG YONG CHOL.

Korea, Republic: Lot 9 and 11, Jalan Nipah, off Jalan Ampang, 55000 Kuala Lumpur; tel. (3) 42512336; fax (3) 42521425; e-mail korem-my@mofat.go.kr; internet mys.mofat.go.kr/eng/index.jsp; Ambassador LEE YONG-JOON.

Kuwait: 229 Jalan Tun Razak, 50400 Kuala Lumpur; tel. (3) 21410033; fax (3) 21456121; e-mail kuwait@streamyx.com; Ambassador MONTHER BADER SULAIMAN AL-EISSA.

Kyrgyzstan: 10th Floor, Wisma Sin Heap Lee, 346 Jalan Tun Razak, 50400 Kuala Lumpur; tel. (3) 21632010; fax (3) 21632024; e-mail embassy@kyrgyzembassy.org.my; internet www .kyrgyzembassy.org.my; Ambassador (vacant).

Laos: 12A Persiaran Madge, off Jalan Ampang Hilir, 55000 Kuala Lumpur; tel. (3) 42511118; e-mail embassylao-kualalumpur@ hotmail.com; Ambassador Dr BOUNTHEUANG MOUNLASY.

Lebanon: 56 Jalan Ampang Hilir, 55000 Kuala Lumpur; tel. (3) 42516690; fax (3) 42603426; Ambassador KHALED AL-KILANI.

Libya: 6 Jalan Madge, off Jalan U Thant, 55000 Kuala Lumpur; tel. (3) 21411293; fax (3) 21413549; Ambassador ABUBAKAR ALMABROUK AL-MANSOURI.

Luxembourg: Menara Keck Seng Bldg, 16th Floor, 203 Jalan Bukit Bintang, 55100 Kuala Lumpur; tel. (3) 21433134; fax (3) 21433157; e-mail emluxem@po.jaring.my; Chargé d'affaires a.i. SAM SCHREINER.

Maldives: Suite 07-01, Menara See Hoy Chan, 374 Jalan Tun Razak, 50400 Kuala Lumpur; tel. (3) 21637244; fax (3) 21647244; e-mail mail@maldives.org.my; internet www.maldives.org.my; High Commissioner MOHAMED ZAKI.

Mauritius: 17th Floor, West Block, Wisma Selangor Dredging, Jalan Ampang, 50450 Kuala Lumpur; tel. (3) 21411870; e-mail maurhckl@streamyx.com; High Commissioner P. KOONJOO (designate).

Mexico: Suite 22-05, 22nd Floor, Menara Tan & Tan, 207 Jalan Tun Razak, 50400 Kuala Lumpur; tel. (3) 21646362; fax (3) 21640964; e-mail embamex@mexico.org.my; internet portal.sre.gob.mx/ malasia; Ambassador JORGE ALBERTO LOZOYA LEGORRETA.

Morocco: Unit 9, 3rd Floor, East Block, Wisma Selangor Dredging, 142B Jalan Ampang, 50450 Kuala Lumpur; tel. (3) 21610701; fax (3) 21623081; e-mail moremb@streamyx.com; internet www .moroccoembassy.org.my; Ambassador AHMED AMAZIANE.

Myanmar: 8C Jalan Ampang Hilir, 55000 Kuala Lumpur; tel. (3) 42516355; fax (3) 42513855; e-mail mekl@tm.net.my; Ambassador TIN LATT.

Namibia: Suite 15-01, Tingkat 15, Menara HLA, 3 Jalan Kia Peng, 50450 Kuala Lumpur; tel. (3) 21433593; e-mail namhckl@streamyx .com; High Commissioner GEBHARD BENJAMIN KANDANGA.

Nepal: Suite 13A-01, 13th Floor, Wisma MCA, 163 Jalan Ampang, 50450 Kuala Lumpur; tel. (3) 21645934; fax (3) 21648659; e-mail info@nepalembassy.com.my; internet www.nepalembassy.com.my; Ambassador RISHI RAJ ADHIKARI.

Netherlands: The Amp Walk, 7th Floor, South Block, 218 Jalan Ampang, POB 10543, 50450 Kuala Lumpur; tel. (3) 21686200; fax (3) 21686240; e-mail kll@minbuza.nl; internet www.netherlands.org .my; Ambassador PAUL BEKKERS.

New Zealand: Menara IMC, 21st Floor, 8 Jalan Sultan Ismail, 50250 Kuala Lumpur; tel. (3) 20782533; fax (3) 20780387; e-mail nzhckl@streamyx.com; internet www.nzembassy.com/malaysia; High Commissioner DAVID PINE.

Nigeria: 85 Jalan Ampang Hilir, 55000 Kuala Lumpur; tel. (3) 42517843; fax (3) 42524302; e-mail info@nigeria.org.my; internet www.nigeria.org.my; Chargé d'affaires NURUDEEN BABATUNDE AYINLA.

Norway: Suite CD, 53rd Floor, Empire Tower, Jalan Tun Razak, 50400 Kuala Lumpur; tel. (3) 21750300; fax (3) 21750308; e-mail emb .kualalumpur@mfa.no; internet www.norway.org.my; Ambassador ARILD BRAASTAD.

Oman: 109 Jalan U Thant, 55000 Kuala Lumpur; tel. (3) 42577378; fax (3) 42571400; e-mail omanemb@po.jaring.my; Ambassador AFLAH BIN SULEIMAN AL-TAEI.

Pakistan: 132 Jalan Ampang, 50450 Kuala Lumpur; tel. (3) 21618877; fax (3) 21645958; e-mail pahickl@gmail.com; internet www.pahickl.com; High Commissioner MASOOD KHALID.

Papua New Guinea: 11 Lingkungan U Thant, off Jalan U Thant, 55000 Kuala Lumpur; tel. (3) 42575405; fax (3) 42576203; High Commissioner VEALI VAGI.

Peru: Wisma Selangor Dredging, 6th Floor, South Block, 142A Jalan Ampang, 50450 Kuala Lumpur; tel. (3) 21633034; fax (3) 21633039; e-mail embperu@streamyx.com; Ambassador WILLIAM BELEVAN MCBRIDE.

Philippines: 1 Changkat Kia Peng, 50450 Kuala Lumpur; tel. (3) 21484233; fax (3) 21483576; e-mail consular@philembassykl.org.my; internet www.philembassykl.org.my; Ambassador JOSE EDUARDO E. MALAYA, III.

Poland: POB 10052, 50704 Kuala Lumpur; tel. (3) 21610780; fax (3) 21649924; e-mail kualalumpur.amb.sekretariat@msz.gov.pl; internet www.kualalumpur.polemb.net; Ambassador ADAM JELONEK.

Qatar: 113 Jalan Ampang Hilir, POB 13118, 55000 Kuala Lumpur; tel. (3) 42565552; fax (3) 42565553; e-mail kualalumpur@mofa.gov .qa; Chargé d'affaires a.i. RASHID MAIRZA AL-MULLA.

Romania: 114 Jalan Damai, off Jalan Ampang, 55000 Kuala Lumpur; tel. (3) 21423172; fax (3) 21448713; e-mail roembdhm@ streamyx.com; internet kualalumpur.mae.ro; Ambassador PETRU PETRA.

Russia: 263 Jalan Ampang, 50450 Kuala Lumpur; tel. (3) 42567252; fax (3) 42576091; e-mail rusembmalaysia@yandex.ru; internet www .malaysia.mid.ru; Ambassador LYUDMILA GEORGIEVNA VOROBYEVA.

Saudi Arabia: Wisma Chinese Chamber, Tingkat 4, 258 Jalan Ampang, 50450 Kuala Lumpur; tel. (3) 42579433; fax (3) 42578751; e-mail saembssy@tm.net.my; Ambassador MOHAMMED REDA HUSSEIN ABU AL-HAMAYEL.

Senegal: 9 Lorong U Thant, off Jalan U Thant, 55000 Kuala Lumpur; tel. (3) 42567343; fax (3) 42563205; e-mail senamb_mal@ yahoo.fr; Ambassador BABACAR DIOP.

Singapore: 209 Jalan Tun Razak, 50400 Kuala Lumpur; tel. (3) 21616277; fax (3) 21616343; e-mail singhc_kul@sgmfa.gov.sg; internet www.mfa.gov.sg/kl; High Commissioner T. JASUDASEN.

Slovakia: 11 Jalan U Thant, 55000 Kuala Lumpur; tel. (3) 21150016; fax (3) 21150018; e-mail emb.kualalumpur@mzv.sk; internet www.mzv.sk/kualalumpur; Ambassador MILAN LAJČIAK.

South Africa: Menara HLA, Suite 22-01, 3 Jalan Kia Peng, 50450 Kuala Lumpur; tel. (3) 21702400; fax (3) 21688591; e-mail sahcadm@ streamyx.com; internet www.sahighcomkl.com.my; High Commissioner THAMSANQA DENNIS MSELEKU.

Spain: 200 Jalan Ampang, 50450 Kuala Lumpur; tel. (3) 21484868; fax (3) 21424582; e-mail emb.kualalumpur@maec.es; internet www .maec.es/embajadas/kualalumpur; Ambassador MARÍA BASSOLS DELGADO.

Sri Lanka: 12 Jalan Keranji Dua, off Jalan Kedondong, Ampang Hilir, 55000 Kuala Lumpur; tel. (3) 42568987; fax (3) 42532497; e-mail slhicom@streamyx.com; internet www.slhc.com.my; High Commissioner NANDA GODAGE.

Sudan: 2A Persiaran Ampang, off Jalan Ru, 55000 Kuala Lumpur; tel. (3) 42569104; fax (3) 42568107; e-mail assalam12@hotmail.com; Ambassador ABDEL RAHMAN HAMZAH ELRAYA.

Swaziland: Suite 22-03 & 22-03A, Menara Citibank, 165 Jalan Ampang, 50450 Kuala Lumpur; tel. (3) 21632511; fax (3) 21633326; e-mail swdkl_2@streamyx.com; High Commissioner MPUMELELO J. N. HLOPE.

Switzerland: 16 Persiaran Madge, 55000 Kuala Lumpur; tel. (3) 21480622; fax (3) 21480935; e-mail kua.vertretung@eda.admin.ch; internet www.eda.admin.ch/kualalumpur; Ambassador Dr ROLF LENZ.

Syria: 93 Jalan U Thant, 55000 Kuala Lumpur; tel. (3) 42516349; fax (3) 42516363; e-mail enquiry@syrianembassy.com.my; internet www.syrianembassy.com.my; Chargé d'affaires a.i. MOHAMED HASANEIN KHADDAM.

Thailand: 206 Jalan Ampang, 50450 Kuala Lumpur; tel. (3) 21488222; fax (3) 21486527; e-mail thaikula@mfa.go.th; internet www.mfa.go.th/web/1830.php?depcode=23000100; Ambassador THANA DUANGRATANA.

Timor-Leste: 62 Jalan Ampang Hilir, 55000 Kuala Lumpur; tel. (3) 42562046; fax (3) 42562016; e-mail embaixada_tl_kl@yahoo.com; Ambassador JOSÉ ANTÓNIO AMORIM DIAS.

Turkey: 118 Jalan U Thant, 55000 Kuala Lumpur; tel. (3) 42572225; fax (3) 42572227; e-mail embassy.kualalumpur@mfa.gov.tr; internet www.kualalumpur.be.mfa.gov.tr; Ambassador SERAP ATAAY.

Ukraine: Suite 22-02, 22nd Floor, Menara Tan & Tan, 207 Jalan Tun Razak, 50400 Kuala Lumpur; tel. (3) 21669552; fax (3)

21664371; e-mail emb_my@mfa.gov.ua; internet www.mfa.gov.ua/malaysia; Ambassador IHOR V. HUMENNYI.

United Arab Emirates: 1 Gerbang Ampang Hilir, off Persiaran Ampang Hilir, 55000 Kuala Lumpur; tel. (3) 42535221; fax (3) 42535220; e-mail uaemal@tm.net.my; Ambassador NASSER SALMAN AL-ABOODI.

United Kingdom: 185 Jalan Ampang, 50450 Kuala Lumpur; tel. (3) 21702200; fax (3) 21702370; e-mail political.kualalumpur@fco.gov.uk; internet ukinmalaysia.fco.gov.uk; High Commissioner SIMON FEATHERSTONE.

USA: 376 Jalan Tun Razak, POB 10035, 50400 Kuala Lumpur; tel. (3) 21685000; fax (3) 21485801; e-mail klconsular@state.gov; internet malaysia.usembassy.gov; Ambassador PAUL W. JONES.

Uruguay: 6th Floor, UBN Tower, 10 Jalan P. Ramlee, 50250 Kuala Lumpur; tel. (3) 20313669; fax (3) 20315669; e-mail urukuala@streamyx.com; Ambassador (vacant).

Uzbekistan: Wisma Chinese Chamber, 2nd Floor, 258 Jalan Ampang, 50450 Kuala Lumpur; tel. (3) 42532406; fax (3) 42535406; e-mail uzbekemb@streamyx.com; internet www.malaysia.mfa.uz; Ambassador SHUKUR SABITOV.

Venezuela: Suite 20-05, 20th Floor, Menara Tan & Tan, 207 Jalan Tun Razak, 50400 Kuala Lumpur; tel. (3) 21633444; fax (3) 21636819; e-mail info@venezuela.org.my; internet www.venezuela.org.my; Ambassador MANUEL ANTONIO GUZMÁN HERNÁNDEZ.

Viet Nam: 4 Jalan Persiaran Stonor, 50450 Kuala Lumpur; tel. (3) 21484036; fax (3) 21483270; e-mail daisevn@putra.net.my; internet www.mofa.gov.vn/vnemb.my; Ambassador NGUYEN HONG THAO.

Yemen: 7 Jalan Kedondong, off Jalan Ampang Hilir, 55000 Kuala Lumpur; tel. (3) 42511793; fax (3) 42511794; e-mail secretary@yemenembassykl.com; internet yemenembassykl.com; Ambassador Dr ABDULLA MOHAMED ALI AL-MONTSER.

Zambia: Suite C, Menara MBF, 5th Floor, Jalan Sultan Ismail, 50250 Kuala Lumpur; tel. (3) 21453512; fax (3) 21453619; e-mail info@zhckl.com.my; internet www.zhckl.com.my; High Commissioner (vacant).

Zimbabwe: 124 Jalan Sembilan, Taman Ampang Utama, 68000 Ampang, Selangor Darul Ehsan; tel. (3) 42516779; fax (3) 42517252; e-mail zhck@tm.net.my; Ambassador CUTHBERT ZHAKATA.

Judicial System

The two High Courts, one in Peninsular Malaysia and the other in Sabah and Sarawak, have original, appellate and revisional jurisdiction as the federal law provides. Above these two High Courts is the Court of Appeal, which was established in 1994 as an intermediary court between the Federal Court (formerly the Supreme Court) and the High Court. When appeals to the Privy Council in the United Kingdom were abolished in 1985 the former Supreme Court became the final court of appeal. Therefore, at that stage only one appeal was available to a party aggrieved by the decision of the High Court; hence, the establishment of the Court of Appeal. The Federal Court has, to the exclusion of any other court, jurisdiction in any dispute between states or between the Federation and any state; it also has special jurisdiction as to the interpretation of the Constitution. The Federal Court is headed by the Chief Justice (formerly the Lord President); the other members of the Federal Court are the President of the Court of Appeal, the two Chief Judges of the High Courts and the Federal Court Judges. Members of the Court of Appeal are the President and the Court of Appeal judges, and members of the High Courts are the two Chief Judges and their respective High Court judges. All judges are appointed by the Yang di-Pertuan Agong on the advice of the Prime Minister, after consulting the Conference of Rulers. In 1993 a Special Court was established to hear cases brought by or against the Yang di-Pertuan Agong or a Ruler of State (Sultans).

The Sessions Courts, which are situated in the principal urban and rural centres, are presided over by a Sessions Judge, who is a member of the Judicial and Legal Service of the Federation and is a qualified barrister or a Bachelor of Law from any of the recognized universities. The criminal jurisdiction of the Sessions Courts covers the less serious indictable offences, excluding those that carry the death penalty. Civil jurisdiction of a Sessions Court is up to RM 250,000. The Sessions Judges are appointed by the Yang di-Pertuan Agong.

The Magistrates' Courts are also found in the main urban and rural centres and have both civil and criminal jurisdiction, although of a more restricted nature than that of the Sessions Courts. The Magistrates consist of officers from the Judicial and Legal Service of the Federation. They are appointed by the State Authority in which they officiate on the recommendation of the Chief Judge.

There are also Syariah (*Shari'a*) courts for rulings under Islamic law. In July 1996 the Cabinet announced that the Syariah courts were to be restructured with the appointment of a Syariah Chief Judge and four Court of Appeal justices, whose rulings would set precedents for the whole country.

Prior to February 1995 trials in the High Courts for murder and kidnapping were heard with jury and assessors, respectively. The amendment to the Criminal Procedure Code abolished both the jury and the assessors systems, and all criminal trials in the High Courts are now heard by a judge sitting alone. In 1988 an amendment to the Constitution empowered any federal lawyer to confer with the Attorney-General to determine the courts in which any proceedings, excluding those before a Syariah court, a native court or a court martial, be instituted, or to which such proceedings be transferred.

Chief Justice of the Federal Court: Tan Sri Dato' ZAKI BIN TUN AZMI, Palace of Justice, Presint 3, 62506 Putrajaya; tel. (3) 88803500; fax (3) 88803507; e-mail cj@kehakiman.gov.my; internet www.kehakiman.gov.my.

President of the Court of Appeal: Tan Sri Dato' ALAUDDIN BIN MOHD SHERIFF; tel. (3) 88803566; fax (3) 88803596; e-mail alauddin@kehakiman.gov.my.

Chief Judge of the High Court in Peninsular Malaysia: Tan Sri ARIFIN BIN ZAKARIA; tel. (3) 88803552; fax (3) 88803556; e-mail cjm@kehakiman.gov.my.

Chief Judge of the High Court in Sabah and Sarawak: Tan Sri Datuk Seri RICHARD MALANJUM, High Court, Jalan Gersik, 93050 Sarawak.

Attorney-General: Tan Sri ABDUL GANI PATAIL.

Religion

Islam is the established religion. While freedom of religious practice is enshrined in the Constitution, Malaysia's parallel Islamic judicial system holds great sway over the Muslim majority on religious issues. In May 2005 21 members of the controversial sect known as 'Sky Kingdom' were arrested for propagating 'devious' teachings said to humiliate Islam. Almost all ethnic Malays are Muslims, representing 60.4% of the total population in 2000. In that year 19.2% of the population followed Buddhism, 9.1% Christianity and 6.3% Hinduism.

Malaysian Consultative Council of Buddhism, Christianity, Hinduism, Sikhism and Taoism (MCCBCHST): Buddhist Maha Vihara, 123 Jalan Berhala, Brickfields, 50470 Kuala Lumpur; tel. (3) 22739304; fax (3) 22739307; e-mail mccbchst@yahoo.com; f. 1981; a non-Muslim group; Pres. Rev. Dr THOMAS PHILIPS.

ISLAM

President of the Majlis Islam: Datuk Haji MOHD FAUZI BIN Haji ABDUL HAMID (Kuching, Sarawak).

Istitut Kefahaman Islam Malaysia (IKIM) (Institute of Islamic Understanding Malaysia): 2 Langgak Tunku, off Jalan Duta, 50480 Kuala Lumpur; tel. (3) 62046200; fax (3) 62014189; e-mail info@ikim.gov.my; internet www.ikim.gov.my; Chair. TUN ABDULLAH BIN AHMAD BADAWI.

Jabatan Kemajuan Islam Malaysia (JAKIM) (Department of Islamic Development Malaysia): Aras 4–9, Blok D7, Pusat Pentadbiran Kerajaan Persekutuan, 62519 Putrajaya; tel. (3) 88864000; fax (3) 88892039; e-mail webmaster@islam.gov.my; internet www.islam.gov.my; Dir-Gen. Haji OTHMAN BIN MUSTAPHA.

BUDDHISM

Malaysian Buddhist Association (MBA): MBA Bldg, 182 Jalan Burmah, 10050 Pinang; tel. (4) 2262690; fax (4) 2263024; e-mail mba.hq@streamyx.com; internet www.malaysianbuddhistassociation.org; f. 1959; the national body for Chinese and English-speaking monks and nuns and temples from the Mahayana, Theravada and Vajrayana tradition; 13 state brs and 33 other brs nation-wide; 30,000 mems; Pres. Ven. SECK JIT HENG.

Buddhist Missionary Society Malaysia (BMSM): 123 Jalan Berhala, off Jalan Tun Sambanthan, 50470 Kuala Lumpur; tel. (3) 22730150; fax (3) 22740245; e-mail bmsm.malaysia@gmail.com; internet www.bmsm.org.my; f. 1962; Pres. Dato' CHEE PECK KIAT.

Buddhist Tzu-Chi Merit Society (Malaysia): 316 Jalan Macalister, 10450 Pulau Pinang; tel. (4) 2281013; fax (2) 2261013; e-mail info@tzuchi.org.my; internet www.tzuchi.org.my.

Malaysian Fo Kuang Buddhist Association: 2 Jalan SS3/33, Taman University, 47300 Petaling Jaya, Selangor; tel. (3) 78776512; fax (3) 78776511; e-mail myfoguang@yahoo.com.

Sasana Abhiwurdhi Wardhana Society: 123 Jalan Berhala, off Jalan Tun Sambanthan, 50490 Kuala Lumpur; f. 1894; the national body for Sri Lankan Buddhists belonging to the Theravada tradition.

Young Buddhist Association of Malaysia (YBAM): 9 Jalan SS25/24, Taman Mayang, 47301 Petaling Jaya, Selangor; tel. (3)

78049154; fax (3) 78049021; e-mail ybam@streamyx.com; internet www.ybam.org.my; f. 1970; 270 mems; Pres. Dr ONG SEE YEW.

CHRISTIANITY

Majlis Gereja-Gereja Malaysia (Council of Churches of Malaysia): 10 Jalan 11/9, 46200 Petaling Jaya, Selangor; tel. (3) 75967092; fax (3) 79560353; e-mail cchurchm@streamyx.org; internet www.ccmalaysia.org; f. 1947; 18 mem. churches; 10 assoc. mems; Pres. Rev. Dr THOMAS PHILIPS (Mar Thoma Syrian Church); Gen. Sec. Rev. Dr HERMEN SHASTRI.

The Anglican Communion

Malaysia comprises three Anglican dioceses, within the Church of the Province of South East Asia.

Primate: Most Rev. Dr JOHN CHEW (Bishop of Singapore).

Bishop of Kuching: Rt Rev. BOLLY ANAK LAPOK, The House of the Epiphany, POB 347, 93704 Kuching, Sarawak; tel. (82) 240187; fax (82) 426488; e-mail bishopk@streamyx.com; has jurisdiction over Sarawak, Brunei and part of Indonesian Kalimantan (Borneo).

Bishop of Sabah: Most Rev. ALBERT VUN CHEONG FUI, Rumah Bishop, Jalan Tangki, POB 10811, 88809 Kota Kinabalu, Sabah; tel. (88) 245846; fax (88) 245942; e-mail dosabah@streamyx.com.

Bishop of West Malaysia: Rt. Rev. NG MOON HING, Bishop's House, 16 Jalan Pudu Lama, 50200 Kuala Lumpur; tel. (3) 20313213; fax (3) 20312728; e-mail anglican@streamyx.com; internet www.anglicanwestmalaysia.org.my.

The Baptist Church

Malaysia Baptist Convention: 2 Jalan Dispensary 2/38, 46000 Petaling Jaya, Selangor; tel. (3) 77823564; fax (3) 77833603; e-mail mbcpj@tm.net.my; internet www.mbc.org.my; Chair. Rev. BERNARD ANG; Gen. Sec. Rev. KOE CHOON HUAN.

The Methodist Church

Methodist Church in Malaysia: 69 Jalan 5/31, 46000 Petaling Jaya, Selangor; tel. (3) 79541811; fax (3) 79541788; e-mail info@methodistchurch.org.my; internet www.methodistchurch.org.my; f. 1885; 164,400 mems; Head Rev. Dr HWA YUNG.

The Presbyterian Church

Presbyterian Church in Malaysia: 7 Jalan Sungai Buaya, Batu 3 1/2, off Jalan Klang Lama, 58100 Kuala Lumpur; tel. (3) 79847361; fax (3) 79809037; e-mail presbych@gmail.com; internet www.gpm.org.my; Moderator Rev. CHUA HUA PENG.

The Roman Catholic Church

Malaysia comprises three archdioceses and six dioceses. At 31 December 2007 approximately 3.0% of the population were adherents.

Catholic Bishops' Conference of Malaysia, Singapore and Brunei

Majodi Centre, 2101 Jalan Masai, Johor; tel. (7) 3871121; fax (7) 3872498; e-mail mpakiam@pd.jaring.my; Pres. Most Rev. MURPHY NICHOLAS XAVIER PAKIAM (Archbishop of Kuala Lumpur).

Archbishop of Kota Kinabalu: Most Rev. JOHN LEE HIONG FUN-YIT HAW, Archbishop's House, POB 10289, 88803, Kota Kinabalu, Sabah; tel. (88) 712297; fax (88) 711954; internet www.kkdiocese.net.

Archbishop of Kuala Lumpur: Most Rev. MURPHY NICHOLAS XAVIER PAKIAM, Archbishop's House, 528 Jalan Bukit Nanas, 50250 Kuala Lumpur; tel. (3) 20788828; fax (3) 20313815; e-mail mpakiam@pd.jaring.my; internet www.archway.org.my.

Archbishop of Kuching: Most Rev. JOHN HA TIONG HOCK, Archbishop's Office, 118 Jalan Tun Abang Haji Openg, POB 940, 93000 Kuching, Sarawak; tel. (82) 242634; fax (82) 425724; e-mail abcofku@pd.jaring.my.

BAHÁ'Í FAITH

Spiritual Assembly of the Bahá'ís of Malaysia: 12 Desa Business Centre, 1–2/F, Jalan 2/109E, Taman Desa, Jalan Klang Lama, 58100 Kuala Lumpur; tel. (3) 79819059; fax (3) 79802058; e-mail nsa-sec@bahai.org.my; internet www.bahai.org.my; f. 1964; mems resident in 800 localities.

The Press

PENINSULAR MALAYSIA DAILIES

English Language

Business Times: Balai Berita 31, Jalan Riong, 59100 Kuala Lumpur; tel. (3) 22822628; fax (3) 22825424; e-mail support@nstp.com.my; internet www.btimes.com.my; f. 1976; morning; Editor SHAHRIMAN JOHARI; circ. 15,000.

The Edge: 1 Menara KLK, Level 3, Jalan PJU 7/6, Mutiara Damansara, 47810 Petaling Jaya, Selangor; tel. (3) 77218000; fax (3) 77218010; e-mail info@bizedge.com; internet www.theedgedaily.com; f. 1996; weekly, with daily internet edition; business and investment news; Editor AU FOONG YEE; circ. 22,821.

Malay Mail: Lot 2A, Jalan 13/2, 46200 Petaling Jaya, Selangor; tel. (3) 79472288; fax (3) 79472323; e-mail mmnews@mmail.com.my; internet www.mmail.com.my; f. 1896; afternoon; Editor-in-Chief YUSHAIMI YAHAYA; circ. 75,000.

Malaysiakini: 48 Jalan Kemuja, Bangsar Utama, 59000 Kuala Lumpur; tel. (3) 22835567; fax (3) 22892579; e-mail enquiries@malaysiakini.com; internet www.malaysiakini.com; f. 1999; Malaysia's first online newspaper; English and Malay; Editor STEVEN GAN.

New Straits Times: Balai Berita 31, Jalan Riong, 59100 Kuala Lumpur; tel. (3) 22823322; fax (3) 22821434; e-mail news@nstp.com.my; internet www.nst.com.my; f. 1845; morning; Group Editor-in-Chief Dato' SYED NADZRI SYED HARUN; circ. 107,513.

The Star: 15 Jalan 16/11, 46350 Petaling Jaya, POB 12474, Selangor Darul Ehsan; tel. (3) 79671388; fax (3) 79550439; e-mail msd@thestar.com.my; internet www.thestar.com.my; f. 1971; morning; Group Chief Editor Datuk WONG CHUN WAI; circ. 302,658.

The Sun: Sun Media Corpn Sdn Bhd, 4th Floor, Lot 6, Jalan 51/217, Section 51, 46050 Petaling Jaya, Selangor Darul Ehsan; tel. (3) 77846688; fax (3) 77835871; e-mail info@thesundaily.com; internet www.thesundaily.com; f. 1993; free tabloid newspaper in print and online formats; Man. Editor CHONG CHENG HAI; circ. 300,587.

Chinese Language

Chung Kuo Pao (China Press): 80 Jalan Riong, off Jalan Bangsar, 59100 Kuala Lumpur; tel. (3) 22896363; fax (3) 22827125; e-mail enews@chinapress.com.my; internet www.chinapress.com.my; f. 1946; Editor POON CHAU HUAY; Gen. Man. NG BENG LYE; circ. 161,794.

Guang Ming Daily: 19 Jalan Semangat, 46200 Petaling Jaya, Selangor; tel. (3) 79658888; fax (3) 79658477; e-mail gmkl@mail.guangming.com.my; internet www.guangming.com.my; Editor-in-Chief YE NING; circ. 94,287.

Kwong Wah Yit Poh: 19 Jalan Presgrave, 11300 Pinang; tel. (4) 2612312; fax (4) 2628540; e-mail editor@kwongwah.com.my; internet www.kwongwah.com.my; f. 1910; morning; Chief Editor HU JINCHANG; circ. 100,000.

Nanyang Siang Pau (Malaysia): 1st Floor, 1 Jalan SS7/2, 47301 Petaling Jaya, Selangor; tel. (3) 78726888; fax (3) 78726800; e-mail editor@nanyang.com.my; internet www.nanyang.com.my; f. 1923; morning and evening; Editor-in-Chief CHONG CHOONG NAM; circ. 180,000 (daily), 220,000 (Sunday).

Sin Chew Jit Poh (Malaysia): 19 Jalan Semangat, POB 367, Jalan Sultan, 46200 Petaling Jaya, Selangor; tel. (3) 79658888; fax (3) 79556881; e-mail editorial@sinchew.com.my; internet www.sinchew-i.com; f. 1929; morning; Group Editor-in-chief SIEW NYOKE CHOW; circ. 440,002 (daily), 230,000 (Sunday).

Malay Language

Berita Harian: Balai Berita, 31 Jalan Riong, 59100 Kuala Lumpur; tel. (3) 22822323; fax (3) 20567081; e-mail bhnews@bharian.com.my; internet www.bharian.com.my; f. 1957; morning; Group Editor Datuk MIOR KAMARUL SHAHID; circ. 166,400.

Mingguan Perdana: 48 Jalan Siput Akek, Taman Billion, Kuala Lumpur; tel. (3) 619133; Group Chief Editor KHALID JAFRI.

Utusan Malaysia: 46M Jalan Lima, off Jalan Chan Sow Lin, 55200 Kuala Lumpur; tel. (3) 92217055; fax (3) 92227876; e-mail corpcomm@utusan.com.my; internet www.utusan.com.my; Editor ABDUL AZIZ ISHAK; circ. 171,582.

Watan: 23-1 Jalan 9A/55A, Taman Setiawangsa, 54200 Kuala Lumpur; tel. (3) 4523040; fax (3) 4523043; circ. 80,000.

Tamil Language

Makkal Osai: 11B Jalan Murai Dua, Batu Kompleks, off Jalan Ipoh, 52000 Kuala Lumpur; tel. (3) 62512251; fax (3) 62535981; f. 1990; est. as a Sunday newspaper after *Tamil Osai* ceased publication; publ. daily since Dec. 2005; Gen. Man. S.M. PERIASAMY; circ. 52,000 (daily), 95,000 (Sunday).

Malaysia Nanban: 544-3 Batu Complex, off Jalan Ipoh, Batu 3 1/4, 51200 Kuala Lumpur; e-mail news@nanban.com.my; internet www.nanban2u.com; tel. (3) 62515981; fax (3) 62591617; circ. 45,000; Editor M. MALAYANDY.

Tamil Nesan: 23, Jalan SBC 5, Taman Sri Batu Caves, 68100 Batu Caves, Selangor Darul Ehsaan; tel. (3) 61841818; fax (3) 61871818; e-mail mytamilnesan@yahoo.com; internet www.tamilnesan.com.my; f. 1924; morning; Editor-in-Chief PADMANATHAN; circ. 35,000 (daily), 60,000 (Sunday).

SUNDAY NEWSPAPERS

English Language

New Sunday Times: Balai Berita 31, Jalan Riong, 59100 Kuala Lumpur; tel. (3) 2822328; fax (3) 2824482; e-mail news@nstp.com.my; f. 1931; morning; Group Editor Datuk HISHAMUDDIN AUN; circ. 191,562.

Sunday Mail: Balai Berita 31, Jalan Riong, 59100 Kuala Lumpur; tel. (3) 2822328; fax (3) 2824482; e-mail smail@nstp.com.my; f. 1896; morning; Editor JOACHIM S. P. NG; circ. 75,641.

Sunday Star: 13 Jalan 13/6, 46200 Petaling Jaya, POB 12474, Selangor Darul Ehsan; tel. (3) 7581188; fax (3) 7551280; f. 1971; Editor DAVID YEOH; circ. 232,790.

Malay Language

Berita Minggu: Balai Berita 31, Jalan Riong, 59100 Kuala Lumpur; tel. (3) 22822323; fax (3) 20567082; e-mail bhnews@bharian.com.my; f. 1957; morning; Group Editor Datuk MIOR KAMARUL SHAHID; circ. 421,127.

Metro Ahad: Balai Berita 31, Jalan Riong, 59100 Kuala Lumpur; tel. (3) 22822328; fax (3) 22821482; e-mail metahad@nstp.com.my; internet www.nstp.com.my/Corporate/nstp/products/productMetroAhd.htm; f. 1995; morning; circ. 136,974.

Mingguan Malaysia: 11A The Right Angle, Jalan 14/22, 46100 Petaling Jaya; tel. (3) 7563355; fax (3) 7577755; f. 1964; Editor MOHD HASSAN MOHD NOOR; circ. 543,232.

PENINSULAR MALAYSIA PERIODICALS

English Language

Her World: Lot 7, Jalan Bersatu 13/4, Section 13, 46200 Petaling Jaya, Selangor Darul Ehsan; tel. (3) 79527000; fax (3) 79600148; e-mail herworld@bluinc.com.my; internet www.herworld.com.my; monthly; Editor ALICE CHEE LAN NEO; circ. 35,000.

The Herald: Archdiocesan Pastoral Centre, 5 Jalan Robertson, 50150 Kuala Lumpur; tel. (3) 20268290; e-mail editor@herald.com.my; internet www.heraldmalaysia.com; weekly; Catholic; Publr Rev. Tan Sri MURPHY PAKIAM; Editor Fr ANDREW LAWRENCE; circ. 14,000.

Malaysia Warta Kerajaan Seri Paduka Baginda (HM Government Gazette): Percetakan Nasional Malaysia Berhad, Jalan Chan Sow Lin, 50554 Kuala Lumpur; tel. (3) 92212022; fax (3) 92220690; e-mail pnmb@po.jaring.my; fortnightly.

Malaysian Agricultural Journal: Ministry of Agriculture and Agro-based Industry, Publications Unit, Wisma Tani, Jalan Sultan Salahuddin, 50624 Kuala Lumpur; tel. (3) 2982011; fax (3) 2913758; f. 1901; 2 a year.

Malaysian Forester: Forestry Department Headquarters, Jalan Sultan Salahuddin, 50660 Kuala Lumpur; tel. (3) 26988244; fax (3) 26925657; e-mail skthai@forestry.gov.my; f. 1931; quarterly; Editor THAI SEE KIAM.

The Planter: Wisma ISP, 29 & 31–33 Jalan Taman U Thant, POB 10262, 50708 Kuala Lumpur; tel. (3) 21425561; fax (3) 21426898; e-mail isphq@tm.net.my; internet www.isp.org.my; f. 1919; publ. by Isp Management (M); monthly; Editor AZIZAN ABDULLAH; circ. 4,000.

The Rocket: 24 Jalan 20/9, 46300 Petaling Jaya, Selangor; tel. (3) 79578022; fax (3) 79575718; e-mail rocket@dapmalaysia.org; internet daprocket.com; monthly; official newsletter of Democratic Action Party; also published in Chinese and Malay; Editor TONY PUA.

Young Generation: 11A The Right Angle, Jalan 14/22, 46100 Petaling Jaya, Selangor; tel. (3) 7563355; fax (3) 7577755; monthly; circ. 50,000.

Chinese Language

Mister Weekly: 2A Jalan 19/1, 46300 Petaling Jaya, Selangor; tel. (3) 7562400; fax (3) 7553826; f. 1976; weekly; Editor WONG AH TAI; circ. 25,000.

Mun Sang Poh: 472 Jalan Pasir Puteh, 31650 Ipoh; tel. (5) 3212919; fax (5) 3214006; bi-weekly; circ. 77,958.

New Life Post: 80M Jalan SS21/39, Damansara Utama, 47400 Petaling Jaya, Selangor; tel. (3) 7571833; fax (3) 7181809; f. 1972; bi-weekly; Editor LOW BENG CHEE; circ. 231,000.

New Tide Magazine: Nanyang Siang Pau Bldg, 2nd Floor, Jalan 7/2, 47301 Petaling Jaya, Selangor; tel. (3) 76202118; fax (3) 76202131; e-mail newtidemag@hotmail.com; f. 1974; monthly; Editor NELLIE OOI; circ. 39,000.

Malay Language

Dewan Masyarakat: Dewan Bahasa dan Pustaka, Jalan Wisma Putra, POB 10803, 50926 Kuala Lumpur; tel. (3) 2481011; fax (3) 2484211; f. 1963; monthly; current affairs; Editor ZULKIFLI SALLEH; circ. 48,500.

Dewan Pelajar: Dewan Bahasa dan Pustaka, Jalan Wisma Putra, POB 10803, 50926 Kuala Lumpur; tel. (3) 2481011; fax (3) 2484211; f. 1967; monthly; children's; Editor ZALEHA HASHIM; circ. 100,000.

Dewan Siswa: POB 10803, 50926 Kuala Lumpur; tel. (3) 2481011; fax (3) 2484208; monthly; circ. 140,000.

Gila-Gila: 38-1, Jalan Bangsar Utama Satu, Bangsar Utama, 59000 Kuala Lumpur; tel. (3) 22824970; fax (3) 22824967; fortnightly; circ. 70,000.

Harakah: 5 Jalan, 65C, Off Jalan Pahang Barat, Pekeliling Business Center, 53000 Kuala Lumpur; tel. (3) 40212009; fax (3) 40212029; e-mail harakahenglish@yahoo.com; internet www.beritaharakah.com; two a week; f. 1980; organ of the PAS; Editor ZULKIFLI SULONG.

Jelita: Berita Publishing Sdn Bhd, 16–20 Jalan 4/109E, Desa Business Park, Taman Desa, off Jalan Klang Lama, 58100 Kuala Lumpur; tel. (3) 76208111; fax (3) 76208026; e-mail jelita@beritapub.com.my; internet www.beritapublishing.com.my; monthly; fashion and beauty magazine; Editor SARIMAH HUSIN; circ. 133,727.

Mangga: 11A The Right Angle, Jalan 14/22, 46100 Petaling Jaya, Selangor; tel. (3) 7563355; fax (3) 7577755; monthly; circ. 56,609.

Mastika: Utusan Karya Sdn Bhd, Lot 6, Jalan P/10, Seksyen 10, 43650 Bandar Baru Bangi, Selangor Darul Ehsan; tel. (3) 89262999; fax (3) 89259277; f. 1941; monthly; illustrated magazine; Editor SAHIDAN JAAFAR; circ. 350,000.

Utusan Radio dan TV: 11A The Right Angle, Jalan 14/22, 46100 Petaling Jaya, Selangor; tel. (3) 7563355; fax (3) 7577755; fortnightly; Editor NORSHAH TAMBY; circ. 115,000.

Wanita: 11A The Right Angle, Jalan 14/22, 46100 Petaling Jaya, Selangor; tel. (3) 7563355; fax (3) 7577755; monthly; women; Editor Nik RAHIMAH HASSAN; circ. 28,651.

Punjabi Language

Navjiwan Punjabi News: 52 Jalan 8/18, Jalan Toman, 46050 Petaling Jaya, Selangor; tel. (3) 7565725; f. 1950; weekly; Assoc. Editor TARA SINGH; circ. 9,000.

SABAH DAILIES

Api Siang Pau (Kota Kinabalu Commercial Press): 24 Lorong Dewan, POB 170, Kota Kinabalu; f. 1954; morning; Chinese; Editor Datuk LO KWOCK CHUEN; circ. 3,000.

Borneo Post (Nountan Press Sdn Bhd): 1 Jalan Bakau, 1st Floor, off Jalan Gaya, 88999 Kota Kinabulu; tel. (88) 238001; fax (88) 238002; internet www.theborneopost.com; English; Chief Editor JIMMY ADIT; circ. 22,533.

Daily Express: News House, 16 Jalan Pasar Baru, POB 10139, 88801 Kota Kinabalu; tel. (88) 256422; fax (88) 238611; e-mail forum@dailyexpress.com.my; internet www.dailyexpress.com.my; f. 1963; morning; English, Bahasa Malaysia and Kadazan; Editor-in-Chief SARDATHISA JAMES; circ. 28,555.

Hwa Chiaw Jit Pao (Overseas Chinese Daily News): News House, 16 Jalan Pasar Baru, POB 10139, 88801 Kota Kinabalu; tel. (88) 256422; fax (88) 238611; e-mail sph@dailyexpress.com.my; internet www.ocdn.com.my; f. 1936; morning; Chinese; Editor HII YUK SENG; circ. 16,489.

Merdeka Daily News: Lot 56, BDC Estate, Mile 1½ North Road, POB 332, 90703 Sandakan; tel. (89) 214517; fax (89) 275537; e-mail merkk@tm.net.my; f. 1968; morning; Chinese; Editor-in-Chief FUNG KON SHING; circ. 8,000.

New Sabah Times: Jalan Pusat Pembangunan Masyarakat, off Jalan Mat Salleh, 88100 Kota Kinabalu; tel. (88) 230055; fax (88) 231155; e-mail chng.boonheng@newsabahtimes.com.my; internet www.newsabahtimes.com.my; English, Malay and Kadazan; Editor-in-Chief CHENG BOON HENG; circ. 22,525.

Syarikat Sabah Times: Kota Kinabalu; tel. (88) 52217; f. 1952; English, Malay and Kadazan; circ. 25,000.

Tawau Jih Pao: POB 464, 1072 Jalan Kuhara, Tawau; tel. (89) 72576; Chinese; Editor-in-Chief STEPHEN LAI KIM YEAN.

SARAWAK DAILIES

Berita Petang Sarawak: Lot 8322, Lorong 7, Jalan Tun Abdul Razak, 93450 Kuching; POB 1315, 93726 Kuching; tel. (82) 480771;

fax (82) 489006; f. 1972; evening; Chinese; Chief Editor HWANG YU CHAI; circ. 12,000.

Borneo Post: 40 Jalan Tuanku Osman, POB 20, 96000 Sibu; tel. (84) 332055; fax (84) 321255; internet www.borneopost.com.my; morning; English; Man. Dir LAU HUI SIONG; Editor NGUOI HOW YIENG; circ. 60,000.

International Times: Lot 2215, Jalan Bengkel, Pending Industrial Estate, POB 1158, 93724 Kuching; tel. (82) 482215; fax (82) 480996; e-mail news@intimes.com; internet www.intimes.com.my; f. 1968; morning; Chinese; Editor LEE FOOK ONN; circ. 24,292.

Malaysia Daily News: 7 Island Rd, POB 237, 96009 Sibu; tel. (84) 330211; tel. (84) 320540; f. 1968; morning; Chinese; Editor WONG SENG KWONG; circ. 22,735.

Sarawak Tribune and Sunday Tribune: Lot 231, Jalan Abell Utara, 93100 Kuching; tel. (82) 424411; fax (82) 415024; e-mail st@tru.my; internet tribune.my; f. 1945; English; licence suspended in Feb. 2006; reappeared in May 2010 as New Sarawak Tribune; Editor (vacant); circ. 29,598.

See Hua Daily News: 40 Jalan Tuanku Osman, POB 20, 96000 Sibu; tel. (84) 332055; fax (84) 321255; f. 1952; morning; Chinese; Man. Editor LAU HUI SIONG; circ. 80,000.

United Daily News: tel. (84) 219251; fax (84) 215037; internet www.eunited.com.my; f. 2004 following merger between Chinese Daily News and Miri Daily News; morning; Chinese; Man. Editor CHRISTINE LIU QING; circ. 35,000.

SARAWAK PERIODICALS

Pedoman Rakyat: Malaysian Information Dept, Mosque Rd, 93612 Kuching; tel. (82) 240141; f. 1956; monthly; Malay; Editor SAIT BIN Haji YAMAN; circ. 30,000.

Pemberita: Malaysian Information Services, Mosque Rd, 93612 Kuching; tel. (82) 247231; internet www.penerangan.gov.my; f. 1950; every 2 months; Iban; Editor PHILIP NYARU BUNDAK; circ. 20,000.

Sarawak Gazette: Sarawak Museum, Jalan Tun Abang Haji Openg, 93566 Kuching; tel. (82) 244232; fax (82) 246680; e-mail museum@po.jaring.my; f. 1870; 2 a year; English; Chief Editor Datu Haji SALLEH SULAIMAN.

Utusan Sarawak: Lot 231, Jalan Nipah, off Jalan Abell Utara, POB 138, 93100 Kuching; tel. (82) 424411; fax (82) 415024; internet www.utusansarawak.com.my; f. 1949; Malay; Editor Haji ABDUL AZIZ Haji MALIM; circ. 32,292.

NEWS AGENCY

Bernama (Malaysian National News Agency): Wisma Bernama, 28 Jalan 1/65A, off Jalan Tun Razak, POB 10024, 50400 Kuala Lumpur; tel. (3) 26939933; fax (3) 26913972; e-mail helpdesk@bernama.com; internet www.bernama.com; f. 1968; general and foreign news, economic features and photo services, public relations wire, screen information and data services, stock market on-line equities service, real-time commodity and monetary information services; daily output in Malay and English; in June 1990 Bernama was given the exclusive right to receive and distribute news in Malaysia; Editor-in-Chief Datuk YONG SOO HEONG.

PRESS ASSOCIATION

Magazine Publishers' Association of Malaysia (MPA): 3-3, Jalan 11/48A, Sentul Blvd, 51000 Kuala Lumpur; tel. (3) 40430500; fax (3) 40437648; e-mail jameselva@brandequity.com.my; internet www.mpamalaysia.org; 16 mems; Chair. ADI SATRIA AHMAD.

Persatuan Penerbit-Penerbit Akhbar Malaysia (Malaysian Newspaper Publishers' Asscn): Unit 706, Blok B, Phileo Damansara 1, 9 Jalan 16/11, off Jalan Damansara, 46350 Petaling Jaya; tel. (3) 76608535; fax (3) 76608532; e-mail mnpa@macomm.com.my; Chair. MOHD NASIR ALI.

Publishers

JOHOR

Penerbitan Pelangi Sdn Bhd: 66 Jalan Pingai, Taman Pelangi, 80400 Johor Bahru; tel. (7) 3316288; fax (7) 3329201; e-mail info@pelangibooks.com; internet www.pelangibooks.com; f. 1979; children's books, guidebooks and reference; Man. Dir SAMUEL SUM KOWN CHEEK.

Perniagaan Jahabersa: 15, Jalan Dataran 3/3, Taman Kempas, Johor Bahru, 81200 Johor; tel. (7) 2351602; fax (7) 2351603; internet www.jahabersa.com.my; f. 1989; Islamist teachings; Man. Dir JAHABAR SATHIK.

KUALA LUMPUR

Arus Intelek Sdn Bhd: Plaza Mont Kiara, Suite E-06-06, Mont Kiara, 50480 Kuala Lumpur; tel. (3) 62011558; fax (3) 62018698; e-mail afusint@streamyx.com; academic; Man. Datin AZIZAH MOKHZANI.

Berita Publishing Sdn Bhd: 16–20 Jalan 4/109E, Desa Business Park, Taman Desa, off Jalan Klang Lama, 58100 Kuala Lumpur; tel. (3) 76208111; fax (3) 76208018; e-mail su@beritapub.com; internet www.beritapublishing.com.my; education, business, fiction, cookery; Chair. A. KADIR JASIN.

Dewan Bahasa dan Pustaka (DBP) (Institute of Language and Literature): Menara DBP, Aras 10, Jalan Dewan Bahasa, 50460 Kuala Lumpur; tel. (3) 21482220; fax (3) 21449614; internet www.dbp.gov.my; f. 1956; textbooks, magazines and general; Vice-Chair. Dato' Dr MOHAMED SALEH BIN YAAPAR.

Jabatan Penerbitan Universiti Malaya (University of Malaya Press): University of Malaya, Lembah Pantai, 50603 Kuala Lumpur; tel. (3) 79574361; fax (3) 79574473; e-mail terbit@um.edu.my; internet umpress.um.edu.my; f. 1954; general fiction, literature, economics, history, medicine, politics, science, social science, law, Islam, engineering, dictionaries; Man. ABDUL MANAF SAAD.

Pustaka Antara Sdn Bhd: Lot UG 07 and 09, Upper Ground Floor, Kompleks Wilayah, 2 Jalan Munshi Abdullah, 50100 Kuala Lumpur; tel. (3) 26980044; fax (3) 26917997; e-mail pantara4@streamyx.com; textbooks, children's, languages, fiction; Man. Dir Datin HAPSAH BINTI MUHAMAD NOR.

Utusan Publications and Distributors Sdn Bhd: 1 and 3 Jalan 3/91A, Taman Shamelin Perkasa, Cheras, 56100 Kuala Lumpur; tel. (3) 92856577; fax (3) 92856341; e-mail rose@utusan.com.my; f. 1976; school textbooks, children's, languages, fiction, general; Exec. Dir WAN MAHMUD WAN TIJAH.

NEGERI SEMBILAN

Bharathi Press: 166 Taman AST, POB 74, 70700 Seremban, Negeri Sembilan Darul Khusus; tel. (6) 7622911; f. 1939; Mans M. SUBRAMANIA BHARATHI, BHARATHI THASAN.

PULAU PINANG

Syarikat United Book Sdn Bhd: 187–189 Lebuh Carnarvon, 10100 Pulau Pinang; tel. (4) 2626891; fax (4) 2626892; textbooks, children's, reference, fiction, guidebooks; Man. Dir CHEW SING GUAN.

SELANGOR

Aras Mega (M) Sdn Bhd: 18, Jalan Damai 2, Taman Desa Damai, Sungai Merab, Kajang, 43000 Selangor; tel. (3) 89258975; fax (3) 89258985; e-mail amsb@arasmega.com; internet www.arasmega.com; f. 1987; Dir ABDUL RAHMAN BIN ABDUL KARIM.

Cemerlang Publications Sdn Bhd: 29 Jalan PBS 14/3, Taman Perindustrian Bukit Serdang, Seri Kembangan, 43300 Selangor; tel. (3) 89417748; fax (3) 89417750; Dir TAN LIN CHAI.

Golden Books Centre Sdn Bhd: Wisma ILBS, 10 Jalan PJU 8/5G, Perdana Business Centre, Petaling Jaya, 47820 Selangor; tel. (3) 77273890; fax (3) 77273884; internet www.goldenbookscenter.com; f. 1982; textbooks; Dir Dr SYED IBRAHIM.

International Law Book Services: 10 Jalan PJU 8/5G, Perdana Business Centre, Bandar Damansara Perdana, 47820 Petaling Jaya, Selangor Darul Ehsan; tel. (3) 77274121; fax (3) 77273884; e-mail gbc@pc.jaring.my; internet www.malaysialawbooks.com; CEO Dato' Dr Haji SYED IBRAHIM.

Karnadya Solution Sdn Bhd: 12A, Jalan BP 6/6, Bukit Puchong Commercial Centre, Puchong, 47100 Selangor; tel. (3) 80684763; fax (3) 80685814; e-mail info@karnadya.com.my; internet www.karnadya.com.my; f. 2005; Dir FAIZ AL-SHAHAB.

Malaya Press Sdn Bhd: 1, Jalan TSB 10, Taman Perindustrian Sungai Buloh, 47000 Selangor; tel. (3) 61573158; fax (3) 61573957; e-mail tmp@tmpsb.com; internet www.malayapress.com.my; f. 1959; education; Man. Dir KOW CHING CHUAN.

Marshall Cavendish (M) Sdn Bhd: Lot 46, Subang Hi-Tech Industrial Park, Batu Tiga, 40000 Shah Alam, Selangor; tel. (3) 56286888; fax (3) 56364620; e-mail eastview@my.marshallcavendish.com; internet www.marshallcavendish.com; f. 1957; fmrly Federal Publications Sdn Bhd; computer, children's magazines, dictionaries, education; Dir DANNY ONG KIM SOO.

Minerva Publications (NS) Sdn Bhd: 51 Jalan SG 3/1, Tan Sri Gombak, Batu Caves, 68100 Selangor; tel. (3) 61882876; fax (3) 61883876; e-mail minerva@streamyx.com; f. 1974; general, children's, reference, medical, law; Dir and Chief Editor SUJAUDEEN; Man. Dir THANJUDEEN.

Oxford Fajar Sdn Bhd: 4 Jalan U1/15, Seksyen U1, Hicom-Glenmarie Industrial Park, 40150 Shah Alam, Selangor; tel. (3) 56294005; fax (3) 56294006; e-mail dcs@oxfordfajar.com.my;

internet www.oxfordfajar.com.my; fmrly Penerbit Fajar Bakti Sdn Bhd; school, college and university textbooks, children's, general; Man. Dir LOKE FOOK YOON.

Pearson Education Malaysia Sdn Bhd: Lot 2, Jalan 215, off Jalan Templer, 46050 Petaling Jaya, Selangor; tel. (3) 78012000; fax (3) 77831906; e-mail inquirymy@pearson.com; internet www.pearsoned.com.my; textbooks, mathematics, physics, science, general, educational materials; Dir WONG WEE WOON; Man. WONG MEI MEI.

Pelanduk Publications (M) Sdn Bhd: 12 Jalan SS 13/3E, Subang Jaya Industrial Estate, 47500 Subang Jaya, Selangor; tel. (3) 56386885; fax (3) 56386575; e-mail pelpub@tm.net.my; internet www.pelanduk.com; f. 1984; politics, history, anthropology, religion, education, language, economics, business and management, culture, self-improvement, women's studies, law; Man. JACKSON TAN.

Penerbit Universiti Kebangsaan Malaysia: Universiti Kebangsaan Malaysia, 43600 UKM, Selangor; tel. (3) 8292840; fax (3) 8254375; e-mail penerbit@ukm.my; internet www.ukm.my/penerbit; Head KAMARUDDIN M. SAID.

Sasbadi Sdn Bhd: Lot 12, Jalan Teknologi 3/4, Taman Sains Selangor 1, Kota Damansara, 47810 Petaling Jaya, Selangor; tel. (3) 61451188; fax (3) 61569080; e-mail enquiry@sasbadi.com; internet www.sasbadi.com; Man. Dir LAW KING HUI.

United Publishing House (M) Sdn Bhd: 5078 Lorong 18/64A, Taman Sri Serdang, Seri Kembangan, 43300 Selangor; tel. (3) 89430631; fax (3) 89436909; e-mail info@uph.com.my; internet www.uph.com.my; f. 1973; children's, dictionaries, textbooks; Dir WONG CHEE KHEONG.

GOVERNMENT PUBLISHING HOUSE

Percetakan Nasional Malaysia Bhd (Malaysia National Printing Ltd): Jalan Chan Sow Lin, 50554 Kuala Lumpur; tel. (3) 92366888; fax (3) 92366999; e-mail inquiries@printnasional.com.my; internet www.printnasional.com.my; fmrly the Nat. Printing Dept; incorporated as a co under govt control in Jan. 1993; Gen. Man. LOTFI AMER BIN ABDUL HAMID.

PUBLISHERS' ASSOCIATION

Malaysian Book Publishers Association: 7-6, Block E2, Jalan PJU, 1/42A, Dataran Prima, 47301 Petaling Jaya, Selangor; tel. (3) 78805840; fax (3) 78805841; e-mail info@mabopa.com.my; internet www.mabopa.com.my; f. 1968; Pres. HUSSAMUDDIN YAACUB; 176 mems.

Broadcasting and Communications

TELECOMMUNICATIONS

Jabatan Telekomunikasi Malaysia (JTM) (Department of Telecommunications): c/o Ministry of Energy, Green Technology and Water, Blok E4–5, Parcel E, Pusat Pentadbiran Kerajaan Persekutuan, 62668 Putrajaya; tel. (3) 88836000; fax (3) 88893712; e-mail webmaster@kttha.gov.my; internet www.jtm.gov.my; regulatory body for telecommunications industry.

Celcom (Malaysia) Sdn Bhd: Menara Celcom, 82 Jalan Raja Muda Abdul Aziz, 50300 Kuala Lumpur; tel. (3) 26883939; fax (3) 36308889; e-mail careline@celcom.com.my; internet www.celcom.com.my; f. 1988; private co licensed to operate mobile cellular telephone service; merged with TM Cellular Sdn Bhd in 2003; Chair. Dato' Sri JAMALUDIN IBRAHIM; CEO Dato' Sri MOHAMMED SHAZALLI RAMLY.

DiGi Telecommunications Sdn Bhd: D'House, Lot 10, Jalan Delima 1/1, Subang Hi-Tech Industrial Park, 40000 Shah Alam, Selangor; tel. (3) 57211800; fax (3) 57210238; internet www.digi.com.my; private co licensed to operate mobile telephone service; Chair. SIGVE BREKKE; CEO HENRIK CLAUSEN.

Maxis Communications Bhd: Menara Maxis, Aras 18, Kuala Lumpur City Centre, off Jalan Ampang, 50088 Kuala Lumpur; tel. (3) 23307000; fax (3) 23300008; internet www.maxis.com.my; f. 1995; provides mobile, fixed-line and multimedia services; approx. 11.4m. subscribers in 2009; Chair. Tan Sri Dato' Seri ARSHAD BIN TUN UDA; CEO SANDIP DAS.

Technology Resources Industries Bhd (TRI): Menara TR, 23rd Floor, 161B Jalan Ampang, 50450 Kuala Lumpur; tel. (3) 2619555; fax (3) 2632018; operates mobile cellular telephone service; Chair. and Chief Exec. Tan Sri Dato' TAJUDIN RAMLI.

Telekom Malaysia Bhd: Tingkat 51, North Wing, Menara Telekom, off Jalan Pantai Baru, 50672 Kuala Lumpur; tel. (3) 22401221; fax (3) 22832415; e-mail help@tm.com.my; internet www.tm.com.my; f. 1984; public listed co responsible for operation of basic telecommunications services; 74% govt-owned; 4.22m. fixed lines (95% of total); Chair. Datuk Dr HALIM SHAFIE; Chief Exec. Dato' Sri MOHD ISA ZAMZAMZAIRANT.

Time dotCom Bhd: 14 Jalan Majistret, U1/26 Hicom Glenmarie Industrial Park, 40150 Shah Alam, Selangor; tel. (3) 50326000; fax (3) 50326010; e-mail customerservice@time.com.my; internet www.time.com.my; f. 1996; est. as Time Telecommunications Holdings Bhd; name changed as above in Jan. 2000; state-controlled co licensed to operate trunk network and mobile cellular telephone service; Chair. ABDUL KADIR MOHAMED KASSIM; CEO AFZAL ABDUL RAHIM.

BROADCASTING

Regulatory Authority

Under the Broadcasting Act (approved in December 1987), the Government is empowered to control and monitor all radio and television broadcasting, and to revoke the licence of any private company violating the Act by broadcasting material 'conflicting with Malaysian values'.

Radio Televisyen Malaysia (RTM): Dept of Broadcasting, Tingkat 2, Wisma TV, Angkasapuri, 50614 Kuala Lumpur; tel. (3) 22887200; e-mail halimaton@rtm.gov.my; fax (3) 22825103; internet www.rtm.gov.my; f. 1946; television introduced 1963; supervises radio and television broadcasting; Dir-Gen. NORHYATI ISMAIL.

Radio

Radio Malaysia: Radio Televisyen Malaysia (see Regulatory Authority), POB 11272, 50740 Kuala Lumpur; tel. (3) 2823991; fax (3) 2825859; f. 1946; domestic service; operates six networks; broadcasts in Bahasa Malaysia, English, Chinese (Mandarin and other dialects), Tamil and Aborigine (Temiar and Semai dialects); Dir of Radio MADZHI JOHARI.

Radio Televisyen Malaysia—Sabah: Jalan Tuaran, 88614 Kota Kinabalu; tel. (88) 213444; fax (88) 223493; f. 1955; television introduced 1971; a dept of RTM; broadcasts programmes over two networks for 280 hours a week in Bahasa Malaysia, English, Chinese (two dialects), Kadazan, Murut, Dusun and Bajau; Dir of Broadcasting JUMAT ENGSON.

Radio Televisyen Malaysia—Sarawak: Broadcasting House, Jalan P. Ramlee, 93614 Kuching; tel. (82) 248422; fax (82) 241914; e-mail pvgrtmsw@tm.net.my; f. 1954; a dept of RTM; broadcasts 441 hours per week in Bahasa Malaysia, English, Chinese, Iban, Bidayuh, Melanau, Kayan/Kenyah; Dir of Broadcasting NORHYATI ISMAIL.

Airtime Management and Programming Sdn Bhd (AMP): All Asia Broadcast Centre, Technology Park, Lebuhraya Puchong, Simpang Besi, Bukit Jalil, 57000 Kuala Lumpur; tel. (3) 95438888; fax (3) 95433888; internet ampradio.my; f. 1997; operates nine stations: Era, Hitz, Lite FM, Mix FM, MY FM, Sinar FM, THR Gegar, THR Raaga and X FM; broadcasts in Chinese, English, Malay and Tamil; Exec. Dir Dato' BORHANUDDIN OSMAN.

Media Prima Bhd: 3 Persiaran Bandar Utama, 47800 Petaling Jaya, Selangor; tel. (3) 77266333; fax (3) 77103876; e-mail communications@mediaprima.com.my; internet www.mediaprima.com.my; owns and operates three networks: Fly FM, Hot FM and One FM; Chair. Datuk JOHAN JAAFFAR; CEO AHMAD IZHAM OMAR.

Rediffusion Sdn Bhd: Rediffusion House, 17 Jalan Pahang, 53000 Kuala Lumpur; tel. (3) 4424544; fax (3) 4424614; f. 1949; two programmes; 44,720 subscribers in Kuala Lumpur; 11,405 subscribers in Pinang; 6,006 subscribers in Province Wellesley; 20,471 subscribers in Ipoh; Gen. Man. ROSNI B. RAHMAT.

Suara Islam (Voice of Islam): Islamic Affairs Division, Prime Minister's Department, Blok Utama, Tingkat 1–5, Pusat Pentadbiran Kerajaan Persekutuan, 62502 Putrajaya; f. 1995; Asia-Pacific region; broadcasts in Bahasa Malaysia on Islam.

Suara Malaysia (Voice of Malaysia): Wisma Radio, Tingkat 3, South Wing, Angkasapuri, 50740 Kuala Lumpur; tel. (3) 22887826; fax (3) 22847594; e-mail suaramalaysia@rtm.gov.my; internet www.vom.com.my; f. 1963; overseas service in Bahasa Malaysia, Arabic, Myanmar (Burmese), English, Bahasa Indonesia, Chinese (Mandarin/Cantonese), Tagalog and Thai; Controller of Overseas Service STEPHEN SIPAUN.

Television

Radio Televisyen Malaysia—Sabah: see Radio.

Radio Televisyen Malaysia—Sarawak: see Radio.

Televisyen Malaysia: Radio Televisyen Malaysia (see Regulatory Authority); f. 1963; operates two national networks, TV1 and TV2; Controller of Programmes ISMAIL MOHAMED JAH.

Measat Broadcast Network Systems Sdn Bhd: All Asia Broadcast Centre, Technology Park Malaysia, Lebuhraya Puchong, Simpang Besi, Bukit Jalil, 57000 Kuala Lumpur; tel. (3) 95434129; fax (3) 95437333; e-mail custcare@astro.com.my; internet www.astro.com.my; nation-wide subscription service; Malaysia's first satellite,

Measat 1, was launched in Jan. 1996; a second satellite was launched in Oct. 1996; Chair. Haji BADRI Haji MASRI.

Media Prima Bhd: see Radio; operates four stations: Metropolitan Television Sdn Bhd (8TV); Sistem Televisyen Malaysia Bhd (TV3); ntv7; and TV9.

Under a regulatory framework devised by the Government, a ban on privately owned satellite dishes was ended in 1996.

Finance

(cap. = capital; auth. = authorized; res = reserves; dep. = deposits; m. = million; brs = branches; amounts in ringgit Malaysia)

BANKING

Following a series of mergers, 10 domestic banking groups and about 30 banks were operating in 2008. In February 2004 53 banks held 'offshore' licences in Labuan.

Central Bank

Bank Negara Malaysia: Jalan Dato' Onn, POB 10922, 50929 Kuala Lumpur; tel. (3) 26988044; fax (3) 26912990; e-mail bnmtelelink@bnm.gov.my; internet www.bnm.gov.my; f. 1959; bank of issue; financial regulatory authority; cap. 100.0m., res 47,992.6m., dep. 234,804.5m. (Dec. 2009); Gov. Tan Sri Dato' Sri Dr ZETI AKHTAR AZIZ; 6 brs.

Regulatory Authority

Labuan Offshore Financial Services Authority (LOFSA): Main Office Tower, Tingkat 17, Financial Park Labuan, Jalan Merdeka, 87000 Labuan; tel. (87) 591200; fax (87) 413328; e-mail communication@lofsa.gov.my; internet www.labuanfsa.gov.my; regulatory body for Int. Offshore Financial Centre of Labuan est. in Oct. 1990; chaired by Gov. of Bank Negara Malaysia; Dir-Gen. Dato' AZIZAN ABDUL RAHMAN.

Commercial Banks

Peninsular Malaysia

Affin Bank Bhd: Menara AFFIN, 17th Floor, 80 Jalan Raja Chulan, 50200 Kuala Lumpur; tel. (3) 20559000; fax (3) 20261415; e-mail head.ccd@affinbank.com.my; internet www.affinbank.com.my; f. 1975; est. as Perwira Habib Bank Malaysia Bhd; name changed to Perwira Affin Bank Bhd in 1994; present name adopted upon merger with BSN Commercial Bank (Malaysia) Bhd in 2001; cap. 1,439.2m., res 1,371.4m., dep. 26,430.5m. (Dec. 2009); Chair. Tan Sri Dato' Seri ISMAIL Haji OMAR; Pres. and CEO Dato' ZULKIFLEE ABBAS BIN ABDUL HAMID; 106 brs.

Alliance Bank Malaysia Bhd: Menara Multi-Purpose, 3rd Floor, Capital Sq., 8 Jalan Munshi Abdullah, 50100 Kuala Lumpur; tel. (3) 26944888; fax (3) 26946200; e-mail info@alliancebg.com.my; internet www.alliancebank.com.my; f. 1982 as Malaysian French Bank Bhd; name changed to Multi-Purpose Bank Bhd 1996; name changed as above Jan. 2001, following acquisition of six merger partners; cap. 600.5m., res 1,215.3m., dep. 22,828.4m. (March 2010); Chair. Dato' THOMAS MUN LUNG LEE; CEO SEOW WAH; 79 brs.

AmBank Bhd: 22nd Floor, Bangunan AmBank Group, 55 Jalan Raja Chulan, 50200 Kuala Lumpur; tel. (3) 20362633; fax (3) 20321914; e-mail ir@ambankgroup.com; internet www.ambankgroup.com; f. 1969; wholly owned subsidiary of AMMB Holdings Bhd; fmrly Arab-Malaysian Bank Bhd; name changed as above 2002; cap. 670.3m., dep. 61,916.4m. (March 2009); Chair. Tan Sri AZMAN HASHIM; Man. Dir CHEA TEK KUANG.

Bangkok Bank Bhd (Thailand): 105 Jalan Tun H. S. Lee, 50000 Kuala Lumpur; tel. (3) 21737200; fax (3) 21737300; e-mail bbb@bangkokbank.com; internet www.bangkokbank.com; f. 1958; cap. 265.0m., res 115.6m., dep. 1,670,5m. (Dec. 2009); Chair. CHATRI SOPHONPANICH; CEO ROBERT LOKE TAN CHENG; 4 brs.

Bank of America Malaysia Bhd: Wisma Goldhill, Jalan Raja Chulan, 50200 Kuala Lumpur; tel. (3) 20321133; fax (3) 20319087; internet www.bankofamerica.com/my; cap. 135.8m., res 318.5m., dep. 1,005.2m. (Dec. 2009); Chair. KRISTJAN DRAKE.

Bank of Nova Scotia Bhd: Menara Boustead, 69 Jalan Raja Chulan, 50200 Kuala Lumpur; tel. (3) 21410766; fax (3) 21412160; e-mail bns.kualalumpur@scotiabank.com; internet www.scotiabank.com.my; f. 1973; cap. 122.3m., res 426.4m., dep. 2,106.8m. (Oct. 2009); Man. Dir RASOOL KHAN.

Bank of Tokyo-Mitsubishi UFJ (Malaysia) Bhd (Japan): Tingkat 9–11, Menara IMC, 8 Jalan Sultan Ismail, 50250 Kuala Lumpur; tel. (3) 20348000; fax (3) 20788870; e-mail edpbtm@tm.net.my; f. 1996est. following merger of Bank of Tokyo and Mitsubishi Bankfmrly known as Bank of Tokyo-Mitsubishi; present name adopted following merger with UFJ; cap. 200m., res 1,056m., dep. 5,094m. (Dec. 2009); Chair. TETSUO TANAKA; Pres. and CEO HAJIME WASHIZU.

CIMB Bank Bhd: Bangunan CIMB, 5th Floor, Jalan Semantan Damansara Heights, 50490 Kuala Lumpur; tel. (3) 20930379; fax (3) 20939688; internet www.cimbbank.com.my; f. 1999; est. as Bumiputra Commerce Bank Bhd, following merger of Bank Bumiputra Malaysia Bhd with Bank of Commerce Bhd; name changed as above 2006; cap. 3,794.2m., res 10,834.2m., dep. 138,170.5m. (Dec. 2009); Chair. Tan Sri Dato' MOHAMED NOR YUSOF; Group CEO Dato' MOHAMED NAZIR ABDUL RAZAK ALI; 230 brs.

Citibank Bhd (USA): 165 Jalan Ampang, POB 11725, 50450 Kuala Lumpur; tel. (3) 23830000; fax (3) 23836666; internet www.citibank.com.my; f. 1959; cap. 121.7m., res 3,153.6m., dep. 33,572m. (Dec. 2009); Country Officer AJAY BANGA; 3 brs.

Deutsche Bank (Malaysia) Bhd (Germany): 18–20 Menara IMC, 8 Jalan Sultan Ismail, 50250 Kuala Lumpur; tel. (3) 20536788; fax (3) 20319822; internet www.db.com/malaysia; f. 1994; cap. 173.5m., res 1,016m., dep. 8,249m. (Dec. 2009); Man. Dir RAYMOND YEOH.

EON Bank Bhd: Menara EON Bank, 12th Floor, 288 Jalan Raja Laut, 50350 Kuala Lumpur; tel. (3) 26941188; fax (3) 26949588; e-mail caf@eonbank.com.my; internet www.eonbank.com.my; f. 1963; fmrly Kong Ming Bank Bhd; merged with Oriental Bank Bhd 2001; cap. 1,329.8m., res 2,328.3m., dep. 34,412.4m. (Dec. 2009); Chair. GOOI HOE SOON; CEO and Exec. Dir MICHAEL LOR CHEE LENG; 95 brs.

Hong Leong Bank Bhd: Wisma Hong Leong, Tingkat 8, 18 Jalan Perak, 50450 Kuala Lumpur; tel. (3) 21648228; fax (3) 21642503; internet www.hlb.com.my; f. 1905; fmrly MUI Bank Bhd; merged with Wah Tat Bank Bhd in 2001; cap. 1,580.1m., res 4,235m., dep. 67,315m. (June 2010); Chair. Tan Sri QUEK LENG CHAN; Man. Dir YVONNE CHIA; 187 local brs, 2 overseas brs.

HSBC Bank Malaysia Bhd (Hong Kong): 2 Leboh Ampang, POB 10244, 50100 Kuala Lumpur; tel. (3) 20753000; fax (3) 20701146; internet www.hsbc.com.my; f. 1860fmrly Hongkong Bank Malaysia Bhdadopted present name in 1999; cap. 114.5m., res 3,689m., dep. 45,232.3m. (Dec. 2009); Chair. PETER WONG TUN SHUN; CEO MAKHTAR HUSSAIN.

Malayan Banking Bhd (Maybank): Menara Maybank, 14th Floor, 100 Jalan Tun Perak, 50050 Kuala Lumpur; tel. (3) 20708833; fax (3) 20702611; e-mail publicaffairs@maybank.com.my; internet www.maybank2u.com.my; f. 1960; acquired Pacific Bank Bhd Jan. 2001; merged with PhileoAllied Bank (Malaysia) Bhd March 2001; cap. 7,078m., res 18,178.8m., dep. 202,500m. (June 2010); Chair. Tan Sri Dato' MEGAT ZAHARUDDIN MEGAT MOHAMED NOR; Pres. and CEO Dato' Sri ABDUL WAHID OMAR; 327 domestic brs, 30 overseas brs.

OCBC Bank (Malaysia) Bhd: Menara OCBC, 18 Jalan Tun Perak, 50050 Kuala Lumpur; tel. (3) 83175000; fax (3) 26984363; internet www.ocbc.com.my; f. 1932; cap. 291.5m., res 3,370m., dep. 43,089.6m. (Dec. 2009); Group Chair. Tan Sri Dato' NASRUDDIN BIN BAHARI; CEO JEFFREY CHEW SUN TEONG; 25 brs.

Public Bank Bhd: Menara Public Bank, 146 Jalan Ampang, 50450 Kuala Lumpur; tel. (3) 21638888; fax (3) 21639917; e-mail pbbcosec@publicbank.com.my; internet www.publicbank.com.my; f. 1965; merged with Hock Hua Bank Bhd March 2001; cap. 3,531.9m., res 8,770.8m., dep. 161,859.0m. (Dec. 2010); Chair. Tan Sri Dato' Dr TEH HONG PIOW; Man. Dir and CEO Tan Sri Dato' Sri TAY AH LEK; 252 domestic brs, 4 overseas brs.

RHB Bank Bhd: Towers Two and Three, Menara AA, 426 Jalan Tun Razak, 50400 Kuala Lumpur; tel. (3) 92878888; fax (3) 92879000; e-mail md_ceo@rhbbank.com.my; internet www.rhbbank.com.my; f. 1997; est. by merger between Development & Commercial Bank Bhd and Kwong Yik Bank Bhd; acquired Sime Bank Bhd 1999; merged with Bank Utama (Malaysia) Bhd 2003; cap. 3,915m., res 3,862m., dep. 81,033.4m. (Dec. 2009); Chair. (non-exec.) Tan Sri AZLAN ZAINOL; Man. Dir Dato' TAJUDDIN ATAN; 148 brs.

The Royal Bank of Scotland Bhd: Menara Maxis, Level 1, Kuala Lumpur City Centre, 50088 Kuala Lumpur; tel. (3) 21609828; fax (3) 21609905; e-mail my.customer.care@rbs.com; internet www.rbs.my; f. 1888; cap. 203m., res 374.2m., dep. 5,536m. (Dec. 2009); Man. Dir HARRY NAYSMITH.

Standard Chartered Bank Malaysia Bhd: Menara Standard Chartered, Level 16, 30 Jalan Sultan Ismail, 50250 Kuala Lumpur; tel. (3) 21177777; fax (3) 27116006; internet www.standardchartered.com.my; 31 brs.

United Overseas Bank (Malaysia) Bhd: Menara UOB, Tingkat 2, Jalan Raja Laut, POB 11212, 50738 Kuala Lumpur; tel. (3) 26924511; fax (3) 26940617; e-mail uob121@uob.com.my; internet www.uob.com.my; f. 1920; merged with Chung Khiaw Bank (Malaysia) Bhd in 1997 and with Overseas Union Bank (Malaysia) Bhd in 2002; cap. 470m., res 2,996.7m., dep. 38,381.5m. (Dec. 2009); Chair. WEE CHO YAW; CEO CHAN KOK SEONG; 37 brs.

Merchant Banks

Affin Merchant Bank Bhd: Menara Boustead, 27th Floor, 69 Jalan Raja Chulan, POB 11424, 50744 Kuala Lumpur; tel. (3) 21423700; fax (3) 21423799; e-mail enquiry@affinmerchantbank.com.my; internet www.affininvestmentbank.com.my; f. 1970; est. as Permata Chartered Merchant Bank Bhd; present name adopted 2001; cap. 222.2m., res 329.2m., dep. 2,856.4m. (Dec. 2009); Chair. Tan Sri YAACOB BIN MOHAMED ZAIN; Man. Dir Datin MAIMOONAH HUSSAIN.

Alliance Investment Bank Bhd (AIB): Menara Multi-Purpose, 19th Floor, Capital Sq., 8 Jalan Munshi Abdullah, 50100 Kuala Lumpur; tel. (3) 26927788; fax (3) 26928787; e-mail eallianceshare@allianceinvestment.com.my; internet www.allianceinvestmentbank.com.my; f. 1974; est. as Amanah-Chase Merchant Bank Bhd; name changed to Alliance Merchant Bank Bhd in 2001, following merger with Bumiputra Merchant Bankers Bhd; name changed as above in 2006, following merger with Kuala Lumpur City Securities (KLCS); cap. 365.0m., res 117.7m., dep. 1,670m. (March 2010); Chair. Dato' THOMAS MUN LUNG LEE; CEO RAFIDZ RASIDDI.

AmInvestment Bank Bhd: 22nd Floor, Bangunan AmBank Group, 55 Jalan Raja Chulan, 50200 Kuala Lumpur; tel. (3) 20362633; fax (3) 20782842; e-mail customercare@ambg.com.my; internet www.ambg.com.my; f. 1975; fmrly Arab-Malaysian Merchant Bank Bhd; later known as AmMerchant Bank Bhd; name changed as above 2006; cap. 200m., res 203.1m., dep. 623,513m. (March 2010); Chair. Tan Sri Dato' AZMAN HASHIM; Group Man. Dir CHEAH TEK KUANG; 5 brs.

CIMB Investment Bank Bhd: Bangunan CIMB, 10th Floor, Jalan Semantan, Damansara Heights, 50490 Kuala Lumpur; tel. (3) 20848888; fax (3) 20848885; e-mail info@cimb.com.my; internet www.cimbbank.com.my; f. 1974; fmrly Commerce Int. Merchant Bankers Bhd; present name adopted 2006; cap. 100m., res 301.7m., dep. 5,916.6m. (Dec. 2009); Chair. Tan Sri Dato' MOHAMED NOR YUSOF.

Maybank Investment Bank Berhad: Menara Maybank, 33rd Floor, 100 Jalan Tun Perak, 50050 Kuala Lumpur; tel. (3) 20591888; fax (3) 20784194; e-mail enquiries@maybank-ib.com; internet www.maybank-ib.com; f. 1973; cap. 50.1m., res 338.3m. (June 2010), dep. 4,095.3m. (June 2009); Chair. Tan Sri Dato' MEGAT ZAHARUDDIN MEGAT MOHAMED NOR; CEO Tengku Dato' ZAFRUL Tengku ABDUL AZIZ; 2 brs.

MIDF Amanah Investment Bank Bhd: Menara MIDF, Level 21, 82 Jalan Raja Chulan, 50200 Kuala Lumpur; tel. (3) 21738888; fax (3) 21738877; e-mail inquiry-feedback@midf.com.my; internet www.midf.com.my; f. 1975; est. as Utama Wardley Bhd; name changed to Utama Merchant Bank Bhd in 1996; present name adopted 2006; cap. 156.5m., res 577.6m., dep. 3,693.2m. (Dec. 2009); Chair. Tan Sri Dato' MAHMOOD BIN TAIB; Group CEO Datuk MOHAMED NAJIB Haji ABDULLAH; 1 br.

MIMB Investment Bank Bhd: Menara EON Bank, 21st Floor, 288 Jalan Raja Laut, 50350 Kuala Lumpur; tel. (3) 26910200; fax (3) 26985388; internet www.mimb.com.my; f. 1970; fmrly Malaysian Int. Merchant Bankers Bhd; wholly owned subsidiary of EON Bank Bhd; cap. 75m., res 176m., dep. 155.3m. (Dec. 2009); Chair. GOOI HOE SOON; 2 brs.

Public Islamic Bank Bhd: Menara Public Bank, 27th Floor, 146 Jalan Ampang, 50450 Kuala Lumpur; tel. (3) 21766341; fax (3) 21639917; e-mail islamicbkg@publicislamicbank.com.my; internet www.publicislamicbank.com.my; f. 1973; est. as Asian Int. Merchant Bankers Bhd; became Sime Merchant Bankers Bhd 1996; present name adopted 2008; cap. 170.2m., res 1,335.6m., dep. 21,124.8m. (Dec. 2009); Chair. Tan Sri Dato' Sri Dr TEH HONG PIOW; CEO ABU HASSAN ASSARI BIN IBRAHIM.

RHB Investment Bank Bhd: Tower Three, 9th Floor, RHB Centre, 426 Jalan Tun Razak, 50400 Kuala Lumpur; tel. (3) 92805475; fax (3) 27118501; e-mail publicaffairs@rhb.com.my; internet www.rhb.com.my; f. 1974; fmrly RHB Sakura Merchant Bankers Bhd; present name adopted 2006; cap. 263.6m., res 479m., dep. 4,340m. (Dec. 2009); Chair. PATRICK CHIN YOKE CHUNG; CEO SHARIFATUL HANIZAH SAID ALI.

Co-operative Bank

Bank Kerjasama Rakyat Malaysia Berhad: Bangunan Bank Rakyat, Jalan Tangsi, Peti Surat 11024, 50732 Kuala Lumpur; tel. (3) 26129600; fax (3) 26129636; internet www.bankrakyat.com.my; f. 1954; 83,095 mems. of which 823 were co-operatives (Dec. 1996); Chair. Tan Sri Dato' Dr SYED JALALUDIN SYED SALIM; Man. Dir Datuk KAMARUZAMAN CHE MAT; 67 brs.

Development Banks

Bank Pembangunan Malaysia Bhd: Menara Bank Pembangunan, 1016 Jalan Sultan Ismail, 50250 Kuala Lumpur; tel. (3) 26113888; fax (3) 26985701; e-mail feedback@bpmb.com.my; internet www.bpmb.com.my; f. 1973; govt-owned; fmrly Bank Pembangunana & Infrastruktur Malaysia Bhd; present name adopted upon merger with Bank Industri & Teknologi Malaysia Bhd in 2005; specializes in infrastructure, maritime and high-technology sectors; cap. 3,078.7m., res 4,051.8m., dep. 8,233m. (Dec. 2009); Chair. Datuk ABDUL SAMAD ALIAS; Pres. Dato' ZAFER HASHIM; 15 brs.

Bank Perusahaan Kecil & Sederhana Malaysia Bhd (SME Bank): Menara SME Bank, Jalan Sultan Ismail, Peti Surat 12352, 50774 Kuala Lumpur; tel. (3) 26152020; fax (3) 26928520; e-mail enq_y@smebank.com.my; internet www.smebank.com.my; f. 2005; wholly owned subsidiary of Bank Pembangunan Malaysia Bhd; provides both financial and non-financial assistance to SMEs; cap. 1,350.0m., res –225.2m., dep 2,033.5m. (Dec. 2009); Chair. Dato' GUMURI HUSSAIN; Man. Dir Datuk MOHD RADZIF MOHD YUNUS.

Sabah Development Bank Bhd: SDB Tower, Wisma Tun Fuad Stephens, km 2.4, Jalan Tuaran, POB 12172, 88824 Kota Kinabalu, Sabah; tel. (88) 232177; fax (88) 261852; e-mail info@sabahdevbank.com; internet www.sabahdevbank.com; f. 1977; wholly owned by Sabah state govt; cap. 430.0m., res 121.8m., dep. 1,335.8m. (Dec. 2009); Chair. PETER SIAU WUI KEE; Man. Dir and CEO Datuk PETER LIM SIONG ENG.

Islamic Banks

Affin Islamic Bank Bhd: Menara Affin, 17th Floor, 80 Jalan Raja Chulan, 50200 Kuala Lumpur; tel. (3) 20559000; fax (3) 20261415; e-mail yourvoice@affinbank.com.my; f. 2006; cap. 260m., res 138m., dep. 5,865.7m. (Dec. 2009); CEO KAMARUL ARIFFIN MOHD JAMIL.

AmIslamic Bank Bhd: Bangunan AmBank Group, 22nd Floor, 55 Jalan Raja Chulan, 50200 Kuala Lumpur; tel. (3) 20362633; fax (3) 20321914; e-mail ir@ambankgroup.com; internet www.ambankgroup.com; f. 1994; wholly owned subsidiary of AmBank Bhd; cap. 403m., res 880.5m., dep. 12,214.5m. (March 2009); CEO Datuk MAHDI MORAD.

Bank Islam Malaysia Bhd: Darul Takaful, 11th Floor, Jalan Sultan Ismail, 50734 Kuala Lumpur; tel. (3) 26935566; fax (3) 26949077; e-mail communications@bankislam.com.my; internet www.bankislam.com.my; f. 1983; cap. 1,725.4m., res –206m., dep. 25,509m. (June 2009); Chair. Dato' ZAMANI ABDUL GHANI; Man. Dir Dato' Sri ZUKRI SAMAT; 90 brs.

Bank Muamalat Malaysia Bhd: Menara Bumiputra, 5th Floor, 21 Jalan Melaka, 50100 Kuala Lumpur; tel. (3) 26988787; fax (3) 20325997; e-mail webmaster@muamalat.com.my; internet www.muamalat.com.my; f. 1999; cap. 1,000m., res 318.4m., dep. 15,036.4m. (March 2010); Chair. Tan Sri Dato' Dr MOHD MUNIR ABDUL MAJID; CEO Dato' Haji MOHD REDZA SHAH ABDUL WAHID; 40 brs.

OCBC Al-Amin Bank Bhd: 25th Floor, Wisma Lee Rubber, 1 Jelan Melaka, 50100 Kuala Lumpur; tel. (3) 83149090; fax (3) 20260825; subsidiary of OCBC Bank Bhd; cap. 65m., res 145.2m., dep. 4,299.5m. (Dec. 2009); CEO SYED ABDULL AZIZ SYED KECHIK.

'Offshore' Banks

AmInternational (L) Ltd: Main Office Tower, Blok 4, Tingkat 12B, Financial Park Labuan, Jalan Merdeka, 87000 Labuan; tel. (87) 413133; fax (87) 425211; e-mail felix-leong@ambankgroup.com.my; internet www.ambankgroup.com; f. 1995; Head of Br. ISKANDAR MOHAMED HAFIDZ.

AmInvestment Bank Bhd, Labuan Branch: Main Office Tower, Blok 4, Tingkat 12B, Financial Park Labuan, Jalan Merdeka, 87000 Labuan; tel. (87) 417891; fax (87) 417898; Man. Dir CHEAH TEK KUANG.

Bank of America, Labuan Branch: Main Office Tower, Tingkat 10, Financial Park Labuan, Jalan Merdeka, 87000 Labuan; tel. (87) 411778; fax (87) 424778; Gen. Man. Pengiran NUR FARHAH OOI ABDULLAH.

The Bank of East Asia Ltd, Labuan Branch: Main Office Tower, Tingkat 10C, Financial Park Labuan, Jalan Merdeka, 87000 Labuan; tel. (87) 451145; fax (87) 451148; e-mail arraisag@hkbea.com; Gen. Man. ALVIN ARRAIS.

Bank Islam Malaysia Bhd: Main Office Tower, Tingkat 15A, Financial Park, Jalan Merdeka, 87000 Labuan; tel. (87) 451802; fax (87) 451800; e-mail engkuafandi@bankislam.com.my; Branch Man. ENGKU AFANDI TAIB.

Bank of Nova Scotia, Labuan Branch: Main Office Tower, Tingkat 10C, Financial Park Labuan, Jalan Merdeka, 87000 Labuan; tel. (87) 451101; fax (87) 451099; Man. NAVEEN CHANDER.

Bank of Tokyo-Mitsubishi UFJ Ltd, Labuan Branch: Main Office Tower, Tingkat 12A, Financial Park Labuan, Jalan Merdeka, 87000 Labuan; tel. (87) 410487; fax (87) 410476; e-mail pulaubtm@tm.net.my; Gen. Man. WATURU TANAKA.

Barclays Bank PLC: Main Office Tower, Tingkat 5A, Financial Park Labuan, Jalan Merdeka, 87000 Labuan; tel. (87) 425571; fax (87) 425575; e-mail barclay@tm.net.my; Man. MIAW SIAW LOONG.

Bayerische Landesbank Girozentrale, Labuan Branch: Office Tower, Blok 4, Tingkat 14C, Financial Park Labuan, Jalan Merdeka, 87000 Labuan; tel. (87) 422170; fax (87) 422175; e-mail blblab@tm.net.my; Exec. Vice-Pres., CEO and Gen. Man. LOUISE PAUL.

BNP Paribas, Labuan Branch: Main Office Tower, Tingkat 9E, Financial Park Labuan, Jalan Merdeka, 87000 Labuan; tel. (87) 422328; fax (87) 419328; e-mail krishna.chetti@asia.bnpparibas.com; internet www.bnpparibas.com.my; Head KRISHNA CHETTI.

Cathay United Bank, Labuan Branch: Main Office Tower, Tingkat 3C, Financial Park Labuan, Jalan Merdeka, 87000 Labuan; tel. (87) 452168; fax (87) 453678; Gen. Man. YEH PIN HUNG.

CIMB Bank (L) Ltd: Main Office Tower, Tingkat 14B, Financial Park Labuan, Jalan Merdeka, 87000 Labuan; tel. (87) 410302; fax (87) 410313; e-mail bumitrst@tm.net.my; Gen. Man. JEMIMA HAZIZ.

Citibank Malaysia (L) Ltd: Main Office Tower, Tingkat 11F, Financial Park Labuan, Jalan Merdeka, 87000 Labuan; tel. (87) 421181; fax (87) 419671; Gen. Man. CLARA LIM AI CHENG.

City Credit Investment Bank Ltd: Main Office Tower, Tingkat 11-D1, Financial Park Labuan, Jalan Merdeka, 87000 Labuan; tel. (87) 582368; fax (87) 582308; e-mail info@ccibl.net; internet www.citycreditinvestmentbank.com; Chair. Tan Sri Dato' HANAFIAH HUSSAIN.

Commercial IBT Bank, Labuan Branch: Tingkat 2, Wisma Lucas Kong, Jalan Merdeka, 87000 Labuan; tel. (87) 411868; fax (87) 416818; e-mail info@cibtbank.com; internet www.cibtbank.com; Pres. Dir Dr ADRIAN ONG CHEE BENG.

Crédit Agricole CIB, Labuan Branch: Main Office Tower, Tingkat 6th Floor B, Financial Park Labuan, Jalan Merdeka, 87000 Labuan; tel. (87) 408331; fax (87) 408335; e-mail hoimeng.chew@ca-cib.com; fmrly known as Crédit Agricole Indosuez, Calyon; Gen. Man. HOI MENG CHEW.

Crédit Industriel et Commercial: Main Office Tower, Tingkat 11C, Financial Park Labuan, Jalan Merdeka, 87000 Labuan; tel. (87) 452008; fax (87) 452009; Gen. Man. YEOW TIANG HUI.

Crédit Suisse AG, Labuan Branch: Main Office Tower, Tingkat 10B, Financial Park Labuan, Jalan Merdeka, 87000 Labuan; tel. (87) 425381; fax (87) 425384; investment banking; Gen. Man. RUDOLF ZAUGG.

Deutsche Bank, Labuan Branch: Main Office Tower, Tingkat 9-G2, Financial Park Labuan, Jalan Merdeka, 87000 Labuan; tel. (87) 439811; fax (87) 439866; internet www.db.com/malaysia; Man. Dir KUAH HUN LIANG.

Development Bank of Singapore (DBS Bank) Ltd, Labuan Branch: Main Office Tower, Tingkat 10A, Financial Park Labuan, Jalan Merdeka, 87000 Labuan; tel. (87) 595500; fax (87) 423376; internet www.dbs.com/my; Gen. Man. JEFFRY LING.

ECM Libra Investment Bank Ltd: Main Office Tower, Tingkat 3-I1, Financial Park Complex, Jalan Merdeka, 87000 Labuan; tel. (87) 408525; fax (87) 408527.

Hongkong & Shanghai Banking Corporation, Offshore Banking Unit: Main Office Tower, Tingkat 11D, Financial Park Labuan, Jalan Merdeka, 87000 Labuan; tel. (87) 417168; fax (87) 417169; Man. PREM KUMAR.

ING Bank NV: Main Office Tower, Tingkat 8B, Financial Park Labuan, Jalan Merdeka, 87000 Labuan; tel. (87) 425733; fax (87) 425734; Gen. Man. MILLY TAN.

J. P. Morgan Chase Bank, Labuan Branch: Main Office Tower, Tingkat 5F, Financial Park Labuan, Jalan Merdeka, 87000 Labuan; tel. (87) 424384; fax (87) 424390; e-mail fauziah.hisham@chase.com; Gen. Man. LEONG KET TI.

J. P. Morgan Malaysia Ltd: Main Office Tower, Tingkat 5, Unit 5F, Financial Park Labuan, Jalan Merdeka, 87000 Labuan; tel. (87) 459000; fax (87) 451328; Gen. Man. LEONG KET TI.

Macquarie Bank Ltd, Labuan Branch: Main Office Tower, Tingkat 3A, Financial Park Labuan, Jalan Merdeka, 87000 Labuan; tel. (87) 583080; fax (87) 583088; Division Dir DARREN WOODWARD.

Maybank International (L) Ltd: Main Office Tower, Tingkat 16B, Financial Park Labuan, Jalan Merdeka, 87000 Labuan; tel. (87) 414406; fax (87) 414806; e-mail millmit@streamyx.com; Chair. Dato' JOHAN ARIFFIN.

Mizuho Corporate Bank Ltd, Labuan Branch: Main Office Tower, Tingkat 9B–C, Financial Park Labuan, Jalan Merdeka, 87000 Labuan; tel. (87) 417766; fax (87) 419766; Gen. Man. ISAKU TANIMURA.

National Australia Bank, Labuan Branch: Main Office Tower, Tingkat 12C, Financial Park Complex, Jalan Merdeka, 87008 Labuan; tel. (87) 426386; fax (87) 428387; e-mail natausm@po.jaring.my; Gen. Man. LIONEL LIM.

Natixis: Main Office Tower, Tingkat 9G, Financial Park Labuan, Jalan Merdeka, 87000 Labuan; tel. (87) 582009; fax (87) 583009; e-mail rizal.abdullah@ap.natixis.com; fmrly Natexis Banque Populaires; Gen. Man. RIZAL ABDULLAH.

OSK Investment Bank (Labuan) Ltd: Lot 3B, Tingkat 5, Wisma Lazenda, Jalan Kemajuan, Labuan; tel. (87) 581885; fax (87) 582885; CEO CHEN HOCK.

Oversea-Chinese Banking Corporation Ltd, Labuan Branch: Main Office Tower, Tingkat 8C, Financial Park Labuan, Jalan Merdeka, 87000 Labuan; tel. (87) 423381; fax (87) 423390; Gen. Man. BERNARD FERNANDO.

Public Bank (L) Ltd: Bangunan Lucas Kong, 5 Jalan Merdeka, 87007 Labuan; tel. (87) 414201; fax (87) 412388; Man. ALEXANDER WONG.

RHB Bank (L) Ltd: Main Office Tower, Tingkat 15B, Financial Park Labuan, Jalan Merdeka, 87000 Labuan; tel. (87) 417480; fax (87) 417484; e-mail rhbl@streamyx.com; Gen. Man. TOH AY LENG.

RUSD Investment Bank Inc: Lot 17, Jalan Kemajuan, 87000 Labuan; tel. (87) 452100; fax (87) 453100; e-mail info@rusdbank.com; internet www.rusdbank.com; Chair. Dr SALEH J. MALAIKAH; Man. Dir NASEERUDDIN A. KHAN.

Société Générale, Labuan Branch: Main Office Tower, Tingkat 11B, Financial Park Labuan, Jalan Merdeka, 87000 Labuan; tel. (87) 421676; fax (87) 421669; Gen. Man. RAMZAN ABU TAHIR.

Standard Chartered Bank Offshore Labuan: Main Office Tower, Tingkat 10F, Financial Park Labuan, Jalan Merdeka, 87000 Labuan; tel. (87) 417200; fax (87) 417202; Gen. Man. EDWARD NG.

Sumitomo Mitsui Banking Corpn, Labuan Branch: Main Office Tower, Tingkat 12B-C, Financial Park Labuan, Jalan Merdeka, 87000 Labuan; tel. (87) 410955; fax (87) 410959; Gen. Man. JUNICHI IKENO.

UBS AG, Labuan Branch: Main Office Tower, Tingkat 4-A1, Financial Park Labuan, Jalan Merdeka, 87000 Labuan; tel. (87) 421743; fax (87) 421746; Man. ZELIE HO SWEE LUM.

United Overseas Bank Ltd, Labuan Branch: Main Office Tower, Tingkat 6A, Financial Park Labuan, Jalan Merdeka, 87000 Labuan; tel. (87) 424388; fax (87) 424389; Gen. Man. HO FONG KUN.

Banking Associations

Association of Banks in Malaysia (ABM): UBN Tower, 34th Floor, 10 Jalan P. Ramlee, 50250 Kuala Lumpur; tel. (3) 20788041; fax (3) 20788004; e-mail banks@abm.org.my; internet www.abm.org.my; f. 1973; Chair. Dato' Sri ABDUL WAHID OMAR; Exec. Dir CHUAH MEI LIN.

Institute of Bankers Malaysia: Wisma IBI, 5 Jalan Semantan, Damansara Heights, 50490 Kuala Lumpur; tel. (3) 20956833; fax (3) 20952322; e-mail ibbm@ibbm.org.my; internet www.ibbm.org.my; f. 1977; professional and educational body for the banking and finance industry; Chair. Tan Sri Dato' AZMAN HASHIM.

Malayan Commercial Banks' Association: POB 12001, 50764 Kuala Lumpur; tel. (3) 2983991.

Persatuan Institusi Perbankan Tanpa Faedah Malaysia (Association of Islamic Banking Institutions Malaysia—AIBIM): Menara Tun Razak, Tingkat 23, Jalan Raja Laut, 50350 Kuala Lumpur; tel. (3) 26948002; fax (3) 26948012; e-mail admin@aibim.com; internet www.aibim.com; f. 1995; Pres. Dato' MOHAMED REDZA SHAH ABDUL WAHID; Exec. Dir MOHAMED SHAMSUDIN.

STOCK EXCHANGE

Bursa Malaysia: Tingkat 10, Exchange Sq., Bukit Kewangan, 50200 Kuala Lumpur; tel. (3) 20347000; fax (3) 20264122; e-mail customerservice@bursamalaysia.com; internet www.bursamalaysia.com; f. 1973; fmrly Kuala Lumpur Stock Exchange (KLSE); present name adopted 2004; merged with Malaysian Exchange of Securities Dealing and Automated Quotation Bhd (MESDAQ) in March 2002; authorized in 1988 the ownership of up to 49% of Malaysian stockbroking cos by foreign interests; 988 listed cos (Jan. 2008); Chair. TUN MOHAMED DZAIDDIN Haji ABDULLAH; CEO Dato' TAJUDDIN ATAN.

Regulatory Authority

Securities Commission (SC): 3 Persiaran Bukit Kiara, Bukit Kiara, 50490 Kuala Lumpur; tel. (3) 62048777; fax (3) 62015078; e-mail cau@seccom.com.my; internet www.sc.com.my; f. 1993; Chair. Tan Sri ZARINAH ANWAR.

INSURANCE

Principal Insurance Companies

Allianz General Insurance Malaysia Bhd: Plaza Sentral, Suite 3A, Level 15, Blok 3A, Jalan Stesen Sentral 5, 50470 Kuala Lumpur; tel. (3) 22641188; fax (3) 22641199; e-mail partner@allianz.com.my;

internet www.allianz.com.my/general; f. 2001; Chair. Tan Sri RAZALI ISMAIL; CEO ZAKRI KHIR.

Allianz Life Insurance Malaysia Bhd: Plaza Sentral, Suite 3A, Level 15, Blok 3A, Jalan Stesen Sentral 5, 50470 Kuala Lumpur; tel. (3) 22641188; fax (3) 22641199; e-mail partner@allianz.com.my; internet www.allianz.com.my; fmrly MBA Life Assurance Sdn Bhd; CEO JENS REISCH.

Commerce Life Assurance Bhd: 338 Jalan Tunku Abdul Rahman, 50100 Kuala Lumpur; tel. (3) 26123600; fax (3) 26987035; f. 1992; est. as AMAL Assurance Bhd; present name adopted 1999.

Great Eastern Life Assurance (Malaysia) Bhd: Menara Great Eastern, 303 Jalan Ampang, 50450 Kuala Lumpur; tel. (3) 42598888; fax (3) 42598000; e-mail wecare@lifeisgreat.com.my; internet www.lifeisgreat.com.my; CEO KOH YAW HUI.

Hong Leong Assurance Sdn Bhd: Petaling Jaya City Development 15A, Menara B, Level 3, Jalan 219, 46100 Selangor; tel. (3) 76501818; fax (3) 76501991; e-mail corpcomm@hla.hongleong.com.my; internet www.hla.com.my; Chair. Tan Sri QUEK LENG CHAN; Man. Dir and CEO LOH GUAT LAN.

ING Insurance Bhd: Menara ING, 84 Jalan Raja Chulan, POB 10846, 50927 Kuala Lumpur; tel. (3) 21617255; fax (3) 27110175; internet www.ing.com.my; f. 1987; fmrly Aetna Universal Insurance Bhd; Chair. Tengku ABDULLAH IBNI AL-MARHUM Sultan ABU BAKAR.

Jerneh Insurance Corpn Sdn Bhd: Wisma Jerneh, 12th Floor, 38 Jalan Sultan Ismail, POB 12420, 50788 Kuala Lumpur; tel. (3) 21163300; fax (3) 21426672; e-mail slim@jerneh.com.my; internet www.jerneh.com.my; f. 1970; general; CEO LIM SUN.

Etiqa Insurance Bhd: Level 12B, Academy Etiqa, 23 Jalan Melaka, 50100 Kuala Lumpur; tel. (3) 26125301; fax (3) 26125068; internet www.etiqa.com.my; life and general; fmrly Malaysia National Insurance Sdn Bhd, name changed as above after merger with Etiqa in 2007; Chair. Dato' MOHAMAD SALLEH Haji HARUN.

Manulife Insurance (Malaysia) Bhd: Menara Manulife RB, 12th Floor, 6 Jalan Gelenggang, Damansara Heights, 50490 Kuala Lumpur; tel. (3) 20948055; fax (3) 20935487; internet www.manulife.com.my; f. 1963; life and non-life insurance; fmrly British American Life and General Insurance Bhd; name then changed to John Hancock Life Insurance (Malaysia) Bhd; present name adopted 2005, following 2004 merger between John Hancock Financial Services, Inc and Manulife Financial Corpn; Chair. Tan Sri Dato' MOHAMED SHERIFF BIN MOHAMED KASSIM.

Mayban Assurance Bhd: Mayban Assurance Tower, Level 15, Dataran Maybank, 1 Jalan Maarof, 59000 Kuala Lumpur; tel. (3) 22972888; fax (3) 22972828; e-mail mayassur@tm.net.my; internet www.maybank2u.com.my; Chair. Dato' JOHAN ARIFFIN.

MBf Insurans Sdn Bhd: Plaza MBf, 5th Floor, Jalan Ampang, POB 10345, 50710 Kuala Lumpur; tel. and fax (3) 2613466; Man. MARC HOOI TUCK KOK.

MCIS Zürich Insurance Bhd: Wisma MCIS Zurich, Jalan Barat, 46200 Petaling Jaya, Selangor; tel. (3) 79552577; fax (3) 79571562; e-mail info@mciszurich.com.my; internet www.mciszurich.com.my; f. 1954; Chair. Dato' BALARAM PETHA NAIDU.

Multi-Purpose Insurans Bhd: Menara Multi-Purpose, 8th Floor, Capital Sq., 8 Jalan Munshi Abdullah, 50100 Kuala Lumpur; tel. (3) 20349888; fax (3) 26945758; e-mail generalenquiries@mpib.com.my; internet www.mpib.com.my; fmrly Kompas Insurans Bhd; Chair. YAHYA BIN AWANG.

Oriental Capital Assurance Bhd: 36 Jalan Ampang, 50450 Kuala Lumpur; tel. (3) 20702828; fax (3) 20724150; e-mail oricap@oricap.com.my; internet www.oricap.com.my; f. 2002; est. by merger of Capital Insurance Bhd and United Oriental Assurance Sdn Bhd; Chair. Dato' VIJAYA KUMAR CHORNALINGAM; CEO LAI POONG SHEN.

Overseas Assurance Corpn (Malaysia) Bhd: Menara Great Eastern, Level 18, 303 Jalan Ampang, 50450 Kuala Lumpur; tel. (3) 42597888; fax (3) 48132737; e-mail enquiry@oac.com.my; internet www.oac.com.my; Chair. FANG AI LIAN.

Progressive Insurance Sdn Bhd: Plaza Berjaya, Menara BGI, 7th, 9th and 10th Floors, 12 Jalan Imbi, 55100 Kuala Lumpur; tel. (3) 21188000; fax (3) 21188101; e-mail progressive@progressiveinsurance.com.my; internet www.progressiveinsurance.com.my; Chair. Datuk DATU HARUN BIN DATU MANSOR.

RHB Insurance Bhd: Tower 1, 8th Floor, RHB Centre, Jalan Tun Razak, 50400 Kuala Lumpur; tel. (3) 92812731; fax (3) 92812729; e-mail rhbi_general@rhbinsurance.com.my; Chair. Haji KHAIRUDDIN BIN AHMAD.

Uni.Asia General Insurance Bhd: Menara Uni.Asia, 10th Floor, 1008 Jalan Sultan Ismail, 50250 Kuala Lumpur; tel. (3) 2938111; fax (3) 26932893; e-mail callcentre@uniasiageneral.com.my; internet www.uniasiageneral.com.my; f. 1931; fmrly South-East Asia Insurance Bhd; Chair. DAVID CHAN MUN WAI.

Trade and Industry

GOVERNMENT AGENCIES

Danamodal Nasional Bhd (Danamodal): 10th Floor, Bangunan Sime Bank, Jalan Sultan Sulaiman, 50000 Kuala Lumpur; tel. (3) 20312255; fax (3) 20310786; e-mail info@danamodal.com.my; f. 1998; est. to recapitalize banks and restructure financial institutions, incl. arranging mergers and consolidations; Chair. Raja Datuk ARSHAD Raja Tun UDA; Man. Dir MARIANUS VONG SHIN TZOI.

Federal Agricultural Marketing Authority (FAMA): Bangunan FAMA Point, Lot 17304, Jalan Persiaran 1, Bandar Baru Selayang, 68100 Batu Caves, Selangor; tel. (3) 61262020; fax (3) 61383650; e-mail fama@fama.gov.my; internet www.fama.gov.my; f. 1965; est. to supervise, co-ordinate and improve marketing of agricultural produce, and to seek and promote new markets and outlets for agricultural produce; Chair. Dato' Paduka Haji BADRUDDIN BIN AMIRULDIN; Dir-Gen. Haji AHMAD B. ISHAK.

Federal Land Development Authority (FELDA): Wisma FELDA, Jalan Perumahan Gurney, 54000 Kuala Lumpur; tel. (3) 26172617; fax (3) 26920087; e-mail upd@felda.net.my; internet www.felda.net.my; f. 1956; govt statutory body formed to develop land into agricultural smallholdings to eradicate rural poverty; involved in rubber, oil palm and sugar-cane cultivation; Chair. Tan Sri MOHD ISA ABDUL SAMAD; Dir-Gen. Dato' AHMAD TARMIZI ALIAS.

Khazanah Nasional: Petronas Twin Towers, Tower 2, Tingkat 33, 50088 Kuala Lumpur; tel. (3) 20340000; fax (3) 20340300; e-mail info@khazanah.com.my; internet www.khazanah.com.my; f. 1994; state-controlled investment co; assumed responsibility for certain assets fmrly under control of the Ministry of Finance; holds 40% of Telekom Malaysia Bhd, 40% of Tenaga Nasional Bhd, 6.6% of HICOM Bhd and 17.8% of Proton; Chair. Dato' Sri MOHD NAJIB BIN Haji ABDUL RAZAK; Man. Dir Tan Sri Dato' AZMAN BIN Haji MOKHTAR.

Malaysia External Trade Development Corpn (MATRADE): Menara MATRADE, Jalan Khidmat Usaha, off Jalan Duta, 50480 Kuala Lumpur; tel. (3) 62077077; fax (3) 62037253; e-mail info@matrade.gov.my; internet www.matrade.gov.my; f. 1993; responsible for external trade devt and promotion; Chair. Dato' MAH SIEW KEONG.

Malaysian Institute of Economic Research: Podium City Point, Level 2, Kompleks Dayabumi, Jalan Sultan Hishamuddin, 50050 Kuala Lumpur; tel. (3) 22725897; fax (3) 22730197; e-mail zakariah@mier.po.my; internet www.mier.org.my; f. 1986; Chair. Tan Sri Dato' MOHAMED SHERIFF MOHAMED KASSIM; Exec. Dir Dr ZAKARIAH ABDUL RASHID.

Malaysian Palm Oil Board (MPOB): 6 Persiaran Institusi, Bandar Baru Bangi, 43000 Kajang, Selangor; tel. (3) 87694400; fax (3) 89259446; e-mail webmaster@mpob.gov.my; internet www.mpob.gov.my; f. 2000; est. by merger of Palm Oil Registration and Licensing Authority and Palm Oil Research Institute of Malaysia; Chair. Dato' Seri SHAHRIR BIN ABDUL SAMAD.

Malaysian Timber Industry Board (Lembaga Perindustrian Kayu Malaysia): 13–17 Menara PGRM, 8 Jalan Pudu Ulu, 56100 Cheras, Kuala Lumpur; tel. (3) 92822235; fax (3) 92851477; e-mail info@mtib.gov.my; internet www.mtib.gov.my; f. 1973; promotes and regulates the export of timber and timber products from Malaysia; Chair. Datuk WILFRED MADIUS TANGAU; Dir-Gen. Dr JALALUDDIN BIN HARUN.

Muda Agricultural Development Authority (MADA): MADA HQ, Ampang Jajar, 05990 Alor Setar, Kedah; tel. (4) 7728255; fax (4) 7722667; e-mail promada@mada.gov.my; internet www.mada.gov.my; Chair. Dato' Seri MAHDZIR BIN KHALID; Gen. Man. Dato' Haji ABDUL RAHIM BIN SALEH.

National Economic Action Council: NEAC-MTEN, Prime Minister's Office, Menara Usahawan, Blok Utama, Tingkat 5, 18 Persiaran Perdana, Pusat Pentadbiran Kerajaan Persekutuan, 62652 Putrajaya; tel. (3) 88886513; fax (3) 88882902; e-mail feedback@neac.gov.my; internet www.neac.gov.my; Chair. Tan Sri AMIRSHAM AZIZ.

National Information Technology Council (NITC): c/o The Ministry of Science, Technology and Innovationi, Aras 1-7, Blok C4–5, Kompleks C, Pusat Pentadbiran Kerajaan Persekutuan, 62662 Putrajaya; tel. (3) 88858000; fax (3) 88884328; internet www.nitc.my; Sec. Datuk Tengku Dr MOHD AZZMAN SHARIFFADEEN.

National Timber Certification Council: C-8-5, Megan Ave II, 12 Jalan Yap Kwan Seng, 50450 Kuala Lumpur; tel. (3) 21612298; fax (3) 21612293; e-mail info@mtcc.com.my; internet www.mtcc.com.my; Chair. Dato' Dr FREEZAILAH CHE YEOM.

Perbadanan Nasional Bhd (PERNAS): Menara Dato' Onn, Level 9B, 45 Jalan Tun Ismail, 50480 Kuala Lumpur; tel. (3) 26986670; fax (3) 26986617; e-mail enquiries@pns.com.my; internet www.pns.com.my; f. 1969; govt-sponsored; promotes trade, banking, property and plantation development, construction, mineral exploration, steel manufacturing, inland container transportation, mining, insurance, industrial development, engineering services, telecommunication equipment, hotels and shipping; cap. p.u. RM 116.25m.; 10 wholly owned subsidiaries, over 60 jointly owned subsidiaries and 18 assoc. cos; Chair. Datuk IDRIS BIN HASHIM; Man. Dir Tuan Syed KAMARULZAMAN BIN Syed ZAINOL KHODKI SHAHABUDIN.

DEVELOPMENT ORGANIZATIONS

Fisheries Development Authority of Malaysia: Plaza Utama Alam Mesra, Kota Kinabalu, Sabah; tel. (3) 26177000; fax (3) 26911931; e-mail info@lkim.gov.my; internet lkim.gov.my; Chair. Dato' Haji JIDIN BIN MOHD SHAFEE; Dir-Gen. Dato' Haji KHAZIN BIN MOHD HAMZAH.

Johor Corporation: Level 2, Persada Johor, Jalan Abdullah Ibrahim, 80000 Johor Bahru; tel. (7) 2232692; fax (7) 2233175; e-mail pdnjohor@jcorp.com.my; internet www.jcorp.com.my; devt agency of the Johor state govt; Chair. Dato' Haji ABDUL GHANI BIN OTHMAN; Chief Exec. Haji KAMARUZZAMAN BIN ABU KASSIM.

Kumpulan FIMA Bhd (Food Industries of Malaysia): Plaza Damansara, Blok C, Tingkat 4, Suite 4.1, 45 Jalan Medan Setia 1, Bukit Damansara, 50490 Kuala Lumpur; tel. (3) 20921211; fax (3) 20925923; e-mail enquiry@fima.com.my; internet www.fima.com.my; f. 1972; fmrly govt corpn; transferred to private sector in 1991; promotes food and related industry through investment on its own or by co-ventures with local or foreign entrepreneurs; oil palm, cocoa and fruit plantation developments; manufacturing and packaging, trading, supermarkets and restaurants; Chair. MUHAMMAD RADZI BIN Haji MANSOR; Man. Dir Encik ROSLAN BIN HAMIR; 1,189 employees.

Majlis Amanah Rakyat (MARA) (Trust Council for the People): Bangunan Medan MARA, 25th Floor, Jalan Raja Laut, 50609 Kuala Lumpur; tel. (3) 26915111; fax (3) 26913620; e-mail webmaster@mara.gov.my; internet www.mara.gov.my; f. 1966; est. to promote, stimulate, facilitate and undertake economic and social development, and to participate in industrial and commercial undertakings and jt ventures; Dir-Gen. IBRAHIM BIN AHMAD.

Malaysian Agricultural Research and Development Institute (MARDI): POB 12301, General Post Office, 50774 Kuala Lumpur; tel. (3) 89437111; fax (3) 89483664; e-mail enquiry@mardi.gov.my; internet www.mardi.gov.my; f. 1969; research and development in food and tropical agriculture; Dir-Gen. Datuk Dr ABD. SHUKOR BIN ABD. RAHMAN.

Malaysian Industrial Development Authority (MIDA): Plaza Sentral, Block 4, 5 Jalan Stesen Sentral, 50470 Kuala Lumpur; tel. (3) 22673633; fax (3) 22747970; e-mail investmalaysia@mida.gov.my; internet www.mida.gov.my; f. 1967; Chair. Tan Sri Dr SULAIMAN MAHBOOB; Dir-Gen. Datuk JALILAH BABA.

Malaysian Industrial Development Finance Bhd (MIDF): Level 21, Menara MIDF, 82 Jalan Raja Chulan, 50200 Kuala Lumpur; tel. (3) 21738888; fax (3) 21738877; e-mail inquiry-feedback@midf.com.my; internet www.midf.com.my; f. 1960 by the Govt; banks, insurance cos, industrial financing, advisory services, project development, merchant and commercial banking services; Chair. Tan Sri Dato' MAHMOOD BIN TAIB; Man. Dir Datuk MOHAMED NAJIB Haji ABDULLAH.

Malaysian Pepper Board: Lot 1115, Jalan Utama, 93916 Kuching, Sarawak; tel. (82) 331811; fax (82) 336877; e-mail info@mpb.gov.my; internet www.mpb.gov.my; f. 2007; govt-owned; est. to replace the Pepper Marketing Bd; responsible for the statutory grading of all Sarawak pepper for export, licensing of pepper dealers and exporters, trading and the development and promotion of pepper grading, storage and processing facilities; Chair. Datuk ALEXANDER NANTA LINGGI; Dir-Gen. GRUNSIN AYOM.

Pinang Development Corporation: 1 Pesiaran Mahsuri, Bandar Bayan Baru, 11909 Bayan Lepas, Pinang; tel. (4) 6340111; fax (4) 6432405; e-mail enquiry@pdc.gov.my; internet www.pdc.gov.my; f. 1969; development agency of the Pinang state government; Gen. Man. Dato' ROSLI JAAFAR.

Sarawak Economic Development Corpn: Menara SEDC, 6th–11th Floors, Sarawak Plaza, Jalan Tunku Abdul Rahman, 93100 Kuching; tel. (82) 416777; fax (82) 424330; e-mail ssedc@po.jaring.my; internet www.sedc.com.my; f. 1972; statutory org. responsible for commercial and industrial development in Sarawak either solely or jtly with foreign and local entrepreneurs; responsible for the development of tourism infrastructure; Chair. Datuk Haji TALIB ZULPILIP.

Selangor State Development Corporation (PKNS): Level 2, Menara HPAIC, Laman Seri Business Park, Seksyen 13, 40100 Shah Alam, Selangor; tel. (3) 55201234; fax (3) 55102149; e-mail wazir@pkns.gov.my; internet www.pkns.gov.my; f. 1964; partially govt-owned; Gen. Man. OTHMAN BIN Haji OMAR.

CHAMBERS OF COMMERCE

Associated Chinese Chambers of Commerce and Industry of Malaysia: Wisma Chinese Chamber, 6th Floor, 258 Jalan Ampang, 50450 Kuala Lumpur; tel. (3) 42603090; fax (3) 42603080; e-mail acccim@acccim.org.my; internet www.acccim.org.my; Pres. Tan Sri WILLIAM CHENG; Sec.-Gen. Datuk DAVID CHUA.

Malay Chamber of Commerce Malaysia: 29 & 31 Jalan Lawan Pedang, 13/27 Shah Alam, 40100 Selangor; tel. (3) 55199110; fax (3) 55120801; e-mail info@dpmmns.com.my; internet www.dpmms.com.my; f. 1957; fmrly Associated Malay Chambers of Commerce of Malaya; present name adopted 1992; Pres. Tan Sri ROZALI ISMAIL BIN; Sec.-Gen. ZAKI SAID.

Malaysian Associated Indian Chambers of Commerce and Industry: Megan Ave II, Blok B, 9th Floor, Unit 1, 12 Jalan Yap Kwan Seng, 50450 Kuala Lumpur; tel. (3) 21712616; fax (3) 21711195; e-mail info@maicci.org.my; internet www.maicci.org.my; f. 1950; Pres. Datuk K. K ESWARAN; 8 brs.

Malaysian International Chamber of Commerce and Industry (MICCI) (Dewan Perniagaan dan Perindustrian Antarabangsa Malaysia): C-8-8, Plaza Mont' Kiara, 2 Jalan Kiara, 50480 Kuala Lumpur; tel. (3) 62017708; fax (3) 62017705; e-mail micci@micci.com; internet www.micci.com; f. 1837; brs in Pinang, Perak, Johor, Melaka and Sabah; 1,000 corp. mems; Pres. CHARLES IRELAND; Exec. Dir STEWART J. FORBES.

National Chamber of Commerce and Industry of Malaysia: Menara MATRADE, Level 3, West Wing, Jalan Khidmat Usaha, off Jalan Duta, 50480 Kuala Lumpur; tel. (3) 62049811; fax (3) 62049711; e-mail enquiry@nccim.org.my; internet www.nccim.org.my; f. 1962; Pres. Tuan Syed ALI MOHAMED ALATTAS; Hon. Sec.-Gen. Dato' Syed HUSSEIN AL-HABSHEE.

Sabah Bumiputera Chamber of Commerce (SBCC): Lot 119, 4th Floor, SBCC Bldg, Locked Bag 154, Jalan Gaya, 88999 Kota Kinabalu; tel. (88) 222442; fax (88) 223454; f. 1972; Pres. Datuk Haji AHMAD ALIP LOPE ABDUL AZIZ; Sec.-Gen. JURIL Haji SUDIN.

Sabah United Chinese Chambers of Commerce (SUCCC): POB 12176, 88824 Kota Kinabalu; tel. (88) 225460; fax (88) 218185; e-mail succc01@tm.net.my; internet www.succc.org; f. 1955; Pres. Datuk Seri Panglima SARI NUAR.

Sarawak Chamber of Commerce and Industry (SCCI): DUBS Commercial Centre, 2nd Floor, Lot 376, Seksyen 54, Jalan Petanak, 93100 Kuching; tel. (82) 237148; fax (82) 237186; e-mail scci@cdc.net.my; internet www.scci.org.my; f. 1950; Chair. Datuk Abang Haji ABDUL KARIM Tun Abang Haji OPENG.

INDUSTRIAL AND TRADE ASSOCIATIONS

Federation of Malaysian Manufacturers: Wisma FMM, 3 Persiaran Dagang, PJU 9 Bandar Sri Damansara, 52200 Kuala Lumpur; tel. (3) 62761211; fax (3) 62741266; e-mail webmaster@fmm.org.my; internet www.fmm.org.my; f. 1968; offers guidance and advice relating to trade and industry; presents problems and concerns to the Govt; 2,117 mems (Jan. 2005); Pres. Tan Sri Datuk MUSTAFA MANSUR; CEO LEE CHENG SUAN.

Federation of Rubber Trade Associations of Malaysia: 138 Jalan Bandar, 50000 Kuala Lumpur; tel. (3) 2384006.

Malayan Agricultural Producers' Association: Plaza Ampang City, 16G-L, Jalan Ampang, 50734 Kuala Lumpur; tel. (3) 2545253; fax (3) 2413158; e-mail mapa@myjaring.net; internet www.mapa.net.my; f. 1997; 406 mem. estates and 108 factories/mills; Pres. Tan Sri Dato' Dr MOHD NOOR BIN ISMAIL; Dir MOHAMAD BIN AUDONG.

Malaysian Automotive Association: F-1-47, Blok F, Jalan PJU 1A/3, 2 Taipan Damansara, Parcel 1, Ara Damansara, 47301 Petaling Jaya, Selangor Darul Ehsan; tel. (3) 78439947; fax (3) 78430847; e-mail secretariat@maa.org.my; internet www.maa.org.my; f. 1960 as Fed. of Malaya Motor Traders' Asscn; renamed following merger with Malaysian Motor Vehicle Assemblers' Asscn in 2000; Pres. Datuk AISHAH AHMAD; Sec.-Gen. GOH CHENG MENG.

Malaysian Iron and Steel Industry Federation: 28E–30E, Tingkat 5, Blok 2, Worldwide Business Park, Jalan Tinju 13/50, Seksyen 13, Shah Alam, 40675 Selangor; tel. (3) 55133970; fax (3) 55133891; e-mail enquiry@misif.org.my; internet www.misif.org.my; Pres. CHOW CHONG LONG; 150 mems.

Malaysian Palm Oil Association (MPOA): Bangunan Getah Asli I, 12th Floor, 148 Jalan Ampang, 50450 Kuala Lumpur; tel. (3) 27105680; fax (3) 27105679; e-mail mpoa@mpoa.org.my; internet www.mpoa.org.my; f. 1999; est. as result of rationalization of plantation industry; secr. for producers of palm oil; Chair. Dato' AZHAR ABDUL HAMID.

Malaysian Pineapple Industry Board: Wisma Nanas, 5 Jalan Padi Mahsuri, Bandar Baru UDA, 81200 Johor Bahru; tel. (7) 2361211; fax (7) 2365694; e-mail umum@mpib.gov.my; internet www.mpib.gov.my; Dir-Gen. Haji SAHDAN BIN SALIM.

Malaysian Rubber Board: POB 10150, 50908 Kuala Lumpur; tel. (3) 92062000; fax (3) 21634492; e-mail general@lgm.gov.my; internet www.lgm.gov.my; f. 1998; implements policies and development programmes to ensure the viability of the Malaysian rubber industry; regulates the industry (in particular, the packing, grading, shipping and export of rubber); Dir-Gen. Dr SALMIAH AHMAD.

Malaysian Rubber Products Manufacturers' Association: 1 Jalan USJ 11/1J, Subang Jaya, 47620 Petaling Jaya, Selangor; tel. (3) 56316150; fax (3) 56316152; e-mail mrpma@po.jaring.my; f. 1952; Pres. Tan Sri Datuk ARSHAD AYUB; 144 mems.

Malaysian Timber Certification Council (MTCC): C-8-5, Megan Ave II, 12 Jalan Yap Kwan Seng, 50450 Kuala Lumpur; tel. (3) 21612298; fax (3) 21612293; e-mail info@mtcc.com.my; internet www.mtcc.com.my; f. 1999; operates a voluntary national timber certification scheme to encourage sustainable forest management; Chair. Dato' Dr FREEZAILAH CHE YEOM.

Malaysian Wood Industries Association: Menara PGRM, 18th Floor, 8 Jalan Pudu Ulu, Cheras, 55100 Kuala Lumpur; tel. (3) 92811999; fax (3) 92828999; e-mail mwia@tm.net.my; internet www.mtc.com.my; f. 1957; CEO CHEA KAM HUAN.

National Tobacco Board Malaysia (Ibu Pejabat Lembaga Tembakau Negara): Kubang Kerian, POB 198, 15720 Kota Bharu, Kelantan; tel. (9) 7652212; fax (9) 7655640; e-mail ltnm@ltn.gov.my; internet www.ltn.gov.my; Dir-Gen. TEO HUI BEK.

Northern Malaya Rubber Millers and Packers Association: 22 Pitt St, 3rd Floor, Suites 301–303, 10200 Pinang; tel. (4) 620037; f. 1919; 153 mems; Pres. HWANG SING LUE; Hon. Sec. LEE SENG KEOK.

Palm Oil Refiners' Association of Malaysia (PORAM): 801 C/802A Blok B, Executive Suites, Kelana Business Centre, 97 Jalan SS7/2, 47301 Kelana Jaya, Selangor; tel. (3) 74920006; fax (3) 74920128; e-mail info@poram.org.my; internet www.poram.org.my; f. 1975; est. to promote the palm oil refining industry; Chair. MOHD ZAIN ISMAIL; CEO MOHD JAAFAR AHMAD; 90 mems.

Rubber Industry Smallholders Development Authority (RISDA): Bangunan RISDA, km 7, Jalan Ampang, Karung Berkunci 11067, 50990 Kuala Lumpur; tel. (3) 4564022; fax (3) 42576726; e-mail webmaster@risda.gov.my; internet www.risda.gov.my; Chair. Tan Sri RAHIM TAMBY CHIK; Dir-Gen. Datuk MOHD IZAT HASAN.

Tin Industry Research and Development Board: West Block, 8th Floor, Wisma Selangor Dredging, Jalan Ampang, POB 12560, 50782 Kuala Lumpur; tel. (3) 21616171; fax (3) 21616179; e-mail mcom@mcom.com.my; Chair. MOHAMED AJIB ANUAR; Sec. MUHAMAD NOR MUHAMAD.

EMPLOYERS' ORGANIZATIONS

Malaysian Employers' Federation: 3A06–3A07, Blok A, Pusat Dagangan Phileo Damansara II, 15 Jalan 16/11, off Jalan Damansara, 46350 Petaling Jaya, Selangor; tel. (3) 79557778; fax (3) 79556808; e-mail mef-hq@mef.org.my; internet www.mef.org.my; f. 1959; Pres. Dato' AZMAN SHAH Dato' Seri HARUN; Exec. Dir Haji SHAMSUDDIN BARDAN; private sector org. incorporating 13 employer orgs and 4,611 individual enterprises, incl.:

Association of Insurance Employers: c/o Royal Insurance (M) Sdn Bhd, Menara Boustead, 5th Floor, 69 Jalan Raja Chulan, 50200 Kuala Lumpur; tel. (3) 2410233; fax (3) 2442762; Pres. NG KIM HOONG.

Commercial Employers' Association of Peninsular Malaysia: c/o The East Asiatic Co (M) Bhd, 1 Jalan 205, 46050 Petaling Jaya, Selangor; tel. (3) 7913322; fax (3) 7913561; Pres. HAMZAH Haji GHULAM.

Malaysian Chamber of Mines: West Block, Wisma Selangor Dredging, 8th Floor, 142C Jalan Ampang, 50450 Kuala Lumpur; tel. (3) 21616171; fax (3) 21616179; e-mail mcom@mcom.com.my; internet www.mcom.com.my; f. 1914; promotes and protects interests of Malaysian mining industry; Pres. MOHAMED AJIB ANUAR; Exec. Dir MUHAMAD NOR MUHAMAD; 100 mems.

Malaysian Textile Manufacturers' Association: C-9-4, Megan Ave 1, 189 Jalan Tun Razak, 50400 Kuala Lumpur; tel. (3) 21621454; fax (3) 21625148; e-mail info@mtma.org.my; internet www.fashion-asia.com; Pres. J. C. SURESH; CEO ANDREW HONG; 100 mems.

Pan Malaysian Bus Operators' Association: 88 Jalan Sultan Idris Shah, 30300 Ipoh, Perak; tel. (5) 2549421; fax (5) 2550858; Sec. TEOH EWE HUN.

Sabah Employers' Consultative Association: Dewan SECA, No. 4, Block A, 1st Floor, Bandar Ramai-Ramai, 90000 Sandakan, Sabah; tel. and fax (89) 272846; Chair. LING AH HONG.

Stevedore Employers' Association: 5 Pengkalan Weld, POB 288, 10300 Pinang; tel. (4) 2615091; Pres. ABDUL RAHMAN MAIDIN.

UTILITIES

Energy Commission of Malaysia: 12 Jalan Tun Hussein, Precinct 2, 62100 Putrajaya; tel. (3) 88708500; fax (3) 88888637; e-mail fauzih@st.gov.my; internet www.st.gov.my; f. 2002; regulatory body supervising electricity and gas supply; Chair. Tan Sri Datuk Dr AHMAD TAJUDDIN ALI; CEO Ir AHMAD FAUZI BIN HASAN.

Electricity

Tenaga Nasional Bhd: 129 Jalan Bangsar, POB 11003, 50732 Kuala Lumpur; tel. (3) 2825566; fax (3) 22833686; e-mail webadmin@tnb.com.my; internet www.tnb.com.my; f. 1990; est. through corporatization and privatization of Nat. Electricity Bd; 53% govt-controlled; generation, transmission and distribution of electricity in Peninsular Malaysia; generating capacity of 7,621 MW (63% of total power generation); also purchases power from 12 licensed independent power producers; Chair. Tan Sri Dato' Amar LEO MOGGIE; Pres. and CEO Dato' Che KHALIB BIN MOHAMAD NOH.

Sabah Electricity Supply Board (SESB): Wisma SESB, Jalan Tunku Abdul Rahman, 88673 Kota Kinabalu; tel. (88) 282500; fax (88) 282314; e-mail webmaster@sesb.com.my; internet www.sesb.com.my; generation, transmission and distribution of electricity in Sabah; Man. Dir Ir BAHARIN BIN DIN.

Syarikat Sesco Bhd (SESCO): POB 149, 93700 Kuching, Sarawak; tel. (82) 441188; fax (82) 444433; e-mail public_enquiry@sesco.com.my; internet www.sesco.com.my; fmrly Sarawak Electricity Supply Corpn; generation, transmission and distribution of electricity in Sarawak; Chair. Datuk ABDUL HAMED SEPAWI.

Gas

Gas Malaysia Sdn Bhd: 5 Jalan Serendah 26/17, Seksyen 26, Peti Surat 7901, 40732 Shah Alam, Selangor Darul Ehsan; tel. (3) 51923000; e-mail ccu@gasmalaysia.com; internet www.gasmalaysia.com; f. 1992; Chair. Tan Sri Datuk Dr HAMZAH BAKAR; CEO MUHAMAD NOOR HAMID.

Water

Under the federal Constitution, water supply is the responsibility of the state Governments. In 1998, owing to water shortages, the National Water Resources Council was established to co-ordinate management of water resources at national level. Malaysia's sewerage system is operated by Indah Water Konsortium, owned by Prime Utilities.

National Water Resources Council: c/o Ministry of Works, Jalan Sultan Salahuddin, 50580 Kuala Lumpur; tel. (3) 2919011; fax (3) 2986612; f. 1998; co-ordinates management of water resources at national level through co-operation with state water boards; chaired by the Prime Minister.

Regulatory Authorities

Johor State Regulatory Body: c/o Pejabat Setiausaha Kerajaan Negeri Johor, Aras 1, Bangunan Sultan Ibrahim, Jalan Bukit Timbalan, 80000 Johor Bahru; tel. (7) 223850; Dir Haji OMAR BIN AWAB.

Kelantan Water Department: Tingkat Bawah, Blok 6, Kota Darul Naim, 15503 Kota Bharu, Kelantan; tel. (9) 7475240; fax (9) 7475220; e-mail jank@kelantan.gov.my; internet www.jank.kelantan.gov.my; Dir Tengku ADLI BIN Tengku ABDULLAH.

Water Supply Authorities

Kedah Public Works Department: Bangunan Sultan Abdul Halim, Jalan Sultan Badlishah, 05582 Alor Setar, Kedah; tel. (4) 7334041; fax (4) 7341616; internet kedah.jkr.gov.my; Dir Ir ROSLAND BIN GHANI.

Kelantan Water Sdn Bhd: Bangunan Perbadanan Menteri Besar Kelantan, Lot 2 & 257, Jalan Kuala Krai, 15050 Kota Bharu, Kelantan; tel. (9) 7437777; fax (9) 7472030; internet www.airkelantan.com.my; Dir PETER NEW BERKLEY.

Kuching Water Board: Jalan Batu Lintang, 93200 Kuching, Sarawak; tel. (82) 240371; fax (82) 244546; e-mail juliab@kwb.gov.my; internet www.kwb.gov.my; Chair. Dato' Sri AHMAD TARMIZI BIN Haji SULAIMAN; Gen. Man. PAUL CHAN PHOO THIEN (acting).

Labuan Public Works Department: Jalan Kg. Jawa, POB 2, 87008 Labuan; tel. (87) 414040; fax (87) 412370; Dir Ir ZULKIFLY BIN MADON.

LAKU Management Sdn Bhd: Menara Soon Hup, 6th Floor, Lot 907, Jalan Merbau, 98000 Miri; tel. (85) 442000; fax (85) 442005; e-mail laku@lakumyy.po.my; internet www.lakumanagement.com.my; f. 1995; serves Miri, Limbang and Bintulu; Chair. HUBERT THIAN CHONG HUI; CEO WONG TIONG KAI.

Melaka Water Corpn: Tingkat Bawah, 1st & 10th–13th Floors, Graha Maju, Jalan Graha Maju, 75300 Melaka; tel. (6) 2821700; fax (6) 2837266; e-mail baharam@pamwtr.gov.my; Dir Ir Haji BAHARAM BIN Haji MOHAMAD.

Negeri Sembilan Water Department: Wisma Negeri, 70990 Seremban; tel. (6) 7610505; fax (6) 7617841; Dir Ir ZULKIFLI IBRAHIM.

Pahang Water Supply Department (Jabatan Bekalan Air Pahang): Kompleks JBA, Bandar Indera Mahkota, 25200 Kuantan, Pahang; tel. (9) 5712222; fax (9) 5712221; e-mail p-jba@pahang.gov.my; internet jba.pahang.gov.my; Dir Ir Haji ISMAIL BIN Haji MAT NOOR.

Perak Water Board: Jalan St John, Peti Surat 589, 30760 Ipoh, Perak; tel. (5) 2551155; fax (5) 2556397; internet www.lap.com.my; Dir Dato' Ir MOHD YUSOF MOHD ISA.

Pinang Water Supply Corpn: Menara KOMTAR, Level 32, Jalan Pinang, 10000 Pinang; tel. (4) 2634200; fax (4) 2613581; e-mail customer@pba.com.my; internet www.pba.com.my; f. 1973; Gen. Man. Ir JASENI BIN MAIDINSA.

Sabah State Water Department: Wisma MUIS, Blok A, Tingkat 6, Beg Berkunci 210, 88825 Kota Kinabalu; tel. (88) 232364; fax (88) 232396; e-mail jans.hq@sabah.gov.my; internet www.sabah.gov.my/air; Man. MOHAMAD TAHIR BIN MOHAMAD TALIB.

SAJ Holdings Sdn Bhd: Bangunan Ibu Pejabat SAJ Holdings, Jalan Garuda, Larkin, POB 262, 80350 Johor Bahru; tel. (7) 2244040; fax (7) 2241990; e-mail support@saj.com.my; internet www.saj.com.my; f. 1999; Exec. Chair. Tan Sri Dato' Paduka Dr SALEHUDDIN MOHAMED.

Sarawak Public Works Department: Wisma Seberkas, Jalan Tun Haji Openg, 93582 Kuching; tel. (82) 203100; fax (82) 429679; internet www.jkr.sarawak.gov.my; Dir Dato' Ir HUBERT THIAN CHONG HUI.

Selangor Water Supply Co: POB 5001, Jalan Pantai Baru, 59990 Kuala Lumpur; tel. (3) 2826244; fax (3) 22955168; e-mail puspel@syabas.com.my; internet www.syabas.com.my; f. 1972; CEO Dato' RUSLAN HASSAN.

Sibu Water Board: Km 5, Jalan Salim, POB 405, 96007 Sibu, Sarawak; tel. (84) 211001; fax (84) 211543; e-mail swbs@swb.gov.my; internet www.swb.gov.my; Gen. Man. DANIEL WONG PARK ING.

Terengganu Water Department: Wisma Negeri, Tingkat 3, Jalan Pejabat, 20200 Kuala Terengganu; tel. (9) 6222444; fax (9) 6221510; Dir Ir Haji WAN NGAH BIN WAN.

MAJOR COMPANIES

The following are among the major industrial undertakings in Malaysia (cap. = capital; res = reserves; m. = million; amounts in ringgit Malaysia):

Aluminium Co of Malaysia Bhd (ALCOM): 3 Persiaran Waja, Bukit Raja Industrial Estate, 41050 Klang, Selangor Darul Ehsan; tel. (3) 33466262; fax (3) 33412793; e-mail sales.alcom@novelis.com; internet www.alcom.com.my; f. 1960; cap. and res 193.6m., revenue 254m. (2009/10); mfrs of aluminium sheet, foil and extruded and fabricated products; Chair. Yang Amat Mulia Tunku Tan Sri IMRAN IBNI AL-MARHUM Tuanku JA'AFAR; Man. Dir SEE-PING TAN; 366 employees.

AMDB Bhd Group: Unit 2.01, PJ Tower, 18 Jalan Persiaran Barat, 46050 Petaling Jaya, Selangor; tel. (3) 79662628; fax (3) 79662629; e-mail cosec@amdbgroup.com; internet www.amdbgroup.com; f. 1965; fmrly Arab-Malaysian Devt Bhd; mfrs and exporters of cotton and finished fabrics; cap. and res 272.7m., sales 176.4m. (2008/09); Chair. AZMI HASHIM; CEO LEE KEEN PONG; 2,175 employees.

Berjaya Group Bhd: Lot 13-01A, Level 13 (East Wing), Berjaya Times Square, 1 Jalan Imbi, 55100 Kuala Lumpur; tel. (3) 21491999; fax (3) 21431685; e-mail corpcom@berjaya.com.my; internet www.berjaya.com.my; f. 1967; mfg, commercial and residential property, insurance and finance; cap. and res 9,988m., sales 6,339m. (2009); Chair. and CEO Tan Sri Dato' VINCENT TAN CHEE YIOUN; Man. Dir Dato' DANNY TAN CHEE SING; 22,300 employees.

British American Tobacco (Malaysia) Bhd: Virginia Park, Jalan Universiti, 46200 Petaling Jaya, Selangor Darul Ehsan; tel. (3) 79566899; fax (3) 79558416; e-mail bat_malaysia@bat.com; internet www.batmalaysia.com; f. 1912; cigarette and other tobacco products mfrs; cap. and res 439.2m., sales 3,923m. (2009); Chair. Tan Sri ABU TALIB BIN OTHMAN; Man. Dir WILLIAM TOH; 1,656 employees.

Carlsberg Brewery Malaysia Bhd: 55 Persiaran Selangor, Section 15, 40200 Shah Alam, Selangor; POB 10617, 50720 Kuala Lumpur; tel. (3) 55226688; fax (3) 55191931; e-mail info@carlsberg.com.my; internet www.carlsbergmalaysia.com.my; brewers of beer and stout; cap. and res 514.7m., sales 1,045.4m. (2009); Chair. Datuk LIM SAY CHONG; Man. Dir SØREN RAVN; 977 employees.

Cement Industries of Malaysia Bhd (CIMA): Bukit Ketri, Mukim of Chuping, 02450 Kangar, Perlis; tel. (4) 9367100; fax (4) 9382722; e-mail coo@pc.jaring.my; internet www.cima.com.my; f. 1975; mfrs of cement and investment holding; Chair. ABDUL KADIR MOHD KASSIM; Man. Dir Che HALIN MOHD HASHIM; 1,328 employees.

CSM Corpn Bhd: Menara Cold Storage, 10th Floor, Jaya Shopping Centre, Jalan Semangat, 46100 Petaling Jaya, Selangor; tel. (3) 79588888; fax (3) 79581289; f. 1903; investment holding co; operates retail supermarkets, pharmacies and shopping arcades; imports and distributes refrigerated and non-refrigerated foods, beverages and pharmaceuticals; Chief Exec. TIEN KOK TAN; 700 employees.

Cycle and Carriage Bintang Bhd: Lot 19, Jalan 219, Section 51A, 46100 Petaling Jaya, Selangor; tel. (3) 78728000; internet www.ccb.com.my; f. 1967; franchise holders for Mercedes Benz and Mazda commercial and passenger vehicles; cap. and res 158.1m., sales 466.3m. (2009); Chair. BENJAMIN WILLIAM KESWICK; CEO WONG KIN FOO; 430 employees.

DMIB Bhd: 4 Jalan Tandang, 46050 Petaling Jaya, 46050 Selangor; tel. (3) 77818833; fax (3) 77825414; e-mail hamdan@dmi.com.my; f. 1961; subsidiary of Continental Sime Tyre Sdn Bhd; mfrs of solid and industrial tyres; Chair. Tunku Tan Sri Dato' Seri AHMAD BIN Tunku YAHAYA; Man. Dir AHMAD ZUBAIR Haji MURSHID; 1,800 employees.

DRB-HICOM Bhd: Level 6, Wisma DRB-HICOM, 2 Jalan Usahawan U1/8, 40150 Shah Alam, Selangor; tel. (3) 20528156; fax (3) 20527891; e-mail info@drb-hicom.com; internet www.drb-hicom.com; f. 1996; automotive manufacturing, assembly and distribution; involved in design and construction of Electrified Double Track Project between Rawang and Ipoh; active in services, property and infrastructure, defence sectors; cap. and res 2,649.2m., sales 276.7m. (2005); Chair. Tan Sri Dato' Seri Syed MOHD BIN Syed MURTAZA; Group Man. Dir Datuk Haji MOHD KAMIL BIN JAMIL; 17,395 employees.

Esso Malaysia Bhd: Menara ExxonMobil, Tingkat 16, Kuala Lumpur City Centre, 50088 Kuala Lumpur; tel. (3) 23803000; fax (3) 23803400; internet www.exxonmobil.com.my; f. 1960; refines and markets all classes of petroleum products, lubricating oils, gas and ammonia; revenue 8,000m. (2009); Chair. HUGH W. A. THOMPSON; 2,000 employees.

FFM Bhd: PT 45125, Batu 15 1/2, Sungai Pelong, Sungai Buloh, 47000 Selangor; tel. (3) 61565888; fax (3) 61579617; e-mail marketing@ffmb.com.my; internet www.ffmb.com.my; f. 1962; fmrly Federal Flour Mills Bhd; flour-milling, soya bean-processing, maize, wheat, palm oil refining and animal feed; wholly owned subsidiary of PPB Group Bhd; Exec. Chair. Datuk OH SIEW NAM; Man. Dir Datuk TAN GEE SOOI; 3,710 employees.

FT Radiosystems Sdn Bhd: 2 Jalan Murai Dua, Batu Complex, 51100 Kuala Lumpur; tel. (3) 62593905; fax (3) 62593925; e-mail info@ftrs.com.my; internet www.ftrs.com.my; mem. of FCW Group of Cos; provision of management services and the trading of telecommunications equipment; Chair. TAN HUA CHOON; 126 employees.

General Corpn Bhd: Plaza Ampang City, 19th Floor, 332A-19 Jalan Ampang, 50450 Kuala Lumpur; tel. (3) 42564599; fax (3) 42578197; e-mail gcorp@tm.net.my; internet www.gcorp.com.my; quarrying, construction, property management and manufacturing; cap. and res 651.6m., revenue 1,571.2m. (2009/10); Chair. Tun MOHAMED HANIF BIN OMAR; Man. Dir LOW KENG BOON.

Genting Plantations Bhd: Wisma Genting, 10th Floor, Jalan Sultan Ismail, 50250 Kuala Lumpur; tel. (3) 21782255; fax (3) 21616149; e-mail gpbinfo@genting.com; internet www.gentingplantations.com; f. 1977; plantation and property devt, food production; fmrly Asiatic Development Bhd; operating revenue 755,567m. (2009); Chair. Tan Sri MOHD AMIN BIN OSMAN; Chief Exec. Tan Sri LIM KOK THAY; 3,259 employees.

Goodyear (Malaysia) Bhd: Persiaran Selangor, Kawasan Perindustrian Shah Alam, 40000 Shah Alam, Selangor Darul Ehsan; tel. (3) 55192411; fax (3) 55103442; e-mail vijaian.k@goodyear.com; internet www.goodyear.com.my; mfrs of passenger car, truck and tractor tyres and tubes; Chair. Dato' SHAHRIMAN BIN Tunku SULAIMAN; Man. Dir NASUTION ABDUL RAHMAN; 720 employees.

Guinness Anchor Bhd: Sungei Way Brewery, POB 144, 46710 Petaling Jaya, Selangor Darul Ehsan; tel. (3) 78614688; fax (3) 78614602; internet www.gab.com.my; mfrs of beer and stout; sales 1,285.4m. (2008/09); Chair. Tan Sri SAW HUAT LYE; Man. Dir CHARLES HENRY IRELAND; 993 employees.

Highlands and Lowlands Bhd: 19th Floor, Wisma Sime Darby, Jalan Raja Laut, 50350 Kuala Lumpur; tel. (3) 26914122; fax (3) 23821075; f. 1975; subsidiary of Synergy Drive Bhd; cultivation and processing of rubber, palm oil, coconut and cocoa; property investment and devt; sales 445.9m. (2006); CEO MOHAMAD HELMY BIN OTHMAN BASHA.

Hume Industries (Malaysia) Bhd: Wisma Hong Leong, 9th Floor, 18 Jalan Perak, 50450 Kuala Lumpur; tel. (3) 21642631; fax (3) 21642514; e-mail IRelations@himb.com.my; internet www.himb.com.my; f. 1961; mfrs of asbestos cement products, steel and concrete pipes, pre-stressed concrete beams and piles, tanks, electrical conduits and other moulded products, pressure vessels, autoclaves and lift gates; cap. and res 870m., sales 590m. (2009); Chair. Tan Sri QUEK LENG CHAN; Pres. and CEO KWEK LENG SAN; 11,868 employees.

IOI Corpn Bhd: 2 IOI Sq., IOI Resort, 62502 Putrajaya; tel. (3) 89478888; fax (3) 89432266; e-mail corp@ioigroup.com; internet www.ioigroup.com; cultivation and processing of oil palm, rubber and cocoa, property devt, production of industrial and medical gases; cap. and res 8,346.2m., revenue 14,600m. (2009); Exec. Chair. and CEO Tan Sri Dato' LEE SHIN CHENG.

Keck Seng (Malaysia) Bhd: Suite 1301, 13th Floor, City Plaza, Jalan Tebrau, 80300, Johor Bahru, Johor; tel. (7) 3322088; fax (7) 3328096; internet www.my.keckseng.com; f. 1958; cap. and res 279.5m., revenue 913,156m. (2009/10); cultivation and processing of oil palm, cocoa, housing devt, property investment; Chair. HO KIAN GUAN; Man. Dir HO KIAN HOCK; 1,500 employees.

Kuala Lumpur Kepong Bhd: Wisma Taiko, 1 Jalan S. P. Seenivasagam, 30000 Ipoh; tel. (5) 2417844; fax (5) 2535018; internet www.klk.com.my; f. 1973; plantations cover 145,967 ha; cap. and res 5,634m., revenue 6,658.3m. (2008/09); Chair. R. M. ALIAS; CEO Tan Sri LEE OI HIAN; 30,892 employees.

Lion Group: Level 11–15, Office Tower, 1 Jalan Nagasari, 50200, Kuala Lumpur; tel. (3) 21420155; fax (3) 21481036; e-mail corpcomm@lion.com.my; internet www.lion.com.my; f. 1924; incl. Lion Diversified Holdings Bhd, Lion Corpn Bhd, Lion Industries Corpn Bhd, Lion Forest Industries Bhd, Parkson Holdings Bhd; also present in Indonesia, Singapore and Hong Kong; mfrs of computer components, property devt, construction, steel-mill operations, retail and trading; revenue 17,321m. (2008/09); Chair. and CEO Tan Sri WILLIAM H. J. CHENG; 23,483 employees.

Malakoff Corpn Bhd: Plaza Sentral, Level 12, Block 3B, 5 Jalan Stesen Sentral, 50470 Kuala Lumpur; tel. (3) 22633388; fax (3) 26333333; e-mail info@malakoff.com.my; internet www.malakoff.com.my; f. 1975; fmrly engaged in the cultivation and processing of natural rubber and oil palm; latterly a leading independent power and water producer; operates six power stations with a combined generating capacity in excess of 5,000 MW; cap. and res 3,445.8m., sales 2,122.0m. (2005); Chair. Tan Sri ABDUL HALIM ALI; CEO and Man. Dir AHMAD JAUHARI YAHYA.

Malaysia Mining Corpn Bhd (MMCB): Level 8, Kompleks Antarabangsa, Jalan Sultan Ismail, 50250 Kuala Lumpur; tel. (3) 21424777; fax (3) 21489887; e-mail cosec@mmc.com.my; internet www.mmc.com.my; f. 1981; est. by merger of Malayan Tin Dredging Co and Malaysia Mining Corpn; the world's largest tin-mining group (active in the exploration, mining, smelting and marketing of tin) until April 1993, when it ceased tin-mining operations, owing to depressed tin prices; plantations and diamond exploration, property and financial services; cap. and res 6,301.7m., sales 8,444m. (2008/09); Chair. Dato' Wira Syed ABDUL JABBAR BIN Syed HASSAN; CEO Malaysia Dato' Haji HASNI HARUN; 2,211 employees.

Malaysian Oxygen Bhd: 13 Jalan 222, 46100 Petaling Jaya, Selangor Darul Ehsan; tel. (3) 79554233; fax (3) 79554491; e-mail ncsc.mox@mox.boc.com; internet www.mox.com.my; f. 1960; mfrs of industrial and medical gases and electrodes, supplies welding, safety, marine, medical and fire-fighting equipment; cap. and res 530.5m., sales 567.0m. (2004/05); Chair. Tan Sri Datuk Dr AHMAD TAJUDDIN ALI; Man. Dir WONG SIEW YAP; 643 employees.

Melewar Industrial Group Bhd (MIG-Maruichi): Suite 17.05, 17th Floor, Menara MAA, 12 Jalan Dewan Bahasa, 50460 Kuala Lumpur; tel. (3) 21481333; fax (3) 21448380; e-mail suhaimi@melewar-mig.com; internet www.melewar-mig.com; f. 1969; fmrly Maruichi Malaysia Steel Tube Bhd; present name adopted 2003; steel pipes and tubes, steel wire, engineering services and share registration services; cap. and res 454.9m., revenue 599.5m. (2009); Exec. Chair. Tunku Dato' YA'ACOB BIN Tunku Tan Sri ABDULLAH; CEO SUHAIMI BIN KAMARALZAMAN; 526 employees.

Mitsubishi Electric (Malaysia) Sdn Bhd (Melco Sales Malaysia): Lot 11, Jalan 219, POB 1036, 46860 Petaling Jaya, Selangor Darul Ehsan; tel. (3) 79552088; fax (3) 79563950; internet melcosales.com.my; f. 1989; mfr of audio and video equipment; Man. Dir MICHOMI HIGUCHI; 1,500 employees.

Motorola Malaysia Sdn Bhd: 14th Floor, Menara Luxor 6B, off Persiaran Tropicana, 47410 Petaling Jaya, Selangor Darul Ehsan; tel. (3) 78039922; e-mail mmscinfo@motorola.com; internet www.motorola.com/my; mfr of electronic components and telecommunications equipment; Pres. MOHD RAUF NASIR; 8,300 employees.

Multi-Purpose Holdings Bhd: 39th Floor, Menara Multi-Purpose, Capital Sq., 8 Jalan Munshi Abdullah, 50100 Kuala Lumpur; tel. (3) 26948333; fax (3) 26941380; e-mail info@mphb.com.my; internet www.mphb.com.my; financial services, property devt and investment, gaming and leisure and utilities; cap. and res 2,178.2m., revenue 3,322m. (2009); Chair. Datuk RAZMAN MOHD HASHIM; Man. Dir Dato' SURIN UPATKOON.

Nylex (Malaysia) Bhd: Persiaran Selangor, Seksyen 15, Shah Alam Industrial Estate, 40200 Shah Alam, Selangor Darul Ehsan; tel. (3) 55191706; fax (3) 55108291; e-mail corp@nylex.com; internet www.nylex.com; cap. and res 189.7m., revenue 1,366m. (2008/09); mfr of vinyl coated fabrics, calendered film, and sheeting and plastic products; Chair. Datuk Haji MOHAMED AL AMIN BIN Haji ABDUL MAJID; Man. Dir Dato' SIEW KA WEI; 1,364 employees.

Rimbunan Hijau: POB 454, 96007 Sibu, Sarawak; tel. (84) 216155; fax (84) 215217; internet www.rhg.com.my; f. 1975; forestry, oil palm, media and hospitality industries; Chair. and Man. Dir Sir TIONG HIEW KING.

SapuraCrest Petroleum Bhd: 7 Jalan Tasik, The Mines Resort City, 43300 Seri Kembangan, Selangor; tel. (3) 86598800; fax (3) 86598811; e-mail investor_relations@sapuracrest.com.my; internet www.sapuracrest.com.my; cap. and res 1,063.2m., revenue 3,257m. (2009/10); Chair. Dato' HAMZAH BAKAR; CEO ROHAIZAD DARUS.

Shell Refining Co (FOM) Bhd: Batu 1, Jalan Pantai, Negeri Sembilan; tel. (6) 6471311; fax (6) 6474622; internet www.shell.com/home/content/src; f. 1960; refining and manufacture of all classes of petroleum products; cap. and res 2,098m., revenue 8,945.7m. (2009); Chair. Dato' SAW CHOO BOON; Man. Dir ROZANO BIN SAAD; 6,400 employees.

Silverstone Bhd: Lot 5831, Kawasan Perusahaan Kamunting II, POB 2, 34600 Kamunting, Taiping, Perak Darul Ridzuan; tel. (5) 8911077; fax (5) 8911079; e-mail silverstone@silverstone.com.my; internet www.silverstone.com.my; revenue 432.1m. (2008/09); f. 1988; tyre mfr; Exec. Dir and CEO NGAN YOW CHONG.

Sime Darby Bhd: Wisma Sime Darby, 19th Floor, Jalan Raja Laut, 50350 Kuala Lumpur; tel. (3) 26914122; fax (3) 26987398; e-mail enquiries@simedarby.com; internet www.simedarby.com; merged with Golden Hope Plantations Bhd, Kumpulan Guthrie Bhd in Nov. 2007; plantation management, manufacturing tyres and trucks, commodity trading, insurance services, oil and gas; cap. and res 21,384.8m., revenue 31,013.9m. (2008/09); Chair. Tun MUSA BIN HITAM; Pres. and Chief Exec. Dato' MOHD BAKKE SALLEH; 26,842 employees.

Tan Chong Motor Holdings Bhd: 62–68 Jalan Ipoh, 51200 Kuala Lumpur; tel. (3) 40478788; fax (3) 40478686; e-mail tcmh@tanchong.com.my; internet www.tanchong.com.my; f. 1972; assembly and distribution of motor vehicles, provision of after-sales services and related financial services; total assets 2,465m., revenue 2,857m. (2009); Chair. SEOW THIAM FATT; Man. Dir Tan ENG SOON; 2,762 employees.

Tasek Corpn Bhd: 6th Floor, Office Block, Grand Millennium Kuala Lumpur, 160 Jalan Bukit Bintang, 55100 Kuala Lumpur; tel. (3) 21446868; fax (3) 21446828; e-mail info@tasek.com.my; internet www.tasekcement.com; fmrly Tasek Cement Bhd; mfr of building materials; cap. and res 908m., revenue 526.7m. (2009); Chair. KWEK LENG PECK; 644 employees.

Top Glove Corpn Bhd: Lot 4969, Jalan Teratai, Batu 6, off Jalan Meru, 41050 Klang, Selangor; tel. (3) 33921992; fax (3) 33921291; e-mail topglove@topglove.com.my; internet www.topglove.com.my; sales 1,529m. (2008/09); mfr and exporter of natural rubber gloves; Chair. Dato' Sri Dr WEE-CHAI LIM; 10,900 employees.

UEM Group Bhd: Jalan Stesen Sentral 5, Kuala Lumpur 50470; tel. (3) 27276868; fax (3) 27272222; e-mail gcc@uemworld.com; internet www.uem.com.my; f. 1966; fmrly United Engineers (Malaysia) Bhd; iron, steel and non-ferrous founders; mechanical, electrical, civil, structural and telecommunication engineers for contract and project schemes; Chair. Tan Sri Dr AHMAD TAJUDDIN ALI; Man. Dir Dato' MOHD IZZADDIN IDRIS; 12,141 employees.

United Plantations Bhd: Jendarata Estate, 36009 Teluk Intan, Perak Darul Ridzuan; tel. (5) 6411411; fax (5) 6411876; e-mail up@unitedplantations.com; internet www.unitedplantations.com; cultivation and processing of oil palm and coconut; cap. and res 1,638m., sales 816.6m. (2009); Chair. Tan Sri Datuk Dr JOHARI BIN MAT; 7,029 employees.

MAJOR INVESTMENT HOLDING COMPANIES

The following are among the major investment holding concerns in Malaysia (cap. = capital; res = reserves; m. = million; amounts in ringgit Malaysia):

ACB Resources Bhd: Menara Citibank, 46th Floor, 165 Jalan Ampang, 50450 Kuala Lumpur; tel. (3) 21622155; fax (3) 21623448; internet www.lion.com.my/WebCorp/acb.nsf/CorpInfo; f. 1977; fmrly known as Amsteel Corpn Bhd; investment holding, mfrs of steel and steel products, assembly of motorcycle engines, etc.; revenue 233.7m. (2008/09); Chair. Tan Sri Dato' ZAIN HASHIM; Man. Dir LIM KANG SENG; 14,649 employees.

AmBank Group: Bangunan Arab-Malaysian, 22nd Floor, 55 Jalan Raja Chulan, 50200 Kuala Lumpur; tel. (3) 20362633; fax (3) 20316453; e-mail ir@ambankgroup.com; internet www.ambankgroup.com; f. 1976; investment holding; cap. and res 9,637.7m., sales 6,828.9m. (2009/10); Chair. Tan Sri Dato' AZMAN HASHIM; Man. Dir CHEAH TEK KUANG; 10,000 employees.

AmcorGroup Bhd: 2nd Floor, AMCORP Tower, AMCORP Trade Centre, 18 Jalan Persiaran Barat, 46050 Petaling Jaya, Selangor Darul Ehsan; tel. (3) 79662300; fax (3) 79662525; e-mail inquiry@amcorp.com.my; internet www.amcorp.com.my; investment holding, operation of rubber and oil palm plantations, management services; fmrly Arab-Malaysian Corpn; name changed as above 2005; cap. and res 1,590.0m., sales 85.3m. (2005/06); Chair. Tan Sri Dato' AZMAN HASHIM; Man. Dir SOO KIM WAI.

Antah Holdings Bhd: 9577 Jalan SS 16/1, Subang Jaya, 47500 Petaling Jaya, Selangor; tel. (3) 27101133; fax (3) 2558464; e-mail info@antah.com.my; internet www.antah.com.my; f. 1976; investment holding and provision of management services; Chair. Tunku NAQUIYUDDIN IBNI Tuanku JA'AFAR; Gen. Man. AZRIN KAMALUDDIN.

Batu Kawan Bhd: Wisma Taiko, 1 Jalan S. P. Seenivasagam, 30000 Ipoh, Perak Darul Ridzuan; tel. (5) 2417844; fax (5) 2548054; e-mail cosec@bkawan.com.my; internet www.bkawan.com.my; f. 1965; investment holding and manufacture of chemicals; cap. and res 2,955m., sales 238.1m. (2008/09); Chair. Tan Sri OI HIAN LEE; Group Man. Dir Dato' HAU HIAN LEE; 548 employees.

Berjaya Sompo Insurance Bhd: 18th Floor, Menara BGI, Plaza Berjaya, 12 Jalan Imbi, 55100 Kuala Lumpur; tel. (3) 21172118; fax (3) 21447297; e-mail info@berjayasompo.com.my; internet www.bgi.com.my; investment holding, property investment and development, hotels, development of resorts and recreational facilities, travel, gaming and lottery management; est. as Berjaya Capital Bhd, name changed as above in 2007; cap. and res 250.3m., sales 437.1m. (2009); Chair. Dato' ABDUL RAHMAN BIN HAMIDON; CEO PATRICK LOH LYE NGOK.

Cahya Mata Sarawak Bhd: Cahya Mata Sarawak Berhad, Wisma Mahmud, Jalan Sungai Sarawak, 93100 Kuching, Sarawak; tel. (82) 238888; fax (82) 338611; e-mail www@hq.cmsb.com.my; internet www.cmsb.com.my; investment holding, management services, construction materials, property development; cap. and res 1,460.4m., sales 874.6m. (2009); Chair. Tan Sri Dato' Seri Syed ANWAR JAMALULLAIL; Group Man. Dir Dato' RICHARD CURTIS; 1,400 employees.

Chemical Co of Malaysia Bhd: 13th Floor, Menara PNB, 201A Jalan Tun Razak, 50400 Kuala Lumpur; tel. (3) 26123888; fax (3) 26123999; internet www.ccm.com.my; f. 1963; subsidiaries engaged in manufacture of fertilizers, chlor-alkali products, pharmaceuticals and health care products; cap. and res 436m., sales 1,571.8m. (2009); Chair. Tan Sri ABDULLAH RAHMAN BIN OMAR; 1,200 employees.

CIMB Group Holdings Bhd: 10th Floor, Bangunan CIMB, Jalan Semantan, Damansara Heights, 50490 Kuala Lumpur; tel. (3) 20848888; fax (3) 20848899; e-mail ir@cimb.com; internet www.cimb.com; f. 1924; fmrly Bumiputra–Commerce Holdings Bhd; investment holding; property management; cap. and res 20,345m., revenue 10,539.7m. (2009); Chair. Tan Sri Dato' MOHAMAD NOR MOHAMAD YUSOF; Exec. Dir and CEO Dato' Sri NAZIR RAZAK; 36,000 employees.

Eng Teknologi Holdings Bhd: 69–70 Pesara Kampung Jawa, Bayan Lepas Industrial Zone, 11900 Pinang; tel. (4) 6440122; fax (4) 6423430; e-mail info@engtek.com; internet www.engtek.com; f. 1992; investment holding; mfr and designer of precision tools; cap. and res 237.5m., revenue 474.9m. (2009); Exec. Chair. Dato' TEH YEONG KEAT; CEO Dato' TEH YONG KHOON; 1,771 employees.

Etiqa Bhd: Level 19, Tower C, 1 Jalan Maarof, 59000 Kuala Lumpur; tel. (3) 27804500; fax (3) 22961799; e-mail info@etiqa.com.my; internet www.etiqa.com.my; f. 1970; investment holding, insurance, takaful, manufacturing and marketing of welding supplies, tin mining; cap. and res 1,081.5m., revenue 1,276.8m. (Etiqa Insurance Bhd, 2008/09); cap. and res 353.3m., revenue 1,674.6m. (Etiqa Takaful Bhd, 2008/09); Chair. Dato' MOHAMED SALLEH Haji HARUN; CEO Dato' AMINUDDIN MOHD DESA.

Genting Bhd: Wisma Genting, 24th Floor, Jalan Sultan Ismail, 50250 Kuala Lumpur; tel. (3) 21782288; fax (3) 21615304; e-mail info@genting.com; internet www.genting.com; gaming operations, hotels and plantations, property development, manufacturing and trading in paper and related products, electricity generation and supply; cap. and res 13,887m., sales 8,893.6m. (2009); Chair. and CEO Tan Sri LIM KOK THAY; 35,000 employees.

Golden Plus Holdings Bhd: Suite 6/7–6/8, Wisma UOA Damansara II, 6 Jalan Changkat Semantan, Damansara Heights, 50490 Kuala Lumpur; tel. (3) 20923311; fax (3) 20947788; e-mail info@gplus.com.my; internet www.gplus.com.my; property development and construction; cap. and res 205.1m., sales 473.1m. (2009); Chair. Dato' Setia ABDUL HALIM BIN Dato'Haji ABDUL RAUF.

Hong Leong Industries Bhd: Wisma Hong Leong, Level 9, 18 Jalan Perak, 50450 Kuala Lumpur; tel. (3) 21642631; fax (3) 21642514; e-mail IRelations@hli.com.my; internet www.hli.com.my; f. 1982; subsidiaries engaged in investment and property holding, property management, manufacture of mosaic and ceramic tiles, steel products, PVC flooring, office products; cap. and res 1,269m., revenue 2,679m. (2008/09); Chair. Tan Sri QUEK LENG CHAN; Pres. and CEO KWEK LENG SAN; 14,052 employees.

Innovest Bhd: Level 9B, Wisma E & C, Damansara Heights, Suite 9B, 2 Lorong Dungun Kiri, Kuala Lumpur 50490; tel. (3) 20933373; investment holding and management services; Exec. Dir Haji MAT HASSAN BIN ESA.

Jaya Tiasa Holdings Bhd: 1–9 Pusat Suria Permata, Lorong Upper Lanang 10A, 96000 Sibu, Sarawak; tel. (84) 213255; fax (84) 213855; e-mail inquiry@jayatiasa.net; internet www.jayatiasa.net; investment holding and management services, manufacture and sales of veneer plywood and sawn timber; cap. and res 1,077.4m., revenue 756.5m. (2008/09); Chair. Tan Sri ABDUL RAHMAN BIN ABDUL HAMID; Man. Dir Dato TIONG CHIONG HOO.

KFC Holdings (Malaysia) Bhd: Tingkat 17, Wisma KFC, 17 Jalan Sultan Ismail, 50250 Kuala Lumpur; tel. (3) 2063388; fax (3) 20728600; internet www.kfcholdings.com.my; f. 1993; investment holding; subsidiaries involved in restaurant operation and poultry breeding and processing; cap. and res 791.7m., revenue 2,297.4m. (2009); Chair. Tan Sri Dato' MUHAMMAD ALI BIN HASHIM; Man. Dir and CEO JAMALUDIN BIN MUHAMMAD ALI; 10,991 employees.

LaFarge Malayan Cement Bhd: Bangunan TH Uptown 3, Tingkat 12, 3 Jalan SS21/39, 47400 Petaling Jaya, Selangor Darul Ehsan; tel. (3) 77238200; fax (3) 77254167; e-mail info@my.lafarge.com; internet www.malayancement.com.my; f. 1950; est. as Malayan Cement Bhd; present name adopted upon acquisition by LaFarge Group in 2003; manufacturing and marketing of cement, ready-mixed concrete and allied products; cap. and res 3,193.6m., sales 2,483.1m. (2009); Chair. Tunku Tan Sri IMRAN IBNI AL-MARHUM Tuanku JA'AFAR; Pres. and Man. Dir BI YONG CHUNGUNCO; 2,615 employees.

Leader Universal Holdings Bhd: Suite 7A and 8A, Menara Northam, 55 Jalan Sultan Ahmad Shah, 10050 Penang; POB 923, 10810 Pinang; tel. (4) 2199888; fax (4) 2292333; e-mail infojoanna@leaderuniversal.com; internet www.leaderuniversal.com; mfr and sale of telecommunication and power cables, copper and aluminium rods and conductors, cable installation and engineering services, power generation and property development; cap. and res 541.3m., revenue 1,949.8m. (2009); Chair. Tan Sri RAZALI ISMAIL; Man. Dir and CEO SEAN H'NG CHUN HSIANG.

Maju Holdings Sdn Bhd: Level 21, Maju Tower, 1001 Jalan Sultan Ismail, 50250 Kuala Lumpur; tel. (3) 27728888; fax (3) 27728899; e-mail profile@maju.com.my; internet www.maju.com.my; manufacturing, engineering, property devt, infrastructure and services; subsidiaries incl. Perwaja Steel Sdn Bhd; Group Exec. Chair. Tan Sri ABU SAHID MOHAMED; Group Man. Dir AMRO AL-KHADRA.

Malayan United Industries Bhd: 5th Floor, Menara PMI, 2 Jalan Changkat Ceylon, 50200 Kuala Lumpur; tel. (3) 21177388; fax (3) 21445209; e-mail muipa@po.jaring.my; internet www.muiglobal.com; activities include retailing, hotels, food and confectionery, financial services, property, and travel and tourism; cap. and res 698.5m., sales 908m. (2009); Chair. and Chief Exec. Tan Sri Dato' Dr KHOO KAY PENG; 11,000 employees.

Malaysian Pacific Industries Bhd: Wisma Hong Leong, Tingkat 9, 18 Jalan Perak, 50450 Kuala Lumpur; tel. (3) 21642631; fax (3) 21642514; e-mail IRelations@mpind.my; internet www.mpind.my; f. 1962; owned by Hong Leong Group; subsidiaries engaged in manufacture of cartons, semiconductors and electronic components; cap. and res 699.3m., sales 1,151m. (2009); Chair. Tan Sri KWEK LENG SAN; Group Man. Dir PETER NIGEL YATES; 3,300 employees.

Malaysian Resources Corpn Bhd: Level 22, 1 Sentral, Jalan Travers, POB 12640, Kuala Lumpur Sentral; tel. (3) 27868080; fax (3) 27805883; e-mail corp.comm-assistline@mrcb.com.my; internet www.mrcb.com.my; f. 1968; property development, construction and civil engineering, telecommunications; cap. and res 671.9m., sales 921.6m. (2008/09); Chair. Datuk AZLAN ZAINOL; Man. Dir and CEO MOHD RAZEEK MOHD HUSSAIN MARICAR; 160 employees.

Metroplex Bhd: 9th Floor, Wisma Equity, 150 Jalan Ampang, Kuala Lumpur; tel. (3) 27158188; fax (3) 21643828; investment holding, hotel and casino operations, property development, quarry operations; Chair. LIM SIEW KIM; Man. Dir LIAN YONG KEE.

Minho (M) Bhd: 31A Jalan Satu Kaw 16, Berkeley Town Centre, off Federal Highway, Klang, 41300 Selangor Darul Ehsan; tel. (3) 33428602; fax (3) 33429162; e-mail enquires@minhobhd.com; internet www.minhobhd.com; activities include manufacture, export and dealing in moulded timber and timber products; cap. and res 202.1m., sales 206.2m. (2009/10); Man. Dir and Dir AN LOO KENG.

Naza Group of Companies: Menara Naza, 115 Jalan Raja Muda Abdul Aziz, Kampung Baru, 56300 Kuala Lumpur; tel. (3) 26177888; fax (3) 26818928; e-mail webmaster@naza.com.my; internet www.naza.com.my; f. 1975; subsidiaries engaged in motor trading and property development; Chair. and CEO Tan Sri S. M. NASIMUDDIN S. M. AMIN.

Nestlé (Malaysia) Bhd: 22-1, Menara Surian, Jalan PJU 7/3, Mutiara Damansara, 47810 Petaling Jaya, Selangor; tel. (3) 79656000; fax (3) 79656767; e-mail InvestorRelations.Malaysia@my.nestle.com; internet www.nestle.com.my; subsidiaries engaged in manufacture and marketing of halal food and beverage products; turnover 3,700m. (2009); Chair. Tan Sri Dato' Seri Syed ZAINOL

ANWAR IBNI Syed PUTRA JAMALULLAIL; Man. Dir PETER R. VOGT; 5,000 employees.

Oriental Holdings Bhd: 1st Floor, 25B Lebuh Farquhar, 10200 Pinang; tel. (4) 2638590; fax (4) 2637152; e-mail corporate@ohb.com.my; internet www.ohb.com.my; f. 1963; subsidiaries engaged in automotive manufacturing, health care, hotels and resorts, manufacture of plastic articles, etc.; cap. and res 3,918.9m., sales 3,438.3m. (2009); Chair. Dato' LOH CHENG YEAN; Man. Dirs Dato' ROBERT WONG LUM KONG, Dato' LIM SU TONG; 9,328 employees.

PacificMas Bhd: Level 19, Menara Prudential, 10 Jalan Sultan Ismail, 50250 Kuala Lumpur; tel. (3) 21761000; fax (3) 20266868; e-mail secretariat@pacificmas.com.my; internet www.pacificmas.com.my; f. 1919; fmrly The Pacific Bank Bhd, acquired by Malayan Banking Bhd and became investment holding company in Jan. 2001; cap. and res 568.5m., revenue 229.8m. (2009); Chair. Tan Sri Dato' NASRUDDIN BIN BAHARI; CEO HON SOON NG.

Perodua Bhd: Sungai Choh, Locked Bag 226, 48009 Rawang, Selangor Darul Ehsan; tel. (3) 60992402; e-mail crd@perodua.com.my; internet www.perodua.com.my; f. 1993; manufacture, assembly and sale of motor vehicles; Man. Dir AMINAR RASHID SALLEH; 10,000 employees.

Petroliam Nasional Bhd (PETRONAS): Tower 1, Petronas Twin Towers, Persiaran KLCC, 50088 Kuala Lumpur; tel. (3) 20515000; fax (3) 20265055; e-mail webmaster@petronas.com.my; internet www.petronas.com.my; f. 1974; national oil co engaged in exploration, production, refining and marketing; Pres. and CEO Dato' SHAMSUL AZHAR ABBAS; 39,236 employees.

PPB Group Bhd: Wisma Jerneh, 17th Floor, 38 Jalan Sultan Ismail, 50250 Kuala Lumpur; tel. (3) 21170888; fax (3) 21170999; e-mail corporateaffairs@ppb.com.my; internet www.ppbgroup.com; fmrly Perlis Plantations Bhd; sugar, flour and feed milling, film distribution, edible oils processing and marketing and computer services; cap. and res 14,086.5m., sales 3,412.4m. (2009); Chair. Datuk OH SIEW NAM; Man. Dir TAN GEE SOOI; 15,492 employees.

Promet Bhd: Level 7, Menara Milenium, Damansara Heights, Jalan Damanlela Pusat, Bandar Damansara 50490, Kuala Lumpur; tel. (3) 20957077; fax (3) 2521911; steel fabrication, civil engineering and construction; Chair. Tan Sri MOHD NGAH SAID; Man. Dir KEAT HIN LEE (acting).

Proton Holdings Bhd: HICOM Industrial Estate, Batu Tiga, 40000 Shah Alam, Selangor; tel. (3) 5191055; fax (3) 5111252; internet www.proton.com; f. 1983; manufacture, assembly and sale of motor vehicles; cap. and res 5,332.9m., sales 8,226.8m. (2009/10); Chair. Dato' MOHD NADZMI BIN MOHD SALLEH; CEO Dato' Haji Syed ZAINAL ABIDIN BIN Syed MOHAMED TAHIR; 10,067 employees.

RHB Banking Group: Level 10, Tower 1, RHB Centre, Jalan Tun Razak, 50400 Kuala Lumpur; tel. (3) 92852233; fax (3) 92819314; e-mail cmc@rhb.com.my; internet www.rhb.com.my; f. 1987; commercial banking, securities, merchant banking, financial and management services, insurance; cap. and res 8,708m., revenue 5,425m. (2009); Chair. Dato' MOHAMED KHADAR MERICAN; Group Man. Dir Dato' TAJUDDIN ATAN; 10,000 employees.

Road Builder (M) Holdings Bhd: Menara John Hancock, Level 16, 6 Jalan Gelenggang, Damansara Heights, 50490 Kuala Lumpur; tel. (3) 20939888; fax (3) 20925488; e-mail info@rb.com.my; internet www.rb.com.my; f. 1992; building, civil construction, quarry operations; cap. and res 1,418.3m., sales 1,025.2m. (2004/05); Chair. Tengku Tan Sri Dato' Seri AHMAD RITHAUDEEN BIN Tengku ISMAIL; Man. Dirs Dato' SHAMSUDIN BIN MOHD DUBI, Dato' LOW KENG KOK; 1,707 employees.

Sarawak Energy Bhd (SECB): 4th Floor, Wisma Sesco, Petra Jaya, Jalan Bako, 93673 Kuching, Sarawak; tel. (82) 441188; fax (82) 313588; e-mail info@sarawakenergy.com.my; internet www.sarawakenergy.com.my; fmrly Serawak Enterprise Corpn Bhd; name changed as above 2007; investment holding; power generation, transmission and distribution; property devt and investment; manufacture and trading of plastic packaging products; cap. and res 3,214.6m., sales 1,375.1m. (2009); Chair. Datuk ABDUL HAMED BIN SEPAWI; CEO TORSTEIN DALE SJOTVEIT.

UMW Holdings Bhd: The Corporate, 3rd Floor, 15/7 Jalan Utas, POB 7052, 40915 Shah Alam, Selangor; tel. (3) 51635000; fax (3) 55193981; e-mail group.pa@umw.com.my; internet www.umw.com.my; automotive equipment, manufacturing and engineering, oil and gas; cap. and res 1,150.1m., revenue 10,720.9m. (2009); Chair. Tan Sri Dato' ASMAT BIN KAMALUDIN; Pres. and CEO Dato' ABDUL HALIM BIN HARUN.

YTL Corpn Bhd: Yeoh Tiong Lay Plaza, 11th Floor, 55 Jalan Bukit Bintang, 55100 Kuala Lumpur; tel. (3) 21426633; fax (3) 21433192; e-mail ctrl@ytl.com.my; internet www.ytl.com.my; property devt, manufacture of industrial products; cap. and res 9,447.1m., revenue 8,892.1m. (2008/09); Chair Tan Sri Dato' Dr YEOH TIONG LAY; Man. Dir Tan Sri Dato' Dr FRANCIS YEOH SOCK PING; 3,016 employees.

TRADE UNIONS

Congress of Unions of Employees in the Public Administrative and Civil Services (CUEPACS): Wisma CUEPACS, 34A, Jalan Gajah, off Jalan Yew, Pudu 55100, Kuala Lumpur; tel. (3) 92856110; fax (3) 92859457; mems: 100 public sector unions; Pres. Haji OMAR BIN Haji OSMAN; Sec.-Gen. LOK YIM PHENG.

Malaysian Trades Union Congress (MTUC): Wisma MTUC, 10-5, Jalan USJ 9/5T, 47620 Subang Jaya, Selangor; POB 3073, 46000 Petaling Jaya, Selangor; tel. (3) 80242953; fax (3) 80243225; e-mail mtuc@tm.net.my; internet www.mtuc.org.my; f. 1949; 247 affiliated unions, representing approx. 500,000 workers; Pres. MOHD KHALID ATAN; Sec.-Gen. ABDUL HALIM MANSOR.

Principal affiliated unions:

All Malayan Estates Staff Union: 29-3, Jalan USJ 1/1A, 47620 Subang Jaya; tel. (3) 80249533; fax (3) 80247822; e-mail amesu@streamyx.com; internet amesu.org; 2,654 mems; Pres. JEYA PASKAR; Gen. Sec. JEY KUMAR.

Amalgamated Union of Employees in Government Clerical and Allied Services: 32A Jalan Gajah, off Jalan Yew, Pudu, 55100 Kuala Lumpur; tel. (3) 92859513; fax (3) 92838632; e-mail auegcas@tm.net.my; internet www.auegcas.org.my; 6,703 mems; Pres. IBRAHIM BIN ABDUL WAHAB; Gen. Sec. MOHAMED IBRAHIM BIN ABDUL WAHAB.

Chemical Workers' Union: 35B Jalan SS15/4B, Subang Jaya, 47500 Petaling Jaya, Selangor; 1,886 mems; Pres. RUSIAN HITAM; Gen. Sec. JOHN MATHEWS.

Electricity Industry Workers' Union: 55-2 Jalan SS15/8A, Subang Jaya, 47500 Petaling Jaya, Selangor; tel. (3) 7335243; 22,000 mems; Pres. ABDUL RASHID; Gen. Sec. P. ARUNASALAM.

Federation of Unions in the Textile, Garment and Leather Industry: c/o Selangor Textile and Garment Manufacturing Employees Union, 9D Jalan Travers, 50470 Kuala Lumpur; tel. (3) 2742578; f. 1989; four affiliates; Pres. ABDUL RAZAK HAMID; Gen. Sec. ABU BAKAR IBRAHIM.

Harbour Workers' Union, Port Klang: 106 Persiaran Raja Muda Musa, Port Klang; 2,426 mems; Pres. MOHAMED SHARIFF BIN YAMIN; Gen. Sec. MOHAMED HAYAT BIN AWANG.

Kesatuan Pekerja-Pekerja FELDA: 2 Jalan Maktab Enam, Melalui Jalan Perumahan Gurney, 54000 Kuala Lumpur; tel. (3) 26929972; fax (3) 26913409; 2,900 mems; Pres. INDERA PUTRA Haji ISMAIL; Gen. Sec. MOHAMAD BIN ABDUL RAHMAN.

Kesatuan Pekerja-Pekerja Perusahaan Membuat Tekstil dan Pakaian Pulau Pinang dan Seberang Prai: 23 Lorong Talang Satu, Prai Gardens, 13600 Prai; tel. (4) 301397; 3,900 mems; Pres. ABDUL RAZAK HAMID; Gen. Sec. KENNETH STEPHEN PERKINS.

Kesatuan Pekerja Tenaga Nasional Bhd: 30 Jalan Liku Bangsar, POB 10400, 59100 Kuala Lumpur; tel. (3) 2745657; 10,456 mems; Pres. MOHAMED ABU BAKAR; Gen. Sec. IDRIS BIN ISMAIL.

Malayan Technical Services Union: 3A Jalan Menteri, off Jalan Cochrane, 55100 Kuala Lumpur; tel. (3) 92851778; fax (3) 92811875; e-mail info@mtsu.org.my; internet www.mtsu.org.my; 6,000 mems; Pres. SHUHAIMI OTHMAN; Gen. Sec. SAMUEL DEVADASAN.

Malaysian Rubber Board Staff Union: POB 10150, 50908 Kuala Lumpur; tel. (3) 42565102; 850 mems; Pres. HASNAH GANI; Gen. Sec. SUBRAMANIAM SINNASAMY.

Metal Industry Employees' Union: Metalworkers' House, 5 Lorong Utara Kecil, 46200 Petaling Jaya, Selangor; tel. (3) 79567214; fax (3) 79550854; e-mail mieum@tm.net.my; 15,491 mems; Pres. SAMUSUDDIN USOP; Gen. Sec. JACOB ENGKATESU.

National Union of Bank Employees (NUBE): 12 NUBE House, 3rd Floor, Jalan Tun Sambanthan 3, Brickfields, 50470 Kuala Lumpur; tel. (3) 22749800; fax (3) 22601800; e-mail nube_hq@streamyx.com; internet www.nube.org.my; f. 1958; 30,000 mems; Gen. Sec. JOSEPH SOLOMON.

National Union of Commercial Workers: Bangunan NUCW, 98A–D Jalan Masjid India, 50100 Kuala Lumpur; POB 12059, 50780 Kuala Lumpur; tel. (3) 26927385; fax (3) 26925930; f. 1959; 11,937 mems; Pres. TAIB SHARIF; Gen. Sec. C. KRISHNAN.

National Union of Plantation Workers: 428A–B Jalan 5/46, Gasing Indah, POB 73, 46700 Petaling Jaya, Selangor; tel. (3) 77827622; fax (3) 77815321; e-mail nupw@tm.net.my; f. 1946; 29,251 mems; Pres. NADARAJA ANAK LAKI KUMARAN; Gen. Sec. Dato' G. SANKARAN.

National Union of PWD Employees: 32B Jalan Gajah, off Jalan Yew, 55100 Kuala Lumpur; tel. (3) 9850149; 5,869 mems; Pres. KULOP IBRAHIM; Gen. Sec. S. SANTHANASAMY.

National Union of Telecoms Employees: Wisma NUTE, 17A Jalan Bangsar, 59200 Kuala Lumpur; tel. (3) 2821599; fax (3) 2821015; 15,874 mems; Pres. MOHAMED SHAFIE B. P. MAMMAL; Gen. Sec. MOHD JAFAR BIN ABDUL MAJID.

Non-Metallic Mineral Products Manufacturing Employees' Union: 99A Jalan SS14/1, Subang Jaya, 47500 Petaling Jaya, Selangor; tel. (3) 56339006; fax (3) 56333863; e-mail nonmet@tm.net.my; 10,000 mems; Pres. ABDULLAH ABU BAKAR; Sec. S. SOMAHSUNDRAM.

Railwaymen's Union of Malaya: Bangunan Tong Nam, 1st Floor, Jalan Tun Sambathan (Travers), 50470 Kuala Lumpur; tel. (3) 2741107; fax (3) 2731805; 5,500 mems; Pres. ABDUL RAZAK MOHD HASSAN; Gen. Sec. S. VEERASINGAM.

Technical Services Union—Tenaga Nasional Bhd: Bangunan Keselamatan, POB 11003, Bangsar, Kuala Lumpur; tel. (3) 2823581; 3,690 mems; Pres. RAMLY YATIM; Gen. Sec. CLIFFORD SEN.

Timber Employees' Union: 10 Jalan AU5C/14, Ampang, Ulu Kelang, Selangor; 7,174 mems; Pres. ABDULLAH METON; Gen. Sec. MINHAT SULAIMAN.

Transport Workers' Union: 21 Jalan Barat, Petaling Jaya, 46200 Selangor; tel. (3) 7566567; 10,447 mems; Pres. NORASHIKIN; Gen. Sec. ZAINAL RAMPAK.

Independent Federations and Unions

Kongres Kesatuan Guru-Guru Dalam Perkhidmatan Pelajaran (Congress of Unions of Employees in the Teaching Services): Johor; seven affiliates; Pres. RAMLI BIN MOHD JOHAN; Sec.-Gen. KASSIM BIN Haji HARON.

Malaysian Medical Association: MMA House, 4th Floor, 124 Jalan Pahang, 53000 Kuala Lumpur; tel. (3) 40411375; fax (3) 40418187; e-mail info@mma.org.my; internet www.mma.org.my; f. 1959; 10 affiliates; Pres. Dr DAVID QUEK KWANG LENG.

National Union of Journalists: 30B Jalan Padang Belia, 50470 Kuala Lumpur; tel. (3) 2742867; fax (3) 2744776; f. 1962; 1,700 mems; Gen. Sec. ONN EE SENG.

National Union of Newspaper Workers: 11A–B Jalan 20/14, Paramount Garden, 46300 Petaling Jaya, Selangor; tel. (3) 78768118; fax (3) 78751490; e-mail nunwl@streamyx.com; f. 1967; 3,000 mems; Pres. RAHIM OMAR; Gen. Sec. R. CHANDRASEKARAN.

Sabah

Sabah Banking Employees' Union: POB 11649, 88818 Kota Kinabalu; tel. (88) 213830; fax (88) 260860; e-mail sbeu2004@streamyx.com; internet www.sbeu.org; 729 mems; Pres. MARGARET CHIN SAT PENG; Gen. Sec. CATHERINE JIKUNAN.

Sabah Civil Service Union: Kota Kinabalu; f. 1952; 1,356 mems; Pres. J. K. K. VOON; Sec. STEPHEN WONG.

Sabah Commercial Employees' Union: Sinsuran Shopping Complex, Lot 3, Block N, 2nd Floor, POB 10357, 88803 Kota Kinabalu; tel. (88) 225971; fax (88) 213815; e-mail sceu-kk@tm.net.my; f. 1957; 980 mems; Pres. CRISPINA FIDELIS; Gen. Sec. REBECCA CHIN.

Sabah Medical Services Union: POB 11257, 88813 Kota Kinabalu; tel. (88) 242126; fax (88) 242127; e-mail smsu65@hotmail.com; 4,000 mems; Pres. KATHY LO NYUK CHIN; Gen. Sec. LAURENCE VUN.

Sabah Petroleum Industry Workers' Union: POB 1087, Kota Kinabalu; tel. (88) 720737; e-mail victorsyb@yahoo.com; internet www.sabah.org.my/spiwu; f. 1966; 168 mems; Pres. PETER LEE YUN LOONG; Gen. Sec. DANY SIBATU.

Sabah Teachers' Union: POB 10912, 88810 Kota Kinabalu; tel. (88) 420034; fax (88) 431633; f. 1962; 3,001 mems; Pres. KWAN PING SIN; Sec.-Gen. PATRICK Y. C. CHOK.

Sarawak

Kepak Sarawak (Kesatuan Pegawai-Pegawai Bank, Sarawak): POB 62, Bukit Permata, 93100 Kuching, Sarawak; tel. (19) 8549372; e-mail kepaksar@tm.net.my; bank officers' union; 1,430 mems; Gen. Sec. DOMINIC CH'NG YUNG TED.

Sarawak Commercial Employees' Union: POB 807, Kuching; 1,636 mems; Gen. Sec. SONG SWEE LIAP.

Sarawak Teachers' Union: Wisma STU, Lot 10964–10966, Jalan Song, 93350 Kuching; tel. (82) 575120; fax (82) 574120; e-mail thomas@stu.org.my; internet stu.org.my; f. 1965; 17,000 mems; Pres. WILLIAM GHANI BINA; Sec.-Gen. THOMAS HUO KOK SEN.

Transport

RAILWAYS

Peninsular Malaysia

The state-owned Malayan Railways had a total length of 1,672 km in Peninsular Malaysia in 1996. The main railway line follows the west coast and extends 782 km from Singapore, south of Peninsular Malaysia, to Butterworth (opposite Pinang Island) in the north. From Bukit Mertajam, close to Butterworth, the Kedah line runs north to the Thai border at Padang Besar where connection is made with the State Railway of Thailand. The East Coast Line, 526 km long, runs from Gemas to Tumpat (in Kelantan). A 21-km branch line from Pasir Mas (27 km south of Tumpat) connects with the State Railway of Thailand at the border station of Sungei Golok. Branch lines serve railway-operated ports at Port Dickson and Telok Anson as well as Port Klang and Jurong (Singapore). Malaysia's first Light Rail Transit (LRT) system was opened in the Kuala Lumpur area in 1996. A second line began operating within the same system in 1998; a second LRT system, comprising one line, also commenced operations in that year. An express rail link connecting central Kuala Lumpur and the new Kuala Lumpur International Airport (KLIA) opened in 2001. The construction of a mass rapid transport system was scheduled to commence in Kuala Lumpur in January 2012, with completion scheduled for 2016.

Keretapi Tanah Melayu Bhd (KTMB) (Malayan Railways): KTMB Corporate Headquarters, Jalan Sultan Hishamuddin, 50621 Kuala Lumpur; tel. (3) 22631111; fax (3) 27105706; e-mail callcenter@ktmb.com.my; internet www.ktmb.com.my; f. 1885; incorporated as a co under govt control in 1992; privatized in 1997; managed by the consortium Marak Unggal (Renong, DRB and Bolton); Chair. Dato' Sri MOHD ZIN BIN MOHAMED.

Sabah

Sabah State Railway: Karung Berkunci 2047, 88999 Kota Kinabalu; tel. (88) 254611; fax (88) 236395; e-mail webmaster.jkns@sabah.gov.my; internet www.sabah.gov.my/railway; 134 track-km of 1-m gauge (2008); goods and passenger services from Tanjong Aru to Tenom, serving part of the west coast and the interior; diesel trains are used; Gen. Man. Ir BENNY WANG.

ROADS

Peninsular Malaysia

Peninsular Malaysia's road system is extensive, in contrast to those of Sabah and Sarawak. In 2004 the road network in Malaysia totalled an estimated 109,333 km, of which 1,821 km were motorways and 16,275 km were highways.

Sabah

Jabatan Kerja Raya Sabah (Sabah Public Works Department): Jalan Sembulan, Locked Bag 2032, 88582 Kota Kinabalu, Sabah; tel. (88) 244333; fax (88) 237234; e-mail jkrweb@sabah.gov.my; internet www.jkr.sabah.gov.my; f. 1881; implements and maintains public infrastructures such as roads, bridges, buildings and sewerage systems throughout Sabah; maintains a road network totalling 15,756.6 km, of which 5,686.5 km are sealed roads; Dir JOHN ANTHONY.

Sarawak

Jabatan Kerja Raya Sarawak (Sarawak Public Works Department): Tingkat 11–18, Wisma Saberkas, Jalan Tun Abang Haji Openg, 93582 Kuching, Sarawak; tel. (82) 203100; fax (82) 429679; e-mail limkh@sarawaknet.gov.my; internet www.jkr.sarawak.gov.my; implements and maintains public infrastructures in Sarawak; road network totalling 10,979 km, of which 3,986 km are sealed roads; Dir HUBERT THIAN CHONG HUI.

SHIPPING

The ports in Malaysia are classified as federal ports, under the jurisdiction of the federal Ministry of Transport, or state ports, responsible to the state ministries of Sabah and Sarawak.

Peninsular Malaysia

The federal ports in Peninsular Malaysia are Klang (the principal port), Pinang, Johor and Kuantan.

Johor Port Authority: 6A1–8A1 Pusat Perdagangan Pasir Gudang, Jalan Bandar, 81700 Pasir Gudang, Johor; tel. (7) 2534000; fax (7) 2517684; e-mail admin@lpj.gov.my; internet www.lpj.gov.my; f. 1976; Gen. Man. Nik AZIZ BIN HUSSAIN.

Johor Port Bhd: POB 151, Wisma Kontena, 81707 Pasir Gudang, Johor; tel. (7) 2535888; fax (7) 2510980; e-mail jpb@johorport.com.my; internet www.johorport.com.my; Chair. Datuk MOHD SIDIK BIN SHAIK OSMAN.

Klang Port Authority: POB 202, Jalan Pelabuhan, 42005 Port Klang, Selangor; tel. (3) 31688211; fax (3) 31689177; e-mail onestopagency@pka.gov.my; internet www.pka.gov.my; f. 1963; Gen. Man. LIM THEAN SHIANG.

Kuantan Port Authority: Tanjung Gelang, POB 161, 25720 Kuantan, Pahang; tel. (9) 5858000; fax (9) 5833866; e-mail lpktn@lpktn.gov.my; internet www.lpktn.gov.my; f. 1974; Gen. Man. Dato' KHAIRUL ANUAR BIN ABDUL RAHMAN.

Penang Port Commission: 3A–6 Sri Weld Bldg, Weld Quay, 10300 Penang; tel. (4) 2633211; fax (4) 2626211; e-mail sppp@penangport.gov.my; internet www.penangport.gov.my; f. 1956; Gen. Man. NOOR ARIF BIN YUSOFF.

Sabah

The main ports, which are administered by the Sabah Ports Authority, are Kota Kinabalu, Sandakan, Tawau, Lahad Datu, Kudat, Semporna and Kunak. Many international shipping lines serve Sabah. Local services are operated by smaller vessels.

Sabah Ports Authority: Bangunan SPA, Jalan Tun Fuad, Tanjung Lipat, Locked Bag 2005, 88617 Kota Kinabalu, Sabah; tel. (88) 538400; fax (88) 223036; e-mail sabport@tm.net.my; internet www.lpps.sabah.gov.my; f. 1968; Gen. Man. Eng. MAYONG OMAR.

Sarawak

There are four port authorities in Sarawak: Kuching, Rajang, Miri and Bintulu. Kuching, Rajang and Miri are state ports, while Bintulu is a federal port. Kuching port serves the southern region of Sarawak, Rajang port the central region, and Miri port the northern region.

Kuching Port Authority: Jalan Pelabuhan, Pending, POB 530, 93450 Kuching, Sarawak; tel. (82) 482144; fax (82) 481696; e-mail hq@kuport.com.my; internet www.kpa.gov.my; f. 1961; Gen. Man. LIU MOI FONG.

Rajang Port Authority: Jalan Pulau, 96000 Sibu, Sarawak; tel. (84) 319004; fax (84) 318754; e-mail rpa@rajangport.gov.my; internet www.rajangport.gov.my; f. 1970; Gen. Man. HELEN LIM HUI SHYAN.

Principal Shipping Companies

Malaysia Shipping Corpn Sdn Bhd: Office Tower, Plaza Berjaya, Suite 14C, 14th Floor, 12 Jalan Imbi, 55100 Kuala Lumpur; tel. (3) 21418788; fax (3) 21429214; Chair. Y. C. CHANG.

Malaysian International Shipping Corpn Bhd (National Shipping Line of Malaysia): Menara Dayabumi, Level 25, Jalan Sultan Hishamuddin, 50050 Kuala Lumpur; tel. (3) 22738088; fax (3) 22736602; e-mail caffairs@miscbhd.com; internet www.misc.com.my; f. 1968; regular services between South-East Asia, South Asia, Australia, Japan and Europe; also operates chartering, tanker, haulage and warehousing and agency services; majority stake owned by Petroliam Nasional Bhd (PETRONAS); Chair. Dato' SHAMSUL AZHAR BIN ABBAS; Pres. and CEO Datuk NASARUDIN BIN MOHD IDRIS.

Perbadanan Nasional Shipping Line Bhd (PNSL): Kuala Lumpur; tel. (3) 2932211; fax (3) 2930493; f. 1982; specializes in bulk cargoes; a wholly owned subsidiary of Konsortium Logistik Bhd; Chair. Tunku Dato' SHAHRIMAN BIN Tunku SULAIMAN; Exec. Dep. Chair. Dato' SULAIMAN ABDULLAH.

Persha Shipping Agencies Sdn Bhd: Bangunan Mayban Trust, Penthouse Suite, Jalan Pinang, 10200 Pinang; tel. (4) 2612400; fax (4) 2623122; Man. Dir MOHD NOOR MOHD KAMALUDIN.

Syarikat Perkapalan Kris Sdn Bhd (The Kris Shipping Co Ltd): POB 8428, 46789 Petaling Jaya, Selangor; tel. (3) 7046477; fax (3) 7048007; domestic services; Chair. Dato' Seri Syed NAHAR SHAHABUDIN; Gen. Man. ROHANY TALIB.

Trans-Asia Shipping Corpn Sdn Bhd: Lot 1A, Persiaran Jubli Perak, Jalan 22/1, Seksyen 22, 40300 Shah Alam, Selangor; tel. (3) 51018888; fax (3) 55488288; e-mail kytan@tasco.com.my; internet www.tasco.com.my; f. 1974; Man. Dir LEE CHECK POH.

CIVIL AVIATION

The new Kuala Lumpur International Airport (KLIA), situated in Sepang, Selangor (50 km south of Kuala Lumpur) began operations in June 1998, with an initial capacity of 25m.–30m. passengers a year, which was projected to rise to 45m. by 2020. An express rail link between central Kuala Lumpur and KLIA opened in early 2001. There are regional airports at Kota Kinabalu, Pinang, Johor Bahru, Kuching and Pulau Langkawi. In addition, there are airports catering for domestic services at Alor Star, Ipoh, Kota Bharu, Kuala Terengganu, Kuantan and Melaka in Peninsular Malaysia, Sibu, Bintulu and Miri in Sarawak, and Sandakan, Tawau, Lahad Datu and Labuan in Sabah. There are also numerous smaller airstrips.

Department of Civil Aviation (Jabatan Penerbangan Awam Malaysia): 27 Persiaran Perdana, Aras 1–4, Blok Podium, 62618 Putrajaya; tel. (3) 88714000; fax (3) 88901640; e-mail webmaster@dca.gov.my; internet www.dca.gov.my; Dir-Gen. Dato' AZHARUDDIN ABDUL RAHMAN.

AirAsia Sdn Bhd: LCC Terminal Jalan KLIA S3, Southern Support Zone, KLIA, 64000 Sepang, Selangor; tel. (3) 86604333; fax (3) 87751100; e-mail tellus@airasia.com; internet www.airasia.com; f. 1993; 85% owned by HICOM; low-cost national carrier with licence to operate domestic, regional and international flights; Chair. ABDUL AZIZ BIN ABU BAKAR; CEO TONY FERNANDES.

Berjaya Air Sdn Bhd: POB 7591, 40720 Shah Alam, Selangor; tel. (3) 78427300; fax (3) 78427330; e-mail admin@berjaya-air.com; internet www.berjaya-air.com; f. 1989; scheduled and charter domestic services; Pres. Tan Sri Dato' Seri VINCENT TAN CHEE YIOUN.

Firefly: Sultan Abdul Aziz Shah Airport, Admin Bldg 1, 3rd Floor, Kompleks A, 47200 Subang, Selangor; e-mail contactus@fireflyz.com.my; internet www.fireflyz.com.my; f. 2007; wholly owned by Malaysia Airlines; low-cost domestic and regional flights; Man. Dir EDDY LEONG.

Malaysia Airlines: Bangunan Pentadbiran 1, Tingkat 3, MAS Kompleks A, Sultan Abdul Aziz Shah Airport, 47200 Subang, Selangor; tel. (3) 78404550; fax (3) 78463932; e-mail tanwf@malaysiaairlines.com.my; internet www.malaysiaairlines.com.my; f. 1971; est. as the Malaysian successor to Malaysia Singapore Airlines (MSA); known as Malaysian Airline System (MAS) until Oct. 1987; 114 international routes and 118 domestic routes; Chair. Tan Sri MOHAMED NOR YUSOF; Man. Dir and CEO AHMAD JAUHARI YAHYA.

Transmile Air Sdn Bhd: Cargo Kompleks, Sultan Abdul Aziz Shah Airport, 47200 Subang, Selangor; tel. (3) 78849898; fax (3) 78849899; e-mail info@transmile.com; internet www.transmile.com; f. 1992; scheduled and charter regional and domestic services for passengers and cargo; Chair. Tan Sri A. RAZAK BIN RAMLI.

Tourism

Malaysia has a rapidly growing tourist industry, and tourism is an important source of foreign-exchange earnings. In 2010 a record 24.6m. tourists visited Malaysia, while receipts from tourism were estimated to total RM $56,500m. Singapore is the main source of visitors, followed by Indonesia and Thailand. Health tourism has significantly expanded in recent years; in 2008 some 370,000 foreign patients sought medical treatment at the 35 participating private hospitals in Malaysia.

Malaysia Tourism Promotion Board (Tourism Malaysia): Menara Dato' Onn, Tingkat 17, Putra World Trade Centre, 45 Jalan Tun Ismail, 50480 Kuala Lumpur; tel. (3) 26158188; fax (3) 26935884; e-mail enquiries@tourism.gov.my; internet www.tourismmalaysia.gov.my; f. 1972; est. to co-ordinate and promote activities relating to tourism in Malaysia; Chair. Datuk Dr VICTOR WEE; Dir-Gen. Dato' MIRZA MOHAMMAD TAIYAB.

Sabah Tourist Association: POB 12181, 88824 Kota Kinabalu, Sabah; tel. and fax (88) 486089; e-mail secretariat@sta.my; internet www.sta.my; f. 1963; independent promotional org.; Chair. LEN PONG LIEW.

Sabah Tourism Board: Mail Bag 112, 88993 Kota Kinabalu, Sabah; tel. (88) 212121; fax (88) 212075; e-mail info@sabahtourism.com; internet www.sabahtourism.com; f. 1976; parastatal promotion org.; Chair. Datuk Seri Tengku ZAINAL ADLIN Tengku MAHAMOOD.

Sarawak Tourism Board: Levels 6 and 7, Bangunan Yayasan Sarawak, Jalan Masjid, 93400 Kuching; tel. (82) 423600; fax (82) 416700; e-mail stb@sarawaktourism.com; internet www.sarawaktourism.com; f. 1995; CEO Datuk RASHID KHAN.

Defence

As assessed at November 2010, the total strength of the armed forces was 109,000; army 80,000 (although this was to be reduced to 60,000–70,000), navy 14,000, air force 15,000; military service is voluntary. Paramilitary forces included the Police-General Operations Force of 18,000 and the People's Volunteer Corps of 240,000. Malaysia is a participant in the Five-Power Defence Arrangements with Singapore, Australia, New Zealand and the United Kingdom.

Defence Expenditure: RM 9,100m. budgeted for 2010.

Chief of the Defence Forces: Gen. Tan Sri Dato' Seri AZIZAN ARIFFIN.

Chief of Army: Gen. Dato' Sri MUHAMMAD ZULKIFELI BIN ZIN.

Chief of Navy Staff: Adm. Tan Sri Dato' Sri ABDUL AZIZ JAAFAR.

Chief of Air Force Staff: Gen. Dato' Seri RODZALI BIN DAUD.

Education

Under the Malaysian education system, free schooling is provided at government-assisted schools for children between the ages of six and 18. There are also private schools, which receive no government financial aid. Education is compulsory for 11 years between the ages of six and 16 years. The Federal Government's development expenditure on education was budgeted at RM 10,827m. in 2009 (21.9% of projected expenditure). Scholarships are awarded at all levels and there are many scholarship-holders studying at universities and other institutes of higher education at home and abroad.

PRIMARY EDUCATION

The national language, Bahasa Malaysia, is the main medium of instruction, although English, Chinese and Tamil are also used. Two-thirds of the total primary school enrolment is in National Schools where Malay is used and the remainder in National-Type Primary Schools where Tamil or Chinese is used. A place in primary school is now assured to every child from the age of six onwards, and parents are free to choose the language of instruction. In 2008 some 3,154,090 students were enrolled in primary education. In 2006/07 the total enrolment at primary level included 96% of all children in the relevant age-group. The primary school course lasts for six years.

SECONDARY EDUCATION

Bahasa Malaysia is the main medium of instruction in secondary schools, while English is taught as a second language and Chinese and Tamil are taught as pupils' own languages. Private Chinese secondary schools are also in operation. Secondary education lasts for seven years, comprising a first cycle of three years and a second of four. In 2008 there were 2,310,660 students enrolled in secondary education. In 2006/07 the total enrolment at the secondary level included 68% of students in the relevant age-group.

HIGHER EDUCATION

In 2008 there were 20 government-funded universities and 33 private universities. In 1995 there were 210,724 students enrolled in tertiary education. In 2002 enrolment at the tertiary level was equivalent to 28% (males 25%, females 31%) of those in the relevant age-group. Malaysia's universities adhere to a quota system (55% of entrants should be Malays and 45% non-Malays), which, in practice, makes it considerably more difficult for non-Malays to gain a place at university. The Government has attempted to encourage foreign universities to establish campuses in Malaysia to improve standards and reduce the cost of sending Malaysian students abroad to study.

Bibliography

General

Barnard, Timothy P. (Ed.). *Contesting Malayness: Malay Identity Across Boundaries.* Singapore, Singapore University Press, 2004.

Cahil, Sharon. *Malaysian Constitutional Law.* Abingdon, Routledge Cavendish, 2006.

Frisk, Sylva. *Submitting to God: Women and Islam in Urban Malaysia.* Copenhagen, NIAS Press, 2009.

Goh, Daniel et al. *Race and Multiculturalism in Malaysia and Singapore.* Abingdon, Routledge, 2009.

Goh, Daniel P. S., Gabrielpillai, Matilda, Holden, Philip, and Gaik Cheng Khoo (Eds). *Race and Multiculturalism in Malaysia and Singapore.* Abingdon, Routledge, 2009.

Hew Cheng Sim. *Women Workers, Migration and Family in Sarawak.* London, RoutledgeCurzon, 2002.

Hoffstaedter, Gerhard. *Modern Muslim Identities: Negotiating Religion and Ethnicity in Malaysia.* Copenhagen, NIAS Press, 2011.

Milner, Anthony. *The Malays.* Oxford, Wiley-Blackwell, 2010.

Nelson, Joan M., Meerman, Jacob, and Embong, Abdul Rahman Haji (Eds). *Globalization and National Autonomy: The Experience of Malaysia.* Singapore, Institute of Southeast Asian Studies, 2008.

Saw Swee-Hock. *Bibliography of Malaysian Demography.* Singapore, Institute of Southeast Asian Studies, 2005.

The Population of Peninsular Malaysia. Singapore, Institute of Southeast Asian Studies, 2007.

Shiraishi, Takashi (Ed.). *Across the Causeway: A Multi-dimensional Study of Malaysia-Singapore Relations.* Singapore, Institute of Southeast Asian Studies, 2009.

Yeoh Seng Guan. *Media, Culture and Society in Malaysia.* Abingdon, Routledge, 2009.

History

Akashi, Yoji, and Yoshimura, Mako. *New Perspectives on the Japanese Occupation in Malaya and Singapore, 1941–1945.* Singapore, Singapore University Press, 2008.

Andaya, Barbara Watson, and Andaya, Leonard. *A History of Malaysia.* 2nd Edn. Honolulu, HI, University of Hawaii Press, 2001.

Cheah Boon Kheng. *Malaysia: The Making of a Nation.* Singapore, Institute of Southeast Asian Studies, 2002.

Cheah Boon Kheng (Ed.). *The Challenge of Ethnicity: Building a Nation in Malaysia.* Singapore, Marshall Cavendish Academic, 2004.

Chio, Vanessa C. M. *Malaysia and the Development Process: Globalization, Knowledge Transfers and Postcolonial Dilemmas.* London, Routledge, 2004.

Comber, Leon. *13 May 1969: A Historical Survey of Sino-Malay Relations.* Singapore, Graham Brash, 2001.

Malaya's Secret Police 1945–60: The Role of Special Branch in the Malayan Emergency. Singapore, Institute of Southeast Asian Studies, 2008.

Daniels, Timothy P. *Building Cultural Nationalism in Malaysia: Identity, Representation and Citizenship.* London, Routledge, 2004.

Hooker, Virginia. *A Short History of Malaysia: Linking East and West.* Sydney, NSW, Allen & Unwin, 2003.

Hussin, Nordin. *Trade and Society in the Straits of Melaka: Dutch Melaka and English Penang, 1780–1830.* Copenhagen, Nordic Institute of Asian Studies, 2007.

Idid, Syed Arabi. *Malaysia at 50: Achievements and Aspirations.* Kuala Lumpur, International Islamic University Malaysia, 2008.

Kathirithamby-Wells, Jeyamalar. *Nature and Nation: Forests and Development in Peninsular Malaysia.* Honolulu, HI, University of Hawaii Press, 2004.

Leigh, Michael B. *Mapping the Peoples of Sarawak.* Kota Samarahan, Sarawak, Institute of East Asian Studies, 2002.

Leow, Rachel. *Contexts of Abolition: The Mui Tsai Controversy in British Malaya, 1878–1938.* Cambridge, University of Cambridge, 2008.

Lim, Regina. *Federal-State Relations in Sabah, Malaysia: The Berjaya Administration, 1976–85.* Singapore, Institute of Southeast Asian Studies, 2008.

Liow, Joseph Chin Yong. *The Politics of Indonesia-Malaysia Relations: One Kin, Two Nations.* Abingdon, Routledge, 2005.

Mohamad, Maznah, Ng, Cecilia, and Tan Beng Hui. *Feminism and the Women's Movement in Malaysia: An Unsung (R)evolution.* Abingdon, Routledge, 2nd Edn, 2009.

Rahman, Noor Aisha Abdul. *Colonial Image of Malay Adat Laws: A Critical Appraisal of Studies on Adat Laws in the Malay Peninsula During the Colonial Era and Some Continuities.* Boston, Brill, 2006.

Riddell, Peter G. *Islam and the Malay-Indonesian World: Transmission and Responses.* Honolulu, HI, University of Hawaii Press, 2001.

Rodan, Garry. *Transparency and Authoritarian Rule in Southeast Asia: Singapore and Malaysia.* London, Routledge, 2004.

Saravanamuttu, Johan. *Malaysia's Foreign Policy: The First Fifty Years.* Singapore, Institute of Southeast Asian Studies, 2010.

Shennan, Margaret. *Out In The Midday Sun: The British in Malaya 1880–1960.* London, John Murray, 2000.

Stubbs, R. *Hearts and Minds in Guerrilla Warfare: The Malayan Emergency 1948–1960.* Singapore, Eastern Universities Press, 2004.

Turnbull, C. M. *The Straits Settlements 1826–67.* London, Athlone Press, 1972.

Verma, Vidhu. *Malaysia: State and Civil Society in Transition.* Boulder, CO, Lynne Rienner Publishers, 2002.

Wadley, Reed L. (Ed.). *Histories of the Borneo Environment: Economic, Political and Social Dimensions of Change and Continuity.* Singapore, Institute of Southeast Asian Studies, 2006.

Weiss, Meredith, and Saliha, Hassan (Eds). *Social Movements in Malaysia: From Moral Communities to NGOs.* London, Routledge Curzon, 2002.

Politics

Abdullah, Kamarulnizam. *The Politics of Islam in Contemporary Malaysia.* Kuala Lumpur, Penerbit Universiti Kebangsaan Malaysia, 2002.

Abraham, Collin. *Speaking Out Loud for National Unity: Social Change and National-Building in Contemporary Malaysia.* Selangor, Gerakbudaya Enterprise, 2008.

Atkins, William. *The Politics of Southeast Asia's New Media.* London, RoutledgeCurzon, 2002.

Chandran, Jeshurun. *Malaysia: Fifty Years of Diplomacy, 1957–2007.* Singapore, Talisman Publishing, 2008.

Chin, C. C., and Hack, Karl (Eds). *Dialogues with Chin Peng: New Light on the Malayan Communist Party.* Singapore, Singapore University Press, 2004.

Gatsiounis, Ioannis. *Beyond the Veneer: Malaysia's Struggle for Dignity and Direction.* Singapore, Monsoon Books, 2009.

Gomez, Edmund Terence (Ed.). *The State of Malaysia: Ethnicity, Equity and Reform.* London, RoutledgeCurzon, 2004.

Politics in Malaysia: The Malay Dimension. Abingdon, Routledge, 2007.

Hilley, John. *Malaysia: Mahathirism, Hegemony and the New Opposition.* London, Zed Books, 2001.

Hooker, Virginia, and Othman, Norani (Eds). *Malaysia: Islam, Society and Politics.* Singapore, Institute of Southeast Asian Studies, 2003.

In-Won Hwang. *Personalized Politics: The Malaysian State Under Mahathir.* Singapore, Institute of Southeast Asian Studies, 2003.

Lee, Julian C. H. *Islamization and Activism in Malaysia.* Singapore, Institute of Southeast Asian Studies, 2010.

Liow, Joseph Chin Yong. *Piety and Politics: Islamism in Contemporary Malaysia.* Melbourne, Oxford University Press, 2009.

Loh Kok Wah, Francis, and Saravanamuttu, Johan (Eds). *New Politics in Malaysia.* Singapore, Institute of Southeast Asian Studies, 2003.

Mandal, Sumit K. *Challenging Authoritarianism in Southeast Asia: Comparing Indonesia and Malaysia.* London, Routledge, 2003.

Milne, R. S., and Mauzy, Diane K. *Malaysian Politics under Mahathir.* London, Routledge, 1999.

Moten, Abdul Rashid. *Government and Politics in Malaysia.* Singapore, Cengage Learning, 2008.

Nair, Shanti. *Islam in Malaysian Foreign Policy.* London, Routledge, 1997.

Ooi Kee Beng. *Era of Transition: Malaysia after Mahathir.* Singapore, Institute of Southeast Asian Studies, 2006.

Lost in Transition: Malaysia Under Abdullah. Singapore, Institute of Southeast Asian Studies, 2008.

Between UMNO and a Hard Place: The Najib Razak Era Begins. Singapore, Institute of Southeast Asian Studies, 2010.

Arrested Reform: The Undoing of Abdullah Badawi. Singapore, Institute of Southeast Asian Studies, 2009.

Ooi Kee Beng, Saravanamuttu, Johan Guan, and Hock, Lee (Eds). *March 8: Eclipsing May 13.* Singapore, Institute of Southeast Asian Studies, 2009.

Othman, Norani. *Sharing the Nation: Faith, Difference, Power and the State, 50 Years After Merdeka.* Petaling Jaya, Strategic Information and Research Development Centre, 2008.

Peletz, Michael G. *Islamic Modern: Religious Courts and Cultural Politics in Malaysia.* Princeton, NJ, Princeton University Press, 2002.

Plate, Tom. *Conversations with Mahathir Mohamad.* Singapore, Marshall Cavendish, 2011.

Saw Swee-Hock and Kesavapany, K. (Eds). *Singapore-Malaysia Relations.* Singapore, Institute of Southeast Asian Studies, 2006.

See, Hoon Peow. *The Law and Child Labour in Malaysia: a Case Study in a Chinese New Village.* Subang Jaya, Selangor Darul Ehsan, Pelanduk Publications, 2007.

Shamsul, A. B. *From British to Bumiputera Rule: Local Politics and Rural Development in Peninsular Malaysia.* Singapore, Institute of Southeast Asian Studies, 2004.

Shome, Tony. *Malay Political Leadership.* Richmond, Curzon Press, 2001.

Stewart, Ian. *The Mahathir Legacy: A Nation Divided, A Region at Risk.* St Leonards, NSW, Allen and Unwin, 2003.

Tan, Andrew T. H. *Security Perspectives of the Malay Archipelago: Security Linkages in the Second Front in the War on Terrorism.* Cheltenham, Edward Elgar Publishing, 2004.

Tan, Jun E., and Zawawi, Ibrahim. *Blogging and Democratization in Malaysia: a New Civil Society in the Making.* Selangor, Strategic Information and Research Development Centre, 2008.

Tan, Nathanial (Ed.). *Mahathir vs. Abdullah: Covert Wars and Challenged Legacies.* Kuala Lumpur, Kinibooks, 2007.

Tan Tai Yong. *Creating 'Greater Malaysia': Decolonization and the Politics of Merger.* Singapore, Institute of Southeast Asian Studies, 2008.

Thompson, Eric C. *Unsettling Absences: Urbanism in Rural Malaysia.* Singapore, Singapore University Press, 2007.

Wain, Barry. *Malaysian Maverick: Mahathir Mohamad in Turbulent Times.* Basingstoke, Palgrave Macmillan, 2009.

Yeoh, Michael (Ed.). *21st Century Malaysia: Challenges and Strategies in Attaining Vision 2020.* London, ASEAN Academic Press, 2002.

Economy

Abdullah, Moha Asri Asri. *Small and Medium Enterprise in Malaysia: Policy Issues and Challenges.* Burlington, VT, Ashgate Publishing Co, 2005.

Alavi, Rokiah. *Industrialization in Malaysia: Import Substitution and Infant Industry Performance.* London, Routledge, 1996.

Ang, James B. *Financial Development and Economic Growth in Malaysia.* Abingdon, Routledge, 2008.

Athukorala, Prema-chandra. *Crisis and Recovery in Malaysia: The Role of Capital Controls.* Cheltenham, Edward Elgar Publishing, 2001.

Baginda, Abdul Razak. *Malaysia in Transition: Politics, Economics and Society.* London, ASEAN Academic Press, 2002.

Barlow, Colin. *Modern Malaysia in the Global Economy: Political and Social Change into the 21st Century.* Cheltenham, Edward Elgar Publishing, 2001.

Barlow, Colin, and Loh Kok Wah, Francis (Eds). *Malaysian Economics and Politics in the New Century.* Cheltenham, Edward Elgar Publishing, 2003.

Barraclough, Simon, and Chee Heng Leng (Eds). *Health Care in Malaysia: The Dynamics of Provision, Financing and Access.* Abingdon, Routledge, 2007.

Bunnell, Tim. *Malaysia, Modernity and the Multimedia Super Corridor: A Critical Geography of Intelligent Landscapes.* London, RoutledgeCurzon, 2004.

Carlos Salazar, Lorraine. *Getting a Dial Tone: Telecommunications Liberalisation in Malaysia and the Philippines.* Singapore, Institute of Southeast Asian Studies, 2007.

Chai, H. C. *The Development of British Malaya 1896–1909.* Kuala Lumpur, Oxford University Press, 1964.

Drabble, J. H. *Rubber in Malaya 1876–1922.* London, Oxford University Press, 1973.

An Economic History of Malaysia, c. 1800–1990: The Transition to Modern Economic Growth. Basingstoke, Palgrave Macmillan, 2000.

Gill, Ranjit. *The Making of Malaysia Inc.: A 25-year Review of the Securities Industry of Malaysia and Singapore.* London, ASEAN Academic Press, 2003.

Gomez, E. T., and Jomo, K. S. *Malaysia's Political Economy: Politics, Patronage and Profits.* Cambridge, Cambridge University Press, 1997.

Hassan, Asan Ali Golam. *Growth, Structural Change, and Regional Inequality in Malaysia.* Burlington, VT, Ashgate Publishing Co, 2004.

Hill, Hal, Tham Siew Yean and Ragayah Haji Mat Zin (Eds). *Malaysia's Development Challenges: Graduating from the Middle.* Abingdon, Routledge, 2011.

Jomo, K. S. *Malaysian Industrial Policy.* Singapore, NUS Press, 2007.

Jomo, K. S. (Ed.). *Malaysian Eclipse: Economic Crisis and Recovery.* London, Zed Books, 2001.

Jomo, K. S., Chang, K. T., and Khoo, K. J. *Deforesting Malaysia: The Political Economy and Social Ecology of Agricultural Expansion and Commercial Logging.* London, Zed Books, 2004.

Jomo, K. S., and Wong, Sau Ngan (Eds). *Law, Institutions and Malaysian Economic Development.* Singapore, University of Singapore Press, 2008.

Mahadevan, Renuka. *Sustainable Growth and Economic Development: A Case Study of Malaysia.* Cheltenham, Edward Elgar Publishing, 2007.

Mahathir Mohamad. *The Malaysian Currency Crisis: How and Why It Happened.* New York, Weatherhill Publishers, 2003.

Navaratnam, Ramon V. *Malaysia's Economic Sustainability: Confronting New Challenges Amidst Global Realities.* Philadelphia, PA, Coronet Books, 2002.

Malaysia's Socioeconomic Challenges: Debating Public Policy Issues. Petaling Jaya, Pelanduk Publications, 2003.

Mehmet, Ozay. *Development in Malaysia: Poverty, Wealth and Trusteeship.* Abingdon, Routledge, 2010.

Nyland, Chris, Smith, Wendy, Smyth, Russell, and Vicziany, Marika (Eds). *Malaysian Business in the New Era.* Cheltenham, Edward Elgar Publishing, 2001.

Pepinsky, Thomas B. *Economic Crises and the Breakdown of Authoritarian Regimes: Indonesia and Malaysia in Comparative Perspective.* Cambridge University Press, 2009.

Saw Swee-Hock and Kesavapany, K. (Eds). *Malaysia: Recent Trends and Challenges.* Singapore, Institute of Southeast Asian Studies, 2005.

Sieh Lee Mei Ling. *Taking on the World: Globalization Strategies in Malaysia.* Kuala Lumpur, McGraw Hill, 2000.

Sundaram, Jomo (Ed.). *Malaysian Eclipse—Economic Crisis and Recovery.* London, Zed Books, 2001.

Tan, Jeff. *Privatization in Malaysia: Regulation, Rent-Seeking and Policy Failure.* Abingdon, Routledge, 2007.

Vincent, Jeffrey R., and Ali, Rozali Mohamed. *Managing Natural Wealth: Environment and Development in Malaysia.* Washington, DC, Resources for the Future, 2004.

Yee Shin Tan. *Political Economy of Budgetary Policy in Malaysia.* Saarbrücken, LAP LAMBERT Academic Publishing, 2011.

Yusuf, Shahid, and Nabeshima, Kaoru. *Tigers Under Threat: The Search for a New Growth Strategy by Malaysia and Its Southeast Asian Neighbors.* Washington, DC, World Bank Publications, 2009.

MONGOLIA

Physical and Social Geography

ALAN J. K. SANDERS

Mongolia occupies an area of 1,564,116 sq km (603,909 sq miles) in east-central Asia. It is bordered by only two other states: the Russian Federation, along its northern frontier (extending for 3,543 km according to a survey completed in December 2001), and the People's Republic of China, along the considerably longer southern frontier (4,709 km).

PHYSICAL ENVIRONMENT

For the purpose of geographical description Mongolia may be divided into five regions. In the west is the Altai area, where peaks covered with eternal snow rise to more than 4,300 m above sea-level. To the east of this lies a great depression dotted with lakes, some of salt water and some of fresh. Some of these, such as Uvs *nuur* (3,350 sq km) and Khövsgöl *nuur* (2,760 sq km) reach a considerable size. The north-central part of the country is occupied by the Khangai-Khentii mountain complex, enclosing the relatively fertile and productive agricultural country of the Selenge-Tuul basin. This has always been the focus of what cultural life existed in the steppes of north Mongolia: the imperial capital of Karakorum lay here and the ruins of other early settlements are still to be seen. To the east again lies the high Mongolian plateau reaching to the Chinese frontier, and to the south and east stretches the Gobi or semi-desert.

Mongolia occasionally suffers severe earthquakes, especially in mountainous regions, but the population is too widely scattered for heavy losses to be caused.

Water is unevenly distributed. In the mountainous north and west of the country large rivers originate, draining into either the Arctic or the Pacific. A continental watershed divides Mongolia, and the much smaller rivers of the south drain internally into lakes or are lost in the ground.

CLIMATE

The climate shows extremes of temperature between the long, cold, dry winter and the short, hot summer during which most of the year's precipitation falls. In Ulan Bator (Ulaanbaatar) the July temperature averages 16.9°C and the January temperature –21.8°C. Annual precipitation is variable but light. Ulan Bator's average is 258.5 mm, with 72.6 mm of rain in July. Rain is liable to fall in sudden, heavy showers or more prolonged outbursts in mid-summer, with severe flooding and damage to towns and bridges. Average snowfall in Ulan Bator in October–March is 16.9 mm. The bitter winter weather is relieved by the almost continuous blue sky and sunshine. The term *zud* is used to describe lack of pasture resulting from drought, frozen snow cover or overgrazing, leading to the death of livestock from starvation.

MINERAL RESOURCES

The alluvial gold of Mongolia's northern valleys was familiar to Russian miners in the early 20th century, but the scale of the country's mineral resources was clarified by Soviet geologists in the post-revolutionary period. Coal from Nalaikh, near Ulan Bator, fed the early power stations and railways. Later, open-cast lignite mines at Baganuur and Sharyn Gol, in northern Mongolia, met the growing demand for electricity. In the new millennium large deposits at Tavantolgoi in the Gobi and Khöshööt near Khovd increased coal exports to China. Concentrates are exported from Erdenet copper mine in northern Mongolia and fluorspar mines in central Mongolia, developed with Soviet aid in the 1970s. More recently, extensive copper and gold deposits at Oyu Tolgoi in the Gobi have been identified and are being exploited in collaboration with international companies. The eastern Gobi oilfields, abandoned by Soviet technicians in the 1950s, are now yielding petroleum from deep wells for export to China. Mongolia also works scattered deposits of silver, zinc and iron, and there is renewed interest in uranium. A parliamentary decree issued in February 2007 listed the country's 15 'strategic' deposits and 39 potential ones. However, deposits are often remote from the transport infrastructure and development requires foreign investment. Phosphate mining has been banned near Lake Khövsgöl, but uncontrolled artisanal gold mining is damaging the environment.

POPULATION

Mongolia is mostly sparsely inhabited. The November 2010 census indicated a population of 2,754,685, or 1.7 persons per sq km. The Mongols are no longer essentially nomadic herdsmen, although seasonal stock-movement *(otor)*, sometimes covering large distances, has been a regular feature of rural life. Of the total population, 63% live in towns, with almost two-thirds of these residing in the capital, Ulan Bator. In December 2010 the resident population of Ulan Bator was estimated at 1.15m. There are 329 rural districts, inhabited by about 36% of the population. The population is, relatively speaking, homogenous. Some 99% of the people are Mongol citizens, and of these the overwhelming majority (82%) belong to the Khalkha (Halh) group. The only important non-Mongol element in the population is that of the Kazakhs, a Turkic-speaking people dwelling mostly in the far west, and representing approximately 3.9% (in 2010) of the whole.

The official language is Mongolian, written in a native vertical script or for everyday purposes in modified Cyrillic. Mongolian is quite different from both Russian and Chinese, its geographic neighbours, but does show certain similarities, perhaps fortuitous, to Turkish, Korean and Japanese. Several Mongolian dialects beside the dominant Khalkha are spoken, and in the province of Bayan-Ölgii the first language is Kazakh, most people being bilingual in Mongolian.

Between 1963 and 1983 the population increased by 74%. The annual growth rate peaked at 2.6% in 1990; it subsequently declined to average 1.2% in 2002–07. A preponderance of young people was recorded at the census of January 2000, when 66% of the population were under 30 years of age. According to official figures, infant mortality declined from 64 per 1,000 births in 1990 to 17.6 in 2007, before rising to 19.4 in 2008, 20.0 in 2009 and to 20.2 in 2010.

History

ALAN J. K. SANDERS

EARLY HISTORY

Today only a minority of ethnic Mongols live in Mongolia, the sole independent Mongol state. Besides the related Buryat and Kalmyk peoples who are to be found within the Russian Federation in their respective republics (near Lake Baikal and on the lower Volga, respectively), many Mongols dwell outside Mongolia, most of them in the Inner Mongolia Autonomous Region of the People's Republic of China and adjacent areas—Heilongjiang, Jilin, Liaoning, Gansu, Ningxia and Xinjiang.

This division came about in the following way: in the early 17th century the Manchus, expanding southwards from Manchuria towards their ultimate conquest of all China, passed through what came to be called Inner Mongolia, which lay across their invasion routes. Many of the Mongol princes allied themselves with the Manchus (sometimes reinforcing such alliances by marriage), others submitted voluntarily to them, while yet others were conquered. In 1636, after the death of Ligdan Khan (the last Mongol Emperor), the subordination of these princes to the new, rising Manchu Qing dynasty was formalized. The princes of Khalkha or Outer Mongolia, in their turn, lost their independence at the Convention of Dolonnor in 1691. Galdan, the ruler of the West Mongol Oirats, who in 1687 attacked the Khalkhas and challenged the Manchus for supremacy, was defeated in 1697. The three great princes of Khalkha and the Javzandamba Khutagt, the Bogd Gegeen or Living Buddha of Urga, the head of the lamaist church in Mongolia, accepted Manchu overlordship. The 1727 Treaty of Kyakhta (Khiagt) defined the western borders between the Russian and Manchu empires, and confirmed Qing rule in Outer Mongolia and Tannu Tuva (Uriankhai).

In Outer Mongolia a fourth princedom (*aimag*) was created in 1725, and soon afterwards the princedoms were renamed leagues and removed from the jurisdiction of the hereditary princes, to be administered instead by Mongol league heads, appointed by the imperial Government in Beijing. Within the league organization Mongolia was divided into about 100 banners. The Living Buddha owned many serfs in a number of scattered temple territories. This structure survived the fall of the Qing in 1911 and lasted until the foundation of the Mongolian People's Republic (MPR) in 1924. However, in spite of their dependence on Beijing, the Mongols always considered themselves allies of the Manchus, not subjects like the Chinese, and made good use of this distinction when the Manchu Qing dynasty lost the throne of China.

AUTONOMOUS MONGOLIA

The beginnings of the existence of modern Mongolia can be traced back to 1911. In that year the fall of the Manchu Qing dynasty enabled the Mongols to terminate their association with China. With some political and military support from Russia, a number of leading nobles proclaimed Mongolia an independent monarchy, and the eighth Javzandamba Khutagt was enthroned as Bogd Khan ('holy emperor'). The Bogd Khan invited all Mongols everywhere to adhere to the new state, but this involved them in conflict with China, which retained control of Inner Mongolia. Nor did they obtain much useful support from Russia, which was bound by secret treaties with Japan not to obstruct the latter's interests in Inner Mongolia, and which in any case was reluctant to engage in a doubtful pan-Mongolist adventure. Sain Noyon Khan Namnansüren was appointed Prime Minister in July 1912. In 1915 Russian, Chinese and Mongol representatives, meeting at Kyakhta on the Russo-Mongol border, agreed to the reduction of Mongolia's would-be independence to autonomy under Chinese suzerainty. Autonomous Mongolia consisted more or less of the territory of present-day Mongolia, the only substantial difference being the accession of Dariganga in the south-east at the time of the 1921 revolution. Inner Mongolia, Barga and the Altai district of Xinjiang were to remain under Chinese control. Tannu Tuva, after a brief period of autonomy as a 'people's republic', was absorbed by the USSR in 1944.

Autonomous Mongolia was a theocratic monarchy and during the few years of its existence very little happened to change the conditions inherited from Manchu times. Russian advisers began to modernize the Mongol army and to bring some sort of order into the fiscal system. Several primary schools and a secondary school were opened, some children (including the future dictator, Khorloogiin Choibalsan) were sent to study in imperial Russia, and the first newspaper appeared; however, the state structure, the feudal organization of society and the administration of justice remained more or less as they had been, while the Buddhist clergy managed to consolidate and enhance its position of privilege. While legally subject to Chinese suzerainty, Mongolia was, in fact, a Russian protectorate. When Russian power and prestige in Central Asia were sapped by the collapse of the tsarist regime and the outbreak of revolution in 1917, this dependence of Mongolia became very apparent, and China lost no time in reasserting its authority. By mid-1919 the abrogation of autonomy was being discussed by the Mongol Government and the Chinese resident in Urga (Niislel Khüree), the capital, but the process was brutally accelerated by the arrival in Mongolia of Gen. Xu Shuzeng who, with a large military force at his disposal, forced the Mongols to relinquish all authority to the Chinese in February 1920.

THE REVOLUTIONARY MOVEMENT

Towards the end of 1919 two revolutionary groups had been founded in Urga; in the following year these amalgamated to form the Mongolian People's Party (MPP). There was no long-standing revolutionary tradition in Mongolia, which was perhaps the reason why the Mongol revolution fell so completely under Soviet control. The members of the groups were men of varied social origin, including lamas (such as Dogsomyn Bodoo, the premier of 1921, government servants, workers, soldiers (such as Damdiny Sükhbaatar) and students who had returned from Russia (such as Khorloogiin Choibalsan). They had the sympathy of several prominent nobles through whom they were able to approach the Bogd Khan, while at the same time they acquired some knowledge of Marxism from their acquaintance with left-wing Russian workers in Urga.

The first real contacts with Soviet Russia took place in early 1920 when a Comintern agent, Sorokovikov, came to Urga to assess the situation. It is therefore not surprising to find that the aims of the revolutionaries were at this time fairly moderate. First of all they desired national independence from the Chinese, then an elective government, internal administrative reforms, improved social justice, and the consolidation of the Buddhist faith. With Sorokovikov's approval they planned to send a delegation to Russia to seek help against the Chinese. They obtained the sanction of the Bogd Khan and carried with them a letter authenticated with his seal. They were, in fact, authorized only to obtain advice from Russia, not to negotiate actual intervention.

The situation was complicated by the incursion into the country of White Russian forces under Baron Roman von Ungern-Sternberg. At first the Mongol authorities and the people welcomed the White Russians who dislodged the oppressive Chinese, and with the help of Ungern, the Bogd Khan was restored to the throne. However, Ungern's brutalities soon turned the Mongols against him. More important, the Soviet agents dealing with the Mongol delegation were able to use Ungern's apparent ascendancy over the Urga regime to extract far-reaching concessions. They made the offer of help conditional upon the subsequent establishment in Urga of a new government well disposed to them.

In March 1921 the first Congress of the MPP was held at Kyakhta on Soviet territory, and a provisional revolutionary Government was formed there, in opposition to the legal authorities in Urga who had sponsored the delegates who now abandoned them. This provisional Government gathered a small band of partisans who, with substantial Soviet forces, entered Mongolia, defeated Ungern and then marched on Urga. Here, in July 1921, a People's Government was proclaimed, headed by Prime Minister Dogsomyn Bodoo. The Bogd Khan was restored, but the monarchy now existed in name only. Mongolia came increasingly under Soviet direction. A secret police force was established, and in 1922 Bodoo was executed in the first of a long series of political purges. Minister of the Army Damdiny Sükhbaatar died in suspicious circumstances in February 1923. In 1924 the Bogd Khan died, and the search for a new incarnation was banned. A People's Republic, with a Soviet-style Constitution, was proclaimed by a popular assembly, the Great Khural. The MPP was renamed the Mongolian People's Revolutionary Party (MPRP) in 1925, at the Comintern's request.

THE MONGOLIAN PEOPLE'S REPUBLIC

Mongolia was now, in name, a people's republic, the second socialist state in the world, but its primitive stage of development posed daunting problems. Buddhism, which commanded deep loyalty from the people, weighed heavily on the economy and was a powerful ideological opponent of communism. Local separatism, especially in the far west, took years to overcome, and in some outlying parts local government could not be established until 1928 or 1929. Moreover, it was easy for disillusioned herdsmen to trek with their herds over the frontiers into China and there were considerable losses of population by emigration. There was widespread illiteracy and many of those who could read and write were lamas whose skill was in Tibetan rather than Mongol.

The country's economy depended exclusively on extensive animal herding. Trade and crafts were in the hands of foreigners, almost all of them Chinese. There was no banking system, no national currency, no industry and no medical service in the modern sense. Finally, most of those men who were politically experienced and capable of running the local administration were lamas or nobles, two classes at whose eventual annihilation the revolutionary regime aimed.

Thus, the stage of economic, social and intellectual development that Mongolia had reached was far below that of Russia. Its capacity for independent action was extremely limited by its one international partner, the immeasurably more powerful USSR. Mongolia was ineluctably linked with Soviet interests and developments, and its history over the next two decades showed the same progression of events as characterized the regime of Stalin, who held power in the USSR from 1924 until his death in 1953.

Initially, until 1928, there was some measure of semi-capitalist development, during which the privileges of the nobility and clergy were not seriously curtailed. In international contacts, too, the Mongols reached out to France and Germany. However, parallel with the rise of Stalin and the movement to the left in the USSR, there developed in Mongolia what came to be known as the 'leftist deviation'. All foreign contacts other than with the USSR were terminated. The USSR monopolized Mongolia's trade, in which it had hitherto had only a modest share. Between 1929 and 1932 an ill-prepared programme of collectivization ruined the country's economy, stocks of cattle falling by at least one-third. A rigorous anti-religious campaign did much to turn people against the MPRP, and in 1932 uprisings broke out, which, particularly in western Mongolia, reached the proportions of civil war and necessitated the intervention of the Soviet army. Thousands of Mongols deserted the country with their herds. This disastrous course was reversed only on the direct instructions of the Comintern in June 1932. Leaders who until then had been enthusiastic leftists, such as Peljidiin Genden, who became Chairman of the Council of Ministers (Prime Minister) and was later 'unmasked' as a 'Japanese spy' and eliminated by Choibalsan, now adopted a more moderate line. Under what was termed the 'New Turn Policy', private ownership of cattle and private trade were again encouraged, and Buddhism was treated more leniently.

However, from 1936 Mongolia fell under the dictatorship of Marshal Choibalsan. Over a period of three years most of the former leadership of revolutionaries, politicians, senior military officers, Buddhist clergy and intellectuals were arrested and shot on charges of 'counter-revolution' and treasonable plotting with the Japanese, which were subsequently acknowledged to have been quite false. Two-thirds of the more than 30,000 victims were lamas, whose monasteries and temples were ransacked and wrecked. In 1939 Choibalsan became Prime Minister, and in 1940 he declared that Mongolia could begin the transition from the 'democratic stage' of the revolution to the socialist stage. Yumjaagiin Tsedenbal was elected General Secretary of the MPRP.

The progress made by 1940 had been mostly negative, consisting of the elimination of old social groupings and the redistribution of wealth confiscated from the former nobles, removed in and after 1929, and the clergy. A certain amount of reconstruction had been achieved, in the fields of education, medical services, communications and industry, but it was not until well after the Second World War that any extensive programme of modernization was to be attempted in Mongolia. One reason for this tardiness was the threat posed by the Japanese in Manchuria, which meant that most of the Soviet expenditure in Mongolia was devoted to a military build-up. It was significant that the only railway to be constructed in pre-war years served the town of Bayantümen, renamed Choibalsan, in eastern Mongolia. Only after the war was Mongolia's main economic region, the area around Ulan Bator, to be connected with the Trans-Siberian railway line.

POLITICAL DEVELOPMENTS SINCE 1945

The Japanese in Manchuria had for some years been probing the defences of eastern Mongolia, and in mid-1939 they provoked a series of battles on the Khalkha River (Khalkhyn Gol) in which they were heavily defeated by Soviet and Mongol troops. From then on a truce reigned until August 1945, when Mongolia followed the USSR in declaring war on Japan. Mongol forces advanced as far as the Pacific coast of China, but were withdrawn soon afterwards, and the only advantage Mongolia gained from its belated participation in the war was the labour of Japanese prisoners. Imports from the USSR almost ceased during the war years, and Mongolia made a heavy contribution to the Soviet war effort in the form of livestock and uniforms, although it was never itself at war with Germany. As a result, there was practically no economic progress over this period.

Following the Allied Powers' agreement in Yalta to preserve the status quo in Mongolia, a plebiscite in October 1945 confirmed the country's wish for independence, which was recognized by China in January 1946. However, Mongolia's international position of isolation, in sole dependence on the USSR, did not change until the communization of Eastern Europe and the success of the communists in China provided it with a new and ready-made field of diplomatic activity. Between October 1948 and March 1950 Mongolia exchanged diplomatic recognition with all the then existing communist states except Yugoslavia, and thereafter with a number of non-aligned countries such as India, Burma (Myanmar) and Indonesia. The United Kingdom was the first Western European state to recognize Mongolia (in 1963). Mongolia was admitted to the UN in 1961.

After the death of Marshal Choibalsan in 1952 General Secretary Yumjaagiin Tsedenbal was appointed Chairman of the Council of Ministers, but in 1954 he lost the leadership of the MPRP to Dashiin Damba, regaining the post only in 1958. The 'thaw' that was initiated in the USSR by Nikita Khrushchev in the 1950s and 1960s was imitated in Mongolia, where several of the leaders who had been executed in the 1930s were 'rehabilitated'. Contacts with non-communist foreigners were permitted, a small tourist industry was developed and controls on publications were slightly relaxed. A feature of this period was the reassertion of feelings of Mongolian nationalism, which for 20 years had been repressed. Since 1936 the existence of pre-revolutionary culture in Mongolia had been systematically denied. Nothing of ancient Mongol literature was taught in schools, no old books were reprinted and manuscripts considered to be contrary to contemporary ideology were destroyed. After 1956 this policy was modified. School curricula, while still insisting that children be given a communist education, were liberalized to the extent that they included the study of extracts from ancient literature once more. The Committee (later Academy) of Sciences was able to begin a programme of research and publication in the fields of literature, history and linguistics, and to organize in 1959 the First International Congress of Mongolists. This was the first occasion on which scholars from the Western world, the Soviet bloc and China conferred together in Mongolia.

This renascence of national sentiment was rebuffed from time to time when it clashed with Soviet requirements of greater international communist conformity. In 1946 the traditional alphabet was abandoned in favour of a form of the Cyrillic script. In 1962 when the Mongols celebrated the 800th anniversary of the birth of Genghis Khan, the unifier of the Mongol tribes and founder of the Mongol Empire, their enthusiasm was regarded by the Soviet Government, and in more orthodox quarters in Mongolia itself, as manifesting excessive feelings of nationalism at the expense of 'proletarian internationalism'. The planned official celebrations were abruptly cancelled and the MPRP Politburo member in charge of them, Daramyn Tömör-Ochir, was dismissed and exiled. (He was murdered in October 1985.) In early 1963 an ideological conference was held in Ulan Bator with the participation of Soviet Politburo member Leonid Ilyichev, in order to reassert the correct political line.

Despite its widening international contacts, Mongolia continued to look mainly to the USSR for guidance and help in its affairs. Mongolia's alignment with the USSR in the Sino-Soviet dispute of the 1960s–70s was predictable, and the official press adopted an uncompromising anti-Beijing line. China was accused, *inter alia*, of carrying out a colonialist policy in its minority areas, including Inner Mongolia, and of openly preparing for war with the USSR and Mongolia. Because of the 'real threat' of Chinese 'great-power expansion', Soviet troops were stationed in the country, under the Mongolian-Soviet treaty of 1966, signed by Tsedenbal and the Soviet leader Leonid Brezhnev in Ulan Bator.

In June 1974 Yumjaagiin Tsedenbal, who had held the post of Chairman of the Council of Ministers since 1952, became Chairman of the Presidium of the People's Great Khural (Head of State), succeeding Jamsrangiin Sambuu, who had died in May 1972. Tsedenbal was strongly pro-Soviet, had a Russian wife and was a great friend of Brezhnev, whose policies and lifestyle he emulated. The new Chairman of the Council of Ministers, Jambyn Batmönkh, was a comparative newcomer to politics. In March 1981 the close links between Mongolia and the USSR were highlighted when a Mongolian cosmonaut, Jügderdemidiin Gürragchaa, was flown by Soviet Soyuz spaceship to the Salyut space station.

In August 1984, following an extraordinary session of the MPRP Central Committee, Tsedenbal, who was in Moscow, was unexpectedly replaced—ostensibly owing to ill health and with his full agreement—as General Secretary of the Central Committee by Batmönkh. Dumaagiin Sodnom was elected to membership of the Politburo and the post of Chairman of the Council of Ministers. Tsedenbal was also removed from the Politburo and relieved of the post of Chairman of the Presidium of the People's Great Khural. Batmönkh was elected to this position in December. The extensive restructuring of a number of government ministries was carried out between 1987 and early 1988, with the aim of improving the efficiency and productiveness of the country's economy.

In November 1988 the MPRP Politburo, obliged to admit that economic renewal was not succeeding because of the need for social reforms, proposed wide-ranging improvements in procedures for party and parliamentary elections and other changes in the name of Gorbachev-style perestroika —*il tod* (openness) and *öörchlön shinechlelt* (renewal). The proposals were reported to have received widespread public approval.

Meanwhile, by 1986 Mongolia's relations with China appeared to have improved significantly, with a visit to Ulan Bator by the Chinese Vice-Minister of Foreign Affairs and the subsequent signing of an agreement on consular relations between the two countries. Mongolia's position as a 'buffer' state between China and the USSR was illustrated in July, when the Soviet leader, Mikhail Gorbachev, in a speech in Vladivostok, offered to withdraw some of the Soviet troops stationed in Mongolia as a step towards the normalization of relations between the USSR and China. A partial withdrawal (of about 20% of the estimated total) took place between April and June 1987, and a second stage began in May 1989. Following a series of senior-level Mongolian-Chinese negotiations, Mongolia and China subsequently declared the normalization of relations, and in May 1990 the Mongolian Head of State, Punsalmaagiin Ochirbat, paid a short visit to Beijing. The final stage of Soviet troop withdrawals was completed in September 1992.

THE BIRTH OF DEMOCRACY

Between December 1989 and March 1990 there was a great increase in political activity, as several newly formed opposition movements organized a series of peaceful demonstrations in Ulan Bator, demanding political and economic reforms. The most prominent of these groups was the Mongolian Democratic Association (MDA), which was founded in December 1989. In January 1990 dialogue was initiated between MPRP officials and representatives of the MDA, including its chief co-ordinator, Sanjaasürengiin Zorig (a lecturer at the Mongolian State University).

The emergence of further opposition groups, together with escalating public demonstrations (involving as many as 20,000 people), led to a crisis of confidence within the MPRP. At a party plenum, held in mid-March 1990, Batmönkh announced the resignation of the entire Politburo as well as of the Secretariat of the Central Committee. Gombojavyn Ochirbat, a former head of the Ideological Department of the Central Committee and a former Chairman of the Central Council of Mongolian Trade Unions, was elected the new General Secretary of the party, heading a new five-member Politburo. The plenum voted to expel the former MPRP General Secretary, Yumjaagiin Tsedenbal, from the party and to rehabilitate several prominent officials who had been removed by Tsedenbal in the 1960s, including Tömör-Ochir and other political rivals.

A session of the People's Great Khural, which was held shortly after the MPRP plenum, adopted amendments to the Constitution, including the removal of references to the MPRP as the 'guiding force' in Mongolian society, approved a new electoral law and brought forward the date of the next parliamentary election from 1991 to 1990.

In April 1990 an extraordinary congress of the MPRP was held, at which more than three-quarters of the members of the Central Committee were replaced. General Secretary Gombojavyn Ochirbat was elected to the restyled post of Chairman of the party. The Politburo was renamed the Presidium, and a new four-member Secretariat of the Central Committee was appointed.

In May 1990 the People's Great Khural approved a law on political parties, which legalized the new 'informal' movements through official registration; it also adopted further amendments to the Constitution, introducing a presidential system with a standing legislature, the State Little Khural, elected by proportional representation of parties.

The 1990 election of 430 deputies to the five-year 12th People's Great Khural was conducted in two stages, with 2,413 candidates standing in the first round held on 29 July, and the two leading candidates in each constituency going into the second round on 26 August. The first round had to be repeated in 30 constituencies and by 3 September, when the new People's Great Khural was convened, 422 deputies had been elected, although their numbers were given as follows: 357 from the MPRP (in some instances unopposed), 16 from the Mongolian Democratic Party (MDP, the political wing of the MDA), nine from the Mongolian Revolutionary Youth League, six from the Mongolian National Progress Party (MNPP), four from the Mongolian Social-Democratic Party (MSDP) and 39 without party affiliation.

In September 1990 the People's Great Khural elected Punsalmaagiin Ochirbat to be the country's first President, with a five-year term of office; the post of Chairman of the Presidium lapsed and Jambyn Gombojav was elected as the chamber's Chairman (Speaker). Radnaasümbereliin Gonchigdorj of the

MSDP was subsequently elected Chairman of the State Little Khural, ex officio becoming Vice-President of Mongolia. Dashiin Byambasüren was appointed Prime Minister (formerly the post of Chairman of the Council of Ministers) and began consultations on the formation of a multi-party government. The newly restyled Cabinet was elected by the State Little Khural in September and October. Under the amended Constitution, the President, Vice-President and cabinet ministers were not permitted to remain concurrently deputies of the People's Great Khural; therefore, by-elections of deputies to the People's Great Khural took place in mid-November.

The 20th Congress of the MPRP, which was held in February 1991, elected a new 99-member Central Committee, which, in turn, appointed a new Presidium. The Central Committee also elected a new Chairman, Büdragchaagiin Dash-Yondon, the Chairman of the Ulan Bator City Party Committee, who had become a member of the Presidium in November 1990.

A new Constitution was adopted by an almost unanimous vote of the People's Great Khural in January 1992 and entered into force in the following month. It provided for the election of a unicameral Mongolian Great Khural, comprising 76 members, to replace the People's Great Khural. The State Little Khural lapsed. The country's official name was changed from the Mongolian People's Republic to Mongolia and the communist gold star was removed from the national flag. Acknowledging the popularity of Genghis Khan, President Ochirbat referred to him as 'a national hero and the pride of the country'.

At the elections to the Mongolian Great Khural in June 1992, a total of 293 candidates stood in 26 constituencies, comprising the 18 *aimag* (provinces), the towns of Darkhan and Erdenet, and Ulan Bator City (six districts). The constituencies had two, three or four seats, according to the size of the local electorate. The MPRP presented 82 candidates, compared with 51 put forward by an alliance of the MDP, the MNPP and the United Party (UP), and 30 by the MSDP; six other parties and another alliance also took part, although with fewer candidates.

A total of 1,037,392 voters (95.6% of the electorate) participated in the elections, although 62,738 ballots were declared invalid. Candidates were elected by a simple majority, provided that they obtained the support of at least 50% of the electorate in their constituency. The MPRP candidates received altogether 1,719,887 votes (some 57%), while the candidates of the other parties (excluding independents) achieved a combined total of 1,205,350 votes (40%), of which the MDP-MNPP-UP alliance won 521,883 votes and the MSDP 304,548. However, the outcome of the elections was disproportionate, the MPRP winning 70 seats (71, including a pro-MPRP independent). The remaining seats were taken by the MDP (two, including an independent), the MSDP, the MNPP and the UP (one each).

The first session of the Mongolian Great Khural opened in July 1992 with the election of officers, the nomination of Puntsagiin Jasrai (who had been a Deputy Chairman of the Council of Ministers and a candidate member of the MPRP Politburo at the end of the communist period) to the post of Prime Minister, and the approval of his Cabinet. Natsagiin Bagabandi, a Vice-Chairman of the MPRP Central Committee, was elected Chairman of the Great Khural. Jambyn Gombojav (Chairman of the People's Great Khural from late 1990 to late 1991) was elected Vice-Chairman of the new Khural. Meanwhile, in June, a National Security Council was established, with the country's President as its Chairman, and the Prime Minister and Chairman of the Great Khural as its members.

In October 1992 the MDP, the MNPP, the UP and the Mongolian Renewal Party amalgamated to form the Mongolian National Democratic Party (MNDP), with a General Council headed by the MNPP leader, Davaadorjiin Ganbold, and including Sanjaasürengiin Zorig and other prominent opposition politicians. In the same month the MPRP Central Committee was renamed the MPRP Little Khural, and its membership was increased to 169 (subsequently to 198). The Presidium was replaced by a nine-member party Leadership Council.

Political life in Mongolia during the first half of 1993 was dominated by the country's first direct presidential election, held in early June. Apparently dissatisfied with the increasingly independent line adopted by the incumbent President, Punsalmaagiin Ochirbat, and angered by presidential vetoes on legislation proposed by the Government, the MPRP Little Khural decided not to support Ochirbat, who had been an MPRP member, and nominated Lodongiin Tüdev as its candidate. Meanwhile, Ochirbat received the nomination of the organizationally weaker opposition coalition of the MNDP and the MSDP. The MPRP expected to win by imposing party discipline on its more numerous supporters, but miscalculated. The outcome of the election was a victory for Ochirbat: 57.8% of the vote, as against 38.7% for Tüdev.

Amendments to the Election Law approved in early 1996 increased the number of constituencies for elections to the Great Khural from 26 to 76; all were to be single-seat constituencies, with representatives elected by the majority vote system. The parliamentary opposition parties, the MNDP and MSDP, supported by the Mongolian Green Party and the Mongolian Believers' (Buddhist) Democratic Party, formed a coalition, the Democratic Alliance, to contest the election of June 1996.

ELECTORAL DEFEAT OF THE MPRP

In the parliamentary elections held at the end of June 1996 the Democratic Alliance confounded most observers by winning 50 of the 76 seats in the Great Khural. The MPRP took only 25 seats, while one seat was won by a candidate of the pro-MPRP Mongolian Traditional United Party (MTUP), also known as the United Heritage (conservative) Party. A total of 1,057,182 voters (officially 92.2% of the electorate) participated in the elections; 47,022 ballots were spoiled. It could be calculated from constituency returns that the Democratic Alliance polled 469,586 votes (46.7%), the MPRP 408,977 (40.6%), and other parties and independents 127,684 (12.7%); the last figure included nearly 4,000 ballots that were blank but ruled as valid votes for no candidate.

The first session of the newly elected Great Khural opened in mid-July 1996 amid confusion. The election of the MSDP leader, Radnaasümbereliin Gonchigdorj (who had been Vice-President of Mongolia during 1990–92), to the post of Chairman of the Great Khural passed without incident. The Democratic Alliance's choice of Prime Minister, Mendsaikhany Enkhsaikhan (head of the Presidential Secretariat), was nominated by President Ochirbat and voted into office by the Great Khural. However, the MPRP had issued a list of demands, including the allocation of the vice-chairmanship of the Khural and two important standing committee chairmanships to MPRP members, and when these demands were rejected by the Democratic Alliance, MPRP members walked out of the Great Khural, leaving it inquorate and unable to function.

The boycott of the Great Khural by the MPRP lasted three days. The Khural elected the MNDP leader, Tsakhiagiin Elbegdorj, to be its Vice-Chairman; thereafter, the political confrontation focused on the six standing committees, the chairmen of which were all members of the Democratic Alliance. Moreover, the Democratic Alliance declared that it intended to remove MPRP officials from all important posts in the administration.

Eight members of Prime Minister Enkhsaikhan's Government were presented to the Great Khural in July 1996 and voted into office. The selection process had been delayed by a ruling of the Constitutional Commission (composed of MPRP appointees) that no member of the Government could remain a member of the Great Khural; the ruling was later annulled by the Great Khural. In the same month the MPRP Little Khural elected a new General Secretary, Nambaryn Enkhbayar, the former Minister of Culture, and a new Leadership Council.

In local government elections, held in October 1996, the Democratic Alliance won 208 seats at provincial council level, while the MPRP achieved 142. However, the Democratic Alliance failed to gain control of Ulan Bator City Council (MPRP 23 seats, MNDP nine, MSDP six, Mongolian Green Party one). At rural and urban district council level, the MPRP won 3,660 seats, the Democratic Alliance secured 3,169 and other parties 29 seats.

For the presidential election of 18 May 1997 the Democratic Alliance nominated the incumbent President, Punsalmaagiin Ochirbat, as its candidate. The MPRP put forward the former

Chairman of the Great Khural (1992–96), Natsagiin Bagabandi, who had been elected MPRP Chairman in February over Enkhbayar's head. The third party in the Mongolian Great Khural, the MTUP, nominated Jambyn Gombojav, who had defected from the MPRP. The election was won by Bagabandi, with 60.8% of the votes, compared with 29.8% for Ochirbat and 6.6% for Gombojav, a result that many observers saw as an expression of popular dissatisfaction with the Democratic Alliance. Meanwhile, the chairmanship of the MPRP passed to Nambaryn Enkhbayar, who, in mid-August, won the by-election for Bagabandi's former seat in the Great Khural.

A CRISIS OF CONFIDENCE

In April 1998 the Democratic Alliance decided that the Cabinet would be headed by the Alliance's leader and, unlike the Enkhsaikhan Cabinet, would comprise members of the Great Khural. Thus, Tsakhiagiin Elbegdorj, leader of the MNDP, was appointed Prime Minister, although the formation of the new Cabinet took a month. The policies of the Elbegdorj Cabinet did not differ much from those of its predecessor, although it sought to project a reformist image.

Soon afterwards the Government became embroiled in a dispute over its amalgamation of the state-owned Reconstruction Bank (which had been declared bankrupt after having overextended its credit) with the private Golomt Bank. The MPRP resorted to another boycott of the Great Khural. When the spring session closed (in August 1998), although the Khural had sat for 103 days, 20 working days had been lost, thus delaying the passage of important legislation, including finance bills.

Insisting that the Democratic Alliance Cabinet should resign, the MPRP returned to the Great Khural in July 1998 to pursue a motion of no confidence in the Government. The vote of no confidence was carried by 42 votes to 33, with 15 members of the Democratic Alliance 'crossing the floor'. The three-month-old Elbegdorj Government resigned, leaving the Democratic Alliance 30 days to choose a new Prime Minister.

Meanwhile, a new altercation arose over the management of the Mongolian-Russian copper-mining joint venture at Erdenet. In February 1998 the Enkhsaikhan Government had become embroiled in a dispute over the reappointment of the Mongolian director-general of the Erdenet enterprise, Shagdaryn Otgonbileg. For many years a member of the MPRP Little Khural, he had been in charge of the enterprise from its inception. The Russians wanted him to be maintained in the post, but Enkhsaikhan refused to reappoint him on the grounds that he had attempted to privatize part of the enterprise illegally. However, President Bagabandi intervened on the Russian side and Otgonbileg's contract was extended.

When Otgonbileg's contract finally ended, he refused to attend the ceremony in August 1998 marking the official transfer to his successor—the former Minister of Defence, Dambyn Dorligjav—and sought a court ruling that his 'dismissal' was illegal. The court's decision in his favour was overruled on appeal by the State Property Committee.

The Elbegdorj Cabinet established a government commission and imposed a 'special regime' on the Erdenet copper enterprise. President Bagabandi then stated that the Government could not impose such a 'special regime' on the enterprise unilaterally, without consulting the Russian co-directors. The government commission accused Otgonbileg of criminal negligence and appealed to the President to withdraw his support for the Russian position. President Bagabandi retorted that the 'special regime' had been imposed in disregard of his opinion, and he issued a statement criticizing anti-Russian reports in the 'official media'. Various MPRP leaders joined him in condemning the 'politicization' of the Erdenet affair as harmful to relations with their 'northern neighbour'. Later in the year a meeting of the full board of Erdenet approved Dorligjav's appointment and the 'special regime' was terminated.

In mid-August 1998 the Democratic Alliance nominated as their choice for the next Prime Minister Davaadorjiin Ganbold, the Chairman of the Economic Standing Committee of the Great Khural, who had served as Chief Deputy Prime Minister in 1990–92 and President of the MNDP in 1992–96. However, President Bagabandi refused to accept Ganbold's nomination, on the grounds that he had done nothing as Chairman of the Economic Standing Committee to resolve the bank merger crisis. Ganbold was nominated a second time, but the President rejected him again. The Democratic Alliance protested that the President had no constitutional right to reject its nomination, but he did so yet again and put forward his own nominee, Dogsomyn Ganbold, whom the Democratic Alliance ignored. After Davaadorjiin Ganbold's nomination had been rejected a sixth time by the President, the Democratic Alliance presented a new nominee, the acting Minister of External Relations, Rinchinnyamyn Amarjargal. His nomination was accepted by President Bagabandi on 31 August 1998 but rejected by the Great Khural on the following day by a majority of only one vote. After a further period of delay, the Democratic Alliance nominated a new candidate, Galsangiin Gankhuyag, who was rejected by the President. In late September Bagabandi rejected a further nominee, Erdeniin Bat-Üül, who had been replaced as Vice-President of the MNDP by Davaadorjiin Ganbold in August.

Sanjaasürengiin Zorig, the Minister of Infrastructure Development and founder of the MDA, was murdered at his home in October 1998. Although never nominated for the post, Zorig had been widely regarded as a potential premier. His murderers were not found. After Zorig's state funeral, President Bagabandi issued the names of six nominees of his own for the premiership, including Dogsomyn Ganbold and the Mayor of Ulan Bator, Janlavyn Narantsatsralt. The Democratic Alliance ignored the presidential list and, for the seventh time, nominated Davaadorjiin Ganbold. Although the nomination was supported by all 48 Democratic Alliance members of the Great Khural, the President again rejected him. Later in the same month the political crisis was deepened by the Constitutional Commission's latest ruling, reaffirming that members of the Great Khural could not serve concurrently in the Government. (The ruling superseded an amendment to the Law on the Status of Great Khural Members adopted in January 1998.) Two months later the Democratic Alliance finally nominated Bagabandi's candidate, Janlavyn Narantsatsralt, who was appointed Prime Minister in early December. The formation of his Government was completed in mid-January 1999.

Narantsatsralt's Government remained in power for just over six months. In July 1999 the Prime Minister was challenged in the Great Khural over a letter that he had written in January to Yurii Maslyukov, First Deputy Chairman of the Russian Government, in which he seemingly acknowledged Russia's right to privatize its share in the Erdenet joint venture without reference to the Mongolian authorities. Unable to offer a satisfactory explanation, in late July Narantsatsralt lost a vote of confidence, in which MSDP members of the Great Khural voted with the opposition MPRP. The Democratic Alliance nominated Rinchinnyamyn Amarjargal for the post of Prime Minister, but the proposal was immediately challenged by President Bagabandi. The President insisted that, following the Constitutional Commission's ruling of late 1998, he could consider Amarjargal's suitability for nomination in the Great Khural only after the candidate had resigned from his parliamentary seat. After several days of arguments, representatives of the Democratic Alliance and the President adopted a formula that allowed the Great Khural's approval of the prime ministerial nomination and the nominee's resignation of his Great Khural seat to take place simultaneously. Amarjargal was elected Prime Minister at the end of July. The ministers of Narantsatsralt's Government remained in office in an acting capacity until early September, when all but one (the Minister of Law) were reappointed. In November Amarjargal replaced Narantsatsralt as President of the MNDP.

The unexpected arrival in Ulan Bator of the ninth Javzandamba Khutagt in July 1999 was welcomed with great enthusiasm by crowds of Mongolian Buddhists. The elderly Jambalnamdol Choijiijantsan, recognized by the Dalai Lama in 1992 as an incarnation of the Bogd Gegeen, had been living in Dharamsala after escaping from Tibet. He was taken to Karakorum to be enthroned, and stayed in Mongolia for several weeks before returning to India. It was unclear whether the Dalai Lama had authorized his visit, and there was some tension in relations with Gandan monastery, long described as the 'centre' of Mongolian Buddhism. In 2009 the 'Ninth Bogd' revisited Mongolia to supervise the enthronement of lesser incarnations or *khutagt,* and in 2011 he adopted Mongolian citizenship and took up permanent residence in the country.

The 1992 Constitution was amended for the first time in December 1999 by a Mongolian Great Khural decree, supported by all three parliamentary parties, which, inter alia, simplified the procedure for the appointment of the Prime Minister and allowed members of the Great Khural to serve as government ministers while retaining their seats in the legislature. However, the President vetoed the decree, stating that the amendments could not be approved by the Great Khural alone. The presidential veto was rejected by the Great Khural in January 2000, but in March a five-member session of the Constitutional Commission ruled that the decree had been unconstitutional. When the Great Khural opened its spring session in April, members rejected the ruling and refused to discuss it.As the next parliamentary elections approached, a breakaway grouping of the MNDP reconstituted the MDP, and a faction of the MSDP founded the Mongolian New Social Democratic Party. Sanjaasürengiin Oyuun, the sister of the murdered minister, Zorig, established the Civil Courage Party (CCP or Irgenii Zorig Party), drawing away from the MNDP several more members of the Great Khural, and formed an electoral alliance with the Mongolian Green Party. The MNDP therefore formed a new Democratic Alliance with the Mongolian Believers' Democratic Party.

THE RETURN TO POWER OF THE MPRP

At the elections, held in early July 2000, three coalitions and 13 parties were represented by a total of 603 candidates, including 27 independents. The MPRP won 72 of the 76 seats in the Great Khural. Prime Minister Rinchinnyamyn Amarjargal and his entire Cabinet lost their seats. The MPRP received 50.2% of the votes cast, the level of participation being 82.4% of the electorate.

The four seats not taken by the MPRP went to Sanjaasürengiin Oyuun (President of the CCP); Badarchiin Erdenebat (Chairman of the Mongolian Democratic New Socialist Party—MDNSP); Lamjavyn Gündalai (independent), a businessman from Khövsgöl Province; and ex-Prime Minister Janlavyn Narantsatsralt (MNDP). The Democratic Alliance, which presented 71 candidates, received 13% of the votes cast; the MDNSP, with 73 candidates, received 10.7% of the votes cast. The 67 MSDP candidates received 8.9% of the votes cast, but won no seats.

When the new Great Khural opened, Lkhamsürengiin Enebish, the MPRP General Secretary, was elected to the post of Chairman of the chamber. However, the nomination of the MPRP Chairman, Nambaryn Enkhbayar, for the post of Prime Minister was rejected by President Natsagiin Bagabandi, on the grounds that priority be given to the constitutional amendments. After a week of discussion a compromise was reached whereby Enkhbayar's nomination was presented to the Great Khural, while the amendments remained in force pending a Great Khural debate and a full nine-member session of the Constitutional Commission. The Great Khural approved Prime Minister Enkhbayar's appointment by 67 MPRP members' votes to three.

Enkhbayar divided the former Ministry of Health and Social Welfare into two separate ministries: the Ministry of Health and the Ministry of Social Protection and Welfare. The Ministry of Law became the Ministry of Justice and Home Affairs and took charge of the border troops. Furthermore, the MSDP alleged that the new Government was acting in violation of the spirit of the Constitution, by dismissing large numbers of civil servants because of their party affiliation. In September 2000 Rinchinnyamyn Amarjargal, leader of the MNDP, and Radnaasümbereliin Gonchigdorj, leader of the MSDP, signed a joint declaration announcing that a conference would be held in December, to formalize the merging of the two parties. This was done with a view to ensuring the necessary parliamentary basis for Gonchigdorj's nomination in the 2001 presidential election. The two parties formed a new Coalition of Democratic Forces (together with four smaller parties) to contest the provincial and Ulan Bator local government elections held on 1 October 2000. None the less, the MPRP won 552 of the 695 seats available in the city and *aimag* (provincial) khurals, with a voter participation rate of almost 60.8% being recorded.

At the conference held in early December 2000, five democratic parties—the MNDP, the MSDP, the MDP, the Mongolian Believers' Democratic Party, and the Mongolian Democratic Renewal Party—decided to disband themselves and form a new Democratic Party (DP). Dambyn Dorligjav, the former Minister of Defence and director of the Erdenet copper combine, was elected Chairman, while ex-Prime Minister Janlavyn Narantsatsralt and former Minister of the Environment Sonomtserengiin Mendsaikhan were elected Vice-Chairmen. Lamjavyn Gündalai, who had been elected to the Great Khural as an independent, also joined the DP. After the formation of the DP's primary organizations nationwide in February 2001, they elected the party's National Consultative Committee (NCC), comprising two members from each of the Great Khural's 76 constituencies. The members included many of the former leaders of the MNDP and MSDP who had failed to be elected in the Great Khural elections of July 2000. In July 2001 the DP's Secretary-General, Zandaakhüügiin Enkhbold, was released to attend a study course in the USA, and his duties were assumed by the former Mongolian ambassador to the United Kingdom, Tsedenjavyn Sükhbaatar. A new Secretary-General, Norovyn Altankhuyag, was elected in September 2001.

In mid-December 2000 the Great Khural readopted unchanged the decree of December 1999 amending the 1992 Constitution for immediate implementation. The President's veto of the decree was rejected, but the Constitutional Commission was unable to meet in full session because the election of replacements for time-expired members was delayed in the Great Khural. President Bagabandi finally placed his seal on the amendments in May 2001, without having approved them.

The MPRP's 23rd Congress was held at the end of February 2001. The Chairman, Nambaryn Enkhbayar, and General Secretary, Lkhamsürengiin Enebish, were both re-elected. Two of the three party secretaries, Taukein Sultaan and Baldangiin Enkhmandakh, were released for diplomatic duties, while Sanjbegziin Tömör-Ochir and Luvsandagvyn Amarsanaa joined the secretariat, although Amarsanaa was shortly afterwards nominated to be the next Mongolian ambassador to China. The membership of the party's Leadership Council was increased from 11 to 15.

The presidential election of May 2001 was won by the MPRP's Natsagiin Bagabandi, who received 574,553 votes (nearly 58.0% of the total ballot), as against 362,684 votes for Radnaasümbereliin Gonchigdorj of the DP (36.6%) and 35,139 votes for Luvsandambyn Dashnyam of the CCP (3.5%).

In January 2001, meanwhile, a member of the Great Khural and former director of the Erdenet copper combine, Shagdaryn Otgonbileg, was killed when an Mi-8 helicopter carrying 23 passengers and crew investigating the *zud* (starvation of livestock) in western Mongolia crashed. The eight dead included several UN staff. In May Otgonbileg was replaced in the Great Khural by his widow, Danzandarjaagiin Tuyaa, who was elected unopposed. The Chairman of the Great Khural, Lkhamsürengiin Enebish, died in September, and was succeeded by Sanjbegziin Tömör-Ochir. Enebish was replaced as General Secretary of the MPRP by Doloonjingiin Idevkhten. In March 2002 Sanjaasürengiin Oyuun's CCP merged with Bazarsadyn Jargalsaikhan's Mongolian Republican Party (MRP) to form the Civil Courage Republican Party, under Oyuun's leadership.

In June 2002 the Great Khural approved the Law on Land and the Law on Land Privatization, both of which were scheduled to enter into force during 2003. Although less than 1% of the country's total territory was to be made available for privatization, the laws generated a great deal of controversy. From November 2002 there were several demonstrations by farmers who were arrested for parking their tractors on Sükhbaatar Square in the centre of Ulan Bator. Headed by Erdeniin Bat-Üül of the DP, President of the Movement for Justice in Land Privatization, they protested that the poor would be denied land by the 'oligarchy'.

Meanwhile, in the predominantly Kazakh province of Bayan-Ölgii, in western Mongolia, dissatisfaction with local leaders led to hunger strikes and demonstrations by up to 4,000 people in February and March 2003. Although poverty and unemployment remained rife, the immediate causes of the protests seemed to be corruption and the abuse of human rights. In May the three Kazakh members of the Great Khural were refused permission to form a national minority group of Great Khural members. The Law on the State Language, adopted by the Great Khural in the same month, was interpreted to mean that Kazakh speakers in Bayan-Ölgii would have to deal with registration and other local government matters in the Mongolian language.

The discovery of the remains of several hundred people at Khambyn Ovoo in the Ulan Bator city suburbs in May 2003 reopened the debate about the political purges of the 1930s. Most of the remains were shown to be of Buddhist lamas shot in the head; it was decided to cremate their bones and build a memorial stupa. Meanwhile, the slow process of exonerating the unjustly condemned victims of Choibalsan's purges and the compensation of victims' relatives was continued by the Rehabilitation Commission, chaired by a deputy chairman of the Great Khural, and the term of the rehabilitation law was extended until 2011.

In June 2003 the Mongolian Great Khural approved the National Latin Script Programme, which declared that drafting of standards for the 'Romanization of the letters of the Mongolian Cyrillic Alphabet' was already under way. The preparatory stage was to remain in force during 2003–04, while the rules for the new Latin script were formulated and plans drawn up for the publication of textbooks, dictionaries and other aids, to be followed by the implementation stage, which was to run during 2005–06. However, the 'standards' were found to be defective and the programme was abandoned.

The National Human Rights Commission's 2003 annual report was highly critical of bureaucracy, corruption and cronyism. The police were accused of numerous cases of brutality, the report stating that the right of detainees to contact a lawyer was widely abused. The National Human Rights Programme was adopted in December. Also in 2003, Damirangiin Enkhbat, who had been resident in France, was reported to have been abducted by Mongolian secret agents and subsequently imprisoned in Mongolia. Attempts were made to force his confession to knowledge of a supposed plot by some National Democratic Party members to murder Sanjaasürengiin Zorig in 1998. He and his lawyer were later sentenced for 'disclosing state secrets'. In early 2004 reports from the human rights organization Amnesty International suggested that Enkhbat had been tortured during interrogation. In June 2005 the UN's Special Rapporteur on Torture and Other Cruel, Inhuman or Degrading Treatment or Punishment, Manfred Nowak, carried out a prison inspection and met Enkhbat and his lawyer. Nowak's report, which was published in December but did not appear in the Mongolian press until a year later, condemned torture in Mongolian prisons and criticized the provisions of the Law on State Secrets for preventing dissemination of information about death sentences. Enkhbat died in February 2006, shortly after his release from prison on the grounds of ill health. (See External Relations)

THE 2004 ELECTION IMPASSE

In the spring of 2004 the political campaigning began for elections to the Mongolian Great Khural, which were held in late June. The new General Election Committee (GEC) incorporated many MPRP nominees. The electorate was calculated to total 1,279,516 persons, but there was no provision for the 70,000 people who were resident abroad to vote. The opposition Motherland-Democracy election pact formed by Mendsaikhany Enkhsaikhan's DP and Badarchiin Erdenebat's Motherland-MDNSP was joined by Sanjaasürengiin Oyuun's Civil Courage Republican Party, minus the followers of Bazarsadyn Jargalsaikhan, who left to re-establish the MRP as the Republican Party (RP).

After the registration of participating political parties and coalitions the GEC set about the registration of candidates, rejecting all Mongolian Youth Party candidates. The final count was 241: 76 each for the MPRP and the Motherland-Democracy coalition, 33 for the RP, 23 for the National Solidarity Party, nine for the MTUP, five for the Mongolian Green Party, four for the Liberal Party and 15 independents.

The parliamentary elections of 27 June 2004 dealt a major reverse to the MPRP and left the political scene in disarray: the MPRP and the Motherland-Democracy coalition had each won about one-half of the seats, leaving neither with the necessary majority of 39 (one-half of the Great Khural seats plus one seat). The three independents elected, although all DP members, were ruled as not counting in this process. The RP won one seat. The number of votes cast was 1,051,812 (82.2% of registered voters). In 25 constituencies there was a straight contest between the MPRP and the Motherland-Democracy coalition.

The GEC submitted the results in 74 of the 76 constituencies to President Bagabandi at the first session of the newly elected Great Khural, which was boycotted by the MPRP. The President stated that, because of the need to address many important issues, it was right to convene the first session, despite the fact that two results had yet to be confirmed. However, the Motherland-Democracy members were not allowed to take the oath. Meeting separately, 70 of the MPRP members elected in 2000 filed a lawsuit against the President on the grounds that he had contravened the Constitution and allowed the Great Khural to meet without a quorum (a minimum of 57 members being present) before the final session of the outgoing Great Khural had been held. The closing session of the legislature released the Great Khural's Deputy Chairman, Jamsrangiin Byambadorj (who had lost his parliamentary seat in the recent election), to take up a vacant seat in the Constitutional Commission and accused the President of acting unconstitutionally in convening the first session of the incoming legislature. All these decisions were vetoed by President Bagabandi in late July 2004 as unconstitutional.

Postponed after another MPRP boycott, the first plenary session of the new Great Khural was held in late July 2004, when 74 members were sworn in. The first business was the election of the new Chairman of the chamber. The MPRP group supported the candidature of the MPRP leader and acting Prime Minister, Nambaryn Enkhbayar, but protracted discussion of this proposal with the Motherland-Democracy members of the Khural continued for days without resolution. In late July the MPRP members of the Great Khural proposed that the Motherland-Democracy members should nominate the next Prime Minister, while the Motherland-Democracy members proposed the formation of a joint working group to draw up a programme for a government of 'national accord'. Meanwhile, the GEC had still not declared the results in the remaining two constituencies, and the Motherland-Democracy coalition threatened to boycott the Khural until it did so.

Eventually, at the end of August 2004 former Prime Minister Nambaryn Enkhbayar of the MPRP was elected Chairman of the Great Khural, and Tsakhiagiin Elbegdorj of the Motherland-Democracy coalition was nominated as Prime Minister. However, the appointment of new government ministers was further delayed. Although the newly elected members of the Mongolian Great Khural agreed on the formation, chairmanship and membership of the Khural's standing committees and sub-committees, discussion of the basic principles for the establishment of a coalition government was protracted. Finally, after months of disagreement between the two main parliamentary groups, in late September a new Government was appointed under the leadership of Elbegdorj. It had been agreed that the terms of office of the Prime Minister and the newly created post of Deputy Prime Minister would be shared between the MPRP and the Motherland-Democracy coalition, implying that Prime Minister Elbegdorj would be required to cede his position to an MPRP prime minister after two years. The deputy ministers, one-half nominated by the Motherland-Democracy coalition and one-half by the MPRP, were appointed in November and December, respectively.

COALITION POLITICS

At the end of December 2004 Radnaasümbereliin Gonchigdorj took the chairmanship of the DP at a meeting of the executive of its NCC and installed his supporters in other senior posts. However, his predecessor, Mendsaikhany Enkhsaikhan, appeared to retain the support of the party's National Assembly. Although a court ruled that the leadership change was contrary to the party's regulations, it declined to intervene. (In March 2005 the NCC confirmed Gonchigdorj's chairmanship.) Badarchiin Erdenebat, the Minister of Defence and leader of the Motherland-MDNSP, withdrew from the Motherland-Democracy coalition, which then collapsed. In January 2005 the leader of the Civil Courage Republican Party, Sanjaasürengiin Oyuun, was obliged to relinquish the post of Deputy Chairwoman of the Great Khural. Erdenebat re-registered his party as the Motherland Party. Prime Minister Elbegdorj took responsibility for the defence portfolio from Erdenebat in February, and a new Minister of Defence, Tserenkhüügiin Sharavdorj, was appointed in March. The Motherland-Democracy coalition's parliamentary group in the Great Khural disbanded, and many DP members, including Gonchigdorj but not Enkhsaikhan, joined the Khural's MPRP group members to form a parliamentary 'combined group', of which Gonchigdorj was elected deputy chairman. Meanwhile, Doloonjingiin Idevkhten was replaced as General Secretary of the MPRP by Sanjaagiin Bayar, the Mongolian ambassador to Russia, on his return to Mongolia.

In February 2005 Jügderdemidiin Gürragchaa (MPRP), Mongolian cosmonaut and former Minister of Defence, was finally declared the winner of the 2004 parliamentary elections in his constituency and was duly sworn in as a member of the Great Khural. Meanwhile, the final result in the constituency of DP candidate Zandaakhüügiin Enkhbold was still being disputed in the courts. Enkhbold had already accepted the post of Chairman of the State Property Committee in the previous December.

The National Human Rights Commission's 2004 annual report noted the need for the rights of vulnerable groups and the human rights activities of legal organizations to remain the 'centre of attention'. The report also indicated that torture and severe punishment were still common and that many police officers equated punishment with physical torture. Provisions of the UN Convention against Torture and other Cruel, Inhumane or Degrading Treatment or Punishment, which Mongolia joined in 2000, were not widely known, and effective measures were not being taken to curb illegal acts, the report stated.

The period March–May 2005 was dominated by the politics of the Mongolian presidential election. The candidates were: Nambaryn Enkhbayar, Chairman of the MPRP and Chairman of the Great Khural; Mendsaikhany Enkhsaikhan, former Prime Minister and former Chairman of the DP; Bazarsadyn Jargalsaikhan, Chairman of the RP; and Badarchiin Erdenebat, Chairman of the Motherland Party. The election, held on 22 May, was won by Enkhbayar, who secured over 53% of the votes cast, more than those for the three other candidates combined.

At the MPRP's congress in June 2005 the Mayor of Ulan Bator, Miyeegombyn Enkhbold, was chosen to replace Enkhbayar as the new party Chairman. The party's Leadership Council was enlarged to 21 members: nine re-elected (with four failing to secure re-election) and 10 new members, including Party Secretary Yondongiin Otgonbayar, the Ministers of External Relations, of Food and Agriculture, and of Health, and six MPRP Great Khural members. Enkhbayar was inaugurated as President of Mongolia on 24 June. At the beginning of July the Great Khural elected the Minister of Justice and Home Affairs, Tsendiin Nyamdorj (of the MPRP), to replace Enkhbayar as Chairman of the Great Khural.

After an attempt by the MPRP to force the Prime Minister to resign, including the expulsion of DP members from the 'combined' MPRP parliamentary group (the 'group of 62'), shortly before the closing of its spring 2005 session the Great Khural voted in favour of the formation of a DP parliamentary group, which 25 party members (headed by Gonchigdorj) joined. The by-election in Enkhbayar's former constituency in August was won by the MPRP Chairman, Miyeegombyn Enkhbold. In the same month a coalition accord had been signed by the DP and the MPRP to 'respect the results of the 2004 elections and maintain the stability of the coalition government'. In September 2005 the Supreme Court finally dismissed the MPRP's appeal against the victory of Zandaakhüügiin Enkhbold in his constituency in the 2004 elections.

Rebuilding of the south front of the State Palace (which houses the Great Khural and government offices) to accommodate a Genghis Khan Memorial and state ceremonial complex began in August 2005. The work was carried out in accordance with presidential and government decrees adopted in May 2001 with a view to celebrating, in August 2006, the 800th anniversary of the founding of the Mongolian state by Genghis Khan. Plans drawn up in March 2003 provided for the demolition of the mausoleum of revolutionary leaders Sükhbaatar and Choibalsan, which stood where the complex was to be built, and for the removal of their remains for burial at the Altan-Ölgii cemetery in Ulan Bator. The Government claimed that it had the consent of the relatives to transfer the remains of Sükhbaatar and Choibalsan. In an overnight operation in August 2005 the remains were secretly removed from the mausoleum and cremated. There was widespread public dissatisfaction that they had been disposed of in such an 'undignified' manner. The partly completed south facade of the complex, with a 5.4-m bronze seated statue of Genghis Khan, was inaugurated by President Enkhbayar at a grand ceremony in July 2006. In November the finished facade was declared open.

In January 2006 a Motherland Party deputy defected to the MPRP, thereby giving the latter its 38th seat in the Great Khural. Following demands by the MPRP for Prime Minister Elbegdorj's resignation, the 10 MPRP ministers in his Cabinet resigned and the 'grand coalition' Government was voted out of office. Miyeegombyn Enkhbold, MPRP Chairman and Mayor of Ulan Bator, was elected Prime Minister. He then formed a new 'national solidarity' Government; this included the leaders of the Motherland Party and the RP, Erdenebat and Jargalsaikhan; ex-DP member Gündalai, who had recently established a new party, the Party of the People; and three DP members, including Enkhsaikhan and Narantsatsralt, who were subsequently expelled from the rump DP, now excluded from the MPRP's new coalition. One newspaper described these politicians as 'unscrupulous'; another claimed that the MPRP's abandonment of its coalition with the DP was intended to halt the progress of a new anti-corruption bill that would focus on corruption within the ruling party's ranks. The new Anti-Corruption Law was finally adopted in July, eight years after the first draft.

Following his appointment in January 2006 to the post of Deputy Prime Minister, Mendsaikhany Enkhsaikhan, and his supporters, began forming a new party, which was named the National New Party at its first congress in May. After the death of Great Khural member Onomoogiin Enkhsaikhan in March, the resultant by-election was won by the Minister of Education, Culture and Science, Ölziisaikhany Enkhtüvshin (MPRP).

The political upheaval of early 2006 also delayed a decision on amendments to the 1997 Minerals Law, introduced at the end of December 2005, which caused disquiet among foreign investors in Mongolia's mining industry. Amid much public debate about the merits of state control of the country's resources and various protests, the Great Khural discussed the amendments, consolidated them in committee and finally adopted a new redaction of the 1997 law in July 2006. Mining licences were to be granted only to companies, not to individuals; foreign and domestic investors in mining were to be taxed at the same rate; stability agreements were to be replaced by investment contracts; and local people in proposed mining areas would be granted greater rights with regard to decisions on exploitation licences. Also, the Government would have the right to acquire up to 50% of the resources of deposits discovered with the help of state funds and to control up to 34% of resources obtained from privately funded deposits. None the less, dissatisfaction with the Minerals Law and the negotiation of the Canadian firm Ivanhoe's terms of management of the Oyu Tolgoi gold and copper deposit were sufficient for final decisions to be postponed.

In February 2007 Danzandarjaagiin Tuyaa of the MPRP was appointed Minister of Health, to replace Lamjavyn Gündalai of the Party of the People, who had been dismissed. The Minister of Social Welfare and Labour, Luvsangiin Odonchimed of the MPRP, resigned and was replaced by another MPRP member,

Damdingiin Demberel. In April Tserengiin Davaadorj was appointed to succeed Bazarsadyn Jargalsaikhan as Minister of Industry and Trade. Meanwhile, in preparation for the parliamentary elections in mid-2008, the Great Khural approved amendments to the Law on Elections restoring large multi-candidate constituencies similar to those prevailing at the time of the 1992 elections and introducing a quota for female members. In early 2007 it emerged that Tsendiin Nyamdorj, the Chairman (Speaker) of the Great Khural, had re-edited legislation, including the Election Law and the Minerals Law, after the final texts had been approved by the Great Khural. Nyamdorj's explanation was accepted by some of his MPRP colleagues, but, following a Constitutional Commission ruling that his actions were unconstitutional, in June he was obliged to resign from his post. He was replaced by the Deputy Chairman, Danzangiin Lündeejantsan.

At the MPRP's 25th Congress in October 2007, delegates expressed their dissatisfaction with Miyeegombyn Enkhbold's performance by voting to remove him from the chairmanship of the party, in favour of General Secretary Sanjaagiin Bayar. The members of a new 255-member MPRP Little Khural and 23-member Leadership Council were later announced; in total, 13 of the 19 Leadership Council members elected in 2005 were replaced and three were re-elected. Former MPRP secretary Yondongiin Otgonbayar was elected General Secretary and six new secretaries were approved, including Enkhbold and Nyamdorj. For the first time intra-party political movements and factions were represented by three Leadership Council members; also of note was the inclusion of four women, one of them a Mongolian Kazakh. The reorganization of the Little Khural had been the subject of wide speculation and was regarded as an important stage in the preparation of the final list of MPRP candidates for the parliamentary elections scheduled for June 2008.

An important consequence of these events was Enkhbold's resignation as Prime Minister in early November 2007, thus allowing Bayar's election to the position later in the month. Bayar's first acts included the appointment of Ravdangiin Bold, ambassador to the USA, to the post of head of the Main Directorate of Intelligence and the dismissal of the ministers responsible for disaster reduction and professional inspection, their portfolios passing to the new Deputy Prime Minister, Enkhbold. After the signing of co-operation agreements with the CCP and the National New Party, Bayar formed a new Cabinet in December. Among the three female appointees was CCP leader Sanjaasürengiin Oyuun, who assumed the role of Minister of External Relations. Meanwhile, the Mayor and Governor of Ulan Bator, Tsogtyn Batbayar, was replaced in December by Tüdeviin Bilegt, head of the Presidential Secretariat.

Janlavyn Narantsatsralt, Minister of Construction and Urban Development and a former Prime Minister, was killed in a car accident in November 2007. He was replaced by Tserendashiin Tsolmon, who also became Chairman of the National New Party in February 2008. In the same month a new political organization, the Mongolian Democratic Movement Party, was registered. The annual report of the Mongolian National Human Rights Commission, published at the end of June, pointed out that the secrecy surrounding death sentences in Mongolia continued to prevent the release of information about appeals for clemency, method of execution, disposal of the corpse and cancellation of civil registration. Mongolian courts had issued a total of 24 death sentences in 2006 and 26 in 2007.

On 29 December 2007, by presidential decree, Mongolia celebrated 'National Freedom Day' for the first time, the anniversary of the 'National Liberation Revolution' of 1911 (the fall of the Qing dynasty and proclamation of Mongolia's independence).

THE ELECTIONS OF 2008 AND BEYOND

At the end of December 2007 the Great Khural amended the country's Election Law to remove the requirement for a 30% quota of female members in the next legislature, and a presidential veto on the amendment was dismissed. Great Khural member Lamjavyn Gündalai abandoned his Party of the People to rejoin the DP. As preparations for the elections commenced and as those senior civil servants standing for election to the Great Khural resigned from their posts, the Main Directorate of Intelligence urged vigilance against 'unregistered self-styled blocs and fronts' engaged in activities against national security, said to be promoting a 'national freedom revolution' and the establishment of an 'all-people's special plenipotentiary court'. The MPRP announced the arrival of two British Labour Party experts to assist with the training of the election managers for the campaign.

The Election Committee's final list of 356 registered candidates, standing in 26 constituencies for 76 seats, was released on 23 June 2008. Candidates represented 11 parties: the MPRP (76 candidates), the DP (also 76), the CCP (29), the MTUP (26), the RP (20), the National New Party (19), the Mongolian Democratic Movement Party (14), the Motherland Party (11), the Freedom Implementer Party (two), the Development Programme Party (one) and the Mongolian Liberal Party (one), as well as the Citizens' Alliance (CA, 36 candidates, representing the Citizens' Movement Party, the Mongolian Green Party and the MSDP). There were 45 independent candidates, some standing unofficially for the above parties. The Party of the People was registered but did not present any candidates.

The elections to the fifth Great Khural took place on 29 June 2008; 74.3% of the electorate were reported to have voted. On the following day the MPRP called a press conference at which MPRP Chairman Bayar thanked the Mongolian people for re-electing the MPRP. 'Observers have concluded that the election was fair . . . However, many complicated situations arose, which needed additional attention during the counting,' he stated. DP Chairman Elbegdorj subsequently held a press conference at which he demanded a recount of the votes, claiming that the MPRP had manipulated the results of the poll. The leader of the CA, Enkhbat, declared that both the DP and the MPRP had been guilty of unethical behaviour.

On 1 July 2008 the newspaper *Zuuny Medee* reported that 48 seats had been awarded to the MPRP and 28 to the DP; another newspaper, *Önöödör*, gave 44 seats to the MPRP, 25 to the DP and one to an independent. The announcement of the provisional results giving victory to the MPRP prompted a riot in Ulan Bator: the MPRP headquarters were set on fire, five people were killed (four by gunshot wounds), hundreds were injured and some 700 people were arrested. President Enkhbayar declared a four-day state of emergency and a night curfew in central Ulan Bator, where armoured cars patrolled the streets. Only stations of the National Public Radio and Television were permitted to broadcast.

The MPRP's publication, *Ünen*, attributed the disorder to DP leader Elbegdorj, and this version of events was repeated by the Russian media. At a press conference on 2 July 2008 the Minister of Justice and Home Affairs, Tsendiin Mönkh-Orgil, accused candidates of the CA and of the DP, namely Jalbaasürengiin Batzandan, Otgonjargalayn Magnai and Radnaagiin Burmaa, of having organized a demonstration. The minister had ordered the temporary closure to traffic of the area around Sükhbaatar Square, the MPRP building and the central post office. Meanwhile, Elbegdorj had held a press conference at DP headquarters in Sükhbaatar Square and then he had met demonstrators. Batzandan, Magnai and RP Chairman Bazarsadyn Jargalsaikhan had led some 500 people to the MPRP headquarters, which had been attacked and then set on fire, Mönkh-Orgil claimed. He announced the formation of a 10-member emergency staff under the National Security Council including himself as chairman, the Governor of Ulan Bator, the Armed Forces Chief of Staff, the Director of Intelligence, the commander of the Border Troops and the acting Chief of Police.

The Chairman of the Election Committee, Bataagiin Battulga, released on Public Television a provisional list of the names of 66 successful election candidates and ballot percentages for all but three of the 26 constituencies, giving 43 seats to the MPRP, 21 to the DP, one to the CCP and one to an independent. The Open Society Forum then reported that Battulga's list comprised 74 election winners, with ballot percentages for all but 11 seats in four constituencies, awarding 44 seats to the MPRP, 27 to the DP, one to the CCP, one to the CA and one to an independent. *Ödriin Sonin*, a daily newspaper, published 'preliminary' election results that listed 75 names and differed from Battulga's list only in the omission (under Bayangol constituency 25) of the name of candidate Sodnomzunduin Erdene, a member of the DP. Political parties continued to protest and to demand recounts in some constituencies. However, there was no further violence, and the state of emergency waslifted on 4 July 2008. Meanwhile, Batzandan and Magnai were arrested and charged under the Criminal Code. (Bazarsadyn Jargalsaikhan, the Chairman of the RP, was also arrested two months later.)

In mid-July 2008 Election Committee Chairman Battulga issued a list of 66 election winners' names and ballot percentages for all but three constituencies, giving 39 seats to the MPRP, 25 to the DP, one to the CCP and one to an independent. On the same day the Open Society Forum posted the 'unified list' of election results, which Battulga had presented to President Enkhbayar. The list contained all winners and losers in their order of registration, with ballot percentages and numbers, as well as constituency voting statistics.

A presidential decree ordered the newly elected fifth Great Khural to hold its first meeting on 23 July 2008. The newly elected DP members attended the opening but walked out of the session, thereby removing the quorum of members, who were unable to register, thus preventing the conduct of any business. Representatives of the MPRP and DP were instructed by President Enkhbayar to hold meetings, with a view to finding a solution to the impasse. DP leader Elbegdorj rejected his party's involvement in the new Great Khural pending the publication of the final full list of election results. The DP then requested that the Prosecutor General investigate the actions of Election Committee Chairman Battulga (who was replaced the following January). Meanwhile, President Enkhbayar left Ulan Bator to attend the opening of the Olympic Games in Beijing.

Following several further unsuccessful attempts to convene the new session of the Great Khural, at the end of August 2008 a total of 67 elected members, including DP representatives, decided to attend, whereupon they were registered. In September the Great Khural elected MPRP member Damdingiin Demberel as its Chairman (Speaker). The outgoing Chairman, Danzangiin Lündeejantsan, was chosen to head the MPRP group in the Great Khural. The legislature subsequently approved the appointment of two Vice-Chairmen (Deputy Speakers), Gavaagiin Batkhüü (a member of the DP) and Nyamaagiin Enkhbold (MPRP). Meanwhile, Elbegdorj resigned from the leadership of the DP and was replaced by Norovyn Altankhuyag. By mid-September the number of declared seats in the legislature had risen to 72; the MPRP's representation in the Great Khural thus increased by two seats to total 44, and the number of DP seats rose by one to reach 26. The final results for three of the four seats of the Ulan Bator 25 Bayangol constituency were declared in January 2009, while the winner in the fourth seat, DP candidate Sodnomzunduin Erdene, was found guilty of fraud in connection with his previous work and imprisoned. On appeal in August he was found not guilty and released, and in September he was declared the winner of his seat. He took the oath of office in October.

Meanwhile, the National Human Rights Committee reported that, of the 716 people arrested during the riot of 1 July 2008, 244 had been found guilty of public disorder, arson or theft, and 86% of those convicted had been given sentences of several years' imprisonment. The '1 July Alliance' was formed by several popular movements and non-governmental organizations to protest against the ill-treatment of demonstrators and to support their families; the Alliance attributed the riots to poverty, unemployment, a popular demand for justice and the 'irresponsibility' of the Bayar Government. The chief of police was replaced, and an investigation commenced into the deaths of the four protesters from gunshot wounds. Some prison sentences were reduced on appeal, and several women and juveniles were released.

The Emergence of the Citizens' Movement

Jalbaasürengiin Batzandan, doctor of law, captured public attention in February 2005 following various statements and interviews given in his capacity as President of the Healthy Society Citizens' Movement (HSCM). The Vice-President (general co-ordinator) of the HSCM was Otgonjargalayn Magnai, an employee of the Ministry of Finance. Magnai gave up the vice-presidency of the HSCM for most of 2007 in order to assume the position of head of secretariat of the CCP. During 2007 Magnai was replaced as Vice-President of the HSCM by Manjaagiin Ichinnorov, a human rights lawyer. In numerous statements and interviews HSCM leaders took up such issues as the rehabilitation of victims of repression and compensation for their relatives. Magnai resigned from the CCP in December 2007 and returned to the HSCM as a member of its Leadership Council, subsequently also resuming the post of Vice-President. In March 2008, as the elections approached, Magnai demanded the resignation of Bataagiin Battulga, Election Committee Chairman and member of the MPRP. Ichinnorov was also a member of the Presidium of the Citizens' Association, its President, Dangaasürengiin Enkhbat, being Chairman (one of two) of the Mongolian Green Party. In 2007 Enkhbat had attempted unsuccessfully to register a Citizens' Party. Enkhbat was President of the so-called Resolute Reform Movement, founded in 2005; during 2006–07 he had been a member of its Leadership Council.

In 2006 there was some discussion of transforming the HSCM into a political party, and in March Batzandan was described several times as Chairman of the Healthy Society Party. In August 2007 the Citizens' Movement Party, which claimed a membership of 1,706, applied for official registration; this was granted in October 2007, with Batzandan as Chairman and Ichinnorov as Deputy Chairman. In February 2008, in preparation for the forthcoming elections to the Great Khural, Batzandan's Citizens' Movement Party and Enkhbat's Mongolian Green Party formed the CA, and the MSDP subsequently joined it. At the elections of June 2008 Batzandan was placed fifth for the CA in No. 22 (Bayanzürkh), a four-seat constituency; Magnai came ninth for the CA in No. 26 (Songinokhairkhan), a four-seat constituency; Ichinnorov came fifth for the CA in No. 19 (Darkhan-Uul), a three-seat constituency; and Enkhbat won a seat for the CA in No. 25 (Bayangol), a four-seat constituency where three official results were not declared until 2009.

In August 2008 Batzandan indicated his wish to join the DP, and several other Citizens' Movement Party leaders followed him. The Citizens' Movement Party reconstituted itself in November, with Nyamaagiin Davaa as Chairman, and Ichinnorov as Deputy Chairman. Davaa was arrested soon after in connection with a bankruptcy investigation into the accounts of Anod Bank, of which he was a director. In 2009 Batzandan was reported to be a member of the Consultative Council of Ulan Bator DP.

In March and April 2010 Batzandan and Magnai led new anti-Government demonstrations in Ulan Bator's Sükhbaatar Square. The first focused on the 1 July 2008 'rebellion of people against power-holders' swindling' and public dissatisfaction with the arrests and prison sentences. The second demonstration protested against the coalition Government's 'broken promises' over the Oyu Tolgoi agreement, and was followed by a week-long hunger strike. President Elbegdorj urged the intervention of members of the Great Khural. Batzandan was variously described as President of the Citizens' Movement and as an activist of the 'Great Khural of United Citizens' Movements to Put the Authorities on Trial'. Batzandan was also named chief co-ordinator of the Ulan Bator branch of the Democratic Forces Association, a DP pressure group headed by Mongolian Great Khural member Zandaakhüügiin Enkhbold.

Joint Government

Sanjaagiin Bayar was formally re-elected as Prime Minister by the Great Khural on 11 September 2008. In accordance with agreements between the MPRP and the DP on the formation of a 'joint' government, the proposed structure of the new administration was approved on 17 September, with 60% of the portfolios being allocated to the MPRP and the remaining 40% to the DP. The proposals envisaged the appointment of a Chief Deputy Prime Minister and a Deputy Prime Minister, and these posts went, respectively, to DP Chairman Norovyn Altankhuyag and former Prime Minister Miyeegombyn Enkhbold of the MPRP. The remit of the Ministry of External

Relations was expanded to include foreign economic relations, trade, credit and aid. Other changes included the establishment of a Ministry of Food, Agriculture and Light Industry; a Ministry of Roads, Transport, Construction and Urban Development; and a Ministry of Mineral Resources, Fuel and Power. The list of ministerial nominees was approved by the Great Khural on 19 September. The selection and appointment of deputy ministers proved to be a prolonged process, each party partner in the coalition Government having to decide its nominees in advance of joint decisions. The drafting of the Government Plan of Action for 2008–12 and the drawing up of a final list of government agencies and their leaders were also protracted processes.

In the October 2008 local elections the MPRP won majorities in 17 provinces and the DP in four. Voter turn-out in Ulan Bator was below the requisite 50%, and the election was therefore repeated in November, when the MPRP won 36 seats in the city assembly and the DP took nine. In December a plenum of the MPRP Little Khural elected Ukhnaagiin Khürelsükh to replace Yondongiin Otgonbayar as General Secretary of the party. In the same month Tüdeviin Bilegt was replaced as Mayor of Ulan Bator by Gombosürengiin Mönkhbayar, and in May 2009 Bilegt also lost his chairmanship of Ulan Bator MPRP Committee.

Undoubtedly the major issue of 2009 was the presidential election, which brought the two parties of the 'joint' Government into direct opposition with one another. The MPRP nominated the incumbent President Enkhbayar as its candidate, while the DP put forward former party Chairman Elbegdorj. There were no other candidates. The election took place on 24 May, with turnout reported at 73.5% of the electorate. In a close contest, Elbegdorj received 562,718 votes (51.2% of the total ballots cast) to defeat Enkhbayar, who garnered 520,948 votes (47.4%). This was a great triumph for the DP, which proclaimed a democratic President 20 years after the advent of democracy in Mongolia. A pro-MPRP newspaper ran a headline stating that 'Enkhbayar won in the country with 50.31%', apparently disregarding the urban vote that had ultimately given Elbegdorj his victory. The MPRP accepted the results, but did not conceal its disappointment; Prime Minister Bayar had been Enkhbayar's election agent. Bayar later admitted, in a conversation with a visiting Social Democrat member of the Bundestag (the German legislature), that the MPRP 'needed serious reform and a change of name'. President Elbegdorj appointed the members of his Presidential Secretariat, and declared that there would be no changes in Mongolia's foreign policy.

A by-election held in mid-October 2009 for the Great Khural seat vacated by Elbegdorj following his election to the post of President was won by Dashdorjiin Zorigt, the Minister of Mineral Resources, Fuel and Power, who defeated former President Nambaryn Enkhbayar in a contest for nomination as the MPRP candidate.

In 2009, after five years of public and parliamentary debates, discussion continued over an agreement with the Ivanhoe mining company on exploitation of the rich Oyu Tolgoi gold and copper deposit. In view of successive governments' inability to address the problem of poverty, the financial return that Mongolia hoped to receive from the mining venture was a huge political issue. Mongolia had been offered 34% of returns from the project, subject to an equivalent investment, for which it did not have the funds. Members of the Great Khural, who had for many months been planning how to spend the Oyu Tolgoi profits, were accused of 'skinning the bear before it's dead'. The Great Khural eventually agreed to let the Government decide the issue, and a new round of negotiations with Ivanhoe began in August 2009. The signing of the Oyu Tolgoi agreement by government ministers and representatives of Ivanhoe Mines and Rio Tinto, in the presence of the President and Prime Minister, finally took place in early October (see also Economy).

The health of Prime Minister Bayar became a matter of public interest during 2009 after several breaks in his work routine. At the end of January he was thrown from his horse during a trip out of Ulan Bator, suffering a suspected cracked vertebra. In February he flew to the South Korean capital of Seoul for treatment. In September and again in October Bayar returned to Seoul for further medical treatment. The brief official releases about his absences did not state the cause of his illness, but he was reported to be undergoing treatment for hepatitis C. In late October Bayar resigned from the premiership and was replaced by Sükhbaataryn Batbold, hitherto the Minister of External Relations. Gombojavyn Zandanshatar, a banker and youth leader, member of the Great Khural and former MPRP Leadership Council member, assumed the vacant cabinet position.

Bayar retained the post of MPRP Chairman until his continuing ill health obliged him to resign, and Batbold replaced him on 8 April 2010. In the previous week Prime Minister Batbold had been the main speaker at a conference in Ulan Bator marking the 70th anniversary of the appointment of Yumjaagiin Tsedenbal to the post of MPRP General Secretary on 8 April 1940. Reporting Batbold's address, the Montsame news agency described Tsedenbal as an outstanding figure under whose leadership the authorities had taken 'far-sighted and wide-ranging measures to strengthen the people's unity'. In fact, some six years after having been dismissed as party leader in 1984, Tsedenbal had been expelled from the MPRP for persecuting his political opponents, adopting an autocratic style of leadership, and allowing the country to decline into political and economic stagnation. Tsedenbal's 'rehabilitation' was presaged by the unveiling of his statue in central Ulan Bator in December 2006. On 17 September 2010 and again in 2011 Batbold and other leaders laid flowers at the Tsedenbal memorial on the 94th and 95th anniversaries of his birth.

In January 2010 President Elbegdorj announced that he was suspending capital punishment in Mongolia pending its abolition by the Great Khural. His announcement was welcomed by several foreign governments and human rights organizations, but not universally within Mongolia. In May the head of the Presidential Secretariat, Dambyn Dorligjav, resigned from his post to take up the appointment of Procurator General. One of his first acts was to accuse the Chairman and Deputy Chairman of the Anti-Corruption Committee of corruption. They were subsequently tried and imprisoned.

In March 2010 Brig.-Gen. Tojoony Dashdeleg, Commander of the Air Defence Forces, announced that Mongolia was acquiring attack helicopters and MiG-29 aircraft for squadrons forming at Nalaikh airfield. It was reported in July that the *National Security Concept* was being revised and updated to meet the new challenges that had emerged since 1994. Meanwhile, Maj.-Gen. Tserendejidiin Byambajav was appointed Chief of Staff of the Mongolian Armed Forces in July 2009.

The Kazakh new year or 'Nowruz', having just been registered by the UN General Assembly as 'intangible heritage', was celebrated in March 2010 by Mongolia's Kazakh community in Bayan-Ölgii in the presence of President Elbegdorj. Mongolia had been criticized by the UN for infringements of the Declaration on Minority Rights in neglecting the Kazakh and Tuvan minorities' right to education in their own language, and this issue was taken up in the 2009 report by the National Human Rights Commission, published in April 2010.

The UN Human Rights Council, meeting in November 2010, recommended that Mongolia should join international human rights conventions, determine a mechanism for implementing national legislation on preventing torture, create a legal environment to protect the rights of women, sexual minorities and the disabled, and combat human trafficking. In the same month Tsevegmidiin Zorig was appointed as the new Chief Justice of the Supreme Court. An administrative court of appeal, headed by Tsendiin Tsogt, was inaugurated in March 2011.

At the beginning of July 2010 President Elbegdorj decreed the use, from July 2011, of the traditional Mongolian vertical script in all official communications addressed to foreign governments and heads of state (with translation attached), and in identity cards, certificates and diplomas (together with Mongolian Cyrillic). In October 2010 the refurbished Victory Square in Ulan Bator was formally renamed Independence Square; a monument commemorating 100 years of Mongolian independence was unveiled in the square in June 2011. In November 2010 President Elbegdorj decreed the celebration in 2011 of the 2,220th anniversary of Modun Shanyui's proclamation (in 209 BC) of the Xiongnu (Hun) state as the anniversary of the 'founding state' (*tulgar tör*) of the Mongols. In his new year and Naadam television broadcasts President Elbegdorj toasted the nation in milk.

The MPRP Little Khural decided to hold the next party congress in November 2010. It had been due in April of that year, but was postponed because of the transfer of power from Bayar to Batbold. The congress, which opened on 4 November, confirmed Batbold's chairmanship, re-elected Ukhnaagiin Khürelsükh to the post of General Secretary and elected five secretaries, including Sanjaagiin Bayar and Miyeegombyn Enkhbold. A Leadership Council of 31 members (including the secretaries) was elected by the party's new Little Khural of 310 members. The congress's most significant decision was to revert to the party's former name, the Mongolian People's Party (MPP), which had been used from the party's foundation in 1920 until 1925. This led to a split within the party when a member of the Great Khural, Tsendiin Shinebayar, established a 'Provisional HQ' to restore the MPRP. Ex-President and former MPRP Chairman Nambaryn Enkhbayar, with the support of members of the 'Justice, Solidarity, Freedom' United Movement, which disapproved of the reversion to the original name, assumed the chairmanship of the MPRP in January 2011 and set about organizing the party's registration. In March Enkhbayar represented the MPRP at a meeting of the 'Motherland-Independence-Justice' National Movement, a loose association of minor political parties, movements and non-governmental organizations. Having initially ignored the application, the Supreme Court approved the registration of the MPRP in June, despite protests by the MPP. The latter initiated court proceedings against the registration on the basis of a law whereby a former party's name could not be reused. Meanwhile, several leading figures in the MPRP relinquished their membership in order to set up a new party 'truer to the ideology'of the (original) MPRP.

In the mean time, CCP leader Sanjaasürengiin Oyuun and Green Party leader Dangaasürengiin Enkhbat, having agreed in January 2011 to amalgamate their parties into the Civil Courage-Green Party under Enkhbat's chairmanship, were refused registration of the new party by the Supreme Court in May. The Alliance of Greens faction subsequently took control of the rump Green Party.

In June 2011 great excitement was created in central Ulan Bator by the establishment in Sükhbaatar Square of an illegal camp with horses, oxen, carts and *gers* (yurts) by the Gal Ündesten ('Fire Nation') association, an environmental pressure group seeking legislation to prevent mining in river basins and forests. Some windows in the State Palace were broken by arrows, and several of the group's leaders were arrested for allegedly firing gunshots at a company's mining machinery.

After five years of discussion, the Great Khural finally approved the Law on Information Transparency and Right and Freedom to Access Information in June 2011. The new legislation required the activities of state agencies, budgetary organizations and legal entities to be open, ensuring citizens' and legal entities' right to access information. Meanwhile, the 'joint' Government continued to debate a new Law on Elections. The MPP was in favour of a majority system of election, while the DP preferred proportional representation. As the spring session drew to a close for the festival of Naadam, it appeared that the persistent disagreement of the two parties would prevent adoption of the new law. The Chairman of the MPP Parliamentary Group, Danzangiin Lündeejantsan, and his deputy resigned from their posts; Ölziisaikhany Enkhtüvshin was selected as the new Chairman. It seemed that the only solution to ending the impasse would be the holding of a referendum, but it remained unclear whether the new law could be implemented in time for the next parliamentary elections scheduled for May 2012.

The 14th Dalai Lama's incarnation was reported in mid-September 2011 to have been revealed as a nine-year-old Mongolian boy whose details were being kept secret for his protection. According to the National Security Council, the ban on discovery of reincarnated 'living Buddhas' in Mongolia remained in force; although a few reincarnations had been announced, there had been no complaints.

EXTERNAL RELATIONS

The dissolution of the USSR in December 1991 had radical repercussions for Mongolia, which was obliged to negotiate separate treaties with the USSR's former constituent parts to ensure the continuation of aid and trade, upon which Mongolia remained largely dependent. In January 1993 President Ochirbat visited the Russian capital of Moscow, where he signed with President Boris Yeltsin a new 20-year Mongolian-Russian Treaty of Friendly Relations and Co-operation to replace the defunct Mongolian-Soviet treaty of 1986. Ochirbat and Yeltsin also issued a joint statement expressing regret at the imprisonment and execution of Mongolian citizens in the USSR during the Stalinist period. Similar treaties of friendly relations and co-operation were concluded with Kazakhstan and Ukraine.

In April 1994 a new Treaty of Friendship and Co-operation was concluded during a visit to Ulan Bator by the Chinese Premier, Li Peng. An agreement on cultural, economic and technical co-operation was also signed.

In July 1994 two important documents outlining Mongolian foreign policy objectives were published, the *National Security Concept* and the *Foreign Policy Concept*. While emphasizing 'complete equality' in its co-operation with Russia and China, Mongolia also focused on the development of relations with its 'third neighbour'—primarily the USA, Japan, Western Europe, the Asia-Pacific region, the UN and international financial bodies. These documents were updated and reissued in July 2010 and February 2011, respectively.

In May 1995 the US Congress issued a statement of support for Mongolia, and in August President Bill Clinton authorized the provision of US military aid to Mongolia. His wife, Hillary Clinton, paid a brief visit to Mongolia in September and announced further aid of US $4.5m. In the same month President Ochirbat flew to Germany and then to the headquarters of the European Union (EU) in Brussels, Belgium, for aid talks. Ochirbat returned to Europe in April 1996 for official visits to France and the United Kingdom; in London he promoted bilateral trade, and was received by Queen Elizabeth. Prime Minister Jasrai had paid an official visit to China at the end of March.

Relations with China were consolidated in 1997 by the visits to Ulan Bator of Qiao Shi, the Chairman of the Standing Committee of the National People's Congress (in April), and of the Minister of Foreign Affairs, Qian Qichen (in August). The Malaysian Prime Minister, Mahathir Mohamad, visited Mongolia in September, but various aid and co-operation projects discussed during his visit were postponed owing to the financial crisis affecting Malaysia.

In July 1998 Mongolia was admitted to the Association of Southeast Asian Nations (ASEAN) Regional Forum (ARF) at its ministerial meeting in Manila, the Philippines. In March 2000 Prime Minister Amarjargal paid an official visit to the United Kingdom. He was followed a fortnight later by a delegation of 10 members of the Mongolian Great Khural. In May Amarjargal attended a conference in Riga, Latvia, where Mongolian membership of the European Bank for Reconstruction and Development (EBRD) was approved. In June 2000 Mongolia became the 24th member of the Parliamentary Union of the Countries of Asia and the Pacific.

In November 2000 Russian President Vladimir Putin made an overnight stop in Ulan Bator on his way to a conference of the Asia-Pacific Economic Cooperation (APEC) in Brunei. He was the first senior-level Russian visitor to Mongolia since Soviet Communist Party General Secretary Leonid Brezhnev's visit in 1974. Presidents Putin and Bagabandi issued a joint declaration that pledged Mongolia and Russia 'not to join any military-political alliances against one another, nor conclude any treaty or agreement with third countries harmful to the interests of the other's sovereignty or independence. Neither side will allow its territory to be used by a third state for purposes of aggression or other acts of violence harmful to the sovereignty, security and public order of the other'. Russia confirmed its adherence to the five nuclear powers' declaration of guarantees for Mongolia's security in connection with its nuclear-weapons-free status.

Enkhbayar travelled abroad as Prime Minister for the first time to the Davos international economic forum in Switzerland in January 2001, then to Japan. Russian premier Mikhail Kasyanov's brief visit to Mongolia in March 2002 raised once more the dispute over Mongolia's repayment to Russia of the large debt for Soviet aid (see Economy).

The seventh British-Mongolian 'Round-Table' Conference in Ulan Bator in September 2002 was attended by a parliamentary secretary of the British Foreign and Commonwealth Office. The Dalai Lama visited Ulan Bator in November, travelling via Japan after Russia refused him a visa and Korean Air, the national carrier of the Republic of Korea, banned him on the grounds that he posed a security threat. Although his visit was at the invitation of Mongolia's Buddhist leaders rather than the Government, the Chinese authorities indicated their displeasure by halting rail traffic on their mutual border for 36 hours. The UN Secretary-General, Kofi Annan, paid a brief visit to Mongolia in October.

Hu Jintao, the Chinese President, visited Ulan Bator in early June 2003; he had discussions with President Bagabandi and Prime Minister Enkhbayar, and addressed the Great Khural on the subject of 'neighbourly partnership of mutual trust', which, besides reiterating respect for each other's independence, sovereignty and territorial integrity, embodied the handling of bilateral relations 'in the spirit of consultation, co-operation and friendship'. China granted Mongolia 50m. yuan for the building of a road across the border between the two countries (from Zamyn-Üüd to Erlian) and offered loans, the exact use of which was to be determined at a later date.

A company of 170 Mongolian soldiers was dispatched to Iraq in September 2003; their duties mainly consisted of working on construction projects and guarding oil pipelines. Further regular contingents were rotated to Iraq as of mid-2008, and contingents of Mongolian soldiers were also sent to Sierra Leone and Chad.

President Natsagiin Bagabandi paid a state visit to China in July 2004, visiting Hainan and Macao, and discussing economic co-operation with President Hu Jintao. Later the same month Bagabandi visited the USA, where he met President George W. Bush and signed a Trade and Investment Framework Agreement. US Assistant Secretary of State James Kelly and Japanese Minister of Foreign Affairs Yoriko Kawaguchi visited Ulan Bator in October, as did delegations from the Inner Mongolia and Tibet Autonomous Regions of China. At the invitation of the President of the Presidium of the Supreme People's Assembly, Kim Yong Nam, President Bagabandi visited the Democratic People's Republic of Korea (North Korea) in December to promote bilateral co-operation. In January 2005 President Bagabandi visited Viet Nam and Laos.

Meanwhile, Nambaryn Enkhbayar, Chairman of the Great Khural, was received by Queen Elizabeth and Prince Philip during his visit to London in November 2004 for a conference of the Alliance of Religion and Conservation, of which he was President. After visits to Austria and Russia in January 2005, Enkhbayar participated in the World Bank's conference on Faith and Development in the Irish capital of Dublin. The eighth British-Mongolian 'Round-Table' Conference, held in London in March 2005, was attended by the new Minister of Industry and Trade, Sükhbaataryn Batbold.

Nambaryn Enkhbayar's first official foreign travel after his inauguration as President of Mongolia was in July 2005 to Astana, the capital of Kazakhstan, where he attended a meeting of the Shanghai Co-operation Organization (SCO) with Russian President Vladimir Putin, Chinese President Hu Jintao and other leaders (Mongolia had been granted observer status). Shortly afterwards he welcomed Turkish Prime Minister Reçep Erdoğan to Ulan Bator. Mongolia's relations with Turkey had been developing on the basis of a co-operation agreement concluded in 1995, which incorporated investment in Mongolia's mining sector. The two countries also shared an interest in the archaeology of the sixth–seventh-century Turkish state.

The US Secretary of Defense, Donald Rumsfeld, visited Ulan Bator briefly in October 2005. He told Mongolians: 'As a free nation, with a free political system and a free economic system, you have contributed to the liberation of 50 million people... In Iraq and Afghanistan the Mongolian army has demonstrated that it is a force worthy of pride and emulation . . . the American people will not forget your friendship'. Standing in front of a statue of Genghis Khan, Rumsfeld informed Minister of Defence Sharavdorj that the USA was 'anxious and willing' to help Mongolia enhance its peace-keeping capabilities. In 2005 the USA provided Mongolia with US $18m. in military assistance, including regular training exchanges and bilateral peace-keeping exercises.

On the first visit to Mongolia by an incumbent US President, in November 2005 George W. Bush spent four hours in Ulan Bator, where he had discussions with President Enkhbayar. In an address President Bush declared that both nations had been settled by pioneers on horseback who 'shook off the yoke of colonial rule and built successful free societies. Today Mongolia and the US are standing together as brothers in the cause of freedom'. A joint presidential statement noted that President Bush welcomed Mongolia's progress towards becoming a mature and stable democracy, which observed human rights and civil liberties, as well as the country's development of a free market economy, led by the private sector. The two Presidents also emphasized their commitment to combating terrorism.

In February 2006, following a closed meeting in Ulan Bator with foreign donors (specifically the World Bank, the Asian Development Bank (ADB), the IMF, the UN, Japan, the USA and Germany), which urged greater accountability, the US Administration issued a statement noting that the US Agency for International Development had found that corruption in Mongolia was increasing at all levels. The Mongolian Government was to be required to draw up lists of specific actions to combat corruption and to detail all the changes needed within existing law in order that Mongolia might comply with the UN Convention Against Corruption (UNCAC).

Prime Minister Miyeegombyn Enkhbold's first foreign trip was to Japan, in March 2006. President George W. Bush sent a message in February to Mongolia's Kazakhs on the occasion of Kurban Ait (Id al-Adha), the first time a US President had done so. The South Korean President, Roh Moo-Hyun, visited Mongolia in May. Russian Prime Minister Mikhail Fradkov visited in July. In August Mongolia received Japanese Prime Minister Junichiro Koizumi, who discussed joint efforts to develop energy resources in Mongolia, as well as issues relating to North Korea. During the same month the Dalai Lama paid his seventh visit to Mongolia at the invitation of local Buddhists and presided over religious ceremonies in Ulan Bator. In November Enkhbold signed a trade and economic co-operation agreement with China, during his first official visit to Beijing since becoming Prime Minister in January. He also visited Urumqi, in the Xinjiang Uygur Autonomous Region, where Mongolia hoped to open a consulate. At the beginning of December President Enkhbayar toured the Buryat and Kalmyk Republics, before flying to Moscow for the first state visit by a Mongolian President in 13 years. Following a meeting with President Putin, a treaty on the border regime and trade and economic agreements were signed.

President Enkhbayar's travels in 2007 took him to France, Japan and the United Kingdom, which he visited in April; he met the Duke of Edinburgh and had discussions with Prime Minister Tony Blair. In July visitors to Mongolia included Kim Yong Nam, President of the Presidium of the Supreme People's Assembly of the Democratic People's Republic of Korea, and the Amir of Kuwait, Sheikh Sabah al-Ahmad al-Jaber as-Sabah. In August President Nambaryn Enkhbayar travelled to Astana for a summit meeting of the SCO, where he had discussions with President Putin, President Nursultan Nazarbayev of Kazakhstan, and other leaders. In October President Enkhbayar visited the USA, meeting the UN Secretary-General and President George W. Bush; Enkhbayar and Bush signed a Millennium Challenge contract, which pledged US $285m. in funds for Mongolia. In the following month Enkhbayar visited Kuwait, Qatar and the United Arab Emirates. Meanwhile, Prime Minister Enkhbold paid a visit to Austria in September and to Luxembourg in October.

In March 2008 President Enkhbayar received Lord Malloch-Brown, leader of the British delegation to the ninth British-Mongolian 'Round-Table' talks in Ulan Bator. Prime Minister Bayar visited Russia in April, when he met Vladimir Putin, former President and now Prime Minister. In the same month President Enkhbayar attended the Bo'ao Forum for Asia where he had a meeting with Chinese President Hu Jintao. In May Enkhbayar visited Israel for talks with Prime Minister Ehud Olmert and in Moscow met President Dimitrii Medvedev. In the same month Sanjaasürengiin Oyuun, the Mongolian Minister of External Relations, paid an official visit to France. In June the Vice-President of China, Xi Jinping, visited Ulan Bator. The Amir of Kuwait visited Mongolia again at the end of July, and President Nursultan Nazarbayev of Kazakhstan in early August. In September 2008 German Federal President Horst Köhler visited Mongolia.

In November 2008 Russian soldiers arrived in Mongolia, for the first time in 16 years, to take part in a joint military exercise, and repair some of the Mongolian Army's Soviet-made equipment. In December Mongolian historians meeting to mark the 800th anniversary of the birth of Batu Khan, ruler of the Golden Horde, criticized Russian historians who, in rewriting the history of Russia, had denied the veracity of the Mongol conquest of Russia and even Batu Khan's very existence. In January 2009 President Enkhbayar had a meeting with Russian Prime Minister Vladimir Putin in Davos, Switzerland, and Prime Minister Bayar had discussions about transport development in Irkutsk, Russia; in March Bayar met Putin in Moscow. In April the Mongolian Ministry of External Relations issued a statement denying rumours that the forthcoming visit to Mongolia by Putin was in any way connected with support for a candidate in the Mongolian presidential election. Putin visited Ulan Bator in mid-May, when he discussed economic co-operation projects with Bayar and Enkhbayar.

Following his visit to Moscow in March 2009, Prime Minister Bayar then flew to Paris, where he met the French premier and inspected a nuclear power station, before travelling on to Luxembourg and Belgium. Continuing a busy schedule, in the same month Bayar had talks about economic co-operation with German Chancellor Angela Merkel, and met representatives of ThyssenKrupp and Siemens. In April Bayar was received in Beijing by Vice-President Xi Jinping. In Ordos municipality, Inner Mongolia, he visited a coal liquefaction plant, then continued to Bo'ao (Sanya, Hainan) where he met Chinese Premier Wen Jiabao. In June Mongolian soldiers participated in a peace-keeping exercise in China for the first time. In the following month Bayar visited Tokyo, where he was received by Prime Minister Taro Aso and Japanese Crown Prince Naruhito. In September Bayar cancelled a scheduled visit to Australia, in order to return to Seoul for medical treatment (see Joint Government).

In June 2009 the Minister of External Relations, Sükhbaataryn Batbold, met US Secretary of State Hillary Clinton to discuss the diversion of promised Millennium Challenge funds after the Russians 'disallowed' their allocation to Mongolian railway development. Following President Elbegdorj's inauguration, the US Senate issued a resolution of support for Mongolia. A visiting delegation from the US House of Representatives thanked Elbegdorj for Mongolia's support in peace-keeping operations. On a visit to Tokyo in July Prime Minister Bayar declared that he wanted Japan to be Mongolia's leading partner; he was received by Japanese Prime Minister Taro Aso. UN Secretary-General Ban Ki-Moon visited Mongolia at the end of July.

Russian President Dmitrii Medvedev visited Mongolia in August 2009, when he stated that Mongolia's 'big debt' for Russian aid had been settled by only 98% in 2003, and that some 'small questions' were outstanding. President Elbegdorj and President Medvedev signed a joint declaration on the development of their 'strategic partnership'. In mid-September President Elbegdorj paid a state visit to India, where he was received by President Pratibha Devisingh Patil and Prime Minister Manmohan Singh, and urged the development of a 'complex partnership' between the two countries. Later in the month President Elbegdorj travelled to the USA for meetings in New York with UN Secretary-General Ban Ki-Moon, former President Bill Clinton and the Vice-President of the Millennium Challenge Corporation. The Mongolian President addressed the UN General Assembly on the issues of the economic crisis and climate change, and had a meeting with South Korean President Lee Myung-Bak. In December President Elbegdorj travelled to Denmark to attend the conference on climate change in Copenhagen.

In February 2010 President Elbegdorj attended the Davos economic conference and visited Brussels on business with the EU. He paid a state visit to China in April–May, which took him to Beijing, Changchun, Shanghai and Inner Mongolia. The President visited Moscow for the Victory Day celebrations in May, and in the following month he travelled to the Turkish city of Istanbul for an Asian confidence-building conference and to Uzbekistan for a meeting of the SCO in Tashkent. In October Elbegdorj paid visits to Belgium, Finland and Denmark. Prime Minister Batbold visited Austria and Hungary in March and attended the Bo'ao conference in China in April. Chinese Premier Wen Jiabao undertook an official visit to Mongolia in June, during which an intergovernmental border regime agreement was signed, renewing an accord signed in 1998. Having addressed the UN General Assembly in New York in September 2010, Prime Minister Batbold then went on to visit Canada. In October the Prime Minister and Prince Mired bin Ra'ad al-Hussein of Jordan, special envoy for the Anti-Personnel Mine Ban Convention, after visiting Mongolian army units and anti-personnel mine stockpiles agreed that Mongolia would sign the Ottawa Treaty banning anti-personnel mines. In December Prime Minister Batbold paid an official visit to Moscow where he had talks with Prime Minister Putin. The two leaders agreed that Mongolia would settle its remaining US $3.8m debt to Russia in one transfer. In addition, contracts were signed on the establishment of the uranium mining joint venture Dornod Uran and the modernization of the Ulan Bator Railway.

In November 2010 President Elbegdorj undertook a state visit to Japan, where he had an audience with Emperor Akihito, had talks with Prime Minister Naoto Kan, attended a business forum and anounced the establishment of a 'strategic partnership'. In the same month, accompanied by Minister of Defence Luvsanvandangiin Bold, the President addressed the NATO summit meeting held in Portugal. In May 2011 in Ulan Bator Elbegdorj received James Appathurai, the NATO Secretary-General's Special Representative for the Caucasus and Central Asia, who described Mongolia as a 'valued contributor' to NATO-led operations. During Appathurai's visit to Mongolia, the two parties agreed to 'develop partnership relations to promote common understanding, interoperability, (and) exchange on emerging security challenges' as well as 'defence capacity building' and crisis management.

President Elbegdorj began his foreign travels in 2011 with a visit in January to Switzerland to observe direct democracy and attend the World Economic Forum in Davos. At the beginning of June he paid a state visit to Russia, where he was received by President Medvedev, met students of the Lomonosov Moscow State University and Russian businesspeople, and had talks with Prime Minister Putin, dealing in particular with the unexpected restriction placed on Russian exports of petroleum products to Mongolia. In St Petersburg the Mongolian President met Russian orientalists and visited a Buddhist temple. Shortly after his trip to Russia, Elbegdorj embarked upon an official visit to the USA, beginning in San Francisco, where he opened a Mongolian consulate-general. He then visited Stanford University before flying to Washington, DC, for a meeting with President Barack Obama. A joint US-Mongolian statement reaffirmed the two states' commitment to a comprehensive partnership. The US Congress issued a Senate resolution to 'acknowledge and celebrate' Mongolia's commitment to democratic reform and to continue to support its economic development. During his US tour, President Elbegdorj also visited New York. In July he travelled to Ukraine and Lithuania. The President of India, Pratibha Devisingh Patil, visited Mongolia at the end of that month.

Prime Minister Batbold visited Kuwait in January 2011, followed by Singapore and Australia in February. The Chinese Minister of Foreign Affairs, Yang Jiechi, visited Ulan Bator in March. In the same month Batbold travelled to the Republic of Korea, where he met Mongolian workers and condemned the recent North Korean attack on a South Korean naval vessel. In June, after attending a regional economic forum in the Indonesian capital of Jakarta, the Prime Minister began an official visit to China in Hong Kong, where he opened a Mongolian consulate-general. Batbold subsequently had official talks in Beijing with his counterpart Wen Jiabao and other officials, following which he signed a joint statement on the establishment of a strategic partnership between the two countries. Other documents signed included a 'soft' loan agreement worth US $500m.

In late 2010 relations between Mongolia and the United Kingdom were strained and a number of joint arrangements, including a visit to London by Prime Minister Batbold scheduled for December, were cancelled. The reason for the tension was the arrest in September at London's Heathrow Airport of Batyn Khurts, head of administration at the Mongolian National Security Council. Khurts claimed that he had been expecting to meet British security officials in London, but the Foreign and Commonwealth Office (FCO) denied this. It later emerged that Khurts was being held on an arrest warrant issued by the German authorities. This warrant related to the alleged kidnapping in France in May 2003 of a Mongolian citizen, Damirangiin Enkhbat, by Khurts and three other Mongolian government agents. Enkhbat was reportedly drugged, transported by car through Belgium and Germany, and held at the Mongolian embassy in Berlin before being secretly flown to Mongolia. There Enkhbat was interrogated about a number of democrat politicians in connection with the murder in 1998 of Sanjaasürengiin Zorig, the Minister of Infrastructure Development (see above). Enkhbat denied all knowledge of the murder and gave details about his kidnapping and interrogation in a video recording made by his lawyer, Lodoisambuugiin Sanjaasüren, which was made available to an Ulan Bator television station and Mongolian newspapers in September 2003. Enkhbat was subsequently charged with 'disclosing Mongolian secrets' (the names of his kidnappers), and in November he was sentenced to three years' imprisonment. Sanjaasüren was also imprisoned for the same offence. Enkhbat died in February 2006, shortly after his release from prison on grounds of ill health.

Refusing to discuss the arrest of Khurts, the FCO limited itself to stating that the City of Westminster Magistrates' Court would decide whether he should be extradited on the German warrant. Supported by the Mongolian ambassador and officials sent to London by the Ministry of External Relations, Khurts claimed that, as he was on an official diplomatic mission, he should be released according to convention. However, the FCO disagreed, asserting that he was not entitled to diplomatic protection. The Mongolians accused the British authorities of entrapment, and of luring Khurts to London with the help of the British ambassador in Ulan Bator, who had been hurriedly retired. In November 2010 Deputy Prime Minister Miyeegombyn Enkhbold demanded the release of Khurts. Meanwhile, the Ministry of External Relations issued a 'note of apology' to the French, Belgian and German Governments containing an admission of the illegality of Khurts' 2003 mission.

The Khurts affair attracted little media attention within the United Kingdom, but created a sensation in Mongolia where the official's arrest was regarded as an outrage. There were demands for the United Kingdom to be 'punished' for imprisoning the Mongolian 'diplomat'. It was claimed that Khurts had merely been doing his duty in 2003. Small demonstrations demanding Khurts' release were held outside the British embassy and the Ministry of External Relations in Ulan Bator. However, a number of Mongolian journalists questioned the wisdom of attempting to defend Khurts at such great financial and political cost, and others pointed out that very senior Mongolian political figures must have been responsible for ordering Khurts' illegal acts. In London the two parties engaged Queen's Counsels to argue their respective cases. Occasional hearings continued into early 2011, while Khurts remained in a London prison, having been denied bail. When the court decided in February that Khurts should be extradited to Germany, Khurts appealed against the decision.

Minister of State at the FCO Jeremy Browne visited Ulan Bator at the end of May 2011, ostensibly to discuss the London 2012 Olympic Games. Deputy Prime Minister Enkhbold asked him about Khurts, 'considering the long years of friendly co-operation' between the two countries. Browne replied that 'no government official can influence the court's decision'. After a two-day hearing in June the appeal court was due to issue a decision 'shortly', but failed to do so. The British appeal court issued a delayed decision to extradite Khurts to Germany, and he was extradited in August. His Mongolian defence team was reorganized to deal with issues of German criminal law. In September the State Procurator's Office began an investigation into the involvement of diplomats, airline personnel, legal staff and police in Enkhbat's kidnapping in 2003. The case was to establish how the name of Khurts and his fellow kidnappers had become public, contrary to the Law on State Secrets. Statements were being taken from the then Chief of Criminal Police, members of the counter-intelligence service, Minister of Justice and Home Affairs Nyamdorj, ex-President Enkhbayar and the former Mongolian ambassador to Germany. The case against Khurts was due to open in Berlin in October, but at the end of September he was unexpectedly released by the German authorities and returned to Ulan Bator. The Mongolian Minister of External Relations was reported to have stated that the release of Khurts was unconnected to the forthcoming visit of Chancellor Merkel to Mongolia.

Economy

ALAN J. K. SANDERS

Between 1948 and 1990 the Mongolian economy was developed under a series of Five-Year Plans, with large-scale assistance from the USSR and other communist countries, principally those that formed the Council for Mutual Economic Assistance (CMEA, dissolved in mid-1991). The two salient features of development during this period were the completion of the transition to the socialist system of production and a rate of economic expansion very much faster than was achieved in the first 30 years of the republic.

In the early 1990s, parallel with the political developments taking place in Mongolia, the Government initiated a series of radical reforms aimed at achieving a market economy and privatization. With a rapidly growing population, there was an increasing demand for foodstuffs and consumer goods. A high rate of infant mortality was disclosed after decades of concealment. Poor living conditions were reported to be responsible for 50% of infant deaths in the 1980s, genetic and ecological conditions for 30% and inadequate medical services for 20%. During the 1980s there was also a severe shortage of convertible currency, necessary to acquire new technology, to stimulate production and export earnings, and to reduce Mongolia's foreign debt. In an attempt to revitalize the economy, Mongolia planned to promote the tourist industry and to secure a relatively small medium-term loan in convertible currency. This was to be used to buy small, mobile mining machinery, in order to exploit the country's deposits of gold and silver and to acquire modern technology for the improvement of livestock-breeding and the associated processing industry.

In 1989, according to official sources, gross national income (GNI) per head was US $473. Reflecting the dislocation of the economy in the transition to a free market, GNI per head had declined to $112 by 1991. Large devaluations of the tögrög subsequently made the exact figure uncertain, but the World Bank estimated GNI per head to be $390 in 1997 and $380 in 1998. In July 2001 the President of Mongolbank (the country's central bank) estimated average annual income per head at $360–$380, although the World Bank estimated GNI per head to have increased to $400 for that year. GNI rose steadily in subsequent years. By 2009, according to World Bank estimates, Mongolia's gross GNI had reached $4,361m., equivalent to $1,630 per head (equivalent to $3,330 per head on an international purchasing-power parity basis). The country's gross domestic product (GDP) expanded by 8.9% in 2008 and declined by 1.6% in 2009, then rose again, by 6.1%, in 2010, according to the Mongolian Statistical Committee. GDP per caput was estimated (following the World Bank method) at $1,649 in 2008, $1,817 in 2009 and $2,251 in 2010. In 2010 22.7% of GDP was derived from the mining sector, 15.9% from the agricultural sector, 15.0% from wholesale and retail trade, and 11.1% from the industrial sector.

AGRICULTURE

After the catastrophe of the period of 'leftist deviation' (1929–32), animal herding, the mainstay of Mongolia's economy, reverted to private enterprise, and, apart from taking compulsory deliveries of produce during the period of the Second World War, the Government did not interfere with herding activity. Small-scale mutual help in carrying out certain tasks was practised, and some herdsmen joined together in small producers' associations, but under the 'New Turn Policy' the formation of co-operatives was discouraged. By 1952 the existing co-operatives contained only 280,000 animals out of a national stock of nearly 23m. However, collectivization of herding had by 1957 again become a matter of policy. Although collectivization was said to have been carried out voluntarily by the herdsmen, the initiative came from the Mongolian People's Revolutionary Party (MPRP), and propaganda and economic compulsion were widely used to persuade people to join. Thus, state loans were granted to newly formed co-operatives, discriminatory rates of taxation were imposed on individuals who owned large herds and similarly differential norms of compulsory deliveries of produce were set.

The collectivization programme reached its height in 1958 and by April 1959 all but a tiny minority of herdsmen had been collectivized. The herdsmen's associations (*negdel*) were quite different in character from the earlier producers' associations. They were of considerable size, and were units of local administration as well as economic units (or goods) according to the work. All families were allowed to retain a certain number of private animals. Produce was purchased by the state, which also granted loans to the co-operatives. Internally, each co-operative was organized into a number of permanent brigades, each with its own territory and headquarters and its own special tasks. The brigade in its turn contained a number of sections (*kheseg*) comprising several bases, each of usually two households living in felt tents and looking after a number of animals.

An innovation in the Mongolian rural economy was the development of large-scale agriculture. This did not affect any previous pattern of economic activity and from the start was organized as a direct state venture. Ten state farms existed in 1940 and 52 state farms in 1988. In and after 1959 the area under cultivation increased sharply as large tracts of virgin land were opened, but the sown area was smaller in 1970 than in 1965. By 1978 1m. ha of virgin land had been ploughed. It was reported that the 1985 grain harvest reached a record 889,400 metric tons, enabling Mongolia to meet its own grain requirements and to export surplus wheat to Siberia. Production amounted to 798,600 tons in 1989, but it subsequently declined annually and by 2002 totalled only 125,860 tons, decreasing further, to 75,500 tons, in 2005. However, cereal production in 2006 rose to 138,572 tons, decreasing in 2007 to 114,800 tons, a level equivalent to 54% of annual consumption. Despite the area sown to crops in 2008 being 2.7% smaller than in 2007, production of cereals in 2008 almost doubled year-on-year to reach 212,900 tons, rose again, to reach 391,700 tons, in 2009, and then declined slightly, to 355,060 tons in 2010.

Increasing attention was paid to mechanization and the introduction of scientific methods of farming. The division of activity between the 255 *negdel* and the 52 state farms was not a strict one. Co-operatives also engaged in field work, especially fodder growing, while state farms were expected to supply good breeding animals. The principal crops produced by the state farms were cereals, potatoes and other vegetables. An apparently successful innovation was the establishment of 17 inter-co-operative production enterprises, in which neighbouring co-operatives combined resources to specialize in particular farm-related activities. A new law on co-operatives came into force in January 1990. This law controlled co-operative activity in small-scale industry, trade and services and transformed the *negdel* into proper co-operatives. In 1991, however, following the new Government's initiation of political and economic reforms, these were privatized and mostly divided into smaller units. All restrictions on private livestock ownership were removed in 1990. Some state farms became joint-stock companies, while others were broken up.

At the annual year-end livestock census in 1995, Mongolia had a total of 28.6m. head of sheep, goats, horses, cows and camels. This was largely due to a 2m. head increase in the number of goats, encouraged by the growth in the cashmere industry. In 1996 the rise in livestock numbers continued, reaching 29.3m., but this was also a reflection of low levels of industrial consumption of meat and hides.

A survey of the herding community at the end of 1996 revealed that, of the 517,700 families in Mongolia, 170,100, or 32.8%, were herding families, with 395,400 herdsmen (16.8% of the population) engaged in livestock raising. Only 9.3% of these families had electricity. Mongolia's livestock herds increased in 1999 to a new record of 33.6m. (compared with 31.3m. in 1997). However, serious drought in late 1999 was followed in early 2000 by several months of *zud* (when drought, frozen snow cover or overgrazing leads to lack of pasture and to the death of livestock from starvation). In consequence, by mid-2000 an estimated 2.5m. head of livestock had died from starvation and cold. In response to government appeals, international donors offered financial aid, and relief teams of the International Committee of the Red Cross (ICRC) were mobilized to take food and medicine to isolated herding families. Almost 2,500 families were believed to have lost all their animals by late June, when survivals of new-born stock numbered 8.4m. head, compared with 10.2m. in 1999.

The December 2000 livestock census recorded a decline in the herds to fewer than 30.1m. head, and in the following months the weakened animals experienced even more severe conditions, with deep snow and exceptionally low temperatures. It was reported at the end of June 2001 that 3.3m. head had died, 27% more than the year before, and that 7,364 households had lost all their animals. Eastern provinces were also affected by foot-and-mouth disease. At the end of 2002 Mongolia's stock of sheep, goats, horses, cattle and camels totalled some 23.7m., after further losses in that year. By the end of 2003 total livestock numbers had recovered to reach 25.4m. Total livestock numbers in 2004 and 2005 rose again, to 28.0m. and 30.4m., respectively. By 2003 the number of goats exceeded the number of sheep for the first time, and this trend subsequently continued. By the end of 2007 the number of goats had risen above 18.3m., while sheep totalled almost 17.0m., with the corresponding figures increasing to 20.0m. and 18.4m., respectively, by the end of 2008.

Prime Minister Nambaryn Enkhbayar expressed concern about the state of the nomadic herding economy, stating that it was important to improve the quality of stock, raise yields and invigorate product processing. Of crucial importance was the intensification of livestock raising to meet the growing needs of large towns, especially Ulan Bator. (The capital's population was estimated at 893,400 in December 2003, with some 100,000–150,000 people commuting into the city daily.)

There was a continuing decline in the numbers of herding households (from 191,526 in 2000 to 168,344 in 2005) and of herdsmen (from 421,392 to 364,293 over the same period), especially of herdsmen aged under 35 years. The number of herding households rose to 171,588 in 2007, before declining slightly to 170,142 in 2009, and more steeply to 160,265 in 2010.The number of herdsmen increased to 366,199 in 2007 (probably reflecting the success of the cashmere sector), decreasing to 349,303 in 2009 and to 327,154 in 2010. Some 28.9% of herdsmen's households had an electricity supply in 2003 (a 5% rise on 2000), but by 2007 the proportion had reached 60%, or 103,900 households, and by 2009 over 77%, or 131,300 households. In the majority of households, the supply came from a petrol-driven generator, rather than a mains source. Although there was a decline in the number of agricultural specialists, the number of vets increased slightly, from 1,800 in 1989 to 2,009 in 2003, before declining to 1,838 in 2006 and 1,748 in 2009. Between 2003 and 2009 the number of tractors declined by about two-thirds and of grain harvesters by more than one-half. Between 2003 and 2009 the number of tractors decreased from 4,193 to 2,898, while grain harvesters declined from 1,072 to 617, then rose again to 967. The number of animal shelters (roofed and fenced) roughly doubled between 1990 and 2003 and reached 129,400 in 2006 and 140,700 in 2009, while the number of wells in operation rose from 34,600 in 1995 to 40,900 in 2003, before decreasing to 38,700 in 2006 and rising again to 42,300 in 2009.

In livestock herding 9.3m. head of new-born stock were raised in 2004 and 2005, but losses of mature stock exceeded 544,000 head in the first six months of 2005, when many provinces were drought-stricken. However, there was good rainfall in the first half of 2006, boosting new-born stock numbers to 10m. At the year-end census the livestock herds exceeded 34.8m. head. In 2007 more than 12m. head of new-born stock were raised, thus increasing the total livestock count to beyond 40m. The 2008 census showed a further rise in total livestock to almost 43.3m., while 13.6m. young were raised in the first six months of 2009, 1.5m. fewer than in the first half of 2008. Meanwhile, there was increasing concern about overgrazing and desertification.

Total livestock at the year-end census in 2009 numbered 44.0m. head, but the severe winter of 2009/10 killed more than 9.7m. mature stock, or some 22% of the herds; one-half of the animals that perished were goats. The United Nations Development Programme (UNDP) allocated US $4m. for the burial of carcasses. More than 750 herding families lost all their stock. In the first six months of 2010 about 7.3m. young animals were raised (71% of those born, compared with the usual average of 89%–95%). At the year-end census the livestock total stood at 32.7m. head. At mid-2011 about 13m. new-born animals were being raised, an above-average survival rate of 97.2%, and it was estimated that the livestock total for that year would reach 43m. head.

INDUSTRY

Large-scale industry has developed only since the 1960s. Before the 1921 Revolution all manufactured items were imported and domestic goods were made locally, mainly by Chinese craftsmen. In the 1920s technicians from Germany were engaged to build a small power station and a brickworks. However, after the movement to the left in 1929, only Soviet aid and expertise were welcome, and in the years prior to the Second World War industrial growth was slow. Only one enterprise of any size was commissioned, the Industrial Combine in Ulan Bator, which in 1934 commenced production of leather goods and felts. Industry developed in two channels. Co-operative industry had a much smaller output than state industry, producing many items needed for domestic use, as well as providing repair services. After the Second World War state-operated industry expanded rapidly and many new enterprises were commissioned.

Mongolia received enormous aid from its political allies—some 10,000m. roubles from the USSR alone between 1945 and 1990—without which its industrial advance, modest though it was in world terms, could not have been envisaged. For a time, in the 1950s, it seemed as if the People's Republic of China was hoping to challenge the USSR's leading position in Mongolia, by means of economic aid. A first gift of 160m. roubles in 1955 was followed by the dispatch of Chinese labourers to supplement Mongolia's inadequate and undertrained labour force. Exact numbers were not available, but in the peak years of 1959 and 1960 several thousand Chinese labourers were working on diverse projects, such as building apartment blocks, laying roads and installing irrigation systems. Many had their families with them. As the Sino-Soviet rift widened, the Chinese workers began to leave Mongolia, until by mid-1964 most had returned home. To some extent the loss of these workmen was made good by the supply of Soviet construction labourers and engineers (some 50,000 at their peak), working principally in Ulan Bator, Darkhan (half-way between the capital and the Russian frontier) and Choibalsan, in eastern Mongolia. However, the break with China had other adverse effects. Chinese consumer goods, in particular silk and cloth, which were plentiful in 1959, were in short supply by 1968. The drastic decrease in railway through-goods traffic between the USSR and China also led to a considerable loss of state revenue.

One of the most important developments in Mongolia's economy was the joint Soviet-Mongolian exploitation of copper and molybdenum deposits at Erdenet in Orkhon Province. The Salkhit–Erdenet railway line, linking the new complex with the trans-Mongolian Ulan Bator Railway, went into operation in October 1975, and the ore concentrator in December 1978. The combine attained its full capacity in November 1983. In the 1990s the Erdenet copper enterprise became Mongolia's largest source of foreign exchange, while Erdenet town emerged as an industrial centre in its own right, with a large carpet factory and other enterprises.

In 1995 copper concentrate exports were sufficient to finance more than 67% of Mongolia's imports. However, in 1995–96 fluctuating world copper prices and the declining metal content of exported concentrate highlighted Mongolia's vulnerability in this area. There was a continuing slow decline in the share of copper in Mongolia's total exports, decreasing from 53.0% in 1995 to 27.6% in 2002. In 2000–01 the Erdenet concern operated at a loss, unable to reduce production costs or to pay government taxes, which had been set too high on world copper price forecasts. However, with the revival of world copper prices, earnings from copper concentrate exports rose steadily from US $284.3m. in 2004 to $835.7m. in 2008; they were worth $501.9m. in 2009 and $770.6m. in 2010.

In July 2008 a Russian presidential decree (signed by President Vladimir Putin but implemented by his successor, Dimitrii Medvedev) transferred the 49% Russian-owned shares in the Erdenet Enterprise and Mongolrostsvetmet joint ventures to the Rostekhnologiya Corporation, which was established in November 2007.

The principal centres of industry—Ulan Bator, Darkhan and Erdenet—are situated in the area of densest population and have direct road and rail communication with Russia. In addition, Ulan Bator has a large, new, open-cast coal mine at Baganuur, linked to the trans-Mongolian railway. These three industrial centres account for most of Mongolia's production in terms of electric power, capital materials such as cement, bricks and wall panels, and consumer goods—food, drink, leather goods, confectionery, soap, etc. A large new cement and lime complex at Khötöl, between Darkhan and Erdenet, which was in the process of being established in 2011, was to produce 100,000 metric tons of lime and 500,000 tons of cement per year, enough to satisfy the country's total requirements. In the mid-1990s, however, the construction industry was working at only some 20% of its capacity. Between 2007 and 2010 annual cement production rose from 179,700 tons to 322,500 tons. A factory producing disposable syringes, financed by the Republic of Korea (South Korea), began production in the mid-1990s.

At the end of the 1990s there was an increase in the output of the knitwear and garment industry. In comparison with the previous year, clothing exports doubled in value to exceed 11% of total exports in 2004. In 2005, however, clothing exports decreased by 60%, after quota restrictions forced China-based producers to halt production in Mongolia, where unemployment in the industry rose sharply as a result. Knitwear production decreased from 4.5m. garments in 2006 to 2.1m. in 2008, and declined further to 639,200 in 2009, before recovering to 801,100 in 2010. There was also a substantial reduction in the number of trousers and shirts being manufactured.

In the mining sector, open-cast extraction of coal, 10.0m. metric tons in 2008 and 14.4m. tons in 2009, almost doubled in 2010 as working began of Tavan Tolgoi mine in the Gobi and Khöshööt mine in Khovd province, both close to the border with China. Output of fluorspar concentrate totalled 142,900 tons in 2008, 115,300 tons in 2009 and 140,700 tons in 2010. Extraction of iron ore has increased substantially, exceeding 3m. tons in 2010, while output of zinc concentrate declined from 141,500 tons in 2009 to 112,600 tons in 2010. The gold-mining industry became increasingly successful from the latter part of the

1990s, with production rising from 4.5 tons in 1995 to 13.7 tons in 2001. Mongolia mined 24.1 tons of gold in 2005 and exported 23.8 tons. Gold output (state procurement) reached almost 22.6 tons in 2006, but subsequently declined:to 17.5 tons in 2007, 15.2 tons in 2008, 9.8 tons in 2009 and 6.0 tons in 2010. Gold exports were worth US $270.1m. in 2006, decreasing to just under $235m. in 2007, before more than doubling to reach $599.9m. in 2008, only to fall back again, to $308.5m. in 2009 and $178.3m. in 2010.

Examination by the Great Khural, the Mongolian parliament, in January 2004 of a draft decree to allow the Government to alter the boundaries of special protected areas (nature reserves) when appropriate for the exploitation of mineral resources led to protests by the Mongolian office of the World Wide Fund for Nature (WWF) and UNDP. It was reported that 3.1m. ha were under threat in the Daguur, Onon-Balj and Gobi Large and Small Reserves, including the habitat of the extremely rare Gobi bear. In April the Government issued a decree to stop illegal gold-mining in the Gobi Small Reserve by hundreds of 'ninjas', as the freelance ('artisanal') miners were called.

In mid-2003 the Canadian company Ivanhoe Mines continued to improve the prospects for developing the Oyu Tolgoi deposit in the Gobi region, upgrading its estimate of copper and gold content and finding plentiful supplies of underground water. Finance was being sought for construction of a road from the deposits to the border with China, but the project was beset by political uncertainties. Following expressions of public dissatisfaction with the terms of the contract being negotiated by the Government with Ivanhoe Mines with regard to the gold and copper deposits at Oyu Tolgoi, in July 2005 draft amendments to the 1997 Minerals Law were proposed in the Great Khural that would reduce tax 'holidays' and the period of validity of operating licences, while increasing licence fees and taxes on mining products. A group campaigning for a bigger share in mining profits for Mongolia pointed out that, under existing rules, a foreign company could completely exhaust a gold deposit before being required to pay any taxes. The Chairman of the Minerals and Petroleum Agency, Luvsanvandangiin Bold, stated that mineral deposit ownership certificates would be replaced during that year by new certificates issued competitively through tendering. In October 2009, in a major development for the country's economy, Mongolian government ministers and directors of Ivanhoe Mines and Rio Tinto signed an investment agreement on the exploitation of the Oyu Tolgoi strategic deposits and associated accords. The Government acquired a 34% interest in the mining enterprise, which would employ several thousand Mongolian workers, and, once in operation, would more than double Mongolia's annual mineral exports to some US $3,000m. by 2014.

The revised Minerals Law was adopted in July 2006. Important points of the amended legislation included a stipulation that exploitation licences could henceforth be issued only to legal entities and not to individuals. Moreover, foreign and domestic investors would pay tax at the same rate, while stability agreements were to be replaced by investment contracts and, furthermore, local people would have more say in the issue of exploration licences. Investors would be obliged to publish full details of their annual income and expenditure, tax payments and 'excavated products'. The Government, meanwhile, would have the right to acquire up to 50% of resources of deposits discovered with the help of Mongolian state funds. However, the revised Minerals Law remained controversial, and in March 2008 Prime Minister Sanjaagiin Bayar and the leader of the main opposition party announced their agreement that Mongolia would own not less than 51% of jointly owned strategic deposits. However, when amendments to the Minerals Law were debated in the Great Khural in June, they were not approved because of disagreements over the size of reserves of 'strategic' deposits, and the matter was deferred until after the election of the new Great Khural, scheduled for the end of the month. Negotiations with some foreign investors remained inconclusive, pending the Great Khural's agreed definition of 'strategic'. Meanwhile, the state-owned Erdenes Mongol company was established, in order to ensure unified coordination of the operations of strategic mineral deposits. The company was also licensed to supervise the Tavan Tolgoi coal mine and Asgat silver mine, pending the establishment of joint ventures.

The revised feasibility study for Oyu Tolgoi was approved by the Mongolian Great Khural, and in May 2010 the State Property Committee nominated to the Oyu Tolgoi board of directors former President Natsagiin Bagabandi and two other Mongolian directors, while Galsangiin Batsükh was appointed as chairman by Ivanhoe Mongolia. In the same month a company to manage the Tavantolgoi coal deposit under the leadership of Erdenes Mongol was established. The Mongol 999 National Association's board of directors was composed of Mongolian businessmen, chaired by D. Bat-Erdene, director of Ajnai Corp. A draft investment agreement was prepared to attract foreign companies, including Russian, Chinese and Japanese consortia, to participate in the Tavan Tolgoi coal-mining project, but it was also intended that ordinary Mongolian citizens should be given 10% of shares in the enterprise, an average of 536 shares per head of the population.

The Government was also under pressure to regulate the thousands of itinerant 'ninjas' in the country, and improve their working conditions. In August 2005 the Government issued a resolution to reinforce the rights of gold-mining companies while controlling mining by 'ninjas'. In July 2006 police forcibly removed some 8,000 people from a gold-mining area at Zaamar, after complaints of encroachment by the Altan Dornod and Monpolimet companies.

Output of petroleum has continued to expand. In 1997 exploratory drilling at Tamsag, in eastern Mongolia, began to yield crude petroleum, at a rate of 1,500 barrels per day. The first consignment was delivered to China for analysis and refining. A clear sign of long-term improvement in government revenues appeared in July 1997, with income of 500m. tögrög from petroleum exploitation included for the first time. The number of wells was scheduled to reach eight in 1998 and 17 in 1999. Production of crude petroleum rose from 44,791 barrels in 1998 to 71,914 barrels in 1999, then declined slightly to 65,522 barrels in 2000. The SOCO oil company had suffered a severe fire at its Tamsag base in eastern Mongolia, but restarted extraction at its three production wells for export to China (73,700 barrels in 2001). Crude petroleum extraction amounted to 139,205 barrels in 2002 and 183,047 barrels in 2003. Extraction figures for 2004 and 2005 were 215,700 and 200,700 barrels, respectively, increasing to 376,500 barrels in 2006 and more than doubling to reach 850,200 barrels in 2007. Extraction amounted to 1,174,200 barrels in 2008, 1,870,000 barrels in 2009 and 2,181,400 barrels in 2010. The PetroChina Daqing Tamsag company, which was established in Mongolia in 2005, conducts mining operations at the Tamsag field and sends all its crude petroleum output to China by truck. Mongolia has evidently closed its small-scale petroleum refining capacity, no production data having been released since 2003, but is expected to build new capacity in the near future.

The 1990s witnessed a resurgence of Chinese business activity in Mongolia. By 2001 companies with Chinese investment accounted for 35.0% of all companies with foreign investment, and companies benefiting from Hong Kong investment for a further 13.7%, while the Republic of Korea accounted for 23.7%.

Investment in Mongolian petroleum production rose from US $123.0m. in 2006 to $238.4m. in 2007. Revenue from extraction of petroleum reached 4,900m. tögrög in 2006, rising to 10,500m. tögrög in 2007. In the latter year exports of crude petroleum amounted to 812,300 barrels, which were worth $88.9m. For 2008 investment in the sector was planned at around $433m., with 200 more wells drilled and extraction reaching 1.5m. barrels. Revenue from exports of mineral fuels rose dramatically from $297.4m. in 2008, to $437.5m. in 2009 and to $1,055.6m. in 2010. Mongolian imports of petroleum products in 2010, nearly all from Russia, were as follows: petrol 284,700 metric tons (compared with 323,000 tons in 2009); diesel 499,400 tons (416,200 tons in 2009); jet fuel 16,200 tons (14,700 tons in 2009); heating oil 5,300 tons (4,600 tons in 2009); and lubricants 3,000 tons (2,900 tons in 2009). These imports cost a total of $713.8m. in 2010. Mongolia imported 4,700 tons of liquefied petroleum gas (LPG) in 2007.

FOREIGN TRADE

Trade was traditionally almost entirely with the countries formerly constituting the 'socialist bloc': in 1989 93.1% of Mongolia's exports went to socialist countries (CMEA 90.3%), which were also the source of 95.6% of imports (CMEA 92.5%). However, the share of Mongolia's total foreign trade conducted with former socialist states had declined to some 74% by 1992. In 2009 the principal source of imports was Russia (costing US $772.8m. and accounting for 36.2% of total imports), followed by China ($538.6m.), the Republic of Korea ($155.1m.) and the USA ($103.7m.). By far the largest market for exports in 2009 was China ($1,393.9m., accounting for 73.9% of the total). Canada, the United Kingdom and Russia were also significant purchasers of Mongolian products in that year. In 2010 China accounted for $3,437.2m. or 56% of total trade turnover (mainly exports) and Russia for $1,129.4m. or 21% (mainly imports).

Mongolia exports mainly primary products, while importing industrial goods and equipment. In 1989 some 42.8% of its exports consisted of fuels, minerals and metals, while raw materials, including foodstuffs, accounted for a further 35.7%. In that year industrial consumer goods accounted for 17.5% of total exports. In 1993 industrial goods accounted for 75.4% of total imports, while consumer goods comprised the remaining 24.6%. Fuel and petroleum accounted for 32.6% of industrial imports.

In 1993 59.9% of imports were conducted by general (convertible currency) trade, 29.5% by barter and 10.6% by other kinds of trade. The breakdown of exports was as follows: 51.6% general trade, 35.2% barter and 13.2% other kinds of trade. Mongolia subsequently aimed to achieve a trade surplus by reducing petroleum imports and promoting the export of cashmere goods, but its international trade recorded a deficit of US $87.4m. in 1996. With world copper prices low, the trade deficit in 1998 was $155.6m., compared with a surplus of $30.2m. in 1997. The trade deficit was estimated by the IMF to have risen from $72.6m. in 2000 to $100.6m. in 2001 and to have increased sharply in 2002 to reach $156.2m. According to the Mongolian Statistical Committee, the trade deficit declined from $185.2m. in 2003 to $151.4m. in 2004 and to $119.4m. in 2005. In 2006 there was a trade surplus of $57.2m. However, in 2008 exports totalled $2,534.5m., and imports amounted to $3,244.5m., resulting in a trade deficit of $710m. The deficit in 2009 was reduced to $252m., with exports totalling $1,885.4m. and imports $2,137.7m. In 2009 the principal imports were machinery and vehicles (costing a total of $689.7m.), fuels and lubricants ($544.4m.) and manufactured goods ($321.7 m.). The principal exports in 2009 were copper concentrate (revenue from which totalled $501.9m.), gold ($308.5m.), and manufactured goods ($46.3m.). In 2010 the trade deficit rose to $291m., with exports totalling $2,908.5m. and imports $3,200.1m. In that year the principal imports were machinery and vehicles (costing a total of $1,261.7m.), refinery products ($713.8m.) and manufactured goods ($414.4 m.). The principal exports in 2010 were petroleum (revenue from which totalled $1,055.6m.), copper concentrate ($770.6m.), gold ($178.3m.) and food and live animals ($60.2m.). In the first six months of 2011 exports totalled $1,992.8m. and imports $2,725.6m.

In 2004 copper concentrate accounted for 33% of exports by value, the price of copper having risen by 75% year-on-year. Gold accounted for 16% of exports by value, and boosted exports to the United Kingdom alone to US $133.7m., a more than 10-fold increase on the usual level. In 2004 70.4% of imports were foreign currency purchases, 9.7% purchases by foreign customers, 9.4% investment goods, and 5.2% foreign aid goods. In the first half of 2006 the volume of copper concentrate exports increased by 18.4%, and their value more than doubled, reflecting the rise in the world price for the commodity from $511 to $870 per metric ton. In 2006 as a whole exports of mineral products (copper, etc.) accounted for 57.9% of all exports, and imports of mineral products (refined petroleum, etc.) for 30.3% of all imports. Coal exports totalled 2.4m. tons in 2006 and 3.3m. tons in 2007, rising to 7.1m. tons in 2009, just under one-half of total extraction. The coal sector grew substantially in 2010 when exports reached 16.7m. tons and total extraction amounted to 25.2m. tons.

The law on the legal status of the free economic zone at Zamyn-Üüd (a railway station on the Chinese border) was adopted in June 2003. The Altanbulag free economic zone (approved in June 2002) on the northern border with Russia, where there is an international road border crossing point, continued its development, with new infrastructure and trade service centres. Another free economic zone, at Tsagaan Nuur on the western border with Russia, where there is also an international road border crossing point, was in the course of approval.

In July 2005 the Minister of Industry and Trade, Sükhbaataryn Batbold, led the Mongolian delegation to the Mongolia-Russia intergovernmental trade, economic, science and technology co-operation commission's meeting in Irkutsk, Russia. The two countries concluded a new trade and economic co-operation programme for the period to 2010 and drew up a plan to reduce infections in Mongolian livestock. The programme was intended to expand trade liberalization, develop Mongolia's Altanbulag free trade zone, increase the added value of Mongolian exports and reduce tariffs on Russian oil exports to Mongolia.

Following the adoption of the Law on Nuclear Energy in July 2009, it emerged that the Mongolians planned to cancel existing exploitation licences issued previously to foreign companies such as Khan Resources, the 58% owner of Central Asia Uranium, and to re-register uranium mining licences. During Russian President Medvedev's visit to Mongolia in August of that year it was agreed to establish a joint venture, Dornod Uran ('Eastern Uranium'), to operate uranium mines in eastern Mongolia. Initially the partners disagreed over their shares in the company, Rosatom wanting 50:50 and the Mongolian side 51:49. Mongolia and Russia also agreed to build a copper smelter, with a feasibility study to commence in 2011 in co-ordination with the Erdenet enterprise.

POWER AND TRANSPORT

Fuel of many types is used in Mongolia. At one end of the scale is the Ulan Bator No. 4 power station, built with Soviet assistance, which went into operation in 1985. Its capacity of 380 MW doubled the country's generating capacity. The station is fuelled by coal from Baganuur. Provincial *(aimag)* centres may have thermal power stations or diesel generators, and in rural centres small diesel generators are common. Long-term plans include the extension of the central grid to outlying regions, but a shortage of generating plants appears imminent. Mongolia has plenty of coal, but nuclear power is another option being considered.

Domestic heating in apartment blocks in Ulan Bator and other large towns is by central town-heating from the local power station. Coal, briquettes, wood, roots, bushes and dried animal dung are burned in stoves for cooking and heating in *ger* (yurt) districts. A new fuel of increasing popularity is LPG, with 12,000 users in Ulan Bator and 20,000 in the countryside as of February 2008.

Transport shows a similar range of sophistication. Ulan Bator has regular air links with Beijing and Hohhot (China), and Ulan-Ude and Irkutsk (in Russia). The one Airbus of the national airline, Mongolian Civil Air Transport (MIAT), flies to Moscow and Berlin and also to Seoul, while two Boeing-727s fly the shorter international routes and a Boeing 737-800 was delivered in 2002. Mongolian railways connect the Trans-Siberian main line with the Chinese railway system, providing a direct route from Moscow to Beijing and an eastern link with the town of Choibalsan. The Mongolian and Chinese gauges are different and goods are trans-shipped at the border station Zamyn-Üüd (for Erenhot). In order to encourage foreign investment, Mongolia is planning long-term road improvements. To mark the millennium the Government launched the building of a road running from west to east across the country, linking Siberian Russia with northern China, and improving communications with Ulan Bator from outlying parts of Mongolia. The route was from Kosh-Agach in the Altai Republic to Ölgii, the Zavkhan valley and through Arkhangai to Ulan Bator, then via Öndörkhaan in Khentii to Sümber (Khalkhyn Gol) and into Inner Mongolia. The project was expected to take about 10 years to complete, but, because of the cost, it was not planned that the road would be hard-topped for its whole length. Meanwhile, long-distance transport is mainly cross-country by lorry or Soviet-built UAZ (jeep-type vehicle). Horse, ox and camel carts are still widely used and camels are employed as beasts of burden.

The amount of freight transported by rail rose steadily in the late 1990s, reaching almost 8.2m. metric tons in 1999. Rail freight totalled 14.6m. tons in 2008, declining to 14.2m. tons in 2009, and rising again to 16.8m. tons in 2010. Transit rail freight decreased from 3.5m. tons in 2007 to an annual 2.3m. tons in 2008–10. Rail passenger traffic declined from 4.3m. passengers carried in 2008 to 3.1m. in 2009, before rising again, to 3.5m., in 2010. The numbers of international passengers carried reached 191,800 in 2006 and 203,700 in 2007, and stood at 144,200 in 2010. During the late 2000s road freight and passengers recorded marginal increases, while air freight and passengers declined slightly.

In connection with the development of the Tavan Tolgoi mine in Ömnögobi Province, in 2010 the Government approved the construction of a broad-gauge railway line from Tavan Tolgoi to Tsagaansuvarga, Züünbayan, Sainshand, Baruun Urt, Khööt and Choibalsan, providing a link to the Trans-Siberian railway. Russian Railways was expected to invest in the project. It was thought that the 1,100-km line could be built within two years.

In September 1995 there were concerns over the state of Mongolia's ageing aviation equipment after a MIAT An-24 twin turbo-prop crashed into a mountain 17 km from Mörön airport in Khövsgöl Province. The civil aviation authority subsequently decided to acquire ground position indicators for the fleet. The crash of a Chinese-built MIAT Yu-12 in June 1997 appeared to have been caused by freak weather conditions. However, in May 1998 another MIAT Yu-12 crashed in the mountains of southern Khövsgöl Province, killing the 28 crew and passengers. MIAT's remaining Yu-12 aircraft were returned to China. By 2005 most of MIAT's An-24 and An-2 aircraft had been taken out of service because of their age. At the end of July 2008 MIAT announced that it was discontinuing its passenger flights on internal routes. The gaps in MIAT's provincial services were filled by new airlines such as Aero Mongolia and Eznis (Easiness) Airways, operating Fokker or SAAB turbo-prop aircraft. MIAT resumed internal flights in mid-2009, introducing its Boeing aircraft on the Ulan Bator–Mörön–Khovd route. Easiness launched a twice-weekly service from Ulan Bator to Hailar, in northern China, to be routed via Choibalsan from September. In May 2010 MIAT was affected by a technicians' strike, which stopped flights for several days. New directors were appointed, who decided that the privatization of MIAT, planned by the Government, would be postponed until 2012.

REFORM AND OTHER DEVELOPMENTS

The regular pattern of Five-Year Plans and CMEA-orientated trade was disrupted in 1990–91 by the collapse of command economies in the USSR and Eastern Europe, by the transition to payments in convertible currencies, and by the first steps towards privatization and a market economy in Mongolia itself. There was a rapid decline in Mongolia's foreign trade, which, with traditional partners, was largely reduced, by the shortage of convertible currencies, to barter transactions. Petroleum, medicines, and some imported foodstuffs and consumer goods were in particularly short supply, owing to Mongolia's inability to pay for all its requirements at prevailing world prices. Industrial production also declined sharply. The rationing of basic foodstuffs, such as flour, pasta, sugar, tea, vodka and meat, was introduced for the urban population. In January 1991 the Government increased wages and private savings two-fold in order to compensate for the expected doubling of retail prices.

In June 1991 a massive devaluation of the tögrög altered the official exchange rate from US $1 = 7.10 tögrög at the end of May to $1 = 40.00 tögrög. A devaluation of the currency on 1 January 1993 from $1 = 40.00 tögrög to 150.00 was followed at the end of May by its flotation at $1 = 400.00 tögrög, stabilizing at 395.00. However, the tögrög decreased from its 1993 flotation value to $1 = 534 tögrög at the official rate of exchange by July 1996. The value of the tögrög declined by 13% in the first half of 1997, decreasing to around US $1 = 830 tögrög in March/April before stabilizing and standing at an average rate of $1 = 840.83 in 1998. In 1999, however, the average rate of exchange declined to $1 = 1,021.87 tögrög. The tögrög continued to weaken, standing at $1 = 1,205.27 in 2005, but subsequently strengthened to reach 1,170.96 in 2007, falling back only slightly in 2008 when it stood at 1,165.74. The average exchange rate in 2009 was 1,440.76, a weakening of 23.2% year-on-year. In 2010 the annual average exchange rate strengthened to 1,355.93.

The Government initiated a programme for the privatization of state property in two stages. The first, involving small-scale enterprises, began in May 1991 with the auctioning of several shops and restaurants in Ulan Bator to private individuals. The privatization of large state industrial enterprises began haltingly in early 1992. However, the Government prohibited the privatization of railways, roads, the airline, the state oil company, gold mines, hunting and forestry enterprises, and large irrigation systems. The state also retained a 51% interest in power stations and transmission lines, mines producing coal and metalliferous ores, communications links, some flour mills, meat-packing plants and cement works, motor transport depots, the brewery and distillery, etc. Although it had been claimed that the members of the *negdel* did not wish them to be dissolved, it was announced in mid-1991 that at least some of the members would leave with their stock, and an Association of Individual Herdsmen was established. The privatization of livestock farming and of internal trade and services had been 80% and 90% completed, respectively, by mid-1993.

A UNDP report, completed in June 1994, stated that privatization in Mongolia had failed to create an environment in which the market mechanism could operate efficiently. Many supposedly privatized enterprises were still partially owned by the state. The report declared that 'the problem is not a low volume of credit but an allocation of credit that responds to political interference and personal private connections rather than to commercial criteria', and stated that the Mongolian Government should have promoted new private sector enterprises, creating additional wealth, rather than simply redistributing assets through the voucher scheme. Substantial aid was forthcoming, the report added, but it was not to be used to sustain consumption rather than investment. UNDP urged price stabilization, lower interest rates, bank regulation and a system of commercial law, as well as a mechanism for the enforcement of contracts.

In November 1994 an IMF report criticized state interference in the allocation of bank credits, which the Government had directed to agriculture and strategic public sector projects without consultation with Mongolbank. This practice had 'adverse consequences for monetary management', constraining private sector activity. Prime Minister Puntsagiin Jasrai's address to Mongolia's first convention of industrialists and business representatives, held in April 1995, was not successful. Delegates complained about government bureaucracy, and criticized middle- and low-ranking officials who were hindering the growth of private businesses with their excessive administrative procedures.

One of the first acts of the Government of Mendsaikhany Enkhsaikhan, which took office in mid-1996, was to remove the ban on the export of raw cashmere. The ban had been imposed in March 1994 to protect the cashmere garment industry's 'added value'. The removal of the ban was welcomed by the IMF, the World Bank and the Asian Development Bank (ADB), which had opposed it on the grounds that it interfered with trade. The Government subsequently abolished customs duty on almost all imports, on the grounds that the imports were needed to boost the country's export production capacity. To protect domestic garment production, a new tax was levied on raw cashmere and camel wool exports.

Prime Minister Enkhsaikhan urged public support for the Democratic Alliance's proposals to transform the state executive and to reform government agencies so as to meet the demands of the market system. The Democratic Alliance's rationalization programme began with the establishment of 'sectoral ministries', which combined (and in some cases relocated and co-sited) ministries of the previous administration. None the less, the Democratic Alliance Government's first year in office produced no real achievements in its efforts to stimulate the free market economic revival for which it had hoped.

The restructuring of the social security 'net', without extra revenue, was not well received by those most in need of financial support, i.e. pensioners, the very poor and the unemployed. The number of registered unemployed reached 64,200 at the end of June 1997, but several estimates put the true figure at around 227,000, if school-leavers, ex-servicemen and others who had never been employed were included. The number of unemployed declined to 39,800 in 1999, representing 4.6% of the economically active population. The rate subsequently fluctuated, and the number of registered unemployed stood at 29,600 in 2008 and 38,300 in 2010 (with the actual total unemployed at around 113,400).

It was reported at the end of December 2003 that the Poverty Reduction Programme, renamed the Sustainable Household Livelihood Programme, was considered a failure after 10 years' operation. Business investment was discouraged by licences, bureaucracy, bribery and excessive taxation, the report stated. The minimum wage was set in January 2004 at 236.68 tögrög per hour or 40,000 tögrög per month; the average civil service salary was 81,750 tögrög, and the minimum state pension was 32,000 tögrög. In February 2006 the minimum wage was raised to 53,000 tögrög. The minimum standard of living was set at 42,800 tögrög (for the Ulan Bator area) in April that year. The average wage in 2005 was 101,200 tögrög, 8.7% more than in 2004. However, it was estimated in 2006 that a family needed a monthly income of 350,000 tögrög to maintain a reasonable standard of living. In June 2006 the basic rate of personal income tax was reduced to 10%. In January 2007 the minimum wage was raised to 69,000 tögrög a month. The minimum standard of living was set regionally from March 2009, the rate for inhabitants of Ulan Bator being a monthly income of 100,100 tögrög. On average 35.2% of the population was classified as poor, while in rural areas the figure was 46%. Meanwhile, there were plans to abolish herdsmen's income tax. In May 2009 the Ministry of Social Welfare and Labour, in conjunction with the ADB, launched a free voucher scheme for obtaining essential commodities such as meat, flour, potatoes, bread and rice. It was reported that 36,800 people had signed up for the scheme. The minimum wage was raised to 140,400 tögrög a month in April 2011.

It was disclosed in June 2004 that the IMF had become aware of Mongolbank and the Mongolian Government 'conducting large quasi-fiscal and/or extra-budgetary operations' in late 2002 and early 2003. The IMF had 'questioned the legality of these operations and cautioned that they could threaten debt sustainability, undermine fiscal transparency and accountability and give rise to misreporting'. The Mongolian authorities took 'significant steps' to address these concerns, relating to the foreign financing of large infrastructure projects—two hydroelectric power stations and a section of the Millennium Road. At the same time, independent supervision of the Board of Mongolbank would be instituted.

Privatization continued to make slow progress, with attention focused on the free disposal of state housing stock and the auction of small businesses, rather than the dispersal of large state-owned enterprises, such as the department store in central Ulan Bator, for which there were no bidders. By the beginning of 1996 more than 91% of trade enterprises had been privatized, as well as 88% of agricultural assets, but over 50% of industrial enterprises remained wholly under state ownership. In September 1997 a radical privatization programme was revealed by the Government, under which it was proposed to sell by auction to the highest bidder the entire state sector except some assets such as the railway.

The Agricultural Bank was sold in February 2003 to a Japanese-financed company for US $6.8m. The 80% state share in the petroleum distributor NIK (Neft Import Kontsern) was sold for $7.32m. to East Oil International Consortium, including Anais Ltd, Irkutsk Oil Co (both of Russia) and a company registered in Cyprus. However, the Government cancelled this sale in September after 'negative reports' about the consortium, and NIK was put out to tender again. In February 2004 the state's share in NIK was sold to the Mongolian distribution company Petrovis, its chief competitor; the director-general of Petrovis, Janchivyn Oyuungerel, had been the manager of NIK during 1990–96 and then a director representing the 20% of private shareholders. The Mongol Daatgal (insurance) company was successfully privatized in December 2003, but a bid for the Gobi cashmere company from Itochu and the Mongolian MCS company in the same month failed on a technicality. In July 2007, however, agreement was reached on a bid by a Japanese investment bank. In the latter part of 2008 the accounts of Anod Bank came under scrutiny when it emerged that there were significant shortages of foreign currency, and in December the bank was placed under the control of Mongolbank. Three of Anod's directors were arrested on suspicion of fraud, including Nyamaagiin Davaa, Chairman of the Citizens' Movement Party. In November 2009 Zoos Bank was declared bankrupt and was reorganized as the State Bank. A cabinet meeting in July 2010 approved the establishment and regulation of the Mongolian Development Bank, with capitalization of 100,000m. tögrög.

The Law on Mongolian Citizens' Ownership of Land, which came into force from 1 May 2003, provided for once-only free privatization of plots of land for locally registered households, which was to be completed within two years. In Ulan Bator each household was entitled free of charge to a maximum of 0.07 ha of land for housing and a further 0.1 ha for growing its own vegetables and fruit. The maximum area for housing in provincial centres was 0.35 ha and in rural district centres 0.5 ha. Land could also be bought, sold or leased freely, but not to foreigners or stateless persons, applications being made through the local governor's office.

As 1 May 2005 approached, it was reported that in Ulan Bator, with 192,900 households (2004), 151,046 households had privatized 9,739.9 ha of land, or around 78%. However, Nyamjavyn Batbayar, Minister of Construction and Urban Development, told the Great Khural that nation-wide the campaign had proceeded 'unsatisfactorily' because of the shortcomings of central and local administrative bodies, lack of information, confusion over privatization of land with buildings standing on it, and big differences between the cost of land privatized and its 'market value'. Members of the Great Khural remarked that citizens had suffered a lot of trouble and inconvenience, which allowed 'opportunities for corruption to flourish'. When amendments to the Law on Mongolian Citizens' Ownership of Land were presented in the Great Khural, Minister Batbayar stated that in the two years of privatization so far altogether 200,000 or so households nationwide had obtained free land, but another 368,000 had yet to do so. The Great Khural agreed to extend the period of privatization by three years, to 1 May 2008. Some residential restrictions were removed. The period was subsequently extended for a further three years.

The annual rate of inflation reached a high point of 183% in 1993, but by 2002 the rate had declined to 3.1%. Inflation in 2003 reached 4.6%, rising to 11.0% in 2004, before decreasing to 9.5% in 2005. The consumer price index (December 2005 base = 100) stood at 106.2 in 2006, rising to 125.0 in 2007 and to 152.6 in 2008, thus resulting in an annual rate of inflation of 22.1% in the most recent year. Consumer prices rose by 6.3% in 2009 and by 10.2% in 2010 (with a 21.5 point increase in the consumer price index in the latter year). A new 20,000 tögrög note entered into circulation in 2007.

According to the IMF, foreign-exchange reserves increased from US $236.1m. at the end of 2004 to $430.10m. in December 2005. Mongolia's reserves continued to strengthen, reaching $1,060.6m. in December 2006 and $1,394.6m. at the end of 2007. They were worth $1,145.3m., equivalent to 25.6 weeks of imports, at the end of 2009, and $2,091.2m., equivalent to 33.3 weeks of imports, at the end of 2010. In June 2010 the Great Khural's budget standing committee reported that government loans in 1991–2009 totalled 2,604,000m. tögrög ($1,900m), and grants received reached $1,800m. As of the end of 2009, government debt amounted to 1,335,000m tögrög, or 14.8% of GDP.

Substantial deficits were incorporated into the budgets for 1996–2002. The budget deficit decreased from the equivalent of 4.5% of GDP in 2003 to only 0.9% in the following year. In 2005 the central government budget recorded a surplus of US $23m., equivalent to 10.2% of GDP. In 2008, following the revision of official figures, a budget deficit of 95,263.9m. tögrög was forecast. In 2009 budgetary revenue amounted to 1,993,995.6m. tögrög and expenditure 2,336,629.7m. tögrög), resulting in a deficit of $342,634.1m. tögrög. The budgetary revenue for 2010 totalled 3,078,418.6m. tögrög and expenditure 3,076,262.8m. tögrög, leading to a surplus of 2,155.8m. tögrög. The budget for 2011 envisaged a deficit of 290,367.2m. tögrög.

Mongolia's total external debt at the end of 2008 was $1,721m. (compared with $1,596.2m. at the end of 2007), of which $1,653m. was public and publicly guaranteed debt. The external debt was equivalent to 98.4% of GNI in 2007, the figure having remained above 90% since 1995. In 2006 the cost of debt-servicing was equivalent to 2.1% of the value of exports of goods and services, in comparison with 29.3% in 2003.

In April 2003 Mongolia joined the 1973 London Convention on Shipping, as part of its preparations to establish its own register of shipping, with help from a Singaporean company, Maritime Chain. In 2010, however, the connection with Maritime Chain was ended. It was reported that Russian Far Eastern shipowners had hurried to register, but there was some concern that the Mongolian authorities might not be able to regulate the safety and insurance of the ships that they registered.

An IMF team visiting Ulan Bator for consultations in June 2005 noted that Mongolia had benefited from the higher world prices of gold and copper. The country's economy was expected to continue its expansion, as new mining capacity became available. Mongolbank's international reserves were also expected to continue increasing. It was reported in mid-July 2005 that Mongolia had been given a ranking of 'B+' by the international credit ratings agency Fitch; previously it had held a rating of 'B' from ratings agency Standard and Poor's. In July 2008 Mongolbank joined the Bank for International Settlements, which promotes co-operation among central banks.

At the end of 2009 there were 358 companies listed on Mongolia's stock exchange; of these 53 were wholly or partly state-owned. Over the course of the 255 trading days of 2009 business to the value of 23,200m. tögrög was conducted. The number of registered companies declined to 336 in 2010, when business worth 62,873m. tögrög was transacted.

EXTERNAL AID

In the early 1990s, in response to an appeal by the Mongolian Government for foreign aid, the USA offered grain credits and, during his visit to Ulan Bator in July 1991, the US Secretary of State, James Baker, pledged further US aid to the value of US $10.6m. Japan also provided wheat, and in August, on the occasion of Prime Minister Toshiki Kaifu's visit to Mongolia, the Japanese Government announced economic assistance worth $15m. and development aid of $7m. for improvements to communications. In September a conference of representatives of the IMF, the ADB (which two bodies Mongolia had joined in February 1991), the European Community (now the European Union—EU) and Japan approved emergency aid totalling $155m. to Mongolia. Another donors' conference, held in Tokyo, Japan, in September 1993, pledged $250m. to Mongolia for 1993–94.

The next international donors' conference, held in Tokyo in November 1994, pledged US $210m. to Mongolia in grants and credits for 1994–95. Apart from the international banks, Japan continued to be the biggest donor, with $82.5m. in grants and $87m. in credits pledged for 1993–95. The next donors' conference, held in Tokyo in February 1996, followed up with new pledges totalling $212.5m. The outgoing Jasrai Government was criticized by Japan for not taking up aid quickly enough. In 1997 there was continued support for Mongolia at the Tokyo international aid donors' conference, held in October, which pledged Mongolia $256.1m. (the ADB and Japan $60m. each, Russia $30m., the World Bank $25m., the Republic of Korea $21m., Germany $17m. and the IMF $15m.).

Convening in Ulan Bator for the first time, the aid donors at the seventh Mongolia Assistance Group Meeting, held in June 1999, pledged a record US $320m. in aid for banking-sector reform, poverty relief and privatization. The Assistance Group urged the Mongolian Government to strengthen the financial sector by increasing transparency and improving conditions for private enterprise, including the privatization of state-owned banks and a legal framework for other financial institutions. Future Assistance Group meetings were to take the form of Consultative Group meetings chaired by the World Bank, the venue rotating between Ulan Bator, Tokyo and the French capital of Paris.

In February 2000, following several months of drought and continuing severe cold, an appeal by the Mongolian Government for international aid was supported by the UN. The climatic conditions of 1999–2000 were believed to have killed millions of livestock (see Agriculture) and directly or indirectly affected the livelihood of at least 500,000 people. Most of the US $5m. received in aid was donated by the Japanese, German, US and British Governments, and the World Bank pledged the balance of $1.3m. from its Poverty Alleviation Programme to Mongolia's relief measures. By mid-2000 a total of $7.4m. had been promised in relief assistance. Mongolia's membership of the European Bank for Reconstruction and Development (EBRD) was approved in May 2000.

The eighth meeting of the Mongolia Consultative Group took place in Paris at the end of May 2001, attended by representatives of 11 countries, the EU, UN, ADB, IMF and World Bank, and three Mongolian ministers. Prime Minister Enkhbayar announced the outcome of the Paris meeting at a press conference in Ulan Bator: Mongolia would receive US $330m. in loans and donations for the coming year, compared with the 1999 meeting's provision of $320m. over 18 months.

On returning to Ulan Bator the Minister of Finance and Economics explained that US $1,900m. of the $2,600m. of Mongolia's development aid for 1991–2000 had been implemented. Interest was payable on 47.6% of this sum; 37% of the money had been allocated to infrastructure, 16.5% to social services, 10.8% to industry and agriculture, and 23% to financial and economic management sectors; 40% of the money came from the ADB, 26% from Japan, 18% from the World Bank, and 6% from Germany.

About 1,700 companies from 65 countries had invested around US $420m. in Mongolia as of June 2001. The leading investors were China, the Republic of Korea, Japan, the USA and Russia. The main sectors of investment were mining, light industry and agricultural processing. Foreign investment had created 50,000 jobs and accounted for 14.2% of Mongolia's tax revenue. Renewed interest in Mongolia's copper and gold resources, especially from China (which had contributed more than one-third of foreign investment), accounted for much of the increased inflows. According to the ADB, foreign direct investment rose from a total of $92.9m. in 2004 to $360.0m. in 2007, increasing substantially in 2008 to reach $682.5m.

The ninth meeting of the Mongolia Consultative Group took place in Ulan Bator at the beginning of July 2002, attended by representatives of 11 countries, the EU, EBRD, ADB, IMF, World Bank and various UN bodies. The meeting pledged US $333m. in aid for the next year, but the IMF and other donors suspended some measures and complained about Mongolia's budget deficits, bureaucracy and the slow pace of reform. The Mongolian Deputy Minister of Finance and Economics told the press that some $2,300m. of the $2,800m. in aid pledged by the previous eight meetings had been implemented. Most of the loans were for 30–40 years at an interest rate of 0.5%–0.75%.

Between 1991 and 2002 Mongolia received US $2,500m. in aid, 52.5% as grants worth $1,200m. (46% of which was for technical assistance) and 47.5% as loans worth $1,140m. (87.9% of which was spent on economic services, including 81.1% on projects, and 12.1% on social services); the amount of loans implemented was $913.1m. In 2002 Japan provided 25.4% of Mongolia's grants and loans, the World Health Organization 8.1%, Germany 5.7%, the ADB 5.4%, the EU 4.2% and the USA 3%; 23% of aid was spent on infrastructure, 12.5% on agriculture and 8.7% on health. The 10th Mongolia Consultative Group meeting held in Tokyo in November 2003 pledged $335m. in grants and loans for the coming year. The donors praised Mongolia's 'effective utilization' of aid. Subsequent meetings were held in camera. Net development assistance for 2005 totalled $212m., equivalent to 11.6% of GNI and 27% of imports. In July 2006 Mongolia became a 'country of operations' of the EBRD, which intended to focus on financial support for the business sector and management advice on restructuring to promote the transition to a market economy.

Meanwhile, Russian premier Mikhail Kasyanov's brief visit to Ulan Bator in March 2002 and the signing of routine co-operation agreements passed in the usual cordial atmosphere. However, the Russian media reported that Kasyanov and Mongolian Prime Minister Enkhbayar had discussed Mongolia's repayment to Russia of its Soviet-era aid debt 'amounting to US $11,600m.'. Enkhbayar stated later that only the terms of repayment had been discussed, not the exact amount, but the Mongolian media and opposition fiercely disputed the equivalence of the defunct transferable Soviet rouble to the US dollar. The issue remained unresolved, although it had been raised at many intergovernmental meetings over the preceding decade. The Mongolian Minister of Finance was reported as saying that Russia was seeking a 90%–95% discount of the debt, with repayment of the remaining $500m. payable over 40 years. However, when the two Prime Ministers met in Moscow in July 2003, Mongolia's repayment of the Soviet-era debt was hardly discussed, and the major outcome of the talks was a new five-year agreement on the operation of the Erdenet copper enterprise that preserved Mongolia's 51% ownership of stock. Russia agreed that Mongolia had already repaid the cost of building the Erdenet plant. Otherwise, Mongolia's main concern was to reduce Russian taxes on imports of Mongolian goods.

At the end of December 2003 Russia announced that it had received Mongolia's payment in settlement of the 'big debt' (as the Mongolians referred to the money Russia claimed it was owed for Soviet aid to Mongolia during 1947–91). Russia had waived 98% of the total debt of 11,400m. transferable roubles and accepted payment of US $250m. Prime Minister Nambaryn Enkhbayar celebrated a political and diplomatic victory for the MPRP Government, but the details of the settlement remained unclear. The two countries had been unable to agree terms for the previous 10 years, especially the equivalence of the now-defunct transferable rouble, but also because of Mongolian opposition pressure to offset the cost of damage done to the environment by Soviet military activity. During a visit to Ulan Bator in August 2009 Russian President Dmitrii Medvedev unexpectedly remarked at a press conference that 'only 98%' of Mongolia's debt to Russia had been paid off in 2003 and that other issues had yet to be settled. Soon afterwards a Russian deputy minister of finance asked Mongolia for the sum of $180m. in settlement of the joint financing of the Mongolrostsvetmet company. As of July 2010 Mongolia continued to assert that the 'big debt' had been paid in full. However, when Prime Minister Batbold made an official visit to Moscow in December 2010 he and Prime Minister Putin agreed that Mongolia would settle its remaining $3.8m debt to Russia in one transfer.

Russian Prime Minister Mikhail Fradkov's visit to Ulan Bator in July 2006 focused on trade and investment issues as well as revisions to the laws relating to joint ventures. Agreements were concluded on aviation search and rescue and the supply to Mongolia of 40,000 metric tons of Russian wheat 'at a reduced price'. Fradkov expressed the hope that more Russian companies would invest in the mining of coal, gold, uranium and copper. However, a fortnight later the Mongolian Government issued a statement denying accusations by Mongolia's Democratic Party that the visit had not met public expectations. The Ministry of Foreign Affairs stated that 'although there were Russian companies that were interested in investing in Mongolia, especially in the mining sector, it was noticed during a business meeting held with the participation of the Prime Ministers that there was a necessity to study Mongolian laws and clear up proposals on implementing big projects'. Mongolia 'would give favourable conditions to Russian companies in the same manner as companies of other countries'.

The issue of Mongolia's debt to Poland of 29.9m. convertible roubles, for loans supplied in 1976, 1981 and 1986, was settled in November 2006: 90% of the debt was cancelled; of the remainder, 70% was set aside to enable Mongolian students to further their studies in Poland, and 30% was allocated to the financing of Polish geological surveys in Mongolia.

In October 2007 President Nambaryn Enkhbayar and US President George W. Bush signed an agreement regarding the implementation of a Millennium Challenge compact assistance programme. Extending over a five-year period and with a total allocation of almost US $285m., the programme was expected to have a significant impact on Mongolia's efforts to reduce poverty. Major improvements to the country's railway operations were also envisaged. However, the director of Russian Railways told his Mongolian partners in the Ulan Bator Railway Company that the Millennium Challenge funding for railway improvements from the USA was 'unacceptable'. Mongolia consequently decided to make new representations to the US Government to divert the money to other projects. An External Partners Technical Meeting, organized jointly with the World Bank, was convened in Ulan Bator in January 2008. At the end of that month the Mongolian legislature approved a draft National Development Policy, encompassing the period to 2021.

During Prime Minister Sanjaagiin Bayar's visit to Russia in April 2008 it was agreed that the two countries would improve the efficiency of the Ulan Bator Railway and with help from Rosatom establish a project to prospect for, extract and process uranium, copper and other metals. During Vice-President Xi Jinping's visit to Ulan Bator in June China agreed to export to Mongolia 10,000 metric tons of petrol per month, mostly through Zamyn-Üüd but also via rural border crossings. It was agreed during President Nursultan Nazarbayev's visit to Ulan Bator in August that Kazakhstan would supply Mongolia with up to 30,000 metric tons of wheat in the coming year.

In April 2009 the IMF approved an 18-month stand-by arrangement for Mongolia worth US $229.2m. An initial allocation of $76.4m. was provided, with the remainder to be disbursed quarterly, subject to review. The funds were to help finance Mongolia's economic stabilization programme, which was to address shortcomings in the banking sector and allow for greater exchange rate flexibility.

The Mongolian-Russian intergovernmental co-operation commission, meeting in Ulan Bator in July 2010, decided to renew the 1949 agreement on the establishment of the Ulan Bator Railway and jointly invest in its further development, to increase Mongolian exports of live animals and meat to Russia, and to proceed with their agreement to establish the Dornod Uran joint venture. Meanwhile, Mongolia began a process of 're-registering' several Western companies that had existing investment in Mongolian uranium mines.

In June 2011 the Foreign Investment and Foreign Trade Agency (FIFTA) released a report indicating how successful Mongolia had been in encouraging investment: as of the end of 2010 a total of 769 companies from 104 countries had invested US $4,840m. since 1990, and in 2010 annual investment exceeded $1,000m. for the first time. The biggest investor was China, which accounted for 51% of total foreign investment, a proportion giving rise to some concern about over-dependency, in view of China's domination of the Mongolian export market (taking 84% of total exports in 2010).

CONCLUSION

Higher tax revenues, boosted by a windfall tax on the copper and gold sectors imposed in 2006, permitted the continuation of the improvement in the Government's fiscal balance. Increasing prices for food (especially imported products) contributed to a rise in the rate of inflation. Despite suggestions that the imposition of the 2006 windfall tax had curtailed growth in production in 2007 and had even encouraged a resurgence in smuggling, strong international prices for gold and copper sustained the performance of the mining sector in 2005–07. Robust GDP growth was maintained in 2008, despite the onset of the global financial crisis in the latter part of the year and the attendant declines in international commodity prices, particularly for copper and cashmere. The deceleration in 2009 of the economy of China, a major purchaser of Mongolian exports, was expected to affect sales.

The founding of the Oyu Tolgoi and Tavan Tolgoi companies in 2010 provided a strong boost of confidence. The launching of the first distribution of cash allocations (70,000 tögrög per citizen) from the Human Development Fund, with more to come in bonds, meant that ordinary people were beginning to enjoy some benefit. An initial US $250m. was invested in Oyu Tolgoi and it was reported that extraction of gold and copper would begin in 2013 (or possibly at the end of 2012). Tavan Tolgoi issued shares, 10% of which were to be distributed free to all citizens (536 per head of the population), while directors of investing companies vied for representation on the Tavan Tolgoi board. Plans for construction of the broad-gauge railway line from Tavan Tolgoi to Choibalsan were slowly progressing, while a standard-gauge line from Oyu Tolgoi to the border with China was also under discussion. At the same time, however, there was concern about the pollution and environmental damage resulting from the transport by truck of large quantities of Mongolian coal and oil across the border into China.

Meanwhile, relatively mild winters had greatly benefited the agricultural sector. However, the unusually severe winter of 2009/10, which resulted in the loss of some 22% of Mongolian herds, was a particularly serious set-back for goat-herders in western Mongolia. Herding families that lost all or most of their animals were hard pressed, despite government relief measures and international aid; finding alternative employment in areas of scattered population was difficult. The half-year reports for 2010 indicated that new-born livestock survival rates were generally lower than usual.

Despite previous efforts to minimize the social impact of the transition to a market economy, the incidence of poverty was estimated at 32.2% in 2006, rising to 35.2% in 2008 and 38.7% in 2009. Mongolia's millennium development index for GDP per head for 2009 at 2.2m. tögrög was marginally less than in the previous year, but rose again in 2010 to reach 2.9m. A massive increase in the unemployment rate of 15–24 year-olds from 3% to 22% was recorded in 2009, but the rate declined slightly to 19.5% in 2010. Meanwhile, some standards of health care and of education were reported to be deteriorating, although considerable statistical variation from year to year is typical. However, developments in 2010 appeared to signal the start of a period of significant GDP growth. The EBRD reported at the end of July 2011 that Mongolia's GDP was forecast to increase by 9% in 2011 and by 12% in 2012, largely owing to raised levels of foreign direct investment and a surge in the prices of mining products.

Statistical Survey

Unless otherwise indicated, revised by Alan J. K. Sanders

Area and Population

AREA, POPULATION AND DENSITY

Area (sq km)	1,564,116*
Population (census results)	
5 January 2000	2,373,493
19 November 2010	2,754,685
Population (official estimate at 31 December)	
2010	2,780,800
Density (per sq km) at 31 December 2010	1.8

* 603,909 sq miles.

POPULATION BY AGE AND SEX

(UN estimates at mid-2011)

	Males	Females	Total
0–14	389,889	381,727	771,616
15–64	944,149	969,956	1,914,105
65 and over	48,210	66,184	114,394
Total	1,382,248	1,417,867	2,800,115

Source: UN, *World Population Prospects: The 2010 Revision*.

ADMINISTRATIVE DIVISIONS

(official population estimates at 31 December 2010)

Province (Aimag)	Area ('000 sq km)	Estimated population ('000)	Provincial centre
Arkhangai	55.3	91.6	Tsetserleg
Bayankhongor	116.0	85.1	Bayankhongor
Bayan-Ölgii	45.7	100.8	Ölgii
Bulgan	48.7	62.6	Bulgan
Darkhan-Uul	3.3	91.7	Darkhan
Dornod (Eastern)	123.6	73.6	Choibalsan
Dornogobi (East Gobi)	109.5	59.5	Sainshand
Dundgobi (Central Gobi)	74.7	46.3	Mandalgobi
Gobi-Altai	141.4	58.4	Altai
Gobi-Sümber	5.5	13.8	Choir
Khentii	80.3	71.8	Öndörkhaan
Khovd	76.1	88.4	Khovd
Khövsgöl	100.6	124.6	Mörön
Orkhon	0.8	85.8	Erdenet
Ömnögobi (South Gobi)	165.4	51.0	Dalanzadgad
Övörkhangai	62.9	117.4	Arvaikheer
Selenge	41.2	106.6	Sükhbaatar
Sükhbaatar	82.3	55.0	Baruun Urt
Töv (Central)	74.0	90.2	Zuun mod
Ulan Bator (Ulaanbaatar)*	4.7	1,151.5	(capital city)
Uvs	69.6	78.2	Ulaangom
Zavkhan	82.5	76.9	Uliastai
Total	1,564.1	2,780.8	

* Ulan Bator, including Nalaikh, and Bagakhangai and Baganuur districts beyond the urban boundary, has special status as the capital city.

ETHNIC GROUPS

(2000 census)

	Number	%
Khalkha (Halh)	1,934,700	81.5
Kazakh (Khasag)	103,000	4.3
Dörvöd (Durbet)	66,700	2.8
Bayad (Bayat)	50,800	2.1
Buryat (Buriat)	40,600	1.7
Dariganga	31,900	1.3
Zakhchin	29,800	1.3
Uriankhai	25,200	1.1
Other ethnic groups	82,600	3.5
Foreign citizens	8,100	0.3
Total	2,373,500	100.0

2010 census (percentage distribution): Khalkha 82.4; Kazakh 3.9; Others 13.7.

PRINCIPAL TOWNS

(estimated population at December)

Ulan Bator (capital)	1,151,500*	Erdenet	74,300†

* 2010.
† 2007.

BIRTHS, MARRIAGES AND DEATHS

	Registered births		Registered marriages*		Registered deaths	
	Number	Rate (per 1,000)	Number	Rate (per 1,000)	Number	Rate (per 1,000)
2003	45,723	18.4	14,572	9.6	16,006	6.4
2004	45,501	18.1	11,242	7.2	16,404	6.5
2005	45,326	17.8	14,993	9.3	16,480	6.5
2006	49,092	19.0	48,996	19.0	16,682	6.5
2007	56,636	21.7	40,965	15.7	16,259	6.2
2008	63,768	24.0	32,982	12.4	15,413	5.8
2009	69,167	25.5	34,071	12.6	16,911	6.2
2010	63,270	22.9	9,349	3.4	18,293	6.6

* Persons aged 18 years and over.

Life expectancy (years at birth): 68.05 (males 64.93; females 72.26) in 2010 (Source: *Mongolian Statistical Yearbook*).

EMPLOYMENT
('000 employees at 31 December)

	2008	2009	2010
Agriculture, forestry and fishing	377.6	348.8	346.6
Industry*	124.1	113.1	119.1
Construction	66.8	49.6	48.8
Transport and communications	46.3	78.9	91.0
Trade	169.7	160.3	146.2
Public administration	50.9	56.1	61.0
Education }	66.2	74.9	85.3
Science, research and development }	—	10.9	9.5
Health	42.3	35.7	40.3
Total (incl. others)	1,041.7	1,006.3	1,033.7

* Comprising manufacturing (except printing and publishing), mining and quarrying, electricity and water.

Source: *Mongolian Statistical Yearbook*.

Mongolians working abroad ('000 in 2009, official estimates): 182.5 (Kazakhstan 90.0; Republic of Korea 31.0) (Source: Montsame—Mongolian News Agency).

Registered unemployed ('000 at 31 December): 32.9 in 2006; 29.9 in 2007; 29.6 in 2008; 38.1 in 2009; 38.3 in 2010 (Sources: Asian Development Bank; Mongolian Statistical Office).

Total unemployed ('000 in 2010): 113.4 (Ulan Bator 34.3) (Source: *Mongolian Statistical Yearbook*).

Health and Welfare

KEY INDICATORS

Total fertility rate (children per woman, 2009)	2.0
Under-5 mortality rate (per 1,000 live births, 2009)	29
HIV/AIDS (% of persons aged 15–49, 2007)	0.1
Physicians (per 1,000 head, 2002)	2.6
Hospital beds (per 1,000 head, 2006)	6.4
Health expenditure (2008): US $ per head (PPP)	131
Health expenditure (2008): % of GDP	3.8
Health expenditure (2008): public (% of total)	81.4
Access to water (% of persons, 2008)	76
Access to sanitation (% of persons, 2008)	50
Total carbon dioxide emissions ('000 metric tons, 2007)	10,574.3
Carbon dioxide emissions per head (metric tons, 2007)	4.0
Human Development Index (2010): ranking	100
Human Development Index (2010): value	0.622

For sources and definitions, see explanatory note on p. vi.

Agriculture

PRINCIPAL CROPS
(metric tons)

	2008	2009	2010
Cereals*	212,894	391,659	355,061
Potatoes	134,773	151,211	167,956
Other vegetables	78,553	77,976	82,266
Hay	1,030,900	912,300	1,137,300

* Mostly wheat, but also small quantities of barley and oats.

LIVESTOCK
(at December census)

	2008	2009	2010
Sheep	18,362,300	19,274,700	14,480,400
Goats	19,969,400	19,651,500	13,883,200
Horses	2,186,900	2,221,300	1,920,300
Cattle	2,503,400	2,599,300	2,176,000
Camels	266,400	277,100	269,600
Pigs	29,285	25,808	24,842
Poultry	259,900	399,400	425,800

LIVESTOCK PRODUCTS
('000 metric tons, unless otherwise indicated)

	2008	2009	2010
Meat	223.1	269.1	204.4
Beef	54.2	58.6	47.5
Mutton and goat meat	122.0	168.9	126.4
Sheep's wool	20.8	22.4	23.5
Cashmere	5.9	6.4	6.3
Hides and skins ('000)	9,762.4	13,076.3	16,784.7
Milk	457.4	493.7	338.4
Eggs (million)	47.9	30.8	47.9

Source: *Mongolian Statistical Yearbook*.

Forestry

ROUNDWOOD REMOVALS
('000 cubic metres)

	2006	2007	2008
Total	574.8	580.5	612.0

Source: *Mongolian Statistical Yearbook*.

SAWNWOOD PRODUCTION
('000 cubic metres, incl. railway sleepers)

	2008	2009	2010
Total	34.1	28.8	32.7

Source: *Mongolian Statistical Yearbook*.

Fishing

(metric tons, live weight)

	2007	2008	2009
Total catch (freshwater fishes)	185	88	90

Source: FAO.

Mining

(metric tons, unless otherwise indicated)

	2008	2009	2010
Salt	115	5	0
Coal ('000 metric tons)	10,072	14,442	25,162
Fluorspar concentrate	142,900	115,300	140,700
Copper concentrate*	362,300	370,900	357,100
Molybdenum concentrate*	4,042	5,125	4,677
Zinc concentrate*	143,600	141,500	112,600
Tungsten concentrate*	142	39	20
Iron ore	1,387,400	1,379,000	3,203,200
Gold (kilograms)	15,184	9,803	6,037
Crude petroleum (barrels)	1,174,200	1,870,000	2,181,400

* Figures refer to the gross weight of concentrates. Copper concentrate has an estimated copper content of 35%, while the metal content of molybdenum concentrate is 47% and that of zinc is 50%; the metal content of tungsten concentrate was not indicated.

Source: *Mongolian Statistical Yearbook*.

Industry

SELECTED PRODUCTS

	2008	2009	2010
Flour ('000 metric tons)	62.0	105.3	143.5
Bread ('000 metric tons)	25.8	23.5	21.7
Confectionery ('000 metric tons)	13.2	12.8	12.9
Sheep's guts ('000 bunches)	641.1	1,057.1	1,288.5
Vodka and wine ('000 litres)	15,277.4	17,410.9	20,396.7
Beer ('000 litres)	19,891.1	32,445.1	44,878.5
Soft drinks ('000 litres)	85,975.8	86,967.9	135,372.0
Cashmere (combed) (metric tons)	1,723.8	1,586.7	824.7
Wool, scoured (metric tons)	1,800.0	1,300.0	2,300.0
Felt ('000 metres)	86.5	128.7	134.9
Camelhair blankets ('000 metres)	35.0	36.9	15.3
Spun thread (metric tons)	28.1	56.4	90.2
Knitwear ('000 garments)	2,148.2	639.2	801.1
Trousers ('000)	1,996.5	163.2	23.5
Shirts ('000)	678.7	0.6	22.6
Carpets ('000 sq metres)	856.5	542.2	609.6
Leather footwear ('000)	5.5	5.3	9.9
Felt footwear ('000 pairs)	6.3	13.0	27.9
Surgical syringes (million)	10.9	10.3	4.0
Bricks (million)	28.9	18.0	27.7
Lime ('000 metric tons)	54.8	43.1	50.2
Cement ('000 metric tons)	269.3	234.8	322.5
Copper (metric tons)	2,586.6	2,470.1	2,746.2
Copper wire (metric tons)	705.8	298.5	147.3
Electricity (million kWh)	4,000.6	4,038.8	4,132.8

Source: *Mongolian Statistical Yearbook*.

Finance

CURRENCY AND EXCHANGE RATES

Monetary Units
100 möngö = 1 tögrög (tughrik).

Sterling, Dollar and Euro Equivalents (31 May 2011)
£1 sterling = 2,055.2 tögrög;
US $1 = 1,245.4 tögrög;
€1 = 1,791.4 tögrög;
10,000 tögrög = £4.87 = $8.03 = €5.58.

Average Exchange Rate (tögrög per US $)
2008 1,165.74
2009 1,437.80
2010 1,357.06

BUDGET
(million tögrög)

Revenue	2008	2009	2010
Tax revenue	1,890,896.6	1,620,549.6	2,673,573.3
Income tax	754,839.9	520,170.6	973,956.2
Excise duty	178,466.9	166,743.3	268,519.9
Taxes on goods and services	562,018.1	508,808.2	863,467.8
Value-added tax	368,049.5	325,956.4	577,275.8
Other current revenue	260,153.2	352,069.7	362,295.4
Social insurance	229,353.2	263,563.4	321,659.1
Grants and transfers	16,118.6	19,067.7	34,561.4
Other revenue	3,201.6	2,308.6	7,988.5
Total	2,170,370.0	1,993,995.6	3,078,418.6

Expenditure	2008	2009	2010
Current expenditure	1,761,190.6	1,788,157.6	2,271,150.0
Goods and services	1,054,940.6	970,143.8	1,193,766.5
Wages and salaries	544,450.3	575,912.4	650,551.7
Interest payments	19,949.0	29,621.6	41,919.7
Subsidies and transfers	686,301.5	788,392.2	1,035,463.7
Capital expenditure	624,389.8	460,564.5	564,710.8
Foreign financed	20,182.5	26,657.3	13,206.1
Lending (net)	81,194.0	87,907.6	240,402.0
Total	2,466,774.4	2,336,629.7	3,076,262.8

Source: *Mongolian Statistical Yearbook*.

2011 (million tögrög, forecasts): Total revenue 2,492,330.3; total expenditure 2,782,697.5 (Source: *Töriin Medeelel*).

INTERNATIONAL RESERVES
(US $ million at 31 December)

	2008	2009	2010
Gold (national valuation)	95.91	32.83	91.56
IMF special drawing rights	0.06	76.42	72.73
Reserve position in IMF	0.21	0.21	0.21
Foreign exchange	561.21	1,217.84	2,123.76
Total	657.39	1,327.3	2,288.3

Source: IMF, *International Financial Statistics*.

MONEY SUPPLY
(million tögrög at 31 December)

	2008	2009	2010
Currency outside depository corporations	328,779	284,994	388,203
Transferable deposits	601,736	738,245	1,535,555
Other deposits	1,292,521	1,810,362	2,728,573
Securities other than shares	47,021	46,432	27,651
Broad money	2,270,056	2,880,034	4,679,981

Source: IMF, *International Financial Statistics*.

COST OF LIVING
(Consumer Price Index at December; base: December 2005 = 100)

	2008	2009	2010
Foods	158.4	157.7	190.1
Clothing and footwear	138.1	143.1	160.4
Rent and utilities	137.7	132.4	149.0
All items (incl. others)	147.3	150.0	171.5

Source: *Mongolian Statistical Yearbook*.

NATIONAL ACCOUNTS

Expenditure on the Gross Domestic Product
('000 million tögrög at current prices, preliminary)

	2007	2008	2009
Government final consumption expenditure	598.6	929.7	848.5
Private final consumption expenditure	2,291.6	3,007.0	3,011.6
Increase in stocks	147.0	732.7	732.7
Gross fixed capital formation	1,703.8	2,407.6	2,234.2
Total domestic expenditure	4,741.0	7,077.0	6,827.0
Exports of goods and services	2,954.9	3,507.1	3,381.3
Less Imports of goods and services	2,888.0	4,447.2	3,792.5
Statistical discrepancy*	–208.3	–117.0	–360.1
GDP in purchasers' values	4,599.5	6,019.8	6,055.8
GDP at constant 2005 prices	3,325.9	3,622.7	3,564.3

* Referring to the difference between the sum of the expenditure components and official estimates of GDP, compiled from the production approach.

Source: Asian Development Bank.

Gross Domestic Product by Economic Activity
(million tögrög at current prices)

	2008	2009	2010
Agriculture, forestry and fishing	1,259,660.8	1,177,380.3	1,312,433.5
Mining and quarrying	1,324,247.7	1,285,899.7	1,800,805.6
Manufacturing	430,179.4	425,000.6	532,925.6
Construction	122,051.0	86,238.7	106,960.0
Electricity, gas, etc.	119,968.0	157,422.9	198,790.1
Water supply, sewerage and waste management	26,015.0	26,356.8	32,503.8
Wholesale and retail trade; repair of motor vehicles and motorcycles	472,226.5	432,646.2	595,254.1
Transport and storage	419,323.2	546,745.5	671,834.8
Hotels and restaurants	38,971.4	43,680.8	54,538.5
Information and communications	221,339.0	215,504.0	261,895.6
Finance and insurance	236,327.4	212,724.0	158,143.8
Real estate and renting	345,984.2	479,635.3	512,399.1
Professional, scientific and technical	76,694.6	65,655.8	70,251.9
Administrative and support services	98,499.8	88,804.4	99,956.3
Public administration and defence; compulsory social security	247,723.6	267,246.3	301,222.9
Education	272,562.3	312,138.4	346,196.9
Health and social work	119,817.4	123,042.0	138,524.5
Arts, entertainment and recreation	23,211.4	27,876.2	30,965.2
Other service activities	27,950.0	24,871.5	27,694.2
Sub-total	5,882,752.4	5,998,869.3	7,253,296.4
Taxes, less subsidies, on products	672,817.0	591,767.8	1,001,764.5
GDP in market prices	6,555,569.4	6,590,637.1	8,255,060.9

Source: *Mongolian Statistical Yearbook*.

BALANCE OF PAYMENTS
(US $ million)

	2008	2009	2010
Exports of goods	2,529.1	1,885.4	2,908.5
Imports of goods	–3,156.3	–2,074.2	–3,088.9
Trade balance	–627.2	–188.8	–180.4
Exports of services	499.4	414.5	485.9
Imports of services	–610.2	–557.8	–780.3
Balance on goods and services	–738.0	–332.0	–474.7
Other income received	16.5	24.3	28.9
Other income paid	–189.3	–219.8	–627.8
Balance on goods, services and income	–910.8	–527.4	–1,073.5
Current transfers received	378.4	260.3	309.4
Current transfers paid	–157.7	–74.6	–122.4
Current balance	–690.1	–341.8	–886.5
Capital account (net)	84.1	160.5	152.2
Direct investment abroad	–6.2	–53.8	–46.6
Direct investment from abroad	844.7	623.6	1,454.7
Portfolio investment assets	–51.2	–138.8	143.3
Portfolio investment liabilities	14.8	56.7	751.0
Other investment assets	64.5	–144.8	–1,040.2
Other investment liabilities	281.2	265.6	107.8
Net errors and omissions	–774.7	127.6	239.3
Overall balance	–233.1	554.7	874.8

Source: IMF, *International Financial Statistics*.

External Trade

PRINCIPAL COMMODITIES
(US $ million, distribution by SITC)

Imports c.i.f.	2008	2009	2010
Food and live animals	344.0	240.4	295.4
Raw materials	14.9	15.6	20.8
Fuels and lubricants	919.0	544.4	713.8
Chemical products	172.3	143.1	195.1
Manufactured goods, classified chiefly by material	485.2	321.7	414.4
Machinery and vehicles	1,060.5	689.7	1,261.7
Miscellaneous manufactured articles	156.8	114.5	211.1
Total (incl. others)	3,244.5	2,137.7	3,200.1

Exports f.o.b.	2008	2009	2010
Food and live animals	27.1	42.7	60.2
Raw materials	1,435.6	1,005.4	1,505.0
Copper concentrate	835.7	501.9	770.6
Fuels and lubricants	297.4	437.5	1,055.6
Chemical products	34.2	1.0	1.3
Manufactured goods, classified chiefly by material	67.4	46.3	53.9
Machinery and vehicles	34.9	23.7	22.8
Miscellaneous manufactured articles	37.5	19.1	27.0
Gold, unwrought or in semi-manufactured forms	599.9	308.5	178.3
Total (incl. others)	2,534.5	1,885.4	2,908.5

Source: *Mongolian Statistical Yearbook*.

PRINCIPAL TRADING PARTNERS
(US $ million)

Imports c.i.f.	2008	2009	2010
China, People's Republic	898.7	538.6	971.0
Germany	92.6	70.3	87.2
Japan	238.5	97.0	196.5
Korea, Republic	194.8	155.1	181.8
Russia	1,242.3	772.8	1,046.7
USA	84.1	103.7	158.9
Total (incl. others)	3,244.5	2,137.7	3,200.1

Exports f.o.b.	2008	2009	2010
Canada	174.6	147.5	141.6
China, People's Republic	1,635.9	1,393.9	2,466.3
Germany	11.0	15.6	22.1
Italy	42.2	31.4	31.8
Russia	86.3	68.2	82.7
United Kingdom	165.8	126.9	67.4
Total (incl. others)	2,534.5	1,885.4	2,908.5

Source: *Mongolian Statistical Yearbook*.

Transport

FREIGHT CARRIED
('000 metric tons)

	2008	2009	2010
Rail	14,646.9	14,171.5	16,804.0
Road	9,255.7	10,563.8	12,610.2
Air	1.8	1.4	1.6
Total (incl. other)	23,904.4	24,736.7	29,415.9

Source: Mongolian Statistical Office.

PASSENGERS CARRIED
(million)

	2008	2009	2010
Rail	4.3	3.1	3.5
Road	226.9	229.0	246.7
Air*	0.4	0.3	0.4
Total	231.6	232.4	250.6

* MIAT only.

Source: Mongolian Statistical Office.

RAILWAYS
(traffic)

	2008	2009	2010
Passengers carried ('000)	4,358.8	3,118.3	3,516.3
Freight carried ('000 metric tons)	14,646.9	14,171.5	16,804.0
Freight ton-km (million)	8,261.4	7,852.1	10,286.7

Source: Mongolian Statistical Office.

ROAD TRAFFIC
(motor vehicles in use)

	2008	2009	2010
Passenger cars	127,538	153,906	172,583
Buses and coaches	15,780	16,136	16,366
Lorries, special vehicles and tankers	47,141	54,026	65,537

Source: Mongolian Statistical Office.

CIVIL AVIATION
(traffic on scheduled services)

	2008	2009	2010
Passengers carried ('000)	365.5	309.3	397.1
International passengers ('000)	262.8	235.9	276.0
Freight carried (tons)	1,847.0	1,369.1	1,641.6

Source: Mongolian Statistical Office.

Tourism

FOREIGN ARRIVALS BY NATIONALITY

Country	2008	2009	2010
China, People's Republic	196,832	229,451	193,370
France	6,688	6,706	7,527
Germany	8,027	6,867	8,095
Japan	14,939	11,401	14,140
Korea, Republic	43,396	38,273	42,231
Russia	109,975	108,105	121,647
United Kingdom	6,781	5,872	6,209
USA	12,474	11,344	12,808
Total (incl. others)	446,446	492,836	456,090

Source: *Mongolian Statistical Yearbook*.

Tourism receipts (US $ million): 213.3 in 2009; 222.4 in 2010 (Source: Ministry of Environment and Tourism, Ulan Bator).

Communications Media

	2008	2009	2010
Television receivers ('000 in use)	454.0	489.5	554.5
Cable television subscribers ('000)	101.3	112.9	120.5
Telephones ('000 main lines in use)	151.6	142.9	143.2
Mobile cellular telephones ('000 subscribers)	1,745.9	2,208.7	2,532.9
Internet users ('000)	42.0	106.0	199.8
Personal computers ('000 in use)	150.9	189.5	234.9
Books (million printers' sheets)	42.1	49.7	55.5
Newspapers (million printers' sheets)	64.8	37.5	42.2

Book production (1994): 128 titles; 640,000 copies.

Newspapers (titles): 170 in 2004 (daily 6, non-daily 164).

Periodicals (titles): 60 in 2004.

Sources: mainly *Mongolian Statistical Yearbook*.

Education

(2010/11)

	Institutions	Teachers	Students ('000)
General education schools:			
Primary (grades 1–3)	65	26,400	265.6
Incomplete secondary (grades 4–9)	147		172.9
Complete secondary (grades 10–11)	539		73.7
Vocational schools			
State-owned	44	2,100	34.7
Private	19		11.4
Universities			
State-owned	9	7,200	98.4
Private	4		16.1
Other higher education			
State-owned	7		6.0
Private	88		49.2

Note: In addition, 700 students were studying abroad through inter-governmental agreements.

Pre-school institutions (2010/11): 839 kindergartens, with 4,651 teachers, attended by 125,700 infants.

Source: *Mongolian Statistical Yearbook*.

2009/10 (official estimates): Student enrolment at all education establishments 736,800; student enrolment abroad 9,550 (Sources: Montsame (Mongolian News Agency) and *Mongolian Statistical Yearbook*).

Pupil-teacher ratio (primary education, UNESCO estimate): 30.4 in 2008/09 (Source: UNESCO Institute for Statistics).

Adult literacy rate (UNESCO estimates): 97.5% (males 97.1%; females 97.9%) in 2009 (Source: UNESCO Institute for Statistics).

Directory

The Constitution

The Constitution was adopted on 13 January 1992 and came into force on 12 February of that year. It proclaims Mongolia (*Mongol Uls*), with its capital at Ulan Bator (Ulaanbaatar), to be an independent sovereign republic that ensures for its people democracy, justice, freedom, equality and national unity. It recognizes all forms of ownership of property, including land, and affirms that a 'multi-structured economy' will take account of 'universal trends of world economic development and national conditions'.

The 'citizen's right to life' is qualified by the death penalty, currently suspended, for serious crimes, and the law provides for the imposition of forced labour. Freedom of residence and travel within the country and abroad may be limited for security reasons. The citizens' duties are to respect the Constitution and the rights and interests of others, pay taxes, and serve in the armed forces, as well as the 'sacred duty' to work, safeguard one's health, bring up one's children and protect the environment.

Supreme legislative power is vested in the Mongolian Great Khural (Assembly), a single chamber with 76 members elected by universal adult suffrage for a four-year term, with a Chairman and Vice-Chairman elected from among the members. The Great Khural recognizes the President on his election and appoints the Prime Minister and members of the Cabinet. A presidential veto of a decision of the Great Khural can be overruled by a two-thirds' majority of the Khural. Decisions are taken by a simple majority.

The President is Head of State and Commander-in-Chief of the Armed Forces. He must be an indigenous citizen at least 45 years old who has resided continuously in Mongolia for the five years before election. Presidential candidates are nominated by parties with seats in the Great Khural; the winning candidate in general presidential elections is President for a four-year term.

The Cabinet is the highest executive body and drafts economic, social and financial policy, takes environmental protection measures, strengthens defence and security, protects human rights and implements foreign policy for a four-year term.

The Supreme Court, headed by the Chief Justice, is the highest judicial organ. Judicial independence is protected by the General Council of Courts. The Procurator General, nominated by the President, serves a six-year term.

Local administration in the 21 *aimag* (provinces) and Ulan Bator is effected on the basis of 'self-government and central guidance', comprising local khurals of representatives elected by citizens and governors (*zasag darga*), nominated by the Prime Minister to serve four-year terms.

The Constitutional Commission, which guarantees 'strict observance' of the Constitution, consists of nine members nominated for a six-year term, three each by the Great Khural, the President and the Supreme Court. It accepts petitions from the public.

The first amendments to the Constitution were adopted by the Mongolian Great Khural in December 1999. Despite opposition from the Constitutional Commission and President Natsagiin Bagabandi, the amendments were finally signed by the President in May 2001. The main effects of the amendments were to clarify the method of appointment of Prime Ministers, enable decision-making by a simple majority vote, and shorten the minimum length of sessions of the Khural from 75 days to 50.

The Government

PRESIDENCY

President and Commander-in-Chief of the Armed Forces: TSAKHIAGIIN ELBEGDORJ (elected 24 May 2009; inaugurated 18 June 2009).

Head of Presidential Secretariat: DASHJAMTSYN BATTULGA.

NATIONAL SECURITY COUNCIL

The President heads the National Security Council; the Prime Minister and the Chairman of the Mongolian Great Khural are its members. The Secretary is the President's national security adviser.

Chairman: TSAKHIAGIIN ELBEGDORJ.

Secretary: TSAGAANDARIIN ENKHTÜVSHIN.

Members: DAMDINGIIN DEMBEREL, SÜKHBAATARYN BATBOLD.

CABINET

(September 2011)

The coalition Government comprises members of the Mongolian People's Party (MPP, formerly the Mongolian People's Revolutionary Party) and the Democratic Party (DP).

Prime Minister: SÜKHBAATARYN BATBOLD (MPP).

Chief Deputy Prime Minister: NOROVYN ALTANKHUYAG (DP).

Deputy Prime Minister: MIYEEGOMBYN ENKHBOLD (MPP).

General Ministries

Minister of External Relations: GOMBOJAVYN ZANDANSHATAR (MPP).

Minister of Finance: SANGAJAVYN BAYARTSOGT (DP).

Minister of Justice and Home Affairs: TSENDIIN NYAMDORJ (MPP).

Sectoral Ministries

Minister of Defence: LUVSANVANDANGIIN BOLD (DP).

Minister of Education, Culture and Science: YONDONGIIN OTGONBAYAR (MPP).

Minister of Environment and Tourism: LÜIMEDIIN GANSÜKH (DP).

Minister of Food, Agriculture and Light Industry: TÜNJINGIIN BADAMJUNAI (MPP).

Minister of Health: SAMBUUGIIN LAMBAA (DP).

Minister of Mineral Resources, Fuel and Power: DASHDORJIIN ZORIGT (MPP).

Minister of Roads, Transport, Construction and Urban Development: KHALTMAAGIIN BATTULGA (DP).

Minister of Social Welfare and Labour: TÖGSJARGALYN GANDI (MPP).

Head of Government Affairs Directorate: CHIMEDIIN KHÜREL-BAATAR (MPP).

MINISTRIES AND GOVERNMENT DEPARTMENTS

All Ministries and Government Departments are in Ulan Bator.

Prime Minister's Office: State Palace, Sükhbaataryn Talbai 6, Ulan Bator; tel. (11) 322356; fax (11) 328329; internet www.pmis.gov .mn.

Ministry of Defence: Government Bldg 7, Dandaryn Gudamj 51, Bayanzürkh District, Ulan Bator; tel. (51) 264818; e-mail mdef@mdef.pmis.gov.mn; internet www.mdef.pmis.gov.mn.

Ministry of Education, Culture and Science: Government Bldg 3, Baga Toiruu 44, Sükhbaatar District, Ulan Bator; tel. (11) 323589; e-mail mecs@mecs.gov.mn; internet www.mecs.gov.mn.

Ministry of Environment and Tourism: Government Bldg 2, Negdsen Ündesnii Gudamj 5/2, Chingeltei District, Ulan Bator; tel. and fax (51) 266171; fax (51) 266286; e-mail contact@mne.gov.mn; internet www.mne.mn.

Ministry of External Relations: Enkh Taivny Örgön Chölöö 7A, Sükhbaatar District, Ulan Bator; tel. (51) 262788; fax (11) 322127; e-mail info@mfat.gov.mn; internet www.mfat.gov.mn.

Ministry of Finance: Government Bldg 2, Negdsen Ündestnii Gudamj 5/1, Chingeltei District, Ulan Bator; tel. and fax (11) 264891; e-mail support@mof.gov.mn; internet www.mof.gov.mn.

Ministry of Food, Agriculture and Light Industry: Government Bldg 9, Enkh Taivny Örgön Chölöö 16A, Bayanzürkh District, Ulan Bator; tel. (51) 262271; e-mail mofa@mofa.gov.mn; internet www .mofa.gov.mn.

Ministry of Health: Government Bldg 8, Olimpiin Gudamj 2, Sükhbaatar District, Ulan Bator; tel. (51) 263913; e-mail admin@moh.gov.mn; internet www.moh.gov.mn.

Ministry of Justice and Home Affairs: Government Bldg 5, Khudaldaany Gudamj 6/1, Sükhbaatar District, Ulan Bator; tel. (11) 267014; fax (11) 325225; e-mail admin@mojha.gov.mn; internet www.mojha.gov.mn.

Ministry of Mineral Resources, Fuel and Power: Government Bldg 2, Negdsen Ündestnii Gudamj 5/2, Chingeltei District, Ulan Bator; tel. (51) 261511; fax (11) 318169; e-mail info@mmre.energy .mn; internet www.mmre.energy.mn.

Ministry of Roads, Transport, Construction and Urban Development: Government Bldg 12, Negdsen Ündestnii Gudamj 5/2, Chingeltei District, Ulan Bator; tel. (11) 310597; fax (11) 310612; e-mail info@mrtcud.mn; internet www.mrtcud.gov.mn.

Ministry of Social Welfare and Labour: Government Bldg 2, Negdsen Ündestnii Gudamj 5, Chingeltei District, Ulan Bator; tel. (11) 264918; fax (11) 328634; e-mail mswl@mongolnet.mn; internet www.mswl.gov.mn.

Government Affairs Directorate (Cabinet Secretariat): State Palace, Sükhbaataryn Talbai 6, Ulan Bator; tel. and fax (51) 262408; e-mail info@cabinet.gov.mn; internet www.pmis.gov.mn/cabinet.

President and Legislature

PRESIDENT

Office of the President: State Palace, Sükhbaataryn Talbai 6, Ulan Bator; fax (11) 311121; internet www.president.mn.

Election, 24 May 2009

Candidate	Votes	%
Tsakhiagiin Elbegdorj (Democratic Party)	562,718	51.21
Nambaryn Enkhbayar (MPRP)	520,948	47.41

MONGOLIAN GREAT KHURAL

Under the fourth Constitution, which came into force in February 1992, the single-chamber Mongolian Great Khural is the State's supreme legislative body. With 76 members elected for a four-year term, the Great Khural must meet for at least 50 working days in every six months. Its Chairman may act as President of Mongolia when the President is indisposed.; State Palace, Sükhbaataryn Talbai, Ulan Bator; e-mail secretariat@parliament .mn; internet www .parliament .mn

Chairman (Speaker): DAMDINGIIN DEMBEREL.

Vice-Chairmen: GAVAAGIIN BATKHÜÜ, NYAMAAGIIN ENKHBOLD.

Secretary-General: TSERENKHÜÜGIIN SHARAVDORJ.

General Election, 29 June 2008

Party	Seats
Mongolian People's Revolutionary Party (MPRP)	45
Democratic Party (DP)	28
Civil Courage Party (CCP)	1
Mongolian Green Party	1
Independent	1
Total	76

Election Commission

General Election Committee: Government Bldg 11, Sambuugiin Gudamj 11, Ulan Bator; tel. (11) 263383; fax (11) 326975; e-mail gecm@mongol.net; internet www.gec.gov.mn; f. 1992; Chair. NAMSRAIJAVYN LUVSANJAV.

Political Organizations

Citizens' Movement Party: Rm 304, National Information and Technology Park, Baga Toiruu 49, Sükhbaatar District, Ulan Bator; tel. (11) 321900; f. 2007; 815 mems; Chair. NYAMAAGIIN DAVAA.

Civil Courage-Green Party (CC-GP): internet www.greenparty .mn; amalgamation of parties begun in March 2011; registration refused May 2011; Chair. DANGAASÜRENGIIN ENKHBAT (Mongolian Green Party); Deputy Chair. SANJAASÜRENGIIN OYUUN (Civil Courage Party).

Civil Courage Party (CCP): Mongolian TU Confederation Bldg, Rm 314, Sükhbaataryn Talbai 3, Ulan Bator; tel. (11) 319006; e-mail izn_ganbat@yahoo.com; internet www.izn.mn; Office Man. G. GANBAT.

Democratic Party (DP): Central Post, POB 578, Sükhbaatar District, Ulan Bator; tel. (11) 322755; fax (11) 323755; e-mail international@demparty.mn; internet www.demparty.mn; f. 2000; est. by amalgamation of the Mongolian National Democratic Party, Mongolian Social-Democratic Party, Mongolian Democratic Party, Mongolian Democratic Renewal Party and the Mongolian Believers' Democratic Party; Mongolian Social-Democratic Party re-est. as independent party in 2004; c. 150,000 mems. (2008); Chair. NOROVYN ALTANKHUYAG; Sec.-Gen. DONDOGDORJIIN ERDENEBAT.

Development Programme Party: Rm 2, Poverty Reduction Programme Foundation Bldg, 14th Sub-District, Sükhbaatar District, Ulan Bator; tel. 96019222; f. 2007; 933 mems (2008); Chair. N. ZUUNNAST.

Freedom Implementer Party: Varyeta Centre, 1st Sub-District, Bayangol District, Ulan Bator (POB 48/117); tel. 88113439; fax (11)

327899; e-mail freedom_ofmn@yahoo.com; 1,600 mems; f. 2006; Chair. SHOOVDORYN TÖMÖRSÜKH.

Mongolian Democratic Movement Party: Rm 306, Ikh Surguuliin Gudamj 3/2, 6th Sub-District, Sükhbaatar District, Ulan Bator (POB 20A/158); tel. 99009093; f. 2008; 850 mems (2008); Chair. T. OYUUNA; Sec.-Gen. M. GANZORIG.

Mongolian Green Party: Internom Block B, Amaryn Gudamj 2, Sükhbaatar District, Ulan Bator; tel. 314560; e-mail info@greenparty.mn; internet www.greenparty.mn; f. 1990; political wing of Alliance of Greens; majority of mems joined Civil Courage-Green Party in 2011; Co-Chair. O. BUM-YALAGCH.

Mongolian Liberal Party: Ulan Bator Higher School of Intellect, 4th Sub-District, Chingeltei District, Ulan Bator (POB 23/320); tel. 99852957; fax (11) 328198; f. 1999 as Mongolian Civil Democratic New Liberal Party, renamed 2004; ruling body Little Khural of 90 mems with Leadership Council of nine; 1,300 mems (2008); Chair. L. ALTANCHIMEG.

Mongolian People's Party (MPP): Baga Toiruu 37/1, Ulan Bator; tel. and fax 65007805; e-mail contact@mpp.mn; f. 1921; est. as Mongolian People's Party; renamed as Mongolian People's Revolutionary Party (MPRP) in 1925; reorganized in the 1990s; reverted to Mongolian People's Party in Nov. 2010; 163,805 mems (2011); ruling body Party Baga Khural (310 mems at Nov. 2010), which elects the Leadership (Steering) Council (31 mems); Chair. SÜKHBAATARYN BATBOLD; Gen. Sec. UKHNAAGIIN KHÜRELSÜKH.

Mongolian People's Revolutionary Party: Ulan Bator; f. 2011; breakaway faction of the Mongolian People's Party; registration in June 2011 challenged by MPP; 20,000 mems; Chair. NAMBARYN ENKHBAYAR.

Mongolian Social-Democratic Party (MSDP): Room 12, No. 5 Bldg, 1st Sub-District, Sükhbaatar District, Ulan Bator (CPOB 680); tel. 99114273; fax (11) 323828; f. 1990; merged in Dec. 2000 to form part of Democratic Party; refounded Jan. 2005; c. 3,000 mems (2008); Chair. ARYAAGIIN GANBAATAR; Gen. Sec. LOSOLYN BYAMBAJARGAL.

Mongolian Traditional United Party (MTUP): Room 3, Mika Hotel, Elchingiin Gudamj, 1st Sub-District, Sükhbaatar District, Ulan Bator (POB 44/5240); tel. (11) 327690; fax (11) 310133; also known as the United Heritage (conservative) Party; f. 1994; est. as an amalgamation of the United Private Owners' Party and the Independence Party; 1,503 mems (2008); ruling body General Political Council; Chair. BATDELGERIIN BATBOLD.

Motherland Party: Motherland Party Central Bldg, Jukovyn Örgön Chölöö 7a, Ulan Bator (POB 49/404); tel. 90150268; fax (11) 453178; internet www.mongol.net/mdnsp; f. 1998; amalgamated with Mongolian Workers' Party 1999; fmrly Mongolian Democratic New Socialist Party, name changed as above in 2005; reported to be disbanding in 2009; c. 160,000 mems (2008); Chair. BADARCHIIN ERDENEBAT.

National Labour Party: Ulan Bator; registration denied by Supreme Court Feb. 2011; Chair. P. ENKHBAYAR; Sec.-Gen. A. PÜREVSÜREN.

Mongolian National New Democratic Party: No. 2 Bldg, Enkh Taivny Örgön Chölöö 12, 1st Sub-District, Sükhbaatar District, Ulan Bator; tel. (11) 260535; fax (11) 312596; f. 2006; registered under above name in Oct. 2011; est. after a split in the leadership of the Democratic Party upon formation of the national solidarity govt; fmrly National New Democratic Party (previously National New Party; 2,400 mems (2008); Chair. MENDSAIKHANY ENKHSAIKHAN; Sec.-Gen. NAMDAGIIN BATTSEREG.

Republican Party (RP): Rm 106, Buyan Holding Co Bldg, 3rd Sub-District, Bayangol District, Ulan Bator; tel. (11) 344844; fax (11) 344843; f. 2004; 50,000 mems (2008); Chair. BAZARSADYN JARGALSAIKHAN; Sec.-Gen. S. BAYARMANLAI.

Diplomatic Representation

EMBASSIES IN MONGOLIA

Bulgaria: Olimpiin Gudamj 8, Ulan Bator (CPOB 702); tel. (11) 322841; fax (11) 324841; e-mail posolstvob@magicnet.mn; Ambassador (vacant).

Canada: Central Tower, 6th Floor, Sükhbaataryn Talbai 2, Sükhbaatar District, Ulan Bator (CPOB 1028); tel. (11) 328285; fax (11) 328289; e-mail ulaan@international.gc.ca; internet www.mongolia.gc.ca; Ambassador GREGORY GOLDHAWK.

China, People's Republic: Zaluuchuudyn Örgön Chölöö 5, Ulan Bator (CPOB 672); tel. (11) 320955; fax (11) 311943; internet mn.chineseembassy.org; Ambassador WANG XIAOLONG.

Cuba: Negdsen Ündestnii Gudamj 5, Ulan Bator (CPOB 710); tel. (11) 323778; fax (11) 327709; Ambassador MARÍA HORTENSIA FEBLES MIRABAL.

Czech Republic: Olimpiin Gudamj 12, Ulan Bator (CPOB 665); tel. (11) 321886; fax (11) 323791; e-mail czechemb@magicnet.mn; internet www.mzv.cz/ulaanbaatar; Ambassador VÁCLAV JILEK.

France: Enkh Taivny Örgön Chölöö 3, Chingeltei District, Ulan Bator (CPOB 687); tel. (11) 324519; fax (11) 319176; e-mail ambafrance@magicnet.mn; internet www.ambafrance-mn.org; Ambassador JEAN-PAUL DUMONT.

Germany: Negdsen Ündestnii Gudamj 7, Ulan Bator (CPOB 708); tel. (11) 323325; fax (11) 323905; internet www.ulan-bator.diplo.de; Ambassador PETER SCHALLER.

India: Zaluuchuudyn Örgön Chölöö 10, Ulan Bator (CPOB 691); tel. (11) 329522; fax (11) 329532; e-mail indembmongolia@magicnet.mn; internet www.indianembassy.mn; Ambassador SATBIR SINGH.

Japan: Olimpiin Gudamj 8, Ulan Bator (CPOB 1011); tel. (11) 320777; fax (11) 313332; e-mail eojmongol@magicnet.mn; internet www.mn.emb-japan.go.jp; Ambassador TAKUO KIDOKORO.

Kazakhstan: Zaisangiin Gudamj 31-6, 1st Sub-District, Khan-Uul District, Ulan Bator (CPOB 291); tel. (11) 315408; fax (11) 341707; e-mail kzemby@mbox.mn; Ambassador ORMAN NURBAYEV.

Korea, Democratic People's Republic: Sambuugiin Gudamj, Ulan Bator (CPOB 1015); tel. (11) 325663; fax (11) 326153; Ambassador RI CHOL GWANG.

Korea, Republic: Olimpiin Gudamj 10, Ulan Bator (CPOB 1039); tel. (11) 321548; fax (11) 311157; e-mail kormg@mofat.go.kr; internet mng.mofat.go.kr; Ambassador CHEUNG IL.

Laos: Ikh Toiruu 59, Ulan Bator (CPOB 1030); tel. (11) 326440; fax (11) 321048; e-mail emblao@magicnet.mn; Ambassador PENG INTHARATH.

Russia: Enkh Taivny Gudamj 6-A, Ulan Bator (CPOB 661); tel. (11) 327191; fax (11) 327018; e-mail embassy_ru@mongol.net; internet www.mongolia.mid.ru; Ambassador VIKTOR V. SAMOILENKO.

Turkey: Enkh Taivny Örgön Chölöö 5, Ulan Bator (CPOB 1009); tel. (11) 311200; fax (11) 313992; e-mail embassy.ulaanbaatar@mfa.gov.tr; internet ulaanbaatar.emb.mfa.gov.tr; Ambassador AHMET ASIM ARAR.

United Kingdom: Enkh Taivny Gudamj 30, Ulan Bator 13 (CPOB 703); tel. (11) 458133; fax (11) 458036; e-mail britemb@mongol.net; internet ukinmongolia.fco.gov.uk; Ambassador THORHILDA MARY VIVIA ABBOTT-WATT.

USA: Ikh Toiruu 59/1, Ulan Bator (CPOB 1021); tel. (11) 329095; fax (11) 320776; e-mail cons@usembassy.mn; internet www.us-mongolia.com; Ambassador JONATHAN S. ADDLETON.

Viet Nam: Enkh Taivny Örgön Chölöö 47, Ulan Bator (CPOB 670); tel. (11) 458917; fax (11) 458923; e-mail vinaemba@magicnet.mn; internet www.vietnamembassy-mongolia.org; Ambassador HOANG TUAN THINH.

Judicial System

Under the fourth Constitution, judicial independence is protected by the General Council of Courts, consisting of the Chief Justice (Chairman of the Supreme Court), the Procurator General, the Minister of Justice and Home Affairs and others. Members of the Supreme Court are nominated by the Council and appointed (or rejected) by the President. The Chief Justice is chosen from among the members of the Supreme Court and approved by the President for a six-year term. Routine civil, criminal and administrative cases are handled by 30 rural district and inter-district courts and eight urban district courts. There are 22 appellate courts at provincial and capital city level. Some legal cases are required by law to be dealt with by the Supreme Court, appellate courts or special courts (military, railway, etc.). The Procurator General and his deputies, who play an investigatory role, are nominated by the President and approved by the Great Khural for six-year terms.

Chief Justice: TSEVEGMIDIIN ZORIG.

Procurator General: DAMBYN DORLIGJAV.

Religion

The 1992 Constitution maintains the separation of Church and State. The Law on State-Church Relations (of November 1993) sought to make Buddhism the predominant religion and restricted the dissemination of beliefs other than Buddhism, Islam and shamanism. During the early years of communist rule Mongolia's traditional Mahayana Buddhism was virtually destroyed. In the early 1990s some 2,000 lamas (monks) established small communities at the sites of 120 former monasteries, temples and religious schools, some of which were being restored. The Kazakhs of western Mongolia are nominally Sunni Muslims. Mosques, also destroyed in the 1930s or closed subsequently, are only now being rebuilt or reopened.

Traces of shamanism from the pre-Buddhist period still survive. In recent years there has been an increase in Christian missionary activity in Mongolia.

BUDDHISM

At the end of 2010 there were 127 Buddhist temples and monasteries in Mongolia, including 52 in Ulan Bator, with 1,899 lamas, 2,559 employees and 867 students in religious schools. According to the November 2010 population census, Mongolia has more than 1m. Buddhist believers.

Living Buddha: The Ninth Javzandamba Khutagt (Ninth Bogd), Jambalnamdolchoijinjaltsan.

Asian Buddhist Conference For Peace: Gandan, Ulan Bator (CPOB 38); tel. and fax (11) 360069; e-mail blgn_abcp@yahoo.com; Sec.-Gen. Dr T. BULGAN.

Gandantegchinlen Monastery: Zanabazaryn Gudamj, Bayangol District, Ulan Bator; tel. (11) 360354; Centre of Mongolian Buddhists; Khamba Lama (Abbot) DEMBERELIIN CHOIJAMTS.

'Good Merit' Buddhist Society: Ulan Bator; Pres. Lama A. ERDENEBAT.

Karmapa Monastery: Khamba Lama (Abbot) DAVAASAMBUUGIIN TAIVANSAIKHAN.

Pethub Buddhist Institute: Ikh Toiruu, Chingeltei District, Ulan Bator (POB 38/105); tel. (11) 321867; fax (11) 320676; e-mail pethubmongolia@magicnet.mn; internet www.pethubmonastery.com; f. 2001 by Ven. Kushok Bakula Rinpoche (Indian Ambassador to Mongolia 1990–2000).

CHRISTIANITY

At the end of 2010 there were 96 Christian congregations in Mongolia, including 72 in Ulan Bator, with 181 priests and ministers, 586 employees and 68 students attending Christian studies. According to the November 2010 population census, Mongolia has 41,000 Christian believers.

Roman Catholic Church

The Church is represented in Mongolia by a single mission. At December 2007, according to Vatican sources, there were 417 Catholics in the country.

Catholic Mission: 18th Sub-District, Bayanzürkh District, Ulan Bator (CPOB 694); tel. (11) 458825; fax (11) 458027; e-mail info@ccmvatican.mn; internet www.ccmvatican.mn; f. 1992; Apostolic Prefect Bishop WENCESLAO PADILLA.

Protestant Church

Association of Mongolian Protestants: f. 1990; Pastor M. BOLDBAATAR.

Mongolian Evangelical Alliance: Jijig Ür Bldg, 3rd Sub-District, Bayanzürkh District, Ulan Bator; tel. 70152040 (mobile); e-mail mea@magicnet.mn; internet www.mea.mn; f. 1998; a branch of the World Evangelical Alliance.

Other Christian Churches

Rich Heart Baptist Church: Ulan Bator (CPOB 1167); tel. 99198221 (mobile); internet www.mongolianteam.org; congregation of 120; Pastor DAMBAKHÜÜGIIN ERDENEBAYAR.

Church of Jesus Christ of Latter-Day Saints (Mormon): Khudaldaany Gudamj, Chingeltei District, Ulan Bator; tel. (11) 312761.

Jesus Reigns Assembly: Ulan Bator; Pastor D. NARANMANDAKH.

Russian Orthodox Church: Holy Trinity Church, Jukovyn Gudamj 55, Bayanzürkh District, Ulan Bator; tel. 99256732; fax 11454425; e-mail fatheraleksei@hotmail.com; internet www.pravoslavie.mn; opened in 1864, closed in 1927; services recommenced 1997 for Russian community; new Holy Trinity Church consecrated in June 2009; Head Father ALEKSEI TRUBACH.

Seventh-day Adventist Church: 5th Sub-District, Bayangol District, Ulan Bator; tel. (11) 688031; fax (11) 688032.

ISLAM

At the end of 2010 there were six Muslim congregations, all but one (in Ulan Bator) in western Mongolia, with 11 clergy, 25 employees and 629 students. A mosque was due to be built in Ulan Bator. It is assumed that the majority of Mongolia's ethnic Kazakh population (numbering 103,000 at the January 2000 census) are Muslim. It was stated in March 2005 that Mongolia had 32 mosques in Bayan-Ölgii and Khovd provinces and in the towns of Darkhan and Nalaikh. Mongolia has 57,000 Muslim believers, according to the population census of November 2010.

Chief Imam (Ölgii): KH. BATYRBEK.

Imam of Gümyr shrine (Ölgii): DÖITENGIIN SHERKHAN.

Association of Mongolian Muslim Societies: f. 2009; Exec. Dir KH. BATYRBEK.

BAHÁ'Í FAITH

Bahá'í Society: Ulan Bator; tel. (11) 321867; f. 1989; Leader A. ARIUNAA.

SHAMANISM

There are 7,000 believers in Shamanism, according to the population census of November 2010.

Darkhad Shamanic Study Centre: Ulan Bator; Leader CH. TSERENBAAVAI.

Tengeriin Süld Shamanic Union: Ulan Bator; Pres. CH. CHINBAT.

The Press

PRINCIPAL NATIONAL NEWSPAPERS

State-owned publications in Mongolia were denationalized with effect from 1 January 1999, although full privatization could not proceed immediately. The number of newspapers published annually decreased from 134.1m. copies in 1990 to 18.5m. copies in 2003. As of January 2010, Mongolia had 139 newspapers and periodicals. A total of 31 provincial and town newspapers were published 36 times a year, with four appearing 48 times a year.

Ardchilal (Democracy): Democracy Palace, 7th Sub-District, Sükhbaatar District, Ulan Bator (POB 20/360); tel. and fax 70110187; e-mail info@ardchilal.com; internet www.ardchilal.com; 260 a year; Editor-in-Chief TSEND-AYUUSHIIN TSOLMON.

Ardyn Erkh (People's Power): Ardyn Erkh Bldg, West of Mongolkino Studio, 5th Sub-District, Bayanzürkh District, Ulan Bator; tel. and fax 99098705; e-mail info@news.mn; f. 2004; original title ceased publication in 1999 (see *Ödriin Sonin*, below); subsequently assumed by new publr; 256 a year; Exec. Dir BAYARMAGNAIN TEMÜÜLEN.

Mongolyn Medee (Mongolian News): Free Press Foundation, Sükhbaatar District, Ulan Bator; tel. and fax 70113551; e-mail mongoliin_medee@yahoo.com; 256 a year; Editor-in-Chief S. GANTOGOO; Sec. B. OYUUNGEREL; circ. 2,900.

Mongolyn Ünen (Mongolian Truth): Mongolyn Ünen Newspaper Bldg, Amaryn Gudamj, Sükhbaatar District, Ulan Bator; tel. (11) 321287; fax (11) 323223; e-mail unen@mongol.net; internet www.unen.imedia.mn; f. 1920; publ. 1925–2010 by MPRP as Ünen; 256 a year; Editor-in-Chief J. MÖNKHBAT; circ. 8,330.

Montsame Medee (Montsame News): Montsame News Agency, Jigjidjavyn Gudamj 8, Ulan Bator (CPOB 1514); tel. (11) 314511; e-mail localnews@montsame.mn; internet www.montsame.mn; daily news digest primarily for govt depts; 248 a year; Editor B. NOMINCHIMED.

Ödriin Sonin (Daily News): Ödriin Sonin Bldg, Ikh Toiruu, Sükhbaatar District, Ulan Bator; tel. 99193519; fax 70134164; e-mail info@dailynews.mn; internet www.dailynews.mn; f. 1924; restored 1990; fmrly Ardyn Erkh, Ardyn Ündesnii Erkh, Ündesnii Erkh and Ödriin Toli; 312 a year; Editor-in-Chief JAMBALYN MYAGMARSÜREN; circ. 14,200.

Öglöönii Sonin (Morning News): 1st Sub-District, Bayanzürkh District, Ulan Bator (POB 46/411); tel. and fax (11) 450640; e-mail ugluuniisonin@yahoo.com; 252 a year; Editor-in-Chief O. MÖNKH-ERDENE.

Önöödör (Today): Mongol News Co Bldg, Juulchny Gudamj 40, Chingeltei District, Ulan Bator; tel. 70111096; fax (11) 330798; e-mail today@mongolnews.mn; internet www.mongolnews.mn; f. 1996; 300 a year; Editor-in-Chief B. NANDINTÜSHIG; circ. 5,500.

Ulaanbaatar Taims (Ulan Bator Times): Credit Bank Centre, 5th Floor, Yörönkhii Said Amaryn Gudamj, Sükhbaatar District, Ulan Bator; tel. (11) 322215; e-mail info@ubtimes.mn; internet www.ubtimes.mn; f. 1929; est. as Ulaanbaatar Khotyn Medee ; renamed Ulaanbaataryn Medee in 1955, Ulaanbaatar in 1990, and Ulaanbaatar Taims in 1999; publ. by Ulan Bator City Govt; 252 a year; Editor-in-Chief DOLGORYN CHULUUNBAATAR; circ. 2,000.

Ündesnii Shuudan (National Post): fmr Ardyn Erkh Bldg, Ikh Toiruu, Ulan Bator; tel. (11) 354632; fax (11) 354631; e-mail undesniishuudan@yahoo.com; 312 a year; Editor-in-Chief BAASANJAVYN GANBOLD.

Zuuny Medee (Century's News): Amaryn Gudamj 1, Ulan Bator; tel. 70116004; fax (11) 321279; e-mail zuuniimedee@yahoo.com; internet www.zuuniimedee.imedia.mn; f. 1991; previously titled Zasgiin Gazryn Medee; 312 a year; Editor-in-Chief DEMCHIGJAVYN OTGONBAYAR; circ 8,000.

OTHER NEWSPAPERS AND PERIODICALS

4 dekh Zasaglal (Fourth Estate): Mongol Sonin Co, Gazar Holding Bldg, Variete Centre, Ulan Bator (POB 46A/81); tel. 99188125; e-mail dorovdekhzasaglal@yahoo.com; 36 a year; Editor A. Enkhbayar.

81-r Suvag (Channel 81): Söüliin Gudamj, Bayangol District, Ulan Bator (POB 46A/81); tel. 96003992; fax (11) 460718; publishes views of the Mongolian Newspaper Asscn; 36 a year; Editor-in-Chief T. Tsogt-Erdene.

Altangadas (Pole Star): AG Töv, Söüliin Gudamj, Bayanzürkh District, Ulan Bator (CPOB 430); tel. (11) 319411; fax (11) 319414; e-mail info@altangadas.mn; internet www.altangadas.mn; monthly political magazine; Editor Norovyn Altankhuyag.

Anagaakh Arga Bilig (The Healthy Way of Yin and Yang): Ulan Bator (CPOB 1053); tel. (11) 321367; e-mail arslny7144@magicnet.mn; 24 a year; Editor Ya. Arslan.

Bagsh (Teacher): Rm 106, Teachers' College, Ulan Bator; tel. 99183398; f. 1989; est. by Ministry of Education; 24 a year.

Biznesiin Medee (Business News): East of Wrestlers Palace, 6th Sub-District, Bayanzürkh District, Ulan Bator (POB 20/335); tel. and fax 70155513; e-mail biznesiin_medee@yahoo.com; 36 a year; Editor-in-Chief S. Khürel.

Bolson Yavdal (Events): Söüliin Gudamj, Sükhbaatar District, Ulan Bator (POB 36/346); e-mail bolsonyavdal@yahoo.com; 36 a year; Editor T. Sangaa.

Business Times: Business Times Bldg, 1st Sub-District, Khan-Uul District, Ulan Bator; tel. and fax (11) 325374; internet www.businesstimes.mn; 36 a year; Editor Batsükhiin Sarantuyaa.

Deed Shüükhiin Medeelel (Supreme Court Information): Mongolian Supreme Court, Ulan Bator; quarterly journal.

Deedsiin Amidral (Elite's Life): Bldg 4, Rm 514, A. Amaryn Gudamj, Ulan Bator (CPOB 356); tel. 91189699; fax (11) 323847; e-mail deedsiinamidral@mongol.mn; 36 a year; Editor-in-Chief B. Otgonbayar.

Deedsiin Khüreelen (Elite's Forum): Ulan Bator (CPOB 1114); tel. and fax (11) 450602; e-mail deed_huree@yahoo.com; 48 a year; Publr M. Sükhbaatar; Editor Kh. Uyanga; circ. 12,000.

Ekh Orny Manaa (Guard of the Motherland): Main Directorate of Border Defence, Ulan Bator; internet bpo.gov.mn; 36 a year.

Emiin Medeelel (Medicine Information): National Health Development Centre, Ministry of Health, Ulan Bator; tel. (11) 321485; fax (11) 320633; e-mail zorig@nchd.mn; bimonthly magazine published by the National Health Development Centre; Editor T. Zorig.

Erüül Mend (Health): Super Zuun Co, Ulan Bator (POB 20/412); tel. 99192239; fax (11) 321278; e-mail dr_jargal_d@yahoo.com; publ. by Ministry of Health; monthly; Editor D. Jargalsaikhan; circ. 5,600.

Khani (Spouse): National Agricultural Co-operative Members' Association Bldg 12, Khiimor Khotkhon, Bayanzürkh District, Ulan Bator (POB 49/600); tel. (11) 460698; fax (11) 458550; e-mail khani_sonin@yahoo.com; women and family issues; 32 a year; Editor-in-Chief Dembereliin Batsükh; circ. 64,920.

Khiimori (Wind-Horse): Ödriin Sonin Bldg, Ikh Toiruu 20, Sükhbaatar District, Ulan Bator; tel. (11) 354565; monthly; Editor-in-Chief A. Erdenetuyaa.

Khödölmör (Labour): Sükhbaataryn Talbai 3, Ulan Bator; tel. (11) 323026; f. 1928; publ. by Confederation of Mongolian Trade Unions; 48 a year; Editor-in-Chief Tsoodolyn Khulan; circ. 64,920.

Khökh Tolbo (Blue Spot): Mon-Azi Co Bldg 54, 4th Sub-District, Chingeltei District, Ulan Bator (POB 24/306); tel. (11) 313405; fax (11) 312794; 36 a year; Publr Batyn Erdenebaatar; Editor-in-Chief E. Enkhtsolmon; circ. 3,500.

Khöröngiin Zakh Zeel (Capital Market): Mongolian Stock Exchange, Sükhbaataryn Talbai 2, Ulan Bator; tel. (11) 313511; fax (11) 325170; e-mail info@mse.mn; monthly; Editor (vacant).

Khuuli Züin Medeelel (Legal Information): National Legal Centre, Chingeltei District, Ulan Bator; tel. (11) 322094; fax (11) 315735; e-mail altantuya.s@legalinstitute.mn; f. 1990; 24 a year; publ. by National Legal Institute.

Khuviin Soyol (Personal Culture): Rm 2, Block 39, behind No. 5 School, Baga Toiruu, Ulan Bator (CPOB 1254); 24 a year; Editor Bekhbazaryn Bekhsüren.

Khümüün Bichig (People and Script): Montsame News Agency, Jigjidjavyn Gudamj 8, Ulan Bator (CPOB 1514); tel. (11) 329486; fax (11) 327857; e-mail khumuun@montsame.mn; current affairs in Mongolian classical script; 48 a year; Editor T. Galdan; circ. 15,000.

Khümüüs (People): Khümüüs Bldg, 1st Sub-District, Bayanzürkh District, Ulan Bator (POB 46/411); tel. 70168363; fax (11) 450323; internet www.humuus.mn; 48 a year; Editor O. Mönkh-Erdene.

Khümüüsiin Amidral (People's Lives): Central Palace of Culture, Ulan Bator (POB 46/411); 48 a year; Editor B. Amgalan.

Mash Nuuts (Top Secret): Mongol Shaazan Bldg, 2nd Sub-District, Sükhbaatar District, Ulan Bator (POB 49/113); tel. and fax (11) 328673; e-mail tsecret@mongolnet.mn; 32 a year; Editor-in-Chief Ononggiin Chinzorig.

Mongoljin Goo (Mongolian Beauty): Mongolian Women's Federation, Ulan Bator (POB 44/717); tel. and fax 7011836; e-mail monwofed@magicnet.mn; internet www.mwf.mn; f. 1990; monthly; Editor J. Erdenechimeg; circ. 3,000.

Mongolyn Anagaakh Ukhaan (Mongolian Medicine): Ulan Bator (CPOB 696); tel. (11) 112306; fax (11) 451807; e-mail nymadawa@hotmail.com; publ. by Scientific Society of Mongolian Physicians and Mongolian Academy of Sciences; 6 a year; Editor-in-Chief Prof. Pagvajavyn Nyamdavaa.

Mongolyn Khödöö (Mongolian Countryside): Agricultural University, Zaisan, Ulan Bator; tel. (11) 345211; e-mail mglhuduu.msun.mn; publ. by Mongolian State University of Agriculture and Academy of Agricultural Sciences; 36 a year; Editor-in-Chief Prof. Begziin Dorj.

Mongolyn Neg Ödör (One Day of Mongolia): Bldg 31, Bayanzürkh District, Ulan Bator (POB 44/764); tel. (11) 450103; fax (11) 460718; e-mail oneday@mongolmedia.com; 48 a year; Editor-in-Chief Sh. Otgonsetseg.

Myangany Zuuch (Millennium Messenger): Mönkh Press Co, West side of Choijin Lama Temple, Sükbataar District, Ulan Bator (POB 46/390); tel. and fax (11) 319745; e-mail monkh@mobinet.mn; 36 a year; Deputy Editor G. Enkhjargal.

Niigmiin Toli (Mirror of Society): Monkord Bldg, 4th Sub-District, Chingeltei District, Ulan Bator; tel. 99049531; e-mail enkhtaivan_987@yahoo.com; internet www.niigmiintoli.mn; 312 a year; Editor-in-Chief Sandagdorjiin Enkhtuul.

Notstoi Medee (Important News): Maximus Press Co, Ulan Bator (POB 20/359); tel. 99113322; 36 a year; Editor B. Galsansükh.

Nyam Garig (Sunday): Mongol News Co Bldg, Juulchny Gudamj, Ulan Bator; tel. (11) 330797; fax (11) 330798; e-mail weekend@mongolnews.mn; weekly supplement of *Önöödör*; Editor-in-Chief B. Boldkhüü.

Onigoo (Jokes): Konsulyn Gudamj 5-13, Bayanzürkh District, Ulan Bator (POB Sky Post 46/50); tel. 70150001; e-mail onigoosonin@yahoo.com; 16 a year; Editor S. Saranchimeg.

Sankhüügiin Medee (Financial News): Ulan Bator; 36 a year; Editor L. Dondog.

Serüüleg (Alarm Clock): Mongol Daatgal Bldg, 15th Sub-District, Bayanzürkh District, Ulan Bator (CPOB 1094); tel. 99151917; fax 70151401; e-mail seruuleg1996@yahoo.com; 48 a year; Editor-in-Chief Bayanmönkhiin Tsoojchuluuntsetseg; circ. 28,600.

Setgüülch (Journalist): Ulan Bator (POB 46/600); tel. (11) 325388; fax (11) 313912; f. 1982; publ. by Union of Journalists; journalism, politics, literature, art, economy; quarterly; Editor Tsendiin Enkhbat.

Shar Sonin (Yellow Newspaper): Ulan Bator (POB 46A/225); tel. (11) 313984; e-mail thesharsonin@yahoo.com; 36 a year; Editor B. Namuun.

Shine Erkh Chölöö (New Freedom): Ödriin Sonin Bldg, Ikh Toiruu, Ulan Bator (CPOB 2590); tel. and fax 70137010; e-mail erkhcholoo2007@yahoo.com; monthly; social and political affairs; Editor-in-Chief Ts. Oyuunchimeg.

Shine Yörtönts (New World): Empathy Centre, Baga Toiruu, 6th Sub-District, Ulan Bator; tel. (11) 313019; internet www.empathy.mn; quarterly; popular science magazine; Editor B. Sarnai.

Shinjlekh Ukhaany Akademiin Medee (Academy of Sciences News): Yörönkhii Said Amaryn Gudamj 1, Ulan Bator (POB 20A/34); tel. and fax (11) 262247; e-mail mas@mas.ac.mn; internet www.mas.ac.mn; f. 1961; publ. by Academy of Sciences; quarterly; Editor-in-Chief Dügeriin Regdel.

Shuurkhai Zar (Quick Advertisement): Enkhtaivny Örgön Chölöö 62, 4th Sub-District, Sükhbaatar District, Ulan Bator (POB 46A/151); tel. and fax (11) 318787; e-mail shzar@mongol.mn; 96 a year; Editor E. Tseyenkhorloo.

Solongo (Rainbow): Green House, 6th Sub-District, Sükhbaatar District, Ulan Bator (POB 23/628); tel. 91887376; internet www.solonggo.net; f. 1992; monthly; Deputy Editor-in-Chief T. Bayanjargal.

Soyombo: Ministry of Defence, Ulan Bator; tel. 91177221; f. 1924; est. as *Ardyn Tsereg* (People's Soldier); renamed *Ekh Orny Tölöö* (For the Motherland), then *Ulaan Od* (Red Star); weekly; Dep. Editor-in-Chief Lt-Col G. Nyamdorj.

Strategi Sudlal (Strategic Studies): Institute of Strategic Studies, National Security Council, Ulan Bator (CPOB 870); tel. (11) 260710; fax (11) 324055; f. 1991; 4 a year; Editor Begziin Davaadorj.

Tavan Tsagarig (Five Rings): Mongol News Co Bldg, Juulchny Gudamj, Chingeltei District, Ulan Bator; tel. (11) 70111095; internet www.mongolnews.mn/tavantsagarig; f. 1995; 100 a year; Editor-in-Chief TSAGAANBAATARYN BYAMBAA.

Tengerleg Khümüüs (Heavenly People): Soyombo Press Co, Partizany Gudamj 17, Sükbaatar District, Ulan Bator (POB 44/716); tel. (11) 325250; fax (11) 330383; 36 a year; Dir-Gen. D. AMBARBAYASGALAN; Editor P. JARGALSAIKHAN.

Tonshuul (Woodpecker): Enkh Taivny Örgön Chölöö 4, Rm 148, Bayanzürkh District (CPOB 322), Ulan Bator; tel. 99118668; fax (11) 459265; e-mail ariun_tonshuul@yahoo.com; fortnightly magazine of cartoons, humour and satire; Editor TS. ARIUNAA.

Töriin Medeelel (State Information): Editorial Office, Rm 124, State Palace, Ulan Bator; tel. (11) 329612; fax (11) 322866; e-mail turiin_medeelel@parliament.mn; internet www.parl.gov.mn; f. 1990; presidential and governmental decrees, state laws; 48 a year; circ. 5,000.

Tsog (Ember): Mongolian Union of Writers, Ulan Bator; literary; quarterly.

Tsonkh (Window): Chingisiin Örgön Chölöö 1, Ulan Bator (CPOB 1085); tel. (11) 310717; publ. by the Democratic Party's Political Department; 6 a year.

Uls Töriin Sonin (Political Newspaper): Delta Centre, Juulchny Gudamj, Chingeltei District, Ulan Bator (POB 46/796); tel. 99095040; fax (11) 312608; f. 2005 following closure of the *Mongol Times*; 48 a year; Editor GANTÖMÖRIIN UYANGA.

Utga Zokhiol Urlag (Literature and Art): Mongolian Union of Writers, Sükhbaataryn Gudamj 11, Ulan Bator (POB 46A/555); tel. 99294530; e-mail info@utgazokhiol.mn; internet www.utgazokhiol.mn; f. 1955; 36 a year; Editor JAMSRANGIIN BAYARJARGAL; circ. 3,000.

Üg (The Word): Bldg 86, Chingeltei District, Ulan Bator; tel. 55152675; fax (11) 329795; e-mail ugsonin@mol.mn; journal of the Mongolian Social-Democratic Party (from 2005); Editor-in-Chief ARYAAGIIN GANBAATAR.

Zar Medee (Advertisement News): Arvit 20 Ail, 4th Sub-District, Chingeltei District, Ulan Bator; tel. 70110008; fax 70110009; e-mail zar_sonin@yahoo.com; internet zarsonin.mn; personal and company adverts; 100 a year; Editor D. BAYASGALAN.

Zindaa (Ranking): Kyokshüyu Tower, 5th Sub-District, Bayangol District, Ulan Bator; tel. 70151619; fax (11) 354555; wrestling news; 36 a year; Editor-in-Chief KH. MANDAKHBAYAR.

FOREIGN LANGUAGE PUBLICATIONS

Inspiring Mongolia: Mongolian National Chamber of Commerce and Industry, Mahatma Gandhi Gudamj, 1st Sub-District, Khan-Uul District, Ulan Bator; tel. (11) 312501; fax (11) 324620; e-mail marketing@mongolchamber.mn; internet www.mongolchamber.mn; magazine in English, publ. twice a year; Editor-in-Chief SAMBUUGIIN DEMBEREL.

Menggu Xiaoxi Bao (News of Mongolia): Montsame News Agency, Ulan Bator (CPOB 1514); tel. (11) 320077; e-mail mgxxbao@chinggis.com; f. 1929; weekly; in Chinese; Sec. P. OYUUNTSETSEG.

The Mongol Messenger: Montsame News Agency, Jigjidjavyn Gudamj 8, Ulan Bator (CPOB 1514); tel. (11) 266740; fax (11) 325512; e-mail monmessenger@magicnet.mn; f. 1991; weekly newspaper in English; owned by Montsame national news agency; Editor-in-Chief INDRA BORKHONDOIN; circ. 2,000.

Mongolian Magazine: Interpress Publishers, Ulan Bator; f. 2004; English-language monthly illustrated magazine about Mongolian history, culture, nature, life and customs.

Mongolia This Week: Ulan Bator; tel. and fax (11) 318339; e-mail mongoliathisweek@mobinet.mn; weekly in English, online daily; Editor-in-Chief D. NARANTUYAA; English Editor ERIC MUSTAFA.

Mongolia Today: Montsame News Agency, Jigjidjavyn Gudamj 8, Ulan Bator (CPOB 1514); quarterly; in English; Editor-in-Chief G. PÜREVSAMBUU.

Mongoliya Segodnya (Mongolia Today): Zoos Goyol Co Bldg, Chingeltei District, Ulan Bator (POB 51/404); tel. 88871402; fax (11) 457968; e-mail ms@mongoliyasegodnya.mn; weekly; in Russian; Editor-in-Chief DÜNGER-YAICHILIIN SOLONGO.

Mongoru Tsushin (Mongolia News): Montsame News Agency, Jigjidjavyn Gudamj 8, Ulan Bator (CPOB 1514); weekly; in Japanese.

Montsame Daily News: Montsame News Agency, Jigjidjavyn Gudamj 8, Ulan Bator (CPOB 1514); tel. (11) 314574; fax (11) 327857; e-mail montsame@magicnet.mn; daily English news digest for embassies, etc.; Editor-in-Chief BAYANBATYN BAYASGALAN.

Novosti Mongolii (News of Mongolia): Montsame News Agency, Jigjidjavyn Gudamj 8, Ulan Bator (CPOB 1514); tel. (11) 310157; fax (11) 327857; e-mail novosty_mongolii@yahoo.co.uk; f. 1942; weekly; in Russian; Editor-in-Chief DÜGERSÜRENGIIN ARIUNBOLD.

The UB Post: Mongol News Co, Juulchny Gudamj, Ulan Bator; tel. (11) 70111095; fax (11) 330798; e-mail ubpost@mongolnews.mn; internet ubpost.mongolnews.mn; f. 1996; 100 a year; in English; Editor-in-Chief G. ÖLZIISAIKHAN; circ. 4,000.

NEWS AGENCIES

Montsame (Mongol Tsakhilgaan Medeenii Agentlag) (Mongolian News Agency): Jigjidjavyn Gudamj 8, Ulan Bator (CPOB 1514); tel. (11) 266904; fax (11) 327857; e-mail montsame@magicnet.mn; internet www.montsame.mn; f. 1921; govt-controlled; Gen. Dir TUGALKHÜÜGIIN BAASANSÜREN; Editor-in-Chief B. NOMINCHIMED.

Mongolyn Medee (Mongolian News): Public Radio and Television, Khuvisgalyn Zam, Ulan Bator; Dir TS. SÜKHBAATAR.

PRESS ASSOCIATIONS

Daily Newspaper Association: c/o Önöödör, Mongol News Co, Juulchny Gudamj, Ulan Bator; f. 2006; Pres. B. TEMÜÜLEN.

Mongolian Newspaper Association: Ulan Bator; Pres. RADNAAGIIN KHADBAATAR.

Press Institute: Ulan Bator; internet www.pressinst.org.mn; f. 1995; Dir M. MÖNKHMANDAKH.

Publishers

The ending of the state monopoly has led to the establishment of several small commercial publishers, including Shuvuun Saaral (Ministry of Defence), Mongol Khevlel and Soyombo Co, Mongolpress (Montsame), Erdem (Academy of Sciences), Süülenkhüü children's publishers, Sudaryn Chuulgan, Interpress, Sükhbaatar Co, Öngöt Khevlel, Admon, Ödsar, Khee Khas Co, etc.

Admon Co: Amaryn Gudamj 2, Sükhbaatar District, Ulan Bator (CPOB 92); tel. (11) 329253; fax (11) 327251; e-mail admon@magicnet.mn; Dir R. ENKHBAT.

Chölööt Khevlel San (Free Press Foundation): Ikh Toiruu 11B, Ulan Bator (POB 20/357); tel. (11) 350016; e-mail mpfnph@magicnet.mn; f. 1996; the country's largest printer of newspapers and the biggest pre-press service provider; Man. Dir BAASTYN GALSANDORJ.

Darkhan Sergelen Co: Naadamchdyn Gudamj, Darkhan; tel. (37) 23049; fax (37) 24741; internet www.munkhiin-useg.mn.

Khevleliin Khüreelen (Press Institute NGO): Ikh Toiruu 11, Sükhbaatar District, Ulan Bator; tel. and fax (11) 350012; e-mail ts_byambaa12@yahoo.com; internet www.owc.org.mn/pressinstitute; Chair. TS. ENKHBAT.

Mongol News Group: Mongol News Group Bldg, Juulchny Gudamj, Ulan Bator; tel. (11) 330797; fax (11) 330798; e-mail mntoday@mobinet.mn; f. 1996; owns newspapers *MN-Önöödör*, *Tavan Tsagarig*, *Nyam Garig* and *The UB Post*, TV Channel 25 and ABM Co printers; Pres. B. NANDINTÜSHIG.

Mönkhiin Üseg Group: Teeverchdiin Gudamj, Songinokhairkhan District, Ulan Bator; tel. (11) 320807; fax (11) 321318; e-mail munuseg@mbox.mn; internet www.munkhiin-useg.mn; Chair. G. BATMÖNKH.

Novum Co: Migma Bldg, Ulan Bator; tel. (11) 319140; fax (11) 319319; e-mail print@mynovum.com; internet www.mynovum.com.

Öngöt Khevlel Co: Amaryn Gudamj 2, Sükhbaatar District, Ulan Bator; tel. (11) 323121; fax (11) 329519; e-mail ungut_khevlel@mongolnet.mn.

Soyombo Printing Co: Natsagdorjiin Gudamj, Sükhbaatar District, Ulan Bator; tel. (11) 325052.

Sükhbaatarprint Co: Amaryn Gudamj 2, Sükhbaatar District, Ulan Bator; tel. and fax (11) 320504; e-mail sukhprint@magicnet.mn.

Zurag Züi Co (Cartography): Ikh Toiruu 15, Ulan Bator; tel. (11) 322164; e-mail cart@magicnet.mn; publr and retailer of maps and atlases.

PUBLISHERS' ASSOCIATIONS

Local Press and Information Association: Ulan Bator; f. 2006; Pres. S. SHARAVDORJ.

Mongolian Book Publishers' Association: Ulan Bator; Exec. Dir S. TSERENDORJ.

Mongolian Free Press Publishers' Association: Ulan Bator (POB 24/306); tel. and fax (11) 313405; Pres. BATYN ERDENEBAATAR.

Broadcasting and Communications

TELECOMMUNICATIONS

Digital exchanges have been installed in Ulan Bator, Darkhan, Erdenet, Sükhbaatar, Bulgan and Arvaikheer, while radio relay lines have been digitalized between: Ulan Bator–Darkhan–Sükhbaatar; Ulan Bator–Darkhan–Erdenet; and Dashinchilen–Arvaikheer. Mobile telephone companies operate in Ulan Bator and other central towns, in addition to Arvaikheer, Sainshand and Zamyn-Üüd. By May 2005 a total of 1,776 km of fibre optic cable had been installed in Mongolia, with plans to lay another 1,400 km by the end of the year. The Ulan Bator–Bulgan cable was under construction.

Bodicom: Ulan Bator; tel. (11) 325144; fax (11) 318486; e-mail bodicom@mongolnet.mn.

Datacom: San Business Centre, 8th Sub-District, Sükhbaatar District, Ulan Bator; tel. (11) 327309; e-mail support@datacom.mn; internet www.datacom.mn; service provider for MagicNet connection to internet; Dir DANGAASÜRENGIIN ENKHBAT.

G-Mobile: Gem International Co, 1st Sub-District, Chingeltei District, Ulan Bator; tel. (11) 333636; e-mail info@g-mobile.mn; internet www.g-mobile.mn; Dir-Gen. TS. TSERENPUNTSAG.

Incomnet: Enkh Taivny Örgön Chölöö, Bayanzürkh District, Ulan Bator (CPOB 582); tel. and fax (11) 480808; e-mail info@incomnet.mn; internet www.incomnet.mn; internet service provider, satellite communications; Gen. Dir N. BUMCHIN.

MagicNet Co: Rm 222, Ground Floor, Science and Technology Information Centre, Ulan Bator; tel. (11) 312061; fax (11) 311496; e-mail info@magicnet.mn; internet www.magicnet.mn; internet service provider.

MCSCom: MCS Plaza, 3rd Floor, Baga Toiruu 49, Ulan Bator; tel. (11) 327854; fax (11) 311323; e-mail sales@mcscom.mn; internet www.mcscom.mn; internet service provider.

Medeelel Kholboo: Central Post Office Bldg, Sükhbaataryn Talbai 1, Chingeltei District, Ulan Bator; tel. and fax 70112519; internet www.icnc.mn; installation of digital radio relays and fibre optic cables for communications and internet, television and radio.

Micom: Central Post Office Bldg, Sükhbaataryn Talbai 1, Chingeltei District, Ulan Bator (CPOB 1124); tel. (11) 313229; fax (11) 322473; e-mail info@micom.mng.mn; internet www.micom.mn; Dir CH. NARANTUNGALAG.

MobiCom: MobiCom Corpn Central Bldg, Sambuugiin Gudamj 7-1, 5th Sub-District, Chingeltei District, Ulan Bator; tel. 95070202; fax (11) 310411; e-mail feedback@mobicom.mn; internet www.mobicom.mn; mobile telephone service provider; Exec. Dir FUMIAKI SHIGA; Dir-Gen. D. BOLOR.

Moncom: Ulan Bator (POB 51/207); tel. (11) 329409; e-mail ch.enkhmend@hotmail.com; pager services.

Mongolia Telecom: Central Post Office Bldg, Sükhbaataryn Talbai 1, Ulan Bator (CPOB 1166); tel. (11) 320597; fax (11) 325412; e-mail mt@mtcone.net; internet www.mongol.net; 54.6% state-owned, 40.0% owned by Korea Telecom; Pres. and CEO OONOIGIIN SHAALUU; Exec. Dir O. BATCHULUUN.

MonSat: New Horizon Bldg, Olimpiin Gudamj 6, 1st Sub-District, Sükhbaatar District, Ulan Bator; tel. (11) 323705; fax (11) 312699; e-mail monsat@mcs.mn; internet www.monsat.mcs.mn; satellite communications, mobile telephone and internet services.

Newcom LLC: Zovkhis Bldg, Söüliin Gudamj 21, Sükhbaatar District, Ulan Bator; tel. (11) 313183; fax (11) 318521; e-mail secretary@newcom.mn; internet www.newcom.mn; Chair. TS. BOLDBAATAR; Exec. Dir B. BYAMBASAIKHAN.

Newtel Co: TEDY Centre, Sambuugiin Gudamj 18, Chingeltei District, Ulan Bator (CPOB 425); tel. and fax (11) 311581; e-mail marketing@ntc.mn; internet www.ntc.mn; Exec. Dir D. BOLOR.

Orbitnet: New Horizon Bldg, Olimpiin Gudamj 6, Sükhbaatar District, Ulan Bator; tel. (11) 323705; fax (11) 312699; e-mail orbitnet@mcs.mn; internet www.orbitnet.mcs.mn.

Railcom: Mongolian Railways (MTZ), Teeverchdiin Gudamj, 3rd Sub-District, Bayangol District, Ulan Bator (CPOB 376); tel. (11) 242601; e-mail info@railcom.mn; internet www.railcom.mn; telephone, TV and internet service provider.

Skynetcom: 1st Sub-District, Chingeltei District, Ulan Bator; tel. (11) 318840; fax (11) 318841; e-mail info@skynetcom.mn; internet www.skynetcom.mn; mobile telephone service provider.

Skytel: Skytel Plaza Centre, Chingisiin Örgön Chölöö 9, Ulan Bator (CPOB 811); tel. (11) 319191; fax (11) 318487; e-mail skytel_comment@yahoo.com; internet www.skytel.mn; mobile telephone and voice mail service provider; Mongolia-Republic of Korea jt venture; Dir-Gen. R. GANBOLD; Marketing Man. G. TÜVSHINTÖGS.

Ulusnet: Zovkhis Bldg, Söüliin Gudamj 21, Sükhbaatar District, Ulan Bator; tel. (11) 321434; fax (11) 322686; e-mail service@ulusnet.mn; internet www.ulusnet.mn; Mongolia's first Wimax service provider.

Unitel: Central Tower, Sükhbaataryn Talbai 2, Sükhbaatar District, Ulan Bator; tel. (11) 328888; fax (11) 330708; e-mail info@unitel.mn; internet www.unitel.mn; f. 2005 by MBSB Telecom, Uangel Corpn (Republic of Korea) and Dream Choice Co (Canada); mobile telephone service provider; Dir-Gen. B. BILGÜÜN.

Univision: Unitel Corpn, Ulan Bator; tel. 77118811; e-mail info@univision.mn; internet www.univision.mn; HD cable TV, internet, mobile telephone service provider; CEO N. NARANBAT.

BROADCASTING

A 1,900-km radio relay line from Ulan Bator to Altai and Ölgii provides direct-dialling telephone links as well as television services for western Mongolia. New radio relay lines have been built from Ulan Bator to Choibalsan, and from Ulan Bator to Sükhbaatar and Sainshand. Most of the population is in the zone of television reception, following the inauguration of relays via satellites operated by the International Telecommunications Satellite Organization (INTELSAT). In 2004 Mongolia had 30 radio stations and 35 television stations.

In 2009 Mongolia had 373 television transmitters and relay stations. However, over 54,600 households continued to receive radio broadcasts by the old wired networks

All provincial centres receive two channels of Mongolian national television, and all district centres can receive television. At the beginning of 2005 the first legislative measures were taken to end state control, with the approval of the Law on Public Broadcasting, the provisions of which entered into force on 1 July 2005, creating an independent public service broadcaster to be known as Public Radio and Television. Also in 2005 it was planned to extend television coverage (UBS, TV-5, TV-9 and Channel 25) to outlying areas of Ulan Bator, including Partizan, Songino and Gachuurt, by installing additional local transmitters. In 2009 Mongolia's first internet television station, Mongol TV, was launched.

Mongolian National Public Radio and Television (ONRT): Mongolian National Public Radio and Television Central Bldg, Khuvisgalyn Zam 3, Bayangol District, Ulan Bator; tel. (11) 322580; f. 2006; replaced the govt-run Directorate of Radio and Television Affairs; Chair. of National Council KHAIDAVYN CHILAAJAV; Dir-Gen. MYANGANBUUGIIN NARANBAATAR; Editor-in-Chief DEMBERELIIN ERDENETSETSEG.

Radio

Mongolian National Public Radio (Mongolradio): Mongolian National Public Radio and Television Central Bldg, Khuvisgalyn Zam 3, Bayangol District, Ulan Bator; tel. (11) 323096; f. 1934; operates for 17 hours daily on three long-wave and one medium-wave frequency, and VHF; programmes in Mongolian (two); part of Public Radio and Television; Dir B. PÜREVDASH; Dep. Dir B. KHANDDOLGOR.

Voice of Mongolia: Ulan Bator (CPOB 365); tel. and fax (11) 325468; e-mail densmaa9@yahoo.com; internet www.vom.mn; f. 1964; external service of Mongolradio; broadcasts in Russian, Chinese, English and Japanese on short wave; Dir B. NARANTUYAA.

AE and JAAG Co: Ikh Toiruu, Sükhbaatar District, Ulan Bator (POB 20/126); tel. 99118563; fax (11) 352463; e-mail aejaag@magicnet.mn; f. 1996; broadcasts for 4.5–5 hours daily; CEO Z. ALTAI.

FM 96.3 Avtoradio: 4th Sub-District, Chingeltei District, Ulan Bator; tel. 98189655; e-mail mongol_media@yahoo.com.

FM 98.9 Royal Radio: Radio Academy, Bayanzürkh District, Ulan Bator; tel. 50006633; e-mail hifi@hi-fi.mn; internet www.hi-fi.mn.

FM 99.3 Ineemseglel (Smile): Central Palace of Culture, Sükhbaatar District, Ulan Bator; tel. 99093713; fax (11) 319789; Dir KH. IKHBAYAR.

FM 100.1 Kiss: Ulan Bator Bank, Chingeltei District, Ulan Bator; tel. (11) 312334; e-mail kiss100_1@yahoo.com.

FM 100.5 Minii Mongol (My Mongolia): Central Palace of Culture, Sükhbaatar District, Ulan Bator; tel. (11) 322199.

FM 100.9 Khökh Tenger (Blue Sky Radio): Mongolian National Television Bldg, Chingeltei District, Ulan Bator; tel. (11) 320522; broadcasts for 12 hours Mon. to Sat. and shorter hours on Sun; shortwave transmitter on 4,850 kHz; Dir L. AMARZAYAA.

FM 101.7 Niisleliin Radio: Narny Titem, 5th Sub-District, Chingeltei District, Ulan Bator; tel. 70110981; fax (11) 322472; Dir U. BULGAN.

FM 102.1 Ekh Oron (Homeland): Central Palace of Culture, Sükhbaatar District, Ulan Bator; tel. (11) 327383; fax (11) 322472; operated by the Open Information Foundation.

FM 103.1: Ulan Bator; BBC World Service Relay.

FM 103.6: TV9 Bldg, Amaryn Gudamj, Sükhbaatar District, Ulan Bator; tel. 70121036; TV-9's radio station; Dir M. BAYANZUL.

FM 104 Life: Business Plaza, Enkhtaivny Örgön Chölöö, 15th Sub-District, Bayanzürkh District, Ulan Bator; tel. and fax (11) 463782; e-mail life_fm104@yahoo.com.

FM 104.5 Ger Büliin Radio (Family Radio): Mamba Datsan, Bayanzürkh District, Ulan Bator; tel. (11) 461045; fax (11) 452987.

FM 105 Tany Derged (Near You): Central Palace of Culture, Sükhbaatar District, Ulan Bator; tel. (11) 319789.

FM 105.5 Necktie: Central Palace of Culture, Sükhbaatar District, Ulan Bator; tel. and fax 70114440; Dir B. TÜVSHINTÖGS.

FM 106.6: Democratic Party Bldg, Chingisiin Örgön Chölöö, Ulan Bator; tel. (11) 329353; Voice of America news and information in Mongolian, English lessons and music.

FM 107.5 Shine Dolgion (New Wave): Namyanjügiin Gudamj 40, Bayanzürkh District, Ulan Bator; tel. and fax (11) 452444; e-mail info@fm1075.mn; internet www.fm1075.mn; relays of Voice of America broadcasts in English and Russian, entertainment programmes; Dir TS. ARIUNAA.

There are seven long- and short-wave radio transmitters and 49 FM stations in 23 towns.

Television

Mongolian Television Association: Ulan Bator; mems: BTV, Channel 25, Eagle, Education, NTV, SBN, TM, TV5, TV8, TV9 and UBS.

Mongolian National Public Television (MNTV): Mongolian National Public Radio and Television Central Bldg, Khuvisgalyn Zam 3, Bayangol District, Ulan Bator (CPOB 365); tel. (11) 327214; fax (11) 328939; e-mail mrtv@magicnet.mn; f. 1967; daily 16-hour transmissions, except Mon; short news bulletins in English Mon., Wed. and Fri; part of Public Radio and Television; Dir TSAGAANY OYUUNDARI.

Bolovsrol (Education) TV Channel: Bayangol District, Behind Mongolian National Public TV Bldg, Ulan Bator; tel. (11) 300722; fax (11) 300710; e-mail develop@edutv.mn; f. 2005; broadcasts 20–22 hours a day; Gen. Dir NATSAGDORJIIN SANJ.

C-1: Supermarket No. 1, Tömörchnii Gudamj, Chingeltei District, Ulan Bator; tel. (11) 312126; fax (11) 325438; e-mail info@c1.mn; internet www.c1.mn; f. 2006; daily 17-hour transmissions; news link with Reuters; Dir BEN MOYLE.

Channel 25: Mongol News Bldg, Juulchny Gudamj, Chingeltei District, Ulan Bator; tel. and fax (11) 321989; daily 18-hour transmissions; Dir ZORIGIIN ALTAI; Gen. Man. AYUUSHIIN AVIRMED.

Eagle Broadcasting Co: Erkhüüd Centre, Lkhagvasürengiin Gudamj, Ulan Bator; tel. (11) 463088; fax (11) 463087; internet www.eagle-tv.mn; f. 1994; several news bulletins a day; Christian message; commenced operations in 1996; broadcasts restarted 2005 after two years off air; Pres. THOMAS TERRY; Dir BALJINNYAMYN BAYARSAIKHAN.

Khiimori Co: Bldg 3A, No. 2 Combined Clinical General Hospital, Ulan Bator; tel. (11) 458531; fax (11) 458569; f. 1995; cable TV service provider.

New TV (NTV): Capital House, Chingisiin Örgön Chölöö, 2nd Sub-District, Khan-Uul District, Ulan Bator; tel. 77117777; fax 77110002; internet www.ntv.mn; Dir M. ULAMBADRAKH.

Sansar KATV: Sansar Bldg, 3rd Sub-District, Chingeltei District, Ulan Bator; tel. (11) 322813; internet www.sansar.mn.

SBN (Supervision Broadcasting Network): Khuvisgalchdyn Gudamj, Bayangol District, Ulan Bator; tel. (11) 301641; fax (11) 301643; internet www.sbn.mn; Exec. Dir B. BAT-ORGIL.

Supervision KATV: SBN TV Bldg, Khuvsgalchdyn Gudamj, Bayangol District, Ulan Bator; tel. (11) 455082; fax (11) 363616; internet www.supervision.mn.

TV-5: Sapporo Centre, 1st Sub-District, Songinokhairkhan District; tel. (11) 680327; fax (11) 680326; e-mail feedback@tv5.mn; internet www.tv5.mn; daily 18-hour transmissions; Editor-in-Chief E. DAGIIMAA.

TV-8: Amaryn Gudamj, 8th Sub-District, Sükhbataar District, Ulan Bator; tel. (11) 315680; fax 70115212; Dep. Dir A. TSASCHIKHER.

TV-9: Amaryn Gudamj, 9th Sub-District, Sükhbaatar District, Ulan Bator; tel. 70110628; fax (11) 70110631; e-mail info@tv9.mn; internet www.tv9.mn; f. 2003; 24-hour broadcaster; Dir TS. ENKHBAT.

UBS (Ulaanbaatar Broadcasting System): Khasbaatar Gudamj 47, Bayangol District, Ulan Bator; tel. (11) 301973; fax (11) 368108; e-mail ext_affairs@ubs.mn; internet www.ubs.mn; f. 1992; fmrly state-owned; privatized in 2005; three channels; Dir-Gen. LKHAGVADORJIIN BALKHJAV.

Cable television companies (29 in total) operate in 19 towns. There are local television stations in Ulan Bator (three), Darkhan, Sükhbaatar and Baganuur. Chinese, Kazakh, Russian, German and French television services are among those that can also be received.

Finance

(cap. = capital; res = reserves; dep. = deposits; m. = million; brs = branches; amounts in tögrög, unless otherwise stated)

BANKING

Restructuring of the banking sector has continued. Plans for the establishment of the Mongolian Development Bank were approved in 2010.

Central Bank

Bank of Mongolia (Mongolbank): Baga Toiruu 9, Ulan Bator; tel. (11) 310413; fax (11) 311471; e-mail ad@mongolbank.mn; internet www.mongolbank.mn; f. 1924; est. as the State Bank of the Mongolian People's Republic; cap. 5,000m., res 103,504m., dep. 2,369,433m. (Dec. 2009); Pres. LKHNAASÜRENGIIN PÜREVDORJ; Chief Vice-Pres. BOLDYN JAVKHLAN.

Other Banks

Capital Bank: Sambuugiin Gudamj 43, Chingeltei District, Ulan Bator; tel. 50115040; fax (11) 310833; e-mail info@capitalbank.mn; internet www.capitalbank.mn; cap. 8,007m., res 16.5m., dep. 66,751.1m. (Dec. 2009); f. 1990; 99% owned by Bishrelt Holding Co; CEO AGVAANJAMBYN ARIUNBOLD; Dep. CEO S. ALTANGEREL; 24 brs.

Capitron Bank: Capitron Bank Bldg, Usny Gudamj 4, Sükhbaatar District, Ulan Bator; tel. (11) 328373; fax (11) 328372; e-mail info@capitronbank.mn; internet www.capitronbank.mn; f. 2001; cap. 8,000.5m., res 333m., dep. 58,530.3m. (Dec. 2009); 49% owned by B. Medree, 46% by P. Mönkhsaikhan; CEO PÜREVJAVYN MÖNKHSAIKHAN.

Chinggis Khaan Bank: New Century Plaza, Chingisiin Örgön Chölöö 15, Sükhbaatar District, Ulan Bator (POB 28/418); tel. (11) 318367; fax (11) 318373; e-mail bank@ckbank.mn; internet www.ckbank.mn; f. 2001; est. by Millennium Securities Management Ltd and Coral Sea Holdings Ltd (British Virgin Islands); cap. 39,373m., dep. 98,820m. (Dec. 2009); Chair. SERGEI GROMOV; CEO (vacant).

Credit Bank: Sükhbaataryn Talbai 20A, Sükhbaatar District, Ulan Bator; tel. (11) 310853; fax (11) 321897; e-mail info@creditbank.mn; internet www.creditbank.mn; f. 1997; owned by Basic Element Finance Ltd, Cyprus; cap. 8,090m., res 20,594m., dep. 12,363m. (July 2006); Propr OLEG DERIPASKA; Exec. Dir B. TSENGEL.

Erel Bank: Chingisiin Örgön Chölöö, Khan-Uul District, Ulan Bator; tel. (11) 344550; fax (11) 343387; e-mail info@erelbank.mn; internet www.erelbank.mn; f. 1997; cap. 4,000m., res 45.9m., dep. 3,163.4m. (Dec. 2005); Owner BADARCHIIN ERDENEBAT; CEO TUMURKHUU DAVAAKHUU.

Golomt Bank of Mongolia: Golomt Bank Central Bldg, Sükhbaataryn Talbai, Ulan Bator; tel. (11) 326231; fax (11) 311958; e-mail mail@golomtbank.com; internet www.golomtbank.com; f. 1995; est. by Mongolian-Portuguese IBH Bodi International Co Ltd; cap. 21,934.1m., res –25.9m., dep. 848,564m. (Dec. 2009); Chair. DANZANDORJIIN BAYASGALAN; Exec. Dir L. BADAMTSETSEG; 14 brs.

Khadgalamjiin Bank (Savings Bank): Kholboochdyn Gudamj 4, Chingeltei District, Ulan Bator; tel. (11) 310103; fax (11) 327467; e-mail contact@savingsbank.mn; internet www.savingsbank.mn; f. 1996; est. as Ardyn Bank; owned by MD Securities Co, a consortium of Chinggis Khaan Bank, Mongol Daatgal Consortium and Bratsk People's Bank (Russian Federation); took over Mongol Shuudan Bank (Post Bank) 2010; cap. 8,031.0m., res 2,544.5m., dep. 65,986.0m. (Dec. 2007); Chair. SH. BATKHÜÜ; Dir L. BADAMTSETSEG; 60 brs.

Khan Bank (KhAAN or Agricultural Bank): Söüliin Gudamj 25, Sükhbaatar District, Ulan Bator (POB 44/192); tel. (11) 332333; fax (11) 70117023; e-mail info@khanbank.com; internet www.khanbank.com; f. 1991; purchased by H and S Securities (Japan) in Feb. 2003; cap. 12,994m., res 14,591.7m., dep. 869,790m. (Dec. 2009); owned by Itochu Corpn and Tavan Bogd Group; Chair. HIDEO SAWADA; CEO SIMON MORRIS; Dep. Exec. Dir R. MÖNKHTUYAA; 380 brs.

National Investment Bank: City Plaza Bldg, Söüliin Gudamj 6 Sükhbaatar District, Ulan Bator; tel. (11) 321995; fax (11) 330434; 55% owned by D. Dagvadorj, 22% by UB Diversified Ltd, and 22% by Firebird Funds; f. 2006; Dir DOLGORSÜRENGIIN SUMYAABAZAR.

State Bank (Töriin Bank): Baga Toiruu 7/1, 1st Sub-District, Chingeltei District, Ulan Bator (POB 44/304); fax (11) 330595; e-mail contact@statebank.mn; internet www.statebank.mn; f. 1999; cap. 14,666.7m., res 11,971m., dep. 159,806m. (Dec. 2008); fmrly Zoos Bank; name changed as above when nationalized in 2009; Exec. Dir J. OTGONBILEG.

Trade and Development Bank of Mongolia (Khudaldaa Khögjliin Bank): Cnr of Juulchny Gudamj 7 and Baga Toiruu 12, Chingeltei District, Ulan Bator; tel. (11) 312362; fax (11) 331155; e-mail sanal@tdbm.mn; internet www.tdbm.mn; f. 1991; carries out Mongolbank's foreign operations; cap. 6,610.1m., res 14,619.2m., dep. 670,631.5m.

(Dec. 2009); 76% equity bought by Banca Commerciale (Lugano) and Gerald Metals (Stanford, CT), May 2002; Chair. D. ERDENEBILEG; Pres. RANDOLPH KOPPA; CEO BALBARYN MEDREE.

Transport and Development Bank (Trans Bank): Delta Centre, Juulchny Gudamj, 1st Sub-District, Chingeltei District, Ulan Bator; tel. (11) 319581; fax (11) 319593; e-mail info@transbank.mn; internet www.transbank.mn; owned by Russian interests; Propr D. ENKHTUYAA; CEO A. E. NOVOZHILOV; Chair. DANZANBALJIRYN ENKHTAIVAN.

Ulaanbaatar City Bank: Sükhbaataryn Gudamj 16, Ulan Bator (POB 46/370); tel. (11) 319041; fax (11) 330508; e-mail info@ubcbank.mn; internet www.ubcbank.mn; f. 1998; est. by Capital City with assistance from the Bank of Taipei (Taiwan); cap. 5,349m., dep. 50,064m. (June 2005); Propr L. ERDENEBILEG; CEO A. ENKHMEND.

XacBank: Yörönkhii Said Amaryn Gudamj, Sükhbaatar District, Ulan Bator (POB 20A/72); tel. (11) 318185; fax (11) 328701; e-mail bank@xacbank.mn; internet www.xacbank.org; f. 2001; cap. 13,290.6m., res 13,605.4m., dep. 148,804.1m. (Dec. 2009); owned by Mercy Corps; Chair. CHULUUNY GANBOLD; Exec. Dir DÜGERSÜRENGIIN BAT-OCHIR.

Bankers' Association

Mongolian Bank Association: Vista Office, Chingisiin Örgön Chölöö 17, Sükhbaatar District, Ulan Bator (CPOB 101); tel. (11) 314105; fax (11) 314104; e-mail monba@mongolnet.mn; internet www.mba.mn; f. 2000; Pres. BALBARYN MEDREE; Exec. Dir ZUUNAIN SHAGDARSÜREN.

STOCK EXCHANGE

Stock Exchange: Sükhbaataryn Talbai 2, Ulan Bator; tel. (11) 313511; fax (11) 325170; e-mail info@mse.mn; internet www.mse.mn; f. 1991; Exec. Dir KH. ALTAI (acting); Dep. Dir D. MÖNKHTÜSHIG.

INSURANCE

Ard Daatgal: Tavan Bogd Plaza, Amaryn Gudamj 8, Ulan Bator; tel. (11) 331185; fax (11) 330083; est. with Omni Whittington Guernsey.

Bodi Daatgal Co: Bodi Tower, Jigjidjavyn Gudamj, Ulan Bator; tel. (11) 323444; fax (11) 326535; e-mail bodi@bodiinsurance.mn; internet www.bodiinsurance.mn; Dir L. BOLDKHUYAG.

Ganzam Insurance: Mongolian Railways (MTZ), Zamchdyn Gudamj, Ulan Bator; tel. and fax (11) 242643.

MIG Daatgal: MIG Bldg, Enkh Taivny Örgön Chölöö, 1st Sub-District, Chingeltei District, Ulan Bator (CPOB 200); tel. (11) 330130; fax (11) 330131; e-mail mig@magicnet.mn; internet www.mig.mn; f. 1997; privately owned; Pres. and CEO JANDAVYN BAT-ORSHIKH.

Mongol Daatgal: Enkh Taivny Örgön Chölöö 13, Ulan Bator; tel. (11) 313615; fax (11) 310347; e-mail insurance@mongoldaatgal.mn; internet www.mongoldaatgal.mn; f. 1934; sold Dec. 2003 to consortium formed by Angara-SKB and Chinggis Khan Bank; Chair. BADARCHIIN ENKHBAT; CEO T. BATZÜL.

National Life Daatgal: Financial Service Corpn, Ambassador Bldg, Enkh Taivny Örgön Chölöö 17A/5, 1st Sub-District, Sükhbaatar District, Ulan Bator (POB 48/35); tel. 70110784; fax 70110781; e-mail national.life@fscomongolia.mn; internet www.fscomongolia.mn; Exec. Dir B. BATBAYAR.

Nomin Daatgal: State Department Store, Enkh Taivny Örgön Chölöö, Ulan Bator; tel. (11) 330023; fax (11) 325528; e-mail insurance@nomin.net; internet www.insurance.nomin.net.

Ochir Undraa Daatgal: Sööliin Gudamj 15/2, 4th Sub-District, Sükhbaatar District, Ulan Bator (POB 44/398); tel. (11) 324248; fax (11) 326466; e-mail insurance@ochir-undraa.com; internet www.ochir-undraa.com.

Tüshig Daatgal Co: Zoos Bank Bldg, Baga Toiruu, Chingeltei District, Ulan Bator; tel. (11) 316119; fax (11) 330578; e-mail insurance@tushigdaatgal.mn; internet www.tushigdaatgal.mn; Exec. Dir M. JALAVDORJ.

UB Daatgal Co: International Trade Centre, Baga Toiruu 37B, Sükbataar District, Ulan Bator (POB 46/385); tel. (11) 324828; fax (11) 322362; e-mail sanal_huselt@ubdaatgal.mn; internet www.ubdaatgal.mn.

INSURERS' ASSOCIATION

Mongolian Insurers' Association: Ulan Bator; Pres. GANZORIG PUREVJAV.

Trade and Industry

GOVERNMENT AGENCIES

Energy Directorate: Ulan Bator; f. 2008; subordinate to Minister of Mineral Resources, Fuel and Power; Head TSENDSÜRENGIIN BAYARBAATAR.

Foreign Capital Investment Directorate: Ulan Bator; f. 2008; subordinate to Minister of External Relations; Head BAASANKHÜÜGIIN GANZORIG.

Mineral Resources Directorate: Government Bldg 12, Barilgachdyn Talbai 3, Chingeltei District, Ulan Bator; tel. (11) 263701; fax (11) 310370; internet mram.gov.mn; f. 2008; subordinate to Minister of Mineral Resources, Fuel and Power; Head DORJPÜREVIIN BATKHUYAG.

Nuclear Energy Directorate: Ulan Bator; f. 2008; subordinate to Prime Minister; Head SODNOMYN ENKHBAT.

Petroleum Directorate: Ulan Bator; f. 2008; subordinate to Minister of Mineral Resources, Fuel and Power; Head DASHZEVEGIIN AMARSAIKHAN.

Small and Medium Enterprise Directorate: Ulan Bator; f. 2008; subordinate to Minister of Food, Agriculture and Light Industry; Head TS. NYAM-OSOR.

DEVELOPMENT ORGANIZATIONS

Agricultural Equipment, Science and Technology Production Association: Zaisan 53, Khan-Uul District, Ulan Bator; tel. (11) 341155; fax (11) 327099; e-mail agrtechcor@magicnet.mn; f. 1997; devt of farm machinery, including biogas plants; 100% state-owned; Exec. Dir J. TÜMEN.

Economics and Market Research Centre: Government Bldg 1, J. Sambuugiin Gudamj 11, Ulan Bator; tel. (11) 324258; fax (11) 324620; e-mail emrc@mongolchamber.mn; internet www.mongolchamber.mn; Dir J. BOZKHÜÜKHEN.

Mongolian Business Development Agency: Yörönkhii Said Amaryn Gudamj, Ulan Bator (CPOB 458); tel. (11) 311094; fax (11) 311092; internet www.mbda-mongolia.org; f. 1994; Gen. Man. D. BAYARBAT.

Mongolian Development Research Centre: Rm 50, Baga Toiruu 13, Chingeltei District, Ulan Bator (POB 20A/63); tel. and fax (11) 315686; internet www.mdrc.mn; f. 1998; Chair. TSEDENDAMBYN BATBAYAR.

National Centre for Renewable Energy: Ulan Bator; Dir N. ENEBISH.

CHAMBERS OF COMMERCE

Mongolian Franchising Council of the Mongolian National Chamber of Commerce and Industry: MNCCI Bldg, Makhatma Gandiin Gudamj, Khan-Uul District, Ulan Bator; tel. (11) 327176; fax (11) 324620; e-mail munkhnast@mongolchamber.mn; internet www.mongolchamber.mn; Chair. SAMBUUGIIN DEMBEREL.

Mongolian National Chamber of Commerce and Industry: Makhatma Gandiin Gudamj 11, 1st Sub-District, Khan-Uul District, Ulan Bator 38; tel. (11) 327176; fax (11) 324620; e-mail chamber@mongolchamber.mn; internet www.mongolchamber.mn; f. 1960; responsible for establishing economic and trading relations, contacts between trade and industrial organizations, both at home and abroad, and for generating foreign trade; organizes commodity inspection, press information, and international exhibitions and fairs at home and abroad; registration of trademarks and patents; issues certificates of origin and of quality; Chair. SAMBUUGIIN DEMBEREL.

INDUSTRIAL AND TRADE ASSOCIATIONS

Association of Exporters of Livestock, Raw Materials and Semi-Processed Products: Ulan Bator; Exec. Dir B. TÖRMÖNKH.

Association of Mongolian Sewn Goods and Knitwear Products Manufacturers: Ulan Bator; Pres. N. DASH-ÖLZII.

Building Materials Industry Association: Ulan Bator; Exec. Dir O. LKHAGVADORJ.

Financial Market Association: Ulan Bator; Pres. Ö. GANZORIG.

Funeral Services Association: Ulan Bator; f. 2008; Pres. G. IDERMAA.

Grain Producers' Association: Ulan Bator; Pres. TSEVEENJAVYN ÖÖLD.

Mongolian Air Traffic Controllers' Association: National Air Traffic Services, Chinggis Khaan International Airport, Buyant-Ukhaa, Ulan Bator; tel. (11) 282008; fax (11) 282108; e-mail monatca@mcaa.gov.mn.

Mongolian Association of Container and Packaging Makers and Users: Ulan Bator; Pres. DEMBERELIIN OTGONBAATAR.

Mongolian Builders' Association: Block 3, Urt Tsagaan, Chingeltei District, Ulan Bator; tel. 99112636; fax (11) 318685; Pres. MÖNKHBAYARYN BATBAATAR.

Mongolian Coal Association: Ulan Bator; tel. and fax (11) 328582; e-mail coalasso@yahoo.com; Exec. Dir NARAN TUVDEN.

Mongolian Entrepreneurs' Association: Ulan Bator; Chair. B. GARMAASÜREN.

Mongolian Exporters' Association: Macro Centre, Erkhüügiin Gudamj 7/1, 7th Sub-District, Sükhbaatar District, Ulan Bator; tel. 99119356; e-mail info@exportmongolia.mn; Exec. Dir DAMBYN GALSANDORJ.

Mongolian Farmers' and Flour Producers' Association: Agro-Pro Business Centre, 19th Sub-District, Bayangol District, Ulan Bator; tel. (11) 300114; fax (11) 362875; e-mail agropro@magicnet.mn; f. 1997; research and quality inspection services in domestic farming and flour industry; Pres. SHARAVYN GUNGAADORJ.

Mongolian Felt Producers' Association: Ulan Bator; Vice-Pres. G. ALZAKHGÜI.

Mongolian Food Producers' Association: Ulan Bator; Pres. L. DAMDINSÜREN.

Mongolian Foodstuffs Traders' Association: Ulan Bator; Exec. Dir KH. GIIMAA.

Mongolian Industrial Geologists' Association: Ulan Bator; Pres. D. BAT-ERDENE.

Mongolian Institute of Internal Auditors: Ulan Bator; tel. (11) 312773; e-mail miia@bizcon.mn; internet www.bizcon.mn/miia; Pres. L. OTGONBAYAR.

Mongolian International Financial Market Association: Ulan Bator; Pres. Ö GANZORIG.

Mongolian Marketing Association: Ulan Bator; tel. 99096400 (mobile); fax 70113756; e-mail bold_dag@yahoo.com; Pres. B. DAVAASÜREN; Exec. Dir D. BOLD.

Mongolian Meat Association: Ulan Bator; Pres. SH. BATKHÜÜ.

Mongolian Metallurgists' Association: School of Technology, Darkhan-Uul Province; tel. (37) 24723; Pres. TS. MÖNKHJARGAL.

Mongolian Mining Engineers' Association: Ulan Bator; Pres. KH. VLADIMIR.

Mongolian Motor Transporters' United Association: Ulan Bator; f. 1996; est. as Mongolian National Society of Motor Transport Owners, amalgamated 2005 with the Mongoltrans Transporters' Asscn; 39 mem. businesses and orgs incl. the Private Bus Owners' Asscn, Taxi Owners' Asscn and Large & Small Bus Asscn; Pres. GAVAAGIIN BATKHÜÜ.

Mongolian National Construction Association: Ulan Bator; Exec. Dir D. TSEND.

Mongolian National Industrialists' Association: Ulan Bator; Pres. NAMJAAGIIN DASHZEVEG.

Mongolian National Mining Association: 501 Geosan Company Bldg, Ikh Surguuliin Gudamj 8, Ulan Bator; tel. (11) 314877; fax (11) 330032; e-mail info@miningmongolia.mn; internet www.miningmongolia.mn; f. 1994; provides legal protection and represents views of mining interests in govt policy and devt of mineral sector; Pres. DAMJINY DAMBA; Exec. Dir NAMGARYN ALGAA.

Mongolian Pig Farmers' Association: Ulan Bator; Exec. Dir M. ZOLZAYAA.

Mongolian Power Engineers' Association: Ulan Bator; Pres. R. GANJUUR.

Mongolian PR Association: Ulan Bator; Chair. D. BOLDKHUYAG.

Mongolian Printing Works Association: Ulan Bator; Pres. E. MYAGMARPÜREV.

Mongolian Skins and Hides Production Association: Ulan Bator; Pres. B. ENKH-AMGALAN.

Mongolian Surveyors' Association: Ulan Bator; Pres. D. DONDOV.

Mongolian Timber Industry Association: Mon-Frukt Co, 1st Sub-District, Bayangol District, Ulan Bator (POB 36/51); tel. 91111191; fax (11) 343145; e-mail tsogoots@gmail.com; f. 1996; Chair. TSOGOO TSEDENPUNTSAG.

Mongolian Wool and Cashmere Federation: Eermel Co Bldg, Khan-Uul District, Ulan Bator; tel. (11) 342950; fax (11) 342814; Pres. D. GANKHUYAG; Vice-Pres. G. YONDONSAMBUU.

National Information and Communications Association: Ulan Bator; Pres. D. BOLOR.

Petroleum Gas Association: Ulan Bator; f. 2005; Pres. SHARAVYN GUNGAADORJ.

Pharmacology Organizations United Association: Ulan Bator; Pres. B. TUYAA.

EMPLOYERS' ORGANIZATIONS

Employers' and Owners' United Association: Rm 401, 4th Floor, Mongolian Youth Association 'B' Bldg, Ulan Bator; tel. (11) 326513; Exec. Dir B. SEMBEEJAV.

Federation of National Small and Medium Enterprise Managers: Ulan Bator; Exec. Dir P. ALTAN-ERDENE.

Federation of Professional Business Women of Mongolia: Ulan Bator; tel. and fax (11) 315638; e-mail mbpw@mongolnet.mn; f. 1992; provides education, training, and opportunities for women to achieve economic independence; Pres. OCHIRBATYN ZAYAA; 7,000 mems, 14 brs.

Forestry and Timber Production Managers' Association: Ulan Bator; tel. (11) 341310; e-mail info@fmwa.mn; internet fmwa.mn; f. 2010; Head D. BAASANBYAMBA.

Immovable Property (Real Estate) Business Managers' Association: Ulan Bator; Pres. J. BYAMBADORJ.

Mongolian Employers' Federation: Baga Toiruu 44A, Ulan Bator 48; tel. and fax (11) 325635; e-mail monef@magicnet.mn; internet www.monef.mn; f. 1990; fmrly Private Industry Owners' Association; 8,100 mems; Pres. KH. GANBAATAR.

Mongolian Food Trade Managers' Association: Ulan Bator; Dir D. NAMSRAI.

Mongolian Gas Managers' Association: Ulan Bator; Chair. N. BAATARJAV.

Mongolian Management Association: 102 and 202, Bldg B, The Academy of Management, Chingisiin Örgön Chölöö, Khan Uul District, Ulan Bator; tel. (11) 341570; e-mail info@mamo.mn; internet www.eng.mamo.mn; Pres. DAGVADORJIIN TSERENDORJ.

Private Business Owners' Association: Tsatsral Mon Bldg, 1st Sub-District, Songinokhairkhan District, Ulan Bator; tel. (11) 682905; Pres. T. NYAMDORJ.

Private Employers' Association: Ulan Bator; Pres. O. NATSAGDORJ.

Refuse Disposal Business Managers' Association: Ulan Bator; Chair. SH. BAASANJAV.

Scrap Business Managers' Association: Ulan Bator; Dir S. ALTANTSETSEG.

Securities Exchange Managers' Association: Ulan Bator; Exec. Dir L. TSEVEENRAVDAN.

Small and Medium Business Directors' United Association: Ulan Bator; Pres. P. ALTAN-ERDENE.

UTILITIES

Electricity

Darkhan-Selenge TsTS Co: Darkhan; management of electric power network in northern Mongolia; Exec. Dir CH. ENKHBOLD.

Dulaan Tsakhilgaan Stants-IV Co: 20th Sub-District, Bayangol District, Ulan Bator; tel. (11) 631768; Mongolia's biggest power station; Exec. Dir B. TSEVEEN.

Ulaanbaatar Power Distribution Network: Chingisiin Örgön Chölöö 45, Khan-Uul District, Ulan Bator; tel. (11) 341674; fax (11) 343061; e-mail info@ubedn.mn; internet www.ubedn.mn; Exec. Dir CH. SARANJAV.

Water

Dulaany Süljee Co: Ulan Bator; tel. (11) 343047; e-mail engineer@dhc.mn; internet www.dhc.mn; supervision of hot water district heating network in Ulan Bator; Exec. Dir DAGVASHADAVYN BYAMBA-OCHIR.

USAG: Khökh Tengeriin Gudamj 5, Ulan Bator; tel. (11) 455055; fax (11) 450120; e-mail usag@magicnet.mn; supervision of water supply network in Ulan Bator; Chair. OSORYN ERDENEBAATAR.

IMPORT AND EXPORT ORGANIZATIONS

Agrotekhimpeks: Ulan Bator; tel. 99119840; imports agricultural machinery and implements, seed, fertilizer, veterinary medicines and irrigation equipment.

Altjin: Ulan Bator; company imports and distributes oil and oil products; manages distilleries; fmrly part of APU; Dir G. ALTAN.

Arisimpex: Ulan Bator; tel. (11) 343007; fax (11) 343008; exports hides and skins, fur and leather goods; imports machinery, chemicals and accessories for leather, fur and shoe industries; Pres. A. TSERENBALJID.

Avtoimpeks: Ulan Bator; f. 1934; state-owned; international trader in motor vehicles; Exec. Dir S. CHULUUNBAT.

Barter and Border: Khuvisgalchdyn Gudamj, Ulan Bator; tel. (11) 324848; barter and border trade operations.

Khorshoololimpeks: Tolgoit, Ulan Bator (CPOB 262); tel. (11) 332926; fax (11) 331128; f. 1964; exports skins, hides, wool and furs,

handicrafts and finished products; imports equipment and materials for housing, and for clothing and leather goods; Dir L. ÖLZIIBUYAN.

Kompleksimport: Enkh Taivny Gudamj 7, Ulan Bator; tel. and fax (11) 688948; f. 1963; imports consumer goods, foodstuffs, sets of equipment and turnkey projects; training of Mongolians abroad; state-owned pending planned privatization; cap. 3,500m. tögrög.

Makhimpeks: 4th Sub-District, Songinokhairkhan District, Ulan Bator; tel. (11) 632471; fax (11) 632517; f. 1946; abattoir, meat processing, canning, meat imports and exports; 51% share privatized in 1999; cap. 7,800m. tögrög; Exec. Dir G. BÜDRAGCHAA.

Materialimpex: Teeverchdiin Gudamj 2B, Bayangol District, Ulan Bator; tel. (11) 365143; fax (11) 367904; e-mail matimpex@mongolnet.mn; internet www.materialimpex.com; f. 1957; exports cashmere, wool products, animal skins; imports glass, roofing material, dyes, sanitary ware, metals and metalware, wallpaper, bitumen, wall and floor tiles; partially privatized Feb. 1999, but most shares still state-owned; Gen. Dir B. ZORIG; 126 employees.

Medimpex International: New Horizon Bldg, Olimpiin Gudamj 6, 1st Sub-District, Sükhbaatar District, Ulan Bator; tel. (11) 319680; fax (11) 318254; e-mail medimpex@mcs.mn; internet www.medimpex.mcs.mn.

Metallimpeks (Metalimpex): Ulan Bator; tel. 70111203; Dir D. GANBAT.

Monfa Trade: Monfarma Trade Co, Khudaldaany Gudamj, 4th Sub-District, Chingeltei District, Ulan Bator; tel. and fax (11) 324420; e-mail monfatrade@mongol.net; procurement and distribution of pharmaceuticals.

Mongoleksport Co Ltd: Government Bldg 7, 8th Fl., Erkh Chölöönii Talbai, Ulan Bator; tel. (11) 327884; exports wool, hair, cashmere, mining products, antlers, skins and hides; Dir-Gen. D. CHIMEDDAMBAA.

Mongolemimpex: Teeverchdiin Gudamj 39, Ulan Bator; tel. (11) 322695; fax (11) 323877; e-mail info@meic.mn; internet www.meic.mn; f. 1923; procurement and distribution to hospitals and pharmacies of drugs and surgical appliances; Dir-Gen. BATBAYARYN BOLORMAA.

Mongolimpeks: Khuvisgalchdyn Örgön Chölöö, Ulan Bator; tel. (11) 326081; exports cashmere, camels' wool, hair, fur, casings, powdered blood and horn, antlers, wheat gluten, alcoholic drinks, cashmere and camels' wool knitwear, blankets, copper concentrate, souvenirs, stamps and coins; imports light and mining industry machinery, scientific instruments, chemicals, pharmaceuticals and consumer goods; state-owned; Dir-Gen. DORJPALAMYN DÖKHÖMBAYAR.

Monnis International: Monnis Tower, Chingisiin Örgön Chölöö 15, Ulan Bator; tel. (11) 311687; fax (11) 323248; e-mail info@monnis.com; internet www.monnis.com; f. 1998; est. as distributor for Nissan Motor Co Ltd; other commercial interests incl. geology, mining, energy, construction, freight forwarding, foreign trade, communications, banking and aviation; CEO B. CHULUUNBAATAR; 700 employees, 8 subsidiaries.

Monnoos: Ulan Bator (POB 36/450); tel. (11) 343201; fax (11) 342591; e-mail monnoos@mongolnet.mn; wool trade enterprise; Dir SANJIIN BAT-OYUUN.

Monos Cosmetics: Monos Group, Bldg 25, 2nd 40,000, 2nd Sub-District, Chingeltei District, Ulan Bator; tel. and fax (11) 633257; e-mail cosmetics@monos.mn; internet www.monoscosmetics.mn; f. 1990; production, export and import of cosmetics; Chair. and CEO BALDANDORJIIN ERDENEKHISHIG; Exec. Dir KH. SOLONGO; 90 employees.

Monos Pharm Trade: Monos Group, Namyanjügiin Gudamj 23, 18th Sub-District, Bayanzürkh District, Ulan Bator; tel. and fax 70114567; fax (11) 463158; internet www.monos.mn; f. 1990; production, export and import of medicine, medical equipment and health food; Dir-Gen. LUVSANGIIN ERDENECHIMEG; 280 employees.

NIK (Neft Import Kontsern): Petrovis Co Bldg, Yörönkhii Said Amaryn Gudamj, Sükhbaatar District, Ulan Bator; tel. (11) 323656; fax (11) 327001; e-mail nic@nic.com.mn; internet www.nic.com.mn; Exec. Dir M. KHALIUNBAT.

Noosimpeks: Ulan Bator; tel. (11) 341577; exports scoured sheep's wool, yarn, carpets, fabrics, blankets, mohair and felt boots; imports machinery and chemicals for wool industry.

Packaging: Tolgoit, Ulan Bator; tel. (11) 31053; exports raw materials of agricultural origin, sawn timber, consumer goods, unused spare parts and equipment, and non-ferrous scrap; imports machinery and materials for packaging industry, and consumer goods.

Petrovis: Petrovis Co Bldg, Yörönkhii Said Amaryn Gudamj 7, Sükhbaatar District, Ulan Bator; tel. (11) 632106; e-mail info@petrovis.mn; internet www.petrovis.mn; oil products importer and distributor; in Feb. 2004 acquired the 80% state-owned shares in the country's biggest distributor NIK (Neft Import Kontsern) for US $8.5m; Exec. Dir O. SEDBILEG.

Raznoimpeks: 3rd Sub-District, Bayangol District, Ulan Bator; tel. (11) 329465; fax (11) 329901; f. 1933; exports wool, cashmere, hides, canned meat, powdered bone, alcoholic drinks, macaroni and confectionery; imports cotton and woollen fabrics, silk, knitwear, shoes, fresh and canned fruit, vegetables, tea, milk powder, acids, paints, safety equipment, protective clothing, printing and packaging paper; state-owned pending planned privatization; cap. 6,100m. tögrög; Exec. Dir TS. BAT-ENKH.

Tekhnikimport: Ulan Bator; tel. (11) 685190; imports machinery, instruments and spare parts for light, food, wood, building, power and mining industries, road-building and communications; state-owned; Dir-Gen. D. GANTSETSEG.

Tüshig Trade Co Ltd: Enkh Taivny Örgön Chölöö, Ulan Bator (POB 44/481); tel. (11) 323206; fax (11) 314052; exports sheep and camel wool, and cashmere goods; imports machinery for small enterprises, foodstuffs and consumer goods; Dir-Gen. D. GANBAATAR.

Whole Sale: Songinokhairkhan District, Ulan Bator; tel. 99112100; fax (11) 632119; e-mail boch30@mobinet.mn; f. 1952; wholesale trader; privately owned; Dir-Gen. OCHBADRAKHYN BALJINNYAM.

YuniGaz: Petrovis Co Bldg, Yörönkhii Said Amaryn Gudamj 8, Sükhbaatar District, Ulan Bator; tel. (11) 457074; fax (11) 327253; e-mail info@unigas.mn; internet www.unigas.mn; petrol, diesel and LPG distributor; Dir-Gen. B. TÜMENTSOGT.

CO-OPERATIVES

Association of Private Herders' Co-operatives: Ulan Bator (POB 21/787); tel. (11) 633601; fax (11) 325935; e-mail mongolherder@magicnet.mn; f. 1991; Pres. R. ERDENE; Exec. Dir TS. MYAGMAR-OCHIR.

Central Association of Consumer Co-operatives: Ulan Bator; tel. and fax (11) 329025; f. 1990; wholesale and retail trade; exports animal raw materials; imports foodstuffs and consumer goods; Chair. G. MYANGANBAYAR.

Mongolian Association of Production Co-operatives: Urt Tsagaan, Khudaldaany Gudamj 12, Chingeltei District, Ulan Bator; tel. (11) 310956; e-mail cumic@mol.mn.

Mongolian Association of Savings and Credit Co-operatives: Bldg 2, State Property Committee, Chingeltei District, Ulan Bator; tel. (11) 313665; Pres. SH. GOOKHÜÜ.

Mongolian Co-operatives Development Centre: Ulan Bator; Dir DANZANGIIN RADNAARAGCHAA.

National Association of Mongolian Agricultural Co-operative Members: Enkh Taivny Örgön Chölöö 18 A/1, Bayanzürkh District, Ulan Bator; tel. (11) 453535; fax (11) 458899; e-mail info@namac.coop; internet www.namac.coop; f. 1992; Pres. NADMIDYN BAYARTSAIKHAN.

Union of Mongolian Production and Services Co-operatives: Bldg 16, 2nd 40,000, 3rd Sub-District, Chingeltei District, Ulan Bator (POB 46/470); tel. (11) 327583; fax (11) 328446; e-mail umpscoop@hotmail.com; f. 1990; Pres. SAMDANY ENKHTUYAA.

MAJOR COMPANIES

Ajnai (Mongol Savkhi): Chingis Khaany Örgön Chölöö, Khan-Uul District, Ulan Bator; tel. (11) 343237; fax (11) 345757; leather processing and garment manufacture; Dir-Gen. A. AMARSAIKHAN.

Altai Holdings: Erönkhii Said Amaryn Gadamj, Ulan Bator (CPOB 513); tel. and fax (11) 358067; precious metal exploration and trading; subsidiaries include Altai Petroleum, Altai Mining, Altai Trading and Altai Travel; Pres. KH. OTGONTUYAA; Exec. Dir L. JAVZMAA.

Altan Dornod Mongol Co: 7th Sub-District, Bayangol District, Ulan Bator; tel. (11) 365536; e-mail zolotoivostok_mongol@mongol.net; f. 1999; gold mining; Dir S. V. PAUSHOK.

Altan Taria: Khünschdiin Gudamj 1, 4th Sub-District, Songinokhairkhan District, Ulan Bator; tel. (11) 632067; fax (11) 632057; e-mail marketing@altantaria.mn; internet www.altantaria.mn; flour milling and retailing; 51% owned by Mongolian-Czech Credit Co; Dir-Gen. P. TSENGÜÜN.

APU: Chingis Khaany Örgön Chölöö 14, Khan-Uul District, Ulan Bator; tel. (11) 344376; fax (11) 343063; e-mail apu@mbox.mn; internet www.apu.mn; vodka, beer and non-alcoholic drinks; privatized in 2002; Exec. Dir TS. ERDENEBILEG.

Bagakhangai Makhny Üildver: No. 6 Bldg, Sükhbaataryn Gudamj, 6th Sub-District, Bagakhangai District, Ulan Bator; tel. and fax (11) 331268; e-mail MPPO_Bagakhangai@yahoo.com; f. 1996; meat packing; Dir PÜREVJAL ENKHBAT.

Baganuur: Baganuur Town, Ulan Bator; tel. (121) 20114; fax (121) 21130; Ulan Bator office; tel. (11) 457717; fax (11) 457715; internet www.baganuurmine.mn; coal-mining co, main supplier of Ulan Bator's power stations; 75% state-owned; Dir D. DAMBAPELJEE.

Bayangol Zochid Buudal: Chingis Khaany Örgön Chölöö 5, Ulan Bator; tel. (11) 312255; fax (11) 326880; e-mail info@bayangolhotel

.mn; internet www.bayangolhotel.mn; f. 1964; 315-room hotel and 5 restaurants; CEO D. GANSÜKH.

Berkh-Uul: Berkh, Khentii Province; fluorspar mining and concentrating; part of Mongolrostsvetmet jt enterprise; state-owned; Exec. Dir M. BOLDBAATAR.

Betonarmatur: Chingis Khaany Örgön Chölöö, Khan-Uul District, Ulan Bator; tel. and fax (11) 342833; ferro-concrete structures.

Biokombinat: Khan-Uul District, Ulan Bator; tel. (11) 492242; fax (11) 492280; e-mail bio_info@mbox.mn; medicines, drugs, veterinary medicines; state-owned; Dir D. BATSÜKH (acting).

Blast Co: Internom Bldg, Amaryn Gudamj 2, Sükhbaatar District, Ulan Bator; tel. (11) 325995; fax (11) 324044; e-mail batmm@chinggis .com; Mongolian-Russian jt enterprise; industrial explosives; Exec. Dir L. DAVAATSEDEV.

Bodi Buyan Co: East side of the Traffic Police Bldg, 1st Sub-District, Sükhbaatar District, Ulan Bator; tel. (11) 99110751; e-mail info@bodibuyan.mn; subsidiary of Bodi International; funeral services.

Bodi International: Bodi Tower, Sükhbaataryn Talbai 3, 4th Floor, Ulan Bator; (POB 20A/11); tel. (11) 311971; fax (11) 329057; financial services, trade, property, gold-mining; Dir-Gen. L. BOLDKHUYAG.

Bolovsrol: Akademich N. Sodnomyn Gudamj 52, Ulan Bator (POB 46/982); tel. and fax (11) 350973; e-mail bboldbaatar@hotmail.com; f. 1990; educational and medical services, food and industrial goods production; Dir-Gen. BYAMBADORJ SÜKHBAT; 100 employees.

Bor-Öndör: Bor-Öndör, Khentii Province; tel. 88099006; e-mail borundur@monros.mn; internet www.borundur.mn; f. 1981; fluorspar mining enterprise under Mongolrostsvetmet; Dir BAYANTÖRIIN BAT-OCHIR.

Boroo Gold: Bodi Tower, Sükhbaataryn Talbai, Ulan Bator; tel. (11) 319056; fax (11) 316100; e-mail bgc@bgc.mn; internet www .centerragold.com; f. 2003; mines in Selenge Province; mines at Boroo (near Baruunkharaa) and Gatsuurt (35 km from Boroo) owned by Canadian Centerra Gold Corpn; Vice-Pres. IGOR KOVARSKY.

Börte: Tömörchnii Gudamj 1, 5th Sub-District, Chingeltei District, Ulan Bator; tel. and fax (11) 324262; e-mail bute@mongol.net; mfr of military uniforms; Dir-Gen. Col KH. BATSAIKHAN.

Bridge Group: Bridge Plaza, Enkh Taivny Örgön Chölöö, 14th Sub-District, Bayanzürkh District, Ulan Bator; tel. (11) 461542; fax (11) 458005; e-mail bridge@bridgegroup.mn; internet www.bridgegroup .mn; Pres. L. DAVAAJARGAL.

Buligaar: Ulan Bator; tel. (11) 344395; tanning, shoemaking; export of shoes to India and China; Exec. Dir OCHIRBATYN RAGCHAA.

Buyan: Khan-Uul District, Ulan Bator; tel. (11) 325413; fax (11) 326755; cashmere and camel-wool processing and garment manufacture; Dir-Gen. B. JARGALSAIKHAN.

Chinggis Khaan Hotel: Tokiogiin Gudamj 10, Ulan Bator (CPOB 513); tel. (11) 313380; fax (11) 312788; e-mail operation_manager@ chinggis-hotel.com; internet www.chinggis-hotel.com; 186 rooms and 400 beds; trade, conference and shopping centres and a casino; Man. Dir SAM SALLAM.

Darkhan Metallurgical Works: Darkhan District, Darkhan-Uul Province (POB 906); tel. (372) 27098; fax (372) 23946; e-mail dmplant@mongol.net; iron mining and casting; Dir T. GANBOLD.

Darkhan Nekhii: Darkhan Nekhii JSC, Industrial Zone, Darkhan-Uul Province (POB Darkhan 901); tel. (372) 27025; fax (372) 23149; f. 1972; cap. US $3.1m.; sheepskin processing and garment manufacture; Exec. Dir E. BATSAIKHAN; 300 employees.

Dornod Uran: Ulan Bator; Mongolian-Russian jt venture; f. 2009; manages devt of uranium mines in eastern Mongolia.

Em Khangamj: Barilgachdyn Talbai, Ulan Bator; tel. and fax (11) 324504; distribution of pharmaceuticals to Ulan Bator retail pharmacies.

Erchim Khüchnii Zasvaryn Üildver: next to No. 4 Power Station, Bayangol District, Ulan Bator; tel. and fax (11) 332626; production, repair and service of equipment and spares for electric power generation; state-owned; Dir CH. TÖMÖR.

Erdenes Mongol (Erdenes MGL): tel. 70110735; state-owned co, est. to ensure unified co-ordination of operations of strategic mineral deposits; initially took charge of Mardai uranium mine; in 2008 also licensed to supervise Tavantolgoi coal mine and Asgat silver mine, pending approval of jt venture; Chair. DULAMYN SUGAR; Dir B. ENEBISH.

Erdenes Tavantolgoi Ltd: Ulan Bator; subsidiary of Erdenes MGL, managing Tavantolgoi coal deposit; 50% state-owned.

Erdenet Enterprise Co: Amaryn Talbai 1, Erdenet, Bayan-Öndör District, Orkhon Province (POB 213900); tel. (352) 73501; fax (352) 23002; Ulan Bator office: Enkh Taivny Örgön Chölöö 14; tel. (11) 320561; fax (11) 312039; internet www.erdenetmc.mn; London office; tel. (0207) 7064413; fax (0207) 7067413; copper and molybdenum mining and concentrating; jt-stock co with Russia (49% owned by Rostekhnologii under Russian presidential decree), 51% state-owned by Mongolia; Jt Chair. of Board DULAMYN SUGAR (Mongolia), SERGEI S. CHEMEZOV (Russia); Dir-Gen. CHIMEDDORJIIN GANZORIG; 7,420 employees.

Erdenet Khivs (Carpet Factory): Engelsiin Gudamj, Bayan-Öndör District, Orkhon Province; tel. (1352) 20111; e-mail g-gantulga@ nomin.net; internet www.carpet.mn; state-owned; wool spinner and woollen carpet mfr; Dir O. GANBAATAR.

Erdmin: Erdenet, Orkhon Province (POB Erdenet 631); tel. (352) 72175; internet www.erdmin.com; f. 1994; Mongolian-US jt venture between Erdenet Concern (51%) and Armada Copper (49%); production since 1997 of pure (A grade) copper cathodes by chemical leaching of low-grade ore from Erdenet mine's waste dump; most sold to Marubeni Corpn; Dir-Gen. J. DAMDINJAV.

Erel Group: Bayanzürkh District, Ulan Bator (POB 51/88); tel. 96054822; internet www.erel.mn; mining, geological research, construction, banking, financial services, investment; Dir-Gen. BADARCHIIN ERDENEBAT.

Gazar Holding Co: Zamchdyn Gudamj, 1st Sub-District, Bayangol District, Ulan Bator; tel. (11) 305164; fax (11) 362889; e-mail contact@gazarmn.com; internet www.gazarmn.com; f. 1991; gold mining.

Gobi: Üildveriin Gudamj, 3rd Sub-District, Khan-Uul District, Ulan Bator (POB 36/434); tel. (11) 342713; fax (11) 343081; e-mail info@ gobi.mn; internet www.gobi.mn; f. 1981; cashmere processing and knitwear production; jt stock co; state-owned 73% shareholding sold to Japanese Toshisooken Invest Bank and HNC Co in 2007; annual capacity of 1,000 tons of cashmere; Exec. Dir TS. BAATARSAIKHAN; 1,500 employees.

Goyo LLC: 3rd Sub-District, Khan-Uul District, Ulan Bator; tel. (11) 344756; fax (11) 344015; e-mail info@goyo-cashmere.com; internet www.goyo-cashmere.com; f. 1993; jt venture between US Amikal Industries (55%) and state-owned Mongolian Temeenii Noos (45%), producing cashmere, goat hair and camel hair; annual capacity approx. 900 metric tons; Man. Dir SENGEE ENKH-AMGALAN.

Gurvan Bilig: Ulan Bator; imports cloth from Hong Kong and exports clothing to the United Kingdom; Dir-Gen. SH. ENKHTSETSEG.

Gurvan Saikhan: Khairkhan, Dundgobi Province; uranium mining; jt venture by Mongolia, USA and Russia; Exec. Dir ALEKSANDR V. RUDCHENKO; Mongolian Dir DASHIIN BAT-ERDENE.

Infrastructure Development: Ulan Bator; 50% owned by Russian Railways, 25% by Mongolian Railways and 25% by Erdenes Mongol; Dir VITALII MOZOROV.

Ivanhoe Mines Mongolia Co: Olimpiin Gudamj, Sükhbaatar District, Ulan Bator; tel. (11) 310785; fax (11) 311469; e-mail immi@ivanhoemines.com; internet www.ivanhoemines.com; gold and copper mining; Exec. Chair. ROBERT M. FRIEDLAND; CEO, Pres. and Dir JOHN MACKEN; Chief Vice-Pres. A. MÖNKHBAT.

Jagar International Co Ltd: Gerel Centre, Ikh Toiruu 53, Ulan Bator; tel. (11) 322823; fax (11) 313289; e-mail erdene@jagar.mn; internet www.jagar.mn; f. 1994; importer and wholesaler of cosmetics, sanitary products, household detergents and motorcycles; production and export of organic fertilizer; Man. Dir JAGARYN ERDENETSOGT.

Khöngön Beton Co: Ajilchdyn Gudamj 8, Khan-Uul District, Ulan Bator; fax (11) 341752; e-mail hungunbeton@magicnet.mn; f. 1966; est. with Polish aid; annual capacity of 30,000 cu m of breeze blocks; Exec. Dir BAT-OCHIRYN ERDENECHIMEG.

Khünstreid: Tolgoit, Songinokhairkhan District, Ulan Bator; tel. (11) 631846; fax (11) 631891; domestic and foreign food trader and wholesaler; state-owned; Dir-Gen. ÜRDEEGIIN TÖMÖRBAATAR.

MCS Holding: Central Tower, Sükhbaataryn Talbai 2, Sükhbaatar District, Ulan Bator; tel. (11) 312625; fax (11) 312175; e-mail mcsgroup@mcs.mn; internet www.mcs.mn; f. 1993; subordinate companies include Intergraphics Advertising, Medimpeks International, Kola and Asia Pacific Brewery; Dir-Gen. J. ODJARGAL.

Mon Tsakhilgaan Tas: 20th Sub-District, Songinokhairkhan District, Ulan Bator; tel. (11) 635760; f. 2002; high- and low-voltage cable manufacturer.

Mon-Uran: Ulan Bator; state-owned; manages Mongolian uranium mines; Dir B. NARANKHÜÜ.

Monel: Ulan Bator; tel. (11) 327546; electronics manufacturer and trader; 40% state-owned.

Monenzim: Research and Production Association of Enzymology and Microbiology, Tolgoit, Ulan Bator; tel. (11) 32431; research, testing and production of enzymes and microbiological products; Dir M. ALTANTSETSEG.

Mongol Alt: Darkhan-Uul Province; tel. 91371274; fax (372) 33263; e-mail mong-alt@mongol.net; gold mining company.

Mongol Altan Tos: Darkhan; tel. 99091020; vegetable oil processor; Dep. Dir KH. ZOLBAYAR.

Mongol Energy Service: Ulan Bator (POB 28/193); tel. (11) 320468; fax (11) 327146; e-mail mes@magicnet.mn; installation and maintenance of electricity generation equipment and district heating pipelines; Mongolian-Russian jt venture; Dir-Gen. B. Shatar.

Mongol Shuudan: Khasbaataryn Gudamj 16/1, Bayangol District, Ulan Bator (CPOB 1106); tel. (11) 330788; fax (11) 304826; e-mail marketing@mongolpost.mn; internet www.mongolpost.mn; handling of letters, parcels, subscriptions to periodicals, book and newspaper retail sales, counter services, printing of postage stamps, rural transport services; Exec. Dir G. Chinzorig.

Mongol Tamga: Sükhbaatar District, Ulan Bator; tel. and fax (11) 350256; e-mail jig_sainjargal@yahoo.com; official seals and stamps; state-owned; Dir Col Jigdengombyn Sainjargal.

Mongolchekhmetall Co: 19th Sub-District, Songinokhairkhan District, Ulan Bator; tel. (11) 631502; fax (11) 631301; e-mail mcsm@mongolnet.mn; mining of gold (Khavchuu) and fluorspar (Chuluut Tsagaan Del); Dir-Gen. Bicheerein Dalai.

Mongolia Mining Corpn: 15th Floor, Central Tower, Sükhbaataryn Talbai 2, Sükhbaatar District, Ulan Bator; internet www.energyresources.mn; f. 2008; fmrly Energy Resource; responsible for construction of broad-gauge railway in Gobi; parent company of ERInvest; state-owned; Chair. J. Odjargal; Exec. Dir G. Battsengel.

Mongolrostsvetmet: Jukovyn Gudamj, Bayanzürkh District, Ulan Bator; tel. (11) 458072; fax (11) 458380; e-mail mailbox@mongolros.mn; internet www.mongolros.mn; f. 1973; fluorspar mining at Bor Öndör, Airag and Örgön, gold mining at Zaamar Placer; jt venture with Russia (49% owned by Rostekhnologii under Russian presidential decree, 51% state-owned by Mongolia); Jt Chair. of Board Dulamyn Sugar (Mongolia), S. V. Sysoyev (Russia); Dir-Gen. Ochiryn Erdenee; 3,985 employees.

Mongolyn Alt (MAK): No. 14 Bldg, 18th Sub-District, Bayanzürkh District, Ulan Bator (POB 48a/237); tel. (11) 455882; fax (11) 458075; e-mail info@mak.mn; internet www.mak.mn; gold-mining, coal mining, agriculture, geology exploration; Pres. B. Nyamtaishir.

Mongolyn Nüürs: Ulan Bator (CPOB 147); tel. and fax (11) 682570; association of Mongolian coal-mines; state-owned; Pres. Dorjiin Dondov; Exec. Dir Toshoony Sambasanchir.

Mongolyn Ünet Tsaasny Khevlekh Üildver (Mongolian Securities Printing Works): Ulan Bator (CPOB 613); tel. (11) 327101; fax (11) 328555; e-mail mnspc@magicnet.mn; jt venture with British company De La Rue; Exec. Dir Ch. Chuluunbaatar.

Monmap Engineering Co Ltd: Sarora Hotel, Rm 502, Söüliin Gudamj 12/6, Ulan Bator; tel. and fax (11) 327824; e-mail msaandar@mongol.net; internet www.monmap.mn; f. 1992; surveying and remote sensing; Chair. M. Saandar.

Monos Group: 23 Namyaanjugiin Gudamj, 18th Sub-District, Bayanzurkh District, Ulan Bator; tel. (11) 450054; fax (11) 455723; internet www.monos.mn; f. 1990; mfr and distributor of pharmaceuticals and cosmetics; manages pharmacies, conducts health research; also financial services and tourism bureau; Dir-Gen. Luvsangiin Khürelbaatar; 1,000 employees.

Monpolimet Co: Tengeriin Tsag Bldg, Olimpiin Gudamj, Sükbataar District, Ulan Bator; tel. (11) 313137; fax (11) 311633; e-mail monopolymet@mongol.net; Dir Gen. Ts. Garamjav.

Monsam: Ulan Bator; tel. (11) 351069; fax (11) 351068; e-mail monsat@magicnet.mn; f. 1995; jt venture with Samsung; surgical syringes and needles; Dir Dr B. Doyoddorj.

Naran Trade Co Ltd: Naran Bldg, Söüliin Gudamj, Ulan Bator; tel. (11) 322855; fax (11) 320396; e-mail info@narantrade.mn; internet www.narangroup.mn; f. 1990; retail and wholesale trade, media, real estate; Man. Dir Sereeteriin Boldkhet.

New Progress Group: New Progress Group Bldg, 4th Sub-District, Songinokhairkhan District, Ulan Bator; tel. (11) 632238; fax (11) 632251; civil engineering, road building, power lines and construction materials.

Niislel Tosgoo: 4th Sub-District, Songinokhairkhan District, Ulan Bator; bricks and tiles; Dir Ch. Sumyaajav.

Ochir Töv: Bolor Business Centre, Chingisiin Örgön Chölöö 11/1, 2nd Sub-District, Sükhbaatar District, Ulan Bator; tel. (11) 330959; fax (11) 330889; e-mail orchirtuv@mongol.net; building materials, buildings, bridges, roads, cable installation, mining, Siemens distributor; Dir-Gen. Dorjdambyn Damba-Ochir; 600 employees.

Oyuuny Undraa: Ulan Bator (POB 46/867); tel. (11) 325496; fax (11) 325495; printing, sale and service of cars and aviation equipment; Dir-Gen. S. Amarsaikhan.

Oyu Tolgoi: Monnis Tower, Chingis Khaany Örgön Chölöö 15, 1st Sub-District, Sükhbaatar District, Ulan Bator; tel. (11) 331880; fax (11) 331890; e-mail immi@ivancorp.net; internet www.ot.mn; f. 2010; supervises devt of Oyu Tolgoi copper and gold deposit in Khanbogd District of Ömnögobi Province; Chair. Galsangiin Batsükh.

Petroleum Production Co: Orkhon Province; f. 2001; est. as Mongolia-Kyrgyzstan jt venture; oil refinery producing petrol, diesel and furnace oil from imported Russian gas condensate; annual capacity 50,000 metric tons.

SAPU: Enkhtaivny Örgön Chölöö, 18th Sub-District, Songinokhairkhan District, Ulan Bator; tel. (11) 636611; fax (11) 636663; e-mail altjin@mongol.net; soft-drinks co; f. 2003; est. with South Korean partnership by ex-director of APU (see above); Dir G. Altan.

Sharyn Gol: Sharyn Gol, Orkhon District, Darkhan-Uul Province; tel. (374) 32235; lignite mine with rail link to Darkhan town; Pres. B. Batmönkh; Gen. Man. S. Altankhuyag.

Shijir Alt: Jukovyn Gudamj 18/6, Bayanzürkh District, Ulan Bator (POB 51/244); tel. (11) 453521; e-mail shijiralt@mongol.net; f. 1995; gold mining in the Tuul river valley.

Shim-Technology Co Ltd: Erdenet Mining Corporation Industrial Area, Erdenet 213900, Orkhon Province; tel. (352) 72262; fax (352) 72261; e-mail shimtech@erdenetmc.mn; f. 2003; molybdenum enrichment; Mongolian-Israeli jt enterprise (70% Metal-Tech Co and 30% Erdenet copper enterprise) with Finnish participation (Outokumpu Co); Resident Representative Tsvi Shva.

Shivee Ovoo: Shiveegobi District, Choir, Gobi-Sümber Province; tel. (542) 23366; fax (542) 23368; lignite mine, extraction began 1991; Dir-Gen. O. Shagdarjav.

Shunkhlai Group: Capital House, Chingsiin Örgön Chölöö 48/1, Ulan Bator; tel. 70073333; fax 70073002; e-mail info@shunkhlai.mn; internet www.shunkhlai.mn; importer and distributor of petroleum products; operator of restaurants and supermarkets; Exec. Dir P. Batkhishig.

Spirt Bal Buram: Mandal District, Züünkharaa, Selenge Province; tel. Züünkharaa 397; tel. Ulan Bator (11) 345506; f. 1942; est. as Züünkharaa distillery, privatized in 1998; producer of alcohol and treacle; Exec. Dir B. Bayarkhüü; Dir. B. Gansükh.

Süü: Üildverchnii Gudamj 13, Songinokhairkhan District, Ulan Bator; tel. (11) 331950; fax (11) 331901; milk and dairy produce; Exec. Dir D. Mönkhjargal.

Talkh Chikher: 18th Sub-District, Songinokhairkhan District, Ulan Bator; tel. (11) 631526; fax (11) 633377; e-mail info@talkh-chikher.mn; internet www.talkh-chikher.mn; f. 1984; bread, confectionery; state-owned; Exec. Dir Kh. Batsooj.

TAS Petroleum: Ulan Bator (POB 46/142); tel. (11) 633347; fax (11) 633349; e-mail taspet@magicnet.mn; f. 1994; CEO Bat Pürevsuren.

Tavan Tolgoi: Ulan Bator; f. 2010; supervises devt of Tavan Tolgoi coal deposit in Tsogttsetsii district of Ömnögobi Province; Chair. D. Bat-Erdene; CEO L. Ariunbold.

Tsairtmineral Co: Tömörtiin Ovoo, Sükhbaatar Province; tel. (512) 31999; zinc mine and concentrator; Mongolian-Chinese jt enterprise; Chief Dep. Dir S. Batkhüü.

Tsakhilgaan Teever: Ulan Bator; capital's trolleybus operator; Dir D. Jargalsaikhan.

Tsement: Darkhan; tel. (37) 4770; fax (37) 4570; output of Portland cement; Dir-Gen. I. Dorjgotov.

Tsement Shokhoi: Khötöl, Selenge Province; tel. Ulan Bator (11) 689921; producer of cement and lime; state-owned; Dir-Gen. A. Shoovdor.

Tüshig Co: Natsagdorjiin Gudamj, Sükhbaatar District, Ulan Bator; parent co of Tüshig Trade and other companies; Dir Ganzorigiin Battüshig.

Ulaanbaatar Barilga: Ajilchny Gudamj, Khan-Uul District, Ulan Bator (CPOB 52); tel. (11) 343357; fax (11) 342806; e-mail info@ubconstruction.mn; building materials, construction; Dir-Gen. B. Jügder.

Ulaanbaatar Buyan Co: Ikh Toiruu, Sükhbaatar District, Ulan Bator; tel. (11) 327607; fax (11) 328036; e-mail info@ulaanbaatarbuyan.mn; internet www.ulaanbaatarbuyan.mn; funeral and cremation services; Chair. G. Idermaa; Exec. Dir M. Zolzayaa.

Ulaanbaatar Khivs: Chingisiin Örgön Chölöö, Khan-Uul District, Ulan Bator; tel. (11) 342559; fax (11) 343311; e-mail ubcarpet@yahoo.com; woollen carpet mfr; Exec. Dir D. Mönkhjargal.

Ulaanbaatar Zochid Buudal: Sükhbaataryn Talbai 14, Ulan Bator; tel. (11) 320620; fax (11) 324485; e-mail info@ubhotel.mn; internet www.ubhotel.mn; 280-bed hotel and restaurants; Exec. Dir Ch. Mönkhtüshig.

Ulsyn Ikh Delgüür: Enkh Taivny Gudamj, Chingeltei District, Ulan Bator; tel. (11) 325720; fax (11) 320792; department store retailing household goods, foodstuffs, clothing, etc.

XL-TA Holding: Ulan Bator (CPOB 981); fax (11) 310133; f. 1990; investment, tourism, banking, trade, security services; Pres. Batdelgeriin Batbold.

Zamar Gold Mining Co: 5th Sub-District, Bayanzürkh District, Ulan Bator; tel. (11) 458072; fax (11) 458430.

TRADE UNIONS

Confederation of Mongolian Trade Unions: Sükhbaataryn Talbai 3, Ulan Bator; tel. (11) 327253; fax (11) 322128; e-mail mpcd@cmtu.mn; internet www.cmtu.mn; brs throughout the country; Chair. SAINKHÜÜGIIN GANBAATAR; Sec.-Gen. M. GANAA.

Mongolian United Confederation of Journalists: Ulan Bator; Pres. T. BAASANSÜREN.

Transport

MTT (Mongol Transport Team): MTT Bldg, 5th Sub-District, Bayangol District, Ulan Bator; tel. (11) 689000; fax (11) 684953; e-mail mtt@mtteam.mn; internet www.mtteam.mn; international freight forwarding by air, sea, rail and road; offices in Beijing, Berlin, Moscow and Prague.

Tuushin Co Ltd: Tuushin Bldg, Yörönkhii Said Amaryn Gudamj, Sükhbaatar District, Ulan Bator; tel. (11) 312092; fax (11) 325570; e-mail tuushin@magicnet.mn; internet www.tuushin.mn; f. 1990; international freight forwarders; transport and forwarding policy and services, warehousing, customs agent; tourism; offices in Beijing, Moscow and Prague; Dir-Gen. N. ZORIGT.

RAILWAYS

Railway Directorate: Chingis Khaany Örgön Chölöö, Sükhbaatar District, Ulan Bator; tel. 976243404; fax 976243405; e-mail osorjamaa.e@railway.gov.mn; internet www.railway.gov.mn; Chair. TÖGSÖÖGIIN BATBOLD.

Mongolyn Tömör Zam (Mongolian Railways): Ulan Bator; f. 2009; state-owned limited co, est. by Erdenes Mongol and Russian Railways (50% each) to modernize Ulan Bator Railway.

Ulan Bator Railway: Söüliin Gudamj 42, Bayangol District, Ulan Bator (CPOB 376); tel. and fax (21) 243012; internet www.ubtz.mn; internet www.mtz.mn; f. 1949; jt-stock co (equal shares) with Russia; Dir TÜVDENGIIN OCHIRKHÜÜ; Chairs O. N. MOROZOV, AMARJARGALYN GANSÜKH.

External Lines: from the Russian frontier at Naushki/Sükhbaatar (connecting with the Trans-Siberian Railway) to Ulan Bator and on to the Chinese frontier at Zamyn-Üüd/Erenhot, connecting with Beijing (total length 1,110 km).

Branches: from Darkhan to Sharyn Gol coalfield (length 63 km); branch from Salkhit near Darkhan, westwards to Erdenet (Erdenetiin-ovoo open-cast copper mine) in Bulgan Province (164 km); from Bagakhangai to Baganuur coal-mine, south-east of Ulan Bator (96 km); from Khar Airag to Bor-Öndör fluorspar mines (60 km); from Sainshand to Züünbayan oilfield (63 km).

Planned railway construction 2011–13: broad-gauge lines (1,040 km) from Tavantolgoi coal mine to Züünbayan, and from Sainshand to Baruun-Urt and Choibalsan (existing link with the Trans-Siberian); standard-gauge line (80 km) from Oyu Tolgoi copper mine to Gants Mod on the Chinese border.

Eastern Railway, linking Mongolia with the Trans-Siberian and Chita via Borzya; from the Russian frontier at Solovyevsk to Choibalsan (238 km), with branch from Chingis Dalan to Mardai uranium mine near Dashbalbar (110 km), possibly inactive.

IFFC (International Freight-forwarding Centre of Mongolian Railways): Mongolian Railways, Söüliin Gudamj 42, Bayangol District, Ulan Bator (CPOB 376); tel. (11) 244845; fax (11) 313165; e-mail iffc@railcom.mn; internet www.iffc.mn; international freight forwarding.

ROADS

Mongolia divides its road system into state-grade and country-grade roads. State-grade roads (of which there were 11,000 km in 2005) run from Ulan Bator to provincial centres and from provincial centres to the border. Country-grade roads account for the remaining roads, but they are mostly rough cross-country tracks. The total length of hard-surfaced roads reached 2,600 km in 2007. To mark the millennium, the Government announced its decision to construct a new east–west road, linking the Chinese and Russian border regions via Ulan Bator. In 2011 some sections of the Millennium Road were to be realigned to avoid areas of permafrost.

Motor Roads Directorate: Ulan Bator; govt agency; Dir B. ENKHTÖR.

Motor Transport Directorate: Ulan Bator; govt agency; Dir B. TSENGEL.

SHIPPING

In 2003 the Government opened a shipping register. By May 2010 more than 1,700 vessels had been registered, with a tonnage exceeding 5m. g.r.t.

Maritime Administration: Ulan Bator; state-owned co, operating until 2010 with Singapore-based Maritime Chain as its agent; Dir DAMDINGIIN GALSANDONDOG.

CIVIL AVIATION

Civil aviation in Mongolia, including the provision of air traffic control and airport management, is the responsibility of the Main Directorate of Civil Aviation, which provides air traffic and airport management services. It also supervises the Mongolian national airline (MIAT) and smaller operators such as Khangarid and Tengeriin Ulaach, which operate local flights. Aeroflot (Russia) and Air China operate flights to Ulan Bator (Chinggis Khaan International Airport). Mongolia has 14 airfields with surfaced runways, and 31 with dirt strips.

Ulan Bator's new international airport, with a 3,600m runway, is under construction at Khöshigiin Khöndii, south of the capital; it will have a 37-km motorway link. Due to enter into service in 2015, the airport will have twice the capacity of Chinggis Khaan (Buyant-Ukhaa) airport, where high ground to the north limits the use of the runway.

Main Directorate of Civil Aviation: Chinggis Khaan International Airport, Buyant-Ukhaa, Ulan Bator; tel. (11) 282051; fax (11) 313151; e-mail webmaster@mcaa.gov.mn; internet www.mcaa.gov.mn; Dir-Gen. SANJAAJAVYN BATMÖNKH.

A-Jet Aviation: Olimpiin Gudamj, 1st Sub-District, Sükhbaatar District, Ulan Bator (POB 46/202); tel. (11) 318480; fax (11) 319780; e-mail aviation@ajet.mn; internet www.aviation.ajet.mn; f. 2000; fmrly Central Mongolia Airways; helicopter services for tourists, aerial surveys and photography; Exec. Dir NYAMBARYN LKHAMJAV.

Aero Mongolia Co Ltd: Chinggis Khaan International Airport, Buyant-Ukhaa, Ulan Bator (POB 34/105); tel. (11) 379616; fax (11) 379943; e-mail management@aeromongolia.mn; internet www.aeromongolia.mn; f. 2001; began operations in 2003; operates scheduled international flights to Irkutsk (Russia), and Hohhot (China), and scheduled internal flights to five provincial centres and Juulchin's South Gobi tourist camp; twice-weekly flights to the Republic of Korea; Dir B. JARGALSAIKHAN.

Blue Sky Aviation: Door 2, Apt S-61, 1st Sub-District, Sükhbaatar District, Ulan Bator; tel. (11) 312085; fax (11) 322857; e-mail bsa@maf-europe.org; internet www.blueskyaviation.mn; jt venture of Mission Aviation Fellowship and Exodus International; operates charter flights and medical emergency services; f. 1999; Dir TOM MASON; Operations Man. BATSUURIIN BAYARJIN.

Eznis (Easiness) Airways: Naiman Zokhis Bldg, Söüliin Gudamj, Sükhbaatar District, Ulan Bator; tel. (11) 313689; fax (11) 314258; internet www.eznis.com; f. 2006; operates internal routes and twice-weekly flights to Hailar (northern China) via Choibalsan; CEO MÖNKHSÜKH SÜKHBAATAR.

Khangarid: Room 210, MPRP Bldg, Baga Toiruu 37/1, Ulan Bator; tel. (11) 320138; fax (11) 311333; e-mail hangard_air_co@magicnet.mn; domestic and international passenger and freight services; Dir L. SERGELEN.

Mongolian Civil Air Transport (MIAT): MIAT Bldg, Chinggis Khaan International Airport, Buyant-Ukhaa, Khan-Uul District, Ulan Bator; tel. (11) 379935; fax (11) 379919; e-mail contact@miat.com; internet www.miat.com; f. 1956; scheduled services to Moscow, Beijing, Seoul, Osaka, Berlin and Tokyo; internal flights to Mörön and Khovd resumed in July 2009; Chair. D. MAKHBAL; Exec. Dir TS. ORKHON.

MIAT Cargo: MIAT Bldg, Chinggis Khaan International Airport, Buyant-Ukhaa, Khan-Uul District, Ulan Bator; tel. (11) 379956; fax (11) 379645; e-mail cargo@miat.com.

Tengeriin Ulaach (Sky Horse Aviation): Chinggis Khaan International Airport, Buyant-Ukhaa, Khan-Uul District, Ulan Bator (POB 34/17); tel. (11) 282023; fax (11) 379765; e-mail skyhorsenew@mbox.mn; internal helicopter transport for tourists and business passengers; Dir L. TÖMÖR.

Trans-Ölgii: Ölgii, Bayan-Ölgii Province; f. 2006; operates on Ölgii–Ulan Bator route twice a week.

Tourism

The country's main attractions are its scenery, wildlife and historical relics. A foreign tourist service bureau was established in 1954, but the tourism sector remained undeveloped. At March 2008 there were 248 tour operators, 326 hotels (with 8,000 beds) and 30 tourist camps (with 6,400 beds). Of the 30 or more hotels in Ulan Bator, all but four are relatively small, and in the peak summer season there is a shortage of rooms. The outlying tourist centres (Terelj, South Gobi, Öndör-Dov and Khujirt) have basic facilities. Tourist arrivals totalled 456,090 in 2010; Chinese and Russian tourists remained the most numerous. Tourism revenue reached US $222m. in 2010.

Juulchin World Tours Corporation: Marco Polo Place, Jamyan Günii Gudamj 5/3, Ulan Bator; tel. (11) 319401; fax (11) 319402; e-mail info@juulchinworld.com; internet www.juulchinworld.com; f. 1954; offices in Berlin, Fairfax, VA and Tokyo; tours, trekking, safaris, jeep tours, expeditions; Pres. SHAGDARSÜRENGIIN NERGÜI; Gen. Man. D. BATNASAN.

Mongolian Adventure Tourism Association: Ulan Bator; Pres. B. JIYAANDORJ.

Mongolian Tourism Association: Shine Tugul Complex D-2, Chingis Khaany Örgön Chölöö, Sükhbaatar District, Ulan Bator; tel. and fax 70111334; e-mail info@mnto.org; internet www.mnto.mn; Chair. BOLDYN INDRA; CEO BATMÖNKHIIN ERDENECHIMEG.

Defence

As assessed at November 2010, according to the International Institute for Strategic Studies, Mongolia's defence forces numbered 10,000, comprising an army of 8,900 (of whom 3,300 were thought to be conscripts), 800 air defence personnel and 300 construction troops. There was a paramilitary force of about 7,200, comprising 1,200 internal security troops and 6,000 border guards under the Ministry of Justice and Home Affairs. Each year a small quota of men can purchase exemption from conscription. In 2010 a total of 1,709 men paid 2.3m. tögrög each. Army reserves numbered an estimated 137,000. Military service is for 12 months (for males aged 18–25 years), but only about 40% of conscripts are found fit for service. There are financial inducements for regular service soldiers, especially those in the best trained and equipped 'élite' battalions, some of whom have served with coalition forces in Iraq and on UN peacekeeping operations elsewhere.

Mongolia has restarted annual military exercises with the Russian army, during which its Soviet-made equipment is serviced and updated. In 2010 Russia was reported to be supplying small numbers of BTR-80 personnel carriers and T-72 tanks, Mi-24M attack helicopters, MiG-29 fighters and missiles.

Defence Expenditure: Defence spending for 2011 was projected at 103,060m. tögrög (some 3.7% of total planned government expenditure in that year).

Chief of Staff of the Mongolian Armed Forces: Maj.-Gen. TSERENDEJIDIIN BYAMBAJAV.

Deputy Chief of Staff, Commander General Purpose Troops: Brig.-Gen. RADNAABAZARYN SÜKHBAT.

Deputy Chief of Staff, Director of Peacekeeping: Brig.-Gen. BYAMBAASÜRENGIIN BAYARMAGNAI.

Commander of Air Defence Troops: Brig.-Gen. TOJOONY DASHDELEG.

Education

General education is state-administered. Eleven-year education is compulsory, and 12-year education is being introduced. In the 2010/11 school year there were an estimated 512,200 pupils receiving general education, and teaching staff totalled 26,400. The 44 state and 19 private vocational schools, with a total of 46,100 students in 2010/11, train personnel for the service industries, including electricians, drivers and machine operators.

The Mongolian State University has three faculties (biology; chemistry; geography and geology) and nine schools (including foreign languages, mathematics, computer science, law, economics and social sciences). The School of Foreign Service provides diplomatic training. A total of 114,500 students were enrolled at the nine state and four private universities in 2010/11.

In 2010/11 there were seven state-owned and 88 private institutes of other higher education; 6,000 students were enrolled at the state institutes and 49,200 at the private institutes of higher education, excluding those studying in Russia, Germany, Turkey, the USA and elsewhere. The student enrolment abroad was estimated at 9,550 in 2009/10.

In July 2010 the Government approved a project for reform of higher education during 2010–12, which included structural change such as the consolidation of some colleges and institutes (e.g. the merger of Ulaanbaatar University and the Higher School of Trade and Industry with the Mongolian State University) and an improved admissions policy in order to raise teaching and research standards to international levels.

The state budget allocation to the Ministry of Education, Culture and Science for 2011 was 655,318.8m. tögrög (23.5% of planned budgetary expenditure).

Bibliography

General and Economy

Avery, Martha. *Women of Mongolia.* Boulder, CO, Asian Art and Archaeology, 2000.

Badarch, Dendeviin, Zilinskas, Raymond A., and Balint, Peter J. (Eds). *Mongolia Today—Science, Culture, Environment and Development.* London, RoutledgeCurzon, 2002.

Bat-Ireedui, J., and Sanders, Alan. *Mongolian-English and English-Mongolian Dictionary of Abbreviations and Acronyms.* Ulan Bator, Zov Zam Books, 2006.

Batbayar, Bat-Erdene (trans. Ed. Kaplonski, C.). *Twentieth Century Mongolia.* Cambridge, White Horse Press, 1999.

Batbayar, Tsedendambyn (Ed.). *Renovation of Mongolia on the Eve of the XXI Century and Future Development Patterns.* Ulan Bator, Mongolian Development Research Centre, 2000.

Batsukh, Jarantai, and Chinzorig, Onon. *Secrets of Mongolian Business Leaders.* Ulan Bator, Mash Nuuts Publishers, 2007.

Becker, Japser. *Travels in the Untamed Land.* London and New York, Tauris Parke, 2008.

Bodio, Stephen J. *Eagle Dreams: Searching for Legends in Wild Mongolia.* Guildford, CT, Lyons Press, 2003.

Bruun, Ole. *Precious Steppe: Mongolian Nomadic Pastoralists in Pursuit of the Market.* Lanham, MD, Lexington Books, 2006.

Bruun, Ole, and Narangoa, Li (Eds). *Mongolia from Country to City.* Nordic Institute of Asian Studies, Copenhagen, 2006.

Bruun, Ole, and Odgaard, Ole (Eds). *Mongolia in Transition: Old Patterns, New Challenges.* Richmond, Curzon Press, 1996.

Bulag, Uradyn E. *Nationalism and Hybridity in Mongolia.* Oxford, Clarendon Press, 1998.

Collaborative Nationalism: The Politics of Friendship on China's Mongolian Frontier. Lanham, MD, Rowman and Littlefield Publishers, 2010.

Bum-Ochir, Dulamyn. *Mongol Shamanic Ritual.* Ulan Bator, Monkhiin Useg Co, 2002.

Chadraa, Baataryn (Ed.). *Mongolyn Ündesnii Nevterkhii Toli* (Mongolian National Encyclopaedia), 3 Vols. Ulan Bator, Mongolian Academy of Sciences, 2009.

Danzan, Narantuya. *Religion in 20th Century Mongolia.* Saarbrücken, VDM Verlag Dr. Muller Aktiengesellschaft & Co, 2008.

Empson, Rebecca (Ed.). *Time, Causality and Prophecy in the Mongolian Cultural Region: Visions of the Future.* Cambridge, Global Oriental, 2006.

Fisher, Brian S. *The Development of Oyu Tolgoi Copper Mine: An Assessment of the Macroeconomic Consequences for Mongolia.* Kingston, School of Economic Studies, National University of Mongolia and BAEconomics Pty Ltd, 2011.

Ganhuu, Batbold. *Mongolia's Transition to Democracy and Market Capitalism.* Saarbrücken, VDM Verlag Dr. Muller Aktiengesellschaft & Co, 2009.

Gaunt, John, and Bayarmandakh, L. *Modern Mongolian: A Course-Book.* London, RoutledgeCurzon, 2004.

Goldstein, Melvyn C., and Beall, Cynthia M. *The Changing World of Mongolia's Nomads.* Hong Kong, The Guidebook Company, 1994.

Griffin, Keith (Ed.). *Poverty and the Transition to a Market Economy in Mongolia.* Basingstoke, Macmillan Press, 1995.

Hibbert, Reginald and Ann. *Letters from Mongolia.* London, Radcliffe Press, 2005.

Humphrey, Caroline, and Onon, Urgunge. *Shamans and Elders.* Oxford, Clarendon Press, 1996.

Janhunen, Juha (Ed.). *The Mongolic Languages.* London, Routledge, 2003.

Jeffries, Ian. *Mongolia: A Guide to Economic and Political Developments.* Abingdon, Routledge, 2007.

Kaplonski, Christopher. *Mongolia: Democracy on the Steppe.* Abingdon, Routledge, 2004.

Truth, History and Politics in Mongolia—The Memory of Heroes. London and New York, RoutledgeCurzon, 2004.

Kotkin, Stephen, and Elleman, Bruce A. (Eds). *Mongolia in the Twentieth Century: Landlocked Cosmopolitan.* London, M. E. Sharpe, 1999.

Man, John. *Gobi: Tracking the Desert.* London, Weidenfeld and Nicolson, 1997.

Genghis Khan: Life, Death and Resurrection. London, Bantam Press, 2004.

Kublai Khan: The Mongol King Who Remade China. London, Transworld Publishers, Bantam Press, 2006.

Mend-Ooyoo, G. (Ed.). *Golden Book of Mongolia: Mongolia's Famous Personalities XXI Century.* Ulan Bator, Mend-Ooyoo Publisher, 2003–04.

Monkhbayar, Ch. *Mongolian 108 Wonders.* Ulan Bator, N. Batjargal Publisher, 2005.

Moser, Achill, and Meinhardt, Olaf. *Land of Genghis Khan.* Munich, C. J. Bucher Verlag, 2007.

Myagmarsuren, D. (Ed.). *Special Protected Areas of Mongolia.* Ulan Bator, Environmental Protection Agency, 2000.

Namjim, Tumuriin. *The Economy of Mongolia from Traditional Times to the Present.* Bloomington, IN, Mongolia Society, 2000.

Namkhainyambuu, Ts. (trans. Rossabi, Mary). *Bounty from the Sheep: Autobiography of a Herdsman.* Cambridge, White Horse Press, 2000.

National Statistical Office. *Mongolian Statistical Yearbook.* Ulan Bator, annually.

Mongolia in a Market System 1989–2002. Ulan Bator, 2004.

Nixson, Frederick, Walters, Bernard, Suvd, B., and Luvsandorj, P. *The Mongolian Economy.* Cheltenham, Edward Elgar, 2000.

Nordby, Judith. *Mongolia.* World Bibliographical Series Vol. 156, Oxford, Clio Press, 1993.

Oleynik, Igor S. (Ed.). *Mongolia: National Security and Defense Handbook.* Washington, DC, International Business Publications USA, 2004.

Pegg, Carole. *Mongolian Music, Dance, and Oral Narrative.* Seattle, WA, and London, University of Washington Press, 2001.

Purev, Otgony. *The Religion of Mongolian Shamanism.* Ulan Bator, GENCO, 2002.

Retejum, Alexey Yu. *Mongolia in Transition: Social, Economic and Environmental Issues.* Bloomington, IN, Indiana University, 2007.

Rossabi, Morris. *Modern Mongolia: From Khans to Commissars to Capitalists.* Berkeley, CA, University of California Press, 2005.

Sanders, A. J. K. *Mongolia: Politics, Economics and Society.* London, Frances Pinter, 1987.

Historical Dictionary of Mongolia. Lanham, MD, and London, Scarecrow Press, 2010 (3rd edn).

Sanders, A. J. K., and Bat-Ireedüy, J. *Colloquial Mongolian.* London, Routledge, 2002 (reprint).

Mongolian Phrasebook. Footscray, Vic, Lonely Planet, 2003 (reprint).

Sermier, Claire. *Mongolia: Empire of the Steppes.* Hong Kong, Odyssey/Airphoto International, 2002.

Severin, Tim. *In Search of Genghis Khan.* London and Sydney, Hutchinson, 1992.

Sneath, David. *The Headless State: Aristocratic Orders, Kinship Society and the Misrepresentation of Inner Asia.* Columbia University Press, New York and Chichester, 2007.

Stewart, Stanley. *In the Empire of Genghis Khan—A Journey among Nomads.* London, HarperCollins, 2000.

Svantesson, Jan-Olof, Tsendina, Anna, Karlsson, Anastasia and Franzén, Vivan. *The Phonology of Mongolian.* Oxford, Oxford University Press, 2005.

Weatherford, Jack. *Genghis Khan and the Making of the Modern World.* New York, Crown Publishers, 2004.

Worden, Robert L., and Savada, Andrea Matles (Eds). *Mongolia: A Country Study.* Washington, DC, Library of Congress, 2nd Edn, 1991.

History

Allsen, Thomas T. *Mongol Imperialism.* Berkeley, CA, University of California, 1987.

Atwood, Christopher P. *Encyclopedia of Mongolia and the Mongol Empire.* New York, Facts on File Inc, 2004.

Barkmann, Udo. *Geschichte der Mongolei* (History of Mongolia). Bonn, Bouvier, 1999.

Batbayar, Tsendendambyn, and Soni, Sharad K. *Modern Mongolia: a Concise History.* New Delhi, Pentagon Press, 2007.

Bawden, Charles R. *The Modern History of Mongolia.* (2nd Edn, with afterword by A. J. K. Sanders). London, Kegan Paul International, 1989.

Biran, Michal. *Qaidu and the Rise of the Independent Mongolian State in Central Asia.* Richmond, Surrey, Curzon Press, 1997.

Bold, Bat-Ochir. *Mongolian Nomadic Society—A Reconstruction of the 'Medieval' History of Mongolia.* Richmond, Curzon Press, 1999.

Buell, Paul D. *Historical Dictionary of the Mongol World Empire.* Lanham, MD, and Oxford, Scarecrow Press, 2003.

Bulag, Uradyn E. *The Mongols at China's Edge: History and the Politics of National Unity.* Lanham, MD, Rowman and Littlefield Publishers, 2002.

Dashpurev, D., and Prasad, Usha. *Mongolia: Revolution and Independence 1911–1992.* New Delhi, Subhash and Associate, 1993.

Dashpurev, D., and Soni, S. K. *Reign of Terror in Mongolia 1920–1990.* New Delhi, South Asian Publishers, 1992.

de Rachewiltz, Igor. *Papal Envoys to the Great Khans.* London, Faber and Faber, 1971.

(Trans. and commentary). *The Secret History of the Mongols—A Mongolian Epic Chronicle of the Thirteenth Century.* Leiden and Boston, MA, Brill, 2004.

Delgado, James. *Khubilai Khan's Lost Fleet.* London, Bodley Head, 2009.

Eisma, Doeke. *Mongol Rule: Reflections on Mongol Sociopolitics.* Leiden, Leiden University Press, 2003.

Ewing, E. E. *Between the Hammer and the Anvil? Chinese and Russian Policies in Outer Mongolia 1911–21.* Bloomington, IN, Indiana University Press, 1980.

Golman, M. I. *Sovremennaya Mongoliya v Otsenkakh Zapadnykh Avtorov* (Modern Mongolia as Evaluated by Western Writers). Moscow, Institute of Oriental Studies, Russian Academy of Sciences, 2010.

Honeychurch, William. *Genghis Khan and the Mongol Empire.* WA, University of Washington Press, 2009.

Jackson, Peter. *The Mongols and the West 1221–1410.* London, Pearson Longman, 2005.

Kaplonski, Christopher, and Sneath, David (Eds). *The History of Mongolia.* Cambridge, Global Oriental, 2007.

Kara, György (trans. John R. Krueger). *Books of the Mongolian Nomads.* Bloomington, IN, Indiana University, 2005.

Kolbas, Judith. *The Mongols in Iran.* Abingdon, Routledge, 2006.

Marshall, Robert. *Storm from the East.* London, BBC Books, 1993.

May, Timothy. *The Mongol Art of War: Chinggis Khan and the Mongol Military System.* Yardley, PA, Westholme, 2007.

Onon, Urgunge (trans.). *Mongolian Heroes of the 20th Century.* New York, AMS Press, 1976.

The Golden History of the Mongols. London, Folio Society, 1993.

The Secret History of the Mongols—The Life and Times of Chinggis Khan. London, RoutledgeCurzon, 2001.

Onon, Urgunge, and Pritchatt, D. *Asia's First Modern Revolution.* Leiden, E. J. Brill, 1989.

Ratchnevsky, Paul (trans. Thomas Haining). *Genghis Khan: His Life and Legacy.* Oxford, Blackwell, 1991.

Roux, Jean-Paul. *Genghis Khan and the Mongol Empire.* London, Thames and Hudson, 2003.

Ruotsala, Antii. *Europeans and Mongols in the Middle of the Thirteenth Century: Encountering the Other.* Helsinki, Finnish Academy of Sciences, 2001.

Rupen, R. A. *Mongols of the Twentieth Century, Vol. 1* (History), *Vol. 2* (Bibliography). The Hague, Indiana University and Mouton and Co, 1964 (reprinted).

Sandag, Shagdariin, and Kendall, Harry H. *Poisoned Arrows: The Stalin-Choibalsan Mongolian Massacres 1921–1941.* Oxford, Westview Press, 2000.

Saunders, J. J. *The History of the Mongol Conquests.* London, Routledge and Kegan Paul, 1971.

Sneath, David (Ed.). *Imperial Statecraft: Political Forms and Techniques of Governance in Inner Asia Sixth–Twentieth Centuries.* Bellingham, Western Washington University and University of Cambridge, 2006.

Sneath, David, and Kaplonski, Christopher (Eds). *The History of Mongolia.* Folkestone, Global Oriental, 2010.

Soni, Sharad K. *Mongolia-Russia Relations (Kiakhta to Vladivostok).* New Delhi, Shipra Publications, 2002.

Mongolia-China Relations: Modern and Contemporary Times. New Delhi, Pentagon Press, 2006.

MYANMAR

(BURMA)

Physical and Social Geography

HARVEY DEMAINE

The Republic of the Union of Myanmar (also known as Burma) covers a total area of 676,552 sq km (261,218 sq miles). It lies to the east of India and Bangladesh and to the south-west of the People's Republic of China, and has a long coastline facing the Bay of Bengal and the Andaman Sea. Much the greater part of its territory, lying between latitudes 28° 50' and 16° N, forms a compact unit surrounded on three sides by a great horseshoe of mountains and focusing on the triple river system of the Ayeyarwady, Chindwinn and Sittoung (or Irrawaddy, Chindwin and Sittang, respectively). In addition, Tanintharyi (Tenasserim), consisting of a narrow coastal zone backed by steep mountains, extends south from the Gulf of Martaban to Victoria Point, only 10° N of the Equator.

PHYSICAL FEATURES

Structurally, the topography of Myanmar falls into three well-marked divisions, of which the first comprises the mid-Tertiary fold mountains of the west. These ranges, forming a great arc from the Hukwang valley to Cape Negrais, appear to represent a southward continuation of the eastern Himalayan series. From north to south these western ranges are known successively as the Patkai, Naga and Chin Hills, and the Arakan Yoma, although this is a misleading description of ranges with summits exceeding 3,650 m in the Patkai and reaching 1,800 m–2,400 m in the Chin and Naga Hills. Further south, in the Arakan Yoma, the summit levels gradually decrease to 900 m–1,500 m. The second major structural unit consists of the eastern mountain ranges, of Mesozoic or earlier origin, which, beginning as a continuation of the Yunnan plateau of China across the Myanma border into the north-eastern corner of Kachin State, extend thence through the Shan and Kayinni (or Karenni) plateaux into more subdued but still rugged upland, which forms the divide between Tanintharyi and peninsular Thailand. In the far north, where this system adjoins the western mountain system, the general plateau level is about 1,800 m, with higher ridges frequently attaining 3,000 m. However, the corresponding altitudes in the Shan area are only about one-half as great, although here also the surface is dissected, with the main rivers, notably the great Thanlwin (Salween), rushing southwards through deep gorges. Between the two main mountain systems lies the third major structural unit, the vast longitudinal trough of central Myanmar, containing the alluvial lowlands. Throughout the length of these lowlands the Ayeyarwady provides the central artery, both of drainage and of communication. To the north it is paralleled by its largest tributary, the Chindwinn, and further south by the Sittoung, which flows separately to the sea on the opposite side of the recent volcanic uplands of the Pegu Yoma. Central Myanmar is a zone of crustal instability; a severe earthquake in July 1975 caused extensive damage. Altogether, the Ayeyarwady drains a total area of some 400,000 sq km, forming a huge delta.

CLIMATE

Apart from the highest uplands in the far north of the country, the climate of practically the whole of Myanmar may be classified as tropical monsoonal, although important regional variations nevertheless occur within that overall category. In all parts of the country the main rains come during the period of the south-west monsoon, i.e. between May and October, and those areas, notably Rakhine (or Arakan) and Tanintharyi, that face the prevailing winds and are backed by steep and high ranges, receive some of the heaviest rainfall in the world (Sittwe, or Akyab, 5,180 mm annually; Kyaikkami, or Amherst, 4,980 mm). Moreover, even the flat and low-lying Ayeyarwady delta receives an annual rainfall of about 2,500 mm, and in all of these three areas mean annual temperatures are around 27°C, although the seasonal range varies from 6.5°C in Sittwe to 35°C in Kyaikkami.

A considerable portion of the interior of the central lowland constitutes a rain-shadow area relative to the south-west monsoon, and here the total annual precipitation is less than 1,000 mm. Although the seasonal incidence is similar to that of other areas, the marked difference in total amount is reflected in a major change of vegetation, from the heavy tropical monsoon forest prevailing elsewhere, to a much more open cover and, in places, a mere thorny scrub. Moreover, the relative aridity is also responsible for a wider range of temperature, as is shown by Mandalay's 21°C in January and 32°C in April, immediately before the onset of the rains. In the eastern plateaux, rainfall is much less than along the western coastal margins, which, combined with temperatures some 6°C–8°C below those of the torrid plains, gives the Shan plateau the most equable climate of any part of the country.

The country is susceptible to cyclones. In May 2008 southern Myanmar was devastated by Cyclone Nargis, which killed almost 150,000 people and left millions homeless.

NATURAL RESOURCES

Myanmar's natural resources include the timber of the humid mountain slopes, particularly teak, and mineral deposits such as coal, lead, zinc, tin and copper. Other important minerals that are commercially exploited include jade, gemstones, gold and silver. By the early 21st century substantial reserves of onshore and offshore gas, as well as petroleum, had been identified. At the end of 2010 Myanmar's proven gas reserves were estimated to total 300,000m. cu m.

POPULATION AND ETHNIC GROUPS

At mid-2011, according to UN estimates, Myanmar's population totalled 48,336,764, giving a density of 71.4 per sq km. The greatest concentration of population occurs in the delta. In the lowlands, including Rakhine and Tanintharyi, the Bamar (Burmans) form the majority element in the population. The uplands are more sparsely inhabited, by minority groups. The Bamar formed some 68% of the total population of Myanmar in 1992; 7% were Shan (the ethnic kinsfolk of the Thai and Lao), while the Arakanese constituted nearly 4% and the Mon 2%. Of the non-Buddhist indigenous groups, the Kayin (Karen—many of whom have adopted Christianity) were the most numerous (6% in 1992). They occupy the uplands between the Shan plateau and Tanintharyi, although many have migrated into the lowlands around Mawlamyine (Moulmein) and to the Ayeyarwady delta. Other upland peoples include the Kachin (2%), Chin (2%), Wa-Palaung, Lolo-Muhso and Naga, who are still mostly animists.

At the census of 31 March 1983 Yangon (Rangoon), the then capital, had a population of 2,513,023. Only seven other towns exceeded 100,000 inhabitants. By mid-2010, according to UN estimates, the population of Yangon had increased to 4,349,604. The functions of the capital city were transferred from Yangon to the new administrative centre of Nay Pyi Taw, located near Pyinmana, in 2006.

History

ROBERT CRIBB

Based on an earlier article by JOSEF SILVERSTEIN

Revised by STEPHEN MCCARTHY

EARLY HISTORY

Modern Myanmar falls into three distinct geopolitical zones: the valley of the Ayeyarwady (Irrawaddy), the hill country that surrounds the valley, and the coastal areas of Rakhine (Arakan) and Tanintharyi (Tenasserim). The long, fertile valley of the Ayeyarwady, which is navigable for 1,400 km from Bhamo to the sea, has witnessed a succession of powerful kingdoms based on both agriculture and trade; but only for brief periods were those kingdoms able to unite the entire valley in a single polity. The earliest kingdoms were founded by the Mon, ethnically close to today's Cambodians, and the Pyus. However, from about the 10th century a Tibeto-Burmese people, the Burmans (now Bamars), entered the valley and eventually conquered the Mon and Pyus, absorbing many elements of those earlier cultures in the process. The hill country, which surrounds the valley in a broad horseshoe of territory, is inhabited by smaller ethnic groups—the Shan (who are closely related to the Thai), the Karen (or Kayin), the Kachin, the Chin and the Naga—which sometimes briefly established kingdoms extending into the valley, but which were more often subject or tributary to the kingdoms of the Mon and Burmans. The third zone, which comprises the coastal strips of Rakhine and Tanintharyi, has remained relatively isolated from the country's heartland and has a long history of maritime engagement with the outside world.

The first large Burman kingdom, Pagan, was founded in the 11th century and it was in the context of this kingdom that Theravada Buddhism was established as the religion of the Burmans. Pagan was destroyed by a Mongol invasion in 1287. Its successor kingdom, Ava, was weakened by fighting with the Mon and the Shan. In the mid-16th century the Toungoo dynasty created an empire that extended briefly from Rakhine in the west to Laos in the east. Spread over too wide an area, the Toungoo empire was unable to defeat counter-attacks from Rakhine and Siam, and subsequently collapsed at the end of the 16th century. Only in the late 18th century did a new dynasty, the Konbaung, unite the country and resume Burma's expansion. However, in doing so, it came into conflict with British power in India, and in three wars between 1824 and 1885 Burma lost first Rakhine and Tanintharyi, then the lower reaches of the Ayeyarwady, and finally the north of the country. The British abolished the Burman monarchy and annexed Burma to British India, inheriting at the same time the Konbaung dynasty's contested claims to the hill regions. The Kachin region in the far north was not fully subdued until 1915, and the British also confronted continuing resistance in the countryside of the Ayeyarwady valley.

BRITISH AND JAPANESE RULE

British rule (which lasted from 1896 to 1948) transformed Burma socially, economically and administratively. The power of the court was removed and that of the aristocracy greatly diminished, while village headmen were included in a new centralized administrative system, leaving the Buddhist monastic establishment (*sangha*) as the country's most powerful indigenous institution and a centre of hostility to foreign rule. Indians began to migrate to Burma in large numbers, as traders and labourers, to the extent that the capital, Rangoon (now Yangon), became a predominantly Indian city. The establishment of Rangoon University in 1920 made Western learning accessible to a new generation of Burmese and with the growth of exports of rice, oil, teak, tin, rubies and cotton, Burma became more integrated than ever before into the global economy. This integration led to serious hardship in Burma during the Great Depression, and discontent was expressed in the Saya San uprising of 1930–31.

As part of British India, Burma was included in the gradual development of democratic institutions. In 1923 the British introduced a partly elected Legislative Council and, under the system known as 'dyarchy', devolved political power in several fields to ministers responsible to the Council. In 1937 the administration of Burma was separated from that of India and Burmese cabinet ministers responsible to an elected parliament took over all areas of government except defence, foreign relations and monetary policy. However, the influence of Burman parliamentarians was circumscribed by the existence of separate, more generously represented electorates for several minorities (Karen, Indians, Anglo-Indians, Chinese and Europeans), so that the four successive Governments that served in office between 1937 and 1942 were all coalitions between Burman and minority representatives. These constitutional arrangements excluded most of the hill regions, which remained under direct British rule.

The modern Burmese nationalist movement that arose in the context of these developments was strongly dominated by ethnic Burmans. The Young Men's Buddhist Association (YMBA), founded in 1906, campaigned initially on religious issues, but subsequently developed into the General Council of Buddhist Associations (GCBA), which pursued a more political agenda. In contrast, the Thakin (master) movement, founded by members of the young intelligentsia in Rangoon in 1930, emphasized a more secular Burmese nationalism which incorporated Marxist elements but which drew strongly on the Burman language, culture and traditions. This movement provided the new generation of leaders who guided the nation through the war and into independence. Throughout the 1930s, while the British tried to lead Burma towards full self-government, the nationalist movement sought the country's independence. Believing that only armed force could overthrow the British, 30 Thakins (the 'Thirty Comrades'), including Aung San, went to Japan in 1940 and returned in 1942 with invading Japanese forces and a small but symbolic Burma Independence Army (BIA).

The Japanese advanced rapidly, driving the British out of most of Burma by mid-1942, but they were unable to press more than a short distance beyond Burma's borders into India. The Japanese ruled Burma with a combination of conciliation and repression. In August 1943, for example, they granted 'puppet' independence to a state headed by the pre-war Burman leader, Dr Ba Maw, and also expanded the BIA into the Burma National Army (BNA). However, they demanded labour and materials for the war effort and were brutal in their repression of the growing resistance movement, especially among the Karen and other hill peoples. In August 1943 the Japanese transferred part of the Shan region to Thailand. In late 1944, with Japan in retreat on its Indian front, Aung San and leaders of the growing Communist movement founded the Anti-Fascist People's Freedom League (AFPFL), turning the BNA against the Japanese in March 1945 and launching a revolt that accelerated the Allied victory in Burma.

The British announced in May 1945 that they were willing to grant Burma independence within the British Commonwealth. However, following the end of Allied military administration in October, this promise was suspended in favour of a period of economic reconstruction. Concerned that such a delay would allow British economic domination to continue, Aung San and other nationalist leaders led a campaign of unrest which forced the British to appoint AFPFL members to the governor's Executive Council and to call elections in April 1947 for a constituent assembly to draft a new constitution. The AFPFL won 171 of the 182 seats contested, and the assembly drafted a constitution, which gave Burma full independence outside the Commonwealth. In July 1947 Aung San and six other members of the Executive Council were assassinated; however, the governor appointed Thakin Nu (later U Nu) as Aung San's successor and allowed the movement towards independence to continue. Burma thus became independent on 4 January 1948.

CONSTITUTIONAL GOVERNMENT, 1948–62

At independence in 1948, the governing party was the socialist AFPFL. Throughout independence negotiations, the United Kingdom had preferred to deal with the non-communist wing of the AFPFL. As a consequence, the communist wing, with strong popular support both in the Ayeyarwady delta and among former members of the BIA, perceived itself to be excluded from power in the new Government. In March 1948, after government incursions against them, the communist element went into revolt, taking significant sections of the army and the militia with it. In 1949 the situation became more complicated when the Karen also launched a revolt. The independent Union of Burma was an unequally balanced federation: alongside the Burman heartland, it included the hill regions as states with varying degrees of autonomy. Shan and Kayah States had the formal right to secede from the Union; Kachin and Karen States had autonomy but no right to secede; the Chin Special Division had only limited autonomy, while a separate status for Arakan was only foreshadowed. The army was also constructed federally, with each unit drawn primarily from one or other of the ethnic groups. However, from the outset the Government in Rangoon tended to concentrate power within its own ranks, and the Karen, who were generally well educated and who had prospered under British rule, grew increasingly discontented. In time, revolts were to break out among almost all the country's minorities. Also, during 1949, the eastern Shan region, which bordered China to the north, was occupied by Chinese Nationalist armies in retreat after the victory of the Chinese Communist Party.

For several months the central Government controlled only Rangoon and a few other centres. Burma's formal unity survived partly because the rebels fought among themselves, partly because they had no significant external support, and partly because U Nu's Government responded vigorously to the crisis. U Nu reformed the army, placing Gen. Ne Win in charge. Ne Win subsequently centralized and enlarged the military, eliminating the ethnic units and placing Burman officers in most command positions. He also operated ruthlessly against the rebels, developing for the army a reputation for brutality against civilian opponents. Meanwhile, U Nu campaigned energetically in the country's heartland, winning support as a charismatic proponent of state Buddhism. By 1951 the Government was once again in control of the Burman heartland and was well established in parts of the hill country, although perhaps 10% of the country remained outside its control.

The AFPFL won national elections in 1951–52 and 1956, and in 1958 the party split into 'Clean' and 'Stable' rival factions. To avert renewed civil war, U Nu invited Gen. Ne Win to form a 'caretaker' government to prepare the country for new elections in 1960. The 18-month interlude of military rule was generally welcomed as a period of law and order, economic growth and the implementation of serious measures against corruption. Although the U Nu-led 'Clean' faction of the AFPFL, renamed the Union Party, won the elections, U Nu soon alienated minorities by declaring Buddhism as the state religion, which provoked a revolt in the Shan and Kachin regions and exacerbated discontent among the Mon and Karen. With corruption and administrative mismanagement plaguing the country once more, the armed forces under Gen. Ne Win carried out a *coup d'état* on 2 March 1962, arresting members of the Government, suspending the Constitution and appointing a Revolutionary Council (RC) to govern Burma by decree.

MILITARY RULE, 1962–74

Following the coup, Gen. Ne Win quickly rescinded U Nu's declaration of Buddhism as the state religion. The democratic institutions of the 1950s were dismantled and power was concentrated in the RC, which comprised a small group of senior officers led by Ne Win. In form and theory, Burma remained a federal state, although for all practical purposes the new leadership treated the country as a unitary state. At the local level, authority was placed under the control of new Security and Administration Committees (SACs), headed by local military commanders. For the next decade, however, the Ne Win Government continued to fight ethnic and communist insurgents in almost all the hill country outside the Burman heartland. Attempts by U Nu to create a coalition of rebel forces under his leadership in 1969–71 failed owing to his lack of popularity among the ethnic minorities. A more serious threat to the Government came from the Communist Party of Burma (CPB), which received substantial support from the People's Republic of China, especially during the latter's Cultural Revolution. From 1970, however, relations between Burma and China improved, and Chinese support for the CPB was reduced. Meanwhile, Ne Win's long-term political aim was to reshape Burma into a socialist one-party state, and to this end he created the Burma Socialist Programme Party (BSPP, also known as Lanzin, from its Burmese name) in June 1962. At the same time, the Government sought to prevent the Buddhist *sangha* (order of monks) from becoming a focus of political opposition, and in 1965 an attempt was made by the Government to require all Buddhist monks to register and to carry identity cards. The BSPP refrained from becoming involved in international conflicts, emphasizing the need for Burma to follow its own path and keeping the country remarkably isolated from the outside world. Ne Win's Government sought to 'Burmanize' the economy, nationalizing land, the banking sector, oil wells, foreign trade, the insurance sector, shipping, wholesale trade, cinemas, and much of the publishing, mining and saw-milling industries in the years between 1963 and 1971, and schools were brought under the closer control of the Ministry of Education from 1966. The economy gradually began to show signs of stagnation, including the emergence of a 'black market'. Formerly a major exporter of rice, Burma ceased to produce rice surpluses. Meanwhile, the reputation of the regime was not helped by growing indications of corruption among members of the RC. The competence of the administration was further diminished by the exclusion of civilians from the Government: whereas Gen. Ne Win had made considerable use of highly qualified civilians in his administration during the 'caretaker' Government of 1958–60, the Government that held office from 1962 to 1974 was dominated by a small group of senior military officers. In those 12 years, only three civilians achieved ministerial rank, while the Council of Ministers—Burma's Cabinet—was reorganized only twice.

In its early stages, the BSPP was a cadre party with a small membership. At the party's inaugural congress, Gen. Ne Win was formally elected as leader. In July 1971 the military leaders announced their intention to draft a new constitution and to transfer power to a civilian government. A recruitment campaign for the party subsequently began in 1972, and within a decade its membership had expanded to 1.5m. Meanwhile, in April 1972, in accord with the progression toward constitutionalism, Ne Win and 20 of his senior commanders retired from the army and became civilian members of the Government. Ne Win became Prime Minister, heading a Cabinet of nine retired officers, three serving officers and two civilians, proclaiming the end of the revolutionary Government and its replacement by the Government of the Union of Burma. This 'civilianization' of Ne Win's rule was completed in early 1974, in which year elections were held, the new Constitution came into effect and the RC was dissolved. Ne Win was elected Chairman of the Council of State and thus became President under the new Constitution. Eleven of the 29 members of the Council of Ministers were carried over from the now-defunct RC.

BSPP RULE, 1974–88

In December 1974 riots broke out in Rangoon and other centres over food shortages, corruption and generally declining economic conditions. (However, the immediate catalyst for the riots had been the perceived lack of proper honour accorded by the Government to the funeral of U Thant, a former Secretary-General of the UN and a close associate of U Nu.) Students in

Rangoon were particularly angry at declining standards and conditions at the universities, and further demonstrations broke out in March 1976. The BSPP responded initially by modifying its socialist programme, approving the idea of foreign aid and investment. The complaints about official corruption were met by new regulations requiring leaders at all levels to disclose their assets. These signs of independent initiative on the part of the BSPP appeared to alarm Ne Win. In October some 50,000 party members were expelled, the party's structure was reformed and more than half the Central Committee resigned, followed by several members of the national Cabinet, including the Prime Minister, Sein Win. Further expulsions took place in September 1977 and February 1978, leaving the upper ranks of the BSPP and much of the Cabinet under the control of serving or retired military officers. In 1977 the Pyithu Hluttaw (People's Assembly) adopted a Private Enterprises Law, which firmly rejected the economic liberalization proposed by the BSPP. The law prohibited private foreign investment in Burma, and only grudgingly permitted local private investment in sectors not yet taken over by the State or the co-operatives. In 1981 Ne Win announced that he would retire as President of the Socialist Republic of the Union of Burma (as the country had been redesignated), while continuing to lead the party. San Yu took over formally as President, although Ne Win in fact continued to control Burmese politics from behind the scenes.

Civilian rule was not merely intended to make military dominance appear more acceptable. Ne Win hoped that the one-party state would provide a format for engaging the public in government and national development but without permitting the political turmoil and drift that had blighted the parliamentary system. In January 1978 and October 1981, therefore, the Government held national elections, although only BSPP candidates were permitted to stand. The BSPP Government presented itself as the protector of Burmese national identity in 1982, by formalizing a citizenship law, which created three categories of citizen—national, associated and naturalized. Resident Indians and Chinese were consigned to the latter categories, under which they had restricted rights in politics and the economy and were not permitted to join the armed forces. The Government also reversed the RC's previous antagonism towards the Buddhist *sangha*: rather than confronting organized Buddhism, the regime provided it with financial and administrative support, establishing a Ministry of Religious Affairs and acknowledging the importance of Buddhist tradition to the history and culture of the nation. In May 1980 the regime sponsored a nation-wide congregation for the purification, propagation and perpetuation of Buddhism. At this convention, representatives created a centralized authority to control the *sangha* throughout the nation and approved the introduction of identification cards for monks and nuns. In 1981 the religious courts, which had been inactive for years, were revived. Two sects were found guilty of teaching heretical doctrines and ordered to be dissolved. These measures seemed to eliminate the potential of the *sangha* to serve as a base for opposition, and gave the Government the confidence to declare an extensive amnesty for U Nu and his followers, who were permitted to return to the country. Thousands of political prisoners were also released.

The return to socialism under a remilitarized BSPP led to continuing economic decline in Burma. In August 1987 Ne Win finally admitted publicly to 'failures and faults' in the management of the economy and announced major reforms. The Government freed the purchase, sale, transport and storage of basic food items from state control, hoping that farmers would increase production to meet local market demands. In early 1988 the Government also terminated its 25-year monopoly on rice exports. These measures were popular, but they were followed by a regulation demonetizing the 25, 35 and 75 kyat currency notes, intended to strike at the wealth of 'black marketeers'. This action, which effectively confiscated money from the public, was deeply resented, and prompted student protests in Rangoon and elsewhere. In March 1988 the police responded with violence to the demonstrations. At least 50 people were killed, leading to mass public demonstrations against the regime. In June security forces brutally suppressed a demonstration by about 5,000 students and others demanding the release of persons detained in March. The Government responded by imposing a curfew and closing universities and schools indefinitely. The regional cities of Taunggyi, Pegu and Prome were also placed under curfew as unrest spread throughout the country. In an atmosphere of crisis, Ne Win and San Yu resigned from their posts in July. Sein Lwin, a close military associate of Ne Win and a known advocate of harsh repressive measures, took over as both BSPP Chairman and State President. Mass strikes and demonstrations against the regime were launched on the supposedly auspicious date of 8 August 1988 (8-8-88), at 8.08 a.m. The protests proceeded peacefully until late in the evening of that day, when security forces resorted to violence in an attempt to disperse the protesters. During the following five days, some 2,000 to 3,000 demonstrators were believed to have been killed as the reform movement was violently suppressed. With unrest continuing, Sein Lwin resigned on 13 August and was replaced by the more moderate Dr Maung Maung, hitherto the Attorney-General. Maung Maung ended martial law, released political prisoners and offered political reforms, which implied that the BSPP was willing to surrender power to the opposition in a peaceful transition.

An emergency meeting of the BSPP held in September 1988 agreed to hold free elections within three months and decided that members of the armed forces, police and civil service could no longer be affiliated to a political party. New political groups—including the All Burma Students Union (ABSU) and the National United Front for Democracy, later renamed the National League for Democracy (NLD)—were permitted to form in preparation for the election. The NLD quickly emerged as the main opposition group, its leaders including Brig.-Gen. Aung Gyi (formerly an associate of Ne Win, but subsequently an outspoken critic of the regime, who was briefly detained under Sein Lwin), Gen. Tin Oo (a former chief of staff and Minister of Defence) and Aung San Suu Kyi, daughter of the assassinated nationalist leader Aung San, whose portraits had been particularly prominent during the demonstrations of 8 August. Even though she had been out of the country since 1960, Suu Kyi increasingly came to represent the peaceful, prosperous country that people imagined Burma might have become but for her father's death. Amid general expectations that the NLD would resoundingly win the coming elections, and with Buddhist monks already taking over municipal administrations in many parts of the country, the military under Gen. Saw Maung launched a coup on 18 September 1988, ostensibly to maintain public order in the approach to the elections. However, Saw Maung immediately created a new ruling body, the State Law and Order Restoration Council (SLORC), comprising 19 senior military officers, with himself as Chairman. All state organs were abolished, demonstrations were banned and a nation-wide dusk-to-dawn curfew was imposed. In the first days after the military coup, more than 1,000 demonstrators were killed by security forces, and thousands more fled to areas along the border with Thailand, where they sought the protection and help of ethnic insurgents.

THE SLORC, 1988–97

The SLORC announced the formation of a nine-member Government, with Saw Maung subsequently appointed Prime Minister. However, it was widely believed that Ne Win retained a controlling influence over the new leaders, all of whom were known to be his supporters. The new Government changed the official name of the country to the Union of Burma (as it had been before 1974). The law maintaining the BSPP as the sole party was abrogated, and by February 1989 a total of 233 new parties had registered. Most were small and based on ethnicity, religion or location. The new parties had little influence; under the Government's martial law regulations, group gatherings were limited to five persons, a curfew existed, and there were restrictions on travel, publication and public meetings. The BSPP was re-established under a new name, the National Unity Party (NUP), with Tha Kyaw, the former Minister of Transport, as Chairman. Although the NLD registered, it was uncertain whether it would contest elections, which, it asserted, could not be held fairly under military rule. In December 1988, owing to disagreements with Aung San Suu

Kyi, Aung Gyi was expelled from the NLD and founded the Union National Democracy Party (UNDP). In May 1989 the Government ratified electoral legislation providing for the holding of multi-party elections in May 1990 and permitting campaigning only in the three months prior to the election date. Stringent campaign regulations were imposed by the SLORC, including restrictions on public rallies and official censorship of speeches. In June 1989 the SLORC reiterated that martial law was still in force, and that it would retain power after the elections until the resulting legislative assembly drafted a new constitution and formed a civilian government. In the same month 3,000 people demonstrated on the anniversary of the student protests of 1988. Troops fired on the crowd and one person was killed.

On 18 June 1989 the name of the country was changed to the Union of Myanmar (Pyidaungsu Myanmar Naingngandaw). The SLORC revealed that the change had been made to avoid the racial connotation of the previous name, Union of Burma, which implied that the population were all Burmans, while, in fact, it included many racial groups. The Roman transliteration of many towns, divisions, states, rivers and nationalities was changed (although the pronunciation remained the same in Burmese). Thus, Rangoon was changed to Yangon, Pegu to Bago and the Irrawaddy River became the Ayeyarwady. The ethnic group known as the Burmans was renamed the Bamars, while the Karen and Karenni were restyled Kayin and Kayinni, respectively.

Tension between the SLORC and the opposition groups increased in July 1989. In an attempt to suppress political dissent, the SLORC established five military tribunals (and a further six in August) to try persons violating martial law regulations (e.g. by failing to observe the curfew or participating in gatherings of more than five people). The tribunals could impose penalties ranging from three years' imprisonment to death. On 19 July, the anniversary of the 1947 assassination of her father, Aung San Suu Kyi planned to lead a protest march through the capital with members of more than 100 of the country's political parties. However, Suu Kyi cancelled the rally, fearing that troops deployed by the Government would open fire on the marchers, as they had done in September 1988. On the next day she and Tin Oo (the Chairman of the NLD) were placed under house arrest. They were accused of attempting to create disunity within the army and 'nurturing public hatred for the military'. In December 1989 Tin Oo was tried and sentenced to three years' imprisonment, with hard labour. Former Prime Minister U Nu was placed under house arrest for his refusal to disband a parallel government that he had proclaimed during the uprising in 1988. Other leaders, especially among the student parties, were either arrested or went 'underground'. When the NLD sought to nominate Suu Kyi as an election candidate, the committee responsible for certifying candidates upheld a challenge by an opposition candidate on the grounds of her marriage to a British citizen. In March 1990 reports began to circulate abroad that the armed forces were forcibly moving people out of certain areas in Yangon, Mandalay and elsewhere to distant new living quarters. Since most of the people moved were believed to be supporters of the NLD, this was seen as an effort by the army to weaken support for the opposition in the cities.

The 1990 Election and its Aftermath

Despite SLORC efforts to weaken opposition leaders and eliminate dissidents, 93 parties presented a total of 2,297 candidates to contest the 492 constituencies. In every constituency there were at least two candidates. Prior to the election, it was widely believed that the armed forces favoured certain parties, particularly the NUP but also Aung Gyi's UNDP. No single party was expected to win a clear majority. Two days before the election, the SLORC unexpectedly issued visas to 61 foreign journalists to report on proceedings. The voting, which took place on 27 May 1990, was orderly, quiet and free. The NLD won an overwhelming victory, taking 392 of the 485 seats that were, in the event, contested, while the NUP won only 10. The remaining seats were allocated to 23 other parties. Parties representing ethnic groups achieved considerable success: the Shan Nationalities League for Democracy (SNLD) won 23 seats, and the Arakan (Rakhine) League for Democracy 11. Following the election, nearly all the parties representing non-Bamar nationalities formed a coalition known as the United Nationalities League for Democracy (UNLD), including 65 elected representatives. The total representation in the assembly of anti-SLORC forces—the NLD, the UNLD, the Party for National Democracy (PND, led by Dr Sein Win, a cousin of Aung San Suu Kyi, which had secured three seats) plus one other elected deputy—was thus 461 of 485 seats, or some 95%.

Following the NLD's electoral victory, its leaders demanded immediate talks with the SLORC, and movement towards popular rule. However, the SLORC announced that the election was intended only to produce a constituent assembly, which was to draft a constitution under the direction of a national convention to be established by the SLORC. In July 1990 the SLORC issued Order 1/90, which stated: that the SLORC had international legitimacy because it was recognized by the UN and individual countries; that it was incumbent on the SLORC to prevent the disintegration of the Union and of national solidarity and to ensure the perpetuity of state sovereignty; and that the SLORC would continue as the de facto Government until a new constitution was accepted by all the races of Myanmar. The elected membership of the NLD responded (independently of their leadership) with the 'Gandhi Hall Declaration'. This proclaimed that the NLD was ready to hold discussions with the SLORC and to convene the national assembly, according to the electoral law; that the national assembly was the highest authority in the State and not simply a constituent assembly; that the NLD had drafted a provisional Constitution by which it could govern and that this provisional Constitution would bring about the transfer of power in accordance with the law, pending the drafting of a new constitution; finally, it demanded the immediate restoration of democratic rights.

In August 1990, at an anti-Government protest in Mandalay commemorating the deaths of thousands of demonstrators in 1988, troops killed four protesters. This led to a decision by various Buddhist orders to withhold their services from members of the military. With the support of other parties, the NLD announced plans to convene a national assembly in September. In early September, however, the SLORC arrested six members of the NLD, including its acting leader, Kyi Maung, and its acting General Secretary, Chit Hlaing, on charges of passing state secrets to unauthorized persons. Both were tried in special tribunals and given 10-year prison sentences. Also in September, NLD representatives discussed plans to declare a provisional government in Mandalay, without the support of the party's central executive committee. Influential monks agreed to support the declaration. However, the plan was abandoned after government troops surrounded the monasteries; the SLORC subsequently banned all but nine Buddhist sects and empowered military commanders to impose death sentences on rebellious monks. More than 50 senior members of the NLD were arrested, and members of all political parties were required to endorse Order 1/90. In acquiescing, the NLD effectively nullified its demand for an immediate transfer of power.

Leaders of other parties were also arrested, disappeared or went into hiding to avoid arrest. Reports of political prisoners being tortured and dying while in detention circulated widely. As a result of the steady repression and threats to the elected members of the national assembly, many of those in the NLD not under arrest assembled secretly in Mandalay in November 1990 and agreed to send some of their members to the border to create a provisional government. In early December eight opposition politicians arrived at Manerplaw, the Kayin (Karen) headquarters, and entered into discussions with the Democratic Alliance of Burma (DAB—a 21-member organization uniting ethnic rebel forces with student dissidents and monks). They subsequently agreed to form the National Coalition Government of the Union of Burma (NCGUB). The aims of the NCGUB were: to wage war against the military rulers; to convene a national conference of all elected leaders, representatives of the DAB, democratic forces and other notable individuals; to draft a new federal constitution; and to form a true democratic government. On 18 December the NCGUB was constituted with Sein Win, the leader of the PND, as its President. The remainder of his cabinet consisted of six elected

NLD representatives and one independent. Other elected members of the national assembly made their way to Manerplaw and gave their support to this rival government. The SLORC quickly denounced the NCGUB and compelled the NLD to do likewise.

Members of the NCGUB agreed to form a Supreme Council of Burma Democratic Forces, known as the Burma Front, in partnership with the minority party leaders. It was to be the policy-making body during the interim period. It consisted of six Bamars and five minority members under the leadership of Gen. Bo Mya, then leader of the Karen (Kayin) National Union (KNU). Although the NCGUB did not receive any official recognition by foreign states, it received funds from non-governmental organizations (NGOs) in Canada, Switzerland and Norway.

In April 1991, following intense pressure from the army, the NLD central executive committee was restructured. Aung San Suu Kyi and Tin Oo, both still under house arrest, were deprived of their former posts of General Secretary and Chairman. Suu Kyi was replaced by U Lwin, a little-known political figure, and Tin Oo by the former acting Chairman, Aung Shwe. In the same month Lt-Gen. (later Gen., then Senior Gen., then Field Marshal) Than Shwe, the Vice-Chairman of the SLORC and the Deputy Commander-in-Chief of the Armed Forces, officially ruled out a transfer of power to those elected in May 1990, condemning the political parties that had taken part in the elections as subversive. In May 1991 34 opposition politicians (25 of them elected representatives) were sentenced to prison terms of up to 25 years, for alleged treason and attempting to establish an alternative government. At the end of May a military tribunal extended the sentences of Kyi Maung and Chit Hlaing to 20 years' imprisonment.

In October 1991 Aung San Suu Kyi was awarded the Nobel Peace Prize. The award ceremony, which took place in Oslo, Norway, in December, was attended by the leader of the NCGUB, Sein Win. In Myanmar students staged demonstrations to coincide with the ceremony; the students were dispersed, and universities and colleges, which had reopened in May, were closed. The now-compliant NLD leadership expelled Suu Kyi from the party.

In April 1992 the SLORC announced the resignation of its Chairman, Saw Maung, on the grounds of ill health (Saw Maung died in July 1997), and his replacement by Than Shwe. Than Shwe was named as Prime Minister, although Maj.-Gen. (later Lt-Gen.) Khin Nyunt, the First Secretary of the SLORC and the head of the intelligence service, was still widely regarded as the most powerful member of the SLORC, owing to Ne Win's patronage. The SLORC permitted Aung San Suu Kyi to receive visits from her husband and sons, and announced that political prisoners who were no longer a threat to the regime would be released; by September more than 500 political prisoners had been released, including U Nu and numerous NLD representatives, although it was estimated that a further 1,600 remained in detention. Meanwhile, in May the SLORC announced that it would convene a co-ordinating meeting for a national convention (the first meeting between representatives of political parties, ethnic groups and members of the SLORC) to develop the principles for a new constitution and to determine who would participate in drawing up the future basic law. In June the co-ordinating meeting convened with 43 delegates, comprising 15 representatives from the SLORC, 15 from the NLD, six from the SNLD, three from the NUP, four from separate ethnic minority parties and one independent.

In August 1992 universities and colleges were reopened, and in September the night curfew, imposed four years previously, was repealed. In the same month a reorganization of the Cabinet included the appointment of two Deputy Prime Ministers and the promotion to ministerial posts of six regional commanders of the armed forces who were known to oppose Khin Nyunt. These appointments, which ended the first overt power struggle under the SLORC, strengthened Khin Nyunt's position by effectively depriving the commanders of their regional power. Following the government reorganization, the SLORC revoked two martial law decrees, which had been in force for three years, although the ban on gatherings of more than five people remained in place.

The National Convention

In January 1993 the National Convention finally assembled. From the outset the Convention was under the firm control of the SLORC: of the initial 702 delegates, only 93 were NLD members (elected as legislators in 1990), while some 80% of all delegates were appointed by the SLORC. The first session was swiftly adjourned, owing to the objections of the opposition members to the SLORC's demand that the armed forces be allocated a leading role in government under the new Constitution. When the National Convention reconvened at the beginning of February, the NLD issued a statement opposing military dominance and proposing a national referendum on whether it should be incorporated in the new Constitution. The Convention was again adjourned. The SLORC reacted to opposition intransigence by suspending its conciliatory gestures; many arrests were reported during January and February. Following several meetings and adjournments of the Convention between March and September, the Chairman of the National Convention's Convening Committee, Aung Toe (the Chief Justice), subsequently announced (seemingly without grounds) that consensus existed in favour of the SLORC's demands, which included: the representation, in both the lower and upper chambers of a proposed parliament, of military personnel (to be appointed by the Commander-in-Chief of the Defence Services); the independent self-administration of the armed forces; and the right of the Commander-in-Chief to exercise state power in an emergency (effectively granting legitimate status to a future coup).

In September 1993 an alternative mass movement to the NUP (which had lost credibility through its election defeat) was formed to establish a civilian front through which the armed forces could exercise control. The Union Solidarity and Development Association (USDA), the aims of which were indistinguishable from those of the SLORC, was not officially registered as a political party, thus enabling civil servants to join the organization, with the incentive of considerable privileges.

In February 1994 a delegation led by a member of the US Congress was granted permission to visit Aung San Suu Kyi (the first time that she had received visitors, other than family members, during the period of her detention). Suu Kyi sent an encouraging message to the democracy movement and appealed for a meeting with the SLORC, expressing her willingness to negotiate on all issues except her exile. On the following day the SLORC announced that Suu Kyi would be detained until at least 1995 (despite the legal maximum of five years under house arrest, whereby Suu Kyi would be released in July 1994), since her first year in detention had only been an 'arrest period'.

Meanwhile, the National Convention's discussions on the draft Constitution resumed in January 1994, and adjourned in April, having determined three significant chapters of the future Constitution. Myanmar was to be renamed the Republic of the Union of Myanmar (Pyidaungsu Thammada Myanmar Naingngandaw). The Republic's territorial organization was to preserve the existing seven *taing* or divisions in central and southern Myanmar (Yangon, Bago, Ayeyarwady, Tanintharyi, Magway, Sagaing and Mandalay), inhabited mainly by Bamars, and seven *pyinay* or states, associated with minority ethnic groups (Rakhine, Chin, Kachin, Shan, Kayinni, Kayin and Mon). The Republic would be headed by an executive President, elected by the legislature for five years; a number of conditions, including one disqualifying any candidate with a foreign spouse or children, were clearly designed to prevent Aung San Suu Kyi from entering any future presidential election (her husband and children were British citizens).

The Convention, which reconvened in early September 1994, again stressed that the central role of the military (as 'permanent representatives of the people') be enshrined in the new Constitution. Proposals by six smaller ethnic minority groups—Naga, Wa, Pa-O, Danu, Kokang and Palaung—for their own self-administered 'national zones' were considered favourably, although comparable demands by several other minority groups were rejected. The establishment of the six 'national zones' was agreed in April 1995, by which time agreement had also been reached on the most important chapters of the Constitution, covering the legislature, judiciary and government, at Union, state and regional level. It was determined that legislative power was to be shared between a bicameral Pyidaungsu Hluttaw (Union Assembly or National Parliament) and regional and state hluttaws, all of which were to include representatives of the military. The Pyidaungsu Hluttaw was to comprise the Pyithu Hluttaw (People's Assembly or House of Representives—the lower chamber) and the Amyotha Hluttaw (National Assembly or House of Nationalities). The former would comprise 330 elected deputies and 110 members of the Tatmadaw (armed forces) and would be elected for five years. The latter would comprise 224 members: 12 elected from each of the 14 divisions and states, as well as 56 members of the Tatmadaw.

In November 1995 the National Convention reconvened. Under instructions from their party, all 86 NLD delegates boycotted this session and were expelled after two days, leaving only a few small elected parties, mainly representing minorities, among the 545 delegates present. The proportion of delegates representing elected parties had declined from over 20% at the start of the Convention to less than 10%; the rest were various categories of SLORC appointees. The Convention was described in *The Nation*, a major Thai newspaper, as 'the world's slowest-operating rubber-stamp body', but in fact it ceased to operate at all after going into recess in 1996, although official statements commonly implied that it would eventually reassemble. It was finally reconvened in May 2004 (see below).

The Opening of Dialogue with Aung San Suu Kyi

In July 1994 Khin Nyunt announced what appeared to be a major change of policy: that the SLORC was prepared to hold talks with Aung San Suu Kyi. In the same month the Minister of Foreign Affairs, Ohn Gyaw, attending a meeting of the Association of Southeast Asian Nations (ASEAN) in Bangkok, Thailand, stated that his Government would accept the invitation of the UN Secretary-General, Dr Boutros Boutros-Ghali, to discuss issues of democratization, national reconciliation and human rights in Myanmar. Following mediation by a senior Buddhist monk between Suu Kyi and leading members of the SLORC, in September Suu Kyi was permitted to leave her house for the first time during her five-year detention to meet Than Shwe and Khin Nyunt. In October Suu Kyi was invited to a second meeting with senior members of the SLORC, and in November she was permitted to meet Tin Oo and Kyi Maung, who were still imprisoned. In February 1995 the fourth round of talks was held in Yangon between leading members of the SLORC and UN Assistant Secretary-General Alvaro de Soto on the range of issues agreed in mid-1994. However, de Soto was prevented from visiting Suu Kyi. Nevertheless, in March 1995 the Government released 31 political prisoners, including Tin Oo and Kyi Maung.

In July 1995, after almost six years under house arrest, Aung San Suu Kyi was unexpectedly released. Some observers suggested that the SLORC had finally yielded to international pressure, while others indicated that the regime could afford to release Suu Kyi at a time when it considered its position stronger than before (largely owing to the defeat or surrender of virtually all the ethnic insurgent groups, see below). Despite the continuing official ban on gatherings of more than five persons, crowds of up to 1,000 supporters of Suu Kyi assembled daily outside her house in Yangon; they were not dispersed by the police.

In public statements and extensive interviews with the foreign media, Aung San Suu Kyi emphasized that her release was only the initial stage of a very long process and that pressure for democratic reforms should be maintained. She appealed to the SLORC for the release of all political prisoners, the gradual easing of martial law restrictions, the recognition of the 1990 election result, and the holding of talks on national reconciliation. In August 1995 de Soto revisited Myanmar, and urged the military leaders to initiate dialogue with Suu Kyi. In the following month Dr Madeleine Albright, then US Permanent Representative to the UN, visited Yangon (the most senior US official to do so since 1988). During talks with leading members of the SLORC, she stated that any change in US policy towards Myanmar would depend on fundamental changes in the regime's treatment of Myanmar's people; Dr Albright also met Suu Kyi. In October the authorities decreed illegal the NLD's reinstatement of Suu Kyi as its General Secretary (with Aung Shwe re-elected as Chairman, and Tin Oo and Kyi Maung as Vice-Chairmen).

In November 1995 23 retired political and military leaders, including Bohmu Aung (one of the 'Thirty Comrades' of 1942, together with Gen. Aung San and Gen. Ne Win), issued an open letter urging dialogue between the SLORC and the NLD. They were severely reprimanded and threatened by the SLORC. Later in that month the remaining NLD delegates boycotted the National Convention and were expelled. The SLORC continued to harass the NLD and arrest its members and supporters throughout 1996, and Aung San Suu Kyi's activities were progressively restricted. In September the military blocked off the area around Suu Kyi's house in University Avenue, rendering impossible the delivery of her regular weekend speeches from her garden. In November the car in which Suu Kyi was travelling was attacked by a 200-strong mob and severely damaged. Meanwhile, in August Win Htein, Suu Kyi's personal assistant, was arrested and sentenced to seven years' imprisonment (subsequently doubled) for allegedly conspiring with groups in India to destabilize the country. Many foreigners, especially journalists, politicians and any groups communicating with the NLD before arrival in the country, or with intentions to meet with Suu Kyi during their visit, found their visas refused or revoked, their aircraft inexplicably delayed and their other scheduled meetings cancelled, while most local people were unable even to approach her house.

In May 1996 the NLD held its first party congress. Prior to its opening, 262 delegates, including 238 of those elected in 1990, were arrested and held until the congress was over; up to 20 remained political prisoners in July. However, the congress proceeded with the attendance of hundreds of NLD members, as well as foreign diplomats and journalists; the main outcome of the congress was the adoption of a resolution to draft an alternative constitution. In June the SLORC intensified pressure on the NLD by issuing an order authorizing the Ministry of Home Affairs to ban any organization holding unlawful gatherings or obstructing the drafting of a new constitution by the National Convention; it was announced that members of a proscribed party could be sentenced to between five and 20 years' imprisonment.

Harassment, detention, arrests, imprisonment and deaths in prison of the middle and lower-level NLD leadership continued in 1997, while government propaganda vilifying the party became more frequent. In July SLORC First Secretary Khin Nyunt held a meeting with the NLD Chairman, Aung Shwe. A further meeting with the SLORC leadership scheduled to take place in September was cancelled by the NLD because the military junta refused to allow Aung San Suu Kyi to participate. The SLORC media continued to assert that the NLD (to which they referred as the 'notorious league for demons') was funded from overseas, although this appeared not to be the case.

THE SPDC

Following the circulation during 1997 of rumours anticipating changes in the membership of the SLORC, on 15 November the leadership unexpectedly announced the dissolution of the SLORC and its immediate replacement by a new State Peace and Development Council (SPDC). The four most senior members of the SLORC retained their positions at the head of the new council: Gen. Than Shwe, despite his deteriorating health, was appointed Chairman of the SPDC (and also remained Prime Minister and Minister of Defence); the Commander-in-Chief of the Army, Gen. Maung Aye, was nominated Vice-Chairman; Lt-Gen. Khin Nyunt, head of military intelligence, was appointed First Secretary and Lt-Gen. Tin Oo Second Secretary (as distinct from the former NLD Chairman, also called Tin Oo). Lt-Gen. Win Myint, the Adjutant-General, was appointed Third Secretary. Unlike the SLORC, the 19-member SPDC was composed entirely of serving military commanders from central and regional levels. Moreover, only the SPDC Chairman, Gen. Than Shwe, concurrently held posts in the Cabinet, of which about half the members were new appointments, many of them younger civilians from the USDA. The formation of the SPDC therefore appeared to be part of the military's slowly developing strategy to outflank the NLD by creating 'safe' political institutions. The USDA in particular expanded rapidly under the sponsorship and funding of the Ministry of Education; its Secretary-General was the Minister of Education, Than Aung, while Than Shwe was its chief patron. By late 1996 the USDA claimed 5m. members (more than 10% of the population), with a further 1m. in affiliated youth organizations. (By mid-2002 the organization claimed 16m. members.) Identified as a protégé of the ageing Gen. Ne Win, Lt-Gen. Khin Nyunt appeared to be the influential force behind the work of a committee responsible to the National Convention, which, in the late 1990s, was said by the Government to be close to completing the draft of a new constitution; in September 1998 he created a Political Affairs Committee, including both civilian and military figures, to oversee this process. A cabinet reorganization effected in November 1998 indirectly further strengthened the position of Khin Nyunt: Ohn Gyaw was replaced as Minister of Foreign Affairs by Win Aung, hitherto the Myanma ambassador to the United Kingdom and reportedly a close ally of Khin Nyunt.

With the gradual stalling of its 1990 democratic mandate, the NLD held a congress in May 1998 and subsequently issued an ultimatum to the SPDC to convene the Pyithu Hluttaw, in accordance with the results of the 1990 election, by 21 August 1998, announcing that it would convene the Assembly itself if the SPDC failed to comply. However, the SPDC rejected the demand and began a series of arrests of NLD deputies and members. By November about 850 deputies and members were reported to be in detention; about half of these were released after they agreed not to take part in an NLD-convened Assembly, but some 270 were given prison sentences. By mid-1999 at least three NLD deputies, including NLD founder member Tin Shwe, had died in prison since 1990. The Government claimed that only 129 of the original 392 NLD parliamentarians still held an electoral mandate; the remainder were reported variously to have died, resigned, left the party or been disqualified. Furthermore, the regime allegedly began a systematic campaign of coercion and intimidation in an attempt to secure the involuntary resignation of vast numbers of NLD members and the closure of a number of regional party headquarters; by the end of 1998 some 40,000 members were reported to have left the party. The junta also began to co-ordinate demands for the party to be declared illegal, thus exposing its members to the risk of imprisonment. Rather than convening the Pyithu Hluttaw under such circumstances, in September 1998 the NLD instead created a Committee Representing the People's Parliament (CRPP) to issue statements on behalf of the Pyithu Hluttaw and to develop policy.

Meanwhile, speculation continued on the subject of whether there were elements within the regime that might be interested in opening a dialogue with the NLD. The SPDC Vice-Chairman, Gen. Maung Aye, was said to be the most vehement opponent of dialogue. It was reported in September that 15 senior military officers had been arrested for seeking contact with Aung San Suu Kyi. In late 1998 the UN reportedly raised the possibility of providing US $1,000m. in aid and assistance to Myanmar if the Government would release political prisoners and begin a dialogue with the NLD, which in turn was to be requested to abandon its demand that the Pyithu Hluttaw convene on the basis of the results of the 1990 election. However, both the SPDC and the NLD angrily rejected the suggestion of any possible compromise. The establishment of genuine dialogue was rendered unlikely by the SPDC's continuation of the SLORC's campaign of attrition against Suu Kyi. In mid-1998 the regime repeatedly used road-blocks to prevent her from attending NLD meetings, and in early 1999 Suu Kyi's British husband, Dr Michael Aris, who had been diagnosed with terminal cancer, was refused permission to enter Myanmar to see Suu Kyi for the last time; he died in March. (Although the junta had encouraged Suu Kyi to visit Aris in the United Kingdom, she declined to do so for fear that she would not be permitted to return to Myanmar.)

In many other respects also, the regime seemed far from conciliatory. After student riots against the Government in December 1996, universities and some high schools were closed indefinitely. Further large-scale anti-Government demonstrations were staged by students in September 1998. In January 1999 four medical schools were reopened, but other areas of the higher education sector remained closed, and plans were announced to transfer several campuses to remote regions before they would be permitted to open again. In July 2000 the ruling junta reportedly allowed some 60,000 university students to resume their education; all returning students were reportedly required to sign an oath, pledging not to engage in political activity. However, it was estimated that many thousands more students remained excluded from education. In August 2001 the Government announced plans for a major expansion in distance education, apparently intended to develop the human capital needed for Myanmar's economic development, while avoiding the political risks associated with campus-based education. In the late 1990s reports emerged of deliberate harassment of religious minorities by government forces, and of the destruction by soldiers, local government officials, and even Buddhist monks, of mosques and churches in order to make way for Buddhist temples. In urban areas, the cemeteries of non-Buddhists were reportedly targeted for redevelopment, and relatives were told to move remains of the deceased at short notice and at their own expense. In 2001 communal riots by opposing groups of Buddhists and Muslims were reported in Taungoo, north of Yangon, and in Rakhine.

Meanwhile, the Tatmadaw increased in size from 175,000 to 400,000 in 1999, according to one estimate (with perhaps an additional 100,000 in the police force and militia groups). The age of recruitment, officially 17, was reportedly lowered in order to increase numbers. The army used local forced labour extensively for portering and logistical support work. In addition, army units were placed in charge of development projects, such as the building of roads, railways and dams, which again relied mainly on forced labour and the labour of prisoners. In principle, non-prison labour was remunerated, but often much of the payment was retained by the military officer in charge.

In April 1999 the UN adopted a unanimous resolution deploring the escalation in the persecution of the democratic opposition. Nevertheless, the harassment and intimidation of NLD members continued throughout 1999 and early 2000, with the resignations from the party of nearly 300 members reported in July 1999; further resignations were reported in November and January 2000, and in December 1999 it was reported that an elected representative of the People's Assembly, Maung Maung Myint, had been forced to resign by the ruling SPDC. The NLD's failure to make any progress against the regime led to increasing tensions within the opposition itself and even, among some elements of the party, to growing dissatisfaction with the uncompromising policy of Aung San Suu Kyi. In April 1999 three senior NLD members wrote to the party Chairman, Aung Shwe, and to Khin Nyunt, urging both the NLD and the Government to be more conciliatory; however, Suu Kyi publicly rejected their suggestion, and the three were suspended from party membership. In August a series of protests was staged by supporters of the democratic opposition to mark the anniversary of the massacre of thousands of demonstrators in 1988 (see above). Local and overseas opposition groups attempted to force a confrontation with the Government on 9 September 1999 (9-9-99), designated an auspicious date by analogy with 8-8-88; however, government forces were well prepared for the protests, and there were no more than small disturbances in several centres. In October 1999 Myanmar's Supreme Court issued a decision rejecting a claim by the NLD that its activities had been 'continuously disrupted, prevented and destroyed' and that hundreds of its members had been illegally detained.

In February 2000 senior Buddhist monks urged the renewal of dialogue between the regime and the opposition, evidently irritating the Government and Aung San Suu Kyi to equal degrees. In late August the regime engaged in a stand-off with Suu Kyi when she attempted to travel from her home in Yangon to conduct party business at other centres. After nine days, troops eventually forcibly removed Suu Kyi from an informal camp she had established at a road-block and returned her to her home. Subsequently, the ruling junta continued to restrict the movements of Suu Kyi and a number of other NLD leaders, holding them under effective house arrest at Suu Kyi's Yangon home and denying diplomatic access to Suu Kyi. Although the restrictions were removed in mid-September, later the same month Suu Kyi was prevented from leaving Yangon by train. Tin Oo and eight other NLD workers, who were planning to accompany Suu Kyi, were detained in a 'government guest house', while Suu Kyi herself was again placed under house arrest. Also in September, the NLD-dominated CRPP announced that it would proceed with developing its own constitution for the country. On the other hand, in October Gen. Khin Nyunt held talks with Suu Kyi, although no results from the discussions were announced. The regime released from detention 85 NLD members, including Tin Oo, in January 2001 and released another NLD leader, Maung Wuntha, in June. Both sides became noticeably more restrained in their comments about the other, and talks continued throughout 2001, mediated by the special envoy of the UN Secretary-General, Malaysian diplomat Tan Sri Razali Ismail. By the end of 2001 some 174 NLD detainees had been released and the party had been permitted to reopen some offices in Yangon.

A minor reorganization of the Cabinet in October 1999 was followed by the forced resignation or dismissal of a number of senior government and military officials between late 1999 and 2001, including former Commander-in-Chief of the Navy and SPDC member Vice-Adm. Nyunt Thein. There was much speculation over the implications of these changes for the political fortunes of the rival factions headed by Gen. Maung Aye—widely perceived as uncompromising in the context of his dealings with the NLD—and Lt-Gen. Khin Nyunt. In August 2002 Maung Aye was promoted to the military rank of deputy senior general, while Khin Nyunt became a full general.

In February 2001 the death in a helicopter crash of SPDC Second Secretary and Army Chief of Staff Lt-Gen. Tin Oo led to speculation as to whether the crash was an accident or an assassination. Also ambiguous was the arrest in March 2002 of the son-in-law and three grandsons of Ne Win, on charges of plotting a coup. The heads of the air force and the national police were both dismissed shortly before the arrests took place. Since there was little evidence of any coup-planning, speculation focused on whether the detentions were related to Ne Win's hostility to any rapprochement with Aung San Suu Kyi, or whether they were prompted by his family's reputed involvement in a criminal gang. There was some suggestion that their real target was Ne Win's unpopular daughter, Sandar Win. In September those arrested were convicted on charges of treason and sentenced to death. Ne Win himself died in December 2002 and was cremated in a private ceremony. In November 2001 10 of the 12 regional commanders had been recalled to Yangon to assume senior positions in the central Government, but only two appeared to have accepted this removal from regional power—the SPDC devolved much administrative and economic decision-making to regional commanders, who were therefore able to develop strong regional economic interests and to build powerful local political bases.

On 6 May 2002 Aung San Suu Kyi was, at last, released unconditionally from detention. Suu Kyi was obliged to inform the authorities about her travel plans but otherwise appeared free to move about the country. A steady stream of 283 NLD prisoners was also released over the following months. However, this process of relative liberalization ended abruptly on 30 May 2003, when Suu Kyi was again placed in detention following a clash between government and NLD supporters. The authorities claimed that she was being held in protective custody for her own safety, and she was not permitted visitors, apart from a brief meeting with Razali in June. NLD offices around the country, which had begun to proliferate, were also closed down.

In August 2003 a cabinet reorganization took place, in which Khin Nyunt became Prime Minister, replacing Than Shwe. Observers were divided over whether this appointment strengthened Khin Nyunt's position as, although his formal powers increased, the appointment removed him from direct military command, which had been an important source of his power. However, he was believed to have retained his position as head of military intelligence. Under Khin Nyunt, the Directorate of Defence Services Intelligence had expanded from being an agency responsible for the collection of intelligence relevant to military operations to become an organization that both devised policy on difficult political issues and closely monitored the activities of military commanders. As such, it gave Khin Nyunt great power, but this drew deep resentment from regional military commanders. Than Shwe remained Chairman of the SPDC and Commander-in-Chief of the Defence Services, as well as Minister of Defence, while also taking on the functions of state President. Maung Aye became responsible for vice-presidential duties. Khin Nyunt was succeeded as First Secretary of the SPDC by Lt-Gen. Soe Win, former Second Secretary. Soe Win was generally believed to be uncompromising in dealings with the NLD. Five other ministers were also replaced during the reorganization. Following his appointment, the new Prime Minister outlined a 'road map', which he promised would lead to a new constitution and to 'free and fair' elections as part of a 'disciplined' democratic system. However, absent from the 'road map' was any gesture towards reconciliation with the NLD.

In September 2003 the regime released Aung San Suu Kyi from detention and confined her under house arrest after she had undergone major surgery, but there was no relaxation of restrictions on the NLD, notwithstanding the release of five members of the NLD's central committee in November 2003 and of a further 29 NLD members in January 2004. The NLD Chairman, Aung Shwe, and the party Secretary, U Lwin, remained under house arrest, while NLD Vice-Chairman Tin Oo was held in prison, before being released into house arrest in February 2004. In December 2003 nine people, including the editor of a sports magazine, were arrested on charges of plotting to assassinate members of the SPDC in a series of bomb attacks.

In early 2004 the Government permitted UN Special Envoy Razali to visit Myanmar to meet both Khin Nyunt and Aung San Suu Kyi, and there was growing optimism that the 'road map' might indeed lead to significant reform. On 17 May the SPDC reconvened the National Convention under the leadership of a senior official of the regime, the SPDC Second Secretary, Lt-Gen. Thein Sein. More than 1,000 delegates were present, but the NLD, which had been allocated only 50 places, refused to participate without the release from house arrest of Suu Kyi and Tin Oo. (It was reported that Khin Nyunt had favoured allowing Suu Kyi to attend the Convention, but that he had been overruled by Than Shwe.) The authorities made it clear that the Convention would proceed from the point at which it had been suspended in 1996, meaning that controversial constitutional provisions, notably the reservation of 25% of parliamentary seats for the military, would not be discussed further. Freedom of debate was also restricted by several rules, including provisions that delegates were not to challenge the role of the SPDC, make 'anti-national' statements, criticize the Convention itself, or stage any form of protest against its proceedings, or discuss proceedings with outsiders.

In September 2004 a minor cabinet reorganization took place, in which the Minister of Foreign Affairs, Win Aung, was replaced by Maj.-Gen. Nyan Win. In October Prime Minister Khin Nyunt left office. The authorities initially reported that he was retiring for health reasons but subsequently revealed that he had been dismissed owing to allegations of corruption against him. It was further stated that Khin Nyunt had disobeyed Field Marshal Than Shwe, and that he had sought to 'break up' the Tatmadaw. This last accusation probably reflected the growing political, professional and economic rivalry between Khin Nyunt's intelligence service and the regular army, including competition over lucrative smuggling routes into and out of the country. In the following months the authorities largely dismantled the intelligence service, beginning with the National Intelligence Bureau, formerly chaired by Khin Nyunt, which had collected and co-ordinated intelligence from several different organizations. A new, less powerful military intelligence body, the Office of Military Affairs Security (OMAS), was created under the Yangon region military commander, Maj.-Gen. Myint Swe. Primary responsibility for intelligence was returned to the 12 regional military commanders. However, the new Prime Minister, Soe Win, and the new SPDC First Secretary, Thein Sein, reaffirmed the Government's commitment to the 'road map' that Khin Nyunt had been instrumental in drafting and promised to uphold the cease-fires with ethnic rebels. By way of demonstration, in late November the Government released nearly 10,000 prisoners, including some well-known dissidents, although Aung San Suu Kyi was not among them. A further 239, mainly former political prisoners, were released in June 2005.

A number of small-scale bomb attacks took place in cities, including Yangon, from late 2004; one of these attacks killed 11 people. In some cases, responsibility was claimed by a small militant group, the Vigorous Burmese Student Warriors (VBSW). In April 2005 a bomb explosion at a Mandalay market killed two civilians, and in May three bomb attacks during a trade fair in Yangon, at two shopping centres and a convention centre, killed 15 civilians and injured many more. Another bomb exploded outside a hotel in Yangon in October, although there were no reported injuries. Meanwhile, the National Convention resumed in February, but the session lasted only six weeks and there was no public announcement of outcomes. From early 2005 there were rumours of deep, even murderous, hostility between SPDC Vice-Chairman Dep. Senior Gen. Maung Aye and Prime Minister Soe Win, but in public the SPDC continued to present a united front.

In July 2005 Khin Nyunt received a suspended sentence of 44 years' imprisonment from a special tribunal that had been established to try him on corruption charges. His sentence was later commuted to house arrest. Khin Nyunt's two sons and 38 intelligence officers were also found guilty and sentenced to prison terms. The National Convention reconvened in December, without the participation of the NLD, the SNLD or the Shan State Kokang Democratic Party. The UN Special Rapporteur on the situation of human rights in Myanmar, Paulo Sérgio Pinheiro, noted in his report to the General Assembly in August that inclusiveness and the removal of restrictions were required before the National Convention and any subsequent constitution would have international credibility.

In November 2005 foreign diplomats in Yangon were informed by the Ministry of Foreign Affairs that the Government's offices had been transferred to Pyinmana, a remote mountainous region approximately 400 km (nearly 250 miles) north of Yangon. The relocation of government ministries by truck convoys began on 6 November. The Tatmadaw had been developing the site for a number of years, but the generals did not inform their ASEAN neighbours of their intentions to relocate the capital beforehand. The first public announcement was given by the Minister of Information, Brig.-Gen. Kyaw Hsan, on the following day; however, no official reasons were given for the secretive move other than that Pyinmana was centrally located and was therefore easily accessible from all parts of the country. The disabling effect of the 1988 pro-democracy demonstrations upon the Government's administrative institutions was likely to have been a contributory factor in the SPDC's decision to relocate its offices away from the general population. Following the 2004–05 bombings in Mandalay and Yangon, the threat of urban terrorism was perhaps another consideration. A number of large-scale projects in the area were begun several years prior to the relocation, including the construction of a large airstrip, government offices, a national headquarters for ethnic groups, a military hospital, a five-star hotel, a golf course, mansions for senior generals and apartments. The International Labour Organization (ILO) reported the extensive use of forced labour on these projects and the forcible relocation of thousands of villagers. In March 2006 Armed Forces Day celebrations were held at the new site and Field Marshal Than Shwe officially named the new capital Nay Pyi Taw ('Royal City' or 'Place of the Kings'). The move suggested a return to the isolationist tendencies of Burmese rulers, both historically and under modern military rule prior to the establishment of the SLORC.

The SPDC also reassessed its attitude towards NGOs following the removal of Khin Nyunt and his military intelligence apparatus in 2004. In February 2006 the SPDC moved to introduce a new set of strict guidelines for UN agencies, international organizations and local and international NGOs designed to facilitate the near-total control by the SPDC of all international agencies' activities in the country—particularly in politically sensitive border regions. Many NGOs found that they were unable to continue operating as before and cancelled projects. The new restrictions on travel and a refusal to renew licences led to the withdrawal of a number of NGOs, including the French section of Médecins Sans Frontières (MSF), which in March ended its medical programmes in Myanmar, citing the imposition of unacceptable conditions by the authorities on the provision of relief to people living in war-affected areas. The SPDC had imposed travel restrictions on MSF personnel and applied pressure on local health authorities not to co-operate with representatives of the organization. Other NGOs reassessed their prospects in view of the restrictive conditions created by the authorities. The World Health Organization became particularly concerned about an outbreak of avian influenza ('bird flu') in central Myanmar; although the disease seemed to have been contained by the end of 2006, another outbreak was reported in March 2007.

The SPDC announced a series of appointments, including a cabinet reorganization, in May 2006, ostensibly to increase efficiency, but also with the purpose of ensuring institutional continuity by attracting younger military officers (the average age of regional commanders was 50 and that of division commanders 47). Major promotions and appointments within the Tatmadaw were made in 2006, including the Chief of Air Defence and chief of Military Affairs Security, seven regional commanders, one deputy regional commander, and 16 division commanders. This continued the Tatmadaw's practice of rotating regional commanders and others on a regular basis in order to prevent local commanders from becoming too powerful. Included in these appointments was the newly established regional command of Nay Pyi Taw. The SPDC also announced a series of major pay rises for civil servants, with approximately 1m. state employees receiving salary increases funded from domestic fuel revenues. The increases, which ranged from 500% for those at the lowest end of the pay-scale to 1,200% for those in the upper echelons, were designed to appease civil servants, many of whom were disgruntled with the transfer to the new administrative centre. However, this decision, combined with major spending on construction at Nay Pyi Taw and price deregulation, contributed to increasing inflationary pressures. In addition, natural disasters, including flooding, landslides and hurricanes, destroyed crops and damaged transport routes in central and southern Myanmar, and were partly responsible for a rise in basic commodity prices of more than 100%—a situation that exacerbated discontent and undermined the SPDC's domestic legitimacy.

The National Convention was suspended in January 2006 but reconvened in October with some 1,070 delegates in attendance. The Tatmadaw secured its institutional autonomy, with the Convention approving the military's draft provisions and decreeing that the post of Commander-in-Chief of the Defence Services was equivalent to the position of Vice-President, controlling one-quarter of the seats in both houses of a future legislature and having the power to appoint holders of the important portfolios of defence, home affairs, and border matters. The Tatmadaw would also assume authority over all armed forces in the country, including the police and paramilitary organizations.

Mass demonstrations in September 2007 attracted worldwide attention and international condemnation. In contrast to previous protests, technological advances allowed the events to receive widespread media coverage and they were well documented by various international organizations. The demonstrations were prompted by sudden price rises and a growing resentment towards SPDC economic policies. While the cost of Nay Pyi Taw's construction had been enormous, it was but one of many major projects and commitments into which the SPDC continued to channel the country's funds. These included dams, bridges and energy projects, as well as civil servants' salary rises and the large military budget. Government expenditure, therefore, far exceeded revenue (including that earned from natural gas exports), leading to high budget deficits, which the IMF and World Bank warned should be lowered. Since the Government resisted curbing expenditure on its favoured major projects, it focused its attention instead

on raising more taxes and reducing fuel subsidies; the latter reform, having been strongly recommended by the IMF for some time, was implemented when a visit by representatives of the Fund was imminent.

In mid-August 2007 the generals chose not to introduce reductions in subsidies gradually, but instead to do so suddenly across the entire system, raising the price of diesel oil by 100% and that of compressed natural gas by almost 500%. This had an immediate impact on the cost of food, transport and electricity generation, exacerbating mounting discontent with the SPDC's economic policies; there had already been a number of rare small protests in Yangon earlier in the year over the rising cost and availability of basic commodities and electricity. Protests involving some 400–500 people, led by the '88 Generation' students' group (named after the 1988 pro-democracy uprising), began four days after the price increases in Tamwe Township in Yangon. The protesters were attacked by members of the USDA and its Swan Arr Shin ('Masters of Force') militia, and the ringleaders, Min Ko Naing and Ko Ko Gyi, were arrested along with around 100 others, including members of the NLD.

Although some monks in Rakhine State had already joined the protests by late August 2007, on 5 September several hundred student monks at a large monastery in Pakokku decided to march in protest against the sudden price rises. Pakokku, lying along the Ayeyarwady River some 480 km north of Yangon and 130 km south of Mandalay, is a centre of Buddhist learning, with the second largest *sangha* community in the country after Mandalay. USDA and Swan Arr Shin militias beat the monks, around 10 of whom were arrested (some reports claiming that another died in the violence), and soldiers were deployed for the first time to disperse the demonstration. An angry crowd of monks and civilians who gathered at Maha Visutarama monastery on the following day prevented a group of visiting local officials from leaving for more than six hours, burned their vehicles and demanded the release of the detained monks.

News of the assaults on the monks at Pakokku rapidly spread through monasteries across the country, after which a newly formed group, the All Burma Monks' Alliance (ABMA), issued a leaflet giving the SPDC until 17 September 2007 to avert the threat of a religious boycott by meeting four demands: an apology to the monks for the Pakokku violence; an immediate reduction in prices for commodities including fuel, rice, and cooking oil; the release of all political prisoners, including Aung San Suu Kyi and those arrested during the current protests; and the initiation of a dialogue with the 'democratic forces' to resolve the suffering of the people. The SPDC ignored these demands, instead offering *sayadaws* (senior abbots) at Pakokku financial compensation, which was refused. The monks were particularly vexed by the local authorities' use of violent militia to suppress peaceful demonstrations, but these gangs remained present and were later armed by the authorities with machetes. Local Tatmadaw commanders also asked leading citizens to persuade the monks not to participate in the boycott.

On 15 September 2007 the ABMA issued a second leaflet urging monks to impose a *pattta nikkuijana kamma*—a refusal to accept alms—on the military, members of the USDA and Swan Arr Shin, and government workers, beginning on 17 September, and to participate in peaceful marches in Yangon, Mandalay and elsewhere on the following day. Although not all monasteries complied, there was certainly sufficient agreement to initiate the marches, which went ahead on 18 September in towns across the country, the largest involving more than 1,000 monks in Yangon. At some monasteries and pagodas the ABMA's religious boycott decree was recited repeatedly.

Over the following week the authorities mostly exercised restraint, photographing and videotaping the demonstrations in order to co-ordinate their retaliation. Since the authorities had not yet responded to any significant degree, thousands of lay citizens soon joined the protests. Although on certain days plain-clothed men had been assigned to block the entrances to major pagodas, denying the marchers the opportunity to gain additional religious significance, on 22 September 2007 a group of 500 monks was inexplicably permitted to pass through road barriers to meet with Aung San Suu Kyi. As a consequence of this meeting, the number of demonstrators expanded considerably overnight across the country, reaching some 20,000 in Yangon, with the number of participating monks doubling; led by monks carrying overturned alms bowls, the marches were joined by nuns, as well as members of the NLD and student groups. In the following days the protests were attended by an estimated 30,000–50,000 monks and a similar number of civilians, many holding flags and banners representing organizations such as the NLD and the banned All Burma Buddhist Monks Union.

On 24 September 2007 the Minister of Religious Affairs, Brig.-Gen. Thura Myint Maung, accused the NLD, the CPB and foreign broadcasters of instigating the demonstrations. On the following day the state-run *New Light of Myanmar* published Directive 93, signed by the Chairman of the State Sangha Maha Nayaka Committee (the governing body of the *sangha*), which, combined with four earlier Directives (dating from 1984, 1990, 1991 and 1996), prohibited monks from participating in secular affairs and party politics, requested *sayadaws* to instruct their disciples to refrain from joining illegal *sangha* organizations (such as the ABMA), and directed *sayadaws* not to shelter monks who had violated these rules. However, this did not prevent the demonstrators from returning, and the authorities amassed large numbers of soldiers and paramilitaries while reinforcing their warnings. A curfew was imposed and widespread arrests began; monasteries were surrounded and shut down on the eve of the suppression of the protests, thus removing the bulk of the *sangha* from the following day's events.

On 26 September 2007 the SPDC used soldiers, the police, the USDA and the Swan Arr Shin to suppress protests around the country—the violence used by the authorities was well documented. Around the country, rebel monasteries were invaded, desecrated and ransacked; thousands of 'bogus monks' (as described by the authorities) were beaten, interrogated, disrobed and imprisoned; and an unknown number of deaths occurred. The authorities would later announce that 10 people had been killed, including a Japanese journalist whose death was reported world-wide, and some 3,000 people (including around 1,000 monks) had been detained. The UN estimated the number of deaths to be at least 31. The abbot leader of the ABMA, U Gambira, was arrested and charged with treason. Notably, in many cases the authorities refused to issue families with death certificates, as a result of which a large number of those believed to have been killed were classified as 'missing'. The SPDC, meanwhile, resumed its approach of combining incentives with warnings to the *sangha*, publicly offering lavish gifts to loyal *sayadaws* and their monasteries, while continuing the occupation of rebel monasteries into 2008. The authorities rescinded the fuel price rises in October 2007.

Meanwhile, the SPDC had announced the completion of its National Convention on a new constitution in early September 2007, claiming that the protesters were undermining the 'road map' to democracy. The Convention had been convening intermittently for 15 years, with representatives being carefully selected from the ethnic minority groups. The NLD had boycotted, and was later expelled from, the National Convention in 1995 (many of its members remained incarcerated), and in 1996 the SLORC had issued Order 5/96 silencing any criticism of the Convention and the constitution being drafted after the NLD threatened to produce its own version. In October 2007 the SPDC held a ceremony attended by 60,000 people to support the National Convention in Hpa-an, Kayin State. Later that month Thein Sein was formally appointed as Prime Minister, following the death of Soe Win, and was replaced as First Secretary of the SPDC by Lt-Gen. Thiha Thura Tin Aung Myint Oo.

In February 2008 the SPDC announced that it would hold a referendum on the draft Constitution in May, and schedule a general election for 2010. While the SPDC may have hoped to defuse the unrest of 2007 with this pronouncement, the fulfilment of its referendum promise provoked widespread international condemnation, not only because it was viewed as a contrived entrenchment of future military rule, but also because it drew attention and much-needed resources away from dealing with the devastation caused by Cyclone Nargis.

On 2–3 May 2008 this powerful cyclone struck southern Myanmar, causing widespread damage to property and crops, particularly in the Ayeyarwady delta, and leaving more than 138,000 people dead or missing and more than 2m. others affected. The SPDC declared an emergency in five administrative regions—Yangon, Ayeyarwady and Bago Divisions, and Kayin and Mon States.

Despite the destruction caused by Nargis, the authorities proceeded with their scheduled constitutional referendum on 10 May 2008, with only a two-week postponement in the areas most directly affected by the cyclone. Troops were recalled from the Ayeyarwady delta to help oversee the running of the referendum. According to official results (excluding those regions where voting had been postponed), the new Constitution, a 235-page document containing 15 chapters of detailed provisions, was endorsed by a remarkable 92.5% of voters. Reports later revealed that some ballots had already been marked and that at some locations people had been required to record their identity on their ballot papers. The new Constitution secured one-quarter of the seats in the national and regional legislatures for the military, and provided for the retention by the Tatmadaw of control over the portfolios of defence and of home affairs; responsibility for appointing the Chairman and Vice-Chairman rested with the Commander-in-Chief of the defence forces, and all members of the military junta were granted immunity from criminal prosecution; and the Commander-in-Chief of the defence forces was given the power to declare a state of emergency during which he would assume all executive, legislative and judicial powers. The NLD declared that it would consider participating in the legislative election scheduled to be held before the end of 2010, provided that its demands were met. These demands included the release of Aung San Suu Kyi and all other political prisoners, the amendment of the Constitution and the monitoring of the election by international observers. However, the NLD stated that it would not commit itself to taking part until the election rules were available (see below).

In late May 2008 Aung San Suu Kyi's detention was extended for a further 12 months. In November the former leader of the ABMA, U Gambira, was sentenced to 68 years' imprisonment for his role in leading the 2007 demonstrations. Win Tin, a former journalist and senior NLD member, was released in September 2008, having been incarcerated for 19 years, making him Burma's longest-serving political prisoner. Win Htein, the former aide of Suu Kyi arrested in 1996 (see above) was released in the same month; however, Amnesty International reported that he was rearrested just a few hours after his release. More than 2,000 other political prisoners remained in gaol, including monks and members of the '88 Generation' students group that had been involved in the 2007 demonstrations. More than 80 people were sentenced during the trials in November 2008, with over one-quarter of them receiving a sentence of 65 years' imprisonment. Many of the longest sentences were delivered on people who had been convicted of using electronic devices to disseminate coverage of the 2007 demonstrations over the internet. The SPDC released Sandar Win from house arrest in December 2008, six years after her arrest in 2002 on suspicion of plotting to overthrow the Government.

Meanwhile, the clean-up operation in the aftermath of Cyclone Nargis was lengthy and fraught with obstacles. While the aid presence had increased dramatically, the regime still tried to control the movements of foreign aid workers, and there were numerous reports of local authorities diverting aid supplies. The most effective distributors of aid in the Ayeyarwady delta were Buddhist monks, whose monasteries provided shelter and relief to large numbers of displaced persons as well as children who had been orphaned by the cyclone. Owing to a lack of potable water and the large number of corpses that had not yet been disposed of, fears of an outbreak of disease were rife. Although this was averted thanks to the efforts of locals and foreign aid workers, the region had lost most of its rice crop owing to the storm surge that flooded nearly all the growing area. Given the fact that the Ayeyarwady delta was Myanmar's primary source of rice, there was concern over the impact that the damage to the crop might have on prices and food shortages in urban areas, leading to the possibility of urban unrest.

In May 2009 Aung San Suu Kyi was accused of breaking the terms of her house arrest when a US national, John Yettaw, swam across Inya Lake to her house in Yangon and stayed for two nights before being apprehended by the authorities upon his departure. Since the current period of Suu Kyi's house arrest was due to expire in May (with the 1975 State Protection Law permitting a maximum of five years' renewable arrest), and with elections scheduled for 2010, the uninvited guest provided a timely pretext for the SPDC to extend the opposition leader's incarceration. Suu Kyi was taken to Insein Prison and was charged under 'Safeguarding the State from the Dangers of Subversive Elements' legislation. She underwent a closed trial inside the prison in July. Suu Kyi was convicted in mid-August and sentenced to three years' imprisonment, which was commuted by Field Marshal Than Shwe to 18 months' house arrest. Suu Kyi's appeal against the extension of her detention was subsequently rejected. Yettaw was sentenced to seven years' imprisonment, although his release was negotiated by US Senator Jim Webb, who visited Than Shwe in Nay Pyi Taw several days afterwards (see Foreign Relations, below).

The SPDC continued to reiterate its commitment to the holding of multi-party national, regional and local elections in 2010, and to changes in the ethno-political and military situation in accordance with the new Constitution, which was to take effect following the elections. Leaders of the ethnic political parties and cease-fire groups (see below), already wary of the new Constitution's provision to reserve 25% of the seats in the national and regional legislatures for the military, were also opposed to the 'unitary' rather than 'union' nature of government that would eventuate. In April 2009 the SPDC declared that all ethnic cease-fire groups would have to transform into new 'Border Guard Force' (BGF) battalions of 326 troops, including a component of 30 Tatmadaw soldiers and one Tatmadaw officer among its commanders. Many of the cease-fire groups resisted the order, including the Myanmar National Democratic Alliance Army (MNDAA) based in the Kokang region of Shan State. Tatmadaw troops were sent to the region to suppress resistance there and support a breakaway faction that had co-operated with its BGF order (see Refugees and Other Migrants, below). Most of the ethnic cease-fire groups were gradually coerced into accepting their fate in the BGF, although pockets of resistance remained. Opinion among the cease-fire ethnic groups over the value of the elections due to be held in 2010 was divided, as was their level of willingness to participate. Although some maintained their opposition to the elections, many argued that refusing to participate would result in their silencing at all levels, while others contended that participation, especially at the regional level, should be pursued, but under new party constructs.

The NLD met to discuss the 2010 elections in April 2009, whereupon it reiterated its earlier demands and issued a statement—the so-called Shwegondaing Declaration—in which it announced that it would take part in the elections only if they were free and fair, genuinely inclusive and monitored by international observers, and if all political prisoners were released and constitutional amendments were forthcoming. This declaration was supported by the SNLD, the leaders of which remained in prison, along with hundreds of NLD members. In March 2010 the SPDC issued a long-awaited series of election laws, which provided for the establishment of an electoral commission with wide-ranging powers to 'supervise and guide' the political parties, and imposed regulations relating to the registration of parties and the eligibility of representatives for the national and regional legislatures. The new legislation banned persons serving prison sentences from standing for political office, thereby prohibiting the involvement in the elections of the imprisoned NLD and SNLD members and leaders, including Aung San Suu Kyi, who remained under house arrest. The NLD central executive committee, which would have been forced to remove Suu Kyi as its leader in order to contest the election, voted later in that month to boycott the polls, citing political repression and unjust electoral laws.

Following the deadline of 6 May 2010 42 parties (including 37 new organizations) were reported to have successfully registered to participate in the elections, more than one-half of

which were representing various ethnic groups around the country. Since the NLD adhered to its pledge not to register for the polls, the party was officially dissolved later that month. However, some 25 former NLD members who did wish to participate in the election had registered a new party, the National Democratic Force (NDF), before the 6 May deadline. The NDF declared that it would be willing to co-operate with other democratic parties, but would not contest seats in ethnic areas. The main pro-SPDC parties were the NUP (which had contested the 1990 election) and the newly formed Union Solidarity and Development Party (USDP), founded in April 2010 by Prime Minister Thein Sein and 26 senior Tatmadaw officers and ministers. Also in April about 20 senior members of the ruling junta, including Thein Sein, were reported to have resigned from their military positions, in an action widely interpreted as an attempt to circumvent the restriction, to 25% of the total, of the number of legislative seats that were to be allocated to military representatives in the forthcoming elections. In July the Government sanctioned the dissolution of the USDA and the transfer of all its assets and offices to the USDP, prompting criticism from many parties that viewed USDA assets as being state-owned and thus argued that the junta's decision afforded an unfair advantage to the new party. In the following month the junta finally announced that the elections were to be held on 7 November, one week before the scheduled expiry of the house arrest of Aung San Suu Kyi.

Local and international scepticism concerning the prospects for free and fair elections intensified in September 2010 when the authorities confirmed the formal dissolution of five parties, including the NLD and the SNLD (the two leading parties in the 1990 general election), which were abolished as a result of their failure to register. Another five parties, mainly representing ethnic minority groups, which had gained initial approval to contest the elections, were also dissolved, owing to their alleged non-compliance with regulations governing the registration of candidates. Furthermore, several opposition parties reported significant difficulties in registering their candidates, citing onerous electoral regulations and expensive registration fees. The Union Election Commission cancelled polling in five ethnic minority-dominated constituencies in Kachin, Kayah, Kayin, Mon and Shan states, ostensibly in response to security concerns in these areas. In October 2010 the SPDC announced a revision of the country's official name from the Union of Myanmar to the Republic of the Union of Myanmar, in accordance with the provisions of the 2008 Constitution, and introduced a new national flag and anthem.

'DISCIPLINED DEMOCRACY'

The multi-party elections to both chambers of the Pyidaungsu Hluttaw, and to the seven state and seven regional assemblies, on 7 November 2010 were the first legislative elections to be held in Myanmar in 20 years; the polls represented the fifth of seven stages on the SPDC's 'road map to disciplined democracy'. Although a total of 37 parties were permitted to take part in the elections, many were unable to present candidates in all constituencies owing to the prohibitively high cost of registration, with some candidates reportedly standing unopposed. Prime Minister Thein Sein's USDP was the only party to field candidates for almost all of the available seats, with more than 1,100 candidates at all three levels, while the other main pro-SPDC party, the NUP, was also well represented. In accordance with the new Constitution, one-quarter of all seats at the national, state and regional levels were reserved for military-appointed representatives. Thus, in the Pyithu Hluttaw (the lower chamber) 110 of the 440 seats were reserved for military representatives, and in the Amyotha Hluttaw (the upper chamber) 56 of the 224 seats were to be occupied by military representatives. At all three levels, including the polls for the 14 state and regional assemblies, the USDP won 76.5% of the seats for which it competed. It dominated the incoming Pyithu Hluttaw, securing 259 of the lower chamber's 330 seats determined by direct election. The Shan Nationalities Democratic Party won 18 seats in the Pyithu Hluttaw, while the NUP took 12 and the Rakhine Nationalities Development Party won nine. Across the 14 state and regional assemblies the ethnic parties achieved mixed results, taking one-half of the seats in Arakan and Shan states. According to official data, voter turnout in polling for the two chambers of the Pyidaungsu Hluttaw was 77.02%, although critics claimed that it was much lower. There were also widespread allegations of electoral irregularities, voter intimidation and other malpractice, particularly by USDP personnel. Six days after the elections Aung San Suu Kyi was released from house arrest.

In mid-January 2011 Gen. Than Shwe appointed 110 military representatives to the Pyithu Hluttaw, 56 to the Amyotha Hluttaw and 222 to the state and regional assemblies, in accordance with the constitutional quotas. Both chambers of the Pyidaungsu Hluttaw convened for the first time on 31 January, with all proceedings being subject to new laws issued by the SPDC in October 2010, which imposed severe restrictions on parliamentary debate, participation and media coverage. While the new laws recognized the right to freedom of expression, legislators were prohibited from making comments deemed to endanger national security or national unity, or to violate the 2008 Constitution, and they could not distribute parliamentary documents or related information. Furthermore, legislators were required to submit parliamentary questions 10 days in advance of a meeting (such questions might not disclose state secrets, undermine the interests of the state or its citizens, or affect Myanmar's international relations), while journalists (other than those employed by state media) were banned from reporting on parliamentary proceedings. The first parliamentary session was initially dominated by the selection and election of the regime's new title holders, and parliamentary questions were deferred for five weeks. Thura Shwe Man, formerly army chief of staff, was elected Speaker of the Pyithu Hluttaw, while fellow USDP member Khin Aung Myint, a former Minister of Culture, was elected Speaker of the Amyotha Hluttaw. At the state and regional levels, all Speakers and Deputy Speakers and Chief Ministers in the 14 assemblies were USDP members or military-appointed representatives; the majority of the Chief Ministers were also former ministers within the SPDC or former senior military officials. Five legislators were nominated as presidential candidates. On 4 February 2011 Thein Sein was elected President of Myanmar, having garnered 408 votes; Tin Aung Myint Oo and Sai Mauk Kham came second and third, respectively, in the election and were duly confirmed as Vice-Presidents.

The first session of the Pyidaungsu Hluttaw concluded on 30 March 2011. As the Constitution stipulated only that the legislature sit regularly at least once a year, it would not be required to reconvene until 2012. On the same day the SPDC was formally dissolved and Thein Sein was sworn in, together with his two Vice-Presidents and 30 new cabinet ministers, 26 of whom were either retired military officers or former SPDC cabinet ministers. Gen. Min Aung Hlaing was appointed as the new Commander-in-Chief of the armed forces, a position that was believed to have been downgraded to a ceremonial role owing to the creation in the same month of an eight-member State Supreme Council (SSC), together with an 11-member National Defence and Security Council (NDSC). Although the creation of the latter was provided for by the 2008 Constitution, the SSC was a new, extra-constitutional body designed to guide the incoming Government and was to be headed by Field Marshal (Senior Gen.) Than Shwe, who would thus effectively remain the most powerful figure in the country. Other members of the SSC included President Thein Sein, Vice-President Tin Aung Myint Oo, former Vice-Chairman of the SPDC Senior Gen. Maung Aye and Speaker of the Pyithu Hluttaw Thura Shwe Man. The NDSC was to be headed by the President, and also to comprise the two Vice-Presidents, the Commander-in-Chief and Vice-Commander-in-Chief of the armed forces, and the Ministers of Defence, of Foreign Affairs and of Border Affairs.

INSURGENTS AND DISSIDENTS

The CPB, located on the Myanma–Chinese border in the northern region of Shan State, posed the most serious military challenge to the Burmese armed forces (Tatmadaw) until 1989. The party was well armed and supported by anti-Government, pro-CPB broadcasts from its China-based secret radio transmitter, the 'Voice of the People of Burma'. In 1984 China's policy changed, and the supply of weapons to the CPB diminished. Owing to its declining fortunes, the CPB allegedly began exporting illicit drugs through Viet Nam and Laos, using the proceeds to purchase Soviet weapons. In early 1989 the CPB was split by internal dissent; certain ethnic factions of the party, critical of its 'narrow racial policies', challenged the central leadership. In April the Wa hill tribesmen and Kokang Chinese, who had served as cadres for the party, mutinied and forced the ageing CPB leaders across the border into China. Thus, the CPB was effectively defunct; its various regional armies divided into ethnic groupings, the most prominent being the Wa, Shan, Kokang Chinese, and Kachin.

Apart from the CPB, several groups of ethnic insurgents have been engaged in low-level warfare against the authorities since independence in 1948. Despite the Government's efforts to eliminate and destroy the various insurgent groups, they survived and united to form the National Democratic Front (NDF) in 1975. The political objective of the NDF was the creation of a truly federal union (as envisaged by the original Constitution of 1947), based on the principles of self-determination, equality and democracy. The NDF hoped to achieve its objective through negotiations with the central Government, but fighting would continue until such talks could be arranged. The NDF formed three commands (northern, central and southern) to co-ordinate the military effort. In 1988 the NDF numbered 10 groups, representing Karen (Kayin), Arakanese (Rakhine), Mon, Karenni (Kayinni), Shan, Kachin, Palaung, Pa-O and Wa. In May 1986 the NDF formed a political and military anti-Government alliance with the CPB, following an NDF conference at Pa Jau in January. This alliance was maintained despite opposition from the Karen (Kayin) National Union (KNU), one of the largest ethnic insurgent groups in the NDF. The Government initially responded with renewed attacks on Karen guerrillas, although this resulted in early victories for the combined forces. By May 1987, however, government forces had gained control of 60 km of border areas previously controlled by the CPB, and had reasserted control over 500 sq km of territory in the north-east. In the same month the Government also launched a major assault against the Kachin, temporarily capturing their military and political headquarters.

In 1988 the unity of the minorities was tested as the Karen and Mon openly fought over control of the 'black market' trade at the Three Pagoda Pass area on the Thai–Burmese border. Through the mediation of the NDF, the fighting ended in August. In April the human rights organization, Amnesty International, issued two long reports documenting human rights violations committed by the Burmese Army in its war against the minorities. These reports drew world attention, but were ignored by the Burmese Government.

The insurgent groups were sympathetic to the anti-Government movements in Rangoon and other major cities in 1988. After the armed forces seized power, an estimated 7,000–10,000 students fled to the border areas to seek refuge and arms in order to continue their struggle against the Government. Despite shortages of weapons and supplies, units of the NDF gave them refuge and some training. At the same time, units of the NDF and the CPB launched attacks on government outposts. During 1989 and 1990 the armed forces' assault against the KNU continued, with the capture of six river enclaves, although the KNU retained its headquarters at Manerplaw. During the same period the Kachin continued to engage the armed forces in their area. The Kachin held most of the countryside in their state, while government forces controlled the two major cities, Bhamo and Myitkyina, and their rail and road connections with the rest of Myanmar.

In the light of the changes in Rangoon, the NDF created a new political grouping, the Democratic Alliance of Burma (DAB), to include Burman students, monks and expatriates in a broad coalition that would, it hoped, eventually incorporate the peoples in the Burmese heartland, on the model of the original post-war nationalist movement, the AFPFL. Maj.-Gen. Bo Mya, the KNU leader, was elected President of the DAB, and Brang Seng, the Kachin leader, was named First Vice-President. At its first convention, in November 1988, 23 separate groups participated. It declared as its main objectives the overthrow of the military Government, the establishment of democratic rule, the ending of the civil war, the restoration of internal peace and national reconciliation, and the creation of a genuine federal union. Student forces within the DAB united to form the All-Burma Student Democratic Front (ABSDF), which operated in border regions and received weapons and training from the KNU and from Kayin rebels. However, the DAB did not replace the NDF; the latter continued to exist and control its own areas and armed forces. In late 1988 it admitted its 11th member, the Chin National Front.

The collapse of the CPB in 1989 provided the SLORC with an opportunity to divide its ethnic opposition and cause some groups to end their participation in the civil war. The Government successfully approached first the Kokang Chinese, and later the Wa, and offered much-needed rice in exchange for support in the government campaign against the NDF and Chang Chi Fu, known as Khun Sa, the 'opium warlord' and leader of the rebel Mong Tai Army (MTA, formerly the Shan United Army), in Shan State. It was reported that the armed forces promised, in addition to food, to allow the Wa to continue to trade opium, the major crop of their area. The SLORC also pledged to initiate a border development programme (including the construction of roads, hospitals and schools) in the former CPB areas. The SLORC also approached members of the NDF, and was successful in securing agreements with the Shan State Progressive Party in September 1989, the Pa-O National Organization in February 1991 and the Palaung State Liberation Organization in April. In July 1991, at its third Congress, the NDF responded by expelling these three organizations, thus reducing the NDF membership to eight.

Following the establishment of the 'parallel' government (the NCGUB, see above) in Manerplaw in December 1990, the SLORC intensified its attacks on KNU positions. In October 1991 the KNU surprised the government armed forces by infiltrating the Ayeyarwady delta area and launching an attack with local support at Bogale, 200 km south-west of Rangoon, now Yangon. Until the attack, the SLORC had considered the area secure. Government forces responded with air and land attacks, and, after nearly one month of fighting, they regained control. In December the SLORC launched a major military campaign to defeat the KNU, attacking Manerplaw and Kawmoora. Its failure either to defeat the KNU in the field or capture its headquarters (owing, in part, to Thailand's actions, see below) led directly to the announcement in April 1992 that it was halting its war against the KNU. In October, however, government troops resumed hostilities.

In February 1993 the Kachin Independence Organization (KIO) agreed to attend peace talks with the Government in the Kachin capital, Myitkyina. The discussions, which took place during February and March, were the result of pressure exerted by China and Thailand. The Kachin (who were the second largest ethnic insurgent force, after the KNU) reportedly demanded a nation-wide cease-fire and that further talks include other rebel groups. However, the KIO finally appeared to have agreed to a bilateral cease-fire with the Government, prior to comprehensive peace talks with all ethnic rebels. The KIO was suspended from the DAB in October for negotiating separately with the SLORC, and the DAB reiterated its conditions for discussions with the SLORC in a series of open letters. The DAB stipulations included: the recognition of the DAB as a single negotiating body (the SLORC insisted on meeting each ethnic group separately); an immediate end to the forcible mass relocation of villages; a new body to draft a constitution; and the release of all political detainees, beginning with Aung San Suu Kyi. The cease-fire agreement between the KIO and the Government was announced in October.

The process of reconciliation continued with the return to the 'legal fold' in May 1994 of the Karenni (Kayinni) National People's Liberation Front, the 11th insurgent group to conclude a cease-fire agreement with the SLORC. This was followed, in July, by the declaration of a cease-fire by the Kayan New Land Party, and in October by the Shan State Nationalities Liberation Organization. In late December government forces launched a new offensive against the KNU, capturing its headquarters at Manerplaw in January 1995 and forcing many hundreds of KNU fighters to retreat across the border into Thailand. The virtual defeat of the KNU forces, after almost 50 years of military resistance, was attributed to their reportedly severe lack of ammunition and funds and to the defection from the Christian-led KNU in December 1994 of a mainly Buddhist faction, which established itself as the Democratic Karen (Kayin) Buddhist Organization (DKBO). The DKBO, which had comprised an estimated 10% of the strength of the KNU's military wing, the Karen (Kayin) National Liberation Army (KNLA), allegedly supported the government forces in their offensive. In February 1995 the Tatmadaw captured another major KNU stronghold, at Kawmoora, and in the following month Bo Mya resigned as the Commander-in-Chief of the KNLA (although he remained the leader of the KNU and was re-elected to the post in August 1995). The SLORC and its proxies, the Democratic Karen (Kayin) Buddhist Army (DKBA, the military wing of the DKBO), continued to attack KNU bases as well as refugee camps inside Thai territory. Discussions between the KNU and the SLORC began in early 1994. Despite the KNU's participation in a series of formal cease-fire negotiations with the SLORC between late 1995 and late 1996, as well as its request for further discussions, the SLORC attacked the KNU in February 1997 and drove its forces from nearly all of their remaining fixed bases. The KNU 16th Battalion Commander, Thamu Hae, surrendered. Unlike the previous offensive, few, if any, DKBA Karen troops were used in 1997. From 1995 the DKBA made frequent incursions into Thai territory, abducting KNU members, attempting to coerce refugees into returning, robbing, raping and destroying villages (including two large Karen refugee villages, Huay Kaloke and Mawker, in March 1998). In March 1999 it was reported that Kayin rebels had executed at least 13 government officials whom they had abducted the previous month.

In the Shan region, after extensive battles with government forces between late 1993 and late 1995, there was great tension within the 20,000-strong MTA between the genuine Shan nationalists among the field officers and the Chinese leaders, who were more interested in the drugs trade. In attempts to prevent a split, the Chinese-Shan leader, Khun Sa—long a prominent figure in the drugs trade—proclaimed an independent Shan State in May 1994, and in mid-1995 established a new Shan State National Congress Party as the political wing of the MTA, with Khun Kan Chit, a Shan, as its nominal leader. This did not prevent a substantial revolt of some northern MTA units led by Karn Yord, who formed the Shan State National Army (SSNA) in July, taking nearly one-quarter of the MTA forces with him. Weakened by this division, as well as by major government attacks, desertions and, reportedly, by his own ill health, Khun Sa, who remained the real MTA leader, agreed to a cease-fire with the SLORC in January 1996. The MTA headquarters at Homong, some other MTA troops at Mong Hsat and a few other locations in the southern region of Shan State surrendered later in January. Most Shan commanders and soldiers of the MTA disapproved of the surrender and continued their resistance, linking up with other Shan groups. This alliance was formalized in September 1997 when the SSNA, remnants of the MTA, and the Shan State Peace Council (SSPC) and its military wing, the Shan State Army (SSA), joined together in an enlarged SSA. As a result, the truce between the Government and the SSPC/SSA broke down, and SSA elements resumed guerrilla activity in various parts of Shan State. Khun Sa subsequently moved to Yangon, like the Kokang drugs-trafficker Lo Hsing-han, and started a number of businesses, including a bus service and an overseas trading company. Having referred to Khun Sa as a 'narco-terrorist' until late 1995, the SLORC Government subsequently used the honorific prefix, U, before his name and refused to extradite him to the USA for prosecution on drugs-trafficking charges (he had been indicted by the USA in 1989 and 1992). Clashes between SSA units and government forces were reported in December 1997. In March 2000, however, following the group's announcement that it wished to seek a peaceful settlement with the ruling junta, the SSA issued a statement outlining cease-fire terms.

The Karenni (Kayinni) National Progress Party (KNPP) cease-fire with the SLORC, which was signed in March 1995, collapsed almost immediately, and government offensives on the KNPP area continued. These attacks intensified from January 1996 after Khun Sa's surrender at Homong, to the north-east of the KNPP area. In that month the KNPP and the KNU agreed to fight together again against the SLORC and both groups continued to exist as guerrilla armies along much of the Myanma border with western Thailand. Following negotiations begun in December 1993, however, the New Mon State Party (NMSP) signed a cease-fire with the SLORC in June 1995. This truce was particularly significant as the NMSP had controlled part of the area where a major gas pipeline to Thailand was under construction. The last members of the NMSP surrendered in May 1997, and the KNU was virtually eliminated from this area. In January 2005 the Tatmadaw launched an attack against the army of the KNPP, with fighting coming close to the Thai border.

The SLORC regularly reported that all ethnic groups except the KNU had ceased armed resistance; however, various small groups in other areas (which were not often mentioned) continued their struggle: several Rohingya Muslim and Rakhine Buddhist groups in Rakhine State, the Chin National Army in Chin State, the National Socialist Council of Nagaland (various factions) in the Naga areas of western Sagaing Division, and a number of breakaway groups from the MTA, which continued resistance after the MTA surrender in January 1996 and formed a substantial Shan alliance in June. Many of the groups with which truces continued to hold were restive, and clashes between SLORC forces and members of the Kachin Independence Army (KIA—the military wing of the KIO) were reported in early 1996. In December 1995 the United Wa State Party (UWSP) was reportedly very discontented at the replacement of MTA forces by Myanma army troops in some areas adjacent to them and at the restrictions that were placed on their movements from early 1996.

ABSDF students in areas controlled by various groups, such as the KIA and KNU, experienced difficulties following the various cease-fires and offensives; the SLORC also attacked them directly, capturing their bases in Myanmar. For years they were also divided by factionalism. With the development of closer relations between Thailand and Myanmar, the Thai security forces increased their harassment, detention, and deportation of the thousands of Myanma refugee students in Thailand; some were moved to a remote camp in western Thailand known as the 'Safe Area'. In September 1996 the ABSDF reunited, with Dr Naing Aung as Chairman and Moe Thee Zun as Vice-Chairman. However, it continued to lose ground militarily. In March 1998 the SPDC (which had replaced the SLORC) detained 40 members of the ABSDF whom it accused of planning terrorist attacks on government buildings and embassies and the assassination of national leaders; the allegations were rejected by the ABSDF.

Various other groups that had signed cease-fires with the SLORC also expanded their involvement in the drugs trade; these included the UWSP and its armed wing, the United Wa State Army (UWSA, reported to have a major amphetamine factory near the Thai border, in addition to its opium and heroin interests), and other former CPB groups in the eastern Shan State, as well as several Chinese groups in the Kokang area of Shan State, notably the Eastern Shan State Army of Lin Min Shin (Sai Lin). The surrender of Khun Sa and the break-up of the MTA did not reduce opium production. Despite the truces, many of the former members of the DAB continued to be in contact; a meeting was held in January 1996, and a DAB congress in April. According to the SLORC, all groups that had signed cease-fire agreements were invited to send observers to the National Convention; apparently few did so.

Following the cease-fires with most ethnic rebels, the Tatmadaw was able to move into many areas where it had had no presence for 20–30 years or more. In some areas, the Tatmadaw forced groups of ethnic soldiers to relocate, contrary to the agreed cease-fire terms. In many zones, especially around the remaining active ethnic rebellions, there was a massive forced movement of villages away from rebel areas and into relocation areas in the plains. Hundreds of thousands of people were displaced from their homes in the eastern states of Shan, Kayah and Karen in 1996 and 1997. In May 1999 it was reported that at least 300,000 Shan had been forced from their villages into resettlement camps by government troops. This population movement severely affected the local support base of the Karen KNU, Karenni KNPP, Pa-O and former MTA, which did not participate in the surrender of early 1996. Many of the villagers who did not wish to relocate in the plains became refugees, especially in Thailand but also in Bangladesh, India and China: the Tatmadaw offensive in Karen State, which started in February 1997, for example, drove an estimated 20,000 additional Karen refugees into Thailand. In many cases, potential refugees were turned back at the Thai, Indian and Chinese borders; in others, people were persuaded to return to Myanmar. Most such people ended up in relocation areas, which some NGOs working along the Thai–Myanma border termed 'concentration camps'. In 1996 Myanmar announced that the local population would be removed from a large tract of land in Tanintharyi (Tenasserim) to create a major nature reserve. However, since the gas pipeline to Thailand was to pass through this region, the announcement was widely interpreted as a security measure, rather than a gesture towards nature conservation.

On 12–14 December 1998 23 ethnic groups met to issue a statement of support for the NLD and for the convening of the elected National Assembly. The SSA and the KNPP announced that they would co-operate to fight the regime. In January 2000 Gen. Bo Mya was succeeded as the leader of the KNU by the former General Secretary of the organization, Saw Ba Thin. Following his appointment as leader, Ba Thin announced that, while the KNU intended to continue its struggle against the ruling SPDC, the movement was prepared to negotiate a political settlement with the military regime. It was subsequently reported by both government and independent sources that an initial but inconclusive round of talks between the KNU and the SPDC was held in February, followed by further discussions in March.

The rapprochement between the SPDC and the NLD in 2001 aroused anxiety among many ethnic groups, which feared that the two sides in Yangon would reach an agreement that gave no place to greater regional autonomy. In September 2001 several ethnic groups formed the National Solidarity and Co-operation Committee to press for a tripartite dialogue.

The breakdown of relations between the SPDC and the NLD in 2003 turned the minorities once more into a potential ally of the regime against the NLD. Particularly after Khin Nyunt became Prime Minister, the SPDC renewed efforts to sign cease-fires with ethnic insurgents and to collect promises from ethnic organizations to participate in the planned new National Convention. The largest group still fighting the Government, the KNU, took part in cease-fire negotiations with government representatives in December 2003 and January 2004. However, once the National Convention had been reconvened in May 2004, and several minority organizations had refused to attend, hostilities between the Tatmadaw and the insurgents flared up again. Although the SPDC had promised to maintain the cease-fires negotiated by ousted Prime Minister Khin Nyunt, and despite special visits by SPDC leaders to some groups to repeat the assurance, tension with both the Karen and the Shan seemed to increase. Illness on the part of Bo Mya, who had headed the group within the KNU that favoured a cease-fire, contributed to the situation, but the authorities themselves detained several ethnic Shan leaders in February 2005 on charges of 'conspiracy against the State'. Those held included Khun Htun Oo, Chairman of the SNLD, and Sai Nyunt Lwin, the party's Secretary-General. Both the SNLD and the Shan State Kokang Democratic Party were absent from the reconvened National Convention in December 2005. The Tatmadaw also launched new operations against rebel groups that had not previously agreed to cease-fires, and clashes were reported between the UWSA and the Tatmadaw in the eastern Shan State.

The Tatmadaw began a dry-season offensive against the KNU in October 2005, testing the limits of the informal cease-fire agreement brokered by Khin Nyunt with Bo Mya in January 2004. The Karen area under attack fell within the territory that the Tatmadaw wished to bring under its control because of its close proximity to the new administrative capital of Nay Pyi Taw. The SPDC also wanted to secure the area to build roads needed to construct five planned dams on the Salween River, which flows through Karen State. While KNU leaders were not prepared to concede that the cease-fire between the SPDC and the KNU had totally broken down, they reiterated that the KNLA would not stand by while Tatmadaw soldiers attacked and burned Karen villages. The Government began an offensive against the 7th Brigade of the KNLA, near the border with Thailand, in early 2006. Both the KNU and the SSA had been weakened by the SPDC's offensive, and there were reports of defections from the SSA—South faction. Meanwhile, the elderly Bo Mya died in a hospital in Mae Sot, Thailand—near the border—in December 2006.

In 2007 the KNU/KNLA Peace Council (a splinter group of the KNU) signed a cease-fire agreement with the SPDC. This group, along with government agents, was thought to be responsible for the assassination of the General Secretary of the KNU, Pado Mahn Sha La Pan, in Mae Sot in February 2008. Pado Mahn Sha, who had been known for his promotion of consensus among the ethnic insurgence groups, was replaced by the KNU's first female General Secretary, Zipporah Sein. Following the referendum in 2008 in favour of the new Constitution, the SPDC asked all cease-fire minority groups to form political parties so that they could participate in the legislative elections scheduled for 2010. Although the new Constitution provided for legislatures in all 14 of the states and divisions, it reserved a large number of the seats in each for the Tatmadaw, as was the case with the national legislature. The ethnic minority groups, therefore, were reluctant to commit to the SPDC's proposal, and concerns were raised by the National Democratic Alliance Army, the NMSP, the UWSP, the KIO and the DKBA. The Tatmadaw began a new offensive against Karen rebels in June 2009, forcing thousands of ethnic Karen villagers to flee across the Thai border (see below). The KNU was accused of supporting the efforts of other anti-Government groups during 2009 and was also blamed for a series of bombings in that year. Yet the KNU, like other militant ethnic national movements that had remained in conflict with the Government (including the Shan and Mon), began to suffer from internal factionalism. Increasingly, the changing policies of neighbouring states toward the ethnic border resistance groups, in part arising from a desire on the part of the former to secure border stability and protect their future investments inside Myanmar, created further problems for the likes of the KNU and, latterly, the Kokang. Not wanting to isolate the Myanma Government, the Chinese authorities were restrained in their criticism of the Tatmadaw's actions against the Kokang Chinese, while the authorities in Thailand were becoming increasingly frustrated by KNU activities along the Thai frontier.

By the end of 2010 only five armed ethnic groups had agreed to join the Government's Border Guard Force (BGF) and to place their armed forces under Tatmadaw control. Fighting broke out between government troops and many of the remaining ethnic groups that were resisting the BGF plan. These groups included: the DKBA and KNLA in Karen State; the MNDAA, the Shan State Army—North (SSA—N) and the Shan State Army—South (SSA—S) in Shan State; the KIO and KIA in Kachin State; and the Arakan Liberation Army and the Chin National Army in Chin State. These areas, including most of the Wa area on the Myanma–Chinese border, were excluded from the legislative election in November. Clashes also occurred with the UWSA, and members of the NMSP were described as 'insurgents' by state media for the first time since the SLORC-brokered cease-fires of the late 1980s and 1990s. In March 2011, in response to escalating violence, a meeting of 12 armed ethnic groups, cease-fire groups and ethnic political groups took place in Chiang Mai, Thailand, where those present agreed to form a coalition, the Union Nationalities Federal Council (UNFC). The alliance included representatives from the Rakhine, Chin, Karen, Karenni, Kachin, Lahu, Mon, Pa-O, Palaung, Shan and Wa groups. The UNFC agreed to establish four military regions in Myanmar; to share their resources if the Tatmadaw attacked any coalition member; and that no member would hold separate cease-fire talks with the Government.

REFUGEES AND OTHER MIGRANTS

As a result of the regime's policies, from the late 1980s large numbers of ethnic minority refugees flooded into every neighbouring country. These included at least 288,000 (or nearly one-half) of the Muslim Rohingya population of Rakhine State, who fled to Bangladesh between 1989 and 1991. In Thailand there were about 70,000 Karen (Kayin) from the KNU areas, about 10,000 Karenni (Kayinni) from the KNPP area, and some 18,000 Mon from the former NMSP areas in the south; most of these fled Myanmar in the early 1990s, but more Karen and Karenni continued to arrive from 1996 onwards. There were also many Kachin refugees (estimated at as many as 15,000) in China, and Chin and Naga refugees (up to 10,000) in north-eastern India. The most recent group of refugees were the Shan from the former MTA area, who arrived in Thailand following the MTA surrender at Homong in January 1996; their number was estimated at up to 100,000, but this was probably an exaggeration. These Shan refugees were not placed in camps but dispersed throughout northern Thailand. The office of the UN High Commissioner for Refugees (UNHCR) was involved in sending more than 200,000 Rohingya back into Myanmar between 1992 and 1997, as they did in 1976–78. In July 1999, however, about 20,000 Rohingya refugees remained in camps in Bangladesh, despite the expiry of the official deadline for their repatriation in August 1997. In April 2000 the International Federation of Human Rights Leagues (FIDH) issued a report condemning the treatment of Rohingya Muslims by the Myanma Government, including forced labour, punitive taxes and extrajudicial killings. The FIDH claimed that the regime was attempting to force the exodus of Rohingyas from their native Rakhine and criticized UNHCR for its effective complicity with the Myanma regime in designating the more recent refugees as economic migrants. The Mon were repatriated in early 1996. Japan offered humanitarian aid to support the repatriation of the Karen on a similar basis. Returning refugees were often concentrated in camps rather than being allowed to return to their homes, or were unable to recover their homes and land.

In addition to these recognized refugees, there were many economic migrants working in Thailand, estimated by some Thai sources to number hundreds of thousands or even 1m.; they provided much of the menial and seasonal labour needs of northern, western and southern Thailand and supplied the Thai sex industry. There were also many more who were internally displaced, either because they had obeyed SLORC demands to move from remote areas and urban centres to relocation zones, or because they had moved away from SLORC-controlled areas. Nearly all such people were undergoing severe hardship, deprived of their traditional homes, land and crops.

Large numbers of people were conscripted into forced labour squads, used by the SLORC to complete infrastructure projects (roads, railways, irrigation systems, etc.) or to carry weapons and supplies for the army, thus also undergoing temporary displacement. The SLORC defended this kind of labour as traditional in Myanmar; but the scale of the works undertaken was the greatest in recent history, and inadequate provision was made for feeding and accommodating the workers, who were required to bring their own tools and sometimes even to feed themselves, while neglecting their own crops or other work for weeks or months at a time. It was usually possible to pay to avoid this labour, but this option was too expensive for many people and only further enriched the local military commanders, who also sometimes received payment for the work done. The mortality rate among such labourers was high, but lower than that for gangs of prisoners (criminal and some political) engaged in such work full-time.

In the first half of 1996 an estimated 70,000–75,000 Kayah were relocated within Kayah State, while about 80,000 Shan were relocated in the former MTA south-western area of Shan State. Similar numbers of Karen were relocated away from the KNU in the first half of 1997. With each relocation, thousands more refugees appeared at the Thai border. Although many, especially Shan, were absorbed into local villages and the local work-force in Thailand, Thai police conducted occasional raids and deported those without Thai documentation. Some, particularly Karen, were placed in refugee camps along the western border. The SLORC on a number of occasions sent DKBA soldiers to burn these camps and kidnap KNU leaders. After the Asian economic crisis began in Thailand in July 1997, Thai soldiers increasingly turned back newly arrived refugees, and also repatriated some existing refugees. Nevertheless, about 98,000 Karen remained in western Thailand, living in camps which they could no longer leave for work, as well as a similar number of more widely dispersed Shan refugees. In December 1999 Thailand expelled tens of thousands of refugees who had been working in the country illegally. In January 2000 it was reported that 800–1,000 Karen had fled across the border into Thailand following clashes between government forces and the KNU.

More than 16,000 Karen villagers from northern and eastern Karen State were displaced following a dry-season offensive by the Tatmadaw launched in October 2005. By mid-2006 about 2,000 displaced villagers had been admitted to Mae Ra Moo refugee camp in Thailand's Mae Hong Son province, while hundreds more camped at a makeshift site on the Myanma side of the Salween River. The Tatmadaw began shelling and burning Karen villages in an effort to secure territory in Karen State for a series of dam projects planned for the Salween River, as well as to secure the area bordering Pyinmana.

In March 2006 the Geneva-based Internal Displacement Monitoring Centre (IDMC), affiliated to the Norwegian Refugee Council, reported that at the end of 2005 Myanmar had the worst internal displacement situation in Asia. The IDMC reported that there were nearly 540,000 internally displaced people in Myanmar and that an estimated 92,000 were hiding in forests. Between May 2004 and May 2005 alone 87,000 villagers were internally displaced in Myanmar owing to conflicts or human rights abuses. An estimated 10,000–20,000 Karen had fled to the Thai–Myanma border area as a result of the military operations against Karen villages near the new administrative centre (later named Nay Pyi Taw) that began in late 2005.

In April 2008 a truck containing 121 Myanma refugees was discovered in Ranong Province, Thailand. It had been abandoned en route to Phuket, where the migrant workers were seeking unskilled employment. A total of 54 bodies were discovered, the migrants having suffocated inside the truck; the survivors were detained by the Thai authorities. The number of Myanma refugees seeking employment in Thailand had increased owing to the damage caused by Cyclone Nargis. In January 2009 Thailand was heavily criticized for its handling of Myanma 'boat people' intercepted off its coastline. These people were Rohingya refugees from the Muslim minority group concentrated in Rakhine State, thousands of whom each year were boarding boats bound for Thailand, where they were either sold into slave labour or continued their journey to Malaysia. This particular group, consisting of 1,000 Rohingyas and Bangladeshis, was captured and detained by the Thai authorities off the coast near Ranong, then forced onto several boats with little food or water and set adrift. More than one-half were believed to be missing or dead, while other large groups were rescued by the Indonesian Navy. An estimated 5,000 such Rohingya refugees were captured by the Thai authorities between 2007 and 2009. The UNHCR continued to press Thailand to grant it access to 126 Rohingya boat people who were believed to remain in detention in that country. The UNHCR also announced the expansion of its mission in Sittwe, the capital of Rakhine State.

More than 3,000 ethnic Karen villagers fled across the border into Thailand in June 2009 following a Tatmadaw offensive. This was the largest movement of refugees across the border since the Tatmadaw's offensive against Karen rebels in 1997. Some of the refugees were from the Ler Per Her camp, which was shelled by the Tatmadaw during their pursuit of Karen rebels. In an effort to gain control of the region, the DKBA had attempted to coerce villagers into recruitment by placing mines close to their rice fields. In response to the sudden influx of refugees, the Thai military sent heavily armed troops to reinforce positions along the border. In August 2009 the SPDC sent Tatmadaw troops to the Kokang region of Shan State to suppress resistance by the MNDAA to its plans to transform cease-fire militant groups into BGF battalions (see above). This led to the deaths of an estimated 200 militants and civilians, and prompted more than 37,000 Kokang Chinese, including their leader, Pheung Kya-shin, to flee across the border into China. In November the Thailand Burma Border Consortium, an international NGO, estimated that 470,000 displaced persons remained in various parts of the eastern borderland area.

The SPDC's ongoing efforts to subdue ethnic militia forces that were resisting its BGF plans intensified from 2010, with violence increasing after the November elections, particularly in Karen and Shan States. Clashes between SPDC troops and Karen insurgents were reported to have led to more than 20,000 villagers being displaced and up to 10,000 fleeing across the Thai border. The Government ended its cease-fire agreement with the SSA—N and carried out operations in March 2011, resulting in the displacement of more than 3,000 villagers in the northern region of Shan State. In early 2011, furthermore, the authorities in Thailand, India and Indonesia reported the arrival and detention of more than 450 Rohingya boat people fleeing alleged repression in Myanmar. In February the UN Special Rapporteur on the situation of human rights in Myanmar, Tomás Ojea Quintana, reported that the grave developments in Myanmar were creating a burden for other countries in the region, owing to the increasing numbers of refugees fleeing to neighbouring countries.

FOREIGN RELATIONS

After attaining independence in 1948, Burma pursued a policy of neutrality and non-alignment in world affairs. Burma declined to join the British Commonwealth and was the first non-communist country to recognize the People's Republic of China in 1949. Cordial relations with China were consolidated by a 1960 agreement to settle outstanding border disagreements, but relations were suspended between 1967 and 1970 over what Burma perceived as attempts to promote the Cultural Revolution among Burmese of Chinese descent. Burma supported the UN, and in 1961 became a founder member of the Non-aligned Movement (it subsequently withdrew from the Movement for a number of years, but was readmitted in 1992). Burma's foreign policy following the military seizure of power in 1962 continued to emphasize independence and non-alignment. Although Ne Win's Government was initially rather isolationist and sought to exclude foreign influences, governments from the 1970s onwards were aware of the importance of foreign contacts and investment for development. They sought to open the country to the West to the extent that this could be done without undermining government authority. Western interest in Burma was prompted especially by the country's importance in the drugs trade. In 1976 Burma began to participate in drug enforcement programmes of the UN and the USA, in an attempt to suppress the cultivation of opium in north-eastern Burma which, together with northern Thailand and north-western Laos, was known as the 'Golden Triangle'. Substantial anti-narcotics assistance, including funds and equipment, failed to halt drug production, as many of the areas cultivated for opium were under the control of insurgent groups that relied on the proceeds of drugs-trafficking to support their anti-Government campaign. The military coup in 1988 prompted the USA to suspend all assistance, and the annual crop increased significantly. The Myanma authorities continued to express willingness to co-operate with the outside world in controlling the trade, arguing that international isolation over human rights issues made this co-operation unnecessarily difficult. In June 1989 Myanmar ratified the 1988 UN Vienna Convention against trafficking in illegal drugs. During the 1990s, however, Myanmar became increasingly important as a regional source of amphetamines and methamphetamines, which were traded especially across the border with China and increasingly through India and Sri Lanka, as well as along more traditional routes through Thailand and the countries of Indo-China. It has been estimated that 50% of the heroin consumed in the USA is of Myanma origin, while earnings from drugs exports are believed to exceed the value of all Myanmar's other exports. Weak supervision of the Myanmar banking system facilitates this trade. Although allegations were persistently heard that the SLORC and later the SPDC were themselves involved in drugs-trafficking (with particular attention being given to claimed links between Gen. Khin Nyunt and Wa producers), regional military commanders appeared to be the most important local figures in the trade. Opium production appeared to increase in Myanmar in 2000 after the Taliban Government in Afghanistan restricted production there, but statistics were unreliable, and the growing importance of the industrial production of amphetamines and methamphetamines meant that the cultivation of opium itself constituted only a small part of the problem. Meanwhile, the ready availability of heroin for injecting within Myanmar, and the social disruption caused by the civil wars, created an environment in which HIV/AIDS spread rapidly. A survey in Kachin State indicated that 90% of heroin users were HIV-positive. It was estimated by the Joint UN Programme on HIV/AIDS (UNAIDS) that 240,000 people in Myanmar were living with HIV in 2007.

The assumption of power by the armed forces in September 1988, and the subsequent brutal suppression of demonstrations by the opposition movement, provoked widespread international censure. Many creditor nations, including Japan, the Federal Republic of Germany, the USA, the United Kingdom and Australia, suspended economic aid, pending an improvement in Burma's human rights record. Among Burma's immediate neighbours, India was the most vocal in its criticism of the military repression; it closed Indian trade routes to Burma and established refugee camps near the border. In March 1993, however, the Indian Minister of External Affairs visited Myanmar and signed bilateral agreements on the suppression of separatist movements and drugs-trafficking along the common border. In 1995–96 two border crossings between India and Myanmar were opened and, in 2002, India agreed with Myanmar to begin the construction of a network of roads linking the two countries; there were also joint military operations against Naga rebel groups. This closer relationship was widely believed to be India's reaction to the growing influence of China in Myanmar. Relations with Bangladesh, with which Myanmar shares a short border, were strained both by the presence of an estimated 21,000 Muslim refugees from Myanmar in camps in Bangladesh and by Myanma plans to dam the shared Naf river.

In response to the events of 1988, the USA halted all non-humanitarian assistance, barred Burma from trade benefits under its Generalized System of Preferences, decertified Burma on narcotics and opposed loans from the World Bank, the IMF and other international financial institutions. It blocked all sales of arms from the USA to Burma and urged other nations to do the same. In 1990 the US Congress adopted, and the President signed into law, the Customs and Trade Act, which empowered the President to restrict trade with Myanmar if it failed to comply with certain conditions, which were to be monitored twice annually. These were: the protection of human rights; an end to martial law and the introduction of democracy; and adherence to the requirements of the 1986 Narcotics Trade Control Act. In conformity with the law, in July 1991 US President George Bush invoked economic sanctions by declining to renew a bilateral textile agreement. (In 1990 textile exports to the USA amounted to nearly one-half of total Myanma exports.) The US Administration retained its tough stance towards the SLORC, and subsequently the SPDC, throughout the 1990s, and continued to condemn the widespread abuse of human rights in Myanmar and to demand the release of all political detainees. In mid-1996 the US Congress approved a law prohibiting new investment and trade with Myanmar; an official ban was announced in April 1997. During 1998 the US Administration criticized the military junta in Myanmar for its treatment of Aung San Suu Kyi and, once again, demanded the release of hundreds of political prisoners. In March 1999 the US Secretary of State, Madeleine Albright, publicly criticized the regime for taking insufficient action to combat the production of, and trade in, narcotics within Myanmar. During the 1990s the European Union (EU) also maintained a common position of refusing to deal with the Myanma authorities, and in October 1998 an existing ban on visas for members of the Myanma Government and their families was extended to cover Myanma citizens working in the tourism industry.

Japan was also critical of the ruling military junta in Myanmar, but like other donors it completed existing aid projects after 1988. Japanese investment and business activities never ceased, and intensified after a Japan Federation of Economic Organizations (Keidanren) visit in June 1994. Substantial new Japanese aid started in mid-1995 after the release of Aung San Suu Kyi, and in April 2001 Japan agreed to provide US $28m. for the rehabilitation of a hydroelectric dam. Other countries, including Australia, Norway and Switzerland, have provided humanitarian aid to refugees outside Myanmar, and more limited humanitarian aid for projects within the country. After resistance to its attempts to observe and reduce human rights abuses, the International Committee of the Red Cross (ICRC) withdrew from Myanmar in July 1995. However, the ICRC subsequently regained permission to visit a limited number of prisons in Myanmar in 1999. Despite visits in 1995 and subsequently, the Asian Development Bank (ADB), IMF and World Bank had not resumed loans by mid-1998. Relations with the USA, the EU, Australia and many other non-Asian countries continued to be difficult. The US Secretary of State denounced Myanmar publicly for its human rights abuses and lack of progress towards democracy at the Ministerial Meeting that followed the ASEAN meeting in July 1997. However, Myanmar was vigorously defended by Prime Minister Mahathir Mohamad of Malaysia. Suu Kyi continued to advocate a diplomatic, economic and tourist boycott of Myanmar under the SLORC (and, subsequently, the SPDC).

Confronting such consistent hostility from the West, the Government of Ne Win placed great emphasis on fostering its relations with its immediate neighbours, especially Thailand. From about 1988, during the boom years before the Asian economic crisis of 1997, Thailand became a major source of foreign investment in Myanmar. The SLORC granted licences to Thai business interests to exploit raw materials in Burma, especially teak and other timber, in return for much-needed foreign exchange, while the Thai Government offered technical training and other assistance. Plans were made for a bridge across the Sai river, which would improve communications between Myanmar and Thailand, for a gas pipeline to Thailand from reserves off the Ayeyarwady delta and for a dam in Shan State to supply water to Thailand.

Although there was no announcement of any official Thai-Myanma agreement, offensives by government forces against rebel groups, particularly the KNU, achieved unprecedented success, with Tatmadaw troops frequently entering Thai territory and attacking insurgent bases from the rear. Partly because of deep-seated historical suspicion between the two countries, these operations led to tension. In early 1992 the Thai Government warned Tatmadaw soldiers not to cross into Thailand in their attempts to capture the KNU headquarters at Manerplaw. Following repeated border violations, there were clashes between Myanma and Thai forces in March as the Thai military forced hundreds of Tatmadaw troops out of entrenched positions that they had taken up to attack the KNU base from the rear. In October, however, government troops resumed hostilities and made several incursions into Thai territory. In December the Thai and Myanmar Governments reached agreement to relocate the Tatmadaw forces, and in February 1993 they resolved to delineate their common border. However, incursions by the Tatmadaw into Thai territory continued in early 1995, leading to a further deterioration in bilateral relations. Tatmadaw shelling of, and incursions into, Thai territory in pursuit of KNU and KNPP rebels occurred frequently, and Thai soldiers, police, paramilitary force members and local Thai villagers were occasionally killed. In December 1998 two Thai naval officers were killed during a clash between two fishing vessels, and in January 1999 a confrontation between naval patrols from the two countries occurred near the Thai city of Ranong. Clashes between Tatmadaw and Thai troops along Thailand's northern border took place between February and May 2001. Thailand also became increasingly concerned at the inflow of drugs, including methamphetamines, from Myanmar.

Myanmar's relations with Thailand were further strained by the large number of Myanma refugees in Thailand. Refugees began reaching Thailand in significant numbers following the military suppression of the pro-democracy movement in 1988, though Thailand was then reluctant to grant them refugee status and in 1990 forcibly repatriated 1,000 Myanma dissidents. By mid-1998 the number of Myanma refugees in Thailand had increased to an estimated 300,000–500,000 (including many economic refugees). Many of these, it was believed, were seeking to escape conscription into forced labour squads used by the Myanma Government for the construction of roads, railways and other infrastructure projects. Others were members of various ethnic or insurgent groups that had been defeated by, or had capitulated to, the SLORC. In early November 1999 Myanma government troops threatened to shoot at least one group of Myanma illegal labourers whom Thai officials were attempting to deport from Thailand. In October 1999 a group of armed Myanma student activists seized control of their country's embassy in Bangkok, demanding the release of all political prisoners in Myanmar and the opening of dialogue between the Government and the opposition. More than 30 hostages, including tourists as well as diplomats, were taken. They were released by the gunmen within 24 hours, in exchange for the Thai Government's provision of helicopter transport to the Thai–Myanma border. Myanmar closed its border with Thailand immediately after the incident. In January 2000 Thai troops shot dead 10 armed Myanma rebels who had taken control of a hospital in Ratchaburi, holding hundreds of people hostage. The rebels, who were reported by some sources to be linked to the Kayin insurgent group, God's Army (a small breakaway faction of the KNU—the KNU itself denied any connection with the rebels), had issued several demands, including that the shelling of their base on the Thai–Myanma border by the Thai military be halted, that co-operation between the Thai and Myanma armies against the Kayins should cease, and that Kayin tribespeople be allowed to seek refuge in Thailand. While the Thai Government denied reports that the perpetrators had been summarily executed after handing over their weapons, the brutal resolution of the incident was praised by the military Government in Myanmar.

None the less, shared economic interests helped to keep Thailand's relations with Myanmar close, despite these strains. Border crossings, which had been closed due to fighting in 1995, were reopened in early 1996, including those at Tachilek and at Myawaddy. Senior Gen. (later Field Marshal) Than Shwe, the head of the SLORC, visited Thailand in December 1995 and his visit was reciprocated in 1996 and 1997. Thai Prime Minister Thaksin Shinawatra made a visit to Yangon in June 2001, during which both sides made it clear that they wished to improve relations, and in September Gen. Khin Nyunt paid a three-day visit to Thailand, which was hailed as establishing a new basis for closer co-operation. In particular, Thailand began to work closely with the Myanma authorities to control the flow of drugs by launching military operations against drugs organizations and by promoting crop substitution programmes in production areas. In January 2002, at a meeting of a joint Thai-Myanma commission (the first to have been held since 1999), the two countries also agreed to establish a task force to aid in the repatriation of illegal workers. In April 2002 Gen. (later Dep. Senior Gen.) Maung Aye made a visit to Bangkok, during which he undertook to help reduce the flow of drugs between the two countries. However, relations deteriorated in the following month when fighting began between Myanma government troops, allied with the UWSA, and the SSA, which had seized four posts on the border. Thai troops were alleged to have fired shells into the country, claiming that the fighting had encroached upon Thai territory. In response, the Myanma Government accused Thailand of supporting the SSA. Shortly afterwards the Thai–Myanma border was closed owing to the escalating tensions, which were compounded by reports that the SPDC had expelled hundreds of Thai workers from the country. Border incursions continued throughout June 2002 as relations worsened. Early in that month masked gunmen, thought to be members of the KNU, opened fire on a Thai school bus travelling close to the border, resulting in the deaths of three children. The KNU denied responsibility for the attack. In August the Thai Minister of Foreign Affairs, Surakiart Sathirathai, met with SPDC leaders in an effort to resolve the tensions. Talks were reported to have been fruitful, and in

October 2002 the border was reopened. By early 2003 relations had improved further, and officials from both countries were engaged in ongoing discussions concerning co-operation over investment and the suppression of drugs-related activity.

From 1988, as Burma's international isolation intensified, China assumed an increasingly important role. In August 1988 the two countries signed a broad cross-border trade agreement, which opened the Burmese market and resources to Chinese exploitation. By 1990 China had become the major supplier of consumer goods, which had previously been purchased mainly from Thailand. In 1991 China also became the SLORC's chief arms supplier, with the sale of weapons valued at more than US $1,000m. It was believed that many of the fighter aircraft that Myanmar purchased from China in the early 1990s were used in the suppression of anti-Government rebel groups. China played a significant role in delaying the passage (both in the UN Commission on Human Rights in Geneva in 1989 and 1990 and at the UN General Assembly in 1990) of strong resolutions criticizing the SLORC's human rights violations. China also improved road and bridge links with northern Myanmar, and Chinese firms became important in the timber industry. In the late 1990s several border towns became the centre of a tourist industry based on gambling, drugs and prostitution. It was reported that in some towns the Myanma kyat had been displaced by the Chinese yuan for virtually all transactions. The Chinese President, Jiang Zemin, visited Myanmar in December 2001, and agreements for economic co-operation in several fields were concluded. During the late 1990s, however, Chinese authorities became increasingly concerned by the flow of drugs from Myanmar into the newly affluent coastal regions of China and began to co-operate more closely with the Myanma Government in attempting to control the trade. In 2000 the Tatmadaw reportedly began to develop closer links with the army of Pakistan.

From the 1980s relations with ASEAN were central to Myanmar's efforts to avoid international isolation. As relatively developed economies, both Malaysia and Thailand were interested in the emerging economic opportunities in Myanmar, while ASEAN as a whole, and Indonesia in particular, was keen to ensure that Myanmar did not fall into China's orbit. In 1991 ASEAN denied a US request to use its influence with Myanmar to help persuade it to end human rights violations and allow democratic government to be restored. ASEAN declared that it pursued a policy of 'constructive engagement' with the SLORC and would not interfere in Myanmar's internal affairs. Trade between Myanmar and ASEAN continued to expand, and in July 1994 Ohn Gyaw, then Myanma Minister of Foreign Affairs, travelled to Bangkok to attend the opening and closing ceremonies of the annual meeting of ASEAN ministers responsible for foreign affairs (the first time that Myanmar had been invited to attend as a guest). Myanmar's links with ASEAN became steadily closer from this time. It signed a treaty of friendship and co-operation with ASEAN members in 1995, and was granted full observer status at the July 1996 ASEAN meeting in the Indonesian capital of Jakarta, also becoming a full member of the ASEAN Regional Forum (ARF). Myanmar applied to join ASEAN in October 1996 and was admitted as a full member on 1 July 1997. It also joined the Bangladesh-India-Sri Lanka-Thailand Economic Co-operation (BIST-EC) Forum in 1997, which subsequently became known as the Bangladesh-India-Myanmar-Sri Lanka-Thailand Economic Co-operation (BIMST-EC) Forum. However, the country was not allowed to participate in the second Asia-Europe Meeting (ASEM) in early 1998, at the insistence of various European states. In early 1999 a meeting between ASEAN and the EU scheduled to take place in February was postponed indefinitely as a result of continued disagreement over the representation of Myanmar at the meeting. ASEAN objected that the EU should not attempt to dictate ASEAN membership and defended its approach of 'constructive engagement'. As EU governments would not permit Myanma senior officials to enter their territory, ASEAN hosted a two-day ministerial summit in Vientiane, Laos, in December 2000, but only junior ministers attended from the European side. The meeting ended with an agreement that an EU delegation would visit Myanmar for discussions with both the Government and Aung San Suu Kyi. The visit took place in January 2001, but produced no formal outcome. In April 1996 James Leander (Leo) Nichols, a businessman, honorary consul of Norway and Denmark and local representative for Sweden, was arrested and imprisoned for having an unauthorized fax machine and additional telephone lines. Despite many vigorous but polite requests for his release on the grounds of old age and ill health, including a visit by the Norwegian, Danish and Swedish diplomatic representatives in Thailand and Singapore, Nichols was kept at Insein prison, notorious for the ill-treatment and torture of prisoners, where he died in June. The SLORC autopsy reported the cause of death as a stroke. Observers believed that the real reason for Nichols' arrest was his close relationship with Suu Kyi. Strong protests about his death were made by Australia (where much of his family lived) as well as Norway, Denmark and Sweden, and Myanmar's hopes for better relations with the EU thus suffered a major set-back.

In September 1999 a diplomatic dispute arose between Myanmar and the United Kingdom, after British consular staff were refused permission to visit two Britons, James Mawdsley and Rachel Goldwyn, being held in prison in Myanmar for their separate involvement in pro-democracy protest action. Goldwyn was released in November; however, Mawdsley was sentenced to 17 years' imprisonment by the ruling junta in September for illegal entry into the country and sedition, and served more than 400 days in solitary confinement before being released in October 2000 as a result of pressure from the British and US Governments, the UN and other international bodies.

The findings of an ILO investigation into forced labour and the suppression of trade unions in Myanmar were published in August 1998: in its report, the ILO found the use of forced labour to be 'pervasive' throughout the whole of the country (and to include women, children, the sick and the elderly), and accused the regime of using beatings, torture, rape and murder in the enforcement of its forced labour policy, constituting a 'gross denial of human rights'. In June 1999 a resolution condemning Myanmar for its widespread use of forced labour was adopted by the member countries of the ILO, and the country was barred from participating in any ILO activities. At the organization's annual conference in Geneva in June 2000, its members voted by an overwhelming majority to adopt measures against Myanmar if the military Government did not halt the practice of forced labour within four months. The sanctions came into effect in November 2000, although their implementation depended on the co-operation of individual countries. The Myanma Government responded by describing the sanctions as 'unfair', 'unreasonable' and 'unjust', and announced that it would cease to co-operate with the ILO. In May 2001 ASEAN labour ministers issued a joint communiqué noting what they described as concrete actions by Myanmar to eradicate forced labour and urging the ILO to end its campaign against Myanmar. The ILO sent a delegation to Myanmar in October 2001 to investigate the claims of improvement; however, it reported that forced labour was still widespread in areas controlled by the military. In March 2002 the ILO established a liaison office in the country, and in 2003 talks were initiated regarding the development of a plan of action for the elimination of forced labour in Myanmar.

Myanmar has also been condemned annually since 1991 by the UN for human rights violations within the country, with increasingly strong resolutions having been adopted by the General Assembly each year. As a result, companies operating in Myanmar may find themselves subject to boycotts and other protest activity, such as that which persuaded Pepsi, Texaco and many others to withdraw completely from the country. Various national governments now encourage companies not to invest in Myanmar, and several local governments, such as that of New York City in the USA, have selective purchasing policies and will not do business with companies that operate in Myanmar. (In June 1998, however, a US court ruled that state and local governments could not impose a boycott on Myanmar by law, since such actions infringed the right of the federal Government to conduct foreign policy.) In November the Republic of Korea (South Korea) became the first Asian country to co-sponsor a UN General Assembly resolution criticizing human rights abuses in Myanmar. In January 2002 the European lingerie manufacturer Triumph decided to close its factory in Myanmar in response to a long campaign in Europe claiming that it was exploiting forced labour.

From late 1998, however, Myanmar's international isolation began, in some respects, to diminish, and Western diplomats began to speak approvingly of the possibility of effecting change in Myanmar through the employment of policies of engagement, rather than isolation, towards its Government. In October 1998 the British Government convened an informal meeting at Chilston Park in the United Kingdom at which ministers of foreign affairs and ambassadors from several countries, together with UN and World Bank officials, began to develop a strategy of engaging with the Myanma Government. These meetings gave rise to the proposal, quickly rejected by the ruling junta, that Myanmar should receive US $1,000m. in aid in return for significant political concessions. A subsequent meeting in Seoul, Republic of Korea, in March 2000, known as Chilston-2, failed to produce any further strategies. None the less, in February 2000 Myanmar hosted a major Interpol conference addressing drugs-related crime. Although the United Kingdom and the USA boycotted the meeting, the military junta convinced some of those attending that it was interested in attacking the trade. The Australian, Japanese and South Korean Governments all made official contact with the Myanma Government to explore possibilities for political change in Myanmar. In November 1999 the Japanese Prime Minister, Keizo Obuchi, met with Senior Gen. Than Shwe during an ASEAN summit meeting in Manila, the Philippines; the meeting was the first between the leader of a major world power and a senior member of the military Government since the junta's suppression of the democratic opposition in 1988. In April 2000 the EU announced the introduction of increased sanctions against Myanmar, but in the second half of 2001, in response to increasing indications that dialogue was taking place between the SPDC and Aung San Suu Kyi, it agreed to allow Myanmar to take part in future ASEAN-EU dialogues and to sponsor a variety of aid programmes, while keeping the sanctions in place. The removal of restrictions on Suu Kyi in May 2002 was welcomed by the international community. The first diplomatic benefit of the release came in August 2002, when the Japanese Minister of Foreign Affairs visited Myanmar. The USA also signalled its willingness to remove sanctions in return for political progress. In January 2003 the EU waived its ban on the granting of visas to members of the SPDC in order to allow the Deputy Minister of Foreign Affairs, Khin Maung Wien, to attend a meeting in Europe. By April, however, the EU was threatening to tighten sanctions unless overt progress towards democratization was made. In February the USA had made similar threats. Following the renewed detention of Suu Kyi in May, the USA expanded its sanctions against Myanmar, banning all imports and 'freezing' SPDC assets in the USA. The EU extended its visa restrictions. Japan, which was Myanmar's largest aid donor, announced that no new aid would be granted until Suu Kyi was freed. In September 2004 the US Senate approved a resolution urging the UN Security Council to take action against Myanmar. In September 2006 the Security Council voted to place Myanmar on its formal agenda, a decision supported by 10 of its 15 members, including the USA, which described the development as a 'major step forward'. Meanwhile, in July 2005 US President George W. Bush signed a bill extending import restrictions under the Burmese Freedom and Democracy Act.

To the surprise of many observers, ASEAN also condemned the detention of Aung San Suu Kyi and urged the resumption of political dialogue. ASEAN leaders appeared to be concerned that Myanmar's poor relations with the West might compromise the efforts of other ASEAN countries to maintain good relations and damage the interests of ASEAN as a whole, since Myanmar was due to chair the Association in 2006. President Megawati Sukarnoputri of Indonesia urged all ASEAN governments to encourage political participation, and a parliamentary caucus to promote democracy in Myanmar was formed in Malaysia. In February 2005, at a meeting in Jakarta, parliamentarians from Cambodia, Indonesia, Malaysia, Singapore and Thailand initiated an inter-parliamentary caucus on Myanmar, aiming for faster progress on political reform. None the less, ASEAN remained committed to a strategy of engagement with, rather than sanctions against, the regime, with the Prime Minister of Thailand, Thaksin Shinawatra, strongly supporting a 'soft' approach. In December 2004 Thaksin commented on Thai radio that Suu Kyi should remain under house arrest because some form of 'turmoil' always followed her release. Thaksin was privately accused of allowing his close business relations with the military Government in Myanmar to influence his political views. Despite private expressions of disappointment with Myanmar's progress towards democracy, therefore, ASEAN limited itself publicly to suggesting involvement of 'all strata of society' in the democratization process. Thailand was particularly keen to maintain good relations with the regime, in order to secure co-operation in its attempts to control the flow of illicit drugs from Myanmar into Thailand. Accordingly, in mid-December 2003 Thailand was host to an international forum, called the 'Bangkok Process', at which the Myanma Minister of Foreign Affairs, Win Aung, presented his Government's 'road map' for democratic progress (see above) to representatives from Australia, Austria, the People's Republic of China, France, Germany, India, Indonesia, Italy, Japan and Singapore, along with UN Special Envoy Razali Ismail. Win Aung announced at this meeting that the first stage of the 'road map'—the reassembly of the National Convention—would take place in early 2004. Myanmar's other main neighbours, India and China, also in competition for influence there, remained reluctant to exert pressure on the Government. The most public pressure on the regime came from UN Secretary-General Kofi Annan, who urged that the transition to democracy foreshadowed in Khin Nyunt's 'road map' be completed by 2006. Annan and Razali Ismail emphasized the need for dialogue with Suu Kyi and the NLD, and Annan expressed dismay that Suu Kyi had not been released to take part in the National Convention in May 2004.

The EU's insistence on not permitting the three newest members of ASEAN (Cambodia, Laos and Myanmar) to join the ASEM forum was placed under strain by the Union's request that its own new members be permitted to participate. ASEAN's official response was that the new European members would be permitted to join only when Cambodia, Laos and Myanmar were admitted. However, behind the scenes there was a protracted search for a formula that might somehow permit ASEM to grow while 'saving face' on both sides. During the first half of 2005 ASEAN members became increasingly concerned that Myanmar would insist on taking its turn to assume the Association's rotating chair in 2006. After private (but quietly publicized) requests from several senior ASEAN officials for the SPDC to demonstrate its good intentions by releasing Aung San Suu Kyi, the Philippine Senate approved a resolution urging that Myanmar be denied the ASEAN chair unless Suu Kyi were freed. Even the Thai Senate approved a similar resolution. In late July 2005 the Government of Myanmar formally announced that the demands of national reconciliation rendered it unable to take its turn as ASEAN chair in 2006. The Philippines agreed to assume the chair for that year in place of Myanmar. Meanwhile, the SPDC also placed some hope in BIMST-EC, now renamed the Bay of Bengal Initiative for Multi-Sectoral Technical and Economic Co-operation. Gen. Khin Nyunt attended the first summit meeting of the grouping in Bangkok in July 2004 to discuss potential co-operation on public health, education, information technology and biotechnology. Plans for a BIMST-EC free trade agreement were envisaged, along with an India–Myanmar–Thailand highway. Senior Gen. Than Shwe visited India shortly after Khin Nyunt's removal in 2004.

The impact of Khin Nyunt's departure on Myanmar's foreign policy was significant. Among the senior generals, he was regarded as the most pragmatic and outward-looking, being more aware of the international sentiments towards the regime's policies. While this may have encouraged his support for Yangon's serving as the host city for ASEAN's 2006 summit meeting, the SPDC relinquished its chairmanship nine months after his departure. Following his removal, responsibility for foreign policy rested with the more inflexible officers—Than Shwe and his protégés. The Government also recalled a large number of ambassadors and minister-counsellors, nearly all of whom were associated either with Khin Nyunt or with his military intelligence, and replaced them with at least 11 brigadier-generals. In July 2005, following Myanmar's announcement that it would not chair ASEAN in 2006, the Chinese Minister of Foreign Affairs, Li Zhaoxing, missed a meeting of the ARF (which discusses regional security issues) in order to visit Myanmar to meet both Senior Gen. Than Shwe and Prime Minister Soe Win. The final communiqué of the ARF expressed concern over the slow pace of democratic reform in Myanmar and urged the Government to begin talks with the NLD. Rumours also circulated that Myanmar was developing closer links with the Democratic People's Republic of Korea (North Korea), although relations had not been formally restored since a bomb attack in 1983 by North Korean agents on a South Korean delegation visiting Myanmar. Myanmar was said to have obtained missiles and other strategic weapons from North Korea, and there was speculation that North Korea might secretly be helping Myanmar to build a nuclear reactor. However, there was little evidence to support any direct nuclear links between the two countries.

The SPDC's relations with its ASEAN neighbours deteriorated following Myanmar's forfeiture of its turn to chair the organization. Prior to the ASEAN summit meeting in Kuala Lumpur, Malaysia, at the end of 2005, a group of South-East Asian parliamentarians had demanded that Myanmar be expelled from ASEAN unless the regime improved its human rights record, urging the permanent inclusion of Myanmar on ASEAN's agenda. ASEAN also noted the increased interest of the international community in developments in Myanmar at the Kuala Lumpur meeting. The Chairman's statement urged the release of those detained without charge, encouraged the country to expedite its 'road map' to democracy, and welcomed Myanmar's invitation to the Malaysian Minister of Foreign Affairs, Datuk Seri Syed Hamid bin Syed Jaafar Albar, to learn first-hand of its progress. Over the next few months, however, the visit of a delegation led by Syed Hamid was postponed twice because, according to the country's Minister of Foreign Affairs, Maj.-Gen. Nyan Win, Myanmar was preoccupied with the relocation of its administrative offices to Pyinmana. The delegation finally arrived in March 2006 but was not permitted to meet with Aung San Suu Kyi and the visit was unexpectedly curtailed.

In 2005 the USA and the United Kingdom attempted to have the issue of Myanmar placed on the agenda of the UN Security Council. Russia, China and Algeria had blocked a previous attempt earlier in the year, but the Philippines' turn on the Security Council facilitated the approval of the latter proposal. A report commissioned in that year by former President of the Czech Republic Václav Havel and Archbishop Desmond Tutu of South Africa recommended that the Security Council adopt a resolution for intervention, requiring that Myanmar work with the UN Secretary-General's office in implementing a plan for national reconciliation and the restoration of a democratically elected government; that the Secretary-General remain vigorously engaged with the resolution process and report back to the Security Council on a regular basis; that Myanmar ensure the immediate, safe and unhindered access to all parts of the country for the UN and international aid organizations to provide humanitarian assistance; and that Aung San Suu Kyi and all prisoners of conscience in Myanmar be released immediately. While the report was heavily criticized by the Myanma Government, in December 2005 the UN Security Council finally heard a briefing by the Under-Secretary-General for Political Affairs, Ibrahim Gambari, and the members agreed to monitor progress.

In February 2006 Prime Minister Soe Win travelled to Beijing to secure China's support and future veto of any UN attempts to impose economic and political sanctions via the Security Council. China expressed vehement opposition to the Security Council's decision to place Myanmar on its formal agenda in September of that year, alleging that this constituted needless interference in Myanmar's internal affairs; Russia, Qatar and the Republic of the Congo also voted against the motion. Meanwhile, in April Dep. Senior Gen. Maung Aye, accompanied by the Minister of Foreign Affairs, Maj.-Gen. Nyan Win, travelled to Moscow to seek the same assurances from the Russian Government. During their visit Maung Aye signed a new co-operation agreement with the Kurchatov nuclear research centre, reviving a project to build a centre for nuclear studies, which was to include the construction of a research nuclear reactor, laboratories and support infrastructure. The project had originally begun in 2001, when Myanmar signed a deal with the Russian Ministry of Nuclear Energy to build a 10-MW nuclear test reactor. Although hundreds of personnel had been sent to Russia for nuclear-technology training, the project had stalled because Myanmar was unable to continue financing the facility's construction. China has assisted Myanmar in the construction of hydropower plants near Pyinmana and of its third international airfield in the Bago Division, and China has also funded the construction of a deep-sea port facing the Indian Ocean along with a highway connecting the port to Yunnan Province. The Chinese Government continued to criticize foreign interference in Myanmar's internal affairs, and the draft resolution concerning Myanmar was eventually vetoed at the UN Security Council in January 2007. Beijing continued to host regular visits by SPDC generals and promoted further co-operation between the Tatmadaw and the Chinese People's Liberation Army (PLA); this was highlighted by a visit from the PLA Chief of General Staff, Gen. Liang Guanglie, in October 2006. In addition to the SPDC's increasing recourse to China for diplomatic advice, Myanmar continued to consolidate relations with India. Following a five-day official visit to India by Senior Gen. Than Shwe in October 2004, India also sent senior-level delegations to Myanmar, including visits by Minister for External Affairs K. Natwar Singh in March 2005 and by President Aavul Pakkiri Jainulabidin Abdul Kalam in March 2006. India's Chief of Staff of the Navy, Adm. Arun Prakash, visited in January 2006, and India held discussions with the SPDC over border security and access to Myanmar's offshore natural gas resources.

The implications of the transfer of administrative headquarters to Nay Pyi Taw were significant for Myanmar's foreign relations, not only because it would greatly inconvenience Yangon-based foreign diplomats and NGOs, but also because the new administrative centre, located in the southern Mandalay Division, is close to the overland river and highway routes connecting Myanmar with China and India. Nay Pyi Taw, hundreds of kilometres from the sea, may be isolated from the West and from many member states of ASEAN, but it is conveniently located in proximity to the Asian continental powers, which are expected to play the most important role in Myanmar's economy.

Frequent visits by Thai civil and military authorities in 2006 focused on gaining access to petroleum deposits in southern Myanmar and on resolving trade and trafficking issues, as well as border security. Although the SPDC had benefited from close relations with the Government of Thai Prime Minister Thaksin Shinawatra, the Myanma Government sent the interim Government of Thailand a congratulatory message following the military coup of December 2006 in Bangkok. Thailand, along with India, China and South Korea, had expressed an interest in gaining access and rights to the drilling and transport of newly discovered natural gas reserves in Rakhine and Chin States in western Myanmar.

In May 2006 the UN sent Ibrahim Gambari to Myanmar to discuss human rights issues and the prospects for restoring democracy. Gambari was the first UN envoy to visit the country since Indonesia's Ali Alatas in 2005. When Razali Ismail resigned in January 2006, having been denied entry for almost two years, he voiced his belief that Myanmar's 'road map' had effectively come to an end with the arrest of Prime Minister Khin Nyunt in 2004. Gambari met with three senior SPDC generals—Than Shwe, Maung Aye and Soe Win—in Pyinmana. During his visit Gambari also became the first foreigner permitted to meet with Aung San Suu Kyi since Razali's visit in 2004. This was also unexpected because, prior to Gambari's visit, the SPDC had accused the NLD of having links to terrorist groups and had threatened to ban the organization. Since the regime was concerned about the UN Security Council placing Myanmar on its agenda, Gambari's visit to the country and his access to Suu Kyi was likely to have been a concession promoted by the Chinese Government, in order that China could continue supporting Myanmar at the UN. Upon his return to the UN, Secretary-General Kofi Annan appealed to Than Shwe to release Suu Kyi, but the SPDC extended her detention under house arrest on the following day. In August 2006 US President Bush renewed the Burmese Freedom and Democracy Act of 2003 for a further three years and extended import restrictions against Myanmar.

In July 2006 Syed Hamid chaired the ASEAN foreign ministers' meeting in Kuala Lumpur and defended the group's joint communiqué as a compromise position on developments in Myanmar. The statement recognized Myanmar's need for time and space to deal with its challenges but voiced concern over the pace of the national reconciliation process; nevertheless, ASEAN expressed its hope that tangible progress would be made by the SPDC towards a peaceful transition to democracy. Syed Hamid insisted that, unless the Myanmar Government's conduct changed, continued pressure for democratic reform would threaten ASEAN's relations with the USA and EU, and he urged China and India to apply pressure on the SPDC accordingly. The ASEAN ministers of foreign affairs reiterated their request for Myanmar to abide by its promised 'road map' to democracy at the January 2007 ASEAN summit meeting held in Cebu, the Philippines. They reaffirmed ASEAN's position on Myanmar—that it should make significant progress toward democratic reform—and also appealed for the release of prominent political prisoners, including the leaders of the NLD. In September 2006 the SPDC had arrested five well-known activists of the '88 Generation' movement, a student grouping that had led the protests of 1988. They were released in January 2007, possibly as a means of circumventing a UN Security Council resolution urging Myanmar to release its political prisoners and improve human rights (in August several of these activists were again taken into custody). ASEAN, along with the UN, the EU and the USA, again urged the release of Aung San Suu Kyi in May 2007, and hundreds of her supporters rallied in Yangon on the 17th anniversary of the NLD's election victory, which was also the day set for her latest detention order to expire. A planned march to the Shwedagon pagoda was blocked by the USDA; the demonstrators returned to the NLD's headquarters to conduct their prayers, and the SPDC extended Suu Kyi's detention for another year.

In April 2007 Myanmar and the Democratic People's Republic of Korea restored diplomatic relations when Kim Yong Il, a North Korean Vice-Minister of Foreign Affairs, visited Yangon and signed an agreement with his counterpart, Kyaw Thu. There was speculation that North Korea was seeking access to Myanmar's natural resources, while the Tatmadaw would benefit from the procurement of military equipment that had been blocked by US and EU sanctions. Relations between the two countries had improved over the previous decade, with several covert senior-level visits between the countries since 2000 to discuss co-operation in the defence industry; Myanmar had reportedly purchased weapons and ammunition from North Korea, as well as receiving technical advice. North Korea provided an alternative to China as a supplier of weapons to the regime, with regard to artillery in particular, although there was no clear evidence to support the claim that Myanmar had sought more than conventional weapons and technology. Since both countries drew condemnation from the West, and particularly the USA, the improvement in their bilateral relations—which was immediately approved by China—was seen by some as a natural alignment of 'pariah' states in need of allies. However, in view of the unlikely nature of a real military threat to Myanmar, the restoration of diplomatic relations with North Korea was more reflective of the generals' suspicion of Western intentions, as well as their dismissive attitude towards Western sanctions, given their strong economic and diplomatic links with China and India. In July 2007 an Amnesty International report revealed that India intended to sell an Advanced Light Helicopter to Myanmar; as many of the helicopter's parts were developed in European countries, such a sale would breach the EU's weapons embargo against Myanmar. The strengthening of relations between Myanmar and North Korea was a concern for ASEAN; ministers had also focused on the North Korean nuclear issue at the Cebu summit meeting in early 2007. In view of North Korea's nuclear test in October 2006, it appeared that Myanmar, an ASEAN member state, had associations with an apparently nuclear 'pariah' state. Myanmar, meanwhile, was also a signatory to ASEAN's Treaty on the South-East Asia Nuclear Weapon-Free Zone. Furthermore, there was speculation that the growing alliance between Myanmar and North Korea might cause problems for Thailand, as the possibility remained that more North Korean asylum-seekers would arrive along its borders with Myanmar and Laos.

The anti-Government demonstrations in September 2007 drew unprecedented world-wide attention from foreign governments and legislatures, the EU, the UN and NGOs, among others. Much of this heightened interest when compared with previous protests could be attributed to the increased availability of internet and satellite coverage of the events recorded by amateur observers equipped with mobile technologies. Despite the regime's best efforts, pictures of the demonstrations were recorded and sent to the international media for world-wide broadcast, some of which became available inside Myanmar. Numerous appeals for restraint on the part of the Myanma authorities, as well as for the release of detained protesters, came from the international community, including the UN, the EU, the European Parliament and some ASEAN countries. Notably, some Western governments turned to Beijing in the hope that Chinese officials might exercise their influence over the regime's leaders and persuade the SPDC to act with moderation.

After force was used against the protesters in late September 2007 (which was again recorded and broadcast by the world's media), ASEAN ministers of foreign affairs issued a statement deploring the violent suppression of the demonstrations, as did the UN Human Rights Council, and Ibrahim Gambari was sent to Myanmar on the first of several visits to meet with Than Shwe and Aung San Suu Kyi. With Chinese and Russian approval, the UN Security Council also issued an unprecedented statement urging the SPDC to address the human rights, humanitarian and economic concerns of its people. Travel and financial transaction restrictions were increased on SPDC officials and their families by the USA, the United Kingdom, Australia, Canada and the EU, and further demands were made for the release of all political prisoners and the initiation of a dialogue with Suu Kyi. Following the shooting of the Japanese journalist Kenji Nagai during the repression of the demonstrations, Japan cancelled some US $4.7m. in funding for a human resources centre at Yangon University, but stopped short of halting all aid. The SPDC appointed a special liaison officer to manage relations with Suu Kyi, and the announcement of a schedule to hold a constitutional referendum in 2008 and elections in 2010 was welcomed by China, Russia and India, although the draft Constitution was criticized by the USA as merely providing an entrenchment of military rule. In October 2007 President Bush expanded economic sanctions to cover further individuals, including financial supporters of the SPDC. Trade sanctions were extended for another year in May 2008, and the US Department of the Treasury was ordered to 'freeze' the assets of state-owned companies in Myanmar.

International condemnation of the SPDC was renewed in May 2008 by the regime's response to Cyclone Nargis. Although multiple offers of humanitarian assistance were initially made to the regime, the SPDC refused to grant entry visas to aid workers, or to allow US, British and French ships carrying aid to dock and unload their cargo. A number of demands for humanitarian intervention based upon the UN's 'responsibility to protect' principle were made by humanitarian and pro-democracy advocates and endorsed by several foreign officials, including the French Minister for Foreign and European Affairs, Bernard Kouchner, as well as some more conservative journalists. Aid organizations were particularly incensed by the SPDC's decision to proceed with its scheduled constitutional referendum on 10 May (only one week after the cyclone had struck), thus drawing valuable financial and human resources away from addressing immediate needs in the Ayeyarwady delta; many believed the regime was withholding full details of the disaster, particularly when it claimed that it had already met the initial requirements for food, water and shelter and was already commencing the 'reconstruction' phase. Moreover, the SPDC had not initially mobilized the Tatmadaw to relieve the situation—comparisons with China's handling of its own natural disaster (a major earthquake) shortly thereafter would be made on this point. The authorities gradually relaxed their stance and allowed some aid flights to land in Yangon, but would not permit unfettered access or distribution of aid, offering instead to monitor and distribute the aid themselves. Some three weeks after Nargis struck the UN Secretary-General Ban Ki-Moon met with Than Shwe in Nay Pyi Taw. As a result of mediation by ASEAN officials, the SPDC eventually agreed to allow all foreign aid workers into the country. However, the regime continued to place major obstacles in the way of foreign relief workers and delayed the granting of visas to foreign nationals seeking access to the delta region.

Following the extension of Aung San Suu Kyi's detention in late May 2008, ASEAN issued a rare strong rebuke to Myanmar at its Ministerial Meeting in Singapore in July. Attending the ARF meeting held later that month, US Secretary of State Condoleezza Rice described the SPDC's plans to restore democracy gradually to Myanmar as a 'mockery'. The USA and the UN had earlier criticized the SPDC's decision to extend Suu Kyi's detention. Also at the ARF meeting, the Australian Minister for Foreign Affairs, Stephen Smith, pledged an additional $A30m. in aid for the survivors of Cyclone Nargis, but insisted to Myanmar's Minister of Foreign Affairs, Nyan Win, that the SPDC should democratize quickly and respect human rights. He also emphasized the need for the SPDC to ensure that the elections in 2010 would be free and fair and involve the participation of the political opposition, including Suu Kyi.

In August 2008 Aung San Suu Kyi refused to meet with visiting UN special envoy Ibrahim Gambari because of his previous lack of success in promoting political dialogue. Gambari was also denied a meeting with Than Shwe. The new UN Special Rapporteur on Human Rights, Tomás Ojea Quintana, visited Myanmar for the first time in August. In December 2008 the SPDC signed an agreement with a consortium of four firms from South Korea (Daewoo and Korea Gas Corporation) and India (ONGC Videsh and GAIL) to pipe natural gas from Myanmar's north-western coast to China. The 30-year deal was to provide natural gas to China's National United Oil Corporation.

The EU extended its sanctions against Myanmar for another year in April 2009, and international condemnation followed the SPDC's committal to trial of Aung San Suu Kyi for breaching the terms of her house arrest in May (see above). ASEAN issued a rare statement expressing 'grave concern' about the trial and stressing that, with the world watching, the honour and credibility of the Myanma Government was at stake and that, as a member of ASEAN, Myanmar had a responsibility to protect and promote human rights. At the ASEAN Summit meeting held earlier in the year, Myanmar and Cambodia had vigorously objected to the presence of human rights groups at the session to discuss the powers of a new human rights body created under the ASEAN Charter. Following ASEAN's statement about Suu Kyi, the Myanma Government accused Thailand (as the current Chair of ASEAN) of interfering in Myanmar's domestic affairs. At the ninth ASEM for ministers responsible for foreign affairs, European ministers urged the immediate release of Suu Kyi. UN Secretary-General Ban Ki-Moon met with Than Shwe in Nay Pyi Taw in June, while Suu Kyi's trial was taking place. He requested but was refused a visit to see Suu Kyi, prompting British Prime Minister Gordon Brown to threaten the possibility of further sanctions against Myanmar.

In July 2009 Myanmar's envoy to the UN announced that some political prisoners were to be granted an amnesty and released in order to stand as candidates in the 2010 elections, as had been requested by Ban Ki-Moon during his visit in the previous month. Also in July a North Korean ship headed for Myanmar was tracked by the US Navy; the vessel turned around of its own accord, but was suspected of carrying weapons for the Myanma regime, although the claims were denied. The ship was liable to inspection under the UN sanctions resolution imposed against North Korea following its nuclear and missile tests two months earlier.

The court handling the trial of Aung San Suu Kyi delayed issuing a verdict until August 2009, possibly to avoid attracting further attention and condemnation at the 42nd meeting of ASEAN foreign ministers and the 16th ARF meeting. While the US Secretary of State, Hillary Clinton, had suggested that Myanmar be expelled from ASEAN if Suu Kyi were not released, the ARF members officially offered to work with Myanmar to promote democracy, human rights and the well-being of its people. After the 18-month extension of Suu Kyi's house arrest was announced, ASEAN issued a statement expressing 'deep disappointment' at her sentence and reiterating appeals made at the meeting of ASEAN foreign ministers for the immediate release of all political prisoners, including Suu Kyi, to enable them to participate in the 2010 legislative elections. According to the statement, the ASEAN Chair believed that 'only free, fair and inclusive General Elections will then pave the way for Myanmar's full integration into the international community'. Nevertheless, ASEAN declared that it would remain constructively engaged with Myanmar and co-operate with the Myanma Government in its efforts to realize full democracy, urging the country's full co-operation with the UN.

Through a number of measures in 2009, including US Secretary of State Clinton's signing of ASEAN's Treaty of Amity and Cooperation in Southeast Asia after the 42nd meeting of ASEAN ministers of foreign affairs in July, the Administration of US President Barack Obama signalled a desire to increase its presence in the Asia-Pacific region. Following the sentencing of Aung San Suu Kyi and John Yettaw in August, the Chairman of the US Senate Foreign Relations Subcommittee on East Asian and Pacific Affairs, Senator Webb, visited Nay Pyi Taw to meet with Than Shwe. Webb successfully negotiated the release of Yettaw and was allowed rare access to Suu Kyi. The Obama Administration had earlier claimed that it would review its policy on Myanmar, and Webb was reputed to favour a policy of constructive engagement over sanctions. Nevertheless, in May 2010 President Obama extended sanctions against Myanmar following the visit to Nay Pyi Taw and Yangon earlier in the month of the US Assistant Secretary of State for East Asian and Pacific Affairs, Kurt Campbell, in order to inspect Myanmar's preparations for the elections. In line with the Obama Administration's policy of 'pragmatic engagement' with the regime, Campbell met with government and USDA officials, as well as leaders of the NLD, including Suu Kyi. (The NLD had been formally dissolved two days prior to Campbell's arrival—see above.) Following his visit (his second to the country in six months), Campbell criticized the regime for exerting pressure on the ethnic groups to comply with its regulations before the polls, and declared that the elections would lack international legitimacy. He was also critical of Myanmar's relations with North Korea, and raised concerns over Myanmar's possible nuclear programme; similar security concerns had been raised by Secretary of State Clinton at the July 2009 ASEAN meeting. In a rare instance of direct involvement in the internal affairs of one of its member states, in July 2010 ASEAN ministers responsible for foreign affairs urged the Myanma Government to hold 'free, fair, and inclusive' elections and offered to send ASEAN observers to oversee the polls. The uncharacteristic appeal reflected strong pressures being applied on the regional grouping by Western states keen to ensure the observance of proper democratic practices in advance of the forthcoming elections.

The Myanma authorities intensified efforts to develop political and economic relations with their two strategic regional partners, China and India. Chinese Premier Wen Jiabao completed a state visit to Myanmar in June 2010, the first such visit in 16 years. A number of agreements on energy projects and aid were reportedly signed. The visit reflected the growing importance of China as an investor and trading partner in Myanmar. Construction work on the Chinese section of a Sino-Myanma oil and gas pipeline project, which would facilitate the transport of fuel from the Middle East and Africa to China's Yunnan Province via Myanmar, commenced in September. Also in September, amid growing international pressure for the establishment of a UN commission of inquiry into alleged human rights abuses and war crimes committed by the regime, Than Shwe embarked on a five-day official visit to China. Meanwhile, in July Than Shwe travelled to India where he held discussions with President Pratibha Devisingh Patil and Prime Minister Manmohan Singh, following which five agreements relating to border security and energy, telecommunications and other infrastructure projects were concluded.

The UN continued to express disappointment and frustration with the SPDC for its lack of co-operation in response to the UN's appeal for the release of political prisoners, the holding of free, fair and fully inclusive elections, and any genuine efforts to achieve national reconciliation. The UN Secretary-General Ban Ki-Moon's Special Adviser on Myanmar, Vijay Nambiar, was denied access to the country in 2010 and was not permitted to visit again until May 2011, when he met with government officials in Nay Pyi Taw and with Aung San Suu Kyi in Yangon. Tomás Ojea Quintana visited Myanmar in February 2010 in his capacity as UN Special Rapporteur on the situation of human rights in Myanmar; in his report issued to the UN Human Rights Council in March, Ojea Quintana outlined a pattern of gross and systematic violation of human rights, recommending the establishment of a commission of inquiry into international crimes in Myanmar. The idea was publicly supported at the UN by some countries, including the USA, with Secretary of State Clinton claiming that this was consistent with the US Government's commitment to seeking accountability for human rights violations in Myanmar. However, the proposal was blocked by China and was not included in the EU's annual resolution on Myanmar. As a result of the critical nature of his report, Ojea Quintana was denied access for any further visits to Myanmar. The operations of international humanitarian organizations were restricted in advance of the November 2010 elections, with staff being denied visas, travel permits and the requisite permission to expand programmes in certain areas. On his return from visiting Myanmar in May 2011, Vijay Nambiar issued a press statement claiming that UN agencies would be better placed to respond to Myanmar's development needs if the existing restrictions on their operations were removed.

International reactions to the legislative elections in Myanmar in November 2010 were mixed. The USA, EU and UN criticized the polls as being insufficiently inclusive or transparent and incompatible with international standards, concluding that the elections had been neither free nor fair. Both the EU and the USA voted to extend sanctions against Myanmar for an additional year, in May and July 2011, respectively. India remained noticeably silent on the question of the elections, avoiding criticism of them, both before and after the event. China, on the other hand, welcomed the polls as an important step in Myanmar's 'road map' for democracy.

ASEAN, chaired by Viet Nam at the time, also welcomed the elections and emphasized the importance of national reconciliation in Myanmar. However, Indonesia and the Philippines criticized Myanmar for its lack of reform, and the Philippines President, Benigno Aquino III, denounced the elections as a farce. At the ASEAN Summit in the Vietnamese capital, Hanoi, in April 2010 the 10 member states of ASEAN had agreed to Indonesia's request to swap its turn to assume the annually rotating chair of the Association, scheduled for 2011, with Brunei. At the following ASEAN summit meeting, held in Jakarta in May 2011, Myanmar's new President, Thein Sein, requested that his country assume the chair of ASEAN in 2014. The request was met with a cautious response, with no decision expected to be made until later in 2011. In his closing statement the summit chairman, Indonesian President Susilo Bambang Yudhoyono, expressed the view that 'ASEAN leaders do not object in principle to the proposal' but stressed that Myanmar would be expected to continue to make tangible progress towards democracy 'so when it becomes chair it does not generate negative views'.

Economy

HTWE HTWE THEIN

INTRODUCTION

The economy of Myanmar (Burma) is predominantly based on agriculture. Although rich in natural and mineral resources, as well as fisheries, the country suffers from the insufficient development of infrastructure, industries and financial institutions. In comparison with neighbouring nations in South-East Asia, Myanmar rates poorly in terms of human development indicators such as purchasing power, health and education. While the legacy of British colonialism is an important factor in understanding the historical development of the economy, post-colonial politics and military governance have been more influential in the formation of economic institutions, policies and development strategies.

A centrally planned 'command' economy was introduced by Gen. Ne Win, who assumed power in a military coup in 1962, effectively terminating the country's experiment with parliamentary democracy. Ne Win followed a self-sufficient path of national economic development through 'the Burmese Way to Socialism', severing most economic and political links with the rest of the world. The country became known as the Socialist Republic of the Union of Burma. The economy declined dramatically during the tenure of Ne Win, and the period was subsequently characterized by many critical scholars as a disastrous turning-point.

Upon assuming control in 1988, the State Law and Order Restoration Council (SLORC) abandoned the Burmese Way to Socialism, stating a preference for transforming the country's economic system into a market economy open to international trade and investment. This historic change in economic development strategy marked an end to the self-imposed economic isolation that had defined preceding decades. However, since gaining power the military regime has been beset by a series of economic and political problems. Although Myanmar was once considered to be the 'rice bowl' of Asia owing to its high level of agricultural productivity, trade and financial sanctions imposed by the USA and the European Union (EU), and the economic mismanagement of the Myanma Government, have severely damaged the country's economy, rendering Myanmar one of the poorest countries in South-East Asia. Myanmar has experienced major macroeconomic imbalances, including excessive inflation, budget deficits and official exchange rates that grossly overvalue the kyat (the national currency). Many observers continue to express scepticism about the prospects for sustained economic growth, suggesting that political repression, ineffective policies and economic mismanagement, poor health and education systems, and infrastructural weaknesses have hindered opportunities for advancement and eroded the nation's human development potential.

The failure of the military junta to restore democracy (see History), in addition to a prevalent narcotics trade and labour rights violations, have continued to restrict Myanmar's external economic relations. The Administration of US President Bill Clinton imposed sanctions against Myanmar in April 1997, amid pressure from human rights and pro-democracy campaigners. However, these sanctions only prohibited new investments by US companies in Myanmar, and applied only to US citizens and companies registered in the USA. At the time these sanctions were considered to be unilateral since the USA was the only country to ban all new investment in Myanmar, although a number of European nations imposed some restrictive measures on trading with Myanmar. In 2003, following further action against political dissidents and the detention of the leader of the National League for Democracy (NLD), Aung San Suu Kyi, the US Government strengthened its 'isolationist' policy stance by banning all imports from Myanmar to the USA, and suspending the US assets controlled by the military junta and individual officials associated with the regime. The new measures included disincentives for the provision of any major loans to Myanmar; they also intensified existing restrictions on the granting of US visas to Myanma government officials and their immediate relatives. In addition to freezing assets, the US sanctions also prohibited financial transactions by selected Myanma authorities and prominent regime-affiliated businesspeople. Following the brutal suppression by the military of pro-democracy demonstrations in September 2007, the US Government further tightened existing sanctions, including the imposition of a ban, from mid-2008 on the import into the USA of jade, rubies and other gemstones from Myanmar. The US Congress has renewed the sanctions on Myanmar every year since the measures were first imposed in 2003, latterly in July 2011, when they were once again renewed for a further year. However, the Administration of US President Barack Obama, which assumed power in January 2009, while continuing to impose sanctions, pronounced itself keen to adopt a policy of constructive engagement with the regime in Myanmar (see History).

The EU 'Common Position' on Myanmar (first adopted in October 1996) imposed a range of measures including a ban on visas and the freezing of assets belonging to senior-ranking officials in the military regime, a weapons embargo and trade restrictions. From the early 2000s pro-democracy groups urged the EU to intensify its measures in a similar manner to the USA. In an attempt to widen the scope of sanctions, such groups urged governments and international institutions to target Myanma government ministries and state-owned enterprises (SOEs), including the Myanma Oil and Gas Enterprise (MOGE), which were thought to be channelling foreign currency to the regime. The appeal to expand sanctions focused not only on individuals and businesses inside the country, but also on foreign companies indirectly engaged in business activity with Myanmar. The Burma Campaign UK, for instance, published in 2008 a report entitled *Insuring Repression*, which criticized foreign insurance companies providing insurance services to companies operating in Myanmar and urged these firms to cease any form of involvement with businesses in the country. Following the Myanma Government's violent repression of demonstrations in September 2007, the EU did indeed increase its restrictions on Myanmar. The new sanctions targeted Myanmar's timber, metal and precious stone industries by placing a ban on the import of these items from Myanmar to EU countries and also on European businesses making new investments in these industries in Myanmar. The EU has subsequently extended its sanctions, most recently in May 2011 for an additional year. Although the EU has maintained its sanctions against the Myanma Government, it also remains supportive of the urgent need to provide humanitarian aid for the country's poor.

While some observers and commentators do not support a system of general sanctions obstructing every industry and business activity, they generally agree on targeted sanctions—in particular, those focusing on the financial interests of regime members and their close associates, and their ability to travel to the West. Some observers have also suggested that, for sanctions to be effective, it would be necessary to ban US and European companies from operating in Myanmar altogether, including several major oil and gas companies with ongoing investments. Global institutions such as the UN, the International Labour Organization (ILO) and the International Trade Union Confederation, together with major international non-governmental organizations (NGOs), have also criticized the Myanma Government over its alleged use of state-imposed forced labour and perpetuation of human rights abuses.

The Association of Southeast Asian Nations (ASEAN) has adopted a different stance from the West, believing a policy of economic and political 'engagement' with Myanmar to be more appropriate and effective in facilitating steady, stable, and gradual change therein. In stark contrast to the isolationist stance adopted by the US Government and the EU, ASEAN made a major commitment to its policy of constructive engagement by admitting Myanmar as a member state in 1997. However, in the years following Myanmar's admission, ASEAN encountered pressure from other international bodies to identify any substantive and meaningful reforms that had been effected in Myanmar as a result of the regional organization's engagement policy. Consequently, there has been evident concern in recent years among several important member states that ASEAN's internal cohesion and international image are at risk.

Following slow economic growth throughout the 1980s, the Myanma economy began to improve in the early 1990s with the introduction of economic liberalization initiatives. Utilizing official statistics reported by the Myanma Government, the IMF estimated that growth in the country's real gross domestic product (GDP) averaged 3.5% annually between 1988 and 1997. During 1999–2003 the economy was reported to have achieved double-digit annual growth rates: 10.9% in 1999; 13.7% in 2000; 11.3% in 2001; 12% in 2002; and 13.8% in 2003. The Government predicted ongoing GDP growth in excess of 10%; however, international observers and economists were cautious with regard to the accuracy of the Government's claims, some going so far as to suggest that there was negative growth in the economy during 2003 and 2004. The generally disappointing performance of the economy, especially during the years prior to 2005, has been due to both domestic and international impediments. According to the Asian Development Bank (ADB), Myanmar's economic stagnation was related to problems concerning the kyat, including high inflation and the dual exchange rate system, to the burden of SOEs, which were operating with huge losses, and to declining output in the agricultural sector, which nevertheless remained the biggest contributor to the GDP. External factors such as fluctuations in foreign direct investment (FDI) and an extremely low level of humanitarian aid (compared with other developing Asian nations) have also affected the economy.

According to the ADB's *Asian Development Outlook 2011*, Myanmar's economic growth slowed to 3.6% in the 2008/09 fiscal year (ending 31 March 2009), compared with 5.5% growth in 2007/08, owing to reduced exports and private consumption (the indirect effect of the global financial crisis in neighbouring countries), depressed commodity prices globally, and the impact of the devastating Cyclone Nargis, which struck southern Myanmar in May 2008 (see Agriculture, Forestry and Fishing, below). However, growth was estimated to have risen to 5.1%, in 2009/10 owing to economic recovery in Myanmar's trade partners, a partial recovery of the country's agricultural sector following Cyclone Nargis, and increased demand from Thailand for Myanmar's gas resources. Growth in 2010/11 was estimated to have increased further, to 5.3%, bolstered by the construction sector and sustained economic recovery in trade partners resulting in higher imports of many goods including food and natural gas.

The economy has continued to be affected by macroeconomic imbalances. Several foreign analysts have attributed the underlying causes of inflation in Myanmar to the Government's monetary policy and persistent budget deficits (see, for example, the US Department of State's *Background Note: Burma*, June 2008). In its *Asian Development Outlook 2008* the ADB contended that the financing of budget deficits through the creation of additional kyat notes had exacerbated inflationary pressures. This report also noted that the Government's fiscal deficit had expanded as a result of massive increases (of up to 1,000%) in the salaries of public servants and military personnel in 2006, as well as costs associated with financing the construction of the new administrative capital, Nay Pyi Taw. Following the announcement of the salary increases, the price of commodities rose by over 10%. Inflation was also exacerbated by increases in government taxes and higher charges for public utilities (water and electricity). According to the ADB, in 2008/09 the Government of Myanmar sought to finance about one-third of the budgetary deficit by issuing Treasury securities, rather than producing additional kyat notes; in January 2010 the Government issued a new two-year Treasury bond, which it hoped would help to control inflationary pressures. According to the ADB, inflation declined from 22.5% in 2008/09 to 8.2% in 2009/10, and further to 7.3% in 2010/11. The kyat significantly appreciated against the US dollar from 2010 and by August 2011 the market exchange rate had reached 752 kyats = US $1, from 1,040 kyats = $1 in January 2010.

Financial reforms are required to address the macroeconomic imbalances detailed above. In 2006–07 the Government implemented several reforms in the banking sector, increasing the limit on deposit-to-capital ratios from 7% to 10%, permitting six private banks to open additional branches and granting 13 foreign banks licences to open representative offices. The Government also signalled the likelihood of foreign banks being permitted to operate branch offices in special economic zones, according to the ADB. In terms of reconciling disparate exchange rate regimes, the Government has, to a limited extent, recognized the reality of the unofficial 'market' exchange rate and has adjusted, in some cases, the official exchange rate to achieve a closer alignment with the market rate. For instance, in early 2007 the Customs Department amended the exchange rate used to calculate duty levies from 850 kyats to the US dollar to around 1,200 kyats to the dollar. None the less, much-needed economic reforms were likely to be significantly delayed given that the first in a series of planned measures, the removal of fuel subsidies in 2007, provoked street demonstrations from citizens protesting against extreme economic hardship. The new 'civilian' Government led by President Thein Sein, who was inaugurated in March 2011, introduced new policy measures including anti-poverty and anti-corruption programmes, as well as tax legislation in place of the former Profit Tax Law. Under the new tax legislation, individuals and companies would have to pay approximately 10% more than under the previous tax regime. The Thein Sein Government also abolished some economic commissions including the Trade Policy Council, which had been established in 1997 and was charged with supervising Myanmar's trade policies in the aftermath of widespread accusations of graft and mismanagement. In recent years the Myanma Government has accelerated the pace of privatization of SOEs across a range of industry sectors, including mining, transportation, dam construction, fuel retailing, and manufacturing. In addition to the sale of government-owned buildings and factories, privatization has also extended to the education and health sectors. In most cases, the buyers of SOEs were predominantly indigenous Burmese private business owners or emerging business conglomerates with close connections with the ruling élite, and most were subject to US and EU sanctions. Privatized businesses have also been purchased by the Union of Myanmar Economic Holdings (UMEH—which, along with the Myanmar Economic Corporation (MEC), is owned by the Directorate of Defence Procurement, a division of the Ministry of Defence) and by prominent military personnel, prompting concerns that the Myanma Government was seeking to reward close associates of the regime through its privatization programme. In addition to widespread unease over such a monopolistic situation, there were additional concerns that such large businesses might be exempted from taxes (in the case of UMEH) or endowed with special privileges and benefits not afforded to smaller businesses lacking 'political' representation.

Assessing the real economic potential of Myanmar has always been a difficult task because of incomplete, and thus unreliable, official statistics issued by its Government. For instance, government statistics concerning FDI inflows typically record the amounts approved under the Union of Myanmar Foreign Investment Law (FIL—see Foreign Investment and Trade, below), rather than actual amounts of 'real' investment inflows. Furthermore, it has been suggested that these amounts also include investments made by companies that subsequently decided to abandon their investment plans or actually divested from Myanmar after initial approval. It is also important to note that some foreign investment did not go through the Myanmar Investment Commission when the FIL was introduced in 1988. Those investments made outside the FIL were legal and often reflected investment from small and medium-sized enterprises. Perhaps more importantly, there is the presence of a thriving and pervasive 'black market', including activities such as narcotics production and jade-trading. The existence of this parallel informal economy, often considered to be of an equivalent size to the 'official' economy, has resulted in the absence of accurate market intelligence and economic analysis, which has proved to be a constant source of frustration for analysts and potential investors.

AGRICULTURE, FORESTRY AND FISHING

Agricultural products (including rice (paddy), pulses, beans, sesame, groundnuts and sugar cane) are major national exports. According to the ADB publication *Key Indicators 2011*, citing official estimates, the agricultural sector contributed 36.4% of total Myanma GDP in 2010/11. According to data published by the USA's Central Intelligence Agency (CIA), the sector employed 70% of the nation's labour force in 2001.

According to the Government's official statistics, Myanmar exported 182,000 metric tons of rice in 2004/05 and 180,000 tons in 2005/06. Myanmar's agricultural exports were reported to have risen rapidly in 2006/07, to a total of US $930m., an increase of more than 75% compared with the previous year. According to the Ministry of Commerce, this increase was attributable to the export of agricultural commodities through border trade, which more than doubled in 2006/07 in comparison with the previous fiscal year. Owing to triple-cropping techniques, Myanmar's agricultural output was expected to rise each year.

The country is the biggest producer of beans and pulses within the Asian region. Myanmar's beans and pulses are of medium quality and the country exports around 70% of its beans and pulses to India, with the remainder sold to Myanmar's Asian neighbours and the Middle East. According to the ADB, compared with the output levels of 10 years earlier, by 2008 production of pulses had increased three-fold. The report attributed the improved performance of the agricultural sector to the liberalization policies implemented in 2007, which allowed the private sector greater autonomy in areas including production, and import and distribution of agricultural raw materials and apparatus. Decreased external demand as a result of the 2008/09 global economic downturn led to a decline in the country's beans and pulses export market; instability in this crucial sector is traditionally thought to have a direct impact on Myanmar's currency exchange market.

In May 2008 Cyclone Nargis caused devastation in the Ayeyarwady (Irrawaddy) Delta region, the main rice-growing region of the country. In the aftermath of the cyclone, farmers in the affected region experienced enormous difficulty in raising sufficient capital to re-establish their livelihoods and recommence farming activities. Rice production from the area in early 2010 was about one-half of that yielded in the corresponding period of previous years. As a result, overall rice exports from Myanmar in the first half of 2010 declined to 276,180 metric tons, according to the Myanmar Chamber of Commerce and Industry, about one-third of the export volume in the corresponding period of 2009. Moreover, there was a decline in demand for agricultural product exports including rice, beans and pulses, and rubber, as major buyers in South-East Asia were affected by the global financial crisis. In January 2010 the Myanmar Rice Industry Association (MRIA) was formed in the hope of improving Myanmar's rice export levels. In mid-2010 the Ministry of Commerce assumed the right to issue rice export permits from the MRIA. The export of rice is conducted by the private sector (60%) and UMEH (40%).However, the low quality of rice continues to impede its export growth potential. A major problem in the agricultural commodity market since 2010 has been the appreciation of the kyat, which has had a negative impact on farmers as exporters have passed on losses and deferred buying agricultural commodities. However, the benefits of lower prices for imported goods have not been passed on to domestic consumers, since exporters (who are very often also importers under Myanma export and import laws) have decided not to reduce the price of imported goods, as a means of compensating for losses incurred as a result of their export activities.

Unavailability of finance is a major impediment to the revitalization of the rice industry in Myanmar. Following the destruction caused by Cyclone Nargis, FAO estimated that reconstruction of coastal embankments (to prevent seawater flooding the paddy fields) alone would cost some US $100m. In the absence of loans from the country's existing banks and the Government, farmers have been dependent on private sector lending, which amounted to thousands of millions of kyat in 2009. Although the Government's Myanmar Agricultural Development Bank has commenced credit schemes to farmers since the legislative elections in November

2010 (see History), the lending processes are reportedly riddled with corruption and taxation is imposed on an arbitrary basis. The rice export market has also suffered from currency instability and the Government's policy mismanagement, including inconsistent policies regarding the openness of the market, the over-controlling of rice export licences, and poor infrastructure.

Some 5,000 metric tons of jatropha oil from Myanmar's plantations were to be exported to the Republic of Korea (South Korea) in 2009 to be converted into biofuel. The Myanma Government has exerted pressure on local farmers to cultivate jatropha plants as it aims to increase the current area under cultivation (estimated at 100,000 acres in late 2008).

Forestry products are a major source of income for the Government, which was reported to have earned more than US $427m. in 2004/05 from timber exports. Timber was the nation's third largest export item in that year, behind minerals and agriculture. Myanmar possesses almost two-thirds of the world's teak reserves. Teak exports in 2004 (at 303,000 cu tons) were the highest in a decade, with an increase of 15.2% on the figure recorded in 2003 (263,000 cu tons). In some regions of Myanmar, ethnic armed groups are reported to control the release of permits to private businesses for logging in their area; consequently, timber production often suffers when conflict intensifies between ethnic armed groups and government troops.

Apart from the production of agricultural goods for export markets, Myanmar has significant natural fisheries and a growing aquaculture industry. According to the Ministry of Livestock and Fisheries, Myanmar exports fish and prawns to more than 40 countries and 30% of its total production to buyers in Asian, European and Middle Eastern markets. From a total of 162,000 ha of farms throughout the country, Myanmar's fishery exports have continued to rise. According to figures from the Ministry of Livestock and Fisheries, in the fiscal year 2005/06 Myanmar exported more than 270,000 metric tons of fishery products, earning US $359m. in export revenue. Export earnings were forecast to increase to $400m. in 2006/07. In 2009 the Myanma authorities were reported to be projecting a substantial increase in production at fisheries in Arakan State to offset the decline in production in the Ayeyarwady Delta region, which continued to suffer from the effects of Cyclone Nargis. However, in mid-2011 a number of seafood-processing plants were temporarily closed owing to declining profitability as the kyat rapidly appreciated against the dollar, damaging fishery exports.

While Myanmar's rich natural environment and fertile lands have produced significant resources for domestic consumption and export markets, the management and exploitation of these resources has, in certain instances, generated international concern. In particular, the logging industry has been criticized by international environmental activist groups. Global Witness (an advocacy group based in the United Kingdom) has produced critical reports detailing the nature of the illegal logging trade in Myanmar, which, it alleges, involves heavy lobbying activities by foreign and local businesses and government officials. Global Witness has alleged that 'severe' logging of teak forests has taken place in Kachin State in areas under the control of the Kachin Independence Organization and has estimated that in 2005 the People's Republic of China imported more than 1.5m. cu m of Myanma timber, worth an estimated US $350m., almost all of which was thought to have been traded illegally. According to FAO, Myanmar's forests have decreased in size by 14% since 1980 as a result of illegal logging.

Another major concern has been the production of narcotics within Myanmar, the US Department of State having rated Myanmar as the most significant producer and trafficker of amphetamine pills in the South-East Asian region. The ethnic Wa groups living in northern Shan State, close to the Myanma–Chinese border, were allegedly responsible for the majority of opium production and trafficking in the area. In 1999 the Government of Myanmar committed itself to a long-term plan intended to eliminate drugs production and trafficking by 2014. Despite initial encouraging results, according to the UN Office on Drugs and Crime (UNODC), Myanmar remained the second largest producer of opium in the world (behind Afghanistan) in 2010, with a global share of 19.5% in that year. Opium cultivation in Myanmar increased in every year during 2006–10, rising from 21,500 ha in 2006 to 38,100 ha in 2010 (although this still represented a reduction in comparison with the corresponding figure for 1996 of some 163,000 ha). Of the total area under cultivation in 2010, some 35,000 ha was thought to be in Shan State. Production of opium was believed to have increased from an estimated 315 metric tons in 2006 to 460 tons in 2007, before declining to 410 tons in 2008 and further to 330 tons in 2009. In 2010 opium production in Myanmar was thought to have increased by 75.8% year-on-year, to 580 tons, attributed by UNODC to the Myanmar military tolerating increased cultivation of opium poppy in some areas of the country. Opiate prevalence increased from 0.6% of the population aged 15 years and above in 2008 to 0.8% in 2010.

ENERGY AND MINING

Myanmar possesses significant natural gas and oil reserves as well as mineral deposits, including coal, copper, gold, nickel, silver, iron, tungsten and zinc. Myanmar also has large deposits of precious and semi-precious stones, including ruby, sapphire and jade. According to the CIA, Myanmar's proven reserves of crude petroleum were estimated at 50m. barrels at January 2010; production totalled 18,800 barrels a day in 2009. Myanmar is a net producer of natural gas, with production estimated at 12,400m. cu m in 2008, while consumption stood at about 3,850m. cu m. In the same year the country exported 8,550m. cu m of natural gas, rendering it the 22nd largest natural gas exporter globally. Proven reserves of natural gas were estimated to be 2,832,000m. cu m at January 2010, ranking Myanmar 41st globally, according to the CIA. Gas exports accounted for 40% of the country's overall export earnings in 2007/08.

Cumulative FDI in Myanmar's oil and gas sector during 1988–2008 totalled US $3,357m., making it the second biggest sector after hydroelectric power (about $6,000m.). There has been extensive international investment and involvement in exploration activities in the development of energy resources, with Asian companies and consortiums particularly prominent in this regard. The Yadana project (which delivers gas to Thailand via a pipeline) was established by France's Total (the sole signatory of the project in June 1992), but later joined by a subsidiary of the US company Unocal (acquired by another US company, Chevron, in 2005), Thailand's PTT Exploration and Production, and the Myanma Government's MOGE. A consortium of foreign companies led by Daewoo International holds exploration and production rights to the Shwe field, while the China National Petroleum Corporation (CNPC) has secured a deal to buy natural gas from blocks A1 and A3 of the field. The CNPC has also been granted permission by the Myanma Government to build a pipeline to transport oil from the Middle East and Africa to China's Yunnan Province via Myanmar's Kyaukpyu deep-sea port in Rakhine (Arakan) State, as well as a second pipeline to transport gas from a newly built port on Myanmar's Ramree Island to China's Yunnan province. In early 2010 Hyundai Heavy Industries was subcontracted by Daewoo International to carry out construction work to facilitate gas production and supply to the gas pipeline. The construction of the pipelines commenced in mid-2010 and was scheduled for completion by 2013, upon which China would replace Thailand as the biggest buyer of Myanma gas. However, human rights groups have warned that such pipeline projects may pose a potential threat to local communities and their livelihoods. Similarly, US, South Korean and European oil and gas companies have attracted criticism from human rights activists who argue that corporate investment in the sector has supported the military junta and damaged the environment in Myanmar.

Russian oil and gas companies have now entered Myanmar's energy sector. In late 2008 Nobel Oil became the fourth Russian company to obtain a licence to explore for petroleum (in Kachin State) in a joint venture arrangement with MOGE. In that year Russia contributed US $94m. in FDI to the sector.

The Myanma Government has signed a number of joint venture agreements with international mining companies to explore and develop large-scale projects to mine gold, nickel and zinc, which has led to predictions that Myanmar has the capacity to become a leading mineral producer within Asia. As with multinational corporations in the energy sector, Western corporations in the mining sector also came under pressure from human rights and environmental activists for complicity in the alleged human rights abuses of the Myanma Government. Furthermore, Myanmar's 1994 mining law was heavily criticized by external observers and activist groups for the absence of policy measures protecting workers and the environment; it was alleged that lax regulations had rendered the cost of mining gold in Myanmar 20% lower than in any other country.

Myanmar is one of the largest producers of jade and gemstones in the world, and the sector has been a significant source of foreign exchange earnings for the Government. According to the Government's Central Statistical Organization (CSO), 25.8m. kg of jade were produced in 2009/10, compared with 11.4m. kg in 2004/05. Myanma rubies are considered to be the finest and most expensive in the world, and comprise about 80% of global supplies. The Government sells its precious stones through the Myanmar Gem Emporium; organized by the Ministry of Mines, the Emporium is held twice a year. According to the Myanmar Gems Enterprise, the sale of gems earned revenues of US $300m. in the financial year 2006/07. However, the value of gemstones illegally smuggled from the country each year is also estimated to be about $300m. To curb the unofficial gem trade, government authorities have increased the frequency of gem fair auctions. There are two dominant operators in the gem-mining industry: Chinese companies and military-controlled companies such as the Union of Myanmar Economic Holdings. Gem production has increased following the signing of peace agreements between the military Government and insurgent groups, especially in Kachin State. Although Myanmar is a major producer of precious stones, a lack of refining and polishing facilities means it exports only raw stones, which are less lucrative.

However, owing to the 'isolationist' approach taken by the USA and the EU, several Western retailers withdrew from gem-trading with the Myanma Government. This voluntary business disengagement from Myanmar was related to military ownership and control of gem mines and gem auctions. However, other jewellers and industry associations have appealed to the US Congress to remove restrictions on the import of Myanma rubies to the USA. Despite these requests, sanctions were in fact strengthened in September 2008, when the import of rubies mined in Myanmar was completely banned. None the less, the effectiveness of such restrictions is questionable, since international jewellery houses usually buy stones from intermediary agents on the international market, rendering it difficult to ascertain the true origin of any given stone.

INFRASTRUCTURE

Deficiencies in modern infrastructure have become a major challenge for economic development in Myanmar, and have affected foreign investors' confidence in entering the market or extending existing commitments. Poor electricity and telecommunication services have rendered many investment and development projects untenable, while airports, seaports, railways and roads have all been reported to be inadequate. Most roads in rural areas, where 70% of the Myanma population live, are inaccessible during the rainy season. As a result, domestic businesses and foreign investors in Myanmar have in the past had to provide their own infrastructure support in order to ensure the viability of projects.

Several large road and port development projects have been instigated in Myanmar. By April 2008 Myanmar's three neighbours (Thailand, India and China) all appeared to have secured bids to develop deep-sea ports along Myanmar's western seaways. A bid won by Thailand in 2008 was to develop a port at Dawei, on the Andaman Sea, although the work was not to commence immediately. In January 2005 it was announced that a deep-sea port (with the capacity to accommodate 2,000 40-ft sea containers) was to be built in Kyaukphyu Harbour on Ramree Island, in Rakhine State. As part of a dual project together with the deep-sea port, the plan also included the construction of a 1,900-km road connecting the Chinese city of Kunming with Mandalay, Kyaukphy and Sittwe. The Chinese Government was to fund the project, raising suggestions that the scheme would allow a significant strategic advantage for China in gaining direct access to the Indian Ocean. Likewise, India has also begun to pursue a similar policy of providing infrastructure in Myanmar's southern waters. In particular, to enable India's north-eastern states, such as Mizoram, to secure access to the sea via Myanmar, an Indian firm, Essar, is to renovate and upgrade the Sittwe port and also to dredge the Kalada river. Reputed to be the largest project in infrastructure development to which India has committed in Myanmar thus far, work on the project began at the end of 2010 and was scheduled for completion by the end of 2013.

Dam construction has traditionally been viewed positively by the Myanma people because these projects have provided irrigation for paddy fields in a country where agriculture remains the predominant economic activity. However, this positive attitude towards irrigation and dam construction has somewhat diminished since Chinese, Thai and Indian companies recently began the construction of a number of hydro-electric power-generating dams, designed primarily for export of the electricity to investors' home countries, while a majority of households in Myanmar remain in darkness owing to the insufficient power grid and a shortage of power supply. Moreover, dam construction in Myanmar has attracted criticism from international human rights and environmental groups, which decry the alleged forced relocation of communities residing along the rivers, as well as the damage caused to local eco-systems.

Amid warnings from international environmental NGOs of potential ecological damage, construction of the Tasang dam (which upon completion would have a generating capacity of 7,100 MW) on the Thanlwin (Salween) river commenced in March 2010; the contract for the project had been awarded to three Chinese SOEs. Chinese firms are also involved in another huge dam project, to be built on the Ayeyarwady (Irrawaddy) river near Myitsone with a 6,000-MW capacity. Dam construction has also brought Chinese labourers to work on these construction sites, a development that is reported to have caused resentment among local ethnic communities. Construction of another dam on the Thanlwin river, the 1,200-MW Hatgyi dam, was to have been overseen by the Thai Ministry of Energy and the Electricity Generating Authority of Thailand (EGAT), but the project has been delayed owing to ongoing pressure from environmentalists and human rights activists. Meanwhile, India has increased its involvement in Myanmar's hydroelectricity-generating dam projects; at mid-2011 India's National Hydroelectric Power Corporation was involved in several such projects, including the Tamanthi and Shwezaye dam projects on the Chindwinn river in western Myanmar (both of which were reported to have stalled in 2008 but were revived in 2010). Bangladesh has also investigated the feasibility of constructing two dams in Myanmar with the aim of supplying electricity to the Bangladeshi capital, Dhaka. Hydropower mega-projects such as those mentioned above are jointly conducted by foreign investors and large privately owned Myanma companies. However, India's ambitions in the field, like those of Thailand, have progressed slowly thus far, owing to rising environmental and human rights concerns with regard to the damaging impact of dam construction on the local communities. Critics have also suggested that the intensification of military operations against ethnic armed groups has been motivated in part by the desire of the Myanma Government to protect these energy projects.

The Government has begun to implement plans to develop special economic zones, free trade zones and border trade zones. Thilawa Free Trade Zone, jointly developed by China and Myanmar, was the first to be established. According to a report in the *New Light of Myanmar* in 2008, a new border trade zone was to open in Myawaddy, near Mae Sot in Thailand. The Myawaddy Border Trade Zone would be the second largest after the existing Muse Border Trade Zone, near China's Yunnan Province. New border trading points along the Indian–Myanma border were also planned.

Electricity production in Myanmar increased from 6,398.0m. kWh in 2007/08 to 7,543.1m. kWh in 2010/11, according to provisional official figures. However, supply nation-wide is at best erratic. Many areas in Yangon and Mandalay have suffered periodic 'black-outs', despite the former capital, Yangon, reportedly receiving one-half of the nation's electricity quota. It has been estimated that Yangon requires about 600 MW of electricity; however, actual supply is not thought to exceed 120 MW. Indeed, insufficient generation capacity in Yangon renders necessary a system of rotating power supply to different sections of the city; as a result, many people in Yangon receive only two or three hours of supply a day. With voltage often declining to as low as 150 volts, voltage regulators are required to operate most electrical appliances and residents also have to turn to small power generators. However, reliance on generators for electricity, in the absence of mains supply, appeared to have become less feasible owing to the rising price of diesel. Electricity in Myanmar is generated from two main sources: hydroelectric (which accounts for 50% of total generation) and gas (40%). The main source of electricity supply for Yangon is a hydroelectric plant in Lawpita (located 350 km north of the city); however, this plant was reportedly unable to function at full capacity owing to insufficient funds for maintenance and repair works. During the dry season, electricity production declines further as around 35% of overall supply is generated by small hydroelectric systems driven by rivers around the country.

Myanmar's telecommunications system and broadcasting sector are underdeveloped, with poor services and generally high charges. According to the International Telecommunication Union (ITU), there were 604,700 main telephone lines and 594,000 mobile cellular telephones in 2010. The Government has relaxed its control of the telecommunications sector by encouraging private companies to participate in constructing control stations in an attempt to expand network coverage. However, the Government still strictly controls supply, with the result that, while the prices of mobile phones in Myanmar have declined in recent years, prices still remain extremely high compared with neighbouring countries. The supply of, and demand for, Global System for Mobile Telecommunications (GSM) telephones has risen rapidly owing to the establishment of relay towers around Yangon and in big cities throughout the country. The quality of reception and the coverage of GSM telephones have also improved as the number of relay towers has increased. GSM network operations are conducted by Myanma Posts and Telecommunictions (MPT) in conjunction with international telecommunications companies. According to ITU, there were 450,000 personal computers in use in 2006 (the vast majority of which were owned by households in urban areas) and 110,000 internet users in 2009. In 2006 Myanmar had two television broadcasting stations and two radio stations, all of which were state-owned. According to World Bank estimates, in 2004 only 3% of households in Myanmar had access to a television, compared with 80% in other countries in the East Asian and Pacific region.

The Government monitors and restricts the media and internet use. In 2005 Reporters Sans Frontières, a France-based international organization concerned with press freedom, rated Myanmar as the country with the fifth least free press in the world, a ranking attributed to the junta's strict censorship of the press and imprisonment of pro-democracy journalists. Control measures implemented by the Myanma Government on internet usage were considered among the most restrictive in the world, and, as a result of this, combined with prohibitively high charges, the number of internet users in Myanmar remains among the lowest in the world. Despite government control measures, advances in telecommunications and internet technology enabled images of the nation-wide demonstrations in September 2007 to be broadcast on international media. Following the protests, the Myanma Government imposed further restrictions on internet usage, limiting access to a select group of local internet cafés. Journalists suspected of working for exiled media stations risk lengthy prison sentences.

FINANCE AND BANKING

The kyat is overvalued and non-convertible, allowing for a large gap between the official rate and the 'black market' rate. While the official exchange rate generally remained stable (standing at 5.2 kyats = US $1 at the end of April 2011), the 'black market' exchange rate increased annually. Exchange rate differentials were a major impediment for many international traders operating in Myanmar, who manoeuvred between the official rate (used for book-keeping purposes) and 'black market' rates (used in actual transactions). The dual exchange rate system also created problems for international traders in that import duties and taxes were calculated on the basis of the official exchange rate while sales transactions occurred at a 'black market' rate. Furthermore, this dual exchange rate system renders statistics issued by the Myanma Government extremely unreliable and unreflective of market realities.

The Government has been reluctant to devalue the kyat, arguing that it would increase the price of imported goods, further exacerbating existing inflationary problems. The Government was also reported to be concerned about the political ramifications of a significant currency devaluation. However, international critics have claimed that the self-interest of the military regime was the principal reason for the lack of financial reforms, arguing that SOEs have benefited from an overvalued exchange rate when purchasing imported goods and services using the official exchange rate. In addition, maintaining an artificial exchange rate that does not reflect the 'real' market value of the kyat has provided the Government with an additional benefit—its large military expenditure and an increasing budget deficit have officially been reported as lower than their true levels. Similarly, the Government has insisted on using the official exchange rate when recording revenues received from the sale of natural gas to Thailand, which resulted in revenues accounting for just 1% of the 2007/08 national budget, compared with an estimated 57% had the market exchange rate been utilized. The IMF has urged the Government to use the market exchange rate in order better to reflect economic reality.

None the less, the Government has introduced some measures to ease the problems caused by maintaining huge differentials between the two exchange rates, the most significant of which was the introduction in 1993 of Foreign Exchange Certificates (FECs) that were based on the model used and subsequently abandoned by China. Local citizens use FECs to pay bills to government departments and other official agencies. FECs are pegged to the US dollar, and are available for use by tourists, foreigners and locals; their introduction was regarded by some as a de facto devaluation of the local kyat.

Inflation has been a persistent problem in Myanmar. Between 1997/98 and 2000/01 the general consumer price index (CPI) increased by almost 50%. The 'black market' price of petrol increased by 600% within less than 12 months in 2002 owing to severe supply shortages. Again in 2005, following the Government 's plans to increase fuel prices from US $0.15 per gallon to $1.25 per gallon, commodity prices escalated in response to rising transport costs. In early 2006 food commodity prices rose alarmingly. Inflationary pressures in the country elevated gold prices as consumers and businesses invested in gold as a safeguard against inflation. However, inflation has subsequently eased. According to the ADB's *Asian Development Outlook 2010*, inflation decreased to 7.9% in the 2009/10 fiscal year (compared with 22.5% in 2008/09), owing to declining prices for food and fuel and a deceleration of economic activity. In this generally inflationary environment, the real market value of the kyat has diminished. By 2005 the exchange rate was 1,015 kyats = $1 and in 2007 it had reached an historic low point of 1,400 kyats = $1. However, the value of the kyat stabilized from 2008, owing to an improved balance of payments position resulting from an increase in natural gas exports, and at January 2010 the exchange rate stood at 1,040 kyats = $1. However, the kyat significantly appreciated from 2010, with the exchange rate standing at 752 kyats = $1 by August 2011. There were several factors in the kyat's sudden appreciation, including the flow of FDI from Asian neighbours into the energy sector; the Government's decreased budget deficit owing to the sale of SOEs; and increased government spending on infrastructural development. Some observers speculated that the appreciation of the kyat against the dollar was also related to trading activities at the Myanma–Chinese border, primarily an increase in revenue from drugs-smuggling and the widespread sale of dollar-denominated savings owing to ongoing conflict between ethnic armed groups and government troops (see History). This prompted concerns that the kyat might appreciate still further if destabilization of border areas continued.

Several foreign analysts have attributed the underlying causes of inflation in Myanmar to the Government's monetary policies and persistent budget deficits. Following the announcement of a 10-fold increase in the salaries of public servants and military personnel in 2006, commodity prices surged by over 10%. Inflation was also exacerbated by increases in government taxes and charges for public utilities. Analysis conducted by the Economist Intelligence Unit (EIU—a research and analysis organization based in the United Kingdom) identified inconsistent export policies, for instance on agricultural commodity exports, as a factor contributing to the high rate of inflation in Myanmar. Moreover, the EIU suggested that monetary policies in Myanmar were inadequate to address the trend of rapid inflation, as the Central Bank of Myanmar was under strict government control and was therefore unable to act independently to adjust interest rates in accordance with the increasing money supply in the country. This situation was deemed to have further reduced consumer confidence in the integrity of the banking system.

In addition to problems deriving from high inflation and the dual exchange rate system, Myanmar also has to contend with the limitations of its banking and financial infrastructure. The banking sector is relatively primitive and remains closely controlled by the Government. In particular, the absence of a capital market has discouraged foreign investors. The Government has often been burdened with considerable foreign debt. According to CIA estimates, Myanmar's external debt totalled US $7,998m. at the end of 2010, while its reserves of foreign exchange and gold increased to $3,762m., from $1,010m. in 2006. There was limited domestic capital with which to finance industrialization and modernization. Four new banks (owned by Burmese indigenous business conglomerates) entered the banking sector in mid-2010. Critics of the sector argued that these new entrants were unlikely to improve the poor lending situation in the country and the private sector might therefore continue to depend on informal/individual money lenders for much-needed credit. The Government's ability to secure foreign capital was further constrained by the Burma Freedom and Democracy Act (BFDA), signed into law by the US Administration in 2003 and renewed in 2006, which banned exports of financial services from the USA to Myanmar. In 2001 Myanmar was included by the Financial Action Task Force on Money Laundering (FATF—an inter-governmental organization formed in 1989, based in Paris, France) on its list of Non-Co-operative Countries and Territories (NCCT), owing to the Myanma Government's failure to provide sufficient co-operation in global efforts to counter money-laundering. However, the task force was somewhat encouraged by the Government's initiatives, which included the introduction of anti-money-laundering (AML) reforms in 2002 and the investigation of two local banks for their alleged links to money-laundering activities. The FATF urged the Myanma Government to accelerate its programme of AML reforms, but continued to advise its members to 'pay special attention' in financial dealings with the country. The FATF removed Myanmar from its NCCT list in October 2006, following further progress in the implementation of AML reforms.

FOREIGN INVESTMENT AND TRADE

After the SLORC took responsibility for national governance from the BSPP in 1988, it began to signal an intention to 'open doors' to foreign trade. The SLORC initiated a series of economic reforms intended to transform the 'socialist' command economy of the previous three decades into a market-orientated system. These reforms included the FIL, implemented in November 1988, which aimed to facilitate FDI inflows. The FIL had both positive and negative features. For potential foreign investors the benefits of the new policy included: a series of tax relief measures and exemptions; a guarantee against nationalization; the right to repatriate foreign capital; permission to lease land and real estate; permission to operate wholly foreign-owned or joint venture enterprises; a relatively uncomplicated screening process for foreign investment; and legal and accounting systems based on the British models. However, the FIL specified that it was illegal to use an exchange rate other than the official exchange rate in converting foreign currencies into kyats, or vice versa. Owing to the huge disparity between the official and unofficial market rates, and the fact that it was the 'black market' rate that was utilized in business transactions, this specification posed a major threat to the viability of international business operations. Moreover, foreign investors were still not entitled to full legal rights and the same protective legislation that would typically operate in their domestic markets to reduce risk and settle commercial disputes, such as intellectual property rights and transparent settlement procedures.

Myanmar's total cumulative FDI during 1998–2008 stood at about US $15,000m. Thailand was the biggest investor (about $7,000m.) followed by the United Kingdom and Singapore (about $1,000m. each). It should be noted that investment by companies based in the British Virgin Islands and Bermuda is included in the United Kingdom figure. Slightly over 50% of total foreign investment in Myanmar was contributed by Asian nations. While US and European enterprises appeared somewhat cautious about investment in Myanmar, in part owing to the political implications of being associated with the regime, Asian businesses (originating, in particular, in China, Thailand, India, Singapore and Malaysia) have developed thriving investment and trade relationships.

Between 2000 and 2005, according to the ADB, foreign investment in Myanmar was reduced by 81%, following the imposition of US trade sanctions. However, in the 2005/06 fiscal year FDI in Myanmar reached the highest level since 1988, primarily owing to Thai investment in the energy sector of US $6,030m., according to trade figures released by the Ministry of National Planning and Economic Development of Myanmar. According to the CIA, in 2009 Myanmar's exports were worth $8,813m., while its imports totalled $4,296m. The principal commodities exported in that year included gas, wood products, beans and pulses, fish, rice, clothing, jade and gems. In the same year primary imported items included petroleum products, fertilizer, machinery, transport equipment and construction materials, and food products. According to the Ministry of Commerce, in the five years subsequent to 2002/03 exports from Myanmar surpassed imports, generating consistent trade surpluses. The export of natural gas to Thailand (estimated to be worth $2,000m. a year) was accredited as the primary contributor to these trade surpluses, followed by exports from the agriculture, mining and fishery sectors. However, in 2008/09 and 2009/10 the current account recorded a deficit owing to declining agricultural product prices, decreased gas exports and reduced foreign remittances. The rapid appreciation of the kyat from 2010 further reduced foreign remittances from Myanma migrant workers.

Myanmar has sought to improve trade relations with its two largest neighbours, China and India. Chinese investments in Myanmar range across numerous sectors including energy, information technology, agriculture, mining and transport. The growth of economic and political links between Myanmar and China has occurred despite ongoing appeals from the USA and international agencies to the global business community to review its investment and trade links with the Myanma Government. In 2004 Myanmar and India signed a memorandum of understanding to increase bilateral trade. In 2008/09 India accounted for 11.85% of Myanmar's exports. Amid growing investment from China and India, Thailand aimed to increase its investment in Myanmar, with plans to develop infrastructural projects such as an international port at Tavoy, in southern Myanmar; roads and bridges at the Myanma–Thai border to facilitate and enhance bilateral border trade; and special economic zones at the border. Meanwhile, trade between Myanmar and Viet Nam was worth more than US $100m. in 2008, representing an 11% increase on 2007, while trade between Myanmar and Indonesia increased by nearly 90% over the same period.

Since the 2000s manufacturing enterprises established by local Myanma families have become more prominent and profitable. Among these enterprises are manufacturers of various consumer goods, including locally made shampoo, toothpaste, soap and herbal medicine, largely targeting mass consumers. With regard to manufacturing by foreign firms in Myanmar, chief among these are Asian garment manufacturers. There have also been some limited investments in motor vehicle assembly. In 2010 India's Tata Motors signed a joint venture agreement with the Myanma Government to invest in a heavy truck factory, and a South Korean state-owned agency, which has provided industrial training in several sectors in Myanmar, announced that it was to establish a new car-manufacturing training centre in the country.

Manufacturing industries in Myanmar have endured several operational difficulties. In particular, manufacturers have often lacked access to quality supplies and essential raw materials, necessitating the acquisition of many such materials from neighbouring Asian countries. A shortage of skilled labour (for example, trained production technicians and managers) also presented a major challenge to export-orientated manufacturers in industries such as garments, forcing them to import foreign labour. Garment exports have dramatically decreased owing to the impact of the economic sanctions imposed by the US Government and the EU. Since the introduction of the BFDA in 2003, which banned the import into the USA of garments made in Myanmar, garment manufacturers have experienced a decline in exports, with exports to the USA decreasing by 50%. During 2010–11 several garment manufacturers were affected by strike action by workers demanding better pay and conditions amid rising consumer prices. As a result of industrial action and the Myanma Government's rejection of a proposal by labour organizations to establish a new national labour union, in mid-2010 the ILO expanded its portfolio in Myanmar, creating a new task force to examine workers' freedom of association in the country.

Since the economic liberalization policy began to take effect in the early 1990s, there has been an influx of imported international consumer goods into Myanmar from both Asian and Western nations. However, as one of the poorest countries in the world, the limited purchasing power of Myanma citizens has imposed a severe restraint on growth within the consumer goods sector. The consumer goods sector has depended on the 'black market' for over three decades, with large quantities of essential goods smuggled in and out of the country. Many importers and distributors of consumer goods have depended on border trade as an import channel, in addition to container trade, simply because of inadequate facilities at Yangon port—and in some cases also to evade some of the import and trade restrictions imposed by the Myanma Government. Aside from import restrictions, international consumer goods businesses have also encountered difficulties in working effectively with government ministries and officials. Such obstacles have reportedly included: an absence of effective rules and regulations; arbitrary government action; bureaucratic delays; corruption; and the heavy involvement and power of close associates of the regime, as well as members of Union of Myanmar Economic Holdings, in Yangon's retail sector. Many international consumer goods companies have withdrawn from the market since the mid-1990s; while some have represented such decisions as a response to appeals from pro-democracy and human rights activists to withdraw, others have directly attributed their market exit to the aforementioned operational difficulties encountered in the country.

FOREIGN AID

After the regime's action against political dissidents in 1988, the Myanma Government ceased to receive funding from many overseas development assistance programmes. Although the World Bank ceased lending to Myanmar in 1987, Myanmar remained a member of the Bank, which has continued to monitor the economic and social situation in the country through the UN, the IMF and other development partners. However, through participation in the Program of Economic Co-operation in the Greater Mekong Subregion (the GMS Program), Myanmar has received significant aid assistance from the ADB; by the end of 2004 the ADB had loaned to Myanmar a total of US $530.9m., which was predominantly used to support development projects in agriculture and natural resources, industry and trade development, water supply, sanitation, waste management and energy. The ADB pledged to offer $1,600m. in loans to support the GMS Program in 2007–09, as part of a wider effort to reduce poverty and achieve the Millennium Development Goals.

Although economic development aid has been restricted by political considerations, Myanmar has continued to receive humanitarian aid from several governments and institutions. The UN Children's Fund (UNICEF) reported that it spent about US $2m. annually on the operation of HIV/AIDS prevention and care programmes in Myanmar. Before the 1988 suppression of the pro-democracy movement, Japanese aid accounted for 72% of all aid funds donated to Myanmar. In 2005 Japan donated a $10.8m. aid 'package' and in 2009 it donated $30m. to assist in technological and economic development. In 2005 the EU increased its humanitarian aid to Myanmar, from $2.4m. to $9.6m., to contribute to areas such as primary health care, malaria control, water supply and sanitation services. Ultimately, governments and donor agencies that continued to provide aid appeared to have accepted the argument that, in a country as poor and underdeveloped as Myanmar, there was a need for ongoing global and regional engagement on humanitarian (health, education and basic infrastructure) grounds. Inevitably, there has been controversy as to the role of the Government in the distribution of these funds and the distinction between 'humanitarian' aid and funds spent on development projects that may benefit local and international business interests.

International aid agencies have been subject to travel restrictions imposed by the military regime. For example, humanitarian workers have experienced lengthy delays in gaining permission from the Government to access sensitive areas, especially in the ethnic regions. In relation to travel restrictions imposed on aid agencies, in 2005 the UN's World Food Programme (WFP) warned of an imminent humanitarian crisis in Myanmar. In particular, WFP expressed concerns about the provision of food to HIV/AIDS sufferers in central Myanmar and to farmers in Shan State who had previously grown opium as a cash crop. UN officials in Yangon also expressed concern about their lines of communication with relevant government departments and officials, following the relocation of the administrative capital to the area of Pyinmana. Citing the adverse impact of travel restrictions imposed on aid agencies, the Global Fund to Fight AIDS, Tuberculosis and Malaria withdrew from Myanmar in 2005. In 2007 the International Committee of the Red Cross announced its decision to downsize its work-force in Myanmar. This followed the Government's further tightening of control over the activities of aid agencies. As is often the case in terms of international businesses and agencies operating in Myanmar, as some depart, others enter. In July 2006 a donor consortium established the Three Diseases Fund (3D Fund) as a substitute for the Global Fund in Myanmar. In the following month the Australian Agency for International Development (AusAID) announced that it was to contribute US $11m. over five years to the 3D Fund. The British Government also donated $36m. to the Fund.

The Myanma Government's mistrust and surveillance of foreign aid agencies became very apparent during the humanitarian crisis caused by Cyclone Nargis in May 2008. Relief efforts were delayed owing to the difficulties in securing entry visas for foreign aid workers and the restrictive bureaucratic controls on their movements and activities imposed by the Myanma Government. Furthermore, a claim emerged that the disaster recovery fund created by the UN in response to Nargis lost 20% of its value owing to the Myanma Government's requirement that donations in foreign currency be converted into FECs. Furthermore, overseas private donors offering funds to Burmese NGOs for Nargis survivors encountered significant difficulty in transferring funds to Myanmar owing to the financial sanctions in place. As a result, in some cases donated funds had to be deposited in private bank accounts in neighbouring nations before their eventual transfer to Myanmar. Regardless of the Government's policies, donor governments were criticized for their insufficient provision of funds to allow for immediate relief to the victims of Nargis and the reconstruction of affected regions. Indeed, despite the cost of reconstruction, estimated at some US $690m., as of April 2009 Myanmar had received only $300m. in international aid. One of the main reasons for the shortfall in international donor support was widely believed to be the lack of trust in the Myanma Government. The international community's proclivity to isolate the Myanma regime appeared to have extended into all forms of engagement, be it business activity or, in this instance, much-needed humanitarian intervention.

TOURISM

Tourist arrivals in Myanmar steadily increased during the early 2000s. According to local sources, the country attracted 660,000 tourists in 2005, earning US $153m. in revenues. More than 60% of tourists to Myanmar were from Asia. According to the research organization Euromonitor International, Asian tourism to Myanmar has been boosted by a number of factors, including geographical proximity and associated low-cost travel and tour 'packages'. According to the CSO, the largest number of tourist arrivals in Myanmar in 2006 came from Thailand (30,400), followed by China (24,893) and Japan (18,945). Thailand also makes a significant contribution to FDI in Myanmar's hotel and tourism industry; in the 2009/10 financial year Thai enterprises invested $30m. in property development in the sector. Euromonitor International expected the number of Eastern European tourists visiting Myanmar to increase because of the country's attraction as a cultural destination. Notably, the number of arrivals from the United Kingdom and the USA, where a tourism boycott campaign has been strongest, were relatively low, especially when compared with a steady growth in tourists from France and Germany. According to the Myanmar Tourism Entrepreneurs Association, there was a 90% decline in tourism in Myanmar in 2008, largely attributable to the regime's suppression of the pro-democracy protesters in 2007 and the devastation caused by Cyclone Nargis in May 2008.

While Myanmar's unspoilt and idyllic natural splendours and architectural heritage offer huge potential, the sustainability of tourism development has been questioned. There are also ethical and political dimensions concerning tourism in Myanmar, as many pro-democracy campaigners (as well as the opposition NLD) have urged international travellers to boycott the country, arguing that tourism supports and prolongs the rule of the military junta. More recently, however, some parties have begun to reconsider the appeal for a general tourism boycott in Myanmar. An alternative view suggests that tourism revenues may have some positive political and economic effects, that tourism does not exclusively benefit enterprises directly linked to the Government and that small local tour operators and family-owned businesses would also gain from the growth of the sector. (According to government statistics, the tourism sector comprised fewer than 12 large joint venture tour companies, with the remainder being locally owned enterprises.) In November 2010 the NLD rescinded its appeal for all international tourists to boycott Myanmar, and the Burma Campaign UK similarly modified its approach to individual tourists wishing to visit Myanmar; however, at mid-2011 it continued to appeal against large 'package' tours to Myanmar on the grounds that these generate substantial amounts of revenue for the Government.

The debate on tourism in Myanmar also highlights an ideological divide between the East and the West. While many in the West, including pro-democracy, human rights and labour activists, ethicists, travel agents and politicians, advocate a boycott against travel to Myanmar, governments and businesses in Asia (particularly in neighbouring countries) support co-operation with the Government of Myanmar in the areas of trade, tourism promotion and infrastructure development.

PROBLEMS AND PROSPECTS

Neither of the strategies adopted by the international community (sanctions and boycotts on the one hand and constructive engagement on the other) has been effective in terms of improving the economic or political situation in Myanmar. Since the first steps towards a market economy in the late 1980s, the regime's failure to engage in effective economic reforms, and to strike a workable political compromise with opposition leader Suu Kyi, has hampered economic progress. Leaving aside debates concerning the effectiveness of 'isolationist' versus 'engagement' strategies for promoting reform, Myanmar has experienced ongoing problems of insufficient economic development and uneven development, and, in health and basic food security, a humanitarian crisis in urgent need of attention. While some nations are exploring ways to engage with the Myanma Government, either to address these humanitarian problems or to attempt to facilitate political reform and dialogue, the military junta's decision in November 2005 to transfer the administrative capital to Nay Pyi Taw served possibly to highlight its increasingly isolated stance, at least at a symbolic level.

Furthermore, both international and local businesses in Myanmar have confronted many challenges and constraints imposed by Myanmar's complex and multifarious domestic problems. Although Myanmar is, in various ways, the 'last frontier' for foreign investment in South-East Asia with long-term market potential, it has shortcomings emanating from an overbearing bureaucracy, the involvement and interference of the regime's family members and close business associates in the country's business sector, restrictive trade policies, and inconsistent policies governing business activity. Moreover, limited infrastructure and operational difficulties, such as the dual exchange rate system and low consumer purchasing power, appeared to have driven many foreign investors from the country.

The manufacturing and service sectors will continue to suffer from inadequate infrastructure, a poor investment environment, insufficient social and human development, especially with regard to health and education, as well as the isolationist economic policies adopted by many Western nations. Initiatives to boost agricultural output and productivity are much needed given the sheer size and importance of the sector to the overall development of the economy of Myanmar.

None the less, there have been some notable areas of growth in Myanmar's economy. The most promising sectors have been its extractive industries (petroleum, gas and minerals) and energy industries (hydroelectric projects), which have attracted continued investment from neighbouring Asian countries and were expected to record strong growth and to deliver significant export revenues. In 2011, however, doubts remained over many issues, including the sustainability of economic development; the limited range of FDI, which was concentrated within the extractive sector; lack of much-needed credit for the agricultural sector; insufficient redistribution of economic benefits; the quasi-monopolistic nature of a small number of large domestic businesses dominating many sectors of the economy; and the limited local employment prospects of the extractive and energy industries.

Statistical Survey

Source (unless otherwise stated): Central Statistical Organization, Ministry of National Planning and Economic Development, Building 32, Nay Pyi Taw; tel. (67) 406325; fax (67) 407265; e-mail cso.stat@mptmail.net.mm; internet www.csostat.gov.mm.

Area and Population

AREA, POPULATION AND DENSITY

Area (sq km)	676,552*
Population (census results)	
31 March 1973	28,885,867
31 March 1983†	
Males	17,507,837
Females	17,798,352
Total	35,306,189
Population (UN estimates at mid-year)‡	
2009	47,601,375
2010	47,963,012
2011	48,336,764
Density (per sq km) at mid-2011	71.4

* 261,218 sq miles.

† Figures exclude adjustment for underenumeration. Also excluded are 7,716 Myanma citizens (males 5,704, females 2,012) abroad.

‡ Source: UN, *World Population Prospects: The 2010 Revision*.

POPULATION BY AGE AND SEX

(UN estimates at mid-2011)

	Males	Females	Total
0–14	6,151,044	6,027,372	12,178,416
15–64	16,558,871	17,095,167	33,654,038
65 and over	1,109,435	1,394,875	2,504,310
Total	23,819,350	24,517,414	48,336,764

Source: UN, *World Population Prospects: The 2010 Revision*.

PRINCIPAL TOWNS

(population at census of 31 March 1983)

Yangon (Rangoon)	2,513,023	Pathein (Bassein)	144,096
Mandalay	532,949	Taunggyi	108,231
Mawlamyine (Moulmein)	219,961	Sittwe (Akyab)	107,621
Bago (Pegu)	150,528	Manywa	106,843

Source: UN, *Demographic Yearbook*.

Mid-2010 (incl. suburbs, UN estimates): Yangon 4,349,604; Mandalay 1,034,167; Nay Pyi Taw 1,024,162 (Source: UN, *World Urbanization Prospects: The 2009 Revision*).

BIRTHS AND DEATHS

(annual averages, UN estimates)

	1995–2000	2000–05	2005–10
Birth rate (per 1,000)	22.3	19.3	17.9
Death rate (per 1,000)	9.3	8.9	8.9

Source: UN, *World Population Prospects: The 2010 Revision*.

Life expectancy (years at birth, WHO estimates): 64 (males 61; females 67) in 2009 (Source: WHO, *World Health Statistics*).

ECONOMICALLY ACTIVE POPULATION*

('000 persons, official estimates)

	1997	1998
Agriculture, hunting, forestry and fishing	11,381	11,507
Mining and quarrying	132	121
Manufacturing	1,573	1,666
Electricity, gas and water	21	48
Construction	378	400
Trade, restaurants and hotels	1,746	1,781
Transport, storage and communications	470	495
Financing, insurance, real estate and business services	577	597
Community, social and personal services†	1,686	1,744
Total employed	17,964	18,359
Unemployed‡	535	452
Total labour force	18,499	18,811

* Excludes members of the armed forces.

† Includes activities not adequately defined.

‡ Persons aged 18 years and over.

Unemployed ('000 persons aged 18 years and over): 183.4 in 2006; 118.7 in 2007; 137.8 in 2008 (Source: ILO).

Mid-2011 ('000 persons, estimates): Agriculture, etc. 18,965; Total labour force 28,418 (Source: FAO).

Health and Welfare

KEY INDICATORS

Total fertility rate (children per woman, 2009)	2.3
Under-5 mortality rate (per 1,000 live births, 2009)	71
HIV/AIDS (% of persons aged 15–49, 2007)	0.7
Physicians (per 1,000 head, 2004)	0.4
Hospital beds (per 1,000 head, 2000)	0.7
Health expenditure (2008): US $ per head (PPP)	27
Health expenditure (2008): % of GDP	2.3
Health expenditure (2008): public (% of total)	7.5
Access to water (% of persons, 2008)	71
Access to sanitation (% of persons, 2008)	81
Total carbon dioxide emissions ('000 metric tons, 2007)	13,179.4
Carbon dioxide emissions per head (metric tons, 2007)	0.3
Human Development Index (2010): ranking	132
Human Development Index (2010): value	0.451

For sources and definitions, see explanatory note on p. vi.

Agriculture

PRINCIPAL CROPS

('000 metric tons)

	2007	2008	2009
Wheat	155	170	179
Rice, paddy	31,451	32,573	32,682
Maize	1,128	1,185	1,226
Millet	191*	195†	185†
Potatoes	508	521	548
Sweet potatoes†	57	58	59
Cassava (Manioc)	282	334	355†
Sugar cane	9,677	9,000†	8,500†
Beans, dry	2,814	3,218	3,000†
Peas, dry	56	60	62†
Chick peas	330	348	398
Cow peas, dry	150	176	180†
Pigeon peas	645	719	765
Arecanuts	99	116	120†
Soybeans (Soya beans)	201	214	240
Groundnuts, with shell	1,222	1,305	1,362

—continued	2007	2008	2009
Coconuts	486	505	420
Sunflower seed	494	692	767
Sesame seed	781	853	868
Onions, dry	918	1,013	1,050†
Garlic	161	197	200†
Plantains	795	789	825†
Tea	28*	29*	31†
Jute	9	3	4†
Tobacco, unmanufactured	27	20	18†
Natural rubber†	45	46	44

* Unofficial figure.
† FAO estimate(s).

Aggregate production ('000 metric tons, may include official, semi-official or estimated data): Total cereals 32,937 in 2007, 34,135 in 2008, 34,284 in 2009; Total roots and tubers 847 in 2007, 913 in 2008, 962 in 2009; Total vegetables (incl. melons) 4,279 in 2007, 4,799 in 2008, 4,903 in 2009; Total fruits (excl. melons) 2,045 in 2007, 2,029 in 2008, 2,093 in 2009.

Source: FAO.

LIVESTOCK
('000 head, year ending September)

	2007	2008	2009*
Horses*	140	140	140
Cattle	12,634	12,929	13,000
Buffaloes	2,842	2,924	3,000
Pigs	7,007	7,677	7,800
Sheep	497	525	535
Goats	2,376	2,624	2,750
Chickens	107,771	122,038	125,000
Ducks	11,144	12,248	12,500
Geese*	685	685	685

* FAO estimates.

Source: FAO.

LIVESTOCK PRODUCTS
('000 metric tons)

	2007	2008	2009*
Cattle meat	130.2	139.6	143.3
Buffalo meat	29.3	31.6	39.8
Goat meat	22.0	23.7	24.0
Pig meat	410.7	463.1	450.0
Chicken meat	726.5	797.5	800.0
Cows' milk	980.3	1,055.8	1,100.0
Buffaloes' milk	220.5	238.7	240.0
Goats' milk*	11.2	12.3	12.8
Hen eggs	231.5	263.4	265.0
Other poultry eggs*	16.0	18.2	22.4

* FAO estimates.

Source: FAO.

Forestry

ROUNDWOOD REMOVALS
('000 cubic metres, excl. bark)

	2003	2004	2005
Sawlogs, veneer logs and logs for sleepers	2,885	2,816	2,849
Other industrial wood	1,353	1,380	1,413
Fuel wood	37,954	37,560	38,286
Total	42,191	41,756	42,548

2006–09: Figures assumed to be unchanged from 2005 (FAO estimates).

Source: FAO.

SAWNWOOD PRODUCTION
('000 cubic metres, incl. railway sleepers)

	2004	2005	2006
Coniferous (softwood)*	77	61	80
Broadleaved (hardwood)	1,056	1,530	1,530†
Total†	1,133	1,591	1,610

* Unofficial figures.
† FAO estimate(s).

2007–09: Production assumed to be unchanged from 2006 (FAO estimates).

Source: FAO.

Fishing

('000 metric tons, live weight)

	2007	2008	2009
Capture*	2,235.6	2,493.8	2,766.9
Freshwater fishes	717.6	814.7	899.4
Marine fishes	1,485.7	1,643.6	1,827.5
Aquaculture*	604.7	674.8	778.1
Common carp	16.7*	18.6	20.9
Roho labeo	389.3*	433.1	488.0
Total catch*	2,840.2	3,168.5	3,545.0

* FAO estimate(s).

Source: FAO.

Mining

(metric tons unless otherwise indicated)

	2007	2008	2009
Coal and lignite	283,703	249,442	245,418
Crude petroleum ('000 barrels)	7,625	7,242	6,881
Natural gas (million cu m)*	13,315	12,445	11,555
Copper ore†	15,100	6,900	8,000‖
Lead ore†‡	2,000	3,000	7,500‖
Zinc ore†	10	20	45
Tin concentrates†	499	499	518
Silver ore (kilograms)†	218	0	249
Gold ore (kilograms)†§‡	100	100	100
Feldspar‡§	10,000	10,000	10,000
Barite (Barytes)	6,813	5,679	7,623
Salt (unrefined, excl. brine)‡	35,000	35,000	35,000
Gypsum (crude)	75,116	82,224	97,518
Rubies, sapphires and spinel ('000 metric carats)§	2,847	3,570	2,767
Jade	20,003	30,896	25,427

* Marketed production.
† Figures refer to the metal content of ores and concentrates (including mixed concentrates).
‡ Estimated production.
§ Twelve months beginning 1 April of year stated.
‖ Preliminary.

Source: US Geological Survey.

Industry

SELECTED PRODUCTS OF STATE-OWNED ENTERPRISES
('000 metric tons unless otherwise indicated)

	2008/09	2009/10	2010/11
Sugar	28.4	20.3	21.4
Beer ('000 gallons)	1,514.4	441.2	n.a.
Cigarettes (million)	2,351.8	n.a.	n.a.
Cotton fabrics ('000 yards)	19.1	20.0	18.5
Cotton yarn ('000 lbs)	13.9	15.1	18.2
Plywood ('000 sq ft)	135.6	160.2	204.8
Fertilizers	106.1	69.8	35.3
Diesel oil ('000 gallons)	50,582	32,843	63,044
Furnace oil ('000 gallons)	17,078	14,243	11,517
Liquefied petroleum gas ('000 gallons)	3,566	3,199	3,291
Motor spirit (petrol, '000 gallons)	103,854	112,615	129,292
Cement	690.8	628.2	547.6
Paper	19.9	13.3	14.7
Soap	76.9	67.4	44.7
Electric energy (million kWh)	6,621.8	6,964.3	7,543.1*

* Provisional figure.

Finance

CURRENCY AND EXCHANGE RATES

Monetary Units
100 pyas = 1 kyat.

Sterling, Dollar and Euro Equivalents (29 April 2011)
£1 sterling = 8.742 kyats;
US $1 = 5.249 kyats;
€1 = 7.800 kyats;
100 kyats = £11.44 = $19.05 = €12.82.

Average Exchange Rate (kyats per US $)
2008 5.388
2009 5.519
2010 5.578

Note: Since January 1975 the value of the kyat has been linked to the IMF's special drawing right (SDR). Since May 1977 the official exchange rate has been fixed at a mid-point of SDR 1 = 8.5085 kyats. On 1 June 1996 a new customs valuation exchange rate of US $1 = 100 kyats was introduced. In September 2001 the free market exchange rate was $1 = 450 kyats.

CENTRAL GOVERNMENT BUDGET
(million kyats, year ending 31 March, excl. capital account)

Current revenue and grants	2003/04	2004/05	2005/06
Tax revenue	170,569	297,104	476,945
Taxes on income, profits and capital gains	91,860	138,866	206,676
Domestic taxes on goods and services	74,107	136,626	251,821
General sales, turnover or value-added tax	58,214	112,543	225,121
Taxes on international trade and transactions	4,602	21,613	18,448
Other revenue	213,542	290,190	342,273
Grants	111	171	316
Total	384,222	587,465	819,534

Current expenditure	2003/04	2004/05	2005/06
General public services, incl. public order	114,195	206,848	354,848
Defence	172,633	173,558	197,792
Education	71,665	101,936	68,676
Health	18,808	26,545	21,963
Social security and welfare	7,865	9,933	8,406
Recreational, cultural and religious affairs	4,112	5,863	4,511
Economic affairs and services	194,354	234,513	346,361
Agriculture, forestry, fishing and hunting	61,056	71,028	93,300
Transportation	119,190	131,839	198,261
Housing and community amenities	7,397	8,622	6,228
Total	591,029	767,818	1,008,785

Source: IMF, *Government Finance Statistics Yearbook*.

INTERNATIONAL RESERVES
(US $ million at 31 December)

	2004	2005	2006
Gold (national valuation)	12.6	11.6	12.2
IMF special drawing rights	0.0	0.2	0.2
Foreign exchange	672.1	770.5	1,235.4
Total	684.7	782.3	1,247.8

IMF special drawing rights: 0.1 in 2008; 113.3 in 2009; 2.6 in 2010.

Source: IMF, *International Financial Statistics*.

MONEY SUPPLY
(million kyats at 31 December)

	2008	2009	2010
Currency outside banks	2,922,503	3,568,431	4,278,691
Demand deposits at deposit money banks	515,204	692,429	1,339,283
Total money (incl. others)	3,437,947	4,262,037	5,618,758

Source: IMF, *International Financial Statistics*.

COST OF LIVING
(Consumer Price Index; base: 2000 = 100)

	2006	2007	2008
Food (incl. beverages)	365.7	493.9	638.3
Fuel and light	370.0	491.7	561.9
Clothing (incl. footwear)	337.6	462.9	583.4
Rent	388.8	518.7	658.6
All items (incl. others)	356.5	481.3	610.3

Source: ILO.

NATIONAL ACCOUNTS
(million kyats at current prices, year ending 31 March)

Expenditure on the Gross Domestic Product

	2005/06	2006/07	2007/08
Final consumption expenditure	10,682,305	14,291,377	19,861,427
Increase in stocks	57,041	23,996	43,470
Gross fixed capital formation	1,563,754	2,282,421	3,390,475
Total domestic expenditure	12,303,100	16,597,794	23,295,372
Exports of goods and services	19,803	29,295	33,995
Less Imports of goods and services	11,514	16,835	18,419
Statistical discrepancy	–24,623	242,504	25,165
GDP in purchasers' values	12,286,765	16,852,758	23,336,113
GDP at constant 2005/06 prices	12,286,765	13,893,395	15,559,413

Gross Domestic Product by Economic Activity

	2007/08	2008/09	2009/10
Agriculture, hunting, forestry and fishing	10,109,849	11,773,735	12,888,806
Mining and quarrying	205,344	254,408	328,488
Manufacturing	3,473,910	4,917,322	6,135,357
Electricity, gas and water	189,790	212,414	251,102
Construction	893,654	1,236,065	1,518,309
Wholesale and retail trade	4,915,159	6,175,063	6,890,046
Transport, storage and communications	2,781,665	3,731,536	4,567,731
Finance	16,948	20,938	22,575
Government services	371,290	399,679	548,674
Other services	378,504	506,375	609,840
GDP in purchasers' values	23,336,113	29,227,535	33,760,928

Source: Asian Development Bank.

BALANCE OF PAYMENTS
(US $ million)

	2004	2005	2006
Exports of goods f.o.b.	2,926.6	3,787.8	4,554.7
Imports of goods f.o.b.	–1,998.7	–1,759.4	–2,343.4
Trade balance	927.9	2,028.4	2,211.3
Exports of services	254.7	259.1	279.5
Imports of services	–459.6	–502.0	–562.9
Balance on goods and services	723.0	1,785.5	1,928.0
Other income received	40.4	55.5	97.8
Other income paid	–785.8	–1,427.3	–1,346.2
Balance on goods, services and income	–22.4	413.8	679.6
Current transfers received	160.6	197.8	161.4
Current transfers paid	–26.7	–23.8	–39.0
Current balance	111.5	587.7	802.0
Direct investment from abroad	213.5	237.2	278.6
Other investment liabilities	–88.3	–71.1	–25.6
Net errors and omissions	–142.7	–610.3	–632.1
Overall balance	94.0	143.6	422.9

Source: IMF, *International Financial Statistics*.

2007 (US $ million): Exports of goods 6,279.3; Imports of goods –3,027.0; *Trade balance* 3,252.3; Services and other income (net) –1,605.2; *Balance on goods, services and income* 1,647.1; Current transfers received 233.2; Current transfers paid –27.3; *Current balance* 1,853.0 (Source: Asian Development Bank).

2008 (US $ million): Exports of goods 6,915.6; Imports of goods –3,887.8; *Trade balance* 3,027.8; Services and other income (net) –1,946.1; *Balance on goods, services and income* 1,081.7; Current transfers received 340.6; Current transfers paid –53.2; *Current balance* 1,369.1 (Source: Asian Development Bank).

2009 (US $ million): Exports of goods 6,673.1; Imports of goods –3,951.4; *Trade balance* 2,721.7; Services and other income (net) –2,254.1; *Balance on goods, services and income* 467.6; Current transfers received 326.0; Current transfers paid –64.0; *Current balance* 729.6 (Source: Asian Development Bank).

External Trade

PRINCIPAL COMMODITIES
(distribution by SITC, million kyats, year ending 31 March)

Imports c.i.f.	2008/09	2009/10	2010/11
Edible vegetable oil and other hydrogenated oils	1,610.0	975.9	934.2
Pharmaceutical products	679.0	797.7	905.3
Base metals and manufactures	1,818.3	1,992.9	2,469.7
Machinery and transport equipment	7,240.2	4,908.2	4,600.5
Electrical machinery and apparatus	948.6	977.1	1,421.5
Paper, paperboard and manufactures	391.7	318.1	309.0
Refined mineral oils	3,192.2	3,674.3	5,046.1
Fabric of artificial materials and synthetics	817.4	780.2	1,053.9
Plastic	908.8	859.2	1,182.0
Total (incl. others)	24,873.8	22,837.4	35,508.4

Exports f.o.b.	2008/09	2009/10	2010/11
Dried beans, peas, etc. (shelled)	4,068.8	5,062.9	4,449.8
Fresh and dried prawns	472.1	346.2	371.3
Fish and fish products	972.3	1,053.3	1,270.9
Teak	1,146.3	1,171.7	1,689.3
Other hardwood	1,065.7	1,518.9	1,499.7
Base metals and ores	176.5	182.7	305.1
Gas	12,995.7	15,853.8	16,020.7
Garments	1,593.9	1,543.7	1,876.0
Total (incl. others)	37,027.8	41,289.1	49,106.8

PRINCIPAL TRADING PARTNERS
(million kyats, year ending 31 March)

Imports	2008/09	2009/10	2010/11
China, People's Republic	6,578.1	6,854.9	12,005.1
Hong Kong	177.7	59.8	46.5
India	796.8	1,058.5	1,079.9
Indonesia	1,139.5	760.4	1,526.1
Japan	908.4	1,412.4	1,417.1
Korea, Republic	1,027.3	1,221.5	1,683.4
Malaysia	1,972.1	871.3	805.0
Singapore	5,712.7	6,593.0	9,116.9
Thailand	2,150.7	2,069.6	3,938.6
Total (incl. others)	24,873.8	22,837.4	35,508.4

Exports	2008/09	2009/10	2010/11
China, People's Republic	3,352.3	3,359.0	6,662.9
Hong Kong	3,611.0	5,162.9	10,530.6
India	4,387.8	5,512.9	4,858.1
Indonesia	155.1	205.3	228.0
Japan	1,005.8	966.1	1,314.0
Malaysia	1,716.0	832.2	2,445.9
Singapore	4,638.4	3,690.9	2,499.9
Thailand	14,340.6	17,431.0	16,065.2
United Kingdom	284.4	202.6	193.0
Total (incl. others)	37,027.8	41,289.1	49,106.8

Transport

RAILWAYS
(traffic, million)

	2008/09	2009/10	2010/11
Passenger-miles	3,405	3,338	3,329
Freight ton-miles	581	658	698

ROAD TRAFFIC
(registered motor vehicles at 31 March)

	2008/09	2009/10	2010/11
Passenger cars	239,895	254,797	279,066
Trucks	58,857	61,132	64,888
Buses	19,683	19,807	20,944
Motorcycles	1,612,423	1,749,083	1,883,958
Others	68,102	62,585	59,665
Total	1,998,960	2,147,404	2,308,521

INLAND WATERWAYS
(traffic by state-owned vessels)

	2008/09	2009/10	2010/11
Passenger-miles (million)	783	820	902
Freight ton-miles (million)	639	687	754

SHIPPING

Merchant Fleet
(registered at 31 December)

	2007	2008	2009
Number of vessels	118	115	117
Displacement ('000 grt)	203.2	165.6	182.5

Source: IHS Fairplay, *World Fleet Statistics*.

International Sea-borne Traffic
('000 metric tons)

	2008/09	2009/10	2010/11
Goods loaded	2,955	4,539	3,256
Goods unloaded	4,123	6,883	8,481

CIVIL AVIATION
(traffic on scheduled services)

	2004	2005	2006
Kilometres flown (million)	19	20	22
Passengers carried ('000)	1,392	1,504	1,621
Passenger-km (million)	1,339	1,448	1,559
Total ton-km (million)	122	132	142

Source: UN, *Statistical Yearbook*.

Passenger-miles (million): 75.3 in 2006/07; 77.6 in 2007/08; 81.9 in 2008/09; 71.9 in 2009/10.

Tourism

TOURIST ARRIVALS BY COUNTRY OF NATIONALITY

	2006	2007	2008
Australia	6,583	6,761	5,374
China, People's Republic	24,893	29,551	30,792
France	15,498	15,521	8,217
Germany	18,003	15,432	8,947
India	7,540	7,675	7,173
Italy	10,774	10,130	3,030
Japan	18,945	15,623	10,881
Korea, Republic	18,265	13,821	12,369
Malaysia	9,588	8,693	8,268
Singapore	10,952	9,310	8,599
Taiwan	15,827	13,707	11,472
Thailand	30,400	35,002	27,311
United Kingdom	7,465	6,356	5,397
USA	18,052	14,862	13,195
Total (incl. others)	263,514	248,076	193,319

Tourism receipts (US $ million, incl. passenger transport): 97 in 2004; 85 in 2005; 59 in 2006.

Source: World Tourism Organization.

Communications Media

	2008	2009	2010
Telephones ('000 main lines in use)	504.4	552.3	604.7
Mobile cellular telephones ('000 subscribers)	367.4	502.0	594.0
Internet subscribers ('000)	21.3	n.a.	n.a.
Broadband subscribers ('000)	10.0	15.0	16.4

Personal computers: 450,000 (9.2 per 1,000 persons) in 2006.

Book production (1999): 227 titles.

Newspapers (1998): 4 dailies (average circulation 400,000).

Radio receivers ('000 in use): 3,157 in 1999.

Television receivers ('000 in use): 344.3 in 2000.

Sources: International Telecommunication Union; UNESCO, *Statistical Yearbook*; UN, *Statistical Yearbook*.

Education

(1994/95, provisional)

	Institutions	Teachers	Students
Primary schools*	35,856	169,748	5,711,202
Middle schools	2,058	53,859	1,390,065
High schools	858	18,045	389,438
Vocational schools	86	1,847	21,343
Teacher training	17	615	4,031
Higher education	45	6,246	247,348
Universities	6	2,901	62,098

* Excluding 1,152 monastic primary schools with an enrolment of 45,360.

2001/02 (provisional): *Primary:* Institutions 36,010; Teachers 143,490; Students ('000) 4,793.5. *General secondary:* Institutions 2,110; Teachers 53,896; Students ('000) 1,600.9. *Tertiary:* Institutions 958; Teachers 15,947; Students ('000) 587.3 (Source: UN, *Statistical Yearbook for Asia and the Pacific*).

2006/07: *Pre-primary:* Teachers 5,279; Students 98,545. *Primary:* Teachers 172,209; Students 5,013,582. *General secondary:* Teachers 81,943; Students 2,686,198. *Tertiary:* Teachers 10,669; Students 507,660 (Source: UNESCO Institute for Statistics).

2007/08: *Pre-primary:* Teachers 6,390; Students 112,268. *Primary:* Teachers 177,331; Students 5,109,630. *General secondary:* Teachers 82,001; Students 2,828,868 (Source: UNESCO Institute for Statistics).

2008/09: *Pre-primary:* Teachers 6,584; Students 120,345. *Primary:* Teachers 179,268; Students 5,094,623. *General secondary:* Teachers 82,204; Students 2,812,866 (Source: UNESCO Institute for Statistics).

Pupil-teacher ratio (primary education, UNESCO estimate): 28.4 in 2008/09 (Source: UNESCO Institute for Statistics).

Adult literacy rate (UNESCO estimates): 92.0% (males 94.7%; females 89.5%) in 2009 (Source: UNESCO Institute for Statistics).

Directory

The Constitution

Following its approval by the electorate in a national referendum, the present Constitution was enacted on 29 May 2008 and entered into force on 31 January 2011.

The official name of the country is the Republic of the Union of Myanmar. The capital is Nay Pyi Taw, which stands as a region directly under the administration of the country's President. The nation is divided into seven regions and seven states of national races, with six self-administered zones of six ethnic minorities.

The President is the Head of State. Of the three candidates for this position, at least one must be a member of the military; and a member of the military must be at least one of the two Vice-Presidents. The President is not answerable to court or to the legislature in exercising his or her duties. The President can declare a state of emergency, during which time the Commander-in-Chief of the defence forces, with the aid of the National Defence and Security Council (six of the 11 members of which are military personnel) assumes legislative, executive and judicial powers.

The Pyidaungsu Hluttaw (Union Assembly or National Parliament) consists of the Pyithu Hluttaw (People's Assembly or House of Representatives—the lower chamber) and the Amyotha Hluttaw (National Assembly or House of Nationalities—the upper chamber). Legislative power is shared by the Union Assembly, state assemblies and regional assemblies, as well as self-administered zones and divisions.

The Pyithu Hluttaw consists of 224 seats, of which 56 are reserved for the military. The Amyotha Hluttaw consists of 440 seats, of which 110 are reserved for the military. Military representatives must comprise one-third of the members of the state and regional assemblies.

Candidates are barred from standing for election if they or their parties accept support from foreign governments or religious organizations. Persons married to a foreign national are barred from holding political office. Members of religious orders and destitute persons are not permitted to vote.

The military has a leading role in the country's national politics. Ministers for defence, home affairs, security and border affairs must be members of the military. The Commander-in-Chief of the defence forces is authorized to exercise all state power should an emergency arise that threatens the disintegration of the union, the disintegration of sovereignty or the loss of national sovereignty. A state of emergency may be extended to a period of at least a year. The military is immune from prosecution for any actions undertaken during emergency rule.

Citizens may not be detained for more than 24 hours without trial, except on security or similar grounds.

The Constitution can be amended only with the approval of 75% of legislators and one-half of the eligible voters.

The Government

HEAD OF STATE

President: THEIN SEIN (took office 30 March 2011).

Vice-Presidents: TIN AUNG MYINT OO, Dr SAI MAUK KHAM.

CABINET
(October 2011)

Minister of Defence: Maj.-Gen. HLA MIN.

Minister of Home Affairs: Lt-Gen. KO KO.

Minister of Border Affairs and Myanma Industrial Development: Maj.-Gen. THEIN HTAY.

Minister of Foreign Affairs: WUNNA MAUNG LWIN.

Minister of Information and Culture: KYAW HSAN.

Minister of Agriculture and Irrigation: MYINT HLAING.

Minister of Forestry: WIN TUN.

Minister of Finance and Revenue: HLA TUN.

Minister of Construction: KHIN MAUNG MYINT.

Minister of National Planning and Economic Development and of Livestock and Fisheries: TIN NAING THEIN.

Minister of Commerce: WIN MYINT.

Minister of Posts and Telecommunications: THEIN TUN.

Minister of Labour and of Social Welfare, Relief and Resettlement: AUNG KYI.

Minister of Mines: THEIN HTIKE.

Minister of Co-operatives: OHN MYINT.

Minister of Transportation: NYAN TUN AUNG.

Minister of Hotels and Tourism and of Sports: TINT SAN.

Minister of Industry (No. 1 and No. 2): SOE THEIN.

Minister of Rail Transportation: AUNG MIN.

Minister of Energy: THAN HTAY.

Minister of Electric Power (No. 1): ZAW MIN.

Minister of Electric Power (No. 2): KHIN MAUNG SOE.

Minister of Education: Dr MYA AYE.

Minister of Health: Dr PE THET KHIN.

Minister of Religious Affairs: THURA MYINT MAUNG.

Minister of Science and Technology: AYE MYINT.

Minister of Immigration and Manpower: KHIN YI.

Ministers of President Office: THEIN NYUNT, SOE MAUNG.

MINISTRIES

Ministry of President Office: Nay Pyi Taw.

Ministry of Agriculture and Irrigation: Bldg 15, Nay Pyi Taw; tel. (67) 410004; fax (67) 140130; e-mail dap.moai@myanmar.com.mm; internet www.moai.gov.mm.

Ministry of Border Affairs: Bldg 14, Nay Pyi Taw; tel. (67) 409022; e-mail pbanrda@mptmail.net.mm; internet www.myanmar.gov.mm/PBNRDA/index.htm.

Ministry of Commerce: Bldg 3, Nay Pyi Taw; tel. (67) 408002; fax (67) 408004; e-mail moc@commerce.gov.mm; internet www.commerce.gov.mm.

Ministry of Construction: Bldg 11, Nay Pyi Taw; tel. (67) 407073; fax (67) 407181; e-mail pwscon@construction.gov.mm; internet www.construction.gov.mm.

Ministry of Co-operatives: Bldg 16, Nay Pyi Taw; tel. (67) 410032; fax (67) 410036; e-mail mcop@mptmail.net.mm; internet www.myancoop.gov.mm.

Ministry of Culture: Bldg 35, Nay Pyi Taw; tel. (67) 408023.

Ministry of Defence: Bldg 20, Nay Pyi Taw.

Ministry of Education: Bldg 13, Nay Pyi Taw; tel. (67) 407131; internet www.myanmar-education.edu.mm.

Ministry of Electric Power (No. 1): Bldg 38, Nay Pyi Taw; tel. (67) 411083.

Ministry of Electric Power (No. 2): Bldg 27, Nay Pyi Taw.

Ministry of Energy: Bldg 6, Nay Pyi Taw; tel. (67) 411046; fax (67) 411114; e-mail myanmoe@mptmail.net.mm; internet www.energy.gov.mm.

Ministry of Finance and Revenue: Bldg 26, Nay Pyi Taw; tel. (67) 410046; internet www.myanmar.com/finance.

Ministry of Foreign Affairs: Bldg 9, Nay Pyi Taw; tel. (67) 412359; e-mail mofa.aung@mptmail.net.mm; internet www.mofa.gov.mm.

Ministry of Forestry: Bldg 28, Nay Pyi Taw; tel. (67) 405004.

Ministry of Health: Bldg 4, Nay Pyi Taw; tel. (67) 411358; internet www.moh.gov.mm.

Ministry of Home Affairs: Bldg 10, Nay Pyi Taw; tel. (67) 412079; internet www.myanmar.gov.mm/ministry/home/default.htm.

Ministry of Hotels and Tourism: Bldg 33, Nay Pyi Taw; tel. (67) 406056; fax (67) 406057; e-mail dg.dht@mptmail.net.mm; internet www.myanmartourism.org.

Ministry of Immigration and Manpower: Bldg 23, Nay Pyi Taw; tel. (67) 404026.

Ministry of Industry (No. 1): Bldg 37, Nay Pyi Taw; tel. (67) 408063; fax (67) 408080; e-mail moi1@myanmar.com.mm; internet www.industry1myanmar.com.

Ministry of Industry (No. 2): Bldg 30, Nay Pyi Taw; tel. (67) 405042; e-mail dmip@mptmail.net.mm; internet www.industry2.gov.mm.

Ministry of Information: Bldg 7, Nay Pyi Taw; tel. (67) 412321.

Ministry of Labour: Bldg 51, Nay Pyi Taw; tel. (67) 404339; e-mail mol@mptmail.net.mm; internet www.mol.gov.mm.

Ministry of Livestock and Fisheries: Bldg 36, Nay Pyi Taw; tel. (67) 408045; e-mail dolf@mptmail.net.mm.

Ministry of Mines: Bldg 19, Nay Pyi Taw; tel. (67) 409001; internet www.energy.gov.mm/MOM_1.htm.

Ministry of Myanma Industrial Development: Nay Pyi Taw.

Ministry of National Planning and Economic Development: Bldg 1, Nay Pyi Taw; tel. (67) 407023; fax (67) 407004; e-mail ministry.nped@mptmail.net.mm; internet www.mnped.gov.mm.

Ministry of Posts and Telecommunications: Bldg 2, Nay Pyi Taw; tel. (67) 407037; internet www.mcpt.gov.mm.

Ministry of Rail Transportation: Bldg 29, Nay Pyi Taw; tel. (67) 405034.

Ministry of Religious Affairs: Bldg 31, Nay Pyi Taw; tel. (67) 406008; internet www.mora.gov.mm.

Ministry of Science and Technology: Bldg 21, Nay Pyi Taw; tel. (67) 404004; fax (67) 404011; internet www.most.gov.mm.

Ministry of Social Welfare, Relief and Resettlement: Bldg 23, Nay Pyi Taw; tel. (67) 404021; e-mail social-wel-myan@mptmail.net.mm; internet www.myanmar.gov.mm/ministry/MSWRR/index.html.

Ministry of Sports: Bldg 31, Nay Pyi Taw; tel. (67) 406028; e-mail MOCYGN.MYA@mptmail.net.mm; internet www.mosports.gov.mm.

Ministry of Transportation: Bldg 5, Nay Pyi Taw; tel. (67) 411033; fax (67) 411420; e-mail dept.transport@mptmail.net.mm; internet www.mot.gov.mm.

Legislature

PYIDAUNGSU HLUTTAW (UNION ASSEMBLY)

The bicameral Pyidaungsu Hluttaw (Union Assembly or National Parliament) comprises the lower chamber of the Pyithu Hluttaw (People's Assembly or House of Representatives), which has 440 seats, and the Amyotha Hluttaw (National Assembly or House of Nationalities), with 224 seats. Prior to the elections of 7 November 2010, 25% of seats in both chambers were reserved under a constitutional provision for appointed representatives of the armed forces. Elections for 14 state and regional assemblies, were held concurrently with the polls for the Pyidaungsu Hluttaw.

Amyotha Hluttaw (National Assembly)

The Amyotha Hluttaw comprises 168 civilian representatives (12 from each of the seven states and seven regions) and 56 military representatives, who are appointed by the Commander-in-Chief of the Defence Services.

Speaker: KHIN AUNG MYINT.

Pyithu Hluttaw (People's Assembly)

Speaker: SHWE MANN.

General Election, 7 November 2010

Party	Seats
Union Solidarity and Development Party	259
Shan Nationalities Democratic Party	18
National Unity Party	12
Rakhine Nationalities Development Party	9
National Democratic Force	8
All Mon Region Democracy Party	3
Pa-O National Organization	3
Chin National Party	2
Chin Progressive Party	2
Phalon-Sawaw Democratic Party	2
Wa Democratic Party	2
Others	10
Appointed members*	110
Total	440

* Military representatives appointed by the Commander-in-Chief of the Defence Services.

Election Commission

Union Election Commission (UEC): Nay Pyi Taw; f. 2010; Chair. Lt-Gen. (retd) TIN AYE; Sec. WIN KO.

Political Organizations

By September 2010 37 parties had successfully registered to participate in the legislative elections of 7 November; these included:

All Mon Region Democracy Party: Lot 7, Holdings Kha 23, 20th St, Myinethaya Ward, Mawlamyine, Mon State; f. 2010; sole party registered for 2010 election representing the Mon ethnic group; advocates democracy and a free-market economy; Chair. NAI NGWE THEIN.

Chin National Party: 277 BPI Rd, West Gyogon Ward, Insein Township, Yangon; tel. (1) 5030870; f. 2010; Chair. PU ZOZAM.

Chin Progressive Party: Room 22, Bldg 2, Pyi Yeik Mon Housing Estate, Narnattaw Rd, Ward 8, Kamayut Township, Yangon; f. 2010; promotes equal rights and economic opportunities for Chin people; Pres. PU NOTHANKAP.

Democratic Party: 6 Kwat Thit St, Yegyaw, Pazundaung Township, Yangon; f. 1988; re-formed 2010; Leader THU WAI.

88 Generation Students and Youth Organization: Room 301, Bldg F, Pearl Condominium, Kaba Aye Pagoda Rd, Bahan, Yangon; f. 2010; Leader YE HTUN.

Kayin People's Party (KPP): 51 Tawwin Rd, Ward 3, Shwe Pyi Tha, Yangon; f. 2001; Leader SIMON THA; Chair. TUN AUNG MYINT.

Lahu National Development Party: 43 Fourth Lane, Parami Rd, Ward 1, Lashio, Shan State; f. 1988; deregistered 1994; reregistered 2010; Leader DANIEL AUNG.

Modern People's Party: Fifth Fl., 255 Bogyoke Aung San Rd, between 39th and 40th Sts, Ward 8, Kyauktada, Yangon; f. 2010; fmrly the New Era People's Party; Leader TUN AUNG KYAW.

Mro (or) Khami National Solidarity Organization (MKNSO): 202 Sartaik Rd, Pyitawtha Ward, Kyauktaw, Rakhine State; f. 1988; Chair. and Leader SAN THA AUNG.

National Democratic Force: Room 103, Bldg 3, Dagonlwin Rd, Mittanyunt Ward, Tamway, Yangon; f. 2010; est. by fmr mems of the National League for Democracy; Chair. Dr THAN NYEIN; Co-Chair. KHIN MAUNG SWE.

National Political Alliance League: 49 16th St, Lanmadaw Township, Yangon; f. 2010; membership includes breakaway factions from the National League for Democracy; Leader OHN LWIN; Chair. TIN TUN MAUNG.

National Unity Party (NUP): 24 Aung Zeya St, Shwe Taung Gyar Ward 1, Bahan, Yangon; tel. (1) 278180; f. 1962; est. as the Burma Socialist Programme Party; sole legal political party until Sept. 1988, when present name was adopted; 15-mem. cen. exec. cttee and 280-mem. cen. cttee; Leader TUN YI; Sec.-Gen. THAN TIN.

Pa-O National Organization: 18 West Circular Rd, Zaypaing Ward, Taunggyi, Shan State; signed a cease-fire agreement with the military junta in April 1991; controls Special Region 6 in southern Shan State; 1,235 mems; Patron AUNG KHAM HTI; Chair. KHUN SAN LWIN; military wing: Pa-O National Army.

Peace and Diversity Party (PDP): 2/2/232 Mahawgani Rd, Htaukkyant, Mingaladon Township, Yangon; tel. 98610719 (mobile); f. 2010; Leader NYO MIN LWIN; Gen. Sec. NAY MYO WAI.

Phalon-Sawaw Democratic Party: Ward 7, Hpa-an Township, Karen State; f. 2010; represents the Karen ethnic group; Chair. KHIN KYAW OO.

Rakhine Nationalities Development Party: Khaung Laung Kyaung Rd, Lanmadaw (South) Ward, Sittwe Township, Rakhine State; f. 2010; Chair. Dr AYE MAUNG.

Shan Nationalities Democratic Party (SNDP): 9 Thitsar Uyin Housing, Thitsar Rd, Ward 8, South Okkalapa, Yangon; tel. (9) 5018229; f. 2010; also known as the White Tiger Party; Chair. SAI AIK PAUNG; Vice-Chair. SAI SAUNG SI.

Taaung (Palaung) National Party: 110 Bogyoke Aung San Rd, Mingala Ward, Namhsan Township, Shan State; f. 2010; 3,300 mems; Gen. Sec. MAI OHN KHAING.

Union Democratic Party: 123 U Chit Maung Rd, North-West Saya San Ward, Bahan, Yangon; f. 2010, following a merger between the Public Democracy Party and the Union Democracy Alliance Party; espouses support for democracy, human rights and national reconciliation; Chair. THEIN HTAY.

Union of Myanmar Federation of National Politics (UMFNP): Bldg F, Rm 301, Pearl Condominium, Kabaraye Rd, Bahan Township, Yangon; tel. (1) 556554; f. 2010; broadly pro-govt group; Leader AYE LWIN.

Union Solidarity and Development Party (USDP): Plot 5, cnr of Yazathingaha Rd and C Rd, Dekkhinathiri Township, Nay Pyi Taw; f. 2010; est. as successor to the Union Solidarity and Development Asscn (USDA—formed in 1993 as civil society group intrinsically linked to the military regime); Leader THEIN SEIN; Chair. AUNG THAUNG.

Wa Democratic Party: tel. 4/7 Hsenwi Rd, Ward 8, Lashio, Shan State; f. 2010.

Wunthanu NLD: NanU Lwin Village, Pathein Gyi, Mandalay; f. 2010; Leader YE MIN.

Deregistered parties include:

Democratic Party for a New Society (DPNS): based in Thailand; e-mail hq@dpns.org; internet www.dpns.org; f. 1988; 8-mem. cen. exec. cttee; Chair. AUNG MOE ZAW; Gen. Sec. KHIN MAUNG TINT.

Kachin State Progressive Party (KSPP): Myothit Quarter, Myitkyina; f. 2009; 150-mem. cen. cttee; registration for 2010 elections withdrawn due to alleged links with the Kachin Independence Organisation; Leader Dr MANAN TUJA.

National League for Democracy (NLD): 97B West Shwegondine Rd, Bahan Township, Yangon; e-mail info@nldla.net; internet www.nldla.net; f. 1988; est. as Nat. United Front for Democracy; name subsequently changed to League for Democracy; above name adopted 1988; cen. exec. cttee of 20 mems; cen. cttee of 108 mems; Gen. Sec. AUNG SAN SUU KYI; Chair. AUNG SHWE; Vice-Chair. TIN OO.

Union Karen (Kayin) League: Saw Toe Lane, Yangon; Leaders SAW MAUNG CHAW, SAW THAN AUNG.

Union Pa-O National Organization: f. 1988; Leader KHUN SEIN WIN HLA.

United Nationalities League for Democracy: Yangon; an alliance of parties representing non-Bamar nationalities; won a combined total of 65 seats at the 1990 election.

Wa National Development Party: Lashio, Shan; dissolved following failure to register for 2010 elections; Chair. LOAP PAUNG; Leader SAW PHILIP SAM.

The following groups are, or have been, in armed conflict with the Government:

Chin National Front: internet www.chinland.org; f. 1988; forces trained by Kachin Independence Army 1989–91; first party congress 1993; carried out an active bombing campaign in 1996–97, mainly in Chin State; joined the Democratic Alliance of Burma (1988), the National Democratic Front (1989) and the Chin National Council (2006); Leader ZING CUNG; military wing: Chin National Army (Leader Col RAL HNIN).

Communist Party of Burma (CPB): internet www.cpburma.org; f. 1939; reorg. 1946; operated clandestinely after 1948; participated after 1986 in jt military operations with sections of the NDF; in 1989 internal dissent resulted in the rebellion of about 80% of CPB members, mostly Wa hill tribesmen and Kokang Chinese; the CPB's military efficacy was thus completely destroyed; leadership exiled in the People's Republic of China; Sec.-Gen. KYIN MAUNG.

Democratic Alliance of Burma (DAB): Manerplaw; f. 1988; formed by members of the NDF to incorporate dissident students, monks and expatriates; Pres. Maj.-Gen. BO MYA; Gen. Sec. TIN MAUNG WIN; remaining organizations include:

All-Burma Student Democratic Front (ABSDF): Dagwin; e-mail absdfhq@csloxinfo.com; internet www.absdf8888.org; f. 1988; in 1990 split into two factions, under MOE THI ZUN and NAING AUNG; the two factions reunited in 1993; Chair. THAN KHE; Sec.-Gen. MYO WIN.

Karen (Kayin) National Union (KNU): f. 1948; Chair. Gen. TAMALA BAW; Vice-Chair. DAVID TAKAPAW; Gen. Sec. ZIPPORAH SEIN; military wing: Karen (Kayin) National Liberation Army (KNLA); c. 6,000 troops; Chief of Staff MU TU.

Karenni (Kayinni) National Progressive Party: agreement with the SLORC signed in March 1995 but subsequently collapsed; resumed fighting in June 1996; Chair. Gen. AUNG THAN LAY; military wing: Karenni (Kayinni) Revolutionary Army.

National Democratic Front (NDF): POB 101, Mae Sot, Tak 63110, Thailand; e-mail ndf.burma@gmail.com; f. 1975; alliance of eight ethnic resistance groups incl. KNU, CNF, NMSP, PSLF; aims to establish a federal union based on national self-determination; Chair., Cen. Exec. Cttee DAVID TAKAPAW.

Palaung State Liberation Front (PSLF): POB 368, Chiang Mai 50000, Thailand; e-mail palaungpslf@gmail.com; f. 1992; est. by mems of Palaung State Liberation Organization opposed to 1991 cease-fire agreement; Sec.-Gen. MAI AIK PHONE.

Shan State Army (SSA): formed in 1964, the original SSA was engaged in an armed rebellion against the military regime until the signing of a cease-fire agreement in 1989; elements led by Sao Sai Lek rejected the cease-fire and came to be known as the **Shan State Army—South (SSA—S)** ; following the dissolution of the separatist Mong Tai Army (MTA), in 1997 the SSA—S formed an alliance with the Shan State National Army (Leader KARN YORD), the Shan United Revolutionary Army and other MTA remnants; operates five bases close to the Thai–Myanma border; Leader Col YAWD SERK; political wing: **Restoration Council of Shan State** (300 mems; cen. cttee of 21 elected mems).

Most of the following groups signed cease-fire agreements, or reached other means of accommodation, with the military junta. In April 2009 the junta declared that all ethnic cease-fire groups would have to transform into new 'Border Guard Force' (BGF) battalions, including a component of 30 soldiers and one officer from the Myanmar Armed Forces; however, many groups resisted the order.

Democratic Karen (Kayin) Buddhist Organization: Manerplaw; breakaway group from the Karen (Kayin) National Union; military wing: Democratic Karen (Kayin) Buddhist Army; transformed into a BGF in Aug. 2010, but breakaway faction rejected agreement and resumed fighting in Nov; Leader THUZANA.

Kachin Defence Army: agreement with junta reached in Jan. 1991; fmrly the 4th Brigade of the Kachin Independence Army; adopted BGF status in Jan. 2010; Leader MAHTU NAW.

Kachin Independence Organization (KIO): agreement with junta reached in Feb. 1994; based in Laiza, Kachin State; rejected the junta's BGF proposal; Chair. LANYAW ZAWNG HRA; military wing: Kachin Independence Army (10,000 regular troops, 10,000 reserves).

Karenni (Kayinni) National People's Liberation Front: agreement with junta reached in May 1994; transformed into a BGF in Nov. 2009; Leader TUN KYAW.

Kayan National Guard: agreement with junta reached in Feb. 1992breakaway faction from the KNLP.

Kayan New Land Party (KNLP): agreement with junta reached in July 1994; rejected the junta's BGF proposal; Leader SHWE AYE.

Myanmar National Democratic Alliance Army (MNDAA): agreement with junta reached in March 1989; est. by fmr mems of the CPB; based in Kokang region of northern Shan State; forcibly removed from its cease-fire zone by govt forces in late 2009; Leader PENG JIA XIANG.

National Democratic Alliance Army (NDAA): agreement with junta reached in June 1989est. by splinter group of the CPBbased in eastern Shan StateLeader SAI LEUN.

New Democratic Army—Kachin (NDA—K): (Dec. 1989); est. by fmr officers of the KIO; adopted BGF status in Nov. 2009; Leader ZAHKUNG TING YING.

New Mon State Party (NMSP): POB 1 Sangkhlaburi, Kanchanaburi 71240, Thailand; e-mail nmsp2006@yahoo.com; internet www.nmsp.info; f. 1958; cease-fire agreement reached, June 1995; Chair. NAI HTAW MON; military wing: Mon National Liberation Army.

Palaung State Liberation Organization: (April 1991); military wing: Palaung State Liberation Army; 7,000–8,000 men.

Shan State Army—North (SSA—N): agreement with junta reached in Sept. 1989; faction of the original SSA that complied with 1989 cease-fire agreement; Chair. Maj.-Gen. LOIMAO.

Shan State Nationalities People's Liberation Organization: agreement with junta reached in Oct. 1994; Chair. THA KALEI.

United Wa State Party: (May 1989); fmrly part of the CPB; rejected the junta's BGF proposal; seeks the establishment of an autonomous Wa state; military wing: United Wa State Army (20,000–30,000 men); Leaders CHAO NGI LAI, PAO YU CHANG.

Since 1991 the National Coalition Government of the Union of Burma, constituted by representatives elected in the general election of 1990, has served as a government-in-exile:

National Coalition Government of the Union of Burma (NCGUB): POB 693, Rockville, MD 20848, USA; tel. (202) 705-6262; e-mail ncgub@ncgub.net; internet www.ncgub.net; Prime Minister Dr SEIN WIN.

Diplomatic Representation

EMBASSIES IN MYANMAR

Australia: 88 Strand Rd, Yangon; tel. (1) 251810; fax (1) 246159; e-mail austembassy.rangoon@dfat.gov.au; internet www.burma.embassy.gov.au; Ambassador BRONTE MOULES.

Bangladesh: 11B Than Lwin Rd, Yangon; tel. (1) 515275; fax (1) 515273; e-mail bdootygn@mptmail.net.mm; Ambassador Maj.-Gen. ANUP KUMAR CHAKMA.

Brunei: 317–319 U Wisara Rd, Sanchaung Township, Yangon; tel. (1) 524285; fax (1) 512854; e-mail myangon.myanmar@mfa.gov.bn; Ambassador Dato' Paduka Haji ABDUR RAHMANI BIN Haji BASIR.

Cambodia: 34 Kaba Aye Pagoda Rd, Bahan Township, Yangon; tel. (1) 549609; fax (1) 541462; e-mail recyangon@myanmar.com.mm; Ambassador SIENG BUNVUTH.

China, People's Republic: 1 Pyidaungsu Yeiktha Rd, Yangon; tel. (1) 221281; fax (1) 227019; e-mail chinaemb_mm@mfa.gov.cn; internet mm.china-embassy.org; Ambassador LI JUNHUA.

Egypt: 81 Pyidaungsu Yeiktha Rd, Yangon; tel. (1) 222886; fax (1) 222865; Ambassador SHERIFF YOUSSEF ABBAS SULEIMAN.

France: 102 Pyidaungsu Yeiktha Rd, POB 858, Yangon; tel. (1) 212523; fax (1) 212527; e-mail ambafrance.rangoun@diplomatie.gouv.fr; internet www.ambafrance-mm.org; Ambassador THIERRY MATHOU.

Germany: 9 Bogyoke Aung San Museum Rd, POB 12, Yangon; tel. (1) 548951; fax (1) 548899; e-mail info@rangun.diplo.de; internet www.rangun.diplo.de; Ambassador JULIUS GEORG LUY.

India: 545–547 Merchant St, POB 751, Yangon; tel. (1) 243972; fax (1) 254086; e-mail indiaembassy@mptmail.net.mm; internet www.indiaembassy.net.mm; Ambassador VILLUR S. SESHADRI.

Indonesia: 100 Pyidaungsu Yeiktha Rd, POB 1401, Yangon; tel. (1) 254465; fax (1) 254468; e-mail kbriygn@indonesia.com.mm; internet www.deplu.go.id/yangon; Ambassador SEBASTIANUS SUMARSONO.

Israel: 15 Khabaung Rd, Hlaing Township, Yangon; tel. (1) 515115; fax (1) 515116; e-mail info@yangon.mfa.gov.il; internet yangon.mfa.gov.il; Ambassador YARON MAYER.

Italy: 3 Inya Myaing Rd, POB 866, Golden Valley, Bahan Township, Yangon 11201; tel. (1) 527100; fax (1) 514565; e-mail ambyang.mail@esteri.it; internet www.ambyangon.esteri.it; Ambassador PAOLO A. BARTORELLI.

Japan: 100 Natmauk Rd, POB 841, Bahan Township, Yangon 11021; tel. (1) 549644; fax (1) 549643; e-mail jembassy@baganmail.net.mm; internet www.mm.emb-japan.go.jp; Ambassador TAKASHI SAITO.

Korea, Republic: 97 University Ave, Bahan Township, POB 1408, Yangon; tel. (1) 515190; fax (1) 513286; e-mail myanmar@mofat.go.kr; internet mmr.mofat.go.kr; Ambassador PARK GI-JONG.

Laos: A1 Diplomatic Quarters, Franser Rd, Yangon; tel. (1) 222482; fax (1) 227446; Ambassador NILAHAT SAYALATH.

Malaysia: 82 Pyidaungsu Yeiktha Rd, Dagon Township, Yangon; tel. (1) 220249; fax (1) 221840; e-mail malyangon@kln.gov.my; internet www.kln.gov.my/web/mmr_yangon; Ambassador Dr AHMAD FAISAL MUHAMMAD.

Nepal: 16 Natmauk Yeiktha Rd, POB 84, Tamwe, Yangon; tel. (1) 545880; fax (1) 549803; e-mail nepemb@mptmail.net.mm; Ambassador GUNALAXMI SHARMA BISWAKARMA.

Pakistan: A4 Diplomatic Quarters, Pyay Rd, Dagon Township, POB 581, Yangon; tel. (1) 222881; fax (1) 221147; e-mail pakistan@myanmar.com.mm; internet www.mofa.gov.pk/myanmar; Ambassador QAZI M. KHALILULLAH.

Philippines: 50 Saya San Rd, Bahan Township, Yangon; tel. (1) 558149; fax (1) 558154; e-mail yangonpe@mptmail.net.mm; Ambassador MARIA HELLEN M. BARBER.

Russia: 38 Sagawa Rd, Dagon Township, Yangon; tel. (1) 241955; fax (1) 241953; e-mail rusinmyan@mptmail.net.mm; internet www.rusembmyanmar.org; Ambassador MIKHAIL M. MGELADZE.

Serbia: 114A Inya Rd, Kamayut Township, POB 943, Yangon; tel. (1) 515282; fax (1) 504274; e-mail serbemb@yangon.net.mn; Chargé d'affaires a.i. NINO MALJEVIĆ.

Singapore: 238 Dhamazedi Rd, Bahan Township, Yangon; tel. (1) 559001; fax (1) 559002; e-mail singemb_ygn@sgmfa.gov.sg; internet www.mfa.gov.sg/yangon; Ambassador ROBERT CHUA.

Sri Lanka: 34 Taw Win Rd, POB 1150, Yangon; tel. (1) 222812; fax (1) 221509; e-mail www.slembyangon.org; internet www.srilankaembassy.net.mm; Ambassador H. R. PIYASIRI (designate).

Thailand: 94 Pyay Rd, Dagon Township, Yangon; tel. (1) 222784; fax (1) 221713; e-mail thaiygn@mfa.go.th; internet www.thaiembassy.org/yangon; Ambassador APIRATH VIENRAVI.

United Kingdom: 80 Strand Rd, Kyauktada Township, POB 638, Yangon; tel. (1) 380322; fax (1) 370866; e-mail BE.Rangoon@fco.gov.uk; internet ukinburma.fco.gov.uk; Ambassador ANDREW HEYN.

USA: 110 University Ave, Kamayut Township, Yangon; tel. (1) 536509; fax (1) 511069; e-mail consularrangoon@state.gov; internet burma.usembassy.gov; Chargé d'affaires LARRY M. DINGER.

Viet Nam: 70–72 Than Lwin Rd, Bahan Township, Yangon; tel. (1) 511305; fax (1) 514897; e-mail vnembmyr@cybertech.net.mm; internet www.vietnamembassy-myanmar.org; Ambassador CHU CONG PHUNG.

Judicial System

Chief Justice of the Supreme Court: TUN TUN OO, Bldg 24, Nay Pyi Taw; tel. (67) 404140.

Attorney-General: Dr TUN SHIN.

Religion

Freedom of religious belief and practice is guaranteed. In 1992 an estimated 87.2% of the population were Buddhists, 5.6% Christians, 3.6% Muslims, 1.0% Hindus and 2.6% animists or adherents of other religions.

BUDDHISM

State Sangha Maha Nayaka Committee: c/o Dept of Promotion and Propagation of the Sasana, Kaba Aye Pagoda Precinct, Mayangone Township, Yangon; tel. (1) 660759.

CHRISTIANITY

Myanmar Naing-ngan Khrityan Athin-dawmyar Kaung-si (Myanmar Council of Churches): 601 Pyay Rd, University PO, Kamayut, Yangon 11041; tel. (1) 537957; fax (1) 296848; e-mail raymond@gmail.com; internet mcc-mm.org; f. 1914; est. as Burma Representative Council of Mission; reconstituted as Burma Council of Churches in 1974; 13 mem. nat. churches, 9 mem. nat. Christian orgs; Pres. Rev. SAW MAR GAY GYI; Gen. Sec. Rt Rev. SMITH N. ZA THAWNG.

The Roman Catholic Church

Myanmar comprises three archdioceses and 11 dioceses. At 31 December 2007 an estimated 1.2% of the total population were adherents.

Catholic Bishops' Conference of Myanmar

292 Pyay Rd, Sanchaung PO, Yangon 11111; tel. (1) 525868; fax (1) 527198; e-mail secrcbcm@myanmar.com.mm.

f. 1982; Pres. Most Rev. PAUL ZINGHTUNG GRAWNG (Archbishop of Mandalay).

Archbishop of Mandalay: Most Rev. PAUL ZINGHTUNG GRAWNG, Archbishop's House, cnr of 82nd and 25th Sts, Mandalay 06011; tel. and fax (2) 33916; e-mail info@mandalayarchdiocese.com; internet www.mandalayarchdiocese.com.

Archbishop of Taunggyi: Most Rev. MATTHIAS U SHWE, Archbishop's Office, Bayint Naung Rd, Taunggyi 06011; tel. (81) 21689; fax (81) 22164; e-mail ushwe1@gmail.com.

Archbishop of Yangon: Most Rev. CHARLES MAUNG BO, Archbishop's House, 289 Theinbyu Rd, Botahtaung PO, Yangon 11161; tel. (1) 246710; fax (1) 379059; e-mail archdygn@myanmar.com.mm.

The Anglican Communion

Anglicans are adherents of the Church of the Province of Myanmar, comprising six dioceses. The Province was formed in February 1970, and contained an estimated 45,000 adherents in 1985.

Archbishop of Myanmar and Bishop of Yangon: Most Rev. STEPHEN THAN MYINT OO, Bishopscourt, 140 Pyidaungsu Yeiktha Rd, Dagon PO, Yangon 11191; tel. (1) 246813; fax (1) 251405; e-mail abcpm@myanmar.com.mm.

Protestant Churches

Lutheran Bethlehem Church: 181–183 Theinbyu St, Mingala Taung Nyunt PO, Yangon 11221; tel. and fax (1) 246585; e-mail jenson-lbc@mail4u.com.mm; Pres. Rev. JENSON RAJAN ANDREWS.

Lutheran Church of Myanmar: 247 Bogkoye St, POB 526, Kyauktada Township, 11182 Yangon; tel. (1) 245626; e-mail lsthanga09@gmail.com; Pres. Rev. Dr LAL SAWI THANGA.

Mara Evangelical Church: Evangelical Mission, 7/86 Chinpyan Rd, Sittaway, Rakhine State; tel. (1) 645955; e-mail mecsd1996@gmail.com; 21,573 mems; Gen. Sec. VICTOR VEU.

Myanmar Baptist Convention: 143 Minye Kyawswa Rd, POB 506, Yangon; tel. (1) 223231; fax (1) 221465; e-mail mbc@mptmail.net.mm; f. 1865; est. as Burma Baptist Missionary Convention; present name adopted 1954; 650,293 mems (2003); Pres. Rev. Dr HONOR NYO; Gen. Sec. Rev. K. D. TU LOM.

Myanmar Lutheran Church: 38D Thar Yar Aye, 1st St, Taung Thu Gone Ward, Insein, Yangon; tel. (1) 642550; e-mail myanmarle@mttmail.net.mm; 2,150 mems; Pres. Rev. ANDREW MANG LONE.

Myanmar Methodist Church: 47 Baho Rd, Thazin Lane, Ah Lone Township 65, Alanpya Pagoda Rd, Dagon, Yangon; Pres. Bishop ZOTHAN MAWIA.

Presbyterian Church of Myanmar: Synod Office, Falam, Chin State; 22,000 mems; Pres. Rev. SUN KANGLO.

Other denominations active in Myanmar include the Lisu Christian Church and the Salvation Army.

The Press

DAILIES

Botahtaung (The Vanguard): 22–30 Strand Rd, Botahtaung PO, POB 539, Yangon; tel. (1) 274310; Myanmar.

Guardian: 392–396 Merchant St, Botahtaung PO, POB 1522, Yangon; tel. (1) 270150; English.

Kyahmon (The Mirror): 77 52nd St, Dazundaung PO, POB 819, Yangon; tel. (1) 282777; internet www.myanmar.com/newspaper/kyaymon/index.html; Myanmar.

Myanmar Ahlin (New Light of Myanmar): 58 Komin Kochin Rd, Bahan PO, POB 21, Yangon; tel. (1) 544309; internet www.myanmar.com/newspaper/myanmarahlin/index.html; f. 1963; fmrly Loktha

Pyithu Nezin (Working People's Daily); organ of the SPDC; morning; Myanmar; Chief Editor WIN TIN; circ. 400,000.

New Light of Myanmar: 22–30 Strand Rd, Yangon; tel. (1) 297028; e-mail webmaster@myanmar.com; internet www.myanmar.com/newspaper/nlm/index.html; f. 1963; fmrly Working People's Daily; organ of the SPDC; morning; English; Chief Editor KYAW MIN; circ. 14,000.

PERIODICALS

A Hla Thit (New Beauty): 46 90th St, Yangon; tel. (1) 287106; international news.

Dana Business Magazine: 72 8th St, Lanmadaw Township, Yangon; tel. and fax (1) 224010; e-mail dana@mptmail.net.mm; economic; Editor-in-Chief WILLIAM CHEN.

Do Kyaung Tha: Myawaddy Press, 184 32nd St, Yangon; tel. (1) 274655; f. 1965; monthly; Myanmar and English; circ. 17,000.

Gita Padetha: Yangon; journal of Myanma Music Council; circ. 10,000.

Guardian Magazine: 392–396 Merchant St, Botahtaung PO, POB 1522, Yangon; tel. (1) 296510; f. 1953; nationalized 1964; monthly; English; literary; circ. 11,600.

Kyee Pwar Yay (Prosperity): 296 Bo Sun Pat St, Yangon; tel. (1) 278100; economic; Editor-in-Chief MYAT KHINE.

Moethaukpan (Aurora): Myawaddy Press, 184 32nd St, Yangon; tel. (1) 274655; f. 1980; monthly; Myanmar and English; circ. 27,500.

Myanma Dana (Myanmar's Economy): 210A 36th St, Kyauktada Post Office, Yangon; tel. (1) 284660; economic; Editor-in-Chief THIHA SAW.

Myanmar Morning Post: Yangon; f. 1998; weekly; Chinese; news; circ. 5,000.

Myanmar Times & Business Review: 379–383 Bo Aung Kyaw St, Kyauktada Township, Yangon; tel. (1) 392928; fax (1) 254158; e-mail management@myanmartimes.com.mm; internet www.mmtimes.com; f. 2000; CEO Dr TIN TUN OO ; Man. Dir BILL CLOUGH (acting).

Myawaddy Journal: Myawaddy Press, 184 32nd St, Yangon; tel. (1) 274655; f. 1989; fortnightly; news; circ. 8,700.

Myawaddy Magazine: Myawaddy Press, 184 32nd St, Yangon; tel. (1) 274655; f. 1952; monthly; literary magazine; circ. 4,200.

Ngwetaryi Magazine: Myawaddy Press, 184 32nd St, Yangon; tel. (1) 274655; f. 1961; monthly; cultural; circ. 3,400.

Pyinnya Lawka Journal: 529 Merchant St, Yangon; tel. (1) 283611; publ. by Sarpay Beikman Management Board; quarterly; circ. 18,000.

Shwe Thwe: 529 Merchant St, Yangon; tel. (1) 283611; weekly; bilingual children's journal; publ. by Sarpay Beikman Management Board; circ. 100,000.

Taw Win Journal (Royal Journal): 149 37th St, Yangon; news; Editor-in-Chief SOE THEIN.

Teza: Myawaddy Press, 184 32nd St, Yangon; tel. (1) 274655; f. 1965; monthly; English and Myanmar; pictorial publ. for children; circ. 29,500.

Thwe Thauk Magazine: Myawaddy Press, 184 32nd St, Yangon; f. 1946; monthly; literary.

Ya Nant Thit (New Fragrance): 186 39th St, Yangon; tel. (1) 276799; international news; Editor-in-Chief CHIT WIN MG.

NEWS AGENCY

Myanmar News Agency (MNA): 212 Theinbyu Rd, Botahtaung, Yangon; tel. (1) 270893; f. 1963; govt-controlled; Chief Editors ZAW MIN THEIN (domestic section), KYAW MIN (external section).

Publishers

Hanthawaddy Press: 157 Bo Aung Kyaw St, Yangon; f. 1889; textbooks, multilingual dictionaries; Man. Editor ZAW WIN.

Knowledge Publishing House: 130 Bo Gyoke Aung San St, Yegyaw, Yangon; art, education, religion, politics and social sciences.

Kyipwaye Press: 84th St, Letsaigan, Mandalay; tel. (2) 21003; arts, travel, religion, fiction and children's.

Myawaddy Press: 184 32nd St, Yangon; tel. (1) 276889; journals and magazines; CEO THEIN SEIN.

Sarpay Beikman Management Board: 529 Merchant St, Yangon; tel. (1) 283611; f. 1947; encyclopaedias, literature, fine arts and general; also magazines and translations; Chair. AUNG HTAY.

Shumawa Press: 146 West Wing, Bogyoke Aung San Market, Yangon; mechanical engineering.

Shwepyidan: 12A Haiaban, Yegwaw Quarter, Yangon; politics, religion, law.

Smart and Mookerdum: 221 Sule Pagoda Rd, Yangon; arts, cookery, popular science.

Thu Dhama Wadi Press: 55–56 Maung Khine St, POB 419, Yangon; f. 1903; religious; Propr TIN HTOO; Man. PAN MAUNG.

GOVERNMENT PUBLISHING HOUSE

Printing and Publishing Enterprise: 365–367 Bo Aung Kyaw St, Kyauktada Township, Yangon; tel. (1) 294645; f. 1880; est. as Govt Printing Office; Man. Dir AUNG NYEIN.

PUBLISHERS' ASSOCIATION

Myanma Publishers' Union: 146 Bogyoke Market, Yangon.

Broadcasting and Communications

TELECOMMUNICATIONS

Posts and Telecommunications Department: Blk 68, Ayeyar Wun Rd, South Dagon Township, Yangon; tel. (1) 591388; fax (1) 591383; e-mail dg.ptd@mptmail.net.mm; internet www.mcpt.gov.mm/ptd/index.htm; regulatory authority responsible for supervising radio communication, telephone, telegraph and post operations; Dir-Gen. TIN HTWE.

Myanma Posts and Telecommunications (MPT): No. 2 Office Bldg, Special Development Zone, Nay Pyi Taw; tel. (1) 407333; fax (1) 407008; internet www.mpt.net.mm; fmrly the Posts and Telecommunications Corpn; Man. Dir THAR OO.

BROADCASTING

Radio

Myanma TV and Radio Department (MTRD): 426 Pyay Rd, Kamayut 11041, Yangon; tel. (1) 531850; fax (1) 530211; f. 1946; broadcasts in Bamar, Arakanese (Rakhine), Shan, Karen (Kayin), Kachin, Kayah, Chin, Mon and English; Dir-Gen. KHIN MAUNG HTAY; Dir of Radio Broadcasting KO KO HTWAY.

Television

Myanma TV and Radio Department (MTRD): 426 Pyay Rd, Kamayut 11041, Yangon; tel. (1) 535553; fax (1) 525428; f. 1946; colour television transmissions began in 1980; Dir-Gen. KHIN MAUNG HTAY; Dir of Television Broadcasting MYINT OO.

TV Myawaddy: Hmawbi, Hmawbi Township, Yangon; tel. (1) 620270; f. 1995; military broadcasting station transmitting public information, education and entertainment programmes via satellite.

In 2005 the Democratic Voice of Burma (DVB) began broadcasting Myanmar language news and educational programmes via satellite from Norway.

Finance

(cap. = capital; res = reserves; dep. = deposits; m. = million; brs = branches; amounts in kyats unless otherwise stated)

BANKING

Central Bank

Central Bank of Myanmar: 26A Settmu Rd, POB 184, Yankin Township, Yangon; tel. (1) 543751; fax (1) 543743; e-mail mofr_it_center@mptmail.net.mm; f. 1947; est. as People's Bank of the Union of Burma; present name adopted 1990; bank of issue; cap. 350m., dep. 13,545m.; Gov. THAN NYEIN; 37 brs.

State Banks

Myanma Economic Bank (MEB): Bldg 34, Nay Pyi Taw; tel. (67) 410449; fax (67) 410331; e-mail mebhoadmin@mpt.net.mm; internet www.mebank.com.mm; f. 1975; provides domestic banking network throughout the country; Man. Dir MYAT MAW.

Myanma Foreign Trade Bank: 80–86 Maha Bandoola Garden St, POB 203, Kyauktada Township, Yangon; tel. (1) 284911; fax (1) 289585; e-mail mftb-hoygn@mptmail-net.mm; f. 1976; handles all foreign exchange and international banking transactions; Chair. and Man. Dir THAN YE; Man. and Sec. HTIN KYAW THEIN.

Development Banks

Myanma Agricultural Development Bank (MADB): 1–7 cnr Latha St and Kanna Rd, Yangon; tel. (1) 226734; f. 1953; est. as State Agricultural Bank; reconstituted as Myanma Agricultural and Rural Devt Bank 1990, and as above 1996; state-owned; Man. Dir CHIT SWE.

Myanma Investment and Commercial Bank (MICB): 170–176 Bo Aung Kyaw St, Botahtaung Township, Yangon; tel. (1) 256871;

fax (1) 250518; e-mail micb.hoygn@mptmail.net.mm; f. 1989; state-owned; cap. 940m., res 890,75m., dep. 25,040m. (March 2007); Chair. and Man. Dir MYA THAN; 1 br.

Private Banks

In mid-2010 it was reported that four additional licences had been issued to private domestic banks.

Asian Yangon Bank Ltd: 319–321 Maha Bandoola St, Botahtaung Township, Yangon; tel. (1) 245825; fax (1) 245865; f. 1994; est. as Asian Yangon Int. Bank Ltd; name changed as above in 2000; Gen. Man. MYO MYINT.

Co-operative Bank Ltd: 334–336, cnr of Strand Rd & 23rd St, Latha Township, Yangon; tel. (1) 372641; fax (1) 240147; e-mail cbbank@mptmail.net.mm; internet www.cbbank.com.mm; f. 1992; Chair. KHIN MAUNG AYE; Gen. Man. NYUNT HLAING; 18 brs.

First Private Bank Ltd (FPB): 619–621, cnr of Merchant St & Bo Soon Pat St, Pabedan Township, Yangon; tel. (1) 251750; fax (1) 242320; e-mail fpb.hq@mptmail.net.mm; internet www.fpbbank-myanmar.com; f. 1992; est. as the first publicly subscribed bank; fmrly Commercial and Devt Bank Ltd; provides loans to private business and small-scale industrial sectors; cap. 5,000m. (March 2008); Chair. Dr SEIN MAUNG; 16 brs.

Innwa Bank Ltd: 554–556 Merchant St, cnr of 35th & 36th Sts, Kyauktada Township, Yangon; tel. (1) 254642; fax (1) 254431; f. 1997; Gen. Man. YIN SEIN.

Kanbawza Bank Ltd: 615/1 Pyay Rd, Kamayut Township, Yangon; tel. (1) 538075; fax (1) 538069; e-mail kbzinfo@kbzbank.asia; internet www.kbzbank.asia; f. 1994; Chair. AUNG KO WIN; 30 brs.

Myanma Citizens Bank Ltd (MCB): 383 Maha Bandoola St, Kyauktada Township, Yangon; tel. (1) 379176; fax (1) 245932; e-mail mcbankygn@mptmail.net.mm; f. 1991; Chair. HLA TIN; Man. Dir AUNG THIN WIN.

Myanma Oriental Bank Ltd (MOB): 166–168 Pansodan St, Kyauktada Township, Yangon; tel. (1) 246594; fax (1) 253217; e-mail mobl.ygn@mptmail.net.mm; f. 1993; Chair. MYAT KYAW; Man. Dir and CEO WIN MYINT.

Myanmar Industrial Development Bank Ltd: 26–42 Pansodan St, Kyauktada Township, Yangon; tel. (1) 249536; fax (1) 249529; f. 1996; cap. US $335m.

Myawaddy Bank Ltd: 24–26 Sule Pagoda Rd, Kyauktada Township, Yangon; tel. (1) 283665; fax (1) 250093; e-mail mwdbankygn@mtpt400.stems.com; f. 1993; Gen. Mans TUN KYI, MYA MIN.

Tun Foundation Bank Ltd: 165–167 Bo Aung Kyaw St, Yangon; tel. (1) 240710; e-mail tfbbank@mptmail.net.mm; f. 1997; Chair. THEIN TUN.

Yadanabon Bank Ltd: 58A 26th St, cnr of 84th & 85th Sts, Aung Myay Thar Zan Township, Mandalay; tel. (2) 23577; f. 1992.

Yangon City Bank Ltd: 12–18 Sepin St, Kyauktada Township, Yangon; tel. (1) 289256; fax (1) 289231; f. 1993; auth. cap. 500m.; 100% owned by Yangon City Devt Cttee; Chair. Col MYINT AUNG.

Yoma Bank Ltd: 1 Kungyan St, Mingala Taung Nyunt Township, Yangon; tel. (1) 242138; fax (1) 246548; f. 1993; Chair. SERGE PUN.

Foreign Banks

By November 2003 18 foreign banks had opened representative offices in Yangon.

STOCK EXCHANGE

Myanmar Securities Exchange Centre: 1st Floor, 21–25 Sule Pagoda Rd, Yangon; tel. (1) 283984; f. 1996; jt venture between MEB and Japan's Daiwa Institute of Research; Man. Dir EIJI SUZUKI.

INSURANCE

At the end of November 2003 there were three representative offices of foreign insurance companies in Myanmar.

Myanma Insurance: 627–635 Merchant St, Yangon; tel. (1) 252373; fax (1) 250275; e-mail myansure@mptmail.net.com; internet www.soft-comm.com/myanma_insurance/index.html; f. 1976; govt-controlled; Man. Dir Col THEIN LWIN.

Trade and Industry

GOVERNMENT AGENCIES

Inspection and Agency Services: 383 Maha Bandoola St, Yangon; tel. (1) 284821; fax (1) 284823; promotes business with foreign cos on behalf of state-owned enterprises; Man. Dir OHN KHIN.

Myanmar Economic Corpn (MEC): 74–76 Shwedagon Pagoda Rd, Dagon Township, Yangon; tel. (1) 254738; (retd) Brig.-Gen. Thura MYINT THIEN.

Myanmar Investment Commission (MIC): Ministry of National Planning and Economic Development, Bldg 32, Nay Pyi Taw; tel. (67) 406334; fax (67) 406333; f. 1994; Chair. MAUNG MAUNG THEIN.

Union of Myanmar Economic Holdings: 72–74 Shwadagon Pagoda Rd, Yangon; tel. (1) 78905; f. 1990; public holding co; auth. cap. 10,000m. kyats; 40% of share capital subscribed by the Ministry of Defence and 60% by members of the armed forces.

CHAMBER OF COMMERCE

Union of Myanmar Federation of Chambers of Commerce and Industry (UMFCCI): 29 Min Ye Kyawswa Rd, Lanmadaw Township, Yangon; tel. (1) 214344; fax (1) 214484; e-mail umcci@mptmail.net.mm; internet www.umfcci.com.mm; f. 1919; est. as Burmese Chamber of Commerce; present name adopted 1999; Pres. WIN MYINT; Gen. Sec. SEIN WIN HLAING.

INDUSTRIAL AND TRADE ASSOCIATIONS

Myanmar Aquaculture and Fisheries Association: 74–86 Bo Sun Pat St, Pabedan Township, Yangon; tel. (1) 243150; fax (1) 248177.

Myanmar Computer Industry Association: Myanmar Info-Tech, Main Bldg, Hlaing University Campus, Hlaing Township, Yangon; tel. (1) 652238; e-mail mcia@mail4u.com.mm; internet www.mcia.org.mm; Pres. WAH WAH HTUN.

Myanmar Construction Entrepreneurs' Association: Thanthumar Rd, cnr Thuwunna Rd, Thingankyun Township, Yangon; tel. (1) 579547; fax (1) 575947.

Myanmar Edible Oil Dealers' Association: 81–82 Kantgaw St, Bayint Naung Warehouse, Mayangon Township, Yangon; tel. (1) 680910; Chair. KO KO GYI.

Myanmar Engineers' Association: Bldg 6, Rm 5, MICT Park, Hlaing Township, Yangon; tel. (1) 652294.

Myanmar Fisheries Federation (MFF): cnr Bayint Naung Rd and Say War Sat Yone St, West Gyo Gone, Insein Township, Yangon; tel. (1) 683652; fax (1) 683662; e-mail fish-fed@mff.com.mm; internet www.fishfedmyanmar.com; six mem. asscns; Pres. HTAY MYINT.

Myanmar Forest Products and Timber Merchants' Association: 29 Min Ye Kyaw Swa St, Lanmadaw Township, Yangon; tel. (1) 214838; e-mail mfptma@mptmail.net.mm; internet www.myanmartimberassociation.org; f. 1993; Chair. SEIN LWIN; Sec.-Gen. NAY HTUN MIN.

Myanmar Garment Manufacturers' Association (MGMA): J V-2 Bldg, between Lanthit St and Wardan St, Seikkan Township, Yangon; tel. (1) 220879; fax (1) 222706; Chair. MYINT SOE.

Myanmar Industries Association: 504–506 Merchant St, Kyauktada Township, Yangon; tel. and fax (1) 241919; f. 1993; Chair. PAW HEIN.

Myanmar Livestock Federation: Livestock Breeding and Veterinary Department Compound, Insein Rd, Insein Township, Yangon; tel. (1) 640820; fax (1) 225955.

Myanmar Rice and Paddy Wholesalers' Association: 504–506 Merchant St, Kyauktada Township, Yangon; tel. (1) 241920.

Myanmar Rice Industry Association: f. 2010; est. to co-ordinate the rice industry, promote private investment and develop the export potential of the sector; provides low-interest loans and improved seeds, fertilizers and technology; 40 exec. mems; Chair. CHIT KHAING.

Myanmar Rice Millers' Association: 69 Theinbyu St, Botahtaung Township, Yangon; tel. (1) 296284; Pres. TIN WIN.

Myanmar Women Entrepreneurs' Association: 288–290 Shwedagon Pagoda Rd, Dagon Township, Yangon; tel. (1) 254400; fax (1) 254566; e-mail mwea2008@gmail.com; internet www.mweamm.org; f. 1995; Pres. YI YI MYINT (acting).

UTILITIES

Electricity

Myanma Electric Power Enterprise (MEPE): 197–199 Lower Kyimyindine Rd, Yangon; tel. (1) 220918; fax (1) 221006; e-mail mepe@mptmail.net.mm; Man. Dir ZAW WIN.

Water

Mandalay City Development Committee (Water and Sanitation Dept): cnr of 26th and 72nd Sts, Mandalay; tel. (2) 36173; f. 1992; Head of Water and Sanitation Dept TUN KYI.

Water Resources Utilization Department (WRUD): Ministry of Agriculture and Irrigation, Office 50, Nay Pyi Taw; tel. (67) 431291; internet wrud15.com; f. 1995; Dir.-Gen. KYI HTUT WIN.

Yangon City Development Committee (Water and Sanitation Dept): City Hall, cnr of Maha Bandoola Rd and Sule Pagoda Rd, Kyauktada Township, Yangon; tel. (1) 248112; fax (1) 246016; e-mail priycdc@mptmail.net.mm; internet www.yangoncity.com.mm/ycdc/index.asp; f. 1992; Head of Water and Sanitation Dept ZAW WIN.

CO-OPERATIVES

In 2003, according to official reports, there were 18,041 co-operative societies.

Central Co-operative Society Ltd: Saya San Plaza, Cnr Saya Rd and New University Ave, Bahan Township, Yangon; tel. (1) 557640; fax (1) 553894; e-mail ccscencoop@gmail.com; internet www.ccsmyanmar.com; Chair. KHIN MAUNG AYE.

Co-operative Department: Ministry of Co-operatives, Bldg 16, Nay Pyi Taw; tel. (1) 410339; fax (1) 410024; e-mail coopdeptdg@mptmail.net.mm; internet www.myancoop.gov.mm/co-department.htm; Dir-Gen. MAUNG HTI.

MAJOR COMPANIES

It was reported that from 2008 a number of state enterprises were in the process of being transferred to private ownership.

State Enterprises

Livestock Feedstuff and Milk Products Enterprise: Station Rd, Insein Township, Yangon; tel. (1) 642019; fax (1) 642023; e-mail livestock@mptmail.net.mm; Man. Dir KHIN MAUNG AYE.

Myanma Agricultural Machinery Industries: 6B Kaba Aye Pagoda Rd, Yankin Township, POB 370, Yangon; tel. (1) 660204; fax (1) 665899; e-mail dmip@mptmail.net.mm; internet www.industry2.gov.mm/mami.htm.

Myanma Agricultural Produce Trading (MAPT): c/o Ministry of Commerce, Bldg 3, Nay Pyi Taw; tel. (67) 408002; fax (67) 408004; e-mail moc@commerce.gov.mm; internet www.commerce.gov.mm/eng/mapt; Man. Dir MIN HLA AUNG.

Myanma Agriculture Service: Kanbe Rd, Yankin Township, Yangon; tel. (1) 663541; fax (1) 283651; f. 1972; fmrly Agriculture Corpn; name changed as above 1989; Man. Dir Dr MYA MAUNG.

Myanma Automobile and Diesel Engine Industries: 56 Kaba Aye Pagoda Rd, Yankin Township, Yangon; tel. (1) 650912; fax (1) 650913; e-mail dmip@mptmail.net.mm; internet www.industry2.gov.mm/madi.htm; Man. Dir MYINT THEIN.

Myanma Ceramic Industries: 192 Kaba Aye Pagoda Rd, Bahan Township, POB 11201, Yangon; tel. (1) 562040; fax (1) 578226; e-mail mci@industry1myanmar.com; internet www.industry1myanmar.com/English/MCI/mci.html; produces cement, glass, pottery, marble, asbestos sheets and bricks; Man. Dir THAN SHWE.

Myanma Cotton and Sericulture Enterprise: Thiri Mingala Lane, off Kaba Aye Pagoda Rd, Yangon; tel. (1) 666067; fax (1) 666065; f. 1994; Man. Dir Dr THEIN HTAY.

Myanma Export-Import Services: 622–624 Merchant St, Yangon; tel. (1) 250270; fax (1) 289587; Man. Dir THAUNG SEIN.

Myanma Farms Enterprise: Pyi Rd, 9th Mile, Yangon; tel. (1) 665138; f. 1957; Man. Dir Col NYUNT MG.

Myanma Foodstuff Industries: Bldg 37, Nay Pyi Taw; tel. (67) 408076; fax (67) 407004; e-mail mfi@industry1myanmar.com; internet www.industry1myanmar.com/English/MFI/mfi.html; produces foodstuffs, incl. soft drinks, biscuits, lagers and distilled spirits; Man. Dir SOE HLAING.

Myanma Gems Enterprise: c/o Ministry of Mines, Head Office Bldg, 19 Nay Pyi Taw; tel. (1) 665169; fax (1) 665092; f. 1976; Man. Dir THEIN SWE.

Myanma General and Maintenance Industries: Bldg 37, Nay Pyi Taw; tel. (67) 408075; fax (67) 408146; e-mail mgmi@industry1myanmar.com; internet www.industry1myanmar.com/English/MGMI/mgmi.html; mfr of shoes, leather products, paper and corrugated cartons; Gen. Man. AYE MAUK.

Myanma Heavy Industries: 56 Kaba Aye Pagoda Rd, POB 370, Yangon; tel. (1) 662880; fax (1) 660465; f. 1960; mfr of vehicles, electrical appliances, electronic goods and agricultural machinery; Man. Dir SOE THEIN.

Myanma Industrial Construction Services: 1 Thitsa Rd, Yankin Township, POB 370, Yangon; tel. (1) 663116; e-mail dmip@mptmail.net.mm; internet www.industry2.gov.mm/mics.htm; f. 1975; Man. Dir SOE WIN.

Myanma Jute Enterprise: 257 Insein Rd, HLG, Yangon; tel. (1) 666059; Man. Dir YE PHONE MYINT.

Myanma Machine Tools and Electrical Industries: Blk 12, Parami Rd, Hlaing Township, Yangon; tel. (1) 660437; fax (1) 660801; e-mail dmip@mptmail.net.mm; internet www.industry2.gov.mm/mtei.htm; Man. Dir KYAW WIN.

Myanma Oil and Gas Enterprise (MOGE): c/o Ministry of Energy, Complex 44, Nay Pyi Taw; tel. (67) 411055; fax (67) 411125; e-mail mogemd@mptmail.net.mm; internet www.energy.gov.mm/upstreampetroleumsubsector.htm; fmrly Myanma Oil Corpn (previously Burma Oil Co); nationalized 1963; Man. Dir SAN LWIN.

Myanma Paper and Chemical Industries: 16B Thukhawady Rd, Yankin, Yangon; tel. (1) 559225; fax (1) 559236; e-mail mpci@industry1myanmar.com; internet www.industry1myanmar.com/English/MPCI/mpci.html; Man. Dir NYUNT AUNG.

Myanma Perennial Crops Enterprise: Thiri Mingala Lane, off Kaba Aye Pagoda Rd, Yangon; tel. (1) 666011; fax (1) 667446; e-mail mpce.moai@mptmail.net.mm; internet www.mpce-moai.gov.mm; f. 1994.

Myanma Petrochemical Enterprise: Complex 44, Nay Pyi Taw; tel. (67) 411349; fax (67) 411343; e-mail mpeho@mptmail.net.mm; internet www.energy.gov.mm/ministryofenergy.htm; f. 1975; Man. Dir HLAING MYINT SAN.

Myanma Petroleum Products Enterprise: Complex 6, Nay Pyi Taw; tel. (67) 411053; fax (67) 411101; e-mail mppe.ho1@mptmail.net.mm; internet www.energy.gov.mm/ministryofenergy.htm; Man. Dir AUNG HLAING.

Myanma Pharmaceutical Industries: Bldg 37, Nay Pyi Taw; tel. (67) 408077; fax (67) 408339; e-mail mpi@industry1myanmar.com; internet www.industry1myanmar.com/English/MPI/mpi.html; Man. Dir TIN HLAING.

Myanma Sugarcane Enterprise: Thiri Mingala Lane, off Kaba Aye Pagoda Rd, Yangon; tel. (1) 666041; fax (1) 666107; f. 1994; Man. Dir MYO MYINT.

Myanma Textile Industries: Bldg 37, Nay Pyi Taw; tel. (67) 408078; fax (1) 573373; e-mail mti@industry1myanmar.com; internet www.industry1myanmar.com/English/MTI/mti.html; produces wide range of fabrics and yarns; sales 23,365,040m. kyats (1998); Man. Dir SAN KYI.

Myanma Timber Enterprise: POB 206, Ahlone, Yangon; tel. (1) 220637; fax (1) 221816; e-mail mdmte@myanmar.com.mm; internet www.myanmatimber.com.mm; f. 1948; extraction, processing, and main exporter of teak and other timber, veneers, plywood and other forest products; Man. Dir WIN TUN.

Myanma Tyre and Rubber Industries: 30 Kaba Aye Pagoda Rd, Mayangone Township, Yangon; tel. (1) 665209; fax (1) 660465; e-mail dmip@mptmail.net.mm; internet www.industry2.gov.mm/mtri.htm.

No. 1 Mining Enterprise: Bldg 19, Nay Pyi Taw; e-mail 1myn@mptmail.net.mm; devt and mining of non-ferrous metals; Man. Dir SAW LWIN.

No. 2 Mining Enterprise: Bldg 19, Nay Pyi Taw; e-mail ME-2@mptmail.net.mm; devt and mining of tin, tungsten and antimony; Man. Dir HLA THEING.

No. 3 Mining Enterprise: Bldg 19, Nay Pyi Taw; e-mail ME3Myanmar@mptmail.net.mm; production of pig iron, steel billet, steel grinding balls, coal, barytes, gypsum, limestone, chromite, antimony, various industrial minerals, etc.; Man. Dir SAN TUN.

Private Companies

Myanmar Daewoo Electronics: 139 MHI Compound, Kaba Aye Pagoda Rd, POB 737, Yangon; tel. (1) 64886; fax (1) 62870; f. 1990; South Korean co in jt venture with Myanma Heavy Industries; mfr of televisions, refrigerators and audio systems; Man. Dir KIM CHANG HUN.

Myanmar International Hotels: 77–91 Sule Pagoda Rd, Yangon; tel. (1) 62857; jt venture between Strand Hotels Int. and Myanmar Hotels and Tourism Services; construction and renovation of hotels.

Myanmar Ivanhoe Copper Co Ltd: 70 I Bo Chein St, Hlaing Township, Pyay Rd, Yangon; tel. (1) 514194; fax (1) 514208; e-mail miccl@miccl.com.mm; internet www.miccl.com.mm; f. 1996; jt venture between Ivanhoe Myanmar Holdings Ltd and No. 1 Mining Enterprise; copper mining; Exec. Officer DAW THIRI.

Myanmar Natsteel Hardware Centre: 262 Seikkantha St, Yangon; tel. (1) 84985; f. 1991; jt venture between Construction and Electrical Stores Trading and Singapore's Natsteel Trade Int; manufacture and marketing of building materials and steel products.

Myanma Traditional Manufacturing Co Ltd: 276 Strand Rd, Pabedan Township, Yangon; tel. (1) 370803; e-mail zmkumbrella@myanmar.com.mm; internet www.myanmarhandmade.com; mfr and exporter of umbrellas, tapestry, painting and jewellery.

Yasmin Enterprise Co Ltd: 3rd Floor, 31 88th St, Mingalar Taung Nyunt Township, Yangon; tel. (1) 394563; fax (1) 379331; e-mail sales@yasminmyanmar.com; internet www.yasminmyanmar.com; f. 1989; exports food products, especially tamarind, imports automotive and bicycle parts, fertilizer, plastics; Dir KYAW NAING TUN.

WORKERS' AND PEASANTS' COUNCILS

Peasants' Asiayone (Organization): Yangon; tel. (1) 82819; f. 1977; Chair. Brig.-Gen. THAN NYUNT; Sec. SAN TUN.

Workers' Unity Organization: Central Organizing Committee, 61 Theinbyu St, Yangon; tel. (1) 284043; f. 1968; workers' representative org.; Chair. OHN KYAW; Sec. NYUNT THEIN.

Transport

All railways, domestic air services, passenger and freight road transport services, and inland water facilities are owned and operated by state-controlled enterprises.

RAILWAYS

The railway network comprised 3,955 km of track in 1996/97, most of which was single track.

Myanma Railways: 361 Theinbyu St, Botahtaung Township, Yangon; tel. (1) 298585; fax (1) 284220; f. 1877; govt-operated; Man. Dir MIN SWE; Gen. Man. HLA YI.

ROADS

In 2005 the total length of the road network in Myanmar was an estimated 27,000 km.

Road Transportation Department: 375 Bogyoke Aung San St, Yangon; tel. (1) 284426; fax (1) 289716; f. 1963; controls passenger and freight road transport; Man. Dir OHN MYINT.

INLAND WATERWAYS

The principal artery of traffic is the River Ayeyarwady (Irrawaddy), which is navigable as far as Bhamo, about 1,450 km inland, while parts of the Thanlwin and Chindwinn rivers are also navigable.

Inland Water Transport: 50 Pansodan St, Kyauktada Township, Yangon; tel. (1) 380753; fax (1) 380752; e-mail iwtnpt@mpt.net.mm; internet www.iwt-myanmar.com; f. 1865; govt-owned; operates cargo and passenger services throughout Myanmar with a fleet of 476 vessels; Man. Dir SOE TINT.

SHIPPING

Yangon is the chief port. Vessels with a displacement of up to 15,000 grt can be accommodated. In December 2009 the Myanma merchant fleet comprised 117 vessels, with a total displacement of 182,500 grt.

Myanma Port Authority: 10 Pansodan St, POB 1, Yangon; tel. (1) 382722; fax (1) 295134; e-mail mpa@mptmail.net.mm; internet www.myanmaportauthority.com; f. 1880; general port and harbour duties; Man. Dir HTIEN HTAY; Gen. Man. HLAING SOON.

Myanma Five Star Line: 132–136 Theinbyu St, POB 1221, Yangon; tel. (1) 295279; fax (1) 297669; e-mail mfslhq@mptmail.net.mm; internet www.mfsl-shipping.com; f. 1959; cargo services to the Far East and Australia; Man. Dir MAUNG MAUNG NYEIN; Gen. Man. WIN PE; fleet of 26 coastal and ocean-going vessels.

CIVIL AVIATION

Mingaladon Airport, near Yangon, is equipped to international standards. Mandalay International Airport was inaugurated in September 2000. In 2002 plans for the construction of a third international airport, to serve Nay Pyi Taw, were approved.

Department of Civil Aviation: Yangon International Airport, Yangon 11021; tel. (1) 533000; fax (1) 533016; e-mail dgdca@dca.gov.mm; internet www.dca.gov.mm; Dir-Gen. TIN NAING TUN.

Air Bagan Ltd: 56 Shwe Taung Gyar St, Bahan Township, Yangon; tel. (1) 514861; fax (1) 515102; e-mail info@airbagan.com.mm; internet www.airbagan.com; f. 2004; domestic services to 17 destinations; Chair. TAY ZA; Man. Dir HTOO THET HTWE.

Air Mandalay: 146 Dhammazedi Rd, Bahan Township, Yangon; tel. (1) 501520; fax (1) 525937; e-mail info@airmandalay.com; internet www.airmandalay.com; f. 1994; jt venture between Air Mandalay Holding and Myanma Airways; operates domestic services and regional services to Thailand and Cambodia; Chair. Dr TUN CHIN; Man. Dir ERIC KANG TIAN LYE.

Myanmar Airways (MA): 104 Kanna Rd, Yangon; tel. (1) 284566; fax (1) 89583; e-mail 8mpr@maiair.com.mm; internet www.mot.gov.mm/ma/index.html; f. 1993; govt-controlled; internal network operates services to 21 airports; Man. Dir TIN MAUNG TUN.

Myanmar Airways International (MAI): 08-02 Sakura Tower, 339 Bogyoke Aung San Rd, Yangon; tel. (1) 255260; fax (1) 255305; e-mail management@maiair.com; internet www.maiair.com; f. 1993; est. by Myanmar Airways in jt venture with RMT company for international schedule services; operates services to Bangkok, Guangzhou, Hong Kong, Kuala Lumpur and Singapore; CEO AUNG GYI.

United Myanmar Air: Summit Parkview Hotel, Yangon; internet www.unitedmyanmar.com; f. 2003; jt venture between Myanmar Airways and Sunshine Strategic Investments Holdings of Hong Kong; international services to Bangkok, Hong Kong, Kuala Lumpur and Singapore; CEO EDWARD TAN.

Yangon Airways: MMB Tower, 5th Floor, 166 Upper Pansodan Rd, Mingalar Taungnyunt Township, Yangon; tel. (1) 383100; fax (1) 383109; e-mail cmya@mmb.com.mm; internet www.yangonair.com; f. 1996; domestic services to 13 destinations; Man. Dir AIK HAUK.

Tourism

Yangon, Mandalay, Taunggyi and Pagan possess outstanding palaces, Buddhist temples and shrines. In 2008 there were 193,319 foreign tourist arrivals. Revenue from tourism (including passenger transport) totalled an estimated US $59m. in 2006.

Myanmar Hotels and Tourism Services: 77–91 Sule Pagoda Rd, Yangon 11141; tel. (1) 282013; fax (1) 254417; e-mail mtt.mht@mptmail.net.mm; govt-controlled; manages all hotels, tourist offices, tourist dept stores and duty-free shops; Gen. Man. TIN HTAY.

Myanmar Tourism Promotion Board: Business Centre, 3rd Floor, 223 Signal Pagoda Rd, Yangon; tel. (1) 242828; fax (1) 242800; e-mail mtpb@mptmail.net.mm; internet www.myanmar-tourism.com; Chair. AUNG MYAT KYAW.

Myanmar Travels and Tours: 118–120 Mahabandoola St, Kyauktada Township, Yangon; tel. (1) 371286; fax (1) 254417; e-mail mtt.mht@mptmail.net.mm; internet www.myanmartravelsandtours.com; f. 1964; govt tour operator and travel agent; handles all travel arrangements for groups and individuals; Gen. Man. HTAY AUNG.

Union of Myanmar Travel Association (UMTA): Bldg 69, Yuzana Condo Tower, 6th Floor, Unit 609B, cnr Shwegonedaing Rd and Kabaraye Pagoda Rd, Bahan Township, Yangon; tel. (1) 559673; fax (1) 545707; e-mail UMTA@mptmail.net.mm; internet www.umtanet.org; f. 2002; organizes private travel agencies and tour operators; Chair. MAUNG MAUNG SWE; Sec. HPONE THANT.

Defence

As assessed at November 2010, the total strength of the armed forces was an estimated 406,000 (army 375,000, navy 16,000, air force 15,000). Military service is voluntary. Paramilitary forces include a people's police force (72,000 men) and a people's militia (35,000 men). The 11-member National Defence and Security Council was established in March 2011.

Defence Expenditure: estimated at US $1,900m. for 2009.

Commander-in-Chief of the Defence Services: Gen. MIN AUNG HLAING.

Commander-in-Chief of the Army: Gen. MIN AUNG HLAING.

Commander-in-Chief of the Navy: Vice-Adm. NYAN TUN.

Commander-in-Chief of the Air Force: Maj.-Gen. MYAT HEIN.

Education

The organization and administration of education is the responsibility of the Ministry of Education. Pre-school education begins at four years of age. Primary education, which is compulsory, lasts for five years between the ages of five and 10. Secondary education, beginning at 10 years of age, comprises a first cycle of four years and a second of two years. In 2007/08 enrolment at primary and secondary schools was equivalent to 82% of children in the relevant age-groups.

In 2001/02 there were 958 tertiary-level institutions, at which an estimated 587,300 students were enrolled. According to provisional estimates, 507,660 students were enrolled in tertiary-level institutions in 2007/08.

In 2005/06 government expenditure on education was 68,676m. kyats (6.8% of total spending).

Bibliography

General

Aung San Suu Kyi. *Freedom from Fear and Other Writings.* Harmondsworth, Penguin, 1991.

Aung San Suu Kyi: Letters From Burma. London, Penguin, 1997.

Aung San Suu Kyi: The Voice of Hope. Conversations with Alan Clements. London, Rider & Co, Revised Edn, 2008.

Becka, Jan. *Historical Dictionary of Myanmar.* Metuchen, NJ, Scarecrow Press, 1995.

Berlie, Jean A. *The Burmanization of Myanmar's Muslims.* Bangkok, White Lotus Press, 2008.

Chao Tzang Yawnghwe. *The Shan of Burma: Memoirs of a Shan Exile.* Singapore, Institute of Southeast Asian Studies, 2010.

Ganesan, N., and Hlaing, Kyaw Yin. *Myanmar: State, Society and Ethnicity.* Singapore, Institute of Southeast Asian Studies, 2007.

Gravers, Mikael (Ed.). *Exploring Ethnic Diversity in Burma.* Honolulu, HI, University of Hawaii Press, 2006.

Horsey, Richard. *Ending Forced Labour in Myanmar—Engaging a Pariah Regime.* Abingdon, Routledge, 2011.

James, Helen. *Governance and Civil Society in Myanmar: Education, Health, and Environment.* 2nd Edn, Abingdon, Routledge, 2009.

Mawdsley, James. *The Heart Must Break: The Fight for Democracy and Truth in Burma.* London, Century, 2001.

Seekins, Donald M. *State and Society in Modern Rangoon.* Abingdon, Routledge, 2010.

Skidmore, Monique (Ed.). *Burma at the Turn of the Twenty-First Century.* Honolulu, HI, University of Hawaii Press, 2005.

Karaoke Fascism: Burma and the Politics of Fear. Honolulu, HI, University of Hawaii Press, 2005.

Skidmore, Monique, and Wilson, Trevor (Eds). *Myanmar: The State, Community and the Environment.* Canberra, Asia Pacific Press, 2007.

Thawnghmung, Ardeth Maung. *Behind the Teak Curtain: Authoritarianism, Agricultural Policies, and Political Legitimacy in Rural Burma/Myanmar.* London, Kegan Paul, 2004.

Thwe, Pascal Khoo. *From the Land of Green Ghosts: A Burmese Odyssey.* London, HarperCollins, 2003.

Tucker, Shelby. *Among Insurgents: Walking through Burma.* London, Flamingo, 2001.

History

Allen, Louis. *Burma: The Longest War 1941–45.* London, Dent, 1985.

Aung San Suu Kyi. *Burma and India: Some Aspects of Intellectual Life Under Colonialism.* Shimla, Indian Institute of Advanced Study, Allied Publishers Pvt Ltd, 1990.

Aung San of Burma. Edinburgh, Kiscadale Publications, 1991.

Badgley, John H. (Ed.). *Reconciling Burma/Myanmar: Essays on US Relations with Burma.* Seattle, WA, National Bureau of Asian Research, 2004.

Charney, Michael W. *A History of Modern Burma.* Cambridge, Cambridge University Press, 2009.

Dijk, Wil O. *Seventeenth-century Burma and the Dutch East India Company, 1634–1680.* Copenhagen, Nordic Institute of Asian Studies, 2006.

Fink, Christina. *Living Silence: Burma under Military Rule.* London, Zed Books, 2001.

Fong, Jack. *Revolution as Development: The Karen Self-Determination Struggle Against Ethnocracy (1949–2004).* Boca Raton, FL, Universal Publishers, 2008.

Ghosh, Parimal. *Brave Men of the Hills: Resistance and Rebellion in Burma, 1825–1932.* London, Hurst & Co, 2000.

Marshall, Andrew. *The Trouser People: A Story of Burma in the Shadow of the Empire.* Boulder, CO, Counterpoint Press, 2002.

Maung Maung. *Burmese Nationalist Movements: 1940–1948.* Honolulu, HI, University of Hawaii Press, 1990.

The 1988 Uprising in Burma. New Haven, CT, Yale University Southeast Asia Studies, 1999.

Myoe, Maung Aung. *Building the Tatmadaw: Myanmar Armed Forces Since 1948.* Singapore, Institute of Southeast Asian Studies, 2009.

Naw, Angelene. *Aung San and the Struggle for Burmese Independence.* Chiang Mai, Silkworm Books, 2001.

Perry, Peter John. *Myanmar (Burma) since 1962: The Failure of Development.* Aldershot, Ashgate, 2007.

Phayre, Arthur P. *History of Burma: From the Earliest Time to the End of the First War with British India.* London, Routledge, 2000.

Rogers, Benedict. *A Land Without Evil: Stopping the Genocide of Burma's Karen People.* Crowborough, Monarch Publications, 2004.

Than Shwe: Unmasking Burma's Tyrant. Chiang Mai, Silkworm Books, 2010.

Seekins, Donald M. *The Disorder in Order: The Army-State in Burma since 1962.* Bangkok, White Lotus Press, 2002.

Burma and Japan since 1940: From 'Co-Prosperity' to 'Quiet Dialogue'. Copenhagen, Nordic Institute of Asian Studies, 2007.

Silverstein, Josef. *The Political Legacy of Aung San.* Ithaca, NY, Cornell University Press, 1993.

Steinberg, David I. *Burma: The State of Myanmar.* Washington, DC, Georgetown University Press, 2001.

Than, Mya. *Myanmar in ASEAN.* Singapore, Institute of Southeast Asian Studies, 2004.

Thant, Myint U. *The Making of Modern Burma.* New York, Cambridge University Press, 2001.

The River of Lost Footsteps. New York, Farrar, Straus and Giroux, 2006.

Tin Maung Maung Than. *State Dominance in Myanmar: The Political Economy of Industrialization.* Singapore, Institute of Southeast Asian Studies, 2006.

Topich, William J., and Leitich, Keith, A. *The History of Myanmar.* Westport, CT, Greenwood Press, 2010.

Tucker, Shelby. *Burma: The Curse of Independence.* London, Pluto Press, 2001.

Tun, Sai Aung. *History of the Shan State: From Its Origins to 1962.* Chiang Mai, Silkworm Books, 2008.

Varey, Bertram S. *The Chin Hills.* New Delhi, Gyan Publishing House, 2004.

Wilson, Trevor (Ed.). *Myanmar's Long Road to National Reconciliation.* Singapore, Institute of Southeast Asian Studies, 2006.

Economy and Politics

Ball, Desmond, and Lang, Hazel. *Factionalism and the Ethnic Insurgent Organisations.* Canberra, Strategic and Defence Studies Centre, Australian National University, 2001.

Brown, Ian. *A Colonial Economy in Crisis: Burma's Rice Delta and the World Depression of the 1930s.* New York, RoutledgeCurzon, 2005.

Burma Campaign UK. *Insuring Repression: Exposing How the Insurance Industry Supports Burma's Dictators.* London, The Burma Campaign UK, 2008.

Callahan, Mary P. *Making Enemies: War and State Building in Burma.* Ithaca, NY, Cornell University Press, 2003.

Political Authority in Burma's Ethnic Minority States: Devolution, Occupation, and Coexistence. Singapore, Institute of Southeast Asian Studies, 2007.

Cheesman, Nick, Skidmore, Monique, and Wilson, Trevor (Eds). *Ruling Myanmar: From Cyclone Nargis to National Elections.* Singapore, Institute of Southeast Asian Studies, 2010.

Collignon, Stefan, and Taylor, Robert H. (Eds). *Burma: Political Economy Under Military Rule.* Basingstoke, Palgrave Macmillan, 2001.

Fujita, Koichi, Mieno, Fumiharu, and Okamoto, Ikuku. *The Economic Transition in Myanmar After 1988: Market Economy versus State Control.* Singapore, Singapore University Press, 2009.

Haacke, Jürgen. *Myanmar's Foreign Policy: Domestic Influences and International Implications.* Abingdon, Routledge/International Institute for Strategic Studies, 2006.

James, Helen. *Security and Sustainable Development in Myanmar.* Abingdon, Routledge, 2006.

Khin Maung Kyi, Findlay, Ronald, and Sundrum, R. M. (Eds). *Economic Development of Burma: A Vision and a Strategy. A study by Burmese Economists.* Singapore, Singapore University Press, 2000.

Kyaw Yin Hlaing, Taylor, Robert H., and Tin Maung Maung Than (Eds). *Myanmar: Beyond Politics to Societal Imperatives.* Singapore, Institute of Southeast Asian Studies, 2005.

Lang, Hazel J. *Fear and Sanctuary: Burmese Refugees in Thailand.* Ithaca, NY, Cornell University Press, 2002.

Li Chenyang and Hofmeister, Wilhelm (Eds). *Myanmar: Prospect for Change.* Singapore, Select Publishing, 2010.

Lintner, Bertil. *Aung San Suu Kyi and Burma's Struggle for Democracy.* Chiang Mai, Silkworm Books, 2011.

Mason, Jana M. *No Way Out, No Way In: The Crisis of Internal Displacement in Burma.* Washington, DC, US Committee for Refugees, 2000.

McCarthy, Stephen. *The Political Theory of Tyranny in Singapore and Burma.* Abingdon, Routledge, 2006.

Mya Than and Gates, Carolyn L. (Eds). *ASEAN Enlargement: Impacts and Implications.* Singapore, Institute of Southeast Asian Studies, 2001.

Mya Than and Myat Thein (Eds). *Financial Resources for Development in Myanmar: Lessons from Asia.* Singapore, Institute of Southeast Asian Studies, 1999.

Myat Thein. *Economic Development of Myanmar.* Singapore, Institute of Southeast Asian Studies, 2004.

Okamoto, Ikuko. *Economic Disparity in Rural Myanmar: Transformation Under Market Liberalization.* Singapore, National University of Singapore Press, 2008.

Pedersen, Morten B. *Promoting Human Rights in Burma: A Critique of Western Sanctions Policy.* Lanham, MD, Rowman and Littlefield, 2007.

Pedersen, Morten B., Rudland, Emily, and May, Ronald J. *Burma-Myanmar: Strong Regime, Weak State?* Adelaide, SA, Crawford House Publishing, 2000.

Rieffel, Lex. *Myanmar/Burma: Inside Challenges, Outside Interests.* Washington, DC, Brookings Institution Press, 2010.

Roberts, Christopher. *ASEAN's Myanmar Crisis.* Singapore, Institute of Southeast Asian Studies, 2010.

Roycee, Alden T. *Burma in Turmoil.* Hauppauge, NY, Nova Science Publishers, 2008.

Sakhong, Lian H. *In Search of Chin Identity: A Study in Religion, Politics and Ethnic Identity in Burma.* Copenhagen, NIAS Press, 2002.

Silverstein, Josef. *Burma: Military Rule and the Politics of Stagnation.* Ithaca, NY, Cornell University Press, 1977.

Burmese Politics: The Dilemma of National Unity. New Brunswick, NJ, Rutgers University Press, 1980.

Independent Burma at Forty Years: Six Assessments. Ithaca, NY, Cornell Southeast Asia Program, 1989.

Singh, Langpoklakpam Suraj. *Movement for Democracy in Myanmar.* New Delhi, Akansha, 2006.

Smith, Martin. *Burma: Insurgency and the Politics of Ethnicity.* London, Zed Books, 1999.

State of Strife: The Dynamics of Ethnic Conflict in Burma. Singapore, Institute of Southeast Asian Studies, 2007.

South, Ashley. *Mon Nationalism and Civil War in Burma: The Golden Sheldrake.* London, RoutledgeCurzon, 2002.

Ethnic Politics in Burma: States of Conflict. Abingdon, Routledge, 2008.

Civil Society in Burma: The Development of Democracy amidst Conflict. Singapore, Institute of Southeast Asian Studies, 2008.

Steinberg, David I. *Turmoil in Burma: Contested Legitimacies in Myanmar.* Norwalk, CT, EastBridge, 2006.

Burma/Myanmar: What Everyone Needs to Know. New York, Oxford University Press, 2009.

Stewart, Whitney. *Aung San Suu Kyi: Fearless Voice of Burma.* Minneapolis, MN, Lerner Publications, 1996.

Taylor, Robert H. *The State in Myanmar.* London, Hurst & Co, Revised Edn, 2009.

Taylor, Robert H. (Ed.). *Burma: Political Economy under Military Rule.* London, St Martin's Press, 2000.

Thawnghmung, Ardeth Maung. *The Karen Revolution in Burma: Diverse Voices, Uncertain Ends.* Singapore, Institute of Southeast Asian Studies, 2008.

Tin Maung Maung Than. *State Dominance in Myanmar: The Political Economy of Industrialization.* Singapore, Institute of Southeast Asian Studies, 2006.

Turnell, Sean. *Fiery Dragons: Banks, Moneylenders and Microfinance in Burma.* Copenhagen, NIAS Press, 2008.

NEW ZEALAND

Physical and Social Geography

A. E. MCQUEEN

New Zealand lies 1,600 km south-east of Australia. It consists of two main islands—North Island with an area of 116,031 sq km (44,800 sq miles) and South Island with an area of 153,540 sq km (59,282 sq miles)—plus Stewart Island (or Rakiura) to the south, and a number of smaller islands. North and South Islands are separated by Cook Strait, which is about 30 km wide at the narrowest point. The total area of New Zealand is 270,534 sq km (104,454 sq miles).

CLIMATE

New Zealand is situated in the westerly wind belt that encircles the globe. The main islands lie between 34°S and 47°S, and are therefore within the zone of the eastward moving depressions and anti-cyclones within this belt. The country's location within a vast ocean means that extremes of temperature are modified by air masses passing across a large expanse of ocean. Abundant moisture is available by evaporation from the ocean, and rainfall is considerable and fairly evenly distributed throughout the year. The mean annual rainfall varies from 330 mm east of the Southern Alps to more than 7,500 mm west of the Alps, but the average for the whole country is between 600 mm and 1,500 mm. A chain of mountains extending from south-west to north-east through most of the country provides a barrier to the movement of air masses, which results in a climatic contrast between east and west. No part of New Zealand is more than 130 km from the sea.

The annual range of mean monthly temperatures in western districts of both islands is about 8°C, while elsewhere it is 9°C–11°C, except in inland areas of South Island where it may be as high as 14°C. The mean temperatures for the year vary from 15°C in the far north to 12°C about Cook Strait and 9°C in the south. Snow is rare below 600 m in North Island, and usually falls for only a few days a year at lower altitudes in South Island. Rainfall and temperature combine to give a climate in which it is possible to graze livestock for all the year at lower altitudes in all parts of the country, and at higher altitudes, even in South Island, for a considerable part of each year. Pasture growth varies according to temperature and season, but ranges from almost continual growth in North Auckland to between eight and 10 months in South Island.

PHYSICAL FEATURES

The Southern Alps (or Ka Tiriti o te Moana), a massive chain including 16 peaks over 3,100 m, extend for almost the entire length of South Island, and the rain shadow effect produces the dry summers of the east coast plains, which are major grain-growing areas. The wide expanses of elevated open country have led to the development of large-scale pastoral holdings. South Island high country produces almost all New Zealand's fine wools, particularly from the Merino sheep. New Zealand rivers are of vital importance for hydroelectric power production. Many of the larger lakes of both islands are also important in power production.

Earthquakes are a particular risk in some areas. In September 2010 a strong earthquake struck South Island, its epicentre being 40 km west of the city of Christchurch. Reported to be the most severe for nearly 80 years, the earthquake caused substantial damage to buildings and infrastructure in the Canterbury area. This was followed in February 2011 by an even more serious earthquake 10 km south-east of Christchurch, which killed at least 65 people and caused further major damage.

NATURAL RESOURCES

In general geological terms, New Zealand is part of the unstable circum-Pacific mobile belt, where volcanoes are active and where the earth's crust has been moving at a geologically rapid rate. Such earth movements, coupled with rapid erosion, have formed the sedimentary rocks that make up about three-quarters of the country. In such a geologically mobile country the constant exposure of new rock has resulted in generally fertile soils.

Various minerals, including gold, have been found, albeit in relatively small deposits. Non-metallic minerals, such as silica, coal, clay, limestone and dolomite became both economically and industrially more important than metallic ores. There are significant ironsand deposits on the west coast of North Island. Exploration and prospecting activities carried out by both local and overseas companies revealed other significant natural resources. A notable discovery in 1970 was a large natural gas field, off the South Taranaki coast. The construction of pipelines to bring the gas to major centres, and of plants to convert this gas into synthetic petrol and methanol, had been completed by 1985. New Zealand also possesses reserves of petroleum, and there are several onshore producing wells. The Tui Area Development, in the Taranaki Basin, is an important project, and the first commercial petroleum began to flow from this offshore field in 2007.

When the first European settlers arrived New Zealand they found two-thirds of the land's surface covered by forest, but by 1991 only 28.5% of the area remained forested, most of it kept as reserve or as national parks. The rest had been felled, much of it with little regard for land conservation principles. By 2010, however, the area under forest was estimated to have increased to 31.4%. Plantations of introduced species provide building timber and raw material for well-established pulp and paper and other forest product industries. These activities are based mainly on the extensive exotic forests of the Bay of Plenty-Taupo region, near the centre of North Island.

POPULATION

The majority of the population is of European origin. At the census of March 1996, 523,374 persons (14.5% of the usually resident population) were enumerated as indigenous Maori; New Zealand's total population stood at 3,681,546. At the census of March 2006 the total population was enumerated at 4,027,947, of whom 565,329 persons (14.6%) were classified as Maori. At mid-2011 the population was estimated at 4,405,300. In terms of international comparison, the population is small, the density (16.3 per sq km in mid-2011) and growth rates are low, and the degree of urbanization is high. Some 85% of the population reside in cities, boroughs or townships with populations greater than 1,000.

For many years after 1945 a high rate of population growth was recorded. This trend was due not only to the high birth rate but also to immigration, which included significant numbers of arrivals from Europe. The birth rate was estimated at 14.6 per 1,000 in 2010. This contrasted with an estimated death rate of 6.5 per 1,000 in the same year, among the lowest levels in the world.

History

JEANINE GRAHAM

THE COLONIAL ERA

New Zealand's earliest migrant population was well established in coastal settlements by the 12th century. Oral tradition tells of voyages from Hawaiiki, the islands of eastern Polynesia, and of subsequent migrations within New Zealand waters. The Maori culture, which was to be of such interest to early European explorers and observers, developed in isolation as one variant of Polynesian culture.

Although the Dutch navigator, Abel Tasman, sailed in 1642–43 along part of the western coastline of the country that he called Staten Landt, it was the three scientific expeditions led by the British naval captain, James Cook (in 1769, 1773 and 1774), that brought New Zealand into prominence. During his first voyage Cook spent more than six months circumnavigating the islands and produced a chart remarkable for its detail and accuracy. Scientists and artists with the expedition recorded their impressions of the nature and habits of the indigenous Maori and New Zealand's unique flora and fauna. Voyages by other 18th- and early 19th-century European explorers were peripheral. The traders, missionaries, scientists and settlers who followed in Cook's wake built on the secure foundations of his achievements.

Sealers, whalers and traders sought to exploit New Zealand's natural resources for economic advantage. Christian missionaries aimed to evangelize the *tangata whenua* (people of the land). The consequences of cultural encounter for the Maori people were varied. Against such diseases as influenza, measles, tuberculosis and whooping cough, the indigenous inhabitants had no immunity. Death rates remained high throughout the 19th century. Tribal receptiveness to new technology, literacy and Christianity was selective. Although the lifestyle of the Maori people was disrupted, it was not, especially in the case of those tribes in locations away from the coast, necessarily undermined. The early Europeans were, in fact, heavily dependent upon Maori co-operation and goodwill, a pattern that persisted during the first two decades after New Zealand became part of the British Empire in 1840.

The New Zealand Co and related organizations founded the settlements of Wellington, Nelson, Wanganui, New Plymouth, Christchurch and Dunedin. Until 1864 the colonial administration was based in Auckland, the character of this town being influenced by its strong links with the Australian colonies. A steady stream of assisted or independent immigrants flowed into New Zealand until the 1880s, with a dramatic influx during the gold rushes of the 1860s and large numbers of labouring-class settlers arriving during the era of public works expansion in the 1870s. A minority in their own land by the late 1850s, the Maori population had declined to 42,000 by 1896, while Pakeha (non-Maori) settlers numbered some 700,000.

The insatiable demand of European settlers for land was a major cause of conflict between Maori and Europeans during the 19th century. Settlers south of the Cook Strait region scarcely felt the impact of racial tension, for relatively few Maori lived there, but many North Island communities were affected. Sporadic and localized fighting in the 1840s was followed by a major outbreak in central and west coast areas of the North Island in the early 1860s. The Treaty of Waitangi, signed on 6 February 1840 by the Lieutenant-Governor-elect, Capt. William Hobson, and subsequently by many of the major Maori chiefs, had acknowledged Maori ownership of land, and accorded *tangata whenua* the status of British subjects. However, post-conflict confiscation of much tribal land and the introduction of a system of individualized land tenure, to replace the traditional communal form of ownership, caused major cultural upheaval during the last decades of the 19th century and effectively undermined the socio-economic base of those tribes most affected. Only since the 1970s have New Zealanders of European origin begun to appreciate that Maori understanding of the Treaty's guarantees had largely been ignored by successive governments for more than a century.

British legislation provided a constitution for New Zealand in 1852. A bicameral General Assembly and six Provincial Councils were functioning by 1854, but responsible government was not granted until 1856. Improved internal and coastal communications, returns from wool and gold exports and the need to co-ordinate loan applications undermined the rationale for separate provincial development. The provincial governments were abolished in 1876 and were replaced by a plethora of local bodies that dominated local government for more than a century and, as with central government, took little cognizance of bicultural values. The granting of the vote to Maori men in 1867 and the establishment of four Maori seats in the House of Representatives in the same year were not sufficient measures to ensure that Maori interests were articulated at parliamentary level and that their needs were satisfied. Inter-tribal initiatives to establish complementary political forums received no parliamentary support.

The economic crises of the 1880s caused many recent immigrants to leave New Zealand for the Australian colonies. Social distress and revelations of 'sweated labour' in the clothing industry fostered a sense of radicalism and protest against the apparently ineffectual, conservative 'continuous ministry'. Politicians espousing a liberal ideology came to form a coherent grouping and took office under the leadership of John Ballance in January 1891. During the ensuing 18 months a hostile, nominated Legislative Council continually blocked reforms, a situation resolved only when the Governor was instructed by the British Secretary of State for the Colonies not to reject the advice of his responsible ministers in making new appointments. Ballance died in early 1893 and was succeeded as Premier by Richard John Seddon. For the next 13 years 'King Dick' Seddon dominated New Zealand life and politics. Assisted initially by some very able colleagues, Seddon carried through legislation that provided for industrial conciliation and arbitration, better factory conditions, accident compensation, shorter working hours and old-age pensions. Maori leaders found Seddon sympathetic to their people's plight, but the initiatives for urgent health reform came from a small group of Maori university graduates. However, liberal policy towards Maori needs remained ambivalent: increased pressure for the further alienation of Maori land in the North Island resulted from measures that were implemented during the 1890s to foster the expansion of small farming, especially dairying. The technology of refrigeration had provided the solution to New Zealand's export difficulties. Such was the new sense of accomplishment and colonial pride that few in New Zealand were disposed to entertain seriously the idea of federation with the Australian colonies. New Zealanders entered the 20th century firmly committed to the ideal of the British Empire, a loyalty that cost the country and its people dearly during the First World War (1914–18).

THE INTER-WAR PERIOD

After 1918, under conditions of general prosperity and full employment, New Zealand resumed a selective, assisted migration policy, which had enlarged the population by nearly 70,000 by 1928, when the intake temporarily ceased. As trade conditions worsened, the Government increasingly intervened to control the nation's economy. As the depression approached, efforts to borrow proved fruitless, and a coalition Government of United and Reform parties took office in September 1931. Orthodox financial solutions were tried. Railway construction was halted and expenditure on defence reduced. Emergency taxes were imposed. Incomes fell by an average of 20%. The depression worsened, and with it the social distress suffered by the growing number of unemployed. An estimated 80,000 people—12% of the labour force—were out of work. Employment schemes, including state forestry planting, provided relatively little relief. Labour unrest was rife throughout the country and short-lived bouts of rioting occurred in the major cities. A noted Maori politician, Sir Apirana Ngata, nevertheless succeeded in promoting a cultural revival among the Maori and addressing issues of Maori poverty through consolidation of fragmented land titles and the establishment of Maori-owned corporations to develop unproductive land.

The election of 1935 resulted in a radical political change. Small farmers combined with urban workers to return the Labour Party to power with a substantial majority. Under its leader, Michael Joseph Savage, the prices of essential commodities were fixed. Dairy farmers were given a guaranteed price for their butter and cheese, which were marketed by the Government both at home and abroad. Unemployment was addressed through the introduction of large-scale public works such as road and railway construction. The state offered the right to work at a fixed basic wage and made trade union membership compulsory. Salary and wage cuts were restored, and a 40-hour week was introduced to increase the demand for labour. An ambitious housing programme was launched. These various undertakings were financed by means of increased taxation and public loans. A political alliance forged in 1936 between Savage and a Maori spiritual leader, Tahupotiki Wiremu Ratana, resulted in Ratana candidates being elected to all four Maori seats; the Ratana movement continued to support Labour until 1979.

In 1938 the Labour Government was re-elected with an increased majority, and immediately began to build upon the social legislation of the 1890s. A Social Security Act provided for free general practitioner services, medicines, hospital treatment and maternity benefits, and for family allowances and increased old-age pensions. To finance such comprehensive insurance a special tax was levied on all incomes and supplemented by grants from ordinary revenue. Such measures were possible because these were years of prosperity and prices for exports were high. By 1939, however, heavy withdrawals to meet overseas commitments, together with the flight of private capital, forced the Government to restrict imports and control the export of capital.

The British declaration of war on Germany in 1939 was felt to be as binding on New Zealand as that of 1914, even though the two countries had differed publicly in their attitude to League of Nations' policy initiatives during the 1930s. A special war cabinet was formed on the basis of a coalition of all parties. The Prime Minister, Peter Fraser, concentrated economic policy around the objective of stabilization, and in this regard he was largely successful. Conscription was introduced for overseas service, essential commodities were rationed and the country's resources were mobilized for the war effort. However, the rationalizing of manpower in 1942 provoked a crisis in the coal-mining industry and led the Government to assume control of the mines. Incensed at what it regarded as the Government's capitulation to the coal miners, the National Party withdrew from the war cabinet. When Japan entered the Second World War (1939–45), New Zealand responded to meet the threat of invasion, but, even after the attack on Pearl Harbor (the US naval base in Hawaii, now a state of the USA) in December 1941, it did not recall its troops from the Middle East. The 40-hour week was suspended, and in 1943 thousands of men were released from the armed forces in order to increase food and factory production and thereby to assist the USA in its Pacific campaign. Employment opportunities, together with the difficulty of providing for a growing population on fragmented landholdings, prompted significant numbers of rural Maori to leave their subsistence lifestyle and migrate to the cities.

THE POST-WAR YEARS

The Labour Party won the election held in November 1946, but by a narrow majority; shortages, rationing, high food prices, poor housing and a reaction against wartime bureaucratic control all undermined the Labour vote. The subsequent introduction of compulsory military training in peacetime further alienated Labour supporters. The National Party, led by Sidney (later Sir Sidney) Holland, capitalized on public dissatisfaction with government regulation, and won a decisive victory at the 1949 election.

With the full approval of the Labour opposition, the Government abolished the Legislative Council, which, as a parliamentary chamber of review, had gradually declined in importance. Subsidies on certain commodities were withdrawn, but attempts to freeze prices failed to prevent inflation. In a climate marked by Cold War fears of communism, the Government severely restricted civil liberties during a prolonged strike by dock workers, and eventually dispatched troops to end the unrest. Among the public there were strong feelings concerning the Prime Minister's handling of the crisis, but in the election called at short notice in 1951 the Government secured an increased parliamentary majority. Growing dissatisfaction with the performance of both parties was reflected three years later in the 1954 election, when the newly formed Social Credit Political League won 11% of the votes cast. While support for its economic policies was always problematic, as a third party Social Credit continued to benefit from tactical and protest voting until the mid-1980s. Electoral legislation in 1956 entrenched the franchise and electoral system and made enrolment compulsory for Maori, as it had been for Europeans since 1924.

Two months before the 1957 election, Holland retired from office because of ill health. Under his successor, Keith (later Sir Keith) Holyoake, the National Party narrowly lost the election. Labour's marginal victory was attributed to its espousal of a new Pay As You Earn (PAYE) system of collecting income tax. Almost immediately the Labour Government, with 75-year-old Walter Nash as Prime Minister, was embarrassed by pressing economic problems. Declining prices for meat and dairy produce led to an adverse balance of trade and to an alarming depletion of the country's overseas reserves. The Government reimposed import licensing and exchange control and thereby raised over £30m. in the United Kingdom and Australia and another £20m. internally. These measures arrested the decline, but the Government's fate was sealed by the 'black budget' of 1958, which, while introducing 3% loans for housing, raising pensions, countering a balance of payments problem and encouraging industry, also increased taxes on beer, spirits, cigarettes and petrol. At the election in 1960 the National Party, led by Holyoake, was returned to power. Among the more important changes that followed was the appointment in 1962 of a Parliamentary Commissioner (ombudsman) to inquire into public complaints arising from governmental administrative decisions. The National Party retained office in an election in 1963. Labour's new leader, Arnold Nordmeyer, had tried unsuccessfully to revive the Labour Party's popularity by denying the social need for class struggle. The formation in 1966 of the small Socialist Unity Party, many of the 60 adherents of which were former members of the New Zealand Communist Party, indicated the persistence of more radical views on the subject of class conflict. Meanwhile, in 1965 Nordmeyer was ousted as Labour's leader by a former party President, Norman Kirk.

Although economic policy was the issue most frequently debated in the 1966 election, attitudes to New Zealand's support of the US forces in Viet Nam transcended party lines and secured a further victory for the National Party. Holyoake's consensus style of politics continued to have electoral appeal, but he retired in February 1972, to be succeeded by John (later Sir John) Marshall, a leader whose urbane demeanour was challenged by ambitious and aggressive younger politicians within the party. Labour gained a decisive victory in November 1972 in an election that had been contested by National, Labour, Social Credit and a newly formed Values Party, one of the world's first 'Green' parties, which, by emphasizing the importance of environmental issues, appealed to many younger voters. As Labour's leader, Kirk was vigorous and forthright, especially in the field of foreign policy, but his leadership was cut short by his untimely death in August 1974. His successor, Wallace (later Sir Wallace) Rowling, opposed by a new leader of the National Party, Robert (later Sir Robert) Muldoon, continued Kirk's policy, but conducted it less forcefully.

In the post-war world, New Zealand's first major step in pursuing a policy independent of British interests was made in 1944 with the signing of the Canberra Pact, a mutual security agreement with Australia. In 1947 New Zealand finally adopted the Statute of Westminster, which gave it complete autonomy and freedom of action in international affairs. As a strong supporter of the UN, in 1950 the Government sent troops to join the UN Command in the Republic of Korea (South Korea). Despite official misgivings about the exclusion of the United Kingdom, in 1952 it signed the Australia, New Zealand and the USA (ANZUS) defence treaty, and two years later New Zealand became a member of the South-East Asia Treaty Organization. New Zealand sent a military unit to Malaya (now Malaysia) in 1955, and combined with Australia in an ANZAC (Australia and New Zealand Army Corps) unit in Viet Nam. Along with those of Australia, its troops in Singapore and Malaysia combined with the remaining British forces to safeguard the political status quo of the region. In 1971 New Zealand joined Australia, Malaysia, Singapore and the United Kingdom in establishing new arrangements for the defence of Malaysia and Singapore, and maintained a presence there until the last troops were withdrawn in 1990.

New Zealand played an increasingly important role in the Pacific after joining the South Pacific Commission (now Pacific Community) as a founder member in 1947. It administered the UN Trust Territory of Western Samoa until 1962, when those islands became independent, and in 1965 it assisted the Cook Islands to achieve self-government in free association with New Zealand. Niue became an associated territory in 1974, while the tiny islands of Tokelau are now New Zealand's only remaining Pacific dependency. When Fiji became independent from the United Kingdom in 1970, New Zealand helped to establish the University of the South Pacific in Suva, and in 1971 it joined the South Pacific Forum (now Pacific Islands Forum), which was founded to promote economic and political co-operation in the region.

SUBSEQUENT DEVELOPMENTS

Political Affairs

Taking advantage of public fears of national economic disaster consequent on the inflationary effects of Labour's policy of heavy overseas borrowing, the opposition leader, Robert Muldoon, campaigned on the promise of a more attractive and egalitarian pensions system than that offered by the Government. At the November 1975 general election a revitalized National Party won 55 of the 87 seats in the House of Representatives. Labour lost 23 seats, including those of five cabinet members.

The National Party retained office in the 1978 election, although its share of the total vote fell, largely owing to the abrasive style of leadership practised by Muldoon as Prime Minister. The Labour Party received more votes than the National Party but won fewer seats, while the Social Credit Political League secured only one seat. The Values Party, with no firm base of appeal, fared poorly (in 1989 it changed its name to the Green Party of Aotearoa). To stabilize the parliamentary representation of the South Island (as its share of the country's population in proportion to that of the North Island had been—and is still—declining), its number of seats was fixed at 25. In 1981 public opinion was highly polarized by the Government's failure to discourage a South African Springbok rugby tour of New Zealand. The National Party narrowly retained office in the election of November. The Social Credit Party (as the Social Credit Political League was restyled in 1982) lost political credibility, but in August 1983 a new third party was founded: the right-wing New Zealand Party, led by a wealthy property owner, Robert (later Sir Robert) Jones. Meanwhile, in February 1983 the Labour Party had replaced its much respected but publicly unimpressive leader, Wallace Rowling, with David Lange, a lawyer with a more vigorous style and greater charisma, who became Prime Minister in July 1984, when Labour capitalized on Muldoon's unpopularity and poor tactics in calling an early general election. The New Zealand Party gained no representation but attracted 12% of the total number of votes cast. The high turn-out of eligible voters (86%) was an indication of public dissatisfaction with the Muldoon administration.

In November 1984 Muldoon was replaced as leader of the National Party by his deputy, former Attorney-General James McLay. The transfer was not effected smoothly, as Muldoon made no pretence of co-operation and maintained a high political profile, undermining the leadership of his successor. In March 1986 McLay was ousted by his deputy leader, James (Jim) Bolger, a farmer from King Country.

Initially, the Labour Government benefited considerably from the opposition's disarray, for the programme of economic restructuring along free market lines was alienating many of Labour's traditional urban-based supporters. The social cost of New Zealand's high level of inflation and worsening balance of payments difficulties, and of Labour's policy initiatives, bore most heavily upon low-income earners and welfare beneficiaries, in which group Maori and Pacific Islanders were heavily represented.

At the general election of August 1987, popular support for the Government's anti-nuclear defence policy, a stance then opposed (but later endorsed) by the National Party, enabled Lange's administration to become the first Labour Government since 1946 to be elected for two successive terms of office. Labour's political euphoria was short-lived, however. Policy disagreements emerged between Minister of Finance Roger Douglas, the architect of Labour's deregulation and free market economics, and David Lange, who wished to prevent the extension of market principles into social policy. Douglas lost his portfolio, but in August 1989 Lange resigned as Prime Minister, his position having been consistently undermined by the continued internal political intriguing of Douglas, and by the formation of the NewLabour Party (led by a former President of the New Zealand Labour Party, Jim Anderton), which aimed to appeal to erstwhile Labour supporters who had become disillusioned with the Government's continued advocacy of privatization. The new Deputy Prime Minister, Helen Clark, a former lecturer in political science, became the first woman to hold such office in New Zealand's parliamentary history. Geoffrey (later Sir Geoffrey) Palmer, previously a professor of law, came to the Prime Minister's position with a reputation for cautious and careful administration and did not find it easy to project a more personable image. Shortly before the next election Palmer resigned from his position. Michael Moore, the Minister of External Relations and Trade (who had contested the August 1989 leadership election), replaced him as Prime Minister.

The National Party secured 67 of the 97 seats in the House of Representatives in the October 1990 election, the Labour Party won 29 seats, and the NewLabour Party one seat. Non-voting increased again, and the incoming National Government actually received fewer votes than had Labour in 1987. Maori voters still had the choice of registering on either the general or the Maori electoral roll, but the Mana Motuhake party, founded in November 1979 by the former member for Northern Maori, Matiu Rata, did not have the resources to contest more than a few seats.

Jim Bolger thus became the country's fourth Prime Minister within 15 months, and the new National Party Government immediately signalled a series of retrenchment measures, designed essentially to reduce the welfare burden, which was to consume 60% of total government spending in the 1991/92 financial year. Under the direction of the Minister of Finance, Ruth Richardson, 'user pays' initiatives in health and education undermined long-cherished principles of a welfare state, while a crisis over pensions funding, with which the Minister of Social Welfare, Jenny Shipley, had to contend, was essentially a result of political decisions made by the National Party at the time of the 1975 general election. The enactment of the Employment Contracts Act in 1991 promoted the rapid deregulation of the labour market and further undermined a trade union movement already weakened by high unemployment. More than 10% of the labour force was out of work in 1992, with the Maori unemployment rate significantly greater than that of Pakeha. By 1992 there was a new political alignment, the Alliance, made up of a coalition of minor parties, including the Greens, NewLabour, Mana Motuhake and the New Zealand Democratic Party (descended from the former Social Credit Party). It also included another new party, the Liberal Party, formed by two dissident ex-National Party members of Parliament (MPs). The maverick political behaviour of the former National and subsequently independent member for Tauranga, Winston Peters, resulted in his expulsion from the National Party; he subsequently formed New Zealand First, a political grouping to which a number of prominent Alliance members defected once it became apparent that Peters would not support the coalition.

Such political manoeuvrings were presented as an argument against electoral reform, for which strong support had been expressed by voters during a referendum in September 1992; but at a second, binding referendum, held in conjunction with the general election of November 1993, the electorate voted in favour of the introduction of a mixed-member proportional representation (MMP) system. The close election results (National 50 seats, Labour 45, Alliance two, New Zealand First two) led to some weeks of political uncertainty, but Bolger continued to govern with his marginal majority because the Alliance rejected Labour proposals that it form a coalition to bring down the Government. The by-election held in August 1994 in the Canterbury constituency of Selwyn, following the unexpected resignation from politics of the former Minister of Finance, Ruth Richardson, confirmed National's position. Labour's poor third-place rating in the polls reflected public reaction to the internecine wrangling that had dominated party affairs after Helen Clark replaced Michael Moore as Labour's leader following the November 1993 election.

As a result of opposition disunity, National was able to continue to govern effectively; no important policy issue encountered a unified challenge, not even that of the ongoing sale of state assets. The growing appeal (in particular among Maori and the elderly) of New Zealand First, the leadership of which was openly critical of overseas investment, Asian immigration and government policies affecting the elderly, continued to erode support for both National and Labour. The increasing dogmatism of both individuals and political parties in the months preceding the 1996 election caused many New Zealanders, desirous of more responsive government, to view the forthcoming change to MMP with considerable scepticism.

At elections for the (further enlarged) House of Representatives in October 1996, the National Party won 44 of the 120 parliamentary seats, the Labour Party 37, New Zealand First 17 and the Alliance 13. An increased number of Maori and women were returned as MPs: 15 and 36, respectively. As no party had secured an outright majority, prolonged negotiations ensued, with both Labour and National endeavouring to establish an alliance with New Zealand First. Eventually, in December, a coalition Government headed by Jim Bolger was formed comprising National and New Zealand First (which together represented 47% of the votes cast). Winston Peters, as well as being appointed Deputy Prime Minister, was assigned the post of Treasurer, giving him substantial control over economic policy. However, Bill Birch, a National MP, remained Minister of Finance.

Older voters, many of whom had supported New Zealand First in protest against National's health and pensions policies, were highly critical of the new coalition, which for National was essentially an arrangement of political convenience. The political inexperience of many New Zealand First MPs and factionalism within that party contributed to its steady decrease in popularity. The leadership change effected by Jenny Shipley and her supporters during Jim Bolger's absence overseas in November 1997 was an indication of National's growing concern that its own standing was being undermined by the reputation and performance of its coalition partner. Differences of economic and social policy, including the continuing privatization of state assets, culminated in Shipley's dismissal of Winston Peters as Deputy Prime Minister and Treasurer in August 1998. The engagement of both parties in an agreed dispute resolution process was a formality. The coalition Government was dissolved four days later. Shipley subsequently led a minority Government that was dependent for its survival upon dissident ex-New Zealand First MPs, independents and the right-wing ACT New Zealand, a party founded by Sir Roger Douglas and led by a former Labour cabinet minister, Richard Prebble. During 1999 Shipley's political reputation was not enhanced by her Government's handling of various controversies concerning substantial severance payments to senior officers within the departments of tourism, the fire service, and work and income support services: the appropriateness of trying to imbue the public service with a corporate ethos continued to be widely debated. In August the withdrawal of the IBM Corporation from further software development of the much-vaunted new police computer system, already $NZ30m. beyond its original $NZ100m. budget and remaining incomplete after five years of effort, was a further political embarrassment for a Government that had pledged a strong policy on law enforcement but appeared to have left its 'front-line' police officers inadequately resourced to cope with the growing rates of drugs- and gang-related crime.

At the election conducted in November 1999, the opposition Labour Party won 38.7% of the votes cast and was allocated 49 of the 120 seats in the House of Representatives, while the National Party, which had won 30.5% of the votes, received 39 seats. The Alliance was allocated 10 seats and ACT New Zealand nine seats. Under the recently introduced system of proportional representation, the Green Party's victory in one constituency automatically entitled it to a further six seats in the legislature. New Zealand First's representation declined to five; the party's leader, Winston Peters, only narrowly retained his seat. United New Zealand took the one remaining seat. Having previously discounted any co-operation with the Green Party, the Labour Party was thus obliged to seek its support, as well as that of the Alliance. The leader of the Labour Party, Helen Clark, therefore became the first female politician to win a New Zealand general election. On 4 April 2001 Dame Silvia Cartwright took office as Governor-General, leading to an unprecedented situation: five important public roles in the country—that of Prime Minister, Leader of the Opposition, Attorney-General, Chief Justice and Governor-General—were all occupied by women, while the influential Kingitanga movement continued under the leadership of Te Arikinui (Dame Te Atairangikaahu, the Maori Queen). In October, however, Bill English replaced Shipley as leader of the National Party.

Clark's minority Government, which incorporated several members of the Alliance, including Jim Anderton as Minister for Regional Development, took office in December 1999. The administration initially functioned relatively harmoniously under the Prime Minister's strong control, although progress on initiatives to address the disparities between Maori and non-Maori communities, particularly in the socio-economic indicators of health, housing, income, education, criminality and domestic violence, was slow. In March 2001 the Government announced *ex gratia* payments of $NZ30,000 per person to survivors of military and civilian Japanese prison camps in the Second World War, or to surviving spouses. In conservation and environmental issues the political influence of the Green Party became apparent, notably in debates over research involving genetic modification.

The disintegration of the Alliance and the clear differences between Labour and the Greens over the continuation of a moratorium banning the commercial release of genetically modified organisms (which expired in October 2003) contributed to Helen Clark's decision to call an early general election, a political strategy used only twice previously in the post-war era, in 1951 and 1984. The Government hoped to take advantage of its popularity and secure sufficient electoral support to function without the need for coalition partners. The growing volatility of the New Zealand electorate was apparent in the outcome: only 77% of registered voters participated on election day in July 2002. Labour polled 41% of the party votes and secured 52 of the 120 seats in the House of Representatives, three more than in 1999, but not sufficient for an outright majority. The Greens secured 7% of the votes cast (nine seats) but the Alliance failed to win any parliamentary representation. Jim Anderton's Progressive Coalition party, a personal grouping formed after the disintegration of the Alliance, won two seats, despite securing only 1.7% of the party votes. The centre-right vote fragmented. New Zealand First received 10% of the votes cast (13 seats), a significant recovery in its political fortunes following adverse reaction to its contribution to the collapse of the 1996–98 coalition Government. ACT New Zealand, the most rightward leaning of the campaigning parties, won 7% (nine seats), and subsequently underwent a peaceful change of leadership in April 2004, when Richard Prebble resigned and was replaced by Rodney Hide. Centre-right support shifted to the centrist alliance of United Future New Zealand, which secured 7% of the votes cast (eight seats). The final outcome was disastrous for the National Party, which lost 12 of its sitting MPs and recorded the worst result of its 66-

year history as a major force in New Zealand politics, winning just 21% of the party vote and only 27 seats.

Subsequent negotiations enabled Clark in August 2002 to announce that her minority coalition Government, comprising Labour and the Progressive Coalition, had enlisted United Future New Zealand's support on matters of confidence and supply. Formed in 1995 through an alliance of United New Zealand with Future New Zealand, a small Christian-based party, United Future New Zealand, led by Peter Dunne, appealed to many middle-class voters because of its emphasis on 'family values'. By remaining outside the Government, Dunne hoped to avoid the fate of the junior coalition partners (New Zealand First and the Alliance, respectively) in the previous two Governments elected under the system of proportional representation. In meeting the expectations of its centre-left supporters, Labour needed to maintain good working relationships with the Greens, the co-leader of which, Jeanette Fitzsimons, lost her electorate seat but was returned to Parliament as a party-list member. After the general election, Helen Clark's firm and effective leadership contributed significantly to Labour's continued popularity in opinion polls. The National Party struggled to re-establish itself as a viable opposition party, while the Alliance virtually disintegrated as a political force. The Greens, however, continued to exert pressure on the Government regarding environmental policies.

In October 2003 Don Brash, a former Governor of the Reserve Bank of New Zealand who had stood successfully as a candidate in the 2002 election, broke with normal National Party convention and publicly announced his challenge to the leadership of Bill English. Despite considerable criticism of both the strategy and his alleged political naivety, Brash won the caucus vote and proceeded to transform National's political fortunes, as indicated by a dramatic rise in the public opinion polls (at considerable cost to ACT New Zealand, which continued to lose many of its conservative supporters to National). In a highly controversial speech addressed, as has become customary for National Party leaders, to the Orewa Rotary Club in January 2004, Brash strongly criticized the fundamental direction of government policy in dealing with issues related to the Treaty of Waitangi, and thereby broke the political consensus that had evolved over past decades. The resultant popular debate, much of it ill informed, revealed deep disquiet over the Labour Government's affirmative action policies, even though many of these initiatives, in areas of health, education and employment especially, had been meeting with considerable success.

The Labour Government's highly controversial legislation, which, in practice, proposed Crown ownership of the foreshore and seabed on behalf of all current and future New Zealanders, while giving recognition and protection to customary rights that Maori currently have under common law, generated both protest and support across society. It seriously undermined Labour's traditional support (since the 1930s) among Maori voters. Thousands of Maori and Pakeha joined in a foreshore and seabed *hikoi* (protest walk), which progressed through the country in late April 2004 and reached Parliament on 5 May, one day before the proposed legislation survived its first reading in the House of Representatives and was sent to a select committee for public submissions. The Associate Minister of Maori Affairs, Tariana Turia, was dismissed because of her decision to vote against the measure; she also resigned from the Labour Party and forced a by-election in which she was returned, in July, as co-leader of the newly formed Maori Party, which was to field candidates against Labour in all seven of the Maori seats in the general election scheduled for September 2005. National contested none of these seats. With the highly respected urban Maori leader and social reformer Dr Pita Sharples as the other co-leader of the party, and with a goal of promoting Maori political unity, the Maori vote in 2005 was expected to be a significant but unpredictable factor affecting the political fortunes of both major parties, especially as National's sole Maori female MP, Georgina Te Heuheu, had been dismissed from her position as party spokesperson for Maori affairs and Treaty of Waitangi issues in February 2004 for criticizing the divisive nature of Brash's Orewa speech.

The emergence in 2003 of a second predominantly Maori and Pacific Islander (Pasifika) political party, Destiny New Zealand, which was closely connected with the new evangelical and socially conservative Destiny Church, was expected to encourage more Pacific Islanders to register a vote against Labour in the forthcoming election. Despite the Clark Government's clear record of achievement in delivering health and housing services to low-income earners, and the success of the 'Pacific Wave' employment project in addressing high levels of Pasifika unemployment in South Auckland, Labour's legalization of prostitution and its promotion of a Civil Union Bill (see below), providing same-sex couples with the same legal protection as married heterosexual couples, had offended communities and individuals who viewed these measures as a challenge to their family and religious values. With the gap between the two major parties narrowing in the opinion polls, particularly after the 2005 budget failed to deliver any immediate reduction in personal income tax levels, the 2005 election seemed again likely to result in a coalition government.

However, the results of the election held on 17 September 2005 confounded most commentators, whose predictions had varied widely. Labour received 41.1% of the popular vote and National 39.1%, giving the two major parties 50 and 48 seats, respectively, in the 121-seat Parliament. New Zealand First polled 5.7% of the vote (giving it seven seats); the Greens 5.3% (six seats); United Future 2.7% (three seats); ACT New Zealand 1.5% (two seats); and Jim Anderton's Progressive Party 1.2% (one seat). The Maori Party obtained 2.1% of the popular vote and wrested four of the Maori seats from Labour incumbents. Many Maori voters appeared to have voted strategically by giving their party vote to Labour, not least because of National's election pledge to abolish the seven Maori seats. Although both Clark and Brash engaged in exploratory discussions with the minority parties, it was widely acknowledged that Labour had the greater likelihood of forming a coalition government of parties committed to a vision of social cohesion, inclusiveness and continuing acknowledgement of past injustice and present aspirations for Maori. The leaders of New Zealand First and of United Future, Winston Peters and Peter Dunne, respectively, confirmed during the campaign that, on matters of confidence and supply, each would support the party that received the most votes. With the Labour Party embarking upon an unprecedented third successive term in office, Clark confirmed the appointment of a coalition Government in which two portfolio holders, Winston Peters as Minister of Foreign Affairs and for Racing and Peter Dunne as Minister of Revenue, remained outside the Cabinet. There was no formal representation of the Maori Party within the coalition. Nor were the Greens included; more devastating for the party was the sudden death in November 2005 of their widely respected co-leader, Rod Donald, a passionate environmentalist.

National's electoral recovery, from winning only 27 seats in 2002, was generally attributed to a skilful campaign strategy, a focus on proposed tax reductions and its leader Don Brash's continuing criticism of Labour's alleged 'special treatment' for minorities, Maori especially. How best to deal with the burgeoning debt of student loans, which had reached $NZ8,000m. by September 2005, was another significant campaign issue. Analysis of voting patterns reflected a provincial/metropolitan division, with voters in rural areas and small towns favouring National. Labour's closure of many small country schools and its urban-orientated priorities of building better roads, public transport and power supply infrastructure for the main urban centres, lost the Government votes during the election. National's appeal to 'mainstream' New Zealanders generated much public debate over who was or was not 'mainstream'; campaign rhetoric over a Treaty 'grievance industry' exposed clear differences of viewpoint between those who supported the redress of historical injustices caused by past Crown policies towards Maori, over land confiscation and purchases especially, and voters who felt that the process had become a 'gravy train' for vested interest groups. However, both major parties declared a commitment to increased resourcing of the Waitangi Tribunal and recommended deadlines for the lodging and settlement of historical claims. The challenge for the incoming coalition Government was to ensure that the differences within New Zealand society that had been exposed during the most vigorous and volatile election campaign in recent history did not become deepening divisions.

Despite National's strong performance in the 2005 election, subsequent dissatisfaction with Don Brash's public performance became increasingly apparent within and beyond the party during 2006. Brash's sudden resignation as leader in November, along with his departure from Parliament shortly afterwards, reflected his assessment that a resolution of both personal and political difficulties might be aided by such action. The former National Party finance spokesman, millionaire John Key, replaced Brash as leader, with Bill English as deputy. Much of National's resurgence in polls throughout 2007 was attributed to the effectiveness of this new leadership team, its espousal of 'compassionate conservatism' and to Key's more personable approach. Despite his relative inexperience in politics, media polls in that year consistently showed greater public support for National, especially after the 2007 budget failed to deliver any major reductions in personal tax rates.

Labour continued to receive political endorsement for many of its social policies: for example, Working for Families, Early Childhood education subsidies, the Kiwisaver superannuation scheme and campaigns to promote healthy eating and reduce obesity. However, the proposed Child Discipline Bill, which aimed to remove Section 59 of the Crimes Act—providing the statutory defence of 'reasonable force' to correct a child—caused nation-wide controversy and a great deal of acrimonious debate about the potential 'criminalizing' of 'good parents'. A compromise amendment, agreed to by Clark and Key, gave police the discretion not to prosecute complaints against a parent or care-giver where the offence of smacking was considered to be inconsequential. In May 2007 the bill passed its third reading in Parliament by 113 votes to seven. However, violence against children remained a serious problem, particularly among ethnic groups whose poor socio-economic circumstances are frequently linked to educational underachievement.

The Government's programme for 2008 continued to prioritize social issues, with particular emphasis on the provision of affordable housing, skills training for young people, early childhood education and health checks for pre-school children. Although in the final year of its term of office, the coalition pressed ahead with policy proposals on contentious issues, including plans for a carbon emissions trading scheme. Reductions in personal income tax announced in the 2008 budget, along with a liberalization of the tax rebate rules for charitable donations, were well received, and the Government's advocacy of paid parental leave and four weeks' annual holiday appealed to employees. Helen Clark's leadership and consistent commitment to making the MMP system work through consultation, co-operation and consensus was crucial to the coalition Government's achievements. However, political polls during 2008 again indicated greater public support for National. Opposition criticism of the 'nanny state' resonated with sector groups critical of what was perceived to be an excessive degree of regulation in areas where personal responsibility should take precedence. In September Clark announced that the next election was to be held on 8 November.

The 2008 election results were unequivocal. National received 44.9% of the votes cast (58 seats in the House of Representatives) and Labour secured 34.0% (43 seats). Of the six minor parties contesting the fifth election to be held under the MMP system, the Greens took 6.7% of the votes (nine seats); ACT 3.7% (five seats); the Maori Party 2.4% (five seats); United Future 0.9% (one seat); and the Progressive Party 0.9% (one seat). New Zealand First failed to win any electorate seats and, with 4.1% of the votes cast, did not reach the 5% threshold required for entry into Parliament through party votes alone. The defeat ended the 27-year career in Parliament of Winston Peters, whose political demise was not unexpected. In the months preceding the election Peters had relinquished his foreign affairs portfolio pending investigations by the Serious Fraud Office, the Electoral Commission and the police into undeclared donations to his party. Although no formal charges resulted, Peters was censured by Parliament's Privileges Committee and lost public credibility and reputation for his prevarication when discussing the issue of the finances of New Zealand First. Prime Minister-elect John Key acted quickly to establish working relationships with several minor parties. As signalled before the election, the United Future leader, Peter Dunne, segued from the Labour-led Government into the National-led administration, retaining his post of Minister of Revenue outside of Cabinet. The confidence and supply agreement signed between National and ACT gave ministerial portfolios outside of Cabinet to the leader of the latter party, Rodney Hide (who assumed responsibility for local government and regulatory reform); and to MP Heather Roy (consumer affairs). Key remained firm to his pre-election stance that Sir Roger Douglas, the former ACT leader, who was returned to Parliament as a party-list MP, would not have any formal role in his Government.

ACT's aspirations for a strong right-wing agenda for the incoming administration were undermined by the centrist Key's pursuit of a political accommodation with the Maori Party, an important new force in Parliament. Given the controversy that had ensued after Don Brash's divisive Orewa speech in January 2004, and National's 2008 election policy platform that the Maori seats should be abolished by 2014 whereas the Maori Party had campaigned for the seats to be entrenched, the speed and relative ease with which political agreement was reached reflected a willingness to compromise on both sides. The Maori Party co-leaders, Dr Pita Sharples and Tariana Turia, secured important social development portfolios, in both ministerial and associate minister roles (Maori affairs, education and corrections; and community and voluntary sector, health, social development and employment, respectively). Although ministers outside of Cabinet, the roles accorded to the Maori Party co-leaders suggested a genuine commitment by Key that major issues affecting Maori would be addressed during his administration.

With the Greens, whose disappointing election results were generally regarded as an electorate reaction against Labour, coupled with concern about the cost of implementing environmental policies at a time of economic recession, National concluded a memorandum of understanding. Both parties committed to establish a working relationship of good faith in which the Greens might consider procedural support for government legislation on a case-by-case basis. Their pre-election stance of not forming a political alliance with National was thereby upheld. Shortly after the election, the founding co-leader of the Greens, Jeanette Fitzsimons, announced that she was to resign from that position. (Maori lawyer Metiria Turei joined Dr Russel Norman as co-leader in mid-2009.) With all political negotiations concluded and his administration sworn into office on 19 November 2008, the new Prime Minister departed to attend his first international conference, the Asia-Pacific Economic Co-operation (APEC) summit meeting in Lima, Peru.

For Labour, major changes ensued rapidly. After nine years as Prime Minister and 15 years as leader of the party, Helen Clark announced her resignation on election night. Her long-time political associate, Deputy Leader Dr Michael Cullen, followed suit shortly afterwards. Phil Goff and Annette King were elected to these respective leadership roles. The smooth transition of power was marked by both Clark and Cullen taking up positions on the back bench, and in April 2009 both delivered their valedictory speeches in the House of Representatives. Clark's appointment to the position of Administrator of the UN Development Programme received cross-party endorsement and acclaim, both locally and internationally. Political opponents and supporters alike acknowledged her energy, intellect, political acumen and commitment to ensuring that New Zealand would be a robust social democracy. Early commentators on the legacy of the Clark years emphasized her serious relationship-building with Asian countries, especially the People's Republic of China, Japan, South Korea, Singapore, Thailand and Viet Nam, and her skill in effecting a diplomatic reconciliation with the USA despite the nuclear issue and the obvious policy differences over the invasion of Iraq.

With Deputy Prime Minister Bill English as his Minister of Finance and of Infrastructure, Key embarked upon a vigorous and diverse 'First 100 Days of Action'. The central election policy promise of lowered personal tax rates took effect on 1 April 2009. However, owing to the realities of a deteriorating economic position, plans for further reductions were deferred until the 2010 budget. The priorities of coalition partners were acknowledged. Hence the Emissions Trading Scheme was sent to a select committee for a complete review, although ACT's insistence that competing views of climate change should also be considered contradicted the stance of National's Minister for Climate Change Issues, Nick Smith, whose understanding of the scientific evidence was well informed. The confusing Electoral Finance Act of 2007, designed to limit excessive party spending on election advertising, was repealed with the support of all parties in the House. A similar consensus resulted in the establishment of a powerful committee to review the ownership issues that had been compounded, rather than resolved, by the Foreshore and Seabed Act, which denied Maori the ability to test the extent of their property rights through the courts. Proposed grants to facilitate home insulation also received cross-party support, since both Labour and the Greens had promoted more energy-efficient housing.

Business leaders and entrepreneurs were invited to a prime ministerial Job Summit in Auckland in April 2009. Public interest in the outcome was high, in view of the rapidly rising rates of redundancy and unemployment. A proposed national cycleway to boost tourism and create employment was one unexpected outcome that met with popular approval. National's move to reinstate the titles of Knight and Dame as part of the New Zealand honour's system resulted in 72 of the 85 recipients opting to take up a title. The Labour Government's decision to phase out incandescent light bulbs was rescinded by the new administration; all government departments were firmly instructed to find ways of reducing expenditure; policy initiatives were signalled in the areas of health, education and correctional services. The latter initiatives included funding of additional elective surgery theatres and more health workers; a proposed implementation of national child literacy and numeracy standards; and the implementation of stricter bail laws and the requirement that repeat offenders serve their full sentences. With New Zealand's high rate of incarceration (8,434 prisoners in custody in July 2009, two-thirds of whom had drug and alcohol problems, and a forecast of 10,700 by 2016), National's announcement that it would increase the present 500-strong capacity of drug treatment units within prisons to 1,000 by 2011 would address, but not solve, a serious social and political issue.

The subsequent enactment of the ACT-inspired 'Three Strikes' Bill, which in effect required judges to impose on third-time offenders the maximum sentence with no possibility of parole, was justifiably criticized for being punitive legislation that not only would be unlikely to deter recidivist offenders, but also would not counteract the adverse domestic conditions in which many at-risk youths were raised. Conversely, a major policy tenet promoted by Tariana Turia, co-leader of National's coalition partner, the Maori Party, offered the possibility of some interventionist solutions provided that the fundamental goal of indigenous empowerment could be attained. The 'Whanau Ora' (safe families) initiative aimed to deliver social services to poor families through non-governmental community organizations, which would have the authority to require co-operation between government social agencies when dealing with at-risk clients. The proposal, variously described as potentially the most valuable or the most disastrous initiative of the National-led Government, was announced in March 2010, although its framework of policy guidelines continued to be a 'work in progress'. There was, nevertheless, growing support for a culturally based initiative that could help to redress the disproportionately high representation of Maori, young people especially, in the negative statistics of poverty, poor health, low educational attainment, high unemployment and criminal offending. With one-half of the entire Maori population aged under 22 years and youth unemployment (45% of the registered unemployed in 2011 were aged between 15 and 24 years) in New Zealand the highest among the countries of the Organisation for Economic Co-operation and Development (OECD), both state and private agencies recognized the importance of becoming more culturally sensitive.

With public interest high following the emergence in 2009 of expenses scandals in the British parliamentary system, the new Speaker of the House of Representatives, Lockwood Smith, convened a cross-party committee on expenses at the behest of the Prime Minister. Payments for accommodation in and outside of Wellington, along with air and surface travel costs, were disclosed for the first time in July and henceforth were to be published quarterly. Considerable public debate ensued, and reconsideration of the system of allowances, for housing and travel especially, was widely anticipated. Details of the misuse of ministerial credit cards during several years prior to 2010 proved both embarrassing and politically damaging to experienced politicians from both major parties. ACT leader Rodney Hide, a renowned 'perk-buster', lost considerable credibility when his own generous use of 'travel perks' was exposed. Given the media scrutiny that inevitably follows such disclosures, henceforth few MPs or local politicians were likely to ignore institutional guidelines or to develop an exaggerated sense of entitlement. In August 2009 the former (expelled) MP for Mangere, Taito Phillip Field (who in 1993 had become the first Pacific Islander to be elected to the New Zealand Parliament) was found guilty of immigration-related bribery and corruption charges during the period between November 2002 and October 2005, and of several counts of perverting the course of justice in a case that raised cultural issues about Pasifika notions of reciprocity and obligation. He was subsequently sentenced to six years' imprisonment, becoming the first New Zealand MP to be incarcerated. National's popular Minister for Ethnic Affairs and of Women's Affairs, Chinese-born Pansy Wong, resigned from her portfolio in November 2010, and subsequently from her parliamentary seat, after revelations that her husband had engaged in private business while accompanying her on taxpayer-funded travel. Although National won the subsequent by-election, politicians from all parties were in no doubt that the New Zealand electorate would not tolerate any further abuse of political privilege, whether unintentional or deliberate.

Throughout 2009 and 2010 the National-led Government's high level of public support was, in no small measure, a reflection of the Prime Minister's consensus-building and relaxed leadership style. Despite periods of tension with both ACT and the Maori Party, John Key's administration sought to steer a middle course and was careful to signal its responsiveness to public opinion—on some issues, at least. When a furore greeted a proposal by the Minister of Energy and Resources, Gerry Brownlee, for exploratory mining in areas of the high-value protected conservation estate and when public submissions were overwhelmingly opposed, the idea was abandoned. Yet in November 2009, when cross-party consensus on climate change measures was both crucial and possible, National pressed ahead with its hastily revised Emissions Trading Scheme. It did so after granting concessions, brokered by the Maori Party, to *iwi* (tribal groups) whose Treaty settlements included the purchase of forestry assets from the Crown, and initiating the development of a system that was beneficial to business and agricultural interests.

As the 2011 election approached, National signalled its intention to pursue a partial privatization of state energy assets, reviving the debate on an issue bitterly contested in Labour's era of 'Rogernomics'; yet National's standing in the polls was barely diminished. While this situation reflected John Key's personal popularity as Prime Minister, it also revealed the electorate's awareness that the cost of the second, and more devastating, earthquake in the Canterbury region in February 2011 (see Other Domestic Affairs, below) required the Government to address an exceptional economic situation.

Labour's lacklustre political performance as the main opposition party could be attributed in part to Phil Goff's difficulty in promoting his own leadership style to the public at large, and to Labour's inability to promote policies that differed substantially from those followed by the centrist Key. These difficulties were made apparent during the November 2010 Mana by-election, occasioned by the retirement of Labour's popular Pasifika MP, Winnie Laban. A safe Labour constituency, where a majority of 6,000 had been achieved at the 2008 election, was reduced by the National candidate to a marginal seat with a Labour majority of just 1,000. There was also discord within Labour Party ranks, most obviously from disaffected Te Atatu MP Chris Carter, whose poorly handled criticism of the leadership resulted in his expulsion from the party in October 2010 and his determination, after a period of stress leave, to complete his term of office as an independent MP.

For ACT the electoral prospects in 2011 were far more unfavourable. Unseemly bids for power within his five-member caucus made public the parliamentary wing's dissatisfaction with Rodney Hide's leadership, while his rigid stance, opposing designated Maori seats on the new Auckland 'Super-City' Council, added to his growing unpopularity. However, in turning to Don Brash for advice and support, Hide did not foresee that he would lose both the ACT leadership and his parliamentary career, and in May Brash secured the leadership of a minority party of which he was not even a member. The erstwhile mayor of Auckland City, John Banks, also a former National MP and a strident voice for law and order, was soon afterwards announced as ACT's candidate for Epson (Hide's Auckland electorate seat) in the November election. ACT's more extreme right-wing stance, especially on issues of race and immigration, was unlikely to resonate with voters in New Zealand's largest and most culturally diverse city.

While ACT was a difficult and ideologically rigid coalition partner for the National-led Government, the Maori Party's participation was the most successful of any minority party since the inauguration of MMP, in view of the number of policy concessions and the amount of funding that it secured for Maori Party initiatives. Ironically, this very success, in working for the empowerment of Maori through consensus and co-operation within government ranks, led to a loss of electoral support from within its own membership. The persistent refusal of controversial Maori Party MP Hone Harawira to observe party discipline and his very public criticism of party co-leaders Tariana Turia and Dr Pita Sharples led finally to Harawira's expulsion from Maori Party ranks in February 2011. He contested the subsequent Te Tai Tokerau by-election as leader of a newly established Mana Party, a left-leaning splinter group with strong appeal to Maori voters who were critical of the Maori Party's decision to join a coalition with National. Thus, despite having secured both the repeal of the controversial Foreshore and Seabed Act (replaced by a Marine and Coastal Areas Act, which abolished Crown title to the foreshore and seabed, and restored the right of Maori to take their claims for customary title and rights to court) and the establishment of a cross-party constitutional review (the comprehensive brief for which included the Maori seats and the role of the Treaty of Waitangi in New Zealand's constitutional arrangements), the Maori Party's strong commitment to consensus-building might well prove to be its weakness from the perspective of many former supporters.

For the Greens, National's minimalistic approach to environmental issues and its failure to establish much-needed national water quality standards (despite being strongly urged to do so by a multi-faceted 2009 Land and Water Forum), suggested that support for the party would be maintained at levels similar to those shown in 2008. However, New Zealand First seemed unlikely to revive its fortunes, despite the efforts of Winston Peters, given the lack of any new policy initiatives and the adoption of a more extreme immigration stance by ACT.

Meanwhile, the election results of 2008 had highlighted two areas of continuing dissatisfaction with the MMP system: the 5% threshold and the seat-winning bonus. It was emphasized that a lowering of the threshold would enable minority parties polling 3% or 4% of the party votes cast to be represented in Parliament. Abolition of the system whereby winning a single constituency seat entitles a party to five MPs in the House of Representatives would result in a fairer distribution of seats, more in accord with voter preference. A referendum to gauge support for MMP was to take place concurrently with the general election scheduled for 26 November 2011. Voters were also to be asked to rank a preferred alternative system: 'first-past-the-post', preferential voting, single transferable vote or supplementary member. Should the electorate vote to retain MMP, a system which, despite its obvious shortcomings, has promoted greater diversity of representation and consensus in policy-making, a review of MMP was to take place before the 2014 general election.

Other Domestic Affairs

Official immigration policies have been a source of electoral concern (exploited most obviously by New Zealand First). The 2006 national census revealed a continuing trend towards ethnic diversity in the country's population: Pacific peoples comprised 6.9% of the total population, while those identifying themselves as Asian totalled 9.2% (compared with 3% in 1991), despite the imposition in October 1996 of a $NZ20,000 fee on immigrants lacking competence in the English language. Appropriate support services were not always in place to assist new migrants. Highly skilled professionals, admitted to New Zealand because of their qualifications, were frequently unable to work in their area of expertise owing to language difficulties, administrative barriers or racial prejudice. Immigration selection policies, introduced in early 2004, targeted areas of skills shortages and aimed to ensure that new arrivals would be gainfully employed in those fields. However, changes to citizenship laws, effective from the beginning of 2006, meant that children born in New Zealand to short-term visitors or migrants without residency would not be granted automatic citizenship rights. According to the 2006 census, Maori totalled 14.6% of the population, while those identifying themselves as European accounted for 67.6% and those identifying themselves as New Zealander, 11.0%. An increase in South African and Croatian immigrants was noticeable within the European category. The median age varied widely across the different ethnic groups, that of Europeans being considerably older (36.8 years) than that of Maori (21.9) and Pacific Peoples (21.0). As the March 2011 census was postponed because of the second Canterbury earthquake in the previous month, statisticians would be unable to update population figures until after 2013, when the deferred census was to be held in time for electoral boundaries to be revised, if necessary, before the 2014 general election.

The ageing of the post-1945 'baby boomers' was expected to begin to have a major impact on the social services, health and superannuation policies by the end of the first decade of the 21st century, as the proportion of children in the total population continued to decline (33% in the 1960s, 21% in 2006). Demographic projections in 2005 indicated that the relative percentages of all ethnic populations in New Zealand would change markedly. In August 2007 a total of 4.18m. New Zealanders were resident in the country, 1.2m. of them in Auckland, while at least 500,000 (and probably far more) Maori and Pakeha New Zealanders lived and worked overseas, particularly in Australia.

During the first half of 2008 an average of 600 New Zealanders a week departed for Australia; in keeping with previous patterns of migration, that number rose substantially after the 2008 election, thus making 2008 the year of the biggest trans-Tasman 'brain drain', with nearly 48,000 New Zealanders migrating west. Australian and New Zealand government officials began to investigate the portability of private retirement savings, a measure that would facilitate the return of those who had spent their working lives in Australia. Agreement was eventually reached in 2009, but concerns over the significant discrepancy in productivity and income led to the appointment in mid-2009 of former National Party leader Don Brash as chairman of an advisory group whose brief was to find ways of closing the income gap with Australia by 2025. The subsequent report was quickly deferred by the National-led Government, which recognized the electoral unpalatability of many of its recommendations. The potential value of expatriate networks in a global economic environment was gradually being acknowledged by government and business agencies, which were previously more concerned with attracting such citizens back to New Zealand. Nevertheless, the continuing loss of highly skilled graduates, in the fields of medicine and science especially, was a major concern to health service providers and to the country's research communities. Rates of trans-Tasman migration accelerated during 2011, influenced in part by the two Canterbury earthquakes, as well as by continuing high unemployment levels in New Zealand, raising the prospect of shortages of skilled professionals and tradespeople to expedite the much-needed repair and reconstruction in Christchurch.

In the early 21st century more than 80% of Maori were urban dwellers, a situation that had caused many to become separated from their tribal background and traditions, despite sustained and vigorous educational efforts to arrest the decline in Maoritanga (Maori culture). In 1985 the Lange Government permitted the Waitangi Tribunal (established in 1975) to consider retrospectively Maori grievances dating back to 1840. The evidence presented by claimants to the Tribunal enabled Maori perspectives on the colonial past to be aired in a public forum, and the findings of the Tribunal, while not binding on the Government, have already contributed significantly towards changing public perceptions on this issue. The importance to Maori of the painstaking and careful process is apparent from the commitment that many small communities have made to have their claim heard. (Some 2,000 applications had been lodged by December 2002.) The strengthening cultural renaissance initially encountered a mixed reception from Pakeha. While the adoption of Maori as an official language in 1987 and the establishment of the *Kohanga Reo* ('language nest') early-childhood programmes in 1981 were soon accepted, the need for affirmative action to redress educational and social disadvantage, much of which was the unforeseen consequence of past policies, was more contentious. National Government promotion of a $NZ2,000m. 'fiscal envelope' scheme as a means of resolving outstanding claims was soundly rejected by Maori at a series of consultative *hui* (gatherings) held throughout the country in 1995. However, direct negotiation with the Crown remained an option, and a 1995 agreement, which included the return of assets and a formal apology by the Crown, with the powerful North Island Tainui tribes, met with a mixed reception from other claimants. In October 1996 a similar settlement was reached with the Ngai Tahu tribes of South Island. The government-initiated Sealord deal, whereby fishing quotas were allocated to coastal tribes, caused dissension about the fairest method of distributing returns within Maoridom. Urban Maori authorities argued that payments according to *iwi* affiliation denied them a share of the resources to which their urban-born membership was entitled. Costly legal action resulted, nevertheless, in an affirmation that an urban Maori authority could not be defined as an *iwi*, even if it served that purpose for its members: affiliation based on *whakapapa* (descent), not on residential location, must be the basis upon which payments are made. Efforts continued to resolve the issue without further redress to the courts.

Disputed rights of ownership over the foreshore and seabed also emerged as a contentious issue in mid-2003. Following a Court of Appeal decision in June that the Maori Land Court could consider an application concerning a tribal proposal for mussel farming in the Marlborough Sounds, and thereby make a ruling on the ownership question, the Labour Government sought to allay public concerns by declaring that the foreshore and seabed were for all New Zealanders. Debates over the recognition of customary title continued: public submissions were invited in late 2003, and the proposed legislation proceeded to select committee hearings in mid-2004. A resolution satisfactory to all parties was not easily attained, because of a public perception that the recreational interests of all New Zealanders would be affected. Government assurances that Maori customary rights would be upheld did not mollify protesters, angered by what they perceived to be a denial of Maori rights to follow due legal process by testing the Court of Appeal's ruling before the Maori Land Court.

As had been predicted, the emergence of the Maori Party—with its array of candidates for the 2005 election—led to more frequent discussion of Maori-related issues in Parliament. This proved to be the case particularly during the National-led administration of John Key and with the establishment of an Iwi Leaders' Forum, which meets regularly with the Prime Minister, Maori Party co-leaders and senior cabinet ministers. Prior to the election, both Labour and National indicated a deadline of 2008 for the registering of historical claims before the Tribunal and suggested a desired timescale for the hearing of all claims. Whether all claims could be heard within the next 10 or 15 years would depend substantially upon the adequate resourcing of the process and the availability of qualified personnel to sit on the lengthy Tribunal hearings. In July 2011 the Tribunal released the long-awaited 1,000-page report on the Wai262 claim, lodged two decades previously in the hope of protecting Maori rights over traditional knowledge, culture and species, and seeking to prevent their commercial exploitation or offensive or derogatory use. The report recommended that some form of guardianship (*kaitiakitanga*) be established, along with a new commission to protect cultural works. In welcoming the report, cultural commentators noted the challenge for the Government and the Office of Treaty Settlements of ensuring that protection did not become ossification of a culture characterized by constant change.

Labour aroused widespread public debate during 2004 over proposed legislation to address the legal inequalities affecting de facto and same-sex couples. MPs were permitted a conscience vote on the Civil Union Bill, which would affect the one in five New Zealanders who, according to the 2001 census, were identified as living in a relationship—heterosexual or homosexual—but were not married. An accompanying Relationships (Statutory References) Bill aimed to remove the legal discrimination that affected all those established in some recognized form of personal partnership. The parliamentary select committees dealing with both issues were inundated with public submissions, and their successful resolution of the issue was a political priority for the Labour administration. However, its legislative achievement came at some cost in terms of electoral support from those members of the public who felt that fundamental personal values were being undermined.

Child poverty, a conspicuous rise in violent crime (much of it drugs-related), youth offending, gang association and drugs-trafficking have become major areas of community anxiety, and Maori and Pasifika youths are over-represented in such statistics. Budgetary measures announced in April 2006 included a 'working for families package' designed to give targeted tax relief and supplementary assistance, where needed, for accommodation and other expenses related to raising a family. Government initiatives such as the 'Fruit in Schools' programme, introduced in 2005 as part of an endeavour to promote healthy eating and increased physical activity, were well supported in the 114 schools in which the scheme was operating. However, a 2006/07 health survey revealed that one in three New Zealand adults were overweight and a further one in four were obese. Pasifika and Maori obesity figures are 2.5 and 1.5 times higher than the national average, respectively, with obvious consequences in terms of the onset of Type 2 diabetes and other weight-related illnesses. High rates of teenage pregnancy, alcohol abuse, methamphetamine addiction (New Zealand has one of the highest rates per caput in the world) and youth suicide (of young males especially) are also matters of social concern. New Zealand's appalling levels of domestic violence and child abuse were highlighted in 2006–07, when a number of child deaths in dysfunctional benefit-dependent households affected by alcohol and drug abuse provoked national outrage and prompted cross-party initiatives to address the issue. Police staffing levels were increased in the Auckland area, and particularly in South Auckland, where sustained efforts to build partnerships with local organizations have expanded the range of youth crime prevention programmes, in a culturally vibrant but economically disadvantaged community where drug and alcohol abuse and gang influence are pervasive. In mid-2008 television campaigns against domestic violence encouraged victims, friends and neighbours to report such abuse. In mid-2011 the publication of a Green Paper for Vulnerable Children by the Minister for Social Development and Employment and of Youth Affairs, Paula Bennett, confirmed that nearly 20% of New Zealand's children lived in poverty. A disproportionately high number of those were in Maori, Pasifika and refugee communities. A Children's Action Plan was to be formulated following public discussion of the Government's proposals to foster responsibility and leadership within communities and to make more child-centred policy and practice changes. For the young people at risk of poor life outcomes, abuse and unemployability, such well-planned intervention could not come soon enough.

A report released in April 2010 by the Law Commission on the reform of New Zealand's liquor laws, entitled *Alcohol in Our Lives: Curbing the Harm*, emphasized the wide range of problems caused by alcohol use, especially the level of criminal offending. The report recommended legislative changes to restrict the ready availability of alcohol to young people. In August the Government announced plans for the adoption, in some form, of 126 of the 153 recommendations made in the Law Commission's report. However, the Government drew considerable criticism for its failure to implement several of the report's more significant proposals, including those on lowering the blood-alcohol limit for all drivers, setting statutory minimum price levels and increasing excise duty on liquor sales. The Government intended partially to adopt recommendations on raising the age limit for purchasing liquor (the limit was lowered to 18 years in 1999); from late 2010 the age limit for 'off-licence' sales only would be increased to 20 years. However, in July the Minister of Transport, Steven Joyce, proposed that the permitted blood-alcohol limit should be zero for drivers under the age of 20 and for those who had previously been convicted of drink-driving; that policy became law in 2011. The adverse impact of heavy drinking on young people's physical and mental well-being is indisputable, but changing a well entrenched culture of youthful (and adult) binge drinking remains both difficult and challenging.

Despite political rhetoric concerning the need for a more skilled work-force in a knowledge-based economy, escalating costs for tertiary education continued to create extremely high levels of indebtedness among the student population, increasing numbers of whom were forced to rely upon bank loans. Shortages of trained staff in the health, education and information technology sectors reflected the trend for recent graduates to seek higher-paid employment abroad in an effort to reduce their burden of debt. In the months leading up to the 2005 election, both major parties identified this problem as one in need of urgent resolution. The coalition Government's budget of April 2006 introduced an interest-free student loan system, but effective solutions had yet to be found to address the problem of the compounding interest, which was an integral part of the original scheme following its inception in 1992.

Other educational issues also proved difficult to address: the introduction of a National Certificate of Educational Achievement (NCEA) to replace former and familiar measurements of secondary school achievement was contentious and onerous in its impact on teachers. The inequalities that emerged in student results from the 2004 scholarship and bursary examinations caused a furore in educational circles: a subsequent official review was strongly critical of the national administration of the new system. Philosophical differences continued to be aired over a qualification system that was moving away from the traditional pass/fail model to one of measuring standards of achievement, initially without giving appropriate recognition of excellence—a shortcoming remedied in 2007. However, under the NCEA fewer students were leaving school without any form of qualification. In 2003, for example, 21% of Pasifika students left school with little or no formal attainment; in 2007 only 6% did so. During 2008 the Government promoted further educational reforms designed to keep all students linked to some form of educational training until the age of 18. In July 2009 the Minister of Maori Affairs, Dr Pita Sharples, announced a new initiative focusing on Maori in industry and trades training. Working in partnership with industry providers, the National-led Government hoped to provide new entrant training and skills improvement for some 1,800 Maori youth when the programme was fully operational. In 2010 the Minister of Education, Anne Tolley, pressed ahead with the implementation of National Standards in literacy and numeracy, confronting serious opposition from primary teachers and principals, who were concerned at the lack of trialling and the probability that the publication of results would lead to 'league tables' in which the performances of primary schools would be compared.

Despite the efforts of successive governments to foster the notion of community responsibility for social welfare, resources, particularly in mental health and care of the aged, remained inadequate. Evoking the precedent of the influential Maori Land March of 1975, in September 1998 the Anglican Church organized an ecumenical Hikoi of Hope, in which marchers from both northern and southern ends of the country converged on Parliament to protest against the trends in social policy. The social cost of the market-led 'reforms' of the late 20th century was no longer a matter of debate. The Labour Government addressed the issue of market-value rents for state housing, a practice that compounded the plight of urban low-income families and contributed to the poor health of their children, particularly in the South Auckland area, with its high concentration of unskilled and unemployed Pacific Island Polynesians. Tax concessions for families and targeted assistance for accommodation were some of the measures adopted to improve living standards in such communities. The closure of rural hospitals, greater privatization and an expensive restructuring of the health service were not perceived by the public at large as delivering improvements in a public health care system that was increasingly reliant on overseas-trained medical and nursing staff to counter the loss of New Zealand graduates working abroad.

Many New Zealanders entered the 21st century with a strong conviction that the individualistic ideology of market forces that had prevailed in the last two decades of the 20th century had not served the country and its people well; however, a divergence of political viewpoints over social reform hindered the implementation of policies designed to redress the obvious inequalities. A change in political rhetoric, from 'closing the gaps' (with its acknowledgement that Maori and Pasifika people were disproportionately represented in the statistics for low standards of income, education and health) to 'needs-based assistance', with minimal or no reference to ethnicity, reflected the Labour-led Government's sensitivity to a level of popular disquiet about policies designed to relieve the inequitable impact of market-driven economic policy. However, during 2007–08 rising food, fuel and energy prices affected mortgaged middle-income households in addition to those on lower fixed incomes. The 'new thrift' measures included a resurgence of home cooking and gardening, greater use of public transport and bicycles, and a higher rate of consultations with budget advisory services. In February 2008 the Government announced a new funding model to support some 850 community organizations delivering essential services to families, children and young people. With a financial commitment of $NZ446m. over the following four years, 'Pathways to Partnership' was publicized as a conscious departure from the competitive and wasteful market-based system. The fact that citizens were prepared to contribute generously to these and other causes was made apparent in the first major report into volunteering in New Zealand, released in 2008. Based on 2004 statistics, it revealed that over 1m. volunteers gave more than 270m. hours of unpaid labour within their communities.

The death of Te Arikinui in August 2006 led to an unprecedented public response from Maori, Pakeha and Pacific people during the six-day *tangihanga* (period of mourning). The Maori Queen's 40-year leadership of the Kingitanga movement had witnessed the cultural resurgence of her Tainui people and the settlement with the Crown, in 1995, of grievances arising from the *raupatu* (unjust confiscation of land) in the 1860s. Her commitment to improving the welfare of all Maori had been repeatedly acknowledged. In accordance with Kingitanga custom, her eldest son, Tuheitia Paki, was chosen to succeed her. He was crowned shortly before her funeral service, which was attended by Prime Minister Helen Clark and Chief Justice Sian Elias. The very positive national reaction to the culturally well-informed coverage of the funeral offered hope that henceforth more would be done by the media to promote greater understanding of Maori *tikanga* (custom). The new Kingitanga leader would be required to address very different challenges from those experienced by his mother. His background in educational administration was expected to be an asset (yet to be demonstrated), a major priority being to increase levels of Maori educational attainment. More tribal organizations were developing significant economic strength through the Treaty settlement process and greater co-operation among the tribes, as demonstrated throughout the *tangihanga*, could significantly enhance their influence within the national economy. Public reaction to Dame Te Ata's death suggested that more Pakeha had become genuinely supportive of Maori political and social aspirations than had been the case four decades previously. The popularity of Maori Television among Pakeha viewers, and widespread endorsement of Maori Language Week, held in July each year, reflected this shift. A milestone of 0.5m. hours of Maori language broadcasting was celebrated in 2008, and Maori Television hosted the first ever World Indigenous Television Broadcasting Conference in Auckland in March.

Controversy developed in October 2009, when the Minister of Broadcasting, Dr Jonathan Coleman, reacted to Maori Television's bid for the Rugby World Cup 2011 broadcasting rights by supporting a combined opposing bid by Television New Zealand (TVNZ) and TV3, ostensibly to ensure guaranteed national coverage of all matches. Intervention by Prime Minister John Key resulted in a necessary compromise: a Maori Television-led multi-network deal involving all three channels. Other preparations for the six-week long tournament, the largest sporting event ever to be held in New Zealand, caused political tensions, particularly over infrastructural developments on Auckland's waterfront. All Christchurch-based games had to be rescheduled after the earthquake of February 2011. Public opinion remained divided over whether the promoted benefits of the event would bear any positive relationship to the cost of hosting it.

While Maori, and particularly Maori youth, remained patently over-represented in the statistics for crime, unemployment, welfare, health, poverty and educational underachievement, the ongoing work of the Waitangi Tribunal and negotiations between the Crown and claimant groups continued to deliver important settlements as redress for past injustices and land alienation. Tribal guardianship of the Waikato River was acknowledged in 2007, and in 2008 settlement negotiations began for the transfer of 176,000 ha of Crown Forest land to the tribal groups comprising the Central North Island Forest Iwi Collective. The leadership of Tumu Te Heuheu, Tuwharetoa's Paramount Chief since 1997, resolved an issue of 20 years' standing. Under the 'Treelords' settlement, eight *iwi* with overlapping and competing interests in the land under negotiation finalized the largest single Treaty settlement achieved to date. The forest land, valued at $NZ196m., was returned to Maori ownership. Crown Forestry Trust rentals accruing since 1989 amounted to $NZ223m. The settlement also included future rental payments of $NZ13m. per year, empowering tribal authorities to resource the education, health, housing and other social and economic initiatives that many had long envisaged. In July 2009, in a settlement involving the wider Wellington region—the Port Nicholson Block (*Taranaki Whanau Ki Te Upoko o Te Ika*) Claims Settlement Bill—the formal apology by the Crown was acknowledged in an official statement of forgiveness by the *iwi* involved, the first that had occurred in the Treaty process.

In the early hours of 4 September 2010 a major earthquake destroyed homes, commercial buildings and infrastructure in the Canterbury region; aftershocks continued for some weeks. Since the epicentre was only 40 km west of Christchurch, New Zealand's second largest city was badly affected, particularly the central retail area; however, there were no deaths and only two serious casualties. With the response co-ordinated through a Civil Defence Emergency Management team, government and local authorities worked closely together to provide immediate assistance; local community effort was equally remarkable. A Regional Rural Recovery Group was established to address the extensive damage in rural areas, in the Waimakariri region in particular. Treasury estimates put the cost of earthquake-related repairs at more than $NZ4,000m.

A second disaster struck a South Island community in November 2010, when an explosion in the Pike River Coal Mine, under the West Coast's Paparoa Range, killed 29 miners. It was New Zealand's worst mining accident in 96 years. A subsequent commission of inquiry was established to investigate the cause of a tragedy that was made all the harder for families to bear because the bodies could not be retrieved owing to the persistence of toxic gas and the danger of fire in the mine.

The magnitude 6.3 earthquake that struck the Canterbury region on 22 February 2011, killing 181 people, destroying the central business district of Christchurch, and rendering hundreds of homes and swathes of suburbs uninhabitable, devastated lives and livelihoods. A national state of emergency was declared for Christchurch city and lasted for almost 10 weeks. International search and rescue personnel contributed generously to the painstaking work of trying to find survivors or bodies in collapsed buildings, as individuals and community groups within and beyond Christchurch sought to provide relief for traumatized residents and visitors. With aftershocks, liquefaction and demolition work continuing for months, the rebuilding of Christchurch would be a long and slow process. Insurance estimates suggested that the cost of this second earthquake would be more than $NZ17,000m.

International Relations

Continuing the more independent foreign policy initiated by Norman Kirk, from 1984 the Lange Government made a determined effort to foster Pacific unity and to build closer relations with New Zealand's Asian neighbours. Strong diplomatic and trading links were established with Japan, South Korea and China. In 1986 the Lange Government was also the first foreign power to give diplomatic recognition to the administration of Corazon Aquino in the Philippines. Support for the policy of creating a nuclear-free zone in the Pacific—in 1972 the Kirk Government sent a naval frigate into the testing zone near Mururoa Atoll, in French Polynesia, in an effort to force French testing to be conducted underground—led to a strengthening of links between New Zealand and the other island nations of the Pacific (see below for relations with France). However, long-term strategies to promote Pacific unity were seriously impeded by the successful military coups in Fiji in May and September 1987. During 1989 New Zealand endeavoured to provide leadership on other issues of mutual concern to South Pacific nations. For example, at a meeting of the South Pacific Forum in Vanuatu in July, New Zealand stated its intention to ban fishing by drift gillnets from its territorial waters and to refuse permission for vessels using such nets to enter its ports. In 1990 the Japanese decision to cease drift gillnet fishing in Pacific waters received general approval; however, Japan's policy of 'scientific whaling' continued to be strongly criticized by New Zealand in the forum of the International Whaling Commission. Other small-power initiatives concerned measures to protect the ozone layer in the atmosphere and to conserve Antarctica's special status; in September 2002, at the major international forum on sustainable development held in South Africa, New Zealand officials strongly advocated policies limiting carbon dioxide emissions. New Zealand's initiative to broker a peace agreement between Bougainville separatists and the Government of Papua New Guinea led to a cessation of hostilities and to the presence of a New Zealand peace-keeping mission on the island of Bougainville throughout 1998. In May 2000 the Labour Government strongly condemned the hostage-taking and eventual overthrow of the Indian-dominated elected Government of Fiji, and also in the early 2000s supported efforts to resolve the civil conflict in Solomon Islands.

In July 1985 the trawler *Rainbow Warrior*, the flagship of the anti-nuclear environmentalist group Greenpeace (which was to have led a flotilla to Mururoa Atoll to protest against French testing of nuclear weapons in the Pacific), was blown up and sunk in Auckland harbour. The vessel's photographer died in the explosion. Alain Mafart and Dominique Prieur, two agents of the French external security division, the Direction générale de la sécurité extérieure, were subsequently arrested and, after being convicted of manslaughter at a court hearing in November, were imprisoned in Auckland. In July 1986, after pressure from France (including the imposition of trade sanctions) that they be released or returned to France, the two agents were transferred to the atoll of Hao in French Polynesia, where they were scheduled to be detained for the remainder of their 10-year sentence. The French Government made a formal apology for the sabotage operation, and paid the New Zealand Government $NZ7m. in compensation. Relations deteriorated in late 1987, however, when Mafart was returned to Paris, ostensibly for medical treatment, and in May 1988 a pregnant Prieur was airlifted back to France immediately prior to the French presidential election. Prieur's promotion to the rank of major on the fourth anniversary of the sinking of the *Rainbow Warrior* and the public decoration of Mafart in July 1991, together with the continuation of French nuclear testing in the

Pacific, showed that protests by New Zealand had little real impact on French policy. President Jacques Chirac's resumption of underground nuclear testing at Mururoa Atoll, in September 1995, outraged world opinion and was vehemently opposed by countries in the South Pacific. In response to public pressure within New Zealand, the Government sent a naval research vessel to Mururoa. Meanwhile, New Zealand attempted unsuccessfully to reopen at the International Court of Justice (in The Hague, Netherlands) its case against France, first presented in 1973 following the earlier nuclear tests.

New Zealand's relationship with Australia was strengthened by the implementation of the Closer Economic Relations (CER) agreement. Inaugurated on 1 January 1983 and taking full effect on 1 July 1990, the arrangement was not without local critics, who pointed to a disparity of access, maintaining that Australian manufacturers had a competitive advantage owing to their unrestricted entry into the open New Zealand market. That disparity continued, as did some restrictive trade practices, the most persistent of which was the Australian refusal to allow New Zealand apples entry into its domestic market, a ban based on commercial considerations, although claiming to be for reasons of protection against a disease that cannot be transmitted on the fruit itself. More significantly, defence links between the two countries were seriously undermined by the dissension that developed within the ANZUS alliance as a consequence of the Labour Government's opposition to nuclear testing and weaponry in the Pacific region. In February 1985 the Lange Government upheld its popular election manifesto by imposing a ban on the entry of any nuclear-capable ships into New Zealand ports. The US Government maintained that such a standpoint rendered the ANZUS treaty inoperable as, for security reasons, it was policy neither to confirm nor to deny that any US vessel was nuclear-propelled or nuclear-armed. New Zealand's access to intelligence-sharing and military co-operation was withheld, and in August 1986 security guarantees to New Zealand under the ANZUS treaty were suspended. In November Lange reaffirmed his Government's decision to impose the ban on nuclear-capable ships. The US Government responded with the announcement, in February 1987, of its decision not to renew a 1982 memorandum of understanding (due to be renegotiated in June 1987), whereby New Zealand was able to purchase military equipment from the USA at concessionary prices.

The New Zealand Government subsequently proposed a new defence strategy, based on increased self-reliance for the country's military forces, in conjunction with continuing co-operation with Australia and greater involvement in the affairs of the South Pacific region. US military aircraft, which, by the nature of their operations, did not need to carry nuclear missiles, were, nevertheless, permitted to continue using the US Antarctic supply base at Christchurch (annual income from which was significant). In June 1987 the ban on nuclear-capable vessels became law, with the enactment of the New Zealand Nuclear Free Zone, Disarmament and Arms Control Bill. The Labour Government's anti-nuclear policy continued to command widespread support within the country, although the National Government, which took office in 1990, appeared to be uncomfortable with such a commitment, as was evidenced by the diplomatic overtures extended towards the USA by the Minister of External Relations, Don McKinnon.

By 1992 the Government was signalling that it wished to amend the anti-nuclear law to allow for the entry of nuclear-powered vessels, following the US announcement in 1991 that it would be removing nuclear weapons from its warships, but the National Party could not risk its slender majority by initiating such a change. The electorate's emotional attachment to a nuclear-free policy returned to political prominence after a meeting between National leader, Don Brash, foreign affairs spokesman Lockwood Smith and a number of prominent US senators in 2004, when Brash declared that the nuclear ban would be 'gone by lunchtime' if National were to enter government. Brash subsequently gave public reassurances that there would be no change of policy without a referendum. Tributes following the death of former Prime Minister David Lange in August 2005 made constant reference to his espousal of the nuclear-free policy and reflected the continuing strong public sentiment in favour of that stance, even if the grounds for support were now regarded by some critics to be based more on nostalgia and symbolism than rational reconsideration of US-New Zealand relations in a changing world environment. Some improvement in the relationship was manifest during the visit to Washington, DC, in July 2006, of Minister of Foreign Affairs Winston Peters, who met with Secretary of State Condoleezza Rice and a number of other senior officials in the US Government. Fifty years of US-New Zealand co-operation in Antarctica were commemorated in January 2007, when Prime Minister Clark and the New Zealand-born world-famous mountaineer Sir Edmund Hillary (who died in January 2008) travelled to Scott Base with a US delegation that included the Assistant Secretary of State, Claudia McMurray, and the US ambassador to New Zealand, William McCormick.

Apart from the common heritage of Commonwealth membership, New Zealand had little diplomatic contact with the African continent until the mid-1980s. Following Prime Minister Lange's visit to Zimbabwe in April 1985, a High Commission was established in the Zimbabwean capital, Harare. Limited promises of aid were also made. In the mid-1990s the National Government sought to improve relations with South Africa, previously compromised by controversy over the apartheid system and the contentious Springbok rugby tour of New Zealand in 1981. The success of President Nelson Mandela's visit to New Zealand in November 1995 was consolidated when New Zealand Prime Minister Bolger opened an embassy in Pretoria in August 1996. While in South Africa, Bolger acknowledged that the 1981 tour had been a costly mistake. In South Asia, the offence caused to the Indian Government by the Muldoon administration's closure in 1982 of the New Zealand High Commission in New Delhi was redressed in 1985 by Lange's appointment of Sir Edmund Hillary as High Commissioner in India.

New Zealand's successful campaign to obtain a seat on the UN Security Council for a two-year term from January 1993 increased the country's international profile and encouraged a greater domestic awareness of foreign policy issues, as did his accession to the position of Commonwealth Secretary-General. At the meeting of Commonwealth heads of government in March 2002, New Zealand officials joined in the condemnation of Zimbabwean President Robert Mugabe's controversial policies of farm seizures and land redistribution. In 2005 Mugabe's politically motivated demolition of urban squatter communities, roundly criticized on humanitarian grounds, also caused lengthy public debate because of a commitment by New Zealand's cricket team to play in Zimbabwe in August. The tour proceeded, since a potential International Cricket Council fine of $NZ2m. would have been financially ruinous to the team, and the New Zealand Government declined to legislate to restrict freedom of movement by its citizens. However, a reciprocal tour by Zimbabwe did not take place, since the Minister of Foreign Affairs, Phil Goff, had already given notice that no visas would be issued to those players.

Members of the armed forces joined the UN peace-keeping force in Bosnia and Herzegovina in the first half of the 1990s, and the National Government agreed to continue involvement despite the escalation of the conflict in the former Yugoslavia. New Zealand's UN role and increasing global support for an international nuclear test ban led to some easing of tension with the USA. Bolger was received in Washington, DC, by President Bill Clinton in early 1995, the first New Zealand Prime Minister to be invited to the White House in a decade. The US President joined other world leaders at the summit meeting of the APEC forum held in Auckland in September 1999. President Clinton announced the end of the 14-year ban on New Zealand's participation in military exercises with the USA, in preparation for the dispatch of a multinational peace-keeping force to East Timor (then part of Indonesia), of which New Zealand troops formed a part throughout 2000. Subsequent (and controversial) government decisions concerning defence expenditure indicated a continuing commitment to such roles in the future.

In December 2001 New Zealand announced that, at the request of the UN transitional administration, its 660 peace-keeping troops would remain in East Timor (now the inde-

pendent state of Timor-Leste) until November 2002. This commitment was subsequently renewed and maintained throughout the civil unrest, in Dili and elsewhere, in May 2006, and reaffirmed in response to the shooting of the Timorese President, José Ramos Horta, in February 2008. In February 2009 Ramos Horta presented the first of 700 medals to New Zealand defence force personnel and 100 to police officers for their peace-keeping actions in April–May 2006. The National-led administration affirmed a continued deployment in both Timor-Leste and Solomon Islands where, in mid-2003, New Zealand defence personnel joined an Australian-led regional intervention force. The multinational South Pacific force, known as the Regional Assistance Mission to Solomon Islands, which also included troops from Fiji, Papua New Guinea, Tonga, Vanuatu and Samoa, was successful in restoring law and order and enforcing a firearms amnesty for illegal weapons. The rebel leader, Harold Keke, surrendered to the international force in August 2003. The military component of the intervention force was significantly reduced at the end of July 2004, although New Zealand subsequently continued to maintain a contingent of police and support personnel in Solomon Islands, and provided aid for the improvement of domestic infrastructure and public sector reform. Substantial financial assistance was also given to Niue following the devastation caused by tropical cyclone Heta on the island in January 2004; and for flood relief in Fiji and Solomon Islands in February 2009.

The need for export markets has been a major influence on New Zealand's foreign policy. New Zealand has sought access to the markets of the European Union (EU), Eastern Europe and the Middle East, and has also become a member of the OECD. Responses to international crises have been tempered by trade considerations. As part of the general protest against the Soviet intervention in Afghanistan, New Zealand temporarily severed diplomatic relations with the USSR and supported the US appeal for a boycott of the Moscow Olympic Games in 1980. In 1982, with considerable swiftness, the Muldoon Government offered aid to the United Kingdom during the crisis over the Falkland Islands, and imposed a boycott on Argentine goods. However, the government-authorized massacre of students in Tiananmen Square, Beijing, in June 1989 received only diplomatic condemnation, as trade with China, especially in wool, had assumed significant proportions since the late 1970s. Official visits to China by Prime Minister Helen Clark in April 2001, and again in 2005, endeavoured to improve New Zealand's trading position with that country prior to and following its accession to the World Trade Organization (WTO). Chinese Premier Wen Jiabao paid a two-day visit to New Zealand in April 2006, during which an agreement to strengthen cultural links between the two countries was signed. (Comparable arrangements existed with France and Italy.) A month previously, the Lithuanian President, Valdas Adamkus, visited New Zealand for the first time. Prime Minister Bolger's state visits to South Korea and Japan in the 1990s, and the accompanying public insistence that New Zealand's trading future was to be found in Asia, led to economic initiatives that were to prove unsustainable. In 1998 the tourism and forestry sectors were particularly badly affected by the Asian economic crisis, thus further exposing the social costs of New Zealand's vulnerable position within the global economy. Again, in 2003 the epidemic of Severe Acute Respiratory Syndrome (SARS, a pneumonia-like virus) not only affected New Zealand's tourism industry but also contributed to a significant decline in the number of international, fee-paying students from Asia attending New Zealand educational institutions.

Responses to world events during 2001 and 2002 reflected New Zealand's non-isolationist stance. The Government was quick to express support for the USA in the aftermath of the terrorist attacks of 11 September 2001 and committed troops from the special combat force to service in Afghanistan, without full parliamentary debate on the decision. In 2001, for humanitarian reasons, the Government accepted 141 of the Afghan refugees rescued at sea by a Norwegian vessel but denied access to the Australian mainland (see the chapter on the Australian territory of Christmas Island). The New Zealand Government continued quietly to accept small numbers of these refugees. In September 2003 a New Zealand Defence Force Provincial Reconstruction Team began work in Bamian (Bamyan) Province, helping to rebuild services and infrastructure in Afghanistan. (The deployment of this force was subsequently extended to the end of September 2011, and the New Zealand Government gave a commitment that the élite New Zealand Special Air Service would serve three more rotations of active service there.) The nature of US policies in the ongoing 'war on terror' remained a source of debate and concern among many New Zealanders. In the preparations for the US-led invasion of Iraq in March 2003, the New Zealand Government's stance in favour of action only through the UN was popularly endorsed, as were the Prime Minister's reputed criticisms of the US Government's approach. Relations with the US Administration were adversely affected, as evidenced by Australia's signing of a free trade agreement with the USA, while New Zealand continued to press, unsuccessfully, for free trade access to US markets. However, international negotiations at the WTO meeting in Geneva, Switzerland, in July–August 2004 resulted in both the EU and the USA agreeing to phase out all agricultural export subsidies. If ever implemented, this commitment would mean a significant rise in New Zealand's export earnings. However, the reintroduction of some EU and US protectionist subsidies in 2009 rendered that possibility unlikely.

In July 2004 New Zealand's relations with Israel deteriorated when it was revealed that two Israelis, convicted on charges related to a fraudulent attempt to obtain a New Zealand passport, were acting on behalf of Israel's intelligence services. Senior-level visits and consultations between the two countries were immediately suspended, and Prime Minister Clark made it clear that she considered a formal apology to be appropriate for this breach of New Zealand sovereignty and international law. That apology was eventually forthcoming one year later. The New Zealand Government also provided strong support to UN efforts to negotiate a settlement of the Middle East crisis that resulted from the conflict in Lebanon in mid-2006. Substantial budgetary increases for the New Zealand Agency for International Development (NZAID), the agency founded in 2002 to co-ordinate and disseminate New Zealand's overseas aid, in the 2007/08 financial year ensured the continuation of humanitarian assistance through international relief agencies working in countries such as Iraq, Somalia, Ethiopia, Kenya, Sudan and Nepal.

The New Zealand Prime Minister's presence at a meeting of the Pacific Islands Forum held in Fiji in early 2002 indicated a renewal of closer relations with that country following its return to democracy. New Zealand expressed disquiet about the level of ongoing violence and civil disorder in Solomon Islands (see above), and about the political unrest that surrounded the general election in Papua New Guinea in mid-2002, concerns that were shared by other Pacific nations. New Zealand also welcomed Australia's increased level of commitment to political and economic development in the Pacific, reflected at the meeting of the Pacific Islands Forum hosted by New Zealand in August 2003. Prime Minister Clark attended the subsequent Pacific Islands Forum meeting held in Apia, Samoa, in August 2004, at which members acknowledged the urgent need for preventive measures against the further spread of HIV/AIDS in the region. At the October 2005 Forum, held in Madang, Papua New Guinea, leaders endorsed the Pacific Plan for strengthening regional co-operation and integration; and adopted a new agreement establishing the Pacific Islands Forum as an intergovernmental organization under international law. Tokelau, which in February 2006 and again in October 2007 voted to remain a New Zealand territory, continued to attend these annual meetings as an observer. The New Zealand Government condemned Cdre Frank (Voreqe) Bainimarama's seizure of power in Fiji in December 2006 and eventually imposed defence, travel and development sanctions. In June 2007 the New Zealand High Commissioner to Fiji was expelled; a series of reciprocal expulsions followed. Along with other Pacific Forum members, New Zealand continued to advocate the restoration of democratic and constitutional government in Fiji, a regional viewpoint reiterated at the Pacific Forum meeting hosted by Niue in August 2008. The National-led Government continued Labour's stance, express-

ing strong criticism of the Commodore's abrogation of the Fiji Constitution in April 2009, his action against the country's judiciary and the imposition of media restrictions.

Through NZAID the Labour-led Government maintained a substantial financial commitment to co-operation and investment in the Pacific, in addition to providing humanitarian aid, such as the recovery assistance delivered after the April 2007 earthquake and tsunami in Solomon Islands. (The Government also contributed to relief efforts following natural disasters in Myanmar and in the Chinese province of Sichuan in May 2008, and New Zealand provided an additional $NZ500,000 towards UN efforts to relieve food shortages in the Democratic People's Republic of Korea—North Korea.) In July 2008, as a gift on the occasion of the coronation of King George Tupou V of Tonga, the Prime Minister's Tonga Coronation Fellowship was established, in order to foster the leadership and governance skills of future generations of island leaders. Similar schemes exist with Samoa, South Korea and Latin America. In December 2008 the National-led Government announced a grant of $NZ1.5m. to support the public education initiatives and democratic reform process in Tonga through the work of the Tongan Constitutional and Electoral Commission, and elections took place in the islands in November 2010. Other co-operation in the Pacific included New Zealand's participation in a multilateral health care initiative for the people of Papua New Guinea, as part of the Pacific Partnership 2008 humanitarian and development project. NZAID links with Papua New Guinea were also recognized in a strategy agreement, signed in July 2008, to improve education and employment opportunities for the latter's citizens.

The strengthening of New Zealand's relationships with Asian countries was signalled in July 2008 with the signing of a free trade agreement with China and the decision to appoint an ambassador to the Association of Southeast Asian Nations (ASEAN). New Zealand's 2008 budget also included a substantial funding increase of approximately $NZ600m. for foreign affairs and trade, designed to redress the adverse effects of the retrenchments of the late 1980s and early 1990s, when, for example, diplomatic posts were closed in Austria, Bahrain, Greece, Peru and Zimbabwe. Formal representation in North American and Australian states has also been deemed to be inadequate, particularly in view of the large numbers of New Zealanders migrating to Australia. In 2008 the establishment of an embassy in Sweden marked the first formal New Zealand representation in the Nordic countries. The proposed 50% increase in the number of diplomats and support staff over the following five years was intended to enhance the country's capacity to engage more effectively in a global context. Visits to New Zealand in January 2009 by the Dutch and South Korean Ministers of Foreign Affairs reflected the new Government's endorsement of this emphasis, although the budget constraints that followed the two Canterbury earthquakes subsequently limited some of these plans. However, the change to NZAID's semi-autonomous status within the Ministry of Foreign Affairs and Trade, and the insistence that aid, as an important component of foreign affairs, should align as much as possible with wider foreign policy interests, and prioritize sustainable economic growth programmes and the Pacific region, were criticized by non-governmental aid agencies, which preferred the previous, more independent, approach. The National-led Government reiterated its stance. However, such objectives needed to take priority when administering the $NZ500m. aid budget, while New Zealand was required to look to increasing its representation in the emerging economies, such as China, India and Brazil.

The peace-keeping orientation of New Zealand defence and foreign policies was emphasized in February 2008, when the country hosted a large international disarmament conference to ban cluster munitions. Attended by 560 delegates from 124 countries, the Wellington Conference on Cluster Munitions was one of several held since the inaugural meeting in Oslo, Norway, in February 2007. Together with the other core states of Norway, Austria, Peru, Mexico, the Holy See and Ireland, New Zealand delegates assisted in the formulation of a treaty to ban the use of the weapons that had caused such civilian trauma and hardship in recent years. The adverse legacy of past wars was also addressed domestically when, in May 2008, Prime Minister Helen Clark delivered a formal apology on behalf of the Crown to the veterans of the Viet Nam war and their families. Tribute08, as the commemoration was known, honoured the 3,500 troops who had served in the Viet Nam conflict. It was acknowledged that their service and subsequent health concerns had not hitherto been recognized.

The brief visit of the US Secretary of State, Condoleezza Rice, in July 2008 and that of the Australian Prime Minister, Kevin Rudd, in August reflected the close interactions that have been maintained and developed despite the failure of the formal ANZUS alliance. New Zealand's growing connection with Latin American countries was demonstrated by the visit of Chile's Minister of Foreign Affairs in July, an expression of the Trans-Pacific Strategic Economic Partnership of Chile, New Zealand, Singapore and Brunei, formed to facilitate trade and economic engagement with Chile.

Barack Obama's election as President of the USA in November 2008 was welcomed at both official and popular levels. The New Zealand Minister of Foreign Affairs, Murray McCully, met with Rice's successor, Hillary Clinton, in April 2009, while in Washington, DC, for a meeting of Antarctic Treaty members. During his first official visit to China in April 2009 Prime Minister John Key confirmed New Zealand's commitment to the consolidation of the bilateral trading relationship. Closer relationships with the USA were manifested by Secretary of State Clinton's visit to New Zealand in November 2010. The ensuing Wellington Declaration committed both countries to work more closely together on practical projects in the Pacific region. it also signalled regular senior-level political dialogue, as demonstrated subsequently by Key's meeting with President Obama at the White House in July 2011.

In May 2010 the Maori Party co-leader, Dr Pita Sharples, signed, on behalf of the New Zealand Government, the UN Declaration on the Rights of Indigenous Peoples. Labour's refusal to endorse the document had been strongly criticized by Maori commentators. However, the National Party expressed its support following a reassurance from the Crown Law Office that the Declaration had no binding authority over domestic policy. In August former Prime Minister Sir Geoffrey Palmer was appointed to chair a UN inquiry into the Israeli military operation against a Gaza-bound aid flotilla in May, during which nine pro-Palestinian Turkish activists were killed.

In September 2011 New Zealand hosted the 40th annual Pacific Islands Forum meeting in Auckland (timed to conclude just as the Rugby World Cup tournament began). Minister of Foreign Affairs McCully visited Vanuatu and Solomon Islands in June, and undertook a Pacific Mission to Tonga, Samoa, the Cook Islands and Niue in July, to discuss regional issues and priorities for the Forum. This emphasis on the Pacific nations in New Zealand's foreign policy and aid programmes reflected the growing proportion of Pasifika people in the country's population.

Economy

KENNETH E. JACKSON

Based on an earlier article by J. W. ROWE

New Zealand is best described as a small, open economy centred on two main islands. According to the last census of 7 March 2006, its population was 4,027,947, rising to an estimated 4,405,300 by mid-2011. The next census was scheduled for March 2011, but this was postponed owing to the Christchurch earthquakes. Although the overall performance of the economy was affected by the earthquake disasters, the impact was not as adverse as it might have been, since the recent recession had left a legacy of some spare capacity to replace damaged and destroyed assets, both public and private. The country's renowned advocacy for, and implementation of, a regime of deregulation, free trade and liberalized investment have remained in place since the mid-1980s, under governments of both the left and the right. Government debt is still low relative to GDP, at around 26% in 2011, making it the fourth lowest among the member countries of the Organisation for Economic Co-operation and Development (OECD), which means that New Zealand is far better placed than Japan to cope with such climatic or natural disasters.

New Zealand is far distant from its traditional markets and relatively distant from its nearest major market, Australia. Export receipts continue to be concentrated upon a very narrow range of primary products. These have been subject to considerable fluctuations in prices, which have been largely determined externally. Overseas market access for agricultural products has increased over time, although current volatile exchange rates have added to commodity price volatility and consequent uncertainty. Despite the liberalization resulting from the establishment of the World Trade Organization (WTO), restrictions on New Zealand exports have remained problematic on the demand side from time to time; an example of this was the protracted dispute over New Zealand apple exports to Australia, which was resolved in 2010. Drought and other constraints on output have intermittently affected supply. The internal market has been restricted by physical obstacles and by the low density of population over much of the country. By the beginning of August 2011 the value of the New Zealand dollar had risen to around 80 US cents, or some 10% above its level of a year earlier, and significantly above the low point of 50 cents recorded in March 2009.

New Zealand's relationship with overseas markets has long been regarded as the cornerstone of the economy, with the farming sector as its basis. Consequently, there is a perceived vulnerability resulting from any potential significant loss of agricultural export receipts. In contrast to its recent liberalization, the New Zealand economy has shown a decline in openness in the very long term. Trade-income ratios have altered substantially since the early 20th century, having decreased to less than 20% of gross domestic product (GDP) by the early 1970s. By 2011 figures suggested that the trade-income ratio was slightly more than 30%, indicating some continuing recovery in trade levels following the difficult conditions of 2008/09; however, this was still not a high level by the standards of a typical small trading country. The growth and development of the economy had come to rely on internal as much as external factors. The low trade-income ratio also reflects a possible explanation of the lessened relative impact of the international financial crisis of 2008/09 on New Zealand. Nevertheless, a technical recession was experienced in New Zealand, where negative growth was exhibited for five successive quarters through to June 2009. The volatility in exchange rates and local stock markets in August 2011 demonstrated that contagion could spread rapidly and effectively.

Debate has continued over the causes of New Zealand's relatively poor macroeconomic performance in comparison with the average of the other OECD countries, and compared with the Australian experience in particular. In the 20th century New Zealand's annual growth rate averaged approximately 1.6%, a figure more similar to that of Argentina than that of the countries normally thought of as being in the same grouping, such as Australia, Canada or the United Kingdom. Australia generally outperforms New Zealand, with wage and corporate tax rate differentials causing perennial concern in political circles, although more recently wage differentials of over 30% have aroused even greater concern. Incomes in New Zealand declined to a position of 22nd in OECD rankings in 2007 (a position it maintained in 2011), as the country's macroeconomic performance began to weaken in comparison with its previous strong growth. Despite the five successive quarterly contractions mentioned above, an overall GDP decline of only 3.0% was recorded for that period. From mid-2009 a weak recovery seemed to be in evidence, with a small rate of GDP growth being recorded in each quarter. In mid-2011 any economic recovery was not the primary cause of inflation; the increase in goods and services tax (GST) in October 2010 raised the rate of inflation above the Reserve Bank of New Zealand's (RBNZ's) target range of 1%–3% (see below), to 5.3%. Migration figures had little or no impact on population growth, with net migration gains of only 3,900 for the year to June 2011. Immigrants continued to settle mainly in the Auckland area. By mid-2011 the RBNZ official cash rate (OCR) stood at 2.5%, having been reduced earlier in the year as the economic recovery faltered in the aftermath of the Christchurch earthquakes. Unless migration levels and economic activity recover, the immediate inflationary threat seems limited.

The development of the New Zealand economy since the initiation of the 1984 reform programme had shown a continuation of many of the previous characteristic features, such as relatively slow growth rates and comparatively high real interest rates, along with a propensity to import (which inclines the economy towards a deficit on the current account of the balance of payments). By March 2011 the current account deficit reached approximately 4% of GDP on an annual basis, with a positive trade balance being offset by net investment and other financial outflows.

Despite the post-1984 campaign for extensive deregulation of the economy, involving deregulation of financial institutions, liberalization of shopping hours and liquor-licensing laws, delicensing of the internal transport system and the meat-processing industry, and the removal of the last vestiges of import licensing, longer-term economic growth rates showed no significant improvement. Farm subsidies were discontinued, and many state trading activities were corporatized, if not privatized. The National Party-led Government promised further privatization, through asset sales and deregulation, if it were re-elected in November 2011. The deregulation model had its critics, but whether other models and prescriptions would have performed any better remained debatable.

The policy measures adopted from 1984, starting with the deregulation of financial and foreign exchange sectors of the New Zealand economy, were part of a broader range of policies avowedly intended to promote more rapid economic adjustment. Not all the desirable aims were, in fact, achieved immediately. Fiscal balance and then a fiscal surplus were accomplished, but only in the longer term. The taxation system was radically altered with the introduction of GST and the reduction of marginal income tax rates on higher incomes. The Government attempted to take a secondary role in economic matters, regarding its function as one of encouraging the efficient operation of markets, competition and an economy able to respond quickly and flexibly to changing circumstances and demands. Initially, a burgeoning fiscal deficit emerged, as taxation revenue stagnated while welfare spending rose. Restructuring resulted in excessive unemployment, at least in the short term, with regional, age and skill disparities appearing in the unemployment figures. Youth unemployment remained a long-term issue of concern.

The pace of liberalization accelerated from late 1990. Greater emphasis was placed on decreasing the fiscal deficit and further reducing inflation, while the Employment Contracts Act (ECA) marked a major shift in negotiating power in the labour market. It reintroduced voluntary unionism and union membership halved. The ECA was claimed to have produced greater flexibility in the labour market, resulting in a significant stimulus to employment and production, notably for export. With the particular impact of individual measures being difficult to distinguish, however, analysis of the overall outcome proved difficult to undertake. At the macro-level the figures were confusing and the choice of start date or benchmark for comparison was an important determinant of the eventual result. Subsequent consequential amendments to the employment law have been made, such as those enacted in October 2000 through the Employment Relations Act, which, among other measures, restored a greater role for collective agreements. In March 2009 a probationary employment period of three months for new employees was introduced, affecting many workplaces.

Close monitoring continued of other public costs, such as health and education, along with institutional changes intended to improve service delivery and accountability. From the early 1990s consistent efforts were undertaken to improve economic performance. Between 1993 and 1996 the economy performed strongly, with unemployment declining and fiscal balance being achieved by mid-1994, largely owing to buoyant tax revenues, but also to spending restraint. A policy of allocating priority to the repayment of overseas public debt from these fiscal surpluses was then implemented, thus improving the country's international credit rating.

Economic problems re-emerged in 1996–97, albeit less serious than those of the 1970s and 1980s. The strength of the New Zealand dollar in the mid-1990s and high interest rates curbed the growth of exports and production generally, while inflation rose slightly. Some decline in the exchange rate gave exporters a boost. Parliamentarians conducted the introduction of the new electoral system of mixed-member proportional representation (MMP, see History) in an unstable manner, which was not highly conducive to economic growth. Economic instability was exacerbated in 1998 by the adverse effects of the Asian financial crisis, which was particularly damaging to the tourism and forestry sectors. Recovery in 1998 and 1999 was somewhat slow and halting, as well as uneven, both geographically and sectorally. A revision of some of the previous reforms emerged following the 1999 election of a new Government, with further reviews occurring after the 2002 general election. The methods and targets of the RBNZ remained under some question, including demands for further rate reductions in 2003 from manufacturers, exporters and trade unions. The changes from a quantity-type control to an interest rate control developed during 1999 and 2000, with the original target band of price inflation being set at 0%–2%, subsequently amended to 1%–3%.The global financial crisis resulted in a lowering of the OCR in 2008/09, to 2.5%. However, it was increased to 2.75% in June 2010, with a further rise, to 3.0%, in July. Difficulties in early 2011 led to a reduction to 2.5%, with little or no prospect of any immediate change until the end of the year. Stability in the OCR contrasted with the volatility shown in the foreign exchange rate and the level of prices on the stock market.

AGRICULTURE, FORESTRY AND FISHING

Agriculture

Farming and associated processing industries play a greater part in the New Zealand economy than in most developed countries. The historic concentration on pastoral products for export income arose partly from preferential access to a large market, the United Kingdom, but production was also favoured by a benign climate. Since soil fertility is not generally high, a scientific approach to the improvement of soil productivity and of stock-breeding and management has been necessary, together with a heavy reliance on (imported) phosphatic fertilizers. Diversification into niche manufacturing and service industries has taken place, contrasting with the traditional manufacturing activity for the small domestic market, with its protection by distance and government intervention. The agricultural sector, along with tourism, has remained fundamentally important for external trade; of necessity, farming is acknowledged to be highly efficient by world standards. Capital intensity, in the guise of large farm size and a high degree of mechanization, has been a major factor in maintaining the international competitiveness of agricultural and pastoral production. Capital intensity is also accompanied by a relatively small proportion of the labour force being directly engaged in agricultural production.

Dairying is the most important sector of farming in New Zealand. Favourable factors have been product and market diversification, increasing average farm size and concentration of processing in a few very large plants. The New Zealand Dairy Board, which had previously played a vital role in improving efficiency in dairying, both on-farm and off-farm, was replaced in 2001 by a new organization, Globalco, which subsequently began trading under the new name of Fonterra, one of the biggest such concerns in the world. By the beginning of the second decade of the 21st century Fonterra accounted for more than 40% of global dairy sales; production was no longer confined to New Zealand farms, and restructuring of the ownership of the organization was under active discussion, with limited share trading proposals being negotiated. Issues relating to overseas competitors' fears of cross-subsidization of export production, as well as local concerns over the long-term implications for efficiency and competition, were expressed at the time of the co-operative's introduction, but farmers largely supported the move. Payments to dairy farmers increased significantly in 2009/10 and have fluctuated since then, as have the underlying export prices for dairy products. Internal concerns led to the announcement of the establishment of a select committee of inquiry into domestic retail milk prices in August 2011. The growth of subsidies by overseas governments also remains an issue affecting prices, with OECD estimating that, in the aftermath of the financial recession, member countries as a whole had increased subsidies, especially to dairy producers, as a result of which 22% of farm receipts were from subsidies. Moreover, concerns have been raised in recent years over foreign purchases of New Zealand dairy farms, but such activity is to be expected in a truly global environment.

Dairy farming has expanded into South Island, in many cases using irrigated pasture, resulting in serious problems regarding water resources. Pastoral farming has remained of major significance, being predominantly export-orientated. Problems of access to some overseas markets, consumer concerns over 'food miles' and limited progress in the processing of products have restricted profitability. Cropping, fruit-growing and horticulture have increased in importance, and there has been a major expansion of viticulture, with significant exports of wine, although New Zealand accounts for only 0.6% of global export receipts. The 2009 grape harvest produced an excellent crop. The value of the crop was reduced by some 7% in 2010, when the harvest decreased to 266,000 metric tons. This decline was then reversed, with more than 300,000 metric tons of grapes produced in the 2011 harvest, a 13% rise in comparison with 2010. The value of wine exports rose by 27% in the 12 months to mid-2010. Fluctuating grape crops have traditionally affected the rate of growth of wine production. The problem of inconsistent production capacity existed previously in this industry, but the development of major producers in newer regions helped to improve the situation. The continuing growth in Asian demand has also been beneficial for producers. Wine accounted for more than 2.5% of total goods export receipts in 2010.

Restructuring of the agricultural sector has been ongoing since the mid-1980s, as part of the programme of economic reform. Despite diversification elsewhere in the economy, exports of farm products of all kinds continued to account for a substantial percentage of total exports and for much of the growth in exports witnessed since 1999. New Zealand's leading export commodities decreased in value in 2009, with cheese, milk powder, casein and butter registering the largest declines, despite an increase in export quantities over the period. This situation was partly turned around in 2009/10, with a dairy products revival leading the way. The most remarkable feature has been the final demise of the country's erstwhile staple wool trade, which by 2010 had declined to 10th place on the list of the country's export products by value. In 2011 exports receipts for commodities increased, the balance of trade registered strong surpluses, and the terms of trade continued to demonstrate the long-term improvement of previous years.

New Zealand welcomed the successful conclusion in December 1993 of the 'Uruguay Round' of GATT negotiations, and actively participated in subsequent bilateral negotiations, which on the whole were reasonably successful. However, agricultural protectionism in Japan, the European Union (EU) and elsewhere remained a problem. In the 12 months to mid-2011 New Zealand continued its extensive and active efforts with regard to bilateral and regional trade agreements, focusing particularly on the Trans-Pacific Partnership agreement, in the absence of any conclusion of WTO agreements. The effective implementation of existing arrangements remained as important an issue for New Zealand as the conclusion of new agreements. Furthermore, there were concerns over the introduction of various measures, which appeared to be tantamount to trade protectionism but were implemented under the guise of environmental protection, especially 'food miles' and associated 'buy local' campaigns in many countries. Although the National Party's revised Emissions Trading Scheme to counter carbon emissions was introduced in late 2009, this appeared to have had little or no discernible impact upon the farming sector by mid-2011.

Forestry

Most parts of New Zealand were still heavily forested when European settlers arrived, although substantial areas had been deforested during the centuries of Maori occupation. Today large tracts remain in indigenous forest, although mainly in rugged terrain. Large-scale clearance of forest cover was utilized for pastoral expansion. Timber from forest clearance was originally used for ships' masts, then as inputs into farming through fencing and construction, a process that extended to urban construction and, later, export to Australia, to supply Melbourne in its late 19th-century building boom for dwellings. In the last decades of the 19th century, clearance was so rapid that much of the timber was burned rather than used.

Today plantation-grown *Pinus radiata* (radiata pine), along with other introduced species, has largely replaced indigenous timber for production purposes. *Pinus radiata*, which in New Zealand produces logs suitable for milling within 25–30 years, also provides the raw material for a widening range of manufactured products—pulp and paper, paperboard and compressed boards of various sorts, as well as exports of sawlogs on a considerable scale. From 1996 there was a major increase in the quantity of wood available for export. The forestry industry's contribution to export earnings has increased, and in 2010 forestry exports accounted for more than 8% of total merchandise export earnings. In the 12 months to mid-2011 timber production rose by 20% and export receipts from the sector were anticipated to exceed $NZ4,000m., although processing capacity expansion continued to require heavy investment. Utilizing plants with spare capacity is relatively straightforward, but significant new expansion is another matter. There was also extensive planting of *Pinus radiata* for land stabilization and environmental, as well as for production, purposes. These underlying developments indicated that forestry should continue to be important in the years ahead. The role of forestry as a carbon sink to mitigate the impact of environmental and climate change is also seen as important, particularly in the emerging debates about the carbon tax and emissions trading schemes.

Legislation relating to native forests increased the level of protection of old-growth forests so that the felling of indigenous trees was significantly reduced, mainly for heritage and conservation reasons. Farm forestry, combining both aesthetic and economic considerations, has reduced the vulnerability of pastoral farming to fluctuations in meat and wool prices. It has also made better use of marginal land and was instrumental in protecting some hill farms from erosion problems. Forestry development was one of the few areas where tax advantages were to be found in New Zealand's deregulated, non-interventionist atmosphere. However, the long-term nature of the investment still tends to deter many potential participants.

Fishing

New Zealand has a wide variety of fish in waters around its long coastline, and many of these are now recognized to be commercially valuable species. The Territorial Sea and Exclusive Economic Zone Act of 1978 gave the country control over the fisheries resources in more than 4m. sq km (1.3m. nautical sq miles) of sea surrounding New Zealand territory, or approximately 13 times the land area of New Zealand. Joint ventures with foreign partners have contributed substantially to the development of the industry, especially in the trawl fisheries of deeper waters. There has also been continuing growth in the domestic finfish industry. Exports of fish were valued at more than $NZ1,500m. in 2009/10, or some 70 times the value of earnings in the early 1970s. Poaching and organized smuggling of paua (abalone) has emerged as a serious threat to the sustained development of such activity. Opposition to bottom-trawling methods by environmentalist groups such as Greenpeace, and by British supermarkets under some pressure from environmental and consumer groups, has also emerged as an issue for the sector.

Since the 1980s fish and shellfish farming and processing have continued to develop, although disputes over property rights in the seabed and foreshore areas (see History) have led to increased uncertainty in the industry. Aquaculture production has been directed primarily at the export market, although an enterprising development on North Island resulted in exotic prawn farming utilizing heated waste water from a geothermal electricity station as an input. With an output of more than 30 metric tons per year, the operation has sold most of its produce on site to domestic and overseas tourists, rather than moving into export sales. Trout, introduced from the northern hemisphere, have not so far been directly commercially exploited, but salmon are farmed, as well as fished recreationally, in parts of the country. Aquaculture, principally involving the production of greenshell mussels, King salmon and Pacific oysters, has become a significant part of total fisheries output. By 2010/11 its total export value was estimated at some $NZ287m., with the direct employment of some 3,000 people. Transferable quota arrangements, introduced in 1986, were developed as a way of dealing with issues relating to the long-term sustainability of common property rights to fish stocks. Allocation of quota to Maori was also undertaken as part of the Treaty of Waitangi process (see History).

MINING

Mining of metallic minerals is limited except for titanomagnetic ironsands from the west coast of North Island, which were exploited originally for export but subsequently also for local steel production. Efforts to revive mining for precious metals, including gold, have been remarkably successful, boosted by strong prices (particularly gold prices), although such operations are capital-intensive and have encountered problems in meeting environmental protection requirements in many cases. From 1991 the Resource Management Act covering environmental requirements made compliance a more expensive undertaking for the mining sector, as well as for many other activities. Government aerial surveys of mineral resources were undertaken in 2010, but proposals for exploratory mining in protected conservation estate encountered substantial public opposition and have been scaled back.

Coal production for use within New Zealand is relatively low, being used mainly by thermal power stations. Initiatives to limit thermal stations, thereby decreasing domestic use of coal even further, have been undertaken. In January 2009, however, the 10-year ban on the construction of new thermal stations was repealed, in order to secure the country's supply of electricity. Household consumption of coal is insignificant. New Zealand has substantial coal reserves, but their economic utilization has not been high. Japan, Chile, India and the People's Republic of China have been the principal export markets. A major loss of life as the result of a coal mine explosion on the West Coast of South Island in November

2010 (see History) affected both production and confidence in the safety practices of the industry.

Natural gas has become increasingly important, especially since the onshore supply was supplemented by offshore gas from the large Maui field, some of which is utilized in the production of synthetic petrol and in thermal power stations. For many years drilling companies failed to make any significant petroleum discoveries, but there are now several onshore producing wells, which together have made a small, yet significant, contribution to meeting New Zealand's oil demands. Concerns were heightened in the mid-2000s over the depletion rates of known reserves. However, the situation changed with the coming on stream of the offshore Tui field in 2007. New Zealand thus produced the equivalent of 35%–40% of its own total usage, although 90% of the petroleum produced was exported rather than consumed locally. Revenue from oil was the fastest growing of all export receipts in 2007/08, albeit from a relatively small base. However, fluctuations in oil prices affected these receipts, resulting in a decline in 2008/09, although they recovered in 2010–11. Nevertheless, oil production has remained static, having declined slightly from a 2008 peak of 52,000 barrels per day. New Zealand's crude petroleum is said to be valued highly in comparison with standard benchmark crudes, and new fields—both onshore and offshore—have helped to sustain oil and gas output.

MANUFACTURING AND CONSTRUCTION

Most of the country's larger industrial enterprises are export-orientated and process pastoral products (milk, livestock and wool), natural gas, logs or ironsand, but there is also a large aluminium smelter using imported alumina. Other major enterprises based on imported raw materials confronted increasing import competition from the 1980s, and some enterprises closed down as border protections were reduced or removed. The global WTO, and the regional grouping Asia-Pacific Economic Cooperation (APEC), as well as the bilateral Closer Economic Relations (CER) agreement with Australia, all played a part in this process, but successive New Zealand governments consistently moved towards the progressive removal of tariffs and non-tariff barriers. This included a unilateral programme aimed at increasing the competitive environment in the domestic market. It also led many manufacturers to relocate their operations off shore. Others became more specialized, while diversification was evident in the expansion of non-traditional manufactured exports. New Zealand has followed the universal trend towards regional and bilateral trade arrangements. Agreements have been concluded with several countries, notably including a major free trade agreement signed with China in 2008.

Since 2008 the Government has acted to increase the levels of openness and expand trade agreements. New Zealand already had fewer non-tariff barriers to imports than was the case in many other countries. Of equal and renewed importance in the period 2008–11 was the issue of the exchange rate, more particularly in relation to the US dollar, which tended to inhibit manufactured exports. The overall trade-weighted exchange rate index declined in mid-2008, before increasing again through to June 2011, at which time volatility increased. Greater trans-Tasman integration has continued, with the ongoing implementation of common food regulations with Australia. However, attempts to gain a single trans-Tasman approach to regulation of non-prescription therapeutic and medical products failed as a result of significant political opposition, as did a proposal to add folic acid to most bread supplies. Achieving easier access to the greater Australian market, combined with improved efficiency, remained important factors for New Zealand's secondary industrial development. The role of PHARMAC, the central purchasing authority for pharmaceuticals, has continued to be a matter of issue in trade negotiations with the USA.

The construction industry in New Zealand has three distinct sectors: the residential construction sector, traditionally timber-framed in single units; commercial and industrial construction, which also uses timber framing as well as steel and concrete; and civil engineering. The Building Activity Survey recorded strong increases from 2000 and into the first half of 2003, despite public and political concern about the so-called 'leaky building syndrome' and a resultant reversion to the use of treated timber for framing and other regulatory changes. By contrast, by 2008/09 the buoyancy in house prices had faltered, as was the case in most OECD countries. The consequences for the construction industry and for household wealth were significant. Global financial linkages to sub-prime mortgage problems (originating in the inability of US borrowers to meet their repayment obligations) affected lending institutions, while fears of substantial decreases in prices and the ongoing effects of the local 'leaky building syndrome' combined to produce a downturn in the New Zealand housing market. Fears exceeded the reality of price decreases, which proved to be somewhat limited. Commercial and industrial construction activity remained strongly positive during 2008, but sales activity declined in the subsequent 12 months. Seasonally adjusted consent figures for June 2009 recorded the lowest monthly level for 21 months, and by June 2010 non-residential consents had decreased in value by more than 18% in comparison with the previous year. Declines in consents continued through to mid-2011. The increase in the residential figures between June 2009 and June 2010 represented only a partial compensation for the industry and to some extent reflected the previous decrease in activity in this sector in 2008, rather than indicating a substantial long-term recovery. It is true to say that any rises in price for existing dwellings in 2011 have been confined to specific locations within particular cities and regions, rather than exhibiting a general national trend.

INFRASTRUCTURE

Energy

New Zealand has substantial hydroelectric generating potential, although limited storage capacity is a weakness, revealed by substantial rises in the 'spot' price at times of shortage, as in the winter of early 2001, and at times of acute shortage, as in 2011 when it appeared that a weak market might be subject to speculative activity. Despite negative forecasts and low lake levels, there were no significant electricity shortages in 2007/08. From 2009 to 2011 lake levels were generally high, resulting in the need to release excess water at times, with lower 'spot' prices appearing in the market. Electricity output reached more than 43,000 GWh per year, with renewable resources such as hydroelectricity and wind power normally contributing approximately 60%–70% of the total. The main thermal stations are fired by a variety of fuels; there are also two large and some smaller geothermal stations contributing some 10% of total output. In 2011 proposals for tidal power were experiencing local opposition, but trial plants seemed likely to proceed. Two-way direct current cables link the two main islands. Although the age and capacity of parts of the system have been called into question, most of the country is served by the grid, even relatively remote areas, as a result of previous subsidized extensions to rural networks.

In a major departure from tradition, in 1989 generation of electricity was separated from the operation of the grid to encourage non-state generation. Until the 1980s such private involvement had been hampered, if not prohibited directly, by government regulation. These changes at the wholesale level were accompanied by the corporatization and some privatization of 'power boards', which previously handled the retail distribution of most electricity. With the development of a wholesale electricity market, electricity retail companies were placed in apparent competition with one another, although the reality was that with existing technology this was difficult to make effective for small consumers. To assist consumers, the supply of so-called smart metering was partially implemented in 2010. In an attempt to control the abuse of monopoly power in the retail market, separate transmission-line companies and retail energy companies were formed. Further refinements to the regulatory system allowed some vertical integration, while attempting to ensure the separating out of the natural monopoly elements of the wholesale and retail distribution networks from generation and retail supply. In 2003, in a further attempt to control monopoly power, the Electricity Commission had been established to regulate and supervise the sector. Various disagreements arose between the regulator and the utility operators, particularly with respect to the national grid. Disputes over retail price rises, which by 2010 had approximately doubled over the previous decade, continued, with electricity generators urging a further increase in prices as a means of raising more funds for new generating capacity. The Electricity Commission was replaced by the Electricity Authority in November 2010. However, the new authority was required to address similar issues to those of its predecessor, as well as having to deal with disputes over volatile 'spot' prices.

Since 1973 considerable efforts have been made to reduce the country's dependence on petroleum products, both crude and refined. Measures such as the expansion and modification of the existing petroleum refinery, the conversion of natural gas to methanol as feed stock for the refinery and moves towards more efficient energy use and use of biofuels for transport have all been employed at various times, to achieve this aim. The substantial increases in international petroleum prices of 2005/06, 2007/08 and 2010/11 have led to demands for further diversification away from a dependence on oil. Such developments, together with rising production from onshore and offshore gas and petroleum wells (see above), and the switch from oil to coal and gas in thermal power stations, greatly increased energy self-sufficiency. Not all of the efforts of the early 1970s were economically sound initiatives, with some developments failing to be subjected to adequate project appraisal in the haste to save on imported energy costs. More recently, energy policy debates have placed a greater emphasis on the reduction of carbon dioxide emissions and their offset by large-scale afforestation in line with predictions of global warming. Discussion continued with regard to the merits or otherwise of New Zealand's ratification of the Kyoto Protocol in 2002 and also the implications of the inconclusive conference held in Copenhagen, Denmark, at the end of 2009. From 2005/06 rising oil prices led to attention being refocused on sustainable alternatives. Wind power was particularly favoured as an alternative source of power, although wind farms had their opponents, especially with regard to their visual impact on some settings. Biofuel production was also the subject of some critical discussion.

Transport and Communications

Historically, the central Government was heavily and directly involved in transport, as with other areas of infrastructure, through its ownership of New Zealand Rail, Air New Zealand and the Shipping Corporation. All were privatized, although Air New Zealand was largely renationalized in October 2001, following the failure of Ansett, its Australian subsidiary carrier. In 2002 the Government held an 82% stake in Air New Zealand, although this had been reduced to 73.7% by 2011. A third major airline, Pacific Blue (a subsidiary of Virgin Blue), began domestic operations within New Zealand in 2007; however, it withdrew from the domestic market in August 2010. Air New Zealand and the remaining international part of Pacific Blue, along with Virgin Australia, entered into an alliance agreement in July 2011, as part of a continuing restructuring within the industry. Direct responsibility for the management of Qantas operations in New Zealand was ceded to Qantas's low-cost carrier, Jetstar, in mid-2009.

The Government has remained involved in transport regulation, notably through the New Zealand Transport Agency, which was formed in 2008 following the merger of Land Transport New Zealand and Transit New Zealand, which previously held responsibility for road safety and main highways, respectively. In mid-1998 debates began with regard to how to apply 'user pays' principles to land transport and how to restructure it. These proposals, which were ongoing in 2011, involved toll roads and moves for public-private partnership approaches. In mid-2009 heavier truck weight limits were proposed for greater efficiency in freight carriage. In other areas of transport, major airports were privatized or corporatized, and in 2007 the public reaction to suggestions of a sale of shares in the Auckland Airport Company clearly demonstrated a strong resistance to foreign ownership. Following a review of the Overseas Investment Act, in September 2010 the Government decided not to amend the legislation, but instead introduced several measures aimed at providing additional clarity and assurances to potential foreign investors, while also safeguarding New Zealand's economic interests.

Reform of port operations was largely complete by the mid-1990s, a period during which transport became more efficient and competitive. Well into the 21st century, however, shipping and air services across the Tasman Sea remained far from totally liberalized. The introduction of new carriers into the trans-Tasman service, such as Emirates (of the United Arab Emirates) in mid-2003, and subsequent low-cost airline competition, as well as a change in Air New Zealand pricing structures, increased the competitive environment.

From the late 1980s equally dramatic changes took place in communications, with the subsequent privatization of telecommunications and the corporatization of postal services. Historically, the Post Office in New Zealand, as a government department, handled postal services and various collections on behalf of other government agencies, as well as telecommunications. It also operated a savings bank catering mainly for small depositors. The Government separated telecommunications services and later re-established banking operations under Kiwibank, which was founded in 2001. NZ Post remained a 'stand-alone', but still state-owned, enterprise, although its monopoly of mail services was removed. National Post and other competitors initially appeared, offering household delivery and separate on-street mail collection boxes. This competition subsequently largely withdrew from the market, as the letter post continued to contract as a result of the increasing use of new communications technology. More recently, the biggest problem in communications has been the slow speed and non-availability of broadband services to much of New Zealand, which again has been viewed as ranking poorly by OECD standards in this regard. Change is only slowly being accomplished, although major upgrades and extensions of broadband services were being planned in 2011.

SERVICE INDUSTRIES

The increase in complexity of the economy has been accompanied by a steady growth in the proportion of the labour force in service industries, some of which rendered specialist services to primary and secondary industries as well as to the community in general. This growth was at the expense of manufacturing in particular, but also of the service-like activities of building and construction and transport and communications (see above). Services have been estimated to account for more than two-thirds of GDP by value.

The general tourism sector is a major component of economic activity, providing jobs for around 10% of the population. Economic expansion in industrial countries generated a significant increase in international tourism, from which New Zealand benefited considerably. In 1987/88 tourism, as officially defined, became the single largest source of foreign exchange earnings, its expansion apparently aided by the increased competitiveness of the industry following the liberalization of the labour market. As might be expected given its proximity, Australia has remained the principal source of overseas visitors, providing almost one-half of the total in 2010. Australia was followed by the United Kingdom, the USA, China, Japan and the Republic of Korea (South Korea) and Germany. The crisis of Severe Acute Respiratory Syndrome (SARS, a pneumonia-like virus) in mid-2003 temporarily depressed visitor numbers, which then continued to fluctuate. The year 2008/09 proved particularly difficult, owing to global recession and swine flu (the H1N1 pandemic of 2009), with visitor numbers from Japan and South Korea declining sharply. The number of Japanese visitors for the month of June 2009 was the lowest recorded since June 1985. Total visitor numbers for the years to June 2010 and to June 2011, however, exceeded 2.5m., and 2.7m. visitors were expected during the major event of the Rugby World Cup in September–October 2011. With visitor numbers from Australia and Asia having recovered from the impact of swine flu, the tourism sector was generally stronger in 2011. The services sector, including the various components of the tourism industry, is notoriously difficult to assess in terms of labour productivity, but its expansion is an essential part of modern economic development.

PUBLIC SECTOR

Until 1991/92 the public sector's claim on national resources was inexorably rising. Within the public sector itself, the central Government came under greater pressure to transfer resources to territorial and other local authorities, because the latter lacked the automatically increasing flow of funds that a relatively fixed and progressive (personal) income tax structure so conveniently provides in an era of rising wages and salaries. At the same time, there was a tendency for local or regional authorities to assume responsibility for a greater proportion of total public sector expenditure. This was given further impetus by the extensive reform of local government undertaken in 1989 and again in the early 21st century. The introduction of a so-called 'super city' or unitary governance structure for the greater Auckland region occurred in 2010, perhaps further extending the trend for local government to assume greater responsibilities; however the final form of such structures, and their impact, will take some time to become evident. The Canterbury area of South Island was significantly affected by earthquake damage in and around Christchurch in September 2010 and February 2011 (see History), and this was a major factor for consideration with respect to future public expenditure and prioritization at both the national and regional level.

As in many other countries, central government deficit-financing was adopted in the early 1980s, with deficits averaging the equivalent of 7% of GDP. In 2011 the deficit stood at just over 4% of GDP, there having been a consistent surplus until the 2008/09 global financial crisis. The Government expects a return to surplus in 2014/15. Despite efforts by successive governments, public sector expenditure, including transfers, was equivalent to more than 40% of GDP by the end of 1990, when the National Party took office. By 2011 the proportion was still approximately 38%, although about one-third of payments represented transfers rather than direct expenditure.

Between 1984 and 1990 the Labour Government had initiated wide-ranging reforms in the public sector, notably by corporatizing many enterprises and privatizing others. This process was continued by the National Party Government. Some of the apparent decline in the share of GDP represented by government expenditure was due to the shifting of these enterprises off the government account. Fiscal surpluses were achieved from 1994 (even when the proceeds of asset sales were excluded). By 2008/09, however, reversion to deficit-financing had become necessary. Public sector debt-to-GDP ratios of 26%, the fourth lowest in the OECD, reduce the concern with responses to the earthquake reconstruction work and stimulus to the economy in recessionary times, when compared with other countries. Tax decreases implemented in April 2009 and April 2010, along with reductions in government pre-funding of future superannuation liabilities, were aimed at countering the recession, at the expense of increasing debt levels. Net public sector debt as a percentage of GDP declined through to the end of 2007, when it reached the equivalent of approximately 18%. Household indebtedness increased consistently in the years to 2004, and subsequently maintained a level comparable to that of other developed nations. The low household savings rate in comparison with other OECD countries remained a matter of concern. Overseas debt for 2010/11, was estimated by the RBNZ to represent in excess of 130% of GDP, having reached a total of some $NZ250m., with the overwhelming proportion being private rather than public.

INTERNATIONAL TRADE

Exports and imports of goods and services are usually roughly equivalent in New Zealand, at approximately 30% of GDP, although a persistent balance of payments deficit remained evident in the early 21st century. In the year to March 2011 the current account deficit represented approximately 4.3% of GDP, despite a monthly trade surplus consistently being recorded in the year to mid-2011. Forestry, agricultural and pastoral exports remained a major component of foreign exchange commodity earnings (above 40%), while petroleum and fruit were of increasing relative importance. Exports of manufactures (other than processed primary products) were also growing steadily, along with information and communication technology (ICT) exports, which in the year to mid-2007 had exceeded $NZ1,500m. for the first time. Earnings of New Zealand technology companies operating overseas have become appreciable, although the figures suggested an ICT trade deficit for 2008/09, in contrast to the reverse situation in Australia. In general, about 50% of New Zealand's foreign exchange earnings still came from the exports of just a few companies, a reflection of the small size of the economy, with approximately 95% of companies essentially not being involved in exporting.

Exports became more diversified, as regards both commodity composition and market destination. In 1950 the United Kingdom purchased nearly two-thirds of New Zealand's exports. By the 1980s it had been overtaken by Australia, the USA and Japan, which remained the three principal export markets until 2009. In 2009/10 China replaced Japan, which thus became the fourth largest recipient of New Zealand's exports, followed by the United Kingdom and South Korea. This order was maintained in 2010/11. The growing importance of India as an export market was also notable by 2011. The trend in imports was similar, the principal suppliers being Australia, China, the USA, and Japan, followed by Germany and Singapore. The increasing interdependence of the Australian and New Zealand economies led the respective Governments to implement the CER agreement, signed by the two countries in December 1982, following three years of negotiations. The bilateral trade agreement took effect in January 1983. Its main objective was to encourage the development of economically strong productive structures in both countries. Two basic mechanisms were set in place by the CER agreement: the phasing out of tariffs in both directions; and the progressive elimination of import-licensing and tariff quotas between Australia and New Zealand. By and large, the CER benefited both countries, perhaps more so New Zealand, and mutual undertakings were generally respected. The CER had a larger impact than the preceding agreement, which had required items for liberalization to be included in the list rather than the CER approach, which stipulated the listing of exceptions. CER remains as the basis for increasing economic integration between New Zealand and Australia.

The New Zealand dollar's previously fixed relationship with the US dollar was ended in July 1973, when the authorities introduced a trade-weighted managed daily 'float' involving weighting against the currencies of New Zealand's main trading partners. In July 1984, immediately following the election of a Labour Government, the currency was devalued by 20%. In March 1985 the New Zealand dollar was then freely 'floated', in response to fears of a renewed 'run' on the currency, which had been caused by a sharp upsurge in inflation following devaluation and the end of a freeze of wages and prices. By mid-1986, contrary to the expectation of many people, the currency remained very close to its average value at the time of the flotation, and it continued to fluctuate around this level until 1991, when the trade-weighted index fell appreciably, giving exporters a welcome boost. In 1993 the New Zealand dollar strengthened again, and in particular appreciated markedly *vis-à-vis* the Australian dollar. It also proved remarkably resilient in view of the turbulence in the exchange rate mechanism of the EU in the early 1990s. These phenomena reflected improvement in the New Zealand economy, as well as relatively high real interest rates.

The new-found strength of the New Zealand dollar at that time was no doubt also attributable to the independence enjoyed by the RBNZ and confidence in the fiscal stance of the National Party Government. Thereafter the New Zealand dollar has been volatile; generally it has appreciated further against the US dollar, and it has remained at around 80 Australian cents. Appreciation has helped to contain inflationary pressures, but rendered New Zealand's exports less competitive internationally. By 2001 the New Zealand dollar had declined to a low of 40 US cents, although the cross rate against the Australian currency was rising at the time. The New Zealand dollar stood at 82 Australian cents by August 2001 (similar to levels attained in the first half of 2011). Relief in terms of additional export revenue was somewhat slower to appear than expected, and there were even calls for the introduction of a common trans-Tasman currency in order to obtain a reduction in transaction costs for traders. The New Zealand dollar demonstrated an upward trend against the US dollar, rising to exceed 65 cents in early 2004. In 2007 high interest rates and a strong 'carry trade' out of Japan (a strategy whereby funds are borrowed and interest paid in order to buy elsewhere at a higher interest rate) resulted in a significant rise in the New Zealand dollar against the Japanese yen, but this trade was weakening by the end of July 2007 and exchange rates eased in the 12 months to mid-2008. From the beginning of 2009, however, the New Zealand dollar again moved upwards against most currencies, and at the beginning of August 2011 it was trading above 80 US cents, about 10% higher than 12 months previously.

DOMESTIC ECONOMY

Throughout the 1950s and 1960s the average rate of growth of real GDP was more than 4% per year, which was not much less than the average for OECD countries. New Zealand's performance in the 1970s, particularly after the first sharp rises in international petroleum prices in 1973 and 1974, was comparatively worse than the OECD average, with the terms of trade deteriorating substantially. Between 1975 and 1982 there was virtually no real growth in GDP. Between 1982 and 1987 there was only modest growth, but even this improvement was not sustained. Large fiscal deficits had emerged in the late 1970s and, together with growing external imbalance, acted to create a mounting burden of debt in which the external component was increasingly important. By the early 1980s economic performance—as measured by a wide range of indicators including growth, unemployment, inflation, external deficit, budgetary imbalance and debt—had deteriorated substantially. In real terms, GDP grew by an average annual rate of 2.5% during the 1990s, although in 1998 GDP actually contracted by 0.3%. Signs of a recovery from the recession had emerged by mid-1999, and GDP expanded by an estimated 3.5% for the year as a whole. Growth of 1.8% was achieved in 2000, with a similar figure recorded in 2001, and GDP growth in 2003, at 3.5%, was easily above the then OECD average of 2.2%. This trend continued in 2004–05, but in the first part of 2006 performance began to weaken. Real GDP growth of only 1.7% was registered in the first quarter of 2007, but a recovery thereafter was strong enough to result in an annual growth rate of 3.0% to the end of the first quarter of 2008. However, in mid-2008 growth rates were again negative, with GDP contracting in the five consecutive quarters to June 2009. Between mid-2009 and mid-2011 a recovery, albeit hesitant, became evident, with annual GDP growth amounting to some 2.0% and 1.4%, respectively, over the two 12-month periods.

Throughout most of the post-1945 period there had effectively been full employment in New Zealand. Unemployment, as indicated by conventional measures, remained virtually non-existent in 1970, and it was only in 1978 that the unemployment rate first rose above 1% of the labour force. Thereafter the rate of unemployment increased to significant levels, notably in 1983 and 1992, exceeding 10% in the latter year. Unemployment levels subsequently appeared to stabilize, with growth in employment being more than offset by rising labour force participation. In the 1998 recession the average rate of unemployment again increased, to 7.5% of the work-force; however, the subsequent trend was downwards, and by March 2008 the rate had declined to 3.6%. Owing to the impact of the recession and subsequent negative growth, in the three months to June 2009 the unemployment rate reached 6.0%, reported to be the largest quarterly increase since July–September 1988. Unemployment peaked at 7.1% at the end of 2009, before declining to 6.0% at the end of the first quarter of 2010. Pessimistic opinion suggests that this was more sample aberration than reality—a view that was borne out by subsequent figures, with the unemployment rate in June 2011 being 6.5%. From the 1970s the rate of inflation rose substantially, with the annual rate averaging 4.8% in 1985–95. Lower rates of inflation were recorded thereafter: consumer prices increased by an annual average of 2.3% in 1996, by 1.2% in 1997 and by 1.3% in 1998. By 1999 some commentators had declared inflation to be defunct: in the first quarter of 1999 the consumer price index (CPI) was negative compared with 12 months previously. In June 2008, however, as international prices for many commodities continued to rise, the CPI stood at an annual rate of 4.0%. A year later this figure had more than halved, and at June 2010 it stood at 1.8%. However, the rise expected in late 2010, owing in large part to a planned increase in GST rates in October (see below), was realized, and the annual inflation rate at June 2011 was 5.3%.

Attempts to reduce the budget deficit without increasing the money supply had led to high real interest rates in the 1980s, and these, in turn, sustained the exchange rate. In accordance with a programme of tax reform that was initiated in 1984, a 10% tax on all goods and services became effective from late 1986 (the GST rate was first raised to 12.5% in July 1989, with another increase, to 15.0%, occurring in October 2010). The original introduction of GST was followed by a reduction in the rate of corporate tax, from 45% to 33%, and the introduction of a basically two-tier rate of personal income tax at 24% and 33%, compared with the former 30% and 48%, respectively. Personal tax thresholds were raised in late 2008, and the highest rate, payable on incomes above $NZ70,000, was reduced to 38% with effect from April 2009. Further changes to the lower tax rates were applied from April 2010, when effectively four tax bands were introduced, in addition to a flat rate increase of 2% for the Accident Compensation Scheme levy. A set of changes to depreciation rules on buildings was also implemented, and further discussion on depreciation rules was conducted amid political arguments as to the merits of a capital gains tax, which essentially is not in place in New Zealand.

Budget surpluses have in the past been used not only to fund tax reductions but also to decrease levels of public debt. In its 2011 budget the Government envisaged a deficit, but its forecast was lower than that for 2009 and deficits were expected to last only until 2014/15. The impact of the 2008/09 recession adversely affected the debt position, with government expenditure undergoing substantial review and retrenchment. The Kiwisaver scheme to encourage savings and superannuation provision was established in mid-2007; its introduction proved successful in terms of membership levels, but there were significant changes in the contribution levels to the scheme, following the appointment of the new Government in late 2008. Moreover, in 2010 there were concerns about the performance of some of the approved scheme providers.

The position in New Zealand with regard to social welfare expenditure is similar to that of most other OECD countries. Benefit payments account for about two-fifths of the Government's total health, education and welfare budget, while health and education each account for about one-quarter. The rate of increase in expenditure in all sectors has tended to outstrip economic growth. Following its election in 2008, the National Party-led administration has made a determined effort to restrain government expenditure, including welfare spending, with some reductions being implemented.

Since the 1980s the indigenous Maori population has made explicit claims for a greater influence over the way in which the country is administered, as well as for ownership of a higher proportion of its resources and output. External economic problems and the changes taking place in New Zealand, together with major demographic and social developments, have been accompanied by adjustmentss in political philosophy and traditional affiliations. The Government of the National Party and its allies introduced significant policy changes, including the closer aligning of foreign aid provision with trade and foreign policy objectives, as well as focusing on the Pacific Islands and economic development.

Statistical Survey

Source (unless otherwise stated): Statistics New Zealand, Aorangi House, 85 Molesworth St, POB 2922, Wellington 1; tel. (4) 931-4600; fax (4) 931-9135; e-mail info@stats.govt.nz; internet www.stats.govt.nz.

Area and Population

AREA, POPULATION AND DENSITY

Area (sq km)	270,534*
Population (census results)†	
6 March 2001	3,737,277
7 March 2006	
Males	1,965,618
Females	2,062,329
Total	4,027,947
Population (official estimates at mid-year)	
2009	4,315,800
2010	4,367,800
2011‡	4,405,300
Density (per sq km) at mid-2011	16.3

* 104,454 sq miles.

† Figures refer to the population usually resident. The total population (including foreign visitors) was: 3,820,749 in 2001; 4,143,282 in 2006.

‡ Provisional.

POPULATION BY AGE AND SEX

(official provisional estimates at mid-2011)

	Males	Females	Total
0–14	458,200	436,400	894,600
15–64	1,438,100	1,485,600	2,923,700
65 and over	268,300	318,700	587,000
Total	2,164,600	2,240,700	4,405,300

Note: Totals may not be equal to the sum of components, owing to rounding.

ADMINISTRATIVE REGIONS

(census of March 2006)

	Area (sq km)	Population	Density (per sq km)
North Island			
Northland	13,296	148,470	11.2
Auckland	5,048	1,303,068	258.1
Waikato	26,170	382,713	14.6
Bay of Plenty	11,428	257,379	22.5
Gisborne	8,355	44,499	5.3
Hawke's Bay Region	13,764	147,783	10.7
Taranaki	7,227	104,124	14.4
Manawatu-Wanganui	22,687	222,423	9.8
Wellington	8,056	448,959	55.7
Total North Island	116,031	3,059,418	26.4
South Island			
Tasman	14,538	44,625	3.1
Nelson	444	42,891	96.6
Marlborough	12,493	42,558	3.4
West Coast	23,351	31,326	1.3
Canterbury	45,845	521,832	11.4
Otago	31,476	193,800	6.2
Southland	25,392	90,876	3.6
Total South Island	153,540	967,908	38.1
Area outside regions	963	618	0.6
Total	270,534	4,027,947	14.9

Note: Totals may not be equal to the sum of components, owing to rounding.

PRINCIPAL CENTRES OF POPULATION

(census of March 2006, enumerated totals, incl. visitors)

Auckland city	404,658	Palmerston North	75,543
Christchurch	348,435	Hastings district	70,842
Wellington (capital)	179,466	Rotorua district	65,901
Hamilton	129,249	Napier	55,359
Dunedin	118,683	Nelson	42,888
Tauranga	103,635		

BIRTHS, MARRIAGES AND DEATHS

	Live births*		Marriages†		Deaths*	
	Number	Rate (per '000)	Number	Rate (per '000)	Number	Rate (per '000)
2003	56,134	13.9	21,419	5.3	28,010	7.0
2004	58,073	14.2	21,006	5.1	28,419	7.0
2005	57,745	14.0	20,470	5.0	27,034	6.5
2006	59,193	14.1	21,423	5.1	28,245	6.8
2007	64,044	15.1	21,494	5.1	28,522	6.7
2008	64,343	15.1	21,948	5.1	29,188	6.8
2009	62,543	14.5‡	21,628	5.0	28,964	6.7‡
2010	63,897	14.6‡	20,940	4.8	28,438	6.5‡

* Data for births and deaths are tabulated by year of registration rather than by year of occurrence.

† Based on the resident population concept, replacing the previous de facto concept.

‡ Provisional.

Life expectancy (years at birth, WHO estimates): 81 (males 79; females 83) in 2009 (Source: WHO, *World Health Statistics*).

IMMIGRATION AND EMIGRATION

	2008	2009	2010
Long-term immigrants*	87,463	86,410	82,469
Long-term emigrants†	83,649	65,157	72,018

* Figures refer to persons intending to remain in New Zealand for 12 months or more, and New Zealand citizens returning after an absence of 12 months or more.

† Figures refer to New Zealand citizens intending to remain abroad for 12 months or more, and overseas migrants departing after a stay of 12 months or more.

ECONOMICALLY ACTIVE POPULATION

('000 persons aged 15 years and over, excl. armed forces)

	2006	2007	2008
Agriculture, hunting and forestry	150.6	153.5	149.4
Fishing	1.8	2.4	2.6
Mining and quarrying	4.8	5.2	4.0
Manufacturing	280.6	279.2	278.0
Electricity, gas and water	8.3	8.8	12.0
Construction	185.1	185.3	179.2
Wholesale and retail trade; repair of motor vehicles, motorcycles and personal and household goods	368.4	377.7	387.1
Restaurants and hotels	97.1	108.2	101.0
Transport, storage and communications	118.7	118.1	123.1
Financial intermediation	70.2	70.8	68.1
Real estate, renting and business activities	246.3	248.7	254.0
Public administration and defence; compulsory social security	136.6	138.1	132.7
Education	166.0	169.6	175.4

—continued	2006	2007	2008
Health and social work	196.2	203.5	207.8
Other community, social and personal service activities	92.4	91.1	99.9
Private households with employed persons	3.3	3.7	2.2
Sub-total	2,126.5	2,163.8	2,176.4
Activities not adequately defined	8.2	10.7	11.8
Total employed	2,134.7	2,174.5	2,188.2
Unemployed	85.4	82.8	95.0
Total labour force	2,220.1	2,257.3	2,283.2
Males	1,188.6	1,206.0	1,214.7
Females	1,031.5	1,051.2	1,068.4

Source: ILO.

Health and Welfare

KEY INDICATORS

Total fertility rate (children per woman, 2009)	2.0
Under-5 mortality rate (per 1,000 live births, 2009)	6
HIV/AIDS (% of persons aged 15–49, 2007)	0.1
Physicians (per 1,000 head, 2002)	2.1
Hospital beds (per 1,000 head, 2002)	6.0
Health expenditure (2008): US $ per head (PPP)	2,655
Health expenditure (2008): % of GDP	9.7
Health expenditure (2008): public (% of total)	80.2
Total carbon dioxide emissions ('000 metric tons, 2007)	32,635.2
Carbon dioxide emissions per head (metric tons, 2007)	7.7
Human Development Index (2010): ranking	3
Human Development Index (2010): value	0.907

For sources and definitions, see explanatory note on p. vi.

Agriculture

PRINCIPAL CROPS
('000 metric tons)

	2007	2008	2009
Wheat	344	343	403
Barley	356	409	435
Maize	186	206	238
Oats	28	25	34
Potatoes*	432	473	490
Peas, dry	22	20	21
Cabbages and other brassicas*	44	39	42
Lettuce and chicory*	34	33	32
Tomatoes*	110	90	92
Cauliflowers and broccoli*	45	41	42
Pumpkins, squash and gourds*	185	175	160
Onions and shallots, green*	206	200	203
Peas, green*	50	47	43
Carrots and turnips*	67	67	65
Maize, green*	90	89	92
Grapes*	190	195	211
Apples*	355	356	357
Pears*	35	33	32
Kiwi fruit*	365	385	390

* FAO estimates.

Aggregate production ('000 metric tons, may include official, semi-official or estimated data): Total cereals 927 in 2007, 999 in 2008, 1,126 in 2009; Total roots and tubers 447 in 2007, 486 in 2008, 502 in 2009; Total vegetables (incl. melons) 1,010 in 2007, 960 in 2008, 950 in 2009; Total fruits (excl. melons) 1,056 in 2007, 1,087 in 2008, 1,105 in 2009.

Source: FAO.

LIVESTOCK
('000 head at 30 June)

	2007	2008	2009
Cattle	9,654	9,715	9,961
Sheep	38,460	34,088	32,384
Goats	112	96	82
Pigs	367	325	323
Horses	80*	63	65
Chickens	19,829	19,733	13,147
Ducks*	170	180	180
Geese and guinea fowls*	80	75	80
Turkeys*	76	76	76

* FAO estimate(s).

Source: FAO.

LIVESTOCK PRODUCTS
('000 metric tons)

	2007	2008	2009
Cattle meat	632.4	634.6	637.0
Sheep meat	573.2	598.1	478.4
Pig meat	50.6	51.4	46.7
Chicken meat	147.3	145.4	135.0
Game meat	32.9	32.3	27.2
Cows' milk	15,618	15,217	15,400*
Hen eggs	46.6	53.2*	54.6*
Other poultry eggs*	2.9	3.0	3.1
Honey	9.7	12.4	8.2*
Wool, greasy	217.9	197.3*	179.2*

* FAO estimate(s).

Source: FAO.

Forestry

ROUNDWOOD REMOVALS
('000 cubic metres)

	2007	2008	2009‡
Sawlogs, veneer logs and logs for sleepers	8,966	8,966‡	8,966
Pulpwood	3,284	3,492	3,119
Other industrial roundwood	7,664	7,852‡	8,125
Total	19,914	20,310	20,210

* FAO estimate(s).

Source: FAO.

SAWNWOOD PRODUCTION
('000 cubic metres, year ending 31 March)

Species	2007/08	2008/09	2009/10
Radiata pine	4,122	3,435	3,551
Other introduced pines	4	2	0
Douglas fir	175	138	115
Rimu and miro	3	3	2
Total (incl. others)	4,341	3,610	3,695

Source: Forestry Statistics Section, Ministry of Agriculture and Forestry, Wellington.

Fishing

('000 metric tons, live weight)

	2007	2008	2009
Capture*	494.5	452.3	437.9
Southern blue whiting	23.9	29.3	39.4
Blue grenadier (Hoki)	101.9	96.0	91.5
Oreo dories	17.8	15.6	16.0
Jack and horse mackerels	46.4	47.3	40.2
Snoek (Barracouta)	28.6	27.4	27.8
Skipjack tuna	33.7	26.1	25.1
Wellington flying squid	70.8	55.6	46.3
Aquaculture	111.9†	112.4†	105.0
New Zealand mussel	99.5	100.1	89.9
Total catch	606.4†	564.7†	542.9

* Excluding catches made by chartered vessels and landed outside New Zealand.

† FAO estimate.

Note: Figures exclude aquatic plants (metric tons, all capture); 192 in 2007; 196 in 2008; 366 in 2009. Also excluded are aquatic mammals (recorded by number rather than by weight). The number of whales and dolphins caught was: 28 in 2007; 5 in 2008; 21 in 2009.

Source: FAO.

Mining

('000 metric tons, unless otherwise indicated)

	2007	2008	2009
Coal (incl. lignite)	4,835	4,909	4,563
Gold (kg)	10,628	13,403	13,442
Crude petroleum ('000 barrels)	15,011	21,436	19,617
Gross natural gas (million cu m)	4,712	4,484	4,644
Liquid petroleum gas ('000 barrels)	1,263	979	900*
Ironsands	1,723	2,020	585
Silica sand	86.5	48.6	43.5
Limestone	5,092	4,810	4,481

* Estimate.

Source: US Geological Survey.

Industry

SELECTED PRODUCTS

(metric tons, unless otherwise indicated)

	2002	2003	2004
Wine (million litres)	89.0	55.0	119.2
Beer (sales, '000 hectolitres)	3,093	3,127	2,902
Chemical wood pulp*	711,361	623,437	743,671
Mechanical wood pulp*	838,963	795,394	852,787
Newsprint*	351,585	362,130	379,913
Other paper and paperboard*	518,155	447,512	537,350
Fibre board (cu m)*	880,301	868,539	873,408
Particle board (cu m)*	204,650	221,855	243,798
Veneer (cu m)*	552,738	637,556	680,687
Plywood (cu m)*	299,056	343,715	402,147
Jet fuels ('000 metric tons)	869	832	930
Motor spirit—petrol ('000 metric tons)	1,530	1,520	1,627
Gas-diesel (Distillate fuel) oils ('000 metric tons)	2,049	2,018	1,763
Residual fuel oils ('000 metric tons)	427	359	350
Cement ('000 metric tons)	1,090	1,100	1,110
Aluminium—unwrought ('000 metric tons):			
primary	335.0	342.0	351.4
secondary†	21.5	21.5	21.5
Electric energy (million kWh)	40,346	40,441	41,813

* Source: Ministry of Agriculture and Forestry, Wellington.

† Estimates.

Sources (unless otherwise stated): UN, *Industrial Commodity Statistics Yearbook* and *Monthly Bulletin of Statistics*; US Geological Survey; New Zealand Wine Online.

2005: Wine (million litres) 102.0; Chemical wood pulp (metric tons, provisional) 747,768; Mechanical wood pulp (metric tons, provisional) 852,961; Newsprint (metric tons) 379,628; Other paper and paperboard (metric tons) 541,711; Fibre board (cu m) 845,663; Particle board (cu m) 229,971; Veneer (cu m) 694,301; Plywood (cu m) 408,635 (Sources: New Zealand Wine Online; Ministry of Agriculture and Forestry, Wellington).

2006: Wine (million litres) 133.2; Chemical wood pulp (metric tons, provisional) 751,349; Mechanical wood pulp (metric tons, provisional) 749,679; Newsprint (metric tons) 367,064; Other paper and paperboard (metric tons) 573,396; Fibre board (cu m) 906,938; Particle board (cu m) 238,205; Veneer (cu m) 665,206; Plywood (cu m) 403,808 (Sources: New Zealand Wine Online; Ministry of Agriculture and Forestry, Wellington).

2007: Wine (million litres) 147.6; Newsprint (metric tons) 292,015; Other paper and paperboard (metric tons) 579,931; Fibre board (cu m) 836,755; Particle board (cu m) 256,239; Veneer (cu m) 688,312; Plywood (cu m) 421,794 (Sources: New Zealand Wine Online; Ministry of Agriculture and Forestry, Wellington).

2008: Wine (million litres) 205.2; Newsprint (metric tons) 285,654; Other paper and paperboard (metric tons) 585,429; Fibre board (cu m) 765,044; Particle board (cu m) 245,309; Veneer (cu m) 512,575; Plywood (cu m) 416,383 (Sources: New Zealand Wine Online; Ministry of Agriculture and Forestry, Wellington).

2009: Wine (million litres) 205.2; Newsprint (metric tons) 291,297; Other paper and paperboard (metric tons) 578,746 (Sources: New Zealand Wine Online; Ministry of Agriculture and Forestry, Wellington).

2010: Wine (million litres) 190.0; Newsprint (metric tons) 305,789; Other paper and paperboard (metric tons) 591,389 (Sources: New Zealand Wine Online; Ministry of Agriculture and Forestry, Wellington).

Finance

CURRENCY AND EXCHANGE RATES

Monetary Units
100 cents = 1 New Zealand dollar ($NZ).

Sterling, US Dollar and Euro Equivalents (31 May 2011)
£1 sterling = $NZ2.016;
US $1 = $NZ1.221;
€1 = $NZ1.757;
$NZ100 = £49.61 = US $81.87 = €56.91.

Average Exchange Rate (New Zealand dollars per US $)

2008	1.4227
2009	1.6002
2010	1.3874

BUDGET
($NZ million, year ending 30 June)

Revenue	2006/07	2007/08*	2008/09*
Taxation	53,064	56,186	55,911
Compulsory fees, fines, penalties and levies	3,496	3,851	4,037
Sales of goods and services	12,613	13,682	14,222
Interest revenue and dividends	2,995	3,203	3,358
Other	2,421	2,891	2,591
Total	74,589	79,813	80,119

Expenditure	2006/07	2007/08*	2008/09*
Social security and welfare	19,829	22,274	22,843
GSF pension expenses	645	714	652
Health	10,661	10,765	12,024
Education	9,853	10,803	11,017
Core government services	4,628	3,163	3,412
Law and order	2,822	3,192	3,341
Defence	1,478	1,524	1,697
Transport and communications	6,990	7,185	8,027
Economic and industrial services	4,723	7,433	7,918
Primary services	1,233	1,404	1,364
Heritage, culture and recreation	2,043	2,366	3,130
Housing and community development	865	965	1,036
Other	74	84	83
Finance costs	2,885	2,954	2,503
Future spending forecast	—	—	249
Adjustment	—	–240	–495
Total (incl. others)	68,729	74,586	78,801

* Forecasts.

2009/10 (estimates): *Revenue:* Tax revenue 55,875; Non-tax revenue 7,328; Capital receipts 1,635; Total 64,838. *Expenditure:* Education 11,740; Health 12,624; Social development 20,394; Total (incl. others) 76,168.

2010/11 (forecasts): *Revenue:* Tax revenue 60,469; Non-tax revenue 7,314; Capital receipts 1,865; Total 69,647. *Expenditure:* Education 11,969; Health 13,574; Social development 21,429; Total (incl. others) 79,283.
Source: New Zealand Treasury, Wellington.

INTERNATIONAL RESERVES
(excl. gold, US $ million at 31 December)

	2008	2009	2010
IMF special drawing rights	22	1,340	1,317
Reserve position in IMF	175	273	273
Foreign exchange	10,855	13,982	15,133
Total	11,052	15,594	16,723

Source: IMF, *International Financial Statistics*.

MONEY SUPPLY
($NZ million at 31 December)

	2008	2009	2010
Currency outside banks	3,526	3,580	3,720
Demand deposits at banking institutions	31,361	31,316	32,760
Total money	34,888	34,896	36,480

Source: IMF, *International Financial Statistics*.

COST OF LIVING
(Consumer Price Index; base: 2000 = 100)

	2007	2008	2009
Food (incl. beverages)	118.8	129.0	137.0
Fuel and light	149.5	160.2	167.0
Clothing (incl. footwear)	101.6	101.5	104.0
Rent	105.2	108.5	110.0
All items (incl. others)	119.6	124.4	127.0

2010: Food (incl. beverages) 138.1; All items (incl. others) 129.9.

Source: ILO.

NATIONAL ACCOUNTS
($NZ million at current prices, year ending 31 March)

Expenditure on the Gross Domestic Product

	2008/09	2009/10	2010/11
Government final consumption expenditure	37,265	38,213	40,156
Private final consumption expenditure	108,603	110,838	115,079
Change in inventories	1,406	–1,448	549
Gross fixed capital formation	40,314	36,845	38,831
Total domestic expenditure	187,589	184,448	194,615
Exports of goods and services	57,196	52,424	57,762
Less Imports of goods and services	59,597	49,690	54,963
Statistical discrepancy	—	—	–40
GDP in market prices	185,188	187,182	197,374

Gross Domestic Product by Economic Activity

	2004/05	2005/06	2006/07
Agriculture	7,666	6,795	7,450
Fishing	257	235	247
Forestry and logging	998	1,005	1,067
Mining and quarrying	1,553	1,830	2,047
Manufacturing	21,759	22,779	23,229
Electricity, gas and water	3,886	4,284	4,502
Construction	7,777	8,473	8,825
Wholesale and retail trade	19,196	20,007	20,282
Hotels and restaurants	2,836	2,939	3,108
Transport, storage and communications	10,592	11,019	11,312
Financial intermediation (incl. insurance)	9,173	10,010	10,780
Property and business activities	22275	24459	25,922
Ownership of dwellings	11,604	12,247	12,671
Public administration and defence	6,363	7,083	7,928
Education	6,167	6,473	6,963
Health and community services	8,124	8,971	9,551
Cultural and recreational services	3,528	3,640	3,720
Personal and other services	2,280	2,391	2,474
Sub-total	146,034	154,640	162,075
Less Financial intermediation services indirectly measured	5,139	5,907	6,552
Gross value added at basic prices	140,896	148,735	155,523
Goods and services tax on production	10,273	10,842	11,472
Import duties	870	997	1,668
GDP in market prices	152,038	160,573	168,663

BALANCE OF PAYMENTS
(US $ million)

	2008	2009	2010
Exports of goods f.o.b.	31,192	25,336	31,884
Imports of goods f.o.b.	-32,897	-24,020	-29,511
Trade balance	-1,705	1,316	2,373
Exports of services	9,264	7,873	8,732
Imports of services	-9,692	-7,932	-9,147
Balance on goods and services	-2,133	1,257	1,959
Other income received	3,787	2,729	3,512
Other income paid	-13,789	-7,877	-11,279
Balance on goods, services and income	-12,136	-3,892	-5,809
Current transfers received	1,695	1,189	986
Current transfers paid	-984	-921	1,553
Current balance	-11,424	-3,624	-3,270
Capital account (net)	-446	271	-217
Direct investment abroad	-973	613	-630
Direct investment from abroad	5,121	-1,259	822
Portfolio investment assets	-702	-3,426	-1,518
Portfolio investment liabilities	-5,696	6,128	4,664
Other investment assets	1,621	-1,650	-1,205
Other investment liabilities	459	3,160	1,111
Net errors and omissions	7,043	3,442	1,090
Overall balance	-4,997	3,653	848

Source: IMF, *International Financial Statistics*.

External Trade

PRINCIPAL COMMODITIES
($NZ million)

Imports c.i.f.	2008	2009	2010
Vehicles, parts and accessories	5,061	3,226	4,267
Boilers, machinery and mechanical appliances	6,218	5,024	5,195
Petroleum, petroleum products, etc.	8,577	5,855	6,487
Electrical machinery and equipment	4,002	3,971	3,630
Paper and paperboard	1,045	955	995
Plastic and plastic articles	1,723	1,488	1,612
Iron and steel and articles	1,762	1,124	1,186
Optical, medical and measuring equipment	1,297	1,371	1,327
Total (incl. others)	48,514	40,221	42,360

Exports f.o.b.	2008	2009	2010
Dairy produce; birds' eggs; natural honey; edible products of animal origin, not elsewhere specified or included	9,285	8,116	10,415
Meat and edible offal	5,145	5,142	5,089
Logs, wood and wood articles	2,184	2,319	2,949
Boilers, machinery and mechanical appliances; parts thereof	1,881	1,658	1,722
Fruit and nuts; peel of citrus fruit or melons	1,445	1,601	1,471
Fish, crustaceans and molluscs	1,217	1,262	1,307
Aluminium and aluminium articles	1,428	883	1,213
Electrical machinery and equipment	1,075	982	1,029
Total (incl. others)*	42,900	39,672	43,532

* Including re-exports.

PRINCIPAL TRADING PARTNERS
($NZ million)

Imports (c.i.f.)*	2008	2009	2010
Australia	8,738	7,397	7,697
Belgium	340	262	290
Canada	727	538	521
China, People's Republic	6,444	6,066	6,762
France	804	1,331	595
Germany	2,076	1,684	1,739
Indonesia	1,155	720	647
Italy	978	728	701
Japan	3,956	2,981	3,107
Korea, Republic	1,318	1,357	1,387
Malaysia	1,986	1,085	1,524
Netherlands	388	337	309
Qatar	1,523	945	825
Saudi Arabia	550	272	305
Singapore	2,252	1,625	1,622
Sweden	378	227	279
Taiwan	973	607	732
Thailand	1,318	1,062	1,372
United Arab Emirates	784	466	885
United Kingdom	1,084	937	955
USA	4,600	4,328	4,393
Total (incl. others)	48,514	40,221	42,360

* Excluding specie and gold.

Exports*	2008	2009	2010
Australia	9,995	9,132	10,025
Belgium	507	490	360
Canada	511	501	497
China, People's Republic	2,534	3,628	4,826
Fiji	363	306	312
France	502	508	457
Germany	895	765	658
Hong Kong	700	794	866
India	543	630	901
Indonesia	1,006	963	930
Italy	471	404	437
Japan	3,613	2,821	3,375
Korea, Republic	1,358	1,240	1,414
Malaysia	949	705	776
Mexico	432	375	363
Netherlands	509	480	494
Philippines	734	570	729
Saudi Arabia	729	475	615
Singapore	863	1,100	826
Taiwan	752	756	843
Thailand	826	453	679
United Kingdom	1,672	1,696	1,528
USA	4,382	3,953	3,759
Venezuela	654	362	463
Total (incl. others)	42,900	39,672	43,532

* Including re-exports, but excluding specie and gold.

Transport

RAILWAYS
(traffic, year ending 30 June)

	2000/01	2001/02	2002/03
Freight ('000 metric tons)	14,461	14,330	14,822
Passengers ('000)	12,714	12,521	12,300*

* Excludes passengers on the Tranz Scenic network.

Source: Tranz Rail Ltd, Wellington.

ROAD TRAFFIC
(vehicles licensed at June)

	2008	2009	2010
Passenger cars	2,311,006	2,330,312	2,337,934
Taxis	7,823	7,855	7,575
Buses and service coaches	18,419	19,067	19,388
Trailers and caravans	446,745	453,488	459,912
Motorcycles and mopeds	75,140	78,217	76,548
Tractors	28,212	28,703	29,030
Trucks	425,894	427,525	426,491

Source: New Zealand Transport Agency.

SHIPPING

Merchant Fleet
(registered at 31 December)

	2007	2008	2009
Number of vessels	174	172	176
Displacement (grt)	210,208	214,142	213,084

Source: IHS Fairplay, *World Fleet Statistics*.

Vessels Handled
(international, '000 grt)

	1993	1994	1995
Entered	37,603	39,700	48,827
Cleared	35,128	37,421	42,985

Source: UN, *Statistical Yearbook*.

International Sea-borne Freight Traffic
('000 metric tons, year ending 30 June)

	2004/05	2005/06	2006/07*
Goods loaded	21,894	21,840	22,986
Goods unloaded	19,164	18,119	18,499

* Provisional.

CIVIL AVIATION
(domestic and international traffic on scheduled services)

	2004	2005	2006
Kilometres flown (million)	176	185	195
Passengers carried ('000)	11,305	11,952	12,382
Passenger-km (million)	24,710	26,093	27,032
Total metric ton-km (million)	3,307	3,486	3,621

Source: UN, *Statistical Yearbook*.

Tourism

VISITOR ARRIVALS

Country of residence	2008	2009	2010*
Australia	976,200	1,082,680	1,154,830
China, People's Republic	112,398	102,259	105,500
Germany	62,300	64,564	66,270
Japan	102,482	78,426	88,190
Korea, Republic	79,061	52,921	66,580
United Kingdom	285,094	258,438	245,430
USA	212,410	197,792	198,120
Total (incl. others)	2,447,208	2,447,346	2,537,680

* Estimates.

Tourism receipts ($NZ million): 5,947 in 2008; 6,187 in 2009; 6,278 in 2010 (estimate).

Source: Tourism Research Council, Wellington.

Communications Media

	2008	2009	2010
Telephones ('000 main lines in use)	1,750	1,870	1,870
Mobile cellular telephones ('000 subscribers)	4,620*	4,700	5,020
Internet subscribers ('000)	1,504	1,415	n.a.
Broadband subscribers ('000)	915	981	1,089

* At September.

Personal computers: 2,200,000 (525.7 per 1,000 persons) in 2006.

Television receivers ('000 in use): 2,130 in 2001.

Radio receivers ('000 in use): 3,750 in 1997.

Daily newspapers: 23 (circulation 739,000 copies) in 2004.

Non-daily newspapers: 129 titles in 2004; 311,380 copies in 2002.

Book production (1999): 4,800 titles.

Sources: partly International Telecommunication Union; UNESCO, *Statistical Yearbook*; UN, *Statistical Yearbook*.

Education

(July 2010 unless otherwise indicated)

	Institutions	Teachers (full-time equivalent)	Students
Early childhood services	5,152	13,294	188,924[1]
Primary schools[2]	2,018	24,853[3]	435,051
Composite schools[4]	155	2,650[3]	50,524
Secondary schools[5]	340	18,970[3]	275,945
Special schools	46	1,038[3]	2,878
Polytechnics	20[6]	4,194[7]	174,964
Colleges of education	4[6]	301[8]	65,005
Universities	8[6]	7,869[7]	156,069
Wananga[9]	3[6]	572[7]	42,293
Private training establishments receiving government grants	522[6]	4,177[6]	59,158[10]

[1] Includes children on the regular roll of kindergartens, playcentres, the Correspondence School, Te Kohanga Reo, Early Childhood Development Unit funded playgroups, Early Childhood Development Unit funded Pacific Islands language groups, education and care centres (including home-based child care).

[2] Primary schools include Full Primary Years 1–8, Contributing Years 1–6, Intermediate Years 7–8.

[3] Teachers employed in state schools at 1 April 2011.

[4] Composite schools provide both primary and secondary education (includes area schools and the Correspondence School).

[5] Secondary schools include Years 7–15, Years 9–15.

[6] 2003 figure.

[7] 2009 figure.

[8] 2006 figure.

[9] Tertiary institutions providing polytechnic and university level programmes specifically for Maori students, with an emphasis on Maori language and culture.

[10] 2004 figure.

Source: Ministry of Education, Wellington.

Pupil-teacher ratio (primary education, UNESCO estimate): 15.3 in 2007/08 (Source: UNESCO Institute for Statistics).

Directory

The Constitution

New Zealand has no written constitution. The political system is closely modelled on that of the United Kingdom (with an element of proportional representation introduced to the legislature in 1996). As in the United Kingdom, constitutional practice is an accumulation of convention, precedent and tradition. A brief description of New Zealand's principal organs of government is given below:

HEAD OF STATE

Executive power is vested in the monarch and is exercisable in New Zealand by the monarch's personal representative, the Governor-General.

In the execution of the powers and authorities vested in him or her, the Governor-General must be guided by the advice of the Executive Council.

EXECUTIVE COUNCIL

The Executive Council consists of the Governor-General and all the Ministers. Two members, exclusive of the Governor-General or the presiding member, constitute a quorum. The Governor-General appoints the Prime Minister and, on the latter's recommendation, the other Ministers.

HOUSE OF REPRESENTATIVES

Parliament comprises the Crown and the House of Representatives. At the 1996 general election, a system of mixed member proportional representation was introduced. The House of Representatives comprises 122 members: 70 electorate members (seven seats being reserved for Maoris) and 52 members chosen from party lists. They are designated 'Members of Parliament' and are elected for three years, subject to the dissolution of the House before the completion of their term.

Everyone over the age of 18 years may vote in the election of members for the House of Representatives. Since August 1975 any person, regardless of nationality, ordinarily resident in New Zealand for 12 months or more and resident in an electoral district for at least one month is qualified to be registered as a voter. Compulsory registration of all electors except Maoris was introduced at the end of 1924; it was introduced for Maoris in 1956. As from August 1975, any person of the Maori race, which includes any descendant of such a person, may enrol on the Maori roll for the particular Maori electoral district in which that person resides.

By the Electoral Amendment Act 1937, which made provision for a secret ballot in Maori elections, Maori electors were granted the same privileges, in the exercise of their vote, as general electors.

In local government the electoral franchise is the same.

The Government

Head of State: HM Queen ELIZABETH II (acceded to the throne 6 February 1952).

Governor-General and Commander-in-Chief: Lt-Gen. Sir JERRY MATEPARAE (assumed office 31 August 2011).

CABINET

(October 2011)

The Government is formed by the National Party, in coalition with ACT New Zealand, the Maori Party and United Future New Zealand.

Prime Minister and Minister of Tourism: JOHN KEY.

Deputy Prime Minister, Minister of Finance and for Infrastructure: BILL ENGLISH.

Minister for Canterbury Earthquake Recovery, for Economic Development and of Energy and Resources: GERRY BROWNLEE.

Minister of Justice, of Commerce and of Consumer Affairs: SIMON POWER.

Minister of Health, for State-Owned Enterprises and of State Services: TONY RYALL.

Minister for the Environment, for Climate Change Issues and for the Accident Compensation Corporation: Dr NICK SMITH.

Minister of Police, of Corrections and of Veterans' Affairs: JUDITH COLLINS.

Minister of Education: ANNE TOLLEY.

Attorney-General and Minister for Treaty of Waitangi Negotiations and for Arts, Culture and Heritage: CHRISTOPHER FINLAYSON.

Minister of Agriculture, for Biosecurity and of Forestry: DAVID CARTER.

Minister of Foreign Affairs and for Sport and Recreation and for the Rugby World Cup: MURRAY MCCULLY.

Minister of Trade: TIM GROSER.

Minister of Defence and of Science and Innovation: Dr WAYNE MAPP.

Minister of Transport, for Communications and Information Technology and for Tertiary Education: STEVEN JOYCE.

Minister for Courts, of Pacific Island Affairs and for Disarmament and Arms Control: GEORGINA TE HEUHEU.

Minister for Social Development and Employment and of Youth Affairs: PAULA BENNETT.

Minister of Fisheries and Aquaculture and of Housing: PHIL HEATLEY.

Minister of Immigration and of Broadcasting: Dr JONATHAN COLEMAN.

Minister of Conservation, of Labour and for Food Safety: KATE WILKINSON.

Minister for Ethnic Affairs and of Women's Affairs: HEKIA PARATA.

MINISTERS OUTSIDE CABINET

Minister for Building and Construction, of Customs, for Land Information, of Statistics and for Small Business: MAURICE WILLIAMSON.

Minister of Civil Defence, for Senior Citizens and for Racing: CRAIG FOSS.

Minister of Internal Affairs: NATHAN GUY.

SUPPORT PARTY MINISTERS

Minister of Local Government and for Regulatory Reform: RODNEY HIDE.

Minister of Maori Affairs: Dr PITA SHARPLES.

Minister for the Community and Voluntary Sector and for Disability Issues: TARIANA TURIA.

Minister of Revenue: PETER DUNNE.

MINISTRIES AND GOVERNMENT DEPARTMENTS

Department of the Prime Minister and Cabinet: Executive Wing, Parliament Bldgs, Wellington 6011; tel. (4) 817-9682; fax (4) 472-3181; e-mail finance@dpmc.govt.nz; internet www.dpmc.govt.nz.

Ministry of Agriculture and Forestry: 25 The Terrace, POB 2526, Wellington 6140; tel. (4) 894-0100; fax (4) 894-0720; e-mail info@maf.govt.nz; internet www.maf.govt.nz.

Department of Building and Housing: Level 6, 86 Customhouse Quay, POB 10-729, Wellington; tel. (4) 494-0260; fax (4) 494-0290; e-mail info@dbh.govt.nz; internet www.dbh.govt.nz.

Ministry of Civil Defence and Emergency Management: Level 9, 22 The Terrace, POB 5010, Wellington; tel. (4) 473-7363; fax (4) 473-7369; e-mail emergency.management@dia.govt.nz; internet www.civildefence.govt.nz.

Department of Conservation: POB 10-420, Wellington 6143; tel. (4) 471-0726; fax (4) 381-3057; e-mail enquiries@doc.govt.nz; internet www.doc.govt.nz.

Ministry of Consumer Affairs: Level 7, 33 Bowen St, POB 1473, Wellington 6140; tel. (4) 474-2750; fax (4) 473-9400; e-mail mcainfo@mca.govt.nz; internet www.consumeraffairs.govt.nz.

Department of Corrections: POB 1206, Wellington 6140; tel. (4) 460-3000; fax (4) 460-3208; e-mail info@corrections.govt.nz; internet www.corrections.govt.nz.

Ministry for Culture and Heritage: POB 5364, Wellington; tel. (4) 499-4229; fax (4) 499-4490; e-mail info@mch.govt.nz; internet www.mch.govt.nz.

Ministry of Defence: Molesworth St, POB 12-703, Wellington 6144; tel. (4) 496-0999; fax (4) 496-0859; e-mail info@defence.govt.nz; internet www.defence.govt.nz.

Ministry of Economic Development: 33 Bowen St, POB 1473, Wellington; tel. (4) 472-0030; fax (4) 473-4638; e-mail info@med.govt.nz; internet www.med.govt.nz.

Ministry of Education: 45–47 Pipitea St, POB 1666, Thorndon, Wellington 6140; tel. (4) 463-8000; fax (4) 463-8001; e-mail enquiries.national@minedu.govt.nz; internet www.minedu.govt.nz.

Ministry for the Environment: POB 10-362, Wellington 6143; tel. (4) 439-7400; fax (4) 439-7700; e-mail info@mfe.govt.nz; internet www.mfe.govt.nz.

Ministry of Fisheries: ASB Bank House, 101–103 The Terrace, POB 1020, Wellington; tel. (4) 819-4600; fax (4) 819-4601; e-mail info@fish.govt.nz; internet www.fish.govt.nz.

Ministry of Foreign Affairs and Trade: Private Bag 18901, Wellington 5045; tel. (4) 439-8000; fax (4) 439-8505; e-mail enquiries@mfat.govt.nz; internet www.mfat.govt.nz.

Ministry of Health: POB 5013, Wellington; tel. (4) 496-2000; fax (4) 496-2340; e-mail emailmoh@moh.govt.nz; internet www.moh.govt.nz.

Department of Inland Revenue: POB 39010, Wellington Mail Centre, Lower Hutt 5045; tel. (4) 978-0779; e-mail nonres@ird.govt.nz; internet www.ird.govt.nz.

Department of Internal Affairs: POB 805, Wellington 6140; tel. (4) 495-7200; e-mail info@dia.govt.nz; internet www.dia.govt.nz.

Ministry of Justice: Vogel Centre, 19 Aitken St, POB 180, Wellington; tel. (4) 918-8800; fax (4) 918-8820; e-mail reception@justice.govt.nz; internet www.justice.govt.nz.

Department of Labour: POB 3705, Wellington; tel. (4) 915-4400; fax (4) 915-4015; e-mail info@dol.govt.nz; internet www.dol.govt.nz.

Ministry of Maori Development (Te Puni Kokiri): POB 3943, Wellington 6140; tel. (4) 819-6000; fax (4) 819-6299; e-mail info@tpk.govt.nz; internet www.tpk.govt.nz.

Ministry of Pacific Island Affairs: POB 833, Wellington 6140; tel. (4) 473-4493; fax (4) 473-4301; e-mail contact@mpia.govt.nz; internet www.mpia.govt.nz.

Ministry of Science and Innovation: POB 5336, Wellington 6145; tel. (4) 917-2900; fax (4) 471-1284; e-mail info@msi.govt.nz; internet www.msi.govt.nz.

Ministry of Social Development: POB 1556, Wellington 6140; tel. (4) 916-3300; fax (4) 918-0099; e-mail information@msd.govt.nz; internet www.msd.govt.nz.

State Services Commission: POB 329, Wellington 6140; tel. (4) 495-6600; fax (4) 495-6686; e-mail commission@ssc.govt.nz; internet www.ssc.govt.nz.

Statistics New Zealand (Tatauranga Aotearoa): POB 2922, Wellington 6140; tel. (4) 931-4600; fax (4) 931-4030; e-mail info@stats.govt.nz; internet www.stats.govt.nz.

Ministry of Tourism: 33 Bowen St, POB 5640, Wellington; tel. (4) 498-7440; fax (4) 498-7445; e-mail info@tourism.govt.nz; internet www.tourism.govt.nz.

Ministry of Transport: POB 3175, Wellington 6140; tel. (4) 439-9000; fax (4) 439-9005; e-mail informationmanagement@transport.govt.nz; internet www.transport.govt.nz.

Treasury: POB 3724, Wellington 6140; tel. (4) 472-2733; fax (4) 473-0982; e-mail info@treasury.govt.nz; internet www.treasury.govt.nz.

Ministry of Women's Affairs: POB 10-049, Wellington; tel. (4) 915-7112; fax (4) 916-1604; e-mail mwa@mwa.govt.nz; internet www.mwa.govt.nz.

Ministry of Youth Development: POB 1556, Wellington 6140; tel. (4) 916-3300; fax (4) 918-0091; e-mail mydinfo@myd.govt.nz; internet www.myd.govt.nz.

Legislature

HOUSE OF REPRESENTATIVES

Speaker: LOCKWOOD SMITH.

General Election, 8 November 2008

Party	Number of party votes	% of votes	Party seats	List seats	Total seats
NZ National Party	1,053,398	44.93	41	17	58
NZ Labour Party	796,880	33.99	21	22	43
Green Party	157,613	6.72	—	9	9
ACT New Zealand	85,496	3.65	1	4	5
Maori Party	55,980	2.39	5	—	5
Progressive Party	21,241	0.91	1	—	1
United Future NZ	20,497	0.87	1	—	1
New Zealand First	95,356	4.07	—	—	—
Total (incl. others)	2,356,536	100.00	70	52	122

Election Commission

Electoral Commission of New Zealand: POB 3050, Wellington 6140; tel. (4) 474-0670; fax (4) 474-0674; e-mail info@elections.govt.nz; internet www.elections.org.nz; f. 2010; independent Crown entity; assumed responsibilities of Chief Electoral Office and previous Electoral Commission in Oct. 2010; Chair. Sir HUGH WILLIAMS; Chief Electoral Officer ROBERT PEDEN.

Political Organizations

In October 2011 16 political parties were registered.

ACT New Zealand: 309 Broadway, POB 99-651, Newmarket, Auckland; tel. (9) 523-0470; fax (9) 523-0472; e-mail info@act.org.nz; internet www.act.org.nz; f. 1994; supports free enterprise, tax reform and choice in education and health; Pres. CHRIS SIMMONDS; Leader DON BRASH.

Green Party of Aotearoa—New Zealand: POB 11652, Wellington; tel. (4) 801-5102; fax (4) 801-5104; e-mail greenparty@greens.org.nz; internet www.greens.org.nz; f. 1989; fmrly Values Party, f. 1972; Co-Leaders RUSSEL NORMAN, METIRIA TUREI.

Maori Party: POB 50-271, Porirua; tel. (4) 471-9900; fax (4) 499-7269; e-mail hekeretari2@maoriparty.com; internet www.maoriparty.org; f. 2004; Co-Leaders Dr PITA SHARPLES, TARIANA TURIA; Pres. PEM BIRD.

NZ Democrats for Social Credit: POB 18-907, New Brighton, Christchurch 8641; tel. and fax (3) 382-9544; e-mail democrats@democrats.org.nz; internet www.democrats.org.nz; f. 1953; est. as Social Credit Political League; subsequently known as New Zealand Democratic Party Inc; liberal; Pres. NEVILLE AITCHISON; Leader STEPHNIE DE RUYTER.

New Zealand First: Albany, North Shore City, POB 301158, Auckland 0752; tel. (7) 827-4932; fax (7) 827-4931; e-mail info@nzfirst.org.nz; internet www.nzfirst.org.nz; f. 1993; est. by fmr Nat. Party mems; Leader WINSTON PETERS; Pres. KEVIN GARDENER.

New Zealand Labour Party: Fraser House, POB 784, Wellington; tel. (4) 384-7649; fax (4) 384-8060; e-mail office@labourparty.org.nz; internet www.labour.org.nz, www.labourparty.org.nz; f. 1916; advocates an organized economy guaranteeing an adequate standard of living to every person able and willing to work; Pres. MOIRA COATSWORTH; Parl. Leader PHIL GOFF; Gen. Sec. CHRIS FLATT.

New Zealand National Party: Willbank House, Level 14, 57 Willis St, POB 1155, Wellington 6001; tel. (4) 472-5211; fax (4) 478-1622; e-mail hq@national.org.nz; internet www.national.org.nz; f. 1936; centre-right; supports private enterprise and competitive business, together with maximum personal freedom; Pres. PETER GOODFELLOW; Parl. Leader JOHN KEY.

Progressive Party: POB 33-243, Christchurch 8030; tel. (3) 377-7679; fax (3) 377-7673; e-mail contact@progressive.org.nz; internet www.progressive.org.nz; f. 2002; est. as Progressive Coalition to contest 2002 general election; name changed as above April 2004; Leader JIM ANDERTON; Gen. Sec. PHIL CLEARWATER.

United Future New Zealand (UFNZ): Bowen House, Parliament Bldgs, Wellington; tel. (4) 471-9410; e-mail frankowen@xtra.co.nz; internet www.unitedfuture.org.nz; f. 1995; est. by 4 mems of Nat. Party, 2 mems of Labour Party and leader of Future New Zealand; Leader PETER DUNNE; Pres. JUDY TURNER.

Other registered parties included the Alliance, the Aotearoa Legalise Cannabis Party, Libertarianz, the Kiwi Party, Conservative Party of New Zealand, Mana Party and New Citizen Party.

Diplomatic Representation

EMBASSIES AND HIGH COMMISSIONS IN NEW ZEALAND

Argentina: Level 14, 142 Lambton Quay, POB 5430, Wellington; tel. (4) 472-8330; fax (4) 472-8331; e-mail enzel@arg.org.nz; internet www.arg.org.nz; Ambassador FERNANDO ESCALONA.

Australia: 72–76 Hobson St, Thorndon, POB 4036, Wellington; tel. (4) 473-6411; fax (4) 498-7135; e-mail nzinbox@dfat.gov.au; internet www.australia.org.nz; High Commissioner PAUL O'SULLIVAN.

Brazil: Deloitte House, Level 9, 10 Brandon St, POB 5432, Wellington 6011; tel. (4) 473-3516; fax (4) 473-3517; e-mail brasemb@brazil.org.nz; internet www.brazil.org.nz; Ambassador RENATE STILLE.

Canada: 125 The Terrace, Level 11, POB 8047, Wellington; tel. (4) 473-9577; fax (4) 471-2082; e-mail wlgtn@international.gc.ca; internet www.canadainternational.gc.ca/new_zealand-nouvelle_zelande; High Commissioner CAROLINE CHRÉTIEN.

Chile: 19 Bolton St, POB 3861, Wellington; tel. (4) 471-6270; fax (4) 472-5324; e-mail echile@embchile.co.nz; internet www.embchile.co.nz; Chargé d'affaires a.i. SEBASTIÁN EDUARDO MOLINA MEDINA.

China, People's Republic: 2–6 Glenmore St, Kelburn, Wellington; tel. (4) 472-1382; fax (4) 499-0419; e-mail administration@chinaembassy.org.nz; internet www.chinaembassy.org.nz; Ambassador XU JIANGUO.

Cuba: 35 Hobson St, Thorndon, POB 3294, Wellington; tel. (4) 472-3748; fax (4) 473-2958; e-mail embajada@xtra.co.nz; Ambassador (vacant).

Fiji: 31 Pipitea St, Thorndon, POB 3940, Wellington; tel. (4) 473-5401; fax (4) 499-1011; e-mail viti@paradise.net.nz; internet www.fiji.org.nz; Head of Mission MERE TORA (acting).

France: Sovereign House, Level 13, 34–42 Manners St, POB 11-343, Wellington 6142; tel. (4) 384-2555; fax (4) 384-2577; e-mail amba.france@actrix.co.nz; internet www.ambafrance-nz.org; Ambassador FRANCIS ETIENNE.

Germany: 90–92 Hobson St, POB 1687, Wellington; tel. (4) 473-6063; fax (4) 473-6069; e-mail info@wellington.diplo.de; internet www.wellington.diplo.de; Ambassador THOMAS H. MEISTER.

Greece: Petherick Tower, Level 11, 38–42 Waring Taylor St, POB 24-066, Wellington; tel. (4) 473-7775; fax (4) 473-7441; e-mail gremb.wel@mfa.gr; internet www.mfa.gr/wellington; Ambassador DIMITRIOS ANNINOS.

Holy See: Apostolic Nunciature, 112 Queens Dr., Lyall Bay, POB 14-044, Wellington 6241; tel. (4) 387-3470; fax (4) 387-8170; e-mail nuntius@ihug.co.nz; Apostolic Nuncio Most Rev. CHARLES D. BALVO (Titular Archbishop of Castello).

India: 180 Molesworth St, POB 4045, Wellington 6015; tel. (4) 473-6390; fax (4) 499-0665; e-mail hicomind@hicomind.org.nz; internet www.hicomind.org.nz; High Commissioner Adm. SUREESH MEHTA.

Indonesia: 70 Glen Rd, Kelburn, POB 3543, Wellington; tel. (4) 475-8698; fax (4) 475-9374; e-mail info@indonesianembassy.org.nz; internet www.indonesianembassy.org.nz; Ambassador ANTONIUS AGUS SRIYONO.

Iran: POB 14733, Kilbirnie, Wellington; tel. (4) 386-2983; fax (4) 939-8108; e-mail info@iranembassy.org.nz; internet www.iranembassy.org.nz; Ambassador SEYED MAJID TAFRESHI KHAMENEH.

Israel: Level 13, Bayley's Bldg, 36 Brandon St, Wellington; tel. (4) 471-0079; fax (4) 498-2959; e-mail info@wellington.mfa.gov.il; internet users.iconz.co.nz/israel; Ambassador SHEMI TZUR.

Italy: 34–38 Grant Rd, Thorndon, POB 463, Wellington; tel. (4) 473-5339; fax (4) 472-7255; e-mail ambasciata.wellington@esteri.it; internet www.ambwellington.esteri.it/ambasciata_wellington; Ambassador Dr GIOACCHINO TRIZZINO.

Japan: POB 6340, Marion Sq., Wellington 6141; tel. (4) 473-1540; fax (4) 471-2951; e-mail japan.emb@eoj.org.nz; internet www.nz.emb-japan.go.jp; Ambassador HIDETO MITAMURA.

Korea, Republic: ASB Bank Tower, Level 11, 2 Hunter St, POB 11-143, Wellington; tel. (4) 473-9073; fax (4) 472-3865; e-mail info@koreanembassy.org.nz; internet www.koreanembassy.org.nz; Ambassador PARK YONG-KYU.

Malaysia: 10 Washington Ave, Brooklyn, POB 9422, Wellington; tel. (4) 385-2439; fax (4) 385-6973; e-mail mwwelton@xtra.co.nz; internet www.kln.gov.my/web/nzl_wellington; High Commissioner Datuk MAZLAN MUHAMMAD.

Mexico: AMP Chambers, Level 2, 185–187 Featherston St, POB 11-510, Wellington; tel. (4) 472-0555; fax (4) 496-3559; e-mail mexico@xtra.co.nz; internet www.sre.gob.mx/nuevazelandia; Ambassador ROSAURA RUEDA GUTIÉRREZ.

Netherlands: POB 840, Wellington 6140; tel. (4) 471-6390; fax (4) 471-2923; e-mail wel@minbuza.nl; internet www.netherlandsembassy.co.nz; Ambassador ARIE VAN DER WIEL.

Pakistan: 182 Onslow Rd, Khandallah, Wellington 6035; tel. (4) 479-0026; fax (4) 479-4315; e-mail pakhcwellington@xtra.co.nz; internet www.mofa.gov.pk/newzealand; High Commissioner SYED IBNE ABBAS.

Papua New Guinea: 279 Willis St, POB 197, Wellington; tel. (4) 385-2474; fax (4) 385-2477; e-mail pngnz@globe.net.nz; internet www.pngnz.org/highcom; High Commissioner WILLIAM DIHM.

Philippines: 50 Hobson St, Thorndon, Wellington 6011; tel. (4) 472-9848; fax (4) 472-5170; e-mail embassy@wellington-pe.co.nz; internet www.philembassy.org.nz; Ambassador Dr VIRGINIA HONRADO BENAVIDEZ.

Poland: City Chambers, Level 9, 142–144 Featherston St, POB 10211, Wellington; tel. (4) 475-9453; fax (4) 475-9458; e-mail polishembassy@xtra.co.nz; internet www.wellington.polemb.net; Ambassador BEATA STOCZYŃSKA.

Russia: 57 Messines Rd, Karori, Wellington; tel. (4) 476-6113; fax (4) 476-3843; e-mail info@rus.co.nz; internet www.russianembassy.co.nz; Ambassador ANDREI A. TATARINOV.

Samoa: 1A Wesley Rd, Kelburn, POB 1430, Wellington; tel. (4) 472-0953; fax (4) 471-2479; e-mail shc@paradise.net.nz; High Commissioner ASI TUIATAGA J. F. BLAKELOCK.

Singapore: 17 Kabul St, Khandallah, POB 13140, Wellington; tel. (4) 470-0850; fax (4) 479-4066; e-mail singhc_wlg@sgmfa.gov.sg; internet www.mfa.gov.sg/wellington; High Commissioner M. P. H. RUBIN.

South Africa: State Insurance Bldg, Level 7, 1 Willis St, POB 25406, Wellington; tel. (4) 815-8484; fax (4) 472-5010; e-mail wellington@foreign.gov.za; High Commissioner ANTHONY LE CLERK KGWADU MONGALO.

Spain: BNZ Trust House Bldg, Level 11, 50 Manners St, POB 24-150, Wellington 6142; tel. (4) 802-5665; fax (4) 801-7701; e-mail emb.wellington@maec.es; internet www.maec.es/subwebs/embajadas/wellington; Ambassador JESÚS MIGUEL SANZ ESCORIHUELA.

Switzerland: POB 25004, Wellington 6146; tel. (4) 472-1593; fax (4) 499-6302; e-mail wel.vertretung@eda.admin.ch; internet www.eda.admin.ch/wellington; Ambassador Dr MARION WEICHELT KRUPSKI.

Thailand: 2 Cook St, Karori, POB 17-226, Wellington; tel. (4) 476-8619; fax (4) 476-8610; e-mail thaiembassynz@xtra.co.nz; internet www.thaiembassynz.org.nz; Ambassador NOPPADON THEPPITAK.

Tonga: 41 Bay St, Petone, Lower Hutt, Wellington 5012; tel. (4) 566-3884; fax (4) 566-3887; e-mail thc.wellington@gmail.com; High Commissioner SIAOSI TAIMANI 'AHO.

Turkey: 15–17 Murphy St, Level 8, POB 12-248, Thorndon, Wellington; tel. (4) 472-1292; fax (4) 472-1277; e-mail turkem@xtra.co.nz; Ambassador ALI YAKITAL.

United Kingdom: 44 Hill St, POB 1812, Wellington; tel. (4) 924-2888; fax (4) 473-4982; e-mail ppa.mailbox@fco.gov.uk; internet ukinnewzealand.fco.gov.uk; High Commissioner VICTORIA TREADELL.

USA: 29 Fitzherbert Terrace, POB 1190, Wellington; tel. (4) 462-6000; fax (4) 499-0490; internet newzealand.usembassy.gov; Ambassador Dr DAVID HUEBNER.

Viet Nam: Grand Plimmer Tower, Level 21, 2–6 Gilmer Terrace, POB 8042, Wellington; tel. (4) 473-5912; fax (4) 473-5913; e-mail embassyvn@clear.net.nz; internet www.vietnamembassy-newzealand.org; Ambassador NGUYEN HONG CUONG.

Judicial System

The Judicial System of New Zealand comprises a Supreme Court, a Court of Appeal, a High Court and District Courts, all of which have civil and criminal jurisdiction, and the specialist courts, the Employment Court, the Family Court, the Youth Court and the Maori Land Court. On 1 January 2004 the newly established Supreme Court replaced the Judicial Committee of the Privy Council in the United Kingdom as the final appellate court. The right to appeal to the Supreme Court was granted only if the Court was satisfied that the case involved a matter of general or public importance or commercial significance, or in order to correct or prevent a substantial miscarriage of justice.

The Court of Appeal hears appeals from the High Court and from District Court Jury Trials, although it does have some original jurisdiction. Its decisions are final, except in cases that may be appealed to the Supreme Court. Appeals regarding convictions and sentences handed down by the High Court or District Trial Courts are by leave only.

The High Court has jurisdiction to hear cases involving crimes, admiralty law and civil matters. It hears appeals from lower courts and tribunals, and reviews administrative actions.

District Courts have an extensive criminal and civil law jurisdiction. They hear civil cases, while Justices of the Peace can hear minor criminal and traffic matters. The Family Court, which is a division of the District Courts, has the jurisdiction to deal with dissolution of marriages, adoption, guardianship applications, domestic actions, matrimonial property, child support, care and protection applications regarding children and young persons, and similar matters.

The tribunals are as follows: the Employment Tribunal (administered by the Department of Labour), Disputes Tribunal, Complaints Review Tribunal, Residential Tenancies Tribunal, Waitangi Tribunal, Environment Court, Deportation Review Tribunal and Motor Vehicles Disputes Tribunal.

In criminal cases involving indictable offences (major crimes), the defendant has the right to a jury. In criminal cases involving summary offences (minor crimes), the defendant may elect to have a jury if the sentence corresponding to the charge is three months or greater.

Attorney-General: CHRISTOPHER FINLAYSON.

Chief Justice: Dame SIAN ELIAS.

THE SUPREME COURT

Judges: Dame SIAN ELIAS, Sir PETER BLANCHARD, Sir ANDREW TIPPING, Sir JOHN MCGRATH, Sir WILLIAM YOUNG, 85 Lambton Quay, Wellington; tel. (4) 918-8222; internet www.courtsofnz.govt.nz/about/supreme.

THE COURT OF APPEAL

President: MARK O'REGAN, cnr Molesworth and Aitken Sts, Wellington; tel. (4) 914-3540; fax (4) 914-3570.

Judges: SUSAN GLAZEBROOK, GRANT HAMMOND, ROBERT CHAMBERS, TERENCE ARNOLD, ELLEN FRANCE, ANTHONY RANDERSON, RHYS HARRISON, LYNTON LAURENCE STEVENS, JOHN RICHARD WILD.

THE HIGH COURT

Permanent Judges: HELEN WINKELMANN (Chief High Court Judge), LOWELL GODDARD, GRAHAM PANCKHURST, LESTER CHISHOLM, WARWICK GENDALL, JUDITH POTTER, JOHN WILD, RODNEY HANSEN, JOHN PRIESTLEY, RONALD YOUNG, PAUL HEATH, GEOFFREY VENNING, PATRICK KEANE, JOHN FOGARTY, ALAN MACKENZIE, FORREST MILLER, MARK COOPER, CHRISTOPHER ALLAN, PATRICIA COURTNEY, SIMON FRANCE, RAYNOR ASHER, GRAHAM LANG, DENIS CLIFFORD, PAMELA ANDREWS, JILLIAN MALLON, PETER WOODHOUSE, AILSA DUFFY, ROBERT ANDREW DOBSON, CHRISTINE FRENCH, EDWIN WYLIE, JOSEPH WILLIAMS, DOUGLAS WHITE, REBECCA ELLIS, TIMOTHY CHARLES BREWER, MARY PETERS, MARK WOOLFORD, CHRISTIAN NATHANIAL WHATA, CHRISTOPHER HOLDEN TOOGOOD, JOHN STEPHEN KÓS.

Religion

CHRISTIANITY

Te Runanga Whakawhanaunga i Nga Hahi o Aotearoa (Maori Council of Churches in New Zealand): Private Bag 11903, Ellerslie, Auckland; tel. (9) 525-4179; fax (9) 525-4346; f. 1982; 4 mem. churches; Administrator TE RUA GRETHA.

The Anglican Communion

The Anglican Church in Aotearoa, New Zealand and Polynesia comprises Te Pihopatanga o Aotearoa and eight dioceses (one of which is Polynesia). In 1996 the Church had an estimated 631,764 members in New Zealand.

Primate of the Anglican Church in Aotearoa, New Zealand and Polynesia, and Bishop of Aotearoa: Rt Rev. WILLIAM BROWN TUREI, POB 568, Gisborne 4040; tel. (6) 867-8856; fax (9) 377-6962; e-mail browntmihi@xtra.co.nz.

General Secretary and Treasurer of the Anglican Church in Aotearoa, New Zealand and Polynesia: Rev. MICHAEL HUGHES, POB 87-188, Meadowbank, Auckland 1742; tel. (9) 521-4439; fax (9) 521-4490; e-mail gensec@ang.org.nz; internet www.anglican.org.nz.

The Roman Catholic Church

For ecclesiastical purposes, New Zealand comprises one archdiocese and five dioceses. At 31 December 2007 there were an estimated 524,645 adherents.

Bishops' Conference

New Zealand Catholic Bishops' Conference, Catholic Centre, 22–30 Hill St, POB 1937, Wellington 6140; tel. (4) 496-1747; fax (4) 496-17461; e-mail adickinson@nzcbc.org.nz; internet www.catholic.org.nz.

f. 1974; Pres. Most Rev. JOHN DEW (Archbishop of Wellington); Sec. Rev. PATRICK DUNN (Bishop of Auckland); Exec. Officer ANNE DICKINSON.

Archbishop of Wellington: Most Rev. JOHN A. DEW, Catholic Centre, 22–30 Hill St, POB 1937, Wellington 6140; tel. (4) 496-1766; fax (4) 496-1330; e-mail g.burns@wn.catholic.org.nz; internet www.wn.catholic.org.nz.

Other Christian Churches

Baptist Churches of New Zealand: 473 Great South Rd, POB 12149, Penrose, Auckland; tel. (9) 526-0333; fax (9) 526-0334; e-mail info@baptist.org.nz; internet www.baptist.org.nz; f. 1882; 22,928 mems; Pres. LYN CAMPBELL; Nat. Leader Rev. RODNEY MACANN.

Congregational Union of New Zealand: 8C Kirrie Dr., Te Atatu South, Auckland; tel. (9) 837-2220; fax (9) 620-8291; e-mail cunzsecretary@xtra.co.nz; internet www.congregational.org.nz; f. 1884; 600 mems, 13 churches; Chair. PETER ECCLES; Sec. LUISA FAITAUA.

Lutheran Church of New Zealand: POB 7606, Wellington 6242; tel. (6) 357-3887; fax (6) 357-3897; e-mail lcnz@clear.net.nz; internet www.lcnz.org.nz; 1,130 mems (2010); Pres. Rev. Dr ROBERT ERICKSON.

Methodist Church of New Zealand: Connexional Office, POB 931, Christchurch 8140; tel. (3) 366-6049; fax (3) 364-9439; e-mail info@methodist.org.nz; internet www.methodist.org.nz; 18,548 mems; Gen. Sec. Rev. DAVID BUSH.

Presbyterian Church of Aotearoa New Zealand: Level 1, Terralink House, 275–283 Cuba St, POB 9049, Wellington; tel. (4) 801-6000; fax (4) 801-6001; e-mail info@presbyterian.org.nz; internet www.presbyterian.org.nz; f. 1840; 30,000 mems; Moderator Rev. PETER CHEYNE; Assembly Convenor Rev. EMMA KEOWN.

There are several Maori Churches in New Zealand, with a total membership of over 30,000. These include the Ratana Church of New Zealand, Ringatu Church, Church of Te Kooti Rikirangi, Absolute Maori Established Church, Destiny Church and United Maori Mission. The Antiochian Orthodox Church, the Assemblies of God, the Greek Orthodox Church of New Zealand, the Liberal Catholic Church and the Society of Friends (Quakers) are also active.

BAHÁ'Í FAITH

National Spiritual Assembly of the Bahá'ís of New Zealand: POB 21-551, Henderson, Auckland 1231; tel. (9) 837-4866; fax (9) 837-4898; e-mail admin@bahai.org.nz; internet www.bahai.org.nz; f. 1957; CEO MURRAY R. SMITH.

The Press

NEWSPAPERS AND PERIODICALS

Principal Dailies

In 2006 there were 28 daily newspapers in New Zealand.

Ashburton Guardian: 161 Burnett St, POB 77, Ashburton; tel. (3) 307-7900; fax (3) 307-7980; e-mail enquiries@theguardian.co.nz; internet www.ashburtonguardian.co.nz; f. 1879; morning; Mon.–Sat.; Editor PETER O'NEILL; Man. Dir BRUCE BELL; circ. 5,243 (2010).

Bay of Plenty Times: 108 Durham St, Private Bag 12002, Tauranga; tel. (7) 577-7770; fax (7) 578-0047; e-mail editor@bopp.co.nz; internet www.bayofplentytimes.co.nz; f. 1872; evening; Mon.–Sat.; Gen. Man. DAVID MACKENZIE; Editor SCOTT INGLIS; circ. 20,352 (2010).

The Daily Post: 1143 Hinemoa St, POB 1442, Rotorua; tel. (7) 348-6199; fax (7) 348-0220; e-mail editor@dailypost.co.nz; internet www.dailypost.co.nz; f. 1885; evening; Gen. Man. GREG ALEXANDER; Editor KIM GILLESPIE; circ. 10,294 (2010).

Dominion Post: Dominion Post House, 40 Boulcott St, POB 3740, Wellington; tel. (4) 474-0000; fax (4) 474-0584; e-mail editor@dompost.co.nz; internet www.dompost.co.nz; f. 2002; est. by merger of *The Evening Post* and *The Dominion*; morning; Mon.–Sat.; Gen. Man. PAUL ELENIO; Editor BERNADETTE COURTNEY; circ. 84,047 (2010).

Gisborne Herald: 64 Gladstone Rd, POB 1143, Gisborne; tel. (6) 869-0600; fax (6) 869-0643; e-mail info@gisborneherald.co.nz; internet www.gisborneherald.co.nz; f. 1874; evening; Man. Dir MICHAEL MUIR; Editor JEREMY MUIR; circ. 7,705 (2010).

Greymouth Star: Werita St, POB 3, Greymouth; tel. (3) 768-7121; fax (3) 768-6205; internet www.greystar.co.nz; f. 1866; Mon.–Sat. (evening); Gen. Man. JOHN GOULDING; Editor PAUL MADGWICK; circ. 4,284 (2010).

Hawke's Bay Today: 113 Karamu Rd, POB 180, Hastings; tel. (6) 873-0800; fax (6) 873-0812; e-mail editor@hbtoday.co.nz; internet www.hbtoday.co.nz; f. 1999; evening; conservative; Gen. Man. RUSSELL BROUGHTON; Editor ANTONY PHILLIPS; circ. 24,682 (2010).

Manuwatu Standard: 57–64 The Square, POB 3, Palmerston North; tel. (6) 356-9009; fax (6) 350-9545; e-mail editor@msl.co.nz; internet www.manawatustandard.co.nz; f. 1880; evening; Gen. Man. CRAIG NASH; Editor MICHAEL CUMMINGS; circ. 17,000 (2010).

Marlborough Express: 62–66 Arthur St, POB 242, Blenheim 7274; tel. (3) 520-8900; fax (3) 520-8911; e-mail smason@marlexpress.co.nz; internet www.marlboroughexpress.co.nz; f. 1866; Gen. Man. ROGER G. ROSE; Editor STEVE MASON; circ. 8,986 (2010).

The Nelson Mail: 15 Bridge St, POB 244, Nelson; tel. (3) 548-7079; fax (3) 546-2802; e-mail mailbox@nelsonmail.co.nz; internet www.stuff.co.nz/nelsonmail; f. 1866; evening; Gen. Man. CRAIG DENNIS; Editor PAUL MCINTYRE; circ. 15,609 (2010).

New Zealand Herald: POB 32, Auckland; tel. (9) 379-5050; fax (9) 373-6421; internet www.nzherald.co.nz; f. 1863; morning; CEO MARTIN SIMONS; Editor-in-Chief TIM MURPHY; circ. 170,677 (2010).

The Northern Advocate: 88 Robert St, POB 210, Whangarei; tel. (9) 470-2899; fax (9) 470-2869; e-mail daily@northernadvocate.co.nz; internet www.northernadvocate.co.nz; f. 1875; evening; 6 a week; Gen. Man. ALEX LAWSON; Editor CRAIG COOPER; circ. 13,292 (2010).

The Oamaru Mail: 80 Thames St, POB 343, Oamaru; tel. (3) 434-9970; fax (3) 433-0549; e-mail news@oamarumail.co.nz; internet www.oamarumail.co.nz; f. 1876; Mon.–Fri.; morning; Gen. Man. TONY NIELSEN; Editor SALLY BROOKER; circ. 2,869 (2010).

Otago Daily Times: 52 Stuart St, POB 517, Dunedin; tel. (3) 477-4760; fax (3) 474-7422; e-mail odt.editorial@alliedpress.co.nz;

internet www.odt.co.nz; f. 1861; morning; 6 a week; Man. Dir JULIAN C. S. SMITH; Editor ROBIN CHARTERIS; circ. 39,097 (2010).

The Press: 22 Cathedral Sq., Private Bag 4722, Christchurch 8140; tel. (3) 379-0940; fax (3) 364-8492; e-mail letters@press.co.nz; internet www.press.co.nz; f. 1861; morning; Gen. Man. ANDREW BOYLE; Editor ANDREW HOLDEN; circ. 81,017 (2010).

Southland Times: 67 Esk St, POB 805, Invercargill; tel. (3) 211-1130; fax (3) 214-9905; e-mail letters@stl.co.nz; internet www.southlandtimes.co.nz; f. 1862; morning; Mon.–Sat.; Gen. Man. GARETH CODD; Editor FRED TULETT; circ. 28,066 (2010).

Taranaki Daily News: 49–65 Currie St, POB 444, New Plymouth; tel. (6) 757-6862; fax (6) 758-4653; e-mail editor@dailynews.co.nz; internet www.stuff.co.nz/dailynews; f. 1857; morning; Gen. Man. MIKE BREWER; Editor ROY PILOTT; circ. 23,005 (2010).

Timaru Herald: POB 46, Timaru; tel. (3) 684-4129; fax (3) 688-1042; e-mail editor@timaruherald.co.nz; internet www.timaruherald.co.nz; f. 1864; morning; Gen. Man. CHRIS MCAUSLIN; Editor DAVID KING; circ. 14,010 (2010).

Waikato Times: Private Bag 3086, Hamilton; tel. (7) 849-6180; fax (7) 849-9554; e-mail editor@waikatotimes.co.nz; internet www.stuff.co.nz/waikatotimes; f. 1872; evening; independent; Gen. Man. GERARD WATT; Editor JONATHAN MACKENZIE; circ. 40,096 (2010).

Wairarapa Times-Age: Cnr Perry St and Chapel St, POB 445, Masterton; tel. (6) 378-9999; fax (6) 378-2371; internet www.times-age.co.nz; f. 1938; evening; 6 a week; Gen. Man. PETER WILSON; Editor DAVE SAUNDERS; circ. 6,566 (2010).

Wanganui Chronicle: 59 Taupo Quay, POB 433, Wanganui; tel. (6) 349-0710; fax (6) 349-0721; e-mail news@wanganuichronicle.co.nz; internet www.wanganuichronicle.co.nz; f. 1856; morning; Gen. Man. ANDY JARDEN; Editor ROSS PRINGLE; circ. 11,217 (2010).

Weeklies and Other Newspapers

Best Bets: 155 New North Rd, Eden Terrace, POB 1327, Auckland; tel. (9) 302-1300; fax (9) 366-4565; e-mail alan.caddy@best-bets.co.nz; Sun. and Thur.; horse-racing, trotting and greyhounds; Editor ALAN CADDY; circ. 10,000.

Herald on Sunday: 58 Albert St, POB 32, Auckland; tel. (9) 373-9323; fax (9) 373-9372; internet www.heraldonsunday.co.nz; f. 2004; Editor BRYCE JOHNS; circ. 96,069 (2010).

MG Business: POB 20-034 Bishopdale, Christchurch 8543; tel. (3) 358-3219; fax (3) 358-4490; internet www.mgpublications.co.nz; f. 1876; fmrly Mercantile Gazette; fortnightly; economics, finance, management, stock market, politics; Editor BILL HORSLEY; circ. 16,300.

The National Business Review: POB 1734, Auckland 1140; tel. (9) 307-1629; fax (9) 373-3997; e-mail editor@nbr.co.nz; internet www.nbr.co.nz; f. 1970; weekly; Editor-in-Chief NEVIL GIBSON; circ. 9,093 (2010).

New Zealand Gazette: POB 805, Wellington 6140; tel. (4) 495-7200; fax (4) 470-2932; e-mail info@dia.govt.nz; internet www.gazette.govt.nz; official govt publ; f. 1840; weekly; Chief Exec BRENDAN BOYLE; circ. 1,000.

New Zealand Truth Weekly: Truth Publications Ltd, POB 9613, Newmarket, Auckland 1149; tel. (9) 909-3660; fax (9) 373-5410; e-mail editor@truth.co.nz; internet www.truth.co.nz; f. 1905; Friday; local news and features, TV and entertainment, sports; owned by Truth Publs Ltd; Editor WAYNE BUTLER; circ. 24,000.

North Shore Times: POB 33-235, Takapuna, Auckland; tel. (9) 489-4189; fax (9) 486-6700; e-mail janet.ainsworth@snl.co.nz; 3 a week; Man. JANET AINSWORTH; Editor PETER ELEY; circ. 69,834 (2010).

The Star: POB 1467, Christchurch; tel. (3) 379-7100; fax (3) 366-0180; e-mail star.reporters@starcanterbury.co.nz; internet www.starcanterbury.co.nz; f. 1868; fmrly Christchurch Star; 2 a week; Editor BARRY CLARKE; circ. 118,170.

Sunday News: POB 1327, Auckland; tel. (9) 302-1300; fax (9) 358-3003; e-mail editor@sunday-news.co.nz; internet www.sundaynews.co.nz; Man. Editor MITCHELL MURPHY; circ. 51,740 (2010).

Sunday Star-Times: POB 1327, Auckland 1140; tel. (9) 302-1300; fax (9) 309-0258; e-mail letters@star-times.co.nz; internet www.stuff.co.nz/sunday-star-times; f. 1994 by merger; Editor DAVID KEMEYS; circ. 160,592 (2010).

Taieri Herald: 92 Gordon Rd, POB 105, Mosgiel; tel. (3) 489-7123; fax (3) 489-7668; e-mail sue.gregory@stl.co.nz; f. 1962; weekly; morning; Editor DARYL HOLDEN; circ. 13,049 (2010).

Wairarapa News: Media House, 89 Chapel St, POB 902, Masterton; tel. (6) 370-5690; fax (6) 370-5699; e-mail editor@wainews.co.nz; f. 1869; weekly; Editor WALT DICKSON; circ. 21,019 (2010).

Other Periodicals

AA Directions: POB 5, Auckland 1010; tel. (9) 966-8800; fax (9) 966-8975; e-mail editor@aa.co.nz; internet www.aa.co.nz/Online; f. 1991; quarterly; official magazine of The New Zealand Automobile Asscn; Editor KATHRYN WEBSTER; circ. 542,242 (2010).

Architecture New Zealand: AGM Publishing Ltd, Private Bag 99-915, Newmarket, Auckland; tel. (9) 846-4068; fax (9) 846-8742; e-mail john.walsh@agm.co.nz; internet www.agm.co.nz; f. 1987; every 2 months; Man. Dir IAN CLOSE; Editor JOHN WALSH; circ. 5,609 (2010).

Australian Women's Weekly (NZ edition): Private Bag 92-512, Wellesley St, Auckland; tel. (9) 308-2945; fax (9) 302-0667; e-mail aww@acpmagazines.co.nz; f. 1987; monthly; Editor LEONIE BARLOW; circ. 80,032 (2010).

Dairying Today: POB 3855, Shortland St, Auckland 1140; tel. (9) 307-0399; fax (9) 307-0122; e-mail sudeshk@ruralnews.co.nz; internet www.ruralnews.co.nz; fortnightly; Editor SUDESH KISSUN; circ. 26,792 (2007).

Fashion Quarterly: ACP Media Centre, Private Bag 92-512, Auckland; tel. (9) 308-2409; fax (9) 302-0667; e-mail fq@acpmagazines.co.nz; f. 1982; 5 a year; Editor FIONA HAWTIN; circ. 25,778 (2010).

Grapevine: Private Bag 92-124, Auckland; tel. (9) 813-4956; fax (9) 813-4957; e-mail info@grapevine.org.nz; internet www.grapevine.org.nz; f. 1981; 4 issues a year; family magazine; Editor JOHN COONEY; circ. 160,000.

Home New Zealand: ACP Media Centre, cnr Fanshawe and Beaumont Sts, Private Bag 92-512, Auckland; tel. (9) 308-2739; e-mail homenewzealand@acpmagazines.co.nz; f. 1936; fmrly *NZ Home and Entertaining*; bi-monthly; design, architecture, lifestyle; Editor JEREMY HANSEN; circ. 13,472 (2010).

Info-Link: AGM Publishing Ltd, 409 New North Rd, Kingsland, Auckland; tel. (9) 846-4068; fax (9) 846-8742; e-mail infolink@agm.co.nz; internet www.info-link.co.nz; quarterly; Publr PARUL SHEOPURI; Editor MARK LONGLEY; circ. 19,303 (2008).

Inwood Magazine: POB 17124, Greenlane, Auckland 1546; tel. (9) 921-257; fax (9) 535-7295; e-mail info@inwoodmag.com; internet www.inwoodmag.com; f. 1993; monthly; forestry; Man. Dir TONY NEILSON; circ. 8,000.

Landfall: Otago University Press, POB 56, Dunedin; tel. (3) 479-4194; fax (3) 479-8385; e-mail wendy.harrex@otago.ac.nz; internet www.otago.ac.nz/press/landfall; f. 1947; 2 a year; new fiction, poetry, biographical and critical essays, cultural commentary; Publr WENDY HARREX; Editor DAVID EGGLETON; circ. 1,200.

Mana Magazine: POB 1101, Rotorua; tel. (7) 349-0260; fax (7) 349-0258; e-mail editor@manaonline.co.nz; internet www.manaonline.co.nz; Maori news magazine; Editor DEREK FOX.

New Idea New Zealand: 48 Greys Ave, 4th Floor, Auckland; tel. (9) 979-2726; fax (9) 979-2721; f. 1992; weekly; women's interest; Editor HAYLEY MCLARIN; circ. 50,563 (2010).

New Zealand Dairy Exporter: 8 Weld St, POB 529, Feilding; tel. (6) 323-7104; fax (6) 323-7101; e-mail amelia.grant@nzx.com; internet www.dairymag.co.nz; f. 1925; monthly; Editor GLENYS CHRISTIAN; circ. 7,201 (2010).

New Zealand Gardener: POB 6341, Wellesley St, Auckland 1141; tel. (4) 909-6800; fax (4) 909-6802; e-mail mailbox@nzgardener.co.nz; internet www.nzgardener.co.nz; f. 1944; monthly; Editor LYNDA HALLIMAN; circ. 48,699 (2010).

New Zealand Horse and Pony: POB 12965, Penrose, Auckland; tel. (9) 634-1800; fax (9) 634-2948; e-mail rowan.dixon@horse-pony.co.nz; internet www.horse-pony.co.nz; f. 1959; monthly; Editor ROWAN DIXON; circ. 10,901 (2010).

New Zealand Management: Mediaweb, Wellesley St, POB 5544, Auckland 1141; tel. (9) 529-3000; fax (9) 529-30016; e-mail editor@management.co.nz; internet www.management.co.nz; f. 1955; monthly; business; Publr TONI MYERS; circ. 7,782 (2010).

New Zealand Medical Journal: Dept of Surgery, Christchurch Hospital, POB 4345, Christchurch; tel. (3) 364-1277; fax (3) 364-1683; e-mail nzmj@cdhb.govt.nz; internet www.nzma.org.nz/journal; f. 1887; publ. by New Zealand Medical Asscn; online publ.; articles free to non-subscribers 6 months after publ; 20 a year; Editor Prof. FRANK A. FRIZELLE; circ. 5,000.

New Zealand Science Review: POB 1874, Wellington; tel. (021) 487-284; e-mail editor@scientists.org.nz; internet www.scientists.org.nz; f. 1942; 4 a year; reviews, policy and philosophy of science; Editor ALLEN PETREY.

New Zealand Woman's Day: Wellesley St, Private Bag 92-512, Auckland; tel. (9) 308-2718; fax (9) 357-0978; e-mail wdaynz@acpmagazines.co.nz; weekly; Editor SIDO KITCHIN; circ. 105,127 (2010).

New Zealand Woman's Weekly: POB 90-119, Victoria St West, Auckland 1142; tel. (9) 373-9400; fax (9) 373-9405; e-mail editor@nzww.co.nz; internet www.nzwomansweekly.co.nz; f. 1932; Mon.; women's issues and general interest; Editor SARAH STUART; circ. 80,439 (2010).

Next: Level 4, cnr Fanshawe and Beaumont Sts, Westhaven, Private Bag 92-512, Auckland 1036; tel. (9) 308-2775; fax (9) 377-6725; e-mail next@acpmagazines.co.nz; internet www.acpmedia.co.nz; f. 1991; monthly; home and lifestyle; owned by ACP Media; Editor CHRISTINA SAYERS WICKSTEAD; circ. 46,489 (2010).

North & South: Wellesley St, Private Bag 92-512, Auckland; tel. (9) 366-5337; fax (9) 308-9498; e-mail northsouth@acpmedia.co.nz; f. 2011; f. 1986; monthly; current affairs and lifestyle; Editor VIRGINIA LARSON; circ. 26,819 (2010).

NZ Catholic: POB 147-000, Ponsonby, Auckland 1034; tel. (9) 360-3067; fax (9) 360-3065; e-mail contact@nzcatholic.org.nz; internet www.nzcatholic.org.nz; f. 1996; fortnightly; Roman Catholic; Man. Editor PETER GRACE; circ. 6,700.

NZ House and Garden: 317 New North Rd, Eden Terrace, Auckland; tel. (9) 909-6913; fax (9) 909-6802; e-mail sally.duggan@nzhouseandgarden.co.nz; internet www.nzhouseandgarden.co.nz; f. 1994; monthly; Editor KATE COUGHLAN; circ. 48,752 (2010).

NZ Listener: POB 90-783, Victoria St West, Auckland 1142; tel. (9) 373-9400; fax (9) 373-9406; e-mail submissions@listener.co.nz; internet www.listener.co.nz; f. 1939; weekly; current affairs and entertainment; Editor PAMELA STIRLING; Publr and Chief Exec. SARAH SANDLEY; circ. 73,404.

Otago Southland Farmer: POB 105, Mosgiel; tel. (3) 489-7123; fax (3) 489-7668; e-mail newspapersales@stl.co.nz; f. 1982; fortnightly; Editor TAM MATANGI; circ. 22,180 (2008).

Pacific Wings: POB 57163, Mana, Porirua 5247; tel. (4) 233-8368; e-mail editor@pacificwingsmagazine.com; internet www.pacificwingsmagazine.com; f. 1932; monthly; aviation; Editor and Publr ROB NEIL; circ. 20,000.

PC World: POB 6813, Wellesley St, Auckland; tel. (9) 926-9108; fax (9) 909-6989; e-mail ted.gibbons@ffxbusinessgroup.co.nz; internet pcworld.co.nz; f. 1988; monthly; Editor ZARA BAXTER; circ. 12,120 (2010).

Prodesign: AGM Publishing Ltd, Private Bag 99-915, Newmarket, Auckland; tel. (9) 846-2722; fax (9) 846-8742; e-mail michael.barrett@agm.co.nz; f. 1992; every 2 months; publ. of the Designers' Institute of New Zealand; Editor MICHAEL BARRETT; circ. 5,717 (2010).

PSA Journal: PSA House, 11 Aurora Terrace, POB 3817, Wellington 6140; tel. (4) 495-7633; fax (4) 917-2051; e-mail enquiries@psa.org.nz; internet www.psa.org.nz; f. 1913; 4 a year; journal of the NZ Public Service Asscn; Pres. PAULA SCHOLES; circ. 52,000.

Reader's Digest: POB 90-487, Mail Service Centre, Auckland; e-mail editor@readersdigest.co.nz; internet www.readersdigest.co.nz; f. 1950; monthly; Editor TONY SPENCER-SMITH; circ. 91,145 (2008).

RSA Review: RNZRSA National Headquarters, POB 27248, Wellington 6030; tel. (6) 384-7994; fax (6) 385-3325; e-mail subscribe@rnzrsa.org.nz; internet www.rsa.org.nz; quarterly; official magazine of the Royal New Zealand Returned and Services' Asscn; Editor BARRY ALLISON; circ. 95,000.

Rural News: POB 3855, Auckland; tel. (9) 307-0399; fax (9) 307-0122; e-mail editor@ruralnews.co.nz; fortnightly; Editor HAMISH CARNACHAN; circ. 81,811 (2007).

Spanz: POB 9049, Wellington; tel. (4) 801-6000; fax (4) 801-6001; e-mail amanda@presbyterian.org.nz; internet www.presbyterian.org.nz; f. 1987; bi-monthly; magazine of Presbyterian Church; circ. 21,500.

Straight Furrow: c/o Rural Press, POB 4233, Auckland; tel. (9) 524-1177; fax (9) 524-1170; e-mail straightfurrow@ruralpress.com; internet www.straightfurrow.co.nz; f. 1933; weekly; Group Editor JEFF SMITH; circ. 85,000.

Time New Zealand: POB 198, Auckland 1015; fax (9) 366-4706; internet www.time.com; weekly; circ. 23,970 (2008).

TV Guide (NZ): 317–319 New North Rd, Eden Terrace, POB 6341, Auckland; tel. (9) 909-6902; fax (9) 909-6912; e-mail julie.eley@tv-guide.co.nz; internet www.stuff.co.nz/entertainment/tv; f. 1986; weekly; Editor JULIE ELEY; circ. 155,591 (2011).

United Nations Association New Zealand: UNANZ, POB 24494, Wellington 6142; tel. (4) 496-9638; e-mail office@unanz.org.nz; internet www.unanz.org.nz; f. 1946; every 2 months; Pres. ANTONY VALLYON.

NEWS AGENCY

South Pacific News Service Ltd (Sopacnews): Lambton Quay, POB 5026, Wellington; tel. and fax (3) 472-8329; e-mail farthing@deepsouth.co.nz; f. 1948; Man. Editor NEALE MCMILLAN.

PRESS COUNCIL

New Zealand Press Council: The Terrace, 79 Boulcott St, POB 10879, Wellington; tel. (4) 473-5220; fax (4) 471-1785; e-mail info@presscouncil.org.nz; internet www.presscouncil.org.nz; f. 1972; Chair. BARRY PATERSON; Exec. Dir M. E. MAJOR.

PRESS ASSOCIATIONS

Commonwealth Press Union (New Zealand Section): POB 1066, Wellington; tel. (4) 472-6223; fax (4) 471-0987; Sec. LINCOLN GOULD.

Newspaper Publishers' Association of New Zealand (Inc): Newspaper House, 93 Boulcott St, POB 1066, Wellington 6015; tel. (4) 472-6223; fax (4) 471-0987; e-mail npa@npa.co.nz; internet www.npa.co.nz; f. 1898; 31 mems; Pres. MICHAEL MUIR; CEO TIM PANKHURST.

Publishers

Auckland University Press: Private Bag 92019, University of Auckland, Auckland; tel. (9) 373-7528; fax (9) 373-7465; e-mail aup@auckland.ac.nz; internet www.auckland.ac.nz/aup; f. 1966; scholarly press; Dir SAM ELWORTHY.

The Caxton Press Ltd: 113 Victoria St, POB 25-088, Christchurch 8013; tel. (3) 366-8516; fax (3) 365-7840; e-mail peter@caxton.co.nz; internet www.caxton.co.nz; f. 1935; human and general interest, local and NZ history, tourist publs; Man. Dir BRUCE BASCAND.

Dunmore Publishing Ltd: POB 250-80, Wellington 6146; tel. (4) 472-2705; fax (4) 471-0604; e-mail books@dunmore.co.nz; internet dunmore.circlesoft.net; f. 1975; non-fiction, educational; Publrs MURRAY GATENBY, SHARMIAN FIRTH.

Hachette New Zealand Ltd: POB 100-749, North Shore Mail Centre, Auckland 0745; tel. (9) 477-5550; fax (9) 477-5560; e-mail admin@hachette.co.nz; f. 1971; fmrly Hachette Livre NZ Ltd; Man. Dir KEVIN CHAPMAN.

HarperCollins Publishers (New Zealand) Ltd: POB 1, Shortland St, Auckland 1140; tel. (9) 443-9400; fax (9) 443-9403; e-mail editors@harpercollins.co.nz; internet www.harpercollins.co.nz; f. 1888; general and educational; CEO MICHAEL MOYNAHAN; Man. Dir TONY FISK.

Learning Media Ltd: POB 3293, Wellington; tel. (4) 472-5522; fax (4) 472-6444; e-mail info@learningmedia.co.nz; internet www.learningmedia.co.nz; f. 1947; est. as School Publs; state-owned enterprise; contract publishing, professional devt services, and educational products in a range of media and languages; Chief Exec. DAVID GLOVER.

Legislation Direct: POB 12357, Wellington 6144; tel. (4) 568-0005; fax (4) 568-0003; e-mail Ldorders@legislationdirect.co.nz; internet www.legislationdirect.co.nz; general publishers and leading distributor of government publs; fmrly Govt Printing Office/GP Publications; Publications Man. WENDY CAYLOR.

LexisNexis NZ Ltd: Level 1, 181 Wakefield St, POB 472, Wellington 6140; tel. (4) 385-1479; fax (4) 385-1598; internet www.lexisnexis.co.nz; legal; Man. Dir HUGO MAHONEY.

McGraw-Hill Book Co, New Zealand Ltd: Private Bag 11904, Ellerslie, Auckland 1005; tel. (9) 526-6200; fax (9) 526-6216; e-mail cservice_auckland@mcgraw-hill.com; internet www.mcgraw-hill.com.au; f. 1974; educational; Man. Dir MURRAY ST LEGER.

New Zealand Council for Educational Research: POB 3237, Wellington 6140; tel. (4) 384-7939; fax (4) 384-7933; e-mail sales@nzcer.org.nz; internet www.nzcer.org.nz; f. 1934; scholarly, research monographs, educational, academic, periodicals; Chair. ALISON GILMORE; Dir ROBYN BAKER.

Otago University Press: POB 56, Dunedin; tel. (3) 479-8807; fax (3) 479-8385; e-mail university.press@otago.ac.nz; internet www.otago.ac.nz/press; f. 1958; publishes titles on New Zealand, the Pacific and Asia, with special emphasis on history, literature, the arts and natural and social sciences; also educational titles and journals; Publr WENDY HARREX.

Pearson Education New Zealand Ltd: Private Bag 102-902, North Shore City, Auckland 0745; tel. (9) 442-7400; fax (9) 442-7401; e-mail customer.service@pearsonnz.co.nz; internet www.pearsoned.co.nz; f. 1968; fmrly Addison Wesley Longman; educational; Dirs ROSEMARY STAGG, P. FIELD.

Penguin Group (NZ) Ltd: Private Bag 102-902, North Shore Mail Centre, Auckland 0745; tel. (9) 442-7400; fax (9) 442-7401; e-mail publishing@penguin.co.nz; internet www.penguin.co.nz; f. 1973; Man. Dir MARGARET THOMPSON.

Wendy Pye Ltd: Sunshine Bookshop, 413 Great South Rd, Ellerslie, 1051 Auckland; tel. (9) 525-3575; fax (9) 525-4205; e-mail sales@sunshine.co.nz; internet www.sunshinebooks.com.au; children's fiction and educational; Man. Dir WENDY PYE.

Random House New Zealand Ltd: Private Bag 102-950, North Shore Mail Centre, Auckland; tel. (9) 444-7197; fax (9) 444-7524; e-mail admin@randomhouse.co.nz; internet www.randomhouse.co.nz; f. 1977; general; Chair. MICHAEL MOYNAHAN; Man. Dir KAREN FERNS.

Victoria University Press: POB 600, Wellington; tel. (4) 463-6580; fax (4) 463-6581; e-mail victoria-press@vuw.ac.nz; internet www.victoria.ac.nz/vup; f. 1970; Publr FERGUS BARROWMAN.

PUBLISHERS' ASSOCIATION

Publishers' Association of New Zealand Inc: Private Bag 102006, North Shore City, Auckland 0745; tel. (9) 477-5589; fax (9) 477-5570; e-mail admin@publishers.org.nz; internet www.publishers.org.nz; f. 1977; Dir ANNE DE LAUTOUR.

Broadcasting and Communications

TELECOMMUNICATIONS

CallPlus: Level 4, 110 Symonds St, POB 108-109, Auckland; tel. (9) 915-7575; e-mail info@callplus.co.nz; internet www.callplus.co.nz; f. 1996; 100% New Zealand owned; full-service telecommunications co; Gen. Man. KELVIN HUSSEY.

Compass Communications Ltd: Level 2, Compass House, 162 Grafton Rd, Grafton, POB 2533, Auckland; tel. (9) 965-2200; fax (9) 965-2270; internet www.compass.net.nz; f. 1995; CEO KARIM HUSSONA.

Kordia: Level 4, Fidelity House, 81 Carlton Gore Rd, Auckland 1023; tel. (9) 916-6400; fax (9) 916-6402; internet www.kordiasolutions.com; fmrly known as THL Group; name changed as above 2006; telecommunications, broadcasting and converged solutions; operates in New Zealand and Australia; Chair. DAVID CLARKE; CEO GEOFF HUNT.

Orcon Internet Ltd: POB 302362, North Harbour, Auckland 0751; tel. (9) 444-4414; e-mail support@orcon.net.nz; internet www.orcon.net.nz; state-owned; provides mobile and internet services; CEO SCOTT BARTLETT.

Telecom Corpn of New Zealand Ltd: Telecom House, 8 Hereford St, Auckland 1011; tel. (4) 801-9000; fax (4) 385-3469; internet www.telecom.co.nz; Chair. WAYNE BOYD; Chief Exec. PAUL REYNOLDS.

Telecommunications Users Association of New Zealand (TUANZ): POB 33-1014, Takapuna North Shore Mail Centre 0740; tel. (9) 488-1888; fax (9) 489-9515; e-mail bernice@tuanz.org.nz; internet www.tuanz.org.nz; f. 1986; non-profit asscn representing corporate telecommunications users; Chair. PAT O'CONNELL; CEO PAUL BRISLEN; 500 corporate mems.

TelstraClear: Private Bag 92-143, Auckland 1142; tel. (9) 913-9150; fax (9) 982-6232; internet www.telstraclear.co.nz; f. 1990; est. as Clear Communications Ltd; merged with TelstraSaturn Ltd 2001; owned by Australian telecommunications co Telstra; business solutions, local and toll services, enhanced internet, etc.; Chair. DAVID THODEY; CEO Dr ALLAN FREETH.

Two Degrees Mobile Ltd: Symonds St, POB 8355, Auckland 1150; tel. 222002000; e-mail info@2degreesmobile.co.nz; internet www.2degreesmobile.co.nz; CEO ERIC HERTZ.

Vodafone New Zealand Ltd: POB 7281, Wellesley St, Auckland 1141; tel. (9) 355-2007; fax (9) 962-9300; internet www.vodafone.co.nz; fmrly Bell South; cellular network; CEO RUSSELL STANNERS.

Woosh Wireless Ltd: 11–15 Railway St, POB 9635, Newmarket, Auckland; tel. (9) 940-0111; fax (9) 520-3447; internet www.woosh.com; f. 1999 as Walker Wireless Ltd; name changed as above 2003; provides internet and telephony services; Chair. ROD INGLIS; CEO KEVIN WILEY.

WorldxChange Communications Ltd: Level 9, Tower Two, 55–65 Shortland St, POB 3296, Auckland; tel. (9) 950-1300; e-mail service@wxc.co.nz; internet www.wxc.co.nz; CEO CECIL ALEXANDER.

Regulatory Authority

Telecommunications Policy Section, Ministry of Economic Development: 33 Bowen St, POB 1473, Wellington; tel. (4) 472-0030; fax (4) 473-4638; e-mail info@med.govt.nz; internet www.med.govt.nz.

BROADCASTING

Radio

Radio Broadcasters' Association (NZ) Inc: POB 3762, Auckland; tel. (9) 378-0788; fax (9) 378-8180; e-mail janine@rba.co.nz; internet www.rba.co.nz; represents commercial radio industry; Exec. Council Chair. JOHN MCELHINNEY; Exec. Dir DAVID INNES; 13 mems.

Radio New Zealand Ltd: RNZ House, 155 The Terrace, POB 123, Wellington; tel. (4) 474-1999; fax (4) 474-1459; e-mail rnz@radionz.co.nz; internet www.radionz.co.nz; f. 1936; Crown-owned entity, operating non-commercial national networks: Radio New Zealand National and Radio New Zealand Concert; parliamentary broadcasts on AM Network; Radio New Zealand News and Current Affairs; short-wave service, Radio New Zealand International; Chair. RICHARD GRIFFIN; CEO PETER CAVANAGH.

The Radio Network of New Zealand Ltd: 54 Cook St, Private Bag 92-198, Auckland; tel. (9) 373-0000; e-mail enquiry@radionetwork.co.nz; internet www.radionetwork.co.nz; operates 129 commercial stations, reaching 1.4m. people; Chief Exec. JOHN MCELHINNEY.

Television

Television New Zealand (TVNZ) Ltd: Television Centre, 100 Victoria St West, POB 3819, Auckland; tel. (9) 916-7000; fax (9) 916-7934; e-mail news@tvnz.co.uk; internet www.tvnz.co.nz; f. 1960; the television service is responsible for the production of programmes for five TV networks: TV One, TV2, TVNZ Sport Extra, TVNZ 6 and TVNZ 7; networks are commercial all week and transmit in colour; channels broadcast 24 hours a day, seven days a week, and reach 99.9% of the population; Chair. Sir JOHN ANDERSON; CEO RICK ELLIS.

Maori Television: 9–15 Davis Cres., POB 113-017, Newmarket, Auckland; tel. (9) 539-7000; fax (9) 539-7199; e-mail info@maoritelevision.com; internet www.maoritelevision.com; f. 2003; owned by the Crown and Te Putahi Paoho; operates two stations; Te Reo station, launched in early 2008, broadcasts Maori-language programmes daily; Maori Television channel broadcasts Maori- and English-language programmes; Chair. GARRY MURIWAI; CEO JIM MATHER.

Private Television

Auckland Independent Television Services Ltd: POB 1629, Auckland.

Sky Network Television Limited: 10 Panorama Rd, POB 9059, Newmarket, Auckland; tel. (9) 579-9999; fax (9) 579-0910; internet www.skytv.co.nz; f. 1990; UHF service on seven channels, satellite service; 720,919 subscribers (Dec. 2007); Chair. PETER MACOURT; CEO JOHN FELLET.

TV3 Network Services Ltd: Symonds St, Private Bag 92-624, Auckland; tel. (9) 377-9730; fax (9) 366-5949; internet www.tv3.co.nz; f. 1989; operated by MediaWorks NZ; Man. Dir RICK FRIESEN.

Finance

(cap. = capital; res = reserves; dep. = deposits; m. = million; br(s). = branch(es); amounts in New Zealand dollars)

BANKING

Central Bank

Reserve Bank of New Zealand (RBNZ): 2 The Terrace, POB 2498, Wellington; tel. (4) 472-2029; fax (4) 473-8554; e-mail rbnz-info@rbnz.govt.nz; internet www.rbnz.govt.nz; f. 1933; cap. 1,600m., res 1,085m., dep. 19,464m. (June 2010); Gov. ALAN BOLLARD; Chair. Dr ARTHUR GRIMES.

Regulatory Authority

Financial Markets Authority: Level 8, Unisys House, 56 The Terrace, POB 1179, Wellington 6140; tel. (4) 472-9830; fax (4) 472-8076; internet www.fma.govt.nz; f. 2011; regulatory body for securities exchanges, financial advisers and brokers, trustees and issuers, and auditors; Chair. SIMON ALLEN; CEO SEAN HUGHES.

Registered Banks

As a result of legislation that took effect in 1987, several foreign banks were incorporated into the domestic banking system. In March 2011 there were 20 registered banks in New Zealand.

ANZ National Bank Ltd: Level 14, ANZ Tower, 215–229 Lambton Quay, Wellington; tel. (4) 470-3142; fax (4) 494-4000; internet www.anz.com/nz; f. 1979; subsidiary of Australia and New Zealand Banking Group Ltd of Melbourne, Australia; fmrly ANZ Banking Group (New Zealand) Ltd; name changed as above 2004 following merger with Nat. Bank of New Zealand Ltd; cap. 9,817m., res 889m., dep. 277,039m. (Sept. 2007); Chair. Sir DRYDEN SPRING; CEO DAVID HISCO; 143 brs and sub-brs.

ASB Bank Ltd: Level 28, ASB Bank Centre, 135 Albert Sts, POB 35, Auckland 1010; tel. (9) 306-3000; fax (9) 358-3511; e-mail helpdesk@asbbank.co.nz; internet www.asbbank.co.nz; f. 1847; est. as Auckland Savings Bank, name changed 1988; cap. 2,798m., res –121m., dep. 58,662m. (June 2010); Chair. G. J. JUDD; Man. Dir BARBARA CHAPMAN; 138 brs.

Bank of India (New Zealand) Ltd: Level 18, PWC Towers, Quay St, Auckland; e-mail boi.nz@bankofindia.co.in; internet www.bankofindia.co.nz.

Bank of New Zealand (BNZ): BNZ Tower, 125 Queen St, Auckland; tel. (9) 302-4955; fax (9) 375-9537; internet www.bnz.co.nz; f. 1861; owned by Nat. Australia Bank; cap. 2,161m., res –3m., dep.

63,366m. (Sept. 2009); Chair. JOHN WALLER; Man. Dir and CEO ANDREW THORBURN; 179 domestic brs and 1 overseas br.

Citibank NA (USA): Level 11, Citibank Centre, 23 Customs St East, POB 3429, Auckland 1140; tel. (9) 307-1902; fax (9) 308-9928; e-mail citinewzealand@citi.com; internet www.citi.co.nz; Chief Country Officer STEPHEN ROBERTS; 2 brs.

Deutsche Bank New Zealand: Level 11, ASB Bank Centre, Wellesley St, POB 6900, Auckland; tel. (9) 351-1000; fax (9) 351-1001; e-mail deutsche-ausnz.press@db.com; internet www.deutsche-bank.co.nz; f. 1986; fmrly Bankers Trust New Zealand; Chair. JOSEPH ACKERNMAN.

Hongkong and Shanghai Banking Corporation Ltd (Hong Kong): 1 Queen St, Level 9, POB 5947, Auckland 1010; tel. (9) 918-8688; fax (9) 918-8797; e-mail premier@hsbc.co.nz; internet www.hsbc.co.nz; CEO DAVID JAMES GRIFFITHS; 6 brs.

Kiwibank Ltd: Private Bag 39888, Wellington Mail Centre, Lower Hutt 5045; tel. (4) 473-1133; fax (4) 462-7922; internet www.kiwibank.co.nz; f. 2002; 100% New Zealand-owned; savings bank for small depositors; cap. 295m., res 60.1m., dep. 10,436.9m. (June 2009); Chair. IAN FITZGERALD; Chief Exec. PAUL BROCK.

Rabobank (New Zealand): POB 38-396, Wellington Mail Centre, Wellington; tel. (4) 819-2700; fax (4) 819-2706; e-mail wellington.enquiry@rabobank.com; internet www.rabobank.co.nz; f. 1996; full subsidiary of Rabobank Nederland; Chair. PIET MOERLAND; CEO BRUCE DICK; 30 brs.

TSB Bank Ltd: POB 240, New Plymouth; tel. (6) 872-2265; fax (6) 968-3815; internet www.tsbbank.co.nz; f. 1850; cap. 10m., res 4.2m., dep. 4,025.1m. (March 2010); Chair. ELAINE GILL; Man. Dir KEVIN MURPHY; 24 brs.

Westpac New Zealand: 188 Quay St, Auckland; tel. (9) 912-8000; fax (4) 498-1350; e-mail customer_support@westpac.co.nz; internet www.westpac.co.nz; acquired Trust Bank New Zealand; New Zealand division of Westpac Banking Corpn (Australia); Chair. PETER WILSON; CEO GEORGE FRAZIS; 200 brs.

Association

New Zealand Bankers' Association: Level 14, Kordia House, 109–125 Willis St, POB 3043, Wellington 6140; tel. (4) 802-3358; fax (4) 473-1698; e-mail nzba@nzba.org.nz; internet www.nzba.org.nz; f. 1891; Chief Exec. SARAH MEHRTENS.

STOCK EXCHANGES

Dunedin Stock Exchange: POB 298, Dunedin; tel. (3) 477-5900; Chair. E. S. EDGAR; Sec. R. P. LEWIS.

New Zealand Exchange Ltd (NZX): Level 2, NZX Centre, 11 Cable St, POB 2959, Wellington 6140; tel. (4) 472-7599; fax (4) 496-2893; e-mail info@nzx.com; internet www.nzx.com; Chair. ANDREW HARMOS; CEO MARK WELDON.

Supervisory Body

New Zealand Securities Commission: POB 1179, Wellington 6011; tel. (4) 472-9830; fax (4) 472-8076; e-mail seccom@seccom.govt.nz; internet www.seccom.govt.nz; f. 1978; Chair. JANE DIPLOCK.

INSURANCE

ACE Insurance NZ Ltd: POB 734, Auckland 1010; tel. (9) 377-1459; fax (9) 303-1909; e-mail michael.poole@ace-ina.com; internet www.aceinsurance.co.nz; CEO GILES WARD.

AMI Insurance Ltd: 29–35 Latimer Sq., POB 2116, Christchurch 8001; tel. (3) 371-9000; fax (3) 371-8340; internet www.ami.co.nz; f. 1926; Chair. KERRY G. L. NOLAN; CEO JOHN B. BALMFORTH.

Atradius: POB 2404, Auckland 1140; tel. (9) 302-4560; fax (9) 353-1244; e-mail info.nz@atradius.com; internet www.atradius.co.nz; f. 1925; fmrly known as Gerling NCM; name changed as above following acquisition by Deutsche Bank and Swiss Re; trade credit insurance services.

AXA New Zealand Ltd: POB 1692, Wellington 6140; tel. (4) 474-4500; fax (4) 161-699; e-mail askus@axa.co.nz; internet www.axa.co.nz; Gen. Man. SID MILLER.

BNZ Life Insurance Ltd: POB 1299, Wellington; tel. (4) 382-2577; fax (4) 474-6883; internet www.bnz.co.nz; Chair. JOHN WALLER; Man. Dir and CEO ANDREW THORBURN.

Farmers' Mutual Group: POB 1943, Palmerston North Central, Palmerston North 4440; tel. (6) 356-9456; fax (6) 356-4603; e-mail contact@fimg.co.nz; internet fmg.co.nz; f. 1905; comprises Farmers' Mutual Finance Ltd and other cos; insurance investment and financial services for the New Zealand rural sector; Chair. GREG GENT.

ING Life (NZ) Ltd: Private Bag 92131, Victoria St West, Auckland 1142; tel. (9) 442-4800; fax (9) 442-4801; e-mail clientserviceslife@onepath.co.nz; internet www.inglife.co.nz; operates ANZ- and The Nat. Bank-branded insurance policies; CEO HELEN TROUP; Man. Dir, Insurance NAOMI BALLANTYNE.

New Zealand Insurance: NZI, Private Bag 92130, Auckland 1030; tel. (9) 969-6000; fax (9) 309-7097; internet www.nzi.co.nz; owned by Insurance Australia Group New Zealand Ltd; Exec. Gen. Man. KARL ARMSTRONG.

New Zealand Local Government Insurance Corporation Ltd (Civic Assurance): POB 5521, Wellington 6145; tel. (4) 978-1250; fax (4) 978-1260; e-mail info@civicassurance.co.nz; internet www.civicassurance.co.nz; f. 1960; local govt insurance provider; fire, motor, all risks, accident; Chief Exec. TIM SOLE.

QBE Insurance (International) Ltd: Level 6, AMP Centre, 29 Customs St West, Auckland; tel. (9) 366-9920; fax (9) 308-8526; internet www.qbe.co.nz/insurance.html; f. 1890; Gen. Man. ROSS CHAPMAN.

Sovereign Ltd: Private Bag Sovereign, Auckland Mail Centre 1142; tel. (9) 487-9000; fax (9) 487-8003; e-mail enquire@sovereign.co.nz; internet www.sovereign.co.nz; f. 1989; life insurance and investment; Chief Exec. CHARLES ANDERSON.

State Insurance Ltd: POB 3233, Wellington 6140; tel. (9) 969-1150; fax (4) 476-9664; internet www.state.co.nz; f. 1905; mem. NRMA Insurance Group; Man. Dir T. C. SOLE.

Tower Insurance Ltd: Level 11, Tower Centre, 22 Fanshawe St, POB 90347, Auckland; tel. (9) 369-2000; fax (9) 369-2040; e-mail contactus@tower.co.nz; internet www.tower.co.nz; f. 1869; fmrly Nat. Insurance Co of New Zealand; Chair. TONY GIBBS; Group Man. Dir ROB FLANNAGAN.

Associations

Insurance Council of New Zealand: iSoft House, Level 7, 111–115 Customhouse Quay, POB 474, Wellington; tel. (4) 472-5230; fax (4) 473-3011; e-mail icnz@icnz.org.nz; internet www.icnz.org.nz; f. 1895; Chief Exec. CHRISTOPHER RYAN.

Investment Savings and Insurance Association of New Zealand Inc: City Chambers, Cnr Johnston and Featherston Sts, POB 1514, Wellington, 6140; tel. (4) 473-8730; fax (4) 471-1881; e-mail isi@isi.org.nz; internet www.isi.org.nz; f. 1996 from Life Office Asscn and Investment Funds Asscn; represents cos that act as manager, trustee, issuer, insurer, etc. of managed funds, life insurance and superannuation; Chair. SEAN CARROLL; Chief Exec. PETER NEILSON.

Trade and Industry

GOVERNMENT AGENCY

New Zealand Trade and Enterprise (NZTE): POB 2878, Wellington 6140; tel. (4) 816-8100; fax (4) 816-8101; e-mail info@nzte.govt.nz; internet www.nzte.govt.nz; f. 2003; national govt devt agency, with global network of offices; provides businesses, organizations and investors with access to goods and services; facilitates partnerships with New Zealand businesses and investment opportunities; Chair. JON MAYSON; CEO PETER CHRISP.

CHAMBERS OF COMMERCE

Auckland Regional Chamber of Commerce and Industry: POB 47, Auckland 1140; tel. (9) 309-6100; fax (9) 309-0081; e-mail auckland@chamber.co.nz; internet www.chamber.co.nz; CEO MICHAEL BARNETT; Chair. JOHN LINDSAY.

Canterbury Employers' Chamber of Commerce: 57 Kilmore St, POB 359, Christchurch 8140; tel. (3) 366-5096; fax (3) 379-5454; e-mail info@cecc.org.nz; internet www.cecc.org.nz; f. 1859; formed through merger of Employers' Fed. and Chamber of Commerce; employment and business support services, incl. legal consultancy and international trade advice, business performance and training, networking and advocacy; Chief Exec. PETER TOWNSEND; Pres. ALLAN POLLARD.

Employers' Chamber of Commerce Central: POB 1087, Wellington 6140; tel. (4) 473-7224; fax (4) 473-4501; e-mail ema@emacentral.org.nz; internet www.eccc.org.nz; f. 1997 as Employers' and Manufacturers' Association (Central Inc); renamed as above following merger with Wellington Regional Chamber of Commerce; CEO KEN HARRIS; 2,200 mems.

Otago Chamber of Commerce Inc: Ground Floor, Burns House, 10 George St, POB 5173, Dunedin 9058; tel. (3) 479-0181; fax (3) 477-0341; e-mail office@otagochamber.co.nz; internet www.otagochamber.co.nz; f. 1861; CEO J. A. CHRISTIE; Pres. M. WILLIS.

Wellington Employers' Chamber of Commerce: POB 1590, Wellington 6140; tel. (4) 473-7224; fax (4) 473-4501; e-mail info@wecc.org.nz; internet www.wecc.org.nz; f. 1856; fmrly Wellington Regional Chamber of Commerce; Chief Exec. KEN HARRIS; Pres. RICHARD STONE; 1,000 mems.

INDUSTRIAL AND TRADE ASSOCIATIONS

Employers' and Manufacturers' Association (Northern Inc): 159 Khyber Pass Rd, Grafton, Private Bag 92066, Auckland; tel. (9) 367-0900; fax (9) 367-0902; e-mail ema@ema.co.nz; internet www.ema.co.nz; f. 1886; fmrly Auckland Manufacturers' Asscn; Chief Exec. ALASDAIR THOMPSON; Pres. GRAHAM MOUNTFORT; 5,000 mems.

ENZA: 405 Williams St, POB 279, Hastings; tel. (9) 878-1898; fax (9) 878-1850; e-mail info@enza.co.nz; internet www.enza.co.nz; f. 1956; owned by Turners and Growers Ltd; fmrly New Zealand Apple and Pear Marketing Bd; export apples, pears and kiwifruit; creates new apple varieties; Man. Dir JEFF WESLEY; Gen. Man. SNOW HARDY.

Federated Farmers of New Zealand (Inc): POB 715, Wellington; tel. (4) 473-7269; fax (4) 473-1081; e-mail receptionwgton@fedfarm.org.nz; internet www.fedfarm.org.nz; f. 1945; Pres. DON NICOLSON; CEO CONOR ENGLISH; 16,000 mems.

Horticulture New Zealand: POB 10232, The Terrace, Wellington 6143; tel. (4) 472-3795; fax (4) 471-2861; e-mail info@hortnz.co.nz; internet www.hortnz.co.nz; est. by merger of New Zealand Fruitgrowers' Fed., New Zealand Berryfruit Fed. and New Zealand Vegetable and Potato Growers' Fed; 7,000 mems; Pres. and Chair. ANDREW FENTON; CEO PETER SILCOCK.

Kiwifruit New Zealand (KNZ): POB 4683, Mt Maunganui South 3149; tel. (7) 572-3685; fax (7) 572-5934; e-mail richard.procter@knz.co.nz; f. 2000; Chair. Sir BRIAN ELWOOD.

Meat and Wool New Zealand: POB 121, Wellington 6140; tel. (4) 473-9150; fax (4) 474-0800; e-mail enquiries@beeflambnz.com; internet www.meatandwoolnz.com; Chair. MIKE PETERSEN; CEO Dr SCOTT CHAMPION.

Meat Industry Association of New Zealand (Inc) (MIA): Level 5, Wellington Chambers, 154 Featherston St, Wellington 6011; tel. (4) 473-6465; fax (4) 473-1731; e-mail info@mia.co.nz; internet www.mia.co.nz; Chair. W. J. (BILL) FALCONER; CEO TIM RITCHE.

National Beekeepers' Association of New Zealand (Inc): Level 6, Adecco House, 330 Lambton Quay, POB 10792, Wellington; tel. (6) 471-6254; fax (6) 499-0876; e-mail secretary@nba.org.nz; internet www.nba.org.nz; f. 1913; 400 mems; Pres. SETH BELSON; Secs JESSICA WILLIAMS, PAULINE DOWNIE.

New Zealand Animal By-Products Exporters' Association: 11 Longhurst Terrace, POB 12-222, Christchurch; tel. (3) 332-2895; fax (3) 332-2825; 25 mems; Sec. J. L. NAYSMITH.

New Zealand Council of Wool Exporters Inc: POB 2857, Christchurch; tel. (3) 353-1049; fax (3) 374-6925; e-mail cwe@woolexport.net; internet www.woolexport.net; f. 1893; Exec. Man. R. H. F. NICHOLSON; Pres. JOHN DAWSON.

The New Zealand Forest Owners' Association: POB 1208, Wellington 6140; tel. (4) 473-4769; fax (4) 499-8893; e-mail nzfoa@nzfoa.org.nz; internet www.nzfoa.org.nz; f. 1926; Pres. PETER BERG; Chief Exec. DAVID RHODES.

New Zealand Fruit Wine and Cider Makers Inc: POB 912, New Plymouth; tel. and fax (6) 769-9009; e-mail admin@fruitwines.co.nz; internet www.fruitwines.co.nz; f. 1985; 40 mems; represents all non-grape wine, cider, perry and mead makers in New Zealand; Chair. JUSTIN HALL; Exec. Officer CHRISTINE GARNHAM.

New Zealand Manufacturers' and Exporters' Association (MEA): POB 13152, Armagh, Christchurch 8141; tel. (3) 353-2540; fax (3) 353-2549; e-mail cma@cma.org.nz; internet www.mea.org.nz; f. 2007; est. by merger of Canterbury Manufacturers' Asscn and New Zealand Engineers' Fed; CEO JOHN L WALLEY; Pres. ALLEN VOSS.

New Zealand Meat Board: POB 121, Wellington 6140; tel. (4) 473-9150; fax (4) 474-0801; e-mail info@nzmeatboard.org; internet www.nzmeatboard.org; f. 1922; Chair. MIKE PETERSEN; 10 mems.

New Zealand Pork Industry Board (New Zealand Pork): Level 4, 94 Dixon St, POB 4048, Wellington; tel. (4) 917-4750; fax (4) 385-8522; e-mail info@pork.co.nz; internet www.pork.co.nz; f. 1937; Chair. C. TRENGROVE; CEO S. MCIVOR.

New Zealand Retailers' Association Inc: POB 12086, Wellington 6144; tel. (4) 805-0830; fax (4) 805-0831; e-mail helpline@retail.org.nz; internet www.retail.org.nz; 6,000 direct mems; Pres. RAY CLARKE; CEO JOHN ALBERTSON.

New Zealand Seafood Industry Council: Private Bag 24901, Manners St, Wellington 6142; tel. (4) 385-4005; fax (4) 385-2727; e-mail info@seafood.co.nz; internet www.seafood.co.nz; CEO PETER BODEKER; Chair. DAVID SHARP.

New Zealand Timber Industry Federation: POB 308, Wellington; tel. (4) 473-5200; fax (4) 473-6536; e-mail inquiries@nztif.co.nz; internet www.nztif.co.nz; f. 1983; 350 mems; Exec. Dir WAYNE. S. COFFEY.

Registered Master Builders' Federation (Inc): Level 6, 234 Wakefield St, POB 1796, Wellington; tel. (4) 385-8999; fax (4) 385-8995; e-mail mbfinfo@masterbuilder.org.nz; internet www.masterbuilder.org.nz; Chief Exec. WARWICK QUINN.

EMPLOYERS' ORGANIZATION

Business New Zealand: Level 6, Lumley House, 3–11 Hunter St, POB 1925, Wellington; tel. (4) 496-6555; fax (4) 496-6550; e-mail admin@businessnz.org.nz; internet www.businessnz.org.nz; f. 2001; Chief Exec. PHIL O'REILLY.

UTILITIES

Energy Efficiency and Conservation Authority (EECA): POB 388, Wellington 6140; tel. (4) 470-2200; fax (4) 499-5330; e-mail info@eeca.govt.nz; internet www.eeca.govt.nz; f. 2000; Chair. ROGER SUTTON; Chief Exec. MIKE UNDERHILL.

Electricity

Following parliamentary approval of the Electricity Industry Bill in September 2010, the new Electricity Authority was established on 1 November in place of the Electricity Commission.

Electricity Authority: Level 7, ASB Bank Tower, 2 Hunter St, POB 10041, Wellington 6143; tel. (4) 460-8860; fax (4) 460-8879; e-mail info@ea.govt.nz; internet www.ea.govt.nz; f. 2010; replaced Electricity Commission; independent regulatory body supervising electricity sector; Chair. Dr BRENT LAYTON; Chief Exec. CARL HANSEN.

Bay of Plenty Energy (BOPE): 52 Commerce St, POB 404, Whakatane; tel. (7) 922-2700; fax (7) 307-0922; e-mail enquiries@bopelec.co.nz; internet www.bope.co.nz; f. 1995; generation, purchase and supply of electricity and natural gas; Commercial Man. CHRIS POWER; CEO DAVID BULLEY.

Contact Energy Ltd: Level 1, Harbour City Tower, 29 Brandon St, POB 10742, Wellington; tel. (4) 449-4001; fax (4) 499-4003; e-mail help@contact-energy.co.nz; internet www.contactenergy.co.nz; f. 1996; generation of electricity, wholesale and retail of energy; Chair. GRANT KING; CEO DENNIS BARNES.

Genesis Energy Ltd: POB 17-188, Greenlane, Auckland 1546; tel. (9) 838-7863; fax (9) 580-4891; internet www.genesisenergy.co.nz; f. 1999; state-owned; generation and retail of electricity and gas; Chair. Dame JENNY SHIPLEY; Chief Exec. ALBERT BRANTLEY.

The Marketplace Co Ltd (M-CO): Level 2, NZX Ltd, NZX Center, 11 Cable St, POB 2959, Wellington 6140; tel. (4) 473-5240; fax (4) 473-5247; e-mail info@m-co.com; internet www.nz.m-co.com; f. 1993; administers wholesale electricity market; acquired by NZX Ltd in 2009; Chief Exec. CARL HANSEN.

Meridian Energy Ltd: POB 2128, Christchurch; tel. (3) 353-9500; fax (3) 353-9501; e-mail contactus@meridianenergy.co.nz; internet www.meridianenergy.co.nz; state-owned; generation and retail of electricity; Chair. CHRIS MOLLER; Chief Exec. TIM LUSK.

Mighty River Power Ltd: Level 14, 23–29 Albert St, POB 90-399, Auckland; tel. (9) 308-8200; fax (9) 308-8209; e-mail enquiries@mightyriver.co.nz; internet www.mightyriverpower.co.nz; f. 1998; electricity generation and retail; cos include Vector Electricity; Chair. JOAN WITHERS; Chief Exec. DOUG HEFFERMAN.

Nova Energy Ltd: POB 10-141, Wellington 6143; tel. (4) 668-236; fax (4) 472-6264; e-mail info@novaenergy.co.nz; internet www.novaenergy.co.nz; fmrly Nova Gas Ltd; supplier of electricity, gas, LPG and solar energy; Group Gas Man. HAMISH TWEEDIE.

Orion New Zealand Ltd: POB 13896, Christchurch 8141; tel. (3) 363-9898; fax (3) 363-9899; e-mail info@oriongroup.co.nz; internet www.oriongroup.co.nz; f. 1998; electricity distribution network; Chair. CRAIG BOYCE; CEO ROGER SUTTON.

Todd Energy Ltd: 95 Customhouse Quay, POB 3141, Wellington; tel. (4) 471-6555; fax (4) 472-2474; e-mail energy@toddenergy.co.nz; internet www.toddenergy.co.nz; Man. Dir and CEO RICHARD TWEEDIE.

Transpower New Zealand Ltd: Level 7, Transpower House, 96 The Terrace, POB 1021, Wellington; tel. (4) 495-7000; fax (4) 495-7100; internet www.transpower.co.nz; f. 1994; manages national grid; Chair. MARK VERBIEST; Chief Exec. PATRICK STRANGE.

TrustPower Ltd: Private Bag 12-023, Tauranga Mail Centre, Tauranga 3143, Auckland; tel. (7) 574-4754; fax (7) 574-4803; e-mail enquiries@trustpower.co.nz; internet www.trustpower.co.nz; f. 1920 as Tauranga Electric Power Board; independent generator; Chair. Dr BRUCE HARKER; CEO VINCE HAWKSWORTH.

Vector Electricity Ltd: Vector, POB 99-882, Newmarket, Auckland 1149; tel. (9) 303-0626; fax (9) 978-7799; e-mail info@vector.co.nz; internet www.vector.co.nz; owned by Vector Ltd; fmrly Mercury Energy Ltd; operates power networks in Auckland, Manukau and Papakura; distributes natural gas in Auckland; Group CEO SIMON MACKENZIE.

Gas

Bay of Plenty Electricity Ltd: see Electricity, above.

E-gas Ltd: Level 13, Forsyth Barr House, cnr Lambton Quay and Johnston St, POB 2577, Wellington; tel. (4) 499-4964; fax (4) 499-

4965; e-mail info@e-gas.co.nz; internet www.e-gas.co.nz; supplier of natural gas.

Genesis Energy Ltd: see Electricity, above.

NGC Holdings Ltd: Level 8, NGC Bldg, 44 The Terrace, Private Bag 39-980, Wellington Mail Centre, Wellington; tel. (4) 462-8700; fax (4) 462-8600; internet www.ngc.co.nz; f. 1992; fmrly Natural Gas Corpn Holdings Ltd; name changed as above 2002; purchase, processing and transport of natural gas; wholesale and retail sales; Chair. MICHAEL STIASSNY; Chief Exec. BRYAN CRAWFORD.

Nova Energy Ltd: see Electricity, above.

Vector Gas Ltd: see Electricity, above.

Wanganui Gas Ltd: 179 Hill St, POB 32, Wanganui; tel. (6) 349-0909; fax (6) 345-4931; e-mail enquiries@wanganuigas.co.nz; internet www.wanganuigas.co.nz; f. 1879; supplier of gas on North Island; Chair. MATTHEW J DOYLE; Chief Exec. TREVOR GOODWIN.

Water

Waste Management NZ Ltd: 86 Lunn Ave, Mt Wellington, Private Bag 14-919, Panmure, Auckland 1741; tel. (9) 527-1300; fax (9) 570-1417; internet www.wastemanagement.co.nz; f. 1985; waste collection, recovery and disposal; liquid waste collection and processing; recycling; Man. Dir GREGG CAMPBELL; Regional Man. KEVIN BONNIFACE.

Watercare Services Ltd: Private Bag 92521, Wellesley St, Auckland 1141; tel. (9) 442-2222; fax (9) 970-1461; e-mail info@water.co.nz; internet www.watercare.co.nz; f. 1993; provides water and waste water services in the Auckland area; Chair. ROSS KEENAN; Chief Exec. MARK FORD.

MAJOR COMPANIES

Construction and Cement

Fletcher Building Ltd: Fletcher House, 810 Great South Rd, Penrose, Auckland 1061; tel. (9) 525-9248; fax (9) 525-9009; e-mail marion.clements@fb.co.nz; internet www.fletcherbuilding.co.nz; f. 2001; total revenue $NZ6,799m. (2009/10); mfr and distributor with operations in concrete, steel, fibreglass insulation, aluminium extrusion, roofing, access flooring systems, sinkware, laminates and panels; also property construction; Chair. RALPH WATERS; CEO and Man. Dir JONATHAN LING; 16,000 employees.

Golden Bay Cement Co Ltd: Level 1, Wright Stephenson House, 585 Great South Rd, Penrose, Auckland 1061; tel. (9) 526-1200; fax (9) 525-9202; e-mail info@goldenbay.co.nz; internet www.goldenbay.co.nz; f. 1909; mfrs of cement; Gen. Man. ANDREW MOSS; 210 employees.

Holcim (New Zealand) Ltd: POB 6040, Christchurch; tel. (3) 339-7500; fax (3) 339-7499; e-mail enquiries-nz@holcim.com; internet www.holcim.co.nz; f. 1888; fmrly Milburn New Zealand Ltd; name changed as above 2002; total sales $NZ262.7m. (2008/09); mfrs of cement and concrete, aggregate lime and associated products; Man. Dir JEREMY SMITH; 550 employees.

Mainzeal Construction & Property Ltd: Level 10, 385 Queen St, POB 3978, Auckland 1140; tel. (9) 375-2100; fax (9) 375-2102; e-mail mzakl@mainzeal.com; internet www.mainzeal.co.nz; f. 1968; subsidiary of Richina Global Real Estate; construction services; Chair. Dame JENNY SHIPLEY; CEO PETER GOMM; 500 employees.

Food and Drink

DB Breweries Ltd: 1 Bairds Rd, Otahuhu, Manukau 2025; tel. (9) 259-3000; fax (9) 259-3001; e-mail db@db.co.nz; internet www.db.co.nz; f. 1930; fmrly DB Group Ltd; owned by Asia Pacific Breweries Ltd; mfrs and distributors of beer, brewers, and bottlers; Man. Dir BRIAN JAMES BLAKE; 500 employees.

Fonterra Co-operative Group Ltd: Private Bag 92-032, Auckland; tel. (9) 374-9000; fax (9) 374-9001; internet www.fonterra.com; f. 2001; New Zealand Dairy Bd (f. 1918) was replaced by a new org., Globalco, in 2001, which subsequently began trading under the above name; cap. and res 4,765m., total revenue $NZ16,035m. (2008/09); collecting and processing of milk, production of dairy products, etc.; Chair. HENRY VAN DER HEYDEN; CEO Theo SPIERINGS; 15,600 employees.

Goodman Fielder NZ Ltd: Private Bag 11913, Ellerslie, Auckland; tel. (9) 580-5300; fax (9) 580-5427; e-mail cac@goodmanfielder.co.nz; internet www.goodmanfielder.co.nz; f. 1986; cap. and res $NZ1,611m., sales $NZ2,848.6m.; mfr and distributor of food products; Australian and NZ operations; 22 production sites in NZ; Chair. MAX OULD; Man. Dir and CEO CHRIS DELANEY; 2,819 employees.

Lion Nathan Ltd (New Zealand): 111 Carlton Gore Rd, Newmarket, Auckland; tel. (9) 357-0111; f. 1923; cap. and res $NZ5,823.2m., total revenue $NZ1,883.1m. (2005/06); brewers, bottlers, wine and spirits merchants; Chair. GEOFF RICKETTS; CEO ROB MURRAY; 3,792 employees.

Pernod Ricard (NZ): 4 Viaduct Harbour Ave, Auckland 1010; tel. (9) 336-8300; fax (9) 336-8472; e-mail info@pernod-ricard-nz.com; internet www.pernod-ricard-nz.com; fmrly Montana Group (New Zealand) Ltd, Allied Domecq Wines (New Zealand) Ltd; subsidiary of Pernod Ricard SA; production and export of wine; Man. Dir FABIAN PARTIGLIANI; 800 employees.

Sanford Ltd: 22 Jellicoe St, Freeman's Bay, Auckland 1010; tel. (9) 379-4720; fax (9) 309-1190; e-mail info@sanford.co.nz; internet www.sanford.co.nz; f. 1904; cap. and res $NZ547.9m., revenue $NZ433m. (2008/09); processing and distribution of seafood; Chair JEFF TODD; Man. Dir E. F. BARRATT; 1,500 employees.

Sealord Group Ltd: POB 11, Nelson 7001; tel. (3) 548-3069; fax (3) 546-0966; e-mail info@sealord.co.nz; internet www.sealord.co.nz; f. 1973; 50% owned by Treaty of Waitangi Fisheries Comm., 50% owned by Nippon Suisan Kaisha (Nissui) of Japan; catching, processing and marketing of seafood; CEO GRAHAM STUART; 1,600 employees.

Forestry, Pulp and Paper

Carter Holt Harvey Ltd: Private Bag 92-106, 173 Captain Springs Rd, Te Papapa, Auckland 1142; tel. (9) 633-0600; fax (9) 633-0601; e-mail chhcontact@chh.com; internet www.chh.com; f. 1971; activities include sawmilling, pulp forestry, tissue, paperboard and plastic packaging; Chair. JOHN H. MAASLAND; CEO PETER SPRINGFORD.

Rayonier Asia Pacific Ltd: 49 Symonds St, POB 9283, Newmarket, Auckland; tel. (9) 302-2988; fax (9) 377-0249; e-mail dave.malone@rayonier.com; f. 1988; forestry products; Gen. Man. (Forest Operations) PAUL NICHOLLS.

Rubicon (NZ): POB 68-249, Newton, Auckland; tel. (9) 356-9800; fax (9) 356-9801; e-mail information@rubicon-nz.com; internet www.rubicon-nz.com; cap. and res $NZ2133m., sales $NZ494m. (2008/09); forestry biotechnology, wood products mfr and distributor; Chair. STEPHEN KASNET; CEO LUKE MORIARTY.

Steel

New Zealand Steel Ltd: Mission Bush Rd, Private Bag 92-121, Auckland 1142; tel. (9) 375-8999; fax (9) 375-8213; e-mail vicki.woodley@bluescopesteel.com; internet www.nzsteel.co.nz; f. 1966; fmrly BHP New Zealand Steel Ltd; name changed as above 2002; owned by BlueScope Steel Ltd; sales $NZ694.9m. (2008/09); suppliers of ironsand concentrate; mfrs of hot- and cold-rolled steel, hollow sections, galvanized flat sheet and coil and pre-painted flat sheet and coil; Pres. SIMON LINGE; 1,670 employees.

Steel and Tube Holdings Ltd: 15–17 Kings Cres., Private Box 30-543, Lower Hutt; tel. (4) 570-5000; fax (4) 569-4218; e-mail info@steelandtube.co.nz; internet www.steelandtube.co.nz; f. 1953; cap. and res $NZ150.1m., sales $NZ484.4m. (2008/09); holding company; 20 subsidiary companies; Chair. DEAN PRITCHARD; CEO DAVE TAYLOR; 881 employees.

Miscellaneous

Bendon Ltd: POB 53-042, Auckland Airport, Auckland; tel. (9) 275-0000; fax (9) 257-1600; e-mail info@bendon.co.nz; internet www.bendon.co.nz; f. 1987; fmrly Ceramco Corpn Ltd; name changed as above 2000; mfrs of underwear and lingerie; COO ANDREA SCOWN; 115 employees.

Cavalier Corporation Ltd: 7 Grayson Ave, Papatoetoe, POB 97-040, South Auckland Mail Centre; tel. (9) 277-6000; fax (9) 278-7417; e-mail dkeown@cavbrem.co.nz; internet www.cavcorp.co.nz; f. 1984; cap. and res $NZ87.5m., sales $NZ246.6m. (2008/09); carpet mfr; Chair. ALLAN JAMES; Man. Dir WAYNE CHUNG; 939 employees.

Donaghys Industries Ltd: 16 Sheffield Cres., POB 20-449, Christchurch; tel. (3) 983-4100; fax (3) 983-4191; e-mail enquiries@donaghys.co.nz; internet www.donaghys.com; f. 1876; cap. and res $NZ19.2m., sales $NZ55.3m. (2004); mfr and distributor of agricultural twines, ropes and cordage and crop packaging; Man. Dir JEREMY SILVA; 120 employees.

EBOS Group Ltd: 108 Wrights Rd, POB 411, Christchurch; tel. (3) 338-0999; fax (3) 339-5111; e-mail ebos@ebos.co.nz; internet www.ebos.co.nz; f. 1922; fmrly known as Early Bros Trading Co Ltd; name changed as above 1986; cap. and res $NZ182.7m., revenue $NZ1,373.3m. (2009/10); suppliers of medical, surgical, dental and scientific products to health care industry; Chair. RICK CHRISTIE; Chief Exec. and Man. Dir MARK WALLER.

Fisher & Paykel Appliances Holdings Ltd: POB 58-732, Botany, Manukau 2163; tel. (9) 273-0600; fax (9) 273-0609; e-mail corporate.enquiries@fp.co.nz; internet www.fisherpaykel.co.nz; f. 1934; cap. and res $NZ601.1m., total revenue $NZ1,027.9m. (2009/10); electricals; Chair. KEITH TURNER; Man. Dir and CEO STUART BROADHURST; 3,300 employees.

Hallenstein Glasson Holding Ltd: POB 91-148, Auckland; tel. (9) 306-2500; fax (9) 306-2523; internet www.hallensteinglasson.co.nz; sales $NZ198.1m. (2008/09); formed through merger of Hallensteins and Glassons Ltd in 1985; fashion retailer; Chair. WARREN JAMES BELL; CEO GRAEME POPPLEWELL.

Hellaby Holdings Ltd: Level 5, 10 Viaduct Harbour Ave, Auckland; tel. (9) 307-6844; fax (9) 307-3559; e-mail info@hellabyholdings.co.nz; internet www.hellabyholdings.co.nz; f. 1984; fmrly Renouf Corpn; cap. and res $NZ100m., revenue $NZ457.4m. (2009/10); principal activities include import and distribution of automotive parts and construction equipment, retail of shoes, outdoor heating products and accessories; Chair. JOHN MAASLAND; CEO JOHN WILLIAMSON; 2,200 employees.

New Zealand Refining Co Ltd: Private Bag 9024, Whangarei; tel. (9) 432-8311; fax (9) 432-8035; e-mail corporate@nzrc.co.nz; internet www.nzrc.co.nz; f. 1961; cap. and res $NZ540m., operating revenue $NZ250.5m. (2009); refines petrol, diesel oils, fuel oils and bitumen; Chair. DAVID JACKSON; CEO KEN RIVERS; 364 employees.

Nufarm New Zealand Ltd: POB 22-407, Auckland 1640; tel. (9) 270-4157; fax (9) 366-1394; e-mail info@nz.nufarm.com; internet www.nufarm.co.nz; f. 1916; fmrly Fernz Corpn Ltd; name changed as above 2000; cap. and res $NZ709.4m., sales $NZ1,680m. (2005/06); mfr and distributor of fertilizers, sulphuric acid, sulphate of alumina, chrome sulphate, agricultural chemicals, animal health products; Country Man. PATRICK CLEMENT.

Nuplex Industries Ltd: 12 Industry Rd, Penrose, Auckland; tel. (9) 579-2029; fax (9) 571-0542; e-mail nuplex@nuplex.co.nz; internet www.nuplex.co.nz; f. 1956; cap. and res $NZ521.6m., sales $NZ1,493.6m. (2009); produces and supplies technical materials and building products; Chair. ROB AITKEN; Man. Dir EMERY SEVERIN.

Pumpkin Patch Ltd: Private Bag 94-310, Pakuranga, Manukau 2140; tel. (9) 274-2233; fax (9) 274-9797; e-mail info@pumpkinpatch.co.nz; internet www.pumpkinpatch.co.nz; f. 1990; cap. and res $NZ88.6m., total revenue $NZ412.3m. (2008/09); retailer of children's clothes; Chair. JANE FREEMAN; Man. Dir MAURICE PRENDERGAST.

Tenon Ltd: Private Bag 92-036, Auckland 1030; tel. (9) 368-4198; fax (9) 368-4197; e-mail info@tenon.co.nz; internet www.tenonglobal.com; f. 1981; est. as Fletcher Challenge Ltd; reorganized as holding co in 1996; name changed as above in 2004; operations in processing, marketing and distribution of timber products; NZ revenue US $91m. (2007/08); Chair. LUKE MORIARTY; COO TONY JOHNSTON.

The Warehouse Group Ltd: 26 The Warehouse Way, Akoranga Dr., Northcote, Auckland; tel. (9) 489-7000; fax (9) 489-7444; e-mail investor@twl.co.nz; internet www.thewarehouse.co.nz; f. 1982; cap. and res $NZ320.8m., sales $NZ1,720.7m. (2008/09); 86 The Warehouse stores, 46 Warehouse Stationery stores; general merchandise retailing; Chair. GRAHAM EVANS; Group CEO MARK POWELL; 8,500 employees.

TRADE UNIONS

In December 2000 a total of 134 unions were in operation; 318,519 workers belonged to a union.

New Zealand Council of Trade Unions: Education House, West Block, 178 Willis St, POB 6645, Wellington 6141; tel. (4) 385-1334; fax (4) 385-6051; e-mail helenk@nzctu.org.nz; internet www.union.org.nz; f. 1937; present name since 1987; affiliated to ITUC; 40 affiliated unions with more than 350,000 mems; Pres. HELEN KELLY; Sec. PETER CONWAY.

Principal Affiliated Unions

Association of Staff in Tertiary Education (ASTE)/Te Hau Takitini o Aotearoa: POB 27141, Wellington; tel. (4) 801-5098; fax (4) 385-8826; e-mail enquiry@aste.ac.nz; internet www.aste.ac.nz; f. 1988; 3,500 mems; Nat. Sec. SHARN RIGGS.

Central Amalgamated Workers Union (CAWU): 307 Willis St, POB 27-291, Wellington; tel. (4) 384-4049; fax (4) 801-7306; e-mail info@cawu.org.nz; internet www.cawu.org.nz; Sec. HAROLD LEWIS.

FinSec Finance and Information Workers Union: POB 27-355, Wellington; tel. (4) 385-7723; fax (4) 385-2214; e-mail union@finsec.org.nz; internet www.finsec.org.nz; Pres. KELVIN PYCROFT; Sec. ANDREW CASIDY.

Maritime Union of New Zealand: POB 2773, Wellington; tel. (4) 385-9288; fax (4) 384-8766; e-mail john.whiting@muno.org.nz; internet www.munz.org.nz; 2,800 mems; Gen. Sec. JOHN WHITING.

New Zealand Dairy Workers Union, Inc: TUC Bldg, 34 Harwood St, POB 9046, Hamilton; tel. (7) 839-0239; fax (7) 838-0398; e-mail nzdwu@nzdwu.org.nz; internet www.nzdwu.org.nz; f. 1992; 7,000 mems; Sec. JAMES RITCHIE; Pres. SINCLAIR WATSON.

New Zealand Educational Institute (NZEI) (Te Riu Roa): 178–182 Willis St, POB 466, Wellington 6140; tel. (4) 384-9689; fax (4) 385-1772; e-mail nzei@nzei.org.nz; internet www.nzei.org.nz; f. 1883; Pres. IAN LECKIE; Sec. PAUL GOULTER.

New Zealand Engineering, Printing & Manufacturing Union (EPMU): POB 14-277, Kilbirnie 7, McGregor St, Rongotai, Wellington; tel. (4) 387-4681; fax (4) 387-4673; e-mail andrew.little@epmu.org.nz; internet www.epmu.org.nz; Sec. ANDREW LITTLE.

New Zealand Meat Workers and Related Trades Union: POB 13-048, Christchurch; tel. (3) 366-5105; fax (3) 379-7763; e-mail nzmeatworkersunion@clear.net.nz; internet www.nzmeatworkersunion.co.nz; 13,788 mems; Pres. MIKE NAHU; Gen. Sec. DAVID EASTLAKE.

New Zealand Nurses' Organisation: POB 2128, Wellington 6140; tel. (4) 931-6730; fax (4) 472-4951; e-mail nurses@nzno.org.nz; internet www.nzno.org.nz; 38,000 mems; CEO GEOFF ANNALS.

New Zealand Post Primary Teachers' Association: POB 2119, Wellington; tel. (4) 384-9964; fax (4) 382-8763; e-mail enquiries@ppta.org.nz; internet www.ppta.org.nz; f. 1952; Pres. ROBIN DUFF; Gen. Sec. KEVIN BUNKER.

New Zealand Public Service Association (PSA): PSA House, 11 Aurora Terrace, POB 3817, Wellington 6140; tel. (4) 495-7633; fax (4) 917-2051; e-mail enquiries@psa.org.nz; internet www.psa.org.nz; 56,000 mems; Pres. PAULA SCHOLES.

Rail & Maritime Transport Union Inc: POB 1103, Wellington; tel. (4) 499-2066; fax (4) 471-0896; e-mail tvalster@rmtunion.org.nz; internet www.rmtunion.org.nz; 4,100 mems; Pres. J. KELLY; Gen. Sec. W. BUTSON.

Service and Food Workers' Union: Private Bag 68-914, Newton, Auckland 1145; tel. (9) 375-2680; fax (9) 375-2681; e-mail info@sfwu.org.nz; internet www.sfwu.org.nz; 23,000 mems; Pres. BARBARA WYETH; Sec. JOHN RYALL.

Tertiary Education Union (TEU): POB 11-767, Wellington 6142; tel. (4) 801-5098; fax (4) 385-8826; e-mail scr.im/nzteu; internet www.teu.ac.nz; fmrly Asscn of University Staff; 6,000 mems; Nat. Pres. TOM RYAN.

Other Unions

Manufacturing & Construction Workers Union: 126 Vivian St, Te Aro, Wellington 6011; tel. (4) 385-8264; fax (4) 384-8007; e-mail m.c.union@tradeshall.org.nz; Gen. Sec. GRAEME CLARKE.

National Distribution Union (NDU): 120 Church St, Private Bag 92-904, Onehunga, Auckland; tel. (9) 622-8355; fax (9) 622-8353; e-mail info@ndu.org.nz; internet www.ndu.org.nz; f. 1986; 18,500 mems; Pres. DENNIS DAWSON; Gen. Sec. ROBERT REID.

New Zealand Building Trades Union: POB 13-594, Christchurch; tel. (4) 366-4033; fax (4) 366-4032; e-mail national@nzbtu.org.nz; internet www.nzbtu.org.nz; f. 1860; Pres. P. REIDY; Sec. DAVID O'CONNELL.

New Zealand Seafarers' Union: Marion Sq., POB 9288, Wellington; tel. (4) 385-9288; fax (4) 384-9288; e-mail admin@seafarers.org.nz; f. 1993; Pres. DAVE MORGAN.

Transport

RAILWAYS

There were 3,898 km of railways in New Zealand in 2003, of which more than 500 km were electrified.

New Zealand Railways Corporation (NZRC—KiwiRail): POB 593, Wellington 6140; tel. 800-801-070; fax (4) 473-1589; e-mail kiwirail@kiwirail.co.nz; internet www.kiwirail.co.nz; f. 2008; state-owned enterprise, est. following Govt's purchase of rail and inter-island ferry operations of Toll NZ Ltd; Chair. JOHN SPENCER; Chief Exec. JIM QUINN.

ROADS

In 2009 there were a total of 93,910 km of maintained roads in New Zealand, including 10,909 km of state highways and motorways, 17,510 km of urban local roads and 65,492 km of rural and special purpose roads.

New Zealand Transport Agency: Victoria Arcade, 44 Victoria St, Private Bag 6995, Wellington 6141; tel. (4) 894-5400; fax (4) 894-6100; e-mail info@nzta.govt.nz; internet www.nzta.govt.nz; f. 2008; formed by merger of Land Transport NZ and Transit NZ; Crown entity charged with contributing to an integrated, safe, responsive and sustainable land transport system; Chair. CHRIS MOLLER; Chief Exec. GEOFF DANGERFIELD.

SHIPPING

There are 13 main seaports, of which the most important are Auckland, Tauranga, Wellington, Lyttleton (the port of Christchurch) and Port Chalmers (Dunedin). In December 2009 the New Zealand merchant fleet comprised 176 vessels, with a total displacement of 213,084 grt.

Principal Companies

Maersk New Zealand: The CPO, Level 3, 12 Queen St, Auckland; tel. (9) 359-3499; fax (9) 359-3488; e-mail nezcsedir@maersk.com; internet www.maerskline.com; f. 1928; CEO Eivind Kolding.

Reef Shipping Ltd: 68 Anzac Ave, Auckland; tel. (9) 302-2204; fax (9) 302-0096; e-mail shipping@reefship.co.nz; internet www.reefship.co.nz; f. 1975; operates services between New Zealand and the Pacific Islands; Gen. Man. Jason Ward.

Sofrana Unilines NZ Ltd: 38 Ponsonby Rd, POB 3614, Auckland; tel. (9) 356-1400; fax (9) 356-1429; e-mail info@sofrana.co.nz; internet www.sofrana.co.nz; Chair. Didier Leroux; Man. Dir Benoit Marcenac.

Other major shipping companies operating services to New Zealand include Blue Star Line (NZ) Ltd and Columbus Line, which link New Zealand with Australia, the Pacific Islands, South-East Asia and the USA.

CIVIL AVIATION

There are international airports at Auckland, Christchurch and Wellington.

Civil Aviation Authority of New Zealand: Asteron Centre, 55 Featherston St, POB 3555, Wellington; tel. (4) 560-9400; fax (4) 569-2024; e-mail info@caa.govt.nz; internet www.caa.govt.nz; Dir of Civil Aviation Steve Douglas.

Principal Airlines

Air Nelson: Private Bag 32, Nelson 7042; tel. (3) 547-8700; fax (3) 547-8788; e-mail airnelsonadmin@airnz.co.nz; internet www.airnelson.co.nz; f. 1979; owned by Air New Zealand; present name adopted 1986; operates services throughout New Zealand; Gen. Man. Grant Kerr.

Air New Zealand: Private Bag 92007, Auckland 1142; tel. (9) 336-2287; fax (9) 366-2664; e-mail investor@airnz.co.nz; internet www.airnewzealand.co.nz; f. 1942; privatized in 1989, recapitalized by the Govt in 2001; 73.7% govt-owned; services to and from Australia, the Pacific Islands, Asia, Europe and North America, as well as regular daily services to regional New Zealand; Chair. John Palmer; CEO Rob Fyfe.

Pacific Blue Airlines (NZ) Ltd: e-mail sales.corporate@virginblue.com.au; internet www.flypacificblue.com; f. 2003; wholly owned subsidiary of Australian Virgin Blue; domestic services and services to Australia and the Pacific Islands; announced plans to terminate domestic services in late 2010; CEO Mark Pitt.

Tourism

New Zealand's principal tourist attractions are its mountains, lakes, forests, volcanoes, hot springs and beaches. The sector makes a substantial contribution to the country's economy, and receipts from tourism totalled an estimated $NZ6,278m. in 2010. In the same year New Zealand received more than 2.5m. international visitors. The majority of visitors are from Australia, the United Kingdom and the USA.

Tourism New Zealand: POB 95, Wellington; tel. (4) 462-8000; fax (4) 915-3817; e-mail reception@tnz.govt.nz; internet www.newzealand.com; f. 1901; responsible for marketing of New Zealand as a tourism destination; offices in Auckland, Wellington and Christchurch; 13 offices overseas; Chair. Kerry Prendergast; Chief Exec. Kevin Bowler.

Defence

As assessed at November 2010, the total strength of the regular forces was 9,673: army 4,905, navy 2,161 and air force 2,607. In addition, there were approximately 2,314 regular reserves (army 1,789, navy 339, air force 186) and 1,789 territorial reserves. Military service is voluntary. New Zealand is a participant in the Five-Power Defence Arrangements with Australia, Malaysia, Singapore and the United Kingdom. In early 2011 New Zealand's overseas deployments included 231 personnel in Afghanistan, 80 in Timor-Leste and 45 in Solomon Islands.

Defence Expenditure: Budgeted at $NZ2,210m. for 2010.

Chief of Defence Force: Lt-Gen. Richard Rhys Jones.

Chief of Army: Maj.-Gen. Tim Keating.

Chief of Navy: Rear-Adm. Antony J. Parr.

Chief of Air Force: Air Vice-Marshal Peter James Stockwell.

Commander Joint Forces New Zealand: Maj.-Gen. Arthur David Gawn.

Education

Education in New Zealand is free and secular in state schools. It is compulsory for all children aged six to 16 years, although in practice almost 100% start at the age of five years. Budgetary expenditure on education by the central Government in 2010/11 was forecast at $NZ11,969m., representing 15.1% of total spending.

In July 2010 there were 188,924 children enrolled in early childhood education services, while 435,051 pupils were enrolled in primary classes at 2,018 schools. A total of 275,945 pupils attended 340 secondary schools. Composite schools, which were attended by 50,524 pupils, provide education at both primary and secondary levels.

PRE-SCHOOL, PRIMARY AND SECONDARY EDUCATION

Local early childhood centres are maintained and controlled by voluntary associations to which the Government gives substantial assistance including grants and subsidies. Since 1 July 1990 all early childhood centres wishing to receive government funding have been required to hold a charter. Those not holding a charter must still be licensed.

Pupils may complete the eight-year primary course at a full primary school (or, in rural areas, an area school) or, as is the case for most pupils, they may proceed to an intermediate school for the final two years. An intermediate school is a centrally located school, usually instructing 300–600 pupils between the ages of 11 and 13 years. These can provide specialist teachers and facilities not normally within the reach of primary schools.

All children are entitled to free secondary education until the end of their 19th year. The majority of pupils leave school at the end of their fourth year. The School Certificate examination is taken at the end of the third or fourth year of secondary school. Pupils who pass subjects in this examination may go on to a year in the sixth form. At the end of the sixth-form year they may obtain the Sixth Form Certificate. Pupils intending to go on to university usually spend a further year in the seventh form to obtain a Higher School Certificate.

RURAL EDUCATION

In order to give children in country districts the advantage of special equipment and the more specialized teaching of larger schools, the consolidation of the smaller rural schools has been undertaken wherever this is practicable. In small rural districts area schools provide primary and secondary education for all pupils in the immediate vicinity, and education from the first to the seventh form is provided in larger districts in separate schools.

CORRESPONDENCE SCHOOL

This school, which had an enrolment of 5,546 in July 2007, serves students who cannot attend school because they live in remote areas, because of illness or for other reasons. It also provides courses for pupils who wish to study subjects not offered at their local school, and adults who do not have access to secondary school classes.

POLYTECHNICS AND TEACHER TRAINING

Since the early 1980s vocational education and training has moved away from the secondary to the continuing education sector, with training formerly provided by technical high schools now provided by polytechnics. Polytechnics provide a diverse range of vocational education resources and cover an increasing number of subjects at various levels of specialization.

In 2004 there were 20 polytechnics, including the Open Polytechnic of New Zealand. This last is the largest polytechnic in the country, with 34,252 students in 2007. In 2010 there were a total of 4,194 full-time equivalent staff and 180,709 students in the polytechnic system.

In mid-2003 there were 11,107 full-time and part-time students undergoing kindergarten, primary and secondary teacher training in four colleges of education. Most pre-school primary teacher trainees follow a three-year course. University graduates take a course lasting one or two years.

UNIVERSITIES

The eight universities are autonomous bodies with their own councils. Some 80% of the universities' funds are state-provided. About 20% of pupils leaving secondary school go to university. In 2010 there were 156,069 students enrolled at the universities. There was a teaching staff of 7,869 full-time equivalent teachers in 2009.

EDUCATION OF MAORI AND PACIFIC ISLAND STUDENTS

Maori and Pacific Island children may attend licensed childcare centres, where there is an emphasis on language development. Te Kohanga Reo ('Language Nests') were established by Maori in the early 1980s to provide an appropriate educational environment. Maori language schools (Kura Kaupapa Maori) have also been established. By 2007 the Kura Kaupapa Maori totalled 68. The three wananga, tertiary institutions providing polytechnic and university level programmes with an emphasis on Maori language and culture, had an enrolment of 42,293 students and 572 full-time teachers in July 2010.

Bibliography

General

The Dictionary of New Zealand Biography, Vols 1–5, 1769–1960. 1990–2000; internet www.dnzb.govt.nz.

Huria, John, and Phillipps, W. J. *Maori Life and Custom.* North Shore, Raupo, 2008.

Jackson, Keith, and McRobie, Alan. *Historical Dictionary of New Zealand.* Auckland, Longman, 1996.

Kirkpatrick, Russell. *Bateman Contemporary Atlas: New Zealand: The Shapes of Our Nation.* Auckland, Bateman, 1999.

McKinnon, Malcolm (Ed.). *New Zealand Historical Atlas: Papatuanuku e Takoto Nei.* Wellington, David Bateman in association with Historical Branch, Department of Internal Affairs, 1997.

McLean, Gavin, and Shoebridge, Tim. *Quarantine!: Protecting New Zealand at the Border.* Dunedin, Otago University Press, 2010.

McLintock, A. H. (Ed.). *An Encyclopaedia of New Zealand.* Wellington, Government Printer, 1966.

Metge, Joan. *Rautahi, The Maoris of New Zealand.* London, Routledge, 2004.

Tuamaka: The Challenge of Difference in Aotearoa New Zealand. Auckland, Auckland University Press, 2010.

Patterson, Brad and Kathryn (Eds). *World Bibliographical Series, Vol. 18, New Zealand.* Oxford, Clio Press, 1998.

Reed, A. W. *An Illustrated Encyclopedia of Traditional Maori Life*, Revised edn by Mikaere, Buddy. London, New Holland Publrs, 2003.

Temple, Philip. *Presenting New Zealand: A Nation's Heritage.* Auckland, New Holland Publishers, 2001.

Website: www.TeAra.govt.nz (*Te Ara Encyclopedia of New Zealand, 2005).*

History and Politics

Alley, Roderic. *New Zealand in World Affairs IV: 1990–2005.* Wellington, Victoria University Press, 2008.

Ballantyne, Tony and Moloughney, Brian (Eds). *Disputed Histories: Imagining New Zealand's Past.* Dunedin, Otago University Press, 2006.

Barclay, Barry. *Mana tuturū: Maori Treasures and Intellectual Property Rights.* Auckland, Auckland University Press, 2005.

Bargh, Maria. *Maori and Parliament: Diverse Strategies and Compromises.* Wellington, Huia, 2010.

Barrington, John. *Separate but Equal? Maori Schools and the Crown, 1867–1969.* Wellington, Victoria University Press, 2008.

Bassett, Michael, and King, Michael. *Tomorrow Comes the Song: A Life of Peter Fraser.* Auckland, Penguin, 2000.

Belgrave, Michael. *Historical Frictions: Maori Claims and Reinvented Histories.* Auckland, Auckland University Press, 2005.

Belich, James. *Making Peoples: A History of the New Zealanders from Polynesian Settlement to the End of the Nineteenth Century.* Auckland, Allen Lane, Penguin Press, 1996.

Paradise Reforged: A History of the New Zealanders from the 1880s to the Year 2000. Auckland, Allen Lane, Penguin Press, 2001.

Replenishing the Earth: The Settler Revolution and the Rise of the Anglo World, 1783–1939. New York, Oxford University Press, 2009.

Binney, Judith (Ed.). *The Shaping of History: Essays from the New Zealand Journal of History 1967–1999.* Wellington, Bridget Williams Books, 2001.

Binney, Judith, Bassett, Judith, and Olssen, Erik. *The People and the Land: Te Tangata me Te Whenua: An Illustrated History of New Zealand, 1820–1920.* Wellington, Allen and Unwin, 1990.

Boast, Richard. *Buying the Land, Selling the Land: Governments and Maori Land in the North Island 1865–1921.* Wellington, Victoria University Press, 2008.

Boast, Richard, and Hill, Richard S. (Eds). *Raupatu: The Confiscation of Maori Land.* Wellington, Victoria University Press, 2009.

Bower, Ernest Z., and Lynch, Brian J. *Pacific Partners: The Future of U.S.-New Zealand Relations* Washington, DC, Center for Strategic and International Studies, 2011.

Brookfield, F. M. *Waitangi and Indigenous Rights.* Auckland, Auckland University Press, Revised Edn, 2006.

Bryder, Linda. *A Voice for Mothers: The Plunket Society and Infant Welfare 1907–2000.* Auckland, Auckland University Press, 2003.

Bush, Graham. *Local Government and Politics in New Zealand.* Auckland, Auckland University Press, 2004.

Byrnes, Giselle. *Boundary Markers: Land Surveying and the Colonisation of New Zealand.* Wellington, Bridget Williams Books, 2002.

(Ed.) *The New Oxford History of New Zealand.* Melbourne, Oxford University Press, 2009.

Calman, Ross. *The New Zealand Wars.* Auckland, Reed Publishing New Zealand, 2004.

Chapman, Robert. *New Zealand Politics and Social Patterns.* Wellington, Victoria University Press, 2001.

Dalley, Bronwyn. *Family Matters: Child Welfare in Twentieth-Century New Zealand.* Auckland, Auckland University Press, 1998.

Dalley, Bronwyn, and Labrum, Bronwyn. *Fragments: New Zealand Social and Cultural History.* Auckland, Auckland University Press, 2000.

Dalley, Bronwyn, and McLean, Gavin (Eds). *Frontier of Dreams: The Story of New Zealand.* Auckland, Hodder Moa Beckett, 2005.

Durie, Mason. *Ngā tai matatū: Tides of Maori Endurance.* Melbourne, Oxford University Press, 2005.

Fairburn, Miles, and Olssen, Erik (Eds). *Class, Gender and the Vote: Perspectives from New Zealand History.* Dunedin, University of Otago Press, 2005.

Gentry, Kynan, and McLean, Gavin (Eds). *Heartlands: New Zealand Historians Write About Where History Happened.* Auckland, Penguin, 2006.

Gustafson, Barry. *His Way: A Biography of Robert Muldoon.* Auckland, Auckland University Press, 2000.

Harper, Glyn, and Richardson, Colin. *In the Face of the Enemy: the Complete History of the Victoria Cross and New Zealand.* Auckland, HarperCollins New Zealand, 2006.

Hill, Richard S. *State Authority/Indigenous Autonomy: Crown-Maori Relations in New Zealand/Aotearoa 1900–1950.* Wellington, Victoria University Press, 2005.

*The State and Indigeneity: Crown Authority and Maori Autonomy in New Zealand/Aoetearoa, 1950–2000.*Wellington, Victoria University Press, 2009.

Howe, Kerry (Ed.). *Vaka Moana: Voyages of the Ancestors: The Discovery and Settlement of the Pacific.* Auckland, David Bateman and Auckland Museum, 2006.

Ip, Manying (Ed.). *Unfolding History, Evolving Identity: The Chinese in New Zealand.* Auckland, Auckland University Press, 2003.

(Ed.). *The Dragon and the Taniwha: Maori and Chinese in New Zealand.* Auckland, Auckland University Press, 2009.

Ip, Manying, and Murphy, Nigel. *Aliens at my Table: Asians as New Zealanders See Them.* Auckland, Penguin, 2005.

Johnson, Henry, and Moloughney, Brian (Eds). *Asia in the Making of New Zealand.* Auckland, Auckland University Press, 2007.

Kawharu H. (Ed.). *Waitangi: Contemporary Maori and Pakeha Perspectives on the Treaty.* Auckland, Oxford University Press, 1989.

Keenan, Danny. *Wars Without End: The Land Wars in Nineteenth-Century New Zealand.* Auckland, Penguin, 2009.

King, Michael. *Death of the Rainbow Warrior.* Harmondsworth, Penguin, 1986.

The Penguin History of New Zealand. Auckland, Penguin, 2003.

Lange, David. *My Life.* Auckland, Penguin, 2005.

Leadbetter, Maire. *Negligent Neighbour: New Zealand's Complicity in the Invasion and Occupation of Timor-Leste.* Nelson, Craig Potton Publishing, 2006.

Levine, Stephen (Ed.). *New Zealand As It Might Have Been.* Wellington, Victoria University Press, 2006.

New Zealand As It Might Have Been II. Wellington, Victoria University Press, 2009.

Levine, Stephen and Roberts, Neil (Eds). *The 2008 New Zealand General Election.* Wellington, Victoria University Press, 2009.

McAra, Sally. *Land of Beautiful Vision: Making a Buddhist Sacred Place in New Zealand.* Honolulu, University of Hawaii Press, 2007.

McClean, Gavin. *The Governors: New Zealand's Governors and Governors General.* Dunedin, Otago University Press, 2006.

McGibbon, Ian. *New Zealand's Vietnam War: A History of Combat, Commitment and Controversy.* Waitakere, Exisle Publishing, 2010.

McGibbon, Ian (Ed.). *The Oxford Companion to New Zealand Military History.* Auckland, Oxford University Press, 2000.

McLauchlan, Gordon. *A Short History of New Zealand.* Auckland, Penguin, 2nd Edn, 2009.

McLeay, Elizabeth (Ed.). *Rethinking Women in Politics.* Wellington, Victoria University Press, 2009.

Mein Smith, Philippa. *A Concise History of New Zealand.* Melbourne, Vic, Cambridge University Press, 2005.

Mein Smith, Philippa, Hempenstall, Peter, and Goldfinch, Shaun. *Remaking the Tasman World.* Christchurch, Canterbury University Press, 2008.

Miller, Raymond (Ed.). *New Zealand Government and Politics.* Melbourne, Oxford University Press, 2006.

Moon, Paul. *This Horrid Practice: The Myth and Reality of Traditional Maori Cannibalism.* Rosedale, Penguin Books, 2008.

Morris, Paul, and Janiewski, Dolores. *New Rights New Zealand: Markets, Moralities and Global Transformation.* Auckland, Auckland University Press, 2005.

Mulgan, Richard. *Politics in New Zealand.* (3rd Edn, updated by Peter Aimer.) Auckland, Auckland University Press, 2004.

Mutu, Margaret. *The State of Maori Rights.* Wellington, Huia, 2011.

Oliver, W. H. *Claims to the Waitangi Tribunal.* Wellington, Daphne Brassell Associates, 1991.

Orange, C. *An Illustrated History of the Treaty of Waitangi.* Wellington, Bridget Williams Books, 2004.

O'Sullivan, Dominic. *Beyond Biculturalism: The Politics of an Indigenous Minority.* Honolulu, University of Hawaii Press, 2007.

Patman, Robert, and Rudd, Chris (Eds). *Sovereignty Under Siege? Globalization and New Zealand.* Aldershot, Ashgate, 2005.

Penetito, Wally. *Maori Education Policy.* Wellington, Victoria University Press, 2009.

Petrie, Hazel. *Chiefs of Industry: Maori Tribal Enterprise in Early Colonial New Zealand.* Auckland, Auckland University Press, 2006.

Phillips, Jock, and Hearn, Terry. *New Zealand Immigrants from England, Ireland and Scotland 1800–1945.* Auckland, Auckland University Press, 2008.

Puckey, Adrienne. *Trading Cultures—A History of the Far North.* Wellington, Huia, 2011.

Rabel, Roberto. *New Zealand and the Vietnam War: Politics, Diplomacy and Society.* Auckland, Auckland University Press, 2005.

Renwick, William (Ed.). *Creating a National Spirit: Celebrating New Zealand's Centennial.* Wellington, Victoria University Press, 2005.

Rice, G. R. (Ed.). *The Oxford History of New Zealand*, 2nd Edn, Auckland, Oxford University Press, 1992.

Richards, Raymond. *Palmer: The Parliamentary Years.* Christchurch, Canterbury University Press, 2011.

Rollo, Arnold. *New Zealand's Burning.* Wellington, Victoria University Press, 1994.

Salmond, Anne. *Two Worlds: First Meetings between Maori and Europeans 1642–1772.* Auckland, Viking, 1991.

Between Worlds: Early Exchanges between Maori and Europeans 1773–1815. Auckland, Viking, 1997.

Sharp, Andrew (Ed.). *Histories, Power and Loss: Uses of the Past—A New Zealand Commentary.* Wellington, Bridget Williams Books, 2002.

Simmons, Laurence (Ed.). *Speaking Truth to Power: Public Intellectuals Rethink New Zealand.* Auckland, Auckland University Press, 2007.

Sinclair, Keith. *A History of New Zealand*, Revised edn with additional material by Raewyn Dalziel. Auckland, Penguin, 2000.

Sinclair, Keith (Ed.). *The Oxford Illustrated History of New Zealand.* Auckland, Oxford University Press, 1990.

Tasman Relations: New Zealand and Australia, 1788–1988. Auckland, Auckland University Press, 1987.

Smith, Anthony L. (Ed.). *Southeast Asia and New Zealand: A History of Regional and Bilateral Relations.* Singapore, Institute of Southeast Asian Studies, 2005.

Stafford, Don. *Tangata Whenua: The World of the Maori.* Auckland, Penguin 2008.

Templeton, Malcolm. *Standing Upright Here: New Zealand in the Nuclear Age 1945–1990.* Wellington, Victoria University Press, 2006.

Trapeznik, Alexander. *Common Ground: Heritage and Public Places in New Zealand.* University of Otago Press, 2000.

Vowles, Jack, Aimer, Peter, Banducci, Susan, Karp, Jeffrey, and Miller, Raymond (Eds). *Voters' Veto: The 2002 Election in New Zealand and the Consolidation of Minority Government.* Auckland, Auckland University Press, 2004.

Walker, Ranginui. *Ka Whawhai Tonu Mataou: Struggle Without End.* Auckland, Penguin, Revised Edn, 2004.

He Tipuna: The Life and Times of Sir Apirana Ngata. Auckland, Viking, 2001.

Ward, Alan. *An Unsettled History: Treaty Claims in New Zealand Today.* Wellington, Bridget Williams Books, 1999.

Wilson, A. C. *New Zealand and the Soviet Union 1950–1991: A Brittle Relationship.* Wellington, Victoria University Press, 2005.

Wilson, J. (Ed.). *From the Beginning: The Archaeology of the Maori.* Auckland, Penguin, 1987.

Wood, G. A., and Rudd, Chris. *The Politics and Government of New Zealand: Robust, Innovative and Challenged.* Dunedin, Otago University Press, 2004.

Websites: www.nz.history.net.nz; www.timeframes.natlib.govt.nz; and www.treatyofwaitangi.govt.nz.

Economy

Callaghan, Paul. *Wool to Weta: Transforming New Zealand's Culture and Economy.* Auckland, Auckland University Press, 2009.

Dalziel, Paul, and Lattemore, Ralph. *New Zealand Macroeconomy*, 3rd Edn, Auckland, Oxford University Press, 1999.

Douglas, Roger. *Unfinished Business.* Auckland, Random House, 1993.

Easton, Brian. *In Stormy Seas—The New Zealand Economy since 1945.* Dunedin, University of Otago Press, 1997.

The Whimpering of the State: Policy after MMP. Auckland, Auckland University Press, 1999.

Erueti, Andrew, and Charters, Claire (Eds). *Maori Property in the Foreshore and Seabed: The Last Frontier.* Wellington, Victoria University Press, 2008.

Goldfinch, Shaun. *Remaking New Zealand and Australian Economic Policy: Ideas, Institution and Policy Communities.* Georgetown University Press, 2000.

Hansen, Paul, and King, Alan (Eds). *Keeping Economics Real: New Zealand Economic Issues.* Auckland, Pearson Education New Zealand, 2004.

Hawke, G. R. *The Making of New Zealand: An Economic History.* Cambridge University Press, 1985.

Hunter, Ian, and Morrow, Diana (Eds). *City of Enterprise: Perspectives on Auckland Business History.* Auckland, Auckland University Press, 2005.

Kelsey, Jane. *The New Zealand Experiment—A World Model for Structural Adjustment.* Auckland, Auckland University Press/ Bridget Williams Books, 1995.

Reclaiming the Future: New Zealand and the Global Economy. University of Toronto Press, 2000.

Lattimore, Ralph, and Eaqub, Shamubeel. *The New Zealand Economy: An Introduction.* Auckland, Auckland University Press, 2011.

Massey, Patrick. *New Zealand—Market Liberalisation in a Developed Economy.* New York, St Martin's Press, 1995.

McKinnon, Michael. *Treasury: A History of the New Zealand Treasury.* Auckland, Auckland University Press, 2003.

Sen, Rahul. *Trade Policy and the Role of Regional and Bilateral FTAs: The Case of New Zealand and Singapore.* Singapore, Institute of Southeast Asian Studies, 2007.

St John, Susan, and Fargher, Scott. *Macroeconomics and the Contemporary New Zealand Economy.* Auckland, Pearson Education New Zealand, 2004.

THE PACIFIC ISLANDS

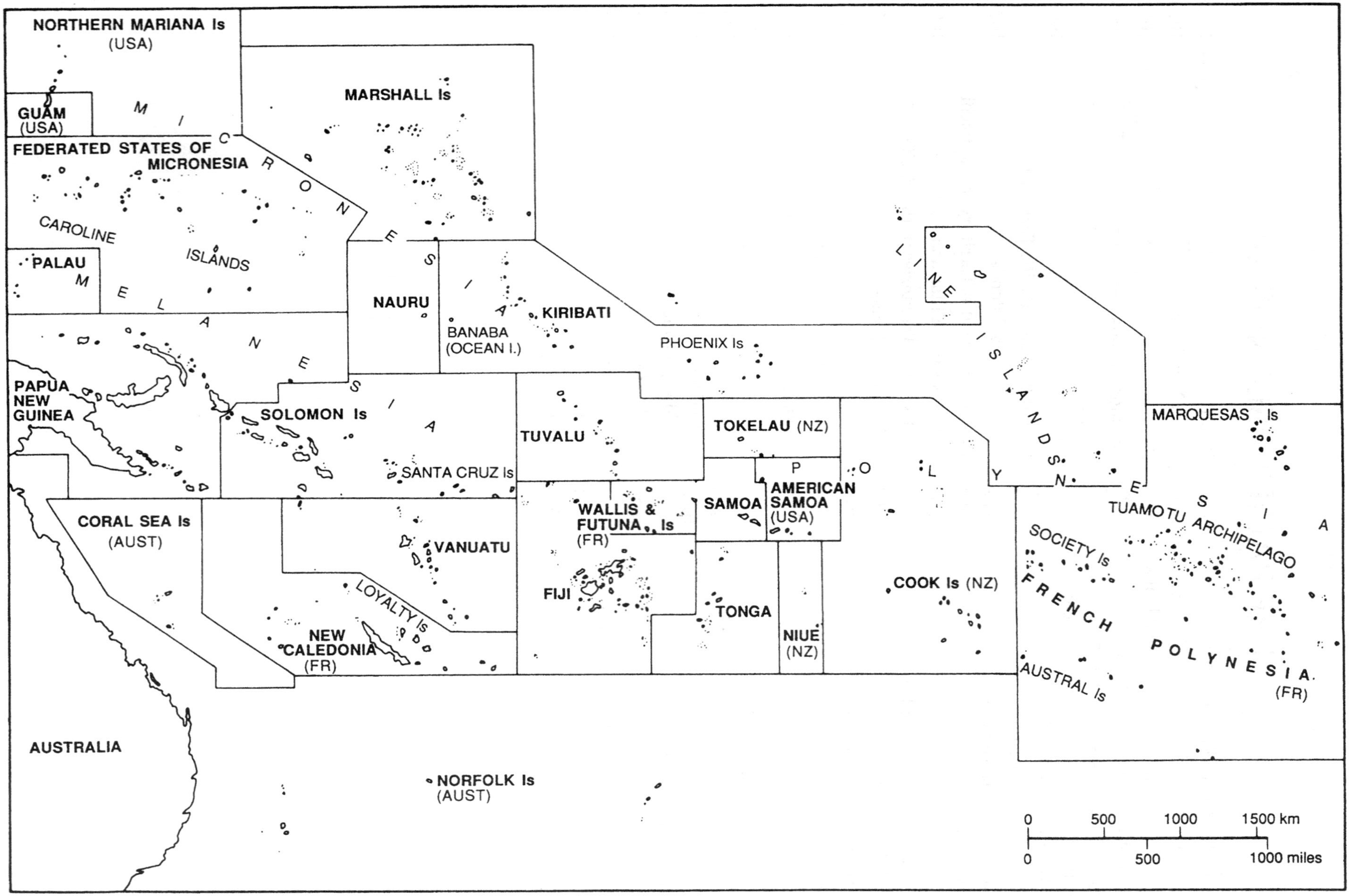

The Pacific Islands

THE PACIFIC ISLANDS

BACKGROUND TO THE PACIFIC ISLANDS

BRYANT J. ALLEN

With subsequent revisions by JENNY J. BRYANT and the editorial staff

PHYSICAL AND SOCIAL GEOGRAPHY

The Pacific Ocean occupies one-third of the earth's surface. Within it are located many thousands of islands, more than in all the rest of the world's seas combined. The large number of the Pacific Islands, and their widespread distribution, gives rise to a great variety of physical, social and economic environments. Their location relative to the continents and larger islands that border the Pacific, which include North and South America, Japan, China, the Philippines, Indonesia, Australia and New Zealand, continues to influence political and economic conditions in them. Their small size and physical isolation have rendered them vulnerable to influences from the rest of the world. Rapid and often traumatic ecological, social, economic and political changes have occurred throughout the Pacific following penetration by European and Asian explorers and colonists, a process that has continued, as communications and the neo-colonialism of mining, investment and tourism have developed.

A number of broad classifications of Pacific Islands exist. The islands may be divided into continental islands, high islands, low islands and atolls. The people of the Pacific may be divided into Melanesians, Polynesians and Micronesians. Melanesians occupy the larger islands in the south-west, Papua (formerly Irian Jaya) and Papua New Guinea, Solomon Islands, Vanuatu, Fiji and New Caledonia. Polynesians live on islands that are located over an immense area from Hawaii in the north to Easter Island in the south-east to New Zealand in the south-west. In the central Pacific, Polynesians occupy the major groups of Tonga, Samoa, the Society Islands including Tahiti, and the Cook Islands, as well as numerous small atolls. The Micronesians live in the north, central and west Pacific in the Mariana, Caroline, Marshall, Gilbert (Tungaru), Phoenix and Line groups.

Physical Features

The Pacific basin is 4–6 km deep and roughly circular in shape. The boundary is, in most places, the continental margin, but elsewhere it is obscured in a jumble of island arcs and fragmented continental blocks. The northern half of the basin forms one relatively deep unit measuring 5–6 km deep, and the southern half another, shallower one. The north is characterized by a number of enormous volcanoes and numerous clusters of smaller ones. The crust here is broken by very long faults. The south is deformed by a series of very long broad arches or rises with associated block and wrench faulting. Island arcs and deep trenches occur along the margins of the basins and parallel to them; archipelagos of volcanic islands and clusters of submarine volcanoes occur in all parts of the basins, but most are in the west and south-west.

These structures give rise to a number of characteristic island types. West of the so-called 'andesite-line', representing the furthest eastward limit of the continental blocks of Asia and Australia, are islands formed on the broken edges of the continental blocks. These continental islands have foundations of ancient folded and metamorphosed sediments which have been intruded by granites. Vulcanism has overlaid these rocks with lavas, tuff and ash, and transgressions by the ocean have laid down softer and younger marine sediments. Erosion has resulted in plains, deltas and swamps along the modern coastline. New Guinea (comprising Papua New Guinea, Papua and surrounding islands) is the best example of these continental islands; it is dominated by a massive central cordillera within which lie dissected and flat-floored montane valleys. The highest peak in the island is over 5,000 m. Active volcanoes exist along the north coast and in the New Guinea islands. North and south of the central mountains are broken hills and vast swamps. The coastal pattern is one of small coastal plains alternating with low river terraces, high marine terraces, coastal hills and steep mountain slopes plunging straight into the sea. The largest rivers of all the Pacific Islands are found here: the Fly and and the Sepik. Other continental islands are Fiji, Solomon Islands, Vanuatu and New Caledonia.

The high islands of the central Pacific are composed almost entirely of volcanic materials, together with reef limestone and recent sediments. The islands are the peaks of the largest volcanoes in the world. The Hawaiian volcano of Mauna Loa, for example, rises 9 km from the ocean floor and is over 200 km in diameter. Characteristic landforms of the high islands are striking peak and valley forms, with old volcanic cores often eroded to form fantastic skylines. Waterfalls, cliff faces and narrow beaches, with fringing coral reefs, complete the pattern. High islands in the Pacific include the Samoas, Tahiti and the Marquesas, Rarotonga in the Cook Islands, Pohnpei in the Eastern Carolines, and the Northern Mariana Islands.

Low islands are of two types: some are volcanic islands, which have been eroded, while others are raised atolls, which resemble sea-level reefs, but which are now elevated above modern sea-level. Caves and sinkholes occur widely. Small pockets of soil occur within the limestone rocks. Surface water is uncommon. Examples of low volcanic islands include Aitutaki, in the Cook Islands, and Wallis Island. Raised coral islands include some of the islands of the Tuamotu, Society, Cook, Line, Tokelau, Marshall, Caroline and Kiribati groups. Low islands with raised reefs are also common. One of the best examples is Mangaia in the Southern Cook group, which has a central core of volcanic rock 180 m high surrounded by an unbroken 1 km-wide band of coral limestone raised 70 m above the present sea-level. A new fringing reef now surrounds the island.

The atolls are the fourth island form, roughly circular reefs of coral limestone, partly covered by seawater, on which there are small islands made up of accumulations of limestone debris, and within each of which there occurs a lagoon of calm water. Atoll islets are commonly less than 3 m above the high-tide level. It is generally agreed that atolls have developed on the tops of volcanoes, which now no longer protrude above sea-level. Atolls vary in size from Rose Island (American Samoa), an atoll about 3 km by 3 km, to the Kwajalein Atoll in the Marshall Islands, which is over 60 km long. Sources of fresh water are rain and a freshwater lens, which is frequently found floating on salt groundwater beneath the islets.

Some of the Pacific Islands, such as Papua New Guinea, Tonga and Vanuatu, are particularly susceptible to earthquakes. Tsunamis also occur in the region from time to time, as demonstrated in September 2009 when Samoa, American Samoa and Tonga were devastated by a series of huge waves that killed nearly 200 people.

Climate

Five atmospheric circulation regions have been identified in the Pacific. A middle latitude area is characterized by the occurrence of extra-tropical cyclones with characteristic distinctive frontal weather systems. The Marianas sometimes receive this type of weather in the northern winter. The trade winds regions, where at least 60% of prevailing winds are from the north-west in the northern hemisphere and the south-east in the southern hemisphere, lie in an arc from the west coast of Mexico through Hawaii to the Marshall Islands in the north, and from the west coast of South America across the Marquesas and Tuamotus to the Society Islands. In these areas distinct wet and dry zones appear on larger islands. The monsoon area occurs to the far west and influences few of the Pacific Islands. However, the weather of Papua New Guinea is affected, and a wet season and a dry season are distinguishable, although they are by no means as sharp as the term 'monsoon' implies. A doldrums area occurs in a poorly defined band south of the Equator in an arc extending east from Solomon Islands to the Phoenix Islands. A cyclone zone exists in the northern Pacific in an arc extending west from Panama and including the Marshall, Caroline and Mariana Islands. A similar zone occurs in the south extending from the Tuamotus west across the Cooks, the Samoas, Tonga and Fiji to the north-east Australian coast. Serious storm damage is sometimes incurred by cyclones.

Rainfall in the Pacific is geographically most variable; some islands are semi-arid while others are very wet. In the northern Pacific, for example, Midway receives a mean annual rainfall of 1,194 mm and Honolulu 550 mm. Further south Yap receives 3,023 mm, Palau 3,900 mm, Pohnpei 4,700 mm and Fanning 2,054 mm. Islands in the eastern Pacific near the Equator are frequently barren. Rainfall decreases from west to east along the Equator: Nauru receives 2,050 mm, Ocean Island (Banaba) 1,930 mm and Christmas Island (Kiritimati) 950 mm. Further south in an arc extending east from New Guinea to the Society Islands in the Central Pacific average annual rainfall varies from between 3,500 mm in the west to 2,000 mm in the east. In Papua New Guinea altitude and local relief influence climate. Areas exposed to the north-west and south-east winds receive over 5,000 mm of rain, while inland areas cut off from moist air masses may receive less than 1,500 mm. On the south-eastern coast, east and west of Port Moresby, average annual rainfall is less than 1,000 mm. (See also below—The Impact of Climate Change.)

Soils, Minerals, Vegetation

Geology, soil, altitude, land-forms, location and climate are all combined in the creation of the widely varying physical environments of Pacific Islands. Continental islands exhibit the widest range of environments, from high alpine grasslands, through montane forest and lowland rain forest to savannah and mangrove swamps. They also contain the richest deposits of minerals: notably nickel in New Caledonia; and gold, copper, nickel and cobalt in Papua New Guinea, which also possesses substantial reserves of petroleum and natural gas. A rich source of minerals with potential for future exploitation are the deep-sea manganese nodules (containing copper, nickel and cobalt), which have been found in the north and south-west Pacific. In mid-2011 it was reported that a team of Japanese geologists had identified substantial deposits of rare earth minerals (used in the manufacture of high-technology appliances) in the Pacific sea-bed, east of Tahiti. Terrain is frequently a limit to cultivation, although soils are in general heavily leached and of low fertility, with low mineral and humus content. Raised coral islands lack groundwater and soils are shallow and often scattered in pockets. Phosphate deposits have been mined from the coralline limestone on Nauru and Banaba (formerly Ocean Island and now part of Kiribati), and also on Makatea in the Society Islands. The atolls contain only sparse resources. Soil development is often nil, fresh water difficult to obtain and foodplants other than coconuts and pandanus nuts difficult to cultivate. Special techniques are used to cultivate taro, but storms or high sea-levels frequently destroy gardens. The atolls provide the most tenuous human existence in the Pacific.

Prehistory, Culture and Early Society

The continental and oceanic Pacific Islands were never linked by land bridges to the Asian continent, and the Indonesian islands east of Bali and west of New Guinea form a frontier zone between a realm of placental mammals and marsupial mammals, the Wallace Line. Many palaeanthropologists argue therefore that man, a placental mammal, is an intruder in the Pacific. The first people to migrate across the Wallace Line are believed to have been *Homo sapiens* approaching the modern form. The inhabitants of the interior of New Guinea are classified as Australoid populations, which are thought to have begun moving into the area more than 40,000 years ago. Archaeological discoveries in Papua New Guinea have provided evidence of agricultural activity more than 9,000 years ago in the central highlands. Archaeological evidence has indicated that the Pacific Islands east of the Bismarck Archipelago were devoid of human settlement until about 3000 BC. In an important archaeological discovery, in 2010 it was reported that campsites dating back 49,000 years had been identified in the highlands of Papua New Guinea. Between 4,000 and 2,000 years ago people who are thought to have lived in north-eastern Indonesia and the Philippines, and who had descended from a Mongoloid stock, spread into the Pacific and along the coasts of the continental islands, intermarrying with the existing Australoid populations of eastern Indonesia and New Guinea. Modern Melanesians, Polynesians and Micronesians are thus, to varying degrees, the outcome of the mixing of these early Australoid and Mongoloid stocks.

Therefore, the Melanesians who inhabit the island chains from Solomon Islands eastwards to Fiji are basically an Australoid group, while the Fijians are a more intermediate group. Polynesians tend towards the Mongoloid end of the continuum and Micronesians more so. However, the actual pattern is far more complex than this simple description.

Origins of the three groups may also be evidenced in their cultures. The Polynesians are culturally and linguistically the most homogenous. Polynesian societies are basically patrilineal and genealogically ranked, with elaborate hierarchical systems of rank and class, best developed on the Hawaiian, Tongan and Society Islands. Micronesian societies are mainly matrilineal, with the exception of those in Yap and Kiribati. Melanesia is culturally the most diverse area of all. Hereditary ranking occurs in Fiji, but in many areas, especially in Papua New Guinea, status is achieved rather than inherited. Most groups are patrilineal, but matrilineal societies occur in New Guinea, Solomon Islands and Vanuatu.

Throughout the Pacific, the pre-contact subsistence economy was based on the vegetative propagation of root and tree crops, together with fishing and some pig husbandry and hunting. The only domesticated animals were dogs, pigs and fowls, but all three were not present everywhere in the region. The major root crops, taro and yam, have Asian origins, but one, the sweet potato, which was grown in New Guinea and in the Hawaii, Marquesas, Society and Easter Island groups prior to European contact, has a South American origin. Shifting cultivation was the main agricultural technique in most areas, although the intensity of land use and the periodicity of cycles varied widely in relation to population densities. In New Caledonia and parts of Polynesia, notably Hawaii, Tahiti and the Cook Islands, taro was cultivated in relatively elaborate, terraced, irrigated gardens.

Short-distance ocean voyaging was well-established in Polynesia and Micronesia before European contact, with large double-hulled canoes and navigation based on stars, wave patterns, bird flights and inherited geographical knowledge. Large ocean-going and coastal canoes were also used in Papua New Guinea and Fiji.

Numerous languages and dialects are spoken in the Pacific Islands (with more than 800 being found in Papua New Guinea alone). They belong to two groups, the non-Austronesian phyla found in Papua New Guinea (and in various areas of Indonesia), and the Austronesian phyla, which are spoken in coastal Papua New Guinea, most of island Melanesia, all of Polynesia and Micronesia (as well as in parts of Indonesia, the Philippines, South-East Asia and Madagascar).

To summarize, evidence that became available in 2010 suggests that Papua New Guinea was settled nearly 50,000 years ago. The ancestral Australoid populations were followed about 3,000 years ago by Austronesian speakers of Mongoloid stock who probably brought pottery, horticulture and pigs to Papua New Guinea. Intermixing occurred, followed by further movements east to New Caledonia and Vanuatu. Fiji was then settled by people who carried with them a pottery technology

previously established in Papua New Guinea and islands to the east, and further movements into the Pacific Ocean took place. During the last 2,500 years further intermixing has occurred in Melanesia, while Polynesian and Micronesian populations have had less interaction.

Population and Socio-Economic Characteristics

By 2011 the population of the 22 countries and territories of the region encompassed by the Pacific Community was estimated to have exceeded 10m., in comparison with 4m. in 1970. About two-thirds of that total were found in Papua New Guinea, which includes the eastern part of New Guinea, the second largest island in the world. The islands of Melanesia together contained some 88% of the region's total population, while Polynesia has 7% and Micronesia 5%. The combined population of the seven smallest island countries and territories totalled some 53,686 in mid-2008. It was predicted that the population of the region would double between 2004 and 2032 if current growth rates continued. The 22 countries and territories occupy about 550,000 sq km of land in 30m. sq km of ocean.

The rate of increase in the population of Pacific nations is near the average for developing countries, but there are wide variations among the islands. During the period 2000–09, for example, the population of Solomon Islands increased at an average annual rate of 2.6%. On Niue a decline of 2.3% was recorded during 1991–2001. On islands with moderate population growth rates, natural increase is partly offset by out-migration to the Pacific rim nations of New Zealand, Australia and the USA. A feature of the Polynesian Pacific, in particular, is that hundreds of thousands of islanders reside in the metropolitan rim countries, where they seek employment, education and generally better standards of living.

The Pacific Islands are becoming increasingly urbanized. In the early 21st century more than 50% of the population in 11 out of 22 island countries and territories lived in urban areas, with urban population growth rates of 8.2% recorded in both American Samoa and the Marshall Islands. The associated problems of overcrowding, housing shortages, the widening economic gap between rural and urban areas, environmental pressures and the need for economic diversification confronted many Pacific nations.

Many of the Pacific countries and territories have a narrow resource base and limited arable land. Those that do possess more diverse resources, such as minerals, timber and the potential for plantation agriculture, have frequently suffered over-exploitation of resources, political turmoil and dislocation of the populations. The susceptibility of the small island nations to cyclones, droughts or the impact of rising sea-levels make them particularly vulnerable.

The majority of the Pacific Islands' labour force continues to be engaged in the agricultural sector. Many islander have depended on mixed subsistence cultivation of coconuts, root crops (taro, sweet potatoes and cassava) and a large number of other tree and leaf crops. Cash-cropping has become a major part of the agricultural sector, with the introduction of oil palm, coffee, cocoa, rice, sugar cane, pumpkins (squash), ginger and nuts, as well as commercial exploitation of crops that are also grown for subsistence purposes, such as taro, pineapples and papayas (pawpaws). Pacific island nations are increasingly dependent upon imported foodstuffs, and the declining nutritional levels of the population reflect this change.

POLITICAL SITUATION

The islands may be divided into politically dependent and independent states. Dependent states that continue to be governed wholly or partially by the former colonial administrations include the Pitcairn Islands (the United Kingdom) and Wallis and Futuna (France). Other dependent states are internally self-governing and include Tokelau, the Cook Islands and Niue (New Zealand), Norfolk Island (Australia) and the Northern Mariana Islands, Guam and American Samoa (USA).

Former dependencies that have achieved full political independence are Samoa, formerly Western Samoa (from New Zealand in 1962); Nauru (from the UN and Australia in 1968); Tonga (from the United Kingdom in 1970); Fiji (from the United Kingdom in 1970); Papua New Guinea (from Australia in 1975); Tuvalu (from the United Kingdom in 1978); Solomon Islands (from the United Kingdom in 1978); Kiribati (from the United Kingdom in 1979); and Vanuatu (from the United Kingdom and France in 1980). The Federated States of Micronesia and the Marshall Islands achieved independence from the USA when the Compact of Free Association took effect in 1991. Palau, the last remaining component of the Trust Territory of the Pacific Islands, achieved independence under a similar agreement in October 1994. The political future of the region's dependent territories was considered in a UN report on decolonization, compiled in 1996, which particularly focused on the status of New Caledonia, Tokelau and Guam. In the late 1990s there were moves towards full autonomy by both New Caledonia and French Polynesia. In 1998 France and New Caledonia signed the Nouméa Accord, which provided for the gradual transfer of powers to local authorities over the next 15 to 20 years. As part of these changes, in 1999 New Caledonia acquired the status of an 'overseas country'. French Polynesia acquired similar status in 2004. Papua (formerly Irian Jaya), the western half of the island of New Guinea, is part of Indonesia and is excluded from this section, as are Hawaii, a state of the USA, and Easter Island, part of Chile.

REGIONAL INITIATIVES

(See also the Regional Organizations section in Part Three)

The Pacific Community

In 1947 the South Pacific Commission was established by the United Kingdom, France, the USA, New Zealand, Australia and the Netherlands. Its aim was to 'promote the economic and social welfare and advancement of the peoples of the region', although some commentators felt that it was more an attempt by Australia and New Zealand to extend their power and to deter others from obtaining access, claiming that organizations such as the SPC served the interests of the metropolitan powers.

In 1950 the South Pacific Conference was established as a separate body for the island nations. The advances towards independence for the island nations in the 1960s and 1970s challenged the role of the South Pacific Conference, which was still controlled by the metropolitan powers. This was most evident in the debates over nuclear testing in the Pacific during 1970, when the French delegation walked out of a meeting of the South Pacific Commission. In May 1997 members of the South Pacific Commission voted to change the name of the organization to reflect the expanded membership of the group. The change to Pacific Community was approved at a meeting of the South Pacific Conference which took place in October 1997, and became effective in February 1998.

The Pacific Islands Forum

In 1971 the South Pacific Forum (SPF) was established. The Pacific Islands Forum (as the SPF was restyled in 2000) has become the most important regional organization in the Pacific, enabling Pacific nations to work towards and foster regional responses to a number of economic, social and political issues which, because of the isolation, distance and small populations of the Pacific nations, might otherwise be ineffectively managed. The Forum comprises the heads of government of the independent and self-governing island countries, as well as Australia and New Zealand. The Forum is a political body, which can raise and discuss any issue. The organization has an administrative, research and development arm, the Pacific Islands Forum Secretariat (called the South Pacific Bureau for Economic Co-operation (SPEC) until 1988 and the South Pacific Forum Secretariat until 2000). At its summit meeting in October 2000 the organization's new title of 'Pacific Islands Forum' was officially adopted, aiming to reflect the group's expanding membership. Following the Forum's endorsement of the Niue Declaration on Climate Change in August 2008, the Pacific Leaders Call for Action on Climate Change was adopted in August 2009, the issue having been identified as the greatest challenge confronting the Pacific Islands. The Pacific Adaptation to Climate Change Project was endorsed by Micronesian nations in July 2011. Meanwhile, Pacific officials were being

instructed to commence work on comprehensive preparations for the relocation of those islanders likely to be affected by rising sea-levels.

Melanesian Spearhead Group

In March 1988 Papua New Guinea, Solomon Islands and Vanuatu formed the Melanesian Spearhead Group, stressing that this was in no way a threat to the SPF (as it was then known). However, it has been seen as a reaction to both the informal formation of a 'Polynesian Community', which has received overt and covert support from France, and to Australian and New Zealand disapproval of Vanuatu's links with Libya, now discontinued. The Melanesian group also supported more radical efforts on the part of the SPF towards the decolonization of French territories in the Pacific. In 1996 a fourth country, Fiji, was admitted to the group. In March 2007 the members of the group signed a constitution at a meeting in Vanuatu.

Pacific Plan

The Pacific Plan was drafted in early 2005. This recommended closer regional co-operation, the free movement of workers throughout the region and the eventual integration of the economies of Pacific island nations. The Prime Ministers of Samoa and Papua New Guinea and the President of the Marshall Islands met New Zealand's Prime Minister Helen Clark in July 2005 to discuss the progress of the draft plan. The Pacific Plan was endorsed by the summit meeting of the Pacific Islands Forum in October 2005. It was also supported by the Pacific Community. In October 2006, meeting in Fiji, Forum members undertook to advance the implementation of the Pacific Plan, focusing on the areas of economic growth, sustainable development and good governance, along with regional security and partnerships.

The Emergence of SPREP

Of increasing significance in the region is the South Pacific Regional Environment Programme (SPREP). SPREP grew out of concern over environmental problems in the region voiced by the South Pacific Conference in the 1960s. In 1982 the South Pacific Commission, with support from the United Nations Environment Programme's Regional Seas Programme and the regional Governments, established SPREP at an intergovernmental conference held in Rarotonga, Cook Islands. SPREP operates on the basis of a Convention and several protocols, which required several rounds of meetings and conferences before they were adopted and ratified. In 1990 the SPREP Convention came into force when ratified by 10 countries. The Convention addresses the threat to marine and coastal environments from all types of pollution (including mining, oil spillages, dumping of toxic wastes and hazardous materials) and the need for co-operation to ensure sustainable resource management. The island Governments have remained firm in their demand for a prohibition of nuclear dumping and testing, but the final Convention excludes a prohibition clause, which is dealt with in the separate Nuclear-Free Zone Treaty (NFZT) banning radioactive waste dumping and testing. The SPREP Convention then allowed for full regional participation, including that of France and its territories. The ratification of the Programme's Convention meant that SPREP became the recipient of a great deal of aid and assistance from bilateral funding agreements.

OTHER REGIONAL AGREEMENTS

Trade Initiatives

In 1981 a trade agreement was signed by Australia, New Zealand and the SPF countries. Known as the South Pacific Regional Trade and Economic Co-operation Agreement (SPARTECA), it was designed to ease import restrictions on island goods into Australia and New Zealand, in an attempt to adjust the massive trade imbalance that exists. On 1 January 1987 new terms of trade came into effect, whereby all duties and quotas on island imports were abolished, with the exception of those on garments, footwear, sugar, steel and motor vehicles. The disparities in size and economic power have presented an obstacle to SPARTECA. Fiji is generally considered to have benefited from regional trade agreements to a greater extent than other, smaller nations which have fewer export resources. The Pacific Island Countries Trade Agreement (PICTA) of 2003 provided for the gradual introduction of a free trade area by Pacific Islands Forum members, which might eventually be expanded to include other countries. By 2005 most of the Forum's member countries had committed themselves to the agreement. By 2008, furthermore, negotiations were under way for a services trade agreement to supplement the existing goods trade agreement.

Fisheries

In 1986 a five-year fisheries treaty was signed by the USA and members of the South Pacific Forum Fisheries Agency, thus ending a protracted dispute that had involved the capture and confiscation of US fishing boats by Papua New Guinea and Solomon Islands. The treaty guaranteed royalties of some US $60m., to be paid over a five-year period, and was renegotiated for a further 10 years in 1992. The fisheries treaty developed out of the lack of return Pacific countries were receiving for tuna taken by distant nations from their waters. The total access fees paid to all countries by the fishing nations were on average less than 3% of the annual market value of tuna caught in the region. In June 1997 the members of the South Pacific Forum Fisheries Agency, together with representatives from several major fishing nations, signed the Majuro Declaration, which contained a commitment to introduce measures for the conservation and management of the region's migratory fish stocks. The South Pacific region was thought to be the only major fishing area in the world not to have adopted such an agreement already. A report by the World Bank, published in 1999, claimed that overfishing posed a serious threat to many Pacific island countries.

A new organization, the Western and Central Pacific Fisheries Commission (WCPFC), was established in June 2004, following several years of regional negotiations. The commission introduced a new tuna conservation convention, which aimed to promote the responsible fishing of shared tuna stocks and to end unregulated fishing on the high seas. The convention was swiftly ratified by 14 countries. A senior Australian government fisheries adviser was appointed to lead the organization in December 2004. The South Pacific Regional Fisheries Management Organisation (RFMO) was initiated in 2006; by 2008 some 20 states had joined the process.

Fishing activities within the exclusive economic zones of the Federated States of Micronesia, Kiribati, the Marshall Islands, Nauru, Palau, Papua New Guinea, Solomon Islands and Tuvaluhave been governed by a sub-regional arrangement, the Parties to the Nauru Agreement (PNA), which was established in 1982. The signatories' restrictions on purse-seine fishing for tuna was extended in October 2010.

The SPNFZ Treaty

In 1962 the French Government transferred its nuclear-testing facilities to Mururoa and Fangataufa atolls, located in the Tuamotu Archipelago, in French Polynesia. Between 1975 and the suspension in 1992 France conducted 135 underground and 52 atmospheric nuclear tests. During 1986 and 1987 continued discussions were held on the implications of the South Pacific Nuclear-Free Zone (SPNFZ) treaty, signed in 1985 by Australia, New Zealand, the Cook Islands, Fiji, Kiribati, Niue, Tuvalu and Western Samoa (now Samoa). (Vanuatu and Solomon Islands had refused to sign, on the grounds that the treaty's provisions were inadequate.) The treaty designates a 'nuclear-free zone' in the South Pacific, and imposes a ban on the manufacture, testing, storage and use of nuclear weapons, and the dumping of nuclear waste, in the region. Both the USSR and the People's Republic of China signed protocols attached to the treaty, but in 1987 the Governments of the USA and the United Kingdom rejected the South Pacific signatories' request for their endorsement of the treaty, a decision that provoked expressions of anger and concern from members of the SPF. Widespread protests against the French Government's programme of nuclear testing on Mururoa Atoll, in French Polynesia, continued until the implementation of a moratorium in 1992. Following France's decision in 1995 to resume its testing programme, in September of that year French Polynesia became the focus of world attention when the first new test took place (see below). After

its final test in January 1996, France signed the SPNFZ treaty, together with the United Kingdom and the USA, and (following its earlier suspension) was reinstated as a dialogue partner to the SPF.

THE IMPACT OF CLIMATE CHANGE

The repercussions of climate change and of rising sea-levels could have devastating consequences for the low-lying islands of the Pacific. Even a half-metre rise in sea-level would mean the flooding of low-lying territories such as the Tokelau group of atolls, Tuvalu, the Marshall Islands and parts of Kiribati. Hilly islands would lose low-lying arable land.

The South Pacific Sea Level and Climate Monitoring Project was launched in 1991 with Australian aid and aimed to allow 11 Pacific island nations to monitor the effects of climate change on their territory. The fourth phase of the programme began in 2006 and, following an extension, was due to end in December 2011. The increasing impact of the greenhouse effect (the heating of the earth's atmosphere as a consequence of pollution) on the Pacific Islands has continued to cause concern in the region. As well as the rise in sea-levels, with its implications for the continued habitability of many low-lying atolls, the phenomenon was also thought to be responsible for a dramatic increase in the frequency of cyclones, tidal waves and other associated natural disasters in the region. The issue dominated the summit meeting of the South Pacific Forum in August 1997 and provoked an unprecedented rift within the group when Australia refused to support recommended reductions in the emission of pollutant gases known to contribute to the greenhouse effect. In 1999 it was announced that two uninhabited islands in Kiribati had disappeared as a result of rising sea-levels. In 2003, following the disappearance of an islet and an increase in the amount of seawater seeping into its crop plantations, Tuvalu began to give serious consideration to the prospect of resettling its citizens elsewhere in the region.

With more frequent high tides and more extensive flooding having led to the increasing encroachment of seawater, the salinization of soil and of drinking water has become a major issue for many islands. In Tuvalu, for example, in late 2007 it was reported that water drawn from wells was becoming increasingly unsuitable for consumption. In response to the threat to the traditional practice of subsistence agriculture, trials of salt-resistant crop varieties have been conducted in Fiji, for example, while mangroves and native grasses have been planted in an attempt to curb the coastal erosion.

In 2009 it was reported from Papua New Guinea that the world's first climate change refugees were in the process of being relocated from the Carteret Islands, which had become uninhabitable. Preparations for similar relocations to higher ground were being made in parts of Solomon Islands and the Federated States of Micronesia. Also to escape the effects of climate change, several families were reported to be moving from Tuvalu to Futuna in 2011. In September of that year the Prime Minister of Solomon Islands, Danny Philip, informed the UN General Assembly that, as seawater was now encroaching to within 5 m of the wall of the country's main hospital in Honiara, the facility was to be relocated to higher ground. To assist the process, Philip urged the swift release of funds from donors.

A report on the effects of climate change on the Pacific Islands, released by the international aid agency Oxfam in July 2009, drew attention to the growing problems of shortages of food and fresh water, the rising incidence of diseases such as malaria and dengue fever, and the increasing frequency of flooding and storm surges. Following heavy rain in Solomon Islands, for example, a state of disaster was declared in February 2009. Torrential rain in Fiji in January, again resulting in many deaths, was described as the worst in the country's history. The Oxfam report emphasized that one-half of the population of the Pacific Islands lived less than 1.5 km from the coast and were thus particularly vulnerable to rising sea-levels. It was projected that by 2050 as many as 8m. Pacific islanders would be forced to relocate, not necessarily within their own country, if climate change were allowed to continue unabated. The agency appealed for urgent action to safeguard Pacific communities. In particular, New Zealand and Australia were urged to reduce their levels of carbon emissions by at least 40% by 2020 and by 95% by 2050. Tuvalu, meanwhile, announced its intention of reducing its carbon output to zero by 2020 through increased use of solar and wind power.

The Global Assessment Report released by the UN at a regional disaster risk management conference held in New Zealand in August 2011 concluded that, although the likelihood of being killed in a natural disaster had been successfully reduced in the past 20 years by improvements in preparedness, the economic impact of such events had increased substantially. The report noted that the Pacific tsunami of 2009 had cost Samoa US $104m., or the equivalent of more than 5% of the country's GDP; the tsunami in Solomon Islands in 2007 had cost the country the equivalent of 90% of its annual budget.

A report published by the Asian Development Bank (ADB) in September 2011 warned of the increasing risk of hunger and malnutrition in the Pacific Islands because of climate change. The ADB's report drew attention to the Pacific Islands' much greater dependence on imported food, urging the region to focus on the production of more climate-resistant crops such as taro, yam and cassava.

A state of emergency was declared in Tuvalu in September 2011 when a shortage of fresh water in parts of the country reached critical levels. Drinking water was rationed, and aid agencies provided supplies of bottled water to the worst affected islanders, on the atoll of Nukulaelae. The New Zealand air force delivered two desalination units and water containers to Tuvalu. Crops of taro, breadfruit and coconuts were reported to have been seriously affected by the protracted dry spell. A similar situation prevailed in Tokelau, which had also received no rainfall for several months. With reserves of drinking water also reduced to precarious levels, supplies were shipped to Tokelau from Samoa, at considerable expense. Samoa itself, American Samoa and Tonga were also reported to be experiencing drought conditions, attributed by many to the climatic phenomenon known as La Niña.

OTHER ISSUES

In addition to the issue of climate change, political and economic events in the region have been increasingly influenced by other environmental concerns. A substantial increase in unsustainable logging activity in the islands (most notably in Solomon Islands, Papua New Guinea and Vanuatu) has caused increasing concern since the early 1990s. The mining operations conducted on several islands, particularly Nauru, Papua New Guinea, Solomon Islands and New Caledonia, have resulted in serious degradation of the environment. (See Environmental Issues of the Pacific Islands for details of deforestation and the impact of mining activities.)

President Jacques Chirac's decision in mid-1995 to resume France's nuclear-testing programme on Mururoa Atoll (see above) was highly controversial. A programme of eight tests was envisaged (subsequently curtailed to six). The announcement of the forthcoming tests led to major demonstrations throughout the region, which intensified when French commandos violently seized *Rainbow Warrior II,* the flagship of the environmentalist group Greenpeace, and its crew, which had been protesting peacefully near the test site. Scientists had also expressed concern at the resumption of testing, as some believed that further explosions at Mururoa could lead to the collapse of the atoll, which had been weakened considerably. In early 1996 the French Government confirmed reports by a team of independent scientists that radioactive isotopes had leaked into the waters surrounding the atoll. The French Government had attracted almost universal criticism for its actions. Following the final test in January 1996, France initiated a series of measures aimed at improving relations with the Pacific Islands, including the doubling of its aid budget to the region. Work to dismantle facilities at the test site was completed in July 1998. As fears for the stability of Mururoa Atoll continued, in early 2011 the French Polynesian Government urged France to conduct a comprehensive assessment of the risks to the population if the atoll were to collapse and release radiation.

Tourism remains vitally important to the Pacific Islands' economy. However, the growth of the industry on many islands is restricted by limited infrastructure and inadequate transport facilities, whereas in those countries that have experienced a rapid expansion in tourist arrivals, damage to the environment has often resulted. Consequently, on some islands the development of 'eco-tourism', which encourages the conservation and appreciation of the natural environment, is being promoted as a more sustainable alternative to traditional tourism.

The development of much of the region, particularly the smaller islands, has been impeded by the lack of efficient communications. Regional airlines have often suffered from problems relating to the islands' small size and populations, their remoteness and the frequent inability of their Governments to subsidize unprofitable routes. In an attempt to address this problem, SPF member nations commissioned a report in 1995 on the possible rationalization of regional air services and established a regular Forum Aviation Policy Meeting. In 1998 representatives adopted a policy framework to manage the region's airspace as a unified area and to replace the numerous bilateral agreements between countries with an integrated regional aviation plan. The resulting Pacific Islands Air Service Agreement drafted by the Pacific Islands Forum (as it had become) proposed the operation of an 'open skies' policy, allowing airlines to compete for routes in order to control air fares and to ensure more viable services. The agreement entered into force in October 2007, by which time 10 countries had signed the agreement and six had ratified it.

HISTORY OF THE PACIFIC ISLANDS

IAN CAMPBELL

BASIC CULTURAL CONFIGURATION

The modern Pacific consists of 25 different political units, ranging from fully independent states to possessions with only a small degree of self-government. Their present status reflects their colonial experience and the consequences of international rivalries in the period since the Second World War (1939–45). To a lesser extent, it also conforms to traditional cultural patterns.

Traditionally, there were three basic cultural areas making up the Pacific islands: Micronesia in the north-west Pacific, Melanesia in the south-west Pacific, and Polynesia in the east. Although modern anthropologists find these categories unsatisfactory because of their indistinct boundaries and shared histories, there were important differences between them that continue to be significant. Melanesian societies on the whole were small, mutually antagonistic and governed by men who acquired their authority through the accumulation of traditional wealth. Sorcery was so common that it was blamed for almost all deaths, coincidental happenings and natural disasters. Various forms of magic were considered necessary for achievement of any kind. Micronesian societies also tended to be small in scale but had a more stable class system, with clearly identified figures of authority whose rank was inherited. Inhabiting for the most part very small, low islands, these people's lives were closely entwined with the sea. Polynesian societies on the whole showed a stronger sense of social class, with more elaborate grades of inherited rank than the other two, and in some cases had exalted chiefs with absolute powers. Warfare was common in most Polynesian societies, which may be described as 'warrior aristocracies'; land and sea territories, as well as population sizes under the command of a single chief, were much greater than in either Micronesia or Melanesia.

These ancient patterns are reflected in their modern societies. Inherited rank continues to be very important in social status, professional achievement and political life in most parts of Polynesia. Democracy functions within a framework of aristocratic assumptions. Modern nations are composed of people who are culturally as well as geographically close to each other. This is also true of Micronesia, but there language divisions are more important and inherited rank less. In Melanesia, the overwhelming problem in modern politics and society is the division of the nations into hundreds of small social units, most of them with their own language. Fragmentation remains the source of some of the most intractable of modern challenges of development and governance.

THE COMING OF EUROPEANS

Exploration

Despite early voyages across the Pacific in the 16th century, beginning with the first global circumnavigation by the expedition led by Ferdinand Magellan (1519–22), discoveries of land were sporadic, isolated and mostly insignificant for 250 years. Systematic exploration did not begin until the voyages of Capt. James Cook (1768–80), who brought for the first time a spirit of scientific enquiry, a passion for accurate, comprehensive information and a concern to establish peaceful, friendly relationships with the people who lived in the islands. Cook's three great voyages verified the location of many of the early discoveries and added major new ones; but it was possibly more important that he made exploration scientific in both its methods and results. Consequently, his voyages were followed by others from several nations including the United Kingdom, France, Russia and the USA from the 1780s to the 1840s. Earlier exploration had previously been incidental to commercial or political purposes, but the age of scientific enquiry associated with Cook freed exploration from national self-interest. Thus, subsequent commercial, evangelical and political intrusion does not reflect the nationality of explorers. To put it another way, the explorers did not initiate any of those processes.

Commercial Enterprises

Trade and evangelism in the eastern Pacific followed Cook's explorations almost simultaneously but were otherwise unrelated to his activities or to each other. Spanish ships called occasionally at Guam in western Micronesia for about 100 years from the 1560s before a serious attempt was made at evangelization. The latter resulted in warfare, which led to conquest, conversion, government and subsequent neglect.

In the eastern Pacific, American and English traders travelling between China and the north-west coast of North America began calling at Hawaii for supplies and refreshment in the mid-1780s, and vessels from the recently established British colony in New South Wales began desultory visits to Tahiti, initially for supplies of salted pork. In Hawaii provisioning gave way to a brief trade in sandalwood for the Chinese incense market, and after a lapse both sandalwood and provisioning were revived after 1812. Both trades lasted for several decades, providing the material basis and the social changes that carried Hawaii through some significant political transitions. Meanwhile, links between New South Wales and Tahiti brought traders into contact with the intermediate archipelagos, especially New Zealand, Tonga and Fiji. Sandalwood was discovered in Fiji, and later in the Marquesas. Both reserves collapsed after intensive exploitation. The next commodity to attract the attention of foreign traders was *bêches-de-mer* (sea-cucumbers), trade in which was concentrated on Fiji from the late 1820s to the late 1850s, until these supplies were also exhausted.

Early trade, therefore, concentrated on Polynesia, despite the greater voyaging distances, and involved commodities that are best described as speculative. Sandalwood and *bêches-de-mer* were both risky commodities for which prices fluctuated enormously. Traders saw their best advantage as being able to obtain as much as they could while they could, and the resources were exploited at unsustainable levels. The removal of both these commodities was also extremely disruptive to island life, needing a major recommitment of island labour for the weeks or months that were required to be devoted to producing a cargo. Village economies did not adapt easily to supplying occasional labour on this scale, which could only be achieved by chiefs compelling their people to work. The chiefs likewise were the major beneficiaries of the trade goods whether they insisted on firearms (as many did) or on more utilitarian or decorative trade goods. Goods demanded in return for sandalwood and *bêches-de-mer* ranged from ornaments and trinkets to cloth, glassware, pottery, pots, axes, knives, fish-hooks, hoop-iron (from which tools could be fashioned) and entire ships. Because the trades were concentrated in particular places and for relatively short times, and because of the chiefs' control of the trades, the material basis of island life did not change significantly as a result.

The more important trades for the Pacific Islands in the 19th century were the less lucrative, less dramatic but more sustainable activities that depended on developments elsewhere. These were the trades in provisions, coconut oil and copra, and also labour. The provisioning trade was associated with the whaling industry, which was at its height in terms of numbers of ships between 1819 and about 1860. Thereafter, whale populations declined markedly and along with them the number of whale hunters. Most whaling vessels were American, sailing out of New England ports, although a small minority were British and French, and there was also some whaling out of Australian ports. At the beginning of the century, a whaler leaving New England and rounding Cape Horn would be back home with a full cargo of oil in approximately two years. Before long that had extended to three years, and by the 1850s it was not uncommon for voyages to last five years. This accounts for the increased contact between foreigners and Pacific islanders: whalers needed regular supplies of fresh water, food and firewood, and it was not long before preferred calling places emerged in all three culture areas. However, the Polynesian ports of Lahaina and Honolulu in Hawaii, Papeete in Tahiti, Apia in Samoa, Kadavu in Fiji and the Bay of Islands in New Zealand received the greatest concentration of visits, and developed into port towns on the basis of the trade. Recreational services also developed, offering alcohol and prostitution.

From the 1830s coconut oil became an increasingly significant supplement to whale oil, and was particularly important for small islands that had no other commodities to offer and, for navigational or other reasons, were unattractive as whaler resorts. Coconut oil was extremely demotic: its production, unlike sandalwood, *bêches-de-mer*, provisioning and prostitution, was a traditional activity, coconuts were ubiquitous, and commercially worthwhile quantities could be produced with no significant disturbance to the traditional village economy. After the 1850s coconut oil was increasingly superseded by copra, the dried kernel of the coconut from which the oil was pressed. This was an even more demotic product because less effort was required to produce it, and its production could be spread out over time more easily because storing the dried nut was easier than storing the oil. Nor was a large work-force or chiefly control necessary: all who had access to coconut trees could produce a quantity of copra, ready for the visit of an itinerant trader or, later, to be sold to a resident trader who kept a trade-store in one of many remote places serviced by a fleet of schooners operated by trading companies that became part of the island scene in the later part of the 19th century. This was the trade that was most responsible for introducing and distributing foreign articles on a wider scale, and was significant in that even resource-poor, small islands could thus gain access to trade.

The decline of the whaling industry, therefore, was matched by this growing trade that was both less disruptive and more successful in changing the material basis of island life. Copra, above all, led to the abandonment of traditional tool-making, the introduction of foreign clothing, cooking utensils and methods, as well as diet, and a reliance on regular access to foreign traders. Contemporary with the copra trade was the growth of trade in labour. From the beginning of commercial contact, islanders had been eager to join foreign ships. By the mid-19th century they formed a significant part of the whale-ship work-force, on some ships comprising more than half of the crew, and even some of the officers were islanders. When the New Hebrides (Vanuatu) sandalwood trade flourished between about 1842 and 1860, it became normal for traders to engage a party of islanders to work on the ships or to cut the wood on islands that were not their own. This had advantages for all parties to the sandalwood trade, but its longer-term significance was that it established a trend of islanders—from the New Hebrides in particular—leaving their homes to work for foreigners for a time, and then returning. In the early 1860s this evolved into a much larger-scale, longer-term labour migration to Queensland, Fiji and Samoa where cotton and later sugar plantations were developing, and to New Caledonia where the demand was both for farm workers and for mining labour. The New Hebrides and the Solomon Islands provided most of the migrant labour, but sizeable contributions also came from the Gilbert Islands (Kiribati) for various destinations, including Hawaii.

The labour trade provided a scale and intensity of contact between islanders and Europeans that was not equalled again for a century, in the era of decolonization. In the 19th century it was not long before the settler societies of Queensland, Samoa, Fiji and Hawaii were well known to islanders; more islanders travelled to those European enclaves than Europeans visited their homelands. Despite popular perceptions of slavery and kidnapping, images propagated at the time and again a century later for political and propaganda purposes, the trade was sustainable and enduring because all parties found that it served their interests. From the islanders' point of view, this included not only the commercial opportunities—that is access to trade goods—but also the opportunity to travel, to escape restrictions at home and to fulfil a growing expectation that a young man should have some experience of the world before marriage. Most islanders returned to their homes able to speak English, or at least an English creole. Some became literate and of these most were converted to Christianity, which some of them then propagated in their homes after their return.

Missionary Enterprise

Trade, as this example shows, could promote Christianity, but the relationship was seldom harmonious or mutually helpful. Missionaries were not far behind traders in following explorers into the Pacific, and in many places went ahead of them. Apart from the Catholic conversion of Guam at the end of the 17th century, and some abortive Catholic attempts in the Caroline Islands subsequently, the Christian history of the Pacific Islands begins with the attempt by the London Missionary Society (LMS), an interdenominational, Protestant group, to evangelize Tahiti, Tonga and the Marquesas Islands in 1797. The missions in Tonga and the Marquesas were brief and unsuccessful. The Tahitian mission suffered many vicissitudes, but within 20 years, most Tahitians had accepted Christianity, and the mission was able to expand, first to the Leeward Islands, and then further west to the southern Cook Islands. Conversion of these places followed quickly, assisted by the formal and informal propagation of the new way by eager converts. By the end of the 1820s the missionary society was able to contemplate new fields, and made its next start in Samoa. In 1839 it lost its most enterprising agent and first martyr, the Rev. John Williams, who was killed on the beach at Tanna, in the New Hebrides.

By this time the conversion of the Pacific Islands had a momentum that appeared irresistible, although not without trials and obstacles to be overcome. The LMS had been joined by the Wesleyan Missionary Society, which began work in Tonga (its second attempt there) in 1826. Hawaii was already in the hands of an American Protestant Mission Society. After a slow start, the Wesleyans achieved rapid success in Tonga and in 1835 quickly moved into Fiji, where success was steady but impeded by political turbulence. Nevertheless, most of Fiji was converted within about 30 years. The LMS continued its expansion westward and northward: from Samoa into the Ellice Islands (now Tuvalu) and the Gilbert Islands, and beyond the New Hebrides into the Loyalty Islands. Much of this expansion was undertaken by island converts who, after receiving some training in their home islands, went to new lands to proclaim the Gospel under the supervision of European missionaries. Most of the preparatory work was done by these men and their wives, who suffered much higher rates of death from violence and disease than their white mentors.

Meanwhile, Catholic missionary orders tried to make up for the opportunities that they had lost to the Protestants. With difficulty and amid controversy they were permitted in the 1840s to maintain bases in Hawaii, Tahiti, Tonga, Samoa and Fiji. Their attempts to evangelize heathen areas in New Caledonia, the Solomon Islands and Papua were not successful.

The momentum of conversion slowed down in Melanesia owing to the greater social and linguistic fragmentation. If it were to be evangelized by the same strategies that had developed in Polynesia, the conversion of Melanesia would take centuries. A fresh approach would be needed, and this came from the Anglican Church Mission Society, which was based in New Zealand. The new strategy was to recruit boys from their homes, take them to New Zealand for education in the faith in English and return them to their homes, where they would be able to explain the principles of Christianity in their own languages. This approach was not immediately successful and needed modification. Over time, however, with the adoption of a Melanesian language as the medium of instruction and the transfer of the school from New Zealand to Norfolk Island (thus eliminating much travelling time), the policy began to yield results. The large Anglican communities in Vanuatu and Solomon Islands derive from this initiative.

Conversion has always been controversial, and the missionary drive likewise. Explaining why Pacific islanders changed their religion so readily is not easy. There are some explanations that may be ruled out. Suggestions that chiefs converted because of threats or inducements offered by foreign governments or naval officers are fallacious. So is the corollary that chiefs, having converted in this way, then delivered their people to the missionaries. Coercion by missionaries, or their requiring conversion in return for medical attention, can also be dismissed. Missionaries were not agents of government, nor were they supported by government patronage. They went to the Pacific as private individuals in response to their calling. Many of them were ill-prepared, under-equipped and inadequately educated, and were in no position to induce people to act contrary to their own wills or perception of advantage. Thus, while political and commercial means may be discounted, there was much in the political and commercial context that encouraged people to consider a religious alternative. The period of early contact was very disturbed, both by traditional conflicts and by external influences. Foreign medicines and manufactured articles, along with the mystery of writing, encouraged islanders to draw their own conclusions about which god or gods offered the best gifts. Social disintegration and a high rate of mortality resulting from introduced disease undermined the people's confidence in the faithfulness and effectiveness of their traditional gods. The inherent attributes of Christianity should not be dismissed: missionaries spoke constantly of love, forgiveness, redemption and the equality of human souls, while the most successful missionaries demonstrated much of this in their own conduct. Their teachings attracted a good deal of interest, and really did seem to many islanders to offer practical, as well as spiritual, solutions to their problems. These problems were often intrinsic to the old religion: burdens of vengeance and retaliation, spiritual tyranny and sorcery, all gave people reasons to consider a religion that offered them an alternative, and in addition to an alternative, spiritual protection.

The missionaries' roles were multiple. Foremost was evangelism, but that was scarcely separable from education, so missionaries provided schools. As people sought relief from strange new diseases, the missionaries were drawn into the provision of medicine and treatment. One of the earliest Wesleyan missionaries was a qualified physician, and missionaries later led the way in providing clinics and hospitals. In the early 19th century missionaries also served as political advisers, not as part of a plan to take secular control but because converted chiefs, such as Pomare in Tahiti and Taufaahau in Tonga, were uncertain as to how to rule their people once conversion removed the old sanctions and the validating effect of the former religion.

FOREIGN SETTLEMENT AND ISLAND POLITICS

By the 1870s the inhabitants of most archipelagos had been affected by profound changes. Many remained untouched, or were reached only indirectly through other islanders. For a great many people the changes were marginal, superficial or inconsequential. European influence was far from uniform in its coverage and far from homogeneous in its content. However, there had been sufficient disturbance to occasion political changes. The disturbance included massive population losses in some places, radical changes in the power structure of island societies, especially in Polynesia, and the intrusion of commercial interests that threatened to erode the structure of social systems, especially in Melanesia. In the first part of the 19th century, Europeans travelled to the Pacific mostly to exchange commodities from shipboard. Small numbers of men settled in order to take advantage of commercial opportunities facilitating such trade or providing services to ships. As these small settlements grew, they acquired interests in property, and they expected protection of their lives and of their assets. Their activities created a need for established systems of law. Contrasting expectations and conventional assumptions between these people and island potentates were a common source of strain and dispute, leading to the first instances of foreign political intervention in island affairs. Naval officers of the various nations responded differently to these occasions according to their personalities or instructions: some by intimidation, some by advice, while others drafted written agreements that purported to bind or protect island chiefs in their dealings with Europeans.

By about 1870, however, a threshold had been crossed in terms of the size and confidence of settler communities. In some archipelagos, and especially in Samoa, Fiji and the New Hebrides, extensive tracts of land had been sold by islanders to foreigners who aspired to establish plantations in order to take advantage of high international prices, especially for cotton. As settler interests increased so did the difficulties of governing them and of ordering their relationships with islanders. Frontier relationships became progressively unsettled, and particularly where power struggles were still taking place among islanders. Transactions in land, and subsequent attempts to use such land, were major sources of conflict. So too was the expectation of settlers that they could employ islanders as farm or plantation labour, a belief that brought them into direct conflict (or less often collaboration) with chiefs. This was a principal motive behind the recruitment of labour from other islands, which was then brought to the plantations under contract for a fixed period.

However, in the absence of conventional laws and law enforcement, the recruitment and employment of such labour was rife with abuse. Missionary and other humanitarian lobbyists drew the attention of foreign governments to the abuses and demanded remedial action. From this point on it became increasingly difficult for foreign governments to refrain from direct political intervention in island affairs.

IMPERIALIST INTERVENTION

Apart from Spain's ineffectual annexation of Guam in 1565 and the Dutch claim to the western part of New Guinea, reasserted in 1828 and 1848, the first political intervention was the British annexation of New Zealand in 1840, primarily as a solution to the growing threat of settler–Maori conflict. In 1842 France annexed the Marquesas Islands on naval advice and, in response to an intermittent dispute between the French consul and the chiefs of Tahiti, established a protectorate there. France made the next move again with the annexation of New Caledonia in 1853, apparently for domestic political reasons rather than because of any compelling issue in the Pacific.

The United Kingdom, its navy having taken the lead in exploration and its citizens having led the evangelical campaign, followed a policy of non-intervention. However, as informal colonization proceeded in the 1860s and early 1870s, this approach came under increasing pressure. As a direct result of these processes, the United Kingdom deviated from this policy and agreed to annex Fiji in 1874. The Pacific Islands' labour trade was a contributory factor, but the United Kingdom strongly affirmed that it would not, indeed, could not, annex other territories simply in order to control labour recruiters and land speculators, nor even missionaries. Instead, it established the Western Pacific High Commission in 1877, in an attempt to assert extra-territorial jurisdiction over British subjects in those western Pacific territories that did not have conventional governments. The emphasis was on controlling British subjects, rather than protecting them. The governments of other nations showed less concern at the activities of their subjects, so the attempt to bring law and order without government achieved only limited success. Their continued activity made it inevitable that government would have to be established by such powers as were capable of doing so. The initiative was taken by Germany.

German subjects had increased rapidly in number and influence across the Pacific since the 1860s, and the most vigorous promoter of German interests was the Hamburg company, Godeffroy and Son, with large interests in Samoa and trading stations across the Pacific. The Godeffroys were anxious to see the establishment of a German government in Samoa and attempted sedulously to bring this about. Then, in the early 1880s, German investors conceived a plan for the development of New Guinea. Rivalry between French and English settlers (and their supporters) in the New Hebrides was strong, and the German move indicated a need to rationalize the intensifying activity. International conferences in 1885 and 1889 resolved actual and potential rivalries by allocating 'spheres of influence', which in effect over the next decade or so partitioned the Pacific among the great powers of the day.

By the end of the century, and after some adjustment to these agreements, colonial governments had been, or were about to be, established in every archipelago. France's foothold in eastern Polynesia was expanded to include the Tuamotu Islands, the Austral Islands and the entire group of Society Islands. The Cook Islands had come under British protection, and in 1900 they were annexed to New Zealand. Niue was treated similarly. Tonga became a British protectorate in 1900, retaining its own government. Samoa was partitioned after an experiment in government by an international commission: the eastern part came under US naval rule, and the western part became German territory. Fiji was already British. The island of Rotuma was added to Fiji. Tokelau and the Ellice and Gilbert Islands became a British protectorate, and later a crown colony. Nauru, the Marshall Islands, the Caroline Islands and the Mariana Islands (except Guam which became a US territory) were administered for Germany by a trading company. Part of the Solomon Islands and north-eastern New Guinea were governed by the German state after a disastrous attempt at government by a chartered company. South-eastern New Guinea was a British protectorate and would pass to Australia in 1906. The Solomon Islands was likewise a British Protectorate; the New Hebrides from 1906 was jointly governed by France and Britain as a condominium, not by partitioning. New Caledonia and the adjacent Loyalty group were French, as were the small islands between Samoa and Fiji, Wallis and Futuna.

This partition came about not so much because of the ambitions of governments, but rather as the result of the personal ambitions of some of their subjects, combined with actual and potential disorder arising from unregulated, unrestrained adventurers working beyond the reach of government and law. However, it was a time of maximum European confidence and technological and organizational superiority, and the ethos of the age favoured the establishment of formal governments where there were none. Recent history had shown that the *laissez-faire* alternative was in no one's interests.

COLONIAL GOVERNMENT

The colonial era falls conveniently into three periods: before the First World War (1914–18), between the two World Wars, and after the Second World War. The pre-1914 period was characterized by the establishment of law and order. European settlers accepted colonial administration readily, even when implemented by a government that was not their own. Pacific islanders resisted colonial government less than they opposed any kind of central government. Those who objected resisted the loss of autonomy rather than Europeans as such, for there was no prevailing sense of nationalism. In most of Polynesia little overt assertion of power was necessary; in Fiji tribal wars had to be terminated and prevented from recurring. In Micronesia there was armed resistance on Pohnpei, but resigned acceptance elsewhere. In many places missions and traders had made such inroads into island society that the establishment of new authority was probably not immediately evident. Nor, for that matter, could representatives of government appear everywhere simultaneously, and often there was nothing for them to assert. If villagers were at peace and controlled by traditional authority, colonial government was in no hurry to disturb or replace.

The greatest difficulties in establishing government were in Melanesia where society was so fragmented, tribal territories were small and indigenous languages numerous—about 80 in the Solomon Islands and more than 900 in British and German New Guinea. In New Caledonia the French had largely ignored the presence of indigenous society and simply expected to be able to move into land and use it for their own purposes. People were herded into smaller landholdings, tribes were forcibly amalgamated and indigenous interests were regarded as being of no importance. New Caledonians were outside the law, neither protected by it nor empowered by it. The situation was not dissimilar in German New Guinea during the period of government by the New Guinea Company. This was basically a land development company, which expected when it bought land to have clear title to it and that the former owners would move away. There was no expectation of providing a government over native people. Needless to say, in both situations, violence was common.

The situation contrasted profoundly with British rule in Fiji: from the beginning Fijians were held to have rights, which were not subordinate to settlers' rights, and they were to be governed by a set of laws adapted to their social and political circumstances rather than by transposed British law. The first Governor, Sir Arthur Gordon, began by upholding the authority of the chiefs over their people, establishing a colony-wide council of chiefs to advise government on native affairs, and preserving their land tenure. To protect Fijians from the disruptive effects of plantation labour, he imported workers from India to operate a developing economy, expecting the Fijians to adapt and evolve at a pace compatible with the preservation of their society and culture.

Gordon's style in Fiji became a model for government elsewhere. German and US government in Samoa bears such close resemblances as to appear to have drawn inspiration from it. The first British Governor of British New Guinea (Sir William MacGregor) was a protégé of Gordon, and while different circumstances required different solutions, his government and legacy was imbued with Gordon's spirit. The pragmatic humanity of later German rule in New Guinea under an imperial governor, Albert Hahl, probably owes nothing directly to Gordon, but like Gordon showed an awareness that there had to be constructive provision for natives in the new order, with their property secured, their societies protected from settlers and each other, and opportunities offered in white society other than as mere labourers and servants.

The First World War brought major changes, the first and most tangible being the removal of Germany from the colonial scene. In usually bloodless military seizures of power, Japan replaced Germany in the Mariana, Caroline and Marshall Islands, Australia did so in New Guinea and Nauru, and New Zealand in Western Samoa. Apart from these events, and the brief threat of action from German raiders, the war did not come close to the Pacific, although small numbers of colonial subjects served in Europe. The former German territories were retained by their conquerors after the war, but more important were the terms on which they were retained. One of the innovations at the peace settlement was the establishment of the League of Nations, an international association of which the primary aim was to prevent future wars. Germany's former colonial possessions were by agreement of the victor nations placed under international supervision of a body established by the League, the Permanent Mandates Commission. The administering powers were required to subscribe to certain principles and standards in their management of the mandated territories, to report annually to the Permanent Mandates Commission and to justify their stewardship. Possibly the most important concept included in these arrangements was that colonial administration was considered to be temporary and that the role of the administering powers was ultimately to prepare the mandated territories for eventual self-government.

Whether the mandatory powers faithfully discharged the obligation of governing in the native interest with a view to eventual independence may be debated. However, it is clear that Japan did not, and that New Zealand made a strenuous effort to do so. In 1935 Japan left the League of Nations but continued for a time to send reports to the Permanent Mandates Commission. New Zealand's efforts were undermined and then defeated by a resistance movement, the Mau, which reduced the New Zealand administration to virtually a caretaker role until after the Second World War.

Possibly as a result of the example of the Permanent Mandates Commission, or possibly because the ideas were already freely circulating in the developed world, colonial administration became more liberal in the period between the two World Wars. The emphasis shifted from pacification and peace-keeping to more creative policies intended to raise the standard of living of indigenous peoples and to cater for their development. Progress was slow and intermittent, but even in New Caledonia the administration began in the 1930s to concede certain indigenous rights and to make basic provision for advancement.

However, there were major constraints everywhere. In the background was the universally accepted conviction that governments had limited roles, primarily related to security, justice and revenue. Governments did not yet assume responsibility for personal or social development. Nevertheless, even such progress as colonial governments wanted to foster was restricted by the economic circumstances of the inter-war years. During the 1920s revenue was depressed by declining, or at best steady, commodity prices, which allowed no expansion of public sectors and restrained private initiatives. Then in 1930 came the sharply falling prices associated with the Great Depression. By 1933 copra, the staple product for most Pacific territories, cost more to produce than it was worth. Business activity contracted sharply, along with government.

However, the colonial assumptions remained firm during these decades. The idea of colonialism as trusteeship was not new, discussion of eventual self-government threatened no vested interests because it seemed unimaginably distant and, despite occasional and scattered indications of native discontent, neither governments nor settlers felt that their time was limited or that colonialism was a passing phase.

DECOLONIZATION

The Second World War (1941–45 in the Pacific) issued a challenge to colonialism, although only in distant terms. The Japanese invaders of New Guinea, Solomon Islands, Nauru and the Gilbert Islands were anything but liberators, and the war is often considered a watershed in Pacific history. For many people their islands and villages had been scenes of fighting and often heavy bombardment. Elsewhere massive numbers of allied troops had moved in, building fortifications and encampments that showed an unprecedented capacity for environmental transformation. Troops waiting for war were free spenders, unconcerned about the social and political consequences of their dealings with islanders. New political and economic possibilities were placed before many islanders. The former German and Japanese territories were now taken over by the USA.

Following the end of the war, demands grew, mainly in metropolitan capitals, for a colonial 'new deal'. The League of Nations was replaced by the United Nations, and the Permanent Mandates Commission by the Trusteeship Council. Oversight of the former German colonies was transferred to the Trusteeship Council, and new trusteeship agreements were drawn up, still with the mission of preparing dependencies for self-government. These arrangements applied only to the mandated territories but, as at the end of the First World War, the articulation of principles of colonial government expressed an implicit expectation of goals for all colonial territories. Australia and New Zealand, in particular, were eager to institute a new colonialism that would promote native welfare and development and in the process enhance the present and future security of their region, while giving larger powers less reason for intervention. To foster this goal, they instigated the formation of an international commission, the South Pacific Commission, which was inaugurated in 1947, as a research and advisory body. All six colonial powers in the Pacific, namely the United Kingdom, the Netherlands (on behalf of West Papua), the USA, Australia, New Zealand and France, were members.

The colonial powers nevertheless did not adopt co-ordinated policies for their dependencies. France instituted immediate political reforms, which were directed at giving islanders equal status within the greater French state. New Zealand almost immediately initiated a programme of rapid political, social and economic development in Western Samoa, which brought the territory to independence within 15 years. This energetic programme carried over into New Zealand's other dependencies, the Cook Islands and Niue. Dutch efforts in West Papua were overshadowed and compromised by its dispute over the territory with Indonesia, which culminated in Indonesian administration in 1963 and annexation in 1969. Australia, after announcing ambitious plans for Papua and New Guinea, faltered in the late 1940s, but in the 1950s invested heavily in development. Nevertheless, by the early 1960s independence still seemed a distant goal, although it came about in 1975. The United Kingdom alone acted as if post-war colonialism was simply a superior form of pre-war colonialism, with similar goals, but better resourced and more expertly implemented. There was no British consensus that its small, usually fragmented territories could reasonably expect to become independent nations. The USA gave greater degrees of self-government to American Samoa and Guam, which were outright possessions. On neither side was there any serious consideration of independence, and development policies were not directed towards creating potentially independent states. In the Trust Territory of the Pacific Islands (Micronesia) development and increasing degrees of autonomy were expected under the trusteeship agreement, and political devolution occurred steadily from the late 1950s, apparently at the pace demanded by Micronesians.

After 1960 assumptions began to change, political goals were adjusted and perceptions of the length of the preparatory period were repeatedly shortened. Colonial powers accepted that they did not have unlimited, or even sufficient, time to overcome the huge development gap between the present state and what they considered necessary for independence. Prior to 1970 only Western Samoa (which became an independent state in 1962), the Cook Islands (self-governing in free association with New Zealand, 1965) and Nauru (independent state, 1968) had ended their formal 'dependency' status. Most of the others followed in the 1970s: Fiji and Tonga in 1970, Tuvalu and Solomon Islands in 1978 and Kiribati in 1979. In controversial circumstances Vanuatu, the former Anglo-French condominium, acceded to independence in 1980.

However, in bringing its trusteeship agreement to an end, the USA was anxious to preserve its strategic position in the islands. Self-government was granted to most of them in the 1970s: the Northern Mariana Islands in 1978; the Republic of the Marshall Islands in 1979 and the Caroline Islands, as the Federated States of Micronesia, also in 1979; and Palau in 1981. The termination of the trusteeship agreement came later, linking the USA and its former wards together in 'compacts of free association', with the exception of the Mariana Islands, which became a US commonwealth territory.

For the most part, independence was achieved as an expression of international expectation and consensus; Pacific islanders were more inclined to be cautious or even reluctant about independence rather than ardent or insistent, but on the whole there were no serious differences of opinion between them and their colonial powers. Nevertheless, there were some notable exceptions. Papuan nationalists were not reconciled to Indonesian rule or to the manner in which it had been attained, and from the 1960s their independence movement opposed an oppressive and intransigent state, which insisted that Papua was an integral part of Indonesia. Indonesia, itself independent only since 1949, never recognized in its own case a distinction between 'colony' and 'administering power'. A similar outlook characterized the French territories. Post-war progressivism was reversed in the late 1950s and became repressive as autonomist movements gathered strength. In French Polynesia autonomists were eventually reconciled after the late 1970s by a combination of liberal reforms and welfare policies, which gave many French Polynesians higher standards of living than their independent neighbours. In New Caledonia the independence movement was more strident and the French Government intransigent, disregarding local demands and international criticism alike. By the late 1980s political violence had reached such a point that some observers spoke of civil war. France subsequently retreated from its position and made concessions that were sufficiently conciliatory, leading to increasing degrees of autonomy within the framework of the French Constitution.

POST-COLONIAL AFFAIRS

There were several constraints inhibiting colonial authorities from contemplating independence at the end of the Second World War. The islands generally had limited land areas, small populations and few developmental prospects. They were distant from markets and international suppliers, and the islands were not located on transit routes for larger economies. In a way they seemed to be a world apart. The early cases of independent countries were sustained by high world prices for copra, which provided adequate incomes for states with modest aspirations. By the early 1970s, however, copra revenues were again in decline. Papua New Guinea's post-independence prosperity was intended to be supported by agricultural diversification and rich mineral discoveries. Nauru and Kiribati had accumulated funds from phosphate royalties which, if prudently managed, could finance national budgets indefinitely. In all cases it was expected that, with independence, subsidies from the former imperial powers would cease. However, island aspirations exceeded immediate economic prospects.

The hope that economies of scale and co-operation, rather than competition, would ease the situation led to the proliferation of regional organizations. Beginning with a trade agreement in 1966, regional approaches to developmental and political issues quickly became accepted, many of them associated with the South Pacific Forum (now the Pacific Islands Forum), which was founded in 1972. The Forum established a shipping line and an airline, and it also fostered telecommunications agreements. One of its greatest successes was the creation of the Forum Fisheries Agency, which was established to provide a regional approach to the management of fish stocks and to establish a licensing regime that enabled member countries to claim royalties on the massive harvest of fish by the 'distant water fishing' nations, mainly the USA, Japan, the Republic of Korea, Taiwan and China.

Emigration was a major economic and social benefit to some states, but not one that lent itself to a regional solution. Cook Islanders and Niueans had constitutionally-guaranteed access to New Zealand, and for historical reasons Samoans and Tongans were able to migrate in large numbers, mainly to New Zealand but also to the USA and Australia. Migration was facilitated unintentionally by temporary work schemes and, besides easing population pressure at home, also became a source of revenue as emigrants generously remitted cash and goods to their families in the islands. By the 1980s remittances were the largest and most reliable source of foreign exchange for several Pacific island states. Kiribati and Tuvalu developed marine training schools and succeeded in attracting large numbers of young men to join the international maritime industry as ships' crew. This too was a regular source of national income. Numerous French Polynesians and people of Wallis and Futuna moved to New Caledonia where economic opportunities appealed, just as people everywhere moved to the larger islands and capital cities of their own states. Other states were less fortunate: Vanuatu, Solomon Islands and Papua New Guinea were not able to arrange generous emigration or work schemes.

Emigration was a palliative, rather than a satisfactory, solution to the problems of underdevelopment. 'Golden handshakes' at independence and agreements for transitional funding soon became exposed as insufficient to match the expectations of people for progress and development. During the 1970s a new era opened up in the subsidy of poor nations by rich, and this applied to the Pacific as it did elsewhere. Development planning and international funding became a global industry in the 1970s, but were still intended to be transitional, to help revitalize sluggish economies and instigate self-sustaining growth. Many of these schemes failed and came under strong criticism as being inflationary, creating a dependency mentality and stimulating the rise of an unproductive but affluent local élite in all countries. By the end of the 1980s there was widespread concern at both the ineffectiveness of aid and what some considered its deleterious effects. Both seemed linked to increasing corruption and declining capacity of governments to deliver the benefits that were expected from the large investment. In the 1990s development assistance was gradually linked to what became known as the 'governance agenda', or political and administrative reforms. The need for reform became increasingly evident. The new states acceded to independence usually with inexperienced civil servants and a political culture that had only superficially imbued the distinction between private gains and public interest. By the time the generation that had been prepared to take responsibility was being replaced or eclipsed by the next generation, the standards of probity in public life and governance seemed to be declining alarmingly. In many ways the late 1980s became a turning point for Pacific affairs.

Beginning with a military coup in Fiji in 1987, followed by the sharp escalation of violence in New Caledonia and then a rebellion on the island of Bougainville, a province of Papua New Guinea, the perception that Pacific islanders could always find negotiated, peaceful solutions to problems through the 'Pacific Way' was severely tested. The 1987 coup in Fiji was perhaps the most portentous of these events in that it created the precedent for the application of force. It was a reaction against the election of a government that for the first time gave a controlling interest to the Indian population, descendants of Sir Arthur Gordon's indentured labourers and later immigrants. To the surprise of many observers beyond the islands, Fiji's neighbours showed no inclination to condemn the overthrow of a democratically elected government. Instead, they sympathized with the argument that it was a valid defence of indigenous interests against the rise of an immigrant population. It was a dilemma that only Fiji (among independent states) confronted, yet in this way the Pacific Islands showed that their adherence to and, to that point, punctilious observance of democratic, constitutional processes, was superficial. It demonstrated that democracy was acceptable and workable to the extent that it did not challenge the national consensus as to who should exercise power. Democracy came under close scrutiny as a 'foreign flower', subordinate and inferior to tradition—or to what Pacific islanders by now believed their traditions to be. In these debates, 'tradition' became a powerful rhetorical aid to the claims to power of élites that so far had been able to manage democracy to their own advantage.

By the late 1990s these debates had receded, overwhelmed by the 'governance agenda' of aid donors. Yet major problems were still, or again, eroding the optimism that had accompanied decolonization. The Bougainville conflict still awaited settlement, ultimately resulting in about 20,000 deaths, and the non-education of a generation became a major issue. Elsewhere in Papua New Guinea, the Government struggled to keep the army under civilian control, while failing to cope with the breakdown of law and order over large areas. Violence was increasing in the neighbouring Indonesian province of Papua as the independence movement there gained local and international attention. The situation in East Timor, another Indonesian annexation (effected in 1975) and ethnically Melanesian, was likewise approaching a climax. The Cook Islands had recently been rescued from near-bankruptcy after becoming involved in a massive tax fraud at the expense of the New Zealand Government. Vanuatu had similarly engaged in dubious international financial arrangements. Nauru had been 'blacklisted' for its money-laundering activities and in the early years of the new millennium was virtually bankrupt, having squandered the very considerable assets accrued from a century of phosphate mining on the island. In 2000 there was another coup in Fiji, again a reaction against the democratic election of a government composed mainly of ethnic Indians. Also in 2000, as if in emulation of the Fiji exemplar, there was a coup in Solomon Islands, the culmination of the failure of the government to deal with inter-tribal violence and rivalries. Critics, reflecting on these events, began to speak of failed and failing states. International peace-keepers were deployed in Bougainville in an attempt to enforce a peace agreement brokered in 1998, and in 2003 an Australian-led international force intervened in Solomon Islands to restore law and order.

Amid the discourse on instability and corruption, as well as discussion of official and private incompetence, the level of foreign aid or 'development assistance' increased and also became more controversial. Yet it may be asked whether these crises have not diverted attention unduly from the very significant and creditable achievements of Pacific islanders in government since independence. In the great majority of cases, throughout the post-colonial period, democratic elections have been held as scheduled, conducted fairly and with decorum; judiciaries functioned honestly and freely; every state had a vigorous, independent and often critical press. What is most apparent is that as islanders adopted Christianity in their own way and for their own reasons, accommodated themselves to a succession of commercial developments in the 19th century, experimented with political forms and offered muted challenges to colonial authority, their recent history similarly evinces a refusal to become a reflection of the Western world, which has done so much for and to them, and a desire to continue to reshape their own affairs.

BIBLIOGRAPHY

See also Bibliography of the Pacific Islands at the end of this section

Bennett, Judith A. *Wealth of the Solomons.* Honolulu, HI, University of Hawaii Press, 1987.

Brookes, Jean I. *International Rivalry in the Pacific Islands.* Berkeley, CA, University of California Press, 1941.

Campbell, Ian. *Island Kingdom: Tonga Ancient and Modern.* Christchurch, University of Canterbury, 2nd edn, 2001.

Davidson, J. W. *Samoa Mo Samoa: the Emergence of the Independent State of Western Samoa.* Melbourne, Oxford University Press, 1967.

Dorney, Sean. *Papua New Guinea: People, Politics and History since 1975.* Sydney, ABC Books, 2nd edn, 2000.

Dunmore, John. *Visions and Realities—France in the Pacific, 1695–1995.* Auckland, Heritage Press, 1997.

Hanlon, David. *Remaking Micronesia. Discourses Over Development in a Pacific Territory, 1944–1982.* Honolulu, HI, University of Hawaii Press, 1998.

Henningham, Stephen. *France and the South Pacific: A Contemporary History.* Sydney, Allen & Unwin, 1992.

Hezel, F. X. *Strangers in Their Own Land: A Century of Colonial Rule in the Caroline and Marshall Islands.* Honolulu, HI, University of Hawaii Press, 1995.

Lal, Brij V. *Broken Waves: A History of the Fiji Islands in the Twentieth Century.* Honolulu, HI, University of Hawaii Press, 1992.

Morrell, W. P. *Britain in the Pacific Islands.* Oxford, Oxford University Press, 1960.

Samson, Jane. *Imperial Benevolence: Making British Authority in the Pacific Islands.* Honolulu, HI, University of Hawaii Press, 1998.

Thomas, Nicholas. *Islanders—The Pacific in the Age of Empire.* New Haven, CT, Yale University Press, 2010.

CONTEMPORARY POLITICS OF THE PACIFIC ISLANDS

STEWART FIRTH

The contemporary politics of the Pacific Islands are best understood against the background of the region's diversity. The 22 Pacific Island states and territories are diverse in geography, size of population, cultural heritage, political status and level of economic development. The total population of the Pacific Islands surpassed 10m. in 2011. Most of the region's people are the Melanesians of the South-West Pacific, the location of the Pacific's three largest countries, Papua New Guinea, Fiji and Solomon Islands. The remainder of the region consists of small states and territories, some with minuscule numbers of people, such as Tuvalu and Niue. Yet population size is not necessarily the most important influence on politics and political stability. Some small islands have experienced as much corruption and instability as some of the larger states. The determining factors are constitutional status, cultural heritage, history, population growth and access to jobs.

SOURCES OF STABILITY AND INSTABILITY

First, the impact of constitutional status should be considered. Some groups of islands are territories, some in free association and some independent. An external constitutional or treaty connection generally means a higher standard of living and greater political stability, although independence movements still present a challenge to the French authorities in both New Caledonia and French Polynesia. The territories of external powers are heavily subsidized by governments in Paris, Washington, DC, and Wellington, the respective capitals of France, the USA and New Zealand. France gives annual direct aid of about US $2,000m. each to French Polynesia and to New Caledonia, and it committed a sum of $50m. to its tiny territory of Wallis and Futuna for the period 2007–11. The USA subsidizes Guam and American Samoa through a wide variety of federal programmes. New Zealand provides about US $24m. a year, through the development agency NZAID, for its last remaining Pacific territory, Tokelau.

The freely associated states of Palau, the Federated States of Micronesia and the Marshall Islands, in association with the USA, and New Zealand's associated states, namely the Cook Islands and Niue, also benefit from subsidies. When the annual budget is to be determined in, for example, the Federated States of Micronesia, Micronesian leaders liaise with the US Office of Insular Affairs in the Department of the Interior in Washington, DC, which administers payments under the Compact of Free Association. The freely associated states also benefit from their citizens' freedom to enter, work and live in the metropolitan states that are their patrons. The vast majority of Cook Islanders, for example, now live in New Zealand, and thousands of Marshall Islanders live in Alabama and other states of the USA. The politics of the territories and freely associated states, therefore, are conducted within the wider framework of the politics of France, the USA and New Zealand. In addition to the eight territories (American Samoa, French Polynesia, Guam, New Caledonia, Northern Mariana Islands, Pitcairn Islands, Tokelau, and Wallis and Futuna) and the five freely associated states (Cook Islands, Niue, Palau, the Federated States of Micronesia and the Marshall Islands), there are nine independent countries, where the majority of Pacific Islanders live (Fiji, Kiribati, Nauru, Papua New Guinea, Samoa, Solomon Islands, Tonga, Tuvalu and Vanuatu).

Independence means surviving on one's own. The budgets of independent Pacific governments are not underwritten by other governments, nor can their people fly to Auckland or Los Angeles in the knowledge that New Zealand and US immigration officials will admit them automatically. Living standards are generally lower in independent Pacific countries than elsewhere in the region, and much lower in Papua New Guinea, Solomon Islands and Vanuatu, where the vast majority of people still obtain most of their food from the land and the sea. In a comparison of 169 countries in the 2010 UN Human Development Index, Solomon Islands ranked 123rd and Papua New Guinea 137th. Living standards are higher further east in the Pacific: Tonga ranked 85th and Fiji 86th. Samoa, which was unranked, is better off than either of these.

Independence also involves a greater risk of political volatility. Three of the nine independent Pacific countries, Samoa, Tuvalu and Kiribati, are models of stable democracy and have been so ever since decolonization. However, Papua New Guinea, Vanuatu, Tonga and Nauru have a consistent record of changing governments constitutionally, but have been forced to address problems such as corruption, weak central authority, lack of accountability and social unrest. Fiji and Solomon Islands have experienced coups, and Fiji can be said to have developed a 'coup culture', with five unconstitutional ruptures within 22 years, the most recent in April 2009.

Second, the effect of cultural heritage on political stability should be examined. Melanesian societies seem peculiarly unsuited to meet the demands of the modern nation-state. The cultures of Melanesia outside Fiji are characterized by small-scale societies of related kin, numerous languages (more than 800 in Papua New Guinea alone), leadership based on achievement rather than ascription, and political loyalties that remain intensely local. In Papua New Guinea, Solomon Islands and Vanuatu, a sense of national identity has been slow to form, and successful politicians are those who respond not to national needs but to the particular demands of the members of the kin group who voted for them. These three Melanesian countries are states defined by territory rather than by national identity, and the result is ineffective or absent government, tantamount almost to state failure in Solomon Islands. They are strong societies (hundreds of them) and weak states. Fiji and the countries of Polynesia and Micronesia, by contrast, were traditionally home to cultures of hierarchy, rank and inherited chiefly authority, often giving rise to larger-scale societies that in some cases came to resemble the state. Here there has been a smoother transition from traditional forms of government to the hierarchy and specialization of the modern state.

Third, the colonial history of Pacific Island countries has left a different legacy in each case. Fiji, Polynesia and Micronesia have a longer history of contact with the outside world than most of Melanesia. Tonga had its own modern Constitution by 1875. Fiji's Council of Chiefs was meeting in regular session, with agendas and minutes, by 1876. Yet, further to the west, in Melanesia, developments of this kind were not to come until the 1950s. Europeans extended control over New Guinea only slowly, taking until the 1930s to reach the Highlands—home to 1m. people—and until the 1950s to exercise authority over the region. Most Highlanders of Papua New Guinea experienced colonial administration as a transient phenomenon lasting a couple of decades before independence in 1975.

Fourth, population growth influences political stability. Rates of population growth differ according to the balance of births, deaths and migration. Fertility is in decline in almost every Pacific country, but remains above four live births per woman in a number of countries, notably Papua New Guinea and Solomon Islands, where half the population has yet to reach adult age. Papua New Guinea has one of the highest fertility rates in the Pacific Islands and is projected to double its population to 12m. by 2032. In both countries cash-paying jobs can be found for only a small minority of young people, and young men in particular are easily recruited to gangs, drawn into criminal activities and attracted to violent political causes. The young man with the gun was a familiar sight on the streets of the Solomon Islands' capital of Honiara during the unrest in that country between 1998 and 2003.

Fifth, access to the best-paying jobs for Pacific Islanders differs from one sub-region of the Pacific to another. These jobs are not in the Islands but in New Zealand, Australia, the USA, the Middle East and elsewhere. Labour migration acts as a safety valve for Pacific countries which have access to employment overseas. Tongans and Samoans have long been able to work in New Zealand and the USA; Fijians have in recent years worked in large numbers for the British army and as guards and escorts for private security firms in Iraq and Afghanistan, taking advantage of employment opportunities created by the conflict there. Many young men of Kiribati and Tuvalu, similarly, work around the world in the merchant marine, and increasing numbers of islanders are leaving Vanuatu to work in New Zealand. In all cases, Pacific Islanders boost the incomes of their families back home by sending remittances, which are major sources of national income in Tonga, Samoa, Fiji, Kiribati, Tuvalu and Vanuatu. Yet the people of the poorest Pacific countries—Papua New Guinea and Solomon Islands—have comparatively little opportunity to work abroad and earn such remittances.

INSTABILITY AND DISORDER IN INDEPENDENT STATES

Four Pacific Islands countries have experienced political instability, social disorder or economic collapse in recent years. They are Fiji, Solomon Islands, Tonga and Nauru. A fifth country, Papua New Guinea, fought a war with a secessionist province from 1989 until 1997 and has lacked authority over another province since 2000.

Fiji

Fiji has a history of coups. Fiji's first two coups occurred in 1987, when an army colonel, Sitiveni Rabuka, seized authority in the name of the rights of the indigenous Fijians. He claimed that the recently elected Government, which included ethnic Indians in senior ministerial positions, threatened the Fijian people and therefore had to be removed in order to ensure that indigenous Fijians continued to rule the country. Another coup followed the 1999 elections, which brought to office Fiji's first Prime Minister of Indian origin, Mahendra Chaudhry. This time a civilian indigenous Fijian, George Speight, initiated the coup with the assistance of a small counter-revolutionary warfare unit of the army. On 19 May 2000, exactly a year after the Government's election, Speight and his allies occupied the Parliament building in Suva and seized the parliamentarians, declaring them to be hostages. Like Rabuka, Speight claimed to protect indigenous rights and the interests of the Fijian people.

Fiji's hostage crisis of 2000 lasted 56 days. The army intervened in the mean time, abrogating the Constitution and imposing a curfew, before arresting Speight and hundreds of his followers. The army then turned to Fiji's Great Council of Chiefs to resolve the crisis. The Council appointed an interim Government. Political influence on this occasion was exercised by the Commander of the Armed Forces, Cdre Frank (Voreqe) Bainimarama. He seemingly imagined that Laisenia Qarase, a banker of Fijian origin whom he appointed as Prime Minister, was an apolitical technocrat who would not hold ambitions of his own and who could be trusted to govern Fiji as the army wished. Instead, Qarase proved to be a man of independent action. He founded a new political party in 2001, the Soqosoqo Duavata ni Lewenivanua (SDL—Fiji United Party), dedicated to unifying indigenous Fijians, and was returned as Prime Minister in his own right in democratic elections held later that year. Bainimarama, having been widely praised for having rescued the country by his intervention, came to regard himself as a national saviour. However, he was the target of an attempted assassination during an army mutiny in November 2000, and some of those implicated were Qarase's political allies. Deep mistrust between army and government thus began to develop.

Relations between Qarase and Bainimarama deteriorated thereafter, and became the perspective through which wider political developments in Fiji since 2001 are seen most clearly, for Fiji now had to exist with the continuing consequences of the turmoil of 2000. Qarase favoured his fellow indigenous Fijians at the expense of Indo-Fijians. In order to achieve a parliamentary majority, he took his SDL party into coalition with a strongly nationalist party that had supported the 2000 coup. Rumours of corruption at senior levels surrounded his Government. Year after year the report of Fiji's Auditor-General to Parliament drew attention to numerous cases of corruption and the lack of accountability in managing public funds, yet demands by the media for the Government to act went largely unheeded. Bainimarama, an indigenous Fijian and a professional military man, came to regard the Government's partiality and corruption as seriously undermining the national interest. He saw himself as a potential saviour of the nation—not only the indigenous Fijians, but the whole nation, with all its citizens irrespective of ethnic origin.

The military forces that emerged from the events of 2000 were no longer accountable to government but were rather an independent power in Fijian politics. Military intervention, which took place on 5 December 2006, led to the installation of an interim government with Bainimarama as Prime Minister and a number of unsuccessful politicians as ministers. The new administration dismissed most heads of government departments and state-owned enterprises, gaining direct military control of the police, prisons, immigration, justice, the postal service, airports and fisheries, and establishing a Military Council which made crucial decisions. In the months that followed the coup the new Government created an atmosphere of intimidation by arresting critics at will and taking them to the army camp in Suva, where they were reportedly threatened and sometimes assaulted. Determined to monitor critics of the coup, Bainimarama's Government was said to have intercepted numerous e-mails. As a radical modernizer, the military commander had no time for traditional Fijian institutions and confronted both the Methodist Church and the Great Council of Chiefs. He imposed states of emergency, curbed the media, expelled the New Zealand High Commissioner and deported two Australian newspaper publishers. Bainimarama created the Fiji Independent Commission Against Corruption; however, he was perceived by many to have used it against his opponents.

Bainimarama's impatience with opposition culminated in a crisis in April 2009, when the Fiji Court of Appeal ruled his seizure of power in 2006 to be illegal. His response was to enact an unprecedented military revolution. Acting through the ailing and compliant President Josefa Iloilo, Bainimarama dismissed the entire judiciary, abrogated the Constitution and transferred complete control of the country to himself and his military forces for the next five years, imposing a state of emergency that remained in force in mid-2011. The regime has continued to issue numerous decrees, which are unchallengeable in any court and are intended to restructure Fiji as its military leader desires. Bainimarama himself, rather than the Great Council of Chiefs, has taken control of the Native Land Trust Board and determines the leasing of Fijian land. Fijian school students are subject to a curfew. Those with telephones, whether mobile or landline, must provide a photograph and personal details before the service can be activated. Under the Regulations of Surfing Areas Decree, surfers are free to enter the water anywhere in Fiji without having to make a payment to tourist resorts or to villagers.

Bainimarama remained in power in mid-2011. His critics included two former Prime Ministers: Laisenia Qarase, who was brought before the courts to answer numerous charges, and Mahendra Chaudhry, who was arrested for breaching emergency regulations by holding a meeting of the National Farmers Union. The Government's Media Industry Development Decree (2010) established a tribunal with extensive powers to investigate media offices and seize materials, order retractions, impose fines and send journalists to prison, and was condemned by governments and journalists' organizations around the world. The decree also forced the sale by News Ltd (the Australian publishing division of News Corporation, chaired by Rupert Murdoch) of Fiji's oldest newspaper, *The Fiji Times*, to one of the country's wealthiest businessmen, further ensuring that the media would report only the news that was favourable to the regime.

Bainimarama promised that elections would take place in 2014, but stated that none of Fiji's three largest established political parties, including those previously in government, would be allowed to participate. He attributed many of Fiji's problems to Australia and New Zealand. Having expelled the high commissioners of both countries in 2009, he expelled yet another Australian high commissioner in 2010. Bainimarama declared that he wanted to break Fiji's traditional ties with Australia, New Zealand and the USA in favour of a closer relationship with the People's Republic of China. China remained far less important than Australia and New Zealand as a trading partner for Fiji, but its loans, on concessionary terms, were financing a number of major projects in Fiji.

The Fiji Government did not receive universal support in 2011, even from some who had originally supported the coup. Bainimarama sent his two most senior military officers on extended leave, and his Minister of Defence and police commissioner resigned, as did the Governor of the Reserve Bank. Numerous senior public servants were dismissed. The most dramatic political defection was by a high-ranking military officer who had been closely involved in the 2006 coup, namely Lt-Col Ratu Tevita Uluilakeba Mara, a battalion commander and son of Fiji's post-independence Prime Minister, the late Ratu Sir Kamisese Mara. He was dismissed by Bainimarama in 2011 for attempting to overthrow the Government, and fled to Tonga, where he was welcomed by relatives in the Tongan aristocracy and took Tongan citizenship. Ratu Tevita embarked on a regional campaign, in part through the internet, to expose what he claimed were the human rights abuses perpetrated by the Bainimarama regime, and when Fiji demanded his extradition from Tonga, the country's Government refused.

Until 2009 Fiji had experienced uniquely Pacific and peaceful coups, which left intact the major institutions inherited from the British administration such as free media, freedom of speech, an independent judiciary and legal profession, and human rights protection for individuals. The 'new legal order' introduced in April 2009 brought radical change. Bainimarama 'militarized' government, and a new class of military officers with a stake in the new order emerged to take charge. Their primary challenge was the economy. The sugar industry was once central to the Fiji economy, but exports declined sharply after the 2006 coup and were continuing to decline five years later, leading to repeated losses by the Fiji Sugar Corporation, which is responsible for milling and export. Required to meet the repayment of a large foreign loan in 2011, the Government of Fiji undertook discussions with the IMF about a possible new loan, but eventually issued government bonds to the value of US $250m., at the high rate of 9%. Tourist numbers grew, but holiday 'packages' were heavily discounted and the industry was not highly profitable. According to the Fiji Reserve Bank, the total output of the country's economy had not returned to 2006 levels by 2011. Inflation affected the country following the devaluation of the Fiji dollar in 2009, and was exacerbated by an increase in value-added tax in the 2010 budget, from 12.5% to 15%. In private many people complained of rising prices for food and other necessities.

Solomon Islands

Solomon Islands is a weak state. A collection of Melanesian islands around which the British and the Germans drew arbitrary borders in the late 19th century, Solomon Islands is a country of small communities and particularist identities, numerous languages (more than 80), and faint national consciousness. When the British administration came to an end in 1978, the country had a small number of university graduates, a few years' experience of the 'Westminster system' of parliamentary democracy (modelled on that of the United Kingdom) and an economy still largely based on subsistence agriculture. Opportunities for development were few. Solomon Islands turned to logging the tropical forests as a solution. Many Asian logging companies then entered the country, paying off local leaders, national politicians and, ultimately, under the prime ministership of Solomon Mamaloni in the 1990s, entire governments. Government regulation of the logging industry existed, but largely in theory only, and the bureaucratic resources needed to ensure environmentally sustainable outcomes did not exist. As companies extracted more and more concessions on taxation, government income declined and Solomon Islands risked insolvency; the country was obliged to accept a structural reform programme formulated by the IMF, the World Bank and the Asian Development Bank in 1997. The Government did little for the villagers, who therefore dealt directly with the logging companies, earning more even from unfavourable agreements than they had ever received from government.

At the same time a burgeoning population encouraged internal migration of Solomon Islanders to the main island of Guadalcanal, site of the capital, Honiara, especially from the island of Malaita. As increasing numbers of Malaitans arrived, tensions grew between them and local landowners of the Guadalcanal plain, leading to the emergence in 1998 of a movement to expel the newcomers and gain compensation. Over the next two years 20,000 Malaitans were forced to return to their home island, and hostilities broke out between militias representing each side in the conflict, the Isatabu Freedom Movement and the Malaita Eagle Force. After raids on the police armoury, pro-Malaitan forces compelled the democratically elected Prime Minister, Bartholomew Ulafa'alu, to resign in June 2000 and replaced with him with Manasseh Sogavare. Foreigners fled, and looters ransacked the houses they left behind. Honiara effectively became a wasteland ruled by young men with guns, and order broke down across much of the main island of Guadalcanal.

A peace agreement brokered by Australia in 2000 failed to resolve the crisis. Militants surrendered smaller guns, under the supervision of an International Peace Monitoring Team, but kept high-powered weapons. The police force, consisting mainly of men from the island of Malaita, was a partisan militia that intimidated the Government into yielding large 'compensation payments' while doing nothing to stop the thugs and criminals who controlled the streets. The economy contracted sharply in 2000–01. Major plantation and mining companies ceased production. Furthermore, the Solomon Islands Government, such as it was, survived on monthly transfers of cash from Taiwan, given in return for diplomatic recognition of Taiwan as the 'Republic of China'. Powerless within its own borders, the Government continued to exist for the purposes of international diplomacy and in the form of a largely corrupt élite.

Australia long claimed that Solomon Islanders should solve their own problems, but it changed policy in 2003, fearing that its Melanesian neighbour was becoming a failed state that might one day endanger Australian security. Under Australian leadership, South Pacific countries organized the Regional Assistance Mission to Solomon Islands (RAMSI), comprising hundreds of police officers, supported by 1,700 military personnel. The mission arrived in July 2003 and achieved remarkable success in arresting and charging militants, removing criminals from within the police force and destroying thousands of weapons. RAMSI then progressed to the more challenging task of constructing a workable state apparatus in Solomon Islands. Australians and personnel from elsewhere in the South Pacific proceeded to work in strategic ministries and government departments in Honiara, with the aim of restoring good governance and efficient administration.

However, 'building the state' and restoring stability to Solomon Islands was no easy task. Serious riots erupted in Honiara following the legislative election of April 2006. The rioters destroyed much of the capital's Chinatown district, forcing the evacuation from the country of hundreds of Chinese who had played a significant role in local commerce. Australia sent 400 troops to stabilize the situation, and 80 remained in mid-2010. By then RAMSI had been in Solomon Islands for seven years. Political parties in Solomon Islands are weak and ideology is absent. When voters cast their ballots, they have no control over what kind of government will emerge. Candidates buy votes with cash, and factions then purchase the support of elected parliamentarians until a government emerges. In 2010 the legislature rejected the Political Parties Reform Bill, which was designed to bring greater political stability to the country by limiting the freedom of parliamentarians to change sides. The 2010 elections therefore produced the same political system as before: 50 members of the National Parliament were elected, one-half of them newcomers to the legislature, and factional negotiations produced a Government led by a new Prime Minister, Danny Philip. Defections by parliamentarians from one side to the other, and threats of no-confidence motions, soon followed.

For reasons such as these, RAMSI, a stabilizing force from outside, enjoys popular support. The People's Survey 2010 interviewed almost 5,000 Solomon Islanders in different parts of the country, and concluded that 84% of them supported the presence of RAMSI in Solomon Islands. This approval may show either that the mission has been successful, or that Solomon Islanders fear that its departure would precipitate a return to earlier divisions and hostilities. The economic outlook for the country is not positive. With the last tropical forests being logged, timber exports account for about 70% of export income, and logging is conducted unsustainably. Experts expect the forests to be exhausted by 2016, whereupon exports, government revenue and employment will decrease drastically.

Tonga

The Kingdom of Tonga is unique in the Pacific. Never fully colonized by a foreign power, Tonga was ruled until 2010 under a constitution that gave full powers to the monarch to govern the country. Elections took place regularly, but commoners could elect only about one-third of the legislature. A pro-democracy movement emerged in the 1990s.

Signs of unrest became increasingly evident in Tonga in 2005 and 2006, years that were notable for protest marches, unprecedented demands for democratization, public complaints about the corruption of the royal family, and a major public service strike. The strike, which began in July 2005 and did not end until September, was provoked by a new stage in the Government's Economic and Public Sector Reform Programme. The strike action succeeded in gaining a commitment to large and unaffordable increases in salaries for employees in the country's overstaffed public service. The reform, which widened salary inequalities and envisaged privatization of public enterprises, might possibly have been acceptable in a different political situation. However, commoner Tongans were outraged at the high salaries being paid to Crown Prince Tupouto'a and to other executives of Shoreline, the privatized Tonga power monopoly. Furthermore, they were aware of the wealth accumulating in the coffers of Princess Salote Mafile'o Pilolevu Tuita, chair of the board of Tongasat, which controlled the country's nine geostationary satellite orbital positions.

The riots of November 2006 were unexpected, not least by the citizens of Tonga, whose history since the formation of the modern kingdom in the 19th century had been one of notable political stability under a succession of hereditary monarchs. The riots were estimated to have caused losses to businesses in Tonga of more than US $60m., with 153 businesses affected, 700 jobs lost and incalculable damage to Tonga's international reputation. In the aftermath of the unrest, Australia dispatched 50 troops and 35 police officers, while New Zealand sent a further 60 troops to secure the airport. Emergency powers were declared, and subsequently extended on a monthly basis (until they were rescinded in August 2008). Hundreds of rioters were arrested, and in February 2007 the authorities closed down a newspaper that had been sharply critical of government corruption. Reconstruction of the capital, Nuku'alofa, was accelerated in 2009 when work began on building a new business centre, funded by a US $58.8m. 'soft' loan from China and undertaken in part by Chinese workers.

An important contribution to reform in the kingdom was made by George Tupou V, who succeeded to the throne in 2006. He supported changes to Tonga's Constitution and voluntarily surrendered some of his powers to the Prime Minister. In 2010 Tonga's Legislative Assembly adopted historic legislation, welcomed by pro-democracy advocates, to increase the number of seats allocated to commoners, to 17 out of 26, and to change electoral boundaries. In November about 40,000 Tongan voters went to the polls on this newly democratic basis. The pro-democracy party, led by 'Akilisi Pohiva, won 12 of the 17 commoner seats, but was unable to form a government. A Tongan aristocrat, Siale 'Ataongo, Lord Tu'ivakano, became Prime Minister.

Nauru

In the 1980s and 1990s the Republic of Nauru, one of the smallest sovereign states in the world, was also one of the richest on a per head basis, with a royalties trust worth more than US $1,000m. Nauru retains the distinction of having the highest rates of obesity in the world, according to the World Health Organization. The source of wealth was the island's phosphate, accumulated over millennia and mined over the last century. High levels of phosphate revenue enabled successive Nauruan governments to invest in real estate and other ventures overseas but also to spend recklessly and without accountability. As Nauru's financial position deteriorated, the Government turned to 'offshore' banking, making Nauru an important location for money-laundering activities by numerous organizations, including some linked to the Russian mafia. By 2004 the country was close to bankruptcy, but the installation of a new Government led to the formulation of a reform strategy aimed at retrenchment and sustainable development.

Australia intervened in Nauru in a number of ways. Under the 2005 Nauru-Australia Memorandum of Understanding (MOU) for Development Assistance to Nauru and Cooperation in the Management of Asylum Seekers, Australia provided civil servants to assist the country in economic reform, education and policing. In return, Nauru agreed to host an offshore refugee-processing centre for illegal immigrants and asylum-seekers. The centre was part of Australia's contentious 'Pacific solution' to illegal immigration, but, in a policy shift, the new Labor Government of Australia closed the facility in 2008. Politics are keenly contested in Nauru, as the population adjusts to living within the country's much reduced means, the economy having contracted substantially in 2007. The Government reduced public spending, and the 18-member Parliament was deadlocked for several months as legislators disputed economic policy. President Marcus Stephen finally declared a state of emergency and called elections for April 2008. Stephen's victory, with a majority of 12 to six, resulted in greater stability. However, Nauru's political system has remained susceptible to deadlock. When a general election was held in April 2010, voters returned 18 members, nine from each camp, with neither side willing to elect a Speaker and therefore to permit the other to form a government. Weeks of stalemate followed until a state of emergency was declared, and another election was held in June. This time a Speaker was proposed, but parliamentarians could not agree on the choice of President. The deadlock was not resolved until November, when a Speaker was finally appointed, Marcus Stephen was re-elected President, the state of emergency was ended and the legislature finally adopted the country's budget.

Australia assists the Nauru Government in drawing up its annual budget and funds various local positions, including that of Secretary of Health and that of Director of Education; the Australian Federal Police and the Attorney-General's Department support the police force, the judiciary and the Ministry of Justice. The Chief Justice, appointed in December 2010, is an Australian. Australia's recent involvement in the affairs of Nauru has increased to such an extent that it is perceived by some to resemble Australia's administration of Nauru prior to the island's independence in 1968.

Papua New Guinea

Papua New Guinea is regarded as the least governable of all Pacific countries. When the Australian administration ended in 1975, the country had a few hundred university graduates, an economy based largely on subsistence agriculture, and whole regions where people had known of the outside world for only a matter of decades. The state has grown weaker since then, the delivery of services less reliable, and the operations of government more open to charges of corruption and malfeasance at every level. Most people lack electricity and piped water, and while schools have multiplied since independence, only a small minority of children progress beyond primary level. Roads are in poor repair, and many villagers' access to markets has diminished. The health system is in disarray. For the ordinary Papua New Guinean, development has stalled. At the same time foreign resource companies have invested heavily in mining, notably the extraction of gold, copper, nickel, cobalt and natural gas, creating enclaves of development for the few fortunate citizens whose land happens to contain such minerals or gas, while delivering riches to the country's élite. Foreign timber companies, especially from Malaysia, have been very active in Papua New Guinea, the location of one of the world's last large reserves of tropical forest.

In a formal sense, Papua New Guinea has been politically stable since independence, with regular five-yearly elections, peaceful changes of government, no military coups and a functioning parliament. Yet, with its origins in Westminster, the political system has been adapted to the Melanesian culture in which it operates. Governments employ parliamentary stratagems that would never be found in the United Kingdom, and the formal description 'stability' does little to capture the 'rough-and-tumble' reality of politics in Papua New Guinea. Political parties do not resemble their counterparts in developed countries. There are numerous parties, but they play little part in elections, which are occasions for voters to elect individuals, usually on the basis of kin or clan loyalty. Once members of the National Parliament gather in the capital, Port Moresby, the parties are used to attract, cajole, bribe and otherwise bring together enough members to form a government. Ideology and policy play no role in this process, which is a pragmatic pursuit of power.

Until 2001 the weakness of parties meant that governments were unstable. No administration in the country's first 25 years survived a full five-year term. Parties lacked discipline and ideology, and their members regularly crossed the floor or brought governments down with votes of no confidence. In 2001, in order to create stability, Papua New Guinea implemented the Organic Law on the Integrity of Political Parties and Candidates. This measure forced a reduction in the number of parties, prevented members of the National Parliament from changing parties, and created post-election 'grace periods' when votes of no confidence were forbidden. The result was that the Government elected in 2002, under Sir Michael Somare, lasted for its full term until 2007, was re-elected and was still in office in 2011, although Somare himself was obliged to resign as Prime Minister in that year because of ill health.

The most important political event of 2010 was the ruling by the Papua New Guinea Supreme Court that important sections of the Organic Law were unconstitutional. The ruling meant that the country would immediately return to the pre-2001 'free-for-all', in which governments were frequently defeated in votes of no confidence. In the immediate aftermath, the Somare Government was alleged to be distributing millions of dollars to its parliamentary supporters in order to maintain their loyalty, and within weeks the Government had brought about a four-month suspension of the legislature in order to avoid being defeated by a vote of no confidence. The National Parliament is constitutionally required to meet for 63 days a year, but commonly meets for only a few days each year.

In 2010 the Papua New Guinea Government enacted two pieces of legislation indicating the direction that the country's political system was taking. The first was an amendment to the Constitution that effectively removed the Ombudsman's power to scrutinize the disbursement of public funds by members of the National Parliament, who receive large amounts of government money each year to distribute among their constituents. In effect, the Government gave tacit approval to the continuation of patronage politics. Public protests against the amendment had no effect. The second piece of legislation prevented landowners from suing either the Government or companies over environmental damage created by resource projects. The reason for this legislation lay in the economic boom that was beginning to emerge in Papua New Guinea. In a project that was expected to double the size of the economy, the resource company ExxonMobil and its venture partners Oil Search and Santos were beginning operations on a project to exploit gas reserves in the Southern Highlands and Western Provinces. The companies intended to build a new town and international airport in Southern Highlands Province, and from 2014 to export the gas to Japan, Taiwan and China from a processing plant to be built near the capital, Port Moresby. The massive investment produced a new confidence in Papua New Guinea. While the Government welcomed the gas project, some observers feared that the scheme would intensify inequality and compound the country's development problems.

Bougainville has been an autonomous province of Papua New Guinea since a secessionist war in the 1990s. Voters cast their ballots in elections in 2010 for the Autonomous Bougainville Government and elected a new President, John Momis, a long-standing Bougainvillean politician. He promised to prepare the province for its referendum on independence in 2015 and to initiate a programme of weapons disposal, a major issue in a part of Papua New Guinea where many people still possess guns.

Elections in Tuvalu, Cook Islands and Samoa

Democratic forms of government, adapted to local cultures, have characterized most of the region since independence in the 1960s and 1970s. In Tuvalu, one of the smallest independent countries in the world, 6,000 citizens went to the polls in 2010 in an election that returned no representatives of political parties, only independent members of Parliament, 15 in all. Parties do not exist in Tuvalu. Maatia Toafa became Prime Minister in September, but was defeated in a vote of no confidence a few months later and replaced by Willie Telavi. Cook Islands, a small territory freely associated with New Zealand, went to the polls in November to elect 24 members of Parliament. The election was won by the Cook Islands Party, led by Henry Puna, who became Prime Minister. In Samoa the March 2011 election indicated a loss of support for Prime Minister Tuila'epa Sailele's Human Rights Protection Party, which lost six seats but retained a majority of 29 of the total of 49 seats in the Legislative Assembly.

EXTERNAL INFLUENCES

Australia is the most important external influence on the region. Australia gives more in official development assistance than any other country, it meets most of the costs of regional institutions, it has strong historical links with the region's largest state, Papua New Guinea, its companies are leading investors in Pacific mining, banking, tourism and other commercial activities, and the Australian dollar is the currency of some smaller Pacific countries.

The 2002 bomb attacks on the Indonesian island of Bali, which killed 88 Australians, focused attention on the security risks of terrorism, and, by extension, the potential dangers created by neighbouring 'failed states' that might one day harbour terrorists. In the following year Australia embarked upon a more intensive Pacific engagement in order to stabilize and reform the region, most dramatically as leader of RAMSI, but also in Papua New Guinea and Nauru, where civil servants from Canberra were working to improve the performance of ineffective governments. Australia's aid to the Pacific has been considerably increased in recent years, totalling US $1,225m. in the financial year 2011/12, with more than one-half going to Papua New Guinea and Solomon Islands. Australia's engagement is comprehensive, encompassing not only bilateral initiatives in Pacific countries, but also the multilateral activities of the Pacific Islands Forum, which is the leading regional organization. Regional policy is being directed towards the Forum's creation of a free trade area that would include Australia and New Zealand and might, in time, adopt the Australian dollar as a currency. Australia is increasing overseas aid as a proportion of gross national income and the Pacific region is a major beneficiary. Australia has signed bilateral development partnership agreements with Pacific countries on condition that those nations make progress towards achieving the UN's Millennium Development Goals.

New Zealand, with a large Maori and Pacific Islander population, is more of a Pacific nation than Australia, culturally and demographically. The people of three Pacific territories—Cook Islands, Niue and Tokelau—are New Zealand citizens, and the Samoan population of New Zealand is two-thirds the size of the population of Samoa itself. One-half of New Zealand's official development assistance goes to the Pacific Islands, and New Zealand's soldiers and police contribute to regional security. Island nations have welcomed New Zealand's Recognised Seasonal Employer scheme, which was introduced in 2007 and brings thousands of workers from the Pacific Islands each year to work in horticulture and viticulture on short-term contracts. The scheme is far more successful than its Australian equivalent, and a New Zealand parliamentary committee has recommended that it be expanded.

The European Union (EU) also has some influence in Pacific regional affairs. All 14 Forum states are members of the Africa, Caribbean and Pacific (ACP) group of countries, and their trade and aid relations with the EU are therefore governed by the Cotonou Agreement of 2000. Under this convention, aid is provided with good governance conditions attached, and trade will soon be compatible with the requirements of the World Trade Organization. Free trade will replace the special arrangements and subsidized commodity prices that have helped to sustain agricultural exports from the Pacific. The EU concluded Economic Partnership Agreements with Fiji and Papua New Guinea in 2007. The impact of the progression towards free trade is severe in Fiji, where the sugar industry has survived on special EU price arrangements since the 1970s and where the EU sugar price is rapidly decreasing.

Taiwan and China have traditionally competed for diplomatic recognition in the Pacific by means of aid and investment. Taiwan is recognized by six Pacific countries—Solomon Islands, Marshall Islands, Palau, Kiribati, Nauru and Tuvalu. Following the improvement in its relations with Taiwan since 2008, China's advance into the Pacific, as well as into Africa and the Caribbean, is motivated less by competition with Taiwan than by the search for reliable supplies of the primary resources that will be needed to power the Chinese economy in the years ahead. China funds the salary of the Melanesian Spearhead Group's Director-General, Rima Ravusiro, and built its headquarters in Port Vila, Vanuatu. Unlike the EU or Australia, China does not link aid to good governance. Among numerous development projects, Chinese companies are building a dam, a bridge and low-cost housing in Fiji, reconstructing the central business district of Nuku'alofa (Tonga—see above), building a six-storey block for government offices in Samoa and upgrading the airport at Niue. The China Metallurgical Construction Company is a major investor in Papua New Guinea's Ramu cobalt-nickel mine.

Japan remains a vital donor of aid to the region, and undertook to provide the Pacific Islands with the sum of US $517m. in development assistance for the period 2009–12.

France has restored its reputation in the Pacific Islands. Nuclear testing in French Polynesia was an issue that once divided France from all the independent Pacific nations, but, following the cessation of the tests in 1996, France has been accepted as a valuable regional partner. The French Government long denied that its nuclear programme endangered health. However, it has now introduced a scheme for workers exposed to radiation during the 30 years of its nuclear testing programme in French Polynesia, and it has identified 18 ailments for which victims may be compensated. At the same time, France is transferring US $200m. per year to French Polynesia under an accord intended to reimburse the territory for the economic impact of the end of testing in 1996.

In the 1980s the independence movement in France's other main Pacific territory, New Caledonia, prompted the French authorities to send 9,000 troops to maintain order. The issue of independence remains on the agenda in the 21st century, but in a calmer political atmosphere. Under the 1998 Nouméa Accord, France is gradually transferring considerable powers to New Caledonia's own popularly elected Government, and a referendum on independence is possible between 2013 and 2018. Under a 2010 agreement, the New Caledonian Government, which is elected on a power-sharing basis, will assume control of primary education, air traffic and maritime transport and security. The majority of indigenous Kanak voters continue to favour independence, but they are a minority community in the territory as a whole. A large new nickel mine, located in the north of the main island of Grande Terre, has attracted thousands of construction workers from China, the Republic of Korea (South Korea), the Philippines and Thailand. The other large French Pacific territory is French Polynesia, where political instability is common. Nine territorial governments have held office since 2004, and France has proposed reform through an organic law that would restrict votes of no confidence (*motions de défiance*) in the territorial assembly in order to give governments greater security of tenure.

The USA customarily looks to Australia and New Zealand to maintain stability in the Pacific Islands south of the equator. The USA's own Pacific focus is on Guam, American Samoa, the Northern Mariana Islands, Palau, the Federated States of Micronesia and the Marshall Islands. All except American Samoa lie north of the equator, and all are firmly within the strategic and financial orbit of the USA. However, after years of minimal interest in the Pacific Islands, the USA is responding directly to China's increased Pacific presence. The Obama Administration chose Suva, Fiji, as the location for the new regional office of the US Agency for International Development (USAID), which operates from a newly built US embassy. The US Secretary of State, Hillary Clinton, visited a number of Pacific countries in 2010, and in 2011 senior US officials, led by the Assistant Secretary for East Asian and Pacific Affairs, Kurt Campbell, held talks with Pacific leaders in Kiribati, Samoa, Tonga, Solomon Islands, Papua New Guinea, Palau, the Federated States of Micronesia and the Marshall Islands, with a view to enhancing US involvement and assistance.

A major military build-up is taking place in Guam, as 8,000 US marines and their dependants are transferred there from the Japanese island of Okinawa: the transfer was originally expected to be completed by 2016. Under the 2003 Compacts of Free Association, the USA was to provide the Marshall Islands and the Federated States of Micronesia with US $3,600m. in assistance between 2004 and 2023. Palau's new Compact of Free Association, which gives the country access to more than 40 federal programmes as well as budgetary assistance until 2024, was signed in September 2010. The extent to which the USA subsidizes these territories and states is demonstrated by the fact that a mere 8% of educational expenditure in the Marshall Islands is derived from local revenue; the remainder comes from external sources, mainly the USA. In the case of the Marshall Islands, the benefit to the USA is strategic. The Marshall Islands host the missile range of the US Space and Missile Defense Command, paying landowners $11m. a year as part of an agreement that could permit the US Army to remain there until 2086. Disputes over compensation between the Kwajalein landowners and the US authorities are a constant feature of Marshall Islands politics.

POLITICAL PROSPECTS

The political prospects for Pacific Islands states and territories cannot be summarized in a single phrase such as 'arc of instability'. In an era of globalization, links to the developed world matter more than ever for Island communities because they mean the difference between standards of living akin to those of New Zealand, as can be found in the Cook Islands or French Polynesia, and standards of living more similar to those of eastern Indonesia, as can be found in parts of Papua New Guinea and Solomon Islands. The aid donors believe the solution for the independent Pacific, which has no constitutional links to the developed world, lies in 'good governance'. Yet the progression to good governance by countries such as Papua New Guinea, Solomon Islands, Vanuatu, Fiji, Tonga and Nauru is difficult, and this must be negotiated in political systems that remain much influenced by Pacific cultures. The good governance programme, in any case, entails free market reforms that widen inequalities, undermining stability in the process. All that can be said with certainty is that the political prospects of some Pacific states and territories diverge widely from those of others. Just as Pacific histories differ, so do Pacific futures.

BIBLIOGRAPHY

Alley, Roderic. *The Domestic Politics of International Relations: Cases from Australia, New Zealand and Oceania.* Aldershot and Burlington, VT, Ashgate, 2000.

Bennett, Judith. *Pacific Forest: A History of Resource Control and Contest in the Solomon Islands, c. 1800 to 1997.* Leiden, Brill, and Cambridge, Whitehorse Press, 2000.

Crocombe, Ron. *Asia in the Pacific Islands: Replacing the West.* Suva, IPS Publications, 2007.

The South Pacific. Suva, IPS Publications, 2008.

Dinnen, Sinclair. *Law and Order in a Weak State: Crime and Politics in Papua New Guinea.* Honolulu, HI, University of Hawaii Press, 2000.

Dinnen, Sinclair, and Firth, Stewart (Eds). *Politics and State-Building in Solomon Islands.* Canberra, Asia Pacific Press, 2008.

Dorney, Sean. *Papua New Guinea: People, Politics and History Since 1975.* Sydney, ABC Books, Revised edn, 2000.

Fraenkel, Jon. *The Manipulation of Custom: From Uprising to Intervention in the Solomon Islands*. Wellington, Victoria University Press, 2004.

Fraenkel, Jon, Firth, Stewart, and Lal, Brij V. (Eds). *The 2006 Military Takeover in Fiji: A Coup to End All Coups?* Canberra, ANU E Press, 2009.

Fry, Greg, and Kabutaulaka, Tarcisius (Eds). *Intervention and State-Building in the Pacific: The Legitimacy of 'Co-operative Intervention'*. Manchester, Manchester University Press, 2008.

Lal, Brij V. *Islands of Turmoil: Elections and Politics in Fiji*. Canberra, Asia Pacific Press, 2006.

Larmour, Peter. *Foreign Flowers: Institutional Transfer and Good Governance in the Pacific Islands*. Honolulu, HI, University of Hawaii Press, 2005.

Lawson, Stephanie. *Tradition Versus Democracy in the South Pacific: Fiji, Tonga and Western Samoa*. Cambridge, Cambridge University Press, 1996.

Lee, Helen, and Francis, Steve Tupai (Eds). *Migration and Transnationalism: Pacific Perspectives*. Canberra, ANU E Press, 2009.

Maclellan, Nic. *Pomp and privatisation: political and economic reform in the Kingdom of Tonga*. Australian Centre for Peace and Conflict Studies, Occasional Papers Series No. 13, March 2009.

May, R. J. (Ed.). *Policy Making and Implementation: Studies from Papua New Guinea*. SSGM Monograph, No. 5, Canberra, ANU E Press, 2009.

Moore, Clive. *Happy Isles in Crisis: The Historical Causes for a Failing State in Solomon Islands, 1998–2004*. Canberra, Asia Pacific Press, 2004.

Regan, Anthony. *Light Intervention: Lessons from Bougainville*. United States Institute of Peace Press, Washington, DC, 2010.

White, Geoffrey M., and Lindstrom, Lamont. *Chiefs Today: Traditional Pacific Leadership and the Postcolonial State*. Palo Alto, CA, Stanford University Press, 1997.

SECURITY ISSUES OF THE PACIFIC ISLANDS

M. ANNE BROWN, VOLKER BOEGE and ANNA NOLAN

INTRODUCTION

Security outlooks can change rapidly and unexpectedly. While outbreaks of serious violence generally have long antecedents, sudden events, such as the terrorist attacks in the USA on 11 September 2001, can also have profound effects on a security situation or on the framework whereby security is assessed. The 2001 attacks in the USA and the subsequent attacks in Indonesia (particularly the bombings on the island of Bali in 2002) had a significant impact on the criteria according to which security in the Pacific Islands region was evaluated within and beyond the region, by focusing attention on a series of more long-standing concerns and by prompting a reassessment of the nature of appropriate response to those concerns. However, despite real problems and serious issues of vulnerability in the region, in recent years there has been no dramatic change in the security situation of the Pacific Islands.

The principal shift in security assessments of the Pacific Islands region was the application of the concept of 'state failure'. The category of failed or failing states, previously applied primarily to parts of Africa, refers to states that are unable to fulfil their fundamental functions, with the important factor being inability to maintain a reasonable level of security or order. Weak and failing states are regarded as potential sources of transnational crime and terrorism, weapons proliferation and other 'non-traditional' security threats, and are thus in a perpetual cycle of violent conflict. Because these influences cannot be confined within borders, failed states are perceived as a threat to their neighbours and as a critical factor in transnational conflict formations. As the perspective of state failure was applied to the Pacific Islands following the 2001 and 2002 bombings, the profile of the region's security issues was raised. There was concern from the greater regional neighbourhood, notably Australia, that the south-west Pacific in particular formed part of an 'arc of instability': a region of failing governance, security vulnerability and economic disintegration that could pose risks not only to itself but to others.

In common with other parts of the developing world, the Pacific Islands struggle with significant patterns of risk. These include: high population growth and the associated youth 'bulge'; low growth in the cash economy and significant unemployment; increasing inequality and poverty; the tension between cash and subsistence economies; patterns of unequal development; unplanned urbanization and squatter settlements; stress on traditional land tenure arrangements and the erosion of traditional mechanisms of social order without the emergence of clear alternatives; serious law and order problems in some parts of the region; political instability; corruption; HIV/AIDS; predatory commercial interests from beyond the region; and resource stripping and environmental degradation. Climate change and rising sea levels are also of pressing concern in a region largely made up of small islands. However, the region is also characterized by relatively high levels of social resilience, based largely on the continuing strength of community life in many Pacific Island societies. While many governments in the region are weak, communities are often peaceable and orderly, with basic functions of security, order and sustenance fulfilled reasonably well at the local level. In broad terms, comparisons with crisis zones in Africa encourage misleading perceptions of Pacific security. The weakness of state institutions and functions in part reflects the reality that while peoples of the region have long histories and traditions, states as such are relatively new. Governments and people are contending with the confusion and pressure of rapid change and with the need to forge states based in their own societies. Many of the region's vulnerabilities and crises reflect these processes. States can be seen as failing, but they can also be regarded as emerging, or still in the early decades of working with a very challenging reality—that of finding ways for state institutions to form a constructive network with the social and economic dynamics of their particular national societies.

Both strengths and weaknesses contribute to the region's security outlook. If the problems are viewed in isolation from the region's strengths, there is a significant risk of misjudgement. The image of states failing is one of pervasive violence and collapse, but this is not an accurate representation of the Pacific Islands. Violent conflict is not the norm, and in much of the region communities continue to provide the foundation of life. The notion of 'failing states' also implies greater vulnerability to transnational conflict than is present and suggests a failure of established state institutions rather than the long process of developing sustainable state institutions based in their own societies and citizenry. Whether regional states are seen as 'failing' or as 'emerging' provides rather different perspectives for understanding the undoubted problems with which they are struggling. The security challenges confronting the region are intra-state and human security issues. While the region's vulnerabilities could be and are exploited by a variety of external forces, such as unscrupulous commercial interests, there is no evidence that the Pacific Islands are as yet particularly vulnerable to terrorist cells. Despite movement of small weapons within Papua New Guinea and across the border between the island of Bougainville and Solomon Islands, the Pacific Islands are not part of a transnational conflict formation. Nor does there appear to be any local constituency for terrorism.

The physical and political geography of the Pacific Islands region are described in greater detail elsewhere in this volume, and are an important part of appreciating the security issues of the region. In brief, the region includes the island groupings held approximately between the tropics of Cancer and Capricorn in the north and south, and reaching from the great mountainous land mass of Papua New Guinea in the west to Rapa Nui (Easter Island, part of Chile) in the east—a sweep of over 30m. sq km, of which 98% is ocean. Comprising 22 states and self-governing territories, the region contains thousands of islands, with some individual political entities consisting of many inhabited islands. Other islands or part-islands such as Rapa Nui, Hawaii (USA), the Torres Strait Islands (Australia) or Papua (or West Papua, a province of Indonesia formerly known as Irian Jaya) are not included in this essay. Distances in the Pacific create challenges and significant costs for transport and communication, despite the tradition of ocean voyaging that characterizes many Pacific cultures. The region is commonly divided into three sub-regions: Melanesia, in the south-west, which is home to approximately 80% of the region's population and is well-endowed with mineral, forest and sea resources; Polynesia to the east; and the more northern islands of Micronesia. While Papua New Guinea has a population of more than 6m., no other state or territory has more than 1m. people. These small national populations are nevertheless characterized by an extraordinary cultural and linguistic diversity, particularly in Melanesia; almost one-third of the world's languages are spoken in the Pacific Islands.

EXTERNAL AND INTER-STATE SECURITY ISSUES

From the international strategic point of view, the security environment of the Pacific Island region has generally been seen as benign. During the protracted period of mutual hostility between the USA and the USSR known as the Cold War, the region was not involved in any significant superpower rivalry, despite some overtures by the Soviet Government. Australia, the major power in the greater region, pursued a policy of strategic denial, endeavouring to exclude unwelcome external powers from the region. In response to nuclear testing in the region by the USA and France, the independent and self-governing countries of the South Pacific (Australia, the Cook Islands, Fiji, Kiribati, Nauru, New Zealand, Niue, Papua New Guinea, Solomon Islands, Tonga, Tuvalu, Vanuatu and Western Samoa) adopted an anti-nuclear stance, signing the South

Pacific Nuclear-Free Zone Treaty (the Rarotonga Treaty) in 1985, a position that helped to define a growing sense of regional identity.

The USA operates a military base on the island of Guam, in the far north-west of the region (the US Pacific Command is headquartered further east, in Hawaii). As the USA focuses greater attention on the strategic potential of the People's Republic of China and possible security developments in the northern Pacific, Guam's significance as a military base is increasing. A massive US military build-up on Guam has commenced, with the size of the population connected to the military base projected to increase from 14,000 in 2009 to more than 40,000 by 2016. This includes transferring personnel and resources from Okinawa in Japan, and relocating about 8,000 US marines and their dependants to Guam. Japan and the USA are sharing the cost of these moves, and in 2010 the US Navy awarded a US-funded contract, worth US $4,000m., to seven contractors for projects related to the transfer to Guam. Despite delays and resistance at various levels the Guam expansion proceeds slowly, but steadily. Local government officials, community representatives and environmental groups have expressed increasing concern at the impact of the build-up on the island's community and infrastructure. The US Air Force, Navy and Army plan to use the expanded base as a major staging ground for security and defence operations throughout the Asia-Pacific region.

Several other self-governing territories in the region also come within the constitutional ambit of the USA: the territories of the Northern Mariana Islands, American Samoa, the Federated States of Micronesia and the Marshall Islands, parts of which remain contaminated by the US nuclear testing that was conducted between 1946 and 1962. The Marshall Islands are still used for non-nuclear weapons testing. French Polynesia and also Wallis and Futuna are overseas territories of France; French Polynesia was the site of French nuclear testing between 1966 and 1996. New Caledonia has 'shared sovereignty' with France; in 2004 only 44% of the population was indigenous. The scene of violent self-determination protests in the 1980s, New Caledonia has subsequently been relatively calm, although social, economic and political divisions within the territory remain. A referendum on independence to be held at some point from 2014 could prompt renewed unrest. A mission of the Melanesian Spearhead Group to New Caledonia in June 2010, led by the Prime Minister of Vanuatu, Edward Natapei, noted concerns relating to the slow rate of progress with the implementation of the 1998 Nouméa Accord, which guaranteed such a referendum.

Papua New Guinea shares a border with Indonesia, a straight line drawn on a map by 19th-century colonial powers, separating Indonesia's Melanesian province of Papua to the west from Papua New Guinea to the east. Ongoing violence and repression over issues of self-determination and the effects of massive mining ventures in western Papua have prompted many to cross the border into Papua New Guinea, at times straining that country's relations with Indonesia. This has not escalated into a serious dispute, although in June 2009 further alleged killings of Papua New Guinean villagers by Indonesian military personnel during incursions over the border prompted local members of Parliament and former military officials within the country to criticize the Papua New Guinea Defence Force and to question its capacity to provide border security for citizens.

China and Taiwan are both increasingly active in the region, where they have been engaged in an intense and often destabilizing 'bidding war' for diplomatic recognition and influence, using aid, investment or immediate cash payments to critical decision-makers. However, improved relations between China and Taiwan (owing to the change of government in Taiwan that followed the 2008 elections) have ameliorated the situation somewhat. The use of such cash inducements in exchange for diplomatic recognition has contributed to the weakening of political accountability and credibility: for example, the suspicion that political campaigns are being funded by Taiwan in Kiribati and Solomon Islands. In April 2006 rioting and the destruction of much of the Chinese quarter of Honiara, capital of Solomon Islands, followed the parliamentary elections and the appointment as Prime Minister of Snyder Rini. He was popularly believed to have secured office through the use of funds from Taiwan, and the events emphasized the additional volatility brought to the region by the rivalry between China and Taiwan. In 1997 China established a satellite-tracking facility on the Micronesian island atoll of Kiribati, amid some speculation that the purpose was to monitor US bases. Although Kiribati subsequently transferred diplomatic recognition to Taiwan, China was able to retain the facility.

Until 2003 Australian foreign policy was a combination of significant bilateral aid and a careful effort at non-interference. In mid-2003, however, in response to both heightened international security concerns and the ongoing crisis in Solomon Islands, important elements of Australian foreign policy with regard to the Pacific Islands underwent a marked policy shift towards more proactive engagement. Critics saw this shift as overbearing, and relations between Australia and neighbouring Pacific states, including Solomon Islands, Papua New Guinea and Fiji, became strained under the conservative Government of John Howard. Labor's accession to power in Australia in November 2007 provided an opportunity to repair Pacific relationships. The Labor Government of Kevin Rudd, which took office in late 2007, actively sought closer relations with Papua New Guinea and Solomon Islands, placing greater emphasis on partnerships and dialogue. However, Australia attracted criticism within the region with regard to its assertive rejection of the failure by the military Government of Fiji to return the country to democracy (see below). The next Australian Prime Minister, Julia Gillard, who replaced Rudd in June 2010, seemed likely to continue her predecessor's policies towards the Pacific Islands.

Within the region there are no significant disputes between states or territories, and only three states, namely Fiji, Papua New Guinea and Tonga, have military forces, Tonga's forces being largely ceremonial in nature. However, in Fiji the country's armed forces were involved in coups in 1987 and 2006 and a mutiny in November 2000. In December 2006 the Commander of the Armed Forces, Cdre Frank (Voreqe) Bainimarama, seized power and became head of government. The size of Fiji's armed forces increased substantially in 2009. In Vanuatu a small paramilitary force, the Vanuatu Mobile Force (VMF), and the Vanuatu Police Force have been involved in illegal activities to exert political pressure. In 2010 a coronial inquiry into the death of a prisoner in March 2009 from injuries sustained during interrogation by VMF officers, and subsequent death threats made against the coroner, exposed major problems with discipline, accountability and government oversight of this force. Uniformed forces across the region tend to suffer from low morale, insufficient training and relatively low professional standards.

INTERNAL SECURITY ISSUES

Self-Determination, Secessionist and Ethnic Tensions

Decolonization, where relevant, has been relatively recent in the region, occurring between 1962 and 1980. Thus, decolonization and self-determination processes are continuing to evolve, with the constitutional status of some territories still in question. In the 1980s violent self-determination struggles in New Caledonia, a territory of France, dominated concerns about regional security. An incident on Ouvéa (Uvea) in 1988, in which 25 people were killed, marked a crisis point in the conflict. Greater inclusion of indigenous people in formal political life and in the economic benefits, as well as the costs, of mining and economic growth, and a deferral of the question of full independence, enabled a political and gradual approach to self-determination to take the place of violent confrontation. However, economic, social and political divisions remain. A vote on New Caledonia's ultimate status will not take place until 2014 at the earliest. In 2009 strikes and street protests organized by the pro-independence Union Syndicale des Travailleurs Kanak et des Exploités (USTKE) at times became violent; the union complained about massive police repression and the danger of the criminalization of the union movement in New Caledonia. Bougainville (see below) was also badly affected by violent inter-communal warfare from 1989 until 1998, articulated in part through demands for greater self-determination. The impact of mining on a massive scale on the environment, land tenure, food security and social relations were critical factors in both conflicts. Bougainville is also making peace. While the form that such self-determination takes is not yet settled in either territory, and could still be the context for violent clashes, both New Caledonia and Bougainville are currently approaching their respective dilemmas gradually and non-violently. Debates about self-determination are also part of the political life of French Polynesia and a number of the US territories, but these are political rather than armed struggles.

Histories of uneven development and disputes over perceived inequity in the distribution of the costs and benefits of natural resource extraction are potent sources of secessionist sentiment, in independent states and self-governing territories alike. Social tension over resource distribution and over access to power has tended to coalesce along lines of regional or ethnic division. These factors contributed significantly to secessionist unrest in Solomon Islands (Western Province) and in parts of Papua New Guinea during the 1990s and early years of the 21st century. Entrenched patterns of uneven development also played a role in relations between the Indo-Fijian and indigenous Fijian communities—the context for a series of coups between 1987 and 2006. The United Kingdom, the former colonial power in Fiji, brought Indians to Fiji as indentured labourers to work sugar plantations in the early part of the 20th century. Colonial policy reinforced economic and political divisions by instituting rigid economic, educational and political 'compartmentalization' between the two groups. At independence in 1970, therefore, the political structure was based on ethnic representation, while economic affairs were divided between subsistence indigenous exchange and the commercial Indo-Fijian economy. As the population of settler Indo-Fijians increased to outnumber indigenous Fijians, competition for resources and efforts to assert indigenous rights further polarized the communities. In this environment, electoral victory by the party associated with Indo-Fijians precipitated three violent coups within a period of 13 years, two in 1987 and one in 2000. While the 2000 coup was not directly successful, the Government was effectively replaced. Social divisions were a complex mixture of economic and political competitions, only partially centred around ethnic identifications. The complexity was highlighted in December 2006, when a fourth, bloodless coup by elements of the military overthrew the elected Government. However, this time the coup was not undertaken in the name of indigenous rights; it arose from the rejection by the military leadership of the amnesty offered to those involved in the 2000 coup and reflected competing views of government. The abolition of the Constitution in April 2009 and the determination of the military-based regime to postpone elections until 2014 were an indication of the increasing deterioration of the internal human security situation in Fiji. The imposition of a new media decree in April 2010, which drastically restricted media freedom, was widely criticized in other countries of the Pacific region and by the International Federation of Journalists.

Inter-communal conflict in Fiji and in Solomon Islands is often represented as ethnic conflict. There are ethnic, cultural and regional frictions across the Pacific Islands. However, while there was an important ethnic element to the violence in the Solomons and the nature of coups in Fiji, conflict was not fundamentally driven by ethnic antagonism. Rather, both conflicts have origins in histories of uneven economic development and in the rapid pace of social, political and economic change, which has severely disrupted traditional structures, values and societies, while new structures are still taking shape.

Land

Self-determination in the region is closely related to indigenous control over land use. Land is crucial to food and social security for most Pacific Islanders; it provides a basis for community life, subsistence and economic independence. As such, it is integral to the social cohesion and order of life in the region. Most Pacific Islanders are engaged in subsistence food production on communally held, customary land. This has enabled the region to avoid the levels of poverty and hunger seen in Africa or Asia. However, population growth is increasing demographic pressure on land, while internal migration and urbanization are changing land usage patterns. As a result, some urban migrants are losing access to their communal land back in the rural areas, while land around urban centres becomes alienated from the original landholders. Such factors contributed to civil conflict in Solomon Islands, for example. Environmental degradation, whether through large-scale resource extraction, insensitive development, urban sprawl or demographic pressure, is threatening the capacity of subsistence food production, thus raising serious concerns for future food security. As yet, in contrast to much of the developing world, there is not a significant problem of landless poor in the region, although the phenomenon is emerging.

The developing cash economy has also led to increasing pressures for the privatization and commodification of land. Pressures with regard to land and also tensions between customary and commercial approaches to land are some of the most immediate causes of conflict, particularly in Melanesia. Some international agencies and commentators argue the need for certainty of tenure for foreign investors as a precondition for investment and view customary tenure as an obstacle to growth in the formal economy. Land registration has been put forward as a mechanism offering greater certainty of tenure. In 2001, however, violent protests in Port Moresby, the capital of Papua New Guinea, by opponents of references to land registration in a World Bank draft agreement, led to the deaths of three demonstrators in clashes with the police. The protesters feared that land registration was a progression towards privatization of land and loss of control, cultural value and economic independence. Resource exploitation brings together issues of land tenure, environmental degradation and resource security—all potent sources of division within communities and between communities and government or developers. Large-scale natural resource extraction practices can destroy ecosystems, devastate local cultures and livelihoods, and contribute to the corruption and vulnerability of governments desperate for foreign investment. Land has been a significant feature in many of the region's more violent conflicts, including that on Bougainville and in Solomon Islands, but there are many small examples. For instance, areas of Vanuatu have witnessed sharp rises in real estate growth since 2006, as foreign tourists and commercial development interests seek to capitalize on sea vistas. The land they seemingly buy is in fact leased under circumstances that are often misleading to local landholders (and possibly to lessees) who, owing to legal ambiguities, are unlikely to be able to regain their holdings. This type of trend has the potential to generate major violence. The persistence of such serious socio-economic fractures can also weaken the legitimacy of governance systems.

Economic Pressures

Economic fragility has also exacerbated concern about regional security. All the island economies are reliant on foreign aid and import more than they export. The region's formal economies are small, open and dependent on the export of a small range of primary commodities: minerals, timber, copra, palm oil, coffee and sugar. Island economies are thus vulnerable to commodity price fluctuations, although the subsistence sector provides some safeguard against fluctuations. The decline in commodity prices in the 1980s and the Asian financial crisis of the late 1990s intensified economic uncertainty in the Pacific, and contributed to political volatility in Papua New Guinea. The loss of preferential trade agreements incompatible with the framework of the World Trade Organization (WTO) will lead to loss of income and employment in the textile and sugar industries of Fiji. Intra-regional trade is slight. Poor economic management and low capacity to manage exportable resources, which can also result in resource predation, are further sources of vulnerability for Pacific Island states. Nauru, which squandered its income from phosphate-mining and is now virtually bankrupt, is a notable example.

Poor to modest growth rates in the formal economies across the region have not kept pace with population growth. Each year in Vanuatu, for example, approximately 5,000 young people enter the local labour market in search of about 500 wage-paying jobs created annually. Neither the formal nor the subsistence sector is able to accommodate the numbers of people looking for work. Population growth has contributed to increased urbanization, as young people move to urban centres or large resource developments looking for work. Urban drift has been associated with squatter settlements, poverty, prostitution, sexually transmitted diseases (including HIV/AIDS) and increasing crime rates in urban centres, with Port Moresby being the most obvious example. As a means of preventing urban drift, Polynesia and Micronesia (and to some extent Fiji) have some access to emigration to metropolitan states, owing to constitutional links with states prepared to offer such routes to mobility (particularly New Zealand and the USA). More Samoans, Tongans and Niueans live elsewhere than in their native land. Labour mobility has a dual function: remittances become a significant contributor to economic well-being, and a path of employment is provided for growing populations. This reduces the pool of unemployed, and thus absorbs an important source of potential instability. Violence in Tonga in 2006, however, was attributed partly to returnees from metropolitan states. Most Melanesian states have not had ready access to either labour mobility schemes or emigration. However, in 2009 Australia followed New Zealand in introducing a labour mobility scheme for some Pacific Island states, including Tonga, Kiribati, Papua New Guinea and Vanuatu.

Law and Order

Life in most of the Pacific Islands region is relatively orderly and peaceful. There are notable exceptions, where levels of social violence are high, and illicit guns and small arms are in circulation, particularly in Port Moresby and the Southern Highlands in Papua New Guinea. In Solomon Islands in 1998–2003 the crisis in Honiara was also compounded by opportunistic criminality and theft of small arms from state-owned armouries. In Papua New Guinea, illicit factories are manufacturing guns, contributing to the country becoming a regional 'hot spot' for small arms and gun-related violence. In a disturbing example, the Chief Ombudsman responsible for investigating political corruption in Papua New Guinea survived a shooting by gunmen outside his home in Port Moresby in December 2009. The erosion of social order is a complex matter. However, the weakening of traditional systems of authority and social control is a major contributory factor to unrest and social violence. When associated with high levels of social tension, often the result of rapid economic and social change and the confusion and disruption that accompany such change, in addition to the introduction of high-powered weaponry, the combination is potent. The three locations mentioned above, two capital cities and one resource-rich province that is the site of major extractive projects, are areas of intense interaction between traditional and globalized economic and social dynamics. Urban drift is characterized by weakening of kin ties to home districts, ties that act as the principal source of normative control. In the Southern Highlands, the availability of high-powered weaponry has distorted the dynamics of semi-ritualized inter-group conflict, while some local politicians manipulated lines of tension for personal advantage; the result is a pervasive gun culture. In Bougainville, the process of post-conflict disarmament and weapons disposal has been only partially successful. Considerable quantities of small arms have remained in the hands of communities and paramilitary groups. From 2009 the problem became more urgent; at the same time new disarmament initiatives by state and civil society representatives commenced. In Solomon Islands, the increasing use of automatic weapons has also undermined traditional compensation processes, which might have helped to break the cycle of violence, and has intensified conflict. However, the campaign of the Regional Assistance Mission to Solomon Islands (RAMSI—see below) to rid the country of illicit weapons resulted in the removal of 6,000 guns, and demonstrated that, with active involvement of civil society groups, local governments and international donor support, Pacific societies are open and can respond well to campaigns to suppress the use of illegal guns. Another area of high social violence in parts of the Pacific Islands is that of violence against women.

Corruption and Political Instability

Drawing on the participative nature of political life in the Pacific Islands region, aspects of democracy have fared well. Judicial institutions are generally robust. In Fiji, however, in April 2009 the entire judiciary was removed (and subsequently only partly reinstated), and the Constitution was suspended by the military Government. The institutional frameworks of liberal governance are very recent in the region, and while government institutions may be acknowledged with some respect, they often carry little weight, purchase or efficacy within communities. State institutions, drawing on weak formal economies and thus very narrow tax bases, offer meagre services. It is not the state, but forms of community, including customary or church-based leadership, that provide order, safety and security at the local level in most rural communities. Friction between liberal modes of governance and local practice creates the conditions for significant problems. Destructive patterns of interaction between indigenous systems of reciprocity and accountability and state and parliamentary systems have led to significant corruption and weakened some national governments. At the same time, customary governance in some contexts has been undermined and corrupted by the interaction. While communities may provide security and cohesion, local governance mechanisms are not equipped to deal with nation-wide patterns of risk. Weak governance, whether state or community governance, undermines the legitimacy of both state and local authorities and their capacity to prevent or resolve conflicts.

RECENT CONFLICTS IN THE REGION

The South Pacific region has been spared large-scale violent conflicts since the end of the Second World War in 1945. There has been no war between states, and the danger that there will be such conflict in the near future is very remote. Even internal wars, which on a global scale have become the most frequent type of wars over the last few decades, have been very rare in the region, arising only in Papua New Guinea and Solomon Islands. However, even in these two cases fighting was confined to a relatively small part of the country: the island of Bougainville in the case of Papua New Guinea and the island of Guadalcanal in the case of Solomon Islands. The 'war of secession' that followed Vanuatu's independence in 1980 was a very short encounter, and the violent clashes in New Caledonia in the 1980s between Kanak supporters of independence and the French colonial authorities did not escalate into a full-scale war. Death, devastation, displacement and starvation on the scale witnessed in Africa or other parts of the developing world are not found in the South Pacific region. However, in relative terms, even violent conflicts that appear to be 'minor cases' from the global perspective do have devastating effects on the comparatively small Pacific Island states. The people of Bougainville and Solomon Islands suffered severely during 'their' wars, and they are struggling hard to rebuild their lives and their communities in the post-conflict period.

Apart from the wars in Bougainville and Solomon Islands, larger-scale politically motivated violence has occurred in the region in the context of coups and attempted coups in Fiji and sporadic riots in several countries, most recently in Tonga and Vanuatu. However, these riots were brief events and mostly were dominated by opportunistic elements without a political agenda. Although the riots in the Tongan capital of Nuku'alofa in November 2006, in which several people died and the business district was burned down, developed out of a protest meeting organized by the country's pro-democracy movement, the rioting and destruction of lives and property was perpetrated by other opportunistic elements. The riot in Port Vila, the capital of Vanuatu, in March 2007 had its cause in conflicts between the communities from the islands of Tanna and Ambrym who live in squatter settlements in Port Vila.

Bougainville

For almost a decade, between 1988 and 1997, the island of Bougainville was the scene of fierce jungle warfare, the bloodiest conflict in the South Pacific since the Second World War. The Bougainville Revolutionary Army (BRA) fought against the security forces of the central Government of Papua New Guinea for an independent Bougainville; however, within this war of secession many other issues and protagonists were involved in a wide range of violent sub-conflicts.

The origin of the violent conflict in Bougainville was a massive mining project, the Panguna gold and copper mine, located in the mountains of central Bougainville. The mine had commenced operations in 1972, and during the 1970s and 1980s was the largest open pit mine in the world. It was operated by the mining company Bougainville Copper Limited (BCL), a subsidiary of the British-Australian mining conglomerate Rio Tinto Zinc/Conzinc Riotinto of Australia (RTZ/CRA, in the mean time merged into Rio Tinto). In the 1970s and 1980s the Panguna mine was the mainstay of Papua New Guinea's economy and the largest single source of income for the central Government. At the same time, for the local people in the immediate mining area and those in adjacent areas the mine had considerable negative effects, particularly owing to the massive environmental degradation and the social disintegration of the communities.

Those affected by the mining project felt economically exploited and socially marginalized. Their demands for environmental protection and compensation for environmental damage and loss of land were rebuffed by the mining company and the central Government; in response, starting in November 1988, young men from the local land-owning clans brought the mine to a standstill through acts of sabotage. When local police were not able to quell the militant protests against the mine, the central Government sent in riot police squads, and in March 1989 its military, the Papua New Guinea Defence Force (PNGDF). Members of the clans in the mine area thus founded the BRA and began fighting the government forces. The BRA swiftly adopted a secessionist stance and demanded self-determination and political independence for Bougainville. The movement emphasized the ethnic differences between Bougainvilleans and other Papua New Guineans, stressing historical and cultural links with neighbouring Solomon Islands, thus repeating demands for secession that had previously been made in the 1960s and 1970s. The central Government rejected the BRA's demands for independence and insisted on the sovereignty and territorial integrity of the state of Papua New Guinea. It was supported by the former colonial power, Australia. Australia feared that Papua New Guinea, where the population consisted of more than 700 ethno-linguistic groups, might disintegrate as a state should the Bougainville secessionists succeed, thus setting a precedent for others. Therefore (and in the interest of the Australian mining company involved) the Australian Government assisted the Government of Papua New Guinea in its action against the secessionist movement.

The BRA managed to seize control of and shut down the Panguna mine at a very early stage in the fighting; the mine subsequently remained closed. Waging guerrilla warfare, the BRA made successful military strikes against the riot squads of the Papua New Guinea police and the PNGDF. In March 1990 the government forces were compelled to withdraw entirely from the island. The central Government then ordered a total blockade of Bougainville; this led to the deaths of thousands of islanders in the following years, mainly as a result of the collapse of the system of medical care. In May 1990 the BRA leadership unilaterally proclaimed the independence of the 'Republic of Bougainville' and established its own authority, the Bougainville Interim Government (BIG). Not one country in the international community recognized the new state.

After 1992 the PNGDF managed to recapture parts of the island with the support of local Bougainvillean auxiliary units, the so-called Resistance Forces. The Resistance Forces developed out of village protection groups formed during the time of unrestrained BRA rule, when the BRA had proved incapable of maintaining law and order at all times and in all places. The Resistance was willing to fight the BRA alongside the PNGDF. It was equipped and supported by the PNGDF, and during the last years of the war it actually bore the brunt of the fighting on the government side, but was at no time formally amalgamated into the government forces. Commanding and controlling the Resistance therefore posed a lasting problem to the military and political leadership of Papua New Guinea. However, its formation partly changed the character of the conflict. From being a war of 'the Bougainvilleans' against 'foreign' government troops, it also became a war among Bougainvilleans themselves, reflecting the fact that the island population itself is deeply divided into extended families, lineages, clans and approximately 20 different ethno-linguistic groups. From that point, issues other than 'the mine' or 'independence' came to the fore as causes of violent conflict. Long-standing traditional conflicts between different clans and other customary groups, which supported either the BRA or the Resistance, were also fought out under the guise of the 'great' war of secession. At times Resistance units would wage their own 'private' small wars against BRA units over merely local issues, especially land disputes. Moreover, it was not unusual for individual Resistance or BRA units to change sides. Fighting followed the logic of 'pay back': revenge had to be taken for losses, in the form of violent attacks on the clan or the family whose members had been responsible. A perpetual cycle of violence was the consequence. Fighting itself became a cause of yet more fighting, and with the protraction of this fighting a culture of violence developed.

Over time the war became increasingly complex, and the frontiers less distinct. There were no two clearly defined sides fighting each other over one single issue as in conventional wars. It was not simply a case of 'the' state (of Papua New Guinea) against 'the' secessionists (or 'the' BRA) who wanted to create their own state; rather, there was an array of parties embroiled in various overlapping conflicts.

For many years neither side made a decisive military advance. The BRA mainly retained its heartland in central Bougainville around the Panguna mine and in the south, while the PNGDF and the Resistance Forces mainly controlled the north, the eastern coastal strip and the neighbouring island of Buka. In 1996 the last major offensive of the PNGDF/Resistance disintegrated after a few weeks. In March 1997 the attempt of Papua New Guinea's Prime Minister, Julius Chan, and his Government to regain control of the Panguna mine and to destroy the BRA by enlisting British-South African mercenary troops from the firms of Sandline International and Executive Outcomes ended in disaster. Huge demonstrations against the mercenaries in Port Moresby and the refusal of the leaders of the PNGDF to co-operate with the mercenaries forced Chan to resign and the mercenaries to leave the country. Thereafter, the war continued at a level of low intensity. Following elections in Papua New Guinea in June, a new Government led by Prime Minister Bill Skate came to power. Skate declared his Government to be willing to negotiate with the secessionists. A decisive factor in this development was the change in the position of Australia, which finally recognized that a 'military solution' to the conflict was impossible.

After almost 10 years of privation and bloodshed, the population of Bougainville was exhausted and war-weary. There was a widespread desire for peace and a return to normality, which neither the BRA nor the Resistance could disregard. Those who had endured the greatest suffering in the jungle war were civilians. About 15,000 persons (out of a population of approximately 200,000) were said to have died in the conflict, only a minority of whom were fighters who had died in combat. The majority of the war-related deaths were among civilians and were due to the effects of the blockade.

In mid-1997 a peace process began, which over the years that followed became a rare example of success in modern post-conflict peace-building. It started with the assistance of the New Zealand Government, which provided the venue for a first session of talks between the conflict parties in June. In October the negotiations resulted in the Burnham Truce. A further round of negotiations in January 1998 led to the Lincoln Agreement on Peace, Security and Development on Bougainville. This agreement provided for a 'permanent and irrevocable' cease-fire, which entered into force on 30 April 1998. This date marked the end of the war on Bougainville. During subsequent years dozens of rounds of further negotiations followed, leading to the Bougainville Peace Agreement of August 2001; this marked the final settlement of the war.

The two core political provisions of the Bougainville Peace Agreement were, first, autonomy for the island in the framework of the state of Papua New Guinea and its Constitution and, second, a referendum on the future political status of Bougainville, that is: independence or autonomy within Papua New Guinea, 10–15 years after the establishment of an autonomous government for Bougainville.

The provisions regarding autonomy are very extensive, granting a political status 'short of independence' for the Autonomous Region of Bougainville, with its own constitution and government, the Autonomous Bougainville Government. After the adoption of a new Constitution for Bougainville (in November 2004) and elections for a Bougainvillean Parliament and President (in May–June 2005), the Autonomous Bougainville Government was finally established in June 2005.

The formation of the Autonomous Bougainville Government as the authority of the 'Autonomous Region of Bougainville' eight years after the cessation of hostilities could be regarded as the final outcome of the war. However, certain security issues had yet to be resolved. Considerable quantities of illicit weapons were still in the hands of communities. In 2010 a heavily armed militant faction of the former secessionist movement (which had renamed itself the Meekamui Defence Force—MDF) remained in control of a 'no-go zone' around the Panguna mine. The followers of the notorious criminal Noah Musingku still roamed free in the south-west of the island. Sporadic clashes between the Musingku group and the MDF on the one hand, and newly established militias (including the Bougainville Freedom Fighters and the Wisai Liberation Force) on the other, led to several deaths. Violent conflicts in the south of Bougainville escalated in 2008 and 2009 and intensified even further in 2010 and the early months of 2011, with rising numbers of skirmishes, ambushes, village raids, abductions and assassinations. Attempts to control and confine the violence in the south by means of talks, negotiations and reconciliations had only very limited success.

In the political sphere, conflicts over the possible reopening of the Panguna mine and over mining in general became more overt from 2008. The sudden death of the Bougainville President, Joseph Kabui, in June 2008 was a major set-back to peace-building and state-building in Bougainville, which were progressing in a positive way. An election for a new President in December 2008 was won by James Tanis, a former BRA commander and close ally of the late Kabui. The new President accorded the reinvigoration of the peace process a high priority, initiating talks with the Meekamui movement and reconciliation processes in the still-volatile areas in southern Bougainville. The process of weapons disposal also made some progress in 2009–10. In May 2010 elections for the Bougainville Presidency and for the Bougainville autonomous assembly were held. Polling proceeded very smoothly, undisturbed by any violence. The elections were deemed free and fair, and the results were accepted by all sides. The incumbent James Tanis lost to John Momis, a contributor to the foundation of Papua New Guinea in the 1970s. Momis included ministers from all regions and all political factions on Bougainville in his cabinet. He declared weapons disposal, the achievement of full autonomy, democracy and good governance to be the main objectives of his presidency. He also spoke out in favour of reopening the Panguna mine, but at the same time made it clear that its reopening would depend on dialogue with the landowners in the mine area. In 2010 and in the first months of 2011 talks about the mine issue at various levels intensified, and leaders of various factions of the Meekamui movement took part. A series of reconciliations in 2010 and 2011 among stakeholders who had been involved in the conflict over the mine prepared the way for substantial and meaningful negotiations about reopening the mine in the future.

Solomon Islands

Solomon Islands is the only other country in the South Pacific region that has had to endure war in recent times. However, compared with the case of Bougainville, the violent internal conflict in Solomon Islands was much more limited and much less costly. It nevertheless placed enormous pressure on the state and its population, and the conflict finally led to the biggest military intervention in the region by forces external to the state concerned since the Second World War.

The violent conflict began in the second half of 1998 on the main island of the Solomons, Guadalcanal, where indigenous Guadalcanal (Guale) people had turned against immigrants from the neighbouring island of Malaita. Malaitans had come to Guadalcanal and particularly the capital of Honiara in large numbers since the Second World War. Eventually, almost 60,000 Malaitans were living on Guadalcanal. They sought employment in the formal sector of the economy and in the public service. Malaitans were over-represented in the administration and particularly in the police force. Sections of the indigenous Guadalcanal population felt disadvantaged by the influx of Malaitans, with regard to employment but also with regard to the land upon which the immigrants had settled. In and around Honiara large Malaitan 'squatter settlements' developed, and conflicts over land rights escalated. Under these conditions anti-Malaitan resentment grew, and an activist militant movement started up among the indigenous Guadalcanal population. This movement assumed responsibility for the long-standing disputes over land and demanded as a 'solution' that the Malaitans return to their own island.

From October 1998 organized gangs attacked the homes of Malaitans in Honiara and surrounding areas. The Royal Solomon Islands Police, dominated by Malaitans, reacted extremely harshly and thus contributed to the escalation of the conflict. On the Guale side, the Guadalcanal Liberation Army was formed: it was later renamed the Isatabu Freedom Movement (IFM—Isatabu being a local name for Guadalcanal). The Government dispatched paramilitary special units (the Police Field Force and the Rapid Response Unit) against the IFM. The IFM harassed the Malaitan population on Guadalcanal and burned down hundreds of houses. A mass exodus of Malaitans ensued; by the end of 1999 more than 20,000 Malaitans had left Guadalcanal for Malaita. At the beginning of 2000 the Malaitans formed the Malaita Eagle Force (MEF), an armed faction that fought against the IFM and now started to harass the Guale people. On 5 June the police and the MEF staged a coup in Honiara, ousted the Government in a so-called 'joint operation' and took control of the capital city. Policemen who did not join the 'joint operation' were disarmed and driven out or fled the capital, whereas the majority of the (Malaitan) police officers joined the MEF, which declared 'total war' on the IFM. Over the next few months the fighting escalated. However, a new central Government under Prime Minister Manasseh Sogavare, which was established at the end of June with the support of the MEF, managed to negotiate a cease-fire in August. In October representatives of the Solomon Islands Government and the conflict parties met in Townsville, Australia, for negotiations, facilitated by the Australian Government. The result was the Townsville Peace Agreement of 15 October. However, by then several hundred people had been killed in the conflicts, and thousands had been displaced.

Although the Townsville Peace Agreement officially ended the MEF–IFM conflict, it was poorly implemented and did not lead to a durable restitution of law and order. The MEF and the IFM officially dissolved, and many combatants returned to their home villages; however, certain sub-groups continued to exist, and most of the weapons were retained by the conflict parties. Honiara remained under the de facto control of various MEF factions, which at times turned against each other; the police force was completely discredited, and the Malaitan members of the force retained their close links to the MEF. Moreover, almost 2,000 ex-combatants were integrated into the police as 'special constables'. On the Guadalcanal side, one faction of the IFM did not accept the peace agreement and reorganized as the Guadalcanal Revolutionary Army (GRA), or Guadalcanal Liberation Front (GLF), under the leadership of Harold Keke. The GLF was particularly active on the remote Weathercoast of Guadalcanal. It fought police and ex-MEF and ex-IFM combatants.

The Townsville Peace Agreement could therefore be regarded as terminating the war between the MEF and the IFM, but it failed to restore law and order. Indeed, Solomon Islands as a state was in danger of disintegrating. It was in these circumstances that the Government of Prime Minister Allan Kemakeza (later Sir Allan), which had been established after the parliamentary election of December 2001, turned to the Australian Government for help and invited Australia (and New Zealand) to intervene. In response, on 30 June 2003 the 16 countries of the Pacific Islands Forum agreed to a multilateral, Australian-led intervention in Solomon Islands. In mid-July the National Parliament of Solomon Islands approved relevant items of legislation and officially requested the Forum's intervention. RAMSI commenced operations on 24 July. More than 2,000 soldiers and several hundred police officers were deployed to Solomon Islands by air and sea, the vast majority of whom were Australian, but also with contingents from New Zealand, Papua New Guinea, Fiji, Tonga and Samoa. The intervention forces rapidly gained control over Honiara, Guadalcanal and Malaita. Australian officers took command of the Solomon Islands police force, which was disarmed. The various armed groups surrendered to this overwhelming force without resistance, and their leaders declared a willingness to co-operate with RAMSI. Even Harold Keke surrendered voluntarily, and the GRA/GLF ceased to exist. Thousands of weapons were handed in and destroyed. The 'special constables' were sent home. Leaders of the militias, as well as some 80 senior-ranking police officers, were arrested and charged. Moreover, several parliamentarians, ministers and other government officials were subsequently charged with corruption and criminal activities during the conflict and its aftermath. By the end of October the supreme command of RAMSI declared the intervention a complete success, and by the end of the year the vast majority of the military intervention forces had been withdrawn. Approximately 600 Australian soldiers remained in Solomon Islands, together with several hundred police officers from Australia and other Pacific Island Forum countries (the Participating Police Force), who had the task of re-establishing the police force of Solomon Islands and of securing law and order in a transitional period. The Solomon Islands Police Force (SIPF), as it was renamed, was completely restructured; approximately 400 officers had to leave the force, and the paramilitary units were disbanded. Furthermore, large numbers of public servants and civilian advisers remained in Honiara, under the auspices of RAMSI, in order to assist in the re-establishment of functioning government institutions, holding positions in central government bodies such as the treasury and finance departments. In 2011 RAMSI was in its ninth year of operation, and a date for the end of the mission had yet to be set: in that year RAMSI comprised approximately 250 Participating Police Force personnel, and about 150 others, including civilian public servants and a small military contingent (the so-called Combined Task Force).

The first stage of RAMSI's operations was successful. The security situation in Solomon Islands was considerably improved, law and order were restored and the political conditions were returned to normal. It remains to be seen whether the objectives of the later stages, particularly the aim of establishing a functioning, effective and legitimate state, can be achieved by means of RAMSI. There is no doubt that the overwhelming majority of Solomon Islanders have continued to support RAMSI and are grateful for the restoration of peace and normality. However, the initial period of goodwill seemed to come to an end, as became apparent after riots in Honiara in April 2006. Following the parliamentary election, Snyder Rini, a member of the 'old guard' of seemingly corrupt politicians, had become Prime Minister. He was perceived by many citizens as deeply discredited because of the part he had played in the war and its aftermath. In response to Rini's appointment as Prime Minister, a large crowd of protesters rioted in Honiara. The disturbances left much of the capital in ruins; large parts of Chinatown were burned down. RAMSI over-reacted to this unexpected outbreak of widespread violence and mishandled the situation.

The events of April 2006 were an indication that the fundamental causes of the conflicts that led to the war had not yet been addressed and that a genuine peace-building process had not yet been pursued. People on Guadalcanal and Malaita remain frustrated and impatient, and a resurgence of violence cannot be discounted. The large numbers of unemployed, disgruntled young men loitering in Honiara, with no prospects and a propensity for violent and criminal behaviour, constitute a serious issue. There are intermittent rumours of ex-MEF and ex-IFM elements reorganizing and preparing for a new spate of violence. The security situation in Solomon Islands, therefore, remains an issue of concern. In recognition of this, the Government introduced a Truth and Reconciliation Commission (TRC) in 2009 to address ongoing tensions. The TRC is an independent body, comprising three national and two international commissioners (from Peru and Fiji). The Commission commenced its work in January 2010 and held its first public hearings in early 2010. Although substantial financial and technical support for the Commission was provided by a range of international organizations (the European Union and United Nations Development Programme among others), bureaucratic and operational constraints have so far hampered TRC activities to a certain extent.

Relations between RAMSI (or, more precisely, the Australian officials leading RAMSI) and the Solomon Islands Government of Manasseh Sogavare (who returned to the post of Prime Minister in May 2006) became severely strained; a dispute between the Australian and Solomon Islands Governments placed RAMSI in a difficult situation throughout 2006 and 2007. It was only after a change of government in Australia in November 2007 and in Solomon Islands in the following month that there was some revival of the initially cordial relationship. Prime Ministers Derek Sikua of Solomon Islands and Kevin Rudd of Australia committed themselves to an improvement in bilateral relations and to making RAMSI a success. Nevertheless, fundamental problems remained, with the dominant role of Australia in RAMSI an ongoing concern. While many Solomon Islanders disagreed with Sogavare's harsh style of confrontation with the Australians, there was also widespread agreement with much of its content. It has become clear over time that the long-term state-building goals of RAMSI will be much more difficult to achieve than the immediate aims of halting violent conflicts and disarming militias and gangs. Although in its role of stabilizing security RAMSI received ongoing broad support, there is a feeling that RAMSI 'is happening' to the country, and that there is no local ownership of the mission. Although RAMSI was presented as a multilateral regional endeavour instigated by the Pacific Islands Forum, the mission has been led and dominated by Australia. New Zealand and Fiji have contributed, but the deployments of other Forum member states have been no more than token participation. RAMSI is driven by an Australian agenda, and this agenda should be viewed in the wider context of Australia's participation in the US-led 'war on terror', which prevailed under President George W. Bush, and later of Australia's concern with state failure. Solomon Islands came to be regarded as a 'failing state'; such 'failed states' are seen as a security threat to their neighbours, as they can become safe havens for terrorists, organized crime and drugs-trafficking activities.

Therefore, there is an obligation to intervene—militarily, if need be. In the context of the 'war on terror', Australia was willing to take responsibility in the Pacific, which was described by then Prime Minister John Howard as 'our patch'. RAMSI only became possible on the basis of the political will in Canberra, and the resources and capacities of the Australian military and police; without Australia there would be no RAMSI. However, RAMSI could no longer be presented as an unambiguously successful venture, nor as a model for future 'co-operative interventions' (in the words of Alexander Downer, Australian Minister for Foreign Affairs, in 2003) in the Pacific region, despite its success in stopping the violent conflict. In 2009–10 Solomon Islanders themselves became more active in preparing and conducting reconciliations between former adversaries at various societal and political levels. Within the provinces of Malaita and Guadalcanal, which had been most severely affected by the violent conflict, numerous reconciliation processes have taken place. However, province-to-province reconciliations, as well as reconciliations that would have to include government and police, are still outstanding. A feeling of insecurity still remains in large sections of the population, because the root causes of the conflicts that led to violent escalation have not yet been properly addressed and because reconciliation at various levels remains incomplete.

Fiji

In comparison with the wars in Bougainville (which resulted in thousands of deaths) and in Solomon Islands (hundreds of deaths), the coups and attempted coups that have taken place in recent times in Fiji were much less serious (approximately a dozen deaths). Nevertheless, in view of the position of Fiji as the biggest South Pacific Island nation and the recurrence of illegal removals of democratically elected governments, the Fijian 'coup culture' gives reason for security concerns. The attempted coup of May 2000, the mutiny of November 2000 and the military seizure of power of December 2006 are expressions of a deep and ongoing crisis in the Fijian state and society.

On 19 May 2000 a number of armed men under the leadership of George Speight, a bankrupt businessman, stormed the parliament building in the capital city of Suva, taking hostage Prime Minister Mahendra Chaudhry, along with numerous members of the Government and other parliamentarians. The rebels (among them members of the Fijian military) demanded that the Government, elected in the previous year, be dismissed from office and that the Constitution of 1997 be repealed. They also demanded special privileges for indigenous Fijians over Fijians of Indian origin. Following the coup, there were riots and violent attacks in Suva and elsewhere on Indo-Fijians and their property. Large sections of the indigenous Fijian population and of the indigenous Fijian élite showed more or less open support for the hostage-takers. On 29 May 2000 the military took power, declared martial law, established an interim Government (dominated by indigenous Fijians) and entered into protracted negotiations with the rebels. On 9 July an agreement, the Muanikau Accord, was signed with them, as a result of which the remaining hostages were set free. The rebels, who had originally been promised immunity from prosecution, were later taken into custody, accused of having broken the Muanikau Accord (by not having completely surrendered their weapons). Later Speight and several other leaders of the attempted coup were sentenced to brief prison terms. However, the vast majority of his followers and other supporters were never charged. The former Chaudhry Government remained dismissed, and an interim Government under Prime Minister Laisenia Qarase took office on 28 July.

On 2 November 2000 the Counter-Revolutionary Warfare Unit (CRW) of the Fijian army mutinied. Many of its officers and members had been involved in the May coup. The aim of the mutiny was to kill the head of the military, Cdre Frank (Voreqe) Bainimarama, to seize political power, to free Speight and the other rebels, and to fulfil all the demands made during the May coup. The mutineers attacked the headquarters of the Fijian army in Suva, killed several loyal soldiers and took hostages. Bainimarama managed to flee, and after heavy fighting loyal troops overcame the mutineers. Five of them were beaten to death, after having been taken prisoner. In the aftermath of the mutiny, the CRW was dissolved and the mutineers sentenced to prison terms. Bainimarama and his followers in the military gained complete control of the force and an even stronger position in Fiji's political life.

The mutiny induced a state of shock among indigenous Fijians, for it revealed the deep divisions within the indigenous community. Hitherto, it had been possible to maintain that the underlying cause of the crisis was the Indo–indigenous divide. This was no longer possible. While rumours and allegations continued to circulate about the involvement of certain political and military officials in the coups of May and November 2000, the full circumstances surrounding these events have remained unclear. Relations between the sections of the population of Indian origin and the indigenous Fijian population continued to be tense in subsequent years, and divisions within the indigenous élite deepened. Although Qarase was installed as Prime Minister with the strong support of the military and its supreme commander, Cdre Bainimarama, the relationship between the military and the Government worsened. Qarase was successful at elections in 2001 and May 2006, much to the disappointment of Bainimarama, who disagreed with the pro-indigenous and anti-Indian politics of the Qarase Governments. Bainimarama was never able to disregard the fact that Qarase and his followers had taken a highly ambiguous stance during the mutiny of November 2000. Qarase subsequently tried to remove Bainimarama on several occasions, without success. The conflict between the Government and the military escalated in the second half of 2006. A major issue of contention was Qarase's intention to introduce legislation that would allow amnesty for the rebels and mutineers of 2000—to which Bainimarama was totally opposed. Finally, on 5 December 2006, the military ousted the Qarase Government and seized power. The main reason given was alleged widespread corruption and abuse of office on the part of the Qarase Government. The bloodless coup did not meet any resistance; indeed, it was welcomed by certain sections of Fijian society, for example the (Indo-Fijian) business community. In contrast to the coups of 1987 and 2000, which were clearly anti-Indian, the seizure of power in December 2006 could be regarded in a way as pro-Indian. Mahendra Chaudhry joined the new interim Government as Minister for Finance, under interim Prime Minister Bainimarama. The interim Government promised to address the issues of entrenched corruption, cronyism, nepotism and abuse of office and stipulated a three-year period as the deadline for the holding of a parliamentary election. Under pressure from external forces (including Australia, the USA and the European Union), in June 2007 the interim Government agreed to hold an election in the first quarter of 2009. However, in the months that followed Bainimarama was ambiguous about an election date. Australia and New Zealand maintained sanctions against the Fijian regime, including travel bans on members of the interim Government and their families, as well as on all who accepted appointments from the Government or were seen as supporting it.

The interim Government attempted to enhance its legitimacy by launching initiatives that were presented as 'stepping stones' to the improvement of governance and democracy, such as a dialogue about electoral reforms, the establishment of a 'National Council for Building a Better Fiji' and the elaboration of a 'People's Charter for Change and Progress'. According to the regime's plans, the charter was to address issues such as good governance, land, the economy, and reform of the civil service and the financial sector, and was to form the basis for future governments in Fiji. However, a number of important political and social actors (Qarase's party among them) refused to participate in deliberations on the charter, and several important personalities from political and public life declined National Council membership (not least owing to fear of the travel bans). The situation in Fiji deteriorated further in 2009 and 2010. On 9 April 2009 the Fiji Court of Appeal ruled that the military takeover of December 2006 had been unconstitutional and declared the interim Government to be unlawful. This stripped the Bainimarama regime of any legal basis, and on the same day Bainimarama resigned as interim Prime Minister. On the following day the Fijian President, Josefa Iloilo, dismissed the Court of Appeal, suspended the Constitution, declared a state of emergency, removed all the country's judges and dismissed the interim Government. On 11 April 2009, however, President Iloilo reappointed Bainimarama as Prime Minister, and Bainimarama formed a new Government. These actions extricated Bainimarama from a difficult political situation, after the ruling of the Court of Appeal, and thus strengthened his (and the military's) position. The military erected roadblocks in the major cities, critics of the regime were put under house arrest and a strict censorship of the media was implemented. The state of emergency was extended several times. Bainimarama announced that the legislative election would be postponed until 2014. Whereas the state of emergency and the military's firm control of power prevented major protests in Fiji itself, the international community responded firmly. The UN, the Commonwealth, and the major regional powers of Australia and New Zealand condemned the abolition of the Constitution, demanded the holding of democratic elections as soon as possible and extended sanctions against the regime. Some neighbouring Pacific Island countries reacted more cautiously, but also showed their disappointment. In May 2009 Fiji's membership of the Pacific Islands Forum was suspended. However, the Fiji regime managed to maintain membership in the Melanesian Spearhead Group. The Governments of the other members of the Group (Papua New Guinea, Vanuatu and Solomon Islands) have endorsed the regime's rule of Fiji and its proposals for a return to democracy, with elections promised for 2014. Furthermore, during 2011 Bainimarama chaired the Melanesian Spearhead Group on behalf of Fiji.

The economic repercussions of the international condemnation and isolation of the regime are becoming more and more evident. The overtly undemocratic and unconstitutional character of the regime and its repressive actions against the media and sections of the public have resulted in the loss of sympathies and support, even among those who thus far have shown some understanding for the concerns of Bainimarama. Moreover, in 2010 and 2011 rifts within the ranks of the Fiji military appeared. Senior military commanders were removed from their positions and charged with planning a mutiny and counter-coup. One of them, Lt-Col Ratu Tevita Mara, commander of the Third Fiji Infantry Regiment and youngest son of the highly respected first Prime Minister and President of Fiji, the late Ratu Sir Kamisese Mara, escaped from Fiji to Tonga aboard a Tongan Navy patrol boat in May 2011. He was picked up by the Tongan vessel in Fijian territorial waters, welcomed by the royal family of Tonga as their guest and placed under the protection of Tonga's King George Tupou V. Fijian requests for extradition of the fugitive were rejected, leading to tensions between Tonga and Fiji. Tevita Mara joined the Fijian opposition in the diaspora and urged regime change in his home country.

Although in 2011 Bainimarama and his military remained in control of politics in Fiji, the potential for further unrest and violence has not been reduced, and the stability of the country may come under renewed pressure in the future.

NON-TRADITIONAL SECURITY ISSUES

While the most serious security threats in the Pacific region have been matters of internal security, other non-traditional security issues have caused major concern across the region, particularly the HIV/AIDS epidemic, natural disasters, resource predation by external protagonists, money-laundering, illegal immigration, organized crime, and trafficking in people, drugs and weapons. In small island populations, with severely strained economies and usually very limited capacity to commit sufficient human and material resources to addressing these problems, their effects have been far more devastating than in more developed regions. Difficulties are also compounded by the weakening or disintegration of traditional forms of social control and cohesion and by the limited capacity of governments effectively to manage or respond to the complex risks involved.

The Impact of HIV/AIDS

HIV/AIDS was of greatest concern in Papua New Guinea, which has the second most serious HIV/AIDS epidemic in the Asia-Pacific region, second only to Thailand, with 34,100 reported cases in 2011. Studies by the World Bank and the Australian Agency for International Development (AusAID) predicted a potential trajectory similar to that of the epidemic in sub-Saharan Africa. Based on numbers of HIV/AIDS cases and deaths in 2005–06, AusAID made a baseline prediction that, if HIV interventions remained at 2006 levels, by the year 2025 there would be a generalized epidemic resulting in over 300,000 adult deaths, more than 500,000 people living with HIV and an HIV prevalence of over 10% of the adult population. The work-force would be reduced by 12.5%, and 70.0% of hospital beds would be occupied by people living with AIDS. The security risks arising from an AIDS epidemic relate to the severe burden on an already inadequate health sector, and the drastic loss of human resources, leading to further weakening of institutional capacity in all sectors of governance, and increased poverty and hardship for people in communities.

Some of the factors that have hindered the campaign against HIV/AIDS in Papua New Guinea include the weak health care system, along with rapid social changes brought by urbanization in the capital and by large influxes of foreigners and their cash in more remote mining areas, accompanied by a disintegration of traditional law and social control, increased violence and sexual violence against women, increased poverty and prostitution, and low levels of awareness and understanding of the impact of HIV/AIDS and the risk of HIV transmission through unprotected sex. At the same time there remains a cultural reluctance to discuss sexuality and sexual health. While unprotected sex is the predominant means of transmission, the Commission on AIDS in the Pacific also identified injecting drug use as a significant issue in Guam, French Polynesia and New Caledonia.

Ensuring access to anti-retroviral drugs is a crucial factor in combating the epidemic, as an international study has found that appropriate treatment can lead to a 96% reduction in risks of further infections. However, in the remote Western Highlands province of Papua New Guinea, where prevalence is high, only about one-third of people reportedly infected are being treated with anti-retroviral medication. Aid donors including the Asian Development Bank (ADB) and the Australian, New Zealand and US Governments have pledged further long-term funding support for a much larger response in the effort to curb the spread of HIV/AIDS in Papua New Guinea and throughout the Pacific. This will be effective only if external aid is successfully channelled through national and provincial levels of government to improve the capacity of the health sector at local sites, and programmes are designed in culturally appropriate ways in order that people in all sectors of society can confront the HIV/AIDS threat and participate in education and intervention programmes. In recognition of the threat that HIV/AIDS poses to the wider region, the Pacific Islands Forum has included discussion of the HIV/AIDS threat and programmes for combating the epidemic at its Regional Security meetings.

Natural Disasters

The vulnerability of the Pacific Islands to natural disasters is one of the main obstacles to economic growth, investment and security. The region regularly experiences earthquakes, tsunamis, volcanic eruptions, cyclones and flooding. In September 2009 a major earthquake led to a tsunami that killed more than 180 people and destroyed parts of Samoa, American Samoa and Tonga. New Caledonia and Vanuatu experienced devastating cyclones in January 2011 and; severe flooding in Fiji and Solomon Islands caused damage to houses, agricultural crops, government facilities and infrastructure. It is often many years before damaged infrastructure can be repaired. Scientists have predicted that the frequency and intensity of cyclones and other extreme weather events are likely to increase with global warming.

Climate Change

The rising sea-levels and increased sea temperatures associated with global warming are threatening many Pacific island countries, including Kiribati, Tuvalu, the Marshall Islands and Nauru. Governments in these countries are confronted with the impending loss of part or all of their lands, which have provided their people's livelihoods and are the basis of their heritage and identity. In Papua New Guinea residents of the Carteret Islands in the Autonomous Region of Bougainville were reported to be the first 'climate refugees' in the Pacific region. The Catholic Church in Bougainville agreed to provide land to the Carteret Islanders, who were to be resettled on mainland Bougainville; the Autonomous Bougainville Government promised to provide a plantation, and the Papua New Guinea Government pledged US $800,000 to aid the relocation. Many of the Carteret Islanders were reluctant to leave, but would risk starvation and a lack of fresh water if they were to stay. Resettlement began in 2009, with the first families from the Carterets arriving in Tinputz in North Bougainville in April. In mid-2009, however, the funding allocated for the relocation had yet to be released, and there were indications of potential for conflicts over the resettlement land. Thus, the relocation could have a negative impact on the stability of Bougainville, making it an early example of the link between climate change and conflict.

The intrusion of seawater onto gardening lands and into scarce freshwater supplies is becomingly increasingly common on islands with large areas of low-lying coast, creating serious impacts on food security in the Pacific region and increasing risks of conflict over land as people are forced to move on to land owned by others. Rising sea temperatures are also having a negative impact on fish stocks, creating further pressure on food security and economic development in the region.

Pacific countries (notably Tuvalu and Kiribati) have been active in international forums, including the UN Climate Change Conference in Copenhagen, Denmark, in December 2009, where Pacific nations, through the Alliance of Small Island States (AOSIS), demanded meaningful reductions in emissions of carbon dioxide and other greenhouse gases, in order to combat global warming. They also appealed for effective financial and other forms of assistance for implementation of adaptation measures, arguing that the effects of climate change, such as forced resettlement and migration, might become serious security challenges. Governments and peoples in the Pacific expressed deep disappointment with the inconclusive results of the Copenhagen Conference, but continued to press their arguments in the media and global forums, including the UN Climate Change Conference held in Bangkok in April 2011.

Resource Stripping

Resource security is a major challenge for Pacific Island countries, with some experiencing very serious environmental degradation from unsustainable mining, logging and fishing activities, particularly in Nauru, Papua New Guinea, Solomon Islands and Vanuatu (see essay on the Environmental Issues of the Pacific Islands). In Solomon Islands, log exports in the year to May 2011 increased by 49% in comparison with those of the previous 12 months, and forests were expected to be entirely depleted within five years. Unsustainable logging and fishing practices by external companies are believed to have contributed to the protracted civil conflict. In a review of logging practices in Papua New Guinea in 2005, the World Bank estimated that 70% of logging was illegal. Regulations such as the requirement to leave buffer zones of forest along rivers and streams are routinely disregarded, creating major erosion problems. In 2008 scientists from Papua New Guinea and Australia released a satellite imagery analysis of the impact of logging, showing that Papua New Guinea has been losing about 1,400 sq miles of rainforest each year; if the current pace continues, more than 80% of the country's accessible forests will be lost by 2020.

In March 2008 the Governments of Papua New Guinea and Australia signed a Forest Carbon Partnership agreement in order to prepare the way for Papua New Guinea to sell carbon credits to Australian companies in future carbon-trading markets. However, for the plan to work, both Governments would need to address the ongoing problem of the export of illegally logged timber from Papua New Guinea, and the need for proper forest management, conservation and enforcement of regulations. Local Papua New Guinea landowners would also need to adopt more sustainable agricultural practices than current methods of clearing forests. The International Tropical Timber Organization pledged financial aid for Papua New Guinea to implement agreed recommendations on forest law enforcement and governance. However, official corruption in this sector in Papua New Guinea, Solomon Islands and Vanuatu continued to be of concern.

Illegal fishing and marine conservation also remained a significant challenge. Countries in the Pacific region hold a total of about 30m. sq km of Pacific Ocean within their 200-nautical mile (370-km) exclusive economic zones (EEZs), but many small island nations lack the capacity to patrol these waters and safeguard fish and marine stocks. As part of co-operative efforts to detect and prosecute illegal operators, the members of the Pacific Islands Forum Fisheries Agency (FFA) signed the 2008 Niue Declaration and are developing a regional monitoring, control and surveillance strategy. The Government of Taiwan also entered into co-operative agreements with New Zealand and the Cook Islands in November 2008 to facilitate the detection of illegal fishing activities, by requiring Taiwanese vessels operating within the Western and Central Pacific Fisheries Commission areas to allow fishery officials or police to board and inspect Taiwanese vessels.

Conflicts around the Porgera gold mine in Enga Province in Papua New Guinea escalated in 2009 and were a reminder of the conflict potential associated with such large-scale mining projects. In April the Government of Papua New Guinea declared a state of emergency in the mine area and sent in 200 additional police officers to deal with the deteriorating security situation. In the course of 'Operation Ipili' in April and May the police burned down between 100 and 300 houses. Hundreds of people were left homeless, and approximately 180 persons were arrested. The reason given for this action was that these homes had been built illegally in the Porgera Special Mining Lease area and that the people were illegal miners. Local residents claimed that at least seven people had been shot dead by police deployed to protect the mine site or by members of the mine's 500-strong private security company, and other serious human rights abuses have allegedly occurred, including rapes, gang rapes and beatings. Landowners continue to press their case for compensation and for an equitable relocation plan for those forcibly removed from their land. Violent conflicts have also continued to mar the development of a major project for the production of liquefied natural gas (LNG) in Papua New Guinea. As disputes between landowning groups along the planned route of the 600-km gas pipeline continued, there were also clashes between landowners and security guards. In February 2010 ExxonMobil suspended related road-building work near Port Moresby, following the deaths of 16 people in fighting between clans whose traditional lands are located near both ends of the proposed pipeline. Police attributed the violence to contested land ownership in anticipation of compensation payments for the LNG developments.

Money-laundering

Campaigns to combat money-laundering activities have been an ongoing concern in the region since the late 1990s. Pacific Islands that were operating 'offshore' financial centres came under intense international pressure, particularly from the USA through the Financial Action Task Force (FATF), to take firm action against money-laundering activities. The FATF banned member states from conducting financial transactions with countries considered to be lax in their efforts to counter the practice of money-laundering. The Organisation for Economic Co-operation and Development (OECD) likewise published 'blacklists' of non-OECD countries believed to be operating as unfair tax havens. From 1999 the FATF and OECD specifically targeted Nauru, Vanuatu, the Cook Islands, Niue, the Marshall Islands, Samoa and Tonga. The impact of these bans was substantial, and most Pacific countries responded proactively by enacting legislation to combat money-laundering, tax evasion and the financing of terrorist activities. Nauru initially resisted this pressure, as its only other main source of income was from the mining of decreasing phosphate deposits on the island; however, in 2004 Nauru also yielded to the pressure and enacted legislation to close down its 'offshore' financial sector and to provide for exchange of information on tax matters and criminal activities.

Since 2006 the USA and other Western nations have adopted a more supportive strategy by offering assistance and technical advice to Pacific Islands Forum countries to help them meet FATF and OECD requirements, as well as relevant UN conventions and Security Council resolutions. In September 2006 the Pacific Anti-Money Laundering Project (PALP) was launched as a joint initiative involving the Pacific Islands, the UN Office on Drugs and Crime (UNODC) and the US Department of State. In August 2006 Australia also established a regional Anti-Money Laundering Assistance Team (AMLAT) to provide in-country technical training and support for member states of the Pacific Islands Forum. By 2007 only the Marshall Islands remained on the OECD 'blacklist' for 'unco-operative' tax practices; it was removed in August of that year. In April 2009, when the OECD released its revised 'blacklist' of states not complying with the global tax standard, no Pacific Islands were identified.

Transnational Crime

Despite fears expressed in the USA and Australia that the Pacific Islands might become havens or staging posts for terrorists, there were no immediate reports of incidents of such activity in the region. In 2008, however, transnational crime was identified as an ongoing human and economic threat in the Pacific region in the Pacific Transnational Crime Assessment report to the Pacific Islands Forum. Papua New Guinea and major tourist centres in Vanuatu, Fiji, Tonga, the Cook Islands, French Polynesia and Micronesia have been targeted by criminal networks involved in trafficking illegal narcotics, including heroin, cocaine, amphetamine precursors and cannabis. Colombian cocaine syndicates are suspected, as well as some Chinese criminal networks. These drugs-trafficking operations have been primarily aimed at international tourists and markets in Australia and New Zealand. People-trafficking and illegal immigration were also identified as a continuing threat to security and human rights in the region. People-trafficking has occurred in the Federated States of Micronesia, Kiribati, Palau, American Samoa, Samoa, Fiji, Papua New Guinea and Solomon Islands, conducted mainly by Chinese and Taiwanese criminal networks involved in prostitution, illegal gambling and drugs-trafficking. US authorities have expressed concern about lack of resources, capacity and efforts to control human-trafficking in Papua New Guinea. The 'Trafficking in Persons' report by the US Department of State, released in June 2011, stated that Asian crime rings, foreign logging companies and other foreign businesses were using fraudulent passports and bribing Papua New Guinean officials to arrange for men, women and girls from Malaysia, Thailand, China and the Philippines to enter Papua New Guinea illegally; they were then taken by traffickers to logging, mining and fishing camps and forced into involuntary labour and prostitution. Some local Papua New Guinean girls and women were also forced into involuntary marriages or prostitution by their families. The report urged the Governments of Papua New Guinea and other Pacific states to develop and implement anti-trafficking legislation and to prosecute offenders and educate the community about the issue. Transnational anti-crime units with responsibility for combating trafficking in people, drugs and illegal weapons have been established in Fiji, Samoa, Tonga, Papua New Guinea, Vanuatu and the Federated States of Micronesia, and have continued to receive assistance from the US Department of Defense and the Australian Federal Police.

MARITIME SECURITY

Maritime safety and security continued to be a focus in the region, in keeping with increased efforts throughout the Pacific and globally to implement the International Maritime Organization (IMO) amendments to the International Convention for Safety of Life at Sea (SOLAS) and new provisions under the International Ship and Port Facility Security Code (ISPS Code). The new procedures entered into force in July 2003, and most Pacific Island countries introduced new arrangements for compliance.

The Australian Government announced a major expansion of its maritime defence capabilities in its Defence White Paper released in May 2009. The report noted the economic emergence of China and India and the prospect of China becoming the dominant military power in the Asia-Pacific region in the 21st century. It emphasized the need for greater engagement and co-operation with China in areas of shared interests.

Officials from 17 countries, including China, the USA, Australia, New Zealand, Fiji, Papua New Guinea and Vanuatu, and six international organizations (including the IMO) met in June 2010 at the 11th Asia-Pacific Heads of Maritime Safety Agencies (APHoMSA) forum in Manila, the Philippines, and agreed to enhance strategic approaches to regional co-operation on maritime safety, security, marine environmental protection, and search and rescue.

REGIONAL SECURITY CO-OPERATION

Mechanisms for regional security co-operation are emerging in the region, but are not yet highly developed. The Pacific Islands Forum is the leading political intergovernmental body and has been pursuing closer co-operation across the region in a number of areas, with a focus on globalization and the international security environment as challenges best addressed collaboratively. The Melanesian Spearhead Group also includes security and economic collaboration within its ambit, but only the Melanesian states participate. The Pacific Islands Forum brings together heads of government and ministers from 16 member states, including Australia and New Zealand, as well as observers from self-governing territories. The active participation of the major powers of the broader region, which are both important aid donors and the leading source of rapidly deployable forces, is logical if the Pacific Islands Forum is to function effectively as a security forum; yet there is a natural tension in a gathering that includes developed economies and majority settler societies on the one hand, and smaller, developing economies and indigenous and customary societies on the other hand. In 2006, after protracted consultation, the Forum produced the Pacific Plan, a 'living document' to help guide regional co-operation. Discussion papers produced under the Plan emphasized the link between social factors and security, and the need to deepen dialogue on, and understanding of, security in the region.

The evolution of a regional approach to security can also be seen through the joint declarations made since the 1990s. Declarations cover co-operative law enforcement, intelligence gathering, and security forces' training, a range of conflict prevention measures (including social, environmental and economic measures), political initiatives for responding to security crises, and commitments to combat terrorism. There have also been some regional responses to national security crises, both through the Melanesian Spearhead Group and the Pacific Islands Forum. However, RAMSI was the first regional response unit to be deployed under the authority of a regional security agreement (the Biketawa Declaration) and with the explicit support of the Forum as well as of the Government concerned. The Forum has been working towards common approaches to conflict and efforts to strengthen conflict prevention. However, the changed nature of the Fijian regime with the military coup of 2006 and the final undermining of civilian control of the military in 2009 have seriously obstructed collaboration, as (in a different way) has the significant tension between the Fijian regime and the Australian and New Zealand Governments. This tension was further entrenched when Fiji's membership of the Pacific Islands Forum was suspended in May 2009 in response to its failure to comply with the Forum's demand to announce a date for the holding of elections in 2009. Australia and New Zealand had demanded Fiji's total exclusion from the regional body. Fiji is the first country ever to be suspended from the Forum. Given Fiji's significant role as a major Pacific Island country, its absence from this most important regional body will inevitably hamper progress in regional co-operation in the near future. The Fiji regime subsequently pursued a policy aimed at strengthening the role of the Melanesian Spearhead Group (at the expense of the Pacific Islands Forum). At its meeting in 2011, under Fijian chairmanship, members of the Melanesian Spearhead Group even decided to establish a rapid response force for Melanesia. The proposed Humanitarian and Emergency Response Force was to address issues such as internal conflicts within Melanesian countries, natural disasters, organized crime and other trans-boundary illicit activities.

OPTIONS FOR HUMAN SECURITY, CONFLICT PREVENTION AND PEACE-BUILDING

In the Pacific there is hardly any threat of war between states of the region, there are no antagonistic national interests that might lead to 'arms races' and into security dilemmas, and there are no external powers threatening countries of the region militarily. Threats to security come from other spheres; they are associated with underdevelopment and maldevelopment, environmental degradation and climate change, epidemics like HIV/AIDS and natural disasters, criminal and domestic violence, predatory commercial behaviour (often by foreign companies and individuals) and, to a lesser extent, organized crime, such as the trafficking of drugs, of weapons and of people, and money-laundering. Violent conflicts are internal, and mostly confined to the local level. Even large-scale internal wars are the exception. Much more common are locally and temporarily confined outbreaks of violence such as riots in the (few) cities of the region, violent disputes between villages, clans or 'tribes' over land and other local issues, or violent conflict over access to resources, seats in a national legislature or demands for compensation. Parts of Papua New Guinea are also marked by serious degradation of law and order. The Autonomous Region of Bougainville remains in a post-conflict situation with potential for renewed violence. Highly divisive issues, such as the question of reopening the Panguna mine or the referendum on the future political status of Bougainville, will be on the agenda and will need sensitive treatment in order to avoid a regression to violence. The situation is similar in parts of Solomon Islands and in New Caledonia. However, it would be misleading to present the Pacific Islands as a region permeated by violence and on the brink of collapse. Most people in the majority of the villages live a generally peaceful existence.

In order to improve the security of people and societies further, one has to consolidate the strength and resilience of the local communities, which are to a large extent based in customary lifestyles. The resilience of communities is an asset for improving human security. As threats to security are mainly internal they have to be addressed in a societal context. This means overcoming a state-centric approach to security. Of course, the state has a responsibility for the internal and external security of its citizens. However, under conditions where external threats are minimal and state institutions are relatively weak, as is the case in the Pacific, other protagonists also have to be involved in the provision of security. Civil society, non-governmental organizations and the churches have a role to play, for instance in conflict prevention and mediation or in addressing domestic violence, as do customary institutions such as village chiefs and elders, healers and community leaders. Custom, customary law and customary institutions remain a significant source of security in the Pacific. The challenge is to organize forms of constructive interaction of state institutions, civil society institutions and customary institutions so that their interplay can provide sustainable peace and security.

BIBLIOGRAPHY

Anderson, Tim. *The Limits of RAMSI.* (Aid/Watch Report). Sydney, Aid/Watch, 2008.

Anwar, D. F., Bouvier, H., Smith, G., and Tol, R. (Eds). *Violent Internal Conflicts in Asia Pacific: Histories, Political Economies and Policies.* Jakarta, Yayasan Obor Indonesia, 2004.

Boege, Volker. *Bougainville and the Discovery of Slowness: an Unhurried Approach to State-Building in the Pacific.* Australian Centre for Peace and Conflict Studies, Occasional Paper No. 3, Brisbane, University of Queensland, 2006.

A promising liaison: kastom and state in Bougainville. Australian Centre for Peace and Conflict Studies, Occasional Paper No. 12, Brisbane, University of Queensland, 2008.

Boege, Volker, Brown, M. Anne, Clements, Kevin P., and Nolan, Anna. *States Emerging from Hybrid Political Orders—Pacific Experiences.* Australian Centre for Peace and Conflict Studies, Occasional Paper No. 11, Brisbane, University of Queensland, 2008.

Braithwaite, J., Charlesworth, H., Reddy, P., and Dunn, L. *Reconciliation and Architectures of Commitment: Sequencing Peace in Bougainville.* Canberra, Australian National University Press, 2010.

Brown, M. Anne. *Security and Development in the Pacific Islands: Social Resilience in Emerging States.* Boulder, CO, Lynne Rienner Publishers, 2007.

Commonwealth of Australia. *A Pacific Engaged: Australia's Relations with Papua New Guinea and the Island States of the South-West Pacific.* Canberra, Senate Foreign Affairs, Defence and Trade References Committee, August 2003.

Defending Australia in the Asia Pacific Century: Force 2030. Canberra, Department of Defence, 2009.

Crocombe, Ron. *The South Pacific.* Suva, Institute of Pacific Studies, University of the South Pacific, 1989 (revised edn, 2001).

Enhancing Pacific Security: Report prepared for the Pacific Islands Forum Regional Security Committee. Suva, Pacific Islands Forum Secretariat, 2000.

Crocombe, Ron, and Ali, Ahmed (Eds). *Politics in Micronesia.* Suva, Institute of Pacific Studies, University of the South Pacific, 1983.

Dauvergne, Peter (Ed.). *Weak and Strong States in Asia-Pacific Societies.* Canberra, Allen & Unwin, 1998.

Dinnen, Sinclair, and Firth, Stewart (Eds). *Politics and State Building in Solomon Islands.* Canberra, Asia Pacific Press, The Australian National University, 2008.

Dinnen, Sinclair, and Ley, Allison (Eds). *Reflections on Violence in Melanesia.* Canberra, Hawkins Press-Asia Pacific Press, 2000.

Dinnen, Sinclair, May, Ron, and Regan, Anthony J. (Eds). *Challenging the State: The Sandline Affair in Papua New Guinea.* Canberra, Australian National University, 1997.

Field, Michael, Tupeni, Baba, and Unaisi, Nabobo-Baba. *Speight of Violence: Inside Fiji's 2000 Coup.* Canberra, Pandanus Books, 2005.

Fry, Greg. *Falling off the Map? The Changing Dynamics of Security in the South Pacific, Strategic Update '99.* Canberra, Australian National University, 1999.

Glenn, Russell W. *Counterinsurgency in a Test Tube: Analyzing the Success of the Regional Assistance Mission to Solomon Islands.* Santa Monica, CA, RAND Corporation, 2007.

Hanson, Fergus. 'China: Stumbling through the Pacific' in *Policy Brief July 2009.* Sydney, Lowy Institute for International Policy, 2009.

Hegarty, David. 'Peace Interventions in the South Pacific: Lessons from Bougainville and Solomon Islands' in *State Society and Governance in Melanesia Working Papers 4/2003.* Canberra, Australian National University, 2003.

Hegarty, David, and Powles, Anna. 'South Pacific Security' in Ayson, Robert, and Ball, Desmond (Eds). *Strategy and Security in the Asia-Pacific.* Crows Nest, Allen & Unwin, 2006.

Heijmans, A., Simmonds, N., and Van de Veen, H. (Eds). *Searching for Peace in Asia Pacific: an Overview of Conflict Prevention and Peacebuilding Activities.* Boulder, CO, Lynne Rienner Publishers, 2004.

Henderson, John, and Watson, Greg (Eds). *Securing a Peaceful Pacific.* Christchurch, Canterbury University Press, 2005.

Henningham, Stephen. *The Pacific Island States: Security and Sovereignty in the Post-Cold War World.* London, Macmillan Publishers Ltd, 1995.

May, Ron J. 'A Brief Overview of Pacific Security Issues' in *State Society and Governance in Melanesia Conference Papers March 2004.* Canberra, Australian National University, 2004.

May, Ron J., and Spriggs, Matthew. (Eds). *The Bougainville Crisis.* Bathurst, Crawford House Press, 1990.

McFarlane, John. 'Organised Crime and Terrorism in the Asia Pacific Region: The Reality and the Response' in *Strategic and Defence Studies Centre Working Paper 370.* Canberra, Australian National University, 2002.

Molloy, Ivan (Ed.). *The Eye of the Cyclone—Issues in Pacific Security.* Sippy Downs, University of the Sunshine Coast, 2004.

Moore, Clive. *Happy Isles in Crisis: the Historical Causes for a Failing State in Solomon Islands, 1998–2004.* Canberra, Asia Pacific Press, 2004.

Pacific Islands Forum. *The Pacific Plan for Strengthening Regional Co-operation and Integration.* Suva, Pacific Islands Forum Secretariat, 2005.

Peebles, Dave. *Pacific Regional Order.* Canberra, Australian National University Press E-book, 2005.

Regan, Anthony J. 'The Bougainville political settlement and the prospects for sustainable peace' in *Pacific Economic Bulletin 17 (1),* 2002.

Regan, Anthony J., and Griffin, Helga M. (Eds). *Bougainville Before the Conflict.* Canberra, Pandanus Books, 2005.

Reilly, Benjamin. 'Internal Conflict and Regional Security in Asia and the Pacific' in *Global Change, Peace and Security 14 (1),* 2002.

Robertson, Robert, and Sutherland, William. *Government by the Gun: The Unfinished Business of Fiji's 2000 Coup.* London, Zed Books, 2002.

US Department of State. *Trafficking in Persons Report.* Washington, DC, Department of State, June 2010.

Van Fossen, Anthony B. 'Money Laundering, Global Financial Instability and Tax Havens in the Pacific Islands', *The Contemporary Pacific 15 (2) Fall,* 2003.

Wehner, Monica, and Denoon, Donald (Eds). *Without a Gun: Australians' Experiences Monitoring Peace in Bougainville, 1997–2001.* Canberra, Pandanus Books, 2001.

ECONOMIC TRENDS IN THE PACIFIC ISLANDS

T. K. JAYARAMAN

Revised by the editorial staff

INTRODUCTION

In the first decade of the new millennium the economic performance of many of the Pacific Islands remained modest. The serious deterioration in the global economy in 2008/09 had a major impact on the region. Although there was some improvement in the majority of Pacific economies in 2010, the extent of the recovery was relatively limited. The UN's annual Economic and Social Survey of Asia and the Pacific, released in May 2011, concluded that most Pacific economies had yet to recover from the impact of the global crisis of 2008/09. The countries of Melanesia appeared to be performing better than their Polynesian counterparts. While Papua New Guinea and Solomon Islands continued to register comparatively high rates of growth in 2010, many regional economies remained stagnant, and Samoa and Tonga continued to contract. Virtually all Pacific economies were forecast by the Asian Development Bank (ADB) to expand in 2011, albeit only moderately in most cases.

The deceleration in the economies of the region's major trading partners, combined with the decline in global commodity prices in the latter part of 2008, greatly reduced the export earnings of the islands. Revenue from the crucial tourism sector was seriously jeopardized by the recessionary conditions that generally prevailed. With the cost of aviation fuel rising, air travel became increasingly expensive; this had an adverse effect on the tourism industry, upon which many of the Pacific Islands remained highly dependent. As employment opportunities in host countries declined, particularly in the USA, remittances from islanders working overseas began to weaken. Furthermore, the value of trust funds, a vital source of financial support for several of the Pacific Islands, was severely affected by the volatility of international financial markets from late 2008, much of the capital from such funds being invested in US stock markets.

Although the inflationary pressures that had resulted from the substantial rises in world prices for fuels and foodstuffs began to ease in 2009, by mid-2011 there was renewed pressure on consumer prices, mainly owing to the upward trends in the costs of the Pacific Islands' imports of essential commodities. A major factor in the increase in the region's import costs in 2011 was the continued strength of the Australian currency in 2011. As a result of the substantial rise in the value of the Australian dollar, the relative cost of the Pacific Islands' imports from Australia had risen sharply, with attendant repercussions for Pacific businesses and for consumers. Receipts from tourism were again jeopardized, as many Australians could more easily afford to travel further afield, notably to Europe and the USA, rather than visit the Pacific Islands.

Various other uncertainties have continued to affect the economies of the Pacific Islands. Political instability has often discouraged the expansion of the private sector, and investment conditions have remained generally unfavourable. Potential foreign investors have been deterred by political turmoil, particularly in Fiji (where the elected Government was ousted in a coup in December 2006), Tonga and Solomon Islands. By 2009 it was clear that Fiji, which was not only a major Pacific Island country with far more skilled human resources and greater manufacturing capacity than others but was also the location of the secretariat of the 16-member Pacific Islands Forum, could not continue to play a leading role in promoting the regional integration of island states. Having been active in efforts to establish a Pacific Islands free trade area, Fiji was no longer a a credible partner in the implementation of the much-heralded Pacific Plan (approved by the Forum in 2005—see below); nor could Fiji lead negotiations with Australia and New Zealand aimed at the creation of a wider free trade area, originally envisaged to be in place by 2015 and to comprise the two metropolitan powers in addition to the 14 Pacific Island members. Fiji's membership of the Pacific Islands Forum was suspended in May 2009, and henceforth the country was excluded from regional trade meetings. Furthermore, in August Cdre Frank Bainimarama, the military leader of Fiji, announced that the country was withdrawing from all regional trade agreements. Although discussions with regard to the establishment of a regional free trade area continued intermittently, the absence of Fiji from such dialogue remained a major obstacle to progress (see Trade and Co-operation, below).

Some of the Pacific Islands have continued to record very high rates of annual population growth, thus impeding any significant rise in terms of gross domestic product (GDP) per head. The continued stagnation of per caput income in many of the Pacific Islands was not an encouraging sign, especially in view of the UN's Millennium Development Goals (MDGs—adopted by the member states of the UN in September 2000). Five of the eight MDGs related to human development, the foremost among them being the reduction of poverty by 50% by 2015. Increasing migration to towns by people in search of jobs as a result of the steady decline in rural incomes over the years, the consequent expansion of squatter settlements, rising crime in urban areas and growing youth unemployment were visible evidence of the poverty experienced in many of the Pacific Islands. Furthermore, there were increases in the numbers of reported cases of HIV/AIDS. A study commissioned by the Commonwealth Secretariat in 2005 indicated that the realization of the MDGs of the eradication of poverty, the reduction of child mortality and the control of the spread of HIV/AIDS and malaria, as well as the achievement of universal education, was proving difficult. This was confirmed by a further study released by the Australian Agency for International Development (AusAID), observing that the Pacific Islands were unlikely to meet the MDGs, as during the 10-year period 1995–2004 they had failed to register an annual per caput income growth rate in excess of 2%, the level indicated by the World Bank as that required for reducing poverty. At the rates of progress prevailing in 2010, therefore, not one country in the Pacific region appeared likely to achieve the MDGs within the recommended time scale.

Fiscal excesses and governance problems have also compounded the constraints on growth. The remoteness and insularity of the widely dispersed multi-island micro-states, combined with the distance from major markets, have resulted in high international and domestic transport costs. In addition to the problem of low volume of cargo, the development of even a small domestic market has been impeded by the distances between settlements and the infrequency of internal transport services. The Pacific Islands' susceptibility to natural disasters and adverse climatic conditions typically have a negative impact upon crop yields, thus affecting the entire region's economy. The relatively small populations of the islands reduce their institutional capacity, which in turn increase the unit costs of services and restrict the potential for private sector growth and investment. Scope for diversification is constrained by the narrow resource base and by the limitations of the domestic markets, resulting in the continuation of unvaried production and exports, and in a weak private sector. The Pacific Islands are heavily dependent upon strategic imports, including fuel and food items such as rice and wheat flour, the costs of which rose substantially in 2008, and to a lesser degree again in 2011. Reliant upon foreign investment and overseas aid to overcome the inherent limitations of scale and resources, the Pacific Islands thus remain vulnerable to external economic developments and to environmental factors, such as the recurrence of devastating cyclones.

The volatility of international petroleum prices from 2006 adversely affected the public finances and foreign-exchange reserves of the Pacific Islands. As fuel prices rose, trade deficits continued to widen. The steep rise in petroleum prices resulted in much higher import bills, with corresponding increases in business costs and household expenses. The high rates of inflation that prevailed in 2008 were unprecedented in many of the islands, thus reducing the purchasing power of households. The impact of increased petroleum prices once again highlighted the need for the Pacific Islands to introduce alternative sources of energy, such as solar power, wind power and biofuels. A coconut oil-diesel fuel blend was being promoted as a biofuel substitute for electricity generation in Vanuatu and Samoa. The Pacific Petroleum Project (see below) was initiated by the Pacific Islands Forum with the objective of reducing the costs of the region's oil imports. A renewable energy project for 11 Pacific Islands, costing US $5.2m., was being conducted by the Secretariat of the Pacific Regional Environment Programme (SPREP) in 2011. Funded by the Global Environment Facility, the Pacific Islands Greenhouse Gas Abatement through Renewable Energy Project (PIGGAREP) included a scheme to introduce solar power to homes in Solomon Islands.

Conversely, being both a producer and a refiner, Papua New Guinea greatly benefited from the particularly sharp rise in world petroleum prices in 2008. As an exporter, Papua New Guinea was also able to take advantage of increasing prices for other minerals, including copper and gold. While most Pacific Islands had to draw down their international reserves in order to pay the higher import bills, Solomon Islands and Vanuatu were able to manage their reserves better because of larger aid inflows.

The issue of food security in the Pacific Islands has become a serious concern. In September 2011 a report released by the ADB warned that climate change was likely to lead to rising levels of hunger and malnutrition in the Pacific Islands, noting that since the mid-1960s the region's dependence on imported food had greatly increased. The ADB urged the Pacific region to focus on the production of more climate-resistant crops and to secure investment for the introduction of new and more robust varieties. The report also recommended more training in plant breeding and resource management.

By the latter part of 2011 several Pacific Islands were being seriously affected by a prolonged lack of rainfall. At considerable expense, emergency supplies were delivered from elsewhere in the region. As drought conditions intensified, the critical shortage of fresh water necessitated the declaration of a state of emergency in Tuvalu. Tokelau was also particularly badly affected, as were the northern Cook Islands. In Samoa output of hydroelectricity was curtailed by the low water levels.

Also in September 2011, the World Health Organization and the Secretariat of the Pacific Community issued a statement warning that the Pacific Islands' economic and social development was being seriously undermined by the increasing pressure being placed on health services by the substantial rise in lifestyle diseases such as diabetes.

Furthermore, a report entitled 'The State of Pacific Youth 2011—Opportunities and Obstacles', published in September of that year jointly by UNICEF and the Secretariat of the Pacific Community, concluded that the situation of the region's young people had changed little since the last report of 2005. Unemployment, the lack of educational opportunities, poverty, hunger and lack of access to services remained major issues for young Pacific islanders.

DEVELOPMENT AID AND INVESTMENT

During 2003–06 an Australian non-governmental policy institution, the Centre for Independent Studies (CIS), issued three reviews on the issue of aid to the Pacific Islands, one of which carried the provocative title 'Aid has Failed the Pacific'. The criticism was based on the empirical findings that poor growth performance was due to the ineffective use of aid, which had totalled US $50,000m. during the previous 30 years, and that most of this aid had been spent on consumption by bureaucracies and government élites, having been diverted from the intended purposes, as aid was often considered fungible.

In the context of significant concerns for security and stability, especially in Melanesia, in early 2007 the Australian Minister for Foreign Affairs announced changes in aid policy, conceding that some of the formulas of the past had not been as successful as hoped. Noting that recent average population growth rates in Papua New Guinea, Solomon Islands and Vanuatu had been 2.5% per year or higher, that more than 40% of the population of Solomon Islands was under 15 years of age and that the incidence of HIV/AIDS in Papua New Guinea was increasing, Australia began to consider ways of refocusing its aid to the Pacific Islands. Australian development assistance to the Pacific Islands rose from $A922.7m. in 2008/09 to an estimated $A1,024.9m. in 2009/10. The projected total for 2010/11 was $A1,085.4m., the largest recipient being Papua New Guinea.

The change of government in Australia in late 2007 opened a new phase in relations between Australia and the Pacific Islands. In March 2008, after discussions with Papua New Guinea, recently appointed Prime Minister Kevin Rudd announced Australia's new policy framework, Pacific Partnerships for Development. The resultant Port Moresby Declaration stated that Australia would work closely with island governments to help them meet the UN's MDGs. In particular, aid programmes would specifically aim at improving economic development and enhancing local employment opportunities through infrastructure projects and broadly based growth. Australia's aid to the Pacific Islands was increased in 2008. Total aid over the subsequent four years, for the improvement of services such as transport, sanitation, waste management, energy and communications, was projected at $A127m. In addition, under a separate Public Sector Capacity Project, $A107m. was to be spent during the next four years, with $A6m. in 2008/09 being allocated to the strengthening of public administration, including management and policy reform. The administration of Julia Gillard, who replaced Kevin Rudd in mid-2010, did not immediately implement any substantial changes of policy towards the Pacific Islands. Australia's commitment to the region was reiterated. During his first official visit to the region in October the new Parliamentary Secretary for Pacific Island Affairs, Richard Marles, emphasized the particular importance of Australia's relationship with Papua New Guinea.

Australia's allocation of official development assistance to Papua New Guinea, the leading recipient, reached an estimated $A445.9m. in 2009/10, with an increase to $A457.2m. projected for 2010/11. Australian aid to Fiji totalled an estimated $A35.9m. in 2009/10, with a sum of $A37.2m. projected for 2010/11. Aid levels for better performers such as Vanuatu, where economic growth remained robust, and Samoa, which continued its reform efforts, were maintained at relatively high levels. Vanuatu received an estimated $A60.3m. from Australia in 2009/10 and was to be allocated a projected $A66.4m. in 2010/11. Vanuatu also benefited from a grant of US $66m., awarded under the US Millennium Foundation Programme, for the period 2007–11. Having reached an estimated $A40.6m. in 2009/10, Australian aid to Samoa was budgeted at $A39.8m. in 2010/11. Solomon Islands received an estimated $A212.5m. in Australian aid in 2009/10, with a total of $A225.7m. being envisaged for 2010/11.

In June 2008 the New Zealand Government announced details of the new Pacific Development Strategy Plan, which encompassed a new approach to bilateral aid. This more focused approach to regional programmes envisaged expenditure in excess of $NZ2,000m. over an eight-year period. New Zealand's official development assistance to the Pacific Islands was to amount to 70% of its total bilateral aid. The aid allocations were expected to make a substantial impact on the improvement of health and education in the Pacific; to address infrastructure shortcomings and to promote economic growth; and to improve governance and leadership. In 2008/09 Solomon Islands and Papua New Guinea received the largest allocations of New Zealand development assistance in the region, being granted $NZ32.8m. and $NZ23.0m., respectively. The new Government that took office in New Zealand in late 2008 upheld the country's commitments to the Pacific Islands, while indicating its intention to bring the provision of development assistance more into line with trade and foreign policy objectives. New Zealand's allocation of official development assistance to the Pacific Islands in 2009/10 was projected to total $NZ253.3m.

Taking advantage of Fiji's strained political relations with neighbouring Australia and New Zealand, China announced rises in aid to Fiji for 2007 and 2008. In 2005 China's aid to Fiji was only US $1m., but by 2007 grants and loans had increased substantially, to reach US $167m. This represented more than one-half of China's total annual aid to the entire Pacific region and was much higher than the total of Australian aid pledged to Fiji in 2007–08. Chinese aid to Fiji included low-interest loans of US $150m. for the purposes of infrastructure development, including a hydropower project. Following the signing in late 2010 of a bilateral agreement confirming China's allocation of US $4.5m., in September 2011 the Chinese President announced that further financial assistance, of $6.2m., was to be provided to Fiji. In the same month it was confirmed that work had commenced on the construction in Veisari of a cement factory, a Chinese company having been one of the first major investors to respond to Cdre Bainimarama's invitation to establish businesses in Fiji. With a 99-year lease, the cement factory agreement represented an investment of $20m.

Owing to the fact that Chinese aid is provided without preconditions relating to issues such as improvements in human rights and governance, China's financial support for various projects in the region has caused concern in the USA and elsewhere. In June 2009 Australia urged greater transparency in the provision of Chinese aid to Fiji and elsewhere. A report released by an Australian institute in April 2011 stated that since 2005 China had pledged a total of US $600m. to the Pacific region. The report also noted that these funds were increasingly taking the form of 'soft' loans, rather than grants.

Amid ongoing suggestions of 'dollar diplomacy', in 2011 several Pacific nations maintained diplomatic relations with Taiwan, which has continued to provide support for various bilateral projects (in areas such as agriculture, fisheries and tourism), along with other aid. However, the use of some of this aid has proved controversial. In November 2005 the Prime Minister of Solomon Islands became involved in controversy with regard to the allocation of Taiwanese financing, and an audit subsequently revealed that millions of dollars could not be accounted for. In March 2010, during an official visit to Solomon Islands, the Taiwanese President reportedly commented that misuse of Taiwanese aid was unacceptable and urged greater transparency. Taiwan has also provided substantial aid to the Marshall Islands. In 2004 it was announced that Taiwan was to contribute more than US $40m. over a 20-year period to a Marshall Islands trust fund. In January 2011, however, the issue of accountability requirements was raised when Taiwan's full disbursement of a quarterly sum intended for development projects in the Marshall Islands was postponed for more than two months, pending the islands' compilation of a satisfactory report relating to the use of a previous quarterly payment. Taiwanese funding was reported to account for almost 8% of total annual budgetary expenditure in the Marshall Islands. In September 2006, following financial difficulties, the national airline of Nauru was able to resume operations after Taiwan provided sufficient funding for the Government's acquisition of an aircraft. In February 2009 the Government of Taiwan provided a stimulus grant of US $3.2m. to Palau, for the purposes of infrastructural improvements.

The acceptance of aid from elsewhere has been similarly controversial. For example, in December 2009 it was reported that in exchange for Russian aid Nauru had granted diplomatic recognition to the secessionist republics of Abkhazia and South Ossetia. Nauru's recognition of these separatist regions of Georgia attracted much international criticism. The Nauruan Minister of Foreign Affairs declined to confirm precise details of the financial arrangements, but the aid in question was believed to total US $50m.

The smaller island states such as Tuvalu and Kiribati have placed their aid resources into trust funds established under parliamentary statutes. The respective acts of parliament stipulated that trust funds should be maintained and invested by internationally reputable financial investment houses; limited the government's recurrent budget that could be financed by revenue earned from the returns on investments; and restricted the use of trust fund money to investment purposes only, with the condition that funds so drawn from the trusts be returned over a given period and that they be maintained in real terms. The trust funds of Tuvalu and Kiribati have served as models for the northern Pacific Islands, namely the Marshall Islands, the Federated States of Micronesia and Palau, which were formerly part of the US Trust Territory of the Pacific Islands. All three countries had been receiving annual grants from the USA under their respective long-term Compacts of Free Association. The Marshall Islands and the Federated States of Micronesia established trust funds to manage the annual aid inflows that were anticipated under the terms of their Compacts. In 1994, one year after gaining its independence, Palau created a trust fund under its first Compact with the USA.

LABOUR MOBILITY

In 2006, following its examination of the issue of the export to Australia and New Zealand of unskilled Pacific islanders as seasonal agricultural labourers on temporary work permits, the World Bank released a report entitled *At Home and Away: Expanding Job Opportunities for Pacific Islanders Through Labour Mobility*. The report recommended the introduction of trial schemes, observing that labour mobility 'could make a significant contribution towards enhancing economic and social stability in the region'. The World Bank initiative arose largely from the recognition of the inability of the smaller Pacific Islands to take full advantage of the greater access to overseas markets offered by trade agreements with other Pacific Islands and the European Union (EU) and from the acknowledgement of their negligible manufacturing capacity and limited natural resources.

New Zealand's official reaction to the World Bank's proposals was more positive than that of Australia. Under intense pressure from New Zealand's farming interests to meet shortages in seasonal labour availability for fruit picking and packaging, the Government ventured to launch pilot schemes, in consultation with Pacific Island countries, with a view to recruiting around 3,000 unskilled farm labourers over a period of three years. Vanuatu was the first beneficiary. Officially designated as the Recognized Seasonal Employer (RSE) scheme, the programme was initiated by the Prime Minister of Vanuatu in April 2007, when the first workers left for New Zealand. According to the Vanuatu Government, New Zealand granted entry to the total of 300 workers permitted under the RSE scheme during 2007. In May 2009 it was reported that Vanuatu had contributed about one-half of the 5,000 seasonal workers eligible for the programme. Tonga, Samoa, Kiribati and Tuvalu also began to participate in the scheme, which was welcomed by the operators of New Zealand's vineyards and orchards. Despite some early difficulties, notably relating to the provision and costs of accommodation in New Zealand, in a report issued in March 2010 the scheme was declared to have been a generally useful and positive initiative.

Similarly, Australian farmers renewed requests to their Government for the introduction of a comparable scheme to meet their shortages of seasonal farm labour. The Government of Kevin Rudd, which took office in late 2007, announced that it would give favourable consideration to a scheme providing for guest workers from the Pacific Islands to work in orchards and plantations after assessing the first year of New Zealand's experience in this regard. Following the successful implementation of the New Zealand scheme, therefore, in November 2008 the Australian Government signed memorandums of understanding (MOUs) with Tonga, Kiribati and Vanuatu. Over a three-year period as many as 2,500 visas were to be granted to Pacific islanders, permitting them to work in the Australian horticultural industry for up to seven months in any 12-month period. In February 2009 a total of 50 Tongans, the first of a projected 800 from the country, travelled to south-eastern Australia to start work there. Evaluations of the effectiveness of the trial scheme were to be conducted after 18 months and after 30 months of operation. However, the weakening of the global economy resulted in the availability of fewer employment opportunities than had originally been envisaged, and by July 2010 only 123 visas had been issued to Tongan workers. In the same month, however, Papua New Guinea and Australia signed an MOU providing for the participation of Papua New Guinean workers in the Pacific Seasonal Worker Pilot Scheme.

Nevertheless, the benefit to local communities of the above arrangements was demonstrated in August 2011 when it was reported from Vanuatu that six seasonal workers had used earnings from their temporary employment in New Zealand to fund the establishment of a health centre in their village.

In September 2011 Australia announced that the seasonal scheme was to be expanded to encompass four additional countries, namely Nauru, Samoa, Solomon Islands and Tuvalu. Meanwhile, Australian employers in the hospitality and tourism industries expressed hopes that the agricultural scheme might be extended to permit Pacific islanders to be engaged for temporary work in their branches of the tertiary sector. Furthermore, legislation to reduce the tax liabilities of seasonal workers was under consideration by the Australian Parliament in the latter part of 2011.

'OFFSHORE' FINANCIAL SERVICES

In the latter part of the 20th century some Pacific Islands, particularly countries such as Vanuatu where little or no revenue was derived from direct tax on either personal incomes or company receipts, encouraged the development of 'offshore' financial centres (OFCs). Following the attacks on the USA in September 2001, however, the Cook Islands, Nauru, Niue, Samoa and Vanuatu came under increasing scrutiny, owing to suspicions of money-laundering and other criminal activities, as well as possible links to terrorist organizations. Aware of the unsolicited adverse publicity, those Pacific Islands with OFCs made efforts to improve their image by conforming to the international standards prescribed by the Paris-based Financial Action Task Force (FATF), the Organisation for Economic Co-operation and Development (OECD) and the IMF.

In October 2005 Nauru became the last of the Pacific Islands to be removed from the FATF list of non-co-operative countries and territories. The region was aware that any islands remaining on the 'black list' would have risked the imposition of sanctions, including higher risk premiums on local firms when making transactions with international companies, the termination of correspondence alliances between local banks and banks based in OECD countries, and the rejection of letters of credit issued by local banks. In April 2009, however, OECD included the Cook Islands on its so-called 'grey list': while committed to the internationally agreed tax standard, the countries and territories listed by OECD had yet to implement substantial measures to combat tax evasion. The Marshall Islands, Nauru and Vanuatu (which had previously been removed from the OECD 'black list') were also included on the 'grey list', as were Niue and Samoa. In response, the Government of the Cook Islands stated that priority would be given to enacting the necessary legislative amendments, and requested assistance from the Group of 20 (G20) leading industrial countries. The Government of the Cook Islands made significant progress throughout 2009 in negotiating agreements on tax information exchange with other nations. By mid-2010 the Cook Islands had signed 11 such agreements, one short of the 12 required to be removed from the 'grey list'. Nevertheless, in February 2010 the French Government included the Cook Islands on a 'black list' of nations accused of a lack of transparency in tax reporting.

TRADE AND CO-OPERATION

Increasing globalization and the new environment of freer trade under the auspices of the World Trade Organization (WTO) have presented further challenges for the Pacific Islands. Widening trade deficits have required additional efforts to explore new export items and to develop niche markets for exclusive products such as noni juice (also known as nonu, a fruit renowned for its medicinal properties), bottled natural water and off-season fruits and vegetables, for example squash sales to the northern hemisphere.

The issue of access to Australian markets under the South Pacific Regional Trade and Economic Co-operation Agreement (SPARTECA, which entered into force in 1981 with the aim of redressing the trade deficit of the Pacific Island countries with Australia and New Zealand) has become less significant. Australian tariffs on imports of products such as copra, coconut milk and cream, and other agricultural products from cheaper sources in other regions were reduced. However, competition from rival economies in Asia continued to increase. Having found themselves unable to attract substantial foreign direct investment in the immediate past, the Pacific Islands sought to co-operate and offer an assured regional market of 7m. consumers. However, various studies have shown that the implementation of free trade in goods with Australia and New Zealand would involve higher adjustment costs than those relating to revised arrangements with the EU (see below), given the greater magnitude of the Pacific Islands' volume of trade with Australia and New Zealand. The revenue losses that would result from the abolition of tariffs on imports from Australia and New Zealand would need to be offset by means of the imposition of other taxes, including value-added tax.

In 2003 the islands of the region signed a Pacific Island Countries Trade Agreement (PICTA), aiming to establish a free trade area among the 14 Pacific Islands by 2010. It was decided that Australia and New Zealand, the two advanced member countries of the Pacific Islands Forum, the regional organization involved, were to be excluded from the free trade area. The Pacific Islands were clearly concerned about the prospect of the immediate removal of trade barriers and the impact that this would have, not only on local consumer goods industries but also on government finances from the resultant loss of tariff revenue. The Pacific Islands believed PICTA to be a move towards a closer relationship with the two advanced members of the Forum, including free trade in goods and services as well as mobility of labour, and Australia and New Zealand tacitly agreed.

Australia and New Zealand were successful in persuading the Pacific Islands to sign another accord, the Pacific Agreement on Closer Economic Relations (PACER), which entered into force in 2002. PACER obliged the Pacific Islands to begin negotiations with Australia and New Zealand by April 2011 with a view to establishing a larger free trade area by 2015.

Partly in response to the problem of the overwhelming complexity of trade arrangements, in 2003 an Eminent Persons Group appointed by the Pacific Islands Forum travelled around the region, meeting numerous leaders from different sectors, and prepared a Pacific Vision report. The Pacific Island leaders met in Auckland, New Zealand, in April 2004 to consider the Group's report, on the basis of which they agreed to develop a Pacific Plan. The Pacific Plan Task Force (PPTF) was also established, with specific terms of reference. Consultation procedures began and a time frame for preparing a draft document was agreed. The final document was presented to the Pacific Island Forum Leaders' Meeting in Port Moresby in Papua New Guinea in December 2005.

The Pacific Plan was based upon four objectives: economic growth, sustainable development, good governance and security. Specifically, with regard to economic growth, the Pacific Plan sought to integrate trade in services, including temporary provisions for the movement of labour during the course of PICTA and PACER negotiations, and to develop the capacity for bulk-purchasing of essential items such as fuel and medicines. While the latter had been on the agenda since 1971 without any progress, the inclusion of trade in services indicated the willingness of the Pacific Islands to consider deeper integration on the right terms. Consequently, the two advanced Forum member countries were obliged to consider relaxing immigration laws for temporary workers from the Pacific Islands seeking employment in Australia and New Zealand on farms and in other unskilled positions that could not be filled by local workers, a situation that had resulted in shortages of manual labour. Greater involvement by Australia and New Zealand in the region addressed the second, third and fourth objectives of the Pacific Plan. Expert advice on financial management and public sector reform was provided.

In response to increasing criticism that preferential trade agreements were incompatible with WTO principles, the EU originally intended to terminate agreements for such preferential treatment of the products of the Pacific Islands by 2007. The Sugar Protocol governing Fiji's exports to the EU under the Cotonou Agreement, signed in 2000 and ratified in 2003 by 77 African, Caribbean and Pacific (ACP) countries, was also due to expire at the end of 2007. The Pacific Islands were therefore obliged to give some consideration to the restructuring of their export industries, such as sugar and tuna-processing, in order to compete with the rest of the world for access to EU markets. It was envisaged that the islands would accelerate and promote regional integration, along similar lines to those of the trade agreement of the Melanesian Spearhead Group (see below). Discussions on Economic Partnership Agreements (EPAs), which were to form an important new element of the Cotonou Agreement, began in 2004. However, the prospect of the EPAs presented difficulties for the Pacific Islands, which came under pressure from the EU to finalize an agreement by the deadline of 31 December 2007. The EU had already announced that it would phase out the preferential price for sugar by 2010 through a 35% reduction over a three-year period. Following an extension of the negotiation period, discussions continued in 2009. By October of that year 25 ACP states had signed, and 11 states had initialled (but not yet signed), full or interim EPAs, covering the liberalization of goods and agricultural products. However, the EPAs attracted some criticism for their focus on trade liberalization and their perceived failure to acknowledge the widespread poverty of ACP countries. The second five-yearly review of the Cotonou Agreement was completed in March 2010.

Efforts to forge a collective regional approach in trade negotiations suffered a serious set-back in November 2007 when Fiji and Papua New Guinea broke ranks and signed independent agreements with the EU. The latter insisted on signing an EPA either before the end of 2007 or at interim dates and on an individual basis. Fiji and Papua New Guinea found it necessary to sign interim agreements to protect their trading interests (sugar exports in the case of Fiji and tuna and coffee exports in the case of Papua New Guinea), as they could not persuade other Pacific Islands to come to a common understanding with regard to services, investment and intellectual property rights, which were added to the agreement at the insistence of the EU. An interim trade agreement with the EU brought great advantages to Fiji. In May 2008 the Fiji Sugar Corporation (FSC) signed a $F2,000m. agreement for the supply of raw sugar at preferential prices for the next seven years. The contract for the supply of 300,000 metric tons of sugar per year was concluded with the traditional EU market buyer Tate & Lyle, the largest cane sugar refiner in the EU and which had been trading with the FSC since the inception of the ACP-EU Sugar Protocol in 1975. (By 2010, however, the FSC was reported to be in serious financial difficulty—see below.)

The Pacific Islands were in fact unlikely to derive great benefit from EPAs, as trade in goods with the EU represented no more than 10% of their combined total trade. Of this total, Fiji and Papua New Guinea generally accounted for some 90%. Moreover, Fiji and Papua New Guinea already had duty-free access to the EU market. The other Pacific Islands, which were designated as least developed countries, were also eligible for tariff-free access to the EU under its 'everything but arms' policy. Thus, the Pacific Islands were not actively interested in EPAs.

The free trade envisaged by the agreement of the Melanesian Spearhead Group, which was signed in 1993 long before PICTA, was disrupted by a disagreement between two of the group's members in early 2008 when the quarantine authorities of Fiji sent back two containers of kava to Vanuatu on the pretext that greater scrutiny was required at the port of origin. (The other members of the Melanesian Spearhead Group are Papua New Guinea and Solomon Islands.) In July 2010, furthermore, the annual meeting of the Melanesian Spearhead Group, which had been scheduled to convene in Fiji, was postponed on account of the political situation in that country. With Fijian leader Cdre Frank Bainimarama thus being unable to assume the chair of the sub-regional grouping, a protracted impasse followed. Having completed its report on the chairmanship issue, in September a three-member Eminent Persons Group submitted its findings to the outgoing Chairman, the Prime Minister of Vanuatu, Edward Natapei. Fiji was permitted to assume the chairmanship, following Natapei's removal from the premiership of Vanuatu in December.

The Pacific Islands Forum Secretariat decided to undertake a feasibility study on the possibility of the establishment of a Pacific Single Market and Economy (PSME), upon which work continued in 2009; however, some analysts remained sceptical about the likelihood of any significant progress being made.

Meeting in Samoa in June 2009, trade ministers from the Pacific Islands, Australia and New Zealand made swift progress in their discussions on the establishment of a free trade area, as a result of which it was unanimously agreed that it would be recommended to their respective leaders that formal negotiations commence. In August, therefore, at a meeting of the Pacific Islands Forum, leaders agreed that negotiations on a new regional trade and economic integration accord, to be known as PACER-Plus, should commence immediately. The initial PACER-Plus negotiations were to be attended by representatives of Australia, the Cook Islands, Kiribati, the Marshall Islands, the Federated States of Micronesia, Nauru, New Zealand, Niue, Palau, Papua New Guinea, Samoa, Solomon Islands, Tonga, Tuvalu and Vanuatu. The process formally commenced in October at a meeting in the Australian city of Brisbane, where regional trade ministers agreed that national consultations should be widened. In October 2010 the Pacific Islands Forum Secretariat conducted its first comprehensive annual consultations with representatives of the private sector and of non-government organizations on the issue of PACER-Plus.

However, progress continued to be impeded by the absence of Fiji, this important regional trading partner having been excluded by its political situation and its failure to hold early democratic elections. Although the continuation of Fiji's suspension from the Pacific Islands Forum was confirmed in September 2011, the country was invited to participate in PACER-Plus discussions; Fiji was reported to have declined the invitation.

Convening in New Zealand in September 2011, the members of the Pacific Islands Forum emphasized the need for a successful conclusion to the EPA negotiations in 2012. Regional leaders also agreed that negotiations on PICTA and PACER-Plus should be advanced as matters of priority, urging those countries that had yet to complete their arrangements to trade under PICTA to do so promptly.

Another major challenge for trade negotiators was the difficulty of maintaining unity, in view of the wide differences among the 16 member economies of the Pacific Islands Forum and the variations in the nature of the individual relationships with Australia and New Zealand. Some Pacific activists, notably those involved with local trade unions, church groups and indigenous rights organizations, maintained that there had been inadequate consultation with the region about the development of the Pacific Islands' trade relationship with Australia and New Zealand. Prior to a meeting of the Pacific Islands Forum held in Vanuatu in August 2010, regional leaders were therefore urged to impose a moratorium on the negotiations for PACER-Plus. Meanwhile, critics claimed that PACER-Plus would not only jeopardize the industries and jobs of the Pacific Islands but also, owing to the projected decrease in receipts from import tariffs, reduce government revenue.

Following the particularly steep increase in international oil prices in 2008, the Pacific Petroleum Project was instigated by the Pacific Islands Forum, with the aim of reducing the region's high energy costs through collective negotiations for the bulk procurement of petroleum supplies and, it was envisaged, economies of scale. By mid-2009 the resultant MOU had been signed by four of the Forum's members, namely the Cook Islands, Nauru, Niue and Tuvalu. The Marshall Islands signed the MOU in August 2010.

Another example of regional co-operation is commercial fishing. Within the eight signatories' exclusive economic zones fishing is regulated by the Parties to the Nauru Agreement (PNA), namely the Federated States of Micronesia, Kiribati, the Marshall Islands, Nauru, Palau, Papua New Guinea, Solomon Islands and Tuvalu. The agreement permits the trading of 'fishing days' among members of the alliance, and in August 2011 the arrangement was reported to be yielding particular benefits to the Marshall Islands and the Federated States of Micronesia, both of which had sold spare capacity to Papua New Guinea and received revenue of US $1m. In September the PNA warned that fishing companies that refused to co-operate with them would lose access to the lucrative tuna fisheries. Amid some controversy, in the latter part of 2011 the Cook Islands was in the process of of finalizing licences for Chinese fishing vessels to explore the possibilities for catches of bigeye tuna, skipjack and swordfish.

COUNTRY ANALYSES

The economy of Fiji was seriously affected by the military coup of December 2006. Foreign investment approvals decreased substantially. In November 2008, as the global economic situation continued to deteriorate, the Government of Fiji announced a reduction in corporation tax. Various islands, including Vanua Levu and Rotuma, were declared tax-free regions, in the hope of stimulating growth through increased investment. Other measures announced as part of the Government's budget for 2009 were tax concessions for capital investment in the tourism industry and the sector's exemption from import duties on essential items. Incentives for the agricultural sector, such as tax concessions for the establishment of new projects in agro-processing activities in addition to commercial farming, were also to be made available.

Fiji's exports have weakened in recent years and the costs of imports have increased, resulting in large trade deficits. The problem of rising deficits was compounded from 2004 by the closure of the country's gold mine and by a decline in sugar production. Consumer items have traditionally been imported from Australia and New Zealand. Singapore has also become an significant source of imports. Fiji's trade deficit reached an estimated US $1,184.1m. in 2008. This was largely due to the increased costs of fuel and food imports in that year. Furthermore, the weak export performance was exacerbated by the decline in garment exports that followed the ending of the US quotas for Fiji's garments under the Multi-fibre Arrangement at the end of 2004. In 2009 the country's sugar industry sustained heavy losses, owing to flood damage early in the year, the immediate impact of the devaluation of the currency in April (see below) and the decline in investment. Moreover, in July 2010, the FSC was reported to be planning the dismissal of 1,000 workers. With the FSC having regularly incurred substantial financial losses since the mid-1990s, the retrenchment programme was expected to be completed by the end of 2011. Pending the restoration of democracy, meanwhile, the EU continued to withhold aid for Fiji's sugar industry. Fiji has therefore been obliged to identify and promote new export products, such as bottled mineral water, in an attempt to offset its growing deficits. Nevertheless, in mid-2011 foreign reserves were reported to have reached US $879m., the highest level ever recorded and sufficient to cover 4.5 months of imports of goods and services.

Fiji's current account deficit reached the equivalent of 18.0% of GDP in 2008, before declining in 2009 and 2010, standing at 7.4% in the latter year. Inward remittances from Fijians working overseas, notably teachers, nurses, security personnel, rugby players and seafarers, have become another significant source of revenue, surpassing receipts from sugar exports. Remittances in 2007 remained at the same level as those in 2006 (about $F250m.). Although the value of remittances was reported to have increased in 2009, this was mainly due to the devaluation of the Fijian dollar (see below). Tourist arrivals decreased significantly in 2006–07, but began to recover in 2008. However, earnings from tourism declined from $F853.8m. in 2008 to $F816.9m. in 2009, before rising to $F979.8m. in 2010. Although there was a strong recovery in terms of visitor numbers in 2010, when arrivals reached 631,868, the deep discounting of prices and the costs of overseas marketing campaigns significantly curbed net revenue from the tourism sector.

Fiji has repeatedly recorded fiscal deficits, equivalent to an estimated 3.6% of GDP in 2010. Borrowing from the public and from institutions, including the Fiji National Provident Fund, financed these deficits. Following the emergence of a crisis at the Fiji National Provident Fund in 2011 as a result of failed investments in the tourism sector, it was announced that substantial reductions were to be made in retirement pensions. A stringent monetary stance adopted by the Reserve Bank of Fiji, the central bank, along with credit 'ceilings' and imposition of exchange controls from early 2007, contributed to exchange rate stability. However, during the political upheaval of April 2009 the central bank building was occupied by the military, and the Governor was peremptorily removed from office. His replacement immediately announced a 20% devaluation of the Fijian currency, with the intention of increasing exports and of revitalizing the tourism sector. Exchange controls were imposed in an attempt to prevent capital flight from the country. The country's rate of inflation rose from 3.7% in 2009 to 7.8% in 2010, with a a similar level anticipated in 2011. Fiji's GDP contracted by 1.3% in 2009 and expanded by only 0.3% in 2010. A modest improvement, with growth forecast by the ADB at 1.2%, was anticipated in 2011. A copper-mining project was scheduled to commence operations in Namosi in 2012. Requiring investment of $F2,000m., the joint venture was expected to provide a major boost to Fiji's economy. In 2011, however, the Governor of the central bank, as well as consumer groups, expressed concern with regard to the high rates of loan interest and the low volume of new lending by the country's banks.

As an exporter of various commodities, Papua New Guinea benefited from the favourable external conditions that prevailed until mid-2008. The oil and gas sector registered strong growth from 2005, as supply responded to rising international prices. Two new gold mines were opened in 2006. In addition, the agricultural sector performed well, achieving increases in output of several exportable products, including coffee, which benefited from higher world prices. The world-wide commodity boom in 2007 contributed in a substantial measure to the country's good performance. Its GDP growth rates remained among the region's highest, at 6.6% in 2008 and 5.5% in 2009, rising to 8.0% in 2010, when the economy expanded for the ninth consecutive year. Papua New Guinea's GDP growth rate was projected to rise to 8.5% in 2011.

A US $10,000m. liquefied natural gas (LNG) project, being undertaken by an international consortium led by ExxonMobil of the USA, was expected to provide a major stimulus to the economy of Papua New Guinea. Preparatory work for the construction of a 700-km pipeline from Southern Highlands to the capital of Port Moresby commenced in 2010, with the project scheduled for completion by 2014. The consortium was expected to allocate more than K2,000m. for the upgrading of the Highlands Highway during the construction stage. It was reported that in the second quarter of 2011 the project workforce had expanded substantially, to reach a total of 9,000 employees. A second major LNG project was under negotiation in late 2010. The development of the Chinese-owned Ramu nickel/cobalt mine in Madang Province, which was expected to provide substantial revenue when fully operational, continued in 2010. Fishing is an important sector in Papua New Guinea: the tuna catch in 2010 reached 749,000 metric tons, reportedly representing about 17% of the world's catch. It was reported in August 2011 that three major fish canneries, which were expected to provide a total of 20,000 jobs, were to be established in the country.

In 2009 a fiscal deficit equivalent to 14.3% of GDP was recorded in Papua New Guinea; however, the deficit was reduced to 0.5% in 2010. The rate of inflation decreased from 6.9% in 2009 to 6.0% in 2010, but was expected to rise in 2011. Public debt declined to 35% of GDP in 2007 (in comparison with 80% in 2002) and was expected to decrease further in 2008–10. The favourable commodity prices for gold, copper, petroleum and timber that prevailed until mid-2008 resulted in an improvement in export earnings, thereby enabling Papua New Guinea to record another current account surplus. The Government also benefited from an increase in its revenue from taxes on the mining sector. The national currency, the kina, based on a floating exchange rate regime, remained strong, having appreciated against major currencies. Increases in international reserves and the strength of the currency provided conditions conducive to investment. The current account moved into deficit in 2009, and in 2010 the deficit was estimated by the ADB to have reached 26.6% of GDP, with an increase to 35.9% forecast for 2011.

Analysts reiterated that the strong revenues earned from commodities should be appropriately invested in Papua New Guinea's infrastructure, public services and urban policing. The challenge for the authorities remained that of how best to utilize export earnings to improve roads and communications, educational opportunities for children and the country's health facilities. The establishment of a sovereign wealth fund was under consideration.

Solomon Islands experienced a slow but remarkable recovery from the aftermath of civil unrest and near-collapse of the economy during 1999–2003. With appropriate policies in place and, from 2003, support from Australia through the Regional Assistance Mission to Solomon Islands (RAMSI), the economy continued to expand in 2008, when GDP rose by 7.3%. Most of the expansion was due to strong performance in the areas of agriculture, construction and trade (both in the wholesale and retail sectors). Exports of logs rose to a new high point of some 1.1m. cu m in 2006, a volume considered to be unsustainable. Log exports accounted for about 66% of total commodity exports in that year, contributing 10% of GDP and 14% of tax revenue. Sales of timber accounted for a similar percentage of export earnings in 2007. However, a substantial reduction in receipts from log exports was subsequently reported. In 2009 the country's GDP contracted by 1.2%. Owing to unexpectedly strong prices for the country's commodity exports, GDP growth reached 7.2% in 2010, with a similar rate of growth envisaged for 2011. In March 2010, with financial assistance from the ADB, a two-year economic recovery support programme was announced.

Substantial aid inflows and technical assistance to the Ministry of Finance and strategic industries under RAMSI enabled the restoration of fiscal stability in Solomon Islands. In 2010 a budget surplus, estimated to be equivalent to 2.4% of GDP, was achieved. Public debt, most of which was external, remained high. The current account, which includes official transfers, remained in deficit in 2007–10, mainly as a result of the higher costs of fuel imports and purchases related to the gold-mining industry. In 2010 the current account deficit was equivalent to 27.6% of GDP, but a reduction was predicted for 2011. With persistent shortages continuing and subsistence agriculture making a slow recovery, the rate of inflation reached a high point of 17.3% in 2008, before declining to 1.0% in 2010. As inflationary pressures re-emerged in 2011, the Solomon Islands dollar was revalued upwards by 5% in June. International creditors agreed on a moratorium on the country's external debt-servicing obligations, with the expectation that the rehabilitation of the once-thriving Guadalcanal Plains Palm Oil company and other enterprises such as Gold Ridge Mining would begin contributing to growth in the coming years. Major challenges lay in the improvement of domestic infrastructure and services in remote islands. Furthermore, the country needed to raise the business skills of its citizens and improve their access to credit, in order to facilitate the establishment of small and medium-sized enterprises.

From 2003 Vanuatu recorded robust rates of GDP growth, in sharp contrast to the contractionary conditions that had prevailed during 2001–02. The improvement was largely due to strong growth in the tourism sector, facilitated by the introduction of additional flights to Vanuatu by Pacific Blue, a newly launched airline based in New Zealand, and a recovery in construction activity. Vanuatu's steady performance continued in 2008, when GDP expanded by 6.2%. Despite the deterioration in the global economy, it was reported that the number of international tourist arrivals in January 2009 was 30% higher than in January of the previous year. The tourism industry was further boosted by the increase in numbers of cruise ship visitors (arrivals by sea having trebled within five years). Vanuatu's tourism sector also benefited from the unrest in Fiji, although by mid-2010 this advantage had largely dissipated. GDP growth was estimated at 3.5% in 2009 and 2.2% in 2010, with an increase of about 3.0% anticipated in 2011.

As revenue collection in Vanuatu showed significant improvement, the budget surplus reached the equivalent of 2.2% of GDP in 2008 and 1.0% in 2009, before returning to deficit (2.1%) in 2010. The rate of inflation declined from 4.3% in 2009 to 2.8% in 2010. International reserves remained at a high level. The current account remained in deficit, reaching the equivalent of 11.1% of GDP in 2008, before declining to 8.2% in 2009 and 5.9% in 2010. The country was expected to pay greater attention to improving its export-earning possibilities, by providing greater access to agricultural produce in remote rural areas in outer islands through the provision of farm roads and links to markets and the construction of new jetties and ports. Major investment in infrastructure projects assisted by the US $65.6m. grant from the US Millennium Challenge Corporation (MCC) was expected to alleviate the long-standing deficiencies. However, in late 2008 the Government decided to defer 11 MCC projects, as the cost estimates for procurement by tendering companies had exceeded the originally approved estimates by the MCC. The cost overrun was mainly due to the weakening of the US currency. After the US Government insisted that all additional expenditures be borne by Vanuatu, the Government sought help from other donors, including Australia and New Zealand.

The successful completion in May 2011 of negotiations on Vanuatu's entry to the WTO, with accession scheduled for later in the year, was expected to lead to the country's closer integration into the global economy and to yield major benefits in the longer term.

From the mid-1990s Samoa's successful record of reform implementation earned the country much international praise. Expansion in the agriculture and fisheries sectors, along with hotel construction activities encouraged by the Tourism and Hotel Development Incentive Act of 2003, contributed to steady growth until 2007. However, the subsequent scaling down of production activities by Yazaki Samoa (a Japanese firm that since 1992 had been manufacturing automotive harness products in its Apia plant, taking advantage of Samoa's cheap labour) had a significant impact on the economy of Samoa, as did a decrease in agricultural output. The economy decelerated sharply in 2008, when GDP contracted by 3.2%.

Partly owing to a rise in visits by cruise-ships, tourist arrivals increased in 2009. However, a state of disaster was declared at the end of September 2009, when Samoa was devastated by a tsunami. The cost of repairing the damage incurred was estimated at US $38m. Subsequent economic activity therefore emanated largely from the construction industry, as repairs to infrastructure and tourist accommodation proceeded, along with other rehabilitation projects. Samoans resident overseas continued to send remittances, which form a significant portion of the country's GDP. Remittances from overseas workers were reported to have decreased by 9% in the year to June 2009. Although such remittances rose in the final quarter of 2009, the higher inflow was largely in response to the tsunami disaster of September, and remittances began to decrease in 2010. Following further contraction, of 1.7% in 2009 and of 0.2% in 2010, GDP growth of 2.1% was expected in 2011.

With revenue collection improving in Samoa, a fiscal surplus, equivalent to 1.2% of GDP, was achieved in 2007, in spite of the large public expenditure programme for the staging of the South Pacific Games, which were held in Samoa in that year. However, a fiscal deficit equivalent to 1.9% of GDP was recorded in 2008, rising to 8.1% in 2010. The rate of inflation decreased from 6.6% in 2009 to 1.2% in 2010, but was expected to rise in 2011. The Strategy for the Development of Samoa (2008–12) envisaged the further expansion of the tourism sector. It was hoped that an increase in tourism earnings would ease the current account situation, as earnings from traditional exports of coconut-based products were likely to continue to diminish. However, the current account recorded a deficit equivalent to 8.1% of GDP in 2010, with an increase to 12.9% anticipated in the following year. In early 2011, furthermore, Air New Zealand's decision to discontinue its service between Apia and the US city of Los Angeles drew much criticism in Samoa, which feared that a significant reduction in tourist arrivals would result (a negligible increase in arrivals having been recorded in 2010). In August 2011 it was reported that a Chinese entrepreneur had concluded a major agreement to import noni juice from Samoa to China. In the following month a Taiwanese company offered to construct a fish storage facility in Apia. Negotiations relating to the arrangements for Samoa's accession to the WTO were approaching completion in late 2011.

Tonga, another Polynesian country, experienced political turmoil in 2005, when mass movements for greater democracy developed; strike action by civil servants lasted for more than a month. The fiscal position deteriorated, as a result of an agreement with the civil service union to raise salaries by 60%–80%. In late 2006 the capital of Nuku'alofa was severely damaged during rioting, which resulted in the destruction of many businesses. China provided financial assistance for the rebuilding of Nuku'alofa. A decrease in tourism and in commercial activities followed in 2007, when GDP contracted by 1.4%. The poor performance of 2007 was also attributable to a decrease in export prices for squash, the country's major commodity, and a decline in Tonga's tuna catch. Having expanded by 2.0% in 2008, GDP contracted by 0.4% in 2009 and by 1.2% in 2010. Despite a rise in inward remittances, which have normally accounted for about one-half of the country's GDP, the current account deficit widened to reach 8.8% of GDP in 2008. A large inflow of remittances from Tongans working in New Zealand and in the US state of California have usually helped to sustain the economy, but such remittances were reported to have declined in real terms in 2007–08, as the deterioration in the economy of the USA reduced the availability of employment opportunities. Although the inflow of remittances remained subdued in 2009–10, the current account deficit decreased to 7.7% of GDP in 2009 and 4.8% in 2010. Tourism receipts have weakened significantly.

Owing to retrenchment in the civil service and to reduced spending, the Government achieved a budget surplus in 2007; this rose to the equivalent of 1.8% of GDP in 2008, but deficits were recorded in in 2009 and 2010. GDP was forecast to expand by only 0.5% in 2011. The annual rate of inflation decreased from 9.8% in 2008 to 5.0% in 2009 and further, to 2.0%, in 2010.

The Government's decision to borrow US $50m. from China for urban infrastructure development raised concerns about the sustainability of the country's debt in terms of future debt-servicing capability. A report released by the IMF in May 2009 drew attention to the country's difficulties in containing the public debt, owing to the recent increases in government borrowing in order to finance reconstruction projects in Nuku'alofa. In the private sector, the availability of credit continued to contract in 2010. The concerns of the IMF were reiterated by the ADB in a report published in March 2011 when attention was again drawn to the country's high level of indebtedness; the public debt was expected to reach 58.5% of GDP in the coming financial year. In June, however, the ADB reported that financial accountability had improved and released the second tranche, of US $5m., for Tonga's Economic Support Programme. During a visit to Australia in August the Prime Minister of Tonga sought additional development assistance to alleviate the debt crisis. Meanwhile, Tonga's debt to China alone was reported to have reached the equivalent of almost one-third of the country's GDP.

Elsewhere in Polynesia, economic growth in the Cook Islands, an associated state of New Zealand, has generally been sustained by the tourism sector. However, the number of tourist arrivals declined in 2008, when GDP contracted by 1.2%. Despite a recovery in tourist numbers in 2009, GDP contracted by 3.5%. The island of Aitutaki, a major tourist destination, suffered serious cyclone damage in February 2010. None the less, in that year total visitor arrivals rose, reaching 104,252. The rate of inflation increased in 2008, reaching 7.8%, but declined to 6.6% in 2009 and to 4.0% in the following year. GDP contracted by 0.1% in 2010; growth of 1.1% was anticipated in 2011.

Pearl oyster farming is an important industry, and in 2007 receipts from pearl exports totalled $NZ2.1m., equivalent to 30.3% of total export earnings in that year. In 2008 the budget deficit was estimated to have reached the equivalent of 0.8% of GDP; this deficit rose to an estimated 11.7% of GDP in 2009, before declining to 0.8% on 2010. The extent of a subsidy provided to Air New Zealand for transporting passengers to Rarotonga from Los Angeles has partly determined the Cook Islands' budget position. Government revenues had declined owing to a reduction in import duties, while outlay on cyclone recovery works raised public expenditure. A withholding tax, taking 15% of all interest earned on bank accounts within the islands, was reintroduced in September 2011. This measure was expected to raise significant revenue, much of which was to be allocated to the Government's continued subsidy of the Los Angeles–Rarotonga air link, vital to the islands' tourism industry. Following continued international criticism of the operations of the Cook Islands' 'offshore' financial sector, in 2009 such financial institutions were in the process of being abolished (see above). In September 2011 the ADB agreed to assist the Government of the Cook Islands in the administration of a programme to reform the public sector. Funded by Japan, the scheme aimed to redefine the size and scope of government.

The GDP of Kiribati contracted by 1.1% in 2008 and by 0.7% in 2009, with growth of 0.5% being estimated for 2010. GDP was expected to expand by 2.0% in 2011. From 2001 Kiribati experienced a steady decline in revenue from its sales of fishing licences to foreign fleets; however, receipts from fishing licences were reported to have risen from $A25.4m. in 2007 to $A32.2m. in 2008, accounting for 20% of total government revenue in the latter year. Kiribati depends heavily upon its fisheries resources and upon seafarers' inward remittances for sustaining levels of national income. Remittances, tuna-fishing licence fees and earnings from the Revenue Equalization Reserve Fund (RERF—an 'offshore' investment fund established with royalties from discontinued phosphate-mining operations) contribute a substantial portion of GDP. The level of emigrants' remittances remained stable in 2008, reaching an estimated US $8m. However, overseas employment opportunities were subsequently restricted by the deterioration in global economic conditions. In 2009 about 20% of I-Kiribati seafarers were reported to have lost their jobs, a development that in turn affected the country's retail sales and government tax receipts. It was hoped that the contraction in remittances from seafarers might be offset by an increase in seasonal demand for agricultural labourers in Australia and New Zealand, under new schemes whereby the two countries provided temporary work permits to Pacific islanders (see Labour Mobility, above).

Kiribati's weak position has been exacerbated by increases in recurrent and development expenditure. Budgetary shortfalls have been serviced by drawdowns from the country's trust fund, but if the assets of the RERF were to be maintained, such drawdowns were unsustainable, particularly in view of the volatility of global stock markets in 2008. (In that year the fund's value was estimated to have decreased by 20%.) However, budget surpluses equivalent to 1.7% and 0.6% of GDP were reported in 2009 and 2010, respectively. As Kiribati uses the Australian dollar as legal tender, and a major proportion of imports are purchased from Australia, the rate of inflation has generally remained low. However, inflation rose to 11.0% in 2008, before declining to 8.8% in 2009. A period of deflation followed in 2010, when consumer prices decreased by 2.8%. The 2008–11 National Sustainable Development Strategy focused on the areas of economic growth, poverty reduction, health and education, the environment, improved governance and the upgrading of the country's infrastructure. The Government embarked upon a programme of privatization in early 2011, with its sale to a Chinese enterprise of the Kiribati Supplies Company, a major provider of construction materials and fittings. A further five public companies were scheduled for reform. Aid from New Zealand was to be substantially increased in 2011/12. With an allocation of US $23m., the programme was to provide financial assistance for various development projects. Having been identified as an area of major potential, the fisheries sector was to receive support for training programmes and the upgrading of facilities.

The GDP of the Marshall Islands, a former US territory, was reported to have contracted by 1.6% in 2008 and by 2.1% in the following year, with growth being estimated at 0.5% in 2010. Under the new financial agreement (2004–29) with the USA as part of the Compact of Free Association, the Marshall Islands received fresh inflows of aid. Government expenditure, mainly on wages and salaries, was supported by Compact funds. The USA's Ronald Reagan Ballistic Missile Defense Test Site, located on Kwajalein Atoll, also continued to contribute to the expenditure component of GDP. However, retrenchment at the military base of Kwajalein led to a reduction in income from this source from 2008. Furthermore, it was feared that substantial reductions in personnel at the base, which at mid-2011 employed about 800 Marshallese workers, would be necessitated by a budget decrease of 13% in that year. Modest GDP growth of 1.0% was predicted for 2011.

A slight improvement in the Marshall Islands' fiscal position was thought to have been achieved in the financial year 2010 when a budget surplus, estimated at the equivalent of 0.3% of GDP, was reported, in contrast to the deficit of the previous year. Remittances from citizens resident in the USA have provided substantial support to the balance of payments. In 2009, however, the current account deficit reached the equivalent of 15.4% of GDP, before declining to 10.5% in the following year. Since the US dollar is legal tender in the Marshall Islands and most of the country's imports are purchased from the USA, the inflation rate has traditionally remained low, but rose sharply in 2008 to reach 14.7%, before decreasing to 1.5% in 2009 and remaining at the same level in 2010. The Marshall Islands were badly affected by the substantial increases in the costs of imports of fuel and foodstuffs in 2008. In July, unable to finance essential imports of fuel and with electricity supplies seriously jeopardized, the Government declared a state of economic emergency. Furthermore, the country's overseas investments, mainly in the USA, lost a significant portion of their value in the stock market volatility of 2008. Between January and November 2008 the value of the Government's trust fund was reported to have declined from US $93.1m. to $72.1m. The trust fund recovered to stand at $140m. at the end of June 2011, but by the end of August, following another period of global volatility, it had lost $14m. In the fiscal year 2012 it was anticipated that funding from the USA would account for almost 70% of the islands' proposed budget. The introduction of a new tax regime, to include the establishment of a value-added tax, was under consideration in late 2011. The tourism sector has continued to decline, partly as a result of the unreliability of the national airline. A four-year national tourism development plan was approved in 2008. In 2010, however, only 4,563 tourists visited the Marshall Islands, the lowest number for 20 years.

The economy of the Federated States of Micronesia, another former US territory, has been constrained by the limitations placed on government expenditure by the reductions in US funding. The country's GDP contracted by 2.3% in 2008 and expanded only modestly, by an estimated 0.5%, in both 2009 and 2010. Some improvement was forecast for 2011, when GDP was expected to expand by 1.0%. The country receives aid from the USA, under the second Compact of Free Association, amounting to US $92m. annually, with the requirement that initially a total of $16m. be saved in a trust fund. US grants usually constitute about 40% of GDP. However, the trust fund remained vulnerable to the volatility of international financial markets; most of the fund's capital was invested in US stock markets. The value of the fund was reported to have decreased by 20% in 2008. The deterioration in global economic conditions in 2008/09, particularly in the USA and Japan (the leading sources of visitors to the islands), had a negative impact on the tourism sector. Remittances from overseas workers were also expected to decrease. However, it was anticipated that the completion of the upgrading of Pohnpei airport in 2011 would provide a stimulus for the tourism sector.

The Federated States of Micronesia failed to manage efficiently the aid inflows from the USA under the first Compact, which expired in 2001. Efforts to establish a trust fund under the second Compact, which took effect in 2004, and to secure overseas borrowing proved difficult. Nevertheless, following the deficit of 2008, the budget moved into surplus in 2009, which was maintained in 2010, when the surplus was estimated at 0.7% of GDP. Bilateral grants from China have become a significant source of support. Inflation reached 7.7% in 2009, before declining to 3.5% in the following year.

The endorsement of the National Trade Policy for the Federated States of Micronesia in early 2011 was regarded as an historic advance, placing emphasis on trade agreements and on issues such as the improvement of investment conditions, the need to encourage import substitution and the promotion of exports of value added goods and services.

In 1994 Palau became the third US-administered Trust Territory to gain independence, following the examples of the Marshall Islands and the Federated States of Micronesia. A trust fund was established into which US aid funds were deposited in order to provide budgetary support from 2009, when the Compact of Free Association (1994–2009) was due to expire. In March 2009 the Compact with the USA was extended for one year from the end of September. By the latter month total US aid to Palau since 1995 was estimated to have exceeded US $852m., with direct assistance under the Compact having accounted for 48% of this. Following protracted negotiations, agreement was reached in early 2010 when Palau accepted a programme of aid totalling $250m. for the next 15 years. Meanwhile, the US General Accountability Office emphasized the need for fiscal reform, noting that an improvement in investment conditions would be conducive to the growth of the private sector. In July 2009 the assets of the trust fund were reported to have exceeded $130.5m. From 1 October Palau was to be permitted to withdraw $15m. annually from the fund. Hotel and retail sector activities showed strong growth until 2007; with the construction of two resorts and a hotel, Palau emerged as an increasingly attractive tourist destination in the north Pacific. However, owing to the global economic downturn, a substantial decrease in tourist arrivals was recorded in 2008 and again in 2009. In 2010 Palau was reported to have received 85,593 visitors. The country's GDP contracted by 4.9% in 2008 and by 2.1% in 2009, with a modest recovery recorded in 2010, when GDP expanded by 0.5%. Expansion of 2.0% was envisaged for 2011.

Palau's macroeconomic stability continued to depend on whether its trust fund, established under the first Compact (1994–2009) with the USA with a view to developing perennial support for annual budgets, would function successfully. However, as domestic revenue collection improved, the budget deficit was steadily reduced from 5.8% of GDP in the 2007 financial year to 2.4% in 2010. Remittances and earnings from tourism are seen as potential sources of financial support upon the expiry of Compact funding, inflows from which have covered 50% of the country's import costs. The tourism sector contributes as much as two-thirds of Palau's GDP. The current account remained in deficit in 2008, in which year the deficit reached 17.9% of GDP, declining to 13.7% in 2009 and 9.5% in 2010. Since Palau uses the US dollar as legal tender and its imports are mostly sourced from the USA, annual inflation has usually remained comparatively low, but it increased substantially in 2008, when the rate reached 11.3%, before declining to 4.6% in 2009 and to 1.5% in 2010.

Nauru experienced serious economic difficulties from the late 1990s, mainly owing to the decline in earnings from the island's phosphate-mining activities. It was hoped that, with the completion of the restoration of the requisite infrastructure and with investment from an Australian company, secondary deposits might yield sufficient phosphate to sustain exports for 20–30 years. However, in mid-2007 phosphate exports were suspended for several months following storm damage to port infrastructure; the port suffered further storm damage in 2009. The ADB estimated that Nauru's GDP contracted by 27.3% in 2007 but grew by 1.0% in 2008. The economy showed no discernible growth in 2009–10. GDP was forecast by the ADB to expand by 4.0% in 2011.

Nauru's economic prospects have remained weak, with the country being totally reliant on its limited phosphate exports. Australia's closure in 2008 of an offshore processing centre for asylum-seekers, from which Nauru had derived substantial revenue, had a major impact on the island's economy. There was no other significant income-generating activity on the island in 2010, apart from subsistence fisheries, and there is little tourism potential. At the first international donor meeting held in November 2005 several alternative sources of income were proposed, including the development of commercial fisheries, in the hope of creating jobs and export potential. Public sector reforms were needed to rationalize public finances. Furthermore, there was a strong need to improve the country's domestic financial system to gain credibility for its business environment. The international debt position of Nauru has been a major concern, as the country's debt has been estimated to be equivalent to around 30 times GDP. Any effort to service the debt would place severe strain on the island's finances. The budget deficit was reduced from 0.6% of GDP in 2008 to 0.4 % in 2009. The rate of inflation decreased from 4.5% in 2008 to 2.2% in 2009, following which deflationary conditions prevailed; consumer prices were estimated to have decreased by 0.5% in 2010.

Tuvalu has tended to record relatively low rates of economic growth. However, its GDP expanded by 7.0% in 2008, mainly owing to new construction activities, including a parliament complex, a new police station and a prison. GDP contracted by 1.7% in 2009 and remained stagnant in 2010. Income from fishing licence fees rose by 18.7% in 2008, while revenues from the '.tv' internet domain facility remained similar to those of the previous year. The Tuvalu Trust Fund (TTF) was established in 1987 with assistance from New Zealand, Australia and the United Kingdom. The TTF generates funding, through overseas investment, for development projects. By September 2006 the assets of the TTF were estimated to total $A77m. The fund supports the Government's recurrent budget. Meanwhile, there was a rise in public expenditure to fund, for example, the construction of the Funafuti power station, which had been completed by 2007, and the upgrading of the Tuvalu Maritime Training Institute. Remittances from Tuvalu's seafarers working on foreign vessels on long contracts are an important source of income, providing much-needed foreign exchange to the country, which has no commodity exports of any kind. GDP was not expected to expand in 2011.

Having demonstrated improved financial management in the early 2000s, notably with regard to the administration of its trust fund, Tuvalu experienced revenue losses as a result of declining sales of fishing licences and telecommunication licences and the reduction in income from the '.tv' domain name. The budget deficit in 2007 reportedly reached the equivalent of 19.0% of GDP, before declining to 8.3% in 2008 and to 7.3% in 2009. The country's debt, all of which was derived from international funding agencies and was hence obtained on concessional terms, stood at 80% of GDP in 2007. Tuvalu, which uses the Australian dollar as its currency and which obtains most of its imports from Australia, recorded an annual inflation rate of 10.4% in 2008. However, consumer prices declined by 0.1% in 2009 and by 1.9% in the following year. A state of emergency was declared in October 2011, owing to the islands' critical shortage of supplies of fresh water. New Zealand and Australia provided desalination plants.

TERRITORY ANALYSES

Macroeconomic stability in the US and French territories has remained the responsibility of the respective sovereign nations. In the US-administered territory of American Samoa, which retains close trade relations with the USA, major employers have included two long-established tuna canneries. In early 2009 the canneries employed almost 5,000 workers, including many from neighbouring Samoa. The majority of American Samoa's exports of processed tuna have been destined for the USA. However, with the advent of free trade arrangements, American Samoa's canned tuna exports became less competitive than the products of some Asian countries, where labour costs were lower but from where access to the US market remained favourable. In September 2009, therefore, one of the two canneries, COS Samoa Packing, was closed down, resulting in heavy job losses, while the operations of the other, StarKist Samoa, which was already reported to be undergoing a programme of retrenchment, were further curtailed by a tsunami disaster that occurred in the same month. In August 2010, furthermore, 380 of the 800 workers remaining at StarKist Samoa were made redundant. In October, however, it was reported that agreement had been reached on the sale of the COS Samoa Packing plant to a US company, TriMarine, and in early 2011 fish-processing operations there were in the process of being resumed. By April 2011 the work-force of StarKist was reported to have been expanded to 2,000, the company's operations being supported by government tax concessions. None the less, the cost of American Samoa's imports far exceed the value of its exports.

Free mobility of labour within the USA has been significant in assisting American Samoa to overcome the disadvantages of being a small economy. The territory's economy has thus been sustained by the inflow of remittances from the US mainland and from Hawaii. Annual fiscal transfers from the US federal Government support the territory's budget. American Samoa's natural constraints, in particular its remote location, limited transport facilities and susceptibility to cyclones, have hindered the islands' development. The annual rate of inflation averaged 3.9% in 2000–07, reportedly rising from 5.3% in the first quarter of 2010 to 7.2% in the first three months of 2011. As the global economy continued to deteriorate, it was announced in March 2009 that American Samoa was to receive the sum of US $19m. from the federal Government; most of this economic stimulus funding was to be used to promote the conservation of energy in the islands. To support the islands' reconstruction programme in the aftermath of the tsunami disaster in September 2009, economic assistance of $10.3m. was approved by the Federal Emergency Management Agency in February 2010. It was announced in July 2011 that a contract to establish and operate a call-centre training facility in American Samoa had been awarded to a company based in California.

In Guam, another US-administered territory, tourism has emerged as a major contributor to the economy, with substantial investments in hotel construction and renovation having been made. In 2008, however, the number of foreign tourist arrivals declined slightly, to fewer than 1.2m., mainly owing to deteriorating economic conditions in Japan, the Republic of Korea and the USA, the three leading sources of visitors. Guam has also begun to attract tourists from China; however, the exclusion of Chinese citizens, as well as Russians, from a federal visa waiver programme was expected to impede Guam's plans to attract more visitors from those countries. Guam has remained largely dependent on US military activities on the island.

As a result of the decline in global economic activity from late 2008, the island's economy was reported to have performed poorly in 2009, being sustained by increased federal expenditure. In particular, continuing adverse economic conditions in Japan, the Republic of Korea and the USA seriously jeopardized Guam's tourism sector. Variations in exchange rates, notably the relative weakness of the South Korean currency, also affected the tourism industry in 2008–09. Consumer prices increased by 1.7% in 2009 and by 3.0% in 2010.

In a major development in October 2005, it was announced that thousands of US marines, along with their dependants, were to be relocated from the Japanese base of Okinawa to Guam over a six-year period. Large-scale infrastructure programmes, including transport schemes and projects for water supply, waste management and health care facilities, have been initiated. With the expansion in military and tourism activities, income per caput has been among the highest in the region. In October 2009 it was reported that the federal Government's allocation of US $734m. to military construction projects on the island for 2009/10 represented a doubling of expenditure in comparison with the previous fiscal year. It was envisaged that as many as 20,000 skilled personnel from the Philippines, mainly engineers, architects and builders, would be engaged to work on the construction of the new military headquarters. The draft federal budget for 2010/11 allocated $566m. to military construction projects on Guam. In September 2010, however, it was announced that the process of the relocation of US troops was unlikely to be completed until 2016, owing to delays in the construction of the new facilities on Guam; the transfer of 8,600 marines and 9,000 dependants would therefore take two years longer than originally anticipated.

The Commonwealth of the Northern Mariana Islands was granted special status under the Covenant Agreement signed with the USA, which entered into force in 1978. The garment industry was formerly a thriving sector. Two trade provisions assisted this industry's performance: quotas were imposed on imports of garments from other low-cost producers, and goods manufactured in the Northern Mariana Islands were exported to the USA tax free. Furthermore, with very few military installations and limited military spending, the Northern Mariana Islands benefited from the autonomous power to control immigration and determine minimum wage levels, thus contributing to economic growth. However, with effect from January 2005, the USA removed import quotas for textiles and clothing. Furthermore, the entry of China into the WTO had a major impact on the islands' clothing industry, as

Chinese garments were cheaper than those of local manufacturers. In early 2009, therefore, the last of the islands' unprofitable garment factories closed down.

The Northern Mariana Islands' economy has since become largely dependent on tourism, and the sector is now a major employer. However, the islands' tourism industry has been intermittently jeopardized, not only by unfavourable economic conditions in Japan (the leading source of tourists) but also by difficulties in the airline industry, notably affecting flights between various Japanese cities and Saipan. The establishment of the Northern Marianas' own airline was under consideration in the latter part of 2011. Visitor numbers decreased by more than 10% in 2009, with some improvement reported in 2010. Although it had been feared that the application of US immigration law to the territory from late 2009 would restrict the numbers of visitors from China and Russia (who were reported to contribute about 20% of the islands' tourist receipts), in October it was announced that they would not be required to apply for US visas prior to arrival and that their right to enter on a special visitor permit would remain in place. It was hoped that the introduction of two additional weekly flights from the Chinese city of Shanghai in November 2011 would further encourage tourists from China.

In April 2009 the islands received more than US $90m. in federal stimulus funding. In the latter part of 2010 a major funding crisis arose after the local legislature failed to agree upon the amendments required to address a shortfall in the annual budget. With the impasse in the islands' legislature unresolved, non-essential government services were suspended in October. The islands' Governor issued an executive order providing for various exemptions from the closures. Consumer prices increased by 3.6% in 2009. As pressure on household budgets continued to increase, in July 2011 it was reported that 12% of the population were in receipt of government assistance in the form of food stamps, while hundreds of others remained on a waiting list. In mid-2011 it was confirmed that the Northern Marianas' GDP had contracted by 12.1% in 2008 and by 19.8% in 2009 to reach $716m., in comparison with an average annual rate of decline 4.2% in 2002–07. In October 2011 it was announced that most government agencies would close every Friday, as part of the austerity measures being implemented for the coming fiscal year.

The economy of French Polynesia was formerly dominated by military-related activities. When nuclear-testing facilities were scaled down in 1996, French Polynesia began focusing on tourism, pearl farming and deep-sea commercial fishing as sources of income. GDP per caput has been among the highest in the region, supported by official grants and inflows of private investment from France. In October 2007, however, a leading international credit ratings agency cited political instability and social unrest as factors in its negative assessment, for the third consecutive year, of French Polynesia. Tourist numbers declined sharply in 2007 and in 2008, decreasing further, by 18%, in 2009, partly owing to the contraction of the economy of the USA, the leading source of visitors. The situation was exacerbated by the weakness of the US dollar against the Pacific franc and by rising competition from other tourist destinations. Tourist arrivals continued to decline in 2010. Furthermore, as a result of lack of profitability, both Air Tahiti Nui and Air France reduced the frequency of their flights to the islands in late 2008, and in early 2009 the Polynesian carrier announced that it was to abandon its New York route completely. In February 2009, owing to the exceptional global economic conditions, the French Government gave its approval to the allocation of the sum of 2,000m. francs CFP from French Polynesia's annual economic development grant for the purpose of addressing the islands' rapidly deteriorating employment situation. In September 2009 it emerged that, in order to finance the 2010 budget, the Government of French Polynesia had been obliged to seek recourse to two bank loans, the projected total of which was 2,983m. francs CFP. A new agreement concluded with metropolitan France in February 2010 provided for the transfer of the equivalent of more than US $200m. annually as part of a new arrangement that took into account the economic legacy of the nuclear weapons tests. About 60% of the funding was to be disbursed by the French Polynesian Government, while about 30% was to be allocated to approved infrastructure projects. Later in February, however, French Polynesia sustained serious cyclone damage, compounding fears for the future of the tourism sector and for the pearl farms of the Tuamotu islands.

In early 2011, amid ongoing political difficulties and as the economy reportedly entered its third year of recession, focus on the need for a fundamental restructuring of the French Polynesian economy was renewed. With the public sector accounting for 70% of GDP and with the system of taxation being based largely on import duties and other indirect taxes, analysts argued that a reduction in government involvement in the economy was crucial. In May 2011 it was announced that France had agreed to lend US $62m. to French Polynesia, subject to conditions that included the urgent restructuring of the economy.

New Caledonia, which is another Pays d'outre-mer (Overseas Country) of France, is believed to hold approximately 25% of the world's known nickel resources. Following two consecutive years of declining output, in 2007 nickel production increased dramatically, by 21.5%. Export receipts from sales of nickel reached an estimated 177,299m. francs CFP in 2007. In 2008, however, export revenues derived from nickel were estimated to total just 102,870m. francs CFP (albeit 94% of total export revenue), owing to weaker world prices for the commodity. In November 2009, in response to the decline in world demand for nickel, New Caledonia's leading producer confirmed its intention to proceed with a programme of redundancies. Meanwhile, legislation approved in March provided a legal framework for mining operations in New Caledonia; it included revised guidelines for environmental controls. A nickel stabilization fund was also established with an initial allocation of 1,500m. francs CFP. It was envisaged that the new fund would mitigate the effects of volatility in global nickel prices.

Only a small proportion of land is suitable for cultivation. Therefore, New Caledonia is heavily dependent on imports for supplies of food and all other essential commodities. Financial support from France generally contributes more than 30% to New Caledonia's GDP. French citizens retiring to the island, and forming a large percentage of the population, also make a significant contribution to consumption, an important component of GDP. Consumer prices rose by less than 0.2% in 2009, but by 2.7% in 2010. Located closer to Australia and New Zealand than other Pacific Islands, New Caledonia has attempted to attract more tourists from these countries through promotional programmes. In 2010, however, France remained by far the leading source of visitors. It was hoped that the Pacific Games, held in New Caledonia in August–September 2011, would revitalize the New Caledonian tourism sector. Meanwhile, the opening in New Caledonia of the first Pacific office of the European Investment Bank was likely to give a much-needed stimulus to construction activities for office accommodation and housing. A report released in October 2011 by a tripartite committee, comprising members of the trade unions, the local legislature and the Government, concluded that 21% of New Caledonians were living in poverty. The committee's recommendations included greater transparency in the area of profit margins and prices (the high cost of living having become a major issue), a review of the tax system and the establishment of a levy on expensive properties.

Norfolk Island is a territory of Australia. In August 2008 the Government of Norfolk Island issued its response to an Australian Senate Committee inquiry into the financial management of the island. The local Government claimed that the existing arrangements remained viable, reiterating its commitment to the continued improvement of the delivery of services on the island. The Government expressed particular concern in relation to its repeated obligation to divert the island's scarce human and financial resources to the task of responding to what was perceived to be constant scrutiny by external committees and consultants, often with regard to issues that it believed to have been adequately addressed on previous occasions. In October the Australian Minister for Home Affairs warned that Norfolk Island was in danger of becoming a 'failed state', a claim that was strongly refuted by the island's Government. The tourism industry has experienced steady growth over the years to become the primary source of revenue on the island. However, arrivals declined from 29,639 in 2008/09 to 24,268 in 2010/11. The agricultural sector has become self-sufficient in the production of beef, poultry and eggs. The island's exports have consisted of postage stamps, seeds of the Norfolk Island pine and of the Kentia palm, and also small quantities of avocados. The global economic downturn of 2008/09 had a significant impact on Norfolk Island, particularly in terms of tourism revenue. In November 2009 the Government reported a decrease in its revenue of $A3.9m. in 2008/09, in comparison with the previous financial year. This decline was attributed to the reduction in tourist arrivals and to an increase in public expenditure of $A1.1m., which was due mainly to wage rises. Norfolk Air, the local airline, recorded a loss of more than $A1m. in the first three months of the 2009/10 financial year. It was announced in September 2011 that Australia was to provide financial support of $A14.1 for Norfolk Island in 2011/12.

Niue attained the status of self-government in free association with New Zealand in 1974, but has remained largely dependent on New Zealand for the management of its public services. The island was devastated by a severe cyclone in January 2004. The Government has remained the island's largest employer, although efforts have been made to decrease government expenditures by reducing the public service by almost one-half. Niue has depended on the agricultural sector for its exports of processed passion fruit juice, lime oil, honey and coconut cream. The sale of postage stamps to foreign collectors is an important source of revenue, and plans for the issue in late 2011 of a series of silver and silver-plated 'Star Wars' coins attracted much international interest. The reintroduction of vanilla cultivation, as well as that of organic nonu, for export was initiated during 2004 as part of the Government's post-cyclone recovery programme. In August 2011 it was announced that the island's noni farm was to undergo major expansion following expressions of interest by Chinese investors. Niue hosted the Pacific Islands Forum Leaders' Summit in August 2008. Topics of discussion included two issues of particular importance to Niue: food and fuel security. Plans for infrastructural investments made during the meeting were expected to be funded by China, which was also considering assisting with the upgrading of Niue's telephone system.

A controversial new consumption tax took effect in Niue in April 2009. Levied at a rate of 12.5%, the tax on goods and services was expected to make a substantial contribution to government revenue. However, the introduction of the tax encountered widespread opposition, owing to its impact on low-income families. Since the 1990s Niue's various other attempts to secure new sources of revenue have included the leasing of the island's telecommunications facilities to foreign companies for use in specialist telephone services. However, this enterprise caused considerable controversy when it was revealed that Niue's telephone code had been made available to companies offering personal services considered indecent by the majority of islanders. The sale of the internet domain name '.nu' also yielded significant revenue but proved similarly controversial. With the objective of providing Niue with an independent source of future revenue, in 2006 the Niue International Trust Fund was established, with a total contribution of $NZ10m. from New Zealand and Australia. By 2010 the trust fund's assets stood at $NZ36m. Revenue from the fund was not expected to be drawn before 2014. A campaign to promote the tourism sector, with the aim of attracting 'up-market' travellers, was announced in mid-2011. A visitor centre was established in Alofi, with financial support from New Zealand. Following Niue's signature of a joint development aid agreement with New Zealand to fund development projects for tourism on the island, in September 2011 New Zealand pledged the sum of $NZ15m., to be disbursed over a three-year period. Meanwhile, with one in three homes on the island unoccupied (their owners having emigrated), plans to convert derelict properties to tourist accommodation were also under consideration. The use of Niue as a retirement village for New Zealanders was another possibility.

Tokelau remains a self-administering territory of New Zealand. With a population of fewer than 1,500 in 2010, Tokelau relies heavily on aid from New Zealand to maintain public services. Following New Zealand's contribution of $NZ15m. in November 2008, the assets of Tokelau's trust fund, established some years previously with the long-term aim of improving the territory's self-reliance, totalled $NZ52m., and by 2010 this sum had risen to $NZ56m. A three-year Economic Support Arrangement was implemented under the direction of the New Zealand Government during 2007–10, with a projected total budget of $NZ43m. Official development assistance from New Zealand was projected to reach $NZ17.3m. in 2010/11. Annual aid is substantially greater than domestic revenue derived from copra, postage stamps, souvenir coins and handicrafts. Inward remittances to families from relatives in New Zealand provide substantial financial support. Owing to a prolonged drought and critical shortage of fresh water, a state of emergency was imposed in September 2011; however, this was removed in late October following substantial rainfall.

CONCLUSION

The unforeseen external developments of recent years, in particular the global economic crisis of 2008/09, and the substantial increases in the costs of essential commodity imports, have emphasized the increasing need for the Pacific Islands to develop a greater degree of resilience in order to withstand such challenges. However, the development of sufficient resilience can be successfully accomplished only in a sound macroeconomic environment. Macroeconomic stability is determined by the annual fiscal position, which in turn affects price levels, interest rates and exchange rates, along with the current account of the balance of payments. External economic conditions will remain beyond the control of the Pacific Islands. The region is unable to influence world markets significantly, given its relatively small contribution to global commodity trade. Attempts to strengthen the Pacific Islands' ability to counter the impact of sudden exogenous events have included measures to promote and sustain a higher degree of self-reliance through the diversification of activities and the adoption of prudent policies. Important objectives include the diversification of the range of globally competitive products, along with the strengthening of the existing infrastructure and the construction of new facilities in order to increase the region's ability to respond to natural disasters.

While political stability has been acknowledged as a critical requirement for steady progress towards the ultimate achievement of the MDGs, the continued vulnerability of the Pacific Islands to the adverse effects of recurrent cyclones, 'king tides' and other natural disasters, including droughts, earthquakes and tsunamis (as demonstrated in September 2009), have made sustainable economic growth very difficult to realize. In addition to these natural disasters, the Pacific Islands have also had to address other unexpected challenges, including sharp decreases in world commodity prices and the consequent reduction in export earnings, along with an increase in the cost of strategic imports, such as petroleum and its products, machinery and transport equipment and other capital goods, as well as in the prices of consumer goods. With their limited range of export items, the Pacific Islands have found it difficult to finance their widening trade deficits. Diversification of activities to reduce dependence on one or two exportable crops cannot be undertaken in isolation. Attempts to diversify and to establish a fundamentally more robust economy clearly require the implementation of a long-term comprehensive strategy. Furthermore, if the Pacific Islands are to benefit from financial globalization, changes are required in other areas, not only in the financial sector. In particular, many would argue that reforms in macroeconomic policies and public financial management are long overdue.

BIBLIOGRAPHY

See also Bibliography of the Pacific Islands at the end of this section

Asian Development Bank. *Asian Development Outlook*. Manila, Asian Development Bank, annually.

Key Indicators for Asia and the Pacific. Manila, Asian Development Bank, annually.

AusAID. *Pacific Island Countries: Analytical Report for the White Paper on Australia's Aid Program.* Canberra, AusAID, 2005.

Australian Aid: Promoting Growth and Stability—White Paper on the Australian Government's Overseas Aid Program. Canberra, AusAID, 2006.

Pacific Economic Survey. Canberra, AusAID, 2008.

Australian Senate Committee. *A Pacific Engaged—Australia's Relations with Papua New Guinea and the Island States of the Southwest Pacific.* Canberra, Commonwealth of Australia, 2003.

Barclay, Kate, and Cartright, Ian. *Capturing Wealth from Tuna: Case Studies from the Pacific.* Canberra, ANU EPress, 2011.

Briguglio, L., Cordina, G., and Kisanga, E. J. (Eds). *Building the Economic Resilience of Small States.* Valletta, Islands and Small States Institute, 2006.

Browne, Christopher, and International Monetary Fund. *Pacific Island Economies.* Washington, DC, International Monetary Fund, 2006.

Bunyaratavej, K., and Jayaraman, T. K. 'Are the Pacific Islands Ready for a Single Currency?', *The Journal of Developing Areas,* 40 (2), 2007, pp. 141–156.

Downes, A. S. 'Progress Towards Achieving the Millennium Development Goals (MDGs) in the Small States of the Commonwealth' in *Small States—Economic Review and Basic Statistics*, Vol. 10. London, Commonwealth Secretariat, 2005, pp. 27–39.

Duncan, Linda, and Webster, Thomas (Eds). *Papua New Guinea's Development Performance 1975–2008.* Boroko, National Research Institute of Papua New Guinea, 2010.

Economist Intelligence Unit. *Country Profile—Pacific Islands 2005.* London.

Fairbairn, T., and Worrell, D. *South Pacific and Caribbean Island Economies: A Comparative Study.* Brisbane, The Foundation for Development Cooperation, 1996.

Grynberg, R. *PICTA, EPA, PACER and the Pacific Plan.* Suva, Pacific Islands Forum Secretariat, 2005.

Hughes, Helen. 'Aid has Failed the Pacific' in *Issue Analysis, No. 33.* Sydney, Centre for Independent Studies, 2003.

'The Pacific is Viable' in *Issue Analysis, No. 53.* Sydney, Centre for Independent Studies, 2004.

Hughes, Helen, and Sodhi, Gaurav. 'Annals of Aid: Vanuatu and the United States Millennium Challenge Corporation' in *Issue Analysis, No. 69.* Sydney, Centre for Independent Studies, 2006.

'Should Australia and New Zealand Open their Doors to Guest Workers from the Pacific? Costs and Benefits' in *Policy Monograph, No. 72.* Sydney, Centre for Independent Studies, 2006.

International Monetary Fund. *International Financial Statistics Yearbook.* Washington, DC, International Monetary Fund, annually.

Jayaraman, T. K. 'Vanuatu's Offshore Financial Centre and its Impact on Growth' in Bowe, M., and Briguglio, L. (Eds). *Banking and Finance in Islands and Small States.* London, Cassells, 1998, pp. 103–133.

Financial Sector Development and Private Investment in Vanuatu. Christchurch, Macmillan Brown Centre for Pacific Studies, University of Canterbury and Suva, Institute of Pacific Studies, University of the South Pacific, 2003.

'A Single Currency for the Pacific Island Countries' in Powles, M. (Ed.). *Pacific Futures.* Canberra, Pandanus Press, 2006, pp. 109–126.

'Macroeconomic Reform and Resilience Building in Small States' in Briguglio, L., Cordina, G., and Kisanga, E. J. (Eds). *Building the Economic Resilience of Small States.* Valletta, Islands and Small States Institute, 2006, pp. 33–58.

'Economic Integration in the Pacific: Review of Past Efforts and Future Prospects' in Kisanga, E., and Danchie, S. J. (Eds). *Commonwealth Small States: Issues and Prospects.* London, Commonwealth Secretariat, 2007, pp. 165–187.

'The Role of Fiscal Policy in Resilience Building: Experiences of Pacific Island Countries' in Briguglio, L., *et al* (Eds). *Small States and the Pillars of Economic Resilience.* London, Commonwealth Secretariat, 2008, pp. 95–117.

Jayaraman, T. K., and Choong, C. 'Public Debt and Economic Growth in the South Pacific Islands' in *Journal of Economic Development*, 31 (2), 2006, pp. 107–121.

Jayaraman, T. K., and Singh, B. 'Impact of Foreign Direct Investment on Employment in Pacific Island Countries: An Empirical Study of Fiji', *Economia Internazionale*, LX (1), 2007, pp. 57–74.

Jayaraman, T. K., and Ward, B. D. 'Economic Growth in a Vulnerable Island Nation: An Empirical Study of Aid-Growth Nexus in Vanuatu', *Asia-Pacific Development Journal,* 13 (2), 2006, pp. 93–112.

Jayaraman, T. K., Ward, B. D., and Xu, Z. I. 'Are the Pacific Islands Ready for a Currency Union? An Empirical Study of Degree of Economic Convergence', *Journal of Asia Pacific Economy,* 12 (4), 2007, pp. 504–521.

May, R. J. (Ed.). *'Arc of Instability'? Melanesia in the Early 2000s.* Christchurch, Macmillan Brown Centre for Pacific Studies, University of Canterbury, 2005.

Powles, M. (Ed.). *Pacific Futures.* Canberra, Pandanus Press, 2006.

Reserve Bank of Fiji. *Monetary Policy Statement, May 2007.* Suva, Reserve Bank of Fiji, 2007.

Scollay, R. *Free Trade Options for the Forum Island Countries.* Suva, Pacific Islands Forum Secretariat, 1998.

United Nations. *Human Development Report.* New York, UN Development Programme, annually.

Statistical Yearbook for Asia and the Pacific. New York, UN, annually.

Economic and Social Survey. Bangkok, UN Economic and Social Commission for Asia and the Pacific (ESCAP), annually.

Improving Employment Opportunities in Pacific Island Developing Countries. Bangkok, UN Economic and Social Commission for Asia and the Pacific (ESCAP), 2008.

Urwin, Greg. *Economic Development of Pacific Island Economies and Regional Cooperation.* Suva, Pacific Islands Forum Secretariat, 2004.

World Bank. *At Home And Away: Expanding Job Opportunities for Pacific Islanders Through Labour Mobility.* Washington, DC, World Bank, 2006.

World Development Indicators. Washington, DC, World Bank, annually.

ENVIRONMENTAL ISSUES OF THE PACIFIC ISLANDS

ROSS STEELE

RICH PHYSICAL AND HUMAN DIVERSITY WITH SHARED ECONOMIC AND ENVIRONMENTAL VULNERABILITY

The Pacific Islands encompass a vast region that stretches from Papua New Guinea in the west to French Polynesia and Pitcairn in the east and from New Caledonia in the south to the Northern Mariana Islands in the north. On the basis of political jurisdiction, this essay excludes the Hawaiian Islands (USA) to the north and Easter Island (Chile) to the east. The whole region is referred to as the Pacific Community. It comprises 22 countries and territories with a total land area of more than 551,000 sq km and a vast 30m. sq km of the Pacific Ocean, an area more than three times larger than the USA or Australia. The islands of the region number almost 30,000, of which about 1,000 are inhabited. They range in size from the largest in the west to the smallest in the east. In mid-2011 the region was home to an estimated 10.01m. people, but if the nation of Papua New Guinea, with the largest land mass and population, is excluded, the land area decreases to 88,549 sq km and the total population to 3.12m. The region has a wide variety of peoples and cultures, with three commonly recognized sub-regional ethnographic groupings—Melanesians, Polynesians and Micronesians—who among them speak more than 2,000 different languages. The Melanesian peoples have strong Australoid origins and occupy the larger islands to the south-west, including Papua New Guinea, Solomon Islands, Vanuatu, Fiji and New Caledonia. Like the Melanesians, Polynesians are believed to have descended from intermarriage between the early Australoid peoples and Mongoloid peoples who had migrated into the Pacific from north-eastern Indonesia and the Philippines, but they tend to be more similar to their Mongoloid ancestors, with the Micronesians even more so. Polynesians inhabit islands spread over a huge area of the Pacific Ocean, stretching from Hawaii in the north to Easter Island in the south-east to New Zealand in the south-west. They occupy the central island groups of Samoa, Tonga, the Society Islands (including Tahiti) and the Cook Islands, as well as many small atolls. The Micronesians inhabit an arc of islands to the north of the Melanesians and Polynesians in the western and central Pacific including the Mariana, Caroline, Marshall, Gilbert (Tungara), Phoenix and Line groups.

For most of the residents of the Pacific Islands, in the early 21st century the reality of daily life is very different from the image of paradise often portrayed elsewhere. Globalization and the modern economic realities that accompany this process have long since caught up with this most pleasant region of the world, with metropolitan powers persistently exploiting the mineral, agricultural, physical and human resources of the islands for the last 150 years, leading to serious environmental consequences for the local populations. In recent decades rapid population growth and increased urbanization, rising aspirations, and increased consumerism and consumption have all combined to create large foreign debt burdens for many of the countries and territories of the Pacific Islands. This burden, and the consequent need to maximize hard-currency revenue, has led to a 'fast-tracking' of tourism, mining and timber extraction development in many of the Pacific Islands. Similar economic and political pressures have forced other islands to act as nuclear-testing sites, sites of refugee camps, missile sites and as dumps for the toxic wastes of regional and metropolitan powers. The ever-present Pacific Ocean influences all aspects of life in the Pacific Island communities, from the development of natural hazards such as tropical cyclones (referred to as hurricanes in the northern hemisphere) over its warm waters, to tsunamis and volcanic eruptions caused by earthquakes and the movement of continental plates and landslides in its deeps, to extreme isolation within its huge expanse. The Pacific Islands have also shared a traditional dependence on marine resources for their daily needs, foods, tools, transport and waste disposal, despite new technologies and lifestyle changes. The waters of the Pacific Ocean contain the highest level of marine diversity in the world, and in the words of the 1999 report of the United Nations Environment Programme (UNEP) 'represent almost the sole opportunity for substantial economic development for nations such as the Marshall Islands, Kiribati and Tuvalu'.

The islands of the Pacific have been classified by Bryant Allen and others into three or four major groupings based on their physiography and geological origins (see Background to the Pacific Islands). The populations of the countries and territories within the region also exhibit marked diversity, but they are all small in a global sense, making their composition and growth rates sensitive to trends in international migration. Over the period 1990–2003 the Pacific Islands' total population grew at the rapid rate of 2.69% per annum, although growth rates have subsequently decreased to 1.9% annually as fertility levels have declined or stabilized. Nevertheless, if projected trends continue, the region's population will have grown by an additional 750,000 people by mid-2015, and will have increased in size by a further 78% to reach 17.88m. by 2050, making already problematic goals of sustainable economic development, adequate levels of welfare and service provision, and the amelioration of serious environmental issues even more difficult to overcome in future decades. Annual population growth rates in 2010–11 in Pacific Island nations such as Solomon Islands and Guam were 2.7%, in Vanuatu they were 2.6%, and in Papua New Guinea and Nauru they were almost as high at 2.1% per annum. Population growth rates of this magnitude, combined with increased aspirations, are considered environmentally unsustainable. The Marshall Islands has similar environmental problems owing to its very limited land mass. Indeed, the resource depletion that may occur on these islands and in their marine environments as a result of continued population growth has the potential to cause serious depopulation almost on the scale of Easter Island, if the 'safety valve' of emigration is not available.

As well as high population growth rates, the Pacific Island nations share other common demographic characteristics such as high but declining or stable fertility rates, increased life expectancy, and higher urban than rural population growth. The regions with the most rapid rates of population growth have the fastest growing urban populations. Parents are leaving inadequate school and medical facilities in the more isolated outer islands or rural villages to migrate to provincial or national urban seats of government in order to provide their children with a better future. Of the 22 Pacific Island countries and territories (PICTs), 10 had 50% or more of their total population resident in urban areas at the time of their last census. According to a background paper on demographic issues prepared for the UN Economic and Social Commission for Asia and the Pacific (ESCAP) Ministerial Conference on Environment and Development in 2000, the Marshall Islands and American Samoa both had annual urban population growth rates of 8.2% in the late 1990s (a doubling time of under nine years), Vanuatu 7.3%, Solomon Islands 6.2%, the Northern Mariana Islands 5.6% and Papua New Guinea 4.2%. By the end of the first decade of the 21st century intercensal annual growth rates of urban populations were lower than in 2000: at 4.7% in Solomon Islands, 3.7% in the Northern Mariana Islands, 3.5% in Vanuatu, 2.8% in Papua New Guinea and 2.6% in the Cook Islands; however, in each of these Pacific Island nations the rates are higher than in the rural populations. Growth rates of this magnitude far exceed the capacity of governments to provide housing and essential urban services such as potable water, sewage disposal and adequate health and dental care. The result has been the creation of crowded shanty towns on the edges of the major urban centres such as Suva, Nadi and Lautoka (in Fiji), Port Moresby and Lae (Papua New Guinea), Port Vila (Vanuatu), Honiara (Solomon Islands), Nouméa (New Caledonia) and Nuku'alofa (Tonga). In these shanty towns crime, homelessness, underemployment and unemployment, intestinal diseases, ear and eye infections, and insect-borne diseases such as dengue fever are prevalent. Population densities in some of the capitals of the atoll nations are very high and comparable to metropolitan cities such as Hong Kong. Tarawa (Kiribati) and Ebeye (the Marshall Islands) are examples, with Ebeye having a density of over 23,000 persons per sq km. High fertility rates are still prevalent in many of the Pacific Islands, with one-half of the 22 countries or territories in the late 1990s still having total fertility rates in excess of twice the replacement rate of 2.1 children per woman. In 2005–07 seven of the 22 PICTs still had fertility rates at this high level: Solomon Islands and Papua New Guinea (with rates of 4.6 and 4.4 children per woman, respectively), Tokelau (4.5), the Marshall Islands and Vanuatu (4.4 and 4.1, respectively), and Samoa and Tonga (4.2). Clearly, in the late 1990s and early 2000s many PICTs were still in the early stages of their fertility transition. Because of their continued high but decreasing fertility and their recent decline in infant mortality, brought about by external medical interventions in the last several decades, the population in many of the Pacific Islands is very youthful, with 12 PICTs having median ages of below 25 years in 2011. This youthful age structure will maintain the momentum of high population growth in the region and sustain the substantial demand for health and education services and for employment in the short-to-medium term, even if fertility rates continue to decline. The growing numbers of young people in this so-called 'youth bulge' have had to adjust to a formal sector incapable of creating sufficient new employment opportunities. The result has been a growth in the numbers of long-term unemployed, underemployed and illegally employed youth who pose increasingly serious social problems and are a source of civil unrest in many PICTS. The World Bank has successfully promoted to the Governments of Australia and New Zealand the development of seasonal employment schemes in the horticultural industries of both countries to employ these young islanders. Although not a panacea for the unemployment and underemployment problems of the PICTs, it is hoped that these schemes will boost the income of islander communities through the receipt of remittances from their absent family members and at the same time ease the labour shortages experienced by these industries.

The relatively rapid transformation from traditional, active lifestyles where islanders were involved in growing, hunting and fishing (providing a diet of predominantly fresh fish, root crops such as taro, breadfruit, coconuts and leafy vegetables, all of which were rich in fibre and complex carbohydrates) to a more modern and sedentary lifestyle, where much of the food is imported, has created serious health problems for many island people. This modern diet includes more cereal-based foods, animal products, fats, oils and high-density energy foods with high sugar and salt content. This change in diet and lifestyle, with increased smoking and drinking, has led to a rise in non-communicable diseases such as hypertension, heart disease, diabetes, cancer, stroke, obesity and undernutrition in the form of Vitamin A and iron deficiencies. The problem has been compounded by the Pacific Islanders' genetic predisposition to store fat for times of scarcity (thrift gene phenotype). Pacific Islanders have paid a hefty cost for this change. They have experienced not only an increase in ill health, but a significant decrease in their life expectancy. A Suva-based study of deaths among mostly male life insurance policy-holders in Fiji found a life expectancy of just 49 years, and although this is not a representative study of all Fijians, or of other Pacific Islanders, it does highlight the problems caused by a change in nutrition and lifestyle and the potential threat that they pose to the region's human resource base. In 2011 males in Papua New Guinea, Nauru and Kiribati had the lowest estimated life expectancies at birth of 54, 55 and 59 years, respectively. During the global commodity shortages of 2008, when the cost of food imports rose substantially, some local experts asserted that Pacific Island Governments needed to reverse the decline in investment in agriculture and safeguard local food security. However, progress has been slow in reducing dependence on imported food staples, such as rice, which are convenient to prepare and store.

Population pressures vary dramatically among different island groups. In many of the Polynesian and Micronesian countries emigration to the Pacific Rim countries (Australia, New Zealand and the USA) and to France, with which they have political associations, is an important population 'safety valve' and has kept population growth rates at moderate levels despite continued high fertility. Examples are Tonga, the Cook Islands, Kiribati, Tokelau and Niue, where remittances comprise a major portion of foreign exchange income. On other islands, such as Guam, Solomon Islands and Nauru, populations have grown rapidly. Over the period 1990–2003 the Melanesian countries had the highest population growth rates at 2.9% annually, followed by Micronesia at a more modest 1.8% and Polynesia with the lowest rate of 1.5%. One reason for this is that the Melanesian people have been more reluctant to emigrate, and populations are rapidly increasing on the Melanesian islands of Papua New Guinea, Solomon Islands, Vanuatu and New Caledonia. Fiji would have experienced similar growth rates, but a racially inspired coup in 1987 encouraged the emigration of many of Fiji's ethnic Indian population. Population growth estimates for 2011 suggested that current annual rates are considerably below the 1990–2003 rates, at 2.0% in Melanesia, 1.5% in Micronesia and 0.7% in Polynesia, but the earlier regional differences persist.

The UNEP *Pacific Islands Environment Outlook* report of 1999 identified the major environmental problems that are placing pressure on the natural resources, lifestyles and economic development of this region as: loss of biological diversity; threats to freshwater resources; degradation of coastal environments; climate change and sea-level rise; and land- and sea-based pollution. However, before examining these and other environmental problems in detail, it needs to be stressed that different areas within this huge region have unique combinations of environmental issues that are an inextricable product of the ecology, natural resources, history, population and ethnic composition of that part of the region. The high islands of the Western Pacific such as Papua New Guinea, Solomon Islands, Vanuatu, New Caledonia and Fiji are rich in mineral and forestry resources and have the largest human populations. Papua New Guinea alone accounted for an estimated 6.9m. (69%) of the region's total population of 10.0m. in 2011. The three countries of Papua New Guinea, Solomon Islands and Vanuatu had at least 75% of their people living in rural settlements as subsistence farmers and most enjoyed an almost undiluted Melanesian culture. The per caput income levels in these three countries were low, as were their rankings on the UN Human Development Index, and each had very high levels of fertility and infant mortality. The French territory of New Caledonia has an ethnically diverse population, comprising peoples of Melanesian, Asian and European backgrounds. The population of Fiji is also ethnically mixed and comprises Melanesians, Polynesians, Indians and Europeans. Both countries have more stable and diversified economies than their Melanesian neighbours, and are more urbanized and more developed economically.

The main environmental problems of all of these high islands are land degradation, unsustainable deforestation, water pollution from mining, invasion of exotic species, local depletion of coastal fisheries and, except for Fiji and New Caledonia, rapid population growth. These countries also confront the issues of rapidly growing urban populations and their attendant problems of unemployment, underemployment, poverty, and poor sanitation and housing. They also regularly endure the natural hazards brought by drought, fire, volcanic eruptions, earthquakes and tsunamis. The mid-sized islands of Polynesia (Tonga, Samoa, and French Polynesia) and Micronesia (Palau and the Federated States of Micronesia) and the high island Territories of the United States (Guam, American Samoa and the Commonwealth of the Northern Mariana Islands) have limited land resources, few commercial forests and no exploitable mineral deposits. Most of the people of Polynesia and Micronesia are agrarian and rural; however, there is considerable variation. For example, Guam is dominated by urban-based, ethnically mixed communities, and Tonga and Samoa receive large remittances from expatriate island communities in Pacific Rim countries. French Polynesia is an overseas territory of France, while Guam, the Northern Mariana Islands and American Samoa are Territories of the USA. These Territories of metropolitan powers enjoy a high standard of living as a result of subsidies, and have few of their own tradable resources and no manufacturing capabilities. Their major environmental problems are: a growing shortage of land, especially of good quality agricultural land that is suitable for the production of food crops; loss of remaining native forest and associated loss of biodiversity; decline of coastal fishery resources; coral reef degradation; invasion of exotic species; solid waste disposal; and pollution of ground water and coastal areas by agricultural chemicals and sewage. The small coral islands and especially the atoll states (the Cook Islands, Kiribati, Tuvalu, the Federated States of Micronesia, the Marshall Islands, Niue and Nauru) have very limited land resources, but are spread over vast areas of the Pacific Ocean. More than 54,000 Marshall Islanders live on 181 sq km of coral islands, with the situation being exacerbated by high population growth rates in the urban areas. In all of the atoll states the situation was slightly better at 0.8 ha per person. On the other hand, each person had economic control over 41.4 sq km of ocean. These low islands are the most vulnerable places on earth to the adverse effects of climate change and sea-level rise, with some of the islands in Tuvalu, Tonga, the Federated States of Micronesia and the Marshall Islands likely to be submerged completely. Coastal erosion, often related to inadequately planned construction work, has caused serious damage to many islands, and two low-lying islands have already eroded below sea level. The most serious environmental problems on these small low islands are: vulnerability to storms and droughts; fresh water availability and the pollution of groundwater with sewage and salt; scarce agricultural land; solid waste disposal; food security; and rapid urban population growth.

LAND DEGRADATION, DEFORESTATION AND LOSS OF BIODIVERSITY

Land Degradation and Commercial Agriculture

Given the recent nature of population growth in the majority of the islands of the Pacific and their relatively well-watered and lush landscapes, most of the region has not experienced the scale of land degradation witnessed in more populous and climatically marginal habitats such as north-western China. There is evidence that local land degradation did occur on some islands where population densities exceeded local resource-carrying capacities, or where destructive land-clearing activities were used. Examples include Easter Island, and the fernlands of Viti Levu in Fiji, and Wallis and Futuna, where excessive burning of land for agriculture denuded soils to such an extent that only ferns could grow. However, for many environmentalists, modern commercial agriculture is regarded as the most environmentally destructive human activity in the Pacific Islands region. The all-pervasive impacts of commercial agriculture result from its disruption of existing ecosystems; biodiversity loss caused by clearing of the natural vegetation (and its replacement by a monoculture of commercial and plantation crops such as sugar cane); drainage of wetlands and accelerated erosion of topsoils and destruction of soil structure; pollution of surface and ground waters with agricultural chemicals; and its contribution to global warming through the loss of trees and the production of methane. Commercial agriculture has also been a contributor to landlessness, as village land traditionally devoted to subsistence cropping was converted to plantation and other commercial crops. These crops were then processed or exported, and the end result was that in many of the Pacific Islands local food production levels in 2002 were lower than or similar to 1989–91 levels, despite significant population increases over the last decade or so. For example, in Fiji, Vanuatu, American Samoa, French Polynesia, Samoa, Tonga and Tuvalu local food production per head of population would appear to be less than a decade ago, meaning that commercial agriculture has not only caused severe environmental problems but also contributed to the health and nutritional problems currently evident in Pacific Island communities. Islanders have become increasingly dependent on imported foods (and their associated additives of fat and salt), rather than traditional and healthier locally produced fresh foods.

Traditional Pacific Island agricultural systems were highly sustainable owing to their discontinuous and limited areal extent amid natural vegetation, their genetic diversity, mixed cropping and minimal tillage practices, and long fallow periods that permitted the replenishment of soil fertility. The 2000 ESCAP background paper on agriculture cited the example of Vanuatu, where the steep slopes of Pentecost and Ambae were traditionally cultivated for a variety of crops, including commercial kava plantations, but because of their small size and traditional practices these gardens did not contribute significantly to soil erosion and degradation. Similarly in Tonga, traditional shifting cultivation, with mixed cropping under a canopy of up to 100 associated tree species, allowed ample fallow time and the regeneration of soils, reduced pest problems and prevented erosion for more than 3,000 years. These environmentally sustainable traditional farming systems decreased in importance as farmers entered the cash-cropping system. Small productive mixed gardens with plentiful tree cover were either burned or bulldozed. The cleared areas were tilled by tractor and exposed to leaching and erosion from the heavy rainfall and seasonal cyclones. The cleared land was replanted with a treeless single species monoculture of densely planted cash crops that inevitably resulted in outbreaks of pests and the need to apply poisons to control them. The yields were boosted with the applications of chemical fertilizers, but pressing commercial imperatives, the growing demand for consumer goods and the cash to buy them have combined with growing population pressures to lead to a shortening of fallow times and further environmental pressures on the limited land resources. Such trends are particularly serious on smaller islands, especially atolls with limited land, poor soils and few other land resources. Land degradation is most evident where populations and economic activity are spatially concentrated together, particularly around towns, and where timber and mineral resources are overexploited. Village cash-cropping is carried out in the same land use and tenure context as subsistence production, but the land requirements for larger plantation ventures compete with those required for the expansion of food production. Crop production is then forced to expand into marginal land that is more susceptible to soil erosion or has lower natural fertility. In Fiji and Samoa, for example, there is already severe pressure on good arable land, and subsistence gardening has been pushed to increasingly marginal soil types and slopes where land has been degraded by water and wind erosion, particularly during cyclonic storms or prolonged drought, such as the intense El Niño event (a periodic warming of the tropical Pacific Ocean) of 1997–98.

In Fiji burning to clear land and remove sugar cane debris altered the characteristics of soils and made them more susceptible to erosion. Clear felling of forests for kava plantations has also reduced the forest habitat in Fiji, a habitat needed for yam and other wild foods that were traditionally important staples during food shortages. The costs of erosion are difficult to estimate, but in Fiji the on-site cost from ginger-farming was estimated by ESCAP in 1995 at US $0.4m.–$1.2m. per year, owing to the loss of 27,000–81,000 metric tons of soil. In other countries, such as Papua New Guinea and Solomon Islands, where only a small proportion of land is currently used for agriculture, increased production mostly comes from an intensification of land use within areas already in production and some movement upslope onto terrain more susceptible to erosion. In these instances, when the systems of land use and their traditional management practices are no longer ecologically suited to the more intensive production levels demanded from them or to their new more marginal sites, land degradation also results. Land degradation by its very nature is usually a gradual and somewhat subtle phenomenon, and so it is perhaps understandable that few Pacific Island countries have developed, and even fewer have implemented, sustainable land-management policies essential to their long-term food self-sufficiency.

Deforestation

In most of the region, deforestation and forest degradation were insignificant prior to European contact because populations were small, commercial activities were absent and steel tools were unknown. This all changed following European contact in the mid- to late 19th century, when deforestation and forest degradation accelerated and as coastal and lowland forests were converted to large-scale commercial coconut, cocoa and banana plantations on many islands. The introduction of steel tools and mechanized transport encouraged the conversion of forest lands to agricultural uses, and in recent decades the introduction of chainsaws combined with increased commercial pressures have encouraged even more rapid removal of forest, with the spread of timber-logging and the development of commercial agriculture. Few data are available on the rates at which natural forest was removed in recent decades. In Samoa UNEP estimated rates of deforestation to be as high as 2% per year in the mid-1990s. In part of the Federated States of Micronesia only 15% of the land was undisturbed forest in 1995, compared with 42% in 1976. The UNEP report of 1999 cited forest cover as a percentage of total land area in 1998 at 50% in Fiji, 64% in Niue, 86% in Papua New Guinea, 65% in Samoa, 85% in Solomon Islands and 74% in Vanuatu. Estimates for 2010 based on the *Global Forest Resources Assessment 2010* (FRA 2010) were released by FAO in late 2010. These most recent estimates are generally much lower in the case of Papua New Guinea (63%), Samoa (60%), Solomon Islands (79%), and Vanuatu (36%), implying dramatically accelerated deforestation since 1998. However, the small but improbable increase in forest cover in Fiji, to 56%, and in Niue to 72%, and the spectacularly large reduction in Vanuatu, imply definitional problems and serious shortcomings in the comparability of the estimates. Nevertheless, there is little doubt that in recent years forest and tree cover has continued to decrease as a result of a combination of population pressures, loss of traditional village-level controls, shifting cultivation and shorter fallow periods, owing to increased population and commercial pressures, pasture development, mining and logging activities.

In recent years the environmental impact of logging in Papua New Guinea and Solomon Islands has received unfavourable publicity, and it is also an issue in Vanuatu, Fiji, Niue, Samoa and Tonga. The loss of forest as a result of agro-deforestation is also significant on those islands with substantial population densities such as the Cook Islands, the Federated States of Micronesia, Kiribati, the Marshall Islands, Tokelau, Tonga, Tuvalu and Samoa, with significant areas of forest lost annually to fire in Fiji, the Federated States of Micronesia, the Cook Islands, Samoa and Guam. The loss of forest cover has had severe adverse impacts on soil conservation and productivity, as well as on the duration of stream flow and its quality, and on the incidence of flash floods. Loss of forest habitat and degradation have a negative impact on wildlife, reduce the availability of medicinal plants and gathered foodstuff, and can have an adverse effect on human nutrition and increase women's workloads. Large- and medium-scale logging operations can also accelerate breakdowns of traditional systems of social sanctions and an increase in alcohol consumption. All of the four larger countries (i.e. Papua New Guinea, Fiji, Solomon Islands and Vanuatu) have developed national codes of logging practice, and Fiji and Papua New Guinea have attempted to implement them in an effort to minimize the adverse effects of logging on the environment. However, analysis of logging programmes in Solomon Islands and Papua New Guinea illustrates the difficulties in trying to implement sustainable forest management policies within the context of the political and economic imperatives that prevail in the Pacific Island nations.

Logging for export began in 1961 in Solomon Islands and has accelerated since the early 1990s. In 1999 UNEP claimed that deforestation rates were so high that harvesting could not be sustained for more than another eight years (i.e. until 2007) and that its cessation would cause a significant decline in national income. An earlier Asian Development Bank (ADB) assessment in 1994 estimated sustainable annual yields of 270,000 cu m, yet logging licences had been granted for up to 1.4m. cu m per year. The ADB suggested that in the more carefully logged areas reafforestation or regeneration of the forests may take 30–40 years, but that the widespread damage to residual forests and forest site productivity may mean that regeneration or reafforestation may take anything from 45 to 200 years. In addition, it was reported that there had been significant under-reporting of the volumes and value of the timber exported and that this had eroded the royalties and export tax returns to Solomon Islands.

With 63% of its original forest cover still untouched by commercial logging, Papua New Guinea's forests represent one of the largest remaining tracts of virgin tropical forest in the world. These forests play a central role in the social, economic and cultural life of most of the country's population who, owing to colonial land policies, still retain traditional ownership over 97% of the country. After independence in 1975, the Papua New Guinea Government restricted the export of sawlogs and required timber producers to establish domestic value-adding processing facilities. By the end of the 1970s the realities of a high-cost and under-performing economy had forced a reassessment, and for the first time forest policies were put in place that emphasized log exports as the nation's principal means of revenue generation and offered large log export quotas to timber developers in exchange for their construction of public infrastructure and the development of follow-up agricultural projects. The next eight years witnessed rapid and largely uncontrolled logging of Papua New Guinea's forests. However, by 1986 accusations that foreign logging companies had engaged in widespread tax evasion, transfer-pricing and abuse of local villagers forced the Government of Papua New Guinea to establish a Royal Commission of Inquiry into the operations of the industry, led by Justice Barnett. Barnett documented in detail a history of systemic fraud, corruption, exploitation and abuse and implicated senior members of the Papua New Guinea Parliament in these practices. The Commission estimated that transfer payments and lost company taxes on hidden profits reached nearly US $32m. during 1986/87, or around 15% of the nation's total earnings from the timber industry in that year. Public outrage forced the Government to invite the World Bank to recommend reforms to the industry, and in mid-1989 both Barnett and the World Bank delivered their findings. A two-year moratorium was immediately placed on new timber permits, and in the next five years forestry policy was completely revised, under a new Forestry Act, to focus on balancing growth with the needs of future generations through the practice of sustained-yield harvesting and the establishment of a comprehensive national forest inventory. The forest bureaucracy was restructured and oversight of the industry was placed under the control of a National Forest Board.

Unfortunately, the impact of the changes remains in doubt, with the interests of indigenous customary landowners being largely excluded from most aspects of forest planning and management. In particular, it was argued that the strategic interrelationships that link Papua New Guinea's traditional communities to their forests were ignored, just as they were in colonial times, and that there was a failure to appreciate the immediate physical impact that logging operations have on the subsistence economies and environment of village communities, in particular on the supply of wild foodstuffs, water sources, building materials and medicinal plants that sustain these communities. The socio-cultural disruptions caused by the loss of the male work-force to logging activities and the subsequent decline in subsistence gardening, along with the loss of important cultural and spiritual resources found within the forests, were also ignored. Instead, the new policies, like their predecessors, viewed forestry as an industrial production-orientated enterprise, controlled by the central Government and its bureaucracy, that excluded landowners from planning and management decisions very early in the production cycle. Like the old, the new policy encouraged the state to play multiple, conflicting roles where it is meant equitably to balance the needs of landowners, but at the same time promote the development of the industry for the revenue that it depends on, work closely with logging contractors, and monitor and regulate logging operations. The net effect was that the new policy virtually guaranteed logging contractors more influence over decision-making processes than it did landowners, while at the same time transferring the greatest costs of logging onto the traditional communities living within forest areas.

A review of the state of Papua New Guinea's forest resources suggested that, despite all these attempts at reform, the logging industry is still not sustainable. The study found that in 2002 Papua New Guinea had approximately 26m. ha of forest, of which about 11m. ha were suitable for commercial logging, and of this 7m. ha had already been allocated for large-scale logging. In the 1970s and early 1980s the large-scale log export industry was focused on the islands of New Britain and New Ireland because of high stocking densities of commercial species and easy access to wharf facilities built along the coastline. Revenue was high and costs low, ensuring substantial profits for the logging companies. The area under concession quadrupled between 1982 and 1991, but there was no corresponding increase in reported log export volumes, suggesting widespread fraud and illegality, as noted by the Barnett Royal Commission. With the exhaustion of these island resources, logging companies were forced onto the mainland, where lower densities of high-value species and poor access necessitated that they acquire ever-larger concessions if they were to remain profitable. The export of logs from Papua New Guinea reached a peak in the mid-1990s at 3m. cu m per year, but there was a decline to around one-half of that figure in 2001, simply because the best commercial forests had already been logged out. It is claimed that the maximum sustainable harvest from the 11m. ha of forest suitable for large-scale exploitation is only 2m. cu m per year. However, this estimate assumes a 40-year cutting cycle that has no scientific basis, and many non-governmental organizations (NGOs) suggest that the forests will take 70, rather than 40, years to regenerate. Less conservative estimates of sustainable cutting cycles were produced in the 1980s by the World Bank, which estimated that Papua New Guinea's forests could sustain logging at an annual rate of 6.0m. cu m, a rate more than double the average achieved since 1985. John McAlpine, a pioneer of satellite mapping of Papua New Guinea's resources, subsequently raised the estimate to 6.3m. cu m. Tim Curtin, an economic adviser, has argued that many species indigenous to Papua New Guinea are capable of yielding much more than assumed by McAlpine, noting that a woodchip project in Madang province has remained in business after 30 years with rotations of 15 years for *Eucalyptus deglupta* and nine years for Acacia. Using the 40-year assumption, some analysts assert that only one-quarter of logging concessions in Papua New Guinea were cutting at or below the sustainable rate and that the remainder were cutting at more than twice the sustainable level. They claim that although timber concessions were intended to last 35–40 years, most were exhausted within 11 or 12 years. Exports were predicted to decline from 400,000 cu m in 2004 to 100,000 cu m by 2010, if no new concessions were granted. Exports could be stabilized at 1.5m. cu m until 2015 if 10 new concessions covering 2.5m. ha of forest previously identified as suitable for commercial logging are brought into production, but after 2015 they would rapidly decline. In a sharp contradiction of this view, Curtin has produced data suggesting that log exports between 1994 and 2005 did not exceed 65% of the maximum sustainable harvesting potential of any of the forests in the provinces of mainland Papua New Guinea, and that most provinces on the mainland were exporting logs at about 30% of the maximum sustainable yield. Other data produced by Curtin found that losses of forest were much greater on the Papua New Guinea islands of New Britain, New Ireland and Manus, with log exports from West New Britain exceeding the maximum sustainable yield by over 20% in 1994 and 1995. A study in 2008 of satellite imagery between 1972 and 2002 undertaken by researchers from the University of Papua New Guinea and the Australian National University showed that Papua New Guinea had lost forest cover at a much faster rate than previously believed. Over the study period 15% of Papua New Guinea's tropical forests were cleared, and 8.8% were degraded through logging. Deforestation was primarily driven by logging and also by clearing for subsistence agriculture, but since 2002 other data have suggested that there has been an increased conversion of forest for industrial agriculture, particularly oil palm plantations. Most deforestation occurred in commercially accessible forest, where the rate of forest loss ranged from 1.1%–3.4% per annum, higher than reported by FAO, but lower than in Borneo and Sumatra. Overall, the nation's primary forest cover contracted from 33.2m. ha to 25.2m. ha between 1972 and 2002 (FRA 2010 gave an estimate of 26.2m. ha for that year), with an additional 2.9m. ha of forest degraded by logging. Clearly there is much dispute about the sustainable yield of Papua New Guinea's forests, but since the 1970s the nation with the largest share of forestry resources in the Pacific Islands region has failed to manage its forest industry in a sustainable manner. As stated by Phil Shearman, lead author of the 2008 study: 'The unfortunate reality is that forests in Papua New Guinea are being logged repeatedly and wastefully with little regard for the environmental consequences and with at least the passive complicity of government authorities'.

Proponents of forestry exports in Papua New Guinea argue that many critics of the forestry industry ignore the fact that most of the country's land mass is unsuitable for anything except forestry and other tree crops such as cocoa, coffee, copra, rubber and oil palm, which accounted for more than 90% of total non-mineral exports in 2005. They also argue that comparative data show that New Zealand exported 7.2m. cu m of logs in 2001, five times more than Papua New Guinea in that year, and that its total roundwood exports were the equivalent of 13m. cu m, 10 times more than Papua New Guinea in 2001, despite New Zealand's smaller total area and even smaller forested area. Curtin has argued that if Papua New Guinea, with its larger land mass and better climatic conditions for rapid tree growth, were to match New Zealand's performance and, similarly to that country, base its exports on a sustainable plantation-based timber industry, then its gross domestic product (GDP) could have been about 28% larger than it actually was in 2005.

A report by Greg Roberts (published in *The Weekend Australian,* 24–25 June 2006) suggested that from early 2005 the Government's own enforcement unit was effectively disbanded, leaving no official responsible for the monitoring of the activities of the logging industry. The report claimed that Malaysian logging companies, which hold concessions to log 8m. ha of rainforest in Papua New Guinea, were operating in contravention of the country's laws. Compliance audits completed by the Papua New Guinea Government's forestry review team found numerous breaches of regulations in all the 11 projects assessed. A report on the Asengseng project, which was claimed to be typical of such schemes, stated that loan conditions negotiated by the Government of Papua New Guinea and the World Bank to improve forestry practices had not been met and that there was political pressure to issue new permits quickly, in defiance of the established government policy to log forests on a sustainable basis. Curtin has strongly disagreed with claims that much of Papua New Guinea's timber exports are illegal and has maintained that the vast majority of the 46 existing and proposed logging projects have met the legal requirements. Reports of illegal logging activities and human rights abuses by the logging industry in Papua New Guinea prompted the Australian Government to ban the import of illegally logged timber from Papua New Guinea and elsewhere. Other international pressure is being mounted on the Papua New Guinea Government from New Zealand and the Wolseley Group in the United Kingdom, which has banned the import of plywood from the People's Republic of China, the main market for Papua New Guinea timber. However, the reports on which these claims of illegality are based, do not verify the illegality of a single shipment of timber products into Australia. Curtin has suggested that rather than trying to deny access to their markets for timber products important to the economies of Papua New Guinea and Solomon Islands, the Australian and British Governments would do better to help those countries develop that resource in accordance with best practice.

In March 2007 Australia committed US $160m. to global forest conservation efforts to help combat illegal logging and to curb global warming. The assistance is being used to create a new fund, the International Forest Carbon Initiative, which aims to reduce deforestation rates and promote reafforestation schemes. It is to be targeted primarily at tropical developing countries where forest loss is the worst, such as Indonesia and Papua New Guinea. The fund was one of the largest ever established by a government for the purposes of the reduction of tropical deforestation, and it was hoped that other developed countries would also contribute. The plan was a response to a proposal put forth by a coalition of developing countries at climate talks in 2005 when the world's industrialized countries were urged to fund forest conservation efforts to offset carbon emissions. Hopefully, this type of transfer of resources from the developed world to the developing world will continue to increase and significantly assist PICTs in forest conservation, but the effectiveness of these schemes will ultimately depend upon the capacity of local governance in the recipient countries. In Papua New Guinea, as in many other developing countries, local officials are frequently engaged in 'unequal partnerships' with multinational companies, which have the capacity to exert tremendous political and economic pressure in order to extract favourable conditions for their business operations. Financial assistance from overseas has the potential to counterbalance some of these pressures, but it will not eliminate them. As Glen Barry, an expert on environmental sustainability policy, emphasized in early 2009, Papua New Guinea 'cannot industrially log, and clear forests for biofuels, and expect to receive at the same time, avoided deforestation payments'. Papua New Guinea will have to 'choose between continued once off rainforest destruction, mostly for foreign advantage, or being paid more, essentially forever, for maintaining the national and global benefits of fully intact rainforests'. Similar deficiencies in forestry management are widespread among the Pacific Island nations, which have already lost, or are in the process of losing, most of their high-value commercial forests. The subsistence communities of the islands are now experiencing the costs of this loss to their traditional lifestyles, societies and cultures, while their environment is being degraded at an accelerating rate. Commenting on a Malaysian logging company's impact in the Vanimo Timber Area in 1999, an environmental and social impact assessment stated that little had changed since 1989 when Judge Barnett had stated: 'In many cases, the timber industry has made life harder for the landowners at all levels. Not only do they have to face destruction of their environment, but they face the destruction of their society.'

Loss of Biodiversity

The Pacific region is one of the world's most biologically diverse regions, the western Pacific alone being considered to have the highest marine diversity in the world, with up to 3,000 species being found on a single reef. The many thousands of islands are surrounded by rich coastal ecosystems comprising mangroves, seagrass beds and estuarine lagoons, along with complex coral reef systems. The extreme isolation of most of the islands and the evolution of island biogeography have led to a high endemism (i.e. unique to that area) in terrestrial species (in excess of 80% on some islands), especially on the larger islands. Ironically, this treasure trove of biodiversity now ranks as one of the most endangered in the world, with perhaps up to 50% of its total biodiversity at risk because of habitat destruction and alien invasive species, according to the South Pacific Regional Environment Programme (SPREP). Isolation and their dependence on very specialized micro-habitats make these species especially vulnerable to rapid extinction caused by fire or deforestation. The destruction began with early human settlement from the Philippines, South America or both some 3,000 years ago. This early settlement resulted in major changes to the biodiversity of the region as forests were cleared and converted to settlements or agricultural land, forest and lagoon resources were exploited and alien species introduced. For example, there is evidence that a number of bird and other animal species were hunted to extinction by the early Pacific Islanders, who had a profound effect on biodiversity even with relatively low population densities and pre-modern technologies. The threats to biodiversity increased enormously with the arrival of European colonization and the introduction of new post-industrial technologies and exploitative commercial values.

In New Caledonia, for example, 75% of the flora and fauna evolved on the islands and several plant species, unique in the world, are limited to only a small area of one mountain. This rich and diverse genetic heritage is of such scientific importance that New Caledonia has been listed as one of only 10 locations in the world where the primary forest is at once exceptional and endangered. The bird life of New Caledonia is the most diverse in the south-west Pacific, with 68 species, of which 22 are endemic to the country. This bird fauna was even more exceptional before the 18th century, when a giant, flightless bird, like the famous (and also extinct) New Zealand moa, was still common. The extinction of these birds began with the arrival of Melanesians about 900 years ago and was probably caused by fire, slash-and-burn agriculture, and hunting. The arrival of European settlers exacerbated the rate of loss through a combination of logging and mining; furthermore, natural drought conditions resulted in massive fires that destroyed a majority of the habitats on the southern part of the main island. Unfortunately for the biodiversity of the main island, it has the world's largest-known deposits of nickel, which today generate about 90% of New Caledonia's foreign exchange. The impact of the open-cast mining has been devastating, causing large expanses of deforestation and habitat destruction, leaving behind bare slopes and waste heaps. The erosion of the mined areas has caused siltation of streams, pollution of water supplies and the destruction of offshore coral reefs. The intentional and accidental introduction of alien species for food or recreational purposes has also been extremely damaging, as these can often out-compete and replace many of the original species. It is estimated by Conservation International Biodiversity Hotspots that there are now approximately 800 alien plant species, 400 alien invertebrates and 36 alien vertebrates established on the islands. An international market for rare species of birds and marine animals such as the Ouvéa (Uvea) parakeet, the horned parakeet and an endemic cephalopod, poses another threat to the islands' rare and unique species. The experience of New Caledonia was repeated throughout the Pacific. In the Marquesas, Polynesian settlers exterminated eight of the 20 species of sea birds and 14 of the 16 land birds. On Easter Island, the early settlers denuded the entire island of trees and exterminated 22 species of sea birds and all six species of land birds. Given recent high rates of population growth, current trends in land degradation and the excessive exploitation of near-shore and offshore marine resources, the high rates of extinctions experienced in the Pacific Islands are expected to continue, despite a growing recognition of the value of biological diversity among the peoples of the region.

A dramatic example of the effects on biodiversity of the accidental introduction of an alien species is found on Guam, where the venomous brown tree snake (*Boiga irregularis*) was accidentally introduced (probably from the Solomon Islands) after the Second World War. The snake lacked natural predators in its new home and, with an ample supply of prey, its population increased substantially. In the 2002 SPREP report the snakes were estimated to number an incredible 18m. Their impact has been devastating on Guam's native species, especially birds, their preferred diet, but also rats, shrews and lizards. Not having evolved with a night-time arboreal (tree-climbing) predator, Guam's native birds had no physical defences against the snake. By the mid-1980s nine of Guam's 11 native forest birds had become extinct and the survival of the others was very tenuous, despite active protection programmes. The Guam experience illustrates the extreme dangers to local biodiversity posed by the introduction of just one alien species. Numerous sightings of the snake have been made on other islands, and an incipient population is probably already established on Saipan, in the Northern Mariana Islands. With Guam continuing its role as a transport hub, it has the potential to cause similar devastation to the biodiversity of many other Pacific Islands, including Hawaii, where repercussions from its introduction could cost over US $100m. Some of the many other uninvited alien species that continue to cause great damage to the local ecosystems are the Merremia vine, which is rapidly smothering Pacific forests; the black rat, which has already eradicated many unique species of birds and lizards; and the giant African snail, which is threatening agriculture and native plants with its voracious eating habits. It is not known exactly how many invasive species there are on the Pacific Islands, but there could be well over 100, according to the International Union for Conservation of Nature (formerly known as the World Conservation Union) Invasive Species Specialist Group. Indigenous bird species appear to be most at risk, with 54% of recent bird extinctions attributed to invasive alien species.

THREATS TO FRESHWATER RESOURCES, DEGRADATION OF COASTAL ENVIRONMENTS, CORAL REEFS AND COASTAL AND OCEANIC FISHERIES

Threats to Freshwater Resources

Occasional water shortages during droughts have been a long-standing problem throughout the Pacific, with the most severe water shortages being on the atolls and raised limestone islands, where there are no streams and thus inhabitants must rely on the groundwater lens floating on top of the seawater for their water needs. As early as 1992, two-thirds of SPREP members reported water supply and storage problems and an even higher number reported groundwater pollution. The region-wide drought in 1998 highlighted problems of water shortage in Papua New Guinea and Samoa and the need to reduce wastage and consumption. Groundwater pollution levels have not been researched in detail, but both solid and liquid waste disposal systems are inadequate and poorly planned. Waste flows are increasing with population growth, local industrial development and tourism, and pollution problems are likely to worsen. Localized pollution and excessive sedimentation, resulting from uncontrolled watershed development, are common problems in Fiji, Samoa and Solomon Islands. In some atoll communities where the water lens used for cooking and drinking water has been polluted, health problems such as diarrhoea and hepatitis are prevalent, along with occasional outbreaks of typhoid, and in Kiribati, Tuvalu and the Marshall Islands cholera has been diagnosed. As the 1999 UNEP report cautions: 'Pumping from the freshwater lens needs to be carefully monitored and controlled in order to provide warning of impending saltwater intrusion and to test water quality for bacteria counts, chemical residues and total dissolved salts.' Freshwater lenses are governed by the interaction of rainfall volume and periodicity, tidal fluctuations, seepage, hydraulic conductivity and abstraction rates. Once the lens, which is in a dynamic state of equilibrium, is contaminated by saltwater intrusion, for example, it may take years to re-establish. If the contamination is land-based from pesticides or leachate, the recovery time may be much longer. For these reasons, detailed research is required into the sustainability of freshwater resources and provision made for greater investment in appropriate water supplies and sanitation services, before new developments such as large tourism resorts are approved by government authorities. There is a growing consensus that global warming may lead to increased energy in the hydrological cycle and consequent greater intensity and frequency of extreme events such as drought and floods which, combined with sea-level rise, may further increase the threats to freshwater resources.

Degradation of Coastal Environments

As the coastal zone and its immediate hinterland is home to most of the region's inhabitants and the focus of critical economic activities—such as fishing, coastal shipping, port and harbour development, water-based recreational activities, road and urban development, infrastructure development, sewage treatment and disposal, rubbish dumping and coastal protection—it is the zone where the environment is most heavily threatened. Imminent threats to the zone include nutrients derived from sewage, soil erosion and chemical fertilizers, solid waste disposal, sedimentation from land clearance and increased erosion, physical alteration caused by destruction of fringing reefs, beaches, wetlands and mangroves for coastal development and by sand and coral extraction, and over-exploitation of coastal food fisheries, particularly through the use of destructive fishing methods such as explosives. Land reclamation and natural erosion owing to wave action are seen as imminent threats to the marine environment by the Cook Islands, Samoa and American Samoa. In many islands sewage discharge has reduced water quality, reef fish are being over-exploited, rubbish is being dumped along the foreshore and sea turtles no longer find the foreshore attractive for nesting. Marine invasive species are also an issue in some ports and coastal habitats, along with ship-sourced marine pollution. Overall, the coastal zone is extremely vulnerable, and many of the impacts such as the destruction of sea-grasses, mangroves and reef habitats and the attendant wave erosion are irreversible.

Coral Reefs

The coral reefs of the region are among the most biologically diverse ecosystems on the planet, with species diversity in corals decreasing from west to east across the Pacific. Unfortunately, many of these unique ecosystems have been destroyed by human activities. It was estimated that in 1998 about 10% of the region's reefs were under a high risk of destruction (19% in Fiji, 12% in Papua New Guinea and 8% in Solomon Islands), 31% were under medium risk (48% Fiji, 42% Solomon Islands and 38% Papua New Guinea), with the remaining reefs (59%) being under a low risk. Assessment criteria included proximity to coastal development, marine pollution, over-exploitation, destructive fishing, and inland pollution and erosion. The less developed regions such as the Marshall Islands and French Polynesia appear to have some of the more pristine reef ecosystems. During the Second World War more than 1,800 ships were sunk in the Asia-Pacific area, many of them on these reef systems, along with a vast load of armaments. On Chuuk, in the Federated States of Micronesia, people have removed explosives from munition dumps to stun and kill fish, and in 1994 it was reported that blasting had killed 10% of the reefs in the lagoon. However, even if these threats are averted, the coral reefs of the region are being heavily stressed by the abnormally high seawater temperatures caused by global warming and severe and frequent El Niño events, which cause widespread coral bleaching and often coral death.

Coastal Fisheries

Subsistence fisheries are of vital importance to the local people, with some 83% of the coastal households in Solomon Islands fishing for home consumption and 35%, 50%, 87% and 99% of the rural households in Vanuatu, Samoa, the Marshall Islands and Kiribati, respectively, also fishing primarily for their own consumption. Prior to the 1980s it was believed that the fish stocks used for subsistence fishing were underfished and thus offered an important route to economic development. A 1999 World Bank report on coastal management revealed that this view was wrong and that overfishing, aggravated by the use of diving equipment and gill nets, poses a major threat to national food security in many Pacific Islands. However, the report also found that the most serious threats to coastal fish stocks were not only from overfishing, but also from pollution and habitat loss, which depressed the ability of inshore stocks to recover even once extraction rates and fishing practices were controlled. The seagrass beds, coral reefs, mangroves and the sea surface microlayer are all critical nursery habitats for marine plants and animals, and serious damage has been done to these habitats by siltation, pesticides, hazardous chemicals, domestic waste, logging and mining. Mangrove habitats have been especially undervalued in the islands of the Pacific where they have been frequently used as municipal dump sites and filled for housing. Destructive fishing practices such as dynamiting and fish poisoning have also posed major problems. Fish stocks of shallow water coral reefs are in good condition away from population centres but, like stocks of important species that are commercially valuable, they have been overfished near villages and urban centres. Valuable commercial species such as giant clams, lobsters, and most large reef fish have been heavily fished even on the more remote reefs. Many countries in the region received financial assistance to increase their fishing fleet for deep-bottom fishing of deep reefs and sea mounts from 100 m to 500 m below the surface, but it was then discovered that the large fish at these depths took decades to reach maturity and that replenishment was so slow that they could not be successfully fished again for many years. Depletion of the sea mounts in Tonga was particularly rapid. Fishers then moved to more distant sea mounts, but increased fuel costs and problems of refrigeration reduced their profits and many loans could not be repaid. Unfortunately, many administrations have excluded the impact of sport fishing, diving, agricultural, forestry, and mining practices from the fisheries development process, and most communities in the Pacific have had limited capacity to control their fish catches and pollution sources. Since the early 1990s the Secretariat of the Pacific Community

(SPC) has helped shift national fishing priorities from increasing commercial fishing capabilities to sustainable management of fisheries resources, and to an increased awareness of the need to involve local communities in self-management programmes.

Oceanic Fisheries

The commercial exploitation of oceanic marine resources in the Pacific Islands region is dominated by the high-technology fishing fleets of distant fishing nations engaged in harvesting migratory tuna. The tuna harvest is worth some US $4,000m. annually, with the tuna fisheries producing more than nine times the amount of fish of all other fisheries in the region combined. In 2004 the environmental group Greenpeace estimated that 95% of the profits from the tuna fisheries go to distant water fishing nations (DWFNs—nations with boats fishing a long way from home, usually because they have overfished their own waters) such as Japan, the Republic of Korea, Taiwan, China, the USA, the Philippines and members of the European Union (EU). Only 10% of the total catch is caught by Pacific Islanders. Despite this unequal distribution of profits and catch, many Pacific Island nations rely on income from access fees paid by foreign vessels for the right to fish the Exclusive Economic Zones (EEZs) that cover 74% of the region's water surface. The annual tuna catch has been estimated at equivalent to 10% of the combined GDP of all countries in the region and to account for one-third of all exports from the region. In six Pacific Island nations the export value of fishery products accounts for 80% or more of all export revenue. The catch is also a major source of employment for Pacific Island nationals, with 12,300 Pacific Islanders working on tuna vessels and in tuna-processing plants. The total direct and indirect employment was estimated to be between 21,000 and 31,000 people, equivalent to 5%–8% of all wage employment in the region.

The Pacific remains one of the world's last healthy fisheries, supplying 72% of the global tuna catch of 4.22m. metric tons a year, of which the western and central Pacific contributed an estimated 2.46m. tons or 58% in 2009: of this, 1.2m. tons came from the waters of island members of the SPC. The tuna catch in 2009 was the highest annual catch ever recorded, and provided evidence of a 319% increase in the region's tuna harvest over the previous 30 years. The most dramatic increase in the tuna harvest began with a doubling of the catch in the 1980s, as the new highly efficient purse-seine fishing vessels that round up schools of tuna in a single net began cruising into the central and western Pacific from the American coast and East Asia. In the period between 1997 and 1998 and 2001 and 2002 the number of registered fishing boats increased from 827 to 1,233, placing even more pressure on fish stocks. In 2002 the catch taken by purse-seine boats was 1.16m. tons, equivalent to 58% of the total catch, with 17% being taken by pole-and-line methods, 11% by longlines and the remaining 14% taken by troll gear and a variety of artisanal gears. By 2009 purse-seine boats took 77% of the catch and longlines 9%. The purse-seine fishery targets skipjack tuna, but also records significant catches of juvenile yellowfin and bigeye tuna. The longline fishery targets adult bigeye, yellowfin and albacore tuna and, although a much smaller catch, its value is relatively high (30% of the total value), with the longline-caught bigeye and yellowfin tuna exported fresh or frozen to sashimi markets in Japan and the USA, while albacore is a premium 'white meat' canned tuna product. In 2009 stock assessments for the four major tuna species indicated significant differences between species in terms of the sustainability of the current catch levels. The assessment for yellowfin tuna in the Western and Central Pacific Ocean was that although catches had increased in recent years, with a resulting loss of biomass, the stock is not considered to be in an overfished state. However, at the subregional level the western equatorial Pacific region that supplied 95% of the catch is at least fully exploited, with no potential for increased catches. The Western and Central Pacific Fisheries Commission (WCPFC) Scientific Committee reiterated earlier advice that there be no increase in catches from the western equatorial Pacific. The 2010 stock assessment showed that bigeye tuna was either slightly overfished or soon would be, and recommended a 29% reduction from recent catch levels. Although the adult biomass of albacore tuna was 60% below its unexploited levels, expert assessment was that while overfishing was not estimated to be occurring, further expansion of the catch was not advisable and that longline catch rates were probably declining. The fast-growing short-lived skipjack tuna, which in 2009 accounted for 72% of the tuna catch in the western and central Pacific Ocean, appeared to be the tuna species most resilient to current levels of fishing, for although it exhibited a 40% depletion of its adult biomass compared with unexploited levels in equatorial waters, expert opinion was that this species could continue to support catches at current levels (1.8m. tons per annum). However, for the first time, owing to a rapid decline in stocks of skipjack tuna, the Scientific Committee emphasized the need for careful monitoring of any increase in fishing activity that may also have an adverse effect on stocks of bigeye and yellowfin tuna. This suggests less scope to increase catches than had previously been thought.

New 'jumbo' class fishing vessels owned by Taiwan, EU nations and the USA are continuing to expand their operations in the region and are threatening the long-term future of the richest tuna stocks in the Pacific Ocean. These new 'super' purse-seine vessels work with sophisticated fish-finding technology and larger nets and can take up to 3,000 metric tons of tuna in a single fishing trip (almost double the entire annual catch of some island countries), or more than 20,000 metric tons of tuna a year. The EU has gained access to this Pacific fishing ground as a reciprocal benefit for giving aid to Pacific countries. With their own waters depleted, fishing fleets from the countries of the EU and elsewhere, including Japan, South Korea, Taiwan and the USA, are now heavily exploiting the fish stocks of Pacific Island nations, where people depend on them for their food, livelihood and future.

Since the early 1990s the Forum Fisheries Agency (FFA) has been representing the small island developing states of the South Pacific in seeking the adoption of an agreement under international law to limit development of tuna fisheries to sustainable levels in the western central Pacific. The aim has been to balance the sovereign rights of coastal states to set catch limits against the need to co-operate to ensure that the collective catch taken within the EEZs of coastal states and on the high seas does not exceed a sustainable agreed level. In June 2004 the Convention on the Conservation and Management of Highly Migratory Fish Stocks in the Western and Central Pacific Ocean (WCP Fisheries Convention) came into force. Fourteen countries of the Pacific Region have ratified the agreement, which gives signatory nations under the UN Fish Stocks Agreement (UNFSA) the right, for the first time, to board and inspect on the high seas within the Convention Area fishing vessels flagged by a state that has also ratified the UNFSA. Although both Australia and New Zealand are among the ratifying countries and both have provided naval and air force resources to monitor the Convention, its ultimate success will depend on the willingness of major DWFNs such as the USA, Japan, China, Taiwan, the Republic of Korea and the countries of the EU to accept its regulations and honour their responsibilities. In the mean time, the threat to the region's fisheries from illegal fishing activities and bilateral licensing agreements between small island nations and powerful DWFNs continues, with EU vessels joining the more than 1,000 Asian and American boats fishing in the EEZs of the region.

In May 2008 fisheries ministers of the Federated States of Micronesia, Kiribati, the Marshall Islands, Nauru, Palau, Papua New Guinea, Solomon Islands and Tuvalu signed the Nauru Agreement, which entailed stricter measures to conserve tuna stocks. Parties to the Nauru Agreement (PNA) decided that foreign fishing boats licensed to fish in their waters would no longer be allowed to fish in high-sea pockets adjacent to the EEZs of PNA members, with 100% of these vessels being required to carry local observers. In April 2010 the PNA announced that, from the beginning of 2011, high seas surrounding these member countries (an area of 4,555,000 sq km) would be closed to purse-seine vessels licensed to fish in their waters. The majority of Pacific tuna comes from these pockets and the EEZs of PNA members. At the same time, in an attempt to restrict the time at sea of foreign vessels and thereby limit their catches, foreign vessels were to be required to retain their full catches on board, whether or not they are tuna stocks. Previously, non-tuna species were thrown overboard to make room in boats' holds for the more valuable tuna species. In addition, the use of fish aggregation devices used to attract juvenile bigeye and yellowfin tuna will be banned in the waters of PNA members for three months of the year. In December 2009 FFA members asked the WCPFC further to increase controls on illegal fishing by ensuring that penalties imposed on illegal vessels are to the satisfaction of the states in which the offence was committed. It was also decided to make countries where the ships are flagged responsible for ensuring that all relevant vessels are on the WCPFC Register. The International Seafood Sustainability Foundation (ISSF) at its January 2011 meeting expressed concern that in 2010 the WCPFC had failed to strengthen its conservation and management measure (CMM-08-01) aimed at ensuring that stocks of bigeye and yellowfin tuna are maintained at levels capable of producing their maximum sustainable yield. This was despite a report by the WCPFC's own Scientific Committee that this measure was not achieving its goal of reducing fishing mortality on the bigeye stock by 30%, and would, according to the most optimistic analyses, result in only a 14% reduction. The ISSF urged the WCPFC at its 2011 meeting to enact meaningful conservation and management measures for 2012 and for subsequent years that would stop overfishing of the bigeye tuna resource. The ISSF also supported a complete closure of the purse-seine fishery, as opposed to the ineffective partial closure under CMM-08-01.

A report prepared by the World Wildlife Fund (WWF) for the review conference of the UNFSA held in May 2006 suggested that, despite the proliferation of Regional Fisheries Management Organizations (RFMOs) such as the WCPFC, these organizations had failed to prevent over-exploitation of straddling and highly migratory fish stocks, to rebuild over-exploited stocks and to prevent degradation of the marine ecosystems in which fishing occurs. According to the WWF, fish stocks in international waters are still being plundered to the point of extinction, with illegal fishing, overfishing and bottom-trawling in deep waters being to blame for most of the damage and not enough being done to enforce quotas or to replenish stocks. Species under severe threat globally include tuna and the orange roughy. The orange roughy is particularly targeted by bottom-trawlers, which drag heavy rollers over the ocean floor, destroying coral and other ecosystems in their path. Given the perilous overall state of marine fisheries resources, the director of the WWF's global marine programme asserted that the need for urgent action is immediate. The WWF report acknowledged that the WCPFC is one of the few RFMOs that have established an ecosystem and bycatch approach to protect other species such as seabirds and turtles and non-target fish species. Despite these preliminary attempts to recognize the problems, research by Larry Crowder of Duke University in the USA has illustrated the current disastrous impact of longline fishing practices on the population of loggerhead and leatherback turtles. Crowder claims that these two endangered species have an annual 40%–60% chance of meeting a longline hook and that thousands are dying annually as a result. In the Pacific, where these two species of turtles are critically endangered, their annual losses as a result of longline fishing are estimated to be greater than the numbers that nest annually in the world's largest ocean. What makes the mortality rates so high is that turtles are not homogeneously distributed throughout the vast expanses of the Pacific; instead they are located at particular sites. New tracking and remote-sensing technologies are revealing that marine organisms, including turtles, congregate along marine 'highways', and these highways or habitats that have now been detected by the high-technology fishing industry are locations where there is intensive fishing.

Recent surveys of the ecological impact of major types of fishing gear have ranked bottom-trawling as the most destructive. This method involves heavy metal rollers pulled by a trawler dragging a heavy net across the ocean floor to pick up slow-growing deep water species such as orange roughy and other marine life. This method ploughs up anything in the way and stirs up clouds of sediment that suffocate any surviving marine life. Photographs of sites that have been bottom-trawled reveal a completely bare ocean floor that appears as if it has been 'vacuum-cleaned' of its marine life and marine habitat. In December 2006 the UN General Assembly carried a resolution aimed at restricting high seas bottom-trawling. In May 2007 more than 20 South Pacific nations, members of the newly created South Pacific Regional Fisheries Management Organization, acted on this resolution and agreed to the implementation of important measures to restrict bottom-trawling on the high seas of the South Pacific. This area contains thousands of underwater sea mountains that are considered to be some of the most ecologically rich habitats in the world. It extends from the Equator to the Antarctic and from Australia and New Zealand to the western coast of South America, an area equivalent to one-quarter of the world's high seas. Observers and ship locator monitoring systems are to be used to enforce the voluntary agreement, which declares that fishing vessels must remain at least five nautical miles from deep-water corals and other vulnerable marine ecosystems. The only exceptions are sites where a prior assessment has been undertaken and highly precautionary protective measures have been implemented. As the new agreement has as its signatories major fishing nations and regional powers such as the USA, Canada, Japan, Russia, South Korea, China, the European Commission, France, Australia, New Zealand, Ecuador, Chile, Colombia and Peru, as well as many PICTs, there is some cause to hope that this may become the major advance for marine conservation intended by its supporters. After reviewing progress in 10 well-studied marine ecosystems from around the world, Boris Worm *et al* introduced some rare optimism into the discussion when they concluded in a report published in 2009 that in one-half of these ecosystems the average exploitation rate had recently declined, and in seven systems it was now at or below the rate predicted to achieve maximum sustainable yield. Some of this recovery was due to the temporary respite provided by the surge in oil prices in mid-2008 that forced many high-seas fishing fleets to return to port as long-range fishing became uneconomic. Despite this improvement, 63% of assessed fish stocks world-wide still required re-establishment in 2009, with even lower exploitation rates needed to reverse the collapse of vulnerable species. The authors suggested that 'a combination of traditional approaches (catch quotas, community management) coupled with strategically placed fishing closures, more selective fishing gear, ocean zoning, and economic incentives holds much promise for restoring marine fisheries and ecosystems'. As noted by Glenn Hurry, the retired founding Chairman of the WCPFC, when speaking of this region in 2010: 'If ever there was a place where sustainable fishing has a chance it is here. The bulk of the fish is caught in the EEZs of the island countries.' According to Hurry, the WCPFC has the best set of tools of any fisheries management agency anywhere in the world: vessel-monitoring; an observer programme; and a boarding and inspection regime to prevent illegal fishing. Hurry's optimism is reinforced by the recent realization by Pacific countries that they can generate revenue from defending their resources, and they are now exhibiting a new-found strength in confronting major powers at international meetings.

CLIMATE CHANGE AND ITS CONSEQUENCES

The evidence of global warming, its causes and general consequences, and the conclusions of the working groups that form part of the Fourth Assessment Report (AR4) to the Intergovernmental Panel on Climate Change (IPCC) have been summarized in Part One, Environmental Issues of the Asia-Pacific Region, and will not be elaborated upon in this essay. From the viewpoint of the peoples of the Pacific Islands and their Governments, whose well-being is so dependent on coastal ecosystems, there are five anticipated consequences of climate change that will be critical to their future: global warming and sea-level rise; an increase in climate-related natural disasters (storms, cyclones, floods and droughts); changes to fisheries; disruption to agriculture owing to changes in temperature, rainfall and winds; and increased health hazards.

Dangers of Sea-level Rise

In its 2001 Third Assessment Report the IPCC predicted a range of global sea-level rises with a central value of 48 cm by the year 2100. In AR4 this estimate of predicted sea-level rises was increased to 65 cm above 2000 levels by 2100. Although changes of this magnitude may appear minor on a global scale, for a region with a large number of low-lying atolls and some atoll-based countries such as Tuvalu, Kiribati and the Marshall Islands, they would be very threatening indeed. AR4 makes special mention of low-lying coastal regions, especially low-lying coastal urban areas, small islands and atolls, as being among the world regions most at risk from climate change due to the threat of sea-level rise and increased occurrence of extreme weather events. It goes on to describe these areas as: '. . . key societal hotspots of coastal vulnerability, occurring where the stresses on natural systems coincide with low human adaptive capacity and high exposure'. However, there is still considerable uncertainty about sea-level rise predictions in the Pacific. Examination of long-term tide-gauge records gave estimated positive relative sea-level trends of 1.07 mm and 0.8 mm per year, but the records were of poor quality, there were likely datum shifts and gaps in the records and the estimates were not adjusted for land movement. A more sophisticated tide-gauge array has now been deployed at 12 sites to monitor sea levels in the region with Australian assistance, but the new SEAFRAME gauges have been in place only since the mid-1990s, an insufficient time span over which to estimate accurately long-term trends in sea-level change. Several years ago, Bill Mitchell of Australia's National Tidal Centre cautioned, 'We are yet to see the acceleration of sea levels that the climatologists have predicted'. Nevertheless, the 15-year record does show a dramatic drop in sea levels associated with the 1997/98 El Niño event. Tuvalu experienced a drop in sea level of almost 40 cm, whereas other countries such as Nauru experienced a sea level rise in the year preceding El Niño, giving a total sea-level variation of over 50 cm from one year to the next. These dramatic changes are likely to have an impact on coastal geomorphic processes, and may cause a movement of sediments towards the lagoon on low-lying atoll islands, rather than a simple readjustment of the beach profile to the new sea level. This is an important consideration for island Governments trying to manage their vulnerability.

Data released by the South Pacific Sea Level and Climate Monitoring Project during June 2009 showed that all 12 monitoring stations indicated a worrying upward trend in sea levels over the past 17 years. Solomon Islands, Tonga and Papua New Guinea exhibited the largest average annual net relative sea level rises (after vertical movements in the observing platform and the inverted barometric pressure effect are taken into account) of between 8.6 mm and 6.5 mm per year. Increases in sea levels in the Cook Islands, Tuvalu, Fiji, Samoa and Vanuatu ranged between 5.7 mm and 4.8 mm per year, whereas increases in Nauru, the Marshall Islands and Kiribati ranged between 4.1 mm and 3.1 mm per year, with records being too short in the Federated States of Micronesia to establish a reliable trend. However, project co-ordinators cautioned that longer-term recordings were needed before firm conclusions could be drawn. Certainly any rise in the mean sea level would increase the zone subject to flooding and intensify the impact of high-tide events, storm waves and cyclones. Coastal erosion would increase and the erosion of fringing reefs would disturb lagoon ecology, mangrove habitats would be damaged and fishing nurseries reduced. Tourism facilities, human settlements and infrastructure would be threatened and possibly damaged. The likely increased frequency of wave overwash owing to rising sea levels would also increase the salinity of the freshwater lens found on most atolls above 1.5 ha in size and reduce its potability, thereby threatening the habitability of many atolls. Another factor complicating the measurement of long-term trends in mean sea level is that much of the monitoring has been conducted in areas affected by human interference such as causeway construction, dredging or reclamation. In Kiribati, for example, international print media highlighted the disappearance of Bikeman islet within Tarawa lagoon in the early 1990s as evidence of the damage already being wreaked by climate change, but other commentators suggested that its disappearance was more likely to have resulted from the construction of a major causeway between two nearby islands that affected current and sand flows.

Other media coverage has been similarly alarmist and lacking in any scientific caution. For example, in February 2002 a routine spring high tide in Funafuti, Tuvalu, was described as proof of inundation caused by global warming, and in the same year a publication in the USA claimed that the nine coral atolls of Tuvalu had already been submerged by the rising waters of the Pacific Ocean. Unfortunately, in the case of Tuvalu the more alarmist and emotive views have been adopted by the local political élite, an understandable stance given that the country's highest point is no more than 5 m above sea level and most areas are well below that. Tuvalu's domestic development options are few, with the small independent state having a total land area of just 26 sq km on three small reef islands and six coral atolls that have poor soils and limited resources, and are frequently exposed to environmental stresses associated with cyclones and droughts. Nevertheless, the aspirations of its estimated 11,000 people have increased considerably, as many have experienced wage employment in Nauru or New Zealand. At the same time emigration has increased, and Tuvalu's economic future has become more dependent on remittances from the 20% of the country's work-force now employed overseas. Internal migration from the outer islands to the main island of Funafuti in search of wage and salary employment has placed enormous environmental stress on the main island, the population of which rose from 871 in 1973 to over 4,000 in the late 1990s, leading to attendant overcrowding, poor sanitation and inadequate fresh water supplies. In effect, the natural hazard of global warming and associated sea-level rise has been embraced by local political leaders as a means of overcoming the challenges of economic development in a very small state, and in recent times even more strident appeals have been made for imminent relocation to Australia or New Zealand, along with threats of litigation against the major emitters of greenhouse gases such as Australia and the USA. The problem with this approach is that emotion and rapid environmental degradation have overwhelmed scientific detachment and with it the need for policy changes in major greenhouse gas-emitting states. At the same time, the critical need to develop appropriate environmental management policies within the atoll states themselves, such as mitigation strategies to combat storm surges, cyclonic damage and groundwater pollution, have been ignored as the islanders see their future as being somewhere else.

A study by analysts Webb and Kench of the physical changes in the area of 27 atoll islands in the central Pacific (that included islands in Kiribati, Tuvalu and the Federated States of Micronesia) over a 19–61 year period, during which time there was an average sea-level rise of 2.0 mm a year, showed that 23 of the islands either maintained the same land area or increased in size, while only four suffered a net loss of land area. These findings contradict existing paradigms that low-lying atolls will erode in response to measured and future sea-level rise and 'will sit there and drown'. Modes of island change identified by Webb and Kench included: 'ocean shoreline displacement toward the lagoon; lagoon shoreline progradation; and, extension of the ends of elongate islands. Collectively these adjustments represent net lagoonward migration of islands in 65% of cases.' The islands are able to grow because they are surrounded by coral reefs that are themselves living and growing and constantly eroded by wave action, with the resulting debris being washed up on the islands. The authors suggest that there are three major implications of this study. 'First, islands are geomorphologically persistent features on atoll reef platforms and can increase in island area despite sea-level change. Second, islands are dynamic landforms that undergo a range of physical adjustments in responses to changing boundary conditions, of which sea level is just one factor. Third, erosion of island shorelines must be reconsidered in the context of physical adjustments of the entire island shoreline as erosion may be balanced by progradation on other sectors of shorelines.' Inundation of many small low-lying islands by seawater is still a major threat, but island nations must place a high priority on predicting the precise styles and rates of change that will occur over the next century and reconsider the implications for adaption.

Climate-related Natural Hazards, Fisheries, Agricultural Production and Health

Another predicted consequence of global warming is an increased incidence of more extreme weather events coupled with El Niño, which would have a severe impact on agricultural productivity through drought and water shortages. The UNEP *Pacific Islands Environment Outlook* claimed that as early as 1999 there was growing evidence of these impacts. The report cited water shortages and drought in Papua New Guinea, the Marshall Islands, the Federated States of Micronesia, American Samoa, Samoa and Fiji, and floods in New Zealand. It also cited research from New Zealand's National Institute of Water and Atmospheric Research suggesting that climate had changed from the mid-1970s in the following regions: Kiribati, the northern Cook Islands, Tokelau and northern French Polynesia had become wetter; New Caledonia, Fiji and Tonga had become drier; Samoa, eastern Kiribati, Tokelau and north-east French Polynesia had become warmer and cloudier; New Caledonia, Fiji, Tonga, the southern Cook Islands and south-west French Polynesia had become warmer and sunnier; and Western Kiribati and Tuvalu had become sunnier.

The accumulation of carbon dioxide and other greenhouse gases in the atmosphere owing to human activities is acting in two major ways to affect fisheries: through global warming and through ocean acidification. First, alterations in ocean temperatures and currents and in the food chains in the open ocean are projected to affect the future location and stocks of tuna species in the Pacific Islands region. Early simulation modelling suggests that the major concentrations of skipjack and bigeye tuna are likely to be located further to the east than in the past. Simulations have yet to be done for yellowfin and albacore. This movement of tuna stocks has the potential to make the EEZs of some Pacific nations more or less attractive to DWFNs engaged in surface fishing for skipjack tuna, with consequences for GDP. Currently, revenues from the sale of fishing rights for tuna make up a greater proportion of GDP in some of the smaller Pacific nations of the central Pacific, such as Kiribati, Tuvalu and Tokelau, than they do in many nations to the west, so any movement eastwards would provide a windfall to these Pacific nations that have few alternative options for generating national income. The larger Melanesian nations in the western Pacific would be comparatively much less affected, although there would be substantial losses in real terms, with their canneries losing some of their comparative cost advantages if they are required to source fish from outside their own EEZs. However, the negative impact on the small western and central Pacific nations of Nauru and the Federated States of Micronesia are likely to be much more serious. Second, coral reefs are predicted to be degraded owing to the synergistic effects of more frequent bleaching, lower levels of carbonate, increased cyclone intensity and greater turbidity of coastal waters that will in turn reduce the productivity of coastal fisheries. Aquaculture is also likely to suffer problems related to floods, increased acidification, and higher temperatures. The report of a scientific panel convened by the International Programme on the State of the Ocean (IPSO), issued in June 2011, warned that owing to the synergistic effects of ocean acidification, warming, local pollution and overfishing, the state of the oceans is so serious that the planet may be entering a phase of extinction of marine species unprecedented in human history.

Increases in the incidence of heavy rainfall and flooding are predicted to raise the rates of water-borne diseases, while higher temperatures and humidity may increase the incidence of vector-borne diseases, such as dengue fever, malaria and yellow fever. Research has shown a strong link between the incidence of El Niño events and dengue fever outbreaks. In 1997/98, during the drought associated with the El Niño event, a dengue fever epidemic affected 24,000 people and killed 13, at a cost of US $3m.–$6m. Drought and water shortages also tend to increase the likelihood of diarrhoea, eye and skin diseases, poor nutrition and a general low level of health, particularly in poorer areas such as urban squatter settlements where clean water supplies and sanitation services are inadequate.

The UNEP report also claimed that cyclones have become more frequent. Tokelau, for example, had suffered only three major storms since 1846, but two cyclones struck in the early 1990s alone. Tuvalu experienced an average of three cyclones per decade from the 1940s until the 1970s, but eight struck the island nation in the 1980s. Events in early 2005 reinforced these concerns. In less than three weeks in February, the Cook Islands was struck by three cyclones (Meena, Nancy and Olaf), with Cyclone Olaf causing substantial damage to property and telecommunications on the west coast of Rarotonga and also to the island of Ta'u in American Samoa. At the end of February 2005 Cyclone Percy caused widespread damage to Tokelau. There is also concern that tropical cyclones may become more intense, which could increase storm surge height. These concerns were underlined in January 2004 when the island of Niue was struck by Cyclone Heta, a Category 5 cyclone (a once-in-1,000-years event), with winds of up to 300 km an hour and a storm surge that brought waves up over 18 m cliffs, leaving 200 of the island's 1,600 residents homeless. Niue's close association with New Zealand and Australia guaranteed that in this case international emergency aid was provided very quickly, but the small size of most of the Pacific Islands, their remoteness and limited financial resources, combined with a steady degrading of traditional coping measures, have made the islanders and the island ecosystems more vulnerable to disasters than in earlier times. Poor farming practices and logging on steep slopes mean that in recent cyclonic conditions massive erosion usually occurs, which in turn pollutes water supplies and deposits massive loads of silt on the coral reefs. Small gardens that were once protected by trees are today large unprotected gardens that can be totally destroyed by cyclonic downpours. In Pohnpei, in the Federated States of Micronesia, for example, after a severe cyclone in 1997 massive landslides caused loss of life, destruction of commercial kava plantations on the upper slopes and damage to coastal reef communities. The cyclone precipitated this disaster, but the large-scale clearing of upland forest for commercial kava plantations had established the ideal pre-conditions.

LAND- AND SEA-BASED POLLUTION

It is a sad irony that governments in an area of the world renowned for the unspoilt beauty of its lagoons and beaches now list the prevention of pollution as their major environmental concern. Indeed, pollution is now so serious that it is recognized as one of the major threats to the sustainable development of the Pacific Islands region, causing damage to its tourism and trade, food supplies, public health and environment. The main types of pollution within the region have been identified by SPREP as shipping-related pollution, hazardous chemicals and hazardous wastes, and inadequate solid waste management and disposal. The region's marine resources are increasingly being threatened by introduced marine species, shipwrecks, marine accidents and spills and ships' waste. There are also increasing quantities of solid waste and a poor control of chemicals imported into the region, and a lack of capacity to manage waste disposal, let alone develop programmes to recycle it. Much of the rubbish slowly breaks down and leaches into the soil and into drinking water supplies, but in the mean time it is dumped on the nearest available government land where there is a proliferation of plastics, paper, glass, metal and even drums of hazardous chemicals. Foul-smelling organic wastes attract disease-carrying pests such as mosquitoes, rats and flies, increasing the incidence of vector-borne disease. In the absence of publicly funded waste disposal systems, piles of household rubbish collect on beaches and in mangrove swamps, detracting from the reputation of the region's famed beaches and waterways. The economic vulnerability and political dependence of many of the countries in the region has exposed their people to the pollution and hazards of nuclear testing, dumping of toxic and radioactive wastes and their shipment, as well as to pollution from mining activities desperately required to bolster meagre foreign exchange earnings.

Land-based Pollution and Waste Management

For most of the last century the impacts of pollution were small and there was little need for waste management in the Pacific

Island countries because most waste products were biodegradable and populations were dispersed. Wastes were usually disposed of through individual dumping in lagoons and rivers or on unused land close to villages. The growth of urban populations and increased imports of non-biodegradable materials and chemicals related to agricultural and manufacturing activities created environmental health problems and the need to manage waste and toxic and hazardous substances. The small size of many Pacific Islands and their dependence on marine resources and a limited land resource base make them very vulnerable to contamination by toxic and hazardous wastes and chemicals and radioactive materials. Although biodegradable material such as vegetable and putrescible waste and garden waste still dominated the household waste stream in most Pacific Island states in 1994, during the 1990s there was a rapid increase in the importation of packaged consumer goods. These have added to the growing amount of non-biodegradable waste such as plastics, glass, cardboard, paper and metals. Increased urbanization placed greater demands on inadequate sanitation systems, resulting in high coliform contamination of surface waters and groundwater near urban centres. Public health has been affected, with diarrhoea the third most common cause of hospitalization in the Pacific Islands. In Kiribati, cholera, diarrhoea and other water-related diseases were the major cause of death. In Ebeye lagoon, in the Marshall Islands, pollution rates reached levels 25,000 times higher than World Health Organization safe levels, and epidemics of gastroenteritis were almost impossible to control. Toxins from industrial waste, effluent from abattoirs, fish canneries or other food-processing plants, leachate from sawmills, and copper-chrome arsenic chemicals used in the preservation treatment of wood have also caused problems. The continued use of chemicals in agriculture and in manufacturing, such as in fibreglass fabrication and the manufacture of plastic packaging, has exacerbated the amount of pollution from toxic and hazardous substances, the presence of which can usually not even be monitored by the inadequate laboratory facilities existing in most Pacific Island countries. A 1999 SPREP/AusAID study of persistent organic pollutants in the region found that considerable stockpiles existed in some countries and that a number of sites had been contaminated through past disposal or storage of these chemicals. For example, even without data from Papua New Guinea and French and US Territories, which were not included in the study, Pacific Island countries had an estimated 130 metric tons of agricultural chemicals (including DDT) that were polluting sites, 220,000 litres of potentially polychlorinated biphenyls (PCB) contaminated transformer oil and another 21 pesticide-contaminated sites. Particular attention is required at the national level to strengthen the capacity of island countries to minimize and prevent pollution, but the small size of local markets and the limited land areas mean that increased international assistance will be required to tackle disposal issues, and to develop programmes to reuse, recycle and reduce wastes and to give effect to the Waigani Convention (see below) and the Global Programme of Action for the Protection of the Marine Environment from Land-Based Activities.

Sea-based Pollution

Sea-based pollution is also a major problem for the Pacific Islands region. The dangers have come from two major sources: shipwrecks sunk in the Pacific Theatre in the Second World War with their unexploded ordnances still on board, and spills of oil and other chemicals from ships visiting or traversing the region. The Pacific was the scene of some of the largest and most famous naval battles of the Second World War, such as Pearl Harbour, Midway, Truk lagoon, Bismarck Sea, Guadalcanal (Iron Bottom Sound) and the Coral Sea. During these and other battles in the early 1940s more than 1,800 ships were sunk in the Asia-Pacific area. The shipwrecks include 23 large aircraft carriers, 213 destroyers, 22 battleships, hundreds of Japanese planes and submarines, and 50 oil tankers. It is the oil tankers that pose the biggest environmental threat. Now, over 50 years since their sinking, these rusting hulks are beginning to discharge their potentially deadly cargo. One tanker alone holds some 19m. litres of fuel oil. Some ships are lying in open water, but others lie within the fringing reef so that any leak is trapped within the island's lagoon. However, the lack of major land-barriers throughout the Pacific, combined with the complex pattern of transoceanic currents, means that in terms of water circulation the Pacific Ocean is perhaps the most highly connected and continuous ocean. These characteristics of the Pacific region compound the seriousness of marine pollution within the region: pollution incidents in one area have potentially serious implications for other areas. SPREP has developed the Pacific Ocean Pollution Prevention Programme (PACPOL), a comprehensive programme to address marine pollution from ship-based sources. By 2002 SPREP, through PACPOL, had set up a regional database that held details on more than 1,500 wrecks across the Pacific region. The next steps will be to identify a generic risk-assessment model to classify the sites, agree on the interventions for each risk category, assess each site and then begin active interventions. Other sea-based threats to the marine environment include anti-fouling paints, introduced rodents or organisms in ballast waters, nutrient enrichment from rusting steel and dispersion of fishing gear that may entangle marine life.

Globalization, the Dumping of Wastes, and Nuclear Testing in the Pacific

With the outbreak of the Pacific War, the region assumed a strategic importance to the major powers, which it has not relinquished since. Unfortunately, this role has come at great environmental cost, and since 1945 the region's huge distances, political dependence and relative isolation from the homelands of the major powers, such as the USA, the United Kingdom and France, have encouraged its use as a nuclear-testing site, as a missile-testing zone, and as a storage and disposal site for chemical weapons. Nuclear testing by the USA began in the region at Bikini and Enewetak atolls in the Marshall Islands, some 4,800 km west of Hawaii and 7,700 km from the West Coast of the USA, in June 1946 and April 1948, respectively. By the time that testing stopped at Bikini atoll in 1958, it had been the site for 23 atmospheric atomic bomb tests. The world's first thermonuclear detonation, a prototype of the hydrogen bomb with a yield of 10.4 megatons (an explosive force 693 times more powerful than the atomic bomb that annihilated Hiroshima in 1945), was conducted at Enewetak atoll in November 1952. The explosion vaporized the island of Elugelab and left behind a 3-km-wide crater and a deeply fractured reef platform that cleaved away and plummeted into the ocean depths after an adjacent thermonuclear test in 1958. This was followed up by the even more powerful Bravo test of a hydrogen bomb at Bikini atoll in February 1954, which at 15 megatons was the most powerful bomb ever exploded by the USA (being 1,000 times more powerful than the atomic bomb dropped on Hiroshima). The force of this bomb was so great that it vaporized three islands and threw radioactive debris over nearly 50,000 sq miles. It also covered the atolls of Rongelap and Utirik and their residents with radioactive fall-out. By the time the USA ceased its nuclear-testing programme in the Marshall Islands in 1958, after 12 years of testing, it had detonated 67 nuclear bombs in and around the land, air and water of the territory. The bombs had a total yield of 108,496 kilotons, over 7,200 times more powerful than the atomic weapons used during the Second World War. The testing totally destroyed six small islands and hundreds of people had been irradiated. The Bikini and Enewetak islanders had been evacuated before the explosions, but peoples of Rongelap, Bikini, Enewetak, Utirik, Ailuk, Likrip and other Marshallese continue to suffer from cancer, miscarriages, and tumours resulting from the radioactive fall-out. Some 84% of those who lived on Rongelap and were aged less than 10 years at the time of the explosions have required surgery for thyroid tumours.

The Bikinians, Rongelapese and the Enjebi community from Enewetak are still 'nuclear nomads' 50 years after the cessation of testing, unable to return to their native atolls and suffering hardships on islands less hospitable than their original homelands. The Enewetakese were unable to return home for 33 years, during which time they were exiled on desolate Ujelang atoll, where the US Government acknowledged that they suffered grave deprivations. On the return of some islanders in 1980, they found a vastly different Enewetak: only 43% of the land area was habitable and some 8% or 154.4 acres had been vaporized. Other tests were carried out in the region on Kiritimati (Christmas) Island (one of the Line Islands and previously part of the British colony of the Gilbert and Ellice Islands—now respectively Kiribati and Tuvalu) by the United Kingdom from 1957 until 1958, and these were resumed again in 1962 at Kiritimati by the United Kingdom and the USA, in a successful attempt to force the USSR to agree to an atmospheric test ban treaty. All testing ceased at Kiritimati in 1962. Tests were also conducted at Johnston Atoll, a US possession 1,900 km to the north-west, from 1958 to 1962. The French Government had also begun atmospheric nuclear testing in the Pacific at Mururoa atoll in the south-east corner of the Tuamotu archipelago in French Polynesia in 1966, and underground tests were begun in 1974. Over the period 1966–92 a total of 41 atmospheric tests and 138 underground tests were conducted. The testing was halted in 1992, in accordance with the Nuclear Non-Proliferation Treaty, but then, despite the outrage of Pacific Island countries, France conducted six more underground tests between 1995 and 1996, when they were finally halted. Although the atmospheric tests at Mururoa, Kiritimati and Johnston increased the risks to humans and aquatic life, they were smaller in yield than those at Bikini and Enewetak. They were also exploded at high altitude, unlike the larger ground-level tests, and appear to have had a less harmful impact on the inhabitants, who were only partly evacuated by the British, US and French authorities. A 1978 study of rats at Enewetak found possible inherited genetic effects caused by radiation, and there were some fears that genetic mutations could have occurred among marine life at Mururoa, where radiation was reputed to have seeped from underground fissures. Certainly, French evidence has shown that years of testing cracked the atoll and probably altered the land plates. In October 2005 the President of French Polynesia claimed that unexpectedly high levels of radioactive contamination were still being discovered in the territory almost a decade after nuclear testing ended on Mururoa Atoll.

Although nuclear testing ceased in most of the Pacific Islands region in 1962 and at Mururoa in 1996, chemical weapons began to be stockpiled at Johnston Atoll in 1971. Incineration of these weapons in 'burnships' began in 1990 and was completed in 2000, with more than 400,000 rockets, projectiles, bombs, mortars and mines being destroyed. A clean-up of the atoll was commenced, and in June 2004 all military personnel departed and the island was transferred to the control of the US Fish and Wildlife Service. However, there is considerable concern that pollution from the plutonium landfill could be absorbed by fish and the threat carried elsewhere. The radioactive rubble left behind has been contained by a sea wall, but the life of that sea wall is predicted to be less than 50 years. The threat of further contamination continues. In the late 1980s, for example, there were at least 10 attempts to use the Pacific Islands as a place to install hazardous waste dumps, incineration sites or storage areas. These proposals were sophisticated and contained a multitude of financial incentives. The independent Governments of the Pacific Island countries rejected the proposals on environmental grounds. The Basel Convention came into force to ensure the safe shipment of hazardous wastes in 1992, and was strengthened in 1994, to outlaw the export of hazardous waste from countries of the Organisation for Economic Co-operation and Development (OECD) to non-OECD countries. In 1995 the South Pacific Forum (now the Pacific Islands Forum) presented to its members the Waigani Convention to ban the import of hazardous and radioactive waste into the territory of its members and to control the transboundary movement of these wastes. Parties to the Waigani Convention are Australia, the Cook Islands, the Federated States of Micronesia, Fiji, Kiribati, Nauru, New Zealand, Papua New Guinea, Samoa, Solomon Islands and Tuvalu.

IMPACT OF MINING ACTIVITIES

Mining has had a significant impact on the environment of many of the Pacific Islands, and, in the extreme case of Nauru, decades of phosphate-mining have made most of the island a lunar landscape that is quite incapable of supporting its population. There are four kinds of mining in the Pacific Islands: mineral extraction (nickel, gold, silver, copper, iron, uranium and titanium); coal-mining; construction mining (for fill, building stone and cement); and petroleum and gas extraction. Papua New Guinea, New Caledonia, Solomon Islands and Fiji are the major mineral mining centres, and Papua New Guinea also produces petroleum and natural gas, mostly from off shore. Mining in these countries has resulted in unavoidable localized damage to the environment from mine tailings, processing fumes and siltation of streams. In the mountainous areas of New Caledonia and Papua New Guinea, strip mining has been particularly damaging. For example, the Panguna copper mine on Bougainville was developed without strict environmental controls and dumped enormous quantities of tailings that turned the fertile Jabs and Kawerong river valleys into wastelands, made the water undrinkable and destroyed coastal fisheries. This caused enormous resentment among local villagers which, combined with the failure of the mining corporation Rio Tinto to pay compensation to the local landowners, contributed to a civil war that led to the closure of the mine in 1989. The Ok Tedi gold and copper mine was set up with numerous controls to avoid the problems of Bougainville, and the agreement even contained clauses on how to close a mine after its resources were exhausted. However, when settlement ponds were destroyed in an earthquake and the mine was allowed to continue operations, the results were much the same, with sediments severely polluting the Fly and other nearby rivers and killing local gardens and fisheries. Tens of thousands of metric tons of tailings containing copper, zinc, cadmium and lead were dumped directly into the Fly and Ok Tedi rivers every day for two decades. Environmental damage was so severe that local landowners attempted to sue the mine owner for $A4,000m. in compensation. The case was dismissed on a technicality, and the Papua New Guinea landholders reluctantly accepted an out-of-court settlement. However, concern about the huge costs involved in the development of a comprehensive waste management scheme forced Australia's BHP Billiton in early 2002 to divest its shares to a local company. Given the importance of the mine to the Papua New Guinea economy (it accounted for 18% of the country's foreign exchange earnings in 2000) and the fact that it employed, both directly and indirectly, 3,500 local villagers in 2002, the Papua New Guinea Government had little choice but to continue to operate the mine until its reserves run out.

However, environmental problems continue at the Ok Tedi mine, and in May 2011 production was halted for a month after leaks were discovered in the tailings waste pipeline along the Tabubil–Kiunga highway. In June 2005 the recently elected Autonomous Bougainville Government agreed unanimously to allow mineral exploration in the island province and urged the Papua New Guinea Government to lift its existing moratorium. Although they denied that this might result in the eventual reopening of the Panguna mine, local leaders were concerned about the financial sustainability of the new Government without mineral revenues. As a referendum on full independence from Papua New Guinea must be held between 2015 and 2020, from early 2010 Bougainvilleans began to consider reopening the massive Panguna mine as a means of funding that independence. The reopening of the mine is expected to cost more than $A3.0m., but it would provide access to reserves worth about $A50,000m., and its reopening is supported in principle by the Bougainville President, John Momis.

The controversy surrounding the development of the Ramu nickel mine, located south of the Ramu River near Madang in Papua New Guinea, has been analysed in previous editions. In December 2007 the Papua New Guinea Government gave approval for the project to proceed. However, copies of the environmental impact assessment were not made public. In June 2009 concerns were raised about the 135-km pipeline being built to carry slurry from the Kurumbukari mine site to the Basamuk refinery on the Rai coast. The route of the pipeline was regarded as too close to the Madang Highway. The pipeline did not have proper foundations; it cut through villages and was constructed just metres above waterways. In early 2010 landowners from the communities affected on the northern coast of Madang province successfully won a court order preventing China's Ramu NiCo company from blasting coral reefs to lay a deep-sea tailings pipeline. The landowners' lawyer pointed out that 99% of the tailings are waste and that it would be more appropriate to return them to where they came from, rather than depositing them in a completely foreign environment under the sea. All of these issues raised environmental and public health concerns. The Chinese state-owned operator of the project, the Metallurgical Construction Company (MCC), was also accused of bringing in illegal workers, thereby depriving local people of job opportunities, of unsafe work practices, of failing to compensate local landowners and of introducing an alien monoculture of hybrid rice cultivation to supply its Chinese work-force. Between August 2008 and May 2009 construction of the mine was halted several times following attacks by angry landowners and fights between employees, which hospitalized injured Chinese workers. Despite delays, the owners claimed that commissioning of the mine would begin on schedule in December 2009; however, by mid-2011 this had not taken place. In a controversial development, in May 2010 the Prime Minister of Papua New Guinea, Sir Michael Somare, at the request of the Chinese owners of the Ramu nickel mine, hastily secured the passage through the National Parliament of amendments to the country's Environment Law, with no consultation or debate. These amendments permitted marine dumping of mine waste and removed landowners' constitutional rights to control what happens on their land and their legal rights to compensation for any environmental damage that is caused. Thus, the Chinese-owned mine would be able to dump hundreds of millions of tons of mine waste into the sea without fear of expensive litigation in the event of environmental damage. In marked contrast, Papua New Guinea's own proposed marine protection laws, which were circulated for public consultation in 2008, were still awaiting enactment by the National Parliament in 2010. An interim injunction temporarily preventing Ramu NiCo from using its deep sea tailings placement offshore facility in Astrolabe Bay was brought by Rai Coast landowners in March 2010. However, in July 2011 the National Court in Madang ruled that toxic dumping could proceed, despite acknowledging the likely adverse impact on the ecology and food chain of the area.

The Porgera Gold Mine in the central highlands of Papua New Guinea has also attracted adverse publicity, owing to conflict with local villagers and to environmental concerns. It is one of the world's leading 10 gold mines: in 2008 it produced 627,000 ounces of gold from a 5,600-acre special mining lease based on open-pit and underground mining methods. It is a highly advanced operation, and is 95% owned by Barrick Gold of Canada, the world's largest gold-mining company. It utilizes the most advanced extraction technologies and uses helicopters to transport people and gold in and out on a daily basis. However, the mine disposes of riverine tailings of processed ore directly into the local river, causing an increased sediment load of 8m. metric tons per year, massive siltation and fears of increased toxicity of major rivers downstream such as the Fly, owing to the significant quantities of cyanide, mercury and other heavy elements that may ultimately enter the food chain. This practice would not be permitted in Canada, Barrick Gold's country of domicile. The mine also has two 'erodible dumps' where soft rock is deposited. The heavy rainfall in this part of the highlands results in much of the sediment in these dumps also being carried into the local rivers, where it may add another 4m.–6m. tons of sediment load per year. Mine management is actively pursuing the possibility of constructing a tailings storage facility as a more environmentally friendly way of disposing of its waste ore. However, this will require additional compensation of local landowners and large alterations of current catchment systems. Furthermore, it would effectively shorten the mine's period of operation, originally estimated to last until 2020. This is because a tailings storage facility can only be constructed to a certain size and once full it would be impossible to revert to riverine discharge. When the mine was first opened, local villagers successfully negotiated the provision of modern health and education services from the mining company, plus payment for the use of the land and of dividends, but the situation began to change in the mid-1990s when the most accessible veins of ore were depleted. The company then turned to open-pit mining, began blasting away the hills, used cyanide and other toxins to leach gold from the rubble and started to dump huge quantities of waste into the local streams. Employment opportunities in the mine and the opportunity to obtain gold from traditional alluvial mining (sometimes illegally from within the company's special mining lease) began attracting tens of thousands of migrants. A 'black market' in guns, drugs, scrap metal, mercury and stolen gold developed, along with an increase in alcoholism, crime, rape and illegal mining. To combat this lawlessness, the company created its own security force of as many as 500 personnel. Local people claim that since 2007 dozens of people have been killed or assaulted by police and security forces, as tensions have escalated between local residents on the one side and police and the company's security forces on the other. In April 2009 the Papua New Guinea Government declared a state of emergency in the mine area and sent in 200 extra police and military forces, who razed at least 300 illegal migrants' shacks constructed within the special mining lease. Barrick Gold has consistently denied these allegations of gross human rights violations and has refused to carry out the full relocation of landowners living within the mine lease area as requested. In May 2010 the Governor of Enga Province suggested that the unique situation in which local people were living within the special mining lease would continue to cause problems unless they were relocated. Overall, despite the positive impact on national revenue, the local impact of the Porgera mine has been similar to that described by local activist Jethro Tulin: 'In one generation, the mine has brought militarization, corruption and environmental devastation to a land that previously knew only subsistence farming and alluvial mining.'

The Panguna, Ok Tedi, Ramu and Porgera mines are examples of the dependence of even the larger Pacific Island economies on major mining ventures and of their limited ability to enforce strict environmental controls in an era of highly mobile international capital that has great capacity to influence local political élites. These environmental issues appear likely to intensify as Papua New Guinea undertakes a massive liquefied natural gas project, which has the potential to double the size of the country's economy. This project requires the construction of a 248-km onshore pipeline, a 407-km offshore pipeline, 26 major water crossings and 138 minor water crossings. The project involves the clearance of primary tropical forests containing biodiversity of global significance, with heightened risks of increased erosion, contamination from construction, groundwater hydrology contamination, direct and indirect impacts on marine life, increased sedimentation rates and toxicity threats. There is also a large potential for future conflict with local landowners similar to the experiences at the Panguna, Ok Tedi, Ramu and Porgera mines, as the project includes no resettlement plan for indigenous people and fails to recognize that many Papua New Guinea indigenous landowners enjoy perpetual customary tribal land rights that are transferred from one generation to the next.

CONCLUSION

This brief survey of the environmental issues and problems of the Pacific Islands region has emphasized the very strong nexus between the geography of the region, its economic and political dependence, and its extreme vulnerability to environmental degradation and pollution. Although the geographic isolation and marginal political importance of most Pacific Island nations should at first sight protect these countries from the acute environmental pressures experienced by the more economically developed and populous countries of the world, the reality has been quite different. Instead, the weakness of their economies, their extreme geographic isolation, their very limited natural resources and their historical links with major colonial powers have conspired to exacerbate their environmental vulnerability. In this context, and in view of rising expectations among their people, the Pacific Islands have been forced to become economically dependent upon a few strategic industries, such as mining, logging and tourism. Foreign fishermen and loggers, frequently from China, the Republic of Korea and Japan, have been hosted by societies characterized by endemic poverty and a disintegration of traditional cultures and values. A UN Children's Fund (UNICEF) report has documented one of the serious social consequences of this interaction in Solomon Islands, where the presence of foreign loggers and fishermen has encouraged the development of a child sex industry. The relative economic and political vulnerability of the Pacific Island nations to outside pressures has led to the exploitation of their marine and land resources and to the use of the region to test nuclear weapons and to store and dispose of chemical weapons. Even their geographical isolation has conspired to maximize the threats to their biological diversity. Many of them are located on the 'Pacific Rim of Fire', which has exposed them to the natural hazards associated with earthquake and volcanic activity and tsunamis. Their tropical waters have also been the breeding ground for major cyclones, which in recent years have devastated many of their island habitats. However, there now appears to be the beginning of a new era of co-operation, self-help and appreciation of their own cultural identity among the Pacific Island nations that, if fostered by genuine financial, technical and political assistance from nearby industrialized countries, may be able to minimize or even overcome their environmental problems.

BIBLIOGRAPHY

See also the following websites: www.biodiversityhotspots.org (Conservation International—Biodiversity Hotspots); www.fao.org (Food and Agricultural Organization); www.ipcc.ch (Intergovernmental Panel on Climate Change); www.unescap.org (United Nations Economic and Social Commission for Asia and the Pacific); www.undp.org (United Nations Development Programme); www.sprep.org (South Pacific Regional Environment Programme).

General

Nukuro, E. 'A Glimpse at the Pacific Island Countries' Population, Development and Environmental Issues'. Nadi, Fiji Islands. Presented at the Millennium Media Conference on the Environment, 24–28 July, 2000.

Steele, Ross. 'Environmental Issues of the Asia-Pacific Region', in *The Far East and Australasia 2012*. 43rd Edn, London, Routledge, 2011.

Thistlethwaite, R., and Votaw, G. *Environment and Development: A Pacific Island Experience*. Manila, Asian Development Bank, 1992.

UN Environment Programme (UNEP). *Pacific Islands Environment Outlook*. London, United Nations Environment Programme, 1999; internet www.grid.unep.ch/geo2000/region/pieo.pdf.

UN Environment Programme (UNEP) and South Pacific Regional Environment Programme (SPREP). *Pacific Environment Outlook*. Special Edition for the Mauritius International Meeting for the 10-year Review of the Barbados Programme of Action for the Sustainable Development of Small Island Developing States, 2005; internet www.unep.org/geo/pdfs/Pacific_EO.pdf.

Demographic and Health Issues

Haberkorn, G. 'Current Pacific population dynamics and recent trends'. Secretariat of the Pacific Community, Demography, Population Programme, July 2004.

Ragogo, M. 'Islanders 'Unhealthy' And Trend Worsening: Need to act now, or else . . .', in *Pacific Magazine and Islands Business*, January 2004.

Secretariat of the Pacific Community, Statistics and Demography Programme. *Pacific Island Populations—Estimates and projections 2005–2015*. Nouméa, New Caledonia, 2006.

2010 Populations and Demographic Indicators, April 2010; internet www.spc.int/sdp/index.php.

UN. *World Population Prospects: The 2008 Revision Population Database*; internet esa.un.org/unpp.

Land Degradation, Deforestation and Loss of Biodiversity

Australian Conservation Foundation and Centre for Environmental Law and Community Rights. *Bulldozing Progress: Human Rights Abuses and Corruption in Papua New Guinea's Large Scale Logging Industry*. Australian Conservation Foundation and CELCOR, August 2006; internet www.acfonline.org.au/uploads/res/res_acf-celcor_full.pdf.

Barnett, T. E. *Report of the Commission of Inquiry into Aspects of the Forest Industry*. Unpublished report to the Government of Papua New Guinea.

Brunton, B. D. *'Underlying Causes of Deforestation and Forest Degradation, Oceania and Pacific: Forest Loss in Papua New Guinea', Compendium of Discussion Papers in the Oceania Region*. World Rainforest Movement, September 1998; internet www.wrm.org.uy/deforestation/Oceania/Papua.html.

Clark, W. C., and Thaman, R. R. (Eds). *Agro-Forestry in the Pacific Islands: Systems for Sustainability*. Tokyo, United Nations University Press, 1993.

Curtin, Tim. 'What constitutes illegal logging?', in *Pacific Economic Bulletin*, Vol. 22, No. 1, pp. 125–134, 2007.

Food and Agriculture Organization of the United Nations. *Global Forest Resources Assessment 2010*. FAO Forestry Paper 163, Rome, 2010.

Forests Monitor Limited and Individual and Community Rights Advocacy Forum Inc (ICRAF). *Environmental and Social Impact Assessment of Logging Operations in the Vanimo Timber Area, Sandaun Province, Papua New Guinea*. Forests Monitor Limited and ICRAF, May 1999.

Montagu, A. S. *Reforming Forest Planning and Management in Papua New Guinea, 1991–94: Losing People in the Process*, Journal of Environmental Planning and Management, Vol. 44, No. 5, pp. 649–662, 2001.

Forest Planning and Management in Papua New Guinea, 1884 to 1995: A Political Ecological Analysis, Planning Perspectives, Vol. 17, pp. 21–40, 2002.

Nunn, P. *Oceanic Islands*. Oxford, Blackwell, 1994.

West, Paige. *Conservation is Our Government Now: The Politics of Ecology in Papua New Guinea*. Durham, NC, Duke University Press, 2006.

Freshwater Resources, Coastal Degradation, Coral Reefs, Coastal and Oceanic Fisheries

Allen, R. *International management of tuna fisheries: Arrangements, challenges and a way forward*. FAO Fisheries and Aquaculture Technical Paper No. 536, Rome, FAO, 2010.

Cleary, P. 'Troubled waters, but fish tide is turning', in *The Weekend Australian*, 5–6 June 2010.

Gillett, R., McCoy, M., Rodwell, L., and Tamate, J. *Tuna: A Key Economic Resource in the Pacific Islands*. Manila, Asian Development Bank and the Forum Fisheries Agency, 2001.

Gillett, R. *Fisheries in the Economies of the Pacific Island Countries and Territories*. Manila, Asian Development Bank, 2009.

Gillett, R., and Cartwright, I. *The Future of Pacific Island Fisheries*. Nouméa, Secretariat of the Pacific Community and Pacific Islands Forum Fisheries Agency, 2010.

Langley, A., Hampton, J., and Williams, P. *The Western and Central Pacific Tuna Fishery: 2002 Overview and Status of Stocks*. Tuna Fisheries Assessment Report No. 5, Nouméa, Oceanic Fisheries Programme, Secretariat of the Pacific Community, 2004.

Secretariat of the Pacific Community (SPC), Oceanic Fisheries Programme (OFP). *Update on Tuna Fisheries, Update 1/2008*; internet www.spc.int/oceanfish/.

Willock, A., and Lack, M. *Follow the leader: Learning from experience and best practice in regional fisheries management organizations*. WWF International and TRAFFIC International, 2006; internet www.traffic.org/fisheries.

Worm, B., et al. 'Rebuilding Global Fisheries', in *Science*, Vol. 325, pp. 578–585, 31 July 2009.

Climate Change and its Consequences for the Pacific Region

Australian Government, Bureau of Meteorology, National Tidal Centre. *The South Pacific Sea Level & Climate Monitoring Project.* Monthly Data Report No. 167, Adelaide, Bureau of Meteorology, May 2009; internet www.bom.gov.au/oceanography.

Barnett, J. *Adapting to Climate Change in Pacific Island Countries: The Problem of Uncertainty*, World Development, Vol. 29, pp. 977–993, 2001.

Connell, J. *Losing ground? Tuvalu, the greenhouse effect and the garbage can*, Asia Pacific Viewpoint, Vol. 44, No. 2, pp. 89–107, August 2003.

Harvey, N., and Mitchell, B. *Monitoring sea-level change in Oceania*, Tiempo, Issue 50, pp. 1–6, December 2003.

McMichael, A., et al. *Human Health and Climate Change in Oceania: A Risk Assessment 2002*. Canberra, Australian Department of Health, 2003.

Rudiak-Gould, Peter. *The Fallen Palm: Climate Change and Culture Change in the Marshall Islands.* Saarbrücken, VDM Verlag Dr. Müller, 2010.

Webb, A. P., and Kench, P. S. 'The dynamic response of reef islands to sea-level rise: Evidence from multi-decadal analysis of island change in the Central Pacific', in *Global and Planetary Change,* 21 May 2010.

Land- and Sea-based Pollution

Nawadra, S., et al. *Improving Ships' Waste Management in Pacific Islands Ports*. Apia, South Pacific Regional Environment Programme (SPREP), 2002.

South Pacific Regional Environment Programme and Australian Agency for International Development (SPREP/AusAID). *Assessment of Persistent Organic Pollution in Pacific Island Countries.* Canberra, SPREP/AusAID, 1999.

Globalization, the Dumping of Wastes, and Nuclear Testing in the Pacific

Johnston Island History; internet www.janeresture.com/johnston, 7 July 2004.

Nuclear Weapons: US Atmospheric Nuclear Tests Page; internet zvis.com/nuclear/ndb/usnuks.shtml.

Republic of the Marshall Islands. *The Republic of the Marshall Islands and the United States: A Strategic Partnership*; internet www.rmiembassyus.org link to 'Nuclear Issues' to obtain details of the impact of nuclear testing on the Marshall Islands and their people.

HEALTH ISSUES OF THE PACIFIC ISLANDS

DAVID A. K. WATTERS

INTRODUCTION

Core Indicators

The health of a population is measured by referring to core indicators, such as the infant mortality rate, the under-five mortality rate, the maternal mortality rate and life expectancy (see the statistical surveys of individual chapters for such figures). The proportion of gross domestic product (GDP) spent on health, amount per caput and doctor/population ratio are also strongly associated with health and the outcomes of health care. Throughout the Pacific Islands there are variations in core health indicators between nations and also between regions within a country. These differences arise as a consequence of how the population is distributed and how well it can access hospitals, clinics, doctors and other health care workers. Compared with their relatively wealthy neighbours, Australia and New Zealand, the Pacific Island nations are poor and generally much less healthy. They spend 20–50 times less on health care, have 3–10 times fewer doctors and 4–20 times worse core indicators.

Demographics and Fertility

The peoples of the Pacific Islands are young, with 35%–40% of the population being less than 15 years of age. Most of the poorer Pacific Islands have crude birth rates in the range of 25–35 per 1,000, Papua New Guinea being at the upper end of this scale and Samoa being just beneath the lowest at 24 per 1,000. The Northern Mariana Islands, New Caledonia, French Polynesia, Fiji, Niue and Palau have relatively low crude birth rates of 17–20 per 1,000. The fertility rate for women aged 15–49 ranges from 4%–5% for the poorer Pacific nations to 1%–3% for the wealthier ones such as New Caledonia, French Polynesia, the Northern Marianas, Palau and Fiji. Fertility rates, education (particularly education of women) and employment make an important impact on the opportunities and desire for good health.

Less than 5% (often less than 3%) of the population are over the age of 65. Life expectancy at birth is only 50–60 years, 20 or more years less than the developed world average of around 80. New Caledonia, French Polynesia and the small island nations of Palau, Niue, Tuvalu and Tokelau have greater proportions of aged people, with the over-65s representing 5%–10%. Life expectancy at birth in these islands is around 70. Life expectancy at birth also approaches 70 in Fiji, but only 3% of its population is over the age of 65. Pacific Islanders feel a sense of belonging and obligation to their extended families with the result that they make arrangements for their aged relatives; thus the care of the elderly has not yet become a major health care issue as it has in the West.

Law and Order

Health services and access to them may sometimes be disrupted by a breakdown of law and order or civil unrest. People may not feel safe to travel, particularly at night, so relatives cannot take their sick family members to hospital. During times of disturbance, belligerent crowds on the streets may also make it dangerous to travel by day. In most Pacific hospitals the well-being of individual patients (food and psycho-social support) is dependent on other family members who stay with or near their sick relative. There may also be a fear of injury in hospital from rival groups. For example, in Solomon Islands, during one period of unrest in the early 2000s, some patients were hacked to death in the wards in front of medical and nursing staff. The Australian-led Regional Assistance Mission to Solomon Islands (RAMSI) restored peace in 2003, although the political turmoil of April 2006 led to rioting, which left much of the capital of Honiara in ruins (see Security Issues of the Pacific Islands). Medical education may also be affected by unrest. For example, as a result of the coup in Fiji in 1987, many medical students were sent home from the islands, some of whom transferred to the University of Papua New Guinea (UPNG). However, during subsequent coups the Fiji School of Medicine (FSM) carried on with its programmes as normal.

Disasters

Although disasters owing to cyclones, volcanic eruptions, and tsunamis are infrequent, they are to be expected, though it is difficult to predict their precise timing. Disasters place extraordinary demands on health services that are already struggling to meet needs, and they also have the potential to destroy the facilities of care. A major volcanic eruption in Papua New Guinea destroyed much of Rabaul in 1994 (but with the loss of only three lives). The health services were transferred from Nonga (Rabaul) to the Catholic Mission Hospital at Vunapope until Nonga was reopened over a year later. The Aitape tsunami of 1998 caused 2,000 deaths, many injuries and the destruction of whole villages. The Australian military were first on the scene (at the invitation of the Papua New Guinea Government) and provided the initial triage and first-line treatment of the injured. Another tsunami destroyed homes and a hospital in the Gizo region of Solomon Islands in April 2007. In September 2009 a tsunami devastated coastal regions in Samoa, American Samoa and Tonga, causing about 200 deaths. Cyclone Heta destroyed Niue's only hospital, Lord Liverpool Hospital, in January 2004. The World Health Organization (WHO) provides courses in Public Health and Emergency Management in Asia and the Pacific (PHEMAP) to enable Pacific Island nations to make preparations in advance for their response to such disasters.

Safe Water and Adequate Sanitation

Safe water and adequate sanitation are essential for health, particularly to avoid acute and chronic gastrointestinal infections. Acute infections threaten life, particularly the lives of children under the age of five, and chronic infections stunt growth or reduce energy, concentration and motivation. In Papua New Guinea fewer than one-half of the country's 7.0m. people (UN population estimate, mid-2011) have access to safe water or adequate sanitation. In Solomon Islands, Vanuatu and Fiji the figures are 60%–70% for safe water but only 30%–60% for sanitation. The figures can be markedly different between the urban and rural areas. For example, adequate sanitation rates are only 30%–50% for the rural populations of Kiribati, the Federated States of Micronesia, Vanuatu, Papua New Guinea and Solomon Islands, compared with 75%–95% for urban populations. Almost 100% of the populations of French Polynesia, Guam, Nauru, the Northern Mariana Islands, Palau and Tuvalu have access to both safe water and adequate sanitation, regardless of whether they reside in an area classified as urban or rural.

THE SYSTEM OF HEALTH CARE

Primary Health Care

Primary health care is provided in the community at first contact and may be preventive, palliative or curative in intent. In the Pacific Islands the primary health care worker may be a nurse or specially trained health extension officer (formerly aid post orderly) who is on the spot in the health centre or village aid post. Such workers are responsible for vaccinations, primary treatment of infection, first aid for trauma, and referral for complex cases, anomalies and malignancies. Manuals help standardize treatments and give advice about whom to refer. Unfortunately, supervision and support for the primary health care work-force is often deficient, resulting in frustration and less efficient delivery of services. In the cities there may also be private general practitioners who provide much of the primary diagnosis and treatment outside the government health system.

Secondary Health Care

Secondary health care is hospital-based and involves diagnosis and treatment of disease, usually by doctors. A functioning district hospital is the 'hub' upon which the success of the health system in a developing country depends. Its 'spokes' are the health centres, clinics and aid posts that it supplies and supports by managing referrals, providing mentorship, continuing medical education and providing quality assurance. A district or regional hospital may be staffed by general medical officers and/or specialists. The services that it provides must incorporate women's health, including the management of complicated deliveries, paediatrics, surgery and general medicine. Mental health services are usually scarce, not as a result of lack of need but owing to the dearth of specifically trained personnel. Anaesthesia may be provided by a doctor anaesthetist or anaesthetically trained medical assistant but rarely by a specialist anaesthetist, this last category being in short supply across the Pacific region. Laboratory support to secondary health care is often rudimentary and limited to a few blood results, a malarial slide and simple microbiology. Histopathology services are available only in the tertiary referral hospital or must be sourced overseas. The doctors working in the hospital are expected to support and make visits to the health centres. However, in reality the obstacles of overwork, lack of incentives, low morale and dearth of transport all need to be overcome to ensure that such 'outreach' actually eventuates. Private health care is provided in major centres by general practitioners and also by national specialists who have abandoned the public system owing to their frustration with working conditions and lack of financial reward. There is a risk that private specialists will ultimately do more and more general practice and provide less and less specialist care, as a result of which after a few years they may become 'deskilled'.

Health Sector Funding

The proportion of GDP spent on health care measured by expenditure per caput can vary widely from 4%–5% (in Papua New Guinea, Fiji, Solomon Islands and Vanuatu) to around 10% or more (in the Marshall Islands, the Federated States of Micronesia, New Caledonia, Kiribati and Niue). The sums spent are far greater in the islands with a high gross national product (GNP), particularly the French and US territories (or former territories). The Melanesian island nations of the Pacific have the worst health indicators, with inadequate health care funding to meet the public's expectations. The cost of health care across the Pacific is made up from public health expenditure, private health care and donor funding. A reasonable estimate of the proportions of each across the region would be 60:20:20, although there is much variation from country to country. Most governments spend 8%–15% of government expenditure on health care. Health insurance schemes are limited. They tend to be available only to some government and major company employees, and the degree of coverage does not have the capacity to make a significant impact. In most islands the private health system is relatively underdeveloped, particularly when it comes to hospital admissions and specialist care. Another reason is that many of the communities in the Pacific live a long way from their referral hospital and/or from private health services. Traditional healers make up a small but unmeasurable proportion of the system, particularly in rural and remote areas.

In most islands the amount actually disbursed for health care does not match the amount budgeted, because of cash flow and other financial problems. This disparity results in delays in procurements, shortages of some essential items, and much frustration for staff and patients alike. It also results in lack of transport for outreach and retrieval, support to peripheral clinics and health promotion.

Specific Country Examples

In Papua New Guinea health services are provided by government and church organizations, which receive public sector funding. There are also enterprise-based services (for example, the mines such as Ok Tedi, Porgera and Lihir) and a small private sector. The National Health Department is responsible for most of the specialists and their training at the 19 provincial or base hospitals (one for each province). The provincial and local governments are responsible for the hospitals, health centres, and aid posts (collectively known as rural health services) within their Province. The churches are responsible for up to 60% of the rural health services. Papua New Guinea trains its own health work-force, having a school of medicine and health sciences within UPNG (see below). The churches administer five of the eight nursing schools and all of the community health worker training schools. Midwifery training was transferred from the health to the education sector (universities) in 2002, but this has resulted in a decline in the number of graduates and the quality of training. Between 1997 and 2001 total health expenditure rose from 3.2% to 4.4% of GDP, but health spending per caput declined from US $32 to $24. In recent years the commodity boom has enabled Papua New Guinea to increase its health expenditure to $30–$35 per caput, although this still only represents about 3.9% of GDP. The private sector is growing and will need to expand further to meet health care demands.

In Fiji there is a significant private sector, with 'out-of-pocket' expenses representing 35% of total health expenditure. FSM has provided medical training for doctors from all around the Pacific. FSM has also managed three schools in health sciences, oral health, and public and primary care for training other health workers. Specialists, doctors and nurses are frustrated by conditions in Fiji, where there is a significant 'brain drain' of trained personnel. There is also inadequate work-force planning, in view of the limited availability of specialists' positions for nationals who have succeeded in their postgraduate qualifications.

In Solomon Islands there are eight public and four private hospitals. The National Referral Hospital is in Guadalcanal, the centre of the unrest of 2006. Some senior doctors departed to work on neighbouring Pacific Islands during the unrest, although most subsequently returned. There is an uneven distribution of doctors, with the hospital in Malaita (responsible for almost one-quarter of the population) being particularly poorly staffed since 2003. Nurses are more evenly distributed. There is a local midwifery-training programme, which by 2004 had produced seven graduates.

In the relatively wealthy country of Palau the US Government and UN agencies provide a major part of the health care budget. In 2006 there were 26 doctors and 117 nurses serving 20,000 people. The development of a local nursing school was expected to improve retention rates among nurses. The US Government provides significant donor funding to Guam, the Marshall Islands and the Northern Mariana Islands. The University of Hawaii offers support in the training of health workers in these islands, and also previously facilitated the Pacific Basin Medical Officers Training Program in the Federated States of Micronesia (see below). Tonga (with a population of more than 100,000) is another of the wealthier Pacific nations: its inhabitants have a life expectancy of some 70 years. Around 30 nurses per year graduate from the local programme. Cardiovascular and respiratory disease, malignancy and diabetes have become the major causes of mortality.

New Caledonia, French Polynesia and Wallis and Futuna receive significant subsidies from France; their doctor and nurse to population ratios are among the best in the Pacific. These islands have already achieved a life expectancy of around 70 years and now confront a significant obesity problem. Neoplasms and cardiovascular diseases are already the two leading causes of death, with accidents, injuries and poisoning third.

Some of the islands, including Niue, Tokelau, Tuvalu and Nauru, are too small to train their own specialists. Nauru has only two national doctors and relies on recruiting expatriates for five other positions. Previously, when Nauru was well endowed with phosphate revenue, large numbers of patients were sent to Australia for treatment, but in recent years, as Nauru has suffered financial difficulties, donor aid has been used to bring specialist teams to provide secondary and tertiary services on the island. Nauru is remarkable in that its population of about 10,000 has such a high prevalence of obesity, and cardiovascular and renal disease. It even established a local renal dialysis programme when the economy was strong and still maintains between 25 and 30 patients on regular haemodialysis. The shunts to enable vascular access are performed by visiting surgical teams (see below).

The public health system in the Pacific region also has to contend with the problem of access to health care for its rural and remote communities. There are significant challenges to be overcome in transporting sick patients to an appropriate hospital. For example, in Tonga there are four hospitals, with a combined 296 beds. Transport problems mean that hospitals tend to serve the population on their respective islands and that acute referrals are uncommon. Similar problems occur wherever the community is spread across many islands and atolls.

Tertiary Health care

National Specialist Capability

The ability to provide tertiary health services depends on the availability and skills of the specialist work-force. The service provided can change markedly with the relocation of one or two individuals. National specialists provide most of the tertiary services in Papua New Guinea and Fiji. Their skills are supplemented and supported by visiting teams, which provide tertiary services for the other Pacific Islands. National specialists already perform a wide range of complex procedures in different fields, and increasingly their expertise is being sought in neighbouring countries. As capabilities develop, the Pacific Island specialists will provide the expert care needed in their own islands. However, the current staff shortage means that Pacific-based specialists are limited in their ability to meet the demand for their services in their own islands and elsewhere.

Visiting Specialist Teams

In the 1980s a number of different surgeons and teams visited Papua New Guinea and the Pacific: ophthalmology (ASPECT), orthopaedics (Orthopaedic Outreach), plastic surgery (Interplast) and cardiac surgery (Operation Open Heart). The Pacific Islands Projects (PIPs), funded by Australian aid, were developed to facilitate the flow of aid to these and other groups and ensure a more systematic, project-orientated approach. The Pacific Islands and Papua New Guinea Tertiary Health Services (PNG THS) Projects commenced in 1995. At the end of 2010, towards the end of the third phase of the PIPs and PNG THS, over 70,000 consultations and more than 20,000 operations had been provided. About two-thirds of these were in the Pacific Islands (Fiji, Samoa, Tonga, the Cook Islands, Vanuatu, Solomon Islands, Tuvalu, Kiribati, the Federated States of Micronesia, the Marshall Islands and Nauru) and one-third in Papua New Guinea. In 2008 some 30 teams were to visit 11 Pacific Islands, and 25 teams were to travel to Papua New Guinea, visiting most of the major centres including Buka and Bougainville. Operation Open Heart screened more than 150 patients and operated on over 60 in 2008. The ongoing success of annual visits was demonstrated by the skill transfer to national surgeons, who dealt with many of the paediatric cases. Each project costs approximately $A1m. a year, although additional fund-raising by Operation Open Heart and donations in kind added a further $A400,000. The primary focus of these projects has been service delivery through the provision of specialist clinical services. However, training and capacity-building have been important by-products, with the medical training programmes in both FSM and the UPNG making use of the teams' expertise for undergraduate and postgraduate medical education. In 2008 both projects were in a 'bridging' phase, while new programmes of tertiary support were being designed with a greater emphasis on capacity-building and local leadership.

Dispatch of Patients Overseas

The funding available to send a small selection of patients overseas is limited. A number of governments allocate a proportion of their health budget for overseas treatment, as they are unable to provide tertiary services. The New Zealand Agency for International Development (NZAID) also funds treatment in New Zealand for a number of Pacific Islands. Rotary Oceania Medical Aid for Children (ROMAC) and other charity groups sometimes arrange hospital care in Australia and New Zealand on a case-by-case basis. Although those treated overseas derive benefit because they are usually selected on the grounds of being curable, the cost of treating one patient is often the equivalent to sending a team for two weeks, who might then consult on 50 patients, operating on 25.

AID AND THE MILLENNIUM DEVELOPMENT GOALS

The major international agencies such as WHO, the World Bank, the Asian Development Bank (ADB) and the United Nations Development Programme (UNDP) have focused on establishing programmes and strategies rather than providing medical care. They have supported the development of individual country plans for the Millennium Development Goals (MDGs), as formulated at the UN Millennium Summit meeting in September 2000. Their focus has been on strategies to reduce childhood deaths and maternal mortality, and combating HIV/AIDS, malaria, tuberculosis and other diseases (including cancer and diabetes), as well as injuries. They have also funded many projects designed to derive the information upon which policy can be determined. AusAID, the Australian aid agency, has also supported a health management project that provided advisers in the health department and key strategic hospitals in Papua New Guinea. It has funded a medical equipment maintenance programme (MEMP) in Papua New Guinea and the other Pacific Islands aimed at standardizing equipment and increasing the capacity to maintain equipment. Various countries, including Japan, have provided funding to build hospitals and replace hospital equipment. Support for the treatment of disease has been from direct budgetary grants and through visiting specialist teams, funded by various agencies (governmental, charities and non-governmental organizations—NGOs) in Australia, New Zealand, France and the USA.

All Pacific Islands have subscribed to the MDGs. They have developed strategies and targets to meet the goals. The eight specific goals are as follows:

Goal 1—to eradicate extreme poverty and hunger;

Goal 2—to achieve universal primary education;

Goal 3—to promote gender equality and empower women;

Goal 4—to reduce child mortality;

Goal 5—to improve maternal health;

Goal 6—to combat HIV/AIDS, malaria and other diseases;

Goal 7—to ensure environmental sustainability;

Goal 8—to promote a global partnership for development.

Each of these goals depends to some extent on the preceding goals, and even Goal 1, the eradication of extreme poverty and hunger, depends upon other prerequisites such as security, climate, economics and food supply. The goals were set with an appreciation of their interdependence: it would be almost impossible to achieve the later ones without significant progress in the earlier ones. Goals 4, 5 and 6 are specifically focused on health. Without a global partnership for development (Goal 8), the supply of anti-retroviral therapy for human immunodeficiency virus (HIV) infection or the human papilloma virus (HPV) vaccination to prevent cervical cancer (the leading cause of cancer related death in women in the Pacific) will not be achieved. If environmental sustainability is not realized, there will be serious implications for the livelihood (and thus health) of rural populations.

The Reduction of Childhood Mortality

Low Birthweight

Goal 4 aims to reduce by two-thirds, between 1990 and 2015, the under-five mortality rate. The perinatal period, the first year, and then the first five years of life, are the critical times that determine child survival. The major risk is infectious diseases, particularly respiratory conditions and gastroenteritis. Perinatal mortality can be minimized by ensuring that delivery takes place in the presence of a skilled birth attendant, trained to recognize foetal distress and maternal complications. Improved antenatal care will reduce the number of low birthweight babies.

Low birthweight is associated with a high infant mortality rate (20 times the risk) and a danger of childhood illnesses, particularly infections. It may also be associated with inhibited growth, cognitive impairment and chronic diseases later in life. Low birthweight is defined as a weight of less than 2,500 g at birth. The rates in the Pacific vary from 4%–18%; indicative rates are 4% in Samoa, 5% in Kiribati and Tuvalu, 11% in Papua New Guinea, 13% in Solomon Islands, 12% in the Marshall Islands and 18% in the Federated States of Micronesia. By comparison the rate is 6%–8% in New Zealand, Australia and Japan. The causative factors are pre-term birth (less than 37 weeks) or restricted intrauterine growth. Malnutrition of the mother during pregnancy may play a role. Birthweight in the absence of complications during pregnancy is affected to some extent by a mother's own foetal growth and her diet in childhood and adolescence, all of which affects her body composition and reserves.

Breast-feeding

It is recommended that infants should, wherever possible, be exclusively fed breast milk until at least four–six months of age. In Papua New Guinea studies in the Eastern Highlands and Madang have suggested that exclusive breast-feeding rates are 85% at four months and 80% at six months of age. Some Pacific Islands report low breast-feeding rates, for example New Caledonia, where less than 50% of babies are being breast-fed at four months of age, and French Polynesia, with only 19% of infants exclusively breast-fed for six months.

Child Growth and Nutritional Problems

Child growth is still affected by malnutrition or ignorance. Children under five are particularly vulnerable to changes in food supply and these effects are usually manifest once breast-feeding is discontinued, owing to custom or the arrival of the next sibling. Child growth is measured in terms of being underweight (less than 80% weight for age), stunted (below 80% height for age) and wasting (less than 90% weight for height). The implication is that impaired child growth is associated with poorer educational performance, greater susceptibility to acute infection and perhaps a propensity to chronic diseases later in life. Wasting or stunting of growth detected in children under five are in the 10%–20% range in the poorer countries such as Papua New Guinea, Solomon Islands and Vanuatu. In Fiji there is a marked difference between the Indian and indigenous Fijian population. The respective figures for Indians and Fijians are: underweight, 15% and 3%; wasted, 15.5% and 2.7%; and stunted, 4.0% and 2.2%.

The annual figures reported may vary according to the rains. For example, a 1998 survey in an area of Papua New Guinea affected by drought as a result of the climatic phenomenon known as El Niño (a periodic warming of the tropical Pacific Ocean) reported that 45% of children under five were underweight. In the richer Pacific nations, such as New Caledonia and French Polynesia, children tend to be overweight.

In Papua New Guinea, a study of hospital deaths in children in the capital of Port Moresby found a case fatality rate of 4.9% (238 cases out of 4,898 admissions over a period of 12 months). While 92% of the children weighed less than 80% of the standard weight for age, 30% weighed less than 60%. Pneumonia, meningitis, measles, septicaemia and HIV infection were the five leading causes of death, all infectious diseases; 75% of these deaths were unavoidable from the time of admission, although two-thirds had treatable causes, if they had been seen and treated early enough. Fewer than one-half of the children in Port Moresby were appropriately immunized for their age.

Anaemia, which arises when haemoglobin levels are too low, reduces energy levels and resistance to infection. It is an indication of poor nutrition, infestation with intestinal parasites and/or, in malaria endemic regions, chronic malarial infection (also manifest by splenomegaly). Anaemia during childhood is common. In Papua New Guinea, for example, blood was taken from children under five as part of a Vitamin A study in three provinces between 1996 and 1997. Two coastal provinces reported anaemia rates of 83% and 91%. In the Western Highlands, where malaria is not endemic, only 35% of children under five were anaemic. A study of two schools in 2001/02 in Solomon Islands reported rates of 25% and 36% for anaemia in schoolchildren. Another study found that more than 70% of children under five in New Caledonia were anaemic. American Samoa, the Federated States of Micronesia and the Marshall Islands have rates of childhood anaemia in the 20%–40% range.

Vitamin A deficiency occurs in populations that rely heavily on staple carbohydrates and do not get sufficient fat-soluble Vitamin A from fish, liver, eggs or dairy products. It is recognized clinically and progresses from night blindness to conjunctival changes, to corneal problems and finally blindness. It is not a major clinical problem in Papua New Guinea (where sub-clinical prevalence rates are around 10%), Solomon Islands, Vanuatu or Fiji, but it is prevalent in the Federated States of Micronesia and the Marshall Islands. In areas affected Vitamin A capsules can be distributed to children of between six months and six years. According to studies conducted in the 1990s, in the Federated States of Micronesia 44% of children in Pohnpei were moderately deficient and 7% were severely deficient in Vitamin A; in Chuuk 18% of children were deficient and 96% sub-clinically deficient. In the Marshall Islands 55% were moderately deficient and 8% severely deficient.

Goitre (enlargement of the thyroid) rates as a result of iodine deficiency are declining, with increasing iodization of salt. In infants and children iodine deficiency leads to mental retardation and cretinism. All salt has been iodized in Papua New Guinea since 1995 and in Fiji since 1996. Much of the early work on endemic goitre was done in the highlands of Papua New Guinea where, in the 1960s, prevalence rates were high. Historically, it was the arrival of Europeans in the highlands of Papua New Guinea from the 1930s that disrupted the salt trade routes and led to the development of iodine deficiency. In 1997 672 school children were studied in two districts. One group had a zero rate of goitre, but a remote mountainous district had a rate of 13.7%. In a Fijian study, the goitre rates approached 50% for school children and 40% and 60% for pregnant women in the Singatoka and Colonial War Memorial hospitals, respectively. Other Pacific Islands have not reported a high incidence of endemic goitre, although there may also be cases in New Caledonia, Solomon Islands and Vanuatu.

Vaccination

The two major causes of childhood death are pneumonia and diarrhoea. The expanded programme on immunization (EPI), begun in 1974, uses vaccines that do not specifically target the organisms that cause pneumonia and diarrhoea, yet there is evidence that the vaccine against measles and the bacillus Calmette-Guérin (BCG) against tuberculosis reduce childhood mortality through non-specific effects, not only by preventing measles and tuberculosis. The BCG vaccine is also effective against leprosy. As a result, all children should receive BCG, measles, diphtheria-pertussis-tetanus and polio vaccines. Another vaccine that has been used with success in Papua New Guinea is pneumococcal vaccine. It is estimated that for a cost of US $1 or less each, immunization of mothers and babies might reduce childhood mortality by 20% at a cost of US $83 per life saved (at 2000 costs). One dose of pneumococcal vaccine given to every Papua New Guinean over five years of age every five years would save approximately 6,600 lives per year at US $121 per life saved. There are plans to administer the *Haemophilus influenzae* Type B vaccine also. However, it is not easy to achieve high immunization rates in Papua New Guinea or other parts of the Pacific region. The barriers to high immunization rates include lack of education and awareness among the mothers of children, the remoteness of many communities and a lack of infrastructure to carry out effective vaccination campaigns. In Papua New Guinea immunizing pregnant women and women of reproductive age against tetanus has been shown to prevent neonatal tetanus. The hepatitis B vaccination early in childhood protects not only against chronic hepatitis infection but also against liver cancer.

Gastroenteritis

Assessing the magnitude of the problem of diarrhoea is fraught with difficulty. The indicators that are often used are the attack rate and mortality rate. Throughout the Pacific region diarrhoea is a common cause of admission to hospital, and community studies have suggested attack rates of between 0.3 and 3.0 episodes per child per year in children under five. The case fatality rate is about 1%–3% in hospitals throughout the Pacific. Rotaviruses are the most important cause of diarrhoea in children under two years of age. An oral vaccine was released in 2006 and was provided as part of the national immunization scheme in Australia from July 2007. Funding will be required to make it available in the Pacific Islands. Other important pathogens include *Shigella flexneri* (dysentery), *Escherichia Coli*, *Salmonella spp* and *Campylobacter jejuni*. *Salmonella typhi*, the organism that causes typhoid fever, may also be encountered but does not always lead to diarrhoea.

The incidence of diarrhoea can be minimized by promoting breast-feeding. Bottle-feeding of infants can lead to infection on account of poor sterilization and contamination of bottles and artificial milk. Safe water and good hygiene are other important factors. Studies have shown that the babies of mothers who do not appreciate that the faeces of their babies might cause disease have a much higher chance of contracting diarrhoea.

Diarrhoea is treated by oral rehydration solutions (ORS), for example the glucose-based ORS promoted by the United Nations Children's Fund (UNICEF). Home-made solutions can be made with salt and sugar (or coconut juice), but in the developing world the correct amounts of salt and sugar can be easily confused, with disastrous consequences. Nasogastric rehydration can be used for dehydrated children who cannot manage to take enough orally or who are vomiting repeatedly. Intravenous fluids are used where the losses cannot be replenished by rehydration through the gastrointestinal tract. Breast-feeding should be continued while the child is being treated. Antibiotics are given only for proven infections such as cholera, dysentery, giardiasis and typhoid fever.

Measles

Measles is a potential childhood killer because it may be complicated by pneumonia or meningitis. It is particularly aggressive in children who are malnourished or debilitated by other chronic infections. It remains a common childhood infection in Papua New Guinea, Solomon Islands, Vanuatu and Fiji. Islands with better vaccination coverage, such as Samoa, Tonga, Kiribati, New Caledonia, French Polynesia, the Federated States of Micronesia, the Northern Mariana Islands and the Marshall Islands, reported no cases in 2006.

Heart Disease in Children

In the Pacific there is still a high prevalence of rheumatic fever, a disease that causes damage to heart valves as a result of infection with Group A streptococci. Streptococcal infections are readily treatable with penicillin. Cardiac teams from Australia visit the South Pacific (Papua New Guinea, Fiji, Samoa, Vanuatu and Solomon Islands) and operate on carefully selected children with congenital heart disease. They usually treat up to 20 cases per visit and achieve very acceptable outcomes, with mortality rates of less than 3%. However, some of the more complex surgery must be performed overseas, at considerable expense, and afterwards there are issues with regard to the management of patients with heart valve replacements, for example, as anti-coagulation is difficult to monitor in the Pacific Islands. Tissue valves were used in six valve replacements in Papua New Guinea in 2008 to avoid the problems of anti-coagulation monitoring.

Pigbel

Pigbel is a colourful name given to the condition of *Enteritis necroticans* in Papua New Guinea. It was first described in 1959, and in the 1960s and 1970s was one of the commonest causes of death in Goroka (Eastern Highlands Province) for children aged over one year. The disease has also been reported in other countries including Solomon Islands, Uganda, Bangladesh and Germany (after the Second World War). It is caused by contamination of food with *Clostridium perfringens* Type C; a changed intestinal environment caused by gorging on animal protein (in the highlands of Papua New Guinea this is pig meat) when the normal diet consists of sweet potatoes and other vegetables; rapid proliferation of *Clostridium perfringens* with production of its B toxin; and low levels of intestinal proteolytic activity resulting from proteolytic inhibitors in the dietary staple—the sweet potato—and/or produced by intestinal parasites, principally the worm *Ascaris lumbricoides*, which fail to destroy the toxin that damages the gut mucosa, resulting in adherence of clostridia with further toxin production, destruction of the intestinal wall and characteristic necrosis. A toxoid vaccine has been produced, which has been highly effective in preventing what was once a common and fatal disease. There are still clusters of pigbel that occur in the highlands of Papua New Guinea today, although the disease is much less common than previously. As a result of the success of the vaccination programme and the reduction in incidence, the vaccine has not been produced in recent years, an issue of concern to health workers in some parts of the highlands where sporadic cases are beginning to recur.

The Improvement of Maternal Health

The target of the fifth MDG is to reduce the maternal mortality ratio by three-quarters between 1990 and 2015. Promoting gender equality and empowering women is fundamental to improving maternal health. A low status for women in society, financial and family constraints and varying cultural values may result in an underutilization of existing maternal health services. Similarly, without education, women may be less likely to attend for antenatal care. The strategy involves improving the availability of essential obstetric care for the management of complications, ensuring skilled attendance at birth and strengthening family-planning services.

Leading causes of maternal death are postpartum haemorrhage, pre-eclampsia (pregnancy-induced hypertension), obstructed labour, puerperal sepsis and complications arising from unsafe abortion. Important indirect causes include anaemia and malaria (the latter in Papua New Guinea and Solomon Islands). In Papua New Guinea anaemia during pregnancy is generally around 40%. The rate of anaemia is 30% in Solomon Islands and more than 50% in pregnant Fijians.

The maternal mortality rate in Papua New Guinea is one of the world's highest at 300 per 100,000. A study of maternal deaths in Goroka found that 48% were due to puerperal sepsis or sepsis resulting from unsafe abortion, and that ruptured ectopic pregnancy and postpartum haemorrhage were other significant causes. Contributory factors included failure to attend antenatal clinics or to use family-planning services. The women who died tended to live in rural locations, in low socio-economic groups with little access to transport and with limited education.

Obstetric Care

The quality of essential obstetric care in developing countries is poor. The proportion of births attended by skilled personnel is variable throughout the Pacific region. This varies from 59% in Papua New Guinea to 99% in Samoa, Tonga and the Cook Islands. WHO Global Monitoring and Evaluation has reported the overall rates as 61% in Melanesia, 93% in Micronesia and 98% in Polynesia, indicative of the relative wealth and health system coverage in the three regions. However, these figures vary from being between two and 10 years out of date. Tonga has an excellent record, with 99% of pregnant women attending antenatal clinics, 98% maternal tetanus toxoid vaccination and 98% delivering in a health facility in 2004. In Fiji, where about 17,000 deliveries take place annually, a trained health worker is reported as being present for all births, with 99% delivering in a health facility in 2005.

Women who deliver in a health facility are well placed should they be one of the 10% or so who develop complications during labour. The Caesarean section rate would be expected to be around 5%, with at least another 15% of cases requiring good supervision of labour to intervene when it is in the best interests of the mother or foetus. A general doctor or surgeon usually performs the procedure as specialist obstetricians are few and far between. Although midwives can assist with decision-making, they have not in the Pacific, as in some parts of sub-Saharan Africa, been trained to do a Caesarean section.

Nevertheless, high standards of maternal care are achievable in the Pacific, at least where health workers can refer complicated or potentially complicated cases to a hospital capable of performing a Caesarean section. In 2009 the National Referral Hospital in Honiara, Solomon Islands, admitted 5,600 obstetric patients, with a Caesarean section rate of 10% of all deliveries. In Vanuatu, a study over a 23-year period in the capital, Port Vila, found the Caesarean section rate to be 5.2% and the instrumental delivery rate 1.8%. The postpartum haemorrhage rate decreased from over 5% to less than 1% between 1979 and 2001. The Port Vila hospital maternal mortality rate was a relatively low seven per 100,000, in contrast with high national maternal mortality rates of 130 in both Solomon Islands and Vanuatu. The first figure represents hospital-based statistics, in contrast to the countryside, where many mothers give birth to their children in the village with only traditional birth attendants to assist.

Family Planning

The use of contraception is low in the Pacific region. Various studies have suggested that it is little more than 5%–10%

among women and much less for men. Fertility rates (4%–5%) are consequently high in many parts of the Pacific, as is the incidence of sexually transmitted diseases. A study in Fiji (1998) suggested that 44% of women in the reproductive age group were using modern contraceptive methods, although only 16.5% were using condoms (2005). A study of risk behaviours in American Samoa, the Northern Mariana and Marshall Islands, Palau and Guam found condom use to be less than 50% in sexually active teenagers. HIV seroprevalence in 15–24 year-old pregnant women is officially reported to be less than 0.1% in Fiji but 1.25% in Papua New Guinea.

Cervical Cancer

After pregnancy and delivery the next greatest threat to a woman's life during her reproductive years is cervical cancer. Mortality rates throughout the Pacific are high. This cancer is associated with HPV, which is spread through unprotected sex. There has been recent progress in developing a vaccine. The US Food and Drug Administration approved the use of the vaccine in the USA in June 2006, and the vaccine was introduced to women aged under 26 in Australia in 2007. In July 2007 the Minister for Health of Papua New Guinea announced a limited study and introduction of the vaccine. There is still some uncertainty about which serosubtypes of HPV are prevalent in Papua New Guinea and the Pacific. Vaccination of prepubertal girls is expected to be introduced in the future. Chlamydial infections may act as a co-factor in carcinogenesis, the effect being mediated by chronic inflammation. Other factors associated, at least in the West, with HPV infection are smoking and long-term use of the contraceptive pill.

In the Pacific region national policies and programmes are needed to promote early detection of reproductive cancers in women. Some islands lack screening services, and in others they are not used because of cultural barriers and inadequate health awareness. In Western countries cervical smears are performed to look for premalignant or malignant changes. Abnormal smears must have further investigation and biopsy. However, on islands with inadequate pathology services to read cervical smears, there may not be the capacity to screen the patients most at risk. The ability further to investigate abnormalities is limited in developing nations. Only the more educated women would be likely to submit themselves to the whole process, which defeats the purpose of offering it to all regardless of socio-economic background. As a result, Papua New Guinea, with a population of more than 6m. (1.5m. women of reproductive age), has not adopted a national screening programme; 80% of the population live in the rural areas and would be unlikely to submit to smear tests or to colposcopy, or to consistently follow up on positive results. A cervical screening programme would benefit only the relatively rich city dwellers, who currently have the most access to doctors and women's services. It will be many years before screening for cervical cancer becomes a reality throughout the Pacific region. It is an option for the future in the wealthier Pacific Island nations, where smaller populations have good access to hospitals. At present the recommendation is to investigate women with symptoms and to accept that cervical cancer screening is not achievable in most island nations. An alternative strategy is to screen at-risk women such as sex workers. In the future, vaccination may be a better approach than attempting to establish a screening programme, but the vaccine is likely to be expensive initially.

Cervical cancer requires radiotherapy to achieve potential cure in early stages (I and II). There is only one radiotherapy unit in the Pacific (at Lae, in Papua New Guinea), but this was not operational between 1998 and 2008. Most patients can only be palliated, as they have no means of accessing radiotherapy overseas. In Papua New Guinea a replacement Cobalt-60 unit for the Lae radiotherapy unit was installed in 2008 and became operational in 2009.

Breast Cancer

Breast cancer incidences are rising. The rates of breast cancer have risen in Papua New Guinea with each decade, and breast cancer affects women of reproductive and middle age rather than the elderly. Rates level out or decline in the elderly when age-specific incidences are calculated. Similar findings have been reported from Fiji and Solomon Islands. The cancers tend to present at an advanced stage and the cure rate is less than 50%. Breast cancer screening is not currently cost-effective in most, if not all, Pacific Islands. Although mammography has been introduced in Fiji and is being considered in the Cook Islands, it is best used for the assessment of symptomatic women. Women of reproductive age, whose mammograms are more difficult to read, can be reasonably assessed by ultrasound, which is inexpensive and more widely available.

Combating HIV/AIDS, Malaria and Other Diseases, Including Non-Communicable Diseases

Communicable diseases are caused by infections and infestations. Non-communicable diseases include conditions such as diabetes, asthma, heart disease, trauma and cancer. The incidence of non-communicable diseases is on the rise throughout the Pacific, and in many countries such conditions are far more important as a cause of sickness or mortality than are infections. However, it is communicable diseases that often make the headlines: these are specified in the Millennium Development goals and are therefore dealt with first.

The Issue of HIV/AIDS

The target of Goal 6 is to halt and begin to reverse the spread of HIV/AIDS by 2015. Acquired immunodeficiency syndrome (AIDS) was first recognized in the early 1980s and is caused by a ribonucleic acid (RNA) retrovirus, HIV. It is transmitted by body fluids, particularly blood and semen. The disease originated in central Africa and spread relatively slowly to the Pacific Islands, the last major region of the world to be affected. The exponential rise in infection rates witnessed in sub-Saharan Africa in the 1980s began in Papua New Guinea in the 1990s, although the first case was identified in 1987. When sub-Saharan African hospitals were full of HIV-infected cases in the 1980s, Pacific Island hospitals encountered them only rarely. The situation has now changed. By 2006 a medical ward round in Port Moresby would always include some patients with AIDS, a phenomenon that was rare a decade previously. In the Pacific the disease is spread mainly by heterosexual contact, and vertically from mother to foetus. Testing of blood for transfusion preceded the pandemic in Papua New Guinea and the rest of the Pacific, so that transfused blood has not been a source of infection.

Some Pacific Islands remain relatively unaffected, at least according to official figures. No country routinely screens its population. Some data are available from antenatal clinics and blood donors. The Pacific epicentre is Papua New Guinea, which has three-quarters of the cases in Oceania, followed by Solomon Islands. Papua New Guinea reports an adult (15–49 years) prevalence of 1%–3%, a rate similar to that of Zimbabwe in 1986. More than 1,000 new cases per year are being reported, and it is estimated that more than 60,000 people have been infected with HIV/AIDS. The urban adult prevalence is around 3.5%. In one study the prevalence among sex workers was 16%. Another study of men and women providing sex for money or favours reported a 19% HIV prevalence rate. High levels of adolescent sexual activity are reported. Condom use in Papua New Guinea and the Pacific region generally is low, especially among the young, and less than 10% even in men visiting sex workers.

In Fiji, where the first four cases were reported in 1989, a total of 294 cases had been reported by February 2009. Recent reports have suggested that the prevalence rate has now exceeded 0.5%, making Fiji the second most affected nation in the Pacific Islands. There have been more women infected than men, suggestive of a heterosexual mode of transmission. Many other Pacific Islands have reported a rate of less than 0.1%. Samoa had reported only 12 and Tonga 14 cases of HIV infection by the end of 2004. Despite AIDS education being promoted in the Pacific since the early 1990s, there has been little impact on the spread of other sexually transmitted infections (STIs). Rates of STIs including chlamydia are relatively high. A study conducted in six nations (Fiji, Kiribati, Samoa, Solomon Islands, Tonga and Vanuatu) described chlamydial infection as a 'silent epidemic', and reported that of over 1,600 women surveyed 26% of pregnant women under 25 years of age and 11.9% over 25 years of age were infected. Gonorrhoea and syphilis infection rates were 1.7% and 3.4%, respectively. The presence of untreated STIs promotes the spread of

HIV through ulceration and discharge from genital mucosal surfaces. Persons with an STI are at greater risk of contracting HIV because both diseases have the same risk factors. The high incidence of STIs creates an environment conducive to the spread of HIV/AIDS across the Pacific. Kiribati is at the eastern end of the Pacific region, relatively far from the epicentre based in Papua New Guinea and Solomon Islands, and the country's official HIV prevalence rate is less than 0.1%. A 2002–03 study of seafarers in Kiribati showed an HIV prevalence of 0.3% and a hepatitis B rate of 22.7%, with high levels of other STIs. Among antenatal women the rate of syphilis was 1.4%, and of hepatitis B 9.2%; there was no case of HIV detected.

HIV infection can be successfully suppressed by anti-retroviral therapy. Unfortunately, treatment is expensive and prolonged, and the majority of those infected do not have access. Improving affordability and access to treatment will play an important part in the control of the disease and management of cases in the future. In 2005 320 people in Papua New Guinea were known to be receiving anti-retroviral therapy, out of an estimated 30,000 living with the infection.

Malaria

The sixth MDG also aims to halt and begin to reverse the incidence of malaria and other major diseases by 2015. Malaria remains a major health problem and a serious cause of mortality and debility in Papua New Guinea, Solomon Islands and, to a lesser extent, Vanuatu. Malaria is not endemic in Fiji, Micronesia or Polynesia. The peak incidence occurs during the rainy season, particularly in coastal areas and river deltas. Malaria does occur in the highlands of Papua New Guinea, although it is less common and the incidence declines with height above sea level. Once an elevation of 1,800 m is reached endemic malaria should not occur, although there are still cases of imported or recurrent malaria, and malaria continues to be reported from every province of Papua New Guinea.

Malaria is transmitted by the *Anopheles* mosquito. Transmission rates can be minimized by sleeping under an impregnated bed net. Increasing the proportion of the population who do so is an important strategy in controlling malaria. Covering up the arms and the use of insect repellent are measures used by tourists, but these are hardly practical methods for the locals. Prophylactic drug regimens are also appropriate for short-term visitors but are unlikely to be adopted by residents.

As regards drug treatment, resistance to chloroquine is about 30%, but resistance to Fansidar (pyrimethamine/sulfadoxine) is rare. There are concerns about the development of resistance to artemether, which has been introduced as a first-line treatment in recent years. Combination therapies, notably artemether-lumefantrine against *P. falciparum*, and dihydroartemisinin-piperaquine against *P. vivax*, have proved effective in children.

Malarial infection during pregnancy can have a major impact on the health of the mother and her baby. Chronic malarial infection results in enlargement of the spleen (big spleen disease), and in the rural endemic areas the majority of village children will have palpably large spleens. Large spleens cause anaemia (the spleen acts as an over-enthusiastic filter for the blood) and are more prone to rupture from insignificant trauma.

Papua New Guinea has contributed to research on malaria and is currently participating in malaria vaccine trials. However, hopes of an effective vaccine for malaria have been frustrated for more than a century.

Tuberculosis

The Asia-Pacific region has the highest prevalence of tuberculosis in the world. The tubercle bacillus is often dormant, awaiting a decline in host immunity such as may occur with HIV infection or later in life. Tuberculosis prevalence rates are high, particularly in Papua New Guinea (448 cases per 100,000 in 2004). The Northern Mariana Islands, the Federated States of Micronesia, Solomon Islands, Guam, New Caledonia and Kiribati have prevalence rates between 50 and 120 cases per 100,000. Fiji, Samoa and Tonga have a prevalence of around 40 cases per 100,000. Dual infection with HIV/AIDS has been recorded at only 3.7% in Papua New Guinea, 2.0% in French Polynesia and Guam and 1.0%–1.5% in Fiji and New Caledonia. The rate of dual infection is expected to rise dramatically as HIV/AIDS spreads. The experience of southern Africa would suggest that it might reach 50%, with HIV/AIDS resulting in a dramatic increase in the number of cases of tuberculosis. By 2006 this trend had not yet been seen. Extrapulmonary tuberculosis occurs in about 20%–25% of cases; the rest are pulmonary or relapses after previous treatment.

Treatment is normally a directly observed treatment schedule (DOTS) with multi-drug anti-tuberculous chemotherapy. The success rates vary from around 50% in Papua New Guinea to more than 80% in Fiji and most other Pacific Islands. Multi-drug resistant tuberculosis occurs in about 1%–3% of cases (2.3% in Papua New Guinea, 1.7% in Solomon Islands). The mortality rate for tuberculosis in Papua New Guinea is 42 deaths per 100,000, whereas it is reported as five or fewer in most other Pacific Islands.

Leprosy

Leprosy rates continue to fall throughout the region as a result of programmes that promote detection and effective treatment of cases using multi-drug regimens. BCG vaccination (for TB) also confers protection against leprosy. Fifty years ago leprosariums were common throughout the Pacific, but most of these hospitals have now closed or been redesignated for other conditions. By 1995 21 countries and territories in the region were close to eliminating leprosy, so that only two, the Federated States of Micronesia and the Marshall Islands, had not yet achieved elimination. In 2010 a total of 33 cases of leprosy were reported from three islands in the Marshalls group.

Dengue Fever

Dengue fever is endemic in many islands of the tropical South Pacific, with sporadic cases and outbreaks occurring. Dengue fever and dengue haemorrhagic fever are caused by arboviruses transmitted by the *Aedes* mosquito. Palau suffered a major epidemic in 1995 with more than 800 cases presenting with the typical symptoms (acute fever, aches with headache and/or vomiting), most of whom tested positive. Another outbreak in Fiji in 1998 resulted in more than 24,000 reported cases. Wallis and Futuna, with a population of only 15,000, reported more than 2,000 cases, with two deaths in 2002. Generally, the attack rate is in the region of 0.001% to 1% of the population, with a case fatality rate for haemorrhagic fever in the range of 1%–5%. No vaccine and no specific treatment are available other than supportive care. The disease is prevented by source reduction. The haemorrhagic form of dengue is rare in Papua New Guinea. WHO figures showed that Fiji reported 100 cases in 2007, Samoa 28 in 2005, Papua New Guinea 22 in 2002. None was reported from Solomon Islands, Vanuatu, Kiribati or Tonga, although this may be a reflection of lack of testing or concern about the disease unless an epidemic is encountered. In 2008, however, outbreaks were reported in Fiji, Samoa, American Samoa and elsewhere, prompting WHO to warn of a regional pandemic. Thousands of cases of dengue fever were reported in New Caledonia and in French Polynesia in the first half of 2009.

Cholera

Cholera is an acute bacterial disease caused by the ingestion of contaminated food or water. Most cases are mild, although it can cause severe disease and tends to present in sporadic epidemics. For example, there was an outbreak of the El Tor biotype of *Vibrio cholerae* on the island of Pohnpei, in the Federated States of Micronesia, in 2000. The risk factors for spread of infection were related to the lack of simple hygienic measures, such as not storing food uncovered outside, using a pit latrine or not washing hands. Protective factors included disinfecting drinking water, having a container to store water, washing hands, using a flush toilet and having access to a refrigerator. Cases also occurred in Guam where imported reef fish and other food products from Pohnpei were responsible. This epidemic demonstrates that the Pacific Islands are susceptible to rapid spread of the disease whenever cases are imported from South-East Asia or elsewhere. During 2009–10 Papua New Guinea experienced its first ever cholera epidemic. Madang, Morobe and the East Sepik Provinces were badly affected, each reporting many hundreds of cases and some deaths. By May 2010 more than 600 cases and seven deaths had been reported in Port Moresby and the surrounding vil-

lages. By the end of 2010 hundreds of cases had been reported in Daru and the South Fly District. This raised concerns in Australia about cholera spreading across the Torres Strait into the Cape York peninsula.

Leptospirosis

Leptospirosis is a zoonosis (transmitted to humans from animals) caused by a spirochaete. Contact with the urine or contaminated soil of domestic animals or rats provides the route for transmission of infection between the animal carrier and the human. The disease is endemic throughout the Pacific. It is characterized by fever, headache and myalgia, and is usually accompanied by blood-shot eyes (conjunctivitis). In severe cases jaundice, meningism, haemorrhages or renal failure may develop, and these sometimes cause fatality. The disease responds to antibiotics, particularly penicillin. Some countries are reporting an alarming rise in the number of cases, including some deaths. Outbreaks have recently occurred in Fiji, Vanuatu, Palau, the Northern Mariana Islands, Wallis and Futuna, French Polynesia and New Caledonia. In New Caledonia, the infection is most common in the Bourail area, a town that lies between between the capital, Nouméa, and the countryside. The incidence has risen in New Caledonia from some 30 cases per 100,000 inhabitants in the early 1990s to more than 100 per 100,000. In Fiji there were 35 cases reported in 2010, but by mid-June 2011 the three major public hospitals had reported more than 50 cases since the beginning of the year, with 10 deaths.

Filiariasis

Filiariasis (Elephantiasis) is caused by a mosquito-borne parasite. There are three species of the nematode responsible world-wide, but cases in the Pacific are usually due to the *Wuchereria bancrofti* worm. The condition presents with lymphoedema, which is often gross, affecting the limbs, breasts or genitalia. Programmes to eradicate the disease employ mass drug administration to a population at risk. Drug regimens used to treat the condition usually include albendazole and diethylcarbamazine or albendazole and ivermectin in various combinations. Surgical resection of the skin and subcutaneous tissue as well as skin grafting may be necessary in particularly severe cases.

Yaws

Yaws (Framboesia) is an endemic disease historically found in humid tropical regions in South America, Africa, Asia and Oceania. In the pre-antibiotic era it was treated with an injection of novarsenobillon, and its prevalence thus offered some immunity against syphilis, as yaws is caused by treponemal infection (*Treponema pertenue*), which is spread by skin-to-skin contact, rather than by sexual transmission. It causes nodular skin lesions and may also deform growing bones and destroy cartilage. The primary nodule(s) or 'yaw(s)' appear as a painless wart, which heals spontaneously after a few months. Months or years later secondary yaws develop; these are usually multiple and extensive, and can ulcerate and are highly infectious, although they also heal. Some victims go on to develop destructive lesions of the nose or face where skin and cartilage are eroded. Today, yaws is treatable with benzyl penicillin; sporadic cases have occurred in rural regions of Papua New Guinea, and the disease has recently re-emerged in an attenuated form on the island of Tanna, in Vanuatu.

Diabetes

When the health ministers of the Pacific Islands met in 2003 in Tonga they noted that non-communicable diseases were the leading cause of mortality and morbidity, with diabetes the most important non-communicable disease. Diabetes develops wherever people have abandoned their traditional lifestyle. A so-called 'thrifty gene', in reality a genetic trait, predisposes Austronesian Pacific Islanders who adopt a Western lifestyle to the development of diabetes. During migration across the Pacific or seasonal starvation (as experienced by the Motu) the 'thrifty gene' offered a survival advantage. However, if food is in constant, plentiful supply the trait promotes diabetes. The specific promotive factors are a change in diet, obesity and reduced physical activity. In the highlands of Papua New Guinea people are accustomed to food supplies all year round, but the 'thrifty gene' is absent and so the rates of diabetes, even with lifestyle changes, are low. Contrast this with the Motu peoples of Koki (Port Moresby) and Wanigela (Central Province) which have some of the highest rates of diabetes in the world. Islanders across the Pacific are similarly affected. The number of diabetics is expected to double between 2000 and 2030. It is anticipated that 5%–15% of the adult population of most Pacific Islands will be affected by around 2025. Already there are a number of communities that have 30% adult prevalence rates, notably Nauru, where traditional lifestyles have been completely abandoned and physical inactivity has become the norm.

Diabetes mellitus is a multi-system disease. Its complications are related to how long the disease has been present and how well it is controlled. These include chronic renal failure, blindness from retinopathy, and accelerated cardiovascular disease. Soft tissue infections are common. Damage to nerves and blood vessels combined with muscle imbalance in the foot result in the so-called 'diabetic foot', which is prone to ulceration, poor healing, infection and ultimately partial or complete amputations. In the 1950s leprosy was the commonest cause of rotting, infected neuropathic feet. Today it is diabetes.

Teamwork and a co-ordinated approach are required to improve individual and population outcomes. A strategy needs to be devised that enables patients to monitor their blood glucose, with supervision of their ability to control their diabetes by a health worker, and minimize complications. The strategy involves education, delivering means of treatment, dietary advice and encouraging more exercise or activity. Each country needs its own national programme for both prevention and management. Educational programmes also need to teach diabetics how to look after their feet to avoid injury, ulceration and infection.

Cardiovascular Disease

Cardiovascular diseases are increasing throughout the Pacific. They are manifested by hypertension, ischaemic heart disease and cerebrovascular accident (stroke). The official figures may be distorted by the final mode of death being recorded as 'heart failure' or 'cardiac arrest' on death certificates, but none the less there is a clear cardiovascular pandemic throughout the Pacific region. Cardiovascular disease is the leading cause of death, notably in Samoa (24.3 deaths per 100,000), Tonga (190.1), the Federated States of Micronesia (116.1), the Northern Mariana Islands (54.1, with 21.0 caused by cerebrovascular diseases), Guam (130.4, with 32.3 caused by cerebrovascular diseases) and French Polynesia (105.0). The incidence is also rising in Papua New Guinea, although there it does not rank in the leading five causes of mortality.

Cancer

In the 1940s cancer was considered a rare condition in South Pacific Islanders. Today it is the second leading cause of death in the Federated States of Micronesia (57.1 deaths per 100,000), Tonga (77.2), the Northern Mariana Islands (39.1), Guam (77.0) and French Polynesia (99.2). In New Caledonia neoplasms are now the leading cause of death (135.6).

In Papua New Guinea oral cancer is one of the leading cancers; it is caused by the chronic inflammation associated with chewing of betel nut mixed with lime and the effects of tobacco. It is the leading cancer in men and third commonest in women. Cervical and breast cancer are the two leading cancers in women (see above). A high incidence of liver cancer is associated with a high prevalence of hepatitis B infection. The introduction of hepatitis B vaccination is reducing the incidence of hepatitis B infection and probably of liver cancer. Lung cancer is one of the emerging cancers of the developing world and, as in the West, is related to smoking. The tobacco industry has developed its market and strongly promoted its product throughout the Pacific region, and thus lung cancer rates are likely to rise.

Burkitt's lymphoma is seen in malaria endemic regions. It is one of the commonest childhood malignancies and is rapidly growing but may also respond well to chemotherapy. It can present in any part of the body but is typically seen as a jaw or facial tumour, or it affects the spine, causing paraplegia.

Prostatic enlargement is a common condition affecting elderly men. Prostatic cancer occurs less frequently than benign prostatic hyperplasia as the reason for middle-aged and elderly

men suffering urinary outflow obstruction. The facilities to treat this disease endoscopically are limited across the Pacific, with only a couple of qualified urologists in the region. General surgeons, performing open surgery which is more prone to complications, are responsible for managing prostatic disease.

The incidence of oesophageal, stomach and colorectal cancers is still relatively low in most parts of the Pacific, although general surgeons treat a few cases of each every year. Bone and soft tissue tumours (osteosarcoma and Ewing's sarcoma) tend to affect the young and rarely present at an early stage. Even when they do, families usually refuse the only chance of cure, amputation. Limb-saving options and adjuvant modalities of treatment are seldom available.

Effective treatment for malignancy is limited by a lack of diagnostic services (pathology and staging) and therapeutic options (chemotherapy and radiotherapy). The only Cobalt-60 unit in the Pacific region, in Papua New Guinea, remained out of operation for 10 years from 1998, but a new unit was installed and services resumed in 2009. There are no oncologists in the Pacific medical work-force, and this will be a training priority for the future. The transfer of patients with malignancy for treatment overseas is not ideal. Potentially curable cases may be delayed, the outcome is uncertain and often dislocates those with incurable disease from the support of their extended family. In some countries the right 'connections' often result in inappropriate cases being referred, where wealth or family ties are more important than stage of pathology or the curability of the cancer.

Thyroid Disease and Nuclear Fall-out

Exposure to radioactivity during childhood and adolescence increases the risk of thyroid cancer later in life. The USA conducted nuclear weapon testing in the Pacific between 1946 and 1958. Subsequent studies have shown an increase in the incidence of thyroid cancer and Hashimoto's thyroiditis, an auto-immune inflammatory disorder of the thyroid in the Marshallese. The effect is due to direct exposure to brief radioactive fall-out. It takes at least five years before tumours develop, and the effect is maximal at 20 years. Adults over 20 years of age at the time of fall-out do not seem to be affected. The incidence continues to decline in the absence of further nuclear testing.

France conducted a number of nuclear tests at the atolls of Mururoa and Fangataufa. Atmospheric tests were conducted between 1966 and 1974 and then underground tests from 1975 to 1991 and finally in 1995–96. The effects have been subject to exaggeration, and the facts have been obscured by the political agenda. It is likely that Tahiti was subject to fall-out, but only from the atmospheric tests conducted, and that the health effects are now also in decline.

Accidents and Injuries

Trauma is the leading cause of surgical admission throughout the Pacific. Morbidity rates are around 200–450 per 100,000, placing injuries among the leading medical conditions. Mortality rates for unintentional injury and violence vary from 29 per 100,000 in Tonga, to around 40 in most Pacific Islands (Fiji, the Cook Islands, Samoa, Palau, Vanuatu, Micronesia), to a high of 104 in Papua New Guinea. In the highlands of Papua New Guinea trauma (from all causes) accounts for up to 50% of surgical admissions; it is the leading cause of death in economically productive adults aged 15–40 throughout the Pacific. When accident or injury occurs there is often no ambulance service, and first aid may consist of bundling victims into a vehicle and driving them to hospital without primary treatment of their injuries. Courses in trauma care (for example, advanced trauma life support—ATLS—or primary trauma care) have been conducted in many Pacific Islands. However, the characteristics of trauma in the Pacific are that the 'golden hour' is missed. Patients who reach hospital alive are to some extent self-selected as having a good chance of survival, single injuries are much more common than multiple and there will be a significant amount of preventable disability owing to lack of skills or equipment to manage the specific injury. Head injuries are the leading cause of death from trauma. Most of the population in the Pacific have no access to a computerized tomography (CT) scan to assess the severity of a head injury, so that all decisions about surgical intervention need to be made on clinical grounds. There are only a couple of CT scanners across the Pacific (in Port Moresby and in the Fijian capital of Suva), and most hospitals do not even have a trained radiologist.

Road accidents account for approximately 10% of trauma cases, although the quoted figures may be higher in official reports. In the Pacific region people travel in the backs of open utility vehicles, often fail to wear seat belts and generally drive without the fear of being breathalysed for alcohol. Studies confirm a high incidence of alcohol intoxication in both drivers and pedestrians. Binge drinking associated with pay-day is the pattern.

There is an increasing problem with urban crime in the cities. Perhaps the worst affected, and certainly the most notorious, is Papua New Guinea. However, even in Port Moresby, the victims of assault are injured by another family member in more than one-half of the cases. Violence against women, and between family members, is a frequent occurrence when viewed from the perspective of an emergency doctor or surgeon. Domestic violence is tolerated to a remarkable extent in the Pacific Islands and this is an issue for society to address in the hope of changing attitudes.

The weapons of assault vary from country to country. Sling darts are commonplace in Micronesia, having been introduced from the Philippines. Bows and arrows are still used in the highlands of Papua New Guinea, where the problems of retained foreign bodies from incompletely removed arrows are repeatedly encountered. In malarial endemic areas blunt trauma injures the enlarged spleen and splenic rupture is the commonest cause of major abdominal trauma. Clubs, knives, machetes and axes make up the armoury. The use of firearms is on the increase.

In the highlands of Papua New Guinea tribal fights still occur and some hospitals charge a 'fight fee', which results in a reluctance to attend even with a serious injury. The injured may rather bypass the hospital with a 'fight fee' for another that charges a lesser or no fee, or opt for traditional treatment in the village. Traditionally, bows and arrows have been used in tribal fights, but since the mid-1990s there has been an increasing trend to use guns, which in turn cause more severe injuries.

Tree-related injuries are common. People fall out of coconut or betel nut trees retrieving the fruit, or coconuts fall onto an unsuspecting victim's head.

Marine-related injuries are caused by sea snakes, sharks, garfish, stonefish and jellyfish. Occasionally a fisherman suffers respiratory distress resulting from a fish obstructing his airway because of the practice of killing a fish by biting off its head. The puffer fish is poisonous and fatal if eaten without properly removing the gonads in preparation. The garfish may be attracted to a light being held in a boat, causing it to jump for the light and inadvertently stab the fisherman.

Snakebite is the commonest reason for mechanical ventilation in Port Moresby General Hospital and is due to a variety of venomous snakes, although mainly the Papuan Taipan (83%). In Polynesia only sea snakes are venomous.

Burns are common among those who have open fires in huts, particularly in highland regions. Epileptics may fall in the fire during a fit. In the Central Province of Papua New Guinea it has long been the custom for distressed young females to pour petrol on themselves and strike a match, suffering severe and usually fatal burns, victims of the 'Kerema syndrome'.

Blindness

The major cause of preventable blindness in adults is cataract, a condition that can be treated by visiting teams or by a visiting local ophthalmic surgeon. There are large numbers of cases waiting to be treated in many parts of the Pacific region. More Pacific Island surgeons need to be trained to perform this operation, to make the cataract service less dependent on visitors. The correction of refractive errors is also a health challenge throughout the Pacific, although spectacles are available at a price in most major centres. Papua New Guinea has made significant progress in training 10 ophthalmologists, along with one for Solomon Islands who, since the period of unrest, has been working in Vanuatu. Diabetic retinopathy is an increasing problem that can be managed by laser therapy.

There will be an increasing need for lasers as the diabetic population of the Pacific increases and ages.

Mental Health

Mental health is fundamentally linked to an individual's achievement and contribution to society, to overall well-being of societies and to physical health. In the Pacific Islands suicide, alcohol and drug use, and other mental health problems are on the increase. Most islands have inadequate mental health resources, with few or no trained health workers, no programmes and no budget. There are few trained psychiatrists, Papua New Guinea being the only country with postgraduate psychiatric programmes for doctors and nurses (six psychiatrists have graduated from UPNG). WHO endorsed a Regional Strategy for Mental Health in 2001, providing general principles and guidance on the challenges of mental health—the approaches outlined are advocacy, service provision, mental health promotion, policy and legislation, encouraging research and suicide prevention. In several of the Pacific Islands policies and legislation are being developed. The first Samoan National Symposium on Mental Health was held in 2003, and a young doctor was selected for psychiatric training in New Zealand. The WHO Pacific Islands Mental Health Network (PIMHnet) was first proposed in March 2005, at the meeting of Ministers of Health for the Pacific Island Countries in Apia, Samoa. The Network, funded by NZAID, was launched in Port Vila, Vanuatu, in 2007 and should result in more training of mental health workers, better access to psychotropic medications and policy development.

Alcohol and Substance Abuse

There is a wide variety of alcoholic home brews in the Pacific. Kava (a narcotic drink made from the root of the same name) is one of the traditional spirits of the South Pacific. It was usually reserved for ceremonial occasions, but it is now consumed more frequently on a casual basis. A study from Vanuatu suggested that low educational levels and residence on Vanuatu's main island were associated with females who drink kava. Heavy kava use can result in skin diseases (kava dermopathy). Weight loss and liver damage are other potential side-effects.

Ethanol has been introduced to the Pacific since contact began with Europeans. Records suggest that the Marshallese learned from outsiders how to ferment *jimanun* (coconut sap). Papua New Guinea had a prohibition policy imposed on its indigenous residents until 1962. Since then the use of alcohol has risen remarkably and, with increasing employment, binge drinking associated with fortnightly pay-days has also increased. Nevertheless, more than one-half of the population of Papua New Guinea abstain from alcohol. In Fiji a similar proportion of the population is abstinent. Alcohol consumption by teenagers in the US Pacific Islands ranged from 30% to 70% in both males and females. The effects of heavy alcohol consumption are generally experienced socio-economically. Alcohol is associated with road accidents, assaults, and sexual and domestic violence across the Pacific. Binge rather than daily drinking seems to be the pattern of use. The contribution of alcohol to cirrhotic liver disease is hard to determine because of the high prevalence of viral hepatitis. Another alcohol, methanol, is used widely as a fuel for cooking but is poisonous when ingested. Sporadic deaths occur, often among prankster-prone youths.

Cannabis is widely used in Papua New Guinea, where it was introduced by Australians after the Second World War and now grows freely. A sharp increase in smoking cannabis probably occurred in the 1990s. Cannabis is also the most popular illicit drug used across the Pacific, and most countries report low rates for the use of heroin, methamphetamines or cocaine. A study in the US-supported Pacific Islands reported rates of less than 5% for use of cocaine, heroin or ecstasy by teenagers, although there were higher rates of around 10% for inhalants such as glue.

Smoking

Most Pacific Island countries report adult smoking rates of 30%–50% in males and 5%–30% in females. The arterial, lung and cardiovascular diseases associated with smoking are anticipated, but cardiovascular disease is probably driven more strongly by hypertension, diabetes, lack of physical activity and obesity than by smoking, which none the less promotes, contributes to and aggravates ill health.

THE HEALTH CARE WORK-FORCE

Undergraduate Medical Education in the Pacific

The predecessor of FSM was founded in 1885. Until 1960 it was the only institution in the Pacific training doctors. Between 1951 and 1964 it also trained 16 national doctors for Papua New Guinea. In 1960 the Papuan Medical College was started, with 44 doctors graduating between 1964 and 1970, seven of whom were from other Pacific Islands. UPNG was founded in 1966, created a Medical Faculty in 1968 and held its first medical graduation in early 1973. Since then UPNG has produced more than 800 doctors, including 132 Pacific Islanders and 52 expatriates. At UPNG in the six years 2000–05, 240 doctors graduated (an average of 40 per year), including 27 Solomon Islanders, three from Vanuatu and two from Tuvalu. The attrition rate of Papua New Guinea doctors from their country's public service is about 50%.

Both UPNG (with the capacity to produce about 50 doctors per year) and FSM (70 annually) have trained doctors from other islands, with FSM having become the principal medical school for the Pacific region. In Fiji 30 of the 70 places per annum are reserved for students from the Pacific Islands and the other 40 are for Fijians. The numbers are insufficient to meet the needs of the ever-increasing population, being only about one-half of what is required, even by conservative estimates. The available teaching staff and resources are fully stretched already and would be unlikely to train more at today's standard.

In order to address shortages in the medical work-force, both Fiji and Papua New Guinea are increasing the numbers of medical students. Towards the end of 2009 FSM was renamed the College of Medicine, Nursing and Public Health, and became part of the Fiji National University. From 2010 the medical student intake was increased to 90 per annum. A second private medical school, the Umanand Prasad School of Medicine, was launched at the University of Fiji in Lautoka. In addition, UPNG is planning to train more medical students on its Goroka campus, and the possibility of medical training at Divine Word University, which already provides physiotherapy and other health worker training, is being considered.

Another strategy introduced to meet the shortage of doctors in the Pacific is the training of medical students in Cuba. Among senior health workers there is still some bewilderment as to how these programmes were agreed, or the students selected, without the involvement of senior doctors. Nevertheless, in 2011 a total of 74 Solomon Islanders, 30 Fijians and a number from Kiribati were already training in rural medicine in Cuba. Quite what the standard of these doctors will be, and what responsibilities they will be given, remains to be determined. Early experience, derived from graduates returning to Timor-Leste after participating in a similar programme, suggests that the students return for clinical experience at home after their overseas academic studies. This will offer an opportunity to ensure that they gain the clinical skills necessary before they are registered by their medical boards for practice in their own countries.

The Pacific Basin Medical Officers Training Program (PBMOTP) was a 10-year programme funded by US government aid and administered by the University of Hawaii (1986–96). It introduced an experimental five-year problem-based learning (PBL) course, with the first three years being spent in rural areas and community health clinics and the last two years being spent in urban hospitals. Because the funding period was limited, it ran for 10 years and produced 70 doctors, 50 of whom were from Micronesia and 20 from Palau, the Marshall Islands and American Samoa. Their degree might not be recognized in Australasia or the USA as a Bachelor of Medicine and Bachelor of Surgery (MBBS) or Medicinae Doctor (MD) equivalent, but it is recognized for entry into postgraduate programmes in Fiji.

Postgraduate and Specialist Training

The benefits of running a local postgraduate programme include keeping the doctor-in-training working for most of the time in his or her own country, learning to diagnose and treat disease with the resources available and being less likely to leave once qualified. Prior to starting a local Master of Medicine (MMed) programme in Fiji in 1997, only five of the 56 doctors who were trained as specialists overseas returned. This led FSM to believe it was training doctors for Australia and New Zealand. Local training seems more appropriate, teaches a broader range of skills than could be acquired in four years in a developed nation and is achieving a high standard of practitioner.

Both Fiji and Papua New Guinea also offer one-year diploma courses in child health, obstetrics and gynaecology, and anaesthesia. Fiji also offers surgery and medical diplomas, while Papua New Guinea offers ophthalmology. Passage to MMed depends upon a good grade at diploma level. Diplomates would be expected to be able to provide a safe service in a rural district or provincial hospital.

University of Papua New Guinea

The main model for specialist training is a university MMed course over four years. The MMed programme started in UPNG in 1975. There are now a number of specialist MMed graduates from UPNG, with the numbers (at the end of 2005) included in parentheses: medicine (17), surgery (52), anaesthesia (17), child health (36), obstetrics and gynaecology (19), psychiatry (six), ear, nose and throat—ENT (nine), ophthalmology (10), radiology (three) and pathology (three). The first emergency medicine specialist graduated in 2006, and one specialist in oral surgery graduated in 2005. The attrition rate from the public sector of specialists has been around 50%, although the majority who have left government service have gone into private practice, politics or health administration within Papua New Guinea. During the years 1994–2006 Papua New Guinea identified the need to train some of its general surgeons in surgical sub-specialties. The specialties selected were orthopaedics (seven), head and neck (four), urology (four), paediatric surgery (three), cardiothoracic surgery (two) and neurosurgery (two). The programmes involve both in-country and overseas training for two to three years after obtaining the MMed. By 2011 a total of 19 surgeons had completed their sub-specialty surgical diplomas (UPNG's higher postgraduate diploma).

Fiji

In Fiji diploma (one year) and MMed (four years) training were begun in 1997, with the first MMed students graduating in 2001. By the end of 2002 74 diplomas had been awarded by FSM (anaesthesia—16; internal medicine—13; obstetrics and gynaecology—eight; paediatrics—17; surgery—16; community and hospital practice—four) and 14 candidates had completed the MMed degree (anaesthesia—one; internal medicine—three; obstetrics and gynaecology—four; paediatrics—two; surgery—four). Of these graduates, 68 with diplomas and 12 with master's degrees were practising in the Pacific Islands. By 2009 over 200 diplomas and 50 MMed degrees had been granted, 25 of which were Fijian. Although Fijian graduates tend to remain in Fiji, a lack of work-force planning results in recent graduates from the specialty programmes having no designated position within the Department of Health work-force. This results in frustration and has contributed to the 'brain drain', although retention rates from the local programme have been better, with the majority of MMed graduates practising in their home country.

AusAID

AusAID, the Australian Government's overseas aid programme, has also supported medical education in the region through the Medical Officers Training Program (Papua New Guinea, 1987–95), Medical Officer, Nursing and Allied Health Science Training Project (MONAHP—Papua New Guinea, 1995–2002), and the Fiji School of Medicine Project (1999–2002). From 2002/03 support to FSM and UPNG was provided directly to the Deans and Project Management Teams in each country. In Papua New Guinea a new five-year programme of support (Health Education and Clinical Services—HECS) commenced in 2009. The programme supports tertiary health services and specialist training, helps build capacity within the school of medicine and health sciences, and is expected to result in greater local leadership of the process. In 1995–2010 the Royal Australasian College of Surgeons (RACS) was the principal agent managing these programmes. Recently, in keeping with the Paris Declaration on Aid Effectiveness (adopted in 2005 by countries convened by the Organisation for Economic Co-operation and Development), there has been a bigger effort to establish local ownership of specialist medical aid programmes and a greater sense of partnership. In Papua New Guinea HECS is chaired by the Dean of Medicine at UPNG and managed by staff from within the country, although many of the specialists are still sourced from overseas, usually Australia. In the Pacific a new arrangement to continue AusAid's PIP programme,entitled Strengthening Specialist Clinical Services in the Pacific (SSCSIP), was established in 2010. The express aim is to support Pacific Island countries in planning to access, host and evaluate specialist clinical services for themselves. A Development and Coordination Team (DaCT) has been established in Suva within FSM. These groups are at an early stage but have great potential to deliver. They are being strongly supported by AusAid's champion for specialist services, RACS.

The Current Work-force

The work-force is about one-half of what is estimated as sufficient to meet current requirements. It is particularly deficient in pathology, radiology and cancer services. Midwifery, radiography, physiotherapy, artificial limb prosthetics and laboratory services are other services that are poorly represented but much needed. The medical work-force comprises doctors who have been trained from a variety of backgrounds:

(i) Locally trained doctors who graduated from six-year MBBS courses from UPNG and FSM. Some of these doctors have also trained as specialists through local MMed programmes or overseas;

(ii) Graduates from the PBMOTP run by the University of Hawaii in the Federated States of Micronesia. Most are working in their home countries in the North Pacific as their degree is recognized nowhere else;

(iii) Doctors from neighbouring Pacific Islands who are employed on contracts that attract better remuneration, if not better hospital facilities, than in their home country;

(iv) Overseas trained doctors, some of whom are volunteers, some associated with missions and some of whom have been recruited by local departments of health or universities. These doctors were the main providers of medical and specialist care until local specialist training programmes began in the 1970s (Papua New Guinea) and 1990s (Fiji). A few have stayed on in specialties where national trainees have not yet filled the available posts (for example, radiology and pathology) or in remote hospitals funded by overseas aid or missions;

(v) Overseas trained doctors from non-English-speaking countries such as the People's Republic of China or Cuba. For example, since 2007 as many as 15 Cuban doctors have been working in Kiribati, while a number of Chinese specialist surgeons and anaesthetists work in Port Moresby, Papua New Guinea. These doctors are inconsistent in their ability to deliver high-quality care and integrate with the local health system. The ones who integrate best are undoubtedly those who learn the language and become part of the health care team rather than just a visible 'aid-presence';

(vi) Visiting specialist teams that travel to one or two centres over a two-week period, performing procedures on cases selected by a specialist nurse, local doctor or specialist. ENT, ophthalmology (mainly cataract), reconstructive surgery, paediatric surgery, urology, neurosurgery and cardiac surgery for congenital heart disease are some of the specialties of these teams. Diabetes specialists also visit to provide support care, education and prevention programmes. They comprise an occasional, inconsistent, but important and popular part of the work-force.

Nursing Numbers and Training

All of the larger countries administer their own nursing training programmes. Some also provide midwifery training, although there is a great need for further training and more midwives to provide essential obstetric care. There are not enough trained nurses and insufficient nursing positions. Nurse to population ratios vary from 12–15 per 10,000 in Solomon Islands, Vanuatu and Papua New Guinea, to 20 per 10,000 in Fiji, 30–34 per 10,000 in Tonga and Tuvalu, 43 per 10,000 in New Caledonia and French Polynesia, and 58 per 10,000 in Palau. The 'brain drain' affects nurses as well as doctors. Nurses produced by Fiji are so well trained that the United Kingdom has sent recruitment teams there in an attempt to persuade nurses to transfer their skills to the British National Health Service. In smaller Pacific Islands nurses trained in neighbouring countries may be tempted to stay, and their services are thus lost to their sponsoring government.

Despite the loss of skills resulting from the 'brain drain', the Pacific Islands derive much-needed foreign exchange from remittances sent home by overseas workers. Thus, a Kiribati nurses' initiative involving cohorts of 30 nursing students has been established with the support of AusAID. Nurses train first in Kiribati but then move to Australia for further training. The first group was due to graduate in 2010 with a view to working overseas. Another part of this project involves upgrading the skills and qualifications of nurses currently registered in Kiribati.

The 'Brain Drain'

A study based on census figures reported that in 2006 there were 652 Pacific Island-born doctors and 3,467 Pacific Island-born nurses and midwives working in Australia and New Zealand. More than one-half were from Fiji, but there were also significant numbers from Papua New Guinea, Samoa and Tonga. There were actually fewer health workers in the domestic work-forces of Tonga and Samoa than Pacific Island-born nationals from those countries working overseas. Fiji had slightly more national-born doctors and nurses working in the country than in Australia and New Zealand. Medical salaries are not competitive with those of neighbouring Australia and New Zealand (for example, the annual salary of a Papua New Guinean doctor is about US $8,000–$20,000, compared with US $50,000–$60,000 in Australia). In the first five years of the 21st century 40% of Fijian graduates went into private practice or left Fiji. The 'brain drain' is due to both 'push' (frustrations, limited positions for promotion, lack of recognition for training and inability to educate children privately) and 'pull' (higher salaries and better health care resources) factors. It affects all the islands, although in Papua New Guinea the majority of doctors disaffected by the public service have opted for private practice rather than going overseas.

Forced Retirements

One way of addressing the cost of salaries for too many public servants has been to encourage or force retirements. An attempt to reduce the inflated public sector in Guam and Solomon Islands has resulted in the loss of well-trained, irreplaceable health workers who were developed at great cost over many years, experienced and providing good service. Neighbouring Pacific Islands readily employed some of these 'retired' doctors. Fortunately Solomon Islands learned from their mistakes and some of the retired doctors have since been re-recruited and are again in public service. Others left the public service and set up in private practice.

CONCLUSIONS

Since the 1970s there has been much progress in Pacific health care, with core indicators improving in most of the islands other than Papua New Guinea. Protein-energy malnutrition rates have fallen. The system of health care lacks resources because of shortfalls in funding, poor infrastructure and inefficiency. Health workers and patients experience many frustrations. Health strategy is focused on reducing childhood mortality, improving maternal health and combating major diseases. However, as infectious diseases are being brought under control (HIV/AIDS and tuberculosis in Papua New Guinea excluded), new challenges have emerged in the field of non-communicable diseases. The populations of the Pacific are becoming obese and suffer an increasing prevalence of diabetes and cardiovascular disease. The incidence of cancer is also rising and has become one of the leading causes of death. Treatment facilities for malignant diseases are limited throughout the Pacific, and although some patients can be treated overseas, the majority who need it do not have access to tertiary care abroad. Accidents and injuries are the leading cause of death in adults aged 15–40 and also result in much untreated disability. There are still many colourful and exotic tropical diseases that attract world-wide interest. Since the 1970s significant progress has also been made in the capacity to train health workers, including doctors, with UPNG and FSM both operating postgraduate programmes for specialist doctors and nurses. As a result, there is less reliance on expatriate recruitment, with national doctors now comprising most of the medical work-force, except in the smaller nations. The supply of doctors and nurses is about one-half of what is required, and medical and nursing training needs to be increased further. The progress made in medical training is offset by a 'brain drain' to neighbouring countries, particularly Australia and New Zealand. However, some countries regard remittances from health workers working overseas as a valuable source of foreign currency.

BIBLIOGRAPHY

Clunie, G. J. A., McCaig, E., and Baravilala, W. 'The Fiji School of Medicine post-graduate training project' in *The Medical Journal of Australia*. Vol. 179, No. 11/12, pp. 631–632, December 2003.

Colagiuri, S., *et al*. 'The prevalence of diabetes in the Kingdom of Tonga' in *Diabetes Care*. Vol. 25, No. 8, pp. 1,378–1,383, August 2002.

Devaney, M. L., Reid, G., Baldwin, S., Crofts, N., and Power, R. 'Illicit drug use and responses in six Pacific Island countries' in *Drug and Alcohol Review 2006*. 25, pp. 387–390.

Dever, G. 'The role of low cost communications in health in the redevelopment of the indigenous physician workforce among selected jurisdictions of the US-associated Pacific Islands' in *Pacific Health Dialog*. Vol. 7, No. 2, pp. 63–67, September 2000.

Dowse, G. K., *et al*. 'Extraordinary prevalence of non-insulin-dependent diabetes mellitus and bimodal plasma glucose distribution in the Wanigela people of Papua New Guinea' in *The Medical Journal of Australia*. 160, pp. 767–774, 1994.

Finau, S. A. 'Appropriate health workforce for sustainable development in the Pacific' in *Pacific Health Dialog*. Vol. 4, No. 1, pp. 143–153, March 1997.

Foliaki, S., and Pearce, N. 'Prevention and control of diabetes in Pacific people' in *The British Medical Journal*. Vol. 327, pp. 437–439, August 2003.

Galbraith, J. E. 'ASPECT in the Pacific: walking the aid tightrope. Australian South Pacific Eye Consultant Teams' in *The Australian and New Zealand Journal of Surgery*. Vol. 64, No, 1. pp. 14–18, January 1994.

Kruske, S. *Papua New Guinea Midwifery Education Report*; internet www.cdu.edu.au/gshp/documents/pngmidwivery reviewfinalreport.pdf.

Lippe, J., Brener, N., Kann, L., Kinchen, S., Harris, W. A., McManus, T., and Speicher, N. 'Youth risk behavior surveillance—Pacific Island United States Territories, 2007' in *MMWR Surveillance Summaries 2008*. 57, pp. 28–56.

Marshall, D. 'The achievements of Interplast' in *The Australian and New Zealand Journal of Surgery*. Vol. 64, No. 1, pp. 19–21, January 1994.

McDonald, D. 'Cannabis in Papua New Guinea' in *Pacific Health Dialog*. Vol. 11, No. 1, pp. 96–101, 2004.

Natuzzi, E. S., Kushner, A., Jagilly, R., Pickacha, D., Agiomea, K., Hou, L., Houasia, P., Hendricks, P. L., Ba'erodo, D. 'Surgical care in the Solomon Islands: A road map for universal surgical care delivery.' in *World Journal of Surgery*. Vol. 35, No. 6, pp 1,183–1,193, June 2011.

Pacific Health Dialog. 'Fiji School of Medicine 1885–2010. Celebrating 125 years' in *Journal of Community Health and Clinical Medicine for the Pacific*. Vol. 16, No. 2, pp. 4–159, September 2010.

Sakaue, M., *et al*. 'Austronesian-speaking people in Papua New Guinea have susceptibility to obesity and Type 2 diabetes' in *Diabetes Care*. No. 26, pp. 955–956, 2003.

Theile, D. E., and Bennett, R. C. 'The Pacific Islands Project: the first 3 years' in *The Australian and New Zealand Journal of Surgery*. Vol. 68, No. 11, pp. 792–8, November 1998.

UN Development Programme (UNDP). *Pacific Islands Regional Millennium Development Goals Report 2004*. New York, United Nations Development Programme and Anse Vata, Secretariat of the Pacific Community, 2004; internet www.spc.int/mdgs/MDGReport/Reg_report.htm.

UN Programme on HIV/AIDS (UNAIDS). *2006 Report on the global AIDS epidemic: May 2006*. Geneva, United Nations Programme on HIV/AIDS, 2006; internet www.unaids.org/en/HIV_data/2006GlobalReport/default.asp.

Watters, D. A. K., *et al*. 'Surgical capability and surgical pathology in Papua New Guinea in the year 2000' in *The Australian and New Zealand Journal of Surgery*. Vol. 71, No. 5, pp. 303–8, May 2001.

Watters, D. A. K., and Scott, D. F. 'Doctors in the Pacific' in *The Medical Journal of Australia*. Vol. 181, No. 11/12, pp. 597–601, December 2004.

Watters, D. A. K., and Theile, D. E. 'The progress of surgical training in Papua New Guinea to the end of the 20th Century' in *The Australian and New Zealand Journal of Surgery*. Vol. 70, No. 4, pp. 302–7, April 2000.

Wilder-Smith, A. 'Current status of "essential obstetric care" activities internationally: A literature review' in *Tropical Doctor*. Vol. 33, No. 3, pp. 135–8, July 2003; internet www.ncbi.nlm.nih.gov/entrez.

Williams, D., Jensen, S., Nimorakiotakis, W., and Winkel, K. D. (Eds). *Venomous Bites and Stings in Papua New Guinea: a guide to treatment for health workers and doctors*. Melbourne, Australian Venom Research Unit, University of Melbourne, 2005.

World Health Organization. *Report: Meeting of Ministers of Health for the Pacific Islands Countries*. Manila, WHO, Regional Office for the Western Pacific, 2003; internet www.wpro.who.int/NR/rdonlyres/8AF5819D-25DF-465-F-8A63-193E5C8F2F1C/0/tonga_meeting_report_2003.pdf.

Global Status Report on Alcohol 2004. Geneva, WHO, 2004.

'Prevalence of diabetes in the WHO Western Pacific Region' in *Diabetes Programme*; internet www.who.int/diabetes/facts/world_figures/en/index6.html.

AUSTRALIAN PACIFIC TERRITORIES

There are two external dependencies or Territories of the Commonwealth of Australia in the Pacific Ocean: the Coral Sea Islands Territory and Norfolk Island, the latter being self-governing. The Australian Attorney-General is responsible for the administration of the dependencies, which lie within the jurisdiction of the Commonwealth Government.

Head of State: HM Queen ELIZABETH II (succeeded to the throne 6 February 1952).

Governor-General: QUENTIN BRYCE (assumed office 5 September 2008).

Attorney-General's Department: Central Office, Robert Garran Offices, National Circuit, Barton, ACT 2600, Australia; tel. (2) 6250-6666; fax (2) 6250-5900; internet www.ag.gov.au.

Attorney-General: ROBERT MCCLELLAND.

CORAL SEA ISLANDS TERRITORY

The Coral Sea Islands became a Territory of the Commonwealth of Australia under the Coral Sea Islands Act of 1969. The Territory lies east of Queensland, between the Great Barrier Reef and longitude 156° 06'E, and between latitude 12°S and 24°S, and comprises several islands and reefs. The islands are composed largely of sand and coral, and have no permanent fresh water supply, but some have a cover of grass and scrub. The area has been a notorious hazard to shipping since the 19th century, the danger of the reefs being compounded by shifting sand cays and occasional tropical cyclones. The Coral Sea Islands have been acquired by Australia by numerous acts of sovereignty since the early years of the 20th century.

Extending over a sea area of approximately 780,000 sq km (300,000 sq miles), all the islands and reefs in the Territory are very small, totalling only a few sq km of land area. They include Cato Island, Chilcott Islet in the Coringa Group, and the Willis Group. In 1997 the Coral Sea Islands Act was amended to include Elizabeth and Middleton Reefs. A meteorological station, operated by the Commonwealth Bureau of Meteorology and with a staff of four, has provided a service on one of the Willis Group since 1921. The other islands are uninhabited. There are eight automatic weather stations (on Cato Island, Flinders Reef, Frederick Reef, Holmes Reef, Lihou Reef, Creal Reef, Marion Reef and Gannet Cay) and several navigation aids distributed throughout the Territory.

The Act constituting the Territory did not establish an administration on the islands, but provides means of controlling the activities of those who visit them. The Lihou Reef and Coringa-Herald National Nature Reserves were established in 1982 to provide protection for the wide variety of terrestrial and marine wildlife, which include rare species of birds and sea turtles (one of which is the largest, and among the most endangered, of the world's species of sea turtle). The Australian Government has concluded agreements for the protection of endangered and migratory birds with Japan and the People's Republic of China. The Governor-General of Australia is empowered to make ordinances for the peace, order and good government of the Territory and, by ordinance, the laws of the Australian Capital Territory apply. The Supreme Court and Court of Petty Sessions of Norfolk Island have jurisdiction in the Territory. The Territory is administered by a parliamentary secretary, who is appointed by the Attorney-General. The area is visited regularly by the Royal Australian Navy.

NORFOLK ISLAND

Introduction

Norfolk Island lies off the eastern coast of Australia, about 1,400 km east of Brisbane, to the south of New Caledonia and 640 km north of New Zealand. The Territory also comprises uninhabited Phillip Island and Nepean Island, 7 km and 1 km south of the main island, respectively. Norfolk Island is hilly and fertile, with a coastline of cliffs and an area of 34.6 sq km (13.4 sq miles). It is about 8 km long and 4.8 km wide. The climate is mild and subtropical, and the average annual rainfall is 1,350 mm, most of which occurs between May and August. The resident population numbered 2,037 at the census of August 2001, and consists of 'islanders' (descendants of the mutineers from *HMS Bounty*, evacuated from Pitcairn Island, who numbered 824 in 1996) and 'mainlanders' (originally from Australia, New Zealand or the United Kingdom). Of the 2,523 residents, 1,863 were living permanently on Norfolk Island in 2006. English is the official language, but Norfuk, a Norfolk Island dialect (a mixture of old English and Tahitian) is also spoken and was given the status of joint official language in 2005. The capital of the Territory is Kingston.

The island was uninhabited when discovered in 1774 by a British expedition, led by Capt. James Cook. Norfolk Island was used as a penal settlement from 1788 to 1814 and again from 1825 to 1855, when it was abandoned. In 1856 it was resettled by 194 emigrants from Pitcairn Island, which had become overpopulated. Norfolk Island was administered as a separate colony until 1897, when it became a dependency of New South Wales. In 1913 control was transferred to the Australian Government.

Under the Norfolk Island Act 1979, Norfolk Island is progressing to responsible legislative and executive government, enabling it to manage its own affairs to the greatest practicable extent. Wide powers are exercised by the nine-member Legislative Assembly and by the Executive Council, comprising the executive members of the Legislative Assembly, who have ministerial-type responsibilities. The Act preserves the Australian Government's responsibility for Norfolk Island as a Territory under its authority, with the Minister for Territories as the responsible minister. The Act indicated that consideration would be given within five years to an extension of the powers of the Legislative Assembly and the political and administrative institutions of Norfolk Island. In 1985 legislative and executive responsibility was assumed by the Norfolk Island Government for public works and services, civil defence, betting and gaming, territorial archives and matters relating to the exercise of executive authority. In 1988 further amendments empowered the Legislative Assembly to select a Norfolk Island Government Auditor (territorial accounts were previously audited by the Commonwealth Auditor-General). The office of Chief Minister was replaced by that of the President of the Legislative Assembly.

In December 1991 a referendum took place at which a proposal by the Australian Government to include Norfolk Island within the Australian federal electorate was overwhelmingly rejected by the islanders. The outcome of the poll led the Australian Government, in June 1992, to announce that it had abandoned the plans. Similarly, in late 1996 a proposal by the Australian Government to combine Norfolk Island's population with that of Canberra for record-keeping purposes was strongly opposed by the islanders.

In late 1997 the Legislative Assembly debated the issue of increased self-determination for the island. Pro-independence supporters argued that the Territory could generate sufficient income by exploiting gas- and oilfields in the island's exclusive economic zone.

In August 1998 a referendum proposing that the Norfolk Island electoral system be integrated more closely with that of mainland Australia (initiated by the Minister for Regional Development, Territories and Local Government) was rejected by 78% of the Territory's electorate. A similar referendum in May 1999 was opposed by 73% of voters.

Frustration with the Australian Government's perceived reluctance to facilitate the transfer of greater powers to the Territory (as outlined in the Norfolk Island Act of 1979, see above) led the island's Legislative Assembly in mid-1999 to vote by seven members to one in favour of full internal self-government. Negotiations regarding the administration of crown land on the island, which continued in 2000, were seen as indicative of the islanders' determination to pursue greater independence from Australia.

Legislation was approved in March 2003 to amend the requirements to vote in Norfolk Island elections. Under the new system Australian, New Zealand and British citizens were to be allowed to vote after a residency period of 12 months (reduced from 900 days). The amendments, which followed a series of occasionally acrimonious discussions with the Australian Government, provoked concern among islanders who feared that succumbing to Australian pressure to reform the Norfolk Island Act would result in the effective removal of authority over electoral matters from island control. Moreover, a report by an Australian parliamentary committee published in July 2003 was critical of Norfolk Island's Government and public services. Many residents believed the report constituted a further attempt by Australia to undermine their autonomy. The Chief Minister refuted the committee's claims, stating that he would refuse any offers of financial assistance from Canberra or any moves to introduce income tax in return for access to services from the mainland.

In February 2006 the Australian Government unexpectedly announced that it was to resume responsibility for matters such as immigration, customs and quarantine, claiming that the existing arrangements under the Norfolk Island Act of 1979 had become too complex and costly for a community of the island's size to sustain. Two main alternative options were to be considered: a form of modified self-government that would allow greater powers for involvement by the Australian Government; and a model of local government whereby Australia might assume responsibility for state-type functions. Other options under consideration included the possibility of an island territory government with the power to legislate on local responsibilities. The island's revenue-raising capacities were also to be reviewed, along with the provision of basic services such as health and education. Following a major review, in December it was confirmed that Norfolk Island was to remain exempt from federal income taxes. Although the Territory would thus retain its attraction as a tax haven for wealthy individuals, many islanders expressed disappointment at the decision.

In August 2008 the Government of Norfolk Island issued its response to an Australian Senate Committee inquiry into the financial management of the island, claiming that the existing arrangements remained viable. In October, however, the Australian Minister for Home Affairs, Bob Debus, warned that Norfolk Island was in danger of becoming a 'failed state'. In December the island's Government submitted its formal response to the concerns raised by Debus, in which it refuted the Minister's claims that the current governance arrangements were operating 'to the disadvantage of many on Norfolk Island'. Meanwhile, the island's Government had commissioned an independent review of the Norfolk Island Act of 1979, following which detailed proposals for the simplification and modernization of the prevailing legislation were presented to Debus. The retention of the role of Administrator was envisaged. The Territories Law Reform Bill 2010 was introduced in March of that year into the House of Representatives in Canberra. While the Norfolk Island Government again acknowledged the need for reform, it regarded the draft legislation as inappropriate and raised numerous concerns, particularly in relation to the proposed reduction in local powers. The Australian Senate subsequently referred the draft law to the Joint Standing Committee on National Capital and External Territories, which was required to conduct an inquiry.

In its report published in May 2010 the Committee concluded that the proposed reforms would lead to improvements in the accountability and transparency of Norfolk Island's governance, recommending that the changes be adopted. It was envisaged that the Governor-General of Australia and the federal minister responsible for Norfolk Island would play a more active role in the drafting and enactment of legislation. The radical reforms were to include provision for the removal of the Chief Minister by the island's Administrator in 'exceptional circumstances'. In November, as the island's financial situation continued to deteriorate, it was announced that, in exchange for federal funding and access to welfare facilities and other services, the local Government had agreed in principle to the implementation of the Territories Law Reform Bill. The stringent conditions attached to the Australian Government's provision of emergency funding included the introduction of federal law in areas such as privacy and freedom of information. The federal Government was to provide up to $A14.1m. in emergency financial support for Norfolk Island in 2011/12.

In October 2010 it was reported that, in collaboration with an Australian university, the world's first trial of a personal carbon trading programme was to commence on Norfolk Island in 2011. In addition to reducing greenhouse gas emissions, it was hoped that the three-year trial would reduce obesity and improve the health of islanders. Residents and visitors to the island were to be offered a carbon credit card, to be used initially when purchasing petrol or power. Frugal users would be able to exchange the remaining units of their annual quota for cash. Researchers hoped to add foodstuffs to the scheme in 2012, ranking products in terms of health as well as carbon costs.

Despite the island's natural fertility, agriculture is no longer the principal economic activity. The main crops are Kentia palm seed, cereals, vegetables and fruit. Cattle and pigs are farmed for domestic consumption. Development of a fisheries industry is restricted by the lack of a harbour. Some flowers and plants are grown commercially. The administration is increasing the area devoted to Norfolk Island pine and hardwoods. In 1985 and 1986 the Governments of Australia and Norfolk Island jointly established the 465-ha Norfolk Island National Park. This was to protect the remaining native forest, which is the habitat of several unique species of flora (including the largest fern in the world) and fauna (such as the Norfolk Island green parrot, the guavabird and the boobook owl). Conservation efforts have included the development of Phillip Island as a nature reserve.

Statistical Survey

Source: The Administration of Norfolk Island, Administration Offices, Kingston, Norfolk Island 2899; tel. 22001; fax 23177; internet www.norfolk.gov.nf.

AREA AND POPULATION

Area: 34.6 sq km (13.3 sq miles).

Population: 2,601 (males 1,257, females 1,344), including 564 visitors, at census of 7 August 2001; 2,523 (males 1,218, females 1,305), comprising 1,863 'ordinarily resident' and 660 visitors, at census of 8 August 2006.

Density (2006 census): 72.9 per sq km.

Population by Age and Sex (2006 census): *0–14:* 359 (males 185, females 174); *15–64:* 1,587 (males 763, females 824); *65 and over:* 561 (males 263, females 298); *Total* 2,523* (males 1,218, females 1,305).

* Including 16 persons (males 7, females 9) of unknown age.

Births, Marriages and Deaths (2005/06 unless otherwise indicated): Live births 22; Marriages 35 (2002/03); Deaths 13.

Employment (ordinarily resident population aged 15 years and over, 2006 census): Agriculture, forestry and fishing 53; Mining and quarrying 13; Manufacturing 30; Electricity, gas and water 37; Construction 104; Wholesale and retail trade 280; Transport and storage 41; Communication 40; Finance, property and business services 49; Public administration and defence 67; Health 59; Education, museum and library services 48; Other community services 28; Restaurants, hotels, accommodation and clubs 206; Other recreational and personal services 97; *Sub-total* 1,152; Activities not stated or not adequately described 31; *Total* 1,183 (males 604, females 579).

FINANCE

Currency and Exchange Rates: Australian currency is used.

Budget (year ending 30 June 2009): Revenue $A26,167,730; Expenditure $A28,039,551.

Cost of Living (Retail Price Index, average of quarterly figures; base: October–December 1990 = 100): All items 159.7 in 2004; 168.6 in 2005; 181.1 in 2006.

EXTERNAL TRADE

2005/06 (year ending 30 June): *Imports:* $A32,065,392, mainly from Australia and New Zealand.

Trade with Australia ($A million, 2006/07): *Imports* 10.

Trade with New Zealand ($NZ '000, 2006/07): *Imports* 7,801. *Exports* 25.

TOURISM

Visitors (year ending 30 June): 29,639 in 2008/09; 26,339 in 2009/10; 24,268 in 2010/11.

COMMUNICATIONS MEDIA

Radio Receivers (1996): 2,500 in use.

Television Receivers (1996): 1,200 in use.

Telephones (2002/03): 2,374 main lines in use.

Internet Users (2002/03): 494.

Non-daily Newspaper (2002): 1 (estimated circulation 1,400).

EDUCATION

Institution (2003): 1 state school incorporating infant, primary and secondary levels.

Teachers (2004/05): Primary 8; Secondary 12.

Students (1999/2000): Infants 79; Primary 116; Secondary 119.

Directory

The Constitution

The Norfolk Island Act 1979 constitutes the administration of the Territory as a body politic and provides for a responsible legislative and executive system, enabling it to administer its own affairs to the greatest practicable extent. The preamble of the Act states that it is the intention of the Australian Parliament to consider the further extension of powers.

The Act provides for an Administrator, appointed by the Australian Government, who shall administer the government of Norfolk Island as a territory under the authority of the Commonwealth of Australia. The Administrator is required to act on the advice of the Executive Council or the responsible Commonwealth Minister in those matters specified as within their competence. Every proposed law passed by the Legislative Assembly must be effected by the assent of the Administrator, who may grant or withhold that assent, reserve the proposed law for the Governor-General's pleasure or recommend amendments.

The Act provides for the Legislative Assembly and the Executive Council, comprising the executive members of the Assembly who have ministerial-type responsibilities. The nine members of the Legislative Assembly are elected for a term of not more than three years under a cumulative method of voting: each elector is entitled to as many votes (all of equal value) as there are vacancies, but may not give more than four votes to any one candidate. The nine candidates who receive the most votes are declared elected.

In November 2010 the implementation of the Territories Law Reform Bill was approved in principle by the Government of Norfolk Island.

The Government

The Administrator, who is the senior representative of the Commonwealth Government, is appointed by the Governor-General of Australia and is accountable to a minister of the federal Cabinet. A form of responsible legislative and executive government was extended to the island in 1979. However, governance arrangements were under review in 2010.

Administrator: OWEN WALSH.

EXECUTIVE COUNCIL
(October 2011)

Chief Minister: DAVID E. BUFFETT.

Attorney-General and Minister for Finance: CRAIG M. ANDERSON.

Minister for Tourism, Industry and Development: ANDRE N. NOBBS.

Minister for Community Services: TIMOTHY J. SHERIDAN.

MINISTRIES

All Ministries are located at:

Old Military Barracks, Quality Row, Kingston, Norfolk Island 2899; tel. 22003; fax 22624; e-mail executives@assembly.gov.nf; internet www.norfolk.gov.nf.

GOVERNMENT OFFICES

Office of the Administrator: POB 201, New Military Barracks, Norfolk Island 2899; tel. 22152; fax 22681.

Administration of Norfolk Island: Administration Offices, Kingston, Norfolk Island 2899; tel. 22001; fax 23177; e-mail records@admin.gov.nf; internet www.norfolkislandgovernment.com; all govt depts; CEO GEORGE PLANT.

Legislature

LEGISLATIVE ASSEMBLY

Nine candidates are elected for not more than three years. The most recent general election was held on 17 March 2010.

Speaker: ROBIN E. ADAMS.

Deputy Speaker: LISLE D. SNELL.

Other Members: TIMOTHY J. SHERIDAN, CRAIG M. ANDERSON, ANDRE N. NOBBS, DAVID E. BUFFETT, MELISSA WARD, MICHAEL W. KING, RHONDA E. GRIFFITHS.

Judicial System

Supreme Court of Norfolk Island: Kingston; appeals lie to the Federal Court of Australia.

Chief Magistrate: WARREN DONALD.

Judges: PETER JACOBSEN (Chief Justice), GARY KEITH DOWNES, BRUCE THOMAS LANDER.

Religion

The majority of the population professes Christianity (66.6%, according to the census of 2001), with the principal denominations being the Church of England (34.9%), the Roman Catholic Church (11.7%) and the Uniting Church (11.2%).

The Press

Norfolk Island Government Gazette: Kingston, Norfolk Island 2899; tel. 22001; fax 23177; internet www.info.gov.nf; weekly.

Norfolk Islander: Greenways Press, POB 248, Norfolk Island 2899; tel. 22159; fax 22948; e-mail news@islander.nf; internet www.norfolkislander.com; f. 1965; weekly; Co-Editors TOM LLOYD, JONATHAN SNELL; circ. 1,350.

Broadcasting and Communications

TELECOMMUNICATIONS

Norfolk Telecom: New Cascade Rd, POB 469, Kingston; tel. 322244; fax 322499; e-mail kim@telecom.gov.nf; internet www.ni.net.nf; mobile services introduced in 2007; Man. KIM DAVIES.

BROADCASTING

Radio

Norfolk Island Broadcasting Service: New Cascade Rd, POB 456, Norfolk Island 2899; tel. 22137; fax 23298; e-mail manager@radio.gov.nf; internet www.norfolk.gov.nf/VL2NI.htm; govt-owned; non-commercial; broadcasts seven days per week; relays television and radio programmes from Australia and New Zealand; Broadcast Man. GEORGE SMITH.

Radio Norfolk: New Cascade Rd, POB 456, Norfolk Island 2899; tel. 22137; fax 23298; e-mail norfolk@radio.gov.nf; internet www.norfolk.gov.nf/VL2NI.htm; f. 1950s; govt-owned; Man. GEORGE SMITH.

Television

Norfolk Island Broadcasting Service: see Radio.

Norfolk Island Television Service: f. 1987; govt-owned; relays programmes of Australian Broadcasting Corpn, Special Broadcasting Service Corpn and Central Seven TV by satellite.

TV Norfolk (TVN): locally operated service featuring programmes of local events and information for tourists.

Finance

BANKING

Commonwealth Bank of Australia (Australia): Taylors Rd, Norfolk Island 2899; tel. 22144; fax 22805.

Westpac Banking Corpn Savings Bank Ltd (Australia): Burnt Pine, Norfolk Island 2899; tel. 22120; fax 22808.

Trade

Norfolk Island Chamber of Commerce Inc: POB 370, Norfolk Island 2899; tel. 22317; fax 23221; e-mail photopress@ni.net.nf; f. 1966; affiliated to the Australian Chamber of Commerce and Industry; 60 mems; Pres. GARY ROBERTSON; Sec. MARK MCGUIRE.

Norfolk Island Gaming Authority: POB 882, Norfolk Island 2899; tel. 22002; fax 22499; e-mail secgameauth@norfolk.net.nf; internet www.gamingauthority.nlk.nf; Dir RODERICK MCALPINE.

Transport

ROADS

There are some 53 km of paved roads and 27 km of unpaved roads.

SHIPPING

Norfolk Island is served by three shipping lines, Neptune Shipping, Pacific Direct Line and Roslyndale Shipping Company Pty Ltd. A small tanker from Nouméa (New Caledonia) delivers petroleum products to the island and another from Australia delivers liquid propane gas.

CIVIL AVIATION

Norfolk Island's airport has two runways and is capable of taking jet-engined aircraft. Work to resurface the main runway, in order to accommodate larger aircraft, was completed in 2006. In 2009 Norfolk Air was operating services to the Australian cities of Brisbane, Sydney, Melbourne and Newcastle, while Air New Zealand provided a twice-weekly service from Auckland. In 2008 Our Airline (formerly Air Nauru) resumed its service to Norfolk Island, in a joint operation with Norfolk Air.

Norfolk Air: POB 209, Norfolk Island 2899; tel. 324272; fax 324276; internet www.norfolkair.com; operated by Norfolk Island Govt; CEO JEFF MURDOCH.

Tourism

Visitor arrivals totalled 24,268 in 2010/11, the majority of whom came from Australia. In 2002/03 tourist accommodation totalled 1,551 beds.

Norfolk Island Tourism: Taylors Rd, Burnt Pine, POB 211, Norfolk Island 2899; tel. 22147; fax 23109; internet www.norfolkisland.com.au; Chair. MARION CHRISTIAN; Gen. Man. WAYNE EMERY.

Education

Education is free and compulsory for all children between the ages of six and at least 15. Pupils attend the one government school from infant to secondary level. In 2002/03 a total of 187 pupils were enrolled at infant and primary levels and 118 at secondary levels. Students wishing to follow higher education in Australia are eligible for bursaries and scholarships. The budgetary allocation for education was more than $A2.4m. in 2006/07.

FIJI

Introduction

The Republic of Fiji lies in the south-west Pacific Ocean, south of the Equator, 1,770 km north of Auckland (New Zealand) and 2,730 km north-east of Sydney (Australia). To the west lies Melanesia: Solomon Islands in the north-west, Vanuatu and New Caledonia. East of Fiji is Tonga and, in the north-east, other Polynesian islands, those of Wallis and Futuna, and Samoa. Tuvalu is to the north. The Fiji group comprises four main islands, Viti Levu (where 70% of the population lives), Vanua Levu, Taveuni and Kadavu, and some 840 smaller islands, atolls and reefs, of which fewer than 100 are inhabited. The island of Rotuma, 386 km (240 miles) north-west of Vanua Levu, and the eight smaller islands of the group also constitute part of the Republic. The total area of the Republic of Fiji is 18,376 sq km (7,095 sq miles). The climate is tropical, with temperatures ranging from 16°C to 32°C (60°F to 90°F). Rainfall is heaviest between November and April, but is more constant on the windward side.

The Fijian islands were settled some 3,500 years ago, by Melanesian and Polynesian peoples. The first Europeans to settle on the islands were sandalwood traders, missionaries and shipwrecked sailors. Under their influence, local fighting and jealousies reached unprecedented heights until, by the 1850s, one Ratu (chief), Thakombau, had gained a tenuous influence over the whole of the western islands. Thakombau ran foul of US interests during the 1850s and turned to the British for assistance, unsuccessfully at first, but in 1874 Britain agreed to a second offer of cession, and Fiji was proclaimed a British possession. The island of Rotuma and its dependencies were added to the territory in 1881. Fiji became independent, within the Commonwealth, on 10 October 1970.

Fiji is characterized by racial diversity. The indigenous Fijian population declined sharply during the 1850s, owing to epidemics of measles and influenza in which thousands died, and only in the 1950s did it begin to rise. The Indian population was originally brought to Fiji as labour for the canefields from 1879. The population at the census of August 1986 was 715,375, of whom 48.7% were Indians and 46.1% Fijians. Following the coups of 1987, there was emigration on a large scale, particularly from among the Indian community. In 1996 it was estimated that ethnic Fijians comprised 51.1% of the population and Indians 43.6%. According to official figures, the population at the census of September 2007 was 837,271, of whom 37.5% were Indians and 56.8% Fijians. According to estimates by the Secretariat of the Pacific Community, the population had reached 851,745 (males 434,400, females 417,344) by mid-2011. In 1996 58% of the population were Christians (mainly Methodists), 34% were Hindus and 7% Muslims. English is the official language, but Fijian (the principal dialect being Bauan) and Hindi (the locally developed dialect being known as Hindustani) are widely spoken. The capital is Suva on Viti Levu.

The racial diversity, compounded by actions of the past colonial administrations, presents Fiji with one of its most difficult problems. The colonial Government consistently favoured the Fijian population, protecting them from exploitation and their land from alienation, but allowed the importation of foreign labour. Approximately 80% of the islands were owned by Fijian communities, but over 90% of the sugar crop, Fiji's largest export, was produced by Indians, usually on land leased from Fijians. Until the mid-20th century Indians were poorly represented politically, while Fijians had their own administrative and judicial systems.

After independence, Fijian politics were, for a long time, dominated by Ratu Sir Kamisese Mara, leader of the Alliance Party (AP). Following tension between the Government and its opposition in Parliament (supported by the labour movement), a meeting of union leaders in May 1985 represented the start of discussions that culminated in the founding of the Fiji Labour Party (FLP). Officially inaugurated in Suva in July 1985 under the presidency of Dr Timoci Bavadra, the party aimed to present a more effective parliamentary opposition.

In 1987 two military coups took place. The first of these, led by Lt-Col (later Maj.-Gen.) Sitiveni Rabuka, occurred in May. Governor-General Ratu Sir Penaia Ganilau refused to recognize Rabuka's administration and established an Advisory Council. The two factions subsequently agreed to form an interim bipartisan Government. However, the implementation of this compromise plan was forestalled in September by a second coup, again led by Rabuka. Ganilau resigned as Governor-General and Fiji was deemed to have left the Commonwealth. Rabuka declared himself Head of State. In December, however, Rabuka resigned as Head of State and Ganilau was appointed the first President of the Fijian Republic. Fiji was readmitted to the Commonwealth at a meeting of member states in October 1997. In the same month Rabuka was granted an audience with Queen Elizabeth II in London, at which he formally apologized for the military coups of 1987.

In February 1988 Rotuma (the only Polynesian island in the country) attempted to declare independence from Fiji, announcing that it did not recognize Fiji's newly declared status as a republic and affirming its continued loyalty to the Commonwealth. Rotumans subsequently received a special status, with one seat in each of the houses of Parliament.

In May 2000 a group of armed men, led by businessman George Speight, invaded the parliament building and ousted the Government, taking hostage Prime Minister Mahendra Chaudhry and 30 other members of the governing coalition. A state of emergency was declared, as Speight's supporters rampaged through the streets of Suva, looting and setting fire to Indian businesses. Speight declared that he had reclaimed Fiji for indigenous Fijians and had dissolved the Constitution. In early 2001 an international panel of judges at the Court of Appeal found the abrogation of the 1997 Constitution to be illegal, and a parliamentary election took place in August 2001.

In December 2006 Prime Minister Laisenia Qarase, who had been returned to power at the parliamentary election held in May, was removed from office in a military coup led by Cdre Frank (Voreqe) Bainimarama, Commander of the Armed Forces. Bainimarama declared himself acting Head of State. Parliament was dissolved, a state of emergency was declared and Fiji was suspended from the Commonwealth. Bainimarama subsequently reinstated the former President, Ratu Josefa Iloilo, and Bainimarama was sworn in as interim Prime Minister. In mid-2007 it was announced that a parliamentary election was to be held in 2009. In August 2008, however, Bainimarama announced that the election schedule was dependent on the implementation of electoral reforms and would therefore be subject to further delays. In May 2009, in response to the lack of progress towards the restoration of democracy, the Pacific Islands Forum suspended Fiji from the group. In April 2009, after the Court of Appeal ruled the interim Government of Bainimarama to be unlawful, President Iloilo revoked the 1997 Constitution. Bainimarama was reinstated as Prime Minister, and the parliamentary election was deferred to 2014. In March 2010 Bainimarama announced that all politicians who had served since 1987 were to be barred from contesting the 2014 election. Furthermore, the imposition in mid-2010 of stringent restrictions on the media drew widespread criticism. The trial of former Prime Minister, Laisenia Qarase on charges of corruption was expected to commence in March 2012.

The removal of the elected Government in the military coup of December 2006 had serious repercussions for the Fijian economy. In September 2006 the forthcoming expiry of the European Union (EU) protocol governing sugar prices, whereby Fiji had been guaranteed the sale of its sugar at preferential rates, prompted the then Government to announce an eight-year reform project aimed at strengthening the country's sugar industry. The programme also envisaged the provision of assistance to sugar farmers for the purposes of diversifying into other activities. However, following the EU's suspension of non-humanitarian aid to Fiji as a result of the coup of December 2006, it was announced in April 2007 that EU funding for the project was to be substantially reduced. In March 2007, furthermore, the Asian Development Bank (ADB) announced that it had suspended funding of US $130m. that had been allocated to various development projects in Fiji. The interim Government identified areas such as forestry, marine products and mineral water, along with information and communications technology, as priority sectors. Tourism has also been affected by political instability. Although the sector recorded a strong recovery in 2010, when visitor numbers increased by 16.5%, the deep discounting of prices and the costs of overseas marketing campaigns were expected to curb net revenue. In December 2010 the Tourist VAT Refund Scheme, to permit visitors to claim back value-added tax paid on goods purchased in Fiji, was enacted; meanwhile, the rate of VAT was raised from 12.5% to 15.0%.

In 2005 Fiji became the first country in the world to sell its carbon emissions credits under the terms of the Kyoto Protocol (which allows countries that are within their permitted limits of carbon emissions to sell their unused allocation to countries that have not met their targets).

Statistical Survey

Sources (unless otherwise stated): Bureau of Statistics, POB 2221, Government Bldgs, Suva; tel. 3315144; fax 3303656; internet www .statsfiji.gov.fj; Reserve Bank of Fiji, POB 1220, Suva; tel. 3313611;

fax 3301688; e-mail info@rbf.gov.fj; internet www.reservebank.gov.fj.

AREA AND POPULATION

Area (incl. the Rotuma group): 18,376 sq km (7,095 sq miles). Land area of 18,333 sq km (7,078 sq miles) consists mainly of the islands of Viti Levu (10,429 sq km—4,027 sq miles) and Vanua Levu (5,556 sq km—2,145 sq miles).

Population: 775,077 at census of 25 August 1996; 837,271 (males 427,176, females 410,095) at census of 16 September 2007; *Mid-2011* (Secretariat of the Pacific Community estimate): 851,745 (Source: Pacific Regional Information System).

Density (at mid-2011): 46.4 per sq km.

Population by Age and Sex (Secretariat of the Pacific Community estimates at mid-2011): *0–14:* 243,020 (males 125,689, females 117,331); *15–64:* 566,997 (males 289,775, females 277,223); *65 and over:* 41,728 (males 18,937, females 22,791); *Total* 851,745 (males 434,400, females 417,344).

Principal Towns (population at 2007 census): Suva (capital) 74,481; Lautoka 43,473; Nadi 11,685; Lami 10,752; Labasa 7,706; Ba 6,826.

Ethnic Groups (2007 census): Fijians 475,739; Indians 313,798; Rotuman 10,771; Chinese 4,704; European 2,953; Others 29,306; Total 837,271.

Births, Marriages and Deaths (registrations, 2009 unless otherwise indicated): Live births 18,854 (birth rate 21.4 per 1,000); Marriages 7,076 in 2004 (marriage rate 8.6 per 1,000); Deaths 3,921 (death rate 4.8 per 1,000). Source: partly UN, *Population and Vital Statistics Report*.

Life Expectancy (years at birth, WHO estimates): 69 (males 66; females 73) in 2009. Source: WHO, *World Health Statistics*.

Economically Active Population (paid employment, persons aged 15 years and over, 2004): Agriculture, hunting, forestry and fishing 89,523; Mining and quarrying 3,222; Manufacturing 43,088; Electricity, gas and water 2,508; Construction 16,950; Trade, restaurants and hotels 66,043; Transport, storage and communications 22,551; Financing, insurance, real estate and business services 10,220; Community, social and personal services 61,936; *Total employed* 316,041. *Mid-2009* (paid employment, '000 persons, unless otherwise indicated): Agriculture 1.7; Industry 39.5; Services 87.6; Total employed 128.8; Unemployed 28.0; Total labour force (incl. subsistence workers) 327.0. Source: partly Asian Development Bank.

HEALTH AND WELFARE

Key Indicators

Total Fertility Rate (children per woman, 2009): 2.7.

Under-5 Mortality Rate (per 1,000 live births, 2009): 18.

HIV/AIDS (% of persons aged 15–49, 2005): 0.1.

Physicians (per 1,000 head, 2003): 0.5.

Health Expenditure (2008): US $ per head (PPP): 168.

Health Expenditure (2008): % of GDP: 3.5.

Health Expenditure (2008): public (% of total): 75.3.

Access to Water (% of persons, 2006): 47.

Access to Sanitation (% of persons, 2006): 71.

Total Carbon Dioxide Emissions ('000 metric tons, 2006): 1,608.5.

Carbon Dioxide Emissions Per Head (metric tons, 2006): 1.9.

Human Development Index (2010): ranking: 86.

Human Development Index (2010): value: 0.669.

For sources and definitions, see explanatory note on p. vi.

AGRICULTURE, ETC.

Principal Crops ('000 metric tons, 2009): Sugar cane 2,089; Coconuts 150.0; Rice, paddy 11.6; Cassava 42.3; Sweet potatoes 4.9; Yams 1.2; Taro 69.9; Aubergines (Eggplants) 3.6; Bananas 3.4; Pineapples 3.6; Ginger 3.0.

Livestock ('000 head, year ending 2009, FAO estimates): Cattle 312; Pigs 145; Sheep 6; Goats 250; Horses 46; Chickens 3,500; Ducks 85; Turkeys 70.

Livestock Products (metric tons, 2009): Poultry meat 12,209; Cattle meat 8,360 (FAO estimate); Goat meat 911; Pig meat 3,983 (FAO estimate); Hen eggs 3,471; Cows' milk 59,000; Honey 395.

Forestry ('000 cubic metres, 2009, FAO estimates): *Roundwood Removals* (excl. bark): Sawlogs and veneer logs 233; Pulpwood 206; Other industrial wood 6; Fuel wood 37; Total 482. *Sawnwood Production* (incl. sleepers): 90.

Fishing ('000 metric tons, live weight, 2009): Capture 39.6 (FAO estimate) (Albacore 7.2; Yellowfin tuna 2.6; Emperors—scavengers 0.8; Other marine fishes 21.0 (FAO estimate); Crustaceans 0.4 (FAO estimate); Molluscs 1.5); Aquaculture 0.2 (FAO estimate); *Total catch* 39.9 (FAO estimate) (excluding corals 1.0).

Source: FAO.

MINING

Production (kg, 2010, estimates): Gold 1,856; Silver 500 (Source: US Geological Survey).

INDUSTRY

Production (metric tons, 2009): Sugar 168,000; Molasses 131,000; Coconut oil 4,977; Flour 89,113; Soap 5,319; Cement 116,000; Paint ('000 litres) 3,217; Beer ('000 litres) 20,000; Soft drinks ('000 litres) 154,111; Cigarettes 367; Matches ('000 gross boxes) 114; Electric energy (million kWh) 809; Ice cream ('000 litres) 2,367; Toilet paper ('000 rolls) 17,179.

FINANCE

Currency and Exchange Rates: 100 cents = 1 Fiji dollar ($F). *Sterling, US Dollar and Euro Equivalents* (31 March 2011): £1 sterling = $F2.906; US $1 = $F1.806; €1 = $F2.565; $F100 = £34.41 = US $55.38 = €38.98. *Average Exchange Rate* ($F per US $): 1.5940 in 2008; 1.9581 in 2009; 1.9185 in 2010.

General Budget ($F million, 2010, provisional): *Revenue:* Current revenue 1,484.7 (Taxes 1,281.0, Non-taxes 203.7); Capital revenue 10.4; Grants 8.6; Total 1,503.7; *Expenditure:* General public services 205.5; Defence 97.0; Education 209.5; Health 113.9; Social security and welfare 3.9; Housing and community amenities 10.5; Economic services 115.5 (Agriculture 19.3; Industry 42.7; Transport, communications and other services 55.4); Total (incl. others) 1,715.5 (Current 1,332.6, Capital 382.9). Source: Asian Development Bank.

International Reserves (US $ million at 31 December 2010): Gold (valued at market-related prices) 1.17; IMF special drawing rights 78.69; Reserve position in IMF 25.02; Foreign exchange 615.63; *Total* 720.51. Source: IMF, *International Financial Statistics*.

Money Supply ($F million at 31 December 2010): Currency outside depository corporations 383.9; Transferable deposits 1,064.0; Other deposits 2,373.9; Securities other than shares 17.4; *Broad money* 3,839.2. Source: IMF, *International Financial Statistics*.

Cost of Living (Consumer Price Index; base: 2005 = 100): All items 115.8 in 2008; 120.0 in 2009; 126.7 in 2010.

Expenditure on the Gross Domestic Product ($F million at current prices, 2009): Government final consumption expenditure 983.5; Private final consumption expenditure 4,087.1; Increase in stocks 140.0; Gross fixed capital formation 1,064.1; *Total domestic expenditure* 6,274.7; Exports of goods and services 2,671.2; *Less* Imports of goods and services 3,414.6; *GDP in purchasers' values* 5,531.3. Source: Asian Development Bank.

Gross Domestic Product by Economic Activity ($F million at current prices, 2009): Agriculture, forestry and fishing 637.2; Mining and quarrying 20.8; Manufacturing 725.7; Electricity, gas and water 41.5; Construction 153.4; Wholesale and retail trade 826.9; Transport and communications 723.6; Finance, real estate, etc. 853.3; Public administration and defence 778.7; *Sub-total* 4,761.1; Indirect taxes, less subsidies 770.2; *GDP in purchasers' values* 5,531.3. Source: Asian Development Bank.

Balance of Payments (US $ million, 2009): Exports of goods f.o.b. 625.9; Imports of goods f.o.b. –1,300.9; *Trade balance* –674.9; Exports of services 706.3; Imports of services –451.1; *Balance on goods and services* –419.8; Other income received 61.3; Other income paid –57.8; *Balance on goods, services and income* –416.3; Current transfers received 227.3; Current transfers paid –49.1; *Current balance* –238.2; Capital account (net) 27.0; Direct investment abroad –3.0; Direct investment from abroad 56.1; Portfolio investment liabilities –1.1; Other investment assets 10.8; Other investment liabilities 163.2; Net errors and omissions 54.0; *Overall balance* 68.8 (Source: IMF, *International Financial Statistics*).

EXTERNAL TRADE

Principal Commodities ($F million, 2010, provisional): *Imports c.i.f.* (distribution by HS): Animals and animal products 205.4; Vegetable products 220.4; Prepared foodstuffs 164.5; Mineral products 1,129.5; Chemical products 209.5; Plastics and rubber 162.4; Textiles and textile articles 171.0; Base metals and articles thereof 174.7; Machinery, mechanical appliances and electrical equipment 447.3; Transportation equipment 182.2; Total (incl. others) 3,450.3. *Exports* *f.o.b.:* Animals and animal products 256.7; Vegetable products 75.1; Prepared foodstuffs 310.7; Mineral products 413.6; Wood and wood products 81.3; Textiles and textile articles 112.6; Pearls, precious or semi-precious stones and metals 94.1; Total (incl. others) 1,549.5.

Principal Trading Partners ($F million, 2010, provisional): *Imports c.i.f.:* Australia 700.2; China, People's Republic 210.3; France 29.1; Germany 4.5; Hong Kong 56.8; India 66.8; Indonesia 31.3; Japan 85.7; Malaysia 66.9; New Zealand 548.7; Singapore 1,146.8; Thailand 85.1; USA 124.1; Total (incl. others) 3,450.3. *Exports:* Australia 276.5; Japan 115.0; New Zealand 93.0; Samoa 31.4; Tonga 35.3; United Kingdom 80.6; USA 178.8; Total (incl. others) 1,549.5.

TRANSPORT

Road Traffic (motor vehicles registered at 31 December 2010): Private cars 89,422; Goods vehicles 43,722; Buses 2,279; Taxis 5,440; Rental vehicles 6,991; Motorcycles 5,127; Tractors 6,161; Total (incl. others) 167,085.

Shipping: *Merchant Fleet* (registered at 31 December 2009): Vessels 58; Total displacement ('000 grt) 35.2 (Source: IHS Fairplay, *World Fleet Statistics). International Freight Traffic* ('000 metric tons, 1990): Goods loaded 568; Goods unloaded 625 (Source: UN, *Monthly Bulletin of Statistics*).

Civil Aviation (traffic on scheduled services, 2010, unless otherwise indicated): Kilometres flown 25 million (2006); Passengers carried 908,651; Passenger-kilometres 2,312 million; Total ton-kilometres 356.6 million. Source: partly UN, *Statistical Yearbook*.

TOURISM

Foreign Visitors by Country of Residence (excluding cruise-ship passengers, 2010): Australia 318,185; Canada 12,970; Japan 12,011; New Zealand 97,857; Pacific Islands 39,198; United Kingdom 23,813; USA 53,122; Total (incl. others) 631,868.

Tourism Receipts ($F million): 853.8 in 2008; 816.9 in 2009; 979.8 in 2010.

COMMUNICATIONS MEDIA

Radio Receivers (1999): 545,000 in use*.

Television Receivers (2000): 92,000 in use†.

Telephones (2010): 137,000 main lines in use†.

Mobile Cellular Telephones (2010): 1,000,000 subscribers†.

Personal Computers: 50,000 (60.4 per 1,000 persons) in 2005†.

Internet Users (2009): 114,200†.

Broadband Subscribers (2010): 16,000†.

Book Production (1980): 110 titles (84 books, 26 pamphlets); 273,000 copies (229,000 books, 44,000 pamphlets).

Daily Newspapers (2004): 3 (estimated combined circulation 44,000)*.

Non-daily Newspapers (2004): 3 (combined circulation 99,000 in 1988)*.

* Source: UNESCO Institute for Statistics.

† Source: International Telecommunication Union.

EDUCATION

Pre-Primary (2002, unless otherwise indicated): 451 schools (2003); 264 teachers; 7,076 pupils.

Primary (at 31 May 2009): 721 schools; 5,173 teachers; 129,444 pupils.

General Secondary (at 31 May 2009): 172 schools; 4,273 teachers; 67,072 pupils.

Vocational and Technical (at 31 May 2009, unless otherwise indicated): 69 institutions; 158 teachers (at 31 May 2008); 2,387 students.

Teacher Training (at 31 May 2009, unless otherwise indicated): 4 institutions; 86 teachers (at 31 May 2008); 633 students.

Medical (1989): 2 institutions; 493 students.

University (2004): 1 institution; 289 teachers; 16,444 students.

Pupil-teacher Ratio (primary education, UNESCO estimate): 26.0 in 2007/08 (Source: UNESCO Institute for Statistics).

Adult Literacy Rate (UN estimates, 1995–99): 92.9% (males 94.5%; females 91.4%). Source: UN Development Programme, *Human Development Report*.

Directory

The Constitution

On 1 March 2001 President Josefa Iloilo reinstated the 1997 Constitution, after the Great Council of Chiefs (Bose Levu Vakaturaga—a traditional body, with some 70 members, consisting of every hereditary chief or Ratu of each Fijian clan) had approved the draft. The Constitution Amendment Bill that was approved in July 1997 included provisions to ensure a multi-racial Cabinet. Following the removal of the country's elected Government in a coup in December 2006, it was declared that the 1997 Constitution was to remain in place. In April 2009, however, after the Court of Appeal ruled that the interim Government of Cdre Frank Bainimarama was unlawful, President Iloilo revoked the Constitution. The following is a summary of the main provisions of the 1997 Constitution:

The Constitution, which declares Fiji to be a sovereign, democratic republic, guarantees fundamental human rights, a universal, secret and equal suffrage and equality before the law for all Fijian citizens. Citizenship may be acquired by birth, descent, registration or naturalization and is assured for all those who were Fijian citizens before 6 October 1987. Parliament may make provision for the deprivation or renunciation of a person's citizenship. Ethnic Fijians, and the Polynesian inhabitants of Rotuma, receive special constitutional consideration. The Judicial and Legal Services Commission, the Public Service Commission and the Police Service Commission are established as supervisory bodies.

THE GREAT COUNCIL OF CHIEFS

The Great Council of Chiefs (Bose Levu Vakaturaga) derives its authority from the status of its members and their chiefly lineage. The Great Council appoints the President of the Republic and selects 14 nominees for appointment to the Senate, the upper chamber of the Parliament.

The Great Council became fully independent of the Government in mid-1999. Following the military coup of December 2006, the Great Council was suspended and later reconstituted with an altered membership. It was dissolved when the Constitution was abrogated in April 2009.

THE EXECUTIVE

Executive authority is vested in the President of the Republic, who is appointed by the Great Council of Chiefs, for a five-year term, to be constitutional Head of State and Commander-in-Chief of the armed forces. The Presidential Council advises the President on matters of national importance. The President, and Parliament, can be empowered to introduce any necessary measures in an emergency or in response to acts of subversion which threaten Fiji.

In most cases the President is guided by the Cabinet, which conducts the government of the Republic. The Cabinet is led by the Prime Minister, who is a Fijian of any ethnic origin and is appointed by the President from among the members of Parliament, on the basis of support in the legislature. The Prime Minister selects the other members of the Cabinet (the Attorney-General, the minister responsible for defence and security and any other ministers) from either the House of Representatives or the Senate on a multiparty and multiracial basis. The Cabinet is responsible to Parliament.

THE LEGISLATURE

Legislative power is vested in the Parliament, which comprises the President, the appointed upper house or Senate and an elected House of Representatives. The maximum duration of a parliament is five years.

The Senate has 32 members, appointed by the President of the Republic for the term of the Parliament. A total of 14 senators are nominated by the Great Council of Chiefs, nine are appointed on the advice of the Prime Minister, eight on the advice of the Leader of the Opposition, and one on the advice of the Rotuma Island Council. The Senate is a house of review, with some powers to initiate legislation, but with limited influence on financial measures. The Senate is important in the protection of ethnic Fijian interests, and its consent is essential to any attempt to amend, alter or repeal any provisions affecting ethnic Fijians, their customs, land or tradition.

The House of Representatives has 71 elected members, who themselves elect their presiding officials and the Speaker from outside the membership of the House, and the Deputy Speaker from among their number (excluding ministers). Voting is communal, with universal suffrage for all citizens of the Republic aged over 21 years. Seats are reserved on a racial basis: 23 for ethnic Fijians, 19 for Indians, three for other races (General Electors), one for Rotuma Islanders and 25 open seats. Elections must be held at least every five years and are to be administered by an independent Supervisor of

Elections. An independent Boundaries Commission determines constituency boundaries.

THE JUDICIARY

The judiciary is independent and comprises the High Court, the Fiji Court of Appeal and the Supreme Court. The High Court and the Supreme Court are the final arbiters of the Constitution. The establishment of Fijian courts is provided for, and decisions of the Native Lands Commission (relating to ethnic Fijian customs, traditions and usage, and on disputes over the headship of any part of the Fijian people, with the customary right to occupy and use any native lands) are declared to be final and without appeal.

The Government

HEAD OF STATE

President: Ratu EPELI NAILATIKAU (appointed Acting President 30 July 2009; inaugurated as President 5 November 2009).

Vice-President: (vacant).

CABINET
(October 2011)

Prime Minister, Minister for Finance, Strategic Planning and National Development and Statistics, Public Service, People's Charter for Change and Progress, Information, Provincial Development, iTaukei, Multi-Ethnic Affairs, Sugar and Acting Minister for Lands and Mineral Resources: Cdre FRANK (VOREQE) BAINIMARAMA.

Attorney-General and Minister for Justice, Electoral Reform, Anti-Corruption, Public Enterprises, Communications, Civil Aviation, Tourism and Industry and International and Internal Trade: AIYAZ SAYED-KHAIYUM.

Minister for Foreign Affairs and International Co-operation: Ratu INOKE KUBUABOLA.

Minister for Health: Dr NEIL SHARMA.

Minister for Women, Social Welfare and Poverty Alleviation: Dr JIKO LUVENI.

Minister for Education, National Heritage, Culture and Arts, Youth and Sports, Labour, Industrial Relations and Employment: FILIPE BOLE.

Minister for Local Government, Urban Development, Housing and Environment: Col SAMUELA SAUMATUA.

Minister for Public Utilities (Water and Energy), Works and Transport: TIMOCI LESI NATUVA.

Minister for Primary Industries and Acting Minister for Defence, National Security and Immigration: JOKETANI COKANASIGA.

MINISTRIES

Office of the President: Government House, Berkley Cres., Government Bldgs, POB 2513, Suva; tel. 3314244; fax 3301645.

Office of the Prime Minister: Government Bldgs, POB 2353, Suva; tel. 3211201; fax 3306034; e-mail pmsoffice@connect.com.fj; internet old.fiji.gov.fj/publish/pm_office.shtml.

Office of the Attorney-General: Government Bldgs, Victoria Parade, POB 2213, Suva; tel. 3309866; fax 3305421; internet www.ag.gov.fj.

Ministry of Communication: Suva.

Ministry of Defence, National Security and Immigration: Government Bldgs, POB 2349, Suva; tel. 3211401; fax 3300346; e-mail infohomaff@govnet.gov.fj.

Ministry of Education: Marela House, Thurston St, PMB, Suva; tel. 3314477; fax 3303511; internet www.education.gov.fj.

Ministry of Finance, Strategic Planning and National Development and Statistics: Government Bldgs, POB 2212, Suva; tel. 3307011; fax 3300834; e-mail psfinance@govnet.gov.fj.

Ministry of Foreign Affairs and International Co-operation: Government Bldgs, POB 2220, Suva; tel. 3309631; fax 3301741; e-mail info@foreignaffairs.gov.fj; internet www.foreignaffairs.gov.fj.

Ministry of Health: Government Bldgs, POB 2223, Suva; tel. 3306177; fax 3306163; e-mail info@health.gov.fj; internet www.health.gov.fj.

Ministry of Industry and Trade: Government Bldgs, POB 2118, Suva; tel. 3305411; fax 3302617; internet www.commerce.gov.fj.

Ministry of Information: Government Bldgs, POB 2225, Suva; tel. 3302102; fax 3305139; e-mail info@fiji.gov.fj; internet www.info.gov.fj.

Ministry of Justice: Government Bldgs, Victoria Parade, POB 2213, Suva; tel. 3309866; fax 3302404.

Ministry of Labour, Industrial Relations and Employment: Government Bldgs, POB 2216, Suva; tel. 3303500; fax 3304701; e-mail callcentre@labour.gov.fj; internet www.labour.gov.fj.

Ministry of Lands and Mineral Resources: POB 2222, Government Bldgs, Suva; tel. 3314399; fax 3305029; e-mail lis@lands.gov.fj; internet www.lands.gov.fj.

Ministry of Local Government, Urban Development, Housing and Environment: Government Bldgs, POB 2131, Suva; tel. 3304364; fax 3303515; e-mail msovaki@govnet.gov.fj.

Ministry of Primary Industries: Government Bldgs, POB 2218, Suva; tel. 3301611; fax 3301595.

Ministry of Provincial Development, iTaukei Affairs and Multi-Ethnic Affairs: Government Bldgs, POB 2100, Suva; tel. 3100909; fax 3312530; e-mail tvolau@govnet.gov.fj.

Ministry of Public Enterprises: Government Bldgs, POB 2278, Suva; tel. 3315577; fax 3315035; e-mail epowell.fj@gmail.com; internet www.publicenterprises.gov.fj.

Ministry of Public Utilities (Water and Energy), Works and Transport: Government Bldgs, POB 2493, Suva; tel. 3384111; fax 3383198.

Ministry of Tourism: Suva.

Ministry of Women, Social Welfare and Poverty Alleviation: POB 14068, Suva; tel. 3312681; fax 3312357.

Ministry of Youth and Sports: Government Bldgs, POB 2448, Suva; tel. 3315960; fax 3305348; e-mail vikash.nand@govnet.gov.fj; internet www.youth.gov.fj.

Legislature

Note: Parliament was dissolved on 6 December 2006, following the military coup of the previous day.

PARLIAMENT

Senate

The Senate was also known as the House of Review. The upper chamber comprised 32 appointed members.

House of Representatives

The lower chamber comprised 71 elected members: 23 representing ethnic Fijians, 19 representing ethnic Indians, three representing other races (General Electors), one for Rotuma Islanders and 25 seats open to all races.

General Election, 6–13 May 2006

	Communal Seats				
	Fijian	Indian	Other*	Open Seats	Total Seats
Fiji United Party (SDL)	23	—	—	13	36
Fiji Labour Party (FLP)	—	19	—	12	31
United People's Party	—	—	2	—	2
Independents	—	—	2	—	2
Total	23	19	4	25	71

* One Rotuman and three General Electors' seats.

Election Commission

Fiji Electoral Commission: Government Bldgs, POB 2528, Suva; tel. 3316225; fax 3302436; e-mail info@elections.gov.fj; internet www.elections.gov.fj; Senior Electoral Officer VILIAME VUIYANUCA; Acting Supervisor of Elections SORO TOUTOU.

Political Organizations

Fiji Indian Liberal Party: Rakiraki; f. 1991; represents the interests of the Indian community, particularly sugar-cane farmers and students; Sec. SWANI KUMAR.

Fiji Labour Party (FLP): Government Bldgs, POB 2162, Suva; tel. 3303317; fax 3303173; e-mail flp@connect.com.fj; internet www.flp.org.fj; f. 1985; Pres. (vacant); Sec.-Gen. MAHENDRA PAL CHAUDHRY.

Fijian Association Party (FAP): Suva; f. 1995; est. by merger of Fijian Assсn (breakaway faction of SVT) and the multiracial All Nationals Congress; Leader Adi KUINI SPEED; Pres. Ratu INOKE SERU.

Janata Party: Suva; f. 1995; est. by fmr mems of NFP and FLP.

National Alliance Party of Fiji: POB 2315, Suva; internet www.alliancefiji.com; f. 2005; Pres. Ratu EPELI GAVIDI GANILAU.

National Federation Party (NFP): POB 13534, Suva; tel. 3305811; fax 3305317; f. 1960; est. by merger of the multiracial (but mainly Indian) Fed. Party and Nat. Democratic Party; Leader ATTAR SINGH; Pres. RAMAN SINGH.

Nationalist Vanua Takolavo Party (NVTLP): Suva; Leader ILIESA DUVULOCO; Pres. VILIAME SAVU.

Party of National Unity (PANU): Ba; f. 1998; est. to lobby for increased representation for the province of Ba; merged with Bai Kei Viti and People's Nat. Party (Leader MELI BOGILEKA) in 2006; Leader Tui Ba Ratu SAIRUSI NAGAGAVOKA.

Soqosoqo Duavata ni Lewenivanua (SDL) (Fiji United Party): c/o House of Representatives, Suva; f. 2001; Leader LAISENIA QARASE; Pres. Ratu KALOKALO LOKI.

Soqosoqo ni Vakavulewa ni Taukei (SVT) (Fijian Political Party): Suva; f. 1990; est. by Great Council of Chiefs; supports constitutional dominance of ethnic Fijians but accepts multiracialism; Pres. Ratu SITIVENI RABUKA; Gen. Sec. EMA DRUAVESI.

United People's Party (UPP): Suva; f. 1998; est. by merger of General Electors' Party and General Voters' Party (fmrly General Electors' Asscn, one of the three wings of the Alliance Party—AP, the ruling party 1970–87); fmrly United General Party; present name adopted in 2004 to be more multiracial in scope; represents the interests of the minority Chinese and European communities and people from other Pacific Islands resident in Fiji; Pres. MICK BEDDOES; Vice-Pres. MARGARET ROUNDS.

Vanua Independent Party: Leader ILIESA TUVALOVO; Sec. URAIA TUISOVISOVI.

The Fiji Democracy and Freedom Movement (Pres. USAIA WAQATAIREWA) was established in Australia in 2009. Based in New Zealand, the Coalition for Democracy in Fiji was formed in 1987. Supporters of secession are concentrated in Rotuma.

Diplomatic Representation

EMBASSIES AND HIGH COMMISSIONS IN FIJI

Australia: 37 Princes Rd, POB 214, Suva; tel. 3382211; fax 3382065; e-mail public-affairs-suva@dfat.gov.au; internet www.fiji.embassy.gov.au; High Commissioner JUDITH ROBINSON (acting).

China, People's Republic: 183 Queen Elizabeth Dr., PMB, Nasese, Suva; tel. 3300215; fax 3300950; e-mail chinaemb_fj@mfa.gov.cn; internet fj.china-embassy.org/chn; Ambassador HUANG YONG.

France: Dominion House, 7th Floor, Thomson St, Suva; tel. 3310526; fax 3323901; e-mail presse@ambafrance-fj.org; internet www.ambafrance-fj.org; Ambassador GILLES MONTAGNIER.

India: POB 471, Suva; tel. 3301125; fax 3301032; e-mail hicomindsuva@is.com.fj; High Commissioner VINOD KUMAR.

Indonesia: Ra Marama Bldg, 6th Floor, 91 Gordon St, POB 878, Suva; tel. 3316697; fax 3316796; e-mail kbrisuva@connect.com; internet www.suva.deplu.go.id; Ambassador AIDIL CHANDRA SALIM.

Japan: Dominion House, 2nd Floor, POB 13045, Suva; tel. 3304633; fax 3302984; e-mail eojfiji@connect.com.fj; internet www.fj.emb-japan.go.jp; Ambassador YUTAKA YOSHIZAWA.

Korea, Republic: Vanua House, 8th Floor, PMB, Suva; tel. 3300977; fax 3308059; e-mail korembfj@mofat.go.kr; internet fji.mofat.go.kr; Ambassador CHEONG HAE-WOOK.

Malaysia: Pacific House, 5th Floor, POB 356, Suva; tel. 3312166; fax 3303350; e-mail mwsuva@connect.com.fj; High Commissioner (vacant).

Marshall Islands: Government Bldgs, 41 Borron Rd, POB 2038, Suva; tel. 3387899; fax 3387115; e-mail amb.rmisuva@gmail.com; Ambassador AMATLAIN KABUA.

Micronesia, Federated States: 37 Loftus St, POB 15493, Suva; tel. 3304566; fax 3304081; e-mail fsmsuva@sopacsun.sopac.org.fj; Ambassador GERSON JACKSON.

Nauru: Ratu Sukuna House, 7th Floor, Government Bldgs, 229-249 Victoria Parade, Suva; tel. 3313566; fax 3318311; e-mail naurulands@connect.com.fj; High Commissioner JARDEN KEPHAS.

New Zealand: Reserve Bank of Fiji Bldg, 10th Floor, Pratt St, POB 1378, Suva; tel. 3311422; fax 3300842; e-mail nzhc@connect.com.fj; internet www.nzembassy.com/fiji; Acting Head of Mission PHILLIP TAULA.

Papua New Guinea: 18 Rakua St, off Nailuva Rd, Govt Bldgs, POB 2447, Suva; tel. 3304244; fax 3300178; e-mail kundufj@is.com.fj; High Commissioner PETER EAFEARE.

Solomon Islands: 34 Reki St, Government Bldgs, POB 2647, Suva; tel. 3100355; fax 3100356; e-mail solohicom@gmail.com; High Commissioner PATTESON OTI.

Tuvalu: 16 Gorrie St, POB 14449, Suva; tel. 3301355; fax 3308479; e-mail s.laloniu@yahoo.com; High Commissioner AUNESE MAKOI SIMATI.

United Kingdom: Victoria House, 47 Gladstone Rd, POB 1355, Suva; tel. 3229100; fax 3229132; e-mail publicdiplomacysuva@fco.gov.uk; internet ukinfiji.fco.gov.uk; Chargé d'affaires a.i. TIMOTHY SMART.

USA: 158 Princess Rd, Tamavua, Suva; tel. 3314466; fax 3308685; e-mail usembsuva@gmail.com; internet suva.usembassy.gov; Ambassador FRANKIE A. REED (designate).

Vanuatu: Town House Apt Hotel, 3 Forster St, Suva; Chargé d'affaires KANAM WILSON NAPLAUI.

Judicial System

Justice is administered by the Supreme Court, the Fiji Court of Appeal, the High Court and the Magistrates' Courts. The Supreme Court of Fiji is the superior court of record, presided over by the Chief Justice. The 1990 Constitution provided for the establishment of Fijian customary courts and declared as final decisions of the Native Lands Commission in cases involving Fijian custom, etc. In April 2009, following the Court of Appeal's finding that the interim Government in place since the 2006 coup was illegal, the President of Fiji dismissed the entire judiciary.

Supreme Court: Suva; tel. 3211335; fax 3305242; e-mail enquiries@judicial.gov.fj; internet www.judiciary.gov.fj; Chief Justice ANTHONY GATES.

Court of Appeal: Victoria Parade, Suva; tel. 3211307; fax 3316284; President of the Court of Appeal (vacant).

High Court: Suva; Chief Registrar GANGA WAKISHTA ARACHCHI (acting).

Magistrates' Courts: there are 15 Magistrates' Courts, which allow for 22 sitting resident magistrates; Chief Magistrate USAIA RATUVILI.

Director of Public Prosecutions: 25 Gladstone Rd, Suva; tel. 3211793; Director AIYESHA JINASENA.

Attorney-General: POB 2213, Government Bldgs, Suva; tel. 3309866; fax 3305421; internet www.ag.gov.fj; Attorney-General AIYAZ SAYED-KHAIYUM (Minister for Justice); Solicitor-General CHRISTOPHER PRYDE.

Religion

CHRISTIANITY

Most ethnic Fijians are Christians. Methodists are the largest Christian group, followed by Roman Catholics. In the census of 1996 about 58% of the population were Christian (mainly Methodists, who comprised 36.2% of the total population).

Fiji Council of Churches: Government Bldgs, POB 2300, Suva; tel. and fax (1) 3313798; e-mail fijichurches@connect.com.fj; f. 1964; nine mem. churches; Pres. Rev. APIMELEKI QILIHO; Gen. Sec. Rev. ISIRELI LEDUA KACIMAIWAI.

The Anglican Communion

In April 1990 Polynesia, formerly a missionary diocese of the Church of the Province of New Zealand, became a full and integral diocese. The diocese of Polynesia is based in Fiji but also includes Wallis and Futuna, Tuvalu, Kiribati, French Polynesia, Cook Islands, Tonga, Samoa and Tokelau. There were an estimated 6,325 adherents in 1996.

Bishop of Polynesia: Archbishop Dr WINSTON HALAPUA, Bishop's Office, POB 35, 8 Desvoeux Rd, Suva; tel. 3304716; fax 3302687; e-mail episcopus@connect.com.fj.

The Roman Catholic Church

Fiji comprises a single archdiocese. At 31 December 2007 there were an estimated 97,692 adherents in the country.

Bishops' Conference: Episcopal Conference of the Pacific Secretariat (CEPAC), 14 Williamson Rd, POB 289, Suva; tel. 3300340; fax 3303143; e-mail cepac@connect.com.fj; f. 1968; 17 mems; Pres. Most Rev. ANTHONY SABLAN APURON (Archbishop of Agaña, Guam); Sec.-Gen. Fr ROGER MCCARRICK.

Archbishop of Suva: Mgr PETERO MATACA, Archdiocesan Office, Nicolas House, 35 Pratt St, POB 109, Suva; tel. 3301955; fax 3301565.

Other Christian Churches

Methodist Church in Fiji & Rotuma (Lotu Wesele e Viti): Epworth Arcade, Nina St, POB 357, Suva; tel. 3311477; fax 3303771; e-mail methodistchhq@connect.com.fj; f. 1835; autonomous since 1964; 212,831 mems (2007); Gen. Sec. Rev. TUIKILAKILA WAQAIRATU; Pres. Rev. AME TUGAUE.

Other denominations active in the country include the Assembly of God (with c. 7,000 mems), the Baptist Mission, the Congregational Christian Church and the Presbyterian Church.

HINDUISM

Most of the Indian community are Hindus. According to the census of 1996, some 34% of the population were Hindus.

ISLAM

In 1996 some 7% of the population were Muslim. There are several Islamic organizations.

Fiji Muslim League: POB 3990, Samabula, Suva; tel. 3384566; fax 3370204; e-mail fijimuslim@connect.com.fj; f. 1926; Nat. Pres. HAFIZUD DEAN KHAN; Gen. Sec. MOHAMMAD TAABISH AKBAR; 26 brs and 3 subsidiary orgs.

SIKHISM

Sikh Association of Fiji: Suva; Pres. MEJA SINGH.

BAHÁ'Í FAITH

National Spiritual Assembly: National Office, POB 639, Suva; tel. 3387574; fax 3387772; e-mail nsafiji@connect.com.fj; mems resident in 490 localities; national headquarters for consultancy and co-ordination.

The Press

NEWSPAPERS AND PERIODICALS

Coconut Telegraph: POB 249, Savusavu, Vanua Levu; f. 1975; monthly; serves rural communities; Editor LEMA LOW.

Fiji Calling: POB 12095, Suva; tel. 3305916; fax 3301930; publ. by Associated Media Ltd; every 6 months; English; Publr YASHWANT GAUNDER.

Fiji Cane Grower: POB 12095, Suva; tel. 3305916; fax 3305256.

Fiji Daily Post: 19 Ackland St, Viria East Industrial Subdivision, Vatuwaqa, Suva; tel. 3275176; fax 3275179; e-mail info@fijidailypost.com; internet www.fijidailypost.com; f. 1987 as *Fiji Post*, daily from 1989; English; 100% govt-owned since Sept. 2003; Chair. MALAKAI NAIYAGA; Editor-in-Chief ROBERT WOLFGRAMM.

Fiji Magic: POB 12095, Suva; tel. 3305916; fax 3302852; e-mail fijimagic@fijilive.com; internet www.fijilive.com/fijimagic; publ. by Associated Media Ltd; monthly; English; Publr YASHWANT GAUNDER; circ. 15,000.

Fiji Republic Gazette: Printing Dept, POB 98, Suva; tel. 3385999; fax 3370203; f. 1874; weekly; English.

Fiji Sun: 12 Amra St, Walubay, Suva; tel. 3307555; fax 3311455; e-mail leonec@fijisun.com.fj; internet www.fijisun.com.fj; re-est. 1999; daily; Editor LEONE CABENATABUA; CEO PETER LOMAS.

Fiji Times: 177 Victoria Parade, Suva; tel. 3304209; fax 3301521; e-mail timesnews@fijitimes.com.fj; internet www.fijitimes.com; f. 1869; fmrly owned by News Ltd (Australia); acquired by Motibhai Group in Sept. 2010 following introduction of legislation limiting foreign ownership of media organizations; daily; English; Publr BRIAN O'FLAHERTY; Editor FRED WESLEY; circ. 34,000.

Fiji Trade Review: The Rubine Group, POB 12511, Suva; tel. 3313944; monthly; English; Publr GEORGE RUBINE; Editor MABEL HOWARD.

Islands Business: 46 Gordon St, POB 12718, Suva; tel. 3303108; fax 3301423; e-mail editor@ibi.com.fj; internet www.islandsbusiness.com; regional monthly news and business magazine featuring the Fiji Islands Business supplement; English; Editor-in-Chief LAISA TAGA; circ. 8,500.

Na Tui: 422 Fletcher Rd, POB 2071, Government Bldgs, Suva; f. 1988; weekly; Fijian; Publr TANIELA BOLEA; Editor SAMISONI BOLATAGICI; circ. 7,000.

Nai Lalakai: 20 Gordon St, POB 1167, Suva; tel. 3304111; fax 3301521; e-mail fijitimes@is.com.fj; f. 1962; publ. by Fiji Times Ltd; weekly; Fijian; Editor SAMISONI KAKAIVALU; circ. 18,000.

Pacific Business: POB 12095, Suva; tel. 3305916; fax 3301930; publ. by Associated Media Ltd; monthly; English; Publr YASHWANT GAUNDER.

Pacific Telecom: POB 12095, Suva; tel. 3300591; fax 3302852; e-mail review@is.com.fj; publ. by Associated Media Ltd; monthly; English; Publr YASHWANT GAUNDER.

PACNEWS: Level 2, Damodar Centre, Gordon St, Suva; tel. 3315732; fax 3317055; e-mail pacnews1@connect.com.fj; internet www.pina.com.fj; daily news service for the Pacific region; Editor MAKERETA KOMAI.

Pactrainer: PMB, Suva; tel. 3303623; fax 3303943; e-mail pina@is.com.fj; monthly; newsletter of Pacific Journalism Development Centre; Editor PETER LOMAS.

The Review: POB 12095, Suva; tel. 3305916; fax 3301930; e-mail review@is.com.fj; publ. by Associated Media Ltd; monthly; English; Publr YASHWANT GAUNDER.

Sartaj: John Beater Enterprises Ltd, Raiwaqa, POB 5141, Suva; f. 1988; weekly; Hindi; Editor S. DASO; circ. 15,000.

Shanti Dut: 20 Gordon St, POB 1167, Suva; f. 1935; publ. by Fiji Times Ltd; weekly; Hindi; Editor NILAM KUMAR; circ. 12,000.

Top Shot: Suva; f. 1995; golf magazine; monthly.

Volasiga: 10–16 Toorak Rd, POB 2071, Suva; f. 1988; weekly; Fijian; publ. by Fiji Daily Post; Gen. Man. ANURA BANDARA (acting); Editor SAMISONI BOLATAGICI.

The Weekender: 2 Denison Rd, POB 15652, Suva; tel. 3315477; fax 3305346; publ. by Media Resources Ltd; weekly; English; Publr JOSEFATA NATA.

PRESS ASSOCIATIONS

Fiji Islands Media Association: c/o Vasiti Ivaqa, POB 12718, Suva; tel. 3303108; fax 3301423; national press assen; operates Fiji Press Club and Fiji Journalism Training Institute; Sec. NINA RATULELE.

Publishers

Fiji Times Ltd: POB 1167, Suva; tel. 3304111; fax 3301521; e-mail timesnews@fijitimes.com.fj; f. 1869; Propr News Corpn Ltd; largest newspaper publr; also publrs of books and magazines; Man. Dir ANNE FESSELL.

Lotu Pasifika Productions: POB 2401, Suva; tel. 3301314; fax 3301183; f. 1973; cookery, education, poetry, religion; Gen. Man. SERU L. VEREBALAVU.

University of the South Pacific: Laucala Campus, Suva; tel. 3231000; fax 3301305; e-mail orga@usp.ac.fj; internet www.usp.ac.fj; f. 1986; education, natural history, regional interests; Pres. RAJESH CHANDRA.

GOVERNMENT PUBLISHING HOUSE

Printing and Stationery Department: POB 98, Suva; tel. 3385999; fax 3370203.

Broadcasting and Communications

TELECOMMUNICATIONS

Digicel Fiji: Kadavu House, Ground Floor, Victoria Parade, POB 13811, Suva; tel. 3310200; fax 3310201; e-mail customercarefiji@digicelgroup.com; internet www.digicelfiji.com; f. 2008; CEO DAVID BUTLER.

Fiji International Telecommunications Ltd (FINTEL): 158 Victoria Parade, POB 59, Suva; tel. 3312933; fax 3305606; e-mail inquiries@fintelfiji.com; internet www.fintel.com.fj; f. 1976; 51% govt-owned; 49% owned by Cable & Wireless Communications Plc (United Kingdom); Group CEO SAKARAIA TUILAKEPA; CEO IOANE KOROIVUKI.

Telecom Fiji Ltd (TFL): PMB, Suva; tel. 3304019; e-mail contact@tfl.com.fj; internet www.telecomfiji.com.fj; owned by Amalgamated Telecom Holdings; Chair. TOM RICKETTS; CEO ROHAN MAIL.

Vodafone Fiji Ltd: PMB, 168 Princes Rd, Suva; tel. 3312000; fax 3312007; e-mail aslam.khan@vodafone.com; internet www.vodafone.com.fj; 51% owned by Amalgamated Telecom Holdings Ltd, 49% by Vodafone International Holdings BV; GSM operator; CEO ASLAM KHAN.

In mid-2007 some 15 companies applied for mobile phone operators' licences.

BROADCASTING

All broadcasting licences were revoked by the interim Government in November 2009. Radio and television stations were issued with temporary licences.

Radio

Fiji Broadcasting Corporation Ltd—FBCL (Radio Fiji): 69 Gladstone Rd, POB 334, Suva; tel. 3314333; fax 3301643; internet www.radiofiji.com.fj; f. 1954; statutory body; jointly funded by govt grant and advertising revenue; Radio Fiji 1 broadcasts nationally on AM in English and Fijian; Radio Fiji 2 broadcasts nationally on AM in English and Hindi; Radio Fiji Gold broadcasts nationally on AM and FM in English; 104 FM and Radio Rajdhani 98 FM, mainly with musical programmes, broadcast in English and Hindi respectively, but are received only on Viti Levu; Bula FM, musical programmes, broadcasts in Fijian, received only on Viti Levu; CEO RIYAZ SAYED KHAIYUM.

Communications Fiji Ltd: 231 Waimanu Rd, PMB, Suva; tel. 3314766; fax 3303748; e-mail cfl@fm96.com.fj; f. 1985; operates three commercial stations; FM 96, f. 1985, broadcasts 24 hours per day, on FM, in English; Navtarang, f. 1989, broadcasts 24 hours per day, on

FM, in Hindi; Viti FM, f. 1996, broadcasts 24 hours per day, on FM, in Fijian; Man. Dir WILLIAM PARKINSON; Gen. Man. IAN JACKSON.

Radio Light/Radio Naya Jiwan/Nai Talai: 15 Tower St, Government Bldgs, POB 2525, Suva; tel. and fax 3319536; e-mail radiolight@connect.com.fj; internet www.radiolight.org; f. 1990; non-profit religious organization; broadcasts in English (Radio Light FM 106, FM 93.6), Hindi (Radio Naya Jiwan FM 94.8) and Fijian (Nai Talai FM 103.4); Gen. Man. DOUGLAS ROSE.

Radio Pasifik: The University of the South Pacific, Suva; tel. 3232131; fax 3312591; e-mail blumel_d@usp.ac.fj; f. 1996; educational, operated by CFDL Multimedia Unit; broadcasts in English, Fijian, French, Bislama, Tongan, Hindi and other Pacific island languages.

Television

Fiji Television Ltd: 20 Gorrie St, POB 2442, Government Bldgs, Suva; tel. 3305100; fax 3305077; e-mail info@fijitv.com.fj; internet www.fijitv.com.fj; f. 1994; operates two services, Fiji 1, a free channel, and Sky Fiji, a three-channel subscription service; Chair. ISOA KALOUMAIRA; Group CEO TARUN PATEL.

Film and Television Unit (FTU): c/o Department of Information, Government Bldgs, Suva; video library; production unit established by Govt and Hanns Seidel Foundation (Germany); a weekly news magazine and local documentary programmes.

Finance

BANKING

(cap. = capital; res = reserves; dep. = deposits; m. = million; brs = branches; amounts in Fiji dollars)

Central Bank

Reserve Bank of Fiji: Pratt St, PMB, Suva; tel. 3313611; fax 3301688; e-mail info@rbf.gov.fj; internet www.reservebank.gov.fj; f. 1984; replaced Central Monetary Authority of Fiji (f. 1973); bank of issue; administers Insurance Act, Banking Act and Exchange Control Act; cap. 2.0m., res 39.1m. (Dec. 2009); Gov. BARRY WHITESIDE.

Commercial Bank

Bank South Pacific: cnr of Renwick Rd and Pratt St, PMB, Suva; tel. 3314400; fax 3318393; internet www.colonial.com.fj; f. 1974; est. as National Bank of Fiji; 51% acquired from Fiji Govt by Colonial Ltd in 1999 and renamed Colonial National Bank; above name adopted after acquisition of the Colonial Group by BSP in 2009; cap. 15.0m., res 0.3m. (June 2003), dep. 317.2m. (June 2004); Country Man. KEVIN McCARTHY; 15 brs; 45 agencies.

Development Bank

Fiji Development Bank: 360 Victoria Parade, POB 104, Suva; tel. 3314866; fax 3314886; e-mail info@fdb.com.fj; internet www.fdb.com.fj; f. 1967; finances devt of natural resources, agriculture, transport, and other industries and enterprises; statutory body; applied for a commercial banking licence in Nov. 2004; cap. 56.1m., res 8.9m. (2005); Chair. ROBERT GORDON LYON; CEO DEVE TOGANIVALU; 9 brs.

Merchant Banks

Merchant Finance and Investment Company Ltd: 91 Gordon St, POB 14213, Suva; tel. 3314955; fax 3300026; e-mail info@mfl.com.fj; internet www.mfl.com.fj; f. 1986; fmrly Merchant Bank of Fiji Ltd; owned by Fijian Holdings Ltd (80%), South Pacific Trustees (20%); CEO UDAY RAJ SEN; 3 brs.

STOCK EXCHANGE

South Pacific Stock Exchange: Level 2, Plaza One, Provident Plaza, 33 Ellery St, POB 11689, Suva; tel. 3304130; fax 3304145; e-mail info@spse.com.fj; internet www.spse.com.fj; fmrly Suva Stock Exchange; name changed as above in 2000; Chair. MESAKE NAWARI; CEO JINITA PRASAD.

INSURANCE

Colonial Fiji Life Ltd: cnr of Renwick Rd and Pratt St, PMB, Suva; tel. 3314400; fax 3318393; internet www.colonial.com.fj; life and health; fmrly Blue Shield (Pacific) Ltd; owned by BSP Group, Australia; Man. Dir Ratu MALAKAI NAIYAG.

Dominion Insurance Ltd: 231 Waimanu Rd, POB 14468, Suva; tel. 3311055; fax 3303475; e-mail enquiries@dominioninsurance.com.fj; internet www.dominioninsurance.com.fj; general insurance; Chair. HARI PUNJA; Exec. Dir GARY S. CALLAGHAN.

FijiCare Insurance Ltd: 9/F, 343–359 FNPF Place, Victoria Parade, Suva; tel. 3302717; fax 3302119; e-mail inquiries@fijicare.com.fj; internet www.fijicare.com.fj; life and health; Chair. ROSS PORTER; Man. Dir PETER McPHERSON.

New India Assurance Co Ltd: Harifam Centre, GPOB 71, Suva; tel. 3313488; fax 3302679; e-mail newindiasuva@connect.com.fj; internet www.niafiji.com; Chief Man. K. VENUKUMAR.

QBE Insurance (Fiji) Ltd: Queensland Insurance Center, 18 Victoria Parade, GPOB 101, Suva; tel. 3315455; fax 3300285; e-mail info.fiji@qbe.com; internet www.qbepacific.com/Insurance.html; owned by Australian interests; fmrly known as Queensland Insurance (Fiji) Ltd, name changed as above 2004; Gen. Man. DAVID PONINGHAUS.

SUN Insurance: Kaunikuila House, Ground Floor, Laucala Bay Rd, Suva; tel. 3313822; fax 3313882; e-mail info@suninsurance.com.fj; internet www.suninsurance.com.fj; f. 1999; general; Chair. PADAM RAJ LALA; CEO ARCHIE SEETO.

Tower Insurance Fiji Ltd: Tower House, Thomson St, GPOB 950, Suva; tel. 3315955; fax 3301376; internet www.towerinsurance.com.fj; owned by New Zealand interests; Gen. Man. PAUL ABSELL.

Trade and Industry

GOVERNMENT AGENCIES

Fiji Islands Trade and Investment Bureau: Civic House, 6th Floor, POB 2303, Victoria Parade, Suva; tel. 3315988; fax 3301783; e-mail info@ftib.org.fj; internet www.ftib.org.fj; f. 1980; restyled 1988, to promote and stimulate foreign and local economic devt investment; Chair. ADRIAN SOFIELD; CEO JITOKO TIKOLEVU.

Training and Productivity Authority of Fiji (TPAF): Beaumont Rd, POB 6890, Nasinu; tel. 3392000; fax 3340184; e-mail info@tpaf.ac.fj; internet www.tpaf.ac.fj; fmrly Fiji National Training Council; present name assumed in 2002; Dir-Gen. JONE USAMATE.

DEVELOPMENT ORGANIZATIONS

Fiji Development Company Ltd: POB 161, FNPF Place, 350 Victoria Parade, Suva; tel. 3304611; fax 3304171; e-mail hfc@is.com.fj; f. 1960; subsidiary of the Commonwealth Development Corpn; Man. F. KHAN.

Fijian Development Fund Board: POB 122, Suva; tel. 3312601; fax 3302585; f. 1951; funds derived from payments from sales of copra by indigenous Fijians; funds used only for Fijian devt schemes; CEO VINCENT TOVATA.

Land Development Authority: POB 5442, Raiwaqa; tel. 3383155; fax 3387157; e-mail rsingh010@govnet.gov.fj; internet www.agriculture.org.fj; f. 1961; co-ordinates devt plans for land and marine resources; Chair. RITESHNI LATA SINGH.

CHAMBERS OF COMMERCE

Ba Chamber of Commerce: POB 99, Ba; tel. 6670134; fax 6670132; Pres. DINESH PATEL.

Fiji Chamber of Commerce and Industry: POB 14803, Suva; tel. 314040; fax 302641; Pres. PETER MASEY.

Labasa Chamber of Commerce: POB 992, Labasa; tel. 8811467; fax 8813009; Pres. ASHOK KARAN.

Lautoka Chamber of Commerce and Industry: POB 366, Lautoka; tel. 6661834; fax 6662379; e-mail vaghco@connect.com.fj; Pres. NATWARLAL VAGH.

Levuka Chamber of Commerce: POB 85, Levuka; tel. 3440248; fax 3440252; Pres. ISHRAR ALI.

Nadi Chamber of Commerce: POB 2735, Nadi; tel. 6701375; fax 6702406; e-mail rraju@connect.com.fj; Pres. RAM RAJU.

Nausori Chamber of Commerce: POB 228, Nausori; tel. 3478235; fax 3400134; Pres. MOTI LAL.

Sigatoka Chamber of Commerce: POB 882, Sigatoka; tel. 6500064; fax 6520006; Pres. TOM WAQA.

Suva Chamber of Commerce and Industry: 8 Dominion House, POB 337, Suva; tel. 3314044; fax 3302188; e-mail secretariat@suvachamber.org; internet www.suvachamber.org; f. 1902; Pres. Dr NUR BANO ALI; 150 mems.

Tavua-Vatukoula Chamber of Commerce: POB 698, Tavua; tel. 6680390; fax 6680390; Pres. SOHAN SINGH.

INDUSTRIAL AND TRADE ASSOCIATIONS

Fiji Kava Council: POB 17724, Suva; tel. 3386576; fax 3371844; Chair. Ratu JOSATEKI NAWALOWALO.

Fiji Sawmillers' Association: Yalalevu; e-mail jayd@islandchill.com; Pres. JAY DAYAL.

Fiji Sugar Corporation Ltd: Western House, 3rd Floor, cnr of Bila and Vidilo St, PMB, Lautoka; tel. 6662655; fax 6664685; nationalized 1974; buyer of sugar cane and raw sugar mfrs; Exec. Chair. ABDUL KHAN.

Mining and Quarrying Council: 42 Gorrie St, Suva; tel. 33313188; fax 3302183; e-mail employer@is.com.fj; Chief Exec. K. A. J. Roberts.

National Trading Corporation Ltd: POB 13673, Suva; tel. 3315211; fax 3315584; f. 1992; govt-owned body; develops markets for agricultural and marine produce locally and overseas; processes and markets fresh fruit, vegetables and ginger products; CEO Apiama Cegumalina.

Native Lands Trust Board: GPOB 116, Suva; tel. 3312733; fax 3312014; e-mail info@nltb.com.fj; internet www.nltb.com.fj; manages holdings of ethnic Fijian landowners; Gen. Man. Alipate Qetaki.

Sugar Cane Growers' Council: Canegrowers' Bldg, 3rd Floor, 75 Drasa Ave, POB 5162, Lautoka; tel. 6650466; fax 6650624; e-mail canegrower@is.com.fj; internet scgcfiji.com; f. 1985; aims to develop the sugar industry and protect the interests of registered growers; closure by interim Govt reported in Aug. 2009; Chair. Jain Kumar; CEO Sundresh Chetty (acting).

Sustainable Forest Industries LTD (SFI): POB 1119, Nabua, Suva; tel. 3384999; fax 3370029; e-mail info@fijimahogany.com; internet www.fijimahogany.com; Man. Dir Christopher Donlon.

EMPLOYERS' ORGANIZATIONS

Fiji Commerce and Employers Federation (FCEF): 42 Gorrie St, GPOB 575, Suva; tel. 3313188; fax 3302183; e-mail employer@fcef.com.fj; internet www.fcef.com.fj; f. 1960; represents 525 major employers with approx. 80,000 employees; fmrly Fiji Employers' Federation; Pres. Digby Bossley; CEO Nesbitt Hazelman.

Fiji Manufacturers' Association: POB 1308, Suva; tel. and fax 3318811; e-mail fma@connect.com.fj; internet fijimanufacturers.org; f. 1971; CEO Desmond Whiteside; 68 mems.

Local Inter-Island Shipowners' Association: POB 152, Suva; fax 3303389; e-mail consortship@connect.com.fj; Pres. Durga Prasad; Sec. Leo B. Smith.

Textile, Clothing and Footwear Council: POB 10015, Nabua; tel. 3384777; fax 3370446; Pres. Kalpesh Solanki.

UTILITIES

Electricity

Fiji Electricity Authority (FEA): PMB, Suva; tel. 3311133; fax 3311882; e-mail ceo@fea.com.fj; internet www.fea.com.fj; f. 1966; govt-owned; responsible for the generation, transmission and distribution of electricity throughout Fiji; CEO Hasmukh Patel.

Water

Water Authority of Fiji: Kings Road, Nasinu, Suva; tel. 3346777; CEO Tony Fullman.

MAJOR COMPANIES

Carlton Brewery (Fiji) Ltd: POB 696, Suva; tel. 3315811; fax 3300408; f. 1957; a subsidiary of Foster's Brewing Group Ltd (Australia); Gen. Man. J. Pickering.

Carter Holt Harvey (Fiji) Ltd: POB 427, Suva; tel. 3410011; fax 3410808; f. 1965; mfrs of polythene bags and paper products; Gen. Man. C. D. Bossley.

Central Manufacturing Co Ltd: POB 560, Suva; tel. 3381144; fax 3370080; f. 1955; mfrs and distributors of cigarettes and tobacco; Gen. Man. Michael Penrose.

Crest Chicken Ltd: POB 83, Nausori; tel. 3478400; fax 3400061; f. 1965; mfrs of animal food; Gen. Man. Don MacLellan.

Dayals Group: 1 Kings Rd, POB 1121, Yalalevu; tel. 6675605; fax 6670479; e-mail info@dayals-fiji.com; internet www.dayals-fiji.com; f. 1940; forestry, mining, water bottling; Dir Prakash Dayal.

Dayals (Fiji) Artesian Waters Ltd: 1 Kings Rd, POB 1121, Ba; tel. 6675605; fax 6670479; e-mail sales@islandchill.com; internet www.islandchill.com; water bottling and exporting; Dir Praneel Dayal.

Dayals Quarries Ltd: Kings Rd, Yalalevu; tel. 6674688; e-mail dol@connect.com.fj.

Dayals Sawmillers Ltd: Kings Rd, POB 1121, Yalalevu; tel. 6675605; fax 6670479; e-mail dayal1@connect.com.fj; internet www.dayals-fiji.com/dsl/index.html; timber producers and exporters; Dir Jay Dayal.

Eddie Hin Industries Ltd: 44 Marine Drive, POB 98, Lautoka; tel. 6661433; fax 6665886; f. 1947; mfrs of non-alcoholic beverages; Man. Dir Eddie Wong.

Fiji Hardwood Corpn Ltd: PMB, Suva; tel. 3372664; fax 3372660; e-mail srbua@fijihardwood.com.fj; f. 1998; govt-owned; mahogany producer; CEO Mark Sanderson.

Fiji Motor Works Ltd: POB 9012, Nadi Airport, Nadi; tel. 723771; fax 723101; e-mail fmw@connect.com.fj; f. 1997; assembly of cars and small commercial vehicles; Man. Dir Richard Bretnal.

Fiji Pine Ltd: POB 521, Lautoka; tel. 6661511; fax 6660359; e-mail rafaele_raboiliku@yahoo.com; f. 1991 to replace Fiji Pine Commission; owned by Govt and Fiji Pine Trust; Chair. Ratu Tevita Uluilakeba Mara; CEO Ilaisa Tulele.

Fiji Ships and Heavy Industries Ltd: GPOB 16695, Sannergren Drive, Korovou, Walu Bay, Suva; tel. 3306426; fax 3309420; e-mail dalealderdice@connect.com.fj; f. 1996 as Shipbuilding Fiji Ltd (SFL); re-registered as Fiji Shipbuilding Corpn Ltd in 2001; present name assumed in 2004; purchased by govt-owned Fiji Ports Corpn Ltd in 2009; govt-owned; builds and services ocean-going vessels; Chair. Leo Smith.

Flour Mills of Fiji Ltd (FMF): GPOB 977, Leonidas St, Walu Bay, Suva; tel. 3301188; fax 3300944; e-mail info@fmf.com.fj; internet www.fmf.com.fj; f. 1971; Chair. Hari Punja; CEO Ram Bajekal.

Foods Pacific Ltd: Lot 30, Wailada Industrial Subdivision, Lami, POB 182, Suva; tel. 3362844; fax 3361155; e-mail info@foodspacific.com; internet www.foodspacific.com; f. 1980; food processing; Man. Dir Arvind Kant Patel.

Future Forests Fiji Ltd: GPOB 704, Suva; tel. 3364201; fax 3364202; e-mail mail@fff.com.fj; internet www.fff.com.fj; f. 2005; teak plantation investment co; Man. Dir Roderic Evers.

Courts Homecentres: POB 3276, Samabula; tel. 3381333; fax 3370483; e-mail hcmerchandise@courts.com.fj; internet www.courts.com.fj; CEO Rajesh Sharma.

Ika Corporation Ltd: POB 1371, Suva; tel. 3361922; fax 3351194; incorporated 1990; govt-owned; tuna-fishing co; exporter of fresh fish; leasing of vessels; Gen. Man. Mitieli Baleivanualala.

Island Brewing Co: POB 11471, Nadi; tel. 6727093; fax 6727127; internet www.islandbrewing.com.fj; f. 2009; Co-owners Jeremy Ullrich, Jonathan Ullrich.

Natural Waters of Viti Ltd: Civic House, Ground Floor, POB 14128, Suva; tel. 3302654; fax 3302714; e-mail legalinfo@fijiwater.com; internet www.fijiwater.com; subsidiary of Fiji Water Co LLC (USA); bottles mineral water under the Fiji Water brand name at a plant in Yaqara, Ra Province.

P. A. Lal & Co Ltd: POB 1242, Suva; f. 1946; builders of buses, trucks, trailers, coaches, furniture and fibreglass work; Dir Richard Lal.

Pacific Fishing Company (PAFCO): Beach St, POB 41, Levuka; tel. 3440055; fax 3440400; e-mail info@pafcofiji.com; internet www.pafcofiji.com; f. 1963; Fiji's largest fish-processing factory; COO Prakash Chandra; Gen. Man. Jean Claude Guenegan.

Pacific Green Industries (Fiji) Ltd: Queens Rd, POB 832, Sigatoka; tel. 6500055; fax 6520014; e-mail pgfiji@connect.com.fj; internet www.pacificgreen.net; exports furniture made from coconut wood; Gen. Man. Ravin Chandra; Dir Peter Ryan.

Rewa Co-operative Dairy Company: Ratu Mara Rd, Suva; tel. 3381288; fax 3370190; f. 1923; processes, packages and supplies dairy produce; CEO Ratu Savenaca Seniloli.

Rewa Rice Ltd: 69 Kings Rd, Nausori; tel. 8812101; fax 8817006; f. 1960; govt-owned; Chair. Hari Pal Singh; Gen. Man. Keshawn Prasad.

South Pacific Distilleries Ltd of Fiji: Navutu Rd, POB 1128, Lautoka; tel. 662088; fax 664631; jt govt and private ownership; Chair. Nuno D'Aquino; Gen. Man. Karai Vuibau; 61 employees.

Toyota Tsusho (South Sea) Co Ltd: POB 355, Suva; tel. 3384888; fax 3370309; f. 1920; fmrly known as BPT (South Sea) Co Ltd; importers and distributors of motor vehicles, machinery and outboard motors; Gen. Man. Ian Thomas McLean.

Vinod Patel and Co Ltd: POB 434, Ba; tel. 3393111; fax 3340255; e-mail enquiry@vinodpatel.com.fj; internet www.vinodpatel.com.fj; f. 1962; hardware retailer and exporter within the South Pacific region; Man. Dir Vinod Patel; associated companies:

Ba Industries Ltd (BIL): Yalalevu, Kings Rd, POB 707, Ba; tel. 6674966; fax 6676700; e-mail admin@baindustriesfiji.com; internet www.baindustriesfiji.com; f. 1973; supplies wire and fencing products; Gen. Man. Sanjay Badgujar (acting).

Tubemakers and Roofmart (South Pacific) Ltd (TRL): 98B Navutu Ind. Sub Division, POB 4336, Lautoka; tel. 6669655; fax 6664024; e-mail trl@connect.com.fj; internet www.tubemakersfiji.com; f. 1987; Gen. Man. Anbalagan Kathiresan.

Viti Foods: POB 165, Suva; tel. 3395888; subsidiary of C. J. Patel and Co Ltd; fish canners.

TRADE UNIONS

Fiji Trades Union Congress (FTUC): 32 Des Voeux Rd, POB 1418, Suva; tel. 3315377; fax 3300306; e-mail ftucl@connect.com.fj;

f. 1952; affiliated to ITUC; 35 affiliated unions; 33,000 mems; Pres. DANIEL URAI MANUFOLAU; Gen. Sec. FELIX ANTHONY.

Principal affiliated unions:

Association of USP Staff (AUSPS): POB U49, Suva; tel. 3232754; fax 3301305; e-mail ausps@usp.ac.fj; internet www.usp.ac.fj; f. 1977; Pres. Dr ROHIT KISHORE; Sec. KRISHNA RAGHUWAIYA.

Communication, Mining and General Workers' Union (CMGWU): 17 Knollys St, Suva; tel. 3300168; f. 1990; fmrly Fiji Post and Telecommunications Employees' Association; Gen. Sec. ATTAR SINGH.

Federated Airline Staff Association: Nadi Airport, POB 9259, Nadi; tel. 6722877; fax 6720068; e-mail fasa@ats.com.fj; Gen. Sec. VILIKESA NAULUMATUA.

Fiji Aviation Workers' Association: FTUC Complex, 32 Des Voeux Rd, POB 5351, Raiwaqa; tel. 3303184; fax 3311805; Pres. VALENTINE SIMPSON; Gen. Sec. ATTAR SINGH.

Fiji Bank and Finance Sector Employees' Union: 101 Gordon St, POB 853, Suva; tel. 3301827; fax 3301956; e-mail fbeu@connect.com.fj; internet www.fbfseu.org.fj; over 1,500 mems; Nat. Sec. PRAMOD K. RAE.

Fiji Electricity and Allied Workers' Union: POB 1390, Lautoka; tel. 6666353; e-mail feawu@connect.com.fj; Pres. LEONE SAKETA; Sec. J. A. PAUL.

Fiji Garment, Textile and Allied Workers' Union: c/o FTUC, Raiwaqa; f. 1992.

Fiji Nursing Association: 26 McGregor Rd, Suva; tel. 3305855; fax 3304881; e-mail fna@connect.com.fj; internet www.fijinursingassociation.com; f. 1957; Pres. S. MATIAVI; Gen. Sec. KUINI LUTUA.

Fiji Public Service Association: 298 Waimanu Rd, POB 1405, Suva; tel. 3311922; fax 3301099; e-mail fpsags@connect.com.fj; f. 1943; 4,000 mems; Pres. REIJIELI NARUMA; Gen. Sec. RAJESHWAR SINGH.

Fiji Sugar and General Workers' Union: 84 Naviti St, POB 330, Lautoka; tel. 6660746; fax 664888; 25,000 mems; Pres. SHIU LINGAM; Gen. Sec. FELIX ANTHONY.

Fiji Teachers' Union: 1–3 Berry Rd, Government Bldgs, POB 2203, Suva; tel. 3314099; fax 3305962; e-mail ftu@connect.com.fj; f. 1930; 4,300 mems; Pres. BALRAM; Gen. Sec. AGNI DEO SINGH.

Fijian Teachers' Association: POB 14464, Suva; tel. 3315099; fax 3304978; e-mail fta@connect.com.fj; internet fta.org.fj/fta; Pres. TEVITA KOROI; Gen. Sec. MAIKA NAMUDU.

Insurance Officers' Association: POB 71, Suva; tel. 3313488; Pres. JAGDISH KHATRI; Sec. DAVID LEE.

Mineworkers' Union of Fiji: POB 876, Tavua; f. 1986; Pres. JOSEPHA SADREU; Sec. KAVEKINI NAVUSO.

National Farmers' Union: POB 522, Labasa; tel. 8811838; 10,000 mems (sugar-cane farmers); Pres. SURENDRA LAL; Gen. Sec. MAHENDRA P. CHAUDHRY; CEO MOHAMMED LATIF SUBEDAR.

National Union of Factory and Commercial Workers: POB 989, Suva; tel. 3311155; fax 3303021; e-mail nufcw@connect.com.fj; 3,800 mems; Pres. CAMA TUILEVEUKA; Gen. Sec. JOHN V. MUDALIAR.

National Union of Hospitality, Catering and Tourism Industries Employees: Nadi Airport, POB 9426, Nadi; tel. 6700906; fax 6700181; e-mail nuhctie@connect.com.fj; Pres. PENI FINAU; Gen. Sec. DANIEL URAI.

Public Employees' Union: POB 781, Suva; tel. 3304501; 6,752 mems; Pres. SEMI TIKOICINA; Gen. Sec. VILIAME KAUTIA.

Transport and Oil Workers' Union: POB 903, Suva; tel. 3302534; f. 1988; est. by merger of Oil and Allied Workers' Union and Transport Workers' Union; Pres. J. BOLA; Sec. MICHAEL COLUMBUS.

There are several independent trade unions, including Fiji Registered Ports Workers' Union (f. 1947; Pres. JIOJI TAHOLOSALE).

Transport

RAILWAYS

Fiji Sugar Corporation Railway: Rarawai Mill, POB 155, Ba; tel. 6674044; fax 670505; for use in cane-harvesting season, May–Dec.; 595 km of permanent track and 225 km of temporary track (gauge of 600 mm), serving cane-growing areas at Ba, Lautoka and Penang on Viti Levu and Labasa on Vanua Levu; Gen. Man. ADURU KUVA.

ROADS

At the end of 2000 there were some 3,440 km of roads in Fiji, of which 49.2% were paved. A 500-km highway circles the main island of Viti Levu.

Land Transport Authority of Fiji: Lot 1, Daniva Rd, Valelevu, Nasinu; tel. 3392166; fax 3390026; e-mail infor@lta.com.fj; internet www.ltafiji.com; f. 1998; responsible for public transport services, vehicle registration, traffic management and road safety; Chair. GREG LAWLOR; CEO NAISA TUINACEVA.

SHIPPING

The principal ports of call are Suva, Lautoka, Levuka, Malau and Wairiki.

Fiji Islands Maritime Safety Administration (FIMSA): FIMSA House, Amra St, Walubay, POB 326, Suva; tel. 3315266; fax 3303251; e-mail mbuli@govnet.gov.fj; internet www.fimsa.gov.fj; regulatory body for maritime sector; Dir JOSATEKI TAGI.

Fiji Ports Corporation Ltd: POB 780, Suva; tel. 3312700; fax 3300064; e-mail fpcl@connect.com.fj; internet www.fijiports.com.fj; f. 2005; management and devt of Fiji's ports; CEO WAQA BAULEKA (acting); Chair. BEN NAIDU.

Ports Terminals Ltd: POB 780, Suva; f. 1998; subsidiary of Fiji Ports Corporation Ltd; stevedoring, pilotage and cargo handling at Suva and Lautoka ports; Gen. Man. EMINONI KURUSIGA.

Consort Shipping Line Ltd: Lot 4, Matua St, Suva; tel. 3313344; fax 3303389; e-mail consortshipping@connect.com.fj; internet www.consortshipping.com.fj; f. 1986; est. following merger of Interport Shipping and Wong's Shipping Co; CEO HECTOR SMITH; Man. Dir JUSTIN SMIT.

Fiji Maritime Services Ltd: c/o Fiji Ports Workers and Seafarers Union, 36 Edinburgh Drive, Suva; f. 1989 by PAF and the Ports Workers' Union; services between Lautoka and Vanua Levu ports.

Pacific Agencies (Fiji) Ltd: Level 2, Gohil Complex, Toorak Rd, Suva; tel. 3315444; fax 3301127; e-mail info@pacshipfiji.com.fj; internet www.pacificagenciesfiji.com; f. 2000 after merger of Burns Philp and Forum Shipping; shipping agents, customs agents and international forwarding agents, crew handling; Gen. Man. MARTIN O'CONNOR.

Transcargo Express Fiji Ltd: POB 936, Suva; tel. 3313266; fax 3303389; e-mail consortship@connect.com.fj; f. 1974; Man. Dir LEO B. SMITH.

CIVIL AVIATION

There is an international airport at Nadi (about 210 km from Suva), a smaller international airport at Nausori (Suva) and numerous other airfields. Nadi is an important transit airport in the Pacific.

Airports Fiji Ltd: Nadi International Airport, Nadi; tel. 6725777; fax 6725161; e-mail info@afl.com.fj; internet www.airportsfiji.com; f. 1999; owns and operates 15 public airports in Fiji, incl. two international airports, Nadi International Airport and Nausori Airport; Chair. RICK RICKMAN; CEO TIMOCI TULSAWAU.

Air Pacific Ltd: Air Pacific Centre, POB 9266, Nadi International Airport, Nadi; tel. 6720777; fax 6720512; e-mail service@airpacific.com.fj; internet www.airpacific.com; f. 1951; est. as Fiji Airways, name changed in 1971; domestic and international services from Nausori Airport (serving Suva) to Nadi, and international services to Tonga, Solomon Islands, Cook Islands, Vanuatu, Samoa, Kiribati, Tuvalu, Hawaii, Japan, Hong Kong, Australia, New Zealand and the USA; 51% govt-owned, 46.05% owned by Qantas (Australia); Chair. NALIN PATEL; CEO and Man. Dir DAVE PFLIEGER.

Pacific Sun: POB 9270, Nadi International Airport, Nadi; tel. 6723555; fax 6723611; e-mail enquiries@pacificsun.com.fj; internet www.pacificsun.com.fj; f. 1980; wholly owned subsidiary of Air Pacific Ltd; acquired Sun Air 2007; scheduled flights to domestic and regional destinations; Gen. Man. SHAENAZ VOSS.

Vanua Air Charters: Labasa; f. 1993; provides domestic charter and freight services; Propr CHARAN SINGH.

Tourism

Scenery, climate, fishing and diving attract visitors to Fiji, where tourism is an important industry. However, the sector has been intermittently affected by political unrest. The number of visitor arrivals increased by 16.5% in 2010 to reach 631,868, of whom 75% were holiday-makers. Most visitors are from Australia, New Zealand, the USA, the United Kingdom and Japan. A total of 9,070 hotel rooms were available in 2006. Receipts from tourism totalled $F979.8m. in 2010.

Fiji Islands Hotels and Tourism Association (FIHTA): 42 Gorrie St, GPOB 13560, Suva; tel. 3302980; fax 3300331; e-mail info@fihta.com.fj; internet www.fihta.com.fj; fmrly Fiji Hotel Association; name changed as above in 2005; 90 active mems, over 300 assoc. mems; Pres. DIXON SEETO; Exec. Officer MICHAEL WONG.

Fiji Islands Visitors' Bureau: Suite 107, Colonial Plaza, Namaka, POB 9217, Nadi; tel. 6722433; fax 6720141; e-mail infodesk@fijifvb.gov.fj; internet www.bulafiji.com; f. 1923; Chair. PATRICK WONG; Chief Exec. (vacant); Dir of Tourism BANUVE KAUMAITOTOYA.

Tourism Fiji: POB 9217, Nadi Airport, Nadi; tel. 6722433; fax 6720141; e-mail marketing@tourismfiji.com.fj; internet www.fijime .com; Chair. DAVID PFLIEGER; CEO JOSEFA TUAMOTO.

Defence

As assessed at November 2010, Fiji's total armed forces numbered 3,500 (3,200 in the army and 300 in the navy). The country's membership of the Commonwealth has entitled Fijians to work in the British armed forces; in mid-2006 about 2,000 Fijian soldiers were serving in Iraq with the British army. In addition, in November 2010 a total of 221 Fijian soldiers were serving in Iraq under the auspices of the United Nations Assistance Mission to Iraq (UNAMI). The country's defence budget for 2011 was an estimated $F100m.

Commander-in-Chief: President of the Republic.

Commander of the Armed Forces: Cdre FRANK (VOREQE) BAINIMARAMA.

Commander of the Land Force: Lt-Col MOSESE TIKOITOGA.

Commander of the Navy: FRANCIS KEAN.

Chief of Staff, Strategic Headquarters: Brig.-Gen. MOHAMMED AZIZ.

Education

Education in Fiji is compulsory and free at primary level. Primary education begins at six years of age and lasts for eight years. Secondary education, beginning at the age of 14, lasts for a further three years. State subsidies are available for secondary and tertiary education in cases of hardship. In May 2009 there were 721 state primary schools (with a total enrolment of 129,444 pupils) and 172 state secondary schools (with an enrolment of 67,072 pupils). There were 69 vocational and technical institutions (with 2,387 enrolled students). In the same year Fiji had four teacher-training colleges (with 633 students). The University of the South Pacific is based in Fiji. In 2004 university students (both on campus and at extension centres) totalled 16,444. The University of Fiji, a privately owned institution, was established in 2004. In January 2010 six government colleges merged to form the Fiji National University. Budgetary expenditure for 2010 allocated $F209.5m. for education, equivalent to 12.2% of total budgetary expenditure.

FRENCH PACIFIC OVERSEAS COLLECTIVITIES

As amended in March 2003, the Constitution of France defines French Polynesia and the Wallis and Futuna Islands as having the status of Overseas Collectivities (collectivités d'outre-mer) within the French Republic. The territories within this category have a greater degree of independence than do the Overseas Departments and Territories, with the particular status of each being defined by an individual organic law. Local assemblies may establish internal legislation. An organic law of February 2004 accords to French Polynesia the unique designation of Overseas Country (pays d'outre-mer), while it retains the legal status of an Overseas Collectivity. French Polynesia was formerly an Overseas Territory, territoire d'outre-mer, of France. Wallis and Futuna are integral parts of the French Republic. Each is administered by a High Commissioner or Chief Administrator, who is the representative of the State and appointed by the French Government. Each permanently inhabited Territory has a Territorial Assembly or Congress (elected by universal adult suffrage) and representation in the Assemblée Nationale (National Assembly) and Sénat (Senate) in Paris. They have varying degrees of autonomy. The French Republic has membership of the Pacific Community (formerly the South Pacific Commission) in respect of its Pacific possessions. The French Government includes a Minister of the Interior, the Overseas Possessions and Territorial Collectivities.

Head of State: President NICOLAS SARKOZY (took office 17 May 2007).

Ministry of the Interior, the Overseas Possessions and Territorial Collectivities: place Beauvau, 75008 Paris, France; tel. 1-40-07-60-60; fax 1-43-59-89-50; e-mail sirp@interieur.gouv.fr; internet www.interieur.gouv.fr.

Minister of the Interior, the Overseas Possessions, the Territorial Collectivities and Immigration: CLAUDE GUÉANT.

FRENCH POLYNESIA

Introduction

French Polynesia is an Overseas Country of France, covering an area of 4,167 sq km (1,609 sq miles—land area of 3,521 sq km), including 35 volcanic islands and 183 coral atolls in five archipelagos: Society, Austral (Tubuai), Tuamotu, Gambier and Marquesas. The Society Islands, to the west, comprise a Windward Islands group (Iles du Vent—including Tahiti and Moorea) and, about 160 km to the north-west, a Leeward Islands group (Iles Sous le Vent—including Raiatea and Bora Bora). The five Austral Islands lie some 160 km to the south of Tahiti and include Tubuai itself; 770 km to the south-east of Tubuai is the separate island of Rapa. The Tuamotu Archipelago is a chain of about 80 atolls stretching from the north of Tahiti, south-east for about 1,500 km, from the islands around Rangiroa (the largest in French Polynesia) towards those beyond Mururoa Atoll, over 1,000 km from Tahiti. The chain is continued in the south-east by the small group of the Gambier Islands, including Mangareva, some 1,700 km from Tahiti. In the north-east, 1,500 km from Tahiti, are the Marquesas, which comprise a southern and a northern group around the chief island of Nuku Hiva. French Polynesia's nearest neighbours are Kiribati to the north-west and the Cook Islands to the west. The small, uninhabited island of Clipperton, located far to the north-east of French Polynesia, some 600 km from Mexico, is administered as a distinct entity, under the direct jurisdiction of the French Government's Minister of the Interior, the Overseas Possessions and Territorial Collectivities.

Temperatures average between 20°C (68°F) and 29°C (84°F), and most rainfall occurs between November and April, the average annual precipitation being 1,625 mm (64 ins). The more mountainous volcanic islands (notably the Society Islands) receive the most rainfall, and the south is generally cooler than the north.

The official languages are French and Tahitian. Polynesian languages and their dialects are spoken by the indigenous population. Christianity is the principal religion, dominated by the Protestant Evangelical Church. The population, which is predominantly Polynesian, includes minorities of French and other Europeans, Chinese and 'Demis' (mixed race—Polynesian with others). The majority of the population are Polynesian or of Polynesian descent, but there is a substantial European minority. According to official estimates, the population totalled 269,972 at the beginning of 2011. At the census of 20 August 2007 almost 88% of the inhabitants lived in the Society Islands, which constitute about one-half of the land area. The population of the capital, Papeete (located on the island of Tahiti), was 26,050 at the time of the 2007 census.

The islands of French Polynesia were already inhabited by the Polynesian Maohi when first visited by Spanish explorers during the 16th century; Dutch, French and British followed during the 1700s. The Tahitian-based kingdom of the Pomare monarchs was made a French protectorate in 1842 and a colony in 1880. All the islands that now constitute French Polynesia had been annexed by the end of the 19th century. Clipperton Island was first claimed by France in 1857. After disputes with the USA and Mexico, the island was restored to France by arbitration in February 1931. The islands were governed from France under a decree of 1885 until 1946, when French Polynesia became an Overseas Territory. The Polynesians were allowed to manage their domestic affairs while France maintained institutional control through a Governor in Papeete. A Territorial Assembly was established in 1957 to assist the Governor.

Between May 1975 and May 1982 a majority in the Territorial Assembly sought independence; a new constitution for the Territory was negotiated with the French Government, and approved by the first fully elected Territorial Assembly in 1977. France retained responsibility over foreign affairs, law and order, defence and money supply, but the powers of the territorial Council of Government were increased, especially in the field of commerce. The French Governor was replaced by a High Commissioner, who presided over the Council; the elected Vice-President was responsible for domestic affairs. An Economic, Social and Cultural Council, responsible for development, was also created.

The Council of Government was replaced in 1984 by a Council of Ministers, the President of which was to be elected from among the members of the Territorial Assembly. In 1990 five consultative Archipelago Councils were established, comprising Territorial and municipal elected representatives. Under a new statute of autonomy, in April 1996 the Territory gained control of areas including fishing, mining and shipping rights, international transport and communications, broadcasting and the 'offshore' economic zone. In March 2004 French Polynesia formally became an Overseas Country (its official status was an Overseas Collectivity), achieving authority over matters including labour law, civil aviation and regional relations. Following several years of political instability characterized by frequent changes of administration, in March 2011 the French Government announced new proposals for reform of the islands' electoral system.

In August 2011, following the resumption of the presidency earlier in the year by the pro-independence Oscar Temaru, the French Polynesian Assembly voted in favour of applying for the reinscription on the UN's decolonization list (from which the territory had been removed by the French Government in 1946). In September, however, the Pacific Islands Forum chose not to endorse the initiative.

The French Government began nuclear testing at Mururoa Atoll in 1966 at the Centre d'Expérimentation du Pacifique (CEP). Between 1975 and 1992 France officially conducted 135 underground and 52 atmospheric nuclear tests. Testing was suspended in April 1992 but resumed in September 1995, in defiance of international opinion and leading to violent local protests. The final test was conducted in January 1996. The French Government later confirmed an independent scientific report that radioactive isotopes had leaked into the waters surrounding the CEP test sites, but it denied that this represented a threat to the environment. In early 1999 a further independent study reported serious radioactive leakage around Mururoa and Fangataufa Atolls. Declassified reports from 1966, published in May 2005, suggested that the French military had deliberately suppressed information about the extent of contamination from the tests. In January 2006 a commission of inquiry, appointed by the Territorial Assembly, found that, contrary to the information given to the public, each of the atmospheric tests between 1966 and 1974 had caused radioactive fall-out on the surrounding islands. In March 2009 it was announced that the French Government was to establish an independent commission to examine individual compensation claims from civilian and military workers affected by the nuclear tests. In December the French legislature voted in favour of compensation payments for those affected by the nuclear tests, and in early 2010 a list of 18 illnesses, including leukaemia and thyroid cancer, was formally recognized by the French Government as having been caused by the nuclear tests.

In February 2010 thousands of islanders were forced to evacuate their homes when the most severe cyclone for decades struck French Polynesia; the Tuamotu Archipelago was the area to be the worst affected. Hundreds of houses were seriously damaged or completely destroyed by Cyclone Oli. The cost of repairs to housing and infrastructure was unofficially estimated to be in the region of 2,000m. francs CFP.

The economy of French Polynesia has been dominated by income from France. The traditional economy was distorted by the large numbers of French personnel working on the nuclear programme. Under the Contract for Development, concluded in 1995, the French Government agreed to provide 28,300m. francs CFP annually, between 1996 and 2006, to compensate for the loss of fiscal and tax revenue resulting from the closure of the CEP. An annual economic development grant of €151m. was introduced in 2003. It was envisaged that this grant, to be paid in perpetuity, would be used for investment in projects such as reconversion and retraining programmes for businesses previously dependent on the CEP, as well as youth employment schemes and infrastructural development. In February 2010 French Polynesia concluded a new agreement with France, which agreed henceforth to release more than US $200m. annually, as part of an arrangement that took into consideration the economic legacy of the nuclear testing programme. About 60% of this funding was to be disbursed by the French Polynesian Government, while more than 30% was to be allocated to approved infrastructure projects. In March 2011, amid renewed fears for the stability of Mururoa Atoll, the local Government urged the French President to dispatch experts to the area to assess the risks to the population if the atoll were to collapse and release radiation. In May, as the French Polynesian economy entered its third year of recession, it was announced that, subject to conditions that included the urgent restructuring of the economy, France had agreed to lend the Territory US $62m.

There is a small manufacturing sector, which is heavily dependent on agriculture, coconuts being the principal cash crop. Coconut oil and copra are thus produced, as are beer, dairy products and vanilla essence. Commercial fishing, principally for tuna, is mainly conducted by licensed Japanese and Korean fleets. The services sector continues to make a substantial contribution to the economy. Tourism remains the primary source of revenue. French Polynesia's major export is cultured pearls, important markets being Hong Kong and Japan. France has remained the principal source of imports. Political instability has continued to deter potential investors.

Statistical Survey

Source (unless otherwise indicated): Institut Statistique de la Polynésie Française, Immeuble Uupa, 1er étage, rue Edouard Ahne, BP 395, 98713 Papeete; tel. 473434; fax 427252; e-mail ispf@ispf.pf; internet www.ispf.pf.

AREA AND POPULATION

Area: Total 4,167 sq km (1,609 sq miles); Land area 3,521 sq km (1,359 sq miles).

Population: 245,516 at census of 7 November 2002; 259,706 (males 133,109, females 126,597) at census of 20 August 2007. *By Island Group* (2007 census): Society Archipelago 227,848 (Windward Islands 194,683, Leeward Islands 33,165); Marquesas Archipelago 8,658; Austral Islands 6,304; Tuamotu-Gambier Islands 16,896; Total 259,706. *2011* (official estimate at 1 January): 269,972.

Density (land area only, at 1 January 2011): 76.7 per sq km.

Population by Age and Sex (UN estimates at mid-2011): *0–14:* 67,843 (males 34,529, females 33,314); *15–64:* 187,865 (males 96,804, females 91,061); *65 and over:* 18,070 (males 8,820, females 9,250); *Total* 273,778 (males 140,153, females 133,625) (Source: UN, *World Population Prospects: The 2010 Revision*).

Ethnic Groups (census of 15 October 1983): Polynesian 114,280; 'Demis' 23,625 (Polynesian-European 15,851, Polynesian-Chinese 6,356, Polynesian-Other races 1,418); European 19,320; Chinese 7,424; European-Chinese 494; Others 1,610; Total 166,753. *1988 Census* ('000 persons): Polynesians and 'Demis' 156.3; Others 32.5.

Principal Towns (population at 2007 census): Faa'a 29,781; Papeete (capital) 26,050; Punaauía 25,399; Moorea-Maiao 16,507; Pirae 14,551; Mahina 14,356; Paea 12,084; Taiarapu-Est 11,538; Papara 10,634.

Births, Marriages and Deaths (2010): Registered live births 4,579 (birth rate 17.0 per 1,000); Marriages 1,330 (marriage rate 5.0 per 1,000); Registered deaths 1,261 (death rate 4.7 per 1,000).

Life Expectancy (official estimates, years at birth, 2010): 75.6 (males 73.2; females 78.3).

Economically Active Population (persons aged 14 years and over, 2007 census, excluding persons in military service): Agriculture, hunting, forestry and fishing 8,809; Mining and manufacturing 6,081; Electricity, gas and water 585; Construction 9,825; Trade, restaurants and hotels 21,064; Transport, storage and communications 7,049; Financial services 1,666; Real estate, housing and services to business 4,391; Other private services 5,326; Education, health and social welfare 15,115; Public administration 15,347; *Total employed* 95,258 (males 56,674, females 38,584); Unemployed 12,668 (males 7,006, females 5,662); *Total labour force* 107,926 (males 63,680, females 44,246). *2009* (salaried workers at 31 December): Agriculture, hunting, forestry and fishing 1,958; Mining and quarrying 170; Manufacturing 4,469; Electricity, gas and water 677; Construction 5,433; Trade, restaurants and hotels 16,861; Transport, storage and communications 6,471; Financial services 1,638; Real estate, housing and services to business 4,915; Public administration 14,885; Education 632; Health and social welfare 3,559; Other community, social and personal services 3,057; Persons employed in private households 1,375; Total 66,100. Note: Figures for 2009 exclude 10,600 non-salaried workers and 11,285 civil servants and armed forces personnel.

HEALTH AND WELFARE

Key Indicators

Total Fertility Rate (children per woman, 2010): 2.1.

Physicians (per 1,000 head, 2009): 1.8.

Total Carbon Dioxide Emissions ('000 metric tons, 2007): 806.1.

Carbon Dioxide Emissions Per Head (metric tons, 2007): 3.1.

For definitions, see explanatory note on p. vi.

AGRICULTURE, ETC.

Principal Crops (metric tons, 2009, FAO estimates): Cassava 3,639; Other roots and tubers 5,067; Sugar cane 3,000; Vegetables and melons 6,946; Pineapples 3,497; Coconuts 97,103; Vanilla 74; Coffee, green 16.

Livestock (year ending September 2009, FAO estimates): Cattle 7,300; Horses 2,200; Pigs 31,000; Goats 16,500; Sheep 440; Chickens 270,000; Ducks 32,000.

Livestock Products (metric tons, 2009): Cattle meat 162; Pig meat 1,219; Goat meat 75 (FAO estimate); Chicken meat 630 (FAO estimate); Cows' milk 1,192; Hen eggs 2,740; Other poultry eggs 82 (FAO estimate); Honey 42 (FAO estimate).

Fishing (metric tons, live weight, 2009): Capture 12,434 (Skipjack tuna 1,282; Albacore 3,170; Yellowfin tuna 1,067; Bigeye tuna 484; Blue marlin 369; Wahoo 214; Common dolphinfish 417; Other marine fishes 5,101); Aquaculture 39; Total catch 12,473. Note: Figures exclude pearl oyster shells: 1,866.

Source: FAO.

INDUSTRY

Selected Products (metric tons, 2010, unless otherwise indicated): Copra 7,879; Coconut oil 6,879; Oilcake 4,461; Electric energy (2009, Tahiti only) 649.3m. kWh. Source: partly Institut d'Emission d'Outre-Mer.

FINANCE

Currency and Exchange Rates: 100 centimes = 1 franc de la Communauté française du Pacifique (franc CFP or Pacific franc). *Sterling, Dollar and Euro Equivalents* (31 May 2011): £1 sterling = 136.902 francs CFP; US $1 = 82.956 francs CFP; €1 = 119.332 francs CFP; 1,000 francs CFP = £7.30 = $12.05 = €8.38. *Average Exchange Rate* (francs CFP per US $): 95.12 in 2006; 87.18 in 2007; 81.47 in 2008. Note: Until 31 December 1998 the value of the franc CFP was fixed at 5.5 French centimes (1 French franc = 18.1818 francs CFP). Since the introduction of the euro, on 1 January 1999, an official exchange rate of 1,000 francs CFP = €8.38 (€1 = 119.332 francs CFP) has been in operation. Accordingly, the value of the franc CFP has been adjusted to 5.4969 French centimes (1 French franc = 18.1920 francs CFP), representing a 'devaluation' of 0.056%.

Territorial Budget (million francs CFP, 2009, budget): *Revenue:* 140,567 (Taxes 107,003, Other revenues 4,087, State grants 18,123, Loans 11,354). *Expenditure:* 140,567 (Current 106,016, Capital 23,900, Debt-servicing 10,651). Source: Institut d'Emission d'Outre-Mer.

French State Expenditure (million francs CFP): 148,618 (incl. military budget 22,315) in 2005; 159,100 (incl. military budget 24,000) in 2006; 169,563 (incl. military budget 21,668) in 2007; 167,809 (incl. military budget 21,662) in 2008; 175,572 (incl. military budget 21,005) in 2009.

Money Supply (million francs CFP at 31 December 2010): Currency in circulation 14,781; Demand deposits 157,218; *Total money* 171,998. Source: Institut d'Emission d'Outre-Mer.

Cost of Living (Consumer Price Index, annual averages; base: 2000 = 100): All items 114.4 in 2008; 114.6 in 2009; 116.1 in 2010. Source: UN, *Monthly Bulletin of Statistics*.

Gross Domestic Product (million francs CFP at constant 2005 prices): 367,556.1 in 2007; 376,575.8 in 2008; 384,320.4 in 2009. Source: UN Statistics Division, National Accounts Main Aggregates Database.

Expenditure on the Gross Domestic Product (million francs CFP at current prices, 2009): Government final consumption expenditure 41,878.4; Private final consumption expenditure 398,672.3; Increase in stocks 852.2; Gross fixed capital formation 98,433.9; *Total domestic expenditure* 539,836.8; Exports of goods and services 70,012.2; *Less* Imports of goods and services 220,176.9; *GDP in purchasers' values* 389,672.1. Source: UN National Accounts Main Aggregates Database.

Gross Domestic Product by Economic Activity (million francs CFP at current prices, 2009): Agriculture, hunting, forestry and fishing 9,967.4; Mining, electricity, gas and water 6,451.8; Manufacturing 22,364.2; Construction 22,377.9; Trade, restaurants and hotels 96,303.7; Transport, storage and communications 29,627.9; Other activities 209,691.5; *Sub-total* 396,784.4; Net of indirect taxes –7,112.3 (obtained as a residual); *GDP in purchasers' values* 389,672.1. Source: UN National Accounts Main Aggregates Database.

Balance of Payments (million francs CFP, 2009): Exports of goods 12,917; Imports of goods –145,851; *Trade balance* –132,934; Exports of services 93,437; Imports of services –61,812; *Balance on goods and services* –101,309; Other income (net) 53,492; *Balance on goods, services and income* –47,817; Current transfers (net) 65,405; *Current balance* 17,587; Direct investment (net) 207; Portfolio investment assets 32,432; Portfolio investment liabilities –43,329; Other investment assets 435,277; Other investment liabilities –460,186; *Overall balance* –18,013. Source: Institut d'Emission d'Outre-Mer.

EXTERNAL TRADE

Principal Commodities (million francs CFP, 2010, excl. military transactions, provisional): *Imports c.i.f.:* Live animals and animal products 7,669.3 (Meat and edible meat offal 7,598.0); Prepared foodstuffs; beverages, spirits and vinegar; tobacco and manufactured substitutes 29,242.5; Mineral products 20,273.5 (Mineral fuels, mineral oils and products of their distillation; bituminous substances; mineral waxes 20,270.5); Products of chemical or allied industries 13,597.7 (Pharmaceutical products 7,254.8); Plastics, rubber and articles thereof 5,710.8; Paper-making materials; paper and paperboard and articles thereof 4,270.6; Textiles and textile articles 4,328.1; Base metals and articles thereof 9,745.5; Machinery and mechanical appliances; electrical equipment; sound and television apparatus 27,627.4 (Nuclear reactors, boilers, machinery, mechanical appliances and parts 13,453.8; Electrical machinery, equipment, etc. 14,173.6); Vehicles, aircraft, vessels and associated transport equipment 16,448.5 (Aircraft and aeronautical craft 695.0; Sea or river vessels 3,833.7; Road vehicles, parts and accessories 11,758.8); Miscellaneous manufactured articles 5,507.3; Total (incl. others) 155,333.1. *Exports f.o.b.:* Fish and crustaceans, molluscs and other aquatic invertebrates 674.3; Prepared foodstuffs; beverages, spirits and vinegar; tobacco and manufactured substitutes 2,463.8 (Preparations of vegetables, fruit, nuts or other parts of plants 754.4); Natural or cultured pearls, precious or semi-precious stones, precious metals and articles thereof; imitation jewellery; coin 8,098.2; Vehicles, aircraft, vessels and associated transport equipment 1,999.7 (Aircraft, spacecraft and parts 244.4); Total (incl. others) 13,868.3.

Principal Trading Partners (million francs CFP, 2010, excl. military transactions, provisional): *Imports:* Australia 4,972.9; Belgium 2,341.2; China, People's Republic 14,670.8; France 43,573.4; Germany 5,234.4; Indonesia 1,464.0; Italy 3,984.3; Japan 4,191.5; Korea, Republic of 2,424.5; Netherlands 1,638.0; New Zealand 12,577.5; Singapore 19,791.4; Spain 1,854.0; Thailand 4,701.1; United Kingdom 1,978.0; USA 15,635.1; Total (incl. others) 155,333.1. *Exports:* Australia 290.1; Belgium 12.3; Canada 45.4; China, People's Republic 309.2; France 1,784.5; Germany 124.4; Hong Kong 4,129.8; Japan 2,777.1; New Caledonia 358.0; New Zealand 219.4; USA 1,597.2; Total (incl. others) 13,868.3.

TRANSPORT

Road Traffic (1987): Total vehicles registered 54,979. *2007 Census:* Private cars 4,602; Vans 3,108; Trucks 80; Special vehicles 19; Two wheelers 3,463; Trailers 20; Total 11,292. *2009:* Four-wheelers 15,909; Two wheelers 2,432; Total 18,341.

Shipping (2009, unless otherwise indicated): *International Traffic:* Passengers carried 27,852 (2003); Freight handled 921,819 (loaded 28,799, unloaded 893,020) metric tons. *Domestic Traffic:* Passengers carried 1,715,455; Total freight handled 397,493 metric tons.

Civil Aviation (2009, unless otherwise indicated): *International Traffic:* Passengers carried 512,169; Freight handled 9,315 metric tons (2009). *Domestic Traffic:* Passengers carried 662,629; Freight handled 2,643 metric tons.

TOURISM

Visitors: 196,496 in 2008; 160,447 in 2009; 153,919 in 2010.

Tourist Arrivals by Country of Residence (2010): Australia 6,945; Canada 5,468; France 36,544; Germany 4,256; Italy 11,208; Japan 13,761; New Caledonia 3,940; New Zealand 5,128; Spain 4,104; Switzerland 519; United Kingdom 2,840; USA 40,735; Total (incl. others) 153,919. Source: Institut d'Emission d'Outre-Mer.

Tourism Receipts (US $ million, incl. passenger transport): 691 in 2006; 807 in 2007; 745 in 2008. Source: World Tourism Organization.

COMMUNICATIONS MEDIA

Radio Receivers (1997): 128,000 in use*.

Television Receivers (2000): 44,000 in use†.

Telephones (2010): 54,900 main lines in use†.

Mobile Cellular Telephones (subscribers, 2010): 215,900†.

Personal Computers (number in use, 2005): 28,000†.

Internet Subscribers (2009): 30,500†.

Broadband Subscribers (2010): 32,200†.

Daily Newspapers (2000): 2.

* Source: UNESCO, *Statistical Yearbook*.

† Source: International Telecommunication Union.

EDUCATION

Pre-primary (2008/09, unless otherwise indicated): 40 schools (2006/07); 408 teachers (1996/97); 14,306 pupils.

Primary (incl. special schools and young adolescents' centres, 2010/11, unless otherwise indicated): 231 schools (incl. pre-primary); 2,811 teachers (1996/97); 39,991 pupils.

Secondary (2010/11, unless otherwise indicated): 51 schools (first and second cycles, 2008/09); 2,035 teachers (general secondary only, 1998/99); 32,418 pupils.

Tertiary (2006/07, unless otherwise indicated): 50 teachers (1999); 681 students.

Source: partly Institut d'Emission d'Outre-Mer.

Directory

The Constitution

The constitutional system in French Polynesia was established under the aegis of the Constitution of the Fifth French Republic and specific laws of 1977, 1984 and 1990. The French Polynesia Statute 1984, the so-called 'internal autonomy statute', underwent amendment in a law of July 1990. A further extension of the Territory's powers under the statute was approved by the French Assemblée nationale (National Assembly) in Paris in December 1995. In January 2000 a constitutional amendment granting French Polynesia a greater degree of autonomy was presented to a joint session of the French Sénat (Senate) and Assemblée nationale for final ratification. In March 2003 both the Assemblée nationale and Sénat ratified amendments to the Constitution providing for French Polynesia (along with Wallis and Futuna) to become an Overseas Country (Pays d'outre-mer). In July the Territorial Assembly and the Government of French Polynesia ratified the amendments. The approval of the French Conseil d'Etat (State Council), the French Government and the Constitutional Council duly followed, and in

March 2004 French Polynesia became known as an Overseas Country.

Although French Polynesia is designated as an Overseas Country of the French Republic, of which it remains an integral part, its official status is that of an Overseas Collectivity (Collectivité d'outre-mer). The High Commissioner, appointed by the French Government, exercises the prerogatives of the State in matters relating to defence, foreign relations, the maintenance of law and order, communications and citizenship. The head of the local executive and the official who represents French Polynesia is the President of the Government, who is elected by the local Assembly from among its own members. The President appoints and dismisses the Council of Ministers and has competence in international relations as they affect French Polynesia and its exclusive economic zone, and is in control of foreign investments and immigration. The local Assembly, which has financial autonomy in budgetary affairs and legislative authority within French Polynesia, is elected for a term of up to five years on the basis of universal adult suffrage. Following the elections of May 2004, it comprised 57 members: 37 elected by the people of the Windward Islands (Iles du Vent—Society Islands), eight by the Leeward Islands (Iles Sous le Vent—Society Islands), three by the Gambier Islands-East Tuamotu Archipelago, three by the West Tuamotu Archipelago, three by the Austral Islands and three by the Marquesas Islands. The Assembly elects a Permanent Commission from among its members, and itself meets for two ordinary sessions each year and upon the demand of the majority party, the President or the High Commissioner. Local government is conducted by the municipalities. There is an Economic, Social and Cultural Council (composed of representatives of professional groups, trade unions and other organizations and agencies that participate in the economic, social and cultural activities of French Polynesia), an Audit Office and a judicial system, which includes a Court of the First Instance, a Court of Appeal and an Administrative Court. The Overseas Country, as a part of the French Republic, also elects two deputies to the Assemblée nationale and two members of the Sénat, and may be represented in the European Parliament.

The Government

High Commissioner: RICHARD DIDIER (took office 24 January 2011).

Secretary-General: ALEXANDRE ROCHATTE.

COUNCIL OF MINISTERS
(October 2011)

The Government is led by Tavini Huiraatira No Te Ao Ma'ohi.

President, also in charge of International and Regional Relations, Tourism and International Air Transport: OSCAR MANUTAHI TEMARU.

Vice-President, also in charge of Budget, Community Development, Digital Economy, Communication, Relations with French Polynesia's Institutions, Government Spokesman: ANTONY GÉROS.

Minister for Economy, Finance, Labour and Employment, in charge of Fiscal Reforms, Vocational Training, Administrative Reforms and Public Service: PIERRE FRÉBAULT.

Minister for Public Utilities, Land Transport, in charge of Ports and Airports: JAMES SALMON.

Minister for Marine Resources, in charge of Pearl Farming Industries, Fisheries, Aquaculture and Green Technologies: TEMAURI FOSTER.

Minister for Education, Youth and Sports, in charge of Higher Education, Research and Associations: TAUHITI NENA.

Minister for Planning and Housing, in charge of Land Affairs and Urban Matters: LOUIS FRÉBAULT.

Minister for Environment, Energy and Mining: JACKY BRYANT.

Minister for Health and Solidarity, in charge of Social Welfare Protection: CHARLES TETARIA.

Minister for Culture, Crafts and Family, in charge of Women's Affairs: CHANTAL TAHIATA.

Minister for Agriculture, Livestock, in charge of Biotechnologies: KALANI TEIXEIRA.

Minister for Outer Islands Development and Transport, in charge of Coconut Plantations Revival: DANIEL HERLEMME.

GOVERNMENT OFFICES

Office of the High Commissioner of the Republic: BP 115, 98713 Papeete; tel. 468686; fax 468689; e-mail courrier@polynesie-francaise.pref.gouv.fr; internet www.polynesie-francaise.pref.gouv.fr.

Office of the President of the Government: ave Pouvana'a A Opa, BP 2551, 98713 Papeete; tel. 472000; fax 472210; internet www.presidence.pf.

Government of French Polynesia: BP 2551, Papeete; tel. 472000; fax 419781.

Economic, Social and Cultural Council (CESC): Immeuble Te Raumaire, ave Bruat, BP 1657, 98713 Papeete; tel. 416500; fax 419242; e-mail cesc@cesc.pf; internet www.cesc.pf; f. 1977; est. as Economic and Social Council; present name adopted in 1990; Pres. RAYMONDE RAOULX; Sec.-Gen. ALEXA BONNETTE.

Ministry of Culture and Handicrafts: BP 2551, 98713 Papeete; tel. 508620; fax 508622; e-mail ambroise.colombani@artisanat.min.gov.pf; internet www.artisanat.gov.pf.

Ministry of Economic Reform, External Trade, Industry and Enterprise: Bâtiment de la Culture, rue des Poilus Tahitiens, Quartier Buillard, Papeete; tel. 484000; fax 484014.

Ministry of Education, Higher Education and Research: rue Tuterai Tane, BP 2551, 98713 Papeete; tel. 544900; fax 544901; e-mail secretariat@education.min.gov.pf; internet www.education.gov.pf.

Ministry of Finance, Budget, Public Expenditure and Fiscal Reform: BP 2551, 98713 Papeete; tel. 484000; fax 484014; e-mail secretariat@finances.gov.pf; internet www.postes.gov.pf.

Ministry of Health and Ecology: Bâtiment de la Direction de la Santé, 1er étage, Papeete; tel. 460099; fax 433942; internet www.sante.gov.pf.

Ministry of Labour and Employment: Bâtiment du Gouvernement, 1er étage, ave Pouvana'a A Opa, Papeete; tel. 472440; fax 855777.

Ministry of Land Affairs, Planning, Housing and Public Works: Bâtiment Administratif A2, 5ème étage, rue du Commandant Destremeau, BP 2551, 98713 Papeete; tel. 468019; fax 483792; e-mail secretariat@equipement.min.gov.pf; internet www.equipement.gov.pf.

Ministry of Maritime Resources: Immeuble Te Fenua, rue Dumont d'Urville, 98713 Papeete; tel. 549575; fax 454343; e-mail secretariat@maritime.min.gov.pf; internet www.mer.gov.pf.

Ministry of Outer Islands Development and Domestic Transport: Immeuble Papineau, 5ème étage, rue Tepano Jaussen, BP 2551, 98713 Papeete; tel. 478350; fax 478357; internet www.transports-interinsulaires.gov.pf.

Ministry of Rural Economy: Bâtiment du Gouvernement, ave Pouvana'a A Opa, Papeete; tel. 504455; fax 504460.

Ministry of Solidarity and Family Affairs: Immeuble Papineau, 6ème étage, rue Tepano Jaussen, BP 2551, Papeete; tel. 478383; fax 478302; e-mail secretariat.mfc@famille.min.gov.pf; internet www.famille.gov.pf.

Ministry of Tourism and International Air Transport: Fare Manihini, rond-point de la Base Marine, blvd Pomare, BP 2551, 98713 Papeete; tel. 803000; e-mail contact@tourisme.min.gov.pf.

Ministry of Youth and Sports: Immeuble ICA, 4ème étage, Colline Putiaoro, Quartier de la Mission, 98713 Papeete; tel. 501075; fax 501077; internet www.jeunesse.gov.pf.

Legislature

ASSEMBLÉE

President: JACQUI DROLLET.

Assembly: Assemblée de la Polynésie Française, rue du Docteur Cassiau, BP 28, 98713 Papeete; tel. 416300; fax 416372; e-mail communication@assemblee.pf; internet www.assemblee.pf.

Election (second round), 10 February 2008*

Party	Seats
To Tatou Ai'a†	27
Union pour la Démocratie (UPLD)‡	20
Tahoera'a Huiraatira	10
Total	57

* Unofficial results. Three of the 57 seats were determined at the first round of voting, held on 27 January 2008, when the requisite absolute majority was secured.

† Coalition led by O Porinetia To Tatou Ai'a.

‡ Coalition led by Tavini Huiraatira.

PARLEMENT

Deputies to the French Assemblée Nationale: MICHEL BUILLARD (Tahoera'a Huiraatira/Union pour un Mouvement Populaire—UMP), BRUNO SANDRAS (Tahoera'a Huiraatira/UMP).

Representatives to the French Sénat: GASTON FLOSSE (Tahoera'a Huiraatira), RICHARD TUHEIAVA (Union pour la Démocratie—UPLD).

Political Organizations

Ai'a Api (New Land): BP 11185, 98709 Mahina, Tahiti; tel. 504596; fax 504598; e-mail courrier@aiaapi.pf; internet www.aiaapi.pf; f. 1982 after split in Te E'a Api; Pres. EMILE VERNAUDON.

Fe'tia Api (New Star): c/o Assemblée de la Polynésie Française, BP 140 512, Arue; tel. 416131; fax 416136; f. 1996; part of Alliance pour une Démocratie Nouvelle coalition; Leader PHILIP SCHYLE.

Heiura-Les Verts Polynésiens: BP 44, Bora Bora; tel. and fax 677174; e-mail heiura@heiura-lesverts.pf; internet www.heiura-lesverts.pf; ecologist; Sec.-Gen. JACKY BRYANT.

Ia Mana Te Nunaa (Power to the People): rue du Commandant Destrémau, BP 1223, Papeete; tel. 426699; f. 1976; advocates 'socialist independence'; Sec.-Gen. JACQUI DROLLET.

No Oe E Te Nunaa (This Country is Yours): Immeuble Fara, rue Nansouty, BP 40205, Fare Tony, 98713 Papeete; tel. 423718; e-mail contact@noetn.com; internet www.noetn.com; favours autonomy; part of Alliance pour une Démocratie Nouvelle coalition; Leader NICOLE MOEA BOUTEAU; Sec.-Gen. ROSALIE TIRIANA ZAVAN.

O Porinetia To Tatou Ai'a (Polynesia, Our Homeland): BP 4061, 98713 Papeete; tel. 584848; fax 504888; e-mail contact@oporinetia.pf; internet www.oporinetia.pf; f. 2007; est. by fmr members of Tahoera'a Huiraatira; leading mem. of To Tatou Ai'a coalition; Pres. GASTON TONG SANG.

Pupu Here Ai'a Te Nunaa Ia Ora: BP 3195, Papeete; tel. 420766; f. 1965; advocates autonomy.

Rautahi (Rally for French Polynesia): BP 60 013, Faa'a Centre; tel. 762000; e-mail rautahi-rpf@mail.pf; internet www.rautahi-be.org; f. 2005; est. by fmr mems of Tahoera'a Huiraatira; Pres. JEAN-CHRISTOPHE BOUISSOU.

Taatiraa No Te Hau: BP 2916, Papeete; tel. 437494; fax 422546; f. 1977; Pres. ROBERT TANSEAU.

Tahoera'a Huiraatira (People's Rally): rue du Commandant Destremeau, BP 471, Papeete; tel. 429898; fax 450004; e-mail courrier@tahoeraahuiraatira.pf; internet tahoeraahuiraatira.pf; f. 1977; fmrly l'Union Tahitienne; supports links with France, with internal autonomy; affiliated to the metropolitan Union pour un Mouvement Populaire (UMP); Pres. GASTON FLOSSE; Pres.-Delegate EDOUARD FRITCH; Sec.-Gen. BRUNO SANDRAS.

Tapura Amui No Te Faatereraa Manahune-Tuhaa Pae: c/o Assemblée de la Polynésie Française, BP 140 512, Arue; represents the Austral Islands; Leader CHANTAL FLORES.

Tavini Huiraatira No Te Ao Ma'ohi/Front de Libération de la Polynésie (Polynesian People's Servant): c/o Assemblée de la Polynésie Française, BP 140 512, Arue; tel. 733865; f. 1977; leading mem. of Union pour la Démocratie (Union for Democracy—UPLD) coalition; independence movement; anti-nuclear; Leader OSCAR TEMARU.

Te' Avei'a (Te Ara): BP 11 362, 98709 Mahina, Tahiti; tel. and fax 851385; e-mail mail@teaveia.pf; internet www.teaveia.pf; f. 2004; est. by fmr mems of Fe'tia Api and Tavini Huiraatira; Pres. ANTONIO PEREZ.

Te Henua Enana Kotoa: Papeete; Leader LOUIS TAATA.

Te Niu Hau Manahune (Principle of Democracy): Rangiroa; f. 2007; Leader TEINA MARAEURA; Sec.-Gen. HINANO TEANOTOGA.

Judicial System

Audit Office: Chambre Territoriale des Comptes, rue Edouard Ahnne, BP 331, 98713 Papeete; tel. 509710; fax 509719; e-mail ctcpf@pf.ccomptes.fr; Pres. JACQUES BASSET; Clerk of the Court MARIE-HÉLÈNE ANDRIOT.

Court of Administrative Law: ave Pouvana'a A Opa, BP 4522, 98713 Papeete; tel. 509025; fax 451724; e-mail tadelapolynesiefrancaise@mail.pf; Pres. CHRISTIAN CAU; Cllrs CHAN-SEREY MUM, MARIE-CHRISTINE LUBRANO, DANIÈLE GONNOT; Clerk of the Court DONA GERMAIN.

Court of Appeal: Cour d'Appel de Papeete, 42 ave Pouvana'a A Opa, BP 101, 98713 Papeete; tel. 415500; fax 424416; e-mail sec.pp.ca-papeete@justice.fr; internet www.ca-papeete.justice.fr; Pres. OLIVIER AIMOT; Attorney-Gen. SERGE SAMUEL; Clerk of the Court RENE ARLANDA.

Court of the First Instance: Tribunal de Première Instance de Papeete, ave Bruat, BP 4633, 78718 Papeete; tel. 415500; fax 454012; e-mail sec.pr.tpi-papeete@justice.fr; internet www.ca-papeete.justice.fr; Pres. GUY RIPOLL; Procurator JOSÉ THOREL; Clerk of the Court KARL LEQUEUX.

Religion

About 54% of the population are Protestants and 38% are Roman Catholics.

CHRISTIANITY

Protestant Church

At mid-2000 there were an estimated 110,000 Protestants.

Maohi Protestant Church: BP 113, Papeete; tel. 460600; fax 419357; e-mail eepf@mail.pf; f. 1884; autonomous since 1963; fmrly l'Eglise Evangélique en Polynésie Française (Etaretia Evaneria I Porinetia Farani); Pres. of Council Rev. TAAROANUI MARAEA; c. 95,000 mems.

The Roman Catholic Church

French Polynesia comprises the archdiocese of Papeete and the suffragan diocese of Taiohae o Tefenuaenata (based in Nuku Hiva, Marquesas Is). At 31 December 2007 there were an estimated 101,090 adherents in French Polynesia. The Archbishop and the Bishop participate in the Episcopal Conference of the Pacific, based in Fiji.

Archbishop of Papeete: (vacant), Archevêché, BP 94, Vallée de la Mission, 98713 Papeete; tel. 420251; fax 424032; e-mail catholic@mail.pf.

Other Churches

Other denominations active in French Polynesia include the Assemblies of God, Church of Jesus Christ of Latter-day Saints (Mormon), Sanito and Seventh-day Adventist missions. At mid-2000 there were an estimated 30,000 adherents to other forms of Christianity.

The Press

La Dépêche de Tahiti: Ave George Clémenceau, BP 50, 98713 Papeete; tel. 464343; fax 464393; e-mail journalistes@ladepeche.pf; internet www.ladepeche.pf; f. 1964; acquired by Groupe France Antilles in 1988; daily; French; Man. Dir and Editor RICHARD BROZAT; circ. 20,500.

Fenua'Orama: BP 629, 98713 Papeete; tel. 475293; fax 475297; e-mail fenuaorama@hersantmedia.pf; publ. by Groupe France Antilles; monthly; women's lifestyle; Editor-in-Chief DANIEL PARDON; circ. 13,700.

L'Hebdo Maohi: Papeete; tel. and fax 4581827; e-mail journal@hebdo.pf; internet www.hebdo.pf; weekly; Man. and Publ. Dir TERII PAQUIER; circ. 3,000.

Journal Officiel de la Polynésie Française: c/o Imprimerie Officielle, 43 rue des Poilus Tahitiens, BP 117, 98713 Papeete; tel. 500580; fax 425261; e-mail imprimerie.officielle@imprimerie.gov.pf; f. 2004 as *Compte Rendu Intégral des Débats de l'Assemblée de la Polynésie Française*; bi-weekly; publ. by the Imprimerie Officielle; Dir CLAUDINO LAURENT; circ. 100.

Les Nouvelles de Tahiti: Immeuble Sarateva, Carrefour de la Fautaua, BP 629, Papeete; tel. 475200; fax 475209; e-mail redac@lesnouvelles.pf; internet www.lesnouvelles.pf; f. 1957; daily; French; Gen. Man. EDMUND TRAN; Editor-in-Chief MURIEL PONTAROLLO; circ. 6,500.

Le Semeur Tahitien: BP 94, 98713 Papeete; tel. 502350; e-mail catholic@mail.pf; f. 1909; 22 a year; French; publ. by the Roman Catholic Church.

Tahiti Beach Press: BP 887, 98713 Papeete; tel. 426850; fax 423356; e-mail tahitibeachpres@mail.pf; internet www.tahitibeachpress.com; f. 1980; monthly; English; Publr G. WARTI; circ. 10,000.

Tahiti Pacifique Magazine: BP 368, Maharepa, Moorea; tel. 562894; fax 563007; e-mail tahitipm@mail.pf; internet tahiti-pacifique.com; monthly; French; Dir and Editor ALEX W. DU PREL; circ. 6,500.

Ve'a Katorika: BP 94, 98713 Papeete; e-mail catholic@mail.pf; f. 1909; monthly; publ. by the Roman Catholic Church.

Ve'a Porotetani: BP 113, Papeete; tel. 460623; fax 419357; e-mail eepf@mail.pf; f. 1921; monthly; French and Tahitian; publ. by the Maohi Protestant Church; Dir TAARII MARAEA; Editor-in-Chief EVA RAAPOTO; circ. 5,000.

Other publications include *Le To'ere*, weekly; *Conso + Info Plus*, *Tahiti Business*, and *Ve'a Ora Magazine*, monthly; and *Dixit* and *Fenua Economie*, annually.

NEWS AGENCIES

Agence France-Presse (AFP): BP 629, Papeete; tel. 508100; fax 508109.

Tahitipresse (Agence Tahitienne de Presse—ATP): Immeuble ICA/TNTV, Vallée de Putiaoro, Quartier de la Mission, BP 4635, 98713 Papeete; tel. 548787; fax 838382; e-mail agence@tahitipresse.pf; internet www.tahitipresse.pf; f. 2001; bilingual French and English news service providing pictures and printed news reports; Chair. NICOLAS BERTHOLON.

Publishers

Editions Haere Pō: BP 1958, Papeete 98713; tel. and fax 480401; e-mail haerepotahiti@mail.pf; internet www.haerepo.org; f. 1981; travel, history, linguistics, literature, culture, anthropology, religion, land tenure and local interest.

Au Vent des Iles: BP 5670, 98716 Pirae; tel. 509595; fax 509597; e-mail mail@auventdesiles.pf; internet www.auventdesiles.pf; f. 1992; South Pacific interest, fiction and trade; Gen. Man. CHRISTIAN ROBERT.

GOVERNMENT PRINTER

Imprimerie Officielle: 43 rue des Poilus Tahitiens, BP 117, 98713 Papeete; tel. 500580; fax 425261; e-mail imprimerie.officielle@imprimerie.gov.pf; f. 1843; printers, publrs; Dir CLAUDINO LAURENT.

Broadcasting and Communications

TELECOMMUNICATIONS

Office des Postes et Télécommunications (OPT): Hôtel des Postes, 8 rue de la Reine Pomare IV, 98714 Papeete; tel. 414242; fax 436767; e-mail contact@opt.pf; internet www.opt.pf; state-owned telecommunications co; subsidiaries incl. Tahiti Nui Telecom (international voice services), Tikiphone (mobile network), Mana (internet service), Tahiti Nui Satellite (satellite broadcaster), ISS (software and network solutions); Chair. FRANÇOIS VOIRIN; Dir-Gen. MANFRED CHAVE.

Tahiti Nui Telecommunications (TNT): Immeuble Aorai, 3ème étage, rue Edouard Ahnne, BP 550, 98713 Papeete; tel. 415400; fax 4303495; e-mail admin.tnt@tahitinui-telecom.com; internet www.tahitinui-telecom.com; f. 2001; owned by OPT; provides international telephone services; Chair. JEAN-CLAUDE TERIIEROOITERAI; Gen. Man. GÉRARD COLAS; 950 employees (2010).

Tikiphone SAS (Vini): POB 440, 98713 Papeete; tel. 481313; fax 487248; internet www.tikiphone.pf; f. 1994; subsidiary of OPT; operates Vini, French Polynesia's first mobile telephone network; more than 208,000 subscribers; Gen. Man. YANNICK TERIIEROOITERAI.

Regulatory Authority

Service des Postes et Telecommunications: Immeuble Fariipiti Iti, rue Marcq Blond de Saint Hilaire, Quartier Fariipiti, BP 5019, 98716 Pirae; tel. 501777; fax 532801; e-mail service.spt@spt.gov.pf; internet www.spt.pf; Dir TAMATOA POMMIER.

BROADCASTING

Radio

RFO Polynésie: Centre Pamatai, Faa'a, BP 60125, 98702 Papeete; tel. 861616; fax 861611; e-mail rfopfr@mail.pf; internet polynesie.rfo.fr; f. 1934; public service radio and television station operated by Réseau France Outre-Mer (RFO), Paris; daily programmes in French and Tahitian; Dir-Gen. GENEVIÈVE GIARD; Regional Dir MICHEL KOPS.

Private Stations

Since 2004 some 17 stations have been licensed. There are currently around 25 commercial radio stations in French Polynesia.

NRJ Tahiti: BP 50, 98718 Papeete; tel. and fax 421042; fax 464346; internet www.nrj.pf; affiliated to NRJ France; French; entertainment; broadcasts 14 hrs daily; Station Man. NADINE RICHARDSON.

Radio Maohi: Maison des Jeunes, Pirae; tel. 819797; fax 825493; e-mail tereo@mail.pf; French and Tahitian; owned by the political party Tahoera'a Huiraatira; ceased broadcasting between March 2008 and May 2009.

Radio One: Fare Ute, BP 3601, 98713 Papeete; tel. 434100; fax 423406; e-mail infos@radio1.pf; internet www.radio1.pf; French; relays Europe 1 news bulletins from Paris; Editor-in-Chief FLORENCE BORDJ.

Radio (Te Reo O) Tefana (La Voix de Tefana): BP 6295, 98702 Faa'a; tel. 819797; fax 825493; e-mail tereo@mail.pf; f. 1987; French and Tahitian; affiliated to the Tavini Huiraatira party; Pres. VITO MAAMAATUAIAHUTAPU; Dir and Station Man. TERIIMATEATA MANA; Editor-in-Chief MICAËL TAPUTU.

Radio Te Vevo O Te Tiaturiraa: 51 rue Dumont d'Urville, BP 1817, 98713 Papeete; tel. 412341; fax 412322; e-mail contacts@mail.pf; religious; affiliated with the Assemblies of God church; Treas. THIERRY ALBERT.

Other radio stations include Pacific FM, Radio Fara, Radio la Voix de l'Espérance (LVDL), Radio Ma'ohi-RTL, Radio Maria No Te Hau, Radio Paofai, Radio Te Vevo No Papara, Star FM and Tiare FM.

Television

RFO Polynésie: see Radio.

TNS (Tahiti Nui Satellite): 8 rue de la Reine Pomare IV, 98714 Papeete; tel. 414370; fax 432707; e-mail tns@opt.pf; internet www.tns.pf; f. 2000; 100% owned by the Office des Postes et Télécommunications; news and entertainment; relays 25 television channels and 6 radio channels, in French, Tahitian and English, incl. TNTV; also relays ABC Asia Pacific Television, Australia, and Canal Plus, France; Man. VETEA TROUCHE-BONNO; over 10,000 subscribers.

TNTV (Tahiti Nui Television): Quartier Mission, BP 348, 98713 Papeete; tel. 473636; fax 532721; e-mail redaction@tntv.pf; internet www.tntv.pf; f. 2000; broadcasts in French and Tahitian 19 hours daily; Chair. JOËL ALLAIN; Dir-Gen. YVES HAUPERT.

Finance

(cap. = capital; res = reserves; dep. = deposits; m. = million; brs = branches; amounts in francs CFP)

BANKING

Commercial Banks

Banque de Polynésie SA: 355 blvd Pomare, BP 530, 98713 Papeete; tel. 466666; fax 466664; e-mail bdp@sg-bdp.pf; internet www.sg-bdp.pf; f. 1973; 80% owned by Société Générale, France; cap. 1,380.0m., res 5,214.3m., dep. 133,725.2m. (Dec. 2009); Chair. JEAN-LOUIS MATTEI; Gen. Man. FRÉDÉRIC COIN; 14 brs.

Banque de Tahiti SA: 38 rue François Cardella, BP 1602, 98713 Papeete; tel. 417000; fax 423376; e-mail contact@bt.pf; internet www.banque-tahiti.pf; f. 1969; owned by Financière Océor (95.4%); merged with Banque Paribas de Polynésie in 1998; cap. 1,814.8m., res 5,271.2m., dep. 180,703.7m. (Dec. 2008); Chair. CHRISTIAN CAMUS; Dir-Gen. PATRICE TEPELIAN; 18 brs.

Banque SOCREDO—Société de Crédit et de Développement de l'Océanie: 115 rue Dumont d'Urville, BP 130, 98713 Papeete; tel. 415123; fax 415283; e-mail socres@bank-socredo.pf; internet www.socredo.pf; f. 1959; public body; in partnership with French cos BNP Paribas, Cardif Assurance and Crédit Agricole, which provide technical assistance; cap. 22,000.0m., res 6,774.9m., dep. 205,874.1m. (Dec. 2009); Pres. MICHEL JACQUIER; Gen. Man. JAMES ESTALL; 26 brs.

Insurance

AGF Vie & AGF IART Polynésie Française: Immeuble Sienne, rue Dumont d'Urville, BP 4452, 98713 Papeete; tel. 549100; fax 549101; e-mail gestion-vie@agf.pf; internet www.allianz.fr; life and general non-life insurance.

GAN Pacifique: 9 ave Bruat, BP 339, 98713 Papeete; tel. 503150; fax 431918; subsidiary of Groupama, France; general non-life insurance; Chair. JEAN-FRANÇOIS LEMOUX; CEO PASCAL ALEXANDRE.

Poe-ma Insurances: Marina Fare Ute, BP 4652, 98713 Papeete; tel. 502650; fax 450097; e-mail info@poema.pf; internet www.poema.pf; f. 1991; general non-life insurance; Man. Dir VINCENT GEORGE.

Trade and Industry

GOVERNMENT AGENCIES

Délégation pour la Promotion des Investissements (DPI): Immeuble Lejeune, 1er étage, bâtiment D, 82 rue du Général de Gaulle, BP 504, 98713 Papeete; tel. 472220; fax 472221; e-mail invest@tahiti-invest.com; internet www.tahiti-invest.com; Dir RICHARD CHIN FOO.

Etablissement Public des Grands Travaux (EGT): 51 rue du Commandant Destremeau, BP 9030, Motu Uta, 98715 Papeete; tel. 508100; fax 508102; e-mail contact@egt.pf; internet www.egt.pf; responsible for public works; Pres. JONAS TAHUAITU; Dir ERIC NOBLE-DEMAY.

Service de l'Artisanat Traditionnel (ART): Ancien Immeuble Royal Confort, 2ème étage, Fare Ute, BP 4451, 98713 Papeete; tel. 545400; fax 532321; e-mail secretariat@artisanat.gov.pf; Dir LAETITIA GALENON.

Service de l'Emploi, de la Formation et de la Insertion Professionnelles (SEFI): Immeuble Papineau, rue Tepano Jaussen, 2ème étage, BP 540, 98713 Papeete; tel. 461212; fax 450280; internet www.sefi.pf; Dir PAUL NATIER.

Service du Commerce Extérieur: 53 rue Nansouty, Immeuble Teissier au 1er étage, BP 20727, 98713 Papeete; tel. 506464; fax 436420; e-mail commerceexterieur@economie.gov.pf; internet www.tahiti-export.pf; Dir WILLIAM VANIZETTE.

Service du Développement de l'Industrie et des Métiers (SDIM): BP 9055, Motu Uta, 98715 Papeete; tel. 502880; fax

412645; e-mail infos@sdim.pf; internet www.sdim.pf; f. 1988; industry and small-business devt administration; Dir DENIS GRELLIER.

Société de Financement du Développement de la Polynésie Française (SOFIDEP): Centre Paofai, Bâtiment BC, 1er étage, blvd Pomare, BP 345, 98713 Papeete; tel. 509330; fax 509333; e-mail sem.sofidep@mail.pf; Dir PIERRE FONTAINE.

DEVELOPMENT ORGANIZATIONS

Agence Française de Développement (AFD): Immeuble Hoku-le'a, 2 rue Cook Paofai, BP 578, 98713 Papeete; tel. 544600; fax 544601; e-mail afdpapeete@pf.groupe-afd.org; internet www.afd.fr; public body; devt finance institute; Dir FRANÇOIS GIOVALUCCHI.

Moruroa e Tatou (Moruroa et Nous): 403 blvd Pomare, BP 5456, 98716 Pirae, Papeete; tel. 460666; e-mail moruroaetatou@mail.pf; internet www.moruroaetatou.com; f. 2001; represents fmr employees of the Centre d'Expérimentation du Pacifique (CEP) and their families; Pres. ROLAND POUIRA OLDHAM; c. 4,500 mems.

SODEP (Société pour le Développement et l'Expansion du Pacifique): BP 4441, Papeete; tel. 429449; f. 1961; est. by a consortium of banks and private interests; regional devt and finance co.

CHAMBERS OF COMMERCE

Chambre de Commerce, d'Industrie, des Services et des Métiers de Polynésie Française (CCISM): 41 rue du Docteur Cassiau, BP 118, 98713 Papeete; tel. 472700; fax 540701; e-mail info@cci.pf; internet www.ccism.pf; f. 1880; Pres. GILLES YAU; Gen. Man. ABNER GILLOUX; 34 mems.

Chambre d'Agriculture et de la Pêche Lagonaire: route de l'Hippodrome, BP 5383, Pirae; tel. 425393; fax 438754; e-mail courrier@vanille.pf; f. 1886; Pres. HENRI TAURAA; Sec.-Gen. JACQUES ROOMATAAROA; 10 mems.

Jeune Chambre Economique de Tahiti: BP 20669, Papeete; tel. 810114; fax 702703; e-mail contact@jcitahiti.com; internet www.jcitahiti.com; Pres. SANDIRA DEROCK.

EMPLOYERS' ORGANIZATIONS

Confédération Générale des Petites et Moyennes Entreprises de Polynésie Française Te Rima Rohi (CGPME): BP 1733, 98713 Papeete; tel. 426333; fax 835608; e-mail courrier@cgpme.pf; internet www.cgpme.pf; Pres. CHRISTOPHE PLÉE; c. 1,000 mems.

Affiliated organizations include:

Chambre Syndicale des Fleuristes de Polynésie Française: tel. 800505; fax 505659; e-mail tahitifleurs@mail.pf; Pres. ALAIN MENARD.

Syndicat des Gérants de Stations Services (SGSS): tel. 455479; fax 427314; Pres. CHRISTIAN BASTIEN.

Syndicat des Restaurants, Bars et Snacks Bars de Polynésie Française (SRBSBPF): Le Mandarin, BP 302, 98713 Papeete; tel. 503350; fax 421632; e-mail charl.beaumont@mail.pf; Pres. CHARLES BEAUMONT.

Syndicat Polynésien des Entreprises et Prestataires de Service (SPEPS): tel. 584629; fax 545641; e-mail rdp@mail.pf; Pres. SÉBASTIEN BOUZARD (acting).

Union Polynésienne de l'Hôtellerie (UPHO): 76 rue Wallis, BP 1733 Motu Uta, Papeete; tel. 426333; fax 429553; e-mail chris.beaumont@mail.pf; Pres. CHRISTOPHE BEAUMONT.

Union Polynésienne des Professions Libérales (UPPL): BP 4554, Papeete; e-mail gibeaux.tahiti@mail.pf; Pres. CHARLIE GIBEAUX.

Conseil des Entreprises de Polynésie Française (CEPF): Immeuble Farnham, rue Clappier, BP 972, 98713 Papeete; tel. 541040; fax 423237; e-mail cepf@cepf.pf; internet www.cepf.pf; f. 1983; fmrly Conseil des Employeurs; affiliated to Mouvement des Entreprises de France (MEDEF); comprises 15 professional and interprofessional orgs, representing 500 cos; Pres. LUC TAPETA-SERVONNAT; Sec.-Gen. JEAN-CLAUDE LECUELLE.

Affiliated organizations include:

Association des Transporteurs Aériens Locaux de Polynésie Française (ATAL): BP 314, 98713 Papeete; tel. 864004; fax 864009; Pres. MARCEL GALENON.

Association Tahitienne des Professionnels de l'Audiovisuelle: Papeete.

Chambre Syndicale des Commissionnaires en Douane, Agents de Fret et Déménageurs de Polynésie Française: BP 972, 98713 Papeete; tel. 541040; fax 423237; e-mail cscdafd@cepf.pf; Pres. TITAINA BOURNE.

Comité de Polynésie de l'Association Française des Banques: Papeete; tel. 426603; fax 26605; Pres. ERIC POMMIER.

Fédération Générale du Commerce: BP 1607, 98713 Papeete; tel. 541042; fax 422359; e-mail fgc@mail.pf; internet www.fgc.pf; Pres. JACQUES BILLON-TYRARD; Sec. PATRICIA LO MONACO.

Organisation Professionnelle du Conseil de l'Intérim et de la Formation: Papeete.

Syndicat des Agences Maritimes au Long Cours: BP 274, 98713 Papeete; tel. 428972; fax 432184; e-mail amitahiti@amitahiti.pf; Pres. MAEVA SIU.

Syndicat des Employeurs du Secteur de l'Assurance (SESA): BP 358, 98713 Papeete; tel. 506262; fax 506263; Pres. ALAIN LEBRIS.

Syndicat des Industriels de Polynésie Française (SIPOF): Immeuble Farnham, BP 3521, 98713 Papeete; tel. 541040; fax 423237; e-mail sipof@cepf.pf; internet www.sipof.pf; f. 1974; represents workers in industry, engineering, manufacturing and printing; Pres. FRANCIS GUEBEL; Sec. SÉBASTIEN MOLLARD; 2,240 mems in 62 cos.

Syndicat Professionnel des Concessionnaires Automobiles: BP 916, 98713 Papeete; tel. 454545; fax 431260; Pres. PAUL YEO CHICHONG.

Union des Industriels de la Manutention Portuaire (UNIM): BP 570, 98713 Papeete; tel. 545700; fax 426262; Pres. JULES CHANGUES.

Groupement Interprofessionnel du Monoï de Tahiti (GIMT): BP 14 165, Arue, Tahiti; tel. 414851; fax 431849; internet www.monoidetahiti.pf; f. 1992; asscn of monoï manufacturers.

UTILITIES

Electricity

Electricité de Tahiti (EDT): route de Puurai, BP 8021, Faa'a-Puurai; tel. 867704; fax 834439; e-mail edt@edt.pf; internet www.edt.pf; subsidiary of Groupe Suez, France; Pres. HERVÉ DUBOST-MARTIN; Gen. Man. CHRISTIAN LEKIEFFRE; c. 60,000 customers (2005).

Water

Société Polynésienne des Eaux et Assainissements: BP 20795, 98713 Papeete; fax 421548; e-mail spea@spea.pf.

MAJOR COMPANIES

Brasserie de Tahiti: pl. Notre Dame, BP 597, 98713 Papeete; tel. 467600; fax 467639; e-mail webmaster@brasseriedetahiti.pf; internet www.brasseriedetahiti.pf; f. 1914; subsidiary of Groupe Martin; revenue €90m. (2005); mfrs and distributors of beer, soft drinks, fruit juices and bottled water; CEO JEAN-PIERRE FOURCADE; c. 350 employees.

CEGELEC Polynésie SA: Z. I. de Fare Ute, BP 5020, Pirae, 98716 Papeete; tel. 414100; fax 414182; e-mail frederic.dock@cegelec.pf; installation and maintenance of electrical and electronic equipment; revenue CFP 3,300m. (2004); Chair. JEAN-PAUL AULAS; 296 employees (2003).

Financière Hôtelière Polynésienne (FHP): BP 718, 98713 Papeete; hotel construction, management and devt; revenue CFP 3,658m. (2004); CEO CHRISTIAN VERNAUDON; c. 430 employees (2003).

SARL Boyer: Z. I. de Tipaerui, 98713 Papeete; tel. 548877; construction and civil engineering; revenue CFP 5,900m. (2004); Man. LAURENT SEIGNOBOS; 400 employees.

SEGC Carrefour: BP 416, 98713 Papeete; f. 1985; subsidiary of Groupe Louis Wane; supermarket retail and distribution; revenue CFP 28,500m. (2004); CEO LOUIS WANE; 710 employees (2003).

SIPAC: Vallée de Tuauru, BP 11984, 98709 Mahina; tel. 540550; fax 482268; e-mail arlindotorrao@sipac.pf; wholesale retail and distribution; revenue CFP 2,803m. (2004); Chair. NADJI OUHARROU; 74 employees (2003).

SODIVA SA: blvd Pomare, Front de Mer, BP 1724, 98713 Papeete; tel. 543900; fax 435274; e-mail sodiva@mail.pf; internet www.sodiva.pf; importers and retailers of motor vehicles; revenue CFP 6,300m. (2004); c. 150 employees (2003).

SOPADEP SA: route de Ceinture, Tipaerui, BP 1617, 98713 Papeete; tel. 475475; fax 475400; e-mail dir@sopadep.pf; internet www.sopadep.pf; importers and retailers of motor vehicles; revenue CFP 7,250m. (2006); Pres. JACQUES SOLARI; 150 employees (2005).

Tahiti Automobiles: 192 ave Georges Clémenceau, BP 1619, 98713 Papeete; internet www.tahitiauto.pf; importers and retailers of motor vehicles; revenue CFP 4,300m. (2004); 110 employees (2003).

Wing Chong SAS: Immeuble Wing Chong, Fare Ute, BP 230, Papeete; tel. 543552; fax 543553; e-mail info@wico.pf; wholesale retail and distribution; CEO LÉON DEVON; 93 employees (2003).

TRADE UNIONS

Under French Polynesian legislation, to be officially recognized, trade unions must receive the vote of at least 5% of the work-force at professional elections.

Chambre Syndicale des Métiers du Génie Civil et des Travaux Publics (CSMGCTP): BP 51120, 98716 Pirae; tel. 502100; fax 436922; Pres. DANIEL PALACZ.

Confédération des Syndicats des Travailleurs de Polynésie/ Force Ouvrière (CSTP/FO): Immeuble Farnham, 1er étage, BP 1201, 98713 Papeete; tel. 426049; fax 450635; e-mail pfrebault@cstp-fo.pf; Pres. COCO TERAIEFA CHANG; Sec.-Gen. PATRICK GALENON.

Confédération des Syndicats Indépendants de la Polynésie Française (CSIP): Immeuble Allegret, 1er étage, ave du Prince Hinoï, BP 468, 98713 Papeete; tel. 532274; fax 532275; Sec.-Gen. CYRIL LE GAYIC.

Confédération Syndicale A Tia I Mua (CFDT): Fare Ia Ora, Mamao, BP 4523, Papeete; tel. 544010; fax 450245; e-mail atiaimua@ifrance.com; affiliated to the Confédération Française Démocratique du Travail; Gen. Sec. JEAN-MARIE YAN TU.

Conseil Fédéral des Syndicats Libres de Polynésie O Oe To Oe Rima: Immeuble Brown, 1er étage, BP 52866, 98716 Pirae; tel. 483445; fax 483445; Gen. Sec. RONALD TEROROTUA.

Union Fédérale des Syndicats Autonomes/Confédération OTAHI (OTAHI UFSA): ancien Immeuble SETIL, 1er étage, ave du Prince Hinoi, BP 148, 98713 Papeete; tel. 450654; fax 451327; Sec.-Gen. LUCIE TIFFENAT.

Transport

ROADS

French Polynesia has 792 km of roads, of which about one-third are bitumen-surfaced and two-thirds stone-surfaced.

Direction des Transports Terrestres: 93 avenue Pomare V, Fariipiti, BP 4586, 98713 Papeete; tel. 502060; fax 436021; e-mail dtt@transport.gov.pf; internet www.transports-terrestres.pf; f. 1988; Dir ROLAND TSU.

SHIPPING

The principal port is at Papeete, on Tahiti.

Port Authority: Port Autonome de Papeete, BP 9164, Motu Uta, 98715 Papeete; tel. 474800; fax 421950; e-mail portppt@portppt.pf; internet www.portdepapeete.pf; Harbour Master MARCEL PELLETIER; Port Dir PATRICK BORDET.

Agence Maritime Internationale de Tahiti: BP 274, 98713 Papeete; tel. 428972; fax 432184; e-mail amitahiti@amitahiti.pf; internet www.amitahiti.com; f. 1978; services from Asia, the USA, Australia, New Zealand and Europe; Gen. Mans JEAN SIU, MAEVA SIU.

CMA CGM Papeete: 2 rue Wallis, BP 96, Papeete; tel. 545252; fax 436806; e-mail ppt.genmbox@cma-cgm.com; fmrly CGM Tour du Monde SA; shipowners and agents; international freight services; Gen. Man. STEPHANE MERCADAL.

Compagnie Polynésienne de Transport Maritime: BP 220, 98713 Papeete; tel. 426242; fax 434889; e-mail aranui@mail.pf; internet www.aranui.com; shipping co; CEO JEAN WONG; Gen. Man. PHILIPPE WONG.

EURL Transport Maritime des Tuamotu Ouest: BP 1816, 98713 Papeete; tel. 422553; fax 422557; inter-island passenger service; Dir SIMÉON RICHMOND.

SA Compagnie Française Maritime de Tahiti: Immeuble Importex, No. 45, Fare Ute, POB 368, 98713 Papeete; tel. 426393; fax 420617; e-mail taporo@mail.pf; Pres. and Man. MORTON GARBUTT.

SARL Société de Transport Insulaire Maritime (STIM): BP 635, 98713 Papeete; tel. 549954; fax 452444; Dir ROLAND PAQUIER.

Société de Navigation des Australes: BP 1890, Papeete; tel. 509609; fax 420609; e-mail snathp@mail.pf; inter-island passenger service; Dir HERVÉ DANTON.

CIVIL AVIATION

There is one international airport, Faa'a airport, 6 km from Papeete, on Tahiti, and there are numerous smaller airports and aerodromes throughout French Polynesia. Since October 2004 the Government has commissioned studies into the possible siting of a new international airport on Tubai in the Austral Islands, or in the Marquesas at either Nuku Hiva or Hiva Oa. International services are operated by Air France, Air Tahiti Nui, Air New Zealand, LAN-Chile, Hawaiian Airlines (USA) and Air Calédonie International.

Service d'Etat de l'Aviation Civile: BP 6404, 98702, Faa'a, Papeete; tel. 861000; fax 861009; e-mail webmaster@seac.pf; internet www.seac.pf; Dir THIERRY RÉVIRON.

Aéroport de Tahiti (ADT): BP 60161, 98702, Faa'a Centre; tel. 866060; fax 837391; e-mail secretariat@tahiti-aeroport.pf; internet www.tahiti-aeroport.pf; f. 2010; 50% govt-owned; management and devt of airports at Faa'a, Bora Bora, Raiatea and Rangiroa; Dir-Gen. ALAIN BERQUEZ.

Air Moorea: BP 6019, 98702 Faa'a; tel. 864262; fax 864269; e-mail direction@airmoorea.pf; internet www.airmoorea.pf; f. 1968; operates internal services between Tahiti and Moorea Island and domestic charter flights; Pres. MARCEL GALENON; CEO FREDDY CHANSEAU.

Air Tahiti: BP 314, 98713 Papeete; tel. 864012; fax 864069; e-mail direction.generale@airtahiti.pf; internet www.airtahiti.aero; f. 1953; Air Polynésie 1970–87; operates domestic services to 46 islands; Chair. CHRISTIAN VERNAUDON; Gen. Man. MARCEL GALENON.

Air Tahiti Nui: Immeuble Dexter, Pont de l'Est, BP 1673, 98713 Papeete; tel. 460303; fax 460290; e-mail fly@airtahitinui.pf; internet www.airtahitinui.com; f. 1996; commenced operations 1998; scheduled services to the USA, France, Japan, New Zealand and Australia; CEO CÉDRIC PASTOUR; Sec.-Gen. STEPHEN HOWAN.

Tourism

Tourism is an important and developed industry in French Polynesia, particularly on Tahiti. However, tourist arrivals decreased from 218,241 in 2007 to 153,919 in 2010. Most visitors were from the USA, France and Japan. The number of hotels increased from 44 in 2001 to 49 in 2005, while the number of available rooms decreased from 4,418 to 3,326 during the same period. In 2008 earnings from tourism were an estimated US $745m.

GIE Tahiti Tourisme: Fare Manihini, blvd Pomare, BP 65, 98713 Papeete; tel. 505700; fax 436619; e-mail info@tahiti-tourisme.pf; internet www.tahiti-tourisme.pf; f. 1966 as autonomous public body; transformed into private corpn in 1993; relaunched Dec. 2005 following merger between GIE Tahiti Tourisme and Tahiti Manava Visitors' Bureau; Chair. HEREMOANA MAAMAATUAIAHUTAPU; Dir-Gen. TEVA JANICAUD.

Service du Tourisme (SDT): Paofai Bldg (Entry D), blvd Pomare, Papeete; tel. 476200; fax 476202; e-mail sdt@tourisme.gov.pf; govt dept; manages Special Fund for Tourist Development; Dir GÉRARD VANIZETTE.

Defence

As assessed at November 2010, France maintained a force of 640 army and 710 navy personnel in French Polynesia. France began testing nuclear weapons at Mururoa and Fangataufa atolls, in the Tuamotu Archipelago, in 1966. The military presence has been largely connected with the Centre d'Expérimentation du Pacifique (CEP) and the Commission d'Energie Atomique (CEA). An indefinite suspension of tests was announced in mid-1993. In June 1995, however, the French Government announced its decision to resume nuclear testing at Mururoa Atoll. The final test was conducted in January 1996. The defence budget for 2006 was 24,000m. francs CFP.

Commander of the French Armed Forces in French Polynesia, of the Pacific Maritime Area and of the Centre d'Expérimentation du Pacifique: Cdre JÉRÔME RÉGNIER.

Education

Education is compulsory for eight years between six and 14 years of age. It is free of charge for day pupils in government schools. Primary education, lasting six years, is financed by the territorial budget, while secondary and technical education are supported by state funds. A total of 14,306 children were enrolled in kindergarten in 2008/09. In 2010/11 39,991 pupils attended primary school. Secondary education was provided by public lycées, public high schools and private or church schools. A total of 32,418 pupils attended secondary school in 2010/11. The French Polynesian Government assumed responsibility for secondary education in 1988. Technical and professional education includes eight technical institutions, a tourism training programme, preparation for entrance to the metropolitan Grandes Ecoles, a National Conservatory for Arts and Crafts and training centres for those in the construction industry, health services, traditional handicrafts, primary school teaching and social work. The French University of the Pacific was established in French Polynesia in 1987. In 1999 it was divided into two separate branches, of which the University of French Polynesia is now based in Papeete. In 2009/10 a total of 2,922 students were enrolled at the Papeete branch. In 2004 French state spending on education, higher education and research amounted to 50,500m. francs CFP.

THE WALLIS AND FUTUNA ISLANDS

Introduction

The French Overseas Collectivity of the Wallis and Futuna Islands comprises two groups: the Wallis Islands, including Uvea (Wallis Island), and 19 volcanic and coralline islets (*motu*) on the surrounding reef; and, 230 km to the south-west, the volcanic and mountainous Futuna (Horn) Islands, comprising the two small islands of Futuna and Alofi (the latter being uninhabited owing to lack of water). The islands are located some 600 km to the north-east of Fiji, south-east of Tuvalu and west of Samoa. The total area is 142 sq km. The Collectivity also includes a group of uninhabited volcanic and coralline islets (18 sq km). Uvea rises to 151 m at Mt Lulu, Futuna to 524 m at Mt Puke, and Alofi to 417 m at Mt Kolofau. Temperatures average between 23°C (73°F) and 30°C (86°F), and there is a cyclone season between December and March.

The inhabitants are mainly Polynesian and nominally Roman Catholic. French is an official language and widely spoken, but the indigenous languages of Uvean (Wallisian) and Futunian are generally used. At the census of July 2003 the population of the islands totalled 14,944, more than two-thirds living on Uvea. The August 2008 census indicated that the population had decreased by approximately 10% since 2003, to 13,445. The capital is the town of Mata'Utu on Uvea.

The islands were originally settled by proto-Polynesian peoples: Wallis by people from Tonga before 1300 BC, and Futuna by those from Samoa and northern Fiji in around 800 BC. Futuna was subsequently discovered by Dutch navigators in 1616, and Uvea by the English in 1767. Three kingdoms later emerged, and in 1837 the first Marist missionaries arrived. By 1842 the majority of the indigenous population had been converted to Christianity. In April 1842 the authorities in Wallis requested French protection. Between 1843 and 1851 there was a *fakauvea* war between the Catholic majority and Methodist minority, assisted by Tonga, which ended when 500 Wallisians left for Tonga. Protectorate status was formalized in 1886 for Wallis and in 1887 for the two kingdoms of Futuna, but customary law remained in force. The islands were never formally annexed but were treated as a dependency of New Caledonia.

During the Second World War Wallis was used as an air-force base by the USA. After the war, many young people began to migrate to New Caledonia and the New Hebrides (now Vanuatu). In 1959, following a request by the traditional Kings and chiefs, a referendum was held at which 94.4% of the electorate voted in favour of integration into the French Republic. The islands formally became an Overseas Territory in July 1961. Government is conducted by the Chief Administrator, the representative of the French State, with the advice of the Territorial Council (including the three Kings) and the Territorial Assembly, elected for the first time in 1961. Wallis and Futuna also has representation in the French Assemblée nationale (National Assembly). Intervention by the French administration in customary affairs is resented and has been a cause of tension. The islands received the status of Overseas Collectivity following a constitutional revision in March 2003.

By 1990 the emigration rate had risen to over 50%: in October of that year 13,705 people lived in the Territory, while 14,186 were resident in New Caledonia. At the 1996 census the number of Wallisians and Futunians resident in New Caledonia had increased to 17,563. The principal reason for emigration was the lack of employment opportunities. In June 2001 senior officials from Wallis and Futuna and New Caledonia agreed to redefine their bilateral relationship under the Nouméa Accord on greater autonomy, signed in 1998. In exchange for controlling immigration, New Caledonia stated that it would make a financial contribution to economic development in Wallis and Futuna. The Nouméa Accord also envisaged a separate arrangement providing for open access to New Caledonia for residents of Wallis and Futuna.

A long-standing dispute over the ownership of a Wallisian settlement in New Caledonia, Ave Maria, led to intense fighting between the Wallisian and indigenous Kanak communities from December 2001. Negotiations mediated by the French High Commissioner to New Caledonia resulted in an agreement to end the violence, which had claimed three lives. There was renewed fighting in June 2003, but by mid-September the remaining Wallisian families had been resettled in Nouméa. A special accord was signed in December governing relations between France, New Caledonia and Wallis and Futuna. It was hoped that Wallis and Futuna would become more self-sufficient in the areas of health and secondary education, and that the islanders would be encouraged to remain there, while those already settled in New Caledonia would become more integrated.

The throne of Sigave, the northern kingdom on the island of Futuna, has been the subject of various disputes. In October 1994 it was reported that the King of Sigave had been deposed by a unanimous decision of the kingdom's chiefs. The action followed the appointment of two customary leaders to represent the Futunian community in New Caledonia, which had led to unrest among the inhabitants of Sigave. In October 2003 Pasilio Keletaona was deposed as King of Sigave by members of his own clan. He was succeeded in March 2004 by Visesio Moeliku. In November 2002 Soane Patita Maituka was enthroned as King of Alo (known as the Tu'i Agaifo), following the deposition of Sagato Alofi in the previous month. In March 1999, meanwhile, festivities were held to commemorate the 40th anniversary of the accession of the King of Wallis Island, Lavelua Tomasi Kulimoetoke. Kulimoetoke passed away in May 2007, and was succeeded by Kapiliele Faupala in July 2008. In February 2008, following criticism of the style of leadership of the King of Alo and a unanimous decision by the four chiefly clans of Alo, the King was removed from office. Petelo Vikena, a former public servant, was subsequently chosen to replace him. However, the choice of Vikena was not supported by some chiefly clans, which criticized the unilateral appointment by the chiefly council and the lack of consensus. In January 2010, amid reports of acts of vandalism against royal property, Petelo Vikena abdicated as King of Alo. Meanwhile, the monarch of Sigave was reported to have relinquished his position in August 2009. The kingdom of Futuna was thus placed in an unusual situation, being required to function without either of its two Kings. In July 2010 Polikalepo Kolivai was crowned King of Sigave; the appointment was reportedly opposed by some chiefly clans on the grounds that they had not been properly consulted.

The economic development of Wallis and Futuna has been limited by the lack of natural resources and of local industry, as well as by the islands' isolated location. Most monetary income on the islands is derived from government employment (accounting for 75% of employees at September 2003) and remittances sent home by islanders employed abroad. There is a high level of unemployment. Agricultural activity is of a subsistence nature. Yams, taro, bananas, cassava and other food crops are cultivated. Pigs and chickens are reared. The domestic fishing catch was estimated at 750 metric tons in 2009. Deep-water fishing fleets from Japan and the Republic of Korea are licensed to catch up to 3,000 metric tons of fish per year. The only significant industry is the manufacture of traditional handicrafts. Traditional food products, mother of pearl and handicrafts are the only important export commodities, with the principal market having been the Wallisian community in New Caledonia. France remained the leading source of imports in 2007. Tourism remains undeveloped. Aid from France over the five-year period 2007–11 was projected at some US $50m. In November 1999 Wallis and Futuna signed a co-operation agreement with the European Union (EU). In March 2008 it was announced that the EU had allocated the sum of €16.49m. to development projects in Wallis and Futuna, under the 10th European Development Fund (EDF) encompassing the period 2008–13. Areas of focus were to include sources of renewable energy, improved management of the islands' natural resources and sustainable development, in addition to the priority sectors of education and health. About 80% of Futuna's crops were reported to have been destroyed by a cyclone in March 2010, leading to serious food shortages. By May, according to the French government minister responsible, a total of US $700,000 had been allocated to the relief effort. The infrastructure of Futuna was badly damaged, requiring the implementation of a major repair programme. Also in 2010, supplies of electricity and water on Wallis were disrupted by a dispute at the local utility company.

Statistical Survey

Source (unless otherwise indicated): Service Territorial de la Statistique et des Etudes Economiques, Immeuble Pukavila, RT1, BP 638, Mata'Utu, Falaleu, 98600 Wallis; tel. 722403; fax 722487; e-mail stats@wallis.co.nc; internet www.spc.int/prism/Country/WF/WFindex.html.

AREA AND POPULATION

Area (sq km): 142. *By Island:* Uvea (Wallis Island) 78; Futuna Island 46; Alofi Island 18. The Collectivity also includes a group of uninhabited volcanic and coralline islets (18 sq km).

Population: Total population 14,944 at census of 22 July 2003. Total population 13,445 (males 6,669, females 6,776) at census of 21 July 2008: Wallis Island—Uvea 9,207; Futuna Island 4,238 (Alo 2,655, Sigave 1,583).

Density (2008 census): 94.7 per sq km.

Population by Age and Sex (2008 census): *0–14:* 4,081 (2,181 males, 1,900 females); *15–64:* 8,387 (4,047 males, 4,340 females); *65* *and over:* 977 (441 males, 536 females); *Total:* 13,445 (6,669 males, 6,776 females).

Principal Villages (population at 2008 census): Mata'Utu (capital) 1,120; Taoa 623; Utufua 622.

Births, Marriages and Deaths (2008): Registered live births 185 (birth rate 13.6 per 1,000); Registered marriages 53 (marriage rate 3.9 per 1,000); Registered deaths 90 (death rate 6.7 per 1,000).

Life Expectancy (years at birth): 74.3 (males 73.1; females 75.5) in 2003.

Economically Active Population (2008 census): Total employed 3,373 (males 1,867, females 1,506); Unemployed persons seeking work 496 (males 296, females 200); Total labour force 3,869 (males 2,163, females 1,706).

HEALTH AND WELFARE

Key Indicators

Total Fertility Rate (children per woman, census of 2008): 2.0.

Under-5 Mortality Rate (per 1,000 live births, average of 2005–2008): 5.2.

Physicians (per 1,000 head, 2003): 0.7.

Access to Sanitation (% of persons, census of July 2003): 80.9.

Access to Water (% of persons, census of July 2003): 68.5.

For definitions, see explanatory note on p. vi.

AGRICULTURE, ETC.

Principal Crops ('000 metric tons, 2009, FAO estimates): Cassava 1.8; Taro (coco yam) 1.9; Yams 0.5; Other roots and tubers 1.1; Coconuts 2.7; Vegetables and melons 0.7; Bananas 5.4. *Aggregate Production* ('000 metric tons, may include official, semi-official or estimated data): Total fruits (excl. melons) 11.1; Total roots and tubers 5.2.

Livestock ('000 head, year ending September 2009, FAO estimates): Pigs 25; Goats 7; Chickens 65.

Livestock Products (metric tons, 2009, FAO estimates): Pig meat 315; Goat meat 15; Chicken meat 48; Cows' milk 48; Hen eggs 41; Honey 10.

Fishing (metric tons, live weight, 2009, FAO estimates): Total catch 750 (Marine fishes 743). Figures exclude Trochus shells (metric tons) 29.

Source: FAO.

INDUSTRY

Selected Products (metric tons, 2009, unless otherwise indicated): Coconut oil 164 (FAO estimate); Copra 252.5 (2006, FAO estimate); Electric energy 19.8m. kWh (Wallis Island 16.7; Futuna Island 3.1) (2010). Sources: FAO; Institut d'Emission d'Outre-Mer.

FINANCE

Currency and Exchange Rates: see French Polynesia.

Territorial Budget (million francs CFP, 2006): *Revenue:* Current 2,683; Capital 189; Fiscal adjustment –14; Total 2,858. *Expenditure:* Current 2,850; Capital 247; Total 3,097.

Aid from France ('000 million francs CFP, 2008): Total expenditure 12.1 (Education 5.7, Health 3.1, Other expenditure by Ministère de l'Outre-Mer 3.3). Source: Institut d'Emission d'Outre-Mer.

Money Supply (million francs CFP at 31 December 2010): Currency in circulation 2,137; Demand deposits 3,581; *Total money* 5,718. Source: Institut d'Emission d'Outre-Mer.

Cost of Living (Consumer Price Index at June; base: June 2008 = 100): All items 100.3 in 2009.

EXTERNAL TRADE

Principal Commodities (million francs CFP, provisional figures): *Imports c.i.f.* (2009): Prepared foodstuff 1,413; Pharmaceutical and cosmetic products 311; Household equipment 214; Transport equipment 327; Mechanical equipment 239; Electrical and electronic equipment 362; Chemicals, rubber and plastic products 237; Fuels 736; Total (incl. others) 4,747.0. *Exports f.o.b.* (2001): Preparations of molluscs and other aquatic invertebrates 0.3; Coral and shells 5.5; Braids and mats of vegetable material 0.9; Total 5.6. *2009:* Total exports 1.0. Source: mainly Institut d'Emission d'Outre-Mer.

Principal Trading Partners: *Imports c.i.f.* ('000 million francs CFP, 2007): Australia 0.7; Fiji 0.3; France (incl. Monaco) 1.5; New Caledonia 0.3; New Zealand 0.5; Singapore 0.8; Total (incl. others) 5.4. *Exports f.o.b.* (million francs CFP, 2004): Italy 4.6; Total 4.6. Source: mainly Institut d'Emission d'Outre-Mer.

TRANSPORT

Road Traffic (vehicles in use, 2001): Scooters 1,093; Cars 1,293. Source: Ministère de l'Agriculture, de l'Alimentation, de la Pêche et des Affaires Rurales, *Recensement agricole du territoire 2001.*

Shipping: *Merchant Fleet* (31 December 2008): Vessels registered 8; Displacement ('000 grt): 92.3. Source: Lloyd's Register-Fairplay, *World Fleet Statistics.*

Civil Aviation (2010): *Domestic Traffic:* Aircraft movements 1,413; Passenger movements 13,191; Freight handled 27.7 metric tons; Mail handled 11.1 metric tons. *International Traffic:* Aircraft movements 332; Passenger movements 28,654; Freight handled 176.2 metric tons; Mail handled 77.3 metric tons. Source: Institut d'Emission d'Outre-Mer.

TOURISM

Foreign Visitors (2006): *Total Arrivals:* 2,456. *Overnight Stays in Hotel Establishments:* 607.

Foreign Visitor Arrivals by Nationality (2006): Australia 37; Fiji 45; France 674; French Polynesia 62; New Caledonia 1,310; Total (incl. others) 2,456.

COMMUNICATIONS MEDIA

Telephones (2010): 3,100 main lines installed.

Internet Users (2009): 1,300.

Broadband Subscribers (2010): 1,100.

Source: International Telecommunication Union.

EDUCATION

Pre-primary (2005): 3 institutions; 260 pupils.

Primary (2010, unless otherwise indicated): 18 institutions (2008); 2,156 pupils (incl. pre-primary). Source: Institut d'Emission d'Outre-Mer.

Secondary (2010, unless otherwise indicated): 7 institutions (2 vocational) (2006); 1,901 students. Source: Institut d'Emission d'Outre-Mer.

Higher (students, 2005/06): 14 in New Caledonia; 60 in metropolitan France; 6 in French Polynesia. Source: Institut d'Emission d'Outre-Mer.

Teachers (2003): Pre-primary and primary 168; Secondary 209.

Adult Literacy Rate (census of July 2003): 78.8% (males 78.2%; females 79.3%).

Directory

The Constitution

The Territory of the Wallis and Futuna Islands has been administered according to a statute of 1961, and subsidiary legislation, under the Constitution of the Fifth Republic. The Statute declared the Wallis and Futuna Islands to be an Overseas Territory of the French Republic, of which they remain an integral part. The Statute established an administration, a Council of the Territory, a Territorial Assembly and national representation. The administrative, political and social evolution envisaged by, and enacted under, the Statute was intended to effect a smooth integration of the three customary kingdoms with the new institutions of the Territory. The Kings are assisted by ministers and the traditional chiefs. The Chief Administrator, appointed by the French Government, is the representative of the State in the Territory and is responsible for external affairs, defence, law and order, financial and educational affairs. The Chief Administrator is required to consult with the Council of the Territory, which has six members: three by right (the Kings of Wallis, Sigave and Alo) and three appointed by the Chief Administrator upon the advice of the Territorial Assembly. This Assembly assists in the administration of the Territory; there are 20 members elected on a common roll, on the basis of universal adult suffrage, for a term of up to five years. The Territorial Assembly elects, from among its own membership, a President to lead it. Wallis and Futuna elects national representatives—one Deputy to the Assemblée nationale (National Assembly), one Senator and one Economic and Social Councillor—and votes for representatives to the European Parliament in Strasbourg. In 2003 both the Assemblée nationale and Sénat (Senate) in Paris ratified amendments to the Constitution providing for Wallis and Futuna (along with French Polynesia) to be designated as an Overseas Country (Pays d'outre-mer). Following the constitutional revisions of 2003, the official status of Wallis and Futuna became that of an Overseas Collectivity (Collectivité d'outre-mer).

The Government

(October 2011)

Chief Administrator (Administrateur Supérieur): MICHEL JEANJEAN.

CONSEIL DU TERRITOIRE

The council is chaired by the Chief Administrator and comprises the members by right (the Kings of Wallis, Sigave and Alo) and three appointed members.

GOVERNMENT OFFICES

Government Headquarters: Bureau de l'Administrateur Supérieur, BP 16, Mata'Utu, Havelu, Hahake, 98600 Uvea, Wallis Islands; tel. 722727; fax 722300; e-mail adsupwf@wallis.co.nc; internet www.adsupwf.org.

Department of Catholic Schools: Direction Diocésaine de l'Enseignement Catholique, BP 80, Mata'Utu, 98600 Uvea, Wallis Islands; tel. 722766; e-mail decwf.wallis@wallis.co.nc; responsible for pre-primary and primary education since 1969.

Department of Cultural Action: BP 131, Mata'Utu, Aka'aka, 98600 Uvea, Wallis Islands; tel. 722667; fax 722563; e-mail culture.wf@mail.wf.

Department of the Environment: BP 294, Mata'Utu, Havelu, Hahake, 98600 Uvea, Wallis Islands; tel. 720351; fax 720597; e-mail senv@mail.wf.

Department of Justice: BP 12, Mata'Utu, Havelu, Hahake, 98600 Uvea, Wallis Islands; tel. 722715; fax 722531; e-mail tpi@wallis.co.nc.

Department of Labour and Social Affairs Inspection (SITAS): BP 385, Mata'Utu, Hahake, 98600 Uvea; tel. 722288; fax 722384; e-mail sitas.wf@mail.wf.

Department of Public Works and Rural Engineering: BP 13, Mata'Utu, Kafika, Hahake, 98600 Uvea, Wallis Islands; tel. 722626; fax 722115; e-mail tpwallis@mail.wf.

Department of Rural Affairs and Fisheries: BP 19, Mata'Utu, Aka'aka, 98600 Uvea, Wallis Islands; tel. 722606; fax 722544; e-mail ecoru.futuna@wallis.co.nc.

Department of Youth and Sports: BP 51, Mata'Utu, Kafika, Hahake, 98600 Uvea; tel. 722188; fax 722322; e-mail jeusport@mail.wf.

Health Agency: Agence de Santé, BP 4G, 98600 Uvea, Wallis Islands; tel. 720700; fax 723399; e-mail sante@adswf.org; operates two hospitals at Sia on Uvea and Kaleveleve on Futuna, respectively.

Legislature

ASSEMBLÉE TERRITORIALE

The Territorial Assembly has 20 members and is elected for a five-year term. Within the Assembly, ministers may form political groupings of five members or more. These groupings are not necessarily formed along party lines, and alliances may be made in support of a common cause. The most recent general election took place on 1 April 2007, at which three new members were elected.

President: VICTOR BRIAL (UMP).

Territorial Assembly: Assemblée Territoriale, BP 31, Mata'Utu, Havelu, Hahake, 98600 Uvea, Wallis Islands; tel. 722004; fax 721807; e-mail cab-pres.at@wallis.co.nc.

PARLEMENT

Deputy to the French National Assembly: ALBERT LIKUVALU (PS).

Representative to the French Senate: Fr ROBERT LAUFOAULU (UMP).

The Kingdoms

WALLIS

(Capital: Mata'Utu on Uvea)

Lavelua, King of Wallis: KAPILIELE FAUPALA.

Council of Ministers (Aliki Fau): The Council is composed of six ministers who assist the King:

Kivalu: the Prime Minister and King's spokesman at official meetings.

Mahe: the second Prime Minister and King's counsel.

Kulitea: responsible for cultural and customary matters.

Uluimonoa: responsible for the sea.

Fotuatamai: responsible for health and hygiene.

Mukoifenua: responsible for land and agriculture.

In addition, the Puliuvea is responsible for the King's security and the maintenance of public order.

The Kingdom of Wallis is divided into three administrative districts (Hihifo, Hahake, Mua), and its traditional hierarchy includes three district chiefs (Faipule), 20 village chiefs (Pule) and numerous hamlet chiefs (Lagiaki).

SIGAVE

(Capital: Leava on Futuna)

Keletaona, King of Sigave: POLIKALEPO KOLIVAI.

Council of Ministers: six ministers, chaired by the King.

The Kingdom of Sigave is located in the north of the island of Futuna; there are five village chiefs.

ALO

(Capital: Ono on Futuna)

Tu'i Agaifo, King of Alo: (vacant).

Council of Ministers: five ministers, chaired by the King.

The Kingdom of Alo comprises the southern part of the island of Futuna and the entire island of Alofi. There are nine village chiefs.

Political Organizations

Alliance: c/o Assemblée Territoriale; f. 2005; coalition of UDF mems and left-wing independents; Pres. APITONE MUNIKIHAAFATA.

Mouvement Démocrate (MoDem): c/o Assemblée Territoriale; fmrly known as Union pour la Démocratie Française; name changed as above in 2007; centrist; based on Uvean (Wallisian) support.

Union pour un Mouvement Populaire (UMP): c/o Assemblée Territoriale; f. 2002; est. as Union pour la Majorité Présidentielle; includes fmr mems of Rassemblement pour la République; centre-right; local br. of the metropolitan party; Territorial Leader ROBERT LAUFOAULU.

Union pour Wallis et Futuna (UPWF): c/o Assemblée Territoriale; f. 1994; est. as Union Populaire pour Wallis et Futuna; affiliated to Parti Socialiste of France since 1998; Leader SILIAKO LAUHEA.

Judicial System

The Statute provided for two parallel judicial systems: customary law, which applied to the indigenous population; and French State law. The competencies of the respective systems are not always clearly defined, which has been a cause of tensions between the indigenous monarchy and the French authorities. On Uvea, under customary law there are separate courts for civil matters (Fono Puleaga) and village matters (Fono Fenua). Disputes over land are dealt with by the Council of the Territory, presided over by the King. A similar system exists on Futuna. Judgments may be referred to a Chambre d'Annulation at the Court of Appeal at Nouméa, New Caledonia.

Court of the First Instance: Tribunal de Première Instance, BP 12, Havelu, Mata'Utu, Hahake, 98600 Uvea, Wallis Islands; tel. 722715; fax 722531; e-mail pr.tpi@wallis.co.nc; f. 1983; Pres. FRANCIS ALARY.

Religion

Almost all of the inhabitants profess Christianity and are adherents of the Roman Catholic Church.

CHRISTIANITY

The Roman Catholic Church

The Territory comprises a single diocese, suffragan to the archdiocese of Nouméa (New Caledonia). The diocese estimated that there were 14,400 adherents at 31 December 2007. The Bishop participates in the Catholic Bishops' Conference of the Pacific, currently based in Fiji.

Bishop of Wallis and Futuna: GHISLAIN MARIE RAOUL SUZANNE DE RASILLY, Evêché Lano, BP G6, Mata'Utu, 98600 Uvea, Wallis Islands; tel. 722932; fax 722783; e-mail eveche.wallis@wallis.co.nc.

The Press

'Uvea Mo Futuna: Tuku'atu Ha'afuasia, Uvea, Wallis Islands; e-mail filihau@uvea-mo-futuna.com; f. 2002; daily; electronic; Editor FILIHAU ASI TALATINI.

The Territory's only newspaper, *Te-Fenua Fo'ou*, was forced to close in April 2002, following a dispute with the King of Wallis. *Fenua Magazine* was launched by a group of local business people in September 2002 but closed in September 2003 owing to a lack of advertising revenue. There is currently no printed press in Wallis and Futuna.

Broadcasting and Communications

TELECOMMUNICATIONS

France Câbles et Radio Wallis et Futuna (FCR WF): Télécommunications Extérieures de Wallis et Futuna, BP 54, Mata'Utu, 98600 Uvea, Wallis Islands; tel. 722436; fax 722255; e-mail fcr@mail.wf; owned by France Telecom; Man. JACQUES PAMBRUN.

Service des Postes et Télécommunications: BP 00, Mata'Utu, 98600 Uvea, Hahake, Wallis Islands; tel. 720809; fax 722662; e-mail pio.tui@wallis.co.nc; internet www.spt.wf; Dir MANUELE TAOFIFENUA; Head of Postage Stamp Section PIO TUI.

BROADCASTING

Radio and Television

France Télévisions Pôle Wallis et Futuna: BP 102, Pointe Matala, Mata'Utu, 98600 Uvea, Wallis Islands; tel. 721300; fax 722446; e-mail rfo.wallis@wallis.co.nc; internet wallisfutuna.rfo.fr; f. 1979; acquired by Groupe France Télévisions in 2004; fmrly Radiodiffusion Française d'Outre-mer, present name adopted in 1998; transmitters at Mata'Utu (Uvea) and Alo (Futuna); programmes broadcast 24 hours daily in Uvean (Wallisian), Futunian and French; a television service on Uvea, transmitting for 12 hours daily in French, began operation in 1986; a television service on Futuna was inaugurated in 1994; satellite television began operation in 2000; Regional Dir JEAN-JACQUES AGOSTINI; Station Man. LOUIS AUGUSTE; Editor-in-Chief NORBERT TAOFIFENUA.

Finance

BANKING

Bank of Issue

Institut d'Emission d'Outre-Mer: BP G5, Mata'Utu, Havelu, Hahake, 98600 Uvea, Wallis Islands; tel. 722505; fax 722003; e-mail direction@ieomwf.fr; internet www.ieom.fr/wallis-et-futuna; f. 1998; Dir RAYMOND COFFRE.

Other Banks

Agence Française de Développement: BP G5, Mata'Utu, 98600 Uvea, Wallis Islands; tel. 722505; fax 722003; e-mail afdmatautu@groupe-afd.org; fmrly Caisse Française de Développement; devt bank; Man. RAYMOND COFFRE.

Banque de Wallis et Futuna: BP 59, Mata'Utu, 98600 Uvea, Wallis Islands; tel. 722124; fax 722156; e-mail maurice.j.lasante@bnpparibas.com; internet nc.bnpparibas.net; f. 1991; 51% owned by BNP Paribas (New Caledonia); CEO MAURICE LASANTE.

Paierie de Wallis et Futuna: BP 29, Mata'Utu, 98600 Uvea, Wallis Islands; tel. 722929; fax 722120; Man. MARCEL BUSH.

Insurance

GAN Assurances: BP 52, Mata'Utu, Hahake, 98600 Uvea, Wallis Islands; subsidiary of GAN Assurances, France; general non-life insurance.

Poe-ma Insurances: Matala'a, Utufua, Mua, BP 728, Vaitupu, 98600 Uvea, Wallis Islands; tel. 450096; fax 450097; e-mail poema@mail.pf.

Trade and Industry

UTILITIES

Electricité et Eau de Wallis et Futuna (EEWF): BP 28, Mata'Utu, 98600 Uvea, Wallis Islands; tel. 721500; fax 721196; e-mail eewf@wallis.co.nc; 32.4% owned by the territory and 66.6% owned by Electricité et Eau de Calédonie (Groupe Suez, France); production and distribution of electricity on Wallis and Futuna; production and distribution of potable water on Wallis since 1986; Dir JEAN-MARC PETIT.

MAJOR COMPANIES

General Import SAS: BP 24, Mata'Utu, 98600 Uvea, Wallis Islands; tel. 722184; fax 722145; e-mail adm@generalimport-wallis.com; f. 1992; importers and distributors of consumer goods; revenue US $34m. (2008); Man. GÉRARD ALPHONSE; 70 employees (2010).

Société Wallisienne et Futunienne d'Entreposage des Produits Pétroliers (SWAFEPP): Mata'Utu, 98600 Uvea, Wallis Islands; f. 1989; 33% owned by Territoire de Wallis & Futuna, 66% owned by Total Pacifique Nouvelle Calédonie; revenue of 299m. francs CFP in 2009; importers and distributors of liquid fuels; 13 employees.

TRADE UNIONS

Union Interprofessionnelle CFDT Wallis et Futuna (UI CFDT): BP 178, Mata'Utu, 98600 Uvea, Wallis Islands; tel. 721880; Sec.-Gen. KALOLO HANISI.

Union Territoriale Force Ouvrière: BP 325, Mata'Utu, 98600 Uvea, Wallis Islands; tel. 721732; fax 721732; Sec.-Gen. CHRISTIAN VAAMEI.

Transport

ROADS

Uvea has a few kilometres of road, one route circling the island, and there is also a partially surfaced road circling the island of Futuna; the only fully surfaced roads are in Mata'Utu.

SHIPPING

There are two wharves on Uvea for bulk goods, at Mata'Utu, and liquid fuels, at Halalo, respectively. There is one wharf at Leava on Futuna. Wallis and Futuna is served by two container ships: the *Southern Moana*, operated jointly by Moana Services of New Caledonia and Pacific Direct Line of New Zealand between Auckland (New Zealand), Nouméa (New Caledonia) and the islands; and the *Sofrana Bligh*, operated by SOFRANA between Auckland and the islands. Plans to expand the harbour facilities at Mata'Utu and to make improvements to the fishing port of Halalo have been subject to delay.

Société Française Navigation (SOFRANA): BP 24, Mata'Utu, 98600 Uvea, Wallis Islands; tel. 720511; fax 720568; f. 1986; subsidiary of Sofrana Unilines, New Zealand; 1 vessel.

CIVIL AVIATION

There is an international airport in Hihifo district on Uvea, about 5 km from Mata'Utu. Air Calédonie International (Aircalin—New Caledonia) is the only airline to serve Wallis and Futuna. The company operates five flights a week from Wallis to Futuna, one flight a week from Wallis to Tahiti (French Polynesia) and two flights a week from Wallis to Nouméa (New Caledonia). The airport on Futuna is at Pointe Vele, in the south-east, in the Kingdom of Alo; work began in 2005 to upgrade Vele airport to receive international traffic, originally scheduled to be completed by the end of 2008. The Compagnie Aérienne de Wallis et Futuna (Air Wallis) was established in 2004, as a joint venture between the Government and local business interests; however, the project was delayed in 2005.

Service d'Etat de l'Aviation Civile de Wallis et Futuna: BP 01, Mata'Utu, Malae, Hihifo, 98600 Uvea, Wallis Islands; tel. 721201; fax 722954; e-mail seac-wf.encadrement@mail.wf; Dir PATRICK PEZZETTA.

Tourism

Tourism remains undeveloped. There are four small hotels on Uvea, Wallis Islands. In 2006 foreign visitors to the islands totalled 2,456. The number of hotel rooms available was expected to increase to 60 in 2006. There are two small guest houses for visitors on Futuna. The 2013 Pacific Mini Games were to be held on Wallis and Futuna.

Defence

Defence is the responsibility of France. The French naval command for the Pacific area is based in French Polynesia.

Education

In 2008 there were 18 primary schools and seven secondary schools (including two vocational schools) in Wallis and Futuna. Primary and pre-primary pupils totalled 2,156 and secondary students 1,901 in 2010. In 2005/06 a total of 80 students were attending various universities overseas.

OTHER FRENCH PACIFIC OVERSEAS TERRITORY

New Caledonia was formerly an Overseas Territory, territoire d'outre-mer, of France. The Nouméa Accord, concluded in 1998, provided for a gradual transfer of powers to New Caledonia. Under its terms, the Territory became an Overseas Country (Pays d'outre-mer), within the French Republic, in 1999. Amendments to the French Constitution, which were approved by Parlement (Parliament) in March 2003 and formed part of the French Government's programme of decentralization, were not to apply to New Caledonia, uniquely among the overseas possessions of the French Republic. New Caledonia has a unique status as a collectivité *sui generis* within the framework of the French Republic.

Head of State: President NICOLAS SARKOZY (took office 17 May 2007).

NEW CALEDONIA

Introduction

New Caledonia is an Overseas Country of France, lying south and slightly west of Vanuatu, some 1,500 km east of Australia and 1,700 km north of New Zealand. It comprises several islands with a total land area of 18,575 sq km (7,172 sq miles). The capital, Nouméa, is located on the main island of New Caledonia itself (Grande Terre), which has a total area of 16,372 sq km (6,321 sq miles). The Bélep Archipelago is to the north, and the Isle of Pines and Huon Islands to the south. The coralline Loyalty Islands chain (including Lifou, Maré and Ouvéa—Uvea) runs parallel to Grande Terre, to the north-east, and the uninhabited Chesterfield Islands lie about 400 km to the north-west. To the south of the Loyalty Islands is Walpole Island; the sporadically active volcanic Matthew and Hunter Islands (also claimed by Vanuatu) lie east of Walpole. Rugged mountains, rising to 1,628 m at Mt Panié, divide Grande Terre lengthwise. Temperatures average about 24°C (75°F). The average rainfall in the east of Grande Terre is about 2,000 mm (80 ins) per year, and in the west about 1,000 mm (40 ins), with a rainy season between December and March. French is an official language; of some 29 indigenous Melanesian Kanak languages the four most common forms are Drehu (Lihou), Nengone (Maré), Aji'e (Houaïlou) and Paicï (Poindimié).

At the 1996 census the population totalled 196,836, comprising Melanesians (44.1%), Europeans (mainly French—34.1%), Wallisians and Tahitians (Polynesian—11.7%) and others, including Indonesians and Vietnamese (3.9%). A total of 341 tribes (with legal status under a high chief—living in reserves that covered 21% of total land) represented about 28.7% of the population. An estimated 55% of the population are Roman Catholics, and there is a substantial Protestant minority. At the census of 27 July 2009 the population had reached 245,580. Some 75% of the population lived in the South Province, 18% in the North and 7% in the Loyalty Islands. The total population was 254,817 in mid-2011, according to UN estimates.

New Caledonia was annexed by France, as a dependency of Tahiti, in 1853. In 1860 a separate administration was established, and in 1885 a Conseil général was elected to defend local interests. The mining of nickel and copper, as well as European cattle-grazing, displaced the indigenous population. There were numerous Kanak rebellions, the last in 1917, and politically motivated violence continued until the 1980s. Separate administrations existed for Kanaks and settlers until New Caledonia became an Overseas Territory in 1946. The first Territorial Assembly was elected in 1956, although the French Governor effectively retained complete control of government until 1976, when the Council of Government (elected from the Territorial Assembly) achieved responsibility for certain internal affairs. The post of Governor was replaced by that of a French High Commissioner.

In 1978 Kanak-supported, pro-independence parties obtained a majority in the Council of Government. In early 1979, however, the French Government dismissed the Council, following its opposition to a 10-year 'contract' between France and New Caledonia, as the plan did not acknowledge the possibility of independence. The Territory was placed under the direct authority of the High Commissioner. With the implementation of a new electoral law, minor political parties were not represented in the Assembly following the election in July.

A new statute in September 1984 gave the Territorial Council of Ministers responsibility over many internal matters, and the High Commissioner was replaced as its President by an elected member. A second legislative chamber was created, with the right to be consulted on development, planning and budgetary issues. Under proposals made in April 1985, New Caledonia was to be divided into four regions, each governed by an elected autonomous council responsible for areas including education, health and welfare, land rights and transport. Council members would serve as regional representatives in a Territorial Congress (to replace the Territorial Assembly). A referendum was scheduled for September 1987, open to all those who had been resident in New Caledonia for at least three years: 98.3% of voters favoured New Caledonia's continuation as part of the French Republic, and only 1.7% of votes were cast in support of independence. Voter participation was almost 59%, but in constituencies inhabited by a majority of Kanaks 90% of the registered electorate abstained.

The Matignon Accord resulted from negotiations in mid-1988, when it was agreed to transfer the administration of the Territory to Paris for 12 months. New Caledonia was to be divided into three administrative Provinces; further provisions addressed economic development, training in public administration for Kanaks and institutional reforms. When the year of direct rule by France ended in July 1989, the Territorial Congress and Provincial Assemblies resumed their functions. In November the French Assemblée nationale approved an amnesty for all who had been involved in politically motivated violence in New Caledonia prior to August 1988.

Talks concerning the future of the Territory continued during 1994–96. Following mass demonstrations and strike action, an agreement was reached for the transfer of nickel interests from a French-owned company to local control by 2005. This became the foundation for the Nouméa Accord, concluded in May 1998, which postponed the referendum on independence for a period of 15–20 years, providing for a gradual transfer of powers to local institutions, and aimed to improve conditions for the Kanak population. Following an election in May 1999, the Congress elected the first President of the Government of New Caledonia. The new Government was elected by proportional representation and replaced the High Commissioner as the executive authority. With responsibility for primary education, labour, external trade and mining having already been granted to the New Caledonian authorities, in November 2009 the local Congress unanimously approved the transfer of responsibility from the French authorities for various other areas; these included secondary education, private primary education, the police and security forces, domestic maritime transport and air services. New Caledonia was expected to assume control of most of these responsibilities during 2011–12. Following several months of political instability, in June 2011 the French Senate approved changes to the electoral law of New Caledonia. Henceforth, an incoming government was be given a grace period of 18 months, thus permitting the exercise of a definite mandate.

Meanwhile, during the visit of the French Prime Minister, François Fillon, to New Caledonia in July 2010, the 'Kanak' flag (regarded as a symbol of the pro-independence movement) was officially raised for the first time concurrently with the French national flag, with the approval of the Congress. In August 2011 French President Nicolas Sarkozy also undertook an official visit to New Caledonia, urging compromise and stating that he would respect the will of the local electorate if it were ultimately to vote in favour of independence.

A protracted dispute over the ownership of the Wallisian settlement of Ave Maria, near Nouméa, led to violence between the Wallisian and indigenous Kanak communities from late 2001. The Kanak community in neighbouring Saint-Louis demanded the departure of all Wallisians. Following the relocation of these Wallisian families, in December 2003 a special accord was signed governing relations between France, New Caledonia and Wallis and Futuna.

New Caledonia's economy is vulnerable to factors affecting the islands' important nickel industry, which have included fluctuations in international prices for the commodity and political unrest. New Caledonia possesses among the world's largest known nickel deposits and is a major producer of ferro-nickel. Receipts from sales of nickel ore, ferro-nickel and nickel matte account for most of New Caledonia's total export revenue. In 2009 new legislation governing the regulation of the nickel industry was enacted. This provided a legal framework for mining operations in New Caledonia, as required by the Nouméa Accord. The legislation included revised guidelines regarding environmental controls. A nickel stabilization fund was also established in order to counter the volatility of global nickel prices. Service industries, notably tourism, continue to make the largest contribution to the New Caledonian economy. The ongoing decline in tourist arrivals by air was believed to have been offset by a substantial increase in cruise-ship visitors in 2010. Exports of marine products, notably prawns, are of some significance. France is the main trading partner. The French Government continues to provide substantial budgetary aid. The sum of €26.4m. was allocated towards protection of natural heritage and as financial assistance in preparation for the 2011 Pacific Games, hosted by New Caledonia. Over the period 2011–15 France was to provide development assistance of 45,000m. francs CFP for New Caledonia. In January 2011 a cyclone seriously damaged a main road leading into Nouméa and also destroyed crops.

Statistical Survey

Source (unless otherwise stated): Institut de la Statistique et des Etudes Economiques, BP 823, 98845 Nouméa; tel. 275481; fax 288148; internet www.isee.nc.

AREA AND POPULATION

Area (sq km): New Caledonia island (Grande Terre) 16,372; Loyalty Islands 1,981 (Lifou 1,207, Maré 642, Ouvéa 132); Isle of Pines 152; Belep Archipelago 70; Total 18,575 (7,172 sq miles).

Population: 230,789 at census of 31 August 2004; 245,580 at census of 27 July 2009. *Population by Province* (census of 2009): Loyalty Islands 17,436; North Province 45,137; South Province 183,007. *2011* (UN estimate at mid-year): 254,817 (Source: UN, *World Population Prospects: The 2010 Revision*).

Density (mid-2011): 13.7 per sq km.

Population by Age and Sex (UN estimates at mid-2011): *0–14:* 63,345 (males 32,404, females 30,941); *15–64:* 170,365 (males 85,166, females 85,199); *65 and over:* 21,107 (males 9,804, females 11,303); *Total* 254,817 (males 127,374, females 127,443) (Source: UN, *World Population Prospects: The 2010 Revision*).

Ethnic Groups (census of 1996): Indigenous Kanaks (Melanesians) 86,788; French and other Europeans 67,151; Wallisians and Futunians (Polynesian) 17,763; Tahitians (Polynesian) 5,171; Indonesians 5,003; Others 14,960.

Principal Towns (population of communes at census of 2009): Nouméa (capital) 97,579; Mont-Doré 25,683; Dumbéa 24,103; Païta 16,358.

Births, Marriages and Deaths (2009, unless otherwise indicated, preliminary): Registered live births 4,112 (birth rate 16.7 per 1,000); Registered marriages 932 (marriage rate 3.8 per 1,000); Registered deaths 1,235 (death rate 5.0 per 1,000).

Life Expectancy (years at birth, 2007): 75.9 (males 71.8; females 80.3).

Economically Active Population (salaried workers, annual averages, 2009): Agriculture, hunting, forestry and fishing 2,198; Mining and quarrying 1,238; Manufacturing 8,473; Electricity, gas and water 842; Construction 8,136; Trade (vehicle repairs and domestic goods) 9,348; Hotels and restaurants 4,171; Transport and communications 5,275; Financing activities 1,899; Real estate and business services 6,564; Education 188; Health and welfare 1,938; Domestic services for households 3,492; Community, social and personal services 2,845; Other services 60; Non-market services 25,565; *Total employed* 82,232; Unemployed 6,981; *Total labour force* 89,213.

HEALTH AND WELFARE

Key Indicators

Total Fertility Rate (children per woman, 2007): 2.2.

Physicians (per 1,000 head, 2008): 2.2.

Hospital Beds (per 1,000 head, 2003): 3.7.

Total Carbon Dioxide Emissions ('000 metric tons, 2007): 2,846.9.

Carbon Dioxide Emissions Per Head (metric tons, 2007): 11.7.

For definitions, see explanatory note on p. vi.

AGRICULTURE, ETC.

Principal Crops ('000 metric tons, 2009): Maize 2.6; Potatoes 1.5; Sweet potatoes 2.6 (FAO estimate); Cassava 2.4 (FAO estimate); Yams 10.3 (FAO estimate); Coconuts 16.5 (FAO estimate); Vegetables (incl. melons) 6.9; Bananas 1.1.

Livestock ('000 head, year ending September 2009, FAO estimates): Horses 12.0; Cattle 90.0; Pigs 37.0; Sheep 2.3; Goats 8.2; Poultry 600.

Livestock Products (metric tons, 2009): Cattle meat 3,194; Pig meat 2,251; Chicken meat 9,000 (FAO estimate); Cows' milk 853 (FAO estimate); Hen eggs 2,159 (FAO estimate).

Forestry ('000 cubic metres, 2009, unless otherwise indicated): *Roundwood Removals:* Sawlogs and veneer logs 12.7; Other industrial wood 2.0 (FAO estimate); Total 14.7. *Sawnwood Production:* 3.3 (all broadleaved) in 1994. *1995–2009:* Sawnwood production assumed to be unchanged from 1995 (FAO estimates).

Fishing (metric tons, live weight, 2009): Capture 3,545 (Albacore 1,649; Yellowfin tuna 487; Other marine fishes 284; Sea cucumbers 364); Aquaculture 1,920 (Blue shrimp 1,860); Total catch 5,465 (excl. trochus shells 277).

Source: FAO.

MINING

Production: Nickel ore (metal content, '000 metric tons) 102.6 in 2008; Nickel ore ('000 wet tons) 8,709 in 2010. Source: Institut d'Emission d'Outre-Mer.

INDUSTRY

Production (2009): Ferro-nickel 38,299 metric tons (nickel content); Nickel matte 13,902 metric tons (nickel content); Electric energy 1,944 million kWh; Cement 138,114 metric tons (Source: US Geological Survey).

FINANCE

Currency and Exchange Rates: see French Polynesia.

French Government Budget Expenditure ('000 million francs CFP, incl. military expenditure): 132.3 in 2007; 137.8 in 2008 (preliminary); 137.0 in 2009 (preliminary).

Territorial Budget (million francs CFP, 2010): *Revenue:* Current 165,753 (Direct taxes 61,082; Indirect taxes 50,159); Capital 6,722; Total 172,475. *Expenditure:* Current 155,569 (Transfers to provinces 61,946); Capital 11,730; Total 167,299.

Money Supply (million francs CFP at 31 December 2010): Currency in circulation 14,666; Demand deposits 245,223; *Total money* 259,889. Source: Institut d'Emission d'Outre-Mer.

Cost of Living (Consumer Price Index for Nouméa, December each year; base: December 1992 = 100): All items 132.1 in 2008; 132.3 in 2009; 135.9 in 2010.

Gross Domestic Product (US $ million at constant 2005 prices): 6,303.2 in 2007; 6,338.7 in 2008; 6,379.7 in 2009. Source: UN Statistics Division, National Accounts Main Aggregates Database.

Expenditure on the Gross Domestic Product (million francs CFP at current prices, 2008, estimates): Government final consumption expenditure 180,037; Private final consumption expenditure 468,234; Gross capital formation 315,536; *Total domestic expenditure* 963,807; Exports of goods and services 134,647; *Less* Imports of goods and services 361,873; *GDP in purchasers' values* 736,582.

Gross Domestic Product by Economic Activity (€ million at current prices, 2005): Agriculture, hunting, forestry and fishing 78; Nickel mining and processing 476; Food processing 91; Miscellaneous manufacturing 170; Electricity, gas and water 82; Construction 409; Trade 573; Transport and telecommunications 346; Banks and insurance 182; Business services 306; Services to households 1,016; Public administration 887; *Sub-total* 4,616; *Less* Financial intermediation services indirectly measured 138; *Gross value added in basic prices* 4,478; Taxes and subsidies on products (net) 536; *GDP in market prices* 5,015. *2008* (million francs CFP, estimates): Gross value added in basic prices 656,312; Taxes on products 81,499; *Less* Subsidies on products 1,228; GDP in market prices 736,582.

Balance of Payments (million francs CFP, 2009): Exports of goods 80,544; Imports of goods –201,615; *Trade balance* –121,071; Exports of services 43,634; Imports of services –95,504; *Balance on goods and services* –172,941; Other income received 53,761; Other income paid –16,107; *Balance on goods, services and income* –135,287; Current transfers received 87,877; Current transfers paid –30,546; *Current balance* –77,956; Capital account (net) 500; Direct investment (net) 93,420; Portfolio investment assets 65,735; Portfolio investment liabilities –51,197; Other investment assets 325,160; Other investment liabilities –362,541; *Overall balance* –6,878. Source: Institut d'Emission d'Outre-Mer.

EXTERNAL TRADE

Principal Commodities (million francs CFP): *Imports* (2010): Food products, beverages and tobacco 33,653; Mineral products 50,176; Chemical products 19,736; Plastic and rubber articles 10,812; Paper and paper articles 4,555; Textiles and textile articles 6,460; Base metals and articles thereof 21,983; Machinery and mechanical appliances, and electrical equipment 49,004; Transport equipment 34,860; Total (incl. others) 298,518. *Exports* (2009): Nickel ore 14,711; Ferro-nickel 44,870; Nickel matte 17,301; Marine products 2,147 (Prawns 1,317); Total (incl. others) 84,503.

Principal Trading Partners (million francs CFP): *Imports* (2010): Australia 28,988; France 66,486; Japan 6,801; New Zealand 11,365; Singapore 38,386; USA 10,274; Total (incl. others) 298,518. *Exports* (2009): Australia 6,063; China, People's Republic 11,218; France 20,789; Japan 10,974; Korea, Republic 8,199; South Africa 1,792; Taiwan 8,805; USA 2,213; Total (incl. others) 84,503.

TRANSPORT

Road Traffic (motor vehicles in use, 2001): Total 85,499.

Shipping (2009): *Domestic Traffic* ('000 metric tons): Freight unloaded 2,906; Freight loaded 90. *International Traffic:* Freight unloaded 1,399 metric tons; Freight loaded 3,735 metric tons. *Merchant Fleet* (vessels registered, '000 grt, at 31 December 1992): 14.

Civil Aviation (La Tontouta international airport, Nouméa, 2009): *Passenger Traffic:* Passengers arriving 231,327; Passengers departing 231,922. *Freight Traffic:* Freight unloaded 5,055 metric tons; Freight loaded 1,395 metric tons (Source: Department of Civil Aviation).

TOURISM

Foreign Arrivals: *Arrivals by Air:* 103,672 in 2008; 99,379 in 2009; 98,562 in 2010. *Cruise-ship Passenger Arrivals:* 124,467 in 2007; 152,250 in 2008; 131,231 in 2009.

Tourist Arrivals by Country of Residence (2010): Australia 17,551; France 24,960; Japan 18,534; New Zealand 6,406; Total (incl. others) 98,562 (Source: Institut d'Emission d'Outre-Mer).

Tourism Receipts (€ million): 152.5 in 2007; 153.0 in 2008 (estimate); 146.0 in 2009 (estimate).

COMMUNICATIONS MEDIA

Radio Receivers (1997): 107,000 in use*.

Television Receivers (2000): 106,000 in use†.

Telephones (2010): 72,200 main lines in use†.

Mobile Cellular Telephones (2010): 220,800 subscribers†.

Internet Subscribers (2009): 33,100†.

Broadband Subscribers (2010): 38,200†.

Personal Computers: 40,000 (170.7 per 1,000 persons) in 2006†.

Daily Newspapers (1999): 1.

* Source: UNESCO, *Statistical Yearbook*.

† Source: International Telecommunication Union.

EDUCATION

Pre-primary (2010, unless otherwise indicated): 83 schools (2004); 12,946 pupils.

Primary (2010, unless otherwise indicated): 286 schools (incl. pre-primary); 1,966 teachers (2009, incl. pre-primary); 23,654 pupils (incl. special education).

Secondary (2009, unless otherwise indicated): 76 schools; 2,763 teachers (2009, incl. higher); 32,490 pupils.

Higher (2005): 4 institutions; 111 teaching staff.

Adult Literacy Rate (1989): Males 94.0%; Females 92.1%.

Directory

The Constitution

The constitutional system in New Caledonia is established under the Constitution of the Fifth French Republic and specific laws, including those enacted in July 1989 in accordance with the terms agreed by the Matignon Accord and the Transitional Provisions appended by legislation on 20 July 1998. A referendum on the future of New Caledonia (originally expected to be conducted in 1998) was postponed for a period of between 15 and 20 years while a gradual transfer of power from metropolitan France to local institutions is effected under the terms of the Nouméa Accord, concluded in 1998. Under the Nouméa Accord, New Caledonia is designated as an Overseas Country (Pays d'outre-mer) of the French Republic, of which it remains an integral part. (Its official status is that of a collectivité *sui generis*.) The High Commissioner is the representative of the State in New Caledonia and is appointed by the French Government. The High Commissioner is responsible for external relations, defence, law and order, finance and secondary education. New Caledonia is divided into three Provinces, of the South, the North and the Loyalty Islands. Each is governed by a Provincial Assembly, which is elected on a proportional basis and is responsible for local economic development, land reform and cultural affairs. Members of the Assemblies (40 for the South, 22 for the North and 14 for the Loyalty Islands) are subject to re-election every five years. A proportion of the members of the three Provincial Assemblies together form the Congress of New Caledonia (32 for the South, 15 for the North and seven for the Loyalty Islands), which is responsible for the New Caledonian budget and fiscal affairs, infrastructure and primary education. The Assemblies and the Congress each elect a President as leader. The Government of New Caledonia is elected by the Congress, and comprises between seven and 11 members. Under the terms of the Nouméa Accord, it replaces the French High Commissioner as New Caledonia's executive authority. Provision is also made for the maintenance of Kanak tradition: there are eight custom regions, each with a Regional Consultative Custom Council. These eight Councils, with other appropriate authorities, are represented on the Customary Senate, which is composed of 16 members (two elected from each regional council for a six-year period); the local Senate is consulted by the Congress and the Government. Local government is conducted by 33 communes. New Caledonia also elects two deputies to the Assemblée nationale (National Assembly) in Paris and one representative to the Sénat (Senate), on the basis of universal adult suffrage. One Economic and Social Councillor is also nominated. New Caledonia may be represented in the European Parliament.

The Government

(October 2011)

STATE GOVERNMENT

High Commissioner: ALBERT DUPUY (took office November 2010).

Secretary-General: THIERRY SUQUET.

LOCAL GOVERNMENT

Secretary-General: JACQUES WADRAWANE.

COUNCIL OF MINISTERS

The coalition Government is led by Avenir Ensemble.

President, responsible for Regional Co-operation, External Relations, Agriculture and Fisheries and International Air Transport: HAROLD MARTIN.

Vice-President and Minister for Mines, Development Plan NC 2025 and Transport (Surface and Marine): GILBERT TYUIENON.

Minister for Defence: PHILIPPE GOMES.

Minister for Energy, Budget and Financial Affairs, Digital Economy, Communication and Broadcasting, Higher Education and Research: SONIA BACKES.

Minister for Economy: ANTHONY LECREN.

Minister for Culture and Citizenship, Women Affairs and Relations with the Communes: DÉWÉ GORODEY.

Minister for Youth and Sports, Primary and Secondary Education and Social Dialogue: JEAN-CLAUDE BRIAULT.

Minister for Civil Services: PHILIPPE DUNOYER.

Minister for Human Resources and Labour and Employment: GEORGES MANDAQUE.

Minister for Health and Society and Vocational Training: SYLVIE ROBINEAU.

Minister for Ecology and Sustainable Development: HELEN IEKAWE.

GOVERNMENT OFFICES

Office of the High Commissioner: Haut-commissariat de la République en Nouvelle-Calédonie, 1 ave du Maréchal Foch, BP C5, 98844 Nouméa Cedex; tel. 266300; fax 272828; e-mail haussariat@nouvelle-caledonie.gouv.fr; internet www.nouvelle-caledonie.gouv.fr.

Secretariat-General of the High Commissioner: 9 bis rue de la République, BP C5, 98844 Nouméa Cedex; tel. 246711; fax 246740; internet www.nouvelle-caledonie.gouv.fr.

New Caledonian Government: Présidence du Gouvernement, 8 route des Artifices, Artillerie, BP M2, 98849 Nouméa Cedex; tel. 246565; fax 246580; e-mail presidence@gouv.nc; internet www.gouv.nc.

Office of the Secretary-General of the Government of New Caledonia: 8 route des Artifices, BP M2, 98849 Nouméa Cedex; tel. 246532; fax 246620; e-mail alain.swetschkin@gouv.nc; internet www.gouv.nc.

GOVERNMENT DEPARTMENTS

Department of the Budget and Financial Affairs (DBAF): 18 ave Paul Doumer, BP M2, 98849 Nouméa Cedex; tel. 256083; fax 283133; e-mail dbaf@gouv.nc.

Department of Civil Aviation: 179 rue Gervolino, BP H01, 98849 Nouméa Cedex; tel. 265200; fax 265202; e-mail dac-nc@aviation-civile.gouv.fr; internet www.dac.nc.

Department of Computer Technology (DTSI): 127 rue Arnold Daly, Magenta Ouemo, BP 15101, 98804 Nouméa Cedex; tel. 275888; fax 281919; e-mail dtsi@gouv.nc.

Department of Cultural and Customary Affairs (DACC): 8 rue de Sébastopol, BP T5, 98852 Nouméa Cedex; tel. 269766; fax 269767; e-mail secretariat.dacc@gouv.nc.

Department of Economic Affairs (DAE): 7 rue du Général Galliéni, BP 2672, 98846 Nouméa Cedex; tel. 232250; fax 232251; e-mail dae@gouv.nc; internet www.dae.gov.nc.

Department of Education (DENC): Immeuble Foch, 19 ave du Maréchal Foch, BP 8244, 98807 Nouméa Cedex; tel. 239600; fax 272921; e-mail denc@gouv.nc; internet www.denc.gouv.nc.

Department of Fiscal Affairs (DSF): Hôtel des Impôts, 13 rue de la Somme, BP D2, 98848 Nouméa Cedex; tel. 257500; fax 251166; e-mail dsf@gouv.nc; internet www.dsf.gouv.nc.

Department of Health and Social Services (DASS): 5 rue Général Galliéni, BP N4, 98851 Nouméa Cedex; tel. 243700; fax 243702; e-mail dass@gouv.nc; internet www.dass.gouv.nc.

Department of Human Resources and Civil Service (DRHFPT): 18 ave Paul Doumer, BP M2, 98849 Nouméa Cedex; tel. 256000; fax 274700; e-mail drhfpt@gouv.nc; internet www.drhfpt.gouv.nc.

Department of Industry, Mines and Energy (DIMENC): 1 ter rue Edouard Unger, 1ère, Vallée du Tir, BP 465, 98845 Nouméa Cedex; tel. 270230; fax 272345; e-mail dimenc@gouv.nc; internet www.dimenc.gouv.nc.

Department of Infrastructure, Topography and Land Transport (DITTT): 1 bis rue Edouard Unger, 1ère, Vallée du Tir, BP A2, 98848 Nouméa Cedex; tel. 280300; fax 281760; e-mail dittt@gouv.nc; internet www.dittt.gouv.nc.

Department of Labour and Employment (DTE): 12 rue de Verdun, BP 141, 98845 Nouméa Cedex; tel. 275572; fax 270494; e-mail dte@gouv.nc; internet www.dtnc.gouv.nc.

Department of Veterinary, Food and Rural Affairs (DAVAR): 209 rue Auguste Bénébig, Haut Magenta, BP 256, 98845 Nouméa Cedex; tel. 255100; fax 255129; e-mail davar@gouv.nc; internet www.davar.gouv.nc.

Department of Vocational Training (DFPC): 19 ave du Maréchal Foch, BP 110, 98845 Nouméa Cedex; tel. 246622; fax 281661; e-mail dfpc@gouv.nc; internet www.dfpc.gouv.nc.

Department of Youth and Sports (DJS): 23 rue Jean Jaurès, BP 810, 98845 Nouméa Cedex; tel. 252384; fax 254585; e-mail djsnc@gouv.nc; internet www.djs.gouv.nc.

Legislature

ASSEMBLÉES PROVINCIALES

Members of the Provincial Assemblies are elected on a proportional basis for a five-year term. Each Provincial Assembly elects its President. A number of the members of the Provincial Assemblies sit together to make up the Congress of New Caledonia. The Assembly of the North Province has 22 members (including 15 sitting for the Congress), the Loyalty Islands 14 members (including seven for the Congress) and the South Province has 40 members (including 32 for the Congress).

North Province: BP 41, 98860 Koné; tel. 417100; fax 472475; e-mail presidence@province-nord.nc; internet www.province-nord.nc; Pres. PAUL NÉAOUTYINE (UNI-FLNKS).

South Province: Hôtel de la Province Sud, route des Artifices, Port Moselle, BP L1, 98849 Nouméa Cedex; tel. 258000; fax 274900; e-mail cabinet@province-sud.nc; internet www.province-sud.nc; Pres. PIERRE FROGIER (Le Rassemblement-UMP).

Loyalty Islands Province: BP 50, Wé, 98820 Lifou; tel. 455100; fax 451440; e-mail presidence@loyalty.nc; internet www.province-iles.nc; Pres. NÉKO HNÉPEUNE (UNI-FLNKS).

Election, 10 May 2009 (provisional results by province)

Party	North	South	Loyalty Islands
Le Rassemblement-UMP	1	15	—
Union Calédonienne-Front de Libération Nationale Kanak Socialiste (UC-FLNKS)	8	—	6
Calédonie Ensemble	—	11	—
Union Nationale pour l'Indépendance (UNI)	9	—	—
L'Avenir Ensemble	—	8	—
Front de Libération Nationale Kanak Socialiste (FLNKS)	—	4	—
Union Nationale pour l'Indépendance-Front de Libération Nationale Kanak Socialiste (UNI-FLNKS)	—	—	4
Parti Travailliste	3	—	2
Dynamique Autochtone (Le Mouvement de la Diversité)	—	—	2
Rassemblement pour la Calédonie	—	2	—
Une Province Pour Tous	1	—	—
Total	22	40	14

Note: in October 2009, following the confirmation of irregularities in the conduct of the election, notably with regard to the use of proxy votes, the results of the Loyalty Islands were declared invalid by the Conseil d'Etat in France. The province thus returned to the polls on 6 December: the UC-FLNKS alliance was reported to have retained six seats, the Parti Travailliste increased its representation to four seats, the Libération Kanak Socialiste (LKS) won two seats and two seats were taken by another pro-independence grouping.

CONGRÈS

A proportion of the members of the three Provincial Assemblies sit together, in Nouméa, as the Congress of New Caledonia. There are 54 members (out of a total of 76 sitting in the Provincial Assemblies).

President: ROCH WAMYTAN, Congrès de la Nouvelle-Calédonie, 1 blvd Vauban, BP P3, 98851 Nouméa Cedex; tel. 273129; fax 270219; e-mail courrier@congres.nc; internet www.congress.nc.

Election, 10 May 2009 (provisional results for New Caledonia as a whole)

Party	Votes	%	Seats
Le Rassemblement-UMP	19,888	20.60	13
Calédonie Ensemble	16,253	16.83	10
Union Calédonienne	11,247	11.65	8
Union Nationale pour l'Indépendance	10,162	10.52	8
L'Avenir Ensemble-Le Mouvement de la Diversité	11,308	11.71	6
Parti Travailliste	7,692	7.97	3
Front de Libération Nationale Kanak Socialiste	5,342	5.53	3
Rassemblement pour la Calédonie	4,304	4.46	2
Libération Kanak Socialiste	1,852	1.92	1
Others	8,510	8.81	—
Total	96,558	100.00	54

PARLEMENT

Deputies to the French National Assembly: PIERRE FROGIER (Le Rassemblement-UMP), HILARION VENDÉGOU (Le Rassemblement-UMP).

Representative to the French Senate: SIMON LOUECKHOTE.

Political Organizations

L'Avenir Ensemble (AE): 2 bis blvd Vauban, 98800 Nouméa; tel. 281179; fax 281011; e-mail avenirensemble@lagoon.nc; internet www.avenirensemble.nc; f. 2004; combined list incl. fmr mems of Rassemblement pour la Calédonie dans la République and Alliance pour la Calédonie; anti-independence party; supports unification of all ethnic groups; Leader HAROLD MARTIN.

Calédonie Ensemble (CE): 13 route de Vélodrome, 98800 Nouméa; tel. 288905; fax 288906; internet www.caledonieensemble.nc; f. 2008; anti-independence party est. by fmr mems of L'Avenir Ensemble; Leader PHILIPPE GOMÈS.

Fédération des Comités de Coordination des Indépendantistes (FCCI): 42 ter rue de Verdun, Nouméa; internet www.fcci-nc.org; f. 1998; est. by breakaway group of FLNKS; includes Front du Développement des Iles Loyauté and Front Uni de Libération Kanak; Leaders LÉOPOLD JORÉDIÉ, RAPHAËL MAPOU, FRANÇOIS BURCK.

Front Calédonien (FC): extreme right-wing; Leader M. SARRAN.

Front de Libération Nationale Kanak Socialiste (FLNKS): 9 rue Austerlitz, Immeuble SAM3, 98800 Nouméa Cedex; tel. 265880; fax 265887; f. 1984; est. following dissolution of Front Indépendantiste; pro-independence; Pres. PAUL NÉAOUTYINE; a grouping of the following parties:

Parti de Libération Kanak (PALIKA): f. 1975; Leader EPÉRI 'DÉWÉ' GORODEY.

Rassemblement Démocratique Océanien (RDO): Nouméa; f. 1994; est. by breakaway faction of Union Océanienne (f. 1989); supports Kanak sovereignty; Pres. ALOISIO SAKO.

Union Calédonienne (UC): 4 rue de la Gazelle, Aérodrome de Magenta, Nouméa; tel. 272599; fax 276257; e-mail info@union-caledonienne.org; internet www.union-caledonienne.org; f. 1952; pro-independence; left FLNKS coalition prior to elections of 2004 but subsequently returned; 11,000 mems; Pres. CHARLES PIDJOT; Sec.-Gen. DANIEL YEIWÉNÉ.

Union Progressiste Mélanésienne (UPM): f. 1974; est. as Union Progressiste Multiraciale; Pres. VICTOR TUTUGORO; Sec.-Gen. RENÉ POROU.

Front National (FN): 12 bis rue du Général Mangin, 98800 Nouméa; tel. 258068; fax 258064; e-mail george@province-sud.nc; internet www.frontnational.com; right-wing; Leader GUY GEORGE.

Génération Calédonienne: f. 1995; youth-based; aims to combat corruption in public life; Pres. JEAN-RAYMOND POSTIC.

Le Groupe MUR: BP 1211, 98845 Nouméa Cedex; tel. and fax 419385; coalition of Mouvement des Citoyens Calédoniens, Union Océanienne (f. 1989) and Rassemblement des Océaniens dans la Calédonie; Jt Pres TINO MANUOHALALO (MCC), MICHEL HEMA (UO), MIKAELE TUIFUA (ROC).

Libération Kanak Socialiste (LKS): Maré, Loyalty Islands; moderate, pro-independence; contested the 2009 elections in the Loyalty Islands as Dynamique Autochtone; Leader NIDOÏSH NAISSELINE.

Le Mouvement de la Diversité (LMD): 98802 Nouméa; tel. 997700; fax 240620; internet www.lmd.nc; f. 2009; allied to L'Avenir Ensemble; Pres. SIMON LOUECKHOTE.

Parti Travailliste: Nouméa; f. 2007; Pres. LOUIS KOTRA UREGEI.

Le Rassemblement-UMP: 13 rue de Sébastopol, BP 306, 98845 Nouméa; tel. 282620; fax 284033; e-mail contact@rassemblement.nc; internet www.rassemblement.nc; f. 1976; est. as Rassemblement pour la Calédonie dans la République; affiliated to the metropolitan Union pour un Mouvement Populaire; in favour of retaining the status quo in New Caledonia; Leader PIERRE FROGIER; Sec.-Gen. ERIC GAY.

A coalition of the following parties:

Centre des Démocrates Sociaux (CDS): f. 1971; Leader JEAN LÈQUES.

Parti Républicain (PR): Leader PIERRE MARESCA.

Rassemblement pour la Calédonie (RPC): Nouméa; f. 2006; Leader (vacant).

Union Calédonienne Renouveau (UC Renouveau): Hôtel de la province des îles Loyauté, BP 50, Wé Lifou; tel. 455100; fax 451440; Leader JACQUES LALIE.

Union Nationale pour l'Indépendance (UNI): c/o Le Congrès de la Nouvelle Calédonie, Nouméa ; Leader PAUL NÉAOUTYINE.

Minor political organizations that participated in the elections of May 2009 included: Avance, Calédonie Mon Pays, Génération Destin Commun, Ouverture Citoyenne, and Patrimoine et Environnement avec les Verts.

Judicial System

Court of Administrative Law: 85 ave du Général de Gaulle, Immeuble Carcopino 3000, 4ème étage, BP 63, 98851 Nouméa Cedex; tel. 250630; fax 250631; e-mail greffe.ta-noumea@juradm.fr; internet www.ta-noumea.juradm.fr; f. 1984; Pres. GUY LAPORTE; Cllrs MICHEL M. BICHET, ARSÈNE IBO, MARIE-THÉRÈSE LACAU.

Court of Appeal: Palais de Justice, BP F4, 98848 Nouméa; tel. 279357; fax 269185; e-mail pp.ca-noumea@justice.fr; internet www.ca-noumea.justice.fr; First Pres. GÉRARD FEY; Procurator-Gen. ANNIE BRUNET-FURSTER.

Court of the First Instance: 2 blvd Extérieur, BP F4, 98848 Nouméa; fax 276531; e-mail p.tpi-noumea@justice.fr; Pres. JEAN PRADAL; Procurator of the Republic CLARE LANET; there are two subsidiary courts, with resident magistrates, at Koné (North Province) and Wé (Loyalty Islands Province).

Customary Senate of New Caledonia: Conseil Consultatif Coutumier, 68 ave J. Cook, BP 1059, Nouville; tel. 242000; fax 249320; e-mail senat-coutumier@gouv.nc; f. 1990; consulted by Local Assembly and French Govt on matters affecting land, Kanak tradition and identity; composed of 16 elected mems (two from the regional council of each of the eight custom areas) for a six-year period; Pres. JULIEN BOANEMOI.

Religion

The majority of the population is Christian, with Roman Catholics comprising about 55% of the total in 2002. About 3% of the inhabitants, mainly Indonesians, are Muslims.

CHRISTIANITY

The Roman Catholic Church

The Territory comprises a single archdiocese, with an estimated 131,000 adherents in December 2007. The Archbishop participates in the Catholic Bishops' Conference of the Pacific, based in Fiji.

Archbishop of Nouméa: Most Rev. MICHEL-MARIE-BERNARD CALVET, Archevêché, 4 rue Mgr-Fraysse, BP 3, 98845 Nouméa; tel. 265353; fax 265352; e-mail archeveche@ddec.nc; internet www.ddec.nc/diocese.

The Anglican Communion

Within the Church of the Province of Melanesia, New Caledonia forms part of the diocese of Vanuatu. The Archbishop of the Province is the Bishop of Central Melanesia (resident in Honiara, Solomon Islands). At mid-2000 there were an estimated 160 adherents.

Protestant Churches

At mid-2000 there were an estimated 30,000 adherents.

Eglise évangélique en Nouvelle-Calédonie et aux Iles Loyauté: BP 277, Nouméa; f. 1960; Pres. Rev. SAILALI PASSA; Gen. Sec. Rev. TELL KASARHEROU.

Other churches active in the Territory include the Assembly of God, the Free Evangelical Church, the New Apostolic Church, the Pentecostal Evangelical Church, the Presbyterian Church and the Tahitian Evangelical Church. At mid-2000 there were an estimated 15,500 adherents professing other forms of Christianity.

The Press

L'Avenir Calédonien: 10 rue Gambetta, Nouméa; organ of the Union Calédonienne; Dir GABRIEL PAÏTA.

La Calédonie Agricole: BP 111, 98845 Nouméa Cedex; tel. 243160; fax 284587; internet www.formagri.nc; quarterly; official publ. of the Chambre d'Agriculture; Pres. GÉRARD PASCO; Man. YANNICK COLLETTE; Chief Editors PIERRE ARDORINO, SOPHIE GOLFIER; circ. 4,000.

Le Chien Bleu: BP 16018, Nouméa; tel. 288505; fax 261819; e-mail courrier@lechienbleu.nc; internet www.lechienbleu.nc; monthly; satirical; Man. Editor ETIENNE DUTAILLY.

Eglise de Nouvelle-Calédonie: BP 3, 98845 Nouméa; fax 265352; f. 1976; monthly; official publ. of the Roman Catholic Church; circ. 450.

Les Infos: 42 route de l'Anse-Vata, BP 8134, 98807 Nouméa; tel. 251808; fax 251882; e-mail lesinfos@lagoon.nc; weekly; Editor-in-Chief THIERRY SQUILLARIO.

Journal Officiel de la Nouvelle-Calédonie: Imprimerie Administrative, BP M2, 98849, Nouméa Cedex; tel. 256001; fax 256021; e-mail webmestre.juridoc@gouv.nc; internet www.juridoc.gouv.nc; f. 1853; est. as *Bulletin Officiel de la Nouvelle-Calédonie*; present name adopted in 1988; only the paper version is official; twice a week; publ. by Govt of New Caledonia; record of state legislative devts in New Caledonia.

Mwà Véé: Centre Tjibaou, BP 378, 98845 Nouméa; tel. 414555; fax 414556; e-mail adck@adck.nc; f. 1993; quarterly; French; publ. by l'Agence de Développement de la Culture Kanak; Kanak history, culture and heritage; Publr EMMANUEL KASARHE'ROU; Editor GÉRARD DEL RIO.

Les Nouvelles Calédoniennes: 41–43 rue de Sébastopol, BP G5, 98848 Nouméa; tel. 272584; fax 281627; e-mail xserre@canl.nc; internet www.lnc.nc; f. 1971; daily; Publr FRÉDÉRIC AURAND; Gen. Man. FRANÇOIS LEVASSOR; Editor-in-Chief XAVIER SERRE; circ. 18,500.

Tazar: Immeuble Gallieni II, 12 rue de Verdun, 98800 Nouméa; tel. 282277; fax 283443; monthly; publ. by Mission d'Insertion des Jeunes de la Province Sud; youth.

Télé 7 Jours: Route de Vélodrome, BP 2080, 98846 Nouméa Cedex; tel. 284598; weekly.

NEWS AGENCY

Agence France-Presse (AFP): 15 rue Docteur Guégan, 98800 Nouméa; tel. 263033; fax 278699; Correspondent FRANCK MADOEUF.

Publishers

Editions d'Art Calédoniennes: 3 rue Guynemer, BP 1626, Nouméa; tel. 277633; fax 281526; art, reprints, travel.

Editions du Santal: 5 bis rue Emile-Trianon, 98846 Nouméa; tel. and fax 262533; history, art, travel, birth and wedding cards; Dir PAUL-JEAN STAHL.

Grain de Sable: BP 577, 98845 Nouméa; tel. and fax 273057; e-mail graindesable@canl.nc; internet www.pacific-bookin.com; literature, travel; Publr LAURENCE VIALLARD.

Ile de Lumière: BP 8401, Nouméa Sud; tel. 289858; history, politics.

Savannah Editeur SNP: Yacht Marianne, BP 3086, 98846 Nouméa; tel. 784711; e-mail savannahmarc@hotmail.com; f. 1994; est. as Savannah Edns; present name adopted in 2006; sports, travel, leisure; Publr JOËL MARC.

Société d'Etudes Historiques de la Nouvelle-Calédonie: BP 63, 98845 Nouméa; tel. 767155; e-mail seh-nc@lagoon.nc; f. 1969; Pres. VALET GABRIEL.

Broadcasting and Communications

TELECOMMUNICATIONS

Citius: Immeuble Administratif, 1 rue du Contre Amiral Joseph Bouzet, Route de Nouville, 98800 Nouméa; tel. 266604; fax 266642; e-mail visio@citius.nc; internet www.citius.nc; f. 2008.

Offices des Postes et Télécommunications (OPT): Le Waruna, 2 rue Monchovet, Port Plaisance, 98841 Nouméa Cedex; tel. 268217; fax 262927; e-mail direction@opt.nc; internet www.opt.nc; provides postal and fixed-line tel. services, and operates Mobilis mobile cellular tel. network (f. 2003); Dir-Gen. JEAN-YVES OLLIVAUD.

BROADCASTING

Radio

NRJ Nouvelle-Calédonie: 41–43 rue Sébastopol, BP G5, 98848 Nouméa; tel. 263434; fax 279447; e-mail nrj@nrj.nc; internet www .nrj.nc; f. 1984; Dir RICARDO GREMY.

Radio Djiido (Kanal K): Résidence La Caravelle, 3 rue Sainte Cécile, Vallée du Tir, BP 10459, 98805 Nouméa Cedex; tel. 778768; fax 272187; e-mail radiodjiido@radiodjiido.nc; internet www.radiodjiido.nc; f. 1985; pro-independence community station; broadcasts in French; socio-cultural programmes; 60% local news, 30% regional, 10% international; Station Man. THIERRY KAMÉRÉMOIN; Editor-in-Chief CÉDRICK WAKAHUGNEME.

Radio Nouvelle-Calédonie: Réseau France Outre-mer (RFO), 1 rue Maréchal Leclerc, Mont Coffyn, BP G3, 98848 Nouméa Cedex; tel. 239999; fax 281252; e-mail internet.nc@rfo.fr; internet nouvellecaledonie.rfo.fr; f. 1942; fmrly Radiodiffusion Française d'Outre-mer (RFO); French; relays Radio Australia's French service; Dir-Gen. GENEVIÈVE GIARD; Regional Dir BERNARD JOYEUX.

Radio Océane: 1 ave d'Auteuil, Lotissement FSH, Koutio, 98835 Dumbéa; tel. 410095; fax 410099; e-mail oceane.fm@lagoon.nc; Dir YANN DUVAL.

Radio Rythme Bleu: 8 ave Foch, BP 578, 98845 Nouméa Cedex; tel. 254646; fax 284928; e-mail rrb@lagoon.nc; f. 1984; music and local, nat. and int. news; Pres. CHRISTIAN PROST; Dir ELIZABETH NOUAR.

Television

RFO-Télé Nouvelle-Calédonie: Réseau France Outre-mer (RFO), 1 rue Maréchal Leclerc, Mont Coffyn, BP G3, 98848 Nouméa Cedex; tel. 239999; fax 239975; internet www.rfo.fr; f. 1965; part of the France Télévisions group, France; three channels; Gen. Man. BERNARD JOYEUX; Editor-in-Chief GONZAGUE DE LA BOURDONNAYE.

Canal+ Calédonie: 30 rue de la Somme, BP 1797, 98845 Nouméa; tel. 265343; fax 265338; e-mail abonnement@canal-caledonie.com; internet www.canalcaledonie.com; subsidiary of Canal Plus, France; subscription service; broadcasts 24 hours daily; CEO SERGE LAMAGNÈRE.

Canal Outre-mer (Canal+): Nouméa; f. 1995; cable service.

Finance

(cap. = capital; res = reserves; dep. = deposits; m. = million; brs = branches; amounts in francs CFP unless otherwise stated)

BANKING

Agence Française de Développement: 1 rue Barleux, BP JI, 98849 Nouméa Cedex; tel. 242600; fax 282413; e-mail afdnoumea@ afd.fr; Man. JEAN-YVES CLAVEL.

Banque Calédonienne d'Investissement (BCI): 54 ave de la Victoire, BP K5, 98849 Nouméa; tel. 256565; fax 274035; e-mail bci@ bci.nc; internet www.bci.nc; f. 1988; cap. 7,500m. (Dec. 2003); Chair. DIDIER LEROUX; Dir-Gen. JEAN-PIERRE GIANOTTI.

Banque de Nouvelle-Calédonie: 10 ave Foch, BP L3, 98849 Nouméa Cedex; tel. 257402; fax 275619; e-mail contact@bnc.nc; internet www.bnc.nc; f. 1974; adopted present name in 2002; 95.8% owned by Financière Océor, France; cap. 3,858.3m., res 1,294.2m., dep. 66,873.0m. (Dec. 2004); Pres. CHRISTIAN CAMUS; Gen. Man. SYLVAIN FAURE; 7 brs.

BNP Paribas Nouvelle-Calédonie (France): 37 ave Henri Lafleur, BP K3, 98849 Nouméa Cedex; tel. 258400; fax 258459; e-mail bnp .nc@bnpparibas.com; internet nc.bnpparibas.net/fr; f. 1969;est. as Banque Nationale de Parispresent name adopted in 2001; cap. €28.0m., res €315.6m. (Dec. 2001); Pres. JEAN-PASCAL DUMANS; Gen. Man. JEAN-FRANCOIS ARACIL; 10 brs.

Société Générale Calédonienne de Banque: 44 rue de l'Alma, Siège et Agence Principale, BP G2, 98848 Nouméa Cedex; tel. 256300; fax 256322; e-mail svp.sgcb@canl.nc; internet www.sgcb .com; f. 1981; total assets 1,086m. (Dec. 2007); Gen. Man. JEAN-PIERRE DUFOUR; Chair. JEAN-LOUIS MATTEI; 21 brs.

INSURANCE

AGF Vie & AGF IART Nouvelle-Calédonie: 99 ave du Générale de Gaulle, BP 152, 98845 Nouméa; tel. 283838; fax 281628; e-mail agfvienc@agfvie.nc; life and general non-life insurance.

GAN Pacifique: 30 route de la Baie des Dames, Immeuble Le Centre-Ducos, BP 7953, 98800 Nouméa Cedex; tel. 243070; fax 278884; e-mail ganoumea@canl.nc; subsidiary of GAN Assurances, France; general non-life insurance; Chair. JEAN-FRANÇOIS LEMOUX; Dir-Gen. PATRICK REYNAUD.

Poe-ma Insurances: 3 rue Sébastopol, BP 8069, 98807 Nouméa; tel. 274263; fax 274267; e-mail info@poema.nc; Bureau Man. FREDERIC DUCOS.

Trade and Industry

DEVELOPMENT ORGANIZATIONS

Agence de Développement de la Culture Kanak (ADCK): Centre Culturel Tjibaou, rue des Accords de Matignon, BP 378, 98845 Nouméa Cedex; tel. 414555; fax 414546; e-mail adck@adck.nc; internet www.adck.nc; Pres. MARIE-CLAUDE TJIBAOU; Dir EMMANUEL KASARHEROU.

Agence de Développement Economique de la Nouvelle-Calédonie (ADECAL): 15 rue Guynemer, BP 2384, 98846 Nouméa Cedex; tel. 249077; fax 249087; e-mail adecal@offratel.nc; internet www.adecal.nc; f. 1995; promotes investment within New Caledonia; Gen. Man. JEAN-MICHEL ARLIE.

Agence de Développement Rural et d'Aménagement Foncier (ADRAF): 1 rue de la Somme, BP 4228, 98847 Nouméa Cedex; tel. 258600; fax 258604; e-mail adraf@adraf.nc; internet www.adraf.nc; f. 1986, reorg. 1989; acquisition and redistribution of land; Chair. MICHEL MATHIEU; Dir-Gen. JULES HMALOKO.

Conseil Economique et Social: 30 route Baie des Dames, Immeuble Le Centre, Ducos, BP 4766, 98847 Nouméa Cedex; tel. 278517; fax 278509; e-mail ces@gouv.nc; internet www.ces.gouv.nc; represents trade unions and other orgs involved in economic, social and cultural life; Pres. ROBERT LAMARQUE; Sec.-Gen. FRANÇOIS-PAUL BUFNOIR.

Institut Calédonien de Participation (ICAP): 1 rue Barleux, BP J1, 98849 Nouméa; tel. 276218; fax 282280; e-mail icap@icap.nc; internet www.icap.nc; f. 1989; est. to finance devt projects and encourage the Kanak population to participate in the market economy; Pres. PAUL NÉAOUTYINE; Man. YVES GOYETCHE.

Institut pour le Développement des Compétences en Nouvelle-Calédonie: 1 rue de la Somme, BP 497, 98845 Nouméa Cedex; tel. 281082; fax 272079; e-mail idc.nc@idcnc.nc; internet www.idcnc .nc; f. 2006; Dir PHILIPPE MARTIN.

Société de Développement et d'Investissement des Iles Loyauté (SODIL SA): 12 rue du Général Mangin, Immeuble Richelieu, BP 2217, 98846 Nouméa Cedex; tel. 276663; fax 276709; e-mail sodil@lagoon.nc; f. 1991; financing, promotion and sustainable devt of industry, tourism and artisanal cos; priority areas are transport, food-processing, aquaculture, and regional and int. tourism; Pres. Hnaejë Hamu; Man. Samuel Hnepeune.

Société d'Equipement de Nouvelle-Calédonie (SECAL): 28 rue du Général Mangin, BP 2517, 98846 Nouméa Cedex; tel. 232666; fax 232676; e-mail contact@secal.nc; internet www.secal.nc; f. 1971; urban management and devt, public sector construction and civil engineering; Pres. Simone Mignard.

Société de Financement et de Développement de la Province Sud (PROMOSUD): BP 295, 98845 Nouméa Cedex; tel. 241972; fax 271326; e-mail info@promosud.nc; internet www.promosud.nc; f. 1991; financing, promotion and economic devt of cos in priority sectors, incl. tourism, fishing and aquaculture, and processing industries; Pres. Pierre Bretegnier; Man. Thierry Payen.

Société de Financement et d'Investissement de la Province Nord (SOFINOR): 85 ave du Général de Gaulle, BP 66, 98800 Nouméa; tel. 281353; fax 281567; e-mail dirgen@smsp.nc; internet www.sofinor.nc; f. 1990; economic devt, management and financing; priority areas include mining and metal production, aquaculture and fishing, tourism, transport, real estate and engineering; Pres. Guigui Dounehote; Man. Louis Mapou.

CHAMBERS OF COMMERCE

Chambre d'Agriculture: 3 rue A. Desmazures, BP 111, 98845 Nouméa Cedex; tel. 243160; fax 284587; e-mail direction@canc.nc; f. 1909; Pres. Gérard Pasco; Dir Yannick Couette; 33 mems.

Chambre de Commerce et d'Industrie: 15 rue de Verdun, BP M3, 98849 Nouméa Cedex; tel. 243100; fax 243131; e-mail cci@cci.nc; internet www.cci.nc; f. 1879; Pres. André Desplat; Gen. Man. Michel Merzeau; 12,000 mems.

Chambre de Métiers et de l'Artisanat: 10 ave James Cook, BP 4186, 98846 Nouméa Cedex; tel. 282337; fax 282729; e-mail cma@cma.nc; internet www.cma.nc; Pres. Jean-Claude Merlet; Sec.-Gen. Paul Sanchez.

EMPLOYERS' ORGANIZATION

MEDEF de Nouvelle-Calédonie (Fédération Patronale des Chefs d'Entreprise en Nouvelle-Calédonie): 6 rue Jean Jaurès, 98800 Nouméa Cedex; tel. 273525; fax 274037; e-mail medefnc@medef.nc; internet www.medef.nc; f. 1936; represents leading cos of New Caledonia in defence of professional interests, co-ordination, documentation and research in socio-economic fields; affiliated to Mouvement des Entreprises de France; Pres. Jean-François Bouillaguet.

UTILITIES

Electricity

Electricité et Eau de Nouvelle-Calédonie (EEC): 15 rue Jean Chalier, PK 4, 98800 Nouméa Cedex; tel. 463636; fax 463510; e-mail clientele@eec.nc; internet www.eec.nc; f. 1929; est. as UNLECO; present name adopted in 1984; subsidiary of Gdf Suez, France; producers and distributors of electricity; Chair. François Guichard; Gen. Man. Yves Morault.

Société Néo-Calédonienne d'Energie (ENERCAL): 87 ave du Général de Gaulle, BP C1, 98848 Nouméa Cedex; tel. 250250; fax 250253; e-mail jbegaud@canl.nc; f. 1955; 16% owned by EDEV, France; production and distribution of electricity; Chair. Jean-Pierre Aifa; Gen. Man. Jean Bégaud.

Water

Société Calédonienne des Eaux (CDE): 13 rue Edmond Harbulot, PK 6, BP 812, 98845 Nouméa Cedex; tel. 413720; fax 438128; e-mail patrick.chantre@cde.nc; water distribution; Gen. Man. Alain Carbonel.

MAJOR COMPANIES

Arbé (Ardimanni Benedetti): 2 blvd Vauban, BP 802, Nouméa; tel. 273266; fax 284382; e-mail arbe@arbe.nc; f. 1967; construction, civil engineering and test drilling; Chair. Albert Ardimanni; Man. Dir and CEO Jean-François Jaubert; c. 200 employees.

Endel NC Suez: BP 1085, 98845 Nouméa Cedex; tel. 272227; fax 275676; e-mail endel@endel.nc; internet www.endel.nc; f. 2002; subsidiary of Groupe Fabricom (Groupe Suez, France); design, installation and maintenance services for the energy, iron and steel, and petrochemical industries; revenue CFP 2,900m. (2001); Dir-Gen. Michel Guepy; 265 permanent employees.

Société de Distribution et de Gestion Carrefour: 10 rue Bichat, Quartier Latin, BP 287, 98845 Nouméa Cedex; supermarket retail and distribution; c. 200 employees.

Société de Participation Minière du Sud Calédonien SAS (SPMSC): f. 2005; holding co managing 10% share in the Goro nickel devt for PROMOSUD, SOFINOR and SODIL; Pres. Philippe Gomès.

Société Immobilière de Nouvelle-Calédonie (SIC): 15 rue Guynemer, Mont Coffyn, BP 412, 98845 Nouméa Cedex; tel. 282316; fax 284356; e-mail sic@sic.nc; internet www.sic.nc; f. 1988; residential and commercial property construction (c. 600 properties per year); Pres. Philippe Gomès; Dir-Gen. Thierry Cornaille; 155 permanent employees.

Société Le Froid: 7 rue des Frères Charpentier, Montravel, BP 1209, 98845 Nouméa Cedex; tel. 272244; fax 283552; internet lefroid.nc; mfrs and distributors of soft drinks, fruit juices and beer; CEO Philippe Caillard; c. 120 employees.

Société Le Nickel (SLN): BP E5, 98840 Nouméa Cedex; tel. 245555; fax 275989; e-mail info@sln.nc; internet www.sln.nc; f. 1880; privatized 1999; 60% owned by the Eramet group, 30% by STCPI, 10% by Nishin Steel, Japan; producers of ferro-nickel and nickel matte; five mines and one refinery; produced 6,873m. metric tons in 2004; sales of €30,000m. (2003/04); Chair. and CEO Patrick Buffet; Gen. Man. Pierre Alla; c. 2,200 employees.

Société Minière du Sud Pacifique (SMSP): BP 66, 98845 Nouméa Cedex; tel. 281353; fax 281567; e-mail dirgen@smsp.nc; internet www.smsp.nc; 87% owned by SOFINOR, 5% by SODIL; nickel-mining co; subsidiaries: Nouméa Nickel (NN), Nickel Mining Corpn (NMC), Koniambo Nickel SAS (KNS—49% owned by Falconbridge, Canada); Chair. and CEO André Dang Van Nha; c. 1,000 employees.

SODIMA Géant Sainte-Marie: 7 rue Henri Schmidt, Vallée des Colons, 98800 Nouméa; tel. 285525; fax 281654; supermarket retail and distribution; c. 300 employees.

Vale Inco Nouvelle-Calédonie: Immeuble Malawi, centre ville, 52 avenue Foch, BP 218, 98845 Nouméa Cedex; tel. 235000; fax 273710; internet www.vale.nc; f. 1999; name changed as above in 2008; 69% owned by Vale Inco, Canada, 21% by Sumic Nickel Netherlands, 10% by SPMSC; nickel and cobalt producers; projected annual capacity: 60,000 metric tons of nickel, 4,300–5,000 metric tons of cobalt; Chair. Tito Martins; CEO Peter Poppinga; c. 2,500 employees.

TRADE UNIONS

Confédération Générale des Travailleurs de Nouvelle-Calédonie (COGETRA): incorporates:

Syndicat de la Fonction Publique Territoriale (SFPT): 3 rue Edouard Unger, Maison des Syndicats, Vallée du Tir, BP 10453, 98805 Nouméa Cedex; tel. and fax 271820; e-mail cogetra_nc@yahoo.fr; f. 1998; Pres. Françoise Armand.

Union des Secteurs Généraux du Commerce et de l'Industrie de Nouvelle-Calédonie: 3 rue Edouard Unger, Maison des Syndicats, Vallée du Tir, BP 1612, 98845 Nouméa Cedex; tel. 276450; fax 245270; e-mail usgcinc@cogetra.nc; f. 1966; Pres. Jean-Pierre Kabar.

Confédération Générale du Travail-Force Ouvrière de Nouvelle-Calédonie (CGT-FO NC): 13 rue Jules Ferry, BP R2, 98851 Nouméa Cedex; tel. 274950; fax 278202; e-mail cgtfonc@lagoon.nc; f. 1984; Sec.-Gen. Jacques Bernaleau.

Confédération Syndicale des Travailleurs de Nouvelle-Calédonie (CSTNC): 49 rue Auer Ducos, 98800 Nouméa; tel. and fax 269648; e-mail cst-nc@laposte.net; Sec.-Gen. Sylvain Néa; grouped with the following orgs.

Fédération des Fonctionnaires, Agents et Ouvriers de la Fonction Publique (FSFAOFP): 3 rue Edouard Unger, Maison des Syndicats, Vallée du Tir, BP 820, 98845 Nouméa Cedex; tel. and fax 273532; fax 273917; e-mail lafede@lagoon.nc; f. 1946; represents civil servants and public sector employees; Sec.-Gen. João d'Almeida.

Union des Syndicats des Ouvriers et Employés de Nouvelle-Calédonie (USOENC): 3 rue Edouard Unger, Maison des Syndicats, Vallée du Tir, BP 2534, 98846 Nouméa Cedex; tel. 259640; fax 250164; e-mail usoenc@canl.nc; f. 1968; affiliated to the Int. Metalworkers' Fed; Sec.-Gen. Didier Guénant-Jeanson; 4,011 mems (2005).

Union Syndicale des Travailleurs Kanak et des Exploités (USTKE): 2 rue Ali Raleb, Vallée du Tir, BP 4372, Nouméa; tel. 277210; fax 277687; e-mail contact@ustke.org; internet www.ustke.org; f. 1981; Pres. Marie-Pierre Goyetche.

Union Territoriale de la Confédération Française de l'Encadrement-Confédération Générale des Cadres (UT-CFE-CGC): Centre Commercial La Belle Vie, 224 rue Jacques Ikékawé, PK 6, BP 30536, 98895 Nouméa Cedex; tel. and fax 410300; fax 410310; e-mail utcfecgc@utcfecgc.nc; internet www.utcfecgc.nc; f. 1996; territorial br. of the Confédération Française de l'Encadrement-Confédération Générale des Cadres; Pres. Christophe Coulson; Sec.-Gen. Jean Marie Armand.

Other unions include the Fédération des Cadres et Collaborateurs en Nouvelle-Calédonie (f. 1968), Syndicat Libre Unité Action (f. 1995),

Syndicat National Personnel Navigant Commercial (f. 1984) and Syndicat des Ouvriers de Travaux Publics et Municipaux (f. 1962).

Transport

ROADS

In 2005 there was a total of 4,926 km of roads in New Caledonia; of these, some 2,559 km were unsealed. There were some 410,680 km of urban roads and 890,450 km of rural tracks. There was a further estimated 350 km of unrecorded urban roads within Nouméa.

Société Anonyme des Voies Express à Péage (SAVEXPRESS): 15 rue de Verdun, BP M3, 98849 Nouméa Cedex; tel. 411930; fax 412899; e-mail savexpress@savexpress.nc; f. 1979; highway management and devt; Pres. GUY GEORGE; Man. MAXIME CHASSOT.

SHIPPING

Most traffic is through the port of Nouméa. Passenger and cargo services, linking Nouméa to other towns and islands, are regular and frequent. There is also a harbour for yachts and pleasure craft at Nouméa.

Port Autonome de la Nouvelle-Calédonie: 34 ave James Cook, BP 14, 98845 Nouméa Cedex; tel. 255000; fax 275490; e-mail noumeaportnc@canl.nc; Port Man. PHILIPPE LAFLEUR; Harbour Master EDMUND MARTIN.

Moana Services: 2 bis rue Berthelot, BP 2099, 98846 Nouméa; tel. 273898; fax 259315; e-mail moana@canl.nc; internet www.moana.nc; f. 2000; shipping and logistics agency; representatives for Moana Shipping (Wallis), Maersk Line (Denmark) and Canadian Steamship Lines (Canada); Gen. Man. LUCIEN BOURGADE.

SEM de la Baie de la Moselle (SODEMO): rue de la Frégate-Nivôse, BP 2960, 98846 Nouméa; tel. 277197; fax 277129; e-mail contact@sodemo.nc; internet www.sodemo.nc; f. 1987; operates Port Moselle for pleasure craft; Pres. JEAN WASMAN; Man. FRANÇOIS LE BRUN.

Sofrana NC: 14 ave James Cook, BP 1602, 98845 Nouméa; tel. 275191; fax 272611; e-mail info@sofrana.nc; internet www.sofrana.nc; f. 1968; subsidiary of Sofrana Holding; shipping agents and stevedores; barge operators; Chair. JEAN-BAPTISTE LEROUX; Gen. Man. FRANÇOIS BURNOUF.

CIVIL AVIATION

There is an international airport, La Tontouta, 47 km from Nouméa, and an internal network, centred on Magenta airport, which provides air services linking Nouméa to other towns and islands. Work on a major expansion of La Tontouta airport, scheduled for completion in 2011, began in early 2008. Air Calédonie International (Aircalin) operates flights to various Asia-Pacific destinations. Other airlines providing services to the island include Air New Zealand, Air Vanuatu and Qantas.

Air Calédonie: Aérodrome de Magenta, BP 212, 98845 Nouméa Cedex; tel. 250302; fax 254869; e-mail direction@air-caledonie.nc; internet www.air-caledonie.nc; f. 1954; services throughout mainland New Caledonia and its islands; operates four aircraft; Pres. NIDOÏSH NAISSELINE; CEO WILLIAM IHAGE.

Air Calédonie International (Aircalin): 47 rue de Sébastopol, BP 3736, 98846 Nouméa Cedex; tel. 265546; fax 272772; internet www.aircalin.com; f. 1983; 27% owned by Agence pour la Desserte Aérienne de la Nouvelle-Calédonie (NC Air Transport Agency), 72% by Caisse Nationale des Caisses d'Epargne et de Prévoyance, 1% by others; services to Sydney and Brisbane (Australia), Auckland (New Zealand), Nadi (Fiji), Papeete (French Polynesia), Wallis and Futuna Islands, Port Vila (Vanuatu), Osaka and Tokyo (Japan) and Seoul (Republic of Korea); Chair. CHARLES LAVOIX; Pres. and CEO JEAN-MICHEL MASSON.

Tontouta Air Service (TAS): La Tontouta International Airport, BP 5, 98840 La Tontouta; tel. 352600; fax 352601; e-mail tas@tas.nc; f. 1995; owned by Endel Group; operates Tontouta airport and freight management services; Exec. Vice-Pres. PHILIPPE DARRASON.

Tourism

The number of visitors arriving by air in New Caledonia declined from 99,379 in 2009 to 98,562 in 2010; in the latter year 25.3% came from France, 18.8% from Japan and 17.8% from Australia. The number of visiting cruise-ship passengers declined from 152,250 in 2008 to 131,231 in 2009. A total of 2,643 hotel rooms were available in 2004. In 2009 receipts from tourism were estimated at €146.0m. New Caledonia hosted the Pacific Games in August–September 2011.

GIE Nouvelle-Calédonie Tourisme Point Sud: Galerie Nouméa Centre, 20 rue Anatole France, BP 688, 98845 Nouméa Cedex; tel. 242080; fax 242070; e-mail info@nctps.com; internet www.nouvellecaledonietourisme-sud.com; f. 2001; Dir-Gen. PATRICK MOISAN.

GIE Nouvelle-Calédonie Tourisme Province Nord: Centre Commercial Le Village, 35 ave du Maréchal Foch, Nouméa Cedex; e-mail info@tourismeprovincenord.nc; internet www.tourismeprovincenord.nc; Gen. Man. HENRY MANIQUANT.

Defence

As assessed at November 2010, France maintained a force of 723 army and 510 navy personnel, as well as a gendarmerie, in New Caledonia. The French naval command for the Pacific area is based in French Polynesia.

Commander of the French Armed Forces in New Caledonia: Brig.-Gen. JEAN-FRANÇOIS PARLANTI.

Education

Education is compulsory for 10 years between six and 16 years of age. Schools are operated by both the State and churches, under the supervision of three Departments of Education: the Provincial department responsible for primary level education, the New Caledonian department responsible for primary level inspection, and the State department responsible for secondary level education. Primary education begins at six years of age, and lasts for five years; secondary education, beginning at 11 years of age, comprises a first cycle of four years and a second, three-year cycle. Overall, in 2006 73.7% of pre-primary and primary pupils, and 67.6% of secondary pupils, were enrolled at public institutions. In 2010 there were 12,946 pupils enrolled in pre-primary education, 23,654 in primary education (including special education) and in 2009 there were 32,463 in secondary education (including vocational training). Four institutions provide higher education. Students may also attend universities in France. In 1987 the French University of the Pacific (based in French Polynesia) was established, with a centre in Nouméa, and divided into two universities in 1999. Several other vocational tertiary education centres exist in New Caledonia, including a teacher-training college and two agricultural colleges. In 2003 total public expenditure on education was 66,914m. francs CFP, of which some 42,362m. francs CFP was provided by the French State.

KIRIBATI

Introduction

The Republic of Kiribati (pronounced 'Kir-i-bas') comprises one island and 32 atolls, in three principal groups, scattered over about 5m. sq km of ocean along the Equator and extending about 3,780 km from east to west and 2,050 km from north to south. The island of Banaba (Ocean Island), a solid coral outcrop 306 km to the east of Nauru, and the 16 Gilbert Islands lie in the west of Kiribati, with Tuvalu to the south and the Marshall Islands to the north. The eight Phoenix Islands, which are largely uninhabited, lie some 1,300 km south-east of the Gilbert group and to the north of Tokelau. In the east, Kiribati also comprises eight of the Line Islands (three others are uninhabited dependencies of the USA), including Kiritimati (Christmas Island), the largest coral atoll in the world, which covers 388 sq km (150 sq miles), or almost one-half of the total 811 sq km (313 sq miles) of dry land in Kiribati. Tahiti, French Polynesia, lies some 900 km to the south-east of the Line Islands.

Most of Kiribati has a maritime equatorial climate, the northern and southern islands being in the tropical zone. Temperature varies very little through the year, and the mean annual temperature ranges from 29°C (84°F) in the southern Gilberts to 27°C (81°F) in the Line Islands. There is a season of north-westerly trade winds from March to October and a season of rains and gales from October to March. Average annual rainfall varies greatly, averaging about 3,000 mm in the islands north of Tarawa, about 1,500 mm on Tarawa and for most of the Gilberts group, and 700 mm in the Line Islands. All the islands are prone to severe drought.

The population, which is mainly Micronesian and Christian, is concentrated in the Gilbert Islands. The principal languages are I-Kiribati (Gilbertese) and English. At the census of November 2000 there were 84,494 people in Kiribati. The total population was enumerated at 92,533 at the census of November 2005. According to estimates by the Secretariat of the Pacific Community, the population had reached 102,697 by mid-2011. The capital is located on Bairiki island, in Tarawa.

The I-Kiribati people first settled the islands of the Gilberts (or Tungaru) group between AD 1000 and 1300. European contact began in the 16th century. In 1892 the United Kingdom established a protectorate over the 16 atolls of the Gilbert Islands and the nine Ellice Islands (now Tuvalu). The two groups were administered together under the jurisdiction of the Western Pacific High Commission (WPHC). Phosphate-rich Ocean Island (Banaba), west of the Gilbert group, was annexed by the United Kingdom in 1900. The Gilbert and Ellice Islands were annexed in 1915, and in January 1916 the protectorate was declared a colony. In that year the new Gilbert and Ellice Islands Colony (GEIC) was extended to include Ocean Island and two of the Line Islands, far to the east. Christmas Island (now Kiritimati), another of the Line Islands, was added in 1919 and the eight Phoenix Islands (then uninhabited) in 1937. A joint British-US administration for two of the Phoenix group, Kanton (Canton) and Enderbury, was agreed in April 1939.

During the Second World War the GEIC was invaded by Japanese forces, who occupied the Gilbert Islands in 1942–43. Tarawa Atoll, in the Gilbert group, was the scene of some of the fiercest fighting in the Pacific between Japan and the USA.

As part of the British Government's programme of developing its own nuclear weapons, the first test of a British hydrogen bomb was conducted near Christmas Island in May 1957, when a device was exploded in the atmosphere. Two further tests took place in the same vicinity later that year.

Preparations for self-government in the GEIC began in 1963. In January 1972 a Governor of the GEIC was appointed to assume almost all the functions previously exercised in the colony by the High Commissioner. At the same time the five uninhabited Central and Southern Line Islands, previously administered directly by the High Commissioner, became part of the GEIC. In 1975 the Ellice Islands were allowed to separate from the GEIC to form a distinct territory, named Tuvalu. The remainder of the GEIC was renamed the Gilbert Islands. The Gilbert Islands obtained internal self-government on 1 January 1977, and on 12 July 1979 the Gilbert Islands became an independent republic, within the Commonwealth, under the name of Kiribati. The country did not become a member of the UN until 1999.

Owing to the high rate of population growth (more than 2% per year), and, in particular, the situation of over-population on South Tarawa and its associated social and economic problems, it was announced in 1988 that nearly 5,000 inhabitants were to be resettled on outlying atolls, mainly in the Line Islands. The migration began in 1989. A further programme of resettlement from South Tarawa to five islands in the Phoenix group was initiated in 1995. In November 2004 the Government announced a major new initiative, supported by the UN Development Programme and the Asian Development Bank (ADB), to establish up to four new urban areas in the outer islands as part of ongoing efforts to ease the overcrowding of South Tarawa. The Kiribati Sustainable Towns Programme was among the topics discussed during President Anote Tong's visit to New Zealand in 2008. Recently established in order to address the issue of rapid urbanization, particularly on South Tarawa, New Zealand intended to allocate to this programme the sum of $NZ15m. over a five-year period.

Open-cast mining of phosphate deposits adversely affected the environment of Banaba to such an extent that most inhabitants were removed from the island during the Second World War and resettled on Rabi Island, 2,600 km away in the Fiji group; they became citizens of Fiji in 1970. However, Banabans remained the landowners of their island, and in 2009 it was reported that rehabilitation work was being undertaken on Bananba. The work was expected to cost $A50m. and to take 20 years to complete, whereupon the Banaban community hoped to return to the island.

According to UN criteria, Kiribati is one of the world's least developed nations. The ending of phosphate production in 1979 had a devastating effect on the economy, as receipts from phosphates had accounted, on average, for about 80% of total export earnings and 50% of government taxation revenue. It was estimated that the country's gross domestic product (GDP) per head was halved between the late 1970s and early 1980s. The investment of some phosphate earnings from 1956 did result in a considerable fund of foreign reserves, which have been maintained since 1979. The Revenue Equalization Reserve Fund (RERF) usually provides the Government with investment income equivalent to around 33% of GDP per year. At October 2006 the value of the RERF was estimated at $A666m., compared with $A97m. in 1984. The Government also holds substantial 'offshore' assets through the Kiribati Provident Fund. However, Kiribati's extremely limited export base (the principal domestic exports being copra, seaweed and shark fins) and dependence on imports of almost all essential commodities result in a permanent (and widening) trade deficit, which in most years has been only partially offset by revenue from fishing licence fees, interest earned on the RERF and remittances from I-Kiribati working overseas. The majority of emigrant workers are seafarers employed on foreign ships. From 2009, however, such employment opportunities were expected to be restricted by the deterioration in global economic conditions. It was hoped that this contraction might be offset by increasing seasonal demand for agricultural labourers in Australia and New Zealand, under new schemes whereby the two countries provided temporary work permits to Pacific islanders. With the creation in 2007 of a large marine reserve (see below) and the banning of commercial fishing in the zone, the sale of fewer fishing licences was expected to lead to a decline in revenue from this source, but it was hoped that this would be offset by payments from a special endowment fund. The 2008–11 National Sustainable Development Strategy accorded priority to strategic areas of economic growth, the reduction of poverty, health and education, the environment, improved governance and the upgrading of the islands' infrastructure. In February 2010 Kiribati joined seven other Pacific nations in a new campaign to secure a greater portion of proceeds from the region's important tuna-fishing industry.

Having been identified as an area of major potential, the fisheries sector of Kiribati was to receive financial support from New Zealand for training schemes and the upgrading of facilities, as part of a wider development programme to be implemented in 2011/12.

In 1989 a UN report on the greenhouse effect listed Kiribati as one of the countries that would completely disappear in the 21st century unless drastic action were taken. None of the land on the islands is more than 2 m above sea-level. A rise in sea-level would not only cause flooding, but would also upset the balance between sea and fresh water (below the coral sands), rendering water supplies undrinkable. In mid-1999 it was announced that two uninhabited coral reefs had sunk beneath the sea as a result of the greenhouse effect. King tides have increased in frequency. These exceptionally high tides, widely attributed to global warming and resultant increased sea levels, can flood coastal areas, destroy crops and damage housing. The severe drought of 2007/08 also highlighted the country's vulnerability to adverse weather conditions.

Further concerns were raised regarding Kiribati's water supply, as it became evident that the islands' ground aquifers were no longer able to meet the population's needs. Although the Government had begun to establish water reserves in some areas, in April 2009 it was revealed that the shortage of drinking water in the southern islands had become so serious that villagers were being forced to abandon their homes. In July 2010 technicians completed a project involving the drilling of boreholes on Tarawa atoll to measure the extent of the underground fresh water supply and assist in preventing contamination by salt water. The work was undertaken as part of the Kiribati Adaptation Program (KAP), financed by the World Bank, Australia and New Zealand. In September President Tong declared that Kiribati lacked the funds to combat coastal erosion caused by rising sea levels. With further international support, the planting of mangroves to alleviate the problem was subsequently undertaken, and in March 2011 it was reported that more than 37,000 mangroves had been planted. In November 2010 Kiribati hosted a conference on climate change, at which the 19 countries and numerous organizations represented drew up a declaration to be submitted at the next UN conference on climate change. The declaration urged the adoption of definite measures to prevent disastrous levels of global warming. In May 2011 it was announced that the World Bank was to provide US $2m. in emergency food aid to residents of the outer islands.

In March 2007 Kiribati formally established a major marine reserve, the Phoenix Islands Protected Area (PIPA). Commercial fishing was banned in the reserve, which afforded protection to hundreds of known species of fauna, including more than 500 fish. A leading US aquarium and an international conservation group assisted in the creation of the reserve, which was extended to 408,250 sq km. In August 2010 PIPA was inscribed by UNESCO on the World Heritage List.

Statistical Survey

Source (unless otherwise stated): Statistics Office, Ministry of Finance and Economic Development, POB 67, Bairiki, Tarawa; tel. 21082; fax 21307; e-mail statistics@mfep.gov.ki; internet www.spc.int/prism/country/KI/Stats.

AREA AND POPULATION

Area: 810.5 sq km (312.9 sq miles). *Principal Atolls* (sq km): Banaba (island) 6.3, Tarawa 31.0 (North 15.3, South 15.8), Abemama 27.4, Tabiteuea 37.6 (North 25.8, South 11.9), Total Gilbert group (incl. others) 285.5; Kanton (Phoenix Is) 9.2, Tabuaeran (Fanning—Line Is) 33.8, Kiritimati (Christmas—Line Is) 388.4, Total Line and Phoenix group 525.0 (Line Is 496.0, Phoenix Is 29.0).

Population: 84,494 at census of 7 November 2000; 92,533 (males 45,612, females 46,921) at census of 7 November 2005. *Principal Atolls* (2005): Banaba (island) 301; Abaiang 5,502; Tarawa 45,989 (North 5,678, South 40,311); Tabiteuea 4,898 (North 3,600, South 1,298); Total Gilbert group (incl. others) 83,683; Kanton (Phoenix Is) 41; Kiritimati 5,115; Total Line and Phoenix Group (incl. others) 8,850. *Mid-2011* (Secretariat of the Pacific Community estimate): 102,697 (Source: Pacific Regional Information System).

Density (mid-2010): 124.4 per sq km.

Population by Age and Sex (Secretariat of the Pacific Community estimates at mid-2011): *0–14:* 35,828 (males 18,439, females 17,389); *15–64:* 63,285 (males 31,120, females 32,165); *65 and over:* 3,584 (males 1,417, females 2,167); *Total* 102,697 (males 50,976, females 51,721) (Source: Pacific Regional Information System).

Ethnic Groups (census of 2000): Micronesians 83,452; Polynesians 641; Europeans 154; Others 247; Total 84,494.

Principal Villages: (population at 2005 census): Betio 12,509; Bikenibeu 6,170; Teaoraereke 3,939; Bairiki (capital) 2,766; Eita 2,399; Bonriki 2,119; Temwaiku 2,011. Note: All of the listed villages are in South Tarawa atoll.

Births, Marriages and Deaths (Secretariat of the Pacific Community estimates, 2010, unless otherwise indicated): Registered live births 2,774 (birth rate 27.8 per 1,000); Marriages (registrations, 1988) 352 (marriage rate 5.2 per 1,000); Registered deaths 827 (death rate 8.3 per 1,000) (Source: mainly Pacific Regional Information System).

Life Expectancy (years at birth, WHO estimates): 68 (males 65; females 70) in 2009. Source: WHO, *World Health Statistics*.

Economically Active Population (paid employees aged 15 years and over, 2005 census): Agriculture, hunting, forestry and fishing 936; Manufacturing 305; Electricity, gas and water 293; Construction 511; Trade, restaurants and hotels 1,873; Transport, storage and communications 1,473; Financing, insurance, real estate and business services 356; Public administration 6,953; *Sub-total* 12,700; Activities not adequately defined 433; *Total employed* 13,133 (males 8,095, females 5,038); Unemployed 2,254 (males 1,130, females 1,124); *Total cash labour force* 15,387 (males 9,225, females 6,162). Note: Subsistence workers (not included) numbered 21,582 (males 10,788, females 10,794). *Mid-2011:* Agriculture, etc. 11,000; Total labour force 49,000 (Source: FAO).

HEALTH AND WELFARE

Key Indicators

Total Fertility Rate (children per woman, 2009): 3.1.

Under-5 Mortality Rate (per 1,000 live births, 2009): 46.

Physicians (per 1,000 head, 2004): 0.2.

Hospital Beds (per 1,000 head, 2005): 1.5.

Health Expenditure (2008): US $ per head (PPP): 304.

Health Expenditure (2008): % of GDP: 12.5.

Health Expenditure (2008): public (% of total): 84.3.

Access to Water (% of persons, 2006): 65.

Access to Sanitation (% of persons, 2006): 33.

Total Carbon Dioxide Emissions ('000 metric tons, 2007): 33.0.

Total Carbon Dioxide Emissions Per Head (metric tons, 2007): 0.3.

For sources and definitions, see explanatory note on p. vi.

AGRICULTURE, ETC.

Principal Crops ('000 metric tons, 2009, FAO estimates): Taro (Cocoyam) 2.2; Other roots and tubers 10.1; Coconuts 131.4; Vegetables 6.2; Bananas 7.3.

Livestock ('000 head, year ending September 2009, FAO estimates): Pigs 12.6; Chickens 480.

Livestock Products (metric tons, 2009, unless otherwise indicated, FAO estimates): Pig meat 888; Poultry meat 539; Hen eggs 303.

Fishing (metric tons, live weight, 2009): Capture 40,221* (Emperors 148; Mullets 353*; Snappers and jobfishes 156; Jacks and crevalles 114; Skipjack tuna 26,810; Yellowfin tuna 6,138; Other marine fishes 500*; Marine molluscs 3,300*); Aquaculture 10; *Total catch* 40,231*. Figures exclude aquatic plants (metric tons, FAO estimate): 1,788 (all aquaculture).

* FAO estimate.

Source: FAO.

INDUSTRY

Copra Production (processed, metric tons): 9,686 in 2006; 8,808 in 2007; 9,135 in 2008.

Electric Energy (million kWh): 22.45 in 2008; 22.19 in 2009; 21.60 in 2010.

Sources: Asian Development Bank; UN Industrial Commodity Statistics Database.

FINANCE

Currency and Exchange Rates: Australian currency: 100 cents = 1 Australian dollar ($A). *Sterling, US Dollar and Euro Equivalents* (31 May 2011): £1 sterling = $A1.541; US $1 = $A0.934; €1 = $A1.343; $A100 = £64.90 = US $107.09 = €74.45. *Average Exchange Rate* (Australian dollars per US $): 1.1922 in 2008; 1.2822 in 2009; 1.0902 in 2010.

Budget (central government operations, $A '000, year ending 30 June 2008): *Revenue*: Current 61,831 (Direct taxes 29,835, Entrepreneurial income 121, Property income 25,822, Fees, etc. 5,981, Other 72); Capital receipts 9; Total 61,840. *Current Expenditure:* General public services 10,571; Public order and safety 7,988; Education 20,533; Health 13,106; Welfare and environment 2,686; Community and culture 2,729; Agriculture, etc. 1,890; Construction affairs 2,749; Communications 3,177; Commerce 1,100; Labour affairs 3,071; Other 13,079; Total 82,679.

Cost of Living (Consumer Price Index; base: 2000 = 100): All items 108.3 in 2006; 112.9 in 2007; 125.3 in 2008. Source: ILO.

Gross Domestic Product ($A '000 at constant 1996 prices): 100,213 in 2006; 100,184 in 2007; 103,971 in 2008.

Expenditure on the Gross Domestic Product ($A million at current prices, 2009): Government final consumption expenditure 117.0; Private final consumption expenditure 150.6; Gross fixed capital formation 138.6; Change in stocks 1.2; *Total domestic expenditure* 407.4; Exports of goods and services 28.3; *Less* Imports of goods and services 267.9; *GDP in purchasers' values* 167.9. Source: UN Statistics Division, National Accounts Main Aggregates Database.

Gross Domestic Product by Economic Activity ($A '000 at current prices, 2010): Agriculture and fishing 36,022; Mining 46; Manufacturing 7,906; Electricity, gas and water 1,469; Construction 2,276; Wholesale and retail trade 10,741; Transport and communications 16,619; Financial intermediation 9,817; Government administration 25,047; Other community, social and personal service activities 38,208; *Sub-total* 148,149; *Less* Imputed bank service charge 5,658; Indirect taxes, less subsidies 11,891; *GDP in purchasers' values* 154,382. Source: Asian Development Bank.

Balance of Payments ($A '000, 2007): Exports of goods 12,096.0; Imports of goods –83,861.4; *Trade balance* –71,765.4; Exports of services and income 85,767.8; Imports of services and income –55,586.7; *Balance on goods, services and income* –41,584.3; Current transfers received 59,517.8; Current transfers paid –11,986.5; *Current balance* 5,947.0 (incl. adjustments); Capital account (net) 36,963.0; Direct investment (net) 363.9; Portfolio investment (net) –4,319.0; Other investments (net) –32,260.9; Net errors and omissions –3,688.6; *Overall balance* 3,005.3. *2010:* Exports of goods 7,066; Imports of goods –80,086; Trade balance –73,020; Exports of services and income 82,671; Imports of services and income –66,214; Current transfers received 26,897; Current transfers paid –5,346; Current balance –35,010. Source: Asian Development Bank.

EXTERNAL TRADE

Principal Commodities ($A '000, 2007): *Imports:* Food and live animals 26,429; Beverages and tobacco 5,434; Crude materials (excl. fuels) 1,327; Mineral fuels, lubricants, etc. 20,849; Chemicals 3,681; Basic manufactures 10,081; Machinery and transport equipment 10,841; Miscellaneous manufactured articles 4,254; Total (incl. others) 83,632. *Exports (incl. re-exports):* Copra 769; Copra cake (meal) 904; Coconut oil (crude) 5,331; Seaweed 220; Total (incl. others) 11,655 (Re-exports 2,218).

Principal Trading Partners (US $ '000, 2010): *Imports:* Australia 18,686; Fiji 30,104; Japan 31,724; New Zealand 3,633; Total (incl. others) 106,935. *Exports:* Ecuador 7,750; Japan 5,750; Thailand 9,960; USA 1,400; Total (incl. others) 35,410. Source: mainly Asian Development Bank.

TRANSPORT

Road Traffic (motor vehicles registered on Tarawa, 2004): Motor cycles 634; Passenger cars 610; Buses 7; Trucks 502; Minibuses 299; Others 18; Total 2,070.

Shipping: *Merchant Fleet* (registered, at 31 December 2009): 104 vessels; total displacement 547,062 grt. (Source: IHS Fairplay, *World Fleet Statistics*). *International Sea-borne Freight Traffic* ('000 metric tons, 1990): Goods loaded 15; Goods unloaded 26 (Source: UN, *Monthly Bulletin of Statistics*).

Civil Aviation (traffic on scheduled services, 1998): Passengers carried 28,000; Passenger-km 11 million; Total ton-km 2 million. Source: UN, *Statistical Yearbook*.

TOURISM

Foreign Tourist Arrivals: 2,004 in 2006; 3,599 in 2007; 3,380 in 2008.

Tourist Arrivals by Country of Residence (by air at Tarawa, 2008): Australia 876; Fiji 561; Japan 192; Nauru 28; New Zealand 319; Solomon Islands 55; Tuvalu 134; USA 35; Total (incl. others) 3,380.

Tourism Receipts ($A million): 2.1 in 1999; 2.2 in 2000; 3.0 in 2001.

COMMUNICATIONS MEDIA

Radio Receivers (1997): 17,000 in use.

Television Receivers (1997): 1,000 in use.

Telephones (main lines in use, 2009): 4,000.

Mobile Cellular Telephones (subscribers, 2009): 1,000.

Personal Computers (2005): 1,000.

Internet Users (2009): 7,800.

Non-daily Newspapers: 2 (estimated combined circulation 3,600) in 2002; 3 in 2004.

Sources: UNESCO, *Statistical Yearbook*; UN, *Statistical Yearbook*; International Telecommunication Union; Australian Press Council.

EDUCATION

Primary (2008): 91 schools; 16,123 students (males 8,044, females 8,079); 645 teachers (males 119, females 526).

Secondary (2005, unless otherwise indicated): 40 schools in 2008; 7,487 students (males 3,716, females 3,771); 665 teachers (males 350, females 315).

Teacher-training (2001): 198 students; 22 teachers.

Vocational (2001): 1,303 students; 17 teachers.

Pupil-teacher Ratio (primary education, UNESCO estimate): 25.0 in 2007/08. Source: UNESCO Institute for Statistics.

Adult Literacy Rate (UNESCO estimates): 92.5% (males 93%; females 92%) in 2001. Source: UNESCO, *Assessment of Resources, Best Practices and Gaps in Gender, Science and Technology in Kiribati*.

Directory

The Constitution

A new Constitution was promulgated at independence on 12 July 1979. The main provisions are as follows:

The Constitution states that Kiribati is a sovereign democratic Republic and that the Constitution is the supreme law. It guarantees protection of all fundamental rights and freedoms of the individual and provides for the determination of citizenship.

The President, known as the Beretitenti, is Head of State and Head of the Government and presides over the Cabinet which consists of the Beretitenti, the Kauoman-ni-Beretitenti (Vice-President), the Attorney-General and not more than eight other ministers appointed by the Beretitenti from an elected parliament known as the Maneaba ni Maungatabu. The Constitution stipulated that the pre-independence Chief Minister became the first Beretitenti, but that in future the Beretitenti would be elected. After each general election for the Maneaba, the chamber nominates, from among its members, three or four candidates from whom the Beretitenti is elected by universal adult suffrage. Executive authority is vested in the Cabinet, which is directly responsible to the Maneaba ni Maungatabu. The Constitution also provides for a Council of State consisting of the Chairman of the Public Services Commission, the Chief Justice and the Speaker of the Maneaba.

Legislative power resides with the single-chamber Maneaba ni Maungatabu, composed of 42 members elected by universal adult suffrage for four years (subject to dissolution), one nominated member (see below) and the Attorney-General as an ex-officio member if he is not elected. The Maneaba is presided over by the Speaker, who is elected by the Maneaba from among persons who are not members of the Maneaba.

One chapter makes special provision for Banaba and the Banabans, stating that one seat in the Maneaba is reserved for a nominated member of the Banaban community. The Banabans' inalienable right to enter and reside in Banaba is guaranteed and, where any right over or interest in land there has been acquired by the Republic of Kiribati or by the Crown before independence, the

Republic is required to hand back the land on completion of phosphate extraction. A Banaba Island Council is provided for, as is an independent commission of inquiry to review the provisions relating to Banaba.

The Constitution also makes provision for finance, for a Public Service and for an independent judiciary (see Judicial System).

The Government

HEAD OF STATE

President (Beretitenti): ANOTE TONG (elected 4 July 2003; re-elected 17 October 2007).

Vice-President (Kauoman-ni-Beretitenti): TEIMA ONORIO.

CABINET
(October 2011)

President and Minister for Foreign Affairs and Immigration: ANOTE TONG.

Vice-President and Minister for Commerce, Industry and Co-operatives: TEIMA ONORIO.

Minister for the Civil Service: TEREREI ABETE-REEMA.

Minister for Public Works and Utilities: KIRABUKE TEIAUA.

Minister for Education, Youth and Sports Development: TOAKAI KORIRINTETAAKE.

Minister for Communications, Transport and Tourism Development: TEMATE ERIATEITI.

Minister for Health and Medical Services: Dr KAUTU TENAUA.

Minister for Environment, Lands and Agricultural Development: AMBEROTI NIKORA.

Minister for Internal and Social Affairs: KOURAITI BENIATO.

Minister for Finance and Economic Development: NATAN TEEWE.

Minister for Fisheries and Marine Resource Development: TABERANNANG TIMEON.

Minister for the Line and Phoenix Islands: TAWITA TEMOKU.

Minister for Labour and Human Resource Development: IOTEBA REDFERN.

Attorney-General: TITABU TABANE.

MINISTRIES

Office of the President (Beretitenti): POB 68, Bairiki, Tarawa; tel. 21183; fax 21145.

Ministry of Commerce, Industry and Co-operatives: POB 510, Betio, Tarawa; tel. 26158; fax 26233; e-mail enquiry@mcic.gov.ki; internet www.mcic.gov.ki.

Ministry of Communications, Transport and Tourism Development: POB 487, Betio, Tarawa; tel. 26003; fax 26193.

Ministry of Education, Youth and Sports Development: POB 263, Bikenibeu, Tarawa; tel. 28091; fax 28222.

Ministry of Environment, Lands and Agricultural Development: POB 234, Bikenibeu, Tarawa; tel. 28507; fax 28334.

Ministry of Finance and Economic Development: POB 67, Bairiki, Tarawa; tel. 21801; fax 21307; e-mail account@mfep.gov.ki; internet www.mfep.gov.ki.

Ministry of Fisheries and Marine Resource Development: POB 64, Bairiki, Tarawa; tel. 21099; fax 21120.

Ministry of Foreign Affairs and Immigration: POB 68, Bairiki, Tarawa; tel. 21342; fax 21466; e-mail mfa@tskl.net.ki.

Ministry of Health and Medical Services: POB 268, Bikenibeu, Tarawa; tel. 28100; fax 28152; e-mail mhfp@tskl.net.ki.

Ministry of Internal and Social Affairs: POB 75, Bairiki, Tarawa; tel. 21092; fax 21133; e-mail homeaffairs@tskl.net.ki.

Ministry of Labour and Human Resource Development: POB 69, Bairiki, Tarawa; tel. 21097; fax 21452; internet www.labour.gov.ki.

Ministry of the Line and Phoenix Islands: Kiritimati Island; tel. 81211; fax 81278.

Ministry of Public Works and Utilities: POB 498, Betio, Tarawa; tel. 26192; fax 26172.

President and Legislature

PRESIDENT

Election, 17 October 2007

Candidate	Votes	% of votes
Anote Tong	15,676	64.3
Nabuti Mwemwenikarawa	8,151	33.4
Patrick Tatireta	356	1.5
Timon Aneri	198	0.8
Total	24,381	100.0

MANEABA NI MAUNGATABU
(House of Assembly)

This is a unicameral body comprising 42 elected members (most of whom formally present themselves for election as independent candidates), and one nominated representative of the Banaban community, along with the Attorney-General in an ex officio capacity (if the latter is not elected). An election was held on 21 October 2011, with a second round of voting being conducted on 28 October.

Speaker: TAOMATI IUTA.

Election Commission

Election Commission: Tarawa; Electoral Commr RINE UEARA.

Political Organizations

Political organizations in Kiribati are not conventional organized bodies but loose groupings of individuals supporting similar policies. In addition to the groupings listed below, also in existence are: the National Progressive Party, led by Teatao Teannaki, and the Liberal Party, led by Tewareka Tentoa.

Boutokan Te Koaua (Pillars of Truth): c/o Maneaba Ni Maungatabu, Tarawa; tel. 21880; fax 21278; mems affiliated to Anote Tong.

Maneaban Te Mauri: c/o Maneaba Ni Maungatabu, Tawara; tel. 21880; fax 21278; mems affiliated to Teburoro Tito and Harry Tong.

Maurin Kiribati Party: c/o Maneaba Ni Maungatabu, Tawara; Sec. NABUTI MWEMWENIKARAWA.

Diplomatic Representation

EMBASSY AND HIGH COMMISSIONS IN KIRIBATI

Australia: POB 77, Bairiki, Tarawa; tel. 21184; fax 21904; e-mail ahc.tarawa@dfat.gov.au; internet www.kiribati.embassy.gov.au; High Commissioner BRETT ALDAM.

New Zealand: POB 53, Bairiki, Tarawa; tel. 21400; fax 21402; e-mail nzhc@tskl.net.ki; High Commissioner MIKE WALSH.

Taiwan (Republic of China): Bairiki, Tarawa; tel. 22557; fax 22535; e-mail Kir@mofa.gov.tw; Ambassador BENJAMIN HO.

Judicial System

There are 24 Magistrates' Courts (each consisting of one presiding magistrate and up to eight other magistrates) hearing civil, criminal and land cases. When hearing civil or criminal cases, the presiding magistrate sits with two other magistrates, and when hearing land cases with four other magistrates. A single magistrate has national jurisdiction in civil and criminal matters. Appeal from the Magistrates' Courts lies, in civil and criminal matters, to a single judge of the High Court, and, in matters concerning land, divorce and inheritance, to the High Court's Land Division, which consists of a judge and two Land Appeal Magistrates.

The High Court of Kiribati is a superior court of record and has unlimited jurisdiction. It consists of the Chief Justice and a Puisne Judge. Appeal from a single judge of the High Court, both as a Court of the First Instance and in its appellate capacity, lies to the Kiribati Court of Appeal, which is also a court of record and consists of a panel of three judges.

All judicial appointments are made by the Beretitenti (President).

Chief Justice of the High Court: Sir JOHN BAPTIST MURIA, POB 501, Betio, Tarawa; tel. 26007; fax 26149.

Judges of the Kiribati Court of Appeal: Sir ROBERT SMELLIE, Sir DAVID TOMPKINS, ROBERT FISHER.

Religion

CHRISTIANITY

Most of the population are Christians: 53.4% Roman Catholic and 39.2% members of the Kiribati Protestant Church, according to the 1990 census.

The Roman Catholic Church

Kiribati forms part of the diocese of Tarawa and Nauru, suffragan to the archdiocese of Suva (Fiji). At 31 December 2007 the diocese contained an estimated 60,686 adherents. The Bishop participates in the Catholic Bishops' Conference of the Pacific, based in Suva (Fiji).

Bishop of Tarawa and Nauru: Most Rev. PAUL EUSEBIUS MEA KAIUEA, Bishop's House, POB 79, Bairiki, Tarawa; tel. 21279; fax 21401; e-mail diocesetarawa@tskl.net.ki.

The Anglican Communion

Kiribati is within the diocese of Polynesia, part of the Anglican Church in Aotearoa, New Zealand and Polynesia. The Bishop in Polynesia is resident in Fiji.

Protestant Church

Kiribati Protestant Church: POB 80, Bairiki, Tarawa; tel. 21195; fax 21453; e-mail kpc@tskl.net.ki; f. 1988; Moderator Rev. BAITEKE NABETARI; Gen. Sec. Rev. MAREWEIA RITETI; over 30,000 mems.

Other Churches

Seventh-day Adventist, Church of God and Assembly of God communities are also represented, as is the Church of Jesus Christ of Latter-day Saints (Mormon).

BAHÁ'Í FAITH

National Spiritual Assembly: POB 269, Bikenibeu, Tarawa; tel. and fax 28074; e-mail natbahaikiribati@gmail.com; 2,400 mems resident in 100 localities in 1995.

The Press

Butim'aea Manin te Euangkerio: POB 80, Bairiki, Tarawa; tel. 21195; e-mail kpc@tskl.net.ki; f. 1913; Protestant Church newspaper; weekly; a monthly publication *Te Kaotan te Ota* is also produced; Editor Rev. TOOM TOAKAI.

Kiribati Business Link: Bairiki, Tarawa; English.

Kiribati Newstar: POB 10, Bairiki, Tarawa; tel. 21652; fax 21671; f. 2000; independent; weekly; English and I-Kiribati; Editor-in-Chief NGAUEA UATIOA.

Te Itoi ni Kiribati: POB 231, Bikenibeu, Tarawa; tel. 28138; fax 21341; f. 1914; Roman Catholic Church newsletter; monthly; circ. 2,300.

Te Mauri: Protestant Church newspaper; Editor BATIRI BATAUA.

Te Uekera: Broadcasting and Publications Authority, POB 78, Bairiki, Tarawa; tel. 21162; fax 21096; e-mail bpa_admin@tskl.net.ki; f. 1945; bi-weekly; English and I-Kiribati; Editor ROOTI TERUBEA; circ. 2,000.

Broadcasting and Communications

TELECOMMUNICATIONS

Telecom Kiribati Ltd: Bairiki, Tarawa; govt-owned; Gen. Man. ENOTA INGINTAU.

Telecom Services Kiribati Ltd: POB 72, Bairiki, Tarawa; tel. 20700; fax 21424; e-mail ceo@tskl.net.ki; internet www.tskl.net.ki; f. 1990; Chair. ELLIOT ALI; CEO BARANIKO TONGANIBEIA.

BROADCASTING

Regulatory Authority

Broadcasting and Publications Authority: POB 78, Bairiki, Tarawa; tel. 21187; fax 21096.

Radio

Radio Kiribati: Broadcasting and Publications Authority, POB 78, Bairiki, Tarawa; tel. 21187; fax 21096; f. 1954; statutory body; station Radio Kiribati broadcasting on SW and MW transmitters; programmes in I-Kiribati (90%) and English (10%); some advertising; Gen. Man. TANIERI TEIBUAKO.

Television

Television Kiribati Ltd: Betio, Tarawa; tel. 26036; fax 26045; internet www.tkl.com.ki; f. 1987; CEO TAOM KAITARA.

Finance

(cap. = capital; dep. = deposits; res = reserves)

BANKING

ANZ Bank (Kiribati) Ltd: POB 66, Bairiki, Tarawa; tel. 21095; fax 21200; e-mail anzkiribati@anz.com; internet www.anz.com/kiribati; f. 1984; 75% owned by ANZ Bank, 25% by Govt of Kiribati; fmrly The Bank of Kiribati Ltd, name changed as above 2009; Chair. JOHN MORSCHEL; Man. Dir TERRENCE LOW; 4 brs.

Development Bank of Kiribati: POB 33, Bairiki, Tarawa; tel. 21345; fax 21297; e-mail dbk@tskl.net.ki; f. 1986; took over the assets of the National Loans Board; identifies, promotes and finances small-scale projects; auth. cap. $A2m.; Gen. Man. KIETAU TABWEBWEITI; 5 brs.

A network of lending entities known as 'village banks' operates throughout the islands, as do a number of credit unions under the management of the Credit Union League.

INSURANCE

Kiribati Insurance Corpn: POB 509, Betio, Tarawa; tel. 253367; fax 25338; e-mail enquire@kic.org.ki; internet www.kic.org.ki; f. 1981; govt-owned; sole insurance co; reinsures overseas; Gen. Man. TEIBABA ABERA.

Trade and Industry

GOVERNMENT AGENCIES

Kiribati Copra Mill Co Ltd: POB 607, Betio, Tarawa; tel. 26831; fax 26635; e-mail kcmc@tskl.net.ki; internet www.kcmcl.ki; f. 2001.

Kiribati Housing Corporation: Bairiki, Tarawa; tel. 21092; operates the Housing Loan and Advice Centre; Chair. TOKOREAUA KAIRORO.

Kiribati Provident Fund: POB 76, Bairiki, Tarawa; tel. 21153; fax 21300; internet www.kpf.com.ki; f. 1977; Chair. TEKIERA ABERA.

CHAMBER OF COMMERCE

Kiribati Chamber of Commerce: POB 550, Betio, Tarawa; tel. 26351; fax 26332; Pres. MARTIN TOFINGA.

UTILITIES

Public Utilities Board: POB 443, Betio, Tarawa; tel. 26292; fax 26106; e-mail ceo.pub@tskl.net.ki; f. 1977; govt-owned; provides electricity, water and sewerage services in Tarawa; CEO TABOIA METUTERA.

Solar Energy Company (SEC): POB 493 Betio, Tarawa; tel. 26058; fax 26210; e-mail sec@tskl.net.ki; a co-operative administering and implementing solar-generated electricity projects in North Tarawa and the outer islands.

CO-OPERATIVE SOCIETIES

Co-operative societies dominate trading in Tarawa and enjoy a virtual monopoly outside the capital, except for Banaba and Kiritimati.

Bobotin Kiribati Ltd (BKL): POB 485, Betio, Tarawa; tel. 26092; fax 26224; replaced Kiribati Co-operative Wholesale Society; govt-owned; Gen. Man. AKAU TIARE.

The Kiribati Copra Co-operative Society Ltd: POB 489, Betio, Tarawa; tel. 26534; fax 26391; e-mail kccs@tskl.net.ki; f. 1976; the sole exporter of copra; seven cttee mems; 29 mem. socs; Chair. RAIMON TAAKE; CEO RUTIANO BENETITO.

MAJOR COMPANIES

Abamakoro Trading Ltd: POB 492, Betio, Tarawa; tel. 26568; fax 26415; e-mail abamakoro@tskl.net.ki; importer and wholesaler of general merchandise.

Atoll Seaweed Co Ltd: POB 528, Betio, Tarawa; tel. 26442; fax 26442; e-mail atoll.seaweed@tskl.net.ki; CEO KEVIN ROUATU.

Betio Shipyard Ltd: POB 468, Betio, Tarawa; tel. 26495; fax 26064; e-mail shipyard@tskl.net.ki; CEO KEVIN ROUATU.

Coconut Products Ltd: POB 280, Betio, Tarawa; mfr of coconut oil soap and cosmetics.

Kiribati Oil Co Ltd: Betio, Tarawa.

Kiribati Supplies Co Ltd: POB 71, Bairiki, Tarawa; tel. 21185; fax 21104; e-mail kscl@tskl.net.ki; public co sold to Chinese enterprise, Wishing Star, in 2011; supplier of construction materials, electrical fittings, plumbing equipment and general hardware.

Marine Export Ltd: Betio, Tarawa.

Tarawa Biscuit Co Ltd: POB 422, Betio, Tarawa; tel. 26078.

Te Mautari Ltd: POB 508, Betio, Tarawa; tel. 26035; fax 26304; e-mail mautari@tskl.net.ki; govt-owned; fishing co; operates five vessels.

TRADE UNIONS

Kiribati Trades Union Congress (KTUC): POB 166, Bairiki, Tarawa; tel. 28157; fax 28712; e-mail ktc@tskl.net.ki; f. 1982; unions and asscns affiliated to the KTUC include: Fishermen's Union, Co-operative Workers' Union, Seamen's Union, Teachers' Union, Nurses' Asscn, Public Employees' Asscn, Bankers' Union, Butaritari Rural Workers' Union, Christmas Island Union of Federated Workers, Pre-School Teachers' Asscn, Makim Island Rural Workers' Org., Nanolelei Retailers' Union, Plantation Workers' Union of Fanning Island and Overseas Fishermen's Union; 2,500 mems; Pres. TATOA KAITEIE; Gen. Sec. TAMARETI TAAU.

Transport

ROADS

Wherever practicable, roads are built on all atolls, and connecting causeways between islets are also being constructed as funds and labour permit.Kiribati has about 670 km of roads that are suitable for motor vehicles; all-weather roads exist in Tarawa and Kiritimati. In March 2011 it was announced that, with a loan of US $12m. from the Asian Development Bank, the road network in South Tarawa was to be upgraded.

SHIPPING

A major project to rehabilitate the port terminal and facilities at Betio, with finance totalling some US $22m. from Japan, was completed in 2000. There are other port facilities at Banaba, Kanton and English Harbour.

Kiribati Shipping Services Ltd (KSSL): POB 495, Betio, Tarawa; tel. 26195; fax 26204; e-mail kssl@tskl.net.ki; govt-owned; operates three passenger/freight vessels on inter-island services connecting Kiribati, Nauru, Tuvalu, the Wallis and Futuna Islands, and Suva (Fiji), and one landing craft and multi-purpose cargo vessels between Fiji, Tuvalu, Nauru and Marshall Islands; Gen. Man. Capt. ITIBWINNANG AIAIMOA.

Nikoraoi Shipping: Betio, Tarawa; tel. 26536; fax 26367.

CIVIL AVIATION

There are five international airports (Bonriki on South Tarawa, Cassidy on Kiritimati, Antekana on Butaritari, as well as two others on Kanton and Tabuaeran) and several other airfields in Kiribati. Air Pacific, the Fijian carrier, operates services to Tarawa and Kiritimati, with links to Nadi (Fiji) and Honolulu (Hawaii, USA).

Air Kiribati Ltd: POB 274, Bonriki, Tarawa; tel. 28533; fax 29716; e-mail admin@airkiribati.net; internet www.airkiribati.com.au; f. 1977; fmrly Air Tungaru; national airline; operates scheduled services to outer islands; Chair. TINIAN REIHER; CEO Capt. IOSABATA NAMAKIN.

Tourism

Kiribati's attractions include fishing and bird-watching opportunities, as well as the sites of Second World War battles. In 1997 Caroline Island, situated close to the recently realigned International Date Line, was renamed Millennium Island, in an attempt to maximize its potential for attracting visitors. The Phoenix Islands Protected Area (PIPA), a 408,250 sq km expanse of marine and terrestrial habitats, was inscribed by UNESCO on its World Heritage List in 2010. PIPA contains about 800 species of fauna, including 200 coral species, 500 fish species, 18 marine mammals and 44 bird species. The objectives of the 2010–15 plan for the development of the tourism sector included an increase in the annual number of visitors to 10,000 by the end of the plan period. A campaign to attract more visitors was launched in April 2010. International visitor arrivals reportedly increased by more than 19% in 2010 to reach 4,701, largely supported by the US, New Zealand and Taiwanese markets.

Kiribati National Tourism Office: Ministry of Communications, Transport and Tourism Development, POB 487, Betio, Tarawa; tel. 25573; fax 26193; e-mail sto@mict.gov.ki; internet www.visit-kiribati.com; Sec. DAVID YEETING; Senior Tourist Officer (vacant).

Defence

Kiribati has no professional defence forces. Assistance is provided by Australia and New Zealand. In 2008 expenditure by Kiribati on the islands' defence totalled nearly $A8.0m. (equivalent to 9.7% of central government spending).

Education

Education is compulsory for children between six and 15 years of age. This generally involves six years at a primary school and at least three years at a secondary school. Every atoll is provided with at least one primary school. In 2008 there were 91 primary schools and 40 secondary schools. There were 16,123 pupils enrolled at primary schools in 2008; 7,487 pupils attended secondary schools in 2005. Teaching staff at primary level numbered 645 in 2008; in 2005 there were 665 secondary-school teachers. In 2001/02 enrolment at primary schools reached 97.4% of pupils in the relevant age-group. In 2006/07 enrolment at secondary schools was equivalent to 87% of students in the relevant age-group. The tertiary sector is based on Tarawa, except for one of the two private colleges, which is based on Abemama. The Government administers a technical college and training colleges for teachers, nurses and seafarers (the last, the Marine Training Centre, trains about 200 students each year for employment by overseas shipping companies). There were 198 students enrolled in teacher-training and 1,303 in other vocational training in 2001. An extra-mural centre of the University of the South Pacific (based in Fiji) is also located on South Tarawa. In 1999 plans for the establishment of a college of advanced education were announced. In 2008 government expenditure on education totalled $A20.5m. (equivalent to 24.8% of total recurrent budgetary expenditure).

THE MARSHALL ISLANDS

Introduction

The Republic of the Marshall Islands consists of two groups of islands, the Ratak ('sunrise') and Ralik ('sunset') chains, comprising 29 atolls (some 1,225 islets) and covering about 180 sq km (70 sq miles) of land. The islands lie within the area of the Pacific Ocean known as Micronesia, some 3,200 km south-west of Hawaii (USA) and about 2,100 km south-east of Guam. The nearest neighbours are Kiribati to the south and the Federated States of Micronesia to the west. The indigenous population comprises a Micronesian people, whose language is known as Marshallese. According to the 1999 census, the population totalled 50,840. The population was estimated at 54,999 in mid-2011.

The first European contact with the Marshall and Caroline Islands was by Spanish expeditions in the 16th century, including those led by Alvaro de Saavedra and Fernão de Magalhães (Ferdinand Magellan), the Portuguese navigator. The islands received their name from the British explorer, John Marshall, who visited them at the end of the 18th century. Spanish sovereignty over the Marshall Islands was recognized by the Vatican in 1886, although in 1914 Japan occupied the islands and received a formal mandate for the territory's administration from the League of Nations in 1920. The territory was intensively colonized. After the capture of the islands by US military forces in 1944 and 1945, most of the Japanese settlers were repatriated. In 1947 the UN established the Trust Territory of the Pacific Islands (comprising the Caroline Islands, the Marshall Islands and the Northern Mariana Islands), to allow the USA to administer the region. The territory was governed by the US Navy from 1947 until 1951, when control passed to a civil administration.

The Marshall Islands' Constitution came into effect on 1 May 1979. In June 1983 the final draft of a Compact of Free Association with the USA was signed, whereby Marshallese citizens were granted the right to live and work in the USA, which would retain its military bases in the Marshall Islands for at least 15 years and, over the same period, was to provide annual aid of US $30m. The Compact came into effect on 21 October 1986. The first President of the Republic of the Marshall Islands was Iroijlaplap (paramount chief) Amata Kabua, who was re-elected on four subsequent occasions, the last of which was in 1995.

On 22 December 1990 the UN Security Council finally ratified the termination of the trusteeship agreement. The Marshall Islands became a member of the UN in 1991. On 1 May 2003 a revised Compact was signed, under which it was envisaged that the Marshall Islands would receive some US $30.5m. per year in US funding; furthermore, a trust fund would be established, to which the USA would contribute $7m. annually in order to provide a means of income after the termination of direct US assistance in 2023. A subsidiary agreement authorized the USA's continued use of Kwajalein Atoll as a missile-testing base until 2066. Agreement with local landowners was finally reached in May 2011.

Bikini and Enewetak Atolls, in the Marshall Islands, were used by the USA for experiments with nuclear weapons, Bikini in 1946–58 and Enewetak in 1948–58, a total of 67 such tests being carried out. Subsequently, the USA agreed to decontaminate Bikini Atoll over a period of 10–15 years. During 1994–95 it emerged that Marshall Islanders had been deliberately exposed to high levels of radiation (through various methods, including atmospheric exposure, tritium and chromium-51 injections, and genetic and bone-marrow transplant experiments) in order that its effects on their health could be studied by US medical researchers. Under the terms of the Compact, the US Administration agreed to establish a US $150m. trust fund to settle claims against the USA resulting from the testing of nuclear devices in the Marshall Islands during the 1940s and 1950s. The Marshall Islands Nuclear Claims Tribunal was established in 1988, and a compensation programme was subsequently implemented.

In September 2000 the Marshall Islands Government petitioned the US Congress for a renegotiation of the settlement agreed under the Compact. The petition sought additional compensation amounting to some US $3,000m. By the end of 2003 compensation awards totalling $83m. had been made. Also, an award of some $578m. had been ordered in May 2000 in respect of a class action brought by the people of Enewetak for loss of and damage to property, and an award of $563m. had been made in March 2002 in settlement of a class action brought by inhabitants of Bikini Atoll. In January 2005 a US State Department report recommended that Congress reject the Marshall Islands' claim for additional compensation payments, citing a lack of a scientific or legal basis for the request. In March 2009 the Marshall Islands renewed its request for additional compensation from the US Government for those affected by the tests. However, in April 2010 the US Supreme Court dismissed without comment the most recent petition from the Marshall Islands. An amended version of a US Senate bill first proposed in September 2007, seeking additional compensation for inhabitants of Bikini, Enewetak, Rongelap and Utrik, was introduced to the upper congressional chamber of the USA in February 2011; the bill was subsequently referred to the Senate Committee on Energy and Natural Resources. A UN General Assembly committee adopted a resolution in April 2010 undertaking to produce by the end of 2011 a comprehensive report examining the effects of the USA's nuclear-testing programme in the Marshall Islands. The listing by UNESCO of Bikini Atoll as a World Heritage Site in 2010 was expected to enhance the atoll's potential for tourism and opportunities for conservation.

In 1989 a UN report on the greenhouse effect (the heating of the earth's atmosphere as a consequence of pollution) predicted a possible resultant rise in sea-level of some 3.7 m by 2030, which would completely submerge the Marshall Islands. In early 2002 the Intergovernmental Panel on Climate Change (IPCC) projected that during the 21st century global sea-level rises would submerge over 80% of Majuro Atoll. The Marshall Islands' susceptibility to adverse climatic conditions was demonstrated by the declaration of a state of emergency in December 2008 after storm surges flooded parts of the capital of Majuro and elsewhere, damaging homes and roads.

Agriculture is mainly on a subsistence level. The industrial sector has declined, especially since the closure of a large tuna-loining factory in 2004. However, the sale of fishing licences is an important source of revenue. The Marshall Islands expected to receive annual revenues of some US $21m. following the renewal of a treaty between the USA and the Forum Fisheries Agency (FFA) group of Pacific island nations in 2003. The economy remains highly dependent on the services sector. The lack of internationally marketable natural resources and the remote location of the islands have presented major challenges for the Marshall Islands Government, and its efforts to revitalize and expand the economy have included the introduction of passport sales and initiatives to promote gambling and 'offshore' financial services. However, such schemes have generated political controversy, both domestically and internationally. In response to global concern that the Marshall Islands had become a significant centre for the laundering of money generated by international criminal activity, in September 2000 legislation was approved to ensure the closer regulation of the banking and financial sector. Following a commendation from the IMF on a series of new measures to combat fraud, in October 2002 the Financial Action Task Force on Money Laundering removed the Marshall Islands from its list of countries judged to be unhelpful in the combating of international financial crime. In February 2006 it was reported that, owing to a shortfall in budgeted government revenues, the Marshall Islands had defaulted on two loan payments to the Asian Development Bank (ADB—which had previously expressed concern in relation to the islands' continued reliance on external aid) and that further spending from the Government's general fund would cease.

Following the establishment in 1998 of diplomatic relations with Taiwan, the Marshalls have received considerable investment and economic aid from the Taiwanese Government. In September 2003 it was announced that Taiwan had agreed to make a substantial contribution to the Marshall Islands' government trust fund, which had been established in May with an initial investment of US $25m. and a deposit of $7m. from the USA. Taiwan planned to transfer a total of $1m. to the fund each year until 2009 and thereafter, until 2023, an annual sum of $2.4m. The assets of the Intergenerational Trust Fund were estimated at more than $30m. in September 2004. Serious concerns with regard to the Marshall Islands' fiscal management re-emerged in early 2011 when, in the first such occurrence, Taiwan's release of a quarterly payment was postponed for more than two months, pending the Marshall Islands' provision of a report complying with accountability requirements in relation to the previous quarter's expenditure. In February, furthermore, as a major investigation into allegations of fraud progressed, the USA threatened to suspend its funding. The country's external debt position also continued to cause concern.

Statistical Survey

Source (unless otherwise indicated): Economic Policy, Planning and Statistics Office (EPPSO), Office of the President, POB 2, Majuro, MH 96960; tel. (625) 3802; fax (625) 3805; e-mail planning@ntamar .net; internet www.spc.int/prism/country/mh/stats.

AREA AND POPULATION

Area: 181.4 sq km (70.0 sq miles) (land only); two island groups, the Ratak Chain (88.1 sq km) and the Ralik Chain (93.3 sq km).

Population: 43,380 at census of 13 November 1988; 50,840 (males 26,026, females 24,814) at census of 1 June 1999. *By Island Group* (1999): Ratak Chain 30,925 (Majuro Atoll 23,676); Ralik Chain 19,915 (Kwajalein Atoll 10,902). *Mid-2011* (Secretariat of the Pacific Community estimate): 54,999 (Source: Pacific Regional Information System).

Density (mid-2011, land area only): 303.2 per sq km.

Population by Age and Sex (Secretariat of the Pacific Community estimates at mid-2011): *0–14:* 22,877 (males 11,820, females 11,057); *15–64:* 30,823 (males 15,809, females 15,014); *65 and over:* 1,299 (males 599, females 700); *Total* 54,999 (males 28,228, females 26,771) (Source: Pacific Regional Information System).

Principal Towns (population of urban places, 1999 census): Ebeye 9,345; Darrit (Djarrot) 7,103; Delap 6,339; Rairok 3,846; Laura 2,256; Uliga 2,044. Note: The country's capital is the combined municipality of Delap-Uliga-Darrit.

Births and Deaths (2006): Registered live births 1,576; Registered deaths 318. Note: Registered live births exclude US military personnel, their dependants and contract employees (Source: UN, *Population and Vital Statistics Report*). *2010* (Secretariat of the Pacific Community estimates): Birth rate 31.1 per 1,000; death rate 5.8 per 1,000 (Source: Pacific Regional Information System).

Life Expectancy (years at birth, WHO estimates): 59 (males 58; females 60) in 2009. Source: WHO, *World Health Statistics*.

Economically Active Population (persons aged 15 years and over, 1999 census): Agriculture and fishery 2,114; Manufacturing 761; Electricity, gas and water 258; Construction 848; Wholesale and retail trade 788; Transport, storage and communications 763; Finance, insurance, real estate and business services 559; Community, social and personal services 3,803; *Sub-total* 9,894; Activities not reported 247; *Total employed* 10,141 (males 7,008, females 3,133); Unemployed 4,536 (males 2,671, females 1,865); *Total labour force* 14,677 (males 9,679, females 4,998). *2006/07* (private sector only): Fishing 281; Manufacturing 60; Construction 782; Wholesale and retail trade 1,791; Total employed (incl. others) 5,491 (Source: IMF, *Republic of the Marshall Islands: Selected Issues and Statistical Appendix* —June 2008). *Mid-2011* (estimates): Agriculture, etc. 6,000; Total labour force 27,000 (Source: FAO).

HEALTH AND WELFARE

Key Indicators

Total Fertility Rate (children per woman, 2009): 3.6.

Under-5 Mortality Rate (per 1,000 live births, 2009): 35.

Physicians (per 1,000 head, 2000): 0.5.

Hospital Beds (per 1,000 head, 1999): 2.1.

Health Expenditure (2008): US $ per head (PPP): 251.

Health Expenditure (2008): % of GDP: 14.0.

Health Expenditure (2008): public (% of total): 97.2.

Access to Water (% of persons, 2008): 94.

Access to Sanitation (% of persons, 2008): 73.

Total Carbon Dioxide Emissions ('000 metric tons, 2007): 98.9.

Carbon Dioxide Emissions Per Head (metric tons, 2007): 1.7.

For sources and definitions, see explanatory note on p. vi.

AGRICULTURE, ETC.

Principal Crop ('000 metric tons, 2009, FAO estimate): Coconuts 27.5.

Livestock ('000 head, year ending September 2003): Pigs 12.9; Poultry 86.0.

Fishing ('000 metric tons, live weight, 2009): Bigeye tuna 2.6; Skipjack tuna 40.3; Yellowfin tuna 1.7; Total catch (incl. others) 46.9.

Source: FAO.

INDUSTRY

Electric Energy (million kWh, Majuro only): 81.0 in 2004; 81.3 in 2005; 78.0 in 2006. Source: Asian Development Bank.

FINANCE

Currency and Exchange Rates: United States currency is used: 100 cents = 1 United States dollar (US $). *Sterling and Euro Equivalents* (31 May 2011): £1 sterling = US $1.6503; €1 = US $1.439; US $100 = £60.60 = €69.52.

Budget (US $ million, year ending 30 September 2009, estimates): *Revenue:* Recurrent 36.6 (Tax 23.1, Non-tax 13.5); Grants 67.1; Total 103.7. *Expenditure:* Recurrent 83.0; Capital (incl. net lending) 21.0; Total 104.0. Source: IMF, *Republic of the Marshall Islands: 2009 Article IV Consultation—Staff Report; a Public Information Notice; and a Statement by the Executive Director of the Republic of Marshall Islands on the Executive Board Discussion* (February 2010).

Cost of Living (Consumer Price Index for Majuro, average of quarterly figures; base: Jan.–March 2003 = 100): All items 112.4 in 2006; 115.8 in 2007; 136.2 in 2008.

Gross Domestic Product (US $ million at constant 2005 prices): 142.4 in 2007; 144.5 in 2008; 144.5 in 2009. Source: UN National Accounts Main Aggregates Database.

Expenditure on the Gross Domestic Product (US $ million at current prices, 2009): Government final consumption expenditure 92.4; Private final consumption expenditure 155.5; Gross capital formation 96.9; *Total domestic expenditure* 344.8; Exports of goods and services 21.2; *Less* Imports of goods and services 195.3; *GDP in purchasers' values* 170.7. Source: UN National Accounts Main Aggregates Database.

Gross Domestic Product by Economic Activity (US $ million at current prices, 2009): Agriculture, hunting, forestry and fishing 16.5; Mining, electricity, gas and water 5.7; Manufacturing 7.2; Construction 18.7; Trade, restaurants and hotels 28.8; Transport, storage and communications 8.8; Other activities 78.9; *Sub-total* 164.7; Net of indirect taxes 6.0 (obtained as a residual); *GDP in purchasers' values* 170.7. Source: UN National Accounts Main Aggregates Database.

Balance of Payments (US $ million, year ending 30 September 2009, estimates): Merchandise exports f.o.b. 14.0; Merchandise imports c.i.f. –85.0; *Trade balance* –71.0; Services (net) –31.7; *Balance on goods and services* –102.7; Other income 30.5; *Balance on goods, services and income* –72.2; Private unrequited transfers (net) 60.1; *Current balance* –12.1. Source: IMF, *Republic of the Marshall Islands: 2009 Article IV Consultation—Staff Report; a Public Information Notice; and a Statement by the Executive Director of the Republic of Marshall Islands on the Executive Board Discussion* (February 2010).

EXTERNAL TRADE

Principal Commodities (US $ million): *Imports* (2000, estimates): Food and live animals 5.0; Beverages and tobacco 6.0; Crude materials, inedible, except fuels 2.6; Mineral fuels, lubricants and related materials 20.4; Animal and vegetable oils and fats 2.4; Chemicals 0.1; Basic manufactures 3.0; Machinery and transport equipment 8.2; Miscellaneous manufactured articles 1.4; Goods not classified by kind 5.8; Total 54.7. *Exports* (year ending September 2007): Coconut oil (crude) 2.0; Copra cake 0.1; Total (incl. others) 20.3. Sources: Asian Development Bank and IMF, *Republic of the Marshall Islands: Selected Issues and Statistical Appendix* (June 2008).

Principal Trading Partners (US $ million): *Imports* (2006): Australia 5.7; Hong Kong 1.2; Japan 5.5; New Zealand 2.2; USA 31.0;

Total (incl. others) 67.7 (Source: Asian Development Bank). *Exports* (2000, estimates): USA 5.2; Total (incl. others) 9.1.

TRANSPORT

Road Traffic (vehicles registered, 1999): Trucks 64; Pick-ups 587; Sedans 1,404; Jeeps 79; Buses 75; Vans 66; Scooters 47; Other motor vehicles 253.

Shipping: *Merchant Fleet* (at 31 December 2009): Vessels 1,376; Displacement ('000 grt) 49,088.3 (Source: IHS Fairplay, *World Fleet Statistics*). *International Sea-borne Freight Traffic** (estimates, '000 metric tons, 1990): Goods loaded 29; Goods unloaded 123 (Source: UN, *Monthly Bulletin of Statistics*).

* Including the Northern Mariana Islands, the Federated States of Micronesia and Palau.

Civil Aviation (traffic on scheduled services, 2006): Kilometres flown 1 million; Passengers carried 30,000; Passenger-km 42 million; Total ton-km 4 million. Source: UN, *Statistical Yearbook*.

TOURISM

Tourist Arrivals: 5,780 in 2006; 7,200 in 2007; 6,022 in 2008.

Arrivals by Country (2008): Japan 1,501; Other Asia 2,535; USA 1,563; Total (incl. others) 6,022.

Tourism Receipts (US $ million, incl. passenger transport): 6.6 in 2006; 4.5 in 2007; 3.0 in 2008.

Source: World Tourism Organization.

COMMUNICATIONS MEDIA

Telephones (main lines in use, estimate): 4,400 in 2010*.

Mobile Cellular Telephones (subscriptions, estimate): 3,800 in 2010*.

Personal Computers: 5,000 in 2005*.

Internet Users: 2,200 in 2009*.

Non-daily Newspaper: 1 (average circulation 3,000 copies) in 2004†.

* Source: International Telecommunication Union.

† Source: UNESCO, *Statistical Yearbook* .

EDUCATION

Pre-primary (2008/09, unless otherwise indicated): 126 teachers (2002/03); 1,524 pupils enrolled.

Primary (2008/09, unless otherwise indicated): 103 schools (1998); 526 teachers (2002/03, estimate); 8,398 pupils enrolled.

Secondary (2008/09, unless otherwise indicated): 16 schools (1998); 387 teachers (2002/03, estimate); 5,229 pupils enrolled.

Higher (2002/03, unless otherwise indicated): 1 college (1994); 49 teachers (estimate); 919 students enrolled (estimate).

Pupil-teacher Ratio (primary education, UNESCO estimate): 14.5 in 2002/03.

Source: UNESCO Institute for Statistics.

Directory

The Constitution

On 1 May 1979 the locally drafted Constitution of the Republic of the Marshall Islands became effective. The Constitution provides for a parliamentary form of government, with legislative authority vested in the 33-member Nitijela. Members of the Nitijela are elected by a popular vote, from 25 districts, for a four-year term. There is an advisory council of 12 high chiefs, or Iroij. The Nitijela elects the President of the Marshall Islands (who also has a four-year mandate) from among its own members. The President then selects members of the Cabinet from among the members of the Nitijela. On 25 June 1983 the final draft of a Compact of Free Association was signed by the Governments of the Marshall Islands and the USA, and the Compact was effectively ratified by the US Congress on 14 January 1986. An amended Compact was signed by the Governments of the two countries on 1 May 2003; final terms were ratified by the US Congress in November, and signed by the US President in December of that year. By the terms of the Compact, free association recognizes the Republic of the Marshall Islands as an internally sovereign, self-governing state, whose policy concerning foreign affairs must be consistent with guide-lines laid down in the Compact. Full responsibility for defence lies with the USA, which undertakes to provide regular economic assistance. The economic and defence provisions of the Compact are renewable after 15 years, but the status of free association continues indefinitely.

The Government

HEAD OF STATE

President: JURELANG ZEDKAIA (took office 26 October 2009; inaugurated 2 November 2009).

CABINET
(October 2011)

Minister in Assistance to the President: RUBEN ZACKHRAS.

Minister of Education: NIDEL LORAK.

Minister of Finance: JACK ADING.

Minister of Transportation and Communication: KENNETH KEDI.

Minister of Health: AMENTA MATTHEW.

Minister of Public Works: MAYNARD ALFRED.

Minister of Internal Affairs: NORMAN MATTHEW.

Minister of Justice: BRENSON S. WASE.

Minister of Resources and Development: MATTLAN ZACKHRAS.

Minister of Foreign Affairs: JOHN SILK.

MINISTRIES

Office of the President: Govt of the Republic of the Marshall Islands, POB 2, Majuro, MH 96960; tel. (625) 3445; fax (625) 4021; e-mail pressoff@ntamar.net; internet www.rmigovernment.org.

Ministry of Education: POB 3, Majuro, MH 96960; tel. (625) 5262; fax (625) 3861; e-mail rmimoe@rmimoe.net; internet www.rmimoe.net.

Ministry of Finance: POB P, Majuro, MH 96960; tel. (625) 3320; fax (625) 3607; e-mail secfin@ntamar.net.

Ministry of Foreign Affairs: POB 1349, Majuro, MH 96960; tel. (625) 3181; fax (625) 4979; e-mail mofasec@ntamar.net.

Ministry of Health: POB 16, Majuro, MH 96960; tel. (625) 3355; fax (625) 3432; e-mail jusmohe@ntamar.net.

Ministry of Internal Affairs: POB 18, Majuro, MH 96960; tel. (625) 8240; fax (625) 5353; e-mail rmihpo@ntamar.net.

Ministry of Justice: c/o Office of the Attorney-General, Majuro, MH 96960; tel. (625) 3244; fax (625) 5218; e-mail agoffice@ntamar.net.

Ministry of Public Works: POB 1727, Majuro, MH 96960; tel. (625) 8911; fax (625) 3005; e-mail secpw@ntamar.net.

Ministry of Resources and Development: POB 1727, Majuro, MH 96960; tel. (625) 3206; fax (625) 7471; e-mail rndsec@ntamar.net; internet rmirnd.net.

Ministry of Transportation and Communication: POB 1079, Majuro, MH 96960; tel. (625) 8869; fax (625) 3486; e-mail rmimotc@ntamar.net.

STATE TRIBUNAL

Nuclear Claims Tribunal: POB 702, Majuro, MH 96960; tel. (625) 3396; fax (625) 3389; e-mail nctmaj@ntamar.net; internet www.nuclearclaimstribunal.com; f. 1988; authorized under Section 177 of the first Compact of Free Association between the Govt of the Marshall Islands and the Govt of the USA to decide all claims arising from the nuclear-testing programme conducted by the USA in the Marshall Islands in 1946–58; Chair. GREGORY DANZ; Defender of the Fund PHILIP A. OKNEY; Public Advocate BILL GRAHAM.

Legislature

THE NITIJELA

The Nitijela (lower house) consists of 33 elected Senators. Following the national election held on 19 November 2007, the Ailin Kein Ad (Our Islands) party, supported by independent candidates, was able to secure a parliamentary majority.

Speaker: ALVIN JACKLICK.

THE COUNCIL OF IROIJ

The Council of Iroij is the upper house of the bicameral legislature, comprising 12 tribal chiefs who advise the Presidential Cabinet and review legislation affecting customary law, land tenure or any traditional practice.

Chairman: Iroij KOTAK LOEAK.

Election Commission

Electoral Commission: POB 18, Majuro, MH 96900; Chief Electoral Officer JOSEPH JORLANG.

Political Organizations

Ailin Kein Ad (Our Islands): Majuro; f. 2002; formed United People's Party coalition following 2007 elections; Chair. CHRISTOPHER LOEAK.

United Democratic Party: Majuro; Chair. RUBEN ZACKHRAS; Pres. KESSAI NOTE.

Diplomatic Representation

EMBASSIES IN THE MARSHALL ISLANDS

Japan: A1 Lojkar Village, POB 300, Majuro, MH 96960; tel. (247) 7463; e-mail royoji@ntamar.net; Ambassador EIICHI SUZUKI (resident in Federated States of Micronesia).

Taiwan (Republic of China): A5–6 Lojkar Village, Long Island, POB 1229, Majuro, MH 96960; tel. (247) 4141; fax (247) 4143; e-mail eoroc@ntamar.net; Ambassador GEORGE T. K. LI.

USA: POB 1379, Majuro, MH 96960; tel. (247) 4011; fax (247) 4012; e-mail publicmajuro@state.gov; internet majuro.usembassy.gov; Ambassador MARTHA CAMPBELL.

Judicial System

The judicial system consists of the Supreme Court and the High Court, which preside over District and Community Courts, and the Traditional Rights Court.

Supreme Court of the Republic of the Marshall Islands: POB 378, Majuro, MH 96960; tel. (625) 3201; fax (625) 3323; e-mail jutrep@ntamar.com; internet www.rmicourts.org; Chief Justice DANIEL N. CADRA.

High Court of the Republic of the Marshall Islands: Majuro; e-mail judrep@ntamar.net; Chief Justice CARL B. INGRAM.

District Court of the Republic of the Marshall Islands: Majuro, MH 96960; tel. (625) 3201; fax (625) 3323; Presiding Judge MILTON ZACKIOS.

Traditional Rights Court of the Marshall Islands: Majuro, MH 96960; customary law only; Chief Judge WALTER K. ELBON.

Religion

The population is predominantly Christian, mainly belonging to the Protestant United Church of Christ. The Roman Catholic Church, Assembly of God, Bukot Nan Jesus, Seventh-day Adventists, the Church of Jesus Christ of Latter-day Saints (Mormons), the Full Gospel and the Bahá'í Faith are also represented.

CHRISTIANITY

The Roman Catholic Church

The Apostolic Prefecture of the Marshall Islands included 5,020 adherents at 31 December 2007.

Prefect Apostolic of the Marshall Islands: Rev. Fr RAYMUNDO SABIO, POB 8, Majuro, MH 96960; tel. (625) 6675; fax (625) 5520; e-mail diocesemarshalls@yahoo.com.

Protestant Churches

The Marshall Islands come under the auspices of the United Church Board for World Ministries (475 Riverside Drive, New York, NY 10115, USA); Sec. for Latin America, Caribbean and Oceania Dr PATRICIA RUMER.

BAHÁ'Í FAITH

National Spiritual Assembly: POB 1017, Majuro, MH 96960; tel. (247) 3512; fax (247) 7180; e-mail nsamarshallislands@yahoo.com; internet www.mh.bahai.org; mems resident in 50 localities; Sec. Dr IRENE J. TAAFAKI.

The Press

Kwajalein Hourglass: POB 23, Kwajalein, MH 96555; tel. (355) 3539; e-mail jbennett@kls.usaka.smdc.army.mil; f. 1954; 2 a week; Editor JIM BENNETT; circ. 2,300.

Marshall Islands Gazette: monthly; govt publ.

Marshall Islands Journal: POB 14, Majuro, MH 96960; tel. (625) 8143; fax (625) 3136; e-mail journal@ntamar.net; internet www.marshallislandsjournal.com; f. 1970; weekly; Editor GIFF JOHNSON; circ. 3,700.

Broadcasting and Communications

TELECOMMUNICATIONS

National Telecommunications Authority (NTA): POB 1169, Majuro, MH 96960; tel. (625) 3676; fax (625) 3952; e-mail info@ntamar.net; internet www.ntamar.net; privatized in 1991; sole provider of local and long-distance tel. services and internet communications in the Marshall Islands; Chair. ALEX BING; Pres. and CEO ANTHONY M. MULLER.

BROADCASTING

Radio

Marshall Islands Broadcasting Co: POB 19, Majuro, MH 96960; tel. (625) 3250; fax (625) 3505; Chief Information Officer PETER FUCHS.

Radio Marshalls V7AB: POB 3250, Majuro, MH 96960; tel. (625) 8411; fax (625) 5353; govt-owned; commercial; programmes in English and Marshallese; Station Man. ANTARI ELBON.

Other radio stations include Micronesia Heatwave and V7AA.

Television

Marshalls Broadcasting Co Television: POB 19, Majuro, MH 96960; tel. (625) 3413; Chief Information Officer PETER FUCHS.

The US Department of Defense operates the American Forces Radio and Television Service for the Bucholz Army Airfield on Kwajalein Atoll.

Finance

(cap. = capital; res = reserves; dep. = deposits; amounts in US dollars)

BANKING

Bank of Guam (USA): POB C, Majuro, MH 96960; tel. (625) 3322; fax (625) 3444; Man. ROMY A. ANGELbrs in Ebeye, Kwajalein and Majuro.

Bank of the Marshall Islands: POB J, Majuro, MH 96960; tel. (625) 3636; fax (625) 3661; e-mail bankmar@ntamar.net; internet www.bomi.biz; f. 1982; 40% govt-owned; cap. 2.1m., res.20m., dep. 39.2m. (Dec. 2009); Chair. GRANT LABAUN; Pres. and Gen. Man. PATRICK CHEN; brs in Majuro, Kwajalein, Ebeye and Santo.

Marshall Islands Development Bank: POB 1048, Majuro, MH 96960; tel. (625) 3230; fax (625) 3309; e-mail rmimidb@ntamar.net; f. 1989; lending suspended in 2003; Man. Dir AMON TIBON.

INSURANCE

Majuro Insurance Company: POB 60, Majuro, MH 96960; tel. (625) 8885; fax (625) 8188; Man. LUCY RUBEN.

Marshalls Insurance Agency: POB 113, Majuro, MH 96960; tel. (625) 3366; fax (625) 3189; Man. TOM LIKOVICH.

Moylan's Insurance Underwriters (Marshall) Inc: POB 727, Majuro, MH 96960; tel. (625) 3220; fax (625) 3361; e-mail marshalls@moylans.net; internet www.moylansinsurance.com; Founder, Chair. and Pres. KURT S. MOYLAN; Br. Man. STEVE PHILLIP.

Trade and Industry

DEVELOPMENT ORGANIZATIONS AND STATE AUTHORITIES

Marshall Islands Development Authority: POB 1185, Majuro, MH 96960; tel. (625) 3417; fax (625) 3158; Gen. Man. DAVID KABUA.

Marshall Islands Environmental Protection Authority (RMIEPA): POB 1322, Majuro, MH 96960; tel. (625) 3035; fax (625) 5202; e-mail eparmi@ntamar.net; internet www.rmiepa.org; Gen. Man. DEBORAH BARKER-MANASE.

Marshall Islands Marine Resources Authority (MIMRA): POB 860, Majuro, MH 96960; tel. (625) 8262; fax (625) 5447; e-mail kiko@mimra.com; internet www.mimra.com; specializes in farming techniques and research and devt; Exec. Dir GLEN JOSEPH.

Tobolar Copra Processing Authority: POB G, Majuro, MH 96960; tel. (625) 3116; fax (625) 7206; e-mail wpcandilas@ntamar.net; Plant Man. WILFREDO CANDILAS.

CHAMBER OF COMMERCE

Marshall Islands Chamber of Commerce: POB 1226, Majuro, MH 96960; tel. (625) 3177; fax (625) 2500; e-mail commerce@ntamar

.net; internet marshallislandschamber.net; fmrly known as Majuro Chamber of Commerce; Pres. Steve Phillips; Sec. Jim McLean.

UTILITIES

Electricity

Marshalls Energy Company: POB 1439, Majuro, MH 96960; tel. (625) 3827; fax (625) 3397; e-mail meccorp@ntamar.net; internet www.mecrmi.net; Gen. Man. David Paul.

Kwajalein Atoll Joint Utility Resource (KAJUR): POB 5819, Ebeye Island, Kwajalein, MH 96970; tel. (329) 3799; fax (329) 3722; Man. Wesley Lemari.

Water

Majuro Water and Sewage Services: POB 1751, Majuro, MH 96960; tel. (625) 8934; fax (625) 3837; Man. Terry Mellan.

MAJOR COMPANY

Robert Reimers Enterprises, Inc: POB 1, Majuro, MH 96960; tel. 6253250; fax 6253505; e-mail administration@rreinc.com; internet www.rreinc.com; hotels, restaurants, automotive repairs and sales, shipping services, water purification and bottling, and aquaculture; CEO Ramsay Reiners.

CO-OPERATIVES

These include the Ebeye Co-op, Farmers' Market Co-operative, Kwajalein Employees' Credit Union, Marshall Is Credit Union, Marshall Is Fishermen's Co-operative, and the Marshall Is Handicraft Co-operative.

Transport

ROADS

Tarmac and concrete roads are found in the more important islands. In 1996 there were 152 km of paved roads in the Marshall Islands, mostly on Majuro and Ebeye. Other islands have stone and coral-surfaced roads and tracks. A road improvement programme was completed in 1999.

SHIPPING

The Marshall Islands operates an 'offshore' shipping register. At the end of 2009 the merchant fleet comprised 1,376 vessels, with a combined displacement of some 49.3m. grt.

Vessel Registry:

International Registries Inc: 11495 Commerce Park Drive, Reston, VA 20191-1506, USA; tel. (703) 620-4880; fax (703) 476-8522; e-mail info@register-iri.com; internet www.register-iri.com; Pres. William R. Gallagher.

The Trust Company of the Marshall Islands Inc: Trust Company Complex, Ajeltake Island, POB 1405, Majuro, MH 96960; tel. (247) 3018; fax (247) 3017; e-mail tcmi@ntamar.net; Pres. Guy Edison Clay Maitland.

Marshall Islands Ports Authority (MIPA): Majuro; tel. 625-8269; fax 625-4269; internet rmipa-aip.org; responsible for seaports and airports; Dir Jack Chong Gum.

CIVIL AVIATION

Air Marshall Islands (AMI): POB 1319, Majuro, MH 96960; tel. (625) 3731; fax (625) 3730; e-mail amisales@ntamar.net; internet www.airmarshallislands.com; f. 1980; internal services for the Marshall Islands; also charter, air ambulance and maritime surveillance operations; agency for Aloha airlines; Chair. Kunio Lamari.

Continental Airlines Micronesia: POB 156, Majuro; tel. (625) 3209; fax (625) 3730; e-mail cmimaj@ntamar.net; international flights between Majuro, the Federated States of Micronesia, Guam and Honolulu; also internal services between Majuro and Kwajalein; based in Hagåtña, Guam; Man. Leo Sion.

Tourism

The islands' attractions include excellent opportunities for diving, game-fishing and the exploration of sites and relics of Second World War battles. Bikini Atoll was listed by UNESCO as a World Heritage site in 2010. In 2008 the Marshall Islands Visitor Authority implemented a four-year tourism development programme focusing on special-interest tourism markets. In the longer term, the Visitor Authority planned to promote the development of small-island resorts throughout the country. A new resort was scheduled to open on Ailinglaplap Atoll in 2012. Tourism receipts totalled US $3.0m. in 2008. In 2010 there were an estimated 4,563 tourist arrivals. The leading sources of visitors include the USA and Japan.

Marshall Islands Visitor Authority: POB 5, Majuro, MH 96960; tel. (625) 6482; fax (625) 6771; e-mail tourism@ntamar.net; internet www.visitmarshallislands.com; f. 1997; Gen. Man. Brenda Alik Maddison.

Defence

Defence is the responsibility of the USA, which maintains a military presence on Kwajalein Atoll. The US Pacific Command is based in Hawaii.

Education

There is a school system, based on that of the USA, operated by the state. However, the development of secondary facilities has been constrained by the limitations of resources. In 1998 there were 103 primary schools, with a total enrolment of 12,421 pupils, but only 16 secondary schools, with a total of 2,667 pupils enrolled. In 2008/09 there were an estimated 8,398 pupils enrolled in primary schools and an estimated 5,229 pupils enrolled in secondary schools. In 2006/07 enrolment at pre-primary schools included 9.3% of pupils in the relevant age-group; enrolment at primary schools included 66.3% of the relevant age-group, and the comparable figure for secondary schools included 44.9% of pupils. The College of the Marshall Islands, which became independent from the College of Micronesia in 1993, is based on Majuro; in 2002/03 there were 919 students enrolled at the College. The Fisheries and Nautical Center offers vocational courses for Marshall islanders seeking employment in the fishing industry or on passenger liners, cargo ships and tankers. In the proposed budget for 2011/12, education was allocated the sum of US $22.2m. (17% of total government expenditure).

THE FEDERATED STATES OF MICRONESIA

Introduction

The Federated States of Micronesia forms (with Palau, q.v.) the archipelago of the Caroline Islands, about 800 km east of the Philippines. The Federated States of Micronesia includes (from west to east) the states of Yap, Chuuk (formerly Truk, renamed in January 1990), Pohnpei (formerly Ponape, renamed in November 1984) and Kosrae, and consists of about 600 islands and atolls, extending for some 2,900 km, with a total land area of 700.8 sq km (270.6 sq miles). The islands of Yap are in the Western Caroline Islands and are about 870 km south-west of Guam. The remaining islands are in the Eastern Carolines and the easternmost island of Kosrae lies some 4,587 km south-west of Hawaii. The indigenous population, which is predominantly Micronesian, consists of various ethno-linguistic groups, the principal ones being Yapese, Ulithian-Woleaian, Chuukese, Pohnpeian, Kosraean and Kapingimarangi-Nukuoroan. English is widely understood. At the census of April 2010, the population totalled 102,624. The federal capital is at Palikir, on Pohnpei.

The Caroline Islands were first settled by the ancestors of the Micronesians some 4,000 years ago. The islands that now constitute the Federated States of Micronesia were then ruled by numerous clan chieftains. In 1525 Portuguese navigators first came upon the islands of Yap and Ulithi. Spanish expeditions subsequently reached the other Caroline Islands. Spain renounced its sovereignty over the territory in 1899, when the Carolines (including Palau) and the Mariana Islands (except the southernmost island of Guam) were sold to Germany. In 1914 this territory of German Micronesia was occupied by the Japanese, who acquired a League of Nations mandate to administer it in 1920. The USA captured the territory in the Second World War and in 1947 agreed to administer it, on behalf of the UN, as the Trust Territory of the Pacific Islands (see the chapter on the Marshall Islands).

Until 1979 the four districts of Yap, Chuuk, Pohnpei and Kosrae were governed by a local Administrator, appointed by the High Commissioner of the Trust Territory. However, on 10 May 1979 the four districts ratified a new Constitution to become the Federated States of Micronesia. The districts of Palau and the Marshall Islands had rejected participation in the federation. In October 1982 the USA signed a Compact of Free Association with the Federated States of Micronesia. The Compact was approved by plebiscite in the Federated States of Micronesia in June 1983, and was ratified by the islands' Congress in September. This took effect on 3 November 1986, at which point the territory was deemed to be subject to the Trusteeship no longer. The UN Security Council ratified the termination of the trusteeship agreement in December 1990, and the Federated States of Micronesia was admitted to the UN in September 1991.

In late 2002 unrest occurred on the Faichuk islands, part of Chuuk, where the Faichuk Commission for Statehood continued its campaign to secede from Chuuk and gain equal status within the Federation. The secessionists believed that independence would bring an improvement in services to the islands. In March 2005 legislation to grant Faichuk the status of the Federation's fifth state was introduced to the national Congress, but several years later had yet to be approved.

A first round of renegotiations of the Compact of Free Association (certain terms of which were due to expire in 2001) was completed in late 1999. The USA and the Federated States of Micronesia pledged to maintain defence and security relations. It was also agreed that the USA would continue to provide economic aid to the islands and assist in the development of the private sector, as well as in promoting greater economic self-sufficiency. In July 2001 the USA offered annual assistance of US $61m. and a trust fund of $13m., while expressing concern that the $2,600m. it had given to Micronesia and the Marshall Islands since 1986 had been mismanaged.

Funding was continued at the Compact's 15-year average level, while negotiations remained in progress. On 1 May 2003 the amended Compact of Free Association was signed. The new Compact envisaged direct annual grants of US $76.2m. in 2004, in addition to a further $16m. annually, which was to be paid into a Trust Fund for Micronesia. From 2007 direct grants were to decrease by some $800,000, with this amount being transferred to the Trust Fund. Under the amended terms, gross financial contributions from the USA were to be $104.9m. annually from September 2005. (The total amount to be paid prior to the expected termination of US assistance in 2023 amounted, in 2004 terms, to some $1,760m.) Furthermore, the Micronesian Government also undertook to provide frequent, strictly monitored audit information on all US funding in order to ensure greater accountability. Final agreement was reached on some outstanding security and immigration issues, and in November 2003 the US Congress approved the amended Compact. US President George W. Bush gave his approval in December, and representatives of the US and Micronesian Governments signed a document of implementation in June 2004. Under the amended Compact, instead of general budgetary grants, US aid would be targeted more towards specific projects and government departments. Also, aid was to be conditional upon the efficiency of its management and use, to be reviewed annually by the Joint Economic Management and Financial Accountability Committee (JEMFAC).

While commending the successful implementation of certain policies, notably the retrenchment in government expenditure and the development of the private sector, concerns were expressed by the Asian Development Bank (ADB—an important source of financial support) regarding the Federated States of Micronesia's overdependence on foreign aid, particularly the adverse impact of this on the islands' progress towards economic self-sufficiency and the restructuring of the economy in preparation for the reduction and eventual withdrawal of direct US aid in 2023. In 2011/12 the USA was to provide a total of US $105.5m. in Compact funding to Micronesia. As demonstrated by the volatility of late 2008, the trust fund established for Micronesia was vulnerable to international economic performance, the majority of this capital being invested in US stock markets. Bilateral grants have been provided by the People's Republic of China and Japan. The National Trade Policy for the Federated States of Micronesia, endorsed by the islands' Congress in February 2011, was regarded as an historic advance for the country's strategy. In addition to emphasis on the importance of trade agreements, the objectives of the policy included the creation of conditions conducive to investment and the wider development of the private sector. The importance of the agricultural sector has diminished. The principal crop is coconut. Fishing access fees, mainly from Japanese fleets, are an important source of income. In November 2002 Micronesia was confirmed as the location of the headquarters for a new multilateral agency to manage migratory fish stocks in the region, to be known as the Tuna Commission. Garments are a major export, but there is little other manufacturing industry. The services sector has assumed greater importance, and the tourism industry has become a significant source of foreign exchange.

Periodic extreme weather formations have caused loss of life and severe damage to crops, property and infrastructure in Micronesia. Following a severe typhoon in December 2002, US President George W. Bush declared Micronesia a federal disaster area and ordered emergency US funding and resources to be allocated to the relief effort. A further typhoon, which struck Yap in April 2004, left 1,200 people homeless; the US Government offered to assume 75% of the cost of the recovery effort. In October 2009 Micronesian President Immanuel Mori addressed European and other world leaders on the issue of climate change at a conference held in Sweden. Declaring that Micronesia was 'on the verge of drowning' he appealed to developed nations to establish and contribute to an Adaptation Fund to assist poorer nations in their efforts to mitigate and adapt to the effects of climate change. At the annual UN Climate Change Conference held in Mexico in late 2010, Micronesia resubmitted a proposal that it had made in the previous year urging governments to take immediate action on the 50% of global warming thought to be caused by gases other than carbon dioxide. It was announced in mid-2011 that, in anticipation of rising sea-levels, the requisite upgrading of the Micronesian infrastructure had commenced. Adaptations included the elevation of the islands' roads.

Statistical Survey

Source (unless otherwise indicated): Statistics Unit, Office of Statistics, Budget and Economic Management, Overseas Development Assistance and Compact Management (SBOC), POB PS-12, Palikir, Pohnpei, FM 96941; tel. 320-2820; fax 320-5854; e-mail fsmstat@sboc.fm; internet www.sboc.fm/index.php.

AREA AND POPULATION

Area: 700.8 sq km (270.6 sq miles): Chuuk (Truk, 294 islands) 127.4 sq km; Kosrae (5 islands) 109.6 sq km; Pohnpei (Ponape, 163 islands) 345.2 sq km; Yap (145 islands) 118.6 sq km.

Population: 107,008 at census of 1 April 2000; 102,624 (males 52,055, females 50,569) at census of 4 April 2010. *By State* (2010): Chuuk 48,651; Kosrae 6,616; Pohnpei 35,981; Yap 11,376.

Density (at 2010 census): 146.4 per sq km.

Population by Age and Sex (at 2010 census): *0–14:* 36,650 (males 18,788, females 17,862); *15–64:* 62,558 (males 31,851, females 30,707); *65 and over:* 3,416 (males 1,416, females 2,000); *Total* 102,624 (males 52,055, females 50,569).

Principal Towns (population of municipalities at 2000 census): Weno (Moen) 13,802; Palikir (capital) 6,444; Nett 6,158; Kitti 6,007. Source: Thomas Brinkhoff, *City Population* (internet: www.citypopulation.de).

Births and Deaths (2003, official estimates): Registered live births 2,568 (birth rate 23.9 per 1,000); Deaths 442 (death rate 4.1 per 1,000). *2006:* Registered live births 2,147. *2005–10* (annual averages, UN estimates): Birth rate 21.3 per 1,000; Death rate 5.4 per 1,000 (Source: UN, *World Population Prospects: The 2010 Revision*).

Life Expectancy (years at birth, WHO estimates): 69 (males 68; females 70) in 2009. Source: WHO, *World Health Statistics*.

Economically Active Population (persons aged 15 years and over, 2000 census): Agriculture, forestry and fishing 15,216; *Total employed* (incl. others) 29,175 (males 16,957, females 12,218); Unemployed 8,239 (males 4,419, females 3,820); *Total labour force* 37,414 (males 21,376, females 16,038). *Mid-2011* (estimates in '000): Agriculture, etc. 12; Total labour force 55 (Source: FAO).

HEALTH AND WELFARE

Key Indicators

Total Fertility Rate (children per woman, 2009): 3.5.

Under-5 Mortality Rate (per 1,000 live births, 2009): 39.

Physicians (per 1,000 head, 2003): 0.6.

Hospital Beds (per 1,000 head, 2006): 3.3.

Health Expenditure (2008): US $ per head (PPP): 408.

Health Expenditure (2008): % of GDP: 13.3.

Health Expenditure (2008): public (% of total): 90.3.

For sources and definitions, see explanatory note on p. vi.

AGRICULTURE, ETC.

Principal Crops ('000 metric tons, 2009, FAO estimates): Coconuts 41; Cassava 8; Sweet potatoes 3; Vegetables 3; Bananas 3.

Livestock ('000 head, year ending September 2009, FAO estimates): Pigs 33; Cattle 14; Goats 4; Chickens 190.

Livestock Products (metric tons, 2009, FAO estimates): Cattle meat 258; Pig meat 876; Chicken meat 140; Hen eggs 211.

Fishing ('000 metric tons, live weight, 2009): Skipjack tuna 16.8; Yellowfin tuna 2.4; Bigeye tuna 1.9; Total catch (incl. others) 27.7 (FAO estimate).

Source: FAO.

FINANCE

Currency and Exchange Rates: United States currency is used: 100 cents = 1 United States dollar (US $). *Sterling and Euro Equivalents* (31 May 2011): £1 sterling = US $1.6503; €1 = US $1.4385; US $100 = £60.60 = €69.52.

Budget (US $ million, year ending 30 September 2009): *Revenue:* Current 59.3 (Tax 31.7, Non-tax 27.6); Grants 123.5; Total 182.8. *Expenditure:* Current 131.4; Capital 46.8; Total 178.2. Note: Figures represent a consolidation of the accounts of the national Government and the four state governments. Source: Asian Development Bank.

International Reserves (US $ '000 at 31 December 2010): IMF special drawing rights 9,555; Reserve position in IMF 0; Foreign exchange 46,208; *Total* 55,763. Source: IMF, *International Financial Statistics*.

Money Supply (US $ '000 at 31 December 2010): Demand deposits at banking institutions 26,988. Source: IMF, *International Financial Statistics*.

Cost of Living (Consumer Price Index, average of quarterly figures; base: April–June 2008 = 100): All items 101.4 in 2008; 109.1 in 2009; 112.9 in 2010. Source: Asian Development Bank.

Gross Domestic Product (US $ million at constant 2005 prices): 239.2 in 2007; 232.2 in 2008; 229.9 in 2009. Source: UN National Accounts Main Aggregates Database.

Expenditure on the Gross Domestic Product (US $ million at current prices, 2009): Government final consumption expenditure 140.1; Private final consumption expenditure 201.7; Gross fixed capital formation 85.3; Changes in inventories 5.4; *Total domestic expenditure* 432.5; Exports of goods and services 46.5; *Less* Imports of goods and services 209.5; *GDP in purchasers' values* 269.6. Source: UN National Accounts Main Aggregates Database.

Gross Domestic Product by Economic Activity (US $ million at current prices, 2009): Agriculture, hunting, forestry and fishing 48.5; Mining, electricity, gas and water 3.8; Manufacturing 3.6; Construction 2.7; Trade, restaurants and hotels 60.9; Transport, storage and communications 11.9; Other activities 122.5; *Sub-total* 253.7; Net of indirect taxes 15.9 (obtained as a residual); *GDP in purchasers' values* 269.6. Source: UN National Accounts Main Aggregates Database.

Balance of Payments (US $ million, year ending 30 September 2006, estimates): Merchandise exports f.o.b. 17.0; Merchandise imports f.o.b. –145.9; *Trade balance* –128.9; Exports of services 20.1; Imports of services –57.5; *Balance on goods and services* –166.2; Other income received 20.5; Other income paid –5.3; *Balance on goods, services and income* –151.0; Private unrequited transfers (net) 5.3; Official unrequited transfers (net) 107.3; *Current balance* –38.4; Capital account (net) 12.0; Other long-term capital (net) 1.9; Other short-term capital (net) 0.8; *Overall balance* (incl. errors and omissions) –23.6. *2009:* Exports of goods 24.9; Imports of goods –152.9; Trade balance –128.0; Exports of services and income 60.1; Imports of services and income –91.6; Balance on goods, services and income –159.4; Current transfers received 122.3; Current transfers paid –14.4; Current balance –51.4; Capital account (net) 70.1; Direct investment (net) 0.6; Portfolio investment (net) –20.9; Other investment (net) –4.2; Overall balance –5.9 (Source: Asian Development Bank).

EXTERNAL TRADE

Principal Commodities (US $ '000, 2007): *Imports c.i.f.:* Mineral products 31,476; Prepared foodstuffs, beverages and tobacco 24,390; Machinery, mechanical appliances and electrical equipment 20,553; Vegetable products 8,538; Animals and animal products 8,755; Transportation equipment 8,480; Chemicals 7,660; Base metals and articles thereof 6,216; Total (incl. others) 142,658. *Exports f.o.b.:* Marine products 12,301; Betel nuts 2,224; Citrus 416; Kava 2,224; Total (incl. others) 16,190.

Principal Trading Partners (US $ '000, 2007): *Imports*: Australia 5,844; China, People's Republic 5,444; Guam 20,512; Hong Kong 8,955; Japan 12,067; Korea, Republic 5,820; Philippines 5,083; Singapore 12,413; USA 58,785; Total (incl. others) 142,658. *Exports*: Guam 3,641; Japan 660; USA (mainland only) 2,790; Total (incl. others) 16,190.

TRANSPORT

Shipping: *Merchant Fleet* (registered at 31 December 2009): Vessels 28; Total displacement ('000 grt) 11.8. Source: IHS Fairplay, *World Fleet Statistics*.

TOURISM

Foreign Tourist Arrivals: 19,136 in 2006; 21,146 in 2007; 25,627 in 2008.

Tourist Arrivals by Country or Region of Residence (2008): Europe 2,788; Japan 2,949; Philippines 2,168; Other Asia 4,121; USA 8,732; Total (incl. others) 25,627.

Tourism Receipts (US $ million, incl. passenger transport): 16.5 in 2004; 17.1 in 2005; 18.3 in 2006.

Source: World Tourism Organization.

COMMUNICATIONS MEDIA

Telephones (main lines in use, 2010): 8,500.

Mobile Cellular Telephones (2010): 27,500 subscribers.

Internet Users (2009): 17,000.

Broadband Subscribers (2010): 100.

Personal Computers: 6,000 (54.8 per 1,000 persons) in 2005.

Radio Receivers (1996): 22,000 in use.

Television Receivers (1996): 19,800 in use.

Source: partly International Telecommunication Union.

EDUCATION

Primary (2006/07, unless otherwise indicated): 174 schools (1995); 1,113 teachers; 18,512 pupils (Sources: UN, *Statistical Yearbook for Asia and the Pacific* and UNESCO Institute for Statistics).

Secondary (2006/07, unless otherwise indicated): 24 schools (1995); 829 teachers; 14,742 pupils (Sources: UN, *Statistical Yearbook for Asia and the Pacific* and UNESCO Institute for Statistics).

Tertiary (1998/99): 1,510 students (Sources: UN, *Statistical Yearbook for Asia and the Pacific* and UNESCO Institute for Statistics).

Pupil-teacher Ratio (primary education, UNESCO estimate): 16.6 in 2006/07 (Source: UNESCO Institute for Statistics).

Adult Literacy Rate (population aged 10 years and over, 2000 census): 92.4% (males 92.9%; females 91.9%).

Directory

The Constitution

On 10 May 1979 the locally drafted Constitution of the Federated States of Micronesia, incorporating the four states of Kosrae, Yap, Ponape (formally renamed Pohnpei in November 1984) and Truk (renamed Chuuk in January 1990), became effective. Each of the four states has its own Constitution, elected legislature and Governor. The Constitution guarantees fundamental human rights and establishes a separation of the judicial, executive and legislative powers. The federal legislature, the Congress of the Federated States of Micronesia, is a unicameral parliament with 14 members, popularly elected. The executive consists of the President, elected by the Congress, and a Cabinet. The Constitution provides for a review of the governmental and federal system every 10 years.

In November 1986 the Compact of Free Association was signed by the Governments of the Federated States of Micronesia and the USA. By the terms of the Compact, the Federated States of Micronesia is an internally sovereign, self-governing state, whose policy concerning foreign affairs must be consistent with guidelines laid down in the Compact. Full responsibility for defence lies with the USA, and the security arrangements may be terminated only by mutual agreement. Furthermore, the Compact guaranteed exclusivity to US military forces in Micronesia's waters. The Governments of the Federated States of Micronesia and the USA signed an amended Compact on 1 May 2003, whereby its terms were renewed until 2023. The agreement was approved by the US Congress in November 2003 and ratified by President George W. Bush in December. The amended Compact came into force in June 2004 and was due to expire in 2023.

The Government

HEAD OF STATE

President: IMMANUEL (MANNY) MORI (took office 11 May 2007; re-elected 11 May 2011).

Vice-President: ALIK L. ALIK.

CABINET
(October 2011)

Secretary of the Department of Finance and Administration: TISER REYNOLD.

Secretary of the Department of Foreign Affairs: LORIN S. ROBERT.

Secretary of the Department of Resources and Development: MARION HENRY.

Secretary of the Department of Health and Social Affairs: Dr VITA AKAPITO SKILLING.

Secretary of the Department of Justice: MAKETO ROBERT.

Secretary of the Department of Transportation, Communication and Infrastructure: FRANCIS I. ITIMAI.

Secretary of the Department of Education: Dr RUFINO MAURICIO.

Public Defender: JULIUS JOEY SAPELALUT.

Postmaster-General: GINGER PORTER MIDA.

GOVERNMENT OFFICES

Office of the President: POB PS-53, Palikir, Pohnpei, FM 96941; tel. 320-2228; fax 320-2785; e-mail ppetrus@mail.fm; internet www.fsmpio.fm.

Department of Education: POB PS-87, Palikir, Pohnpei, FM 96941; tel. 320-2643; fax 320-5500.

Department of Finance and Administration: POB PS-158, Palikir, Pohnpei, FM 96941; tel. 320-2640; fax 320-2380; e-mail fsmsofa@mail.fm.

Department of Foreign Affairs: POB PS-123, Palikir, Pohnpei, FM 96941; tel. 320-2641; fax 320-2933; e-mail foreignaffairs@mail.fm; internet www.fsmgov.org/ovmis.html.

Department of Health and Social Affairs: POB PS-70, Palikir, Pohnpei, FM 96941; tel. 320-2872; fax 320-5263; e-mail fsmhealth@mail.fm.

Department of Justice: POB PS-105, Palikir, Pohnpei, FM 96941; tel. 320-2644; fax 320-2234; e-mail pdochuuk@mail.fm.

Department of Resources and Development: POB PS-12, Palikir, Pohnpei, FM 96941; tel. 320-2648; fax 320-5854; e-mail fsmrd@dea.fm; internet www.fsminvest.fm.

Department of Transportation, Communication and Infrastructure: POB PS-2, Palikir, Pohnpei, FM 96941; tel. 320-2865; fax 320-5853; e-mail transcom@mail.fm; internet www.ict.fm.

Office of the Public Auditor: POB PS-05, Palikir, Pohnpei, FM 96941; tel. 320-2863; fax 320-5482; e-mail hhainrick@fsmopa.fm; internet www.fsmopa.fm.

Office of the Public Defender: POB PS-174, Palikir, Pohnpei, FM 96941; tel. 320-2648; fax 320-5775.

Public Information Office: POB PS-34, Palikir, Pohnpei, FM 96941; tel. 320-2548; fax 320-4356; e-mail fsmpio@mail.fm.

Legislature

CONGRESS OF THE FEDERATED STATES OF MICRONESIA

The Congress comprises 14 members (Senators): four Senators-at-Large (one for each of the four states), who are elected for a four-year term; and 10 Senators who serve a two-year term. The most recent election was held on 8 March 2011. There are no formal political parties.

Speaker: ISAAC V. FIGIR.

STATE LEGISLATURES

Chuuk State Legislature: POB 189, Weno, Chuuk, FM 96942; tel. 330-2234; fax 330-2233; Senate of 10 mems and House of Representatives of 28 mems elected for four years; Gov. JOHNSON ELIMO.

Kosrae State Legislature: POB 187, Tofol, Kosrae, FM 96944; tel. 370-3002; fax 370-3162; e-mail kosraelc@mail.fm; unicameral body of 14 mems serving for four years; Gov. ROBERT J. WEILBACHER.

Pohnpei State Legislature: POB 114, Kolonia, Pohnpei, FM 96941; tel. 320-2753; fax 320-2754; e-mail legislature@mail.fm; internet www.fm/pohnpeileg; 27 representatives elected for four years (terms staggered); Gov. JOHN EHSA.

Yap State Legislature: POB 39, Colonia, Yap, FM 96943; tel. 350-2108; fax 350-4113; 10 mems, six elected from the Yap Islands proper and four elected from the Outer Islands of Ulithi and Woleai, for a four-year term; Gov. SEBASTIAN L. ANEFAL.

Election Commission

National Election Commission: POB 1685, Kolonia, Pohnpei 96941; tel. 320-4283; fax 320-7805; e-mail ned@mail.fm; Dir ALBERT T. WELLY.

Political Organizations

There are no formal political parties in the Federated States of Micronesia.

Diplomatic Representation

EMBASSIES IN THE FEDERATED STATES OF MICRONESIA

Australia: POB S, Kolonia, Pohnpei, FM 96941; tel. 320-5448; fax 320-5449; e-mail australia@mail.fm; internet www.fsm.embassy.gov.au; Ambassador MARTIN QUINN.

China, People's Republic: POB 1530, Kolonia, Pohnpei, FM 96941; tel. 320-5575; fax 320-5578; e-mail chinaemb@mail.fm; internet fm.chineseembassy.org/eng; Ambassador ZHANG WEIDONG.

Japan: Pami Bldg, 3rd Floor, POB 1837, Kolonia, Pohnpei, FM 96941; tel. 320-5465; fax 320-5470; internet www.micronesia.emb-japan.go.jp; Ambassador EIICHI SUZUKI.

USA: POB 1286, Kolonia, Pohnpei, FM 96941; tel. 320-2187; fax 320-2186; e-mail usembassy@mail.fm; internet kolonia.usembassy.gov; Ambassador PETER ALAN PRAHAR.

Judicial System

Supreme Court of the Federated States of Micronesia: POB PS-J, Palikir Station, Pohnpei, FM 96941; tel. 320-2357; fax 320-2756; e-mail fsmsupcourt@mail.fm; internet www.fsmlaw.org; Chief Justice MARTIN G. YINUG.

State Courts and Appellate Courts have been established in Yap, Chuuk, Kosrae and Pohnpei.

Religion

The population is predominantly Christian, mainly Roman Catholic. The Assembly of God, Jehovah's Witnesses, Seventh-day Adventists, the Church of Jesus Christ of Latter-day Saints (Mormons), the United Church of Christ, Baptists and the Bahá'í Faith are also represented.

CHRISTIANITY

The Roman Catholic Church

The Federated States of Micronesia forms a part of the diocese of the Caroline Islands, suffragan to the archdiocese of Agaña (Guam). The Bishop participates in the Catholic Bishops' Conference of the Pacific, based in Fiji. At 31 December 2007 there were 79,199 adherents in the diocese.

Bishop of the Caroline Islands: Most Rev. AMANDO SAMO, Bishop's House, POB 939, Weno, Chuuk, FM 96942; tel. 330-2399; fax 330-4585; e-mail diocese@mail.fm.

Other Churches

Calvary Baptist Church: Kolonia, Pohnpei, POB 2179, FM 96941; tel. 320-2830; fax 320-3887; e-mail cca_pohnpei@yahoo.com; Pastor ISAMO WELLES.

Liebenzell Mission: Rev. Seigbert Betz, POB 9, Weno, Chuuk, FM 96942; tel. 330-3869; e-mail missions@liebenzellusa.org; internet www.liebenzellusa.org.

Truth Independent Baptist Church: Kolonia, Pohnpei, POB 65, FM 96941; tel. 320-3643; fax 320-6769; Pastor RICARDO P. VERACRUZ.

United Church of Christ in Pohnpei: Kolonia, Pohnpei, POB 864, FM 96941; tel. 320-2271; fax 320-4404; Pres. BERNELL EDWARD.

The Press

Da Rohng: Jano News Service, POB 510, Kolonia, Pohnpei FM 96941; tel. 320-6494; fax 320-4200; e-mail darohng2005@yahoo.com; Editor MARTIN JANO.

The Island Tribune: Pohnpei, FM 96941; f. 1997; fortnightly.

Kaselehlie Press: POB 2222, Pohnpei, FM 96941; tel. 320-6547; fax 320-6571; e-mail kpress@mail.fm; internet www.kpress.info; f. 2001; fortnightly; Man. Editor BILL JAYNES.

Micronesian Alliance: POB 543, Tofol, Kosrae, FM 96944; tel. 370-6131; e-mail equatormedia@yahoo.com.

Broadcasting and Communications

TELECOMMUNICATIONS

FSM Telecommunication Corporation: POB 1210, Kolonia, Pohnpei, FM 96941; tel. 320-2740; fax 320-2745; e-mail customerservice@telecom.fm; internet www.fm; provides domestic and international services; Pres. and CEO JOHN D. SOHL.

BROADCASTING

Radio

Federated States of Micronesia Public Information Office: POB PS-34, Palikir, Pohnpei, FM 96941; tel. 320-2548; fax 320-4356; e-mail fsmpio@mail.fm; internet www.fsmpio.fm/pio.htm; govt-operated; four regional stations, each broadcasting 18 hours daily; Information Officer PATRICK BLANK.

Station V6AH: POB 1086, Kolonia, Pohnpei, FM 96941; programmes in English and Pohnpeian; Man. WEIDEN MANUEL.

Station V6AI: POB 117, Colonia, Yap, FM 96943; tel. 350-2174; fax 350-4426; programmes in English, Yapese, Ulithian and Satawalese; Man. SEBASTIAN F. TAMAGKEN.

Station V6AJ: POB 147, Tofol, Kosrae, FM 96944; tel. 370-3040; fax 370-3880; e-mail kosraebroadcast@yahoo.com; programmes in English and Kosraean; Man. MCDONALD ITTU.

Station V6AK: Wenn, Chuuk, FM 96942; tel. 330-2596; programmes in Chuukese and English; Man. JOE COMMOR.

WSZA Yap: Dept of Youth and Civic Affairs, POB 30, Colonia, Yap 96943; tel. 350-2174; Media Dir PETER GARAMFEL.

WSZD Pohnpei: POB 1086, Kolonia, Pohnpei 96941; tel. 320-2296; programmes in English and Pohnpeian; Man. FRANCIS ZARRED.

Television

Island Cable TV—Pohnpei: POB 1628, Pohnpei, FM 96941; tel. 320-2671; fax 320-2444; e-mail ictv@mail.fm; f. 1991; Gen. Man. DAVID O. CLIFFE.

TV Station Chuuk (TTTK): Wenn, Chuuk, FM 96942; tel. 330-4475; commercial.

TV Station Pohnpei (KPON): Central Micronesia Communications, POB 460, Kolonia, Pohnpei, FM 96941; f. 1977; commercial; Tech. Dir DAVID CLIFFE.

TV Station Yap (WAAB): Colonia, Yap, FM 96943; tel. 350-2160; fax 350-4113; govt-owned; Man. LOU DEFNGIN.

Finance

BANKING

Regulatory Authority

Federated States of Micronesia Banking Board: POB 1887, Kolonia, Pohnpei, FM 96941; tel. 320-2015; fax 320-5433; e-mail fmbb@mail.fm; f. 1980; Chair. ALEXANDER NARRUHN; Commissioner WILSON F. WAGUK.

Banks are also supervised by the US Federal Deposit Insurance Corporation.

Commercial Banks

Bank of the Federated States of Micronesia: POB 98, Kolonia, Pohnpei, FM 96941; tel. 320-2838; fax 320-5359; cap. US $4.6m., dep. US $74.8m. (Dec. 2010); brs in Kosrae, Yap, Pohnpei and Chuuk.

Bank of Guam (USA): POB 367, Kolonia, Pohnpei, FM 96941; tel. 320-2550; fax 320-2562; e-mail bogpohn@mail.fm; internet www.bankofguam.com; Br. Mans JOANNE H. AKINAGA, VIDA B. RICAFRENTE; brs in Chuuk and Pohnpei.

Yap Credit Union: POB 610, Colonia, Yap; tel. 350-2142.

Development Bank

Federated States of Micronesia Development Bank: POB M, Kolonia, Pohnpei, FM 96941; tel. 320-2840; fax 320-2842; e-mail info@fsmdb.fm; internet www.fsmdb.fm/index; f. 1979; total assets US $35.6m. (2007); Chair. IHLEN JOSEPH; Pres. ANNA MENDIOLA; 4 brs.

Banking services for the rest of the islands are available in Guam, Hawaii and on the US mainland.

INSURANCE

Actouka Executive Insurance: POB 55, Kolonia, Pohnpei; tel. 320-5331; fax 320-2331; e-mail mlamar@mail.fm.

Caroline Insurance Underwriters: POB 37, Chuuk; tel. 330-2705; fax 330-2207.

FSM Insurance Group: Kosrae; tel. 370-3788; fax 370-2120.

Islands Insurance: POB K, Kolonia, Pohnpei; tel. 320-3422.

Moylan's Insurance Underwriters: POB 1448, Kolonia, Pohnpei, FM 96941; tel. 320-2118; fax 320-2519; e-mail pohnpei@moylans.net; Pres. and Gen. Man. MELNER ISAAC.

Oceania Insurance Co: POB 1202, Weno, Chuuk, FM 96942; tel. 330-3036; fax 330-3764; e-mail oceanpac@mail.fm; also owns and manages Pacific Basin Insurance; Region Man. ERICSON MARAR.

Pacific Islands Insurance Underwriters: POB 386, Colonia, Yap; tel. 350-2340; fax 350-2341.

Transpacific Insurance: POB 510, Kolonia, Pohnpei; tel. 320-5525; fax 320-5524.

Yap Insurance Agency: POB 386, Colonia, Yap; tel. 350-2340; fax 350-2341; e-mail tachelioyap@mail.fm.

Trade and Industry

GOVERNMENT AGENCIES

Coconut Development Authority: POB 297, Kolonia, Pohnpei, FM 96941; tel. 320-2892; fax 320-5383; e-mail fsmcda@mail.fm; f. 1981; responsible for all purchasing, processing and exporting of copra and copra by-products in the islands; Gen. Man. NAMIO NANPEI.

FSM National Fisheries Corporation: POB R, Kolonia, Pohnpei, FM 96941; tel. 320-2529; fax 320-2239; e-mail nfcairfreight@mail.fm; internet www.fsmgov.org/nfc; f. 1984; established in 1990, with the Economic Devt Authority and an Australian co, the Caroline Fishing Corpn (three vessels); promotes fisheries development; Pres. NICK SOLOMON.

National Oceanic Resource Management Authority (NORMA): POB PS-122, Palikir, Pohnpei, FM 96941; tel. 320-2700; fax 320-2383; e-mail info@norma.fm; internet norma.fm; fmrly Micronesian Fisheries Authority; name changed 2002; responsible for conservation, management and development of tuna resources and for issue of fishing licences; Exec. Dir PATRICK MACKENZIE; Deputy Dir EUGENE PANGELINAN.

Office of Compact Management: 253 Palikir Station, Pohnpei FM 96941; tel. 320-8375; fax 320-8377; Exec. Dir EHPEL ILON.

Pohnpei Economic Development Authority: POB 738, Kolonia, Pohnpei, FM 96941; tel. 320-2298; fax 320-2775; e-mail eda@mail.fm; chaired by the President of the Federated States of Micronesia; Exec. Dir SHELTEN NETH.

CHAMBERS OF COMMERCE

Chuuk Chamber of Commerce: POB 700, Weno, Chuuk, FM 96941; tel. 330-2318; fax 330-2314; e-mail larry.bruton@mail.fm; Pres. WILLIAM STINNETT.

Kosrae Chamber of Commerce: POB 877, Tofol, Kosrae, FM 96944; tel. 370-3483; e-mail info@kosraechamberofcommerce.org; internet www.kosraechamberofcommerce.org; Chair. WITSON PHILLIP.

Pohnpei Chamber of Commerce: POB 405, Kolonia, Pohnpei, FM 96941; tel. 320-2452; fax 320-5277; e-mail amc@mail.fm; Pres. LEON SENDA.

Yap Chamber of Commerce: Colonia, Yap, FM 96943; tel. 350-2298; Pres. PHILLIP RANGANBAY.

UTILITIES

Chuuk Public Works (CPW): POB 248, Weno, Chuuk, FM 96942; tel. 330-2242; fax 320-4815.

Kosrae Utility Authority: POB 277, Tofol, Kosrae, FM 96944; tel. 370-3799; fax 370-3798; e-mail info@kosraepower.com; internet kosraepower.com; corporatized in 1994; Gen. Man. FRED N. SKILLING.

Pohnpei Utilities Corporation: POB C, Kolonia, Pohnpei, FM 96941; tel. 320-2374; fax 320-2422; e-mail info@puc.fm; internet www.puc.fm; f. 1992; provides electricity, water and sewerage services; Gen. Man. FELICIANO PERMAN.

Yap State Public Service Corpn (YSPSC): POB 621, Colonia, Yap, FM 96943; tel. 350-2175; fax 350-2331; f. 1996; provides electricity, water and sewerage services; Gen. Man. FAUSTINO R. YANGMOG.

CO-OPERATIVES

Chuuk: Chuuk Co-operative, Faichuk Cacao and Copra Co-operative Asscn, Pis Fishermen's Co-operative, Fefan Women's Co-operative.

Pohnpei: Pohnpei Federation of Co-operative Asscns (POB 100, Pohnpei, FM 96941), Kapingamarangi Copra Producers' Asscn, Kitti Minimum Co-operative Asscn, Kolonia Consumers' and Producers' Co-operative Asscn, Kosrae Island Co-operative Asscn, Metalanim Copra Co-operative Asscn, Mokil Island Co-operative Asscn, Ngatik Island Co-operative Asscn, Nukuoro Island Co-operative Asscn, PICS Co-operative Asscn, Pingelap Consumers' Co-operative Asscn, Pohnpei Fishermen's Co-operative, Pohnpei Handicraft Co-operative, Uh Soumwet Co-operative Asscn.

Yap Co-operative Association Inc: POB 159, Colonia, Yap, FM 96943; tel. 350-2209; fax 350-4114; e-mail yca@mail.fm; internet yapcoop.com; f. 1952; Pres. FAUSTINO YANGMOG; Gen. Man. TONY GANNGIYAN; 1,832 mems.

Transport

ROADS

In 2000 the Federated States of Micronesia had a total road network of 240 km. Tarmac and concrete roads are found in the more important islands. Other islands have stone- and coral-surfaced roads and tracks.

SHIPPING

Pohnpei, Chuuk, Yap and Kosrae have deep-draught harbours for commercial shipping. The ports provide warehousing and transshipment facilities.

Caroline Fisheries Corporation (CFC): POB 7, Kolonia, Pohnpei, FM 96941; tel. 320-3926; fax 320-4733; e-mail cfc@mail.fm; Gen. Man. MILAN KAMBER.

Pacific Shipping Agency: POB 154, Lelu, Kosrae FM 96944; tel. 370-3956; fax 370-3750; e-mail KosraeAce@mail.fm; f. 1990; Gen. Man. SMITH SIGRAH.

Pohnpei Transfer & Storage, Inc: POB 340, Kolonia, Pohnpei FM 96941; tel. 320-2552; fax 320-2389; e-mail fsmlinejv@mail.fm; Gen. Man. JOE VITT.

Truk Transportation Company (TRANSCO): POB 99, Weno, Chuuk FM 96942; tel. 330-2143; fax 330-2726; e-mail transco@mail.fm; f. 1964; Pres. MYRON HASHIGUCHI; Gen. Man. GIDEON BISALEN.

Waab Transportation Company: POB 177, Colonia, Yap FM 96943; tel. 350-2301; fax 350-4110; e-mail waabtrans@mail.fm; agents for PM & O Lines (USA); Man. LOUIS GAW.

CIVIL AVIATION

The Federated States of Micronesia is served by Continental Micronesia, Our Airline (formerly Air Nauru) and Continental Airlines (USA). Pacific Missionary Aviation, based in Pohnpei and Yap, provides domestic air services. There are international airports on Pohnpei, Chuuk, Yap and Kosrae, and airstrips on the outer islands of Onoun and Ta in Chuuk. The extension of the runway at Pohnpei airport, to accommodate larger aircraft, was scheduled for completion in 2011.

Tourism

The tourist industry is a significant source of revenue, although it has been hampered by the lack of infrastructure. Visitor attractions include excellent conditions for scuba-diving (notably in Chuuk Lagoon), Second World War battle sites and relics (many underwater) and the ancient ruined city of Nan Madol on Pohnpei. The number of tourist arrivals was estimated to total 25,627 in 2008. Tourist receipts totalled an estimated US $18.3m. in 2006.

Federated States of Micronesia Visitors Board: National Government, PO Box PS-12, Palikir, Pohnpei, FM 96941; tel. 320-5133; fax 320-3251; e-mail fsminfo@visit-fsm.org; internet www.visit-micronesia.fm.

Chuuk Visitors Bureau: POB FQ, Weno, Chuuk, FM 96942; tel. 330-4133; fax 330-4194; e-mail cvb@mail.fm.

Kosrae Visitors Bureau: POB 659, Tofol, Kosrae, FM 96944; tel. 370-2228; fax 370-3000; e-mail kosrae@mail.fm; internet www.kosrae.com.

Pohnpei Department of Tourism and Parks: POB 66, Kolonia, Pohnpei, FM 96941; tel. 320-2421; fax 320-6019; e-mail tourismparks@mail.fm; Deputy Chief BUMIO SILBANUZ.

Pohnpei Visitors Bureau: POB 1949, Kolonia, Pohnpei, FM 96941; tel. 320-4851; fax 320-4868; e-mail pohnpeiVB@mail.fm; internet www.visit-pohnpei.fm.

Yap Visitors Bureau: POB 988, Colonia, Yap, FM 96943; tel. 350-2298; fax 350-7015; e-mail yvb@mail.fm; internet www.visityap.com; Chair. ALPHONSO GANANG; Gen. Man. LAURENCE KENBAROY.

Defence

Defence and security are the responsibility of the USA. The US Pacific Command is based in Hawaii.

Education

Primary education, which begins at six years of age and lasts for eight years, is compulsory. Secondary education, beginning at 14 years of age, comprises two cycles, each of two years. The education system is based on the US pattern of eight years' attendance at an elementary school and four years' enrolment at a high school. The Micronesia Maritime and Fisheries Academy, which was opened in Yap in 1990, provides education and training in fisheries technology at secondary and tertiary levels. The College of Micronesia offers two- and three-year programmes leading to a degree qualification. In 2006/07 there were 18,512 pupils enrolled in primary education and 14,742 pupils enrolled in secondary education. In 2005/06 approximately 2,283 pupils were studying at college level.

NAURU

Introduction

The Republic of Nauru is a small island in the central Pacific Ocean, lying about 4,000 km north-east of Sydney, Australia, and 306 km west of Banaba (Ocean Island), in Kiribati, its nearest neighbour. Covering an area of 21.3 sq km (8.2 sq miles), Nauru is a low-lying island (its highest point is 65 m—213 ft), comprising a narrow, coastal strip of fertile land surrounding coralline cliffs rising to a plateau of phosphatic rock which covers more than three-fifths of the land area. Nauru has a tropical climate, with a westerly monsoon season from November to February, during which time most rainfall occurs. Annual rainfall averages 2,060 mm (80 ins), but there are marked variations from year to year. In 1989 a UN report on the greenhouse effect (the heating of the earth's atmosphere and a resultant rise in sea-level, as a consequence of pollution) listed Nauru as one of the countries that might disappear beneath the sea in the 21st century, unless drastic action were taken. Indigenous Nauruans are of mixed Polynesian, Micronesian and Melanesian descent, but are predominantly Polynesian. Nauruan is the official language, although English is widely used and generally understood. At the 1992 census the population was 9,919, rising to 10,065 at the census of 2002. By mid-2011 the population had increased slightly, to 10,186, according to estimates from the Secretariat of the Pacific Community. There is no capital as such, but Parliament House and most government offices are in Yaren district.

The first European to discover Nauru was Capt. John Fearn, whose whaling ship, *Hunter*, reached the island in 1798. The territory, which he named Pleasant Island, was described as being inhabited by relatively large numbers of predominantly Polynesian people, organized in 12 clans. The arrival of traders during the 19th century and the subsequent introduction of firearms and alcohol on to the island, however, led to unrest between the tribes and precipitated 'The Ten-Year War': a civil war in which more than one-third of the population was killed. When the island was eventually annexed by Germany in 1888, its inhabitants numbered little more than 900 in total. In 1914, shortly after the outbreak of the First World War, the island was captured by Australian forces. It continued to be administered by Australia under a League of Nations mandate (granted in 1920) which also named the United Kingdom and New Zealand as co-trustees. Between 1942 and 1945 Nauru was occupied by the Japanese, who deported 1,200 islanders to Truk (now Chuuk), Micronesia, where some 500 died as a result of starvation and bombing. In 1947 the island was placed under UN Trusteeship, with Australia as the administering power on behalf of the Governments of Australia, New Zealand and the United Kingdom. The UN Trusteeship Council proposed in 1964 that the indigenous people of Nauru be resettled on Curtis Island, off the Queensland coast. The Nauruans, however, elected to remain on the island. Nauru received a considerable measure of self-government in January 1966, with the establishment of Legislative and Executive Councils, and proceeded to independence on 31 January 1968 (exactly 22 years after the surviving Nauruans returned to the island from exile in Micronesia). In 1999 Nauru attained full membership of the Commonwealth and became a member of the UN.

Phosphate extraction was conducted largely by indentured labour, notably by I-Kiribati and Tuvaluan workers. After gaining independence in 1968, Nauru benefited from sole control of phosphate earnings and, as a result, its income per head was among the highest in the world. This, however, had serious repercussions for the country, which became excessively dependent on imported labour, foreign imports and convenience foods, precipitating severe social problems. About one-third of the adult Nauruan population is believed to suffer from diabetes (by far the worst incidence of the disease anywhere in the world), while obesity, heart-disease, alcoholism and other illnesses attributable to social and dietary problems are also prevalent.

In February 1987 the British, Australian and New Zealand Governments officially terminated the functions of the British Phosphate Commissioners, who from 1919 until 1970 had managed the mining of Nauru's phosphate deposits. President Hammer DeRoburt subsequently expressed concern over the distribution of the Commissioners' accumulated assets, which were estimated to be worth $A55m. His proposal that part of this sum be spent on the rehabilitation of areas of the island that had been mined before Nauru gained independence was rejected by the three Governments involved. The ensuing dispute became known as the 'Matter of Rehabilitation'. In August 1987 DeRoburt established a government commission of inquiry to report on proposals for rehabilitation, and in the following year proposed that the three Governments each provide one-third of the estimated rehabilitation costs of $A216m. (As a result of extensive phosphate mining, 80% of the surface of the island had become uninhabitable and impossible to cultivate.) In 1989, because of Australia's refusal to contribute to the rehabilitation of former phosphate mining areas, Nauru appealed to the International Court of Justice (ICJ) in The Hague, Netherlands, for compensation for damage to its environment. (New Zealand and the United Kingdom deposited instruments with the ICJ that prevented them from being sued by Nauru.) Australia agreed to comply with the eventual ruling of the ICJ. However, in 1993 a Compact of Settlement was signed, under which the Australian Government was to pay a total of $A107m. to Nauru. New Zealand and the United Kingdom subsequently agreed to contribute $A12m. each towards the settlement. In 1995 a report commissioned by the Nauruan Government was published, which gave details of a rehabilitation programme extending over the next 20–25 years and costing $A230m. In 1997 Parliament approved the Nauru Rehabilitation Corporation (NRC) Act, providing for the establishment of a corporate body to manage the rehabilitation programme. The programme, which began in May 1999, was expected to transform the mined areas into sites suitable for agriculture and new housing.

Measures to reform Nauru's financial sector, in response to allegations that the country's 'offshore' banking services were being abused for the purposes of money-laundering, were announced in 2000. However, serious allegations of money-laundering re-emerged in 2001, when the Paris-based Financial Action Task Force (FATF) declared Nauru to be one of the worst international offenders. The FATF imposed countermeasures (which remained in place until October 2004), prescribing increased monitoring, surveillance and transparency in financial transactions. Nauru remained on the FATF list until October 2005. In December 2003, meanwhile, the country was also removed from a list of unco-operative tax havens issued by the Organisation for Economic Co-operation and Development (OECD).

Controversy ensued in December 2009 when it was reported that, in exchange for Russian aid of US $50m., Nauru had accorded diplomatic recognition to the secessionist republics of Abkhazia and South Ossetia. Nauru's recognition of these separatist regions of Georgia drew much criticism. The Nauruan Minister of Foreign Affairs subsequently confirmed the provision of the development aid, but withheld details of the financial arrangements.

In 2006, following the development of new production techniques and the upgrading of processing facilities, Nauru's first major shipment of primary phosphate for nearly 10 years was exported. The mining of secondary phosphate resources was expected to sustain the industry for up to 40 years. Strong expansion was subsequently recorded in the phosphate sector, which further benefited from the high international price for the commodity. Meanwhile, revenue from phosphate sales was invested partly in a long-term trust fund, the Nauru Phosphate Royalties Trust (NPRT). The value of the NPRT was estimated at some $A300m. in 2003, compared with $A1,300m. in 1991, and by mid-2004 Nauru's remaining trust fund assets were in the possession of receivers. The establishment of a new trust fund was under consideration in 2011. In November 2005 Nauru hosted an international donor meeting, attended by representatives of about 20 donor nations and agencies, at which it requested support for its National Sustainable Development Strategy. The aims of this programme included an increase in revenue from phosphate production, better use of fish resources and the encouragement of agricultural activities, with particular emphasis on local food production. Nevertheless, Nauru's short-term economic outlook remained poor, and the situation was exacerbated by the closure in 2008 of a refugee-processing centre, from which the island had derived significant revenue from the Australian Government. The economy was further impeded by the suspension of Parliament for much of 2010, as a result of which the enactment of the annual budget was delayed by four months. In October 2010 Nauru applied to the International Seabed Authority for permission to explore for deep sea minerals in an area of the north-east Pacific Ocean reserved for developing states.

Statistical Survey

Source (unless otherwise indicated): Bureau of Statistics, Ministry of Finance, Government Offices, Yaren District; tel. (674) 444-3142; fax (674) 444-3125; e-mail statistics@naurugov.nr; internet www.spc.int/prism/country/nr/stats.

AREA AND POPULATION

Area: 21.3 sq km (8.2 sq miles).

Population: 8,042 (Nauruan 4,964, Other Pacific Islanders 2,134, Asians 682, Caucasians—mainly Australians and New Zealanders—262) at census of 13 May 1983; 9,919 (males 5,079, females 4,840) at census of 17 April 1992; 10,065 (males 5,136, females 4,929) at census of 23 September 2002. *Mid-2011* (Secretariat of the Pacific Community estimate): 10,186 (Source: Pacific Regional Information System).

Density (at mid-2011): 478.2 per sq km.

Population by Age and Sex (Secretariat of the Pacific Community estimates at mid-2011): *0–14:* 3,607 (males 1,840, females 1,767); *15–64:* 6,445 (males 3,271, females 3,174); *65 and over:* 134 (males 64, females 70); *Total* 10,186 (males 5,175, females 5,011) (Source: Pacific Regional Information System).

Principal Districts (population, 2002 census): Denigomudu 2,381; Meneng 1,323; Aiwo 1,051; Boe 731; Yaren (capital) 632; Buada 673.

Births, Marriages and Deaths (1995): Registered live births 203 (birth rate 18.8 per 1,000); Registered marriages 57 (marriage rate 5.3 per 1,000); Registered deaths 49 (death rate 4.5 per 1,000). *2006* (unless otherwise indicated): Registered live births 120; Registered deaths 75 (2002).

Life Expectancy (years at birth, WHO estimates): 60 (males 56; females 65) in 2009. Source: WHO, *World Health Statistics*.

Economically Active Population (census of 17 April 1992): 2,007 (Elementary occupations 401, Clerks and office workers 355, Craft and related workers 299, Service, shop and market sales workers 250, Professionals 208, Plant, machine operators and assemblers 136, Technicians and associate professionals 115, Legislators, senior officials and managers 18, Agriculture and related workers 2, Not classified 223). *2002* (census of 23 September): Total employed 2,534; Unemployed 746; Total labour force 3,280. *Mid-2011* (estimates): Agriculture, etc. 1,000; Total labour force 5,000 (Source: FAO).

HEALTH AND WELFARE

Key Indicators

Total Fertility Rate (children per woman, 2009): 3.2.

Under-5 Mortality Rate (per 1,000 live births, 2009): 44.

Physicians (per 1,000 head, 2004): 0.8.

Hospital Beds (per 1,000 head, 2004): 5.9.

Health Expenditure (2008): US $ per head (PPP): 440.

Health Expenditure (2008): % of GDP: 14.0.

Health Expenditure (2008): public (% of total): 78.4.

For sources and definitions, see explanatory note on p. vi.

AGRICULTURE, ETC.

Principal Crop and Livestock (2009, FAO estimates): Coconuts 2,179 metric tons; Pigs 3,000 head; Chickens 5,000 head.

Livestock Products (metric tons, 2009, FAO estimates): Pig meat 72; Chicken meat 4; Hen eggs 16.

Fishing (metric tons, live weight of capture, 2009, FAO estimates): Yellowfin tuna 9; Bigeye tuna 3; Skipjack tuna 10; Total catch (incl. other marine fishes) 220.

Source: FAO.

MINING

Phosphate Rock ('000 metric tons, estimates): 84 in 2003; 22 in 2004; 11 in 2005. The phosphoric acid content ('000 metric tons, estimates) was: 26 in 2003; 7 in 2004; 3 in 2005. Source: US Geological Survey.

INDUSTRY

Electric Energy (million kWh): 33 in 2006; 34 in 2007; 35 in 2008. Source: UN Industrial Commodity Statistics Database.

FINANCE

Currency and Exchange Rates: Australian currency: 100 cents = 1 Australian dollar ($A). *Sterling, US Dollar and Euro Equivalents* (31 May 2011): £1 sterling = $A1.5410; US $1 = $A0.9338; €1 = $A1.3433; $A100 = £64.89 = US $107.09 = €74.45. *Average Exchange Rate* (Australian dollars per US $): 1.1922 in 2008; 1.2822 in 2009; 1.0902 in 2010.

Budget ($A '000, year ending 30 June 2007, budget forecasts): *Total Revenue:* 22,288 (Tax revenue 8,646, Non-tax revenue 13,643); *Total Expenditure:* 22,226 (Employee expenses 5,890, Operating expenses 8,543, Property expenses 505, Current transfers 2,150, Gross fixed capital formation 4,682, Other 457).

Gross Domestic Product ($A '000, year ending 30 June at current prices): 27,630 in 2007; 49,520 in 2008; 69,540 in 2009. Source: Asian Development Bank.

Gross Domestic Product by Economic Activity ($A million at current prices, year ending 30 June 2009): Agriculture, hunting and fishing 2.8; Mining 10.2; Manufacturing 17.3; Electricity, gas and water 5.8; Construction 2.3; Trade 6.7; Transport and communications 6.4; Finance 2.9; Public administration 4.9; Other services 10.3; *GDP in market prices* 69.5. Source: Asian Development Bank.

EXTERNAL TRADE

Principal Commodities (US $ '000, year ending 30 June 2005): *Imports:* Food and live animals 4,548; Beverages and tobacco 1,891; Crude materials (except food and fuel) 1,741; Mineral fuels and lubricants 1,528; Animal fats and vegetable oils 1,698; Chemical products 3,300; Manufactured goods 11,898; Machinery and transport equipment 5,375; Miscellaneous manufactured articles 1,705; Total (incl. others) 33,683. *Exports:* Food and live animals 293; Crude materials (except food and fuel) 1,489; Chemical products 408; Manufactured goods 2,039; Machinery and transport equipment 616; Miscellaneous manufactured articles 113; Total (incl. others) 4,959.

Principal Trading Partners (US $ million, year ending 31 December 2010): *Imports:* Australia 13.1; Fiji 0.9; Russia 76.4; USA 2.4; Total (incl. others) 96.2. *Exports:* Australia 5.1; India 16.1; Korea, Republic 3.9; New Zealand 8.9; Total (incl. others) 42.5. Source: Asian Development Bank.

Trade Totals (US $ million, year ending 31 December): *Imports c.i.f.:* 90.1 in 2008; 102.5 in 2009; 96.2 in 2010. *Exports f.o.b.:* 121.4 in 2008; 24.9 in 2009; 42.5 in 2010. Source: Asian Development Bank.

TRANSPORT

Road Traffic (1989): 1,448 registered motor vehicles.

Shipping: *Merchant Fleet* (displacement, '000 grt at 31 December): 15 in 1991 (at 30 June); 5 in 1992; 1 in 1993. Source: Lloyd's Register of Shipping. *International Freight Traffic* (estimates, '000 metric tons, 1990): Goods loaded 1,650; Goods unloaded 59. Source: UN, *Monthly Bulletin of Statistics*.

Civil Aviation (traffic on scheduled services, 2006): Kilometres flown (million) 4; Passengers carried ('000) 219; Passenger-km (million) 376; Total ton-km (million) 37. Source: UN, *Statistical Yearbook*.

COMMUNICATIONS MEDIA

Radio Receivers (1997): 7,000 in use*.

Television Receivers (1997): 500 in use*.

Telephones (main lines, 2009): 1,900 in use†.

Mobile Cellular Telephones (2005): 1,500 subscribers†.

Internet Users: 300 in 2005†.

* Source: UNESCO, *Statistical Yearbook*.
† Source: International Telecommunication Union.

EDUCATION

Pre-primary (2008, unless otherwise indicated): 4 schools (2007); 42 teachers; 663 pupils.

Primary (2008, unless otherwise indicated): 2 schools (2007); 56 teachers; 1,254 pupils.

Secondary (2008, unless otherwise indicated): 4 schools (2007); 57 teachers; 816 pupils.

Vocational (2003, unless otherwise indicated): 2 schools (2004); 4 teachers; 38 students.

Pupil-teacher Ratio (primary education, UNESCO estimate): 22.4 in 2007/08 (Source: UNESCO Institute for Statistics).

Note: Nauruans studying at secondary and tertiary levels overseas in 2001 numbered 85.

Source: Department of Education, Yaren, Nauru.

Directory

The Constitution

The Constitution of the Republic of Nauru came into force at independence on 31 January 1968, having been adopted two days previously. It protects fundamental rights and freedoms, and vests executive authority in the Cabinet, which is responsible to a popularly elected Parliament. The President of the Republic is elected by Parliament from among its members. The Cabinet is composed of five or six members, including the President, who presides. There are 18 members of Parliament, including the Cabinet. Voting is compulsory for all Nauruans who are more than 20 years of age, except in certain specified instances.

The highest judicial organ is the Supreme Court and there is provision for the creation of subordinate courts with designated jurisdiction.

There is a Treasury Fund from which monies may be taken by Appropriation Acts.

A Public Service is provided for, with the person designated as the Chief Secretary being the Commissioner of the Public Service.

Special mention is given to the allocation of profits and royalties from the sale of phosphates.

The Government

HEAD OF STATE

President: MARCUS STEPHEN (elected by Parliament 19 December 2007; re-elected 29 April 2008 and 1 November 2010).

CABINET
(October 2011)

President and Minister of Public Service, Home Affairs, Police, Prisons and Emergency Services, and the Nauru Phosphate Royalties Trust: MARCUS STEPHEN.

Minister of Finance, Foreign Affairs and Trade and Minister Assisting the President: Dr KIEREN KEKE.

Minister of Commerce, Industry and Environment, and Utilities: DOMINIC TABUNA.

Minister of Education, Youth Affairs and Fisheries: ROLAND KUN.

Minister of Health, Sport and Justice: MATTHEW BATSIUA.

Minister of Information and Communications Technology and Transport: SPRENT DABWIDO.

MINISTRIES

Office of the President: Yaren; tel. 444-3772; fax 444-3776; e-mail the.president@naurugov.nr.

Ministry of Commerce, Industry and Resources: Yaren; tel. 444-3133; fax 444-3188; e-mail minister.cir@naurugov.nr.

Ministry of Education: Yaren; tel. 444-3130; fax 444-3718; e-mail minister.education@naurugov.nr.

Ministry of Finance: Government Offices, Yaren; tel. 557-3133; e-mail minister.finance@naurugov.nr.

Ministry of Fisheries: e-mail minister.fisheries@naurugov.nr.

Ministry of Foreign Affairs and Trade: Government Offices, Yaren; tel. 444-3133; e-mail minister.foreignaffairs@naurugov.nr.

Ministry of Health: Yaren; tel. 444-3133; fax 444-3188; e-mail minister.health@naurugov.nr.

Ministry of Home Affairs: ; fax 444-3891; e-mail minister.homeaffairs@naurugov.nr.

Ministry of Justice: Yaren; tel. 444-3160; fax 444-3108; e-mail minister.justice@naurugov.nr.

Ministry for the Nauru Phosphate Royalties Trust: e-mail minister.nprt@naurugov.nr.

Ministry of Police: e-mail minister.police@naurugov.nr.

Ministry of Public Service: e-mail minister.publicservice@naurugov.nr.

Ministry of Sport: e-mail minister.sport@naurugov.nr.

Ministry of Telecommunications: e-mail minister.telecommunications@naurugov.nr.

Ministry of Transport: Yaren; tel. 444-3133; fax 444-3136; e-mail minister.transport@naurugov.nr.

Ministry of Utilities: e-mail minister.utilities@naurugov.nr.

Ministry of Youth Affairs: e-mail minister.youthaffairs@naurugov.nr.

Legislature

PARLIAMENT

Parliament comprises 18 members. The general election held on 24 April 2010 failed to produce a conclusive result, with all 18 incumbent legislators being returned to office. A fresh election was therefore conducted on 19 June, when one of the nine opposition members was defeated. However, with Parliament unable to function owing to its failure to select a new Speaker, a state of emergency remained in place until the beginning of November when the impasse was ended.

Speaker: LUDWIG SCOTTY.

Political Organizations

Democratic Party of Nauru: c/o Parliament House, Yaren; f. 1987; revival of Nauru Party (f. 1975); Leader KENNAN ADEANG.

Naoero Amo (Nauru First): c/o Parliament House, Yaren; e-mail visionary@naoeroamo.com; f. 2001; Co-Leaders DAVID ADEANG, KIEREN KEKE.

Diplomatic Representation

EMBASSY AND HIGH COMMISSION IN NAURU

Australia: MQ45 NPC OE, Aiwo; tel. 444-3380; fax 444-3382; e-mail george.fraser@dfat.gov.au; High Commissioner BRUCE COWLED.

Taiwan (Republic of China): Civic Centre, 1st Floor, Aiwo; tel. 444-3239; fax 444-3846; e-mail nru@mofa.gov.tw; internet www.taiwanembassy.org/nr; Ambassador TIMOTHY HSIANG.

Judicial System

The Chief Justice presides over the Supreme Court, which exercises original, appellate and advisory jurisdiction. The Resident Magistrate presides over the District Court, and he also acts as Coroner under the Inquests Act 1977. The Supreme Court is a court of record. The Family Court consists of three members, one being the Resident Magistrate as Chairman, and two other members drawn from a panel of Nauruans. The Chief Justice is Chairman of the Public Services Appeals Board and of the Police Appeals Board.

Chief Justice of the Supreme Court: GEOFFREY EAMES (non-resident) Yaren; tel. 444-3163; fax 444-3104.

Resident Magistrate of the District Court: G. N. SAKSENA.

Chairman of the Family Court: G. N. SAKSENA.

Religion

Nauruans are predominantly Christians, adhering either to the Nauruan Protestant Church or to the Roman Catholic Church.

Nauruan Protestant Church: Head Office, Nauru; Moderator (vacant).

Roman Catholic Church: POB 16, Nauru; tel. and fax 444-3708; Nauru forms part of the diocese of Tarawa and Nauru, comprising Kiribati and Nauru. The Bishop resides on Tarawa Atoll, Kiribati.

The Press

Central Star News: Nauru; f. 1991; fortnightly.

Nasero Bulletin: Nauru; tel. 444-3847; fax 444-3153; e-mail bulletin@cenpac.net.nr; fortnightly; English; local and overseas news; Editor SEPE BATSIUA; circ. 500.

The Nauru Chronicle: Nauru; Editor RUBY DEDIYA.

Broadcasting and Communications

TELECOMMUNICATIONS

A mobile telephone service was introduced in 2009.

Nauru Telecommunications Service: ICT Centre, Civic Centre Complex, Aiwo, Nauru; tel. 444-3324; fax 444-3111; e-mail director .ict@naurugov.nr; Dir (vacant).

BROADCASTING

Radio

Nauru Broadcasting Service: Information and Broadcasting Services, Chief Secretary's Department, POB 77, Nauru; tel. 444-3133; fax 444-3153; f. 1968; state-owned and non-commercial; broadcasts in the mornings in English and Nauruan; operates Radio Nauru; Station Man. RIN TSITSI; Man. Dir GARY TURNER.

Television

Nauru Television (NTV): Nauru; tel. 444-3133; fax 444-3153; began operations in June 1991; govt-owned; broadcasts 24 hrs per day on 3 channels; most of the programmes are supplied by foreign TV companies via satellite or on videotape; a weekly current affairs programme is produced locally; Man. MICHAEL DEKARUBE; Dir of Media GARY TURNER.

Finance

(cap. = capital; res = reserves; dep. = deposits; m. = million; amounts in Australian dollars unless otherwise stated)

BANKING

State Bank

Bank of Nauru: Civic Centre, POB 289, Nauru; tel. 444-3238; fax 444-3203; e-mail bonauru@yahoo.com; f. 1976; state-owned; reported to be insolvent; Chair. NAGENDRA GOSWAMI.

INSURANCE

Nauru Insurance Corporation: POB 82, Nauru; tel. 444-3346; fax 444-3731; f. 1974; sole licensed insurer and reinsurer in Nauru; Chair. NIMES EKWONA.

Trade and Industry

GOVERNMENT AGENCIES

Nauru Agency Corporation: Civic Centre, 1st Floor, POB 300, Aiwo; tel. 444-3782; fax 444-3730; e-mail info@nauruoffshore.com; internet www.nauruoffshore.com; f. 1972; management service to assist entrepreneurs in the incorporation of holding and trading corpns and the procurement of trust and insurance licences; CEO R. MOSES.

Nauru Corporation: Civic Centre, Yaren; f. 1925; operated by the Nauru Council; the major retailer in Nauru; Gen. Man. A. EPHRAIM.

Nauru Fisheries and Marine Resources Authority: POB 449, Aiwo; tel. 444-3733; fax 444-3812; e-mail nfmra@cenpac.net.nr; f. 1997; CEO CHARLESTON DEIYE.

Nauru Phosphate Royalties Trust (NPRT): Nauru; statutory corpn; invests phosphate royalties to provide govt revenue; extensive int. interests, incl. hotels and real estate; assets put into receivership in 2004; Sec. NIRAL FERNANDO.

Nauru Rehabilitation Corporation (NRC): Camp Ibaganiquane, Meneng; tel. and fax 444-3200; e-mail nrcadmin8464@gmail.com; f. 1999; manages and devises programmes for the rehabilitation of those parts of the island damaged by the overmining of phosphate; CEO VINCI CLODUMAR.

UTILITIES

Eigigu Holding Corporation: Civic Centre, Aiwo; public works, water and waste management; also has interests in supermarket retail and television broadcast distribution; Chair. LESSI OLSSON.

Nauru Central Utilities (Nauru Utilities Authority): Aiwo; tel. 444-3247; fax 444-3521; e-mail wayne.brearley@naurugov.nr; f. 1968; sole electricity provider; CEO APISAKE SOAKAI.

RONPhos Corporation (Republic of Nauru Phosphate Company): Aiwo; tel. 444-3839; fax 444-2752; f. 1967; est. as Nauru Phosphate Corpn; has operated the phosphate industry and several public services of the Republic of Nauru (including provision of electricity) on behalf of the Nauruan people; present name adopted in 2005 following reorganization; Chair. RIDDELL AKUA; Gen. Man. LESI OLSSON.

Transport

RAILWAYS

There are 5.2 km of 0.9-m gauge railway serving the phosphate workings.

ROADS

A sealed road, 16 km long, circles the island, and another serves Buada District.

SHIPPING

In 1998 finance was secured from the Japanese Government for the construction of a harbour in Anibare district, which was opened in 2000.

Nauru Pacific: Government Bldg, Yaren; tel. 444-3133; f. 1969; operates cargo charter services to ports in Australia, New Zealand, Asia, the Pacific and the west coast of the USA; Man. Dir (vacant).

CIVIL AVIATION

Our Airline: Directorate of Civil Aviation, Government Offices, POB 40, Yaren; tel. and fax 444-3746; e-mail info@ourairline.com.au; internet www.ourairline.com.au; f. 1970; fmrly Air Nauru; name changed as above in 2006; operates passenger and cargo services to Kiribati, Fiji, Solomon Islands and Australia; Chair. Capt. KEVIN POWER; CEO KARAM CHAND.

Tourism

There is no tourism industry on the island.

Defence

Nauru has no defence forces. Under an informal agreement, Australia is responsible for the defence of the island.

Education

Education is free and compulsory for children between the ages of six and 16. In 2007 the island had four pre-primary schools, with 663 pupils and 42 teachers in 2008. In 2007 the island had two primary schools and four secondary schools. In 2008 a total of 1,254 pupils were enrolled in primary education with 56 teachers, and 816 pupils in secondary education with 57 teachers. In addition, there were two vocational training schools in 2004. An extension centre of the University of the South Pacific, based in Suva, Fiji, was opened in Nauru in the late 1980s.

NEW ZEALAND PACIFIC TERRITORY

Tokelau is the only remaining Island Territory of New Zealand, of which it is an integral part. New Zealand is a member of the Pacific Islands Forum (formerly the South Pacific Forum), both in its own right and in respect of its Pacific dependencies. The cabinet minister responsible is the Minister of Pacific Island Affairs.

Head of State: HM Queen ELIZABETH II (succeeded to the throne 6 February 1952).

Governor-General: Lt-Gen. Sir JERRY MATEPARAE (took office 31 August 2011).

Ministry of Pacific Island Affairs: POB 833, Wellington 6140, New Zealand; tel. (4) 473-4493; fax (4) 473-4301; e-mail contact@mpia.govt.nz; internet www.mpia.govt.nz.

Minister of Pacific Island Affairs: GEORGINA TE HEUHEU.

TOKELAU

Introduction

Tokelau is located in the central Pacific Ocean, about 480 km north of Apia in Samoa, its nearest neighbour. Tuvalu lies to the west and Kiribati to the north and east. The Territory consists of three atolls with a total area of 12.2 sq km (4.7 sq miles). The central atoll of Nukunonu is the largest; Atafu, the smallest, lies 64 km to the north-west and Fakaofo lies 92 km to the south-east of Nukunonu. Each atoll consists of a number of reef-bound islets, or *motu*, encircling a lagoon. The *motu* vary in size but are never wider than 200 m or higher than 5 m, although they can be up to 6 km in length. The average annual temperature is 28°C (82°F), July being the coolest month and May the warmest. Rainfall is heavy but inconsistent, and occasionally there are severe storms. In February 2005 Cyclone Percy, coinciding with 'king tides', caused widespread damage to housing, infrastructure and food crops. The indigenous inhabitants are a Polynesian people, and Tokelauan is the official language, although English is widely spoken. The population is almost entirely Christian, being either Protestant (just over two-thirds) or Roman Catholic. The total population was 1,487 at the 1996 census, declining to 1,074 at the census of October 2006. The population was estimated at 1,162 in mid-2011. Tokelau has no official capital, each atoll having its own administrative centre. However, the seat of Government is recognized as 'the capital' and is rotated on a yearly basis among the three atolls.

The islands now comprising Tokelau were inhabited by Polynesians, closely related to the people of Samoa, before becoming a British protectorate in 1877. At the request of the inhabitants, the United Kingdom annexed the territory, then known as the Union Islands, in 1916 and included it within the Gilbert and Ellice Islands Colony (now Kiribati and Tuvalu respectively). The British Government transferred administrative control of the islands to New Zealand through legislation enacted in 1925, effective from February 1926. In 1946 the group was officially designated the Tokelau Islands, and in 1948 sovereignty was transferred to New Zealand. From 1962 until the end of 1971 the High Commissioner for New Zealand in Western Samoa (now Samoa) was also the Administrator of the Tokelau Islands. In November 1974 the administration of the Tokelau Islands was transferred to the Ministry of Foreign Affairs in New Zealand. In 1976 the Tokelau Islands were officially redesignated Tokelau.

New Zealand has undertaken to assist Tokelau towards increased self-government and economic self-sufficiency. The Territory was visited by the UN Special Committee on Decolonization in 1976 and 1981, but on both occasions the missions reported that the people of Tokelau did not wish to change the nature of the existing relationship between Tokelau and New Zealand. This opinion was reiterated by an emissary of the General Fono, the Territory's highest advisory body, in 1987, and by the Official Secretary in 1992. A report by the UN Special Committee in 2002 listed Tokelau as one of 16 dependent territories it was seeking to encourage towards independence. However, a UN decolonization mission that visited the islands in September of that year was informed that the majority of Tokelauans wanted to remain part of New Zealand and that the Territory was far too dependent on that country to change its status.

A programme of constitutional change, agreed in 1992 and formalized in January 1994, provided for a more defined role for Tokelau's political institutions, as well as for their expansion. A process of relocating the Tokelau Public Service (hitherto based in Apia, Western Samoa, now Samoa) to the Territory began in 1994, and by 1995 most government departments had been transferred to Tokelauan soil. However, the Tokelau Apia Liaison Office (formerly the Office for Tokelau Affairs) was to remain in Western Samoa, owing to the country's more developed communications facilities.

In June 1994 the General Fono adopted a National Strategic Plan, which gave details of Tokelau's progression (over the next five to 10 years) towards increased self-determination and, possibly, free association with New Zealand. The executive and administrative powers of the Administrator were formally transferred, in that year, to the General Fono and, when the Fono was not in session, to the Council of Faipule. A draft Constitution was subsequently drawn up. In May 1996 the New Zealand House of Representatives approved the Tokelau Amendment Bill, granting the General Fono the power to enact legislation, to impose taxes and to declare public holidays, effective from 1 August 1996 (although New Zealand was to retain the right to legislate for Tokelau).

Under legislation approved in 1999, management of the islands' public service was formally transferred to Tokelau in July 2001. In July 2003 responsibility for the islands' budget was transferred to the General Fono. In October of that year a number of constitutional changes were instituted. The Council of Faipule was renamed the Tokelau Council for Ongoing Government, henceforth to comprise the three Faipule and the three Pulenuku.

At a referendum on the issue of the future status of Tokelau held in February 2006 the requisite two-thirds' majority in favour of the proposed change to free association with New Zealand was not received, contrary to the expectations of the latter: 349 votes were cast in favour of greater self-government, while 232 voters wanted Tokelau to remain a Dependent Territory. The result was regarded as a major set-back for the New Zealand Government. In October, furthermore, the decision to appoint a New Zealand diplomat to the position of Tokelau's Administrator gave rise to some controversy. Meanwhile, in June it was announced that the General Fono had agreed to the holding of another referendum on the issue of Tokelau's status. In November regional inter-governmental groups, led by the Secretariat of the Pacific Community (SPC), began a fact-finding operation in Tokelau. The mission aimed to identify the islands' particular needs and priorities and to formulate a three-year strategy. In February 2007, following similar visits to the Tokelauan communities in Hawaii, American Samoa and New Zealand, an official delegation from Tokelau travelled to Samoa in order to discuss with expatriate Tokelauans the various issues relating to the next referendum. It was emphasized that if they wished to participate in the second referendum, Tokelauans resident overseas would be required to return to the islands three months prior to the poll. In March the Faipule of Fakaofo, Kolouei O'Brien, declared that if the requisite majority in favour of greater autonomy were to be secured at the next referendum then Tokelau would wish to enter immediate negotiations with the USA regarding the return of Swains Island, which had remained part of American Samoa. However, at the second referendum, conducted in October 2007, support for self-government was not sufficient to produce the requisite two-thirds' majority, with 246 out of 692 voters rejecting the proposal.

Under the Administrative Assistance scheme (part of the Principles of Partnership agreement with New Zealand signed in 2003), the limited capacity of the Tokelau Public Service is supplemented by the resources of various New Zealand government departments. Tokelau's agricultural development has been constrained by the lack of suitable cultivable soil and by the adverse effects of inclement weather, particularly cyclones. The Territory's small size, remote situation, lack of land-based resources and the population's continuing migration to New Zealand severely hinder economic development. It was hoped that Tokelau would derive greater benefits from its fisheries resources as a result of a plan initiated by the SPC in 2004. A five-year development plan for the fisheries sector encompassed the period 2006–10. The sale to foreign fleets of fishing licences permitting them to operate in Tokelau's exclusive economic zone (EEZ) has provided an important, albeit fluctuating, source of income. In 2001 the sum of $NZ0.68m. derived from the income from fisheries licensing was used to found the Tokelau Trust Fund (TTF). The fund was established with assistance from New Zealand and with the aim of enhancing the Territory's long-term self-reliance. It was hoped that eventually the fund would attract international contributions. Contributions have been made by Australia and the United Kingdom. Following New Zealand's contribution of $NZ15m. in November 2008, the assets of the TTF totalled $NZ52m. Under the direction of the New Zealand Government, a three-year Economic Support Arrangement was to be implemented during 2007–10. The programme's total budget was projected at $NZ43m.; areas targeted for development included transport, communications, education and health. In April 2010 Tokelau announced that it hoped to ban whaling in its territorial waters. The establishment of a 320,000 sq km shark sanctuary in the islands' EEZ was declared by Tokelau in September 2011.

Also in September 2011 it emerged that reserves of drinking water had been reduced to critical levels by a prolonged drought, a situation that was attributed by many to the climatic phenomenon known as La Niña. Emergency supplies of fresh water were shipped to Tokelau from Samoa.

Meanwhile, following the purchase of the islands' internet domain address '.tk' by a Dutch entrepreneur in 2001, more than 1.6m. names had been registered to the facility by 2007. The services of this joint venture with TeleTok, the islands' communications company, were reported to be proving highly profitable, although the Government's precise earnings from Dot TK were not disclosed. In March 2007, however, a leading information technology publication reported that '.tk' was the most insecure web domain in the world. A content-filtering system was subsequently installed, in an attempt to reduce the risks. In March 2008 an international software security company reported that, along with Niue, in per caput terms Tokelau was one of the world's worst offenders with regard to the relaying of unsolicited e-mails. In October 2011 it was announced that Tokelau was to transfer from the east to the west of the International Date Line. Like Samoa, which had made a similar decision earlier in the year, Tokelau hope to benefit from being in a similar time zone to Australia and New Zealand, its main business partners.

Statistical Survey

Source (unless otherwise indicated): Tokelau Apia Liaison Office, POB 805, Apia, Samoa; tel. 20822; fax 21761; e-mail f.aukuso@clear.net.nz; internet www.spc.int/prism/country/tk/stats/.

AREA AND POPULATION

Area: Atafu 3.5 sq km; Nukunonu 4.7 sq km; Fakaofo 4.0 sq km; Total 12.2 sq km (4.7 sq miles).

Population: 1,537 (males 761, females 776) at census of 11 October 2001; 1,074 (males 543, females 531) at census of 19 October 2006 (excluding 392 persons usually resident but absent on census night). *By Atoll* (2006 census): Atafu 417; Nukunonu 287; Fakaofo 370; Total 1,074. Note: Data for census of 19 October 2006 refer to the population usually resident on census night; actual population count was 1,151. *Mid-2011* (Secretariat of the Pacific Community estimate): 1,162 (Source: Pacific Regional Information System).

Density (mid-2011): 95.2 per sq km.

Population by Age and Sex (Secretariat of the Pacific Community estimates at mid-2011): *0–14:* 378 (males 191, females 187); *15–64:* 686 (males 353, females 333); *65 and over:* 98 (males 45, females 53); *Total* 1,162 (males 589, females 573) (Source: Pacific Regional Information System).

Births and Deaths (1996): Birth rate 33.1 per 1,000; Death rate 8.2 per 1,000. *2010* (Secretariat of the Pacific Community estimates): Live births 26 (birth rate 22.1 per 1,000); Registered deaths 9 (death rate 7.6 per 1,000) (Source: Pacific Regional Information System).

Life Expectancy (years at birth, 1996, official estimates): Males 68; Females 70. Source: Ministry of Foreign Affairs and Trade, Wellington.

Economically Active Population (2001 census, persons aged 15 years and over): Construction 78; Retail trade 12; Hotels and restaurants 4; Transport 7; Communications 20; Village services 182; Public administration 59; Education 53; Medical 23; Total 438. *2006 Census:* Total in paid employment 375.

HEALTH AND WELFARE

Key Indicators

Access to Water (% of households, 2004): 88.

Access to Sanitation (% of households, 2004): 78.

For sources and definitions, see explanatory note on p. vi.

AGRICULTURE, ETC.

Crop Production (metric tons, 2009, FAO estimates): Coconuts 3,566; Roots and tubers 193; Bananas 19.

Livestock (year ending September 2009, FAO estimates): Pigs 1,000; Chickens 5,000.

Livestock Products (metric tons, 2009, FAO estimates): Pig meat 19; Chicken meat 4; Hen eggs 8.

Fishing (metric tons, live weight, 2009, FAO estimate): Total catch 70.

Source: FAO.

INDUSTRY

Production (1990, estimate): Electric energy 300,000 kWh.

FINANCE

Currency and Exchange Rates: New Zealand currency is legal tender. Tokelau souvenir coins have also been issued. New Zealand currency: 100 cents = 1 New Zealand dollar ($NZ); *Sterling, US Dollar and Euro Equivalents* (31 May 2011): £1 sterling = $NZ2.0158; US $1 = $NZ1.2214; €1 = $NZ1.7571; $NZ100 = £49.61 = US $81.87 = €56.91. *Average Exchange Rate* ($NZ per US $): 1.4227 in 2008; 1.6002 in 2009; 1.3874 in 2010.

Budget ($NZ, year ending 30 June 1998): *Revenue:* Local 734,950; New Zealand subsidy 4,600,000; Total 5,334,950. *Expenditure:* Total 5,208,449.

Overseas Aid (projection, $NZ '000, 2002/03): Official development assistance from New Zealand 8,100 (of which Budget support 4,750, Projects and training 2,650). *2010/11:* Total development assistance from New Zealand $NZ17.25m.

EXTERNAL TRADE

Principal Commodities ($NZ, 2002): *Imports:* Food and live animals 923,766; Mineral fuels, lubricants, etc. 194,779; Animal and vegetable oils, fats and waxes 50,012; Chemicals and related products 45,429; Manufactured goods 183,488; Total (incl. others) 1,673,389.

COMMUNICATIONS MEDIA

Radio Receivers (1997, estimate): 1,000 in use.

EDUCATION

Schools (1999): 3 (one school for all levels on each atoll).

Teachers (2003): Primary 23; Secondary 17.

Pupils (2003): Primary 182; General secondary 176.

Students Overseas (1999): Secondary 22; Tertiary 20.

Pupil-teacher Ratio (primary education, UNESCO estimate): 5.8 in 2003/04 (Source: UNESCO Institute for Statistics).

Directory

The Constitution

Tokelau is administered under the authority of the Tokelau Islands Act 1948 and subsequent amendments and regulations. The Act declared Tokelau (then known as the Tokelau Islands) to be within the territorial boundaries of New Zealand. The Administrator is the representative of the Crown and is responsible to the Minister of Foreign Affairs and Trade in the New Zealand Government. The office of Administrator is normally held conjointly with that of New Zealand's Secretary of Foreign Affairs and Trade, but provision is made for the offices to be held separately. Most of the powers of the Administrator are delegated to the Tokelau Apia Liaison Office, the General Fono and the Tokelau Council for Ongoing Government (formerly the Council of Faipule). The chief representative of the Administrator (and the Crown) on each atoll is the highest elected official, the Faipule, who exercises executive, political and judicial powers. The three Faipule, who hold ministerial portfolios and along with the three Pulenuku (Village Mayors) form the six-member Tokelau Council of Faipule, act as the representatives of the Territory in dealings with the administration and at international meetings, and choose one of their number to hold the title Ulu-O-Tokelau (Head of Tokelau) for a term of one year. The Ulu-O-Tokelau chairs sessions of the territorial assembly, the General Fono. The General

Fono is a meeting of 20 delegates (including the Faipule and the Pulenuku from each atoll), representing the entire Territory. There are three or four meetings each year, which take place on the atoll of the Ulu-O-Tokelau. The General Fono is the highest advisory body and the administration must consult it about all policy affecting the Territory. The assembly has responsibility for the territorial budget and has the power to enact legislation, to impose taxes and to declare public holidays. There are a number of specialist committees, such as the Budget Committee and the Law Committee.

Tokelau is an association of three autonomous atoll communities. Local government consists of the Faipule, the Pulenuku and the Taupulega (Island Council or Council of Elders). The Faipule, the Pulenuku and delegates to the General Fono are elected every three years on the basis of universal adult suffrage (the age of majority being 21). The Faipule represents the atoll community, liaises with the administration and the Tokelau Public Service, acts as a judicial commissioner and presides over meetings of the Taupulega. The Pulenuku is responsible for the administration of village affairs, including the maintenance of water supplies and the inspection of plantations, and, in some instances, the resolution of land disputes (practically all land is held by customary title, by the head of a family group, and may not be alienated to non-Tokelauans). The Taupulega is the principal organ of local government. The Taupulega also appoints the Failautuhi (Island Clerk), to record its meetings and transactions. The Taupulega in Atafu consists of the Faipule, the Pulenuku and the head of every family group; in Nukunonu it consists of the Faipule, the Pulenuku, the elders of the community and the nominated heads of extended families; in Fakaofo it consists of the Faipule, the Pulenuku and the elders (meetings of all the heads of family groups take place only infrequently).

The Government

(October 2011)

Administrator: JONATHAN KINGS (took office in 2011).

FAIPULE

The title of Ulu-O-Tokelau (Head of Tokelau) is held on a one-year rotational basis by each Faipule in turn. At elections held on Atafu on 19 January and on Nukunonu on 20 January 2011 new Faipule were chosen on both atolls.

Faipule of Fakaofo: FOUA TOLOA.

Faipule of Nukunonu: SALESIO LUI.

Faipule of Atafu: KELISIANO KALOLO.

PULENUKU

At elections in January 2011 a new Pulenuku (Village Mayor) was chosen on Atafu, while the incumbent Pulenuku of Nukunonu was re-elected.

Pulenuku of Fakaofo: OTINIELU TUUMULI.

Pulenuku of Nukunonu: PANAPA SAKARIA.

Pulenuku of Atafu: SAASETAI TAUMANU.

GOVERNMENT OFFICES

Council for the Ongoing Government of Tokelau: POB 3298, Apia, Samoa; tel. 32325; fax 32338; e-mail jsuveinakama@yahoo.com; internet www.tokelau.org.nz; Gen. Man. JOVILISI SUVEINAKAMA.

Tokelau Apia Liaison Office/Ofiha o Fehokotakiga Tokelau Ma Apia: POB 865, Savalalo, Apia, Samoa; tel. 20822; fax 21761; e-mail maka@lesamoa.net; internet www.tokelau-govt.info; responsible for transport, accounting and consular functions; Gen. Man. FALANI AUKUSO.

The Tokelau Public Service has seven departments, divided among the three atolls, with a supervising administrative official located in each village. Two departments are established on each atoll, while the seventh department, the Council for the Ongoing Government of Tokelau (formerly the Council of Faipule), rotates on a yearly basis in conjunction with the position of Ulu-O-Tokelau. Management of the Tokelau Public Service was formally transferred to Tokelau in July 2001.

Legislature

GENERAL FONO

The General Fono, or territorial assembly, is a meeting of delegates representing the Territory, and includes the Faipule and Pulenuku; it is the highest advisory body and must be consulted by the administration about all policy affecting the Territory. The General Fono has responsibility for the territorial budget and has the power to enact legislation, impose taxes and declare public holidays. The assembly is elected by universal suffrage and, since the legislative elections of 2002, the number of representatives from each atoll has been determined by its proportion of the total population. Members of the General Fono elect a Chairman, and hold between three and four sessions a year on the Ulu-O-Tokelau's atoll.

Chairman: MOSE PELASIO.

Judicial System

Tokelau's legislative and judicial systems are based on the Tokelau Islands Act 1948 and subsequent amendments and regulations. The Act provided for a variety of British regulations to continue in force and, where no other legislation applies, the law of England and Wales in 1840 (the year in which British sovereignty over New Zealand was established) was to be applicable. New Zealand statute law applies in Tokelau only if specifically extended there. In 1986 legislation formalized the transfer of High Court civil and criminal jurisdiction from Niue to New Zealand. Most cases are judged by the Commissioner established on each atoll, who has limited jurisdiction in civil and criminal matters. Commissioners are appointed by the New Zealand Governor-General, after consultation with the elders of the atoll.

Commissioner of Fakaofo: PENEHE TULAFONO.

Commissioner of Nukunonu: IOANE TUMUA.

Commissioner of Atafu: SALASOPA SEMU IUPATI.

Religion

On Atafu almost all inhabitants are members of the Congregational Christian Church, on Nukunonu all are Roman Catholic, while both denominations are represented on Fakaofo. In the late 1990s some 70% of the total population adhered to the Congregational Christian Church, and 30% to the Roman Catholic Church.

CHRISTIANITY

Roman Catholic Church

The Church is represented in Tokelau by a Mission, established in 1992. There were an estimated 500 adherents at 31 December 2007.

Superior: Mgr OLIVER P. ARO, Catholic Mission, Nukunonu, Tokelau (via Apia, Samoa); tel. 4160; fax 4236; e-mail dr.tovite@clear.net.n3.

Broadcasting and Communications

Each atoll has a radio station to broadcast shipping and weather reports. Radio-telephone provided the main communications link with other areas until the late 1990s. A new telecommunications system established at a cost of US $2.76m. (US $1m. of which was provided by New Zealand) and operating through an earth station, linked to a communications satellite, on each atoll, became operational in 1997. A new weekly radio programme, called Vakai, broadcast by Samoa Broadcasting Service to Tokelau's three atolls, began in October 2004.

TELECOMMUNICATIONS

Telecommunications Tokelau Corporation (TeleTok): Fenuafala, Fakaofo; tel. 3100; fax 3108; e-mail apvitale@clear.net.nz; f. 1996; govt-owned; Gen. Man. AUKUSITINO VITALE.

Finance

There are no banks in operation in Tokelau; however, the Office of Tokelau Affairs provides a facility for deposits and withdrawals, and pays interest on accounts. Commercial and other banking facilities are available in Apia, Samoa.

Trade and Industry

A village co-operative store was established on each atoll in 1977. These stores are operated by village management committees, which work with the public service administration to reduce the costs of imported goods. Most imports are purchased from Samoa, with an increasing amount coming from New Zealand and Fiji. Local industries include copra production, woodwork and plaited craft goods, and the processing of tuna. Electricity is provided by diesel generators based in the village on each atoll.

Transport

There are no roads or motor vehicles. Unscheduled inter-atoll voyages, by sea, are forbidden because the risk of missing landfall is too great. Passengers and cargo are transported by vessels that anchor off shore, as there are no harbour facilities. A scheme to provide wharves (primarily to facilitate the export of fish) was proposed in September 2002. Most shipping links are with Samoa, but a monthly service from Fiji was introduced in 1986. The vessel *Forum Tokelau*, operated by Pacific Forum Line, began a monthly service between Tokelau and Apia, Samoa, in mid-1997. A New Zealand-funded inter-atoll vessel commenced service in 1991, providing the first regular link between the atolls for 40 years. Plans to construct an airstrip on each atoll were postponed in 1987 in favour of the development of shipping links. Proposals for the introduction of air links have encountered resistance from the island communities.

Education

Education is provided free of charge, and attendance is virtually 100%. Kindergarten facilities are available for children from the age of three years, while primary education takes place between the ages of five and 14. The provision of an additional year of schooling, for those aged 15, is rotated among the Territory's three schools every five years. In 2003 there were 23 primary school teachers and 17 secondary school teachers. Pupil enrolment in that year at primary level totalled 182 and at secondary level totalled 176. The New Zealand Department of Education provides advisory services and some educational equipment. The Education Department of Samoa organizes daily radio broadcasts. Scholarships are awarded for secondary and tertiary education, and for vocational training, in New Zealand, Australia and other Pacific countries. Link arrangements exist between Tokelau and the Fiji-based University of the South Pacific, which has an outpost on each atoll that is electronically connected. In 2004 a total of 53 Tokelauans over the age of 15 years were studying overseas under the Tokelau Sponsorship Scheme (34 in Samoa, 12 in New Zealand and seven in Fiji). In 2001 there were some 169 Tokelauan pupils enrolled at the Samoa Secondary School. Australia also provides scholarships.

NEW ZEALAND PACIFIC: ASSOCIATED STATES

The Associated States of New Zealand, the Cook Islands and Niue, were formerly Island Territories and integral parts of New Zealand. They now enjoy full self-government but continue in free association with New Zealand. New Zealand remains responsible for defence and represents the dependencies at the UN and in whichever external relations not conducted by the local Government.
Head of State: HM Queen ELIZABETH II (succeeded to the throne 6 February 1952).

Governor-General: Lt-Gen. Sir JERRY MATEPARAE (took office 31 August 2011).

THE COOK ISLANDS

Introduction

The 13 inhabited and two uninhabited islands of the Cook Islands are located in the southern Pacific Ocean. The territory lies between American Samoa, to the west, and French Polynesia, to the east. The total area of all the islands is 236.7 sq km (91.4 sq miles), but they extend over about 2m. sq km (more than 750,000 sq miles) of ocean, and form two groups: the Northern Cooks, which are all atolls and include Pukapuka (Danger Islands), Rakahanga (Rierson Island) and Manihiki (Humphrey Island), and the Southern Cooks, including Aitutaki, Mangaia and Rarotonga, which are all volcanic islands. From December to March the climate is warm and humid, with the possibility of severe storms; from April to November the climate is mild and equable. The average annual rainfall on Rarotonga is 2,134 mm (84 ins). The official language is English, but Polynesian languages are also spoken. The principal religion is Christianity, with the majority of the population adhering to the Cook Islands Christian Church. The population was 18,027 in December 2001, according to the provisional results of the census; of these, 14,900 were estimated to be permanent residents. In that year some 52,569 Cook Islands Maori were resident in New Zealand. The total population was 19,569 in December 2006, according to preliminary census results. According to official estimates, the population was 23,300 in mid-2010. The capital is Avarua, on Rarotonga.

The islands were already settled by Polynesian (Maori) clans when the first Europeans, Spaniards, visited the territory in the late 16th and early 17th centuries. The Cook Islands are named after the leader of a British expedition of 1773, Capt. James Cook. The first islands were proclaimed a British protectorate in 1888. The first British Resident, in 1891, established an Elective Federal Parliament and a Federal Executive Council (the latter comprising Arikis or hereditary chiefs). This system was dissolved when the Cook Islands were annexed to New Zealand in 1901. Subsequent legislation developed government and representative institutions, and a Legislative Assembly was established in 1957. In 1962 the New Zealand Government presented the Assembly with four choices for constitutional development.

Following negotiations on the details and the enactment of the Constitution, the Cook Islands became a self-governing territory in free association with New Zealand on 4 August 1965. The people are New Zealand citizens. In May 1981 an Amendment Bill made several changes in the Cook Islands' Constitution, increasing the membership of the Parliament, from 22 to 24, and extending the parliamentary term from four to five years.

New Zealand is ultimately responsible for the defence and foreign relations of the Cook Islands, although the territory has progressively assumed control over much of its foreign policy (a Ministry of Foreign Affairs was established in 1983). In January 1986, after the virtual disintegration of the ANZUS military alliance linking Australia, New Zealand and the USA, Premier Sir Thomas Davis declared the Cook Islands a neutral country, because he considered that New Zealand was no longer in a position to defend the islands. In 1989 and 1990 the Government of Geoffrey Henry sought to improve links with the neighbouring territory of French Polynesia (Cook Islanders and Tahitians are related) and secured French co-operation in the policing of the Cook Islands' exclusive economic zone (EEZ). In 1990 an agreement was signed that settled the exact delimitation of the EEZs of the Cook Islands and French Polynesia (the two claims overlapped). In 1991 the Cook Islands signed a treaty of friendship and co-operation with France. The establishment of closer relations with France was widely regarded as an expression of the Cook Islands' Government's dissatisfaction with existing arrangements with New Zealand. However, relations deteriorated considerably when the French Government resumed its programme of nuclear-weapons testing at Mururoa Atoll in September 1995. The tests were concluded in January 1996, and bilateral relations subsequently improved.

A reported increase in the number of Russian nationals opening bank accounts in the Cook Islands led to allegations in early 1999 that the islands' 'offshore' financial centre was being used extensively by criminal organizations for 'laundering' the proceeds of their activities. In June 2000 the naming of the islands by the Paris-based Financial Action Task Force (FATF) as one of a number of countries and territories that had failed to co-operate in regional efforts to combat money-laundering, along with the islands' identification by the Organisation for Economic Co-operation and Development (OECD) as a tax haven that lacked financial transparency, led to increased international pressure on the Government to implement stricter controls over its 'offshore' financial centre. Consequently, legislation was approved in August of that year providing for the creation of the Money Laundering Authority and the introduction of new regulations aimed at reducing criminal activity in the sector. In February 2005 the Cook Islands were finally removed from the FATF list of non-co-operative countries and territories. In April 2009 however, OECD included the Cook Islands on its so-called 'grey list' of countries that, while committed to the internationally agreed tax standard, had yet to implement substantial measures to combat tax evasion. In response, the Government made significant progress in negotiating agreements on tax information exchange with other nations, and by mid-2010 the Cook Islands had signed 11 such agreements, one short of the 12 required to be removed from the 'grey list'. The Banking Amendment Bill was approved by islands' Parliament in August 2010, with the closure of all 'offshore' banks operating without the requisite domestic licence envisaged by mid-2011.

The rate of emigration has continued to cause concern. In late 2000 it was announced that some 1,400 residents had left the islands during that year (compared with 641 in the previous year). This resulted in a reduction in the population of the islands to its lowest level in more than 50 years, the majority of the loss being from the outer islands, and prompted the Government to campaign in Australia and New Zealand to encourage former residents to return to the Cook Islands. Another major challenge for the Government has been that of delivering basic services to the outer islands.

The National Sustainable Development Plan and the Infrastructure Master Plan, the latter to encompass a 20-year period, were announced in 2007. These long-term programmes envisaged substantial capital expenditure. The Cook Islands continue to be supported by development assistance from New Zealand and Australia. Under the Cotonou Agreement with the European Union, the islands were also to receive €3.3m. per year between 2008 and 2013 (to be spent on improvements to the environment, water supply and sanitation, including waste disposal). The Cook Islands' acceptance of a large loan from the People's Republic of China, to finance preparations for the hosting of the 2009 South Pacific Mini Games, aroused considerable controversy. The Government announced an audit into the finances of the enterprise responsible for organizing the event.

The islands are vulnerable to cyclones and suffered considerable damage in February and March 2005, when five cyclones struck in just over four weeks. Aquaculture, in the form of giant clam farming and pearl oyster farming, was developed from the 1980s and, despite serious cyclone damage in 1997 and the impact of a pearl shell disease, in the early 2000s pearls remained one of the islands' most important export commodities. The export of fresh and chilled fish is also significant. The tourism sector has expanded considerably since the late 1980s. In 2011 the Government of the Cook Islands continued to subsidize Air New Zealand flights on the Los Angeles–Rarotonga route, in order to ensure the continuation of the carrier's vital service to the islands. The inauguration of direct flights from the Australian city of Sydney in 2010 also enhanced the capacity of the tourism sector. Meanwhile, however, the dramatic increase in tourist arrivals to the islands had led to expressions of concern that

Rarotonga, in particular, was unable to sustain the growth, with reports indicating that waste disposal and energy provision were proving inadequate. In Febuary 2010 the island of Aitutaki, a major tourist destination, was devastated by a cyclone.

Statistical Survey

Sources (unless otherwise stated): Cook Islands Statistics Office, Ministry of Finance and Economic Management, POB 41, Rarotonga; tel. 29511; fax 21511; e-mail info@stats.gov.ck; internet www.stats.gov.ck; Prime Minister's Department, Government of the Cook Islands, Avarua, Rarotonga; tel. 29300; fax 22856.

AREA AND POPULATION

Area: 236.7 sq km (91.4 sq miles).

Population: 18,027 (males 9,303, females 8,724) at census of 1 December 2001 (resident population 14,990); 19,342 (males 9,816, females 9,526) at census of 1 December 2006. *Cook Island Maoris Resident in New Zealand* (New Zealand census of 6 March 2001): 52,569. *By Island* (resident population at 2006 census): Rarotonga (including the capital, Avarua) 10,226; Aitutaki 1,975; Atiu 558; Mangaia 631; Manihiki 344; Mauke 372; Mitiaro 193; Nassau 75; Palmerston (Avarua) 62; Penrhyn (Tongareva) 254; Pukapuka 507; Rakahanga 127; Total 15,324. *Mid-2010* (official estimate, provisional): 23,300.

Density (mid-2010): 98.4 per sq km.

Population by Age and Sex (resident population at 2006 census): *0–14:* 5,049 (males 2,619, females 2,430); *15–64:* 12,821 (males 6,430, females 6,391); *65 and over:* 1,472 (males 767, females 705); *Total* 19,342 (males 9,816, females 9,526).

Principal Town (UN population estimate at mid-2003, incl. suburbs): Avarua (capital) 12,507. Source: UN, *World Urbanization Prospects: The 2003 Revision*.

Births, Marriages and Deaths (2010, provisional): Registered live births 279 (birth rate 12.0 per 1,000); Registered marriages 846 (marriage rate 36.3 per 1,000); Registered deaths 95 (death rate 4.1 per 1,000).

Life Expectancy (years at birth, WHO estimates): 76 (males 72; females 80) in 2009. Source: WHO, *World Health Statistics*.

Economically Active Population (resident population aged 15 years and over, 2001 census): Agriculture, hunting, forestry and fishing 427; Mining and quarrying 3; Manufacturing 357; Electricity, gas and water 79; Construction 347; Trade, restaurants and hotels 1,938; Transport, storage and communications 587; Financing, insurance, real estate and business services 323; Community, social and personal services 1,867; *Total employed* 5,928 (males 3,386, females 2,542); Unemployed 892 (males 449, females 443); *Total labour force* 6,820 (males 3,835, females 2,985). *Mid-2011* (estimates): Agriculture, etc. 2,000; Total labour force 8,000 (Source: FAO).

HEALTH AND WELFARE

Key Indicators

Total Fertility Rate (children per woman, 2009): 2.5.

Under-5 Mortality Rate (per 1,000 live births, 2009): 15.

Physicians (per 1,000 head, 2004): 1.2.

Hospital Beds (per 1,000 head, 2005): 6.3.

Health Expenditure (2008): US $ per head (PPP): 361.

Health Expenditure (2008): % of GDP: 4.3.

Health Expenditure (2008): public (% of total): 91.1.

Access to Water (% of persons, 2006): 95.

For sources and definitions, see explanatory note on p. vi.

AGRICULTURE, ETC.

Principal Crops (metric tons, 2009, FAO estimates): Cassava 1,035; Sweet potatoes 645; Coconuts 1,850; Tomatoes 1,038; Watermelons 72; Guavas, mangosteens and mangoes 172; Papayas 608; Bananas 76; Oranges 74. *Aggregate Production* (metric tons, may include official, semi-official or estimated data): Roots and tubers 3,295; Vegetables (incl. melons) 2,620; Fruits (excl. melons) 1,297.

Livestock (head, year ending September 2009, FAO estimates): Cattle 125; Pigs 32,200; Goats 1,010; Poultry 20,000; Horses 305.

Livestock Products (metric tons, 2009, FAO estimates): Hen eggs 33; Pig meat 555; Chicken meat 20.

Forestry ('000 cu m, 2009, FAO estimate): Roundwood removals (excl. bark) 5.

Fishing (metric tons, live weight, 2009): Albacore 1,707; Yellowfin tuna 297; Bigeye tuna 214; Total catch (incl. others) 2,852 (FAO estimate).

Source: FAO.

INDUSTRY

Electric Energy (production, million kWh): 34 in 2007; 34 in 2008; 33 in 2009.

FINANCE

Currency and Exchange Rates: New Zealand currency is legal tender. In mid-1995 it was announced that the Cook Islands dollar (formerly the local currency, at par with the New Zealand dollar) was to be withdrawn from circulation. New Zealand currency: 100 cents = 1 New Zealand dollar ($NZ); for details of exchange rates, see Tokelau.

Budget ($NZ '000, year ending 30 June 2009, provisional): *Revenue:* Total revenue 95,491 (Tax 80,963, Other current 7,857, Capital 6,671). (Note: Revenue excludes grants of 21,174). *Expenditure:* Total expenditure 124,355 (Current 109,330, Capital 15,025).

Overseas Aid ($NZ '000): Official development assistance from New Zealand (incl. $A1.5m. annual contributions from Australia, but administered by New Zealand) 51,000 for 2009/10–2011/12. Source: Ministry of Foreign Affairs and Trade, Wellington.

Cost of Living (Consumer Price Index for Rarotonga, average of quarterly figures; base: December 2006 = 100): All items 110.4 in 2008; 117.7 in 2009; 117.4 in 2010.

Gross Domestic Product ($NZ '000 at constant 2006 prices): 289,097 in 2007; 278,937 in 2008; 268,977 in 2009.

Gross Domestic Product by Economic Activity ($NZ '000 in current prices, 2009): Agriculture and fishing 16,857; Mining, quarrying and manufacturing 12,556; Electricity, gas and water 7,425; Construction 14,667; Wholesale and retail trade 66,204; Restaurants and hotels 52,602; Transport and communications 59,034; Finance and business services 41,586; Education and health services 18,268; Public administration 28,841; Other community, social and personal services 9,767; Ownership of dwellings 20,128; *Sub-total* 347,935; *Less* Imputed bank service charge 17,451; *GDP in purchasers' values* 330,486.

EXTERNAL TRADE

Principal Commodities ($NZ '000, 2009, estimates): *Imports c.i.f.:* Food and live animals 35,477; Mineral fuels, lubricants, etc. 91,001; Chemicals 10,077; Basic manufactures 34,854; Machinery and transport equipment 55,208; Miscellaneous manufactured articles 39,227; Total (incl. others) 290,228. *Exports f.o.b.:* Fish, fresh or chilled 1,950; Pearls 1,197; Total (incl. others) 4,396.

Principal Trading Partners ($NZ '000, 2009, estimates): *Imports:* Australia 19,675; Fiji 51,240; Japan 6,660; New Zealand 182,243; USA 7,662; Total (incl. others) 290,228. *Exports:* Australia 130; Japan 2,164; New Zealand 290; USA 89; Total (incl. others) 4,396. *2010:Exports*: Australia 793; China, People's Repub. 1,017; Japan 3,557; New Zealand 277; USA 72; Total (incl. others) 7,163 (Source: Asian Development Bank).

TRANSPORT

Road Traffic (registered vehicles, April 1983): 6,555. *New Motor Vehicles Registered* (Rarotonga, 2009): Motorcycles 442; Cars and jeeps 163; Vans and pick-ups 73; Trucks and buses 25; Others 19; *Total* 722.

Shipping: *Merchant Fleet* (registered at 31 December 2009): 107 vessels, displacement 150,020 grt (Source: IHS Fairplay, *World Fleet Statistics*); *International Sea-borne Freight Traffic* ('000 metric tons, estimates): Goods unloaded 32.6 (2001); Goods loaded 9; Goods unloaded 32 (1990) (Source: UN, *Monthly Bulletin of Statistics*).

Civil Aviation (2009): *Aircraft Movements:* 732 departures. *Freight Traffic* (metric tons): Goods loaded 75; Goods unloaded 1,056.

TOURISM

Foreign Tourist Arrivals: 94,776 in 2008; 101,229 in 2009; 104,252 in 2010.

Tourist Arrivals by Place of Residence (2010): Australia 16,841; Canada 2,260; Europe 10,547; New Zealand 67,487; USA 4,327; Total (incl. others) 104,252.

Tourism Revenue (US $ million, incl. passenger transport): 90 in 2006; 107 in 2007; 105 in 2008. Source: World Tourism Organization.

COMMUNICATIONS MEDIA

Radio Receivers (1997): 14,000 in use*.

Television Receivers (1997): 4,000 in use*.

Telephones (main lines, 2010): 7,200 in use†.

Mobile Cellular Telephones (2010): 7,800 subscribers†.

Internet Subscribers (2009): 1,900†.

Broadband Subscribers (2010): 1,700†.

Daily Newspaper (2004, unless otherwise indicated): 1; circulation 2,000 (1996)*.

Non-daily Newspaper (1996): 1; circulation 1,000*.
* Source: UNESCO, *Statistical Yearbook*.
† Source: International Telecommunication Union.

EDUCATION

Pre-primary (2010, unless otherwise indicated): 26 schools (1998); 31 teachers; 452 pupils.

Primary (2010, unless otherwise indicated): 28 schools (1998); 123 teachers; 1,841 pupils.

Secondary* (2010, unless otherwise indicated): 23 schools (1998); 117 teachers; 1,893 pupils.

Higher (1980): 41 teachers; 360 pupils†.
* Includes high school education.
† Source: UNESCO, *Statistical Yearbook*.

Pupil-teacher Ratio (primary education, UNESCO estimate): 15.0 in 2009/10 (Source: UNESCO Institute for Statistics).

Directory

The Constitution

On 4 August 1965 a new Constitution was proclaimed, whereby the people of the Cook Islands have complete control over their own affairs in free association with New Zealand, but they can at any time move into full independence by a unilateral act if they so wish.

Executive authority is vested in the British monarch, who is Head of State, and exercised through an official representative. The New Zealand Government also appoints a representative (from 1994 redesignated High Commissioner), resident on Rarotonga.

Executive powers are exercised by a Cabinet consisting of the Prime Minister and between five and seven other ministers including a Deputy Prime Minister. The Cabinet is collectively responsible to Parliament.

Legislation approved in September 2003 resulted in the abolition of the seat for one member elected by voters living overseas and consequently Parliament consists of 24 members elected by universal suffrage and presided over by the Speaker. Moreover, as a result of a referendum held concurrently with the general election of September 2004, the parliamentary term was shortened from five years to four. The House of Ariki comprises up to 15 members who are hereditary chiefs; it can advise the Government, particularly on matters relating to land and indigenous people, but has no legislative powers. The Koutu Nui is a similar body composed of sub-chiefs, which was established by an amendment in 1972 of the 1966 House of Ariki Act.

Each of the main islands, except Rarotonga (which is divided into three tribal districts or *vaka*), has an elected mayor and a government representative who is appointed by the Prime Minister. In January 2000 it was announced that the post of Government Representative in the outer islands was to be phased out over two years.

The Government

Queen's Representative: Sir FREDERICK GOODWIN.

New Zealand High Commissioner: JOHN CARTER.

CABINET
(October 2011)

The Government is formed by the Cook Islands Party.

Prime Minister and Minister for the Public Service Commission, Office of the Head of State, Attorney-General, Parliamentary Services, Police, Minister of Justice, Ombudsman, National Environment Service, Energy and Renewable Energy, and Emergency Management: HENRY PUNA.

Deputy Prime Minister and Minister of Foreign Affairs, Immigration, Transport, and Mineral and Natural Resources: TOM MARSTERS.

Minister of Finance and Economic Management, Business Trade and Investment Board, Cook Islands Investment Corporation, Internal Affairs, Commerce Commission, Financial Intelligence Unit, Telecommunication, Financial Services Development Authority, Financial Supervisory Commission, National Superannuation, and Public Expenditure and Review Committee Audit (PERCA): MARK BROWN.

Minister of Infrastructure and Planning, Cultural Development and House of Ariki: TEARIKI HEATHER.

Minister of Health and Agriculture: NANDI GLASSIE.

Minister of Education, Marine Resources, Tourism, and National Human Resource Development: TEINA BISHOP.

GOVERNMENT OFFICES

Office of the Queen's Representative: POB 134, Titikaveka, Rarotonga; tel. and fax 29311; e-mail queenrep@oyster.net.ck.

Office of the Prime Minister: Government of the Cook Islands, Private Bag, Avarua, Rarotonga; tel. 25494; fax 20856; e-mail coso@pmoffice.gov.ck; internet www.pmoffice.gov.ck.

Office of the Public Service Commissioner: POB 24, Rarotonga; tel. 29421; fax 21321; e-mail epati@psc.gov.ck; internet www.psc.gov.ck.

New Zealand High Commission: 1st Floor, Philatelic Bureau Bldg, Takuvaine Rd, Avarua, POB 21, Rarotonga; tel. 22201; fax 21241; e-mail nzhcraro@oyster.net.ck.

Ministries

Ministry of Agriculture: POB 96, Rarotonga; tel. 28711; fax 21881; e-mail cimoa@oyster.net.ck; internet www.agriculture.gov.ck.

Ministry of Cultural Development: POB 8, Rarotonga; tel. 20725; fax 23725; e-mail sonny@oyster.net.ck; internet www.mocd.gov.ck.

Ministry of Education: POB 97, Rarotonga; tel. 29357; fax 28357; e-mail cieducat@oyster.net.ck; internet www.education.gov.ck.

Ministry of Energy: POB 72, Rarotonga; tel. 24484; fax 24483; e-mail punanga@energy.gov.ck.

Ministry of Finance and Economic Management: POB 120, Rarotonga; tel. 22878; fax 23877; e-mail etuatina@mfem.gov.ck; internet www.mfem.gov.ck.

Ministry of Foreign Affairs and Immigration: POB 105, Rarotonga; tel. 29347; fax 21247; e-mail secfa@mfai.gov.ck.

Ministry of Health: POB 109, Rarotonga; tel. 29664; fax 23109; e-mail aremaki@health.gov.ck; internet www.health.gov.ck.

Ministry of Infrastructure and Planning: POB 102, Rarotonga; tel. 20034; fax 21134; e-mail t.taoro@moip.gov.ck; internet www.moip.gov.ck.

Ministry of Internal Affairs: POB 98, Rarotonga; tel. 29370; fax 23608; e-mail secintaff@intaff.gov.ck.

Ministry of Justice: POB 111, Rarotonga; tel. 29410; fax 29610; e-mail offices@justice.gov.ck.

Ministry of Marine Resources: POB 85, Rarotonga; tel. 28721; fax 29721; e-mail I.Bertram@mmr.gov.ck.

Ministry of Transport: POB 61, Rarotonga; tel. 28810; fax 28816; e-mail transport@oyster.net.ck.

National Environment Service: POB 371, Rarotonga; tel. 21256; fax 22256; e-mail resources@environment.org.ck; internet www.environment.org.ck.

Advisory Chambers

House of Ariki: POB 13, Rarotonga; tel. 26500; fax 21260; Pres. TRAVEL TOU ARIKI.

Koutu Nui: POB 13, Rarotonga; tel. 29317; fax 21260; e-mail nvaloa@parliament.gov.ck; Pres. TETIKA MATAIAPO DORICE REID.

Legislature

PARLIAMENT

Parliamentary Service

POB 13, Rarotonga; tel. 26500; fax 21260; e-mail nvaloa@parliament.gov.ck.

Speaker: Sir GEOFFREY HENRY.

General Election, 17 November 2010

Party	Seats
Cook Islands Party (CIP)	16
Democratic Party (DP)	8
Total	24

Political Organizations

Cook Islands Labour Party: Rarotonga; f. 1988; anti-nuclear; Leader RENA ARIKI JONASSEN.

Cook Islands Party (CIP): Rarotonga; f. 1965; Leader HENRY PUNA; Deputy Leader MARK BROWN.

Democratic Party (DP): POB 73, Rarotonga; tel. 21224; e-mail demo1@oyster.net.ck; internet www.democookislands.com; f. 1972; Pres. SEAN WILLIS; Leader ROBERT WIGMORE.

Party Tumu: c/o Parliament, POB 13, Rarotonga; f. 2010; est. as Cook Islands Party Tumu; obliged to change name as above following court ruling; Leader ALBERT NICHOLAS.

Te Kura O Te Au: Rarotonga; f. 2010; based upon People's Movement; advocates reform in accordance with spiritual and cultural values; opposed to Sunday flights to Aitutaki; Leader TARAOTA TOM.

Judicial System

The judiciary comprises the Privy Council, the Court of Appeal and the High Court. The High Court exercises jurisdiction in respect of civil, criminal and land titles cases on all the islands, except for Mangaia, Pukapuka and Mitiaro, where disputes over land titles are settled according to custom. The Court of Appeal hears appeals against decisions of the High Court. The Privy Council, sitting in the United Kingdom, is the final appellate tribunal for the country in civil, criminal and land matters.

Attorney-General: HENRY PUNA.

Solicitor-General: TINGIKA ELIKANA.

President of the Court of Appeal: Sir IAN BARKER.

Chief Justice of the High Court: TOM WESTON, Avarua, Rarotonga; e-mail offices@justice.gov.ck.

Judges of the High Court: GLENDYN CARTER, COLIN NICHOLSON, HETA HINGSTON, CHRISTINE GRICE.

Religion

CHRISTIANITY

The principal denomination is the Cook Islands (Congregational) Christian Church, to which the majority of islanders belong.

Religious Advisory Council of the Cook Islands: POB 763, Rarotonga; tel. 23778; fax 21767; e-mail tpere@oyster.net.ck; f. 1972; six mem. churches; Pres. Pastor TUTAI PERE.

The Roman Catholic Church

The Cook Islands form the diocese of Rarotonga, suffragan to the archdiocese of Suva (Fiji). At 31 December 2007 the diocese contained an estimated 2,471 adherents. The Bishop participates in the Catholic Bishops' Conference of the Pacific, based in Suva.

Bishop of Rarotonga: Rev. PAUL DONOGHUE, Catholic Diocese, POB 147, Avarua, Rarotonga; tel. 20817; fax 29817; e-mail sbish@oyster.net.ck.

The Anglican Communion

The Cook Islands are within the diocese of Polynesia, part of the Church of the Province of New Zealand. The Bishop of Polynesia is resident in Fiji.

Protestant Churches

Cook Islands Christian Church: Takamoa, POB 93, Rarotonga; tel. 26452; 11,193 mems (1986); Pres. Rev. TANGIMETUA TANGATATUTA; Gen. Sec. WILLIE JOHN.

Seventh-day Adventists: POB 31, Rarotonga; tel. 22851; fax 22852; e-mail umakatu@oyster.net.ck; 732 mems (1998); Pres. UMA KATU.

Other churches active in the islands include the Assembly of God, the Church of Latter-day Saints (Mormons), the Apostolic Church, the Jehovah's Witnesses and the Baptist Church.

BAHÁ'Í FAITH

Administrative Committee of the Bahá'ís of Cook Islands: POB 1, Rarotonga; tel. 20658; e-mail nsacooks@bahai.org.ck; mems resident in six localities; Sec. JANE LAMB.

The Press

Cook Islands Herald: POB 126, Tutakimoa, Rarotonga; e-mail bestread@ciherald.co.ck; internet www.ciherald.co.ck; weekly; Publr GEORGE PITT; Editor CHARLES PITT.

Cook Islands News: POB 15, Rarotonga; tel. 22999; fax 25303; e-mail editor@cookislandsnews.com; internet www.cinews.co.ck; f. 1954; est. by Govt; transferred to private ownership in 1989; 6 a week; mainly English; Editor JOHN WOODS; circ. 2,100.

Cook Islands Star: POB 798, Rarotonga; tel. 29965; e-mail jason@oyster.net.ck; fortnightly; Chief Reporter JASON BROWN.

Broadcasting and Communications

TELECOMMUNICATIONS

Telecom Cook Islands Ltd: POB 106, Avarua, Rarotonga; tel. 29680; fax 26174; e-mail sales@telecom.co.ck; internet www.telecom.co.ck; CEO JULES MAHER.

BROADCASTING

Radio

Cook Islands Broadcasting Corpn (CIBC): POB 126, Avarua, Rarotonga; tel. 29460; fax 21907; f. 1989; est. to operate new TV service, and radio service of former Broadcasting and Newspaper Corpn; state-owned; Gen. Man. EMILE KAIRUA.

Radio Cook Islands: tel. 20100; e-mail tunein@radio.co.ck; internet www.radio.co.ck; broadcasts in English and Maori 18 hours daily.

KC Radio: POB 521, Avarua, Rarotonga; tel. 23203; f. 1979; est. as Radio Ikurangi; commercial; operates station ZK1ZD; broadcasts 18 hours daily on FM; Man. Dir and Gen. Man. DAVID SCHMIDT.

Television

Cook Islands Broadcasting Corpn (CIBC): see Radio.

Cook Islands TV (CITV): POB 126, Rarotonga; tel. 29460; fax 21907; f. 1989; operated by Elijah Communications; broadcasts nightly, in English and Maori; 10 hours of local programmes per week; remainder provided by Television New Zealand.

Finance

(cap. = capital; dep. = deposits; m. = million; brs = branches)

Financial Supervisory Commission: POB 594, Avarua, Rarotonga; tel. 20798; fax 21798; e-mail Inquire@fsc.gov.ck; internet www.fsc.gov.ck; f. 1981; est. as Cook Islands Monetary Bd; present name adopted 2003; supervises banks and insurance cos; licenses trustee cos; registers international cos, limited liability cos, trusts, financial institutions, etc.; Commr JOHN HOBBS; Chair. RAYMOND NEWNHAM.

Trustee Companies Association (TCA): Rarotonga; controlling body for the 'offshore' financial sector; Sec. LOU COLVEY.

BANKING

Legislation was adopted in 1981 to facilitate the establishment of 'offshore' banking operations.

Development Bank

Bank of the Cook Islands (BCI): POB 113, Avarua, Rarotonga; tel. 29341; fax 29343; e-mail cash@bci.co.ck; internet www.bci.co.ck; f. 2003; est. by merger of Cook Islands Devt Bank and Cook Islands Savings Bank; 100% state-owned; finances devt projects in all areas of the economy and helps islanders to establish small businesses and industries by providing loans and management advisory assistance; Man. Dir VAINE ARIOKA; 10 brs throughout the Cook Islands.

Commercial Banks

ANZ Cook Islands: ANZ House, Maire Nui Dr., POB 907, Avarua, Rarotonga; tel. 21750; fax 21760; e-mail murphyp@anz.co.uk; internet www.anz.com/cookislands; Gen. Man. PHIL HAYNES.

Capital Security Bank Ltd: POB 906, ANZ House, Rarotonga; tel. 22505; fax 22506; e-mail info@csb.co.ck; internet www.capitalsecuritybank.com; cap. US $1.2m., res US $.4m., dep. US $166.5m. (Dec. 2009); Chair. BRIAN MASON.

Westpac Banking Corpn (Australia): Main Rd, POB 42, Avarua, Rarotonga; tel. 22014; fax 20802; e-mail westpaccookislands@westpac.com.au; internet www.westpac.co.ck/pacific; Man. TERRY SMITH.

INSURANCE

Cook Islands Insurance: POB 44, Rarotonga.

International General Insurance (Cook Islands) Ltd: POB 11, Avarua, Rarotonga; tel. 20514; fax 20667; e-mail info@internationalgeneral.com; internet www.internationalgeneral.com; f. 1982.

Trade and Industry

GOVERNMENT AGENCIES

Business Trade Investment Board: Private Bag, Avarua, Rarotonga; tel. 24296; fax 24298; e-mail info@btib.gov.ck; internet www.btib.gov.ck; f. 1996; est. as replacement for Devt Investment Council; present name adopted 2009, following a merger between the Development Investment Board (DIB) and Small Business Enterprise Centre (SBEC); promotes, monitors and regulates foreign investment, promotes international trade, advises the private sector and Govt, and provides training in business skills; Chair. JAMES BEER; CEO TERRY RANGI.

Cook Islands Investment Corporation: Rarotonga; tel. 29391; fax 29381; e-mail ciic@oyster.net.ck; f. 1998; manages govt assets and shareholding interests; Chair. JULIAN DASHWOOD; CEO JOHN TINI.

Cook Islands Public Service Commission: POB 24, Rarotonga; tel. 29421; fax 21321; e-mail epati@psc.gov.ck; internet www.psc.gov.ck; Commr NAVY EPATI; CEO PRISCILLA MARUARIKI.

Cook Islands Trading Corporation (CITC): Private Bag 1, Avarua, Rarotonga; tel. 22000; fax 20857; e-mail directors@citc.co.ck; internet kiaorana.net/citc; f. 1891; principal importer, distributor, wholesaler and retailer of products in the Cook Islands; Exec. Chair. TREVOR CLARKE; Gen. Man. GAYE WHITTA.

CHAMBER OF COMMERCE

Chamber of Commerce: POB 242, Rarotonga; tel. 20925; fax 20969; e-mail chamber@commerce.co.ck; internet www.cookislandschamber.org; f. 1956; represents the private sector in the Cook Islands; Pres. STEVE ANDERSON.

INDUSTRIAL AND TRADE ASSOCIATION

Pearl Guild of the Cook Islands: POB 257, Rarotonga; tel. 21902; fax 21903; e-mail trevon@oyster.net.ck; f. 1994; monitors standards of quality within the pearl industry and develops marketing strategies; Pres. TREVON BERGMAN.

UTILITIES

Electricity

Te Aponga Uira O Tumutevarovaro (TAUOT) (Rarotonga Electricity Authority): POB 112, Rarotonga; tel. 20054; fax 21944; Chair. TAMARII TUTANGATA.

Water

Water Supply Department: POB 102, Arorangi, Rarotonga; tel. 20034; fax 21134.

MAJOR COMPANIES

Cook Islands Fish Exports Ltd: Nikao, Rarotonga; f. 2003; blast freezing, ice production and chilled storage of fish (mainly tuna) for export; Propr BRETT PORTER; Man. GLEN ARMSTRONG.

Island Craft Ltd: Marine Drive, Avarua, POB 28, Rarotonga; tel. 22009; fax 22031; e-mail sales@islandcraft.co.ck; internet islandcraft.com; f. 1943; traditional carvings, perfumes, floral services; Dir FLETCHER MELVIN.

TRADE UNIONS

Airport Workers' Association: Rarotonga Int. Airport, POB 90, Rarotonga; tel. 25890; fax 21890; e-mail jessie@airport.gov.ck; f. 1985; Pres. (vacant).

Cook Islands Industrial Union of Waterside Workers: Avarua, Rarotonga.

Cook Islands Workers' Association (CIWA): POB 403, Avarua, Rarotonga; tel. 24422; fax 24423; e-mail ciwa@oyster.net.ck; largest union in the Cook Islands; Pres. ANTHONY TURUA; Gen. Sec. TUAINE MAUNGA; 700 mems (2006).

Transport

ROADS

On Rarotonga a 33-km sealed road encircles the island's coastline. A partly sealed inland road, parallel to the coastal road and known as the Ara Metua, is also suitable for vehicles. In February 2006 it was announced that construction of a cyclone-proof road, which would encompass the flood-prone area west of Rarotonga airport, was to be initiated with aid from the People's Republic of China. Roads on the other islands are mainly unsealed.

SHIPPING

The main ports are on Rarotonga (Avatiu), Penrhyn, Mangaia and Aitutaki. The Cook Islands National Line operates a three-weekly cargo service between the Cook Islands, Tonga, Samoa and American Samoa. In August 2002 the Government approved proposals to enlarge Avatiu Harbour. The project received additional funding from the Ports Authority and from New Zealand. In October 2008 plans further to upgrade Avatiu Wharf, to enable large ships to berth in the harbour, were endorsed by the Government. The Asian Development Bank agreed to lend US $15.5m. for the three-year project.

Apex Maritime: POB 378, Rarotonga; tel. 27651; fax 21138.

Cook Islands National Line: POB 264, Rarotonga; tel. 20374; fax 20855; 30% govt-owned; operates three fleet cargo services between the Cook Islands, Niue, Samoa, Norfolk Island, Tonga and New Zealand; Dirs CHRIS VAILE, GEORGE ELLIS.

Cook Islands Shipping Ltd: POB 2001, Arorangi, Rarotonga; tel. 24905; fax 24906.

Ports Authority: POB 84, Rarotonga and Aitutaki; tel. 21921; fax 21191; e-mail info@ports.co.ck; internet www.ports.co.ck; Gen. Man. BIM TOU.

Reef Shipping Ltd: operates services between New Zealand and the Pacific Islands.

Taio Shipping Ltd: Teremoana Taio, POB 2001, Rarotonga; tel. 24905; fax 24906.

Triad Maritime (1988) Ltd: Rarotonga; fax 20855.

CIVIL AVIATION

An international airport was opened on Rarotonga in 1974. An airport rebuilding project was completed in 2010. Air New Zealand is among the airlines operating services between Rarotonga and other airports in the region. Air Pacific (Fiji) began a twice-weekly service between Nadi and Rarotonga in June 2000, and in August of that year Air New Zealand began a direct service from Rarotonga to Los Angeles, USA.

Airport Authority, Cook Islands: POB 90, Rarotonga; tel. 25890; fax 21890; e-mail aaci@airport.gov.ck; f. 1986; CEO JOE NGAMATA.

Air Rarotonga: POB 79, Rarotonga; tel. 22888; fax 23288; e-mail admin@airraro.co.ck; internet www.airraro.com; f. 1978; privately owned; operates internal passenger and cargo services and charter services to Niue and French Polynesia; Man. Dir EWAN F. SMITH.

Tourism

Tourism is the most important industry in the Cook Islands. In 2010 the number of foreign tourist arrivals reached 104,252, the majority of whom came from New Zealand. Australia and Europe are also important sources of tourists. There were 1,874 beds available at hotels and similar establishments in the islands in 1999. Most of the tourist facilities are to be found on Rarotonga and Aitutaki, but the outer islands also offer attractive scenery. Revenue from tourism was estimated at some US $105m. in 2008.

Cook Islands Tourism Corporation: POB 14, Rarotonga; tel. 29435; fax 21435; e-mail tourism@cookislands.gov.ck; internet www.cookislands.travel; Chair. EWAN F. SMITH; CEO CARMEL BEATTIE.

Education

Free secular education is compulsory for all children between six and 15 years of age. In 1998 there were 26 pre-primary schools, 28 primary schools and 23 secondary schools. In 2010 there were 452 pupils enrolled in pre-primary education, 1,841 in primary education and 1,893 in secondary education. Under the New Zealand Training Scheme, the New Zealand Government offers overseas scholarships in New Zealand, Fiji, Papua New Guinea, Australia and Samoa for secondary and tertiary education, career-training and short-term in-service training. There is an extension centre of the University of the South Pacific (based in Fiji) in the Cook Islands. Budgetary expenditure on education was estimated at $NZ14.7m. in 2007/08, equivalent to 15.4% of total expenditure.

NIUE

Introduction

Niue is a coral island of 261.5 sq km (101 sq miles) located about 480 km east of Tonga and 930 km west of the southern Cook Islands. The island is mainly covered with bush and forest and, because of the rocky and dense nature of the terrain, fertile soil is not plentiful. Agriculture is further made difficult because there are no running streams or surface water. Rainfall occurs predominantly during the hottest months, from December to March, when the average temperature is 27°C (81°F). Average annual rainfall is 7,715 mm (298 ins). The restricted nature of local resources has led many islanders to migrate to New Zealand. The population declined from 5,194 in September 1966 to 2,088 at the census of August 1997 and to 1,625 at September 2006. According to provisional census results, the population totalled 1,615 in September 2011. The official languages are Niuean (a Polynesian language of the indigenous inhabitants) and English. Both are widely spoken. Most of the population are Christian, mainly Protestant. The capital and administrative centre (with a population of 540 in mid-2010) is Alofi, on the west coast.

The first Europeans to discover Niue, which was inhabited by a Polynesian people related to the Tongans and Samoans, were members of a British expedition, led by Capt. James Cook, in 1774. Missionaries visited the island throughout the 19th century. In 1876 the clans and families of Niue elected a king, and in 1900 the island was declared a British protectorate. In 1901 Niue was formally annexed to New Zealand as part of the Cook Islands, but in 1904 it was granted a separate administration.

In October 1974 Niue attained the status of 'self-government in free association with New Zealand'. Niueans retain New Zealand citizenship, and 14,556 Niueans were resident in New Zealand in 1991. Robert (from 1982, Sir Robert) Rex, who had been Niue's political leader since the early 1950s, was the island's Premier when it became self-governing, and retained the post following three-yearly general elections in 1975–90.

The migration of Niueans to New Zealand has been a cause of increasing concern, and in 1985 the Government of New Zealand announced its intention to review its constitutional relationship with Niue, with the specific aim of preventing further depopulation of the island. In 1987 a six-member committee, comprising four New Zealanders and two Niueans, was formed to examine Niue's economic and social conditions, and to consider the possibility of the island's reverting to the status of a New Zealand-administered territory. It was hoped that the replacement of national superannuation by Guaranteed Retirement Income (GRI) in the July 1989 New Zealand budget would encourage the return of the Niueans resident in New Zealand, since all those eligible for GRI would immediately be able to receive 50% of the entitlement if they resided overseas for more than six months of the year.

In March 2000 a Niue-New Zealand joint consultative committee met, for the first time, in Alofi to consider the two sides' future constitutional relationship. Later that year the committee proposed to conduct a survey of islanders' views and to consider all options, from reintegration with New Zealand to full independence. A meeting of the joint committee took place in March 2001 in Wellington at which the issues of New Zealand aid and reciprocal immigration laws were discussed, as well as options for Niue's future constitutional status.

Niue's economic development has been adversely affected by inclement weather and the inadequacy of transport services, as well as by the high rate of emigration to New Zealand. Two-thirds of the land surface is uncultivable, and marine resources are variable. In 1994 the Niue Assembly approved legislation allowing the island to become an 'offshore' financial centre. In 1999, however, allegations that Niue was being used by criminal organizations for 'laundering' the proceeds of their illegal activities were strongly denied by Premier Sani Lakatani. In a report published in June 2000, the Paris-based Financial Action Task Force (FATF) on Money Laundering (established in 1989 on the recommendation of the Group of Seven (G7) industrialized nations) named the island as one of a number of countries and territories that had 'failed to co-operate' in regional efforts to combat money-laundering. As a result the Government suspended the issue of any further 'offshore' banking licences. In early 2001 the USA imposed sanctions on Niue (including a ban on transactions with US banks), claiming that the island had not implemented all the recommendations of the report. Lakatani appealed directly to US President George W. Bush to end the embargo, and in June the Government engaged a US law firm in an attempt to persuade two banks, Chase Manhattan and Bank of New York, to remove their bans on the transfer of some $NZ1m. to Niue via a business registry in Panama that the Government used for 'offshore' tax activity. Having failed to meet an FATF deadline in August 2001, in February 2002 the Government announced proposals to repeal the 'offshore' banking legislation. The FATF announced in April 2002 that, in view of the island's commitment to improving the transparency of its tax and regulatory systems, the organization was to remove Niue from its list of non-co-operative territories; the decision was duly implemented in October. The bank-licensing legislation was repealed in June.

Other attempts to secure additional sources of revenue in Niue have included the leasing of the island's telecommunications facilities to foreign companies for use in specialist telephone services. However, this enterprise (which earned the island an estimated $NZ1.5m. per year) caused considerable controversy when it was revealed that Niue's telephone code had been made available to companies offering personal services considered indecent by the majority of islanders. In addition, the island earned some US $0.5m. between 1997 and 2000 from the sale of its internet domain name '.nu', although similar controversy ensued when a report published in July 2004 claimed that the island was hosting some 3m. pages of pornographic material via its '.nu' domain. In March 2008, furthermore, an international software security company reported that, along with Tokelau, in per caput terms Niue had become one of the world's worst offenders with regard to the relaying of unsolicited e-mails. In addition to the annual development assistance provided by New Zealand, an aid programme totalling $NZ20m. over five years was announced in late 2004 and a trust fund was established with $NZ10m. from New Zealand and Australia. By mid-2005 the trust fund's assets stood at $NZ12m.

Niue's entire economy was severely affected by Cyclone Heta, which struck the island in January 2004 causing extensive damage to housing, crops and infrastructure. The subsequent recovery programme, known as New Niue or Niue Foou, emphasized rebuilding works and the development of a major fish-processing project. A major programme to extend the Matavai Resort, Niue's main hotel, was under way in 2011. The refurbishment project was to be funded by New Zealand aid of almost US $5m., and a trust company was established to oversee the project. The establishment of a casino on Niue was under consideration in 2011. In February of that year China was reported to have provided funding for an extension of Niue's airport terminal and other improvements, and a Chinese-financed hotel was scheduled to open in 2012.

In August 2008 Niue hosted the annual summit meeting of the Pacific Islands Forum, at which the Niue Declaration on Climate Change was endorsed. Niue also hosted a meeting of the Pacific Island Forum ministers responsible for economic affairs in October 2010 and the Pacific Climate Change Roundtable in March 2011.

Statistical Survey

Source (unless otherwise indicated): Statistics Unit, Economics, Planning, Development Office, Government of Niue, POB 95, Alofi; tel. 4219; fax 4148; e-mail statsniue@mail.gov.nu; internet www.spc .int/prism/country/nu/stats.

AREA AND POPULATION

Area: 261.5 sq km (100.9 sq miles).

Population: 1,625 (males 802, females 823) at census of September 2006 (an estimated 22,473 Niueans lived in New Zealand at the time of the 2006 census); 1,615 at census of 10 September 2011 (provisional result).

Density (at 2011 census): 6.2 per sq km.

Population by Age and Sex (official estimates at mid-2010, on-island residents): *0–14:* 383 (males 187, females 196); *15–64:* 929 (males 482, females 447); *65 and over:* 182 (males 85, females 97); *Total* 1,494 (males 754, females 740).

Ethnic Groups (2001 census, declared ethnicity): Niuean 1,399; Caucasian 81; Pacific Islander 182; Niuean/Caucasian 28; Niuean/ Pacific Islander 42; Asian 4.

Principal Villages (population at mid-2010, official estimates): Alofi (capital) 540; Hakupu 138; Avatele 137; Tamakautoga 115; Tuapa 105.

Births, Marriages and Deaths: *2009* (including Niueans temporarily resident in New Zealand): Live births 31; Marriages 12; Deaths 12. *2010* (Secretariat of the Pacific Community estimate): Birth rate 14.8 per 1,000; Death rate 9.7 per 1,000 (Source: Pacific Regional Information System).

Life Expectancy (years at birth, WHO estimates): 72 (males 66; females 80) in 2009. Source: WHO, *World Health Statistics*.

Immigration and Emigration (2009): Arrivals 6,380; Departures 6,426.

Economically Active Population (2006 census, persons aged 15 years and over): Agriculture, forestry and fishing 119; Mining, electricity, gas, water and construction 61; Manufacturing 67; Trade, restaurants and hotels 84; Transport, storage and communications 43; Finance, real estate, business activities 33; Public administration 180; Education and health 117; Community, social and personal services 43; *Total employed* 747. Note: figures exclude subsistence workers. *Paid Employment* (December 2004): Government sector 512 (males 294, females 218); Private sector (estimates) 269 (males 143, females 126).

HEALTH AND WELFARE

Key Indicators

Total Fertility Rate (children per woman, 2006): 2.6.

Under-5 Mortality Rate (per 1,000 live births, 2009): 17.

Physicians (per 1,000 head, 2004): 2.0.

Hospital Beds (per 1,000 head, 2006): 4.9.

Health Expenditure (2008): US $ per head (PPP): 2,360.

Health Expenditure (2008): % of GDP: 13.5.

Health Expenditure (2008): public (% of total): 98.6.

For sources and definitions, see explanatory note on p. vi.

AGRICULTURE, ETC.

Principal Crops (metric tons, 2009, FAO estimates): Taro 3,634; Sweet potatoes 239; Yams 110; Coconuts 2,601; Bananas 101; Lemons and limes 139. *Aggregate Production* ('000 metric tons, may include official, semi-official or estimated data): Vegetables (incl. melons) 131; Fruits (excl. melons) 920.

Livestock (year ending September 2009, FAO estimates): Cattle 115; Pigs 2,100; Chickens 15,000.

Livestock Products (metric tons, 2009, FAO estimates): Pig meat 52; Chicken meat 18; Cows' milk 54; Hen eggs 15; Honey 6.

Forestry (cu m, 1985): Roundwood removals 613; Sawnwood production 201.

Fishing (metric tons, live weight, 2009, FAO estimate): Total catch 192.

Source: FAO.

INDUSTRY

Production (2008, estimate): Electric energy 3 million kWh. Source: UN Industrial Commodity Statistics Database.

FINANCE

Currency and Exchange Rates: 100 cents = 1 New Zealand dollar ($NZ). For details, see Tokelau.

Budget ($NZ '000, year ending 30 June 2006, provisional): Internal revenue 14,206; New Zealand budgetary support 6,953; *Total revenue* 21,159; Recurrent expenditure 21,417; Capital 90; *Total expenditure* 21,507. *2006/07* ($NZ '000, forecasts): Internal revenue 16,499; New Zealand budgetary support 6,915; Total revenue 23,414; Recurrent expenditure 23,364; Capital projects 50; Total expenditure 23,414. *2008/09* ($NZ '000, forecasts): Total revenue 20,441; Total expenditure 20,259.

Overseas Aid ($NZ '000, 2010/11, provisional): Official development assistance from New Zealand 19,000. Source: Ministry of Foreign Affairs and Trade, Wellington.

Cost of Living (Consumer Price Index, average of quarterly figures; base: July–Sept. 2003 = 100): All items 123.9 in 2008; 138.3 in 2009; 145.7 in 2010.

Gross Domestic Product ($NZ '000 in current prices): 17,771 in 2004; 19,441 in 2005; 20,541 in 2006.

Gross Domestic Product by Economic Activity ($NZ '000 in current prices, 2006): Agriculture, forestry and fishing 4,913; Mining and quarrying 47; Manufacturing 282; Electricity, gas and water 494; Construction 196; Trade 2,344; Restaurants and hotels 819; Transport, storage and communications 1,057; Financial and business services, real estate, etc. 1,596; Public administration 6,941; Other community, social and personal services 534; *Sub-total* 19,223; *Less* Imputed bank service charge 334; *GDP at factor cost* 18,889; Indirect taxes *Less* Subsidies 1,664; *GDP in purchasers' values* 20,541.

EXTERNAL TRADE

Principal Commodities ($NZ '000, 2008): *Imports c.i.f.:* Animals and animal products 679; Prepared foodstuffs 1,250; Mineral products 4,206; Chemical products 321; Plastics and rubber 195; Wood and wood products 403; Base metals and articles thereof 1,176; Machinery, mechanical appliances and electrical equipment 915; Miscellaneous manufactured articles 461; Total (incl. others) 10,968. *Exports f.o.b.:* Taro 24; Coconut 2; Vanilla 1; Total (incl. others) 27.

Principal Trading Partners ($NZ '000, 2008): *Imports c.i.f.:* China, People's Republic 113; Japan 296; New Zealand 10,478; Total (incl. others) 10,968. *Exports f.o.b.:* Total 27.

TRANSPORT

Road Traffic (2001 census): Passenger cars 323; Motorcycles 134; Vans 170; Trucks 74; Pick-ups 76; Buses 11.

International Shipping: *Ship Arrivals* (1989): Yachts 20; Merchant vessels 22; Total 42. *Freight Traffic* (metric tons, 1989, official estimates): Unloaded 3,410; Loaded 10.

Civil Aviation: *Passengers* (1992): Arrivals 3,500; Departures 3,345. *Freight Traffic* (metric tons, 1992): Unloaded 41.6; Loaded 15.7.

TOURISM

Foreign Tourist Arrivals (by air): 3,463 in 2007; 4,748 in 2008; 4,662 in 2009.

Tourist Arrivals by Country of Residence (2009): Australia 461; New Zealand 2,690; United Kingdom 47; USA 157; Total (incl. others) 4,662.

Tourism Receipts (US $ million, incl. passenger transport): 1.1 in 2006; 1.6 in 2007; 2.0 in 2008. Source: World Tourism Organization.

COMMUNICATIONS MEDIA

Telephones (2010): 1,200 main lines in use*.

Mobile Cellular Telephones (2009): 1,100 units in use*.

Radio Receivers (2006 census): 373 per 1,000 persons.

Television Receivers (2006 census): 519 per 1,000 persons.

Personal Computers (2001 census): 77 in use.

Internet Users (2009): 1,100*.

Daily Newspaper (2004): 1.

Non-daily Newspaper (2004): 1†.

* Source: International Telecommunication Union.

† Source: UNESCO.

EDUCATION

Pre-primary and Primary (2006): 1 school; 212 pupils (males 104, females 108); 20 teachers (males 3, females 17).

Secondary (2006): 1 school; 191 pupils (males 102, females 89); 31 teachers (males 9, females 22).

Source: Department of Education, Niue.

Pupil-teacher Ratio (primary education, UNESCO estimate): 11.9 in 2004/05. Source: UNESCO Institute for Statistics.

Directory

The Constitution

In October 1974 Niue gained self-government in free association with New Zealand. The latter, however, remains responsible for Niue's defence and external affairs and will continue economic and administrative assistance. Executive authority in Niue is vested in the British monarch as sovereign of New Zealand but exercised through the government of the Premier, assisted by three ministers. Legislative power is vested in the Niue Assembly or Fono Ekepule, which comprises 20 members (14 village representatives and six elected on a common roll), but New Zealand, if requested to do so by the Assembly, will also legislate for the island. There is a New Zealand representative in Niue, the High Commissioner, who is charged with liaising between the Governments of Niue and New Zealand.

The Government

New Zealand High Commissioner: MARK BLUMSKY.

Secretary to Government: RICHARD HIPA.

CABINET
(October 2011)

Premier, Chairman of the Cabinet and Minister responsible for Finance, Customs and Revenue and Government Assets, Premier's Department (Civil Aviation, Crown Law, External Affairs, Planning, Economic Development and Statistics), Infrastructure, Transport, Public Service Commission, Police and National Security, Tourism, Posts and Telecommunications and Immigration and Population: TOKE TUFUKIA TALAGI.

Minister of Education, Agriculture, Forestry and Fisheries and Administrative Services: POKOTOA SIPELI.

Minister of Public Works, Niue Power Corpn, Justice, Lands and Survey and Bulk Fuel: KUPA MAGATOGIA.

Minister of Health, Community Affairs, and Niue Broadcasting Corpn: JOAN VILIAMU.

GOVERNMENT OFFICES

All ministries are in Alofi.

Office of the New Zealand High Commissioner: POB 78, Tapeu, Alofi; tel. 4022; fax 4173; e-mail sog.hipa@mail.gov.nu; internet www.gov.nu.

Office of the Secretary to Government: POB 40, Alofi; tel. 4220; fax 4232; e-mail ctatui.sog@mail.gov.nu.

Legislature

ASSEMBLY

The Niue Assembly or Fono Ekepule has 20 members (14 village representatives and six members elected on a common roll). The most recent general election was held on 7 May 2011.

Speaker: AHOHIVA LEVI.

Political Organizations

There have been no active political parties on Niue since the disbanding, in 2003, of the Niue People's Pary (f. 1987—Niue's sole political party to date). All politicians on the island are de facto independents.

Judicial System

The Chief Justice of the High Court, which exercises civil and criminal jurisdiction, and the Judge of the Land Court, which is concerned with litigation over land and titles, visit Niue quarterly. In addition, locally appointed lay justices exercise limited criminal and civil jurisdiction. Appeals against High Court judgments are heard in the Court of Appeal of Niue, while appeals against Land Court judgments are heard in the Land Appellate Court. Established in 1992, sessions of the Court of Appeal of Niue are usually held in the New Zealand capital of Wellington. In April 2009, however, for the first time the four New Zealand judges heard various cases, including several land disputes, on Niue itself.

Chief Justice of the High Court: PATRICK SAVAGE.

Registrar of the High Court: JUSTIN KAMUPALA.

Religion

About 63% of the population belong to the Ekalesia Niue, a Protestant organization, which had 1,093 adherents at the time of the 2001 census. Within the Roman Catholic Church, which had 128 adherents (equivalent to 7.4% of the population) in 2001, Niue forms part of the diocese of Tonga. The Church of Jesus Christ of Latter-day Saints (Mormon—which had 158 adherents in 2001), the Seventh-day Adventists, the Jehovah's Witnesses and the Church of God of Jerusalem are also represented.

Ekalesia Kerisiano Niue: Head Office, POB 25, Alofi; tel. 4195; fax 4352; e-mail ekalesia.niue@niue.nu; f. 1846; est. by London Missionary Society, became Ekalesia Niue in 1966; Pres. Rev. ARTHUR PIHIGIA; Gen. Sec. Rev. PETESA SIONETUATO.

The Press

Niue Business News: 20 Lautamina Rd, Mutalau 110175; tel. 3317; fax 4010; e-mail sioneholof@gmail.com; f. 2000; owned by Tropical Suppliers; electronic; previously publ. in print as *Niue Economic Review*; CEO FRANK SIONEHOLO.

Niue Star: weekly; Niuean and English; publ. in Alofi until destruction of office by Cyclone Heta in 2004; operations transferred to Auckland, New Zealand; Publr MIKE JACKSON; circ. 800.

Broadcasting and Communications

TELECOMMUNICATIONS

In 2003 Niue became the first location in the world to have a national wireless internet system allowing access from anywhere on the island by means of solar-powered aerials attached to coconut palms. A four-fold expansion of the island's internet capacity was announced in March 2010. A mobile telephone service was introduced in 2011.

Director of Posts and Telecommunications: POB 37, Alofi; tel. 4000; fax 4010.

Telecom Niue: POB 37, Alofi; tel. 4002; Dir RICHARD HIPA.

BROADCASTING

Radio

Broadcasting Corporation of Niue: POB 68, Alofi; tel. 4026; fax 4217; operates radio and TV services; govt-owned; Chair. NEAL MORRISSEY; CEO TREVOR TIAKIA; Gen. Man. PATRICK LINO.

Radio Sunshine: broadcasts in English and Niuean between 6 a.m. and 10 p.m. Mon.–Sat.

Television

Broadcasting Corporation of Niue: see Radio.

Television Niue broadcasts in English and Niuean six days a week from 5 p.m. to 11 p.m.

Finance

DEVELOPMENT BANK

Niue Development Bank: POB 34, Alofi; tel. 4335; fax 4290; e-mail devbank@niue.nu; f. 1993; govt-owned; began operations July 1994; Chair. MISIATA TASMANIA; Gen. Man. VAINE PASISI.

COMMERCIAL BANK

Bank South Pacific Ltd: POB 76, Main St, Alofi; tel. 4220; fax 4043; e-mail bsp@niue.nu; internet www.bsp.com.pg/niue/niue.htm; acquired from Westpac Banking Corpn in Sept. 2004; Man. ANN PESAMINO.

Trade and Industry

GOVERNMENT AGENCIES

Business Advisory Service: Alofi; tel. 4228.

Office of Economic Affairs, Planning and Development, Statistics and Trade and Investment: POB 42, Alofi; tel. 4148; e-mail business.epdsu@mail.gov.nu; responsible for planning and financing activities in the agricultural, tourism, industrial sectors, business advisory and trade and investment.

CHAMBER OF COMMERCE

Niue Chamber of Commerce: POB 160, Alofi; tel. 4399; fax 4010; e-mail chamber@niue.nu; internet live.niuechamber.com; Pres. AVI RUBIN.

UTILITIES

Niue Power Corporation: POB 198, Alofi; tel. 4119; fax 4385; e-mail gm.npc@mail.gov.nu; Gen. Man. SPEEDO HETUTU.

MAJOR COMPANY

NU Domain Ltd: Alofi; e-mail support@nic.nu; internet www.nunames.nu; f. 1997; responsible for the sale of Niue's internet domain name; Admin. Man. STAFFORD GUEST; Tech. Man. RICHARD ST CLAIR.

TRADE UNION

Public Service Association: Alofi.

Transport

ROADS

There are 123 km of all-weather roads and 106 km of access and plantation roads. A total of 788 motor vehicles were registered in 2001. The road network was extensively damaged by Cyclone Heta in January 2004. In mid-2004 it was estimated that some 48 km of sealed roads were clear and in good condition.

SHIPPING

The best anchorage is an open roadstead at Alofi, the largest of Niue's 14 villages. Work to extend a small wharf at Alofi began in 1998 with

US assistance. The New Zealand Shipping Corporation operates a monthly service between New Zealand, Nauru and Niue. Fuel supplies are delivered by a tanker (the *Pacific Explorer*) from Fiji. In December 2002 the Government signed an agreement with Reef Shipping Ltd to provide a service to New Zealand every three to four weeks.

CIVIL AVIATION

Hanan International Airport has a total sealed runway of 2,350 m, following the completion of a 700 m extension in 1995, with New Zealand assistance. In 2005 Air New Zealand began a weekly service between Auckland and Niue. In early 2011 the provision of funding by the People's Republic of China, to finance improvements that included the extension of the airport terminal, was confirmed.

Tourism

Niue has a small but significant tourism industry (specializing in holidays based on activities such as diving, rock-climbing, caving and game fishing), which has benefited from an increase in the frequency of flights between the island and New Zealand. The Matavai Resort provides the main tourist facilities; the resort was in the process of being extended in 2011. A second hotel, financed by Chinese interests, was expected to open in 2012. In September 2011 it was announced that over a three-year period New Zealand was to provide a total of $NZ15m. for the purposes of tourism development projects. Tourist receipts (including passenger transport) totalled US $2.0m. in 2008. A total of 4,662 people arrived by air to visit Niue in 2009. Most visitors are from New Zealand. In comparison with the previous year, visitor arrivals were reported to have increased by 33.3% in 2010, with arrivals from Germany and the United Kingdom estimated to have doubled.

Niue Tourism Office: POB 42, Alofi; tel. 4224; fax 4225; e-mail niuetourism@mail.gov.nu; internet www.niueisland.com; Dir of Tourism TANYA LIAMOTU (acting).

Education

Education is free and compulsory between six and 16 years of age (the school-leaving age having been raised from 14 in 1998). In 1987 the island's seven village primary schools were closed and a single national primary school was opened at Halamahaga. In 2006 this bilingual (Niuean/English) primary school had 20 teachers and an enrolment of 212 pupils. There was one secondary school at Paliati, with a teaching staff of 31 and a total enrolment of 191 pupils in 2006. Higher education takes place at the Niue Extension Centre of the University of the South Pacific (based in Fiji), on government training schemes or by correspondence. Some study overseas, in the Pacific region and New Zealand. A private medical school opened in Niue in 2000 but closed in the following year. A private university offering online business and information technology courses opened in late 2003.

PALAU

Introduction

The Republic of Palau (also known as Belau) consists of eight principal and 252 smaller islands, in a chain about 650 km long, stretching from the small groups of islands around Tobi and Sonsorol, north-east to the main group, which extends from Angaur to Kayangel Atoll and covers a total area of 508 sq km (196 sq miles). This latter group includes the main island of Babeldaob (Babelthuap), the second largest island in Micronesia (after Guam), which has a total area of 409 sq km (158 sq miles). Palau lies about 7,150 km south-west of Hawaii and about 1,160 km south of Guam. The territory's nearest neighbour is Yap to the east, one of the Federated States of Micronesia. The Philippines lie to the west and Indonesia to the south and south-west. With the Federated States of Micronesia (q.v.), Palau forms the archipelago of the Caroline Islands. Palau is subject to heavy rainfall, and seasonal variations in precipitation and temperature are generally small. The indigenous population is Micronesian, most of whom speak Palauan, a language with little variation in dialect, although some linguists class Sonsorolese-Tobian (from south-west Palau) as a separate language. English is also an official language, and many people still speak Japanese. At the April 2005 census the population totalled 19,907, of whom some 54% resided in Koror, on Koror Island. Koror served as the provisional capital until the completion of the new capital of Ngerulmud, located on the less-developed island of Babeldaob, in Melekeok state, in October 2006. According to estimates from the Secretariat of the Pacific Community, the population totalled 20,643 in mid-2011.

The earliest settlement of the islands of Palau occurred some 4,500 years ago, probably from Indonesia. A complex society of warring, matrilineal clans emerged. There was a considerable degree of social stratification, with every individual born to a definite rank in society. The clans came to be grouped into two loose confederations. As part of the Carolines, Palau was in the Spanish sphere of influence from the 16th century, but it was not formally annexed to the Spanish Crown until 1886. Until that date, from the late 18th century, the British had dominated trade with the islands. European contacts resulted in the population being devastated by dysentery and influenza. In 1899, following its defeat in the Spanish–American War of 1898, Spain sold the Caroline Islands (including Palau) and the Northern Mariana Islands (i.e. all the Marianas except Guam) to Germany. This area, together with the Marshall Islands, became known as German Micronesia (because of German trading rights in the region) until the First World War began in 1914, when Japan occupied the territory.

Japan's formal administration began in 1920, under a mandate from the League of Nations. The islands were colonized and greatly developed, with the influx of more than 100,000 permanent Japanese settlers (compared with some 40,000 indigenous inhabitants). In Palau alone, by 1940, there were some 35,000 people, of whom only about 7,500 were Palauan. Micronesia was captured by the USA in 1944, and the former Japanese territory, with its settlers repatriated, became the only strategic trusteeship of the 11 trusteeships established by the UN in 1947. The USA was named the administering authority of the Trust Territory of the Pacific Islands, which included Palau (see the chapter on the Marshall Islands).

From 1965 there were increasing demands for local autonomy within the Trust Territory. In that year the Congress of Micronesia was formed, and in 1967 a commission to examine the future political status of the islands was established. In 1970 it declared Micronesians' rights to sovereignty over their own lands, self-determination, the right to devise their own constitution and the right to revoke any form of free association with the USA.

In Palau a referendum in July 1979 approved a proposed local Constitution, which took effect on 1 January 1981, when the district became known as the Republic of Palau. The USA signed a Compact of Free Association with the Republic of Palau in August 1982. More than 60% of Palauans voted in February 1983 to support their Compact, but fewer than the required 75% approved changing the Constitution to allow the transit and storage of nuclear materials. A revised Compact, which contained no reference to nuclear issues, was approved by 66% (again short of the requisite 75%) of voters in a plebiscite in September 1984. In January 1986 representatives of the Palauan and US administrations reached a preliminary agreement on a new Compact, whereby the USA consented to provide US $421m. in economic assistance to the islands. The new Compact was approved by only 72% of Palauan voters at another referendum in February. A fifth plebiscite on Palau's proposed Compact with the USA, held in June 1987, failed to secure the 75% vote in favour required by the Constitution.

The House of Delegates (the lower house of the Palau National Congress) agreed to a further referendum in August 1987. In this referendum an amendment to the Constitution was approved, ensuring that a simple majority would be sufficient to approve the Compact. This was duly achieved in a further referendum in the same month. However, a writ was entered with the Supreme Court challenging the result. The ensuing violence and allegations of corruption and intimidation on the part of the Palau Government resulted, in February 1988, in the opening of an investigation by the US General Accounting Office (GAO). In April Palau's Supreme Court declared invalid the procedure by which the Compact had been approved in the previous August. A seventh referendum on the issue of the Compact was held in February 1990. The level of participation was low, and only 60% of voters approved the Compact. In July the US Department of the Interior declared its intention to impose stricter controls on the administration of Palau, particularly in financial matters. Nevertheless, on 1 October 1994 Palau achieved independence under the Compact of Free Association. President Kuniwo Nakamura (who had been elected in late 1992) appealed to opponents of the Compact to support Palau's new status. This date marked the termination of the Trust Territory of the Pacific Islands, of which Palau was the final component. Palau was admitted to the UN in December 1994.

Palau maintains strong diplomatic links with Japan, which has been a leading source of tourist revenue, investment and aid. Following the establishment of diplomatic relations with Taiwan, in early 2000 a bilateral agreement to develop projects in a number of areas, including agriculture, fisheries and tourism was signed. In February 2009 the Government of Taiwan provided a stimulus grant of US $3.2m. to Palau, for the purposes of infrastructural improvements. Fishing licences are sold to foreign fleets, including those of Taiwan, the USA, Japan and the Philippines. Palau introduced more stringent regulations to curb illegal fishing in May 2002, and introduced a comprehensive marine protection law in September 2003. In September 2009 the President of Palau announced the establishment of the world's first shark sanctuary, which was to encompass an area of 600,000 sq km.

Upon implementation of the Compact of Free Association with the USA in 1994, Palau became eligible for an initial grant of US $142m. and for annual aid of $23m. over a period of 14 years. The cessation of compact grants was scheduled for 2008/09. In March 2009, however, the Compact with the USA was extended for one year from the end of September. Following protracted negotiations, agreement on a new long-term arrangement was reached in early 2010, when Palau accepted a $250m. aid programme for the next 15 years. Pending approval by the US Congress; the first sub-committee hearing took place in October. In February 2011 the Compact was introduced into the US Senate, from where it was referred to the Senate's Committee on Energy and Natural Resources.

The only manufacturing activity of any significance is the garment sector. Service industries dominate Palau's economy, with tourism an important source of foreign exchange. The Government is also a major employer. The islands record a persistent budget deficit. The economy continued to be sustained by externally financed infrastructure projects, the tourism sector and associated hotel construction activities. Palau's trust fund remained vulnerable to the volatility of global stock markets. The US General Accountability Office continued to draw attention to the need for fiscal reform and for an improvement in investment conditions, in order to encourage the growth of the private sector. In January 2011 it was announced that (as in the previous year) the Government of Taiwan was to provide stimulus funding of US $10m. for the purposes of economic development: the 22 projects thus financed by Taiwan again included agricultural schemes and infrastructural improvements such as the rehabilitation of the road network. At a referendum conducted in June, voters rejected the proposed establishment of casino gaming in the country.

Statistical Survey

Source (unless otherwise indicated): Office of Planning and Statistics, Ministry of Finance, POB 6011, Koror; tel. 767-1269; fax 767-5642; e-mail ops@palaugov.net; internet www.palaugov.net/stats/index.htm.

AREA AND POPULATION

Area: 508 sq km (196 sq miles); Babeldaob (Babeldaop, Babelthuap) island 409 sq km (158 sq miles).

Population: 19,129 at census of 15 April 2000; 19,907 (males 10,699, females 9,208) at census of 1 April 2005. *Mid-2011* (Secretariat of the Pacific Community estimate): 20,643 (Source: Pacific Regional Information System).

Density (at mid-2011): 40.6 per sq km.

Population by Age and Sex (Secretariat of the Pacific Community estimates at mid-2011): *0–14:* 4,136 (males 2,123, females 2,013); *15–64:* 15,288 (males 8,395, females 6,893); *65 and over:* 1,219 (males 536, females 683); *Total* 20,643 (males 11,054, females 9,589) (Source: Pacific Regional Information System).

Principal Towns (population at 2005 census): Koror (capital) 10,743; Meyuns 1,153. Source: Thomas Brinkhoff, *City Population* (internet www.citypopulation.de).

Births and Deaths (2006): Registered live births 259 (birth rate 12.9 per 1,000); Registered deaths 144 (death rate 7.2 per 1,000).

Life Expectancy (years at birth, WHO estimates): 72 (males 68; females 77) in 2009. Source: WHO, *World Health Statistics*.

Economically Active Population (persons aged 16 years and over, 2005 census): Agriculture 451; Forestry and fishing 310; Mining 34; Manufacturing 225; Utilities and sanitary services 208; Construction 1,365; Transport and communications 561; Trade, restaurants, etc. 1,670; Finance, insurance and real estate 132; Public administration 1,734; Professional and related services 1,466; Private households 915; Other personal services 387; Other services 319; *Total employed* 9,777 (males 5,982, females 3,795); Unemployed 426 (males 232, females 194); *Total labour force* 10,203 (males 6,214, females 3,989).

HEALTH AND WELFARE

Key Indicators

Total Fertility Rate (children per woman, 2009): 1.8.

Under-5 Mortality Rate (per 1,000 live births, 2009): 15.

Physicians (per 1,000 head, 2000): 1.6.

Hospital Beds (per 1,000 head, 2006): 5.9.

Health Expenditure (2008): US $ per head (PPP): 991.

Health Expenditure (2008): % of GDP: 10.8.

Health Expenditure (2008): public (% of total): 78.1.

Total Carbon Dioxide Emissions ('000 metric tons, 2007): 212.5.

Carbon Dioxide Emissions Per Head (metric tons, 2007): 10.5.

For sources and definitions, see explanatory note on p. vi.

AGRICULTURE, ETC.

Fishing (metric tons, live weight, 2009, FAO estimates): Marine fishes 920; Total catch (incl. others) 1,012. Source: FAO.

INDUSTRY

Production (2008): Electric energy 152 million kWh (estimate). Source: UN Industrial Commodity Statistics Database.

FINANCE

Currency and Exchange Rates: United States currency is used: 100 cents = 1 United States dollar (US $). *Sterling and Euro Equivalents* (31 May 2011): £1 sterling = US $1.6503; €1 = US $1.4385; US $100 = £60.60 = €69.52.

Budget (US $ million, year ending 30 September 2010): *Revenue:* Current revenue 39.0 (Taxes 31.4, Non-tax revenue 7.7); Grants 50.0; Total 89.0. *Expenditure:* Current expenditure 75.3; Capital expenditure 19.0; Total 94.3. Source: Asian Development Bank.

Cost of Living (Consumer Price Index, base: June 2008 = 100): All items 90.1 in 2007; 100.9 in 2008; 102.3 in 2009.

Gross Domestic Product (US $ '000 at current prices, provisional): 170,144 in 2007; 187,140 in 2008; 203,620 in 2009. Source: Asian Development Bank.

Gross Domestic Product by Economic Activity (US $ '000 at current prices, 2009): Agriculture and fishing 6,481; Mining (incl. electricity, gas and water) 6,663; Manufacturing 723; Construction 33,375; Trade (including hotels and restaurants) 65,190; Transport and communications 16,905; Other services 71,062; *Sub-total* 200,398; Taxes on imports, less imputed bank service charges 3,221; *GDP in purchasers' values* 203,620. Source: Asian Development Bank.

Balance of Payments (US $ million, year ending September 2010): Exports of goods f.o.b. 12.3; Imports of goods f.o.b. −113.4; *Trade balance* −101.1; Services and income (net) 62.0; *Balance on goods, services and income* –39.1; Current transfers (net) 18.3; *Current balance* –20.8; Capital and financial account (net) 20.9; *Overall balance* 0.1. Source: Asian Development Bank.

EXTERNAL TRADE

Principal Commodities (US $ '000): *Imports f.o.b.* (2004): Food and live animals 10,862; Beverages and tobacco 4,947; Mineral fuels, lubricants, etc. 30,061; Chemicals 5,772; Basic manufactures 8,597; Machinery and transport equipment 47,405; Miscellaneous manufactured articles 7,129; Total (incl. others) 116,499. *Exports* (2004/05): 13,414 (including trochus shells, tuna, copra and handicrafts). *2009* (year ending 30 September, provisional): Total imports 103,500; Total exports 11,800. Source: Asian Development Bank.

Principal Trading Partners (US $ '000, year ending September 2004): *Imports:* Japan 8,531; Korea, Republic 5,411; Philippines 6,934; Singapore 29,885; Taiwan 5,343; USA (incl. Guam) 48,225; Total (incl. others) 107,280. *Exports:* Total 5,882.

TRANSPORT

International Shipping (freight traffic, metric tons, 2006): Goods loaded 8,767; Goods unloaded 94,693.

Civil Aviation (2006): Aircraft movements 1,054; Passengers enplaned 98,808; Cargo loaded 2,170,648 lbs.

TOURISM

Tourist Arrivals: 84,566 in 2007; 75,829 in 2008; 68,329 in 2009.

Tourist Arrivals by Country of Residence (2009): Guam 2,779; Japan 26,340; Korea, Republic 12,901; Philippines 626; Taiwan 16,105; USA (mainland) 4,236; Total (incl. others) 68,329.

Tourism Receipts (US $ million, incl. passenger transport): 97 in 2004; 97 in 2005; 90 in 2006.

Source: World Tourism Organization.

COMMUNICATIONS MEDIA

Radio Receivers (1997): 12,000 in use.

Television Receivers (1997): 11,000 in use.

Telephones (2010): 7,000 main lines in use.

Mobile Cellular Telephones (2010): 14,500 subscribers.

Internet Subscribers (2009): 1,000.

Broadband Subscribers (2010): 200.

Source: partly International Telecommunication Union.

EDUCATION

Pre-primary (public institutions only, 2006/07): 13 schools; 30 teachers; 509 pupils.

Enrolment (2006/07): *Elementary:* Total 2,683 (Public 2,135, Private 548). *Secondary:* Total 1,309 (Public 810, Private 499).

Teachers (1999/2000, estimates): *Elementary:* 124. *Secondary:* 126.

Institutions (2006/07): *Elementary:* Total 21 (Public 19, Private 2). *Secondary:* Total 6 (Public 1, Private 5).

Tertiary (Palau Community College): 54 teachers (full-time and part-time, 2005/06); 545 students (at 2005 census).

Pupil-teacher Ratio (primary education, UNESCO estimate): 12.5 in 2004/05 (Source: UNESCO Institute for Statistics).

Directory

The Constitution

In October 1994 Palau, the last remaining component of the Trust Territory of the Pacific Islands (a United Nations Trusteeship administered by the USA), achieved independence under the Compact of Free Association. Full responsibility for defence lies with the USA, which undertakes to provide regular economic assistance.

From 1986 the three polities of the Commonwealth of the Northern Mariana Islands, the Republic of the Marshall Islands and the Federated States of Micronesia ceased, de facto, to be part of the Trust Territory. In December 1990 the United Nations Security Council agreed formally to terminate the Trusteeship Agreement for all the territories except Palau. The agreement with Palau was finally terminated in October 1994.

The islands became known as the Republic of Palau when the locally drafted Constitution came into effect on 1 January 1981. The Constitution provides for a democratic form of government, with executive authority vested in the directly elected President and Vice-President. Presidential elections are held every four years. Legislative power is exercised by the Olbiil era Kelulau, the Palau National

Congress, which is an elected body consisting of the Senate and the House of Delegates. The Senators represent geographical districts, determined by an independent reapportionment commission every eight years, according to population. The number of Senators was increased to 13 at the elections of 2008. The House of Delegates comprises 16 members, one elected to represent each of the 16 states of the Republic. The states are: Kayangel, Ngerchelong, Ngaraard, Ngardmau, Ngaremlengui, Ngiwal, Melekeok, Ngchesar, Ngatpang, Aimeliik, Airai, Koror, Peleliu, Angaur, Sonsorol and Tobi. Each state elects its own Governor and legislature.

The Government

HEAD OF STATE

President: JOHNSON TORIBIONG (took office 15 January 2009).

Vice-President and Minister of Administration and of Finance: KERAI MARIUR.

CABINET
(October 2011)

Minister of Health: Dr STEVENSON KUARTEI.

Minister of Public Infrastructure, Industries and Commerce: JACKSON NGIRAINGAS.

Minister of Natural Resources, Environment and Tourism: HARRY FRITZ.

Minister of Education: MASA-AKI EMESIOCHEL.

Minister of Justice: JOHNNY GIBBONS.

Minister of Community and Cultural Affairs: FAUSTINA K. REHUHER-MARUGG.

Minister of State: VICTOR YANO.

COUNCIL CHIEFS

The Constitution provides for an advisory body for the President, comprising the 16 highest traditional chiefs from the 16 states. The chiefs advise on all traditional laws and customs, and on any other public matter in which their participation is required.

Chairman: Ibedul YUTAKA GIBBONS (Koror).

GOVERNMENT OFFICES AND MINISTRIES

Office of the President: POB 6051, Koror, PW 96940; tel. 488-2403; fax 488-1662; e-mail pres@palaunet.com.

Department of the Interior, Office of Insular Affairs (OIA): OIA Field Office, POB 6031, Koror, PW 96946; tel. 488-2601; fax 488-2649; internet www.doi.gov/oia/Islandpages/palaupage.htm; Field Rep. (vacant); Co-ordinator HAURO WILLTER.

Ministry of Community and Cultural Affairs: POB 100, Koror, PW 96940; tel. 767-1126; fax 767-3354; e-mail mcca@palaunet.com.

Ministry of Education: POB 819, Koror, PW 96940; tel. 767-1464; fax 767-1465; e-mail moe@palaumoe.net; internet www.palaumoe.net.

Ministry of Finance: POB 6011, Koror, PW 96940; tel. 767-2501; fax 767-2168; e-mail bpss@palaugov.net.

Ministry of Health: POB 6027, Koror, PW 96940; tel. 767-5552488; fax 767-0722; e-mail moh@palau-health.net; internet www.palau-health.net.

Ministry of Justice: POB 3022, Koror, PW 96940; tel. 488-3198; fax 488-4567; e-mail justice@palaunet.com.

Ministry of Natural Resources, Environment and Tourism: Exec. Bldg, 1st Floor, Ngerulmud, PW 96939; tel. 767-5435; fax 767-3380; e-mail mnret@palaugov.net.

Ministry of Public Infrastructure, Industries and Commerce: POB 1471, Ngerulmud, PW 96940; tel. 767-2111; fax 767-3207; e-mail mincat@palaunet.com.

Ministry of State: Ngerulmud, Melekeok; tel. 767-2509; fax 767-2443; e-mail state@palaugov.net.

All national government offices were transferred from Koror to the new capital Ngerulmud, in the state of Melekeok, in October 2006. Each state has its own administrative headquarters.

President and Legislature

PRESIDENT

At the presidential election held on 4 November 2008, Johnson Toribiong defeated his opponent, Elias Camsek Chin, by a narrow margin. Toribiong secured 5,040 votes, and Chin received 4,828.

OLBIIL ERA KELULAU
(Palau National Congress)

The Palau National Congress comprises two chambers, the Senate and the House of Delegates. The Senate has 13 elected members, and the House of Delegates consists of 16 elected members. The most recent election was held on 4 November 2008.

President of the Senate: MLIB TMETUCHL.

Vice-President of the Senate: KATHY KESOLEI.

Speaker of the House of Delegates: NOAH IDECHONG.

Vice-Speaker of the House of Delegates: ALEXANDER MEREP.

National Congress: National Capitol Bldg, Ngerulmud, Melekeok State; tel. 767-2455; fax 767-2633; e-mail senate@palaunet.com; internet www.palauoek.net.

Election Commission

Palau Election Commission: POB 826, Koror, PW 96940; tel. 488-1554; fax 488-3327; Chair. SANTOS BORJA.

Political Organizations

(There are currently no active political parties in Palau)

Palau Nationalist Party: c/o Olbiil era Kelulau, Koror, PW 96940; inactive; Leader JOHNSON TORIBIONG.

Ta Belau Party: c/o Olbiil era Kelulau, Koror, PW 96940; inactive; Leader KUNIWO NAKAMURA.

Diplomatic Representation

EMBASSIES IN PALAU

Japan: POB 6050, Palau Pacific Resort, Arakebesang, Koror, PW 96940; tel. 488-6455; fax 488-6458; internet www.palau.emb-japan.go.jp; Ambassador YOSHIYUKI SADAOKA.

Philippines: Minami Bldg, 2nd Floor, Iyebukel Hamlet, POB 1447, Koror, PW 96940; tel. 488-5077; fax 488-6310; e-mail philkor@palaunet.com; Ambassador RAMONCITO MARIÑO.

Taiwan (Republic of China): WCTC Bldg, Of. 3F, POB 9087, Koror, PW 96940; tel. 488-8150; fax 488-8151; e-mail roc@palautelecoms.com; Ambassador MAGGIE TIEN.

USA: POB 6028, Koror, PW 96940; tel. 587-2920; fax 587-2911; e-mail usembassykoror@palaunet.com; internet palau.usembassy.gov; Ambassador HELEN REED-ROWE.

Judicial System

The judicial system of the Republic of Palau consists of the Supreme Court (including Trial and Appellate Divisions), presided over by the Chief Justice, the National Court (inactive), the Court of Common Pleas and the Land Court.

Supreme Court of the Republic of Palau: POB 248, Koror, PW 96940; tel. 488-4979; fax 488-1597; e-mail cjngiraklsong@palaunet.com; Chief Justice ARTHUR NGIRAKLSONG.

Office of the Attorney-General: 1365 Koror, PW 96940; tel. 488-2481; fax 488-3329; e-mail agoffice@palaunet.com; Attorney-Gen. ERNESTINE RENGIIL.

Religion

The population is predominantly Christian, mainly Roman Catholic. The Assembly of God, Baptists, Seventh-day Adventists, the Church of Jesus Christ of Latter-day Saints (Mormons), and the Bahá'í and Modignai (or Modeknai) faiths are also represented.

CHRISTIANITY

The Roman Catholic Church

Palau forms part of the diocese of the Caroline Islands, suffragan to the archdiocese of Agaña (Guam). The Bishop, who is resident in Chuuk, Eastern Caroline Islands (see the Federated States of Micronesia), participates in the Catholic Bishops' Conference of the Pacific, based in Suva, Fiji.

MODIGNAI FAITH

Modignai Church: Koror, PW 96940; an indigenous, non-Christian religion; also operates a high school.

The Press

Moonshadow Publications: POB 9006, Koror, PW 96940; tel. 488-8655; fax 779-3440; e-mail jerome@palaunet.com; internet jerometemengil.synthasite.com; Publr JEROME TEMENGIL.

Palau Gazette: POB 100, Koror, PW 96940; tel. 488-3257; fax 488-1662; e-mail roppresoffice@palaunet.com; newsletter publ. by Govt; monthly; Publr ROMAN YANO.

Roureur Belau: POB 477, Koror, PW 96940; tel. 488-6365; fax 488-4810; e-mail myu@palaunet.com; weekly; Publr CLIFFORD 'SPADE' EBAS.

Tia Belau (This is Palau): POB 477, Koror, PW 96940; tel. 488-6365; fax 488-4810; e-mail tiabelau@palaunet.com; f. 1992; weekly; English and Palauan; Editor RAOUL G. BRIONES; Publr MOSES ULUDONG; circ. 1,500.

Broadcasting and Communications

TELECOMMUNICATIONS

Palau National Communications Corpn (PNCC): POB 99, Koror, PW 96940; tel. 587-9000; fax 587-1888; e-mail pncc@palaunet.com; internet www.palaunet.com; f. 1982; mem. of the Pacific Islands Broadcasting Asscn; telephone, internet and digital television operator; 24 hrs daily; Chair. LEILANI REKLAI; Gen. Man. RICHARD L. MISECH.

Palau Mobile Corpn (PMC): POB 8084, Koror, PW 96940; tel. 488-4088; fax 488-2111; e-mail marklin@palaumobile.com; internet www.palaumobile.com; mobile telephone operator.

BROADCASTING

Radio

High Adventure Ministries: POB 66, Koror, PW 96940; tel. 488-2162; fax 488-2163; e-mail hamadmin@palaunet.com; f. 1992; broadcasts religious material; Engineering Man. BENTLEY CHAN.

KRFM: Sure Save Store, Koror, PW 96940; tel. 488-1359; e-mail rudimch@palaunet.com.

T8AA (Eco Paradise): POB 279, Koror, PW 96940; tel. 488-2417; fax 488-1932; broadcasts news, entertainment and music; govt-owned.

WSZB Broadcasting Station: POB 279, Koror, PW 96940; tel. 488-2417; fax 488-1932; Station Man. ALBERT SALUSTIANO.

WWFM: POB 1327, Koror, PW 96940; tel. 488-4848; fax 488-4420; e-mail wwfm@palaunet.com; internet www.brouhaha.net/palau/wwfm.html; Man. ALFONSO DIAZ.

Television

PNCC Digital Television: POB 39, Koror, PW 96940; tel. 587-3515; fax 587-1888; e-mail pncc@palaunet.com; internet www.palaunet.com; owned by the Palau Nat. Communications Corpn; fmrly Island Cable Television.

STV-TV Koror: POB 2000, Koror, PW 96940; tel. 488-1357; fax 488-1207; broadcasts 12 hrs daily; Man. DAVID NOLAN; Technical Man. RAY OMELEN.

Finance

(cap. = capital; res = reserves; amounts in US dollars)

BANKING

Bank of Guam: POB 338, Koror, PW 96940; tel. 488-2696; fax 488-1384; internet www.bankofguam.com; Man. KATHERINE LUJAN.

Bank of Hawaii (USA): POB 340, Koror, PW 96940; tel. 488-2602; fax 488-2427; internet www.boh.com.

Bank Pacific: Lebuu St, Tngerongel Hamlet, Koror; tel. 488-5635; fax 488-4752; internet www.bankpacific.com; Sr Country Officer JOSEPH KOSHIBA.

National Development Bank of Palau: POB 816, Koror, PW 96940; tel. 587-2578; fax 587-2579; e-mail ndbp@palaunet.com; internet www.ndbp.com; f. 1982; cap. and res 11.5m. (Sept. 2002); 100% govt-owned; Pres. KALEB ADUI, Jr; Chair. RINGSANG RECHIREI.

INSURANCE

Century Insurance Co: POB 318, Koror, PW 96940; tel. 488-8580; fax 488-8632; e-mail knakamura@palaunet.com.

Moylan's Insurance Underwriters Palau: POB 156, Koror, PW 96940; tel. 488-2765; fax 488-2744; e-mail palau@moylans.net; internet www.moylansinsurance.com; Branch Man. KENJI DENGOKL.

NECO Insurance Underwriters Ltd: POB 129, Koror, PW 96940; tel. 488-2325; fax 488-2880; e-mail necogroup@palaunet.com.

Poltalia National Insurance: POB 12, Koror, PW 96940; tel. 488-2254; fax 488-2834; e-mail psata@palaunet.com; f. 1974; Pres. and CEO EPHRAM POLYCARP.

Trade and Industry

CHAMBER OF COMMERCE

Palau Chamber of Commerce: POB 6021, Koror, PW 96940; tel. 488-4581; fax 488-2732; e-mail reklai@reklai.com; f. 1984; Pres. SURANGEL WHIPPS, Jr.

CO-OPERATIVES

These include the Palau Fishermen's Co-operative, the Palau Boatbuilders' Asscn and the Palau Handicraft and Woodworkers' Guild. In 1990, of the 13 registered co-operatives, eight were fishermen's co-operatives, three consumers' co-operatives (only two in normal operation) and two farmers' co-operatives (one in normal operation).

DEVELOPMENT ORGANIZATION

Palau Conservation Society: POB 1811, Koror, PW 96940; tel. 488-3993; fax 488-3990; e-mail pcs@palaunet.com; internet www.palauconservation.org; f. 1994; sustainable devt, environmental protection; Chair. MAURA GORDON; Exec. Dir ELBUCHEL SADANG.

Transport

ROADS

Tarmac and concrete roads are found in the more important islands. Other islands have stone- and coral-surfaced roads and tracks. The Government is responsible for 36 km (22 miles) of paved roads and 25 km (15 miles) of coral- and gravel-surfaced roads. Most paved roads are located on Koror. A major project to construct a new 85-km (53-mile) road around Babeldaob was completed in 2007, funded with US $150m. from the Compact of Free Association.

SHIPPING

Most shipping in Palau is government-organized. However, the Micronesia Transport Line operates a service from Sydney (Australia) to Palau. A twice-weekly inter-island service operates between Koror and Peleliu. There is one commercial port at Malakal Harbor, which is operated by the privately owned Belau Transfer and Terminal Company.

CIVIL AVIATION

There is an international airport on Babeldaob. Domestic airfields (former Japanese military airstrips) are located on Angaur and Peleliu. Continental Micronesia (Northern Mariana Islands and Guam) provides daily flights to Koror from Guam, and twice-weekly flights from Manila (Philippines). Cebu Pacific operates direct flights from Davao (Philippines) to Koror. In May 2008 China Airlines began operating charter flights between Taiwan and Palau. Palau Trans Pacific also operates from Taiwan. In July 2008 two South Korean carriers, Korean Air and Asiana Airlines, reached an agreement with the Palau Government, allowing for up to seven passenger flights and four cargo flights per week. Following the suspension by Japan Airlines of its charter flights from Tokyo, US carrier Delta Airlines inaugurated a regular service between the Japanese capital and Palau in December 2010.

Pacific Flier: POB 37, Koror, PW 96940; tel. 488-2604; e-mail palautravel@palaunet.com; internet www.pacificflier.com.

Rock Island Airlines: managed by Aloha Airlines (Hawaii).

Tourism

Tourism is becoming increasingly important in Palau. The islands are particularly rich in their marine environment, and the Government has implemented measures to conserve and protect these natural resources. The myriad Rock Islands, now known as the Floating Garden Islands, are a noted reserve in the lagoon to the west of the main group of islands. There were 959 hotel rooms in 2004. In 2010 Palau reportedly received 85,593 visitors, most of whom were from Taiwan, Japan and the Republic of Korea. Tourist revenue reached US $90m. in 2006. The Seventh Micronesian Games were held in Palau in August 2010.

Belau Tourism Association: POB 9032, Koror, PW 96940; tel. 488-4377; fax 488-1725; e-mail bta@palaunet.com; Pres. MARY FRANCES VOGT.

Palau Visitors' Authority: POB 256, Koror, PW 96940; tel. 488-2793; fax 488-1453; e-mail pva@visit-palau.com; internet www.visit-palau.com; f. 1982; Man. Dir DARIN DE LEON.

Defence

The USA is responsible for the defence of Palau, according to the Compact of Free Association implemented in October 1994, and has exclusive military access to Palau's waters, as well as the right to operate two military bases on the islands. The US Pacific Command is based in Hawaii.

Education

The educational system is similar to that of the USA. The Government of Palau is now responsible for the state school system, which most children attend. Education is free and compulsory between the ages of six and 14, and secondary education may be obtained at the public High School or one of the five private ones.

In 2006/07 there were 509 pupils enrolled in pre-primary public schools, 2,683 in primary schools, and 1,309 in secondary schools. According to the results of the 2005 census, there were 545 students in tertiary education in that year. In 2006/07 government schools totalled 20, one of which was a secondary school. The Micronesian Occupational College, based in Koror, provides two-year training programmes. Government expenditure on education totalled US $9.1m. in 1999/2000, equivalent to 10.7% of total budgetary expenditure.

PAPUA NEW GUINEA

Introduction

Papua New Guinea lies east of Indonesia and north of the north-eastern extremity of Australia. It comprises the eastern part of the island of New Guinea, the western section of which, Papua (formerly Irian Jaya), is part of Indonesia, and some smaller islands including the Bismarck Archipelago (mainly New Britain, New Ireland and Manus) and the northern part of the Solomon Islands (mainly Bougainville and Buka). It covers a total area of 462,840 sq km (178,704 sq miles). The climate is hot and humid throughout the year, with an average maximum temperature of 33°C (91°F) and an average minimum of 22°C (72°F). Rainfall is heavy on the coast but lower inland: the annual average varies from about 1,000 mm (40 ins) to 6,350 mm (250 ins).

The census of July 2000 recorded a population of 5,190,786. The UN estimated the population to be 7.013,829 at mid-2011. In February 2000 it was announced that about 25,000 inhabitants of the Duke of York Islands, which are situated in East New Britain province, were expected to be resettled by the Government, following the publication of a UN report indicating that the islands were becoming uninhabitable owing to rising sea-levels resulting from the greenhouse effect (the heating of the earth's atmosphere as a consequence of pollution).

New Guinea was visited by European navigators from the early 16th century onwards, but exploration and colonial settlement did not begin until the mid-19th century. The western part of New Guinea was administered until 1949 as part of the Netherlands East Indies and from 1949 until 1962 as the Nederlands Nieuw Guinea. In 1963, after military action by Indonesia, the territory was redesignated Daerah Irian Barat and declared a part of Indonesia by an 'act of free choice' in August 1962. It is now known as Papua, a province of Indonesia formerly known as Irian Jaya (or West Papua).

The southern part of eastern New Guinea became British New Guinea in 1906, following the establishment of a British protectorate in 1884 and annexation in 1886. Australia administered what became the Territory of Papua until 1949, when it was joined, under a unified administration, with the Trust Territory of New Guinea. In 1884 the northern part of eastern New Guinea came under German administration as Schutzgebiet Kaiser-Wilhelmsland und Bismarck-archipel, later becoming known as German New Guinea. In 1914 the Germans were removed from the territory by Australian troops, and Australia subsequently administered the area under a League of Nations mandate until 1942. Between 1942 and 1945, during the Second World War, parts of both territories were occupied by Japanese forces. In 1945 the territory returned to Australian administration under UN trusteeship arrangements. A Legislative Council was established in November 1951 and was replaced by a House of Assembly, with an elected indigenous majority, in June 1964. The territory was renamed Papua New Guinea in July 1971. In December 1973 the Territory of Papua New Guinea became internally self-governing, and on 16 September 1975 it became the independent nation of Papua New Guinea. The House of Assembly became the National Parliament. Michael (later Sir Michael) Somare, who from 1972 had served as Chief Minister in an interim coalition Government, became Prime Minister on independence. He remained in office until 1980, serving again in 1982–85 and also in 2002–11.

The status of the province of Bougainville was brought into question in the late 1980s, and the issue developed into a long-term national crisis. In April 1988 landowners on the island of Bougainville submitted compensation claims, for land mined by Bougainville Copper Ltd at Panguna since 1972. When no payments ensued, acts of sabotage were perpetrated in late 1988 by the Bougainville Revolutionary Army (BRA). The BRA's demands increasingly favoured secession for the island of Bougainville (and North Solomons Province) from Papua New Guinea. In July 1997 discussions were held in New Zealand between secessionists and representatives of the Bougainville Transitional Government (established by the Charter of Mirigini, signed in November 1994). The resultant 'Burnham Declaration' recommended the withdrawal of government troops from Bougainville and the deployment of a neutral peace-keeping force. The Bougainville Transitional Government was later replaced by the Bougainville Reconciliation Government following a parliamentary vote in October 1998, which approved the amendment of the Constitution. Elections to the Bougainville People's Congress (BPC, formerly the Bougainville Reconciliation Government) were held in May 1999. In March 2000 an agreement, known as the Loloata Understanding, was signed, allowing for the eventual holding of a referendum on independence, once full autonomy had been implemented, and the formal establishment of the Bougainville Interim Provincial Government (BIPG). In February 2001 agreement on the terms of the referendum was finally reached. The agreement stated that the referendum would be held within 10–15 years and would contain the option of independence. In the interim the provincial government was to be granted increased autonomy and the BRA would be expected to disarm. In January 2003 it was announced that the BIPG and the BPC would be merged to form the Bougainville Constituent Assembly. Elections for the first autonomous government of Bougainville were held in mid-2005. Joseph Kabui was subsequently declared to be Bougainville's first President, and remained in the role until his death in June 2008. John Momis defeated the incumbent President James Tanis at the elections of May 2010. At the concurrent legislative election more than three-quarters of sitting members were reported to have lost their seats in Bougainville's House of Representatives.

A major cause for concern has been the high rate of serious crime in Papua New Guinea. The marked increase in ownership of illegal firearms, particularly in the Highlands region, has become a significant problem. Furthermore, the country has continued to experience serious problems of ethnic and inter-tribal violence, which has resulted in numerous deaths. Foreign investment has been discouraged not only by the country's high levels of crime and the intermittent ethnic unrest but also by the problems of corruption.

Papua New Guinea has been largely dependent on aid from international donors for its economic development. Papua New Guinea receives grants for budgetary aid from Australia. In 2010/11 official development assistance from Australia was projected at $A457.2m. New Zealand is also a significant aid donor. In May 2007 it was announced that the European Union (EU) was to allocate US $159m. to various development projects in Papua New Guinea, over a six-year period commencing in 2008. The country's difficult terrain, lack of infrastructure and the limitations of the domestic market have impeded Papua New Guinea's progress, as has its vulnerability to extreme climatic conditions (such as droughts and tidal waves). Development has also been constrained by a shortage of skilled workers. In the early 2000s it was estimated that at least 70% of the population were within the subsistence sector of the economy. Moreover, an increase in migration from rural areas has led to a high rate of urban unemployment, estimated by some sources to be as high as 70%. The proportion of the labour force employed in the formal sector remains comparatively low. Only one in 10 of the total labour force was estimated to be in paid employment in 2006. These difficulties have been compounded by the country's exceptionally high rate of population growth. The leading agricultural exports include palm oil, coffee, tea, cocoa and vanilla. Exports of canned tuna are also significant. Forestry is an important activity, and Papua New Guinea is one of the world's largest exporters of unprocessed tropical timber. However, there is serious concern about the environmental damage caused both by extensive logging activity in the country (much of which is illegal) and by mining operations. The economy remains susceptible to fluctuations in world commodity prices. Plans to revitalize the coffee industry over the period 2008–18 were to be implemented, in an attempt to counter the variations in global coffee prices and the recent changes in the country's climatic conditions. None the less, the intermittent strength of prices for commodities such as gold, copper, petroleum and timber has been very advantageous to Papua New Guinea. The country possesses large deposits of nickel and cobalt. However, work on the development of the Chinese-owned Ramu nickel/cobalt mine in Madang Province was disrupted in 2009–10 by disputes related to labour conditions and land ownership. Papua New Guinea also has substantial reserves of natural gas. The country's long-term economic prospects have been greatly enhanced by plans for a major liquefied natural gas project (LNG) project and export facility, being developed in collaboration with an international consortium. A 700-km pipeline from Southern Highlands to the proposed processing facilities near the capital of Port Moresby was to be constructed, and work on the project commenced in 2010. Production of LNG for export was expected to commence in 2014 or 2015.With negotiations for a second LNG scheme under way in late 2010, and in view of the substantial revenue that would ultimately be derived from the country's LNG production, the establishment of a sovereign wealth fund was under consideration. The Government's Medium-Term Development Plan for 2011–15 focused on the effective utilization of the substantial revenue inflows expected from the US $16,000m. LNG project (see above). The Government planned to open up a number of state-owned enterprises, such as electricity provision and ports, to private sector competition.

Statistical Survey

Source (unless otherwise stated): Papua New Guinea National Statistical Office, POB 337, Waigani, NCD; tel. 3011200; fax 3251869; e-mail pmaime@nso.gov.pg; internet www.nso.gov.pg.

Area and Population

AREA, POPULATION AND DENSITY

Area (sq km)	462,840*
Population (census results)	
11 July 1990†	3,607,954
9 July 2000	
Males	2,691,744
Females	2,499,042
Total	5,190,786
Population (UN estimates at mid-year)‡	
2009	6,703,361
2010	6,858,266
2011	7,013,829
Density (per sq km) at mid-2011	15.2

* 178,704 sq miles.

† Excluding North Solomons Province (estimated population 154,000).

‡ Source: UN, *World Population Prospects: The 2010 Revision*.

POPULATION BY AGE AND SEX
(UN estimates at mid-2011)

	Males	Females	Total
0–14	1,407,746	1,308,931	2,716,677
15–64	2,085,222	2,014,098	4,099,320
65 and over	84,848	112,984	197,832
Total	3,577,816	3,436,013	7,013,829

Source: UN, *World Population Prospects: The 2010 Revision*.

PRINCIPAL TOWNS
(census of 9 July 2000, provisional)

Port Moresby (capital)	254,158	Mount Hagen	27,782
Lae	78,038	Madang	27,394
Arawa	36,443	Kokopo/Vunamami	20,262

Source: Thomas Brinkhoff, *City Population* (internet www.citypopulation.de).

Mid-2009 (incl. suburbs, UN estimate): Port Moresby 313,593 (Source: UN, *World Urbanization Prospects: The 2009 Revision*).

BIRTHS AND DEATHS
(annual averages, UN estimates)

	1995–2000	2000–05	2005–10
Birth rate (per 1,000)	35.8	33.7	31.5
Death rate (per 1,000)	9.5	8.7	7.9

Source: UN, *World Population Prospects: The 20010 Revision*.

2003 (incomplete registration): Registered live births 192,817; Registered deaths 7,054 (Source: UN, *Population and Vital Statistics Report*).

Life expectancy (years at birth, WHO estimates): 63 (males 62; females 65) in 2009 (Source: WHO, *World Health Statistics*).

ECONOMICALLY ACTIVE POPULATION
(census of 9 July 2000, persons aged 10 years and over)

Agriculture, hunting and forestry	1,666,247
Fishing	30,024
Mining and quarrying	9,282
Manufacturing	25,557
Electricity, gas and water	2,208
Construction	48,312
Wholesale and retail trade; repair of motor vehicles, motorcycles and personal and household goods	353,186
Hotels and restaurants	4,395
Transport, storage and communications	24,513
Financial intermediation	3,670
Real estate, renting and business activities	27,459
Public administration and defence; compulsory social security	32,043
Education	27,118
Health and social work	12,341
Other community, social and personal service activities	31,409
Private households with employed persons	15,523
Extra-territorial organizations and bodies	163
Activities not adequately defined	31,284
Total employed	2,344,734
Unemployed	68,623
Total labour force	2,413,357
Males	1,256,887
Females	1,156,470

Source: ILO.

Mid-2011 (estimates in '000): Agriculture, etc. 2,155; Total labour force 3,135 (Source: FAO).

Health and Welfare

KEY INDICATORS

Total fertility rate (children per woman, 2009)	4.0
Under-5 mortality rate (per 1,000 live births, 2009)	68
HIV/AIDS (% of persons aged 15–49, 2007)	1.5
Physicians (per 1,000 head, 2000)	0.05
Hospital beds (per 1,000 head, 1990)	4.0
Health expenditure (2008): US $ per head (PPP)	70
Health expenditure (2008): % of GDP	3.2
Health expenditure (2008): public (% of total)	80.1
Access to water (% of persons, 2008)	40
Access to sanitation (% of persons, 2008)	45
Total carbon dioxide emissions ('000 metric tons, 2007)	3,363.6
Carbon dioxide emissions per head (metric tons, 2007)	0.5
Human Development Index (2010): ranking	137
Human Development Index (2010): value	0.431

For sources and definitions, see explanatory note on p. vi.

Agriculture

PRINCIPAL CROPS
('000 metric tons, FAO estimates)

	2007	2008	2009
Cassava (Manioc)	145	132	100
Sweet potatoes	580	485	534
Yams	310	426	262
Taro (Cocoyam)	285	323	314
Sugar cane	320	320	320
Coconuts	783	910	930
Oil palm fruit	1,400	1,700	1,730
Pineapples	16.7	18.8	17.9
Bananas	940	936	1,187
Coffee, green	58.1	61.7	60.2
Cocoa beans	49.3	51.5	51.0
Tea	7.1	7.6	6.5
Natural rubber	7.2	7.9	7.5

Aggregate production ('000 metric tons, may include official, semi-official or estimated data): Total cereals 11.9 in 2007, 15.4 in 2008, 15.7 in 2009; Total oil crops 530 in 2007, 632 in 2008, 641 in 2009; Total vegetables (incl. melons) 493 in 2007, 489 in 2008, 496 in 2009; Total fruits (excl. melons) 2,004 in 2007, 2,130 in 2008, 2,324 in 2009.

Source: FAO.

LIVESTOCK
('000 head, year ending September, FAO estimates)

	2005	2006	2007
Horses	2	2	2
Cattle	92	93	94
Pigs	1,800	1,800	1,800
Sheep	7	7	7
Goats	3	3	3
Chickens	4,000	4,000	4,000

2008–09: Figures assumed to be unchanged from 2007 (FAO estimates).

Source: FAO.

LIVESTOCK PRODUCTS
('000 metric tons, FAO estimates)

	2007	2008	2009
Cattle meat	3.2	3.1	3.2
Pig meat	68	68	68
Chicken meat	5.7	5.9	5.9
Game meat	365	358	302
Hen eggs	5.4	6.2	5.0

Source: FAO.

Forestry

ROUNDWOOD REMOVALS
('000 cubic metres, excluding bark)

	2005	2006	2007
Sawlogs, veneer logs and logs for sleepers	2,536*	2,908*	2,958†
Pulpwood	78	82	82†
Fuel wood†	5,533	5,533	5,533
Total†	8,147	8,523	8,573

* Unofficial figure.
† FAO estimate(s).

2008–09: Production assumed to be unchanged from 2007 (FAO estimates).

Source: FAO.

SAWNWOOD PRODUCTION
('000 cubic metres, including railway sleepers, unofficial figures)

	2007	2008	2009
Coniferous (softwood)	10	10	10
Broadleaved (hardwood)	51	51	71
Total	61	61	81

Source: FAO.

Fishing

('000 metric tons, live weight)

	2007	2008	2009
Capture	247.3	222.3	229.6
Mozambique tilapia*	2.3	2.3	2.3
Other freshwater fishes*	6.7	6.7	6.7
Sea catfishes*	1.9	1.9	1.9
Skipjack tuna	181.5	147.0	160.8
Yellowfin tuna	42.6	53.3	44.7
Aquaculture	0.2	0.2	0.2
Total catch*	247.5	222.5	229.8

* FAO estimates.

Note: Figures exclude crocodiles, recorded by number rather than weight. The number of estuarine crocodiles caught was: 12,675 in 2007, 14,074 in 2008, 11,910 in 2009. The number of New Guinea crocodiles caught was: 15,904 in 2007, 16,955 in 2008, 18,840 in 2009. Figures also exclude shells ('000 metric tons): 0.4 in 2007, 0.4 in 2008, 0.3 in 2009.

Source: FAO.

Mining

	2007	2008	2009*
Petroleum, crude ('000 barrels)	15,418	13,993	12,806
Copper ('000 metric tons)†	169.2	159.7	166.7
Silver (metric tons)†	48.7	51.3	50.0
Gold (metric tons)†	57.5	67.5	63.6

* Preliminary figures.
† Figures refer to metal content of ore.

Source: US Geological Survey.

Industry

SELECTED PRODUCTS
('000 metric tons, unless otherwise indicated)

	2007	2008	2009
Beer of barley*	60	65	60
Palm oil*	382	465	470
Raw sugar	35	35	n.a.
Electric energy (million kWh)	3,112†	3,131	n.a.

* Unofficial figures.
† Estimate.

Wood products ('000 cu m, excl. furniture): 1,611 in 2003.

Sources: FAO; UN Industrial Commodity Statistics Database; Asian Development Bank.

Finance

CURRENCY AND EXCHANGE RATES

Monetary Units
100 toea = 1 kina (K).

Sterling, Dollar and Euro Equivalents (31 May 2011)
£1 sterling = 3.925 kina;
US $1 = 2.378 kina;
€1 = 3.421 kina;
100 kina = £25.48 = $42.05 = €29.23.

Average Exchange Rate (kina per US $)
2008 2.7001
2009 2.7551
2010 2.7193

Note: The foregoing information refers to the mid-point exchange rate of the central bank. In October 1994 it was announced that the kina would be allowed to 'float' on foreign exchange markets.

BUDGET
(million kina)

Revenue*	2009	2010	2011†
Taxation	4,974.5	6,481.0	7,331.0
Personal tax	1,241.8	1,497.4	1,727.1
Company tax	1,121.4	2,690.9	2,996.6
Other direct tax	1,156.5	518.4	568.7
Import duties	143.7	189.7	218.0
Excise duties	493.9	611.6	702.8
Export tax	108.7	153.9	172.2
Goods and services tax	703.0	812.8	938.3
Other indirect tax	5.5	6.3	7.2
Non-tax revenue	244.8	409.6	411.1
Dividends	138.0	299.1	289.4
Interest revenue/fees	6.9	4.0	4.0
Other internal revenue	99.9	106.5	117.7
Total	5,219.3	6,890.6	7,742.1

Expenditure‡	2009	2010	2011†
Recurrent expenditure	4,169.7	4,164.9	5,291.2
National departmental	2,403.4	2,436.8	3,432.3
Provincial governments	1,046.6	1,071.7	1,109.3
Interest payments	449.2	387.0	430.4
Foreign	59.2	53.0	60.9
Domestic	390.0	334.0	369.5
Other grants and expenditure	270.5	269.4	319.2
Development expenditure	2,348.7	3,430.3	4,041.0
National projects	1,879.0	2,744.24	3,232.8
Provincial projects	469.7	686.06	808.2
Additional priority expenditure	—	653.3	—
Reappropriation to trust account	172.5	—	—
Total	6,690.0	8,244.5	9,328.2

* Excluding grants received from abroad, tax credits and trust accounts (million kina): 1,432.0 in 2009; 1,353.9 in 2010; 1,586.1 in 2011 (budget figure).

† Budget figures.

‡ Excluding net lending (million kina): -3.3 in 2009; -4.0 in 2010; -4.0 in 2011 (budget figure).

Source: Bank of Papua New Guinea, Port Moresby.

INTERNATIONAL RESERVES

(US $ million at 31 December)

	2008	2009	2010
Gold (national valuation)	33.73	46.40	58.40
IMF special drawing rights	0.11	182.19	15.50
Reserve position in IMF	0.67	0.69	0.67
Foreign exchange	1,952.62	2,377.73	3,017.56
Total	1,987.13	2,607.01	3,092.13

Source: IMF, *International Financial Statistics*.

MONEY SUPPLY

(million kina at 31 December)

	2008	2009	2010
Currency outside depository corporations	675.93	788.95	954.91
Transferable deposits	4,843.68	5,443.73	6,688.71
Other deposits	4,180.78	5,537.23	5,323.39
Securities other than shares	—	52.66	66.91
Broad money	9,700.39	11,822.57	13,033.92

Source: IMF, *International Financial Statistics*.

COST OF LIVING

(Consumer Price Index; base: 1977 = 100)

	2008	2009	2010
Food	969.6	1,039.1	1,094.9
Clothing and footwear	525.6	531.2	544.2
Rent, fuel and power	429.2	384.8	406.8
All items (incl. others)	910.7	973.6	1,032.2

NATIONAL ACCOUNTS

(million kina at current prices)

National Income and Product

	2004	2005	2006
Compensation of employees	2,450.5	2,491.1	2,550.9
Operating surplus	9,163.8	10,505.1	11,994.5
Domestic factor incomes	11,614.3	12,996.2	14,545.4
Consumption of fixed capital	828.9	876.7	985.0
Gross domestic product (GDP) at factor cost	12,443.2	13,872.9	15,530.4
Indirect taxes less subsidies	1,016.3	1,221.8	1,366.2
GDP in purchasers' values	13,459.3	15,094.7	16,896.5
Net factor income from abroad	-1,408.8	-1,670.0	-2,462.0
Gross national product	12,050.7	13,424.7	14,434.6
Less Consumption of fixed capital	828.9	876.7	985.0
National income in market prices	11,221.8	12,548.0	13,449.6

Source: Bank of Papua New Guinea, Port Moresby.

Expenditure on the Gross Domestic Product

	2004	2005	2006
Government final consumption expenditure	2,237.6	2,437.6	2,837.6
Private final consumption expenditure	7,047.5	7,239.2	7,959.0
Increase in stocks	580.2	150.0	350.0
Gross fixed capital formation	2,294.3	2,489.3	2,302.6
Total domestic expenditure	12,159.6	12,316.1	13,449.2
Exports of goods and services	9,143.4	11,245.7	13,986.2
Less Imports of goods and services	7,843.7	8,467.1	10,538.9
GDP in purchasers' values	13,459.3	15,094.7	16,896.5
GDP at constant 1998 prices	8,299.1	8,625.2	8,823.1

Source: Bank of Papua New Guinea, Port Moresby.

Gross Domestic Product by Economic Activity

(million kina, provisional)

	2008	2009	2010
Agriculture, hunting, forestry and fishing	6,916.7	7,207.9	8,056.0
Mining and quarrying	5,894.9	4,714.9	5,801.2
Manufacturing	1,247.6	1,328.8	1,500.1
Electricity, gas and water	404.1	461.7	534.5
Construction	2,226.2	2,844.2	3,453.2
Wholesale and retail trade	1,393.3	159.9	1,872.6
Transport, storage and communications	440.3	603.7	749.0
Finance, insurance, real estate and business services*	760.0	929.0	1,083.4
Community, social and personal services (incl. defence)	1,818.8	2,010.1	2,211.4
Sub-total	21,101.9	20260.2	25,261.4
Import duties, *less* subsidies	499.4	1,946.8	575.8
GDP in purchasers' values	21,601.3	22,207.0	25,837.2

* Including services of owner occupied dwellings.

Source: Asian Development Bank.

BALANCE OF PAYMENTS
(million kina)

	2008	2009	2010
Exports of goods f.o.b.	15,675	12,101	15,599
Imports of goods f.o.b.	–8,479	–7,909	–9,597
Trade balance	7,196	4,192	6,002
Exports of services	980	511	844
Imports of services	–4,727	–5,070	–7,497
Balance on goods and services	3,449	–367	–651
Other income received	230	128	114
Other income paid	–1,970	–1,849	–1,724
Balance on goods, services and income	1,709	–2,088	–2,261
Current transfers received	1,060	1,046	1,192
Current transfers paid	–624	–569	–676
Current balance	2,145	–1,611	–1,745
Capital account (net)	67	74	101
Direct investment abroad	—	–12	–1
Direct investment from abroad	–82	1,166	79
Portfolio investment assets	941	414	–284
Portfolio investment liabilities	—	–1	0
Financial derivatives assets	–356	58	–21
Other investment assets	–2,579	1,232	3,236
Other investment liabilities	–787	363	–55
Net errors and omissions	53	42	–245
Overall balance	–598	1,725	1,065

Source: Bank of Papua New Guinea, Port Moresby.

External Trade

PRINCIPAL COMMODITIES
(US $ million)

Imports f.o.b.*	2002	2003	2004
Food and live animals	176.8	192.4	237.3
Meat and meat preparations	32.9	34.8	40.8
Cereals and cereal preparations	81.4	94.6	122.7
Rice	53.2	61.5	90.8
Milled or semi-milled rice	23.5	20.5	88.6
Mineral fuels, lubricants and related materials	153.9	173.2	264.5
Petroleum and petroleum products	150.0	169.9	262.1
Chemicals and related products	90.6	109.6	128.9
Basic manufactures	239.2	233.6	247.5
Iron and steel	35.5	39.2	41.2
Manufactures of other metals	100.1	82.0	80.2
Machinery and transport equipment	399.9	454.3	541.6
Power-generating machinery and equipment	36.1	51.2	57.1
Machinery specialized for particular industries	89.5	90.6	123.6
General industrial machinery and equipment	84.3	92.4	102.4
Electrical machinery, apparatus and appliances, etc.	40.3	46.7	48.1
Road vehicles and parts†	63.2	68.1	101.0
Motor vehicles for goods transport	24.0	24.2	43.1
Other transport equipment and parts†	27.9	46.4	52.8
Miscellaneous manufactured articles	90.3	100.7	102.6
Total (incl. others)	1,186.0	1,302.4	1,567.2

Exports f.o.b.	2002	2003	2004
Food and live animals	206.3	285.0	280.4
Coffee, tea, cocoa and spices, etc.	127.9	193.2	192.0
Crude materials, inedible, except fuels	588.8	1,107.2	753.3
Cork and wood	96.4	54.3	167.6
Metalliferous ores and metal scrap	478.9	1,043.4	572.8
Ores and concentrates of precious metals	263.2	645.0	91.3
Mineral fuels, lubricants and related materials	367.8	459.3	543.1
Crude petroleum and oils obtained from bituminous materials	367.7	458.1	513.3
Animal and vegetable oils, fats and waxes	107.0	146.5	140.2
Palm oil	86.0	122.8	113.2
Gold, non-monetary, unwrought or semi-manufactured	278.7	143.9	880.7
Total (incl. others)	1,625.1	2,260.2	2,722.2

* Figures include migrants' and travellers' dutiable effects, but exclude military equipment and some parcel post.

† Data on parts exclude tyres, engines and electrical parts.

Source: UN, *International Trade Statistics Yearbook*.

2005 (million kina): *Imports c.i.f.*: Total 4,732. *Exports f.o.b.*: Gold 2,834; Crude petroleum 2,283; Copper 2,498; Forestry products 476; Coffee beans 471; Palm oil 391; Cocoa 199; Total (incl. others) 10,168 (Source: Asian Development Bank).

2006 (million kina): *Imports c.i.f.*: Total 6,084. *Exports f.o.b.*: Gold 3,091; Crude petroleum 2,989; Copper 4,330; Forestry products 527; Coffee beans 337; Palm oil 430; Cocoa 204; Total (incl. others) 12,752 (Source: Asian Development Bank).

2007 (million kina): *Imports c.i.f.*: Total 7,603. *Exports f.o.b.*: Gold 3,672; Crude petroleum 2,984; Copper 4,173; Forestry products 631; Coffee beans 408; Palm oil 672; Cocoa 261; Total (incl. others) 13,866 (Source: Asian Development Bank).

2008 (million kina): *Imports c.i.f.*: Total 8,413.3. *Exports f.o.b.*: Gold 4,669.3; Crude petroleum 3,506.1; Copper 3,616.7; Forestry products 537.9; Total (incl. others) 15,423.4 (Source: Bank of Papua New Guinea, Port Moresby).

2009 (million kina): *Imports c.i.f.*: Total 7,890.0. *Exports f.o.b.*: Gold 5,419.2; Crude petroleum 1,645.3; Copper 2,025.9; Forestry products 476.8; Total (incl. others) 12,079.8 (Source: Bank of Papua New Guinea, Port Moresby).

2010 (million kina): *Imports c.i.f.*: Total 9,576.2. *Exports f.o.b.*: Gold 6,380.3; Crude petroleum 2,224.8; Copper 3,089.3; Forestry products 743.7; Total (incl. others) 15,579.5 (Source: Bank of Papua New Guinea, Port Moresby).

PRINCIPAL TRADING PARTNERS
(US $ million)

Imports c.i.f.	2008	2009	2010
Australia	1,469.0	1,620.6	2,067.9
China, People's Republic	378.1	571.7	387.9
Indonesia	89.1	97.2	169.1
Japan	198.8	173.1	324.2
Korea, Republic	34.5	37.7	47.9
Malaysia	149.0	143.1	181.7
New Zealand	107.8	107.4	151.1
Singapore	538.8	359.3	645.6
Thailand	98.8	96.5	154.5
USA	76.9	239.6	210.9
Total (incl. others)	3,491.5	3,864.1	4,910.5

Exports f.o.b.	2008	2009	2010
Australia	2,469.5	2,314.9	2,778.4
China, People's Republic	464.7	324.8	709.5
Germany	311.8	197.7	255.3
India	246.9	93.0	111.7
Italy	63.6	99.0	110.8
Japan	814.3	621.3	906.0
Korea, Republic	207.9	194.0	246.4
Philippines	132.3	229.1	303.0
Spain	143.4	109.8	98.8
United Kingdom	106.8	76.8	n.a.
USA	101.7	97.5	92.0
Total (incl. others)	9,098.1	7,896.4	9,968.8

Note: Data reflect the IMF's direction of trade methodology and, as a result, the totals may not be equal to those presented for trade in commodities.

Source: Asian Development Bank.

Transport

ROAD TRAFFIC
('000 vehicles in use)

	1999	2000	2001
Passenger cars	18.8	24.9	24.9
Commercial vehicles	87.0	87.8	87.8

Source: UN, *Statistical Yearbook*.

2007 ('000 vehicles in use at 31 December): Passenger cars 38,173; Coaches and buses 6,561; Vans and lorries 11,333; Motorcycles and mopeds 1,193 (Source: IRF, *World Road Statistics*).

SHIPPING

Merchant Fleet
(registered at 31 December)

	2007	2008	2009
Number of vessels	125	124	135
Total displacement ('000 grt)	85.2	90.3	97.8

Source: IHS Fairplay, *World Fleet Statistics*.

International Sea-borne Freight Traffic

	1997	1998	1999
Cargo unloaded ('000 metric tons)	2,208.6	2,209.0	2,062.8
Cargo loaded ('000 metric tons)	735.9	823.3	788.1

Source: Papua New Guinea Harbours Board, *Monthly Shipping Register Form*.

CIVIL AVIATION
(traffic on scheduled services)

	2004	2005	2006
Kilometres flown (million)	12	12	14
Passengers carried ('000)	763	819	919
Passenger-km (million)	667	695	771
Total ton-km (million)	84	92	100

Source: UN, *Statistical Yearbook*.

2007: Passenger carried ('000) 918.7 (Source: World Bank, World Development Indicators database).

2008: Passenger carried ('000) 904.9 (Source: World Bank, World Development Indicators database).

Tourism

FOREIGN TOURIST ARRIVALS

Country of origin	2006	2007	2008
Australia	40,642	54,098	58,724
Canada	981	1,385	1,745
Germany	818	1,492	1,408
Japan	3,966	3,347	3,865
Malaysia	3,155	4,490	4,772
New Zealand	2,867	4,643	5,399
Philippines	3,784	6,478	7,661
United Kingdom	1,783	3,515	3,800
USA	6,228	6,159	6,109
Total (incl. others)	77,730	104,122	114,182

Receipts from tourism (US $ million, incl. passenger transport): 5.9 in 2004; 3.7 in 2005.

Source: World Tourism Organization.

Communications Media

	2008	2009	2010
Telephones ('000 main lines in use)	66.8	91.1	121.2
Mobile cellular telephones ('000 subscribers)	874.0	1,417.5	1,909.1
Internet users ('000)	120	125	n.a.
Broadband subscribers ('000)	3.0	4.5	6.1

Personal computers: 391,000 (63.9 per 1,000 persons) in 2005.

Daily newspapers (2004): 2 (combined circulation 51,000 copies).

Radio receivers (1997): 410,000 in use.

Television receivers (2001): 110,000 in use.

Sources: UNESCO, *Statistical Yearbook*; International Telecommunication Union.

Education

(2005/06, unless otherwise indicated)

	Institutions*	Teachers	Students
Pre-primary	29	2,697†	95,121†
Primary	2,790	14,860	532,250
Secondary	n.a.	8,420‡	173,214‡
Tertiary§	n.a.	815	13,761

* 1994/95 figures.
† 2001/02 figure.
‡ 2002/03 figure.
§ 1998/99 figures.

Sources: National Department of Education, *The State of Education in PNG* (March 2001); UN, *Statistical Yearbook for Asia and the Pacific*; UNESCO Institute for Statistics.

Pupil-teacher Ratio (primary education, UNESCO estimate): 35.8 in 2005/06 (Source: UNESCO Institute for Statistics).

Adult Literacy Rate (UNESCO estimates): 60.1% (males 63.6%; females 56.5%) in 2009 (Source: UNESCO Institute for Statistics).

Directory

The Constitution

The present Constitution came into effect on 16 September 1975, when Papua New Guinea became independent. The main provisions of the Constitution are summarized below:

PREAMBLE

The national goals of the Independent State of Papua New Guinea are: integral human development, equality and participation in the development of the country, national sovereignty and self-reliance, conservation of natural resources and the environment and development primarily through the use of Papua New Guinean forms of social, political and economic organization.

BASIC HUMAN RIGHTS

All people are entitled to the fundamental rights and freedoms of the individual whatever their race, tribe, place of origin, political opinion, colour, creed or sex. The individual's rights include the right to freedom, life and the protection of the law, freedom from inhuman treatment, forced labour, arbitrary search and entry, freedom of conscience, thought, religion, expression, assembly, association and employment, and the right to privacy. Papua New Guinea citizens also have the following special rights: the right to vote and stand for public office, the right to freedom of information and of movement, protection from unjust deprivation of property and equality before the law.

THE NATION

Papua New Guinea is a sovereign, independent state. There is a National Capital District which shall be the seat of government.

The Constitution provides for various classes of citizenship. The age of majority is 19 years.

HEAD OF STATE

Her Majesty the Queen of the United Kingdom of Great Britain and Northern Ireland is Queen and Head of State of Papua New Guinea. The Head of State appoints and dismisses the Prime Minister on the proposal of the National Parliament and other ministers on the proposal of the Prime Minister. The Governor-General and Chief Justice are appointed and dismissed on the proposal of the National Executive Council. All the privileges, powers, functions, duties and responsibilities of the Head of State may be exercised or performed through the Governor-General.

Governor-General

The Governor-General must be a citizen who is qualified to be a member of Parliament or who is a mature person of good standing who enjoys the respect of the community. No one is eligible for appointment more than once unless Parliament approves by a two-thirds' majority. No one is eligible for a third term. The Governor-General is appointed by the Head of State on the proposal of the National Executive Council in accordance with the decision of Parliament by simple majority vote. He may be dismissed by the Head of State on the proposal of the National Executive Council in accordance with a decision of the Council or of an absolute majority of Parliament. The normal term of office is six years. In the case of temporary or permanent absence, dismissal or suspension he may be replaced temporarily by the Speaker of the National Parliament until such time as a new Governor-General is appointed.

THE GOVERNMENT

The Government comprises the National Parliament, the National Executive and the National Judicial System.

National Parliament

The National Parliament, or the House of Assembly, is a single-chamber legislature of members elected from single-member open or provincial electorates. The National Parliament has 109 members elected by universal adult suffrage. The normal term of office is five years. There is a Speaker and a Deputy Speaker, who must be members of Parliament and must be elected to these posts by Parliament. They cannot serve as government ministers concurrently.

National Executive

The National Executive comprises the Head of State and the National Executive Council. The Prime Minister, who presides over the National Executive Council, is appointed and dismissed by the Head of State on the proposal of Parliament. The other ministers, of whom there shall be not fewer than six nor more than a quarter of the number of members of the Parliament, are appointed and dismissed by the Head of State on the proposal of the Prime Minister. The National Executive Council consists of all the ministers, including the Prime Minister, and is responsible for the executive government of Papua New Guinea.

National Judicial System

The National Judicial System comprises the Supreme Court, the National Court, Local Courts and Village Courts. The judiciary is independent.

The Supreme Court consists of the Chief Justice, the Deputy Chief Justice and the other judges of the National Court. It is the final court of appeal. The Chief Justice is appointed and dismissed by the Head of State on the proposal of the National Executive Council after consultation with the minister responsible for justice. The Deputy Chief Justice and the other judges are appointed by the Judicial and Legal Services Commission. The National Court consists of the Chief Justice, the Deputy Chief Justice and no fewer than four nor more than six other judges.

The Constitution also makes provision for the establishment of the Magisterial Service and the establishment of the posts of Public Prosecutor and the Public Solicitor.

THE STATE SERVICES

The Constitution establishes the following State Services which, with the exception of the Defence Force, are subject to ultimate civilian control.

National Public Service

The Public Service is managed by the Department of Personnel Management which is headed by a Secretary, who is appointed by the National Executive Council on a four-year contract.

Police Force

The Police Force is subject to the control of the National Executive Council through a minister and its function is to preserve peace and good order and to maintain and enforce the law.

Papua New Guinea Defence Force

The Defence Force is subject to the superintendence and control of the National Executive Council through the Minister for Defence. The functions of the Defence Force are to defend Papua New Guinea, to provide assistance to civilian authorities in a civil disaster, in the restoration of public order or during a period of declared national emergency.

The fourth State Service is the Parliamentary Service.

The Constitution also includes sections on Public Finance, the office of the Auditor-General, the Public Accounts Commission and the declaration of a State of National Emergency.

The Government

HEAD OF STATE

Queen: HM Queen ELIZABETH II.

Governor-General: MICHAEL OGIO (sworn in 25 February 2011).

NATIONAL EXECUTIVE COUNCIL

(October 2011)

The cabinet includes members of the People's National Congress (PNC), National Alliance (NA), the United Resources Party (URP), People's Party, Papua New Guinea Party and the United Party.

Prime Minister: PETER O'NEILL.

Deputy Prime Minister and Minister for Forestry and Climate Change: BELDEN NAMAH.

Minister for Foreign Affairs and Immigration: ANO PALA.

Minister for Finance and Treasury: DON POLYE.

Minister for Trade, Commerce and Industry: CHARLES ABEL.

Minister for Defence: GUMA WAU.

Minister for Internal Security: JOHN BOITO.

Minister for Justice and Attorney-General: Dr ALLAN MARAT.

Minister for Agriculture and Livestock: Sir PUKA TEMU.

Minister for Communications and Information: JIM MIRINGTORO.

Minister for Arts, Culture and Tourism: BENJAMIN PHILIP.

Minister for Environment and Conservation: THOMPSON HAROKAQVEH.

Minister for Mining: BYRON CHAN.

Minister for Fisheries: JOB POMAT.

Minister for Public Service: BART PHILEMON.

Minister assisting the Prime Minister on Constitutional Matters: WAKE GOI.

Minister for Health: JAMIE MAXTONE-GRAHAM.

Minister for Education: THEO ZURENUOC.

Minister for Higher Education, Research, Science and Technology: DAVID ARORE.

Minister for Housing and Urban Development: KEN FAIRWEATHER.

Minister for Inter-Government Relations and District Development: MARK MAIPAKAI.

Minister for Labour and Industrial Relations: MARTIN AINI.

Minister for National Planning: SAM BASIL.

Minister for Petroleum and Energy: WILLIAM DUMA.

Minister for Public Enterprise: Sir MEKERE MORAUTA.

Minister for Lands and Physical Planning: LUCAS DEKENA.

Minister for Civil Aviation: PURI RUING.

Minister for Bougainville Affairs: STEVEN KAMA PIRIKA.

Minister for Community Development, Religion and Family Affairs: ANDREW MALD.

Minister for Sports: SALI SUBAM.

Minister for Correctional Services: SAI SAILON BESEO.

Minister for Transport and Works: FRANCIS AWESA.

Minister of Implementation and Rural Development: MOSES MALADINA.

GOVERNMENT DEPARTMENTS AND OFFICES

Office of the Prime Minister: POB 639, Waigani, NCD; tel. 3277316; fax 3277328; e-mail chiefsectogov@pmnec.gov.pg; internet www.pm.gov.pg.

Department of Agriculture and Livestock: POB 417, Konedobu 125; tel. 3231848; fax 3230563; e-mail dalit@daltron.com.pg; internet www.agriculture.gov.pg.

Department of the Attorney-General: POB 591, Waigani, NCD; tel. 3230138; fax 3230241.

Department of Communications and Information: POB 1122, Waigani, NCD; tel. 3250148; fax 3250412; e-mail hiduhu@gopng.gov.pg.

Department of Community Development: POB 7354, Boroko, NCD; tel. 3244526; fax 3250133; internet www.pngfamilies.gov.pg.

Department of Defence: Murray Barracks, Free Mail Bag, Boroko 111, NCD; tel. 3242494; fax 3277480; internet www.defence.gov.pg.

Department of Education: Fincorp Haus, POB 446, Waigani, NCD; tel. 3013555; fax 3254648; internet www.education.gov.pg.

Department of Environment and Conservation: POB 6601, Boroko 111, NCD; tel. 3250182; fax 3250180; e-mail wamini@dec.gov.pg; internet www.dec.gov.pg.

Department of Family and Church Affairs: Ori Lavi Haus, Nita St, POB 7354, Boroko, NCD; tel. 3254566; fax 3251230.

Department of Finance: POB 710, Waigani, Vulupindi Haus, NCD; tel. 3288455; fax 3232239; e-mail inquires@finance.gov.pg; internet www.finance.gov.pg.

Department of Fisheries and Marine Resources: POB 2016, Port Moresby; tel. 3271799; fax 3202074.

Department of Foreign Affairs and Trade: POB 422, Waigani 131, NCD; tel. 3156047; fax 3254263.

Department of Health: POB 807, Waigani, NCD; tel. 3013827; fax 3013742; internet www.health.gov.pg.

Department of Housing and Urban Resettlement: POB 1550, Boroko, NCD; tel. 3247200; fax 3259918.

Department of Justice: POB 591, Waigani, NCD.

Department of Labour and Industrial Relations: POB 5644, Boroko, NCD; tel. 3235758; fax 3256655; e-mail enquiries@workpermits.gov.pg; internet www.workpermits.gov.pg.

Department of Lands and Physical Planning: Aopi Centre, Tower 2, Levels 2, 3 and 4, Waigani Drive, Boroko, NCD; tel. 3013206; fax 3013205; e-mail onnoj@lands.gov.pg; internet www.lands.gov.pg.

Department of Mining: PMB, Port Moresby Post Office, Port Moresby 121; tel. 3214011; fax 3217958; internet www.mineral.gov.pg.

Department of National Planning and Monitoring: POB 631, Waigani, NCD; tel. 3288302; fax 3288444; e-mail dnpm_enquiries@planning.gov.pg; internet www.planning.gov.pg.

Department of Personnel Management: POB 519, Wards Strip, Waigani, NCD; tel. 3276422; fax 3250520; e-mail perrtsiamalili@dpm.gov.pg.

Department of Petroleum and Energy: POB 1993, Port Moresby, NCD; tel. 3224200; fax 3224222; e-mail enquiry@petroleum.gov.pg; internet www.petroleum.gov.pg.

Department of Police: Police Headquarters, POB 85, Konedobu, NCD; tel. 3226100; fax 3226113.

Department of Provincial and Local Government Affairs: POB 1287, Boroko, NCD; tel. 3011002; fax 3250553; e-mail paffairs@dalton.com.pg; internet www.dplga.gov.pg.

Department of Social Welfare and Development, Youth and Women: POB 7354, Boroko, NCD; tel. 3254967; fax 3213821.

Department of State: Haus To Makala, 5th Floor, Post Office, Wards Strip, Waigani, NCD; tel. 3276758; fax 3214861.

Department of Transport and Civil Aviation: POB 1489, Port Moresby; tel. 3222580; fax 3200236.

Department of Treasury: POB 542, Waigani 131, NCD; tel. 3128817; fax 3128844; e-mail enquiries@treasury.gov.pg; internet www.treasury.gov.pg.

Department of Works and Implementation: POB 1108, Boroko 111, NCD; tel. 3222500; fax 3200236; e-mail webmaster@works.gov.pg; internet www.works.gov.pg.

Correctional Service: POB 6889, Boroko, NCD III; tel. 3231437; fax 3230407; e-mail rsikani@hq.cs.gov.pg.

Papua New Guinea Forest Authority: POB 5055, Boroko, NCD; tel. 3277841; fax 3254433; e-mail info_general@pngfa.gov.pg; internet www.forestry.gov.pg.

Legislature

NATIONAL PARLIAMENT

The unicameral legislature has 109 elective seats: 89 representing open constituencies and 20 representing provincial constituencies. There is constitutional provision for up to three nominated members.

Speaker: FRANCIS MARUS (acting).

General Election, 30 June–15 July 2007 (provisional results)

Party	Seats
National Alliance	27
Papua New Guinea Party	8
People's Action Party	6
Pangu Pati	5
People's Democratic Movement	5
United Resource Party	5
New Generation Party	4
People's National Congress	4
People's Progress Party	4
Rural Development Party	4
People's Party	3
Melanesian Liberal Party	2
People's Labour Party	2
PNG Country Party	2
United Party	2
Melanesian Alliance Party	1
National Advance Party	1
Pipol First Party	1
PNG Conservative Party	1
PNG Labour Party	1
PNG National Party	1
Independents and others	20
Total	109

Note: in many cases party affiliations were subject to review in the immediate aftermath of the election. The National Alliance was subsequently reported to have secured the support of 30 members of the legislature.

Autonomous Region

BOUGAINVILLE ASSEMBLY

In March 2004 the Bougainville Interim Provincial Government (BIPG) approved legislation to establish the Bougainville Constituent Assembly (BCA). The organization, which was composed of the members of both the BIPG and the Bougainville People's Congress (BPC), was convened for the first time on 30 March 2004, to approve the third and final draft of the proposed Constitution for Bougainville. Following its consideration by the Bougainville Constitutional Commission in August, in November the BCA recommended the proposed Constitution to the National Government, which approved the document in January 2005. Elections for the President of the incoming Autonomous Bougainville Government (and for the island's first autonomous assembly were held during May–June 2005.

Elections for 39 of the 40 seats in Bougainville's second autonomous assembly and for the President of the Autonomous Bougainville Government took place over a period of two weeks commencing on 7 May 2010. John Momis of the New Bougainville Party was elected President of the ABG, winning 52.3% of the total votes cast, thus defeating the incumbent James Tanis (20.9%) and five other candidates. More than three-quarters of incumbent legislators lost their seats in the House of Representatives. Independent candidates were reported to have won 23 seats and the New Bougainville Party 14 seats. Three of the 39 seats are reserved for women and three for former combatants. The President occupies the 40th seat in the assembly. The incoming President and the House of Representatives were inaugurated on 15 June 2010.

President: JOHN MOMIS.

Vice-President: PATRICK NISIRA.

Speaker: ANDREW MIRIKI.

Election Commission

Election Commission of Papua New Guinea: POB 5348, Boroko, NCD; tel. 3258187; fax 3258650; e-mail info@pngec.gov.pg; internet www.pngec.gov.pg; Electoral Commr ANDREW TRAWEN.

Political Organizations

Bougainville Revolutionary Army (BRA): f. 1988; demands full independence for island of Bougainville; Leader ISHMAEL TOROAMA.

Christian Democratic Party: Leader Dr BANARE BUN.

Customary Land Rights-holders Party: f. 2011; promotes wealth creation, co-operation and equal devt among all customary land rights-holders and citizens; Pres. PETER DONIGI; Sec.-Gen. EMMANUEL MUNGU.

Melanesian Alliance (MA): Port Moresby; tel. 3277635; f. 1978; socialist; Chair. Sir MOI AVEI; Gen. Sec. FABIAN WAU KAWA.

Melanesian Labour Party: Port Moresby; Leader PAUL MONDIA.

Movement for Greater Autonomy: Manus Province; Leader STEPHEN POKAWIN.

National Alliance (NA): c/o National Parliament, Port Moresby; f. 1996; est. to combat corruption in public life; Pres. SIMON KAIWI; Parliamentary Leader DON POLYE.

National Party (NP): Private Bag, Boroko, NCD; f. 1979; fmrly People's United Front; Leader MICHAEL MEL.

New Bougainville Party (NBP): Bougainville; f. 2005; aims to combat corruption, review peace process and issue of disposal of guns, and to involve youths, women, church groups and businesses in devt of Bougainville; Leader JOHN MOMIS; Pres. LINUS SAHOTO.

New Generation Party: c/o National Parliament, Port Moresby; Leader BART PHILEMON.

Pangu Pati (PANGU) (Papua New Guinea Unity): POB 289, Waigani, NCD; tel. 3277628; fax 3277611; f. 1968; urban- and rural-based; Leader ANDREW KUMBAKOR; Deputy Leader PHILEMON EMBEL.

Papua New Guinea Greens Party: f. 2001; Pres. DOROTHY TEKWIE.

Papua New Guinea Party: f. 2007; Leader BELDEN NAMAH.

People's Action Party (PAP): Boroko, NCD; tel. 3251343; f. 1985.

People's Democratic Movement (PDM): POB 972, Boroko, NCD; f. 1985; merged with Advance PNG Party in 2001; Leader PAIAS WINGTI.

People's National Congress (PNC): c/o National Parliament, Port Moresby; Leader PETER O'NEILL.

People's National Party: Port Moresby.

People's Party: Leader PETER IPATAS.

People's Progress Party (PPP): POB 6030, Boroko, NCD; f. 1970; Parliamentary Leader JULIUS CHAN; Nat. Pres. ALEX ANISI; Gen. Sec. EMOS DANIELS.

Rural Development Party: Leader MOSES MALADINA.

Social Democratic Party: f. 2010; est. as United Democratic Front; aims to eliminate corruption and 'power politics, power-play and politics of convenience'; Leader POWES PARKOP; Pres. WESLEY SANARUP.

United Party: c/o National Parliament, Port Moresby; Leader BOB DADAE.

United Resources Party (URP): Port Moresby; f. 1997; aims to secure greater representation in govt for resource owners; Leader WILLIAM DUMA.

Other parties that contested the 2007 election included the Melanesian Liberal Party, the National Advance Party, the People's Labour Party, the Pipol First Party, the PNG Conservative Party, the PNG Country Party (Leader Jamie Maxtone-Graham), the PNG Labour Party and the PNG National Party.

Diplomatic Representation

EMBASSIES AND HIGH COMMISSIONS IN PAPUA NEW GUINEA

Australia: Godwit Rd, Waigani, NCD; tel. 3259333; fax 3256647; internet www.png.embassy.gov.au; High Commissioner IAN KEMISH.

China, People's Republic: POB 1351, Boroko, NCD; tel. 3259836; fax 3258247; e-mail chinaemb_pg@mfa.gov.cn; internet www.chinaembassy.org.pg; Ambassador QIU BOHUA.

Fiji: Defens Haus, 4th Floor, Champion Parade, Port Moresby; tel. 3211914; fax 3217220; High Commissioner Dr NIUMAIA TABUNAKAWAI.

France: Defens Haus, 6th Floor, Champion Parade, POB 1155, Port Moresby; tel. 3215550; fax 3215549; e-mail ambfrpom@global.net.pg; internet www.ambafrance-pg.org; Ambassador ALAIN WAQUET.

Holy See: POB 98, Port Moresby; tel. 3256021; fax 3252844; e-mail nunciaturepng@datec.net.pg; Apostolic Nuncio Most Rev. FRANCISCO MONTECILLO PADILLA (Titular Archbishop of Nebbio).

India: Lot 20, Section 8, Unit 2, Tanatana St, Boroko, NCD; tel. 3254757; fax 3253138; e-mail hcipom@datec.net.pg; High Commissioner A. M. GONDANE.

Indonesia: POB 7165, Boroko, NCD; tel. 3253116; fax 3250535; e-mail kbripom@daltron.com.pg; internet www.deplu.go.id/portmoresby; Ambassador ANDREAS SITEPU.

Japan: POB 1040, Port Moresby; tel. 3211800; fax 3214868; e-mail sceoj@online.net.pg; Ambassador HIROHARU IWASAKI.

Korea, Republic: POB 381, Port Moresby; tel. 3215822; fax 3215828; e-mail embpng@mofat.go.kr; internet png.mofat.go.kr; Ambassador LEE WHIE-JIN.

Malaysia: POB 1400, Port Moresby; tel. 3252076; fax 3252784; e-mail malpmresby@kln.gov.my; internet www.kln.gov.my/web/png_port-moresby; Ambassador Datin BLANCHE OLBERY.

New Zealand: POB 1051, Waigani, NCD; tel. 3259444; fax 3250565; e-mail nzhcpom@dg.com.pg; High Commissioner MARION CRAWSHAW.

Philippines: POB 5916, Boroko, NCD; tel. 3256414; fax 3231803; e-mail pompe@datec.net.pg; internet www.philembassypng.tk; Ambassador BIENVENIDO V. TEJANO.

Solomon Islands: Waigani, Port Moresby; e-mail sihicomm@daltron.com.pg; High Commissioner (vacant).

United Kingdom: Locked Bag 212, Waigani 131, NCD; tel. 3251677; fax 3253547; e-mail ukinpng@datec.net.pg; internet www.ukinpng.fco.gov.uk; High Commissioner JACQUELINE BARSON.

USA: POB 1492, Port Moresby; tel. 3211455; fax 3211593; e-mail png@state.gov; internet portmoresby.usembassy.gov; Ambassador TEDDY TAYLOR.

Judicial System

The Supreme Court is the highest judicial authority in the country, and deals with all matters involving the interpretation of the Constitution, and with appeals from the National Court. The National Court has unlimited jurisdiction in both civil and criminal matters. All National Court Judges (except acting Judges) are Judges of the Supreme Court. District Courts are responsible for civil cases involving compensation, for some indictable offences and for the more serious summary offences, while Local Courts deal with minor offences and with such matters as custody of children under the provision of Custom. There are also Children's Courts, which judge cases involving minors. Appeal from the District, Local and Children's Courts lies to the National Court. District and Local Land Courts deal with disputes relating to Customary land, and Warden's Courts with civil cases relating to mining. In addition, there are other courts with responsibility for determining ownership of government land and for assessing the right of Customary landowners to compensation. Village Courts, which are presided over by Magistrates with no formal legal qualification, are responsible for all Customary matters not dealt with by other courts.

Chief Justice of the Supreme Court of Papua New Guinea: Sir SALAMO INJIA, POB 7018, Boroko, NCD; tel. 3245700; fax 3234492; internet www.pngjudiciary.gov.pg.

Attorney-General: Dr ALLAN MARAT.

Religion

The belief in magic or sorcery is widespread, even among the significant proportion of the population that has adopted Christianity (nominally 97% in 1990). Pantheism also survives. There are many missionary societies.

CHRISTIANITY

Papua New Guinea Council of Churches: POB 1015, Boroko, NCD; tel. 3259961; fax 3251206; f. 1965; seven mem. churches; Chair. EDEA KIDU; Gen. Sec. SOPHIA W. R. GEGEYO.

The Anglican Communion

Formerly part of the Province of Queensland within the Church of England in Australia (now the Anglican Church of Australia), Papua New Guinea became an independent Province in 1977. The Anglican Church of Papua New Guinea comprises five dioceses and had 246,000 members in 2000.

Archbishop of Papua New Guinea and Bishop of Popondota: Most Rev. JOSEPH KIFAU KOPAPA, POB 26, Popondetta, Oro Province; tel. 3297194; fax 7297476; e-mail acpngpop@online.net.pg.

General Secretary: RICHARD RABIAFI, POB 673, Lae, Morobe Province; tel. 4724111; fax 4721852; e-mail acpnggensec@global.net.pg.

The Roman Catholic Church

For ecclesiastical purposes, Papua New Guinea comprises four archdioceses and 15 dioceses. At 31 December 2007 there were 1,826,012 adherents.

Catholic Bishops' Conference of Papua New Guinea and Solomon Islands

POB 398, Waigani, NCD; tel. 3259577; fax 3232551; e-mail cbcgensec@catholic.org.pg; internet www.catholicpng.org.pg.

f. 1959; Pres. Most Rev. JOHN RIBAT (Bishop of Bereina); Gen. Sec. LAWRENCE STEPHENS.

Archbishop of Madang: Most Rev. STEPHEN JOSEPH REICHERT, Archbishop's Residence, POB 750, Madang 511; tel. 8522599; fax 8522596; e-mail Kurtz_caom@global.net.pg.

Archbishop of Mount Hagen: Most Rev. DOUGLAS YOUNG, Archbishop's Office, POB 54, Mount Hagen, Western Highlands Province 281; tel. 5421285; fax 5422128; e-mail dwyoung@global.net.pg.

Archbishop of Port Moresby: Most Rev. JOHN RIBAT, Archbishop's House, POB 1032, Boroko, NCD 111; tel. 3251192; fax 3256731; e-mail archpom@daltron.com.pg.

Archbishop of Rabaul: Most Rev. FRANCESCO PANFILO, Archbishop's House, POB 357, Kokopo 613, East New Britain Province; tel. 9828369; fax 9828858; e-mail abkhesse@online.net.pg.

Other Christian Churches

Baptist Union of Papua New Guinea Inc: POB 705, Mount Hagen, Western Highlands Province; tel. 5522364; fax 5522402; e-mail bupng@global.net.pg; f. 1976; Gen. Sec. JOHN KAENKI; 48,000 mems.

Evangelical Lutheran Church of Papua New Guinea: Bishop Rt Rev. GIEGERE WENGE, POB 80, Lae, Morobe Province; tel. 4723711; fax 4721056; e-mail bishop.admin@global.net.pg; internet www.elcpng.org; f. 1956; ALBERT TOKAVE; 900,000 mems.

Gutnius Lutheran Church of Papua New Guinea: Bishop Rev. DAVID P. PISO, POB 111, 291 Wabag, Enga Province; tel. 5471280; fax 5471235; e-mail dpisoglc@online.net.pg; f. 1948; Gen. Sec. RICHARD R. MOSES; 149,455 mems.

Papua New Guinea Union Mission of the Seventh-day Adventist Church: POB 86, Lae, Morobe Province 411; tel. 4721488; fax 4721873; internet pngum.adventist.org.pg; Sec. LEIGH RICE; 200,000 adherents.

The United Church in Papua New Guinea: POB 1401, Port Moresby; tel. 3211744; fax 3214930; e-mail ucpng@daltron.com.pg; internet www.ucpng.com; f. 1968; formed by union of the Methodist Church in Melanesia, the Papua Ekalesia and United Church, Port Moresby; Moderator Sir SAMSON LOWA; 700,000 mems; Gen. Sec. Rev. SIULANGI KAVORA.

BAHÁ'Í FAITH

National Spiritual Assembly: PMB 9, Boroko, NCD; tel. 3250286; fax 3236474; e-mail nsasecretary@bahai.org.pg; internet www.bahai.org.pg.

ISLAM

In 2000 the Muslim community in Papua New Guinea numbered about 1,500, of whom approximately two-thirds were believed to be expatriates. The religion was introduced to the island in the 1970s. The country's first mosque was opened in 2000 at Poreporena Highway, Hohola, Port Moresby; Imam MIKHAIL KORAH (acting).

The Press

There are numerous newspapers and magazines published by government departments, statutory organizations, missions, sporting organizations, local government councils and regional authorities. They are variously in English, Tok Pisin (Pidgin), Motu and vernacular languages.

Ailans Nius: POB 1239, Rabaul, East New Britain Province; weekly.

Foreign Affairs Review: Dept of Foreign Affairs, Central Government Offices, Kumul Ave, Post Office, Wards Strip, Waigani, NCD; tel. 3271401; fax 3254886.

Hailans Nius: Mount Hagen, Western Highlands Province; weekly.

Lae Nius: POB 759, Lae, Morobe Province; 2 a week.

The National: POB 6817, Boroko, NCD; tel. 3246888; fax 3246868; e-mail national@thenational.com.pg; internet www.thenational.com.pg; f. 1993; daily; Editor DANIEL KORIMBAU; circ. 30,000.

Papua and New Guinea Education Gazette: Dept of Education, Fincorp Haus, POB 446, Waigani, NCD; tel. 3272413; fax 3254648; monthly; Editor J. OBERLENTER; circ. 8,000.

Papua New Guinea Post-Courier: POB 85, Port Moresby; tel. 3091000; fax 3212721; e-mail postcourier@ssp.com.pg; internet www.postcourier.com.pg; f. 1969; daily; English; published by News Corpn; Editor YEHIURA HRIEHWAZI; circ. 25,044.

Sunkamap Times: POB 322, Buka, Bougainville, North Solomons Province; e-mail stephen@viscom.co.nz; internet www.viscom.co.nz/SunkamapTimes; monthly; f. 2004; community newsletter.

Wantok (Friend) Niuspepa: POB 1982, Boroko, NCD; tel. 3252500; fax 3252579; e-mail word@global.net.pg; f. 1970; weekly in New Guinea Pidgin; mainly rural readership; Publr ANNA SOLOMON; Editor NEVILLE CHOI; circ. 10,000.

Publishers

Gordon and Gotch (PNG) Pty Ltd: POB 107, Boroko, NCD; tel. 3254855; fax 3250950; e-mail ggpng@online.net.pg; f. 1970; books, magazines and stationery; Gen. Man. PETER G. PORTER.

Scripture Union of Papua New Guinea: POB 280, University, Boroko, NCD; tel. and fax 3253987; f. 1966; religious; Chair. RAVA TAVIRI.

Word Publishing Co Pty Ltd: POB 1982, Boroko, NCD; tel. 3252500; fax 3252579; e-mail word@global.net.pg; f. 1982; 60% owned by the Roman Catholic Church, 20% by Evangelical Lutheran, 10% by Anglican and 10% by United Churches; Gen. Man. JEREMY BURGESS.

Broadcasting and Communications

TELECOMMUNICATIONS

Department of Information and Communication: POB 1122, Waigani; tel. 3250148; fax 3250412; e-mail hiduhu@gopng.gov.pg; internet www.communication.gov.pg; Sec. HENAO IDUHU.

Digicel (PNG) Ltd: POB 1618, Port Moresby, NCD; e-mail customercarepng@digicelgroup.com; internet www.digicelpng.com; GSM services; CEO JOHN MANGOS.

Pacific Mobile Communications Company Ltd: POB 6973, Boroko, NCD; tel. 3232555; fax 3232554; e-mail pmc@tiare.net.pg; internet www.pacificmobile.com.pg; Chair. Dr FLORIAN GUBON.

Papua New Guinea Radiocommunications and Telecommunications Technical Authority (Pangtel): POB 8444, Boroko, NCD; tel. 3258633; fax 3256868; e-mail licensing@pangtel.gov.pg; internet www.pangtel.gov.pg; f. 1997; CEO CHARLES PUNAHA.

Telikom PNG Pty Ltd: POB 291, Waigan, Port Moresby, NCD; tel. 3004010; fax 3250665; e-mail webadmin@telikompng.com.pg; internet www.telikompng.com.pg; Chair. GEREA AOPI; CEO PETER LOKO.

In 2006 Green Communications (GreenCom), an Indonesian company, acquired a licence to expand into Papua New Guinea.

BROADCASTING

Radio

National Broadcasting Corporation of Papua New Guinea: POB 1359, Boroko, NCD; tel. 3255233; fax 3256296; e-mail info@nbc.com.pg; internet www.nbc.com.pg; f. 1973; commercial and free govt radio programmes services; broadcasting in English, Melanesian, Pidgin, Motu and 30 vernacular languages; Chair. CHRIS RANGATIN; Man. Dir Dr MEMAFU KAPERA.

Kalang Service (FM): POB 1359, Boroko, NCD; tel. 3255233; commercial radio co established by National Broadcasting Commission; Chair. CAROLUS KETSIMUR.

Nau FM/Yumi FM: POB 774, Port Moresby; tel. 3201996; fax 3201995; f. 1994; Gen. Mans MARK ROGERS, JUSTIN KILI.

Television

EM TV: POB 443, Boroko, NCD; tel. 3257322; fax 3254450; e-mail emtv@emtv.com.pg; internet www.emtv.com.pg; f. 1988; operated by Media Niugini Pty Ltd; Gen. Man. GLENN ARMSTRONG.

Media Niugini Pty Ltd: POB 443, Boroko, NCD; tel. 3257322; fax 3254450; e-mail emtv@emtv.com.pg; internet www.emtv.com.pg; f. 1987; owned by Fijity Ltd; Gen. Man. GLENN ARMSTRONG.

Finance

(cap. = capital; res = reserves; dep. = deposits; m. = million; brs = branches; amounts in kina unless otherwise stated)

BANKING

Central Bank

Bank of Papua New Guinea: POB 121, Port Moresby 121; tel. 3227200; fax 3211617; e-mail info@bankpng.gov.pg; internet www.bankpng.gov.pg; f. 1973; bank of issue since 1975; sold to Bank of South Pacific in 2002; cap. 145.5m., res 246.8m., dep. 4,926.6m. (Dec. 2008); Gov. LOI MARTIN BAKANI; Deputy Gov. BENNY POPOITAI.

Commercial Banks

Australia and New Zealand Banking Group (PNG) Ltd: POB 1152, Port Moresby 121; tel. 3211079; fax 3223302; e-mail cshdpg@anz.com; internet www.anz.com/Png; f. 1976; cap. 5.0m., res 2.2m., dep. 3,055.3m. (Sept. 2008); Chair. JOHN MORSCHEL; Man. Dir GARRY TUNSTALL; 12 brs.

Bank of South Pacific Ltd: POB 78, Cnr Douglas and Musgrave Sts, Port Moresby; tel. 3211999; fax 3211954; e-mail servicebsp@bsp.com.pg; internet www.bsp.com.pg; f. 1974; acquired from National Australia Bank Ltd by Papua New Guinea consortium (National Investment Holdings, now BSP Holdings Ltd) in 1993; merged with Papua New Guinea Banking Corpn in 2002; 10% stake acquired by International Finance Corporation in mid-2010; cap. 318.0m., res 66.4m., dep. 6,771.8m. (Dec. 2009); Chair. NOREO BEANGKE; CEO IAN B. CLYNE; 35 brs.

Finance Corpn Ltd (FinCorp): Aopi Centre, Ground Floor, Waigani Dr., Port Moresby; tel. 3232399; fax 3230167; e-mail sales@fincorp.com.pg; internet www.fincorp.com.pg; Chair. KERENGA KUA; Man. Dir and CEO TONY WITHAM; 5 brs.

Maybank (PNG) Ltd: Cnr Waigani Rd and Islander Dr., POB 882, Waigani, NCD; tel. 3258028; fax 3256128; e-mail maybankpom@datec.net.pg; internet maybank.com.my/maybank-worldwide/papua-new-guinea; f. 1995; Chair. ALISTER MAITLAND.

Westpac Bank—PNG—Ltd: POB 706, Port Moresby; tel. 3220511; fax 3220636; e-mail westpacpng@westpac.com.au; internet www.westpac.com.pg; f. 1910; est. as Bank of New South Wales, present name adopted 1982; 93.5% owned by Westpac Banking Corpn (Australia); cap. 5.8m., res 78.5m., dep. 2,206m. (Sept. 2010); Man. Dir GAIL KELLY; 16 brs.

Development Bank

National Development Bank (NDB): POB 686, Waigani, NCD; tel. 3247500; fax 3259817; e-mail rbank@devbank.com.pg; internet www.ndb.com.pg; f. 1967; est. as Agriculture Bank of Papua New Guinea; later known as Rural Development Bank of Papua New Guinea; name changed as above in 2007; statutory govt agency; Chair. WILLIAM LAMUR; Man. Dir RICHARD MARU; 18 brs.

Savings and Loan Societies

Registry of Savings and Loan Societies: Bank of Papua New Guinea, Banking Supervision Dept, POB 121, Port Moresby; tel. 3227200; fax 3214548; e-mail gawap@bankpng.gov.pg; internet www.bankpng.gov.pg; 21 savings and loan societies; 243,003 mems (2010); total funds 756.8m., loans outstanding 219.4m., investments 341.1m. (Dec. 2010); Man. GEORGE AWAP.

STOCK EXCHANGE

Port Moresby Stock Exchange (POMSoX) Ltd: POB 1531, Port Moresby; tel. 3201980; fax 3201981; e-mail pomsox@pomsox.com.pg; internet www.pomsox.com.pg; f. 1999; Chair. GEREA AOPI; Gen. Man. VINCENT IVOSA.

INSURANCE

Capital Life Insurance Co: Tisa Haus, 2nd Floor, Wardship, Waigani, Port Moresby; tel. 3234036; fax 3232533; e-mail marketing@tsl.org.pg; f. 1993; fmrly Pan Asia Pacific Assurance (PNG); 100% owned by Teachers' Savings & Loan Society Ltd (TISA).

Kwila Insurance Corpn: POB 1457, Boroko, NCD; tel. 3258811; fax 3112867; e-mail jmcllvena@kwilainsurance.com.pg; internet www.kwilainsurance.com.pg; f. 1977; Gen. Man. JASON R. MCILVENA.

Pacific MMI Insurance Ltd: POB 331, Port Moresby; tel. 3214077; fax 3218437; e-mail enquiries@pacificmmi.com; internet www.pacificmmi.com; f. 1998; fmrly Niugini Insurance Corpn Ltd; jt venture; general and life insurance; financial services; Chair. Dr JOHN MUA; Man. Dir WAYNE DORGAN.

There are branches of several Australian and United Kingdom insurance companies in Port Moresby, Rabaul, Lae and Kieta.

Trade and Industry

GOVERNMENT AGENCIES

Independent Public Business Corpn (IPBC): POB 320, Port Moresby, NCD; tel. 3212977; fax 3212916; e-mail ipbc@ipbc.com.pg; internet www.ipbc.com.pg; f. 2002; assets manager of all govt enterprises of Papua New Guinea; Chair. GEREA AOPI; Man. Dir GLENN BLAKE.

Investment Promotion Authority (IPA): POB 5053, Boroko, NCD 111; tel. 3213900; fax 3213049; e-mail ipa@ipa.gov.pg; internet www.ipa.gov.pg; f. 1992; est. following reorganization of National Investment and Development Authority; statutory body responsible for the promotion of foreign investment; recommends priority areas for investment to the Govt; also co-ordinates investment proposals; Man. Dir IVAN POMALEU.

Mineral Resources Authority (MRA): POB 1906, Port Moresby; tel. 3213511; fax 3215711; e-mail info@mra.gov.pg; internet www.mra.gov.pg; f. 2006; Man. Dir KEPAS WALI.

DEVELOPMENT ORGANIZATION

Industrial Centres Development Corporation (ICDC): POB 1571, Boroko, NCD; tel. 3112211; fax 3112212; e-mail henlytaka@hotmail.com; internet www.icdc.gov.pg; f. 1990; owned by govt of Papua New Guinea under the Ministry of Commerce and Industry; promotes foreign investment in non-mining sectors through establishment of industrial estates; Sr Marketing Officer HENLY TAKA.

CHAMBERS OF COMMERCE

Lae Chamber of Commerce Inc: POB 265, Lae, Morobe Province; tel. 4722340; fax 4726038; e-mail lcci@global.net.pg; internet www.lcci.org.pg; Pres. ALAN MCLAY.

Papua New Guinea Chamber of Commerce and Industry: POB 1621, Port Moresby; tel. 3213057; fax 3210566; e-mail pngcci@global.net.pg; internet www.pngcci.org.pg; Pres. JOHN LEAHY; Vice-Pres. MICHAEL MAYBERRY.

Port Moresby Chamber of Commerce and Industry: POB 75, Port Moresby; tel. 3213077; fax 3214203; e-mail bizcentre@pomcci.org.pg; internet www.pomcci.com; Pres. RON SEDDON; Chief Exec. DAVID CONN.

INDUSTRIAL AND TRADE ASSOCIATIONS

Cocoa Board of Papua New Guinea: POB 532, Rabaul, East New Britain Province; tel. 9829083; fax 9828712; e-mail l.tautea@global.net.pg; f. 1974; Chair. JIMMY SIMITAB; CEO LAVATAU TAUTEA.

Coffee Industry Corpn Ltd: POB 137, Goroka, Eastern Highlands Province; tel. 7321266; fax 7321214; e-mail cicgka@daltron.com.pg; internet www.coffeecorp.org.pg; CEO NAVI ANIS.

Fishing Industry Association (PNG) Inc: POB 5860, Boroko, NCD; tel. 3258222; fax 3258994; e-mail netshop1@daltron.com.pg; Pres. PETE CELSO.

Forest Industries Association: POB 229, Waigani, NCD; internet www.fiapng.com; Pres. ANTHONY HONEY; CEO ROBERT TATE.

Kokonas Indastri Korporesen (KIK): POB 81, Port Moresby; tel. 3211133; fax 3214257; e-mail infor@kik.com.pg; regulates and markets all copra and coconut products in Papua New Guinea; represents producers; fmrly Copra Marketing Board of Papua New Guinea (f. 1950s); name changed as above 2002; govt-owned; Chair. JOE ARARUA; Man. Dir TORE OVASURU.

Manufacturers' Council of Papua New Guinea: POB 598, Port Moresby; tel. 3259512; fax 3230199; e-mail pngmade@global.com.pg; Chair. WAYNE GOLDING; CEO BRUCE REVILLE.

Mineral Resources Development Corporation: POB 1076, Port Moresby, NCD 121; tel. 3255822; fax 3252633; e-mail enquiry@mrdc.com.pg; internet www.mrdc.com.pg; f. 1975; manages landowner and provincial govt interests in major mineral resources projects; subsidiaries incl. Mineral Resources Star Mountains Ltd, Mineral Resources Ok Tedi No 2 Ltd, Mineral Resources Enga Ltd, Petroleum Resources Kutubu Ltd, Petroleum Resources Gobe Ltd and Petroleum Resources Moran Ltd; Chair. SIMON TOSALI; Man. Dir AUGUSTINE SANGA MANO.

National Fisheries Authority: POB 2016, Port Moresby; tel. 3212643; fax 3202061; e-mail nfa@fisheries.gov.pg; internet www.fisheries.gov.pg; Man. Dir SYLVESTER POKAJAM.

National Housing Corpn (NHC): POB 1550, Boroko, NCD; tel. 3252124; fax 3259918; e-mail managingdirector@nhc.gov.pg; f. 1990; man. and promotion of nat. housing projects; Man. Dir TARCISSIUS MUGANAUA (acting).

Palm Oil Producers Association: Port Moresby; Chair. BROWN BAI.

Papua New Guinea Chamber of Mines and Petroleum: POB 1032, Port Moresby; tel. 3212988; fax 3217107; e-mail conf@

pngchamberminpet.com.pg; internet www.pngchamberminpet.com.pg; Exec. Dir GREG ANDERSON; Pres. Dr ILA TEMU.

Papua New Guinea Forest Authority: POB 5055, Boroko, NCD; tel. 3277800; fax 3254433; e-mail info_general@pngfa.gov.pg; internet www.forestry.gov.pg; Man. Dir KANAWI POURU; Chair. JOSEPH LELANG.

Papua New Guinea Growers Association: POB 14, Kokopo, East New Britain Province 613; tel. 9829123; fax 9829264; e-mail growers@global.net.pg; Pres. PAUL ARNOLD; Exec. Dir DAVID LOH.

Rural Industries Council: POB 1530, Port Moresby; tel. 3215773; fax 3217223; e-mail ric@daltron.com.pg; Chair. BROWN BAI.

UTILITIES

Electricity

PNG Power Ltd (PPL): POB 1105, Boroko, NCD; tel. 3243200; fax 3250072; e-mail marketing@pngpower.com.pg; internet www.pngpower.com.pg; prev. PNG Electricity Commission (Elcom); Commission privatized and name changed to above in 2002; undertakes regulatory role on behalf of Consumer and Competition Commission; Chair. WILLIAM KENJIBI; Chief Exec. TONY KOIRI.

Water

Eda Ranu (Our Water): PMB, Waigani, NCD; tel. 3122100; fax 3122194; e-mail info@edaranu.com.pg; internet www.edaranu.com.pg; fmrly Port Moresby Water Supply Company; Gen. Man. BILLY IMAR.

PNG Waterboard: POB 2779, Boroko, NCD; tel. 3235700; fax 3256298; e-mail pamini@pngwater.com.pg; f. 1986; govt-owned; operates 17 water supply systems throughout the country; Man. Dir PATRICK AMINI.

MAJOR COMPANIES

Food, Drink and Tobacco

Associated Mills Ltd: Speybank St, POB 1906, Lae, Morobe Province; tel. 4723555; fax 4723424; flour milling; operates two mills in Lae and Port Moresby; subsidiary of Goodman Fielder PNG; Gen. Man. JIM GREGG.

British American Tobacco Papua New Guinea: POB 632, Port Moresby; tel. 3201416; fax 3201412; internet www.bat.com; cigarettes and tobacco.

W. R. Carpenter & Co Estates: cnr Hagen Dr. and Benzin Rd, POB 94, Mount Hagen, Western Highlands Province; tel. 5422700; fax 5421616; e-mail sales@wrcarpenters.com.pg; internet www.wrcarpenters.com.pg; coffee, cocoa and tea processing; Gen. Man. RAMESH VASUDEVAN.

Kongo Coffee Ltd: POB 388, Kundiawa, Chuave, Simbu Province; tel. 2757518; fax 2757521; e-mail info@kongocoffee.com.pg; internet kongocoffee.com.pg; coffee exporters; Man. Dir JERRY KAPKA.

Niugini Coffee, Tea and Spice Co Ltd: POB 2531, Lae, Morobe Province; tel. 4725633; fax 4725614; e-mail niuginicoffee@global.net.pg; Div. Man. ALYOSHA REILLY.

SP Brewery Ltd (South Pacific Brewery): POB 6550, Boroko, NCD; tel. 3128200; fax 3250656; internet www.sp.com.pg; f. 1951; beer; Chair. J. TAUVASA; Gen. Man. STAN JOYCE; c.300 employees.

Laga Industries Ltd: POB 1441, Lae, Morobe Province; tel. 4757344; fax 3233599; internet www.lagaindustries.com.pg; f. 1975; subsidiary of Steamships Trading Co Ltd; ice cream and other dairy and frozen products, vegetable oils, condiments and seasonings.

Petroleum, Gas and Minerals

Barracuda Pty Ltd: Level 8, Pacific Place, cnr Champion Parade and Musgrave St, POB 1139, Port Moresby, NCD; tel. 3212633; fax 3212847; owned by Santos Ltd (Australia); exploration for petroleum.

BOC Gases Papua New Guinea: c/o 10 Julius Ave, N Ryde, Sydney, NSW 2113, Australia; tel. (2) 8874-4400; fax (2) 9886-9000; e-mail contact@boc.com; internet www.boc.com.au; industrial gases, oxygen, dissolved acetylene, nitrogen, argons, medical gases, pestigas, insectigas and deodour gas; cutting and welding equipment and consumables; Man. Dir BARRY BURKE.

Bougainville Copper Ltd: Pacific Place, Level 6, cnr Champion Parade, POB 1274, Port Moresby; tel. 3092800; fax 3213634; e-mail info@bcl.com.pg; internet www.bougainvillecopper.com.pg; f. 1967; 53.6% owned by Rio Tinto Ltd (Australia), 19.1% state-owned, 27.3% owned by public shareholders; mine production suspended in 1989; Chair. and Man. Dir PETER TAYLOR; Sec. PAUL D. COLEMAN.

Esso Highlands Ltd: Level 5, Credit House, Cuthbertson St, GPO Box 118, Port Moresby NCD; tel. 3222111; fax 3203457; e-mail png.lng.ncm@exxonmobil.com; internet www.pnglng.com; subsidiary of ExxonMobil Corpn (USA); construction and operation of the PNG LNG project; commercial production scheduled to commence in 2014; Man. Dir PETER GRAHAM.

Highlands Pacific Ltd: POB 1486, Port Moresby, NCD 121; tel. 3235966; fax 3235990; e-mail info@highlandspacific.com; internet www.highlandspacific.com; exploration for gold, nickel, cobalt, copper and other minerals; Chair. KEN MACDONALD; Man. Dir JOHN GOODING.

Lihir Gold Ltd: Pacific Place, Level 7, Cnr Champion Parade, POB 789, Port Moresby; tel. 3217711; fax 3214705; e-mail denise.allan@lihir.com.pg; internet www.newcrest.com.au; mining; gold mining on Lihir Island; merged with Newcrest Mining Ltd (Australia) in September 2010; Chair. Dr ROSS GARNAUT; Man. Dir and CEO ARTHUR HOOD.

Mobil Oil New Guinea Ltd: Credit Corp Bldg, 5th Floor, Cuthbertson St, POB 485, Port Moresby; tel. 3212055; fax 3222100; sale and distribution of fuel; operation of service stations; Area Man. NAMAR T. MAWASON.

Niugini Mining Ltd: Mogoru Moto Bldg, Level 4, Champion Parade, Port Moresby; tel. 3092000; fax 3092099; wholly owned subsidiary of Lihir Gold Ltd; developers of the Lihir Island gold project; CEO JOSEPH BAYLISS; Chair. IAN BAYER.

Oil Search Ltd: Credit House, 7th Floor, Cuthbertson St, POB 842, Port Moresby; tel. 3225599; fax 3225566; e-mail general.enquiries@oilsearch.com; internet www.oilsearch.com; f. 1929; oil and gas exploration; Chair. BRIAN HORWOOD; Man. Dir PETER R. BOTTEN.

Ok Tedi Mining Ltd (OTML): POB 1, Tabubil, Western Province; tel. 5483311; fax 5482033; e-mail info@oktedi.com; internet www.oktedi.com; copper and gold mining; 52% stake owned by BHP (Australia) transferred to PNG Sustainable Development Programme Ltd in 2002; 18% owned by Inmet Mining Corpn (Canada), 30% owned by PNG govt; Chair. ALAN ROBERTS; Man. Dir ALAN BREEN; 2,000 employees.

Origin Energy (PNG) Pty Ltd: Port Moresby; tel. 3234033; fax 3233017; e-mail william_lamur@originenergy.com.pg; internet www.originenergy.com.au/120/Papua-New-Guinea; distribution of LPG; Gen. Man. WILLIAM LAMUR.

Pacrim Energy Ltd: Brian Bell Plaza, Level 2, Turumu St, POB 6861, Boroko, NCD 111; tel. 3257611; fax 3259389; e-mail info@pacrimenergy.com.au; internet www.pacrimenergy.com.au; f. 1988; owned by Pacarc NL; oil, gas, gold and mineral exploration; Chair. Sir BARRY BLYTHE HOLLOWAY; Man. Dir RODNEY DAVID FOSTER.

Parker Drilling Co (PNG): Deloitte Tower, 8th Floor, Douglas St, Port Moresby, NCD; tel. 3213322; fax 3213213; e-mail pom-ops@daltron.com.pg; internet www.parkerdrilling.com; owned by Parker Drilling Co (USA); drilling contractor; Operations Mans MARK ANDREWS, HERB VIGEANT.

Ramu NiCo Ltd: Pacific Place, Level 3, POB 1825, Port Moresby; tel. 3213270; fax 3213276; e-mail info@mccgrd.com; internet www.ramunico.com; f. 2000; nickel mining; Pres. LUO SHU.

Shell Papua New Guinea Ltd: POB 169, Port Moresby; tel. 3228700; fax 3211842; aviation fuel, other fuels, lubricants and industrial chemicals; Gen. Man. DON MANOA.

United Pacific Drilling (PNG) Pty Ltd: Fikus St, POB 108, Madang; tel. 8522411; fax 8522830; e-mail wkh@upd.com.pg; mineral exploration; Gen. Man. WILLIAM HUGHES.

Timber and Palm Oil

Hargy Oil Palms Ltd: POB 21, Bialla, West New Britain Province; tel. 9831005; fax 9831191; e-mail harg@online.net.pg; internet www.hargy.com.pg; 100% owned by the Société Internationale de Plantations et de Finance (SIPEF); production of palm oil; Gen. Man. DAVID MATHER.

Higaturu Oil Palms Pty Ltd: POB 28, Popondetta, Oro Province; tel. 3297177; fax 3297137; f. 1976; controlled by New Britain Palm Oil Ltd from mid-2010; major producer of palm oil and cocoa; Gen. Man. DAVID MATHER.

Japan New Guinea Timber Pty Ltd (JANT): POB 714, Madang; tel. 8522700; fax 8523017; e-mail jant@daltron.com.pg; wood chips, milled timber.

Milne Bay Estates Pty Ltd: POB 36, Alotau; tel. 6411211; fax 6411324; palm oil production; controlled by New Britain Palm Oil Ltd from mid-2010; Gen. Man. RAJU.V VENGIDDAPPA.

New Britain Palm Oil Ltd (NBPOL): PMB, Kimbe, West New Britain; tel. 9852177; fax 9852178; e-mail info@nbpol.com.pg; internet www.nbpol.com.pg; f. 1967; controlled by Kulim (Malaysia) Bhd; fmrly Ramu Agri-Industries Ltd, fmrly Ramu Sugar Ltd; sugar, beef and oil palm processing; CEO NICK THOMPSON; Sec. HIMSON WANINARA.

Open Bay Timber Pty Ltd: POB 48, Rabaul 611, East New Britain Province; tel. 9821633; fax 9821636; e-mail obtohira@global.net.pg; milled timber, mouldings, scantlings, log and sawn timber export, reafforestation; Gen. Man. TOSHIHARU SHINOHARA; Man. Dir TOSHIFUMI OHIRA.

PNG Forest Products Ltd: POB 88, Bulolo, MP 423; tel. 4745201; fax 4745365; e-mail administration@pngfp.com; internet pngfp.com; plywood, mouldings, milled timber, furniture, kitset buildings; Man. Dir TONY HONEY; c. 1500 employees.

Rimbunan Hijau (PNG) Group: POB 102, Port Moresby, NCD; tel. 3257677; fax 3230522; e-mail pr_dept@rhpng.com.pg; internet www.rhpng.com.pg; subsidiary of Rimbunan Hijau (Malaysia); producer and processor of timber and wood; other interests incl. transport, trading, media and property devt; Gen. Sec. J. K. BALASUBRAMANIAM.

Stettin Bay Lumber Co Pty Ltd: POB 162, Kimbe, West New Britain Province; tel. 9854066; fax 9854028; e-mail ccsia@daltron.com.pg; timber merchants; Man. Dir S. W. LONG.

Miscellaneous

Bishop Bros Engineering Pty Ltd: POB 81, Waigani, Port Moresby NCD; tel. 3252900; fax 3254104; e-mail sales@bishopbros.com.pg; internet www.bishopbros.com.pg; all types of civil engineering; Gen. Man. MARK HIRD.

Buka Metal Fabricators Ltd: POB 224, Buka 335; tel. 9739805; fax 9739163; e-mail info@bukametalfab.com.pg; Dir MATHIAS HORN.

Coconut Products Ltd: POB 94, Rabaul, East New Britain Province; tel. 9839310; fax 9839308; e-mail pjamison@datec.com.pg; internet www.carpenters.com.pg; coconut oil and copra; owned by W. R. Carpenter (PNG) Group of Companies; Gen. Man. G. DOWNS.

Collins and Leahy Holdings Ltd: ANZ House, 2nd Floor, Central Avenue, Lae; tel. 7313204; fax 7322350; f. 1970; became a wholly owned subsidiary of John Swire and Sons (PNG) Ltd in 2000; Chair. Sir MICHAEL BROMLEY; Sec. C. I. CUNNINGHAME.

Hebou Constructions (PNG) Pty Ltd: POB 6207, Boroko, NCD; tel. 3253077; fax 3253441; e-mail reception@hebou.com.pg; internet www.hebou.com.pg; f. 1969; building, civil construction, sand and gravel, timber, hotels; Gen. Man. MITCH LUTSCHINI.

HG Group: POB 828, Waigani, Port Moresby, NCD; tel. 3251503; fax 3258590; internet www.hgconstruction.com.pg; f. 1989; construction, quarrying, property devt.

Hornibrook NGI Pty Ltd: Malaita Street, Lae, Morobe Province, NCD; tel. 4723599; fax 4725083; e-mail hngi@hornibrook.com.pg; internet www.hornibrook.com.pg; civil works and building construction, steel manufacture, pre-fabricated buildings, bridges, tubular fabrications, plant hire; f. 1991; Man. Dir MALCOLM LEWIS.

Pacific Helicopters Ltd: Airport Rd, POB 342, Goroka, Eastern Highlands Province; tel. 7321833; fax 7321503; e-mail enquiries@pacifichelicopters.aero; internet www.pacifichelicopters.aero; f. 1975; helicopter services, hotels, real estate, construction; CEO TERRY PALMER.

Steamships Trading Co Ltd: POB 1, Champion Parade, Port Moresby, NCD 121; tel. 3220222; fax 3213595; internet www.steamships.com.pg; f. 1919; cap. and res 326.8m., sales 465.8m. (2008); hotels, department stores, food and hardware, wholesale and retail; quarrying, manufactures building materials, fibreglass products and UHT products; stevedoring, shipping; road transport, automotive distributors and car rentals; property management; Chair. W. L. ROTHERY; Exec. Dir D. H. COX.

TRADE UNIONS

Papua New Guinea Trade Unions Congress (PNGTUC): POB 4279, Boroko, NCD; tel. 3257642; fax 3257890; e-mail tucl@daltron.com.pg; Pres. MICHAEL MALABAG; Gen. Sec. JOHN PASKA; 52 affiliates, 76,000 mems.

The following are among the major trade unions:

Bougainville Mining Workers' Union: POB 777, Panguna, North Solomons Province; tel. 9958272; Pres. MATHEW TUKAN; Gen. Sec. ALFRED ELISHA TAGORNOM.

Central Province Building and Construction Industry Workers' Union: POB 265, Port Moresby.

Central Province Transport Drivers' and Workers' Union: POB 265, Port Moresby.

Employers' Federation of Papua New Guinea: POB 6057, Boroko, NCD; tel. 3258266; fax 3258272; e-mail information@efpng.org.pg; internet www.efpng.org.pg; f. 1963; Pres. ROBERT DEBROUWERE; Exec. Dir FLORENCE WILLIE.

National Federation of Timber Workers: Madang; f. 1993; Gen. Sec. MATHIAS KENUANGI (acting).

Papua New Guinea Communication Workers' Union: Pres. BOB MAGARU; Gen. Sec. EMMANUEL KAIRU.

Papua New Guinea National Doctors' Association: Pres. Dr BOB DANAYA; 225 mems.

Papua New Guinea Teachers' Association: POB 1027, Waigani, NCD; tel. 3409291; fax 3261514; e-mail pngta@gmail.com; f. 1971; Pres. TOMMY HECKO; Gen. Sec. UGWALUBU MOWANA; 20,049 mems.

Papua New Guinea Waterside Workers' and Seamen's Union: POB 76, Kimbe 621; tel. 9835603; f. 1979; an amalgamation of four unions; Sec. DOUGLAS GADEBO.

Police Association of Papua New Guinea: tel. 3214172; f. 1964; Pres. ROBERT ALI; 4,596 mems.

Port Moresby Council of Trade Unions: POB 265, Boroko, NCD; Gen. Sec. JOHN KOSI.

Port Moresby Miscellaneous Workers' Union: POB 265, Boroko, NCD.

Printing and Kindred Industries Union: Port Moresby.

Public Employees' Association: POB 965, Boroko, NCD; tel. 3252955; fax 3252186; f. 1974; Pres. NAPOLEON LIOSI; Gen. Sec. JACK N. KUTAL; 28,000 mems.

Transport

There are no railways in Papua New Guinea. The capital city, Port Moresby, is not connected by road to other major population centres. Therefore, air and sea travel are of particular importance.

ROADS

In 2000 there were an estimated 19,600 km of roads in Papua New Guinea, of which 3.5% were paved.

National Roads Authority: Lae, Morobe Province; f. 2004; statutory authority; maintains the road network, particularly the Highlands Highway; Chair. ALLAN MCLAY.

SHIPPING

Papua New Guinea has 16 major ports and a coastal fleet of about 300 vessels.

PNG Ports Corporation Ltd: POB 671, Port Moresby, NCD; tel. 3084200; fax 3211546; e-mail business@pngports.com.pg; internet www.pngports.com.pg; CEO BRIAN RICHES.

Port Authority of Kieta: POB 149, Kieta, North Solomons Province; tel. 9956066; fax 9956255; Port Man. CHARLES TARURAVA.

Port Authority of Lae: POB 563, Lae, Morobe Province; tel. 4723464; fax 4723543; Port Man. SAKEUS GEM.

Port Authority of Port Moresby: POB 671, Port Moresby; tel. 211400; fax 3211546; Gen. Man. BEN PUKAI.

Port Authority of Rabaul: POB 592, Rabaul, East New Britain Province; tel. 9821533; fax 9821535; Port Man. JOHN TUNGAPIK.

Shipping Companies

Coastal Shipping Co Ltd: Sulphur Creek Rd, POB 423, Rabaul, East New Britain Province; tel. 9821746; fax 9821734; e-mail coastco@global.net.pg; f. 1967; Man. Dir HENRY CHOW.

Lutheran Shipping: POB 789, Madang; tel. 8522577; fax 8522180; e-mail finance.luship@global.net.pg.

Morehead Shipping Pty Ltd: POB 1908, Lae, Morobe Province; tel. 4423602.

New Guinea Australia Line Pty Ltd: POB 145, Stanley Esplanade, Port Moresby, NCD 121; tel. 3212377; fax 3201825; f. 1952; est. by The China Navigation Co, a fully owned shipping wing of John Swire & Sons (PNG) Ltd; operates regular container services between Australia, Papua New Guinea, Singapore, Indonesia, Vanuatu, Tuvalu and Solomon Islands; Chair. JAMES HUGHES-HALLETT.

P & O Maritime Services (PNG) Ltd: MMI House, 3rd Floor, Champion Parade, POB 1403, Port Moresby; tel. 3229200; fax 3229251; e-mail jhulse@pom.popng.com.pg; owned by P & O (Australia); Country Man. JOHN HULSE.

Papua New Guinea Shipping Corporation Pty Ltd: POB 634, Port Moresby; tel. 3220290; fax 3212815; e-mail shipping@steamships.com.pg; f. 1977; owned by Steamships Trading Co Ltd; provides a container/break-bulk service to Australia and the Pacific islands; Chair. CHRISTOPHER PRATT; Man. Dir JOHN DUNLOP.

South Sea Lines Proprietary Ltd: POB 5, Lae, Morobe Province; tel. 4423455; fax 4424884; Man. Dir R. CUNNINGHAM.

Steamships Trading Co Ltd: Champion Parade, POB 1, Port Moresby; tel. 3220222; fax 3213595; internet www.steamships.com.pg; f. 1924; Chair. W. L. ROTHERY; Man. Dir D. H. COX.

Western Tug & Barge Co P/L: POB 1403, Port Moresby; tel. 3229290; fax 3229251; division of P & O PNG; operates 24 vessels.

CIVIL AVIATION

There is an international airport, Jackson's Airport, at Port Moresby. International services also operate from Lae and Mount Hagen airports. There are more than 400 other airports and airstrips throughout the country. In mid-2011 it was announced that the

Asian Development Bank was to invest US $480m. over eight years to upgrade the country's airports.

Air Niugini: POB 7186, Boroko, NCD; tel. 3259000; fax 3273482; e-mail airniugini@airniugini.com.pg; internet www.airniugini.com.pg; f. 1973; govt-owned national airline; operates scheduled domestic cargo and passenger services within Papua New Guinea and international services to Australia, Fiji, Solomon Islands, Philippines, Hong Kong, Singapore and Japan; fleet comprises 20 aircraft (2010); Chair. JIM TJOENG; CEO WASANTHA KUMARASIRI.

Airlines PNG: POB 170, Boroko, NCD; tel. 3252011; fax 3252219; e-mail apng@apng.com; internet www.apng.com; f. 1984; est. as Milne Bay Air (MBA); operates domestic scheduled and charter services; Chair. SIMON WILD; CEO GARRY TOOMEY.

National Aviation Services: Boroko, NCD; f. 2005; provides services between all small airstrips in Central, Oro, Gulf and Western Provinces, primarily for the transport of agricultural products to markets; Operations Man. GILBERT YENBARI; Propr and CEO TED DIRO.

Tourism

Papua New Guinea's attractions include the tribal customs, spectacular scenery and abundant wildlife. Foreign visitor arrivals reportedly rose from 125,891 in 2009 to 146,928 in 2010. The industry earned an estimated US $3.7m. in 2005.

PNG Tourism Promotion Authority: POB 1291, Port Moresby; tel. 3200211; fax 3200223; e-mail info@pngtourism.org.pg; internet www.pngtourism.org.pg; CEO PETER VINCENT.

Tour Operators Association of Papua New Guinea (TOAPNG): tel. 3200211; fax 3200223; e-mail toapng@pngtourism.org.pg; internet www.toa.org.pg; f. 2005; Pres. MICHAEL BULEAU; Treas. AARON HAYES.

Defence

As assessed at November 2010, the Papua New Guinea Defence Force had a total strength of some 3,100 (army 2,500, navy 400 and air force 200). Military service is voluntary. Australian training forces stationed in the country totalled 38. Government expenditure on defence in 2010 was budgeted at K116m.

Commander-in-Chief of Papua New Guinea Defence Force: Brig.-Gen. FRANCIS WANGI AGWI.

Education

Most education facilities have remained inadequate and unevenly distributed. In August 2011, however, it was announced that from the beginning of 2012 elementary education was to be provided free of charge and that 75% of the cost of higher education was to be subsidized by the Government. In 2005/06 there were 2,790 primary schools, with 532,250 pupils and 14,860 teachers. In 1986 there were 116 secondary schools and 103 technical and vocational schools. Secondary-school pupils totalled 173,214 and the teachers numbered 8,420 in 2002/03. There are two universities.

Children attend school from seven years of age. At the age of 13 they move from community schools to provincial high schools for a further three years and are then eligible to spend another two years at the national high schools, where they are prepared for entrance to tertiary education.

In 2005/06 the total enrolment at primary schools was equivalent to 55% of that school-age population (males 59%; females 50%). In 1995 secondary enrolment was equivalent to only 14% of children in the relevant age-group (boys 17%; girls 11%). In some areas, such as East New Britain and Port Moresby, almost all eligible children attend primary schools, whereas in others, such as the Highlands provinces, attendance is as low as 34%. Access to secondary education ranges from 7% in the Eastern Highlands to almost 50% in East New Britain. In 2007, according to UNESCO estimates, adult literacy averaged 57.8% (males 62.1%; females 53.4%).

Budgetary expenditure on education by the central Government in 2006 totalled an estimated K43m.

SAMOA

Introduction

The Independent State of Samoa (formerly Western Samoa) comprises the two large islands of Savai'i and Upolu and seven small islands, of which five are uninhabited. Their total area is 2,831 sq km (1,093 sq miles). These high volcanic islands, with rugged interiors and little flat land except along the coasts, lie in the South Pacific, about 2,400 km north of New Zealand. The country's nearest neighbour is American Samoa, to the east. The climate is tropical, with temperatures generally between 23°C (73°F) and 30°C (86°F). The rainy season is from November to April.

The islands are populated by Polynesians and are thought to have been the origin of many of the people who now occupy islands further east. The Samoan language is believed to be the oldest extant form of Polynesian speech. Samoan society developed an intricate hierarchy of graded titles comprising titular chiefs and orator chiefs. One of the striking features of modern Samoa is the manner in which these titles and the culture prior to European contact remain a dominant influence. Most of the population have become Christians. At the census of November 2006 the population of Samoa totalled 180,741. About 75% of the population resided on the island of Upolu. The population of Apia, the capital, totalled an estimated 36,433 in mid-2009. According to estimates from the Secretariat of the Pacific Community, in mid-2011 Samoa's population had reached 183,617.

The Samoan islands were first visited by Europeans in the 1700s, but it was not until 1830 that missionaries from the London Missionary Society settled there. The eastern islands (now American Samoa) were ceded to the USA in 1904 but Western Samoa (as it was known until July 1997), a former German colony, was occupied by New Zealand in 1914 and the League of Nations granted a mandate over the territory to New Zealand in 1920. In 1946 the UN assumed responsibility for the Territory of Western Samoa through its Trusteeship Council, with New Zealand as the administering power. From 1954 measures of internal self-government were gradually introduced, culminating in the adoption of an independence Constitution in October 1960. This was approved by a UN-supervised plebiscite in May 1961 and the islands became independent on 1 January 1962. The office of Head of State was to be held jointly by two of the paramount chiefs but, upon the death of his colleague in April 1963, Malietoa Tanumafili II became sole Head of State for life.

Samoa has had a Legislative Assembly (Fono) since 1947. Since independence the islands have been governed under a parliamentary system, with a Prime Minister and Cabinet. Until 1991, only two of the 47 seats in the Fono were decided by universal suffrage, the rest being decided by the Matai (elected clan chiefs). In May 1997 the Prime Minister proposed a constitutional amendment in the Fono to change the country's name to Samoa. (The country has been known simply as Samoa at the UN since it was admitted to the organization in 1976.) On 3 July the Fono voted by 41 votes to one to approve the change, which came into effect on the next day when the legislation was signed by the Head of State. The neighbouring US territory of American Samoa, however, expressed dissatisfaction with the change (which was believed to undermine the Samoan identity of its islands and inhabitants), and in September introduced legislation to prohibit the recognition of the new name within the territory. In March 1998 the House of Representatives in American Samoa voted against legislation that proposed not to recognize Samoan passports (thereby preventing Samoans from travelling to the territory), but decided to continue to refer to the country as Western Samoa and to its inhabitants as Western Samoans.

Samoa maintains strong links with New Zealand, where many Samoans now live and where many others receive their secondary and tertiary education. An appeal against attempts to curb the high level of migration to New Zealand led the Privy Council in London to rule in July 1982 that all Western Samoans born between 1924 and 1949, and their male children, were entitled to New Zealand citizenship. The ruling was estimated to affect about 100,000 Western Samoans. However, in August 1982 the New Zealand and Western Samoan Governments agreed to annul the ruling, declaring in its stead that illegal immigrants already in New Zealand would be allowed to apply for citizenship, and that a quota of 1,100 migrants per year would be accepted into New Zealand.

In June 2002 New Zealand formally apologized for the mistakes it had committed while administering Samoa during 1914–62. These injustices included New Zealand's poor handling of the 1918 influenza pandemic (which had killed 22% of Samoa's population within a fortnight, the virus having been brought in on a ship from New Zealand); the murder of a Samoan paramount chief and independence leader, Tupua Tamasese Lealofi III, and the killing of nine other supporters of the pacifist Mau movement during a non-violent protest in 1929 and the banishment of native leaders, who were also stripped of their chiefly titles. The apology, while accepted, drew mixed reactions from Samoans, many of whom were more concerned with the issue of the restoration of their rights to New Zealand citizenship, as upheld by the Privy Council in 1982. Moreover, in March 2003 large protest marches took place in Samoa and New Zealand demanding the repeal of the 1982 law, which ended Samoans' automatic right to New Zealand citizenship. In May 2004 a parliamentary select committee rejected a 100,000-signature petition seeking a repeal of the law and upheld the principles of the 1982 ruling. In May 2007 the Samoan Head of State, Malietoa Tanumafili II, died at the age of 95. In the following month the Fono elected former Prime Minister Tuiatua Tupua Tamasese Efi as Head of State, for a term of five years.

The principal cash crops are coconuts and taro (the latter also the country's primary staple food). Coconut oil, cream and copra make a significant contribution to the country's exports. (A programme for the generation of electricity from coconut oil commenced in early 2009.) Exports of nonu fruit are also significant. The country's commercial fishing industry expanded considerably in the late 1990s. The manufacturing sector also recorded strong expansion in the early 1990s with the establishment of a Japanese-owned factory, Yazaki EDS Samoa, producing electrical components for road motor vehicles; however, production has been intermittently affected by adverse global factors and concomitant variations in demand. Despite the global downturn of 2008/09, the tourism sector as a whole has continued to perform well, partly owing to an increase in visits by cruise-ships. The economy has also been sustained by remittances from overseas emigrants, although such inflows have been affected by the reduction in job opportunities for Samoans in the USA. The Strategy for the Development of Samoa (2008–12), supported by Australia and New Zealand, placed particular emphasis on the development of the private sector. However, the Samoan economy was seriously disrupted by a major tsunami disaster in September 2009. Subsequent economic growth emanated largely from increased activity in the construction industry, as repairs to infrastructure and tourist accommodation proceeded, along with other rehabilitation projects. As a result of the disaster, Samoa's transition from the UN list of Least Developed Countries to that of Developing Countries was postponed from 2011 to 2014. The transfer of Samoa to the western side of the International Date Line, in a bid to facilitate the conduct of business with Australia and New Zealand, was to take effect at the end of 2011.

The islands are highly vulnerable to natural disasters. The dramatic increase in the incidence of cyclones occurring in the region since the late 20th century has been widely attributed to climatic change caused by the greenhouse effect (the heating of the earth's atmosphere as a consequence of pollution). In January 2004 serious damage to buildings, infrastructure and the agricultural sector was caused by Cyclone Heta. Following the tsunami disaster of September 2009, in which about 150 people were killed, the Samoan Government urged villagers to rebuild their homes on higher ground.

Statistical Survey

Source (unless otherwise indicated): Samoa Bureau of Statistics, Ministry of Finance, Government Building (MFMII), POB 1151, Apia; tel. 24384; fax 24675; e-mail info.stats@sbs.gov.ws; internet www.sbs.gov.ws.

AREA AND POPULATION

Area: Savai'i and adjacent small islands 1,708 sq km; Upolu and adjacent small islands 1,123 sq km; Total 2,831 sq km (1,093 sq miles).

Population: 176,710 at census of 5 November 2001; 180,741 (males 93,677, females 87,064) at census of 5 November 2006. *By Island* (2006 census): Savai'i 43,142; Upolu 137,599 (Apia Urban Area 37,708, North West Upolu 56,122, Rest of Upolu 43,769). *Mid-2011* (Secretariat of the Pacific Community estimate): 183,617 (Source: Pacific Regional Information System).

Density (at mid-2011): 64.7 per sq km.

Population by Age and Sex (Secretariat of the Pacific Community estimates at mid-2011): *0–14:* 69,441 (males 36,165, females 33,276); *15–64:* 104,899 (males 55,073, females 49,825); *65 and over:* 9,277 (males 4,199, females 5,078); *Total* 183,617 (males 95,437, females 88,180) (Source: Pacific Regional Information System).

Principal Towns (population at 2006 census, provisional results): Apia (capital) 37,237 (urban area); Vaitele 6,294; Faleasi'u 3,548; Vailele 3,174; Le'auva'a 3,015. *Mid-2009:* Apia (capital) 36,433 (Source: UN, *World Urbanization Prospects: The 2009 Revision*).

Births, Marriages and Deaths (registrations, 2001): Live births 3,516; Marriages 821; Deaths 339. *2004:* Live births 1,679; Deaths 547. Note: Registration is incomplete. *2005–10* (annual averages, UN estimates): Birth rate 25.9 per 1,000; Death rate 5.5 per 1,000 (Source: UN, *World Population Prospects: The 2010 Revision*).

Life Expectancy (years at birth, WHO estimates): 70 (males 68; females 72) in 2009. Source: WHO, *World Health Statistics*.

Economically Active Population (persons aged 15 years and over, 2006 census): Agriculture, hunting and forestry 17,196; Fishing 1,903; Manufacturing and handicrafts (incl. mining) 10,548; Electricity, gas and water supply 872; Construction 2,476; Wholesale and retail trade; repair of motor vehicles, motorcycles and personal and household goods 3,947; Hotels and restaurants 2,018; Transport, storage and communications 3,255; Financial intermediation 967; Real estate, renting and business activities 472; Public administration and defence; compulsory social security 2,706; Education 2,842; Health and social work 833; Other community, social and personal service activities 2,437; Private households with employed persons 811; Extra-territorial organizations and bodies 279; *Sub-total* 53,562; Activities not adequately defined 366; *Total employed* 53,928 (males 36,478, females 17,450); Unemployed 707 (males 418, females 289); *Total labour force* 54,635 (males 36,896, females 17,739).

HEALTH AND WELFARE

Key Indicators

Total Fertility Rate (children per woman, 2009): 3.9.

Under-5 Mortality Rate (per 1,000 live births, 2009): 25.

Physicians (per 1,000 head, 2003): 0.3.

Hospital Beds (per 1,000 head, 2005): 1.0.

Health Expenditure (2008): US $ per head (PPP): 264.

Health Expenditure (2008): % of GDP: 5.9.

Health Expenditure (2008): public (% of total): 84.7.

Total Carbon Dioxide Emissions ('000 metric tons, 2007): 161.2.

Carbon Dioxide Emissions Per Head (metric tons, 2007): 0.9.

Human Development Index (2007): ranking 94.

Human Development Index (2007): value 0.771.

For sources and definitions, see explanatory note on p. vi.

AGRICULTURE, ETC.

Principal Crops ('000 metric tons, 2009, FAO estimates): Taro 20; Yams 3.0; Other roots and tubers 2.9; Coconuts 155; Bananas 29.0; Papayas 2.9; Pineapples 4.0; Guavas, mangoes and mangosteens 3.8; Avocados 1.2; Other fruits 8.9; Vegetables 1.2; Cocoa beans 0.5.

Livestock ('000 head, year ending September 2009, FAO estimates): Pigs 202; Cattle 30; Horses 1.9; Chickens 620.

Livestock Products (metric tons, 2009, FAO estimates): Cattle meat 1,100; Pig meat 4,500; Chicken meat 594; Cows' milk 1,617; Hen eggs 380; Honey 217.

Forestry ('000 cubic metres, 2006): *Roundwood Removals* (excl. bark): Sawlogs and veneer logs 3; Other industrial roundwood 3; Fuel wood 70; Total 76. *Sawnwood Production* (incl. sleepers): 1. *2006–09* (FAO estimates): Annual output as in 2006.

Fishing (metric tons, live weight, 2009): Albacore 2,805; Yellowfin tuna 412; Other marine fishes 6,239; Marine crustaceans 402; Marine molluscs 2,204; Sea-urchins and other echinoderms 7; Total capture (incl. others) 13,265 (FAO estimate); Aquaculture 5 (FAO estimate); *Total catch* 13,270 (FAO estimate).

Source: FAO.

INDUSTRY

Electric Energy (million kWh): 113.5 in 2006; 119.6 in 2007; 109.9 in 2008. Note: Figures relate only to government-owned power schemes. Source: Treasury Department of Samoa. *2010:* 112 (Source: Asian Development Bank).

FINANCE

Currency and Exchange Rates: 100 sene (cents) = 1 tala (Samoan dollar). *Sterling, US Dollar and Euro Equivalents* (31 May 2011): £1 sterling = 3.732 tala; US $1 = 2.261 tala; €1 = 3.253 tala; 100 tala = £26.80 = US $44.22 = €30.74. *Average Exchange Rate* (tala per US $): 2.6442 in 2008; 2.7308 in 2009; 2.4866 in 2010.

Budget (million tala, year ending 30 June 2006): *Revenue:* Tax revenue 273.1 (Income tax 47.2; Excise tax 69.0; Taxes on international trade 40.9; Value-added gross receipts and services tax 108.6); Other revenue 42.2; Total 315.4, excl. external grants received (71.8). *Expenditure:* Current expenditure 281.9 (General administration 69.5, Law and order 20.2, Education 55.3, Health 47.3, Social security and pensions 14.0, Agriculture 11.7, Public works 29.6, Natural resources 12.4, Other economic services 2.6, Interest on public debt 4.3, Other purposes 29.7, *Less* Value-added gross receipts and services tax payable by government 14.7); Development expenditure 86.1; Total 368.0, excl. net lending (23.7) (Source: IMF, *Samoa: Selected Issues and Statistical Appendix*—June 2007). *2008/09* (million tala): Total revenue 492.0 (Domestic receipts 381.4, External grants 110.7); Total expenditure 552.5 (Domestically financed 358.8). *2009/10* (million tala): Total revenue 525.2 (Domestic receipts 372.4, External grants 152.8); Total expenditure 631.7 (Domestically financed 347.0). (Source: Ministry of Finance, *Quarterly Economic Review*).

International Reserves (US $ million at 31 December 2010): IMF special drawing rights 19.41; Reserve position in IMF 1.07; Foreign exchange 188.97; *Total* 209.45. Source: IMF, *International Financial Statistics*.

Money Supply (million tala at 31 December 2010): Currency outside banks 58.45; Transferable deposits 206.16; Other deposits 490.37.*Broad money* 754.99. Source: IMF, *International Financial Statistics*.

Cost of Living (Consumer Price Index, excluding rent; base: 2005 = 100): All items 122.1 in 2008; 129.9 in 2009; 130.9 in 2010. Source: IMF, *International Financial Statistics*.

Gross Domestic Product (million tala at constant 2002 prices, fiscal year ending 30 June): 1,116.8 in 2007/08; 1,059.8 in 2008/09; 1,059.6 in 2009/10.

Expenditure on the Gross Domestic Product (million tala in current prices, fiscal year ending 30 June 2010): Final consumption expenditure 1,466.8 (Households 1,050.9, Non-profit institutions serving households 69.3, General government 346.6); Gross fixed capital formation 393.1; Changes in inventories 29.7; *Total domestic expenditure* 1,889.6; Exports of goods and services 471.2; *Less* Imports of goods and services 762.6; Statistical discrepancy –151.6; *GDP in market prices* 1,446.6.

Gross Domestic Product by Economic Activity (million tala in current prices, fiscal year ending 30 June 2010): Agriculture and fishing 160.8; Manufacturing 138.8; Electricity, gas and water 73.2; Construction 187.1; Trade 290.8; Hotels and restaurants 50.9; Transport and communications 203.4; Finance and business services 125.8; Public administration 125.5; Ownership of dwellings 48.4; Other services 60.8; *Sub-total* 1,465.5; *Less* Financial intermediation services indirectly measured 18.9; *Total* 1,446.6.

Balance of Payments (US $ million, 2010): Exports of goods f.o.b. 35.07; Imports of goods f.o.b. –280.0; *Trade balance* –244.9; Exports of services 159.9; Imports of services –87.6; *Balance on goods and services* –172.6; Other income received 6.8; Other income paid –25.7; *Balance on goods, services and income* –191.5; Current transfers received 140.7; Current transfers paid –8.1; *Current balance* –58.9; Capital account (net) 85.3; Direct investment from abroad 2.0; Portfolio investment assets –1.7; Portfolio investment liabilities 0.0; Other investments assets –36.0; Other investment liabilities 48.8; Net errors and omissions –15.2; *Overall balance* 24.3. Source: IMF, *International Financial Statistics*.

EXTERNAL TRADE

Principal Commodities (million tala, 2010): *Imports c.i.f.:* Food and live animals 177.8; Crude materials (excl. fuels) 22.1; Mineral fuels, etc. 138.1; Chemicals 48.6; Basic manufactures 129.9; Machinery and transport equipment 189.6; Miscellaneous manufactured articles 64.1; Total (incl. others) 786.4. *Exports (incl. re-exports) f.o.b.:* Food and live animals 22.3; Beverages and tobacco 4.3; Basic manufactures 0.9; Machinery and transport equipment 114.3; Total (incl. others) 151.4.

Principal Trading Partners (million tala, 2010): *Imports:* Australia 153.9; China, People's Republic 48.1; Japan 66.0; New Zealand 241.8; USA 90.2; Total (incl. others) 786.4. *Exports (incl. re-exports):* Australia 116.7; New Zealand 16.5; USA 2.9; Total (incl. others) 151.4.

TRANSPORT

Road Traffic (motor vehicles registered, 2007): Private cars 5,189; Pick-ups 4,136; Taxis 1,916; Trucks 2,375; Buses 251; Motorcycles 104; Tractors 45; Total (incl. others) 16,215.

International Shipping (freight traffic, '000 metric tons, 2009): Goods loaded 207.2; Goods unloaded 45.6. *Merchant Fleet* (at 31 December 2009): Vessels 10; Total displacement ('000 grt) 10.5 (Source: IHS Fairplay, *World Fleet Statistics*).

Civil Aviation (traffic on scheduled services, 2006): Kilometres flown 6 million; Passengers carried 288,000; Passenger-kilometres

384 million; Total ton-kilometres 36 million. Source: UN, *Statistical Yearbook*.

TOURISM

Visitor Arrivals: 122,163 in 2008; 129,238 in 2009; 129,500 in 2010.

Visitor Arrivals by Country (2010): American Samoa 23,737; Australia 23,415; Fiji 2,636; New Zealand 57,837; USA 8,658; Total (incl. others) 129,500.

Tourism Receipts (million tala, incl. passenger transport): 262.5 in 2007; 288.4 in 2008; 304.3 in 2009.

COMMUNICATIONS MEDIA

Telephones (2010): 35,300 main lines in use*.

Personal Computers: 4,200 (23.5 per 1,000 persons) in 2006*.

Internet Users (2009): 9,000*.

Broadband Subscribers (2010): 200*.

Mobile Cellular Telephones (2010): 167,400 subscribers*.

Radio Receivers (1997): 410,000 in use†.

Television Receivers (2001): 26,000 in use*.

Daily Newspapers (2004): 2†.

Non-daily Newspapers (1988): 5 (estimated circulation 23,000)†.

* Source: International Telecommunication Union.
† Source: UNESCO, *Statistical Yearbook*.

EDUCATION

Pre-primary (2008/09): 299 teachers; 4,080 pupils.

Primary (2008/09, unless otherwise indicated): 167 schools (2005); 936 teachers; 29,663 pupils.

Secondary (2008/09): 1,206 teachers; 25,429 pupils.

Universities and other Higher (2001): 140 teachers; 1,179 students.

Source: mainly UNESCO Institute for Statistics.

Pupil-teacher Ratio (primary education, UNESCO estimate): 31.7 in 2008/09. Source: UNESCO Institute for Statistics.

Adult Literacy Rate (UNESCO estimates): 98.8% (males 99.0%; females 98.5%) in 2009. Source: UNESCO Institute for Statistics.

Directory

The Constitution

A new Constitution was adopted by a constitutional convention on 28 October 1960. After being approved by a UN-supervised plebiscite in May 1961, the Constitution came into force on 1 January 1962, when Western Samoa became independent. A constitutional amendment adopted in July 1997 shortened the country's name to Samoa. The main provisions of the Constitution are summarized below:

HEAD OF STATE

The office of Head of State was occupied (from 5 April 1963, when his co-ruler died) by HH Malietoa Tanumafili II, who held this post until his death in May 2007. After that the Head of State was to be elected by the Fono (Legislative Assembly) for a term of five years.

EXECUTIVE

Executive power lies with the Cabinet, consisting of the Prime Minister, supported by the majority in the Fono, and ministers selected by the Prime Minister. Cabinet decisions are subject to review by the Executive Council, which is made up of the Head of State and the Cabinet.

LEGISLATURE

The Fono consists of 49 members. It has a five-year term and the Speaker is elected from among the members. Beginning at the election of 5 April 1991, members are elected by universal adult suffrage: 47 members of the Assembly are elected from among the Matai (elected clan leaders) while the remaining two are selected from non-Samoan candidates.

The Government

HEAD OF STATE

O le Ao o le Malo: TUIATUA TUPUA TAMASESE EFI (elected by the Fono 15 June 2007).

CABINET

(October 2011)

The Government is formed by the Human Rights Protection Party.

Prime Minister and Minister of Foreign Affairs, Trade and Tourism: TUILA'EPA SAILELE MALIELEGAOI.

Deputy Prime Minister and Minister of Commerce, Industry and Labour: FONOTOE PIERRE LAUOFO.

Minister of Women, Community and Social Development: TOLOFUAIVALELEI FALEMOE LEI'ATAUA.

Minister of Police and Prisons: SALA FATA PINATI.

Minister of Works, Transport and Infrastructure: MANU'ALESAGALALA POSALA ENOKATI .

Minister of Natural Resources and Environment: FA'AMOETAULOA FA'ALE TU'UMALI'I.

Minister of Finance: FAUMUINA TIATIA LIUGA.

Minister of Customs and Revenue: TUILOMA PULE LAMEKO.

Minister of Health: Dr TUITAMA TALALELEI TUITAMA.

Minister of Communications and Information Technology: TUISUGALETAUA SOFARA AVEAU.

Minister of Education, Sports and Culture: MAGELE MAUILIU MAGELE.

Minister for Justice and Courts Administration: FIAME NAOMI MATA'AFA.

Minister of Agriculture and Fisheries: LE MAMEA ROPATI.

MINISTRIES

Prime Minister's Department: POB L 1861, Apia; tel. 63222; fax 21339; e-mail presssecretariat@samoa.ws; internet www.govt.ws.

Ministry of Agriculture and Fisheries: POB 1874, Apia; tel. 22561; fax 21865; e-mail tai.matatumua@maf.gov.ws; internet www.maf.gov.ws.

Ministry of Commerce, Industry and Labour: Apia; tel. 20441; fax 20443; e-mail mpal@mcil.gov.ws; internet www.mcil.gov.ws.

Ministry of Communications and Information Technology: Private Bag, Apia; tel. 26117; fax 24671; e-mail mcit@mcit.gov.ws; internet www.mcit.gov.ws.

Ministry of Education, Sports and Culture: POB 1869, Apia; tel. 21911; fax 21917; e-mail samoamesc@lesamoa.net; internet www.mesc.gov.ws.

Ministry of Finance: Private Bag, Apia; tel. 34333; fax 21312; e-mail information@mof.gov.ws; internet www.mof.gov.ws.

Ministry of Foreign Affairs and Trade: POB L 1859, Apia; tel. 21171; fax 21504; e-mail mfat@mfat.gov.ws; internet www.mfat.gov.ws.

Ministry of Health: Private Bag, Apia; tel. 68100; fax 24496; e-mail moh@health.gov.ws; internet www.health.gov.ws.

Ministry of Justice and Courts Administration: POB 49, Apia; tel. 22671; fax 21050; e-mail ceojustice@samoa.ws; internet www.mjca.gov.ws.

Ministry of Natural Resources and Environment: Private Bag, Apia; tel. 23800; fax 23176; e-mail info@mnre.gov.ws; internet www.mnre.gov.ws.

Ministry of Police: Apia; tel. 28055; fax 21319; e-mail anisi.tua@police.gov.ws; internet www.police.gov.ws.

Ministry for Revenue: POB 1877, Apia; tel. 20411; fax 20414; e-mail info_services@revenue.gov.ws; internet www.revenue.gov.ws.

Ministry of Women, Community and Social Development: Private Bag, Apia; tel. 20854; fax 23665; internet www.mwcsd.gov.ws.

Ministry of Works, Transport and Infrastructure: Private Bag, Apia; tel. 21611; fax 21990; e-mail enquiries@mwti.gov.ws; internet www.mwti.gov.ws.

Election Commission

Office of the Electoral Commissioner: POB 219, Apia; tel. 25967; fax 24309; internet www.oec.gov.ws; Electoral Commr TANUVASA ISITOLO LEMISIO.

Legislature

FONO

(Legislative Assembly)

The Assembly has 47 Matai members, representing 41 territorial constituencies, and two individual members. Elections are held every five years. A total of 158 candidates contested the general election of 4 March 2011. The ruling Human Rights Protection Party (HRPP) was returned to office, winning the support of 36 newly elected legislators, including seven independent members of the Fono. In June 2011 four parliamentarians were disqualified. The HRPP won all four by-elections in July, thus maintaining its majority. The Tautua Samoa Party held 12 seats.

Speaker: LA'AULIALEMALIETOA LEUATEA POLATAIVAO FOSI.

Political Organizations

Human Rights Protection Party (HRPP): c/o The Fono, Apia; f. 1979; Western Samoa's first formal political party; Leader TUILA'EPA SAILELE MALIELEGAOI; Gen. Sec. LAULU DAN STANLEY.

The People's Party (TPP): f. 2008; Leader SOLOMONA TOAILOA.

Samoa Christian Party: Leader TUALA TIRESA MALIETOA.

Samoa Democratic United Party (SDUP): POB 1233, Apia; tel. 23543; fax 20536; f. 1988; est. as Samoa National Development Party (SNDP); coalition party comprising Christian Democratic Party (CDP) and several independents; assumed present name after 2001 election, following merger of SNDP and Samoa Independent Party; Leader (vacant); Sec. VALASI TAFITO.

Samoa Progressive Political Party: Leader TOEOLESULUSULU SIUEVA.

Tautua Samoa Party (TSP): Apia; f. 2008; Leader PALUSALUE FAAPO.

Diplomatic Representation

EMBASSIES AND HIGH COMMISSIONS IN SAMOA

Australia: Beach Rd, POB 704, Apia; tel. 23411; fax 23159; internet www.samoa.embassy.gov.au; High Commissioner Dr STEPHEN HENNINGHAM.

China, People's Republic: Private Bag, Vailima, Apia; tel. 22474; fax 21115; e-mail tce@samoa.net; Ambassador ZHAO WEIPING .

New Zealand: Beach Rd, POB 1876, Apia; tel. 21711; fax 20086; e-mail nzhcapia@samoa.ws; High Commissioner NICK HURLEY.

USA: POB 3430, Matafele, Apia; tel. 21631; fax 22030; e-mail AmEmbApia@state.gov; internet samoa.usembassy.gov; Ambassador Dr DAVID HUEBNER (resident in New Zealand).

Judicial System

The Supreme Court, which is composed of six local judges and presided over by the Chief Justice, has full jurisdiction for both criminal and civil cases. Appeals lie with the Court of Appeal, which sits twice a year and is presided over by three overseas judges. The Magistrates' Court was replaced by two District Courts in 1998. The Land and Titles Court has jurisdiction in respect of disputes over land ownership and Samoan titles. It consists of the President and two Samoan judges appointed by the President.

Attorney-General: MING LEUNG WAI.

Chief Justice of the Supreme Court: PATU TIAVA'ASU'E FALEFATU SAPOLU.

President of the Court of Appeal: WILLIAM DAVID BARAGWANATH (non-resident).

District Court Judges: VAEMOA VAAI, TAUILIILI HARRY SCHUSTER.

President of the Land and Titles Court: TAGALOA KERSLAKE.

Religion

Almost all of Samoa's inhabitants profess Christianity.

CHRISTIANITY

Fono a Ekalesia i Samoa (Samoa Council of Churches): POB 574, Apia; f. 1967; four mem. churches; Sec. Rev. EFEPAI KOLIA.

The Anglican Communion

Samoa lies within the diocese of Polynesia, part of the Church of the Province of New Zealand. The Bishop of Polynesia is resident in Fiji, while the Archdeacon of Tonga and Samoa is resident in Tonga.

Anglican Church: POB 16, Apia; tel. 20500; fax 24663; Rev. PETER E. BENTLEY.

The Roman Catholic Church

The islands of Samoa constitute the archdiocese of Samoa-Apia. At 31 December 2007 there were an estimated 40,500 adherents in the country. The Archbishop participates in the Catholic Bishops' Conference of the Pacific, based in Fiji.

Archbishop of Samoa-Apia: Cardinal ALAPATI L. MATA'ELIGA, Archbishop's House, Fetuolemoana, POB 532, Apia; tel. 20400; fax 20402; e-mail archdiocese@samoa.ws.

Other Churches

Church of Jesus Christ of Latter-day Saints (Mormon): Samoa Apia Mission, POB 1621, Apia; tel. 64230; fax 64241; f. 1888; Pres. ALEMA S. FITISEMANU; f. 1888; 65,000 mems.

Congregational Christian Church in Samoa: Tamaligi, POB 468, Apia; tel. 22279; fax 20429; e-mail cccsgsec@lesamoa.net; f. 1830; 100,000 mems; Gen. Sec. Rev. MAONE F. LEAUSA.

Congregational Church of Jesus in Samoa: 505 Borie St, Honolulu, HI 96818, USA; Rev. NAITULI MALEPEAI.

Methodist Church in Samoa (Ekalesia Metotisi i Samoa): POB 1867, Apia; tel. 22283; fax 22203; e-mail afereti@samoa.ws; f. 1828; 37,000 mems; Pres. Rev. TUPU FOLASA, II; Gen. Sec. Rev. ELISAIA TUITOLOVA'A.

Seventh-day Adventist Church: POB 600, Apia; tel. 20451; f. 1895; covers Samoa and American Samoa; 5,000 mems; Pres. Pastor SAMUELU AFAMASAGA; Sec. UILI SOLOFA.

BAHÁ'Í FAITH

National Spiritual Assembly: POB 1117, Apia; tel. 23348; fax 21363; e-mail secretariat@bahaisamoa.ws.

The Press

Newsline: POB 2441, Apia; tel. 24216; fax 23623; twice a week; Editor PIO SIOA.

Samoa News: POB 1160, Apia; daily; merged with the weekly *Samoa Times* (f. 1967) in Sept. 1994; Publr RHONA ANNESLEY.

The Samoa Observer: POB 1572, Apia; tel. 21099; fax 21195; e-mail samoaobserver@yahoo.com; internet www.samoaobserver.ws; f. 1979; 5 a week; independent; English and Samoan; also publ. in New Zealand twice a week; Editor-in-Chief SAVEA SANO MALIFA; Editor KENI LESA; circ. 4,500.

Samoa Weekly: Saleufi, Apia; f. 1977; weekly; independent; bilingual; Editor LANCE POLU; circ. 4,000.

Savali: POB L 1861, Apia; tel. 26938; fax 21339; e-mail savalinews@samoa.ws; publ. of Lands and Titles Court; monthly; govt-owned; Samoan edn f. 1904; Editor FALESEU L. FUA; circ. 6,000; English edn f. 1977; circ. 500; bilingual commercial edn f. 1993; circ. 1,500; Editor TUPUOLA TERRY TAVITA.

South Seas Star: POB 800, Apia; tel. 23684; weekly.

PRESS ASSOCIATION

Journalists' Association of Samoa (JAWS): Apia; tel. 7773776; e-mail jawsexec@yahoo.com; internet jawsamoa.blogspot.com; f. 1980; Pres. UALE PAPALII TAIMALELAGI.

Broadcasting and Communications

TELECOMMUNICATIONS

Digicel Samoa Ltd: Vaimea, Apia; fax 28005; e-mail customercaresamoa@digicelgroup.com; internet www.digicelsamoa.com; f. 2006; est. following acquisition of Telecom Samoa by Digicel Group; 90% owned by Digicel Group, 10% govt-owned; CEO PEPE CHRISTIAN FRUEAN.

SamoaTel: Maluafou, Private Bag, Apia; tel. 67846; fax 24000; internet www.samoatel.ws; corporatized in 1999; in process of privatization in 2011; 70% stake sold to Blue Sky (American Samoa) in Jan; telecommunications and postal services provider; Chair. Rev. IUTISONE SALEVAO; CEO MIKE JOHNSTONE.

Samoa.ws: Lotemau Centre, Apia; tel. 20926; e-mail helpdesk@samoa.ws; internet www.samoa.ws; locally owned internet service provider.

BROADCASTING

Radio and Television

Samoa Broadcasting Corpn: Apia; tel. 21420; fax 21072; f. 1948; govt-controlled, with commercial sponsorship; operates SBC Radio 1 and SBC Television 1; CEO FAIASEA LEI SAM MATAFEO.

Graceland Broadcasting Network: POB 3444, Apia; tel. 20197; fax 25487; e-mail gbn@lesamoa.net; internet www.welcome.to/gbn; f. 1992; telecommunications, television and radio.

Magik 98 FM: POB 762, Apia; tel. 25149; fax 25147; e-mail magic98fm@samoa.net; f. 1989; privately owned; operates on FM wavelengths 98.1 and 99.9 MHz; Man. COREY KEIL.

Star Television: Apia; f. 2009; Man. Dir APULU LANCE POLU.

Finance

(cap. = capital; res = reserves; dep. = deposits; m. = million; brs = branches; amounts in tala, unless otherwise indicated)

BANKING

Central Bank

Central Bank of Samoa: Private Bag, Apia; tel. 34100; fax 20293; e-mail centralbank@cbs.gov.ws; internet www.cbs.gov.ws; f. 1984; cap. 10.0m., res 18.0m. (Nov. 2009); Gov. ATELINA EMMA ENARI.

Commercial Banks

ANZ Bank (Samoa) Ltd: Beach Rd, POB L 1885, Apia; tel. 69999; fax 69972; e-mail samoa@anz.com; internet www.anz.com/samoa; f. 1959; est. as Bank of Western Samoa, name changed 1997; 100% owned by ANZ Funds Pty Ltd; cap. 1.5m., res 28.4m., dep. 246.1m. (Sept. 2001); CEO STEPHEN ROGERS; 1 br.

National Bank of Samoa: ACB Bldg, 1st Floor, Beach Rd, Apia 00685; tel. 26766; fax 23477; internet www.nbs.ws; f. 1995; owned by consortium of private interests in Samoa, American Samoa and the USA; Chair. SALA EPA TUIOTI; CEO MALCOLM JOHNSTON; 15 agencies; 5 brs.

Samoa Commercial Bank: POB L 602, Apia; tel. 31233; fax 30250; e-mail info@scbl.ws; internet www.scbl.ws; f. 2003; CEO RAY AH LIKI.

Westpac Bank Samoa Ltd: Beach Rd, POB 1860, Apia; tel. 20000; fax 22848; e-mail westpacsamoa@westpac.com.au; internet www.westpac.com.ws; f. 1977; est. as Pacific Commercial Bank Ltd, current name adopted 2001; first independent bank; 93.5% owned by Westpac Banking Corpn (Australia); cap. 1.2m., res 1.1m., dep. 215.7m. (Sept. 2009); Chair. ALAN WALTER; Gen. Man. JASON GREEN; 3 brs.

Development Bank

Development Bank of Samoa: POB 1232, Apia; tel. 22861; fax 23888; e-mail dbs@dbsamoa.ws; internet www.dbsamoa.ws; f. 1974; est. by Govt to foster economic and social development; Chair. TUPAIMATUNA LULAI LAVEA; CEO TUIASAU SAUMANI WONGSIN.

INSURANCE

National Pacific Insurance Ltd: DBS Bldg, Level 5, Beach Rd, Apia; tel. 20481; fax 23374; e-mail NationalPacificInsurance@npisamoa.ws; internet www.nationalpacificinsurance.com; f. 1977; Gen. Man. DARRYL WILLIAMSON.

Progressive Insurance Company: POB 620, Lotemau Centre, Apia; tel. 26110; fax 26112; e-mail progins@samoa.ws; f. 1993; Gen. Man. I. O. FILEMU.

Samoa Life Assurance Corporation: POB 494, Apia; tel. 23360; fax 23024; e-mail info@samoalife.ws; internet www.samoalife.ws; f. 1977; Gen. Man. A. S. CHAN TING.

Trade and Industry

CHAMBER OF COMMERCE

Samoa Chamber of Commerce and Industry: Le Sanalele Complex, 1st Floor, Saleufi, POB 2014, Apia; tel. 31090; fax 31089; e-mail chamber@samoa.ws; internet www.samoachamber.ws; f. 1938; represents the interests of the private sector; Pres. NAMULAUULU SAMI LEOTA.

INDUSTRIAL AND TRADE ASSOCIATIONS

Samoa Coconut Products: Apia.

Samoa Forest Corporation: Apia.

UTILITIES

Electricity

Electric Power Corporation: POB 2011, Apia; tel. 65246; fax 23748; e-mail fepuleait@epc.ws; internet www.epc.ws; f. 1972; autonomous govt-owned corpn; part of Public Works Dept, known as Electric Power Scheme, until 1972; Gen. Man. MUAAUSA JOSEPH WALTER.

Water

Samoa Water Authority: POB 245, Apia; tel. 20409; fax 21298; e-mail taputoa@swa.gov.ws; internet www.swa.gov.ws; Chair. AFIOGA TUISUGALETAUA AVEAU SOFARA AVEAU.

MAJOR COMPANIES

Alexar Corp Ltd: Carruthers Bldg, Beach Rd, POB 1882, Apia; tel. 29357; fax 21416; e-mail info@alexar.com; internet www.alexar.com; personnel, property, finance, e-commerce services; Chair. KOLONE VAAI.

CCK Trading Ltd: POB 3043, Apia; tel. 24467; fax 24447; e-mail cck@lesamoa.net; internet www.ccksamoa.ws; f. 1985; leading producer and exporter of nonu products, retailer of clothing, travel goods and jewellery and car hire provider; Man. Dir KENNETH NEWTON; c. 80 employees.

Le Vai Ltd: POB 2091, Apia; tel. 20779; fax 23881; e-mail levai@ipasifika.net; internet www.levaisamoa.com; f. 1994; suppliers of purified water; Dir FATIMA STRICKLAND.

Samoa Breweries Ltd: POB 3015, Apia; tel. 20200; fax 22929; e-mail fomai@vailima.ws; internet www.vailima.ws; f. 1978; govt-private jt ownership; produces and bottles alcoholic and non-alcoholic drinks; Gen. Man. LEI SAM FOMAI.

Wilex CCP Ltd: Apia; tel. 23377; fax 24518; e-mail wilex@wilex.ws; operates chocolate factory; Gen. Man. EDDIE WILSON.

Yazaki EDS Samoa Ltd: Apia; tel. 65200; fax 25075; e-mail oliva-vaai@yazaki.ws; f. 1995; facility of Australian Arrow Pty Ltd (AAPL), wholly owned subsidiary of Yazaki Corpn (Japan); manufacturers of automotive components; Gen. Man. FUNEFEAI OLIVA VA'AI; 950 employees.

TRADE UNIONS

Samoa Association of Manufacturers and Exporters (SAME): POB 3428, Apia; tel. 23377; fax 26895; e-mail info@same.org.ws; internet www.same.ws; f. 1981; Pres. EDDIE WILSON.

Samoa Nurses' Association (SNA): POB 3491, Apia; tel. 24439; fax 26976; e-mail sna@lesamoa.ne; internet www.samoanursing.ws; Pres. FAAMANATU NIELSEN; 252 mems.

Samoa Trade Union Congress (STUC): POB 1515, Apia; tel. 24134; fax 20014; f. 1981; affiliate of ITUC; Pres. FALEFATA TUANIU PETAIA; Dir MATAFEO R. MATAFEO; 5,000 mems.

Transport

Public Works Department: Private Bag, Apia; tel. 20865; fax 21927; e-mail pwdir@lesamoa.net; Dir of Works ISIKUKI PUNIVALU.

ROADS

In 1999 there were 790 km of roads on the islands, of which some 42% were paved. In 2004 the Government announced a programme of road-building, including new roads from Apia to the airport and to the inter-island wharves.

SHIPPING

There are deep-water wharves at Apia and Asau. Regular cargo services link Samoa with Australia, New Zealand, American Samoa, Fiji, New Caledonia, Solomon Islands, Tonga, US Pacific coast ports and various ports in Europe.

Samoa Ports Authority: POB 2279, Apia; tel. 64400; fax 25870; e-mail spa@spasamoa.ws; internet www.spasamoa.ws; f. 1999; Gen. Man. TOLEAFOA ELON BETHAM.

Samoa Shipping Corporation Ltd: Private Bag, Shipping House Matautu-tai, Apia; tel. 20935; fax 22352; e-mail info@samoashipping.com; internet www.samoashipping.com; Man. Dir PAPALI'I WILLIE NANSEN.

Samoa Shipping Services Ltd: POB 1884, Apia; tel. 20790; fax 20026; e-mail sss@lesamoa.net; internet www.sssl.ws.

CIVIL AVIATION

There is an international airport at Faleolo, about 35 km from Apia, and an airstrip at Fagali'i, 4 km east of Apia Wharf, which receives light aircraft from American Samoa.

Polynesian Blue: internet www.polynesianblue.com; f. 2005; 49% owned by the Samoan Govt, 49% owned by Virgin Blue, 2% owned by independent Samoan shareholder; flies between Samoa, Australia and New Zealand; replaced the services of Polynesian Airlines upon that carrier's cessation of international operations in 2005; CEO JOHN BARTLETT.

Polynesian Ltd: SNPF Bldg, 2nd Floor, Beach Rd, POB 599, Apia; tel. 21261; fax 20023; e-mail enquiries@polynesianairlines.com; internet www.polynesianairlines.com; f. 1959; 100% govt-owned; operates service to American Samoa and offers charter services between the islands of Upolu and Savai'i; Chair. TUILA'EPA SAILELE MALIELEGAOI; CEO TAUA FATU TIELU.

Tourism

The principal attractions are the scenery and the pleasant climate. Samoa has traditionally maintained a cautious attitude towards tourism, fearing that the Samoan way of life might be disrupted by an influx of foreign visitors. Tourist arrivals were reported to have risen from 122,163 in 2008 to 128,804 in 2009, partly owing to an increase in cruise-ship visits, rising to an estimated 129,487 in 2010. Most visitors come from New Zealand, American Samoa, Australia and the USA. Tourist receipts (including passenger transport) totalled an estimated 304.3m. tala in 2009.

Samoa Tourism Authority: POB 2272, Apia; tel. 63500; fax 20886; e-mail info@samoa.travel; internet www.samoa.travel; f. 1986; CEO MATATAMALI'I SONJA HUNTER.

Samoa Hotel Association: POB 3973, Apia; tel. 30160; fax 30161; e-mail info@samoa-hotels.ws; internet www.samoa-hotels.ws; f. 1999; owned by Asscn of Accommodation Providers; Pres. STEVE YOUNG.

Defence

In August 1962 Western Samoa (as it was then known) and New Zealand signed a Treaty of Friendship, whereby the New Zealand Government, on request, acts as the sole agent of the Samoan Government in its dealings with other countries and international organizations. In April 2009 Samoa and Australia renewed a bilateral programme of defence co-operation. In the year ending June 2008 expenditure on defence amounted to 26.8m. tala (equivalent to 7.0% of total budgetary expenditure).

Education

The education system is divided into pre-primary, primary, intermediate and secondary and is based on the New Zealand system. In 2008/09 there were 4,080 pupils at pre-primary schools and 29,663 pupils at primary schools. In the same year 25,429 pupils were undergoing secondary-level education. Teaching staff at primary level numbered 936 in 2008/09; in the same year there were 299 pre-primary teachers and 1,206 secondary-school teachers. There are also a trades training institute, a teacher-training college and a college for tropical agriculture. About 99% of the adult population are literate. The National University of Samoa was founded in 1988, and had an initial intake of 328 students. By 2001 some 1,179 students were enrolled in university and other higher education. Samoa joined other governments in the region in establishing the University of the South Pacific, based in Fiji, in 1977. Current government expenditure on education in the year ending 30 June 2008 was an estimated 106.1m. tala (27.7% of total current expenditure). With support from Australia and New Zealand, the Government was in the process of implementing a programme of free education in 2009/10.

SOLOMON ISLANDS

Introduction

Solomon Islands is a scattered Melanesian archipelago covering a land area of 27,556 sq km (10,639 sq miles) in the south-western Pacific Ocean, east of Papua New Guinea and north of Vanuatu. The country includes most of the Solomon Islands (those to the north-west being part of Papua New Guinea), Ontong Java Islands (Lord Howe Atoll), Rennell Island and the Santa Cruz Islands, about 500 km to the east. There are 21 large islands and numerous small ones. The principal islands, all in the main group, are Choiseul, Santa Isabel (Boghotu), New Georgia, Malaita, Guadalcanal and San Cristobal (Makira). The climate is equatorial, with small seasonal variations governed by the trade winds. Much of the country is mountainous and of volcanic origin, with steep terrain which remains under dense tropical rain forest; extensive tracts of native and introduced grassland cover the northern plains of Guadalcanal. The smaller islands are mainly coralline.

Most of the population are Melanesian, and they speak about 80 dialects and languages. Pidgin English (Pijin—much of the vocabulary is derived from standard English, but used in a Melanesian grammatical form and with different intonations) is the lingua franca and is widely understood, but standard English is the official language. Solomon Islands has an extremely high rate of population growth, which averaged an annual rate of 2.6% in 2000–09. In mid-2011 the population was officially estimated at 553,254. The capital is Honiara, on the island of Guadalcanal.

The Solomon Islands were named by a Spanish navigator, Alvaro de Mendaña, in 1568. In the 19th century traders, whalers and missionaries began to establish outposts on the main islands. Forcible recruiting of labour ('blackbirding') spread from the New Hebrides (now Vanuatu) to the Solomon Islands during the 1860s. The northern Solomon Islands became a German Protectorate in 1885 and the southern Solomons a British Protectorate in 1893. Rennell Island and the Santa Cruz Islands were added to the British Protectorate in 1898 and 1899. Germany ceded most of the northern Solomons and Ontong Java Islands to the United Kingdom between 1898 and 1900. The whole territory, known as the British Solomon Islands Protectorate, was placed under the jurisdiction of the Western Pacific High Commission (WPHC), with its headquarters in Fiji. The High Commissioner for the Western Pacific was represented locally by a Resident Commissioner.

The Solomon Islands were invaded by Japan in 1942 but, after a fierce battle on Guadalcanal, most of the islands were recaptured by US forces in 1943. After the Second World War the Protectorate's capital was moved from Tulagi, on Ngella (Florida Islands), to Honiara, on Guadalcanal, which was near to a major wartime airfield. In January 1953 the headquarters of the WPHC also moved to Honiara. Meanwhile, elected local councils were established on most of the islands and by 1966 almost the whole territory was covered by such councils. The introduction of responsible local government was initially prompted by the challenge of the Maa'sina (brotherhood) Ruru movement, also known by the anglicized form 'Marching Rule'. This originated in Malaita in 1927, but grew during and after the Second World War. It favoured strictly controlled, custom-based communities living in large villages and practising a communal agricultural economy, and opposed close co-operation with the colonial administration or the dominant churches. The WPHC at first attempted to accommodate the movement, but its influence continued to spread and its suppression took place between 1948 and 1950.

Under a new Constitution, introduced in October 1960, a Legislative Council and an Executive Council were established for the Protectorate's central administration. Initially, all members of both bodies were appointed but from 1964 the Legislative Council included elected members, and the elective element was gradually increased as successive legislative and administrative bodies were created by new Constitutions in March 1970 and April 1974. The Constitution of April 1974 instituted a single Legislative Assembly with 24 members who chose a Chief Minister with the right to appoint his own Council of Ministers. A new office of Governor of the Protectorate was also created to assume almost all the functions previously exercised in the territory by the High Commissioner for the Western Pacific. Solomon Mamaloni, leader of the newly founded People's Progressive Party (PPP), was appointed the first Chief Minister in August 1974. The territory was officially renamed the Solomon Islands in June 1975, although it retained protectorate status.

In January 1976 the Solomon Islands received internal self-government, with the Chief Minister presiding over the Council of Ministers in place of the Governor. In June elections were held for an enlarged Legislative Assembly and in July the Assembly elected one of its new members, Peter (later Sir Peter) Kenilorea, to the position of Chief Minister. Following a constitutional conference in London in September 1977, Solomon Islands (as it was restyled) became an independent state, within the Commonwealth, on 7 July 1978. The Legislative Assembly became the National Parliament and designated Kenilorea the first Prime Minister.

From the late 1990s ethnic tensions, mainly between the inhabitants of Guadalcanal and Malaita provinces, resulted in increasing unrest in Honiara. The alienation of land by the Government since independence and the financial burden imposed upon Guadalcanal by its hosting of the capital had led to widespread resentment. A protracted campaign of militancy to force the Government to relocate the capital ensued. In October 2000 a peace treaty was signed by two of the rebel movements, the Solomon Islands Government and the Provincial Governments of Malaita and Guadalcanal. The two provinces were to be granted a greater degree of administrative autonomy, and Malaita Province was to receive additional funding to reflect the demands placed on it by the influx of 20,000 displaced persons from Guadalcanal. The country's precarious peace process suffered a major reversal in February 2003 when a leading member of the National Peace Council, Sir Frederick Soaki, was assassinated. In July 2003, following a serious deterioration in the situation, an Australian-led regional intervention force, the Regional Assistance Mission to Solomon Islands (RAMSI) as it became known, was deployed in the country to restore law and order. Meanwhile, housing and welfare payments to displaced victims of the Guadalcanal unrest had placed a serious strain on the country's economy.

In April 2006 the appointment of Snyder Rini as Prime Minister led to widespread protests, culminating in two days of the most serious rioting witnessed in the country for many years. The country's management of Taiwanese financial aid (a source of much controversy and a major factor in the downfall of Rini) subsequently came under increasing scrutiny. During an official visit to Solomon Islands in March 2010 Taiwanese President Ma Ying-jeou reportedly commented that misuse of aid was unacceptable. The islands' Prime Minister subsequently confirmed that greater transparency in relation to Taiwanese funding would be required.

In April 2009 the Government officially established the Solomon Islands Truth and Reconciliation Commission. The panel was charged with investigating the causes of the violent conflict in Guadalcanal that occurred between 1997 and 2003. Also in April 2009, an official report into the 2006 riots found the Royal Solomon Islands Police responsible for the violence, owing to incompetence and a failure properly to fulfil its duty. However, the report concluded that there was no conspiracy connected to the violence. Public hearings by the Solomon Islands Truth and Reconciliation Commission commenced in March 2010, when victims of the ethnic conflict gave their testimonies.

The destruction of numerous local businesses (owned predominantly by Chinese entrepreneurs) in the rioting of 2006 was a major deterrent to potential investors in Solomon Islands. Economic development has also been impeded by the inadequacy of transport facilities, inclement weather and by fluctuations in prices on the international market for the major agricultural exports, such as copra and cocoa, as well as for round logs. The islands depend for much of their export revenue on the controversial logging industry. Environmental concerns over the exploitation of the country's natural resources by unscrupulous foreign operators have increased. In April 2008 the new Government announced various measures to counter the detrimental impact on the nation's forests. Henceforth all companies, including those engaged in the mining and agricultural sectors, were to be required to obtain a public environment report prior to commencing operations. A report issued in April 2010 described numerous illegal practices perpetrated with impunity by logging companies, together with corruption, social problems and conflict among traditional landowning communities as a result of the companies' activities. Meanwhile, in March the National Parliament adopted legislation on establishing protected areas and conserving biodiversity in Solomon Islands' remaining areas of forest and elsewhere. In March 2011 the Government stated that it would further promote the replacement of the natural forest with the establishment of plantations (by both smallholders and by the large-scale logging companies) in an effort to counterbalance the excessive deforestation activities. Various mineral resources have been identified. In March 2010 the Australian-owned Gold Ridge gold mine, on Guadalcanal, which had been forced by ethnic unrest to close 10 years previously, was formally reopened following a ceremony of reconciliation among local land-owning communities; the resumption of the mine's operations in early 2011 was expected to make a major contribution to the country's economy. The Government's budget for 2011 emphasized the need for clarification of the complex land tenure system, in an attempt to attract greater investment in Solomon Islands.

Statistical Survey

Source (unless otherwise indicated): National Statistics Office, Ministry of Finance, P.O. Box G6, Honiara; tel. (677) 27835; fax (677) 23951; e-mail Stats_management@mof.gov.sb; internet www.spc.int/prism/country/sb/stats.

AREA AND POPULATION

Area: 27,556 sq km (10,639 sq miles).

Population: 409,042 (males 211,381, females 197,661) at census of 21–22 November 1999; 515,870 at census of 21–22 November 2009. *Mid-2011* (Secretariat of the Pacific Community estimate): 553,254 (males 286,578, females 266,676) (Source: Pacific Regional Information System).

Density (mid-2011): 20.1 per sq km.

Population by Age and Sex (Secretariat of the Pacific Community estimates at mid-2011): *0–14:* 218,420 (males 113,692, females 104,728); *15–64:* 316,148 (males 163,178, females 152,970); *65 and over:* 18,686 (males 9,708, females 8,978); *Total* 553,254 (males 286,578, females 266,676) (Source: Pacific Regional Information System).

Ethnic Groups (census of November 1986): Melanesians 268,536; Polynesians 10,661; Micronesians 3,929; Europeans 1,107; Chinese 379; Others 564.

Principal Towns (population at 1999 census): Honiara (capital) 49,107; Noro 3,482; Gizo 2,960 (Source: Thomas Brinkhoff, *City Population*—internet www.citypopulation.de). *Mid-2009* (incl. suburbs, UN estimate) Honiara 71,921 (Source: UN, *World Urbanization Prospects: The 2009 Revision*).

Births and Deaths (annual averages, 2005–10, UN estimates): Birth rate 33.3 per 1,000; Death rate 6.2 per 1,000 (Source: UN, *World Population Prospects: The 2010 Revision*).

Life Expectancy (years at birth, WHO estimates): 71 (males 69; females 72) in 2009. Source: WHO, *World Health Statistics*.

Employment (excluding informal sector, 2004, estimates): Agriculture 6,342; Forestry 3,482; Fishing 5,114; Manufacturing (incl. mining and quarrying) 1,476; Electricity and water 469; Construction 1,397; Trade, restaurants and hotels 3,274; Transport, storage and communications 1,246; Finance, insurance, real estate and business services 806; Administration 6,758; Other community, social and personal service activities 21,757; *Total* 52,121. *2006* (excluding informal sector, estimate): Total employed 59,161. Source: IMF, *Solomon Islands: Tax summary and Statistical Appendix* (November 2008).

HEALTH AND WELFARE

Key Indicators

Total Fertility Rate (children per woman, 2009): 3.8.

Under-5 Mortality Rate (per 1,000 live births, 2009): 36.

Physicians (per 1,000 head, 2003): 0.1.

Hospital Beds (per 1,000 head, 2005): 1.5.

Health Expenditure (2008): US $ per head (PPP): 139.

Health Expenditure (2008): % of GDP: 5.3.

Health Expenditure (2008): public (% of total): 93.4.

Access to Water (% of persons, 2006): 70.

Access to Sanitation (% of persons, 2006): 32.

Total Carbon Dioxide Emissions ('000 metric tons, 2007): 197.9.

Carbon Dioxide Emissions Per Head (metric tons, 2007): 0.4.

Human Development Index (2010): ranking: 123.

Human Development Index (2010): value: 0.494.

For sources and definitions, see explanatory note on p. vi.

AGRICULTURE, ETC.

Principal Crops ('000 metric tons, 2009, FAO estimates): Coconuts 384 (unofficial figure); Oil palm fruit 190; Rice, paddy 4.4; Cocoa beans 4.7; Sweet potatoes 80; Yams 27; Taro 48; Vegetables (incl. melons) 8.2; Fruits (excl. melons) 30.6.

Livestock ('000 head, year ending September 2009, FAO estimates): Cattle 14.5; Pigs 54; Chickens 235.

Livestock Products (metric tons, 2009, FAO estimates): Cattle meat 740; Pig meat 2,320; Chicken meat 280; Hen eggs 488; Cows' milk 1,425.

Forestry ('000 cu m, 2009): *Roundwood Removals* (excl. bark): Sawlogs and veneer logs 1,233 (FAO estimate); Fuel wood 127 (FAO estimate); Total 1,360. *Sawnwood Production:* 27 (FAO estimate, all broadleaved, incl. railway sleepers).

Fishing (metric tons, live weight, 2009): Skipjack tuna 9,557; Yellowfin tuna 8,133; Bigeye tuna 193; Total catch (incl. others): 27,938 (FAO estimate). Note: Figures exclude FAO estimates of capture data for trochus shells (18 metric tons) and of aquaculture data for aquatic plants (150 metric tons).

Source: FAO.

MINING

Production (kilograms, 2006): Gold 10. Source: US Geological Survey.

INDUSTRY

Production (metric tons, 2007, unless otherwise indicated): Copra 28,000; Coconut oil 741,000; Palm oil 22,000; Electric energy 79 million kWh (2010). Source: Asian Development Bank.

FINANCE

Currency and Exchange Rates: 100 cents = 1 Solomon Islands dollar (SI $). *Sterling, US Dollar and Euro Equivalents* (31 May 2011): £1 sterling = SI $12.944; US $1 = SI $7.84; €1 = SI $11.282; SI $100 = £7.73 = US $12.75 = €8.86. *Average Exchange Rate* (SI $ per US $): 7.7479 in 2008; 8.0550 in 2009; 8.0645 in 2010.

Budget (SI $ million, 2010): *Revenue:* Taxes 1,603.1; Non-tax revenue 140.4; Grants 518.1; Total 2,261.6. *Expenditure:* Total 1,871.9 (Current expenditure 1,515.3, Capital expenditure 356.6). Source: Asian Development Bank.

Official Development Assistance (US $ million, 2000): Bilateral 22.1; Multilateral 46.3; Total 68.4 (Grants 69.7, Loans –1.3). *2007:* Total 246.1. Source: UN, *Statistical Yearbook for Asia and the Pacific*.

International Reserves (excl. gold, US $ million at 31 December 2010): IMF special drawing rights 14.26; Reserve position in IMF 0.85; Foreign exchange 250.73; *Total* 265.84. Source: IMF, *International Financial Statistics*.

Money Supply (SI $ million at 31 December 2010): Currency outside depository corporations 411.83; Transferable deposits 891.97; Other deposits 770.81; *Broad money* 2,074.62. Source: IMF, *International Financial Statistics*.

Cost of Living (Consumer Price Index for Honiara, average of quarterly figures; base: October–December 1992 = 100): 433.0 in 2008; 463.8 in 2009; 468.2 in 2010. Source: Asian Development Bank.

Gross Domestic Product (SI $ million at constant 2005 prices): 372.5 in 2007; 399.8 in 2008; 391.1 in 2009. Source: UN Statistics Division, National Accounts Main Aggregates Database.

Expenditure on the Gross Domestic Product (SI $ million at current prices, 2009): Government final consumption expenditure 2,117.4; Private final consumption expenditure 4,254.9; Changes in inventories 72.3; Gross fixed capital formation 727.9; *Total domestic expenditure* 7,172.5; Exports of goods and services 2,004.1; *Less* Imports of goods and services 3,127.2; Statistical discrepancy –295.7; *GDP in purchasers' values* 5,753.7. Source: UN Statistics Division, National Accounts Main Aggregates Database.

Gross Domestic Product by Economic Activity (SI $ million at current prices, 2009): Agriculture, hunting, forestry and fishing 2,012.4; Mining, manufacturing and utilities 384.7 (Manufacturing 298.7); Construction 38.9; Trade, restaurants and hotels 780.5; Transport, storage and communications 536.8; Other services 1,893.5; *Gross value added* 5,646.8; Net taxes on products 106.9 (obtained as residual); *GDP in market prices* 5,753.7. Source: UN Statistics Division, National Accounts Main Aggregates Database.

Balance of Payments (US $ million, 2009): Exports of goods f.o.b. 163.42; Imports of goods f.o.b. –239.19; *Trade balance* –75.78; Exports of services 72.48; Imports of services –98.92; *Balance on goods and services* –102.22; Other income received 12.91; Other income paid –138.12; *Balance on goods, services and income* –227.42; Current transfers received 31.80; Current transfers paid –12.28; *Current balance* –207.90; Capital account (net) 27.09; Direct investment abroad –2.98; Direct investment from abroad 117.65; Other investments assets 13.88; Other investment liabilities 14.90; Net errors and omissions 6.52; *Overall balance* –30.85. Source: IMF, *International Finance Statistics*.

EXTERNAL TRADE

Principal Commodities (SI $ '000, 2007): *Imports c.i.f.:* Food and live animals 231,381; Mineral fuels, etc. 434,324; Basic manufactures 95,429; Machinery and transport equipment 206,847; Total (incl. others) 1,836,334. *Exports f.o.b.:* Fish 151,392; Copra 36,768; Palm oil 105,281; Timber 838,693; Cocoa 70,838; Total (incl. others) 1,285,651.

Principal Trading Partners (US $ million, 2010): *Imports:* Australia 115.3; China, People's Republic 31.3; Fiji 13.8; India 1.1; Japan 13.2; Malaysia 13.3; New Zealand 24.2; Papua New Guinea 13.5; Singapore 86.1; Thailand 7.7; Total (incl. others) 387.2. *Exports:* Australia 5.0; China, People's Republic 260.9; Italy 14.2; Japan 8.5; Korea, Republic 11.9; Malaysia 5.0; Philippines 5.6; Spain 9.1; Thailand 14.8; Total (incl. others) 420.0. Note: Data reflect the IMF's direction of trade methodology and, as a result, the totals may not be equal to those presented for trade in commodities.

Source: Asian Development Bank.

TRANSPORT

Road Traffic (motor vehicles in use at 30 June 1986): Passenger cars 1,350; Commercial vehicles 2,026.

Shipping: *Traffic* (international traffic, '000 metric tons, 1990): Goods loaded 278; Goods unloaded 349 (Source: UN, *Monthly Bulletin of Statistics*). *Merchant Fleet* (registered at 31 December 2009): Vessels 38; Total displacement ('000 grt) 12.9 (Source: IHS Fairplay, *World Fleet Statistics*).

Civil Aviation (traffic on scheduled services, 2006): Kilometres flown 3 million; Passengers carried 101,000; Passenger-km 85 million; Total ton-km 8. Source: UN, *Statistical Yearbook*.

TOURISM

Visitor Arrivals by Country (2008): Australia 7,413; Japan 589; New Zealand 1,097; Papua New Guinea 906; United Kingdom 457; USA 1,105; Vanuatu 518; Total (incl. others) 16,264.

Tourism Receipts (US $ million, excl. passenger transport, unless otherwise indicated): 10.3 in 2006 (incl. passenger transport); 3.5 in 2007; 3.5 in 2008.

Source: World Tourism Organization.

COMMUNICATIONS MEDIA

Non-daily Newspapers (1996): 3; estimated circulation 9,000.

Radio Receivers (1997): 57,000 in use.

Television Receivers (2001): 12,000 in use.

Telephones (2010): 8,400 main lines in use.

Mobile Cellular Telephones (2010): 30,000 subscribers.

Personal Computers: 22,000 (46.4 per 1,000 persons) in 2005.

Internet Users (2009): 10,000.

Broadband Subscribers (2010): 2,000.

Sources: UNESCO, *Statistical Yearbook*; International Telecommunication Union.

EDUCATION

Pre-primary (2002/03): 16,469 pupils.

Primary: 523 schools (1993); 3,014 teachers (1999); 83,232 pupils (2006/07).

Secondary: 23 schools (1993); 1,337 teachers (2000); 27,332 pupils (2006/07).

Overseas Centres (1988): 405 students.

Source: UNESCO, *Statistical Yearbook*; UNESCO Institute for Statistics.

Adult Literacy Rate (estimate based on census data): 76.6% in 2003. Source: UN Development Programme, *Human Development Report*.

Directory

The Constitution

A new Constitution came into effect at independence on 7 July 1978.

The main provisions are that Solomon Islands is a constitutional monarchy with the British sovereign (represented locally by a Governor-General, who must be a Solomon Islands citizen) as Head of State, while legislative power is vested in the unicameral National Parliament composed of 50 members (increased from 47 in 1997), elected by universal adult suffrage for four years (subject to dissolution), and executive authority is exercised by the Cabinet, led by the Prime Minister. The Governor-General is appointed for up to five years, on the advice of Parliament, and acts in almost all matters on the advice of the Cabinet. The Prime Minister is elected by and from members of Parliament. Other ministers are appointed by the Governor-General, on the Prime Minister's recommendation, from members of Parliament. The Cabinet is responsible to Parliament. Emphasis is laid on the devolution of power, and traditional chiefs and leaders have a special role within these arrangements. Legislation approved in August 1996 provided for the abolition of the provincial government system and the transfer of legislative and administrative powers from the nine provincial governments to 75 area assemblies and councils controlled by central Government.

The Constitution contains comprehensive guarantees of fundamental human rights and freedoms, and provides for the introduction of a 'leadership code' and the appointment of an Ombudsman and a Public Solicitor. It also provides for 'the establishment of the underlying law, based on the customary law and concepts of the Solomon Islands people'. Solomon Islands citizenship was automatically conferred on the indigenous people of the islands and on other residents with close ties with the islands upon independence. The acquisition of land is reserved for indigenous inhabitants or their descendants.

In mid-1999 it was announced that two review committees had been established to amend the Constitution. They were expected to examine ways in which the traditions of the various ethnic groups could be better accommodated.

The Government

HEAD OF STATE

Queen: HM Queen Elizabeth II.

Governor-General: Frank Ofagioro Kabui (sworn in 7 July 2009).

CABINET

(October 2011)

The Government is formed by the National Coalition for Reform and Advancement, which includes the Reformed Democratic Party, the Independent Democratic Party, the Solomon Islands Democratic Party, OUR Party, independents and others.

Prime Minister: Danny Philip.

Deputy Prime Minister and Minister for Home Affairs: Manasseh Maelanga.

Minister for Foreign Affairs and Trade Relations: Peter Shanel Agovaka.

Minister for Finance and Treasury: Gordon Darcy Lilo.

Minister for Commerce, Industry and Employment: Elijah Doro Muala.

Minister for Development Planning and Aid Co-ordination: Snyder Rini.

Minister for Agriculture and Livestock: Connelly Sandakabatu.

Minister for Fisheries and Marine Resources: John Moffat Fugui (acting).

Minister for Forestry: Bradley Tovosia.

Minister for Communication and Aviation: Andrew Hanaria Keniasina.

Minister for Culture and Tourism: Samuel Manetoali.

Minister for Education and Human Resources Development: Dickson Ha'amori.

Minister for Energy, Mines and Rural Electrification: Moses Garu.

Minister for Environment, Conservation and Meteorology: John Moffat Fugui.

Minister for Health and Medical Services: Charles Sigoto.

Minister for Infrastructure Development: Jackson Fiulaua.

Minister for Justice and Legal Affairs: Commins Aston Mewa.

Minister for Lands, Housing and Survey: Joseph Onika.

Minister for National Unity, Peace and Reconciliation: Hypolite Taremae.

Minister for Police, National Security and Correctional Services: Clay Forau Soalaoi.

Minister for Provincial Government and Institutional Strengthening: Walter Folotalu.

Minister for Public Service: Ricky Houeniopwela.

Minister for Women, Youth and Children's Affairs: Dickson Mua.

Minister of Rural Development and Indigenous Affairs: Lionel Alex.

MINISTRIES

Office of the Prime Minister: POB G1, Honiara; tel. 21867; fax 26088; internet www.pmc.gov.sb.

Ministry of Agriculture and Livestock Development: POB G13, Honiara; tel. 27987; fax 28365; e-mail psagriculture@pmc.gov.sb.

Ministry of Commerce, Industries, Labour and Immigration: Honiara; tel. 28614; fax 25084; e-mail commerce@commerce.gov.sb; internet www.commerce.gov.sb.

Ministry of Communication and Aviation: Honiara; tel. 28049; fax 28054.

Ministry of Culture and Tourism: POB G26, Honiara; tel. 26848; fax 26875.

Ministry of Development Planning and Aid Co-ordination: Honiara; tel. 28608; fax 30163.

Ministry of Education and Human Resources: POB G28, Honiara; tel. 28643; fax 22042; e-mail pseducation@pmc.gov.sb.

Ministry of Energy, Mines and Rural Electrification: POB G37, Honiara; tel. 28609; fax 25811; e-mail psmines@pmc.gov.sb.

Ministry of Environment, Conservation and Meteorology: Honiara; tel. 28611; fax 28735; e-mail psforestry@pmc.gov.sb.

Ministry of Finance and Treasury: POB 26, Honiara; tel. 24102; fax 28619; e-mail psfinance@pmc.gov.sb.

Ministry of Fisheries and Marine Resources: POB G13, Honiara; tel. 39143; e-mail psfisheries@pmc.gov.sb.

Ministry of Foreign Affairs and External Trade: POB G10, Honiara; tel. 28612; fax 20351; e-mail psforeign@pmc.gov.sb.

Ministry of Forestry: POB G13, Honiara; tel. 28611; fax 28735.

Ministry of Health and Medical Services: POB 349, Honiara; tel. 20830; fax 20085; e-mail pshealth@pmc.gov.sb.

Ministry of Home Affairs: POB G11, Honiara; tel. 28602; fax 25591; e-mail psaffairs@pmc.gov.sb.

Ministry of Infrastructure Development: POB G30, Honiara; tel. 28605; fax 28705; e-mail kudu@mnpd.gov.sb.

Ministry of Justice and Legal Affairs: Honiara; tel. 21632; fax 22702; e-mail hclibrary@courts.gov.sb.

Ministry of Lands, Housing and Survey: POB G38, Honiara; tel. 22750; fax 27298; e-mail pslands@pmc.gov.sb.

Ministry of National Unity, Reconciliation and Peace: POB 1548, Honiara; tel. 28616.

Ministry of Police, National Security and Correctional Services: POB G1723, Honiara; tel. 28607; fax 28423; e-mail pspolice@pmc.gov.sb.

Ministry of Provincial Government and Institutional Strengthening: POB G35, Honiara; tel. 28606; fax 28708; e-mail psprovincial@pmc.gov.sb.

Ministry of Public Service: POB G1, Honiara; tel. 28617; fax 25559; e-mail pspublic@pmc.gov.sb.

Ministry of Rural Development and Indigenous Affairs: Honiara; tel. 25238; fax 22170.

Ministry of Women, Youth and Children's Affairs: Honiara; tel. 28602; fax 23547.

Legislature

National Parliament

POB G19, Honiara; tel. 21751; fax 23866; internet www.parliament.gov.sb.

Speaker: Sir Allan Kemakeza.

General Election, 4 August 2010 (provisional results)

Party	Seats
Solomon Islands Democratic Party	12
Ownership, Unity and Responsibility (OUR) Party	3
Solomon Islands Party for Rural Advancement	3
Independent Democratic Party	1
National Party	1
Rural and Urban Political Party	1
Solomon Islands Liberal Party	1
Independents and others	28
Total	50

Note: in many cases party affiliations were subject to review in the immediate aftermath of the election.

Election Commission

Electoral Commission: Ministry of Home Affairs, POB 1500, Honiara; tel. 21198; fax 26161; Chair. Sir Peter Kenilorea; Chief Electoral Officer Polycarp Haununu.

Political Organizations

Parties in the National Parliament can have a fluctuating membership and an influence disproportionate to their representation. There is a significant number of independents who are loosely associated in the amorphous, but often decisive, 'Independent Group'. The following parties represent the main groupings:

Autonomous Solomon Islanders Party: Honiara; f. 2010; advocates return of Solomon Islands' ownership to the people; Pres. Elijah Owa.

Independent Democratic Party: c/o National Parliament, POB G19, Honiara; f. 2004; fmrly the Asscn of Independent Members of Parliament; Sec.-Gen. Snyder Rini; Pres. Sir Thomas Chan.

National Party: c/o National Parliament, POB G19, Honiara; f. 1996; Leader Francis Billy Hilly.

Ownership, Unity and Responsibility (OUR) Party: c/o National Parliament, POB G19, Honiara; f. 2010; est. by opponents of Govt of Derek Sikua; Pres. Manasseh Sogavare; Interim Gen. Sec. Patterson Oti.

People's Alliance Party (PAP): Honiara; f. 1979; est. by merger of People's Progressive Party (f. 1973) and Rural Alliance Party (f. 1977); advocates establishment of a federal republic; Pres. James Mekab; Sec. Edward Kingmele.

People's Congress Party: Honiara; f. 2010; advocates reform of the Rural Constituency Development Fund; Leader Fred Fono.

People's Federation Party: Honiara; f. 2010; aims to improve national infrastructure, education, health and medical services, and the stability of the political culture; Sec.-Gen. Ruddolf Dorah.

Reformed Democratic Party: c/o National Parliament, POB G19, Honiara; f. 2010; Pres. Danny Philip.

Rural and Urban Political Party (RUPP): Honiara; f. 2010; Pres. Samuel Manetoali.

Solomon Islands Democratic Party: c/o National Parliament, POB G19, Honiara; campaigns for self-reliance and for ending of country's dependence on external aid; Leader Steve William Abana; Gen. Sec. John Keniapisia.

Solomon Islands Liberal Party (SILP): c/o National Parliament, POB G19, Honiara; f. 1976; est. as National Democratic Party (NADEPA); present name adopted in 1986; Leader Richard Ulufa'alu.

Solomon Islands Party for Rural Advancement (SIPRA): Honiara; f. 2006; advocates the decentralization of powers and the recognition of community governance structures and traditional values; Pres. and Leader Job Dudley Tausinga; Deputy Pres. Gordon Darcy Lilo.

Other parties that contested the 2010 election included the Direct Development Party (f. 2010 by Dick Ha'amori), New Nations Solomon Islands Party (f. 2010 by Belani Tekulu), People's Power Action Party (f. 2010 by Robert Wales Feratelia), Rural Congress People's Party (f. 2010 by Rev. Milton Talasasa), United Party (interim Pres. Joel Konofilia), Twelve Pillars to Peace and Prosperity Party (TP4, f. 2010 by Delmah Nori to represent the views of women).

Diplomatic Representation

EMBASSIES AND HIGH COMMISSIONS IN SOLOMON ISLANDS

Australia: Hibiscus Ave, POB 589, Honiara; tel. 21561; fax 23691; e-mail austhoniara.enquiries@dfat.gov.au; internet www.solomonislands.embassy.gov.au; High Commissioner Matthew Anderson.

Japan: Mendana Ave, POB 560, Honiara; tel. 22953; fax 21006; Chargé d'affaires Akira Iwanade.

New Zealand: Mendana Ave, POB 697, Honiara; tel. 21502; fax 22377; e-mail nzhicom@solomon.com.sb; High Commissioner Mark Ramsden.

Papua New Guinea: POB 1109, Honiara; tel. 20561; fax 20562; High Commissioner Brian Yombon-Copio.

Taiwan (Republic of China): Bairiki, Tarawa; tel. 22557; fax 22535; e-mail Kir@mofa.gov.tw; Ambassador Benjamin Ho.

United Kingdom: Telekom House, Mendana Ave, POB 676, Honiara; tel. 21705; fax 21549; e-mail bhc@solomon.com.sb; internet ukinsolomonislands.fco.gov.uk; High Commissioner Timothy Smart.

Judicial System

The High Court is a Superior Court of Record with unlimited original jurisdiction and powers (except over customary land) as prescribed by the Solomon Islands Constitution or by any law for the time being in force in Solomon Islands. The Judges of the High Court are the Chief Justice, resident in Solomon Islands and employed by its Government, and the Puisne Judges (of whom there are usually three). Appeals from this Court go to the Court of Appeal, the members of which are senior judges from Australia, New Zealand and Papua New Guinea. The Chief Justice and judges of the High Court are ex officio members of the Court of Appeal.

In addition there are Magistrates' Courts staffed by qualified and lay magistrates exercising limited jurisdiction in both civil and criminal matters. There are also Local Courts staffed by elders of the local communities, which have jurisdiction in the areas of established native custom, petty crime and local government by-laws. In 1975 Customary Land Appeal Courts were established to hear land appeal cases from Local Courts, which have exclusive original jurisdiction over customary land cases.

Office of the Registrar: High Court and Court of Appeal, POB G21, Honiara; tel. 21632; fax 22702; Registrar of the High Court GAVIN WITHERS.

President of the Court of Appeal: Sir ROBIN AULD.

Chief Justice of the High Court: Sir ALBERT ROCKY PALMER.

Attorney-General: BILLY TITIULU.

Religion

More than 95% of the population profess Christianity, and the remainder follow traditional beliefs. According to the census of 1976, about 34% of the population adhered to the Church of Melanesia (Anglican), 19% were Roman Catholics, 17% belonged to the South Seas Evangelical Church, 11% to the United Church (Methodist) and 10% were Seventh-day Adventists. Most denominations are affiliated to the Solomon Islands Christian Association. In many areas Christianity is practised alongside traditional beliefs, especially ancestor worship.

CHRISTIANITY

Solomon Islands Christian Association: POB 1335, Honiara; tel. 23350; fax 26150; e-mail essica@solomon.com.sb; f. 1967; five full mems, seven assoc. mem. orgs; Chair. Most Rev. ADRIAN SMITH; Gen. Sec. EMMANUEL IYABORA.

The Anglican Communion

Anglicans in Solomon Islands are adherents of the Church of the Province of Melanesia, comprising eight dioceses: six in Solomon Islands (Central Melanesia, Malaita, Temotu, Ysabel, Hanuato'o and Central Solomons, which was established in May 1997) and two in Vanuatu (one of which also includes New Caledonia). The Archbishop is also Bishop of Central Melanesia and is based in Honiara. The Church had an estimated 180,000 members in 1988.

Archbishop of the Province of Melanesia: Rt Rev. DAVID VUNAGI, Archbishop's House, POB 19, Honiara; tel. 21137; fax 21098; e-mail dvunagi@comphq.org.sb.

General Secretary: GEORGE KIRIAU, Provincial Headquarters, POB 19, Honiara; tel. 21892; fax 21098; e-mail gkiriau@comphq.org.sb.

The Roman Catholic Church

For ecclesiastical purposes, Solomon Islands comprises one archdiocese and two dioceses. At 31 December 2007 there were an estimated 101,564 adherents in the country. The Bishops participate in the Bishops' Conference of Papua New Guinea and Solomon Islands (based in Papua New Guinea).

Archbishop of Honiara: Most Rev. ADRIAN THOMAS SMITH, Holy Cross, GPOB 237, Honiara; tel. 21943; fax 26426; e-mail chancery@solomon.com.sb.

Other Christian Churches

Assembly of God: POB 928, Honiara; tel. and fax 25512; f. 1971; Gen. Supt Rev. JERIEL OTASUI.

Christian Fellowship Church: Church, Paradise, Munda, Western Province; f. 1960; over 5,000 mems in 24 villages; runs 12 primary schools in Western Province; Rev. IKAN ROVE.

Seventh-day Adventist Mission: POB R145, Ranandi, Honiara; tel. 39267; fax 30653; e-mail sim@adventist.org.sb; internet www.adventist.org.sb; over 9,000 mems on Guadalcanal and over 6,800 on Malaita (Oct. 2000); Pres. WAYNE BOEHM; Sec. SAMUEL PANDA.

South Seas Evangelical Church: POB 16, Honiara; tel. 22388; fax 20302; Pres. ERIC TAKILA; Gen. Sec. CHARLES J. RAFEASI.

United Church in Solomon Islands: POB 82, Munda, Western Province; tel. 62125; fax 62143; e-mail ucsihq@solomon.com.sb; internet www.unitedchurchsi.com; a Methodist church; Moderator Rev. DAVID BARAKANA HAVEA; Gen. Sec. ISAAC VULA DAKEI.

BAHÁ'Í FAITH

National Spiritual Assembly: POB 245, Honiara; tel. 22475; fax 25368; e-mail secretary@bahai.org.sb.

ISLAM

Solomon Islands Muslim League: POB 219, Honiara; tel. 21773; fax 24243; Gen. Sec. Dr MUSTAPHA RAMO; 66 mems.

The Press

Agrikalsa Nius (Agriculture News): POB G13, Honiara; tel. 21211; fax 21955; f. 1986; monthly; Editor ALFRED MAESULIA; circ. 1,000.

Citizens' Press: Honiara; monthly.

Link: Solomon Islands Development Trust, POB 147, Honiara; tel. 21130; fax 21131; pidgin and English; 3 or 4 a year.

Solomon Nius: POB 718, Honiara; tel. 22031; fax 26401; monthly; Dept of Information publication; Editor-in-Chief THOMAS KIVO; monthly; circ. 2,000.

Solomon Star: POB 255, Honiara; tel. 22062; fax 25290; e-mail solstar@solomon.com.sb; internet www.solomonstarnews.com; f. 1982; daily; English; Dir JOHN W. LAMANI; Editor EDNAL PALMER; circ. 7,000.

Solomon Times: POB 707, Honiara; tel. 23272; fax 39197; internet www.solomontimes.com; daily; online newspaper; Chief Editor and Man. Dir EDWARD KINGMELE.

Solomon Voice: POB 1235, Honiara; tel. 20116; fax 20090; f. 1992; weekly; circ. 10,000; Editor CAROL COLVILLE.

Broadcasting and Communications

TELECOMMUNICATIONS

The Telecommunications Bill 2009, approved by Parliament in August of that year, ended the long-standing monopoly of the Solomon Telekom Company. In December 2010 the Telecommunications Commission announced plans to invite bids for a third telecommunications licence.

Regulatory Authority

Telecommunications Commission of the Solomon Islands (TCSI): POB 2180, Honiara; tel. 23855; fax 23860; internet www.tcsi.org.sb; f. 2010; Commr BERNARD HILL.

Service Providers

Bemobile: 50% owned by Telikom PNG Pty Ltd; provides mobile telephone services; commenced operations in August 2010; CEO MICHAEL AH KOY.

Telekom (Solomon Telekom Company Ltd): Mendana Ave, POB 148, Honiara; tel. 21576; fax 23110; e-mail info@ourtelekom.com.sb; internet www.solomon.com.sb; 64.74% owned by Solomon Islands National Provident Fund, 32.58% by Cable and Wireless plc, 2.68% by Investment Corpn of Solomon Islands; operates national and international telecommunications links; Chair. JOHN BEVERLEY; Chief Exec. LOYLEY NGIRA.

BROADCASTING

Radio

Solomon Islands Broadcasting Corporation: POB 654, Honiara; tel. 20051; fax 23159; e-mail sibcnews@solomon.com.sb; internet www.sibconline.com.sb; f. 1976; daily transmissions in English and pidgin; broadcasts total 112 hours per week; Chair. AUGUSTINE TANEKO; Gen. Man. CORNELIUS RATHAMANA; Editor WALTER NALANGU.

Finance

BANKING

(cap. = capital; res = reserves; dep. = deposits; brs = branches; amounts in Solomon Islands dollars)

Central Bank

Central Bank of Solomon Islands: POB 634, Honiara; tel. 21791; fax 23513; e-mail info@cbsi.com.sb; internet www.cbsi.com.sb; f. 1983; sole bank of issue; cap. 20m., res 248.1m., dep. 359.5m. (Dec. 2008); Gov. DENTON RARAWA; Deputy Gov. GANE SIMBE.

Development Bank

Development Bank of Solomon Islands: POB 911, Honiara; tel. 21595; fax 23715; e-mail dbsi@welkam.solomon.com.sb; f. 1978; declared insolvent in Sept. 2004 and placed under the administration of the Central Bank of Solomon Islands; Chair. JOHN MICHAEL ASIPARA; Man. Dir LUKE LAYMAN ETA; 4 brs; 5 sub-brs.

Commercial Banks

Australia and New Zealand Banking Group Ltd (Australia): Mud Alley, POB 10, Honiara; tel. 21111; fax 26937; e-mail solomons@anz.com; internet www.anz.com/SolomonIslands; Gen. Man. BARRY SOWMAN.

Bank South Pacific Ltd (Papua New Guinea): tel. 21874; fax 24674; e-mail bsp@solomon.com.sb; internet www.bsp.com.sbfmrly National Bank of Solomon Islands Ltdbecame br. of Bank of South Pacific Ltd following acquisition in 2007; Gen. Man. MARK CORCORAN.

Westpac Banking Corporation (Australia): National Provident Fund Bldg, 721 Mendana Ave, POB 466, Honiara; tel. 21222; fax 23419; e-mail westpacsolomons@westpac.com.au; internet www.westpac.com.sb; Man. GIAN TAVIANI.

INSURANCE

A number of British and Australian insurance companies maintain agencies in Solomon Islands.

Trade and Industry

GOVERNMENT AGENCY

Investment Corporation of Solomon Islands: POB 570, Honiara; tel. 22511; fax 21263; holding company through which the Government retains equity stakes in a number of corporations; Chair. (vacant).

DEVELOPMENT ORGANIZATION

Solomon Islands Development Trust (SIDT): POB 147, Honiara; tel. 23409; fax 21131; e-mail sidt@welkam.solomon.com.sb; f. 1982; development org.; Exec. Dir ABRAHAM BAENESIA.

CHAMBER OF COMMERCE

Solomon Islands Chamber of Commerce and Industry (SICCI): NPF Bldg, 2nd Floor, POB 650, Honiara; tel. 39542; fax 39544; e-mail sicci@solomon.com.sb; internet www.solomonchamber.com.sb; 69 member cos (July 2004); Chair. JAMES KIM; CEO CALVIN ZIRU.

INDUSTRIAL AND TRADE ASSOCIATIONS

Association of Mining and Exploration Companies: c/o POB G24, Honiara; f. 1988; Pres. NELSON GREG YOUNG.

Commodities Export Marketing Authority: POB 54, Honiara; tel. 22528; fax 21262; e-mail cema@solomon.com.sb; regulator of agricultural commodities such as coconut, cocoa, coffee, palm oil, spices and ngali nut products; agencies at Honiara, Noro and Yandina; Chair. (vacant); Gen. Man. PITAKIA MOSES PELOMO.

Livestock Development Authority: POB 525, Honiara; tel. 29649; fax 22214; f. 1977; privatized 1996; Man. Dir WARREN TUCKER.

Solomon Islands Small Business Enterprise Centre: POB 972, Honiara; tel. 26650; fax 26653; e-mail manager.sbec@solomon.com.sb; Man. RILEY MESEPITU.

Solomon Islands Forest Industries Association: POB 1617, Honiara; tel. 26026; fax 20267; Chair. and Sec. KAIPUA TOHI.

EMPLOYERS' ORGANIZATIONS

Chinese Association: POB 1209, Honiara; tel. 22351; fax 23480; asscn of business people from the ethnic Chinese community.

Federation of Solomon Islands Business: POB 320, Honiara; tel. 22902; fax 21477.

UTILITIES

Electricity

Solomon Islands Electricity Authority (SIEA): POB 6, Honiara; tel. 39422; fax 39472; e-mail mike@siea.com.sb; internet www.siea.com.sb; f. 1961; autonomous, govt-owned entity responsible for generation, transmission, distribution and sale of electrical energy; Chair. Hon. FRANCIS ZAMA; CEO MICHAEL NATION.

Water

Solomon Islands Water Authority (SIWA): POB 1407, Honiara; tel. 23985; fax 20723; f. 1994; Chair. (vacant); Gen. Man. DONALD MAKINI.

CO-OPERATIVE SOCIETIES

Central Co-operative Association (CCA): Honiara.

Salu Fishing Co-operative Association: POB 1041, Honiara; tel. 26550.

Solomon Islands Consumers Co-operative Society Ltd: Honiara; tel. 21798; fax 23640.

Western General Co-operative Association (WGCA): Gizo, Western Province.

MAJOR COMPANIES

Evergreen Forest Industries: POB 771, Honiara; tel. 30778.

Gold Ridge Mining: POB 1556, Honiara; tel. 25807; fax 25872; e-mail admin@solomonsgold.com.au; internet www.solomonsgold.com.au; f. 1998; managed by Australian Solomon Gold Ltd since May 2005, gold mining on Guadalcanal and New Georgia; operations suspended in 2000, in process of resumption in 2010; Country Man. VAL BENIUK.

Guadalcanal Plains Palm Oil Ltd: Honiara; re-est. 2005 to rehabilitate oil palm plantations on Guadalcanal; fmrly Solomon Islands Plantations Ltd, which suspended operations in 1999; jt ownership between New Britain Palm Oil Ltd of Papua New Guinea (80%) and the Guadalcanal Plains Landowners Association (20%); operated by Kulim (Malaysia) Bhd; Gen. Man. HARRY BROCK.

Honiara Timber Exporters: POB 959, Honiara; tel. 39200; fax 39199.

Kolombangara Forest Products Ltd: POB 382, Honiara; tel. 60230; fax 60020; e-mail legassicke@kfpl.com.sb; internet www.kfpl.com.sb; sustainable forestry; mahogany, teak, eucalyptus, gmelina; 100% owned by Investment Corpn of Solomon Islands; FSC-certified company; Gen. Man. SIMON LE GASSICKE.

Linkali Timber Development Co Ltd: f. 1988; jtly owned by Xing Ling Timber Co Ltd and the Kalikoqu tribe.

Melanesian Handicraft: BJS Corporate Headquarters, Commonwealth St, Honiara; tel. 22189; fax 21027; e-mail handicraft@bjs.com.sb; internet www.melanesianhandicraft.com.sb.

National Fisheries Developments Ltd: Honiara; tel. 21506; fax 21459; f. 1977; sold by Govt in 1990; Singaporean-owned; operates fishing vessels and exports tuna; Gen. Man. PHIL ROBERTS.

Pacific Timbers: POB 201, Honiara; tel. 31100; fax 30062; e-mail movers@welkam.solomon.com.sb.

Russell Islands Plantation Estates Ltd: PO Yandina, Russell Islands, Central Province; tel. 21779; fax 21785; e-mail ripelyan@solomon.com.sb; coconut products; cocoa; livestock.

SolBrew: POB 848, Honiara; Chair. STEPHEN DOWLING; Man. Dir. CHRISTOPH STEINWEHE.

Solomon Islands Tobacco Co Ltd: POB 13, Honiara; tel. 30127; fax 30463; subsidiary of British American Tobacco; Gen. Man. ALLAN FAULDS.

Solomon Soaps Ltd: POB 326, Honiara; tel. 30266; fax 39958; Gen. Man. EWALD TISCHLER.

Solrice: Honiara; 100% owned by Ricegrowers' Co-operative of Australia; Gen. Man. BRIAN HUTCHINSON.

Soltai Fishing and Processing Ltd: POB 965, Honiara; tel. 21664; fax 23462; e-mail akukui@soltai.com.sb; f. 2001; 51% owned by Tri Marine Fish Co and 29% owned by Solomon Islands National Provident Fund; Chair. JOE HAMBY; Gen. Man. THOMAS DORKU.

South Pacific Oil: Honiara; tel. 21839; e-mail humphreyt@solomon.com.sb; internet www.spo.com.sb; 75% owned by the Solomon Islands National Provident Fund; fuel storage and distribution, aviation facilities, engineering services; Chair. JOSES TUHANUKU; Gen. Man. CARSON KOROWA; 54 employees.

TRADE UNIONS

There are 14 registered trade unions in Solomon Islands.

Solomon Islands Council of Trade Unions (SICTU): National Centre for Trade Unions, POB 271, Honiara; tel. 22566; fax 23171; f. 1986; Pres. DAVID P. TUHANUKU; Sec. TONY KAGOVAI; the principal affiliated unions are:

Media Association of Solomon Islands (MASI): POB 654, Honiara; tel. 20051; fax 23300; e-mail sibcnews@welkam.solomon.com.sb; Pres. GEORGE HERMING.

Solomon Islands Medical Association: Honiara.

Solomon Islands National Teachers' Association (SINTA): POB 967, Honiara; f. 1985; Pres. K. SANGA; Gen. Sec. JOHN HOUAINIMA.

Solomon Islands Post and Telecommunications Union: Honiara; tel. 21821; fax 20440; Gen. Man. SAMUEL SIVE.

Solomon Islands Public Employees' Union (SIPEU): POB 360, Honiara; tel. 21967; fax 23110; Pres. Martin Karani; Sec.-Gen. Paul Belande.

Solomon Islands Seamen's Association: POB G32, Honiara; tel. 24942; fax 23798.

Transport

ROADS

There are about 1,391 km of roads maintained by the central and provincial governments. In addition, there are 800 km of privately maintained roads mainly for plantation use. Honiara has a main road running about 65 km each side of it along the north coast of Guadalcanal, and Malaita has a road 157 km long running north of Auki and around the northern end of the island to the Lau Lagoon, where canoe transport takes over; and one running south for 35 km to Masa. On Makira a road links Kira Kira and Kakoranga, a distance of 35 km.

SHIPPING

Regular shipping services (mainly cargo) exist between Solomon Islands and Australia, New Zealand, Hong Kong, Japan, Singapore, Taiwan and European ports. The four main ports are at Honiara, Yandina, Noro and Gizo.

Solomon Islands Ports Authority: POB 307, Honiara; tel. 22646; fax 23994; e-mail ports@solomon.com.sb; f. 1956; responsible for the ports of Honiara and Noro; Chair. (vacant); Gen. Man. William Barile.

Sullivans (SI) Ltd: POB 3, Honiara; tel. 21643; fax 23889; e-mail shipping@sullivans.com.sb; shipping agents, importers, wholesalers; CEO Kevin Chant.

Tradco Shipping Ltd: POB 114, Honiara; tel. 22588; fax 23887; e-mail tradco@solomon.com.sb; f. 1984; shipping agents; Man. Dir Gerald Stenzel.

CIVIL AVIATION

Two airports are open to international traffic and a further 25 serve internal flights. Air Niugini (Papua New Guinea) and Qantas (Australia) fly to Honiara International Airport (located 13 km from the capital).

Director of Civil Aviation: Demetrius T. Piziki.

Solomon Airlines Limited: POB 23, Honiara; tel. 20031; fax 20232; e-mail it.man@flysolomons.com; internet www.flysolomons.com; f. 1968; govt-owned; international and domestic operator; scheduled services between Honiara and Port Moresby (Papua New Guinea), Nadi (Fiji), Brisbane (Australia) and Port Vila (Vanuatu); Chair. Bill Tyson; CEO Ron Sumsum.

Tourism

The development of the tourism sector is hindered by the relative inaccessibility of the islands and the inadequacy of tourist facilities. In 2008 tourism receipts (excluding passenger transport) amounted to an estimated US $3.5m. Tourist arrivals were reported to have risen from 13,748 in 2007 to 16,264 in 2008.

Solomon Islands Tourism Industry Association (SITIA): Honiara; tel. 26848; fax 26875; f. 2008; Pres. Wilson Maelaua.

Solomon Islands Visitors Bureau: POB 321, Honiara; tel. 22442; fax 23986; e-mail info@sivb.com.sb; internet www.visitsolomons.com.sb; f. 1980; Gen. Man. Michael Tokuru; Marketing Man. Freda Unusi.

Defence

In July 2003, as the security situation on Guadalcanal deteriorated, the Regional Assistance Mission to Solomon Islands (RAMSI), an Australian-led force comprising more than 2,500 troops and police from various countries in the region, arrived in Solomon Islands to restore law and order. Assisting the local security forces, some 80 RAMSI personnel remained in the country at mid-2010.

Commissioner of Police: Walter Kola (acting).

Education

About two-thirds of school-age children receive formal education, mainly in state schools. About 30% of the children who complete a primary school education receive secondary schooling, either in one of eight national secondary schools (at least one of which is run by the Government and the remainder by various churches) or in one of 12 provincial secondary schools, which are run by provincial assemblies. The provincial secondary schools provide curricula of a practical nature, with a bias towards agriculture, while the national secondary schools offer more academic courses.

In 1993 there were 523 primary schools and 23 secondary schools. In 2002/03 pre-primary pupils numbered 16,469. In 2006/07 primary pupils totalled 83,232 and secondary students numbered 27,332. In 2003 the Church of Melanesia announced plans to establish a new secondary school in each of the country's six dioceses. There are two teacher-training schools and a technical institute. According to the 1999 census, 57% of children aged between five and 14 attended school. In 2006/07 the total enrolment at primary schools was equivalent to 67% of children in the relevant age group, while enrolment in secondary schools included only 30% of children in the relevant age-group. The introduction of free basic education in 2009 was reported to have led to a substantial increase in primary enrolment. Scholarships are available for higher education at various universities overseas. In 1977 the Solomon Islands Centre of the University of the South Pacific (based in Fiji) opened in Honiara.

TONGA

Introduction

The Kingdom of Tonga, which is located in the central South Pacific, about 650 km (400 miles) east of Fiji and south of Samoa, comprises more than 170 islands, totalling 748 sq km (289 sq miles) in area. The islands consist of two chains, those to the west being volcanic and those to the east being coral islands. They are divided into three groups: Vava'u in the north, Ha'apai and Tongatapu in the south. Only 36 of the islands are permanently inhabited. The climate is mild, with temperatures generally in the range 16°C–21°C (61°F–71°F) for most of the year, although usually hotter (27°C, or 81°F) in December and January. The population is predominantly Polynesian, and Tongan is the language of the indigenous inhabitants. English is also widely spoken and is the language of education and administration. Most of the population are Christians, and the leading denomination is Wesleyan. According to the census of 30 November 2006, the population of Tonga was 101,991. In mid-2011, according to the Secretariat of the Pacific Community, the population had increased to an estimated 103,682. About two-thirds of the population are resident on the largest island, Tongatapu, where the capital of Nuku'alofa is situated.

From about the 10th century Tongan society developed a lineage of sacred chiefs, who gradually became effective rulers. Following European contact the chiefs became known as kings. The Kingdom of Tonga adopted its first Constitution in 1875, during the reign of King George Tupou I, who had reunited the islands. As a result of increasing unrest, Tonga negotiated a treaty with the United Kingdom in 1900, whereby it came under British protection. Queen Salote Tupou III came to the throne in 1918 and ruled Tonga until her death in December 1965. Her son, Prince Tupouto'a Tungi, who had been Prime Minister since 1949, succeeded her. He took the title of King Taufa'ahau Tupou IV and appointed his brother, Prince Fatafehi Tu'ipelehake, to be Prime Minister. In 1958 a treaty of friendship was signed between Tonga and the United Kingdom, providing for the appointment of a British commissioner and consul to be responsible to the Governor of Fiji, who held the office of British Chief Commissioner for Tonga. Tonga gained greater control over internal affairs in 1967 and became fully independent, within the Commonwealth, on 4 June 1970. Tonga was formally admitted to the UN in September 1999.

The Legislative Assembly continued to be dominated by traditionalist conservatives: the majority of legislators were appointed by the King, with a number of seats being occupied by nobles. However, following the elections for the nine commoners' seats in February 1987, some of the Government's harshest critics were reported to be among the six newcomers to the legislature. In September 1989 the commoners tabled a motion demanding an increase in the number of parliamentary seats determined by popular election. In early 1990 'Akilisi Pohiva, the leader of the pro-reform commoners, and his colleagues were re-elected by substantial majorities, and at parliamentary elections in February 1993 reformists won six of the nine commoners' seats. In August 1994 Tonga's first official political party was formed when the Pro-Democracy Movement (which had been recognized in 1992, the group having been formed in the early 1970s as the Human Rights and Democracy Movement in Tonga—HRDMT) established the People's Party, under the chairmanship of a local businessman, Huliki Watab.

In January 2000 the King appointed Prince 'Ulukalala-Lavaka-Ata as Prime Minister, replacing Baron Vaea. In March of that year a report published by the US Department of State claimed that Tonga's system of government was in breach of UN and Commonwealth human rights guidelines. At the legislative election of March 2002, the Tonga Human Rights and Democracy Movement won seven of the nine commoners' seats. In September, having repeatedly failed to secure government approval for the group's registration under that name, the organization once again became known as the HRDMT.

In March 2005, with nine seats having been filled by nobles, the elections for the nine commoners' seats were contested by a record 60 candidates. For the first time, two newly elected members from each group were appointed to positions in the Cabinet, and the by-election for the four seats thus vacated took place in May. Following a separate by-election, the former cabinet minister and member of the newly formed People's Democratic Party (PDP), Clive Edwards, became a member of the Legislative Assembly. The PDP had been launched in April by a breakaway group from the HRDMT, which had stated its intention to pursue political reform in a more aggressive manner (and which in late 2005 assumed the name of Friendly Islands Human Rights and Democracy Movement—FIHRDM—Inc).

In July 2005 public servants voted to approve the first national strike in Tonga's history. The strike ended in early September when an agreement allowing for salary increases of between 60% and 80% was signed. More significantly, however, the agreement also provided for the establishment of a commission to review the country's Constitution and to examine possibilities for a more democratic form of government.

In February 2006 Prince 'Ulukalala resigned as Prime Minister. He was replaced by Dr Feleti (Fred) Sevele, a commoner and advocate of constitutional reform, whose appointment was widely welcomed. On 11 September King Taufa'ahau Tupou IV died at the age of 88. Crown Prince Tupouto'a was formally declared to be his successor, assuming the title of King George Tupou V. In contrast to the conservative approach of his father, the new King was believed to favour reform. In October a government committee, established following the strike of 2005 to examine the issue of constitutional reform, recommended the popular election of all members of the Legislative Assembly. However, the apparent slow pace of democratic reform led in November 2006 to serious rioting in Nuku'alofa and to the destruction of many buildings in the capital. Several deaths were reported, and a state of emergency was declared. In response to the Tongan Government's appeal for assistance in the restoration of law and order, Australia and New Zealand dispatched a total of about 150 soldiers and police officers. It was subsequently announced that a new, modified programme of reform had been approved. This envisaged a 30-member legislature comprising 21 people's representatives and nine nobles' representatives. The Prime Minister, it was agreed, would be elected by the legislature. Pro-democracy candidates secured a majority of the commoners' seats at elections in April 2008. In July, as part of the process of democratic reform, the Legislative Assembly approved the establishment of the Constitution and Electoral Commission, which submitted its final report in November 2009. The Commission recommended that the elected membership of the Assembly be increased to 26, of whom nine would be elected by and from among the hereditary nobles (as before), and 17 would be chosen in a general election (compared with nine previously). The term of the legislature was to be increased from three to four years. The executive power of the King was to be considerably reduced. The Prime Minister was to be appointed by the King, but nominated by the legislature. At the parliamentary elections held in November 2010, therefore, for the first time the majority of legislators were elected by the general populace. Lord Tu'ivakano, a member of the nobility, was subsequently appointed as Prime Minister. The state of emergency, which had remained in place since late 2006, was removed in February 2011.

Tonga's economic development has been adversely affected by inclement weather, inflationary pressures, a high level of unemployment, large-scale emigration and over-reliance on the agricultural sector. The country remains vulnerable to fluctuations in international prices for squash (pumpkin). Remittances from Tongans resident overseas are an important source of income. However, these inflows were reported to have declined in real terms in 2007–08, and remittances were subsequently subdued by the deterioration in global economic conditions, which reduced the availability of employment opportunities in countries such as the USA. The Economic and Public Sector Reform Programme (EPSRP) was supported by a loan worth US $10m. over 24 years (the first tranche of which was released in 2002) and technical assistance from the Asian Development Bank (ADB). The programme's aims included the improvement of the performance of the civil service and the development of better investment conditions. Tonga's terms of accession to the World Trade Organization (WTO—to which Tonga was formally admitted in July 2007), concluded in December 2005, were criticized by some on the grounds that the country would be forced to implement drastic reductions in trade tariffs, hitherto a vital source of revenue for the financing of areas such as health and education. The rioting of November 2006 had an adverse effect on the economy, with the costs of reconstruction projected to exceed 50m. pa'anga. Furthermore, concern regarding the country's debt service ratio intensified in late 2007 when Tonga accepted a loan of US $50m. from the People's Republic of China for the purposes of financing reconstruction work. Under an economic and technical co-operation agreement signed in March 2011, China undertook to provide aid of US $11m. to Tonga. In a report released in March 2011, the ADB reiterated concerns with regard to Tonga's high level of public debt and urged the Government to restrain its expenditure. In the same month similar concerns were expressed by the IMF, which also recommended a reduction in government borrowing and in current expenditure, while noting that inflows of remittances from overseas had begun to stabilize.

Statistical Survey

Source (unless otherwise indicated): Tonga Government Department of Statistics, POB 149, Nuku'alofa; tel. (676) 23300; fax (676)

24303; e-mail dept@stats.gov.to; internet www.spc.int/prism/country/to/stats.

AREA AND POPULATION

Area: 748 sq km (289 sq miles).

Population: 97,784 at census of 30 November 1996; 101,991 (males 51,772, females 50,219) at census of 30 November 2006. *By Island Group* (2006 census): Tongatapu 72,045; Vava'u 15,505; Ha'apai 7,570; 'Eua 5,206; Niuas 1,665; Total 101,991. *Mid-2011* (Secretariat of the Pacific Community estimate): 103,682 (Source: Pacific Regional Information System).

Density (at mid-2011): 138.6 per sq km.

Population by Age and Sex (Secretariat of the Pacific Community estimates at mid-2011): *0–14:* 39,265 (males 20,452, females 18,813); *15–64:* 58,414 (males 29,487, females 28,927); *65 and over:* 6,003 (males 2,660, females 3,343); *Total* 103,682 (males 52,599, females 51,083) (Source: Pacific Regional Information System).

Principal Towns (population at 2006 census, provisional): Nuku'alofa (capital) 23,658; Neiafu 4,123; Haveluloto 3,405; Tofoa-Koloua 3,213; Vaini 3,091 (Source: Thomas Brinkhoff, *City Population*—internet www.citypopulation.de). *Mid-2009* (incl. suburbs, UN estimate): Nuku'alofa 24,260 (Source: UN, *World Urbanization Prospects: The 2009 Revision*).

Births, Marriages and Deaths (2006, unless otherwise indicated): Registered live births 2,945 (birth rate 28.6 per 1,000); Registered marriages (2004, provisional) 677 (marriage rate 6.6 per 1,000); Registered deaths 709 (death rate 6.9 per 1,000). Source: mainly UN, *Demographic Yearbook* and *Population and Vital Statistics Report*.

Life Expectancy (years at birth, WHO estimates): 71 (males 72; females 70) in 2009. Source: WHO, *World Health Statistics*.

Economically Active Population (persons aged 15 years and over, 2003): Agriculture, forestry and fishing 11,000; Mining and quarrying 60; Manufacturing 8,530; Electricity, gas and water 530; Construction 1,440; Trade, restaurants and hotels 3,560; Transport, storage and communications 1,580; Financing, insurance, real estate and business services 770; Public administration and defence 2,590; Education 1,780; Health and social work 660; Other community, social and personal services 1,330; Private households with employed persons 610; Extra-territorial organizations 90; Not adequately defined 30; *Total employed* 34,560 (males 20,420, females 14,140); Unemployed 1,890 (males 760, females 1,130); *Total labour force* 36,450 (males 21,180, females 15,270). Note: Figures are rounded to the nearest 10 persons. *Mid-2011* (estimates): Agriculture, etc. 11,000; Total labour force 42,000 (Source: FAO).

HEALTH AND WELFARE

Key Indicators

Total Fertility Rate (children per woman, 2009): 3.9.

Under-5 Mortality Rate (per 1,000 live births, 2009): 19.

Physicians (per 1,000 head, 2002): 0.3.

Hospital Beds (per 1,000 head, 2004): 2.9.

Health Expenditure (2008): US $ per head (PPP): 194.

Health Expenditure (2008): % of GDP: 5.0.

Health Expenditure (2008): public (% of total): 75.4.

Access to Sanitation (% of persons, 2008): 97.

Total Carbon Dioxide Emissions ('000 metric tons, 2007): 175.9.

Carbon Dioxide Emissions Per Head (metric tons, 2007): 1.7.

Human Development Index (2010): ranking 85.

Human Development Index (2010): value 0.677.

For sources and definitions, see explanatory note on p. vi.

AGRICULTURE, ETC.

Principal Crops ('000 metric tons, 2009, FAO estimates): Sweet potatoes 6.3; Cassava 6.7; Taro 4.2; Yams 4.0; Other roots and tubers 2.1; Coconuts 59.2; Pumpkins, squash and gourds 21.3; Other vegetables and melons 5.7; Bananas 1.1; Plantains 3.1; Oranges 0.9; Lemons and limes 2.8.

Livestock ('000 head, year ending September 2009, FAO estimates): Pigs 81; Horses 12; Cattle 11; Goats 13; Chickens 330.

Livestock Products (metric tons, 2009, FAO estimates): Pig meat 1,561; Hen eggs 300; Honey 11; Cows' milk 400.

Forestry ('000 cu m, 2000): *Roundwood Removals* (excl. bark): 4; *Sawnwood Production:* 2 (FAO estimate). *2001–09:* Annual output as in 2000 (FAO estimates).

Fishing (metric tons, live weight, 2009): Marine fishes 1,404 (FAO estimate) (Snappers and jobfishes 77; Albacore 126; Bigeye tuna 38; Yellowfin tuna 109); Marine crustaceans 403 (FAO estimate); Total catch (incl. others, FAO estimate) 2,038.

Source: FAO.

INDUSTRY

Electric Energy (production, million kWh): 55 in 2008; 51 in 2009; 51 in 2010. Source: Asian Development Bank.

FINANCE

Currency and Exchange Rates: 100 seniti (cents) = 1 pa'anga (Tongan dollar or $T). *Sterling, US Dollar and Euro Equivalents* (29 April 2011): £1 sterling = $T2.906; US $1 = $T1.745; €1 = $T2.593; $T100 = £34.42 = US $57.32 = €38.57. *Average Exchange Rate* (pa'anga per US $): 1.9424 in 2008; 2.0345 in 2009; 1.9060 in 2010.

Budget ('000 pa'anga, year ending 30 June 2010): *Revenue:* Taxation 114,633; Non-tax revenue 28,921; Total 143,554 (excl. grants received from abroad 39,164). *Expenditure:* Current expenditure 193,325; Capital expenditure 7,016; Total 200,341 (excl. net lending 488). Source: Asian Development Bank.

International Reserves (US $ million at 31 December 2010): IMF special drawing rights 10.90; Reserve position in the IMF 2.64; Foreign exchange 90.99; *Total* 104.53. Source: IMF, *International Financial Statistics*.

Money Supply ('000 pa'anga at 31 December 2010): Currency outside depository corporations 28,388; Transferable deposits 78,699; Other deposits 203,751; *Broad money* 310,838. Source: IMF, *International Financial Statistics*.

Cost of Living (Consumer Price Index, excl. rent; base: 2005 = 100): All items 124.5 in 2008; 126.2 in 2009; 130.7 in 2010. Source: IMF, *International Financial Statistics*.

Gross Domestic Product (million pa'anga at constant 2000/01 prices, year ending 30 June): 381.8 in 2007/08; 378.1 in 2008/09; 379.3 in 2009/10 (preliminary).

Expenditure on the Gross Domestic Product (million pa'anga at current prices, year ending 30 June 2010, preliminary): Government final consumption expenditure 128.6; Private final consumption expenditure 619.7; Non-profit institutions serving households 45.3; Gross fixed capital formation 165.6; Change in stocks 31.6; *Total domestic expenditure* 990.8; Exports of goods and services 90.2; *Less* Imports of goods and services 402.9; Statistical discrepancy –6.3; *GDP in purchasers' values* 671.9.

Gross Domestic Product by Economic Activity (million pa'anga at current prices, year ending 30 June 2010, preliminary): Agriculture, forestry and fishing 119.5; Mining and quarrying 1.7; Manufacturing 44.2; Electricity, gas and water 17.3; Construction 41.4; Trade, restaurants and hotels 91.2; Transport, storage and communications 25.9; Finance and real estate 52.1; Public administration 89.1; Other services 117.4; *Sub-total* 599.8; *Less* Imputed bank service charges 12.2; *Gross value added in basic prices* 587.6; Indirect taxes, less subsidies 84.4; *GDP at market prices* 671.9.

Balance of Payments (US $ '000, 2009): Exports of goods f.o.b. 8,435; Imports of goods f.o.b. –139,640; *Trade balance* –131,205; Exports of services 35,141; Imports of services –48,601; *Balance on goods and services* –144,665; Other income received 10,037; Other income paid –6,190; *Balance on goods, services and income* –140,819; Current transfers received 96,669; Current transfers paid –10,066; *Current balance* –54,216; Capital account (net) 54,867; Direct investment from abroad –36; Financial derivatives assets 1,657; Other investment assets 10,381; Other investment liabilities 5,648; Net errors and omissions –37,266; *Overall balance* –18,965. Source, IMF, *International Financial Statistics*.

EXTERNAL TRADE

Principal Commodities ('000 pa'anga, 2010): *Imports:* Animals and animal products 34,792; Vegetable products 9,622; Prepared foodstuffs 42,381; Mineral products 72,532; Chemical products 12,717; Wood and wood products 11,084; Wood pulp, paper and paperboard 9,462; Base metals and articles thereof 20,267; Machinery, mechanical appliances and electrical equipment 46,309; Transportation equipment 13,385; Miscellaneous manufactured articles 6,289; Works of art, collectors' pieces and antiques 1,875; Total (incl. others) 301,754. *Exports* (including re-exports): Animal and animal products 10,145; Vegetable products 3,849; Chemical products 681; Wood and wood products 406; Total (incl. others) 15,626.

Principal Trading Partners ('000 pa'anga, 2010): *Imports:* Australia 27,635; China, People's Republic 16,231; Fiji 32,281; Japan 7,135; New Zealand 96,199; USA 39,215; Total (incl. others) 301,754.

Exports: Australia 612; Japan 1,657; New Zealand 2,571; USA 2,516; Total (incl. others) 15,626.

TRANSPORT

Road Traffic (registered motor vehicles, 2004): Passenger cars 6,580; Light goods vehicles 5,183; Heavy goods vehicles 2,698; Buses 114; Taxis 845; Total (incl. others) 16,748.

Shipping: *International Traffic* ('000 metric tons, 1998, unless otherwise indicated): Goods loaded 13.8; Goods unloaded 80.4. Vessels entered ('000 net registered tons) 1,950 in 1991 (Source: UN, *Statistical Yearbook*). *Merchant Fleet* (registered at 31 December 2009): Vessels 50; Total displacement ('000 grt) 68.2 (Source: IHS Fairplay, *World Fleet Statistics*).

Civil Aviation (traffic on scheduled services, 2004): Kilometres flown 1 million; Passengers carried 75,000; Passenger-km 19 million; Total ton-km 2 million. Source: UN, *Statistical Yearbook*.

TOURISM

Foreign Tourist Arrivals (excl. cruise-ship passengers): 39,451 in 2006; 46,040 in 2007; 49,405 in 2008.

Tourist Arrivals by Country (2008): Australia 11,428; New Zealand 22,835; USA 5,836; Total (incl. others) 49,405.

Tourism Receipts (US $ million, excl. passenger transport): 16 in 2006; 14 in 2007; 20 in 2008.

Source: World Tourism Organization.

COMMUNICATIONS MEDIA

Radio Receivers (1997): 61,000 in use.

Television Receivers (1997): 2,000 in use.

Telephones (2010): 31,000 main lines in use.

Mobile Cellular Telephones (2010): 54,300 subscribers.

Personal Computers: 6,000 (58.9 per 1,000 persons) in 2005.

Internet Users (2009): 8,400.

Broadband Subscribers (2010): 1,000.

Daily Newspapers (1996): 1; estimated circulation 7,000.

Non-daily Newspapers (2004 unless otherwise indicated): 3; estimated circulation 13,000 (2001).

Sources: UNESCO, *Statistical Yearbook*; UN, *Statistical Yearbook*; Audit Bureau of Circulations, Australia; and International Telecommunication Union.

EDUCATION

Primary (2007, unless otherwise indicated, provisional): 117 schools (1999); 665 teachers; 16,892 pupils.

General Secondary (2007, unless otherwise indicated, provisional): 39 schools (1999); 982 teachers; 14,580 pupils.

Technical and Vocational: 4 colleges (2001); 45 teachers (1990); 467 students (1999).

Teacher-training (1999, unless otherwise indicated): 1 college; 22 teachers (1994); 288 students.

Universities, etc. (1985): 17 teachers; 85 students.

Other Higher Education: 36 teachers (1980); 620 students (1985); 230 students were studying overseas on government scholarships (1990).

Pupil-teacher Ratio (primary education, UNESCO estimate): 22.3 in 2005/06 (Source: UNESCO Institute for Statistics).

Adult Literacy Rate: 99.0% (males 99.0%; females 99.1%) in 2006 (Source: UNESCO Institute for Statistics).

Directory

The Constitution

The Constitution of Tonga is based on that granted in 1875 by King George Tupou I. Following the enactment of constitutional reforms in 2010, executive power was transferred from the Sovereign to the Cabinet. The King remains as Head of State and continues to preside over the Privy Council, which has advisory powers. The unicameral Legislative Assembly (which formerly included the King) has 26 elected members: 17 chosen by direct election by all adult Tongan citizens; and nine elected by and from among the hereditary nobles. In addition to the 26 elected representatives, the Prime Minister may nominate a further four members. The Prime Minister is elected by the members of the Legislative Assembly, which serves a four-year term.

The Government

HEAD OF STATE

The Sovereign: HM King GEORGE TUPOU V (succeeded to the throne 11 September 2006).

CABINET
(October 2011)

Prime Minister and Minister of Foreign Affairs, Defence, Information and Communication: Lord TU'IVAKANO.

Deputy Prime Minister and Minister of Transport and Works: SAMIU KUITA VAIPULU.

Minister of Finance and Revenue Services: SUNIA MANU FILI.

Minister of Justice and Public Enterprises: WILLIAM CLIVE EDWARDS.

Minister of Education, Women's Affairs and Culture: Dr ANA MAUI TAUFE'ULUNGAKI.

Minister of Labour, Commerce and Industries: 'ISILELI PULU.

Minister of Police, Prisons and Fire Services: LISIATE 'ALOVEITA 'AKOLO.

Minister of Lands, Survey, Natural Resources, Environment and Climate Change: Lord MA'AFU.

Minister of Health: ULITI UATA.

Minister of Training, Employment, Youth and Sports: FE'AOMOEATA VAKATA.

Minister of Agriculture, Food, Forestry and Fisheries: Lord VAEA.

Minister of Tourism: Dr VILIAMI LATU.

Attorney-General: BARRIE SWEETMAN (acting).

The Governors of Ha'apai and of Vava'u serve as ex officio members of the Cabinet.

GOVERNMENT MINISTRIES AND OFFICES

Office of the Prime Minister: POB 62, Nuku'alofa; tel. 24644; fax 23888; e-mail pmomail@pmo.gov.to; internet www.pmo.gov.to.

Palace Office: Salote Rd, Kolofo'ou, Nuku'alofa; tel. 21000; fax 24102; internet www.palaceoffice.gov.to.

Ministry of Agriculture, Food, Forestry and Fisheries: Administration Office, Vuna Rd, Kolofo'ou, Nuku'alofa; tel. 23038; fax 23039; e-mail pvea@kalianet.to.

Ministry of Education, Women's Affairs and Culture: POB 61, Vuna Rd, Kolofo'ou, Nuku'alofa; tel. 23511; fax 23596; e-mail moe@kalianet.to; internet www.tongaeducation.gov.to.

Ministry of Environment and Climate Change: Nuku'alofa.

Ministry of Finance and National Planning: Treasury Bldg, POB 87, Vuna Rd, Nuku'alofa; tel. 23066; fax 26011; e-mail info@finance.gov.to; internet www.finance.gov.to.

Ministry of Foreign Affairs: National Reserve Bank Bldg, 4th Floor, Salote Rd, Kolofo'ou, Nuku'alofa; tel. 23600; fax 23360; e-mail secfo@candw.to.

Ministry of Health: POB 59, Taufa'ahau Rd, Tofoa, Nuku'alofa; tel. 28233; fax 24921; e-mail tpaea@health.gov.to; internet www.health.gov.to.

Ministry of Information and Communications: POB 1380, Nuku'alofa; tel. 28170; fax 24861; e-mail enquiries@mic.gov.to; internet www.mic.gov.to.

Ministry of Justice: POB 130, Railway Rd, Kolofo'ou, Nuku'alofa; tel. 21055; fax 23098; internet www.justice.gov.to.

Ministry of Labour, Commerce and Industries: POB 110, Nuku'alofa; tel. 23688; fax 23887.

Ministry of Lands, Survey and Natural Resources: POB 5, Vuna Rd, Kolofo'ou, Nuku'alofa; tel. 23611; fax 23216; internet www.lands.gov.to.

Ministry of Police, Prisons and Fire Services: POB 8, Nuku'alofa; tel. 23233; fax 23036; e-mail polcombr@kalianet.to.

Ministry of Public Enterprises: Nuku'alofa.

Ministry of Revenue Services: POB 7, Nuku'alofa; tel. 23444; fax 25018; internet www.revenue.gov.to.

Ministry of Transport: Dupincia Lodge, Ma'ufanga, Nuku'alofa; tel. 24144; fax 24145; e-mail info@mca.gov.to; internet www.mca.gov.to.

Ministry of Works and Disaster Relief Activities: POB 52, Nuku'alofa; tel. 23100; fax 25440; e-mail mowtonga@kalianet.to.

Legislative Assembly

The number of directly elective seats was increased from a minority of nine to a majority of 17 at the 2010 election. The term of the Legislative Assembly was increased from three to four years.

Speaker: Lord LASIKE.

Election, 25 November 2010

Party	Seats
Democratic Party of the Friendly Islands	12
Independents	5
Nobles' Representatives	9
Total	26

The nine Nobles' Representatives were elected from among their peers in a separate ballot. An additional four members may be appointed by the Prime Minister.

Election Commission

Electoral Commission: Nuku'alofa; f. 2010; Chair. BARRIE SWEETMAN; Supervisor of Elections PITA VUKI.

Political Organizations

Democratic Party of the Friendly Islands (DPFI): c/o Legislative Assembly, Nuku'alofa; f. 2010; est. as electoral vehicle by mems of Human Rights and Democracy Movement; advocates transparent government, further constitutional reform, greater accountability and economic reform; Leader 'AKILISI POHIVA.

Friendly Islands Human Rights and Democracy Movement Inc (FIHRDM Inc): POB 843, Nuku'alofa; tel. 25501; e-mail demo@kalianet.to; f. late 1970s; est. and recognized in 1992 as the Pro-Democracy Movement; application in 1998 for incorporation under new name of Tonga Human Rights and Democracy Movement refused by Govt; reverted to the name of Human Rights and Democracy Movement in Tonga (HRDMT) in 2002; assumed present name in Nov. 2005; advocates democratic reform; Leader 'ULITI UATA.

Paati Langafonua Tu'uloa (PLT) (Sustainable Nation-Building Party): f. 2007; Pres. SIONE FONUA.

People's Democratic Party: Nuku'alofa; f. 2005; breakaway group from HRDMT; Pres. SIONE TEISINA FUKO; Vice-Pres. SIONE TU'ALAU MANGISI.

Tongan Democratic Labour Party: Nuku'alofa; f. 2010; Chair. Dr PITA TAUFATOFUA.

Diplomatic Representation

EMBASSIES AND HIGH COMMISSIONS IN TONGA

Australia: Salote Rd, Private Bag 35, Nuku'alofa; tel. 23244; fax 23243; e-mail ahctonga@dfat.gov.au; internet www.tonga.embassy.gov.au; High Commissioner THOMAS ROTH.

China, People's Republic: Vuna Rd, POB 877, Nuku'alofa; tel. 24554; fax 24595; e-mail chinaemb_to@mfa.gov.cn; Ambassador WANG DONGHUA.

Japan: NRBT Bldg, 5th Floor, POB 330, Nuku'alofa; tel. 22221; fax 27025; e-mail emb-japan@nu.mofa.go.jp; internet www.ton.emb-japan.go.jp; Ambassador YASUO TAKASE.

New Zealand: cnr Taufa'ahau and Salote Rds, POB 830, Nuku'alofa; tel. 23122; fax 23487; e-mail nzhcnuk@kalianet.to; High Commissioner JONATHAN AUSTIN.

Judicial System

There are eight Magistrates' Courts, the Land Court, the Supreme Court and the Court of Appeal. Appeal from the Magistrates' Courts lies to the Supreme Court, and from the Supreme Court and Land Court to the Court of Appeal (except in certain matters relating to hereditary estates, where appeal lies to the Privy Council). The Chief Justice and Puisne Judge are resident in Tonga and are judges of the Supreme Court and Land Court. The Court of Appeal is presided over by the Chief Justice and consists of three judges from other Commonwealth countries. In the Supreme Court, the accused in criminal cases, and either party in civil suits, may elect trial by jury. In the Land Court, the judge sits with a Tongan assessor. Proceedings in the Magistrates' Courts are in Tongan, and in the Supreme Court and Court of Appeal in Tongan and English.

Chief Justice: MICHAEL DISHINGTON SCOTT, Supreme Court, POB 11, Nuku'alofa; tel. 23599; fax 22380; e-mail cj_tonga@kalianet.to.

Puisne Judge: ROBERT SHUSTER.

Chief Registrar of the Supreme Court: MANAKOVI PAHULU.

Religion

The Tongans are almost all Christians, and about 36% of the population belong to Methodist (Wesleyan) communities. There are also significant numbers of Roman Catholics (15%) and Latter-day Saints (Mormons—15%). Anglicans (1%) and Seventh-day Adventists (5%) are also represented. Fourteen churches are represented in total.

CHRISTIANITY

Kosilio 'ae Ngaahi Siasi 'i Tonga (Tonga National Council of Churches): POB 1205, Nuku'alofa; tel. 23291; fax 27506; e-mail tncc@kalianet.to; f. 1973; three mem. churches (Free Wesleyan, Roman Catholic and Anglican); Chair. Rt Rev. ALIFALETI MONE; Gen. Sec. Rev. SIKETI TONGA.

The Anglican Communion

Tonga lies within the diocese of Polynesia, part of the Church of the Province of New Zealand. The Bishop of Polynesia is resident in Fiji.

Archdeacon of Tonga and Samoa: The Ven. SAM KOY, The Vicarage, POB 31, Nuku'alofa; tel. 22136.

The Roman Catholic Church

The diocese of Tonga, directly responsible to the Holy See, comprises Tonga and the New Zealand dependency of Niue. At 31 December 2007 there were an estimated 15,384 adherents in the diocese. The Bishop participates in the Catholic Bishops' Conference of the Pacific, based in Fiji.

Bishop of Tonga: SOANE PATITA MAFI, Toutaimana Catholic Centre, POB 1, Nuku'alofa; tel. 23822; fax 23854; e-mail cathbish@kalianet.to.

Other Churches

Church of Jesus Christ of Latter-day Saints (Mormon): Mission Centre, POB 58, Nuku'alofa; tel. 23437; fax 23763; 53,000 mems; Pres. LYNN C. MCMURRAY.

Church of Tonga: Nuku'alofa; f. 1928; a branch of Methodism; 6,912 mems; Pres. Rev. FINAU KATOANGA.

Free Church of Tonga: POB 23, Nuku'alofa; tel. 23896; fax 24458; e-mail kmakakaufaki@yahoo.co.nz; f. 1885; 20,175 mems (2009); brs in Australia, New Zealand and USA; Pres. Rev. SEMISI FONUA.

Free Wesleyan Church of Tonga (Koe Siasi Uesiliana Tau'ataina 'o Tonga): POB 57, Nuku'alofa; tel. 23522; fax 24020; e-mail fwc@kalianet.to; internet www.fwc.to; f. 1826; 36,500 mems; Pres. Rev. Dr FINAU 'AHIO.

Tokaikolo Christian Fellowship: Nuku'alofa; f. 1978; breakaway group from Free Wesleyan Church; 5,000 mems.

BAHÁ'Í FAITH

National Spiritual Assembly: POB 133, Nuku'alofa; tel. 21568; fax 23120; e-mail nsatonga@patco.to; mems resident in 142 localities.

The Press

Eva, Your Guide to Tonga: POB 958, Nuku'alofa; tel. 25779; fax 24749; e-mail editor@matangitonga.to; internet www.matangitonga.to; f. 1989; 4 a year; publication suspended under media restrictions in Jan. 2004; Publr and Editor PESI FONUA; circ. 4,500.

Ko e Kele'a (Conch Shell): POB 1567, Nuku'alofa; tel. 25501; fax 26330; internet www.planet-tonga.com/tongatimes/kelea; f. 1986; monthly; activist-orientated publication, economic and political; Editor MATENI TAPUELUELU; circ. 3,500.

Lali: Nuku'alofa; f. 1994; monthly; English; national business magazine; Publr KALAFI MOALA.

Lao and Hia: POB 2808, Nuku'alofa; tel. 14105; weekly; Tongan; legal newspaper; Editor SIONE HAFOKA.

Matangi Tonga: POB 958, Nuku'alofa; tel. 25779; fax 24749; e-mail editor@matangitonga.to; internet www.matangitonga.to; f. 1986; monthly; national news magazine ceased publication following suspension of licence in Jan. 2004 and subsequently published solely on internet; Man. Editor MARY FONUA.

'Ofa ki Tonga: c/o Tokaikolo Fellowship, POB 2055, Nuku'alofa; tel. 24190; monthly; newspaper of Tokaikolo Christian Fellowship; Editor Rev. LIUFAU VAILEA SAULALA.

Taumu'a Lelei: POB 1, Nuku'alofa; tel. 27161; fax 23854; e-mail tmlcath@kalianet.to; f. 1931; monthly; Roman Catholic; Editor Dr SOANE LILO FOLIAKI.

The Times of Tonga/Ko e Taimi'o Tonga: POB 880, Nuku'alofa; tel. 27477; e-mail times@kalianet.to; internet www.taimionline.com; f. 1989; twice-weekly; English edn covers Pacific and world news,

Tongan edn covers local news; part of Taimi Media Network; Publr KALAFI MOALA; Editor FAKA'OSI MAAMA; circ. 8,000.

Tohi Fanongonongo: POB 57, Nuku'alofa; tel. 26533; fax 24020; e-mail fwctf@kalianet.to; monthly; Wesleyan; Editor Rev. TEVITA PAUKAMEA TIUETI.

Tonga Chronicle/Kalonikali Tonga: POB 197, Nuku'alofa; tel. 23302; fax 23336; e-mail chroni@kalianet.to; f. 1964; govt-sponsored; weekly; Tongan and English; Editor JOSEPHINE LATU; circ. 3,000.

Publisher

Vava'u Press Ltd: POB 958, Nuku'alofa; tel. 25779; fax 24749; e-mail vapress@matangitonga.to; internet www.matangitonga.to; f. 1980; books and magazines; Pres. PESI FONUA.

Broadcasting and Communications

TELECOMMUNICATIONS

Tonga Communications Corporation: Private Bag 4, Nuku'alofa; tel. 20000; fax 26701; internet www.tcc.to; f. 2000; responsible for domestic and international telecommunications services; Man. Dir TIMOTE KATOANGA.

Digicel Tonga Ltd: Fatafehi Rd, POB 875, Nuku'alofa; fax 24978; e-mail Paul.Stafford@digicelgroup.com; internet www.digiceltonga.com; f. 2008; CEO PAUL STAFFORD.

Tongasat—Friendly Islands Satellite Communications Ltd: POB 2921, Nuku'alofa; tel. 24160; fax 23322; e-mail info@tongasat.com; internet www.tongasat.com; f. 1988; 80% Tongan-owned; private co but co-operates with Govt in management and leasing of orbital satellite positions; Chair. Princess SALOTE MAFILE'O PILOLEVU TUITA; Man. Dir SEMISI PANUVE.

BROADCASTING

Radio

Tonga Broadcasting Commission (TBC): POB 36, Tungi Rd, Fasi-moe-afi, Nuku'alofa; tel. 23550; fax 28921; internet www.tonga-broadcasting.com; independent statutory board; commercially operated; operates two free-to-air TV channels and three radio stations, with programmes in Tongan and English; Gen. Man. ELENOA AMANAKI.

93FM: Pacific Partners Trust, POB 478, Nuku'alofa; tel. 23076; fax 24970; broadcasts in English, Tongan, German, Mandarin and Hindi.

A3V The Millennium Radio 2000: POB 838, Nuku'alofa; tel. 25891; fax 24195; e-mail a3v@tongatapu.net.to; broadcasts on FM; musical programmes; Gen. Man. SAM VEA.

BroadCom—TMN Group: Ngele'ia; f. 2009; operates one radio station, FM 88.1, and one TV channel, TMN TV2; Founders MAKA TOHI, KATALINA TOHI.

Tonga News Association: Nuku'alofa; Pres. PESI FONUA.

Television

DigiTV: Fatafehi Rd, POB 875, Nuku'alofa; tel. 876-1000; fax 24978; e-mail customercaretonga@digicelgroup.com; internet www.digiceltonga.com; fmrly Tonfon TV; acquired by Digicel Group and renamed as above in 2007; operates 20 channels; CEO (Digicel Tonga) PAUL STAFFORD.

Oceania Broadcasting Network: POB 91, Nuku'alofa; tel. 23314; fax 23658; reportedly ceased operations in late 2006.

Television Tonga: Fasi-moe-afi, Nuku'alofa; f. 2000; 60% of programmes in English; 40% of programmes in Tongan.

Finance

(cap. = capital; res = reserves; dep. = deposits; m. = million; brs = branches; amounts in Tongan dollars)

BANKING

Central Bank

National Reserve Bank of Tonga: Private Bag 25, Nuku'alofa; tel. 24057; fax 24201; e-mail nrbt@reservebank.to; internet www.reservebank.to; f. 1989; assumed central bank functions of Bank of Tonga; issues currency; manages exchange rates and international reserves; cap. 5.0m., res 13.1m., dep. 101.1m. (June 2009); Gov. SIOSI MAFI; Chair. Princess PILOLEVU TUITA.

Other Banks

Australia and New Zealand Banking Group Ltd: POB 910, Nuku'alofa; tel. 20500; fax 23870; e-mail anztonga@anz.com; internet www.anz.com/Tonga; Gen. Man. ARTHUR HUBBARD.

MBf Bank Ltd: POB 3118, Nuku'alofa; tel. 24600; fax 24662; e-mail info@mbfbank.to; internet www.mbfbank.to; f. 1993; 93.35% owned by MBf Asia Capital Corpn Holdings Ltd, 4.75% owned hitherto by King George Tupou V, 0.95% owned by Tonga Investments Ltd, 0.95% owned by Tonga Co-operative Federation Society; Gen. Man. H. K. YEOH.

Tonga Development Bank: Fatafehi Rd, POB 126, Nuku'alofa; tel. 23333; fax 23775; e-mail ssefanaia@tdb.to; internet www.tdb.to; f. 1977; est. to provide credit for developmental purposes, mainly in agriculture, fishery, tourism and housing; cap. 10.5m., res 6.9m. (Dec. 2010); Man. Dir SIMIONE SEFANAIA; 5 brs.

Westpac Bank of Tonga: POB 924, Nuku'alofa; tel. 23933; fax 25066; e-mail westpactonga@westpac.com.au; internet www.westpac.to; f. 1973; est. as Bank of Tonga; name changed as above in 2002; owned by Westpac Banking Corpn (Australia); cap. 23.5m., res 10.6m., dep. 168.8m. (Sept. 2009); Gen. Man. MISHKA TU'IFUA; 6 brs.

Trade and Industry

DEVELOPMENT ORGANIZATIONS

Tonga Investments Ltd: POB 27, Nuku'alofa; tel. 24388; fax 24313; f. 1992; est. to replace Commodities Board; govt-owned; manages five subsidiary cos; Man. Dir ANTHONY WAYNE MADDEN.

Tonga Association of Small Businesses: Nuku'alofa; f. 1990; est. to cater for the needs of small businesses; Chair. SIMI SILAPELU.

CHAMBER OF COMMERCE

Tonga Chamber of Commerce and Industry: Tungi Arcade, POB 1704, Nuku'alofa; tel. 25168; fax 26039; e-mail chamber@kalianet.to; internet www.tongachamber.org; Pres. ALOMA JOHANSSON.

TRADE ASSOCIATIONS

Tonga Kava Council: Nuku'alofa; promotes the development of the industry both locally and abroad; Chair. TO'IMOANA TAKATAKA.

Tonga Squash Council: Nuku'alofa; promotes the development of the industry; introduced a quota system for exports in 2004; Pres. TSUTOMU NAKAO; Sec. STEVEN EDWARDS.

UTILITIES

Shoreline Power Group: POB 47, Taufa'ahau Rd, Kolofo'ou, Nuku'alofa; tel. 23311; fax 23632; provides electricity via diesel motor generation; took control of operations from the Tonga Electric Power Board in 2004; purchased by Tongan Govt in 2008; CEO SOANE RAMANLAL.

Tonga Water Board: POB 92, Taufa'ahau Rd, Kolofo'ou, Nuku'alofa; tel. 23298; fax 23518; operates four urban water systems, serving about 25% of the population; Man. SAIMONE P. HELU.

MAJOR COMPANIES

Nautilus Minerals Tonga: Kupu House, 2nd Floor, Fatafehi Rd, POB 893, Nuku'alofa; tel. 21733; fax 21734; Country Man. PAULA TAUMOEPEAU.

Royal Beer Co Ltd: POB 20 Nuku'alofa; tel. 25554; e-mail denis@royalbeer.to; internet www.royalbeer.to; Gen. Man. DES CARTER.

Sea Star Fishing Co Ltd: POB 2291, Ma'ufanga, Nuku'alofa; tel. 25458; fax 24779; e-mail seastar@canfor.to; tuna fishery and marketing; Man. Dir GEORGE NAKAO.

TRADE UNIONS

Association of Tongatapu Squash Pumpkin Growers: Nuku'alofa; f. 1998.

Public Servants' Association (PSA): Nuku'alofa; Pres. FINAU TUTONE; Gen. Sec. MELE AMANAKI.

Tonga Nurses' Association and Friendly Islands Teachers' Association (TNA/FITA): POB 859, Nuku'alofa; tel. and fax 23972; e-mail fita@candw.to; Pres. FINAU TUTONE; Gen. Sec. TOKANKAMEA PULEIKU.

Transport

ROADS

Total road length was estimated at 680 km in 2000, of which some 27% were all-weather paved roads. Most of the network comprises fair-weather-only dirt or coral roads.

SHIPPING

The chief ports are Nuku'alofa, on Tongatapu, and Neiafu, on Vava'u, with two smaller ports at Pangai and Niuatoputapu.

Shipping Corporation of Polynesia Ltd: Queen Salote Wharf, Vuna Rd, POB 453, Nuku'alofa; tel. 23853; fax 23250; e-mail info@olovaha.com; internet www.olovaha.com; govt-owned; regular inter-islands passenger and cargo services; Chair. 'ALISI TAUMOEPEAU.

Uata Shipping Lines: 'Uliti Uata, POB 100, Nuku'alofa; tel. 23855; fax 23860.

Warner Pacific Line: POB 93, Nuku'alofa; tel. 21088; services to Samoa, American Samoa, Australia and New Zealand; Man. Dir MA'AKE FAKA'OSIFOLAU.

CIVIL AVIATION

Tonga is served by Fua'amotu International Airport, 22 km from Nuku'alofa, and airstrips at Vava'u, Ha'apai, Niuatoputapu, Niuafo'ou and 'Eua. A government agency, Tonga Airports Ltd (TAL), assumed responsibility for the management of all airports in 2007. Air New Zealand provides a regular service to Australia and New Zealand and a regional carrier, Reef Air, operates between Tonga, Niue and Fiji. The New Zealand-based low-cost airline Pacific Blue commenced direct flights to Tonga, from Sydney, Australia, and from Auckland, New Zealand, in 2005.

Airlines Tonga: c/o Teta Tours, cnr of Railway St and Wellington St, Nuku'alofa; tel. 23690; fax 23238; e-mail tetatour@kalianet.to; internet www.airfiji.com.fj/pages.cfm/home/airlines-tonga.html; f. 2006; jt venture between Teta Tours of Tonga and Air Fiji Ltd; sole operator of domestic services in Tonga from Nov. 2006; Man. SITAFOOTI 'AHO.

Chathams Pacific (The Friendly Islands Airline): POB 907, Nuku'alofa; tel. 28000; fax 23447; e-mail sales@chathamspacific.com; internet www.chathamspacific.com; f. 2008; owned by Air Chathams (New Zealand); Gen. Man. RUSSELL JENKINS.

Tourism

Tonga's attractions include scenic beauty, a pleasant climate and whale-watching opportunities. Visitor arrivals increased from an estimated 46,040 in 2007 to 49,405 in 2008. In 2008 revenue from the industry totalled US $20m. The majority of tourists were from New Zealand, the USA and Australia.

Tonga Tourist Association: POB 74, Nuku'alofa; tel. 23344; fax 23833; e-mail royale@kalianet.to; Pres. PAPILOA FOLIAKI; Sec. KOLOLIANA NAUFAHU.

Tonga Visitors' Bureau: Vuna Rd, POB 37, Nuku'alofa; tel. 25334; fax 23507; e-mail info@tvb.gov.to; internet www.tongaholiday.com; f. 1978; CEO SAKOPO LOLOHEA.

Tourism Tonga Inc: Nuku'alofa; f. 2009.

Defence

Tonga has its own defence force, the Tonga Defence Services, consisting of both regular and reserve units. The island also has a defence co-operation agreement with Australia. As part of the multinational operation, a contingent of 55 Tongan soldiers was serving in Afghanistan in 2011. Projected government expenditure on defence in 2004/05 was $T3.9m.

Commander of the Tonga Defence Services: Brig.-Gen. TAU'AIKA 'UTA'ATU.

Education

Free state education is compulsory for children between five and 14 years of age, while the Government and other Commonwealth countries offer scholarship schemes enabling students to go abroad for higher education. In 2007 there were 16,892 primary pupils and 14,580 secondary pupils, according to provisional figures. In 1999 a total of 467 students attended technical and vocational colleges, of which there were four in 2001. There was one teacher-training college in 1999, with 288 students. Some degree courses are offered at the university division of 'Atenisi Institute. A new establishment offering higher education, the 'Unuaki 'o Tonga Royal Institute (UTRI), opened in 2004. Recurrent government expenditure on education in 2004/05 was an estimated $T19.0m.

TUVALU

Introduction

Tuvalu is a scattered group of nine small atolls (five of which enclose sizeable lagoons), extending 560 km from north to south and covering a land area of 26 sq km (10 sq miles) in the western Pacific Ocean. Its nearest neighbours are Fiji to the south, Kiribati to the north and Solomon Islands to the west. The climate is warm and pleasant, with a mean annual temperature of 29°C (84°F), and there is very little seasonal variation. The average annual rainfall is 3,000 mm. The inhabitants are a Polynesian people who speak Tuvaluan and English. Almost all profess Christianity, and about 98% are Protestants. The population was estimated by the Secretariat of the Pacific Community to be 11,206 at mid-2011. The capital is on Funafuti Atoll.

Tuvalu was formerly known as the Ellice (or Lagoon) Islands. Between about 1850 and 1875 many of the islanders were captured by slave-traders and this, together with European diseases, reduced the population from about 20,000 to 3,000. In 1877 the United Kingdom established the Western Pacific High Commission, with its headquarters in Fiji, and the Ellice Islands and other groups were placed under its jurisdiction. In 1892 a British protectorate was declared over the Ellice Islands and the group was linked administratively with the Gilbert Islands to the north. In 1916 the United Kingdom annexed the protectorate, which was renamed the Gilbert and Ellice Islands Colony (GEIC). During the Japanese occupation of the Gilbert Islands in 1942–43, the administration of the GEIC was temporarily moved to Funafuti in the Ellice Islands (see the chapter on Kiribati).

A series of advisory and legislative bodies prepared the GEIC for self-government. In May 1974 the last of these, the Legislative Council, was replaced by the House of Assembly, with 28 elected members (including eight Ellice Islanders) and three official members. A Chief Minister was elected by the House and chose between four and six other ministers, one of whom had to be from the Ellice Islands.

In January 1972 the appointment of a separate GEIC Governor, who assumed most of the functions previously exercised by the High Commissioner, increased the long-standing anxiety of the Ellice Islanders over their minority position as Polynesians in the colony, dominated by the Micronesians of the Gilbert Islands. In a referendum held in the Ellice Islands in mid-1974, over 90% of voters favoured separate status for the group, and in October 1975 the Ellice Islands, under the old native name of Tuvalu ('eight standing together', which referred to the eight populated atolls), became a separate British dependency. The Deputy Governor of the GEIC took office as Her Majesty's Commissioner for Tuvalu. The eight Ellice representatives in the GEIC House of Assembly became the first elected members of the new Tuvalu House of Assembly. They elected one of their number, Toaripi Lauti, to be Chief Minister. Tuvalu was completely separated from the GEIC administration in January 1976. The remainder of the GEIC was renamed the Gilbert Islands and achieved independence, under the name of Kiribati, in July 1979.

Tuvalu's first separate elections were held in August 1977, when the number of elective seats in the House of Assembly was increased to 12. An independence Constitution was finalized at a conference in London in February 1978. After five months of internal self-government, Tuvalu became independent on 1 October 1978, with Lauti as the first Prime Minister. The pre-independence House of Assembly was redesignated Parliament. Tuvalu is a 'special member' of the Commonwealth, taking part in functional activities but not represented at meetings of Heads of Government. Tuvalu was admitted to the UN in September 2000. In February 1979 Tuvalu signed a Treaty of Friendship with the USA, which renounced its claim, dating from 1856, to the four southernmost atolls.

Following parliamentary elections in September 1981, Lauti was replaced as Prime Minister by Dr Tomasi (later Sir Tomasi) Puapua, who was re-elected in September 1985 before being replaced in September 1989 (and being appointed Governor-General in 1998).

In February 1986 a nation-wide poll was conducted to establish public sentiment as to whether Tuvalu should remain a constitutional monarchy, with the British monarch at its head, or become a republic. On only one atoll did the community appear to favour republican status. Under a revised Constitution that took effect on 1 October 1986, the Governor-General's ability to veto government measures was abolished. In 1991 the Government announced that it was to prepare a compensation claim against the United Kingdom for the allegedly poor condition of Tuvalu's economy and infrastructure at the time of the country's accession to independence in 1979. Moreover, Tuvalu was to seek additional compensation for damage caused during the Second World War when the United Kingdom gave permission for the USA to build airstrips on the islands (some 40% of Funafuti had been rendered uninhabitable by the construction of an airstrip on the atoll).

In December 1994, in what was widely regarded as a significant rejection of its political links with the United Kingdom, the Tuvaluan Parliament voted to remove Britain's union flag from the Tuvalu national flag. A new design was selected and the new flag was inaugurated in October 1995. Speculation that the British monarch would be removed as Head of State intensified during 1995, following the appointment of a committee to review the Constitution. The three-member committee was to examine the procedure surrounding the appointment and removal of the Governor-General, and, in particular, to consider the adoption of a republican system of government. In late 1996, however, when Bikenibeu Paeniu replaced Kamuta Latasi as Prime Minister, the new premier acted promptly to restore the country's original flag.

A referendum on Tuvalu's system of government was conducted at the end of April 2008. The level of participation was reported to be only 21% of the electorate. The majority of voters rejected proposals for a republican system, whereby the appointment of a president as head of state had been envisaged: according to reports, 1,260 voters (or 65%) out of a total of 1,939 preferred the retention of the existing system of constitutional monarchy. The issue of the lack of female members in Parliament came to the fore in May 2010 when a consultation group recommended the creation of two seats specifically to be reserved for women.

Tuvalu has been increasingly affected by the impact of climate change. A report published by the UN Environment Programme (UNEP) in 1989 warned that Tuvalu was one of five island groups that were particularly threatened, and which, unless drastic measures were taken, might be completely submerged by the mid-21st century. In February 2005 high tides flooded homes, government buildings and the airport, and caused damage to agricultural produce. It was reported in late 2007 that water from Tuvalu's wells was becoming increasingly unsuitable for consumption. At a climate change convention held in the Australian town of Cairns in April 2011, Tuvalu's representative appealed for regional assistance in addressing the issue of the country's increasingly frequent annual flooding from high tides. In September a state of emergency was declared, owing to the critical shortages of fresh water. The New Zealand air force delivered two desalination units and water containers to Tuvalu. Crops of taro, breadfruit and coconuts were reported to have been seriously affected by the protracted drought conditions.

Tuvalu's economic development has also been impeded by the shortcomings of the islands' infrastructure. With the exception of copra production, agriculture (including fishing) is of a basic subsistence nature. Revenue from the sale of fishing licences, furthermore, has become increasingly vulnerable to the fluctuations in fish stocks caused by the greater frequency of the climatic phenomena known as El Niño and La Niña. Amid reports that in the previous year Tuvalu had received only 5% of the revenue derived from local fishing activities, in late 2010 New Zealand expressed its support for a four-year fisheries programme that was expected to require funding of nearly US $3m. Manufacturing is confined to the small-scale production of coconut-based products, soap and handicrafts. The Government is an important employer, and consequently the services sector makes a relatively large contribution to Tuvalu's economy. In the late 1990s the Government began to explore the possibility of leasing the country's national internet suffix. The sale of the '.tv' suffix to a US company in February 2000 substantially increased the islands' revenue. Another important source of revenue has been provided by remittances from Tuvaluans working abroad, notably seafarers employed on foreign merchant ships. However, with numerous seafarers having lost their jobs as global economic conditions deteriorated, these inflows were reported to have declined in 2009. Tuvalu has remained reliant on income from overseas and has continued to depend on foreign assistance for its development budget. In 1987 the Tuvalu Trust Fund (TTF) was established, with assistance from New Zealand, Australia and the United Kingdom, to generate funding, through overseas investment, for development projects. A priority for successive governments has been the need to reduce the disparities in living standards between Funafuti and the outer islands. Tuvalu's remote situation and lack of amenities have hindered the development of a tourist industry. In an attempt to turn the arrival of the annual high tide to the islands' advantage by raising awareness of the issue of rising sea-levels, in February 2010 Tuvalu held its first King Tide Festival. The Government hoped to increase revenue from tourism through initiatives such as this.

Statistical Survey

Source (unless otherwise indicated): Central Statistics Division, Ministry of Finance, Economic Planning and Industries, PMB, Vaiaku, Funafuti; tel. 20107; fax 21210; e-mail statistics@tuvalu.tv; internet www.spc.int/prism/country/tv/stats/.

AREA AND POPULATION

Land Area: 25.6 sq km (9.9 sq miles).

Population: 9,043 at census of 17 November 1991; 9,561 (males 4,729, females 4,832) at census of 1 November 2002 (*By Atoll:* Funafuti 4,492; Vaitupu 1,591; Nanumea 664; Niutao 663; Nanumaga 589; Nukufetau 586; Nui 548; Nukulaelae 393; Niulakita 35). *Mid-2011* (Secretariat of the Pacific Community estimate): 11,206 (Source: Pacific Regional Information System).

Density (at mid-2011): 437.7 per sq km.

Population by Age and Sex (Secretariat of the Pacific Community estimates at mid-2011): *0–14:* 3,553 (males 1,840, females 1,713); *15–64:* 7,060 (males 3,501, females 3,560); *65 and over:* 593 (males 240, females 353); *Total* 11,206 (males 5,582, females 5,626) (Source: Pacific Regional Information System).

Principal Towns (population at 2002 census): Alapi 1,024; Fakaifou 1,007; Senala 589; Teone 540; Vaiaku (capital) 516; Motufoua 506. Source: Thomas Brinkhoff, *City Population* (internet www.citypopulation.de).

Births and Deaths (2007): Registered live births 155; Registered deaths 47 (provisional).

Life Expectancy (years at birth, WHO estimates): 64 (males 64; females 63) in 2009. Source: WHO, *World Health Statistics*.

Economically Active Population: In 1979 there were 936 people in paid employment, 50% of them in government service. In 1979 114 Tuvaluans were employed by the Nauru Phosphate Co, with a smaller number employed in Kiribati and about 255 on foreign ships. At the 1991 census the total economically active population (aged 15 years and over) stood at 2,383 (males 1,605, females 778). *Mid-2011* (estimates): Agriculture, etc. 1,000; Total labour force 4,000 (Source: FAO).

HEALTH AND WELFARE

Key Indicators

Total Fertility Rate (children per woman, 2009): 3.2.

Under-5 Mortality Rate (per 1,000 live births, 2009): 35.

Physicians (per 1,000 head, 2003): 0.9.

Hospital Beds (per 1,000 head, 2001): 5.6.

Health Expenditure (2008): US $ per head (PPP): 266.

Health Expenditure (2008): % of GDP: 9.7.

Health Expenditure (2008): public (% of total): 99.7.

Access to Sanitation (% of persons, 2008): 81.

For sources and definitions, see explanatory note on p. vi.

AGRICULTURE, ETC.

Principal Crops (metric tons, 2009, FAO estimates): Coconuts 1,700; Roots and tubers 145; Vegetables 543; Bananas 354.

Livestock ('000 head, year ending September 2009, unless otherwise indicated, FAO estimates): Pigs 13.6; Chickens 45; Ducks 15 (2008).

Livestock Products (metric tons, 2009, FAO estimates): Chicken meat 53; Pig meat 91; Hen eggs 28; Honey 6.

Fishing (metric tons, live weight, 2009): Total catch 4,198 (FAO estimate) (Skipjack tuna 3,135; Yellowfin tuna 399).

Source: FAO.

FINANCE

Currency and Exchange Rates: Australian and Tuvaluan currencies are both in use. Australian currency: 100 cents = 1 Australian dollar ($A). *Sterling, US Dollar and Euro Equivalents* (31 May 2011): £1 sterling = $A1.541; US $1 = $A0.934; €1 = $A1.343; $A100 = £64.89 = US $10.71 = €74.45. *Average Exchange Rate* ($A per US dollar): 1.1922 in 2008; 1.2822 in 2009; 1.0901 in 2010.

Budget ($A '000, 2008): Current revenue 16,790 (Revenue from taxation 6,772, Non-tax revenue 10,018); Grants 28,567; Total revenue and grants 45,357; Total expenditure 42,936.

Official Development Assistance (US $ million, 2002): Bilateral 11.2; Multilateral 0.5; Total 11.7 (all grants). *2007:* Total assistance 11.7. Source: UN, *Statistical Yearbook for Asia and the Pacific*.

Cost of Living (Consumer Price Index; base: November 2006 = 100): All items 98.7 in 2006; 99.2 in 2007; 100.2 in 2008. Source: Asian Development Bank.

Gross Domestic Product (US $ million at constant 2005 prices): 23.6 in 2007; 24.1 in 2008; 24.6 in 2009. Source: UN Statistics Division, National Accounts Main Aggregates Database.

Expenditure on the Gross Domestic Product (US $ million at current prices, 2009): Government final consumption expenditure 19.5; Private final consumption expenditure 27.7; Gross fixed capital formation 2.2; *Total domestic expenditure* 49.4; Exports of goods and services 5.2; *Less* Imports of goods and services 22.6; Statistical discrepancy –4.7 *GDP in purchasers' values* 27.3. Source: UN Statistics Division, National Accounts Main Aggregates Database.

Gross Domestic Product by Economic Activity (US $ million at current prices, 2009): Agriculture, hunting, forestry and fishing 5.2; Mining, manufacturing and utilities 2.7 (Manufacturing 1.1); Construction 1.4; Trade, restaurants and hotels 3.8; Transport, storage and communications 3.2; Other services 13.6; *Gross value added* 29.8; Net taxes on products –2.5 (obtained as residual); *GDP in purchasers' values* 27.3. Source: UN Statistics Division, National Accounts Main Aggregates Database.

Balance of Payments ($A '000, 2003): Exports of goods f.o.b. 444; Imports of goods f.o.b. –28,995; *Trade balance* –28,552; Exports of services and other income 7,403; Imports of services and other income –17,687; *Balance on goods, services and income* –38,836; Current transfers (net) 20,833; *Current balance* –18,003. Source: Asian Development Bank.

EXTERNAL TRADE

Principal Commodities ($A '000, 2005): *Imports:* Animals and animal products 1,473.8; Vegetable products 1,224.2; Prepared foodstuffs 2,385.1; Mineral products 3,661.2; Chemical products 734.5; Textiles and textile articles 759.2; Base metals and articles thereof 695.1; Machinery, mechanical appliances and electrical equipment 2,318.9; Transportation equipment 884.8; Total (incl. others) 16,908.3. *Exports:* Mineral products 5.9; Wood and wood products 10.0; Base metals and articles thereof 12.3; Machinery, mechanical appliances and electrical equipment 13.9; Transportation equipment 9.3; Instruments—measuring, musical 14.9; Total (incl. others) 80.0. *2006:* Total imports 17,903.0; Total exports 130.0. *2007:* Total imports 18,503.0; Total exports 120.0. Source: Asian Development Bank.

Principal Trading Partners (US $ million, 2010, preliminary): *Imports:* Australia 1.94; China, People's Republic 8.36; India 0.27; Japan 45.28; Malaysia 1.42; New Zealand 1.73; Total (incl. others) 94.21. *Exports:* Australia 0.44; India 0.06; Indonesia 1.07; Japan 1.26; Total (incl. others) 3.53.

Source: Asian Development Bank.

TRANSPORT

Shipping: *Merchant Fleet* (registered at 31 December 2009): Vessels 181; Total displacement ('000 grt) 1,098.2. Source: IHS Fairplay, *World Fleet Statistics*.

TOURISM

Tourist Arrivals: 1,085 in 2005; 1,135 in 2006; 1,130 in 2007.

Tourist Arrivals by Country of Residence (2007): Australia 138; Fiji 218; Japan 227; New Zealand 105; United Kingdom 35; USA 54; Total (incl. others) 1,130.

Source: World Tourism Organization.

COMMUNICATIONS MEDIA

Non-daily Newspapers (2004, unless otherwise stated): 1; Estimated circulation 300 in 1996*.

Telephones (main lines, 2010): 1,600 in use†.

Mobile Cellular Telephones (subscribers, 2010): 2,500.

Internet Users (2009): 4,300.

Radio Receivers (1997): 4,000 in use*.

* Source: UNESCO, *Statistical Yearbook*.

† Source: International Telecommunication Union.

EDUCATION

Pre-school (2005/06, unless otherwise indicated): 57 teachers (2004/05); 711 pupils.

Primary (2001, unless otherwise indicated): 9 government schools, 1 private school; 103 teachers (2006); 2,093 pupils (2007).

General Secondary (2005): 2 government schools; 56 teachers; 593 pupils.**Pupil-teacher Ratio** (primary education, UNESCO estimate): 19.2 in 2003/04. Source: UNESCO Institute for Statistics.

Directory

The Constitution

A new Constitution came into effect at independence on 1 October 1978. Its main provisions are as follows:

The Constitution states that Tuvalu is a democratic sovereign state and that the Constitution is the Supreme Law. It guarantees protection of all fundamental rights and freedoms and provides for the determination of citizenship.

The British sovereign is represented by the Governor-General, who must be a citizen of Tuvalu and is appointed on the recommendation of the Prime Minister. The Prime Minister is elected by Parliament, and up to four other ministers are appointed by the Governor-General from among the members of Parliament, after consultation with the Prime Minister. The Cabinet, which is directly responsible to Parliament, consists of the Prime Minister and the other ministers, whose functions are to advise the Governor-General upon the government of Tuvalu. The Attorney-General is the principal legal adviser to the Government. Parliament is composed of 15 members directly elected by universal adult suffrage for four years, subject to dissolution, and is presided over by the Speaker (who is elected by the members). The Constitution also provides for the operation of a Judiciary (see Judicial System) and for an independent Public Service. Under a revised Constitution that took effect on 1 October 1986, the Governor-General no longer has the authority to reject the advice of the Government.

The Government

HEAD OF STATE

Sovereign: HM Queen ELIZABETH II.

Governor-General: Sir IAKOBA TAEIA ITALELI (took office May 2010).

CABINET
(October 2011)

Prime Minister and Minister of Home Affairs: WILLIE TELAVI.

Minister of Foreign Affairs, Environment, Trade, Labour and Tourism: APISAI IELEMIA.

Minister of Finance: LOTOALA METIA.

Minister of Communications: KAUSEA NATANO.

Minister of Education and Sports: FALESA PITOI.

Minister of Health: TAOM TANUKALE.

Minister of Works and Natural Resources: (vacant).

MINISTRIES

Office of the Prime Minister: PMB, Vaiaku, Funafuti; tel. 20101; fax 20820.

Ministry of Education, Sports and Health: POB 37, Vaiaku, Funafuti; tel. 20405; fax 20832.

Ministry of Finance, Economic Planning and Industries: PMB, Vaiaku, Funafuti; tel. 20202; fax 20210.

Ministry of Foreign Affairs: Vaiaku, Funafuti; tel. 20102; fax 20820.

Ministry of Home Affairs and Rural Development: PMB, Vaiaku, Funafuti; tel. 20172; fax 20821.

Ministry of Natural Resources and Environment: PMB, Vaiaku, Funafuti; tel. 20827; fax 20826.

Ministry of Public Utilities and Industries: PMB, Vaiaku, Funafuti.

Ministry of Works, Communications and Transport: PMB, Vaiaku, Funafuti; tel. 20052; fax 20772; e-mail tuvmet@tuvalu.tv.

Legislature

PARLIAMENT

Parliament has 15 members, who hold office for a term of up to four years. At the general election held on 16 September 2010, 10 of the 15 previous incumbents were re-elected. There are no political parties.

Speaker: ISAIA TAEIA.

Diplomatic Representation

There are no embassies or high commissions in Tuvalu. The British High Commissioner in Fiji is also accredited as High Commissioner to Tuvalu. Other Ambassadors or High Commissioners accredited to Tuvalu include the Australian, New Zealand, US, French and Japanese Ambassadors in Fiji.

Judicial System

The Supreme Law is embodied in the Constitution. The High Court is the superior court of record, presided over by the Chief Justice, and has jurisdiction to consider appeals from judgments of the Magistrates' Courts and the Island Courts. Appeals from the High Court have traditionally been heard by the Court of Appeal in Fiji or, in the ultimate case, with the Judicial Committee of the Privy Council in the United Kingdom.

There are eight Island Courts with limited jurisdiction in criminal and civil cases.

Chief Justice of the High Court: GORDON WARD, Vaiaku, Funafuti; tel. 20837.

Attorney-General: ESELEALOFA APINELU, Funafuti; tel. 20823; fax 20819; e-mail agoffice@tuvalu.tv.

Religion

CHRISTIANITY

Te Ekalesia Kelisiano Tuvalu (The Christian Church of Tuvalu): POB 2, Funafuti; tel. 20755; fax 20651; f. 1861; autonomous since 1968; derived from the Congregationalist foundation of the London Missionary Society; some 91% of the population are adherents; Pres. Rev. TOFIGA FALANI; Gen. Sec. Rev. TAFUE M. LUSAMA.

Roman Catholic Church: Catholic Centre, POB 58, Funafuti; tel. and fax 20527; e-mail cathcent@tuvalu.tv; 131 adherents (31 Dec. 2006); Superior Fr JOHN IKATAERE RARIKIN.

Other churches with adherents in Tuvalu include the Church of Jesus Christ of Latter-day Saints (Mormons), the Jehovah's Witnesses, the New Apostolic Church and the Seventh-day Adventists.

BAHÁ'Í FAITH

National Spiritual Assembly: POB 48, Vaiaku Side, Funafuti; tel. 20860; e-mail natsectuv@yahoo.com; mems resident in 8 localities.

The Press

Te Lama: Ekalesia Kelisiano Tuvalu, POB 2, Valuku, Funafuti; tel. and fax 20755; e-mail gs_ekt@yahoo.com; quarterly; religious; Pres. Rev. TOFIGA FALANI; Editor Rev. KITIONA TAUSI; circ. 1,000.

Tuvalu Echoes: Broadcasting and Information Office, Vaiaku, Funafuti; tel. 20138; fax 20732; f. 1984; fortnightly; English; Editor MELAKI TAEPE; circ. 250.

Broadcasting and Communications

TELECOMMUNICATIONS

Tuvalu Telecommunications Corporation: Vaiaku, Funafuti; tel. 20001; fax 20800; f. 1994; Gen. Man. SIMETI LOPATI.

BROADCASTING

Tuvalu Media Corporation: PMB, Vaiaku, Funafuti; tel. 20731; fax 20732; e-mail media@tuvalu.tv; internet www.tuvalu-news.tv/tmc; f. 1999; govt-owned; Chief Broadcasting and Information Officer PUSINELLI LAAFAI.

Radio

Radio Tuvalu: Broadcasting and Information Office, PMB, Vaiaku, Funafuti; tel. 20138; fax 20732; f. 1975; daily broadcasts in Tuvaluan and English, 43 hours per week; Programme Producer RUBY S. ALEFAIO.

Finance

BANKS
(cap. = capital; dep. = deposits; m. = million)

Development Bank of Tuvalu: POB 9, Vaiaku, Funafuti; tel. 20199; fax 20850; f. 1993; replaced the Business Development Advisory Bureau; Gen. Man. TAUKAVE POOLO.

National Bank of Tuvalu: POB 13, Vaiaku, Funafuti; tel. 20803; fax 20802; e-mail nbt@tuvalu.tv; f. 1980; commercial bank; govt-owned; ($A '000) cap. 471.0, dep. 23,725 (Dec. 2008); Chair. AUNESE SIMATI; Gen. Man. SIOSE P. TEO; brs on all atolls.

Trade and Industry

GOVERNMENT AGENCIES

National Fishing Corporation of Tuvalu (NAFICOT): POB 93, Funafuti; tel. 20724; fax 20152; fishing vessel operators; seafood-processing and -marketing; agents for diesel engine spare parts, fishing supplies and marine electronics; Gen. Man. SEMU SOPOANGA TAAFAKI.

Tuvalu Philatelic Bureau: POB 24, Funafuti; tel. 20224; fax 20712.

CHAMBER OF COMMERCE

Tuvalu Chamber of Commerce: POB 27, Vaiaku, Funafuti; tel. 20846; fax 20800; Chair. MATANILE IOSEFA; Sec. TEO PASEFIKA.

UTILITIES

Electricity

Tuvalu Electricity Corporation (TEC): POB 32, Vaiaku, Funafuti; tel. 20352; fax 20351; Gen. Man. MAFALU LOTOLUA.

CO-OPERATIVE

Tuvalu Co-operative Society Ltd: POB 11, Funafuti; tel. 20747; fax 20748; e-mail mlaafai@tuvalu.tv; f. 1979; est. by amalgamation of the eight island socs; controls retail trade in the islands; Gen. Man. MONISE LAAFAI; Registrar AUNESE MAKOI.

TRADE UNION

Tuvalu Overseas Seamen's Union (TOSU): POB 99, Funafuti; tel. 20609; fax 20610; e-mail tosu@tuvalu.tv; f. 1988; Sec.-Gen. FEPUALI KITISENI.

Transport

ROADS

Funafuti has some impacted-coral roads totalling some 8 km in length; elsewhere, tracks exist.

SHIPPING

There is a deep-water lagoon at the point of entry, Funafuti, and ships are able to enter the lagoon at Nukufetau. Irregular shipping services connect Tuvalu with Fiji and elsewhere. The Government operates an inter-island vessel.

CIVIL AVIATION

In 1992 a new runway was constructed with aid from the European Union to replace the grass landing strip on Funafuti. Air Marshall Islands operates a three-weekly service between Funafuti, Nadi (Fiji) and Majuro (Marshall Islands). The Government of Tuvalu purchased a substantial shareholding in Air Fiji in 2001, but the carrier terminated all operations in 2009. Air Pacific commenced a twice-weekly service from Fiji in August 2008.

Tourism

In 2004 there was one hotel, with 16 rooms, on Funafuti and three guest houses. Visitor arrivals were estimated to total 1,130 in 2007. The majority of visitors are from Fiji, Australia, Japan and New Zealand. In a new initiative to attract tourists, in February 2010 Tuvalu held its first King Tide Festival, celebrating the arrival of the annual high tide.

Tuvalu Tourism Office: Ministry of Finance, Economic Planning and Industries, PMB, Funafuti; tel. 20055; fax 20722; e-mail tourism@tuvalu.tv; internet www.timelesstuvalu.com; Tourism Officer LONO LENEUOTI.

Education

Education is provided by the Government, and is compulsory between the ages of six and 15 years. In 2001 there were nine government and one private primary schools, with a total of 2,093 pupils in 2007 and 103 teachers in 2006. There were two secondary schools with 56 teachers and 593 pupils in 2005. The only tertiary institution is the Maritime Training School at Amatuku on Funafuti, with vocational, technical and commerce-related courses. About 60 people graduate from the school annually. Further training or vocational courses are available in Fiji and Kiribati. The University of the South Pacific (based in Suva, Fiji) has an extension centre on Funafuti offering diploma and vocational courses and the first two years of degree courses (the latter requiring completion in Suva). A programme of major reforms in the education system in Tuvalu, begun in the early 1990s, resulted in the lengthening of primary schooling (from six to eight years) and a compulsory two years of secondary education, as well as the introduction of vocational, technical and commerce-related courses at the Maritime Training School. Total government expenditure on education in 2001 was equivalent to some 35% of total budgetary expenditure.

UNITED KINGDOM PACIFIC TERRITORY

There is only one British Dependent Territory remaining in the Pacific, which is the Crown Colony of Pitcairn, Henderson, Ducie and Oeno Islands. Until the end of 1995 the United Kingdom maintained membership of the South Pacific Commission (now Pacific Community) in respect of the Pitcairn Islands. The British Minister responsible for overseas possessions is the Secretary of State for Foreign and Commonwealth Affairs.

Head of State: HM Queen ELIZABETH II (succeeded to the throne 6 February 1952).

Foreign and Commonwealth Office: King Charles St, London, SW1A 2AH; tel. (20) 7008-1500; internet www.fco.gov.uk.

Secretary of State for Foreign and Commonwealth Affairs: WILLIAM HAGUE.

THE PITCAIRN ISLANDS

Introduction

The British Dependent Territory of Pitcairn, Henderson, Ducie and Oeno Islands is commonly known as Pitcairn (after the one inhabited island) or the Pitcairn Islands. Pitcairn Island is situated at 25°04 ' S and 130°06 ' W, about midway between Panama and New Zealand and 2,172 km (1,350 miles) east-south-east of Tahiti (French Polynesia). It is a rugged and fertile island of volcanic origin, which rises to a height of some 330 m (1,100 ft) and has an area of 4.35 sq km (1.75 sq miles). Even at the only landing place, access from the sea is difficult. The climate is equable, with mean monthly temperatures ranging from 19°C (66°F) in August to 24°C (75°F) in February, and average annual rainfall of 2,000 mm. There is a large population of some 1,500 descendants of Pitcairn Islanders, most of whom live in New Zealand (an estimated 171 in 2002) and Australia. The resident population has been in decline since 1937 (when it reached a high point of 233), and in December 2010 numbered 58. It was estimated in 1990 that fewer than 500 people had been born on Pitcairn since 1790. The official language is English, but most of the islanders use Pitcairnese or Pitkern, a dialect based on 18th-century seafarers' English and Tahitian. The islanders are adherents of the Seventh-day Adventist Church. The chief settlement is Adamstown on Pitcairn Island.

The other three islands of the Territory are uninhabited, although the islanders regularly visit Henderson and Oeno Islands, the former being a large, raised atoll of 30 sq km (11.6 sq miles), 169 km east-north-east of Pitcairn, which provides miro wood, and the latter an atoll of less than 1 sq km and 121 km north-west of Pitcairn. Ducie Island (471 km east of Pitcairn) is the smallest of the four islands, and is largely inaccessible.

Pitcairn Island was discovered in 1767, when it was uninhabited, although there is evidence of previous occupation by Polynesian peoples. The island was first settled by the British in 1790, when it was occupied by nine mutineers of *HMS Bounty* (led by Fletcher Christian), accompanied by 12 women and six men from Tahiti. Despite the violence of the first decade (by 1800 the only surviving adult male was John Adams, who led the community until his death in 1829), the population increased steadily. Concern about the size of the population led to a temporary evacuation to Tahiti in 1831 and, when numbers reached 194 in 1856, the entire community was evacuated to a new home, provided by the British Government, on Norfolk Island. By 1864 a total of 43 Pitcairners had returned to the island, which has been permanently settled ever since. Pitcairn officially became a British settlement in 1887. In 1893 a parliamentary form of government was adopted, and in 1898 responsibility for administration was assumed by the High Commissioner for the Western Pacific. Pitcairn came under the jurisdiction of the Governor of Fiji in 1952, and, from 1970 onwards, of the British High Commissioner in New Zealand acting as Governor, in consultation with the Island Council, presided over by the Island Magistrate (who is elected triennially) and comprising one ex-officio member (the Island Secretary), five elected and three nominated members.

In 1987 the British High Commissioner in Fiji, acting on behalf of Pitcairn, the United Kingdom's last remaining dependency in the South Pacific, joined representatives of the USA, France, New Zealand and six South Pacific island states in signing the South Pacific Regional Environment Protection Convention, the main aim of which is to prevent the disposal of nuclear waste in the region.

In April 1993, during an official visit to Pitcairn, the Governor was presented with a document expressing dissatisfaction with British policy towards the islands and raising the question of a transfer of sovereignty. Following some structural changes in the local government of Pitcairn, Steve Christian was elected to the position of Mayor in December 1999, presiding over the Island Council (a role previously fulfilled by the Island Magistrate). The British Overseas Territories Act, which entered into effect in May 2002, granted citizenship rights in the United Kingdom to residents of the Overseas Territories, including Pitcairn. The legislation also entitled Pitcairn Islanders to hold British passports and to work in the United Kingdom and elsewhere in the European Union.

Consultations on amendments to the Constitution, which were explicitly to state Pitcairn Islanders' rights and responsibilities, commenced in 2009. Emphasis was to be placed on partnership values as the basis of Pitcairn's relationship with the United Kingdom. Advice on human rights and other constitutional matters was provided by the Commonwealth Foundation, and islanders' comments on the proposed revisions were to be submitted to the Governor by the end of October. The constitutional amendments were enacted in February 2010. New provisions included: the formal incorporation of the Island Council into the Constitution; a requirement that the Island Council be consulted with regard to all draft legislation; the creation of the role of Ombudsman, who was to be responsible for investigating any complaints of government maladministration; the establishment of a Supreme Court; and the appointment of an independent attorney-general. The new Constitution was proclaimed in March.

In 2003, following an investigation by British and New Zealand detectives into allegations of systematic sexual abuse, nine Pitcairn men were charged with a total of 64 offences, some of which dated back about 40 years. In June a further four men, all now resident in New Zealand, were charged with a total of 32 offences. Among those convicted in October 2004 was the Mayor of Pitcairn, Steve Christian, who was found guilty of five counts of rape. Subsequent appeals against the convictions by the men, who argued that they were not British subjects and that English law did not apply on Pitcairn, were rejected by the Pitcairn Supreme Court (sitting in Auckland, New Zealand) and ultimately by the United Kingdom's highest court, the Privy Council. In October 2008 the Foreign and Commonwealth Office announced that the victims of sexual abuse would be eligible to apply for compensation. The compensation paid would be comparable to amounts awarded in similar cases in the United Kingdom. The closing date for the submission of applications for compensation was 31 March 2009.

In April 2009, after the majority of islanders voted in favour of the proposal, the Governor signed a law to remove the ban on the consumption of alcohol, subject to various caveats. The prohibition had remained in force since the 1830s.

A reafforestation scheme, begun in 1963, concentrated on the planting of miro trees, which provide a rosewood suitable for handicrafts. In 1992 an exclusive economic zone (EEZ), designated in 1980 and extending 370 km (200 nautical miles) off shore, was officially declared.

Development projects have been focused on harbour improvements, power supplies, telecommunications and road-building. Pitcairn's first radio-telephone link was established in 1985, and a modern telecommunications unit was installed in 1992. A new health clinic was established, with British finance, in 1996. Major improvements to the jetty and slipway at Bounty Bay and to the Hill of Difficulty road, which leads to the landing area, were carried out in 2005. In the same year a museum was constructed on the island to house some of Pitcairn's historical artefacts, including the *Bounty* cannon, which had been raised from Bounty Bay with assistance from an Australian team in 1999 and was returned to the island in 2009. New Zealand currency is used. There is no taxation (except for small licensing fees on guns and vehicles), and government revenue has been derived mainly from philatelic sales and from interest earned on investments. Hopes that Pitcairn might find an additional source of revenue through the sale of website addresses were boosted in 2000 when the island won a legal victory to gain control of its internet domain name suffix '.pn'. In 2008 the telephone system was upgraded and islanders were given constant internet access, while television became available for the first time. Pitcairn's potential for tourism (particularly ecotourism) is considered as a possible source of future revenue. Following the British Government's provision of funding for a bee-keeping expert to spend six months on Pitcairn, assisting the islanders with the expansion of their honey industry, by 2010 the number of beehives had been increased to 150. It was reported that the product was being supplied to exclusive food retailers in the United Kingdom.

In 1989 uninhabited Henderson Island was included on the UNESCO 'World Heritage List'. The island, 169 km east-north-east of Pitcairn, was to be preserved as a bird sanctuary. As well as many endemic plants, there are five species of bird unique to the island: the flightless rail or Henderson chicken, the green Henderson fruit dove, the Henderson crake, the Henderson warbler and the Henderson lorikeet. In August 2010, however, with the number of rats on Henderson Island estimated to have reached 30,000, UNESCO emphasized the need for urgent action to address the rodent problem and warned of the possibility of the removal of Henderson Island's World Heritage status. With the objective of saving the Henderson petrel from ultimate extinction, an operation to eliminate the rats, which were reported to be consuming 95% of petrel chicks, commenced in mid-2011.

Statistical Survey

Source: Office of the Governor of Pitcairn, Henderson, Ducie and Oeno Islands, c/o British Consulate-General, Pitcairn Islands Administration, Private Box 105-696, Auckland, New Zealand; tel. (9) 366-0186; fax (9) 366-0187; e-mail pitcairn@iconz.co.nz.

AREA AND POPULATION

Area: 35.5 sq km. *By Island*: Pitcairn 4.35 sq km; Henderson 30.0 sq km; Oeno is less than 1 sq km and Ducie is smaller.

Population: 66 at census of 31 December 1991. *31 December 2010* (annual census): 58. Note: Figure excludes 10 off-island residents.

Density (Pitcairn only, 31 December 2010): 13.3 per sq km.

Employment (able-bodied men, 2002): 9.

FINANCE

Currency and Exchange Rates: 100 cents = 1 Pitcairn dollar. The Pitcairn dollar is at par with the New Zealand dollar ($NZ). New Zealand currency is usually used.

Budget ($NZ, 1998/99): Revenue 492,000; Expenditure 667,000.

EXTERNAL TRADE

Trade with New Zealand ($NZ '000): *Imports:* 791.4 in 2008; 1,253.3 in 2009; 626.1 in 2010. *Exports:* 45.4 in 2008; 88.8 in 2009; 137.8 in 2010.

Trade with the USA (US $ '000): *Imports:* 0.0 in 2008; 568.2 in 2009; 3.7 in 2010. *Exports:* 0.8 in 2008; 26.0 in 2009; 4.1 in 2010.

TRANSPORT

Road Traffic (motor vehicles, 2002): Passenger vehicles 30 (two-wheeled 1, three-wheeled 6, four-wheeled 23); Tractors 3; Bulldozer 1; Digger 1.

Shipping: *Local Vessels* (communally owned open surf boats, 2000): 3. *International Shipping Arrivals* (visits by passing vessels, 1996): Ships 51; Yachts 30.

COMMUNICATIONS

Telephones (2002): a party-line service with 15 telephones in use; 2 public telephones; 2 digital telephones. Most homes also have VHF radio.

Directory

The Constitution

Pitcairn is a British settlement under the British Settlements Act 1887, although the islanders reckon their recognition as a colony from 1838, when a British naval captain instituted a Constitution with universal adult suffrage and a code of law. That system served as the basis of the 1904 reformed Constitution and the wider reforms of 1940, effected by Order in Council. The Constitution of 1940 provided for a Governor of Pitcairn, Henderson, Ducie and Oeno Islands (who, since 1970, is concurrently the British High Commissioner in New Zealand), representing the British monarch. A Mayor was elected every three years to preside over the Island Council. The Local Government Ordinance 1964 constituted an Island Council of 10 members: in addition to the Mayor, five members were elected annually; three were nominated for terms of one year (the Governor appointing two of these members at his own discretion); and the Island Secretary was an ex-officio member. In addition to the Island Council, there was an Island Magistrate who presided over the Magistrate's Court of Pitcairn, and was appointed by the Governor. Liaison between the Governor and the Island Council is conducted by a Commissioner, usually based in the Office of the British Consulate-General in Auckland, New Zealand.

Customary land tenure provides for a system of family ownership (based upon the original division of land in the 18th century). Alienation to foreigners is not forbidden by law, but in practice this is difficult. There is no taxation, and public works are performed by the community.

The constitutional amendments enacted in February 2010 *inter alia* formally incorporated reference to the Island Council. The revised Constitution also provided for: the establishment of a Supreme Court, which was to be the superior court of record; the appointment of an independent attorney-general, who was to be the principal legal adviser to the Government; and the creation of the role of Ombudsman, who was to be responsible for the investigation of any complaint of maladministration.

The Government

Governor of Pitcairn, Henderson, Ducie and Oeno Islands: VICTORIA TREADELL (British High Commissioner in New Zealand—took office May 2010).

Office of the Governor of Pitcairn, Henderson, Ducie and Oeno Islands: c/o British High Commission, 44 Hill St, POB 1812, Wellington 6011, New Zealand; tel. (4) 924-2888; fax (4) 473-4982; e-mail ppa.mailbox@fco.gov.uk; Gov. VICTORIA TREADELL.

Pitcairn Islands Office: Private Box 105-696, Auckland, New Zealand; tel. (9) 366-0186; fax (9) 366-0187; e-mail admin@pitcairn.gov.pn; internet www.government.pn.

ISLAND COUNCIL
(October 2011)

Mayor: MICHAEL WARREN.

Deputy Mayor: SIMON YOUNG.

Governor's Representative (ex officio): LUCY FOSTER.

Other Members: DAVE BROWN, LEA BROWN, BRENDA CHRISTIAN, JAY WARREN, PAUL WARREN.

Elections to the Island Council take place each December. Meetings are held at the Court House in Adamstown.

Office of the Island Secretary: The Square, Adamstown.

Judicial System

The constitutional amendments enacted in February 2010 provided for the establishment of the Pitcairn Supreme Court and for the appointment of an independent Attorney-General.

Chief Justice: CHARLES BLACKIE.

Island Magistrate: SIMON YOUNG.

Public Prosecutor: SIMON MOORE.

Public Defender: PAUL DACRE.

Attorney-General: PAUL RISHWORTH.

Religion

CHRISTIANITY

Since 1887 many of the islanders have been adherents of the Seventh-day Adventist Church.

Pastor: JOHN O'MALLEY, SDA Church, The Square, POB 24, Adamstown; fax 872-7620/9763.

The Press

Pitcairn Miscellany: e-mail admin@miscellany.pn; internet www.miscellany.pn; monthly four-page mimeographed news sheet; f. 1959; edited by the Education Officer; Editor P. FOLEY; circ. 1,400 (2002).

Finance, Trade and Industry

There are no formal banking facilities. A co-operative trading store was established in 1967. Industry consists of handicrafts, and the production of honey and dried fruit.

Transport

ROADS

There are approximately 14 km (9 miles) of dirt road suitable for two-, three- and four-wheeled vehicles. In 2002 Pitcairn had one conventional motor cycle, six three-wheelers and 22 four-wheeled motor cycles, one four-wheel-drive motor car, three tractors, a five-ton digger and a bulldozer; traditional wheelbarrows are used occasionally. In 1995 a total of £79,000 was received from individual donors for work to improve the road leading to the jetty at Bounty Bay. Work to concrete the road, known as the Hill of Difficulty, was completed in mid-2006.

SHIPPING

No passenger ships have called regularly since 1968, and sea communications are restricted to cargo vessels operating between New Zealand and Panama, which make scheduled calls at Pitcairn three times a year, as well as a number of unscheduled calls. A shipping route between French Polynesia and Pitcairn was opened in 2006. There are also occasional visits by private yachts. The number of cruise ships calling at Pitcairn increased in the late 1990s, and 10 such vessels visited the island in 2000 (compared with just two or three annually in previous years). Two cruise ships called at Pitcairn in April 2005 before stopping at Oeno Island for the tourists to witness a solar eclipse near the island. Bounty Bay, near Adamstown, is the only possible landing site, and there are no docking facilities; in mid-2007 plans to build a breakwater at Bounty Bay were announced. In 1993 the jetty derrick was refitted with an hydraulic system. The islanders have three aluminium open surf boats. Major work to repair the slipway and jetty was carried out by the islanders in mid-2005.

Tourism

The tourism sector has yet to be developed. The development of eco-tourism, to include activities such as whale-watching, has been identified as offering particular potential for the islands. Henderson Island was declared a UNESCO World Heritage Site in 1988 and has been designated as a bird sanctuary.

Pitcairn Island Tourism Dept: Adamstown; e-mail tourism@pitcairn.pn; internet www.visitpitcairn.pn; Co-ordinator HEATHER MENZIES.

Education

Free primary education is provided on the island under the direction of a qualified schoolteacher, recruited in New Zealand. Scholarships, provided by the Pitcairn Government, are available for post-primary education or specialist training in New Zealand. In February 2004 there were seven children (four primary and three secondary) being educated on Pitcairn.

UNITED STATES COMMONWEALTH TERRITORY IN THE PACIFIC

There are two US Commonwealth Territories, the Northern Mariana Islands, in the Pacific Ocean, and Puerto Rico, in the Caribbean Sea. A Commonwealth is a self-governing incorporated territory that is an integral part of, and in full political union with, the USA. The Secretary of the Interior, in the federal Government, is responsible for relations with the Government of the Northern Mariana Islands. Within the US Department of the Interior, the Assistant Secretary for Policy, Management and Budget is responsible for the Office of Insular Affairs and exercises authority on behalf of the Secretary in all matters pertaining to the insular governments and territories. The USA maintains membership of the Pacific Community (formerly the South Pacific Commission), the Colombo Plan and the UN's Trusteeship Council (the operations of which were suspended in 1994) and its Economic and Social Commission for Asia and the Pacific (ESCAP).

Head of State: President BARACK HUSSEIN OBAMA (took office 20 January 2009).

Department of the Interior, Office of Insular Affairs: 1849 C St, NW, Washington, DC 20240, USA; tel. (202) 208-6816; fax (202) 219-1989; internet www.doi.gov/oia.

Assistant Secretary of the Interior for Insular Affairs: ANTHONY M. BABAUTA.

Director, Office of Insular Affairs: NIKOLAO A. PULA.

THE NORTHERN MARIANA ISLANDS

Introduction

The Commonwealth of the Northern Mariana Islands (CNMI) comprises 16 islands (all the Mariana group except Guam), most being of volcanic origin, lying in the western Pacific Ocean. The territory has a land area of 457 sq km (177 sq miles) and is situated about 5,300 km west of Honolulu (Hawaii) and due south of Japan, some 2,300 km from Tokyo. Its nearest neighbours are Guam and the Federated States of Micronesia. The climate is tropical and there is little seasonal variation in temperature, the mean annual temperature being some 28°C (82°F). Mean annual rainfall is some 2,120 mm (84 ins), the driest months being January–May. The Mariana Islands can be affected by monsoons between August and November. English, Chamorro and Carolinian are the official languages of the Commonwealth. The chief settlements, and the administrative centre of Capitol Hill, are on Saipan. The population was estimated by the Secretariat of the Pacific Community to be 63,517 at mid-2011.

The islands, already settled for more than 2,000 years by a Polynesian people now known as the Chamorros, were claimed for Spain by Fernão de Magalhães (Ferdinand Magellan) in 1521. They were known as the Ladrone Islands until 1668, when they were named the Mariana Islands in honour of Mariana of Austria, widow of Philip IV of Spain. The islands were sold by Spain to Germany in 1899. During the 20th century the islands were administered successively by Germany, Japan and the USA, from 1947 as part of the UN Trust Territory of the Pacific Islands.

The islands voted for separate status as a US Commonwealth Territory in June 1975. In March 1976 the US President, Gerald Ford, signed the 'Covenant to Establish a Commonwealth of the Northern Mariana Islands in Political Union with the USA'. In October 1977 US President Jimmy Carter approved the Constitution of the Northern Mariana Islands, which provided that, from January 1978, the former Marianas District would become internally self-governing. The Northern Marianas formally entered political union with the USA on 3 November 1986, upon the termination of the Trusteeship. The residents of the Commonwealth became citizens of the USA. The US federal Government is responsible for the islands' defence and foreign relations.

In January 1999 the Office of Insular Affairs (OIA) published a report in which it concluded that the Government's attempts to eradicate abuses of labour and immigration laws had been unsuccessful. In particular, it had failed to reduce the territory's reliance on alien workers, to enforce US minimum wage laws and to curb evasions of trade legislation governing the export of garments to the USA. In the same month former employees of 18 US clothing retailers initiated legal action against the companies, which were accused of failing to comply with US labour laws in Saipan. In April 2000 a settlement was reached with the garment manufacturers, providing some US $8m. in compensation for the workers. The companies also agreed to conform to regulations established by an independent monitoring system in Saipan.

Many of the economic and social problems of the Northern Marianas have been largely attributed to the dramatic increase in the islands' population (from some 17,000 in 1979 to 69,221 at the census of 2000). Rapid industrial growth in the 1980s led to a shortage of local labour in the expanding garment factories and a substantial increase in immigrant workers, particularly from the Philippines. The number of non-resident alien workers increased by 655% between 1980 and 1989 alone, and by the early 1990s had exceeded the permanent population of the islands. While companies benefited from US regulations that permitted duty-free and quota-free imports of garments from the Commonwealth and while advantageous local regulations allowed manufacturers to certify garments as having been 'made in the USA', the influx of migrant labour depressed wage levels, and there were widespread complaints of poor working conditions. In February 2000 the US Senate approved a bill granting permanent residency in the Northern Marianas to some 40,000 immigrant workers. However, the legislation also included provisions for limiting the stay of all future guest workers. In December 2000 the Governor of the Northern Marianas announced that he was to oppose the decision by the US Government to bring the islands' labour and immigration laws under federal control, arguing that this would have a negative impact on the Commonwealth's economy. In May 2001, following intense lobbying by the Northern Marianas Government, the US Congress abandoned the bill. In January 2007 the Northern Marianas were finally included in new minimum wage legislation ensuring parity with the US wage increase to US $7.25 an hour, while various tax concessions were provisionally approved to ease any resultant losses incurred by small businesses. The legislation also sought to allow qualified immigrant workers to apply for permanent residency. However, within the Northern Marianas strong opposition to the federal legislation continued. In December 2009 US President Barack Obama signed legislation postponing from May until September 2010 the implementation of the next scheduled increase in the minimum wage in the Northern Mariana Islands. Meanwhile, in February 2009 Saipan's two remaining garment factories were closed down, bringing an end to the production of clothing on the islands.

In early 2004 the Northern Marianas requested provision for the appointment of a non-voting delegate to the US Congress from the islands. (Unlike other US territories such as American Samoa and Guam, the Northern Marianas had continued to be represented in the federal legislature by the islands' Resident Representative in Washington, DC.) Upon the US House of Representatives' approval of the Northern Mariana Islands Immigration, Security, and Labor Act in December 2007, the bill was transferred to the US Senate, which returned it to the House of Representatives with amendments in April 2008. The legislation brought the Northern Marianas under federal immigration laws, also creating a delegate seat for the Territory in the US House of Representatives. (Elections for the first congressional delegate took place in November 2008.) In September the islands' Governor filed legal proceedings against the US Government in an attempt to prevent the implementation in the Northern Marianas of the federalization law, introducing new restrictions on immigration policy. However, the transition to US immigration laws commenced in November 2009. Partly in response to the ending of the islands' exemption from federal immigration and minimum wage laws, in March 2010 the islands' Governor accused the federal Government of systematically suppressing the provisions originally enshrined in the Covenant that had been intended to protect the Northern Marianas' economy. Amid further controversy, in January 2011 the US House of Representatives voted to rescind the 'symbolic' voting rights of territorial delegates in the 'Committee of the Whole House on the State of the Union', a means by which the House was able to expedite consideration of certain legislation, particularly amendments.

After the devastation of the sugar industry in 1944, during the Second World War, agriculture was subsequently based on smallholdings. Although there is little domestic commercial fishing in the islands, there is a major tuna transshipment facility at Tinian harbour. The services sector has continued to make a vital contribution to the economy. In 1995 a US company opened the Northern Marianas' first casino on Tinian. Revenue from the casino was to be invested in infrastructure projects and health services. A second casino subsequently opened on Rota. However, plans for the establishment of a luxury casino resort on Tinian were abandoned in October 2011 after the South Korean company involved in the project encountered financial difficulties. Although intermittently affected by global factors, tourism receipts remain significant, with the majority of visitors coming from Japan. The inauguration of new flights from the Chinese cities of Shanghai and Guangzhou in May 2011 was expected significantly to boost tourist arrivals from mainland China. In April 2009, in response to the sharp deterioration in the global economy, the islands received more than $90m. in federal stimulus funding. A state of emergency was declared in October 2010 and public services were temporarily suspended after the islands' legislature failed to endorse the budget for 2010/11.

In 2002 and 2003 there were frequent reports of chemical contamination owing to US military activity. A US court order filed by the Center for Biological Diversity, an environmental lobby group, forced military training on the uninhabited island of Farallon de Medinilla to be suspended for 30 days in mid-2002. Despite environmentalists' concerns about the impact and legality of US military activity, in particular the testing of ordnance, upon the island's wildlife, the Northern Marianas Chamber of Commerce expressed fears that the substantial revenue generated by the visiting US armed forces might be jeopardized.

Statistical Survey

Source: (unless otherwise stated): Department of Commerce, Central Statistics Division, POB 10007, Saipan, MP 96950; tel. 664-3000; fax 664-3001; internet www.commerce.gov.mp.

AREA AND POPULATION

Area: 457 sq km (176.5 sq miles). *By Island*: Saipan 120 sq km; Tinian 102 sq km; Rota 85 sq km; Pagan 48 sq km; Anatahan 32 sq km; Agrihan 30 sq km; Alamagan 11 sq km; Asuncion 7 sq km; Aguijan (Goat Is) 7 sq km; Sarigan 5 sq km; Guguan 4 sq km; Farallon de Pajaros 3 sq km; Maug 2 sq km; Farallon de Medinilla 1 sq km.

Population: 69,221 at census of 1 April 2000; 53,883 at census of 1 April 2010. *By Island* (2010 census): Saipan 48,220; Rota 2,527; Tinian (with Aguijan) 3,136; Northern Islands 0.

Density (at 2010 census): 117.9 per sq km.

Population by Age and Sex (Secretariat of the Pacific Community estimates at mid-2011): *0–14:* 16,610 (males 8,785, females 7,825); *15–64:* 44,628 (males 22,259, females 22,369); *65 and over:* 2,279 (males 1,075, females 1,204); *Total* 63,517 (males 32,119, females 31,398). Note: Mid-2011 estimates not adjusted to take account of results of 2010 census (Source: Pacific Regional Information System).

Ethnic Groups (2000 census): Filipino 18,141; Chinese 15,311; Chamorro 14,749; part-Chamorro 4,383; Total (incl. others) 69,221.

Principal Towns (population at 2000 census): San Antonio 4,741; Garapan (capital) 3,588; Koblerville 3,543; San Vincente 3,494; Tanapag 3,318; Chalan Kanoa 3,108; Kagman 3,026. Source: Thomas Brinkhoff, *City Population* (internet www.citypopulation.de).

Births and Deaths (2002): Registered live births 1,289 (birth rate 17.4 per 1,000); Registered deaths 164 (death rate 2.2 per 1,000). *2008:* Live births 1,260; Deaths 176 (Source: UN, *Population and Vital Statistics Report*).

Employment (2000 census, persons aged 16 years and over): Agriculture, forestry, fisheries and mining 623; Manufacturing 17,398; Construction 2,785; Transport, communication and utilities 1,449; Trade, restaurants and hotels 9,570; Financing, insurance and real estate 1,013; Community, social and personal services 9,915; *Total employed* 42,753 (males 19,485, females 23,268); Unemployed 1,712 (males 888, females 824); *Total labour force* 44,465 (males 20,373, females 24,092). *2007* (US economic census, paid employment only, excl. public administration): Total employed 22,622 (Manufacturing 7,094; Wholesale and retail 3,642; Hotels and restaurants 4,772). *Mid-2011:* Agriculture, etc. 7,000; Total labour force 30,000 (Source: FAO).

HEALTH AND WELFARE

Key Indicators

Access to Water (% of persons, 2008): 98.

Access to Sanitation (% of persons, 2006): 94.

For sources and definitions, see explanatory note on p. vi.

AGRICULTURE, ETC.

Principal Crops (crops harvested for sale, '000 lb, 2007): Cassava 30.3; Taro 221.6; Yams 67.7; Sweet potatoes 352.3; Beans, yard long 40.2; Chinese cabbage 38.2; Cucumbers 93.8; Aubergines (Eggplant) 47.3; Pumpkins and squash 68.0; Watermelons 150.2; Bananas 146.9; Breadfruits 4.8; Papayas 50.7; Betel nuts 88.3; Coconuts 42.9; Ginger 1.5.

Livestock (2007): Cattle 1,395; Pigs 1,483; Goats 276; Poultry birds 12,390.

Livestock Products (sales of dozens, 2007): Hen eggs 195,510.

Fishing (metric tons, live weight, 2009): Total catch 142 (Parrotfishes 11; Skipjack tuna 59; Yellowfin tuna 11; Common dolphinfish 9; Scads 11; Other marine fishes 19). Source: FAO.

FINANCE

Currency and Exchange Rates: United States currency is used: 100 cents = 1 United States dollar (US $). *Sterling and Euro Equivalents* (31 May 2011): £1 sterling = US $1.650; €1 = US $1.439; US $100 = £60.60 = €69.52.

Federal Direct Expenditures (US $ million, year ending September 2009): Retirement and disability 34; Total (incl. others) 241 (Source: US Census Bureau, *Consolidated Federal Funds Report*).

Budget (US $ million, 2009): General fund revenue 154.7 (Taxes 112.6, Fees, charges and other revenues 30.0, Net transfers from other funds 12.1); Total expenditure 168.1.

Cost of Living (Consumer Price Index for Saipan; quarterly averages; base: 2000 = 100): All items 111.9 in 2007; 117.3 in 2008; 121.5 in 2009. Source: ILO.

Gross Domestic Product (US $ million in current prices): 1,073 in 2005; 1,007 in 2006; 962 in 2007 (Source: Bureau of Economic Analysis, US Department of Commerce).

Expenditure on the Gross Domestic Product (US $ million in current prices, 2007): Government consumption expenditure and gross investment 354; Personal consumption expenditure 566; Private fixed investment 22; *Total domestic expenditure* 942; Exports of goods and services 548; *Less* Imports of goods and services 529; *GDP in purchasers' values* 962 (Source: Bureau of Economic Analysis, US Department of Commerce).

EXTERNAL TRADE

Principal Commodities (US $ million): *Imports* (1997): Beverages 12.8; Tobacco 5.4; Automobiles (incl. parts) 42.1; Clothing 309.2; Total (incl. others) 836.2. *Exports* (2000): Total 1,000. *Value of Garment Exports* (US $ million): 486.5 in 2006; 307.6 in 2007; 145.8 in 2008.

Principal Trading Partners (US $ million, 1997): *Imports*: Guam 298.0; Hong Kong 200.5; Japan 118.3; Korea, Republic 80.6; USA 63.3; Total (incl. others) 836.2.

Sources: partly UN, *Statistical Yearbook for Asia and the Pacific* and *Statistical Yearbook*.

TRANSPORT

Road Traffic (registered motor vehicles, 2001): 17,900.

Shipping: *Registered Fleet* (2001): 1,029 vessels (791 fishing vessels); *Traffic* ('000 short tons, 1997): Goods loaded 184.1; Goods unloaded 425.9.

Civil Aviation (Saipan Int. Airport, year ending September 1999): 23,853 aircraft landings; 562,364 boarding passengers. *2007:* Passenger arrivals 470,013, Passenger departures 473,249. Source: Commonwealth Ports Authority.

TOURISM

Visitor Arrivals: 389,261 in 2007; 396,410 in 2008; 353,956 in 2009.

Visitor Arrivals by Country (2009): China, People's Republic (incl. Hong Kong) 29,814; Japan 191,111; Korea, Republic 89,132; USA (incl. Guam) 29,259; Total (incl. others) 353,956.

Tourism Receipts (US $ million): 407 in 1999; 430 in 2000; 225 in 2002 (approximate figure). Source: Bank of Hawaii, *Commonwealth of the Northern Mariana Islands Economic Report* (October 2003).

COMMUNICATIONS MEDIA

Radio Receivers (households with access, census of 2000): 10,684.

Television Receivers (estimate, 1995): 15,460 in use.

Telephones (main lines in use, 2010): 25,500.

Mobile Cellular Telephones (2004): 20,500 subscribers (Source: International Telecommunication Union).

EDUCATION

Pre-primary (2002/03, state schools, Headstart programme): 12 schools; 98 teachers; 606 pupils.

Primary (2002/03, state schools): 12 schools; 283 teachers; 5,849 students.

Secondary (2002/03, state schools): 9 schools; 248 teachers; 4,705 students.

Higher (2000/01): 1 college; 1,641 students (full- and part-time students).

Private Schools (2002/03): 18 schools; 186 teachers; 2,326 students.

Directory

The Constitution

The Northern Mariana Islands became part of the US-administered UN Trust Territory of the Pacific Islands in 1947. In 1975 the Northern Mariana Islands voted for separate status as a US Commonwealth Territory; the Covenant to Establish a Commonwealth of the Northern Mariana Islands (CNMI) in Political Union with the United States was approved by the US Congress in 1976 and took effect fully in 1986. According to the Covenant, CNMI comes under federal law, with certain exceptions including customs. In 1977 the Government of the CNMI adopted a new Constitution, and in the following year the Territory became self-governing. Under the terms of the Constitution, executive authority is vested in the Governor, who is elected by popular vote for a four-year term. Legislative authority is vested in the bicameral Legislature, comprising the nine-member Senate and the 20-member House of Representatives. The Constitution also provides for a Lieutenant-Governor and a judicial system including a Superior Court and a Supreme Court. The Northern Mariana Islands elect a non-voting Delegate to the federal legislature.

The Government

(October 2011)

Governor: BENIGNO R. FITIAL (took office 9 January 2006; re-elected 23 November 2009).

Lieutenant-Governor: ELOY INOS.

DEPARTMENT SECRETARIES

Secretary of the Department of Finance: LARRISA LARSON.

Secretary of the Department of Community and Cultural Affairs: MELVIN FAISAO.

Secretary of the Department of Labor: GIL M. SAN NICOLAS.

Secretary of the Department of Lands and Natural Resources: ARNOLD I. PALACIOS (acting).

Secretary of the Department of Public Lands: OSCAR M. BABAUTA.

Secretary of the Department of Public Works: MARTIN C. SABLAN.

Secretary of the Department of Commerce: SIXTO K. IGISOMAR (acting).

Commissioner of the Department of Public Safety: RAMON C. MAFNAS.

Secretary of the Department of Public Health: JOSEPH KEVIN P. VILLAGOMEZ.

GOVERNMENT OFFICES

Office of the Governor: Caller Box 10007, Capitol Hill, Saipan, MP 96950; tel. 664-2200; fax 664-2211; e-mail gov.frosario@saipan.com; internet cnmigov.net.

Department of the Interior, Office of Insular Affairs (OIA): Field Office of the OIA, Dept of the Interior, POB 502622, Saipan, MP 96950; tel. 234-8861; fax 234-8814; e-mail jeff.schorr@pticom.com; internet www.doi.gov/oia/Islandpages/cnmipage.htm; OIA representation in the Commonwealth; Field Representative JEFFREY SCHORR.

Department of Commerce: Caller Box 10007, Capitol Hill, Saipan, MP 96950; tel. 664-3000; fax 664-3067; e-mail deptcommerce@pticom.com; internet www.commerce.gov.mp.

Department of Community and Cultural Affairs: Capitol Hill, Saipan, MP 96950; tel. 664-2576; fax 664-2570; e-mail faisaom_dcca.deputysecretary@pticom.com.

Department of Finance: POB 5234, Capitol Hill, Saipan, MP 96950; tel. 664-1100; fax 664-1115; e-mail finance.edp@cnmiarra.net; internet www.cnmidof.net.

Department of Labor: POB 10007, Saipan, MP 96950; tel. 236-0900; fax 236-0991; e-mail webmaster@marianaslabor.net; internet www.marianaslabor.net.

Department of Lands and Natural Resources: Capitol Hill, Saipan, MP 96950; tel. 322-9830; fax 322-2633.

Department of Public Health: POB 500409 CK, 1 Hospital Way, Saipan, MP 96950; tel. 234-8950; fax 236-8756; e-mail joseph.kevin@dph.gov.mp; internet www.dph.gov.mp.

Department of Public Lands: POB 500380, Capitol Hill, Saipan, MP 96950; tel. 234-3751; fax 234-3755; e-mail dpl@dpl.gov.mp; internet www.dpl.gov.mp.

Department of Public Safety: Jose M. Sablan Bldg, POB 500791, Susupe, Saipan, MP 96950; tel. 664-9022; fax 664-9027; internet www.dps.gov.mp.

Department of Public Works: Caller Box 10007, Capitol Hill, Saipan, MP 96950; tel. 235-5827; fax 235-6346; e-mail dpwadmin@pticom.com; internet www.dpw.gov.mp.

Legislature

NORTHERN MARIANAS COMMONWEALTH LEGISLATURE

Legislative authority is vested in the Northern Marianas Commonwealth Legislature, a bicameral body consisting of the Senate and the House of Representatives. There are nine senators, elected for four-year terms, and 20 members of the House of Representatives, elected for two-year terms. The most recent legislative election was held on 7 November 2009. The Republican Party won nine seats in the House of Representatives, the Covenant Party seven seats and independent candidates four seats. Meanwhile, four Republican Party candidates and two independent candidates were elected to the six Senate seats that were contested.

Senate President: PAUL ATALIG MANGLONA.

Speaker of the House: ELI D. CABRERA.

Commonwealth Legislature: CNMI Legislative Bureau, POB 500586, Capitol Hill, Saipan, MP 96950; tel. 664-8954; fax 322-6840; e-mail semanp@cnmileg.gov.mp; internet www.cnmileg.gov.mp.

CONGRESS

Since 2008 the Northern Mariana Islands have been able to elect a non-voting Delegate to the US House of Representatives. The first election for this position was held on 4 November 2008. At the election to the post in November 2010, incumbent Congressman Gregorio K. C. Sablan was re-elected for a two-year term.

Delegate of the Northern Mariana Islands: GREGORIO K. C. SABLAN, POB 504879 Saipan, MP 96950; tel. 323-2647; fax 323-2649; e-mail kilili@mail.house.gov; internet sablan.house.gov.

Election Commission

Commonwealth Election Commission: POB 500470, Saipan, MP 96950-0470; tel. 664-8683; fax 664-8689; e-mail info@votecnmi.gov.mp; internet www.votecnmi.gov.mp; Chair. FRANCES SABLAN; Exec. Dir ROBERT A. GUERRERO.

Political Organizations

Covenant Party: c/o Commonwealth Legislature, Capitol Hill, Saipan, MP 96950; Leader BENIGNO R. FITIAL; Chair. GREGORIO 'KACHUMA' CAMACHO.

Democratic Party of the Commonwealth of the Northern Mariana Islands, Inc: Saipan, MP 96950; tel. 234-7497; fax 233-0641; Pres. Dr CARLOS S. CAMACHO; Chair. LORENZO CABRERA.

Republican Party of the Northern Marianas: POB 500777, Saipan, MP 96950; tel. and fax 233-1288; e-mail dpwpio@vzpacifica.net; State Chair. DAVID ATTAO; Exec. Dir (vacant).

Judicial System

The judicial system in the Commonwealth of the Northern Mariana Islands (CNMI) consists of the Superior Court, the Commonwealth Supreme Court (which considers appeals from the Superior Court) and the Federal District Court. Under the Covenant, federal law applies in the Commonwealth, with some exceptions: for example, the CNMI is not part of the US Customs Territory, and it may enact its own taxation laws.

Chief Justice of the Commonwealth Supreme Court: (vacant), POB 502165, Saipan, MP 96950.

Presiding Judge of the Superior Court: ROBERT C. NARAJA, POB 500307, Saipan, MP 96950.

Attorney-General: EDWARD T. BUCKINGHAM.

US Attorney: ALICIA GARRIDO LIMTIACO.

Public Defender: ADAM HARDWICKE.

Religion

The population is predominantly Christian, mainly Roman Catholic. There are small communities of Episcopalians (Anglicans—under the jurisdiction of the Bishop of Hawaii, in the USA) and Protestants.

CHRISTIANITY

The Roman Catholic Church

The Northern Mariana Islands comprise the single diocese of Chalan Kanoa, suffragan to the archdiocese of Agaña (Guam). The Bishop participates in the Catholic Bishops' Conference of the Pacific, based in Suva, Fiji. At 31 December 2007 there were 43,000 adherents, including temporary residents, in the Northern Mariana Islands.

Bishop of Chalan Kanoa: (vacant), Bishop's House, Chalan Kanoa, POB 500745, Saipan, MP 96950; tel. 234-3000; fax 235-3002; e-mail diocese@pticom.com; internet www.dioceseofchalankanoa.com.

The Press

The weekly *Focus on the Commonwealth* is published in Guam, but distributed solely in the Northern Mariana Islands.

Marianas Observer: POB 502119, Saipan, MP 96950; tel. 233-3955; fax 233-7040; weekly; Publr JOHN VABLAN; Man. Editor ZALDY DANDAN; circ. 2,000.

Marianas Review: POB 501074, Saipan, MP 96950; tel. and fax 234-7160; f. 1979 as *The Commonwealth Examiner*; weekly; English and Chamorro; independent; Publr LUIS BENAVENTE; Editor RUTH L. TIGHE; circ. 1,700.

Marianas Variety: POB 6338, Tamuning 96931; tel. 234-9272; fax 234-9271; e-mail editor@mvariety.com; internet www.mvariety.com; Mon.–Fri.; English and Chamorro; independent; f. 1972; Publr ABED E. YOUNIS; Editor ZALDY DANDAN; circ. 8,000.

North Star: Chalan Kanoa, POB 500745, Saipan, MP 96950; tel. 234-3000; fax 235-3002; e-mail nstar@pticom.com; internet www.dioceseofchalankanoa.com; weekly; English and Chamorro; Roman Catholic; f. 1976; Publr Bishop TOMAS A. CAMACHO; Man. Editor Fr CELSO MAGBANUA, Jr; circ. 3,000.

Pacific Daily News (Saipan bureau): POB 500822, Saipan, MP 96950; tel. 234-6423; fax 234-5986; Publr LEE WEBBER; circ. 5,000.

Pacific Star: POB 505815 CHRB, Saipan, MP 96950; tel. 288-0746; fax 288-0747; weekly; Operational Man. NICK LEGASPI; circ. 3,000.

Pacifica: POB 502143, Saipan, MP 96950; monthly; Editor MIKE MALONE.

Saipan Tribune: CIC Centre, 2nd Floor, Beach Rd, Saipan; tel. 235-6397; fax 235-3740; e-mail editor.tribune@saipan.com; internet www.saipantribune.com; 2 a week; Publr LYNN KNIGHT; Editor JAYVEE L. VALLEJERA; circ. 3,500.

Broadcasting and Communications

TELECOMMUNICATIONS

Docomo Pacific Inc: Gualo Rai Commercial Center, Main Bldg, Gualo Rai, Middle Rd, Saipan; tel. 483-2273; fax 235-7640; e-mail service@guamcell.net; internet docomopacific.com/saipan; fmrly Saipan Cellular & Paging; name changed to SAIPANCELL Communications in 1992; present name adopted 2008; mobile cellular services; Pres. JAY SHEDD.

IT & E Overseas Inc: POB 500306 CK, Saipan, MP 96950; tel. 682-1060; fax 682-4555; internet www.pticom.com; fmrly Pacific Telecom Inc; name changed as above in 2009; mobile cellular and internet services; Pres. and CEO RICKY DELGADO.

BROADCASTING

Radio

Far East Broadcasting Co, Inc: POB 500209, Saipan, MP 96950; tel. 322-9088; fax 322-3060; e-mail saipan@febc.org; internet www.febc.org; f. 1946; non-commercial, religious broadcasts; Pres. GREGG HARRIS; Field Dir ROBERT L. SPRINGER.

KFBS-SW: POB 500209, Saipan, MP 96950; tel. 322-9088; fax 322-3060; e-mail saipan@febc.org; internet www.febc.org; f. 1946; international broadcasts in Chinese, Indonesian, Russian and Vietnamese; owned by Far East Broadcasting Co, Inc; Pres. GREGG HARRIS.

Inter-Island Communications, Inc: POB 500914, Saipan, MP 96950; tel. 234-7239; fax 234-0447; f. 1984; commercial; station KCNM-AM, or KZMI-FM in stereo; Gen. Man. HANS W. MICKELSON; Programme Dir KEN WARNICK; CEO ANGEL OCAMPO.

KRNM: POB 501250, Saipan, MP 96950; tel. 234-5498; fax 235-0915; internet www.krnm.org; f. 1994; public station based on Northern Marianas College campus; Gen. Man. CARL POGUE.

Magic 100.3: Magic Studio, 1st Floor, Naru Bldg, Susupe; tel. 234-5929; fax 286-5483; e-mail Kwaw100.3@Magic100Radio.com; internet www.magic100radio.com; contemporary music; Man. Dir LEO JUN GANACIAS.

Power 99: POB 10000, Saipan, MP 96950; tel. 235-7996; fax 235-7998; e-mail tpalacios@spbguam.com; Station Man. TINA PALACIOS; Gen. Man. CURTIS DANCOE.

The Rock 97.9: POB 10000, Saipan, MP 96950; tel. 235-7996; fax 235-7998; e-mail cdancoe@spbguam.com; Man. ALBERT JUAN.

Television

KMCV-TV: POB 501298, Saipan, MP 96950; tel. 235-6365; fax 235-0965; f. 1992; 52-channel commercial station, with 8 pay channels, broadcasting 24 hours a day; US programmes and local and international news; 5,650 subscribers; Gen. Man. WAYNE GAMBLIN.

Marianas CableVision: POB 501298, Saipan, MP 96950; tel. 235-4628; fax 235-0965; e-mail mcv.service@saipan.com; internet www.mcvcnmi.com; 55-channel cable service provider, broadcasting US and Pacific Rim programmes; Pres. JOHN CRUIKSHANK; Gen. Man. MARK BIRMINGHAM.

Finance

BANKING

Bank of Guam (USA): POB 500678, Saipan, MP 96950; tel. 233-5000; fax 233-5003; internet www.bankofguam.com; Gen. Man. MARCIE TOMOKANE; 5 brs.

Bank of Hawaii: Bank of Hawaii Bldg, El Monte Ave, Garapan, POB 500566, Saipan, MP 96950; tel. 237-2900; fax 322-4210; internet www.boh.com; Man. JOHN SHEATHER; 2 brs.

Bank of Saipan: POB 500690, Saipan, MP 96950; tel. 234-6260; fax 235-1802; e-mail bankofsaipan@gtepacifica.net; internet www.bankofsaipan.com; dep. US $23m. (Dec. 2004); Pres. JON BARGFREDE; 4 brs.

City Trust Bank: Gualo Rai, POB 501867, Saipan, MP 96950; tel. 235-7701; fax 234-8664; e-mail citytrustbank@ctbsaipan.com; Asst Vice-Pres. and Acting Man. MARIA LOURDES JOHNSON.

First Hawaiian Bank: Gualo Rai Commercial Center, Middle Rd, Gualo Rai, Saipan 96950; tel. 235-3090; fax 236-8936; internet www.fhb.com; Area Man. JUAN LIZAMA.

Guam Savings and Loan Bank: POB 503201, Saipan, MP 96950; tel. 233-2265; fax 233-2227; Gen. Man. GLEN PEREZ.

INSURANCE

Allied Insurance/Takagi and Associates, Inc: PPP 602, Box 10000, Saipan, MP 96950; tel. 233-2554; fax 670-2553; Gen. Man. PETER SIBLY.

Aon Insurance: Aon Insurance Micronesia (Saipan) Inc, POB 502177, Saipan, MP 96950; tel. 234-2811; fax 234-5462; e-mail rod.rankin@aon.com.au; internet www.aon.com/saipan; Communications Officer RODNEY RANKIN.

Associated Insurance Underwriters of the Pacific, Inc: POB 501369, Saipan, MP 96950; tel. 234-7222; fax 234-5367; e-mail aiup@pticom.com; Gen. Man. MAGGIE GEORGE.

Calvo's Insurance Underwriters, Inc: Oleai Centre Bldg, Saipan, MP 96950; tel. 234-5690; fax 234-5693; e-mail eli.buenaventura@calvosinsurance.com; internet www.calvosinsurance.com; affiliated to Tokio Marine & Nichido Fire Insurance Co, Japan; Man. ELI C. BUENAVENTURA.

Century Insurance (Tan Holdings Corpn): Century Insurance PMB 193, POB 10000, Saipan, MP 96950; tel. 234-0609; fax 234-1845; e-mail nel_matanguihan@cicspn.com; internet www.cicspn.com; Gen. Man. NEL MATANGUIHAN.

General Accident Insurance Asia Ltd (Microl Insurance): POB 502177, Saipan, MP 96950; tel. 234-2811; fax 234-5462; Man. Dir MICHAEL W. GOURLAY.

Marianas Insurance Co Ltd: POB 502505, Saipan, MP 96950-2505; tel. 234-5091; fax 234-5093; e-mail admin@marianasinsurance.com; internet www.marianasinsurance.com; f. 1989; Gen. Man. ROSALIA S. CABRERA.

Midland Insurance Underwriters, Inc: PMB 219, POB 10000, Capitol Hill, Saipan, MP 96950; tel. 235-3598.

Moylan's Insurance Underwriters (Int.), Inc: POB 500658, Saipan, MP 96950; tel. 234-6571; fax 234-8641; e-mail saipan@moylans.net; internet www.moylansinsurance.com; Branch Man. CATHY TENORIO.

Pacifica Insurance Underwriters Inc: POB 500168, Saipan, MP 96950; tel. 234-6267; fax 234-5880; e-mail piui@pacificains.com; internet www.pacificains.com; f. 1972; affiliated to Tokio Marine & Nichido Fire Insurance Co, Japan; Pres. NORMAN T. TENORIO.

Primerica Financial Services: POB 500964, Saipan, MP 96950; tel. 235-2912; fax 235-7910; Gen. Man. JOHN SABLAN.

Royal Crown Insurance: Royal Crown Bldg, Beach Road, Chalan LauLau, POB 10001, Saipan, MP 96950; tel. 234-2256; fax 234-2258.

StayWell Saipan, Inc: POB 502050, Saipan, MP 96950-2050; tel. 323-4260; fax 323-4263; e-mail saipan.office@staywellguam.com; internet www.staywellguam.com; Branch Man. ERIC PLINSKE.

Trade and Industry

GOVERNMENT AGENCIES

Commonwealth Development Authority: POB 502149, Wakins Bldg, Gualo Rai, Saipan, MP 96950; tel. 234-6245; fax 235-7147; e-mail administration@cda.gov.mp; internet www.cda.gov.mp; govt lending institution; funds capital improvement projects and private enterprises; offers tax incentives to qualified investors; Chair. PEDRO I. ITIBUS; Exec. Dir MANUEL A. SABLAN.

CHAMBER OF COMMERCE

Saipan Chamber of Commerce: Chalan Kanoa, POB 500806 CK, Saipan, MP 96950; tel. 233-7150; fax 233-7151; e-mail saipanchamber@saipan.com; internet www.saipanchamber.com; Pres. DOUGLAS BRENNAN; Exec. Dir KYLE CALABRESE.

EMPLOYERS' ASSOCIATIONS

Association of Commonwealth Teachers (ACT): POB 5071, Saipan, MP 96950; tel. and fax 256-7567; e-mail cnmiteachers@netscape.net; supports the teaching profession and aims to improve education in state schools.

Saipan Garment Manufacturers' Association (SGMA): POB 10001, Saipan, MP 96950; tel. 235-7699; fax 235-7899; e-mail sgmaemy@vzpacifica.net; Exec. Dir (vacant).

UTILITIES

Commonwealth Utilities Corporation (CUC): POB 501220, Saipan, MP 96950; tel. 235-7025; fax 235-6145; e-mail cucedp@gtepacifica.net; internet www.cuccnmi.com; Exec. Dir ABE UTU MALAE.

TRADE UNION AND CO-OPERATIVES

International Brotherhood of Electrical Workers: c/o Micronesian Telecommunications Corpn, Saipan, MP 96950; local branch of US trade union based in Washington, DC.

The Mariana Islands Co-operative Association, and the Rota Producers and Tinian Producers Associations operate on the islands.

Transport

RAILWAYS

There have been no railways operating in the islands since the Japanese sugar industry railway, on Saipan, ceased operations in the Second World War.

ROADS

In 1991 there were 494 km (307 miles) of roads on the islands, 320 km (199 miles) of which are on Saipan. First grade roads constitute 135 km (84 miles) of the total, 99 km (62 miles) being on Saipan. There is no public transport, apart from a school bus system.

SHIPPING

The main harbour of the Northern Mariana Islands is the Port of Saipan, which underwent extensive renovation in the mid-1990s. There are also two major harbours on Rota and one on Tinian. Several shipping lines link Saipan, direct or via Guam, with ports in Japan, Asia, the Philippines, the USA and other territories in the Pacific.

Commonwealth Ports Authority (CPA): POB 501055, Saipan, MP 96950; tel. 237-6500; fax 234-5962; e-mail cpa.admin@pticom.com; internet www.cpa.gov.mp; Exec. Dir EDWARD DELEON GUERRERO.

Mariana Express Lines: POB 501937, CTS Bldg, Saipan, MP 96950; tel. 322-1690; fax 323-6355; e-mail desmond_aw@mariana-express.com; internet www.mariana-express.com; services between Saipan, Guam, Japan and Hong Kong; Man. DESMOND AW.

Saipan Shipping Co Inc (Saiship): Saiship Bldg, Charlie Dock, POB 500008, Saipan, MP 96950; tel. 322-9706; fax 322-3183; e-mail darlene_cabrera@saipanshipping.com; f. 1956; weekly barge service between Guam, Saipan and Tinian; monthly services to Japan and Micronesia; Gen. Man. DARLENE CABRERA.

Westpac Freight: POB 2048, Puerto Rico, Saipan, MP 96950; tel. 322-8798; fax 322-5536; e-mail westpac@gtepacifica.net; services between Saipan, Guam and the USA; Man. MICHIE CAMACHO.

CIVIL AVIATION

Air services are centred on the main international airport, Isley Field, on Saipan. There are also airports on Rota and Tinian.

Continental Micronesia: POB 508778, A.B. Won Pat International Airport, Tamuning, GU 96911, Guam; tel. 647-6595; fax 649-6588; internet www.continental.com; f. 1968, as Air Micronesia, by Continental Airlines (USA); name changed 1992; subsidiary of Continental Airlines; hub operations in Saipan and Guam; services throughout the region and to destinations in the Far East and mainland USA; Pres. CHARLES DUNCAN.

Freedom Air: POB 500239 CK, Saipan, MP 96950; tel. 234-8328; e-mail freedom@ite.net; internet www.freedomairguam.com; scheduled internal flights.

Tourism

Tourism is one of the most important industries in the Northern Mariana Islands, earning some US $225m. in 2002. In that year there were 4,313 hotel rooms. Most of the islands' hotels are Japanese-owned, and in 2009 more than 50% of tourists came from Japan. The Republic of Korea, the People's Republic of China and the USA are also important sources of tourists. The islands received a total of 396,410 visitors in 2008; tourist arrivals declined, to 353,956, in 2009. Arrivals on Saipan, Tinian and Rota were reported to have increased to 370,091 in 2010. The islands of Asuncion, Guguan, Maug, Managaha, Sarigan and Uracas (Farallon de Pajaros) are maintained as uninhabited reserves. Visitors are mainly attracted by the white, sandy beaches and the excellent diving conditions. There is also interest in the *Latte* or *Taga* stones (mainly on Tinian), pillars carved from the rock by the ancient Chamorros, and relics from the Second World War.

Hotel Association of the Northern Mariana Islands: POB 5075 CHRB, Saipan, MP 96950; tel. 233-6964; fax 233-1424; e-mail lynn_knight@tanholdings.com; internet www.saipanhotels.org; f. 1983; Chair. NICK NISHIKAWA.

Marianas Visitors Authority (MVA): POB 500861 CK, Saipan, MP 96950; tel. 664-3200; fax 664-3237; e-mail mva@mymarianas.com; internet www.mymarianas.com; f. 1976; responsible for the promotion and devt of tourism in the Northern Mariana Islands; Chair. MARIAN ALDAN-PIERCE; Man. Dir PERRY TENORIO.

Defence

The USA is responsible for the defence of the Northern Mariana Islands. The US Pacific Command is based in Hawaii (USA).

Education

School attendance is compulsory from six to 16 years of age. In 2002/03 there were 12 state primary schools, with a total of 5,849 pupils enrolled, and there were nine state secondary schools, with a total enrolment of 4,705 pupils. There was a total of 18 private schools, with a total enrolment of 2,326 pupils. There was one college of further education in 2000/01, with 1,641 students. Budgetary expenditure on education totalled US $49.6m. in 2000, equivalent to 22.0% of total government expenditure.

UNITED STATES EXTERNAL TERRITORIES IN THE PACIFIC

Most of the external or unincorporated territories of the USA (except the US Virgin Islands and uninhabited Navassa Island, in the Caribbean Sea) are located in the Pacific Ocean. There are two territories with differing degrees of self-government. The Trust Territory of the Pacific Islands was terminated on 1 October 1994, when the Republic of Palau achieved independence from the USA under the Compact of Free Association. Most of the seven remaining island jurisdictions were annexed to the USA by the Guano Act of 1856, together with other, now-relinquished claims. In the federal Government, the Secretary of the Navy is ultimately responsible for Kingman Reef and for Johnston Atoll, and the Secretary of the Air Force for Wake Island. Otherwise, the Secretary of the Interior is the responsible authority for the territories, although the administration may be exercised by another federal agency. Within the Department of the Interior, the Assistant Secretary for Policy, Management and Budget is responsible for the Office of Insular Affairs and acts on behalf of the Secretary in all matters relating to the insular governments and territories. The USA maintains membership, in its own right and in respect of its territories, of the Pacific Community (formerly the South Pacific Commission), the Colombo Plan and the UN's Economic and Social Commission for Asia and the Pacific (ESCAP).

Head of State: President BARACK HUSSEIN OBAMA (took office 20 January 2009).

Department of the Interior, Office of Insular Affairs: 1849 C St, Washington, DC 20240, USA; tel. (202) 208-6816; fax (202) 219-1989; internet www.doi.gov/oia.

Assistant Secretary of the Interior for Insular Affairs: ANTHONY M. BABAUTA.

Director, Office of Insular Affairs: NIKOLAO A. PULA.

Department of Defense: The Pentagon, Washington, DC 20301, USA; tel. (703) 545-6700; fax (703) 428-1982; internet www.defense.govfor details of service departments, see under relevant insular possessions.

AMERICAN SAMOA

Introduction

American Samoa comprises the five islands of Tutuila, Ta'u, Olosega, Ofu and Aunu'u, and the atolls of Swains Island (Olohenga) and uninhabited Rose Island. The islands lie in the South Central Pacific along latitude 14°S at about longitude 170°W, some 3,700 km south-west of Hawaii (USA). Swains Island, administered as part of American Samoa since 1925, lies 340 km to the north-west of the main group. The territory's nearest neighbour is Samoa (formerly known as Western Samoa). The five principal islands are high and volcanic with rugged interiors and little flat land except along the coasts. The area of the islands is 201 sq km (77.6 sq miles).

At the 2000 census the population was 57,291, of whom the majority lived on Tutuila, where the main town and capital, Pago Pago, is situated (the officially designated seat of government is the village of Fagatogo). Approximately 91,000 American Samoans are resident in the USA. In mid-2011 the population was estimated at 66,692.

The islands are peopled by Polynesians and are thought to have been the origin of many of the people who now occupy islands further east. The Samoan language is believed to be the oldest extant form of Polynesian speech. Samoan society developed an intricate hierarchy of graded titles comprising titular chiefs and orator chiefs. The basis of Samoan society remains the aiga, or extended family unit, headed by a chiefly Matai. One of the striking features of modern Samoa is the manner in which this system and the culture of the islands prior to European contact remains a dominant influence. It is referred to as *fa'a Samoa*, the Samoan Way. Most of the population are Christians.

The Samoan islands were first visited by Europeans in the 1700s, but it was not until 1830 that missionaries from the London Missionary Society settled there. In 1872 the Kingdom of Samoa, then an independent state, ceded Pago Pago harbour to the USA as a naval coaling station. The United Kingdom and Germany were also interested in the islands, but a treaty signed in 1889 by these powers and the USA guaranteed the neutrality of Samoa. The British withdrew in 1899, and in the same year, following internal conflicts among rival chiefs, the kingship was abolished and a further tripartite treaty left the Western islands for Germany to govern, while the Eastern islands passed under US influence. In 1900 the high chiefs, or Matai, of Tutuila formally ceded the islands of Tutuila and Aunu'u to the USA and, in 1904, the chiefs of the islands of Ta'u, Olosega, Ofu and Rose (Manu'a District) followed suit. These deeds of cession and American Samoa's annexation as a US territory were enacted by Congress in the 1920s. The President of the USA was empowered to provide for the executive, legislative and judicial administration of the territory, this responsibility being vested in the Secretary of the Navy until 1951, and subsequently in the Secretary of the Interior. The federal Government of the USA remains responsible for defence and foreign affairs.

Since 1925 Swains Island has also been administered by the USA as part of American Samoa. From 1951 until 1978 American Samoa was administered by a Governor appointed by the US Department of the Interior, and a legislature comprising a Senate and a House of Representatives. In November 1977 the first popular vote to elect a Governor was held.

In October 1986 a constitutional convention completed a comprehensive rewriting of the American Samoan Constitution. The draft revision, however, had yet to be submitted to the US Congress in the mid-2000s. In April 2004 it was announced that the Political Status Study Commission was to examine the status of the territory and submit its recommendations prior to the next constitutional convention.

In September 2002 the Territory's immigration procedures were amended to give the Attorney-General, rather than the Immigration Board, the ultimate authority to grant permanent residency status to aliens. The House of Representatives also approved a resolution to repeal legislation automatically conferring US citizenship in the Territory to children of foreign parents. A delegation was dispatched to American Samoa by the US General Accountability Office in January 2010, charged with the task of identifying potential risks for American Samoa and the rest of the USA arising from existing customs and immigrations policies and practices.

Proposed amendments to the Constitution of American Samoa were discussed at a convention held in mid-2010. Among the proposals endorsed was a new stipulation that members of the Fono should be US nationals of American Samoan ancestry, which provoked considerable censure owing to its perceived discriminatory and unconstitutional nature. At a popular referendum held concurrently with the legislative elections of November 2010, the proposed amendments were rejected by a majority of voters, amid criticism that the electorate's only option was to reject or to approve the entire list of proposed constitutional amendments, rather than being able to express an opinion on the individual proposals. Further controversy arose in January 2011 when the US House of Representatives voted to rescind the 'symbolic' voting rights of territorial delegates in the 'Committee of the Whole House on the State of the Union', a means by which the House was able to expedite consideration of certain legislation, particularly amendments.

The decision in July 1997 by the Government of neighbouring Western Samoa to change the country's name to simply Samoa caused some controversy in the territory, as it was viewed by many islanders as serving to undermine their own Samoan identity. Legislation prohibiting citizens of the former Western Samoa from owning land in American Samoa was approved in response to the change. Nevertheless, moves towards rapprochement have continued. Although in March 2005 the Samoan Government announced plans to open a consulate in American Samoa and the US State Department subsequently approved the proposal, the opening of the consulate (originally scheduled for March 2006) was postponed indefinitely.

Fish-canning has been the dominant industrial activity, accounting for most export revenue, with tuna-canning plants at Pago Pago processing fish from US, Taiwanese and South Korean vessels. The

StarKist Samoa and (until its closure in September 2009—see below) COS Samoa Packing plants were among the largest in the world. Other activities include meat-canning, handicrafts, dairy farming, orchid farming and the manufacture of soap, perfume, paper products and alcoholic beverages. A garment factory began operations at Tafuna in 1995, and by the following year employed more than 700 people (although almost one-half of these employees were foreign workers). In 2002 the management of the Daewoosa clothing manufacturer was ordered by the authorities to pay compensation for the poor working conditions to its employees, and in early 2003 the factory's South Korean owner was convicted of human trafficking. Service industries engage the majority of the employed labour force in American Samoa, with the Government engaging a substantial percentage of workers. The tourist industry has developed steadily. In addition to the regular flights from Hawaii, a new twice-weekly service between the US city of Los Angeles and Pago Pago, scheduled to commence in late 2011, was expected to provide local employment opportunities, as well as attract more tourists to the islands.

American Samoa's minimum wage structure has caused much controversy. As stipulated in the US Fair Labor Standards Act, American Samoa was exempt from the general minimum wage of mainland USA and, instead, applies industry-specific rates set by a special industry commission. The situation (whereby American Samoa had considerably lower minimum hourly rates of pay than the rest of the USA) was largely attributed to the presence of the two tuna-canning plants on the islands, which exerted substantial influence over the setting of wage levels. A US recommendation for modest increases in wage levels, implemented in mid-1996, was strongly opposed by the American Samoan Government, which argued that, with higher costs, the territory's tuna-canning industry would be unable to compete with those in other parts of the world. In October 2006 the minimum hourly wage for five industry categories was increased. However, plans to raise the hourly rate for the cannery sector encountered strong opposition from the business community and from the Government itself, which argued that the decision would adversely affect companies' cost effectiveness. In 2007 the remit of mainland US minimum wage legislation was extended to American Samoa. However, in December 2009 US President Barack Obama signed legislation postponing from May until September 2010 the implementation of the next scheduled increase in the minimum wage in American Samoa.

In March 2009, following the serious deterioration in the global economy, it was announced that American Samoa was to receive US $19m. in federal economic stimulus funding. Following the closure of one of the two tuna canneries in 2009, in October 2010 agreement was reached on the sale of the plant to a US company; its fish-processing operations were therefore resumed, and by April 2011, with the help of government tax concessions, the work-force of the cannery was reported to have been expanded to 2,000.

The economy of American Samoa was disrupted in September 2009 when the islands were devastated by a tsunami, which killed more than 30 people in the territory. American Samoa was declared a federal disaster area. To facilitate the reconstruction of public infrastructure, economic assistance of US $10.3m. was approved by the Federal Emergency Management Agency in February 2010. In March 2011 it was reported that a newly endorsed 2% increase in personal income tax, being introduced in an attempt to reduce the government deficit, was to be backdated to 1 January.

Statistical Survey

Source (unless otherwise indicated): Statistics Division, Department of Commerce, Pago Pago, AS 96799; tel. 633-5155; fax 633-4195; internet www.spc.int/prism/Country/AS/ASindex.html.

AREA AND POPULATION

Area: 201 sq km (77.6 sq miles); *By Island* (sq km): Tutuila 137; Ta'u 46; Ofu 7; Olosega 5; Swains Island (Olohenga) 3; Aunu'u 2; Rose 1.

Population: 57,291 (males 29,264, females 28,027) at census of 1 April 2000; 55,519 at census of 1 April 2010. *By Island* (2010): Western district 30,720; Eastern district 23,639; Manu'a District (Ta'u, Olosega and Ofu islands) 1,143; Swains Island (Olohenga) 17.

Density (at 2010 census): 276.2 per sq km.

Population by Age and Sex (Secretariat of the Pacific Community estimates at mid-2011): *0–14:* 23,089 (males 11,947, females 11,142); *15–64:* 40,524 (males 20,643, females 19,881); *65 and over:* 3,080 (males 1,445, females 1,635); *Total* 66,692 (males 34,035, females 32,657). Note: Mid-2011 estimates not adjusted to take account of results of 2010 census (Source: Pacific Regional Information System).

Ethnic Groups (2000 census): Samoan 50,545; part-Samoan 1,991; Asian 1,631; Tongan 1,598; Total (incl. others) 57,291.

Principal Towns (population at 2000 census): Tafuna 8,409; Nu'uuli 5,154; Pago Pago (capital) 4,278; Leone 3,568; Ili'ili 2,513.

Births, Marriages and Deaths (2006): Registered live births 1,442 (birth rate 21.6 per 1,000); Registered marriages 171; Registered deaths 267 (death rate 4.0 per 1,000). *2010:* Registered live births 1,542 (birth rate 23.5 per 1,000); Registered deaths 294 (death rate 4.5 per 1,000).

Life Expectancy (years at birth, 2007): 75.9 (Males 71.8; Females 80.3).

Economically Active Population (persons aged 16 years and over, 2000 census): Agriculture, hunting, forestry, fishing and mining 517; Manufacturing 5,900; Construction 1,066; Trade, restaurants and hotels 2,414; Transport, storage, communications and utilities 1,036; Financing, insurance, real estate and business services 311; Community, social and personal services 5,474; *Total employed* 16,718 (males 9,804, females 6,914); Unemployed 909 (males 494, females 415); *Total labour force* 17,627 (males 10,298, females 7,329) (Source: US Department of Commerce, *2000 Census of Population and Housing*). *2003* (estimates): Total employed 14,319; Unemployed 1,681; Total labour force 16,000 (Source: US Department of State). *2005* (official estimates): Basic employment 8,428 (Fish-processing 4,546, Government employment—supported by federal grants 3,282, Other 600); Non-basic employment 8,916; Total employment 17,344. *Mid-2011* (estimates): Agriculture, etc. 8,000; Total labour force 29,000 (Source: FAO).

AGRICULTURE, ETC.

Principal Crops ('000 metric tons, 2009, FAO estimates): Coconuts 5.6; Taro 9.3; Bananas 1.0.

Livestock (year ending September 2009, FAO estimates): Pigs 10,500; Cattle 110; Chickens 40,000.

Livestock Products (metric tons, 2009, FAO estimates): Pig meat 315; Chicken meat 24; Cows' milk 26; Hen eggs 40.

Fishing (metric tons, live weight, 2009): Total catch 5,051 (Albacore 3,918; Yellowfin tuna 390; Wahoo 136; Bigeye tuna 320).

Source: FAO.

INDUSTRY

Production (2008): Electric energy 199 million kWh. Source: UN Industrial Commodity Statistics Database.

FINANCE

Currency and Exchange Rates: United States currency is used: 100 cents = 1 United States dollar (US $). *Sterling and Euro Equivalents* (31 May 2011): £1 sterling = US $1.650; €1 = US $1.439; US $100 = £60.60 = €69.52.

Federal Direct Expenditures (US $ million, year ending September 2009): Retirement and disability payments 59; Grants 213; Total (incl. others) 368 (Source: US Census Bureau, *Consolidated Federal Funds Report*).

Budget (US $ '000, year ending September 2005): *Revenue:* Taxes 50,397; Licences and permits 1,160; Intergovernmental 111,783; Charges for services 8,438; Fines and fees 1,869; Total (incl. others) 182,015. *Expenditure:* General government 45,555; Public safety 11,827; Public works 5,801; Health and recreation 31,952; Education and culture 65,881; Economic development 20,083; Capital projects 7,411; Debt-servicing 3,989; Total 192,499.

Cost of Living (Consumer Price Index; base: 2000 = 100): All items (excl. rent) 116.1 in 2004; 122.1 in 2005; 125.7 in 2006. Source: ILO.

Gross Domestic Product (US $ million at current prices): 572 in 2007; 605 in 2008; 703 in 2009 (Source: Bureau of Economic Analysis, US Department of Commerce).

Expenditure on the Gross Domestic Product (US $ million at current prices, 2009): Government consumption expenditure and gross investment 293; Personal consumption expenditure 403; Private fixed investment 17; Change in private inventories –10; *Total domestic expenditure* 703; Exports of goods and services 536; *Less* Imports of goods and services 537; *GDP in purchasers' values* 703 (Source: Bureau of Economic Analysis, US Department of Commerce).

Gross Domestic Product by Economic Activity (US $ million at current prices, 2002): Agriculture and fishing (excl. fish-processing) 54.3; Fish-processing 107.3; Wholesale and retail trade 36.6; Government services 100.0; Other services 111.3; Other non-services 71.9; *Total* 481.4. Note: Recorded accounts are not available; figures represent the findings of the American Samoa National Income and Product Accounts Task Force, established to produce reliable economic statistics for the territory.

EXTERNAL TRADE

Principal Commodities (US $ million): *Imports* (excl. government purchases and cannery goods, year ending September 2006): Food 141.3 (Fish 74.4); Fuel and oil 35.8 (Diesel fuel 14.4); Textiles and clothing 6.6; Machinery and transport equipment 21.8 (Road motor vehicles and parts 13.7); Miscellaneous manufactured articles 113.7 (Tin plates 48.0); Construction materials 17.5; Total (incl. others) 341.5. *Exports:* Total exports 438.5 (Canned tuna 431.5; Pet food 7).

Principal Trading Partners (US $ million, year ending September 2006): *Imports* (excl. government purchases and cannery goods): Australia 8.4; Fiji 22.5; Japan 2.0; Korea, Republic 21.2; New Zealand 31.1; Samoa 17.0; Singapore 27.2; USA 133.4; Total (incl. others) 341.5. *Exports:* Total 438.5 (almost entirely to the USA).

TRANSPORT

Road Traffic ('000 registered motor vehicles, year ending September 2006): Passenger cars 7.8; Total 9.2.

International Sea-borne Shipping (freight traffic, '000 metric tons, year ending September 2006): Goods loaded 148; Goods unloaded 400.

Civil Aviation (Pago Pago Int. Airport, year ending September 2006): Flights 4,344; Passengers (excl. transit) 157,023 (Boarding 81,907, Disembarking 75,116); Transit 385; Freight and mail ('000 lb): Loaded 3,893, Unloaded 3,939.

TOURISM

Tourist Arrivals by Country (2006): Australia 950; China, People's Republic 439; Fiji 345; New Zealand 3,224; Philippines 230; Samoa 11,313; Tonga 450; United Kingdom 148; USA 7,037; Total (incl. others) 25,347. *2008:* Total arrivals 30,268.

Tourism Receipts (US $ million): 9 in 1996; 10 in 1997; 10 in 1998.

Source: World Tourism Organization.

COMMUNICATIONS MEDIA

Daily Newspapers (1996): 2; estimated circulation 5,000*.

Non-daily Newspapers (1996): 1; estimated circulation 3,000*.

Radio Receivers (1997): 57,000* in use.

Television Receivers (1999): 15,000* in use.

Telephones ('000 main lines in use, 2010): 10.4.

Mobile Cellular Telephones (2006): 8,525 subscribers.

* Sources: UNESCO, *Statistical Yearbook*; American Samoa Telecommunications Authority; International Telecommunication Union.

EDUCATION

Pre-primary (2006): 40 schools; 140 teachers; 2,038 pupils.

Primary (2006): 35 schools; 450 teachers; 11,100 pupils.

Secondary (2006): 12 high schools; 213 teachers; 5,074 pupils.

Higher (2006): American Samoa Community College 1,607 students.

Source: American Samoa Department of Education.

Directory

The Constitution

American Samoa is an Unincorporated Territory of the USA. Therefore, not all the provisions of the US Constitution apply. As an unorganized territory it has not been provided with an organic act by Congress. Instead the US Secretary of the Interior, on behalf of the President, has plenary authority over the Territory and enabled the people of American Samoa to draft their own Constitution.

According to the 1967 Constitution, executive power is vested in the Governor, whose authority extends to all operations within the Territory of American Samoa. The Governor has veto power with respect to legislation passed by the Fono (Legislature). The Fono consists of the Senate and the House of Representatives, with a President and a Speaker presiding over their respective divisions. The Senate is composed of 18 members, elected, according to Samoan custom, from local chiefs, or Matai, for a term of four years. The House of Representatives consists of 20 members who are elected by popular vote for a term of two years, and a non-voting delegate from Swains Island. The Fono meets twice a year, in January and July, for not more than 45 days and at such special sessions as the Governor may call. The Governor has the authority to appoint heads of government departments with the approval of the Fono. Local government is carried out by indigenous officials. In August 1976 a referendum on the popular election of a Governor and a Lieutenant-Governor resulted in an affirmative vote. The first gubernatorial elections took place on 8 November 1977 and the second was held in November 1980; subsequent elections were to take place every four years.

American Samoa sends one non-voting Delegate to the US House of Representatives, who is popularly elected every two years.

The Government

(October 2011)

Governor: TOGIOLA TALALELEI A. TULAFONO (took office March 2003, re-elected 16 November 2004 and 18 November 2008).

Lieutenant-Governor: FAOA IPULASI AITOFELE TOESE FITI SUNIA.

GOVERNMENT OFFICES

Governor's Office: Executive Office Bldg, 3rd Floor, Utulei, Pago Pago, AS 96799; tel. 633-4116; fax 633-2269; e-mail jacinta@americansamoa.gov; internet americansamoa.gov/governor.

Department of the Interior, Office of Insular Affairs (OIA): Field Office of the OIA, Dept of the Interior, POB 1725, Pago Pago, AS 96799; tel. 633-2800; fax 633-2415; internet www.doi.gov/oia/Islandpages/asgpage; Field Representative LYDIA FALEAFINE NOMURA.

Office of the Representative to the Government of American Samoa: Amerika Samoa Office, 1427 Dillingham Blvd, Suite 210, Honolulu, HI 96817, USA; tel. (808) 847-1998; fax (808) 847-3420; e-mail ahawaiioffice@aol.com; Representative SOLOALI'I FA'ALEPO, Jr.

Department of Administrative Services: American Samoa Government, Executive Office Bldg, Utulei, Pago Pago, AS 96799; tel. 633-4158; fax 633-1841; e-mail adminservices@americansamoa.gov; internet americansamoa.gov/departments/admin/department-administrative-services; Dir NU'UTAI SONNY THOMPSON.

Department of Agriculture: American Samoa Government, Executive Office Bldg, Utulei, Pago Pago, AS 96799; tel. 699-9272; fax 699-4031; e-mail agriculture@americansamoa.gov; internet americansamoa.gov/departments/agriculture/department-agriculture; Dir LEFITI AITULAGI PESE.

Department of Commerce: American Samoa Government, Executive Office Bldg, 2nd Floor, POB 1147, Utulei, Pago Pago, AS 96799; tel. 633-5155; fax 633-4195; e-mail doc@americansamoa.gov; internet americansamoa.gov/departments/doc/department-commerce; Dir FALESEU ELIU PAOPAO.

Department of Education: American Samoa Government, Executive Office Bldg, Utulei, Pago Pago, AS 96799; tel. 633-5237; fax 633-4240; e-mail webmaster@doe.as; internet www.doe.as; Dir Dr JACINTA GALEA'I.

Department of Health: American Samoa Government, Pago Pago, AS 96799; tel. 633-4606; fax 633-5379; e-mail publichealth@americansamoa.gov; internet americansamoa.gov/departments/doh/department-health; Dir ELISAPETA PONAUSUIA.

Department of Homeland Security: POB 4567, Pago Pago, AS 96799; tel. 633-2827; fax 633-2979; e-mail mrsala@americansamoa.gov; internet americansamoa.gov/asdhs/index.htm; Dir MICHAEL SALA.

Department of Human Resources: American Samoa Government, Executive Office Bldg, Utulei, Pago Pago, AS 96799; tel. 633-4485; fax 633-1139; e-mail hr@americansamoa.gov; internet americansamoa.gov/departments/hr/department-human-resources; Dir EVELYN VAITAUTOLU LANGFORD.

Department of Human and Social Services: American Samoa Government, Pago Pago, AS 96799; tel. 633-1187; fax 633-7449; e-mail hss@americansamoa.gov; internet americansamoa.gov/departments/dhss/department-human-social-services; Dir LEILUA STEVENSON.

Department of Legal Affairs: American Samoa Government, Executive Office Bldg, Utulei, Pago Pago, AS 96799; tel. 633-4163; fax 633-1838; e-mail legalaffairs@americansamoa.gov; internet americansamoa.gov/departments/legal-affairs/department-legal-affairs; Dir Attorney-General FEPULEA'I AFA RIPLEY, Jr.

Department of Local Government (Office of Samoan Affairs): American Samoa Government, Pago Pago, AS 96799; tel. 633-5201; fax 633-5590; e-mail localgov@americansamoa.gov; internet americansamoa.gov/departments/samoan-affairs/local-government; Dir NANAI AFUOLA (acting).

Department of Marine and Wildlife Resources: American Samoa Government, Executive Office Bldg, Utulei, Pago Pago, AS 96799; tel. 633-4456; fax 633-5944; e-mail marine@americansamoa.gov; internet americansamoa.gov/departments/mwr/department-marine-wildlife-resources; Dir UFAGAFA RAY TULAFONO.

Department of Parks and Recreation: American Samoa Government, Pago Pago, AS 96799; tel. 699-9614; fax 699-4427; e-mail parks@americansamoa.gov; internet americansamoa.gov/departments/parks/department-parks-recreation; Dir SAMANA SEMO VE'AVE'A.

Department of Planning and Budget: tel. 633-4201; fax 633-1148; e-mail budget@americansamoa.gov; internet americansamoa.gov/departments/budget/department-planning-budget; Dir MALEMO TAUSAGA.

Department of Port Administration: American Samoa Government, Pago Pago, AS 96799; tel. 633-4251; fax 633-5281; e-mail matagi.mcmoore@americansamoa.gov; internet americansamoa.gov/departments/port/department-port-administration; Dir MATAGI MAILO RAY MCMOORE.

Department of Procurement: American Samoa Government, Tafuna, AS 96799; tel. 699-1170; fax 699-2387; e-mail procurement@americansamoa.gov; internet americansamoa.gov/procurement/index.htm; Dir PAT TERVOLA.

Department of Public Information: American Samoa Government, Pago Pago, AS 96799; tel. 633-4191; fax 633-1044; e-mail kvzk@americansamoa.gov; internet americansamoa.gov/departments/kvzk/department-public-information; Dir PAOLO SIVIA SIVIA.

Department of Public Safety: American Samoa Government, Pago Pago, AS 96799; tel. 633-1111; fax 633-7296; e-mail publicsafety@americansamoa.gov; internet americansamoa.gov/departments/dps/department-public-safety; Dir TUAOLO M. E. FRUEAN.

Department of Public Works: American Samoa Government, Pago Pago, AS 96799; tel. 633-4141; fax 633-5958; e-mail publicworks@americansamoa.gov; internet americansamoa.gov/departments/dpw/department-public-works; Dir PUNAOFO TILEI.

Department of Treasury: American Samoa Government, Executive Office Bldg, Utulei, Pago Pago, AS 96799; tel. 633-4155; fax 633-4100; e-mail lmagalei@asg.as; internet americansamoa.gov/departments/treasury/department-treasury; Dir LOGOVI'I MAGALEI.

Department of Youth and Women's Affairs: American Samoa Government, Executive Office Bldg, Utulei, Pago Pago, AS 96799; tel. 633-2836; fax 633-2875; e-mail youthandwomen@americansamoa.gov; internet americansamoa.gov/departments/youth/youth-womens-affairs; Dir Leiataua Dr LEUGA TURNER.

Environmental Protection Agency: American Samoa Government, Executive Office Bldg, Utulei, Pago Pago, AS 96799; tel. 633-2304; fax 633-5801; e-mail toafa.vaiagae@asepa.gov; internet asepa.gov; Dir Fanuatele Dr TOA'FA VAIAGA'E.

Office of Protection and Advocacy for the Disabled: POB 3937, Pago Pago, AS 96799; tel. 633-2441; fax 633-7286; e-mail opad@americansamoa.gov; internet americansamoa.gov/departments/OPAD/office-protection-and-advocacy-disabled; Dir Dr LALOULU TAGOILELAGI.

Office of the Public Defender: American Samoa Government, Executive Office Bldg, 3rd Floor, Utulei, Pago Pago, AS 96799; tel. 633-1286; fax 633-4745; e-mail public_defender@americansamoa.gov; internet americansamoa.gov/departments/pd/public-defender; Dir RUTH RISCH.

Legislature

FONO

Senate

The Senate has 18 members, elected, according to Samoan custom, from local chiefs (*Matai*) for a term of four years.

President: GAOTEOTE PALAIE GAOTEOTE.

House of Representatives

The House has 20 members who are elected by popular vote for a term of two years, and a non-voting delegate from Swains Island.

Speaker: SAVALI TALAVOU ALE.

CONGRESS

Since 1980 American Samoa has been able to elect, for a two-year term, a Delegate to the Federal Congress, who may vote in committee but not on the floor of the House of Representatives. At the election to the post in November 2010, incumbent Congressman Eni F. Hunkin Faleomavaega was re-elected for a record 12th two-year term.

Delegate of American Samoa: ENI F. HUNKIN FALEOMAVAEGA, US House of Representatives, 2422 Rayburn House Office Bldg, Washington, DC 20515, USA; tel. (202) 225-8577; fax (202) 225-8757; e-mail faleomavaega@mail.house.gov; internet www.house.gov/faleomavaega.

Election Commission

Government Election Office: POB 3970, Pago Pago, AS 96799; tel. 699-3571; fax 699-3574; e-mail info@americansamoaelectionoffice.org; internet www.americansamoaelectionoffice.org; Chief Election Officer SOLIAI T. FUIMAONO.

Political Organizations

While the USA's Democratic Party and the Republican Party have local chapters in American Samoa, most politicians in the Territory remain non-partisan.

Judicial System

The judicial system of American Samoa consists of the High Court, presided over by the Chief Justice and assisted by an Associate Justice (appointed by the Secretary of the Interior), and a local judiciary in the District and Village Courts. The judges for these local courts are appointed by the Governor, subject to confirmation by the Senate of the Fono. The High Court consists of three Divisions: Appellate, Trial, and Land and Titles. The Appellate Division has limited original jurisdiction and hears appeals from the Trial Division, the Land and Titles Division and from the District Court when it has operated as a court of record. The Trial Division has general jurisdiction over all cases. The Land and Titles Division hears cases involving land or *Matai* titles.

The District Court hears preliminary felony proceedings, misdemeanours, infractions (traffic and health), civil claims less than US $3,000, small claims, Uniform Reciprocal Enforcement of Support cases, and *de novo* trials from Village Courts. The Village Courts hear matters arising under village regulations and local customs.

Chief Justice of the High Court: MICHAEL KRUSE, Office of the Chief Justice, High Court, Pago Pago, AS 96799; tel. 633-1261; fax 633-1318; e-mail hcourt@samoatelco.com.

Associate Justice of the High Court: LYLE L. RICHMOND.

Attorney-General: FEPULEAI AFA RIPLEY, Jr.

Judges of the District Court: JOHN L. WARD II, ELVIS PATEA, POB 427, Pago Pago, AS 96799; tel. 633-1101; fax 633-5127.

Judge of the Village Court: FAISIOTA TAUANU'U, Pago Pago, AS 96799; tel. 633-1102.

Religion

The population is largely Christian, more than 50% being members of the Congregational Christian Church and about 20% being Roman Catholics.

CHRISTIANITY

American Samoa Council of Christian Churches: c/o CCCAS Offices, POB 1537, Pago Pago, AS 96799; f. 1985; six mem. churches; Pres. (vacant); Gen. Sec. Rev. ENOKA L. ALESANA (Congregational Christian Church in American Samoa).

The Roman Catholic Church

American Samoa comprises the single diocese of Samoa-Pago Pago, suffragan to the archdiocese of Samoa-Apia and Tokelau. At 31 December 2007 there were 15,000 adherents in the islands. The Bishop participates in the Catholic Bishops' Conference of the Pacific, based in Suva, Fiji.

Bishop of Samoa-Pago Pago: Rev. JOHN QUINN WEITZEL, Diocesan Pastoral Center, POB 596, Fatuoaiga, Pago Pago, AS 96799; tel. 699-1402; fax 699-1459; e-mail quinn@samoatelco.com.

The Anglican Communion

American Samoa is within the diocese of Polynesia, part of the Church of the Province of New Zealand. The Bishop of Polynesia is resident in Fiji.

Protestant Churches

Congregational Christian Church in American Samoa (CCCAS): POB 1537, Pago Pago, AS 96799; tel. 699-9810; fax 699-1898; e-mail cccasgs@samoatelco.com; internet www.efkas.org; f. 1980; 39,000 mems (incl. congregations in New Zealand, Australia and USA) in 2011; Chair. Rev. LEATULAGI T. FAALEVAO.

Other active Protestant groups include the Baptist Church, the Christian Church of Jesus Christ, the Methodist Church, Assemblies of God, Church of the Nazarene and Seventh-day Adventists. The Church of Jesus Christ of Latter-day Saints (Mormons) is also represented.

The Press

American Samoa Tribune: 5 a week; circ. 4,500 (2006).

News Bulletin: Department of Public Information, American Samoa Government, Pago Pago, AS 96799; tel. 633-5490; daily (Mon.–Fri.); English; non-commercial; Editor PHILIP SWETT; circ. 1,800.

Samoa Journal and Advertiser: POB 3986, Pago Pago, AS 96799; tel. 633-2399; weekly; English and Samoan; Editor MICHAEL STARK; circ. 3,000.

Samoa News: POB 909, Pago Pago, AS 96799; tel. 633-5599; fax 633-4864; e-mail webmaster@samoanews.com; internet www.samoanews.com; owned by Osini Faleatasi Inc dba Samoa News; 6 a week; English and Samoan; Publr VERA M. ANNESLEY; circ. 6,000.

Broadcasting and Communications

TELECOMMUNICATIONS

American Samoa Telecommunications Authority: Box M, Pago Pago, AS 96799; tel. 633-1126; internet www.samoatelco.com.

Blue Sky Communications: 478 Laufou Shopping Center, Pago Pago, AS 96799; tel. 699-2759; fax 699-6593; e-mail webmaster@bluesky.as; internet www.bluesky.as; mobile telecommunications provider; Pres. and CEO ADOLFO MONTENEGRO.

BROADCASTING

Radio

KSBS-FM (Island 92): POB 793, Pago Pago, AS 96799; tel. 633-7000; fax 622-5727; e-mail info@ksbsfm92.com; internet www.ksbsfm92.com; commercial; Gen. Man. ESTHER PRESCOTT.

V103: POB 6758, Pago Pago, AS 96799; tel. 633-7793; fax 633-4493; e-mail thepeople@wvuv.com; internet www.wvuv.com; fmr govt-administered station leased to Radio Samoa Ltd in 1975; commercial; English and Samoan; 24 hours a day; Gen. Man. JOEY CUMMINGS.

Television

KVZK-TV: POB 3511, Pago Pago, AS 96799; tel. 633-4191; fax 633-1044; e-mail kvzk@americansamoa.gov; f. 1964; govt-owned; non-commercial; English and Samoan; broadcasts 18 hours daily on two channels; Gen. Man. PAOLO SIVIA SIVIA; Technical Dir JEFFREY ALWIN.

Malama TV: Malama Communications, Inc, POB AB, Pago Pago 96799; tel. 699-5999; fax 699-6006; e-mail webmaster@malama.tv; internet malama.solupress.com.

Finance

(cap. = capital; dep. = deposits; m. = million; amounts in US dollars)

BANKING

Commercial Banks

ANZ Amerika Samoa Bank: POB 3790, Pago Pago, AS 96799; tel. 633-1151; fax 633-5057; internet www.anz.com.au/americansamoa; f. 1979; fmrly Amerika Samoa Bank; joined ANZ group in April 2001; Pres. and CEO DAVID WHITBY; 3 brs.

Bank of Hawaii (USA): POB 69, Pago Pago, AS 96799; tel. 633-4226; fax 633-2918; f. 1897; District Man. HOBBS LAWSON; 3 brs.

Development Bank

Development Bank of American Samoa: POB 9, Pago Pago, AS 96799; tel. 633-4031; fax 633-1163; e-mail dbasinfo@dbas.org; internet www.dbas.org; f. 1969; govt-owned and non-profit-making; Chair. (vacant); Pres. LOLO MOLIGA.

INSURANCE

American International Underwriters (South Pacific) Ltd: Pago Pago, AS 96799; tel. 633-4845.

Mark Solofa, Inc: POB 3149, Pago Pago, AS 96799; tel. 699-5902; fax 699-5904; e-mail marksalofainc@yahoo.com.

National Pacific Insurance Ltd: Centennial Bldg, POB 1386, Pago Pago, AS 96799; tel. 633-4266; fax 633-2964; e-mail contact@npipago.as; f. 1977; Country Man. JASON THOMAS.

Oxford Pacific Insurance Management: POB 1420, Pago Pago, AS 96799; tel. 633-4990; fax 633-2721; e-mail progressive_oxford@yahoo.com; f. 1977; represents major international property and life insurance cos; Pres. GREG F. DUFFY.

South Seas Financial Services Corporation: POB 1448, Pago Pago, AS 96799; tel. 633-7896; fax 633-7895; e-mail ssfs@samoatelco.com.

Trade and Industry

DEVELOPMENT ORGANIZATIONS

American Samoa Development Corporation: Pago Pago, AS 96799; tel. 633-4241; f. 1962; financed by private Samoan interests.

American Samoa Economic Advisory Commission: Pago Pago; Chair. JOHN WAIHEE.

Department of Commerce: see Government Offices; Dir FALESEU ELIU PAOPAO.

CHAMBER OF COMMERCE

Chamber of Commerce of American Samoa: POB 6758, Pago Pago, AS 96799; tel. 633-7793; fax 633-4493; e-mail info@amsamoachamber.com; internet www.amsamoachamber.com; 1979; Chair. JOEY CUMMINGS.

UTILITIES

American Samoa Power Authority: POB PPB, Pago Pago, AS 96799; tel. 699-1234; fax 699-4783; internet www.aspower.com; supplies water and electricity throughout the islands; also manages sewer and solid waste collection; Chair. ASAUA FUIMAONO; CEO ANDRA SAMOA.

MAJOR COMPANIES

BP Oil South-West Pacific: POB 5620, Pago Pago, AS 96799; tel. 633-7386; fax 633-7389; internet www.bp.com; petroleum suppliers; Gen. Man. MATT ELLIOT.

G.H.C. Reid & Co, Ltd: POB 1269, Pago Pago, AS 96799; tel. 699-1854; fax 699-2869; e-mail ghcreid@ghcreid.com; import and distribution of beverages.

Haleck Enterprises, Inc.: POB 670, Pago Pago, AS 96799; tel. 688-1922; fax 688-1217; e-mail hei@haleck.com; internet www.haleck.com; f. 1922; consulting, automobiles, food, beverages, building materials, devt and philanthropy.

Origin Energy: POB 159, Pago Pago, AS 96799; tel. 699-2948; fax 699-1852; e-mail pacific.banyo@originenergy.com.au.

Samoa Tuna Processors: POB Y, Suite 208B, Fagatogo Sq., Pago Pago, AS 96799; tel. 731-5913; e-mail tomi@trimarinegroup.com; owned by Tri Marine International (USA); tuna-canning; fmrly COS Samoa Packing; Corporate Sec. DAN KING.

StarKist Samoa, Inc: Pago Pago, AS 96799; tel. 644-4231; fax 644-2440; tuna-canning; owned by Dongwon Group (South Korea); f. 1963; Pres. and CEO IN-SOO CHO; c. 2,000 employees.

Transport

ROADS

There are about 150 km (93 miles) of paved and 200 km (124 miles) of secondary roads. Non-scheduled commercial buses operate a service over 350 km (217 miles) of main and secondary roads. There were an estimated 8,100 registered motor vehicles in the islands in 2004.

SHIPPING

There are various passenger and cargo services from the US Pacific coast, Japan, Australia (mainly Sydney) and New Zealand that call at Pago Pago, which is one of the deepest and most sheltered harbours in the Pacific. Inter-island boats provide frequent services between Samoa and American Samoa.

PM&O Line: Suite 202, Fagatogo Sq., POB 5023, Pago Pago, AS 96799; tel. 633-4527; fax 633-4530; e-mail paige@blueskynet.as; f. 1978.

Polynesia Shipping: POB 1478, Pago Pago, AS 96799; tel. 633-1211; fax 633-1265.

Samoa Pacific Shipping: Samoan Sports Bldg, 1 Main St, Fagatogo, POB 1417, Pago Pago, AS 96799; tel. 633-4665; fax 699-4667; e-mail spsi@samoatelco.com; internet www.hamburgsud.com; f. 1988; Gen. Man. VA'A UITUALAGI.

CIVIL AVIATION

There is an international airport at Tafuna, 11 km (7 miles) from Pago Pago, and smaller airstrips on the islands of Ta'u and Ofu. International services are operated by Hawaiian Airlines and Polynesian Blue.

Samoa Aviation: POB 280, Pago Pago Int. Airport, Pago Pago, AS 96799; tel. 699-9106; fax 699-9751; f. 1986; operates service between Pago Pago and Samoa, Tonga and Niue; Pres. ANDRE LAVIGNE.

Tourism

The tourist industry is encouraged by the Government, but its development has been impeded by the cost and paucity of air services. A total of 29,060 tourists visited the islands in 2010, 1,645 fewer than in the previous year. The majority of tourists came from Samoa, the USA and New Zealand. The industry earned an estimated US $10m. in 1998.

American Samoa Visitors Bureau: POB 4240, Pago Pago, AS 96799; tel. 699-9805; fax 699-9806; e-mail info@americansamoa.travel; internet www.americansamoa.travel; Exec. Dir DAVID VAEAFE.

Office of Tourism: Convention Center, POB 1147, Tafuna, Pago Pago, AS 96799; tel. 699-9411; fax 699-9414; e-mail asgtourism@samoatelco.com; Deputy Dir VIRGINIA SAMUELU.

Pago Pago Visitors Association (PPVA): f. 2004; Pres. TOM DRABBLE.

Defence

The USA is responsible for the defence of American Samoa. The US Pacific Command is based in Hawaii, but the territory receives regular naval visits and assistance in surveillance of its waters.

Education

The Government's early childhood education division provides facilities for all children between three and five years of age. Education is compulsory for children between six and 18 years of age. The education system is based on the US pattern of eight years' attendance at an elementary school and four years' enrolment at a high school. In 2006 there were 11,100 pupils enrolled at the 35 primary schools and 5,074 at the 12 secondary schools. The American Samoa Community College had 1,607 students in 2006.

GUAM

Introduction

Guam, the largest and southernmost of the Mariana Islands, covers an area of 549 sq km (212 sq miles). The island comprises a northern, coralline, limestone plateau and a mountainous area in the south, of volcanic origin, rising to some 395 m. It is situated about 2,400 km east of the Philippines, and its nearest neighbour is the Northern Mariana Islands, to the north. Guam has a tropical climate, with a mean annual temperature of 30°C (85°F), the hottest months being May and June. Most rain falls from July to October, and the island is sometimes subject to tropical storms and typhoons. The population is multiracial: some 45% are the indigenous Chamorro, 25% Filipino and 15% US immigrants. Chamorro and, particularly, English are widely spoken and are both official languages. The population was officially estimated at 192,090 in mid-2011. In 1998 the US authorities approved changing the name of the capital from Agaña to Hagåtña, to reflect more accurately the original Chamorro language name for the town.

The ancestors of the Micronesians first settled in Guam and the other Mariana Islands some 4,000 years ago. A society of matrilineal clans evolved. Members of a Spanish expedition, under the Portuguese navigator Fernão Magalhães (Ferdinand Magellan), were the first Europeans to discover Guam, visiting the island in 1521, during a voyage that accomplished the first circumnavigation of the globe. The island was claimed by Spain in 1565, and the first Jesuit missionaries arrived in 1668. The present-day Chamorro population are the descendants of the Micronesians, mingled with Spaniards and immigrant Filipinos. Following the Spanish–American War of 1898, Spain ceded Guam to the USA, and then sold the other Mariana Islands to Germany. Japan obtained a League of Nations mandate over the German islands, including the Caroline and Marshall Islands, in 1919. Japanese forces seized Guam in 1941, but the island was recaptured by US troops in 1944.

Guam is an Unincorporated Territory of the USA: the population are US citizens, but do not take part in US presidential elections, and not all the provisions of the US Constitution apply. The territory has been organized, however, under a constitutional or organic act. Previously the responsibility of the US Navy, the island was transferred to the Department of the Interior in 1950, when the territory was granted its Constitution, and formally placed under the Secretary of the Interior's full jurisdiction in 1951. In 1970 the island elected its first Governor, and in 1972 a new law gave Guam one Delegate to the US House of Representatives. The Delegate may vote only in committee.

In a referendum held in September 1976 voters decided that Guam should maintain close links with the USA, but that negotiations should be held to improve the island's status. In a further referendum in 1982, in which only 38% of eligible voters participated, the status of commonwealth was the most favoured of six options, attracting 48% of the votes cast. In August 1987, in a referendum held on the provisions of a draft law aimed at conferring the status of Commonwealth on the Territory, voters approved the central proposal, while rejecting articles empowering the Guam Government to restrict immigration and granting the indigenous Chamorro people the sole right to determine the island's future political status. In a further referendum, later that year, both outstanding provisions were approved. Negotiations between the Guam Commission for Self Determination and the USA continued, and in 1995 it was reported that US President Bill Clinton had appointed a team of negotiators to review the draft Guam Commonwealth Act. In 1997 Guam's self-styled Commission on Decolonization was established, headed by the Governor. The next plebiscite on the political status of Guam was repeatedly postponed.

In November 2002 the US Congress approved the Guam War Claims Review Commission Act, which provided for the creation of a body to investigate events on the island following its occupation by the Japanese during the Second World War. The Commission was also to determine whether the USA had offered the islanders sufficient compensation for their mistreatment prior to Guam's liberation in 1944. The War Claims Review Commission, appointed in September 2003, acknowledged the hardship and suffering of the people of Guam, their 'courageous loyalty to the USA' and the inequality in compensation payments as regards similar claims. In May 2004 the US State Department's Radiation Exposure Compensation Program declared Guam eligible for compensation for the effects of nuclear tests carried out in the Pacific region during the long period of mutual hostility between the USA and the Soviet Union known as the 'Cold War'. However, a report by the US Government in April 2005 concluded that, although Guam had been exposed to radiation through wind-borne particles, this exposure had not significantly increased the incidence of cancers and other radiation-related illnesses.

In March 1998 delegates from several Pacific island nations and territories met in Hawaii to discuss methods of controlling the increasing population of brown tree snakes in Guam. The venomous reptile, which was accidentally introduced to the island from New Guinea after the Second World War, has been responsible for frequent power cuts (it ascends electricity poles and short-circuits the lines), as well as major environmental problems (including the decimation of native bird, rodent and reptile populations). Various offensives against the infestation were subsequently conducted. In a new initiative by the US Department of Agriculture in September 2010, dead mice containing poisonous chemicals, which it was hoped would attract and kill the snakes, were dropped by helicopter into the jungle area around the US naval base. The US Geological Survey has estimated the density of tree snakes on Guam to be roughly 13,000 per sq mile of forested land (see Environmental Issues of the Pacific Islands for further details).

Fruit and vegetables are grown mainly for local consumption. The fishing industry expanded greatly during the late 1980s, and by the late 1990s there were more than 1,000 vessels operating from Guam (mainly Japanese, South Korean and Taiwanese, fishing in the waters of the Federated States of Micronesia). Industrial enterprises include textile and garment firms. Guam is a duty-free port and an important distribution point for goods destined for Micronesia. Re-exports constitute a high proportion of Guam's exports, major commodities being petroleum and petroleum products, along with iron and steel scrap. Increased foreign investment, notably from Japan and the Republic of Korea (also important sources of visitors), resulted in the rapid expansion of the island's tourism industry. During a visit to Guam in October 2010 US Secretary of State Hillary Clinton pledged her support for a proposal to waive visa requirements for Chinese and Russian nationals in a bid to boost Guam's tourism industry. However, the tsunami disaster in Japan in March 2011 was expected to lead to a considerable decline in tourist arrivals from that country in subsequent months. In April, with the aim of supporting the island's tourist industry, the Government of Guam issued a US $90m. bond, which was to be repaid by means of receipts from a tax on hotel rooms. Of this total, $55m. was to be used for the financing of a new museum and cultural centre, along with other projects of benefit to the tourism sector.

The island's importance as a strategic military base has greatly increased. As part of a major redeployment of its forces, in 2006 the USA began the process of transferring thousands of troops to Guam from the US base of Okinawa in Japan. The relocation of such large numbers of US marines and their families to Guam and a further US military proposal to station a Global Strike Task Force at Andersen air force base on Guam (the projected cost of which was US $2,000m.) were likely to have profound repercussions for the island's economy. Notwithstanding the objections of some anti-war and Chamorro rights activists, the increased military presence on Guam has been widely welcomed as an important source of new investment and employment. However, this significant increase in Guam's population compelled government agencies to review the capacity of the island's infrastructure, following which the sum of $25m. was committed towards the establishment of a mass transit system. In mid-2009 the USA pledged $1,000m. to fund a new road between northern and southern Guam. The modernization of the island's port was also to be accorded priority. A new naval hospital was to be built at a projected cost of $259m. US President Barack Obama allocated $566m. to military construction projects on Guam in his proposed budget for 2010/11. In September 2010 Japan agreed to disburse $497.8m. for 2010/11 towards the transfer of troops to Guam, primarily to be allocated to the development of facilities and infrastructure on the island, including the construction of a fire station and a medical clinic. Also in September 2010 the US Department of Defense confirmed that, owing to delays in the construction of the requisite facilities on Guam, the transfer of 8,600 marines and 9,000 dependants would take two years longer than originally anticipated; the relocation was therefore not likely to be completed until 2016. In January 2011 the USA and Japan agreed to relocate to Guam military drills involving 20 of the 50 F-15 fighter jets based in Okinawa.

Statistical Survey

Sources (unless otherwise stated): Guam Bureau of Statistics and Plans, PO Box 2950, Hagåtña; tel. 472-4201; fax 477-1812; internet www.bsp.guam.gov.

AREA AND POPULATION

Area: 549 sq km (212 sq miles).

Population: 154,805 (males 79,181, females 75,624) at census of 1 April 2000; 159,358 at census of 1 April 2010.

Density (at 2010 census): 290.3 per sq km.

Population by Age and Sex (Secretariat of the Pacific Community estimates at mid-2011): *0–14:* 50,967 (males 26,361, females 24,606); *15–64:* 127,892 (males 66,737, females 61,155); *65 and over:* 13,231 (males 6,335, females 6,896); *Total* 192,090 (males 99,433, females 92,657). Note: Mid-2011 estimates not adjusted to take account of results of 2010 census (Source: Pacific Regional Information System).

Ethnic Groups (2000 census): Chamorro 57,297; Filipino 40,729; White 10,509; Other Asian 9,600; part-Chamorro 7,946; Chuukese 6,229; Total (incl. others) 154,805.

Regions (population at 2000 census): North 80,466; Central 45,382; South 28,957.

Principal Towns (population at 2000 census): Tamuning 10,833; Mangilao 7,794; Yigo 6,391; Astumbo 5,207; Barrigada 4,417; Hagåtña (capital) 1,122.

Births, Marriages and Deaths (2010 unless otherwise indicated, preliminary): Registered live births 3,421 (birth rate 18.9 per 1,000); Registered marriages (2009) 1,394 (marriage rate 7.8 per 1,000); Registered deaths 873 (death rate 4.8 per 1,000).

Life Expectancy (years at birth, estimates): 79.4 (males 76.9; females 82.1) in 2010.

Economically Active Population (persons aged 16 years and over, excl. armed forces, 2002 estimates): Agriculture, forestry, fishing and mining 290; Manufacturing 1,570; Construction 3,420; Transport, storage and utilities 4,590; Wholesale and retail trade 12,690; Finance, insurance and real estate 2,450; Public administration 16,500; Education, health and social services 14,510; *Total employed* 56,020; Unemployed 7,070; *Total labour force* 63,090. *2011* (payroll data at June, preliminary): Agriculture, forestry, fishing and mining 270; Manufacturing 1,730; Construction 6,100; Transport, storage and utilities 4,380; Wholesale and retail trade 13,450; Finance, insurance and real estate 2,750; Public administration 15,060; Other services 16,940; Total employed 60,680 (Source: Guam Department of Labor).

AGRICULTURE, ETC.

Principal Crops (metric tons, 2009, FAO estimates): Coconuts 59,378; Roots and tubers 2,412; Cucumbers and gherkins 402; Watermelons 2,383; Other melons 391; Bananas 441.

Livestock (head, year ending September 2009, FAO estimates): Chickens 200,000; Pigs 5,200; Goats 700.

Livestock Products (metric tons, 2009, FAO estimates): Chicken meat 120; Pig meat 156; Hen eggs 809.

Fishing (metric tons, live weight, 2009): Common dolphinfish 70; Skipjack tuna 150; Other marine fishes 261; Total capture (incl. others) 488; Mozambique tilapia 80; Milkfish 35; Total aquaculture (incl. others) 136; *Total catch* 624.

Source: FAO.

INDUSTRY

Electric Energy (million kWh, estimates): 1,891 in 2006; 1,879 in 2007; 1,870 in 2008. Source: UN Industrial Commodity Statistics Database.

FINANCE

Currency and Exchange Rates: US currency is used. For details, see section on the Northern Mariana Islands.

Federal Direct Expenditures (US $ million, year ending September): 1,479 (Defence 507) in 2007; 1,533 (Defence 789) in 2008; 1,396 (Defence 567) in 2009. Source: US Census Bureau, *Consolidated Federal Funds Report*.

General Fund Budget (US $ million, year ending September 2010): *Revenue:* Taxes 431.4 (Income tax 239.2, Gross receipts 188.6, Other 3.6); Licences, fees and permits 4.5; Use of money and property 0.4; Total (incl. others) 491.0. *Expenditure:* General government 47.8; Public order 78.9; Public health 17.1; Community services 4.1; Recreation 2.9; Individual and collective rights 11.4; Public education 204.2; Economic development 3.2; Debt service 43.0; Total (incl. others) 499.9.

Cost of Living (Consumer Price Index; annual averages, base: October–December 2007 = 100): All items 104.3 in 2008; 106.1 in 2009; 109.3 in 2010.

Gross Domestic Product (US $ million at current prices): 4,141 in 2007; 4,255 in 2008; 4,491 in 2009 (Source: Bureau of Economic Analysis, US Department of Commerce).

Expenditure on the Gross Domestic Product (US $ million at current prices, 2009): Government consumption expenditure and gross investment 2,816; Personal consumption expenditure 2,924; Private fixed investment 237; *Total domestic expenditure* 5,977; Exports of goods and services 720; *Less* Imports of goods and services 2,206; *GDP in purchasers' values* 4,491 (Source: Bureau of Economic Analysis, US Department of Commerce).

Gross Island Product by Economic Activity (US $ million, 1995): Construction 379.02; Trade 622.86; Public administration 965.97; Other services 486.94; Other non-services 544.61; *Total* 2,999.40.

EXTERNAL TRADE

Principal Commodities (US $ million, 2008): *Imports f.o.b.:* Food and non-alcoholic beverages 66.5 (Meat and edible offal of beef 5.9; Meat and edible offal of poultry 4.7; Bread and bakery products 3.8; Water, containing sugar 8.2); Alcoholic beverages 8.5 (Malt beer 6.0); Home appliances, equipment, etc. 5.3; Transportation and parts 52.1 (Motor cars 40.0); Construction materials 14.4 (Structures of iron and steel 3.4); Men's and women's apparel 12.5; Plastics, leather and paper 28.9 (Travel goods, handbags, etc. 19.4); Miscellaneous manufactured imports 36.6 (Perfumes and toilet waters 8.0; Articles of jewellery 3.5; Watches 4.9); Total 224.9. *Exports (incl. re-exports) f.o.b.:* Food and non-alcoholic beverages 20.6 (Fish—fresh, chilled, frozen and preserved 19.2); Transportation and parts 49.8 (Motor cars 48.1); Construction materials 9.3 (Iron and steel 3.4; Aluminium waste, scraps, tubes and fittings 3.2); Plastics, leather and paper 5.0 (Travel goods, handbags, etc. 3.6); Miscellaneous manufactured imports 18.1 (Perfumes and toilet waters 3.8; Articles of jewellery 8.5; Watches 2.1); Total (incl. others) 104.9.

Principal Trading Partners: *Imports* (US $ '000, 2002): Australia 9,770; Hong Kong 36,240; Japan 96,450; Korea, Republic 9,688; New Zealand 5,520; Philippines 1,437; Singapore 180,076; Total (incl. others) 527,000 (Source: UN, *Statistical Yearbook for Asia and the Pacific*). *Exports* (US $ million, 2008): China, People's Republic 7.7;

Finland 5.7; Germany 20.1; Hong Kong 15.1; Japan 22.9; Micronesia, Federated States 6.5; Philippines 6.0; Singapore 6.5; Total (incl. others) 104.9.

TRANSPORT

Road Traffic (registered motor vehicles, 2007): Private cars 65,062; Taxis 293; Buses 665; Goods vehicles 24,774; Motorcycles 1,545; Total (incl. others) 98,416. Source: Department of Revenue and Taxation, Government of Guam.

International Sea-borne Shipping (estimated freight traffic, '000 revenue tons, 2008): Goods loaded 213.7; Goods unloaded 1,269.6; Goods transshipped 576.5. *Merchant Fleet* (total displacement, '000 grt at 31 December 1992): 1 (Source: Lloyd's Register-Fairplay, *World Fleet Statistics*).

Civil Aviation (Guam International Airport): *Passengers* (year ending May 2008): Arrivals 933,364; Departures 934,263; Transit 285,762. *Cargo* (metric tons, 2008): Unloaded 17,528; Loaded 11,616. *Mail* (metric tons, 2008): Incoming 4,111; Outgoing 1,104. *Aircraft Movements* (year ending May 2008): 14,093. Source: Guam International Airport Authority.

TOURISM

Foreign Tourist Arrivals ('000): 1,140.5 in 2008; 1,052.9 in 2009; 1,196.5 in 2010.

Tourist Arrivals by Country of Residence ('000, 2008): Japan 849.8; Korea, Republic 110.5; Philippines 10.9; Taiwan 22.6; USA 52.8; Total (incl. others) 1,140.5. Source: World Tourism Organization.

Tourism Receipts (US $ million): 2,361 in 1998; 1,908 in 1999. Source: World Tourism Organization.

COMMUNICATIONS MEDIA

Radio Receivers (1997): 221,000 in use.

Television Receivers (1999): 110,000 in use.

Telephones (2010): 65,500 main lines in use.

Mobile Cellular Telephones (2008, estimate): 98,000 subscribers.

Internet Users (2009): 90,000.

Broadband Subscribers (2010): 3,000.

Daily Newspapers (1997): 1 (circulation 24,457).

Non-daily Newspapers (1988): 4 (estimated circulation 26,000).

Sources: International Telecommunication Union; UN, *Statistical Yearbook for Asia and the Pacific*.

EDUCATION

Institutions (2008/09): Primary (incl. kindergarten, grades 1–8) 44 (public 29, private 15); Secondary (grades 9–12) 11 (public 5, private 6).

Teachers (2005/06): Primary 1,917 (public 1,405, private 512); Secondary 1,108 (public 470, private 638).

Enrolment (2008/09, unless otherwise specified): Kindergarten (grades 1–5) 18,474 (public 13,851, private 4,623); Primary (grades 6–8) 9,241 (public 6,845, private 2,396); Secondary (grades 9–12) 12,160 (public 9,633, private 2,527); High school (graduates) 2,085 (public 1,492, private 593); Guam Community College (2005/06) 10,268; University of Guam 3,387.

Sources: Department of Education, Guam Community College, Office of Insular Affairs, *Guam Statistical Yearbook*; University of Guam.

Directory

The Constitution

Guam is governed under the Organic Act of Guam of 1950, which gave the island statutory local power of self-government and made its inhabitants citizens of the United States, although they cannot vote in presidential elections. Their Delegate to the US House of Representatives is elected every two years. Executive power is vested in the civilian Governor and the Lieutenant-Governor, first elected, by popular vote, in 1970. Elections for the governorship occur every four years. The Government has 48 executive departments, whose heads are appointed by the Governor with the consent of the Guam Legislature. The Legislature consists of 15 members elected by popular vote every two years (members are known as Senators). It is empowered to pass laws on local matters, including taxation and fiscal appropriations.

The Government

(October 2011)

Governor: EDWARD B. CALVO (Republican—took office 3 January 2011).

Lieutenant-Governor: RAY TENORIO.

GOVERNMENT DEPARTMENTS

Government departments are located throughout the island.

Office of the Governor: POB 2950, Hagåtña, GU 96932; tel. 472-8931; fax 477-4826; e-mail governor@mail.gov.gu; internet governor .guam.gov.

Department of the Interior, Office of Insular Affairs (OIA): Hagåtña, GU 96910; tel. 472-7279; fax 472-7309; internet www .interior.gov/oia/Islandpages/gumpage.htm; Field Representative KEITH A. PARSKY.

Department of Administration: POB 884, Hagåtña, GU 96932; tel. 475-1101; fax 475-6788; e-mail doadir@mail.gov.gu; internet www.doa.guam.gov; Dir BENITA MANGLONA (acting).

Department of Agriculture: 163 Dairy Rd, Mangilao, GU 96913; tel. 734-3942; fax 734-6569; internet www.agriculture.guam.gov; Dir MARIQUITA TAITAGUE.

Department of Chamorro Affairs: POB 2950, Hagåtña, GU 96910; tel. 475-4278; fax 475-4227; internet www.dca.guam.gov; Pres. JOSEPH CAMERON.

Department of Corrections: POB 3236, Hagåtña, GU 96932; tel. 473-7021; fax 473-7009; internet www.doc.guam.gov; Dir JOSÉ A. SAN AGUSTIN.

Department of Education: POB DE, Hagåtña, GU 96932; tel. 475-0457; fax 472-5003; e-mail nbunderwood@gdoe.net; internet www .gdoe.net; Supt NERISSA BRETANIA UNDERWOOD.

Department of Integrated Services for Individuals with Disabilities: Suite 702, 238 Archbishop F. C. Flores St, Pacific News Bldg, Hagåtña, GU 96910; tel. 475-4646; fax 477-2892; internet www .disid.guam.gov; Dir BENITO S. SERVINO.

Department of Labor: 414 West Soledad Ave, GCIC Bldg, Hagåtña, GU 96910; tel. 475-7000; fax 475-7045; e-mail connent@ ite.net; internet www.dol.guam.gov; Dir LEAH BETH NAHOLOWAA.

Department of Land Management: POB 2950, Hagåtña, GU 96932; tel. 649-5263; fax 649-5383; e-mail dlmdir@dlm.guam.gov; internet dlm.guam.gov; Dir ANISIA B. TERLAJE.

Department of Mental Health and Substance Abuse: tel. 647-5330; fax 649-6948; e-mail info@guamdmhsa.com; internet dmhsa .guam.gov; Dir WILFRED AFLAGUE.

Department of Military Affairs: 430 Army Dr., Bldg 300, Barrigada; tel. 735-0406; fax 649-8775; internet dma.guam.gov; Dir Maj.-Gen. BENNY M. PAULINO.

Department of Parks and Recreation: 490 Chalan Palasyo, Agaña Heights, GU 96910; tel. 475-6296; fax 477-0997; e-mail parks@ns.gov.gu; internet www.dpr.guam.gov; Dir PETER CALVO (acting).

Department of Public Health and Social Services: 123 Chalan Kareta, Route 10, Mangilao, GU 96913-6304; tel. 735-7173; fax 734-5910; internet dphss.guam.gov; Dir JAMES GILLAN.

Department of Public Works: 542 North Marine Dr., Tamuning, GU 96913; tel. 646-3131; fax 649-6178; e-mail joanne.brown@dpw .guam.gov; internet www.dpw.guam.gov; Dir JOANNE M. BROWN.

Department of Revenue and Taxation: POB 23607, Guam Main Facility, GU 96921; tel. 635-1835; fax 633-2643; e-mail pinadm@ revtax.gov.gu; internet www.guamtax.com; Dir JOHN P. CAMACHO.

Department of Youth Affairs: POB 23672, Guam Main Facility, GU 96921; tel. 735-5010; fax 734-7536; e-mail adonis.mendiola@dya .guam.gov; internet dya.guam.gov; Dir ADONIS MENDIOLA.

Legislature

GUAM LEGISLATURE

The Guam Legislature has 15 members, known as Senators, who are directly elected by popular vote for a two-year term. Elections took place on 2 November 2010, when the Democratic Party secured a majority of seats.

Speaker: JUDITH WON PAT.

CONGRESS

Guam elects a non-voting Delegate to the US House of Representatives. An election was held on 2 November 2010, when the Democratic candidate, Madeleine Z. Bordallo, was re-elected for a fifth term as Delegate.

Delegate of Guam: MADELEINE Z. BORDALLO, Cannon House Office Bldg, 427, Washington, DC 20515-5301, USA; tel. (202) 225-1188; fax (202) 226-0341; e-mail madeleine.bordallo@mail.house.gov; internet www.house.gov/bordallo.

Election Commission

Guam Election Commission: Guam Capital Investment Corpn Bldg, 414 West Soledad Ave, Suite 200, Hagåtña 96910; tel. 477-9791; fax 477-1895; e-mail director@gec.guam.gov; internet www.gec.guam.gov; Chair. FREDERICK J. HORECKY; Exec. Dir JOHN BLAS.

Political Organizations

The Territory has a two-party system, comprising local chapters of the US Democratic Party and Republican Party. However, at the local level, non-partisan candidates may seek election.

Judicial System

Attorney-General: LEONARDO M. RAPADAS.

US Attorney: ALICIA GARRIDO LIMTIACO.

Supreme Court of Guam: Suite 300, Guam Judicial Center, 120 West O'Brien Dr., Hagåtña, GU 96910; tel. 475-3162; fax 475-3140; e-mail justice@guamsupremecourt.com; internet www.justice.gov.gu/supreme.html; Chief Justice ROBERT J. TORRES, Jr.

District Court of Guam: US Courthouse, 4th Floor, 520 West Soledad Ave, Hagåtña, GU 96910; tel. 473-9180; fax 473-9118; e-mail judith_hattori@gud.uscourts.gov; internet www.gud.uscourts.gov; judge appointed by the President of the USA; the court has the jurisdiction of a federal district court and of a bankruptcy court of the USA in all cases arising under US law; appeals may be made to the Court of Appeals for the Ninth Circuit and to the US Supreme Court; Magistrate Judge JOAQUIN V. E. MANIBUSAN.

Superior Court of Guam: 120 West O'Brien Drive, Hagåtña, GU 96910; tel. 475-3250; internet www.justice.gov.gu/superior.html; judges are appointed by the Governor of Guam for an initial eight-year term and are thereafter retained by popular vote; the Superior Court has jurisdiction over cases arising in Guam other than those heard in the District Court; Presiding Judge ALBERTO C. LAMORENA, III.

There are also Probate, Traffic, Domestic, Juvenile and Small Claims Courts.

Religion

The majority of the population are Roman Catholic, but there are also members of the Episcopal (Anglican) Church, the Baptist churches and the Seventh-day Adventist Church. There are small communities of Muslims, Buddhists and Jews.

CHRISTIANITY

The Roman Catholic Church

Guam comprises the single archdiocese of Agaña. The Archbishop participates in the Catholic Bishops' Conference of the Pacific, based in Suva, Fiji, and the Federation of Catholic Bishops' Conferences of Oceania, based in Wellington, New Zealand.

At 31 December 2007 there were 141,177 adherents in Guam.

Archbishop of Agaña: Most Rev. ANTHONY SABLAN APURON, Chancery Office, Cuesta San Ramón 196B, Hagåtña, GU 96910; tel. 472-6116; fax 477-3519; e-mail archbishop@mail.archdioceseofagana.com; internet www.archdioceseofagana.com.

BAHÁ'Í FAITH

National Spiritual Assembly: POB Box BA, Hagåtña, GU 96932; tel. 472-9100; fax 472-9101; e-mail bahaioffice@marianas.bahai.org; internet marianas.bahai.org; mems resident in 19 localities in Guam and 10 localities in the Northern Mariana Islands.

The Press

NEWSPAPERS AND PERIODICALS

Bonita: POB 11468, Tumon, GU 96931; tel. 632-4543; fax 637-6720; f. 1998; monthly; Publr IMELDA SANTOS; circ. 3,000.

Directions: POB 27290, Barrigada, GU 96921; tel. 635-7501; fax 635-7520; f. 1996; monthly; Publr JERRY ROBERTS; circ. 3,800.

Guam Business: POB 3191, Hagåtña, GU 96932; tel. 649-0883; fax 649-8883; e-mail glimpses@glimpsesofguam.com; internet www.guambusinessmagazine.com; f. 1983; quarterly; Publr MAUREEN N. MARATITA; Man. Editor FRANK WHITMAN; circ. 2,600.

Hospitality Guahan: POB 8565, Tamuning, GU 96931; tel. 649-1447; fax 649-8565; e-mail info@ghra.org; internet www.ghra.org; f. 1996; quarterly; circ. 3,000.

Marianas Business Journal: POB 3191, Hagåtña, GU 96932; tel. 649-0883; fax 649-8883; e-mail glimpses@glimpsesofguam.com; internet www.mbjguam.net; f. 2003; fortnightly; Publr MAUREEN N. MARATITA; Editor PATRICIA SHOOK; circ. 3,000.

Pacific Daily News and Sunday News: POB DN, Hagåtña, GU 96932; tel. 472-1736; fax 472-1512; e-mail cblas@guampdn.com; internet www.guampdn.com; f. 1950; Publr RINDRATY LIMTIACO; Man. Editor DAVID CRISOSTOMO; circ. 28,520 (weekdays), 26,237 (Sunday).

The Pacific Voice: POB 2553, Hagåtña, GU 96932; tel. 472-6427; fax 477-5224; f. 1950; Sunday; Roman Catholic; Gen. Man. TEREZO MORTERA; Editor Rev. Fr HERMES LOSBANES; circ. 6,500.

TV Guam Magazine: 237 Mamis St, Tamuning, GU 96911; tel. 646-4030; fax 646-7445; f. 1973; weekly; Publr DINA GRANT; Man. Editor EMILY UNTALAN; circ. 15,000.

NEWS AGENCY

United Press International (UPI) (USA): POB 1617, Hagåtña, GU 96910; tel. 632-1138; Correspondent DICK WILLIAMS.

Broadcasting and Communications

TELECOMMUNICATIONS

Guam Educational Telecommunication Corporation (KGTF): POB 21449, Guam Main Facility, Barrigada, GU 96921; tel. 734-2207; fax 734-3476; e-mail kgtfl2@ite.net; internet www.kgtf.org.

Guam Telephone Authority: 624 North Marines Corps Dr., POB 9008, Tamuning, GU 96913; tel. 644-4482; fax 649-4821; e-mail ask@gta.net; internet www.gta.net; acquired by TeleGuam Holdings LLC in Dec. 2004; CEO and Pres. DAN MOFFAT.

BROADCASTING

Radio

K-Stereo: 1868 Halsey Dr., Piti, GU 96915; tel. 477-9448; fax 477-6411; e-mail ksto@ite.net; operates on FM 24 hours a day; Pres. and Gen. Man. EDWARD H. POPPE.

KOKU-FM: 424 West O'Brien Drive, Julale Center, Hagåtña, GU 96910; tel. 477-5658; fax 472-7663; e-mail marketing@hitradio100.com; operates on FM 24 hours a day; Pres. KURT S. MOYLAN; Marketing and Sales Man. VINCE LIMUACO.

KPRG FM: KPRG, UoG Station Mangilao, GU 96923; tel. 734-8930; fax 734-2958; e-mail kprg@kprg.org; internet www.kprg.org; operated by the University of Guam; news and music; Chair. MARIE MESA-KERLIN; Chairs TOD THOMPSON, NICK CAPTAIN; Gen. Man. CHRIS HARTIG (acting).

Radio Guam (KUAM): 600 Harman Loop, Dededo, GU 96912; tel. 637-5826; fax 637-9865; e-mail generalmanager@kuam.com; internet www.kuam.com; f. 1954; operates on AM and FM 24 hours a day; Pres. PAUL M. CALVO; Gen. Man. JOEY CALVO.

Sorensen Media Group: Suite 800, 111 Chalan Santo Papa, Hagåtña, GU 96910; tel. 477-5700; fax 477-3982; e-mail rex@spbguam.com; internet www.pacificnewscenter.com; f. 1981; privately owned; Chair. and CEO REX SORENSEN.

Trans World Radio Pacific (TWR): POB CC, Hagåtña, GU 96932; tel. 477-9701; fax 477-2838; e-mail ktwr@twr.org; internet www.guam.net/home/twr; f. 1975; broadcasts Christian programmes on KTWR and one medium-wave station, KTWG, covering Guam and nearby islands, and operates five short-wave transmitters reaching most of Asia, Africa and the Pacific; Chair. THOMAS J. LOWELL; Pres. Dr DAVID G. TUCKER; Station Dir MICHAEL DAVIS.

Television

KGTF—TV: POB 21449 Guam Main Facility, Barrigada, GU 96921; tel. 734-3476; fax 734-5483; e-mail kgtf12@kgtf.org; internet www.kgtf.org; f. 1970; cultural, public service and educational programmes; Gen. Man. SHIRLEY M. SUOZA (acting); Operations Man. BENNY T. FLORES.

KTGM—TV: 692 Marine Dr., Tamuning 96911; tel. 649-8814; fax 649-0371.

KUAM—TV: 600 Harmon Loop, Dededo, Hagåtña, GU 96912; tel. 637-5826; fax 637-9865; e-mail generalmanager@kuam.com; internet www.kuam.com; f. 1956; operates channels 8 and 11; News Dir SABRINA SALAS.

Finance

(cap. = capital; res = reserves; dep. = deposits; m. = million; brs = branches; amounts in US dollars)

BANKING

Commercial Banks

Allied Banking Corpn (Philippines): Suite 104, Bejess Commercial Bldg, 719 South Marine Drive, Tamuning, GU 96913; tel. 649-5001; fax 649-5002; e-mail abcguam@kuentos.guam.net; Asst Vice-Pres. MARIO R. PALISOC; 1 br.

ANZ Guam Inc: 424 West O'Brien Dr., 112 Julale Shopping Center, Hagåtña, GU 96910; tel. 479-9000; fax 479-9092; internet www.anz.com/guam; mem. of ANZ Group; fmrly Citizens Security Bank (Guam) Inc, name changed as above in 2009; cap. 8.5m., dep. 148.7m. (Dec. 2010); CEO DAVID MCCALL; 4 brs.

Bank of Guam: POB BW, 111 Chalan Santo Papa, Hagåtña, GU 96932; tel. 472-5300; fax 477-8687; e-mail customerservice@bankofguam.com; internet www.bankofguam.com; f. 1972; cap. 1.8m., dep. 904.3m. (Dec. 2010); Chair. LOURDES A. LEON GUERRERO; Exec. Vice-Pres. WILLIAM D. LEON GUERRERO; 19 brs.

Bank of Hawaii (USA): 134 West Soledad Ave, Hagåtña, GU 96910; tel. 479-3500; fax 479-3893; Vice-Pres. RODNEY KIMURA; 3 brs.

BankPacific, Ltd: 151 Aspinall Ave, Hagåtña, GU 96910; tel. 472-6704; fax 477-1483; e-mail philipf@bankpacific.com; internet www.bankpacific.com; f. 1954; Pres. and CEO PHILIP J. FLORES; Exec. Vice-Pres. MARK O. FISH; 4 brs in Guam; 1 br. in Palau; 1 br. in Northern Mariana Islands.

Citibank NA (USA): 402 East Marine Dr., Hagåtña, GU 96910; tel. 477-2484; fax 477-9441; internet www.citibank.com/guam; Country Man. AGUSTIN DAVALOS; 2 brs.

First Commercial Bank (Taiwan): POB 2461, Hagåtña, GU 96932; tel. 472-6864; fax 477-8921; e-mail fcbgu@ite.net; Gen. Man. JENN-HWA WANG; 1 br.

First Hawaiian Bank (USA): Compadres Mall 562, Harmon Loop Rd, Dededo, GU 96912; tel. 632-9381; fax 637-9686; internet www.fhb.com; Regional Man. LAURA-LYNN DACANAY; 3 brs.

HSBC Ltd: POB 27C, Hagåtña, GU 96932; tel. 647-8588; fax 646-3767; CEO GUY N. DE B. PRIESTLEY; 2 brs.

Metropolitan Bank and Trust Co: 665 South Marine Drive, Tamuning, GU 96911; tel. 649-9555; fax 649-9558; e-mail mbguam@metrobank.com.ph; f. 1975; Sen. Man. JOSEPHINE M. PAPELERA.

Union Bank of California (USA): 194 Hernan Cortes Ave, POB 7809, Hagåtña, GU 96910; tel. 477-8811; fax 472-3284; Man. KINJI SUZUKI; 2 brs.

INSURANCE

American National Insurance Co: POB 3340, Hagåtña, GU 96910; tel. 477-9600.

Chung Kuo Insurance Co: GCIC Bldg, Suite 707, 414 West Soledad Ave, Hagåtña, GU 96910; tel. 477-7696; fax 477-4788; e-mail chungkuo@ite.net; internet www.cki.com.tw.

Midland National Life Insurance Co: Winner Bldg, Suite 20N, Tamuning, GU 96911; tel. 649-0330; internet www.mnlife.com; f. 1906 as Dakota Mutual Life Insurance Company; name changed as above in 1925.

Moylan's Insurance Underwriters, Inc: Suite 102 Julale Shopping Center, 424 West O'Brien Dr., Hagåtña, GU 96910; tel. 477-8613; fax 477-1837; e-mail agana@moylans.net; internet www.moylansinsurance.com; Pres. KURT S. MOYLAN; CEO CESAR GARCIA.

Nanbo Insurance: 434 West O'Brien Dr., Hagåtña, GU 96910; tel. 477-9754; internet www.nanbo.com.

Pioneer Pacific Financial Services, Inc of Guam: POB EM, Hagåtña, GU 96910; tel. 477-6400.

Trade and Industry

DEVELOPMENT ORGANIZATION

Guam Economic Development Authority (GEDA): Guam International Trade Center Bldg, Suite 511, 590 South Marine Dr., Tamuning, GU 96913; tel. 647-4332; fax 649-4146; e-mail help@investguam.com; internet www.investguam.com; f. 1965; Admin. ANTHONY C. BLAZ.

CHAMBER OF COMMERCE

Guam Chamber of Commerce: Ada Plaza Center, Suite 101, 173 Aspinall Ave, POB 283, Hagåtña, GU 96932; tel. 472-6311; fax 472-6202; e-mail gchamber@guamchamber.com; internet www.guamchamber.com.gu; f. 1924; Chair. DAVID J. JOHN; Pres. DAVID P. LEDDY.

EMPLOYERS' ORGANIZATION

The Employers' Council: 718 North Marine Dr., Suite 201, East-West Business Center, Upper Tumon, GU 96913; tel. 649-6616; fax 649-3030; e-mail tecinc@teleguam.net; internet www.guamemployers.org; f. 1966; private, non-profit asscn providing management devt training and advice on personnel law and labour relations; Exec. Dir ANDY ANDRES.

UTILITIES

Electricity

Guam Energy Office: 548 North Marine Corps Dr., Tamuning, GU 96913; tel. 646-4361; fax 649-1215; e-mail lucybk@teleguam.net; internet www.guamenergy.com; Dir J. LAWRENCE M. CRUZ.

Guam Power Authority: POB 2977, Hagåtña, GU 96932; tel. 648-3225; fax 649-3290; e-mail webmaster@guampowerauthority.com; internet www.guampowerauthority.com; f. 1968; autonomous govt agency; supplies electricity throughout the island; Gen. Man. JOAQUIN FLORES.

Water

Guam Waterworks Authority: 578 North Marine Corps Dr., Tamuning, GU 96913-4111; tel. 647-2603; fax 646-2335; e-mail heidi@guamwaterworks.org; internet www.guamwaterworks.org; Gen. Man. Dr LEONARD J. OLIVE.

TRADE UNIONS

Many workers belong to trade unions based in the USA such as the American Federation of Government Employees and the American Postal Workers' Union.

Guam Federation of Teachers (GFT): Local 1581, POB 2301, Hagåtña, GU 96932; tel. 735-4390; fax 734-8085; e-mail mrector@gftunion.com; internet www.gftunion.com; f. 1965; affiliate of American Federation of Teachers; Pres. MATT RECTOR; 2,000 mems.

Guam Hotel and Restaurant Association: POB 8565, Tamuning, GU 96931; tel. 649-1447; fax 649-8565; e-mail president@ghra.org; internet www.ghra.org; 37 mem. restaurants and hotels; Pres. MARY P. TORRE.

Guam Landowners' Association: Hagåtña; Pres. ANTONY SABLAN; Sec. RONALD TEEHAN.

Transport

In September 2008 the Government announced that the sum of US $25m. was to be allocated to the creation of a mass transit network on the island, to accommodate the projected rise in the population that would result from the relocation of thousands of US marines to Guam.

ROADS

There are 885 km (550 miles) of public roads, of which some 675 km (420 miles) are paved. A further 685 km (425 miles) of roads are classified as non-public, and include roads located on federal government installations.In February 2009 a $140m. project to upgrade the island's road network was announced. In the same month the US Government announced that it was committing $1,000m. to fund a new road to link US military facilities in northern and southern Guam. The works were expected to be completed by 2014.

SHIPPING

Apra, on the central western side of the island, is one of the largest protected deep-water harbours in the Pacific. Plans for the modernization of the port were under way in 2009.

Port Authority of Guam: 1026 Cabras Highway, Suite 201, Piti, GU 96925; tel. 477-5931; fax 477-4445; e-mail webmaster@portguam.com; internet www.portguam.com; f. 1975; govt-operated port facilities; Gen. Man. PEDRO A. LEON GUERRERO, Jr.

Ambyth, Shipping and Trading, Inc: 1026 Cabras Highway, Piti, GU 96915; tel. 477-7250; fax 472-1264; e-mail ops@ambyth.guam.net; internet www.ambyth.com; agents for all types of vessels and charter brokers; Pres. ALFRED LAM; Gen. Man. ANDREW MILLER.

Atkins, Kroll, Inc: 443 South Marine Dr., Tamuning, GU 96913; tel. 649-6410; fax 646-9592; e-mail atkins_kroll@akguam.com; internet www.akguam.com; f. 1914; vehicle distribution; Pres. DAN CAMACHO.

COAM Trading Co Ltd: PAG Bldg, Suite 110, 1026 Cabas Highway, Piti, GU 96925; tel. 477-1737; fax 472-3386.

Dewitt Moving and Storage: Suite 100, 165-1, Guerrero St, Tamuning, GU 96913; tel. 648-1800; fax 648-0034; e-mail ezdewitt@dewittguam.com; internet www.dewittguam.com; Pres. JOHN BURROWS.

Guam Shipping Agency: POB GD, Hagåtña, GU 96932; tel. 477-7381; fax 477-7553; Gen. Man. H. KO.

Interbulk Shipping (Guam) Inc: Bank of Guam Bldg, Suite 502, 111 Chalan Santo Papa, Hagåtña, GU 96910; Man. S. GYSTAD.

Maritime Agencies of the Pacific Ltd: Piti, GU 96925; tel. 477-8500; fax 477-5726; e-mail rehmapship@kuentos.guam.net; f. 1976; agents for fishing vessels, cargo, dry products and construction materials; Pres. ROBERT E. HAHN.

Pacific Navigation System: POB 7, Hagåtña, GU 96910; f. 1946; Pres. KENNETH T. JONES, Jr.

Seabridge Micronesian, Inc: 1026 Cabras Highway, Suite 114, Piti, GU 96925; tel. 477-7345; fax 477-6206; Gen. Man. PAUL L. BLAS.

Sea-Land Service, Inc: POB 8897, Tamuning, GU 96931; tel. 475-8100; internet www.horizon-lines.com; CEO CHARLES RAYMOND.

Tucor Services: 180 Guerrero St, Harmon Industrial Park, POB 6128, Tamuning, GU 96911; tel. 646-6947; fax 646-6945; e-mail boll@tucor.com; general agents for numerous dry cargo, passenger and steamship cos; Pres. MICHELLE BOLL.

CIVIL AVIATION

Guam is served by A. B. Won Pat International Airport.

Guam International Airport Authority: POB 8770, Tamuning, GU 96931; tel. 646-0300; fax 646-8823; e-mail lizb@guamairport.net; internet www.guamairport.com; Chair. MARTIN GERBER; Exec. Man. MARY C. TORRES.

Asia Pacific Airlines (APA): POB 24858, Guam Main Facility, Barrigada, Guam 96921; fax 647-8440; e-mail info@flyapa.com; internet www.flyapa.com; f. 1999; affiliate of Tan Holdings Corpn (Commonwealth of the Northern Mariana Islands); cargo; serving Guam, Hawaii (USA), Hong Kong, Marshall Islands, Federated States of Micronesia, Palau and the Philippines.

Continental Micronesia Airlines: POB 8778, Tamuning, GU 96931; tel. 645-8182; internet www.continental.com; f. 1968, as Air Micronesia, by Continental Airlines (USA); hub operations in Guam and Saipan (Northern Mariana Islands); services throughout the region and to destinations in the Far East and the mainland USA; Pres. CHARLES DUNCAN.

Freedom Air: POB 1578, Hagåtña, GU 96932; tel. 647-8359; fax 646-7488; e-mail freedom@ite.net; internet www.freedomairguam.com; f. 1974; Man. Dir JOAQUIN L. FLORES, Jr.

Tourism

Tourism is the most important industry on Guam. Visitor arrivals were reported to have increased by more than 13% in 2010, to total 1,196,500. Most visitors are from Japan, the Republic of Korea, the USA and Taiwan. The majority of Guam's hotels are situated in, or near to, Tumon, where amenities for entertainment are well-developed. Numerous sunken wrecks of aircraft and ships from Second World War battles provide interesting sites for divers. There were 7,561 hotel rooms on Guam in 2004.

Guam Visitors Bureau: 401 Pale San Vitores Rd, Tumon, GU 96913; tel. 646-5278; fax 646-8861; e-mail guaminfo@visitguam.org; internet www.visitguam.org; Chair. DAVID B. TYDINGCO; Gen. Man. JOANN G. CAMACHO (acting).

Defence

Guam is an important strategic military base for the USA. In 2004 a new hangar for B-52 and B-2 bombers was completed. In May 2005 the US Government announced plans substantially to increase military spending in 2005/06 in Guam, with some US $162m. allocated for new construction projects. As assessed at November 2010, a total of 2,982 members of the US Air Force were stationed on Guam, in addition to a US naval base. As part of a wider programme of redeployment of its overseas personnel, the USA intended to transfer some 8,000 troops to Guam from its bases in Japan.

Education

School attendance is compulsory from six to 16 years of age. There were 44 kindergarten and primary schools (29 public, 15 private) and 11 secondary schools (five public, six private) operating on the island in 2008/09. In that year total enrolment at kindergarten schools amounted to 18,474 students; the comparable figures for primary and secondary schools were 9,241 and 12,160 students, respectively. Enrolment in tertiary education has expanded in recent years, with 10,268 students enrolled at the Guam Community College for 2005/06 and 3,387 students enrolled at the University of Guam for 2008/09. In 2000 the rate of adult illiteracy was estimated at 1.0%. Government expenditure on public education was US $204.2m. in 2009/10 (equivalent to 40.8% of total expenditure).

Other United States Territories

Baker and Howland Islands

The Baker and Howland Islands lie in the Central Pacific Ocean, about 2,575 km (1,600 miles) south-west of Honolulu, Hawaii; they comprise two low-lying coral atolls without lagoons, and are uninhabited. Both islands were mined for guano in the late 19th century. Settlements, known as Meyerton (on Baker) and Itascatown (on Howland), were established by the USA in 1935, but were evacuated during the Second World War, owing to Japanese air attacks. The islands are National Wildlife Refuges, and since 1974 have been administered by the US Fish and Wildlife Service. In 1990 legislation before Congress proposed that the islands be included within the boundaries of the State of Hawaii. In January 2009 President George W. Bush established by proclamation the Pacific Remote Islands Marine National Monument, which included Baker and Howland Islands. The islands are administered by the US Department of the Interior, US Fish and Wildlife Service, Refuge Complex Office, POB 50167, Honolulu, Hawaii 96850; internet www.fws.gov.

Jarvis Island

Jarvis Island lies in the Central Pacific Ocean, about 2,090 km (1,300 miles) south of Hawaii. It is a low-lying coral island and is uninhabited. The island was mined for guano in the late 19th century. A settlement, known as Millersville, including a weather station for the benefit of trans-Pacific aviation, was established by the USA in 1935, but was evacuated during the Second World War. Legislation before Congress in 1990 proposed that the island be included within the State of Hawaii. In January 2009 Jarvis Island became part of the Pacific Remote Islands Marine National Monument (see above). The island is a National Wildlife Refuge and is administered by the US Department of the Interior, US Fish and Wildlife Service (details as above, under Baker and Howland Islands).

Johnston Atoll

Johnston Atoll lies in the Pacific Ocean, about 1,319 km (820 miles) west-south-west of Honolulu, Hawaii. It comprises Johnston Island, Sand Island (uninhabited) and two man-made islands, North (Akua) and East (Hikina), with a total area of 2.6 sq km (1 sq mile). Johnston Atoll was designated a Naval Defense Sea Area and Airspace Reservation in 1941, and is closed to public access. In 1985 construction of a chemical weapons disposal facility began on the atoll, and by 1990 it was fully operational. In 1989 the US Government agreed to remove artillery shells containing more than 400 metric tons of nerve gas from the Federal Republic of Germany, and destroy them on Johnston Island. In late 1991, following expressions of protest to the US Government by the nations of the South Pacific Forum (now Pacific Islands Forum), together with many environmental groups, a team of scientists visited the chemical disposal facility to monitor the safety and environmental impact of its activities. In May 1996 it was reported that all nerve gases stored on the atoll had been destroyed. However, 1,000 tons of chemical agents remained contained in landmines, bombs and missiles at the site. In December 2000 it was announced that the destruction of the remaining stock of chemical weapons had been completed (the original deadline for the destruction of 40,000 weapons stored on the island had been August 1995). The closure and decontamination of the facility was completed in 2004; in June of that year all military personnel left and control of the atoll was transferred to the US Fish and Wildlife Service, which has reported its intention eventually to create a nature reserve on the atoll. In March 2005 the Department of Defense announced the termination of the Air Force mission in Johnston Atoll. A facility capable of performing atmospheric tests of nuclear weapons remains operational on the atoll. The atoll had an estimated population of 173 in 1990, although this increased to approximately 1,000, mainly military, personnel during weapons disposal operations in previous years. In January 2009 Johnston Atoll became part of the Pacific Remote Islands Marine National Monument (see above, under Baker and Howland Islands). Johnston Atoll falls under the jurisdiction of the Department of the Interior, US Fish and Wildlife Service (details as above, under Baker and Howland Islands). Operational control is the responsibility of the US Air Force. Permission to land on Johnston Island must be obtained from the US Air Force. The residing military commander of Johnston Island acts as the agent for the Defense Threat Reduction Agency (DTRA).

Kingman Reef

Kingman Reef lies in the Pacific Ocean, about 1,500 km (925 miles) south-west of Hawaii, and comprises a reef and shoal measuring about 8 km (5 miles) by 15 km (9.5 miles). In 2000 administrative control was transferred from the US Navy to the Department of the Interior. In 2001 the waters around the reef were designated a National Wildlife Refuge, under the jurisdiction of the US Fish and Wildlife Service (details as above, under Baker and Howland Islands). In January 2009 Kingman Reef became part of the Pacific Remote Islands Marine National Monument (see above, under Baker and Howland Islands).

Midway Island

Midway Atoll lies in the northern Pacific Ocean, about 1,850 km (1,150 miles) north-west of Hawaii. A coral atoll, it comprises Sand Island, Eastern Island and several small islets within the reef, and has a total area of about 5 sq km (2 sq miles). The islands had a population of 2,200 in 1983, but by 1990 this had declined to 13. Since the transfer of the islands' administration from the US Department of Defense to the Department of the Interior in October 1996, limited tourism is permitted. There is a National Wildlife Refuge on the Territory, which is home to many species of birds. In March 2011 it was reported that thousands of seabirds, including albatrosses and other endangered species, had been killed by the tsunami that followed the powerful earthquake of the east coast of Japan. Legislation before Congress in 1990 proposed the inclusion of the Territory within the State of Hawaii. The islands are administered by the US Department of the Interior, US Fish and Wildlife Service (details as above, under Baker and Howland Islands).

Palmyra

Palmyra lies in the Pacific Ocean, about 1,600 km (1,000 miles) south of Honolulu, Hawaii. It comprises some 50 low-lying islets, has a total area of 100 ha, is uninhabited and is privately owned. Since 1961 the Territory has been administered by the US Department of the Interior. In 1990 legislation before Congress proposed the inclusion of Palmyra within the boundaries of the State of Hawaii. In mid-1996 it was announced that the owners (the Fullard-Leo family in Hawaii) were to sell the atoll to a US company, which, it was believed, planned to establish a nuclear waste storage facility in the Territory. The Government of neighbouring Kiribati expressed alarm at the proposal, and reiterated its intention to seek the reinclusion of the atoll within its own national boundaries. However, in June one of the Hawaiian Representatives to the US Congress proposed legislation in the US House of Representatives to prevent the establishment of such a facility, and a US government official subsequently announced that the atoll would almost certainly not be used for that purpose. Palmyra was purchased by The Nature Conservancy (internet www.tnc.org) in December 2000. Designated a National Wildlife Refuge, the lagoons and surrounding waters within the 12 nautical mile zone of US territorial seas were transferred to the US Fish and Wildlife Service (details as above, under Baker and Howland Islands) in January 2001; the US Fish and Wildlife Service subsequently undertook negotiations to purchase part of the 680 acres of emergent lands owned by The Nature Conservancy. In November 2005 an international team of scientists joined with The Nature Conservancy to establish a new station on the Palmyra Atoll in order to undertake environmental research. In January 2009 Palmyra became part of the Pacific Remote Islands Marine National Monument (see above, under Baker and Howland Islands).

Wake Island

Wake Island lies in the Pacific Ocean, about 2,060 km (1,280 miles) east of Guam. It is a coral atoll comprising the three islets of Wake, Wilkes and Peale, with an area less than 8 sq km (3 sq miles) and a population estimated to be almost 2,000 in 1988. Legislation before Congress in 1990 proposed the inclusion of the islands within the Territory of Guam. However, the Republic of the Marshall Islands, some 500 km (310 miles) south of Wake, exerted its own claim to the atoll (called Enenkio by the Micronesians), which is a site of great importance for the islands' traditional chiefly rituals. Plans by a US company, announced in 1998, to establish a large-scale nuclear waste storage facility on the atoll were condemned by environmentalists and politicians in the region. In August 2006 Hurricane Loke severely damaged much of the island's infrastructure. The US Air Force had previously evacuated all 188 residents. In January 2009 Wake Island became part of the Pacific Remote Islands Marine National Monument (see above, under Baker and Howland Islands). Since 1972 the group has been administered by the US Department of Defense, Department of the Air Force (Pacific/East Asia Division), The Pentagon, Washington, DC 20330; tel. (202) 694-6061; fax (703) 696-7273; internet www.af.mil.

VANUATU

Introduction

The Republic of Vanuatu (formerly the New Hebrides) comprises an archipelago of some 80 islands covering a land area of 12,190 sq km (4,707 sq miles), including the Banks and Torres Islands, stretching from south of Solomon Islands to Hunter and Matthew Islands, east of New Caledonia, 900 km in all. The islands range in size from 12 ha to 3,600 sq km. The islands have rugged mountainous interiors, with narrow coastal strips where most of the inhabitants dwell. Three islands have active volcanoes on them. The climate is tropical. Temperatures in Port Vila, the capital, range from 16°C (61°F) to 33°C (92°F). There is a rainy season between November and April, and the islands are vulnerable to cyclones during this period; south-east trade winds blow between May and October. At the November 2009 census the population totalled 234,023, which represented an average annual growth rate of 2.3% since 1999. The population was estimated at 251,748 in mid-2011. Most of the inhabitants (approximately 95%) are Melanesians, and there are small numbers of Europeans, Micronesians and Polynesians. The national language is Bislama (a Pidgin English), and English and French are also official languages. Most of the population profess Christianity, the largest denomination being Presbyterian. The capital of Port Vila is located on the island of Efate. The population of Port Vila increased dramatically during the late 1980s and early 1990s, and was estimated to total 44,040 by November 2009.

The New Hebrides were governed until 1980 by an Anglo-French condominium, which was established in 1906. Under this arrangement there were three elements in the structure of administration: the British national service, the French national service and the condominium (joint) departments. Each administering power was responsible for its own citizens and other non-New Hebrideans who chose to be *ressortissant* of either power. Indigenous New Hebrideans were not permitted to claim either British or French citizenship. The result of this was two official languages, two police forces, three public services, three courts of law, three currencies, three national budgets, two resident commissioners in Port Vila and two district commissioners in each of the four districts.

After the Second World War (1939–45) New Hebridean concern regarding the alienation of native land (more than 36% of the New Hebrides was owned by foreigners) prompted local political initiatives. Na-Griamel, one of the first political groups to emerge, had its source in cult-like activities. In 1971 Na-Griamel leaders petitioned the UN to prevent more land sales at a time when territory was being sold to US interests for development as tourist resorts. In 1972 the New Hebrides National Party (NHNP) was formed with encouragement from Protestant missions and covert support from British interests. In 1974 French interests established the Union des communautés néo-hébridaises and the Advisory Council, which had been established in 1957, was replaced by a Representative Assembly. Although 29 of the Assembly's 42 members were directly elected, this did not fulfil nationalist aspirations, and following a boycott by the NHNP (which had changed its name to the Vanuaaku Pati—VP), in early 1977 the Representative Assembly was dissolved. However, the VP succeeded in reaching an agreement with the condominium powers on the holding of new elections for the Representative Assembly, based on universal suffrage for all seats.

In July 1977 it was announced, at a conference of New Hebridean, British and French delegates, that the New Hebrides would become independent in 1980, following a referendum and elections. The VP, demanding immediate independence, boycotted this conference, refused to participate in the November 1977 elections and declared a 'people's provisional government'. A smaller, 39-member Assembly was none the less elected, and a degree of self-government was introduced in early 1978, with the creation of a Council of Ministers and of the office of Chief Minister, together with the inauguration of a single New Hebrides public service to replace the French, British and condominium services. In December 1978 a Government of National Unity was formed, with Fr Gérard Leymang, a Roman Catholic priest, as Chief Minister.

In November 1979 new elections resulted in victory for the VP, which secured 26 of the Assembly's 39 seats. The outcome provoked rioting on Espiritu Santo by Na-Griamel supporters, who threatened non-Santo 'foreigners'. In late November Fr Walter Lini, the President of the VP, was elected Chief Minister. In June 1980 Jimmy Stevens, the leader of Na-Griamel, declared Espiritu Santo independent of the rest of the New Hebrides, renaming the island the 'Independent State of Vemarana'. Members of his movement, armed with bows and arrows (and allegedly assisted by French *colons* and supported by private US business interests), detained government officers and police, who were later released and allowed to leave the island, together with other European and indigenous public servants. The dispatch of a peace-keeping force comprising about 200 British troops to Espiritu Santo was strongly criticized by the French authorities, which would not permit Britain's unilateral use of force on Espiritu Santo.

In mid-July 1980, however, agreement was reached between the two condominium powers and Lini. On 30 July 1980 the New Hebrides became independent within the Commonwealth, under the name of Vanuatu. The former Deputy Chief Minister, George Kalkoa, who adopted the surname Sokomanu ('leader of thousands'), assumed the largely ceremonial post of President. Walter Lini became the country's first Prime Minister. Shortly after independence, Vanuatu signed a defence pact with Papua New Guinea, and in August units of the Papua New Guinea defence force replaced the British and French troops on Espiritu Santo and arrested the Na-Griamel rebels. Periods of extreme political instability have sometimes ensued, as exemplified in June 2011 when Sato Kilman assumed the premiership for the third time since late 2010.

The country's status as an 'offshore' financial centre aroused international controversy. It was claimed that the country was being used to 'launder' the proceeds of illegal activities of the Russian mafia and drug cartels. Vanuatu remained on a list of unco-operative tax havens drawn up by the Paris-based Organisation for Economic Co-operation and Development (OECD) until May 2003.

Vanuatu's agricultural sector, which includes the production and export of copra, is vulnerable to adverse weather conditions and fluctuations in international commodity prices. Other major sources of export revenue are beef and timber. Attempts to diversify the economy have been hampered by a shortage of skilled indigenous labour and a weak infrastructure. Nevertheless, Vanuatu has come to depend heavily on the services sector. The tourism industry and a shipping registry (providing a 'flag of convenience' to foreign-owned vessels), as well as 'offshore' banking facilities, have made significant contributions to the economy. In March 2006 Vanuatu and the US Millennium Challenge Corporation signed an agreement providing the country with a grant of US $66m., to be disbursed between 2007 and 2011, for the purposes of financing various infrastructural projects. Since 2007 seasonal arrangements permitting Pacific islanders to work in the horticultural industries of New Zealand and Australia have provided wider overseas employment opportunities for ni-Vanuatu. Along with Australia, the People's Republic of China is an important provider of development assistance, and in 2009 China provided a new jointly owned fish-processing plant near Port Vila. An ongoing challenge for successive Governments has been the need to address the persistent problem of rural hardship and to reverse the decline in income; in the early years of the new millennium the country's gross domestic product (GDP) per head was estimated to be below the level of the mid-1980s. Although steady GDP growth was recorded for the eighth consecutive year in 2010, sustained by a good performance in the tourism and property sectors, the very high rate of population growth continued to impede any comparable rise in the country's income per head. Vanuatu's accession to the World Trade Organization (WTO), scheduled for the latter part of 2011 following the successful completion of negotiations in May, was expected to lead to the country's closer integration into the global economy and to yield major benefits in the longer term.

Statistical Survey

Source (unless otherwise indicated): National Statistics Office, Ministry of Finance and Economic Management, PMB 9019, Port Vila; tel. (678) 22110; fax (678) 24583; e-mail stats@vanuatu.com.vu; internet www.spc.int/prism/country/vu/stats.

AREA AND POPULATION

Area: 12,190 sq km (4,707 sq miles); *By Island* (sq km): Espiritu Santo 4,010; Malekula 2,024; Efate 887; Erromango 887; Ambrym 666; Tanna 561; Pentecost 499; Epi 444; Ambae 399; Vanua Lava 343; Gaua 315; Maewo 300.

Population: 186,678 at census of 16 November 1999; 234,023 (males 119,090, females 114,933) at census of 16 November 2009. *Mid-2011* (Secretariat of the Pacific Community estimate): 251,784 (Source: Pacific Regional Information System). *By Island* (mid-1999, official estimates): Espiritu Santo 31,811; Malekula 19,766; Efate 43,295; Erromango 1,554; Ambrym 7,613; Tanna 26,306; Pentecost 14,837; Epi 4,706; Ambae 10,692; Vanua Lava 2,074; Gaua 1,924; Maewo 3,385. Source: partly Pacific Regional Information System.

Density (mid-2011): 20.7 per sq km.

Population by Age and Sex (Secretariat of the Pacific Community estimates at mid-2011): *0–14:* 93,910 (males 48,965, females 44,945); *15–64:* 148,069 (males 74,499, females 73,570); *65 and over:* 9,804 (males 5,098, females 4,706); *Total* 251,784 (males 128,563, females 123,221) (Source: Pacific Regional Information System).

Principal Towns (population at 2009 census): Port Vila (capital) 44,039; Luganville (Santo) 13,156.

Births and Deaths (annual averages, 2005–10, UN estimates): Birth rate 30.4 per 1,000; Death rate 5.1 per 1,000. Source: UN, *World Population Prospects: The 2010 Revision*.

Life Expectancy (years at birth, WHO estimates): 71 (males 69; females 72) in 2009. Source: WHO, *World Health Statistics*.

Economically Active Population (census of May 1989): Agriculture, forestry, hunting and fishing 40,889; Mining and quarrying 1; Manufacturing 891; Electricity, gas and water 109; Construction 1,302; Trade, restaurants and hotels 2,712; Transport, storage and communications 1,030; Financing, insurance, real estate and business services 646; Community, social and personal services 7,891; *Sub-total* 55,471; Activities not adequately defined 11,126; *Total labour force* 66,597 (males 35,692, females 30,905). *1999 Census* (persons aged 15 to 64 years): Subsistence farmers 51,309; Total employed (incl. others) 75,110; Unemployed (seeking work) 1,260; Total labour force 76,370 (males 42,072, females 34,298). *Mid-2011:* Agriculture, etc. 39,000; Total labour force 130,000 (Source: FAO).

HEALTH AND WELFARE

Key Indicators

Total Fertility Rate (children per woman, 2009): 3.9.

Under-5 Mortality Rate (per 1,000 live births, 2009): 16.

Physicians (per 1,000 head, 2004): 0.1.

Hospital Beds (per 1,000 head, 2005): 4.1.

Health Expenditure (2008): US $ per head (PPP): 170.

Health Expenditure (2008): % of GDP: 3.9.

Health Expenditure (2008): public (% of total): 83.5.

Access to Water (% of persons, 2008): 83.

Access to Sanitation (% of persons, 2008): 53.

Total Carbon Dioxide Emissions ('000 metric tons, 2007): 102.6.

Carbon Dioxide Emissions Per Head (metric tons, 2007): 0.4.

Human Development Index (2007): ranking: 126.

Human Development Index (2007): value: 0.693.

For sources and definitions, see explanatory note on p. vi.

AGRICULTURE, ETC.

Principal Crops ('000 metric tons, 2009, FAO estimates): Coconuts 309; Roots and tubers 46.0; Vegetables and melons 11.6; Bananas 18.3; Groundnuts, with shell 2.6; Maize 0.8.

Livestock ('000 head, year ending September 2009, FAO estimates): Cattle 170; Pigs 89; Goats 19; Horses 3; Chickens 800.

Livestock Products (metric tons, 2009, FAO estimates): Cattle meat 2,560; Pig meat 3,500; Chicken meat 460; Cows' milk 3,150; Hen eggs 400.

Forestry ('000 cu m, 2009): *Roundwood Removals* (excl. bark): Sawlogs and veneer logs 28; Fuel wood 91; Total 119. *Sawnwood Production* (all broadleaved, incl. railway sleepers): Total 14.

Fishing ('000 metric tons, live weight, 2009): Marine fishes 57.6 (Skipjack tuna 40.8; Yellowfin tuna 4.6; Bigeye tuna 4.0; Albacore 8.2); Marine crustaceans 250.0; Total catch (incl. others) 144.6.

Source: FAO.

FINANCE

Currency and Exchange Rates: Currency is the vatu. *Sterling, Dollar and Euro Equivalents* (28 February 2011): £1 sterling = 151.122 vatu; US $1 = 93.090 vatu; €1 = 128.781 vatu; 1,000 vatu = £6.62 = $10.74 = €7.77. *Average Exchange Rate* (vatu per US $): 101.33 in 2008; 106.74 in 2009; 96.91 in 2010.

Budget (million vatu, 2010): *Revenue:* Tax revenue 10,888; Other current revenue 1,089; Capital assets 5; Total 11,982, excluding grants from abroad (4,484). *Expenditure:* Current expenditure 15,105; Capital expenditure 2,748; Total (incl. others) 17,852. Source: Asian Development Bank.

International Reserves (US $ million at 31 December 2010): IMF special drawing rights 2.39; Reserve position in IMF 3.84; Foreign exchange 155.15; *Total* 161.38. Source: IMF, *International Financial Statistics*.

Money Supply (million vatu at 31 December 2010): Currency outside depository corporations 4,542; Transferable deposits 17,591; Other deposits 34,407; *Broad money* 56,539. Source: IMF, *International Financial Statistics*.

Cost of Living (Consumer Price Index; base: 2005 = 100): All items 118.5 in 2007; 124.2 in 2008; 129.8 in 2009. Source: ILO.

Gross Domestic Product (million vatu at constant 1983 prices): 17,906 in 2005; 19,236 in 2006; 20,550 in 2007.

Expenditure on the Gross Domestic Product (million vatu at current prices, 2008): Government final consumption expenditure 9,360; Private final consumption expenditure 36,671; Gross fixed capital formation 19,779; Increase in stocks 690; Statistical discrepancy 1,441; *Total domestic expenditure* 67,941; Exports of goods and services 30,016; *Less* Imports of goods and services 35,204; *GDP in purchasers' values* 62,753. Source: Asian Development Bank.

Gross Domestic Product by Economic Activity (million vatu at current prices, 2009): Agriculture, forestry and fishing 12,425; Mining 26; Manufacturing 1,915; Electricity, gas and water 1,125; Construction 3,162; Wholesale and retail trade 9,392; Transport, storage and communications 6,847; Finance and insurance 4,623; Public administration 8,140; Others 10,071; *Sub-total* 57,726; Taxes, less subsidies, on products 8,208; *Less* Imputed bank service charge 2,910; *GDP in purchasers' values* 63,024. Source: Asian Development Bank.

Balance of Payments (US $ million, 2010): Exports of goods 50.1; Imports of goods –240.1; *Trade balance* –190.0; Exports of services and income 305.0; Imports of services and income –181.6; *Balance on goods, services and income* –66.6; Current transfers received 29.0; Current transfers paid –3.3; *Current balance*–40.9; Capital account (net) 20.8; Direct investment (net) 37.7; Portfolio investment (net) –0.7; Other investments (net) –9.6; Net errors and omissions –3.3; *Overall balance* 4.0. Source: Asian Development Bank.

EXTERNAL TRADE

Principal Commodities (million vatu, 2010): *Imports c.i.f.* (excl. imports for re-export): Food and live animals 5,108; Beverages and tobacco 1,023; Mineral fuels, lubricants, etc. 3,751; Chemicals 2,923; Basic manufactures 3,817; Machinery and transport equipment 7,252; Miscellaneous manufactured articles 2,735; Total (incl. others) 27,391. *Exports f.o.b.* (excl. re-exports): Cocoa 384; Copra 579; Beef 494; Timber 26; Coconut oil 933; Shells 31; Kava 508; Total (incl. others) 4,504.

Principal Trading Partners (million vatu, 2010, unless otherwise indicated): *Imports c.i.f.* (excl. imports for re-export): Australia 8,540; Fiji 2,138; France 661; Japan 1,007; New Zealand 3,725; Singapore 3,456; Total (incl. others) 27,391. *Exports f.o.b.* (2008, excl. re-exports): Australia 126; European Union countries 783; Japan 241; New Caledonia 350; New Zealand 194; Total (incl. others) 3,566.

TRANSPORT

Road Traffic ('000 motor vehicles in use, 2001, estimates): Passenger cars 2.6; Commercial vehicles 4.4. Source: UN, *Statistical Yearbook*.

Shipping: *Merchant Fleet* (registered at 31 December 2009): Vessels 445; Total displacement ('000 grt) 2,144.6 (Source: IHS Fairplay, *World Fleet Statistics*). *International Sea-borne Freight Traffic* ('000 metric tons, 1990, estimates): Goods loaded 80; Goods unloaded 55 (Source: UN, *Monthly Bulletin of Statistics*).

Civil Aviation (traffic on scheduled services, 2006): Kilometres flown (million) 3; Passengers carried ('000) 117; Passenger-km (million) 241; Total ton-km (million) 23. Source: UN, *Statistical Yearbook*.

TOURISM

Foreign Tourist Arrivals: 81,345 in 2007; 90,657 in 2008; 100,675 in 2009. Note: Figures refer to arrivals by air only; arrivals from cruise-ships were: 106,138 in 2008; 124,818 in 2009; 140,468 in 2010.

Tourist Arrivals by Country of Residence (2010): Australia 58,760; New Caledonia 11,410; New Zealand 11,927; Other Pacific 4,719; Europe 4,888; North America 2,395; Total (incl. others) 97,180.

Tourism Receipts (US $ million, incl. passenger transport): 104 in 2005; 109 in 2006; 142 in 2007 (Source: World Tourism Organization).

COMMUNICATIONS MEDIA

Radio Receivers (1997): 62,000 in use*.

Television Receivers (1999): 2,000 in use†.

Telephones (2010): 5,000 main lines in use‡.

Mobile Cellular Telephones (2010): 285,300 subscribers‡.

Internet Subscribers (2009): 2,600‡.

Broadband Subscribers (2010): 300‡.

Personal Computers: 3,000 (13.9 per 1,000 persons) in 2005‡.

Non-daily Newspapers (2004): 1 (estimated circulation 3,000)*.

* Source: UNESCO, *Statistical Yearbook*.
† Source: UN, *Statistical Yearbook*.
‡ Source: International Telecommunication Union.

EDUCATION

Pre-primary (1992, unless otherwise indicated): 252 schools; 49 teachers (1980); 5,178 pupils.

Primary (2007, unless otherwise indicated): 374 schools (1995); 1,614 teachers (2002); 38,026 pupils.

Secondary (2007, unless otherwise indicated): 27 schools (1995); 591 teachers (2002); 15,132 students.

Tertiary (2002): 2,124 students.

Secondary (Teacher Training): 1 college (1989); 13 teachers (1983); 124 students (1991).

Pupil-teacher Ratio (primary education, UNESCO estimate): 23.8 in 2006/07 (Source: UNESCO Institute for Statistics).

Adult Literacy Rate (UNESCO estimates): 82.0% (males 83.7%; females 80.3%) in 2009 (Source: UNESCO Institute for Statistics).

Directory

The Constitution

A new Constitution came into effect at independence on 30 July 1980. The main provisions are as follows:

The Republic of Vanuatu is a sovereign democratic state, of which the Constitution is the supreme law. Bislama is the national language and the official languages are Bislama, English and French. The Constitution guarantees protection of all fundamental rights and freedoms and provides for the determination of citizenship.

The President, as head of the Republic, symbolizes the unity of the Republic and is elected for a five-year term of office by secret ballot by an electoral college consisting of Parliament and the Presidents of the Regional Councils.

Legislative power resides in the single-chamber Parliament, consisting of 39 members (amended to 46 members in 1987, to 50 in 1995 and further to 52 in 1998) elected for four years on the basis of universal franchise through an electoral system that includes an element of proportional representation to ensure fair representation of different political groups and opinions. Parliament is presided over by the Speaker elected by the members. Executive power is vested in the Council of Ministers which consists of the Prime Minister (elected by Parliament from among its members) and other ministers (appointed by the Prime Minister from among the members of Parliament). The number of ministers, including the Prime Minister, may not exceed a quarter of the number of members of Parliament.

Special attention is paid to custom law and to decentralization. The Constitution states that all land in the Republic belongs to the indigenous custom owners and their descendants. There is a National Council of Chiefs, composed of custom chiefs elected by their peers sitting in District Councils of Chiefs. It may discuss all matters relating to custom and tradition and may make recommendations to Parliament for the preservation and promotion of the culture and languages of Vanuatu. The Council may be consulted on any question in connection with any bill before Parliament. Each region may elect a regional council and the Constitution lays particular emphasis on the representation of custom chiefs within each one. (A reorganization of local government was initiated in May 1994, and resulted in September of that year in the replacement of 11 local councils with six provincial governments.)

The Constitution also makes provision for public finance, the Public Service, the Ombudsman, a leadership code and the judiciary (see Judicial System).

The Government

HEAD OF STATE

President: IOLU ABBIL JOHNSON (appointed 2 September 2009).

COUNCIL OF MINISTERS
(October 2011)

The Government includes members of the Green Confederation Party, the Land and Justice Party (LJP), National Community Association Party (NCAP), the People's Progressive Party (PPP), Union of Moderate Parties (UMP), the Vanuaaku Party (VP), the Vanuatu Republikan Pati (VRP) and the National United Party (NUP).

Prime Minister and Minister for Public Service: SATO KILMAN (PPP).

Deputy Prime Minister and Minister of Trade, Industry and Tourism: HAM LINI (NUP).

Minister of Foreign Affairs: ALFRED CARLOT (VRP).

Minister of Infrastructure and Public Utilities: HARRY IAUKO (VP).

Minister of Internal Affairs: GEORGE WELLS (NCAP).

Minister of Justice and Social Affairs: RALPH REGENVANU (LJP).

Minister of Agriculture, Quarantine, Forestry and Fisheries: JAMES NGWANGO (PPP).

Minister of Health: WILLIE RUBEN ABEL (VP).

Minister of Education: MARCELLINO PIPITE (VRP).

Minister of Finance and Economic Management: MOANA CARCASSES KALOSIL (Green Confederation Party).

Minister of Lands and Natural Resources: STEVEN KALSAKAU (UMP).

Minister of Ni-Vanuatu Business Development and Co-operatives: DON KEN (Ind.).

Minister of Youth Sports and Training: MORKIN STEVENS (NUP).

MINISTRIES AND DEPARTMENTS

Prime Minister's Office: PMB 9053, Port Vila; tel. 22413; fax 26301; internet www.governmentofvanuatu.gov.vu.

Deputy Prime Minister's Office: PMB 9056, Port Vila; tel. 27045; fax 27832.

Ministry of Agriculture, Quarantine, Forestry and Fisheries: PMB 9039, Port Vila; tel. 23406; fax 26498.

Ministry of the Comprehensive Reform Programme: POB 9088, Port Vila; tel. 25816; fax 25815.

Ministry of Co-operative and Ni-Vanuatu Business Development: PMB 9056, Port Vila; tel. 26220; fax 25677.

Ministry of Education: PMB 9028, Port Vila; tel. 22309; fax 24569.

Ministry of Finance and Economic Management: PMB 9058, Port Vila; tel. 23032; fax 27937.

Ministry of Foreign Affairs and External Trade: PMB 9051, Port Vila; tel. 27045; fax 27832.

Ministry of Health: PMB 9042, Port Vila; tel. 22545; fax 26113.

Ministry of Infrastructure and Public Utilities: PMB 9057, Port Vila; tel. 22790; fax 27714.

Ministry of Internal Affairs: PMB 9036, Port Vila; tel. 22252; fax 27064.

Ministry of Justice and Social Welfare: PMB 9036, Port Vila; tel. 22252; fax 27064.

Ministry of Lands and Natural Resources: PMB 9090, Port Vila; tel. 22892; fax 27708; e-mail molvanuatu@gmail.com; internet www.mol.gov.vu.

Ministry of Sports and Youth Development: POB 9006, Port Vila; tel. 25298; fax 26879.

Ministry of Trade, Industry, Commerce and Tourism: PMB 9056, Port Vila; tel. 25674; fax 25677.

Legislature

PARLIAMENT

Speaker: DUNSTAN HILTON.

General Election, 2 September 2008

	Seats
Vanuaaku Pati	11
National United Party	8
Union of Moderate Parties	7
Vanuatu Republikan Pati	7
People's Progressive Party	4
Green Confederation Party	2
Others	9
Independents	4
Total	52

Election Commission

Vanuatu Electoral Commission: PMB 033, Port Vila; tel. 23914; fax 26681; Principal Electoral Officer MARTIN TETE.

Political Organizations

Efate Laketu Party: Port Vila; f. 1982; regional party, based on the island of Efate.

Green Confederation Party: POB 538, Port Vila; tel. 7778069; e-mail moanakalosil6@gmail.com; f. 2001; est. by breakaway group of the UMP; Leader MOANA CARCASSES KALOSIL.

Land and Justice Party: Port Vila; f. 2010; aims to protect customary land ownership and to address issue of foreign ownership of local businesses; Leader RALPH REGENVANU.

Melanesian Progressive Pati (MPP): POB 39, Port Vila; tel. 23485; fax 23315; f. 1988; est. by breakaway group of the VP; Chair. BARAK SOPE; Sec.-Gen. GEORGES CALO.

National Community Association Party (NCAP): Port Vila; f. 1996; advocates land reform.

National Democratic Party (NDP): Port Vila; f. 1986; advocates strengthening of links with France and the United Kingdom; Leader JOHN NAUPA.

National United Party (NUP): Port Vila; f. 1991; est. by supporters of Walter Lini, following his removal as leader of the VP; Pres. HAM LINI; Sec.-Gen. WILLIE TITONGOA.

People's Democratic Party (PDP): Port Vila; f. 1994; est. by breakaway faction of the NUP.

People's Progressive Party (PPP): Port Vila; f. 2001; formed coalition with the NUP and Fren Melanesia to contest 2002 elections; Pres. SATO KILMAN; Sec.-Gen. WILLIE LOP.

Tu Vanuatu Kominiti: Port Vila; f. 1996; espouses traditional Melanesian and Christian values; Leader HILDA LINI.

Union of Moderate Parties (UMP): POB 698, Port Vila; f. 1980; Pres. SERGE VOHOR; Vice-Pres. CHARLOT SALWAI.

Vanuaaku Pati (VP) (Our Land Party): POB 472, Port Vila; tel. 22584; f. 1971; est. as the New Hebrides National Party; advocates 'Melanesian socialism'; Pres. EDWARD NATAPEI; First Vice-Pres. IOLU ABBIL JOHNSON; Sec.-Gen. SELA MOLISA.

Vanuatu Independent Alliance Party (VIAP): Port Vila; f. 1982; supports free enterprise; Leaders THOMAS SERU, GEORGE WOREK, KALMER VOCOR.

Vanuatu Independent Movement: Port Vila; f. 2002; Pres. WILLIE TASSO.

Vanuatu Labour Party (VLP): Port Vila; f. 1986; trade-union based; Leader JOSHUA KALSAKAU.

Vanuatu Progressive Development Party: Epi; f. 2011; promotes devt in rural sector; Pres. ROBERT BOHN; Sec.-Gen. PETER MAWA.

Vanuatu Republikan Pati (VRP): Port Vila; f. 1998; est. by breakaway faction of the UMP; Leader MAXIME CARLOT KORMAN; Sec.-Gen. MARCELLINO PEPITE.

The Na-Griamel (Leader FRANKLEY STEVENS), Namangie Aute Tan Union (Leader VINCENT BULEKONE) and Fren Melanesia (Leader ALBERT RAVUTIA) represent rural interests on the islands of Espiritu Santo and Malekula. The John Frum Movement represents interests on the island of Tanna.

Diplomatic Representation

EMBASSIES AND HIGH COMMISSIONS IN VANUATU

Australia: Winston Churchill Ave, POB 111, Port Vila; tel. 22777; fax 23948; e-mail australia_vanuatu@dfat.gov.au; internet www.vanuatu.highcommission.gov.au; High Commissioner JEFF ROACH.

China, People's Republic: PMB 9071, Rue d'Auvergne, Nambatu, Port Vila; tel. 23598; fax 24877; e-mail publicinfo@chinese-embassy.com.vu; internet vu.china-embassy.org; Ambassador CHENG SHUPING.

France: Kumul Highway, POB 60, Port Vila; tel. 28700; fax 28701; e-mail ambafra@vanuatu.com.vu; internet www.ambafrance-vu.org; Ambassador FRANÇOISE MAYLIÉ.

New Zealand: La Casa d'Andrea e Luciano, Rue Pierre Lamy St, POB 161, Port Vila; tel. 22933; fax 22518; e-mail kiwi@vanuatu.com.vu; internet www.nzembassy.com/vanuatu; High Commissioner BILL DOBBIE.

Judicial System

The Supreme Court has unlimited jurisdiction to hear and determine any civil or criminal proceedings, and is the court of first instance in constitutional matters. It consists of the Chief Justice, appointed by the President of the Republic after consultation with the Prime Minister and the leader of the opposition, and three other judges, who are appointed by the President of the Republic on the advice of the Judicial Service Commission. The Court of Appeal is constituted by two or more judges of the Supreme Court sitting together.

Magistrates' Courts have limited jurisdiction to hear and determine any civil or criminal proceedings. Island Courts have been established in several local government regions, and are constituted when three justices are sitting together to exercise civil or criminal jurisdiction, as defined in the warrant establishing the court. A magistrate nominated by the Chief Justice acts as Chairman. The Island Courts are competent to rule on land disputes.

In 2001 legislation was introduced to establish a new Land Tribunal, in order to expedite the hearing of land disputes. The tribunal was to have three levels, and no cases were to go beyond the tribunal and enter either the Supreme Court or the Island Courts.

Chief Justice of the Supreme Court: VINCENT LUNABEK, PMB 041, rue de Querios, Port Vila; tel. 22420; fax 22692.

Public Prosecutor: KAYLEEN TAVOA.

Attorney-General: ISHMAEL KALSAKAU.

Religion

Most of Vanuatu's inhabitants profess Christianity. Presbyterians form the largest Christian group (with about one-half of the population being adherents), followed by Anglicans and Roman Catholics.

CHRISTIANITY

Vanuatu Christian Council: POB 13, Luganville, Santo; tel. 03232; f. 1967; est. as New Hebrides Christian Council; five mem. churches, two observers; Chair. Rt Rev. JAMES LIGO; Sec. SHEM TEMA.

The Roman Catholic Church

Vanuatu forms the single diocese of Port Vila, suffragan to the archdiocese of Nouméa (New Caledonia). At 31 December 2007 there were an estimated 32,500 adherents in the country. The Bishop participates in the Catholic Bishops' Conference of the Pacific, based in Fiji.

Bishop of Port Vila: JOHN BOSCO BAREMES, Evêché, POB 59, Port Vila; tel. 22640; fax 25342; e-mail catholik@vanuatu.com.vu.

The Anglican Communion

Anglicans in Vanuatu are adherents of the Church of the Province of Melanesia, comprising eight dioceses: Vanuatu (which also includes New Caledonia), Banks and Torres and six dioceses in Solomon Islands. The Archbishop of the Province is the Bishop of Central Melanesia, resident in Honiara, Solomon Islands. In 1985 the Church had an estimated 16,000 adherents in Vanuatu.

Bishop of Vanuatu: Rt Rev. JAMES LIGO, Bishop's House, POB 238, Luganville, Santo; tel. 37065; fax 36331; e-mail comdov@vanuatu.com.vu.

Bishop of Banks and Torres: Rt Rev. NATHAN TOME, Bishop's House, POB 19, Sola, Torba Province; tel. and fax 38520.

Protestant Churches

Presbyterian Church of Vanuatu (Presbitirin Jyos long Vanuatu): POB 150, Port Vila; tel. 27184; fax 23650; f. 1948; 56,000 mems (1995); Moderator Pastor OBED MOSES; Assembly Clerk Pastor FAMA RAKAU.

Other denominations active in the country include the Apostolic Church, the Assemblies of God, the Churches of Christ in Vanuatu and the Seventh-day Adventist Church.

BAHÁ'Í FAITH

National Spiritual Assembly of the Bahá'ís of Vanuatu: POB 1017, Port Vila; tel. 22419; e-mail nsavanuatu@vanuatu.com.vu; f. 1953; Sec. CHARLES PIERCE; mems resident in 233 localities.

The Press

Hapi Tumas Long Vanuatu: POB 1292, Port Vila; tel. 23642; fax 23343; quarterly tourist information; English; Publr MARC NEIL-JONES; circ. 12,000.

Pacific Island Profile: Port Vila; f. 1990; monthly; general interest; English and French; Editor HILDA LINI.

Port Vila Presse: Raffea House, 1st Floor, POB 637, Port Vila; tel. 22200; fax 27999; e-mail marke@presse.com.vu; internet www.presse.com.vu; f. 2000; daily; English and French; Publr MARKE LOWEN; Editor RICKY BINIHI.

Vanuatu Daily Post: POB 1292, Port Vila; tel. 23111; fax 24111; e-mail tpost@vanuatu.com.vu; internet www.dailypost.vu; daily; English; Publr MARC NEIL-JONES; Editor ROYSON WILLIE; circ. 2,000.

Vanuatu Weekly: PMB 049, Port Vila; tel. 22999; fax 22026; f. 1980; weekly; govt-owned; Bislama, English and French; circ. 1,700.

Vanuatu Wikli Post: f. 2008; weekly; Bislama; Editor RICKY BINIHI.

Viewpoints: Port Vila; weekly; newsletter of Vanuaaku Pati; Editor PETER TAURAKOTO.

Wantok Niuspepa: POB 1292, Port Vila; tel. 23642; fax 23343.

Broadcasting and Communications

TELECOMMUNICATIONS

Digicel Vanuatu: PMB 9103, Ellouk Plateau, Port Vila; tel. 27692; fax 27865; e-mail customercarevanuatu@digicelgroup.com; internet www.digicelvanuatu.com; Gen. Man. TANYA MENZIES.

Telecom Vanuatu Ltd (TVL): POB 146, Port Vila; tel. 22185; fax 22628; e-mail sales@tvl.net.vu; internet www.tvl.vu; f. 1989; national and international telecommunications services; Man. Dir MICHEL DUPUIS.

BROADCASTING

Radio

Vanuatu Broadcasting and Television Corpn (VBTC): PMB 049, Port Vila; tel. 22999; fax 22026; internet www.vbtc.com.vu; fmrly Government Media Services, name changed in 1992; Gen. Man. FRED VUROBARAVU; Chair. GODWIN LIGO.

Radio Vanuatu: PMB 049, Port Vila; tel. 22999; fax 22026; f. 1966; govt-owned; broadcasts in English, French and Bislama; Dir JOE BOMAL CARLO.

Television

Vanuatu Broadcasting and Television Corpn (VBTC): see Radio

Television Blong Vanuatu: PMB 049, Port Vila; f. 1993; govt-owned; French-funded; broadcasts for four hours daily in French and English; Gen. Man. CLAUDE CASTELLY; Programme Man. GAEL LE DANTEC.

Finance

(cap. = capital; res = reserves; dep. = deposits; brs = branches; amounts in vatu unless otherwise indicated)

BANKING

Central Bank

Reserve Bank of Vanuatu: PMB 9062, Port Vila; tel. 23333; fax 24231; e-mail enquiries@rbv.gov.vu; internet www.rbv.gov.vu; f. 1981; est. as Central Bank of Vanuatu; name changed as above in 1989; govt-owned; cap. 100.0m., res 613.6m., dep. 7,722.1m. (Dec. 2006); Gov. ODO TEVI.

Development Bank

Development Bank of Vanuatu: Rue de Paris, POB 241, Port Vila; tel. 22181; fax 24591; f. 1979; govt-owned; Man. Dir AUGUSTINE GARAE.

National Bank

National Bank of Vanuatu: POB 249, Rue de Paris, Port Vila; tel. 22201; fax 27227; e-mail nationalbank@vanuatu.com.vu; internet www.nbv.vu; f. 1991; est. upon assumption of control of Vanuatu Co-operative Savings Bank; govt-owned; cap. 600m., dep. 7,793.5m. (Dec. 2008); Chair. DUDLEY ARU; Man. Dir BOB HUGHES; 21 brs.

Foreign Banks

ANZ Bank (Vanuatu) Ltd: PMB 9003, Port Vila; tel. 26355; fax 22230; e-mail vanuatu@anz.com; internet www.anz.com/vanuatu; f. 1971; cap. 3.7m., res 317.7m., dep. 24,734.2m. (Sept. 2003); Man. Dir GAYLE STAPLETON; brs in Port Vila and Luganville.

European Bank Ltd (USA): International Bldg, Fr Walter Lini Highway, POB 65, Port Vila; tel. 27700; fax 22884; e-mail info@europeanbank.net; 'offshore' and private banking; cap. US $0.75m., res US $1.25m., dep. US $44.76m. (Dec. 2008); Chair. THOMAS MONTGOMERY BAYER; Pres. ROBERT MURRAY BOHN.

Westpac Banking Corporation (Australia): Lini Highway, Port Vila; tel. 22084; fax 24773; e-mail westpacvanuatu@westpac.com.au; internet www.westpac.vu; Man. R. B. WRIGHT; 2 brs.

Financial Institutions

The Vanuatu Financial Centre Association: POB 1128, Port Vila; tel. 23410; fax 23405; e-mail VFCA@vanuatu.com.vu; internet www.fca.vu; f. 1980; group of banking, legal, accounting and trust cos administering 'offshore' banking and investment; Chair. MARK STAFFORD; Sec. THOMAS BAYER.

Vanuatu Financial Services Commission (VFSC): Bougainville St, PMB 9023, Port Vila; tel. 22247; fax 22242; e-mail info@vfsc.vu; internet www.vfsc.vu; f. 1993; regulation and supervision of non-banking financial services; Commr GEORGE ANDREWS.

INSURANCE

Pacific Insurance Brokers: POB 229, Port Vila; tel. 23863; fax 23089.

QBE Insurance (Vanuatu) Ltd: La Casa D'Andrea Bldg, POB 186, Port Vila; tel. 22299; fax 23298; e-mail info.van@qbe.com; Gen. Man. GEOFFREY R. CUTTING.

Trade and Industry

GOVERNMENT AGENCY

Vanuatu Investment Promotion Authority: PMB 9011, Port Vila; tel. 24096; fax 25216; e-mail ataritambe@vanuatu.gov.vu; internet www.investinvanuatu.com; fmrly the Vanuatu Investment Board, name changed as above in 2000; CEO SMITH TEBU.

CHAMBER OF COMMERCE

Chamber of Commerce and Industry of Vanuatu: POB 189, Port Vila; tel. 27543; fax 27542; e-mail vancci@vanuatu.com.vu; internet www.vanuatuchamber.org; Pres. JACQUES NIOTEAU.

MARKETING BOARD

Vanuatu Commodities Marketing Board: POB 268, Luganville, Santo; f. 1982; sole exporter of major commodities, including copra, kava and cocoa; plans to cease operations were mooted in mid-2010; Chair. JACK LOWANI.

UTILITIES

Utilities Regulatory Authority: Port Vila, Efate; internet www.ura.gov.vu; f. 2008; regulates electricity and water supply; Pres. JOHNSON NAVITI MARAKIPULE.

Union Electrique du Vanuatu (Unelco Vanuatu Ltd): POB 26, rue Winston Churchill, Port Vila; tel. 22211; fax 25011; e-mail unelco@unelco.com.vu; f. 1939; private org. contracted for the generation and supply of electricity in Port Vila, Luganville, Tanna and Malekula, and for the supply of water in Port Vila; fully owned subsidiary of GDF Suez, France; Dir-Gen. JEAN FRANÇOIS BARBEAU.

MAJOR COMPANIES

Port of Palekula: POB 237, Santo; tel. 36319; fmrly South Pacific Fishing Co; renamed in 2000; jt venture between the National Fishermen's Co-operative Ltd (NFC) and Vanuatu Lampa Co (VLC) Group Ltd; Man. Dir RAY CHITTY.

Tuna Fishing (Vanuatu) Ltd: POB 1640, Port Vila; tel. 25887; fax 25608; e-mail tunafishing@vanuatu.com.vu; Man. Dir CHRISTOPHER EMELEE.

Vanuatu Brewing Ltd: POB 169, Port Vila; tel. 22435; fax 22152; e-mail tusker@vanuatu.com.vu; f. 1990; purchased by a New Caledonian co, Froico, in 2008; production of Pripps Lager and Vanuatu Tusker Beer; Gen. Man. LIONEL RAMANA.

Vanuatu Maritime Services Ltd: POB 102, Port Vila; tel. 22454; fax 22884; e-mail security@vila.net; internet www.vanuatuships.com; provides registry and administration of maritime services.

Vanuatu Registries Ltd: e-mail info@acshk.com; marketing and promotion of Vanuatu as a jurisdiction for company registration and ship registration; brs in Singapore and Hong Kong.

Volcanic Earth Ltd: POB 1642, Port Villa; tel. 7746112; e-mail enquiries@volcanicearth.com; internet www.volcanicearth.com; producer and exporter of organic skincare products; Export Man. BARRY ROCHE.

TRADE UNIONS

Vanuatu Council of Trade Unions (VCTU): POB 287, Port Vila; tel. 26903; fax 23679; e-mail carlo@vanuatu.com.vu; Pres. OBED MASINGIOW; Sec.-Gen. EPHRAIM KALSAKAU.

National Union of Labour: Port Vila.

The principal trade unions, of which the majority were reported to be inactive at mid-2011, include:

Oil and Gas Workers' Union: Port Vila; f. 1984.

Vanuatu Airline Workers' Union: Port Vila; f. 1984.

Vanuatu National Workers' Union: PMB 9089, Port Vila; tel. 23679; fax 26903; Nat. Sec. EPHRAIM KALSAKAU.

Vanuatu Public Service Association: Port Vila.

Vanuatu Teachers' Union: Port Vila; Gen. Sec. CHARLES KALO; Pres. WILFRED LEO.

Vanuatu Waterside, Maritime and Allied Workers' Union: Port Vila.

Transport

ROADS

There are about 1,070 km of roads, of which 54 km, mostly on Efate Island, are sealed.

SHIPPING

The principal ports are Port Vila and Luganville. Various shipping lines operate services to Vanuatu. At the end of 2009 the merchant fleet comprised 445 vessels, with a total displacement of 2,144,600 grt. A shipping registry, based in Singapore, provides a 'flag of convenience' to foreign-owned vessels.

Vanuatu Maritime Authority: POB 320, Marine Quay, Port Vila; tel. 23128; fax 22949; e-mail iantchichine@vma.com.vu; domestic and international ship registry, maritime safety regulator; Commissioner of Maritime Affairs JOHN T. ROOSEN; Chair. LENNOX VUTI.

Ports and Harbour Department: PMB 9046, Port Vila; tel. 22339; fax 22475; e-mail nhamish@vanet.com; Harbour Master Capt. LUKE BEANDI; Dir NORRIS HAMISH.

Burns Philp (Vanuatu) Ltd: POB 27, Port Vila.

Ifira Shipping Agencies Ltd: POB 68, Port Vila; tel. 22929; fax 22052; f. 1986; Man. Dir CLAUDE BOUDIER.

Sami Ltd: Kumul Highway, POB 301, Port Vila; tel. 24106; fax 23405.

South Sea Shipping: POB 84, Port Vila; tel. 22205; fax 23304.

Vanua Navigation Ltd: POB 44, Port Vila; tel. 22027; f. 1977; est. by the Co-operative Federation and Sofrana Unilines; Chief Exec. GEOFFREY J. CLARKE.

CIVIL AVIATION

The principal airports are Bauerfield (Efate, for Port Vila) and Pekoa (Espiritu Santo, for Luganville). There are airstrips on all Vanuatu's principal islands, and also an international airport at White Grass on Tanna. In 2000 it was announced that a further three airports were to be built on the islands of Pentecost, Malekula and Tanna. Major improvements providing for the accommodation of larger aircraft at both Bauerfield and Pekoa airports began in 2000. Moreover, in September 2000 plans for a new international airport at Teouma (Efate) were announced, with finance from a private Thai investor. In late 2003 plans for the construction of an international air terminal at Pekoa (Espiritu Santo) costing US $1.6m. were announced.

Civil Aviation Authority: POB 131, Port Vila; tel. 25111; fax 25532.

Air Vanuatu: 3rd Floor, Air Vanuatu House, Rue de Paris, Port Vila; tel. 23838; fax 23250; e-mail sales@airvanuatu.com.vu; internet www.airvanuatu.com; f. 1981; govt-owned national carrier since 1987; regular services between Port Vila and Sydney, Brisbane and Melbourne (Australia), Nadi (Fiji), Nouméa (New Caledonia), Auckland (New Zealand) and Honiara (Solomon Islands); CEO PETER FOGARTY.

Dovair: Port Vila; privately owned; operates domestic services.

Tourism

Tourism is an important source of revenue. Visitors are attracted by the islands' scenery and rich local customs. There were some 120 hotels and guest houses in 2003, providing more than 1,300 rooms. In 2010 foreign visitor arrivals (including cruise-ship passengers) were estimated to have increased by more than 5% to reach 237,648. The majority of visitors are from Australia and New Zealand. Receipts from tourism totalled some US $142m. in 2007. The development of the tourist industry has hitherto been concentrated on the islands of Efate, Espiritu Santo and Tanna, but other islands are also being promoted.

Vanuatu Hotels and Resorts Association: POB 5151, Port Vila; tel. 22040; fax 27579; internet www.vanuatuhotelsandresortsassociation.com; Chair. FAHAD HAYAT.

Vanuatu Tourism Office: Lini Highway, POB 209, Port Vila; tel. 22685; fax 23889; e-mail tourism@vanuatu.com.vu; internet www.vanuatutourism.com; Gen. Man. ANNIE NIATU; Chair. BEN TARI.

Defence

Upon Vanuatu's achievement of independence in 1980, a defence pact with Papua New Guinea was signed. A 300-strong paramilitary force, the Vanuatu Mobile Force, exists. In 2003 Vanuatu sent 50 defence personnel to join the Australian-led regional intervention force in Solomon Islands. In 2007 the Government allocated 1,380m. vatu for defence, equivalent to 11.7% of total recurrent budgetary expenditure.

Education

In 2009 the central Government launched a policy to provide free primary education from the beginning of the 2010 school year. The policy, which was made possible with financial assistance from Australia and New Zealand, was in response to evidence that many children were denied access to education because their parents could not afford school fees. At 2007 it was estimated that 87% of children between the ages of six and 11 were enrolled at primary institutions. Secondary education begins at 12 years of age, and comprises a preliminary cycle of four years and a second cycle of three years. In 2007 there were 38,026 pupils enrolled in primary schools (which numbered 374 in 1995) and 15,132 pupils attended the country's secondary schools (which numbered 27 in 1995). Vocational education and teacher-training are also available.

An extension centre of the University of the South Pacific was opened in Port Vila in 1989. Students from Vanuatu can also receive higher education at the principal faculties of that university (in Suva, Fiji), in Papua New Guinea or in France.

In 2004 the country's first pre-school (the Vila North Model Pre-School) was opened. The pre-school, which had been built with funding of 5.6m. vatu from the European Union, was to have a staff of four teachers and was expected to serve as a centre for training other pre-school teachers.

The 2007 budget allocated an estimated 3,156m. vatu to education (26.7% of total recurrent expenditure by the central Government).

Bibliography of the Pacific Islands

Akram-Lodhi, A. Haroon (Ed.). *Confronting Fiji Futures*. Canberra, Australian National University, 2000.

Aldrich, Robert. *The French Presence in the South Pacific, 1842–1940*. London, Macmillan, 1990.

France and the South Pacific since 1940. London, Macmillan, 1993.

Aldrich, Robert, and Connell, John. *France's Overseas Frontier*. Cambridge, Cambridge University Press, 1992.

Alkire, William H. *An Introduction to the Peoples and Cultures of Micronesia*. Menlo Park, CA, Cummings Publishing Co, 1977.

American Samoa Economic Advisory Commission. *Transforming the Economy of American Samoa: A Report to the President of the United States of America through the U. S. Department of the Interior*. Pago Pago, April 2002 (revised July 2002).

Angleviel, Frédéric (Ed.). *La Nouvelle-Calédonie, Terre des Recherches—Bibliographie Analytique des Thèses et Memoires*. Nouméa, Association Thèse-Pac, 1995.

101 Mots Pour Comprendre l'Histoire de la Nouvelle-Calédonie. Nouméa, Ile de Lumière, 1997.

Angleviel, Frédéric, Atoloto, Malau, and Atonio, Takasi (Eds). *101 Mots Pour Comprendre Wallis et Futuna*. Nouméa, Ile de Lumière, 1999.

Angleviel, Frédéric, Coppell, William, and Charleux, Michel (Eds). *Bibliographie des Thèses sur le Pacifique*. Bordeaux, CRET, CEGET, Université de Bordeaux, 1991.

Angleviel, Frédéric, and Levine, Stephen. *New Zealand–New Caledonia: Neighbours, Friends, Partners*. Wellington, Victoria University Press, 2008.

Antheaume, Benoît, and Bonnemaison, Joël. *Atlas des Iles et Etats du Pacifique Sud*. Montpellier-Paris, GIP Reclus/Publisud, 1988.

Asian Development Bank. *Cook Islands 2008 Social and Economic Report: Equity in Development*. Manila, Asian Development Bank, 2008.

Skilling the Pacific. Manila, Asian Development Bank, 2008.

Transforming Tonga: A Private Sector Assessment. Manila, Asian Development Bank, 2008.

Kiribati Social and Economic Development Report 2008. Manila, Asian Development Bank, 2009.

Australian Joint Parliamentary Committee on Foreign Affairs, Defence and Trade. *Australia's Relations with Papua New Guinea*. Canberra, 1991.

Australian National University. *Pacific History Bibliography and Comment, 1979–1987, Journal of Pacific History Bibliography 1988–97, Journal of Pacific History*. Canberra, Australian National University.

Baba, T., Field, M., and Nabobo-Baba, U. *Speight of Violence: inside Fiji's 2000 coup*. Auckland, Reed Publishing (NZ), 2005.

Bachimon, Philippe. *Tahiti Entre Mythes et Réalités: Essai d'Histoire Geographique*. Paris, Comité des Travaux Historiques et Scientifiques, 1989.

Ballard, J. A. (Ed.). *Policy-Making in a New State: Papua New Guinea 1972–77*. Melbourne, Oxford University Press, 1981.

Banks, Glenn, Bonnell, Susanne, and Filer, Colin (Eds). *Dilemmas of Development: the social and economic impact of the Porgera gold mine 1989–1994*. Canberra, Asia Pacific Press, Australian National University, 2000.

Barclay, Kate. *A Japanese Joint Venture in the Pacific: Foreign Bodies in Tinned Tuna*. Abingdon, Routledge, 2008.

Barclay, Kate, and Cartright, Ian. *Capturing Wealth from Tuna: Case Studies from the Pacific*. Canberra, ANU EPress, 2011.

Barillot, Bruno. *L'héritage de la bombe: Sahara, Polynésie (1960–2002): les faits, les personnels, les populations*. Lyon, Centre de documentation et de recherche sur la paix et les conflits, 2002.

Bates, S. *The South Pacific Island Countries and France: A Study in International Relations*. Canberra, Australian National University, 1990.

Bayliss-Smith, T., Bedford, R., Brookfield, H., Latham, M., with Brookfield, M. *Islands, Islanders and the World: The Colonial and Post-Colonial Experience of Eastern Fiji*. Cambridge, Cambridge University Press, 1988.

Bellwood, Peter S. *The Polynesians: Prehistory of an island People*. London, Thames and Hudson, 1987.

Bellwood, Peter S. (Ed.). *The Austronesians: Historical and Comparative Perspectives*. Canberra, Australian University Press, 1995.

Bennett, Judith A. *Wealth of the Solomons*. Honolulu, HI, University of Hawaii Press, 1987.

Natives and Exotics: World War II and Environment in the Southern Pacific. Honolulu, HI, University of Hawaii Press, 2009.

Bensa, Alban. *Nouvelle-Calédonie, un paradis dans la tourmente*. Paris, Gallimard, 1990.

Bensa, Alban, and Leblic, Isabelle. *En Pays Kanak*. Paris, Edition de la Maison des Sciences de L'Homme, Mission du Patrimoine Ethnologique, Collection Ethnologie de la France, Cahier 14, 2000.

Bird, I. *The Hawaiian Archipelago*. London, Picador, 1998.

Birkett, Dea. *Serpent in Paradise*. New York, NY, Doubleday, 1997.

Bolyanatz, Alexander H. *Pacific Romanticism: Tahiti and the European Imagination*. Westport, CT, Praeger, 2004.

Bonnemaison, J., Huffman, K., Kauffmann, C., and Tryon, D. *Arts of Vanuatu*. Bathurst, NSW, Crawford House Press, 1997.

Borofsky, Robert (Ed.). *Remembrance of Pacific Pasts: an invitation to remake history*. Honolulu, HI, University of Hawaii, 2000.

Brady, Anne-Marie (Ed.). *Looking North, Looking South: China, Taiwan, and the South Pacific*. Singapore, World Scientific Publishing, 2010.

Bril, Isabelle. *Dictionnaire nêlêmwa-nixumwak-français-anglais: avec introduction grammaticale et lexiques*. Paris, Peeters, 2000.

Brookfield, H. C. *Melanesia, a Geographical Interpretation of an Island World*. London, Methuen, 1971.

Colonialism, Development and Independence; the Case of the Melanesian Islands in the South Pacific. London, Methuen, 1972.

The Pacific in Transition: a Geographical Perspective on Adaptation and Change. Canberra, Australian National University, 1973.

Brown, Anne M. (Ed.). *Security and Development in the Pacific Islands: Social Resilience in Emerging States*. Boulder, CO, Lynne Rienner Publishers, 2007.

Browne, C., and Scott, D. A. *Economic Development in Seven Pacific Island Countries*. Washington, DC, International Monetary Fund, 1989.

Bullard, Alice. *Exile to Paradise: Savagery and Civilization in Paris and the South Pacific, 1790–1900*. Stanford, CA, Stanford University Press, 2000.

Burt, Ben, and Clerk, Christian (Eds). *Environment and Development in the Pacific Islands*. Canberra, Australian National University, 1994.

Cameron, I. *Lost Paradise: the Exploration of the Pacific*. Massachusetts, Salem House, 1987.

Campbell, Ian. *Island Kingdom: Tonga Ancient and Modern*. Christchurch, University of Canterbury Press, 2nd Edn, 2001.

Worlds Apart: A History of the Pacific Islands. Christchurch, Canterbury University Press, 2nd Edn, 2011.

Campbell, Ian C., and Latouche, Jean-Pierre. *Les insulaires du Pacifique—histoire et situation politique*. Paris, Puf, 2001.

Capie, D. *Under the Gun: The Small Arms Challenge in the Pacific*. Wellington, Victoria University Press, 2003.

Carano, P., and Sanchez, P. C. *A Complete History of Guam*. Rutland, VT, Charles E. Tuttle, 1964.

Carrier, James. *History and Tradition in Melanesian Anthropology*. Berkeley, CA, University of California, 1992.

Chappell, David. *Double Ghost: Oceanian Voyagers on Euro-American Ships*. London, Armonk, 1997.

Chauvet, Lisa, Collier, Paul, Hoeffler, Anke. 'Paradise Lost: The Costs of State Failure in the Pacific', in *Journal of Development Studies, Volume 46, Issue 5*. Abingdon, Routledge, 2010.

Chesneaux, Jean, and Maclellan, Nic. *La France dans le Pacifique, De Bougainville à Moruroa*. Paris, La Découverte, 1992.

After Mururoa—France in the South Pacific. Melbourne, Ocean Press, 1998.

Clark, R. S., and Sann, M. (Eds). *The Case against the Bomb: Marshall Islands, Samoa and Solomon Islands before the International Court of Justice*. Mansfield, OH, Book Masters, 1996.

Clifford, James. *Person and Myth: Maurice Leenhardt in the Melanesian World*. Los Angeles, University of California Press, 1982.

Cochrane, S. *Contemporary Art in Papua New Guinea*. Sydney, Craftsman House, 1997.

Colbert, Evelyn. *The Pacific Islands: Paths to the Present*. Boulder, CO, Westview Press. 1997.

Cole, Rodney V. (Ed.). *Pacific 2010—Challenging the Future*. Canberra, Development Studies Centre, Australian National University, 1993.

Cole, Rodney V., and Cuthbertson, S. *Population Growth in the South Pacific Island States—Implications for Australia*. Canberra, Bureau of Immigration, 1995.

Cole, Rodney V., and Parny, T. G. (Eds). *Selected Issues in Pacific Island Development*. Canberra, Development Studies Centre, Australian National University, 1986.

Connell, John. *New Caledonia or Kanaky? The Political History of a French Colony*. Canberra, Development Studies Centre, Australian National University, 1987.

Papua New Guinea: The Struggle for Development. London, Routledge, 1997.

Connell, John et al. *Encyclopedia of the Pacific Islands*. Canberra, Australian National University, 1999.

Connell, John, and Lea, John (Eds). *Planning the Future: Melanesian Cities in 2010*. Canberra, Development Studies Centre, Australian National University, 1993.

Urbanisation in Polynesia. Canberra, Development Studies Centre, Australian National University, 1996.

Urbanization in the Island Pacific. London, Routledge, 2002.

Connell, John, and McCall, G. (Eds). *A World Perspective on Pacific Islander Migration: Australia, New Zealand and the USA*. Centre for Pacific Studies, University of New South Wales, 1992.

Coutau-Bégarie, H. *Géostratégie du Pacifique*. Paris, Economica, 1987.

Craig, Robert D. *Historical Dictionary of Polynesia*. Metuchen, NJ, Scarecrow Press, 1994.

Craig, Robert, and King, Frank (Eds). *Historical Dictionary of Oceania*. London, Greenwood Press, 1981.

Crocombe, Ron. *The South Pacific*. Suva, Institute of Pacific Studies, University of the South Pacific, 1989 (revised 2001).

The Pacific Islands and the USA. Suva, Institute of Pacific Studies, 1995.

Asia in the Pacific Islands: Replacing the West. Suva, Institute of Pacific Studies Publications, 2007.

Crocombe, Ron, and Ali, A. *Politics in Melanesia*. Suva, Institute of Pacific Studies, University of the South Pacific, 1982.

Crocombe, Ron, and Mason, Leonard (Eds). *Micronesian Politics*. Suva, Institute of Pacific Studies, University of the South Pacific, 1988.

Culbertson, Philip, Agee, Margaret N., and Makasiale, Cabrini 'Ofa (Eds). *Penina Uliuli: Contemporary Challenges in Mental Health for Pacific Peoples*. Honolulu, HI, University of Hawaii Press, 2007.

Daniel, P., and Sims, R. *Foreign Investment in Papua New Guinea: Policies and Practices*. Canberra, Development Studies Centre, Australian National University, 1986.

D'Arcy, Paul (Ed.) *Peoples of the Pacific: The History of Oceania to 1870*. Aldershot, Ashgate, 2008.

Davidson, J. W. *Samoa Mo Samoa: the Emergence of the Independent State of Western Samoa*. Melbourne, Oxford University Press, 1967.

Davis, T. *Island Boy, an Autobiography*. Suva, Institute of Pacific Studies, University of the South Pacific, 1992.

Daws, G. *Shoal of Time. A History of the Hawaiian Islands*. Honolulu, HI, University of Hawaii Press, 1968.

A Dream of Islands. Queensland, Jacaranda Press, 1980.

De Deckker, Paul. *Le Peuplement du Pacifique et de la Nouvelle-Calédonie au XIXè siècle*. Paris, L'Harmattan & U.F.P., 1994.

De Deckker, Paul, and Faberon, Jean-Yves (Eds). *Custom and the Law*. Canberra, Asia Pacific Press 2001.

De Deckker, Paul, and Kuntz, Laurence. *La Bataille de la Coutume*. Paris, L'Harmattan, 1997.

De Deckker, Paul, and Tryon, Darell (Eds). *Identités en Mutation dans le Pacifique à l'Aube du Troisième Millénaire, Iles et Archipels No. 26*. Cret, Coll., Université de Bordeaux III, 1998.

De Deckker, Paul et al. *L'outre-mer français dans le Pacifique (Nouvelle-Calédonie, Polynésie française, Wallis-et-Futuna)*. Paris-Nouméa, L'Harmattan-CDP, 2003.

De Vries, Pieter, and Seur, Han. *Moruroa and Us: Polynesians' Experiences during Thirty Years of Nuclear Testing in the French Pacific*. Lyon, Centre de Documentation et de Recherche sur la Paix et les Conflits, 1997.

Debsky, R. *The Organization of Development in the South Pacific*. Honolulu, Pacific Islands Studies Program, Center for Asian and Pacific Studies, 1986.

Decentralisation in the South Pacific: Local, Provincial and State Government in Twenty Countries. Suva, University of the South Pacific, 1986.

Delgado, James P. *Ghost fleet: The Sunken Ships of Bikini Atoll*. Honolulu, HI, University of Hawaii Press, 1996.

Dening, Greg. *Beach Crossings: Voyaging across Times, Cultures and Self*. Melbourne, Miegunyah Press, 2004.

Denoon, Donald. *A Trial Separation: Australia and the Decolonisation of Papua New Guinea*. Canberra, Pandanus Books, 2005.

Denoon, Donald, Firth, S., Linnekin, J., Meleisea, M., and Nero, K. *The Cambridge History of the Pacific Islanders*. Cambridge, Cambridge University Press, 1997.

Denoon, Donald, and Mein-Smith, Philippa. *A History of Australia, New Zealand and the Pacific*. Malden, Blackwell, 2000.

Dervieux, Karen. *Archives kanak: guide des sources, 1774-1958*. Nouméa, Gouvernement de la Nouvelle-Calédonie, 2004.

Detudamo, Timothy. *Legends, Traditions and Tales of Nauru*. Suva, Institute of Pacific Studies, University of South Pacific, 2008.

Diamond, J. *Guns, Germs and Steel—The Fate of Human Societies*. New York, W. W. Norton, 1997.

Diaz, Vincente M. *Native Pacific Cultural Studies on the Edge*. Honolulu, HI, University of Hawaii Press, 2001.

Dibblin, Jane. *Day of Two Suns: US Nuclear Testing and the Pacific Islanders*. New York, NY, New Amsterdam Books, 1990.

Dinnen, Sinclair. *Law and Order in a Weak State—Crime and Politics in Papua New Guinea, Pacific Islands Monograph Series, No.17*. Honolulu, HI, The University of Hawaii Press, 2001.

Dinnen, Sinclair, and Firth, Stewart (Eds). *Politics and State Building in Solomon Islands*. Canberra, Asia Pacific Press, 2008.

Dinnen, Sinclair, and Ley, Alison (Eds). *Reflections on Violence in Melanesia*. Canberra, Asia Pacific Press, Australian National University, 2000.

Dinnen, Sinclair, May, Ron, and Regan, Anthony J. (Eds). *Challenging the State: The Sandline Affair in Papua New Guinea*. Canberra, Australian National University, 1998.

Diolé, P. *The Forgotten People of the Pacific*. London, Cassell, 1976.

Dobbin, Jay, and Hezel, Francis. *Summoning the Powers Beyond: Traditional Religions in Micronesia*. Honolulu, HI, University of Hawaii Press, 2011.

Dorney, Sean. *The Sandline Affair: Politics and Mercenaries and the Bougainville Crisis*. Sydney, ABC Books, 1998.

Papua New Guinea: People, Politics and History since 1975. Sydney, ABC Books, 2nd Edn, 2000.

Dorrance, John C. *The United States and the Pacific Islands*. Westport, CT, Praeger, 1992.

Douglas, Bronwen. *Across the Great Divide—Journeys in History and Anthropology*. Amsterdam, Harwood Academic Publishers, 1998.

Douglas, Ngaire, and Norman, Douglas (Eds). *Pacific Islands Yearbook*. Suva, Fiji Times Ltd.

Doumenge, F. *L'Homme dans le Pacifique Sud; Etude Géographique*. Paris, Société des Océanistes, 1966.

Doumenge, J. P. *Du Terroir à la Ville, les Mélanésiens et leurs espaces en Nouvelle-Calédonie*. Bordeaux, CRET, CEGET, Université de Bordeaux, 1982.

Dubois, Marie-Joseph. *Les Chefferies de Maré*. Paris, Librarie, H. Champion, 1977.

Dunmore, John. *Who's Who in Pacific Navigation*. Honolulu, HI, University of Hawaii Press, 1991.

Visions and Realities—France in the Pacific, 1695–1995. Auckland, Heritage Press, 1997.

Duroy, L. *Hienghène, Le désespoir calédonien*. Barrault, 1988.

Dwyer, Deborah, Dwyer, Terence, and Ellis, Graham. *A Compensation Claims Procedure for Papua New Guinea*. Canberra, Asia Pacific Press, 2000.

Dye, Bob (Ed.). *World War Two in Hawaii from the pages of 'Paradise of the Pacific'*. Honolulu, HI, University of Hawaii Press, 2001.

Emberson-Bain, A. *Labour and Gold in Fiji*. Cambridge, Cambridge University Press, 1994.

Emberson-Bain, A. (Ed.). *Sustainable Development of Malignant Growth? Perspectives of Pacific Island Women*. Suva, Marama Publications, 1995.

Ernst, Manfred. *Winds of Change*. Suva, Pacific Conference of Churches, 1994.

Ewins, Rod. *Staying Fijian: Vatulele Island Barkcloth and Social Identity*. Honolulu, HI, University of Hawaii Press, 2009.

Fairbairn, T. I. J. *Island Economies: Studies From the South Pacific*. Suva, Institute of Pacific Studies, University of the South Pacific, 1985.

Fairbairn, T. I. J., Morrison, C., Baker, R., and Groves, S. *The Pacific Islands*. Honolulu, HI, University of Hawaii Press, 1991.

Farran, Sue. *Human Rights in the South Pacific—Challenges and Changes*. Abingdon, Routledge-Cavendish, 2010.

Field, Michael. *Black Saturday: Killings in Samoa*. Auckland, Reed Publishing (NZ) Ltd, 2006.

Figiel, S. *Where We Once Belonged*. Auckland, Pasifika Press, 1997.

Finnegan, Ruth, and Orbell, Margaret. *South Pacific Oral Traditions*. Bloomington, IN, Indiana University Press, 1995.

Firth, Stewart (Ed.). *Globalisation and Governance in the Pacific Islands*. Canberra, Australian National University Press, 2006.

Fischer, Steven Roger. *A History of the Pacific Islands*. Basingstoke, Palgrave Global Publishing, 2002.

Fleming, Euan, and Hardaker, Brian. *Pacific 2010: Strategies for Melanesian Agriculture for 2010: Tough Choices*. Canberra, National Centre for Development Studies, Australian National University, 1994.

Flynn, Dennis O., and Giraldez, Arturo (Eds). *The Pacific World: Lands, Peoples and History of the Pacific, 1500–1900*. 17 vols. Aldershot, Ashgate, 2009.

Foerstel, L., and Gilliam, A. (Eds). *Confronting the Margaret Mead Legacy: Scholarship, Empire and the South Pacific*. Philadelphia, Temple University Press, 1992.

Forbes, David W. (Ed.). *Hawaiian National Bibliography, 1780–1900, Vol. 2: 1831–1850*. Honolulu, HI, University of Hawaii Press, 2001.

Foster, Robert (Ed.). *Nation-making Emergent Identities in Post-colonial Melanesia*. Ann Arbor, University of Michigan Press, 1995.

Fraenkel, Jon. *Manipulation of Custom: From Uprising to Intervention in the Solomon Islands*. Canberra, Pandanus Books, 2005.

Fraenkel, Jon, and Firth, Stewart (Eds). *From Election to Coup in Fiji: The 2006 Campaign and its Aftermath*. Asia Pacific Press, ANU EPress and IPS Publications, University of the South Pacific, 2007.

Fraenkel, Jon, Firth, Stewart, and Lal, Brij V. (Eds). *The 2006 Military Takeover in Fiji: A Coup to End All Coups?* Canberra, Australian National University Press, 2009.

Franceschi, M. *La Démocratie Massacrée: Consensus ou Mystification à Nouméa?* Paris, Pygmalion, 1998.

Freeman, Derek. *Margaret Mead and Samoa: The Making and Unmaking of an Anthropological Myth*. Harmondsworth, Penguin, 1983.

Freeman, Donald. *The Pacific*. Abingdon, Routledge, 2009.

Friedlaender, Jonathan S. (Ed.). *Genes, Languages, and Culture History in the Southwest Pacific*. New York, Oxford University Press, 2007.

Frost, Lionel (Ed.). *Urbanization and the Pacific World, 1500–1900*. Aldershot, Ashgate, 2005.

Fry, Gerald, and Rufino, Mauricio (Eds). *Pacific Basin and Oceania, World Bibliographical Series, Vol. 70*. Oxford. Clio Press, 1987.

Galipaud, Jean-Christophe, and Lilley, Ian (Eds). *Le Pacifique de 5000 à 2000 avant le présent—Suppléments à L'Histoire d'une Colonisation*. Paris, Edition de l'Institut de Recherche pour le Développement, 1999.

Gannicott, Ken. *Pacific 2010—Women's Education and Economic Development in Melanesia*. Canberra, National University Centre for Development Studies, 1994.

Garrett, John. *Island Exiles*. Melbourne, ABC Books, 1996.

To live among the stars—Christian origins in Oceania. Suva, University of the South Pacific, 1982.

Footsteps in the Sea—Christianity in Oceania Since World War II. Suva, University of the South Pacific, 1992.

Where Nets Were Cast—Christianity in Oceania Since World War II. Suva, University of the South Pacific, 1997.

Geddes, W. H., et al. *Atoll Economy: Social Change in Kiribati and Tuvalu, Islands on the Line Team Report No. 1*. Canberra, Australian National University Press, 1982.

Gewertz, Deborah B., and Errington, Frederick K. *Emerging Class in Papua New Guinea: The Telling of Difference*. Cambridge, Cambridge University Press, 2008.

Ghai, Y. *Law, Politics and Government in Pacific Island States*. Suva, University of the South Pacific, 1988.

Gill, W. W. *Cook Islands Customs*. Cook Islands, University of the South Pacific and the Ministry of Education, 1979.

Gille, Bernard, et Toullelan, Pierre Yves. *De la Conquête à l'Exode—Histoire des Océaniens et de leurs Migrations dans le Pacifique. Tome 1. Les Migrations Contraintes en Océanie, Terres de Colonisation et D'immigration*. Papeete, Tahiti, Au Vent des Iles, 1999.

Goetzfridt, Nicholas. *Indigenous Literature of Oceania—A Survey of Criticism and Interpretation*. Westport, CT, Greenwood Press, 1995.

Goodman, R., Lepani, C., and Morawetz, D. *The Economy of Papua New Guinea: An Independent Review*. Canberra, Development Studies Centre, Australian National University, 1985.

Gorman, G. E., and Mills, J. J. (Eds). *Fiji, World Bibliography, Volume 173*. Oxford, Clio Press, 1992.

Gostin, O. *Cash Cropping, Catholicism and Change: Resettlement among the Kuni of Papua*. Canberra, Development Studies Centre, Australian National University, 1986.

Grynberg, Roman. *Rules of Origin Issues in Pacific Island Development*. Canberra, Asia Pacific Press, Australian National University, 1998.

Gunson, W. N. (Ed.). *The Changing Pacific: Essays in Honour of H. E. Maude*. Melbourne, Oxford University Press, 1978.

Haley, Nicole, and May, R. J. (Eds). *Conflict and Resource Development in the Southern Highlands of Papua New Guinea*. Canberra, Australian National University Press, 2007.

Hanlon, David, and White, Geoffrey. *Voyaging through the Contemporary Pacific*. New York, NY, Rowman, Littlefield and Publishers, 2000.

Remaking Micronesia. Discourses Over Development in a Pacific Territory, 1944–1982. Honolulu, HI, University of Hawaii Press, 1998.

Harding, Thomas, Lockwood, Victoria, and Wallace, Ben (Eds). *Contemporary Pacific Societies: Studies in Development and Change*. Englewood Cliffs, Prentice Hall, 1993.

Hau'ofa, E., Naidu, V., and Waddell, E. (Eds). *A New Oceania: Rediscovering Our Sea of Islands*. Suva, University of the South Pacific, 1993.

Hayes, P., Zarskey, L., and Bello, W. *American Lake: Nuclear Peril in the Pacific*. Harmondsworth, Penguin, 1986.

Henningham, Stephen. *France and the South Pacific: A Contemporary History*. Sydney, Allen & Unwin, 1992.

Henningham, Stephen, and May, R. J. *Resources, Development and Politics in the Pacific Islands*. Bathurst, Crawford House Press, 1992.

Heyerdahl, Thor. *Green was the Earth on the Seventh Day*. London, Little Brown, 1997.

Hezel, F. X. *Strangers in Their Own Land: A Century of Colonial Rule in the Caroline and Marshall Islands*. Honolulu, HI, University of Hawaii Press, 1995.

The New Shape of Old Island Cultures—A Half Century of Social Change in Micronesia. Honolulu, HI, University of Hawaii Press, 2001.

Hintjens, Helen M., and Newitt, M. D. (Eds). *The Political Economy of Small Tropical Islands: The Importance of Being Small*. Exeter, University of Exeter Press, 1992.

Hongo, G. *Volcano: A Memoir of Hawai'i*. Washington, Knopf, 1995.

Hooper, Antony (Ed.). *Culture and Sustainable Development in the Pacific*. Canberra, Australian National University, 2000.

Howard, Michael. *Mining, Politics and Development in the South Pacific*. Boulder, Westview Press, 1991.

Howe, Kerry. *The Loyalty Islands—A History of Culture Contacts 1840–1900*. Honolulu, HI, University of Hawaii Press, 1977.

Where the waves fall: A new South Seas islands history from first settlement to colonial rule. Honolulu, HI, University of Hawaii Press, 1984.

Nature, Culture and History—The 'Knowing' of Oceania. Honolulu, HI, University of Hawaii Press, 2000.

Howe, Kerry, Kiste, Robert, and Lal, Brij (Eds). *Tides of History: The Pacific Islands in the Twentieth Century*. Sydney, Allen & Unwin, 1994.

Huffer, Elise, and So'o, Asofou (Eds). *Governance in Samoa*. Canberra, Asia Pacific Press, Australian National University, 2000.

Huntsman, Judith, and Hooper, Antony. *Tokelau, A Historical Ethnography*. Honolulu, HI, University of Hawaii Press, 1997.

Huntsman, Judith, and Kalolo, Kelihiano. *The Future of Tokelau: Decolonising Agendas, 1975–2006*. Honolulu, HI, University of Hawaii Press, 2007.

Institute of Pacific Studies, University of the South Pacific, and Ministry of Education, Training and Culture, Kiribati. *Kiribati: Aspects of History*. Suva, Institute of Pacific Studies, University of the South Pacific, 1979.

Jackson, Keith, and McRobie, Alan. *Historical Dictionary of New Zealand, No.5*. Metchuen, NJ, Scarecrow Press, 1996.

Jones, Peter D. *From Bikini to Belau: The Nuclear Colonization of the Pacific*. London, War Resisters International, 1988.

Jowitt, Anita, and Newton Cain, Tess. *Passage of Change: Law, Society and Governance in the Pacific*. Canberra, ANU EPress, 2011.

Kaeppler, Adrienne, and Nimmo, Arlo H. (Eds). *Directions in Pacific Traditional Literature*. Honolulu, HI, Bishop Museum Press, 1976.

Kamisese, Ratu. *The Pacific Way: a Memoir*. Honolulu, HI, University of Hawaii Press, 1997.

Kaul, M. M. *Pearls in the Ocean: Security Perspectives in the South-West Pacific*. New Delhi, UBSPD, 1993.

Keating, Elizabeth. *Power Sharing—Language, Rank, Gender and Social Space in Pohnpei, Micronesia*. Oxford, Oxford University Press, 1999.

Kernahan, M. *White Savages in the South Seas*. London, Verso, 1996.

King, D., and Ranck, S. *Papua New Guinea Atlas*. Robert Brown and University of Papua New Guinea, 1982.

Kirch, Vinton. P. (Ed.). *Island Societies—Archeological Approaches to Evolution and Transformation*. Cambridge, Cambridge University Press, 1986.

Kirch, Vinton P. *On the Road of the Wind—An Archeological History of the Pacific Islands before the European Contact*. Berkeley, CA, University of California Press, 2nd Edn, 2002.

Kirch, Vinton P., and Hunt, Terry L. (Eds). *Historical Ecology in the Pacific Islands: Prehistoric Environmental and Landscape Change*. New Haven, CT, Yale University Press, 1997.

Klein II, D. A. (Ed.). *Marshall Islands Legends and Stories*. Honolulu, HI, Bess Press, 2003.

Kluge, P. F. *The Edge of Paradise: America in Micronesia*. New York, NY, Random House, 1991.

Koburger, Charles W. *Pacific Turning Point: The Solomon Islands Campaign, 1942–1943*. London, Greenwood Publishing, 1995.

Kramer, Anthony. *The Samoa Islands*. Auckland, Pasifika Press, 1994.

Kramer, Augustin. *The Samoa Islands: Volume 1: Constitution, Pedigrees and Traditions*. Honolulu, HI, University of Hawaii, 2000.

Krieger, M. *Conversations with the Cannibals: the End of the Old Pacific*. Hopewell, NJ, Ecco Press, 1994.

Lacey, Rod. *'Whose voices are heard? Oral history and the Decolonisation of History'* in *Emerging from Empire?—Decolonisation in the Pacific*. Canberra, Australian National University, 1997, pp. 180–186.

Lal, Brij V. *Girmitiyas: the Origin of Fiji Indians*. Canberra, Journal of Pacific History, 1983.

Politics in Fiji: Studies in Contemporary History. Hawaii, Brigham Young University, Institute for Polynesian Studies, 1986.

Power and Prejudice: The Making of the Fiji Crisis. Wellington, New Zealand Institute of International Affairs, 1989.

A Vision for Change: A. D. Patel and the Politics of Fiji. Canberra, Asia Pacific Press, Australian National University, 1997.

Another Way: the Politics of Constitutional Reform in Post-Coup Fiji. Canberra, Australian National University, 1998.

Islands of Turmoil: Elections and Politics in Fiji. Canberra, Asia Pacific Press, Australian National University, 2006.

Lal, Brij V., and Fortune, K. (Eds). *The Pacific Islands: An Encyclopedia*. Honolulu, HI, University of Hawaii Press, 2000.

Broken Waves: A History of the Fiji Islands in the Twentieth Century. Honolulu, HI, University of Hawaii Press, 1992.

Larmour, Peter (Ed.). *Governance and Reform in the South Pacific*. Canberra, Development Studies Centre, Australian National University, 1997.

Larmour, Peter. *Foreign Flowers: Institutional Transfer and Good Governance in the Pacific Islands*. Honolulu, HI, University of Hawaii Press, 2005.

Latukefu, S. *Church and State in Tonga*. Canberra, Australian National University, 1974.

Laux, Claire. *Les Théocraties Missionnaires en Polynésie (Tahiti, Hawaii, Cook, Tonga, Gambier, Wallis et Futuna) au XIVè siècle. Des Cités de Dieu dans les Mers du Sud?* Paris, L'Harmattan, 2000.

101 mots pour comprendre l'Océanie. Nouméa, Ile de Lumière 2002.

Lawson, Stephanie. *Tradition versus Democracy in the South Pacific: Fiji, Tonga and Western Samoa*. Cambridge, Cambridge University Press, 1996.

Leckie, Jacqueline. *To Labour with the State: The Fiji Public Service Association*. Dunedin, University of Otago Press, 1997.

Leibowitz, A. *Defining Status: A Comprehensive Analysis of the United States' Territorial Relations*. Hingham, MA, Kluwer Academic Publishers, 1989.

Levantis, Theodore. *Papua New Guinea: employment, wages and economic development*. Canberra, Australian National University, 2000.

Levesque, Rodrigue (Ed.). *History of Micronesia. A Collection of Source Documents.*, Series, Québec, Levesque Publications.

Levine, Stephen. *Pacific Ways: Government and Politics in the Pacific Islands*. Wellington, Victoria University Press, 2010.

Levy, Neil M. *Micronesia Handbook*. Emeryville, CA, Moon Publications, 1999.

Lewis, D. *The Voyaging Stars—Secrets of the Pacific Island Navigators*. Sydney and London, Collins, 1978.

Lieber, M. D. (Ed.). *Exiles and Migrants in Oceania*. Honolulu, HI, University of Hawaii Press, 1977.

Lindstrom, Lamont. *Knowledge and Power in a South Pacific Society*. Washington, DC, Smithsonian Institute Press, 1990.

Lobban, Christopher, and Schefter, Maria. *Tropical Pacific Island Environments*. Hagåtña, University of Guam Press, 1998.

Löffler, E. *Geomorphology of Papua New Guinea*. Canberra, Australian National University, 1977.

Lummis, Trevor. *Life and Death in Eden: Pitcairn Island and the Bounty Mutineers*. London, Phoenix, 2000.

Lynch, John, and Mugler, France. *Pacific Languages in Education*. Suva, University of the South Pacific, 1996.

Macdonald, Barrie. *Cinderellas of the Empire: Towards a History of Kiribati and Tuvalu*. Suva, Institute of Pacific Studies, University of the South Pacific, 2002.

Macdonald, Ross. *Money Makes You Crazy: Custom and Change in the Solomon Islands*. Dunedin, Otago University Press, 2003.

Maclellan, Nic, and Chesneaux, Jean. *After Moruroa: France in the South Pacific*. Melbourne, Ocean Press, 1998.

Macpherson, Cluny, and Macpherson, La'avasa. *The Warm Winds of Change: Globalisation in Contemporary Samoa*. Auckland, Auckland University Press, 2010.

Mageo, Jeanette, M. *Cultural Memory—Reconfiguring History and Identity in the Postcolonial Pacific*. Honolulu, HI, University of Hawaii Press, 2001.

Mahadevan, Renuka, and Asafu-Adjaye, John. *Agricultural Development and Trade Liberalisation: Implications for a Small Island State*. Hauppauge, NY, Nova Science Publishers Inc, 2008.

Makihara, Miki, and Schieffelin, Bambi B. (Eds). *Consequences of Contact: Language Ideologies and Sociocultural Transformations in Pacific Societies*. Oxford, Oxford University Press, 2008.

Marchal, H (Ed.). *De Jade et de Nacre—Patrimonie Artistique Kanak*. Paris, Réunion des Musées Nationaux, 1990.

Marck, Jeff. *Topics in Polynesian Language and Culture History*. Canberra, Australian National University, 2000.

Marshall, M. *Beyond the Reef: The Transformation of a Micronesian Community*. Boulder, CO, Westview Press, 2004.

McConnel, Frasier (Ed.). *Papua New Guinea. World Bibliography, Volume 90*. Oxford, Clio Press, 1990.

McGillivray, Mark, Naudé, Wim, and Santos-Paulino, Amelia. 'Vulnerablility, Trade, Financial Flows and State Failure in Small Island Developing States', in *Journal of Development Studies, Volume 46, Issue 5*. Abingdon, Routledge, 2010.

McInnes, D. (Ed.). *Encyclopaedia of Papua New Guinea*. Mount Waverley, Dellasta Pacific, 1996.

McKnight, Tom Lee. *Oceania—The Geography of Australia, New Zealand and the Pacific Islands*. Englewood, Prentice Hall, 1995.

Meleisea, M. *Lalaga: A Short History of Western Samoa*. Suva, University of the South Pacific, 1987.

Meller, Norman. *Constitutionalism in Micronesia*. Honolulu, HI, University of Hawaii Press, 1986.

Miles, J., and Shaw, E. *The French Presence in the South Pacific 1838–1990*. Auckland, Greenpeace, 1990.

Miles, John. *Infectious Diseases—Colonising the Pacific?* Dunedin, University of Otago Press, 1997.

Mills, Peter R. *Hawaii's Russian Adventure: A New Look at Old History*. Honolulu, HI, University of Hawaii Press, 2002.

Mitchell, Jean, Noveczek, Irene, and Veitayaki, Joeli (Eds). *Pacific Voices: equity and sustainability in Pacific island fisheries*. Suva, Institute of Pacific Studies, University of the South Pacific, 2005.

Moala, Kalafi. *Island Kingdom Strikes Back: The Story of an Independent Island Newspaper*. Auckland, Pacmedia Publishers, 2003.

Moore, Clive. *Happy Isles in Crisis: the Historical Causes for a Failing State in the Solomon Islands 1998-2004*. Canberra, Asia Pacific Press, 2005.

Moorehead, A. *The Fatal Impact: The Invasion of the South Pacific 1767–1840*. London, Hamish Hamilton, 1966.

Morrell, W. P. *Britain in the Pacific Islands*. Oxford, Oxford University Press, 1960.

Murray, Spencer. *Pitcairn Island: The First 200 Years*. La Canada, CA, Bounty Sagas, 1992.

Naepels, Michel. *Histoires de Terres Kanakes—Conflits Fonciers et Rapports Sociaux dans la Région de Houaïlou (Nouvelle Calédonie)*. Paris, Belin, 1998.

Najita, Susan Y. *Decolonizing Cultures in the Pacific: Reading History and Trauma in Contemporary Fiction*. Abingdon, Routledge, 2006.

Narakobi, Bernard Mullu. *The Melanesian Way*. Suva, Institute of Pacific Studies University, 1980.

Neemia, U. *Cooperation and Conflict: Costs, Benefits and National Interests in Pacific Regional Cooperation*. Suva, University of the South Pacific, Institute of Pacific Studies, 1986.

Newbury, C. *Tahiti Nui*. Honolulu, HI, University of Hawaii Press, 1980.

New Politics in the South Pacific. Suva, Institute of Pacific Studies, 1994.

Nicolson, Robert. *The Pitcairners*. Honolulu, HI, University of Hawaii Press, 1997.

Nordyke, E. C. *The Peopling of Hawaii*. Honolulu, HI, University of Hawaii Press, 1977.

Nunn, Patrick, and Waddell Eric (Eds). *The Margin Fades—Geographical Itineraries on a World of Islands*. Suva, University of the South Pacific, 1994.

O'Callaghan, Mary-Louise. *Enemies Within: Papua New Guinea, Australia and the Sandline Crisis*. Sydney, Doubleday Australia, 1998.

Oliver, Douglas L. *Native Cultures of the Pacific Islands*. Honolulu, HI, University of Hawaii Press, 1989.

The Pacific Islands. Honolulu, HI, University of Hawaii Press, 1989.

Black Islanders—A Personal Perspective of Bougainville 1937–1991. Melbourne, Hyland House Publishing, 1991.

Polynesia in Early Historic Times. Honolulu, HI, University of Hawaii Press, 2002.

Otto, Ton, and Borsboom, Ad. *Cultural Dynamics of Religious Change in Oceania*. Leiden, Netherlands, KITLV Press, 1997.

Overton, John, and Scheyvens, Regina (Eds). *Strategies for Sustainable Development—Experiences from the Pacific*. Sydney, University of New South Wales Press, 1999.

Papoutsaki, Evangelia, and Harris, Usha Sundar. *South Pacific Islands Communication: Regional Perspectives, Local Issues*. Singapore, Institute of Southeast Asian Studies, 2008.

Parmentier, R. J. *The Sacred Remains: Myth, History and Polity in Belau*. Chicago, University of Chicago Press, 1987.

Peltzer, Louise. *Chronologie des événements politiques, sociaux et culturels de Tahiti et des archipels de la Polynésie française*. Papeete, Au Vent des Iles, 2002.

Peterson, G. *Ethnicity and Interest at the 1990 Federated States of Micronesia Constitutional Convention*. Canberra, Australian National University, 1994.

Pitts, Maxine. *Crime, Corruption and Capacity in Papua New Guinea*. Canberra, Asia Pacific Press, Australian National University, 2002.

Poirine, Bernard. *Les Petites Economies Insulaires: Théories et Stratégies de Développement*. Paris, L'Harmattan, 1995.

Pollock, Nancy J. *These Roots Remain: Food Habits in Islands of the Central and Eastern Pacific since Western Contact*. Honolulu, HI, University of Hawaii Press, 1992.

Poyer, Lin, Falgout, Suzanne, and Carucci, Laurence, M. (Eds). *The Typhoon of War, Micronesian Experiences of the Pacific War*. Honolulu, HI, University of Hawaii Press, 2001.

Prasad, Biman, C., and Tisdell, Clem. *Institutions, Economic Performance and Sustainable Development: A Case Study of the Fiji Islands*. Suva, University of the South Pacific, 2006.

Quadling, P. *Bougainville—The Mine and the People*. Sydney, Centre for Independent Studies, 1991.

Quanchi, M. *Atlas of the Pacific Islands*. Honolulu, HI, Bess Press, 2003.

Quanchi, M., and Adams, R. (Eds). *Culture Contact in the Pacific: Essays on Contact Encounter and Response*. New York, Cambridge University Press, 1992.

Rainier, Chris, and Taylor, Meg. *Where Masks Still Dance: New Guinea*. London, Little, Brown, 1997.

Rannels, J. *PNG—A Modern Fact Book on Papua New Guinea*. Melbourne, Oxford University Press, 1995.

Rapaport, Moshe (Ed.). *The Pacific Islands—Environment and Society*. Hawaii, HI, University of Hawaii Press, 1999.

Ravuvu, A. D. *Development or Dependence: The Pattern of Change in a Fijian Village*. Suva, Institute of Pacific Studies, University of the South Pacific, 1988.

Regan, Anthony, and Griffin, Helga. *Bougainville Before the Conflict*. Canberra, Pandanus Books, 2005.

Regenvanu, Sethy. *Laef Blong Mi: From Village to Nation*. Suva, Institute of Pacific Studies, University of the South Pacific, 2004.

Reid, Anthony (Ed.). *The Chinese Diaspora in the Pacific*. Aldershot, Ashgate, 2008.

Rensel, J. and Rodman, M. *Home in the Islands: housing and social change in the Pacific*. Honolulu, HI, University of Hawaii Press, 1998.

Revue Tiers-Monde. *Le Pacifique Insulaire—Nations, Aides, Espaces, Numéro Special de la Revue Tiers-Monde, Tome XXXVIII, No. 149*. Paris, Université de Paris, 1997.

Ridgell, Reilly. *Pacific Nations and Territories*. Honolulu, HI, University of Hawaii Press, 1998.

Rio, Knut Mikjel. *The Power of Perspective: Social Ontology and Agency on Ambrym Island, Vanuatu*. Oxford, Berghahn Books, 2007.

Robert, Craig, and King, Frank. *Historical Dictionary of Oceania*. London, Greenwood Press, 1981.

Robie, D. *Eyes of Fire: The Last Voyage of the Rainbow Warrior*. Auckland, Lindon Publishing, 1986.

Robie, D. (Ed.). *Tu Galala—Social Change in the Pacific*. Wellington, Bridget Williams Books, 1992.

Robillard, A. B. (Ed.). *Social Change in the Pacific Islands*. London, Kegan Paul International, 1992.

Rodman, Margaret C. *Houses Far From Home—British Colonial Space in the New Hebrides*. Honolulu, HI, University of Hawaii Press, 2001.

Rogers, R. F. *Destiny's Landfall: A History of Guam*. Honolulu, HI, University of Hawaii Press, 1996.

Rose, R. G. *Hawaii: The Royal Isles*. Honolulu, HI, Bishop Museum, 1980.

Ross, K. *Regional Security in the South Pacific: the Quarter-Century 1970–95*. Canberra, Strategic and Defence Studies Centre, Australian National University, 1993.

Rubinstein, H. J., and Zimmet, P. *Phosphate, Wealth and Health in Nauru: a study of lifestyle change*. Caulfield, Brolga Press, 1993.

Rumsey, Alan, and Weiner, James. *Emplaced Myth—Space, Narrative and Knowledge in Aboriginal Australia and Papua New Guinea*. Honolulu, HI, University of Hawaii Press, 2001.

Sacks, O. *The Island of the Colorblind*. London, Picador, 1997.

Saffu, Y. (Ed.). *The 1992 Papua New Guinea Election—Change and Continuity in Electoral Politics*. Canberra, Australian National University, 1996.

Sahlins, M. *How 'Natives' Think: About Captain Cook, For Example*. Chicago, University of Chicago, 1996.

Samson, Jane. *Imperial Benevolence: Making British Authority in the Pacific Islands*. Honolulu, HI, University of Hawaii Press, 1998.

Sand, Christophe. *Le Temps d'Avant—La Préhistoire de la Nouvelle Calédonie*. Paris, L'Harmattan, 1995.

Saura, Bruno. *Tinito, la communauté chinoise de Tahiti: installation, structuration, intégration*. Papeete, Au Vent des Iles, 2002.

Des Tahitiens, des français. Leurs représentations réciproques aujourd'hui. Papeete, Au Vent des Iles, 2004.

Scarr, Deryck. *A History of the Pacific Islands: Passages through Tropical Time*. London, Curzon Press, 2001.

Schoeffel, Penelope. *Sociocultural Issues and Economic Development in the Pacific Islands*. Manila, Asian Development Bank, Pacific Studies Series, 1996.

Segal, G. *Rethinking the Pacific*. London, Oxford University Press, 1990.

Seward, Robert. *Radio Happy Isles: Media and Politics at Play in the Pacific*. Honolulu, HI, University of Hawaii Press, 1998.

Sharphan, J. *Rabuka of Fiji: the Authorised Biography of Major-General Sitiveni Rabuka*. Queensland, Central Queensland University Press, 2000.

Shennan, Jennifer, and Tekenimatang, Makin Corrie (Eds). *One and a Half Pacific Islands: Stories the Banaban People Tell of Themselves*. Wellington, Victoria University Press, 2005.

Shineberg, Dorothy. *They came for Santalwood—A Study of the Santalwood Trade in the South-West Pacific, 1830–1865*. Melbourne, Melbourne University Press, 1967.

The People Trade—Pacific Island Laborers and New Caledonia, 1865–1930, Pacific Island Monograph series No.16. Honolulu, HI, University of Hawaii Press, 1999.

Short, F. G. *Sinners and Sandalwood*. North Leura, NSW, Jomaru Press, 1997.

Short, Iaveta, Crocombe, Ron, and Herrmann, John. *Reforming the Political System of the Cook Islands: Preparing for the Challenges of the 21st Century*. Suva, Institute of Pacific Studies, University of the South Pacific, 1998.

Siaguru, Sir Anthony. *In-House: In Papua New Guinea with Anthony Siaguru*. Canberra, Asia Pacific Press, Australian National University, 2002.

Singh, Rup. *A Macroeconometric Model for Fiji*. Hauppauge, NY, Nova Science Publishers Inc, 2008.

Sissons, J. *Nation and Destination: Creating a Cook Islands Identity*. Suva, Institute of Pacific Studies, University of South Pacific, 1999.

Skully, M. T. (Ed.). *Financial Institutions and Markets in the Southwest Pacific*. London, Macmillan, 1985.

Skully, M. T., and Fairbairn, T. I. J. *Private Sector Development in the South Pacific: Options for Donor Assistance*. Sydney, Centre for South Pacific Studies, University of New South Wales, 1992.

Smith, Bernard. *European Vision and the South Pacific*. New Haven, CT, Yale University Press, 1989.

Smith, Gary. *Micronesia: Decolonization and US Military Interests in the Trust Territories of the Pacific Islands*. Canberra, Australian National University, 1991.

Smith, R. A., and Meehl, G. A. *Pacific Legacy*. New York, Abbeville Press, 2003.

Somare, M. T. *Sana, an Autobiography*. Port Moresby, Niugini Press, 1975.

So'o, Asofou. *Universal Suffrage in Western Samoa: the 1991 General Elections*. Canberra, Australian National University, 1994.

Spate, O. H. K. *The Pacific Since Magellan*. Canberra, Australian National University. Vol. 1: The Spanish Lake, 1981; Vol. 2: Monopolists and Freebooters, 1983.

Speiser, F. *Ethnology of Vanuatu*. Bathurst, NSW, Crawford House Press, 1991.

Spickard, Paul (Ed.). *Pacific Diaspora: island peoples in the United States and across the Pacific*. Honolulu, HI, University of Hawaii Press, 2002.

Stanley, D. *South Pacific Handbook*. Emeryville, CA, Moon Publications, 1989.

Tahiti—Polynesia Handbook. Emeryville, CA, Moon Publications, 1999.

Fiji Islands Handbook. Emeryville, CA, Moon Publications, 2001.

Tahiti, including the Cook Islands. Emeryville, CA, Moon Publications, 2003.

Stewart, Pamela J., and Strathern, Andrew. *Religious and Ritual Change: Cosmologies and Histories*. Durham, NC, Carolina Academic Press, 2009.

Subramani. *South Pacific Literature—From Myth to Fabulation*. Suva, Institute of Pacific Studies, University of the South Pacific, 1992.

Swain, Tony, and Trompf, Gary. *The Religions of Oceania*. London, Routledge, 1995.

Syed, Saifullah, and Mataio, Ngatokorua. *Agriculture in the Cook Islands—New Directions*. Suva, Institute of Pacific Studies, and University of the South Pacific, 1993.

Tait, M. (Ed.). *The Papua New Guinea Handbook*. Canberra, Australian National University, irregular.

Taylor, M. (Ed.). *Fiji: Future Imperfect?* Sydney, Allen & Unwin, 1987.

Tcherkézoff, Serge, and Douaire-Marsaudon, Françoise (Eds). *The Changing South Pacific: Identities and Transformations*. Canberra, Pandanus Books, 2005.

Temu, Ila (Ed.). *Papua New Guinea: a 20/20 vision*. Canberra, Australian National University, 1997.

Terrell, J. E. *Prehistory in the Pacific Islands: a study in variation in language, customs and human biology*. Cambridge, Cambridge University Press, 1988.

Thakur, R. (Ed.). *The South Pacific: Problems, issues and prospects*. Macmillan and the University of Otago, 1991.

Thawley, John (Ed.). *Australasia and South Pacific Islands Bibliography, Area Bibliographies No. 12*. London and Lanham, MD, Scarecrow Press, 1997.

Thomas, Nicholas. *In Oceania: Visions, Artifacts, Histories*. Durham, NC/London, Duke University Press, 1997.

Marquesan Societies—Inequality and Political Transformation in Eastern Polynesia. Oxford, Clarendon Press, 1990.

Islanders—The Pacific in the Age of Empire. New Haven, CT, Yale University Press, 2010.

Tjibaou, Jean-Marie. *La Presence Kanak*. Paris, O. Jacob, 1996.

Tjibaou, Jean-Marie, and Missotte, P. *Kanak, Melanésien de Nouvelle Calédonie*. Papeete, Tahiti, Les Editions du Pacifique, 1976.

Kanaké—the Melanesian Way. Papeete,Les Editions du Pacifique, with Suva, Institute of Pacific Studies, University of the South Pacific, 1982.

Tolron, Francine. *La Nouvelle-Zélande—Histoire et Représentations*. Avignon, Université d'Avignon, 2000.

Toohey, John. *Captain Bligh's Portable Nightmare*. London, Fourth Estate, 1998.

Treadgold, M. L. *Bounteous Bestowal: The Economic History of Norfolk Island*. Canberra, Development Studies Centre, Australian National University, 1988.

Trnka, Susanna. *State of Suffering: Political Violence and Community Survival in Fiji*. Ithaca, NY, Cornell University Press, 2008.

Tudor, J. (Ed.). *Pacific Islands Year Book and Who's Who*. Sydney, Pacific Publications, Ltd.

Turner, Ann (Ed.). *Historical Dictionary of Papua New Guinea No.4*. Metuchen, NJ, Scarecrow Press, 1994.

University of the South Pacific. *South Pacific Bibliography 1981, 1982, 1983, 1984, 1985, 1988, 1989-90, 1991, 1992–93, 1994–95*. Suva, Pacific Information Centre, University of the South Pacific.

South Pacific Bibliography 1996–97. Suva, Pacific Information Centre, University of the South Pacific, 1998.

Uriam, K. K. *In Their Own Words—History and Society in Gilbertese Oral Tradition*. Canberra, Journal of Pacific History, 1996.

Usher, L. *Letters from Fiji 1987–1990*. Suva, Fiji Times Ltd, 1992.

Viviani, N. *Nauru*. Canberra, Australian National University, 1970.

Vltchek, André. *Oceania*. Groningen, V.O.F. Expathos, 2009.

Waddell,Eric. *Jean-Marie Tjibaou: Kanak Witness To The World: An Intellectual Biography*. Honolulu, HI, University of Hawaii Press, 2008.

Waiko, John Dademo. *A Short History of Papua New Guinea*. Oxford, Oxford University Press, 1995.

Walker, Scott. 'Human Rights and South Pacific: A New Voice in the Global Dialogue', in *Journal of Human Rights, Volume 10, Issue 2*. Abingdon, Routledge, 2011.

Ward, R. G. (Ed.). *Man in the Pacific Islands: Essays on Geographical Change in the Pacific Islands*. Oxford, Clarendon Press, 1972.

Ward, R. G., and Kingdom, Elizabeth (Eds). *Land, Custom and Practice in the South Pacific*. Cambridge, Cambridge University Press, 2007.

Ward, R. G., and Proctor, A. W. *South Pacific Agriculture: Choices and Constraints. South Pacific Agricultural Survey 1979*. Canberra, Australian National University, and Asian Development Bank, 1980.

Weeramantry, C. *Nauru—Environmental Damage Under International Trusteeship*. Melbourne, Oxford University Press, 1992.

Weightman, B. *Agriculture in Vanuatu: A Historical Review*. Cheam, British Friends of Vanuatu, 1989.

Weir, Tony, and Virani, Zahira. 'Three Linked Risks for Development in the Pacific Islands: Climate Change, Disasters and Conflict', in *Climate and Development, Volume 3, Issue 3*. Abingdon, Taylor and Francis, 2011.

Wenkam, R., and Baker, B. *Micronesia*. Honolulu, HI, University of Hawaii Press, 1971.

White, Geoffrey M. *Identity Through History*. Cambridge, Cambridge University Press, 2003.

White, Geoffrey M., and Lindstrom, Lamont (Eds). *Chiefs Today—Traditional Pacific Leadership and the Postcolonial State*. Cambridge, Cambridge University Press, 1998.

Williams, Glyndwr. *Buccaneers, Explorers and Settlers: British Enterprise and Encounters in the Pacific, 1670–1800*. Aldershot, Ashgate, 2005.

Wilson, Lynn. *Speaking to Power: Gender and Politics in the Western Pacific*. New York, Routledge, 1995.

Wilson, Margaret, and Hunt, Paul (Eds). *Culture, Rights and Cultural Rights: Perspectives from the South Pacific*. Wellington, Huia Publishers, 2006.

Winchester, S. *The Pacific*. London, Hutchinson, 1991.

Wittersheim, Eric. *Melanesian Elites and Modern Politics in New Caledonia and Vanuatu, National Centre for Development Studies, Discussion and Policy Papers, No.3*. Canberra, Australian University Press, 1998.

Wurm, S. A., and Hattori, S. *Language Atlas of the Pacific Area. Part 1: New Guinea Area, Oceania, Australia*. Canberra, Australian Academy of the Humanities, and Tokyo, Japan Academy, Pacific Linguistics Series C, No. 66, 1981.

THE PHILIPPINES

Physical and Social Geography

HARVEY DEMAINE

The land area of the 7,100 islands that constitute the Republic of the Philippines totals 300,000 sq km (115,831 sq miles). Many of these multitudinous islands are uninhabited. With the intervening seas, most of which are classified as Philippine territorial waters, the country extends over a considerably larger area, from above 18°N to below 6°N, lying between the South China Sea and the Pacific Ocean. The two largest islands, namely Luzon in the north, covering 104,688 sq km, and Mindanao in the south, with an area of 94,630 sq km, account for 66% of the Philippines' territory, and this figure exceeds 92% if the next nine largest (Samar, Negros, Palawan, Panay, Mindoro, Leyte, Cebu, Bohol and Masbate) are also included.

PHYSICAL FEATURES

The Philippines forms part of the vast series of island arcs that fringe the East Asian mainland and also include Japan, the Ryukyus and Taiwan to the north, and extend into Sulawesi, Papua (formerly Irian Jaya) and other Indonesian territories to the south. Two main and nearly parallel lines of Tertiary folding run roughly north–south through Luzon, extend approximately north-west–south-east through the smaller islands surrounding the Sabayan, Visayan and Mindoro seas, and resume a north–south trend in Mindanao. A less pronounced north-east–south-west pair extend from the central Philippines through Panay and the smaller islands of the Sulu archipelago, ultimately linking up with the similar Tertiary structures of the north-eastern tip of Borneo.

These major lines of folding largely determine the broad pattern of relief throughout the country. More than a dozen major volcanoes are still active. Nearly all the larger islands have interior mountain ranges, typically attaining heights of 1,200 m–2,400 m above sea-level, but, apart from narrow strips of coastal plain, few have any extensive lowlands. The central plain of Luzon, which represents the only significant exception, has therefore assumed a dominant role.

CLIMATE

Owing to its mountainous character and its alignment across the south-west monsoon and the north-east trade winds, the Philippines shows considerable regional variation in both the total amount and the seasonal incidence of rainfall. Thus, in general, the western side of the country receives most of its rain during the period of the south-west monsoon (late June–late September) whereas on most of the eastern side the wettest period of the year is from November to March when the influence of the north-east trades is at its greatest, although here, in contrast to the west, there is no true dry season. These differences can be seen by comparing Manila (on the west side of Luzon), which, out of an annual total of 2,100 mm, receives 1,100 mm in July–September and only 150 mm in December–April, with Surigao (in the north-east of Mindanao), which receives an annual total of 3,560 mm, 2,230 mm between the months of November and March, but with no monthly total falling below the August figure of 120 mm. However, in some sheltered valleys annual totals may be as low as 1,020 mm, which, in association with mean annual sea-level temperatures that are rarely much below 26.7°C (80°F) anywhere in the country, makes farming distinctly precarious. On the other hand, a different kind of climatic hazard affects many of the more exposed parts of the country as a result of their exposure to typhoons, which are most common in the later months of the year and tend to be most severe in eastern Luzon and Samar.

NATURAL RESOURCES

The central lowlands of Luzon provide by far the best major food-producing region within the country, and although many of the smaller lowlands are also intensively cultivated, their soils are, in most cases, of only average fertility. The southern island of Mindanao has become more densely populated, and the once extensive resources of tropical hardwoods have been disappearing.

The cultivation of rice is important, but in several of the islands, partly because of their relatively low rainfall and partly because of the close cultural link with Latin America, maize is the leading food crop. Coconuts, bananas, pineapples and sugar cane are widely grown for export.

The Philippines has a fairly wide range of metallic mineral deposits, the most important of which are copper (with reserves mainly found on Cebu and at Marinduque), chromite, nickel, gold and silver. Petroleum was discovered off the island of Palawan in 1977, and new reserves were subsequently identified. Natural gas is produced, and coal is also extracted. Hydroelectric power and geothermal energy are significant, the latter being the product of the unstable geological structure of the archipelago.

POPULATION AND ETHNIC GROUPS

At September 1995 the country had an average population density of 228.7 per sq km, which was nearly double the South-East Asian average and, in the region, exceeded only by that of Singapore. The August 2007 census recorded a total population of 88,566,732, in comparison with the 68,616,536 recorded at the September 1995 census., By mid-2011, according to UN estimates, the population had risen to 94,852,031. With its average population density of 316.2 per sq km, that of the Philippines is among the highest in South-East Asia. The shortage of lowland means that much the greater part of the population is concentrated in a relatively small area, and, particularly in the lowlands of central Luzon, the resultant pressure has become a serious problem and is likely to remain so, owing to the high rate of population growth (estimated at 1.8% in 2005–10).

Despite the existence of several regional languages spoken by the lowland Filipinos, the latter, who form the great majority of the population, share what is essentially a common culture, which is much influenced by Roman Catholicism. Tagalog, the language of central Luzon, has been developed as a national language (Filipino), although English is also widely used. Other than the Christian Filipinos, the only large indigenous group comprises the Muslim Moros inhabiting the southern and south-western peripheries of the country, who form approximately 5% of the total population. There are small communities of animist hill peoples, principally in the remoter parts of Luzon and Mindanao, who together form perhaps 6% of the total. There is also an ethnic Chinese minority in the Philippines.

Manila is the nation's capital, with a population of 1,660,714 at the 2007 census. However, the boundaries of the administrative unit of Manila's National Capital region (NCR) encompass a large number of former towns and districts, including Quezon City (population of 2,679,450 in 2007), and contained a total population of 11,566,325 at the census. However, other macro-regions of the country also have their urban focuses, with Davao City in south-east Mindanao, Cebu City in the Visayas and Zamboanga City in south-west Mindanao being the largest.

History

MICHAEL PINCHES

Based on an earlier article by IAN BROWN

Revised by DONNA AMOROSOand for this edition by the editorial staff

HISTORICAL BACKGROUND

In March 1521 a Spanish expedition, led by the Portuguese navigator Fernão Magalhães (Ferdinand Magellan), which had sailed west from Spain in September 1519, in search of the Spice Islands, landed at Samar in the central Philippine archipelago. In April 1565 the first Spanish settlement was established in Cebu by Miguel López de Legaspi. By the early 1570s Spanish control extended over Cebu, Leyte, Panay, Mindoro and central Luzon; the capital of the new Spanish dominion was Manila, captured in May 1571. The extremely fragmented nature of indigenous political organization at that time made large-scale co-ordinated resistance impossible. Political authority was focused on the *barangay*, commonly a kinship community that contained between 30 and 100 families. These restricted communities were frequently at war with each other, but no nation-wide state organization emerged from these conflicts. Thus, the pre-colonial archipelago did not sustain the great indigenous empire, or powerful traditional kingdom, that provided a foundation for the modern nation-state in the rest of South-East Asia.

The principal aim of Spanish rule in the Philippines was religious conversion. In this, Spain exerted a profound influence over the indigenous population, although the animists of northern Luzon and, more particularly, the Muslims of Mindanao and Sulu effectively resisted Roman Catholicism; even in regions of widespread conversion, animist beliefs were by no means expelled. Spanish rule was financed primarily by the galleon trade; silver dollars and bullion were brought to Manila from Acapulco (Mexico) to be exchanged for Chinese silks, porcelain, bronzes and jade. The Spanish made little attempt to exploit the economic resources of the archipelago, and, by restriction and monopoly, prevented any other Europeans from doing so—at least until the beginning of the 19th century.

In 1834 the port of Manila was opened to unrestricted commerce, irrespective of nationality. Between 1855 and 1873 six provincial ports, including Iloilo and Cebu, were also opened, for the Spanish were now permitting other Westerners to engage in agriculture and manufacturing on the islands. From these initiatives there emerged the production and export of the crops—sugar, coconuts, Manila hemp (abaca) and tobacco—that were to become the foundation of the economy for the remaining decades of colonial rule and into the post-independence period. These economic changes had important repercussions, both socially and politically. An increase in agricultural production, from the middle of the 19th century onwards, encouraged the settlement of a vigorous Chinese entrepreneurial class in the regions. As time passed, a *mestizo*, or mixed race, élite emerged (sons of Chinese fathers and native mothers, brought up as natives and Roman Catholics). The *mestizo* derived their wealth and influence from land ownership, and frequently sent their children, known as *ilustrados* (enlightened ones), to universities in Manila and Europe. The *ilustrados* became the channels for Spanish culture and liberal thought in the Philippines. By the close of the 19th century they were also to challenge the repressive orthodoxy and exclusiveness of Spanish rule in the islands, as exposed in the writings of Dr José Rizal (1861–96). The *ilustrados* sought reform through a so-called 'Propaganda Movement', but the mass of rural and urban Filipinos, impoverished by loss of land, exploitative labouring wages and unemployment, were moving towards armed revolt against the colonial power.

The Philippine revolution erupted in late August 1896, launched by a secret society, the Katipunan (Association of Sons of the People), under the leadership of Andres Bonifacio, who had been born in the Tondo slum district of Manila. Although Rizal played no part in the revolt, he was subsequently seized by the Spanish, and tried on charges of rebellion, sedition and illicit association. In December 1896 he was executed by a firing squad. Rizal's death provoked a major upsurge in revolutionary fervour. The most important initial military successes against the Spanish were achieved in the province of Cavite, south of Manila, under the leadership of Emilio Aguinaldo, the mayor of the town of Kawit. That success ensured a shift in the leadership of the revolution, away from Bonifacio and his dispossessed followers, to Aguinaldo and the provincial landed élite, the *principalia*; divisions also emerged in the revolutionary movement at this time. In May 1897 Bonifacio was executed, having been sentenced to death by a military court that Aguinaldo had appointed. The struggle then turned against the Filipinos; and in December 1897 Aguinaldo and the *principalia* ceased hostilities, in return for exile in Hong Kong and a financial settlement. In the Philippines itself, the struggle was maintained.

In late April 1898 the USA declared war on Spain, following the sinking of the *USS Maine* in the harbour at Havana, Cuba. In May the US Asiatic Squadron sailed into Manila Bay and destroyed the Spanish fleet. Aguinaldo, with US encouragement and assistance, returned to the Philippines, and on 12 June 1898 proclaimed Philippine independence. However, from this time onwards, a rift developed between the USA and its Filipino 'allies'. The US armed forces colluded with the Spanish colonial administration to stage a mock battle for Manila, so that the capital would be surrendered solely to US forces. On 14 August 1898 the Spanish capitulated; in the following December Spain ceded the Philippines to the USA for the payment of US $20m., under the terms of the Treaty of Paris.

On 23 January 1899 the Philippine Republic was inaugurated at Malolos, and Aguinaldo was sworn in as President. Early in the following month skirmishes occurred between the republican army and US occupying forces, leading rapidly to open conflict. For a year the new Republic fiercely resisted the US forces, but by early 1900 Aguinaldo's troops had been forced into retreat, in the mountains of northern Luzon. When Aguinaldo was captured in March 1901, major resistance was at an end. In April Aguinaldo took his oath of allegiance to the USA, and urged his fellow Filipinos to do the same. However, sporadic fighting by guerrillas, still motivated by the vision of *kalayaan* (freedom), which had inspired the initial outbreak of revolution in late 1896, continued to occur during the following decade.

US RULE

Under US dominance, the Philippines became even more heavily dependent on agricultural exports, and the rural masses found no relief from rigorously exploitative conditions of tenancy. Superficially, the US political administration did appear to constitute a decisive break with the past. While the Spanish had denied Filipinos even the prospect of political advancement, the new US administration acted rapidly to make political and bureaucratic positions accessible to them. Municipal elections were instituted in 1901; provincial government elections in 1902; an elective Lower-House Legislature in 1907; and an Upper House in 1916. By 1903 Filipinos occupied 49% of bureaucratic positions, although mainly at the lower levels; by 1913 they accounted for 71% of such positions; and by 1928 virtually the whole colonial Government (from clerks to cabinet ministers) was controlled by Filipinos. Crucially, however, these appointees were drawn almost exclusively from the ranks of the *ilustrados*, who, as soon as the leadership of the revolution had been wrested from the dispossessed in early 1897, had begun to collaborate closely with the new colonial power. The USA had strongly reinforced the dominant position of the *ilustrados* within Filipino society, in the interests of effective colonial administration. It was primarily for this reason that no significant attempt was made to reduce the extremely high levels of tenancy in the major regions of export production, for land reform would have threatened to destroy the foundation of *ilustrado* wealth and influence. Even colonial education policy, which was characterized by a major expansion of educational opportunity in the islands, reinforced the position of the *ilustrados* and their US promoters: the use of English as the medium of instruction in schools, and the introduction of a US-style school curriculum, brought an influx of US cultural values into the Philippines, which, in time, dissipated the intense indigenous identity that had animated the Filipino masses during the revolution and the resistance to US occupation.

Filipino politics were dominated in the period of US administration by the Nacionalista Party (NP), led firstly by Sergio Osmeña, and then by Manuel L. Quezon; on numerous occasions the Nacionalista ranks were divided by the fierce personal ambitions of its leadership. In public, Nacionalista leaders fiercely demanded 'immediate, complete and absolute independence', but they were fully aware that they largely owed their power and privileged position to their relationship with the USA. As the prosperity of the islands increasingly came to depend on the free entry of its agricultural exports to the US market, dependence on the colonial power was reinforced. By the 1930s, whatever their public stance, the élite regarded the prospect of independence with increasing unease.

In the event, Philippine independence was secured less by Filipino agitation than by the USA's domestic rejection of its colonial role. Important elements in US society found it difficult to reconcile the proud heritage of independence in the USA with the acquisition of empire. As the USA plunged deeply into depression at the end of the 1920s, these elements were joined by the farming and labour lobbies in demanding protection against the free import of Philippine agricultural commodities—or, in effect, Philippine independence.

Under the Tydings-McDuffie Act, signed by President Franklin Roosevelt on 24 March 1934 and subsequently accepted by the Philippine legislature, the Philippines was to achieve full independence on 4 July 1946. This was to be preceded by a 10-year transitional period of internal self-government, during which the Philippine Commonwealth would remain under US control as far as foreign relations and national defence were concerned; the President of the USA would also be empowered to veto any constitutional amendment or any legislation affecting currency, coinage, imports or exports during this period. In July 1934 a commission was elected to draft a Philippine constitution. The Constitution was approved by the US President and ratified by the Filipino electorate in May 1935. The Philippine Commonwealth was formally inaugurated on 15 November 1935, with Manuel L. Quezon as President and Sergio Osmeña as Vice-President.

During the 1920s and 1930s abuses on the part of landowners led to the emergence of large peasant unions, principally in central Luzon; the founding of the Partido Komunista ng Pilipinas (PKP—the Communist Party of the Philippines) in 1930; and the establishment of the *Sakdal* (Accusation) movement, which campaigned against the inequitable distribution of property, excessive taxes, and the large landholdings of the Roman Catholic Church, and demanded complete and immediate independence. In May 1935 the *Sakdalistas*, drawn from the discontented peasantry in the provinces around Manila, began an uprising, but it was rapidly crushed. President Quezon responded to growing agrarian unrest by introducing a programme of 'Social Justice', which established, *inter alia*, minimum wages for industrial and agricultural labourers, and written contracts between landowners and tenants. However, Quezon's legislative programme proved virtually impossible to enforce against landed interests, who dominated both local administration and national politics.

In December 1941 Japanese forces landed in the Philippines. Manila was occupied in early January 1942. The political and bureaucratic élite remained largely intact during the occupation, except for Quezon, who escaped to Australia. On 14 October 1943 the Japanese declared the Philippines an independent Republic within the 'Greater East Asia Co-Prosperity Sphere'; the new President of the Republic was José P. Laurel. Japan's occupation did not go unchallenged. Particularly important here was the *Hukbalahap*, or *Huks* (People's Army Against Japan), formed in March 1942, and drawing its forces, in particular, from the militant peasant movement that had been approaching revolt in the late 1930s. Operating in central and southern Luzon, the *Huks* continuously harried Japanese forces. In October 1944 US forces, under Gen. Douglas MacArthur, landed on Leyte island; US troops entered Manila in early February 1945 and operations continued for several months thereafter. In many areas, the US military advance was prepared by guerrilla groups, under the leadership of former officers of the US Armed Forces in the Far East and the *Huks*.

THE PHILIPPINE REPUBLIC

With a major part of the country's physical capital destroyed by the occupation and liberation, with the export economy in urgent need of rehabilitation, and with Filipino political life riven with charges and denials of wartime collaboration with the Japanese, the Philippines moved towards the attainment of full political independence on 4 July 1946. In the mean time, interim Commonwealth rule was re-established on 27 February 1945, under President Sergio Osmeña, who had succeeded Quezon as head of the Government-in-exile on the latter's death in the USA in August 1944. In the presidential election of April 1946, Osmeña was narrowly defeated by Manuel Roxas (from the liberal wing of the NP), who had been a cabinet minister during the occupation, and a director of the wartime rice procurement agency which supplied the Japanese army, but who was now strongly supported by Gen. MacArthur. Roxas's principal concern was to secure the Philippines' economic relationship with the USA. In March 1947 the USA and the new Republic concluded an agreement on military bases, whereby the USA received a 99-year lease on 23 bases in the islands. The lease was shortened to 25 years in subsequent negotiations. The principal military bases were Subic Bay Naval Base and Clark Air Base, both situated on the main island of Luzon. This agreement controversially gave the US authorities extensive legal jurisdiction over Filipinos living within the bases.

Despite their resistance to the Japanese, the *Huks* were regarded with suspicion: the politicians who had collaborated with the Japanese during the war were aware that the *Huks'* open resistance could further expose them; landowners knew that, during the occupation, the *Huks* had been as ruthless with their class as with the Japanese; and the US Administration, as well as the Philippine government élite, recognized the strong communist inspiration of the *Huks*. As the war came to a close, these forces combined in a strenuous attempt to suppress the movement. *Huk* units were disarmed, usually by force. In mid-1945 a group of *Huks* was seized and executed by government forces, with the knowledge of the US military police; a major part of the leadership was arrested, but subsequently released. In the immediate post-war months the *Huks*, working principally through the opposition Democratic Alliance (DA), sought entry into formal politics. In the April 1946 presidential and congressional elections, the *Huks* supported President Osmeña, while seven DA candidates (including the *Huk* leader, Luis Taruc) were elected to the legislature by the central Luzon peasantry. In mid-1946 Taruc offered to negotiate a cease-fire agreement with the Government of President Roxas, but the negotiations broke down over the demand that *Huks* surrender their weapons. Roxas then engineered the exclusion of successful DA candidates from the legislature, while Philippine army and police units launched a fierce and brutal campaign against the *Huks*. On 6 March 1948 Roxas declared the *Hukbalahap* to be an illegal organization.

Roxas died suddenly in April 1948. He was succeeded by his Vice-President, Elpidio Quirino. The new President immediately sought a truce with the *Huks*: indeed, agreement for an amnesty and surrender of arms was reached, and Taruc was finally able to take his seat in the Philippine Congress. In

August, however, Taruc suddenly left Manila, accusing the authorities of duplicity, primarily over the surrender of arms. The *Huks* were now in open revolt. Taruc announced that he had become a member of the PKP, and in April 1949 he publicly declared, for the first time, that the *Hukbalahap* sought the overthrow of the Government.

Quirino sought re-election in 1949 as the Liberal candidate for the presidency, against the NP nominee, José Laurel, the wartime collaboration leader. After an election marred by fraud, violence and intimidation, Quirino was returned to office, to confront a deepening economic crisis and an intensified campaign of insurgency by the *Huks*. A new Secretary of National Defense, Ramon Magsaysay, pursued a dual policy: the excesses of the armed forces (which had done much to secure support for the *Huks* in rural districts) were sharply curtailed, and a programme for the rehabilitation of rebels who surrendered was instituted. In October 1950 the central committee of the *Hukbalahap* was seized in a number of army and police raids across Manila. The removal of a major part of the leadership, coupled with the Government's more calculated military strategy and more constructive response to rural grievances, including the first stage of a tenancy reform programme in Luzon, resulted in the elimination of the *Huks* as a political entity. In May 1954 Taruc surrendered to the authorities. The urgency of demands for genuine agrarian reform waned and little further progress was made.

The disintegration of the *Hukbalahap* secured Magsaysay's prominence in Quirino's Cabinet. When it became clear that Quirino would seek re-election in 1953, Magsaysay left the Liberal Party and became the presidential candidate of the Nacionalistas, winning a convincing majority. President Magsaysay reinforced the Philippines' relationship with the USA; in 1954 the Philippines became a founder-member of the US-inspired South East Asia Treaty Organization (SEATO), and in 1956 US parity with Filipinos in the exploitation of the Philippines' natural resources was extended to all economic activities until 1974, under the Laurel-Langley Agreement. In domestic policy, Magsaysay strongly emphasized his desire to improve the lot of the *tao* (common man) through land reform and agricultural and community development projects. When Magsaysay died in an air accident in March 1957 he was succeeded by his Vice-President, Carlos P. Garcia, who won the presidential election held later that year. Garcia's presidency was initially characterized by austerity measures, and by a policy of economic nationalism (the 'Filipino First' policy) that was intended to lessen the Philippines' economic dependence on the USA, in particular. However, as Garcia's term of office came to a close, his Government foundered on the issues of rampant corruption, graft and financial scandal. In the 1961 presidential election Garcia was defeated by the Liberal Party nominee, Diosdado Macapagal. The new President instituted far-reaching economic reforms, encouraged by the USA and the IMF. Macapagal's Government established a Philippine claim to Sabah, on the eve of its inclusion in the new Federation of Malaysia in August 1963. This act caused the Philippine Government to sever diplomatic relations with Malaysia in September; relations were not resumed until June 1966.

THE MARCOS YEARS

In the presidential election of November 1965, Macapagal was defeated by Ferdinand E. Marcos, the Senate President, who had earlier left the Liberal Party to become the Nacionalista candidate. During his first term there was an increase in government expenditure on infrastructure, financed by foreign loans. By the end of the 1960s the principal and interest payments fell due and the country confronted a balance of payments crisis, which was aggravated by massive election spending in 1969. Marcos was re-elected by a large majority. In the late 1960s and early 1970s student activists emerged, demanding social justice and national sovereignty. There was also an increasing challenge to central authority from the Moro National Liberation Front (MNLF), a Muslim secessionist movement based on the southern islands of Mindanao and Sulu. Dissension within the communists' ranks led in 1968 to a split in the PKP. A Maoist breakaway group, led by Jose Maria Sison, formed the Communist Party of the Philippines (CPP), whose military wing, the New People's Army (NPA), frequently clashed with government military forces. An umbrella organization, the National Democratic Front (NDF), which included the CPP, was formed in the early 1970s. The PKP, meanwhile, condemned the use of violence and continued to operate within the parliamentary framework.

Acts of political intimidation and violence, frequently perpetrated by private armies under the control of political figures, increased alarmingly after 1969. The number and size of student demonstrations escalated and they were violently dispersed, leaving scores of students dead. As the political and social fabric of the Republic disintegrated, a convention began the task of preparing a new constitution. Reports of corruption by Marcos and his wife, Imelda, were widespread and included allegations of bribery of members of the convention to extend Marcos's term of office, which, by the terms of the Constitution, had to end in 1973. In August 1971 many died when an opposition rally was bombed. Marcos suspended the writ of habeas corpus. In September 1972, claiming a conspiracy between right-wing oligarchs and Maoist revolutionaries, Marcos declared martial law. Leading left- and right-wing opponents to Marcos, including politicians and journalists, were arrested and detained, among them a former senator, Benigno S. Aquino, Jr. The new Constitution, which conferred the offices of both President and Prime Minister on Marcos (who was also empowered to determine when the interim National Assembly would be convened), received ratification in January 1973 from Citizens' Assemblies throughout the Philippines. Martial law continued. The first elections to the interim Assembly were held in April 1978; local elections followed, in January 1980. On both occasions, the ruling Kilusan Bagong Lipunan (KBL—New Society Movement—formed in 1978 by Marcos and other former NP members) was successful, although there were claims by the opposition of widespread electoral malpractice. Marcos followed his electoral success with a period of slight political relaxation; Benigno Aquino was released in May 1980, enabling him to undergo medical treatment in the USA. Martial law was ended in January 1981, although Marcos's powers remained largely intact. In the following April a national plebiscite approved constitutional amendments which, in effect, replaced the parliamentary form of regime with a mixed presidential-parliamentary Government, and César Virata was appointed Prime Minister.

In the mid-1970s the Muslim secessionist movement in the southern Philippines provoked a military confrontation between government troops and the MNLF. Although the secessionists were initially successful, the movement was neutralized in the late 1970s by the Tripoli Agreement, sponsored by Col Muammar al-Qaddafi of Libya. Marcos defeated the MNLF by ostensibly granting regional autonomy to the Muslim areas and by allegedly paying huge sums of money to some Moro leaders.

In August 1983 Benigno Aquino returned to the Philippines from exile in the USA. As he came down the steps of his aircraft, he was assassinated; the alleged assassin, Rolando Galman, was immediately shot by military guards. Benigno Aquino's death precipitated a major political crisis. Large-scale street demonstrations and labour strikes followed, demanding the resignation of Marcos. This pressure led to the appointment of an independent commission of inquiry into the assassination. In its report, published in October 1984, the commission concluded that Galman was not the assassin, and that Benigno Aquino had been the victim of a military conspiracy. It indicted 25 military officers (including the Chief of Staff of the Philippine Armed Forces, Gen. Fabian Ver), and a trial opened in February 1985.

It was widely believed that the President's immediate circle of associates, if not the President himself and his wife, Imelda, were implicated in Benigno Aquino's death. Rumours of the vast personal wealth that the Marcos family and their associates had accrued through questionable practices, and of the gross extravagance of Imelda Marcos, now began to circulate more openly. Human rights violations, including torture and killings, were documented by both the human rights organization Amnesty International and the US Congress. The communists and the legal opposition co-operated in daily demonstrations against the beleaguered regime. At the same time, the massively indebted national economy was on the verge of collapse. Domestic political instability caused foreign creditors to suspend the short-term loans that had sustained the economy from the late 1970s onwards. New investment was curtailed, and capital fled the country. The Government of the USA brought pressure to bear on Marcos, urging him to submit his regime to electoral test.

On 3 November 1985 Marcos announced that the next presidential election, scheduled for May 1987, would be brought forward to early 1986. Corazon Aquino (the widow of Benigno Aquino) was chosen as the presidential candidate of the United Nationalist Democratic Organization (UNIDO—an alliance of opposition groups formed in 1982), while Salvador Laurel, the President of the alliance, became its vice-presidential candidate. Corazon Aquino's candidacy had received particular support from Lakas ng Bayan (the People's Power Movement, founded by Benigno Aquino in 1978) and the Pilipino Democratic Party (PDP), which had formed an alliance (PDP-Laban) in 1983, and which formed part of UNIDO. During the election campaign Gen. Ver and other military escorts of Benigno Aquino were acquitted of murder, in a trial that appeared to have been manipulated by Marcos.

Confusion followed the election, which was held on 7 February 1986, when the two monitoring bodies, the National Movement for Free Elections (Namfrel), financed by the US-based National Endowment for Democracy, and the Government's Commission on Elections (Comelec), each alleged that the other had manipulated the enumeration of votes. Namfrel, basing its result on 70% of total votes, declared that Corazon Aquino had won a majority, while Comelec recorded Marcos in the lead from the outset, and completed the count, whereupon it declared Marcos's victory. A few days later, Marcos was recognized by the *Batasang Pambansa* (National Assembly) as the winner of the elections.

On 14 February 1986 a pastoral statement, issued by the Roman Catholic Church, declared that the election had been 'a fraud unparalleled in history'. Two days later Corazon Aquino announced a campaign of non-violent civil disobedience in protest at the outcome of the election. On the evening of 21 February Juan Ponce Enrile, the Minister of National Defense, retreated to his office at Camp Aguinaldo, where he decided to resist his arrest by Marcos, following news that a coup plot by members of the Rebolusyonaryong Alyansang Makabayan (RAM—Nationalist Revolutionary Alliance—also known as the Reform the Armed Forces Movement), a group of right-wing reformist military officers, had been discovered. He was joined at Camp Aguinaldo by Lt-Gen. (later Gen.) Fidel Ramos, the Deputy Chief of Staff of the armed forces, and on 22 February both men announced that they had withdrawn their support from Marcos. Following an appeal by Cardinal Jaime Sin, the Archbishop of Manila, for the populace to come to the aid of the two men, thousands of Filipinos flocked into the streets, effectively blocking the way of Marcos's troops. On 24 February the Government of the USA declared that it supported Enrile and Ramos. What had begun as a military revolt against Marcos had developed into a 'snap revolution', in which the strength of civilian support rendered Marcos's troops helpless. Enrile later declared that it was only because of the strength of civilian support for Corazon Aquino, manifested in 'people power', that he and Ramos had relinquished their own intention to form a government, including some civilians, and decided to ally with her. In spite of these events, Marcos insisted on a formal inauguration on 25 February, before being flown to safety in Hawaii, USA, together with his family and associates, in two aircraft supplied by the US Air Force.

THE GOVERNMENT OF CORAZON AQUINO

Corazon Aquino was inaugurated as President of the Philippines in a separate ceremony, also on 25 February 1986. Among those appointed to her Cabinet were Enrile, who retained the position of Minister of National Defense, and Ramos, who became the new Chief of Staff of the armed forces. Two new commissions were created: the Presidential Commission on Good Government, which was given the onerous task of recovering Marcos's ill-gotten wealth, and the Presidential Commission on Human Rights, which was formed to investigate allegations of violations of human rights under the Marcos regime, and to seek redress for the victims.

More than 500 political detainees were released within days of Aquino's inauguration (the release of communist leaders, including Jose Maria Sison, alarming the armed forces and the US Government); the right of habeas corpus was restored; censorship of the media was abolished; and elderly pro-Marcos military officers were retired. However, there was some concern that President Aquino's powers were virtually dictatorial: she abolished the legislature, under an interim Constitution, and demanded the resignation of several Supreme Court judges and dismissed local officials. She also abolished the position of Prime Minister, within a few days of conferring it on Laurel.

By mid-1986 there was growing doubt concerning the President's ability to produce a cohesive economic policy from the widely varying opinions represented within her administration. Civil unrest was a serious problem and street rioting by pro-Marcos supporters frequently required armed intervention by the authorities. Marcos himself maintained daily contact with his Manila supporters from his base in Hawaii, where he directed anti-Aquino operations. There were continuous rumours of impending political and military coups.

In June 1986 Aquino announced the beginning of formal negotiations with the outlawed NDF, which would aim to establish agreement for a cease-fire in the 17-year campaign by the NPA. However, the pessimistic attitude of both the armed forces and the NDF doomed the peace initiatives to failure and two temporary cease-fires in the second half of the year were broken. In addition, the new Government sought to end the 16-year secessionist war being conducted by the MNLF in the southern Philippines. In August Agapito Aquino, the President's brother-in-law, and Nur Misuari, the Chairman of the MNLF, met in Saudi Arabia and, as a result, the Aquino Government agreed to grant autonomy to four mainly Muslim-populated provinces in Mindanao. A month later, Misuari returned to the Philippines and agreed to a truce, although there was doubt as to whether this would be observed by some factions within the MNLF. The initiatives were criticized by another Muslim secessionist grouping, the Moro Islamic Liberation Front (MILF), which was not included in the negotiations but claimed a wider membership than the MNLF.

In July 1986, while Aquino was on a visit to Mindanao, Arturo Tolentino, Marcos's vice-presidential candidate in the February election, proclaimed himself acting president from the Manila Hotel, which had been seized by 300 rebel troops. He claimed to be acting on the instructions of Marcos and appointed a cabinet that included Enrile. The Minister of National Defense immediately dissociated himself from the rebels, and ordered troops loyal to Aquino to surround the hotel; Tolentino and his supporters surrendered. Over the next two months, however, disagreement within the new Government intensified. By mid-October Enrile and Laurel, with some support from Ramos, were insisting upon the holding of a new presidential election and the adoption of a more forceful policy against the insurgents. In early November, following his appearance at an anti-Aquino rally, there were rumours of an impending coup by Enrile and his army supporters. Tensions increased with the assassination of Rolando Olalia, a trade union leader and prominent opponent of Enrile. Subsequent investigations implicated officers close to Enrile. On the night of 22–23 November there was a poorly co-ordinated uprising by officers at several military camps. Aquino reacted swiftly, dismissing Enrile and demanding the resignation of the rest of the Cabinet.

A new Constitution was approved by Aquino's Cabinet on 12 October 1986, and was endorsed in a national referendum, held on 2 February 1987 by 76% of voters. In essence, the new charter returned the Philippines to the constitutional form that had operated (except for the war years) from 1935 to 1973, with a US-style bicameral legislature and an executive presidency. The House of Representatives was to have 200 directly elected members and up to 50 presidential 'appointees' chosen from party lists, interest groups (including labour and women's organizations) and tribal minorities. The members of the 24-

seat Senate were to be directly elected in national elections. The Constitution provided for an extension of the term of the Presidential Commission on Good Government and formally recognized 'People Power' organizations. Under the new Constitution, Aquino and Vice-President Laurel were given a mandate to govern until 30 June 1992. Subsequent Presidents would serve terms of six years, and would not be eligible for re-election. However, the Constitution did empower the President to declare martial law in times of national emergency. The Constitution also stipulated that there should be no installation of nuclear weapons in the Philippines, thus directly threatening the maintenance and future of the US military bases.

The weeks immediately prior to the holding of the constitutional referendum had been unusually tense. On 22 January 1987 some 10,000–15,000 demonstrators, gathered at the Mendiola Bridge in Manila in support of demands for accelerated land reforms, were attacked by government security forces, and at least 20 people were killed. The 'Mendiola Massacre' seriously damaged the reputation of the Aquino Government. The NDF immediately withdrew from peace talks with the Government. Civil unrest intensified during the following days, and on 27 January troops belonging to secret organizations within the armed forces attacked military and civilian targets in Manila. Troops loyal to Aquino quashed the insurrection within hours, although a complete surrender by the rebels did not take place until four days had elapsed. On 28 January US officials thwarted an attempt by Marcos to return to Manila in order to take advantage of the disorder resulting from the attempted coup. Thirteen officers and 359 troops were subsequently detained by Ramos, pending their trial by court martial. Aquino's position was considerably strengthened, both in her negotiations with the communists and in her relationship with the armed forces, by the strength of public support for the new Constitution. Shortly after the plebiscite, all members of the armed forces swore an oath of allegiance to the new Constitution; this was followed by an order disbanding military fraternities, such as the RAM, because they 'encouraged divisiveness'. Congressional elections held on 11 May resulted in a victory for Aquino's Lakas ng Bayan alliance, which secured 180 of the 200 elective seats in the House of Representatives and 22 of the 24 senatorial seats.

Meanwhile, talks between the Government and MNLF leaders in late 1986, under the auspices of the Organization of the Islamic Conference (OIC), resulted in an undertaking by MNLF leaders, in January 1987, to relinquish demands for complete independence in Mindanao and to accept autonomy. However, in western Mindanao fierce fighting ensued, instigated by members of the MILF. Although the new Constitution provided for the eventual granting of autonomy to Muslim provinces in Mindanao, MNLF leaders claimed that this would not be sufficient to meet their demands, and in March the MILF reiterated that it would not recognize any agreement between the Government and the MNLF concerning the future of Mindanao. Following a deadlock in talks regarding autonomy provisions, in August the Government announced that it would no longer consult MNLF leaders.

In April 1987 government forces overcame an abortive coup by rebel soldiers. In July Marcos was forbidden to leave Hawaii by US officials, following the discovery of a pro-Marcos coup plot in Manila; and in the same month the Philippine Government initiated legal proceedings against Marcos, his family and associates (including Enrile) in a Manila court, claiming damages of US $22,500m. for the sufferings of the Filipino people as a result of the Marcos Government's alleged corruption. Following the assassination of Jaime Ferrer, the Secretary of Local Government, by the NPA in August, there was an outbreak of strikes and violence in Manila. On 28 August Ramos and troops loyal to President Aquino averted a fifth attempted coup, when rebel officers, led by Col Gregorio Honasan (a former leader of the RAM and closely associated with Enrile), occupied the army headquarters. In subsequent fighting 53 people were killed. On the next day Honasan and his supporters fled, successfully evading capture until December.

In January 1988 Ramos was appointed Secretary of National Defense. The government campaign against communist insurgents was immediately intensified, although the President continued to resist demands from the armed forces that a state of emergency be declared. Among numerous CPP officials captured by the army were its General Secretary, Rafael Baylosis, and the Commander-in-Chief of the NPA, Romulo Kintanar (who escaped from custody in November). There were almost 2,000 deaths in insurgency-related violence during the first six months of 1988, and, despite the intensification of the government campaign, Aquino was criticized by the military for not dealing sufficiently robustly with rebel elements.

The politically sensitive issue of US military bases in the Philippines came to the fore in 1988. Under an agreement signed in 1983 by the US and Philippine Governments, the continued use of six military bases, including Clark Air Base and Subic Bay Naval Base (both on Luzon island), had been permitted until 1989. The 1987 Constitution stated that foreign military bases would not be allowed in the country after 1991, unless under the provisions of a treaty approved by the Senate and ratified by voters in a referendum. Despite the strong nationalist feelings aroused by this issue, the bases had proved a useful source of employment and government revenue, and negotiations for a two-year extension to 1991 were successfully concluded in October 1988. Under the new agreement, the Philippine Government was to receive annual economic and military aid totalling US $481m., representing almost 2.5 times the previous level of receipts. The USA also secured the right for its military aircraft and warships to use the Philippines' facilities without a contingent obligation to declare the presence of nuclear weaponry.

In June 1988 the Government introduced a Comprehensive Agrarian Reform Programme (CARP), providing for an extensive redistribution of agricultural lands, over a 10-year period, to untenured farmers and farm workers. However, the extended timetable, together with numerous exemptions and complicated provisions for legal appeals, seriously impeded its implementation. These provisions were included in the programme as a result of the numerical domination of Congress, particularly the House of Representatives, by landowners. Also in June the PDP and Lakas ng Bansa formed a new pro-Aquino alliance, the Laban ng Demokratikong Pilipino (LDP).

In August 1988 Vice-President Laurel announced his leadership of a broadly based opposition front, the Union for National Action, and demanded the President's resignation. He also initiated a campaign against alleged corruption in the Aquino Government and among members of the President's family. In May 1989 the NP was revived, with Laurel elected as President and Enrile appointed Secretary-General.

In February 1989 the NDF offered to begin peace talks with the Government, if Aquino agreed not to renew the lease on US bases after 1991. After the Government's refusal of this offer, attacks were made by the NPA on US personnel and facilities. During the year the Government responded to accusations of human rights abuses by exposing atrocities allegedly committed by the NPA. In June 1989 revelations of irregularities in the administration of the CARP gave further embarrassment to the Government. Aquino's ensuing attempts to appoint as Secretary for Agrarian Reform Miriam Defensor Santiago (who had previously been in charge of the Commission on Immigration and Deportation and who had a reputation for combating corruption) were repeatedly rejected by members of the Commission on Appointments, influenced by landowning interests.

In September 1989 the Philippine Government began the first of 35 planned civil suits against former President Marcos, in his absence, with the aim of regaining embezzled funds. At the end of the month, however, Marcos died in Hawaii. The Supreme Court prohibited (in the interests of national security) the return of Marcos's body for burial in the Philippines, as demanded by his supporters. (The trial of Imelda Marcos, on charges of fraud and of illegal transfer of stolen funds into the USA, began in New York in April 1990: she was acquitted of all charges in July.)

In November 1989 a plebiscite was held in 13 provinces and nine cities in Mindanao, on proposed legislation that envisaged the autonomy of these provinces and cities, with direct elections to a unicameral legislature in each province; this contrasted with the MNLF's demand for autonomy in 23 provinces, to be granted without a referendum. The MNLF appealed, with considerable success, to the Muslim population (about 28% of the inhabitants of the region) to abstain from participating in the referendum. The Christian inhabitants (about 66% of the regional population) were largely opposed to autonomy. Four provinces (Lanao del Sur, Maguindanao, Tawi-Tawi and Sulu) voted in favour of the government proposal and formed the Autonomous Region of Muslim Mindanao (ARMM).

In December 1989 an abortive coup was staged by members of two élite military units, the Marines and the Scout Rangers, in collusion with the illicit RAM and officers loyal to Marcos. Rebel soldiers captured an armed forces base and the air force headquarters, which enabled them to launch air-strikes on government strongholds and on the presidential palace. The progress of the coup prompted Aquino to request US air support to deter further aerial attacks by the rebels. This aim was achieved by the mere presence in the air of units of the US Air Force, which did not fire on rebel troops. Most of the rebel strongholds were captured within 24 hours. The coup was thought to involve many officers who had graduated with Honasan. Aquino subsequently accused Laurel and Enrile (who were both included in an eight-member provisional junta named by the rebels) of involvement in the coup attempt. Suspicion also fell on her estranged cousin, Eduardo Cojuangco, who had fled to the USA with Marcos in 1986 and returned secretly from exile shortly before the coup.

In February 1990 Enrile was arrested, on charges of 'rebellion complexed with murder'. He was also charged with harbouring Honasan, prior to the coup attempt. In March Rodolfo Aguinaldo, who had been suspended as Governor of Cagayan in January for supporting the attempted coup, launched an unsuccessful rebellion, following an attempt to arrest him. Arrests of those implicated in the attempted coup continued. In April Lt-Commdr Bilbastro Bibit, a suspected leader of the coup, was freed from prison by masked rebel soldiers. The soldiers claimed to be members of a military movement called the Young Officers' Union (YOU), which was alleged to have played an important role in the December 1989 coup attempt. In June 1990 the Supreme Court ordered the charge of 'rebellion complexed with murder' against Enrile and 22 other alleged rebels to be amended to 'simple rebellion' or 'illegal possession of firearms' since the original charge had been removed from the statute book in 1986 by presidential decree. Aguinaldo consequently surrendered and was formally charged.

In September 1990, following a trial lasting more than three years, a special court convicted 16 members of the armed forces of the murder of Benigno Aquino and Rolando Galman, the alleged assassin, and acquitted 20 defendants. However, it was recognized that those responsible for planning the assassination had not been brought to justice.

In November 1990 it was announced that all US fighter aircraft and more than 1,800 military personnel would be withdrawn from the Philippines by the end of 1991. It was also announced that the two sides were to negotiate a new agreement to replace the existing security treaty, drafted in 1947. In August 1991 the Philippines and the USA provisionally agreed a military bases treaty providing for a new 10-year lease on Subic Bay Naval Base, with generous US compensation for the Philippines. Aquino, the armed forces and many business groups campaigned to gain the constitutionally necessary support of a two-thirds' majority in the Senate. In September the NDF pledged an immediate cease-fire, pending a commitment by the Senate to reject the treaty. This commitment was subsequently given and the unilateral cease-fire duly implemented. Despite widespread popular support for the US installations, the Senate rejected the treaty by 12 votes to 11. However, the Government rescinded the formal notice on termination of the previous lease, which had been served in May 1990, effectively extending the lease for another year. Meanwhile, in July 1991 the armed forces had captured the NPA's most important base, Camp Venus in Sagada, Mountain Province, representing a major success in the struggle against the communist insurgency, and in early August Romulo Kintanar, the Commander-in-Chief of the NPA, became the 10th communist leader to be captured in two weeks. In September Lt-Gen. Lisandro Abadio, the Chief of Staff of the armed forces since April, suspended all operations against Honasan and other military rebels in a concerted attempt to achieve national reconciliation. Abadio met Honasan twice in August and released 68 rebel soldiers as a gesture of goodwill.

In July 1991 Aquino announced that Imelda Marcos and her family would be permitted to return to the Philippines, following a ruling of the Swiss Supreme Court in December 1990, which stated that the transfer of funds held in Swiss bank accounts to the Philippines was conditional on Imelda Marcos being brought to trial for fraud in a Philippine court before December 1991. In October Aquino relaxed the ban on the return of Marcos's remains, but stipulated that the burial should take place in his home province of Ilocos Norte, rather than in Manila, with no state or military honours. (Marcos's funeral finally took place in July 1993.) In November 1991 Imelda Marcos returned to the Philippines, and in December she pleaded 'not guilty' to charges of tax evasion. During the ensuing months more than 80 civil and criminal charges were brought against her. In July 1993 she was convicted of corruption and sentenced to 18 years' imprisonment (although she remained at liberty pending an appeal).

During 1991 there was much political manoeuvring with a view to the presidential election, to be held in May 1992. In April 1991 Ramos officially joined the ruling LDP to compete with the Speaker of the House of Representatives, Ramon Mitra, for the party nomination. Although Ramos's candidacy elicited much support from the commercial sector, it was Mitra who was selected as the LDP's presidential candidate in November. Ramos then resigned from the LDP and formed a new party, the Partido Lakas Tao (People Power Party—PPP).

In January 1992 President Aquino endorsed the presidential candidacy of Ramos, thus ending speculation that (despite repeated denials) she might seek re-election. In the same month Ramos discarded the PPP and registered a new party, EDSA-LDP, with the support of 25 former LDP members of Congress. (EDSA was the popular acronym for Epifanio de los Santos Avenue, the main site of the uprising of February 1986.) The party subsequently altered its title to Lakas ng EDSA (Power of EDSA), and formed an electoral alliance with Raul Manglapus's National Union of Christian Democrats (NUCD) and the Partido Democratiko Sosyalista ng Pilipinas (Philippine Democratic Socialist Party). The grouping was subsequently known as Lakas-NUCD.

On 11 May 1992 elections took place to select the President, Vice-President, 24 senators, 200 members of the House of Representatives and 17,014 local government councillors. Although more than 100 people were killed in election-related violence, the contest was regarded as relatively orderly, in comparison with previous occasions. Accusations of widespread electoral malpractice appeared to be largely unsubstantiated. Fidel Ramos emerged victorious, with only 23.6% of the votes. His closest rivals were Miriam Defensor Santiago (who was supported by the newly formed People's Reform Party, with 19.7%) and Eduardo Cojuangco (18.2%). Joseph Estrada (a senator and former film actor) was elected Vice-President. The success of Ramos and the high degree of support for Santiago (whose electoral campaign had emphasized the need for eradicating corruption) were regarded as a rejection of traditional party politics, since neither candidate was supported by a large-scale party organization. However, in the legislative elections, the LDP (the only party that had local bases in every province) won 16 of the 24 seats in the Senate, and 89 of the 200 elective seats in the House of Representatives.

THE GOVERNMENT OF FIDEL RAMOS

Ramos's ascent to the presidency was supported by three important political groups: retired yet still powerful military officers; business executives and technocrats, some of whom had served under the Aquino Government; and traditional politicians from Lakas-NUCD. The principal appointees to Ramos's Cabinet, established after his inauguration on 30 June 1992, consequently came from these groups. Ramos declared that his administration's priorities were to restore political and civil stability through national reconciliation and an amnesty programme; to deregulate the economy and encourage foreign investment by dismantling monopolies; and to curb criminality and corruption.

In July 1992 Lakas-NUCD gained leadership in Congress by expanding its membership through defections from the LDP and other parties and by forging a 'Rainbow Coalition' with the Liberal Party, Cojuangco's Nationalist People's Coalition (NPC) and the KBL to form a new majority. The Secretary-General of Lakas-NUCD, Jose de Venecia, a close ally of Ramos, assumed the post of Speaker of the House of Representatives. However, the LDP retained control of the Senate, with Neptali Gonzales remaining as Senate President. In the same month Ramos submitted to Congress four initiatives to support his reconciliation programme: the repeal of the Anti-Subversion Law, which would in effect legalize the CPP and similar organizations; the granting of an amnesty to 4,485 former rebels; the creation of a National Unification Commission (NUC) to help frame the Government's peace and amnesty strategy; and the review of all cases of rebels under detention or serving a sentence. (Congress formally approved these initiatives seven months later, in February 1993.) Ramos announced that his administration would pursue peace talks on three fronts: with the communist insurgents; the Muslim secessionists; and the military rebels.

In July 1992 Ramos appointed a member of the House of Representatives, Jose Yap, as an official emissary to the NDF, thus giving government sanction to informal talks that were already taking place between Yap and rebel representatives. In August Ramos authorized Yap to start exploratory talks with the expatriate leaders of the NDF, Luis Jalandoni and Jose Maria Sison, in the Netherlands. Ramos ordered the temporary release from prison of five communist leaders, including Romulo Kintanar and NDF negotiator Saturnino Ocampo, as well as 16 military rebels. Government and NDF emissaries held preliminary discussions in the Netherlands on 31 August and 1 September (the first since the failure of the peace talks in 1987). They agreed to recommend to their respective principals the resumption of formal talks in an attempt to secure a negotiated settlement of the insurgency. The Chairman of the NDF, Manuel Romero, immediately accepted the proposal, while Ramos promised to submit it to the NUC, which was created later in September. Ramos appointed Haydee Yorac, an elections commissioner and human rights lawyer, as head of the NUC, and selected members from the legislature (including Yap), the Cabinet and the Catholic and Protestant churches. The NUC began its series of public consultations in October. Meanwhile, a breakthrough was made in the negotiations with the MNLF: a member of the NUC met MNLF Chairman Nur Misuari in Tripoli, Libya, where the latter indicated his willingness to return home to hold peace talks with the Government. Two weeks later Ramos agreed to negotiate with the MNLF, with the OIC acting as an observer. At the end of October, following a series of separate talks with rebel leaders Honasan and Jose Maria Zumel, Yorac announced that the military rebels had submitted a framework for negotiations.

In November 1992 the USA completed its withdrawal from Subic Bay Naval Base and formally transferred command and control of the 56,000-ha facility to the Philippine Government. The Subic Bay Metropolitan Authority was established to oversee the conversion of the area to commercial use. In the same month Ramos urged a review of the 1951 Mutual Defense Treaty between the Philippines and the USA, declaring that it was not clear about the terms on which the USA would come to the aid of the Philippines in the event of an external attack.

In January 1993 Edgardo Angara of the LDP was elected as Senate President, replacing Neptali Gonzales (also of the LDP) after realignments in the chamber brought together LDP and Lakas-NUCD senators in a new pro-Ramos majority. In another show of political dominance, the gubernatorial candidate supported by Ramos, Liningding Pangandaman, won 72% of the votes cast at elections in the ARMM on 25 March.

The rift within the CPP, which had started in 1992 as a result of a Maoist purge initiated by the Chairman, Sison, worsened in 1993. In July the CPP's Metro Manila-Rizal organization declared its secession from the central leadership. Five months earlier, in November 1992, the party's Executive Committee had ordered the dissolution of the region's leading committee and its armed unit, the Alex Boncayao Brigade, purportedly for factionalism and military excesses. In October 1993 four communist leaders, including Romulo Kintanar, were expelled from the CPP and the NPA for refusing to recognize the authority of Sison.

Despite progress in early 1993, which had facilitated the reintegration of mutinous soldiers into active service, in February 1994 the military rebels announced that peace negotiations between the Government, the RAM and the YOU would continue to be suspended, pending the release of six military detainees. In the following month Ramos proclaimed a general amnesty for all rebels and for members of the security forces charged with offences committed during counter-insurgency operations, as recommended by the NUC. However, crimes of torture, arson, massacre, rape and robbery were exempted from the pardon. The RAM rejected the amnesty, on the grounds that it failed to address the causes of the rebellion, and reiterated its commitment to electoral, military, social and economic reform. Saturnino Ocampo also dismissed the proclamation, claiming that it was biased against communist rebels, since 80% of them had been charged with common crimes not covered by the amnesty.

The first formal negotiations between the Government and the MNLF took place in October 1993 in Jakarta, Indonesia, following two phases of exploratory talks earlier in the year. The MNLF demanded the creation of an autonomous Islamic state in the south, as provided for under the 1976 Tripoli Agreement. In November the two sides signed a memorandum of understanding (MOU) and an interim cease-fire was agreed. In January 1994 the terms of the cease-fire were agreed, stipulating that both government and rebel forces should remain in place and refrain from provocative action. Nur Misuari subsequently gave an assurance that MNLF demands for a transitional government in Mindanao would not affect the terms of office of the officials of the existing ARMM, due to expire in 1996. The second round of formal peace negotiations between the Government and the MNLF took place in Jakarta in April 1994.

In February 1994 a federal court in Hawaii awarded US $1,200m. in punitive damages to 10,000 Filipinos who had been tortured under President Marcos's administration. Imelda Marcos announced that she would appeal against the decision. Lawyers acting for the Philippine Government also filed counter-claims to the money, citing an Aquino decree that stipulated that all properties recovered from the Marcoses should be used only to finance the Government's agrarian reform programme. In January 1995 the Hawaiian court ordered the estate of Marcos to pay a further $774m. in compensatory damages to the 10,000 victims. At the end of that month the Philippine Supreme Court restored a freeze on the assets of more than 500 companies controlled by former associates of Marcos, which had been revoked on technical grounds in 1991. In August 1995 the Swiss authorities approved the transfer of about $475m. from Swiss bank accounts held by Marcos to an account in the Philippines.

In June 1994 the Government launched an offensive against Abu Sayyaf, an Islamist secessionist group, which was responsible for terrorist activities, including kidnapping, on the southern islands of Jolo and Basilan. In retaliation for the military assault, Abu Sayyaf planted a bomb in Zamboanga City, in south-western Mindanao, injuring 28 civilians. On the following day the armed forces captured the group's headquarters on Jolo Island, prompting Abu Sayyaf's seizure of 74 Christian hostages on Basilan. Many hostages were swiftly released, but 15 were killed in retaliation for government 'summary executions'. In mid-June all but one of the remaining 21 hostages were released following the alleged payment of a ransom by the local authority and the intercession of the MNLF. Government troops subsequently captured the group's main headquarters in Basilan; the remaining hostage, a Roman Catholic priest, was later released unharmed.

In July 1994 the majority leader of the House of Representatives, Ronaldo Zamora, defected from Lakas-NUCD to the NPC. A few days later he and 19 other members of the NPC resigned from the ruling coalition. However, in August Lakas-

NUCD and the LDP formed an alliance, known as Lakas-Laban; the ruling coalition, which also comprised the NP, the Liberal Party and PDP-Laban, thus controlled 158 of the 215 seats in the House of Representatives and 19 of the 23 occupied seats in the Senate. The priority of Lakas-Laban was to present a common list for the 12 seats in the Senate that were to be contested in 1995, but Ramos would also benefit from support in the Senate to expedite the passage of vital legislation.

In August 1994 the RAM agreed to support government programmes that would benefit the population. Later that month it signed an agreement with the ruling administration on electoral reform. In July 1995 negotiations between the Government, the RAM and the YOU resumed, following a three-month hiatus owing to the elections (see below). The military groupings pledged that they would refrain from organizing any further coup attempts.

In October 1994 negotiations resumed between the Government and the NDF in the Netherlands, but collapsed owing to disagreements over the NDF's insistence on granting immunity to government negotiators for future talks to be held in areas of the Philippines claimed by the NDF to be under its control. Peace talks in Belgium in June 1995 were curtailed by the Government following NDF demands for the release of a leading NDF member, Sotero Llamas, who had been arrested in May. The Government subsequently announced that it would guarantee safe passage to all members of the NDF panel for future negotiations in the Philippines, but that it was no longer prepared to attend meetings overseas, as the discussions frequently collapsed owing to the unreasonable demands made by the insurgents. The NDF rejected the new conditions, and Sison announced that peace negotiations would be postponed until the expiry of Ramos's term of office in 1998.

Negotiations between the Government and the MNLF proceeded in Mindanao in January 1995, at the end of which it was announced that the Government had agreed to the establishment of an MNLF provisional government in Mindanao, subject to congressional approval and the holding of a referendum. In April an attack by about 200 guerrillas on the largely Christian town of Ipil in Mindanao, in which more than 50 civilians were massacred, was attributed to Abu Sayyaf. Members of an MNLF splinter group, the Islamic Command Council, were alleged to have taken part in the attack on Ipil, which was denounced by Misuari as an attempt to sabotage the peace talks. However, Ramos pledged to continue negotiations with the MNLF.

On 8 May 1995 elections were held to contest 12 of the 24 seats in the Senate and the 204 elective seats in the House of Representatives; 76 provincial governorships and more than 17,000 local government positions were also contested. Prior to the elections, in which an estimated 80% of all eligible voters participated, more than 80 people were killed in campaign violence. In Mindanao widespread violence caused voting to be postponed until 27 May, when 30,000 troops were dispatched to the island to ensure security. In the event, the ruling coalition won the vast majority (about 70%) of seats in the House of Representatives and Lakas-Laban won nine of the 12 seats in the Senate. One of the three opposition seats was secured by Honasan, despite a campaign by Aquino against his candidacy. In his opening address to Congress in July Ramos urged the adoption of radical legislation to reduce public bureaucracy and eliminate corruption in the police force and in the judicial system.

In January 1996 the LDP withdrew from its alliance with Lakas-NUCD in protest against proposed anti-terrorist legislation, which it described as tantamount to the introduction of martial law, intended to facilitate Ramos's extension of his term of office. The withdrawal left Ramos with a minority in the Senate, which threatened to undermine his reform programme, but still with a substantial majority in the House of Representatives. Ramos's administration had become increasingly unpopular as a result of rising crime, a national rice shortage (owing largely to mismanagement) and increasing inflation. Furthermore, controversial extended value-added tax (VAT) legislation took effect in January, and in February an increase in the price of petrol was announced.

Formal peace negotiations continued between the Government and the MNLF in Jakarta. In August 1995 Misuari agreed for the first time to a referendum (as stipulated under the Constitution) prior to the establishment of an expanded autonomous zone in Mindanao, but demanded the immediate establishment of a provisional MNLF government to ensure that the referendum was conducted fairly. In April 1996 two bomb explosions in Zamboanga City were widely attributed to Abu Sayyaf or to other groups similarly opposed to the peace negotiations. In June it was announced that the MNLF and the Government had finally reached agreement on a proposal by Ramos for the establishment of a transitional administrative council, to be known as the Southern Philippines Council for Peace and Development (SPCPD), which was to derive powers from the Office of the President. The five-member SPCPD, which was to be headed by Misuari, was to co-ordinate peacekeeping and development efforts in 14 provinces and 10 cities in Mindanao, with the assistance of an 81-member Consultative Assembly and a religious advisory council. After a period of three years a referendum was to be conducted in each province and city to determine whether it would join the existing ARMM. (The MNLF had abandoned its demands for autonomy in 23 provinces in Mindanao.) In July government officials announced that, under the peace agreement, Muslims were to be allocated one cabinet post, and were to be granted representation in state-owned companies and constitutional commissions. In addition, Ramos offered to support the candidacy of Misuari in the forthcoming gubernatorial election in the ARMM.

In September 1996 the Government and the MNLF signed a final draft of the peace agreement in Jakarta; discussions continued regarding the integration of some 7,500 members of the MNLF's military wing into the national army and security forces (this commenced in March 1997), the establishment of a regional security force in Mindanao and the administrative structure of the SPCPD. The MILF refused to endorse the settlement, continuing to demand separate status for 23 provinces in Mindanao. On 9 September 1996 elections took place peacefully in Muslim Mindanao for the region's Governor and Assembly; Misuari, who, as agreed, contested the gubernatorial election with the support of Lakas-NUCD, was elected unopposed. (Critics of Misuari subsequently maintained that he was not permitted by law concurrently to chair the SPCPD and hold office as Governor of the ARMM.) Following his election as Governor, Misuari demanded reforms in the Senate whereby the number of seats would be increased from 24 to 72 (with 24 senators elected from Mindanao). In October he was officially appointed Chairman of the SPCPD.

MILF and government officials had met for preliminary peace discussions for the first time in August 1996, following the MILF's rejection of the peace agreement concluded by the MNLF. Clashes between government and MILF forces, which resulted in several deaths, were reported in October in North Cotabato and Maguindanao. Nevertheless, peace talks reconvened in January 1997, resulting in the announcement of a temporary cease-fire, but the abduction, allegedly by MILF rebels, of some 40 workers from the Philippine National Oil Co in mid-June resulted in the collapse of the peace talks and a renewed outburst of fierce fighting between government and MILF forces in Mindanao, with many thousands of civilians forced to evacuate the area. In an attempt to encourage the resumption of peace negotiations and to allow the citizens to return to their homes, President Ramos ordered a suspension of military offensives by the armed forces in early July. During a meeting between MILF leaders and Misuari later in the month, the MILF reiterated its demands for the withdrawal of government forces from the region, and a new cease-fire agreement was subsequently signed by the Government and the MILF.

During 1996–97 Ramos repeatedly dissociated himself from efforts by his supporters to amend the constitutional stipulation that restricted the President to a single term in office. However, his attempt to transform Congress into a constituent assembly to revise the 1987 Constitution in early September prompted Cardinal Sin and Aquino to organize a protest demonstration on 21 September, the 25th anniversary of Marcos's declaration of martial law. Recognizing the support that the protest movement was already commanding (in the event, some 500,000 people took to the streets of Manila),

Ramos issued a statement several hours before the demonstration was due to commence, declaring that he still believed that the Constitution should be amended, but that it should be changed after the 1998 presidential election, and that he was categorically not intending to offer his candidature.

The unsuccessful moves to introduce constitutional changes that would have enabled President Ramos to stand for a second term greatly weakened the capacity of the ruling Lakas-NUCD to contest the presidential election. There was widespread apprehension within Lakas-NUCD, and more widely within the élite and business community, that Ramos was the only candidate able to defeat the populist Vice-President, Estrada, who had been nominated as the candidate of his own small party, the Partido ng Masang Pilipino (Party of the Filipino Masses). In early 1998 a former senator, Gloria Macapagal Arroyo, the only candidate seriously to rival Estrada in opinion polls, withdrew from the presidential race, and from her own party, to become Lakas-NUCD's vice-presidential candidate. In June 1997 Estrada's party formed a coalition with two leading opposition parties, the LDP and the NPC. The resultant party, Laban ng Makabayang Masang Pilipino (LaMMP—the Struggle of Nationalist Filipino Masses), endorsed Estrada as its presidential candidate in December.

The election on 11 May 1998 was one of the country's most peaceful (there were 53 deaths) and fair. As the opinion polls had predicted, the presidency was won by the former film actor, Estrada, with 39.9% of the votes cast; his nearest rival was de Venecia, who secured 15.9%. Estrada incorporated his family name into his professional name, becoming President Joseph Ejercito Estrada, and the LaMMP, which gained 66 seats in the House of Representatives (compared with 106 for Lakas-NUCD), was renamed Laban ng Masang Pilipino (LMP—Struggle of Filipino Masses). Exit polls showed that Estrada's strongest vote came from among lower socio-economic groups. Estrada had built his public reputation and his campaign around his identity with the *masa* (masses). Despite a comfortable, educated middle-class background and decades of political experience as a former mayor, senator and Vice-President, he had, unlike many other politicians in the post-Marcos era, avoided being stigmatized as a 'traditional politician'. Indeed, the 1998 elections continued a post-Marcos trend, the rise of populist politicians and a decline in what had always been a weak party system. Along with Estrada, several other film actors and celebrities were elected to positions of national and local authority. While Lakas-NUCD candidates won a majority of congressional seats, over one-half defected to Estrada's LMP soon after the election results were announced, as had occurred with the LDP after Ramos's election in 1992.

THE GOVERNMENT OF JOSEPH ESTRADA

President Estrada's Cabinet and coterie of advisers were reminiscent of the 'rainbow coalition' that marked the early period of Aquino's presidency. Among them were wealthy, mainly ethnic Chinese business executives, former Marcos cronies and political allies, friends from Estrada's mayoral days in San Juan, and activists formerly linked with the communist movement and left-wing non-governmental organizations (NGOs). In a post-election spirit of reconciliation, Ramos accepted a position as Senior Adviser, modelled on that of Singapore's former Prime Minister, Lee Kuan Yew. One of the most powerful figures to re-emerge alongside Estrada was a former close ally of Marcos, Eduardo 'Danding' Cojuangco, to whom Estrada was 'running mate' in 1992. In July 1998 Cojuangco became Chairman and CEO of the San Miguel corporation, the position that he had held during the Marcos years, and it appeared that the Government was to abandon its legal cases against him and another Marcos crony, Lucio Tan. Estrada announced his intention to reach a compromise with the Marcos family over government claims to Marcos's Swiss bank accounts. However, Estrada prompted a public outcry when he agreed to allow the body of former President Marcos to be buried in the Cemetery of National Heroes and was forced to back down. While Estrada adopted a more conciliatory stance towards the leaders of the Marcos era than his two predecessors, he also attempted to reassure the business community that he would continue the economically successful policies of liberalization, deregulation and privatization put in place under Ramos.

While some former communists were participating in the Estrada Government, the leadership of what remained of the CPP-NDF condemned the new regime, much as it did that of Aquino and Ramos. Not long after taking office, on 30 July 1998 President Estrada approved a human rights agreement that had been negotiated with the NDF under Ramos, and invited the exiled NDF leadership to the Philippines for a resumption of peace negotiations. With the NDF demanding a reversal of the Government's liberalization policies, the next round of negotiations on social and economic reforms was likely to be difficult.

With continued Muslim secessionist pressures in western Mindanao, one of the foremost bills in Estrada's legislative agenda was an amendment to the Organic Act of the ARMM. A plebiscite was scheduled for the southern Philippines in 1999, with the intention of widening the ARMM beyond the four provinces it covered. However, with continuing disquiet over the implementation of the Organic Act and Nur Misuari's governorship of the ARMM, there were even threats from two provincial Governors that they would withdraw from the regional body. Alternating hostilities and short-term cease-fire agreements continued to characterize relations between the national Government and the secessionist MILF over the latter half of 1997 and 1998. Despite the 1996 settlement with the MNLF, this period witnessed the largest deployment of military personnel to western Mindanao since the mid-1970s.

Over the course of his first year in office, President Estrada proved himself a much more adept leader than many had anticipated. Not only did he maintain his mass popularity, but he also won the grudging acceptance of many opponents, notably from within the business community. Estrada's coalition party, the LMP (relaunched as the Lapian ng Masang Pilipino—LaMP, Party of the Filipino Masses—in August 1999), continued to hold the great majority of seats in both houses of Congress. While hardly spectacular, the Philippine economy continued its recovery under Estrada, and political stability was maintained. Where Ramos was noted for his work ethic and attention to detail, Estrada proved his skill in cultivating and drawing upon a range of experienced, generally well-respected advisers, who assumed important positions in the government and state bureaucracy. While factional tensions developed between some of the most powerful of these figures—notably the Executive Secretary, Ronaldo Zamora, and the Chief of the Presidential Management Staff, Leonora Vasquez de Jesus—Estrada was able to negotiate a balance.

Some claimed that this system of particularistic authority had allowed Estrada to reduce bureaucratic inefficiency, but it also exposed him to accusations of cronyism. Rather than pursuing his predecessor's policies of liberalization, some critics argued that Estrada had overseen the creation of new monopolies, for instance in the petrochemical industry and port services, as well as a reconcentration of power in the area of telecommunications. Remaining at the centre of these accusations were former Marcos cronies Eduardo Cojuangco and Lucio Tan, the majority owner of the heavily indebted Philippine Airlines. Estrada was also censured for his relative inaction in seeking the recovery of the Marcos family's ill-gained wealth, although the cases against the Marcoses continued to be dealt with through the courts. In March 1999 the Supreme Court upheld a 1990 decision by the Bureau of Internal Revenue against the Marcos heirs for US $600m. in unpaid inheritance taxes. Later in the year an anti-graft court blocked an earlier $150m. damages agreement between the Marcos family and 10,000 victims of human rights abuses during the Marcos incumbency. The victims had agreed to abandon further claims in exchange for this settlement, but the court ruled against the release of funds from the $590m. sequestered by the Government from Swiss bank accounts.

Just as Estrada's record on economic liberalization was uneven and even contradictory, so too was the stance of the mainstream political opposition. Under the leadership of former President Aquino and the head of the Catholic Church, Cardinal Sin, this opposition continued to define itself as the defender of the democratic gains made following the overthrow of the Marcos regime. Amid mounting concerns that Estrada's presidency was beginning to undermine these gains, a 'Rally for Democracy' was held on 20 August 1999, demanding an end to cronyism, presidential interference in the print media and government action to amend the 1987 Constitution.

For many, the biggest expectations of the Estrada Government centred on its 'pro-poor' platform. The principal aim was 'food security', which was to be achieved through agricultural modernization. To this end, the Agricultural and Fisheries Modernization Act was approved, with an increased budget allocation to fund such projects as rural credit and the improvement of irrigation, roads and other infrastructure. To complement this, the enclave development of Subic Bay was reorientated better to provide for its depressed Luzon hinterland. However, the dramatic increase in agricultural output in the early part of 1999 was largely a result of recovery from the effects of the natural disasters that marred the previous year, rather than a measure of successful rural reform. There also appeared to have been little progress in the Government's plans to redistribute the remaining 1.3m. ha of land set aside under CARP. One of the few achievements under the pro-poor programme by mid-1999 was the rehousing of some 25,000 urban poor in Manila.

While Estrada still enjoyed wide popular support, his Government's continued failure to put its pro-poor rhetoric into practice threatened to bring significant political consequences. The communist movement remained small and fragmented, and, although its influence did not compare with that of a decade previously, it was recruiting growing numbers of people disillusioned with the mainstream political process and the social inequalities that continued to affect Philippine society. The NDF withdrew from peace negotiations with the Government in May 1999, following the Senate's ratification of a defence treaty with the USA (see below); Estrada then assumed a position of outright hostility towards the movement. Nor did the Estrada Government succeed in placating the rural poor who were the major constituency of the MILF in the southern Philippines. Indeed, Estrada's stance towards the MILF vacillated between peace negotiations and promises of agricultural development, and declarations of war. In early 1999, for example, the armed forces launched a major offensive on the MILF's main training camp in Maguindanao, with many killed or wounded, and thousands displaced. Peace negotiations resumed, but the national Government's standing among Muslim Filipinos remained tenuous. The national Government continued to delay the ARMM plebiscite that it hoped would extend its authority over the region. Although the Estrada Government made negligible progress in dealing with the communist and Muslim secessionist movements, it did achieve success in reducing crime, most notably in reducing the number of kidnappings, largely owing to measures jointly formulated by Estrada and the Chinese business community.

In response to mounting pressure and criticism, in January 2000 Estrada announced that constitutional change had been put on hold. While Estrada thus placated some opponents, others emerged within the trade union movement, whose wage claims Estrada rejected, and among teachers, whose promised bonuses were withdrawn. Opposition was also mounting among powerful sectors of the business community, represented by the Makati Business Club, which were critical of Estrada's tardiness in pushing further liberalization and privatization reforms through Congress. Allegations of indecisiveness and inaction also surfaced increasingly in relation to Estrada's 'pro-poor' programme. World Bank funds intended for development projects, ostensibly aimed at benefiting the poor, were withdrawn in December 1999 because they had not been used, and almost a year later, in September 2000, similar funds from the Asian Development Bank (ADB) and the Japan Bank for International Development were also unused, apparently because of government inaction. Despite Estrada's continued populist rhetoric, dissatisfaction was growing among the rural and urban poor, his main constituency. In March 2000, for example, oil price rises, which were affecting the whole region, resulted in widespread protests among Manila jeepney drivers, and the Government's continued failure to implement significant agricultural land reform also resulted in growing rural discontent. From a low point of 6,000 armed guerrillas in 1994, the communist NPA had, by mid-2000, expanded its numbers to an estimated 9,500, mainly drawn from disaffected rural and urban youth.

Persistent accusations of corruption and favouritism also contributed to Estrada's growing unpopularity, particularly among the middle classes and the élite. Especially damaging, both to Estrada's claims to even-handedness and good economic management, was the accusation that he had intervened to protect one of his business associates from the charge of insider trading in March 2000, the result of which had been the near collapse of the Philippine Stock Exchange. While Estrada reorganized his Cabinet and dismissed several of his closest advisers in January 2000, partly in an effort to address accusations of favouritism and indecision, these allegations continued to plague his Government. By April opinion polls showed that Estrada's net approval rating had fallen to 5%, compared with 65% less than one year earlier, and rumours were circulating that he would not complete his term of office. Yet the principal formal opposition party, Lakas, lacked unity, occupying only a small minority of seats in Congress, and its leader, Vice-President Gloria Arroyo, remained in Estrada's Cabinet and declared her continued support for the President.

Of all the crises witnessed hitherto by the Philippines under the Estrada Government, the most serious and costly, but also the one that regained some popularity for Estrada, involved the sharp escalation of hostilities in the Muslim south from the early months of 2000. Despite promises of ongoing dialogue and the provision of greater development assistance, the Government's attitude towards the MILF increasingly assumed the profile of a military offensive. In February government aircraft bombed the MILF's Camp Omar and a secondary camp was seized, the military claiming that this was in retaliation for an earlier ambush. In May, after weeks of fierce fighting, government troops took control of an MILF-controlled section of highway near its headquarters in Camp Abubakar, Maguindanao, and continued their attack on MILF positions despite the offer of a cease-fire. By now hundreds had been killed, mostly on the MILF side, and well over 300,000 civilians, mainly Muslim peasants, had been forced to flee to evacuation centres. In May bombs exploded in two Manila shopping malls, killing one person and wounding others. Though widely attributed to Muslim terrorists, they were just as likely to have been the work of military elements seeking further public support for their war in the south.

In July 2000, after further offensives into MILF-controlled territory, government soldiers finally captured and destroyed much of Camp Abubakar. Now in retreat, and with no major camps left intact, the MILF leadership issued a call for a *jihad* (holy war) against the Philippine state. While government officials and the Catholic Church had long been anxious not to represent the war in the south in religious terms, a dangerous shift seemed to be taking place as more self-proclaimed Christian vigilantes had begun killing and terrorizing ordinary Muslims. Estrada announced plans to turn Camp Abubakar into a special economic zone for the mainly Muslim population of the region and, after initially putting a price on their heads, offered an amnesty to the MILF leadership. Rejecting these proposals, but with most of its approximately 15,000-strong fighting force now fragmented, the MILF turned, once again, to guerrilla warfare, its leadership unbowed in its quest for an independent Islamic state.

In the Sulu archipelago to the west of Mindanao, Abu Sayyaf resumed its campaign of terrorism with the kidnapping, in March 2000, of some 30 students and teachers, threatening to kill them unless various demands were met. A few weeks later, in April, as government troops were closing in, one Abu Sayyaf unit kidnapped 21 tourists and staff, many of them European, from the island resort of Sipadan in eastern Malaysia, not far from Abu Sayyaf strongholds in Basilan and Jolo. Foreign journalists and a group of Filipino Christian evangelists who travelled to Jolo, with the aim of ending the crisis through prayer, were also taken hostage. In May 15 of the original Filipino hostages were freed by the military, but four others were found dead. By the end of September, after months of periodic military assaults, numerous civilian casualties and intermittent negotiation, nearly all of the remaining hostages had been released. Most were freed in exchange for millions of dollars in ransom, much of it paid by the Libyan Government as 'development aid'.

In October 2000 the Philippines was engulfed by a political crisis that arose as a result of allegations, made to an investigative committee of the Senate by the Governor of Ilocos Sur, Luis Singson, that President Estrada had accepted large sums of money as bribes from illegal gambling businesses and from provincial tobacco taxes. Despite the President's denial of these allegations in a televised statement to the nation, opposition parties announced their intention to begin, in late October, the process of impeaching the President. Earlier in the month Vice-President Gloria Arroyo had announced her resignation from the Cabinet, in which she served as Secretary for Social Welfare and Development. The fact that she did not relinquish the vice-presidency at the same time led to speculation that she was preparing to succeed President Estrada in the event of his forced removal from office. On 13 November Estrada was impeached on charges of bribery, corruption, betrayal of public trust and culpable violation of the Constitution. The Speaker of the House of Representatives, Manuel Villar, ordered the transmittal of the articles of impeachment to the Senate without a vote, on the grounds that more than the required one-third of members had signed a petition endorsing impeachment. Villar and the President of the Senate, Franklin Drilon, were both replaced in their positions as they had resigned from the ruling coalition and urged Estrada's removal. A majority of two-thirds of the Senate, 15 of the 22 members, would be required to remove Estrada (who refused to resign) from office.

While the impeachment trial promised a balanced set of formal procedures to resolve the political uncertainties surrounding the corruption charges levelled against the President, a more volatile, extra-parliamentary process unfolded. The anti-Estrada street protests, which had begun with Singson's accusations, continued as growing numbers of Estrada allies withdrew their support, and public figures, like former President Fidel Ramos, repeated their demands for Estrada's resignation. On 30 December 2000, two weeks after the trial had started, Manila was rocked by five separate bomb explosions, resulting in 22 deaths and many more injured. While government sources blamed Estrada's political opponents or Muslim separatists, others attributed blame to Estrada's supporters, arguing that such violence was intended either to intimidate witnesses or to create an opportunity for the Government to declare martial law. However, the trial continued and damning testimony against Estrada emerged, notably that of Equitable PCI Bank's Senior Vice-President, Clarissa Ocampo, who alleged that she had been instructed to prevent the discovery of a bank account containing millions of dollars controlled by the President. Despite such testimony, the pro-Estrada majority in the Senate blocked a proposal by the prosecutors to open an envelope said to contain evidence of Estrada's corrupt banking practices.

With prosecutors resigning in protest, the trial came to an abrupt halt, more of Estrada's allies abandoned him, and the centre of political gravity moved to the street protests taking place at Manila's People Power monument, the scene of Marcos's overthrow in 1986. Covert lobbying by political, church and business leaders led the military and the police force to withdraw their support from Estrada in favour of Vice-President Gloria Arroyo. Finally, on 20 January 2001, Estrada departed from the presidential palace and Arroyo was sworn in as his successor.

THE GOVERNMENT OF GLORIA ARROYO

Named People Power II by its supporters, the transition was welcomed by many, but it also aroused significant criticism because Estrada still appeared to have majority support, principally among his main constituency of urban and rural poor, and the transition created another political precedent, weakening the institutions of electoral democracy and the stability of the new regime. Although Estrada maintained his claim to the presidency and, hence, to immunity from prosecution, in March 2001 the Supreme Court ruled against both claims, reaffirmed Arroyo as President and opened the way for charges of corruption, bribery and economic plunder to be brought against Estrada. In late April Estrada was imprisoned, awaiting trial.

Shortly afterwards, on 1 May 2001, mass protests were again staged in Manila, this time by Estrada's supporters. These disturbances were violent, resulting in several deaths and many injuries. President Arroyo responded by declaring a week-long 'state of rebellion', and arrest orders, in response to an alleged aborted coup, were issued for Senators Juan Ponce Enrile and Gregorio Honasan, and for Estrada's former national police chief, Panfilo Lacson. Although Arroyo withstood this challenge, doubt remained over her authority. However, at elections for 13 of the 24 seats in the Senate, to the House of Representatives and to local administrations, on 14 May, Arroyo emerged with a majority in both houses of Congress. While veteran senator Juan Ponce Enrile lost his seat, both Honasan and Lacson, who remained in hiding, were returned to the Senate.

While Estrada's removal had much to do with the distaste that he aroused among the élite and middle class, these represented President Arroyo's principal, but not only, base of support: as the winning vice-presidential candidate in 1998 she had demonstrated a broad appeal, gaining the single largest number of votes of any candidate and thereby repeating an earlier performance in 1995, when she had received the most votes in elections to the Senate. In addition to her élite social and political credentials, Arroyo (who had a doctorate in economics) was admired by many in the business community, having drafted many bills aimed at liberalizing the economy during the era of President Ramos. Indeed, figures such as Ramos and organizations such as the powerful Makati Business Club, which favoured ongoing liberalization of the economy, were among Arroyo's staunchest supporters. Like former President Aquino, but in contrast to Estrada, Arroyo also had a reputation as a devout and conservative Catholic, which gained her strong support from the upper echelons of the Catholic Church.

Following her inauguration in January 2001, President Arroyo pledged to return the Philippines to the course that had been planned under the presidencies of Aquino and Ramos: more stable democratic institutions, a campaign against official corruption, a war on poverty and steady economic growth based on policies of increased liberalization. However, in her efforts to fulfil these promises, Arroyo was confronted by major problems. One was the difficult task of accommodating within her administration the disparate interests and personalities who had supported her in the overthrow of Estrada: the Catholic Church, the business élite, the military, militant trade unions, a range of left-orientated NGOs and a number of former Estrada cronies. Policies ranging from economic liberalization to family-planning aroused opposing views within this broad coalition, with potential impediments to the implementation of the reform agenda that many regarded as necessary in the Philippines. Many of those appointed to Arroyo's Cabinet were associates of Aquino and Ramos, such as the former Secretary of the Budget under Aquino and new Secretary of Finance, Alberto Romulo, and the former Secretary of National Defense under Ramos and incoming Chief Security Adviser and Executive Secretary, Gen. (retd) Renato de Villa. However, Arroyo was also obliged to rely on many former supporters of Estrada who had changed their allegiance in the final days of his presidency. Notably, Luis Singson, whose exposure of Estrada's bribe-taking prompted the impeachment trial, was appointed as the new Government's gambling consultant. Such appointments raised doubts about the new President's capacity to eradicate corruption, a problem compounded by accusations that her husband, Mike Arroyo, had misused public lottery funds. However, the Arroyo administration persisted in bringing several corruption charges against Estrada, the most serious being the embezzlement of US $80m. in state funds, a charge punishable by death.

The politicized class divide that seemed evident during the transition from Estrada to Arroyo appeared to fade in the aftermath of the May 2001 elections, but the new President still confronted the seemingly impossible task of implementing the liberal economic reforms of the Ramos era while, at the same time, addressing the deteriorating circumstances of the rural and urban poor. The Government's commitment to further liberalization appeared to be confirmed by the enactment, on 4 June 2001, of legislation, pending for five years, privatizing electric power supply. With regard to measures to combat poverty, President Arroyo made a number of promises, undertaking fully to implement the CARP, in particular its land reform provisions. The President also pledged to implement a housing and livelihood programme for the urban poor, and stated that the Government would grant loans and scholarships to the needy. However, Arroyo's administration continued to be impeded by the high budget deficit.

By mid-2002 President Arroyo had fulfilled, or made substantial progress in implementing, many of the numerous pledges presented in her first State of the Nation address. Most surprisingly, in view of her own and her predecessor's respective bases of support, she had delivered more material benefits to the poor than had President Estrada. Notably, her Government was reported to have distributed more than 200,000 ha of land under the agrarian reform programme, to have provided security of tenure to over 180,000 urban poor families, and to have constructed some 150,000 houses for workers and others among the rural and urban poor. In addition, it had initiated a number of stores selling basic commodities at subsidized prices, and had established a national health insurance system (in which some 2.2m. had enrolled), which was largely designed to benefit the urban poor. The Arroyo administration had also maintained its success, under new legislation, in promoting private sector involvement in infrastructural development, most notably in rural electrification, although excessive increases in power prices prompted widespread protests.

Despite these successes, government efforts continued to be impeded by a large budgetary deficit, inadequate tax collection and a series of social and political problems. One of these was the continued widespread support enjoyed by detained former President Estrada, whose trials on charges of corruption and economic sabotage proceeded extremely slowly, protracted by appeals to the Supreme Court and the dismissal of trial judges and defence lawyers, amid claims by Estrada that he remained the legitimate President. In the mean time, from his military hospital prison, Estrada campaigned for the holding of an immediate presidential election and delivered an alternative State of the Nation speech to that of Arroyo.

President Arroyo's Lakas-NUCD party continued to command a majority in the lower house, but its control of the Senate remained tenuous. Indeed, as a consequence of the defection of one senator in June 2002, and the absence abroad of another, proceedings in the Senate, and consequently the Government's legislative agenda, were suspended for nearly two months. Arroyo's presidency also suffered through the resignation at about the same time of two of her leading cabinet members, the Secretary of Foreign Affairs, Teofisto Guingona, and the Secretary of Education, Culture and Sports, Raul Roco, over the government decision to allow the deployment of US troops in the Philippines, and corruption charges, respectively. Both politicians claimed that Arroyo's management of these issues was also as much the cause of their resignations, reflecting a criticism that had been levelled more widely at the President's technocratic style of leadership.

The main areas in which President Arroyo had little success were in curbing official corruption and escalating crime, particularly on the part of kidnap-for-ransom syndicates. Both posed a growing threat to local and foreign business confidence in the country, and in her second State of the Nation address in mid-2002, Arroyo identified these problems as requiring special attention. Among other measures, she established a new task force (replacing two earlier bodies for combating corruption and crime), transferred the police force to the authority of local government, and authorized the establishment of citizen self-defence units, but with little apparent impact. Corruption was curtailed in the highest political echelons, but continued to prove extremely difficult to eradicate within the state bureaucracy, while law enforcement agencies made little progress against organized crime. Despite a formal policy of non-negotiation with kidnappers, lucrative ransoms continued to be collected, while hostages were frequently killed, particularly by Abu Sayyaf. President Arroyo continued to deploy the armed forces in attempts to free hostages held by Abu Sayyaf, but virtually abandoned the pursuit of a military solution to the conflicts with the MILF (see below) and the NPA.

The CPP and NPA became more active under the Arroyo presidency: apart from conventional guerrilla warfare, the NPA was believed to have supported some 400 candidates in the July 2002 local elections. It was also reported that NPA militias had been instructed to open fire on US troops at the start of the Balikatan campaign (see below), although this did not, in fact, happen. In August 2002 the US authorities declared the CPP and the NPA to be international terrorist organizations, thereby subjecting their supporters in the USA to the same legal sanctions as those associated with the al-Qa'ida organization of Osama bin Laden. Soon afterwards, the Dutch, British and Canadian authorities followed the US Government's example in freezing the assets of NPA groups and of their leaders, including Sison and many others who were exiled in the Netherlands. Although there had been ongoing efforts on both sides to reactivate peace talks between the Philippine Government and the CPP, Sison maintained that discussions would not resume while Arroyo remained President. At the same time as these developments, various left-wing groups that had broken away from the CPP in the years following the overthrow of Marcos announced that they were to unite as the Partido ng Manggagawang Pilipino (PMP—Filipino Workers' Party).

Concerns over corruption, lawlessness and political instability continued to shape political and economic life in the Philippines throughout 2003. In January Arroyo announced a national campaign against corruption, allocating public funds to such projects as the computerization of vote-counting and reforms to the Bureau of Internal Revenue and the Customs Office. A number of kidnap-for-ransom syndicates, some involving renegade police and military officers, were apprehended, and four officials from the Bureau of Internal Revenue were dismissed. In May the Supreme Court upheld the Government's earlier cancellation of the contract for Manila's new international air terminal, on the grounds that it had been fraudulently awarded to Filipino and German joint venture contractors under the Government's build-operate-transfer (BOT) policy. In July the Supreme Court also deemed that the funds held in Marcos's Swiss bank accounts belonged to the Philippine Government, a ruling later upheld by the Swiss authorities. In September Congress approved a number of economic reform bills, providing, among other measures, for a better and more efficient system of tax collection. Despite these and other initiatives, the success of which was partly assessed through an increase in state revenues, corruption continued to undermine government promises further to alleviate poverty, to attract foreign investment and, in other ways, to pursue its programme of national development. In August 2003, in a survey of 66 countries conducted by the ADB, the Philippines ranked second in terms of the detrimental impact of corruption upon business in the country.

Rival allegations of corruption also came to dominate political debate at the expense of arguments over development policy. The corruption trial of former President Estrada continued to proceed, slowly, in the courts; Estrada himself filed impeachment complaints against eight justices of the Supreme Court. Meanwhile, Estrada's supporters threatened to impeach President Arroyo on charges of corruption, while the former national police chief under Estrada, Senator Panfilo Lacson, and Arroyo's husband, Mike Arroyo, continued to clash over allegations of money-laundering, racketeering and connections to drug syndicates.

While opposition efforts to undermine the credibility of President Arroyo had only a limited impact, they appeared to have been part of a wider campaign of destabilization undertaken by forces associated with Estrada. In late July 2003 the most immediate threat was presented by an attempted coup involving over 300 members of the Philippine armed forces, who took control of the Oakwood residential and shopping complex in the Manila business district of Makati and wired it with explosives. Reported to be part of a more serious plot discovered one week earlier, the mutiny was quickly quashed, in part owing to the lack of wider support that had been expected by some of its leaders. The soldiers involved were detained, but not before they had publicly aired their grievances, most notably the claim that high-ranking military personnel were guilty of systematic corruption in selling arms to, and otherwise profiting through collusion with, Muslim rebels in the southern Philippines. Secretary of National Defense Gen. (retd) Angelo Reyes was forced to resign, and several known associates of Estrada were charged with rebellion, including the former military coup leader Senator Gregorio Honasan. In contrast to the relaxed treatment of military mutineers under the administration of Corazon Aquino, the soldiers involved in the coup attempt had criminal charges filed against them, and the state of rebellion imposed by the Government during the mutiny remained in force two months later, amid rumours of further attempts at political destabilization.

Concerns over corruption and instability were increased by the activities of various parties seeking to gain an advantage in the period prior to the May 2004 presidential election. In an apparent effort to limit the negative impact that such efforts were having on government, in December 2002 President Arroyo announced that she would not stand as a candidate at the election and would focus instead on implementing the reforms that she had promised during her remaining period in office. However, by September 2003 the President was reconsidering her decision, buoyed by respectable economic growth, a reported drop in poverty levels, and an improvement in her popular opinion ratings; the latter was partly attributed to the firm manner in which she was perceived to have dealt with the coup attempt of July.

The Philippines continued to be affected by the ongoing rebellion of the NPA and Muslim separatists in the southern Philippines. The NPA continued to increase in size and to engage government troops and local authorities in many parts of the country. It assumed responsibility for a number of attacks on government and private infrastructural installations, including the bombing of several mobile telephone relay stations, which was claimed by the Government to be a response to the failure of private companies to pay 'revolutionary taxation'. In an effort to reopen dialogue, in September 2003 plans were mooted for the holding of exploratory talks in Oslo, Norway, between Netherlands-based CPP officials and Philippine government representatives.

Following the passage of legislation in February 2003, absentee Filipino overseas workers would, for the first time, be able to vote in elections, scheduled for 10 May, to select the President, Vice-President, 12 members of the Senate, 212 members of the House of Representatives and more than 17,000 local officials, although only a small number had registered. After considerable speculation and manoeuvring, five candidates were left to contend the presidential election: the incumbent President Arroyo, who had reversed her earlier decision not to stand; a well-known film actor, Fernando Poe, Jr; Senators Lacson and Roco, and the leader of the Jesus Is Lord Church, evangelist Eddie Villanueva. However, only Arroyo and Poe emerged as serious contenders, with Poe leading in popular opinion polls for much of the campaign period. Like his friend Joseph Estrada, he had been a film idol, a former supporter of the Marcos regime and had failed to complete his secondary education. He was, if anything, a more popular public figure than Estrada, but had never been a politician. For his opponents, particularly within the intelligentsia and business community, this and his limited formal education were a major deficiency in his candidature; for his supporters, these qualities made him a 'man of the people', untarnished by the dishonest behaviour commonly associated with traditional politicians. Unlike Estrada, Poe had a reputation for marital fidelity and clean living, making him much less of a target for the Catholic Church than Estrada had been. Indeed, under the leadership of Cardinal Gaudencio Rosales, the Catholic Church played a less prominent role in the election campaign than had been the case under Cardinal Sin, who after 30 years in office as Archbishop of Manila retired in September 2003. Popular support for Poe was particularly evident in Manila, but more generally he assumed Estrada's supporter base, the members of which were still angered by the way in which their President had been removed from office and by his continued detention. Poe also advanced a similar pro-poor policy platform, although it was less pronounced and less developed during this campaign than in that of 1998. Indeed, the campaign in general was bereft of serious policy debate and centred rather on personality and manoeuvres such as the unsuccessful attempt by the Arroyo camp to have Poe excluded from the election because of his alleged alien citizenship.

Owing to the Government's failure to deliver on its promise of introducing a computerized counting system, and the fact that this helped to precipitate various charges of fraud by a number of losing candidates, the outcome of the elections was not made public until six weeks after the vote, by which time more than 100 people had been killed in electoral violence, more than in 1998, but most of it associated with the simultaneous local elections. Although Poe warned of another 'people power' backlash when it became clear that he would lose the presidential election, the street demonstrations that followed were relatively small and were not sustained, and even many of his supporters thought his campaign had been poorly managed. In part, Arroyo's victory, with 40.0% of the votes cast to Poe's 36.5%, was a consequence of her party's ability to secure as her running mate the highly popular celebrity politician Noli de Castro and the effective block vote of the Iglesia ni Cristo church, which had formerly supported Estrada.

Although the election was close, Arroyo's victory gave her a mandate that she did not formerly enjoy, having not originally been elected into the presidency. Moreover, the immediate dangers of a military coup, rumoured throughout most of her last incumbency, had significantly diminished. Her party, Lakas-Christian Muslim Democrats (Lakas-CMD, as Lakas-NUCD had restyled itself in 2003), formally received majority support in both houses of Congress, and her 10-point plan for the nation, articulated in her inauguration and State of the Nation speeches, won broad endorsement from the principal political parties. President Arroyo promised to address state inefficiency, not only by reducing the size of the bureaucracy, but also by replacing congressional government with a parliamentary system. This, too, had broad support among legislators, but would require constitutional change, which neither of her predecessors had been able to achieve owing to wide public opposition. Plans to introduce a parallel federal system of government, in order to devolve more of the inordinate power concentrated in Congress and in Manila, were similarly likely to prove difficult to implement, as were constitutional amendments aimed at attracting more foreign investment into industries such as mining.

Another major problem confronting the new Arroyo Government was domestic rebellion, in large part a reflection of the need for social, legislative and constitutional reform. In November 2003 two men, one a former senior aviation official, occupied the control tower of the Ninoy Aquino International Airport in Manila in order to draw attention to the national consequences of ceaseless political feuding. Although the siege was brief and the men were shot dead by the police, this event, like the earlier hotel siege by disaffected military officers, indicated the level of discontent felt among many Filipinos and their preparedness to challenge state authority openly. The NPA continued to engage government troops in battle in many parts of the country, with over 200 killed in just six months of fighting to June 2004. As a consequence of the CPP's shortage of income, following its branding as an international terrorist organization by the USA, the NPA further increased its imposition of 'revolutionary taxation' on candidates during the May elections, as well as on various business interests, notably cellular telephone companies (a number of their communication towers were bombed). Peace negotiations between the CPP and the Philippine Government had commenced in Oslo in February, but were suspended by the party in August, with a promise that attacks on the new Arroyo Government would be intensified.

During the final months of 2004 the Arroyo Government concentrated some of its energy on internal administrative and fiscal reform, including the downsizing of government bureaucracy and the approval of legislation that abolished the Priority Assistance Fund, otherwise known as the 'pork barrel fund', through which members of Congress had traditionally rewarded their particular constituencies. This fund had long been viewed as a major vehicle of corruption, and it was hoped that its removal would be regarded as part of a more transparent and accountable system of public spending. A government probe was also directed at corruption among senior military officers, leading to a number being charged and detained. Mounting foreign debt and inadequate state revenue were to be addressed both by new austerity measures affecting government spending and by the introduction of eight new bills aimed at increasing taxes and improving revenue collection. In January 2005 Congress approved a higher rate of VAT, which was to be increased from 10% to 12%, on consumer goods. In July the implementation of the measure was suspended amid concerns over its constitutionality, but it was subsequently reinstated by the Philippine Supreme Court in September and took effect in February 2006. President Arroyo also pledged to complete the Government's programme of rural electrification and water supply provision, the area receiving the largest budgetary allocation in her 10-point development and poverty alleviation agenda. During the course of 2004 the Government also claimed to have provided homes for more than 640,000 poor families, and to have reduced kidnappings to the lowest level in over a decade. It also appeared that the Arroyo administration was making progress on the prolonged dispute over the unused, but almost completed, Terminal 3 of the Ninoy Aquino International Airport when it took possession of the facility in December.

Notwithstanding some clear progress in policy implementation, the Arroyo Government found itself embroiled in mounting political crisis during the course of 2005. Concerns about the corruption inquiry into the military were said to have angered some within the armed forces, leading to rumours of a mutiny, while former President Estrada, who remained on trial and under house arrest, claimed that he was forming a new 'shadow' government in view of data suggesting that there was growing poverty and hunger in the country. Opposition against the Government escalated during April and May. Supporters of Fernando Poe, Jr, who continued to claim that government malpractice had cheated him of victory in the May 2004 elections, held street protests intended to interrupt the 112th Inter-Parliamentary Union Assembly held in Manila, while various opposition groups organized protests for 1 May, the anniversary of 'Edsa-III' (the popular street rebellion in Manila that had sought to reinstate Estrada following his overthrow by Arroyo supporters). In the same month a retired general launched the Coalition of National Salvation, the aim of which was to replace the Arroyo administration with a transitional government. The new legitimacy that Arroyo had appeared to enjoy following her electoral victory was further undermined by corruption allegations directed at her husband, son and brother-in-law, who were said, like Estrada before them, to be receiving large sums of money from operators of *jueteng*—illegal lottery syndicates. Under mounting pressure from a senate investigation and growing media scrutiny, the President's husband, Mike Arroyo, went into self-imposed exile in the USA, but was reported to have returned to the Philippines just a few days later.

In June 2005 the Arroyo administration was cast into a much deeper crisis when a tape recording emerged of an alleged conversation between Arroyo and a senior Comelec official during the 2004 presidential election, in which the apparent voice of Arroyo was heard trying to influence the vote-counting process. Appearing to support Fernando Poe, Jr's complaint, dismissed in the Supreme Court, that he had been cheated of electoral victory, the new evidence precipitated numerous demands for Arroyo's resignation from opposition politicians, newspaper editors, NGO activists, the Makati Business Club and even the Christian Brothers of one of the country's leading universities, De La Salle. Arroyo subsequently publicly admitted that she had spoken to an election official, but strenuously denied having tried to determine the outcome of the vote count. As a campaign of almost-daily street rallies was mounted over the following months, impeachment proceedings developed in Congress, coup rumours surfaced within the military and in early July several members of Arroyo's Cabinet resigned in protest, including, notably, Secretary of Finance Cesar Purisima and Secretary of Trade and Industry Juan Santos. (The resignations followed that of Arthur Yap, former Secretary of Agriculture, in the previous month, who stated that he was leaving the post in order to concentrate on challenging tax evasion charges brought against his family company following the purchase of property in Pasig City.) Corazon Aquino, the former President and leader of previous 'people power' campaigns, took to the streets. Yet again a Philippine President appeared to be on the brink of removal from office. That this did not occur was testament both to Arroyo's steadfast refusal to concede and to an opposition that was disunited and lacking the requisite leadership that had emerged in the past. Despite coup rumours, the military continued to support Arroyo, as for the most part did the business community and the Catholic Church. Cardinal Sin, who had been such an important political force on previous such occasions, had not only retired but then passed away only days after the emergence of the crisis. Major political opponents had also died—Fernando Poe, Jr, in December, and Raul Roco in August—and while Estrada continued to speak of uniting the opposition, he stated that he no longer wanted to assume the leadership and that there was no significant desire to give it to him. Namfrel, the independent electoral monitoring body that had played a crucial role in the demise of Marcos, claimed that it had no evidence of widespread electoral fraud, and in September Congress voted to reject the impeachment motions against Arroyo. Finally, although opinion polls showed that Arroyo's popularity had plummeted, opposition leaders were singularly unsuccessful in attracting onto the streets similar numbers of demonstrators (especially those of the middle class) that had pressed for the removal of Marcos and, to a lesser extent, Estrada.

While Arroyo survived, both the Government and the national economy were left weakened; yet the crisis also generated some consensus on the initiative for constitutional change to replace the presidential system with a parliamentary framework. The proposed change had broad support across a number of political parties for its potential to make government more responsive, legislation easier to enact and unsatisfactory leadership removable without recourse to extra-constitutional measures. Charter change was advocated not only by Arroyo but also, conditionally, by Estrada and some other opposition figures. It was particularly promoted by former President Fidel Ramos, who suggested that the transition to parliamentary government could provide Arroyo with a 'graceful exit'. In September 2005 the President appointed a Consultative Commission, the 55 members of which were to assist Congress in drafting a modified Constitution that would set in motion the transformation.

The campaign against Arroyo continued during the latter months of 2005 and most of 2006, while the President remained steadfast in her refusal to resign or to hold an early election. In January 2006 the influential 120-member Catholic Bishops' Conference expressed strong support for continued investigations into the allegations against the President, owing to the undermining of such efforts thus far by 'acts of evasion and obstruction of truth'. In the following month, however, the National Bureau of Investigation announced that it had closed its own investigation of the affair owing to insufficient evidence (the tape recording of the conversation between Arroyo and the election official had been adjudged to have been tampered with). Relatively small street rallies were held frequently under the leadership of left-wing activists and Estrada loyalists, as well as prominent figures such as former President Corazon Aquino and Jejomar Binay, Mayor of Makati City. Although a second impeachment motion against Arroyo was easily defeated in Congress in August 2006, opposition members staged a 'People's Court' and a 'Citizen's Congress' for the 'impeachment' trial. Numerous rumours of coup plots emerged, in some cases apparently circulated by opposition politicians in an attempt to undermine Arroyo's authority. In February 2006, on the 20th anniversary of the overthrow of Ferdinand Marcos, a more tangible challenge was mounted by mutinying soldiers, including some who had participated in the Oakwood rebellion of July 2003 (see above) and had escaped military custody. At the core of the revolt was a group calling itself the Young Officers' Union—new generation (YOUng), subsequently reported by the Government to have been co-ordinated by Senator Honasan. Like its predecessor, this coup attempt was suppressed. Dozens of military officers and soldiers were arrested and charged with rebellion, while

Honasan remained in hiding, with an increased bounty being offered by the Philippine authorities for his capture.

While the main complaints voiced by opposition politicians and mutinying soldiers related to government corruption, in particular on the apparent evidence of vote manipulation by Arroyo in the 2004 elections, dissatisfaction was growing over the increasingly authoritarian government response to opposition. Some feared that it was a precursor to the imposition of martial law. Journalists were subjected to mounting pressure, and many of those reporting from the front lines of conflict were killed. The Government shifted from a liberal stance on street rallies to a pre-emptive policy that strictly enforced the requirement for a protest permit. In several cases rallies were dispersed by police using water cannons, and opposition leaders were arrested. Also targeted were six members of Congress identified with the left who were said to have acted as accomplices of the military coup plotters of February 2006. One of these congressmen, Crispin Beltran, representative for the electoral wing of the militant labour federation Kilusang Mayo Uno (KMU), was detained on rebellion charges, while the others were placed under house arrest. Military sources claimed to possess evidence proving that all were members of the CPP or the outlawed NDF. However, the greatest anathema to many was the declaration in March 2006 of a state of emergency in response to a 'clear threat' to national security following the failed February coup plot, although this was rescinded by the President after only one week. Arroyo continued to receive the official support of the Catholic Church, but many within the clergy and elsewhere were critical of her shift to more repressive rule.

The most troubling development was the Government's apparent disregard for—or even, possibly, complicity in—extra-judicial killings that targeted various legal leftist organizations such as Bayan Muna (People First), Partido ng Bayan (New People's Alliance) and the KMU. Human rights groups identified as many as 800 violent deaths, believed to have occurred between 2001 and early 2007, of journalists, activists, local government officials (including 20 of the nation's mayors), indigenous people and other critics of the Government. Bayan Muna, which had entered Congress through the party-list system in 2001, was reportedly among the worst affected, claiming that 132 of its members had been killed by mid-2007; many of the alleged murders took place in Bicol, Southern Tagalog and Central Luzon, where the party won most of its votes. However, the armed forces insisted that the victims were members of the CPP or NPA who had been killed in an internal purge. The Government, which claimed on several occasions that it would eradicate the NPA by the end of Arroyo's term in 2010, dismissed any suggestion of military involvement. Although the campaign seemed initially to gain legitimacy from the US Government's classification of the CPP as a terrorist organization, national and international pressure grew against what the Commission on Human Rights described as 'an emerging culture of impunity'. In August 2006 Arroyo created the Melo Commission to investigate the killings. The Commission's report, which was made public under pressure from a UN special envoy in February 2007, declared the military's claim of an internal purge 'improbable'; the killings were apparently 'well-organized and the killers adequately equipped' and the general in command of the units allegedly responsible had a 'cavalier attitude towards the killings'. The report, which did not apportion responsibility, moved neither the Government nor the armed forces toward resolution of past killings or prevention of further violence.

In parallel to the opposition's vociferous but ineffective efforts to oust Arroyo, the Government's campaign for charter change dominated politics in 2006. The Consultative Commission had submitted proposals in December 2005 recommending the establishment of a unicameral legislature with a party-elected prime minister and the transformation of the unitary republic into a federation. In addition, the Commission suggested electoral and judicial reforms, 'anti-turncoat' measures to strengthen political parties, the opening of the natural resource sector to foreign investment and ownership and, controversially, a transitory period of government with the cancellation of the May 2007 elections and the retention of all incumbents until 2010. Most opposition to the proposals came from those who regarded Arroyo's removal from office, rather than charter change, as the country's most pressing need; it was feared that any transitory period scheme would allow Arroyo's allies in the House of Representatives to draft a constitution perpetuating their own (and perhaps her) power. In particular, opposition was increased in the Senate, where the members, elected nationally under the 1987 Constitution, would have difficulty competing for seats from local constituencies.

The Commission's proposals were impossible to legislate, and in March 2006 the Government began a 'people's initiative'—a signature campaign demanding a plebiscite to decide whether to cancel the 2007 elections and allow the incumbent Congress, sitting as a Constituent Assembly, to draft a new constitution. The members of the Senate, who would be outnumbered in a combined assembly, approved two resolutions in response. The first asserted that under the 1987 Constitution, the two chambers were required to vote separately to introduce amendments to the Constitution, and the second deemed the proposed plebiscite illegal in the absence of enabling legislation. Constitutional experts also maintained that a people's initiative was inadequate to change the entire system of government; it was intended to effect specific changes and then only after an enabling act (the Supreme Court had decided as much in 1997). Nevertheless, the Government implemented the campaign through local government assemblies, and in May 2006 the required signatures (12% of registered voters nation-wide and 3% per legislative district) were submitted to Comelec for validation. Meanwhile, opinion polls suggested that 67% of respondents (54% of those satisfied with Arroyo's performance) would vote against changes to the Constitution in a plebiscite and that six out of 10 respondents who had been asked to sign the petition had not been shown the text of the proposed amendments. In August Comelec rejected the petition based on the 1997 precedent, and in October 2006 the Supreme Court narrowly (by eight to seven) upheld Comelec's decision. The year culminated in a failed and highly controversial effort by Arroyo's allies to circumvent the Senate, convene the House of Representatives as a Constituent Assembly and create an interim legislature immediately. Although the movement for charter change was not wholly defeated at the end of 2006 (the Makati Business Club and the Catholic Church still expressed interest in a popularly elected Constitutional Convention), the Government was forced to suspend its immediate plan in order to prepare for the local and congressional elections of May 2007.

Having narrowly avoided cancellation, the mid-term elections effectively became a referendum on the Arroyo presidency. The fragmented opposition virtually conceded many of the 219 contested seats in the House of Representatives, which had historically been controlled by the sitting administration through patronage, and the ruling coalition indeed increased its strength in that chamber. However, the campaign for 12 seats in the Senate was influenced by deep public dissatisfaction with the President (the only post-Marcos head of state to register negative satisfaction ratings, from October 2004 to March 2007) and her divisive style of leadership. The latter was evident in her use of her own grouping, Kabalikat ng Malayang Pilipino (Kampi, originally founded in 1997), to compete alongside the administration-affiliated Lakas-CMD. Instead of preventing candidate defections, ensuring local victories and delivering votes to the administration's senatorial list, the existence of two factions led to intense rivalry, and Arroyo did not (or could not) arbitrate. The other unsuccessful campaign tactic was the appropriation of Senate candidates, which left the opposition smaller but more coherent. Finally, at the last minute, the opposition added to its Senate list Antonio Trillanes IV, the Oakwood coup leader seen by many as an anti-corruption crusader. Campaigning from prison with no mechanism and scant media coverage, Trillanes unexpectedly won a seat. Two of the three leading recipients of votes were also known for their anti-Arroyo and anti-corruption stance, while some strong candidates suffered upsets that were attributed in part to their closeness to Arroyo. The resulting strength of the opposition in the Senate was the most striking mid-term repudiation of a sitting government since that of Marcos in 1971. The highly divergent House of Representatives and

Senate results reflected the country's growing urbanization, as more of the nation voted along the same lines as Manila's typically anti-Government voters. With the exception of Loren Legarda, the former broadcast journalist and Senator who was placed first in her re-election bid, celebrities fared poorly in the polls, reversing a decade-long trend.

Finally, the 2007 election was notable for the country's general mistrust of Comelec (still led by officials suspected of assisting Arroyo in 2004) and for increased vigilance by the media, the Catholic Church, teachers and Namfrel. With the help of computer colleges and student volunteers, the media conducted 'quick counts' in important constituencies to maintain the pressure on Comelec, and teachers (staffing the polls as part of their duties) fought attempts to manipulate the ballot. Elections in the ARMM, which had operated as a 'reservoir of votes' for national candidates, were closely monitored; Comelec later declared polls in the province of Maguindanao a failure. (Special elections held in some towns subsequently changed the province's 'statistically improbable' result of 12–0 for the Government's senatorial list to 6–5 for the opposition.) Widespread fraud and violence prompted the proposal of electoral reforms urgently needed before the 2010 election. The most widely agreed-upon proposals included the reform of the system of appointment of commissioners to Comelec, the professionalization and diversification of the composition of Comelec (hitherto dominated by lawyers), and progress toward automation of either tabulation (of paper ballots) or voting itself.

After the election, unresolved issues returned to the fore. Amnesty International urged the Government to address the country's deteriorating human rights situation, and the international NGO Human Rights Watch found 'strong evidence of a 'dirty war' by the armed forces against left-leaning activists and journalists'. The latter noted that such killings had escalated in 2006 after Arroyo accused legal leftist organizations of supporting military coup plotters and declared 'all-out war' on the NPA (which marked its 38th anniversary in March 2007). Both reports drew attention to high-level complicity in the failure to prosecute the activists' killers.

In June 2007 the Supreme Court dismissed the Government's case against the arrested leftist legislators. (In April it had also freed Bayan Muna representative Saturnino Ocampo, who had been arrested on 15 charges of murder in connection with NPA purges in Leyte province over 20 years earlier.) Human rights activists condemned the implementation of the Human Security Act of 2007 (or 'anti-terror law') in July, which had been approved by the previous Congress. It was argued that the law's definition of terrorism was overly broad and vague and would lead to more abuses of human rights. This sentiment led to a multi-sector judicial summit meeting that appealed to the President to order an end to political killings and for new laws to help investigators search for victims. Nevertheless, the Government and the Philippine National Police—which had pressed for the enactment of the law—insisted that it was necessary, and reiterated that it included stricter sanctions on police officers violating human rights.

It emerged in mid-2007 that a contract signed in April with China's ZTE Corporation for the construction of a national broadband network had been overpriced by some US $130m. The resulting investigation by the Senate revealed a spectacle of cronyism that increased public distrust of the Arroyo administration. Attention initially focused on the alleged role of the Comelec Chairman, Benjamin Abalos (widely suspected of having helped Arroyo to win the 2004 election), in transferring $70m. of the excess cost to a 'mystery' broker. The scandal widened in September when the losing bidder for the broadband contract, the son of the Speaker of the House of Representatives, Jose de Venecia, testified before the Senate that the President's husband, Mike Arroyo, was that broker. The former Director-General of the National Economic and Development Authority, Romulo Neri, who had approved the contract, subsequently testified that he had declined a bribe offered by Abalos and shared that information with President Arroyo, but invoked executive privilege in refusing to respond to the question of whether or not the President had instructed him to authorize the contract anyway. By the end of the year the contract had been cancelled, Abalos had resigned as Comelec Chairman, the testimony of the younger de Venecia had cost his father the office of speaker, and the Supreme Court had upheld the principle of executive privilege. President Arroyo had survived yet again.

Public trust in another government institution was eroded in mid-2008 when a special Supreme Court tribunal investigating eight Court of Appeals justices found that five had committed improprieties in adjudicating a takeover bid for the Manila Electric Company (Meralco), the country's largest power distributor, by the Government Service Insurance System (GSIS). Justice Vicente Roxas was dismissed from the Court in September for violations of its code of conduct, dishonesty, undue interest in the case and conduct prejudicial to the best interests of the service. Another justice, Jose Sabio, received a two-month suspension. This investigation, and another into the alleged bribery of Justice Consuelo Ynares-Santiago, revealed a degraded culture of politicized appointments and questionable ethics among many of the 69 justices of the Court of Appeals.

The ability of the armed forces to modernize their equipment and upgrade their training became crucial in 2008. A 210,000m. peso Capability Upgrade Programme, which had commenced in 2006 and was in its first phase, sought to make field battalions 'mission-capable'. Using weapons, vehicles and communications equipment that had been 'state of the art' when Marcos was President, the 72 army battalions and 12 marine battalions were estimated to require over 40,000m. pesos just to reach their 1992 level of capability. The programme was underfunded owing to the loss of expected profits from the Bases Conversion and Development Authority and hampered by a 2006 procurement law that prohibited multi-year contracts. Not only were the Philippine armed forces inferior to their regional counterparts, but they also began to run out of ammunition after only two weeks of fighting Moro rebels in August 2008 (see below).

From late 2008 politics focused on two main issues. First, speculation and advertisements began to emerge about likely candidates for the positions of President and Vice-President in elections scheduled to be held in 2010. Among the possible pairings were Senators Loren Legarda and Francis Escudero of the NPC; NP President Manuel Villar (who had been elected Senate President in July 2007) and party Vice-President Noli de Castro; and Senators Manuel Roxas II and Francisco Pangilinan of the Liberal Party. By early 2009 former President Estrada was also considering a candidacy, and by mid-year President Arroyo had brought about the creation of a coalition, the Lakas-Kampi-CMD, to support an administration candidate.

The second issue related to persistent attempts at constitutional reform by the Arroyo administration and its allies, which cast doubt on whether the presidential election would take place at all. Reform efforts were interpreted by the President's opponents as a means of extending her term of office through cancellation of the election or the creation of the post of Prime Minister, to be assumed by Arroyo. At the very least, these efforts kept the opposition on the defensive, and staved off the development of 'lame duck' status and the usual fractures in the ruling coalition as the end of Arroyo's term approached. In August 2008 the administration supported a federalism resolution in the Senate, in anticipation of a settlement with the MILF; when that failed, the Government and its allies renewed their efforts to constitute the House of Representatives as a constituent assembly. Although the intention of pursuing term extension through charter change was disavowed, significant opinion-makers joined the Senate in opposition to it, including potential presidential candidates, media figures, some military groups, the Catholic hierarchy, and leaders of the Jesus Is Lord movement and El Shaddai (a Catholic Charismatic Renewal movement). Even erstwhile supporter former President Ramos argued that it was too late in Arroyo's term to pursue constitutional reform. A public consensus emerged by 2009 that any reform to the Constitution should be postponed until after the 2010 election or through the election of a Constitutional Convention at that time.

Meanwhile, President Arroyo survived a fourth impeachment attempt in November 2008; however, the proceedings drew renewed attention to allegations of corruption at Malacañang Palace, the President's headquarters. Also in November, Villar was forced to resign from the presidency of the Senate, owing to a lack of support in the upper house, his unpopularity having further increased when it had emerged that provision for a road project in Villar's home province had been inserted twice into the budget; Juan Ponce Enrile was immediately nominated as Villar's replacement and swiftly sworn in. Villar had become a leading presidential candidate, and his ousting from the position of President of the Senate was widely regarded as an attempt to undermine his candidacy.

The Supreme Court was an important factor in politics; if a constituent assembly bill was approved by the House of Representatives, it would have to withstand Supreme Court scrutiny of its constitutionality. Chief Justice Reynato Puno was widely considered a source of vexation to the Arroyo administration after he had convened a summit meeting on extra-judicial killings in 2007 to address the issue of the murder and disappearance of political activists. Furthermore, in the same year Puno had promulgated the 'writ of amparo', which enabled relatives of victims of alleged extra-judicial killings to demand to see military records, and which, supporters of the writ argued, had contributed to a subsequent notable decline in the number of extra-judicial killings. Puno had voted against the majority that upheld executive privilege in the ZTE case of 2007 and led the court in declaring unconstitutional the Memorandum of Agreement on Ancestral Domain (MOA-AD) with the MILF in 2008 (see below). As Chief Justice, Puno was also a member of the Judicial and Bar Council (JBC), which produced the shortlist from which the President was required to fill vacancies on the bench. A constitutional crisis was narrowly averted in August 2009 when Arroyo made a last-minute appointment from the list, after a request that the JBC include additional names was rebuffed.

Another issue relating to the 2010 presidential election was the fate of election automation and other reforms to prevent fraud. Comelec was still regarded as highly politicized, unaccountable and unprepared to update the national voter list before May 2010. The technology proposed by Comelec to automate elections encountered opposition from many parties; however, it seemed likely to reduce the opportunities for the introduction of irregularities into the vote-counting process. Some 80,000 precinct count optical scan (PCOS) machines would collect and scan completed ballot papers and convert them into a digital tally on the spot. These tallies would be transmitted to a central database for compilation and would also be printable at the local level. In March 2009 both houses of Congress approved the necessary supplementary budget to proceed with the automation process. In July, after a bidding process that was deemed fair and transparent by observers, Comelec signed a contract for the joint venture between a Philippine company, Total Information Management, and Smartmatic International Corporation.

In June 2009 the two main political themes, preparation for elections and constitutional reform, converged. Arroyo's new party was unable to persuade the most popular candidate, Noli de Castro, to stand for the presidency under the Lakas-Kampi-CMD banner, probably owing to Arroyo's personal unpopularity with voters. Arroyo, meanwhile, was said to be considering running for Congress from the province of Pampanga, a plan that fitted into a constitutional reform scenario and confirmed that the President anticipated a continuation of her political career. Then, apparently under orders from Arroyo herself, the House of Representatives approved Resolution 1109, which urged its members to convene as a constituent assembly for constitutional reform. As expected, this action was condemned by the Senate, and the constitutionality of the resolution was challenged before the Supreme Court.

The political scene was altered by the death in August 2009 of former President Corazon Aquino, whose tenure had restored electoral democracy to the Philippines and who had been outspoken against the Arroyo Government's intention of amending the 1987 Constitution, which the administration of Corazon Aquino had introduced. Tens of thousands of people took to the streets to pay their last respects to the former President, and a movement emerged to support her son, Benigno Aquino, III of the Liberal Party, for the position of President. Commentators touted Aquino's legacy of effecting a peaceful transfer of power to her successor and raised the spectre of renewed 'people power' should Arroyo fail to do the same. Administration officials assured the public that the President would leave office at the end of her term, but at the same time members of the House of Representative began to distance themselves from Resolution 1109. Hopes of charter change appeared once again to have been extinguished.

Meanwhile, in June 2009 Congress approved a five-year extension of the CARP, originally implemented by the administration of Corazon Aquino in 1988. The extension allocated 150,000m. pesos for the acquisition and distribution of at least 1m. ha of land to more than 700,000 beneficiaries, although some economists believed that this would do little to alleviate poverty in the country. By July 2009 the Responsible Parenthood, Reproductive Health and Population and Development Bill—controversial draft legislation that sought to curb the country's population growth by expanding access to a variety of contraceptive methods and improving health education in schools—had gained 130 supporters in the House of Representatives, but was strongly opposed by the Catholic Bishops' Conference of the Philippines; in a public poll conducted in October 2008 63% of those surveyed supported the bill. The Philippine population was growing at an annual rate of more than 2%, one of the highest rates of expansion in Asia.

In August 2009 the Government and the CPP agreed to renew peace talks after the former released two prominent CPP leaders. Observers suggested that the CPP was being forced back to the negotiating table by the success of government counter-insurgency operations against its political infrastructure. Others regarded the renewal of peace talks as a tactical compromise to enable both the CPP and political allies of President Arroyo to win more seats in the 2010 elections. However, talks failed to materialize as both parties focused their efforts on their respective election campaigns. The NPA continued to impose 'revolutionary taxes' on mining operations and 'permit to campaign' fees on mainstream politicians in the areas under its control. Fees were said to range from 30m. pesos for a presidential candidate to 5,000 pesos for a local council candidate.

By October 2009 Benigno Aquino, Villar, former President Estrada and President Arroyo's Lakas-Kampi-CMD standard-bearer, Gilbert Teodoro (formerly Secretary of National Defense and Lakas-Kampi-CMD Chairman), had emerged as the leading presidential candidates. Aquino, whose popularity had increased significantly following the death in August of his mother, maintained a commanding lead over Villar in pre-election opinion polls, while Estrada and Teodoro oscillated between third and fourth place. Arroyo's own candidacy for a seat in the House of Representatives was approved in January 2010 by Comelec. As the date of the polls approached, local media reported delays in the delivery of the PCOS machines, as well as in the training of school teachers to use the machines and in the printing of ballot papers. There was also concern regarding both the possibility of mobile phones interfering with the transmission of data and a lack of telecommunication facilities in some areas.

President Arroyo sought to protect her post-election future by appointing Renato Corona, her former Presidential Chief of Staff, as successor to Supreme Court Chief Justice Reynato Puno, who was scheduled to retire one week after the election. In a close vote, from which Puno had excused himself, the court decided in March 2010 to rescind its 1998 ban on the appointment of public officials in the two months before an election and until the end of a President's term, the so-called 'midnight appointments'. The Arroyo administration's subsequent authorization of a plethora of appointments to state bodies and government-controlled corporations provoked widespread opposition condemnation.

Nevertheless, by most measures the 2010 elections, held as scheduled on 10 May, were a resounding success. Logistically, the main problem related to the long queues of voters at polling stations. Aquino turned this issue to his advantage by being seen to eschew the VIP line and queue for many hours with ordinary voters while waiting to cast his own ballot. According to an audit that compared the tally transmitted by the PCOS machines with a manual count in selected precincts, the PCOS machines counted ballots with a 99.6% degree of accuracy. The percentage of citizens who believed that Comelec had freely and fairly counted the votes increased from 55% in the 2007 election to 83%, with 65% attributing reduced levels of cheating in the vote count to the new automated system. For the first time, Filipinos learned major election results within hours of the polls closing. According to final results, released several weeks later, Aquino won 41.9% of the votes cast, Estrada unexpectedly secured second place with 26.1%, while Villar was placed third with 15.4% and Teodoro fourth with 11.3%. In the vice-presidential election, Estrada's running mate, Jejomar Binay, narrowly defeated the leading contender, Manuel Roxas II, who had initially intended to stand as the Liberal Party's presidential candidate for the presidency but had stepped aside to make way for Aquino. Arroyo was elected as the congressional representative of the second district of Pampanga, having defeated her three rivals by a significant margin.

The nine-year presidency of Gloria Arroyo came to an end in June 2010, leaving a mixed legacy. Her supporters cited a 5% decrease in the poverty rate between 2005 and 2008, the inflow of US $11,200m. in foreign direct investment and the creation of 1m. new jobs; progress in talks with the MILF and peace within the armed forces; new infrastructure outside Metro Manila and cheaper inter-island shipping; continued deregulation of the airline industry and the encouragement of domestic holiday travel. Arroyo's critics, on the other hand, countered that economic growth was faster in several other South-East Asian countries and that the Philippines still relied heavily on remittances from foreign workers, who collectively accounted for about 10% of the Philippines' population and included at least 10,000 doctors, thus depriving the country of valuable, skilled personnel. They also drew attention to the failure of Congress during 2008–10 to approve the Responsible Parenthood, Reproductive Health and Population and Development Bill and the birth of 1.8m. Filipinos during that time; and to persistent inequality and the continued threat of the CPP and the NPA. However, what was largely undisputed was that Arroyo had increased government effectiveness, strengthened policy-making and accrued power to the executive at the expense of the legislative and judicial branches of central government. This was achieved by means of stringent control of the budgetary process that distributed rewards to local allies and withheld funds from political rivals. This pattern of alliance with local power-holders was demonstrated by the 'Maguindanao Massacre' of November 2009 (see below).

THE GOVERNMENT OF BENIGNO AQUINO

Benigno Aquino was sworn in as President on 30 June 2010. In his inauguration speech, the new President hailed 'the end of a regime indifferent to the needs of the people' and identified a number of priorities for his administration, including combating corruption, addressing the persistent budgetary deficit, reducing bureaucracy in order to render the country more attractive to potential investors, enhancing national infrastructure and improving the education system. On the previous day Aquino had announced the composition of his new Cabinet, which was dominated by members of the Liberal Party, technocrats and representatives of the business sector. Alberto Romulo retained the foreign affairs portfolio, while Voltaire Gazmin was appointed Secretary of National Defense; both men had been close allies of Corazon Aquino. Other notable members of the incoming Cabinet included Cesar Purisima, who resumed responsibility for the finance portfolio, and Leila de Lima, hitherto Chairperson of the Commission on Human Rights of the Philippines, who became Secretary of Justice, an appointment that was welcomed by human rights and anti-corruption groups.

On 1 July 2010 Arroyo filed a congressional resolution appealing for a constitutional convention to propose changes to the Constitution, furthering concerns among her critics that she was seeking the introduction of a parliamentary system of government with a view to returning to power in a prime-ministerial position. Some observers, while supportive of constitutional reform, questioned whether Arroyo was the right person to file the resolution, arguing that her unpopularity would likely result in the resolution being defeated, while others suggested that Arroyo's decision to file the resolution reflected an addiction to power on the part of the former President. A presidential spokesperson stated that constitutional change was 'not a priority' and that debates on the proposal would distract attention from the Aquino administration's primary objectives of combating poverty and corruption, while Feliciano Belmonte, who was elected Speaker of the House of Representatives in mid-July, argued that the issue of constitutional reform was 'time-consuming and divisive'. Aquino himself stated that he would not endorse proposals to reform the Constitution unless there was proof that such action was urgently required.

At the end of July 2010 Aquino revoked by executive order some 977 'midnight appointments' authorized by the Arroyo administration during its final weeks, and formally established the Philippines Truth Commission of 2010, which was to investigate alleged human rights abuses and other anomalies from the Arroyo presidency. However, concerns were raised about the apparently limited scope of the Commission, and several further extra-judicial killings were reported during the early weeks of Aquino's tenure. (In July 2011 Human Rights Watch claimed that it possessed evidence of military involvement in seven extra-judicial killings and three enforced disappearances since Aquino took office in June 2010, and urged the Philippine Government to conduct full and proper investigations into such cases.) A small group of legislators, known allies of Arroyo, filed a petition with the Supreme Court in August seeking to nullify the Commission, claiming that it was unconstitutional and encroached upon the respective remits of the Department of Justice and the Office of the Ombudsman. In December the Court ruled that the Commission was unconstitutional since it 'singled out' an individual, Arroyo. Aquino expressed concern at the ruling, which he denounced as a set-back for anti-graft reform, but vowed to continue his efforts undeterred. The Secretary of Justice dismissed the ruling as being politically motivated, an apparent reference to the fact that 14 of the 15 Supreme Court justices had been appointed by Arroyo, including the Chief Justice, Renato Corona, whose 'midnight appointment' in April had not been challenged by the incoming Aquino administration. In October a petition filed by Bai Omera Dianalan-Lucman appealing against the revocation of his 'midnight appointment' was upheld by the Supreme Court, prompting an angry response from Aquino, who urged the Court to reconsider its ruling, which, the President argued, would have 'far-reaching consequences' throughout the executive branch of government.

Meanwhile, the first crisis of the Aquino administration presented itself when eight Hong Kong tourists were killed and a further seven injured following the hijacking of a bus in Manila in mid-August 2010 by a former Filipino police officer, Rolando Mendoza, who had recently been dismissed on suspicion of extortion and brutality. An 11-hour siege was finally concluded when armed police officers approached the bus at close quarters and fatally shot Mendoza. Aquino issued a public apology for the outcome of the affair and pledged to reprimand those found to be responsible. However, the Government attracted criticism for its handling of the incident, with local police officers and government officials apparently having been left to tackle the situation without direct federal assistance. Furthermore, witnesses stated that negotiation efforts appeared to have been leading to a peaceful resolution to the impasse when the authorities decided to approach the bus and that it was the advance of the police officers that had provoked Mendoza into opening fire on his hostages; the strategy had been intended to carry the element of surprise, but, unbeknown to the authorities, had been broadcast live on television and watched by Mendoza on a monitor aboard the bus. Of further embarrassment to the Philippine authorities was the revelation by Secretary of Justice de Lima in September that the Government was investigating the theory that some of the tourists killed might have been shot by the police officers trying to rescue them. In the same month investigators recommended that criminal charges be brought against 12 people deemed to have been responsible for the violent conclusion to the siege, including police officers, the mayor of Manila and two journalists; three national broadcasting networks, which had relayed live images of the police operation, were also identified as having been culpable.

In October 2010 Aquino announced a presidential proclamation granting amnesty to rebel soldiers involved in the military uprisings of 2003 and 2006. Senator Antonio Trillanes IV was among those released from prison in December 2010, and was able to take up his seat in the Senate for the first time in January 2011. Shortly after Aquino had taken office, Nicanor Faeldon, one of several military officers who in November 2007 had walked out of court during their trial on charges of staging a coup in July 2003 and occupied a hotel in protest against the perceived illegitimacy of Arroyo's presidency, voluntarily surrendered to the authorities 'in recognition of the legitimacy' of Aquino's presidency.

In January 2011 the US district court of Hawaii approved the disbursement of US $1,000 to each of 7,526 victims of human rights abuses perpetrated during the regime of former President Ferdinand Marcos; the compensation payments commenced in late February, and by mid-April some 6,500 victims had received their monies. The US court also held Imelda Marcos and Ferdinand Marcos, Jr in contempt for violating a court order requesting information on assets belonging to the Marcos estate, and fined them $353.6m., which was to fulfil in part the $2,000m. ruling against the Marcos estate in 1994. In April 2011 a Philippine court ordered Imelda Marcos to reimburse the state with 12m. pesos that her late husband was found to have misappropriated from the Government's National Food Authority in 1983.

In February 2011 Albert del Rosario was appointed acting Secretary of Foreign Affairs, in place of Alberto G. Romulo; del Rosario was confirmed in the post at the end of May. Edcel Lagman was elected as National Chairman of Lakas-Kampi-CMD, in place of Gloria Arroyo, while Ramon Bong Revilla, Jr was chosen as the party's National President.

The issue of corruption continued to attract much attention throughout the first year of Aquino's administration, which appeared keen to use public scandals dating from Arroyo's presidency to its political advantage. In February 2011 former cabinet minister Angelo Reyes, a close ally of Arroyo who had served as army chief of staff in 2000–01, died in an apparent suicide shortly prior to a scheduled appearance before a congressional committee investigating allegations of corruption within the military. Reyes was alleged by Lt-Col George Rabusa, a former military budget officer, to have received 50m. pesos diverted from state coffers upon his departure from his military post, but he had denied any wrongdoing. Rabusa claimed that all departing chiefs of staff had received large sums of money in this way, and that Carlos Garcia, former army comptroller, had received some 160m. pesos, having ordered Rabusa to make 16 separate withdrawals of 10m. pesos on his behalf. The diverted funds, Rabusa alleged, had been intended for combat equipment, military intelligence, soldiers' wages and a military hospital. The accused denied all charges against them. According to the results of a survey published in March 2011, nearly one-half of Filipinos considered the military to be the most corrupt public entity. In the same month Aquino pledged to punish those officers found to have embezzled state funds and charged his newly appointed military chief of staff, Lt-Gen. Eduardo Oban, with effecting radical reform of the military so as to eradicate large-scale vice, insisting that corruption would no longer be tolerated as, Aquino claimed, it had been by his predecessor. Also in March the House of Representatives voted to impeach the Ombudsman, Merceditas Gutierrez, another close ally of Arroyo, on the charge of betraying public trust, by 210 votes to 46. The motion accused Gutierrez of failing properly to address corruption allegations against Arroyo and other senior officials during her presidency, including the recent military graft scandal as well as the scandal emanating from the tape recording during which the voice of Arroyo was apparently heard trying to influence the vote-counting process during the 2004 presidential election (see above). Citing the likelihood of protracted impeachment proceedings against her distracting attention from important legislative considerations, Gutierrez announced her resignation at the end of April 2011, and was replaced in an interim capacity by Orlando Casimiro. In his 2011 State of the Nation address, given in late July, Aquino announced that Conchita Carpio-Morales, hitherto an associate justice in the Supreme Court, had been appointed as the new Ombudsman.

In June 2011 the United Church of Christ, a Protestant church grouping, filed a civil lawsuit against Arroyo, claiming that during her administration security forces had detained and tortured many of its members and had killed at least six. A report published by Amnesty International in the previous month claimed that more than 200 disappearances and at least 305 extra-judicial killings that took place during the Arroyo administration remained unresolved.

At mid-2011 both legislative chambers were debating controversial legislation, first introduced in 2005, which sought to promote awareness, and to increase availability, of contraceptives; if approved, the legislation would require the Government to provide reproductive health education in schools. Critics of the Responsible Parenthood, Reproductive Health and Population and Development Bill argued that it would lead to an increase in the number of abortions and a decline in moral values. Tens of thousands of people attended a rally in Manila in March 2011 to protest against the draft legislation, which was due to be voted on later in the year. However, others contended that the legislation was necessary in order to reduce both the national population growth rate (and in turn the rate of poverty) and the incidence of medical complications arising from the practice of unsafe abortions (abortion being illegal in the Philippines). Meanwhile, in October 2010 the Supreme Court had upheld the constitutionality of the Human Security Act, which was known to have been invoked just twice since its implementation in July 2007. Several human rights groups and legislators had lodged separate petitions seeking to revoke the legislation, arguing that its definition of 'terrorism' was too broad-based and that it posed a significant threat to civil liberties.

Upon assuming power, the Aquino administration had emphasized its commitment to concluding a peace settlement with the NDF, the NPA and the CPP. In July 2010 Aquino announced the formation of two government 'peace panels', one to facilitate negotiations with the NDF, the NPA and the CPP, and the other to focus on the peace process with the MILF. The NDF continued to appeal for the release of all political prisoners and meaningful land reform, while sporadic violent clashes were reported throughout 2010. In mid-December 10 government soldiers were killed in an ambush by NPA rebels, two days prior to the scheduled commencement of an 18-day cease-fire between government troops and the NPA, the longest cease-fire agreed in some 10 years. Nevertheless, the cease-fire appeared to be observed by both sides. Following its conclusion in early January 2011, senior NPA leader Tiro Alcantara (alias Ka or Comrade Bart) was arrested and charged with more than 20 counts of murder. Formal peace talks were convened in February, under the auspices of the Norwegian Government, and were reported to have been constructive, with both the Philippine Government and the NPA expressing their resolve to conclude a comprehensive settlement by June 2012. Further talks were due to have been held in June 2011. However, in a letter sent early in the month to Alex Padilla, the Government's chief negotiator, Luis Jalandoni, Padilla's NDF counterpart, warned that the continued detention of 17 NDF members 'seriously prejudiced' the peace talks and urged that the process be suspended until they were released.

RECENT DEVELOPMENTS IN MINDANAO

Although the armed strength of the MILF had declined as a result of military action by the Estrada regime, it remained a potent force, with a strong recruitment base among ordinary Muslim Filipinos struggling with poverty and prejudice. In July 2001 in Tripoli, Libya, a cease-fire between the Government and the MILF was concluded, and an accord—containing basic principles and an agenda for future negotiations on security, rehabilitation and development, and ancestral domain—was signed in August. Meanwhile, sporadic fighting between government and MILF forces continued. Moreover, the plebiscite held on 14 August in Mindanao, which the Government had hoped would increase the authority of the

ARMM, was marked by a low level of participation and an emphatic rejection, except in Basilan and Marawi City.

In May 2002 an agreement was reached between the Government and the MILF, whereby the former would provide reparations for damaged MILF property and establish a state-funded aid body, to be administered by the MILF, in order to assist the many thousands of Muslims displaced by fighting in Mindanao. This agreement even included plans to relinquish control of the MILF stronghold at Abubakar for non-military purposes, but these plans were abandoned owing to strong opposition from within the military and Congress. Moreover, despite the cease-fire agreement negotiated in 2001, sporadic military encounters continued, and by late 2002 the pace of peace discussions had slowed. Indeed, the future of relations between the Government and the MILF, and the Arroyo doctrine of a non-military solution, came under increasing pressure following repeated claims that the MILF, rather than Abu Sayyaf, had the strongest links to international terrorist groups.

Despite an apparent decline in hostilities involving Abu Sayyaf members, violence between government soldiers and Muslim separatists continued intermittently. Several bomb attacks took place in 2002–03, including two blasts in Zamboanga City in October 2002, in which several people were killed and some 150 were injured. In February 2003 important transmission pylons were destroyed, leaving the whole of Mindanao without power, and in the same month a bomb explosion at Awang airport in Cotabato City killed one soldier and injured six civilians. In March 21 civilians were killed and 134 injured when bombs were detonated outside Davao Airport. These and other attacks were thought to have been carried out by Abu Sayyaf or other breakaway factions of the MNLF or the MILF, although the leadership of the latter consistently denounced attacks on civilian targets.

In June 2003 the MILF declared a unilateral cease-fire supported by Local Monitoring Teams in 13 conflict-affected provinces, and in July the Philippine Government asked Malaysia to host peace talks amid pressures from the USA to have the MILF designated an international terrorist organization, a proposal against which President Arroyo campaigned. In July the Chairman of the MILF, Hashim Salamat, died of natural causes. His replacement, Al-Haj Murad Ebrahim, while a devout Muslim, was not considered a religious ideologue; he continued to insist on the MILF's local orientation and organizational independence. Although peace negotiations continued, the MILF's change in leadership, along with continued efforts by Indonesian and Malaysian members of the regional Islamist organization Jemaah Islamiah (JI) to recruit and establish training camps in Mindanao, created tensions within the MILF; according to some sources, these tensions were leading to its fragmentation.

Abu Sayyaf re-emerged in February 2004 with a bombing that sank a new super-ferry, resulting in 116 deaths. This was reportedly perpetrated in conjunction with the Manila-based Rajah Solaiman Movement (RSM), an organization formed in 2002 and predominantly comprising Muslim converts. In August 2004 a total of 17 members of Abu Sayyaf, found guilty of kidnapping offences, were sentenced to death. In December Abu Sayyaf claimed responsibility for an explosion in General Santos City that killed 14 civilians, and in February 2005 it was reported to be responsible for a series of simultaneous bomb explosions in General Santos City, Davao City and Metro Manila, killing about the same number and injuring hundreds more. While small numbers of alleged Abu Sayyaf members were killed or captured, its membership appeared to be growing and so too was its association with JI and RSM. The latter's founding leader, Ahmad Santos, was one of eight men arrested by the Philippine authorities in October 2005 on suspicion of organizing militant attacks in the country's south. In August relatively peaceful elections were held in the ARMM, although MNLF renegades loyal to Nur Misuari, the former Governor of the region who had been imprisoned in 2002 for inciting rebellion, continued to challenge the Philippine authorities.

By contrast, the MILF assisted the Philippine military in tracking down Abu Sayyaf and JI activists, in part as an attempt to dispel US and Philippine military claims that it was sheltering international terrorists. In October 2004 an International Monitoring Team (IMT), led by Malaysia and including members from Libya and Japan, began working with the Local Monitoring Teams. Subsequently, alleged cease-fire violations declined from some 500 in 2002–04 to 37 in 2005, with a continuing downward trend in both violent and non-violent incidents in 2006. Nevertheless, MILF splinter groups did appear to have been engaged in such activities, and in January 2005 were suspected to be responsible for the first major breakdown of the 2003 cease-fire. In the ensuing fighting and air-strikes, more than 60 people were killed, most of them on the Moro side.

However, by and large the MILF and the armed forces continued to liaise with each other and the IMT through a Joint Monitoring Assistance Center (JMAC) established in July 2005. The relative success of the security arrangements allowed for progress in the areas of rehabilitation and development. The IMT was able to engage in medical assistance and resettlement of displaced families in conflict-affected areas. In March 2006 the World Bank-led Mindanao Trust Fund-Reconstruction and Development Program (MTF-RDP) was created to begin capacity-building activities even before the signing of a final peace agreement. This first phase of the MTF-RDP was to be funded by New Zealand, Canada, Australia, Sweden and the World Bank, while Japan directly funded the construction of school buildings, post-harvest facilities, a livelihood training centre for Bangsamoro women and potable water systems. The commitment of the parties and their international partners to development before peace reflected the experience gained from the governance failures of the ARMM following the MNLF's 1996 peace agreement with the Government.

Negotiations in 2006, hosted by Malaysia, reached an impasse over the final and most difficult issue—ancestral domain—in September. Both parties acknowledged the need for more preliminary work on the delineation of territory and wider public support for the peace process. In November the Government's principal negotiator, Silvestre Afable, informally offered the MILF broad self-determination—within constitutional limits and excluding areas such as foreign affairs and defence—once the territory was defined, and talks were to resume after the May 2007 elections. However, Afable resigned from the Government's peace panel in June 2007, citing lack of support from the President and cabinet security officials, who appeared to rescind the offer of self-determination in August. He was replaced by Gen. (retd) Rodolfo Garcia.

Conditions for negotiation were also marred by serious incidents of violence in mid-2007. In July marines searching for a kidnapped Italian priest (suspected to be held by Abu Sayyaf) were ambushed in MILF territory in Basilan, leaving 14 dead (10 of whom were beheaded). The MILF admitted to ambushing the soldiers, but denied mutilating their bodies. An independent investigation swiftly revealed the probable motive for the beheadings: before the recent elections, the marine unit had strictly enforced a gun ban and angered local politicians. The incident highlighted how the interaction of secessionist, criminal and political violence could easily escalate and disrupt the fragile peace. Then, in early August, the armed forces quietly began a campaign in Sulu. Soldiers were told that they were pursuing Abu Sayyaf personnel, but later reported taking part in operations against the MNLF. The latter claimed that all the casualties on the Moro side were its own, while the armed forces maintained that its enemies were Abu Sayyaf fighters who were collaborating with 'rogue' MNLF combatants. By mid-August the armed forces had suffered 27 fatalities in Sulu. With more than 6,000 troops pursuing fewer than 500 armed fighters in Sulu and Basilan, these losses raised questions about the high level of tactical errors and the effect of constant operations on weary troops. In late August a massive reorganization of the upper echelons of the armed forces was announced.

Despite these set-backs, the cease-fire remained in force and informal negotiations resumed on the delineation of territory for a Bangsamoro Juridical Entity (BJE), including quiet consultation with political and religious leaders of affected communities. The urgent need to move towards a resolution was underlined in May 2008, when Malaysia withdrew 29 of its unarmed peace monitors from the IMT in protest at delays. Finally, the details of a MOA-AD, which had been initialled by the Government and the MILF in July, were revealed a few days in advance of a formal signing ceremony scheduled for 5 August in Kuala Lumpur, Malaysia. The MOA-AD recognized the Bangsamoro as a 'first nation' with an ancestral domain distinct from the public domain of the Philippines. It identified this domain—subject to approval in a plebiscite—as the whole of the ARMM, together with specified areas in Palawan, Zamboanga del Norte, Zamboanga del Sur, Zamboanga Sibugay, North Cotabato, Sultan Kudarat and Sarangani provinces, including parts of the cities of Iligan, Zamboanga and Isabela. The MOA-AD also outlined expanded responsibility and authority for the BJE, especially in economic and fiscal matters.

The contents of the MOA-AD and the secretive manner in which it had been formulated drew immediate protests from leaders of cities and provinces proposed for whole or partial inclusion in the BJE. Several legislators filed petitions with the Supreme Court to stop the Government from signing and implementing the agreement, arguing that the MOA-AD was 'patently unconstitutional . . . eroding, as it does, the national sovereignty and territorial integrity of the Philippine state', and that the Government had abused and exceeded its authority in negotiating the accord. The Supreme Court issued a temporary restraining order on 4 August 2008, preventing the signing ceremony from taking place, after which Liberal Party leader Manuel Roxas II condemned the agreement in a widely publicized Senate speech. In subsequent weeks the Manila-based media reflected rising anti-MOA-AD and anti-Muslim sentiments.

At first, the MILF's chief peace negotiator, Mohagher Iqbal, insisted that the initialled MOA-AD was 'binding on the contracting parties', while the Government's Solicitor-General told the Supreme Court that it was 'merely a codification of consensus points reached between both parties', the implementation of which depended on the enactment of legislation, constitutional amendment, and the holding of a plebiscite. However, events soon overshadowed the disagreement over legal nuances. Fighting broke out between the Bangsa Moro Islamic Armed Forces (the MILF's military wing) and government forces after the former occupied, looted and burned 20 villages in North Cotabato, displacing 165,000 people. In a dramatic escalation on 18 August 2008, MILF commanders Ombra Kato and Abdullah Macapaar (alias Commander Bravo) ambushed an army convoy in Lanao del Sur and raided towns in Lanao del Norte and Sarangani, killing civilians with gunfire and machetes. The Government demanded that the MILF surrender the rebel commanders, which it refused to do, while members of the opposition urged a military response and a halt to the peace process. As the atmosphere in Manila became more hostile, the Government declared the MOA-AD defunct and requested that the Supreme Court dismiss the petitions against it; however, the Court ruled in October that the agreement was unconstitutional.

In September 2008 the Government disbanded its peace panel, ending 11 years of official negotiation and prompting fears that the cease-fire would collapse. By this time, the National Disaster Co-ordinating Council had reported the deaths of 70 people (including 62 civilians) and the displacement of a further 500,000 owing to the hostilities. However, the Co-ordinating Committee on the Cessation of Hostilities and the IMT remained in place, the latter now comprising a diminished group of 12 Malaysians (whose mission had been extended at the end of August for a further three months), along with 10 Bruneians, eight Libyans and one Japanese development worker.

The unsuccessful MOA-AD had revealed weaknesses on both sides of the dispute: the MILF's inability to control its commands, and the degree to which all parties distrusted the central Government. During the following 12 months, no peace talks were held as the Government continued to search for the rebel commanders and shifted its engagement strategy with armed groups (including the NPA) from political settlement to 'disarmament, demobilization and rehabilitation'. A number of kidnappings were carried out by Abu Sayyaf, including the abduction in January 2009 of three aid workers of the International Committee of the Red Cross, who were held for between three and six months before being released. There was an increasing incidence of bombings of public places using improvised explosive devices. In July the Government suspended offensive military action against the MILF, which reciprocated in kind, and both sides announced that they were working toward the resumption of formal peace talks. It was announced in August that several members of the OIC, as well as one or two European countries, were to join an International Contact Group to monitor and help implement any agreement signed by the Government and the MILF. However, clashes broke out in the same month in Basilan, which were reported to have claimed the lives of 23 government troops, 21 Abu Sayyaf members and 10 MILF fighters.

In late 2009 national and international attention focused on an unprecedented election-related massacre in the ARMM province of Maguindanao in November. En route to file a certificate of candidacy for the provincial governorship on behalf of local politician Ismael Mangudadatu, a convoy of his supporters (including his wife and two sisters), together with lawyers and journalists, drove into territory controlled by armed militia loyal to the powerful provincial Ampatuan clan, headed by the incumbent Maguindanao Governor, Andal Ampatuan, Sr. The convoy was intercepted and directed to a deserted area by a group of about 100 armed men, allegedly led by Andal Ampatuan, Jr, who had been widely expected to stand, unopposed, for election to the Maguindanao governorship, in place of his father. Some members of the convoy managed to call for help, but the complicity of locally assigned army and police personnel, including some senior officers, supported by so-called CVOs (civilian volunteer organizations under police command), hampered any timely response. Eyewitnesses to the incident described seeing the armed men shoot the victims at close range, before dumping them in shallow graves. The authorities eventually recovered 57 bodies, many of which showed signs of sexual assault and mutilation. At least 30 members of the media were among the victims—the highest number of journalists ever killed in a single incident anywhere in the world.

In the aftermath of the brazen massacre, a significant Ampatuan arsenal was confiscated, martial law was briefly imposed in Maguindanao (with military control subsequently continuing) and the main suspects, identified by eyewitnesses, were arrested and held without bail, including Ampatuan, Sr, together with Ampatuan, Jr and his brother, ARMM Governor Zaldy Ampatuan. All three were expelled from Lakas-Kampi-CMD; Ampatuan, Sr and Zaldy Ampatuan were both removed from their respective governorships. However, such measures did not conceal the systemic nature of the incident. The Ampatuan clan was closely allied with the Arroyo administration, which had long traded weapons and revenue allocations in exchange for valuable votes with which it had secured its tenure. In April 2010 the Acting Secretary of Justice, Alberto Agra, directed prosecutors to dismiss multiple murder charges against Zaldy Ampatuan and his cousin, Akmad Ampatuan, the mayor of Mamasapano, owing to an apparent lack of evidence. However, following protests by relatives of the victims of the massacre and by the Department of Justice's own prosecutors, the decision was soon reversed. Nevertheless, the elections in May appeared to signal that the clan's political power would continue unabated: although Mangudadatu secured election to the post of Governor of Maguindanao (defeating two known allies of the Ampatuan clan), 15 Ampatuans (of the 68 candidates) won seats throughout the province. With less than one-half of the 196 charged persons in custody by the time the trial formally opened in September 2010, there were widespread reports of attempts to intimidate investigators and witnesses by supporters of the Ampatuan clan. At least five people known to have provided, or to have agreed to provide, incriminatory testimony against the Ampatuans were reported to have been killed prior to the commencement of the trial. Given the naming of 200 witnesses by the prosecution and of a further 300 by the defence, the trial was not expected to be concluded rapidly.

A rift between the public prosecutors and the private lawyers of the victims' relatives became increasingly apparent as the trial progressed, and precipitated the resignation, in March 2011, of two public prosecutors, both of whom cited an 'intolerable' working environment. Meanwhile, a report published by

Human Rights Watch in November 2010 claimed that during the previous 20 years the Ampatuan clan had been responsible for at least 56 killings in addition to those of the Maguindanao massacre; the international human rights organization urged the Philippine Government to conduct a full investigation into the allegations. In June 2011 the Philippine Court of Appeals ordered that assets of US $23m. in bank accounts, businesses and property belonging to the Ampatuan family be frozen, pending an investigation into how the family's wealth had been accumulated.

Meanwhile, in April 2010 an MOU emphasizing the intention of both the MNLF and the Government to work towards 'just, meaningful and lasting peace and development in Mindanao' was signed in Libya, and in the following month arrangements for the Bangsamoro Development Assistance Fund were concluded in Surabaya, Indonesia. In December consensus points for proposed amendments to the 1996 ARMM peace accord were initialled by government and MNLF representatives meeting at the Indonesian embassy in Manila. A number of issues of contention remained, but both sides welcomed the initialling of consensus points as a sign of significant progress.

The change of presidential administration in June 2010, following Benigno Aquino's election in May, similarly brought fresh impetus to the peace process with the MILF. In July Marvic Leonen, an environmental and community activist and dean of the University of the Philippines College of Law, was chosen to lead the government negotiating team, while the MILF retained Mohagher Iqbal as its chief negotiator. In September Aquino announced the formation of an advisory body to assist the Government's negotiating team and to facilitate 'greater transparency and accountability' during the forthcoming peace negotiations. An attack by MILF rebels later that month on a military outpost on Mindanao, which resulted in an exchange of gunfire with government soldiers, was interpreted by some observers as an attempt by certain elements within the MILF to disrupt the peace process. Tensions as a result of the incident, together with a disagreement over the Malaysian facilitator, resulted in a delay in the resumption of the talks. The Philippine Government claimed that Othman Razak, who had been facilitating the peace talks between the Government and the MILF since 2003, was biased towards the latter, and demanded his replacement with an intermediary who would remain impartial; the MILF denied that Razak had demonstrated any such bias and insisted that he be allowed to continue as facilitator in order to ensure continuity in the talks.

The arrest of a senior MILF leader, Abraham Yap Alonto, in October 2010 was condemned by the MILF leadership as 'a direct blow to the early resumption of the negotiations'. In the same month a bomb explosion on a bus in North Cotabato province in the southern Philippines, which claimed the lives of eight people and injured a further 10, was believed by the authorities to have been carried out by a splinter group of JI in an attempt further to delay the resumption of peace talks between the Government and the MILF. A bomb attack on a bus terminal in North Cotabato in November, which killed one person and injured two others, was similarly attributed to Islamist militants seeking to disrupt the peace process. In January 2011 a further bomb explosion on a bus, in Manila, killed five people and injured 13 others; no claim of responsibility was immediately issued, but the authorities stated that the device used in the bombing was similar to those used in recent attacks on Mindanao. In January–February some 3,000 local villagers were reported to have been displaced by violent clashes between hundreds of rival MNLF and MILF members, which killed at least 13 rebels and injured about a dozen others. Further bomb attacks and kidnappings were reported in mid-2011, notably the abduction in April of 13 people, including one child, by local militia in Mindanao's Agusan del Sur province; all the hostages were released unharmed five days later after the kidnappers' demand—namely, the release of tribal leader Jobert 'Ondo' Perez—appeared to have been met by the local authorities.

Despite the ongoing violence, formal negotiations between the MILF and the Philippine Government were reconvened in Kuala Lumpur in February 2011, with both sides expressing confidence that a peace agreement could be concluded within 12 months. The MILF presented its 'comprehensive compact' for peace, which the Government subsequently confirmed did not include the demand for independence. A second round of negotiations was held in April, brokered by a new facilitator, Tengku Dato' Ab Ghafar Tengku Mohamed, former secretary of Malaysia's National Security Council; both sides expressed support for the appointment. During the discussions, the MILF submitted a draft proposal for the creation of Bangsamoro sub-state in Mindanao. A third round of talks was held in late June, but was cut short after the Government announced that it was to defer the presentation of its counter-proposal until the following round of talks, which was scheduled to be held later in the year. Meanwhile, shortly before the resumption of talks in February it was revealed that a splinter group of the MILF had been formed. Headed by Ustadz Ameril Umbra Kato, the so-called Bangsamoro Islamic Freedom Fighters (BIFF) was identified as a threat to the peace process by both the MILF and the Government. The MILF leadership was reported in April to have expelled Kato from the MILF after he refused to disband his armed grouping. In July the MILF issued a statement urging those engaged in 'anti-MILF seminars'—widely believed to be a reference to Kato and other BIFF commanders—to cease all efforts to obstruct the peace process, and accusing such individuals and groups of undermining 'the legitimate aspirations of the Bangsamoro people'.

Meanwhile, in early August 2010 an apparent suicide bombing at Zamboanga airport claimed the lives of two people, including the perpetrator, and injured 24 others, among them the Governor of Sulu, Sakur Tan. Shortly after the attack, which was believed to have been an attempt to assassinate Sakur Tan, who had spearheaded campaigns targeting members of the Abu Sayyaf grouping, the US ambassador to the Philippines cancelled a scheduled visit to Zamboanga.

In March 2011 Ricardo Ayeras, a founding member of the RSM, was reported to have been captured by the Philippine authorities in Manila. Ayeras was alleged to have been involved in a number of terrorist attacks, including the bombing in 2003 at Awang airport and a foiled plot to bomb several business establishments in the capital in 2005.

RECENT FOREIGN RELATIONS

The regional relations of the Philippines have been impeded by a protracted dispute over sovereignty of the Spratly Islands in the South China Sea, the other claimants being the People's Republic of China, Taiwan, Viet Nam, Brunei and Malaysia. In February 1995 it was revealed that Chinese forces had occupied an area of the disputed islands claimed by the Philippines (the first time that China had seized territory in the South China Sea from a country other than Viet Nam). The Philippine Government lodged a formal diplomatic protest with the Chinese Government, which had established several permanent structures on Mischief Reef, located about 200 km from the Philippine island of Palawan. Although the Philippines ruled out the use of force to regain the territory, air and sea patrols in the region were increased, 62 Chinese fishermen and five Chinese vessels were detained in the area and Chinese territorial markers were destroyed. In August the Chinese Government agreed for the first time to settle disputes in the South China Sea according to international law, rather than insisting that historical claims should take precedence. The Chinese and Philippine Governments issued a joint statement agreeing on a code of conduct to reduce the possibility of a military confrontation in the area. A similar agreement was signed with Viet Nam in November 1995. In March 1996 the Philippines and China agreed to co-operate in combating piracy, which was also a source of tension between the two countries since pirate vessels in the area often sailed under Chinese flags. In May, however, the Philippines, together with other nations in the region, expressed concern after the Chinese Government announced new territorial claims.

Relations between the Philippines and China improved slightly in late 1996 when the Chinese President, Jiang Zemin, visited the Philippines in November and the two countries agreed to exchange military attachés. However, the construction of an airstrip by the Philippines on one of the Spratly Islands was criticized by China. The entry of Chinese warships into the waters around the Spratly Islands in April 1997 prompted a formal protest from the Philippine Government. Tension was heightened in May, when a Chinese flag that had been raised on one of the islands was replaced by the Philippine flag. Several Chinese fishermen, who had entered Philippine waters, were arrested by the Philippine authorities, and in late May negotiations were held between the two countries to resolve the situation.

The escalating conflict over the Spratly Islands constituted the most urgent international issue confronting the Philippines during the first year of office of President Estrada. In November 1998 the Philippines protested to China over its construction of fort-like buildings on Mischief Reef, which the Philippines claimed to be within its exclusive economic zone. The Philippine navy responded by arresting Chinese fishermen for illegal fishing in nearby waters, and impounded their boats; however, China refused to dismantle the structures. Relations deteriorated further in May 1999 when China claimed that one of its fishing vessels had sunk after being deliberately rammed by a Philippine navy boat. A further Chinese fishing vessel sank in a collision with a Philippine navy vessel in July. In the mean time, Philippine relations with fellow Association of Southeast Asian Nations (ASEAN) claimants of the Spratly Islands varied. Joint troop operations in the islands were agreed with Viet Nam, and in mid-1999 Malaysia intensified its dispute with the Philippines with the construction of a two-storey building on Investigator Shoal, a reef claimed by both countries. The Philippines and Viet Nam drafted a new code of conduct for claimants of the Spratlys, which was approved by ASEAN.

As a result of China's expansionist policy in the South China Sea, relations between the Philippines and the USA improved considerably. Despite protests by the Catholic Church and the nationalist left, the May 1999 session of the Philippine Senate ratified the Visiting Forces Agreement (VFA) between the Philippines and the USA, thereby allowing joint military operations to take place in the Philippines. President Estrada campaigned strenuously for the ratification, despite his earlier support for the dismantling of the US military bases in 1992. Rationalized as an integral element to the modernization of the Philippine armed forces, the VFA also appeared to be part of the Government's strategy for dealing with its problems in the Spratly Islands and internal conflicts with the MILF and the communist movement.

In Manila, in November 1999, China rejected the code, prepared by ASEAN, for international conduct in the South China Sea, but subsequently softened its stance by circulating its own modified code in early 2000. During a state visit to China in May 2000 President Estrada concluded a number of agreements and issued a joint statement with China's President Jiang in which they undertook to seek the peaceful resolution of regional disputes. President Estrada subsequently visited the USA, but was forced to abandon his visit owing to the Abu Sayyaf hostage crisis in the Philippines (see above). Earlier, in January 2000, the first joint military exercises between the USA and the Philippines for five years took place, amid local protests, under the new VFA. Although it was not publicly acknowledged, US military personnel were reported to have been directly involved in attempts to resolve the Abu Sayyaf hostage crisis.

Moro separatist activities continued to be at the forefront of international relations. During the latter part of the Estrada period, the MILF was reported to have been training radical Muslim fighters from Indonesia, while the bombing, in August 2000, of the Philippine ambassador's residence in Jakarta was believed by some to have been carried out by Indonesian supporters of the MILF. Conversely, under Arroyo, who assumed the presidency in early 2001, cease-fire agreements with the MILF were brokered through Libya and Malaysia. During this period President Arroyo made her first state visit to Malaysia. Abu Sayyaf had continued to move in and out of Sabah with impunity, and in September 2000 had kidnapped three Malaysians from the resort of Pandanan, adding to the others whom it still held captive. The military freed a US hostage in April 2001, but in May Abu Sayyaf members took three more US citizens hostage, along with 17 Filipinos, from a luxury resort in Palawan. Abu Sayyaf later claimed to have beheaded one of the US captives. What most drew international attention to the activities of Abu Sayyaf was the hunt for members of al-Qa'ida, following attacks, allegedly by that organization, on New York and Washington, DC, in September 2001. It was well known that Abu Sayyaf had been assisted by this group, some of whose members from the Middle East had spent time in the Philippines. Declaring her support for the US-led alliance against the al-Qa'ida network, President Arroyo agreed to grant the USA access to Philippine military bases and airspace, while the Congress adopted legislation aimed at combating money-laundering.

Not only was there continuing concern over Abu Sayyaf links to al-Qa'ida, but poor law enforcement in the Philippines appeared to make the country a potential haven for international terrorists. However, anti-Islamic sentiment among the majority Christian population and President Arroyo's strident support for the US Government's position also made the Philippines the initial focus of the new US military presence in South-East Asia. In December 2001 the USA pledged US $100m. in military aid. In February 2002 660 US troops were deployed to the southern Philippines as part of the six-month Balikatan campaign with the Philippine military to suppress Abu Sayyaf operations, although their role was to be limited to training, advice, surveillance and infrastructure development. While their presence attracted sharp criticism from the left, and from some nationalist politicians, surveys indicated widespread popular support, at least among the Christian population. At the end of the six months the Balikatan campaign was declared a success, with the total number of active Abu Sayyaf members reported to have declined from 4,000 to about 100, and the government forces stationed in the south were believed to have improved in fighting power and discipline. While some hostages held by Abu Sayyaf were released during the campaign, at least two (one US national and one Filipino) were killed, and other hostages were seized just before and soon after the campaign's completion. Indeed, two Filipinos were beheaded shortly after the departure of US forces. At the height of the campaign, US troops in the south were reinforced to number about 1,000, while a large contingent was engaged in military manoeuvres in the north.

In May 2002 the Government signed an agreement with Indonesia and Malaysia, which was aimed at preventing cross-border terrorist activity, with particular focus on members of JI, which was reported to be furthering al-Qa'ida objectives in South-East Asia. In January, and again in March, the Philippine authorities arrested several Indonesian nationals suspected of producing or transporting bombs, while arrests of foreign nationals were made elsewhere in the region. In November 2001 the Malaysian Government arrested, and then transferred to the custody of the Philippine authorities, former MNLF leader Nur Misuari, who earlier had led a violent, but unsuccessful, attack on a military outpost in Jolo, after being forced to relinquish his position as Governor of the ARRM. Malaysia also continued to play a significant role in the peace negotiations between the Philippine Government and the MILF.

In an attempt to exercise tighter control over its population and borders, the Malaysian Government introduced stringent new immigration laws in August 2002, aimed at the estimated 80,000 illegal Filipino workers and residents, most of them Muslims, who had long been settled in Sabah. As thousands of Filipinos were assembled in detention centres and deported to the Philippines, reports emerged of their abuse and mistreatment by the Malaysian authorities. Also confronted with the difficult prospect of accommodating these large numbers, mainly in Mindanao, the Philippine authorities protested to Malaysia, while some Filipino politicians urged a revival of the Philippines' long-standing claims on Sabah. Following the intervention of President Arroyo and the protests of employers and human rights activists in Malaysia, that country's Prime Minister, Dr Mahathir Mohamad, suspended the mass deportations in September. However, from early 2005 the Malaysian Government introduced further measures to control illegal foreign residents, leading to the forced repatriation of tens of thousands of undocumented Filipino workers.

Meanwhile, as US forces escalated their 'war on terror' in early 2003 by leading an invasion of Iraq with the intention of ousting the regime of Saddam Hussain, President Arroyo remained one of the USA's staunchest allies in South-East Asia. In February, in response to US pressure and citing intelligence reports on links between Iraqi agents and Abu Sayyaf, the Philippine Government expelled a number of Iraqi diplomats, embassy employees and businessmen. Meanwhile, in December 2002 the Philippines signed a five-year military agreement with the USA under which the Philippines would be provided with heavy equipment, training and logistical support in its efforts to address local and international terrorism.

The focus of these international measures was the growth of JI, which reputedly used the Philippines as its principal training ground. Included among those of its agents who had trained in the southern Philippines were several men arrested in Indonesia for the October 2002 bombing of a tourist resort on the island of Bali, which killed more than 200 people, mainly Indonesians and Australians. While the MILF steadfastly denied any support for, or organizational linkage to, JI, its leadership acknowledged that it might have unintentionally trained JI personnel. In May 2003 Saifullya Yunos, a former MILF member, was arrested on the basis of army intelligence reports that he had formed a JI 'cell' in the Philippines with the alleged manufacturer of the bombs used in the Bali attack, Rohman al-Ghoza, who was already in custody. Together with the alleged leader of JI, the Indonesian Hambali, who was later arrested in Bangkok, Thailand, Yunos and al-Ghoza were charged with having been responsible for a number of bombings in Manila and Mindanao. Al-Ghoza had already been convicted on one of these charges and was sentenced to a 10-year prison term. However, in July, on the same day that the Australian Prime Minister arrived in Manila to sign an anti-terrorist agreement, al-Ghoza escaped from custody, along with two Abu Sayyaf prisoners, apparently by bribing prison officials. Following a number of other escapes from police custody of high-profile terrorist suspects, the incident was not only an embarrassment to the Philippine authorities, but supported the claim made in some quarters that the Philippines provided a safe haven to international terrorists. In October al-Ghoza was located and killed by Philippine soldiers in Mindanao.

US concerns over the Philippines stance on the 'war on terror' escalated in July 2004, when President Arroyo agreed to bring home, slightly ahead of schedule, a small police and military contingent from Iraq in response to threats by kidnappers to execute a Filipino truck driver. Reacting to strong domestic pressure to save the life of a man who had come to symbolize the 1.3m. Filipino civilian workers employed in the Middle East, including hundreds in Iraq, Arroyo's decision drew considerable local approval, but was sharply condemned by fellow 'allies of the willing', the USA and Australia. In the same month a US envoy to the Philippines warned of ongoing concerns over intelligence reports noting the continued establishment of JI training camps in Mindanao. Shortly afterwards, US and Filipino troops commenced 'training exercises' in North Cotabato, amid claims of increased US surveillance activities in Mindanao. At the same time, US troops arrived for joint naval exercises in the northern Philippines. Arroyo herself was reported to have been saved from a thwarted JI terrorist attack on her inauguration ceremony on 30 June. The Philippines was also forced to tighten security at its foreign embassies following threats, issued in Sweden, from sources identified with al-Qa'ida.

Meanwhile, the Spratly Islands continued to arouse regional tensions, despite a 'declaration on the conduct of parties in the South China Sea' signed by China and the relevant ASEAN countries in November 2002, but, unusually, the Philippines was only mildly critical of its neighbours' transgressions. Moreover, a state visit by Arroyo to China in September 2004 resulted in the two countries signing a Defence Co-operation Agreement. Later, in March 2005, China announced a programme of military aid to the Philippines. In March 2006 the Chinese Government granted the Philippine administration US $3m., intended to support the establishment of a Chinese-language military training programme in the Philippines, in return for that country's continued adherence to the 'one China' policy, which recognized Taiwan as an integral part of the People's Republic of China. The Chinese Government also invited the Philippines to participate in joint naval exercises.

Concerns that Muslim groups in the southern Philippines were providing sanctuary and training facilities for JI militants prompted the USA and a number of other countries to issue travel warnings in the mid-2000s. In September 2004 the Australian Government even went as far as declaring its preparedness for pre-emptive strikes on terrorist training camps in Mindanao, an announcement that drew much criticism from the Philippines. In early 2005 Australian security officials met with MNLF representatives to discuss their concerns, while the USA announced a substantial increase in the number of military exercises that it planned in that year with the Philippine military. Periodic reports were issued announcing the presence or capture of Indonesian and Malaysian members of JI, some of them suspects in the Bali bombing of 2002.

Despite pressure from the USA, anti-terrorism bills remained blocked in Congress during 2005–06, partly as a consequence of civil liberties campaigns but also owing to the impasse between President Arroyo and the opposition-controlled Senate. (The Human Security Act was eventually approved in February 2007 and implemented in July—see above.) In the early months of 2006 about 7,000 US troops entered the Philippines for joint exercises in the largest display of force in the region since the Viet Nam War. Australia, too, conducted joint naval exercises in Philippine waters and dispatched troops there to assist in the hunt for JI members. In the mean time, the Philippines participated in ASEAN and Asia-Pacific Economic Cooperation (APEC) talks aimed at strengthening regional military and intelligence co-operation.

The pursuit of bilateral agreements with regional neighbours was another significant area of foreign policy activity. In September 2006 President Arroyo and the Japanese Prime Minister, Junichiro Koizumi, signed the Japan-Philippines Economic Partnership Agreement (JPEPA), the Philippines' first bilateral free trade and investment treaty since the Parity Rights Agreement concluded with the USA in 1946 (which accorded equal rights to US and Filipino nationals in the exploitation of Philippine natural resources). JPEPA would eliminate tariffs for 94% of bilateral trade value and allow the Philippines to send nurses and carers to Japan to address a significant shortage of such workers in that country. Proponents stated that the agreement would most benefit the country's agricultural sector. Although its constitutionality, terms and environmental impact were fiercely contested by leftist critics, the Senate ratified JPEPA in October 2008 and it came into effect in December.

Economic agreements with China also proved controversial. After the Philippines hosted the 10th ASEAN-China Summit in January 2007, President Arroyo and Premier Wen Jiabao signed the Framework Agreement on Expanding and Deepening Bilateral Economic and Trade Cooperation. This agreement was expected to expand co-operation on agriculture, fisheries, public works and infrastructure, housing, mining, energy and trade promotion, in pursuit of a mutual trade goal of US $30,000m. by 2010. In April 2007 the two countries also signed agreements on economic and technical co-operation, the provision of $4,000m. in loans and construction contracts, including those for two railway lines and a national broadband network in the Philippines. The broadband contract with the Chinese ZTE Corporation became the subject of intense scrutiny and was cancelled in October (see above), while the Northrail project to connect Manila to Clark was suspended following allegations of overpricing and non-compliance with Philippine procurement laws.

In the aftermath of the August 2008 MILF attacks in North Cotabato, Lanao del Norte and Sarangani (see above), the US ambassador reaffirmed US commitment to supporting the peace process. However, when an air-strike by the Philippine armed forces in Maguindanao killed six civilians, public suspicion was aroused by the possibility that US forces had provided their Philippine counterparts with faulty intelligence. The Executive Director of the Presidential Commission on the VFA denied that US intelligence was provided in this case, claiming that the air force had fired in retaliation, but clarified that such 'real-time information' would be welcome and had earlier been deemed legitimate by the Supreme Court. In late 2008 the Government sought to reassure the Legislative Oversight Committee on the VFA that US troops were neither engaged in combat operations nor 'overstaying', but were merely engaged in 'a continuing exercise over the years'.

The alleged rape of a Filipina woman by a US marine in late 2005 had repercussions that continued into 2009. Lance-Corporal Daniel Smith was convicted of rape by the Makati City Regional Trial Court in December 2006 and sentenced to 40 years' imprisonment. Pending appeal, he was transferred by the Department of Interior and Local Government from the Makati City Jail to the US embassy. This controversial move reflected the acquiescence of the Philippine Departments of Justice and of Foreign Affairs to the US embassy's interpretation of the VFA and contradicted the order of the presiding court to hold Smith in Philippine custody. In March 2009 Smith's accuser swore an affidavit declaring that she 'entertain(ed) doubts' about her previous account, and dismissed her activist attorneys. She was soon bound for the USA on an immigrant fiancée visa, for which she claimed to have applied much earlier. However, the development aroused suspicion that a deal had been struck. In April the Court of Appeals overruled Smith's conviction and he was released. However, the reversal was not made on the basis of the recantation; the decision was reached much earlier and was based on the Court's finding of both technical and substantive shortcomings in the original conviction.

In October 2008 the Philippines became the eighth member of ASEAN to ratify the Association's new Charter, adopted in Manila in late 2007. The Charter stated ASEAN's commitment to 'strengthen democracy, enhance good governance and the rule of law' and 'promote human rights and fundamental freedoms'. A significant element was the call for a regional human rights body, although this recommendation was weakened in the final draft owing to opposition from Myanmar. ASEAN as a group continued to adhere to a strict policy of non-intervention in members' internal affairs, but in 2009–10 the Philippines urged Myanmar on numerous occasions to free all political prisoners and honour its commitment to democratization. At an ASEAN summit meeting held in Hanoi, Viet Nam, in October 2010, the Philippine delegation communicated the view of the Aquino administration that the forthcoming legislative election in Myanmar, which was held in November, was 'a farce to democratic values', following recent developments that indicated that the poll would be neither free nor fair (see the chapter on Myanmar). Meanwhile, in July 2009 a document of terms of reference (TOR) for the ASEAN Inter-governmental Commission on Human Rights (AICHR) was signed in Phuket, Thailand, albeit with some modifications. The TOR included no means to investigate or punish violators, but observers noted that the very establishment of the body—which was inaugurated in October at the annual ASEAN summit, held in Hua Hin, Thailand—represented a significant development for the region. To make the AICHR meaningful, the Philippines urged ASEAN to address regional human rights problems and to protect 'basic freedoms'.

The expansion of Chinese power in the Asia-Pacific region in recent years has led to an emerging rivalry with the USA, a development that was emphasized by major naval visits by both China and the USA to the Philippines in April and September 2009, respectively; both navies conducted public relations and goodwill activities during their visits. On her final foreign visit as President, Arroyo travelled to the Chinese city of Shanghai in June 2010, on the 35th anniversary of the establishment of diplomatic relations between the two countries; various political, economic and cultural exchanges and events were held to mark the anniversary.

President Arroyo's successor, Benigno Aquino, travelled to the USA in September 2010, in his first official overseas visit; during his stay, Aquino addressed the UN General Assembly and attended the second US-ASEAN Leaders' Meeting. Aquino had his first, albeit very brief, meeting with US President Barack Obama and conducted discussions with Vietnamese President Nguyen Minh Triet and the Prime Ministers of Malaysia and Singapore, Najib Tun Razak and Lee Hsien Loong. Aquino also witnessed the signing of a US $434m. development grant from a US governmental aid agency. However, the central aim of the visit was to promote foreign investment in the Philippines' economy, with Aquino asserting that his Government was introducing measures to ensure that the country was 'open for business'.

Meanwhile, the Philippines' relations with China were threatened in August 2010 by the killing in Manila of eight tourists from Hong Kong by a former police officer (see above). The Aquino administration's perceived mishandling of the incident provoked severe criticism by the Chinese and Hong Kong Governments. Hong Kong Chief Executive Donald Tsang described the management of the incident by the Philippine authorities as 'disappointing', and his administration issued a warning against all travel to the Philippines. However, bilateral economic relations did not appear to suffer, as Chinese investments continued to enter the country. In September Beidahuang Group, a Chinese agricultural corporation, announced an initial investment of 100m. pesos in hybrid rice-farming, and government officials stated that the China Mining Association had shown interest in mining projects collectively worth some US $600m. Bilateral trade with China had risen significantly in recent years, and the implementation of the China-ASEAN free trade agreement in January 2010 was expected to further this trend.

Proposals to formulate a binding Code of Conduct for the Spratly Islands were espoused in October 2010, and discussions to this end remained ongoing between China and ASEAN at mid-2011. However, tensions between the Philippines and China (and, to a lesser extent, Viet Nam) over sovereignty of the islands intensified from early 2011, with the Philippine Government alleging numerous incursions into its territorial waters by Chinese vessels. In April the Philippines announced that it had lodged a formal protest with the UN against China's claims, formally submitted to the organization in 2009, to the Spratly Islands and surrounding waters. In June President Aquino announced that he was to visit China in late August to discuss the ongoing dispute, among other issues. Bilateral tensions were further heightened later in June 2011 by the holding of Chinese navy exercises, including live fire drills, in the disputed waters, and by the Philippines' expulsion of a senior Chinese diplomat from foreign ministerial meetings, on the grounds that his conduct was 'unbecoming of a diplomat'. During a visit to Washington, DC, in late June, the Secretary of Foreign Affairs, Albert del Rosario, had discussions with US Secretary of State Hillary Clinton. In a joint press conference with the visiting Philippine minister, Clinton urged all parties to seek a swift and peaceful resolution to the territorial dispute through concerted diplomacy. However, she also stressed the continued relevance of the US-Philippine Mutual Defense Treaty and the US Administration's 'commitment to the defence of the Philippines', appearing to indicate tacit US support for the Philippines; Clinton also noted that the USA had helped the Philippines to establish a coastal radar system to enable the South-East Asian country to monitor its waters more closely. To the consternation of the Chinese Government, joint US-Philippines naval exercises were held close to the disputed Spratly Islands at the end of June. In the following month del Rosario met with his Chinese counterpart during a visit to Beijing, but no significant developments on the territorial dispute were reported. A visit to Pagasa Island in mid-July by a five-member Philippine delegation prompted an angry response from Chinese government officials; a spokesperson for the Ministry of Foreign Affairs contended that the visit of the Philippine officials seriously infringed upon China's 'indisputable sovereignty' over the Spratly Islands and the surrounding waters.

Economy

EDITH HODGKINSON

Since independence in 1946 the overall record of the Philippine economy has been one of underperformance—both in relation to other countries in the region and in terms of its potential for growth. Initially, its rate of development was close to that of Japan, and it shared many characteristics with the countries of Asia that graduated to newly industrialized status in the latter part of the 20th century—Taiwan, the Republic of Korea (South Korea) and Singapore—with the added advantage of a plentiful natural resource base and a potentially enormous domestic market. Yet it has only intermittently matched the rapid economic expansion recorded by the 'tiger' economies of the region, both the initial group and the second group from the 1980s on (comprising Thailand, Malaysia, Indonesia and Viet Nam). The less rapid progress of the Philippine economy was a result of major and basic structural deficiencies. Among these were: a dependence on imported intermediate and capital goods, following a period of protectionism; a grossly inequitable distribution of wealth; a tendency for wealth to be acquired through ownership of monopoly privileges, derived from connections with influential persons, rather than entrepreneurship; and pervasive corruption, which distorted the design and implementation of economic policy. The Government that came to power after the overthrow of President Ferdinand Marcos in 1986 espoused policies that would mitigate these features, and they were pursued with greater vigour and success by the administration of Gen. Fidel Ramos, who succeeded President Corazon Aquino in mid-1992. The economy was developed through the dismantling of domestic monopolies and the liberalization of the terms of entry of foreign goods and capital (notably in the banking sector). With investment rising, boosted by inflows of funds from the Philippine community overseas, and strong external markets for the country's manufactures, growth in gross national income (GNI) increased steadily in the mid-1990s, reaching 7.2% in 1996, and the Philippines at last seemed likely to match the very rapid growth of other economies in the region.

However, this advance was interrupted by the regional financial and currency crisis in mid-1997, and it was not until the mid-2000s that the Philippine economy was again able to realize growth comparable to the rates achieved before this setback. Growth remained highly sensitive to external forces (particularly the price of oil and demand in the two major export markets—the USA and Japan—as well as in the rapidly growing Chinese economy). The country is also vulnerable to weather phenomena, notably the El Niño current, which periodically appears along the Pacific coast of South America, causing drought in the Philippines. None the less, supported by strong, consistent growth in private consumer spending, which was sustained by rising inflows of remittances from the large Filipino community overseas, GNI growth accelerated in 2006 and 2007, reaching a new high point of 7.5% in the latter year. However, the pace of growth began to decelerate from the second half of 2007, slowing to 6.4% in 2008 and 3.7 % in 2009. This reflected the deterioration in the world economy precipitated by the mortgage credit crisis in the USA in late 2007, which had developed into a global recession by 2009. The strengthening of Philippine exports as the global economy recovered in 2010, combined with a surge in government spending in an attempt to sustain domestic demand, boosted GNI growth to a record 8.2% in that year. However, the pace of growth began to ease in the latter half of 2010, and in the first three months of 2011 the annual rate of increase had declined to just 3.6% as export growth decelerated and government spending contracted.

GROWTH WITHOUT REFORM, 1946–85

On independence in 1946 the Philippines maintained the broad character of its economic policies as a US colony: freedom of trade with the USA, preferential entry for Philippine commodities into the US market and preferential treatment for US investment in the Philippines. However, with the vast increase in demand after the ravages of war, and despite reconstruction aid from the USA, import spending rose to levels far beyond the country's financing capacity. Consequently, import controls were imposed in 1949, and the country adopted the industrialization by import-substitution policy, which was to become the pattern among newly independent developing countries. Very high tariffs on manufactured goods and quantitative controls were combined with a preferential exchange rate for the import of intermediate and capital goods, and interest 'ceilings', which underpriced capital. This set of measures served as a strong stimulus to manufacturing production, which grew by 12% a year in the 1950s, making the Philippines both the most industrialized country in South-East Asia by the end of the decade and the fastest growing economy. The misuse of resources engendered by the policy of import-substitution, notably the recourse to capital-intensive processes in a country where labour was skilled and low-cost, was not immediately perceived. This was due to strong international prices for the country's agricultural exports, while the low population-to-land ratio allowed an expansion in the area under cultivation and, therefore, an increase in production. The Philippines was thus able to earn the foreign exchange needed to fund its dependence on imports.

At the beginning of the 1960s, however, the prospects for a sustained growth in export earnings receded as a land constraint emerged. With rising imports threatening to create a balance of payments crisis, the Philippine Government implemented two significant measures towards stimulating export-manufacturing based on the country's factor endowment: the peso was devalued by around 100% and exchange controls were eliminated. However, other protectionist features were retained: high tariff rates, quantitative controls, and regulated and low interest rates. Thus, there was little incentive to switch from capital-intensive, domestic-orientated activities to labour-intensive export manufacture.

It was only after the introduction of martial law in 1972 that the Government implemented an effective policy, mainly through tax and tariff incentives, of encouraging export manufacture and attracting foreign investment. Coinciding with a period of buoyant world demand, the policy proved highly successful, increasing earnings from non-traditional manufactures by 25%–30% a year in 1973–78. With commodity prices rising rapidly in the 1970s, the rate of economic growth accelerated to an average of 6.9% a year in 1973–79.

This record of success, and the ready availability of foreign funds as commercial banks sought to recycle 'petrodollars', prompted the Government to embark on a programme to widen the country's industrial base. The initiation of large-scale, mainly heavy industrial, projects was essentially aimed at enhancing self-sufficiency (only one was directed at export markets), but required massive inputs of foreign capital and technology. As a result, the foreign debt rose eight-fold between 1975 and 1982. The debt-servicing payments required proved unsustainable when the international recession of the early 1980s brought a slowing in the growth in demand for Philippine manufactures. As a result, two-fifths of the country's foreign exchange earnings were needed to cover the debt repayment and interest costs in 1982.

The deterioration in external economic conditions focused attention on one of the characteristics of economic management under President Marcos: the concentration of ownership and control among members of the President's family and a group of close associates, in a system that came to be dubbed 'crony capitalism'. Marketing monopolies were set up for the coconut and sugar industries, while subsidies and special privileges (including preferential access to bank credit and government guarantees for foreign borrowing) were awarded to companies owned by 'crony' interests. The failings of this pattern of economic management were masked when the economy was expanding rapidly, but as growth slowed sharply in the early 1980s, to an average of 2.4% a year in 1981–83, many of the 'crony' companies, including commercial banks, found themselves in severe financial difficulties. In August 1983 the assassination of President Marcos's leading opponent, Benigno Aquino, Jr precipitated a downturn in the economy. It immediately produced a crisis of confidence both domestically, prompting a flight of capital, and among the country's foreign creditors, who refused to renew short-term financing. The already fragile balance of payments situation thus tipped into crisis. As the economy moved into deep recession in 1984 and 1985, with GNI contracting by almost one-quarter, a number of companies failed. This in turn undermined the viability of the big government banks, the portfolios of which included a high and growing proportion of non-performing assets, and which consequently recorded massive losses in these two years.

The first set of measures introduced to address the crisis were emergency ones, designed to halt the steep decline in foreign exchange reserves. A moratorium was declared on the repayment of external debts, rigorous exchange controls were imposed and the peso was devalued by almost one-quarter. This devaluation, which had long been urged by the IMF and the World Bank, allowed negotiations to begin on a rescheduling of foreign debt and the provision of new funds by the IMF and the commercial banks. The Philippines was required to implement a severe austerity programme, with harsh reductions in government spending, restrictions on the liquidity of banks and a steep rise in interest rates.

In addition to its short-term stabilization objective, the programme agreed with the IMF had a long-term aim: the development of a more efficient economy, based on the exploitation of the country's factor endowment, in labour and in agricultural resources. The distortions represented by an overvalued currency, high import tariffs and quantitative controls, and interest subsidies were to be removed, and the role of market forces enhanced through the reduction of government intervention in the economy, specifically through the ending of the agricultural monopolies and the restructuring of government financial institutions.

LIBERALIZATION OF THE ECONOMY

Economic reform was only intermittently implemented by President Marcos, since it weakened the power system that he operated. It was adopted with greater commitment after his overthrow in February 1986. Within months the coconut and sugar marketing monopolies were dismantled and a wide range of tax exemptions eliminated. Non-performing assets were removed from the portfolios of the government banks, their operations rationalized and their special privileges removed to place them on an equal footing with private banks. Government corporate holdings were put up for sale.

Supported by the country's international creditors, the new Government was able to embark on a rapid restimulation of the economy, mainly through an increase in spending on infrastructure and on an emergency rural employment programme. The boost from the fiscal side was reinforced by the sharp improvement in world coconut prices in both 1986 and 1987. Strong demand for Philippine export manufactures, combined with increasing levels of investment, contributed to another period of robust economic expansion, with GNI growth averaging 6% a year in 1987–89.

This process was abruptly halted at the end of 1989. The economy encountered the familiar problem of a burgeoning deficit on the current account of the balance of payments, as the increase in exports was exceeded by import growth, boosted by the surge in petroleum prices following the Iraqi invasion of Kuwait in August 1990. From a modest US $390m. in 1988, the current account deficit had risen to $2,697m. in 1990. However, the most serious reverse was the severe shortfall of power in Luzon, the country's industrial centre (see below). The situation was compounded by the austere budgetary stance, which was the condition of IMF support, and GNI growth declined to about 1%–2% in 1991–93. It was only after electricity-generating capacity was rapidly expanded to meet the supply deficit that economic growth improved, increasing to just over 5% in both 1994 and 1995, and rising to 7.2% in 1996.

This surge in growth was in part due to the major structural reforms that were implemented by the Ramos administration. These included the removal of nearly all foreign exchange controls, the termination of monopolies in telephones, aviation and inter-island shipping, and the ending of the 45-year ban on the entry of foreign banks. Privatization, which had been a major feature of the administration of Corazon Aquino (30% of the country's largest bank, the government-owned Philippine National Bank—PNB, was transferred to the private sector, and the national airline was privatized), was extended to the refining and marketing of petroleum, and steel manufacture. Moreover, the private sector was brought in to relieve one of the most serious constraints on economic growth, the inadequacy of the physical infrastructure, which could not be corrected by the public sector while budget finances were still precarious. The 'fast track' programme of capacity expansion that resolved the electricity supply crisis in 1993 employed a system of build-operate-transfer (BOT) schemes, under which private firms finance the installation of new facilities and contract to operate them for a fixed period, at the end of which they are transferred to government ownership. The same mechanism was extended to other sectors, such as roads and commuter railways. The franchise for the operation of the capital's water system was awarded to two private consortia. Not all the liberalization targets had been achieved by the end of the Ramos administration in mid-1998, but the economy had been transformed from its state in 1986 when President Marcos left office.

Economic liberalization continued under the next two Presidents, Joseph Estrada and Gloria Arroyo, although at a slower pace. The ban on foreign participation in retail trade was removed in 2000, and 100% foreign ownership of local banks was permitted under certain circumstances. In 2001 legislation was approved for the privatization of the state-owned electricity utility, the National Power Corporation (NAPOCOR). It was envisaged that 70% of NAPOCOR's generating capacity in Luzon and the Visayas, as well as the operating franchise for the electricity transmission network, would be sold off within three years. In the event, the latter was not awarded until December 2007 and the former was not achieved until July 2009. The final condition for the liberalization of electricity supply—the transfer of 70% of NAPOCOR's contracts with independent power producers—was scheduled to be met by the end of 2011.

The most important structural reform achieved by the Arroyo presidency was the significant increase in tax revenue, through an expansion in the coverage of value-added tax (VAT) from November 2005 and an increase in its rate from February 2006. This allowed the Government to increase spending while reducing the budget deficit to near zero in 2007 (see Government Finance, below).

POVERTY AND INCOME DISPARITY

A distinguishing feature of the Philippine economy, which is linked to its underperformance and to persistent civil unrest, is the high level of poverty. This is accompanied by gross inequality in income distribution. In 2009 the richest 10% of households had an income 18 times that of the poorest 10%, a ratio that had changed very little during the previous two decades. Those living in poverty—defined as having an annual per caput income below 16,841 pesos (equivalent to US $353, or 98 cents a day)—were officially estimated at 26.5% of the population in 2009, i.e. 23.1m. people. (A different method of assessment suggested a much higher rate of poverty incidence in that year, at 37.3%.) Under both measures the ratio was higher than in 2003, despite the economy having grown by 32% in real terms during 2003–09. Upon assuming office at the end of June 2010, the administration of President Benigno Aquino implemented an expansion of the Pantawid Pamilyang Pilipino Program, which provides conditional monthly cash grants to poor households that comply with basic health and educational criteria, as part of its efforts to tackle poverty issues. Introduced in 2007, this programme reached 1m. families in 2010 and this was projected to increase to 2.3m. in 2011. A planned increase of a further 700,000 households in 2012 would, if achieved, raise coverage to around three-quarters of all poor households.

National averages conceal very wide disparities among regions, which is another characteristic of the Philippine economy. In the National Capital Region (NCR, or Metropolitan Manila), gross domestic product (GDP) per caput in 2009 stood at US $5,175, three times the national average, while in the provinces that make up the Autonomous Region of Muslim Mindanao (ARMM) GDP per caput stood at just under one-quarter of the national average, at $397. This disparity reflects the concentration of investment in physical and social infrastructure in the Manila area and nearby regions in Luzon and the growth in higher-income economic activity (notably manufacturing), which both generates, and is in turn stimulated by, this investment. The economic disparity among regions has thus tended to worsen over time.

Poverty incidence is exacerbated by major structural faults: the concentration of economic power and income opportunities within a small élite, further entrenched by corruption; and the high rate of population growth, which has in most years exceeded the growth in jobs, so that recorded unemployment has for decades stood at around 10% while underemployment was estimated at 17%–22% in 2000–07. Under the more restricted definition subsequently used, the unemployment rate was put at 7.2% in April 2011 and underemployment at 19.4%. Poverty and the endemic labour surplus are the main factors in the high level of emigration (an average of 78,000 per year in 2006–08) and the much higher numbers (not classified as emigrants) who undertake contract work abroad. Overseas placements of Filipino workers averaged just under 2m. in 2009–10, equivalent to about 5% of the domestic labour force. Some 11m. Filipinos were estimated by the Government to be living abroad, of whom about 30% were resident in the USA.

AGRICULTURE, FORESTRY AND FISHING

The agriculture, forestry and fishing sector contributed 12.3% of GDP in 2010, and engaged 33% of the employed labour force at April 2011. Its share of GDP has been exceeded by that of manufacturing since the 1980s, and as early as the mid-1970s the agricultural sector had lost its primacy as an export earner. The farming system is extremely diverse and includes a large number of rice, maize and coconut holdings that are cultivated by agricultural tenants or workers, as well as sugar *haciendas* and large plantations, devoted mainly to non-traditional export crops such as bananas and pineapples.

Agriculture experienced a period of relatively strong growth in the 1970s, averaging annual expansion of 5%, stimulated by measures to achieve self-sufficiency in food grains as well as by the rise in the area under crops, particularly through the clearing of virgin forest in Mindanao. The pace of expansion then slowed to an average of only around 2% a year in the 1980s through to the mid-1990s, as a land constraint reappeared, government investment in infrastructure favoured urban areas, and the marketing monopolies operated under the Marcos administration depressed producer prices. Rural income was supported by measures introduced by the Government of Corazon Aquino, such as the removal of export taxes on agricultural commodities and the dismantling of monopolies, while government investment in rural infrastructure and services for farmers has tended to rise, making the sector less vulnerable to adverse weather conditions. Agricultural growth consequently strengthened to an average annual rate of around 3% in 2000–10.

Rice is the principal food crop, currently grown on around one-third of the cultivated area. The introduction of higher-yielding strains and an expansion in the supply of fertilizer and pesticides have increased the Philippines' output of rice. However, the country still relies on imports to meet about 10% of internal demand, and the Government does not expect self-sufficiency to be attained until 2013.

Coconuts are the most important cash crop, and the Philippines is the world's leading exporter of coconut products. Between 1975 and 1982 there was a rapid rise in annual output, from 1.9m. metric tons (copra equivalent) to 3.4m. tons. After 1983 output declined, largely owing to the ageing of trees, which reduced overall yields. A major replanting and rehabilitation programme initiated in the late 1980s helped to restore output to 2m.–3m. tons a year by the mid-1990s, a level that has subsequently been broadly maintained.

Sugar, which was once a leading export crop, is now of minor importance. For many years a guaranteed share of the US market, at a fixed price, protected the Philippine sugar industry from the effects of a long-term decline in productivity, but a lengthy period of world price weakness prompted a switch to higher-value crops and fish-farming in the 1980s. With rising domestic demand, imports of sugar have become necessary to supply the premium US market. Sugar has been far exceeded as a source of dollar earnings by bananas and pineapples, mainly grown on plantations developed in Mindanao by multinational companies. The production of mangoes and rubber has also increased in significance.

Agrarian Reform

One of the major requirements for sustained and broadly based economic growth in the Philippines is land reform. Since independence, pressure for such a redistribution of resources has been continually resisted by the landed élite, who also constitute the political élite. In 1972 President Marcos launched a limited programme of agrarian reform covering land under rice and maize in holdings of 7 ha or more. By 1986 more than one-half of the 600,000-ha area covered by the programme still remained to be distributed. The Comprehensive Agrarian Reform Programme (CARP), introduced by the Government of Corazon Aquino in 1988, covered 80% of cultivable land (both publicly and privately owned), with redistribution of land scheduled to be effected over a period of 10 years. Landowners were allowed to retain 5 ha and their direct heirs 3 ha, but large estates could remain intact if they were made into corporate holdings with stock transfers substituting for land. Owing to obstruction by vested interests and reductions in government funding for landholder compensation, redistribution remained well below target. The programme was extended by 10 years in 1998, and subsequently—after a one-year moratorium on compulsory acquisition—by a further five years, to the end of June 2014. At mid-2010 1.49m. ha had yet to be distributed. The country's failure to implement comprehensive land reform supported by adequate extension services is a major factor in the economy's persistent underperformance.

Fishing

The Philippines has extensive fishing resources, both marine and inland. Production increased rapidly to account for about 5% of GDP by the late 1980s. The fishing sector became a major source of foreign exchange earnings, principally through the export of shrimps and prawns to Japan. While neither freshwater ponds nor most of the marine waters have been fully developed, productivity in some areas has deteriorated because of pollution of coastal waters as the result of population growth, mining activities and destructive methods of exploitation. The infrastructure remains highly inadequate. Nevertheless, the total catch increased gradually through the 1990s and 2000s, reaching 3.3m. metric tons in 2009.

Forestry

Forests were in the past one of the country's major resources, but suffered very severe depletion as the result of population pressure, shifting cultivation, illegal logging and inadequate reafforestation. In 1945 there were 15m. ha of virgin forest, but by 1999 the area was estimated at only 700,000 ha. A ban on logging in areas of virgin forest, introduced in 1991, proved largely ineffectual, and two decades later few such areas remained. Nevertheless, in February 2011 the Government announced an extension of the ban to cover logging in all natural and residual forest.

Government policy in the 1980s was to phase out exports of hardwood logs in order to stimulate the development of the local processing industry. An export ban has been in place since 1986, but substantial quantities of logs are believed to be illegally exported. Reflecting the overall decline in output as the resource base narrowed, officially recorded lumber export earnings have decreased sharply, to an average of only US $11m. per year in 2000–10.

MINING

The Philippines has extensive deposits of gold, silver, copper, nickel, lead and chromium. Lesser, but still important, minerals include zinc, cobalt and manganese. However, around one-quarter of the land area has yet to be surveyed and some of the richest deposits remain unexploited. During the 1970s the Government gave high priority to the development of minerals, which resulted in a rapid growth of the sector. From the mid-1980s, however, mining entered two decades of decline, owing to weak prices and an unstable system of taxes and incentives. With investment in the sector depressed by bureaucratic delays and legal challenges, mining remained underdeveloped, accounting for only 1% of GDP in 2004, one-half of the level in 1985, and engaging a mere 0.4% of the employed labour force. By 2004 output of copper ore and concentrates, copper being the country's leading mineral, had decreased to around 7% of its 1980 level, at 15,984 metric tons (metal content), although output subsequently increased moderately, reaching 22,900 tons in 2007 and 49,1000 tons in 2009. Output of gold, of which the Philippines is also a significant producer, tended to follow the same pattern since it is largely a by-product of copper mining; output stood at 38,800 kg in 2007. The non-metallic sector performed better, with the output of coal stimulated by energy conversion in the cement and mining industries. Averaging some 1.2m. tons per year in the 1990s, coal production increased strongly from the early 2000s to reach 4.69m. tons in 2009.

The sector's outlook was transformed in the mid-2000s, with the stimulus of surging demand from the People's Republic of China and the consequent rise in world metal prices. In addition, in late 2004, the Supreme Court (in a reversal of an earlier ruling) confirmed the constitutionality of legislation introduced in 1995 that improved access for foreign investment. The Government actively sought such investment in 24 large-scale projects, with a target of investment totalling US $10,000m. by 2010. Some $1,400m. was invested in mining in 2005–07, including a polymetallic mine at Rapu Rapu, a gold and copper project at Didipio (both involving Australian companies), a nickel mine at Coral Bay (involving a Canadian company) and the rehabilitation by Atlas Consolidated, the country's leading mining company, of its copper mine at Toledo, which had ceased operations in 1994. The realization of additional production capacity in the Philippines occurred as world prices for minerals strengthened. In 2006–07 export earnings from minerals averaged $2,303m. a year, compared with an annual average of around $800m. during 2004–05. The contribution of mining to GDP had risen to 1.5% by 2007. However, as minerals prices weakened as a result of the global economic crisis of 2008/09, investment during 2008–10 stood at just $1,856m., far below levels required to meet the target of $10,000m. by the end of the decade. A new target of investment totalling $13,000m. was set for the period to 2013; however, this seemed unlikely to be achieved since the industry's prospects have been depressed both by strong local opposition (led by the Catholic Church) to its environmental and social impact, and by deficiencies in the approval and regulatory structure, which are exacerbated by interference by local government. An extreme example of the latter was the implementation in April 2011 of a ban on open-cast mining by the provincial government of South Cotabato, in Mindanao, thereby jeopardizing a massive copper and gold development proposed for Tampakan, representing total investment of some $5,900m. The contribution of mining to GDP stood at 1.4% in 2010.

ENERGY

In 1973, at the time of the first major increase in international petroleum prices, the Philippines was dependent on imported oil for 95% of its energy consumption. This level had declined to 32% by 2009, owing to the development of various domestic sources of energy, notably coal, hydroelectric power, natural gas, geothermal steam and non-conventional sources (mainly bagasse, agricultural waste and dendrothermal).

The contribution of domestic petroleum production has been very limited. Output from petroleum deposits off the island of Palawan reached a peak in its first year of operation, in 1979, of 42,000 barrels per day (b/d). Despite the entry into production of other commercial oilfields and new drillings stimulated by rising oil prices, output had declined to 24,000 b/d by 2007, covering just 8% of domestic demand. However, new facilities at the Galoc offshore oilfield came on stream in October 2008, supplying between 12,000 b/d and 14,000 b/d in 2009. Natural gas reserves at the offshore gasfield at Malampaya were estimated at more than 3,000,000m. cu ft. Commercial operations started in 2002, reaching 138,030m. cu ft in 2009 and serving three power plants with a total capacity of 2,763 MW. By 2005 natural gas had superseded coal as the leading source of electricity generation.

The exploitation of geothermal resources has been actively pursued: in 2006 the Philippines had an installed capacity of 1,953 MW (a total exceeded only by the USA). Considerable resources remain to be exploited: some estimates suggest that the total potential exceeds 35,000 MW.

The Ramos administration embarked on a 'fast track' programme to expand electricity-generating capacity, which had achieved its aim of ending daily power cuts in Luzon by late 1993. However, further substantial new investment in the sector has been impeded by the slow pace of power privatization and by delays in the introduction of a new regulatory framework. As a result, supply shortages were experienced in all three island networks in 2010, exacerbated by the drought associated with the El Niño phenomenon.

MANUFACTURING

Philippine manufacturing developed relatively early, its contribution to GDP reaching 22%–25% by the 1960s, a share that it has since broadly maintained; the sectoral contribution to GDP in 2010 stood at 21.4%. Manufacturing engaged 8.5% of the employed labour force at April 2011. The sector was supported initially by exchange controls and, from the early 1960s, by tariffs and import quotas, which tended to promote production of consumer goods for the domestic market. Manufacturing for the export market was stimulated from the 1970s by the introduction of tax and duty exemptions for export producers and the establishment of four export-processing zones where 100% foreign ownership was permitted and companies were allowed to pay below the minimum wage. As a consequence, there was a rapid growth of labour-intensive manufacturing, mainly textile products and electronic components, produced in many cases by Filipino enterprises working for multinationals on a subcontracting basis (these industries remained heavily dependent on imported inputs).

In the early 1980s the Government implemented a programme to develop the country's intermediate and heavy industrial base through 11 capital-intensive projects. Only four of these projects became operational: a copper smelter, a coco-chemical manufacturing project, a phosphate fertilizer project and the manufacture of diesel engine components. Nevertheless, despite these developments and the elimination of import quotas in the late 1980s and extensive reductions in tariffs since, Philippine manufacturing remains orientated towards the provision of consumer goods for the domestic market. Its performance has thus been very responsive to movements in domestic demand. The external market for Philippine manufacturers is, nevertheless, significant, with the export-processing zone model introduced at four government-owned sites in the late 1970s replicated at special economic centres established by the private sector since the early 1990s; these centres have attracted the bulk of investment and boosted the zones' contribution to export receipts to four-fifths of the total in 2008. The conversion to special economic zones of the two major military bases from which the USA withdrew in 1992 represented a significant advance. The former naval base at Subic Bay has become a centre for transshipment, shipbuilding and ship repairs, as well as export manufacture; investment therein was estimated to have reached US $7,200m. by the end of 2010. The former air base at Clark, where a second airport for Manila is being developed, has become a centre for electronics. Growth in investment in the special economic zones has fluctuated in line with foreign demand for Philippine goods. Approved investment reached a peak of $5,423m. in 1997 before declining to a low point of $524m. (excluding Subic Bay and Clark) in 2003. Thereafter it recovered fitfully, but at $3,682m. in 2009 was still below its 1997 level. This moderate performance was largely due to the strong competition for foreign investment in export-orientated manufacturing from other countries in the region.

INFRASTRUCTURE

The country's physical infrastructure is characterized by marked regional disparity, which both reflects and reinforces the concentration of modern economic activity in Metropolitan Manila and regions immediately adjacent. Its efficiency was in decline from the mid-1980s as a result of reductions in budget expenditure under the austerity programme of that period. While considerable improvements were made in the 1990s as BOT contracts mobilized private funds (both domestic and foreign) for investment in the transport infrastructure, overall the poor state of physical infrastructure has remained a major constraint on economic growth. The Government of Benigno Aquino hoped to ease this constraint through the implementation of a public-private partnership (PPP) programme—an enhancement of the BOT model—with seven projects scheduled to be awarded before the end of 2011, for road, airport and commuter rail developments.

The road network in the Philippines accommodates about 60% of freight and 80% of passenger traffic. In 2009 there were 213,151 km of roads, of which only 25.6% were paved. Feeder roads are in poor condition. However, new urban highways are being built in Metropolitan Manila and adjacent areas.

The rail system is limited, with just 740 km of single-line track in Luzon, the condition of which has been deteriorating for decades. The network carried only 64,000 passengers in 2005. However, a major programme of rehabilitation and expansion of the northern line, supported by credit from China, began in 2006, when work commenced on the reconstruction of the 32-km double-track line extending from Metropolitan Manila to Bulacan. The next stages planned were a 48-km extension to the Clark Special Economic Zone and a branch line to Subic. The first of these was scheduled to enter into service in 2010–11; essential maintenance and reconstruction work was also due to take place on the 479-km southern rail line, for which China had promised concessional funding for the first 77 km. However, work on the programme was interrupted in 2009 by a dispute over cost overruns and design changes. Subsequent negotiations failed to reactivate the project, which was formally suspended in May 2011, with just under one-quarter of the work completed. Planned interconnections with the existing mass transit system in Metropolitan Manila were thus also at a standstill at mid-2011. The mass transit system began operation in 1984, and has been undergoing extensive expansion since the late 1990s, with further extensions proposed under the Benigno Aquino administration's PPP programme.

The seaport network services about 40% of freight and carries 10% of passenger traffic. The most important ports are Manila and Cebu; both have container facilities. The inter-island fleet is old, safety regulations are poor and maritime navigational aids inadequate.

There are 85 national airports; international airports include Manila, Cebu, General Santos and Clark, the former US facility, which is being developed as a joint principal airport for the capital with the Ninoy Aquino International Airport.

GOVERNMENT FINANCE

Fiscal imbalance has been endemic in the Philippines for decades, with budget income very rarely enough to cover spending and never sufficient to allow for adequate levels of investment in physical and social infrastructure. The tax effort—the ratio of tax revenue to GDP—has always been low, at around 15% in the late 1990s and declining in every year from 1998 to 2003, when it reached 12.5%. In large part this reflected a massive failure in tax collection. The Department of Finance has estimated that revenue agencies receive only 73% of personal income tax due, 40% of corporate income tax and 49% of VAT. Owing to congressional resistance to tax increases, and with sales of assets constituting only a limited option, the spending side has usually borne the brunt of the deficit reduction effort. Under President Marcos there was a steady rise in government expenditure, associated with ambitious programmes of public investment, often in urban-based capital-intensive projects, in an effort to sustain growth. Tax revenues failed to keep pace with the expanded expenditure, largely because of the proliferation of exemptions, inefficiency in tax administration and widespread evasion, generating persistent and rising fiscal deficits. The administration of Corazon Aquino reduced the deficit, both absolutely and as a percentage of GNI from the 4.2% recorded in 1986 to 1.2% in 1992, aided by proceeds from asset sales, such as the highly successful privatization of the country's national airline in that year.

Under President Ramos, who took office in mid-1992, the budgetary balance moved into surplus for the first time, reaching 0.9% of GNI in 1994. Supported by the proceeds of privatization and the declining cost of servicing a diminishing debt, this surplus was sustained, albeit at declining levels, in the following three years. The slowing in economic growth and the rise in interest payments following the currency and financial crisis in 1997 returned the budget to deficit in 1998, equivalent to 1.8% of GNI. The combination of higher spending, to stimulate weak domestic demand, and shortfalls in tax collection increased the deficit to 3.6% of GNI in 1999. Persistent tax shortfalls, together with higher interest rates (introduced to counter the depreciation of the peso during 2000–01), increased the budgetary deficit to a record 5.0% of GNI in 2002. From 2003 to 2007 there was a sustained decline in the budget deficit, which was largely attributable to increases in tax revenue. Alcohol and tobacco excise duties were raised in 2005, and the coverage of VAT was extended from November 2005, with its rate increased by two percentage points in February 2006, to 12%. These changes, together with a rise in the rate of corporate income tax, allowed an increase of more than one-fifth in tax revenue in 2006. Overall, tax revenue was equivalent to 14.3% of GDP in that year, the highest ratio realized since 1999.

While the pace of growth in tax revenue faltered in 2007, with its ratio to GDP decreasing marginally, to 14%, the tax shortfall was more than offset by major disposals of government assets, notably the residual equity in the Philippines National Oil Company-Energy Development Corporation, which yielded a total of 90,629m. pesos. As a result, the budget deficit was reduced to near zero, at 12,441m. pesos or only one-fifth of the planned figure. The Government envisaged a balanced budget for 2008, but was forced to abandon this target as the economy slowed as a result of the world recession; budgetary spending was boosted by an additional 93,600m. pesos in mid-2008 as subsidies were extended to poor households and outlays on infrastructure increased. With a partial offset from the sale of the Government's equity in Petron Corporation, the country's leading petroleum refiner, a budget deficit of some 68,117m. pesos (equivalent to 0.8% of GNI) was recorded in 2008. This reversal of trend continued in 2009, as much slower economic growth and tax reliefs that were introduced to boost domestic demand produced a 6.4% decline in tax revenues and a 12.2% ratio of tax to GDP. With the spending stimulus maintained, the budget deficit widened to 298,532m. pesos, equivalent to 2.8% of GNI. For 2010 the Government envisaged only a marginal narrowing of the deficit, but by mid-year the deficit was already some 30% above target, despite stronger than forecast economic growth (and hence tax receipts), largely owing to an increase in budgetary spending in advance of the legislative elections in May. The incoming administration of Benigno Aquino set a new deficit target of 325,000m. pesos for 2010, but, with spending restrained, the deficit was held to 314,458m. pesos (equivalent to 2.6% of GNI); the ratio of tax to GDP declined marginally, to 12.1% of GDP. Despite a planned increase in budgetary expenditure of 6.4%, underspending continued through the first half of 2011, with a year-on-year decline of 11.4%, largely because of delays in the disbursement of infrastructure spending. With a target of a 15.3% increase in revenue nearly being achieved, the deficit, at 17,231m. pesos, was only around one-tenth of the anticipated figure. Nevertheless, the Government's projected deficit for 2011 remained unchanged at 300,000m. pesos.

The Government has made significant progress in reducing the burden of public sector debt since the mid-2000s. Decades of persistent and substantial deficits on the budget and the drain from government-owned or -controlled corporations (GOCCs) operating at a loss had increased public sector (non-financial) debt to a record 5,297,600m. pesos, equivalent to 100.8% of GNI, at the end of 2004. A subsequent easing in the Government's budget borrowing requirement helped initially to reverse this trend, a reversal that has been consolidated as the drain from GOCC operations has diminished, with results at NAPOCOR—the major GOCC—improving as the proceeds from the privatization of its assets were used to pay off debt. In addition, economic growth has strengthened. The ratio of public sector debt to GNI had declined to 51% by the end of 2008 (at 4,495,500m. pesos), while the ratio of government debt to GNI had decreased to 43.1% (at 4,223,130m. pesos); the latter ratio had declined further to 39.3% (4,716,200m. pesos) by the end of 2010. Moreover, the burden of debt repayment has been eased through a series of bond swaps, which have lengthened the maturity of government liabilities. As a result, the Philippines has become better able to withstand adverse movements in interest rates or in economic output.

The Financial Sector

The banking and financial sector is still relatively undeveloped for an economy as large as that of the Philippines. Of the 38 commercial banks in operation at the end of 2010, 18 had assets of less than 50,000m. pesos, and a number were still family-owned. However, the sector has been developing rapidly since the mid-1990s, stimulated by its liberalization, which has included the privatization of what was then the largest commercial bank, the PNB, the removal in 1994 of the ban on the establishment of foreign banks, and legislation raising the maximum foreign ownership level of local banks. As a result of the regional financial and currency crisis of 1997/98, the ratio of bad loans in commercial banks' portfolios increased from 2.4% at the end of 1996 to 19.4% by the end of 2001. The introduction in 2003 of tax incentives on the sale of non-performing assets to asset management companies had brought the ratio down to below 4% before the end of 2008, and it had nearly returned to its pre-crisis level by the end of 2010. In addition, the strengthening of the supervisory and regulatory system after 1997, together with enhanced capital requirements, meant that Philippine banks were better shielded from the global financial crisis in 2008/09, sustaining only minor damage.

The local securities market is still small and speculative, although it underwent a period of rapid expansion in the early 1990s. The market capitalization of the Philippine Stock Exchange (PSE) was US $80,645m. at the end of 1996, six times the level at the end of 1992. This reflected new listings and growing foreign confidence in the Philippines. This process was reversed in 1997, as the regional crisis affected both foreign fund inflows and domestic corporate results, causing a decline of 61% (in dollar values) in the PSE's capitalization, to $31,270m. at the end of the year. Market capitalization had recovered to $51,562m. by the end of 2000 and fluctuated around this level in the three subsequent years. A very marked rise was registered in 2004–07, partly owing to a surge in initial public offerings, and market capitalization stood at $192,328m. at the end of 2007. As a result of the onset of the global financial crisis, the stock market's capitalization more than halved, to $85,695m., in 2008. However, a full recovery ensued, with market capitalization increasing rapidly to $202,030m. by end-2010, in line with global trends.

TRADE AND THE BALANCE OF PAYMENTS

Merchandise trade is constantly in deficit, reflecting the economy's dependence on foreign capital goods and intermediates. The shortfall is thus extremely sensitive to variations in GDP. Sudden surges in economic growth have, in the past, led to unsustainable increases in imports. For example, as economic growth gained momentum in the mid-1990s, the trade deficit rose nearly every year, reaching a record of US $11,342m. in 1996 (equivalent to 13% of GNI in that year). However, within two years it was virtually eliminated (at $28m. in 1998) as import demand was suppressed by the sharp depreciation of the peso and the steep rise in credit costs resulting from the regional financial crisis and the downturn in the economy. The recovery in economic growth in 1999 raised the trade deficit to $6,207m. This level was broadly maintained in 2000–04 as foreign demand for Philippine manufactured goods (in particular electronics and transport equipment) remained strong, while imports increased in response to buoyant domestic consumption (supported by rising remittances from Filipino workers overseas), higher oil prices and the import requirements of the electronics export sector. The deficit generally increased during 2005–08, mainly reflecting the trend in demand for electronics, the growth of which initially slowed and then became negative in 2008. In that year the trade deficit increased to a new high point of $12,885m., owing to the surge in oil and food import prices. The contraction in global demand produced a sharp decline in exports, of 22.3%, in 2009, but this was offset by a concomitant decrease in domestic demand for inputs into export manufacture; consequently, the trade deficit declined by almost one-third, to $8,842m. A strong and sustained recovery in exports became evident during the final months of 2009 and continued through 2010, slightly outpacing the rate of increase in imports. However, as a result of the higher base for imports, the trade gap widened further, to $10,384m. in 2010. The trade deficit increased further still during the first three months of 2011, with exports growing by 8.1% year-on-year (subdued by a downturn in the sale of electronics) and imports by 13.9% (raised by higher prices for oil and raw materials). Compared with the corresponding period in 2010, the trade deficit during the first quarter of 2011, at $3,947m., increased by about one-third.

Japan and the USA have traditionally dominated Philippine international trade, with the level of transactions sustained by aid and private investment inflows at significant volumes. However, the most rapid growth in trade in recent years has been with China/Hong Kong and with fellow members of the Association of Southeast Asian Nations (ASEAN). In 2010 China and Hong Kong surpassed Japan and the USA on both sides of the account, taking 19.5% of exports and providing 11.1% of imports, compared with 4.7% and 5.9%, respectively, in 2000. Trade with ASEAN has grown from a mere 2% on both sides of the account in the early 1970s to 22.4% of exports and 28.2% of imports in 2010.

Exports and Imports

The commodity composition of the Philippines' export trade has been transformed since the 1970s, when four primary commodities—coconut products, sugar, timber and copper—accounted for about one-half of the total. The general decline in world prices of these commodities and/or the contraction in the volume of production coincided with the development of the export manufacturing sector and the diversification of agricultural production, with the result that in 2009–10 the four traditional exports accounted for only 4.9% of the total, while manufactures accounted for 86.4%. One category alone, electronic products, secured nearly two-thirds of all export earnings.

Changes in imports have been less marked, although the decline in world prices and some changes in energy use reduced the proportion represented by crude petroleum to only 6% in 1996–98 from the 23% recorded in 1983. The steep rise in world petroleum prices between 2003 and 2008 raised the country's oil costs to 13% of total imports in the latter year, but the ratio has since eased, to an average of 8.8% in 2009–10. The most important spending category is semi-processed raw materials and intermediates, at 33.2% of the total in 2009–10, reflecting the high import component of the leading export, electronics. Import spending is therefore sensitive to trends in foreign demand for Philippine electronics.

Invisible Transactions

Invisible transactions (services, investment income and unrequited transfers) have always registered a significant surplus, owing primarily to inflows of remittances from Filipinos working abroad. These have tended to rise, reflecting the dependence of Philippine households on foreign wages and the strength of foreign demand for Filipino labour. In 2009–10 remittances from workers abroad, channelled through the banking system, averaged US $18,056m. per year, equivalent to two-fifths of merchandise export earnings. These receipts serve as a significant stabilizer of growth when other economic sectors are under pressure, as was the case in 2008–09. The business process outsourcing (BPO) industry is a rapidly growing source of services income, with the Philippines able to offer an English-speaking work-force with cultural affinity to the USA. It has made a significant contribution to the economy's resilience in recent years. Foreign revenue from BPO reached some $6,100m. in 2010, 75% above its level in 2006. Tourism makes a useful, if smaller, contribution, at around an average gross $3,600m. a year in 2007–10. After fluctuating around the 2m. level in the early 2000s, visitor numbers rose to exceed 3m. a year in 2008–09, increasing further to 3.5m. in 2010. There has been particularly strong growth in arrivals from Asian countries in recent years, with South Korea surpassing the USA as the leading source of tourists in most years since 2006, while visitors from China have been increasing rapidly (albeit from a low base level).

Since 2003 inflows from remittances, BPO and tourism have offset the deficits recorded on the merchandise trade balance to produce growing current account surpluses on the balance of payments, which reached a peak of US $7,119m. in 2007, equivalent to 4.5% of GNI. Sharp variations in the trade deficit during 2008–10 had marked effects on the current account surplus, first halving it to $3,633m. in 2008, before raising it to a record-high $9,358m. in 2009. This was followed by a reduction to $8,465m. in 2010, in which year the surplus was equivalent to 3.2% of GNI.

Capital Transactions

Traditionally, the capital account has been in surplus, largely as the result of foreign borrowing. Although long-term loans remained the most significant inflow, the contribution of foreign investment, both direct and indirect, increased in the mid-1990s in response to the liberalization of the investment environment, political stability and sustained economic growth. Portfolio investment was by far the most important component, attracted by the strength of the peso and high domestic interest rates, but direct investment also rose rapidly, stimulated by the opportunities presented by strong external demand for Philippine manufactures. Like other long-term trends this was interrupted in 1997–98, as the regional financial crisis reduced the surplus on the capital account to near zero in the latter year. With a sharp rise in medium- and long-term borrowing in 1999, the capital account moved back into substantial surplus in that year, to stand at US $3,363m. In subsequent years net capital flows have fluctuated widely in response to international and regional economic trends, the interest differential on peso assets and concerns regarding the political stability of the Philippines (all these factors contributed to the volatility of portfolio investment). A surge in both direct and portfolio investment in 2005 produced a $2,229m. surplus on the capital account, but this was almost eliminated in 2006 (when an overall surplus of only $20m. was recorded), mainly owing to trends in transfers between companies. A marked recovery occurred in 2007, when the capital account recorded a surplus of $3,527m., with much of the improvement attributable to companies increasing their foreign borrowing during a period of considerable appreciation in the peso's value. Owing to the global financial crisis, the capital account moved into deficit (reaching $1,802m.) in 2008, with a net portfolio investment outflow of $3,798m. Although the latter decreased in 2009, the capital account deficit remained virtually unchanged, at $1,627m. However, a robust recovery in portfolio investment inflows in 2010, reflecting a general trend toward emerging economies, produced a surplus of $7,948m. on the capital account; the overall balance of payments consequently recorded an unprecedented surplus of $14,403m.

CURRENCY

After the sharp correction in the value of the peso in the aftermath of the regional crisis of 1997/98, when its value against the US dollar decreased by more than one-third over a six-month period, the Philippine currency has been broadly stable, supported by generally improved economic performance and sustained by inflows of foreign remittances. However, there have been relatively sharp falls during periods of political instability, such as the period prior to the removal of President Estrada in January 2001; the attempted military coup in July 2003; the candidacy of the populist film actor, Fernando Poe, Jr, in the May 2004 presidential election; and the challenge to that election result. The Philippine currency declined to a record low point of US $1 = 56.4 pesos in mid-June 2004. It then entered a period of sustained appreciation, supported by rising inflows of remittances and continuing progress in reducing the budget deficit, but also reflecting the overall weakening of the US dollar against major currencies. The peso rose by 8.2% against the US dollar in 2006 and by 18.0% in 2007, when it was the fastest-appreciating Asian currency, registering $1 = 41.4 pesos by the end of that year. The trend was reversed in 2008, when the peso's value declined by 12.8% against the US dollar, owing to the sharp rise in consumer price inflation as a result of the surge in world prices of oil and rice, and to the widening in the budget deficit, as the Government sought to sustain household spending power. The peso resumed its modest appreciation against the US dollar in 2009, as the steep decrease in export earnings and the continuing high budgetary deficit were offset by the resilience of BPO services and of inflows from remittances from overseas workers. BPO services continued to sustain the peso through 2010, in which year the marked rise in inflows of portfolio investment, combined with the holding of successful presidential elections in May, also served as significant sources of support for the Philippine currency. The peso consequently rose against the US dollar by 5.6% in 2010, although this slowed to 1.4% in the first half of 2011.

FOREIGN DEBT

Following the removal of President Marcos, the Philippines was left with massive foreign indebtedness (equivalent to 96.4% of GNI at the end of 1986, with a high short-term component) and an unsustainable debt-servicing burden (34.6% of earnings from exports of goods and services in the same year). Thus, the administrations of both Corazon Aquino and Fidel Ramos were obliged to seek regular rounds of debt relief, the cost of which was compliance with IMF requirements on structural change and fiscal austerity. The debt relief took the form of rescheduling of both official and commercial credits, with grace periods when only interest payments were due. A new feature in 1990 was the 'buy-back' of debt, under which commercial banks sold Philippine debt to the Government at the secondary market rate, with the IMF, the World Bank and the USA providing funding. At the same time, the commercial banks agreed to provide new money, by buying 15-year government bonds at a reduced interest margin. A similar arrangement was agreed in 1992. The Government finally returned to the international capital market in 1993, with its first sovereign bond issue since before the 1983 payments crisis (see above). At the end of 1996 foreign debt, while still substantial, at US $40,146m., represented much less of a burden. It was then equivalent to 47% of GNI, while long-term debt to private creditors was predominantly in bonds rather than loans.

The reduced level of debt (in terms of the size of the economy), the stabilization of the current account deficit, the increase in inflows of direct investment and the substantial growth in foreign currency reserves were all indicative of the improvement in the Philippines' payments position. However, owing to the regional financial crisis of 1997/98, the Philippines had to turn to the IMF for assistance. The award of a two-year stand-by arrangement in March 1998, the policy implications of a continuing relationship with the Fund, and the promise of policy continuation under the Estrada administration helped to maintain foreign confidence in the Philippines during an uncertain period for the whole regional economy. The Philippines was therefore able to return to the international bond market to help fund its budget deficits. Foreign indebtedness has therefore generally followed an upward trend, but sustained economic growth has meant that as a ratio to GNI it has been in decline, from 60.9% (US $62,549m.) at the end of 2003 to an estimated 24% ($63,800m.) in 2010. With the share of short-term debt, according to the central bank, at well under one-half of the 25.8% registered in 1997, and given the persistent and sizeable current account surplus, at mid-2011 the country's external debt situation appeared robust.

Statistical Survey

Source (unless otherwise stated): National Statistics Office, Solicarel 1, R. Magsaysay Blvd, Santa Mesa, 1008 Metro Manila; tel. (2) 7160807; fax (2) 7137073; internet www.census.gov.ph.

Area and Population

AREA, POPULATION AND DENSITY

Area (sq km)	300,000*
Population (census results)	
1 May 2000	
Males	38,524,266
Females	37,979,811
Total	76,504,077
1 August 2007†	88,566,732
Population (UN estimates at mid-year)‡	
2009	91,703,090
2010	93,260,798
2011	94,852,031
Density (per sq km) at mid-2011	316.2

* 115,831 sq miles.

† Includes 2,279 Filipinos in Philippine embassies, consulates and missions abroad.

‡ Source: UN, *World Population Prospects: The 2010 Revision*.

POPULATION BY AGE AND SEX

(UN estimates at mid-2011)

	Males	Females	Total
0–14	17,028,635	16,239,020	33,267,655
15–64	29,060,472	29,017,964	58,078,436
65 and over	1,477,609	2,028,331	3,505,940
Total	47,566,716	47,285,315	94,852,031

Source: UN, *World Population Prospects: The 2010 Revision*.

REGIONS

(population at 2007 census)

	Population
National Capital Region	11,566,325
Ilocos (Region I)	4,546,789
Cagayan Valley (Region II)	3,051,487
Central Luzon (Region III)	9,709,177
CALABARZON (Region IV-A)*	11,757,755
MIMAROPA (Region IV-B)*	2,559,791
Bicol (Region V)	5,106,160
Western Visayas (Region VI)	6,843,643
Central Visayas (Region VII)	6,400,698
Eastern Visayas (Region VIII)	3,915,140
Zamboanga Peninsula (Region IX)†	3,230,094
Northern Mindanao (Region X)	3,952,437
Davao (Region XI)‡	4,159,469
SOCCSKSARGEN (Region XII)§	3,830,500
Cordillera Administrative Region	1,520,847
Autonomous Region of Muslim Mindanao	4,120,795
Caraga	2,293,346
Total	88,566,732‖

* Southern Tagalog region prior to September 2001.

† Western Mindanao region prior to September 2001.

‡ Southern Mindanao region prior to September 2001.

§ Including area designated Central Mindanao region prior to September 2001.

‖ Total includes Filipinos in Philippine embassies, consulates and missions abroad (2,279 persons).

PRINCIPAL TOWNS

(population at 2007 census)

Manila (capital)*	1,660,714	Bacolod City	499,497
Quezon City*	2,679,450	Muntinlupa City*	452,943
Caloocan City*	1,381,610	Marikina City	424,610
Davao City	1,366,153	Iloilo City	418,710
Cebu City	799,762	Pasay City*	403,064
Zamboanga City	774,407	Mandaue City	318,577
Pasig City*	627,445	Angeles City	317,398
Valenzuela City	568,928	Iligan City	308,046
Makati City*	567,349	Mandaluyong City*	305,576
Cagayan de Oro City	553,966	Baguio City	301,926
Parañaque City	552,660	Butuan City	298,378
Las Piñas City	532,330	Cotabato City	259,153
Gen. Santos City	529,542	Olongapo City	227,270

* Part of Metropolitan Manila.

BIRTHS, MARRIAGES AND DEATHS*

	Registered live births		Registered marriages		Registered deaths	
	Number	Rate (per 1,000)	Number	Rate (per 1,000)	Number	Rate (per 1,000)
1996	1,608,468	23.0	525,555	7.5	344,363	4.9
1997	1,653,236	23.1	562,808	7.9	339,400	4.7
1998	1,632,859	22.3	549,265	7.5	352,992	4.8
1999	1,613,335	21.6	551,445	7.4	347,989	4.7
2000	1,766,440	23.1	577,387	7.5	366,931	4.8
2001	1,714,093	22.0	559,162	7.2	381,834	4.9
2002	1,666,773	21.0	583,167	7.3	396,297	5.0
2003	1,669,442	20.6	593,553	7.3	396,331	4.9
2004	1,710,994	20.7	582,281	7.0	403,191	4.9

* Registration is incomplete. According to UN estimates, the average annual rates per 1,000 were: births 30.2 in 1995–2000, 29.0 in 2000–05, 25.9 in 2005–10; deaths 6.1 in 1995–2000, 6.0 in 2000–05, 5.9 in 2005–10 (Source: UN, *World Population Prospects: The 2010 Revision*).

2005: Registered live births 1,688,918 (20.1 per 1,000); Registered marriages 518,595 (6.2 per 1,000); Registered deaths 676,156 (5.1 per 1,000).

2006: Registered live births 1,663,029 (19.1 per 1,000); Registered marriages 492,666 (5.7 per 1,000).

2007: Registered live births 1,749,878 (19.7 per 1,000); Registered marriages 490,054 (5.5 per 1,000); Registered deaths 441,956 (5.1 per 1,000).

2008: Registered live births 1,784,316; Registered marriages 486,514.

Life expectancy (years at birth, WHO estimates): 70 (males 67; females 73) in 2009 (Source: WHO, *World Health Statistics*).

ECONOMICALLY ACTIVE POPULATION

('000 persons aged 15 years and over)

	2006	2007	2008
Agriculture, hunting and forestry	10,254	10,342	10,604
Fishing	1,428	1,444	1,426
Mining and quarrying	139	149	158
Manufacturing	3,053	3,059	2,926
Electricity, gas and water	128	135	130
Construction	1,677	1,778	1,834
Wholesale and retail trade; repair of motor vehicles, motorcycles and personal and household goods	6,202	6,354	6,446
Hotels and restaurants	887	907	953
Transport, storage and communications	2,483	2,599	2,590
Financial intermediation	344	359	368
Real estate, renting and business activities	783	885	953
Public administration and defence; compulsory social security	1,485	1,551	1,676

—continued	2006	2007	2008
Education	999	1,035	1,071
Health and social work	359	373	391
Other community, social and personal services	801	849	833
Private households with employed persons	1,612	1,740	1,729
Extra-territorial organizations and bodies	2	2	2
Total employed	32,636	33,560	34,089
Unemployed	2,829	2,653	2,716
Total labour force	35,465	36,213	36,805
Males	21,811	22,217	22,673
Females	13,653	13,996	14,131

Source: ILO.

2009 ('000 persons aged 15 years and over): Total employed 35,062; Unemployed 2,831; Total labour force 37,893.

2010 ('000 persons aged 15 years and over): Total employed 36,047; Unemployed 2,859; Total labour force 38,906.

Health and Welfare

KEY INDICATORS

Total fertility rate (children per woman, 2009)	3.0
Under-5 mortality rate (per 1,000 live births, 2009)	33
HIV/AIDS (% of persons aged 15–49, 2005)	<0.1
Physicians (per 1,000 head, 2004)	0.58
Hospital beds (per 1,000 head, 2006)	1.3
Health expenditure (2008): US $ per head (PPP)	129
Health expenditure (2008): % of GDP	3.7
Health expenditure (2008): public (% of total)	34.7
Access to water (% of persons, 2008)	91
Access to sanitation (% of persons, 2008)	76
Total carbon dioxide emissions ('000 metric tons, 2007)	70,858.1
Carbon dioxide emissions per head (metric tons, 2007)	0.8
Human Development Index (2010): ranking	97
Human Development Index (2010): value	0.638

For sources and definitions, see explanatory note on p. vi.

Agriculture

PRINCIPAL CROPS

('000 metric tons)

	2007	2008	2009
Rice, paddy	16,240	16,816	16,266
Maize	6,737	6,928	7,034
Potatoes	118	121	119
Sweet potatoes	574	573	561
Cassava (Manioc)	1,871	1,942	2,044
Taro	114	116	120*
Yams	29	24	25*
Sugar cane	22,235	26,601	22,933
Beans, dry	29	30	28
Groundnuts, with shell	31	30	31
Coconuts	14,853	15,320	15,668
Oil palm fruit	414	466	516
Cabbages and other brassicas	123	129	125
Tomatoes	188	196	199
Pumpkins, squash and gourds	259	253	248
Aubergines (Eggplants)	210	200	201
Onions, dry	146	129	127
Watermelons	126	103	97

—continued	2007	2008	2009
Bananas	7,484	8,688	9,013
Grapefruit and pomelos	38	37	40*
Guavas, mangoes and mangosteens	1,024	884	771
Avocados	25	24	25*
Pineapples	2,016	2,209	2,198
Papayas	164	183	177
Coffee, green	98	97	96
Ginger	28	28	27
Tobacco, unmanufactured	34	32	36
Natural rubber	404	411	391

* FAO estimate.

Aggregate production ('000 metric tons, may include official, semi-official or estimated data): Total cereals 22,977 in 2007, 23,744 in 2008, 23,301 in 2009; Total roots and tubers 2,779 in 2007, 2,850 in 2008, 2,943 in 2009; Total vegetables (incl. melons) 5,963 in 2007, 5,791 in 2008, 5,705 in 2009; Total fruits (excl. melons) 14,475 in 2007, 15,668 in 2008, 15,961 in 2009.

Source: FAO.

LIVESTOCK

('000 head, year ending 30 June)

	2007	2008	2009
Cattle	2,566	2,566	2,586
Pigs	13,459	13,070	13,596
Buffaloes	3,384	3,339	3,321
Horses*	232	235	240
Goats	4,046	4,174	4,222
Sheep*	30	30	30
Chickens	135,640	158,663	158,372
Ducks	10,162	10,508	10,577

* FAO estimates.

Source: FAO.

LIVESTOCK PRODUCTS

('000 metric tons)

	2007	2008	2009
Cattle meat	178	180	184*
Buffalo meat	110.2	99.2	100.0*
Pig meat	1,616.7	1,606.0	1,710.4*
Chicken meat	661.8	740.7	752.0*
Cows' milk	13.4	13.8	14.3
Hen eggs†	470	550	555
Other poultry eggs†	73.0	72.0	74.0

* Unofficial figure.

† FAO estimates.

Source: FAO.

Forestry

ROUNDWOOD REMOVALS
('000 cubic metres, excl. bark)

	2007	2008	2009
Sawlogs, veneer logs and logs for sleepers*	648	474	689
Pulpwood	227	338	109
Other industrial wood*	2,295	3,000	3,000
Fuel wood*	12,698	12,581	12,469
Total	15,868	16,393	16,267

* FAO estimates.

Source: FAO.

SAWNWOOD PRODUCTION
('000 cubic metres, incl. railway sleepers)

	2007	2008	2009
Total (all broadleaved)	362	358	300

Source: FAO.

Fishing

('000 metric tons, live weight)

	2007	2008	2009
Capture	2,499.7	2,561.2	2,602.5
Scads (Decapterus)	437.3	414.0	379.0
Sardinellas	313.1	369.2	467.9
Frigate and bullet tunas	191.5	156.3	152.3
Skipjack tuna	185.9	222.0	251.5
Yellowfin tuna	135.8	169.4	152.9
Indian mackerel	89.6	91.3	87.4
Aquaculture	709.7	741.1	737.4
Nile tilapia	180.1	188.1	189.4
Milkfish	349.7	350.8	347.6
Total catch	3,209.4	3,302.3	3,339.9

Note: Figures exclude aquatic plants ('000 metric tons): 1,505.5 (capture 0.4, aquaculture 1,505.1) in 2007; 1,667.0 (capture 0.4, aquaculture 1,666.6) in 2008; 1,740.4 (capture 0.4, aquaculture 1,740.0) in 2009.

Source: FAO.

Mining

('000 metric tons unless otherwise indicated)

	2007	2008	2009
Coal	3,401	3,610	4,687
Crude petroleum ('000 barrels)	184	965	2,920
Chromium ore (gross weight)	31.6	15.3	16.0*
Copper ore†	22.9	21.2	49.1
Salt (unrefined)	438	510	516
Nickel ore†	91.4	80.6	137.4
Gold (metric tons)†	38.8	35.7	37.0
Silver (metric tons)†	27.8	14.2	33.8
Dolomite	1,092.7	1,150.0	1,177.0
Limestone‡	26,419	31,528	33,090

* Estimated production.
† Figures refer to the metal content of ores and concentrates.
‡ Excludes limestone for road construction.

Source: US Geological Survey.

Industry

SELECTED PRODUCTS
('000 metric tons unless otherwise indicated)

	2006	2007	2008
Plywood ('000 cubic metres)	317	281	235
Mechanical wood pulp*	38	38	38
Chemical wood pulp	147	147	147
Paper and paperboard*	1,097	1,097	5,000
Jet fuels	714	771	716
Motor spirit—petrol	1,590	1,470	1,520
Kerosene	162	166	133
Distillate fuel oils	3,575	3,659	3,301
Residual fuel oils	3,057	3,206	2,413
Liquefied petroleum gas	327	253	305
Cement	12,033	13,048	n.a.
Smelter (unrefined) copper	162	162	n.a.
Electric energy (million kWh)	56,784	59,612	60,821

* Estimates.

2009: Electric energy (million kWh) 61,379 (preliminary); Plywood ('000 cubic metres) 253; Mechanical wood pulp 38 (FAO estimate); Chemical wood pulp 147; Paper and paperboard 5,000 (FAO estimate).

Sources: FAO; UN Industrial Commodity Statistics Database; Asian Development Bank.

Finance

CURRENCY AND EXCHANGE RATES

Monetary Units
100 centavos = 1 Philippine peso.

Sterling, Dollar and Euro Equivalents (31 May 2011)
£1 sterling = 71.44 pesos;
US $1 = 43.29 pesos;
€1 = 62.27 pesos;
1,000 Philippine pesos = £14.00 = $23.10 = €16.06.

Average Exchange Rate (pesos per US $)
2008 44.323
2009 47.680
2010 45.110

GENERAL BUDGET
(million pesos)

Revenue*	2003	2004	2005†
Tax revenue	537,684	596,408	677,707
Taxes on net income and profits	243,735	278,848	319,102
Taxes on property	712	798	914
Taxes on domestic goods and services	186,784	203,779	225,041
General sales tax	82,444	93,727	109,094
Excises on goods	56,865	51,433	50,699
Taxes on international trade	106,453	112,983	132,650
Non-tax revenue	87,748	79,491	80,239
Bureau of the Treasury income	56,657	40,735	45,369
Fees and charges	29,375	22,993	24,643
Privatization	1,716	1,000	500
Other non-tax revenue	—	14,763	9,726
Total	625,432	675,898	757,945

Expenditure‡	2003	2004	2005†
Economic services	169,881	155,585	159,158
Agriculture	32,932	25,262	25,941
Natural resources and the environment	6,752	6,776	6,803
Trade and industry	2,722	2,833	3,020
Tourism	1,182	1,200	1,412
Power and energy	1,099	1,999	1,512
Water resources, development and flood control	7,007	6,180	6,471
Transport and communications	67,149	54,908	54,949
Other economic services	1,688	7,077	5,982
Allotment to local government units	49,350	49,350	53,068
Social services	237,532	247,888	254,297
Education, culture and training	128,995	133,321	135,470
Health	12,400	12,880	12,927
Social security, welfare and employment	39,096	38,381	40,080
Housing and community development	3,019	2,577	1,739
Land distribution	907	4,284	4,422
Other social services	945	4,275	3,558
Allotment to local government units	52,170	52,170	56,101
Defence	44,439	43,847	44,193
General public services	141,233	137,278	140,650
General administration	43,442	42,254	40,143
Public order and safety	52,565	53,213	54,290
Other general public services	5,746	2,331	3,763
Allotment to local government units	39,480	39,480	42,454
Interest payments	226,408	271,531	301,692
Total	819,493	856,129	899,990

* Excluding grants received (million pesos): 1,198 in 2003; 511 in 2004; 527 in 2005 (forecast).

† Forecasts.

‡ Excluding net lending (million pesos): 5,620 in 2003; 5,500 in 2004; 7,600 in 2005 (forecast).

2006: *Revenue:* Tax revenue 859,857; Non-tax revenue 119,598; Total revenue 979,455 (excl. grants 183). *Expenditure:* Allotment to local government units 174,713; Interest payments 310,108; Subsidy 13,810; Equity 3,561; Tax expenditures 15,577; Others 526,529; Total expenditure 1,044,298 (excl. net lending 131).

2007: *Revenue:* Tax revenue 932,937; Non-tax revenue 203,473; Total revenue 1,136,410 (excl. grants 150). *Expenditure:* Allotment to local government units 193,712; Interest payments 267,800; Subsidy 27,336; Equity 3,729; Tax expenditures 24,984; Others 621,690; Total expenditure 1,139,251 (excl. net lending 9,750).

2008: *Revenue:* Tax revenue 1,049,189; Non-tax revenue 153,591; Total revenue 1,202,780 (excl. grants 125). *Expenditure:* Allotment to local government units 222,995; Interest payments 272,218; Subsidy 21,109; Equity 1,691; Tax expenditures 49,717; Others 688,899; Total expenditure 1,256,629 (excl. net lending 14,393).

2009: *Revenue:* Tax revenue 981,631; Non-tax revenue 141,389; Total revenue 1,123,020 (excl. grants 191). *Expenditure:* Allotment to local government units 264,645; Interest payments 278,866; Subsidy 17,439; Equity 1,359; Tax expenditures 45,231; Others 809,139; Total expenditure 1,416,679 (excl. net lending 5,064).

2010: *Revenue:* Tax revenue 1,093,643; Non-tax revenue 113,877; Total revenue 1,207,520 (excl. grants 406). *Expenditure:* Allotment to local government units 279,552; Interest payments 294,244; Subsidy 21,005; Equity 2,149; Tax expenditures 39,693; Others 876,483; Total expenditure 1,513,126 (excl. net lending 9,258).

INTERNATIONAL RESERVES

(US $ million at 31 December)

	2008	2009	2010
Gold*	4,358	5,460	7,010
IMF special drawing rights	11	1,141	1,121
Reserve position in IMF	135	138	251
Foreign exchange	33,047	37,504	53,991
Total	37,551	44,243	62,373

* Valued at market-related prices.

Source: IMF, *International Financial Statistics*.

MONEY SUPPLY

('000 million pesos at 31 December)

	2008	2009	2010
Currency outside depository corporations	432.98	461.49	478.43
Transferable deposits	651.32	773.88	899.32
Other deposits	3,393.10	3,635.63	3,948.54
Securities other than shares	111.09	113.87	201.78
Broad money	4,588.48	4,984.88	5,528.07

Source: IMF, *International Financial Statistics*.

COST OF LIVING

(Consumer Price Index; base: 2000 = 100)

	2008	2009	2010
Food (incl. beverages and tobacco)	152.3	161.2	166.1
Fuel, light and water	193.9	188.8	213.8
Clothing (incl. footwear)	130.1	133.4	136.0
Housing and repairs	139.6	143.6	146.1
Services	180.5	180.1	188.0
Miscellaneous	126.1	129.4	131.2
All items	155.0	160.0	166.1

NATIONAL ACCOUNTS

('000 million pesos at current prices)

Expenditure on the Gross Domestic Product

	2007	2008	2009
Government final consumption expenditure	653.8	697.7	809.7
Private final consumption expenditure	4,611.9	5,281.1	5,675.0
Gross fixed capital formation	977.2	1,090.5	1,130.1
Change in inventories	45.2	45.6	–5.4
Total domestic expenditure	6,288.1	7,114.9	7,609.4
Exports of goods and services	2,826.6	2,736.3	2,431.4
Less Imports of goods and services	2,810.2	2,842.0	2,364.8
Statistical discrepancy	342.8	400.2	3.0
GDP in purchasers' values	6,647.3	7,409.4	7,678.9
GDP at constant 1985 prices	1,366.5	1,417.1	1,432.1

Gross Domestic Product by Economic Activity

	2007	2008	2009
Agriculture, hunting, forestry and fishing	943.3	1,102.5	1,138.3
Mining and quarrying	108.3	111.0	119.2
Manufacturing	1,459.1	1,654.6	1,566.7
Electricity, gas and water	230.9	235.6	242.5
Construction	299.9	346.6	390.4
Wholesale and retail trade, restaurants and hotels	981.5	1,088.2	1,115.4
Transport, storage and communications	478.4	508.8	514.3
Financial intermediation	362.0	404.9	443.5
Public administration	473.3	507.2	574.4
Other services	1,310.8	1,450.0	1,574.0
GDP in purchasers' values	6,647.3	7,409.4	7,678.9

Source: Asian Development Bank.

BALANCE OF PAYMENTS
(US $ million)

	2008	2009	2010
Exports of goods f.o.b.	48,253	37,610	50,684
Imports of goods f.o.b.	–61,138	–46,452	–61,068
Trade balance	–12,885	–8,842	–10,384
Exports of services	9,717	11,014	13,243
Imports of services	–8,557	–8,900	–11,297
Balance on goods and services	–11,725	–6,728	–8,438
Other income received	5,973	5,712	6,093
Other income paid	–5,868	–5,905	–5,785
Balance on goods, services and income	–11,620	–6,921	–8,130
Current transfers received	15,780	16,910	17,419
Current transfers paid	–533	–631	–824
Current balance	3,627	9,358	8,465
Capital account (net)	53	104	98
Direct investment abroad	–259	–359	–487
Direct investment from abroad	1,544	1,963	1,713
Portfolio investment assets	789	–2,715	–3,442
Portfolio investment liabilities	–4,416	2,090	9,745
Financial derivatives assets	541	403	429
Financial derivatives liabilities	–654	–371	–620
Other investment assets	4,305	–1,967	–2,273
Other investment liabilities	–3,544	–2,784	5,068
Net errors and omissions	–1,889	–1,310	–2,009
Overall balance	97	4,411	16,687

Source: IMF, *International Financial Statistics*.

External Trade

PRINCIPAL COMMODITIES
(distribution by SITC, US $ million)

Imports c.i.f.	2007	2008	2009
Food and live animals	3,713.1	5,866.2	4,806.9
Mineral fuels, lubricants, etc.	9,883.0	12,803.6	7,654.2
Petroleum, petroleum products, etc.	8,834.3	11,582.0	6,635.5
Crude petroleum oils, etc.	5,832.0	7,683.6	3,354.6
Chemicals and related products	4,229.2	5,166.6	4,482.7
Basic manufactures	4,729.5	4,893.9	3,639.5
Textile yarn, fabrics, etc.	1,189.2	872.5	604.2
Machinery and transport equipment	31,706.1	27,896.9	21,540.8
Office machines and automatic data-processing equipment	5,204.5	4,757.6	3,989.4
Parts and accessories for office machines, etc.	4,915.0	4,435.4	3,663.6
Telecommunications and sound equipment	1,234.5	1,297.8	1,200.8
Other electrical machinery, apparatus, etc.	20,091.9	16,118.5	11,638.7
Thermionic valves, tubes, etc.	18,080.4	14,126.8	9,897.7
Electronic microcircuits	5,118.5	5,123.8	4,243.8
Parts for electronic microcircuits	12,675.2	8,693.4	5,434.7
Road vehicles and parts (excl. tyres, engines and electrical parts)	1,827.5	2,093.8	2,044.4
Miscellaneous manufactured articles	1,762.9	1,730.9	1,603.5
Total (incl. others)	57,995.7	60,419.7	45,877.7

Exports f.o.b.	2007	2008	2009
Food and live animals	2,021.1	2,340.6	2,079.5
Basic manufactures	3,746.2	3,958.3	2,678.1
Machinery and transport equipment	35,224.4	33,030.8	26,623.7
Office machines and automatic data-processing equipment	10,209.0	9,016.4	8,210.1
Automatic data-processing machines and units	7,941.3	6,852.0	5,753.1
Digital automatic data-processing machines and units thereof	1,250.0	1,447.1	1,397.2
Digital central storage units, separately consigned	2,082.6	1,651.4	1,106.0
Parts and accessories for data-processing machines	2,135.2	2,013.4	2,346.9
Telecommunications and sound equipment	996.8	1,061.9	841.5
Other electrical machinery, apparatus, etc.	21,156.6	19,741.5	14,710.8
Thermionic valves, tubes, etc.	17,672.5	15,572.7	11,066.7
Diodes, transistors, etc.	1,860.6	1,789.3	1,458.0
Electronic microcircuits	15,226.6	13,165.2	8,815.8
Road vehicles and parts (excl. tyres, engines and electrical parts)	1,808.1	2,213.6	1,567.3
Miscellaneous manufactured articles	4,442.9	4,090.5	3,381.0
Clothing and accessories (excl. footwear)	2,294.4	1,979.0	1,534.1
Total (incl. others)	50,465.7	49,077.5	38,435.8

Source: UN, *International Trade Statistics Yearbook*.

2010 (US $ million): Total imports 54,492.9; Total exports 51,431.7.

PRINCIPAL TRADING PARTNERS
(US $ million)

Imports f.o.b.	2007	2008	2009
Australia	760.6	956.8	784.7
China, People's Republic	4,232.9	4,561.1	4,060.4
France (incl. Monaco)	626.9	821.3	546.4
Germany	1,291.9	1,148.4	1,008.0
Hong Kong	2,325.8	2,101.6	1,547.6
India	514.5	654.3	532.3
Indonesia	1,357.2	1,602.3	1,915.1
Iran	200.3	292.7	106.0
Ireland	1,435.0	644.2	185.4
Japan	7,219.1	7,121.9	5,764.9
Korea, Republic	3,403.9	3,128.5	3,160.9
Malaysia	2,370.1	2,583.2	1,787.1
Saudi Arabia	3,592.3	5,154.4	1,558.5
Singapore	6,411.3	6,217.9	3,931.1
Thailand	2,402.5	2,997.6	2,595.7
Viet Nam	906.5	1,800.7	1,401.7
United Arab Emirates	1,297.9	1,377.9	807.6
USA	8,115.3	7,738.1	5,488.2
Total (incl. others)	57,995.7	60,419.7	45,877.7

Exports f.o.b.	2007	2008	2009
Australia	528.4	470.8	296.3
Belgium	666.3	639.8	492.5
China, People's Republic	5,749.5	5,469.2	2,933.9
Germany	2,149.3	2,440.1	2,505.6
Hong Kong	5,803.5	4,987.5	3,213.3
Indonesia	524.5	602.7	382.7
Japan	7,304.1	7,707.1	6,208.4
Korea, Republic	1,783.7	2,522.5	1,828.2
Malaysia	2,506.7	1,957.6	1,359.9
Netherlands	4,149.5	3,708.4	3,743.5
Singapore	3,138.7	2,606.7	2,477.3
Thailand	1,403.0	1,509.0	1,236.1
United Kingdom	479.0	482.8	296.7
USA	8,601.4	8,216.4	6,797.1
Total (incl. others)	50,465.7	49,077.5	38,435.8

Source: UN, *International Trade Statistics Yearbook*.

2010 (US $ million): Total imports 54,492.9; Total exports 51,431.7.

Transport

RAILWAYS
(traffic)

	2002	2003	2004
Passenger-km (million)	93	83	84
Freight ton-km ('000)	63	69	76

Source: UN, *Statistical Yearbook*.

ROAD TRAFFIC
(registered motor vehicles)

	2008	2009	2010
Passenger cars	761,919	780,252	808,583
Utility vehicles	1,595,162	1,643,878	1,700,795
Sports utility vehicles (SUVs)	198,497	221,980	261,213
Buses	29,745	33,033	34,933
Trucks	296,276	311,582	317,903
Motorcycles and mopeds*	2,982,511	3,200,968	3,482,149
Trailers	27,162	28,740	29,279

* Including tricycles.

Source: Land Transportation Office, Manila.

SHIPPING

Merchant Fleet
(registered at 31 December)

	2007	2008	2009
Number of vessels	1,768	1,808	1,823
Total displacement ('000 grt)	5,066.2	5,029.2	5,219.3

Source: IHS Fairplay, *World Fleet Statistics*.

International Sea-borne Shipping
(freight traffic)

	1994	1995	1996
Vessels ('000 net registered tons):			
entered	53,453	61,298	n.a.
cleared	53,841	61,313	n.a.
Goods ('000 metric tons):			
loaded	14,581	16,658	15,687
unloaded	38,222	42,418	51,830

CIVIL AVIATION
(traffic on scheduled services)

	2004	2005	2006
Kilometres flown (million)	82	87	87
Passengers carried ('000)	7,388	8,057	8,305
Passenger-km (million)	15,739	17,123	16,800
Total ton-km (million)	1,929	2,085	2,040

Source: UN, *Statistical Yearbook*.

Tourism

TOURIST ARRIVALS

Country of residence	2006	2007	2008
Australia	101,313	112,466	121,514
Canada	80,507	91,308	102,381
China, People's Republic	133,585	157,601	163,689
Germany	51,402	55,894	55,303
Hong Kong	96,296	111,948	116,653
Japan	421,808	395,012	359,306
Korea, Republic	572,133	653,310	611,629
Singapore	81,114	94,008	100,177
Taiwan	114,955	112,206	118,782
United Kingdom	68,490	79,670	87,422
USA	567,355	578,983	578,246
Total (incl. others)*	2,843,345	3,091,993	3,139,422

* Including Philippine nationals permanently resident abroad.

Tourism receipts (US $ million, incl. passenger transport, unless otherwise indicated): 5,520 in 2007; 4,990 in 2008; 2,329 in 2009 (excl. passenger transport, provisional).

Source: World Tourism Organization.

2009 (foreign visitor arrivals by country of residence): Australia 132,330; Canada 99,012; China, People's Republic 155,019; Germany 55,912; Hong Kong 122,786; Japan 324,980; Korea, Republic 497,936; Malaysia 68,679; Singapore 98,305; Taiwan 102,274; United Kingdom 91,009; USA 582,537; Total (incl. others) 3,017,099. Note: Including Philippine nationals permanently resident abroad (Source: Department of Tourism, Manila).

2010 (foreign visitor arrivals by country of residence): Australia 40,928; Canada 106,345; China, People's Republic 187,446; Germany 58,725; Hong Kong 133,746; Japan 358,744; Korea, Republic 740,622; Malaysia 79,694; Singapore 121,083; Taiwan 142,455; United Kingdom 96,925; USA 600,165; Total (incl. others) 3,520,471. Note: Including Philippine nationals permanently resident abroad (Source: Department of Tourism, Manila).

Communications Media

	2008	2009	2010
Telephones ('000 main lines in use)	4,076.1	6,783.4	6,783.4
Mobile cellular telephones ('000 subscribers)	68,117.2	75,586.6	79,895.6
Internet subscribers ('000)	3,545.7	3,600.0	n.a.
Broadband subscribers ('000)	1,045.7	1,722.4	1,722.4

Personal computers: 6,300,000 (72.3 per 1,000 persons) in 2006.

Radio receivers ('000 in use): 11,500 in 1997.

Television receivers ('000 in use): 13,500 in 2001.

Book production (titles, excluding pamphlets): 1,380 in 1999.

Daily newspapers: 82 (with average circulation of 6,514,102 copies) in 2004.

Non-daily newspapers: 498 (with average circulation of 971,220 copies) in 2004.

Sources: International Telecommunication Union; UN, *Statistical Yearbook*; UNESCO, *Statistical Yearbook*.

Education

(2009/10 unless otherwise stated, estimates)

	Institutions	Teachers	Pupils
Pre-primary	44,846	410,386	1,474,644
Primary schools			13,934,172
Secondary schools	10,384	197,684	6,806,079
University and other tertiary education*	1,619	111,225	2,402,315

* 2004/05 figures.

Sources: Department of Education; Commission on Higher Education.

Pupil-teacher ratio (primary education, UNESCO estimate): 33.7 in 2006/07 (Source: UNESCO Institute for Statistics).

Adult literacy rate (UNESCO estimates): 95.4% (males 95.0%; females 95.8%) in 2008 (Source: UNESCO Institute for Statistics).

Directory

The Constitution

A new Constitution for the Republic of the Philippines was ratified by national referendum on 2 February 1987. Its principal provisions are summarized below:

BASIC PRINCIPLES

Sovereignty resides in the people, and all government authority emanates from them; war is renounced as an instrument of national policy; civilian authority is supreme over military authority.

The State undertakes to pursue an independent foreign policy, governed by considerations of the national interest; the Republic of the Philippines adopts and pursues a policy of freedom from nuclear weapons in its territory.

Other provisions guarantee social justice and full respect for human rights; honesty and integrity in the public service; the autonomy of local governments; and the protection of the family unit. Education, the arts, sport, private enterprise, and agrarian and urban reforms are also promoted. The rights of workers, women, youth, the urban poor and minority indigenous communities are emphasized.

BILL OF RIGHTS

The individual is guaranteed the right to life, liberty and property under the law; freedom of abode and travel, freedom of worship, freedom of speech, of the press and of petition to the Government are guaranteed, as well as the right of access to official information on matters of public concern, the right to form trade unions, the right to assemble in public gatherings, and free access to the courts.

The Constitution upholds the right of habeas corpus and prohibits the intimidation, detention, torture or secret confinement of apprehended persons.

SUFFRAGE

Suffrage is granted to all citizens over 18 years of age, who have resided for at least one year previously in the Republic of the Philippines, and for at least six months in their voting district. Voting is by secret ballot.

LEGISLATURE

Legislative power is vested in the bicameral Congress of the Philippines, consisting of the Senate and the House of Representatives, with a maximum of 274 members (subsequently increased to 299). All members shall make a disclosure of their financial and business interests upon assumption of office, and no member may hold any other office. Provision is made for voters to propose laws, or reject any act or law passed by Congress, through referendums.

The Senate shall be composed of 24 members; Senators are directly elected for six years by national vote, and must be natural-born citizens, at least 35 years of age, literate and registered voters in their district. They must be resident in the Philippines for at least two years prior to election, and no Senator shall serve for more than two consecutive terms. One-half of the membership of the Senate shall be elected every three years. No treaty or international agreement may be considered valid without the approval, by voting, of at least two-thirds of members.

A maximum of 250 Representatives (increased to 275 at the 2007 election) may sit in the House of Representatives. Its members may serve no more than three consecutive three-year terms. Representatives must be natural-born citizens, literate, and at least 25 years of age. Each legislative district may elect one representative; the number of legislative districts shall be determined according to population and shall be reapportioned following each census. Representatives must be registered voters in their district, and resident there for at least one year prior to election. In addition, one-fifth of the total number of representatives shall be elected under a party list system from lists of nominees proposed by indigenous, but non-religious, minority groups (such as the urban poor, peasantry, women and youth).

The Senate and the House of Representatives shall each have an Electoral Tribunal which shall be the sole judge of contests relating to the election of members of Congress. Each Tribunal shall have nine members, three of whom must be Justices of the Supreme Court, appointed by the Chief Justice. The remaining six members shall be members of the Senate or of the House of Representatives, as appropriate, and shall be selected from the political parties represented therein, on a proportional basis.

THE COMMISSION ON APPOINTMENTS

The President must submit nominations of heads of executive departments, ambassadors and senior officers in the armed forces to the Commission on Appointments, which shall decide on the appointment by majority vote of its members. The President of the Senate shall act as ex-officio Chairman; the Commission shall consist of 12 Senators and 12 members of the House of Representatives, elected from the political parties represented therein, on the basis of proportional representation.

THE EXECUTIVE

Executive power is vested in the President of the Philippines. Presidents are limited to one six-year term of office, and Vice-Presidents to two successive six-year terms. Candidates for both posts are elected by direct universal suffrage. They must be natural-born citizens, literate, at least 40 years of age, registered voters and resident in the Philippines for at least 10 years prior to election.

The President is Head of State and Chief Executive of the Republic. Bills (legislative proposals) that have been approved by Congress shall be signed by the President; if the President vetoes the bill, it may become law when two-thirds of members in Congress approve it.

The President shall nominate and, with the consent of the Commission on Appointments, appoint ambassadors, officers of the armed forces and heads of executive departments.

The President is Commander-in-Chief of the armed forces and may suspend the writ of habeas corpus or place the Republic under martial law for a period not exceeding 60 days when, in the President's opinion, public safety demands it. Congress may revoke either action by a majority vote.

The Vice-President may be a member of the Cabinet; in the event of the death or resignation of the President, the Vice-President shall become President and serve the unexpired term of the previous President.

THE JUDICIARY

The Supreme Court is composed of a Chief Justice and 14 Associate Justices, and may sit *en banc* or in divisions comprising three, five or seven members. Justices of the Supreme Court are appointed by the President, with the consent of the Commission on Appointments, for a term of four years. They must be citizens of the Republic, at least 40 years of age, of proven integrity, and must have been judges of the lower courts, or engaged in the practice of law in the Philippines, for at least 15 years.

The Supreme Court, sitting *en banc*, is the sole judge of disputes relating to presidential and vice-presidential elections.

THE CONSTITUTIONAL COMMISSIONS

These are the Civil Service Commission and the Commission on Audit, each of which has a Chairman and two other Commissioners, appointed by the President (with the approval of the Commission on Appointments) to a seven-year term; and the Commission on Elections, which enforces and administers all laws pertaining to elections and political parties. The Commission on Elections has seven members, appointed by the President (and approved by the Commission on Appointments) for a seven-year term. The Commission on Elections may sit *en banc* or in two divisions.

LOCAL GOVERNMENT

The Republic of the Philippines shall be divided into provinces, cities, municipalities and barangays. The Congress of the Philippines shall enact a local government code providing for decentralization. A region may become autonomous, subject to approval by a majority vote of the electorate of that region, in a referendum. Defence and security in such areas will remain the responsibility of the national Government.

ACCOUNTABILITY OF PUBLIC OFFICERS

All public officers, including the President, Vice-President and members of Congress and the Constitutional Commissions, may be removed from office if impeached for, or convicted of, violation of the Constitution, corruption, treason, bribery or betrayal of public trust.

Cases of impeachment must be initiated solely by the House of Representatives, and tried solely by the Senate. A person shall be convicted by a vote of at least two-thirds of the Senate, and will then be dismissed from office and dealt with according to the law.

SOCIAL JUSTICE AND HUMAN RIGHTS

The Congress of the Philippines shall give priority to considerations of human dignity, the equality of the people and an equitable distribution of wealth. The Commission on Human Rights shall investigate allegations of violations of human rights, shall protect human rights through legal measures, and shall monitor the Government's compliance with international treaty obligations. It may advise Congress on measures to promote human rights.

AMENDMENTS OR REVISIONS

Proposals for amendment or revision of the Constitution may be made by:

i) Congress (upon a vote of three-quarters of members);

ii) A Constitutional Convention (convened by a vote of two-thirds of members of Congress);

iii) The people, through petitions (signed by at least 12% of the total number of registered voters).

The proposed amendments or revisions shall then be submitted to a national plebiscite, and shall be valid when ratified by a majority of the votes cast.

MILITARY BASES

Foreign military bases, troops or facilities shall not be allowed in the Republic of the Philippines following the expiry, in 1991, of the Agreement between the Republic and the USA, except under the provisions of a treaty approved by the Senate, and, when required by Congress, ratified by the voters in a national referendum.

The Government

HEAD OF STATE

President: Benigno Aquino, III (assumed office 30 June 2010).

Vice-President: Jejomar Binay.

CABINET
(October 2011)

The Cabinet comprises members of the Liberal Party and numerous unaffiliated representatives of the public and private sectors.

Executive Secretary: Paquito Ochoa, Jr.

Secretary of the Interior and Local Government: Jesse Robredo.

Secretary of Foreign Affairs: Albert del Rosario.

Secretary of Finance: Cesar Purisima.

Secretary of Justice: Leila L. de Lima.

Secretary of National Defense: Voltaire Gazmin.

Secretary of Education: Brother Armin A. Luistro.

Secretary of the Budget and Management: Florencio Abad.

Secretary of Agriculture: Proceso V. Alcala.

Secretary of Energy: Jose Rene V. Almendras.

Secretary of the Environment and Natural Resources: Ramon Paje.

Secretary of Health: Dr Enrique T. Ona.

Secretary of Labor and Employment: Rosalinda Baldoz.

Secretary of Public Works and Highways: Rogelio Singson.

Secretary of Science and Technology: Dr Mario G. Montejo.

Secretary of Social Welfare and Development: Corazon Soliman.

Secretary of Tourism: Ramon Jimenez, Jr.

Secretary of Trade and Industry: Gregory L. Domingo.

Secretary of Transportation and Communications: Manuel Roxas, II.

Secretary of Agrarian Reform: Virgilio de los Reyes.

Secretary of Presidential Communications Development and Strategic Planning: Ramon Carandang.

Secretary of the Presidential Communications Operations Office: Herminio Coloma.

Director-General of the National Economic and Development Authority: Cayetano L. Paderanga, Jr.

There are a further 11 officials of cabinet rank.

MINISTRIES

Office of the President: New Exec. Bldg, Malacañang Palace Compound, J. P. Laurel St, San Miguel, Metro Manila; tel. (2) 7356201; fax (2) 9293968; e-mail opnet@ops.gov.ph; internet www.president.gov.ph.

Office of the Vice-President: PNB Financial Center, 7th Floor, President Diosdado Macapagal Blvd, Pasay City, 1300 Metro Manila; tel. (2) 8333311; fax (2) 8316676; e-mail vp@ovp.gov.ph; internet www.ovp.gov.ph.

Department of Agrarian Reform: DAR Bldg, Elliptical Rd, Diliman, Quezon City, Metro Manila; tel. (2) 9287031; fax (2) 9293088; e-mail info@dar.gov.ph; internet www.dar.gov.ph.

Department of Agriculture: DA Bldg, 4th Floor, Elliptical Rd, Diliman, Quezon City, Metro Manila; tel. (2) 9288741; fax (2) 9203987; e-mail usec.gonzales@da.gov.ph; internet www.da.gov.ph.

Department of the Budget and Management: DBM Bldg, Gen. Solano St, Malacañang, San Miguel, Metro Manila; tel. (2) 7354933; fax (2) 7354809; e-mail dbmtis@dbm.gov.ph; internet www.dbm.gov.ph.

Department of Education: DepED Complex, Meralco Ave, Pasig City, 1600 Metro Manila; tel. (2) 6321361; fax (2) 6388634; internet www.deped.gov.ph.

Department of Energy: Energy Center, Merritt Rd, Fort Bonifacio, Taguig, 1201 Metro Manila; tel. and fax (2) 8402278; e-mail info@doe.gov.ph; internet www.doe.gov.ph.

Department of the Environment and Natural Resources: DENR Bldg, Visayas Ave, Diliman, Quezon City, 1100 Metro Manila; tel. (2) 9296626; fax (2) 9204352; e-mail osec@denr.gov.ph; internet www.denr.gov.ph.

Department of Finance: DOF Bldg, BSP Complex, Roxas Blvd, 1004 Metro Manila; tel. (2) 5236051; fax (2) 5268474; e-mail hotline@dof.gov.ph; internet www.dof.gov.ph.

Department of Foreign Affairs: DFA Bldg, 2330 Roxas Blvd, Pasay City, 1330 Metro Manila; tel. (2) 8344000; fax (2) 8321597; e-mail webmaster@dfa.gov.ph; internet www.dfa.gov.ph.

Department of Health: San Lazaro Compound, Rizal Ave, Santa Cruz, 1003 Metro Manila; tel. (2) 7438301; fax (2) 7431829; e-mail ftduque@co.doh.gov.ph; internet www.doh.gov.ph.

Department of the Interior and Local Government: A. Francisco Gold Condominium II, Epifanio de los Santos Ave, cnr Mapagmahal St, Diliman, Quezon City, 1100 Metro Manila; tel. (2) 9250349;

fax (2) 9250386; e-mail dilgmail@dilg.gov.ph; internet www.dilg.gov.ph.

Department of Justice: Padre Faura St, Ermita, 1000 Metro Manila; tel. (2) 5238481; fax (2) 5267643; e-mail info@doj.gov.ph; internet www.doj.gov.ph.

Department of Labor and Employment: DOLE Exec. Bldg, 7th Floor, Muralla Wing, Muralla St, Intramuros, 1002 Metro Manila; tel. (2) 5273000; fax (2) 5273494; e-mail osec@dole.gov.ph; internet www.dole.gov.ph.

Department of National Defense: DND Bldg, 3rd Floor, Camp Aguinaldo, Quezon City, 1110 Metro Manila; tel. (2) 9116402; fax (2) 9111651; e-mail webmaster@dnd.gov.ph; internet www.dnd.gov.ph.

Department of Public Works and Highways: DPWH Bldg, Bonifacio Dr., Port Area, Metro Manila; tel. (2) 3043000; fax (2) 5275635; e-mail bonoan.manuel@dpwh.gov.ph; internet www.dpwh.gov.ph.

Department of Science and Technology: DOST Compound, Gen. Santos Ave, Bicutan, Taguig, 1631 Metro Manila; tel. (2) 8372071; fax (2) 8373161; e-mail efa@dost.gov.ph; internet www.dost.gov.ph.

Department of Social Welfare and Development: Batasang Pambansa, Constitution Hills, Quezon City, Metro Manila; tel. (2) 9318101; fax (2) 9318191; e-mail lfp@dswd.gov.ph; internet www.dswd.gov.ph.

Department of Tourism: T. F. Valencia Circle, T. M. Kalaw St, Rizal Park, Metro Manila; tel. (2) 5238411; fax (2) 5256538; e-mail amflor@tourism.gov.ph; internet www.wowphilippines.com.ph.

Department of Trade and Industry: Industry and Investments Bldg, 385 Sen. Gil J. Puyat Ave, Buendia, Makati City, 1200 Metro Manila; tel. (2) 7510384; fax (2) 8956487; e-mail mis@dti.dti.gov.ph; internet www.dti.gov.ph.

Department of Transportation and Communications: Columbia Tower, 17th Floor, Ortigas Ave, Mandaluyong City, 1555 Metro Manila; tel. (2) 7277960; fax (2) 7234925; e-mail webmaster@dotc.gov.ph; internet www.dotc.gov.ph.

National Economic and Development Authority (NEDA—Department of Socio-Economic Planning): NEDA-sa-Pasig Bldg, 12 St Josemaria Escriva Dr., Ortigas Center, Pasig City, 1605 Metro Manila; tel. (2) 6313747; fax (2) 6313282; e-mail info@neda.gov.ph; internet www.neda.gov.ph.

Philippine Information Agency (Office of the Press Secretary): PIA Bldg, Visayas Ave, Diliman, Quezon City, 1101 Metro Manila; tel. (2) 9204345; fax (2) 9204390; e-mail angie.villapando@gmail.com; internet www.pia.gov.ph.

President and Legislature

PRESIDENT

Election, 10 May 2010

Candidate	Votes	% of votes
Benigno Aquino III (Liberal Party—LP)	15,208,678	41.87
Joseph Estrada (Pwersa ng Masang Pilipino—PMP)	9,487,837	26.12
Manuel Villar (Nacionalista Party—NP)	5,573,835	15.35
Gilberto Teodoro (Lakas-Kampi-CMD)	4,095,839	11.28
Eduardo Villanueva (Bangon Pilipinas)	1,125,878	3.10
Richard Gordon (Bagumbayan-VNP)	501,727	1.38
Vetellano Acosta (Kilusang Bagong Lipunan—KBL)	181,985*	0.50
Nicanor Perlas (Independent)	54,575	0.15
Jamby Madrigal (Independent)	46,489	0.13
John Carlos de los Reyes (Ang Kapatiran)	44,244	0.12
Total	36,321,087	100.00

* Candidate was disqualified after ballot papers had been printed; all votes for Vetellano Acosta were therefore deemed invalid.

THE CONGRESS OF THE PHILIPPINES

Senate

President of the Senate: JUAN PONCE ENRILE.

Elections for 12 of the 24 seats were held on 10 May 2010. The LP and the NP-Nationalist People's Coalition (NPC) alliance both won three seats, while Lakas-Kampi-CMD and the PMP secured two seats each, and the People's Reform Party took one. The remaining seat was secured by an independent candidate.

House of Representatives

Speaker of the House: FELICIANO BELMONTE.

General Election, 10 May 2010, provisional results

	Seats
Lakas-Kampi-CMD	105
Liberal Party (LP)	42
Nationalist People's Coalition (NPC)	31
Nacionalista Party (NP)	25
Independents	7
Pwersa ng Masang Pilipino (PMP)	5
Others	46
Undeclared	25
Total	286

Note: The total includes 57 seats reserved for members of minority and cause-orientated groups allocated under the concurrent party list elections.

Autonomous Region

MUSLIM MINDANAO

The Autonomous Region of Muslim Mindanao (ARMM) originally comprised the provinces of Lanao del Sur, Maguindanao, Tawi-Tawi and Sulu. The Region was granted autonomy in November 1989. Elections took place in February 1990, and the formal transfer of limited executive powers took place in October of that year. In August 2001 a plebiscite was conducted in 11 provinces and 14 cities in Mindanao to determine whether or not they would become members of the ARMM. The city of Marawi and the province of Basilan subsequently joined the Region. The Regional Legislative Assembly was expanded to 24 seats, from 21 previously, at elections held on 8 August 2005. A total of six candidates contested the concurrent gubernatorial election; Zaldy Ampatuan, the candidate of Lakas ng EDSA-Christian Muslim Democrats (Lakas-CMD), won an estimated 63.7% of the votes cast, defeating Mahid Mutilan of the Ompia Party, a Muslim grouping, and Ibrahim Paglas of the Liberal Party, who received 24.3% and 11.8% of the votes respectively. Ampatuan was re-elected Governor on 11 August 2008. However, owing to his alleged involvement in the killing of 57 people on Mindanao in November 2009, Ampatuan was subsequently suspended from office and replaced by his deputy, Ansaruddin Adiong, in an acting capacity.

Governor: ANSARUDDIN ALONTO ADIONG (acting).

Vice-Governor: REJIE SAHALI-GENERALE (acting).

Election Commission

Commission on Elections (COMELEC): Postigo St, Intramuros, 1002 Metro Manila; tel. (2) 5275581; e-mail asd@comelec.gov.ph; internet www.comelec.gov.ph; f. 1940; Chair. SIXTO BRILLANTES, Jr.

Political Organizations

Akbayan (Citizens' Action Party): 36B Madasalin St, Teacher's Village West, Diliman, Quezon City, 1101 Metro Manila; tel. (2) 4336933; fax (2) 9252936; e-mail secretariat@akbayan.org; internet www.akbayan.org; f. 1998; left-wing party list; Chair. PERCIVAL CENDANA; Pres. RONALD LLAMAS; Sec.-Gen. CONRAD CASTILLO.

Aksyon Demokratiko (Democratic Action Party): 16th Floor, Strata 2000 Bldg, F. Ortigas Jr Rd, Ortigas Center, Pasig City, 1600 Metro Manila; tel. (2) 6385381; fax (2) 6343072; e-mail senator@raulroco.com; internet 203.115.161.138/library/raulroco/aksyond/aksyond.htm; f. 1997; est. to support presidential candidacy of RAUL ROCO; joined Alyansa ng Pag-asa in 2003 to contest 2004 elections; Chair. SONIA M. ROCO; Pres. JAIME GALVEZ-TAN; Sec.-Gen. LORNA KAPUNAN.

Bagumbayan-Volunteers for a New Philippines (Bagumbayan-VNP): Unit 3C, Classica Condominium I, H. V. Dela Costa St, Makati City, Metro Manila; tel. (2) 813-1257; e-mail join@bagumbayan-vnp.com; f. 2009; Chair. RICHARD GORDON; Pres. LEON B. HERRERA.

Bangon Pilipinas (Rise Philippines): 8th Floor, Dominion Bldg, 833 Arnaiz Ave, Legaspi Village, Makati City, 1200 Metro Manila; tel. (2) 8113355; fax (2) 8111110; e-mail feedback@bangonpilipinas.org; internet bangonpilipinas.com; Pres. CIELITO F. HABITO; Chair. EDUARDO VILLANUEVA.

Bayan Muna (People First): 153 Scout Rallos St, Kamuning, Quezon City, 1103 Metro Manila; tel. (2) 4251045; fax (2) 9213473; e-mail information@bayanmuna.net; internet www.bayanmuna.net; f. 1999; Pres. SATUR C. OCAMPO; Chair. Dr REYNALDO LESACA, Jr.

Kilusang Bagong Lipunan (KBL) (New Society Movement): Metro Manila; f. 1978 by Pres. MARCOS and fmr mems of the Nacionalista Party; Chair. FERDINAND 'BONG BONG' MARCOS, Jr.

Laban ng Demokratikong Pilipino (LDP) (Fight of Democratic Filipinos): 3-B, Osmena Bldg, 1991 A. Mabini St, Malate, Metro Manila; internet www.edangara.com; f. 1987; reorg. 1988 as an alliance of Lakas ng Bansa and a conservative faction of the PDP-Laban Party; mem. of Lapian ng Masang Pilipino (LAMP) until Jan. 2001; split into two factions, led by EDGARDO ANGARA and AGAPITO AQUINO, to contest 2004 elections; Angara faction joined Koalisyon ng Nagkakaisang Pilipino (KNP) in Dec. 2003 to support presidential candidacy of FERNANDO POE, Jr; Aquino faction supported presidential candidacy of PANFILO LACSON; Pres. EDGARDO ANGARA.

Lakas-Kampi-CMD: 6th Floor, CLMC Bldg, Greenhills East, Mandaluyong City; tel. (2) 7250872; fax (2) 7250736; f. 2009; est. by merger of Lakas ng EDSA-Christian Muslim Democrats (fmrly Lakas-National Union of Christian Democrats/Lakas-NUCD) and of Kabalikat ng Malayang Pilipino (Kampi); Nat. Chair. EDCEL LAGMAN; Nat. Pres. RAMON BONG REVILLA, Jr.

Liberal Party (LP): 2nd Floor, Matrinco Bldg, Chino Roces Ave, Makati City, 1231 Metro Manila; tel. (2) 8937483; fax (2) 8930218; e-mail liberalpartyphils@gmail.com; internet www.liberalparty.ph; f. 1946; represents centre-liberal opinion of the fmr Nacionalista Party, which split in 1946; joined Koalisyon ng Katapatan at Karanasan sa Kinabukasan (K-4) in Jan. 2004 to contest 2004 elections; Chair. FRANKLIN M. DRILON; Pres. MANUEL ROXAS, II.

Nacionalista Party (NP): 2nd Floor, Starmall EDSA, cnr Shaw Blvd, Mandaluyong City, 1552 Metro Manila; tel. (2) 7224727; fax (2) 7274223; e-mail secretariat@nacionalistaparty.com; internet www.nacionalistaparty.com; formed alliance with NPC in April 2010 to contest election in May; Pres. MANUEL VILLAR; Sec.-Gen. ALAN PETER CAYETANO.

Nationalist People's Coalition (NPC): 8 Bouganvilla St, cnr Balete Dr., Mariana, Quezon City, 1112 Metro Manila; tel. (2) 5847518; fax (2) 5847568; e-mail npcparty@gmail.com; internet npcparty.org; f. 1991; breakaway faction of the NP, with which it formed an alliance in April 2010, in advance of the legislative election in May; mem. of Lapian ng Masang Pilipino (LAMP) from 1997 until Jan. 2001; Chair. FAUSTINO DY, Jr; Pres. FRISCO SAN JUAN.

Partido Demokratiko Pilipino-Lakas Ng Bayan (PDP-Laban): 721 J. P. Rizal St, Makati City, Metro Manila; internet www.pdplaban.org; tel. (2) 8901792; fax (2) 8900858; f. 1983; est. following merger of Pilipino Democratic Party (f. 1982 by fmr mems of the Mindanao Alliance) and Laban (Lakas ng Bayan—People's Power Movement, f. 1978 and led by BENIGNO S. AQUINO, Jr, until his assassination in 1983); centrist; formally dissolved in Sept. 1988, following formation of the LDP, but a faction continued to function as a political movement; formed United Opposition (UNO) alliance with the PMP in advance of the May 2010 elections; Pres. JEJOMAR BINAY; Sec.-Gen. AQUILINO PIMENTEL, III.

Partido Demokratiko Sosyalista ng Pilipinas (PDSP) (Philippine Democratic Socialist Party): 45 Melchor St, Varsity Hills, Quezon City, Metro Manila; tel. and fax (2) 4161325; fax 9286678; e-mail secretariat@pdsp.net; internet pdsp.net; f. 1981; formed by mems of the Batasang Pambansa allied to the Nacionalista (Roy faction), Pusyon Visaya and Mindanao Alliance parties; joined People Power Coalition (PPC) in Feb. 2001; Chair. NORBERTO GONZALES.

Partido ng Manggagawang Pilipino (Filipino Workers' Party): e-mail pinoy_bolshevik@yahoo.com; internet manggagawangpilipino.tripod.com; f. 2002; est. by fmr supporters of the CPP.

Partido para sa Demokratikong Reporma: Chateau Bldg, Pasig City, Metro Manila; joined People Power Coalition (PPC) in Feb. 2001; Chair. RENATO DE VILLA; Sec.-Gen. RAFAEL COLET.

People's Reform Party (PRP): Narsan Bldg, 4th Floor, 3 West Fourth St, West Triangle Quezon Ave, Quezon City, Metro Manila; e-mail miriam@miriam.com.ph; f. 1991; formed by MIRIAM DEFENSOR SANTIAGO to support her candidacy in the 1992 presidential election; Santiago re-elected to Senate for a third term in 2010; Pres. MIRIAM DEFENSOR SANTIAGO.

Probinsya Muna Development Initiatives (PROMDI): 7 Pasteur St, Lahug, Cebu City; tel. (32) 2326692; fax (32) 2313609; f. 1997; Leader EMILIO ('LITO') OSMEÑA.

Pwersa ng Masang Pilipino (PMP): 409 Shaw Bld, Mandaluyong City, Metro Manila; e-mail pmp_power@yahoo.com; formed United Opposition (UNO) alliance with PDP-Laban in advance of the May 2010 elections; Pres. JOSEPH EJERCITO ESTRADA; Sec.-Gen. JOSEPH VICTOR EJERCITO.

United Negros Alliance (UNA): Negros Occidental; formed alliance with the NPC in advance of the May 2010 elections; Chair. ALFREDO MARAÑON, Jr.

The following organizations are, or have been, in conflict with the Government:

Abu Sayyaf (Bearer of the Sword): Mindanao; radical Islamist group seeking the establishment of an Islamic state in Mindanao; breakaway grouping of the MILF; est. strength 1,500 (2000); Leader YASSER IGASAN.

Alex Boncayao Brigade (ABB): communist urban guerrilla group, fmrly linked to CPP; formed alliance with Revolutionary Proletarian Party in 1997; est. strength 500 (April 2001); Leader NILO DE LA CRUZ.

Islamic Command Council (ICC): Mindanao; splinter group of MNLF; Leader MELHAM ALAM.

Maranao Islamic Statehood Movement: Mindanao; f. 1998; armed grouping seeking the establishment of an Islamic state in Mindanao.

Mindanao Independence Movement (MIM): Mindanao; claims a membership of 1m; Leader REUBEN CANOY.

Moro Islamic Liberation Front (MILF): Camp Abubakar, Lanao del Sur, Mindanao; aims to establish an Islamic state in Mindanao; comprises a faction that broke away from the MNLF in 1978; its armed wing, the Bangsa Moro Islamic Armed Forces, has c. 12,500 armed regulars; Chair. Al-Haj MURAD EBRAHIM.

Moro Islamic Reform Group: Mindanao; breakaway faction from MNLF; est. strength of 200 in 2000.

Moro National Liberation Front (MNLF): internet mnlf.net; seeks autonomy for Muslim communities in Mindanao; signed a peace agreement with the Govt in Sept. 1996; its armed wing, the Bangsa Moro Army, comprised an est. 10,000 mems in 2000; Chair. and Pres. of Cen. Cttee Dr NUR MISUARI.

Moro National Liberation Front—Islamic Command Council (MNLF—ICC): Basak, Lanao del Sur; f. 2000; Islamist separatist movement committed to urban guerrilla warfare; breakaway faction from MNLF.

National Democratic Front (NDF): a left-wing alliance of 14 mem. groups; Chair. MARIANA OROSA; Spokesman GREGORIO ROSAL.

The NDF includes:

Communist Party of the Philippines (CPP): f. 1968; breakaway faction of the Partido Komunista ng Pilipinas (PKP, f. 1930); legalized Sept. 1992; in July 1993 the Metro Manila-Rizal and Visayas regional committees, controlling 40% of total CPP membership (est. 15,000 in 1994), split from the Central Committee; Chair. JOSE MARIA SISON; Gen. Sec. BENITO TIAMZON.

New People's Army (NPA): f. 1969; est. as the military wing of the CPP; based in central Luzon, but operates throughout the Philippines; est. strength 9,500; Leader JOVENCIO BALWEG; Spokesman GREGORIO ROSAL.

Revolutionary Proletarian Party: Metro Manila; f. 1996; comprises mems of the Metro Manila-Rizal and Visayas regional committees, which broke away from the CPP in 1993; has a front organization called the Bukluran ng Manggagawang Pilipino (Association of Filipino Workers); Leader ARTURO TABARA.

Rajah Solaiman Movement (RSM): Mindanao; f. 2002; radical Islamist group seeking to establish an Islamic state in the Philippines; predominantly composed of converts to Islam.

Workers and Peasants Party (WPP): Unit 113, Legaspi Suites, 11th Floor, 178 Salcedo St, Legaspi Village, Makati City, Metro Manila; fmrly known as Lapiang Mangagawa; Pres. JOSE MALVAR VILLEGAS, Jr; Sec.-Gen. FRANK PASION.

Diplomatic Representation

EMBASSIES IN THE PHILIPPINES

Argentina: 8th Floor, Liberty Center, 104 H. V. de la Costa St, Salcedo Village, Makati City, 1227 Metro Manila; tel. (2) 8453218; fax (2) 8453220; e-mail embarfil@eastern.com.ph; Ambassador JOAQUIN DANIEL OTERO.

Australia: 23rd Floor, Tower II, RCBC Plaza, 6819 Ayala Ave, Makati City, 1200 Metro Manila; tel. (2) 7578100; fax (2) 7578268; e-mail public-affairs-MNLA@dfat.gov.au; internet www.australia.com.ph; Ambassador ROD SMITH.

Austria: Prince Bldg, 4th Floor, 117 Rada St, Legaspi Village, POB 2411, Makati City, 1200 Metro Manila; tel. (2) 8179191; fax (2) 8134238; e-mail manila-ob@bmeia.gv.at; internet www.aussenministerium.at/manila; Ambassador WILHELM DONKO.

Bangladesh: Universal-Re Bldg, 2nd Floor, 106 Paseo de Roxas, Legaspi Village, Makati City, Metro Manila; tel. (2) 8175001; fax (2)

8164941; e-mail bdemb.manila@yahoo.com; Ambassador IKHTIAR MOMIN CHOWDHURY.

Belgium: Multinational Bancorporation Center, 9th Floor, 6805 Ayala Ave, Makati City, Metro Manila; tel. (2) 8451869; fax (2) 8452076; e-mail manila@diplobel.fed.be; internet www.diplomatie.be/manila; Ambassador CHRISTIAN MEERSCHMAN.

Brazil: 16th Floor, Liberty Center, 104 H. V. de la Costa St, Salcedo Village, Makati City, 1227 Metro Manila; tel. (2) 8453651; fax (2) 8453676; e-mail brascom@info.com.ph; internet www.brasemb.org.ph; Ambassador ALCIDES G. R. PRATES.

Brunei: Bank of the Philippine Islands Bldg, 11th Floor, Ayala Ave, cnr Paseo de Roxas, Makati City, 1227 Metro Manila; tel. (2) 8162836; fax (2) 8916646; Ambassador MALAI Hajah HALIMAH MALAI YUSSOF.

Cambodia: Unit 7A, 7th Floor, Country Space One Bldg, Sen. Gil J. Puyat Ave, Makati City, Metro Manila; tel. (2) 8189981; fax (2) 8189983; e-mail phnompenhpe@ezecom.com.kh; Ambassador HOS SEREYTHONH.

Canada: 6th–8th Floors, Tower 2, RCBC Plaza, 6819 Ayala Ave, POB 2098, Makati City, 1200 Metro Manila; tel. (2) 8579000; fax (2) 8431082; e-mail manil@dfait-maeci.gc.ca; internet www.canadainternational.gc.ca/philippines; Ambassador CHRISTOPHER THORNLEY.

Chile: 17th Floor, Liberty Center, 104 H. V. de la Costa St, cnr Leviste St, Salcedo Village, Makati City, 1227 Metro Manila; tel. (2) 8433461; fax (2) 8431976; e-mail echileph@eastern.com.ph; internet www.embachileph.com; Ambassador ROBERTO MAYORGA LORCA.

China, People's Republic: 4896 Pasay Rd, Dasmariñas Village, Makati City, Metro Manila; tel. (2) 8443148; fax (2) 8452465; e-mail chinaemb_ph@mfa.gov.cn; internet ph.chineseembassy.org; Ambassador LIU JIANCHAO.

Cuba: 101 Aguirre St, cnr Trasierra St, Cacho-Gonzales Bldg Penthouse, Legaspi Village, Makati City, Metro Manila; tel. (2) 8171192; fax (2) 8164094; e-mail embacuba@pldtdsl.net; Ambassador JUAN CARLOS ARENCIBIA CORRALES.

Czech Republic: 30th Floor, Rufino Pacific Tower, 6784 Ayala Ave, 1200 Makati City, Metro Manila; tel. (2) 8111155; fax (2) 8111020; e-mail manila@embassy.mzv.cz; internet www.mzv.cz/manila; Ambassador JOSEF RYCHTAR.

Egypt: 2229 Paraiso St, cnr Banyan St, Dasmariñas Village, Makati City, Metro Manila; tel. (2) 8439232; fax (2) 8439239; Ambassador AHMED MAHMOUD MAHER ABBAS.

Finland: 21st Floor, BPI Buendia Center, Sen. Gil J. Puyat Ave, POB 2447, MCPO, Makati City, 1264 Metro Manila; tel. (2) 8915011; fax (2) 8914107; e-mail sanomat.mni@formin.fi; internet www.finland.ph; Ambassador HEIKKI HANNIKAINEN.

France: Pacific Star Bldg, 16th Floor, Makati Ave, cnr Sen. Gil J. Puyat Ave, 1200 Makati City, Metro Manila; tel. (2) 8576900; fax (2) 8576951; e-mail consulat@ambafrance-ph.org; internet www.ambafrance-ph.org; Ambassador THIERRY BORJA DE MOZOTA.

Germany: 25th Floor, Tower 2, RCBC Plaza, 6819 Ayala Ave, Makati City, Metro Manila; tel. (2) 7023000; fax (2) 7023015; e-mail deboma@pldtdsl.net; internet www.manila.diplo.de; Chargé d'affaires a.i. RALPH TIMMERMAN.

Greece: 12th Floor, Sage House, 110 Herrera St, Legaspi Village, Makati City; tel. (2) 8174444; fax (2) 8120202; e-mail gremb.man@mfa.gr; Ambassador POLYXENI STEFANIDOU.

Holy See: 2140 Taft Ave, POB 3364, 1099 Metro Manila (Apostolic Nunciature); tel. (2) 5210306; fax (2) 5211235; e-mail nuntiusp@info.com.ph; Apostolic Nuncio Most Rev. GIUSEPPE PINTO.

India: 2190 Paraiso St, Dasmariñas Village, POB 2123, Makati City, MCPO, Metro Manila; tel. (2) 8430101; fax (2) 8158151; e-mail info@embindia.org.ph; internet www.embindia.org.ph; Ambassador Shri YOGENDRA KUMAR.

Indonesia: 185 Salcedo St, Legaspi Village, POB 1671, MCPO, Makati City, Metro Manila; tel. (2) 8925061; fax (2) 8925878; e-mail fungsipensosbud@yahoo.com.ph; internet www.kbrimanila.org.ph; Ambassador YOHANNES KRISTIARTO SOERYO LEGOWO.

Iran: 2224 Paraiso St, cnr Pasay Rd, Dasmariñas Village, Makati City, Metro Manila; tel. (2) 8884757; fax (2) 8884777; e-mail mrouzbehani@gmail.com; Ambassador (vacant).

Israel: Trafalgar Plaza, 23rd Floor, 105 H. V. de la Costa St, Salcedo Village, Makati City, 1227 Metro Manila; tel. (2) 8940441; fax (2) 8941027; e-mail info@manila.mfa.gov.il; internet manila.mfa.gov.il; Ambassador MENASHE BAR-ON.

Italy: Zeta II Bldg, 6th Floor, 191 Salcedo St, Legaspi Village, Makati City, Metro Manila; tel. (2) 8924531; fax (2) 8171436; e-mail informazioni.manila@esteri.it; internet www.ambmanila.esteri.it; Ambassador LUCA FORNARI.

Japan: 2627 Roxas Blvd, Pasay City, 1300 Metro Manila; tel. (2) 5515710; fax (2) 5515780; e-mail jicc-mnl@japanembassy.ph; internet www.ph.emb-japan.go.jp; Ambassador TOSHINAO URABE.

Korea, Republic: 10th Floor, Pacific Star Bldg, Sen. Gil J. Puyat Ave, cnr Makati Ave, Makati City, 1226 Metro Manila; tel. (2) 8116139; fax (2) 8116148; e-mail philippines@mofat.go.kr; internet embassy_philippines.mofat.go.kr; Ambassador LEE HYE-MIN.

Kuwait: 1230 Acacia Rd, Dasmariñas Village, POB 2033, Makati City, Metro Manila; tel. (2) 8876880; fax (2) 8876887; Ambassador WALEED AHMAD AL-KANDARI.

Laos: 34 Lapu-Lapu St, Magallanes Village, Makati City, Metro Manila; tel. and fax (2) 8525759; Ambassador LEUANE SOMBOUNKHAN.

Libya: 1644 Dasmariñas St, cnr Mabolo St, Dasmariñas Village, Makati City, Metro Manila; tel. (2) 8177331; fax (2) 8177337; e-mail lpbmanila@skynet.net; Chargé d'affaires a.i. MOHAMMAD HANDER.

Malaysia: 107 Tordesillas St, Salcedo Village, Makati City, 1200 Metro Manila; tel. (2) 8640761; fax (2) 8640727; e-mail mwmanila@indanet.com; internet www.kln.gov.my/perwakilan/manila; Ambassador IBRAHIM SAAD.

Mexico: 150 Legaspi St, G. C. Corporate Plaza, Legaspi Village, Makati City, Metro Manila; tel. (2) 8122211; fax (2) 8927635; e-mail embmxfil@info.com.ph; internet portal.sre.gob.mx/filipinaseng; Ambassador TOMAS JAVIER CALVILLO UNNA.

Myanmar: Gervasia Corporate Center, 8th Floor, 152 Amorsolo St, Legaspi Village, Makati City, Metro Manila; tel. (2) 8931944; fax (2) 8928866; e-mail myanila@mydestiny.net; Ambassador AUNG KHIN SOE.

Netherlands: Equitable PCI Bank Tower, 26th Floor, 8751 Paseo de Roxas, Makati City, Metro Manila; tel. (2) 7866666; fax (2) 7866600; e-mail man@minbuza.nl; internet www.netherlandsembassy.ph; Ambassador ROBERT BRINKS.

New Zealand: BPI Buendia Center, 23rd Floor, Sen. Gil J. Puyat Ave, POB 3228, MCPO, Makati City, Metro Manila; tel. (2) 8915358; fax (2) 8915357; e-mail nzmanila@nxdsl.com.ph; internet www.nzembassy.com/philippines; Ambassador REUBEN LEVERMORE.

Nigeria: 2211 Paraiso St, Dasmariñas Village, POB 3174, Makati City, 1271 Metro Manila; tel. (2) 8439866; fax (2) 8439867; e-mail embassy@nigeriamanila.org; internet www.nigeriamanila.org; Chargé d'affaires a.i. STEVIE ALDRIN OGENYI EGURUBE.

Norway: Petron Mega Plaza Bldg, 21st Floor, 358 Sen. Gil J. Puyat Ave, Makati City, 1209 Metro Manila; tel. (2) 8863245; fax (2) 8863384; e-mail emb.manila@mfa.no; internet www.norway.ph; Ambassador KNUT SOLEM.

Pakistan: Alexander House, 6th Floor, 132 Amorsolo St, Legaspi Village, Makati City, Metro Manila; tel. (2) 8172776; fax (2) 8400229; e-mail pakrepmanila@yahoo.com; internet www.cpsctech.org/~pkembphil; Ambassador MOHSIN RAZI.

Palau: Marbella Condominium II, Unit 101, Ground Floor, 2071 Roxas Blvd, Malate, Manila; tel. (2) 5221982; fax (2) 5210402; e-mail ropembassy-pi@pldtdsl.net; Ambassador RAMON RECHEBEI.

Panama: 10th Floor, MARC 2000 Tower, 1973 Taft Ave and San Andres St, cnr Quirino Ave, Malate, 1004 Metro Manila; tel. (2) 5212790; fax (2) 5215755; e-mail panamaph@pldtdsl.net; Ambassador IVAN J. CRESPO.

Papua New Guinea: 3rd Floor, Corinthian Plaza Condominium Bldg, cnr Paseo de Roxas and Gamboa St, Makati City, Metro Manila; tel. (2) 8113465; fax (2) 8113466; e-mail kundumnl@pngembmnl.com.ph; Ambassador CHRISTIAN ANTHONY VIHRURI.

Qatar: 1398 Cabellero St, cnr Lumbang St, Dasmariñas Village, Makati City, Metro Manila; tel. (2) 8874944; fax (2) 8876406; e-mail gemanila2000@yahoo.com; Ambassador ABDULLAH AHMED YOUSIF AL-MUTAWA.

Romania: 1216 Acacia Rd, Dasmariñas Village, Makati City, Metro Manila; tel. (2) 8439014; fax (2) 8439063; e-mail amarom@zpdee.net; Ambassador VALERIU GHEORGHE.

Russia: 1245 Acacia Rd, Dasmariñas Village, Makati City, Metro Manila; tel. (2) 8930190; fax (2) 8109614; e-mail RusEmb@i-manila.com.ph; internet www.philippines.mid.ru; Ambassador NIKOLAI R. KUDASHEV.

Saudi Arabia: Saudi Embassy Bldg, 389 Sen. Gil J. Puyat Ave Ext., Makati City, Metro Manila; tel. (2) 8564444; fax (2) 8953493; e-mail phemb@mofa.gov.sa; internet www.saudiembassy.com.ph; Ambassador ABDULLAH AL-HASSAN.

Singapore: 505 Rizal Drive, Bonifacio, 1634 Taguig City, Metro Manila; tel. (2) 8569922; fax (2) 8569932; e-mail singemb_mnl@sgmfa.gov.sg; internet www.mfa.gov.sg/manila; Ambassador A. SELVERAJAH.

South Africa: 29th Floor, Yuchengco Tower, RCBC Plaza, 6819 Ayala Ave, Makati City, 1227 Metro Manila; tel. (2) 8899383; fax (2) 8899337; e-mail manila@foreign.gov.za; Ambassador AGNES NYAMANDE-PITSO.

Spain: 27th Floor, Equitable Bank Tower, 8751 Paseo de Roxas, 1226 Metro Manila; tel. (2) 8176676; fax (2) 8174892; e-mail emb.manila@mae.es; Ambassador JORGE DOMECQ.

Sri Lanka: 7th Floor, G. C. Corporate Plaza, 150 Legaspi St, Legaspi Village, Makati City, Metro Manila; tel. (2) 8120124; fax (2) 8120126; e-mail slembmanila@pldtdsl.net; internet www.slembmanila.ph; Ambassador NAWALAGE B. COORAY.

Switzerland: Equitable Bank Tower, 24th Floor, 8751 Paseo de Roxas, Makati City, 1226 Metro Manila; tel. (2) 7579000; fax (2) 7573718; e-mail man.vertretung@eda.admin.ch; internet www.eda.admin.ch/manila; Ambassador IVO SIEBER.

Thailand: 107 Rada St, Legaspi Village, Makati City, 1229 Metro Manila; tel. (2) 8154220; fax (2) 8154221; e-mail infomnl@pldtdsl.net; internet www.thaiembassymnl.ph; Ambassador PRASAS PRASASVINITCHAI.

Timor-Leste: 17th Floor, Centerpoint Condominium, Rm 1703, cnr Julia Vargas Ave, Ortigas Center, Pasig City, 1605 Metro Manila; tel. (2) 637-9405; fax (2) 637-9408; e-mail timorlesteembassyinmanila@yahoo.com; Ambassador FRANCISCO CEPEDA.

Turkey: 2268 Paraiso St, Dasmariñas Village, Makati City, Metro Manila; tel. (2) 8439705; fax (2) 8439702; e-mail turkembm@info.com.ph; Ambassador HATICE P. IŞIK.

United Arab Emirates: Renaissance Bldg, 2nd Floor, 215 Sakedo St, Legaspi Village, Makati City, Metro Manila; tel. (2) 8173906; fax (2) 8183577; Ambassador MUSA ABDUL WAHED ABDUL GHAFAR AL-KHAJA.

United Kingdom: Locsin Bldg, 15th–17th Floors, 6752 Ayala Ave, cnr Makati Ave, Makati City, 1226 Metro Manila; tel. (2) 5808700; fax (2) 8197206; e-mail uk@info.com.ph; internet www.ukinthephilippines.fco.gov.uk; Ambassador STEPHEN LILLIE.

USA: 1201 Roxas Blvd, Ermita, 1000 Metro Manila; tel. (2) 3012000; fax (2) 3012399; internet manila.usembassy.gov; Ambassador HARRY THOMAS, Jr.

Venezuela: Unit 17A, Multinational Bancorporation Center, 6805 Ayala Ave, Makati City, Metro Manila 1226; tel. (2) 8452841; fax (2) 8452866; e-mail venezemb@info.com.ph; Chargé d'affaires a.i. MANUEL VICENTE PÉREZ ITURBE.

Viet Nam: 670 Pablo Ocampo St, Malate, Metro Manila; tel. (2) 5216843; fax (2) 5260472; e-mail vnembph@yahoo.com; internet www.vietnamembassy-philippines.org; Ambassador NGUYEN VU TU.

Judicial System

The Philippine judicial system comprises the Supreme Court, the Court of Appeals, Regional Trial Courts, Metropolitan Trial Courts, Municipal Courts in Cities, Municipal Courts and Municipal Circuit Trial Courts. There is also a special court for trying cases of corruption (the Sandiganbayan). The Office of the Ombudsman (Tanodbayan) investigates complaints concerning the actions of public officials. Islamic *Shari'a* courts were established in the southern Philippines in July 1985 under a presidential decree of February 1977. They are presided over by three district magistrates and six circuit judges.

SUPREME COURT

The February 1987 Constitution provides for the establishment of a Supreme Court comprising a Chief Justice and 14 Associate Justices; the Court may sit *en banc* or in divisions of three, five or seven members. Justices of the Supreme Court are appointed by the President from a list of a minimum of three nominees prepared by a Judicial and Bar Council.

Chief Justice: RENATO CORONA, New Supreme Court Bldg Annex, 3rd Floor, Padre Faura St, Ermita, 1000 Metro Manila; tel. (2) 5225090; fax (2) 5268129; e-mail pio@sc.judiciary.gov.ph; internet sc.judiciary.gov.ph.

COURT OF APPEALS

Consists of a Presiding Justice and 68 Associate Justices.

Presiding Justice: ANDRES B. REYES, Jr, Maria y Orosa St, Ermita, 1000 Metro Manila; tel. (2) 524-1241; e-mail ca_manila@yahoo.com; internet ca.judiciary.gov.ph.

Religion

According to the results of the 2000 census, 81.1% of the population were Roman Catholics and 11.6% belonged to other Christian denominations. The Islamic community constituted 5% of the population, Buddhists accounted for 0.1%, while indigenous and other religious traditions comprised a further 1.7%. Atheists and persons who did not state a religious preference accounted for 0.5%.

CHRISTIANITY

Sangguniang Pambansa ng mga Simbahan sa Pilipinas (National Council of Churches in the Philippines): 879 Epifanio de los Santos Ave, West Triangle, Quezon City 1104, Metro Manila; tel. (2) 9293745; fax (2) 9267076; e-mail library@nccphilippines.org; internet www.nccphilippines.org; f. 1963; 10 mem. churches, 9 assoc. mems; Gen. Sec. Rev. REX R. B. REYES, Jr.

The Roman Catholic Church

For ecclesiastical purposes, the Philippines comprises 16 archdioceses, 55 dioceses, six territorial prelatures, one military ordinate and seven apostolic vicariates. At 31 December 2007 approximately 81.2% of the population were adherents.

Catholic Bishops' Conference of the Philippines (CBCP)
470 General Luna St, Intramuros, 1076 Metro Manila; tel. (2) 9414471; fax (2) 5279634; e-mail cbcpmonitor@cbcpworld.net; internet cbcponline.net.

f. 1945; statutes approved 1952; Pres. Most Rev. PEDRO QUITORIO, III

Archbishop of Caceres: Most Rev. LEONARDO Z. LEGASPI, Archbishop's House, Elias Angeles St, POB 6085, 4400 Naga City; tel. (54) 4738483; fax (54) 4738383; e-mail chancerynaga@yahoo.com.

Archbishop of Cagayan de Oro: Most Rev. ANTONIO J. LEDESMA, Archbishop's Residence, POB 113, 9000 Misamis Oriental, Cagayan de Oro City; tel. (8822) 722375; fax (8822) 726304; e-mail acdo_chancery@yahoo.com.

Archbishop of Capiz: Most Rev. ONESIMO C. GORDONCILLO, Chancery Office, POB 44, 5800 Roxas City; tel. (36) 6215595; fax (36) 6211053.

Archbishop of Cebu: Most Rev. JOSÉ SEROFIA PALMA, Archbishop's Residence, cnr P. Gomez St and P. Burgos St, POB 52, 6000 Cebu City; tel. (32) 2541861; fax (32) 2530123; e-mail adelito@skynet.net.

Archbishop of Cotabato: Most Rev. ORLANDO B. QUEVEDO, Archbishop's Residence, 158 Sinsuat Ave, POB 186, 9600 Cotabato City; tel. (64) 4212918; fax (64) 4211446.

Archbishop of Davao: Most Rev. FERNANDO R. CAPALLA, Archbishop's Residence, 247 Florentino Torres St, POB 80418, 8000 Davao City; tel. (82) 2275992; fax (82) 2279771; e-mail bishopdavao@yahoo.com.

Archbishop of Jaro: Most Rev. ANGEL N. LAGDAMEO, Archbishop's Residence, Jaro, 5000 Iloilo City; tel. (33) 3294442; fax (33) 3293197; e-mail abpjaro@yahoo.com.

Archbishop of Lingayen-Dagupan: Most Rev. SOCRATES B. VILLEGAS, Archbishop's House, Jovellanos St, 2400 Pangasinan, Dagupan City; tel. (75) 5235357; fax (75) 5221878; e-mail maximo82158@gmail.com; internet www.lingayen-dagupan.org.

Archbishop of Lipa: Most Rev. RAMON C. ARGÜELLES, Archbishop's House, St Lorenzo Ruiz Rd, Lipa City, 4217 Batangas; tel. (43) 7562572; fax (43) 7560005; e-mail chancery@batangas.net.ph; internet www.archlipa.org.

Archbishop of Manila: Most Rev. GAUDENCIO B. ROSALES, Arzobispado, 121 Arzobispo St, Intramuros, POB 132, 1099 Metro Manila; tel. (2) 5277631; fax (2) 5273956; e-mail rcamaoc@yahoo.com; internet www.rcam.org.

Archbishop of Nueva Segovia: Most Rev. ERNESTO A. SALGADO, Archbishop's House, Vigan, 2700 Ilocos Sur; tel. (77) 7222018; fax (77) 7221591; e-mail nschancery@yahoo.com.ph.

Archbishop of Ozamis: Most Rev. JESUS A. DOSADO, Archbishop's House, POB 2760, Rizal Ave, Banadero, 7200 Ozamis City; tel. (65) 5212820; fax (65) 5211574.

Archbishop of Palo: (vacant), Archdiocesan Chancery, Palo, 6501 Leyte; POB 173, Tacloban City, 6500 Leyte; tel. (53) 3232213; fax (53) 3235607; e-mail rcap@mozcom.com.

Archbishop of San Fernando (Pampanga): Most Rev. PACIANO B. ANICETO, Chancery Office, San José, San Fernando, 2000 Pampanga; tel. (45) 9612819; fax (45) 9616772; e-mail rca@pamp.pworld.net.ph; internet www.rcasf.com.

Archbishop of Tuguegarao: Most Rev. SERGIO LASAM UTLEG, Archbishop's House, Rizal St, Tuguegarao, 3500 Cagayan; tel. (78) 8441663; fax (78) 8462822; e-mail chancerycat@lycos.com.

Archbishop of Zamboanga: Most Rev. ROMULO G. VALLES, Sacred Heart Centre, POB 1, Justice R. T. Lim Blvd, 7000 Zamboanga City; tel. (62) 9911329; fax (62) 9932608; e-mail zambochancery-10@yahoo.com.

Other Christian Churches

Convention of Philippine Baptist Churches: POB 263, 5000 Iloilo City; tel. (33) 3290621; fax (33) 3290618; e-mail gensec@iloilo.net; f. 1935; Gen. Sec. HUDSON HERVILLA; Pres. DAN L. PEDROSA.

Episcopal Church in the Philippines: POB 10321, Broadway Centrum, Quezon City, 1102 Metro Manila; tel. (2) 7228481; fax (2)

7211923; e-mail ecpnational@yahoo.com.ph; internet www.episcopalchurchphilippines.org; f. 1901; six dioceses; Prime Bishop Most Rev. EDWARD MALECDAN.

Iglesia Evangélica Metodista en las Islas Filipinas (Evangelical Methodist Church in the Philippines): Beulah Land, Iemelif Center, Greenfields 1, Subdivision, Marytown Circle, Novaliches, Quezon City, 1123 Metro Manila; tel. (2) 9356519; fax (2) 4185017; f. 1909; 40,000 mems (2003); Gen. Supt Bishop NATHANAEL P. LAZARO.

Iglesia Filipina Independiente (Philippine Independent Church): POB 2484, 1000 Metro Manila; tel. (2) 5237242; fax (2) 5213932; e-mail gensec@ifi.ph; internet www.ifi.ph; f. 1902; 34 dioceses; 6.0m. mems; Obispo Maximo (Supreme Bishop) Most Rev. EPHRAIM S. FAJUTAGANA.

Iglesia ni Cristo: 1 Central Ave, New Era, Quezon City, 1107 Metro Manila; tel. (2) 9814311; fax (2) 9814333; f. 1914; 5m. mems; Exec. Minister Brother EDUARDO V. MANALO.

Lutheran Church in the Philippines: 4461 Old Santa Mesa, 1008 Metro Manila; POB 507, 1099 Metro Manila; tel. (2) 7157084; fax (2) 7142395; internet www.lutheranphilippines.org; f. 1946; Pres. Rev. JAMES CERDEÑOLA.

Union Church of Manila: cnr Legaspi St and Rada St, Legaspi Village, Makati City, Metro Manila; tel. (2) 8126062; fax (2) 8172386; e-mail ucmweb@unionchurch.ph; internet www.unionchurch.ph; Senior Pastor Rev. STEVE RUESTCHLE.

United Church of Christ in the Philippines: 1667 A. Vasquez St, Malate, Metro Manila; tel. (2) 9240215; fax (2) 9240207; e-mail uccpnaof@manila-online.net; internet uccp.org.ph; f. 1948; 900,000 mems (1996); Gen. Sec. Rev. ELIEZER PASCUA (Bishop).

Among other denominations active in the Philippines are the Iglesia Evangélica Unida de Cristo and the United Methodist Church.

ISLAM

Some 14 different ethnic groups profess the Islamic faith in the Philippines. Mindanao and the Sulu and Tawi-Tawi archipelago, in the southern Philippines, are predominantly Muslim provinces, but there are 10 other such provinces, each with its own Imam, or Muslim religious leader. More than 500,000 Muslims live in the north of the country (mostly in, or near to, Manila).

Islamic Da'wah Council of the Philippines (IDCP): Suite 400, FUBC Bldg, Escolta, Metro Manila; tel. (2) 2458456; fax (2) 2415142; e-mail info@halalislamicdawah-ph.com; internet www.halalislamicdawah-ph.com; f. 1982; federation of 95 mem. orgs; Pres. ABDUL RAHAM R. T. LINZAG.

BAHÁ'Í FAITH

National Spiritual Assembly: 1070 A. Roxas St, cnr Bautista St, Singalong Subdiv., Malate, 1004 Metro Manila; POB 4323, 1099 Metro Manila; tel. (2) 5240404; fax (2) 5232449; e-mail nsa.bahai.ph@gmail.com; internet bahai.ph; mems resident in 129,949 localities; Chair. ALFREDO RAMIREZ; Sec.-Gen. MA ADORACION NEWMAN.

The Press

The Office of the President implements government policies on information and the media. Freedom of the press and freedom of speech are guaranteed under the Constitution.

METRO MANILA

Dailies

Abante: 167 Liberty Bldg, Roberto S. Oca St, Port Area, Metro Manila; tel. (2) 5276722; fax (2) 5280147; e-mail abante@abante-tonite.com; internet www.abante.com.ph; morning; Filipino and English; Man. Editor NICOLAS V. QUIJANO, Jr; circ. 417,000.

Abante Tonite: 167 Liberty Bldg, Roberto S. Oca St, Port Area, Metro Manila; tel. (2) 5276722; fax (2) 5279838; e-mail tonite@abante-tonite.com; internet www.abante-tonite.com; afternoon; Filipino and English; Man. Editor NICOLAS V. QUIJANO, Jr; circ. 277,000.

Balita: Liwayway Publishing Inc, 2249 Pasong Tamo, Makati City, Metro Manila; tel. (2) 5278121; fax (2) 4000095; e-mail balitamb@yahoo.com; f. 1972; morning; Filipino; Publr HERMOGENES P. POBRE; circ. 151,000.

BusinessMirror: Dominga Bldg (Annex), 2nd Floor, 2113 Chino Roces Ave, cnr De La Rosa St, Makati City, Metro Manila; tel. (2) 8179467; fax (2) 8137025; e-mail news@businessmirror.com.ph; internet www.businessmirror.com.ph; f. 2005; Editor-in-Chief LOURDES M. FERNANDEZ; Man. Editor VLADIMIR S. BUNOAN.

BusinessWorld: Raul L. Locsin Bldg I, 95 Balete Dr. Ext., New Manila, Quezon City, 1112 Metro Manila; tel. (2) 5359901; fax (2) 5359926; internet www.bworldonline.com; f. 1987; Exec. Editor ARNOLD E. BELLEZA; Man. Editor WILFREDO G. REYES; circ. 54,000.

Daily Tribune: Penthouse Suites, GLC Bldg, T. M. Kalaw St, cnr A. Mabini St, Ermita, Metro Manila; tel. (2) 5215584; fax (2) 5215522; e-mail nco@tribune.net.ph; internet www.tribune.net.ph; f. 2000; English; Publr and Editor-in-Chief NINEZ CACHO-OLIVARES.

Malaya Business Insight: Leyland Bldg, 20th St, cnr Railroad St, Port Area, Metro Manila; tel. (2) 3393324; fax (2) 5271839; e-mail malayanews@yahoo.com; internet www.malaya.com.ph; f. 1981; originally Filipino; English since 1983; Exec. Editor ENRIQUE P. ROMUALDEZ; Editor-in-Chief JOY DE LOS REYES; circ. 175,000.

Manila Bulletin: Bulletin Publishing Corpn, Muralla St, cnr Recoletos St, Intramuros, POB 769, 1002 Metro Manila; tel. (2) 5278121; fax (2) 5277510; e-mail bulletin@mb.com.ph; internet www.mb.com.ph; f. 1900; English; Publr HERMOGENES P. POBRE; Editor-in-Chief Dr CHRIS J. ICBAN, Jr; circ. 265,000.

Manila Standard Today: Leyland Bldg, 21st St, cnr Railroad St, Port Area, Metro Manila; tel. (2) 5278351; fax (2) 5246649; e-mail mst@manilastandardtoday.com; internet www.manilastandardtoday.com; f. 1987 as Manila Standard; name changed as above in 2005, following merger with rival newspaper *Today*; morning; English; Editor-in-Chief JOJO ROBLES; circ. 96,000.

Manila Times: 371A Bonifacio Dr., Port Area, Metro Manila; tel. (2) 5245664; fax (2) 3019552; e-mail newsboy1@manilatimes.net; internet www.manilatimes.net; f. 1945; morning; English; Publr and Editor-in-Chief FRED DELA ROSA.

People's Journal: Universal-Re Bldg, 6th Floor, 106 Paseo de Roxas, cnr Perea and Gallardo Sts, Legaspi Village, Makati City, Metro Manila; tel. (2) 5278421; fax (2) 5274627; internet www.journal.com.ph; English and Filipino; Editor AUGUST B. VILLANUEVA; circ. 219,000.

People's Taliba: 6th Floor, Universal-Re Bldg, 106 Paseo de Roxas, cnr Perea and Gallardo Sts, Legaspi Village, Makati City, Metro Manila; fax (2) 5274627; Filipino; Editor BENJAMIN DEFENSOR; circ. 229,000.

People's Tonight: 6th Floor, Universal-Re Bldg, 106 Paseo de Roxas, cnr Perea and Gallardo Sts, Legaspi Village, Makati City, Metro Manila; tel. (2) 5278421; fax (2) 5274627; f. 1978; English and Filipino; Editor FERDIE RAMOS; circ. 500,000.

Philippine Daily Inquirer: Philippine Daily Inquirer Bldg, Chino Roces Ave, cnr Mascardo and Yague Sts, Pasong Tamo, POB 2353, Makati City, 1263 Metro Manila; tel. (2) 8978808; fax (2) 8974793; e-mail feedback@inquirer.com.ph; internet www.inquirer.com.ph; f. 1985; English; Editor-in-Chief LETTY JIMENEZ-MAGSANOC; circ. 250,000.

Philippine Star: 202 Railroad St, cnr 13th St, Port Area, 1016 Metro Manila; tel. (2) 5276856; fax (2) 5276851; e-mail editor@philstar.com; internet www.philstar.com; f. 1986; Editor ISAAC BELMONTE; circ. 275,000.

Pilipino Star Ngayon: 202 Railroad St, cnr 13th St, Port Area, 1016 Metro Manila; tel. (2) 5272389; fax (2) 5272403; e-mail psngayon@philstar.net.ph; internet www.philstar.com; f. 1986; Filipino tabloid; Chief Editor ALFONSO G. PEDROCHE; circ. 286,452.

Tempo: Bulletin Publishing Corpn, Muralla St, cnr Recoletos St, Intramuros, POB 769, 1002 Metro Manila; tel. (2) 5278121; fax (2) 5277510; internet www.tempo.com.ph; f. 1982; English and Filipino; Editor-in-Chief BAMBANG HARYMURTI; circ. 230,000.

United Daily News: 812–818 Benavides St, Binondo, 1006 Metro Manila; tel. (2) 2447171; e-mail united_dailynews@yahoo.com; f. 1973; Chinese; Editor-in-Chief CHUA KEE; circ. 85,000.

Selected Periodicals

Weeklies

Bannawag: c/o Manila Bulletin Publishing Corpn, Muralla St, cnr Recoletos St, Intramuros, Metro Manila; tel. (2) 5278121; fax (2) 5277510; f. 1934; Ilocano; Editor DIONISIO S. BULONG; circ. 42,900.

Bisaya: c/o Manila Bulletin Publishing Corpn, Muralla St, cnr Recoletos St, Intramuros, Metro Manila; tel. (2) 5278121; fax (2) 5277510; f. 1934; Cebu-Visayan; Editor EDGAR S. GODIN; circ. 90,000.

Liwayway: c/o Manila Bulletin Publishing Corpn, Muralla St, cnr Recoletos St, Intramuros, Metro Manila; tel. (2) 5278121; fax (2) 5277510; f. 1922; Tagalog; circ. 102,400.

Panorama: Manila Bulletin Publishing Corpn, Muralla St, cnr Recoletos St, Intramuros, POB 769, Metro Manila; tel. and fax (2) 5277509; e-mail panorama@mb.com.ph; internet www.panorama.com.ph; f. 1968; English; Editor RANDY V. URLANDA; circ. 239,600.

Philippine Starweek: 13th St, cnr Railroad St, Port Area, Metro Manila; tel. (2) 5277901; fax (2) 5275819; e-mail feedback@philstar.net.ph; internet www.philstar.com; English; Editor JOSEPH NACINO; circ. 268,000.

SELECTED PROVINCIAL PUBLICATIONS

The Aklan Reporter: 1227 Rizal St, Kalibo, Panay, 5600 Aklan; tel. (36) 2684158; f. 1971; weekly; English and Aklanon; Editor SUNRA ROJO; circ. 1,000.

Baguio Midland Courier: 16 Kisad Rd, POB 50, Baguio City; tel. (74) 4422444; fax (74) 4439485; e-mail baguiomidlandcourier@yahoo .com; internet www.baguiomidlandcourier.com.ph; f. 1947; weekly; English; Publr CHARLES M. HAMADA; circ. 24,500.

Bayanihan Weekly News: Bayanihan Publishing Co, P. Guevarra Ave, Santa Cruz, Laguna; f. 1966; Mon.; Filipino and English; Editor ARTHUR A. VALENOVA; circ. 1,000.

Bohol Chronicle: 56 B. Inting St, Tagbilaran City, 6300 Bohol; tel. and fax (38) 5010077; fax (38) 4113100; e-mail editor@boholchronicle .com; internet www.boholchronicle.com; f. 1954; 2 a week; English and Cebuano; Editor and Publr ZOILO DEJARESCO; circ. 5,500.

The Bohol Times: 100 Gallares St, Tagbilaran City, 6300 Bohol; tel. (38) 4112961; fax (38) 4112656; e-mail boholtimes@yahoo.com; Publr Dr LILIA A. BALITE; Editor-in-Chief SALVADOR D. DIPUTADO.

The Ilocos Times: Barangay 23, M. H. del Pilar St, 2900 Laoag City; tel. (77) 7720976; fax (77) 7711378; e-mail publisher@ilocostimes .com; internet www.ilocostimes.com; f. 1920; weekly; publ. by Ilocos Publishing Corpn; English and Iluko; Publr and Editor EFREN S. RAMOS, Jr; circ. 5,000.

The Kapawa News: L. V. Moles and Jose Abad Santos Sts, Tangub, POB 365, 6100 Bacolod City; tel. and fax (34) 4441941; e-mail LM-Kapawa@eudoramail.com; f. 1966; weekly; Sat.; Hiligaynon and English; Publr HENRY G. DOBLE; circ. 2,000.

Mindanao Post: Blk 16, Lot 3, SIR New Matina, Davao City, Mindanao; f. 1999; Editor-in-Chief DOMING ROSAL.

Mindanao Times: UMBN Bldg, Ponciano Reyes St, Davao City, Mindanao; tel. 2273252; e-mail editorial.mtimes@gmail.com; internet www.mindanaotimes.com.ph; daily; Editor-in-Chief AMALIA B. CABUSAO; circ. 5,000.

Pagadian Times: 0519 Alano St, 7016 Pagadian City; tel. (62) 2141721; fax (62) 2151504; e-mail pagtimes@mozcom.com; f. 1969; weekly; English; Publr PEDE G. LU; Editor REMAI ALEJADS; circ. 7,000.

Panay News: Panay News Complex, Q. Abeto St, Mandurriao, Iloilo City; tel. (33) 3212749; fax (33) 5094159; e-mail pnnews@ panaynewsphilippines.com; internet www.panaynewsphilippines .com; Editor-in-Chief DANNY FAJARDO.

Sorsogon Today: 2903 Burgos St, East District, 4700 Sorsogon; tel. and fax (56) 4215306; fax (56) 2111340; e-mail sortoday@yahoo.com; f. 1977; weekly; Publr and CEO MARCOS E. PARAS, Jr; circ. 2,250.

Sun Star Cebu: Sun Star Bldg, 3rd Floor, cnr of P. del Rosario St and P. Cui St, Cebu City; tel. (32) 2546100; fax (32) 2537256; e-mail centralnewsroom@sunstar.com.ph; internet www.sunstar.com.ph/ cebu; f. 1982; daily; English; Editor-in-Chief PACHICO A. SEARES; Gen. Man. JULIUS NERI.

Superbalita Davao: 5–6 Granland Business and Warehouse Center, R. Castillo St, Agdao, Davao City; tel. (82) 2351004; fax (82) 2351006; e-mail ssdavao@gmail.com; internet www.sunstar.com.ph/ superbalitadavao; daily; Editor-in-Chief STELLA ESTREMERA.

The Tribune: Jarlego & Sons Bldg, Maharlika Highway, 2301 Cabanatuan City, Luzon; f. 1960; weekly; English and Filipino; Editor and Publr ORLANDO M. JARLEGO; circ. 8,000.

The Valley Times: Daang Maharlika, San Felipe, Ilagan, Isabela; f. 1962; weekly; English; Editor AUREA A. DE LA CRUZ; circ. 4,500.

The Visayan Tribune: 1973 Mezzanine Floor, Masonic Temple Bldg, Plaza Libertad 5000, Iloilo City; f. 1959; weekly; English; Editor HERBERT L. VEGO; circ. 5,000.

The Voice of Islam: Davao City; f. 1973; monthly; English and Arabic; official Islamic news journal; Editor and Publr NASHIR MUHAMMAD AL'RASHID AL HAJJ.

NEWS AGENCY

Philippines News Agency: PIA Bldg, 2nd Floor, Visayas Ave, Diliman, Quezon City, Metro Manila; tel. (2) 9206551; fax (2) 9206566; e-mail bert.panganiban@gmail.com; internet www.pna .gov.ph; f. 1973; Gen. Man. VITTORIO V. VITUG; Exec. Editor DANILO C. TAGUIBAO (acting).

PRESS ASSOCIATION

National Press Club of the Philippines: National Press Club Bldg, Magallanes Drive, Intramuros, 1002 Metro Manila; tel. (2) 3010521; fax (2) 5219300; e-mail ad-nationalpressclub@yahoo.com; f. 1952; Pres. BENNY ANTIPORDA; Vice-Pres. ROLLY GONZALO; 1,405 mems.

Publishers

Abiva Publishing House Inc: Abiva Bldg, 851 Gregorio Araneta Ave, Quezon City, 1113 Metro Manila; tel. (2) 7120245; fax (2) 7120486; e-mail mmrabiva@i-manila.com.ph; internet www.abiva .com.ph; f. 1937; reference and textbooks; Pres. JORGE GARCIA.

Ateneo de Manila University Press: Bellarmine Hall, Ateneo de Manila University, Katipunan Ave, Loyola Heights, Quezon City, Metro Manila; tel. (2) 4265984; fax (2) 4265909; e-mail unipress@ admu.edu.ph; internet www.ateneopress.org; f. 1972; literary, textbooks, humanities, social sciences, reference books on the Philippines; Dir MARICOR E. BAYTION.

Bookman, Inc: 373 Quezon Ave, Quezon City, 1114 Metro Manila; tel. (2) 7123587; fax (2) 7408108; e-mail sales@bookmanphilippines .com; internet bookmanphilippines.com; f. 1945; textbooks, reference, educational; Pres. LINA PICACHE-ENRIQUEZ.

Capitol Publishing House, Inc: 13 Team Pacific Bldg, Jose C. Cruz St, cnr F. Legaspi St, Barrio Ugong, Pasig City, Metro Manila; tel. (2) 6712662; fax (2) 6712664; e-mail cacho@mozcom.com; f. 1947; Gen. Man. MANUEL L. ATIENZA.

Heritage Publishing House: 33 4th Ave, cnr Main Ave, Cubao, Quezon City, POB 3667, Metro Manila; tel. (2) 7216218; fax (2) 7220468; e-mail heritage@skydsl.com.ph; art, anthropology, history, political science; Pres. MARIO R. ALCANTARA; Man. Dir GEORGE B. ALCANTARA.

The Lawyers' Co-operative Publishing Co Inc: 1071 Del Pan St, Makati City, 1206 Metro Manila; tel. (2) 5634073; fax (2) 5642021; e-mail lawbooks@info.com.ph; f. 1908; law, educational; Pres. ELSA K. ELMA.

Manila Bulletin Publishing Corpn: Muralla cnr Recoletos, Intramuros, 1002 Metro Manila; tel. (2) 5278121; fax (2) 5277510; e-mail bulletin@mb.com.ph; internet www.mb.com.ph; f. 1900; Chair. Dr EMILIO T. YAP; Pres. HERMOGENES P. POBRE.

Mutual Books Inc: Rm 208, Jovan Condominium, 600 Shaw Blvd, Mandaluyong City, Metro Manila; tel. (2) 5329656; fax (2) 5342665; internet mutualbooks.com; f. 1959; textbooks on accounting, management and economics, computers and mathematics; Pres. ALFREDO S. NICDAO, Jr.

Reyes Publishing Inc: Mariwasa Bldg, 4th Floor, 717 Aurora Blvd, Quezon City, 1112 Metro Manila; tel. (2) 7221827; fax (2) 7218782; e-mail reyespub@skyinet.net; f. 1964; art, history and culture; Pres. LOUIE REYES.

SIBS Publishing House Inc: Phoenix Bldg, 927 Quezon Ave, Quezon City, Metro Manila; tel. (2) 3764041; fax (2) 3764034; e-mail sibsbook@sibs.com.ph; internet www.sibs.com.ph; f. 1996; science, language, religion, literature and history textbooks; Pres. MA. ERLINDA SIBAL.

Sinag-Tala Publishers Inc: GMA Lou-Bel Plaza, 6th Floor, Chino Roces Ave, cnr Bagtikan St, San Antonio Village, Makati City, 1203 Metro Manila; tel. (2) 8971162; fax (2) 8969626; e-mail stpi@info.com .ph; internet www.sinagtala.com; f. 1972; educational textbooks; business, professional and religious books; Man. Dir LUIS A. USON.

University of the Philippines Press: Epifanio de los Santos St, U. P. Campus, Diliman, Quezon City, 1101 Metro Manila; tel. (2) 9266642; fax (2) 9282558; e-mail press@up.edu.ph; internet uppress.com.ph; f. 1965; literature, history, political science, sociology, cultural studies, economics, anthropology, mathematics; Dir MARIA LUISA T. CAMAGAY.

Vibal Publishing House, Inc: 1253 G. Araneta Ave, cnr Maria Clara St, Talayan, Quezon City, Metro Manila; tel. (2) 7122722; fax (2) 7118852; e-mail inquire@vibalpublishing.com; internet www .vibalpublishing.com; f. 1953; linguistics, social sciences, mathematics, religion; Pres. and Gen. Man. ESTHER A. VIBAL.

PUBLISHERS' ASSOCIATIONS

Philippine Educational Publishers' Asscn: 84 P. Florentino St, Santa Mesa Heights, Quezon City, 1113 Metro Manila; tel. (2) 7402698; fax (2) 7115702; e-mail info@pepa.org.ph; internet www .pepa.org.ph; Pres. DOMINADOR D. BUHAIN.

Publishers' Association of the Philippines Inc: Unit 206 Cityland 8, 98 Sen. Gil Puyat Ave, Makati City 1200, Metro Manila; tel. (2) 8929278; fax (2) 8944687; e-mail papi@gawab.com; internet papiphilippines.org; f. 1974; more than 1,000 mems; Pres. JUAN P. DAYANG.

Broadcasting and Communications

TELECOMMUNICATIONS

National Telecommunications Commission (NTC): NTC Bldg, BIR Rd, East Triangle, Diliman, Quezon City, 1104 Metro Manila;

tel. (2) 9244042; fax (2) 9244048; e-mail bsd@ntc.gov.ph; internet www.ntc.gov.ph; f. 1979; supervises and controls all private and public telecommunications services; Commr GAMALIEL A. CORDOBA.

BayanTel: Diliman Corporate Center, Bayan Bldg, Maginhawa St, cnr Malingap St, Teacher's Village East, Quezon City, 1101 Metro Manila; tel. (2) 4121212; fax (2) 4492174; e-mail bayanserve@bayantel.com.ph; internet www.bayantel.com.ph; 359,000 fixed lines (1999); Chair. OSCAR M. LOPEZ; Pres. and CEO EUGENIO L. LOPEZ III.

Bell Telecommunications Philippines (BellTel): Pacific Star Bldg, 3rd Floor, Sen. Gil J. Puyat Ave, cnr Makati Ave, Makati City, Metro Manila; tel. (2) 68002355; fax (2) 8915618; e-mail info@belltel.ph; internet www.belltel.ph; f. 1997; Pres. EDGARDO REYES.

Capitol Wireless Inc: Dolmar Gold Tower, 6th Floor, 107 Carlos Palanca, Jr, St, Legaspi Village, Makati City, Metro Manila; tel. (2) 8159961; fax (2) 8941141; Pres. EPITACIO R. MARQUEZ.

Digital Telecommunications Philippines Inc (DIGITEL): 110 Eulogio Rodriguez Jr Ave, Bagumbayan, Quezon City, 1110 Metro Manila; tel. and fax (2) 3978888; e-mail customerservice@digitel.ph; internet digitel.webready.ph; provision of fixed line telecommunications services; over 400,000 fixed lines; Pres. and CEO JAMES L. GO.

Digital Mobile Philippines Inc: 110 Eulogio Rodriguez Jr Ave, Bagumbayan, Quezon City, 1110 Metro Manila; tel. (2) 3958000; e-mail customerservice@digitel.ph; internet www.suncellular.com.ph; f. 2003; wireless services under the brand name Sun Cellular; CEO CHARLES LIM.

Domestic Satellite Philippines Inc (DOMSAT): Solid House Bldg, 4th Floor, 2285 Pasong Tamo Ext., Makati City, 1231 Metro Manila; tel. (2) 8105917; fax (2) 8671677; Pres. SIEGFRED MISON.

Globe Telecom (GMCR) Inc: Globe Telecom Plaza 1, 5th Floor, Pioneer St, cnr Madison St, 1552 Mandaluyong City, Metro Manila; tel. (2) 7301000; fax (2) 7390072; e-mail custhelp@globetel.com.ph; internet www.globe.com.ph; fixed line and mobile telecommunication services; 23.2m. mobile telephone subscribers (2009); Chair. JAIME AUGUSTO ZOBEL DE AYALA; Pres. and CEO ERNEST CU.

Philippine Communications Satellite Corpn (PhilcomSat): 12th Floor, Telecoms Plaza, 316 Sen. Gil J. Puyat Ave, Makati City, Metro Manila; tel. (2) 8158406; fax (2) 8159287; internet philcomsat.com.ph; Pres. MANUEL H. NIETO.

Philippine Global Communications, Inc (PhilCom): 8755 Paseo de Roxas, Makati City, 1259 Metro Manila; tel. (2) 8451101; fax (2) 8189720; e-mail helpdesk@philcom.com; internet www.philcom.com; Chair. WILLY N. OCIER; CEO SALVADOR M. CASTILLO.

Philippine Long Distance Telephone Co (PLDT): Ramon Cojuangco Bldg, Makati Ave, POB 2148, Makati City, Metro Manila; tel. (2) 8168024; fax (2) 8446654; e-mail customercare@pldt.com; internet www.pldt.com.ph; f. 1928; monopoly on overseas telephone service until 1989; transferred to private sector in 2007; major fixed line and wireless services provider; 44.7m. subscribers (2010); Chair. MANUEL V. PANGILINAN; Pres. and CEO NAPOLEON L. NAZARENO.

Smart Communications, Inc (SCI): SMART Tower, 6799 Ayala Ave, Makati City, 1226 Metro Manila; tel. (2) 8881111; fax (2) 8488830; e-mail customercare@smart.com.ph; internet www.smart.com.ph; 43.2m. subscribers (2010); Pres. and CEO NAPOLEON L. NAZARENO.

Pilipino Telephone Corpn (Piltel): SMART Tower, 25th Floor, 6799 Ayala Ave, Makati City, 1200 Metro Manila; tel. (2) 8913888; fax (2) 8171121; subsidiary of Smart Communications, Inc; major cellular telephone provider; 400,000 subscribers (1999); Chair. MANUEL V. PANGILINAN; Pres. and CEO NAPOLEON L. NAZARENO.

BROADCASTING

Radio

Bureau of Broadcast Services (BBS) (Philippine Broadcasting Service): Media Centre Bldg, 4th Floor, Visayas Ave, Diliman, Quezon City, 1100 Metro Manila; tel. (2) 9203968; fax (2) 9203961; e-mail pbs.inquiry@gmail.com; internet www.pbs.gov.ph; f. 1952; est. as Philippine Broadcasting Service; govt-operated; 32 radio stations; Dir JOHN S. MANALILI.

Cebu Broadcasting Co: Star City Complex, Vicente Sotto St, Roxal Blvd, Pasay City; tel. (2) 8326134; fax (2) 8326133; e-mail ed_montilla@hotmail.com; Chair. HADRIAN ARROYO.

Far East Broadcasting Co Inc: 62 Karuhatan Rd, Karuhatan, Valenzuela City, 1441 Metro Manila; tel. (2) 2921152; fax (2) 2925790; e-mail info@febc.org.ph; internet www.febc.org.ph; f. 1948; 18 stations; operates a classical music station, eight domestic stations and an overseas service in 64 languages throughout Asia; Pres. DAN ANDREW CURA.

Filipinas Broadcasting Network: Legaspi Towers 200, Room 306, Paseo de Roxas, Makati City, Metro Manila; tel. (2) 8176133; fax (2) 8177135; six stations; Gen. Man. DIANA C. GOZUM.

GMA Network Inc: GMA Network Center, EDSA cnr Timog Ave, Diliman, Quezon City, 1103 Metro Manila; tel. and fax (2) 9287021; e-mail investor_relations@gmanetwork.com; internet www.gmanetwork.com; f. 1950; fmrly Republic Broadcasting System Inc; 21 stations; Chair., Pres. and CEO FELIPE L. GOZON; Exec. Vice-Pres. GILBERTO R. DUAVIT, Jr.

Manila Broadcasting Co: Star City Complex, Vicente Sotto St, Roxas Blvd, Pasay City; tel. (2) 8326142; fax (2) 8326143; internet www.mbcsales.com.ph; f. 1946; affiliate of Philippine Broadcasting Service; 16 stations; Chair. FRED J. ELIZALDE; Pres. RUPERTO NICDAO, Jr.

Nation Broadcasting Corpn: 8th–9th Floors, Jacinta Bldg 2, Edsa Guadalupe, Makati City; tel. (2) 8821622; fax (2) 8821400; e-mail radio@philexport.com; f. 1963; 13 stations; Pres. MANUEL PANGILINAN.

Newsounds Broadcasting Network Inc: 2406 Nobel, cnr Edison St, Makati City, 3117 Metro Manila; tel. (2) 8430116; fax (2) 8430122; 10 stations; Gen. Man. E. BILLONES; Office Man. HERMAN BASBANO.

Pacific Broadcasting System: c/o Manila Broadcasting Co, Star City Complex, Vicente Sotto St, Roxas Blvd, Metro Manila; tel. (2) 8326142; fax (2) 8326143; three stations; Pres. RUPERTO NICDAO, Jr; Vice-Pres. RUDOLPH JULARBAL.

PBN Broadcasting Network Inc: Ersan Bldg, 3rd Floor, 32 Quezon Ave, Quezon City, Metro Manila; tel. (2) 7120190; fax (2) 7438162; e-mail pbnbroadcasting@yahoo.com; internet www.pbnbicol.com; f. 1958; five radio stations, two TV stations; Chair. JORGE D. BAYONA.

Philippine Federation of Catholic Broadcasters: 201 Sunrise Condominium, 226 Ortigas Ave, North Greenhills, San Juan, Metro Manila 1503; tel. (2) 7249850; fax (2) 7249962; e-mail cmnftd@cmn-ftd.org; internet www.catholicmedianetwork.org; f. 1965; operates under the brand name Catholic Media Network (CMN); all 51 radio stations are united by the Dream Satellite; Chair. Bishop BERNARDINO CORTEZ; Pres. Fr FRANCIS LUCAS.

Radio Philippines Network, Inc: Broadcast City, Capitol Hills, Diliman, Quezon City, Metro Manila; tel. (2) 9318618; fax (2) 4357403; e-mail dody_lacuna@yahoo.com; internet www.rpn9.com; f. 1969; 14 radio stations; Pres. ANTONIO ALBANO; Gen. Man. FELIPE G. MEDINA.

Radio Veritas Asia: Buick St, Fairview Park, POB 2642, Quezon City, Metro Manila; tel. (2) 9390011; fax (2) 9381940; e-mail rveritas-asia@rveritas-asia.org; internet www.rveritas-asia.org; f. 1969; Catholic short-wave station; broadcasts in 14 languages; owned by Philippine Radio Educational and Information Center, Inc; Pres. and Chair. Cardinal GAUDENCIO B. ROSALES; Gen. Man. Fr ROBERTO M. EBISA (SVD).

UM Broadcasting Network: cnr P. Reyes and Palma Gil Sts, Davao City; tel. (82) 2279535; fax (82) 2217824; e-mail umbndvo@mozcom.com; internet www.umbn.com.ph; 14 stations; Exec. Vice-Pres. WILLY TORRES.

Vanguard Radio Network: Cityland Pasong Tamo Tower, Rm 520, Chino Roces Ave, Makati City; tel. (2) 7161233; fax (2) 7160899; Pres. MANUEL GALVEZ.

Television

ABC Development Corpn: APMC Bldg, 136 Amorsolo St, cnr Gamboa St, Legaspi Village, Makati City, Metro Manila; tel. (2) 8923801; fax (2) 8128840; CEO EDWARD U. TAN.

ABS-CBN Broadcasting Corpn: ABS-CBN Broadcasting Center, Sgt E. Esguerra Ave, cnr Mother Ignacia St, Quezon City, 1103 Metro Manila; tel. (2) 9244101; fax (2) 4163567; e-mail feedback_web@abs-cbn.com; internet www.abs-cbn.com; Chair. EUGENIO LOPEZ III; Pres. ROSARIO SANTOS-CONCIO.

AMCARA Broadcasting Network: ABS-CBN Broadcasting Centre, Mother Ignacia St, cnr Sgt Esguerra Ave, Quezon City, 1103 Metro Manila; tel. (2) 4152272; fax (2) 4121259; e-mail studio23@abs.pinoycentral.com; internet www.studio23.tv; Man. Dir LEONARDO P. KATIGBAK.

Channel V Philippines: 89 Timog Ave, South Triangle, Quezon City; tel. (2) 9292151; e-mail feedback@channelv.ph; internet www.channelv.ph; Pres. JOEL JIMENEZ; Gen. Man. MON ALCARAZ.

GMA Network, Inc: (see Radio) transmits nation-wide through 46 VHF and 2 affiliate stations and in Asia, Australia and Hawaii through Measat-2 satellite.

Intercontinental Broadcasting Corpn: Broadcast City Complex, Capitol Hills, Diliman, Quezon City, Metro Manila; tel. (2) 9318781; fax (2) 9524002; e-mail ibcpres@ibc.com.ph; 5 stations; Pres. ROBERTO DEL ROSARIO.

National Broadcasting Network (NBN): Broadcast Complex, Visayas Ave, Quezon City, Metro Manila; tel. (2) 9204389; fax (2) 9204342; internet ptni.tv/nbn; f. 1992; public television network; fmrly People's Television Network (PTV4); CEO JOSE S. ISABELO.

Radio Mindanao Network: State Condominium, 4th Floor, 1 Salcedo St, Legaspi Village, Makati City, Metro Manila; tel. (2)

8191073; fax (2) 8163680; e-mail sales@rmn.com.ph; f. 1952; 2 stations; Chair. HENRY CANOY; Pres. ERIC S. CANOY.

Radio Philippines Network, Inc: (see Radio) operates 7 TV stations.

Rajah Broadcasting Network, Inc (RJ TV 29): Save a Lot Bldg, 3rd Floor, 2284 Pasong Tamo Ext., Makati City, Metro Manila; tel. (2) 8932360; fax (2) 8933404; e-mail rjofc@compass.com; f. 1993; Gen. Man. BEA J. COLAMONICI.

Southern Broadcasting Network, Inc: Suite 2902, Jollibee Plaza, 29th Floor, Ortigas Jr Rd, Ortigas Center, Pasig City, Metro Manila; tel. (2) 6363286; fax (2) 6363288; e-mail gemceo@sbnphilippines.net; four stations; Pres. and CEO TEOFILO A. HENSON; Vice-Pres. GERMELINA DINOPOL.

United Broadcasting Network: FEMS Tower 1, 11th Floor, 1289 Zobel Roxas, cnr South Superhighway, Malate; tel. (2) 5216138; fax (2) 5221226; Gen. Man. JOSEPH HODREAL.

Broadcasting Association

Kapisanan ng mga Brodkaster ng Pilipinas (KBP) (Association of Broadcasters in the Philippines): LTA Bldg, 6th Floor, 118 Perea St, Legaspi Village, Makati City, 1226 Metro Manila; tel. (2) 8151990; fax (2) 8151993; e-mail info@kbp.org.ph; internet www.kbp.org.ph; f. 1973; est. in order to regulate the broadcasting industry, elevate standards, disseminate govt information and strengthen relations with advertising industry; Chair. BASBAÑO HERMAN; Pres. RUPERTO NICDAO, Jr.

Finance

(cap. = capital; res = reserves; dep. = deposits; m. = million; brs = branches; amounts in pesos, unless otherwise stated)

BANKING

In 1994 legislation providing for the establishment in the Philippines of additional foreign bank branches was enacted. By the end of 2008 the number of foreign banks had increased to 21; at that time some 38 principal commercial banks were operating in the Philippines.

Central Bank

Bangko Sentral ng Pilipinas (Central Bank of the Philippines): A. Mabini St, cnr Pablo Ocampo St, Malate, 1004 Metro Manila; tel. (2) 5247011; fax (2) 5236210; e-mail bspmail@bsp.gov.ph; internet www.bsp.gov.ph; f. 1993; cap. 10,000m., surplus and res 164,419.5m., dep. 661,015.1m. (Dec. 2007); Gov. AMANDO M. TETANGCO, Jr; 18 brs.

Principal Commercial Banks

Allied Banking Corpn: 6754 Allied Bank Centre, Ayala Ave, cnr Legaspi St, Makati City, 1200 Metro Manila; tel. (2) 8163311; fax (2) 8160921; e-mail info@alliedbank.com.ph; internet www.alliedbank.com.ph; f. 1977; cap. 3,302.4m., res 1,654.1m., dep. 152,543.6m. (Dec. 2009); Chair. DOMINGO T. CHUA; Pres. ANTHONY Q. CHUA; 285 brs.

Banco de Oro Unibank Inc: 7899 Makati Ave, Makati City, 0726 Metro Manila; tel. (2) 8407000; e-mail irandcorplan@bdo.com.ph; internet www.bdo.com.ph; f. 1996; fmrly known as Banco de Oro Universal Bank; name changed as above following merger with Equitable PCI Bank in 2007; acquired 1st e-Bank June 2003; cap. 23,096.6m., res 36,743.7m. (Dec. 2007), dep. 694,678m. (Dec. 2009); Chair. TERESITA T. SY; Pres. NESTOR V. TAN; 185 brs.

Bank of Commerce: Phil First Bldg, 6764 Ayala Ave, Makati City, 1226 Metro Manila; tel. (2) 8120000; fax (2) 8300651; e-mail mscallangan@bankcom.com.ph; internet www.bankcom.com.ph; f. 1983; fmrly Boston Bank of the Philippines; merged with Traders Royal Bank 2001; cap. 5,211.4m., res 2,264m., dep. 91,029m. (Dec. 2009); Chair. RAUL B. DE MESA; Pres. and CEO VIRGILIO MARTIN GOQUINGCO; 117 brs.

Bank of the Philippine Islands: BPI Bldg, 6768 Ayala Ave, Makati City, 1226 Metro Manila; tel. (2) 8185541; fax (2) 8910170; e-mail expressonline@bpi.com.ph; internet www.bpiexpressonline.com; f. 1851; merged with Far East Bank and Trust Co in April 2000; merged with DBS Bank Philippines, Inc, 2001; cap. 32,467m., res 1,171m., dep. 618,065m. (Dec. 2009); Pres. and Dir AURELIO R. MONTINOLA, III; Chair. JAIME ZOBEL DE AYALA, II; 896 local brs; 1 overseas br.

China Banking Corpn: CBC Bldg, 8745 Paseo de Roxas, cnr Villar St, Makati City, 1226 Metro Manila; tel. (2) 8855555; fax (2) 8920220; e-mail online@chinabank.com.ph; internet www.chinabank.ph; f. 1920; cap. 9,750.8m., res 20,350.1m., dep. 197,585m. (Dec. 2009); Chair. GILBERT U. DEE; Pres. and CEO PETER S. DEE; 206 brs.

ChinaBank Savings Inc (CBS): 6772 Ayala Ave, Makati City, 1226 Metro Manila; tel. (2) 7516000; fax (2) 8645016; internet www.chinabank.ph; f. 1999; est. as Manila Banking Corpn; present name adopted following acquisition by China Banking Corpn in 2007; cap. 531m., res 2,288m., dep. 6,704m. (Dec. 2006); Pres. SAMUEL L. CHIONG; Chair. RICARDO R. CHUA; 6 brs.

Development Bank of the Philippines: DBP Bldg, Makati Ave, cnr Sen. Gil J. Puyat Ave, Makati City, 1200 Metro Manila; tel. (2) 8189511; fax (2) 8934311; e-mail info@dbp.ph; internet www.dbp.ph; f. 1947; est. as the Rehabilitation Finance Corpn; govt-owned; provides medium- and long-term loans for strategic devt projects; cap. 39,984m., dep. 124,015m. (Dec. 2009); Chair. JOSÉ A. NUÑEZ, Jr; Pres. and CEO FRANCISCO F. DEL ROSARIO, Jr; 81 brs.

East West Banking Corpn: PBCOM Tower, 20th Floor, 6795 Ayala Ave, cnr Herrera St, Salcedo Village, Makati City, 1226 Metro Manila; tel. (2) 8150233; fax (2) 3250412; e-mail service@eastwestbanker.com; internet www.eastwestbanker.com; f. 1994; Chair. JONATHAN T. GOTIANUN; Pres. and CEO ANTONIO C. MONCUPA, Jr; 89 brs.

Export and Industry Bank Inc (Exportbank): Exportbank Plaza, Chino Roces Ave, cnr Sen. Gil J. Puyat Ave, Makati City, 1200 Metro Manila; tel. (2) 8780190; fax (2) 8879969; e-mail expertinfo@exportbank.com.ph; internet www.exportbank.com.ph; merged with Urban Bank, Inc, 2002; cap. 4,787m., dep. 12,479m. (June 2007); Chair. JAIME GONZALEZ; Pres. JUAN VICTOR S. TANJUATCO; 50 brs.

Land Bank of the Philippines: POB 2284, Manila Central Post Office, Metro Manila; tel. (2) 5220000; fax (2) 5288580; e-mail landbank@mail.landbank.com; internet www.landbank.com; f. 1963; specialized govt bank with universal banking licence; cap. 11,971m., res 17,787.6m., dep. 428,715.1m. (Dec. 2009); Chair. CESAR V. PURISIMA; Pres. and CEO GILDA E. PICO; 324 brs.

Maybank Philippines Inc: Legaspi Towers 300, Pablo Ocampo St, cnr Roxas Blvd, Malate, 1004 Metro Manila; tel. (2) 5237777; fax (2) 5218514; e-mail mayphil@maybank.com.ph; internet www.maybank2u.com.my/philippines/index.shtml; f. 1961; cap. 4,542.2m., res 122.5m., dep. 20,174.7m. (Dec. 2009); Chair. Dato' MOHD SALEH Haji HARUN; Pres. and CEO ONG SEET JOON; 45 brs.

Metropolitan Bank and Trust Co (Metrobank): Metrobank Plaza, Sen. Gil J. Puyat Ave, Makati City, 1200 Metro Manila; tel. (2) 8988000; fax (2) 8176248; e-mail customercare@metrobank.com.ph; internet www.metrobank.com.ph; f. 1962; acquired Global Business Bank (Globalbank) 2002; cap. 36,145.4m., res 11,670m., dep. & bonds 649,556m. (Dec. 2008); Chair. ANTONIO S. ABACAN; Pres. ARTHUR TY, Jr; 700 local brs, 35 overseas brs.

Philippine Bank of Communications: PBCOM Tower, 6795 Ayala Ave, cnr V. A. Rufino St, Makati City, 1226 Metro Manila; tel. (2) 8307000; fax (2) 8182598; e-mail info@pbcom.com.ph; internet www.pbcom.com.ph; f. 1939; merged with AsianBank Corpn in 1999; cap. 8,259.9m., res 519.8m., dep. 35,978m. (Dec. 2009); Chair. ENRIQUE LUY; Pres. and CEO HENRY Y. UY; 66 brs.

Philippine National Bank (PNB): PNB Financial Center, President Diosdado Macapagal Blvd, Pasay City, 1300 Metro Manila; tel. (2) 5738888; fax (2) 5734580; e-mail customercare@pnb.com.ph; internet www.pnb.com.ph; f. 1916; partially transferred to the private sector in 1996 and 2000; 10.93% govt-owned; cap. 26,490m., res 3,939.5m., dep. 221,041m. (Dec. 2009); Chair. FLORENCIA G. TARRIELA; Pres. and CEO CARLOS A. PEDROSA; 324 local brs, 5 overseas brs.

Philippine Veterans Bank: PVB Bldg, 101 V. A. Rufino St, cnr de la Rosa St, Legaspi Village, Makati City, Metro Manila; tel. (2) 9021600; fax (2) 9021700; e-mail corpcomm@veteransbank.com.ph; internet www.veteransbank.com.ph; cap. 4,200m., assets 29,600m. (Dec. 2006); Chair. EMMANUEL V. DE OCAMPO; Pres. and CEO RICARDO A. BALBIDO, Jr; 45 brs.

Philtrust Bank (Philippine Trust Co): Philtrust Bank Bldg, United Nations Ave, cnr San Marcelino St, Ermita, 1045 Metro Manila; tel. (2) 5249061; fax (2) 5217309; e-mail ptc@philtrustbank.com; internet www.philtrustbank.com; f. 1916; cap. 6,617m., res 263m., dep. 73,960m. (Dec. 2009); Pres. ANTONIO H. OZAETA; Chair. JAIME C. LAYA; 46 brs.

Rizal Commercial Banking Corpn: Yuchengco Tower, RCBC Plaza, 6819 Alaya Ave, Makati City, 0727 Metro Manila; tel. (2) 8949000; fax (2) 8949958; e-mail customercontact@rcbc.com; internet www.rcbc.com; f. 1960; cap. 10,112.5m., res 11,111.3m., dep. 236,895m. (Dec. 2009); Chair. HELEN Y. DEE; Pres. and CEO LORENZO V. TAN, Jr; 287 brs.

Security Bank Corpn: 6776 Ayala Ave, Makati City, 0719 Metro Manila; tel. (2) 8676788; fax (2) 8911079; e-mail ccad@securitybank.com.ph; internet www.securitybank.com; f. 1951; fmrly Security Bank and Trust Co; cap. 4,186.3m., res 3,136.5m., dep. 119,610.2m. (Dec. 2009); Pres. and CEO ALBERTO S. VILLAROSA; Chair. FREDERICK Y. DY; 125 brs.

Union Bank of the Philippines: Union Bank Plaza, Meralco Ave, cnr Onyx and Sapphire Sts, Ortigas Center, Pasig City, 1605 Metro Manila; tel. (2) 6676388; fax (2) 6325259; e-mail online@unionbankph.com; internet www.unionbankph.com; f. 1982; cap.

6,414.2m., res 24,866.1m., dep. 200,600.8m. (Dec. 2009); Chair. and CEO JUSTO A. ORTIZ; Pres. VICTOR B. VALDEPEÑAS; 111 brs.

United Coconut Planters Bank (UCPB): UCPB Bldg, 7907 Makati Ave, Makati City, 0728 Metro Manila; tel. (2) 8119000; fax (2) 8119706; e-mail crc@ucpb.com; internet www.ucpb.com; f. 1963; cap. 1,484.8m., res 9,661m., dep. 137,897.8m. (Dec. 2009); Chair. CARLOS C. EJERCITO; Pres. and CEO RAMON Y. SY; 178 brs.

United Overseas Bank Philippines: 17th Floor, Pacific Star Bldg, Sen. Gil J. Puyat Ave, cnr Makati Ave, Makati City, Metro Manila; tel. (2) 67008686; fax (2) 8115917; e-mail info@uob.com.ph; internet www.uob.com.ph; f. 1999; cap. 920m., res –725m., dep. 2,208.2m. (Dec. 2009); Pres. and CEO EMMANUEL MANGOSING; 67 brs.

Rural Banks

Small private banks have been established with the assistance of the Government in order to promote the rural economy. Their principal objectives are to provide credit facilities on reasonable terms and, in co-operation with other agencies of the Government, to give advice on management.

Thrift Banks

Thrift banks mobilize small savings and provide loans to lower-income groups. The thrift banking system comprises savings and mortgage banks, stock savings and loan associations, and private development banks.

Development Bank

Pampanga Development Bank: MacArthur Highway, Dolores San Fernando, Pampanga, Luzon; tel. (45) 9612786; fax (45) 9633931; e-mail pdb@ag.triasia.net; originally Agribusiness Development Bank; name changed as above 1995; cap. 75.0m., res 4.3m., dep. 125.8m. (Dec. 2006); Pres. JOSE ERIBERTO H. SUAREZ.

Islamic Bank

Al-Amanah Islamic Investment Bank of the Philippines: 4th Floor, DBP Bldg, Makati Ave, Makati City, Metro Manila; tel. (2) 8934350; fax (2) 8195249; e-mail info@al-amanahbank.com; internet www.al-amanahbank.com.ph; f. 1989; Chair. and CEO ENRIQUE D. BAUTISTA.

Banking Associations

Bankers Association of the Philippines: Sagittarius Cond. Bldg, 11th Floor, H. V. de la Costa St, Salcedo Village, Makati City, Metro Manila; tel. (2) 8103858; fax (2) 8103860; e-mail secretariat@bap.org.ph; Pres. AURELIO R. MONTINOLA, III; Exec. Dir CESAR O. VIRTUSIO.

Bankers Institute of the Philippines, Inc (BAIPhil): TRB Tower, 6th Floor, Unit 66, Paseo de Roxas, Makati City, Metro Manila; tel. (2) 8534457; fax (2) 8530889; e-mail secretariat@baiphil.org; internet www.baiphil.org; f. 1941; est. as Nat. Asscn of Auditors and Comptrollers; name changed to Bank Administration Institute in 1968, and as above in 2001; Pres. EMMANUEL E. BARCENA.

Chamber of Thrift Banks: Cityland 10 Condominium Tower 1, Unit 614, H. V. de la Costa St, Salcedo Village, Makati City, Metro Manila; tel. (2) 8126974; fax (2) 8127203; internet www.ctb.com.ph; Pres. PATRICK D. CHENG.

Offshore Bankers' Association of the Philippines, Inc: MCPO 3088, Makati City, 1229 Metro Manila; tel. (2) 8103554; Chair. TERESITA MALABANAN.

Rural Bankers' Association of the Philippines: RBAP Bldg, A. Soriano Jr Ave, cnr Arzobispo St, Intramuros, Metro Manila; tel. (2) 5272968; fax (2) 5272980; e-mail info@rbap.org; internet www.rbap.org; Pres. CORAZON L. MILLER.

STOCK EXCHANGES

Securities and Exchange Commission: SEC Bldg, Epifanio de los Santos Ave, Greenhills, Mandaluyong City, Metro Manila; tel. (2) 5840923; fax (2) 5845293; e-mail mis@sec.gov.ph; internet www.sec.gov.ph; f. 1936; Chair. TERESITA J. HERBOSA.

Philippine Stock Exchange: Philippine Stock Exchange Center, Exchange Rd, Ortigas Center, Pasig City, 1605 Metro Manila; tel. (2) 6887600; fax (2) 6345113; e-mail pirs@pse.com.ph; internet www.pse.com.ph; f. 1994 following the merger of the Manila and Makati Stock Exchanges; 237 listed cos (Dec. 2005); Chair. JOSE T. PARDO; Pres. HANS B. SICAT.

INSURANCE

At the end of 2000 a total of 156 insurance companies were authorized by the Insurance Commission to transact in the Philippines. Foreign companies were also permitted to operate in the country.

Principal Domestic Companies

Ayala Life Assurance Inc: Ayala Life-FGU Center, 14th–15th Floors, 6811 Ayala Ave, Makati City, Metro Manila; tel. (2) 8885433; fax (2) 8180171; e-mail customer.service@ayalalife.com.ph; internet www.ayalalife.com.ph; Chair. XAVIER LOINAZ.

BPI/MS Insurance Corpn: Ayala Life-FGU Center, 11th Floor, 6811 Ayala Ave, Makati City, 1226 Metro Manila; tel. (2) 8409000; fax (2) 8409099; e-mail insure@bpims.com; internet www.bpims.com; f. 2002; est. by merger of FGU Insurance Corpn and FEB Mitsui Marine Insurance Corpn; jt venture of Bank of the Philippine Islands and Sumitomo Insurance Co (Japan); cap. 731m. (2006), sales 2,140m.; Chair. AURELIO R. MONTINOLA, III; Pres. TAKAAKI UEDA.

Central Surety & Insurance Co: 2nd Floor, Universal-Re Bldg, 106 Paseo de Roxas, Legaspi Village, Makati City, 1200 Metro Manila; tel. (2) 8174931; fax (2) 8170006; f. 1945; bonds, fire, marine, casualty, motor car; Pres. FERMIN T. CASTAÑEDA.

Commonwealth Insurance Co: BDO Plaza, 10th Floor, 8737 Paseo de Roxas, Makati City, Metro Manila; tel. (2) 8187626; fax (2) 8138575; e-mail info@cic.com.ph; internet www.cic.com.ph; f. 1935; Pres. MARIO NOCHE.

Co-operative Insurance System of the Philippines: CISP Bldg, 80 Malakas St, Diliman, Quezon City, Metro Manila; tel. (2) 4359100; fax (2) 4333211; e-mail cisplife@cisplife.com; internet www.cisplife.com; Chair. LEONIDA V. CHAVEZ; Pres. AMBROSIO M. RODRIGUEZ.

Empire Insurance Co: Prudential Life Bldg, 2nd Floor, 843 Arnaiz Ave, Legaspi Village, Makati City, 1229 Metro Manila; tel. (2) 8159561; fax (2) 8152599; e-mail empire_ins_co@yahoo.com; f. 1949; fire, bonds, marine, accident, motor car, extraneous perils; Pres. and CEO JOSE MA G. SANTOS.

Equitable Insurance Corpn: Equitable Bank Bldg, 4th Floor, 262 Juan Luna St, Binondo, POB 1103, Metro Manila; tel. (2) 2430291; fax (2) 2415768; e-mail info@equitableinsurance.com.ph; internet www.equitableinsurance.com.ph; f. 1950; fire, marine, casualty, motor car, bonds; Pres. NORA T. GO; Exec. Vice-Pres. ANTONIO C. OCAMPO.

Great Domestic Insurance Co of the Philippines: 5th Floor, Champ Bldg, Anda Circle, Bonifacio Drive, Port Area, Manila; tel. (2) 5273044; fax (2) 5273052; e-mail grdomic@intertasia.com.ph; internet www.greatdomesticph.com; f. 1946; cap. 10m.; Pres. and Chair. MAR S. LOPEZ.

Insular Life Assurance Co Ltd: Insular Life Corporate Center, Insular Life Drive, Filinvest Corporate City, Alabang, 1781 Muntinlupa City; tel. (2) 5821818; fax (2) 7711717; e-mail corplan@insular.com.ph; internet www.insularlife.com.ph; f. 1910; members' equity 14,000m. (Dec. 2009); Chair. and CEO VICENTE R. AYLLÓN.

Makati Insurance Co Inc: BPI Buendia Center, 19th Floor, Sen. Gil J. Puyat Ave, Makati City, 1200 Metro Manila; tel. (2) 8459576; fax (2) 8915229; f. 1965; non-life; Pres. and Gen. Man. JAIME L. DARANTINAO; Chair. OCTAVIO V. ESPIRITU.

Malayan Insurance Co Inc: Yuchengco Tower I, 4th Floor, 484 Quintin Paredes St, Binondo, 1099 Metro Manila; tel. (2) 2428888; fax (2) 2412188; e-mail malayan@malayan.com; internet www.malayan.com; f. 1949; cap. 100m.; insurance and bonds; Pres. YVONNE S. YUCHENGCO; Chair. ADELITA VERGEL DE DIOS.

Manila Surety & Fidelity Co Inc: 66 P. Florentino St, Quezon City, Metro Manila; tel. (2) 7122251; fax (2) 7124129; f. 1945; cap. p.u. 50m., members' equity 85m. (Dec. 2003); Pres. MARIA LOURDES V. PEÑA; Vice-Pres. MARIA EDITHA PEÑA-LIM; 4 brs.

Metropolitan Insurance Corpn Co: Ateneum Bldg, 3rd Floor, 160 L. P. Leviste St, Salcedo Village, Makati City, Metro Manila; tel. (2) 8672888; fax (2) 8162294; f. 1933; non-life; Pres. JOSE M. PERIQUET, Jr; Exec. Vice-Pres. ROBERTO ABAD.

National Life Insurance Co of the Philippines: National Life Insurance Bldg, 6762 Ayala Ave, Makati City, Metro Manila; tel. (2) 8100251; fax (2) 8178718; f. 1933; Pres. BENJAMIN L. DE LEON; Sr Vice-Pres. DOUGLAS MCLAREN.

National Reinsurance Corpn of the Philippines: AXA Life Center, 18th Floor, Sen. Gil J. Puyat Ave, cnr Tindalo St, Makati City, 1200 Metro Manila; tel. (2) 7595801; fax (2) 7595886; e-mail nrcp@nrcp.com.ph; internet www.nrcp.com.ph; f. 1978; Chair. HELEN Y. DEE; Pres. and CEO ROBERTO B. CRISOL.

Paramount Life and General Insurance Corpn: Sage House, 14th and 15th Floors, 110 V. A. Rufino St, Legaspi Village, Makati City, 1229 Metro Manila; tel. (2) 8127956; fax (2) 8131140; e-mail insure@paramount.com.ph; internet www.paramount.com.ph; f. 1950; fmrly Paramount General Insurance Corpn; name changed to Paramount Union Insurance Corpn in 2001; name changed as above in 2002; fire, marine, casualty, motor car; Chair. PATRICK L. GO; Pres. GEORGE T. TIU.

Philippine American Life and General Insurance Co (Philamlife): Philamlife Bldg, United Nations Ave, Metro Manila; POB

2167, 0990 Metro Manila; tel. (2) 5269404; fax (2) 5222863; e-mail philamwebmaster@aig.com; internet www.philamlife.com; Pres. TREVOR BULL.

Philippine AXA Life Insurance Corpn: Philippine AXA Life Centre, Sen. Gil J. Puyat Ave, cnr Tindalo St, Makati City, Metro Manila; tel. (2) 5815292; fax (2) 8192631; e-mail customer.service@axa.com.ph; internet www.axa.com.ph; Pres. and CEO SEVERINUS HERMANS.

Philippine Charter Insurance Coprn: Skyland Plaza, Sen. Gil J. Puyat Ave, cnr Tindalo St, Makati City 1203; tel. (2) 5806800; fax (2) 8154797; e-mail customerservice@philcharter.com.ph; internet www.philcharter.com.ph; f. 1960; Chair. BIENVENIDO E. LAGUESMA; Pres. MELECIO MALLILLIN.

Pioneer Insurance and Surety Corpn: Pioneer House Makati, 108 Paseo de Roxas, Legaspi Village, Makati City, 1229 Metro Manila; tel. (2) 8127777; fax (2) 8171461; e-mail info@pioneer.com.ph; internet www.pioneer.com.ph; f. 1954; cap. 5,441m. (2009); Pres. and CEO DAVID C. COYUKIAT.

Rizal Surety and Insurance Co: Prudential Life Bldg, 3rd Floor, 843 Arnaiz Ave, Legaspi Village, Makati City, Metro Manila; tel. (2) 8159561; fax (2) 8152599; e-mail rizalsic@mkt.weblinq.com; f. 1939; fire, bond, marine, motor car, accident, extraneous perils; Chair. and Pres. S. CORPUS.

Standard Insurance Co Inc: Petron Mega Plaza Bldg, 28th Floor, Sen. Gil J. Puyat Ave, Makati City, Metro Manila; tel. (2) 9886388; f. 1958; Chair. LOURDES T. ECHAUZ; Pres. PATRICIA CHILIP.

Sterling Insurance Co: Zeta II Annex Bldg, 6th Floor, 191 Salcedo St, Legaspi Village, Makati City, Metro Manila; tel. (2) 8923794; fax (2) 8923794; f. 1960; fmrly Dominion Insurance Corpn; renamed as above Nov. 2001; fire, marine, motor car, accident, engineering, bonds; Pres. RAFAEL GALLAGA.

Tico Insurance Co Inc: Trafalgar Plaza, 7th Floor, 105 H. V. de la Costa St, Salcedo Village, Makati City, 1227 Metro Manila; tel. (2) 8140143; fax (2) 8140150; f. 1937; fmrly Tabacalera Insurance Co Inc; Chair. and Pres. CARLOS CATHOLICO.

UCPB General Insurance Co Inc: UCPB Bldg, 5th Floor, 7907 Makati Ave, Makati City; tel. (2) 8111788; fax (2) 2773333; e-mail ucpbgen@ucpbgen.com; internet www.ucpbgen.com; f. 1963; non-life; Pres. ISABELO P. AFRICA; Chair. JULITA S. MANAHAN.

Universal Reinsurance Corpn: Ayala Life Bldg, 9th Floor, 6786 Ayala Ave, Makati City, Metro Manila; tel. (2) 7514977; fax (2) 8173745; f. 1949; life and non-life; Chair. JAIME AUGUSTO ZOBEL DE AYALA II; Pres. HERMINIA S. JACINTO.

Regulatory Body

Insurance Commission: 1071 United Nations Ave, Metro Manila; tel. and fax (2) 5238461; e-mail pubassist_ic@yahoo.com.ph; internet www.insurance.gov.ph; regulates the private insurance industry by, among other things, issuing certificates of authority to insurance companies and intermediaries and monitoring their financial solvency; Commr EMMANUEL F. DOOC.

Trade and Industry

GOVERNMENT AGENCIES

Board of Investments: Industry and Investments Bldg, 385 Sen. Gil J. Puyat Ave, Makati City, 1200 Metro Manila; tel. (2) 8901332; fax (2) 8961166; e-mail nerbac@boi.gov.ph; internet www.boi.gov.ph; Chair. GREGORY L. DOMINGO.

Bureau of Domestic Trade (BDT): Trade and Industry Bldg, Ground Floor, 361 Sen. Gil J. Puyat Ave, Makati City, Metro Manila; tel. (2) 7513223; fax (2) 7513324; e-mail bdt@dti.gov.ph; Dir MEYNARD R. ORBETA.

Cagayan Economic Zone Authority: Westar Bldg, 7th Floor, 611 Shaw Blvd, Pasig City, 1603 Metro Manila; tel. (2) 6365774; fax (2) 6313997; e-mail info@ceza.gov.ph; internet ceza.gov.ph; Administrator and CEO JOSÉ MARI B. PONCE.

Clark Development Corpn: Bldg 2122, C. P. Garcia St, Clark Freeport Zone, Pampanga; tel. (45) 5999000; fax (45) 5992507; e-mail info@clark.com.ph; internet www.clark.com.ph; Pres. and CEO BENIGNO N. RICAFORT.

Industrial Technology Development Institute: DOST Compound, Gen. Santos Ave, Bicutan, Taguig, 1631 Metro Manila; tel. (2) 8372071; fax (2) 8373167; e-mail adiv@dost.gov.ph; internet itdibiz.com; Dir Dr NUNA E. ALMANZOR.

Maritime Industry Authority (MARINA): Parkview Plaza, 984 Taft Ave, cnr T. M. Kalaw St, Ermita, Manila; tel. (2) 5239078; fax (2) 5242746; e-mail oadm@marina.gov.ph; internet www.marina.gov.ph; f. 1974; development of inter-island shipping, overseas shipping, shipbuilding and repair, and maritime power; Administrator MARIA ELENA H. BAUTISTA, Jr.

National Tobacco Administration: NTA Bldg, Scout Reyes St, cnr Panay Ave, Quezon City, Metro Manila; tel. (2) 3743987; fax (2) 3742505; e-mail mis@nta.gov.ph; internet www.nta.da.gov.ph; f. 1987; Administrator CARLITOS S. ENCARNACION.

Philippine Coconut Authority (PCA): PCA Compound, Elliptical Rd, Diliman, Quezon City, 1100 Metro Manila; tel. (2) 9284501; fax (2) 9216173; e-mail pca_cpo@yahoo.com.ph; internet www.pca.da.gov.ph; f. 1973; Chair. ARTHUR C. YAP; Administrator OSCAR G. GARIN.

Philippine Council for Advanced Science and Technology Research and Development (PCASTRD): DOST Main Bldg, Gen. Santos Ave, Bicutan, Taguig, 1631 Metro Manila; tel. (2) 8377522; fax (2) 8373168; e-mail pcastrd@dost.gov.ph; internet www.pcastrd.dost.gov.ph; f. 1987; Exec. Dir Dr REYNALDO V. EBORA.

Philippine Economic Zone Authority: Roxas Blvd, cnr San Luis St, Pasay City, Metro Manila; tel. (2) 5513454; fax (2) 8916380; e-mail info@peza.gov.ph; internet www.peza.gov.ph; f. 1995; Dir-Gen. Dr LILIA B. DE LIMA.

Privatization and Management Office: Department of Finance, 104 Gamboa St, Legaspi Village, Makati City, 1229 Metro Manila; tel. (2) 8932383; fax (2) 8933453; e-mail pmo@eastern.com.ph; internet www.pmo.gov.ph; f. 2002; formed to handle the privatization of govt assets; succeeded Asset Privatization Trust; Chief Privatization Officer GUILLERMO N. HERNANDEZ.

Subic Bay Metropolitan Authority: Administration Bldg, 229 Waterfront Rd, Subic Bay Freeport Zone, 2222 Zambales; tel. (47) 2524000; fax (47) 2524216; e-mail webteam@sbma.com; internet www.sbma.com; Chair. FELICIANO G. SALONGA; CEO and Administrator ARMAND C. ARREZA.

DEVELOPMENT ORGANIZATIONS

Bases Conversion and Development Authority: Bonifacio Technology Center, 2nd Floor, 31st St, Cres. Park West, Bonifacio Global City, POB 42, Taguig, 1634 Metro Manila; tel. (2) 8166666; fax (2) 8160996; e-mail bcda@bcda.gov.ph; internet www.bcda.gov.ph; f. 1992; est. to facilitate the conversion, privatization and development of fmr military bases; Chair. ALOYSIUS R. SANTOS; Pres. and CEO NARCISO L. ABAYA.

Bureau of Land Development: DAR Bldg, Elliptical Rd, Diliman, Quezon City, Metro Manila; tel. (2) 9287031; fax (2) 9260971; Dir EUGENIO B. BERNARDO.

Capital Market Development Council (CMDC): Unit 1901, 19th Floor, 139 Corporate Center, Valero St, Salcedo Village, Makati City, Metro Manila; tel. (2) 8114052; fax (2) 8114185; e-mail cmdcphil@yahoo.com.ph; internet www.cmdc-phil.net; f. 1991; Chair. ABELARDO V. CORTEZ; Exec. Dir RESCINA BHAGWANI.

Cooperative Development Authority: CDA Bldg, Ground Floor, 827 Aurora Blvd, Immaculate Conception Village, Quezon City, Metro Manila; tel. (2) 3736894; fax (2) 3712077; e-mail cda.oed@gmail.com; internet www.cda.gov.ph; Chair. LECIRA V. JUAREZ; Exec. Dir NIEL A. SANTILLAN.

Micro, Small and Medium Enterprise Development Council: Oppen Bldg, 3rd Floor, 349 Sen. Gil J. Puyat Ave, Makati City, Metro Manila; tel. and fax (2) 8967916; e-mail bsmbd@mnl.sequel.net; f. 2008; est. to replace Small and Medium Enterprise Devt Council; initiates and implements programmes and projects addressing the specific needs of micro, small and medium enterprises in areas concerning entrepreneurship, institutional development, productivity improvement, organization, financing and marketing; chaired by Sec. of Trade and Industry; Vice-Chair. JOSE CONCEPCION, III.

Bureau of Micro, Small and Medium Enterprise Development (BMSMED): Trade and Industry Bldg, 5th Floor, 361 Sen. Gil J. Puyat Ave, Makati City, Metro Manila; tel. (02) 8971693; fax (02) 8967916; e-mail bmsmed@dti.gov.ph; f. 2008, to replace Bureau of Small and Medium Business Development; Secr. of the MSMED Council.

National Development Co (NDC): NDC Bldg, 8th Floor, 116 Tordesillas St, Salcedo Village, Makati City, 1227 Metro Manila; tel. (2) 8404838; fax (2) 8404862; e-mail info@ndc.gov.ph; internet www.ndc.gov.ph; f. 1919; govt-owned corpn engaged in the organization, financing and management of subsidiaries and corpns, incl. commercial, industrial, mining, agricultural and other enterprises assisting national economic devt; also jt industrial ventures with other ASEAN countries; Chair. PETER B. FAVILA; Gen. Man. LOURDES F. RUBUENO.

Philippine National Oil Co (PNOC): PNOC Bldg 6, Energy Center, Merritt Rd, Fort Bonifacio, Taguig City, Metro Manila; tel. (2) 7897662; internet www.pnoc.com.ph; f. 1973; state-owned energy devt agency mandated to ensure stable and sufficient supply of oil products and to develop domestic energy resources; Chair. ANGELO T. REYES; Pres. and CEO ANTONIO M. CAILAO.

Southern Philippines Development Authority: Basic Petroleum Bldg, 104 Carlos Palanca, Jr, St, Legaspi Village, Makati City, Metro Manila; fax (2) 8183907; Chair. ROBERTO AVENTAJADO; Manila Rep. GERUDIO 'KHALIQ' MADUENO.

CHAMBERS OF COMMERCE AND INDUSTRY

Cebu Chamber of Commerce and Industry (CCCI): CCCI Center, cnr 11th and 13th Ave, North Reclamation Area, 6000 Cebu City; tel. (32) 2321421; fax (32) 2321422; internet www.cebubusinesswebportal.com; f. 1913; Pres. SAMUEL L. CHIOSON.

Chamber of Mines of the Philippines: Rm 809, Ortigas Bldg, Ortigas Ave, Pasig City, 1605 Metro Manila; tel. (2) 6354123; fax (2) 6354160; e-mail info@chamberofmines.com.ph; internet www.chamberofmines.com.ph; f. 1975; Chair. ARTEMIO F. DISINI; Pres. BENJAMIN PHILIP G. ROMUALDEZ.

Federation of Filipino-Chinese Chambers of Commerce and Industry Inc: Federation Center, 6th Floor, Muelle de Binondo St, Binondo, POB 23, Metro Manila; tel. (2) 2419201; fax (2) 2422361; internet www.ffcccii.com.ph/main.html; f. 1954; Pres. TAN CHING.

Philippine Chamber of Coal Mines (Philcoal): Rm 1007, Princeville Condominium, S. Laurel St, cnr Shaw Blvd, 1552 Mandaluyong City, Metro Manila; tel. (2) 5330518; fax (2) 5315513; f. 1980; Exec. Dir BERTRAND GONZALES.

Philippine Chamber of Commerce and Industry (PCCI): 3rd Floor, ECC Bldg, 355 Sen. Gil Puyat Ave, Makati City, Metro Manila; tel. (2) 8964549; fax (2) 8991727; e-mail pcci@philippinechamber.com; internet www.philippinechamber.com; f. 1978; Chair. MIGUEL B. VARELA; Pres. EDGARDO G. LACSON.

FOREIGN TRADE ORGANIZATIONS

Bureau of Export Trade Promotion (BETP): New Solid Bldg, 6th Floor, 357 Sen. Gil J. Puyat Ave, Makati City, 1200 Metro Manila; tel. (2) 8904707; fax (2) 8904693; e-mail infobetp@dti.gov.ph; internet www.tradelinephil.dti.gov.ph; Dir FERNANDO P. CALA, II.

Bureau of Import Services (BIS): Tara Bldg, 3rd Floor, 389 Sen. Gil J. Puyat Ave, Makati City, Metro Manila; tel. (2) 8964431; fax (2) 8964430; e-mail bis@dti.gov.ph; Dir LUIS M. CATIBAYAN.

Garments and Textile Export Board (GTEB): New Solid Bldg, 2nd and 3rd Floors, 357 Sen. Gil J. Puyat Ave, Makati City, Metro Manila; tel. (2) 8978723; fax (2) 4904653; e-mail gtebebs@dti.gov.ph; manages and supervises the garment textile quota system; Exec. Dir FELICITAS R. AGONCILLO REYES.

Philippine International Trading Corpn (PITC): NDC Bldg, 5th Floor, 116 Tordesillas St, Salcedo Village, 1227 Metro Manila; tel. (2) 8189801; fax (2) 8920782; e-mail pitc@pitc.com.ph; internet www.pitc.gov.ph; f. 1973; state trading company to conduct international marketing of general merchandise, industrial and construction goods, raw materials, semi-finished and finished goods, and bulk trade of agri-based products; also provides financing, bonded warehousing, shipping, cargo and customs services; Chair. PETER B. FAVILA; Pres. and CEO JORGE MENDOZA JUDAN.

INDUSTRIAL AND TRADE ASSOCIATIONS

Beverage Industry Association of the Philippines: SMPC Bldg, 23rd Floor, St Francis St, Mandaluyong City, Metro Manila; tel. (2) 6346840; fax (2) 6318672; e-mail rbkmlo@mnl.sequel.net; f. 1988; Pres. HECTOR GUBALLA.

Chamber of Automotive Manufacturers of the Philippines (CAMPI): Suite 1206, 12th Floor, Jollibee Center, San Miguel Ave, Ortigas Center, Pasig City, 1600 Metro Manila; tel. (2) 6329733; fax (2) 6339941; e-mail campi@globelines.com.ph; internet www.campiauto.org; f. 1995; 13 mems; Pres. ELIZABETH H. LEE.

Construction Industry Authority of the Philippines (CIAP): Jupiter I Bldg, 4th Floor, Jupiter St, Makati City, Metro Manila; tel. (2) 8979336; e-mail pocb@skynet.net; Officer-in-Charge KATHERINE T. DELA CRUZ.

Cotton Development Administration (CODA): ATI Bldg, 1st Floor, Elliptical Rd, Diliman, Quezon City, 1100 Metro Manila; tel. (2) 9208878; fax (2) 9209238; e-mail coda@da.gov.ph; internet www.coda.da.gov.ph; f. 1998; Administrator Dr EUGENIO D. ORPIA, Jr.

Federation of Philippine Industries (FPI): Unit 701, Atlanta Center, 31 Annapolis St, Greenhills, San Juan City, Metro Manila; tel. (2) 7223409; fax (2) 7229737; e-mail fpi@fpi.ph; internet www.fpi.ph; f. 1991; 129 mems; Chair. MENELEO J. CARLOS, Jr; Pres. JESUS L. ARRANZA.

Fiber Industry Development Authority: Asiatrust Bank Annex Bldg, 1424 Quezon Ave, Quezon City, Metro Manila; tel. (2) 3737494; fax (2) 4944126; e-mail fida@pldtdsl.net; internet www.fida.da.gov.ph/home.html.html; f. 1977; Administrator CECILIA GLORIA J. SORIANO.

Philippine Association of Electrical Industries: Banks of the Philippines Bldg, Suite 702, Plaza Cervantes, Binondo, Metro Manila; tel. and fax (2) 2421144; Pres. RICARDO SY.

Philippine Fisheries Development Authority: PCA Annex Bldg, 2nd Floor, 1 Elliptical Rd, Diliman, Quezon City, 1109 Metro Manila; tel. (2) 9258472; fax (2) 9256444; e-mail oagm@pfda.gov.ph; internet www.pfda.da.gov.ph; f. 1976; Gen. Man. PETRONILO B. BUENDIA.

Philippine Liquefied Petroleum Gas Association: 218 San Vicente St, Binondo, Metro Manila; tel. (2) 2412668; fax (2) 6337781; f. 1966; Pres. JOSELITO ASENTERO.

Semiconductor and Electronic Industries in the Philippines (SEIPI): Unit 902, RCBC Plaza, Tower 2, Ayala Ave, cnr Sen. Gil J. Puyat Ave, Makati City, 1200 Metro Manila; tel. (2) 8449028; fax (2) 8449037; e-mail philippine.electronics@seipi.org.ph; internet www.seipi.org.ph; f. 1984; 226 mems; Pres. ERNESTO B. SANTIAGO.

EMPLOYERS' ORGANIZATIONS

Cement Manufacturers' Association of the Philippines (CeMAP): Corporal Cruz St, cnr E. Rodriguez Jr Ave, Bagong Ilog, Pasig City, Metro Manila; tel. and fax (2) 6717585; e-mail cementinfo@cemap.org.ph; internet www.cemap.org.ph; f. 1957; est. as Cement Institute of the Philippines; renamed in 1965 as Cement Asscn of the Philippines, in 1973 as Philippine Cement Corpn, and in 1980 as Philippine Cement Mfrs' Corpn; present name adopted in 2003; 14 mems; Chair. RENATO SUNICO; Pres. ERNESTO M. ORDOÑEZ.

Employers' Confederation of the Philippines (ECOP): ECC Bldg, 2nd Floor, 355 Sen. Gil J. Puyat Ave, Makati City, Metro Manila; tel. (2) 8904845; fax (2) 8958623; e-mail ecop@webquest.com; internet www.ecop.org.ph; f. 1975; Chair. MIGUEL B. VARELA; Pres. SERGIO ORTIZ-LUIS, Jr.

Filipino Shipowners' Association: Victoria Bldg, Rm 503, 429 United Nations Ave, Ermita, 1000 Metro Manila; tel. (2) 5227318; fax (2) 5243164; e-mail filiship@info.com.ph; internet www.filipinoshipowners.com.ph; f. 1950; 24 mems, incl. 6 assoc. mems; Chair. CARLOS C. SALINAS; Exec. Sec. AUGUSTO Y. ARREZA, Jr.

Philippine Coconut Producers' Federation, Inc: Wardley Bldg, 2nd Floor, 1991 Taft Ave, cnr San Juan St, Pasay City, 1300 Metro Manila; tel. (2) 5230918; fax (2) 5211333; e-mail cocofed@pworld.net.ph; Pres. MARIA CLARA L. LOBREGAT.

Philippine Retailers' Association (PRA): Unit 2610, Jollibee Plaza, F. Ortigas Jr Rd, Ortigas Center, Pasig City, Metro Manila; tel. (2) 6874180; fax (2) 6360825; e-mail philretailers@gmail.com; internet www.philretailers.com; f. 1976; est. as Chamber of Philippine Dept Stores and Retailers, Inc; present name adopted 1991; Pres. JORGE MENDIOLA.

Philippine Sugar Millers' Association Inc: 1402 Security Bank Centre, 6776 Ayala Ave, Makati City, 1226 Metro Manila; tel. (2) 8911138; fax (2) 8911144; e-mail psma@psma.com.ph; internet www.psma.com.ph; f. 1922; Chair. JULIO O. SY; Pres. PEDRO E. ROXAS.

Textile Mills Association of the Philippines, Inc (TMAP): Ground Floor, Alexander House, 132 Amorsolo St, Legaspi Village, Makati City, 1229 Metro Manila; tel. (2) 8186601; fax (2) 8183107; e-mail tmap@pacific.net.ph; f. 1956; 11 mems; Pres. HERMENEGILDO C. ZAYCO; Chair. JAMES L. GO.

Textile Producers' Association of the Philippines, Inc: Downtown Center Bldg, Rm 513, 516 Quintin Paredes St, Binondo, Metro Manila; tel. (2) 2411144; fax (2) 2411162; Pres. GO CUN UY; Exec. Sec. ROBERT L. TAN.

UTILITIES

Energy Regulatory Commission: Pacific Center Bldg, San Miguel Ave, Ortigas Center, Pasig City, 1600 Metro Manila; tel. (2) 9145000; fax (2) 6315818; e-mail info@erc.gov.ph; internet www.erc.gov.ph; f. 2001; Chair. and CEO ZENAIDA CRUZ-DUCUT; Exec. Dir FRANCIS SATURNINO C. JUAN.

Electricity

Davao Light and Power Co: 163–165 C. Bangoy Sr St, 8000 Davao City; tel. (82) 2293572; internet www.davaolight.com; f. 1929.

Manila Electric Co (Meralco): Lopez Bldg, 2nd Floor, Meralco Center, Ortigas Ave, Pasig City, 0300 Metro Manila; tel. (2) 6312222; fax (2) 6315591; e-mail finplan.inv.relations@meralco.com.ph; internet www.meralco.com.ph; f. 1903; partially privatized in 1991; 34% govt-owned; supplies electric power to Manila and seven provinces in Luzon; largest electricity distributor, supplying 54% of total consumption in 2000; Chair. and CEO MANUEL M. LOPEZ; Pres. JOSE P. DE JESUS.

National Power Corpn (NAPOCOR): Quezon Ave, cnr BIR Rd, Quezon City, Metro Manila; tel. (2) 9213541; fax (2) 9212468; e-mail webmaster@napocor.gov.ph; internet www.napocor.gov.ph; f. 1936; state-owned corpn supplying electric and hydroelectric power throughout the country; partially privatized in 2007; Pres. FROILAN TAMPINCO.

Gas

First Gen Corpn: Benpres Bldg, 3rd Floor, Exchange Rd, cnr Meralco Ave, Pasig City, Metro Manila; tel. and fax (2) 4496400; fax (2) 6378366; e-mail info@firstgen.com.ph; internet www.firstgen.com.ph; f. 1998; major interests in power generation and distribution; Chair. OSCAR M. LOPEZ; Pres. FEDERICO R. LOPEZ.

Water

Regulatory Authority

Metropolitan Waterworks and Sewerage System: 4th Floor, Administration Bldg, MWSS Complex, 489 Katipunan Rd, Balara, Quezon City, 1105 Metro Manila; tel. (2) 9223757; fax (2) 9212887; e-mail info@mwss.gov.ph; internet www.mwss.gov.ph; govt regulator for water supply, treatment and distribution within Metro Manila; Administrator GERARDO ESQUIVEL (acting).

Distribution Companies

Davao City Water District: Km 5, Jose P. Laurel Ave, Bajada, 8000 Davao City; tel. (82) 2219400; fax (82) 2264885; e-mail dcwd@davao-water.gov.ph; internet www.davao-water.gov.ph; f. 1973; public utility responsible for the water supply of Davao City; Chair. EDUARDO A. BANGAYAN; Gen. Man. Eng. RODORA N. GAMBOA.

Manila Water: MWSS Administration Bldg, 489 Katipunan Rd, Balara, Quezon City, 1105 Metro Manila; tel. (2) 9267999; fax (2) 9818164; e-mail info@manilawater.com; internet www.manilawater.com; f. 1997 following the privatization of Metro Manila's water and wastewater services; responsible for water supply and wastewater services to Manila East until 2037; Pres. and CEO GERARDO C. ABLAZA, Jr.

Maynilad Water: MWSS Compound, 489 Katipunan Rd, Balara, Quezon City, 1105 Metro Manila; tel. (2) 9813333; fax (2) 9223759; e-mail customer.helpdesk@mayniladwater.com.ph; internet www.mayniladwater.com.ph; f. 1998; est. following the privatization of Metro Manila's water services; responsible for water supply, sewage and sanitation services for Manila West until 2021; Pres. ROGELIO SINGSON.

Metropolitan Cebu Water District: Magallanes St, cnr Lapulapu St, 6000 Cebu City; tel. (32) 2548434; fax (32) 2545391; e-mail mcwd@cvis.net.ph; internet www.mcwd.gov.ph; f. 1974; public utility responsible for water supply and sewerage of Cebu City and surrounding towns and cities; Chair. JUAN SAUL F. MONTECILLO; Gen. Man. ARMANDO H. PAREDES.

MAJOR COMPANIES

(Amounts in pesos, unless otherwise stated)

A Soriano Corpn (Anscor): 7th Floor, Pacific Star Bldg, cnr Makati Ave and Gil J. Puyat Ave, Makati City, Metro Manila; tel. (2) 8190251; fax (2) 8115652; e-mail info@anscor.com.ph; internet www.anscor.com.ph; f. 1930; cap. and res 7,453.8m., revenue 1,736.2m. (2009); investment holding co; Chair. and CEO ANDRES SORIANO, III.

Aboitiz Equity Ventures Inc: Aboitiz Corporate Center, Gov. Manuel A. Cuenco Ave, Kasambagan, 6000 Cebu City; tel. (32) 4111800; fax (32) 2314037; e-mail aev@aboitiz.com; internet www.aboitiz.com.ph; f. 1989; construction and fabrication; banking, power distribution; interests in shipping, shipyards, production of gases; operator of container terminal; cap. and res 8,307m., revenue 46,230m. (2009); Chair. JON RAMON ABOITIZ; Pres. and CEO ERRAMON I. ABOITIZ.

Alaska Milk Corpn: Corinthian Plaza, 6th Floor, 121 Paseo de Roxas, Makati City, 1220 Metro Manila; tel. (2) 8404500; fax (2) 8944929; e-mail investorrelations@alaskamilk.com.ph; internet www.alaskamilk.com.ph; f. 1972; mfr of milk and milk products; cap. and res 4,677m., revenue 10,580m. (2009); Chair. ANTONIO H. OZAETA, Sr; Pres. and CEO WILFRED STEVEN UYTENGSU, Jr.

Alliance Global Group Inc: 1880 Eastwood Ave, 7th Floor, Eastwood City Cyberpark, 188 E. Rodriguez Jr Ave, Bagumbayan, Quezon City, 1110 Metro Manila; tel. (2) 9112949; fax (2) 4210851; e-mail jhao@megaworldcorp.com; internet www.allianceglobalinc.com; food and beverages, real estate, restaurants; cap. and res 82,100.9m., revenue 15,230.5m. (2009); Chair. and CEO ANDREW L. TAN.

Alliance Select Foods International Inc: Suite 1206/1405, East Tower, Philippine Stock Exchange Center, Exchange Rd, Ortigas Center, Pasig City, 1600 Metro Manila; tel. (2) 6355241; fax (2) 6355235; e-mail info@alliancetuna.com.ph; internet www.allianceselectfoods.com; f. 2004; tuna processing, canning and export; cap. and res US $20.8m., revenue US $50.9m. (2009); Chair. GEORGE E. SYCIP; Pres. and CEO JONATHAN DEE.

Alsons Consolidated Resources Inc: Alsons Bldg, 2nd Floor, 2286 Pasong Tamo Ext., Makati City, 1231 Metro Manila; tel. (2) 8175506; fax (2) 8940655; e-mail legal@alcantaragroup.com; internet www.acr.com.ph; f. 1974; est. as Victoria Mining Corpn; energy and power, property devt, product distribution; cap. and res 6,807.7m., revenue 2,476.2m. (2009); Chair. and Pres. TOMAS ALCANTARA.

Anchor Land Holdings Inc: Unit 11B, 11th Floor, L. V. Locsin Condominium Bldg, 6752 Ayala Ave, Makati City, 1228 Metro Manila; tel. (2) 8886688; fax (2) 8857349; e-mail inquiries@anchorlandholdings.com; internet www.anchorlandholdings.com; f. 2004; real estate devt and marketing; cap. and res 1,638m., revenue 1,630m. (2009); Chair. STEPHEN LEE; Pres. IMELDA SZE.

Asian Terminals, Inc: Bonifacio Drive, South Harbor, Port Area, 1018 Metro Manila; tel. (2) 5286000; fax (2) 5273647; e-mail webmaster@asianterminals.com.ph; internet www.asianterminals.com.ph; f. 1986; cap. and res 6,043m., sales 4,212.7m. (2009); Chair. KUN WAH WONG; Pres. EUSEBIO TANCO.

Atlas Consolidated Mining and Development Corpn: Quad Alpha Centrum Bldg, 7th Floor, 125 Pioneer St, Mandaluyong City, 1554 Metro Manila; tel. (2) 6327847; e-mail info@atlasphilippines.com; internet www.atlasphilippines.com; f. 1953; mining of copper ore and recovery of by-products of gold, silver and pyrite at Cebu mines; mining of gold ore (with silver) at Masbate Gold Operations; total assets 13,935m., revenue 4,185.52m. (2009); 10,558 employees; Chair., Pres. and CEO ALFREDO C. RAMOS.

Ayala Corpn: Ayala Triangle, Tower 1, 34th Floor, Ayala Ave, Makati City, 1226 Metro Manila; tel. (2) 8485643; fax (2) 8485846; e-mail acquery@ayala.com.ph; internet www.ayala.com.ph; f. 1834; real estate, financial services, telecommunications, electronics, utilities, automobiles, information technology, etc.; cap. and res 102,260m., revenue 76,293m. (2009); Chair. and CEO JAIME AUGUSTO ZOBEL DE AYALA; 120 employees.

Ayala Land Inc: Tower One, Exchange Plaza, Ayala Triangle, Ayala Ave, Makati City, 1226 Metro Manila; tel. (2) 8485643; fax (2) 8485336; e-mail ir@ayalaland.com.ph; internet www.ayalaland.com.ph; f. 1988; real estate and hotel operations; cap. and res 59,194m., revenue 30,455m. (2009); 510 employees; Chair. FERNANDO ZOBEL DE AYALA.

CADP Inc: Barangay Lumbangan, Nasugbu, Batangas; tel. (43) 9312302; fax (43) 9312327; f. 1918; sugar production; wholly owned subsidiary of Roxas and Company Inc; Chair. PEDRO ROXAS; Pres. and CEO FRANCISCO F. DEL ROSARIO, Jr.

Central Azucarera de Tarlac: Cojuangco Bldg, 119 de la Rosa St, Makati City, Metro Manila; tel. (2) 8183911; fax (2) 8179309; e-mail info@cat-luisita.com; internet www.cat-luisita.com; f. 1927; sugar producer and mfr of sugar products; cap. and res 825.2m., revenue 653.1m. (2008/09); 1,734 employees; Pres. and Chair. PEDRO COJUANGCO.

Chemical Industries of the Philippines Inc: Chemphil Bldg, 851 Antonio S. Arnaiz Ave, Legaspi Village, Makati City, Metro Manila; tel. (2) 8188711; fax (2) 8174803; e-mail chemphilgroup@chemphil.com.ph; internet www.chemphil.com.ph; f. 1958; manufacture and distribution of industrial chemicals; cap. and res 1,021m., revenue 335m. (2009); Chair. ANTONIO GARCIA; Pres. and CEO ANA MARIA ORDOVEZA.

Chemrez Technologies Inc: 65 Industria St, Bagumbayan, Quezon City, 1110 Metro Manila; tel. (2) 6350680; fax (2) 6376099; e-mail info@chemrez.com; internet www.chemrez.com; f. 1989; fmrly Corrocoat Inc; mfr of powder coatings; cap. and res 3,508.5m., revenue 5,115.4m. (2009); Chair. RENATO PARAS; Pres. and CEO LEON LAO.

Cityland Development Corpn: Cityland Condominium 10, Tower 1, 2nd Floor, 156 H. V. Dela Costa St, Ayala North, Makati City, Metro Manila; tel. (2) 8936060; fax (2) 8928656; e-mail admin@cityland.net; internet www.citylandcondo.com; f. 1978; fmrly Statehouse Land Devt Corpn; real estate devt; cap. and res 3,971.8m., revenue 2,439.3m. (2009); Chair. SYCIP WASHINGTON; Pres. GRACE LUISON.

Cosmos Bottling Corpn: 1890 Paz Guazon Ave, Otis, Paco, Manila; tel. (2) 6885888; fax (2) 6323364; e-mail acelia.velena@ccbpi.com; internet www.cosmosbottling.com.ph; f. 1918; manufactures, markets and distributes soft drinks; cap. and res 1,172.4m., revenue 6,478.8m. (2009); Chair. WILLIAM SCHULTZ; Pres. and Dir BARING OLAFSSON.

DMCI Holdings Inc: Dacon Bldg, 3rd Floor, 2281 Don Chino Roces Ave Ext., Makati City, 1231 Metro Manila; tel. (2) 8883000; fax (2) 8167362; e-mail investor_inquiries@dmcinet.com; internet www.dmciholdings.com; f. 1995; cap. and res 20,468.2m., revenue 29,711m. (2009); Chair. DAVID M. CONSUNJI; Pres. and CEO ISIDRO A. CONSUNJI.

EEI Corpn: 12 Manggahan St, Bagumbayan, Quezon City, 1110 Metro Manila; tel. (2) 6350843; fax (2) 6350861; e-mail eeicenter@eei.com.ph; internet www.eei.com.ph; f. 1931; industrial construction;

general trading; overseas construction services; cap. and res 3,256m., revenue 6,267m. (2009); 11,594 employees; Chair. RIZALINO S. NAVARRO; Pres. and CEO ROBERTO JOSE L. CASTILLO.

Empire East Land Holdings Inc: The World Centre, 21st Floor, 330 Sen. Gil Puyat Ave, Makati City, 1227 Metro Manila; tel. (2) 8678351; fax (2) 8678013; e-mail empire@empire-east.com; internet www.empire-east.com; f. 1994; devt and marketing of affordable housing; cap. and res 17,083.2m., revenue 2,171.2m. (2009); Chair. ANDREW TAN; Pres. ANTHONY YU.

Energy Development Corpn (EDC): EDC Bldg 5, Energy Center, Merritt Rd, Fort Bonifacio, Taguig, Metro Manila; tel. (2) 8936001; fax (2) 8401575; e-mail edc@energy.com.ph; internet www.energy.com.ph; f. 1976; fmrly PNOC Energy Development Corpn; exploration, devt and optimization of geothermal steamfields; power generation; cap. and res 28,802.1m., revenue 22,066.9m. (2009); Chair. OSCAR LOPEZ; CEO PAUL AQUINO.

Euro Med Laboratories Philippines Inc: PPL Bldg, 2nd Floor, United Nations Ave, cnr San Marcelino St, Metro Manila; tel. (2) 5240091; fax (2) 5260977; e-mail corporate@euromedlab.net; internet www.euromedlab.net; cap. and res 3,927m., sales 4,376.6m. (2009); Chair. Dr WILLIAM G. PADOLINA; Pres. GEORGIANA S. EVIDENTE.

Filinvest Development Corpn: FDC Bldg, 173 P. Gomez St, San Juan, Metro Manila; tel. (2) 7270431; fax (2) 7224797; e-mail ir@filinvestgroup.com; internet www.filinvestgroup.com; f. 1973; real estate devt; cap. and res 47,633.3m., revenue 16,032.9m. (2009); Chair. JONATHAN GOTIANUN; Pres. and CEO LOURDES JOSEPHINE G. YAP.

Ginebra San Miguel Inc: 3rd & 6th Floors, San Miguel Properties, St Francis Ave, Mandaluyong City, 1500 Metro Manila; tel. (2) 6899100; fax (2) 6342211; e-mail smc.stsc@sanmiguel.com.ph; internet www.ginebrasanmiguel.com; f. 1987; manufacture and sale of alcoholic beverages; cap. and res 8,166.7m., sales 19,548.5m. (2009); Chair. and CEO EDUARDO COJUANGCO; Pres. GERARDO PAYUMO.

Holcim Philippines Inc: 7th Floor, 2 World Square, Mckinley Hill, Fort Bonifacio, Taguig City, 1634 Metro Manila; tel. (2) 4593333; fax (2) 45934444; internet www.holcim.ph; f. 2000; est. as Union Cement Corpn; acquired by the Swiss-based Holcim Group and name changed as above in 2003; cap. and res 18,005.4m., revenue 21,861.6m. (2009); Chair. OSCAR J. HILADO; Pres. Dir MAGDALENO B. ALBARRACIN.

Interphil Laboratories Inc: Canlubang Industrial Estate, 4025 Barrio Pittland, Cabuyao, 4025 Laguna; tel. (49) 5492345; fax (49) 8172435; f. 1974; mfr of chemicals and pharmaceuticals; cap. and res 660.2m., revenue 2,106.3m. (2007); Chair. RICARDO ROMULO; Pres. FRANCISCO BILLANO.

Ionics Inc: Plant 2, Block 2 and 3, Carmelray Industrial Park of the Philippines 2, Barangay Tulo, Calamba City, 4027 Laguna; tel. (49) 5081111; fax (49) 5080073; e-mail rose.vicente@ionics-ems.com; internet www.ionics-ems.com; f. 1974; mfr of electronic components; cap. and res US $40.0m., revenue US $72.3m. (2009); Chair. and CEO LAWRENCE QUA.

IPVG Corpn: RCBC Plaza, Tower 2, 34th Floor, 6819 Ayala Ave, Makati City, 1200 Metro Manila; tel. (2) 9764784; fax (2) 8866510; e-mail info@ipvg.com; internet www.ipvg.com; computer games, business process outsourcing, information technology, telecommunications; cap. and res 808.1m., revenue 1,274.4m. (2009); Chair. and Pres. JAIME GONZALEZ; CEO ENRIQUE GONZALEZ.

J. G. Summit Holdings Inc: 42nd Floor, Robinsons-Equitable Tower, ADB Ave, cnr Poveda St, Pasig City, 1600 Metro Manila; tel. (2) 26337631; fax (2) 6339208; e-mail jgsir@jgsummit.com.ph; internet www.jgsummit.com.ph; f. 1990; retailers of food and agro-industrial products; property, power generation, electronics manufacturing, etc.; cap. and res 83,157.7m., revenue 107,955.1m. (2009); 14,865 employees; Chair. and CEO JAMES L. GO; Pres. LANCE Y. GOKONGWEI.

Jollibee Foods Corpn: Jollibee Plaza Bldg, 9th Floor, F. Ortigas Jr Rd, Pasig City, 1605 Metro Manila; tel. (2) 8988181; fax (2) 6341191; e-mail feedback@jollibee.com.ph; internet www.jollibee.com.ph; f. 1975; operation of fast-food chain; cap. and res 16,462.5m., revenue 47,957.6m. (2009); Chair., Pres. and CEO TONY TAN CAKTIONG; 14,243 employees.

Lafarge Cement Services (Philippines) Inc (LCSPI): The Salcedo Tower, 25th Floor, 169 H. V. Dela Costa Ave, Salcedo, Makati City, 1226 Metro Manila; tel. (2) 8854599; fax (2) 8152668; f. 1955; owns Republic Cement Corpn; owned by Lafarge Group; mfr of cement; cap. and res 11,785.4m., revenue 13,816.0m. (2007); Chair. BRUNO LAFONT.

Lepanto Consolidated Mining Co: BA-Lepanto Bldg, 21st Floor, 8747 Paseo de Roxas, Makati City, 1226 Metro Manila; tel. (2) 8159447; fax (2) 8105583; e-mail info@lepantomining.com; internet www.lepantomining.com; f. 1936; copper, gold, silver and calcines; cap. and res 4,659.8m., revenue 1,455.9m. (2009); Chair. and CEO FELIPE U. YAP; Pres. BRYAN U. YAP; 2,015 employees.

Liberty Flour Mills Inc: Liberty Bldg, 6th Floor, 835 Antonio Arnaiz Ave, Makati City, 1200 Metro Manila; tel. (2) 8925011; fax (2) 8932644; e-mail info@libertygroup.com.ph; f. 1958; mfr of flour and flour products; cap. and res 1,590.3m., revenue 1,897.9m. (2009); Chair. WILLIAM CARLOS UY; Pres. FELIX MARAMBA, Jr.

Lopez Holdings Corpn: Benpres Bldg, 4th Floor, cnr Exchange Rd and Meralco Ave, Pasig City, 1600 Metro Manila; tel. (2) 4492345; fax (2) 6313107; e-mail ir@benpres.com.ph; internet www.lopez-holdings.ph; f. 1993; broadcasting, telecommunications, entertainment, power generation, infrastructure devt, etc.; fmrly Benpres Holdings Corpn; cap. and res 22,604m., revenue 24,849m. (2009); Chair. and CEO MANUEL M. LOPEZ.

MacroAsia Corpn: 12th Floor, Allied Bank Bldg, 6754 Ayala Ave, Makati City, 1226 Metro Manila; tel. (2) 8402001; fax (2) 8401892; e-mail info@macroasiacorpn.com; internet www.macroasiacorp.com; f. 1970; aviation support services; cap. and res 2,810.6m., revenue 1,121.7m. (2009); Chair. WASHINGTON SYCIP; Pres. and CEO JOSEPH CHUA.

Mariwasa Siam Holdings Inc: Barangay San Antonio, Santo Tomas, Batangas 4234; tel. (43) 7782936; fax (43) 7782934; e-mail hotline@mariwasa.com; internet www.mariwasa.com; f. 1963; mfr of ceramic tiles; fmrly Mariwasa Manufacturing Corpn; above name adopted after merger with Siam Cement Group, Thailand; cap. and res 629.8m., revenue 2,493.9m. (2009); Chair. REGINA CO SETENG; Pres. SURASAK KRAIWITCHAICHAROEN.

Megaworld Corpn: The World Centre, 28th Floor, 330 Sen. Gil J. Puyat Ave, Makati City, 1227 Metro Manila; tel. (2) 8678826; fax (2) 8678803; e-mail jhao@megaworldcorp.com; internet www.megaworldcorp.com; f. 1989; property devt; cap. and res 49,111.8m., revenue 17,758.6m. (2009); Chair. and Pres. ANDREW TAN.

Metro Pacific Investments Corpn: MGO Bldg, 10th Floor, cnr de la Rosa St, Legaspi Village, Makati City, 0721 Metro Manila; tel. (2) 8880888; fax (2) 8880813; e-mail info@mpic.com.ph; internet www.mpic.com.ph; fmrly Metro Pacific Corpn; name changed and restructured in 2006; principal activities include water utilities, toll operations and health care; cap. and res 51,265.4m., revenue 16,107.7m. (2009); Chair. MANUEL V. PANGILINAN; Pres. and CEO JOSE MARIE K. LIM.

Panasonic Manufacturing Philippines Corpn: Barrio Mapandan, Ortigas Ave, Extension Taytay, Rizal, 1920 Metro Manila; tel. (2) 6352260; fax (2) 28422; e-mail pmpc_op@ph.panasonic.com; internet www.panasonic.com.ph; f. 1963; fmrly Festival Manufacturing Corpn; mfr and distributor of electrical appliances and machinery; cap. and res 3,593.9m., revenue 6,460.4m. (2009/10); Chair. MASARU MARUO; Pres. and CEO NAOYA NISHIWAKI.

Paxys Inc: 18th Floor, 6750 Ayala Office Tower, Ayala Ave, Makati City, 1227 Metro Manila; tel. (2) 8568201; fax (2) 8405181; e-mail ir@paxys.com.ph; internet www.paxys.com; f. 1952; fmrly Fil-Hispano Holdings Corpn; business process outsourcing; cap. and res 2,300m., revenue 3,632.7m. (2009); Chair. and Pres. TARCISIO MEDALLA.

Pepsi-Cola Products Philippines Inc: Km 29 National Rd, Barrio Tunasan, Muntinlupa City, 1773 Metro Manila; tel. (2) 8507901; fax (2) 8507910; internet www.pepsiphilippines.com; f. 1989; mfr of soft drinks; cap. and res 5,894.4m., revenue 16,128.8m. (2009/10); Chair. and CEO MICKY YONG.

Petron Corpn: San Miguel Head Office Complex, 40 San Miguel Ave, Mandaluyong City, 1550 Metro Manila; tel. (2) 8863888; fax (2) 8863064; e-mail contactus@petron.com; internet www.petron.com; petroleum refining; 40% owned by Ashmore Group, 51% owned by San Miguel Corpn; cap. and res 37,291m., revenue 176,531m. (2009); 1,250 employees; Chair. and CEO RAYMON S. ANG; Pres. ERIC O. RECTO.

Philex Mining Corpn: Philex Bldg, 27 Brixton St, Pasig City, 1600 Metro Manila; tel. (2) 6311381; fax (2) 6344441; e-mail philex@philexmining.com.ph; internet www.philexmining.com.ph; mining; f. 1955; cap. and res 16,983.2m., revenue 8,377.9m. (2009); Chair. MANUEL V. PANGILINAN; Pres. JOSE ERNESTO VILLALUNA, Jr; 2,245 employees.

Philippine National Construction Corpn (PNCC): PNCC Bldg, Epifanio de los Santos Ave, cnr Reliance St, Mandaluyong City, Metro Manila; tel. (2) 6318431; fax (2) 6315362; e-mail pnccnet@globelines.com.ph; internet www.pncc.com.ph; f. 1966; 80% govt-owned; tollway operation and maintenance, general construction, mfr of steel products; Chair. ARTHUR AGUILAR; Pres. and CEO THERESA DEFENSOR-ASUNCION.

Philippine National Oil Co (PNOC): see under Development Organizations.

Philippine Seven Corpn: The Columbia Tower, 7th Floor, Ortigas Ave, Mandaluyong City, 1550 Metro Manila; tel. (2) 7244441; fax (2) 7055209; e-mail psc-corp@7-eleven.com.ph; internet www.7-eleven.com.ph; f. 1982; operation of convenience stores; cap. and res

907.9m., revenue 6,688.5m. (2009); Chair. VINCENTE PATERNO; Pres. and CEO JOSE VICTOR PATERNO.

Phinma Corpn: Phinma Plaza, 12th Floor, 39 Plaza Dr., Rockwell Center, Makati City, 1200 Metro Manila; tel. (2) 8700100; fax (2) 8700456; e-mail Ciophn@phinma.com.ph; internet www.phinmacorp.com.ph; f. 1957; mfr of iron sheets, real estate, education, property investment; fmrly Bacnotan Consolidated Industries Inc; name changed as above in 2010; total assets 4,282.1m., revenue 2,743.5m. (2008); Chair. OSCAR HILADO; Pres. RAMON DEL ROSARIO, Jr.

Phoenix Petroleum Philippines Inc: Phoenix Bulk Depot, Lanang, Davao City 8000; tel. (82) 2358888; internet www.phoenixphilippines.com; f. 2002; fmrly Davao Oil Terminal Services Corpn; name changed as above in 2006; trade of refined petroleum products, operation of oil depots and allied services; cap. and res 1,528.8m., revenue 5,873m. (2009); Chair. DOMINGO UY; Pres. and CEO DENNIS UY.

PICOP Resources Inc: Moredel Bldg, 2nd Floor, 2280 Pasong Tamo Ext., Makati City, Metro Manila; tel. (2) 8135308; fax (2) 8937195; e-mail picop.inc@gmail.com; f. 1952; mfr of paper and timber products; cap. and res –962.0m., revenue 987.4m. (2007); 2,100 employees; Chair. ROBERTO ATENDIDO; Pres. and CEO TEODORO BERNARDINO.

Prime Orion Philippines Inc: LKG Tower, 20th Floor, 6801 Ayala Ave, Makati City, 1200 Metro Manila; tel. (2) 8841106; fax (2) 8841409; e-mail popi-corporate@primeorion.com; internet www.primeorion.com; principal activities of group include investment holding, real estate, manufacturing and distribution of Pepsi Cola products; cap. and res –317m., revenue 1,293.6m. (2008/09); Chair. FELIPE YAP; Pres. and Chief Exec. YUEN PO SENG.

Robinsons Land Corpn: Level 2, Galleria Corporate Center, EDSA, cnr Ortigas Ave, Quezon City, 1100 Metro Manila; tel. (2) 3971888; e-mail investor.relations@robinsonsland.com; internet www.robinsonsland.com; f. 1980; property devt; cap. and res 25,446.6m., total revenue 10,733.5m. (2009); Chair. and CEO JAMES GO; Pres. FREDERICK GO.

Roxas Holdings Inc: Cacho Gonzales Bldg, 6th Floor, 101 Aguirre St, Legaspi Village, Makati City, 1226 Metro Manila; tel. (2) 8108901; fax (2) 8171875; e-mail ir_corpcomm@roxas.com.ph; internet www.roxas.com.ph; f. 1927; fmrly Central Azucarera Don Pedro; sugar processing; cap. and res 5,670.3m., sales 5,864.6m. (2008/09); Chair. PEDRO ROXAS; Pres. and CEO RAMON PICORNELL, Jr.

San Miguel Corpn: 40 San Miguel Ave, Mandaluyong City, 1550 Metro Manila; tel. (2) 6323000; fax (2) 6323099; e-mail smc_stsc@smg.sanmiguel.com.ph; internet www.sanmiguel.com.ph; f. 1890; breweries, food-processing, packaging; cap. and res 213,817m., sales 174,213m. (2009); Chair. and CEO EDUARDO COJUANGCO; 14,600 employees.

San Miguel Pure Foods Co: JMT Corporate Condominium, 23rd Floor, ADB Ave, Ortigas Center, Pasig City, Metro Manila; tel. (2) 7025000; fax (2) 9148746; e-mail smc.stsc@sanmiguel.com.ph; internet www.sanmiguelpurefoods.com; f. 1956; est. as Pure Foods Corpn; name changed as above in 2002, following 2001 acquisition by San Miguel Corpn; cap. and res 15,244.9m., sales 75,042.9m. (2009); Chair. and CEO EDUARDO M. COJUANGCO, Jr; Pres. FRANCISCO ALEJO; 3,520 employees.

Semirara Mining Corpn: DMCI Plaza Bldg, 2nd Floor, 2281 Chino Roces Ave Extension, Makati City, 1231 Metro Manila; tel. (2) 8673377; fax (2) 8167185; internet semiraraminingcorp.com; f. 1980; coal mining; cap. and res 9,847.1m., revenue 11,943.6m. (2009); Chair. DAVID CONSUNJI; CEO ISIDRO CONSUNJI.

SM Development Corpn (SMDC): One E-com Center, 10th Floor, Harbor Drive, Mall of Asia Complex, Pasay City, 1300 Metro Manila; tel. (2) 8311371; fax (2) 8336244; e-mail info@smdevelopment.com; internet www.smdevelopment.com; f. 1974; fmrly Alaya Fund Inc; property devt; cap. and res 10,937.2m., revenue 5,261.8m. (2009); Chair. HENRY SY, Sr; Pres. ROGELIO CABUÑAG.

SM Prime Holdings Inc: Bldg A, J. W. Diokno Blvd, Mall of Asia Complex, Pasay City, 1300 Metro Manila; tel. (2) 8311000; fax (2) 8341800; e-mail info@smprime.com; internet www.smprime.com; f. 1994; operation of shopping malls; cap. and res 47,349.1m., revenue 20,497.4m. (2009); Chair. HENRY SY, Sr; Pres. HANS SY.

Splash Corpn: Ground Floor, HBC Corporate Center, 548 Mindanao Ave, Quezon City, 1116 Metro Manila; tel. (2) 9845555; e-mail splashcare@splashcorp.com; internet www.splash.com.ph; f. 1991; mfr of cosmetics; cap. and res 2,600m., revenue 2,719.2m. (2009); Chair. and CEO ROLANDO HORTALEZA; Pres. ERIC ROEL E. DOMAGAS.

Stream Global Services Inc: Stream Quezon City, 6th Floor, SM City North EDSA, 1105 Quezon City; tel. (2) 9081300; internet www.stream.com; f. 1999; call centre operations; est. as eTelecare Global Solutions; above name adopted after merger with Stream Global Services in 2009; Chair. and CEO KATHRYN MARINELLO.

Swift Foods Inc: RFM Corporate Centre, 2nd Floor, Pioneer cnr Sheridan St, Mandaluyong City, 1603 Metro Manila; tel. (2) 6318101; fax (2) 6315064; e-mail swiftagri@swiftfoods.com.ph; internet myswiftfoods.com.ph; mfr of processed meat products, poultry products and commercial feeds; cap. and res 145.1m., revenue 912.2m. (2009); Chair. and CEO JOSE A. CONCEPCION III; Pres. LUIS BERNARDO CONCEPCION.

Tanduay Holdings Inc: 348 J. Nepomuceno St, San Miguel District, 1001 Manila; tel. (2) 7339301; fax (2) 7339090; e-mail tanduay@tanduay.com; internet www.tanduay.com; f. 1937; fmrly Asia Pacific Wine Merchants; liquor distillation and bottling; cap. and res 5,595.9m., revenue 10,202.2m. (2009); Chair. and CEO LUCIO TAN; Pres. MICHAEL TAN.

TKC Steel Corpn: Unit 3C, Zone 4, 3rd Floor, Corinthian Plaza, 121 Paseo de Roxas, Legaspi Village, Makati City, 1227 Metro Manila; tel. (2) 8640734; fax (2) 8933702; e-mail freddie_gamboa@tkcsteel.com; internet www.tkcsteel.com; f. 1996; fmrly SQL Wizard Inc; manufacture and sale of steel products; cap. and res 2,679.4m., revenue 2,493.2m. (2009); Chair. BEN TIU; Pres. ANTHONY DIZON.

Universal Robina Corpn: POB 13879, Ortigas Center, Pasig City, Metro Manila; tel. (2) 6337631; fax (2) 6345276; e-mail JGSIR@JGSummit.net; internet www2.urc.com.ph; f. 1954; mfr of snacks, chocolates, candies, biscuits, pasta and ice cream; cap. and res 35,913.2m., sales 50,452.9m. (2008/09); Chair. and CEO JAMES L. GO, Jr; Pres. LANCE Y. GOKONGWEI; 8,938 employees.

Victorias Milling Co Inc: POB 71, Negros Occidental, 6119 Victorias City; tel. and fax (34) 3993378; internet www.victoriasmilling.com; f. 1919; sugar mfrs and refiners, agribusiness, engineering; cap. and res –704.2m., revenue 3,106.9m. (2008/09); Chair. OMAR BYRON MIER; Pres. HUBERT TUBIO.

Vista Land and Lifescapes Inc: 15th Floor, Tower 1, The Enterprise Center, cnr Ayala Ave and Paseo de Roxas Ave, Legaspi Village, Makati City, 1226 Metro Manila; tel. (2) 8872264; fax (2) 8894690; e-mail inquiry@vistaland.com.ph; internet www.vistaland.com.ph; f. 2007; housing construction; cap. and res 35,624.6m., revenue 10,766.7m. (2009); Chair. MARCELINO MENDOZA; Pres. and CEO BENJAMARIE THERESE SERRANO.

Vitarich Corpn: MacArthur Highway, Abangan Sur Marilao, Bulacan; tel. and fax (2) 8433033; fax (2) 8430297; e-mail info@vitarich.com; internet www.vitarich.com; f. 1962; mfr of animal feeds; cap. and res 594.6m., revenue 2,630.7m. (2009); Chair. and CEO ROGELIO M. SARMIENTO.

TRADE UNION FEDERATIONS

Katipunang Manggagawang Pilipino (KMP-TUCP) (Trade Union Congress of the Philippines): TUCP Training Center Bldg, TUCP-PGEA Compound, Masaya St, cnr Maharlika St, Diliman, Quezon City, 1101 Metro Manila; tel. (2) 9247551; fax (2) 9219758; e-mail secrtucp@tucp.org.ph; internet www.tucp.org.ph; f. 1975; 1.0m. mems; Pres. DEMOCRITO T. MENDOZA; Gen. Sec. ERNESTO F. HERRERA; 39 affiliates, incl.:

Associated Labor Union for Metalworkers (ALU—METAL): TUCP-PGEA Compound, Diliman, Quezon City, 1101 Metro Manila; tel. (2) 9222575; fax (2) 9247553; e-mail alumla@info.com.ph; 29,700 mems; Pres. DEMOCRITO T. MENDOZA.

Associated Labor Union for Textile Workers (ALU—TEXTILE): TUCP-PGEA Compound, Elliptical Rd, Diliman, Quezon City, 1101 Metro Manila; tel. (2) 9222575; fax (2) 9247553; e-mail alumla@info.com.ph; 41,400 mems; Pres. DEMOCRITO T. MENDOZA.

Associated Labor Unions (ALU—TRANSPORT): 1763 Tomas Claudio St, Baclaran, Parañaque, Metro Manila; tel. (2) 8320634; fax (2) 8322392; 49,500 mems; Pres. ALEXANDER O. BARRIENTOS.

Associated Labor Unions—Visayas Mindanao Confederation of Trade Unions (ALU—VIMCONTU): ALU Bldg, Quezon Blvd, Port Area, Elliptical Rd, cnr Maharlika St, Diliman, Quezon City, 1101 Metro Manila; tel. (2) 9222185; fax (2) 9247553; e-mail alumla@info.com.ph; f. 1954; 350,000 mems; Pres. DEMOCRITO T. MENDOZA.

Associated Professional, Supervisory, Office and Technical Employees Union (APSOTEU): TUCP-PGEA Compound, Elliptical Rd, Diliman, Quezon City, 1101 Metro Manila; tel. (2) 9222575; fax (2) 9247553; e-mail alumla@info.com.ph; Pres. CECILIO T. SENO.

Association of Independent Unions of the Philippines: Vila Bldg, Mezzanine Floor, Epifanio de los Santos Ave, Cubao, Quezon City, Metro Manila; tel. (2) 9224652; Pres. EMMANUEL S. DURANTE.

Association of Trade Unions (ATU): Antwel Bldg, Room 1, 2nd Floor, Santa Ana, Port Area, Davao City; tel. (82) 2272394; 2,997 mems; Pres. JORGE ALEGARBES.

Confederation of Labor and Allied Social Services (CLASS): Doña Santiago Bldg, TUCP Suite 404, 1344 Taft Ave, Ermita, Metro Manila; tel. (2) 5240415; fax (2) 5266011; f. 1979; 4,579 mems; Pres. LEONARDO F. AGTING.

Federation of Agrarian and Industrial Toiling Hands (FAITH): Kalayaan Ave, cnr Masigla St, Diliman, Quezon City, Metro Manila; tel. (2) 9225244; 220,000 mems; Pres. RAYMUNDO YUMUL.

Federation of Consumers' Co-operatives in Negros Oriental (FEDCON): Bandera Bldg, Cervantes St, Dumaguete City; Chair. MEDARDO VILLALON.

Federation of Unions of Rizal (FUR): Suite 307, Buenavista Bldg, 3rd Floor, 82 Quirino Ave, cnr Rivera St, Parañaque City, Metro Manila; tel. and fax (2) 8320110; 10,853 mems; Pres. EDUARDO ASUNCION.

Lakas sa Industriya ng Kapatirang Haligi ng Alyansa (LIKHA): 32 Kabayanihan Rd Phase IIA, Karangalan Village, Pasig City, Metro Manila; tel. and fax (2) 6463234; e-mail jbvlikha@yahoo.com; Pres. JESUS B. VILLAMOR.

National Association of Free Trade Unions (NAFTU): Rm 404, San Luis Terrace, T. M. Kalaw St, Ermita, Metro Manila; tel. (2) 598705; 7,385 mems; Pres. JAIME RINCAL.

National Congress of Unions in the Sugar Industry of the Philippines (NACUSIP): 7431A Yakal St, Barangay San Antonio, Makati City, Metro Manila; e-mail nacusip@compass.com.ph; 32 affiliated unions and 57,424 mems; Nat. Pres. ZOILO V. DELA CRUZ, Jr.

National Mines and Allied Workers' Union (NAMAWU): Unit 201, A. Dunville Condominium, 1 Castilla St, cnr Valencio St, Quezon City, Metro Manila; tel. (2) 7265070; fax (2) 4155582; 13,233 mems; Pres. ROBERTO A. PADILLA.

Pambansang Kilusan ng Paggawa (KILUSAN): TUCP-PGEA Compound, Elliptical Rd, Diliman, Quezon City, 1101 Metro Manila; tel. (2) 9284651; 13,093 mems; Pres. AVELINO V. VALERIO; Sec.-Gen. IGMIDIO T. GANAGANA.

Philippine Agricultural, Commercial and Industrial Workers' Union (PACIWU): 5 7th St, Lacson, Bacolod City; fax (2) 7097967; Pres. ZOILO V. DELA CRUZ, Jr.

Philippine Federation of Labor (PFL): Metro Manila; fax (2) 5272838; 8,869 mems; Pres. ALEJANDRO C. VILLAVIZA.

Philippine Federation of Teachers' Organizations (PFTO): BSP Bldg, Rm 112, Concepcion St, Ermita, Metro Manila; tel. (2) 5275106; Pres. FEDERICO D. RICAFORT.

Philippine Government Employees' Association (PGEA): TUCP-PGEA Compound, Elliptical Rd, Diliman, Quezon City, Metro Manila; tel. (2) 9261573; fax (2) 6375764; e-mail eso_pgea@hotmail.com; f. 1945; 120,000 mems; Pres. ESPERANZA S. OCAMPO.

Philippine Integrated Industries Labor Union (PIILU): Mendoza Bldg, Rm 319, 3rd Floor, Pilar St, Zamboanga City; tel. (992) 2299; f. 1973; Pres. JOSE J. SUAN.

Philippine Labor Federation (PLF): ALU Bldg, Quezon Blvd, Port Area, Cebu City; tel. (32) 71219; fax (32) 97544; 15,462 mems; Pres. CRISPIN B. GASTARDO.

Philippine Seafarers' Union (PSU): TUCP-PGEA Compound, Elliptical Rd, cnr Maharlika Ave, Diliman, Quezon City, 1101 Metro Manila; tel. (2) 9222575; fax (2) 9247553; e-mail psumla@info.com.ph; internet www.psu.org.ph; f. 1984; 10,000 mems; Pres. DEMOCRITO T. MENDOZA; Gen. Sec. ERNESTO F. HERRERA.

Philippine Transport and General Workers' Organization (PTGWO—D): Cecilleville Bldg, 3rd Floor, Quezon Ave, Quezon City, Metro Manila; tel. (2) 4115811; fax (2) 4115812; f. 1953; 33,400 mems; Pres. VICTORINO F. BALAIS.

Port and General Workers' Federation (PGWF): Manila; Pres. FRANKLIN D. BUTCON.

Public Services Labor Independent Confederation (PSLINK): 15 Clarion Lily St, Congressional Ave, Quezon City, 1100 Metro Manila; tel. (2) 9244710; fax (2) 9281090; e-mail annie.geron@pslink.org; internet www.pslink.org; f. 1987; est. as Public Sector Labor Integrative Center; 35,108 mems; Pres. JARAH HAMJAH; Gen. Sec. ANNIE ENRIQUEZ-GERON.

United Sugar Farmers' Organization (USFO): SPCMA Annex Bldg, 3rd Floor, 1 Luzuriaga St, Bacolod City; Pres. BERNARDO M. REMO.

Workers' Alliance Trade Unions (WATU): Metro Manila; tel. (2) 9225093; fax (2) 975918; f. 1978; 25,000 mems; Pres. TEMISTOCLES S. DEJON, Sr.

INDEPENDENT LABOUR FEDERATIONS

The following organizations are not affiliated to the KMP-TUCP:

Associated Marine Officers and Seamen's Union of the Philippines (AMOSUP): Seaman's Centre, cnr Cabildo and Sta Potenciana Sts, Intramuros, Metro Manila; tel. (2) 5278491; fax (2) 5273534; e-mail s_center@amosup.org; internet www.amosup.org.ph; f. 1960; 23 affiliated unions with 55,000 mems; Pres. GREGORIO S. OCA.

Federation of Free Workers (FFW): FFW Bldg, 1943 Taft Ave, Malate, Metro Manila; tel. (2) 5219435; fax (2) 4006656; internet www.ffw.org.ph; f. 1950; affiliated to Int. Trade Union Confed. (ITUC); 300 affiliated local unions and 400,000 mems; Pres. ANTONIO ASPER.

Kilusang Mayo Uno (KMU): 63 Narra St, Barangay Claro, Quezon City, 1102 Metro Manila; tel. (2) 4210986; fax (2) 4210768; e-mail obrero@kilusangmayouno.org; internet www.kilusangmayouno.org; f. 1980; Chair. ELMER LABOG; Sec.-Gen. WILSON BALDONAZA.

Lakas ng Manggagawa Labor Center: Metro Manila; tel. and fax (2) 5280482; a grouping of 'independent' local unions; Chair. OSCAR M. ACERSON.

Manggagawa ng Komunikasyon sa Pilipinas (MKP): 22 Libertad St, Mandaluyong City, Metro Manila; tel. (2) 5313701; fax (2) 5312109; f. 1951; Pres. PETE PINLAC.

National Confederation of Labor: Suite 402, Carmen Bldg, Ronquillo St, cnr Evangelista St, Quiapo, Metro Manila; tel. and fax (2) 7334474; f. 1994 by fmr mems of Kilusang Mayo Uno; Pres. ANTONIO DIAZ.

Philippine Social Security Labor Union (PSSLU): Carmen Bldg, Suite 309, Ronquillo St, Quiapo, Metro Manila; f. 1954; Nat. Pres. ANTONIO B. DIAZ; Nat. Sec. OFELIA C. ALAVERA.

Samahang Manggagawang Pilipino (SMP-NATOW) (National Alliance of Teachers and Office Workers): 236 J. Romualdez St, Mandaluyong City, Metro Manila; tel. and fax 9176242569 (mobile); e-mail smpnatow@smpnatow.org; internet smpnatow.org; Pres. JOSEPH JOVELLANOS; Sec.-Gen. MILAGROS C. OGALINDA.

Solidarity Trade Conference for Progress: Rizal Ave, Dipolog City; tel. and fax (65) 2124303; Pres. NICOLAS E. SABANDAL.

Trade Unions of the Philippines and Allied Services (TUPAS): Med-dis Bldg, Suites 203–204, Solana St, cnr Real St, Intramuros, Metro Manila; tel. (2) 493449; affiliated to the World Fed. of Trade Unions; 280 affiliated unions and 75,000 mems; Nat. Pres. DIOSCORO O. NUÑEZ; Pres. VLADIMIR R. TUPAZ.

Transport

RAILWAYS

The railway network is confined mainly to the island of Luzon. Following a dispute over costs and other issues, work on a major programme of network improvements and expansion, which was to include an extension to the Clark Special Economic Zone and a branch line to Subic, was suspended in May 2011.

Light Rail Transit Authority (Metrorail): Adm. Bldg, LRTA Compound, Aurora Blvd, Pasay City, Metro Manila; tel. (2) 8530041; fax (2) 8316449; e-mail lrtamain@lrta.gov.ph; internet www.lrta.gov.ph; managed and operated by Light Rail Transit Authority (LRTA); electrically driven mass transit system; Line 1 (15 km, Baclaran to Monumento) began commercial operations in Dec. 1984; Line 2 (13.8 km, Santolan to Recto) became fully operational in Oct. 2004; Line 1 South Extension (12 km, Baclaran to Bacoot) planned; Administrator RAFAEL S. RODRIGUEZ.

Philippine National Railways: PNR Exec. Bldg, Mayhaligue St, Tondo, Metro Manila; tel. (2) 3190041; fax (2) 3190169; e-mail info@pnr.gov.ph; internet www.pnr.gov.ph; f. 1887; govt-owned; northern line services run from Manila to Caloocan, 6 km (although the track extends to San Fernando, La Union); southern line services run from Manila to Legaspi, Albay, 479 km; Chair. GERARD L. RABONZA; Gen. Man. MANUEL D. ANDAL.

ROADS

In 2009 there were 213,151 km of roads in the Philippines, of which 29,898 km were national roads and 183,253 km were covered by provincial, city, municipal and barangay roads; an estimated 53,596 km of the total network were paved. Bus services provided the most widely used form of inland transport.

Department of Public Works and Highways: Bonifacio Dr., Port Area, Metro Manila; tel. (2) 3043300; e-mail singson.rogelio@dpwh.gov.ph; internet www.dpwh.gov.ph; responsible for the construction and maintenance of roads and bridges; Sec. ROGELIO L. SINGSON.

Land Transportation Franchising and Regulatory Board: East Ave, Diliman, Quezon City, Metro Manila; tel. (2) 9257191; fax (2) 4262515; e-mail officeofthechairman@ltfrb.gov.ph; internet www.ltfrb.gov.ph; f. 1987; Chair. DANTE M. LANTIN.

Land Transportation Office (LTO): East Ave, Quezon City, 1100 Metro Manila; tel. (2) 9219072; fax (2) 9219071; e-mail ltombox@lto.gov.ph; internet www.lto.gov.ph; f. 1987; plans, formulates and implements land transport rules, regulations and safety measures;

registration of motor vehicles; issues licences; Asst Sec. VIRGINIA TORRES; Exec. Dir RICARDO E. ALFONSO, Jr.

SHIPPING

In 2000 there were 102 national and municipal ports, 20 baseports, 58 terminal ports and 270 private ports. The eight major ports are Manila, Cebu, Iloilo, Cagayan de Oro, Zamboanga, General Santos, Polloc and Davao.

Pangasiwaan ng Daungan ng Pilipinas (Philippine Ports Authority): Bonifacio Dr., South Harbour, Port Area, 1018 Metro Manila; tel. (2) 5274856; fax (2) 5274853; e-mail info@ppa.com.ph; internet www.ppa.com.ph; f. 1977; supervises all ports within the Philippine Ports Authority port system; Gen. Man. JUAN C. SANTA ANA.

Philippine Shippers' Bureau (PSB): Trade and Industry Bldg, 2nd Floor, 361 Sen. Gil J. Puyat Ave, Makati City, Metro Manila; tel. and fax (2) 7513304; fax (2) 7513305; e-mail psb@dti.gov.ph; shipping facilitator for international and domestic trade; promotes and protects the interests of shippers, exporters, importers and domestic traders; Dir PEDRO VICENTE C. MENDOZA.

Domestic Lines

Aboitiz Transport System Corpn: 12th Floor, Times Plaza Bldg, United Nations Ave, cnr Taft Ave, Ermita, Metro Manila; tel. (2) 5287171; e-mail corporate_communications@atsc.com.ph; internet www.atsc.com.ph; f. 1996 following the merger of William Lines, Aboitiz Shipping and Carlos A. Gothong Lines; fmrly WG & A Philippines; passenger and cargo inter-island services; Chair. JON RAMON ABOITIZ; Pres. ENRIQUE M. ABOITIZ.

Albar Shipping and Trading Corpn: 2649 Molave St, cnr East Service Rd, United Hills Village, Parañaque, 1713 Metro Manila; tel. (2) 8232391; fax (2) 8233046; e-mail info@albargroup.com.ph; internet www.albargroup.com.ph; f. 1974; manning agency (maritime), trading, ship husbanding; Chair. AKIRA S. KATO; Pres. JOSE ALBAR G. KATO.

Candano Shipping Lines, Inc: Victoria Bldg, 6th Floor, 429 United Nations Ave, Ermita, 2802 Metro Manila; tel. (2) 5238051; fax (2) 5211309; f. 1953; inter-island and Far East chartering, cargo shipping; Pres. and Gen. Man. TRINIDAD CANDANO.

Delsan Transport Lines Inc: Magsaysay Center Bldg, 520 T. M. Kalaw St, Ermita, Metro Manila; tel. (2) 5219172; fax (2) 2889331; Pres. VICENTE A. SANDOVAL; Gen. Man. CARLOS A. BUENAFE.

Eastern Shipping Lines, Inc: ESL Bldg, 54 Anda Circle, Port Area, POB 4253, 2803 Metro Manila; tel. (2) 5277841; fax (2) 5273006; e-mail eastship@skyinet.net; f. 1957; services to Japan; Pres. ERWIN L. CHIONGBIAN; Exec. Vice-Pres. ROY L. CHIONGBIAN.

Loadstar Shipping Co Inc: Loadstar Bldg, 1294 Romualdez St, Paco, 1007 Metro Manila; tel. (2) 5238381; fax (2) 5218061; Pres. and Gen. Man. TEODORO G. BERNARDINO.

Lorenzo Shipping Corpn: 20th Floor, Times Plaza Bldg, United Nations Ave, cnr Taft Ave, Ermita, Metro Manila; tel. (2) 5672180; fax (2) 5672030; internet www.lorenzoshipping.com; Pres. ROBERTO UMALI.

Luzteveco (Luzon Stevedoring Corpn): Magsaysay Bldg, 520 T. M. Kalaw St, Ermita, Metro Manila; f. 1909; two brs; freight-forwarding, air cargo, world-wide shipping, broking, stevedoring, salvage, chartering and oil-drilling support services; Pres. JOVINO G. LORENZO; Vice-Pres. RODOLFO B. SANTIAGO.

National Shipping Corpn of the Philippines: Metro Manila; tel. (2) 473631; fax (2) 5300169; services to Hong Kong, Taiwan, Korea, USA; Pres. TONY CHOW.

Negros Navigation Co Inc: Pier 2, North Harbor, Metro Manila; tel. and fax (2) 5548777; fax (2) 5548721; e-mail gcabalo@negrosnavigation.ph; internet www.negrosnavigation.ph; Chair. and CEO SULFICIO O. TAGUD.

Philippine Pacific Ocean Lines Inc: Delgado Bldg, Bonifacio Drive, Port Area, POB 184, Metro Manila; tel. (2) 478541; Vice-Pres. C. P. CARANDANG.

Philippine President Lines, Inc: PPL Bldg, 1000–1046 United Nations Ave, POB 4248, Metro Manila; tel. (2) 5249011; fax (2) 5251308; trading world-wide; Chair. EMILIO T. YAP; Pres. ENRIQUE C. YAP.

Sulpicio Lines, Inc: Don Sulpicio Go Bldg, Sulpicio Go St, Reclamation Area, POB 137, 6000 Cebu City; tel. (32) 2325361; fax (32) 2321216; internet www.sulpiciolines.com; Chair. ENRIQUE S. GO; Man. Dir CARLOS S. GO.

Transocean Transport Corpn: Magsaysay Bldg, 8th Floor, 520 T. M. Kalaw St, Ermita, POB 21, Metro Manila; tel. (2) 506611; Pres. and Gen. Man. MIGUEL A. MAGSAYSAY; Vice-Pres. EDUARDO U. MANESE.

United Philippine Lines, Inc: Plaza Santiago Bldg, Santa Clara St, Intramuros, POB 127, Metro Manila; tel. (2) 5277491; fax (2) 3380087; e-mail mailadmin@uplines.net; internet www.uplines.net; services world-wide; Pres. FERNANDO V. LISING.

CIVIL AVIATION

In addition to the international airports in Metro Manila (Ninoy Aquino International Airport), Cebu (Mactan International Airport), Angeles City (Clark International Airport) and Olongapo City (Subic Bay International Airport), there are five alternative international airports: Laoag City, Ilocos Norte; Davao City; Zamboanga City; Gen. Santos (Tambler) City; and Puerto Princesa City, Palawan. There are also numerous domestic and private airports. By late 2006 the development of new airports in Silay City, Iloilo City and Bohol was under way.

Civil Aviation Authority: MIA Rd, Pasay City, Metro Manila; tel. (2) 8799104; fax (2) 8340143; e-mail information@mis.caap.gov.ph; internet www.caap.gov.ph; implements govt policies for the development and operation of a safe and efficient aviation network; Dir-Gen. ALFONSO G. CUSI.

Civil Aeronautics Board: CAB Bldg, Old MIA Rd, Pasay City, Metro Manila; tel. (2) 8537259; fax (2) 8516911; e-mail tmanalac@cab.gov.ph; internet cab.gov.ph; exercises general supervision and regulation of, and jurisdiction and control over, air carriers, their equipment facilities and franchise; Exec. Dir LEANDRO R. MENDOZA.

Manila International Airport Authority (MIAA): Metro Manila; tel. (2) 8322938; fax (2) 8331180; e-mail gm@miaa.gov.ph; internet www.miaa.gov.ph; Gen. Man. Maj.-Gen. (retd) JOSE ANGEL HONRADO.

Air Philippines: R1 Hangar, APC Gate 1, Andrews Ave, Nichols, Pasay City, Metro Manila; tel. (2) 8517601; fax (2) 8517922; e-mail info@airphilippines.com.ph; internet www.airphils.com; f. 1995; domestic and regional services; Chair. LUCIO TAN; Pres. DAVID LIM.

Cebu Pacific Air: Airlines Operations Center Bldg, Manila Domestic Airport Complex, Pasay City, Metro Manila; tel. (2) 2905271; fax (2) 8512871; e-mail customerservice@cebupacificair.com; internet www.cebupacificair.com; f. 1995; domestic and international services; Chair. RICARDO J. ROMULO; Pres. and CEO LANCE Y. GOKONGWEI.

Grand Air: Mercure Hotel, Philippines Village Airport Compound, 8th Floor, Pasay City, 1300 Metro Manila; tel. (2) 8313001; fax (2) 8917682; f. 1994; Pres. REBECCA PANLILI.

Philippine Airlines Inc (PAL): PNB Financial Center, Pres. Diosdado Macapagal Ave, CCP Complex, Pasay City, Metro Manila; tel. (2) 5562220; fax (2) 5562221; e-mail webmgr@pal.com.ph; internet www.philippineairlines.com; f. 1941; in Jan. 1992 67% of PAL was transferred to the private sector; operates domestic, regional and international services to destinations in the Far East, Australasia, the Middle East, the USA and Canada; Chair. and CEO LUCIO TAN; Pres. JAIME J. BAUTISTA.

Spirit of Manila Airlines: Roxas Sea Front Garden, Roxas Blvd, cnr Ortigas St, Pasay City; tel. (2) 7844888; fax (2) 5567377; e-mail sales@spiritofmanilaairlines.com; internet www.spiritofmanilaairlines.com; regional and international passenger services from Manila to destinations in Asia and Middle East; Pres. and CEO BASILIO P. REYES.

Zest Airways Inc: General Aviation Area, Pasay City; e-mail customerrelations@zestair.com.ph; internet www.zestair.com.ph; f. 1995; est. as Asian Spirit; following takeover by AMY Holdings, renamed as above 2008; operates services to about 20 domestic destinations, and international services to the Republic of Korea (South Korea); three aircraft; Chair. DONALD DEE; Pres. and CEO ALFREDO YAO.

Tourism

Although intermittently affected by political unrest, tourism remains an important sector of the economy. In 2009 visitor arrivals totalled 3,017,099 (including 197,921 Filipinos permanently resident overseas), compared with 3,139,422 in the previous year. According to provisional figures, tourist receipts, excluding passenger transport, totalled US $2,329m. in 2009.

Philippine Convention and Visitors' Corpn: Legaspi Towers, 4th Floor, 300 Roxas Blvd, 1004 Metro Manila; tel. (2) 5259318; fax (2) 5253314; e-mail pcvcnet@dotpcvc.gov.ph; internet www.dotpcvc.gov.ph; Chair. JOSEPH H. DURANO; Exec. Dir DANIEL G. CORPUZ.

Philippine Tourism Authority: Department of Tourism Bldg, T. M. Kalaw St, Teodoro F. Valencia Circle, Ermita, 1000 Metro Manila; tel. (2) 5247141; fax (2) 5218113; e-mail info@philtourism.gov.ph; internet www.philtourism.com; Gen. Man. and CEO MARK T. LAPID.

Defence

As assessed at November 2010, the total strength of the armed forces was estimated at 125,000: army 86,000, navy an estimated 24,000 (including 8,300 Marines), air force an estimated 15,000. Active paramilitary forces, comprising the Philippine National Police (under the Department of Interior and Local Government), numbered 40,500. The Citizen Armed Forces Geographical Units (CAFGU), which replaced the civil home defence force, numbered about 50,000. Military service is voluntary.

Defence Expenditure: Budgeted at an estimated 105,000m. pesos for 2011.

Chief of Staff of the Armed Forces: Lt-Gen. Eduardo Oban.

Chief of Staff (Army): Lt-Gen. Arturo Ortiz.

Chief of Staff (Navy): Rear-Adm. Alexander Pama.

Chief of Staff (Air Force): Lt-Gen. Oscar Rabena.

Education

The 1987 Constitution commits the Government to provide free elementary and high school education; elementary education is compulsory. The organization of education is the responsibility of the Department of Education.

There are both public and private schools. The private schools are either sectarian or non-sectarian. Education in the Philippines is divided into four stages: pre-school (from the age of three); elementary school, which begins at seven years of age and lasts for six years; secondary or high school, which begins at 13 and lasts for five years (extended in 1994 from four years); and higher education, normally lasting four years. The public schools offer a general secondary curriculum and there are private schools that offer more specialized training courses. There is a common general curriculum for all students in the first and second years and more varied curricula in the third and fourth years leading to either college or technical vocational courses.

There were 44,846 pre-primary and primary schools in 2009/10. In that year there were 1,474,644 pupils enrolled at pre-primary schools and 13,934,172 pupils enrolled at primary schools. Total enrolment at pre-primary level in 2007/08 included 39% (males 39%; females 38%) of children in the relevant age-group. In the same year 92% (males 91%; females 93%) of all children in the relevant age-group were enrolled at primary schools. In 2009/10 there were a total of 10,384 secondary schools, at which 6,806,079 pupils were enrolled. In 2007/08 enrolment at secondary level included 61% of children in the relevant age group(males 55.0%; females 66.0%). In 2009/10 there were a total of 1,619 tertiary level institutions, at which 2,402,315 pupils were enrolled. In 2005/06 total enrolment at tertiary level was equivalent to 28.0% (males 25%; females 32%) of the relevant age-group. Instruction is in both English and Filipino at elementary level, and English is the usual medium at the secondary and tertiary levels. The 2005 budget allocated 135,470m. pesos (15.1% of total national expenditure) to education, culture and training.

Bibliography

General

Abueva, Jose V. (Ed.). *The Making of the Filipino Nation and Republic.* Metro Manila, University of the Philippines Press, 1999.

Barreveld, Dirk J. *Terrorism in the Philippines: The Bloody Trail of Abu Sayyaf, Bin Laden's East Asian Connection.* San Jose, CA, Writers Club Press, 2002.

Bauzon, Kenneth E. *Islam in the Philippines.* Abingdon, Routledge, 2009.

Billig, Michael S. *Barons, Brokers and Buyers: The Institutions and Cultures of Philippine Sugar.* Honolulu, HI, University of Hawaii Press, 2002.

Bryant, Raymond L. *Nongovernmental Organizations in Environmental Struggles: Politics and the Making of Moral Capital in the Philippines.* New Haven, CT, Yale University Press, 2005.

Gonzalez, Joaquin Jay. *Filipino American Faith in Action: Immigration, Religion, and Civic Engagement.* New York, New York University Press, 2009.

Guevarra, Anna Romina. *Marketing Dreams, Manufacturing Heroes: The Transnational Labor Brokering of Filipino Workers.* Piscataway, NJ, Rutgers University Press, 2009.

Milligan, Jeffrey Ayala. *Islamic Identity, Postcoloniality, and Educational Policy: Schooling and Ethno-Religious Conflict in the Southern Philippines.* London, Palgrave Macmillan, 2005.

Moreno, Antonio F. *Church, State, and Civil Society in Post-Authoritarian Philippines: Narratives of Engaged Citizenship.* Quezon City, Ateneo de Manila University Press, 2006.

Umehara, Hiromitsu, and Bautista, Germelino M. *Communities at the Margins: Reflections on Social, Economic and Environmental Change in the Philippines.* Quezon City, Ateneo de Manila University Press, 2005.

History

Abinales, Patricio N. *Orthodoxy and History in the Muslim-Mindanao Narrative.* Quezon City, Ateneo de Manila University Press, 2009.

Arcilla, Jose S. *Sueldo and Bayad: Essays on Philippine Lifestyle.* Honolulu, HI, University of Hawaii Press, 2009.

Arnold, James R. *The Moro War: How America Battled a Muslim Insurgency in the Philippine Jungle, 1902-1913.* London, Bloomsbury Publishing, 2011.

Bankoff, Greg. *Cultures of Disaster: Society and Natural Hazards in the Philippines.* London, RoutledgeCurzon, 2002.

Bankoff, Greg, and Weekley, Kathleen. *Post-Colonial National Identity in the Philippines: Celebrating the Centennial of Independence.* London, Ashgate Publishing Company, 2002.

Barnes, Mark. *The Spanish–American War and Philippine Insurrection, 1898–1902: An Annotated Bibliography.* Abingdon, Routledge, 2010.

Blanco, John D. *Frontier Constitutions: Christianity and Colonial Empire in the Nineteenth-Century Philippines.* Berkeley, CA, University of California Press, 2009.

Co, Edna C. A., Tigno, Jorge V., Lao, Maria Elissa Jayne, and Jayo, Margarita A. *Philippine Democracy Assessment: Free and Fair Elections and the Democratic Role of Political Parties.* Honolulu, HI, University of Hawaii Press, 2006.

Dery, Luis Camara. *Pestilence in the Philippines: A Social History of the Filipino People, 1571-1800.* Quezon City, New Day, 2006.

Edgerton, Ronald K. *People of the Middle Ground: A Century of Conflict and Central Mindanao, 1880-1980s.* Quezon City, Ateneo de Manila University Press, 2009.

Go, Julian. *American Empire and the Politics of Meaning: Elite Political Cultures in the Philippines and Puerto Rico During US Colonialism.* Durham, NC, Duke University Press, 2008.

Go, Julian, and Foster, Anne. *The American Colonial State in the Philippines.* Durham, NC, Duke University Press, 2003.

Guillermo, Artemio R. *Historical Dictionary of the Philippines.* Lanham, MD, Rowman and Littlefield Publishers, 2005.

Hamilton-Paterson, James. *America's Boy: The Rise and Fall of Ferdinand Marcos and Other Misadventures of US Colonialism in the Philippines.* New York, Henry Holt, 1999.

Harris, Susan K. *God's Arbiters: Americans and the Philippines, 1898-1902.* New York, Oxford University Press, 2011.

Juan, E. San. *US Imperialism and Revolution in the Philippines.* Basingstoke, Palgrave Macmillan, 2007.

Lico, Gerard. *Edifice Complex: Power, Myth and Marcos State Architecture.* Honolulu, HI, University of Hawaii Press, 2003.

Linn, Brian MacAllister. *The Philippine War, 1899–1902.* Lawrence, KS, University Press of Kansas, 2002.

McFerson, Hazel M. (Ed.). *Mixed Blessing: the Impact of the American Colonial Experiences on Politics and Society in the Philippines (Contributions in Comparative Colonial Studies).* Westport, CT, Greenwood Publishing, 2002.

Muslim, M. *The Moro Armed Struggle in the Philippines.* Marawi City, Mindanao State University, 1994.

Nadeau, Kathleen M. *The History of the Philippines.* Westport, CT, Greenwood Press, 2008.

Newson, Linda A. *Conquest and Pestilence in the Early Spanish Philippines.* Honolulu, HI, University of Hawaii Press, 2009.

Quibuyen, Floro C. *A Nation Aborted: Rizal, American Hegemony and Philippine Nationalism.* Quezon City, Ateneo de Manila University Press, 2009.

Reid, Robert H., and Guerrero, Eileen. *Corazon Aquino and the Brushfire Revolution*. Baton Rouge, LA, Louisiana State University Press, 1996.

Rood, Steven. *Forging Sustainable Peace in Mindanao: The Role of Civil Society*. Singapore, Institute of Southeast Asian Studies, 2005.

Salman, Michael. *The Embarrassment of Slavery: Controversies over Bondage and Nationalism in the American Colonial Philippines*. Berkeley, CA, University of California Press, 2001.

San Juan, Jr, Epifanio. *U.S. Imperialism and Revolution in the Philippines*. Basingstoke, Palgrave Macmillan, 2008.

Shaw, Angel V., and Francia, Luis H. (Eds). *Vestiges of War: the Philippine-American War and the Aftermath of an Imperial Dream 1899–1999*. New York, New York University Press, 2002.

Simbulan, Dante C. *The Modern Principalia: The Historical Evolution of the Philippine Ruling Oligarchy*. Honolulu, HI, University of Hawaii Press, 2006.

Tan, Samuel K. *A History of the Philippines*. Manila, University of the Philippines, 2009.

Wilson, Andrew R. *Ambition and Identity: Chinese Merchant Elites in Colonial Manila, 1880–1916*. Honolulu, HI, University of Hawaii Press, 2004.

Economy

Balisacan, Arsenio M., and Hill, Hal (Eds). *Philippine Economy: Development, Policies and Challenges*. Oxford, Oxford University Press, 2002.

Canlas, Dante B., Khan, Muhammad E., and Zhuang Juzhong (Eds). *Diagnosing the Philippine Economy*. London, Anthem Press, 2009.

Carlos Salazar, Lorraine. *Getting a Dial Tone: Telecommunications Liberalisation in Malaysia and the Philippines*. Singapore, Institute of Southeast Asian Studies, 2007.

Corpuz, O. D. *An Economic History of the Philippines*. Quezon City, University of the Philippines Press, 1999.

Eaton, Kent. *Politicians and Economic Reform in New Democracies: Argentina and the Philippines in the 1990s*. Philadelphia, PA, University of Pennsylvania Press, 2002.

Estanislao, Jesus P. *The Philippine Economy: An Emerging Asian Tiger*. Singapore, Institute of Southeast Asian Studies, 1997.

International Alert. *Breaking the Links Between Economics and Conflict in Mindanao*. London, 2003.

Krinks, P. *The Economy of the Philippines*. London, RoutledgeCurzon, 2002.

McKay, Steven C. *Satanic Mills or Silicon Islands?: The Politics of High-Tech Production in the Philippines*. Ithaca, NY, Cornell University Press, 2006.

Rola, Agnes C. *An Upland Community in Transition: Institutional Innovations for Sustainable Development in Rural Philippines*. Singapore, Institute of Southeast Asian Studies, 2011.

Tyner, James A. *Made in the Philippines*. London, RoutledgeCurzon, 2003.

The Philippines: Mobilities, Identities, Globalization. Abingdon, Routledge, 2008.

UN Development Programme. *Energy and Poverty in the Philippines: Challenges and the Way Forward*. UNDP, New York, 2008.

Van Den Top, Gerhard. *The Social Dynamics of Deforestation in the Philippines: Actions, Options and Motivations*. Copenhagen, Nordic Institute of Asian Studies, 2002.

Walden, Bello, Docena, Herbert, and de Guzman, Marissa. *The Anti-Development State: The Political Economy of Permanent Crisis in the Philippines*. London, Zed Books, 2005.

Politics and Government

Abinales, P. (Ed.). *The Revolution Falters: The Left in Philippine Politics after 1986*. Ithaca, NY, Cornell University Press, 1996.

Making Mindanao: Cotabato and Davao in the Formation of the Philippine Nation-State. Quezon City, Ateneo de Manila University Press, 2001.

Abinales, Patricio N., and Amoroso, Donna J. *State and Society in the Philippines*. Lanham, MD, Rowman and Littlefield Publishers, 2005.

Alejo, Albert E. *Generating Energies in Mount Apo: Cultural Politics in a Contested Environment*. Honolulu, HI, University of Hawaii Press, 2001.

Balisacan, Arsenio M., and Hill, Hal (Eds). *The Dynamics of Regional Development: The Philippines in East Asia*. Cheltenham, Edward Elgar Publishing, 2007.

Banlaoi, Rommel. *Philippine Security in the Age of Terror: National, Regional and Global Challenges in the Post-9/11 World*. Abingdon, Routledge, 2009.

Bernas, Joaquin G. *A Living Constitution: The Troubled Arroyo Presidency*. Quezon City, Ateneo de Manila University Press, 2007.

Bonner, Raymond. *Waltzing with a Dictator: The Marcoses and the Making of American Policy*. New York, Times Books, 1987.

Coronel, Sheila S. (Ed.). *Pork and Other Perks*. Manila, Philippine Center for Investigative Journalism, 1998.

EDSA 2: A Nation in Revolt. Manila, AsiaPix/Anvil, 2001.

Investigating Estrada: Millions, Mansions and Mysteries. Manila, Philippine Centre for Investigative Journalism, 2001.

Delmendo, Sharon. *The Star-Entangled Banner: One Hundred Years of America in the Philippines*. Piscataway, NJ, Rutgers University Press, 2004.

Enriquez, Elizabeth L. *Appropriation of Colonial Broadcasting: A History of Early Radio in the Philippines, 1922–1946*. Quezon City, University of the Philippines Press, 2009.

Franco, Jennifer C., and Kerkvliet, B. J. T. *Elections and Democratization in the Philippines (Comparative Studies of Democratization)*. New York, Garland Publishing, 2001.

Gutierrez, Edgardo V., Gutierrez, Ricardo V., and Tiongson, Jr, Antonio T. (Eds). *Positively No Filipinos Allowed: Building Communities and Discourse*. Philadelphia, PA, Temple University Press, 2006.

Hedman, Eva-Lotta. *In the Name of Civil Society: From Free Election Movements to People Power in the Philippines*. Honolulu, HI, University of Hawaii Press, 2005.

Hedman, Eva-Lotta, and Sidel, John T. (Eds). *Philippine Politics and Society in the Twentieth Century: Colonial Legacies, Post-Colonial Trajectories*. London, Routledge, 2000.

Hodder, Rupert. *Between Two Worlds—Society, Politics and Business in the Philippines*. London, Curzon Press, 2002.

Nadeau, Kathleen M. *Liberation Theology in the Philippines: Faith in a Revolution*. Westport, CT, Praeger Publications, 2001.

Pesigan, Guillermo, and MacDonald, Charles J. (Eds). *Old Ties and New Solidarities: Studies on Philippine Communities*. Honolulu, HI, University of Hawaii Press, 2001.

Philippine Center for Investigative Journalism. *People Power Uli! A Scrapbook About EDSA 2*. Manila, 2001.

Rasul, Amina (Ed.). *Muslim Perspectives on the Mindanao Conflict: The Road to Peace and Reconciliation*. Makati City, AIM Policy Center, Asian Institute of Management, 2003.

Rodil, B. R. *The Minoritization of the Indigenous Communities of Mindanao and the Sulu Archipelago*. Davao City, Alternate Forum for Research in Mindanao, 2004.

Severino, Rodolfo C. *Where in the World is the Philippines? Debating Its National Territory*. Singapore, Institute of Southeast Asian Studies, 2010.

Severino, Rodolfo C., and Carlos Salazar, Lorraine (Eds). *Whither the Philippines in the 21st Century?* Singapore, Institute of Southeast Asian Studies, 2007.

Tadiar, Neferti Xina M. *Fantasy Production: Sexual Economies and Other Philippine Consequences for the New World Order*. Hong Kong, Hong Kong University Press, 2003.

Tordesillas, Ellen, and Hutchinson, Greg. *Hot Money, Warm Bodies: The Downfall of Philippine President Joseph Estrada*. Manila, Anvil, 2001.

Vitug, Marites Danguilan, and Gloria, Glenda. *Under the Crescent Moon: Rebellion in Mindanao*. Manila, Ateneo Center for Social Policy and Public Affairs/Institute for Popular Democracy, 2000.

Williams, Udo Moses. *The Philippine Presidency*. Philadelphia, PA, Xlibris Corpn, 2007.

SINGAPORE

Physical and Social Geography

HARVEY DEMAINE

The Republic of Singapore is an insular territory, with an area of 710.3 sq km (274.2 sq miles), lying to the south of the Malay peninsula, to which it is joined by a causeway, 1.2 km long, carrying a road, a railway and a water pipeline across the intervening Straits of Johor. Singapore Island, which is situated less than 1.5° north of the Equator, occupies a focal position at the turning-point on the shortest sea-route from the Indian Ocean to the South China Sea.

PHYSICAL FEATURES

The mainly granitic core of the island, which rises in a few places to summits of over 100 m, is surrounded by lower land, much of it marshy, though large areas are now intensively cultivated. Singapore City has grown up on the firmer ground adjacent to the Mt Faber ridge, the foreshore of which provides deep water anchorage in the lee of two small offshore islands, Pulau Sentosa and Pulau Brani. In recent years suburban growth has been rapid towards the north and along the eastern foreshore, and since 1961 a large expanse of mangrove swamp to the west of the dock area has been reclaimed to provide industrial estates for the Jurong Town Corporation.

The climate, like that of the Malay peninsula, is hot and humid, with no clearly defined seasons, although February is usually the sunniest month and December often the least sunny. Rainfall averages 2,367 mm annually, and the average daytime temperature is 26.6°C, decreasing to an average minimum of 23.7°C at night.

POPULATION

According to the census of 30 June 2000, the population (including non-residents) was 4,017,733. Of the total population (excluding non-residents) at the 2000 census, 76.8% were Chinese, 13.9% Malay and 7.9% Indian. In 2009 the birth rate was estimated at 9.9 per 1,000 (compared with 18.2 in 1990) and the death rate at 4.3 per 1,000. At mid-2010 the population was officially estimated at 5,076,700, giving a population density of 7,147.3 per sq km, one of the highest in the world.

There are four official languages: Chinese (in 2000, as a first language, Mandarin was spoken by 35% of the population, Chinese dialects by 24%), English (used by 23% in 2000), Malay (14%) and Tamil (3%).

History

C. M. TURNBULL

Revised by MICHAEL D. BARR

ORIGINS AND EARLY DEVELOPMENT

The island of Singapore has a record of human habitation going back possibly some 2,000 years, but its early history is obscure, and the very name of Singapura (Sanskrit for 'Lion City') is unexplained, since the lion is not native to the region. The original seaport, Temasek, may have been part of the great Sumatran maritime empire of Srivijaya, which disintegrated in the 13th century. The earliest historical chronicle, the *Malay Annals*, described 14th-century Temasek as a prosperous trading centre. At about this time it became known as Singapura. However, the island's prosperity brought it into the sphere of rival expanding empires: Thai Ayudhya and Javanese Majapahit. Attacked by both and torn further by internal strife, the city was destroyed in the final years of the 14th century. The ruler and his followers fled to found a more auspicious settlement at Melaka (Malacca), which became the centre of a renowned Empire.

Following this violent episode, Singapore remained almost deserted for more than 400 years, home of a few tribes of *orang laut* (boat people), who lived by fishing, piracy and petty trading and owed allegiance to the Malay Riau-Johor Empire, centred nearby in the Riau archipelago. Soon all that remained of the old city were a few crumbling ramparts and the neglected graves of its former rulers on the hill above the Singapore river. Riau itself was a prosperous emporium for regional commerce, but Singapore merely battened on the piratical fringe of that trade.

In the early 19th century the Straits of Melaka and the southern part of the Malay peninsula assumed a new commercial and strategic importance when Britain's East India Co sought bases to protect its China trade and to challenge the Dutch commercial monopoly in the Malay peninsula and archipelago. In 1819 Sir Stamford Raffles, an official of the East India Co, obtained permission, from the Sultan of Johor and the local chief, to establish a trading post at the mouth of the Singapore river, and five years later the two Malay chiefs ceded the island in perpetuity to the East India Co and its successors, in return for payments of money and for pensions.

The Straits Settlements

In 1826 the East India Co united Singapore with its two other dependencies on the west coast of the Malay peninsula: Pinang (Penang), acquired in 1786, and Melaka, ceded by the Dutch in 1824. These scattered territories remained one political entity, known as the Straits Settlements, for the next 120 years. Under the protection of the East India Co, the new port, conveniently situated and free from customs duties or restrictions, attracted traders and settlers from all over the region. They came first from the nearby ports of Riau, Melaka and Pinang, but soon others began to arrive from further afield in the Indonesian archipelago, and from Thailand, Indo-China, Burma (now Myanmar), Borneo, the Philippines, India, China and Europe.

In 1833 the East India Co lost its monopoly of the China trade, after which it had no further use for the Straits Settlements. It continued to administer them, but on a severely constrained budget. The very laxness of government and freedom from taxation attracted further steady immigration and trade, but the European merchants of Singapore became increasingly dissatisfied with administrative inefficiency and the lack of representative institutions. In 1857 Singapore's merchants petitioned that the Straits Settlements be separated from India and brought under direct British rule, and in 1867 the Straits Settlements became a crown colony, with a constitution that remained basically unchanged until the Second World War. A Governor, appointed by the British Government, ruled with the assistance of an Executive and a Legislative Council, the latter comprising a majority of officials with unofficial members nominated by the Governor. Over the years the number of 'unofficials' and of Asian councillors increased, so that by the 1920s there were equal numbers of officials and 'unofficials' on the Legislative Council, with the Governor having the casting vote. By that time some 'unofficials' were nominated by the chambers of commerce but there were no elected members as such.

The transfer of the Straits Settlements to direct colonial rule was soon followed by two events which gave a new impetus to Singapore's development: the opening of the Suez Canal in 1869, and the first treaties of protection made between the British and rulers of the Malay states in 1874. With the opening of the Suez Canal, the India–Melaka Straits route, on which Singapore was situated in a dominating position, became the main highway from Europe to the Far East. The 1874 treaties with the west coast Malay states of Perak, Selangor and Sungei Ujong marked the first stage in bringing all the Malay states under British protection. Singapore provided a political focal point as the base of the Governor of the Straits Settlements Colony, who was also High Commissioner of the Malay States and the chief authority for the three British-protected Borneo states of Sarawak, North Borneo and Brunei.

In the late 19th and early 20th century Singapore became the commercial and financial centre for the whole region. Growing Western interests in South-East Asia, the increasing use of steamships (which from the 1880s replaced sailing ships as the main carriers) and the development of telegraphs all put Singapore, with its fine natural sheltered harbour, at the hub of international trade in South-East Asia. It became a vital link in the chain of British ports which stretched from Gibraltar, through the Mediterranean Sea and the Indian Ocean, to the Far East.

The 60 years from the opening of the Suez Canal to the onset of the Great Depression in 1929 were a time of almost unbroken peace, steady economic expansion and population growth in Singapore. A more sophisticated administration gradually brought the population within the jurisdiction of the Government and the law courts. In the early years the different immigrant groups lived in specified districts of the town, largely supervised by their own community leaders or *kapitans*. As early as 1827 the Chinese were the biggest single community in Singapore and by the beginning of the 20th century constituted three-quarters of the population, a proportion which has remained fairly constant since that time. Most Chinese came from the troubled Guangdong and Fujian Provinces of southern China, representing a variety of dialect groups, chiefly Fukien, Cantonese, Teochew, Hakka and, in the later years of the century, Hainanese. Most were young adult men who aimed to make money abroad and return to their native China, so that, well into the 20th century, the population was transitory and shifting, with very few women, children or old people. As the years passed more women came to Singapore, and a large number of immigrants settled permanently and raised families. By the early 20th century there was a sizeable Straits-born Asian community, who were British subjects and sometimes English-educated. Some Straits-born Asians collaborated with the colonial establishment as Legislative and Municipal Councillors or Justices of the Peace, while many others worked as clerks and assistants. In the 1930s the colonial regime created a Straits civil service, Straits legal service and Straits medical service, which offered the first openings to Asian British subjects in professional government work, but only at subordinate levels. All senior administrative and technical posts in Singapore were held by British European officials.

There was little interest in local politics. From the mid-1920s a Legislative Councillor, Tan Cheng Lock, began to urge elected representation on the Legislative Council for those who had made the Straits Settlements their home, but he found little backing even among his fellow Straits Chinese. There was no indigenous nationalist movement or desire for independence and any political interest was directed more to China or India.

Immigration reached a high point in 1927, when an all-time record of 360,000 Chinese landed in Singapore. However, the Great Depression of 1929–33 affected Singapore badly, leading to the first restrictions. In 1930 an Immigration Restriction Ordinance imposed a quota on Chinese men, but it did not affect women for some years, which encouraged the trend towards permanent family settlement.

THE SECOND WORLD WAR AND JAPANESE OCCUPATION

After the First World War, Singapore acquired a new strategic significance as a naval and military base. However, this did not deter Japan from attacking Malaya in December 1941 as part of a campaign to seize the raw materials it needed from South-East Asia. After a swift campaign down the Malay peninsula, culminating in a week of fighting on the island itself, Singapore capitulated to the Japanese in February 1942.

Renamed Syonan, or 'Light of the South', Singapore remained under Japanese occupation for more than three years. Japan intended to retain Singapore as a permanent colony and military base, a focal point in its proposed 'Greater East Asia Co-Prosperity Sphere', but wartime priorities and difficulties prevented the Japanese from developing this concept. They destroyed the colonial economy but did not replace it with an Asian alternative; and they tried to suppress the English language and colonial education without increasing the use of Japanese in its place. Japan did nothing to promote indigenous politics in Singapore, although the island for a time became the regional base for the collaborationist Indian National Army and the Indian Independence League. The occupation was a time of misery, hunger and fear, which came to an abrupt end in August 1945, when Japan surrendered after atom bombs were dropped on two of its own cities, thus sparing Singapore the ordeal of an Allied invasion.

THE POST-WAR PERIOD

In September 1945 the British established a temporary military administration in preparation for a return to colonial government under a new structure. They aimed to unite the peninsula by creating a Malayan Union comprising all the Malay states, together with Pinang and Melaka, but separating Singapore as a crown colony. In April 1946 civil rule was restored and the Malayan Union and Singapore Crown Colony came into being. These decisions were taken because of Singapore's special position as a free port, its importance as a military base and the complications of trying to absorb it into a Malaya embarking on the road to self-government and independence. However, Singapore's separation was not intended to be permanent.

The proposals provoked protest in Singapore, leading in 1945 to the creation of its first political party, the Malayan Democratic Union (MDU), which campaigned for the island's incorporation in the Malayan Union. The party joined other opposition groups in the peninsula to form the All-Malaya Council of Joint Action, which put forward proposals for the inclusion of Singapore in a Malayan federation. However, these proposals were rapidly cast aside by the intensity of peninsular Malay nationalism; reaction against the Malayan Union, the loss of state identity and the proposed liberal granting of citizenship to immigrants was strong. As a result, in 1948 a Federation of Malaya replaced the Malayan Union. Singapore remained separated, but this time on racial grounds, since the Malay leaders did not want to upset the ethnic balance of the federation by including a predominantly Chinese Singapore.

Constitutional Development, 1948–65

Meanwhile, Singapore was being prepared for eventual self-government, and in 1948 the first elections were held for six members of the Legislative Council. The MDU, now heavily communist-infiltrated, boycotted the election, and most of the elected seats went to the Singapore Progressive Party. This upper-middle-class English-educated group supported British plans for gradual constitutional reform while maintaining the economic status quo. There was little popular enthusiasm for this experiment. Voting was confined to British subjects, registration was voluntary, and the activities of the English-speaking Legislative Council were remote from the majority of the population, with their problems of poverty, unemployment, bad housing and inadequate vernacular education. The outbreak of a communist 'Emergency' in the Federation of Malaya in 1948 led to a period of severe repression of all radical politics in Singapore. While the colony was not directly involved in the revolt, the same emergency regulations were enforced. The Malayan Communist Party was proscribed in 1948 and the MDU disbanded itself.

As the Malayan 'Emergency' was brought under control, the authorities permitted a greater level of political activity in Singapore. In 1955 a new Constitution was granted in an effort to speed up constitutional reform and encourage a sense of real participation and responsibility. The new Legislative Assembly had an elected majority (25 out of 32 members), voters were registered automatically, and the leader of the largest party in the Assembly, as Chief Minister, would form a Council of Ministers responsible to the Assembly.

Two new rival left-of-centre parties were created to contest the election, both headed by lawyers: the Labour Front under David Marshall and the People's Action Party (PAP), led by Lee Kuan Yew. Unexpectedly, these two parties routed the Progressives and other conservatives, and Marshall's Labour Front formed a minority Government. However, in 1955–56 the communist-linked left wing of the PAP made a determined bid for power through the trade union movement and Chinese middle schools. For a time they even wrested control of the PAP Central Executive Committee away from Lee Kuan Yew. The Labour Front Government curbed them by using emergency regulations to imprison their leaders and by taking measures to remove genuine grievances. A 1957 Education Ordinance gave parity to the four main language streams; in the same year citizenship was offered on generous terms to nearly all residents, and a new public services commission was set up to achieve rapid localization of the civil service. In 1958 terms were agreed for full internal self-government, and at elections held in 1959 to implement this, the PAP won an outright majority (43 out of 51 seats). Lee Kuan Yew took office as Prime Minister, and the party was to remain in power into the 21st century.

The new Government committed itself to a programme of rapid industrialization and social reform, with ambitious schemes for education, housing and a radical Women's Charter. It also aspired within its four-year term to achieve full independence through a merger with the Federation of Malaya, which had itself secured independence in 1957. Such a union was seen as vital to provide the military security and free access to a Malayan market that were considered essential for Singapore's survival. However, the implementation of this policy quickly led to dissension in the party, and to challenges from the extreme left wing, which threatened to rupture the party and plunge Singapore into chaos.

The conservative, Malay-dominated Government of the Federation of Malaya, which was originally reluctant to draw closer to Singapore because of its large Chinese population and left-wing tendencies, decided it needed to exercise direct control over its unstable neighbour. To do this, in May 1961 the Malayan Prime Minister, Tunku Abdul Rahman, proposed a closer association between the federation and Singapore, by bringing in the three Borneo territories to achieve racial equilibrium. The PAP leadership eagerly took up this idea, but the prospect of merging Singapore in a conservative, anti-communist Malayan federation so alarmed members of the party's radical left wing that in July 1961 they made a bid to topple Lee Kuan Yew's Government. Having failed by a narrow margin at a dramatic all-night session of the Assembly, the rebels then broke away to form an opposition socialist front, the Barisan Sosialis (BS).

Following an intensive, government-sponsored campaign in its favour, the Malaysia Agreement was signed in July 1963, under which Singapore was to join Malaya, Sarawak and Sabah (North Borneo) in forming the Federation of Malaysia on 31 August 1963. The implementation was deferred until mid-September to enable UN representatives to ascertain the wishes of the people of the Borneo states. Singapore took advantage of this delay to declare its own unilateral independence from colonial rule and to call an election. Having survived the 1961 crisis, the moderate element of the PAP had reorganized and strengthened the party, and profited from the success of the Malaysia merger to secure a comfortable victory.

However, the association was strained. 'Confrontation' by Indonesia, which objected to the formation of the Malaysian federation, severely damaged Singapore's trade and led to acts of violence by Indonesian saboteurs. Simultaneously, the central Government and Singapore clashed over what each perceived as undue interference in the other's internal affairs. In July and September 1964 communal riots in Singapore further strained relations with Kuala Lumpur, while the ruling Alliance Party in Malaysia objected to the PAP's contesting the 1964 general elections. Finally, Lee Kuan Yew's attempts to unite all Malaysian opposition parties brought the crisis to a head, and on 9 August 1965, the central Government forced Singapore to agree to a separation.

REPUBLIC OF SINGAPORE

In this way Singapore became independent against the declared wishes of its own leaders, although it later emerged that Prime Minister Lee Kuan Yew and Minister for Finance Goh Keng Swee had, in fact, negotiated the terms of Singapore's supposed expulsion from the Federation, having already become disillusioned with Malaysia. Singapore then joined the UN in September 1965 and was admitted as a member of the Commonwealth the following month. The new Republic was committed to multi-racial, non-communist, democratic socialist policies, and to co-operation with Malaysia, particularly in economic and defence matters.

Politically, the transition to full independence was smooth. The machinery of government remained almost intact, with minor constitutional amendments, notably the appointment of a non-executive President as Head of State. Effective power rested with the Prime Minister and his Cabinet, responsible to the single-chamber Parliament (formerly the Legislative Assembly), which was elected for a five-year term by all adult Singapore citizens. Other adjustments were more difficult. Few, if any, had visualized a separate independent Singapore on the grounds that such a tiny state, with a large population and no natural resources, could neither sustain its economy nor defend itself. Initially, the British defence 'umbrella' continued to protect Malaysia and Singapore, but in 1966 the United Kingdom decided to withdraw its bases from 'east of Suez' during the mid-1970s. Singapore introduced compulsory national service and was working to build up a credible defence force when, less than two years later, the British Government advanced the withdrawal date to 1971. The accelerated timetable threatened Singapore's economy, since the bases accounted for 20% of the country's gross national income (GNI), but the Government took advantage of the situation to call an election in 1968, when it won a mandate to pass far-reaching labour legislation curbing trade union activity, to provide the right conditions for foreign investment. As hopes for access to the Malaysian market receded, Singapore intensified its efforts to achieve rapid export-orientated industrialization. To attract foreign and local capital and expertise, the Government rejected doctrinaire socialism in favour of a mixed economy, largely privately owned and managed, but with a sizeable public ownership stake used by the Government to give impetus and direction to industrialization.

With independence suddenly thrust upon it, Singapore needed to create a sense of nationhood. In the early years this was done by stressing the unique qualities and differences that distinguished Singapore from its neighbours, resulting in an abrasive foreign policy. While the Republic was a founder member of the Association of Southeast Asian Nations (ASEAN), formed in 1967 along with Malaysia, Thailand, Indonesia and the Philippines (and joined in 1984 by Brunei, in 1995 by Viet Nam, in 1997 by Myanmar and Laos, and in 1999 by Cambodia), at first it made little practical contribution to regional co-operation. However, the British withdrawal, the sharp increase in oil prices in 1974 (petroleum refining being Singapore's largest industry), and the fall of South Viet Nam to the communists in 1975, induced Singapore to draw closer to its neighbours, and it subsequently led the way in supporting regional solidarity.

Any desire to be readmitted to the Federation of Malaysia disappeared with growing confidence in the country's viability as an independent state and the maturing sense of nationhood. After an initially troubled period, in the early 1970s the relationship between the two countries improved, and they maintained close co-operation in matters of mutual concern: combating subversion and illicit trading in narcotic drugs, and protecting the Straits of Melaka.

Independence was followed by eight years of rapid international expansion, when Singapore achieved an 'economic miracle' in industrialization. Official policy aimed to improve living standards without creating a welfare state: it encouraged full employment and subsidized education, housing and public health. Social reform was initially accompanied by a strict policy of family limitation and population control, together with stringent immigration curbs. In the 1960s and 1970s a vigorous education programme concentrated on promoting bilingualism in primary and secondary schooling, while developing technical skills appropriate to the Republic's economy. English became increasingly accepted as the language of development and modernization. An energetic programme of urban renewal and the construction of new townships meant that by the end of the century about 90% of households owned their homes, the highest rate of home ownership in the world.

After the 1961 crisis, the Government pursued a consistently anti-communist policy, using the emergency regulations—a legacy of colonial times—to imprison 'hard-core' subversives. The BS refused to acknowledge Singapore's independence in 1965, and boycotted the Parliament, opting to oppose the Government by extra-constitutional means. After the communist victories in Indo-China in 1975, the extreme left wing re-grouped to attempt a resurgence in Singapore and Malaysia, but the Government arrested leading cadres of the Malayan National Liberation Front, the militant satellite of the Communist Party of Malaya.

From 1968 until October 1981 the PAP held every seat in Parliament, and the party leadership maintained a remarkable cohesion, which contributed to the country's stability but tended to stifle criticism. Radio and television services were state-owned. Newspapers, all concentrated under the ownership of one public company, Singapore Press Holdings Ltd, required annual licences and inclined towards self-censorship. This concentration of power and patronage, and the acknowledgement of the considerable achievements and success of PAP policies, emphasized the lack of credible alternatives. Seven opposition parties contested the 1980 parliamentary elections, but the ruling party achieved its widest margin of victory, winning all seats for the fourth successive election and capturing nearly 78% of the votes. In two decades of remarkable economic progress, Singapore had achieved the third highest per caput income in Asia (excluding the Middle East), after Brunei and Japan. The Republic was also acquiring a sense of nationhood; the 1980 census showed that more than 78% of the population were Singapore-born. In the more relaxed climate, numbers of political prisoners were released, leaving only a small band of committed left-wingers in detention.

However, a nation that had begun to take its relatively high standard of living for granted became less tolerant of the more arbitrary aspects of PAP policies. The victory of J. B. Jeyaretnam, the Secretary-General of the opposition Workers' Party, at a parliamentary by-election in 1981 was an unsettling event for the ruling PAP. At the 1984 general election the PAP's share of the total vote declined to below 63% and the party lost a second seat, this time to Chiam See Tong, founder and Secretary-General of the Singapore Democratic Party (SDP). This reverse caused consternation among the PAP's leadership. While two opposition members in Parliament posed no serious threat to the Government (Jeyaretnam subsequently lost his seat in 1986 and was disbarred from Parliament for five years, following his conviction for perjury), and there was still no viable alternative to the PAP, the period of the party's unchallenged dominance was over. After the 1984 election Lee Kuan Yew remained as Prime Minister but delegated daily government administration to younger men, led by Goh Chok Tong, the First Deputy Prime Minister. Lee Kuan Yew's elder son, Brig.-Gen. Lee Hsien Loong, was appointed a junior minister in 1985 and Minister for Trade and Industry in the following year.

In 1987 a New Population Policy was introduced, since strict population control had resulted in a decline in fertility to below replacement levels. Early marriage was encouraged, as was a return to three-child families, particularly among the more prosperous and better-educated groups. The 1990 census recorded a resident population of 2.7m., and in 1991 an official Concept Plan set a target of 4m. by 2010.

The Government placed even greater emphasis on the need for political stability, in order to attract investors. In 1986 press laws were extended to reduce the circulation of those foreign publications that were considered to be unduly critical of Singapore. These were invoked against several journals, and in 1990, following a dispute between the Government and three foreign publications, which had allegedly interfered in Singapore's politics, the Newspaper and Printing Presses Act was amended: all publications of which the 'contents and editorial policy were determined outside Singapore' and which dealt with politics and current events in South-East Asia would be required to obtain a ministerial licence, renewable annually and limiting the number of copies sold. Punitive damages were awarded against *The International Herald Tribune* and the author of articles that were published in 1994 implying nepotism and the Government's use of a compliant judiciary to suppress opposition by bankrupting rival opposition politicians. This increased caution in reporting on Singapore by journals that circulated locally, although Singapore continued to attract opposition from the US liberal media.

In 1987 the Government alleged that it had discovered a 'Marxist network' that had infiltrated student and church groups and the Workers' Party, and arrested a group of alleged activists under the Internal Security Act, which permitted indefinite detention, without trial, of persons suspected by the authorities of subversion. Mainly young, English-speaking university-educated professionals, the detainees differed from political dissidents of former years. In 1988 the Internal Security Act was tightened to put detention beyond the review of the law courts. Despite the most vigorous campaigning for 20 years, Chiam See Tong of the SDP was again the only successful non-PAP candidate in the 1988 general election. With the expansion of population and migration to new towns, constituencies were redelineated and the number of elective parliamentary seats was increased from 58 in 1967 to 83 in 1997.

In 1988 MPs were allocated a role as town councillors in managing new towns, and 39 constituencies were reorganized into 13 Group Representation Constituencies (GRCs). These were contested by teams of three from the same party, including at least one candidate from a minority community. (This was changed in 1991 to a minimum of three and a maximum of four candidates, and in 1996 the maximum was raised to six, in a measure that the Government claimed would facilitate town council operations, but that also made it more difficult for opposition parties to present electoral teams.) In 1990 Parliament approved legislation enabling the Government to appoint up to two unelected MPs for a two-and-a-half year term. This scheme was later expanded to provide for six and subsequently nine Nominated Members of Parliament (NMPs). Independent, well-educated people, successful in the fields of business and industry, the professions, the labour movement, social and community organizations, the media, arts and sport, or tertiary education institutions, these NMPs were expected to provide constructive non-partisan criticism and to improve the quality of parliamentary debate. They had the right to vote on all legislative proposals except those concerning financial and constitutional affairs. When the term of office of the six NMPs expired in 1994, the system was made permanent on the basis of two-year appointments, with the possibility of reappointment.

Goh Chok Tong's Premiership

In November 1990 Lee Kuan Yew resigned as Prime Minister in favour of Goh Chok Tong; however, he remained in the Cabinet as Senior Minister, retained his influential post of PAP Secretary-General and continued to travel extensively abroad promoting Singapore's interests. Lee Hsien Loong and Ong Teng Cheong, formerly the Second Deputy Prime Minister (and also the Secretary-General of the National Trades Union Congress—NTUC), were appointed Deputy Prime Ministers of supposedly equal rank, but Lee Hsien Loong was to act in the Prime Minister's absence.

Goh offered a more open political system and, at his inauguration, invited 'fellow citizens to join me, to run the next lap together'. An official programme, entitled *The Next Lap*, which was published in 1991, promised to make Singapore 'more prosperous, gracious and interesting over the next 20 to 30 years', as befitted an affluent, well-educated society. Censorship of films, television and magazines was relaxed, the new Prime Minister embarked on an extensive programme of community visits and exhorted the public to participate and express its views. This gained him considerable support among the Malay and Indian minorities, who were traditionally wary of the PAP. However, the changes represented a difference of style rather than of substance. Goh still stressed the virtues of hard work, meritocracy, sound education, economic growth, the need to avoid the pitfalls of a welfare state and a defence policy based on national resilience. The public was invited to offer constructive criticism, but not to advocate radical change. Restrictions on the foreign press remained in force. Although all political detainees were released from prison by June 1990, Goh refused to repeal the Internal Security Act, and it was only in November 1998 that the final residential restrictions were removed on the movements of Chia Thye Poh, Singapore's last political prisoner, who had been arrested in 1966. Even then he was prohibited from engaging in politics.

Seeking popular endorsement for his style of government, the Prime Minister called an early election in August 1991, two years ahead of schedule, arguing that consensus and national unity precluded the need for a formal opposition. The opposition parties, in a plan conceived by Chiam See Tong, decided to contest only 40 out of the 81 seats, conceding victory to the ruling PAP by default, but inviting voters to create a strong opposition. In the event, the PAP's share of the vote dropped to 61.0% (from 63.2% in 1988), and the party won 77 seats, compared with 80 in 1988. Jeyaretnam was unable to contest the election as his disqualification still remained in force, but the Workers' Party won in one constituency while Chiam's SDP secured three seats. During the election campaign the Prime Minister warned that there would be a return to a more authoritarian and paternalistic form of government if he failed to receive a popular mandate. However, Goh subsequently announced that he would continue his style of government but would implement reforms more slowly.

In November 1992 the Government announced that both Deputy Prime Ministers were suffering from cancer. Lee Hsien Loong relinquished his office, and the illness of both men gave urgency to holding a by-election, which the Prime Minister had pledged to stage to counter Jeyaretnam's claim that he had been deliberately excluded by the early timing of the 1991 general election. In an astute move, Goh held the contest in his own four-member GRC in December 1992; Jeyaretnam was unable to enter the contest, since the Workers' Party did not have the required minimum of four candidates. The PAP secured 72.9% of the vote; this result, combined with Lee Hsien Loong's indisposition and Goh's unanimous election earlier in the month as Secretary-General of the PAP (replacing Lee Kuan Yew), strengthened the rather fragile personal power of the Prime Minister considerably.

Following many years of public discussion, in 1991 Parliament approved a constitutional change in the presidency. Instead of a ceremonial figurehead appointed by Parliament, the new-style President was chosen directly by the electorate, and was empowered to safeguard the large financial reserves that had been accumulated over the previous 30 years and to veto senior civil service and judicial appointments. Only those who had served as cabinet ministers, chief justice, senior civil servants or the head of a large company would be eligible as presidential candidates.

In 1993 Ong Teng Cheong was elected President for a six-year term, securing 58.7% of the votes cast. The election of Ong, who had been nominated by the NTUC and who enjoyed strong PAP support, was almost a foregone conclusion; however, the only other candidate, a former accountant-general, Chua Kim Yeow, who adopted an apolitical platform, attracted a significant 41.3% of the vote.

In January 1994 Goh reorganized the Cabinet, appointing Lee Hsien Loong to supervise both the trade and industry and the defence portfolios. By mid-1994 senior ministers were once more expressing concern about the difficulty of recruiting able people into public service and, most particularly, into the Cabinet. The consequent decision to increase ministerial salaries to a level comparable with private sector leaders provoked some protest, especially from the SDP. The ruling party also encouraged junior MPs simultaneously to hold posts as professionals and senior business executives, provided there were no conflicts of interest.

Under the slogan 'Singapore 21: make it our best home', the Prime Minister contested the general election of January 1997 on three key issues: his own impressive track record; a solid programme offering political stability, economic growth, high-quality education and rising living standards; and a capable leadership being prepared for the 21st century. On the eve of the election seven opposition parties came to an agreement to avoid splitting the anti-PAP vote in most constituencies, but, despite their promising performance in the 1991 general election, the opposition was in an unstable state. The SDP was divided by personal feuds and became more confrontational under the leadership of Chee Soon Juan, a former university lecturer, who was elected Secretary-General in 1995. Chee's book, *Dare to Change*, which he had published in 1994 as a counterbalance to the PAP's *The Next Lap*, argued for greater democracy and was adopted as the SDP's policy. Articulate and vocal, the new SDP leaders received substantial coverage in the local press, but their strident anti-Government censure was frequently criticized by journalists and many of the public as unpatriotic. Meanwhile, Chiam was expelled from the party and in July 1995 formed the Singapore People's Party, which aimed to revive the original moderate policy of the early SDP. The new party sought to liberalize publishing and the internal security laws and to create a 'caring and civic society in which people could enter politics without fear'.

Unopposed in 47 of the 83 seats in the January 1997 general election, the PAP was assured of being returned to power. Nevertheless, Goh conducted an energetic campaign, emphasizing the successes of his six years in office. He insisted that the principal role of government was to improve the quality of life by providing a stable and secure environment. At the same time he proposed to give Singaporeans more say in municipal affairs and in determining their living environment by creating geographic communities with mayors and Community Development Councils.

Overall in 1997 the PAP achieved its best result since the 1984 general election, winning all but two seats, increasing its share of the contested votes to 65% (up from 61% in 1991), and regaining two opposition seats. Low Thia Kiang of the Workers' Party retained his seat with a slightly increased vote, Chiam was returned for a fourth term but as leader of the Singapore People's Party with a reduced majority, while Chee and the SDP were completely routed. Jeyaretnam was declared a Non-Constituency MP, under a constitutional amendment that provided for the highest-scoring losers to be admitted to Parliament if there were fewer than three opposition members; Non-Constituency MPs were prohibited from voting on constitutional and financial matters.

The new Cabinet incorporated no important changes in the senior posts but introduced several younger ministers. The Prime Minister appealed for unity following the election, but acrimonious court disputes ensued. The Prime Minister, Senior Minister and other PAP leaders issued writs for defamation against Tang Liang Hong, an unsuccessful parliamentary candidate of the Workers' Party who had accused PAP leaders of lying during the election campaign after they accused him of being anti-Christian and of promoting Chinese interests over those of ethnic minorities. Tang subsequently fled to Johor, declaring that he had received threats against his life. In his absence, the court ordered Tang to pay a record S $8m. in damages and costs. The Court of Appeal later substantially reduced the damages, but Tang refused to pay and was declared bankrupt. The PAP leadership also sued Jeyaretnam, following remarks made at an election rally concerning two police reports submitted by Tang that accused the PAP leadership of criminal conspiracy and of lying. Jeyaretnam insisted that the legal suits were an attempt to bankrupt him and thus disqualify him from Parliament. The High Court found against Jeyaretnam, but ordered the payment of only modest damages of S $20,000 (10% of the amount claimed by Prime Minister Goh) and 60% of the costs. However, the Court of Appeal upheld the Prime Minister's appeal for higher damages: Jeyaretnam's damages were multiplied five-fold, to S $100,000, and full costs were awarded against him.

The number of NMPs was increased to nine in 1997, by which time Parliament comprised 93 representatives, of whom six were women and 17 were selected from the minority communities. The Prime Minister urged a change of attitude: instead of expecting every initiative to come from a few political leaders, all Singaporeans should feel responsible for solving local issues and shaping their own communities. Nine Community Development Councils were created to encompass all constituencies, including the two opposition wards; however, opposition MPs could not be chairmen of the councils or have power to disburse funds.

In February 1998 the Government banned political parties from making videos and from promoting their views on television, with the reported aim of maintaining the propriety of political debate. At that time 22 opposition parties were registered, of which 13 were dormant and the remainder rarely met. The SDP was devastated by its general election defeat. In early 1999 Chee was convicted twice under the Public Entertainment Act after deliberately refusing to apply for licences to make two public speeches, in which he criticized government policy; he served two brief spells in prison for refusing to pay the fines. In July 2005 the existing ban on political videos was used as the basis for preventing the SDP from showing a video on Hong Kong politics at the launch of Chee's new book, *The Power of Courage*, in which Chee urged Singaporeans to take a pro-active stance against the PAP in the hope of effecting social and political change through non-violent means.

The Workers' Party was active immediately after the 1997 election, with Jeyaretnam meeting the public at regular weekly sessions, but he ended these when he became involved in legal proceedings. In addition to the damages and costs owed to the PAP leaders, in November 1998 10 members of a Tamil Language Committee won defamatory damages from Jeyaretnam and the Workers' Party for an article published in the party's journal, *The Hammer*. An appeal against the order was rejected, and Jeyaretnam was finally declared bankrupt in January 2001, consequently losing his non-constituency seat and becoming barred from contesting the next general election. The PAP leaders repeatedly refused to remove Jeyaretnam's bankruptcy order, and an appeal at the Court of Appeal in October 2004 also failed to secure Jeyaretnam an early discharge. In May 2001, at the age of 76, he relinquished the post of Secretary-General of the Workers' Party, which he had held for 30 years, and was succeeded by the former Assistant Secretary-General, Low Thia Khiang, MP. (Jeyaretnam was finally released from bankruptcy in April 2007 upon receipt of assistance from a group of benefactors led by one of his sons; he promptly announced plans to found a new political party, which came to fruition in July 2008 with the official registration of the Reform Party; he died in September and in April 2009 his son, Kenneth Jeyaretnam, announced that he was assuming leadership of the party.) Meanwhile, associations began to form outside the formal political arena. The Association of Women for Action and Research aimed to achieve full equality for women in public and private life and was influential in gaining significant amendments to the Women's Charter, which widened the provisions protecting families in case of violence and divorce. The Association of Muslim Professionals (AMP) sought to raise the educational, economic and social status of the Malay/Muslim community. 'Roundtable', a discussion group of young professionals, urged a review of the Societies, Internal Security and Public Entertainments Acts.

In June 1999 President Ong Teng Cheong, whose six-year mandate was due to expire in September, announced that he did not intend to seek a second term in office, citing the difficulties he had experienced as Singapore's first elected President: notably, restrictions placed on the presidential right of veto, official obstruction of his efforts to establish the details of the Republic's financial reserves, and disappointment at not being approached to release the funds needed to help Singapore through the recession. In response, the Government insisted that net investment income lay outside the President's jurisdiction and that the surplus accumulated during the current Parliament would be sufficient to finance measures to be implemented up to the year 2000 without the need to use reserves. In July 1999 Parliament endorsed a set of rules agreed between Ong and the Prime Minister to ensure a smooth future working relationship: it was decreed that a President could block the sale of land holdings and prohibit unreasonable disposals, but could not fetter the day-to-day operations of government; furthermore, the President would be obliged to give warning before blocking any transaction, while the Government, in turn, undertook regularly to furnish the President with information. Public speculation about the potential impact of the appointment of a new President was quickly dispelled by Senior Minister Lee Kuan Yew, who emphasized that there could be only one centre of executive power and that the powers of the President were largely ceremonial and confined to preventing an irresponsible administration from squandering the reserves or making unsuitable appointments. S. R. Nathan, a former Singaporean ambassador to the USA, whose presidential candidature was supported by the Cabinet and welcomed by the NTUC, was chosen as the new President without an election being held, since the two other potential contestants failed to meet the stringent criteria for nomination. Reviewing Singapore's position in 1999, the Prime Minister concluded that although the Republic had prospered since independence, it was still a fragile society with racial divisions. The 'Singapore 21' concept, which was the result of two years' wide-ranging consultation, was embodied in a book, entitled *Singapore 21: Together We Make The Difference*, and debated in a marathon parliamentary session in May 1999. It aspired to be a 'total vision', providing for the country's future in the next millennium. This went beyond mere material achievement to developing a partnership between the public and private sectors and the citizens of the Republic, with the aim of building—over one or two generations—a multi-racial nation, in which each community would have its own distinctive identity but overlap with other communities, and in which English would be the common language and equal opportunities would be enjoyed by all. The population target of 4m. envisaged in the 1991 Concept Plan was achieved in 1999, 11 years ahead of schedule, principally as the result of an influx of foreign immigrants, and the target was raised to 5m. by the middle of the 21st century.

In celebrating National Day in August 1999 Goh Chok Tong outlined a vision of Singapore as a 'world-class renaissance city', with excellence in education, arts and sport to match a world-class economy, which would attract foreign talent and encourage Singaporeans to remain in the country. In October he declared consultation and participation to be among the Government's main objectives, encouraging citizens to turn the republic into 'a nation of ideas'. In September 2000 a 'Speakers' Corner' was designated, which would be open seven days a week for any Singapore citizen to register and speak freely, provided that they did not endanger law and order, respected racial and religious sensitivities, and avoided libel. Opposition politicians were wary, and the initial public interest soon waned. None the less, the PAP leaders maintained their stance that politics was the domain of elected politicians, since they alone had a popular mandate and were accountable to the electorate. Goh Chok Tong had insisted that 'meaningful politics must mean joining a political party', and Lee Kuan Yew repeated a warning about would-be critics crossing 'out of bounds markers'. The Prime Minister insisted that the press should inform and educate but was not entitled to set the national agenda. In May 2000 a Political Donations Bill was approved, which aimed to keep Singaporean politics free of foreign interference. Political parties were required to keep lists of donors, accept donations only from Singaporean and local companies, and declare any single donation exceeding S $10,000. Associations promoting purely social causes would not be affected, but any organization would be gazetted as political if its activities related wholly or mainly to politics in

Singapore or if it pressed for changes in the political or legal structure. While agreeing that foreigners should be kept out of Singaporean politics, all three opposition MPs registered spirited resistance to the Bill, arguing that it would place a heavy burden on small parties to keep detailed records and would deter donors, who were often reluctant to make their support for opposition parties known.

Singapore was in a better position than its neighbours to withstand the economic crisis that beset the region from mid-1997. Both the Prime Minister and the leader of the NTUC stressed giving priority to full employment by adjusting wages in order to curb costs and to save jobs. By November Singapore was formally in recession, and the Government introduced radical measures to reduce business costs, which included wage reductions and the halving of employers' Central Provident Fund (CPF) contributions from 20% to 10%. By May 1999 Singapore was technically no longer in recession, and the economy experienced greater growth than expected for the rest of the year and throughout 2000. This prompted the National Wages Council to recommend wage increases, bonus payments and the restoration, at a more rapid rate than the proposed five-year period, of the 10% CPF reduction. Some 2% of the CPF decrease was restored in April 2000, and a further 4% in January 2001.

Singapore celebrated National Day in August 2000 in an optimistic mood, but the Prime Minister warned of 'grave problems', notably falling fertility, emigration, and a widening gap between rich and poor. Despite the introduction of tax incentives in the mid-1980s to encourage the educated classes to have more children, the fertility rate had declined sharply to less than 1.5 and was still falling; already one-quarter of the population were non-Singaporeans. In August further incentives were announced in the form of bonus payments and improved maternity leave for those parents producing a second and third child. To compound the fertility problem, competition from other countries to recruit talent in a global economy was encouraging many Singaporeans to emigrate, thus raising salaries among the most highly paid echelons. This was a particular threat to the public service and, in July 2000, in order to curb rising resignations, the Government announced a radical overhaul of civil service rewards. All ministers and senior officials were given substantial salary increases and enhanced bonuses, linked partly to personal performance and partly to the national economy. Life-long tenure was to be replaced by fixed 10-year appointments, and outstanding young officials could expect accelerated promotion. Opposition MPs objected to the large increases, urging that public service demanded some sacrifice, but the press gave cautious approval.

While the upsurge in the economy created many new jobs for professionals and technicians, unemployment continued to increase among the unskilled, who had suffered most during the 1997–98 crisis. The gap between those earning 'First World' salaries and 'Third World' wages was widening, and in the midst of affluence, the number of Singaporeans living in poverty was growing perceptibly. While rejecting the Workers' Party demand for widespread welfare measures, which it believed would encourage dependency, in August 2000 the Government announced a grants programme, providing for, in particular, help for the elderly, the poor and families with young children, and including CPF and medical insurance 'top-up' sums and Housing and Development Board mortgage discounts. Furthermore, there was to be continued emphasis on areas such as education, retraining and upgrading skills. While a very high proportion of Singaporeans were educated to upper secondary and tertiary level, the Government remained concerned at the low academic standards and high drop-out rates at some private schools, notably in *madrasahs* (Islamic religious schools).

Appalled by the attacks on the USA on 11 September 2001, the Singapore Government immediately pledged its support for the US effort to create a world-wide alliance to counter terrorism, urging in particular that Muslim and developing countries should be included in the coalition. The Republic undertook to co-operate on intelligence, eliminate terrorist networks and monitor financial transactions.

In order to gain a strong mandate and convince foreign and local investors that the PAP had the electorate's confidence to address the economic recession and terrorist threat, the Government decided to bring forward the date of the general election (which was required to be held no later than August 2002). The election was scheduled for 3 November 2001, allowing only the minimum legal nine-day notice period, prompting protests from the opposition. After lengthy research the PAP had prepared a new electoral team, comprising prospective cabinet ministers from the senior ranks of the private sector, together with well-qualified younger candidates, including a number of women and representatives of ethnic minorities. In July 2001 three opposition parties, the Singapore People's Party, the National Solidarity Party and the Singapore Malay National Organization, had formed a Singapore Democratic Alliance (SDA), under the leadership of Chiam See Tong, but both Low Thia Khiang's Workers' Party and Chee Soon Juan's SDP refused to join the new coalition. A Workers' Party team, which planned to contest a GRC, was disqualified by its failure to submit the correct nomination papers. At the elections the PAP was unopposed in 55 of the 84 elective seats and consequently returned to power with the largest number of outright victories since the 1968 election. Nevertheless, the party contested the election with customary vigour, campaigning on its good record, promising to overcome recession and to have a strong new leadership in place by the next election in five years' time. Unlike previous parliamentary contests, the campaign was not marred by racial or religious discord, but inaccurate allegations about a proposed loan to Indonesia, directed at Goh Chok Tong and Lee Kuan Yew by Chee Soon Juan, caused controversy.

On 3 November 2001 the PAP won an overwhelming 73.3% of votes cast in the poll, the biggest margin since the 1980 election. This represented a 10% transfer of the vote since the 1997 election, and the party emerged with 82 of the 84 elective seats. Low Thia Khiang and Chiam See Tong retained their seats, but with smaller majorities. Chiam, who had represented his constituency for 17 years, was now the longest ever serving opposition member, but his majority fell to 52.4%. Low won for the third time, but his proportion of the vote had declined from 58% to 55%. As the losing candidate with the highest number of votes, Steve Chia of the SDA became a Non-Constituency MP. Although the SDP was overwhelmingly defeated, Chee Soon Juan declared that he would not relinquish the leadership of the party. However, the Prime Minister and Lee Kuan Yew refused to accept Chee's apology for the false allegations made during the general election campaign. Following protracted legal proceedings, the damages awarded against him were upheld on appeal in April 2003.

Goh announced that he would remain in office throughout the period of recession, but would resign prior to the next general election in favour of a younger team. Immediately after the election, the Prime Minister appointed his new Cabinet. The Deputy Prime Minister, Lee Hsien Loong, assumed control of the Ministry of Finance, and Dr Tony Tan Keng Yam continued as Second Deputy Prime Minister and Minister for Defence. Five first-term MPs were appointed Ministers of State; in contrast to the previous procedure whereby Ministers of State had tended to be government officials or military officers, all five appointees were young and from the private sector. However, no women were appointed to senior office.

In November 2001, implementing a concept first proposed by Goh five years earlier, Singapore was divided into five districts, each with a mayor (who would become an MP with the same rank as a Minister of State), and managed by their own Community Development Councils. The aim was to improve community spirit and to allow local government to administer social services, such as welfare, health and sports.

Following the election the Government embarked immediately upon addressing the nation's economic problems, giving greatest priority to combating unemployment, which in December 2001 reached its highest level for 15 years. 'New Singapore shares' were issued to all citizens, with a greater proportion being allocated to the poor. An Economic Review Committee was appointed, under the chairmanship of Lee Hsien Loong, with seven sub-committees chaired by prominent politicians and businessmen. The Committee's remit was to recommend long-term economic restructuring to meet the changes in the global economy, notably the increasing influence of the People's Republic of China and the transfer in emphasis to North-East Asia, which threatened to marginalize the South-East Asian markets. In April 2002 the committee recommended a major revision of taxation and employment benefits, in order to liberalize the labour market and create jobs. It proposed the reduction of direct corporate and personal taxes, including income tax, in favour of increasing indirect general sales taxes. These recommendations were implemented in the budget in May, but with the stipulation that, in order to lessen the impact on the poor of the transfer to indirect taxation, at least five years' financial aid would be required, such as in rebates on public housing service charges. Addressing the issue of company structure, the Economic Review Committee recommended that, in principle, the Government should remain involved only in strategic areas, such as the Port of Singapore, and withdraw gradually and methodically from enterprises that the private sector could manage. Regarding the CPF, in July the Committee proposed the imposition of a permanent 'freeze' on employers' contributions at the level of 16% for the age group of over 50 years, in order to keep jobs competitive for older workers, a measure that was accepted with reservations by the trade unions.

A parallel 'Remaking Singapore Committee' was established in February 2002, comprising younger citizens under the chairmanship of the Minister of State for National Development. Continuing the research of the Singapore 21 Committee, this body was to make a comprehensive review of political, social and cultural affairs, including the arts and censorship. In March the PAP invited its MPs to speak and vote according to their personal views, except on matters of critical national importance, such as the budget, the Constitution or security. For the first time the expertise of NMPs appointed in 2002, including the President of the 'Roundtable' political discussion group and five women, was extended to include the areas of community activities, the media and sports, and academia. The greater relaxation in party control resulted in some unusually vigorous criticism in Parliament in July over the Government's decision to increase public transport fares, but official reaction, while conciliatory in tone, was not influenced into modifying the policy. Most of the recommendations of the Remaking Singapore Committee were finally accepted in April 2004, although there was a general sense of disappointment that those rejected were the ones that could have liberalized Singapore's political system.

The atmosphere in Singapore following the 11 September 2001 attacks on the USA remained calm. Muslim leaders condemned terrorism, and there was no harassment of Muslims by other communities. Nevertheless, the authorities feared that the peace was fragile, that Singapore itself was vulnerable to attack and that the international terrorist network al-Qa'ida, believed to be responsible for the attacks, had links with neighbouring Indonesia, Malaysia and the Philippines. A new national security secretariat was created, and in December 15 alleged terrorists were arrested, of whom 13 received two-year sentences of imprisonment under the Internal Security Act. Of these, all but one were middle-class Singapore citizens, while none of them had been educated at *madrasahs* or involved in mosque activities or Muslim community organizations, and six had served as full-time national servicemen. They were believed to be members of Jemaah Islamiah (JI), a secret network of at least three active groups, part of a larger network in Malaysia and Indonesia, which had been established in 1995 with the aim of creating a Java-based Islamic state, incorporating Indonesia, Malaysia, Singapore, Brunei and the southern Philippines. The group was alleged to be linked to al-Qa'ida, and some JI members were trained in Afghanistan and led by Indonesian militants. The arrests foiled JI's long-planned action against targets in Singapore, including, it was alleged, the hijacking of an aeroplane to crash into Changi Airport, attacks against US service personnel and US naval vessels, suicide bombing of US, British, Israeli and Australian diplomatic missions, and a simultaneous offensive against US embassies in Singapore, Kuala Lumpur and Jakarta.

Singapore's Muslim leaders expressed strong support for the Government's actions against the suspected terrorists and, despite the high-profile arrests, relations between Singapore's Muslim and non-Muslim communities remained stable. Goh, in his Chinese New Year message in February 2002, emphasized that security was a more long-standing problem than the current economic crisis and depended on racial harmony. The Government sought even greater national cohesion, urging compliance with legislation such as that banning Malay girls in primary schools from wearing the head covering (*tudung*), which provoked protests from some parents. In January 2002 new 'grassroots' community groups, known as 'Inter-racial Confidence Circles' were established in each constituency, and Goh, together with Lee Hsien Loong and other senior ministers, organized a confidential meeting of some 1,700 community leaders to discuss the impact of the arrests of JI suspects.

During the following months further arrests were made in the Philippines and Oman of individuals suspected of involvement in the alleged conspiracy to attack Singapore, and in September 2002 there was a second wave of arrests in the Republic. A total of 21 Singaporeans were taken into custody, of whom 18 were detained for two years and three were placed under restriction orders. All 'blue-collar' workers, these were junior operatives, instructed by Singaporean and Malaysian leaders under direction from Indonesia. The arrests disrupted the JI network in Singapore, but the regional organization remained a threat. Singapore was also frustrated by the refusal of the Indonesian Government to extradite Indonesian cleric Abu Bakar Bashir, allegedly the spiritual leader of the regional JI network. In the aftermath of the September arrests, the Minister in charge of Muslim Affairs, Dr Yaacob Ibrahim, pleaded for citizens, Muslim and non-Muslim alike, to unite against terrorism, and in October Goh proposed a draft Code on Religious Harmony at a meeting with community leaders. In January 2003 Parliament held a three-day debate over a government 'White Paper' detailing JI and its international links, which concluded that, while Singapore could not eliminate terrorism, it could police its ideological spread, strengthen social cohesion and religious harmony, and encourage the Muslim community to curb extremism in religious education. The country's principal Islamic religious body, the Islamic Religious Council of Singapore (MUIS), was recruited to play a central role in this project. After the September 2001 attacks MUIS began to offer *imams* and *ulama* an ongoing series of high-quality seminars and academic forums that promoted 'moderate' Islam. It increased the sophistication of the draft sermons that it offered to the island's mosques for Friday prayers, and also appointed Western-trained 'executive *imams*' to work within the heart of the Muslim community. More long-term goals included the ongoing improvement of the professional standards of staff working in *madrasahs*.

Meanwhile, the Republic suffered its longest and deepest recession since independence. Overall, the economy contracted in 2001, and hopes for a return to pre-recession levels of growth in 2002 were tempered by external factors. In February 2003, for the first time in its history, the Port of Singapore Authority (PSA) made a large part of its work-force redundant, and civil service salaries were reduced further, with senior officials and ministers suffering the greatest decreases. The economy in general, and tourism in particular, suffered from the repercussions of the terrorist attack on Bali in October 2002 (see the chapter on Indonesia) and, in March 2003, from the commencement of the US-led campaign to oust the regime of Saddam Hussain in Iraq, together with a serious epidemic of Severe Acute Respiratory Syndrome (SARS). In mid-2003 Singapore Airlines imposed drastic pay cuts and retrenchment. The immediate campaign in Iraq was brief, and public co-operation with the stringent measures imposed by the Government quickly contained the SARS epidemic. Although SARS was believed to have been eliminated by the end of August, it re-emerged almost immediately in the form of a lone case originating in a supposedly sterile SARS laboratory. While most sectors of Singapore's economy had recovered from the repercussions of SARS before the end of the year, the threat that it, or another epidemic, might again occur remained a new and influential factor in national planning, one consequence of which was a reduction in employers' contributions to the CPF from 16% to 13%. By July consumer confidence was returning and output from manufacturing rising, and the 2004 budget bore testament to Singapore's ongoing economic recovery.

Minister for Finance Lee Hsien Loong announced tax reductions and increased investment in services, although he was still unable to promise a budgetary surplus, thus putting the budget in deficit for the third time in four years. He also failed to assuage ongoing popular discontent concerning increases in the cost of living brought about by rises in government charges, persistently high levels of unemployment and the large numbers of skilled foreign workers commonly perceived to be taking jobs in the country at the expense of Singaporean citizens.

After the general election of late 2001, the opposition parties took little active role in politics, supporting the Government's stance on anti-terrorism measures and acquiescing in general to its programme for the revival of the economy. In November 2002 Chiam See Tong gave up his law practice in order to concentrate fully on his parliamentary ward. He urged opposition politicians to acknowledge the failure of individual parties and the need to combine in order to produce an effective two-party system, and invited the Workers' Party and SDP to join the SDA. However, this proposal did not attract Low Thia Khiang's Workers' Party, celebrating its 45th anniversary that month, although the party continued to criticize the political system as being flawed, lacking checks and balances, and ignoring social justice in its quest for economic growth.

In June 2004 independent civil society was restricted even further when the Societies Act was amended in order to control more stringently the registration of societies. Since 1999 discretionary decisions concerning registration had rested with the directly elected President of Singapore. The amendment awarded this discretion to a government minister. This incremental change confirmed the pattern of restrictions on civil society that had taken place under Goh's premiership.

At the beginning of 2002 seven new ministers were awarded junior cabinet portfolios by Deputy Prime Minister Lee. In a cabinet reorganization announced in April 2003 (effective from August of that year), three of the seven—Dr Ng Eng Hen, Khaw Boon Wan and Tharman Shanmugaratnam—were promoted to senior portfolios: Dr Ng was appointed Minister for Manpower, while Khaw assumed the health portfolio on an acting basis and Shanmugaratnam was appointed acting Minister for Education. These three ministers were clearly identified as 'rising stars' in the forthcoming Government of Lee Hsien Loong. Other notable changes announced in April included the appointment of Deputy Prime Minister and former Minister for Defence Tan to the newly created position of Co-ordinating Minister for Security and Defence in the Prime Minister's Office, and that of Teo Chee Hean, hitherto Minister for Education, as the new Minister for Defence.

Lee Hsien Loong's Premiership

In mid-2004 the succession of Lee Hsien Loong to the premiership was confirmed through a complex process whereby Goh Chok Tong's official endorsement of Lee as his successor was confirmed by a meeting of PAP MPs and the PAP Central Executive Committee. This exercise seemed superfluous to most observers, but Goh hoped to institutionalize the selection of the Prime Minister and, to some extent, begin the process of removing the personal elements of political power. Certainly, Lee Hsien Loong's first year as premier was more remarkable for the continuity that it signalled with his two predecessors than for any radical initiatives or personal mark, although when he revived discussion of the importance of Singapore's 'élite' in a speech to university students, he was clearly showing a stronger affinity with his father's views than with those of Goh.

Prime Minister Lee's first Cabinet formally assumed office on 12 August 2004 and the new Government was distinguished by the retention of former Prime Ministers Goh Chok Tong and Lee Kuan Yew as Senior Minister and 'Minister Mentor', respectively. Dr Tan was retained as a Deputy Prime Minister, to be replaced by Minister for Home Affairs Wong Kan Seng in mid-2005 following the former's retirement (which was subsequently postponed to September, ostensibly so that he could complete a major restructuring of the tertiary education sector). Prof. Shanmugam Jayakumar was also appointed a Deputy Prime Minister, becoming Singapore's first citizen of Indian origin to hold the post. (Upon Tan's retirement in September, Jayakumar was given the additional role of Co-ordinating Minister for National Security—formerly the position of Co-ordinating Minister for Security and Defence.) Lee retained the finance portfolio, but appointed Goh Chok Tong as his replacement as Chairman of the Monetary Authority of Singapore (MAS). At the same time Tharman Shanmugaratnam was also promoted to the deputy chairmanship of the MAS, but in 2005 Ng Eng Hen was appointed Second Minister for Defence, clearly positioning him ahead of Shanmugaratnam in the hierarchy. He filled a vacancy left by Cedric Foo, the former Minister of State for Defence, who became the first of the 2002 intake of new ministers to be removed.

In August 2005 S. R. Nathan's term as President of the Republic ended, but he was retained as the government candidate for the next five-year term of office, despite being 81 years old and in poor health. He was elected unopposed after the other three candidates were ruled ineligible for nomination. The only major initiative that distinguished Lee Hsien Loong's first year in office was the decision to abandon the Government's long-standing opposition to gambling and to open two major casino resorts, in a concerted bid to reclaim Singapore's share of this lucrative area of the tourism market. The unpopularity of this move, especially but not exclusively with Muslims and Christians, forced the new Prime Minister to abandon plans to call an early election to endorse his rule. However, these political considerations did not delay the plans for the casinos, and by the end of 2006 tenders for these had been awarded to consortia based in Malaysia and the USA (see Economy).

Meanwhile, in July 2005 an unexpected political crisis emerged when the National Kidney Foundation (NKF) became embroiled in a very public scandal about the misuse of charitable donations. The NKF was a government-endorsed charity, upon which the Government relied to provide subsidized dialysis for Singaporeans. The Government's sensitivity on this issue was heightened on account of existing anger over the recent withdrawal of polyclinic services in the evenings—a development that left Singaporeans with no alternative to expensive private doctors, which for many was not a feasible option. In his 2005 National Day Rally speech in August, Prime Minister Lee announced two measures that were designed to deflect some of this concern: a new housing grant for low-income earners and a partial relaxation of the restrictions on how the elderly might pay for medical treatment. A few months later Minister for Health Khaw Boon Wan vowed to tighten the regulatory controls on all charities, admitting that the Government had failed in its duty as regulator and that his professional reputation had been tarnished by the NKF débâcle.

Following his appointment as acting Minister for Education in August 2003, Tharman Shanmugaratnam instituted a range of reforms within the education sector, some of which appeared to have weakened Singapore's commitment to Mandarin as the country's second language, and even moderated the Singaporean fixation on examinations and scholarships. In 2005 a new, easier curriculum for teaching Chinese in primary schools was announced. The then Senior Minister Lee Kuan Yew confirmed in June 2004 that, after 40 years of effort, he had abandoned his goal of trying to make Singapore's citizens bilingual. However, this weakening of Chinese-language education was balanced by attempts to create a much smaller cohort (in the region of 200 per year) of bilingual Chinese graduates capable of 'engaging China'. In 2005 Prime Minister Lee Hsien Loong announced a plan to provide every pupil with post-secondary education, and further reforms of the tertiary education sector were initiated. Furthermore, the Government hoped to develop Singapore as a regional educational hub.

As the parliamentary election of May 2006 approached, for the first time since 1988 the opposition contested a majority of seats, as a result of which the Government was not returned by default on Nomination Day. The opposition parties also came to an agreement that successfully averted tripartite contests. The PAP's strategies during the campaign were familiar: senior government officials suing opposition candidates; Minister Mentor Lee's effort to make the election campaign focus on the issue of the integrity of a single opposition candidate—on this occasion, James Gomez of the Workers' Party over a misplaced form connected with the nomination process; and denying access to government funds for the upgrade of housing estates that refused to vote for the PAP (targeted at the opposition-held wards of Potong Pasir and Hougang).

In the event, the PAP won all but two seats (excluding the seat of Sylvia Lim of the Workers' Party, who was appointed a Non-Constituency MP after the election). However, somewhat disquieting for Prime Minister Lee was the fact that the vote for his personal election team in Ang Moh Kio GRC (66.1%) was slightly below the average for PAP candidates (66.6%). Following the election, no new appointments were made to the Cabinet, although there was a significant rearrangement of portfolios, with Tharman Shanmugaratnam and Raymond Lim Siang Keat moving decisively up the hierarchy. Shanmugaratnam relinquished his position as Deputy Chairman of the MAS to become Second Minister for Finance, but retained the education portfolio. Lim became Minister for Transport, while continuing as Second Minister for Foreign Affairs (but left the positions of Second Minister for Finance and Minister in the Prime Minister's Office). The Minister for Community Development, Youth and Sports, Dr Vivian Balakrishnan, was also appointed to the position of Second Minister for Information, Communications and the Arts (but relinquished the post of Second Minister for Trade and Industry).

In August 2006 Prime Minister Lee's annual National Day Rally speech highlighted four areas of critical activity for the Government: the economy, the population (increasing the birth rate and the intake of 'foreign talent'), reaping the benefits and 'managing the risks' of digital technologies, and increasing the emotional ties—the 'heartware'—of Singaporeans for their homeland. However, the speech conveyed an unusually defensive tone.

By 2006, therefore, the tenure of Lee Hsien Loong had not resulted in the political openness that some had anticipated. In fact, there were signs of increased levels of repression: a full police investigation was conducted against a group of schoolgirls who had erected cardboard cut-outs of white elephants to protest against the delays in the opening of a railway station; and, for the first time in many years, a popular newspaper column was discontinued in July 2006 after its author was publicly rebuked by the Government for one of his articles. During 2006 the internet also came under closer government regulation, with 'bloggers' being prosecuted under the Sedition Act for posting racist comments on their websites, and an ineffectual attempt to ban webcasts during the election campaign. In September 2006 the *Far Eastern Economic Review*, an influential Hong Kong-based journal, was banned in Singapore for breaching the country's media laws. In the previous month its editors and publisher were sued in relation to the publication of an interview with Chee Soon Juan.

Perhaps the most notable immediate change arising from Lee Hsien Loong's premiership was an unprecedented acknowledgement of the reality of, and concern about, the effects of racial discrimination against the minority communities in the area of employment, which was voiced by Lee himself and two of his ministers throughout the latter half of 2005. There was also a significant extension of efforts, which had modest beginnings during the premiership of Goh Chok Tong, to help alleviate poverty, with a number of welfare and 'workfare' measures being implemented by Lee's administration. The significance of workfare—cash rewards to low-income earners—was increased in December 2006 with Lee's announcement that the scheme was to become a permanent feature of Singapore's 'safety net' for the poor, alongside the CPF, the health system and housing subsidies. This was followed in 2007 by a partial restoration of employers' contributions to the CPF from 13.0% to 14.5%. The rate was increased further to 15.5% in May 2010.

In December 2007 Shanmugaratnam became Minister for Finance (replacing Lee Hsien Loong), while retaining the education portfolio. However, in a major cabinet reorganization announced in late March 2008, Shanmugaratnam relinquished the education portfolio to Dr Ng Eng Hen, who nevertheless continued as Second Minister for Defence. After many years of being overlooked for office, K. Shanmugam, a senior lawyer, entered the Cabinet from May as Minister of Law (succeeding Jayakumar, who remained Deputy Prime Minister and Co-ordinating Minister for National Security) and Second Minister for Home Affairs, while Gan Kim Yong replaced Dr Ng, in an acting capacity, as Minister for Manpower.

Meanwhile, in 2006 there was a resurgence of the threat from JI. Four more suspected JI members were arrested between November 2006 and April 2007, after they had allegedly undergone terrorist training in the Philippines, Pakistan or Malaysia. The unexpected detention of an allegedly 'self-radicalized' suspect, a former lawyer and lecturer who was believed to have been recruited to *jihad* through his exposure to extremist websites, was reported in mid-2007. He was arrested in Afghanistan, where he was allegedly attempting to join a Lashkar-e-Taiba training camp in Pakistan. All five men were placed under detention without trial. The campaign against JI appeared to be progressing steadily until February 2008, when Mas Selamat Kastari, the suspected leader of JI in Singapore, who had been captured in Indonesia in February 2003 and extradited to Singapore in 2006, escaped from the detention centre in which he was being held under the Internal Security Act. This extraordinary lapse of security was investigated by a committee of inquiry appointed by the Deputy Prime Minister and Minister for Home Affairs, Wong Kan Seng. In April the committee absolved Wong and the senior members of his ministry of all responsibility. On the following day Prime Minister Lee confirmed that Wong and the 'top management' of the Ministry of Home Affairs 'were not to blame'. Disciplinary proceedings were subsequently instigated against nine guards and Internal Security Department officers, including the superintendent of the detention centre. Mas Selamat was finally recaptured by the Malaysian authorities in the Malaysian town of Johor Bahru in May 2009.

Prime Minister Lee's National Day Rally speech in August 2008 was distinctive for its defensiveness on two economic issues: the rising cost of living in general, but particularly increased costs for health care and transport; and the pressure on wages and jobs created by the presence of lower-paid foreign workers. In the English version of his speech the Prime Minister devoted considerable attention to delivering a mixed message on political restrictions on the internet. While justifying the need for ongoing restrictions, he argued that many of those already in place were neither effective nor sensible. This was followed by a promise to legalize some political audio and video podcasts and more political internet sites.

In 2009 some political outcomes were for the first time shaped by developments in internet-based communities, reflecting the rising significance of the 'new media', notably *The Temasek Review* (www.temasekreview.com) and *The Online Citizen* (www.theonlinecitizen.com). Singaporeans vented anger online over issues such as the payment of huge bonuses to civil servants and mayors during the global financial crisis, a suggestion by Minister for Health Khaw Boon Wan that elderly Singaporeans might be transferred to Malaysia to reduce expenditure, and Temasek Holdings' performance and its links to the family of Minister Mentor Lee Kuan Yew (see below); the discontent in each case flowed through to the mainstream media, eliciting responses from serving politicians. Significantly, much of the online commentary consisted of detailed examinations of ministers' and other politicians' speeches, a feature that had always been conspicuously absent in the mainstream media. The ruling party responded by developing a strong online presence of its own, and it reminded people that 'anonymity is an illusion in cyberspace'. Meanwhile, some of the restrictions on political content published on the internet were eased, as promised by Prime Minister Lee Hsien Loong in 2008. Conversely, in April 2009 Parliament approved a new Public Order Act, which greatly increased the Government's powers, granting courts the power to declare a single person in any public place to be an 'illegal assembly'. Police were given the power to prevent people from leaving their homes if it was suspected that they intended to attend a rally.

A cabinet reorganization, which came into effect on 1 April 2009, was described by Prime Minister Lee as 'another step in the long process of self-renewal'. Teo Chee Hean was promoted to Deputy Prime Minister, replacing Jayakumar, who became Senior Minister and retained his special responsibilities in national security and foreign policy. Gan Kim Yong was confirmed as Minister for Manpower, while Lim Hwee Hua became Singapore's first female full cabinet minister, being appointed Minister in the Prime Minister's Office and Second Minister for Finance and Transport. Lui Tuck Yew was made Minister for Information, Communications and the Arts, on an acting basis, following the retirement of Lee Boon Yang.

The cabinet reorganization was followed in May 2009 by the unexpected announcement that the number of non-constituency MPs was to be raised from a maximum of six to a maximum of nine, bringing them into line with the number of NMPs. The categories of people invited to become NMPs was also increased, with a new category—'the people sector'—to be considered alongside the existing professional and representative fields. Moreover, the NMP scheme, which hitherto had been submitted to Parliament for approval after every election, was made permanent. In August Senior Minister Goh indicated that the search for Lee Hsien Loong's eventual replacement as Prime Minister was under way, with plans being laid five to 10 years in advance.

Temasek Holdings—one of the Government's sovereign wealth funds, and the holding company for virtually all of Singapore's government-linked companies—attracted some attention in 2009. In February it was announced that Prime Minister Lee's wife, Ho Ching, was relinquishing the post of CEO and Executive Director, to be replaced by Charles (Chip) Goodyear, former CEO of the Anglo-Australian mining conglomerate BHP Billiton. Ho had presided over some extraordinary losses while head of Temasek, which had recently lost around 30% of its value (according to official statements), mostly owing to investments in failing investment banks and other financial institutions since the onset of the global financial crisis, although the company had recovered this lost ground by the end of 2010 through more conventional investments, mainly in Asia. Goodyear's appointment was viewed in the international business community as a step towards the introduction of professional standards and a much-needed distancing of Temasek Holdings from the Singapore Government; however, just five months after taking up the position Goodyear resigned owing to 'strategic differences', and Ho returned to the position, ostensibly while the search for a replacement was conducted. She remained in the post more than one year later. In the interim Temasek found itself at the centre of a corporate governance crisis at Malaysia's Alliance Bank, whose CEO had been chosen by Temasek in its capacity as the key shareholder. The CEO took extended leave while the bank conducted an internal inquiry that was later reported to be concerned with matters of 'due diligence', and resigned several months later—although without any public disclosure of the issues that were being investigated.

As the global financial crisis worsened, the Temasek débâcle compounded the political challenges for the Government. Reports emerged of unprecedented scenes of acrimony at official 'feedback' sessions, and the Government mooted the idea of dipping into its reserves, even proposing a constitutional amendment to allow it to exceed the existing borrowing limits. In January 2009 Senior Minister Goh had announced that the preservation of jobs was the Government's most important priority.

Prime Minister Lee's 2009 National Day Rally speech, in August, was notable for its defensive and pleading tone, rather than for its initiatives, reflecting the challenges of the previous 12 months. Apart from a section that foreshadowed some health reforms, the messages emphasized surviving the global financial crisis and maintaining social cohesion across racial and religious groups. However, the National Day Rally speech (which retained its iconic status in Singapore, comparable to the State of the Union Address in the USA) was very nearly overshadowed by Minister Mentor Lee Kuan Yew's address to his local constituency's National Day Dinner a few days earlier. The Minister Mentor's speech focused on calming tensions between Singaporean citizens and the 30% of 'Singaporeans' who were Permanent Residents and Permit Holders—most of whom do not speak English but who have become a dominant presence in retail and service industries—and on Singapore's need to welcome these 'new citizens' in order to maintain the ethnic Chinese majority's proportion of both the population in general and the armed forces in particular. Immigration continued to be a highly sensitive issue for the Government, and the one that elicited the most vociferous reaction from the general population during 2009–11. Both the Prime Minister and the Minister Mentor had seemed unsure of how best to respond to the mounting concerns about immigration, oscillating between defending the current high levels on the one hand, and, on the other hand, promising to reduce immigration in the long term. Prime Minister Lee pledged to implement various constraints and restrictions on immigrants—including the introduction of English-language tests and residential quotas in housing estates—but the Government failed satisfactorily to engage with the growing restiveness among sizeable elements of the population, and consequently the issue threatened severely to compromise the Government's standing within its core constituencies.

A series of comparatively minor domestic and municipal issues that took on a public role beyond their real significance also threatened the Government's position in 2010. One of these was entirely of the Government's own creation: having announced plans to review the emphasis on the mother-tongue language policy in primary education, which requires students to achieve proficiency in the language of their ethnic group, the Government effected a *volte-face* almost immediately upon being confronted by uncharacteristically forceful opposition from several language interest groups (particularly Chinese- and Malay-language groups). This followed an explicit admission by Minister Mentor Lee in November 2009 that the bilingualism policy that he had enforced in schools until 2004 had been wrong and had caused much damage.

Another such domestic issue was recurrent serious flooding in retail and residential areas, which caused damage costing millions of dollars and raised serious questions about the effectiveness of the Government's ability to deliver basic services. Unlike the mother-tongue language policy affair, the Government was able to maintain a reasonable level of control over this issue by imposing a de facto ban on media photographs of the floods, although it took the arrest of a photographer from a prominent newspaper to ensure that the ban was upheld. This repressive approach was part of a wider intensification of government efforts to combat dissent, which included the arrest of practitioners of Falun Gong (a religious movement outlawed in China in 1999), a ban on a video recording of a speech made by a former political detainee who had been released in 1981, a ban on a public appearance by another former detainee at an academic forum, and the arrest, imprisonment and eventual deportation (in July 2011) of the British author of a book criticizing Singapore's use of the death penalty. Furthermore, the Attorney-General, Walter Woon Cheng Ming, was dismissed in April 2010, soon after he had attracted public censure from Minister Mentor Lee and his daughter, Lee Wei Ling, for ordering a prosecution that they did not wish to see pursued; Sundaresh Menon, a former judicial commissioner, was named as Woon's replacement, effective from October, with Koh Juat Jong assuming the role in an acting capacity in the interim.

In his 2010 National Day Rally speech Prime Minister Lee continued to focus on immigration, which was the main element of both the Malay and the English sections of the speech. In advance of parliamentary elections due in 2011, the main initiative announced in the speech was a direct response to concerns about the immigration issue: the creation of a new Population and Talent Division in the Prime Minister's Office, to be overseen by Deputy Prime Minister Wong Kan Seng. A series of education reforms, reinforcing the multi-track schooling system that the Government had been developing since the early 2000s, was also announced. Under this system, talented children are identified in primary school and then 'fast-tracked' to university, by removing a series of examinations from their academic pathway and allowing them to proceed directly to 'Advanced' Levels or alternative qualifications such as the International Baccalaureate. The Prime Minister also announced the expansion of alternative educational routes, whereby 'less academically inclined students' are also identified in primary school and directed into paths that lead to technical colleges or vocational training. One of the destinations for such students was to be the Singapore Institute of Technology, which opened in 2010.

In April 2011 it was announced that parliamentary elections were to be conducted in early May. The campaign period was dominated by sentiments of popular discontent over a wide range of basic issues, most of which were related, directly or indirectly, to concerns about immigration. The main issues included access to education, inadequate infrastructure and housing, the cost of living and the cost of health services. Other prevalent issues were concerns over the size of ministerial salaries (Singapore's government ministers being among the best paid in the world) and doubts about ministerial competence. All these issues were set against a new standard of accountability, primarily resulting from the greater freedom of expression afforded by the internet, and a newly invigorated and professional opposition that contested 82 out of 87 seats and whose frontline candidates included a significant number of scholars and populists. Prior to the election, Minister Mentor Lee published a new book; however, for the first time, his prominence, together with that of Senior Minister Goh, was seen as an electoral liability for the PAP, with a significant proportion of the population believed to be seeking a new generation of Singaporean leadership.

The results of the election held on 7 May 2011 were unexpected, to a degree. Although the PAP's victory was never in question, the ruling party's share of the vote was reduced to its lowest level since independence, at 60.1%, down from 66.6% in 2006. Furthermore, for the first time ever, the opposition secured control of a GRC (that of Aljunied, in north-eastern Singapore), which was won by a five-member Workers' Party team, headed by party Secretary-General Low Thia Khiang. The Workers' Party also retained Low Thia Khiang's former seat in Hougang constituency, which was won, with an increased majority, by Yaw Shin Leong, taking the opposition party's total number of seats to six. However, the SDA lost control of its one seat, in Potong Pasir, which was regained by the PAP.

Although the PAP retained an overwhelming parliamentary majority, the ruling party acknowledged the 'watershed' nature of the elections and pledged to carry out appropriate internal reform in response to public concerns. Despite the generally disappointing results for the PAP, Prime Minister Lee's authority over the Cabinet and the wider political arena was strengthened, both because his personal vote in his constituency increased, in contrast to the national PAP trend, and because he was able to apportion the blame for the party's general decline to others, including Minister Mentor Lee, Senior Minister Goh and a number of under-performing ministers.

Prime Minister Lee announced the composition of his new Cabinet in mid-May 2011; nine of the 21 ministers who comprised the outgoing Cabinet were not retained: Minister of Foreign Affairs George Yeo and Minister in the Prime Minister's Office Lim Hwee Hua both lost their seats in Aljunied; Minister Mentor Lee, Senior Minister Goh, Deputy Prime Minister Wong Kan Seng, Minister for National Development Mah Bow Tan and Minister for Transport Raymond Lim Siang Keat all resigned from the Cabinet after the election. Senior Minister S. Jayakumar and Minister in the Prime Minister's Office Lim Boon Heng had announced their respective retirements prior to the polls. Tharman Shanmugaratnam was promoted to Deputy Prime Minister and also assumed the manpower portfolio, while retaining the finance portfolio, and Deputy Prime Minister Teo Chee Hean was appointed to serve concurrently as Co-ordinating Minister for National Security and Minister for Home Affairs. Khaw Boon Wan, hitherto Minister for Health, was transferred to head the Ministry of National Development, while Minister for Law K. Shanmugam was allocated additional responsibility for foreign affairs. Yaacob Ibrahim was promoted from Minister for the Environment and Water Resources to the position of Minister for Information, Communications and the Arts, Gan Kim Yong was promoted to the post of Minister for Health and Lui Tuck Yew took responsibility for transport in place of Raymond Lim Siang Keat. Vivian Balakrishnan, hitherto Minister for Community Development, Youth and Sports, was transferred, in an effective demotion, to the environment and water resources portfolio. Balakrishnan was replaced in an acting capacity by one of three new entrants to the Cabinet, Chan Chun Sing (in his first parliamentary term), who was also appointed as Minister of State for Ministry of Information, Communications and the Arts. The other two newcomers to the Cabinet were S. Iswaran, who was appointed Minister in the Prime Minister's Office and Second Minister for Home Affairs,Trade and Industry, and Heng Swee Keat, who was appointed Minister for Education.

The resignations from the Cabinet of Lee Kuan Yew and Goh Chok Tong marked the end of an era. In a joint statement, the two erstwhile leaders declared that they had decided to step down to allow Prime Minister Lee and a younger generation of leaders 'a fresh clean slate'. Lee Kuan Yew also resigned from the chairmanship of the GIC (a position that was subsequently filled by the Prime Minister) but was appointed Senior Advisor to the GIC. Meanwhile, Goh was appointed Senior Advisor to the MAS. Both Lee and Goh remained as MPs.

Prime Minister Lee's 2011 National Day Rally speech conveyed his new-found confidence and determination to address widespread discontent. His address focused on practical measures to redress, or at least to ameliorate, the causes of popular grievances, including: improving the affordability and availability of flats for Singaporeans, increasing the number of university places for local students, the imposition of new limitations on the entry of foreign workers, and improving access to health care for the elderly.

The presidential election held on 27 August 2011 also set a new precedent: with S. R. Nathan having announced, in July, his intention to step down at the end of his second term, four candidates were successfully nominated to replace the outgoing President: the first time in Singapore's history that more than two candidates had ever contested a presidential election, and the first time since 1993 that a presidential election had been contested at all. Former Deputy Prime Minister Tony Tan, former PAP MP Tan Cheng Bock, Goh Chok Tong's former Principal Private Secretary (and also an SDP candidate in the legislative election of May 2011), Tan Jee Say, and a former CEO of NTUC Income Insurance, Tan Kin Lian, were all awarded certificates of eligibility to contest the election. According to the official results, Tony Tan received only 35.19% of the total votes cast, but under Singapore's 'first-past-the-post' electoral system this was sufficient to secure election, narrowly defeating Tan Cheng Bock, who attracted 34.85% of the votes. Tan Jee Say received 25.04% of the ballot, while Tan Kin Lian was placed a distant fourth, with just 4.91%.

FOREIGN RELATIONS

Singapore's dealings with Malaysia have always been dominated by the uneasy proximity of the two countries and their mutual dependency. With this exception, the sole objective of Singapore's foreign policy has always been to develop cordial international relationships, the only significant variation being times when issues of security or profit were the primary motivation. From 2001 the increased awareness of the threat of terrorism afforded fresh prominence to security concerns. The threat gave even greater impetus to Singapore's intention to establish good relations with neighbouring countries. Regional co-operation in addressing terrorism developed slowly.

During the 1990s the Republic had focused more on considerations of profit within the context of its foreign policy. It consistently supported the promotion of the proposed ASEAN Free Trade Area, which had been agreed upon at the summit meeting held in Singapore in 1992, and the fostering of regional security. The Republic welcomed the entry of Viet Nam, Myanmar, Laos and Cambodia as members of ASEAN in the 1990s. Singapore supported ASEAN's policy of 'constructive engagement' and gentle persuasion to reform Myanmar's autocratic military regime, in contrast to economic sanctions recommended by the EU, a policy that was reiterated by the new Minister for Foreign Affairs, Brig.-Gen. (retd) George Yong-Boon Yeo, in July 2005. Singapore was anxious to restore the influence of ASEAN, which collectively had failed to address the 1997 regional economic crisis; relations between its member states had suffered as a result of increased pressure, dissipating the confidence of overseas investors as a consequence. At meetings of ASEAN, Singapore was foremost in securing substantial measures to increase regional trade and attract capital back to South-East Asia. At the ASEAN summit in 2000 the Republic pressed for further economic integration and persuaded ASEAN to undertake a feasibility study on proposals to link the regional economies to those of China, Japan and the Republic of Korea (South Korea). The Asian economic crisis strained relations between Singapore and its immediate neighbours but, at the National Day rally in August 1998, Prime Minister Goh emphasized Singapore's dependence upon Indonesia and Malaysia. Goh also took the initiative in promoting the development of the Singapore-Johor-Riau 'Growth Triangle'. While this would benefit both Malaysia and Indonesia, it was particularly crucial to Singapore, offering the Republic's economy the opportunity to compensate for the geographical constraints of land and labour shortages.

In January 1999 Singapore signed a long-term trade agreement with Indonesia for the supply of natural gas from West Natuna to Singapore. The Singapore authorities co-operated closely with the Government of President Suharto on economic enterprises. Political relations were sometimes strained with his successors, President B. J. Habibie, who took office following the resignation of Suharto in May 1998, and Abdurrahman Wahid, who became President in 1999. However, Senior Minister Lee Kuan Yew accepted Indonesia's invitation to join an international advisory council to help accelerate the country's recovery; Singapore took the initiative in encouraging investment in Indonesia, and President Wahid and Goh launched the West Natuna gas pipeline in January 2001. Nevertheless, the Singapore Government welcomed the end of Wahid's 'wayward presidency' in July, followed by the swift and peaceful transition to power of the new Indonesian President, Megawati Sukarnoputri, with her appeal for unity. In February 2002 Singapore proposed the extension of the free trade agreement (FTA) being negotiated with the USA to Indonesia, to support its manufacturing base and attract investment. Relations were strained for a time after Lee Kuan Yew publicly reprimanded the Indonesian Government for allegedly allowing terrorists to remain at large, provoking Indonesian protests of interference, but the Singapore Government welcomed the more stringent anti-terrorist laws enacted by Indonesia after the Bali bombing, followed by the immediate arrest of cleric Abu Bakar Bashir in October. In December Prime Minister Goh became the first foreign leader to visit Indonesia after the Bali attack; the two leaders pledged to work together to combat terrorism and to revive the region's economy. This co-operation yielded results in February 2003, when the Indonesian authorities arrested and imprisoned Mas Selamat Kastari, the Indonesian-born Singaporean who was believed to be the former leader of JI in Singapore.

In 2004 Singapore began pressing for US and regional co-operation in patrolling the Melaka Straits in order to guard against the potentially disastrous effects of a hijacking or terrorist attack in this narrow stretch of water, through which passes one-third of the world's global trade and one-half of the world's oil supply. Despite US reluctance, Indonesia, Malaysia and Singapore began co-ordinating their naval patrols in July of that year, and in May 2005 Singapore joined with Indonesia in initiating a new maritime monitoring system designed to allow the Singaporean and Indonesian navies to share common surveillance data on the waters immediately to the south of Singapore. In August Thailand announced that it was to join Singapore, Indonesia and Malaysia in co-ordinated air patrols and enhanced sea patrols of the Melaka Straits. The Singaporean navy joined the annual Rim of the Pacific (RIMPAC) joint exercise for the first time in 2008, engaging in combat practice with the navies of Australia, Canada, Chile, Japan, South Korea, the Netherlands, Peru, the United Kingdom and the USA.

Despite their common desire to address the threat of terrorism, tensions continued to exist between Singapore and Malaysia. The two countries had grown closer in the mid-1990s, agreeing to settle all their differences amicably and to work together to promote investment in emerging Asian economies. In 1995 the two countries launched a bilateral defence forum, signed a Defence Co-operation Pact, and agreed on the permanent boundary of their territorial waters after 15 years of negotiations. By mid-1996 Singapore was well on the way to becoming the leading investor in Malaysia, but indiscreet disparaging remarks at that time by Lee Kuan Yew relating to Johor Bahru provoked a ferocious response from the Malaysian press and the United Malays National Organization (UMNO), the dominant element in the Malaysian ruling coalition. After several meetings between Goh Chok Tong and the Malaysian Prime Minister, Dr Mahathir Mohamad, by early 1998 it appeared that Singapore and Malaysia had put aside their differences. The two Prime Ministers discussed ways to help restore economic confidence in the region, and agreed to co-operate in the areas of banking and finance and to encourage private investment in each other's economies. Mahathir announced that bilateral problems could be solved, given flexibility. However, friction escalated over conflicting interpretations of the Points of Agreement, signed by the two countries in 1990, covering the status and development of Malayan Railway land in Singapore, under the terms of which land at Tanjong Pagar, Kranji and Woodlands would be developed jointly by the two countries. In accordance with a long-standing arrangement, Singapore prepared to transfer railway customs, immigration and quarantine facilities from Tanjong Pagar to the frontier at Woodlands in August 1998; however, Malaysia refused to do likewise and ended talks with Singapore abruptly at the end of July. In September Malaysia imposed restrictions on the use of its airspace by Singaporean military aircraft, complained that Malaysian ports were losing trade to Singapore and withdrew from a Five Power Defence Arrangement exercise, citing tensions with Singapore as well as economic difficulties. In September 1998 the publication of the first volume of Lee Kuan Yew's memoirs, which contained a contentious section devoted to Singapore's separation from Malaysia in 1967, revived traditional antagonisms and provoked protests from the Malaysian leadership.

However, Singapore's politicians continued to emphasize the need for good relations with Malaysia and the importance of maintaining racial harmony in Singapore. In November 1998 Goh visited Malaysia at the invitation of Mahathir, and at the ASEAN summit meeting in Hanoi, Viet Nam, in the following month the two Prime Ministers agreed upon an arrangement to settle all outstanding issues. Officials met several times over the next few months, but discussions were abandoned in May 1999. Contact was resumed unexpectedly by Senior Minister Lee Kuan Yew, who paid a four-day informal visit to Malaysia in August 2000 for the first time in 10 years. After receiving a very cordial welcome, including meetings with Mahathir and other ministers, Lee declared that, given compromise on both sides, all disputes could be settled within a few months. Lee's second volume of memoirs, published in September 2000, was warmly received in Malaysia, and the two Prime Ministers had discussions at the time of the ASEAN summit meeting in Singapore in November 2000. A joint naval exercise was held in that month, and in February 2001 the Malaysian Deputy Prime Minister brought a large delegation for informal discussions, at which a compromise over the railway facilities was agreed in principle, and ideas were mooted for a new bridge to replace the causeway and an undersea rail tunnel. Meeting in Kuala Lumpur in August 2001, the Malaysian Prime Minister and Senior Minister Lee Kuan Yew agreed a compromise in principle on all outstanding issues, leaving the detailed arrangements to be worked out by officials.

However, the negotiations were fraught with difficulties. The main issue of contention was the price of water supplied by Malaysia under two agreements, made in 1961 and 1962, which were guaranteed under the 1965 Separation Agreement and were due to remain in force until 2011 and 2061, respectively. Malaysia had undertaken to supply raw water at a cost of 3 sen (Malaysian cents) per 1,000 gallons and to receive treated water back from Singapore. While provision was included in the agreements to vary the price after 25 years, Malaysia had not proposed this at the relevant times in 1986 and 1987, but first raised complaints about the price early in 2001. In September of that year Singapore offered to pay 45 sen for the period between 2011 and 2061 (although not legally required to do so), and Malaysia pledged to continue the supply after 2061 at an increased price, which would be reviewed every five years. Despite a conciliatory visit by Lee Hsien Loong to Kuala Lumpur, Malaysia's national press and politicians continued what Singapore's Minister for Foreign Affairs described as 'psychological warfare'. Complaints about Singapore profiting from cheap water were followed for several months from February 2002 by vociferous objections to Singapore's reclamation projects at Tuas and Pulau Tekong in the Johor Strait. Singapore insisted that the reclamation would cause no damage and was entirely within the Republic's territorial waters. The two Governments also came into conflict over the nature of a possible replacement for the causeway and the sovereignty of Pedra Branca (a rocky outcrop off the eastern Johor coast on which Singapore had constructed and maintained a lighthouse since the mid-19th century).

Singapore aimed to resolve nearly all outstanding issues in one settlement, which would include water, the location of Customs, Immigration and Quarantine facilities in Singapore, the redevelopment of Malaysian railway land in Singapore, the early release of CPF money to West Malaysian contributors, the use of Malaysian airspace and the construction of a bridge to replace the causeway. However, at the first meeting of officials, held in July 2002, Malaysia argued that the water issue should be settled first; in October Prime Minister Mahathir notified Singapore that Malaysia had decided to abandon the idea of resolving all outstanding issues at the same time. Later that month officials met in Johor Bahru to discuss the water issue, but no progress was made; both sides then aired their grievances in public. The two countries had agreed in 1998 to refer the issue of sovereignty over Pedra Branca to international arbitration, but in December 2002 Mahathir accused Singapore of continuing to develop the disputed island. Meanwhile, Singapore criticized Malaysia for delaying the signing of the Special Agreement concerning referral of the issue, which had already been concluded, but which needed formal signature before it could be submitted to the International Court of Justice (ICJ) in The Hague, Netherlands.

In January 2003 Singapore's Minister for Foreign Affairs, Prof. Shanmugam Jayakumar, presented to Parliament the published details of all the correspondence between the two Governments, describing it as 'the Republic's most significant statement on bilateral relations since independence'. Jayakumar stressed that the water dispute was not an issue of money but one of national sovereignty, since the Water Agreements were included in the Constitution, registered with the UN, and could not be changed unilaterally by either party. Kuala Lumpur objected to the release of the documents. Goh Chok Tong insisted throughout that relations with Malaysia were not beyond repair, and the Agreement referring the Pedra Branca issue to the ICJ was signed in February, but the dispute continued. Meanwhile, Singapore sought to reduce its dependence on Malaysia by implementing long-term plans to construct desalination facilities and thus make the Republic self-sufficient in water. Relations with Malaysia continued to be strained in 2003, but eased with the succession of Abdullah Badawi to the Malaysian premiership. The dispute over land reclamation in the Strait of Johor was resolved in April 2005 after successful bilateral negotiations, and the dispute over rebuilding the causeway eased when Abdullah Badawi abandoned his predecessor's building plans. Relations between the two Governments became increasingly cordial. In 2006 a high level of Singaporean involvement and investment was forthcoming in the Iskander Malaysia development project—a major housing, commercial and industrial project in the Malaysian state of Johor. The Pedra Branca dispute was finally resolved by the ICJ in May 2008: Singapore was confirmed as the owner of Pedra Branca itself, but Malaysia was awarded sovereignty over Middle Rocks, Pedra Branca's rocky northern outcrop. Neither side was satisfied with this result, but they both accepted the outcome and gave every appearance of being determined to make the settlement work.

Singapore's relations with other members of ASEAN have remained mostly harmonious, despite some areas of discord, notably with Indonesia. In September 2006 Minister Mentor Lee caused a rupture in relations with Indonesia and Malaysia when he suggested that they were subjugating their Chinese minorities. Meanwhile, India took the unusual action of preventing Temasek Holdings (which was owned by the Singapore Government and overseen by the wife of Prime Minister Lee) and the Government of Singapore Investment Corporation (GIC) from increasing their combined stake in ICICI, a major Indian bank, in accordance with Reserve Bank of India regulations.

In early 2007 the Indonesian Government imposed a ban on the sale of sand to Singapore, placing intense pressure on the city-state's construction industry and land reclamation programme, neither of which could function without a steady supply of large quantities of sand. Although the Indonesian Government formally denied that there was any connection with other diplomatic issues, it quickly became clear that the issue of the sand was being used to bring an extradition treaty to a swift conclusion. Indonesia had been accusing Singapore of laundering Indonesian money that had been illegally removed from the country, but negotiations to settle the matter had been slow. The sand ban brought the matter to a conclusion, and both the extradition treaty and a defence co-operation agreement were signed in April. Singapore also began diversifying its sourcing of sand to decrease its reliance upon Indonesia. An emerging pattern of Indonesian intransigence seemed to establish itself two months later, when the Indonesian Government unexpectedly raised late objections to the defence co-operation agreement, which would have given Singapore extensive rights to train and engage in exercises on Indonesian soil. In late 2007 the defence co-operation agreement was suspended 'indefinitely', the Singapore Government attributing this directly to 'the complex dynamics of Indonesia's domestic debate' over the extradition treaty and the defence accord. Singapore suffered a further set-back in the Indonesian courts in May 2008, when an earlier ruling against Temasek Holdings—to the effect that different investment and corporate arms of the Singapore Government should be regarded as one entity under Indonesia's anti-monopoly laws—was upheld. However, despite these problems, bilateral co-operation on matters such as combating terrorism and piracy has continued, and in March 2009 the two countries successfully concluded four years of negotiations on the maritime border between the two countries.

Full diplomatic relations had been restored between Singapore and the Philippines in January 1996, following an acrimonious dispute in the previous year, which had caused the deepest rift between ASEAN partners for more than a quarter of a century, after Singapore insisted in March 1995 on hanging a Filipina woman found guilty of murder, despite pleas from President Fidel Ramos for a stay of execution. When President Joseph Estrada of the Philippines visited Singapore in October 1998, a few months after his election, the Republic welcomed his pledge to retain an open economy and pro-market policies. At the ASEAN summit meeting (held in Hanoi) in December, the two countries signed a Philippine-Singapore Action Plan to develop closer bilateral co-operation in trade.

Goh Chok Tong welcomed the efforts of the Thai Prime Minister, Thaksin Shinawatra, to revive the Thai economy, and in February 2002 proposed an extension of their existing co-operation in the form of the Singapore-Thailand Enhanced Economic Relationship (STEER). In August 2003 the Republic commended the arrest in the Thai capital, Bangkok, of Hambali, the alleged operational head of JI. At the annual ASEAN summit meeting held in Phnom-Penh, Cambodia, in November 2002, Goh Chok Tong, with the strong support of Thailand, proposed a single ASEAN market with free movement of goods and services and no tariffs. In 2006 the sale of a 49.25% share in Shin Corporation, the iconic Thai telecommunications and media company, to Temasek Holdings provoked public outrage in Thailand, ultimately contributing to a bloodless military coup against Thaksin. It was not known how much value had been stripped from Shin Corporation in the aftermath of the purchase. The Singapore Government compounded the complications arising from this incident when Deputy Prime Minister Shanmugam Jayakumar met Thaksin in January 2007. The Thai transitional Government responded by summoning the Singapore ambassador and abruptly cancelling a planned visit by Singapore's Minister for Foreign Affairs, George Yeo.

Having accorded diplomatic recognition to the People's Republic in 1990, Singapore continued to maintain cordial relations with China. By 2001 earlier problems over the progress of Suzhou Industrial Park, a Sino-Singaporean joint venture in China, from which Singapore had contemplated withdrawing, had been resolved, and Singapore continued to encourage investment and commercial links. Lee Kuan Yew travelled frequently to China, always receiving a warm welcome. In April 2000 Goh Chok Tong paid an official visit, reaffirming co-operation with China, and in 2001 Singapore established institutions for closer business links, following China's admission to the World Trade Organization (WTO). In April 2002 Chinese Vice-President Hu Jintao made an official visit to Singapore. He and Goh agreed to establish a senior-level joint council to investigate potential areas of practical co-operation, such as an early start to negotiations for a China-ASEAN free trade area, and Beijing also offered Singapore military training facilities on Hainan Island as an alternative to Taiwan. In 2003 and 2004 the Singapore Government intensified its attention towards China, regarding it as being crucial to Singapore's prosperity as well as its 'main challenger'. Clear indications of the focus on Sino-Singaporean relations included: ministerial visits; the opening of a replica of Singapore's Raffles City in Shanghai; a new, positive focus on development of the Suzhou Industrial Park; and plans to begin talks concerning a bilateral FTA. However, the seemingly ineluctable progress of the movement towards ever closer bilateral relations was temporarily interrupted in July 2004 by Deputy Prime Minister Lee Hsien Loong's misjudged 'private' visit to Taiwan, which provoked unexpectedly strong protests from the mainland Chinese Government. In 2005 harmonious relations with China seemed likely to grow stronger with the formal development of the 'ASEAN + 3' group (the 10 member states of ASEAN, plus China, Japan and South Korea) into the East Asia Summit. Not even the detention by China of a Singapore-based journalist was allowed to obstruct bilateral goodwill: by late 2005 Prime Minister Lee was once again visiting China in an official capacity, and Minister for Foreign Affairs George Yeo was speaking with confidence of plans to expand Singapore's consular presence in China. Bilateral free trade talks between China and Singapore commenced in October 2006 and were successfully concluded in September 2008.

Anxious to avoid conflict in the region, Singapore hoped that Taiwan would reach an agreement with China, with a view to reunification. Singapore had hosted the first Taiwan-China talks in 1993. In October 2001 Lee Kuan Yew made a four-day visit to Taiwan (his first in six years) on his own initiative, and not at the invitation of the Taiwan Government. He was received with respect, although his views differed from those of President Chen Shui-bian. Lee Kuan Yew argued that Taiwan should accept the 'one China' reunification principle on the terms proposed by the Chinese Government.

The maintenance of good relations with the USA continued to be of crucial importance to Singapore. The Republic had distanced itself from the hostile stance towards China adopted by the US Administration of President Bill Clinton (1993–2001), and during 1993–96 the Clinton Administration relegated Singapore to *persona non grata* status following the sentence of caning imposed on a young US national who had been convicted of vandalism. However, the measures taken by the Singapore Government to mitigate the Republic's financial problems following the onset of the regional economic crisis in 1997 won praise in the US press. Goh Chok Tong was the first South-East Asian leader to meet President George W. Bush in Washington in June 2001, when he urged a permanent US interest in South-East Asia. In recognition of Singapore's strong support after the 11 September terrorist attacks, the US Government designated Singapore 'a friendly foreign country', with privileged access to technology and eligibility to take part in co-operative programmes in research, development and defence. In October 2002 a new Singapore Congressional Caucus was established in the US House of Representatives, with the objective of strengthening security and economic links. The US alliance has remained a central tenet of Singapore's foreign policy—for both strategic and trade purposes—and in 2005 bilateral relations were further consolidated when Prime Minister Lee met President Bush during a visit to the USA. The Republic had previously welcomed the Joint Declaration for Co-operation to Combat International Terrorism agreed between ASEAN and the USA and signed by the US Secretary of State, Colin Powell, in Brunei in July 2002. The agreement, reached at meetings of ASEAN ministers responsible for foreign affairs and their 13 dialogue partners, provided for sharing intelligence, blocking terrorist funds, and tightening border security, without increasing the number of US troops in the region or creating new military bases. While giving the final keynote speech at the World Economic Forum's East Asia Economic Summit, held in Kuala Lumpur in October 2002, Goh Chok Tong appealed for the closer economic integration of ASEAN. He urged the formation of an East Asian community, potentially similar to the EU, with a common currency and single market, in order to combat terrorism and to keep abreast of global economic change. One of Prime Minister Goh's last foreign policy ventures before his retirement was a tour of the Middle East in 2004, whereby he hoped to progress towards opening up a new area of commercial activity for the Republic.

Under Lee Hsien Loong's premiership, Singapore's foreign policy focused firmly on three goals: maintaining and increasing political relations with, and market access to, the USA and China; maintaining good relations with ASEAN and other near neighbours; and securing access to new and emerging markets such as the Middle East and India. Despite the inevitable emergence of various problems and set-backs, Singapore remained on course in all these areas.

Singapore maintained very close relations with the US Administration of President Bush, and was one of the first to declare its support for the US-led coalition's invasion of Iraq in 2003. The election of Barack Obama to the US presidency in November 2008 made no discernible difference to bilateral relations, with both the Obama Administration and the Singapore Government sufficiently realist in outlook to continue business as usual.

Singapore's relations with the new Malaysian Government of Najib Tun Razak, who assumed the premiership in April 2009, began poorly when Najib made a series of statements that seemed to be reviving points of contention from the Mahathir era. However, the Singapore Government successfully defused tension by sending Minister Mentor Lee on a one-week visit to Malaysia in June to engage in discussions with a wide range of senior officials, including Malaysia's Yang di-Pertuan Agong ('Supreme Head of State'), Sultan Tuanku Mizan Zainal Abidin, and also Prime Minister Najib's wife.

Relations with Malaysia improved steadily during 2010, and by mid-2011 bilateral ties were at their healthiest for quite some time. The most significant development was a land exchange agreement, signed in June 2010, under the terms of which Malaysia was to transfer its railway line and station at Tanjong Pagar, in central Singapore, to a location closer to the causeway linking the two countries across the Strait of Tebrau. An agreement was also concluded on the establishment of a joint company to redevelop land in Singapore scheduled to be vacated by the Malaysian railway company, Keretapi Tanah Melayu Bhd (KTMB). The relocation was effected in September 2011, and signalled the resolution of the final outstanding matter from a bilateral agreement signed in 1990. Following another bilateral summit meeting in September 2010 it was announced that Prime Ministers Lee and Najib had agreed to settle through the international Permanent Court of Arbitration all outstanding issues concerning the KTMB land redevelopment project. Bilateral relations were further enhanced when, during the same summit, the Malaysian authorities confirmed the extradition of Mas Selamat Kastari, the suspected leader of JI in Singapore, who had been captured in Malaysia in April 2009 following his escape from Singaporean custody in 2008 (see above).

The likelihood of renewed friction between Singapore and Malaysia continued to diminish as the city-state decreased its reliance upon Malaysia for fresh water. The country's 15th reservoir (Marina Reservoir) was opened in November 2010. This reservoir was distinctive because it was in the middle of the city and had a totally urban catchment, and yet was expected to provide some 10% of Singapore's total water supply. Declaring water self-sufficiency to be 'a strategic priority', Prime Minister Lee announced in July 2011 that desalination and recycling plants were expected to account for 80% of Singapore's water supply before the expiry, in 2061, of the second water treaty with Malaysia.

In October 2010 Singapore and Viet Nam signed agreements to the value of US $300m.; most of these accords pertained to residential real estate development projects in Ho Chi Minh City. Singapore had already been heavily investing in Viet Nam, but this agreement, and the fact that it was signed by the two countries' respective Prime Ministers, indicated a deepening of bilateral relations.

Singapore's relations with Indonesia also improved during 2010, and remained stable at mid-2011. Closer co-operation was manifest in a bilateral leaders' retreat held in November 2009, increased joint patrols of the Melaka Straits announced in March 2010, and the creation in May of that year of six new joint working groups designed to enhance bilateral economic co-operation and investment.

During 2011 Singapore's foreign affairs were dominated by the continuation of its attention to relations with the USA and China. Senior-level visitors were exchanged with both countries, including visits to Singapore by China's Vice-President Xi Jinping to commemorate the 20th anniversary of the establishment of diplomatic relations, and by US Navy Secretary Raymond Mabus.

Economy

TILAK ABEYSINGHE

INTRODUCTION

Singapore's ascent from 'third world' to 'first world' status has been spectacular, particularly in view of the country's lack of natural resources. The island's only assets have been its relatively minuscule population and its excellent geographical location. In terms of annual real per caput income, measured on the basis of purchasing-power parity at 2005 constant prices, Singapore had reached the level of Switzerland by the mid-1990s, earlier than had been anticipated. By 2009 Singapore had attained an income level of US $47,000, about US $7,000 more than the corresponding figure for Switzerland. This stood in stark contrast to the situation in 1965, in which year the per caput income of Singapore was about US $4,700, compared with about US $22,000 in Switzerland. In 2010 Singapore's gross national income (GNI) per head (excluding foreign workers) was about US $42,000. Owing to the 2008/09 global economic downturn, per caput income declined to about US $35,800 in 2008 and US $32,300 in 2009. In 2009 per caput household net wealth stood at about US $200,600. Even in terms of other development indicators, the country's progress since 1965, when Singapore left the Malaysian Federation and acceded to independence, is unsurpassed. The infant mortality rate, which was above 26 per 1,000 live births in 1965, had declined to 2.0 per 1,000 by 2010, among the lowest in the world. Between 1965 and 2007 the proportion of people living in and owning publicly provided housing units increased from 4% to 80%, with total home-ownership exceeding 90%; the adult literacy rate improved from 73% to 96%; the number of participants in the labour force educated to secondary level increased from 14% to 50%; the labour force with tertiary education went up from 2% to 36%; and life expectancy at birth improved from 66 to 81 years.

When questioned about the success of Singapore, the response of the founding leader, Lee Kuan Yew, was: 'there was no secret; we had no choice but to take a chance and sail into rough waters'. The Government's development ideology has been growth-driven, purely pragmatic and adaptable to changing circumstances. As a result, a uniquely Singaporean system has emerged, which may not be easily emulated by other countries. On the one hand, Singapore is a tightly regulated, planned economy; on the other hand it stands out as a 'beacon' of the free market system. The pioneering economic architect of Singapore, Goh Keng Swee, described Singapore as 'a socialist economy that works'. The present-day Singapore may be described as a 'market-driven guided economy'.

Singapore is not without its critics. The contention arises primarily with regard to the lack of political freedom and the uncompromising approach that the Government has adopted in handling political opponents and dissenting views. The racial riots, political turmoil and bloodshed that was witnessed in other newly independent countries such as India and Sri Lanka, and Singapore's own turbulent beginnings, emphasized to the island's leaders the importance of political stability for the achievement of economic progress. In the words of Goh Keng Swee: 'The role of government is pivotal. Non-economic factors, which have yet to be reduced to a coherent multi-disciplinary system, are more important than economic variables'. Amartya Sen, the Nobel laureate, reiterated these views by arguing that good governance, not less governance, is crucial to addressing the challenges of economic inequality, environmental degradation and terrorism. The importance of good governance and political stability was again emphasized in *The Growth Report: Strategies for Sustained Growth and Inclusive Development*, which was released in May 2008 by the Commission on Growth and Development, chaired by Nobel laureate Michael Spence.

After a brief account of Singapore's recent growth record, this essay will focus on the main reasons for the country's success. In a typical production function analysis, the focus is placed on factor inputs, mainly labour and capital. In an economy such as that of Singapore, which is driven primarily by international investments, capital is essentially an intermediate input; and what makes Singapore attractive to this capital are the factors that need to be examined. These elements can be captured in three broad categories: human resources, infrastructure and international competitiveness. Furthermore, the composition of these elements is a product of government policies. Unless otherwise stated, all growth rates provided are calculated on a year-on-year basis.

RECENT GROWTH RECORD

With the exception of the recession of 1985/86, the Singapore economy recorded impressive growth rates from the mid-1970s until the onset of the Asian financial crisis in mid-1997 and the subsequent instability. The regional crisis was followed by the sharp downturn in the electronics sector in 2001 and by the setback resulting from the emergence of a hitherto-unknown virus, Severe Acute Respiratory Syndrome (SARS), in 2003. Despite this, the economy made a quick recovery and then started to accelerate, recording gross domestic product (GDP) growth rates of 9.0% in 2004, 7.3% in 2005, 8.6% in 2006 and 8.5% in 2007. However, this proved to be a brief period of expansion. In the latter months of 2008 the world economic downturn, precipitated by the US 'sub-prime' mortgage crisis, had an impact on the Singapore economy before that of its regional neighbours, and resulted in the deepest recession that Singapore had experienced since independence. Entities severely affected by the global financial crisis included the Government of Singapore Investment Corporation and Temasek Holdings, an investment company owned by the Singapore Government. The economy weakened rapidly in 2008, contracting in the second half of the year, and resulting in meagre GDP growth of 1.5% for the year as a whole. The recession continued into 2009, with the Singapore economy registering an unprecedented 8.4% contraction in the first quarter of the year. Although the economy recovered slowly in the second half of 2009, a contraction of 0.8% was recorded for the year as a whole. Unlike previous periods of financial difficulty in Singapore, during which some sectors were badly affected while others continued to perform relatively well, the 2008/09 recession was not only deep but also widespread across the whole economy. By contrast, during the 2001 economic crisis, while the electronics sector experienced a severe downturn, the services sector continued to fare comparatively well; similarly, during the 1997/98 Asian financial crisis a relatively strong performance by the manufacturing sector helped to offset the decline in financial services and commerce, and during the 1985/86 recession the contraction in the manufacturing and construction industries was counterbalanced to some extent by a comparatively robust services sector. The recovery in 2010 was spectacular, with the economy expanding by 14.5%. The manufacturing sector recorded a stellar performance, posting growth of 29.7%, while services also recovered robustly and expanded by 10.5%.

The manufacturing sector had helped to propel the Singapore economy to its heights, but by 2008 had also become the source of volatility. Having steadily expanded from 2004, registering a 12.6% increase in the first quarter of 2008, the manufacturing sector entered a period of significant decline, contracting by 5.6%, 11.0% and 10.7% in the second, third and fourth quarters of 2008, respectively, and by an extraordinary 23.8% in the first quarter of 2009. However, the sector made an unexpectedly strong recovery in the first half of 2010, recording 37.2% growth in the first quarter and 45.2% in the second quarter. Although these impressive growth rates were partly due to the low base of 2009, the strong momentum continued through the second half of 2010, with growth of 13.7% and 25.5%, respectively, in the third and fourth quarters of the year. Furthermore, from this much stronger base, there was further robust growth, of 13.1%, in the first quarter of 2011. Although the manufacturing sector has become less dependent on the electronics industry, another volatile sub-sector, biomedical production, has come to account for a substantial share of manufacturing exports. Despite volatility, the manufacturing sector has retained its dominance in the economy, contributing on average about 25% of GDP; the sector's GDP contribution reached 27% in 2010, having increased from 23% in 2009.

The services sector, which accounted for 66% of GDP in 2008, did much to offset the contraction in manufacturing in that year, registering a 4.3% expansion. However, in 2009 the services sector succumbed to the effects of the global recession and contracted by 0.7%, with the most severe sub-sectoral contractions appearing in wholesale and retail trade (6.0%), transport and storage (9.0%) and hotels and restaurants (1.6%). Financial services, which contracted by 4.0% in the first quarter of 2009, registered growth of 4.3% in 2009 as a whole. The services sector made a strong recovery in 2010, recording growth of 10.5% in that year, and expanding by a further 7.3% in the first quarter of 2011. The burgeoning tourism sector, with the number of visitors to Singapore reaching 10.3m. in 2007, started to decelerate rapidly in the second half of 2008; arrivals for 2008 as a whole declined to 10.12m. and further declined to 9.68m. in 2009. In 2010 visitor arrivals recovered to reach 11.64m.

The only sector that registered an impressive performance during the recessionary period was that of construction. After a long period of stagnation, the construction sector started to recover in 2006, in which year it expanded by 2.6%, with growth accelerating to 16.3% in 2007 and further to 20.1% in 2008. This momentum continued into 2009, with a number of major construction projects that were brought forward by the Government as part of its counter-cyclical measures helping to boost sectoral growth to 17.1% in that year. However, the construction sector, which accounted for less than 4% of GDP and employed a large foreign work-force, was of insufficient significance within the Singapore economy as a whole to be able to counter the downturn. In any case, sectoral growth decelerated subsequently, growing by 6.1% in 2010 and by just 2.4% in the first quarter of 2011.

On the demand side, the growth of private consumption expenditure decelerated from 6.5% in 2007 to 3.2% in 2008, declining further to just 0.2% in 2009, before recovering to 4.2% in 2010, albeit from the low base of 2009. An enigmatic development in Singapore has been a decline in the share of private consumption expenditure in GDP. This share has decreased from 61% in 1970 to 35% in 2010. In general, private consumption expenditure is the most stable aggregate demand component and accounts for about two-thirds of GDP in developed economies. As this integral stabilizing element is eroded, the economy's trajectory of growth becomes more uncertain, owing to the volatility of the other demand components, private investment expenditure and exports. Studies have shown that Singapore's declining consumption share has resulted primarily from rising property and car prices; when these prices decrease the consumption share tends to rise.

Gross fixed capital formation decelerated from growth of 20% in 2007 to 14% growth in 2008, before contracting by 2.9% in 2009. It expanded modestly by 5.1% in 2010, but unexpectedly contracted by about 9.5% in the first quarter of 2011.

Despite the economic downturn, Singapore continued to draw steady inflows of foreign direct investment (FDI) in 2008; the manufacturing sector attracted a total of S $18,046m. in investment commitments, representing an increase of 5% from 2007. However, in 2009 investment commitments declined to S $11,754m., a year-on-year contraction of 35%, with the contribution of foreign investors to total investment commitments declining from about 90% in 2008 to 71% in 2009. Interestingly, investment commitments by local firms increased in 2009, despite the overall decline. In 2010 investment commitments rose modestly, to S $12,854m., of which 84% was from foreign investors.

The driving force in the Singapore economy has been external demand, with exports of goods and services being of vital importance. The significance of exports is well reflected in the ratio of exports to GDP. Between 2005 and 2010 the merchandise exports to GDP ratio was about 170%, and the domestic merchandise exports (excluding re-exports) to GDP ratio was more than 90%. The most significant value-adding export item is non-oil domestic (merchandise) exports, which accounted for 37% of total exports (including re-exports) during 2005–10. External demand, which accounted for more than 75% of total demand during 2005–10, is the primary determinant in growth fluctuations within Singapore. Non-oil domestic exports contracted by 8% in 2008, and by a further 11% in 2009; against this low base, the 23% expansion recorded by non-oil domestic exports in 2010 appeared less impressive. Although intra-regional trade among Singapore's Asian trading partners has increased substantially over the last decade, the belief of some commentators that the region had become decoupled from the US economy has been dispelled by the 2008/09 global economic downturn. It should be noted that the increase in intra-regional trade has been largely a result of growth, in volume terms, in the trade of parts and components. Demand is still largely driven by the USA, the European Union (EU) and Japan. The weakening of demand and the trade-financing constraints had a severe impact on cross-border production networks in Asia. As a result, Singaporean exports, as well as those of its regional trading partners, declined rapidly from early 2008.

Singapore has recorded consistent balance of payments surpluses over many decades. In the early phase of Singapore's development the current account was in deficit, and this was financed by large capital inflows, mainly FDI. Since 1988 the current account has recorded surpluses, averaging about 12% of GNI. Over this period FDI inflows continued, and there was a substantial outflow of domestic savings, primarily public savings, in the form of portfolio investments. The outflow of domestic savings and inflow of foreign savings have constituted a unique feature of Singapore's balance of payments since about 1988. Furthermore, exports and imports are closely linked because a substantial proportion of products imported by Singapore are intermediate products needed for the production of exports. Consequently, when exports contracted in 2009 so too did imports, and a merchandise trade surplus of S $42,458m. was recorded. This, together with a positive service balance, led to an overall current account surplus of S $50,769m., equivalent to about 18% of GDP. In 2010 the merchandise balance improved to S $63,596m., while the service balance increased to S $20,542m. The capital and finance account recorded a deficit of S $39,016m., in 2009; in 2010 the deficit declined to S $9,458m. As a result, the overall balance of payments improved from a surplus of S $16,456m. in 2009 to S $57,480m. in 2010, which strengthened Singapore's foreign reserve position.

Despite the decline in exports in 2008–09, the job market demonstrated its customary delayed response. In fact, some 221,600 new jobs were created in 2008; total employment in that year stood at 2.86m. workers (including foreign workers), and the unemployment rate decreased to 2.2%, down from a peak of 4.0% in 2003. However, unemployment started to increase from the third quarter of 2009, with the resident unemployment rate peaking at 4.8% in September of that year. This had declined to 3.3% by mid-2010, at which time total employment stood at 3.05m. A further 28,300 new jobs were created during the first quarter of 2011; at March 2011 the unemployment rate had decreased to 1.9%, although this increased slightly, to 2.1%, at June, with many employers adopting a cautious approach to expansion and job creation. As a result of the anticipated severity of the downturn, the Government had released the 2009 budget in mid-January, well in advance of the start of the fiscal year (1 April), and offered it primarily as a 'resilience package' aimed predominantly at protecting jobs, especially under the so-called Jobs Credit Scheme, an innovative measure intended to protect jobs. The stimulus programme played a significant role in mitigating job losses. In 2010 the services sector accounted for 78% of total employment of resident workers, while manufacturing accounted for only 15% and construction employed a mere 5%.

The strong economic growth between 2004 and 2007 was accompanied by a substantial increase in employment, mostly imported labour. However, job creation has been at the cost of decreasing productivity; value-added per worker rose by a meagre 0.1% in 2007, decreased by 7.5% in 2008 and by 3.4% in 2009, before increasing by 10.7% in 2010. The decline in labour productivity created a substantial disparity with the rate of wage growth. Owing to increasing demand for labour, nominal wages in 2007 grew by 6.2%. In the same year consumer prices increased by 2.6%, leading to a real wage increase of 3.6%. In 2008 nominal wages grew by 5.4%. Owing to sharp rises in international commodity prices and to other domestic cost pressures in the first half of that year, consumer prices increased by 6.5% and as a result real wages declined by 1.1%. In 2009 nominal wages contracted by 2.6%. However, the rate of increase in the consumer price index (CPI) also decelerated, to 0.6%, resulting in a real wage contraction of 3.2%. In 2010 nominal wages grew by 5.6% and the CPI increased by 2.8%, leading to real wage growth of a modest 2.8% despite the substantial growth in labour productivity and the wider economy. The most highly paid jobs in 2010, as in previous years, were in financial services, with monthly earnings averaging S $7,656, compared with S $4,263 in manufacturing. As a result of mounting wage pressures, the economy-wide unit labour cost (ULC) index increased steadily from 2005, following a decline in both 2003 and 2004. Although a large influx of foreign labour kept wage cost pressures under control, rising nominal wages and decreasing labour productivity generated a 4.7% increase in the ULC index in 2008. However, as wage pressures eased in 2009, the ULC index rose by only 0.6% in that year, and it declined by 2.7% in 2010.

Apart from wage costs, overall domestic costs grew rapidly in the first half of 2008, driven by a substantial increase in property rentals, other service costs and government rates and charges. The unit business cost index in manufacturing increased by 11.1% in 2008, compared with a 2.1% increase in 2007. Increasing domestic costs, combined with high import costs resulting from rising food, oil and other commodity prices, and an increase of two percentage points in the goods and services tax (GST) in July 2007, translated into CPI inflation of 6.6% and 7.5% in the first and second quarter of 2008, respectively—a substantial increase from 2.1% in 2007 and 1.0% in 2006. As commodity prices and property rentals started to decline from the second half of 2008, CPI growth began to decelerate in 2009, with the annual average standing at 0.6%. However, as the economy started to recover in the first half of 2010, CPI inflation began to rise again, reaching 4.0% (year-on-year) by the end of that year, and rising by a further 5.2% in the first half of 2011.

Driven by the high growth performance of 2004–07, the property market was revitalized, after a decade of relative inactivity, and re-entered a period of frenzy, contributing to a 'bubble' situation similar to the one that had ended abruptly in 1996. After a 7% increase in 2006, private residential property prices started to escalate rapidly in 2007; the four quarters of 2007 registered increases of 14%, 21%, 28%, and 31%, respectively. The first three quarters of 2008 also registered further increases of 30%, 20% and 8%, respectively, but these prices declined by 14% in 2009. However, the decline was brief and prices gathered momentum again in 2010, registering a 26% rise, before slowing to a 12% increase in the first half of 2011. Public housing resale flats followed similar price trends, although they continued to increase in 2009, by 7.4%, and increased further by 14.2% in 2010 and by 12.3% in the first half of 2011. With the affordability of housing eroding quickly, the Government introduced some drastic measures in September 2010 in an effort to contain the soaring property prices, including: an extension of sellers' stamp duty to those who resell within three years of purchase; an extension, to five years, of the minimum occupancy period for resale public housing accommodation; limiting mortgage loans to 70% of the purchase price; and requiring private property owners, both within Singapore and overseas, purchasing public housing accommodation to sell their private property within six months of buying their new public housing. The main objective of these measures was to separate the public and private housing markets from one another and to reduce investment and speculative activities in the public housing market in an attempt to ensure that public housing is exclusively for owner occupation. However, the measures are generally perceived to be overly restrictive.

Despite the robust economic growth recorded in 2010 and the first half of 2011, the short-term outlook for the rest of the year remained uncertain. A sustained recovery in Singapore's export-led economy remained dependent on the economies of the USA, the EU and Japan gathering momentum.

DEVELOPMENT STRATEGY

Development Experience and Institutions

Since the achievement of self-government in 1959 and independence in 1965, Singapore has passed through a number of phases in its development process. The Government implemented strategic plans in 1960 (First Plan), 1980 (Second Plan), 1985 (Economic Committee Report), 1991 (Strategic Economic Plan), 1998 (Competitiveness Report), 1999 (Industry 21; Manpower 21), 2002 (Economic Review Committee) and 2010 (Economic Strategies Committee). Through a forward-looking strategy, the Government of Singapore has responded to new economic challenges quickly and capitalized very well on the 'first-mover' advantages.

Despite its current standing as a developed economy, Singapore had to address many initial challenges. Although at independence Singapore received an efficient entrepôt trade system from the colonial administration, it also inherited a large pool of unemployed workers (more than 10% of the labour force being unemployed in 1960), a low-skilled work-force and wretched housing conditions. The institutional structure that the Government put in place to address these issues, although evolved over time, continues to this day. The Government took initiatives to tackle these problems simultaneously. The education policy was geared towards training in skills that were needed for the emerging industries. The Housing and Development Board (HDB) was established in 1960 to provide adequate public housing at subsidized rates. The Economic Development Board (EDB) was founded in 1960 to lead the industrialization drive.

A major challenge for the Government was to transform Singapore from a re-export economy to an export economy. This initially appeared to be an insurmountable task for three reasons. First, unlike Hong Kong and Taiwan, which had benefited from an exodus of entrepreneurs from communist China, at the early stages Singapore confronted a severe dearth of industrial (as opposed to commercial) entrepreneurs.

Second, the lack of domestic savings exacerbated the situation further. Third, the regional markets for Singapore's exports were not that viable because they were likely to impose trade barriers in order to help their own industries. This meant that Singapore had to look beyond the regional market.

The solution to these problems was aggressively to seek FDI from the industrial world, in order to develop the manufacturing base of Singapore. The foreign companies brought in not only investment and entrepreneurship but also access to the markets for their products. The Government ensured that Singapore was as attractive as possible for foreign investors, providing them with financial incentives such as tax concessions and accelerated depreciation allowances, as well as an agreeable labour force. This latter objective was achieved by weakening the power of militant labour unions and establishing the National Trade Union Congress (NTUC), which worked co-operatively with the Government and employers. The Government also mobilized domestic savings through the compulsory savings scheme under the CPF, which the colonial administration had started in 1955, initially for civil servants. The basic structure thus established has remained in place to this day.

A number of institutions have played a very important role in transforming the Singapore economy. Apart from leading Singapore's industrialization drive by attracting FDI, the EDB was also engaged in developing local entrepreneurship and, since the 1990s, in promoting Singapore's regionalization drive. The NTUC is also a multi-tasking institution. In addition to the important role mentioned above, it also administers a grocery chain, a taxi service and an insurance service. As a virtual branch of the Government, therefore, the NTUC services have acquired public trust. In 2002 International Enterprise Singapore was created by expanding the role of the former Trade Development Board (established in 1983) to promote trade and internationalization of Singapore-based companies. The Urban Redevelopment Authority (URA), founded in 1974, is the major institution that makes plans (under its 10-year Concept Plan) for land usage. Under a land acquisition act, the Government acquired private land at low prices. The government ownership of land increased from 44% in 1960 to 85% in 2000. The National Wages Council, established in 1972, brings together the Government, employers and trade unions to set wage guidelines. In addition to the many statutory boards, there are government holding companies and a large number of government-linked companies (GLCs) that play major roles in Singapore.

Diversification

One important element of Singapore's development strategy has been historical continuity and 'branching off'. A serious mistake made by a number of newly independent countries was either the severance or weakening of colonial economic links, which resulted in a decline into economic degradation. In the industrialization process, Singapore did not break away from the entrepôt trade system that it inherited from the colonial administration. In fact, entrepôt trade still plays a very important role in Singapore. The value of re-exports has increased sharply, from S $3,300m. in 1960 to S $254,560m. in 2010 (at 2006 prices), following a temporary decline in 2009 as a result of the global economic downturn. However, the relative importance of entrepôt trade in the economy has changed in recent years. As a share of total exports, re-exports accounted for only 49% during 2006–10, compared with 94% in 1960. The country had thus evolved from a re-export economy to a manufactured export economy.

Even within manufacturing, further diversification from electronics to other areas, such as chemicals and biomedical manufacturing (especially pharmaceuticals), has taken place over the decade since the Asian financial crisis. Between 2006 and 2010 electronics accounted for 32% of manufacturing value-added, compared with more than 50% in 1995. With the emergence of chemicals and biomedical manufacturing as leading industries, accounting for 7% and 19%, respectively, of value-added during 2006–10, the manufacturing sector has become more broadly based. Unlike the electronics industry, chemicals and biomedical production are highly capital- and skills-intensive. In terms of employment in the manufacturing sector, in 2006–10 electronics absorbed 23% of the manufacturing workforce, whereas chemicals and biomedical sectors accounted for only 4% and 1%, respectively. For these sectors the Government has made substantial infrastructure investments in Biopolis and the Tuas Biomedical Park. These heavy investments represented a calculated risk that the Government decided to take.

With rising competition for manufacturing from low-cost competitors, the Singapore Government embarked on a further diversification into new areas; one of these initiatives was to develop an 'external wing', and another was to develop Singapore as a regional service hub. While both of these were emerging as natural outcomes of Singapore's development process, the former received special government attention in the early 1990s and the latter from about 2000.

Under its regionalization programme, the Government designed an incentive scheme for Singapore companies to invest in the region and beyond. Direct investment is an effective way to penetrate protected markets. The emerging transition economies, such as the People's Republic of China, Viet Nam and Cambodia, provided more opportunities for such investment. India and the Middle East are also markets actively targeted by Singapore investors. Outside Asia, countries like Mexico and the states of Central and Eastern Europe were also emphasized, because of their proximity to the USA and the EU, respectively. Private companies, as well as GLCs, with the support of institutions such as the EDB, were encouraged to take advantages of these opportunities. The EDB also arranges training schemes for managers under its Initiatives in New Technology (Rationalization) Programme. Notwithstanding the economic downturn, at the end of 2009 Singapore's direct equity investment abroad amounted to about S $300,491m., representing a 16% increase from the 2008 level of investment and a substantial increase in comparison with the 1990 level of S $13,600m. During this period equity investment grew by more than 20% per year, with the exception of 1998 when there was a contraction as a result of the Asian financial crisis. In 2009 total direct investment, including net lending to overseas affiliates, amounted to S $359,348m., of which 16% went to China, 12% to the United Kingdom, 10% to the British Virgin Islands, 8% to Malaysia and 7% to Indonesia. About 50% of this investment in 2009 was in financial and insurance services and 23% was in the manufacturing sector. In terms of returns, Singapore's factor income from the rest of the world was about 13% of GDP in 2010, declining from about 19% in 2007. Obviously, these returns were minuscule in relation to what accrues to foreign residents and institutions in Singapore. As a result, Singapore's GDP remains higher than its gross national product.

As part of its promotion as a service hub, Singapore is aiming to move into non-traditional service areas as quickly as possible, because the traditional sectors, such as aviation, logistics, finance and tourism, are also being increasingly exposed to intense regional competition. For example, Singapore's attraction to tourists lies primarily in its aviation hub status, a stop-over point for many travellers en route to more popular tourist destinations in the region. There is a strong correlation between tourism in the region and in Singapore. Moreover, the average length of stay for tourists in Singapore is only about three days, compared with about two weeks in Thailand. As these competitors improve their aviation services and can also offer relatively cheap retail shopping, Singapore may lose a large proportion of its stop-over business. In the area of financial services, the Chinese city of Shanghai is trying to capture a large proportion of the market. However, the major obstacle to Shanghai in this regard is its serious pollution problem. Competition from Malaysia's Tanjong Pelapas port made Singapore re-evaluate its approach to the management of its port services.

As with the manufacturing sector, the intense competition in traditional services has prompted Singapore to move into the area of non-traditional services quickly, before competitors are able to catch up. The Government has focused on developing two major areas; on making Singapore a 'global schoolhouse' and on developing the country as a medical hub for various treatments. Promoting Singapore as a learning centre in the region, the Government is planning to attract at least 150,000 international students by 2015. The country is in fact well placed to achieve or even surpass this target. In 2009 Singapore hosted about 97,000 international students, an increase of 77% in comparison with the 2003 figure. Students came from more than 120 countries, but the majority were from China, which has now overtaken the traditional sources of Malaysia and Indonesia. At around S $8,000m. in 2008, this sector's contribution to the economy represented about 3.4% of GDP. The Government's aim is to increase this to 5.0% of GDP by 2015. The Government launched its plans for this endeavour in 2002, as recommended by the Economic Review Committee, to take advantage of Singapore's English-speaking background, as well as its multi-lingual society, high education standards, cosmopolitan character, global connectivity and safe environment. About 20 reputed foreign academic institutions were operating in Singapore in early 2007, and the Singapore Tourism Board has been holding exhibitions in many overseas cities to promote Singapore both for tourism and other services.

In its aims to develop the island as a medical hub, the Government hopes to attract about 1m. foreign patients to Singapore for treatments by 2012. The record thus far has been impressive. Unofficial figures indicate that more than 410,000 foreign patients were undergoing treatment in 2006, suggesting annual growth of 20%. However, the number had decreased to 348,000 in 2007. Despite this decline, medical tourist spending increased by 30% in 2007, to reach S $1,700m. With the projected arrival of 1m. patients, it was envisaged that revenue would reach S $3,000m. and create an additional 13,000 jobs by 2012, thus making a substantial contribution to the economy. While the Singhealth cluster of hospitals (Singapore General Hospital, Changi General Hospital and KK Women's and Children's Hospital) and National Healthcare Group (NHG—Tan Tock Seng Hospital, Alexandra Hospital and National University Hospital) provide subsidized care to Singaporeans, the private operations like Parkway Holdings (East Shore, Gleneagles and Mount Elizabeth) and Raffles Medical Group cater primarily to non-subsidized patients, including foreign patients. Apart from traditional regional markets, the Government's aim is also to attract patients from the USA, where health care costs have increased sharply. For example, a heart bypass operation that may cost more than US $130,000 in the USA would cost about US $18,500 in Singapore. However, Singapore confronts a serious challenge from India, which boasts much lower medical costs. For example, a cardiac surgery procedure that costs about US $14,000 in Singapore may cost as little as US $4,000 in India; a liver transplant, which costs about US $75,000 in Singapore, costs in the region of US $45,000 in India. More competition may help to bring down costs in Singapore. The medical services received a further boost after the Singapore Medical Association removed fee guidelines in early 2007, in response to a recommendation for wider competition by the Competition Commission of Singapore, which was established in 2005.

A third, and controversial, area of services into which the Government has ventured, is that of the casino business. Construction of two integrated casino resorts, one in Marina Bay and the other on Sentosa Island, commenced in 2007. The first hotels at the Resort World Sentosa, the total cost of which was estimated at S $6,590m., opened in January 2010, and the casino opened in February. The Marina Bay Sands project, costing an estimated US $5,500m., opened in June. The two resorts immediately attracted huge crowds to their respective casinos and entertainment sites, and were expected to add more than S $5,000m. to Singapore's GDP and to create about 60,000 jobs by 2015. The two integrated resorts have delivered substantial profits, and Singapore was expected to overtake the US city of Las Vegas to become the world's second largest gambling hub, after Macao, within just two years of the opening of the resorts. The Government's final acceptance of casinos on the island was regarded as an outcome of the lack of alternative choices, resulting from increasing competition in the region for Singapore's established industries.

Research and Development Policy

Another area in which Singapore is trying to press ahead, and thereby move towards the creation of a knowledge-based economy, is that of research and development (R & D). Recognizing the importance of an innovation-driven growth strategy, the Government compiled the first five-year National Technology Plan in 1991. A total of S $2,000m. was allocated for infrastructure development, R & D efforts and the training of the human resources needed in nine areas—information technology and telecommunications; microelectronics and semiconductors; electronic systems; manufacturing technology; materials and chemicals technology; environmental technology; energy, water and resources; biotechnology, food and agrotechnology; and medical science. A second (1996–2000) and a third (2001–05) five-year plan of science and technology followed, and the Government made further commitments to strengthen the R & D effort. Under the Technopreneurship 21 initiative, the Government further formalized and liberalized the business regulations to encourage entrepreneurship.

Furthermore, in 2000 the Agency for Science, Technology and Research (A*STAR) was created by reorganizing the National Science and Technology Board. The Government has been setting aside substantial, and increasing, funds for fundamental research and innovations, promoting entrepreneurship and attracting foreign talents. As of 2009 total R & D expenditure stood at S $6,043, having decreased from S $7,128m. in 2008, as a result of the global economic downturn. As a percentage of GDP, Singapore's R & D expenditure stood at 2.7% in 2008, still lagging behind larger protagonists such as Japan (3.4%), the Republic of Korea (South Korea—3.2%) and the USA (2.8%), and even the smaller economies such as Switzerland and Taiwan (both 2.9% in 2005). In 2006 the Government established the National Research Fund. In the 2007 and 2008 budgets the Singapore Government undertook to increase R & D expenditure to 3% of GDP. In the 2008 budget the Government further increased funds available for R & D and introduced wide-ranging incentives for companies, such as deductions and allowances, to enhance and encourage research activities. While falling short of the Government's 3% target, R & D expenditure did increase modestly to 2.7% of GDP in 2008. In 2010 the Economic Strategies Committee again emphasized the importance of innovations and productivity improvements in Singapore's attempts to remain globally competitive.

Given the long-term nature of these investments, it is difficult to measure their impact on the economy directly. Nevertheless, indirect indicators show that Singapore is progressing rapidly in the area of R & D. In terms of human resources, the number of research scientists and engineers in Singapore rose by about 12% per year from 1997 to reach 26,608 by 2009. This equates to about 90 researchers per 10,000 workers, compared with fewer than 30 in 1990. There has also been a steady increase in patents granted in Singapore since 1998, with the number reaching 6,067 in 2009. These are essentially input indicators of the R & D campaign, and the value-added should be measured indirectly.

EDUCATION AND HUMAN RESOURCES

The deployment of human resources for industrial needs has played a central role in Singapore's economic progress. The country's policies with regard to education and human resources are intertwined. Mindful of the experience of countries such as Sri Lanka, where unemployment among the educated youth was conducive to the development of communist sentiments, at an early stage the Government recognized the importance of targeted education. An important aspect of Singapore's education system is its bilingual policy, with English used as the medium of instruction, the language of commerce, technology and administration, and a mother tongue (Chinese, Malay or Tamil) to encourage students to keep in touch with their cultural heritage.

The evolution of the education policy can be grouped into three periods: the early industrialization phase; the post-1979 industrial restructuring phase; and the post-Asian crisis phase of knowledge-driven economy. During the early phase, the emphasis was on providing sufficient vocational and technical training and discipline to meet the needs of the new industries and to maintain industrial harmony. To address the massive problem of unemployment, the Government also adopted an anti-natalist policy during this period. Known as the 'stop at two' policy, this involved many disincentives to extending a family to beyond two children. Unfortunately, further reinforced by rapid industrialization and education, the anti-natalist policy exceeded its target of zero population growth too early, and by 1977 the total fertility rate (TFR) had declined to 1.8, below the replacement level. The situation of labour surplus thus turned into one of labour shortage, with the average unemployment rate decreasing to about 2% over the decade prior to the onset of the Asian financial crisis in 1997.

The second and third phases of industrial restructuring towards high value-added production and services moved on with educational reforms. The Government established the Council for Professional and Technical Education in 1979. Making projections in the area of human resources and recommendations were among the main tasks of the Council. Educational wastage was another important issue that the Government addressed at this time. In the late 1970s the attrition rate was 29% for the primary level and 36% for the secondary level students. To reduce these numbers, the Government introduced streaming of students in 1980, with an allowance for lateral transfers between streams. Although streaming created some unhappiness among parents, it led to a substantial increase in the pass rates at national examinations. The pass rate at the Primary School Leaving Examination (PSLE) rose steadily from 83.3% in 1980 to more than 98% since 2004. The pass rate at General Certificate of Education (GCE—Ordinary Level) also increased, from 68.6% in 1980 to 80%–83% since 2001, while the pass rate at GCE (Advanced Level) improved from 67.9% in 1980 to about 91% since 2003.

To address the labour shortage, since 1980 the Government has adopted a pro-natalist and pro-immigration policy. The incentives for procreation beyond two children were provided on a selective basis; the emphasis was on high-income well-educated families to procreate more, but to restrict the family size for low-income less educated families. In August 2000 the Government introduced a further incentive known as 'baby bonus' to encourage procreation. This involved the creation of a Children Development Account, into which the Government was to deposit S $1,500 annually for a second child and S $3,000 for a third, until the child reached six years of age. In addition, for every Singapore dollar placed in the account by the parents, the Government would make a matching dollar-for-dollar contribution of up to S $1,000 a year for the second child and up to S $2,000 for the third child. Parents can decide freely how to use the funds. In August 2004 the Government announced an additional incentive payment of S $10,000 on the birth of a couple's third and fourth child. Despite all these incentives, the pro-natalist policy recorded little success. The TFR generally declined steadily over the years, with the exception of some sharp increases in 'dragon years' (regarded as particularly auspicious in the Chinese zodiac), and reached 1.15 in 2010. At the National Day Rally speech in August 2008, the Prime Minister announced another wide range of incentives to encourage marriage and parenthood. Singapore has one of the lowest TFRs in the world. As with other developed nations, this paradoxical (non-Malthusian) opposite movement of family income and family size is partly a result of the increasing costs of children for educated mothers. Even with the provision of low-cost childcare facilities, tax rebates on maid services and other financial incentives, the non-reversal of the declining fertility trend can be attributed to rising material aspiration levels outpacing the growth in family income.

Given the difficulty of raising fertility levels, the Government had no option other than to rely on imported labour to meets the needs of the expanding industries. In the 1970s the main source of foreign workers, except for professionals, was Malaysia. Subsequently, however, the Government had to grant access to workers from other countries such as Thailand, Indonesia, China and the Philippines, as well as the Indian sub-continent. Although detailed data on foreign workers are not available from public sources, the substantial growth of total employment beyond the increase in the resident population indicates the extent of the use of foreign workers in the Singapore economy. For example, during the boom years of the 1990s total employment grew by more than 6% annually, while the resident population (Singapore citizens and permanent residents) increased by less than 2%. Singapore's total resident population increased to 5.1m. by July 2010, of which 3.2m. were Singapore citizens, 0.5m. were permanent residents and 1.3m. were foreign residents. In 2008 the total labour force was 2.94m., of whom 1.01m. (or about 34%) were foreigners. The foreign work-force plays a dual role in the Singapore economy: one is to meet the shortfall in the resident labour force, and the other is to keep wages at a competitive level. The Government uses the flow of foreign workers as a controlling mechanism on wages. The levy on foreign workers is also an important source of revenue for the Government.

In the 1970s the emphasis was on reaching a population target of 3.2m. by 2030. In the 1990s the Government revised the target to 4.3m.; and in 2001 this was raised to 5.5m. In early 2007 the Government set a target population for Singapore of 6.5m. by 2050. Given the population of 5.1m. at mid-2010, and if Singapore's TFR were to remain constant at 1.3, by 2050 about 40% of Singapore's population would comprise new immigrants. This also means that Singaporeans would have to cope with an increasing population density: more than 9,000 people per sq km by 2050, compared with the already dense 7,147.3 per sq km at mid-2010. Should tourist arrivals increase beyond the 10m. level recorded in 2007 and 2008, the population density in the business district may increase to uncomfortable levels. The substantial increase in the foreign population has generated widespread discontent among Singapore citizens, for both economic and social reasons (see Immigration, below).

INFRASTRUCTURE

A major factor in Singapore's substantial growth has been the island's infrastructure, a point that is often overlooked in standard growth-accounting exercises. The quality of the physical infrastructure, combined with a highly efficient services framework and political stability, provided Singapore with an advantage over its competitors in attracting FDI, despite the cost disadvantages. The provision of physical infrastructure alone will not define its quality; the efficient use of it is also important. The outstanding efficiency of Singapore's Changi International Airport is a prime example in this regard. Another exemplary case is Singapore's method of managing its vehicle numbers without allowing the traffic to congest the road network.

Singapore is one of the most efficient economies in the world. With its promotion of an innovation-driven economy, Singapore has been developing another type of infrastructure to make the country attractive for innovative activities. Some have come to differentiate between these two types of infrastructure by categorizing them as 'efficiency infrastructure' and 'innovation infrastructure'. The latter requires facilities and the legal framework for R & D, as well as a conducive environment for creative work. Obviously, except for conceptual clarity, these two are inseparable entities.

Efficient use of land is of paramount importance to the small island, which through land reclamations has increased in size from 581.5 sq km in 1960 to 710.3 sq km in 2009. Changi International Airport was built on reclaimed land. Jurong Island, the location of the petrochemical industries, was created by combining seven small islands. As stated above, the Government owns more than 85% of the land; the URA, through its Concept Plan and Master Plan, makes projections on the future use of land and allocates the land accordingly.

Improvements to public housing, the road and rail networks and port facilities are regular features in Singapore's programme of infrastructure development. In particular, Changi International Airport underwent a major upgrading exercise in 2006. The new Terminal 3 came into operation in early 2008, thereby increasing the airport's annual handling capacity by 20m. passengers, to a total of 67m. Jurong Island was scheduled for a S $1,000m. improvement programme. This included new living quarters to house about 12,000 workers, an ambitious project to create nearly 3m. cu m of underground storage capacity for oil, concentrates and naphtha, a fire station that can respond to emergencies within eight minutes, and enhanced transport networks for better security and the smooth flow of traffic. About 57,000 people worked on the island in 2009, compared with about 30,000 in 2007. In the 2007 budget the Government announced further plans to improve Singapore's living environment, to make it a garden city with many waterways. The number of public sector construction contracts awarded is an excellent indicator of infrastructure development activities that the Government is undertaking over the long term. The number of these contracts awarded rose significantly from the second quarter of 2007; in 2007 as a whole the number of contracts increased by 52% and in 2008 this soared by a remarkable 172%. By contrast, the number of private sector contracts awarded in 2008 increased by just 7% year-on-year. In 2009, however, the number of public sector contracts declined by 10% and the comparable figure for the private sector decreased by 57%, largely owing to the economic downturn and a steep increase in building material prices. In 2007 the concrete sand price index increased by a massive 213%, while the granite price index increased by 91%. Cement and steel bar prices continued to rise in 2008. However, in 2009 building material prices decreased by about 20%. In 2010 public sector contracts decreased by 42%, while private sector contracts increased by 102%. Construction work at the Marina Bay Sands project remained ongoing at mid-2011.

The innovation infrastructure mentioned above requires amenities that can foster creative minds. In this regard the Government is committed to taking a holistic approach in infrastructure development, which involves harnessing the synergy between scientific research and a creative atmosphere. Science parks and amenities for cultural and artistic work are being established. The One North project is an important initiative in the creation of a scientific-cultural hub. One North, signifying Singapore's location in the world (i.e. one degree north of the equator), is a three-phased megaproject that the Government is planning to complete within about 20 years.

A negative aspect of these infrastructure developments is that they are built following the demolition of existing structures that are in perfectly good condition. This is a result of the limited land area that constrains Singapore. Nevertheless, from a global perspective, this approach involves a substantial waste of resources and environmental costs.

INTERNATIONAL COMPETITIVENESS

The Global Competitiveness Report 2010–2011, published by the World Economic Forum, ranked the Singapore economy in third place, out of 132 countries, in terms of overall competitiveness. Ahead of Singapore were Switzerland and Sweden. Apart from providing extremely efficient and high-quality institutions and infrastructure, the challenge of maintaining international cost competitiveness has been a major priority for policy-makers; Singapore's sustained growth depends critically on international factor inflows and external trade. The Government has been addressing this issue in two ways; the first is by containing cost pressures during downturns, and the second is through long-term productivity improvements.

The Government's approach to addressing the short-term cost competitiveness has been both direct and indirect. The exchange rate policy is directed towards containing imported inflation (see below). An important policy device that the Government has used in direct interventions is adjustment to the CPF contribution rates. To combat the 1985–86 recession, the Government drastically reduced the employer's CPF contribution rate from 25% to 10%, while retaining the employee's contribution rate at 25%. As the economy gained its growth momentum, the employer's rate was adjusted steadily upwards and the employee's rate was adjusted downwards, both reaching 20% by 1994. In response to the Asian financial crisis of 1997/98, the Government again reduced the employer's rate, to 10%, in 1999. This was later restored to 16%, but decreased again to 13%, after the outbreak of SARS. The rate was raised to 14.5% in July 2007 and to 15.0% in September 2010, to 15.5% in March 2011, and to 16.0% in September 2011 thereby increasing the total employer-employee contribution rate to 36%. The cost reduction programmes included many other measures such as decreasing the utility rates and tax rebates to companies. In the 2009 budget, the Government introduced a number of non-CPF measures to enhance cost competitiveness (see The 2009–11 Budgets, below).

The Government intervenes indirectly to reduce wage pressures by controlling the inflow of foreign workers. Apart from this, a unique institutional feature that Singapore has put in place to make wages more flexible is to attach a variable component to the wage system. This variable component can increase or decrease, depending on the performance of the company and of the Singapore economy as a whole. Emulating the practice of the public sector, many private companies have adopted this adjustable wage system.

The achievement of long-term competitiveness through productivity improvements is a challenge that the Government has been trying to address since the early 1980s. Developments in the areas of education and skills, along with the restructuring of the economy towards high value-added industries, have taken priority in recent years. The above-mentioned R & D programme is a concerted effort in productivity improvements. When labour productivity is measured in terms of value-added per worker, Singapore's productivity growth rate has been impressive (with the exception of the turbulent period between 1997 and 2004 and 2007–09, when the Government allowed a large inflow of foreign workers). Overall, the annual growth rate of GDP per worker has been about 4% since 1980. However, the value-added per worker overstates the productivity gains, since Singapore (and East Asian) employees tend to work more hours in comparison with their counterparts in the countries of the Organisation for Economic Co-operation and Development (OECD). In the absence of reliable data on hours worked, it is difficult to assess these productivity trends. Nevertheless, data published by the Singapore Department of Statistics show that value-added per worker hour increased by about 3% annually between 2000 and 2006. However, value-added per worker contracted by 0.1% in 2007, 7.5% in 2008 and 3.4% in 2009, but expanded by 10.7% in 2010.

MONETARY SYSTEM AND POLICY

In June 1967, nearly two years after independence, Singapore broke away from the currency union with Malaysia and Brunei and established its own currency board (Board of Commissioners of Currency, Singapore—BCCS), subsequently issuing its own currency, the Singapore dollar. Until 1973 the Malaysian ringgit, Brunei dollar and Singapore dollar were interchangeable at par. In June 1973, when the Singapore dollar was floated, it was delinked from the Malaysian ringgit but remained exchangeable at par with the Brunei dollar. Until the BCCS was merged with the Monetary Authority of Singapore (MAS) in October 2002, the BCCS remained the issuer of the Singapore dollar. The MAS, which was established in 1971, is Singapore's de facto central bank and the regulator of the banking and financial institutions. In 1981 the Government of Singapore Investment Corporation (GIC) was established to manage and invest long-term government reserve assets, a function that MAS had previously handled.

As classified by the World Economic Forum, Singapore ranks among the leading 10 most sophisticated financial markets in the world. A 2009 study by the commercial 'think tank' Z/Yen Group (based in the United Kingdom) ranked Singapore in third place, behind London and New York, as a financial centre. At mid-2011 a total of 2,908 financial institutions were operating in Singapore, offering a wide range of products. A distinguishing feature of Singapore's banking sector is the Asian Dollar Market (ADM), which was established in 1968 as a counterpart to the Eurodollar Market with the aim of carrying out non-Singapore dollar financial transactions known as Asian Currency Units (ACUs). The ADM proved to be an immense success and contributed to Singapore's transformation into the fourth largest foreign-exchange market in the world, after London, New York and Tokyo. By mid-2011 there were 115 foreign banks operating in Singapore, in contrast to only six domestic banks. In 1999 the Government created the Singapore Exchange (SGX) by merging the Singapore Stock Exchange (SES) and the Singapore International Monetary Exchange (SIMEX) to enable the country further to develop its equity, foreign exchange and derivatives markets. Singapore's bond market remained relatively less prominent because bond financing was not important for either the Government or the corporate sector. The Government operated with a budget surplus from 1980, while retained earnings, sophisticated bank lending and equity markets provided sufficient funds for companies. However, since the mid-1990s there has been a considerable growth in the bond market, owing to the implementation by the Government of many incentive schemes. Singapore Government Securities (SGS), Asian Dollar Bond and SDCB markets are the major segments of Singapore's bond market.

Over the years, the MAS liberalized its rules and regulations on the financial market, thus enabling it to capture an increasing proportion of the world's financial transactions. Except for its regulation of the banking and financial system and money-market operations in order to maintain liquidity in the system, the MAS does not engage in the control of interest rates or money supply. The main monetary policy instrument that the MAS uses is the exchange rate for the purposes of controlling imported inflation.

Interest rates in Singapore closely follow those of the USA, and the money supply fluctuates in response to demand. As the effects of the US financial crisis spread and the US Federal Reserve tried to ease monetary policy by reducing the target federal funds rate, the US dollar three-month Singapore Interbank Offered Rate (SIBOR) decreased from 5.36% in the second quarter of 2007 to 0.26% in May 2011. The domestic Singapore dollar three-month interbank rate followed this trend closely, declining to 0.44% in May 2011. The longer-term interest rates also followed a similar trend: the benchmark 10-year Singapore Government Securities rate declined from more than 3% in early 2007 to 2.21% in January 2008; following a recovery to 2.58% by mid-2009, the rate subsequently declined again, to 1.77% in August 2011. By contrast, the average prime lending rate remained stable, increasing modestly from 5.33% at the beginning of 2007 to 5.38% since the second quarter of 2008. The average savings deposit rate had fallen below 0.12% by mid-2011. With price inflation exceeding 5%, the real interest rates on deposits were negative during this period.

Exchange Rate and Inflation

Although Singapore has adopted a managed float for the exchange rate, studies show that changes in the value of the US dollar tend to determine the Singapore dollar. Between 1988 and 1997 the US dollar received a weight of about 0.7, with the remainder being largely taken by the Deutsche Mark and the Japanese yen. However, the weight placed on the US dollar diminished after the 1997/98 Asian financial crisis, and it further decreased to about 0.46 after the global economic crisis of 2008/09. The weight placed on the euro diminished from 0.24 before 2009 to near-zero as a result of the global economic downturn, while the weight on the yen remained unchanged. The Australian dollar has emerged as an important currency, with a weight of about 0.25. The MAS policy towards the exchange rate since 1981 has been to allow it to appreciate sufficiently to counter imported inflation. Singapore has recorded a consistent balance of payments surplus, and the resultant excess demand for the Singapore dollar has set the exchange rate on an appreciating trajectory.

The MAS regulates the exchange rate by allowing it to fluctuate within an undisclosed band set against a trade-weighted nominal effective exchange rate. In general, however, the MAS policy has been to stabilize the fluctuations of the exchange rate and to permit the market to determine the trend. During the Asian financial crisis of the late 1990s the MAS widened the band and allowed the Singapore dollar to depreciate substantially. The powerful instrument that the MAS uses to keep the exchange rate within the band is the accumulation of foreign exchange reserves amassed over the years. By July 2011 Singapore's official foreign reserves, among the largest in Asia, stood at S $299,851m. (US $249,149m.). In view of this reserve position, and given the long-standing policy of discouraging the internationalization of the Singapore dollar, the MAS is able to inflict losses on speculators quickly through interventions in the foreign exchange market. (However, the non-internationalization rules have been relaxed over the years.) Market interventions are carried out by means of buying and selling US dollars against the Singapore dollar. Foreign exchange swaps (an arrangement whereby central banks allow each other credit in their respective currencies) are the main mechanism that the MAS uses to offset the effect of accumulations of foreign reserves on the domestic money supply. Excess domestic savings accumulated through CPF savings and government savings also work in a similar way. Despite persistent balance of payment surpluses and the accumulation of foreign reserves, Singapore's monetary base has remained very much delinked from foreign reserves.

In the early 1980s the Singapore dollar rate against the US dollar was about S $2 to US $1. Before the onset of the Asian financial crisis the Singapore dollar had appreciated to about S $1.40 : US $1. Following the crisis, the Singapore dollar depreciated to reach more than S $1.80 : US $1 in 2001 and then resumed an appreciating trajectory. The MAS allowed the Singapore dollar to appreciate much more swiftly from late 2007 because of the rapid increase in imported commodity prices. By mid-2011 the Singapore dollar had appreciated by about 27% since 2005 to reach S $1.20 : US $1.

There are two points worth emphasizing with regard to the impact of the exchange rate on export competitiveness. First, in view of the high import content in merchandise exports and the country's position as a relatively small trader and as a price-taker in the world market, the appreciating Singapore dollar does not greatly affect merchandise exports. However, the currency appreciation damages service exports, since the protective effect of import content is low in such exports. Nevertheless, the professed policy of the MAS has been that it is better to enhance export competitiveness through reduced business costs and improved productivity than through exchange rate depreciations. Second, on a longer term basis the real exchange rate (REER) has remained stable without seriously eroding Singapore's export competitiveness.

Given that Singapore uses other instruments to improve export competitiveness, the MAS has used the exchange rate mainly to reduce imported inflation. An important determinant of Singapore's CPI is the price of imports. Exchange rate fluctuations are transmitted fully into domestic prices of imports within about a year, depending on the import category. Although domestic prices of imports have declined in general until the onset of commodity price escalation towards the end of 2007, the CPI has moved upwards over the years, reflecting the important role played by non-traded goods and services in the determination of the domestic inflation rate. Despite the cost pressures resulting from the strong economic growth since 2004, the rate of inflation remained subdued, at below 1%, before the rapid rise experienced from the fourth quarter of 2007. Owing primarily to rising food prices, the CPI reached a high point of 7.5% in the second quarter of 2008, before slowing steadily; by June 2011, however, inflation had risen again, to reach 5.2%. As mentioned above, domestic cost pressures from wages, rentals and government rates and charges pushed up domestic costs substantially. Although it is argued that, with more than 90% home-ownership, the implicit rental component of owner-occupied housing tended to overstate the housing cost in the CPI when residential property prices escalated from early 2007, the cost of outstanding mortgages, which vary across age groups, should not be disregarded. Although data on this are not available, it is difficult to contend that the housing cost for home-owners is zero or negligible.

FISCAL POLICY

The pivotal role that the public sector has played in Singapore's transformation is well acknowledged. Despite such heavy involvement, based on the philosophy of fiscal prudence, the Singapore Government has kept both government revenue and expenditure at relatively low levels, around 15% of GDP. By contrast, in 2007 government revenue as a percentage of GDP among the OECD economies was 42%, while primary government expenditure was 40%. Despite its comparatively low levels of revenue and expenditure, the Singapore Government has generated strong and consistent budget surpluses. However, on the revenue side the Government has adopted an unconventional accounting method by excluding two items: receipts from the sale of land and capital goods; and the net income produced by the investment of government reserves.

Up to 50% only of the latter is included in the budget. If these items were taken into account, the actual budget surplus would be much larger than that reported. For example, in 2005 the reported budget surplus was S $430m., whereas the true surplus would have been as high as S $10,000m. Although the official surplus varied between the equivalent of –2% and 8% of GDP over the period 1990–2005, the adjusted surplus remained positive and varied from 3% to 19% of GDP. These surpluses resulted in a robust fiscal position for Singapore, with total public assets standing at S $649,564m. at the end of March 2010. It is interesting to note that conservative budget forecasting by the Government has contributed, to some extent, to creating these surpluses. In the 2007 fiscal year, for example, the projected budget balance was a deficit of S $700m., but in the event a basic surplus of S $6,051m. was recorded. As a result of the anticipated global economic downturn and the Singapore Government's stimulus programme, the projected budgetary deficit widened to S $14,900m. in 2009, although the actual recorded basic deficit was of a much smaller magnitude, at S $8,500m.

Tax Policy

In general, the Government's fiscal measures have been pro-business. The corporate tax rate was steadily reduced from 40% prior to 1986 to 20% in 2005. In view of the competitive pressures from economies like that of Hong Kong, where the corporate tax rate in 2007 was 17.5%, and other economies with even lower rates, the Singapore Government reduced its corporate tax rate to 18%, with effect from the 2008 fiscal year. A further reduction to 17% was implemented in 2010. Businesses also receive many other incentives such as investment tax credits, accelerated depreciation allowances and firm-specific benefits to reduce their tax burden substantially.

The Government also reduced the personal marginal income tax rate steadily over the years in order to encourage the work effort. The highest marginal income tax rate in 1980 was 55% for assessed income in excess of S $600,000. Since 2007 this has been 20% for assessed income in excess of S $320,000. The income-share weighted average marginal income tax rate declined from about 10% in 1980 to less than 7% since 2003. Effectively, an average Singaporean worker pays very little income tax in comparison with a counterpart employed in an OECD country. However, there are many other tax and non-tax charges (including the GST) that would add up to a much higher effective tax rate. Moreover, Singapore does not have a social welfare network similar to that of many OECD countries, and only recently has the Government begun to address this issue openly.

Corporate income tax constituted the largest revenue item, accounting for 26% of total revenue in 2010. The second largest revenue item was previously personal income tax. However, the Government has not only reduced personal income tax rates but also increased rebates and deductions, the largest deduction being the CPF contributions. Moreover, only about one-third of the labour force pays income tax. Therefore, to offset the reduction in income tax revenue resulting from reduced corporate and personal income tax rates, the Government has been periodically raising the GST rate. The GST was introduced in April 1994, at an initial rate of 3%. It was subsequently increased to 4% and then to 5%. As a result of these changes, by the 2004 fiscal year the position of these two tax items had reversed. In July 2007 the GST rate was further raised to 7%. In 2010 GST accounted for 19% of total revenue, while personal income tax accounted for 16%. Some 38% was derived from other tax and non-tax charges; among these were radio and TV licence fees, which were abolished after the 2011 budget.

Among other revenue items, two are somewhat unique to Singapore. One is the foreign worker levy, introduced in 1980, which the Government uses to regulate the inflow of low-skilled foreign workers and thereby the market wage rate. The employer has to pay the levy to the Government when it engages low-skilled workers. The other revenue item is motor vehicle taxes, which the Government uses to control vehicle numbers in Singapore. This involves taxes and charges on both ownership and usage. The charges on ownership include a market-determined price of Certificate of Entitlement (introduced in May 1990), import duties (Singapore is largely duty-free), registration fees, GST and annual road taxes. On the usage side are fuel taxes, parking fees, and road charges based on an electronic road-pricing system. Car ownership in Singapore is the most expensive in the world, and as a result the possession of a car has become a status symbol. On the other hand, peak-hour traffic congestion in Singapore is the lowest among the wealthy cities of the world. However, yielding to public pressure, the Government reduced the cost of car ownership. For example, an average 1.6-litre Toyota Corolla that cost about S $110,000 (some US $64,000) in 2000 was available for about S $64,000 (US $47,000) in early 2008. This led to a substantial rise in car ownership (of about 35%), creating unexpected traffic congestion. To counter this, the Government resorted to reducing the car quota, as well as increasing both the usage cost of cars and the frequency of trains and buses.

Expenditure Policy

Government consumption expenditure constitutes about 10% of GDP and investment expenditure about 4%, most of which goes to infrastructure developments. In view of the high savings and import 'leakages', the multiplier effect of government expenditure in Singapore is extremely low. Nevertheless, the Government uses infrastructure spending and off-budget 'packages' as counter-cyclical measures. Infrastructure spending obviously entails more long-term beneficial effects that are not easily assessed.

Among the principal expenditure items in Singapore is defence spending. In the 2011 budget this was projected to account for 26% of total expenditure (the largest single item, S $12.075m.) and 4%–5% of GDP. Although some in Singapore consider such a high level of spending on defence as unnecessary, the Government's position is that it is a premium that needs to be paid to sustain Singapore's progress, and that security cannot be taken for granted. The second largest single item in the 2011 budget was education expenditure (S $10,910m.), accounting for 23% of total expenditure and 3%–4% of GDP.

One item that was conspicuously absent from Singapore budget accounts was (welfare) transfers. The Singapore Government has always been averse to the concept of a welfare state. The Government considers that welfare payments not only deplete fiscal resources but also erode work ethics and create a mentality of entitlement. The basic philosophy of the Government has been to provide equal opportunity for every individual to enhance his or her human capital and to become self-reliant. Responsibility for welfare is left to the individual, the family and the community. Government subsidies are designed essentially along these lines. Public education is almost free of charge up to the university level. Public housing is provided at highly subsidized rates. Health care is basically a co-pay system, but it is also subsidized for low-income groups; subsidies in public hospitals range from 80% to 20%. Beyond this, there has been very little provision of social welfare until recently.

In view of the changing demographic situation, in particular the ageing of the population and increasing income disparities, Singapore has begun seriously to reconsider its position on social welfare. Since the mid-1990s the Government has put in place some special transfers on a piecemeal basis. Since most of these transfers were on an ad hoc basis, the amounts allocated have varied widely. For example, between 1998 and 2009 the lowest figure was S $52m., recorded in 1998, and the highest was S $7,099m., in 2008. The budgets since 2008 also included an extensive array of special transfers. A transfer that the Government has made mostly on a regular basis was CPF 'top-ups' for Singapore citizens. The 2009 budget was an exception because it was formulated as a 'resilience package'.

Central Provident Fund and Social Security

With the exception of a state-funded pension scheme for some civil servants, the mandatory savings in the CPF is the only formal social security scheme that Singapore has in place at present. The CPF is essentially a retirement fund that can be withdrawn, subject to maintaining a minimum sum, by members upon reaching the age of 55, or upon death, permanent disability or departure from Singapore. Prior to 1986 the contribution rate reached a peak of 50%: 25% from the employer and 25% from the employee, subject to a maximum.

With changing economic circumstances, the Government varied these rates; in 2006 the employer's rate was 13% and the employee's rate 20%. The Government raised the employer's rate to 14.5% in July 2007 and implemented a tiered system for low-income workers, to allow them to take home a larger percentage of their pay. From September 2010 the employer's contribution rate was raised to 15% and the total compulsory savings rate for those aged 50 or under was set at 35%, subject to income tiers and maximum thresholds. The CPF contribution rates for those above the age of 50 were: 29% (employer 11% and employee 18%) for those aged between 50 and 55, 20.5% (employer 8.0% and employee 12.5%) for those between 55 and 60, 13% (employer 5.5% and employee 7.5%) for those between 60 and 65, and 10.5% (employer 5.5% and employee 5.0%) for those above the age of 65.

For health care financing, in 1984 the Government added a compulsory Medisave account, which draws a pre-specified percentage from CPF contributions. The account has a minimum sum and an upper limit, which have varied over time. The Government later introduced two additional features for health care financing: Medishield (a low-cost insurance scheme for catastrophic illnesses); and a Medifund (a health endowment fund for the poor). Together these are known as the 3M system. The Medishield is implemented on an 'opt-out' basis. For higher-income groups, the Government introduced a Medishield Plus scheme on an 'opt-in' basis. For the elderly who may need long-term care, an Eldershield scheme has been implemented by the Government. However, health care in Singapore is largely a private responsibility. The Government claims that the system incorporates the best features of the US insurance model and the British taxation model.

The CPF now consists of four accounts: Ordinary, Special, Medisave and Retirement. The last three accounts are commonly known as SMRA and the first OA. The retirement account becomes accessible when the person retires; withdrawals from the CPF accounts are subject to holding a minimum sum in the retirement account. Over the years the Government liberalized the usage of the CPF funds in the ordinary account for other purposes, such as for house mortgages and some approved investments. The adequacy, or rather the non-adequacy, of the CPF for retirement and health care is an intensely debated topic in Singapore. Some have argued that the CPF is a mortgage finance scheme and not a pension scheme. In fact, the per caput (of resident population) net CPF balance in 2010 was a mere S $46,800. The capital within a house is not available for the financing of retirement, and the discretionary savings among low-income groups are virtually zero.

Enhancing financial security in retirement has received considerable attention in policy discussions since 2007. In the 2008 budget the Government announced tax reliefs and incentives to increase voluntary CPF 'top-ups' to the minimum sum required. The Government also announced a major longevity insurance plan, CPF LIFE, which essentially converts the CPF minimum sum into an annuity with the proviso, unlike commercial annuities, that the unused balance upon death can be withdrawn by a nominated beneficiary. By 2013 CPF members with a CPF balance of at least S $40,000 will automatically join the scheme upon reaching the age of 55. CPF LIFE involves a substantial amount of transfers (termed Life Bonus) to low-income groups to boost their CPF balances, and also offers these incentives to encourage those outside the scheme to participate.

In a move aimed at further improving the CPF system, the Government changed the CPF interest rate structure in 2008. From 1999 CPF balances in the ordinary account (OA) earned 2.5% in interest and other accounts 4.0%, far higher rates than the savings deposit rate offered in commercial banks, which in mid-2011 was 0.12%. From January 2008 onwards the Government allowed the CPF interest rate to float by pegging it to the 12-month average yield of the 10-year Singapore Government security bond (10YSGS) plus 1%. This rate was expected to earn better returns than the fixed rate that CPF members had received in the past. However, to protect members from anticipated low rates in the immediate future, the Government imposed a 'floor rate' of 4% for the SMRA for two years and a rate of 2.5% for all accounts thereafter. Furthermore, an additional 1% was to be paid on the first S $60,000 held in all accounts, including up to S $20,000 in the ordinary account.

To help the low-income Singaporeans, who are mostly older workers, in 2006 the Government introduced, instead of welfare, a 'workfare' bonus scheme. In place of an unemployment allowance, an individual receives the 'workfare' allowance only if he or she is earning. In the 2007 budget the Government expanded this scheme under the Workfare Income Supplement (WIS) programme and implemented it as a more permanent feature. These transfers (somewhat similar to the earned income tax credit scheme of the USA) depend on age, income level and whether or not the recipient has had employment for at least three months within the six-month period prior to the claim. Again, to save more for retirement most of the 'workfare' transfers are made to the individual's CPF account; in 2007 the Government set the cash to CPF ratio at 1:2.5. Although the WIS initiative was a welcome development, setting aside too much in the CPF was regarded as of little help to the poor who are struggling with the costs of their daily subsistence. The Government's position on this is to set aside more funds to help these people upgrade their skills and improve their earning capacity. Various proposals to address old-age social security and health care in Singapore have been under discussion since 2007. To ensure that subsidized health care is not misused, the Government adopted, after a thorough debate, means-testing for health care provision. In August 2011 the Government announced a major reform of health subsidies in order to encompass more Singaporeans, in the Primary Care Partnership Scheme. Previously, only those aged 65 years or above with a per caput monthly household income of S $800 or less qualified for the subsidy. Under the new scheme, the age limit was lowered to 40 years and the monthly income limit was raised to S $1,500. Qualifying patients can claim the subsidy when they visit their local doctors for the treatment of eight chronic ailments, including asthma, diabetes and hypertension. Meanwhile, in 2009 the Government introduced a reverse mortgage scheme for elderly public home-owners, enabling them to monetize their housing wealth without having to sell their property.

The 2009–11 Budgets

In response to the global financial crisis, the budget of 2009 was characterized by a commitment to a range of innovative measures intended to protect jobs, companies and low-income families in advance of the anticipated economic downturn. The most innovative feature of the budget was the Jobs Credit Scheme (JCS), which aimed to encourage employers to retain employees by means of cash grants based on companies' CPF contributions. (In response to public feedback, the Government announced in October that it was to extend the scheme for an additional six months; the final grants were awarded, and the JCS ended, in June 2010.) The 2009 budget was unique not only because of its innovative relief measures but also, for the first time, because of its recourse to Singapore's accumulated reserves. The budget measures had a huge mitigating impact; although the economy contracted by 1.3% in 2009, the decline would have been significantly worse had the budget measures not been implemented.

The budget of 2010 largely reflected the recommendation of the Economic Strategies Committee—established in May 2009—to effect a transition from crisis management to investing in skills, innovations and productivity for 'inclusive growth' that improves the living standard of all citizens. In a report published by the Committee in 2010, it also emphasized the need to make Singapore a distinctive city that would be a good platform from which to reach out to the rest of Asia.

Other issues addressed in the 2010 budget included climate change, higher education and care for the elderly. Under the Sustainable Singapore Blueprint, the Government allocated S $1,000m. over five years to improve energy efficiency in industry, transport, housing and construction, and undertook to reduce carbon emissions by 7%–11% by 2020.

The 2010 budget aimed to upgrade the educational profile of the resident work-force: at least 50% were projected to possess a diploma by 2020, including 35% with degrees. Higher education not only improves labour productivity but also brings other social benefits, such as lower crime rates and better social cohesion to a multi-racial and multi-religious society such as that of Singapore. Another objective of the emphasis on higher education is to enhance domestic research capabilities. Since around 2000 the existing universities have shifted their focus to research. A new university, the Singapore University of Technology and Design, established in close collaboration with the Massachusetts Institute of Technology (MIT) of the USA and Zhejiang University of China, is also envisioned to be a world-class, research-intensive university. The next area emphasized in the 2010 budget was long-term care for the elderly. The projections are that the resident population aged 65 and above will triple from 300,000 in 2010 to 900,000 by 2030. Therefore, about one in five residents will fall into this category by 2030, compared with one in 11 in 2010. Currently, the Government spends about 0.1% of GDP on long-term care, whereas the OECD countries allocate about 1%–2% of GDP. The 2010 budget emphasized the need for increasing long-term care expenditure and focusing more on preventive care. The final area of the budget's emphasis was 'leveraging networks for public service delivery'. During the first decade of the 21st century almost all government services were transformed into electronic services, thereby saving substantial amounts of time for both individuals and firms. The Government is now examining strategies for the next stage of innovations for e-government services.

Provisions of the 2011 budget included a significant range of benefits intended to assist poor Singaporean households. An important feature of the budget was the enhancement of the productivity and innovation credit scheme that was introduced in 2010. Under the scheme, companies that incur expenditure on R & D, design work, acquisition or registration of intellectual property rights, automation through technology or software or training of employees would be able to obtain a 400% tax deduction, subject to a limit of S $400,000 for each activity. The new scheme, combined with other recently introduced benefits, will allow companies to make substantial gains by pressing ahead with productivity improvements. However, concerns have arisen with regard the extent to which small businesses will benefit from the scheme. Increases in foreign worker levies have substantially intensified cost pressures. Although big companies may be able to offset the increase in the wage bill by engaging in some productivity improvement activities and claiming the resultant 400% tax deduction, small businesses such as restaurants generally do not have much room to manoeuvre on the productivity side. Given that about 60% of employment is provided by small and medium-sized enterprises (SMEs), if wage pressures force them to downsize, or to close, it would lead to a significant increase in the rate of unemployment.

IMMIGRATION

One highly contentious issue is that of 'foreign talent' or the question of whether there are 'too many foreigners' in Singapore. As noted above, by mid-2010 there were 1.3m. foreign residents and 0.5m. permanent residents in Singapore. Many Singaporeans have expressed their discontent at greater competition for jobs, overcrowded public transport systems, rising residential property prices and undesirable social effects. Many Singaporeans who previously did not differentiate between themselves and permanent residents have now begun to place permanent residents in the same category as foreign residents. Prime Minister Lee Hsien Loong referred to the issue in his 2010 and 2011 National Day Rally Speeches, contending that Singapore will be disadvantaged if foreign workers are excluded, before highlighting policy measures that accord priority to Singaporeans.

In 2010 the Government reduced permanent resident visas by about one-half and tightened the criteria on the granting of foreign worker visas. For low-skilled workers, Singapore issues a work permit, which is valid for two years. Work permit holders, who generally engage in jobs that are shunned by most Singaporeans, are not allowed to bring family members into Singapore on a dependant's pass. Highly skilled workers are issued with an employment pass, and can apply for permanent residence. In August 2011 the Government announced a further tightening of the restrictions governing the issue of employment passes and increased the minimum qualifying salary for the various categories of employment passes. With these much higher salary thresholds, companies will henceforth not be able to employ cheap foreign labour at the expense of Singaporeans. With the economy operating at near-full employment, there were concerns that many SMEs might not be able to cope with the additional wage pressures.

While foreign residents do not qualify for any subsidies, some existing and forthcoming policies are intended to differentiate more between citizens and permanent residents. In education, the fee differential between citizens and permanent residents was to increase three-fold by 2012, while citizens are granted an extra ballot for primary school selection. In health care, the fee differential was widened by 20% in July 2011. Permanent residents do not qualify for any childcare subsidy, baby bonus or paid maternity leave. They cannot buy subsidized new HDB flats, nor do they qualify for public housing grants, mortgage loans or subsidies for renovations; moreover, no more than 8% of resale HDB flats in a housing block may be occupied by permanent residents. Proposals were even mooted to retract residency if a permanent resident declined to take up citizenship upon an invitation to apply.

There is a risk of adverse selection resulting from such attempts to differentiate too greatly between citizens and permanent residents. The objective of the immigration policy is to attract 'foreign talent' and incentivize them to become permanent residents and then citizens. Talented people are highly mobile and may move elsewhere if they feel that they are welcome in Singapore only if they become citizens. Moreover, since Singapore does not allow dual citizenship and if permanent residency is not a welcome choice, foreign workers have to choose between remaining in Singapore as temporary foreign residents or working elsewhere, where they may be made to feel more welcome. As a result, not only will the talent pool within Singapore's permanent resident population in all likelihood contract, but also those who take up citizenship may not be the most talented people that the Government might otherwise have been able to attract.

MEDIUM-TERM PROSPECTS

The era of steady high growth in Singapore ended with the onset of the Asian financial crisis in 1997. Since then the economy has become more vulnerable to unexpected external factors and growth rates have become more volatile. There are two possible ways to stabilize the growth rate. One method would be to try to raise the consumption expenditure share of GDP. Given that property prices are several times higher than the affordable income levels, further rises in these prices would place a strain on households, and they would reduce their consumption in order to pay loans and to accumulate some savings. Since residential properties are the most important asset of a household, an appreciation of the value of this asset without an erosion of housing affordability is extremely important for the health of the economy.

The other counteracting effect appeared likely to emerge from the new policy of promotion of the services sector detailed above. Most of the service industries in Singapore had a close link with manufacturing activities. As a result, business cycles in manufacturing created similar cycles in services. With diversification into new service areas that are not heavily linked to manufacturing, the synchrony in the business cycles of manufacturing and of services may be reduced and even reversed.

Despite the volatility of growth rates, as demonstrated during the global downturn of 2008/09, the Singapore economy surpassed all expectations in 2010 to record a robust recovery. However, the worsening debt crisis in the USA and Europe were expected to subdue growth in the immediate future. Singapore had been entering emerging markets such as China and India quickly. With sustained growth in such trading partner countries, the Singapore economy was expected to maintain its expansion. As efforts are made to increase productivity with lower dependence on low-skilled imported labour, the Government's targets of productivity growth of 2%–3% and GDP growth of 3%–5% over the next decade are likely to be realized.

Statistical Survey

Source (unless otherwise stated): Department of Statistics, 100 High St, 05-01 The Treasury, Singapore 179434; tel. 63327686; fax 63327689; e-mail info@singstat.gov.sg; internet www.singstat.gov.sg.

Area and Population

AREA, POPULATION AND DENSITY

Area (sq km)	710.3*
Population (census results)†	
30 June 2000	
Males	2,061,800‡
Females	1,955,900‡
Total	4,017,733
30 June 2010	5,076,700‡
Density (per sq km) at 2010 census	7,147.3

* 274.2 sq miles.
† Includes non-residents, totalling 754,524 in 2000 and 1,305,000 in 2010.
‡ Rounded figure.

POPULATION BY AGE AND SEX

('000 persons at 2010 census)*

	Males	Females	Total
0–14	334.4	320.0	654.4
15–64	1,377.0	1,401.5	2,778.9
65 and over	149.5	188.8	338.3
Total	1,861.1	1,910.6	3,771.7

Note: Totals may not be equal to the sum of components, owing to rounding.
* Resident population of Singapore only; the total population was recorded at 5,076,700.

ETHNIC GROUPS

('000 persons at 30 June 2010)*

	Males	Females	Total
Chinese	1,370.1	1,423.9	2,794.0
Malays	250.9	253.0	503.9
Indians	180.3	167.8	348.1
Others	59.8	65.9	125.8
Total	1,861.1	1,910.6	3,771.7

* Figures refer to the resident population of Singapore only.

BIRTHS, MARRIAGES AND DEATHS*

	Registered live births		Registered marriages		Registered deaths	
	Number	Rate (per 1,000)	Number	Rate (per 1,000)	Number	Rate (per 1,000)
2003	37,485	10.5	21,962	5.2	16,036	4.5
2004	37,174	10.3	22,189	5.2	15,860	4.4
2005	37,492	10.2	22,992	5.3	16,215	4.4
2006	38,317	10.3	23,706	n.a.	16,393	4.4
2007	39,490	10.3	23,966	n.a.	17,140	4.5
2008	39,826	10.2	24,596	n.a.	17,127	4.4
2009	39,570	9.9	26,081	n.a.	17,101	4.3
2010	37,967	9.3	24,363	n.a.	17,610	4.4

* Data are tabulated by year of registration, rather than by year of occurrence.

Life expectancy (years at birth, WHO estimates): 82 (males 79; females 84) in 2009 (Source: WHO, *World Health Statistics*).

ECONOMICALLY ACTIVE POPULATION

('000 residents aged 15 years and over, at June of each year)*

	2008	2009	2010
Agriculture, fishing, mining and quarrying, utilities, sewage and waste management	22.7	20.9	37.6
Manufacturing	311.9	293.6	291.4
Construction	105.5	113.8	104.0
Wholesale and retail trade; repair of motor vehicles, motorcycles and personal and household goods	269.5	272.4	281.7
Hotels and restaurants	120.0	124.9	128.9
Transport and storage	182.4	179.9	191.3
Information and communications	87.0	94.3	99.9
Financial intermediation	123.6	121.9	126.0
Real estate, renting and business activities	237.5	243.4	253.4
Community, social and personal services	391.9	404.4	448.6
Total employed	1,852.0	1,869.4	1,962.9
Unemployed	76.2	116.3	84.4
Total labour force	1,928.3	1,985.7	2,047.3

* Data refer to Singapore citizens and permanent residents, but exclude foreign workers temporarily resident.

Health and Welfare

KEY INDICATORS

Total fertility rate (children per woman, 2009)	1.3
Under-5 mortality rate (per 1,000 live births, 2009)	3
HIV/AIDS (% of persons aged 15–49, 2007)	0.2
Physicians (per 1,000 head, 2004)	1.5
Hospital beds (per 1,000 head, 2006)	3.2
Health expenditure (2008): US $ per head (PPP)	1,833
Health expenditure (2008): % of GDP	3.3
Health expenditure (2008): public (% of total)	34.1
Total carbon dioxide emissions ('000 metric tons, 2007)	54,146.6
Carbon dioxide emissions per head (metric tons, 2007)	11.8
Human Development Index (2010): ranking	27
Human Development Index (2010): value	0.846

For sources and definitions, see explanatory note on p. vi.

Agriculture

PRINCIPAL CROPS

('000 metric tons)

	2007	2008	2009
Groundnut oil*	1,816	1,674	1,674
Sesame oil*	2,436	2,631	2,631
Soybean oil*	3,094	3,213	3,213
Cabbages and other brassicas	566	464	499
Spinach	2,012	1,890	2,105

* FAO estimates.

Total vegetables (incl. melons, '000 metric tons, may include official, semi-official or estimated data): 19.0 in 2007–09.

Source: FAO.

LIVESTOCK
('000 head, year ending September, FAO estimates)

	2007	2008	2009
Pigs	260	260	260
Chickens	3,000	3,000	3,200
Ducks	712	720	750

Source: FAO.

LIVESTOCK PRODUCTS
('000 metric tons)

	2007	2008	2009
Pig meat	19.2	19.3	17.5
Chicken meat*	83.1	82.6	86.2
Hen eggs	22.4	20.3	20.0

* FAO estimates.

Source: FAO.

Forestry

SAWNWOOD PRODUCTION
('000 cubic metres, incl. railway sleepers, FAO estimates)

	1990	1991	1992
Coniferous (softwood)	5	10	5
Broadleaved (hardwood)	50	20	20
Total	55	30	25

1993–2009: Annual production assumed to be unchanged since 1992 (FAO estimates).

Source: FAO.

Fishing

(metric tons, live weight)

	2007	2008	2009
Capture	3,522	1,623	2,121
Prawns and shrimps	505	132	244
Aquaculture	4,503	3,518	3,567
Indonesian snakehead	235	175	157
Milkfish	1,303	917	961
Green mussel	1,852	1,488	1,299
Total catch	8,025	5,141	5,688

Note: Figures exclude crocodiles, recorded by number rather than by weight. The number of estuarine crocodiles caught was: 1,653 in 2007; 1,877 in 2008; 1,086 in 2009.

Source: FAO.

Industry

PETROLEUM PRODUCTS
('000 metric tons)

	2006	2007	2008
Liquefied petroleum gas	678	673	608
Naphtha	4,621	4,490	4,405
Motor spirit (petrol)	7,361	8,405	9,300
Kerosene	601	584	573
Jet fuel	9,667	10,416	9,997
Gas-diesel (distillate fuel) oils	13,433	14,364	14,968
Residual fuel oil	7,691	7,794	6,902
Lubricating oils	2,487	2,581	2,837
Petroleum bitumen (asphalt)	1,745	1,982	2,030

Source: UN Industrial Commodity Statistics Database.

SELECTED OTHER PRODUCTS

	1988	1989	1990
Paints ('000 litres)	48,103.6	52,746.9	58,245.9
Broken granite ('000 metric tons)	6,914.0	7,007.5	6,371.7
Bricks ('000 units)	103,136	116,906	128,386
Soft drinks ('000 litres)	269,689.4	252,977.6	243,175.1
Plywood, plain and printed ('000 sq m)	31,307.0	28,871.3	26,106.9
Vegetable cooking oil (metric tons)	75,022	103,003	102,854
Animal fodder (metric tons)	110,106	115,341	104,541
Gas (million kWh)	681.1	722.4	807.1
Cassette tape recorders ('000 sets)	15,450	14,006	18,059

Source: UN, *Industrial Commodity Statistics Yearbook*.

Plywood ('000 cu m, estimates): 280 per year in 1991–2009 (Source: FAO).

Electric energy (million kWh): 41,138 in 2007; 41,717 in 2008; 41,801 in 2009 (Source: Asian Development Bank).

Finance

CURRENCY AND EXCHANGE RATES

Monetary Units
100 cents = 1 Singapore dollar (S $).

Sterling, US Dollar and Euro Equivalents (31 May 2011)
£1 sterling = S $2.0345;
US $1 = S $1.2328;
€1 = S $1.7734;
S $100 = £49.15 = US $81.12 = €56.39.

Average Exchange Rate (Singapore dollars per US $)
2008 1.4149
2009 1.4545
2010 1.3635

BUDGET
(S $ million)

Revenue*	2008	2009	2010
Tax revenue	37,519	35,272	40,662
Income tax	18,559	16,884	18,077
Corporate and personal income tax	16,403	16,861	17,206
Contributions by statutory board	2,156	23	420
Assets taxes	2,891	2,004	2,598
Taxes on motor vehicles	2,003	1,787	1,893
Customs and excise duties	2,083	2,080	2,090
Betting taxes	1,777	1,726	2,120
Stamp duty	1,838	1,989	3,097
Goods and services tax	6,632	6,633	7,699
Others	1,736	2,170	2,889
Fees and charges	3,726	2,423	3,779
Total (incl. others)	41,377	37,872	44,581

Expenditure	2008	2009	2010
Operating expenditure	28,590	29,871	32,755
Security and external relations	13,588	13,548	14,311
Social development	12,568	13,465	15,400
Education	7,298	7,419	8,517
Health	2,295	2,764	3,070
Community development and sports	1,173	1,404	1,793
Environment and water resources	560	662	661
Economic development	1,436	1,785	1,914
Trade and industry	624	652	673
Transport	374	372	420
Government administration	998	1,071	1,130
Development expenditure	8,880	10,612	11,295
Total	37,470	40,482	44,050

*Figures refer to operating revenue only; the data exclude investment income and capital revenue.

INTERNATIONAL RESERVES
(US $ million at 31 December)

	2008	2009	2010
Gold and foreign exchange	173,649	186,005	223,890
IMF special drawing rights	370	1,537	1,527
Reserve position in the IMF	174	262	297
Total	174,193	187,803	225,714

Source: IMF, *International Financial Statistics*.

MONEY SUPPLY
(S $ million at 31 December)

	2008	2009	2010
Currency outside banks	18,997	20,217	22,300
Demand deposits at commercial banks	56,706	73,255	90,166
Total money	75,703	93,472	112,466

Source: IMF, *International Financial Statistics*.

COST OF LIVING
(Consumer Price Index; base: 2009 = 100)

	2007	2008	2010
Food	90.7	97.7	101.3
Transport	99.1	103.2	110.3
Clothing and footwear	97.6	99.0	100.4
Housing	86.7	98.3	102.0
Education	96.0	99.2	102.7
Health	92.9	98.0	101.9
All items (incl. others)	93.2	99.4	102.8

NATIONAL ACCOUNTS
(S $ million at current prices)

Expenditure on the Gross Domestic Product

	2008	2009	2010
Government final consumption expenditure	28,847.0	28,563.6	32,426.0
Private final consumption expenditure	106,424.7	107,019.8	115,180.2
Change in inventories	5,143.1	–6,078.5	–3,530.3
Gross fixed capital formation	75,780.9	76,367.9	75,903.7
Statistical discrepancy	–4,340.3	–2,212.8	–1,529.8
Total domestic expenditure	211,855.4	203,660.0	218,449.8
Exports of goods and services	625,462.0	533,090.6	640,901.3
Less Imports of goods and services	569,365.5	470,091.4	555,698.9
GDP in market prices	267,951.9	266,659.2	303,652.2
GDP at constant 2005 prices	250,516.1	248,587.0	284,560.7

Gross Domestic Product by Economic Activity

	2008	2009	2010
Agriculture, fishing and quarrying	107.6	107.3	104.1
Manufacturing	52,476.8	54,128.8	63,463.9
Electricity, gas and water	3,886.0	3,812.9	4,392.7
Construction	11,296.6	13,675.2	12,961.5
Wholesale and retail trade	44,447.7	41,496.7	47,160.2
Hotels and restaurants	6,010.5	5,534.6	6,320.7
Transport and storage	25,511.2	21,343.1	24,448.7
Information and communications	9,713.1	9,885.6	10,380.7
Financial services	30,568.7	31,078.8	34,155.0
Business services	34,408.2	35,089.5	40,033.4
Owner-occupied dwellings	10,641.9	11,231.6	11,781.1
Other services	24,651.6	25,368.4	30,716.3
Sub-total	253,719.9	252,752.5	285,918.3
Taxes on products (net)	14,232.0	13,906.7	17,733.9
GDP in market prices	267,951.9	266,659.2	303,652.2

BALANCE OF PAYMENTS
(US $ million)

	2007	2008	2009
Exports of goods f.o.b.	302,822	342,776	273,411
Imports of goods f.o.b.	–256,859	–316,161	–243,180
Trade balance	45,963	26,615	30,231
Exports of services	84,889	100,965	90,920
Imports of services	–74,747	–87,361	–82,425
Balance on goods and services	56,105	40,218	38,726
Other income received	57,333	56,126	52,676
Other income paid	–64,159	–57,522	–55,738
Balance on goods, services and income	49,279	38,822	35,665
Current transfers received	157	163	158
Current transfers paid	–2,352	–2,975	–3,196
Current balance	47,084	36,011	32,628
Capital account (net)	–259	–308	–305
Direct investment abroad	–27,645	8,478	–5,979
Direct investment from abroad	35,777	10,912	16,809
Portfolio investment assets	–37,229	–28,145	–24,444
Portfolio investment liabilities	19,349	–12,136	–5,716
Other investment assets	–78,316	–48,387	–4,105
Other investment liabilities	56,714	45,309	3,160
Net errors and omissions	4,165	1,333	–241
Overall balance	19,640	13,067	11,808

Source: IMF, *International Financial Statistics*.

External Trade

PRINCIPAL COMMODITIES
(S $ million)

Imports c.i.f.	2008	2009	2010
Mineral fuels, lubricants, etc.	128,792	89,001	115,592
Chemicals and related products	23,723	21,444	28,630
Basic manufactures	35,020	26,079	26,492
Machinery and equipment	210,232	170,767	196,902
Electronic components and parts	75,151	61,861	79,952
Miscellaneous manufactured articles	29,074	24,810	29,634
Total (incl. others)	450,893	356,299	423,221

Exports f.o.b.*	2008	2009	2010
Mineral fuels, lubricants, etc.	115,479	78,398	103,511
Petroleum products	87,339	59,192	76,886
Chemicals and related products	48,514	46,598	56,644
Basic manufactures	22,331	16,836	18,905
Machinery and equipment	242,702	203,295	244,933
Electronic components and parts	104,273	91,139	119,327
Miscellaneous manufactured articles	29,885	27,502	33,410
Total (incl. others)	476,762	391,118	478,840

* Including re-exports (S $ million); 229,144 in 2008; 191,115 in 2009; 230,231 in 2010.

PRINCIPAL TRADING PARTNERS
(S $ million)

Imports c.i.f.	2008	2009	2010
Australia	6,459	5,804	4,711
China, People's Republic	47,595	37,585	4,004
France	11,118	12,185	10,119
Germany	13,023	11,424	12,125
Hong Kong	4,909	3,894	4,004
India	11,922	8,157	12,566
Italy	4,873	3,967	3,830
Japan	36,580	27,148	33,262
Korea, Republic	25,335	20,339	24,515
Kuwait	9,222	4,006	3,607
Malaysia	53,814	41,336	49,490
Netherlands	5,819	4,608	7,280
Philippines	6,929	7,475	12,523
Saudi Arabia	20,692	11,752	15,297
Switzerland	3,643	3,585	6,181
Taiwan	23,195	18,577	25,239
Thailand	15,923	11,907	14,001
United Arab Emirates	8,908	6,206	8,693
United Kingdom	6,606	6,545	7,603
USA	52,847	41,436	47,515
Total (incl. others)	450,893	356,299	423,222

Exports f.o.b.*	2008	2009	2010
Australia	19,537	15,317	17,111
China, People's Republic	43,818	38,125	49,468
France	5,846	5,155	7,531
Germany	9,378	6,013	8,370
Hong Kong	49,526	45,274	56,081
India	16,835	13,429	18,101
Japan	23,487	17,804	22,332
Korea, Republic	17,318	18,219	19,548
Malaysia	57,639	44,809	57,114
Netherlands	10,217	7,204	8,388
Philippines	10,265	7,313	9,775
Taiwan	13,411	12,600	17,442
Thailand	18,612	14,613	17,284
United Arab Emirates	5,858	5,389	5,183
United Kingdom	9,284	7,168	8,334
USA	33,452	25,485	30,871
Viet Nam	12,280	10,114	10,061
Total (incl. others)	476,762	391,118	478,841

* Including re-exports (S $ million); 229,144 in 2008; 191,115 in 2009; 230,231 in 2010.

Transport

ROAD TRAFFIC
(registered vehicles)

	2008	2009	2010
Cars*	552,846	579,371	597,746
Motorcycles and scooters	146,120	147,215	148,160
Motor buses	15,327	16,023	16,309
Taxis	24,300	24,702	26,073
Goods and other vehicles (incl. private)	156,089	158,207	157,541
Total	894,682	925,518	945,829

* Including private, company, tuition and private hire cars.

SHIPPING

Merchant Fleet
(at 31 December)

	2007	2008	2009
Number of vessels	2,257	2,451	2,563
Displacement ('000 grt)	36,251.7	39,885.8	41,046.6

Source: IHS Fairplay, *World Fleet Statistics*.

International Sea-borne Shipping

	2008	2009	2010
Vessels entered	131,695	130,575	127,299
Total cargo ('000 metric tons)	515,415	472,300	503,342

Source: Maritime and Ports Authority of Singapore.

CIVIL AVIATION

	2008	2009	2010
Passengers:			
arrived	18,185,230	18,026,026	20,486,452
departed	18,102,820	18,062,970	20,437,264
in transit	1,406,774	1,114,982	1,115,061
Mail (metric tons):			
landed	12,721	12,113	11,165
dispatched	14,234	14,945	16,027
Freight (metric tons):			
discharged	951,939	846,671	941,403
loaded	905,002	787,120	872,406

Source: partly Civil Aviation Authority of Singapore.

Tourism

FOREIGN VISITOR ARRIVALS
(incl. excursionists)

Country of nationality	2008	2009	2010
Australia	833,156	830,299	880,558
China, People's Republic	1,078,742	936,747	1,171,493
Germany	175,280	183,681	209,263
Hong Kong	278,115	294,420	387,579
India	778,303	725,624	828,994
Indonesia	1,765,404	n.a.	n.a.
Japan	571,040	489,987	528,951
Korea, Republic	423,018	271,987	360,703
Malaysia	647,339	n.a.	n.a.
Philippines	418,920	n.a.	n.a.
Taiwan	175,924	156,761	191,186
Thailand	333,892	n.a.	n.a.
United Kingdom	492,933	469,756	461,769
USA	396,618	370,704	417,195
Total (incl. others)	10,116,050	9,682,690	11,641,700

Tourism receipts (US $ million, excl. passenger transport): 9,179 in 2007; 10,583 in 2008; 9,187 in 2009 (provisional) (Source: World Tourism Organization).

Communications Media

(at 31 December)

	2008	2009	2010
Telephones ('000 main lines in use)	1,876.0	1,925.6	1,983.9
Mobile cellular telephones ('000 subscribers)	6,414.8	6,879.8	7,307.3
Internet subscribers ('000)	1,132.1	1,247.2	n.a.
Broadband subscribers ('000)	1,023.8	1,170.8	1,257.4

Personal computers: 3,410,000 (743.1 per 1,000 persons) in 2007.

Radio receivers ('000 in use): 2,550 in 1997.

Television receivers ('000 in use): 1,200 in 2000.

Daily newspapers: 11 (with average circulation of 1,542,000 copies) in 2004.

Non-daily newspapers: 9 (with average circulation of 1,134,000 copies) in 2004.

Sources: mainly International Telecommunication Union; UNESCO, *Statistical Yearbook*; UNESCO Institute for Statistics; UN, *Statistical Yearbook*.

Education

(2010)

	Institutions	Teachers	Students
Primary	173	13,318	256,801
Secondary	155	12,183	196,220
Mixed levels*	15	2,572	37,225
Pre-university	13	1,789	20,468
Institute of Technical Education	3	1,645	24,789
Polytechnics	5	5,059	83,542
National Institute of Education	1	716	4,965
Universities†	4	4,220	74,534

* Referring to schools with multiple levels, encompassing full schools (P1–S4/5), sixth-form schools (S1–JC2) and JC-plus levels (S3–JC2).

† Student and teacher numbers are not available for Singapore's fourth university (SIM University), which opened in 2005.

Pupil-teacher ratio (primary education, UNESCO estimate): 17.4 in 2008/09 (Source: UNESCO Institute for Statistics).

Adult literacy rate (official estimate): 95.9% in 2010.

Directory

The Constitution

A new Constitution entered into force on 3 June 1959, with the establishment of the self-governing State of Singapore. This was subsequently amended as a consequence of Singapore's affiliation to Malaysia (September 1963 to August 1965) and as a result of its adoption of republican status on 22 December 1965. The Constitution was also amended in January 1991 to provide for the election of a President by universal adult suffrage, and to extend the responsibilities of the presidency, which had previously been a largely ceremonial office. A constitutional amendment in October 1996 placed restrictions on the presidential right of veto. The main provisions of the Constitution are summarized below:

HEAD OF STATE

The Head of State is the President, elected by universal adult suffrage for a six-year term. He normally acts on the advice of the Cabinet, but is vested with certain functions and powers for the purpose of safeguarding the financial reserves of Singapore and the integrity of the Public Services.

THE CABINET

The Cabinet, headed by the Prime Minister, is appointed by the President and is responsible to Parliament.

THE LEGISLATURE

The Legislature consists of a Parliament of 84 elected members, presided over by a Speaker who may be elected from the members of Parliament themselves or appointed by Parliament although he may not be a member of Parliament. Members of Parliament are elected by universal adult suffrage for five years (subject to dissolution) in single-member and multi-member constituencies. A constitutional amendment was introduced in May 1988, whereby 39 constituencies were merged to form 13 'group representation constituencies', which would return 'teams' of three Members of Parliament. At least one member of each team was to be of minority (non-Chinese) racial origin. In January 1991 the Constitution was further amended, stipulating that the number of candidates contesting 'group representation constituencies' should be a minimum of three and a maximum of four. The maximum was increased to six by constitutional amendment in October 1996.

Additionally, a constitutional amendment approved in 1984 provided for up to six 'non-constituency' seats to be offered to opposition parties. A further amendment in April 2010 increased to nine the maximum number of 'non-constituency' seats available to the opposition. Also, legislation approved in 1990, and amended in 1997, enabled the Government to nominate up to nine additional, politically neutral members for a term of two years; these members have restricted voting rights.

A 21-member Presidential Council, chaired by the Chief Justice, examines material of racial or religious significance, including legislation, to see whether it differentiates between racial or religious communities or contains provisions inconsistent with the fundamental liberties of Singapore citizens.

CITIZENSHIP

Under the Constitution, Singapore citizenship may be acquired either by birth, descent or registration. Persons born when Singapore was a constituent State of Malaysia could also acquire Singapore citizenship by enrolment or naturalization under the Constitution of Malaysia.

The Government

HEAD OF STATE

President: Dr Tony Tan Keng Yam (elected 27 August 2011).

CABINET

(October 2011)

The Cabinet comprises members of the People's Action Party.

Prime Minister: Brig.-Gen. (retd) Lee Hsien Loong.

Deputy Prime Minister, Co-ordinating Minister for National Security and Minister for Home Affairs: Teo Chee Hean.

Deputy Prime Minister and Minister for Finance and Manpower: Tharman Shanmugaratnam.

Minister for Trade and Industry: Lim Hng Kiang.

Minister in the Prime Minister's Office: Lim Swee Say.

Minister for Information, Communications and the Arts: Yaacob Ibrahim.

Minister for National Development: Khaw Boon Wan.

Minister for Defence: Dr Ng Eng Hen.

Minister for the Environment and Water Resources: Dr Vivian Balakrishnan.

Minister for Foreign Affairs and Law: K. Shanmugam.

Minister for Health: Gan Kim Yong.

Minister for Transport and Second Minister for Foreign Affairs: Lui Tuck Yew.

Minister in the Prime Minister's Office and Second Minister for Home Affairs, Trade and Industry: S. Iswaran.

Minister for Education: Heng Swee Keat.

Acting Minister for Community Development, Youth and Sports and Minister of State for Ministry of Information, Communications and the Arts: Chan Chun Sing.

MINISTRIES

Office of the President: The Istana, Orchard Rd, Singapore 238823; e-mail istana_general_office@istana.gov.sg; internet www.istana.gov.sg.

Office of the Prime Minister: The Istana, Orchard Rd, Singapore 238823; tel. 62358577; fax 68356621; e-mail pmo_hq@pmo.gov.sg; internet www.pmo.gov.sg.

Ministry of Community Development, Youth and Sports: 512 Thomson Rd, MCYS Bldg, Singapore 298136; tel. 62589595; fax 63536695; e-mail mcys_email@mcys.gov.sg; internet www.mcys.gov.sg.

Ministry of Defence: Gombak Dr., off Upper Bukit Timah Rd, Mindef Bldg, Singapore 669645; tel. 67608844; fax 67646119; internet www.mindef.gov.sg.

Ministry of Education: 1 North Buona Vista Dr., MOE Bldg, Singapore 138675; tel. 68722220; fax 67755826; e-mail contact@moe.edu.sg; internet www.moe.gov.sg.

Ministry of the Environment and Water Resources: 40 Scotts Rd, 24-00 Environment Bldg, Singapore 228231; tel. 67319000; fax 67319456; e-mail mewr_feedback@mewr.gov.sg; internet www.mewr.gov.sg.

Ministry of Finance: 100 High St, 06-03 The Treasury, Singapore 179434; tel. 62259911; fax 63327435; e-mail mof_qsm@mof.gov.sg; internet www.mof.gov.sg.

Ministry of Foreign Affairs: MFA Bldg, Tanglin, off Napier Rd, Singapore 248163; tel. 63798000; fax 64747885; e-mail mfa@mfa.gov.sg; internet www.mfa.gov.sg.

Ministry of Health: 16 College Rd, College of Medicine Bldg, Singapore 169854; tel. 63259220; fax 62241677; e-mail moh_info@moh.gov.sg; internet www.moh.gov.sg.

Ministry of Home Affairs: New Phoenix Park, 28 Irrawaddy Rd, Singapore 329560; tel. 64787010; fax 62546250; e-mail mha_feedback@mha.gov.sg; internet www.mha.gov.sg.

Ministry of Information, Communications and the Arts: 140 Hill St, 02-02 MICA Bldg, Singapore 179369; tel. 62707988; fax 68379480; e-mail mica@mica.gov.sg; internet www.mica.gov.sg.

Ministry of Law: 100 High St, 08-02 The Treasury, Singapore 179434; tel. 63328840; fax 63328842; e-mail contact@mlaw.gov.sg; internet www.mlaw.gov.sg.

Ministry of Manpower: 18 Havelock Rd, 07-01, Singapore 059764; tel. 64385122; fax 65344840; e-mail mom_hq@mom.gov.sg; internet www.mom.gov.sg.

Ministry of National Development: 5 Maxwell Rd, 21/22-00 Tower Blk, MND Complex, Singapore 069110; tel. 62221211; fax 63257254; e-mail mnd_hq@mnd.gov.sg; internet www.mnd.gov.sg.

Ministry of Trade and Industry: 100 High St, 09-01 The Treasury, Singapore 179434; tel. 62259911; fax 63327260; e-mail mti_email@mti.gov.sg; internet www.mti.gov.sg.

Ministry of Transport: 460 Alexandra Rd, 39-00 PSA Bldg, Singapore 119963; tel. 62707988; fax 63757734; e-mail mot@mot.gov.sg; internet www.mot.gov.sg.

President and Legislature

PRESIDENT

Presidential Election, 27 August 2011

Candidate	Votes	% of votes
Tony Tan Keng Yam	744,397	35.19
Tan Cheng Bock	737,128	34.85
Tan Jee Say	529,732	25.04
Tan Kin Lian	103,931	4.91
Total	2,115,188	100.00*

* Adjusted for rounding.

PARLIAMENT

Parliament House

1 Parliament Place, Singapore 178880; tel. 63326666; fax 63325526; e-mail parl@parl.gov.sg; internet www.parliament.gov.sg.

Speaker: MICHAEL PALMER.

General Election, 7 May 2011

Party	Seats
People's Action Party	81*
Workers' Party	6
Total	87

* Five seats were uncontested.

Election Commission

Elections Department of Singapore (ELD): Prime Minister's Office, 11 Prinsep Link, Singapore 187949; fax 63323428; internet www.elections.gov.sg; govt body; Chair. LEE SENG LUP.

Political Organizations

National Solidarity Party (NSP): 397 Jalan Besar, 02-01A, Singapore 209007; tel. 83823961; fax 63968645; e-mail nsp-cec@yahoogroups.com; internet www.nsp.sg; f. 1987; Pres. SEBASTIAN TEO; Sec.-Gen. HAZEL POA.

People's Action Party (PAP): Blk 57B, PCF Bldg, 01-1402 New Upper Changi Rd, Singapore 463057; tel. 62444600; fax 62430114; e-mail paphq@pap.org.sg; internet www.pap.org.sg; f. 1954; governing party since 1959; 18-mem. Cen. Exec. Cttee; Chair. KHAW BOON WAN; Sec.-Gen. LEE HSIEN LOONG.

Pertubuhan Kebangsaan Melayu Singapura (PKMS) (Singapore Malay National Organization): PKMS Bldg, 4th Floor, 218F Changi Rd, Singapore 1441; tel. 64470468; fax 63458724; f. 1950; est. as United Malay Nat. Org. (UMNO) of Malaysia; renamed UMNO Singapore in 1954; present name adopted 1967; seeks to advance the implementation of the special rights of Malays in Singapore, as stated in the Constitution; to safeguard and promote the advancement of Islam; and to encourage racial harmony and goodwill in Singapore; joined SDA in July 2001; Pres. OSMAN HASSAN, MOHD AZ-ZAHARI AMMAD KAMIL.

Reform Party: 18A Smith St, Singapore 058932; tel. 65349641; fax 65349640; e-mail enquiries@thereformparty.net; internet www.thereformparty.net; f. 2008; Chair. ANDY ZHU LAI CHENG; Sec.-Gen. KENNETH JEYARETNAM.

Singapore Democratic Alliance (SDA): Singapore; f. 2001; est. to contest 2001 general election, as coalition of PKMS, SPP, NSP and SJP; NSP left coalition in 2007; Chair. CHIAM SEE TONG; Sec.-Gen. DESMOND LIM BAK CHUAN.

Singapore Democratic Party (SDP): 1357A Serangoon Rd, Singapore 328240; tel. and fax 63981675; e-mail speakup@yoursdp.org; internet www.yoursdp.org; f. 1980; 12-mem. Cen. Cttee; Chair. GANDHI AMBALAM; Sec.-Gen. CHEE SOON JUAN.

Singapore Justice Party (SJP): Singapore; f. 1972; joined SDA in July 2001; Pres. A. R. SUIB; Sec.-Gen. AMINUDDIN BIN AMI.

Singapore People's Party (SPP): 22A Upper Weld Rd, Singapore 207379; tel. 68585771; fax 62970138; e-mail feedback@spp.org.sg; internet www.spp.org.sg; f. 1993; breakaway faction of SDP, espousing more moderate policies; joined SDA in July 2001; 12-mem. Cen. Exec. Cttee; Chair. SIN KEK TONG; Sec.-Gen. CHIAM SEE TONG.

Socialist Front: 24 Peck Seah St, 05-09-11 Nehsons Bldg, Singapore 079314; e-mail contact@socialistfront.org; internet www.socialistfront.org; f. 2010; encourages participation and ownership in politics; promotes equal opportunities for citizens; Chair. NG TECK SIONG; Sec.-Gen. CHIA TI LIK.

United Singapore Democrats (USD): Singapore; f. 2010; est. by fmr mems of SDP (q. v.); Pres. NARAYANASAMY GOGELAVANY; Sec. JASLYN GO.

Workers' Party: 216G Syed Alwi Rd 02-03, Singapore 207799; tel. 62984765; fax 64544404; e-mail webmaster@wp.sg; internet www.wp.org.sg; f. 1961; active as opposition party in Singapore since 1957; merged with Barisan Sosialis (Socialist Front) in 1988; seeks to establish a democratic socialist govt with a constitution guaranteeing fundamental citizens' rights; Chair. SYLVIA LIM SWEE LIAN; Sec.-Gen. LOW THIA KHIANG.

Other parties include the Alliance Party Singapura, the Democratic People's Party, the Democratic Progressive Party, the National Party of Singapore, the Partai Rakyat, the Parti Kesatuan Ra'ayat (United Democratic Party), the People's Front, the People's Republican Party, the Persatuan Melayu Singapura, the Singapore Chinese Party, the Singapore Indian Congress, the Singapore National Front, the United National Front, the United People's Front and the United People's Party.

Diplomatic Representation

EMBASSIES AND HIGH COMMISSIONS IN SINGAPORE

Angola: 9 Temasek Blvd, 44-03 Suntec Tower Two, Singapore 038989; tel. 63419360; fax 63419367; e-mail embangola@pacific.net.sg; Ambassador FIDELINO LOY DE JESUS FIGUEIREDO.

Australia: 25 Napier Rd, Singapore 258507; tel. 68364100; fax 67375481; e-mail enquiries-sg@dfat.gov.au; internet www.australia.org.sg; High Commissioner DOUG CHESTER.

Bangladesh: 91 Bencoolen St, 06-01, Sunshine Plaza, Singapore 189652; tel. 62550075; fax 62551824; e-mail bdoot@singnet.com.sg; internet www.bangladesh.org.sg; High Commissioner KAMRUL AHSAN.

Belgium: 8 Shenton Way, 14-01, Singapore 068811; tel. 62207677; fax 62226976; e-mail Singapore@diplobel.fed.be; internet www.diplomatie.be/singapore; Ambassador ROLAND VAN REMOORTELE.

Brazil: 101 Thomson Rd, 10-05 United Sq., Singapore 307591; tel. 62566001; fax 62566619; e-mail cinbrem@brazil.org.sg; internet www.brazil.org.sg; Ambassador LUIS FERNANDO DE ANDRADE SERRA.

Brunei: 325 Tanglin Rd, Singapore 247955; tel. 67339055; fax 67375275; e-mail singapore.singapore@mfa.gov.bn; High Commissioner ABDUL GHAFAR BIN ISMAIL.

Cambodia: 400 Orchard Rd, 10-03/04 Orchard Towers, Singapore 238875; tel. 63419785; fax 63419201; e-mail cambodiaembasy@pacific.net.sg; internet www.recambodia.net; Ambassador SEREY SIN.

Canada: 1 George St 11-01, Singapore 049145; tel. 68545900; fax 68545930; e-mail spore@international.gc.ca; internet www.canadainternational.gc.ca/singapore-singapour; High Commissioner DAVID SEVIGNY.

Chile: 105 Cecil St, 25-00 The Octagon Bldg, Singapore 069534; tel. 62238577; fax 62250677; e-mail contacto@chileabroad.gov.cl; internet chileabroad.gov.cl/republica-de-singapur; Ambassador LUIS FERNANDO DANÚS CHARPENTIER.

China, People's Republic: 150 Tanglin Rd, Singapore 247969; tel. 64712117; fax 64795345; e-mail chinaemb_sg@fmprc.gov.cn; internet www.chinaembassy.org.sg; Ambassador WEI WEI.

Costa Rica: 271 Bukit Timah Rd, 04-08 Balmoral Plaza, Singapore 259708; tel. 67380566; fax 67380567; e-mail info@costaricaembassy-sg.net; internet www.costaricaembassy-sg.net; Ambassador JUAN FERNANDO CORDERO ARIAS.

Denmark: 101 Thomson Rd, 13-01/02 United Sq., Singapore 307591; tel. 63555010; fax 62533764; e-mail sinamb@um.dk; internet www.ambsingapore.um.dk; Ambassador OLE LISBORG.

Egypt: 75 Grange Rd, Singapore 249579; tel. 67371811; fax 67323422; e-mail admin@egyptemb-sin.org; Ambassador NASSER HAMDY.

Finland: 101 Thomson Rd, 21-03 United Sq., Singapore 307591; tel. 62544042; fax 62534101; e-mail sanomat.sin@formin.fi; internet www.finland.org.sg; Ambassador ARI HEIKKINEN.

France: 101–103 Cluny Park Rd, Singapore 259595; tel. 68807800; fax 68807801; e-mail consulat@ambafrance-sg.org; internet www.ambafrance-sg.org; Ambassador OLIVIER CARON.

Germany: 12-00 Singapore Land Tower, 50 Raffles Place, Singapore 048623; tel. 65336002; fax 65331132; e-mail consul@sing.diplo.de; internet www.singapur.diplo.de; Ambassador ANGELIKA VIETS.

Hungary: 250 North Bridge Rd, 29-01 Raffles City Tower, Singapore 179101; tel. 68830882; fax 68830177; e-mail mission.sin@kum.hu; internet www.mfa.gov.hu/kulkepviselet/SG; Ambassador Dr CSABA A. FARAGÓ.

India: 31 Grange Rd, India House, Singapore 239702; tel. 67376777; fax 67326909; e-mail indiahc@pacific.net.sg; internet www.hcisingapore.com; High Commissioner T. C. RAGHAVAN.

Indonesia: 7 Chatsworth Rd, Singapore 249761; tel. 67377422; fax 67375037; e-mail info@kbrisingapura.com; internet www.kbrisingapura.com; Chargé d'affaires a.i. KENSSY EKANINGSIH.

Ireland: Ireland House, 541 Orchard Rd, 08-00 Liat Towers, Singapore 238881; tel. 62387616; fax 62387615; e-mail singaporeembassy@dfa.ie; internet www.embassyofireland.sg; Ambassador JOE HAYES.

Israel: 24 Stevens Close, Singapore 257964; tel. 68349200; fax 67337008; e-mail press@singapore.mfa.gov.il; internet singapore.mfa.gov.il; Ambassador AMIRA ARNON.

Italy: 101 Thomson Rd, 27-02 United Sq., Singapore 307591; tel. 62506022; fax 62533301; e-mail ambasciata.singapore@esteri.it; internet www.ambsingapore.esteri.it; Ambassador ANACLETO FELICANI.

Japan: 16 Nassim Rd, Singapore 258390; tel. 62358855; fax 67331039; e-mail eojsingfv@vsystem.com.sg; internet www.sg.emb-japan.go.jp; Ambassador YOICHI SUZUKI.

Kazakhstan: 20 Raffles Pl., 14-06 Ocean Towers, Singapore 048620; tel. 65366100; fax 64388990; e-mail office@kazakhstan.org.sg; internet www.kazakhstan.org.sg; Ambassador YERLAN BAUDARBEK-KOZHATAYEV.

Korea, Democratic People's Republic: 7500 Beach Rd, 09-320 The Plaza, Singapore 199591; tel. 64403498; fax 63482026; e-mail embdprk@singnet.com.sg; Ambassador JONG SONG IL.

Korea, Republic: 47 Scotts Rd, 08-00 Goldbell Towers, Singapore 228233; tel. 62561188; fax 62543191; e-mail info@koreaembassy.org.sg; internet sgp.mofat.go.kr; Ambassador OH JOON.

Kuwait: c/o The Ritz-Carlton Millenia Singapore, 7 Raffles Ave, Suite 3108, Singapore 039799; tel. 68847401; fax 64345387; e-mail embassy@kuwait.org.sg; internet www.kuwait.org.sg; Ambassador ABDULAZIZ AHMED S. AL-ADWANI.

Laos: 51 Newton Rd, 13-04/05 Goldhill Plaza, Singapore 308900; tel. 62506044; fax 62506014; e-mail laoembsg@singnet.com.sg; Ambassador THOUANE VORASARN.

Malaysia: 301 Jervois Rd, Singapore 249077; tel. 62350111; fax 67336135; e-mail mwspore@singnet.com.sg; internet www.kln.gov.my/perwakilan/singapore; High Commissioner Dato' MOHAMMED HUSSIN NAYAN.

Maldives: 101 Thomson Rd, 30-01A United Sq., Singapore 307591; tel. 67209012; fax 67209014; e-mail info@maldiveshighcommission.sg; High Commissioner MOHAMED KHALEEL.

Mexico: 152 Beach Rd, 06-07 Gateway East Tower, Singapore 189721; tel. 62982678; fax 62933484; e-mail embamexsing@embamexsing.org.sg; internet portal.sre.gob.mx/singapur; Ambassador ANTONIO GUILLERMO VILLEGAS VILLALOBOS.

Mongolia: 600 North Bridge Rd, 24-08 Parkview Sq., Singapore 188778; tel. 63480745; fax 63481753; e-mail singapore@mfat.gov.mn; internet www.singapore.mfat.gov.mn; Chargé d'affaires a.i. TULGA NARKHUU.

Myanmar: 15 St Martin's Dr., Singapore 257996; tel. 67350209; fax 67356236; e-mail ambassador@mesingapore.org.sg; internet www.mesingapore.org.sg; Ambassador TIN OO LWIN.

Netherlands: Tanglin, POB 447, Singapore 912415; tel. 67371155; fax 67371940; e-mail sin@minbuza.nl; internet www.mfa.nl/sin; Ambassador JOHANNES W. GUNIVORTUS JANSING.

New Zealand: 391 Orchard Rd, Tower A, 15-06/10 Ngee Ann City, Singapore 238873; tel. 62359966; fax 67339924; e-mail enquiries@nz-high-com.org.sg; internet www.nzembassy.com/singapore; High Commissioner PETER HAMILTON.

Nigeria: 143 Cecil St, 15-01 GB Bldg, Singapore 069542; tel. 67321743; fax 67321742; e-mail nigerhighcommission@yahoo.com.sg; internet www.nigeriahcsinga.org.sg; High Commissioner DANJUMA NANPON SHENI.

Norway: 16 Raffles Quay, 44-01 Hong Leong Bldg, Singapore 048581; tel. 62207122; fax 62202191; e-mail emb.singapore@mfa.no; internet www.norway.org.sg; Ambassador JANNE JULSRUD.

Pakistan: 1 Scotts Rd, 24-02/04 Shaw Centre, Singapore 228208; tel. 67376988; fax 67374096; e-mail secyhc@pakhicom.org.sg; internet www.parep.org.sg; High Commissioner SYED HASAN JAVED.

Panama: 16 Raffles Quay, 41-06 Hong Leong Bldg, Singapore 048581; tel. 62218677; fax 62240892; e-mail general@panamaemb.org.sg; internet www.panamaemb.org.sg; Ambassador JOSÉ ANTONIO RUIZ BLANCO.

Peru: 390 Orchard Rd, 12-03 Palais Renaissance, Singapore 238871; tel. 67388595; fax 67388601; e-mail embperu@pacific.net.sg; internet www.embassyperu.org.sg; Ambassador ARMANDO RAÚL PATIÑO ALVISTUR.

Philippines: 20 Nassim Rd, Singapore 258395; tel. 67373977; fax 67339544; e-mail php@pacific.net.sg; internet www.philippine-embassy.org.sg; Ambassador MINDA CRUZ.

Poland: 435 Orchard Rd, 17-02/03 Wisma Atria, Singapore 238877; tel. 62359478; fax 62359479; e-mail secretary@pacific.net.sg; internet www.singapore.polemb.net; Ambassador WALDEMAR DUBANIOWSKI.

Qatar: 8 Temasek Blvd, 41-02 Suntec Tower 3, Singapore 038988; tel. 65939900; fax 68365731; Ambassador RASHID BIN ALI HASSAN AL-KHATER.

Romania: 1 Claymore Dr., Singapore 229594; tel. 67355023; fax 67355021; e-mail comofrom@starhub.net.sg; Chargé d'affaires ALEXANDRU IRIMIA.

Russia: 51 Nassim Rd, Singapore 258439; tel. 62351834; fax 67334780; e-mail mail@russia.org.sg; internet www.russia.org.sg; Ambassador ANDREY N. ROZHKOV.

Rwanda: 6 Temasek Blvd, 27-01 Suntec Tower 4, Singapore 038986; tel. 68844621; fax 68844206; e-mail info@rwandaembassy.org.sg; internet www.rwandaembassy.org.sg; High Commissioner JEANINE KAMBANDA.

Saudi Arabia: 163 Penang Rd, 03-02/03 Winsland House 2, Singapore 238463; tel. 67345878; fax 67385291; e-mail enquiries@saudiembassy.org.sg; Ambassador Dr JAMIL MAHMOUD MERDAD.

South Africa: 331 North Bridge Rd, 15-01/06 Odeon Towers, Singapore 188720; tel. 63393319; fax 63396658; e-mail hom@southafricahc.org.sg; internet www.southafricahc.org.sg; High Commissioner Dr SIMEON SELBY RIPINGA.

Spain: 7 Temasek Blvd, 39-00 Suntec City Tower 1, Singapore 038987; tel. 67259220; fax 63333025; e-mail emb.singapur@maec.es; internet www.maec.es/Subwebs/Embajadas/singapur; Ambassador FEDERICO PALOMERA GUEZ.

Sri Lanka: 13-07/12 Goldhill Plaza, 51 Newton Rd, Singapore 308900; tel. 62544595; fax 62507201; e-mail slhcs@lanka.com.sg; internet www.lanka.com.sg; High Commissioner FERIAL ISMAIL ASHRAFF.

Sweden: 111 Somerset Rd, 05-01 Singapore Power Bldg, Singapore 238164; tel. 64159720; fax 64159747; e-mail ambassaden.singapore@foreign.ministry.se; internet www.swedenabroad.com/singapore; Ambassador BENGT INGEMAR DOLFE.

Switzerland: 1 Swiss Club Link, Singapore 288162; tel. 64685788; fax 64668245; e-mail sin.vertretung@eda.admin.ch; internet www.eda.admin.ch/singapore; Ambassador JÖRG ALOIS REDING.

Thailand: 370 Orchard Rd, Singapore 238870; tel. 67372158; fax 67320778; e-mail consular@thaiembassy.sg; internet www.thaiembassy.sg; Ambassador NOPADOL GUNAVIBOOL.

Turkey: Shenton Way, 10-03 SGX Centre Tower 1, Singapore 068804; tel. 65333390; fax 65333360; e-mail turksin@singnet.com.sg; internet singapur.be.mfa.gov.tr; Ambassador ŞAFAK GÖKTÜRK.

Ukraine: 50 Raffles Pl., 16-05 Singapore Land Tower, Singapore 048623; tel. 65356550; fax 65352116; e-mail emb_sg@mfa.gov.ua; internet www.mfa.gov.ua/singapore; Ambassador PAVLO SULTANSKY.

United Arab Emirates: 600 North Bridge Rd, 09-01 Parkview Sq., Singapore 188778; tel. 62388206; fax 62380081; e-mail emarat@singnet.com.sg; internet www.uaeembassy-sg.com; Ambassador MOHAMMED AHMED HAMIL AL-QUBAISI.

United Kingdom: 100 Tanglin Rd, Singapore 247919; tel. 64244200; fax 64244218; e-mail consular.singapore@fco.gov.uk; internet www.ukinsingapore.fco.gov.uk; High Commissioner ANTONY PHILLIPSON.

USA: 27 Napier Rd, Singapore 258508; tel. 64769100; fax 64769340; e-mail singaporeusembassy@state.gov; internet singapore.usembassy.gov; Ambassador DAVID ADELMAN.

Uzbekistan: 20 Kramat Lane, 04-01/02 United House, Singapore 228773; tel. 67343943; fax 67345849; e-mail info@uzbekistan.org.sg; internet www.uzbekistan.org.sg; Ambassador ALISHER A. KURMANOV.

Venezuela: 3 Killiney Rd, 07-03 Winsland House 1, Singapore 239519; tel. 64911172; fax 62353167; e-mail embassy@embavenez.org.sg; Ambassador ALFREDO TORO HARDY.

Viet Nam: 10 Leedon Park, Singapore 267887; tel. 64625938; fax 64625936; e-mail vnemb@singnet.com.sg; internet www.vietnamembassy-singapore.org; Ambassador TRAN HAI HAU.

Judicial System

The judicial power of Singapore is vested in the Supreme Court and in the Subordinate Courts. The Judiciary administers the law with complete independence from the executive and legislative branches of the Government; this independence is safeguarded by the Constitution. The Supreme Court consists of the High Court and the Court of Appeal. The Chief Justice is appointed by the President if the latter, acting at his discretion, concurs with the advice of the Prime Minister. The other judges of the Supreme Court are appointed in the same way, in consultation with the Chief Justice. Under a 1979 constitutional amendment, the position of judicial commissioner of the Supreme Court was created 'to facilitate the disposal of business in the Supreme Court'. A judicial commissioner has the powers and functions of a judge, and is appointed for such period as the President thinks fit.

The Subordinate Courts consist of District Courts and Magistrates' Courts. In addition, there are also specialized courts such as the Coroner's Court, Family Court, Juvenile Court, Mentions Court, Night Court, Sentencing Courts and Filter Courts. The Primary Dispute Resolution Centre and the Small Claims Tribunals are also managed by the Subordinate Courts. The Subordinate Courts have also established the Multi-Door Courthouse, which serves as a one-stop centre for the screening and channelling of any cases to the most appropriate forum for dispute resolution.

District Courts and Magistrates' Courts have original criminal and civil jurisdiction. District Courts try offences for which the maximum penalty does not exceed 10 years of imprisonment and in civil cases where the amount claimed does not exceed S $250,000. Magistrates' Courts try offences for which the maximum term of imprisonment does not exceed three years. The jurisdiction of Magistrates' Courts in civil cases is limited to claims not exceeding S $60,000. The Coroners' Court conducts inquests. The Small Claims Tribunal has jurisdiction over claims relating to a dispute arising from any contract for the sale of goods or the provision of services and any claim in tort in respect of damage caused to any property involving an amount that does not exceed S $10,000. The Juvenile Court deals with offences committed by young persons aged under 16 years.

The High Court has unlimited original jurisdiction in criminal and civil cases. In its appellate jurisdiction it hears criminal and civil appeals from the District Courts and Magistrates' Courts. The Court of Appeal hears appeals against the decisions of the High Court in both criminal and civil matters. In criminal matters, the Court of Appeal hears appeals against decisions made by the High Court in the exercise of its original criminal jurisdiction. In civil matters, the Court of Appeal hears appeals against decisions made by the High Court in the exercise of both its original and appellate jurisdiction.

With the enactment of the Judicial Committee (Repeal) Act 1994 in April of that year, the right of appeal from the Court of Appeal to the Judicial Committee of the Privy Council in the United Kingdom was abolished. The Court of Appeal is now the final appellate court in the Singapore legal system.

Supreme Court: 1 Supreme Court Lane, Singapore 178879; tel. 63360644; fax 63379450; e-mail supcourt_qsm@supcourt.gov.sg; internet www.supcourt.gov.sg.

Attorney-General: SUNDARESH MENON.

Chief Justice: CHAN SEK KEONG.

Judges of Appeal: V. K. RAJAH, ANDREW PHANG BOON LEONG, CHAO HICK TIN.

Religion

According to the 2010 census, 57.4% of ethnic Chinese, who constituted 74% of the population, professed either Buddhism or Daoism (including followers of Confucius, Mencius and Lao Zi) and 20.1% of Chinese adhered to Christianity. Malays, who made up 13.3% of the population, were 98.7% Muslim. Among Indians, who constituted 9.2% of the population, 58.9% were Hindus, 21.7% Muslims, 12.8% Christians and 5.7% Sikhs, Jains or adherents of other faiths. There are small communities of Zoroastrians and Jews. Freedom of worship is guaranteed by the Constitution.

BAHÁ'Í FAITH

The Spiritual Assembly of the Bahá'ís of Singapore: 55 Cantonment Rd, Singapore 089754; tel. 62226200; fax 62229166; e-mail webmaster@bahai.org.sg; internet www.bahai.org.sg.

BUDDHISM

Buddhist Union: 28 Jalan Senyum, Singapore 418152; tel. 62419419; fax 64443280; e-mail thebu@singnet.com.sg.

Singapore Buddhist Federation: 59 Lorong 24A, Geylang, Singapore 398583; tel. 67444635; fax 67473618; e-mail buddhist@singnet.com.sg; internet www.buddhist.org.sg; f. 1948; Pres. KWANG SHENG.

Singapore Buddhist Sangha Organization: 88 Bright Hill Drive, Singapore 579644.

CHRISTIANITY

National Council of Churches: 1 Coleman St, B1-27 The Adelphi, Singapore 179803; tel. 63368177; fax 63368178; e-mail admin@nccs.org.sg; internet www.nccs.org.sg; f. 1948; Pres. Rev. Dr ROBERT SOLOMON; Gen. Sec. LIM K. TAN.

Singapore Council of Christian Churches (SCCC): Singapore; f. 1956.

The Anglican Communion

The Anglican diocese of Singapore (also including Indonesia, Laos, Thailand, Viet Nam and Cambodia) is part of the Province of the Anglican Church in South-East Asia.

Bishop of Singapore: The Rt Rev. Dr JOHN HIANG CHEA CHEW, 01-01, St Andrew's Vill., 1 Francis Thomas Dr., Singapore 359340; tel. 62888944; fax 62885538; e-mail bpoffice@anglican.org.sg; internet www.anglican.org.sg.

Orthodox Churches

The Orthodox Syrian Church and the Mar Thoma Syrian Church are both active in Singapore.

The Roman Catholic Church

Singapore comprises a single archdiocese, directly responsible to the Holy See. In December 2007 there were an estimated 177,775 adherents in the country, representing 3.9% of the total population.

Archbishop of Singapore: Most Rev. NICHOLAS CHIA, Archbishop's House, 31 Victoria St, Singapore 187997; tel. 63378818; fax 63334735; e-mail nc@catholic.org.sg; internet www.veritas.org.sg.

Other Christian Churches

Brethren Assemblies: Bethesda Hall (Ang Mo Kio), 601 Ang Mo Kio Ave 4, Singapore 569898; tel. 64587474; fax 64566771; e-mail bethesdahall@gmail.com; internet www.bethesdahall.com; f. 1864; Hon. Sec. WONG TUCK KEONG.

Evangelical Fellowship of Singapore (EFOS): 06-03 Morningstar Centre, 12 New Industrial Rd, Singapore 536202; e-mail tonyyeo@gdop.sg; internet www.efosingapore.org; f. 1980; Chair. Dr LAWRENCE CHIA.

Lutheran Church in Singapore: 28-30 Duke's Rd, Singapore 268912; tel. 64646337; fax 64646323; e-mail lutheran@lutheran.org.sg; internet www.lutheran.org.sg.

Methodist Church in Singapore: 70 Barker Rd, Singapore 309936; tel. 64784784; fax 64784794; e-mail mcs@methodist.org.sg; internet www.methodist.org.sg; f. 1885; 38,000 mems (Dec. 2010); Leader Bishop Dr ROBERT SOLOMON.

Presbyterian Church: 3 Orchard Rd, cnr Penang Rd, Singapore 238825; tel. 63376681; fax 63391979; e-mail orpcenglish@orpc.org.sg; internet www.orpc.org.sg; f. 1856; services in English, Chinese (Mandarin), Indonesian and German; 2,000 mems; Moderator Rev. DEREK KINGSTON (acting).

Singapore Baptist Convention: 01 Goldhill Plaza, 03-19 Podium Blk, Singapore 308899; tel. 62538004; fax 62538214; e-mail info@baptistconvention.org.sg; internet www.baptistconvention.org.sg; f. 1974; Chair. Rev. EDWIN LAM HON MUN; Exec. Dir PETER TANG.

Other denominations active in Singapore include the Lutheran Church and the Evangelical Lutheran Church.

HINDUISM

Hindu Advisory Board: c/o 397 Serangoon Rd, Singapore 218123; tel. 62963469; fax 62929766; e-mail heb@pacific.net.sg; f. 1985; Chair. R. BAJAWEE; Sec. S. RAMESH.

Hindu Endowments Board: 397 Serangoon Rd, Singapore 218123; tel. 62963469; fax 62929766; e-mail heb@pacific.net.sg; internet www.heb.gov.sg; f. 1968; Chair. S. RAJENDRAN; Sec. P. AVADIAR.

ISLAM

Majlis Ugama Islam Singapura (MUIS) (Islamic Religious Council of Singapore): Singapore Islamic Hub, 273 Braddell Rd, Singapore 579702; tel. 63591199; fax 62537572; e-mail info@muis.gov.sg; internet www.muis.gov.sg; f. 1968; Pres. Haji MOHD ALAMI MUSA; Sec. ABDUL RAZAK MARICAR.

Muslim Missionary Society Singapore (JAMIYAH): 31 Lorong, 12 Geylang Rd, Singapore 399006; tel. 67431211; fax 67450610; e-mail info@jamiyah.org.sg; internet www.jamiyah.org.sg; Pres. Haji ABDUL KARIM BIN MAIDIN; Sec.-Gen. MOHD YUNOS BIN MOHD SHARIFF.

SIKHISM

Central Sikh Gurdwara Board (CSGB): c/o 2 Towner Rd, 03-01, Singapore 327804; tel. 62993855; e-mail csgb@sikhs.org.sg; internet www.sikhs.org.sg; Pres. KARPAL SINGH MEHLI.

The Press

DAILIES

English Language

The Business Times: 1000 Toa Payoh North, Podium Blk, Level 3, Singapore 318994; tel. 63195318; fax 63198277; e-mail btocs@sph.com.sg; internet www.businesstimes.com.sg; f. 1976; morning; Editor ALVIN TAY; circ. 34,368.

The New Paper: 1000 Toa Payoh North, Annexe Blk, Level 6, Singapore 318994; tel. 63196319; fax 63198266; e-mail tnp@sph.com.sg; internet www.tnp.sg; f. 1988; afternoon tabloid; Editor DOMINIC NATHAN; circ. 102,616.

The Straits Times: 1000 Toa Payoh North, Singapore 318994; tel. 63195397; fax 67320131; e-mail stonline@sph.com.sg; internet www.straitstimes.com; f. 1845; morning; Editor-in-Chief PATRICK DANIEL; circ. 359,989.

Today: Caldecott Broadcast Centre, Andrew Rd, Singapore 299939; tel. 63333888; fax 65344217; e-mail news@newstoday.com.sg; internet www.todayonline.com; f. 2000; merged with *Streats*, a rival free morning tabloid, in 2004; Editor WALTER FERNANDEZ; circ. 584,000.

Chinese Language

Lianhe Wanbao: 1000 Toa Payoh North, Podium Blk, Level 4, Singapore 318994; tel. 63196319; fax 63198133; e-mail wanbao@sph.com.sg; f. 1983; evening; Editor CHUA CHIM KANG; circ. 97,082.

Lianhe Zaobao: 1000 Toa Payoh North, Podium Blk, Level 4, Singapore 318994; tel. 63196319; fax 63198228; e-mail zaobao@web1.asia1.com.sg; internet www.zaobao.com; f. 1923; Editor LIM JIM KOON; circ. 169,420.

My Paper: 1000 Toa Payoh North, News Centre, Singapore 318994; tel. 63192222; fax 63198115; e-mail mypaper@sph.com.sg; internet www.mypaper.sg; f. 2006; free tabloid aimed at bilingual working adults aged between 20 and 40 yrs; Editor APRIL PUNG KOON KING; circ. 250,000.

Shin Min Daily News (S) Ltd: 1000 Toa Payoh North, Podium Blk, Level 4, Singapore 318994; tel. 63196319; fax 63198166; e-mail shinmin@sph.com.sg; f. 1967; evening; Editor KOH LIN HOE; circ. 136,127.

Malay Language

Berita Harian: 1000 Toa Payoh North, Annexe Blk, Level 3, Singapore 318994; tel. 63195137; fax 63198255; e-mail aadeska@sph.com.sg; internet cyberita.asia1.com.sg; f. 1957; morning; Editor MOHD GUNTOR SADALI; circ. 59,193.

Tamil Language

Tamil Murasu: SPH Media Centre, 82 Genting Lane 06-07, Singapore 349567; tel. 63196319; fax 63194001; e-mail murasu4@cyberway.com.sg; internet www.tamilmurasu.com.sg; f. 1935; Editor NIRMALA MURUGAIAN; circ. 13,766.

WEEKLIES

English Language

The Edge Singapore: 150 Cecil St 13-00, Singapore 069543; tel. 62328622; fax 62328620; e-mail theedgespore@bizedge.com; internet www.theedgesingapore.com; business and investment; Editor BEN PAUL; circ. 17,870.

The New Paper on Sunday: 1000 Toa Payoh North, Annexe Blk, Level 6, Singapore 318994; tel. 63196319; fax 63198266; e-mail tnp@sph.com.sg; internet www.tnp.sg; f. 1999; tabloid; Editor DOMINIC NATHAN; circ. 125,107.

The Sunday Times: 1000 Toa Payoh North, Singapore 318994; tel. 63195397; fax 67320131; e-mail stonline@sph.com.sg; internet www.straitstimes.com; f. 1931; Editor IGNATIUS LOW; circ. 372,809 (Singapore only).

Weekend Today: Caldecott Broadcast Centre, Andrew Rd, Singapore 299939; tel. 63333888; fax 65344217; e-mail today@mediacorp.com.sg; internet www.todayonline.com; f. 2002; Editor P. N. BALJI; circ. 150,000.

Chinese Language

Thumbs Up: 1000 Toa Payoh North, Annexe Blk, Level 5, Singapore 318994; tel. 63196319; fax 63198111; e-mail thumbsup@sph.com.sg; f. 2000; newspaper aimed at primary school students; Editor LIM SOON LAN; circ. 37,445.

Malay Language

Berita Minggu: 1000 Toa Payoh North, Annex Blk, Level 3, Singapore 318994; tel. 63195665; fax 63198255; e-mail aadeska@sph.com.sg; internet cyberita.asia1.com.sg; f. 1960; Sunday; Editor ISMAIL PANTEK; circ. 65,608 (Singapore only).

SELECTED PERIODICALS

English Language

8 Days: 10 Ang Mo Kio St 65, 01-06/08 Techpoint, Singapore 569059; tel. 62789822; fax 62724800; e-mail feedback@8daysonline.com; internet www.8days.sg; f. 1990; weekly; Editor-in-Chief LAU KUAN WEI; circ. 113,258.

Female: SPH Media Centre, 82 Genting Lane, Level 7, Singapore 349567; tel. 63196319; fax 63196345; e-mail magfemale@sph.com.sg; internet www.femalemag.com.sg; f. 1974; monthly; circ. 60,000.

FHM Singapore: 01-06/08, 10 Ang Mo Kio St 65, Singapore 569059; tel. 64845212; e-mail info@fhm.com.sg; internet www.fhm.com.sg; Sr Editor DAVID FURHMANN-LIM.

Her World: SPH Media Centre, 82 Genting Lane, Singapore 349567; tel. 63196319; fax 63196345; e-mail magherworld@sph.com.sg; internet www.herworld.com; f. 1960; monthly; women's; Editor NIKI BRUCE.

Her World Brides: SPH Media Centre, 82 Genting Lane, Singapore 349567; tel. 63196319; fax 63196345; e-mail maghwbrides@sph.com.sg; internet www.hwbrides.com.sg; f. 1998; quarterly; circ. 13,193.

Home and Decor: SPH Media Centre, 82 Genting Lane, 5th Floor, Singapore 349567; tel. 63196319; fax 63196345; e-mail hdecor@sph.com.sg; internet www.homeanddecor.com.sg; f. 1987; 6 a year; Editor SOPHIE KHO; circ. 27,000.

NSman: SAFRA National Service Association, 5200 Jalan Bukit Merah, Singapore 159468; tel. 63779835; fax 63779898; e-mail hq@safra.sg; internet www.safra.sg; f. 1972; est. as *Reservist*; renamed 1994; bi-monthly; publ. of SAFRA Nat. Service Asscn; Gen. Sec. TAN KOK YAM; circ. 150,000.

Pioneer: 5 Depot Rd, 05-06 Defence Technology Tower B, Singapore 109681; tel. 63731114; fax 63731111; e-mail pioneer@starnet.gov.sg; internet www.mindef.gov.sg/imindef/publications/cyberpioneer/index.html; f. 1996; monthly; publication of the Singaporean Armed Forces.

Republic of Singapore Government Gazette: Toppan Leefung Pte Ltd, 1 Kim Seng Promenade, 18-01 Great World City East Tower, Singapore 237994; tel. 68269600; fax 68203341; e-mail egazinfo@toppanleefung.com; internet www.egazette.com.sg; weekdays.

SimplyHer: SPH Media Centre, 82 Genting Lane, Level 7, Singapore 349567; tel. 63196319; fax 63196345; e-mail magsimplyher@sph.com.sg; internet www.simplyher.com.sg; f. 2004; monthly; women's; Editor PENELOPE CHAN; circ. 21,000.

Singapore Medical Journal: Singapore Medical Asscn, Level 2, Alumni Medical Centre, 2 College Rd, Singapore 169850; tel. 62231264; fax 62247827; e-mail smj@sma.org.sg; internet www.sma.org.sg/smj; f. 1959; monthly; Editor Prof. TEO ENG KIONG; circ. 5,000.

Torque: SPH Media Centre, 82 Genting Lane, Level 7, Singapore 349567; tel. 63196319; fax 63196345; e-mail seowlka@sph.com.sg; internet www.torque.com.sg; f. 1990; monthly; automobile; Editor LEE NIAN TJOE.

Young Parents: SPH Media Centre, 82 Genting Lane, Level 7, Singapore 349567; tel. 63196319; fax 63196345; e-mail magyoungparents@sph.com.sg; internet www.youngparents.com.sg; f. 1987; monthly; family; Editor STEPHANIE YEO; circ. 20,000.

Chinese Language

Characters: 1 Kallang Sector, 04-04/05 Kolam Ayer Industrial Park, Singapore 349276; tel. 67458733; fax 67458213; f. 1987; monthly; television and entertainment; Editor SAM NG; circ. 45,000.

The Citizen: People's Association, 9 Stadium Link, Singapore 397750; tel. 63405138; fax 63468657; monthly; English, Chinese, Tamil and Malay; Man. Editor OOI HUI MEI.

Icon: SPH Media Centre, 82 Genting Lane, Level 7, Singapore 349567; tel. 63196319; fax 63196345; e-mail magicon@sph.com.sg; internet www.iconsingapore.com; f. 2005; monthly; Chinese language; lifestyle; Man. Editor ELSIE YAH.

i-weekly: 10 Ang Mo Kio St 65, 01-06/08 Techpoint, Singapore 569059; tel. 64837837; fax 64837257; e-mail i-weekly@mediacorp.com.sg; f. 1981; weekly; lifestyle and entertainment; Editor-in-Chief JACKIE LIU; circ. 232,000.

NuYou: SPH Media Centre, 82 Genting Lane, Level 7, Singapore 349567; tel. 63196319; fax 63196345; internet www.nuyou.com.sg; f. 1976; monthly; Editor-in-Chief GRACE LEE.

Punters' Way: 4 Ubi View (off Ubi Rd 3), Pioneers and Leaders Centre, Singapore 408557; tel. 67458733; fax 67458321; e-mail pnlhldg@pnl-group.com; internet www.pnl-group.com; f. 1977; bi-weekly; English and Chinese; horse racing; Editor T. S. PHAN; circ. 90,000.

Racing Guide: 1 Scotts Rd, 26-03 Shaw Centre, Singapore 228208; tel. 67340111; e-mail inquiries@asiapacificpublishing.com; internet www.racingguide.com.sg; f. 1987; 2 a week; English and Chinese; sport; Editorial Consultant BENNY ORTEGA; Chinese Editor KUEK CHIEW TEONG; circ. 20,000.

Singapore Literature: Singapore Literature Society, 122B Sims Ave, Singapore 1438; quarterly; Pres. YAP KOON CHAN; Editor LUO-MING.

UW (U-Weekly): Focus Publishing Ltd,1000 Toa Payoh North, News Centre, Singapore 318994; tel. 63196319; fax 63198124; e-mail youmail@sph.com.sg; f. 2001 as You Weekly; renamed as above 2005; weekly; entertainment and lifestyle; circ. 80,000.

Young Generation: 1 New Industrial Rd, Times Centre, Singapore 536196; tel. 62139276; fax 68463440; e-mail kelenkoh@tpl.com.sg; internet www.panpaceducation.com; monthly; children's; Editor EVELYN TANG; circ. 80,000.

Malay Language

Manja: 10 Ang Mo Kio St 65, 01-06/08 Techpoint, Singapore 569059; tel. 64837118; fax 64812098; e-mail hello@manja.sg; internet www.manja.sg; f. 2000; monthly; entertainment and lifestyle; Editor RUSLINA AFFENDY.

NEWS AGENCIES

Foreign Bureaux

Various foreign bureaux operate in Singapore.

Publishers

ENGLISH LANGUAGE

Butterworths Asia: 3 Killiney Rd, 08-08 Winsland House 1, Singapore 239519; tel. 67331380; fax 67331175; e-mail help.sg@lexisnexis.com; internet www.lexisnexis.com.sg/butterworths-online; f. 1932; law texts and journals; Gen. Man. DEAN CORKERY.

Caldecott Publishing Pte Ltd: 10 Ang Mo Kio St 65, 01-06/08 Techpoint, Singapore 569059; tel. 64837118; fax 64837286; f. 1990; Editorial Dir MICHAEL CHIANG; Group Editor TAN LEE SUN.

FEP International Pte Ltd: 3A Phillips Ave, Singapore 546921; tel. 62814185; fax 67375561; f. 1960; textbooks, reference, children's and dictionaries; Gen. Man. RICHARD TOH.

Flame of the Forest Publishing Pte Ltd: Blk 5, Ang Mo Kio Industrial Park 2A, 07-22/23, AMK Tech II, Singapore 567760; tel. 64848887; fax 64842208; e-mail mail@flameoftheforest.com; internet www.flameoftheforest.com; f. 1989; Man. Dir ALEX CHACKO.

Graham Brash Pte Ltd: 45 Kian Teck Drive, Blk 1, Level 2, Singapore 628859; tel. 62624843; fax 62621519; e-mail evelyn@grahambrash.com.sg; internet www.grahambrash.com.sg; f. 1947; general, academic, educational; English, Chinese and Malay; Publr and Man. Dir CHUAN I. CAMPBELL; Gen. Man. EVELYN LEE.

Institute of Southeast Asian Studies: 30 Heng Mui Keng Terrace, Pasir Panjang Rd, Singapore 119614; tel. 67780955; fax 67756259; e-mail pubsunit@iseas.edu.sg; internet www.iseas.edu.sg; f. 1968; scholarly works on contemporary South-East Asia and the Asia-Pacific region; Chair. Prof. WANG GUNGWU; Dir K. KESAVAPANY.

Intellectual Publishing Co: 113 Eunos Ave 3, 04-08 Gordon Industrial Bldg, Singapore 1440; tel. 67466025; fax 67489108; f. 1971; Man. POH BE LECK.

Marshall Cavendish International (Singapore) Pte Ltd: Times Centre, 1 New Industrial Rd, Singapore 536196; tel. 62139300; fax 62889254; e-mail timesales@sg.marshallcavendish.com; internet www.marshallcavendish.com/education; f. 1957; fmrly Times Media Pte Ltd; academic texts; Group Publr SHANE ARMSTRONG; Publr DURIYA AZIZ.

NUS Press (Pte) Ltd: National University of Singapore, 3 Arts Link, AS3-01/02, Singapore 117569; tel. 67761148; fax 67740652; e-mail nusbooks@nus.edu.sg; internet www.nus.edu.sg/nuspress; f. 1971; scholarly; Man. Dir PAUL KRATOSKA.

Pearson Education South Asia Pte Ltd: 23–25 First Lok Yang Rd, Jurong Town, Singapore 629733; tel. 63199388; fax 62651033; e-mail info@pearsoned.com.sg; internet www.pearsonlongman.com.sg; educational; Dir, Business Support, South Asia RASMIATI HARTANTO.

Stamford Media International Pte Ltd: 209 Kallang Bahru, Singapore 339344; tel. 62947227; fax 62944396; e-mail info@stamford.com.sg; internet www.stamford.com.sg; f. 1963; est. as Stamford College Publrs; renamed Stamford Press Pte Ltd in 1983; present name adopted 2001; general, educational and journals; Man. LAWRENCE THOMAS.

Times Publishing Ltd: Times Centre, 1 New Industrial Rd, Singapore 536196; tel. 62139288; fax 62131186; e-mail tpl@tpl.com.sg; internet www.tpl.com.sg; f. 1978; political, social and cultural books, general works on Asia; Chair. LIM KIM SAN; CEO GOH SIK NGEE.

World Scientific Publishing Co Pte Ltd: 5 Toh Tuck Link, Singapore 596224; tel. 64665775; fax 64677667; e-mail wspc@wspc.com.sg; internet www.worldscientific.com; f. 1981; academic and research texts and science journals; Chair. and Editor-in-Chief Prof. K. K. PHUA; Man. Dir DOREEN LIU.

MALAY LANGUAGE

Malaysia Press Sdn Bhd (Pustaka Melayu): Singapore; tel. 62933454; fax 62911858; f. 1962; textbooks and educational; Man. Dir ABU TALIB BIN ALLY.

Pustaka Nasional Pte Ltd: 548 Changi Rd, Singapore 419931; tel. 67454321; fax 67452417; e-mail enquiry@pustaka.com.sg; internet www.pustaka.com.sg; f. 1963; Arabic, English, Malay and Islamic religious books and CD-Roms; Dir SYED ALI SEMAIT.

CHINESE LANGUAGE

Shanghai Book Co (Pte) Ltd: 231 Bain St, 02-73 Bras Basah Complex, Singapore 180231; tel. 63360144; fax 63360490; e-mail shanghaibook@pacific.net.sg; f. 1925; educational and general; Man. Dir MA JI LIN.

Shing Lee Publishers Pte Ltd: 120 Hillview Ave, 05-06/07 Kewalram Hillview, Singapore 669594; tel. 67601388; fax 67623247; e-mail info@shinglee.com.sg; internet www.shinglee.com.sg; f. 1935; educational and general; Man. PEH SOH NGOH.

Union Book Co (Pte) Ltd: 231 Bain St, 03-01 Bras Basah Complex, Singapore 180231; tel. 63380696; fax 63386306; e-mail youlian@singnet.com.sg; internet www.unionbook.com.sg; f. 1952; general and reference; Gen. Man. MARGARET XIAOMIN.

TAMIL LANGUAGE

EVS Enterprises: 16 Cuff Rd, Singapore 209727; tel. 62915334; fax 62952105; f. 1967; children's books, religion and general; Man. E. V. SINGHAN.

GOVERNMENT PUBLISHING HOUSE

Toppan Leefung Pte Ltd: 1 Kim Seng Promenade, 18-01 Great World City East Tower, Singapore 237994; tel. 68269600; fax 68203341; e-mail enquiries@toppanleefung.com; internet www.toppanleefung.com; f. 1973; fmrly SNP Corpn Ltd; present name adopted following acquisition by Toppan Printing Co Ltd in 2008; printers and publrs; Pres. and CEO YEO CHEE TONG.

PUBLISHERS' ORGANIZATIONS

National Book Development Council of Singapore (NBDCS): 50 Geylang East Ave 1, Singapore 389777; tel. 68488290; fax 67429466; e-mail info@bookcouncil.sg; internet www.bookcouncil.sg; f. 1969; independent non-profit org.; promotes reading, writing and publishing; offers professional training programmes; Chair. Prof. SERENE WEE.

Singapore Book Publishers' Association: 86 Marine Parade Central, 03-213, Singapore 440086; tel. 63447801; fax 64470897; e-mail info@singaporebookpublishers.sg; internet www.singaporebookpublishers.sg; 75 mems; Pres. TRIENA ONG.

Broadcasting and Communications

TELECOMMUNICATIONS

Infocomm Development Authority of Singapore (IDA): 8 Temasek Blvd, 14-00 Suntec Tower Three, Singapore 038988; tel. 62110888; fax 62112222; e-mail info@ida.gov.sg; internet www.ida.gov.sg; f. 1999; formed as result of merger of Nat. Computer Bd and Telecommunication Authority of Singapore; the national policy maker; regulator of telecommunications and promoter of information and communication technologies in Singapore; CEO Dr CHRISTOPHER CHIA.

MobileOne (M1): 10 International Business Park, Singapore 609928; tel. 68951111; fax 68993929; e-mail ir@m1.com.sg; internet www.m1.com.sg; f. 1997; Chair. TEO SOON HOE; CEO KAREN KOOI.

Netrust Pte Ltd: 70 Bendemeer Rd, 05-03, Luzerne, Singapore 339940; tel. 62121388; fax 62121366; e-mail infoline@netrust.net; internet www.netrust.net; f. 1997; the only licensed Certification Authority (CA) in Singapore, jtly formed by Nat. Computer Bd and Network for Electronic Transfers; verifies the identity of parties doing business or communicating in cyberspace through the issuing of electronic identification certificates, in order to enable govt orgs and private enterprises to conduct electronic transactions in a secure manner; CEO FOO JONG AI.

Singapore Technologies Telemedia: 51 Cuppage Rd, 09-01 Starhub Centre, Singapore 229469; tel. 67238777; fax 67207266; e-mail contactus@stt.st.com.sg; internet www.sttelemedia.com; Pres. and CEO LEE THENG KIAT.

Singapore Telecommunications Ltd (SingTel): 19-00 Comcentre, 31 Exeter Rd, Singapore 239732; tel. 68383388; fax 67328428; e-mail contact@singtel.com; internet info.singtel.com; f. 1992; postal and telecommunications service operator and holding co for a number of subsidiaries, serving both the corporate and consumer markets; 61.79%-owned by Temasek Holdings (Pvt) Ltd (a govt holding co), 38.21% transferred to the private sector; Chair. CHUMPOL NALAMLIENG; Group CEO CHUA SOCK KOONG.

StarHub Pte Ltd: Head Office, 51 Cuppage Rd, 01-02/03 StarHub Centre, Singapore 229469; tel. 68255000; fax 67205000; e-mail corpcomms@starhub.com; internet www.starhub.com; f. 2000; telecommunications service provider; consortium includes Singapore Technologies Telemedia Pte Ltd, Singapore Power Ltd, Nippon Telegraph and Telephone Corpn (NTT) and British Telecom (BT); CEO NEIL MONTEFIORE.

BROADCASTING

Regulatory Authority

Media Development Authority (MDA): 3 Fusionopolis Way, 16-22 Symbiosis, Singapore 138633; tel. 63773800; fax 65773888; internet www.mda.gov.sg; f. 1994; fmrly Singapore Broadcasting Authority; present name adopted 2003; licenses, regulates and promotes the devt of the media industry in Singapore; ensures the provision of an adequate range of media services to serve the interests of the general public, maintains fair and efficient market conduct and effective competition in the media industry, ensures the maintenance of a high standard of media services, regulates public service broadcasting; Chair. Dr TAN CHIN NAM; CEO Dr CHRISTOPHER CHIA.

Radio

Far East Broadcasting Associates (FEBA Ltd): 30 Lorong Ampas, 07-01 Skywaves Industrial Bldg, Singapore 328783; tel. 62508577; fax 62508422; e-mail febadmin@febaltd.com; f. 1960; Chair. GOH EWE KHENG; Exec. Dir LEE CHI KWAN (acting).

Media Corporation of Singapore: Caldecott Broadcast Centre, Andrew Rd, Singapore 299939; tel. 63333888; fax 62515628; e-mail feedback@mediacorp.com.sg; internet www.mediacorp.com.sg; f. 1994; est. as Singapore Int. Media (SIM), following corporatization of Singapore Broadcasting Corpn; holding co for 7 operating cos—Television Corpn of Singapore (TCS), Singapore Television Twelve (STV12), Radio Corpn of Singapore (RCS), MediaCorp Studios, MediaCorp News, MediaCorp Interactive and MediaCorp Publishing; Chair. TEO MING KAN; CEO SHAUN SEOW.

Radio Corpn of Singapore Pte Ltd (RCS): Caldecott Broadcast Centre, Radio Bldg, Andrew Rd, Singapore 299939; tel. 63597307; fax 63597500; e-mail feedback@mediacorp.com.sg; internet www.mediacorpradio.sg; f. 1936; operates 13 domestic services—incl. in English (six), Mandarin (three), Malay (two) and Tamil (one)—and three international radio stations (manages Radio Singapore International (RSI)—services in English, Mandarin and Malay for three hours daily and service in Bahasa Indonesia for one hour daily); Man. Dir LEO GOH.

Rediffusion (Singapore) Pte Ltd: 12 New Industrial Rd, 03-03 Morningstar Centre, Singapore 536202; tel. 63832633; fax 62850421; e-mail md@rediffusion.com.sg; internet www.rediffusion.com.sg; f. 1949; commercial audio wired broadcasting service and wireless digital audio broadcasting service; broadcasts 15 regional and international channels; Man. Dir WONG BAN KUAN.

SAFRA Radio: Bukit Merah Central, POB 1315, Singapore 911599; tel. 63731924; fax 62783039; e-mail power98@pacific.net.sg; internet www.power98.com.sg; f. 1994; broadcasts in Mandarin and English.

SPH UnionWorks Pte Ltd: 1000 Toa Payoh North, News Centre, Podium Blk, Level 3, Singapore 318994; tel. 63191900; fax 63191099; e-mail webadm@sphuw.com.sg; internet www.sphuw.com.sg; f. 1991; fmrly Radio Heart and UnionWorks Pte Ltd; first private radio station; broadcasts in English and Mandarin; 2 channels covering news, music and entertainment.

Television

CNBC Asia Business News (S) Pte Ltd: 10 Anson Rd, 06-01 International Plaza, Singapore 079903; tel. 63230488; fax 62230020; e-mail contactus@cnbcasia.com; internet asia.cnbc.com; f. 1998; cable and satellite broadcaster of global business and financial news; US-controlled; broadcasts in English (24 hours daily) and Mandarin; Pres. and Man. Dir SATPAL BRAINCH.

Media Corporation of Singapore: see Radio.

Singapore Television Twelve Pte Ltd (STV12): 12 Prince Edward Rd, 05-00 Bestway Bldg, Singapore 079212; tel. 62258133; fax 62203881; internet www.stv12.com.sg; f. 1994; terrestrial TV station; 2 channels—Suria (Malay, 58 hours weekly) and Central (110.5 hours weekly); COO WOON TAI HO.

SPH MediaWorks Ltd: 1000 Toa Payoh North, News Centre, Singapore 318994; tel. 63196319; fax 63198150; e-mail sphcorp@sph.com.sg; internet www.sph.com.sg; f. 2000; subsidiary of Singapore Press Holdings Ltd (SPH); two channels—Channel U (Mandarin) and Channel i (English); also owns two radio stations; CEO ALAN CHAN HENG LOON.

Starhub CableVision Ltd: 51 Cuppage Rd, 01-02/03 Cuppage Centre, Singapore 229469; tel. 68255000; fax 67205000; internet www.starhub.com; f. 1992; fmrly Singapore CableVision Ltd; present name adopted 2002 following acquisition by Starhub Ltd; broadcasting and communications co, subscription television service; launched cable service in June 1995; offers 83 digital channels

(March 2005); offers broadband access services; CEO NEIL MONTEFIORE.

Television Corpn of Singapore (TCS): Caldecott Broadcast Centre, Andrew Rd, Singapore 299939; tel. 63333888; fax 62515628; e-mail feedback@mediacorp.com.sg; internet www .mediacorp.sg; f. 1994; est. following the corporatization of Singapore Broadcasting Corpn; eight channels; broadcasts in English, Mandarin, Malay and Tamil; teletext service on one channel; also owns TVMobile, Singapore's first digital TV channel, and Digital TV; Chair. HO KWON PING; CEO LUCAS CHOW.

Finance

(cap. = capital; res = reserves; dep. = deposits; m. = million; brs = branches; amounts in Singapore dollars)

BANKING

The Singapore monetary system is regulated by the Monetary Authority of Singapore (MAS) and the Ministry of Finance. The MAS performs all the functions of a central bank and also assumed responsibility for the issuing of currency following its merger with the Board of Commissioners of Currency in October 2002. In May 2011 there were 120 commercial banks (six local, 114 foreign) and 33 representative offices in Singapore. Of the foreign banks, 26 had full licences, 50 had wholesale licences and 38 had 'offshore' banking licences.

Government Financial Institution

Monetary Authority of Singapore (MAS): 10 Shenton Way, MAS Bldg, Singapore 079117; tel. 62255577; fax 62299229; e-mail webmaster@mas.gov.sg; internet www.mas.gov.sg; merged with Board of Commissioners of Currency Oct. 2002; cap. 17,000.0m., res 18,321.3m., dep. 139,498.4m. (March 2010); Chair. GOH CHOK TONG; Man. Dir THARMAN SHANMUGARATNAM.

Domestic Full Commercial Banks

Bank of Singapore: 63 Market St, 22-00 Bank of Singapore Centre, Singapore 048942; tel. 65598000; fax 65598180; internet www .bankofsingapore.com; cap. US $596.3m., dep. US $4,680.6m. (Dec. 2009); subsidiary of Oversea-Chinese Banking Corpn Ltd; fmrly ING Asia Private Bank Ltd; CEO RENATO DE GUZMAN.

DBS Bank (Development Bank of Singapore Ltd): 6 Shenton Way, DBS Bldg, Tower One, Singapore 068809; tel. 68788888; fax 64451267; e-mail dbs@dbs.com; internet www.dbs.com/sg; f. 1968; merged with Post Office Savings Bank in 1998; 29% govt-owned; cap. 12,096m., res 7,110m., dep. 121,662m. (Dec. 2006); Chair. PETER SEAH LIM HUAT; CEO PIYUSH GUPTA; 107 local brs, 9 overseas brs.

Far Eastern Bank Ltd: 80 Raffles Place, UOB Plaza, Singapore 048624; tel. 62219055; fax 62242263; internet www.uobgroup.com; f. 1959; subsidiary of United Overseas Bank Ltd; cap. 100m., res 69.8m., dep. 645.7m. (Dec. 2006); CEO WEE EE CHEONG; 3 brs.

Oversea-Chinese Banking Corpn Ltd (OCBC): 65 Chulia St, 09-00 OCBC Centre, Singapore 049513; tel. 65357222; fax 65337955; e-mail info@ocbc.com.sg; internet www.ocbc.com.sg; f. 1932; merged with Keppel TatLee Bank Ltd in 2001; cap. 5,480.9m., res 7,923.3m., dep. 89,639.5m. (Dec. 2006); Chair. Dr CHEONG CHOONG KONG; CEO DAVID PHILBRICK CONNER; 56 local brs, 52 overseas brs.

Singapore Island Bank: POB 1900, Robinson Rd Post Office, Singapore 903750; tel. 64383883; fax 64383718; e-mail clientservice@finatiq.com; internet www.finatiq.com; f. 1954; subsidiary of Oversea-Chinese Banking Corpn Ltd; fmrly Bank of Singapore Ltd, name changed as above in Jan. 2010; Chair. DAVID PHILBRICK CONNER.

United Overseas Bank Ltd: 80 Raffles Pl., UOB Plaza, Singapore 048624; tel. 65339898; fax 65342334; internet www.uobgroup.com; f. 1935; merged with Overseas Union Bank Ltd in Jan. 2002 and with Industrial and Commercial Bank Ltd in Aug. 2002; cap. 2.013.7m., res 8,080.1m., dep. 118,501.6m. (Dec. 2007); Chair. WEE CHO YAW; CEO WEE EE CHEONG; 61 local brs, 21 overseas brs.

Foreign Banks

Full Commercial Banks

Australia and New Zealand Banking Group Ltd (Australia): 50 Raffles Place, 01-03 Singapore Land Tower, Singapore 048623; tel. 62268899; fax 63493976; internet www.anz.com/singapore; f. 1974; CEO VISHNU SHAHANEY.

Bangkok Bank Public Co Ltd (Thailand): 180 Cecil St, Bangkok Bank Bldg, Singapore 069546; tel. 64100400; fax 62255852; e-mail kanchana.kon@bangkokbank.com; internet www.bangkokbank .com; Sr Vice-Pres. and Gen. Man. KHUN KANCHANA KONGVANANON.

Bank of America NA (USA): 9 Raffles Place, 18-00 Republic Plaza Tower 1, Singapore 048619; tel. 62393888; fax 62393068; CEO ALAN KOH.

Bank of China (People's Republic of China): 4 Battery Rd, Bank of China Bldg, Singapore 049908; tel. 65352411; fax 65343401; e-mail Service_SG@bank-of-china.com; internet www.bank-of-china.com; Gen. Man. LIU YANFEN.

Bank of East Asia Ltd (BEA) (Hong Kong): 60 Robinson Rd, Bank of East Asia Bldg, Singapore 068892; tel. 66027702; fax 62251805; e-mail info@hkbea.com.sg; internet www.hkbea.com.sg; Gen. Man. YAP GAY SIN.

Bank of India (India): 01-01 to 03-01, Corporate Office Bldg, 138 Robinson Rd, Singapore 068906; tel. 62220011; fax 62271275; e-mail boi.singapore@bankofindia.co.in; internet www.boi.com.sg; Chief Exec. MUNIR ALAM.

PT Bank Negara Indonesia (Persero) Tbk (Indonesia): 39 Robinson Rd, 01-02 and 06-01/04 Robinson Point, Singapore 068911; tel. 62257755; fax 62254757; internet www.ptbni.com.sg; f. 1955; Gen. Man. HADI SUTARYO.

Bank of Tokyo-Mitsubishi UFJ Ltd (Japan): 9 Raffles Place, 01-01 Republic Plaza, Singapore 048619; tel. 65383388; fax 65388083; internet www.bk.mufg.jp; Gen. Man. YUICHI OKURA; Dep. Gen. Man. HITOSHI MIKAWA.

BNP Paribas (France): 20 Collyer Quay, Tung Centre, Singapore 049319; tel. 62101288; fax 62243459; internet www.bnpparibas.com .sg; Regional Man. JEAN-PIERRE BERNARD.

Citibank NA (USA): 3 Temasek Ave, 12-00 Centennial Tower, Singapore 039190; tel. 62255221; fax 63286882; internet www .citibank.com.sg; f. 1902; CEO MICHAEL ZINK.

HL Bank (Malaysia): 20 Collyer Quay, 01-02 Tung Centre, Singapore 049319; tel. 63498338; fax 65339340; internet www.hlb.com.my; Country Head GAN HUI TIN.

Hongkong and Shanghai Banking Corpn Ltd (Hong Kong): 01-01 HSBC Bldg, 21 Collyer Quay, Singapore 049320; tel. 4722669; fax 62250663; e-mail direct@hsbc.com.sg; internet www.hsbc.com.sg; f. 1877; CEO ALEX HUNGATE.

ICICI Bank Ltd (India): 9 Raffles Place, 50-01 Republic Plaza, Singapore 048619; tel. 67239288; fax 67239268; e-mail globalinvest@icicibank.com; internet www.icicibank.com.sg; Chief. Exec. BAGAWATISWAR KRISHNA IYER.

Indian Bank (India): 3 Raffles Place, Bharat Bldg, Singapore 048617; tel. 65343511; fax 65331651; e-mail indbksg@pacific.net .sg; internet indianbank-singapore.com; f. 1941; Chief Exec. S. K. BANDOPADHYAY.

Indian Overseas Bank (India): 64 Cecil St, IOB Bldg, Singapore 049711; tel. 62251100; fax 62244490; e-mail iobrem@iob.com.sg; internet iobsingapore.com; f. 1941; Chief Exec. KANDASAMY SETHU.

JP Morgan Chase Bank (USA): 168 Robinson Rd, 17-01 Capital Tower, Singapore 068912; tel. 68822888; fax 68821756; internet jpmorganchase.com; CEO JAMES DIMON.

Mizuho Corporate Bank Ltd (Japan): 168 Robinson Rd, 13-00 Capital Tower, Singapore 068912; tel. 64230330; fax 64230012; Gen. Man. KATSUYUKI MIZUMA.

RHB Bank Bhd (Malaysia): 5th Floor, 90 Cecil St, Singapore 069531; tel. 63200602; fax 62255296; e-mail contactus@rhbbank .com.sg; internet rhb.com.sg; f. 1961; Country Head JASON WONG; 7 brs.

Standard Chartered Bank (UK): 6 Battery Rd, Singapore 049909; tel. 62258888; fax 67893756; internet www.standardchartered.com .sg; f. 1859; Chief Exec. RAY FERGUSON.

State Bank of India (India): 135 Cecil St, 01-00, Singapore 069536; tel. 65064220; fax 62281115; e-mail cecilstreet@sbising.com; internet www.sbising.com; CEO ANIL KISHORA.

Sumitomo Mitsui Banking Corpn (Japan). (SMBC): 3 Temasek Ave, 06-01 Centennial Tower, Singapore 039190; tel. 68820000; fax 68870220; internet www.smbc.co.jp; CEO MASAYUKI SHIMURA.

UCO Bank (India): 3 Raffles Place, Bharat Bldg, Singapore 048617; tel. 65325944; fax 65325044; e-mail general@ucobank.com.sg; internet www.ucobank.com.sg; f. 1951; Chief Exec. MAITRAYEE BANERJEE; 2 brs.

Wholesale Banks

Bank of Communications (People's Republic of China): 50 Raffles Place, 26-04 Singapore Land Tower, Singapore 048623; tel. 65320335; fax 65320339; Gen. Man. NIU KE RONG.

Bank of Nova Scotia (Canada): 1 Raffles Quay, 20-01 North Tower, Singapore 048583; tel. 63058388; fax 65347817; Group Head ANATOL VON HAHN.

Barclays Bank PLC (UK): 23 Church St, 13-08 Capital Sq., Singapore 049481; tel. 63953000; fax 63953139; Regional Head VIKRAM MALHOTRA; Country Man. QUEK SUAN KIAT.

China Construction Bank Corpn (People's Republic of China): 9 Raffles Place, 33-01/02 Republic Plaza, Singapore 048619; tel. 65358133; fax 65356533; e-mail enquiry@ccb.com.sg; internet www.ccb.com.sg; Gen. Man. Jin Yu.

Commerzbank AG (Germany): 8 Shenton Way, 42-01 Temasek Tower, Singapore 068811; tel. 63110000; fax 62253943; e-mail info@commerzbank.com.sg; internet www.commerzbank.com.sg; f. 1978; Man. Jürgen Schmieding.

Commonwealth Bank of Australia (Australia): 22-04 Singapore Land Tower, 50 Raffles Place, Singapore 048623; tel. 62243877; fax 62245812; Gen. Man. Robert Lewis Buchan.

Crédit Industriel et Commercial (France): 63 Market St, 15-01, Singapore 048942; tel. 65366008; fax 65367008; internet www.cic.com.sg; Gen. Man. Jean-Luc Anglada.

Crédit Suisse (Switzerland): 1 Raffles Link, 05-02, Singapore 039393; tel. 62126000; fax 62126200; e-mail ask.us@credit-suisse.com; internet www.cspb.com.sg; Br. Man. Salman Shoaib.

Deutsche Bank AG (Germany): 1 Raffles Quay, 17-00 South Tower, Singapore 048583; tel. 64238001; fax 62259442; internet www.db.com/singapore; f. 1971; Gen. Man. Ronny Tan Chong Tee.

DnB NOR (Norway): 8 Shenton Way, 48-02 Temasek Tower, Singapore 068811; tel. 62206144; fax 62249743; e-mail dnbnor.singapore@dnbnor.no; internet www.dnbnor.no; Gen. Man. Erik Borgen.

First Commercial Bank (Taiwan): 77 Robinson Rd, 01-01, Singapore 068896; tel. 62215755; fax 62251905; e-mail fcbsin@singnet.com.sg; Gen. Man. Lai Jen-yu.

Habib Bank Ltd (Pakistan): 3 Phillip St, 01-03 Commerce Pt, Singapore 048693; tel. 64380055; fax 64383244; e-mail rizwan@hblsg.com; Regional Gen. Man. Rizwan Haidar.

HSBC Pvt Bank SA (Switzerland): 21 Collyer Quay, 21-01 HSBC Bldg, Singapore 049320; tel. 62248080; fax 62237146; CEO Nancie Dupier.

Industrial and Commercial Bank of China (People's Republic of China): 6 Raffles Quay, 12-01 John Hancock Tower, Singapore 048580; tel. 65381066; fax 65381370; e-mail icbcsg@icbc.com.sg; Chair. and Pres. Jiang Jianqing.

ING Bank NV (Netherlands): 9 Raffles Place, 19-02 Republic Plaza, Singapore 048619; tel. 65353688; fax 65338329; Country Head J. Kestemont.

Intesa Sanpaolo SpA (Italy): 6 Temasek Blvd, 42/04-05 Suntec Tower Four, Singapore 038986; tel. 63338270; fax 63338252; e-mail singapore.sg@intesasanpaolo.com; internet www.intesasanpaolo.com; Gen. Man. Giovanni Fiorendi.

KBC Bank NV (Belgium): 30 Cecil St, 12-01/08 Prudential Tower, Singapore 049712; tel. 63952828; fax 65342929; e-mail reception@kbc.com.sg; f. 1993; Gen. Man. Thierry Mezeret.

Korea Exchange Bank (Republic of Korea): 30 Cecil St, 24-03/08 Prudential Tower, Singapore 049712; tel. 65361633; fax 65382522; e-mail kebspore@keb.co.kr; Gen. Man. Jeong Oo Yeoung.

Landesbank Baden-Württemberg (Germany): 25 International Business Park, 01-72 German Centre, Singapore 609916; tel. 65627722; fax 65627729; Man. Dr Wolfhart Auer van Herrenkirchen.

Mega International Commercial Bank Co Ltd (Taiwan): 80 Raffles Place, 23-20 UOB Plaza II, Singapore 048624; tel. 65366311; fax 65360680; Gen. Man. Hsiang Yen-ping.

National Australia Bank Ltd (Australia): 5 Temasek Blvd, 15-01 Suntec Tower Five, Singapore 038985; tel. 64196875; fax 63380039; f. 1981; Gen. Man. Frank Olsson.

National Bank of Kuwait SAK (Kuwait): 9 Raffles Place, 24-02 Republic Plaza, Singapore 048619; tel. 62225348; fax 62245438; f. 1984; Gen. Man. Richard McKegney.

Natexis Banques Populaires (France): 50 Raffles Place, 41-01, Singapore Land Tower, Singapore 048623; tel. 62241455; fax 62248651; Gen. Man. Philippe Petitgas.

Norddeutsche Landesbank Girozentrale (Germany): 6 Shenton Way, 16-00 DBS Bldg Tower Two, Singapore 068809; tel. 63231223; fax 63230223; e-mail nordlb.singapore@nordlb.com; internet www.nordlb.de; f. 1994; Gen. Man. Heinz Werner Frings.

Northern Trust Company (USA): 1 George St, 12-06, Singapore 049145; tel. 64376666; fax 64376609; e-mail LA16@ntrs.com; internet www.northerntrust.com; f. 1889; Sr Vice-Pres. Lawrence Au.

Rabobank International (Netherlands): 77 Robinson Rd, 09-00 SIA Bldg, Singapore 068896; tel. 65363363; fax 65363236; Regional Man. (Asia) Rob Van Zadelhoff.

Royal Bank of Scotland PLC (UK): 50 Raffles Place, 08-00 Singapore Land Tower, Singapore 048623; tel. 64168600; fax 62259827; Gen. Man. Alan Roy Goodyear.

Société Générale (France): 80 Robinson Rd, 25-00, Singapore 068898; tel. 62227122; fax 62252609; Chief Country Officer Eric Wormser.

State Street Bank and Trust Co (USA): 8 Shenton Way, 33-03 Temasek Tower, Singapore 068811; tel. 63299600; fax 62259377; Br. Man. Lee Yow Fee.

UBS AG (Switzerland): 5 Temasek Blvd, 18-00 Suntec City Tower, Singapore 038985; tel. 64318000; fax 64318188; e-mail rolf-w.gerber@wdr.com; Man. Dir Brad Orgill.

UniCredito Italiano SpA (Italy): 80 Raffles Pl., 51-01 UOB Plaza 1, Singapore 048624; tel. 62325728; fax 65344300; e-mail singaporebranch@gruppocredit.it; Gen. Man. Maurizio Brentegani.

VTB Capital PLC (Russia): 9 Battery Rd, 27-01 Straits Trading Bldg, Singapore 049910; tel. 62209422; fax 62250140; internet www.vtbcapital.comfmrly Moscow Narodny Bank Ltd; Man. Dir John Peter Cardosa.

Westpac Banking Corpn (Australia): 77 Robinson Rd, 19-00 SIA Bldg, Singapore 068896; tel. 65309898; fax 65326781; e-mail yhlee@westpac.wm.au; Gen. Man. Christopher David Rand.

'Offshore' Banks

Agricultural Bank of China (People's Republic of China): 80 Raffles Place, 27-20 UOB Plaza 2, Singapore 048624; tel. 65355255; fax 65387960; e-mail aboc@abchina.com.sg; Gen. Man. Sun Meiyu.

Arab Bank PLC (Jordan): 80 Raffles Place, 32-20 UOB Plaza 2, Singapore 048624; tel. 65330055; fax 65322150; e-mail abplc@pacific.net.com.sg; Exec. Vice-Pres. Kim Eun-Young.

PT Bank Mandiri (Persero) (Indonesia): 16 Collyer Quay, 28-00 Hitachi Tower, Singapore 049318; tel. 65320200; fax 65320206; Gen. Man. Muhadjir Sangidu.

Bank of New York Mellon (USA): 1 Temasek Ave, 02-01 Millenia Tower, Singapore 039192; tel. 64320222; fax 63374302formed through merger of Bank of New York with Mellon Financial Corpn in 2007; Sr Vice-Pres. and Man. Dir Jai Arya.

Bank of New Zealand (New Zealand): 5 Temasek Blvd, 15-01 Suntec City Tower, Singapore 038985; tel. 63322990; fax 63322991; Gen. Man. Vivien Koh.

Bank of Taiwan (Taiwan): 80 Raffles Place, 28-20 UOB Plaza 2, Singapore 048624; tel. 65365536; fax 65368203; Gen. Man. Chiou Yechin.

Canadian Imperial Bank of Commerce (Canada): 16 Collyer Quay, 04-02 Hitachi Tower, Singapore 049318; tel. 65352323; fax 65357565; Br. Man. Norman Sim Chee Beng.

Chang Hwa Commercial Bank Ltd (China): 1 Finlayson Green, 08-00, Singapore 049246; tel. 65320820; fax 65320374; Gen. Man. Yang Jih-Cheng.

Dexia Banque Internationale à Luxembourg (Luxembourg): 9 Raffles Place, 42-01 Republic Plaza, Singapore 048619; tel. 62227622; fax 65360201; Gen. Man. Alexandre Josset.

Hana Bank (Republic of Korea): 8 Cross St, 23-06 PWC Bldg, Singapore 048424; tel. 64384100; fax 64384200; Gen. Man. Cho Young-Seok.

Hang Seng Bank Ltd (Hong Kong): 21 Collyer Quay, 14-01 HSBC Bldg, Singapore 049320; tel. 65363118; fax 65363148; e-mail sgp@hangseng.com; Country Man. Anthony Kam Ping Leung.

HSH Nordbank AG (Germany): 3 Temasek Ave, 32-03 Centennial Tower, Singapore 039190; tel. 65509000; fax 65509003; e-mail info@hsh-nordbank.com.sg; Gen. Man. and Regional Head Klaus Heiner Boritzka.

Hua Nan Commercial Bank Ltd (Taiwan): 80 Robinson Rd, 14-03, Singapore 068898; tel. 63242566; fax 63242155; e-mail accounting@hncb.com.sg; internet sg.hncb.com; Gen. Man. Huang Yun-lung.

Korea Development Bank (Republic of Korea): 8 Shenton Way, 07-01 Temasek Tower, Singapore 068811; tel. 62248188; fax 62256540; Gen. Man. Kim Byoung Soo.

Krung Thai Bank Public Co Ltd (Thailand): 65 Chulia St, 32-05/08 OCBC Centre, Singapore 049513; tel. 65336691; fax 65330930; e-mail br.singapore@ktb.co.th; Gen. Man. Pumin Leelayoova.

Land Bank of Taiwan: UOB Plaza 1, 34-01 Raffles Place, Singapore 048624; tel. 63494555; fax 63494545; Gen. Man. Wilson W. B. Lin.

Lloyds TSB Bank PLC (UK): 1 Temasek Ave, 18-01 Millenia Tower, Singapore 039192; tel. 65341191; fax 65322493; e-mail mktg@lloydstsb.com.sg; internet www.lloydstsb.com.sg; Country Head Wallace Wong.

Mitsubishi Trust and Banking Corpn (Japan): 50 Raffles Place, 42-01/06 Singapore Land Tower, Singapore 048623; tel. 62259155; fax 62241857; Gen. Man. Mikio Kobayashi.

Nordea Bank Finland Plc (Finland): 3 Anson Rd, 22-01 Springleaf Tower, Singapore 079909; tel. 63176500; fax 63275616; e-mail singapore@nordea.com; Gen. Man. THOR ERLING KYLSTAD.

Norinchukin Bank (Japan): 80 Raffles Place, 53-01 UOB Plaza 1, Singapore 048624; tel. 65351011; fax 65352883; Gen. Man. AKITA KURIHARA.

Philippine National Bank (Philippines): 96 Somerset Rd, 04-01/04 UOL Bldg, Singapore 238183; tel. 67374646; fax 67374224; e-mail singapore@pnb.com.ph; Vice-Pres. and Gen. Man. RODELO G. FRANCO.

Raiffeisen Zentralbank Österreich Aktiengesellschaft (Austria): 50 Raffles Place, 45-01 Singapore Land Tower, Singapore 048623; tel. 62259578; fax 62253973; Gen. Man. RAINER SILHAVY.

Royal Bank of Canada (Canada): 20 Raffles Place, 27-03/08 Ocean Towers, Singapore 048620; tel. 65369206; fax 65322804; Gen. Man. TREVOR DAVID WYNN.

Shinhan Bank (Republic of Korea): 50 Raffles Place, 04-02/03 Singapore Land Tower, Singapore 048623; tel. 65361144; fax 65331244merged with Chohun Bank 2006; Gen. Man. CHOI HEUNG MIN.

Siam Commercial Bank Public Company Ltd (Thailand): 16 Collyer Quay, 25-01 Hitachi Tower, Singapore 049318; tel. 65364338; fax 65364728; Gen. Man. BANDIT ROJANAVONGSE.

Skandinaviska Enskilda Banken AB Publ (Sweden): 50 Raffles Place, 36-01 Singapore Land Tower, Singapore 048623; tel. 62235644; fax 62253047; Gen. Man. SVEN BJÖRKMAN.

Sumitomo Trust & Banking Co Ltd (Japan): 8 Shenton Way, 45-01 Temasek Tower, Singapore 068811; tel. 62249055; fax 62242873; Gen. Man. MASAYUKI IMANAKA.

Svenska Handelsbanken AB (publ) (Sweden): 65 Chulia St, 21-01/04 OCBC Centre, Singapore 049513; tel. 65323800; fax 65344909; Gen. Man. JAN BIRGER DJERF.

Toronto-Dominion (South East Asia) Ltd (Canada): 15-02 Millenia Tower, 1 Temasek Ave, Singapore 039192; tel. 64346000; fax 63369500; Br. Dir AKHILESHWAR LAMBA.

Union de Banques Arabes et Françaises (UBAF) (France): 6 Temasek Blvd, 25-04/05 Suntec Tower Four, Singapore 038986; tel. 63336188; fax 63336789; e-mail ubafsg@singnet.com.sg; Gen. Man. ERIC REINHART.

Woori Bank (Republic of Korea): 5 Shenton Way, 17-03 UIC Bldg, Singapore 068808; tel. 62235855; fax 62259530; e-mail combksp@singnet.com.sg; Gen. Man. PARK DONG YOUNG.

Bankers' Association

The Association of Banks in Singapore: 10 Shenton Way, 12-08 MAS Bldg, Singapore 079117; tel. 62244300; fax 62241785; e-mail banks@abs.org.sg; internet www.abs.org.sg; f. 1973; Chair. DAVID P. CONNOR.

STOCK EXCHANGE

Singapore Exchange Ltd (SGX): 2 Shenton Way, 19-00 SGX Centre One, Singapore 068804; tel. 62368888; fax 65356994; e-mail query@sgx.com; internet www.sgx.com; f. 1999; demutualized and integrated securities and derivatives exchange; Chair. J. Y. PILLAY; CEO MAGNUS BÖCKER; Chief Finance Officer SECK WAI KWONG.

INSURANCE

The insurance industry is supervised by the Monetary Authority of Singapore (see Banking). In May 2011 there were 157 insurance companies, comprising 62 direct insurers (10 life insurance, 46 general insurance, six composite insurers), 28 professional reinsurers (three life reinsurers, 16 general reinsurers, nine composite reinsurers), six authorized reinsurers (two life reinsurers, three general reinsurers, one composite reinsurer) and 61 captive insurers.

Domestic Companies

Life Insurance

Axa Life Insurance Singapore Pte Ltd: 8 Shenton Way, 27-02, Singapore 068811; tel. 68805500; fax 68805501; e-mail comsvc@axa.com.sg; internet www.axalife.com.sg; CEO GLENN JOHN WILLIAMS.

Friends Provident International Ltd (Singapore): 63 Market St, 06-05, Singapore 048942; tel. 63274019; fax 63274020; e-mail singapore.enquiries@fpiom.com; internet www.fpinternational.com; Prin. Officer CHRISTOPHER GAVIN GILL.

Great Eastern Life Assurance Co Ltd: 1 Pickering St, 13-01 Great Eastern Centre, Singapore 048659; tel. 62482000; fax 65322214; e-mail wecare@lifeisgreat.com.sg; internet www.lifeisgreat.com.sg; f. 1908; CEO TAN BENG LEE.

International Medical Insurers Pte Ltd: 585 North Bridge Rd, 13-00, Raffles Hospital, Singapore 188770; tel. 62982266; fax 63112396; e-mail enquiries@imi.sg; internet www.imi.sg; f. 1996; Prin. Officer VICTOR LYE.

Manulife (Singapore) Pte Ltd: 491B River Valley Rd, 07-00 Valley Pt, Singapore 248373; tel. 67371221; fax 62359158; e-mail service@manulife.com; internet www.manulife.com.sg; acquired John Hancock Life Assurance Co Ltd in Dec. 2004; Pres. and CEO ANNETTE LOUISE KING.

Royal Scandia Life Assurance Ltd : Level 25, North Tower, 1 Raffles Quay, Singapore 048583; tel. 66225402; fax 66225400; internet www.royalskandia.com; Prin. Officer DAVID MACDONALD.

Swiss Life Private Placement (Singapore) Pte Ltd: 250 North Bridge Rd, 37–03/04 Raffles City Tower, Singapore 179101; tel. 65806680; fax 65806683; e-mail slpp@swisslife.com; internet www.sl-pp.com; f. 2008; Prin. Officer THOMAS VONRUETI.

Tokio Marine Life Insurance Singapore Ltd: 20 McCallum Street, 07-01 Tokio Marine Centre, Singapore 069046; tel. 65926100; fax 62239120; internet www.tokiomarine-life.sg; CEO DAVID JOHN BEYNON.

Transamerica Life (Singapore) Ltd: 1 Finlayson Green, 13-00, Singapore 049246; tel. 62120620; fax 62120621; internet www.transamerica.com.sg; wholly owned subsidiary of Transamerica Occidental Life Insurance Co; Prin. Officer PETER MONKSFIELD.

Zurich International Life (Singapore) Ltd: 50 Raffles Pl., 29-05 Singapore Land Tower, Singapore 048623; tel. 68766750; fax 68766751; e-mail helppoint.singapore@zurich.com; internet www.zurich.com/international/singapore; Regional Dir NEAL PALMER ARMSTRONG.

General Insurance

Allianz Insurance Company of Singapore Pte Ltd: 3 Temasek Ave, 09-01 Centennial Tower, Singapore 039190; tel. 62972529; fax 62971956; e-mail askme@allianz.com.sg; internet www.allianz.com.sg; est. by merger between Allianz Insurance (Singapore) Pte Ltd and AGF Insurance (Singapore) Pte Ltd; CEO KEVIN M H. LEONG.

Axa Insurance Singapore Pte Ltd: 8 Shenton Way, 27-01 AXA Tower, Singapore 068811; tel. 68804741; fax 68804740; e-mail customer.service@axa.com.sg; internet www.axa.com.sg; CEO CHUA KIM SOON.

China Taiping Insurance (Singapore) Pte Ltd: 105 Cecil St, 18-00 and 19-00 The Octagon, Singapore 069534; tel. 63896111; fax 62221033; internet www.sg.cntaiping.com; f. 1939; fmrly known as China Life Insurance Co Ltd; name changed as above in 2009; Gen. Man. LI WEIGUO.

Cosmic Insurance Corpn Ltd: 410 North Bridge Rd, 04-01 Cosmic Insurance Bldg, Singapore 188726; tel. 63387633; fax 63397805; e-mail query@cosmic.com.sg; internet www.cosmic.com.sg; f. 1971; Gen. Man. SWEE LEE CHUN.

ECICS Ltd: 7 Temasek Blvd, 10-03 Suntec City Tower 1, Singapore 038987; tel. 63374779; fax 63389267; e-mail principalofficer@ecics.com.sg; internet www.ecics.com.sg; CEO LUA TOO SWEE.

First Capital Insurance Ltd: 6 Raffles Quay 21-00, Singapore 048580; tel. 62222311; fax 62223547; e-mail enquiry@first-insurance.com.sg; internet www.first-insurance.com.sg; CEO RAMASWAMY ATHAPPAN.

India International Insurance Pte Ltd: 64 Cecil St, 04-00/05-00 IOB Bldg, Singapore 049711; tel. 63476100; fax 62244174; e-mail insure@iii.com.sg; internet www.iii.com.sg; f. 1987; all non-life insurance; CEO ISH KUMAR.

Liberty Insurance Pte Ltd: 5 Shenton Way, 03-00 UIC Bld, Singapore 068808; tel. 62218611; fax 62236434; e-mail feedback@libertycitystate.com.sg; internet www.libertyinsurance.com.sg; division of Liberty Mutual Group (USA); fmrly Citystate Insurance Pte Ltd; Man. Dir MARTIN BRIDGER.

MSIG Insurance (Singapore) Pte Ltd: 4 Shenton Way, 21-01 SGX Centre 2, Singapore 068807; tel. 68277888; fax 68277800; internet www.msig.com.sg; f. 2010; est. following the merger of MSIG Insurance (Singapore) Pte Ltd and Mitsui Sumitomo Insurance Singapore; CEO PAUL FAULKNER.

QBE Insurance International Ltd Singapore: 60 Anson Rd, 11–01 Mapletree Anson, Singapore 079914; tel. 62246633; fax 65333270; e-mail info.sing@qbe.com; internet www.qbe.com.sg; Prin. Officer MICHAEL GOODWIN.

Royal & Sun Alliance Insurance (Singapore) Ltd: 77 Robinson Rd, 17-00 Robinson 77, Singapore 068896; tel. 64230888; fax 65339291; e-mail customer.service@sg.rsagroup.com; internet www.rsagroup.com.sg; Man. Dir and CEO MARK MITCHELL.

SHC Capital Ltd: 302 Orchard Rd, 09-01 Tong Bldg, Singapore 238862; tel. 68299199; fax 68299249; e-mail shccapital@shcsb.com.sg; internet www.shccapital.com.sg; f. 1956; fmrly The Nanyang Insurance Co Ltd; name changed as above following takeover in June 2004; Dir and Prin. Officer QUEK SUN HUI.

Singapore Aviation and General Insurance Co (Pte) Ltd: 25 Airline Rd, 06-A Airline House, Singapore 819829; tel. 65423333; fax 65450221; f. 1976; Man. GEORGE VARUGHESE.

Standard Steamship Owners' Protection and Indemnity Association (Asia) Ltd: 140 Cecil St, 15-00 PIL Bldg, Singapore 069540; tel. 65062896; fax 62211082; e-mail p&i.singapore@ctcplc.com; internet www.standard-club.com; Director NICK SANSOM.

Tenet Insurance Co Ltd: 11 Collyer Quay, 09-00 The Arcade, Singapore 049317; tel. 62212211; fax 62213302; e-mail emailus@tenetinsurance.com; internet www.tenetinsurance.com; CEO STELLA TAN YIAN HUA.

Tokio Marine Insurance Singapore Ltd: 20 McCallum Street, 09-01 Tokio Marine Centre, Singapore 069046; tel. 62216111; fax 62240895; internet www.tokiomarine.com.sg; f. 1957; est. as The Tokio Marine and Fire Insurance Company (Singapore) Pte Ltd; name changed as above following merger with TM Asia Insurance Singapore Ltd in 2008; Prin. Officer CHER AH KOW.

United Overseas Insurance Ltd: 3 Anson Rd, 28-01 Springleaf Tower, Singapore 079909; tel. 62227733; fax 63273870; e-mail contactus@uoi.com.sg; internet www.uoi.com.sg; f. 1971; Man. Dir DAVID CHAN MUN WAI.

Zürich Insurance (Singapore) Pte Ltd: 50 Raffles Place, 29-01 Singapore Land TowerSingapore 048623; tel. 62362210; fax 65384184; Prin. Officer and Man. Dir CHAN TAT YOONG.

Composite Insurance

American International Assurance Co Ltd: 1 Robinson Rd, AIA Tower, Singapore 048542; tel. 62918000; fax 65385802; internet www.aia.com.sg; Prin. Officer TAN HAK LEH.

Aviva Ltd: 4 Shenton Way, 01-01 SGX Centre 2, Singapore 068807; tel. 68279929; fax 68277900; e-mail globalsolutions_sg@aviva-asia.com; internet www.aviva.com.sg; f. 2002; CEO SIMON NEWMAN.

HSBC Insurance (Singapore) Pte Ltd: 10 Eunos Rd 8, 11-01 Singapore Post Centre, Singapore 408600; tel. 62256111; fax 62212188; e-mail e-surance@hsbc.com.sg; internet www.insurance.hsbc.com.sg; Prin. Officer WALTER MARK DE OUDE.

NTUC Income Insurance Co-operative Ltd: 75 Bras Basah Rd, NTUC Income Centre, Singapore 189557; tel. 63363322; fax 63381500; e-mail inbox@income.wm.sg; internet www.income.com.sg; f. 1970; CEO TAN SUEE CHIEH; Gen. Man. ALOYSIUS TEO SENG LEE.

Overseas Assurance Corpn Ltd: 1 Pickering St, 01-01 Great Eastern Centre, Singapore 048659; tel. 62482000; fax 65322214; e-mail wecare@lifeisgreat.com.sg; internet www.lifeisgreat.com.sg; f. 1920; wholly owned subsidiary of Great Eastern Holdings; Chair. CHRISTOPHER WEI.

Prudential Assurance Co Singapore (Pte) Ltd: 30 Cecil St, 30-01 Prudential Tower, Singapore 049712; tel. 65358988; fax 65354043; e-mail customer.service@prudential.com.sg; internet www.prudential.com.sg; f. 1931; CEO KEVIN LEE HOLMGREN.

Associations

General Insurance Association of Singapore: 112 Robinson Rd, 05-03 HB Robinson, Singapore 068902; tel. 62218788; fax 62272051; e-mail feedback@gia.org.sg; internet www.gia.org.sg; f. 1965; Pres. DEREK TEO; Exec. Dir MARK LIM.

Life Insurance Association, Singapore: 20 Cross St, 02-07/08 China Court, China Sq. Central, Singapore 048422; tel. 64388900; fax 64386989; e-mail lia@lia.org.sg; internet www.lia.org.sg; f. 1967; Pres. HAK LEH TAN.

Reinsurance Brokers' Association: 69 Amoy St, Singapore 069888; tel. 63723189; fax 62241091; e-mail secretariat@rbas.org.sg; internet www.rbas.org.sg; f. 1995; Chair. RICHARD AUSTEN.

Singapore Insurance Brokers' Association: 138 Cecil St, 15-00 Cecil Court, Singapore 069538; tel. 62227777; fax 62220022; e-mail siba@stcsamasmgt.com.sg; Pres. ANTHONY LIM; Vice-Pres. DAVID LUM.

Singapore Reinsurers' Association: 85 Amoy St, Singapore 069904; tel. 63247388; fax 62248910; e-mail secretariat@sraweb.org.sg; internet www.sraweb.org.sg; f. 1979; Chair. CHRISTOPHER HO SIOW SOONG.

Trade and Industry

Temasek Holdings Pte Ltd: 60B Orchard Rd, 06-18 Tower 2, The Atrium@ Orchard, Singapore 238891; tel. 68286828; fax 68211188; internet www.temasek.com.sg; f. 1974; 100% govt-owned; active shareholder and investor in banking and financial services, real estate, transport, infrastructure, telecommunications, media, bioscience and health care, education, consumer services, engineering and technology, energy and resources; revenue S $79,615m. (2008/09); Chair. S. DHANABALAN; Exec. Dir and CEO HO CHING.

GOVERNMENT AGENCIES

Housing and Development Board: 480 Lorong 6, Toa Payoh, Singapore 310480; tel. 64901111; fax 64901033; e-mail hdbmailbox@hdb.gov.sg; internet www.hdb.gov.sg; f. 1960; public housing authority; Chair. JAMES KOH CHER SIANG; CEO TAY KIM POH.

Singapore Land Authority (SLA): 55 Newton Rd, 12-01 Revenue House, Singapore 307987; tel. 63239829; fax 63239937; e-mail SLA_enquiry@sla.gov.sg; internet www.sla.gov.sg; f. 2001; est. by merger of Land Office, Singapore Land Registry, Survey Dept and Land Systems Support Unit; responsible for management and devt of state land resources; Chair. CHALY MAH; CEO VINCENT HOONG SENG LEI.

Urban Redevelopment Authority (URA): 45 Maxwell Rd, URA Centre, Singapore 069118; tel. 62216666; fax 62275069; e-mail ura_email@ura.gov.sg; internet www.ura.gov.sg; f. 1974; est. to replace Urban Renewal Dept (f. 1967); statutory board; responsible for national planning; Chair. ALAN CHAN HENG LOON; CEO NG LANG.

DEVELOPMENT ORGANIZATIONS

Agency for Science, Technology and Research (A*STAR): 1 Fusionopolis Way, 20-10 Connexis North Tower, Singapore 138632; tel. 68266111; fax 67771711; e-mail contact@a-star.edu.sg; internet www.a-star.edu.sg; f. 1991; fmrly National Science and Technology Board; statutory board; responsible for the devt of science and technology; Chair. LIM CHUAN POH; Man. Dir LOW TECK SENG.

Applied Research Corpn (ARC): Singapore; f. 1973; independent non-profit-making research and consultancy org. aiming to facilitate and enhance the use of technology and expertise from tertiary institutions to benefit industry and businesses.

Asian Infrastructure Fund (AIF): Singapore; f. 1994; promotes and directs investment into regional projects; Chair. MOEEN QURESHI.

Economic Development Board (EDB): 250 North Bridge Rd, 28-00 Raffles City Tower, Singapore 179101; tel. 68326832; fax 68326565; e-mail clientservices@edb.gov.sg; internet www.edb.gov.sg; f. 1961; statutory body for industrial planning, devt and promotion of investments in manufacturing, services and local business; Chair. LEO YIP SENG CHEONG; Man. Dir Dr BEH SWAN GIN.

Government of Singapore Investment Corpn Pte Ltd (GIC): 168 Robinson Rd, 37-01 Capital Tower, Singapore 068912; tel. 68898888; fax 68898722; e-mail contactgic@gic.com.sg; internet www.gic.com.sg; f. 1981; Chair. LEE HSIEN LOONG; Exec. Dir Dr TONY TAN KENG YAM.

Infocomm Development Authority of Singapore (IDA): see under Telecommunications.

International Enterprise Singapore: 230 Victoria St, Level 10, Bugis Junction Office Tower, Singapore 188024; tel. 63376628; fax 63376898; e-mail enquiry@iesingapore.gov.sg; internet www.iesingapore.gov.sg; f. 1983; formed to develop and expand international trade; fmrly Trade Development Board; statutory body; Chair. SUNNY VERGHESE; CEO CHONG LIT CHEONG.

JTC Corpn: The JTC Summit, 8 Jurong Town Hall Rd, Singapore 609434; tel. 65600056; fax 65655301; e-mail askjtc@jtc.gov.sg; internet www.jtc.gov.sg; f. 1968; statutory body responsible for planning, promoting and developing industrial space; Chair. CEDRIC FOO; CEO MANOHAR KHIATANI.

Standards, Productivity and Innovation Board Singapore (SPRING): 1 Fusionopolis Way, 01-02 South Tower, Solaris, Singapore 138628; tel. 62786666; fax 62786667; e-mail enterpriseone@spring.gov.sg; internet www.spring.gov.sg; f. 1996; est. as Singapore Productivity and Standards Bd (PSB), following merger of Singapore Institute of Standards and Industrial Research and the Nat. Productivity Bd; present name adopted 2001; work-force devt, training, productivity and innovation promotion, standards devt, etc.; assistance for SMEs; Chair. PHILIP YEO; Chief Exec. PNG CHEONG BOON.

CHAMBERS OF COMMERCE

Singapore Business Federation (SBF): 10 Hoe Chiang Rd, 22-01 Keppel Towers, 089315 Singapore; tel. 68276828; fax 68276807; internet www.sbf.org.sg; f. 2002; est. following restructuring of Singapore Fed. of Chambers of Commerce and Industry; Chair. TONY CHEW LEONG CHEE; represents over 15,000 cos; constituent mems incl. the following:

Singapore Chinese Chamber of Commerce and Industry: 47 Hill St, 09-00 Singapore 179365; tel. 63378381; fax 63390605; e-mail corporate@sccci.org.sg; internet www.sccci.org.sg; f. 1906; Pres. TEO SIONG SENG; Sec.-Gen. LIM SAH SOON.

Singapore Indian Chamber of Commerce and Industry: 31 Stanley St, SICCI Bldg, Singapore 068740; tel. 62222855; fax 62231707; e-mail sicci@sicci.com; internet www.sicci.com; f. 1924; Chair. RANGARAJAN NARAYANAMOHAN; CEO HERNAIKH SINGH.

Singapore International Chamber of Commerce: 6 Raffles Quay, 10-01 John Hancock Tower, Singapore 048580; tel. 65000988; fax 62242785; e-mail general@sicc.com; internet www.sicc.com.sg; f. 1837; Chair. JENNIE CHUA.

Singapore Malay Chamber of Commerce and Industry (SMCCI): 15 Jalan Pinang, Singapore 199147; tel. 62979296; fax 63924527; e-mail inquiry@smcci.org.sg; internet www.smcci.org.sg; f. 1956; Pres. ABDUL ROHIM SARIP.

Singapore Manufacturers' Federation (SMa): 2 Bukit Merah Central, 03-00 SPRING Singapore Bldg, Singapore 159835; tel. 68263000; fax 68263008; e-mail hq@smafederation.org.sg; internet www.smafederation.org.sg; f. 1932; est. as Singapore Manufacturers' Asscn; renamed Singapore Confed. of Industries in 1996; name changed as above in 2002; Pres. GEORGE HUANG; Sec.-Gen. GWEE SENG KWONG.

INDUSTRIAL AND TRADE ASSOCIATIONS

Association of Singapore Marine Industries (ASMI): 30 Tuas Ave 10, 07-01 Freight Links E-Logistics Technopark, Singapore 639150; tel. 68633038; fax 68632881; e-mail admin@asmi.com; internet www.asmi.com; f. 1968; 12 hon. mems, 70 assoc. mems, 51 ordinary mems (Oct. 2003); Pres. WONG WENG SON.

Singapore Commodity Exchange (SICOM): 2 Shenton Way, 19-00 SGX Centre 1, Singapore 068804; tel. 62368888; fax 65366648; internet www.sicom.com.sg; f. 1968; est. as Rubber Asscn of Singapore; adopted present name in 1994; regulates, promotes, develops and supervises commodity futures trading in Singapore, including the establishment and dissemination of official prices for various grades and types of rubber; provides clearing facilities; endorses certificates of origin and licences for packers, shippers and mfrs; Chair. MAGNUS BOCKER; CEO JEREMY ANG PENG LEONG.

EMPLOYERS' ORGANIZATION

Singapore National Employers Federation (SNEF): 22-00 Keppel Towers, 10 Hoe Chiang Rd, Singapore 089315; tel. 68276827; fax 68276800; e-mail webmaster@snef.org.sg; internet www.sgemployers.com; f. 1948 as Fed. of Industrialists and Traders in Singapore; name changed to Singapore Employers Fed. in 1953; present name adopted in 1980 following merger with Nat. Employers Council; Pres. STEPHEN LEE CHING YEN.

UTILITIES

Electricity and Gas

Singapore Power Ltd: 111 Somerset Rd 10-01, Singapore 238164; tel. 68238888; fax 68238188; e-mail spservices@singaporepower.com.sg; internet www.singaporepower.com.sg; incorporated in 1995 to take over the piped gas and electricity utility operations of the Public Utilities Board (see Water), which now acts as a regulatory authority for the privately owned cos; 100% owned by government holding co, Temasek Holdings Pte Ltd; f. 1995; subsidiaries incl. PowerGrid, PowerGas, SP Services, Singapore Power International, Singapore District Cooling and SP Telecommunications; Chair. NG KEE CHOE; CEO QUEK POH HUAT.

Water

Public Utilities Board: 40 Scotts Rd, 22-01 Environment Bldg, Singapore 228231; tel. 62358888; fax 62840363; e-mail pubone@singnet.com.sg; internet www.pub.gov.sg; f. 1963; statutory board responsible for water supply; manages Singapore's water system to optimize use of water resources; develops additional water sources; Chair. TAN GEE PAW; Chief Exec. KHOO TENG CHYE.

MAJOR COMPANIES

(cap. = capital; res = reserves; m. = million; amounts shown are in Singapore dollars unless otherwise stated)

Building and Building Materials

Holcim (Singapore) Pte Ltd: 16 Jalan Tepong, Singapore 619331; tel. 62651933; fax 62684027; internet www.holcim.sg; mfrs of cement; CEO SUJIT GHOSH; 182 employees.

Hong Leong Asia Ltd: 16 Raffles Quay, 26-00 Hong Leong Bldg, Singapore 048581; tel. 62208411; fax 62200087; e-mail tkteo@hlasia.com.sg; internet www.hlasia.com.sg; f. 1982; cap. and res 708m., revenue 4,448.1m. (2009); mfr and retailer of concrete, metal packaging, plastic packaging and containers; Chair. KWEK LENG BENG; CEO TONG KOOI TEO; 2,400 employees.

Lee Kim Tah Holdings Ltd: 20 Jalan Afifi, 07-01 CISCO Centre, Singapore 409179; tel. 67453318; fax 67451218; e-mail info@leekimtah.com; internet www.leekimtah.com; cap. and res 295.3m., sales 148.3m. (2009); investment holding co with subsidiaries engaged in manufacture of precast concrete building products and other building materials, building and civil engineering construction and property development; Chair. LEE SOON TECK; 700 employees.

Low Keng Huat (S) Ltd: 80 Marine Parade Rd, 18-05/09 Parkway Parade, Singapore 449269; tel. 63442333; fax 63457841; e-mail info@lkhs.com.sg; internet www.lkhs.com.sg; cap. and res 209.5m., revenue 274.6m. (2008/09); property management, construction and building materials; Chair. Tan Sri Dato' LOW KENG HUAT; Man. Dir LOW KENG BOON.

Tuan Sing Holdings Ltd: 9 Oxley Rise, 03-02 The Oxley, Singapore 238697; tel. 62237211; fax 62241085; e-mail enquiry@tuansing.com; internet www.tuansing.com; f. 1969; cap. and res 492.2m., revenue 252.9m. (2009); investment holding co with interests in property, manufacturing, construction and trading; Chair. PATRICK YEOH KHWAI HOH; CEO WILLIAM LIEM; 4,200 employees.

Chemicals and Petroleum

BP Singapore Pte Ltd: 02-01 Keppel Bay Tower, 1 Harbour Front Ave, Singapore 098632; tel. 63718888; fax 63718855; e-mail gohl@bp.com; internet www.bp.com; f. 1964; retailer of petroleum products; Pres. PEK HAK BIN; 640 employees.

Caltex Singapore Pte Ltd: 30 Raffles Place, 25-00 Caltex House, Singapore 048622; tel. 65333000; fax 64391790; e-mail enquiries@caltexoil.com.sg; internet www.caltex.com.sg; f. 1989; retailing and refining of petroleum products; 800 employees.

Chemical Industries (Far East) Ltd: 3 Samulun Rd, Singapore 629127; tel. 62650411; fax 62656690; e-mail chemical.ind@cifel.com.sg; cap. and res 68.6m., revenue 92.9m. (2009/10); mfrs and retailers of chemicals; Chair. and Man. Dir LIM SOO PENG; 120 employees.

ExxonMobil Asia Pacific Pte Ltd: 1 HarbourFront Place, 06-00 HarbourFront Tower 1, Singapore 098633; tel. 68858000; fax 68858799; internet www.exxonmobil.com.sg; f. 1963; petroleum refining; retailing of petroleum products; Gen. Man. DARRIN TALLEY; 640 employees.

Idemitsu Lube (Singapore) Pte Ltd: 37 Pandan Rd, Singapore 609280; tel. 62655672; fax 62655610; e-mail general@idemitsu-ils.com.sg; internet www.idemitsu-ils.com.sg; retailer of petroleum products; Man. Dir Z. SUDA.

Itochu Petroleum Co (Singapore) Pte Ltd: 9 Raffles Place, 41-01, Republic Plaza, Singapore; tel. 62300400; fax 62300560; e-mail info@itochu.com.sg; f. 1984; retailer of petroleum products.

Marubeni International Petroleum (S) Pte Ltd: 7 Temasek Blvd, 09-02A Suntek Tower One, Singapore 38987; tel. 63368815; fax 63365835; f. 1988; subsidiary of Marubeni Corpn, Japan; retailer of petroleum and related products; CEO MASASHI KOMINE.

Nippon Oil (Asia) Pte Ltd: 6 Battery Rd, 29-02/03, Singapore 049909; tel. 62236732; fax 62248921; f. 1980; retailer of petroleum products; Man. Dir N. TAKAYAMA.

Nissho Iwai Petroleum Pte Ltd: 77 Robinson Rd, 33-00 SIA Bldg, Singapore 065896; tel. 64382566; fax 64382577; f. 1991; petroleum and petroleum products; Man. Dir S. JIMBO.

Shell Singapore: Shell House, 83 Clemenceau Ave, Singapore 239920; tel. 63848000; fax 63848373; e-mail tell-shell@shell.com; internet www.shell.com.sg; businesses incl. Shell Eastern Petroleum (Pte) Ltd, Shell Eastern Trading (Pte) Ltd, Seraya Chemicals Singapore Pte Ltd, Shell Research Eastern (Pte) Ltd, Shell Singapore Trustees Pte Ltd; Chair. LEE TZU YANG; 1,700 employees.

Singapore Petroleum Co Ltd: 1 Maritime Sq., 10-10 Harbour Front Centre, Singapore 099253; tel. 62766006; fax 62756006; e-mail spccc@spc.com.sg; internet www.spc.com.sg; f. 1969; cap. and res 1,700.8m., revenue 11,123.7m. (2008); petroleum refining, tanker transport, trading, distribution and marketing; investment in oil and gas development and production; Chair. CHOO CHIAU BENG.

SK International: 4 Shenton Way, 11-02 SGX Centre 2, Singapore 068807; tel. 62201266; fax 62211225; e-mail jinhur@skenergy.com; owned by Malaysia-based SK Energy; fmrly Yukong Int. Pte Ltd; petroleum products; Man. Dir C. K. LEE.

Electrical and Electronics

Beyonics Technology Ltd: 30 Marsiling Industrial Estate, Rd 8, Singapore 739193; tel. 63490600; fax 63490500; e-mail btl@sg.beyonics.com; internet www.beyonics.com; f. 1981; mfr of precision components for computer and electronics industries; investment holding; cap. and res 299m., revenue 1,574.2m. (2009); CEO GOH CHAN PENG; 2,500 employees.

CarrierNet Global Ltd: 300 Beach Rd, 29-01 The Concourse, Singapore 199555; tel. 63099088; fax 63050489; e-mail corporate@arianecorp.com; internet www.carriernetglobal.com; f. 1984; fmrly ArianeCorp Ltd and Vikay Industrial Ltd; mfrs of electronic products, fibre optics and telecommunications equipment; cap. and res –15.4m., revenue 44.7m. (2009); Chair. LEW SYN PAU; CEO RICHARD CHAN SING EN; 3,688 employees.

China Auto Corpn Ltd: 17 Jurong Port Rd, Singapore 619092; tel. 62687733; fax 62663998; f. 1965; fmrly Acma Ltd; cap. and res 122.1m., revenue 64.7m. (2009); mfrs of tooling, injection moulding, die-casts etc.; Chair. QUEK SIM PIN; 200 employees.

Creative Technology Ltd: 31 International Business Park, Creative Resource, Singapore 609921; tel. 68954000; fax 68954999; internet sg.creative.com; f. 1983; cap. and res US $289.1m., sales US $275.3m. (2009/10); multimedia products peripherals; Chair. and CEO SIM WONG HOO.

Elec & Eltek International Co Ltd: 4 Leng Kee Rd, 03-02 SiS Bldg, Singapore 159088; tel. 62260488; fax 62202377; internet www.eleceltek.com; f. 1993; cap. and res 368.1m., sales 435m. (2009); investment holding, with subsidiaries engaged in design, manufacture and distribution of circuit boards; Chair. CHEUNG KWOK WING; 11,588 employees.

Flextronics International: 2 Changi South Lane, Singapore 486123; tel. 68907188; e-mail investor_relations@flextronics.com; internet www.flextronics.com; design, engineering and manufacture of electronic components; cap. and res US $1,984.5m., revenue US $24,110.7m. (2009/10); Chair. H. RAYMOND BINGHAM; CEO MIKE MCNAMARA.

General Magnetics Ltd: 625 Lorong 4, Toa Payoh, Singapore 319519; tel. 62595511; fax 62593723; e-mail sales@genmag.com.sg; internet www.genmag.com.sg; cap. and res 20.7m., sales 6.8m. (2008); mfrs and retailers of magnetic media and related products and telecommunication equipment; Chair. and Man. Dir OH LOON LIAN; 400 employees.

Giken Sakata (S) Ltd: 7 Second Chin Bee Rd, Singapore 618774; tel. 62599133; fax 62599822; e-mail enquiry@giken.com.sg; internet www.giken.com.sg; f. 1979; cap. and res 6.5m., sales 73.0m. (2008/09); parts for electronics equipment; Chair. SIEW GIM CHIN; Pres. and CEO KAY GUAN TAN; 4,886 employees.

GP Batteries International Ltd: 97 Pioneer Rd, Singapore 639579; tel. 65599800; fax 65599801; e-mail gpbi@gpbatteries.com.sg; internet www.gpbatteries.com.sg; f. 1964; cap. and res 308.6m., revenue 799m. (2009/10); batteries and related products; Chair. and CEO ANDREW SUNG ON NG; 9,800 employees.

Hewlett-Packard Singapore (Pte) Ltd: 450 Alexandra Rd, Singapore 119960; tel. 62733888; fax 62756839; e-mail hpdirect_sgp@hp.com; internet www.hp.com.sg; f. 1970; mfrs of opto-electronic components, inkjet printers and peripherals, personal computers, imaging products, hand-held devices and integrated circuits; Vice-Pres. and Man. Dir (Singapore) YEN YEN TAN; 9,000 employees.

Hitachi Home Electronics Asia (S) Pte Ltd: 438A Alexandra Rd 01-01/02, Alexandra Technopark, Singapore 119967; tel. 65362520; fax 65362521; e-mail enquiries@hitachiconsumer.com; internet www.hitachiconsumer.com.sg; f. 1972; mfrs of TV and radio receivers, tape-recorders, vacuum cleaners, air purifiers; Man. Dir M. MATSUNAGA; 1,000 employees.

Infineon Technologies Asia Pacific Pte Ltd: 8 Kallang Sector, Singapore 349282; tel. 68762888; fax 68763122; e-mail RnD.Singapore@infineon.com; internet www.infineon.com; f. 1970; mfr of electronic components; Man. Dir TIEN TEE POW; 2,700 employees.

IPC Corpn Ltd: 23 Tai Seng Dr., 06-00, IPC Bldg, Singapore 535224; tel. 67442688; fax 67430691; e-mail info@ipc.com.sg; internet www.ipc.com.sg; f. 1985; cap. and res 139.9m., revenue 20m. (2009); mfrs and retailers of computers and electronic products; Chair. and CEO MIA JE PATRICK NGIAM.

Matsushita Electronic Components (S) Pte Ltd: 3 Bedok South Ave, Singapore 469269; tel. 64437744; fax 64453168; e-mail mesaki@singnet.com.sg; f. 1977; mfrs of radio receivers, tape-recorders and stereophonic equipment; Man. Dir KASHIMA KELVIN; 2,200 employees.

Micron Semiconductor Asia Ltd: 990 Bendemeer Rd, Singapore 339942; tel. 62903000; fax 62903639; e-mail inverel@micron.com; internet www.micron.com; provider of semiconductor memory solutions; US-owned; Man. Dir JEN KWONG HWA; 3,000 employees.

Motorola Electronics Pte Ltd: 12 Ang Mo Kio Ind. Park 3, St 64, Singapore 569088; tel. 64812000; fax 64813081; internet www.motorola.com/sg; f. 1983; mfr of mobile telephones, pagers, cable modems; Man. Dir ARTHUR CHEN WAN SHOU; 2,445 employees.

PCI Ltd: 386 Jalan Ahmad Ibrahim, Singapore 629156; tel. 62658181; fax 62653333; e-mail sales@pciltd.com.sg; internet www.pciltd.com; f. 1988; cap. and res 61m., sales US $153.3m. (2009); mfr of printed circuit boards, liquid crystal displays, cordless telephones and other turnkey products; Chair. PEH KWEE CHIM; CEO TEO ENG LIN; 3,400 employees.

Philips Electronics Singapore Pte Ltd: 620A Lorong 1, Toa Payoh, Singapore 319762; tel. 63502000; fax 62533395; internet www.philips.com.sg; f. 1951; mfrs of consumer electronic products, domestic appliances and telecommunications equipment; Chair. and CEO LUP WAI WONG; 5,570 employees.

Pioneer Electronics (S) Pte Ltd: 253 Alexandra Rd, 04-01 Comco Bldg, Singapore 159936; tel. 64727555; fax 64727472; internet www.pioneer.com.sg; f. 1988; marketing and sales of electronic goods; Man. Dir MAKOTO TAKANO; 6,000 employees.

Qioptiq Singapore Pte Ltd: 8 Tractor Rd, Singapore 627969; tel. 64997766; fax 62651479; est. as Avimo Group Ltd and later became Thales Electro Optics Pte Ltd; name changed as above following takeover by Qioptic Group, Luxembourg in 2005; photonic products and solutions; CEO DAVID MARKS.

Samsung Asia Pte Ltd: 83 Clemenceau Ave, 08-06 UE Sq., Singapore 239920; tel. 68333402; fax 68333100; internet www.samsung.com/sg; f. 1988; retailers of semiconductors and telecommunications equipment; CEO GREGORY LEE.

Sanmina-SCI Systems (Singapore) Pte Ltd: 3 Depot Close, Singapore 109840; tel. 62784800; fax 62749741; e-mail it.asiapacific@sanmina-sci.com; internet www.sanmina-sci.com; 1,000 employees.

Sanyo Asia Pte Ltd: 6 Commonwealth Lane, 03-01/02, GMTI Bldg, Singapore 149547; tel. 62657777; fax 63781231; internet ap.sanyo.com; f. 1966; mfrs of electrical household appliances; Man. Dir YOSHINORI NAKATANI; 500 employees.

Schneider Electric Singapore Pte Ltd: 10 Ang Mo Kio, St 65, 02-17/20 Tech Point, Singapore 569059; tel. 64847877; fax 64847800; e-mail customercare@sg.schneider-electric.com; internet www.schneider-electric.com.sg; f. 1991; fmrly Clipsal Industries (Holdings) Ltd, name changed as above after acquisition by Schneider Electric Group in 2003; energy distribution, electrical installation systems, automation and control systems; Pres. and CEO JEAN-PASCAL TRICOIRE; 2,400 employees.

ST Microelectronics Asia Pacific (Pte) Ltd: 5A Serangoon North Ave 5, Singapore 554574; tel. 62165000; fax 64834153; internet www.st.com; f. 1969; manufacturing, marketing and sales, design of integrated circuits; Vice-Pres. and CEO, Asia Pacific FRANÇOIS GUIBERT; 4,479 employees.

Thakral Corpn Ltd: 20 Upper Circular Rd, 03-06 The Riverwalk, Singapore 058416; tel. 63368966; fax 63367225; e-mail enquiries@thakralcorp.com.sg; internet www.thakralcorp.com; cap. and res 227.6m., sales 438.8m. (2009); investment holding, distributor of consumer electronic and home entertainment products with operations in Hong Kong and China; Chair. KARTAR SINGH THAKRAL; Man. Dir INDERBETHAL SINGH THAKRAL; 769 employees.

Toshiba Asia Pacific Pte Ltd: 152 Beach Rd, 16-00 Gateway East, Singapore 189721; tel. 62970990; fax 62975510; e-mail wee_kee_tay@tea.toshiba.ceo.jp; internet www.asia.toshiba.com/tapl/singapore; electronic components retailers; Man. Dir SHOJI YOSHIOKA; 80 employees.

Venture Corporation Ltd: 5006 Ang Ko Mio Ave 5, 05-01/12 Techplace II, Singapore 569873; tel. 64821755; fax 64820122; e-mail contact-us@venture.com.sg; internet www.venture.com.sg; f. 1984 under the name Venture Manufacturing (Singapore) Ltd; name changed as above in 2002; mfrs and traders for companies in electronic and computer-related industries; cap. and res 1,862.7m., revenue 3,412.5m. (2009); Chair. and CEO WONG NGIT LIONG; Exec. Dir TAN CHOON HUAT.

Western Digital (S. E. Asia) Pte Ltd: 300 Tampines Ave 5, 05-07 NTUC Income Tampines Junction, Singapore 529653; tel. 64419989; fax 64419909; mfr of personal computer components; Dir, Sales and Marketing CRAIG DAVIS.

Food and Beverages

Asia Pacific Breweries (S) Pte Ltd: 21-00 Alexandra Pt, 438 Alexandra Rd, Singapore 119958; tel. 63189393; fax 62710811; e-mail corporatecommsgp@apb.com.sg; internet www.apb.com.sg; f. 1931 as Malayan Breweries Limited (MBL); name changed as above in 1990; cap. and res 1,032.3m., revenue 2,040.2m. (2008/09); brewers of beer and stout; Chair. SIMON ISRAEL; CEO ROLAND PIRMEZ; 5,750 employees.

Auric Pacific Group Ltd: 78 Shenton Way, 22-02 Lippo Centre, Singapore 079120; tel. 63362262; fax 63362272; e-mail corporate@auric.com.sg; internet www.auric.com.sg; f. 1988; cap. and res 217.9m., revenue 405.9m. (2009); food manufacturing; Chair. ALBERT SAYCHUAN CHEOK; Man. Dir YAO CHE WAN; 2,068 employees.

Cerebos Pacific Ltd: 18 Cross St 12-01/08, China Sq. Central, Singapore 048423; tel. 62120100; fax 62262126; e-mail contactus@cerebos.com.sg; internet www.cerebos.com; cap. and res 437.5m., revenue 1,194.8m. (2009/10); subsidiaries engaged in manufacture and marketing of food products; Chair. TEO CHIANG LONG; Pres. and Group CEO EIJI KOIKE; 2,635 employees.

Cold Storage Singapore Ltd: 21 Tampines North Dr. 2, 03-01, Singapore 528765; tel. 68918000; fax 63374019; e-mail service@coldstorage.com.sg; internet www.coldstorage.com.sg; f. 1960; retailers and distributors of food, mfrs of food and beverages; Chair. MICHAEL P. K. KOK; CEO LIM BOON CHEONG; 3,000 employees.

Fraser and Neave Ltd: 21-00 Alexandra Pt, 438 Alexandra Rd, Singapore 119958; tel. 63189393; fax 62717936; e-mail jenniferyu@fngroup.com.sg; internet www.fraserandneave.com; f. 1883; est. as The Singapore and Straits Aerated Water Co; name changed as above 1898; cap. and res 7,679.6m., sales 5,332.5m. (2008/09); investment holding company with subsidiaries involved in food and beverages, properties, publishing and printing; Chair. HSIEN YANG LEE; 18,000 employees.

Kuok Oils and Grains Pte Ltd: 1 Kim Seng Promenade, Great World City, 07-01, Singapore 237994; tel. 67333600; fax 67333188; e-mail corporate@kuokgroup.com.sg; internet www.kuokgroup.com.sg; f. 1989; mfr of edible oils and fats; Man. Dir KWOK KIAN HAI; 130 employees.

Network Foods International Ltd: 12 Woodlands Link, Singapore 738740; tel. 67577678; fax 67570300; e-mail enquiry@networkfoods.com; internet www.networkfoods.com; mfrs, distributors and marketers of chocolate and other cocoa-based products, biscuits and confectioneries; Marketing Exec. CHARVIN LAU.

Prima Ltd: 201 Keppel Rd, Singapore 099419; tel. 62728811; fax 62732933; e-mail support.flourmills@prima.com.sg; internet www.prima.com.sg; f. 1961; producers of wheat flour, wheat bran and pollard; fish and meat; Chair. and CEO CHENG CHIH KWONG; 235 employees.

QAF Ltd: 150 South Bridge Rd, 09-04 Fook Hai Bldg, Singapore 058727; tel. 65382866; fax 65386866; e-mail info@qaf.com.sg; internet www.qaf.com.sg; f. 1958; cap. and res 294m., revenue 854.9m. (2009); mfrs, wholesalers and retailers of food and beverages; trading, distribution and logistics; Chair. DIDI DAWIS; Man. Dir TAN KONG KING; 4,200 employees.

Yeo Hiap Seng Ltd: 3 Senoko Way, Singapore 758057; tel. 67522122; fax 67565625; e-mail enquiries@yeos.com; internet www.yeos.com.sg; cap. and res 379.4m., revenue 402.2m. (2009); mfrs and distributors of food and beverages; Chair., Man. Dir and CEO PHILIP NG CHEE TAT; Pres. TJONG YIK MIN.

Metals and Engineering

Amtek Engineering Ltd: 1 Kian Teck Drive, Singapore 628818; tel. 62640033; fax 62652510; e-mail sales@amtek.com.sg; internet www.amtek.com.sg; f. 1980; cap. and res 288.3m. (2004/05), sales 912.5m. (2005/06); mfrs and stampers of precision metal parts; precision rubber components and moulds; mechanical assemblies; computer enclosures; Chair. LEE AH BEE; CEO LAI FOOK KUEN; 44,813 employees.

CROWN Asia Pacific Holdings Ltd: 10 Hoe Chiang Rd, 19-01/02 Keppel Towers, Singapore 089315; tel. 64239798; e-mail Janet.Swee@crowncork.com.sg; internet www.crowncork.com; fmrly CarnaudMetalbox Asia Ltd; investment holding co and mfrs of metal packaging; Chair. and CEO WILLIAM HENRY VOSS; 3,000 employees.

Grand Banks Yachts Ltd: 541 Orchard Rd, 18-01 Liat Towers Singapore 238881; tel. 65452929; fax 67331527; e-mail gbsin@grandbanks.com; internet www.grandbanks.com; cap. and res 76.9m., sales 113.8m. (2007/08); investment holding co with subsidiaries engaged in manufacture and retailing of diesel-powered cruisers, sailing boats; yacht repairers; Chair. ROBERT W. LIVINGSTON; 870 employees.

Hitachi Zosen Singapore Ltd: 41 Science Park Rd, 04-01C (Lobby B), The Gemini, Singapore Science Park II, Singapore 117610; tel. 68631490; fax 68985429; f. 1970; ship-building and repair, steel structures, industrial engineering; Man. Dir FOO MENG KEE.

Jurong Engineering Ltd: 25 Tanjong Kling Rd, Singapore 628050; tel. 62653222; fax 62684211; e-mail marketing@jel.com.sg; internet www.jel.com.sg; cap. and res 63.9m., sales 336.5m. (2005); construction and engineering services; Chair. BOB TAN BENG HAI; Man. Dir and CEO SEIICHI DAITA.

Keppel Corpn Ltd: 1 HarbourFront Ave, 18-01, Keppel Bay Tower, Singapore 098632; tel. 62706666; fax 64136452; e-mail keppelgroup@kepcorp.com; internet www.kepcorp.com; f. 1859; cap. and res 4,596.2m., revenue 11,805.4m. (2008); Chair. BOON YANG LEE; CEO CHIAU BENG CHOO; 15,947 employees.

Keppel Offshore and Marine Ltd: 50 Gul Rd, Singapore 629531; tel. 68637200; fax 62617719; internet www.keppelom.com; f. 2002 following merger of Keppel FELS Ltd and Keppel Hitachi Zosen Ltd; subsidiary of Keppel Corpn Ltd; builders and repairers of offshore production facilities; Chair. and CEO CHIAU BENG CHOO; Man. Dir CHONG HEONG TONG; 1,970 employees.

Liang Huat Aluminium Ltd: 51 Benoi Rd, Blk 8, 08-05 Liang Huat Industrial Complex, Singapore 629908; tel. 68622228; fax 68624962; e-mail lhg_corpadm1@pacific.net.sg; internet www.lianghuatgroup.com.sg; f. 1978; cap. and res 11.5m., revenue 9.2m. (2007); aluminium products; Man. Dir PETER TAN YONG KEE; 1,000 employees.

Lion Asiapac Ltd: 10 Arumugam Rd, 10-00 Lion Industrial Bldg, Singapore 409957; tel. 67459678; fax 67425753; e-mail tshella@liongroup.com.sg; internet www.lionapac.com; f. 1974; cap. 47.5m., res 47.5m., sales 105.7m. (2007/08); mfrs and retailers of containers, and investment holding; Chair. OTHMAN WOK; Exec. Dir KGAI MUN LOH; 286 employees.

NSL Ltd: 77 Robinson Rd, 27-00, Singapore 068896; tel. 65361000; fax 65361008; e-mail enquiries@nsl.com.sg; internet www.nsl.com.sg; f. 1961; fmrly Natsteel Ltd, fmrly National Iron and Steel Mills; cap. and res 500.3m., revenue 347.8m. (2008); manufacturing and marketing of chemicals, engineering and construction products; Chair. TAO SOON CHAM.

SembCorp Industries: 30 Hill St, 05-04, Singapore 179360; tel. 67233113; fax 68223254; e-mail gcr@sembcorp.com; internet www.sembcorp.com.sg; f. 1998; est. following merger of Singapore Technologies Industrial Corpn and Sembawang Corpn Ltd; cap. and res 2,594.2m., sales 9,928.4m. (2008); investment holding with subsidiaries involved in engineering and construction, environmental engineering, logistics and utilities; Chair. PETER SEAH LIM HUAT; Pres. and CEO TANG KIN FEI; 9,767 employees.

Sembcorp Marine Ltd: 29 Tanjong Kling Rd, Singapore 628054; tel. 62651766; fax 62610738; internet www.sembcorpmarine.com.sg; f. 1968; cap. and res 1,318.0m., sales 5,063.9m. (2008); fmrly Jurong Shipyard Ltd; maritime services, shipping, civil construction, construction of oil rigs and specialized marine equipment; also active in industrial and venture sectors; Chair. GOH GEOK LING; Pres. and CEO WENG SUN WONG; 1,800 employees.

Singapore Technologies Engineering Ltd (ST Engineering Ltd): 51 Cuppage Rd, 09-08, StarHub Centre, Singapore 229469; tel. 67221818; fax 67202293; e-mail comms@stengg.com; internet www.stengg.com; cap. and res 1,580.4m., sales 5,344.5m. (2008); fmrly Singapore Technologies Aerospace Ltd; maintenance, modification and refurbishment of military and civilian aircraft, engines and components; Chair. PETER SEAH; Pres. PHENG HOCK TAN; 4,772 employees.

The Straits Trading Co Ltd: 18 Cross St, 15-01, Singapore 048423; tel. 65139288; fax 65347202; e-mail straits@stc.com.sg; internet www.stc.com.sg; f. 1887; cap. and res 1,196.8m., revenue 1,250.1m. (2008); tin smelting; Pres. and CEO NORMAN IP KA CHEUNG; Chair. CHEW GEK KHIM.

Superior Multi-Packaging Ltd: 7 Benoi Sector, Singapore 629842; tel. 62683933; fax 62657151; e-mail general@smpl.com.sg; internet www.smpl.com.sg; cap. and res 64.6m., sales 122.4m. (2007); fmrly Superior Metal Printing Ltd; mfrs of metal containers and flexible packaging; Chair. GOH HUP JIN; Group Gen. Man. WANG GEE HOCK.

United Engineers Ltd: 83 Clemenceau Ave, 18-01 UE Sq., Singapore 239920; tel. 68308383; fax 68308398; e-mail business@uel.com.sg; internet www.uel.com.sg; cap. and res 765.8m., sales 624.6m. (2008); civil, mechanical, electrical and environmental engineering; fabrication of industrial, construction and agricultural machinery; Chair. NGIAP JOO TAN; Group Man. Dir and CEO JACKSON CHEVALIER YAP KIT SIONG; 2,000 employees.

Wood and Paper Products

Asia Pulp and Paper Co Ltd: 1 Maritime Sq., 10-01 World Trade Centre, Lobby B, Singapore 099253; tel. 2729288; fax 3749249; internet www.asiapulppaper.com; f. 1994; mfrs and distributors of paper products; majority stakeholder Sinar Mas Group, Indonesia; CEO TJIE GOAN OEI.

Hiap Moh Corpn Ltd: Block 162, Bukit Merah Central, 08-3545, Singapore 150162; tel. 62735333; fax 62789707; e-mail hiapmoh@pacific.net.sg; internet www.hiapmoh.com; cap. and res 36.0m., revenue 42.7m. (2007); mfrs and traders of paper products; Chair. MICHAEL WEE SOON LOCK; Man. Dir NG KAH LIN; 267 employees.

United Pulp and Paper Co Ltd: 35 Tuas View Crescent, Singapore 637608; tel. 68610018; fax 68613318; e-mail uppgroup@singnet.com.sg; cap. and res 77.7m., revenue 51.1m. (2008); investment holding co with subsidiaries engaged in manufacture and retail of paper products; Chair. KIM KOH HUAT; Pres. and CEO KOH WAN KAI; 300 employees.

Miscellaneous

Alliance Technology and Development Ltd: 139 Joo Seng Rd, 06-01, ATD Centre, Singapore 368362; tel. 67491090; fax 62825377; investment holding co with subsidiary engaged in manufacture of contact lenses and related eye-care products, property investment and development, leisure and entertainment, hospitality and Underwater World; Chair. CHANG CHING CHUAN; Exec. Vice-Chair. and CEO CHANG WHE HAN.

AsiaMedic Ltd: 350 Orchard Rd, 08-00 Shaw House, Singapore 238868; tel. 67898888; fax 67384136; internet www.asiamedic.com.sg; f. 1987; cap. and res 14.3m., revenue 12.3m. (2008); precision plastic moulding, mould manufacture and medical services; Chair. LOW CZE HONG; CEO KHOR CHIN KEE.

Aztech Group Ltd: 31 Ubi Rd 1, Aztech Bldg, Singapore 408694; tel. 65942288; fax 67491198; e-mail pavanin@aztech.com; internet www.aztech-group.com; f. 1986; electronics, construction and marine logistics; cap. and res 112.3m., revenue 280.3m. (2009); Chair. and CEO MICHAEL MUN YEW HONG.

Bonvests Holdings Ltd: 541 Orchard Rd, 16-00 Liat Towers, Singapore 238881; tel. 67325533; fax 67379166; e-mail marketing@bonvests.com.sg; internet www.bonvests.com.sg; f. 1982; cap. and res 619.9m., revenue 244.0m. (2008); investment holding co with subsidiary engaged in property development and rental, hotel and fast food chain ownership and management, waste collection and cleaning services; Chair. and Man. Dir HENRY NGO; 1,992 employees.

British-American Tobacco Co (Singapore) Ltd: 15 Senoko Loop, Singapore 758168; tel. 67588555; fax 67557798; f. 1978; investment holding co with subsidiaries engaged in manufacturing, importing and retailing tobacco products; Dir, Asia-Pacific JOHN DALY; 500 employees.

Bukit Sembawang Estates Ltd: 65 Chulia St, 49-05 OCBC Centre, Singapore 049513; tel. 68900333; fax 65361858; internet www.bukitsembawang.sg; cap. and res 488.9m., revenue 75.6m. (2007/08); property development; Chair. CECIL VIVIAN RICHARD WONG; CEO NG CHEE SENG.

Capitaland Commercial Ltd: 168 Robinson Rd, 30-01 Capital Tower, Singapore 068912; tel. 68233200; fax 68202202; e-mail ask_us@capitalandcommercial.com; internet www.capitaland.com; f. 2000; est. by merger of Pidemco Land Ltd and DBS Land Ltd; cap. and res 9,940.9m. (2007), revenue 2,752.3m. (2008); property investment and devt; Chair. Dr TSU TAU HU; Pres. and CEO LIEW MUN LEONG; 2,390 employees.

City Developments Ltd: 9 Raffles Place, 36-00 Republic Plaza, Singapore 048619; tel. 64380880; fax 64380800; e-mail enquiries@cdl.com.sg; internet www.cdl.com.sg; cap. and res 5,429.7m., sales 2,945.2m. (2008); property ownership and development; Chair. KWEK LENG BENG; Man. Dir KWEK LENG JOO; 317 employees.

ComfortDelGro Corpn Ltd: 205 Braddell Rd, Singapore 579701; tel. 63838833; fax 62870311; e-mail info@comfortdelgro.com; internet www.comfortdelgro.com; f. 1993; est. as Comfort Group Ltd; name changed as above in 2003 following merger with DelGro Corpn; cap. and res 1,690m., revenue 3,051.8m. (2009); passenger land transport co; fleet of 44,100 vehicles; Chair. JIT POH LIM; Man. Dir and CEO HONG PAK KUA; 22,300 employees worldwide.

Datacraft Asia Ltd: 6 Temasek Blvd, 26-01 to 05 Suntec Tower Four, Singapore 038986; tel. 3226688; fax 3237933; e-mail ask@datacraft-asia.com; internet www.datacraft-asia.com; f. 1974; wholly owned subsidiary of Dimension Data plc (United Kingdom); cap. and res US $118.4m. (2007/08), total revenue US $605.6m. (2008/09); management and investment holding, data communication systems; Chair. PATRICK QUARMBY; CEO BILL PADFIELD; 1,473 employees.

DKSH Singapore Pte Ltd: 34 Boon Leat Terrace, Singapore 119866; tel. 64711466; fax 64799104; internet www.dksh.com.sg; fmrly Diethelm Trading Co Ltd, above name adopted in 2010; market expansion services for consumer goods, healthcare and technology; Man. Dir LEONARD TAN; over 550 employees.

Frasers Centrepoint Ltd: 438 Alexandra Rd, 02-00 Alexandra Point, Singapore 119538; tel. 62764882; fax 62757732; e-mail feedback@fraserscentrepointhomes.com; internet www.fraserscentrepointhomes.com; f. 1963; fmrly Centrepoint Homes; property ownership and devt; Chair. Dr MICHAEL FAM.

Goldtron Ltd: 21 Serangoon North Ave 5, 06-02, Singapore 554864; tel. 67471616; fax 67413525; e-mail skong@singnet.com.sg; f. 1962; cap. and res 44.9m., revenue 112.4m. (2007/08); investment holding co with subsidiaries engaged in manufacture and retail of telecommunication products; Chair. MOKHZANI BIN MAHATHIR; CEO ONG SOON KIAT; 1,462 employees.

GP Industries Ltd: 97 Pioneer Rd, Singapore 639579; tel. 63950850; fax 63950860; e-mail gpind@gp-industries.com; internet www.gp-industries.com; f. 1995; cap. and res 403.9m., revenue 242.4m. (2008/09); mfr of car radios; Chair. VICTOR LO CHUNG WING; 4,550 employees.

Haw Par Corpn Ltd: 401 Commonwealth Dr., 03-03 Haw Par Technocentre, Singapore 149598; tel. 63379102; fax 63369232; internet www.hawpar.com; f. 1969; cap. and res 1,320.1m., revenue 122.1m. (2008); investment holding co with subsidiaries engaged in property, investments and manufacture of industrial products, sports products and pharmaceutical products; Chair. WEE CHO YAW; Pres. and CEO WEE EE LIM; 449 employees.

Hotel Properties Ltd: 50 Cuscaden Rd, 08-01 HPL House, Singapore 249724; tel. 67345250; fax 67320347; e-mail contactus@hotelprop.com; internet www.hotelprop.com; cap. and res 1,184.2m., sales 612.0m. (2008); hotels; leisure; food retailing; Chair. JOSEPH GRIMBERG; Man. Dir ONG BENG SENG; 200 employees.

Htl International Holdings Ltd: 11 Gul Circle, Singapore 629567; tel. 67475050; fax 67478497; e-mail investorrelations@htlinternational.com; internet www.htlinternational.com; f. 1976; cap. and res 213.7m., sales 646.2m. (2008); furniture, fabrics; Chair. PHUA YONG PIN; Man. Dir PHUA YONG TAT.

Hwa Hong Corpn Ltd: 38/40 South Bridge Rd, Singapore 058672; tel. 65385711; fax 65333028; e-mail finance@hwahongcorp.com; internet www.hwahongcorp.com; cap. and res 317.7m., revenue 80.2m. (2008); investment holding co with subsidiaries engaged in general insurance and related activities, packaging of edible oil products, construction and engineering; Chair. HANS HUGH MILLER; Man. Dir ONG CHOO ENG; 800 employees.

Jardine Cycle and Carriage Ltd: 239 Alexandra Rd, Singapore 159930; tel. 64733122; fax 64757088; internet www.jcclgroup.com; f. 1969; fmrly Cycle and Carriage Ltd; name changed as above 2004; cap. and res US $2,263m., revenue US $11,192m. (2008); retailer of motor vehicles; property investment; Chair. ANTHONY NIGHTINGALE; Man. Dir BENJAMIN KESWICK; 100,000 employees.

Jasper Investments Ltd: 30 Raffles Place, 20–01 Caltex House, Singapore 048622; tel. 65136888; fax 65572132; e-mail corp@jasperinvests.com; internet www.jasperinvests.com; f. 1993 as Econ International Ltd; name changed as above in 2006 following a change in its strategic direction and business focus, from building and construction to investment holding; cap. and res 33.9m., revenue 45.3m. (2007/08); Chair. SEAMUS DAWES; Exec. Dir GEOFFREY YEOH.

Keppel Land Ltd: 230 Victoria St, 15-05 Bugis Junction Towers, Singapore 188024; tel. 63388111; fax 63377168; e-mail stoh@kepland.com.sg; internet www.keppelland.com.sg; property investment and devt; property fund management; hotel and resort operations; Chair. CHIAU BENG CHOO; Man. Dir and CEO KEVIN WONG; 3,572 employees.

Kim Eng Holdings Ltd: 9 Temasek Blvd, 39-00 Suntec Tower 2, Singapore 038989; tel. 63369090; fax 63396003; e-mail helpdesk@kimeng.com; internet www.kimeng.com; cap. and res 882.7m., revenue 353.7m. (2008); sharebrokers, stockbrokers and investment holding co; Chair., Man. Dir and CEO THEAN THAT OI.

Leeden Ltd: 1 Shipyard Rd, Singapore 628128; tel. 62664868; fax 62662026; e-mail enquiry@leedenlimited.com; internet www.leedenlimited.com; fmrly Ace Dynamics Ltd; cap. and res 61.0m., revenue 157.2m. (2008); investment holding co, with subsidiaries engaged in distribution of industrial welding and safety equipment and the manufacture and supply of industrial gases; Chair. and CEO STEVEN THAM WENG CHEONG; 220 employees.

MCL Land Ltd: 78 Shenton Way, 33-00, Singapore 079120; tel. 62218111; fax 62253383; e-mail contactus@mclland.com.sg; internet www.mclland.com.sg; f. 1963; cap. and res US $393.9m., revenue US $343.1m. (2008); investment holding, property investment and management; Chair. Y. K. PANG; CEO KOH TECK CHUAN.

MPH Ltd: 47 Scotts Rd, 18-02 Goldbell Towers, Singapore 228233; tel. 67341515; fax 67322241; f. 1927; fmrly Jack Chia-MPH Ltd; investment holding co; activities of subsidiaries: publication, distribution and retail of books and magazines, manufacture and distribution of confectionery products, residential home building; Chair. and Man. Dir SIMON CHEONG; 2,065 employees.

Olam International Ltd: 9 Temasek Blvd, Suntec Tower Two, Singapore 038989; tel. 63394100; fax 63399755; e-mail info@olamnet.com; internet www.olamonline.com; cap. and res 638.4m., revenue 8,111.9m. (2007/08); global supply chain manager; sources and delivers agricultural products incl. cocoa, coffee, rice and wood; Chair. RANGAREDDY JAYACHANDRAN; Group Man. Dir and CEO SUNNY GEORGE VERGHESE.

Orchard Parade Holdings Ltd: 14 Scotts Rd, 06-01 Far East Plaza, Singapore 228213; tel. 62352411; f. 1967; cap. and res 818.2m., revenue 69.0m. (2008); management and investment holding, property investment and development; Chair. CHEE TAT NG; 228 employees.

Overseas Union Enterprise Ltd: 333 Orchard Rd, Overseas Union Bldg, 6th Floor, Singapore 238867; tel. 62357788; fax 62356688; e-mail info@oue.com.sg; internet www.oue.com.sg; f. 1964; advertising; hotels and leisure; property; cap. and res 805.8m., revenue 148.7m. (2008); Chair. CHRISTOPHER JAMES WILLIAMS; CEO and Group Man. Dir GIM HOCK THIO; 1,120 employees.

Parkway Holdings Ltd: TripleOne Somerset, 111 Somerset Rd, 15-01, Singapore 238164; tel. 63077880; fax 67338156; e-mail grpcorpcomms@parkway.sg; internet www.parkway.com.sg; cap. and res 1,284.3m., sales 645.4m. (2008); hospital ownership and management; wholesale of medicines and medical products; Chair. RICHARD SEOW YUNG LIANG; Man. Dir and CEO Dr LIM CHEOK PENG.

Rothmans Industries Ltd: 15 Senoko Loop, Singapore 758168; tel. 63388998; fax 63388181; investment holding co with subsidiaries engaged in manufacture, import and retail of cigarettes, pipe tobaccos, cigars and other tobacco-related products; Chair. ALAN YEO CHEE YEOW.

San Teh Ltd: 701 Sims Drive, 06-01 LHK Bldg, Singapore 387383; tel. 67496386; fax 67473456; f. 1979; cap. and res 279.3m., revenue 155.3m. (2008); mfrs of specialized silicone rubber products; Chair. and CEO KAO SHIN PING; 217 employees.

Singapore Press Holdings Ltd: 1000 Toa Payoh North, Singapore 318994; tel. 63196319; fax 63198282; e-mail sphcorp@sph.com.sg; internet www.sph.com.sg; cap. and res 2,088.9m., revenue 1,014.3m. (2007/08); publishing, printing and distribution of newspapers and magazines; Chair. Dr TONY TAN KENG YAM; CEO ALAN CHAN HENG LOON; 3,277 employees.

SM Summit Holdings Ltd: 45 Ubi Rd 1, Summit Bldg, Singapore 408696; tel. 67453288; fax 67489612; e-mail co@smsummit.com.sg; internet www.smsummit.com.sg; f. 1981; cap. and res 72.4m., revenue 83.4m. (2007); investment holdings, mfrs and retailers of compact discs (CDs), digital versatile discs (DVDs) and related products; Chair. and Man. Dir LEE KERK CHONG; 750 employees.

Sumitomo Corporation (Singapore) Pte Ltd: 20 Cecil St, 23-01/08 and 24-01/08, Equity Plaza, Singapore 049705; tel. 65337722; fax 65339693; e-mail general@sumitomocorp.com.sg; internet www.sumitomocorp.com.sg; retailing and project management; Man. Dir MASAO TETSUYA; 151 employees.

Toepfer International Asia Pte: 100 Beach Rd, 31-01 Shaw Towers, Singapore 189702; tel. 62932366; fax 62927556; e-mail tiaspu@pacific.net.sg; sale of commodities; Chair. SOH KIM SIANG.

United Industrial Corpn Ltd: 5 Shenton Way, 02-16 UIC Bldg, Singapore 068808; tel. 62201352; fax 62240278; internet www.uic.com.sg; cap. and res 3,219.1m., sales 892.3m. (2008); investment holding co with subsidiaries engaged in manufacture of detergent products, toiletries and electronic systems; Chair. WEE CHO YAW; Pres. and CEO LIM HOCK SAN; 1,027 employees.

United Overseas Land Ltd: 101 Thomson Rd, 33-00 United Sq., Singapore 307591; tel. 62550233; fax 62529822; e-mail uol@pacific.net.sg; internet www.uol.com.sg; cap. and res 3,394.7m., sales 899.2m. (2008); property development; hotels; Chair. WEE CHO YAW; Pres. and CEO GWEE LIAN KHENG; 3,451 employees.

Wearnes Ltd (WBL Corpn): 801 Lorong 7, Toa Payoh, 07-00 Wearnes Bldg, Singapore 319319; tel. 65333444; fax 65341443; e-mail info@wbl.com.sg; internet www.wbl.com.sg; cap. and res 991.3m., sales 2,072.8m. (2008); investment holding co with subsidiaries engaged in manufacture of vehicles, industrial machinery, electronic components and products, building materials and precision engineering products, property development and investment, provision of management services; Chair. WONG NANG JANG; CEO TAN CHOON SENG.

Wheelock Properties (Singapore) Ltd: 501 Orchard Rd, 04-01/03 Lane Wheelock Place, Singapore 238880; tel. 67388660; fax 67359833; internet www.wheelockproperties.com.sg; f. 1972; fmrly Marco Polo Developments Ltd; cap. and res 2,053.6m., revenue 454.6m. (2008); property devt; Chair. PETER K. C. WOO; Man. Dir DAVID J. LAWRENCE; 600 employees.

Wing Tai Holdings Ltd: 3 Killiney Rd, 10-01, Winsland House I, Singapore 239519; tel. 62809111; fax 67363486; internet www.wingtaiasia.com.sg; cap. and res 1,605.5m., revenue 428.2m. (2007/08); investment holding co with subsidiaries engaged in property development and hospitality, trading in fabrics, garments and architectural products and the provision of internet-related services; Chair. and Man. Dir CHENG WAI KEUNG.

TRADE UNIONS

At the end of 2003 there were 68 employees' trade unions and associations, with 417,166 members, and three employer unions, with 2,052 members.

National Trades Union Congress (NTUC): NTUC Centre, 1 Marina Blvd 10-01, Singapore 018989; tel. 62138008; fax 63273740; e-mail membership@ntuc.org.sg; internet www.ntuc.org.sg; f. 1961; 60 affiliated unions, 6 affiliated assocs and approx. 540,000 mems (2009); Pres. JOHN DE PAYVA; Sec.-Gen. LIM SWEE SAY.

Transport

RAILWAYS

Singapore is linked to the Malaysian railway system via the Johor causeway. Branch lines provide a link to the industrial estate at Jurong.

The Mass Rapid Transit (MRT) system opened in 1990. In 2002 the extension of the East–West line to Changi Airport was completed. A 33.3-km orbital line was to link all the radial lines into the city with the last phase of construction scheduled for completion in 2012. In early 2010 the rail length of the MRT was 109.4 km.

Singapore's first Light Rapid Transit (LRT) system, the Bukit Panjang LRT, opened in 1998. Construction of the 2.1-km Sentosa Express monorail system was completed in June 2006, and operations commenced in January 2007. In 2008 the LRT covered 28.8 km of the total rail length.

Land Transport Authority: 1 Hampshire Rd, Singapore 219428; tel. 63757100; fax 63757200; internet www.lta.gov.sg; f. 1995; planning, devt and man. of the land transport system; Chair. MICHAEL LIM CHOO SAN; Chief Exec. CHEW HOCK YONG.

SMRT Corpn Ltd: 251 North Bridge Rd, Singapore 179102; tel. 63311000; fax 63340247; e-mail corpcomms@smrt.com.sg; internet www.smrt.com.sg; f. 1987; operates the MRT and LRT rail systems, a fleet of more than 950 buses and more than 2,500 taxis (2010); Chair. KOH YONG GUAN; Pres. and CEO SAW PHAIK HWA.

ROADS

In 2007 Singapore had a total of 3,297 km of roads, of which 153 km were motorway; in that year 100% of the road network was paved.A system of electronic road pricing, whereby vehicles are charged according to road use, is in operation. The 12-km Kallang–Paya Lebar expressway (with approximately 9 km of the expressway under ground) became fully operational in September 2008.

SHIPPING

Singapore is one of the world's busiest ports. The Port of Singapore Authority operates six cargo terminals: Tanjong Pagar Terminal, Keppel Terminal, Brani Terminal, Pasir Panjang Terminal (where the final two phases of construction were scheduled for completion in 2013), Sembawang Terminal and Jurong Port. In December 2009 the Singapore merchant fleet comprised 2,563 vessels, with a total displacement of 41,046,600 grt.

Maritime and Port Authority of Singapore: 460 Alexandra Rd, 18-00 PSA Bldg, Singapore 119963; tel. 63751600; fax 62759247; e-mail shipping@mpa.gov.sg; internet www.mpa.gov.sg; f. 1996; regulatory body responsible for promotion and development of the port, overseeing all port and maritime matters in Singapore; Chair. LUCIEN WONG; Chief Exec. LAM YI YOUNG.

PSA International Pte Ltd: 460 Alexandra Rd, 38th Floor, PSA Bldg, Singapore 119963; tel. 62747111; fax 62794677; e-mail gca@psa.com.sg; internet www.internationalpsa.com; f. 1964; est. as Port of Singapore Authority; made a corporate entity in 1997 in preparation for privatization; present name adopted 2003; wholly owned by Temasek Holdings Pte Ltd; responsible for the provision and maintenance of port facilities and services; participates in 28 port projects in 16 countries in Asia, Europe and the Americas; Group Chair. SIEW WAH FOCK; Group CEO EDDIE TEH.

Major Shipping Companies

American President Lines Ltd (APL): 456 Alexandra Rd, 08-00 NOL Bldg, Singapore 119962; tel. 62789000; fax 62784900; e-mail erep_asia@apl.com; internet www.apl.com; container services to North and South Asia, the USA and the Middle East; Pres. ENG AIK MENG.

Glory Ship Management Private Ltd: 24 Raffles Place, 17-01/02, Clifford Centre, Singapore 048621; tel. 65361986; fax 65361987; e-mail gene@gloryship.com.sg.

Guan Guan Shipping Pte Ltd: 2 Finlayson Green, 13-05 Asia Insurance Bldg, Singapore 049247; tel. 65343988; fax 62276776; e-mail golden@golden.com.sg; f. 1955; shipowners and agents; cargo services to East and West Malaysia, Indonesia, Pakistan, Sri Lanka, Bengal Bay ports, Persian (Arabian) Gulf ports, Hong Kong and China; Man. Dir RICHARD THIO.

IMC Shipping Co Pte Ltd: 5 Temasek Blvd, 37-01 Suntec City Tower, Singapore 038987; tel. 64119800; fax 63379715; e-mail corpcomms@imcpaa.com; internet www.imcshipping.com; Chair. FRANK TSAO WEN KING.

Maersk Singapore Pte Ltd: 200 Cantonment Rd, 10-100, Southpoint, Singapore 089763; tel. 63238323; fax 62247649; e-mail sinlinmng@maersk.com; f. 1929; operates under the brand name of Maersk Line; Head, Asia Pacific THOMAS KNUDSEN.

Neptune Orient Lines Ltd: 456 Alexandra Rd, 05-00 NOL Bldg, Singapore 119962; tel. 62789000; fax 62784900; e-mail nol_group_corp_comms@nol.com.sg; internet www.nol.com.sg; f. 1968; liner containerized services on the Far East/Europe, Far East/North America, Straits/Australia, South Asia/Europe and South-East Asia, Far East/Mediterranean routes; logistics services and terminals; Chair. CHENG WAI KEUNG; Group Pres. and CEO RON WIDDOWS.

Ocean Tankers (Pte) Ltd: 37 Tuas Rd, Singapore 638503; tel. 68632202; fax 68639480; e-mail corporate@oceantankers.com.sg; internet www.oceantankers.com.sg; Marine Supt V. LIM.

Osprey Maritime Ltd: 8 Cross St, 24-02/03 PWC Bldg, Singapore 048424; tel. 62129722; fax 65570450; CEO PETER GEORGE COSTALAS.

Pacific International Lines (Pte) Ltd: 140 Cecil St, 03-00 PIL Bldg, POB 3206, Singapore 069540; tel. 62218133; fax 62273933; e-mail sherry.chua@sgp.pilship.com; internet www.pilship.com; shipowners, agents and managers; international liner services; container services to South-East Asia; world-wide chartering, freight forwarding, etc.; Exec. Chair. Y. C. CHANG; Man. Dir S. S. TEO.

Petroships Private Ltd: 460 Alexandra Rd, 25-04 PSA Bldg, Singapore 119963; tel. 62731122; fax 62732200; e-mail gen@petroships.com.sg; Man. Dir KENNETH KEE.

Syabas Tankers Pte Ltd: 10 Anson Rd, 34-10 International Plaza, Singapore 0207; tel. 62259522.

Tanker Pacific Management (Singapore) Private Ltd: 1 Temasek Ave, 38-01 Millenia Tower, Singapore; tel. 64335888; fax 63365311; internet www.tanker.com.sg; Chair. and CEO ALASTAIR MCGREGOR.

CIVIL AVIATION

Singapore's international airport at Changi was opened in 1981. Construction of a terminal solely for the use of budget carriers was completed in 2006, thereby increasing the airport's total capacity to 64m. passengers a year. Construction of a third main terminal was completed in 2008. A second airport at Seletar operates as a base for charter and training flights.

Civil Aviation Authority of Singapore: Singapore Changi Airport, POB 1, Singapore 918141; tel. 65421122; fax 65421231; e-mail thennarasee_R@caas.gov.sg; internet www.caas.gov.sg; responsible for regulatory and advisory services, air services development, airport management and development, and airspace management and organization; Chair. LEE HSIEN YANG; Dir-Gen. YAP ONG HENG.

Jetstar Asia Airways: Singapore Changi Airport T1, POB 323, Singapore 918144; tel. 93470208; internet www.jetstar.com; f. 2004; 49% owned by Qantas (Australia); service to regional destinations; merged with ValuAir in 2005; continues to operate under the Jetstar name; CEO CHONG PHIT LIAN.

SilkAir: 371 Beach Rd Unit, 17-08, Singapore 199597; tel. 62238888; fax 65426286; internet www.silkair.com; f. 1975; fmrly Tradewinds Private; wholly owned subsidiary of Singapore Airlines Ltd; began scheduled services in 1989; Chair. GOH CHOON PHONG; CEO MARVIN TAN.

Singapore Airlines Ltd (SIA): Airline House, 25 Airline Rd, Singapore 819829; tel. 65415880; fax 65456083; e-mail investor_relations@singaporeair.com.sg; internet www.singaporeair.com; f. 1972; passenger services to over 90 destinations in about 40 countries; Chair. STEPHEN LEE CHING YEN; CEO CHEW CHOON SENG.

Tiger Airways: Singapore Changi Airport, POB 82, Singapore 918143; tel. 68222300; fax 68222310; internet www.tigerairways.com; f. 2003; 49% owned by Singapore Airlines, 24% owned by US co Indigo Partners, 11% owned by Temasek Holdings Pte Ltd; services to 10 regional destinations; Chair. GERARD EE HOCK KIM; CEO CHIN YAU SENG (acting).

ValuAir: Singapore Changi Airport T1, POB 323, Singapore 918144; tel. 93470208; internet www.jetstar.com/vf/en/index.aspx; f. 2003; merged with Jetstar Asia in 2005; continues to operate under the ValuAir name; provides low-cost services between Singapore and Indonesia; CEO CHONG PHIT LIAN.

Tourism

Singapore's tourist attractions include its blend of cultures and excellent shopping facilities. In 2005 the Government legalized gambling on the island, rescinding a 40-year ban and allowing for the construction of two major casino resorts, at Marina Bay and on Sentosa Island. The first hotels and the casino at the Sentosa resort opened in early 2010. A phased opening of the Marina Bay resort commenced in June 2010. The resorts were expected significantly to increase the number of visitors to Singapore. Foreign visitor arrivals rose from fewer than 9.7m. in 2009 to exceed 11.6m. in 2010. Receipts from tourism (excluding passenger transport) totalled an estimated US $9,187m. in 2009.

Singapore Tourism Board: Tourism Court, 1 Orchard Spring Lane, Singapore 247729; tel. 67366622; fax 67369423; e-mail feedback@stb.com.sg; internet www.stb.com.sg; f. 1964; Chair. SIMON ISRAEL; Chief Exec. AW KAH PENG.

Defence

As assessed at November 2010, the total strength of the armed forces was 72,500 (including 39,000 conscripts): army 50,000 (35,000 conscripts), navy an estimated 9,000 (1,000 conscripts), air force 13,500 (3,000 conscripts). Military service lasts 24 months. Army reserves numbered an estimated 312,500. Paramilitary forces of an estimated 93,800 comprised the Singapore police force, marine and Gurkha guard battalions, and a civil defence force (numbering an estimated 81,800, including 3,200 conscripts). Singapore is a participant in the Five-Power Defence Arrangements with Malaysia, Australia, New Zealand and the United Kingdom.

Defence Expenditure: Budgeted at S $12,300m. for 2011.

Chief of the Defence Forces: Maj.-Gen. NEO KIAN HONG.

Chief of the Army: Brig.-Gen. CHAN CHUN SING.

Chief of the Air Force: Brig.-Gen. NG CHEE MENG.

Chief of the Navy: Rear-Adm. NG CHEE PENG.

Education

From 2003 education in Singapore became compulsory for the first time at primary level, the six years of which are granted free to all children. Less able pupils are afforded an additional two years in which to complete primary education, under the New Primary Education System implemented in 1979.

Despite schooling being optional at the time, in 1996 the number of children attending primary schools was equivalent to 94% of children in the relevant age-group (males 95%; females 93%) and secondary school enrolment was equivalent to 74% of children in the relevant age-group. Government expenditure on education in 2010 was estimated at S $8,517m. (19.3% of total expenditure). In 2010 there were 173 primary institutions, at which 256,801 students were enrolled; and 155 secondary institutions, at which 196,220 students were enrolled. In the same year there were 15 mixed-level schools, at which 37,225 students were enrolled, and a further 13 pre-university institutions, at which 20,468 students were enrolled.

The policy of bilingualism ensures that children are taught two languages, English and one of the other official languages, Chinese, Malay or Tamil. The option to study French, German or Japanese is offered in secondary schools to interested pupils with linguistic ability as a third language, and as a second language to pupils not of Chinese, Malay or Tamil ethnic origin.

Primary education focuses on the core subjects of English, mathematics and the mother tongue (Chinese, Malay or Tamil). Students take the Primary School Leaving Examination (PSLE) on completion of their primary education and are streamed, depending on their performance in the PSLE, into the Special/Express course (four years), the Normal course (four years), or the Normal Technical Course (four years). Pupils of Special/Express courses will take the Singapore-Cambridge General Certificate of Education (GCE) 'Ordinary' ('O') Level Examination. Normal and Normal Technical course pupils will sit the GCE 'Normal' Level Examination after four years. Normal course pupils who do well may extend their studies by a year in order to take the GCE 'O' Level. Based on 'O' Level results, pupils may follow a two-year or three-year pre-university course leading to the GCE 'Advanced' Level Examination. More able pupils may participate in the Integrated Programme (IP), which spans secondary and junior college education. Pupils on this course do not sit 'O' levels, but instead proceed directly to 'Advanced' Levels or alternative qualifications such as the International Baccalaureate. Students interested in technical and commercial studies may continue their education in the technical or commercial institutes under the Institute of Technical Education. In 2004 57.8% of resident non-students aged 15 years and over held secondary or higher qualifications.

There were 13 tertiary institutions in 2010, including the National University of Singapore, the Nanyang Technological University, the Ngee Ann Polytechnic, the Singapore Polytechnic, the Nanyang Polytechnic and the Temasek Polytechnic. In 2010 total enrolment in the universities and colleges (not including SIM University, which opened in 2005) was 187,830. The Singapore Institute of Technology, which was to provide industry-orientated qualifications in partnership with several overseas universities, opened in 2010. The Institute of Technical Education provides and regulates vocational training. It conducts institutional training for school-leavers, offers part-time continuing education and training programmes and registers apprentices. It is also responsible for setting national skills standards, the conduct of public trade testing and certification of skills.

Bibliography

General and History

Abdul Rahman, Noor Aisha, and Lai Ah Eng (Eds). *Secularism and Spirituality: Seeking Integrated Knowledge and Success in Madrasah Education in Singapore.* Singapore, Institute of Policy Studies, 2006.

Amitav, Acharya. *Singapore's Foreign Policy: The Search for Regional Order.* Singapore, World Scientific Publishing Co, 2007.

Arora, Mandakini (Ed.). *Small Steps, Giant Leaps: A History of Aware and the Women's Movement in Singapore.* Singapore, Association of Women for Action and Research, 2007.

Barr, Michael D. *Lee Kuan Yew: The Beliefs Behind the Man.* Kuala Lumpur, New Asian Library, 2nd Edn, 2009.

Barr, Michael D., and Skrbis, Zlatko. *Constructing Singapore: Elitism, Ethnicity and the Nation-building Project.* Copenhagen, NIAS Press, 2008.

Barr, Michael D., and Trocki, Carl A. *Paths Not Taken: Political Pluralism in Post-war Singapore.* Singapore, Singapore University Press, 2008.

Bose, Romen. *The End of the War: Singapore's Liberation and the Aftermath of the Second World War.* Singapore, Times, 2006.

Chan Heng Chee. *Singapore: Politics of Survival 1965–1967.* Singapore, Oxford University Press, 1971.

A Sensation of Independence: Singapore's David Marshall. Singapore, Oxford University Press, 1984.

Chee Soon Juan. *Dare to Change.* Singapore, 1994.

Singapore: My Home Too. Singapore, Melodies Press Co, 1995.

Cherian, George. *Singapore: The Air-Conditioned Nation—Essays on the Politics of Comfort and Control, 1990–2000.* Singapore, Landmark Books, 2001.

Chew, Ernest C. T., and Lee, Edwin (Eds). *A History of Singapore.* Singapore, Oxford University Press, 1991.

Chong, Terence (Ed.). *Management of Success: Singapore Revisited.* Singapore, Institute of Southeast Asian Studies, 2010.

da Cunha, Derek. *Singapore in the New Millennium: Challenges Facing the City-State.* Singapore, Institute of Southeast Asian Studies, 2001.

Ern Ser Tan. *Does Class Matter? Social Stratification and Orientations in Singapore.* Singapore, World Scientific Publishing Co, 2004.

Farrel, Brian, and Hunter, Sandy (Eds). *Sixty Years On: The Fall of Singapore Revisited.* Singapore, Times Academic Press, 2003.

Francesh-Huidobro, Maria. *Government, Politics and the Environment: A Singapore Study.* Singapore, Institute of Southeast Asian Studies, 2008.

Ganesan, Narayanan. *Realism and Dependence in Singapore's Foreign Policy.* Abingdon, Routledge, 2005.

Goh, Daniel P. S., Gabrielpillai, Matilda, Holden, Philip, and Gaik Cheng Khoo (Eds). *Race and Multiculturalism in Malaysia and Singapore.* Abingdon, Routledge, 2009.

Gomez, James. *Self-Censorship: Singapore's Shame.* Singapore, Think Center, 2000.

Hack, Karl, and Blackburn, Kevin. *Did Singapore Have to Fall?: Churchill and the Impregnable Fortress.* London, RoutledgeCurzon, 2003.

Han Fook Kwang, Fernandez, Warren, and Tan, Sumiko. *Lee Kuan Yew: The Man and his Ideas.* Singapore, 1997.

Ho Khai Leong. *Shared Responsibilities, Unshared Power: The Politics of Policy-Making in Singapore.* Singapore, Times Academic Press, 2000.

Hong Liu and Sin Kiong Won. *Singapore Chinese Society in Transition: Business, Politics and Socio-Economic Change 1945–1965.* New York, NY, Peter Lang Publishing, 2004.

Hong Lysa and Huang Jianli. *The Scripting of a National History: Singapore and Its Pasts.* Washington, DC, University of Washington Press, 2008.

Kau Ah Keng, Tambayah Siok Kuan, Tan Soo Jiuan and Jung Kwon. *Understanding Singaporeans: Values, Lifestyles, Aspirations and Consumption Behaviours.* Singapore, World Scientific Publishing Co, 2004.

Kaur, Arunajeet. *The Sikhs in Singapore.* Singapore, Institute of Southeast Asian Studies, 2010.

Kenley, David. *New Culture in a New World: The May Fourth Movement and the Chinese Diaspora in Singapore, 1919–1932.* London, Routledge, 2003.

Khun Eng, Pearce. *State, Society and Religious Engineering: Towards a Reformist Buddhism in Singapore.* Singapore, Eastern Universities Press, 2003.

Lai Ah Eng (Ed.) *Religious Diversity in Singapore.* Singapore, Institute of Southeast Asian Studies, 2008.

Latif, Asad Ul-Iqbal. *Between Rising Powers: China, Singapore, India.* Singapore, Institute of Southeast Asian Studies, 2007.

Lim Kim San: A Builder of Singapore. Singapore, Institute of Southeast Asian Studies, 2009.

Lee, Edwin. *Singapore—The Unexpected Nation.* Singapore, Institute of Southeast Asian Studies, 2008.

Lee Kuan Yew. *The Battle for Merger.* Singapore, Ministry of Culture, 1961.

The Singapore Story: Memoirs of Lee Kuan Yew. Prentice Hall/ Simon & Schuster Asia, Singapore, 1998.

From Third World to First: The Singapore Story: 1965–2000. Singapore, Times Media Private and Straits Times Press, 2000.

Lee, Terence. *The Media, Cultural Control and Government in Singapore.* Abingdon, Routledge, 2010.

Leifer, Michael. *Singapore's Foreign Policy—Coping with Vulnerability.* London, Routledge, 2000.

Lian Kwen Fee and Chee Kiong Tong (Eds). *Social Policy in Post-Industrial Singapore.* Leiden, Netherlands, Brill Academic Publishers, 2008.

Lyons, Lenore. *State of Ambivalence: The Feminist Movement in Singapore.* Leiden, Netherlands, Brill Academic Publishers, 2004.

Mahizhnan, Arun, and Lee Tsao Yuan (Eds). *Singapore: Re-Engineered Success.* Oxford, Oxford University Press, 2002.

Makepeace, Walter, Brooke, Gilbert E., and Braddell, Roland St J. (Eds). *One Hundred Years of Singapore.* 2 vols, 1921, 1991.

McCarthy, Stephen. *The Political Theory of Tyranny in Singapore and Burma.* Abingdon, Routledge, 2006.

Milne, R. S., and Mauzy, Diane K. *Singapore: The Legacy of Lee Kuan Yew.* Boulder, CO, Westview Press, 1990.

Singapore Politics Under the People's Action Party. London, Routledge, 2002.

Mulliner, Kent. *Historical Dictionary of Singapore.* Lanham, MD, Scarecrow Press, 2002.

Murfett, Malcolm H., et al. *Between Two Oceans: A Military History of Singapore from First Settlement to Final British Withdrawal.* Singapore, Times Academic Press, 2004.

Mutalib, Hussin. *Parties and Politics: A Study of Opposition Parties and the PAP in Singapore.* Singapore, Eastern Universities Press, 2003.

Nasir, Kamaludeen Mohamed, Pereira, Alexius, and Turner, Bryan. *Muslims in Singapore: Piety, Politics and Policies.* Abingdon, Routledge, 2009.

Ng, Irene. *The Singapore Lion: A Biography of S. Rajaratnam.* Singapore, Institute of Southeast Asian Studies, 2010.

Ooi Kee Beng. *In Lieu of Ideology: An Intellectual Biography of Goh Keng Swee.* Singapore, Institute of Southeast Asian Studies, 2010.

Ortmann, Stephan. *Politics and Change in Singapore and Hong Kong: Containing Contention.* Abingdon, Routledge, 2010.

Plate, Tom. *Conversations with Lee Kuan Yew: Citizen Singapore—How to Build a Nation.* Singapore, Marshall Cavendish, 2010.

Preston, Peter. *Singapore in the Global System: Relationship, Structure and Change.* Abingdon, Routledge, 2008.

Rahim, Lily Zubaidah. *Singapore in the Malay World.* Abingdon, Routledge, 2009.

Rappa, Antonio L. *Modernity and Consumption: Theory, Politics and the Public in Singapore and Malaysia.* Singapore, World Scientific Publishing Co, 2002.

Reisman, David. *Social Policy in an Ageing Society: Age and Health in Singapore.* Cheltenham, Edward Elgar Publishing, 2009.

Saw Swee Hock. *Population Policies and Programmes in Singapore.* Singapore, Institute of Southeast Asian Studies, 2005.

The Population of Singapore. Singapore, Institute of Southeast Asian Studies, 2nd Edn, 2007.

Bibliography of Singapore Demography. Singapore, Institute of Southeast Asian Studies, 2005.

Singapore Government. *The Next Lap.* Singapore, 1991.

Shadrake, Alan. *Once a Jolly Hangman: Singapore Justice in the Dock.* Petaling Jaya, Strategic Information and Research Development Center, 3rd Edn, 2010.

Song Ong Siang. *One Hundred Years' History of the Chinese in Singapore.* Oxford University Press, 1923, 1967, 1984.

Suryadinata, Leo. *Ethnic Chinese in Singapore and Malaysia.* Singapore, Times Academic Press, 2002.

Tan, Kevin Y. L., and Thio, Li-Ann (Eds). *Evolution of a Revolution: 40 Years of the Singapore Constitution.* Abingdon, Routledge Cavendish, 2008.

Tan Tarn How (Ed.). *Singapore Perspectives: A New Singapore.* Singapore, World Scientific Publishing Co, 2008.

Tan, Yong Soon, Jean, Lee Tung, and Tan, Karen. *Clean, Green and Blue: Singapore's Journey Towards Environmental and Water Sustainability.* Singapore, Institute of Southeast Asian Studies, 2008.

Teo, Peggy, Mehta, Kalyani, Thang Leng Leng and Chan, Angelique. *Ageing in Singapore: Service Needs and the State.* Abingdon, Routledge, 2006.

Teo, Youyenn. *Neoliberal Morality in Singapore: How Family Policies Make State and Society.* Abingdon, Routledge, 2011.

Tong Chee Kiong. *Rationalizing Religion: Religious Conversion, Revivalism, and Competition in Singapore Society.* Leiden and Boston, Brill Academic Publishers, 2007.

Tong Chee Kiong and Lian Kwen Fee (Eds). *The Making of Singapore Sociology: Society and State.* Leiden, Netherlands, Brill Academic Publishers, 2003.

Trocki, Carl A. *Singapore: Wealth, Power and the Culture of Control.* Abingdon, Routledge, 2005.

Turnbull, C. M. *A History of Singapore 1819–1988.* Oxford University Press, 1989.

A History of Malaysia, Singapore, and Brunei. Sydney, Allen and Unwin, 1989.

The Straits Settlements, 1826–67. London, Athlone Press, and Kuala Lumpur, Oxford University Press, 1972.

Dateline Singapore: 150 Years History of the Straits Times. Singapore, Singapore Press Holdings, 1995.

Vasil, Raj. *Governing Singapore: A History of National Development and Democracy.* Singapore, Institute of Southeast Asian Studies, 2000.

Velayutham, Selvaraj. *Responding to Globalization: Nation, Culture, and Identity in Singapore.* Singapore, Institute of Southeast Asian Studies, 2007.

Wijeysingha, Vincent. *Social Engineering in Singapore: Social Policy, State Making and the Quest for Economic Success.* Abingdon, RoutledgeCurzon, 2006.

Worthington, Ross. *Governance in Singapore.* London, Routledge Curzon, 2002.

Yao, Sauchou. *Singapore: The State and the Culture of Excess.* Abingdon, Routledge, 2007.

Yeoh, Brenda S. A. *Contesting Space in Colonial Singapore: Power Relations and the Urban Built Environment.* Singapore, Singapore University Press, 2003.

Zahari, Said. *Dark Clouds at Dawn: A Political Memoir.* Kuala Lumpur, INSAN, 2001.

Zhang Wei-Bin. *Singapore's Modernization: Westernization and Modernizing Confucian Manifestations.* New York, Nova Science Publishers, 2002.

Economy

Abeysinghe, Tilak, and Choy Keen-Meng. *The Singapore Economy: An Econometric Perspective.* Abingdon, Routledge, 2008.

Basu Das, Sanchita. *Road to Recovery: Singapore's Journey through the Global Crisis.* Singapore, Institute of Southeast Asian Studies, 2010.

Bhaskaran, Manu. *Re-inventing the Asian Model: The Case of the Singapore Economy.* Singapore, Times Academic Press, 2003.

Chia Wai Mun and Sng Hui Ying (Eds). *Singapore and Asia in a Globalized World: Contemporary Economic Issues and Policies.* Singapore, World Scientific Publishing Co, 2008.

Dent, Christopher. *The Foreign Economic Policies of Singapore, South Korea and Taiwan.* Cheltenham, Edward Elgar Publishing, 2002.

Freeman, Nick, Chia Siow Yue, Venkatesan, R., and Malvea, S. V. (Eds). *Growth and Development of the IT Industry in Bangalore and Singapore: A Comparative Study.* Singapore, Institute of Southeast Asian Studies, 2001.

Ghesquiere, Henri. *Singapore's Success: Engineering Economic Growth.* Singapore, Thomson Learning, 2007.

Hon Sui Sen. *Singapore's Economic Success.* Singapore, Times Academic Press, 2004.

Institute of Southeast Asian Studies. *Energy Perspectives on Singapore and the Region.* Singapore, Institute of Southeast Asian Studies, 2007.

Kumar, Sree, Siddique, Sharon, and Hedrick-Wong, Yuwa. *Mind the Gaps: Singapore Business in China.* Singapore, Institute of Southeast Asian Studies, 2005.

Mirza, Hafiz. *Multinationals and the Growth of the Singapore Economy.* Abingdon, Routledge, 2011.

Murray, Geoffrey, and Perera, Audrey (Eds). *Singapore: The Global City State.* Richmond, Surrey, Curzon Press, 1996.

Ng, Weng Hoong. *Singapore, the Energy Economy: From The First Refinery To The End Of Cheap Oil, 1960–2010.* Abingdon, Routledge, 2011.

Pang, Eul-Soo. *The U.S.-Singapore Free Trade Agreement: An American Perspective on Power, Trade and Security in the Asia Pacific.* Singapore, Institute of Southeast Asian Studies, 2011.

Peebles, Gavin, and Wilson, Peter. *The Singapore Economy.* Cheltenham, and Brookfield, USA, Edward Elgar Publishing, 1996.

Economic Growth and Development in Singapore: Past and Future. Cheltenham, and Brookfield, USA, Edward Elgar Publishing, 2002.

Rajan, Ramkishen S. (Ed.). *Sustaining Competitiveness in the New Global Economy: The Experience of Singapore.* Cheltenham, and Brookfield, USA, Edward Elgar Publishing, 2003.

Rajan, Ramkishen S., Sen, Rahul, and Siregar, Reza. *Singapore and Free Trade Agreements: Economic Relations with Japan and the United States.* Singapore, Institute of Southeast Asian Studies, 2001.

Sen, Rahul. *Trade Policy and the Role of Regional and Bilateral FTAs: The Case of New Zealand and Singapore.* Singapore, Institute of Southeast Asian Studies, 2007.

Sng Hui Ying and Chia Wai Mun (Eds). *Crisis Management and Public Policy: Singapore's Approach to Economic Resilience.* Singapore, World Scientific Publishing Co, 2011.

Sung, Johnny. *Explaining the Economic Success of Singapore: The Developmental Worker as the Missing Link.* Cheltenham, Edward Elgar Publishing, 2006.

Tan Chwee Huat. *Singapore Financial and Business Sourcebook.* Singapore, Singapore University Press, 2002.

Financial Services in Singapore. Singapore, Singapore University Press, 2004.

Financial Markets and Institutions in Singapore. Singapore, Singapore University Press, 2006.

Tan Ern Ser, Yeoh, Brenda S. A., and Wang, Jennifer (Eds). *Tourism Management and Policy: Perspectives from Singapore.* Singapore, World Scientific Publishing Co, 2002.

Tan Sook Yee. *Private Ownership of Public Housing in Singapore.* Singapore, Times Academic Press, 1998.

Toh Mun Heng and Tan Kong Yam (Eds). *Competitiveness of the Singapore Economy: A Strategic Perspective.* Singapore, Singapore University Press and World Scientific Publishing Co, 1998.

Wilson, Peter. *Challenges for the Singapore Economy After the Global Financial Crisis.* Singapore, World Scientific Publishing Co, 2011.

Wong Tai Chee and Guillot, Xavier. *A Roof Over Every Head: Singapore's Housing Policy Between State Monopoly and Privatization.* Singapore, Institute of Southeast Asian Studies, 2005.

Yahya, Faizal bin. *Economic Cooperation Between Singapore and India: An Alliance in the Making?* Abingdon, Routledge, 2008.

TAIWAN

Physical and Social Geography

The Republic of China has, since 1949, been confined mainly to the province of Taiwan (comprising one large island and several much smaller ones), which lies off the south-east coast of the Chinese mainland. The territory under the Republic's effective jurisdiction consists of the island of Taiwan (also known as Formosa) and nearby islands, including the P'enghu (Pescadores) group, together with a few other islands that lie just off the mainland and form part of the province of Fujian (Fukien), west of Taiwan. The largest of these is Kinmen (Jinmen), also known as Quemoy, which (with three smaller islands) is about 10 km from the port of Xiamen (Amoy), while five other islands under Taiwan's control, notably Matsu (Mazu), lie further north, near Fuzhou. The island of Taiwan itself is separated from the mainland by the Taiwan Strait, which is about 220 km wide at its broadest point and 130 km at the narrowest point. Taiwan is 36,188 sq km (13,972 sq miles) in area, measuring 394 km from north to south and, at its widest point, 144 km from east to west. The island straddles the Tropic of Cancer. The Central Range of mountains occupies almost 50% of the island, extending 270 km from north to south. At 3,952 m, Mount Jade is the island's highest point. Owing to the mountainous character of the relief, in 2005 only 23% of the land area was cultivated, while forests covered 58%. The climate is subtropical in the north and tropical in the south, being strongly modified by oceanic and relief factors. Apart from the mountainous core, winter temperatures average 15°C and summer temperatures about 26°C. Monsoon rains visit the north-east in winter (October to March) but come to the south in summer, and are abundant, the mean annual average rainfall being 2,580 mm. Typhoons are often serious, particularly between July and September, when windward mountain slopes may receive as much as 300 mm of rain within 24 hours.

Taiwan is not well endowed with natural resources. Small amounts of petroleum and natural gas are produced. Marble is mined, and modest reserves of coal are located in the north of the island.

The population totalled 23,162,000 at 31 December 2010. This gave Taiwan a population density of 640.0 per sq km, one of the highest in the world. The crude birth rate in 2009 was 7.2 per 1,000 (compared with 44.8 per 1,000 in 1956), and the crude death rate in 2010 was 6.3 per 1,000 (compared with 8.0 per 1,000 in 1956). The death rate is one of the lowest in Asia, as is the infant mortality rate (deaths under five years of age per 1,000 live births), which stood at 6.1 in 2006. In 2009 nearly 16.3% of Taiwan's population were estimated to be under 15 years of age; 69.1% were aged between 15 and 64; and 14.6% of the population were 65 and over (compared with 2.5% in 1962). With the expansion of industry, Taiwan's population has become increasingly urbanized. Between 1966 and 2002 the proportion living in towns of 100,000 or more inhabitants increased from 31.0% to 60.6%.

History

HISTORICAL BACKGROUND

The geographic location of the island of Taiwan has determined its history. Situated between the Malay archipelago, China and Japan, the island has had an eventful past. The original inhabitants were tribes of Malayan origin. China's relations with the island date from AD 607, but the first small Chinese settlements were not established there until the 14th century. During the 17th century Portuguese, Spanish and Dutch traders visited the island from time to time. In 1624 the Dutch settled the southern part. Two years later came the Spanish, who occupied the northern part. In 1642 the Dutch expelled the Spanish, and in 1661 the Dutch were, in turn, driven out by the Chinese Ming loyalist Zheng Cheng Gong (Coxinga) who ruled, with his sons, for 22 years. In 1663 the Qing emperor, Kang Xi, invaded and conquered the island, which became a part of his empire until it was ceded to the Japanese at the end of the Sino-Japanese war of 1895. During the period of independence and Qing rule, massive immigration from the mainland established the ethnic Chinese character of the island.

Following Japan's defeat in the Second World War of 1939–45, Taiwan became one of the provinces of the Republic of China, ruled by the Kuomintang (KMT, Nationalist Party). The leader of the KMT was Gen. Chiang Kai-shek, President of the Republic since 1928. Virtually all of Taiwan's exportable surpluses went to the Chinese mainland. In 1947 misgovernment by mainland officials led to a large-scale, but peaceful, political uprising, which was repressed with great brutality. In early 1949 the KMT regime, driven from the mainland by the Communists, moved to Taiwan's capital, Taipei, along with approximately 2m. soldiers, officials and their dependants. Thus, the island's population increased from 6.8m. to 7.5m. in 1950, excluding military personnel numbering 600,000. The KMT regime continued to assert that it was the rightful Chinese Government, in opposition to the People's Republic of China (proclaimed by the victorious Communists in 1949), and declared its intention to recover control of the mainland from the Communists. (For further details of events prior to 1949, see the chapter on the People's Republic of China.)

THE ESTABLISHMENT OF CHINESE NATIONALIST RULE AND SUBSEQUENT FOREIGN RELATIONS

Although its effective control was limited to Taiwan, the KMT regime continued to be dominated by politicians who had formerly been in power on the mainland. In support of the regime's claim to be the legitimate government of all China, Taiwan's legislative bodies were filled mainly by surviving mainland members, and the representatives of the island's native Taiwanese majority occupied only a minority of seats. Unable to replenish their mainland representation, the National Assembly (last elected fully in 1947) and other organs extended their terms of office indefinitely, although fewer than one-half of the original members were alive on Taiwan by the 1980s. While it promised eventually to reconquer the mainland, the KMT regime was largely preoccupied with ensuring its own survival, and promoting economic development, on Taiwan. Under the KMT Government, Taiwan achieved a remarkable record of economic growth, although the island's regeneration in the period after 1949 was assisted by massive US aid. The years 1951 and 1952 were notable for government reorganization. There followed a four-year (1953–56) period of adjustment and planning. In 1957 and 1958 the cumulative effect of domestic reform and US aid brought a great improvement in economic and other fields. The prominent developments of this period include the land reform programme, the rapid development of industry and the establishment of a system of nine-year free public education. The political domination of the island by immigrants from the mainland caused resentment among the Taiwanese, and led to demands for increased democratization and for the recognition of Taiwan as a state independent of China. However, the KMT consistently rejected demands for independence, constantly restating the party's long-standing policy of seeking political reunification, under KMT terms, with the mainland.

Membership of International Organizations and Diplomatic Recognition

The KMT Government continued to represent China at the UN (and as a permanent member of the UN Security Council) until October 1971, when the People's Republic of China was admitted in place of Taiwan. Nationalist China was subsequently expelled from several other international organizations. In June 1995 Taiwan offered to make a donation of US $1,000m., to be used for the establishment of an international development fund, if the island were permitted to rejoin the UN. However, Taiwan's attempts to secure re-entry to the UN continued to be rejected. Nevertheless, the Taiwanese leadership pledged to continue the island's campaign to gain re-entry, stating that henceforth it would make its application under the name of Taiwan, rather than the 'Republic of China'. In July 2007, however, the application under this alternative name was rejected. The leadership had attempted to argue that, as the world's 18th largest economy and the seventh largest investor, Taiwan should no longer be excluded from the organization. In September 2008, for the 16th consecutive year, the UN rejected a proposal urging Taiwan's participation. Taiwan subsequently began to consider the adoption of a different approach to the issue of UN representation, and it was expected to focus henceforth on securing representation in selected UN specialized agencies. In September 2009 the Ministry of Foreign Affairs confirmed that it was renouncing its immediate quest for a seat at the UN. This change of strategy was confirmed in August 2010.

In November 1991 Taiwan joined the Asia-Pacific Economic Cooperation (APEC) forum as 'Chinese Taipei'. As 'Taipei, China', Taiwan also remained a member of the Asian Development Bank (ADB). In September 1992, under the name of the 'Separate Customs Territory of Taiwan, P'enghu, Kinmen and Matsu', Taiwan was granted observer status at the General Agreement on Tariffs and Trade (GATT), and discussions on its application for full membership of the successor World Trade Organization (WTO) followed. Taiwan was finally approved for membership of the body in late September 2001, and on 1 January 2002 Taiwan formally became a member of the WTO. In April 1997 the Minister of Foreign Affairs announced that Taiwan had applied to be an observer of the World Health Organization (WHO) and would be seeking similar status in other UN agencies. However, its application was unsuccessful, as was a second attempt to gain observer status in May 1998 and subsequent annual attempts. In May 2003 the People's Republic of China strongly opposed a US proposal that Taiwan be permitted to participate in WHO. The People's Republic reiterated its view in May 2008, when for the 12th time the World Health Assembly (the WHO governing body) rejected a proposal, supported by The Gambia and by the Pacific nation of Palau, that Taiwan be granted observer status in WHO. In April 2009, in an important sign of improving bilateral relations, China abandoned its objections to Taiwan's attendance as an observer, under the name of Chinese Taipei. In May 2011, however, the Taiwanese President claimed that China had exerted pressure on WHO to refer to Taiwan as a Chinese province in its documentation.

After 1971 a number of countries broke off diplomatic relations with Taiwan and recognized the People's Republic of China. The British Government established full diplomatic relations with the People's Republic in March 1972. When the Japanese Government sought a rapprochement with China in September 1972, Taiwan broke off diplomatic relations with Japan. In August 1992 the Republic of Korea (South Korea) accorded recognition to the People's Republic of China, but unofficial links were to be maintained. The USA maintained diplomatic relations with Taiwan until 1978. Various changes in diplomatic allegiance followed, particularly on the part of Caribbean, Pacific and African nations (see below). Despite this lack of formal recognition in the international community, Taiwan's commercial relations with numerous countries continued to flourish, and in 2008 around 50 countries without full diplomatic relations with Taiwan maintained representative offices or visa-issuing centres on the island. In mid-2011 the Government of Taiwan was recognized by 23 countries.

Relations with the USA

In 1954 the USA, which had refused to recognize the People's Republic of China, signed a mutual security treaty with the KMT Government, pledging to protect Taiwan and the Pescadores. In 1955 the islands of Kinmen (Quemoy) and Matsu, lying just off shore from the mainland, were included in the protected area. However, US documents declassified in 2002 revealed that in 1971 the USA had secretly pledged to China that it would not support Taiwan's independence, in exchange for Chinese assistance in ending the Viet Nam War. In February 1973 the US Government announced that it would continue to maintain diplomatic relations with Taiwan but, at the same time, would establish an 'American mission' in Beijing and allow a 'Chinese liaison office' to open in Washington, DC. In December 1978, however, prior to a visit to Washington by Deng Xiaoping, the leader of the People's Republic, there was a dramatic change in US policy towards Taiwan. Diplomatic recognition was withdrawn from Taiwan as constituting the Republic of China, and the US embassy was closed. Nevertheless, Taiwan, as an unrecognized but existing state, remained assured of continuing US protection and trade until some form of reconciliation between China and Taiwan could be brought about. The USA also terminated the mutual security treaty with Taiwan. However, commercial links were maintained, and Taiwan's purchase of armaments from the USA became a controversial issue. In August 1982 a joint Sino-US communiqué was published, in which the USA pledged to reduce gradually its sale of armaments to Taiwan. In April 1984 the US President, Ronald Reagan, gave an assurance that he would continue to support Taiwan, despite the improved relations between the USA and the People's Republic. In mid-1989 US relations with the People's Republic deteriorated sharply, following the Tiananmen Square massacre in Beijing. In September 1992 President George Bush announced the sale of up to 150 F-16 fighter aircraft to Taiwan, and in December Carla Hills, the US trade representative, became the first senior US government official to visit the island since the severance of diplomatic relations in early 1979.

In September 1994 the USA announced a modification of its policy towards Taiwan, henceforth permitting senior-level bilateral meetings to be held in US government offices. In December the US Secretary of Transportation visited the Ministry of Foreign Affairs in Taipei, the first US official of cabinet rank to visit Taiwan for more than 15 years. In June 1995 Taiwanese President Lee Teng-hui was permitted to make a four-day unofficial visit to the USA, where he met members of the US Congress, following which China recalled its ambassador from Washington.

In March 1996, as China began a series of missile tests off the Taiwanese coast (see below), the USA stationed two naval convoys in waters east of the island. US President Bill Clinton agreed to the sale of defensive weaponry. In September President Lee and the US Deputy Treasury Secretary, Lawrence Summers, met in Taipei for discussions. In November Taiwan welcomed the pledge of the US Department of State to continue to sell defensive weapons to the island. However, some controversy arose in late 1996 when irregularities in the financing of President Clinton's re-election campaign, involving Taiwanese donors, were reported. Furthermore, it was alleged that a senior KMT official had offered an illicit contribution of US $15m. to the Democratic Party in Washington. In early 1997 the first of the *Patriot* anti-missile air defence systems, purchased from the USA under an arrangement made in 1993, were reported to have been deployed on Taiwan. The first of the F-16s were delivered to the island in April 1997. However, in mid-1998 a statement by President Clinton affirming that the USA would not support Taiwan's membership of the UN was sharply criticized. In October the Taiwanese Chief of Staff, Gen. Tang Fei, made a secret two-week visit to the USA. This was regarded as an extremely sensitive matter, in view of the fact that Koo Chen-fu (see Relations with the People's Republic, below) had recently met with President Jiang Zemin. In the following month the People's Republic complained to the USA following the visit of the US Secretary of Energy to Taiwan.

In January 1999 the People's Republic was antagonized by Taiwan's proposed inclusion in the US-led Theater Missile Defense (TMD) anti-missile system. In August the USA reaffirmed its commitment to defend Taiwan against Chinese military action. In October of that year the island welcomed the adoption, albeit in modified form, of the Taiwan Security Enhancement Act (TSEA), establishing direct military links, by the International Relations Committee of the US House of Representatives, despite opposition from the Clinton Administration. The House of Representatives overwhelmingly approved the Act in February 2000. In April, however, the US Senate postponed consideration of the Act at the behest of the Taiwanese President-elect, Chen Shui-bian, in order not to antagonize China during the sensitive period preceding his inauguration. In the same month the US Government announced that it had decided to defer the sale of four naval destroyers to Taiwan. In September the USA granted a transit visa to Taiwanese Vice-President Annette Lu to stay in New York en route to Central America. In October China condemned a resolution approved by the US Congress that supported Taiwan's participation in the UN and other international organizations.

The election of George W. Bush to the US Presidency in late 2000 was widely expected to boost Taiwan's relations with the USA at the expense of the latter's relations with the mainland. Bush's uncompromising stance against China became more apparent after the crisis over the detention of a US spy plane and its crew following its collision with a Chinese fighter plane in April 2001. The USA subsequently agreed to sell Taiwan military equipment and armaments worth a total of US $4,000m., and President Bush declared that the USA would do whatever was necessary to defend Taiwan, in the event of an invasion by the mainland. China was further antagonized by the visit of President Chen Shui-bian to the USA in May 2001, when he met business leaders and members of the US Congress. Chen's visit was followed by that of his predecessor, Lee Teng-hui, in June, as well as by a group of Taiwanese military and intelligence officials on an exchange programme, the first such exchange since 1979. Also in June 2001, Taiwan successfully tested its US-made *Patriot* air defence missiles for the first time. In August two US Navy aircraft carrier battlegroups staged a one-day exercise in the South China Sea, coinciding with Chinese military exercises in the Taiwan Strait. In December the US House of Representatives approved the 2002 Defense Authorization Act, which included weapons sales to Taiwan.

In January 2002 a delegation from a US 'think tank', consisting of retired generals and officials, visited the mainland, and subsequently Taiwan, where they met President Chen and other senior officials and discussed the island's security. Also in January, Vice-President Annette Lu made a brief stopover in New York, en route to South America. In March the Minister of National Defense, Gen. (retd) Tang Yao-ming visited the USA to attend a private three-day defence and security conference in Florida, where he met the US Deputy Secretary of Defense, Paul Wolfowitz, and Assistant Secretary of State James Kelly. Tang was the first incumbent to make a non-transit visit to the USA since 1979. Meanwhile, the scandal in late March concerning former President Lee Teng-hui's co-operation with the island's intelligence services in secretly establishing an unauthorized fund (see below) embarrassed Taiwan and several US lobbying groups, which had received sums of this money. In April, however, the US Under-Secretary of Commerce for International Trade, Grant Aldonas, became the most senior official of George W. Bush's Administration to visit Taiwan, where he had a meeting with President Chen Shui-bian.

In September 2002 the Taiwanese Government urged the state-owned China Airlines (CAL) to place a US $2,000m. order for US-manufactured Boeing aircraft for its fleet, rather than the rival European-manufactured Airbus. However, in October CAL awarded the contract to Airbus, while also purchasing 10 Boeing aircraft. Also in September 2002, the US Congress approved the Foreign Relations Authorization Act, Fiscal Year 2003, which for the first time allowed US Department of State and other government agencies' staff to work at the American Institute in Taiwan, the unofficial US mission to the island. Previously, US officials were required to embark upon sabbatical leave before serving at the institute. US military officers would also be allowed to work there, albeit not in uniform. Furthermore, the bill recognized Taiwan as a major non-NATO ally of the USA. In August 2003 plans for Taiwan's purchase of four naval destroyers from the USA were finalized. Taiwan also made an advance payment towards the acquisition of eight new diesel submarines from the USA. In November President Chen undertook a visit to New York, in the course of which he was permitted to make a public speech.

In April 2004 Therese Shaheen, head of the American Institute in Taiwan, resigned after reportedly having misrepresented US policy on Taiwanese independence. Her departure prompted the resignation of Taiwanese Minister of Foreign Affairs. In June the Executive Yuan (cabinet) approved a special defence budget for the purchase of weapons from the USA, which had been agreed in April 2001. Following public opposition in Taiwan to the special defence budget, the USA warned that there would be serious implications if the armaments purchase were not approved by the Taiwanese legislature. However, in late 2005 the opposition parties in the Legislative Yuan continued to obstruct the special defence budget, despite significant reductions in the overall scale of the proposed purchase. In January 2006 the US Government described as 'inflammatory' President Chen's proposals for the abolition of the National Unification Council (NUC) and the reunification guidelines established by it (see below). The US Department of State emphasized that it supported the maintenance of the status quo in cross-Straits relations, within the overall framework of a 'one China' policy.

In May 2006 Deputy US Trade Representative, Karan Bhatia, visited Taiwan to discuss trade issues. In the following month the USA reacted positively to the announcement of a programme of direct charter flights to the mainland (see below). Meanwhile, the USA continued to press Taiwan to purchase its weapons, with US officials expressing 'grave concern' over Taiwan's defence capabilities when two legislators of the Democratic Progressive Party (DPP) visited Washington, DC, in August. (The remarks followed the Taiwanese opposition's rejection in April, for the 50th time, of the special defence budget to permit the procurement of US weapons—see below.) The two legislators also received a sharp rebuff with regard to Taiwan's renewed request to open negotiations on a bilateral free trade agreement (FTA). Nevertheless, the two sides were to continue to focus on discussions under the joint Trade and Investment Framework Agreement (TIFA). As President Chen became increasingly embroiled in various scandals, the director of the American Institute in Taiwan, Stephen Young, entered the fray to state that the USA wished Chen to remain in power for the sake of the stability of the island. The USA's commitment to the security of Taiwan was confirmed in February 2007 when the US Department of Defense announced the sale of more than 450 missiles to the island. In May, furthermore, Young reiterated his appeal to the Taiwanese legislature to grant approval to the outstanding defence budget that would permit the purchase of weaponry from the USA (aspects of the sale were expected to proceed following the legislature's approval of an amended budget in June 2007).

The USA continued to exert pressure on Taiwan to give up its efforts to join the UN under the proposed name of Taiwan. In August 2007 the US Deputy Secretary of State, John Negroponte, declared that it would be 'a mistake' if Taiwan were to proceed with a proposal to submit to referendum the issue of UN membership concurrently with the 2008 presidential election, urging the Government to respect the status quo. The referendums were duly conducted in March 2008 (although the required turn-out of 50% was not achieved—see below). Taiwan's President-elect, Ma Ying-jeou, maintained that he would work to improve relations with the USA. Meanwhile, Taiwan's purchase of various types of US defence equipment, which had been approved by the Taiwan legislature in 2007, made little progress until October 2008, when the Bush Administration confirmed its intention to sell weaponry worth almost US $6,500m., although the agreement excluded the advanced F-16 fighter aircraft and diesel submarines requested by Taiwan. The announcement of the sale was welcomed by

Senator Barack Obama as being consistent with the USA's obligations under the Taiwan Relations Act. No immediate change in US policy towards Taiwan followed Obama's inauguration as US President in early 2009.

In October 2009, upholding a ruling by the US Court of Appeals in April, the US Supreme Court refused to hear a case brought by Roger Lin, a Taiwanese activist who, in the hope that former President Chen Shui-bian's recent conviction on charges of corruption (see below) might be quashed, had attempted to argue that the USA remained the principal occupying power of Taiwan and therefore retained control of the island. Chen instigated his own unsuccessful case in the US Court of Appeals for the Armed Forces.

The lack of any reference to the Taiwan Relations Act in a joint statement issued by Presidents Hu Jintao and Barack Obama during the latter's visit to China in November 2009 aroused much concern on the island. Although a reference to the Act was made by Obama at a subsequent press conference in Beijing, President Ma was urged to seek immediate clarification of US policy towards Taiwan. None the less, the USA remained the leading supplier of weaponry to the island, and in January 2010 the Obama Administration's decision to proceed with the sale of defence equipment to the value of US $6,400m., which included 60 helicopters, was welcomed by Taiwan. However, the announcement provoked an unusually strong reaction from the Chinese Government. In May 2011 a KMT member of the Taiwanese legislature appeared to confirm the postponement of the purchase of the equipment, ostensibly owing to budget constraints, and in June President Ma acknowledged that Taiwan's renewed attempts to purchase from the USA advanced F-16 fighter aircraft (to replace the island's rapidly ageing fleet of F-16s) were not proceeding smoothly. Tsai Ing-wen, presidential candidate of the opposition pro-independence DPP, visited the USA in September in order to discuss bilateral issues and establish channels of communication, in preparation for the possibility of a change of government in Taiwan. Although Tsai's approach to the issue of independence was regarded as more moderate than that of Taiwan's last DPP President, the Obama Administration indicated that the recent improvement in cross-Straits relations might be jeopardized if the DPP were to take power following the elections of early 2012.

Relations with Japan

In February 1993, for the first time since the rupture in diplomatic relations in 1972, the Taiwanese Minister of Foreign Affairs paid a visit to Japan, leading to a strong protest from the People's Republic. In September 1994 pressure from China resulted in the withdrawal of President Lee's invitation to attend the forthcoming Asian Games in Hiroshima. Instead, however, the Taiwanese Vice-Premier was permitted to visit Japan. Similarly, in July 1995 Japan announced that the Taiwanese Vice-Premier would not be permitted to attend a meeting of APEC members to be held in Osaka in November. Instead, President Lee was represented by Koo Chen-fu, Chairman of the Straits Exchange Foundation (SEF, see below). Taiwan's relations with Japan were also strained by the issue of adequate compensation for the thousands of Asian (mostly Korean) women used by Japanese troops for sexual purposes during the Second World War. In October 1996 Taiwan rejected a Japanese offer of nominal compensation for such Taiwanese women.

Taiwan's relations with Japan were also affected by a dispute relating to a group of uninhabited islets in the East China Sea: known as the Tiaoyutai (Diaoyu Dao) in Chinese, or Senkaku in Japanese, and situated about 200 km north-east of Taiwan and 300 km west of the Japanese island of Okinawa, the islands were claimed by Taiwan, China and Japan. In July 1996, following the construction of a lighthouse on one of the islands by a Japanese right-wing group, the Taiwanese Ministry of Foreign Affairs lodged a strong protest over Japan's decision to incorporate the islands within its 200-mile (370-km) exclusive economic zone. Further tensions related to the issue of Taiwanese fishing rights within the disputed waters. In October 1997 it was reported that Japanese patrol boats were forcibly intercepting Taiwanese fishing vessels. In November 1999, however, the Governor of Tokyo paid an official visit to Taiwan. In March 2002 it was revealed that Japanese politicians, including former Prime Minister Ryutaro Hashimoto, had received money from an unauthorized fund established by former President Lee Teng-hui in order to procure influence in Japan. However, the incident did not damage commercial relations. In January 2003 Taiwan, along with China, condemned Japan's attempts to assert sovereignty over the Tiaoyutai Islands by renting them out to private companies. In September 2003 the second Taiwan-Japan Forum opened in Tokyo, at which issues of mutual concern were discussed. In February 2005, as part of a revised strategic understanding with the USA, Japan identified Taiwan's security as a 'common strategic objective' for the first time. In January 2007 the Taiwanese Government announced that it would designate 2007 as 'Taiwan-Japan Cultural Exchange Year'. In June a visit by former President Lee to the Yasukuni Shrine, a controversial war memorial in Japan, further antagonized the mainland.

The dispute over the sovereignty of the Tiaoyutai Islands, and disagreements over fishing rights, continued, with Taiwanese fishermen repeatedly complaining of harassment by Japanese patrol boats. In June 2005 an armed naval frigate, carrying the Taiwanese Minister of National Defense, the President of the Legislative Yuan and 15 legislators, was dispatched to the region, reportedly in response to these complaints of harassment. Subsequent negotiations between Taiwan and Japan over fishing rights, the 15th round of talks on the issue since 1996, concluded without agreement in July 2005. In September the Taiwanese President's Secretary-General, Yu Shyi-kun, attended a forum on relations between Taiwan and Japan in Tokyo, thus becoming the most senior Taiwanese official to visit Japan since the withdrawal of diplomatic recognition in 1972. In June 2008, following an accident involving a Taiwanese boat and a vessel of the Japanese coastguard off the Tiaoyutai Islands, Taiwanese protesters entered the islands' territorial waters, accompanied by the Taiwanese coastguard. The newly elected President, Ma Ying-jeou, reiterated Taiwan's sovereignty over the islands shortly afterwards.

In July 2009, in a major concession to expatriate Taiwanese, the Japanese legislature approved a revision of immigration law to permit Taiwanese resident in Japan henceforth to declare Taiwan, rather than China, as their nation of citizenship when submitting an application for residence in Japan. The removal of the incumbent Liberal-Democratic Government of Japan at legislative elections in August 2009, after more than 50 years of near-uninterrupted rule, was not expected to have a major impact on Taiwan's relations with Japan. Like its predecessor, the incoming administration of the Democratic Party of Japan did not support Taiwanese independence but opposed the use of force by the People's Republic against the island. With the inauguration of a new air link, in October 2010 Shinzo Abe, the former Japanese Prime Minister, flew to Taiwan, where he had discussions with President Ma. In April 2011, however, the Taiwanese Government formally protested against Japan's renewal of its claim over the Tiaoyutai Islands. Taiwan also protested to Japan in June following an incident in which a Taiwanese fishing vessel, conveying activists participating in a protest about the Tiaoyutai Islands, was reportedly prevented by Japanese patrol vessels from sailing to the disputed islands.

Relations with South-East Asia

Despite the lack of formal diplomatic links and repeated obstruction from mainland China, Taiwan continued its attempts to develop good relations with the countries of South-East Asia. In March 1989 President Lee undertook a state visit to Singapore, the first official visit overseas by a Taiwanese head of state for 12 years. (In October 1990, however, Singapore established diplomatic relations with the People's Republic of China.) In February 1994 President Lee embarked upon an eight-day tour of South-East Asia. His itinerary incorporated the Philippines, Indonesia and Thailand, all three of which maintained diplomatic relations with the People's Republic of China. Although the tour was described as informal, President Lee had meetings with the three countries' heads of state, leading to protests from China.

In September 1996 the Taiwanese Minister of Foreign Affairs was obliged to curtail an ostensibly private visit to Jakarta (where he was reported to have had discussions with his Indonesian counterpart), following objections from China. The Malaysian and Singaporean Prime Ministers met their Taiwanese counterpart in Taiwan in November 1997. In January 1998 the Taiwanese Premier, Vincent Siew, met senior officials during a visit to the Philippines and Singapore. The Premier's negotiations with the Malaysian Deputy Prime Minister and Minister of Finance, held in Taiwan in February1998, concentrated on issues. Vincent Siew undertook a reciprocal visit to Malaysia in April. China was highly critical of these visits, accusing Taiwan of seeking to gain political advantage from the regional economic crisis through its offers of financial support. Vice-President Lu also visited Indonesia in August 2002 and met several cabinet ministers. While in Indonesia, Lu discussed possible liquefied natural gas projects, investment and migrant labour. In December, however, President Chen was forced to cancel a trip to Indonesia after that country came under heavy pressure from China.

Taiwan's relations with the Philippines were seriously jeopardized in August 1999 when the Government threatened to refuse entry to Filipino labourers, in apparent retaliation for the Philippine Government's unilateral termination of its aviation agreement with Taipei. Flights to the Philippines were intermittently suspended in subsequent months. In June 2000 the Taiwanese Government imposed a three-month ban on new work permits for Philippine nationals. In September, however, a new aviation agreement was signed. Bilateral relations were severely tested again in February 2011 when, despite Taiwan's request that they be repatriated to their homeland, 14 Taiwanese citizens suspected of fraud were deported to China by the Philippine authorities, along with 10 mainland Chinese alleged to be their accomplices. Taiwan recalled its representative from the Philippines and demanded a formal apology for the incident. A presidential envoy was dispatched to Taipei by the Philippine Government in an attempt to restore good relations.

The question of the sovereignty of the Spratly Islands, situated in the South China Sea and to which five countries as well as Taiwan laid claim, remained unresolved. Believed to possess petroleum and gas resources, in addition to encompassing rich fishing areas, the grouping comprises more than 100 small islands and reefs. A contingent of Taiwanese marines has been maintained on Taiping Island, the largest of the disputed islands, located some 1,574 km south-west of Taiwan. A satellite telecommunications link between Taiping and Kaohsiung was inaugurated in October 1995. In December 1998 the Legislative Yuan approved the first legal definition of Taiwan's sea borders. The Spratly Islands were claimed, as were the disputed Tiaoyutai Islands (see above), within the 12- and 24-nautical mile zones. In November 2002, in Phnom-Penh, Cambodia, members of the Association of Southeast Asian Nations (ASEAN) signed a 'declaration on the conduct of parties in the South China Sea', which aimed to avoid conflict in the area. Under this agreement, which was similar to one drafted in late 1999 but not implemented, claimants would practise self-restraint in the event of potentially hostile action (such as inhabiting the islands), effect confidence-building measures and give advance notice of military exercises in the region. However, the agreement did not include the Paracel Islands. In August 2003 Minister of the Interior Yu Cheng-hsien visited Taiping Island and reaffirmed Taiwanese sovereignty. In February 2008 President Chen Shui-bian visited Taiwanese forces stationed on Taiping, where he inaugurated a new airstrip and proposed a 'Spratly Initiative', urging claimant countries to disregard the issue of sovereignty and to co-operate in the protection of the islands' environment and resources. The Philippines and Viet Nam had been particularly critical of Taiwan's construction of the airstrip. In April 2011, in response to China's agreement with Viet Nam to co-operate in the area (which prompted an official complaint to the UN from the Philippines), Taiwan announced that it was to reinforce its coastguard deployment in the area of the Spratly Islands. Taiwan reiterated its claim to sovereignty of the islands in July 2011, following a visit to the area by a group of Philippine legislators.

Other Foreign Relations

At the beginning of the 21st century a total of five Pacific nations, namely the Marshall Islands, Nauru, Palau, Solomon Islands and Tuvalu, recognized Taiwan, which was increasingly vying with China for influence in the region. Taiwan maintained several embassies in the Pacific Islands and provided considerable financial support to these nations. In addition, Kiribati granted diplomatic recognition to Taiwan in November 2003. Diplomatic relations were briefly established with Vanuatu in late 2004. In January 2005 President Chen undertook an official visit to Palau, thus becoming the first Taiwanese President to visit the Pacific nation. He also travelled to Solomon Islands and to the US territory of Guam. In May Chen became the first head of any foreign state to visit the Marshall Islands in an official capacity, as part of a diplomatic tour of Pacific nations, during which the Taiwanese President also became the first foreign head of state to visit Kiribati and Tuvalu. However, he controversially altered his published itinerary to visit Fiji, a country that maintained diplomatic relations with the People's Republic of China. Also in May 2005, diplomatic relations with Nauru, which had been terminated in July 2002 after the country established relations with China, were re-established.

As competition with China for diplomatic support in the Pacific region continued, in May 2008 two senior members of the Taiwanese Government, Vice-Premier Chiou I-jen and the Minister of Foreign Affairs, Huang Chih-fang, were forced to resign (see above) over a funding scandal involving an alleged attempt to influence the allegiance of Papua New Guinea, a country with which Taiwan had briefly succeeded in establishing diplomatic relations in 1999. Meanwhile, in June 2007 President Kessai Note of the Marshall Islands embarked upon his sixth visit to Taiwan, and in August 2008 President Ma Ying-jeou received Note's successor, Litokwa Tomeing, in Taipei. During 2009 President Ma held discussions with the heads of government of Palau, Tuvalu and Solomon Islands during their respective state visits to Taiwan. In March 2010 President Ma embarked upon his first official visit to the Pacific Islands. His itinerary incorporated all six diplomatic allies: the Marshall Islands, Kiribati, Tuvalu, Nauru, Solomon Islands and Palau. The Prime Minister of Tuvalu, Apisai Ielemia, undertook an official visit to Taiwan in April. In June the various bilateral projects were also among the topics discussed with their Taiwanese counterpart during the respective visits to Taipei of Kiribati President Anote Tong and Marshallese President Jurelang Zedkaia. In the following month President Ma also received King Mswati III of Swaziland.

In September 2006 a summit meeting attended by the President of Taiwan and the leaders of its six Pacific allies was convened in Palau. The Second Taiwan-Pacific Allies Summit took place in the Marshall Islands in October 2007. The 2008 Summit was cancelled following the recent return to power of the KMT, which had insufficient time to prepare. The meeting scheduled to be held in Solomon Islands in October 2009 was also cancelled, to allow the Taiwanese authorities to focus on addressing the aftermath of Typhoon Morakot.

Taiwan's relations with Africa have been similarly governed by competition with China for influence. In May 1994 President Lee of Taiwan visited South Africa and Swaziland. In January 1997 the Taiwanese Minister of Foreign Affairs embarked upon a tour of seven African nations, including South Africa, in an attempt to consolidate relations. In January 1998, however, South Africa's transfer of diplomatic recognition from Taiwan to China was a major set-back to Taiwan. In February the Minister of Foreign Affairs visited eight African countries, and in April it was announced that Taiwan's overseas aid budget was to be substantially increased, in an attempt to retain diplomatic support. In August 2000 the new Taiwanese President, Chen Shui-bian, embarked upon a tour of diplomatic allies in West Africa. The Taiwanese Vice-President visited The Gambia in December 2001. President Chen completed a four-nation tour of Africa in July 2002, having visited Senegal, São Tomé and Príncipe, Malawi and Swaziland. In subsequent years Taiwan suffered several reverses in Africa. In October 2003 Liberia transferred its diplomatic recognition to the People's Republic of China. Relations with Senegal were also terminated when that country re-established diplomatic links with the People's Republic of China in October 2005. In August 2006, furthermore, Chad also transferred diplomatic recognition to the People's Republic, announcing this decision less than 24 hours before Premier Su Tseng-chang was due to embark upon an official visit to the African nation. Nevertheless, the Taiwanese Minister of Foreign Affairs visited several other African states in 2007, and in September Taiwan hosted the first Taiwan-Africa Summit, which was attended by its five African allies. In January 2008, however, it was announced that Malawi had severed diplomatic relations with Taiwan. President Yahya Jammeh of The Gambia undertook his eighth state visit to Taiwan in April 2009.

Similar trends characterized Taiwan's relations with the countries of Central America and the Caribbean. In July 1997, following the Bahamas' establishment of diplomatic relations with the People's Republic of China, the Taiwanese Minister of Foreign Affairs undertook an extensive tour of the countries of Central America and the Caribbean, in an effort to maintain their support. In September, during a tour of Central America (the six nations of the region having become the core of Taiwan's remaining diplomatic allies), President Lee attended an international conference on the development of the Panama Canal. In May 1998 Vice-President Lien Chan visited Taiwan's Central American and Caribbean allies. In August 2000 the new Taiwanese President, Chen Shui-bian, embarked upon a tour of diplomatic allies in Central America. As Taiwan continued to seek diplomatic recognition in return for aid and investment, in May 2001 President Chen began a tour of five Latin American nations: El Salvador, Guatemala, Panama, Paraguay and Honduras. While in El Salvador, Chen met eight regional leaders, who pledged support for Taiwan. Vice-President Lu visited Nicaragua and Paraguay in January 2002. In March 2004, however, Dominica withdrew its diplomatic recognition of Taiwan, as did Grenada in January 2005. In 2007 Saint Lucia restored recognition in May, but Costa Rica terminated diplomatic links in June. Following his assumption of office in the previous year, in mid-2009 President Ma Ying-jeou undertook official visits to Belize, Guatemala, El Salvador, Panama and Nicaragua. In January 2010 President Ma visited Honduras and the Dominican Republic.

In the 1990s relations with Europe were dominated by the issue of purchases of French defence equipment. In January 1993 official confirmation of Taiwan's purchase of 60 Mirage fighter aircraft from France provoked strong protest from China. Taiwan suffered a reverse in January 1994 when (following pressure from the People's Republic) France recognized Taiwan as an integral part of Chinese territory and agreed not to sell weapons to the island. In March 1995, however, it was reported that Taiwan was to purchase anti-aircraft missiles from a French company; the sale was subsequently confirmed. In 1996 the first delivery of Mirage aircraft to Taiwan from France took place. It was confirmed that, as agreed in 1991, France would proceed with the sales of six frigates to Taiwan; delivery of these was completed in March 1998. There were tensions in Taiwan's relations with France in early 2004 after President Jacques Chirac expressed his support for China's opposition to a proposed referendum in Taiwan (see above) during a visit by Chinese President Hu Jintao to Paris. Two visits by Taiwanese ministers to France were subsequently cancelled, and joint military exercises between the French and mainland Chinese navies were held in March off Taiwan's northern coast. In May 2010, ruling that the payment of commission to intermediaries involved in the sale of the six French frigates to the island in the 1990s had been a breach of the terms of the contract, an international court of arbitration ordered France and the company concerned to pay the sum of €630m. to Taiwan in compensation. Some of the defendants in the case were subsequently acquitted, although in late 2010 prosecutors declared their intention to continue their pursuit of the bribery charges against a retired naval captain and a weapons dealer.

In January 1997 the Taiwanese Vice-President was received by the Pope during a visit to the Holy See, the only European state that continued to recognize Taiwan. A visit to Europe in October by Vice-President Lien Chan was curtailed when pressure from China forced the Spanish Government to withdraw an invitation. In November 2001 Wu Shu-jen, wife of President Chen, travelled to Strasbourg, France, to accept the 'Prize for Freedom' awarded to her husband by Liberal International, a world grouping of liberal parties. Chen himself had been refused a visa by the European Union (EU). In March 2003 President Chen was again refused a visa by the EU, and was thus unable to travel to Belgium to address members of the European Parliament in Brussels. In early 2010 Taiwan's proposed purchase of three helicopters from the European Aeronautic Defence and Space Company, a corporation based in the Netherlands, attracted some controversy. Although the aircraft were ostensibly being acquired for civilian purposes, observers noted that the Taiwanese air force, rather than the police or coastguard, was to receive the helicopters.

RELATIONS WITH THE PEOPLE'S REPUBLIC

The Government of Taiwan repeatedly rejected proposals from the People's Republic of China for reunification, whereby Taiwan would become a 'special administrative region' of China and would enjoy a high degree of autonomy, including the retention of its own armed forces. Limitations on this autonomy would be that the People's Republic would represent China in international affairs. In October 1984, following the agreement between the People's Republic of China and the United Kingdom that the former would regain sovereignty over Hong Kong in 1997, mainland Chinese leaders urged Taiwan to accept similar proposals for reunification on the basis of 'one country, two systems'. However, the KMT Government insisted that Taiwan would never negotiate with China until the mainland regime renounced communism, thus reasserting the rigid and fundamental 'three no's' policy (of 'no compromise, no contact and no negotiation with the mainland') on which its relationship with the People's Republic was based. In May 1986 Taiwan was induced to adopt a more flexible policy after a Taiwanese cargo aircraft was diverted to the mainland by a pilot who wished to defect; representatives from the airlines of the two sides held negotiations in Hong Kong, leading to the return of the aircraft (and two other crew members) to Taiwan. These discussions represented the first-ever direct contact between the two sides (although Taiwan insisted that the talks were for humanitarian reasons only). In March 1987, however, Taiwan declared the agreement that had been concluded between the People's Republic of China and Portugal, regarding the return of Macao to Chinese sovereignty, to be null and void.

Questions of Taiwan's political evolution and of its future relations with the People's Republic of China were the principal determinants of the pace at which the KMT proceeded with the programme of political reform. While the opposition parties and liberal elements within the KMT generally recognized that Taiwan should adopt a more pragmatic foreign policy if it were to end its diplomatic isolation, the KMT was, until its 13th National Congress in July 1988, dominated by 'conservative' members who had fled the mainland with Chiang Kai-shek in 1947, and who feared that reform would undermine the *raisons d'être* of the KMT: that it constituted 'the legitimate Government of all China and that Taiwan formed a province of this polity', not an independent state. They thus opposed the increasing dominance of the KMT by native Taiwanese.

In October 1987 the Government announced the repeal of the 38-year ban on visits to the mainland by Taiwanese citizens, with the exception of civil servants and military personnel. (The latter regulations were relaxed in November 1998.) Between November 1987 and October 1990, according to the mainland authorities, almost 1.8m. Taiwanese visited (mainly via Hong Kong) the People's Republic. However, reconciliation initiatives were abruptly halted by the violent suppression of the pro-democracy movement in Beijing in June 1989. The actions of the Chinese Government were strongly condemned by Taiwan. Nevertheless, in May 1990 President Lee suggested the opening of direct dialogue on a government-to-government basis with the People's Republic. The proposal was rejected by China, which continued to maintain that it would negotiate only on a party-to-party basis with the KMT.

The National Unification Council (NUC), under the chairmanship of the President of Taiwan, was formed in October 1990. In the same month the Mainland Affairs Council, comprising heads of government departments and led by the Vice-Premier of the Executive Yuan, was founded. In December 1990 President Lee announced that Taiwan would formally end the state of war with the mainland; the declaration of emergency was to be rescinded by May 1991. In February 1991 the NUC put forward radical new proposals whereby Taiwan and the People's Republic of China might recognize each other as separate political entities. In April a delegation from the SEF, established in late 1990 to deal with bilateral issues, travelled to Beijing for discussions, the first such delegation ever to visit the People's Republic. Also in April, Taiwanese President Lee announced the end of the state of war with the People's Republic, and 10 amendments to the Constitution were promulgated.

Two senior envoys of the mainland Chinese Red Cross were allowed to enter Taiwan in August 1991 on a humanitarian mission, the first ever visit by official representatives of the People's Republic of China. As the mainland Government continued to warn against independence for Taiwan, in September the island's President asserted that conditions were not appropriate for reunification with the mainland and that Taiwan was a de facto sovereign and autonomous country. In December the non-governmental Association for Relations across the Taiwan Straits (ARATS) was established in Beijing. In January 1992 the SEF protested to the People's Republic over the detention of a former pilot of the mainland air force who had defected to Taiwan in 1965 and, upon returning to his homeland for a family reunion in December 1991, had been arrested. He subsequently received a 15-year prison sentence.

In July 1992 President Lee urged the establishment of 'one country, one good system', and statutes to permit the further expansion of economic and political links with the People's Republic were adopted by the Legislative Yuan. Delegates from the SEF and the ARATS met in Hong Kong in October for discussions. However, the Chairman of the Mainland Affairs Council, which had been established two years previously (comprising heads of Taiwanese government departments and led by the island's Vice-Premier), insisted that the People's Republic renounce the use of military force prior to any dialogue on the reunification question.

In 1993 divisions between Taiwan's business sector and political groupings (the former advocating much closer links with the People's Republic, the latter urging greater caution) became evident. In January, and again later in the year, the Secretary-General of the SEF resigned, following disagreement with the Mainland Affairs Council.

Historic talks between the Chairmen of the SEF and of the ARATS were held in Singapore in April 1993. Taiwan and the People's Republic agreed on the establishment of a formal structure for future negotiations on economic and social issues. Following a series of aircraft hijackings to Taiwan from the mainland, an SEF-ARATS meeting was held in Taiwan in December, in an attempt to address the issue of the repatriation of hijackers. Further meetings between delegates of the SEF and the ARATS were held in early 1994. In April, however, 24 Taiwanese tourists were among those robbed and killed on board a pleasure boat plying Qiandao Lake, in mainland China.

In August 1994 the SEF-ARATS talks were resumed when Tang Shubei, Vice-Chairman and Secretary-General of the ARATS, flew to Taipei for four days of discussions with his Taiwanese counterpart, Chiao Jen-ho. The two sides reached tentative agreement on several issues, including the repatriation of hijackers and illegal immigrants from Taiwan to the mainland. Procedures for the settlement of cross-Straits fishing disputes were also established. In mid-November relations were strained once again when, in an apparent accident during a training exercise, Taiwanese anti-aircraft shells landed on a mainland village, injuring several people. Nevertheless, in late November a further round of SEF-ARATS talks took place in Nanjing, at which agreement in principle on the procedure for the repatriation of hijackers and illegal immigrants was confirmed. Further progress was made at meetings in Beijing in January 1995. In March the Mainland Affairs Council approved a resolution providing for the relaxation of restrictions on visits by mainland officials and civilians.

In April 1995 President Lee proposed a 'six-point' programme for cross-Straits relations, the objectives of which included unification in accordance with the reality of separate rules and increased trade relations. However, a meeting between the SEF Chairman, Koo Chen-fu, and his mainland counterpart, Wang Daohan, was postponed by the ARATS, in protest at President Lee's recent visit to the USA. In July, furthermore, the People's Republic unexpectedly announced that it was about to conduct an eight-day programme of guided missile and artillery-firing tests off the northern coast of Taiwan. A second series of exercises took place in August. In January 1996 the Taiwanese Premier again urged the early resumption of cross-Straits dialogue, but in March the People's Republic began a new series of missile tests. Live artillery exercises continued in the Taiwan Strait until after the island's presidential election, arousing international concern.

In November 1996 the Mainland Affairs Council announced that the permanent stationing of mainland media representatives in Taiwan was to be permitted. President Lee's renewed offer to travel to the People's Republic was rejected and, despite repeated SEF requests, Tang Shubei of the ARATS continued to assert that cross-Straits discussions could not resume owing to Taiwan's pursuit of its 'two Chinas' policy (a reference to President Lee's attempts to raise the diplomatic profile of the island). In January 1997, however, shipping representatives of Taiwan and of the People's Republic reached a preliminary consensus on the establishment of direct sea links. Under the terms of the agreement, which permitted mainland cargoes to be transshipped at the Taiwanese port of Kaohsiung for onward passage to a third country but did not allow goods to enter the island's customs, five Taiwanese and six mainland shipping companies were granted permission to conduct cross-Straits cargo services. In April 1997, following the arrival in Kaohsiung of the first ship in 48 years to sail directly from the Chinese mainland to the island, the first Taiwanese-owned (but Panamanian-registered) vessel set sail for the port of Xiamen on a similarly historic voyage across the Taiwan Strait. In July 1997, upon the reversion to Chinese sovereignty of the British colony of Hong Kong, President Lee firmly rejected the concept of 'one country, two systems' and any parallel with Taiwan.

In March 1997 a six-day visit to Taiwan by the Dalai Lama, the first to the island by the exiled spiritual leader of Tibet, was strongly condemned by the People's Republic of China, which denounced a meeting between President Lee and the exiled spiritual leader of Tibet as a 'collusion of splittists'. The Dalai Lama's subsequent visits to Taiwan were similarly criticized by China.

The declaration by an ARATS official, in January 1998, that Taiwan did not need to recognize the Government of the People's Republic as the central Government as a precondition for dialogue was regarded as a significant concession on the part of the mainland authorities. However, Taiwan continued to insist that China abandon its demand that talks be conducted under its 'one China' principle. In April a delegation chaired by the newly appointed Deputy Secretary-General of the SEF, Jan Jyh-horng, visited the People's Republic. Following negotiations with the ARATS, it was announced that the Chairman of the SEF would visit the People's Republic later in 1998 formally to resume the dialogue, suspended since 1995. The visit was regarded as an important step towards restoring stability to Taiwan-China relations. The arrest on the mainland in May 1998 of four Taiwanese business executives on charges of espionage threatened to reverse the improvement in relations, but in July the Chinese Minister of Science and Technology visited Taiwan, the first such visit by a mainland minister since the civil war. This was followed later in the month by a formal visit to Taiwan by the Deputy Secretary-General of the ARATS. The kidnap and murder in August in the People's Republic of a Taiwanese local government official caused serious concern. Furthermore, later in that month a Beijing court convicted the four Taiwanese businessmen on charges of espionage. In October Koo Chen-fu, the SEF Chairman, duly travelled to the People's Republic. Koo's meeting with President Jiang Zemin represented the most senior level of bilateral contact since 1949. Koo also had discussions with his mainland counterpart and other senior officials. A four-point agreement was reached, allowing for increased communications between the two sides. In April 1999 President Lee reaffirmed that China should recognize Taiwan as being of equal status. An SEF group went to Beijing in March, and preliminary agreement was reached that Wang Daohan would visit Taiwan in either mid-September or mid-October. In August, however, the ARATS suspended contacts with the SEF, following President Lee's insistence on the 'two-state theory' (see below).

Meanwhile, China was becoming increasingly demonstrative in its opposition to Taiwan's inclusion in the TMD system (see above). Ballistic missiles were deployed in mainland coastal regions opposite Taiwan, and in July 1999 the People's Republic announced that it had developed a neutron bomb, after declaring itself ready for war should Taiwan attempt to gain independence. This declaration was prompted by a radio interview by President Lee, during which he asserted that relations with the People's Republic were 'state-to-state'. Chinese military exercises took place in the Taiwan Strait later in that month, and in August the USA reaffirmed its readiness to defend Taiwan. Also in August the ruling KMT incorporated the 'two-state theory' into the party resolution. In September, following a severe earthquake in Taiwan that killed or injured several thousand people, China was among the many countries to offer emergency assistance to the island; however, Taiwan accused the People's Republic of contravening humanitarian principles by trying to force other countries to seek its approval before offering help.

In February 2000 the People's Republic threatened to attack Taiwan if it indefinitely postponed reunification talks. In April the Vice-President-elect, Annette Lu, was denounced by the Chinese media after she made 'separatist' remarks, televised in Hong Kong, declaring that Taiwan was only a 'remote relative and close neighbour' of China. In October China published a policy document on its national defence, which confirmed that the People's Republic would use force to prevent Taiwanese secession. In November, however, there were signs of an improvement in relations when Wu Po-hsiung, the Vice-Chairman of the KMT, travelled to Beijing and met unofficially with Chinese Vice-Premier Qian Qichen. Wu was the most senior KMT official to visit mainland China for more than 50 years. Also in November Taiwan announced that journalists from the People's Republic were to be granted permission to stay in Taiwan for periods of up to one month. In December plans were announced for 'mini three links' with China, providing for direct trade, transport and postal links between Kinmen and Matsu islands and the mainland, albeit subject to rigorous security checks. In January 2001 groups sailed from Kinmen and Matsu to Xiamen and Fuzhou, respectively, in the People's Republic. Economic links continued to develop, with many Taiwanese companies investing on the mainland. In August President Chen endorsed a plan to expand commercial links with the People's Republic, a reversal of the previous Government's policy of limiting trade with the mainland.

In October 2001 Taiwan boycotted the APEC summit meeting in Shanghai, following China's refusal to allow Taiwan's chosen delegate, former Vice-President Li Yuan-tsu, to attend, on the grounds that he was not an 'economic' official. Despite this, the opposition DPP deleted from its charter a vow to achieve the island's formal independence, since it was already a de facto separate entity. In January 2002 the Government announced a list of more than 2,000 items that would thenceforth be legally importable from the mainland. In March China announced that, for the first time, two Taiwanese banks would be permitted to open offices on the mainland. Taiwan would allow mainland banks to establish offices on the island. The Taiwanese Government also eased restrictions on the island's companies investing in computer-chip manufacturing on the mainland, although restrictions would remain on the number of plants established and type of chips produced, mainly owing to security concerns.

In July 2002 the Taiwanese Ministry of National Defense warned in a biannual report that China's military spending was accelerating rapidly and that it would possess 600 short-range missiles targeting the island by 2005. President Chen further antagonized the mainland in August 2002 by supporting demands for a referendum to determine the island's future. Taiwan then cancelled planned military exercises as a gesture of good faith, but Chen's comments delayed the introduction of direct transport links. At the end of July the Government announced that Chinese products could be advertised on the island and that Chinese employees of Taiwanese or foreign companies would be allowed to work in Taiwan. A Taiwanese semiconductor manufacturer also announced plans to build a new factory on the Chinese mainland, in Shanghai. However, bilateral relations remained volatile, and in September President Chen described the mainland's threats against the island as a form of 'terrorism'. China accused Taiwan of allowing the banned Falun Gong sect to use the island as a base for disrupting mainland Chinese television and satellite broadcasts.

During 2002 Taiwan and China acquired advanced weaponry from the USA and Russia, respectively. In January 2003 President Chen stated that Taiwan was a sovereign state, and would never accept a Hong Kong-style solution nor federate with the mainland. At the same time, Vice-President Lu described China as being of a 'terrorist nature', referring to its missile build-up across the Taiwan Strait. In late January, none the less, the first Taiwanese airliner in more than 50 years flew to mainland China, via Hong Kong, and landed in Shanghai. The flight was one of 16 charter operations organized by the Taiwanese carrier, CAL, to transport Taiwanese visitors in China home for Chinese New Year celebrations. In February the Minister of National Defense stated that Taiwan would not reduce weapons purchases from the USA in return for the dismantling of Chinese missiles targeting the island. His remarks followed Chinese President Jiang Zemin's offer of such an arrangement, made to President Bush in October 2002.

An outbreak on the mainland of severe acute respiratory syndrome (SARS), a pneumonia-like virus, spread to Taiwan in early 2003. Taiwan accused the Chinese authorities of concealing the seriousness of the outbreak. In August the island's authorities arrested two Taiwanese citizens and a Taiwanese American on charges of spying for China. Also in August, a Chinese surveillance vessel was seen to the north of Taiwan. Military exercises simulating an attack on Taiwan by China were conducted in early September. The announcement in the same month that Taiwan was to issue new passports for its citizens that for the first time would have 'Taiwan' printed on the front (ostensibly to distinguish Taiwanese passports more clearly from mainland documents) heightened cross-Straits tensions, as did mass protests in Taipei demanding that the name 'Taiwan' be used officially by government agencies and private companies (see below). In October the Taiwanese Legislative Yuan approved the so-called Act Governing Relations between Peoples of the Taiwan Area and the Mainland Area, which was to provide a framework for the regulation of travel and business links between Taiwan and the mainland.

In November 2003 the Taiwanese legislature approved a bill allowing referendums to take place on the island (see below). Although the legislation in its final version prohibited a vote on Taiwan's sovereignty except in the event of an external attack, China feared that the new law might lead to the holding of a vote on Taiwan's independence. In December the issue of Taiwan dominated a visit by Chinese Premier Wen Jiabao to Washington, DC, with Wen seeking assurance from the USA that it would not support moves towards Taiwanese independence. President Chen defended plans to hold a referendum in March 2004 on the subject of a proposed request to China that it remove hundreds of missiles aimed at the island. In January Chen stated that the referendum might include 'counter-proposals' such as direct transport links between Taiwan and China if the latter were to withdraw its missiles. In February, furthermore, the Taiwanese President suggested the establishment of a demilitarized zone between the mainland and Taiwan in order to facilitate joint discussions. Chen also stated that he would not declare Taiwanese independence, were he to win the forthcoming presidential election, although his attitude to relations with the Chinese mainland, for example in rejecting the 'one country, two systems' model advocated by

China, was regarded by some as tantamount to stating that independence already existed.

The Chinese Government did not attempt directly to influence the election when it was held in March 2004, resulting in a narrow victory for Chen. However, following widespread controversy and protests over the election result, the Chinese Government stated that it would not tolerate social instability in Taiwan. In the event, President Chen's referendum, held concurrently with the presidential election, did not produce a valid result (see below). In August the President of Taiwan cancelled a military exercise scheduled for September after China removed 3,000 troops from the island of Dongshan owing to a typhoon threat. Anti-secession legislation, drafted with the intention of preventing Taiwan from declaring independence, was approved by the National People's Congress (NPC) in Beijing in March 2005.

In January 2005 it was announced that, for the first time, direct flights between Taipei and the Chinese mainland would be permitted over the forthcoming Lunar New Year period. The first direct commercial flights between Taipei and Beijing duly took place at the end of the month. In late April, in the first such visit since 1949, the Chairman of the opposition KMT, Lien Chan, embarked upon an official visit to the mainland, where he and Chinese President Hu Jintao agreed to remain opposed to Taiwanese independence. Following Chan's visit, in May 2005 the Government of the People's Republic offered Taiwan a pair of giant pandas (see below), along with a series of concessions that included the easing of restrictions for mainland Chinese tourists visiting Taiwan. Also in May, James Soong, leader of the PFP, an ally of the KMT within the opposition 'pan-blue' alliance, visited the People's Republic and met with President Hu. In June the Chinese Government announced that regulations restricting employment by Chinese companies of residents of Taiwan (as well as Hong Kong and Macao) were to be relaxed. The approval of a series of constitutional amendments by the Taiwanese National Assembly in June (see below) enabled future constitutional changes, including any declaration of independence, to be endorsed by referendum.

In a New Year speech on 1 January 2006 President Chen reiterated his commitment to achieving a new constitution, ratified by referendum, by 2008, with the implication that this would enshrine Taiwan's independence and sovereignty. The objective was repeated by Chen on the occasion of the Chinese Lunar New Year, when he also proposed the abolition of the NUC, along with the guidelines for unification proposed by the council and accepted by the Executive Yuan in 1991. Chen also stated his intention of reapplying for membership of the UN under the name of 'Taiwan', instead of the 'Republic of China'. In March tens of thousands of protesters participated in a rally in Taipei to protest against the perceived threat of domination by the People's Republic. In April former KMT Chairman Lien Chan made a further, controversial trip to Beijing to meet with President Hu Jintao, who urged the restoration of bilateral talks at the most senior level.

In June 2006 it was announced that up to 168 charter passenger flights would operate between the island and the mainland at four important annual holiday periods and that cargo and humanitarian flights would be licensed on an individual basis. (One month later the first non-stop cargo charter flight was made from Taiwan to Shanghai.) At a two-day Conference on Sustaining Taiwan's Economic Development, held in July, it was decided that investment limits might be relaxed for some Taiwanese companies operating on the mainland. However, during the forum President Chen emphasized that cross-Straits trade should be seen as part of the 'entire framework of international trade'. In August the Mainland Affairs Council established the Taiwan Strait Tourism and Travel Association, in response to China's foundation earlier in the month of the Cross-Strait Tourism Exchange Association.

Meanwhile, bilateral economic and trading links continued to expand unabated. By mid-2006 official Chinese statistics showed that 70,256 Taiwanese companies had invested on the mainland (excluding companies that had invested via third territories, such as Hong Kong). This investment was estimated to have reached a total of US $50,800m., despite measures introduced by the Taiwanese Government in May to ensure stricter supervision. As concerns persisted that many of the island's business people were contravening existing Taiwanese investment regulations, the Government remained under heavy pressure from the business community, which was becoming increasingly frustrated at the inability of Taiwanese companies to deal more directly with China. In September the Mainland Affairs Council announced that it was to raise the limit on the number of Chinese visitors attending business meetings in Taiwan from 30 to 50. By the end of the year, furthermore, tourists from the mainland would be able to visit Taiwan without first passing through a third location. In November a spokesman from the mainland's Taiwan Affairs Office urged the island to reduce its control over cross-Straits tourism.

In a defence document published in December 2006, however, China described Taiwan as a 'major threat'. Cross-Straits relations suffered further in January 2007, when President Chen used his New Year speech to reiterate his views on Taiwan's status, declaring that the island's sovereignty belonged to its people. In the same month Taiwan announced revisions to school history textbooks, in which references to 'the mainland' and 'our country' were to be replaced by simply 'China', thus implying that Taiwan and China were not part of the same country, with a common history. In March the Taiwanese President's confirmation that he wished the island to pursue independence, draft a new constitution and change its official designation from the 'Republic of China' to Taiwan prompted the mainland Chinese Minister of Foreign Affairs to refer to such statements as 'criminal'. On the same day Chinese Premier Wen Jiabao expressed a willingness to open a dialogue with Taiwan on condition that the island recognized the 'one China' principle. In February Taiwan declined to confirm reports that it had test-fired a missile that had a range of 1,000 km and was therefore capable of reaching Shanghai. In a further development, Taiwan's National Day celebrations in October featured a parade that displayed its military capabilities, including a ship-to-ship missile and anti-ballistic missile. The event, the first of its kind since the early 1990s, appeared to constitute a response to the perceived threat of military action from the mainland. Also in October, at the 17th Congress of the Chinese Communist party (CCP) convened in Beijing, President Hu Jintao reaffirmed Premier Wen's position, stressing the need for a dialogue to attain 'peaceful reunification'. Meanwhile, preparations in Beijing for the 2008 Olympic Games were a source of further tension, with Taiwan refusing to accept the proposed route of the Olympic torch in April 2007, based on the implications of an itinerary that sent the torch to Hong Kong and Macao after Taiwan; for Taiwan's Olympic Committee, this 'domestic route' represented an 'attempt to downgrade (Taiwan's) sovereignty'. After several months of difficult discussions, the International Olympic Committee (IOC) announced in September that the route would omit Taiwan completely.

Relations with the People's Republic improved considerably following the election of the KMT candidate, Ma Ying-jeou, as President of Taiwan in March 2008. Ma, who was born in Hong Kong, emphasized the importance of economic and transport links with China and distanced himself from his predecessor's policies, but maintained that a peace treaty could not be agreed while an estimated Chinese missiles were directed at Taiwan. In April a meeting between the Taiwanese Vice-President-elect, Vincent Siew, and President Hu Jintao, at the Boao Forum for Asia, was described as the most senior-level encounter ever to take place between Taiwan and China. In May the Chairman of the KMT, Wu Poh-hsiung, attended an historic meeting with President Hu in China, and formal talks between representatives of the two sides recommenced, following a long hiatus, in June. As a result of these SEF-ARATS negotiations, the two parties agreed to establish offices on each other's territory; to initiate 36 (and eventually 96) regular direct charter flights between China and Taiwan every weekend; and to allow entry to a total of 3,000 tourists per day in each direction. Soon after, President Ma proposed that bilateral agreements should expand into areas such as taxation and investment, through a process of 'economic normalization'. From late June, banks began offering the conversion of Chinese yuan into New Taiwan dollars.

Emergency aid was swiftly mobilized by Taiwanese charity organizations and religious groups to support the victims of the earthquake in Sichuan Province in May 2008. In the first such cross-Straits relief operation ever mounted, more than 150 metric tons of aid were delivered by air from Taiwan to the mainland within a week. At the end of May the Taiwanese Government announced that it planned to allocate a total of US $67m. in emergency relief funds. In addition, by the end of the month private Taiwanese donations had exceeded US $80m.

In early November 2008 Chiang Pin-kung, Chairman of the SEF, and Chen Yunlin, President of the ARATS, signed a series of agreements in Taipei. Chen was the most senior mainland Chinese official to travel to Taiwan since 1949, although his five-day visit was opposed by demonstrators (see below). The agreements included the expansion of bilateral transport links, permitting the establishment of daily direct flights, shipping and postal services between Taiwan and mainland China. The two sides also agreed, in view of increasing concerns with regard to the safety of Chinese products, to co-operate in the area of food safety. In mid-December 2008 the first regular direct flights and cargo shipping services began. No longer required to operate via an intermediary point such as Hong Kong, more than 100 regular passenger flights a week, serving eight cities in Taiwan and more than 20 on the mainland, were envisaged.

Following the return to power of the KMT, negotiations resumed with regard to China's offer of two pandas, traditionally the most esteemed diplomatic gift. The offer had been declined in 2006 on the grounds that Taiwan lacked the requisite facilities for panda care. In December 2008, following the preparation of a special enclosure at Taipei Zoo, amid heavy security two pandas were flown in a specially chartered aircraft to the island. The Taiwanese Government's acceptance of this highly symbolic gift was criticized by the opposition DPP.

In December 2008 the Taiwanese Government announced that the restrictions hitherto imposed on mainland spouses, notably with regard to issues such as the right to work and the processing of applications for permanent residency on the island, were to be relaxed. At the end of December President Hu Jintao urged the adoption of a more pragmatic approach to the issue of Taiwan. He also indicated some support for Taiwan's ongoing efforts to attain membership of various international organizations. At the annual session of the NPC convened in Beijing in March 2009, Premier Wen Jiabao stated his willingness to negotiate with Taiwan on political and military issues, reiterating that any discussions would be based on the 'one China' principle. In response, the Taiwanese Government expressed its preference to focus on economic matters.

In April 2009 Chiang Pin-kung of the SEF and Chen Yunlin of the ARATS signed agreements to permit further cross-Straits investment. The two sides pledged to 'realize the normalization of cross-strait economic ties'. Also in April, at the third session of discussions between Chiang and Chen, held in Beijing, agreement was reached on several important issues, including the combating of crime, judicial assistance and financial co-operation. A substantial expansion of cross-Straits air transport was also agreed, providing for the addition of six new airport destinations in mainland China and an increase in the number of weekly flights from 108 to 270. By May, one year after President Ma Ying-jeou's assumption of office, a total of nine bilateral agreements on economic co-operation had been signed. Furthermore, in an unprecedented bilateral exchange in late July, President Hu Jintao sent a message of congratulation to President Ma Ying-jeou following the latter's election as Chairman of Taiwan's ruling Kuomintang (KMT).

However, the Dalai Lama's five-day visit to Taiwan in late August 2009, following the typhoon earlier in the month (see below), provoked condemnation from the mainland. Having stressed the humanitarian nature of his visit, the spiritual leader of Tibet offered comfort to the victims of the disaster, visiting the village of Hsiaolin in southern Taiwan, where almost 500 people had been killed in a mudslide. However, mindful of the importance of the island's economic relations with the People's Republic, President Ma declined to meet the Dalai Lama.

In September 2009 the Taiwanese Government refused entry to Rebiya Kadeer, a Uygur businesswoman who had been imprisoned by the mainland Chinese authorities in 1999; upon her release in 2005 she had gone into exile in the USA. Denounced as a Muslim separatist, more recently Kadeer had been accused of inciting violence in the Chinese autonomous region of Xinjiang, where 200 people had been killed in rioting between Uygurs and Han Chinese in July 2009.

In a report issued in October 2009, the Taiwanese Ministry of National Defense warned that its efforts to improve relations with the Chinese military continued to be impeded by the mainland's confrontational stance. The report urged the withdrawal of missiles aimed at the island (the number of which was estimated by Taiwanese officials to have risen to 1,500) and suggested the establishment of a 'hotline' between Taipei and Beijing. The document also drew attention to the increasing frequency of military exercises being conducted on the mainland. President Ma, meanwhile, remained in favour of a formal peace accord with the mainland.

Despite military tensions, bilateral economic relations continued to expand. In November 2009 Taiwan and China signed a memorandum of understanding that provided for better access to financial services. Negotiations with regard to the conclusion of a free trade pact continued to progress. During four days of discussions held in Taiwan in December Chiang Pin-kung of the SEF and his mainland counterpart concluded a series of economic agreements. In June 2010 Taiwan and China reached consensus on the details of an historic Economic Co-operation Framework Agreement (ECFA). This major accord provided for the eventual removal of many trade tariffs and permitted wider access to the two respective markets. However, there was much domestic opposition to the agreement in Taiwan, and the passage of the requisite legislation was seriously disrupted. None the less, the legislation was finally approved in August, and the ECFA took effect in the following month.

In May 2010, meanwhile, the first semi-official Taiwanese presence in mainland China was established, when a representative office of the Taiwan Strait Tourism Association, headed by a senior government official, was inaugurated. In the same month the mainland Cross-Strait Tourism Association opened an office in Taipei. In July the KMT and the CCP reached agreement on the expansion of co-operation between the two ruling parties in the areas of culture, education, sports and economic development. In September Cai Wu, the mainland Minister of Culture, undertook an official visit to Taiwan, only the second official of cabinet rank to visit the island.

In December 2010 a delegation of the ARATS, led by Chen Yunlin, attended the sixth round of bilateral discussions at senior level, convened in Taipei. In February 2011, when Chen returned for a six-day visit at the head of a delegation of more than 50 business people and government officials, his itinerary incorporated major enterprises in southern Taiwan. However, in the southern city of Kaohsiung his visit prompted protests by pro-independence activists. Nevertheless, bilateral agreement was reached on permitting larger numbers of mainland tourists to visit Taiwan on an individual basis (the first individual tourists arriving on the island in June). In April, amid much domestic controversy, the Taiwanese authorities accepted the first applications from mainland students wishing to further their higher education on the island.

In May 2011, following his attendance at a bilateral forum in the Chinese city of Chengdu, Wu Poh-hsiung, honorary Chairman of the KMT, was received in Beijing by President Hu Jintao. In the same month, however, following the revelation by an opposition legislator that China had apparently exerted pressure on WHO to refer to Taiwan as a province of China in its documentation, the Taiwanese President issued a strong protest to China.

Following his conviction on charges of espionage, bribery and extortion, at the end of April 2011 an intelligence officer at the Taiwanese Ministry of National Defense, Col Lo Chi-cheng, was sentenced to life imprisonment. Col Lo had apparently collaborated with Lo Pin, a Taiwanese businessman based on the mainland, to gather intelligence for the People's Republic of China. In July a general of the Taiwanese army, Lo Hsien-che, was also sentenced to life imprisonment, having been found guilty of supplying classified data to mainland Chinese agents in exchange for bribes on five occasions during 2002–05, while serving as a military attaché in Thailand. Furthermore, it was reported in September 2011 that a Taiwanese academic had been detained by prosecutors on suspicion of espionage. Wu Chang-yu, an associate professor of political science, was alleged to have gathered information pertaining to mainland Chinese pro-democracy activists, those actively seeking independence for Tibet and followers of Falun Gong, a banned spiritual sect.

The next SEF-ARATS meeting was scheduled to be held in the mainland Chinese city of Tianjin in August 2011, when Chiang Pin-kung and Chen Yunlin were to sign accords relating to nuclear power safety and investment protection. However, the meeting was postponed until late October, pending final agreement on various points relating to the protection of investors.

INTERNAL POLITICAL DEVELOPMENTS

President Chiang Kai-shek remained in office until his death in April 1975. He was succeeded by the former Vice-President, Dr Yen Chia-kan, as head of state, and by his son, Gen. Chiang Ching-kuo (who had been Premier since May 1972), as Chairman of the KMT. Chiang Ching-kuo succeeded Dr Yen as President in May 1978, when Sun Yun-suan became Premier.

Meanwhile, legislative elections were held in December 1972, for the first time in 24 years, to fill 53 seats in the National Assembly. The new members, elected for a fixed term of six years, joined 1,376 surviving 'life-term' members of the Assembly. In the December 1983 elections for 71 local seats in the Legislative Yuan, in which the original republican membership had been reduced by attrition from 760 to 274 (with an average age of 77), the ruling KMT won 62 seats. In addition, 27 supplementary vacancies for overseas Chinese were filled by presidential appointment. Younger, well-qualified Taiwan-orientated members thus entered the Legislative Yuan. In March 1984 President Chiang Ching-kuo was re-elected for a second six-year term by the National Assembly. Lee Teng-hui, hitherto Governor of Taiwan Province, was elected as Vice-President. Yu Kuo-hwa, a former Governor of the Central Bank, was appointed Premier in May, in place of Sun Yun-suan, and a major reorganization of the Executive Yuan brought several younger politicians into the Government. At local elections in November 1985 the KMT won 80% of the seats.

The Ending of Martial Law and Progress towards Democracy

In 1986 the KMT announced its readiness to discuss four controversial issues: the possible establishment of new political parties, the status of the martial law (which had remained in force since 1949), the structure of provincial government in Taiwan and the problem of the ageing political leadership. In September 135 leading opposition politicians formed the DPP, in defiance of the KMT, and in preparation for the legislative elections that were due to be held in December. In October the KMT announced its intention to suspend martial law. The formation of rival political groups was also permitted. During 1987 three such organizations emerged: the Chinese Freedom Party (CFP), favouring improved relations with mainland China; the Democratic Liberal Party (DLP); and the Kungtang, or Labour Party. The Chinese Republican Party (CRP) was formed in 1988.

Elections for 84 seats in the National Assembly and 73 seats in the Legislative Yuan were held in December 1986. The KMT won 68 seats in the National Assembly and 59 in the Legislative Yuan, but the DPP received about one-quarter of the total votes cast, winning 11 seats in the Assembly and 12 in the Legislative Yuan, thus more than doubling the non-KMT representation. Following the opening of a new session of the Legislative Yuan in February 1987, the KMT began to implement its programme of reform. The most significant change was the termination of martial law, and its replacement in July by a new national security law, whereby political parties other than the KMT were permitted, civilians were removed from the jurisdiction of military courts, and military personnel no longer had the right to determine the acceptability of persons entering and leaving Taiwan. Despite the fact that the removal of martial law had been the principal aim of the DPP, the party remained opposed to the conditions with which opposition groups had to comply in order to gain legal recognition. The new law stated that opposition parties should honour the Constitution, support the Government's anti-communist policy and oppose separatism, but many DPP leaders argued that acceptance of these conditions would effectively recognize the right of the ruling KMT to regulate its own opposition. The question of the DPP's legal status thus remained unresolved.

The KMT also attempted to rejuvenate Taiwan's ageing leadership. Within the party, younger members advocating reform were promoted to positions of influence, and in April 1987 secured seven major posts in a reorganization of the Executive Yuan. Among the younger members of the KMT, a strong movement in favour of the increased democratization of Taiwan's parliamentary system developed. In February 1988 a plan to restructure the legislative bodies, which had been initiated by President Chiang Ching-kuo in 1986, was approved by the Central Standing Committee of the KMT. Under its provisions, 'life-term' members of the Legislative Yuan and the National Assembly would be progressively reduced in number through death and voluntary retirement. Seats in the National Assembly and the Legislative Yuan would no longer be reserved for representatives of mainland constituencies, and there would be a corresponding increase in members representing Taiwanese constituencies.

Chiang Ching-kuo died in January 1988, and was succeeded by the Vice-President, Lee Teng-hui, who was designated to serve the remaining two years of President Chiang's term of office. Before his death, President Chiang had stated that Taiwan's future leadership should be provided by constitutional means, thus signalling the end of the Chiang 'dynasty'. President Lee was the first native Taiwanese to serve as President and was thus, potentially, at variance with the 'old guard' of mainland-orientated members of the KMT and the Legislative Yuan. The new President sought to strengthen the KMT's commitment to the programme of political reform and to the rejuvenation and 'Taiwanization' of the country's leadership. However, the slow pace at which the Government proceeded attracted criticism, not only from the DPP, but also from liberal elements within the KMT. In January 1988 the DPP sought to obstruct the adoption of two draft laws regarding the freedom of assembly and demonstration, and the formation of new political parties, claiming that their provisions would regulate too strictly the activities of the opposition. In April liberal representatives of the KMT in the Legislative Yuan began to intensify the campaign for a restructuring of the party, demanding that all 150 members of its Central Committee, and at least some of the 31 members of its Central Standing Committee, be elected to office. In May an initially peaceful demonstration by farmers in Taipei resulted in the most serious riots in Taiwan's recent history.

At the 13th National Congress of the KMT, held in July 1988, Lee promised to accelerate reform and to fortify 'the substance and function of democracy'. The party congress confirmed him in the chairmanship of the party and went on to elect most of his 180 nominees for membership of an expanded Central Committee. Two-thirds of the members of the new Central Committee were chosen, for the first time in the history of the KMT, by free elections and had not previously been members. The proportion of members who were native Taiwanese also increased sharply, from one-fifth to almost two-thirds. President Lee's appointments to the Central Standing Committee followed the same trend, in that 12 of its 31 members were replaced by representatives of the younger, liberal faction of the KMT. For the first time, also, the number of members of the Central Standing Committee who were native Taiwanese was greater than that of those born on the mainland. A reorganization of the Executive Yuan in late July reflected the changes that had been accomplished at the National Congress of the KMT: new ministerial appointments resulted in a government comprising younger members. At the same time, President Lee promoted three urgent legislative measures: a draft revision of regulations concerning the registration of civic organizations and political parties; a retirement plan (with generous pensions) for those members of the Legislative Yuan, the Control Yuan and the National Assembly who had been elected by mainland constituencies in 1947; and a new law to give greater autonomy to the Taiwan Provincial Government and its assembly.

The three measures became law in January 1989. In the following month the KMT became the first political party to register under the new legislation. Despite its objections to the size of the retirement pensions being offered and to the terms of the Civic Organizations Law, which required political parties to reject communism and any notion of independence for Taiwan, the DPP applied for official registration in April 1989. In May Yu Kuo-hwa resigned as Premier of the Executive Yuan and was replaced by Lee Huan, the Secretary-General of the KMT.

Partial elections to the Legislative Yuan and the Taiwan Provincial Assembly were held in December 1989. A total of 101 seats in the Legislative Yuan were contested by the KMT, the DPP and several independent candidates. The KMT obtained 72 seats and the DPP won 21. By virtue of achieving more than 20 seats, the DPP secured the prerogative to propose legislation in the Legislative Yuan. In February 1990 the opening of the National Assembly's 35-day plenary session, convened every six years to elect the country's President, was disrupted by DPP members' violent action in a protest against the continuing domination of the Assembly by elderly KMT politicians, who had been elected on the Chinese mainland prior to 1949 and who had never been obliged to seek re-election. At the Legislative Yuan, demonstrators attempted to prevent senior KMT members from entering the building, and the election of a KMT veteran as President of the legislature had to be postponed, when opposition members deliberately delayed the procedure. More than 80 people were injured during the ensuing street clashes between riot police and demonstrators.

In March 1990 DPP members were barred from the National Assembly for refusing to swear allegiance to the 'Republic of China', attempting instead to substitute 'Taiwan' upon taking the oath. A number of amendments to the Temporary Provisions, which for more than 40 years had permitted the effective suspension of the Constitution, were approved by the National Assembly in mid-March. Revisions included measures to strengthen the position of the mainland-elected KMT members, who were granted new powers to initiate and veto legislation, and also an amendment to permit the National Assembly to meet annually. The revisions were opposed not only by the DPP but also by more moderate members of the KMT, and led to a large protest rally in Taipei, which attracted an estimated 10,000 demonstrators, who continued to demand the abolition of the National Assembly and the holding of direct presidential elections. Nevertheless, President Lee was duly re-elected, unopposed, by the National Assembly for a six-year term, two rival KMT candidates having withdrawn from the contest. In April President Lee and the Chairman of the DPP met for discussions.

There was renewed unrest in May 1990, following President Lee's unexpected appointment as Premier of Gen. (retd) Hau Pei-tsun, the former Chief of the General Staff and, since December 1989, the Minister of National Defense. Outraged opposition members prevented Hau from addressing the National Assembly, which was unable to approve his nomination until the session was reconvened a few days later, police being summoned to the Assembly to restore order. Angry demonstrators, fearing a reversal of the process of democratic reform, again clashed with riot police on the streets of Taipei. A new Executive Yuan was appointed at the end of the month, and included a civilian as Minister of National Defense. New Ministers of Foreign Affairs and of Finance were appointed, but the majority of ministers retained their previous portfolios.

The National Affairs Conference (NAC), convened in late June 1990, was attended by 150 delegates from various sections of society. At the historic meeting, proposals for reform were presented for discussion. A Constitutional Reform Planning Group was subsequently established. The NAC also reached consensus on the issue of direct presidential elections, which would permit the citizens of Taiwan, rather than the ageing members of the National Assembly, to select the head of state. Conservative members of the KMT were strongly opposed to this proposal.

Meanwhile, the Council of Grand Justices had ruled that elderly members of the National Assembly and of the Legislative Yuan should step down by the end of 1991. Constitutional reform was to be implemented in several stages: in April 1991 the Temporary Provisions, adopted in 1948, were to be abolished; in late 1991 a new National Assembly was to be elected by popular vote, the number of members being reduced and all elderly mainland-elected delegates being obliged to relinquish their seats; elections to the new Legislative Yuan were to take place in 1992. Meanwhile, in early December 1990 Huang Hwa, the leader of a faction of the DPP and independence activist, had received a 10-year prison sentence upon being found guilty of 'preparing to commit sedition'.

In April 1991 the National Assembly was convened, the session again being marred by violent clashes between KMT and DPP members. The DPP subsequently boycotted the session, arguing that a completely new constitution should be introduced and that elderly KMT delegates, who did not represent Taiwan constituencies, should not have the right to make amendments to the existing Constitution. As many as 20,000 demonstrators attended a protest march organized by the DPP. Nevertheless, the National Assembly duly approved the constitutional amendments, and at midnight on 30 April the 'period of mobilization for the suppression of the Communist rebellion' and the Temporary Provisions were formally terminated. The existence, but not the legitimacy, of the Government of the People's Republic was officially acknowledged by President Lee. Furthermore, Taiwan remained committed to its 'one China' policy. Martial law remained in force until November 1992 on the islands of Kinmen (Quemoy) and Matsu where, owing to their proximity to the mainland, it had not been removed in mid-1987 as elsewhere in Taiwan. In May 1991 widespread protests, following the arrest of four advocates of independence, led to the abolition of the Statute of Punishment for Sedition. The law had been adopted in 1949 and had been frequently employed by the KMT to suppress political dissent.

A senior UN official arrived on the island in August 1991, the first such visit since Taiwan's withdrawal from the organization in 1971. Large-scale rallies to demand the holding of a referendum on the issue of Taiwan's readmission to the UN took place in September and October, resulting in clashes between demonstrators and the security forces.

In August 1991 the opposition DPP officially announced its alternative draft constitution for 'Taiwan', rather than for the 'Republic of China', thus acknowledging the de facto position regarding sovereignty. In late September, only one day after being reinstated in the Legislative Yuan, Huang Hsin-chieh, the Chairman of the DPP, relinquished his seat in the legislature and urged other senior deputies to do likewise. Huang Hsin-chieh had been deprived of his seat and imprisoned in 1980, following his conviction on charges of sedition. At the party congress in October 1991, Huang Hsin-chieh was replaced as DPP Chairman by Hsu Hsin-liang. Risking prosecution by the authorities, the DPP congress adopted a resolution henceforth to advocate the establishment of 'the Republic of Taiwan'.

Elections to the new 405-member National Assembly, which was to be responsible for amending the Constitution, were held on 21 December 1991. The 225 seats open to direct election were contested by a total of 667 candidates, presented by 17 parties. The campaign was dominated by the issue of independence. The KMT secured a total of 318 seats (179 of which were won by direct election), while the DPP won 75 seats (41 by direct election).

In February 1992 20,000 demonstrators took part in a march in Taichung. The protesters' demands included the abolition of the sedition laws and the holding of a referendum on the issue of independence for the island. In the same month the Government released a report on the 1947 massacre of 18,000–28,000 civilians. For the first time the KMT leadership admitted responsibility for the violent suppression of the alleged communist rebels. In March 1992, at a plenary session of the KMT Central Committee, agreement was reached on several issues, including a reduction in the President's term of office from six to four years. However, the important question of arrangements for future presidential elections remained unresolved. Liberal members continued to advocate direct election, while conservatives favoured a complex proxy system. In April street demonstrations were organized by the DPP to support demands for direct presidential elections. In May the National Assembly adopted eight amendments to the Constitution, one of which empowered the President to appoint members of the Control Yuan.

The First Full Elections and KMT Disunity

Taiwan's first full elections since the establishment of Nationalist rule in 1949 were held in December 1992. The KMT retained 102 of the 161 seats in the Legislative Yuan. However, the DPP garnered 31% of the votes and more than doubled its representation in the legislature, winning 50 seats. Following this set-back, the Premier and the KMT Secretary-General resigned. In February 1993 President Lee nominated the Governor of Taiwan Province, Lien Chan, for the premiership. The Legislative Yuan duly approved the appointment of Lien Chan, who thus became the island's first Premier of Taiwanese descent. The incoming Executive Yuan incorporated numerous new ministers.

There were violent scenes in the National Assembly in April 1993, when deputies of the DPP (which in recent months had modified its aggressive pro-independence stance, placing greater emphasis on the issues of corruption and social welfare) accused members of the KMT of malpractice in relation to the election of the Assembly's officers.

In May 1993 the growing rift between conservative and liberal members of the ruling party was illustrated by the resignation from the KMT of about 30 conservative rebels, and their formation of the New Alliance Nationalist Party. Furthermore, in June the Government was defeated in the Legislative Yuan, when a group of KMT deputies voted with the opposition to approve legislation on financial disclosure requirements for elected and appointed public officials. The unity of the KMT was further undermined in August, when six dissident legislators belonging to the New Kuomintang Alliance, which had registered as a political group in March, announced their decision to leave the ruling party in order to establish the New Party (NP). The rebels included Wang Chien-shien, the former Minister of Finance. Nevertheless, at the KMT Congress in August, Lee Teng-hui was re-elected Chairman of the party. A new 31-member Central Standing Committee and 210-member Central Committee, comprising mainly Lee's supporters, were selected. In a conciliatory gesture by the KMT Chairman, four vice-chairmanships were created, the new positions being filled by representatives of different factions of the party.

In September 1993, following a series of bribery scandals, the Executive Yuan approved measures to combat corruption. In the same month a KMT member of the Legislative Yuan was sentenced to 14 years' imprisonment for bribery of voters during the 1992 election campaign; similar convictions followed. At local government elections held in November 1993, although its share of the votes declined to 47.5%, the KMT fared better than anticipated, securing 15 of the 23 posts at stake. The DPP, which accused the KMT of malpractice, received 41.5% of the votes cast, but won only six posts; it retained control of Taipei County. The DPP Chairman, Hsu Hsin-liang, resigned, and was replaced by Shih Ming-teh. Following allegations of extensive bribery at further local polls in early 1994 (at which the DPP and independent candidates made strong gains), the Ministry of Justice intensified its campaign against corruption. Proposals for constitutional amendments to permit the direct election in 1996 of the Taiwanese President by popular vote (rather than by electoral college) and to limit the powers of the Premier were approved by the National Assembly in July 1994.

At gubernatorial and mayoral elections in December 1994 the DPP took control of the Taipei mayoralty, in the first such direct polls for 30 years, while the KMT succeeded in retaining the provincial governorship of Taiwan, in the first ever popular election for the post, and the mayoralty of Kaohsiung. The NP established itself as a major political force, its candidate for the mayoralty of Taipei receiving more votes than the KMT incumbent. Almost 77% of those eligible voted in the elections. A government reorganization followed.

In March 1995, in response to continuing allegations of corruption (the number of indictments now having exceeded 2,000), President Lee announced the appointment of a committee to investigate the financial activities of the KMT. In the same month, following the President's formal apology at a ceremony of commemoration in February, the Legislative Yuan approved a law granting compensation to the relatives of the victims of the massacre by Nationalist troops in 1947 (the 'February 28 Incident'), in which thousands of native Taiwanese had been killed. (In June 1997 the Executive Yuan approved draft legislation to grant an amnesty to those involved in the incident.)

Less than 68% of those eligible voted at the elections to the Legislative Yuan held in December 1995. A major campaign issue was that of corruption. The KMT received only 46% of the votes cast, and its strength declined to 85 of the 164 seats. The ruling party fared particularly badly in Taipei. Although it performed less well than anticipated, the DPP increased its representation to 54 seats. The NP, which favoured reconciliation with the mainland, secured 21 seats. At the Legislative Yuan's first session in February 1996, Liu Sung-pan of the KMT only narrowly defeated a strong challenge from Shih Ming-teh of the DPP to secure re-election as the chamber's President.

The Presidential Election of 1996 and Beyond

The first direct presidential election was scheduled for March 1996, to coincide with the National Assembly polls. President Lee had declared his intention to stand for re-election in August 1995. In January 1996 Lien Chan offered to resign as Premier in order to support President Lee and to concentrate on his own vice-presidential campaign. He remained in office in an interim capacity. Other contenders for the presidency included the independent candidate and former President of the Judicial Yuan, Lin Yang-kang, supported by former Premier Hau Pei-tsun (both conservative former KMT Vice-Chairmen having campaigned on behalf of NP candidates at the December elections and therefore having had their KMT membership revoked); Peng Ming-min of the DPP; and Chen Li-an, former President of the Control Yuan and previously Minister of National Defense, an independent Buddhist candidate. Wang Chien-shien of the NP withdrew his candidacy in favour of the Lin-Hau alliance. The campaign was dominated by the issue of reunification with the mainland. In mid-March a DPP demonstration on the streets of Taipei, in support of demands for Taiwan's independence, was attended by 50,000 protesters.

At the presidential election, held on 23 March 1996, the incumbent President Lee received 54.0% of the votes cast, thus securing his re-election. His nearest rival, Peng Ming-min of the DPP, took 21.1% of the votes. The independent candidates, Lin Yang-kang and Chen Li-an, received 14.9% and 10.0% of the votes, respectively. At the concurrent elections for the National Assembly, the KMT garnered 55% of the votes and took 183 of the 334 seats. The DPP won 99 seats and the NP 46 seats. The Chairman of the DPP, Shih Ming-teh, resigned and Hsu Hsin-liang subsequently returned to the post.

On 20 May 1996 President Lee was sworn in for a four-year term. In June, however, the President's announcement of the composition of the new Executive Yuan aroused much controversy. Although several members retained their previous portfolios, the President (apparently under pressure from within the KMT and disregarding public concern at the rising levels of corruption and organized crime) demoted the popular Ministers of Justice (Ma Ying-jeou) and of Transportation and Communications, both of whom had exposed malpractice and initiated campaigns against corruption. Other changes included the replacement of the Minister of Foreign Affairs, Fredrick Chien (who became Speaker of the National Assembly), by John Chang, the grandson of Chiang Kai-shek. However, the most controversial nomination was the reappointment as Premier of Lien Chan, despite his recent election as the island's Vice-President. Opposition members of the Legislative Yuan, along with a number of KMT deputies, demanded that the President submit the membership of the

Executive Yuan to the legislature for approval. In October the Constitutional Court opened its hearing regarding the question of the island's Vice-President serving concurrently as Premier.

In October 1996 the Taiwan Independence Party was established by dissident members of the DPP. In the same month the Legislative Yuan approved the restoration of funding for a controversial fourth nuclear power plant, construction of which had been suspended in 1986. Thousands of anti-nuclear protesters demonstrated at the legislature, clashing with police and preventing Lien Chan from entering the building.

In December 1996 the multi-party National Development Conference (NDC), established to review the island's political system, held its inaugural meeting. The convention approved KMT proposals to abolish the Legislative Yuan's right to confirm the President's choice of Premier, to permit the legislature to introduce motions of no confidence in the Premier and to empower the President to dismiss the legislature. The Provincial Governor, (James) Soong Chu-yu, subsequently tendered his resignation in protest at the NDC's recommendations that elections for the provincial governorship and assembly be abolished, as the first stage of the dissolution of the provincial apparatus. An historical legacy duplicating many of the functions of central and local government, the Provincial Government was responsible for the entire island, with the exception of the cities of Taipei and Kaohsiung. In January 1997 President Lee refused to accept the Governor's resignation, but the affair drew attention to the uneasy relationship between the island's President and its Governor.

In May 1997 more than 50,000 demonstrators, protesting against the Government's apparent inability to address the problem of increasing crime, demanded the resignation of President Lee. Three members of the Executive Yuan resigned, including the popular Minister without Portfolio and former Minister of Justice, Ma Ying-jeou, who expressed his deep shame at recent events. The appointment of Yeh Chin-feng as Minister of the Interior (the first woman to oversee Taiwan's police force) did little to appease the public, which remained highly suspicious of the alleged connections between senior politicians and the perpetrators of organized crime. In mid-May thousands of protesters, despairing of the rapid deterioration in social order, again took to the streets of Taipei, renewing their challenge to President Lee's leadership and demanding the immediate resignation of Premier Lien Chan. In June, prior to the return to Chinese sovereignty of Hong Kong, a 'Say No to China' rally attracted as many as 70,000 supporters.

In July 1997 the National Assembly approved various constitutional reforms, including the freezing of the Provincial Government. (The Provincial Government was abolished in December 1998.) Other revisions that received approval were to empower the President of Taiwan to appoint the Premier without the Legislative Yuan's confirmation; the legislature was to be permitted to hold a binding vote of no confidence in the Executive Yuan, while the President gained the right to dissolve the Legislative Yuan. In August the Premier and his entire Government resigned in order to permit a reallocation of portfolios. Vincent Siew, former Chairman of the Council for Economic Planning and Development and also of the Mainland Affairs Council, replaced Lien Chan as Premier. (The latter retained the post of Vice-President.) John Chang was appointed Vice-Premier, and the new Minister of Foreign Affairs was Jason Hu. Following the installation of the new Executive Yuan, the Premier pledged to improve social order, further develop the economy, raise the island's standard of living and improve links with the People's Republic of China. In the same month President Lee Teng-hui was re-elected unopposed as Chairman of the ruling KMT.

The KMT experienced a serious set-back in elections at mayoral and magistrate levels, held on 29 November 1997. The opposition DPP, which had campaigned on a platform of more open government, secured 43% of the total votes, winning 12 of the 23 constituency posts contested, while the KMT won only 42% (eight posts). Voter turn-out was 65.9%. More than 70% of Taiwan's population would thus come under DPP administration. The Secretary-General of the KMT resigned, and was replaced by John Chang. A major reorganization of the party followed. Liu Chao-shiuan was appointed Vice-Premier in place of Chang.

At local elections, held in January 1998, the KMT won an overwhelming majority of the seats contested, while the DPP, in a reversal of fortune, performed badly. A minor reorganization of the Executive Yuan was carried out in early February.

In late March the Minister of Transportation and Communications resigned, assuming responsibility for two aeroplane crashes in Taiwan in early 1998, in which more than 200 people had died. In the following month the Minister of Justice tendered, and then subsequently withdrew, his resignation, citing pressure from lawmakers with connections to organized crime. However, in July he was forced to resign, following his mishandling of an alleged scandal concerning the acting head of the Investigation Bureau.

In June 1998 the first-ever direct election for the leadership of the DPP was held. Lin Yi-hsiung won a convincing victory, assuming the chairmanship of the party in August. Meanwhile, in local elections in June, the KMT suffered a set-back, winning fewer than 50% of the seats contested. Independent candidates performed well. In August 17 new members were elected to the KMT Central Standing Committee, the 16 others being appointed by President Lee.

The Legislative Elections of December 1998 and Constitutional Issues

Elections to the newly expanded 225-member Legislative Yuan took place in December 1998; 68.1% of the electorate participated in the poll. The KMT won 46.4% of the votes cast, securing 125 seats, the DPP received 29.6% of the votes and won 72 seats, while the pro-unification NP obtained only 7.1% of the votes and took 11 seats. The New Nation Alliance, a breakaway group from the DPP (formed in September), won only one seat (with 1.6% of the votes cast). In the simultaneous election for the mayor of Taipei, the KMT candidate, Ma Ying-jeou, defeated the DPP incumbent, Chen Shui-bian. However, the DPP candidate for the office of mayor of Kaohsiung, Frank Hsieh, narrowly defeated the KMT incumbent. The KMT retained control of both city councils.

Owing to the DPP's poor performance at the elections, Lin Yu-hsiung offered his resignation as Chairman of the DPP, but withdrew it following overwhelming party support for his leadership. However, Chiou I-jen resigned as DPP Secretary-General in December 1998 and was replaced by Yu Shyi-kun. Later in that month Chao Shu-po, a Minister without Portfolio, was appointed Governor of Taiwan Province, replacing the elected incumbent, James Soong, as part of the plans to dismantle the Provincial Government, agreed in 1997. A minor reorganization of the Executive Yuan took place in late January 1999.

In March 1999 an unprecedented vote of no confidence in the leadership of Premier Vincent Siew was defeated in the Legislative Yuan. The motion was presented by the opposition following Siew's decision to reduce the tax on share transactions, apparently as a result of pressure from President Lee. In September the National Assembly approved a controversial constitutional amendment, which, *inter alia*, extended the terms of the deputies from May 2000 to June 2002. Election to the Assembly was henceforth to be on the basis of party proportional representation. Several politicians and critical citizens condemned the move as being 'against the public will'. Shortly afterwards, the KMT leadership expelled the Speaker of the National Assembly, Su Nan-cheng, from the party on the grounds that he had violated its policy on the tenure extension, thereby also removing him from his parliamentary seat and the post of speaker. In March 2000, however, the Council of Grand Justices of the Judicial Yuan ruled the National Assembly's action to be unconstitutional. The DPP and the KMT then reached an agreement on the abolition of the National Assembly and the cancellation of elections scheduled for early May. In April the National Assembly convened, and approved a series of constitutional amendments, which effectively deprived the body of most of its powers, and reduced it to an ad hoc institution. The capacity to initiate constitutional amendments, to impeach the President or Vice-President, and to approve the appointment of senior officials, was transferred to the Legislative Yuan. The National Assembly was to retain the functions of ratifying constitutional amendments and impeachment proceedings, in which case 300 delegates, appointed by political parties according to a system of proportional representation, would convene for a session of a maximum duration of one month.

The Presidential Election of 2000 and Beyond

In November 1999 it was announced that a presidential election was to be held in March 2000. Five candidates registered: Lien Chan (with Vincent Siew as candidate for Vice-President) was the KMT nominee, while Chen Shui-bian, a former mayor of Taipei, was to stand for the DPP (with the feminist Annette Lu as vice-presidential candidate), and Li Ao was to represent the NP; the former DPP Chairman, Hsu Hsin-liang, qualified as an independent candidate, as did James Soong, who was consequently expelled from the KMT, along with a number of his supporters. Jason Hu resigned as Minister of Foreign Affairs in November 1999 in order to direct the KMT's election campaign. He was replaced by Chang Che-shen, hitherto Director-General of the Government Information Office. It became evident in the following month, when Soong was publicly accused of embezzlement, that the election would be bitterly contested. Although Soong denied the charges, his popularity was affected. In January 2000 Lien Chan proposed that the KMT's extensive business holdings be placed in trust and that the party terminate its direct role in the management of the numerous companies in which it owned shares. The KMT adopted the proposal shortly afterwards. In a reflection of the tense political situation between Taiwan and China, Chen Shui-bian of the DPP modified the party's stance and pledged not to declare formal independence for the island unless Chinese forces attacked.

The presidential election of 18 March 2000 was won by Chen Shui-bian, who obtained 39.3% of the votes cast. James Soong, his closest rival, received 36.8% of the votes. (On the day after the election he founded the People First Party (PFP), in an attempt to take advantage of his popularity.) Lien Chan of the KMT secured only 23.1% of the votes. The remaining candidates obtained less than 1%. The poll attracted a high level of participation, 82.7% of the electorate taking part. (Upon his inauguration in May, Chen would thus become Taiwan's first non-KMT President since 1945.) Violence erupted as disappointed KMT supporters besieged the party's headquarters, attributing the KMT's defeat to the leadership's expulsion of James Soong and the resultant division of the party. Lee Teng-hui subsequently resigned from the chairmanship of the party, and Lien Chan assumed the leadership. However, as the KMT continued to dominate the Legislative Yuan, the party did not entirely relinquish its influence, and in early April gave permission for Tang Fei, a KMT member and hitherto Minister of National Defense, to serve as Premier (although he was to be suspended from party activities while in the post). Following protracted negotiations, the membership of the new Executive Yuan, which incorporated 11 DPP members and 13 KMT members, was approved in early May. The incoming Government largely lacked ministerial experience. Furthermore, the DPP's lack of a legislative majority impeded the passage of favourable legislation. The size of the budget deficit also made it difficult for the DPP to fulfil specific electoral pledges on health, housing and education. In July Frank Hsieh replaced Lin Yi-hsiung as Chairman of the DPP.

In July 2000 the Government was heavily criticized after a river accident in which four workers, stranded by a flash flood, drowned as a result of the authorities' failure to provide a rescue helicopter. While the various government departments deliberated over the allocation of responsibility, the victims' final hours were broadcast live on national television. The Vice-Premier and Chairman of the Consumer Protection Commission, Yu Shyi-kun, subsequently resigned, as did senior officials of the emergency services. The Premier's offer of resignation was refused by President Chen Shui-bian. In October 2000, however, Tang Fei resigned as Premier, ostensibly owing to ill health. It was suggested that his departure from the post was due to the Government's failure to agree upon the fate of Taiwan's fourth nuclear power plant, the DPP being opposed to the project. (Later that month the Executive Yuan announced that construction of the plant was to be halted.) Vice-Premier Chang Chun-hsiung was appointed Premier, and a minor government reorganization was effected. Changes included the appointment of Yen Ching-chang as Minister of Finance.

Political disputes over the construction of Taiwan's fourth nuclear power plant intensified later in October 2000. The Minister of Economic Affairs, Lin Hsin-yi, was expelled from the KMT after he had demonstrated his support for the cancellation of the project. At the end of the month it was announced that the Executive Yuan had decided to halt construction of the plant for financial reasons. The outraged KMT rejected the Government's right to cancel a project previously approved by the legislature, and, together with the NP and the PFP, began collecting legislators' signatures for the recall (dismissal) of President Chen Shui-bian. Despite Chen's subsequent apology, the Legislative Yuan approved revised legislation on the process for presidential impeachment. KMT member Vincent Siew refused to act as the President's representative to the annual APEC forum in Brunei in November. The business community, furthermore, issued an unprecedented public statement that economic recovery should take priority over political differences, but in December some 10,000 protesters in Taipei demanded that Chen resign. In November the Government requested a constitutional interpretation of the issue from the Council of Grand Justices, which in January 2001 ruled that the Government should have sought the legislature's approval before terminating the project. The Government therefore decided to resume construction of the nuclear plant. In March a minor government reorganization was effected. The most notable change was the appointment of Hu Ching-piao, hitherto a Minister without Portfolio, as Chairman of the Atomic Energy Council, replacing Hsia Der-yu.

In July 2001 the KMT issued a radical policy document arguing that Taiwan's best option in terms of its relations with China was to form a 'confederation' with the mainland. However, the KMT's Central Standing Committee in late July refrained from adopting the proposal, reflecting the party's uncertainty over mainland policy. In August a new political party, the Taiwan Solidarity Union (TSU), was formally established with the support of former President Lee Teng-hui. Led by the former Minister of the Interior, Huang Chu-wen, and consisting of breakaway members of the KMT and DPP, the party hoped to secure for President Chen a majority in the forthcoming legislative elections. Lee was expelled from the KMT in September.

The Legislative Elections of December 2001 and Subsequent Events

At the elections held on 1 December 2001 the DPP emerged as the biggest single party in the new legislature, having won 36.6% of the votes cast and 87 of the 225 seats. The KMT won 31.3% of votes and 68 seats, thereby losing its dominance of the Legislative Yuan for the first time in its history. The PFP came third, winning 20.3% of the votes and 46 seats, while the newly formed TSU came fourth, with 8.5% of the votes and 13 seats. The NP won only 2.9% of the votes and one seat, while independents took nine seats. The level of voter participation was registered as 66.2%.

In January 2002 President Chen reorganized the Executive Yuan, appointing his hitherto Secretary-General, Yu Shyi-kun, as Premier. Other notable appointments included Chen Shih-meng, hitherto deputy governor of the Central Bank, as the Secretary-General to the President, replacing Yu. Lin Hsin-i, hitherto Minister of Economic Affairs, was appointed Vice-Premier and Chairman of the Council for Economic Planning and Development; and Eugene Y. H. Chien was appointed as Minister of Foreign Affairs, and Lee Yung-san became Minister of Finance. The new administration incorporated several members of the KMT, including Gen. Tang Yao-ming, hitherto Chief of the General Staff, who became Minister of National Defense. Tang was the first native-born Taiwanese to hold the newly augmented defence post in a military dominated hitherto by mainlanders. The ministers in charge of mainland and overseas Chinese affairs were retained.

At elections for provincial city and town councils held in January 2002, the KMT won the largest number of seats. In February an alliance of the KMT and PFP ('pan-blue' camp) successfully blocked the candidate of the DPP-TSU ('pan-green' camp) for the post of Vice-President of the Legislative Yuan, electing Chiang Ping-kun of the KMT to that position. At the same time, the incumbent President of the legislature, Wang Jin-pyng of the KMT, was re-elected to his post. The KMT-PFP alliance immediately challenged the new Government by attempting to force it to accept revisions to local budget allocations, which had been hastily approved by the outgoing Legislative Yuan, but the alliance failed to secure the majority necessary in the new legislature. However, an early set-back for the DPP administration occurred in March 2002 when the Minister of Economic Affairs, Christine Tsung, resigned, citing a hostile political environment. She was replaced by her deputy, Lin Yi-fu.

A major scandal emerged in March 2002 when it was reported that the Government of former President Lee Teng-hui had, in co-operation with the island's intelligence service (National Security Bureau—NSB), clandestinely established an unauthorized fund of US $100m. in order to finance covert operations on the mainland and to further Taiwanese interests among influential lobby groups abroad. It was widely believed that the source of the 'leaks' was a former NSB colonel who had embezzled US $5.5m. and then fled the island.

In April 2002 the Executive Yuan approved plans to abolish the posts of Speaker and Deputy Speaker of the National Assembly, and replace them with that of a chairman of the session. In May the Government revealed plans to reform the electoral system, which would reduce the number of seats in the Legislative Yuan from 225 to 150 and extend the term of legislators from three to four years. Some 90 seats would be filled from single-seat constituencies (thereby eliminating the need for candidates from the same party to compete against each other, as in the existing multi-seat constituencies), with the remaining seats divided proportionally among parties that gained more than 5% of the total vote. Also in May, KMT Chairman Lien Chan announced that his party would form an official alliance with the PFP in order to strengthen opposition to the ruling DPP. However, plans for a joint candidacy in the 2004 presidential elections were hampered by regulations stipulating that the presidential and vice-presidential candidates should belong to the same party. Meanwhile, in mid-May thousands of people demonstrated in favour of changing Taiwan's official name from the 'Republic of China' to 'Taiwan'.

In June 2002 Premier Yu Shyi-kun appointed Liu Shyh-fang as the first female Secretary-General of the Executive Yuan, replacing Lee Ying-yuan, who was standing as the DPP's candidate in elections for the mayoralty of Taipei, in December. In July President Chen Shui-bian formally assumed the chairmanship of the DPP. In September the Executive Yuan approved drafts of the new Political Party Law, which would ban political parties from operating or investing in profit-making enterprises, and allow the Government to investigate and confiscate assets unlawfully obtained by political parties. Although ostensibly intended to create greater political fairness and financial openness, the draft legislation was viewed as being directed at the KMT which, during the decades of its rule, had by 2001 amassed a vast commercial fortune, estimated NT $53,750m. As a result, the KMT might be forced to sell many of its assets.

A new political dispute emerged in late September 2002 over planned reforms of the debt-ridden agricultural and fishermen's credit co-operatives. The Government sought to reduce the activities of these local financial bodies, which had traditionally been used as a source of funds and influence for local KMT politicians. However, opposition to the reforms was so intense that by late November President Chen was forced to suspend the plans. At the same time, more than 120,000 farmers and fishermen marched through Taipei to protest against the reforms, in what was the largest demonstration on the island since Chen took office. Premier Yu Shyi-kun offered to resign, but was retained by Chen, who instead accepted the resignations of the Minister of Finance, Lee Yung-san, and the Chairman of the Council of Agriculture, Fan Chen-tsung. They were replaced by Lin Chuan and Lee Chin-lung, respectively. The departure of the respected Lee Yung-san, and the appointment of the third finance minister in as many years, raised concerns about political stability.

Meanwhile, attention began to focus on elections for the mayoralties of Taipei and Kaohsiung, which took place in early December 2002. In Taipei the incumbent mayor, Ma Ying-jeou of the KMT, defeated his DPP rival, Lee Ying-yuan, winning 64.1% of the votes cast. Thus he immediately emerged as a potential presidential candidate. His popularity complicated efforts by the KMT and PFP to select one of their respective party chairmen, Lien Chan or James Soong, as the joint presidential candidate of the 'pan-blue' camp. In Kaohsiung the incumbent mayor, Frank Hsieh of the DPP, narrowly defeated his KMT rival Huang Chun-ying, by 50.0% to 46.8% of the votes cast.

In February 2003 President Chen appointed Chiou I-jen, hitherto Secretary-General of the National Security Council, as Secretary-General to the President, while Kang Ning-hsiang, hitherto Vice-Minister of National Defense, succeeded Chiou in his former position. Following criticism of his handling of the outbreak of SARS, the Minister of Health, Twu Shiing-jer, resigned in May 2003. By June the virus had killed more than 80 people on the island.

The issue of Taiwan's very identity came to the fore once again in September 2003, when as many as 150,000 independence activists, led by former President Lee Teng-hui, rallied in Taipei to demand that the island's name be formally changed from the 'Republic of China' to 'Taiwan'. The continued use of the former had remained the source of much international confusion, and it was believed that the adoption of 'Taiwan' would facilitate wider diplomatic recognition. A rival rally, attended mainly by veterans of the civil war and their descendants (who continued to favour eventual reunification with the mainland), attracted several thousand supporters. Also in September, President Chen proposed the drafting of a new constitution for Taiwan.

In November 2003 Taiwan's legislature approved a new law to allow referendums to be held on the island, prompting strong criticism from China (see above). The approval of the legislation followed President Chen's formal declaration of his intention to stand for re-election in the 2004 presidential election. In December 2003 President Chen announced plans to hold a referendum on the issue of China's deployment of missiles against Taiwan (see above), to coincide with the forthcoming presidential poll. Also in December 2003, President Chen confirmed that Vice-President Annette Lu, a vocal supporter of Taiwanese independence, would stand for re-election. Opposition presidential candidate Lien Chan and vice-presidential candidate James Soong, of the KMT and of the allied PFP, respectively, as well as the popular mayor of Taipei, Ma Ying-jeou of the KMT, expressed strong opposition to the proposed referendum. In February 2004 demonstrations involving more than 70,000 people took place in southern Taiwan in support of the referendum. At the end of February, in Taiwan's largest-ever demonstration, an estimated 1.5m. people formed a 500-km 'human chain', linking hands across the island to protest against China's deployment of missiles. Meanwhile, the wording of the referendum question had been modified to ask voters whether, in the event of China's refusal to withdraw its missiles, they would favour a strengthening of Taiwan's defence system.

The Presidential and Legislative Elections of 2004 and Beyond

In a dramatic development on the day before the presidential election, while campaigning in Tainan both President Chen and Vice-President Lu were injured in a shooting incident. (The alleged assailant, Chen Yi-hsiung, was an unemployed man who was reported to have committed suicide shortly afterwards; however, further doubts with regard to these events were subsequently raised—see below). Neither Chen nor Lu was seriously injured in the apparent assassination attempt, and the poll proceeded as planned on 20 March 2004. President Chen was re-elected by a narrow margin of 29,518 votes, equivalent to only 0.2% of valid votes, with 337,297 ballot papers being declared invalid. A turn-out of 80.28% of the electorate was recorded. However, in the concurrent referendum on the issue of Taiwan's response to the deployment of mainland missiles, the majority of citizens declined to vote on President Chen's proposals, thus indicating widespread division within Taiwan on the issue of the island's relationship with China. President Chen's re-election was immediately challenged by opposition candidate Lien Chan, who claimed that there had been irregularities in the electoral process, and demanded a recount of the votes. Supporters of Lien rioted in Taipei and other cities. President Chen's re-election was none the less confirmed by Taiwan's Central Election Commission. In April the Minister of the Interior, Yu Cheng-hsien, resigned, citing the failure to prevent the shooting of President Chen during the election campaign as the reason for his departure. In the same month Minister of Foreign Affairs Eugene Chien resigned in connection with the departure of the head of the American Institute in Taiwan (see above). A recount of votes cast in the presidential election was completed on 19 May. It was estimated that 38,000 ballots were controversial, and that of these 23,000 were votes for Chen. Nevertheless, President Chen was inaugurated for a second term on 20 May, and on the same day announced appointments to his new Executive Yuan. Yu Shyi-kun was retained as Premier.

In July 2004 remarks by Vice-President Annette Lu suggesting a resettlement of Taiwan's aboriginal communities to South America caused widespread offence among the island's indigenous population. In the same month a new political party, the pro-independence Formosa Party, was inaugurated. In August the Legislative Yuan approved a bill on constitutional changes, which included plans for a reduction in the number of legislators and for reform of the electoral system. Also in August there was controversy surrounding the establishment of an independent committee to investigate the shooting of President Chen, with the President of the Judicial Yuan claiming that the investigatory powers being given to this body were unconstitutional. In September protests took place in Taipei against the special budget of NT $610,800m. for the purchase of US weapons, which had been approved by the Executive Yuan in June.

In the election for the Legislative Yuan held on 11 December 2004 the 'pan-green alliance' of the DPP and the TSU secured 101 seats, whereas the 'pan-blue alliance', comprising the KMT, the PFP and the NP, secured 114 seats. The resulting opposition majority in the legislature was expected to hinder President Chen's plans for constitutional changes. Chen resigned as DPP Chairman after the election, taking responsibility for the party's failure to secure a larger number of seats. Meanwhile, disputes over the legitimacy of President Chen's victory in March continued, with the High Court rejecting two opposition attempts, in November and December, respectively, to nullify the presidential election result.

In January 2005 the Executive Yuan approved a draft amendment to the referendum law (see above), requiring any changes to Taiwan's boundaries to be approved by the population. Later in January Premier Yu Shyi-kun and all members of the Executive Yuan resigned prior to the first meeting of the new Legislative Yuan. President Chen subsequently appointed Frank Hsieh, mayor of Kaohsiung and a leading member of the DPP, as Premier. Most outgoing ministers were reappointed. Also in January Secretary-General Su Tseng-chang was appointed Chairman of the DPP, replacing Chen; former Premier Yu Shyi-kun was subsequently appointed Secretary-General in his place. In February Premier Hsieh appointed Wu Rong-i as Vice-Premier and Minister of the Consumer Protection Commission.

In March 2005 a large rally, attended by President Chen, took place in Taipei in protest at the approval of anti-secession legislation by China's NPC (see above). On 14 May elections were held for an ad hoc National Assembly, which was to convene in order to ratify or reject the range of constitutional amendments approved by the Legislative Yuan in August 2004. The DPP secured 127 of the Assembly's 300 seats, having received 42.5% of votes cast, while the KMT won 117 seats. When the Assembly came to vote in the following month, 248 members were in favour of the amendments, 23 more than the two-thirds' majority required for ratification. The amendments to the Constitution thus passed into law included a reduction in the number of seats in the Legislative Yuan (from 225 to 113), reforms to the electoral system, the transfer of the power to impeach the President and Vice-President from the National Assembly to the Judicial Yuan, and the ratification of all future constitutional amendment proposals by popular referendum (requiring the approval of 50% of eligible voters, following approval by 75% of the Legislative Yuan). These reforms were due to take effect prior to the next legislative elections. Meanwhile, in June and again in September 2005 the Supreme Court rejected the appeals of the 'pan-blue' alliance to have the results of the 2004 presidential election declared invalid. In July Ma Ying-jeou, the mayor of Taipei, was elected Chairman of the KMT, in the party's first leadership election. Ma received 72.4% of votes cast by party members to defeat Wang Jin-pyng, President of the Legislative Yuan.

The mid-term elections for city and county magistrates held in December 2005 resulted in significant gains for the KMT, which took 14 of the 23 contested constituencies, leading to considerable embarrassment for the DPP, which won in only six. The KMT also outperformed the DPP in elections for county councillors and township governors, which for the first time were held simultaneously with the elections for magistrates. Following the elections, Su Tseng-chang resigned from the post of Chairman of the DPP. Yu Shyi-kun, the former Premier and latterly Secretary-General to the President, was elected as his replacement in the following month.

In January 2006 Frank Hsieh resigned as Premier, citing the failure of the legislature to approve his proposed budget for 2006 as the main reason for his departure, while also hinting at policy disagreements with President Chen; in his farewell speech Hsieh warned Chen that the policy of a separate sovereign identity for Taiwan was not supported by the majority of the population. The DPP's poor electoral performance was also regarded by some as a contributory factor in his resignation, as was a scandal over allegations of corruption and exploitation surrounding the construction of the metro system in Kaohsiung, where hundreds of Thai construction workers had reportedly rioted in August 2005 in protest at their poor living and working conditions. President Chen appointed Su Tseng-chang to replace Hsieh; the new appointee thereby became Chen's fifth Premier since the President's accession to power in 2000. The new Executive Yuan was sworn in on 25 January 2006. Tsai Ing-wen became Vice-Premier and Minister of the Consumer Protection Commission, Lee Yi-yang was appointed Minister of the Interior, Huang Chih-fang was the new Minister of Foreign Affairs, and Joseph J. C. Lyu took the post of Minister of Finance. In all, 14 new appointments were made, while the remaining 29 members of the Executive Yuan were retained from the previous administration. Meanwhile, President Chen appointed the former Minister of Foreign Affairs, (Mark) Chen Tan-sun, as presidential Secretary-General, after the post was reportedly refused by Hsieh, who stated his intention to withdraw from politics.

President Chen's reiteration in January 2006 of his commitment to the ratification by referendum of a new constitution by 2008, his proposed abolition of the NUC and his declaration that he intended to reapply for membership of the UN under the name of 'Taiwan' (see above) drew strong criticism from the opposition. Joseph Wu, Minister of the Mainland Affairs Council, noted that the NUC had not in fact convened since 1999 and was so poorly funded as to be effectively useless. In February 2006 the DPP administration announced its intention to change Taiwan's official name, its flag, its national anthem and the definition of its territory. In April Chen participated in an unprecedented televised meeting with Ma Ying-jeou. On the following day the special defence budget proposed in June 2004 was opposed for the 50th time by the 'pan-blue' alliance in the Legislative Yuan.

In May 2006 President Chen's authority was greatly undermined by the detention of his son-in-law, Chao Chien-ming, on charges of insider dealing. It was alleged that in 2005 Chao had purchased in his mother's name, 20m. shares of the Taiwan Development Corporation, a state-owned property company, having learned that the value of the company's stock was about to increase. Chao relinquished his membership of the DPP in an attempt to protect the party's image. (Subsequently indicted, along with his father and three others, Chao was sentenced to six years' imprisonment in December.) Although Chen had apologized to the nation for his family's involvement in the affair, the PFP instigated a campaign to remove the President from office.

In May 2006 former DPP legislator Shen Fu-hsiung confirmed an allegation that in the 1990s, during his campaign for the mayoralty of Taipei, President Chen had received no fewer than six political donations from the fugitive tycoon Chen You-hao. (Former head of the Tuntex group, Chen You-hao had fled Taiwan in 2002 when Tuntex was in financial difficulties, and was subsequently accused of embezzling funds from the group.) Shen also claimed that he had accompanied Chen You-hao on a visit to the President's wife, Wu Shu-jen (also a former legislator), to whom the tycoon had given nearly US $200,000, an accusation that Wu had previously denied. Two days later the 'pan-blue' alliance submitted a recall motion to the legislature in the hope of removing President Chen.

On 1 June 2006, under intense political pressure, President Chen ceded much of his authority to Premier Su Tseng-chang. Henceforth the President would no longer have the power to dictate policy or appoint members of the Executive Yuan, but would remain in charge of foreign and defence policy and would oversee relations with the People's Republic. The President also announced that he would play no further active role within the DPP. However, opposition politicians continued to demand Chen's resignation; protest rallies were held in the days that followed in an effort to increase pressure on the President to stand down. In a live televised speech Chen defended his administration and denied the allegations that had been made against his family. The motion of recall was voted upon in late June: despite gaining some support from the KMT (90 votes, including that of Wang Jin-pyng, the President of the Legislative Yuan, who was supposed to remain neutral), the 'pan-blue' alliance received just 119 votes, thus falling short of the number of votes (two-thirds of the seats currently occupied) required to put the motion to a national referendum. However, it was thought that the opposition might subsequently attempt to remove the Government by tabling a vote of no confidence in the Premier.

At the end of June 2006 it was announced that Ho Chih-chin, an academic, would succeed Joseph J. C. Lyu as Minister of Finance. Lyu, who had come under criticism for his handling of negotiations over the management of Mega Financial Holding (a major provider of financial services), retained a position within the Executive Yuan, as Minister without Portfolio. In early July party factions within the DPP unanimously approved the candidacy of former Premier Frank Hsieh in the forthcoming Taipei mayoral election.

Controversy surrounding President Chen continued. In July 2006 prosecutors questioned his wife, Wu Shu-jen, in relation to allegations that she and her doctor, Huang Fang-yen, had acted on behalf of businessmen who wished to acquire the Sogo department store and that in return Wu had accepted vouchers worth about US $185,000. A newspaper report claimed that forged receipts to the value of around US $600,000 had been submitted for reimbursement under the special allowances budget of the Office of the President. This was confirmed by a KMT legislator, Chiu Yi, who accused the President of having embezzled the money, although Chiu failed to provide any evidence to support his allegation. The Office of the President also came under scrutiny for the alleged improper use of taxpayers' money from May 2000 to pay the wages of the housekeeper at an apartment occupied by the President before his move to his official residence in January 2001, and which subsequently became the home of his daughter. DPP legislators in turn accused KMT Chairman Ma Ying-jeou of remitting a proportion of his official allowance as mayor of Taipei into his personal account for private use, and reported their suspicions to the National Audit Office. Meanwhile, Premier Su Tseng-chang appeared to be consolidating his position within the DPP after the Conference on Sustaining Taiwan's Economic Development, held in late July 2006, during which he gained the support of local business groups and trade unions. At the DPP convention, also held in July, the party voted by a small majority to dissolve its factions in an attempt to promote unity.

In August 2006 the Executive Yuan underwent a further reorganization when the Minister of Economic Affairs, Hwang In-san, who had resigned on the grounds of ill health, was replaced by his deputy, Chen Ruey-long. Also in August, the Minister of Transportation and Communications, Kuo Yao-chi, offered to resign, in order to take responsibility for a scandal that had arisen from the controversial awarding of a contract for an electronic motorway toll collection system. She was replaced by Tsai Duei. Prosecutors began to question President Chen over the alleged misuse of public funds. Meanwhile, the President continued to antagonize the KMT (and mainland China) by reiterating that he intended to draft a new constitution, and that Taiwan should apply to join the UN as an observer under the name of 'Taiwan'. In early August the PFP announced that it would begin an attempt to impeach Chen. Shih Ming-teh, a former DPP chairman, subsequently announced the formation of a 'one million people' mass movement to remove the President from office. Within days Shih's campaign had attracted more than 1m. supporters, each of whom donated NT $100 to show their commitment to the cause. Shih vowed that he and his supporters would stage a round-the-clock protest outside the presidential office in the following month and that they would not disperse until the President resigned. Neither the KMT nor the PFP was prepared officially to participate in the campaign, instead encouraging party members to attend the rallies.

In September 2006 at least 100,000 demonstrators rallied on the streets of Taipei, wearing red to signify their anger at Chen's alleged corruption. Despite inclement weather conditions, around 4,000 spent the night in front of the presidential office, and many stayed for several days until a march in mid-September. The DPP organized a rival rally the next day. The PFP again attempted to initiate a recall motion against the President, and in late September the Legislative Yuan voted by 106 to 82 to refer the motion for review by a parliamentary committee prior to a full debate in the chamber in October. By mid-October the momentum against the President had increased, with violent skirmishes (including a scuffle between two rival legislators from the DPP and KMT) marring the official National Day celebrations. Demonstrators caused serious disruption of the events, obstructing Chen's motorcade, blocking roads and effectively besieging the presidential office. None the less, the next recall motion against Chen again failed when the opposition secured only 116 votes, still short of the requisite two-thirds' majority. Later in October the opposition once more blocked a controversial arms bill involving multi-million dollar weapons purchases from the USA (see above).

In early October 2006 President Chen's wife, Wu Shu-jen, had been cleared by prosecutors of wrongdoing during the takeover of the Sogo department store (see above) on the basis of lack of evidence. In early November, however, prosecutors declared that they had sufficient evidence to charge Chen with misuse of public funds and that they were prevented from doing so only by his presidential immunity. No such immunity surrounded Wu Shu-jen, who was indicted along with three former presidential aides on charges of forgery and corruption. According to the prosecutors, Wu and the three senior aides had misappropriated NT $14.8m. from the 'state affairs fund'. While the prosecutors accepted Chen's explanation that in two of the six cases being investigated the funds had been used for secret diplomatic missions, they concluded that the use of such assets in four other cases could not be verified. Opposition members immediately demanded Chen's resignation and urged the DPP to join them in approving a motion of recall against the President, who attributed the apparent irregularities in the use of the state affairs fund to poorly defined regulations. Meanwhile, thousands of protesters once more took to the streets of Taipei, again demanding the President's resignation. The demonstration was spurned by the PFP and the KMT; however, the latter warned that the President could be impeached only by formal legal proceedings. The opposition then initiated a third recall motion against the President. Furthermore, disagreements began to emerge within the ranks of the DPP, when two members resigned from the Legislative Yuan in order to demonstrate dissatisfaction with their party's handling of the scandal. DPP legislators filed a lawsuit against Ma Ying-jeou, accusing him of embezzling public funds.

When the crucial recall vote was held in late November 2006, the DPP again rallied to support its leader, boycotting the vote and thus preventing the motion from obtaining the requisite two-thirds' majority. Moreover, at mayoral elections held in Taipei and Kaohsiung in December the DPP performed better than anticipated. Although the DPP candidate in Taipei, Frank Hsieh, lost to his KMT rival, Hau Long-bin, Hsieh nevertheless garnered 40.9% of the votes, an increase of 5.0% in comparision with the mayoral election of 2002. In Kaohsiung the DPP candidate, Chen Chu, won by a narrow margin to become the island's first female mayor.

Party differences were temporarily put aside in late December 2006 when the KMT voted with the Government to place the long-stalled arms procurement bill (see above) on the legislative agenda. The proposed legislation, which the KMT had previously boycotted along with the PFP, would provide for the purchase of US weapons from the annual budget of the Ministry of Defense, rather than from a special budget. In June 2007 budget legislation, which encompassed funding for military procurement that had been debated and altered by the Legislative Yuan, was finally approved.

In January 2007 the KMT and PFP formalized a party alliance, undertaking to present a single candidate in each district in the legislative election scheduled for early 2008. In March Lee Jye, Minister of National Defense, was expelled from the KMT as a result of a dispute regarding a government order to remove statues of Chiang Kai-shek from military premises, a decision with which Lee had complied. Ma Ying-jeou had resigned from the chairmanship of the KMT in February following accusations of forgery and of the embezzlement of NT $11.2m. during his tenure of the mayoralty of Taipei. Although Ma was replaced as KMT Chairman in April by Wu Poh-hsiung, in May the party confirmed Ma's candidacy for the presidency of Taiwan, and in August 2007 he was acquitted of all charges. Meanwhile in May 2007, following his defeat by former Premier Frank Hsieh in the contest for the nomination of the DPP presidential candidate, Su Tseng-chang resigned as Premier. President Chen appointed Chang Chun-hsiung, who had served as Premier in 2000–02, to replace Su. Premier Chang Chun-hsiung subsequently effected a government reorganization, although many of the incumbent members of the Executive Yuan were retained; notable exceptions included Tsai Ing-wen, who was succeeded by Chiou I-jen as Vice-Premier and Minister of the Consumer Protection Commission, and Lee Jye, who was replaced by Lee Tien-yu in the position of Minister of National Defense.

In September 2007 several prominent members of the DPP, including Chairman Yu Shyi-kun, Vice-President Annette Lu and former Minister of Foreign Affairs (Mark) Chen Tan-sun, were indicted on charges of corruption and forgery. Yu Shyi-kun, who resigned from the DPP chairmanship with immediate effect, was charged with the misuse of funds, which he claimed had been spent on public, rather than private, affairs. Meanwhile, similar charges against the DPP's presidential candidate, Frank Hsieh, and his vice-presidential candidate, Su Tseng-Chang, were withdrawn. President Chen returned to the position of DPP Chairman in October. In September the DPP had adopted a resolution affirming Taiwan's separate identity and appealing for a new constitution and a referendum on the issue of sovereignty; the name of 'Taiwan', it was stated, should enter into common usage without necessarily abolishing the official designation of the 'Republic of China'. The DPP continued its campaign against the commemoration of Chiang Kai-shek, cancelling two public holidays honouring the former President in August, and removing Chiang's name from a memorial hall in Taipei in December.

The Legislative and Presidential Elections of 2008 and Subsequent Events

Legislative elections held on 12 January 2008 resulted in a resounding victory for the KMT, which secured 81 seats (out of a reduced total of 113 seats in accordance with the constitutional amendments of 2005); the DPP, with only 27 seats, was thus defeated by a considerable margin. The Non-Partisan Solidarity Union (NPSU) won three seats and the KMT's alliance partner, the PFP, only one. Turn-out was extremely low in comparison with previous elections, at approximately 58%. Wang Jin-pyng was subsequently re-elected President of the Legislative Yuan. Voters were also presented with two proposals at referendums, both of which were rejected: the first proposed measure was the seizure of state assets allegedly appropriated by the KMT during and after its assumption of power in 1945; the second, submitted by the KMT, entailed additional anti-corruption measures. The results were widely regarded as an indication of public opposition to the DPP's forceful stance on sovereignty and Taiwan's status, as well as of the fear of jeopardizing relations with the mainland and of alienating the island's strategic allies. Following the DPP's defeat, Chen resigned as the party's Chairman and was replaced by Frank Hsieh. Premier Chang Chun-hsiung and the other members of the Executive Yuan submitted their resignations, but President Chen refused to accept these, citing a need for stability. In February, however, the Premier accepted the resignation of Lee Tien-yu from the post of Minister of National Defense, owing to criticism of his role in the establishment of a weapons company, the majority of which was privately owned. In mid-March the Minister of Finance, Ho Chih-chin, resigned, following his involvement in a scuffle at the offices of the DPP's presidential candidate, Frank Hsieh. Meanwhile, the election pledges of presidential candidate Ma Ying-jeou included an undertaking to pursue neither unification nor independence.

On 22 March 2008 Ma Ying-jeou of the KMT was elected the island's President, having received almost 58.5% of the votes cast, thus defeating Frank Hsieh, who subsequently announced that he would resign as Chairman of the DPP. At 76.3%, the level of participation by voters in the presidential election was high. However, the results of two concurrent referendums on the issue of the island's application for membership of the UN were declared invalid: although the number of votes in favour of each proposal exceeded 50% of the ballots cast, the total number of votes exercised failed to reach the requisite threshold of 50% of the registered electorate. The first proposal, which sought approval for the island's application under the name of Taiwan, was supported by the DPP; the KMT urged that this referendum be boycotted. The second referendum, initiated by the KMT, asked voters if they supported an application to return to the UN as 'the Republic of China' or alternatively as Taiwan or under any other suitable designation. Liu Chao-shiuan, a former Vice-Premier and hitherto President of Soochow University, was subsequently nominated as the island's Premier by the President-elect. In early May, just weeks before the swearing in of the new Government, Vice-Premier Chiou I-jen and Minister of Foreign Affairs Huang Chih-fang submitted their resignations as a result of a funding controversy: it was alleged that an attempt in 2006 to persuade Papua New Guinea to transfer diplomatic recognition from China to Taiwan, using almost US $30m. in aid, had failed, and that one of the intermediaries had absconded with the money. As the scandal widened, President Chen also denied his involvement in the affair; however, he and several others were subsequently prosecuted and brought to trial (see below). It was feared that the scandal had damaged Taiwan's reputation by drawing international attention to the practice of so-called 'chequebook diplomacy'.

Ma Ying-jeou was sworn in as President on 20 May 2008. Important appointments to the Executive Yuan, led by incoming Premier Liu Chao-shiuan and incorporating many who had served as ministers in the previous KMT administration, included that of Li Sush-der as Minister of Finance and that of Francisco H. L. Ou as Minister of Foreign Affairs. The new cabinet also included a record 11 women, notably Wang Ching-feng as Minister of Justice. Almost immediately, his presidential immunity having been removed upon his departure from office, it emerged that a corruption inquiry involving former President Chen had been instigated; in August, amid further allegations of financial impropriety, Chen left the DPP. Meanwhile, in May Tsai Ing-wen, a former Vice-Premier, was elected Chairwoman of the DPP, replacing Frank Hsieh.

In the latter part of 2008, as the island's economy began to deteriorate, large anti-Government protests were held. In October an estimated 600,000 Taiwanese attended a rally in Taipei, organized by the opposition DPP, to protest against the policies of President Ma Ying-jeou. The demonstrators were highly critical not only of the President's conduct of the economy but also of his policy of wider engagement with mainland China. In November about 150 police officers and dozens of protesters were reported to have been injured in violent clashes in Taipei during the visit of a senior mainland official, Chen Yunlin (see above), whose presence on the island provoked renewed protests against President Ma Ying-jeou's policy of developing closer relations with the People's Republic.

The Taiwanese Minister of the Department of Health, Lin Fang-yue, resigned in September 2008, taking responsibility for the Government's tardy response to the revelation that some milk products imported from mainland China had been contaminated. In October his successor, Yeh Ching-chuan, was reportedly hospitalized, following his alleged assault by opposition DPP legislators angered by the threat to health from the tainted Chinese produce.

In July 2008 the 15-year prison sentence imposed on Yen Wan-chin, former Vice-Minister of the Interior in the DPP administration, was reduced by the High Court when one of the bribery charges upon which he had been convicted in September 2007 was successfully challenged. Nevertheless, public concern about the issue of corruption continued to increase. Former Vice-Premier Chiou I-jen was arrested on charges of embezzlement at the end of October 2008; the senior DPP member was accused of having misappropriated diplomatic funds totalling US $500,000 in 2004.

In November 2008 former President Chen Shui-bian was taken into custody on suspicion of having embezzled public funds. After being detained for a month, Chen was formally indicted in December on charges of forgery, corruption, embezzlement and money-laundering. He was returned to prison, after being briefly released from detention. Chen's wife, son, daughter-in-law and 10 former colleagues were indicted on similar charges. In February 2009 Wu Shu-jen, the former President's wife (who, owing to ill health, had been unable to attend her trial in 2006—see above), pleaded guilty to charges of money-laundering and forgery, but she continued to deny charges of embezzlement. Her son, Chen Chih-chung, and other defendants also pleaded guilty to money-laundering charges. The trial of former President Chen, who had been an outspoken critic of the KMT Government, opened in March 2009, amid suggestions that it was politically motivated and related to his support for the independence of Taiwan. In September Chen was sentenced to life imprisonment upon his conviction by the Taipei District Court on various charges of corruption related to his misuse between 2000 and 2008 of public funds totalling the equivalent of US $15m. Chen's wife, who earlier in September had been found guilty of perjury, also received a life sentence. Found guilty of money-laundering, Chen Chih-chung and the former President's daughter-in-law received relatively short prison terms, while other relatives were given suspended sentences. Two former advisers were sentenced to 16 and 20 years' imprisonment.

Following his conviction, Chen made an unsuccessful attempt to claim that technically Taiwan remained under US military occupation and that the island's Government therefore had no legal right to place him on trial (see above). Later in September 2009, furthermore, prosecutors issued a series of new indictments against the former President and four others, including former Vice-Premier Chiou I-jen, alleging that funds allocated to the advancement of diplomatic relations had been embezzled (see above), but in June 2010 Chen was acquitted on the charge of misapproriating diplomatic funds. (Meanwhile, in February of that year Chen was indicted on fresh charges of abetting his subordinates to give false testimony, and in June the former President's appeal against his conviction was rejected by the High Court; however, on the basis that the sum involved was less than previously contended, his prison sentence was reduced to 20 years, as was that of his wife.)

In May 2009, meanwhile, as the first anniversary of President Ma Ying Jeou's assumption of office approached, thousands of protesters again demonstrated on the streets of Taipei against the Government's policy of greater engagement with the mainland. Tsai Ing-wen, Chairwoman of the opposition DPP, claimed that Taiwanese sovereignty was being seriously compromised and stated that the DPP would seek the holding of a referendum on the issue of Ma's plans for an FTA with China. Tsai led a march to the presidential office, where an overnight 'sit-in' protest was held. Thousands more participated in demonstrations in Kaohsiung and elsewhere.

In August 2009 Taiwan was struck by a devastating typhoon. More than 600 people were killed in the resultant mudslides and flooding, which was reported to be the worst for 50 years, with two metres of rain having fallen in a single weekend. The Government appealed for international assistance, in particular large cargo aircraft capable of transporting digging equipment, cranes and other machinery to the remote mountain areas affected by Typhoon Morakot. Although the army was swiftly mobilized, the rescue effort was hampered by the continuation of heavy rain. The Government was subsequently criticized for the shortcomings in its response to the disaster. On 7 September Premier Liu Chao-Shiuan unexpectedly announced that President Ma Ying-jeou had accepted his resignation, submitted in mid-August in order to take responsibility for the failings in the Government's handling of the aftermath of the typhoon. Liu was replaced by Wu Den-yih, hitherto the Secretary-General of the ruling Kuomintang. Chu Li-luan was appointed as Vice-Premier. In a major reorganization of the Executive Yuan, veteran diplomat Timothy Yang replaced Francisco Ou as Minister of Foreign Affairs. Other appointments included that of Jiang Yi-huah as Minister of the Interior and Kao Hua-chu as Minister of National Defense. The Minister of Finance, Li Sush-der, retained his portfolio. The appointment in late September of Shen Lyu-shun as Deputy Minister of Foreign Affairs drew intense criticism from the opposition DPP, owing to his involvement in an embezzlement scandal relating to his tenure during 2003–08 as head of Taiwan's representative office in Switzerland.

In July 2009 President Ma Ying-jeou was elected unopposed by party members as Chairman of the KMT, to replace Wu Po-hsiung in mid-October. As Chairman of the ruling party, therefore, Ma would be in a position to exercise greater control over the legislature, particularly with regard to the approval of appointments. On a party-to-party basis, Ma would also be able to exert more influence over Taiwan's relations with mainland China.

At local elections held in December 2009 the DPP won a much larger percentage of votes than that secured at previous local polls. A significant factor in the decline in support for the KMT was thought to be President Ma's focus on closer relations with mainland China, which many believed would ultimately jeopardize the island's sovereignty as well as lead to job losses. Shortly after the polls, King Pu-tsung replaced Chan Chun-po as Secretary-General of the KMT. Also, having returned to the post only eight months previously, Wu Nai-jen resigned as Secretary-General of the DPP on the grounds of ill health; he was subsequently replaced by Su Jia-chyuan. Amid increasing fears about Taiwan's growing economic dependency on China, later in December an estimated 30,000 Taiwanese joined a march through the city of Taichung to protest against the visit of senior mainland official Chen Yulin, who had travelled from Beijing to attend negotiations on a bilateral trade agreement (see above). The KMT suffered further reverses at by-elections in early 2010, when it lost six of seven seats contested to the DPP. Although the latter's representation in the Legislative Yuan was increased to 33 seats, the KMT nevertheless retained a large majority in the legislature. In March, however, the KMT also performed less well than anticipated at local elections to choose the speakers and vice-speakers of county and city councils. Nevertheless, in June the KMT fared better than the DPP at local elections in 17 counties and cities.

Wang Ching-feng, the Minister of Justice, unexpectedly resigned in March 2010, owing to her opposition to the removal of the five-year moratorium on the implementation of the death penalty. A former human rights activist, Wang had refused to approve the enforcement of the penalty on 44 prisoners who awaited execution, her stance being at variance with that of the Government. She was replaced by Tseng Yung-fu. Other new appointments to the Executive Yuan included that of Emile Chi-jen Sheng, who assumed the post of Minister of the Council for Cultural Affairs. Also in March, the Minister of the Department of Health, Yaung Chih-liang, withdrew his resignation, submitted earlier in the month but rejected by the Premier, with whom he had disagreed about the scale of increases in health insurance costs.

There were violent scenes in the Legislative Yuan in April 2010, when opponents clashed during a debate on the issue of the opening of Taiwanese institutes of higher education to students from mainland China. In May, in order to pursue his election campaign for a mayoralty, Vice-Premier Eric Chu resigned from the Executive Yuan. He was replaced by Sean Chen, hitherto the Chairman of the Financial Supervisory Commission, who also assumed his predecessor's responsibility for the Consumer Protection Commission. Chen Yu-chang was appointed to chair the Financial Supervisory Commission, and Christina Liu became Minister of the Council for Economic Planning and Development, succeeding Tsai Hsun-hsiung.

In late June 2010 tens of thousands of demonstrators, including former President Lee Teng-hui, rallied in Taipei to protest against the Government's proposals for the new trade agreement with China (see Relations with the People's Republic—above). The opposition DPP and TSU maintained that the proposed ECFA would not only jeopardize Taiwanese manufacturing industries, by permitting a substantial increase in imports of inexpensive products from the mainland, but also undermine the island's separate political identity; however, the parties' demands for the holding of referendum on the issue of the ECFA were repeatedly rejected. In the following month several members of the Legislative Yuan were injured and the Premier was prevented from delivering his speech when the opposition disrupted the introduction of the law into the chamber. The Speaker then ruled that the bill should proceed directly to its second reading, thereby circumventing the committee stage. In response to this omission of the process of detailed examination, the DPP declared that it would boycott all forthcoming parliamentary proceedings.

In July 2010 the President of the Judicial Yuan, Lai In-jaw, and the body's Vice-President resigned in response to the arrest of three high court judges and one prosecutor in connection with a new corruption scandal. It was alleged that the senior judges had collectively accepted bribes, totalling as much as NT $1m., in exchange for the acquittal of a former KMT legislator and county magistrate (whose whereabouts subsequently became unknown) on charges of financial impropriety related to the development of a science park. In August, following an extensive operation by the authorities, several additional suspects were detained in connection with the allegations. In July, meanwhile, with public concern about the involvement of senior functionaries in such cases rising, President Ma announced the establishment of a new agency to combat official corruption. The agency, which was to form part of the Ministry of Justice, was to comprise four departments, one of which was to be responsible for government ethics. Legislation providing for the establishment of the Agency Against Corruption received parliamentary approval in April 2011. Meanwhile, a human rights commission, headed by Vice-President Vincent Siew, was established in December 2010.

In September 2010 eight incumbent and former members of the Legislative Yuan received prison sentences of between seven and 10 years, following their conviction on charges of bribery. Six of the defendants had been acquitted in a previous trial. In the following month the new President of the Judicial Yuan, Lai Hau-min, expressed his determination to eradicate corruption. In November a total of 13 officials were indicted in connection with the judicial corruption case. In January 2011 the Commander of the Air Force, Gen. Lei Yu-chi, was removed from his post, following the revelation that he had enlisted air force personnel to serve at lavish celebrations for the wedding of his son. Lei was replaced by Gen. Yen Ming. In March impeachment proceedings began against the three high court judges and the prosecutor arrested on charges of bribery.

Former President Chen's appeal against his conviction was rejected by the High Court in June 2010. However, on the basis that the sum involved was less than previously stated, his sentence was reduced from life imprisonment to 20 years, as was that of his wife. In November Chen was acquitted of bribery charges relating to a bank merger and to money-laundering activities. Wu Shu-jen and other family members, along with several others, were also acquitted on related charges. In the same month, however, the Supreme Court upheld Chen's conviction in connection with two other bribery cases. In December the High Court ruled that the former President serve a maximum combined sentence of 17 years and six months. In February 2011, having recently received an additional sentence upon her conviction of further charges of bribery, the frail Wu Shu-jen was deemed unfit to remain in prison and released from detention. Meanwhile, her husband returned to court to answer new bribery charges. In August Chen received an additional prison term of two years and eight months, having been found guilty of charges of money-laundering and of the forging of documents. In September the former President's son, Chen Chih-chung, began a period of community service in lieu of a three-month prison term following his sentencing on charges of perjury in June.

At the end of June 2011 another former DPP President, Lee Teng-hui, was charged with embezzling NT $238m. from state funds. Similar to the charges upon which former President Chen had been convicted, the allegations related to the existence of a clandestine account reportedly used for the purposes of financing covert diplomatic initiatives. In July one of the first high-profile cases to be referred to the newly established Agency Against Corruption was that of a senior Taiwanese envoy to Fiji. Victor Chin resigned from his post and was subsequently suspended from the Ministry of Foreign Affairs, amid allegations of irregularities that included the use of public funds to finance an extra-marital affair with a Japanese diplomat who had also been stationed in Fiji.

Campaigning for the mayoral elections of November 2010 was marred by the shooting of Lien Chen-wen, the son of former Vice-President Lien Chan, and the killing of a bystander. Although it was widely believed that the attack was politically motivated, it was subsequently reported that Lien was not the intended target of the assailant, who was apparently involved in a dispute relating to a land transaction. In what was regarded as a major test for President Ma, the KMT won three important mayoralties, including that of Taipei, while the opposition DPP took the southern cities of Kaohsiung and Tainan. The KMT was also successful in elections for local speaker and vice-speaker posts in December, when the DPP won only that of Tainan. Also in December, having been persuaded to return to the position in May, Wu Nai-jen confirmed his retirement as Secretary-General of the DPP. Su Jia-chyuan agreed to resume the post. The DPP was encouraged by its resounding success at by-elections to fill two vacant seats in the Legislative Yuan, held in Kaohsiung and Tainan in March 2011.

In January 2011 King Pu-tsung resigned as Secretary-General of the KMT, in order to lead President Ma Ying-jeou's campaign for re-election in 2012; King was replaced by Liao Liao-yi. At the beginning of February a minor cabinet reorganization included the appointment of Chiu Wen-ta as Minister of the Department of Health, in place of Yaung chi-liang who had resigned in early January. At the end of April President Ma was nominated unopposed as the KMT's presidential candidate. Ma subsequently chose Premier Wu Den-yih as his vice-presidential candidate. On the same day Tsai Ing-wen became Taiwan's first female presidential candidate when she defeated former Premier Su Tseng-chang to secure the nomination of the DPP. After the unsuccessful Su declined an offer of candidacy for the island's vice-presidency, in September Tsai selected Su Jia-chyuan as her partner. However, the tardy nature of Tsai's decision with regard to her vice-presidential candidate incurred some criticism.

The establishment of the Taiwanese National Party (TNP) was announced in July 2011, with the aim of promoting Taiwanese identity. The objectives of the TNP included the holding of a referendum on the issue of self-determination for Taiwan. Huang Hua, erstwhile adviser to former President Chen, was appointed Chairman of the new party. Although the TNP planned to nominate its own candidates for the forthcoming legislative elections, the party declared its intention to endorse the candidacy of the DPP's Tsai Ing-wen in the contest for the Taiwanese presidency.

The latter part of 2011 was thus dominated by the forthcoming legislative and presidential elections. In a departure from tradition, the two elections were to be held simultaneously, on 14 January 2012.

Economy

ROBERT F. ASH

INTRODUCTION

Since 1949 the economic development of Taiwan has been significantly influenced by historical and international geo-strategic factors, as well as by the familiar demands and dictates of domestic growth and improved material and social welfare. The main historical influences have been two-fold. First, Taiwan's early post-1949 development capacity was enhanced by the legacy of important economic initiatives, undertaken by Japan during its colonization of Taiwan between 1895 and 1945. Second, the defeat during the Chinese Civil War of the forces of the Chinese Nationalist Party (Kuomintang—KMT) by those of the Chinese Communist Party, and the subsequent transfer, in 1949, of the Government of the Republic of China to Taiwan were cathartic events that prompted and facilitated fundamental shifts in economic strategy. These shifts were eventually translated into the establishment of a free market economy, based on private ownership and private enterprise.

From 1949 until the 1970s mainland China's alienation from the USA, Japan and most Western European countries served Taiwan's economic interests well by enabling the island to forge increasingly close economic links with the capitalist world. Thereafter, however, almost universal recognition of the People's Republic as the sole legitimate Government of China left Taiwan's international diplomatic and political status seriously exposed. Nevertheless, the positive momentum of economic growth was maintained into and beyond the 1980s, by which time Taiwan's economic maturity had come to be demonstrated in terms of both the structure and level of its development. A noteworthy feature of its performance was the attainment of rapid and sustained growth alongside an equitable distribution of income. Such features of the island's growth record have prompted some to view Taiwan's as a development model for other newly industrializing countries in Asia and elsewhere.

With the benefit of hindsight, in terms of its economic development Taiwan can be seen to have passed several notable watersheds during the last six decades. The first of these was the abandonment, starting in the late 1950s, of a strategy of inward-orientated import-substitution in favour of one of outward-orientated export promotion. This important shift signalled the beginning of a process that witnessed Taiwan's emergence as one of the most important trading nations in the world. A second watershed, dating from the 1980s, was the development of a comparative advantage in knowledge-intensive industries. This was made possible by maximizing the benefits of tertiary education in order to generate high-technology human resources, and by engaging in investment in research and development (R & D). By such means, Taiwan has become one of the global powerhouses of information technology (IT) development, especially in the design and manufacture of semiconductors. However, by far the most important watershed was the Government's lifting of martial law (in July 1987) and the process of economic rapprochement with mainland China to which this decision gave rise. The outcome has been the accelerated integration, since the late 1980s, of Taiwan's economy with that of China. The most dramatic recent manifestation of this process was the signing in June 2010 of a cross-Straits preferential trade agreement, the Economic Co-operation Framework Agreement (ECFA). Whatever one's views of the threats and opportunities inherent in Taiwan's growing economic dependence on China, there is no doubt that Taiwan's economic fate is now inextricably linked with that of its mainland neighbour.

As well as history and geo-strategic forces, natural and geographical factors have played an important part in Taiwan's economic development. The island lacks mineral and energy resources in any significant quantities, making it necessary to import most of the raw materials needed by domestic industry. The geo-strategic dimension is captured in Taiwan's geographical location on trade routes between Japan, Korea, China and countries of South-East Asia, which has long given it a central, strategically important position in the Asia-Pacific trading region. The small size of Taiwan's economy has also significantly shaped its development trajectory. In terms of surface area, the island ranks 139th out of 250 countries included in the US Central Intelligence Agency's *World Factbook*, although the same source shows it to be the 50th largest in terms of population. Thus, in contrast to mainland China's traditional inward-looking stance and associated quest for economic self-sufficiency, Taiwan's inherent natural and market constraints have forced it to look outwards in its pursuit of economic growth and modernization. In short, its strong external orientation since the early 1960s has been a characteristic feature, as well as a critical determinant, of Taiwan's post-1949 economic development.

From a post-Second World War developmental perspective, Taiwan's growth and overall economic performance is one of the most remarkable in the world. However, viewed from a more recent regional perspective, comparisons of Taiwan's economic growth with that of other East and South-East Asian countries highlight the downturn in the island's growth record prior to the onset of the global financial crisis. In 2007, for example, data issued by Taipei's Directorate-General of Budget, Accounting and Statistics (DGBAS) show that gross domestic product (GDP) growth in Taiwan exceeded that of Japan, the Republic of Korea (South Korea) and Thailand, but was lower than that of China, Hong Kong, India, Indonesia, Malaysia, the Philippines and Singapore. Nevertheless, in the same year economic growth remained significantly higher than that of France, Germany, Italy, the United Kingdom and the USA. However, the global economic recession has taken a serious toll on Taiwan's economy (see below), and IMF estimates published in April 2010 indicated that real GDP growth in 2008 was below that of all the comparator East and South-East Asian countries cited above, except Japan. In 2009 growth remained negative and was lower than in those same countries, except Hong Kong. However, in 2010 a sharp recovery raised the rate of GDP increase to 10.9%—ahead even of mainland China and India, and in East and South-East Asia exceeded only by Singapore.

Despite its recent more disappointing growth performance, at least judged in the context of its own impressive record, Taiwan remains one of the world's most important economic and trading nations. In 2010 it ranked 19th in the world in terms of the size of its GDP on a purchasing-power parity basis (but 33rd in per caput terms), and was the 17th largest importer and 18th largest exporting nation. At the end of the same year the island held the fifth largest reserves of foreign exchange and gold in the world after China, Japan, Russia and Saudi Arabia, and ranked 22nd in terms of its cumulative stock of outward foreign direct investment (FDI). The 2011 'world competitiveness scoreboard', published by the International Institute for Management Development (based in Lausanne, Switzerland), ranked Taiwan sixth (two places higher than in the 2010 rankings). Meanwhile, reports published by the World Economic Forum in 2010–11 showed Taiwan in 13th place in terms of global competitiveness (one place lower than in the previous year), 11th in terms of higher education and training, and 20th in terms of technological readiness. The Economist Intelligence Unit (EIU—a research and analysis organization based in the United Kingdom) placed Taiwan 16th in its 'digital economy' rankings.

HISTORICAL CONTEXT OF ECONOMIC DEVELOPMENT

Following China's defeat by the Japanese in 1895, Taiwan was ceded, supposedly in perpetuity, to Japan. During the next half-century, until Japan's own defeat at the end of the Second World War led to the retrocession of the island to the Chinese Government, initiatives sponsored by Japanese colonial rulers had a major positive impact on the island's economy. Such developments took place against the background of a major surge in population growth, reflecting a sharp decline in the death rate unaccompanied by any similar decrease in birth rate. The outcome of these demographic changes was that between 1910 and 1940 Taiwan's total population rose from 3.3m. to 5.9m., registering an average annual rate of growth of almost 2%.

Economic growth under Japanese rule accelerated sharply. By 1936 net domestic product had risen by almost 200% above that of 1911, implying an average rate of growth of 4.2% per year. Concealed in this figure was buoyant growth of both agriculture (rising by well over 3% a year) and, albeit from a negligible base, industry (around 6% annually). In economic terms, Japan viewed Taiwan primarily as an agricultural base: above all, as a source of food (rice and sugar) in order to help meet the rising demand of its own rapidly growing population. The implications of this agricultural orientation were profound. Most directly, Japan's focus on food production facilitated the modernization of Taiwanese agriculture itself, through the introduction of new rice varieties, the increased application of modern farm inputs (e.g. chemical fertilizers) and the promotion of infrastructural construction (e.g. irrigation extension). Japan also helped to promote modern industrialization through the strong impetus it gave to the development of a modern sugar-refining industry in Taiwan. Finally, through the rapid expansion of rice and sugar shipments to Japan, it helped to transform Taiwan into a major export economy. Thus, between 1900–09 and 1930–39 not only did Taiwan's exports increase, on average, by almost 9% annually, but the share of such exports shipped to Japan rose from less than one-third to more than 90%. Meanwhile, the share of agricultural exports in the total also increased; by the 1930s farm products accounted for more than 85% of all Taiwan's exports.

In contrast to the experience of Korea under Japanese colonial rule, accelerated farm output growth seems to have benefited not only Japan's population, but also that of Taiwan. For example, estimates indicate that the surplus of food available to the indigenous population after the deduction of exports to Japan was sufficient to allow improvements in welfare, at least judged by levels of calorie intake. The social impact of the Japanese presence was also positive, owing to improvements in education and increased literacy among the Taiwanese population. None of this is to deny that colonial rule had negative consequences, too. Social policies were, for example, implemented without regard for Taiwan's own cultural traditions and values—even to the extent that Taiwanese children were forced to learn Japanese in preference to Chinese. Political control also resided unambiguously with the Japanese colonial authorities, with little or no scope for involvement in decision-making by Taiwanese. Nevertheless, there is a strong case for arguing that, even allowing for the destruction wrought by the Second World War, the legacy of colonial rule made a significant and positive contribution to Taiwan's post-War development.

The impact of the Second World War was considerable. US bombing caused immense damage to the island's physical infrastructure: by 1945 railways and harbours were operating at half-capacity. Production levels throughout the economy had also declined sharply. In agriculture, total rice output was less than two-thirds of its previous peak level; in industry, electric power had declined to 40% of its previous high point, while fertilizer and steel production were a mere 32% and 17%, respectively, of their corresponding levels. Inflationary pressures were also severe, the wholesale price index (WPI) having risen nearly 15-fold since 1942.

Japan's defeat in 1945 forced more than 250,000 Japanese to return to their homeland from Taiwan. Their exodus and the imposition of military rule from the mainland by the Nationalist Government under Chiang Kai-shek caused a major deterioration in economic and social conditions on the island. The new administration, headed by Governor-General Ch'en Yi, confiscated many Taiwanese industrial facilities and other property, which they added to Japanese assets that had already been seized. It used command economy methods to procure food and other agricultural goods, which it stockpiled for rationing purposes. Such actions encouraged a return to subsistence farming, led to the proliferation of black markets and severely impeded economic recovery. They also exacerbated price rises, giving rise to hyperinflation: between 1945 and 1949 the WPI increased by well over 5,600%. In general, because of the economic and social disruption associated with the 'inter-regnum' of military rule under Ch'en Yi, economic recovery from war-time dislocation was not to be completed until the early 1950s.

EVOLUTION OF ECONOMIC STRATEGY

By the end of 1949, following their defeat by the Chinese Communist forces, the Nationalist central Government and the remnants of its army had moved to Taiwan. The economy that the new Government inherited from the previous provincial administration of Ch'en Yi was in disarray. Inflationary pressures remained severe (in the first half of 1949 the retail price index rose by more than 50%); production levels were still sufficiently depressed to cause serious commodity shortages; and foreign exchange was scarce. The arrival of some 1.6m. civilians and military personnel from the mainland meanwhile exacerbated existing and widespread unemployment.

The first economic measures adopted by the new Government sought to address these problems. They embraced the introduction of centralized fiscal and monetary controls, as well as the imposition of strict regulation of foreign trade. By such means, the Government sought to re-establish economic discipline through more effective management of budgetary allocations.

Recourse to state-led methods of economic management accorded with the 'commandist' instincts of the KMT. During its years of power in mainland China the KMT had shown itself to be a keen advocate and practitioner of centralized economic decision-making. Moreover, in Taiwan itself, at the end of the war against Japan not only did the State take control of most of the large-scale manufacturing firms previously managed by Japanese entrepreneurs, but also new government monopolies were established. The belief that industrialization and economic growth were most effectively nurtured within a framework of state ownership and management was one that continued to enjoy widespread support within KMT circles after the Government's removal to Taiwan in 1949. It is a salutary reminder of the statist thrust of initial post-1949 economic strategy that until the second half of the 1950s less than one-half of industrial output was generated by the private sector.

The evidence suggests that in the early 1950s Chiang Kai-shek was uncertain of the direction of Taiwan's future economic strategy. The choice was between the establishment of a command economy, in which state-owned industrial enterprises would dominate, or the promotion of a competitive, capitalist market system. Chiang's solution was effectively to devolve the decision to a small group of close officials, whose responsibility it became to formulate the economic principles and create the institutions that would most effectively facilitate industrialization and growth. In addition to Chiang Kai-shek himself, without whose support the new strategic thrust would have been impossible, the most important agents of economic change were Ch'en Ch'eng, Yan Jiagan (C. K. Yen) and Yin Zhongrong (K. Y. Yin).

During the early 1950s the principal tasks of these economic policy-makers were to revive farm and industrial production, expand employment and reduce inflationary pressures. Between 1950 and 1952 they successfully fulfilled these goals by focusing their efforts on a number of carefully selected firms in the state enterprise sector that were best equipped and had the requisite resources to become the core of a small, but efficient, industrial sector, capable of raising output and expanding employment. The underlying rationale was that the activities of these enterprises would elicit increased demand from other firms, and eventually generate a virtuous circle of increased savings and investment throughout the manufacturing sector. Meanwhile, with a view to post-recovery growth, K. Y. Yin also encouraged state ministries and agencies to extend special assistance to 'infant' industries that were thought to have potential for expansion. In this way, a strategy of import-substituting industrialization (ISI) was initiated.

In the event, compared with other developing economies of the time, Taiwan's unmodified ISI phase was fairly brief and its associated policies quite mild. Until well into the second half of the 1950s, GDP growth was driven by the expansion of labour-intensive, low-technology light manufacturing industries. The goal of economic policy at the time was to reduce import costs by encouraging domestic production of basic necessities, such as cement, fertilizers and textiles. By contrast, production for export was a low priority. The range of exported goods was limited and mainly confined to agricultural commodities (rice, sugar, tea, etc.), the production of which had been encouraged by the Japanese colonial administration. These policies were supported by high tariffs, a high rate of protection for domestic producers and the imposition of exchange rate controls.

With regard to its longer-term impact, the most important policy initiative in the early 1950s was the implementation of land reform, comprising rent reduction, the distribution of public land and the reallocation of landlords' arable land (see also below). The Government's decision to espouse land redistribution was motivated by social, as much as economic, concerns. Above all, Chiang was determined to avoid rural instability of the kind that had been so effectively mobilized by the Chinese Communist Party on the mainland. However, in contrast to the violent campaigns that characterized land reform in China in the early 1950s, the dislocative impact of land redistribution in Taiwan was minimized. Not only were landlords allowed to retain land for their own farming purposes, but they were also compensated for land that was repossessed by being given shares in four major privatized industrial concerns.

Towards the end of the 1950s many of the former ISI policies were dismantled, as the Taiwanese economy was opened up and reorientated towards international markets. Under the impact of important new policy initiatives, Taiwan's economy began to change from an import-substituting regime characterized by modest expansion into one of accelerated export-driven GDP growth.

The first major policy initiative embraced exchange rate reform. Under the ISI regime, Taiwan had maintained a multiple exchange rate system characterized by overvaluation. In 1958 the New Taiwan Dollar (NT $) was devalued from NT $24.7 per US $1 to NT $40. At the same time, multiple exchange rates were abolished in favour of a single rate. The underlying intent of these measures, to reduce import demand and to increase exports, was emphasized two years later, when the Government, influenced by US thinking, introduced its Nineteen-Point Programme for Economic and Financial Reform. This watershed document effectively ended Taiwan's ISI strategy. It embodied a commitment to privatization, to be underpinned by increased domestic investment funded by higher savings; it sought to rationalize the government budget; and it gave added force to the earlier exchange rate reform by promoting measures to increase exports.

Taiwan's new strategic thrust was further highlighted by the enactment, in September 1960, of the Statute for the Encouragement of Investment, which offered tax benefits to export firms, including those in government-sponsored 'pioneer' sectors, such as electronics. Although it was to undergo several revisions, this Statute was to provide the legislative framework in which Taiwan's industrialization and export expansion would take place during the next 30 years until, in 1990, it was replaced by the Statute for the Promotion of Industrial Upgrading. Meanwhile, as the 1960s progressed, the 1958 and 1960 radical reforms were supplemented by further initiatives. These included the extensive use of import tax rebates and the extension of low-interest credit to exporting firms. Most important of all among these supplementary initiatives was the establishment of Export Processing Zones (EPZs), designed to facilitate the export activities of both domestic and foreign investors. The first EPZ was opened in Kaohsiung in 1965, and by the beginning of the 1970s 177 export-orientated firms were operating in the island's three EPZs, generating exports worth US $163m. The zones were especially effective in facilitating the inflow of foreign investment (already worth US $31m. by 1971 and destined to reach more than $350m. by 1990). Significant too was the Government's establishment of 'industrial estates' throughout Taiwan. These were designed to make the best possible use of the island's abundant labour force, and numerous companies benefited from them. Taken together, the EPZs and industrial estates encouraged the creation of new firms and laid the foundation for what has become one of the distinctive hallmarks of Taiwan's industrialization, namely the dominance of small and medium-sized enterprises (SMEs—see below), rather than the concentration of large firms, such as the Japanese *zaibatsu* and South Korean *chaebol*.

An important element in Taiwan's early development was the provision of large-scale aid from the USA. Between 1951 and 1964, when it began to be phased out, the cumulative total of US aid was US $1,280m. Its significance in the early post-1949 period is captured in the finding that in 1955 such disbursements were the equivalent of 9.5% of the island's GDP, and two-thirds of its imports. In the absence of US aid, the Government in Taipei would have confronted a difficult choice between lowering its defence budget and reducing its budgetary support for economic development. Although much US aid was defence-related, it is estimated that between 1952 and 1958 it also contributed significantly to capital formation in many indigenous firms.

As a result of the Government's export promotion strategy, during the 1960s labour-intensive, export-orientated industries became the main engine of Taiwan's economic growth. By the beginning of the 1970s, however, concern about the perceived 'shallowness' of the economy, as well as an aspiration to meet more of the island's rising demand for intermediate inputs for its expanding industries from domestic sources, encouraged economic officials to embark on a programme of heavy and chemical industrialization (HCI). Such economic considerations were given added force by political factors: the loss of Taiwan's UN seat in 1971 and the early stages of the process of rapprochement between the USA and China, symbolized by US President Richard Nixon's visit to China in the following year. With the benefit of hindsight, it is apparent that the impact of the HCI initiative was much less marked than that of the similar, but much more extensive, strategy pursued in South Korea at about the same time. This was to have two important consequences. First, Taiwan avoided massive foreign borrowing and reliance on big business in order to implement the policy of HCI, and thereby avoided the problems of high inflation, huge foreign debt and deteriorating income distribution that subsequently confronted South Korea. Second, Taiwan's milder HCI prevented the emergence of dominant, large-scale conglomerates and, instead of basic and petrochemical industries becoming the mainstay of the economy, Taiwan's industrial and export base continued to be dominated by small-scale labour-intensive activities, such as textiles, garment and consumer electronics production.

Taiwan's heavy industry programme, which was essentially a public sector initiative involving the creation of new state-owned enterprises, focused on four major sectors: steel, petrochemicals, shipbuilding and cars. Among these, the most significant developments were in the steel and petrochemical sectors. Following the construction of a large-scale, integrated steel mill, China Steel became an important industrial force on the island. From 1978 its production rose rapidly. Its efficiency and ability to provide a high-quality product forced the closure of many small-scale producers. During the 1980s China Steel doubled its annual production capacity, and by the first half of the 1990s it ranked 24th in the world in terms of crude steel output. Petrochemicals also expanded rapidly in the 1980s, under the aegis of the China Petroleum Corpn (CPC). It was estimated that by 1986 Taiwan's petrochemical industry was generating more than 15% of GDP, and around 25% including downstream industries. (Later, privatization changed the structure of the petrochemical industry; environmental concerns also encouraged producers to move overseas.)

The very nature of Taiwan's heavy industrialization placed a premium on access to energy at precisely the time when the two price surges (in 1974 and 1978) had hugely increased the cost of oil. Therefore, when demand for further industrial upgrading became evident in the early 1980s, there was a perception that future industrial structural change should be focused towards more knowledge- and technology-intensive industries, such activities having the advantage of minimizing demand for high-cost overseas oil. Out of such deliberation emerged a new strategic focus for Taiwan's industrial sector: namely, the expansion of machinery and electronics: high value-added activities with good market potential and the possibility of favourable domestic linkage effects, and an emphasis on technology rather than energy inputs (to the benefit of the environment). Other high-technology sectors were subsequently added to the list.

The development of these industries marked another important watershed in Taiwan's economic and social development. In 1979 the Government introduced its first Science and Technology Research Plan (1979–81), and oversaw the establishment of the Institution for Information Industry—a non-governmental organization with public and private sector involvement, designed to promote the development of the IT industry. The single most important institutional initiative was the creation, in December 1980, of the Hsinchu Science Park (sometimes referred to as Taiwan's 'Silicon Valley'), which has continued to play an outstanding role in promoting R & D and facilitating IT industrial expansion to the present day.

Under the impact of these and other initiatives, the IT industry underwent rapid expansion, most notably in the production of semiconductors and computers (see below). Crucial to this success was the implementation of a comprehensive range of support measures, including tax incentives, concessionary loans, R & D sponsorship and technology transfer. The rise of the semiconductor sector was attributable to a variety of factors, including the existence of buoyant global demand for components for the computer industry, access to a 'reverse brain drain' of Taiwanese-born, but US-trained, experts (many of whom had experience of having worked in California's 'Silicon Valley'), and the benefits of the flexibility and adaptability of SMEs to the industry's short product cycle. Meanwhile, the Government's continuing role in facilitating technology transfer and technology diffusion did much to help generate rapid growth.

The last and unfinished part of the evolution of Taiwan's post-1949 economic strategy dates from the late 1980s, when the Government in Taipei removed previous restrictions on cross-Straits trade and investment in mainland China. The full implications of this decision have yet to become evident. However, what is already clear is that by precipitating a rapid and ongoing increase in economic relations between the two countries a major new economic dimension to the political discourse on Taiwan's evolving relationship with China has been added (for detailed consideration of cross-Straits economic relations, see below). The issue has remained a source of ongoing debate and concern. In particular, during the two Democratic Progressive Party (DPP) administrations of President Chen Shui-bian (2000–08), it was at the centre of acrimonious inter-party disputes over economic policy. Following the presidential election of 2000, in which the DPP secured victory over a divided KMT by the most slender of margins, fears that the incoming Chen administration might actively espouse Taiwanese independence (a stance with which the DPP was closely associated) exacerbated the political impasse between the KMT and the DPP. President Chen's re-election in March 2004 merely served to increase inter-party political tensions, as well as those between Taiwan and China. The decisive return of a KMT Government under President Ma Ying-jeou did not remove domestic political differences, but the KMT's more accommodating attitude towards the mainland placed political relations between the two sides on a firmer basis and also resulted in accelerated progress towards further integration of the two economies. This was confirmed by the signing in mid-2010 of the ECFA between Taiwan and China.

ECONOMIC GROWTH AND STRUCTURAL CHANGE

Between the early 1950s and the first half of the 1960s Taiwan succeeded in laying the foundations of self-sustaining growth. Economic growth rates were among the highest in the world (real GDP growth, in constant 1996 NT dollars, averaged 8.3% annually during 1952–65), while inflationary pressures remained modest. Until the mid-1960s, however, a large part of the increase in output was absorbed by a rapid rise in population, as the rate of natural increase remained high (averaging 3.4% a year). Even so, real per caput GDP growth of 4.9% per year meant that average income rose more than two-and-a-half times between 1952 and 1965. All sectors shared in this buoyant performance, with agriculture, industry and services growing by 5.0%, 12.5% and 10.4%, respectively.

Whether viewed through estimates of per caput income or through more aggregate measures of national product, investment, exports and growth, data for the late 1960s and throughout the 1970s offer evidence of an even more buoyant economic performance. Between 1966 and 1980 GDP grew at an average annual rate of 9.8%, while per caput income growth accelerated even more sharply, to 7.1%, owing to a reduction in population expansion from 2.7% to 1.8% annually.

During the 1950s changes in the structure of GDP were fairly modest. The shares of both agriculture and services in GDP contracted (from 32.2% to 28.5%, and from 48.1% to 44.6%, respectively), while the contribution of industry increased from 19.7% to 26.9%. Thereafter, economic structural change accelerated under the impact of first, the process of industrial deepening, and second, that of industrial upgrading and diversification. The economic implications of these initiatives were evident in terms of their impact on markets, ownership and industrial composition. By 1980 the agricultural sector's contribution to GDP had contracted to 7.7%, while that of industry had expanded to 45.7%. By contrast, the share of the tertiary sector remained fairly stable.

Although Taiwan's economic growth slowed down after 1980, GDP expansion during the next two decades remained buoyant (averaging 7.9% annually during 1981–90 and 6.4% during 1991–2000). By the 1980s the growth contribution of the agricultural sector had become insignificant, and the strong momentum of economic expansion was sustained by manufacturing and, increasingly, services. Manufacturing output more than doubled in the 1980s, and increased by a further 69% in the following decade; the corresponding figures for the tertiary sector were 147% and 108%, respectively. Perhaps most noteworthy of all was the expansion of financial services, the average annual growth of which was 9.4% between 1980 and 2000. Such figures highlight the increasing maturity of Taiwan's economy as it shifted from one based on manufacturing industry to one driven by high valued-added services. By 2000 the service sector accounted for two-thirds of GDP (23% from financial services alone), while the industrial share had contracted to 32.4% (26.4% from manufacturing). Within these figures is also the finding that, unlike most of its East and South-East Asian neighbours, Taiwan emerged relatively unscathed from the Asian financial crisis of the late 1990s. Between 1997 and 1998 real GDP growth declined from 6.6% to 4.6%, the lowest level since 1982. However, this growth contraction was much less severe than that of the other three first-echelon Asian 'dragon economies' (Hong Kong, South Korea and Singapore).

In 1999 and 2000 the Taiwanese economy maintained its buoyant growth momentum, with GDP expansion averaging around 5.8%. In the following year, however, in the aftermath of the bursting of the IT 'bubble' in the USA, Taiwan suffered a dramatic downturn in its economic position as it confronted recessionary conditions. In 2001, for the first time in its post-1949 history, GDP growth was negative: in real terms, it declined by 1.7%. Underlying this bleak performance was an unprecedented contraction in Taiwan's merchandise trade, with exports and imports both decreasing sharply (by 10% and 17%, respectively, compared with declines of 20% and 28% in the USA). Meanwhile, private final consumption, which had grown by 6% annually during the previous five years, rose by little more than 0.5% in 2001, while gross capital formation recorded a real decline of 20%. Unemployment too increased sharply: from 293,000 in 2000 to 450,000 in 2001 (i.e. from 3.5% to 4.6% of the labour force).

In the event, the recession was brief and in 2002 positive growth resumed; thereafter, until the onset of the global financial crisis, annual GDP averaged 4.7% in 2002–07. During these years manufacturing recorded quite buoyant growth (averaging 5.2% per year), but its contribution to GDP continued to decline relative to that of services. Thus, by 2007 the tertiary sector's contribution to GDP had reached more than 70%, while that of industry (construction, as well as manufacturing) had decreased to less than 25%, and agriculture to a mere 1.5%.

With the onset of the global economic downturn, annual GDP growth in 2008 declined to a mere 0.7% (after 2001, the second lowest figure on record since 1949). Initially, conditions worsened in 2009, when a pronounced decline, of 9.1%, in year-on-year quarterly growth was in evidence in the first quarter. Thereafter, however, a recovery slowly began to get under way. In the second and third quarters GDP continued to contract, but in the final quarter substantial growth of 9.1% was registered; nevertheless, in 2009 as a whole there was an overall contraction in GDP, of 1.9%. The most important factor in Taiwan's economic downturn following the global financial crisis was the steep decline in both foreign trade and domestic investment. In 2008 and 2009 gross fixed capital formation decreased by more than 11% in each year. The contraction in foreign trade was most apparent in 2009, when exports and imports declined, respectively, by 9.1% and 13.4%. By contrast, consumption was much less affected. In both years government consumption growth remained positive, albeit at a low rate; although private consumption declined by 0.6% in 2008, it expanded by 1.4% in 2009, in part owing to stimulatory measures introduced by the Government to encourage spending.

From the perspective of mid-2010, signs of recovery in the global economy were expected to generate stronger GDP growth in Taiwan. Indeed, between March and June 2010 DGBAS raised its annual growth forecast from 4.7% to 6.1%, although the latter figure was significantly lower than the 8.5% predicted by the EIU in its June 2010 *Country Report*. In the event, both projections fell short of the mark, with annual GDP growth rising by 10.9%. Meanwhile, per caput gross national product (GNP) increased by 10.3% to reach US $19,155. As of June 2011, Taiwanese projections of annual GDP growth, published in the regular quarterly situation report issued by the Council for Economic Planning and Development (CEPD), ranged from 4.3% to 5.7%. Although these projections forecast that domestic investment would contract by 1.8% in 2011, rises in domestic consumption (up by an expected 4.0%) and, above all, exports (up by 6.9%) were expected to drive the continued buoyant momentum of growth. Against the background of a rise in the consumer price index (CPI) by 1% in 2010, it was expected that inflationary pressures would intensify, generating an annual increase of between 1.5% and 2.5% in 2011.

POPULATION AND LABOUR

Among countries with a population of 10m. or more, Taiwan is the second most densely populated, after Bangladesh, in the world. Average population density was about 640 persons per sq km in 2010, but more than 2,600 per sq km in cities. In December of the same year Taiwan's total population was 23.16m. The main sources of post-1949 demographic pressures lie in the influx of more than 1.5m. mainlanders during 1948–49 and a subsequent, albeit quite short-term, rise in the birth rate (in the early 1950s Taiwan's birth rate was among the highest in the world). According to estimates published in the CEPD's 2011 edition of the *Taiwan Statistical Data Book* (*TSDB*), in 2010 the crude birth rate was 7.2 per 1,000, the crude death rate was 6.3 per 1,000, and the rate of natural increase was 0.9 per 1,000. The US Population Reference Bureau estimated the total fertility rate to be a mere 0.9 live births per female in 2010, the lowest in the world (the global average was 2.5).

In and after the 1960s deliberate fertility control measures led to a sharp decline in population growth, enabling Taiwan rapidly to complete its demographic transition. Underlying these demographic changes there has been a major contraction in the percentage of the population under the age of 15 (from 40% to 15.6% of total population between 1970 and 2010). However, as life expectancy has increased (to more than 78 years), so the proportion aged above 65 years has risen (from 3.0% to 10.7%, a relatively high figure by international standards). Taiwan's overall dependency ratio in 2010 was 0.358. This last figure is unlikely to alter much in the short term, although its underlying structure will change as the declining proportion of those under 15 years of age is offset by a continuing rise in the corresponding share of the over-65s (the number of Taiwan's over-65s has now reached almost 2.5m., and since 1995 the aged dependency ratio has risen from 11% to about 15%). Since more men than women fled the mainland after the KMT defeat in the Civil War, there is still an imbalance of males over females in Taiwan (101 males to 100 females in 2010, but almost 109 males to 100 females for live births), although it is thought that within a few years the number of females will have overtaken that of males. Official projections suggest that Taiwan's population will reach a high point of around 23.8m. towards the end of the 2020s, after which it will decline to fewer than 22m. by 2050. Slowing population growth and an increasing dependency ratio, especially among the elderly, have become matters of concern in Taiwan. As a result, family-planning policy has shifted away from the former advocacy of one-child families to encouragement to couples to 'give their child a companion'.

Accelerated economic modernization has been accompanied by increasing urbanization of Taiwan's population. In 1920, during the period of Japanese colonization, the urban share of total population was a mere 4%, a figure that changed little in succeeding decades. Not until the 1960s did rising farm productivity and expanding industrialization start to facilitate rural–urban migration on a significant scale. Thereafter, such was the pace of economic structural change that by the early 1970s Taiwan's population had already become about two-thirds urban. By 1980 78% of Taiwanese lived in cities with a population of 50,000 or more, a higher proportion than in either Japan or the USA. Official estimates indicate that large metropolitan areas are now home to about 80% of Taiwan's total population, and almost one-half of that population is concentrated in just four cities, namely Taipei, Kaohsiung, Taichung and Tainan.

In 1952 Taiwan's labour participation rate (labour force as a proportion of the population between the ages of 15 and 64) was 66.5%. Such was the impact of subsequent demographic change that this figure has not subsequently been reattained, and in May 2010 it was 55%. Between 1952 and 1980 the total labour force more than doubled, rising from 3.1m. to 6.6m. (an average annual growth rate of 2.8%). During the next three decades the rate of expansion slowed considerably, to 1.7% per year, and at mid-2010 the total labour force numbered 11.07m. From 1965 until 2000 the unemployment rate never exceeded 3.0%, and as recently as 1995 it was as low as 1.8%. In the more recent past, however, new pressures have been brought to bear on employment. One of these has been the relocation of many previously indigenous industrial activities to the Chinese mainland, the so-called 'hollowing out' of the domestic economy, which has displaced significant numbers of industrial workers. Even more serious was the profound impact of two external developments. First, the bursting of the IT 'bubble' took a heavy toll on jobs, resulting in the unemployment rate rising from 3% to 5.2% between 2000 and 2002. Notwithstanding subsequent job recovery (between 2002 and 2007 the number of unemployed declined by almost 100,000 to 419,000), the impact of the second development, the global financial crisis, was such that by August 2009 the rate of unemployment had reached 6.1%, with 672,000 people out of work. However, by the end of the year the number of unemployed had decreased to 639,000 (5.9%), and in 2010 both figures continued to decline (to 577,000 and 5.2%, respectively). A source of particular concern in recent years has been the rise in graduate unemployment: for example, between 1998 and 2008 the unemployment rate among college and university graduates increased from 2.7% to 4.8% (the corresponding figures for the entire work-force were 2.7% and 4.1%, respectively).

Since the 1950s the Government has sought to generate not only rapid, but also efficient, economic growth. Crucial to the fulfilment of this goal has been the provision of a highly skilled work-force. To a significant extent, a country's skill endowment reflects its educational attainments. In Taiwan improvements in education have consistently assumed a high priority among human resource development policies, although these policies have met with varied success. Since the late 1960s all children have received nine years of compulsory education, while a wide range of educational opportunities has been made available for those who have left school. Government spending on education rose steadily to reach 5.6% of GDP by the beginning of the 1990s (the corresponding figure in 2009 was 4.7%). The private sector has also played a large part in meeting the growing demand for tertiary education: in 2005 more than two-thirds of graduates were from private institutions. Despite criticisms of the higher education sector for its supposed inflexibility and failure to address Taiwan's economic and social needs, it is noteworthy that in recent years there has been a sharp increase in the number of students taking degree courses in mathematics and technical subjects, such as engineering and computer science. In 2007 (the most recent year for which comprehensive data were available in mid-2011) the disciplines that attracted the most students were: engineering (275,755 students), commerce and business administration (272,781), mathematics and computer science (142,444), and medical science (127,346).

Alongside the expansion of domestic higher education, the number of Taiwanese studying abroad has also risen rapidly in recent years. At the end of the 1980s fewer than 10,000 Taiwanese were enrolled in foreign colleges and universities; by 2007 the corresponding figure had reached more than 33,000 (although this was 11% below the peak level of 37,171 recorded in 2006). Ministry of Education statistics showed that 45% of those studying abroad in 2007 were enrolled in courses in the USA, with a further 22% taking up places in the United Kingdom. Other popular destinations were Australia, Japan and Canada, each of which accounted for between 6% and 8% of overseas Taiwanese students.

In 1990 Taiwan liberalized its foreign labour policy in an attempt to address emerging domestic labour shortages. At the end of 2000 310,000 foreign workers were employed on the island, 59% of whom were engaged in manufacturing and 13% in the construction industry. Most overseas workers came from Thailand, although the Philippines was also a major source of domestic helpers. Foreign workers also play an important role in nursing, health care and catering activities. In 2010 there were 418,802 foreigners resident in Taiwan (3.7% more than in 2009, but 3.3% fewer than in 2007). More than one-third of all foreign residents were from Indonesia, while South-East Asia accounted for more than 90% of the total. Their positive economic contribution notwithstanding, foreign workers have at times been viewed as a threat to local employment, and at the end of 1998 the Government signalled its intention to reduce the foreign labour quota for manufacturing industries by 10% in order to combat the rising level of domestic unemployment. In 1999 promulgation of the Immigration Act provided for the establishment of a National Immigration Agency (NIA), although this body was formally established only in January 2007. Although stringent employment conditions have encouraged both the legal and illegal entry of foreign workers, their role has remained a controversial topic. Thus, the suggestion made in April 2006 by the then Premier, Su Tseng-chang, to the effect that immigrant labour should only be allowed to fill jobs for which domestic workers were not available elicited a hostile reaction from some members of the Taiwanese legislature. The movement of people from the Chinese mainland to Taiwan has also become a significant issue in recent years. This too has both a legal and illegal dimension. On the one hand, there has been a rise in the trafficking of prostitutes from China. On the other hand, there has also been an increase in the number of Chinese spouses married to Taiwanese citizens. According to the NIA Chairman, by the end of 2006 some 238,000 Chinese immigrant spouses were living in Taiwan (in addition to 80,000 Vietnamese spouses), a figure that had risen to some 264,000 by mid-2009. Such figures highlight the political ramifications of migration issues, which have added to the difficulties confronting the NIA in fulfilling its responsibilities of controlling and monitoring foreign workers. Meanwhile, Chinese spouses have been increasingly vociferous in their opposition to existing discriminatory treatment *vis-à-vis* other immigrants in terms of the demands that they have to meet before being given a Taiwan identity card.

AGRICULTURE

The inherited post-1949 economy was dominated by the agricultural sector. In 1952 agriculture accounted for almost one-third of Taiwan's GDP, well over one-half of all jobs and, in raw or processed form, more than 90% of total exports. Its economic contribution persisted well into the 1960s: in 1965 farming still generated almost one-quarter of GDP, almost one-half of total employment and more than one-half of exports. Subsequently, however, the role of agriculture as a force of economic growth diminished rapidly under the impact of accelerated industrialization. By 2010 the agricultural sector employed 550,000 people (just over 5% of total employment), and generated 1.6% of GDP and barely 1.0% of exports.

Institutional and technical factors, as well as supportive government policy, lie behind Taiwan's agricultural success. The most important institutional initiative was land reform, which transformed the agricultural sector into one dominated by owner-occupiers (their share of the agricultural population rising from 38% to 85% between 1952 and 2009—but 96% if part-owners are included). With arable land resources diminishing and a serious labour constraint (the farm population has been in decline since the 1970s), farming has become increasingly mechanized. The increased provision of working, as well as fixed, capital has also made farming more efficient.

The structure of farm production has changed markedly. In the 1970s crop production dominated farming activities; thereafter, however, the output of livestock and fish grew much more rapidly. In particular, the output of rice, which was once the mainstay of the agricultural economy, has declined sharply: from 1.9m. metric tons in 2000 to just 1.5m. tons in 2008 (a decrease of more than 23%). Data published by the Council of Agriculture show that in 2008 the share of crop cultivation in total agricultural production was 42.9%; the corresponding figures for livestock and fisheries were, respectively, 35% and 22% (0.1% came from forestry). In the livestock sector, pig-farming is the dominant activity, followed by poultry and dairy production. Deep-sea fishing accounts for about one-half of the total value of production in the fisheries sector. A major influence on agricultural development was Taiwan's accession, in January 2002, to the World Trade Organization (WTO). On the eve of joining the WTO, official sources acknowledged the significant challenges that were likely to confront farmers, especially rice and fruit producers, as pressures would increase to liberalize the agricultural sector by reducing tariffs and broadening market access. Measures by the Council of Agriculture have helped to mitigate the impact of WTO membership, but have not been able to prevent varying degrees of decline in output growth. As of 2008, for example, the value of overall crop production was 10.5% below the 2001 level, while the corresponding figures for livestock and fisheries were –11.3% and between –40.2% (offshore fishing) and +7.6% (aquaculture), respectively.

INDUSTRY AND MANUFACTURING

In 1952 the industrial sector generated one-fifth of Taiwan's GDP, and the manufacturing sector 'proper' accounted for a mere 13%. The corresponding figures for agriculture and services were 32% and 48%, respectively. Until the 1960s farm-processing remained the main industrial and export activity in Taiwan. However, following the shift from ISI to a much more overtly outward-orientated strategy, manufacturing production expanded rapidly, and by the end of the 1970s its contribution to GDP (in nominal price terms) had risen to 36%. Its peak share (37.5%) was attained in 1986, since when, under the impact of rapid tertiary sector growth, it has once more declined (in 2010 it generated 26.3%).

The changing pattern of industrial growth in Taiwan has followed a trajectory common to all four first-echelon Asian newly industrialized economies (NIEs). Initially, its growth was centred on the production of labour-intensive goods, such as textiles, plastics, plywood and electronic products. Subsequently, the shift to higher value-added activities was reflected in the accelerated expansion of capital-intensive, heavy industrial goods, including synthetic fibres, steel, machinery, cars and ships—a process given further impetus by the HCI programme (see above). The most recent and, in terms of its economic impact, most significant change was towards knowledge- and skill-intensive production, exemplified in the emergence of Taiwan's IT sector. With labour costs rising and the price of capital declining, the pattern of industrial growth inherent in these structural shifts reflects the operation of the principle of comparative advantage.

Since 2000 recessionary conditions have twice had serious repercussions for the manufacturing sector. Between 2000 and 2001 production contracted sharply, decreasing in constant 2006 price terms by 9%, a decline that was carried entirely by light industry (heavy industry showed a marginal increase in 2001). On this occasion, recovery was swift, and between 2002 and 2007 manufacturing output grew by more than 40% (more than 7.5% annually). In the second half of 2008 the sharp deterioration in global economic conditions once more exerted a downward influence on growth. In both 2008 and 2009 manufacturing production experienced negative growth, declining by 1.6% and 8.0%, respectively. However, recovery was again swift, and in 2010 manufacturing output rose by 28.6%. In April the EIU predicted that annual industrial growth (of which manufacturing is by far the biggest component) would be 4% in 2011, rising to 5.5% in 2012.

The role of R & D in supporting the expansion of knowledge- and skill-intensive activities is self-evident, and raising R & D expenditure is critically important to fulfilling Taiwan's aspiration to maintain its position as a global IT force. Between the mid-1990s and 2007 R & D spending in Taiwan increased by about 8% annually to reach some NT 331,386m. As a result, R & D expenditure as a share of GDP rose from 1.8% in 1993 to 2.6%, and by 2009 it had reached more than 2.9% (higher than in the USA, Germany, France and the United Kingdom (2.8%, 2.8%, 2.2% and 1.9%, respectively), but below that of South Korea (an estimated 3.3%) and Japan (3.4%); the corresponding figure for mainland China was 1.8%. About three-quarters of R & D spending is focused on engineering, and a further 10% on natural sciences. Since 2000 the number of personnel engaged in R & D in Taiwan has almost doubled (in 2009 it stood at 196,893). Owing to institutional and fiscal support measures, considerable success has also been achieved in recent years in reducing the Government's share of R & D expenditure in Taiwan, although compared with that of major industrialized countries the private business sector's contribution (69.7% in 2009) remained low.

SMEs have made a vital contribution to industrial development in Taiwan. Indeed, they have become the mainstay of Taiwan's industrial economy. By the mid-1980s their contribution to manufacturing output had reached almost 50%, their share of non-farm employment was more than 60% and they contributed a similar proportion of export earnings. Their resilience, especially in manufacturing, has been remarkable. Even today they account for around 98% of all enterprises in Taiwan, generating more than three-quarters of total employment, almost 30% of the total sales value of all domestic enterprises and more than 15% of the value of all exports. Not only have they contributed more to foreign trade growth than their larger-scale counterparts, but, unlike large firms, they have done so without having been major recipients of government protection and incentives. The SMEs' strong outward orientation is highlighted in the finding that up to two-thirds of their output is exported, compared with just over one-third for large-scale enterprises.

The structure of SMEs may be likened to a pyramid. The base comprises a large number of tiny family firms, with a workforce of no more than 10 employees. Typically, these are involved in just one stage of a production process, making use of quite simple technologies to produce a single component of a larger and more complex product. One stage removed from such 'micro' firms are enterprises, which employ between 10 and 30 people and have a broader production base. Finally, firms with up to 100 employees, engaged in even more complex production activities, constitute the largest category of SMEs. Firms at the top of the pyramid are likely also to have more complex management structures.

By encouraging competition within a network of sub-contracting relationships and by minimizing the discretionary element in industrial policy, the promotion of SMEs has quite effectively obviated the threat posed by the emergence of 'predatory capitalism' in Taiwan. SMEs have also maximized their potential for creativity and flexibility in production, thereby enabling them to adjust quickly to changes in market conditions. At the same time, however, they have sometimes confronted serious financial constraints. In particular, their small size and limited resources, as well as the legacy of a mindset that has traditionally focused on standardized, large-volume activities, have inhibited their involvement in R & D. One consequence is that in recent years Taiwan's SMEs have lost ground to their more competitive Chinese and Indian counterparts.

Textiles

During most of the colonial period Taiwan relied on imports, especially from Japan, to meet its textile needs. At the end of the 1940s, however, the tiny scale of indigenous activities was enlarged as equipment and expertise began to be shifted to Taiwan from the mainland, and production capacity and output thereafter steadily increased. Between 1950 and the end of the 1970s the textile and apparel industries constituted the largest share of manufacturing employment and generated more exports than any other single manufacturing activity. The importance of the industry during this period was demonstrated by the fact that by the early 1970s textiles (including apparel) accounted for almost 13% of manufacturing GDP, and, at their peak, 30% of net exports. Initially, textiles benefited from the availability of abundant supplies of cheap labour. The resilience of the sector's export performance in view of the quota restrictions imposed in the 1960s by the USA and by members of the European Union (EU) on the import of textile products reflected the success of Taiwanese producers in shifting from export-orientated production of cotton textile goods to synthetic fibre products (exempted from the restrictions). By contrast, the impact of the Multi-Fibre Arrangement, introduced in 1974, was more serious and presaged a period of uncertainty for the industry.

As recently as the mid-1980s, textiles (fibres, yarn, apparel and accessories) accounted for around one-fifth of the net value of Taiwan's exports. Thereafter, however, the sector's export contribution declined steadily: by 2000 it had decreased to 10% and by 2010 to less than 4%. One major factor that has contributed to the decline in textile exports has been the erosion of Taiwan's competitiveness *vis-à-vis* other countries. According to data published by management consultants Werner International, in 2008 the average hourly cost of labour in Taiwan's textile and apparel industry was US $7.89, compared with $0.31 in Bangladesh, $0.57 in Viet Nam, $0.85 in India, $1.44–$1.88 in China, depending on the region, and $4.27 in Turkey. Such figures help to explain why since the 1990s many of Taiwan's textile and apparel factories have moved off shore, many of them relocating to mainland China (especially to the Pearl River Delta region of Guangdong Province), as well as to South-East Asia. Reflecting this geographical shift in production has been a steady decline in domestic output. Between 2002 and 2010, for example, the output of apparel decreased by almost three-quarters, while textile mill production declined by more than one-third.

General Machinery and Machine Tools

Machine tools are one of the most important heavy industries in a developing economy. In Taiwan's case, not only have they generated important forward linkages with the rest of the economy, but they have also contributed much to its defence infrastructure. Machine tool production grew rapidly in the 1970s, and by the following decade had gained a significant share in the world market, eliciting a request from the USA that it introduce export restrictions. Machine tools are the most important component of the general machinery industry, which produces a wide range of goods, including industrial machinery, fans, pumps and compressors, engines, etc. Although widely regarded as a large-scale, heavily capital-intensive industry, machine tool firms in Taiwan are predominantly small scale, and their success has reflected their flexibility and ability to deliver high-quality products punctually. In 1981 the Government designated machine production as a strategic industry.

The general machine industry's recent performance has been buoyant. Between 2000 and 2008 output grew, in nominal terms, by 8.8% per year; however, owing to the impact of the global downturn, production declined by one-quarter in 2009. Export expansion during the same period was also quite impressive, rising, on average, by 7.4% annually from NT $256,109m. in 1998 to NT $521,940m. in 2008. In 2009, however, exports contracted by 28%. The performance of machine tools has been even more impressive. Between 1997 and 2008 output growth averaged more than 10% per year, while the value of exports almost tripled to reach NT $116,777m. (NT $68,457m. in net terms). Implied in these figures is an export rate of 77%. Total exports of machine tools were expected to rise by around 20% in 2011, driven by a rapid expansion in orders from mainland China; as a result, Taiwan was poised to overtake Italy to become the third most important export producer in the world (behind Germany and Japan).

Metallurgical Industry (Steel)

Taiwan has no significant mineral reserves. Until the 1970s domestic production of steel was entirely undertaken by small-scale plants, and output remained insufficient to meet rapidly growing demand. In 1971 China Steel Corporation (CSC) was established, but not until seven years later did it begin production, following the construction of Taiwan's first large-scale integrated steel mill. Initially, more than one-half of China Steel's production was exported, although the domestic share of output gradually increased, reaching about 80% by the mid-1990s. At this time, Taiwan ranked 24th in the world as a steel producer. However, such was the pace of continuing growth that by 2009 its global ranking had risen to 12th; and its regional ranking within Asia to fifth (after China, Japan, India and South Korea). Estimates by the World Steel Association showed that between 2000 and 2007 total steel output rose from 16.9m. metric tons to 20.9m. tons, registering average annual growth of 3.1%. In 2008, however, there was a marginal decline in output, and in 2009 production contracted much more sharply (by 20%), to 15.9m. tons. Only in 2010 did a recovery take place, with annual production rising by some 23% to reach 19.6m. tons. As recovery continued in 2011, by the end of July steel output had already reached nearly 12.3m. tons. In 2010 Taiwan was the fourth largest steel exporter in Asia (9.8m. tons), and the sixth largest importer (8.3m. tons).

CSC remains easily the largest producer of steel in Taiwan, and in 2010 ranked 21st in the world among steel producers. It is also Taiwan's only producer of pig iron. It has an annual production capacity of about 13m. metric tons (excluding the 0.6m. tons of capacity of Dragon Steel, of which CSC became the outright owner in 2008), or about 65% of the island's total capacity. Steel production is overwhelmingly concentrated in Kaohsiung, although there are also production facilities in Taichung. Meanwhile, owing to environmental opposition, in 2006 the Formosa Group was forced to abandon plans to construct an iron and steel plant, with a projected annual capacity of 8m. tons, in Yunlin County (central western Taiwan). Agreement was subsequently reached with the Government of Viet Nam to build the plant in the Ha Tinh Province of that country.

Shipbuilding

The shift towards an export-orientated strategy in the 1960s encouraged the Government to establish an indigenous shipbuilding industry. In 1973 the newly established China Shipbuilding Corpn (CSBC) inaugurated Taiwan's first modern shipyard, a large-scale venture with a construction capacity of 1.6m. metric tons and matching repair facilities. It was Taiwan's misfortune that the completion of this venture coincided with the first oil crisis, which caused a slump in the shipbuilding market and left a surplus of oil tankers and other shipping vessels. One consequence was the cancellation of major construction orders, eventually forcing the Government to assume sole ownership of CSBC. Subsequently, the focus of CSBC operations shifted to the construction of offshore drilling rigs and other ancillary activities, although this was only partially successful in helping to revive the company's fortunes.

In the 1990s CSBC was listed for privatization, but progress continued to be hampered by the poor financial basis of the company. Not until 2008 was the process of privatization completed. Today CSBC, renamed CSBC Corpn, provides naval and commercial shipbuilding services (including the construction of tankers, bulk carriers and container ships). In March 2011 a report noted that Taiwan's shipbuilding market remained depressed, and suggested that the industry would not experience a significant recovery until 2012.

Motor Vehicles (Cars and Motorcycles)

The performance of the motor vehicle industry (mainly cars, but also buses and trucks) has, by Taiwan's own standards, been disappointing. Production began in the 1960s and, despite the failure to launch two planned joint ventures (with Toyota of Japan and General Motors of the USA), output subsequently expanded rapidly. For example, from a tiny production base of fewer than 3,300 vehicles in 1965, production grew to more than 436,000 vehicles by 1992. Thereafter, in response to the vagaries of changing domestic demand, output growth was more erratic. Recessionary conditions in 2001 resulted in a sharp decline in production, of 28%, to the lowest level since 1989. Subsequent recovery was swift and a new peak output level (more than 446,000 vehicles) was reached in 2005. However, this level of production was not maintained, and data made available by the Taiwan Transportation Vehicle Manufacturers Association (TTVMA) showed that by 2008 total output had declined by 59% to just under 183,000 vehicles. Only in 2009 was this downward trend reversed, with production rising to 226,356 motor vehicles. By 2010 output had returned to the level of 2006, with some 303,456 vehicles produced (an annual increase of more than one-third).

Almost all cars produced in Taiwan are sold to domestic consumers. In 2010, for example, domestic sales accounted for 87% of total sales, which meant that fewer than 37,000 vehicles were exported. Among domestic producers, TTVMA statistics revealed that Kuozui Motors had the largest market share in 2010 (34.5%), followed by China Motor Corpn (19.7%) and Taiwan Honda (11.1%).

In general, growing affluence has made car ownership increasingly popular in Taiwan in recent decades. At the end of 2010 the total number of registered passenger cars was more than 5.6m., almost all of these being for private use. Motorcycles have remained a popular alternative to cars, and motorcycle ownership reached almost 15m. at the end of 2010. The peak level of motorcycle production (1.7m. units) was recorded in 1995. According to TTVMA statistics, between 1995 and 2001 output decreased by 40%, but thereafter recovered; indeed, in 2008 it was one of the few industries to maintain positive growth, with production rising by 3% to 1,555,042 units. In 2009, however, output declined by more than one-third, to just over 1m. motorcycles, and it remained at this level in 2010.

Unlike cars, a significant proportion of domestically produced motorcycles is exported. In 2009 almost 542,000 units, a little more than one-half of total output, were sold overseas. Data for 2010 showed that the most important export markets were Italy (21% by export value, but only 15% in terms of physical shipments) and Japan (20% by value, but 23% in physical terms), followed by Belgium and Spain. The success of Taiwanese motorcycle exporters reflects their high R & D expenditure, which has not only enabled them to meet the low pollution and high performance criteria of overseas markets in developed countries, but also released them from their earlier dependence on Japanese partners or parent firms. Both domestic and overseas sales are dominated by three motorcycle producers: Kwang Yang Motor Co (accounting for 37% of domestic sales and 40% of foreign sales in 2010), San Yang Industry (27% and 31%, respectively) and Taiwan Yamaha (32% and 20%, respectively).

Petrochemicals

By the 1960s the rapid growth of textiles and plastic goods had encouraged the construction of large-scale chemical production facilities, and in 1968 the state-owned CPC built Taiwan's first naphtha-cracking plant. The 1973 energy crisis gave further impetus to domestic petrochemical production, including the construction by CPC of two more naphtha-cracking plants. Owing to subsequent rapid output growth, by the end of the 1990s the industry's annual production value had exceeded US $12,000m. Between 1997 and 2007 the output of chemical materials grew, on average, by 6.4% per year (in constant 2006 price terms). Since then, production has decreased quite sharply owing to the impact of the global economic downturn, contracting by 8% in 2008 alone. Even so, Taiwan remains one of the most important petrochemical producers in the world.

Since the mid-1990s Taiwan's petrochemical industry has undergone a major transformation, as it has shifted from domestic-orientated to export-orientated production. Official data attest to the industry's impressive export performance. From a negligible base, between 1982 and 1995 the value of chemical exports increased by more than 19% annually, to reach US $3,238.1m. Even more remarkably, from a much higher base, during the next 13 years export growth averaged almost 14% annually, so that by 2008 overseas sales of chemicals totalled US $17,240.6m. (6.7% of the total value of Taiwan's exports). In 2009, however, exports declined by almost 20%, to US $13,930.4m., before recovering to reach a new peak of $19,227.4m. in 2010.

Taiwan's petrochemicals industry comprises about 50 upper and middle-stream producers, based mainly in Kaohsiung. The most important domestic companies are CPC (originally established in 1946 in Shanghai, in mainland China), Formosa Plastics Corpn (first established in 1954 and the most important private enterprise in the industry), Chi Mei Corpn (established in 1959 and now the largest producer of acrylonitrile butadiene styrene—ABS—resins in the world), and Lee Chang Yung Chemical Corpn (founded in 1965).

Another factor that has shaped the industry's recent trajectory has been the removal, for both economic and environmental reasons, of much downstream petrochemical production activity from Taiwan to China and South-East Asia. The strength of the environmental lobby was evident as recently as April 2011, when, after six years of fierce debate, the Taiwanese Government announced that it had decided not to support the construction of a US $20,000m. petrochemical plant in an ecologically sensitive wetland area of the island. As a result of this decision, it was recognized that ethylene imports would have to increase.

Meanwhile, cross-Straits economic rapprochement has facilitated increasing involvement by Taiwanese producers in mainland China's petrochemical sector. Such involvement was previously confined to downstream activities. However, in the more open and liberal atmosphere that has characterized cross-Straits relations under the Ma Ying-jeou administration, this has now been extended to embrace upstream activities as well. Not least, the signing of the ECFA is expected to enhance the competitiveness of Taiwan's petrochemicals industry and increase sales in China.

Information Technology

The development of high-technology industries in Taiwan had its origins in a number of important institutional and policy initiatives launched in the late 1970s and early 1980s. Four of these may be noted here: first, the convening of the first National Conference for Science and Technology (1978) and subsequent adoption of a Science and Technology Development Programme (1979); second, the establishment of the Institution for Information Industry (1979), designed to help nurture the development of an information industry in Taiwan; third, construction of a manufacturing plant by United Microelectronics Corpn (1980); and fourth, the beginning of operations at Taiwan's first science-based industrial park at Hsinchu (also 1980). This last initiative not only provided a location where an increasing number of research-based companies could be sited (70 by the end of the 1980s), but also facilitated a 'reverse brain drain', as Taiwanese researchers who had found jobs overseas (especially in the USA) returned home. The 1990s witnessed the establishment of a second government-sponsored science park in Tainan, while private sector sites, such as the one opened near Taipei by the Formosa Plastics Corpn, also contributed to the development of high-technology manufacturing. Such facilities, assisted by the Industrial Technology Research Institute of the Ministry of Economic Affairs (MoEA) and the institute's offshoot, the Electronic Research and Service Organization, were the principal means whereby technologies were developed and transferred to domestic private enterprises. Overall, it can be said that Taiwan's IT industry has upgraded in 'classic' fashion, shifting from less sophisticated, lower-value to more sophisticated, higher-value activities. Such adjustments have also reflected the determination of successive governments to make Taiwan a knowledge-based economy.

By the end of the 1990s Taiwan had established itself as the world's third largest manufacturer of IT products, behind the USA and Japan. With a total production value of US $39,900m., measured in terms of combined domestic and overseas revenue, the IT industry had also become the single most important source of foreign exchange. Taiwan's 900 computer hardware manufacturers provided jobs for some 100,000 employees. Meanwhile, laptop computers, monitors, desktop personal computers (PCs) and motherboards had come to dominate the IT industry, accounting for around 80% of its production value. The rapid expansion of these and other IT activities is highlighted in the following average annual rates of output growth between 1995 and 2008: mobile phones, 123.7%; computer disks, 91.5% (1995–2007; in 2008 production declined by one-third); integrated circuit (IC) packages, 13.4%; foundry wafers, 11.6%; printed circuit boards, 10.9%; and thin-film-transistor liquid-crystal display (TFT-LCD) panels, 63.7% (2000–08). The shift towards higher-end activities is reflected in the fact that at various points since 2000 the domestic output of mobile phones, LCD monitors, PCs, computer disks, interface cards and motherboards have all declined. The most spectacular example of such contraction is that of laptop computers, the production of which increased from 45,000 to 14.5m. between 1988 and 2002, only to decline precipitately to 760,571 in 2008 (and to a mere 327,000 in 2010). However, such statistics should emphatically not be interpreted as indicating the demise of Taiwan's laptop industry. On the contrary, it has retained its leading role, albeit from production facilities now sited on the Chinese mainland. Overall, data for 2010 attest to the remarkable vitality of Taiwan's IT industry, and show a rapid recovery from the downturn of 2009 that followed the onset of the global financial crisis. For example, production levels of TFD-LCD panels, IC packages, foundry wafers and printed circuit boards were all at historic peaks.

Taiwan's impressive record in high-technology development is highlighted in the finding that it now ranks as the world's second largest producer, after mainland China, of information and communications technology (ICT) goods. Moreover, as indicated above, a high proportion of ICT goods produced in China was, in fact, manufactured in Taiwanese plants established on the mainland. For example, more than 90% of all notebook computers are today produced by Taiwanese companies in China. Taiwanese original design manufacturers are also the most important mobile phone producers in mainland China.

One recent important focus of growth has been flat panel displays (FPDs), of which Taiwan is the leading producer in the world, accounting for 45.9% of global production of large-screen FPDs in 2006 (compared with South Korea's share of 40.4%). FPD activities highlight Taiwanese producers' continuing ability to move into new technologies in order to respond to market changes. However, the flexibility of indigenous producers notwithstanding, the extent to which the industry's buoyant performance can be maintained will partly depend on factors beyond Taiwan's control. In this respect, the potential for China to become a serious IT market competitor poses an obvious challenge. The Chinese dimension is also important in interpreting changing trends in the domestic output of a wide range of IT products, bearing in mind that many Taiwanese manufacturers have relocated their production activities to the Chinese mainland in recent years.

The strength of the IT industry was confirmed in the finding that, measured by sales value, in 2005 five out of Taiwan's 10 leading companies, namely Quanta Computer Inc, Asustek Computer Inc, Acer Inc, Taiwan Semiconductor Manufacturing Co Ltd (TSMC) and Compal Electronics Inc, were IT firms. In general, high-technology companies dominate Taiwan's leading 50 rated corporations. The 2009 list of Asia's 'Fab 50 Companies', compiled by US media corporation Forbes, included five from Taiwan (compared with three from Hong Kong, two from South Korea and one from Singapore), all of which were high-technology firms. The strength of Taiwan's IT industry is also reflected in the high global market shares that it has attained in strategic areas; in addition to being the world's biggest producer of large-screen FPDs, even allowing for recent contraction in domestic production (to a significant extent, a reflection of the relocation of production activities to mainland China), Taiwan is still the largest global supplier of notebook PCs, mask ROMs, LEDs, motherboards and LCD monitors.

The impressive foreign-exchange contribution of IT and related products was illustrated by the fact that associated exports increased almost 20-fold between 1986 and 2000, registering an average annual growth rate of 21.4%. Following the bursting of the US technology 'bubble' and increasing competition both from existing IT companies and newly established firms (not least in China), Taiwan's IT industry has come under increasing competitive pressure. Nevertheless, the continuing buoyancy of the industry was evident in a report by the Government Information Office in Taipei, which revealed that in 2006 Taiwan's global sales of IT manufactures in Taiwan and China had totalled US $88,600m.

The development over 30 years of the semiconductor industry has been a major element in Taiwan's emergence as a global force in IT activities. The two largest contract chip manufacturers in the world, TSMC and United Microelectronics Corpn (UMC), are located on the island. UMC is the older of the two companies, having been founded in 1979, and is a global leader in the development of foundry technology. It employs some 12,000 people world-wide and, as of 2010, had assets of US $3,218m. TSMC was established in 1987 and has since grown into the world's largest dedicated semiconductor foundry. In 2010 its manufacturing capacity was 11.33m. 8-inch equivalent wafers. In Taiwan, it operated two advanced 12-inch wafer fabs, four 8-inch fabs and one 6-inch fab (in addition, it managed two 8-inch fabs at wholly owned subsidiaries—one in the USA, the other in mainland China). TSMC employs 33,000 people world-wide, and in 2010 its total assets were valued at NT $701,240m.

In response to the potential market threat to Taiwan posed by the recent establishment of start-up foundries in China, both UMC and TSMC have established their own chip fabrication facilities in China. The initial decision, in 2003, to allow TSMC to open a plant in Shanghai was controversial, but burgeoning demand on the mainland (already worth well in excess of US $15,000m. a year, and projected to reach $40,000m. by 2025) offered Taiwanese semiconductor manufacturers a way of maintaining revenue sales by penetrating the mainland Chinese market and offsetting possible contractions in demand elsewhere in the world. Even so, the DPP Government made strenuous efforts to control the use of the most advanced technologies in foundries located on the mainland. From this perspective, its decision in December 2006 to allow the transfer of 0.18-micron technology to China for use in 8-inch wafer plants was an important development. However, in view of China's ability to secure advanced technologies from other countries and, no less important, the incumbency of a new KMT administration, which aims to achieve economic normalization with China, restrictions on semiconductor-manufacturing investments in China can be expected gradually to be abandoned. This process is already under way: not only has the limit on investment in China been raised from 40% to 60%, but in July 2008 it was announced that Taiwan's semiconductor industry would be allowed to establish 12-inch wafer factories on the mainland. Recent evidence also suggests a shift in emphasis, as Taiwan focuses more on design and logistics, managing production and distribution for multinational companies from Taiwanese-owned enterprises on the mainland.

Another significant development was the establishment, in March 2007, of the Taiwan Robot Industry Association. Underlying this initiative was the intention to make Taiwan a global force in the production of intelligent robots by 2014–20, by which time the value of annual output was expected to have reached some NT $250,000m. In support of Taiwan's robotics industry, the former DPP Government undertook to invest NT $2,000m. over a five-year period.

According to a survey of 145 countries made by the World Bank, in 2009 Taiwan ranked 18th in the Knowledge Economy Index—three places higher than in 2008. This was the highest ranking of any Asian country, placing Taiwan ahead of Japan, Singapore and Hong Kong. Taiwan's pre-eminence in this regard owes most to its very strong showing in terms of ICT (10th highest in the world), but also of education and innovation.

Domestic enterprises have established around 100 R & D centres in Taiwan. Another 40 similar centres have been established on the island by global multinational corporations, including Dell, Ericsson, IBM, Intel, Microsoft and Sony.

INFRASTRUCTURE

Taiwan benefited from important infrastructural initiatives undertaken by the Japanese during the period of colonial rule. Between the mid-1950s and the end of the 1970s the Government directed large-scale investment funds towards extending Taiwan's physical economic infrastructure. Most important of all were the 'Ten Major Construction Projects' implemented between 1973 and 1980, which facilitated major improvements in roads, and air and sea transport. In the 1980s infrastructural initiatives were accorded much lower priority, as a result of which quite serious problems of congestion began to emerge. Accordingly, in the second half of the decade economic plans once more gave a high priority to infrastructural construction, but with added emphasis on the need to accommodate environmental pressures.

At the start of the 21st century such initiatives have continued to be regarded as a vital factor in generating economic growth. The importance of infrastructural upgrading was highlighted as long ago as June 2004, when the CEPD acknowledged that inadequate infrastructure remained a major impediment to further improvements in Taiwan's economic competitiveness. The DPP administration of Chen Shui-bian demonstrated its commitment to improving Taiwan's basic infrastructure through the expansion of airport passenger and cargo transport capacities, the extension of link roads between airports and harbours, and the construction of broadband networks. Under a six-year development plan ('Challenge 2008') announced in 2002, the Government embarked on a NT $2,650,000m. public projects spending programme, including construction of a high-speed 345-km rail link between Taipei and Kaohsiung (described as the largest build-operate-transfer project in the world and formally inaugurated in March 2007), and of an express rail service between central Taipei and the capital's Taoyuan International Airport, scheduled for completion in 2012. The administration of President Ma Ying-jeou has similarly highlighted the need for infrastructural upgrading as one of its priority objectives. Stimulus spending measures designed to address the consequences of the global recession have given a further boost to infrastructural activity: in February 2009, for example, the Executive Yuan (cabinet) approved a government public works programme, including urban regeneration measures, the extension of Taiwan's national highway system and other major projects.

From 1995 successive Taiwanese Governments sought to promote the development of Taiwan into an Asia-Pacific Regional Operations Centre (APROC). The aim of this plan was to transform Taiwan into a business and investment hub in the region, embracing services and high technology, and providing multinational corporations with the manufacturing, air and sea transport, financial, telecommunications and media facilities essential for their efficient operation. It was believed that the successful implementation of the project would greatly enhance Taiwan's regional economic status and, by making it a centre for transshipment, financial and communications activities, improve its strategic security. APROC's implementation was premised on further realizing Taiwan's core strengths: its strategic location within the Asia-Pacific region, its well-educated and highly skilled work-force, and its high level of scientific and technological expertise. In the event, progress in fulfilling this ambitious goal was halting, highlighting the difficulties confronting Taiwan in its efforts successfully to compete with other service and high-technology hubs, such as Hong Kong, Shanghai and Singapore.

The most important recent infrastructural initiative was the 'i-Taiwan 12 Projects', launched by the CEPD in January 2010. This large-scale programme prioritized 12 construction projects, embracing transport, port construction, industrial innovation, urban and industrial renewal, farm and coastal regeneration, and environmental protection. Projected investment was estimated at NT $3,990,000m. over eight years, involving the creation of some 120,000 jobs per annum.

Transport and Communications

From the 1950s until the mid-1980s the growth of transport was rapid (an index published by the CEPD indicated an average annual rate of expansion of 10.2% during 1952–84). Subsequently, however, progress was much slower, and in many years it ceased altogether. Meanwhile, in recent years telecommunications have expanded significantly: another index pointed to average growth of more than 9% per year between 1996 and 2010.

Between 1952 and 1975 the road network expanded by a mere 1,553 km (i.e. by 9.9%). Thereafter, the pace of road-building accelerated sharply, and by 2010 the total length of roads throughout the island had more than doubled to 41,383 km. Highways—some 21,804 km—account for more than one-half of total road length, and more than one-half of all highways are rural. The pressure on major trunk routes is severe and, in particular, major national highways, such as the Sun Yat-sen Freeway (the country's principal north–south route, connecting Taipei and Keelung), are often congested. Further improvements in the road network therefore remain a major priority.

The expansion of Taiwan's rail network has been much less impressive than that of its roads, at least until relatively recently. Between 1952 and 2000 total track length increased from 1,695 km to 2,851 km; subsequently, the rate of expansion of new track accelerated, and by 2010 the total length of the rail network had risen to 3,915 km. In addition, the opening of a high-speed rail link between Taipei and Kaohsiung (see above) made available an important new transport artery. In 2010 Taiwan's roads carried 1,046m. passengers—a figure that had changed little during the previous decade—and more than 635m. metric tons of freight (a record amount). The corresponding figures for rail transport were 779m. passengers and 15.1m. tons of freight. The likelihood is that transport will dominate infrastructural spending in Taiwan for the foreseeable future, with particular emphasis on further extending and upgrading the railway network (it was estimated that in 2010 more than 90% of transport investment would be allocated to rail projects).

Taiwan's seven international ports (Keelung, Kaohsiung, Taichung, Hualien, Suao, Anping and Taipei) are capable of handling marine traffic and of servicing ocean vessels of all sizes. According to the *TSDB*, in 2010 the total volume of cargo handled (loaded and unloaded) by all Taiwan's international ports was an unprecedented 655.4m. revenue tons (more than 8% higher than in 2009, but almost 8% below the peak level of 2007). The single most important Taiwanese port—and the sixth largest container port in the world—is Kaohsiung, which, in 2010, accounted for almost two-thirds of Taiwan's total container traffic. Next in importance are Taichung, Keelung and Taipei. From the 1960s there was a rapid rise in the scale of Taiwan's merchant marine, the gross registered tonnage of its shipping increasing from a mere 1.1m. tons in 1970 to a high point of 6.6m. tons in 1993. Subsequently, gross tonnage of the merchant fleet contracted sharply, and in 2010 its gross displacement was just 2.79m. tons. Between 2000 and 2007 the volume of goods imported and exported through Taiwan's ports increased from 173.6m. tons to 224.5m. tons. Between 2007 and 2009 there was a 10% contraction, to 202.8m. tons, although by the end of 2010 this figure had recovered to 218.1m. tons. In 2010 Taiwanese vessels carried 22m. tons of merchandise trade, or 10% of total shipping tonnage.

There are two international airports in Taiwan: one is Taiwan Taoyuan International Airport (formerly Chiang Kai-shek International Airport), which serves Taipei and northern regions of the island; the other is Kaohsiung International Airport, which serves the south. During his election campaign in 2006 the Mayor of Taipei advocated transforming the capital's Songshan Airport from a domestic into a third international airport, to focus on carrying passengers between Taiwan and China. The immediate response of the Taiwanese civil aviation authority to the proposal was not enthusiastic, but some commentators believe that Songshan could usefully fulfil an international role in the future. The number of airlines using Taiwanese airspace peaked at 51 in 1996; Ministry of Transport and Communications data show that by 2008 the corresponding figure had declined to 35 (12 national and 23 foreign carriers), although this subsequently increased to 51, with the number of foreign carriers having risen to a record 35. Between the 1950s and the second half of the 1990s the numbers of domestic and international flights increased steadily. Since 1997, however, while the number of international flights has continued to rise, that of domestic flights has contracted sharply. In 2010 171,086 domestic flights were recorded (in 1997 the corresponding figure had reached a peak of more than 580,000), almost all of which used the Taoyuan and Kaohsiung Airports. Domestic air passenger numbers declined from 37.4m. in 1997 to 12.7m. in 2007 and to 9.73m. in 2010. The sharp contraction in domestic air passenger traffic is mainly a reflection of the popularity of the high-speed rail link between Taipei and Kaohsiung. Meanwhile, except for 2003, when international air passenger traffic decreased by one-quarter as a result of the outbreak of severe acute respiratory syndrome (SARS), the number of international passengers has risen more steadily and consistently: from a mere 235,000 in 1965 to 9.7m. in 1990, increasing further to 27.7m. in 2010 (the highest on record). The global economic downturn appears to have had a fairly modest impact on Taiwan's international passenger traffic, with numbers declining by 5.5% during 2007–09. Air freight traffic also reached a record level of 1,864.2m. metric tons in 2010.

Tourism has the potential to be an important foreign-exchange earner for Taiwan. However, although the number of tourist visitors more than doubled between 2000 and 2010 (from 2.6m. to a record 5.6m.), receipts from tourism still account for little more than 1% of GDP. By far the largest proportion (just over three-quarters) of tourists visiting Taiwan in 2010 were from Asian countries; more than 40% were Overseas Chinese. More than 1m. visitors arrived from Japan, and a further 700,000 from Hong Kong and Macao. Outside Asia, the USA provided the largest number of visitors (391,000). However, the most important recent development has been the dramatic increase in visitor numbers from mainland China (see below).

With just under 12.7m. subscribers in 2010, fixed telephone line penetration in Taiwan reached about 60% and seemed likely to remain at about that level, or perhaps slowly decline. The most significant recent change in telecommunications has been the dramatic increase in the ownership of mobile phones, the penetration of which has risen from a mere 6.7% in 1997 to more than 100% in 2010 (third in Asia after Hong Kong and Singapore). The change in usage was highlighted in statistics showing that while the number of landline subscribers increased from 10.9m. to 12.7m. between 1997 and 2010 (an average annual rate of increase of just 1.2%), during the same period the number of mobile telephone users increased from 1.5m. to 27.8m. (rising by an average of more than 25% annually). Further expansion in the mobile phone market will be mainly dependent on technological advances, such as the extended use of 3G technology (which permits users to receive and deliver internet data and video images on cellular handsets). Between 1995 and 2003 the number of internet service subscribers increased from 429,000 to 8.0m. (more than one-half of them with broadband connections), making Taiwan's internet penetration among the highest in the world. However, that number has subsequently declined, to 5.9m. in 2010, and the focus of future developments is likely to be the continuing shift by subscribers to broadband use.

ENERGY

Taiwan has very limited natural resources, forcing it to import most of its raw materials and virtually all its energy (99.4% of supplies were imported in 2010). Coal reserves, which are found in northern Taiwan, are negligible; in 1989 775,000 metric tons of steam coal were domestically produced, but by 2000 output had declined to less than 83,000 tons and thereafter it dwindled to virtually nothing. Domestic petroleum and natural gas supplies are also scarce—estimated at 190,000 kilolitres and 8.2m. cu m, respectively—and are concentrated mainly in two northern counties of the island (Hsinchu and Miaoli). Total hydroelectric potential has been estimated at around 5,000 MW; in 2010 installed hydroelectric capacity was about 4,579 MW.

A national energy policy for Taiwan was first endorsed by the Executive Yuan in 1973. In view of domestic and international developments (for example, the oil crises of the 1970s and 1980s, the 1990–91 Gulf War, and the challenges of liberalization of the domestic energy industry and of environmental concerns) underlying guidelines have since been revised. Today, the Bureau of Energy describes the overriding goal of Taiwan's energy policy as being to establish 'a liberal, orderly, efficient and clean sustainable energy demand and supply system'. To these ends, priority measures include the intensification of energy research and development, as well as the implementation of appropriate policies in order to stabilize supplies, and enhance energy efficiency and security.

According to statistics published by the Bureau of Energy, between 1982 and 1990 total primary energy supplies available to Taiwan rose from 31.6m. to 58.5m. kilolitres of oil equivalent (KLOE). By 2000 they had almost doubled, to reach 103.8m. KLOE, and they subsequently continued to rise to 146.1m. KLOE in 2007. Thereafter, however, supplies declined to 138.2m. KLOE in 2009, before once more rising to 145.6m. KLOE in 2010. Concealed in these figures was a rise in average per caput energy consumption from 2,401.1 LOE in 1989 to more than 5,000 LOE in 2010. Noteworthy too is the fact that average per caput carbon dioxide emissions have more than doubled since 1990, from 5.4 metric tons to around 11 tons by 2010.

Coal and oil have traditionally been the principal sources of energy, although their relative importance has changed significantly as Taiwan sought to reduce its oil dependence; between 1980 and 2010 the contribution of coal to total energy supplies doubled (from 15% to 32%), while that of crude petroleum and petroleum products contracted from 71% to 49%. In 2009 nuclear energy accounted for 8.3% of total energy supplies, natural gas (including liquefied natural gas) 10.2%, hydropower 0.3%, and geothermal, wind, solar and solar thermal sources 0.1%. During 1980–2010 energy consumption increased, on average, by 4.8% per year to reach 120.3m. KLOE. The fact that this figure was slightly below the annual rate of GDP expansion suggested some improvement in conservation and/or efficiency in energy use, although industrial restructuring may also have lessened the energy-to-GDP ratio. Official data do, in fact, show that energy consumption growth has slowed in recent years, to an average annual rate of 3.8% between 2000 and 2007 (reaching 2.6% during 2000–10, demonstrating the impact of the global financial crisis). Meanwhile, since the end of the 1980s final demand for electricity has almost tripled, reaching 58.5m. KLOE in 2010. Taiwan Power (Taipower) was, until 1994, the monopoly provider of electricity in Taiwan, and it still dominates the electric power sector. Before the onset of the global recession, fears that continuing growth of electricity consumption would generate excess demand in the near future encouraged the electricity generation industry to be opened up to overseas investment in order to increase production.

In 1955 domestic sources provided almost three-quarters of Taiwan's total energy supplies, 60% of which were derived from domestically produced coal. By 1970 well over one-half of energy needs were being met from imports, and the contribution from overseas subsequently continued to rise steadily. Since the mid-1980s Taiwan's energy imports have risen by about 6% annually, and by 2010 they accounted for 99.4% of total commercial energy supplies, compared with 86.4% and 95.3%, respectively, in 1980 and 1990. In 2009 energy imports included the purchase of 71.4m. KLOE of crude petroleum (about three-quarters of which came from the Middle East) and 46.7m. KLOE of coal, most of which came from China, Indonesia and Australia. The cost of crude petroleum imports has risen sharply in recent years, from US $8,132.9m. in 2000 to a peak of $33,088.4m. in 2008 (as of 2010, the corresponding figure had declined to $25,676.9m.). In 2010 overseas purchases of oil were the third largest import category, accounting for 10.2% of Taiwan's total imports.

Between the late 1970s and the second half of the 1980s there was a sharp increase in the share of nuclear energy in total commercial energy consumption, from 4.9% in 1979 to 16.4% in 1987. From the 1980s, however, plans to extend Taiwan's nuclear energy capacity became increasingly controversial, and eventually, in 2000, the Government announced its decision to halt construction of a fourth nuclear power plant at Lungmen. In the event, construction work recommenced in 2001, and the two reactors being built at Lungmen were expected to begin operations in December 2011 and December 2012, respectively. Meanwhile, there are currently six nuclear power reactors in operation in Taiwan (at Chinshan, Kuosheng and Maanshan), all of which are run by Taipower. Since the late 1980s the contribution of nuclear power to total energy supplies has declined, and in 2010 it was 8.3%.

The biggest demand for energy has come from the industrial sector. According to the Bureau of Energy, in 2010 its share of total domestic consumption was 53.8%. Within the industrial sector, by far the largest user is chemicals, accounting for about one-half of energy use. Other significant users are: transport (12.9%); services (10.9%); residential housing (10.7%); and the energy sector itself (7%). By contrast, in 2010 the agricultural sector accounted for a mere 0.8% of energy consumption.

FOREIGN TRADE

Overview

Heavy reliance on foreign trade was a predictable consequence of the small scale of Taiwan's economy. With the benefit of hindsight, the abandonment of ISI policies at the end of the 1950s can be seen to have marked one of the major turning points in the island's post-1949 development trajectory. From that point through to the present day, foreign trade (especially export promotion) has made a critical contribution to Taiwan's economic growth. Together with the other first-echelon Asian NIEs (i.e. Hong Kong, South Korea and Singapore) Taiwan's development record during the last half-century exhibited many traditional characteristics of trade dependence. Foreign investment has also played an important role in Taiwan's economic transformation. Since the late 1980s cross-Straits interactions have added a new, crucial and ultimately dominant dimension to Taiwan's external economic relations. As they have evolved, such interactions have both complemented and challenged the island's economic links with other parts of the world.

The exhaustion of ISI policies by the late 1950s and the increasingly severe constraints imposed by limited domestic markets left little alternative but to look overseas for new markets. Accordingly, at the end of the 1950s, the Government embarked on a more aggressive external-orientated strategy. This embraced a variety of measures, including lowering tariffs for domestic producers, devaluing the exchange rate, extending preferential treatment to exporters and establishing export-processing zones. Education and labour training were also accorded high priority in order to promote the growth of export-orientated manufacturing production.

The subsequent expansion of Taiwan's foreign trade was remarkable. During the 1960s the nominal US dollar-denominated value of its merchandise trade (exports plus imports) averaged annual growth of 21.8%, compared with a mere 5.4% between 1952 and 1960. Concealed in these figures was an acceleration in export growth from 4.4% to 20.6% per year. Although import growth in the 1960s was slower than that of exports (averaging 17.8% annually), such growth was from a higher base. As a result, the balance of merchandise trade for the time remained in modest deficit.

The momentum of trade expansion accelerated further in the 1970s: the average annual rate of growth of merchandise trade was 29.4%, almost identical to that of exports (29.6%). However, such rapid growth could not be maintained, and from the 1980s foreign trade growth began to slow. In the 1980s and 1990s merchandise trade growth averaged 11.9% and 9.2%, respectively; the corresponding figures for exports were 13% and 8.5%, respectively. Meanwhile, after 1975 Taiwan's trade balance moved into surplus, where it has consistently remained to the present day. Between 1980 and 1987 the merchandise trade surplus rose from US $78m. to $18,695m. (a level that was not to be exceeded until 2002). By 1984 the total value of Taiwan's foreign trade had reached well over US $50,000m., making it the 10th largest exporter and 15th largest trading nation in the world. By the beginning of the 1980s Taiwan was trading even more than Japan relative to the size of its economy: the value of its merchandise trade constituted 95% of GNP in 1980, compared with about 30% for Japan. Taiwan's export share alone was around 48%.

Geo-strategic factors ensured that until the late 1980s the direction of Taiwan's foreign trade was overwhelmingly towards capitalist industrial countries, particularly the USA and Japan. However, fears that Taiwan might fall prey to the pessimistic predictions of dependency theory proved unfounded. Indeed, a major problem experienced by Taiwan was the burgeoning scale of its trade surplus with the USA, which grew from US $171m. in 1975 to reach a record $16,037m. in 1987. The size of this bilateral surplus elicited protests from the US Administration, which led to the subsequent removal of Taiwan from preferential tariff treatment by the USA. This was the context in which, starting in 1986, the Government introduced a range of trade liberalization measures. In particular, the decision to allow the NT dollar to float led to an appreciation of the exchange rate. The impact on Taiwan's trade balance was swiftly evident: by the end of 1987 the Taiwanese currency had risen by 42% against the US dollar. In line with a more general trend, Taiwan's global trade surplus steadily declined, and its bilateral surplus *vis-à-vis* the USA also decreased sharply. By the early 1990s it had almost halved, having declined to US $7,801m. in 1992. Only after the NT dollar devaluation in 1997 did Taiwan's trade surplus with the USA once more rise significantly (from US $6,318m. to $11,521m. between 1997 and 1999). Since then it has once again declined, reaching a low point of US $4,464m. in 2008, but rising to $6,087m. in 2010.

Taiwan's balance of trade with Japan has consistently deteriorated since the 1950s. By the mid-1980s its bilateral deficit averaged about US $3,000m.; by the end of that decade it had exceeded $6,000m., and at the end of the 1990s it was $18,594m. Having reached US $30,943m. in 2005, it subsequently decreased to $21,718m. in 2009, before rising to a record level of $33,911m. in 2010. It is a salutary reminder of the continuing importance of the economic axis between Taiwan and Japan that in 2010 the total value of bilateral merchandise trade was US $69,923m., 23% higher than the value of trade with the USA, although almost 40% below that with mainland China.

Until the beginning of cross-Straits economic rapprochement towards the end of the 1980s, the USA and Japan dominated Taiwan's foreign trade. The rest of Asia accounted for around 15% of Taiwan's total foreign trade, and the remaining balance was roughly shared between Western Europe and the Middle East. At the end of the 1980s the initiation for the first time since 1949 of indirect trade links with the Chinese mainland (see below) became a shaping, and eventually the dominant, influence of Taiwan's foreign trade trajectory.

In global terms, Taiwan has recorded a trade surplus in every year since 1976, although had it not been for the remarkable expansion of trade with China, a return to a global trade deficit would have taken place some years ago. In 1987 Taiwan's global surplus had reached US $18,695m., although as a result of NT dollar revaluation it subsequently contracted to US $8,564m. in 1994. Since then it has displayed quite significant annual fluctuations. It attained its all-time peak, US $29,304m., in 2009 (in 2010 the corresponding figure was $23,364m.). Meanwhile, Taiwan has also accumulated sizeable foreign-exchange reserves. They increased from US $2,205m. at the end of 1980 to $72,441m. in 1990, expanding further to $106,742m. in 2000. Reserves have continued to rise, and at the end of June 2011 they reached a record level of US $400,330m, giving Taiwan the fifth largest reserves in the world (after China, Japan, Russia and Saudi Arabia).

In 1998, following the Asian financial crisis, Taiwan's foreign trade contracted by 9.0%. However, recovery was swift, and by 2000 further growth had taken the value of merchandise trade to a new record level of US $292,682m. In 2001 the bursting of the IT 'bubble' had a severe impact, causing trade to decline by more than 20% (exports contracting by 17% and imports by 23%). Once again, a rapid recovery took place, and between 2002 and 2008 Taiwan's merchandise trade recorded average annual growth of 10.6%, to reach a record US $496,077m. Although merchandise trade grew by 6.5% in 2008, this figure concealed a sharp downturn in both exports and imports during the second half of the year. In particular, a sharp decline in external demand caused a 20% decrease in exports in real terms in the final quarter of 2008. Demand remained depressed during much of 2009, and, despite a recovery in the final months of that year, the value of Taiwan's merchandise trade decreased by almost one-quarter to US $378,045m., the lowest level since 2003. The annual contraction in exports was 20%, while imports declined by 27.5%. Nevertheless, there were signs of trade recovery in the final months of 2009, and in 2010 Taiwan's merchandise trade increased by almost 40% to reach a record level of US $525,837m.

Exports

The structure of Taiwan's exports has changed dramatically since the 1960s, when raw and processed agricultural goods began to be replaced by manufactured products as the dominant export category. For example, whereas agricultural products had accounted for two-thirds of total exports in 1960, by 1970 79% of exports were industrial goods. This change reflected major declines in overseas sales of rice, sugar and tea (their share of total exports decreasing from 38% to 4% between 1961 and 1971), alongside big rises in those of textiles, plastic products, and electrical and other machinery (their share rising from 16% to 54% in the same period). Subsequently, the dominant position of manufactured goods among exports became even more apparent. In 2010 industrial products accounted for 98.9% of total exports, with 83.3% deriving from heavy industry.

Concealed in these structural changes has been a shift from labour-intensive to capital-intensive exports, and subsequently to knowledge- and technology-intensive exports. In 2010 the most important category of foreign exports was electronic products, which earned US $77,306.1m., followed by basic metals and associated products ($25,884.4m.), precision instruments ($23,623.6m.), plastics and related products ($19,652.1m.), chemicals ($19,227.4m.) and machinery ($16,725.4m.). The value of exports of information and communication products was US $14,095.4m. Other significant sources of export earnings were textiles and apparel (US $10,838.3m.) and transport equipment ($9,333.2m.).

The geographical destination of exports has also changed over time. Between the 1950s and 1980s the USA accounted for an increasing share of Taiwan's overseas sales, rising from a mere 4.4% in 1955 to a peak of 48.8% in 1984. Subsequently, however, the US share steadily contracted, declining to just 11.5% in 2010 (lower than in any year since the early 1960s). Until the late 1960s Japan was also a major purchaser of Taiwanese goods, although its share was already declining, and it has continued to contract to the present day (from a high point of 59.5% in 1955 to 6.6% in 2010). There was an especially sharp decrease in exports to Japan—cumulatively, by 31%—in 1997 and 1998, although recovery was swift and, in value terms, exports reached a record level (not exceeded until 2008) of US $16,887m. in 2000. This turnaround reflected recovery in exports of Taiwanese IT products to Japan, as well as a rise in the output of Taiwanese-Japanese joint ventures, mainly producing electrical items and electronics, based in Taiwan. Meanwhile, from the second half of the 1980s, the importance of Hong Kong, which had always been a significant export destination, grew; by the end of the 1990s its share of total exports (23.5% in 1997) was almost as large as that of the USA, although it has since contracted once more (to 13.8% in 2010).

Taiwanese exporters have also targeted European markets. Between 1960 and 1980 Europe's share in total exports increased from 6% to 16%, and remained at about that level for the next two decades. Since 2000, however, the European share has declined, and in 2010 was 10.7%. In descending importance, Germany, the Netherlands (owing to the entrepôt role of Rotterdam) and the United Kingdom are the three main

European destinations for Taiwanese goods, these three countries accounting for about one-half of the value of EU consignments. Taiwan's trade with Europe is overwhelmingly dominated by the EU, which is Taiwan's fourth largest trading partner and accounts for almost 95% of all its trade with Europe. Conversely, Taiwan is the EU's 10th largest partner throughout the world, and the fourth biggest in Asia after China, Japan and South Korea. In order to overcome EU trade restrictions, several of Taiwan's largest companies have gained footholds in the EU by merging with existing local companies or by establishing independent electronics and IT manufacturing facilities there.

More recently, six members of the Association of Southeast Asian Nations (ASEAN), namely Indonesia, Malaysia, the Philippines, Singapore, Thailand and Viet Nam, have come to represent an increasingly important export market, accounting for 15.1% of overseas sales in 2010. However, by far the most important recent development has been the opening of the mainland Chinese market to Taiwanese exporters. Between 1997 and 2010 China's share of total exports increased from 0.5% to 28%, overtaking the USA in 2004 to become Taiwan's single most important destination for exports. In 2010 the value of Taiwan's exports to China was almost two-and-a-half times greater than that of sales to the USA.

The recent global financial crisis took a severe toll on Taiwan's exports. The value of exports decreased by one-fifth in 2009, from US $255,628.7m. to $203,674.6m. Some products were less affected than others: for example, textile sales declined by 14%, whereas exports of base metals and associated products were down by almost one-third. However, by the final months of 2009 a recovery was under way, and this continued into 2010. Indeed, the value of Taiwan's global exports in 2010 reached a record level of US $274,601m. (an annual increase of more than one-third). A CEPD report noted that the impetus provided by the ECFA, as well as rising demand for electronic and machinery products as a result of increasing labour costs in mainland China, had facilitated a rise of almost 11% in exports of goods and services during the first quarter of 2011. The same source predicted that the rate of increase in exports for the year as a whole would reach almost 7%.

Imports

Most of Taiwan's imports have comprised raw materials and semi-finished goods required for production, with the balance made up by imports of consumer goods. In 2010 raw materials accounted for 75.5% of the value of all imports (the peak figure was 79.4% in 2008), compared with 16.6% and 7.9%, respectively, for capital goods and consumer products. According to the CEPD, in 2010 Asian countries were the origin of 56.9% of Taiwan's imports (the value of such purchases was US $142,296m.). Next in importance were North America (US $26,913m., or 10.7% of the total) and, almost identically, Europe ($26,005m., or 10.4% of the total, with almost all European imports coming from EU member states). Japan is still easily the single most important source of imports: in 2010 the value of purchases from Japan was a record US $51,917m., or almost 21% of the total. In recent years the importance of China has also increased, and in 2006 the value of merchandise imports from the mainland (US $24,783.1m.) for the first time exceeded the value of shipments from the USA ($22,264m.). By 2010 imports from China had reached US $35,946m. (also a record).

In 2010 the three most important categories of shipments to Taiwan were machinery, electrical equipment, and basic metals and related products (the aggregate cost of which was US $93,397m., accounting for 37.2% of total overseas purchases). Crude petroleum purchases alone accounted for more than one-10th of the value of all Taiwan's imports. Also significant were imports of chemicals (US $29,339.1m., or 11.7%) and precision instruments ($10,857.9m., or 4.3%).

Just as exports suffered a sharp decline as a result of the global financial crisis of 2008–09, so too did imports. Indeed, the reduction in the value of imports in 2009—down by 27.5% to US $174,370.5m.—was considerably greater than that of exports. Most severely affected were imports of base metals and associated products (down by 47.5%), and minerals (down by 40%). The beginning of import recovery was evident in late 2009 and continued into 2010, with rising export-induced demand and surging raw material prices. For 2010 as a whole, imports increased by a remarkable 44% to reach a record level of US $251,236.2m. The CEPD predicted that in 2011 the corresponding rate of growth would be 1.9%.

Foreign Investment

Taiwan has been both a net recipient and net source of foreign investment, the turning point occurring in the mid-1980s, when Taiwan ceased to be a capital-poor country and became 'cash-rich'. In the 1950s Taiwan was a net beneficiary of foreign capital, the main form of which was US aid. Later, Taiwan's economic success encouraged foreign firms and private entrepreneurs to undertake large-scale investment on the island. Between 1969 and 1972, for example, almost 10% of investment undertaken in the manufacturing sector came from overseas—a figure that was higher than in other developing countries. The impact of such capital inflows was considerable: by the end of the 1970s foreign firms accounted for more than 8% of GDP, while exports of foreign firms contributed 20% of all exports. No less important was the economic contribution of foreign investment as a result of technology transfer, as foreign investors introduced new production and management techniques. In the mid-1980s Taiwan became the source of a net outflow of capital and such outward FDI subsequently came to play an important role in domestic economic restructuring, while also facilitating closer relations with other Asia-Pacific countries. Taiwan had already been a significant source of investment in the USA, especially in residential and commercial real estate. However, from the mid-1980s new economic opportunities encouraged Taiwanese entrepreneurs to take advantage of low labour and land costs and invest in South-East Asia, especially in countries with large ethnic Chinese communities that had close historical relations with Taiwan. Appreciation of the NT dollar was another factor that encouraged domestic producers to establish operations in such countries as Viet Nam, the Philippines, Indonesia, Thailand and Malaysia. However, important as such developments have been, the most profound factor influencing outward investment in recent years occurred during and after the 1990s, when cross-Straits economic rapprochement made mainland China the pre-eminent destination for Taiwanese capital (see below).

CROSS-STRAITS ECONOMIC RELATIONS

Trade relations with the mainland were historically extremely close, and in the early 1930s such exchanges probably accounted for about one-half of Taiwan's total trade, excluding Japan. Cross-Straits economic relations were interrupted in 1949 by the establishment of the People's Republic of China and were resumed only in the second half of the 1980s, following an official announcement in July 1985 that, while neither direct trade nor entrepreneurial contact would be permitted across the Taiwan Strait, entrepôt trade would no longer be prohibited.

Cross-Straits economic links have developed against a background of China and Taiwan in pursuit of different imperatives. Without discounting the inherent economic value of closer relations, China seeks also to use economic rapprochement as a means of fulfilling political objectives: in other words, to achieve reunification. From Taiwan's perspective, the situation is more complicated because of the more overt tension between the wishes of entrepreneurs, seeking to maximize profits through closer economic integration, and those of the Government, which (depending on the administration) has shown varying degrees of caution in pursuing economic rapprochement. At the beginning of his presidency, for example, Chen Shui-bian came under increasing pressure to relax investment restrictions. In October 2001 the DPP announced its decision to replace the supposedly outmoded 'no haste, be patient' policy on investment in China with a strategy of 'active opening and effective management'. Associated with this were an easing of previous restrictions on single investments of over US $50m. and a reduction in restricted investment categories, including PCs and semiconductors. In 2006 this strategy was, in turn, replaced by one of 'pro-active management, effective liberalization'. There is a perception that under Chen Shui-bian's two administrations the strengthening of economic links across the Taiwan Strait was impeded by Chen's preoccupation with establishing an independent identity for Taiwan, as well as by the fear that closer economic relations would merely serve to increase the island's political vulnerability *vis-à-vis* China. Be that as it may, during these eight years there was an almost three-fold increase in cross-Straits trade, while Taiwanese investment in the mainland rose almost four-fold. In general, the DPP's continued wariness of the political consequences of any undue acceleration in the development of economic relations with China contrasted with the more open position of the KMT, the latter being most dramatically demonstrated by the unprecedented meeting that took place in the Chinese capital of Beijing in 2005 between mainland President Hu Jintao and the former KMT Chairman, Lien Chan.

It was always clear that a KMT victory in the 2008 presidential and parliamentary elections would presage an easing of tensions across the Taiwan Straits, and in his inaugural address President Ma Ying-jeou spoke of his desire to 'normalize' bilateral economic relations. Barely a month after Ma's inauguration, in June 2008 representatives of the two sides (Chen Yunlin, Chairman of the Association for Relations across the Taiwan Straits—ARATS) and Chiang Pin-kung (Chairman of the Straits Exchange Foundation—SEF) met in Beijing for the first cross-Straits talks to take place for nine years. Two major agreements emerged from the discussions: one was to establish reciprocal representative offices in Beijing and Taipei; the other was to initiate non-stop direct weekend flights across the Taiwan Strait. From an economic perspective, no less significant was the subsequent announcement by the Taiwanese Premier, Liu Chao-shiuan, that the Government would relax restrictions on investment in China by allowing firms to invest up to 60% (instead of the 20%–40% permitted under existing rules) of their net worth in the mainland. The Government also revealed that it was to remove the ban on companies with 20% or more Chinese equity from investing in Taiwan. Such initiatives dramatically highlighted the new, more open official stance towards Taiwan's economic relations with China.

In November 2008 Chen Yunlin travelled to Taipei for the second round of ARATS-SEF discussions. This was the highest level visit to Taiwan by a mainland Chinese representative since 1949. The talks resulted in the signing of four agreements: on direct air transport, direct sea transport, postal co-operation and food safety. According to the Taiwanese authorities, the opening of direct air travel would halve the flight time from Taipei to Shanghai to less than one-and-a-half hours, and save an estimated 40%–45% in fuel costs. Meanwhile, direct sea transport would reduce the length of each voyage by between 16 and 27 hours, and reduce shipping costs by 15%–30%.

The third round of talks, held in the mainland city of Nanjing in April 2009, led to three further agreements: on judicial assistance and combating crime; financial co-operation; and cross-Straits air transport, providing for the opening of six new destinations in China and an increase in the number of weekly flights from 108 to 270. A fourth round of discussions was hosted by Taiwan in Taichung in December and resulted in the signing of another three co-operation agreements: on agricultural quarantine and inspection; standards, metrology, inspection and accreditation; and fishing crew affairs.

The climax of negotiations came in the fifth round of talks (held in Beijing in June 2010), when SEF and ARATS representatives agreed the terms of the landmark ECFA, which was duly signed at a ceremony in Chongqing, China, on 29 June. (The same talks also generated an agreement on intellectual property rights protection and co-operation.) The two sides then published 'early harvest lists' of agreed tariff reductions. China listed 539 early harvest items, on which tariffs would be reduced over a three-year period (2011–13). Just four sectors accounted for 70% of the items (petrochemicals, textiles, machinery and transport equipment) and reflected activities in which Taiwan was challenged by intense competition from ASEAN countries, as well as Japan and South Korea. Taiwanese government sources also noted that the items included in the Chinese list offered significant opportunities for Taiwanese farmers and SMEs to expand their exports to the mainland. According to Chinese customs data, the value of Taiwanese exports of the 539 items in 2009 was US $13,838m., or 16.1% of total exports to the mainland. The export value of the 267 early harvest items listed by Taiwan in 2009 was US $2,858m., or 10.5% of total Chinese exports to Taiwan. Significantly, no agricultural products were included in Taiwan's list, reflecting the Taiwanese Government's determination to protect the agricultural sector. Taiwanese banks would also be allowed to start conducting business in Chinese renminbi after one year of opening branches in China, rather than waiting for the two years required by WTO rules.

The sixth round of talks between SEF and ARATS representatives took place in Taipei in December 2010, and resulted in the signing of an agreement on medical and health co-operation. It had been hoped that the two sides would also sign an investment protection agreement. In the event, however, although progress was reported also to have been made on this issue, that agreement remained unsigned.

In February 2011 Chen Yunlin led a delegation of mainland businesspeople to Taiwan. During his visit Chen urged the Taiwanese Government to review its policy of restricting mainland investment on the island. He pointed out that such investment, in just 73 projects, currently stood at a mere US $153m., compared with reverse flows from Taiwan of $51,700m. Increased investment by mainland companies would, he stated, generate new jobs to the benefit of the island's economy.

Although polls showed considerable popular support for the ECFA (a poll conducted in December 2010 by the Mainland Affairs Council—MAC—revealed that more than 73% of respondents endorsed cross-Straits negotiations as being conducive to peace and stability between the two countries), analysts and especially politicians remained divided on its advisability. In particular, the opposition DPP expressed considerable scepticism about the ECFA, with party Chairwoman Dr Tsai Ing-wen stating that it would 'hand the key for Taiwan's economic prosperity over to China' and cause Taiwan to 'lose the independence of its economy and financial system'. By contrast, the KMT administration hoped that the ECFA would not only have beneficial effects on trade and the economy, but would also encourage other countries—most immediately, the member nations of ASEAN—to sign similar agreements with Taiwan. Over time, however, many members of the DPP have recognized that economic integration between Taiwan and the mainland has become an irreversible process. During Chen Yunlin's visit to Taiwan in February 2011, the DPP broke with past practice by not organizing demonstrations in protest against the visit.

Chinese and Taiwanese sources give widely varying estimates of the value of cross-Straits trade. MAC statistics showed that the value of such trade was US $120,784.5m. in 2010—17% below the corresponding figure ($145,370.5m.) cited by Chinese Customs. What is not in doubt is the rapid increase in merchandise trade that has taken place since 1990. According to data published by the MAC, between 1990 and 2007 total merchandise trade grew, on average, by 19.2% per year (from US $5,160m. to $102,260.9m.). This figure conceals annual export growth of 18.1%, and annual import growth of 23.6%. MAC estimates also showed that in 2008–09 there was a significant reduction in cross-Straits trade: Taiwanese exports to the mainland declined from US $74,245.9m. in 2008 to $62,090.9m. in 2009, a contraction of more than 16%; imports, having risen to a record $31,391.3m. in 2008, declined to $24,423.5m. in 2009, down by 22%. However, there was a sharp recovery and indeed net growth in 2010, with bilateral trade rising year-on-year by a remarkable 40% (with export growth of 36.6%, and import growth of 47.2%).

Taiwan has consistently enjoyed a bilateral trade surplus *vis-à-vis* the mainland. MAC data revealed that Taiwan's bilateral surplus rose from US $3,629.2m. in 1990 to a peak of $46,230.9m. in 2007. During the next two years it declined quite sharply, contracting by almost 19% to US $37,587.2m. in 2009. Despite more rapid import growth, compared with that of exports, in 2010 Taiwan's surplus totalled a record US $48,880m., a year-on-year increase of 30%. The rapid expansion in Taiwanese exports to China in the last two decades has been driven by increasing shipments of electrical machinery, equipment and parts, which have come to account for well over 40% of total shipments to the mainland. The significance of Taiwan's large surplus *vis-à-vis* China was captured in the finding that, in its absence, Taiwan's global trade surplus (US $23,364m. in 2010) would have been transformed into a sizeable deficit.

It is also clear that since the end of the 1980s Taiwan has become increasingly trade-dependent on the mainland. MAC statistics indicated that between 1987 and 2010 Taiwan's total trade dependency ratio in relation to China increased dramatically, from an insignificant 1.7% to 23%. In interpreting the figures, it is important to differentiate Taiwan's relatively low degree of import dependence (14.3%), and the much higher—some would say alarming—reliance (29.7%) on the mainland as an export market. The pattern of increasing trade, especially export, dependence on China is one that Taiwan shares with many other countries and regions, including the USA, the EU, ASEAN and Japan. However, the extent of Taiwan's export dependence on the mainland is uniquely high. By contrast, China's trade dependence on Taiwan is much lower. MAC data showed that, having increased to a high point of 15.8% in 1997, Taiwan's share of China's global imports declined to just 6.1% in 2010. The island's share of China's global exports peaked at 2.8% in 2004, but had decreased to 2.3% by 2010. Even so, it is instructive that, following accession by both China and Taiwan to the WTO, the latter has become the third largest origin of imports purchased by China, after Japan and South Korea.

In recent years huge amounts of FDI have also flowed to China from Taiwan. Quantifying these capital flows is extremely difficult, and a major problem is that much investment by Taiwanese entrepreneurs flows through the British Virgin and Cayman Islands. Official mainland sources indicated that these British Caribbean territories improbably accounted for about 15% of all inward FDI to China in 2009. There was little doubt, however, that at least one-half of such flows (and probably considerably more) originated in Taiwan. As with merchandise trade flows, there are wide variations in different sources' estimates of Taiwanese FDI to China. Taiwanese estimates published by the Investment Commission of the MoEA indicated that up to the end of April 2011 FDI destined for China was cumulatively worth US $102,118.71m. This contrasted with a figure of US $52,809.24m., more than 50% below the MoEA estimate, published by the Chinese Ministry of Commerce (although this figure excluded Taiwanese FDI that originated in the Virgin and Cayman Islands). Both Taiwanese and Chinese sources agreed that FDI flows to the mainland declined in 2009; however, whereas the MoEA pointed to a dramatic contraction (by one-third), official Chinese statistics indicated only a marginal decline of less than 1%. Both sources recorded a significant increase in FDI in 2010, but again in sharply differing degrees. Notwithstanding the difficulties in quantifying investment flows, there is no doubt that China has become by far Taiwan's single most important investment destination: MoEA data (excluding investment routed through the British Caribbean) showed that between 1991 and 2010 the mainland absorbed 60.9% of the island's global outward investment, and in January–April 2011 the corresponding figure was more than 83%.

The Lower Yangtze River Delta (the regions of Jiangsu and Shanghai), Zhejiang, Guangdong and Fujian have been the main investment destinations within China. Cumulatively, these regions were estimated by the MoEA to have absorbed more than 85% of all Taiwanese FDI in China during 1991–2010. During this period Jiangsu was the biggest single Chinese provincial recipient of FDI, taking more than one-third of the total (US $33,383.3m.); and, if Shanghai were included, this figure would rise to one-half (some $47,000m.). In the most recent past, the importance of the Pearl River Delta as a recipient of FDI has given way to that of 'Greater Shanghai', although in cumulative terms Guangdong has received more than one-fifth of all Taiwanese FDI since 1991. The geographical concentration of Taiwanese FDI was shown by the fact that between 1991 and 2010 less than 5% of the island's outward bound capital was destined for Beijing and Tianjin, while under 10% was allocated to interior provinces.

The manufacturing industry remains the dominant sectoral destination of Taiwanese FDI in China. Individual industries that accounted for more than 5% of total FDI inflows during 1991–2010 included: electronic parts and components for the manufacturing sector (19.6% of cumulative FDI); computers, and electronic and optical products (14.5%); electrical equipment manufacturing (8.5%); and fabricated metal products (5.9%). The cumulative share of services remains tiny, although in future years China seems likely to become increasingly attractive to Taiwanese investors in tertiary sector activities (for example, banking, retail activities, advertising and legal services).

The extent of Taiwan's involvement in the mainland is also highlighted by the sheer number of Taiwanese business executives who live and work there. Finding a precise estimate of this number is extremely difficult, but authoritative sources suggest that it is no fewer than 3m. and some estimates suggest a considerably higher figure. Reflecting the geographical pattern of Taiwanese investment in the mainland, the vast majority of Taiwanese residents in China live in the Lower Yangtze and Pearl River delta regions. It was also estimated that in 2000–02 Taiwan directly employed at least 5m. Chinese workers, a figure that has since increased significantly and that would be even higher if related ancillary employment were included. In recent years there has also been a rapid expansion in the level of remittances from mainland China to Taiwan: at the end of 2008 the cumulative total of remittances was US $389,355m. Since then they have increased steadily, to reach US $705,900m. by April 2011 (an increase of more than 80%).

WTO membership always seemed likely eventually to end Taiwan's long-standing bans on direct shipping and air links across the Straits, since impediments to such links were widely regarded as being incompatible with the principle of most-favoured-nation treatment that lies at the core of WTO rules. Within the framework of the so-called 'mini-three links', from 2001 there was a steady increase in the number of round trips made annually by Taiwanese vessels plying two routes: between Kinmen and Xiamen, and between Matsu and Fuzhou. However, the most significant recent breakthrough came in June 2008, when representatives of SEF and ARATS reached a watershed agreement providing for an expansion in tourist visits by mainland residents to Taiwan (since 1987 Taiwanese had made almost 50m. visits in the opposite direction). The terms of the agreement granted permission, in the first instance, for parties of 10–40 persons to travel to Taiwan, subject to an upper limit of 3,000 people per day. Following the inauguration of cross-Straits direct flights in December 2008, the number of mainland visitors to the island rose dramatically—from 288,511 in 2008 to 1,580,099 in 2010. Within this figure was a three-and-a-half-fold increase in the number of mainland visitors engaged in trade and other kinds of economic activity. However, the rise in the number of tourists was even more remarkable, increasing by some 1,200%, from 90,000 to almost 1.2m. There can be little doubt that the scale of tourist visits from China to Taiwan will continue to rise significantly in the coming years. In the first four months of 2011 a further 426,000 tourists arrived in Taiwan from the Chinese mainland. The cumulative total of Taiwanese tourists to the mainland has been even more spectacular, reaching more than 61m. by the end of 2010.

Trade and investment data highlight the extent to which cross-Straits economic integration has become a reality. China has become an important link in the production chain of many Taiwanese firms, and their business association with Chinese partners has meanwhile facilitated their emergence as global exporters to major international markets. It is clear that Taiwan's economic destiny has become increasingly dependent on China. Many, especially in Taiwan's 'pan-green' camp, argue that such dependence leaves Taiwan dangerously exposed to political pressure from China. That any serious interruption in cross-Straits economic links would have a severe, even catastrophic, economic impact on Taiwan is not in doubt. However, it deserves stating that the process of economic integration under way since the late 1980s has brought benefits to both sides, and the economic effects of any disruption would be severely damaging to China, as well as to Taiwan. Re-exports by Taiwanese-owned companies account for a significant share of China's global exports. Taiwan's role as the second largest source of FDI to the mainland and, in particular, its pre-eminent contribution to the further development of China's most important growth hub (Greater Shanghai and the Lower Yangtze Region) also emphasizes the major economic sacrifice that would be entailed by the disruption of cross-Straits economic relations.

FINANCE

Taiwan's financial sector remained under tight central control until the end of the 1970s. In the following decade, however, changing circumstances (not least the impact of the international oil crisis) dictated the first measures that were taken with regard to financial liberalization. Accordingly, price deregulation, including the abolition of interest rate controls, began to take place, and restrictions on capital movements were relaxed. Foreign-exchange reforms were also introduced. Such changes served to facilitate more competitive financial behaviour and more efficient management. It was against this background that, in 1989, Taiwan's Banking Law was revised, the principal effect being to remove controls on deposit and lending interest rates.

Membership of the WTO imposed new financial pressures on Taiwan, and from the late 1990s the Government introduced more financial deregulatory initiatives in anticipation of its accession. It also adopted a more accommodating attitude towards the privatization of banks (especially the three main commercial banks), most of which had traditionally been under state ownership or control. Despite opposition from some quarters, legislative and institutional initiatives helped to accelerate this process. In general, the ability of the Government to divest itself of bank ownership has been an ongoing and important factor shaping the success of financial sector privatization and restructuring in Taiwan.

In October 2000 an amendment to the Banking Law relaxed restrictions on the investment activities of Taiwanese banks, while increasing the ownership limit in other banks or financial companies from 15% to 25%. In December, in an attempt to encourage mergers involving foreign as well as domestic institutions, the Merger Act of Financial Institutions was approved. In 2001 new financial reform laws were proposed, involving further liberalization and an acceleration of the consolidation of domestic banks. The Financial Holding Company Law sought to permit the establishment of integrated financial groups capable of offering a wide range of services, including banking, insurance and brokering. Insurance companies also gained more freedom to formulate investment policies and develop new products. No less significant, in September 2001 control of 35 local financial institutions was transferred to 10 commercial banks. In 2008 financial reform remained a priority for the incoming KMT Government, as it had been for the DPP administration, although the even more urgent imperative of combating the effects of the global financial crisis temporarily relegated it to a lower priority status. It remains to be seen to what extent the KMT's large majority in the Legislative Yuan will facilitate more rapid progress than has hitherto been achieved.

A matter of growing concern in the 1990s was the deterioration in the financial position of Taiwan's banking sector. By the end of 1998 overdue bank loans had reached 4.4% of total lending, and, while the major banks remained in profit, they felt compelled to set aside large reserves to meet lending losses. In 2000 some 10 Taiwanese banks were reported to have made losses, totalling NT $16,600m. According to Taiwan's central bank, the Central Bank of China (subsequently the Central Bank of the Republic of China), by the end of that year non-performing loans (NPLs) had risen to total NT $773,522m., equivalent to 5.3% of all domestic bank loans; at the end of the first quarter of 2002 the figure had reached an unprecedented NT $1,147,470m. (11.3%). Subsequently, large-scale sales of NPLs, mainly to global investors through public auctions, led to a steady improvement in the situation. By the end of 2004 the NPL ratio had declined to 2.8% of total loans, and since 2007 the figure has remained below 2%. Indeed, a report by the Financial Supervisory Commission noted that at the end of 2010 the ratio had decreased to an all-time low point of 0.61%.

Until the onset of the global financial crisis, another source of concern had been the mounting problem of consumer debt, highlighted in the finding that during 2006 lenders in Taiwan wrote off more than US $3,000m. of 500,000 consumers' bad credit card loans, or 60% of total overdue debt on credit and cash cards. In a further effort ostensibly to encourage greater transparency, although interpreted by many as a politically motivated initiative, in March 2007 the Financial Supervisory Commission announced that all banks would henceforth be compelled to disclose details of borrowers with loan defaults greater than NT $100m. The announcement elicited critical comment not only from within Taiwan, but also from overseas, on the grounds that it infringed the principle of bank confidentiality.

An event that further undermined confidence in Taiwan's regulatory capabilities was the collapse of a major conglomerate, the Rebar Group, which filed for insolvency protection in December 2006. The flight from Taiwan to Singapore of the Chairman of Rebar, Wang You-theng, allied to rumours of insider trading and the perceived inefficiency of the Financial Supervisory Commission in dealing with Rebar's problems, precipitated a financial crisis. In the first week of January 2007 the Government took control of The Chinese Bank (a subsidiary of Rebar), following the loss of more than one-quarter of its deposits.

In the mid-1980s a relaxation of central bank controls generated a sharp acceleration in the rate of money supply expansion. By the end of the decade more stringent control had been reimposed, and money supply growth was subsequently constrained. Indeed, between 2000 and 2002 the slow growth of money supply (M0, the stock of notes and coins in circulation, and M2, notes and coins plus the value of current accounts and also some deposit or interest-bearing accounts) became a source of anxiety, encouraging the central bank to ease its monetary policy. In the recessionary conditions of 2001, firms' demand for investment credit slackened, while the level of NPLs did little to encourage a proactive lending stance by commercial banks. Quite significant increases in most money aggregates in 2003 and 2004 were followed by a period of much slower growth, and, on some measures, money supply contraction. The onset of the global financial crisis had inevitable implications for monetary policy. For example, in the aftermath of the instability in global financial markets, between June 2008 and February 2009 the central bank made seven reductions in the discount rate, lowering it from 3.625% to 1.25%. It remained at this level until June 2010, when domestic economic recovery was deemed sufficient to raise it to 1.375%. Confidence that the Taiwanese economy had returned to a more stable growth trajectory enabled the central bank to make further increases, and at the end of 2010 the rate stood at 1.625%.

In 2004 the CPI experienced its biggest increase since 1998, rising by 1.6%, and in the following year the rate of increase accelerated to 2.3%. One reason that the CPI has not risen more strongly in recent years has been the weakness of the Taiwanese property market. Since late 2005 the central bank has shown increasing concern about the potential effect of rising international oil prices on consumer price inflation, although the Government has argued that a 10% annual rise in domestic oil prices would translate into a mere 0.2% increase in the CPI. In the event, consumer price inflation in 2006 declined to 0.6%. Although it remained low in early 2007, the annual rate of increase in consumer prices for the year as a whole rose sharply to reach 3.8%. Consumer price inflation intensified in the first half of 2008 before moderating in the second half of the year to generate an annual increase of 1.3%. In 2009 the CPI rose marginally by 0.4%. In 2010 consumer prices increased by 1.4%, and the EIU predicted that the rate of CPI growth for 2011 would be 1.8%.

In response to the global financial crisis, during 2008–09 the Government adopted various fiscal stimulus measures. In May 2008 the Executive Yuan approved a budgetary disbursement of NT $103,420m., intended to raise domestic demand through increased local construction. In January 2009 consumption vouchers worth NT $3,600 were distributed to each member of

Taiwan's population in an attempt to help stimulate demand. The cost of the programme was NT $58,700m. In the same month the Government announced a public works programme, designed to channel NT $500,000m. into the economy over a four-year period. The consensus in 2010 was that these measures had proved effective in helping to facilitate domestic economic recovery.

In the 1990s financial liberalization was accompanied by a parallel process in Taiwan's stock exchange, which was opened to direct investment by foreign institutions in 1991 and to foreign individuals in 1996. Many domestic households now own stocks, although only a quite small proportion of business firms in Taiwan seek to issue shares for public trading. However, despite the earlier initiatives, in October 1997 little more than 3% of Taiwan's stocks were owned by foreigners. In the event, this no doubt protected Taiwan from damaging capital flight of the kind that was so detrimental to other economies during the Asian crisis. However, conditions subsequently changed, not least owing to the impact of further legislative initiatives designed to facilitate share ownership by foreigners. From the early 1990s the number of activities that remained closed to overseas investors declined from more than 100 to 18 as of mid-2003. The process of stock market deregulation has since continued, and investors' share of the stock market has risen to more than one-third.

The domestic stock market experienced an eventful year in 1997. Following a 50% rise over three months to take the Taiwan Stock Exchange (TAIEX) Weighted Index to a record high of 10,256 points (1966 average = 100), it then suffered as a result of panic selling associated with the onset of the Asian financial crisis. By the end of 1997 the index had decreased to 8,228 points, and by the end of 1998 to 6,418 points. Efforts by the DPP Government to halt the stock market decline were not wholly successful. The huge scale of capital outflows after 1997, combined with ongoing securities liberalization, led some members of Taiwan's business community to question the logic of greater exposure to international markets. Stock market volatility continued around a downward trend, and by October 2001 the TAIEX index had declined to 3,446 points. Between February 2000 and October 2001 the market decreased by more than 60%. Recovery, initially halting but subsequently more sustained, then took place, as a result of which the TAIEX Index reached a new peak of 9,810 points in October 2007. Between the first and third quarters of 2008 the index declined by 11.5%, a rate of decrease that accelerated sharply under the impact of global financial instability in the final quarter of 2008 and the first quarter of 2009 (by which point the index had decreased to 4,591 points). However, optimistic expectations of a continuing improvement in cross-Straits relations, as well as of renewed growth in demand for Taiwanese electronics products, subsequently generated quite rapid recovery. By the end of July 2009 the TAIEX Index had reached 8,188 points—a year-on-year increase of almost 80%—and by June 2010 it had risen further, to 8,257 points. The momentum was maintained, and by the end of the year the index had reached 8,972.5 points; however, having reached more than 9,000 points in June 2011, it subsequently declined and by the second week of September was below 7,400 points.

Statistical Survey

Source (unless otherwise stated): Directorate-General of Budget, Accounting and Statistics (DGBAS), 1, Section 1, Jhongsiao East Rd, Taipei 10058; tel. (2) 23803542; fax (2) 23803547; e-mail sicbs@dgbas.gov.tw; internet www.dgbas.gov.tw.

Area and Population

AREA, POPULATION AND DENSITY

Area (sq km)	36,192*
Population (census results)	
16 December 1990	20,393,628
16 December 2000	
Males	11,386,084
Females	10,914,845
Total	22,300,929
Population (official figures at 31 December)	
2008	23,037,031
2009	23,119,772
2010†	23,162,000
Density (per sq km) at 31 December 2010	640.0

* 13,974 sq miles.

† Figure rounded to the nearest thousand persons.

POPULATION BY AGE AND SEX
(official estimates at 31 December 2009)

	Males	Females	Total
0–14	1,970,302	1,807,716	3,778,018
15–64	8,039,423	7,933,921	15,973,344
65 and over	1,627,009	1,741,401	3,368,410
Total	11,636,734	11,483,038	23,119,772

PRINCIPAL TOWNS
(population at 31 December 2009)

Taipei (capital)	2,607,428	Keelung	388,321
Kaohsiung	1,527,914	Sanchong	388,304
Taichung	1,073,635	Jhongli	365,109
Tainan	771,060	Fongshan	339,952
Banciao	552,884	Sindian	294,602
Jhunghe	414,535	Chiayi	273,861
Hsinchu	411,587	Tucheng	238,897
Taoyuan	401,096	Jhanghua	237,160
Sinjhuang	400,848	Yonghe	236,812

BIRTHS, MARRIAGES AND DEATHS
(registered)

	Live births		Marriages		Deaths	
	Number	Rate (per 1,000)	Number	Rate (per 1,000)	Number	Rate (per 1,000)
2003	227,070	10.06	171,483	7.60	130,801	5.80
2004	216,419	9.56	131,453	5.80	135,092	5.97
2005	205,854	9.06	141,140	6.21	139,398	6.13
2006	204,459	8.96	142,669	6.25	135,839	5.95
2007	204,414	8.92	135,041	5.89	141,111	6.16
2008	198,733	8.64	154,866	6.73	143,624	6.25
2009	191,310	8.29	117,099	5.07	143,582	6.22
2010*	166,886	7.20	138,819	6.00	145,772	6.30

* Preliminary.

Life expectancy (years at birth, 2010, provisional): 79.2 (males 76.2; females 82.7).

ECONOMICALLY ACTIVE POPULATION

(annual averages, '000 persons aged 15 years and over)*

	2008	2009	2010
Agriculture, forestry and fishing	535	543	550
Mining and quarrying	6	5	4
Manufacturing	2,886	2,790	2,861
Construction	842	788	797
Electricity and gas supply	28	29	29
Water supply and remediation services	71	73	78
Services	6,036	6,051	6,174
Trade	1,770	1,735	1,747
Hotels and restaurants	687	693	727
Transport and storage	414	402	404
Information and communication	203	207	208
Finance and insurance	411	413	428
Education	605	613	619
Public administration, defence and compulsory social security	343	382	389
Total employed	10,403	10,279	10,493
Unemployed	450	639	577
Total labour force	10,853	10,917	11,070
Males	6,173	6,180	6,242
Females	4,680	4,737	4,828

*Excluding members of the armed forces and persons in institutional households.

Health and Welfare

KEY INDICATORS

Total fertility rate (children per woman, 2010)	0.9
Under-5 mortality rate (per 1,000 live births, 2006)	6.06
HIV/AIDS (% of persons aged 15–49, 2006)	0.03
Physicians (per 1,000 head, 2008)	1.83
Hospital beds (per 1,000 head, 2010)	6.86
Health expenditure (2009): NT $ per head	37,224
Health expenditure (2009): % of GDP	6.9
Health expenditure (2005): public (% of total)	62.90
Human Development Index (2004): value	0.925

For definitions, see explanatory note on p. vi.

Note: Data are mainly from Directorate-General of Budget, Accounting and Statistics (DGBAS).

Agriculture

PRINCIPAL CROPS

('000 metric tons)

	2007	2008	2009
Potatoes	47.4	59.7	n.a.
Rice, paddy	1,363.5	1,457.2	1,578.2
Sweet potatoes	200.1	212.8	229.0
Sorghum	4.9	2.5	0.7
Maize	118.9	118.1	n.a.
Tea	17.5	17.4	16.8
Tobacco	1.7	1.7	1.9
Groundnuts	51.9	55.1	56.9
Sugar cane	720.9	707.1	613.2
Vegetables	2,595.2	2,640.7	n.a.
Fruits	2,654.0	2,577.6	n.a.
Bananas	241.7	207.7	172.6
Pineapples	476.8	452.1	434.8

LIVESTOCK

('000 head at 31 December)

	2006	2007	2008
Cattle	134.8	137.1	134.0
Buffaloes	3.5	3.5	3.6
Pigs	7,068.6	6,620.8	6,427.6
Goats	267.4	249.4	229.5
Chickens	109,633	103,499	100,298
Ducks	11,912	11,000	9,177
Geese	2,841	2,318	1,990
Turkeys	163	156	147

LIVESTOCK PRODUCTS

	2006	2007	2008
Beef (metric tons)	5,626	5,480	5,683
Pig meat (metric tons)	930,609	913,824	861,836
Sheep and goat meat (metric tons)	3,896	3,548	3,183
Chickens ('000 head)*	346,153	333,504	315,896
Ducks ('000 head)*	37,741	36,862	31,730
Geese ('000 head)*	6,723	5,873	5,149
Turkeys ('000 head)*	335	301	280
Cow's milk (metric tons)	323,165	322,220	315,559
Duck eggs ('000)	466,232	507,328	483,878
Hen eggs ('000)	6,620,415	6,659,584	6,469,671

* Figures refer to numbers slaughtered.

Forestry

ROUNDWOOD REMOVALS

('000 cubic metres)

	2006	2007	2008
Industrial wood	27.0	26.4	25.1
Fuel wood	9.2	7.2	6.1
Mill wood	0.0	1.5	0.0
Total	36.2	35.1	31.2

Fishing

('000 metric tons, live weight)

	2006	2007	2008
Tilapias	72.6	76.1	81.0
Other freshwater fishes	10.2	10.0	n.a.
Japanese eel	23.8	24.8	21.0
Milkfish	56.1	53.2	46.9
Pacific saury	60.6	87.3	139.5
Skipjack tuna	194.4	214.0	168.9
Albacore	40.1	47.5	37.6
Yellowfin tuna	77.7	67.7	71.3
Bigeye tuna	59.1	69.9	53.8
Chub mackerel	54.8	49.9	56.0
Sharks, rays, skates, etc.	49.1	48.6	39.8
Marine shrimps and prawns	37.7	34.4	n.a.
Other crustaceans	7.1	6.7	n.a.
Pacific cupped oyster	28.5	28.1	34.4
Common squids	8.9	7.3	5.0
Argentine shortfin squid	148.1	300.0	240.3
Sailfish	28.6	27.4	24.2
Total catch (incl. others)	1,282.3	1,498.2	1,339.3

Note: Figures exclude aquatic plants, totalling (in '000 metric tons, preliminary): 6.1 in 2006; 9.6 in 2007; n.a. in 2008.

Mining

(metric tons unless otherwise indicated)

	2004	2005	2006
Crude petroleum ('000 litres)	44,562	32,389	23,565
Natural gas ('000 cu m)	706,991	486,646	411,524
Sulphur*	222,760	267,790	245,789
Marble (raw material)*	22,970,546	24,069,551	25,492,633
Dolomite*	114,598	173,986	61,224

* Preliminary figures.

Crude petroleum ('000 litres): 17,778 in 2007; 16,097 in 2008; 15,996 in 2009; 14,229 in 2010.

Natural gas ('000 cu m): 370,522 in 2007; 317,654 in 2008; 311,701 in 2009; 263,291 in 2010.

Industry

SELECTED PRODUCTS

('000 metric tons unless otherwise indicated)

	2007	2008	2009
Carbonated beverages ('000 litres)	302,869	284,024	310,554
Alcoholic beverages—excl. beer ('000 hectolitres)	368.0	361.6	624.6
Paperboard	3,406.5	2,909.6	2,775.3
Spun yarn	223.6	185.1	153.4
Cement	18,957.3	17,330.3	15,918.5
Steel ingots	19,838.7	19,222.1	15,566.4
Sewing machines ('000 units)	1,356.5	1,416.4	1,118.4
Electric fans ('000 units)	7,114.5	5,267.8	4,393.7
Personal computers ('000 units)	1,262.8	760.6	378.7
Mobile phones ('000 units)	22,669.0	25,692.6	15,983.5
LCD displays ('000 units)	1,225.8	849.4	887.4
Integrated circuits (million units)	5,033.4	5,577.6	4,376.7
Electronic condensers (million units)	242,938	252,515	166,372
Global positioning systems	17,784	21,333	20,661
Telephone sets ('000 units)	687.0	514.4	351.8
Passenger motor cars ('000 units)	213.1	137.6	178.2
Trucks, buses and commercial vans ('000 units)	68.8	41.5	46.9
Bicycles ('000 units)	5,120.5	6,131.7	4,778.9
Electric energy (million kWh)	228,806	225,258	216,921

2006: Wheat flour 784.3; Granulated sugar and molasses 392.3; Cigarettes (million) 22,073.3; Cotton yarn 286.1; Paper 836.0; Sulphuric acid 1,265; Television sets and VCRs 1,829,000; Audio units for cars 682,100; Loud-speakers and microphones 49,038,000; Ships (value of sales, NT $ million) 26,435.5; Refined petroleum (million litres) 59,460.2.

2007: Wheat flour 811.0.

2010: Carbonated beverages ('000 litres) 297,099; Paperboard 2,850.4; Cement 16,301.0; Steel ingots 20,498.4; Personal computers ('000 units) 326.9; LCD displays ('000 units) 1,171; Integrated circuits (million units) 7,408; Electronic condensers (million units) 199,886; Global positioning systems 21,157; Passenger cars, trucks and buses (units) 305,273; Electric energy (million kWh) 232,365.

Finance

CURRENCY AND EXCHANGE RATES

Monetary Units

100 cents = 1 New Taiwan dollar (NT $).

Sterling, US Dollar and Euro Equivalents (31 May 2011)

£1 sterling = NT $47.482;
US $1 = NT $28.772;
€1 = NT $41.389;
NT $1,000 = £21.06 = US $34.76 = €24.16.

Average Exchange Rate (NT $ per US $)

2008 31.517
2009 33.056
2010 31.547

GENERAL GOVERNMENT BUDGET

(NT $ million, year ending 31 December)

Revenue	2007	2008	2009
Current revenue	2,189,035	2,181,188	2,041,406
Taxes	1,685,875	1,710,617	1,483,518
Income tax	730,160	834,988	640,967
Business tax	246,137	243,961	223,503
Fees	96,579	94,302	91,963
Fines and indemnities	44,646	46,690	41,395
Public enterprise and utilities surplus	291,799	264,918	330,928
Public properties profits	15,103	14,249	14,111
Donations, etc.	7,845	8,862	8,658
Other	47,188	41,550	70,834
Capital revenue	55,724	50,425	72,137
Total	2,244,758	2,231,614	2,113,543

Expenditure	2007	2008	2009
General administration	343,950	350,500	354,981
National defence	255,854	262,150	297,746
Education, science and culture	492,625	495,515	537,310
Economic development	383,298	432,335	445,037
Agriculture	106,788	112,827	133,210
Industry	16,004	34,001	36,071
Transport and communication	218,338	234,604	213,404
Other	42,167	50,902	62,352
Social welfare	372,202	368,136	387,446
Social insurance	162,548	147,651	189,268
Social relief	23,245	25,559	23,333
Benefit service	151,322	158,275	136,719
Employment service	2,480	2,252	2,485
Medical care	32,607	34,400	35,641
Community development and environmental protection	87,282	82,157	86,333
Community development	24,520	13,514	18,941
Environmental protection	62,762	68,643	67,392
Pensions and survivors' benefits	200,677	202,228	205,289
Obligations	139,380	134,697	129,484
Miscellaneous	14,901	15,867	17,331
Total	2,290,169	2,343,585	2,460,958
Current	1,801,511	1,811,308	1,896,804
Capital	488,658	532,278	564,154

INTERNATIONAL RESERVES

(US $ million at 31 December)

	2008	2009	2010
Gold (national valuation)	4,682	4,769	5,202
Foreign exchange	291,707	348,198	382,005
Total	296,389	352,967	387,207

MONEY SUPPLY

(NT $ '000 million at 31 December)

	2008	2009	2010
Currency outside banks	833.5	912.6	995.9
Demand deposits at deposit money banks	7,320.2	9,599.0	10,461.3
Total money	8,153.7	10,511.6	11,457.1

COST OF LIVING

(Consumer Price Index; base: 2006 = 100)

	2008	2009	2010
Food	111.7	111.2	111.8
Clothing	104.9	104.8	107.3
Housing	102.4	102.1	102.6
Transport and communications	104.1	99.9	102.7
Medicines and medical care	106.2	106.8	107.5
Education and entertainment	101.9	100.1	100.1
All items (incl. others)	105.4	104.5	105.5

NATIONAL ACCOUNTS

(NT $ million in current prices)

National Income and Product

	2008	2009	2010
Domestic factor incomes	10,035,650	9,913,725	10,860,817
Consumption of fixed capital	1,909,114	1,945,767	2,008,242
Gross domestic product (GDP) at factor cost	11,944,764	11,859,492	12,869,059
Indirect taxes, *less* subsidies	675,386	617,690	734,418
GDP in purchasers' values	12,620,150	12,477,182	13,603,477
Net factor income from abroad	314,646	413,597	417,114
Gross national product (GNP)	12,934,796	12,890,779	14,020,591
Less Consumption of fixed capital	1,909,114	1,945,767	2,008,242
Statistical discrepancy	–4,857	–56,701	–1,445
National income in market prices	11,020,825	10,888,311	12,010,904
Other current transfers from abroad (net)	–88,233	–68,194	–84,373
National disposable income	10,932,592	10,820,117	11,926,531

Expenditure on the Gross Domestic Product

	2008	2009	2010
Government final consumption expenditure	1,563,634	1,617,455	1,659,935
Private final consumption expenditure	7,609,995	7,579,888	7,895,553
Gross capital formation	2,826,311	2,203,436	3,077,335
Total domestic expenditure	11,999,940	11,400,779	12,632,823
Exports of goods and services	9,208,653	7,796,555	10,018,572
Less Imports of goods and services	8,588,443	6,720,152	9,047,918
GDP in purchasers' values	12,620,150	12,477,182	13,603,477
GDP at constant 2006 prices	13,070,681	12,818,935	14,213,925

Gross Domestic Product by Economic Activity

	2008	2009	2010
Agriculture, hunting, forestry and fishing	201,799	215,869	214,622
Mining and quarrying	20,734	51,691	63,001
Manufacturing	3,132,252	2,960,300	3,573,474
Construction	363,274	332,724	377,341
Electricity, gas and water	148,587	251,889	248,972
Transport, storage and communications	850,782	837,891	886,813
Trade, restaurants and hotels	2,641,468	2,574,238	2,742,067
Finance, insurance and real estate*	2,024,032	1,934,850	2,034,852
Public administration, defence, health and social work	1,322,592	1,345,659	1,399,321
Education	603,213	619,336	628,107
Other services	952,674	972,435	1,032,155
Sub-total	12,261,407	12,096,882	13,200,725
Value added tax	221,321	206,405	249,198
Import duties	132,565	117,194	152,109
Statistical discrepancy	4,857	56,701	1,445
GDP in purchasers' values	12,620,150	12,477,182	13,603,477

* Including imputed rents of owner-occupied dwellings.

BALANCE OF PAYMENTS

(US $ million)

	2008	2009	2010
Exports of goods f.o.b.	254,897	203,399	273,823
Imports of goods f.o.b.	–236,419	–172,846	–247,310
Trade balance	18,478	30,553	26,513
Exports of services	36,829	31,774	40,516
Imports of services	–34,982	–29,783	–37,867
Balance on goods and services	20,325	32,544	29,162
Other income received	23,277	20,339	23,133
Other income paid	–13,299	–7,827	–9,686
Balance on goods, services and income	30,303	45,056	42,609
Current transfers received	5,526	4,902	5,251
Current transfers paid	–8,324	–7,047	–7,961

—continued	2008	2009	2010
Current balance	27,505	42,911	39,899
Capital account (net)	–334	–96	–116
Direct investment abroad	–10,287	–5,877	–11,553
Direct investment from abroad	5,432	2,805	2,492
Portfolio investment assets	3,527	–31,699	–33,487
Portfolio investment liabilities	–15,777	21,372	12,824
Financial derivatives assets	7,938	5,344	4,792
Financial derivatives liabilities	–6,349	–4,492	–4,166
Other investment assets	10,621	25,663	11,932
Other investment liabilities	3,235	353	17,232
Net errors and omissions	763	–2,158	324
Overall balance	26,274	54,126	40,173

External Trade

PRINCIPAL COMMODITIES

(US $ million)

Imports c.i.f.	2008	2009	2010
Mineral products	65,245.2	39,335.4	55,326.2
Crude petroleum	33,016.3	19,638.7	25,676.9
Products of chemical or allied industries	26,591.5	20,424.8	29,339.1
Organic chemicals	10,021.3	7,085.8	10,675.1
Base metals and articles thereof	28,922.4	15,195.4	24,352.5
Iron and steel products	16,405.2	7,619.5	12,433.6
Machinery and mechanical appliances; electrical equipment; sound and television apparatus	70,575.0	59,004.6	86,522.7
Electronic products	35,086.1	31,285.8	42,719.2
Machinery	17,657.4	14,645.2	26,325.0
Electrical machinery products	6,930.4	4,705.1	6,932.9
Information and communication products	5,072.8	4,545.7	5,719.6
Vehicles, aircraft, vessels and associated transport equipment	4,380.4	4,175.3	6,132.8
Optical, photographic, cinematographic, measuring, precision and medical apparatus; clocks and watches; musical instruments	10,819.3	7,464.7	10,857.9
Total (incl. others)	240,447.8	174,370.5	251,236.2

Exports f.o.b.	2008	2009	2010
Chemicals	17,240.6	13,930.4	19,227.4
Plastics, rubber and articles thereof	19,674.0	16,523.3	22,254.7
Textiles and textile articles	10,900.4	9,344.3	11,301.5
Fibre and yarn	8,118.8	6,935.4	8,493.8
Base metals and articles thereof	28,220.5	19,359.3	25,884.4
Iron and steel	18,247.6	12,322.0	16,376.9
Machinery and mechanical appliances; electrical equipment; sound and television apparatus	114,246.5	95,215.0	131,276.9
Electronic products	63,456.3	56,664.1	77,306.1
Machinery	16,038.1	10,987.1	16,725.4
Electrical machinery products	13,247.7	9,316.5	11,282.1
Information and communication products	10,167.5	9,192.2	14,095.4
Vehicles, aircraft, vessels and associated transport equipment	9,094.8	7,727.5	9,333.2
Total (incl. others)	255,629.2	203,674.9	274,600.8

PRINCIPAL TRADING PARTNERS
(US $ million)

Imports c.i.f.	2008	2009	2010
Angola	2,017.0	1,061.2	2,878.1
Australia	8,270.6	5,965.9	8,921.4
Chile	2,021.8	1,343.8	2,105.0
China, People's Republic	31,391.3	24,423.5	35,946.0
France	2,292.8	1,784.2	2,250.2
Germany	7,474.3	5,672.9	8,264.1
Hong Kong	1,492.8	1,122.6	1,627.6
India	2,333.2	1,623.2	2,837.5
Indonesia	7,289.0	5,183.7	6,020.2
Iran	5,039.1	1,974.5	2,714.4
Iraq	2,192.0	1,973.8	1,928.9
Japan	46,508.0	36,220.0	51,917.4
Korea, Republic	13,168.4	10,506.8	16,058.8
Kuwait	8,074.2	4,555.7	6,124.8
Malaysia	6,762.7	4,552.7	7,695.0
Netherlands	2,353.5	1,862.8	3,199.9
Philippines	2,240.6	1,613.7	2,319.9
Russia	2,686.8	2,192.0	2,335.8
Saudi Arabia	15,172.7	8,657.9	11,859.2
Singapore	4,825.2	4,809.2	7,636.1
Thailand	3,252.0	2,681.7	3,829.0
United Arab Emirates	4,611.0	2,480.0	3,511.6
United Kingdom	1,917.6	1,230.3	1,672.9
USA	26,326.6	18,153.9	25,379.4
Total (incl. others)	240,447.8	174,370.5	251,236.4

Exports f.o.b.	2008	2009	2010
Australia	3,486.6	2,353.4	3,132.1
China, People's Republic	66,883.5	54,248.7	76,935.1
Germany	5,729.7	4,695.9	6,511.6
Hong Kong*	32,689.9	29,445.2	37,807.1
India	3,007.1	2,531.5	3,628.4
Indonesia	3,566.0	3,226.3	4,509.6
Italy	2,449.7	1,786.6	2,447.2
Japan	17,556.0	14,502.3	18,006.0
Korea, Republic	8,705.8	7,302.5	10,681.6
Malaysia	5,513.8	4,060.1	5,947.9
Netherlands	4,565.5	4,229.4	5,261.1
Philippines	4,780.1	4,432.8	5,982.0
Singapore	11,675.8	8,613.8	12,096.4
Thailand	4,906.0	3,826.8	5,288.5
United Kingdom	3,630.5	2,980.2	3,621.4
USA	30,791.0	23,552.9	31,466.0
Viet Nam	7,946.9	5,987.9	7,533.5
Total (incl. others)	255,628.7	203,674.6	274,600.5

* The majority of Taiwan's exports to Hong Kong are re-exported.

Transport

RAILWAYS
(traffic)

	2008	2009	2010
Passengers ('000)	689,880	718,515	778,779
Passenger-km ('000)	19,065,567	19,277,397	20,930,785
Freight ('000 metric tons)	16,583	14,144	15,106
Freight ton-km ('000)	933,341	776,023	872,520

ROAD TRAFFIC
(motor vehicles in use at 31 December)

	2008	2009	2010
Passenger cars	5,674,426	5,704,312	5,803,413
Buses and coaches	27,339	27,667	29,030
Goods vehicles	973,671	986,767	993,550
Motorcycles and scooters	14,365,442	14,604,330	14,844,932

SHIPPING

Merchant Fleet
(at 31 December)

	2007	2008	2009
Number of vessels	629	637	641
Total displacement ('000 grt)	2,749.6	2,671.9	2,636.0

Source: IHS Fairplay, *World Fleet Statistics*.

International sea-borne freight traffic

	2007	2008	2009
Vessels entered ('000 grt)	480,700	471,040	525,502
Vessels cleared ('000 grt)	498,593	486,700	515,483
Goods loaded ('000 metric tons)	50,810	45,745	45,750
Goods unloaded ('000 metric tons)	191,892	189,261	170,013

CIVIL AVIATION
(traffic on scheduled services)

	2008	2009	2010
Passengers carried ('000)	33,053	32,329	37,469
Freight carried ('000 metric tons)	1,072.1	969.9	1,200.6

Tourism

TOURIST ARRIVALS BY COUNTRY OF ORIGIN

	2007	2008	2009
Australia	51,270	57,725	56,697
Canada	56,554	59,605	59,490
Germany	39,372	40,129	39,372
Hong Kong and Macao	79,548	78,628	84,685
Indonesia	95,327	110,017	106,272
Japan	1,164,446	1,084,888	998,973
Korea, Republic	222,347	247,815	164,152
Malaysia	140,720	155,073	166,354
Philippines	80,117	83,056	73,182
Singapore	204,015	204,967	194,129
Thailand	89,137	83,685	77,344
United Kingdom	39,758	48,176	44,619
USA	395,036	383,747	365,266
Total (incl. others)	2,988,815	2,962,536	2,770,082

Note: Figures exclude arrivals of Overseas Chinese (i.e. those bearing Taiwan passports) resident abroad (especially Hong Kong and Macao): 727,248 in 2007; 882,651 in 2008; 1,624,922 in 2009.

Total visitor arrivals: 3,716,063 in 2007; 3,845,187 in 2008; 4,395,004 in 2009.

Tourism receipts (US $ million): 5,214 in 2007; 5,936 in 2008; 6,816 in 2009.

Communications Media

	2008	2009	2010
Book production (titles)	41,083	40,478	43,282
Newspapers (titles)	198	189	193
Magazines	982	1,018	1,078
Telephone subscribers ('000)	13,082	12,821	12,696
Mobile telephones ('000 in use)	25,413	26,959	27,840
Internet subscribers ('000)	6,027	5,668	5,888
Broadband subscribers ('000)*	5,024	4,998	5,265

* Source: International Telecommunication Union.

Television receivers (2006): 152.3 colour television receivers per 100 households; 79.9 cable television receivers per 100 households.

Education

(2009/10 unless otherwise indicated)

	Schools	Full-time teachers	Students
Pre-school*	3,154	16,904	182,049
Primary	2,661	99,541	1,519,456
Secondary (incl. vocational)	1,231	105,154	1,682,958
Higher	163	50,684	1,343,603
Special	24	1,790	7,006
Supplementary*	834	1,488	240,392

* 2008/09.

Pupil-teacher ratio (primary education, official estimate): 15.3 in 2009/10.

Adult literacy rate (official estimate): 93.0% (males 96.3%; females 89.5%) in 2008.

Directory

Note: the issue of the implementation of a uniform system of romanization of Taiwanese names has remained unresolved; the central Government favours the use of a system of Pinyin similar to that employed in mainland China but with certain differences (Tongyong), while local authorities in Taiwan remain divided between usage of the standard mainland Pinyin system (Hanyu) and a form of the traditional Wade-Giles system.

The Constitution

On 1 January 1947 a new Constitution was promulgated for the Republic of China. When the Chinese Communist Party established the People's Republic of China on the Chinese mainland in 1949, the Government of the Republic of China, led by the Kuomintang (KMT), relocated to Taiwan, where it maintained jurisdiction over Taiwan, Penghu, Kinmen, Matsu and numerous other islets. The two sides of the Taiwan Strait have since been governed as separate territories. The form of government that was incorporated in the Constitution is based on a five-power system and has the major features of both cabinet and presidential government. A process of constitutional reform, initiated in 1991, continued in the early 21st century. The following is a summary of the Constitution, as subsequently amended:

PRESIDENT

The President shall be directly elected by popular vote for a term of four years. Both the President and Vice-President are eligible for re-election to a second term. The President represents the country in all state functions, including foreign relations; commands land, sea and air forces, promulgates laws, issues mandates, concludes treaties, declares war, makes peace, declares martial law, grants amnesties, appoints and removes civil and military officers, and confers honours and decorations. The President, subject to certain limitations, may issue emergency orders to deal with national calamities and ensure national security; may dissolve the Legislative Yuan; and also appoints the Premier and the officials of the Judicial Yuan, the Examination Yuan and the Control Yuan.

EXECUTIVE YUAN

The Executive Yuan is the highest administrative organ of the nation and is responsible to the Legislative Yuan; it has two categories of subordinate organization:

Executive Yuan Council (policy-making organization)

Ministries and Commissions (executive organizations), of which there are currently 37, including other agencies.

LEGISLATIVE YUAN

The Legislative Yuan is the highest legislative organ of the State, empowered to hear administrative reports of the Executive Yuan, and to advise on government policy, statutory and budgetary issues. It may hold a binding vote of no confidence in the Executive Yuan. It comprises 113 members: 73 are chosen by direct election from single-member constituencies; 34 members are elected on the basis of proportional representation from a nation-wide constituency, with seats being allocated only to parties that have garnered more than 5% of the total votes in this second, supplementary ballot; the remaining six members are elected from and by aborigines. Members serve for a term of four years and are eligible for re-election.

JUDICIAL YUAN

The Judicial Yuan is the highest judicial organ of state and has charge of civil, criminal and administrative cases, and of cases concerning disciplinary measures against public functionaries (see Judicial System).

EXAMINATION YUAN

The Examination Yuan supervises examinations for entry into public offices, and deals with personnel matters of the civil service, implements training and protection measures for public functionaries, and supervises the public service pension fund. The Examination Yuan is also responsible for certification examinations for professionals and technologists.

CONTROL YUAN

The Control Yuan is the highest control organ of the State, exercising powers of impeachment, censure and audit, comprising 29 members serving a six-year term. (According to the Additional Articles of the Constitution of the Republic of China as amended in April 2000, the members of the Control Yuan shall be nominated by the President of the State, and with the consent of the Legislative Yuan.) The Control Yuan may impeach or censure a public functionary at central or local level, who is deemed guilty of violation of law or dereliction of duty, and shall refer the matter to the civil courts for action in cases involving a criminal offence; the Control Yuan may propose corrective measures to the Executive Yuan or to its subordinate organs.

The Government

HEAD OF STATE

President: MA YING-JEOU (inaugurated 20 May 2008).

Vice-President: VINCENT C. SIEW.

Secretary-General: WU CHIN-LIN.

EXECUTIVE YUAN

(October 2011)

The Government is formed by the Kuomintang.

Premier: WU DEN-YIH.

Vice-Premier and Minister of the Consumer Protection Commission: SEAN C. CHEN.

Secretary-General: LIN JOIN-SANE.

Ministers without Portfolio: YIIN CHII-MING, OVID J. L. TZENG, CHANG JIN-FU, LEE HONG-YUAN, JAMES C. T. HSUEH, LIN JUNQ-TZER , CYRUS C. Y. CHU.

Minister of the Interior: JIANG YI-HUAH.

Minister of Foreign Affairs: TIMOTHY CHIEN-TIEN YANG.

Minister of National Defense: KAO HUA-CHU.

Minister of Finance: LI SUSH-DER.

Minister of Education: WU CHING-JI.

Minister of Justice: TSENG YUNG-FU.

Minister of Economic Affairs: SHIH YEN-SHIANG.

Minister of Transportation and Communications: MAO CHI-KUO.

Minister of the Mongolian and Tibetan Affairs Commission: LUO YING-SHAY.

Minister of the Overseas Compatriot Affairs Commission: WU YING-YIH.

Governor of the Central Bank: PERNG FAI-NAN.

Minister of the Directorate-General of Budget, Accounting and Statistics: SHIH SU-MEI.

Minister of Central Personnel Administration: WU TAI-CHENG.

Minister of the Government Information Office: PHILIP Y. M. YANG.

Minister of the Department of Health: CHIU WEN-TA.

Minister of the Environmental Protection Administration: STEPHEN SHU-HUNG SHEN.

Director of the National Palace Museum: CHOU KUNG-SHIN.

Minister of the Mainland Affairs Council: LAI SHIN-YUAN.

Minister of the Council for Economic Planning and Development: CHRISTINA LIU.

Minister of the Public Construction Commission: LEE HONG-YUAN.

Minister of the Veterans' Affairs Commission: TSENG JING-LING.

Minister of the National Youth Commission: JACK YUN-JIE LEE.

Minister of the Atomic Energy Council: TSAI CHUEN-HORNG.

Minister of the National Science Council: LEE LOU-CHUANG.

Minister of the Research, Development and Evaluation Commission: CHU CHIN-PENG.

Minister of the Council of Agriculture: CHEN WU-HSIUNG.

Minister of the Council for Cultural Affairs: EMILE CHI-JEN SHENG.

Minister of the Council of Labor Affairs: WANG JU-HSUAN.

Chairperson of the Fair Trade Commission: WU SHIOW-MING.

Minister of the Sports Affairs Council: TAI HSIA-LING.

Minister of the Council of Indigenous Peoples: SUN TA-CHUAN.

Minister of the Coast Guard Administration: WANG GINN-WANG.

Minister of the Council for Hakka Affairs: HUANG YU-CHENG.

Chairperson of the Central Election Commission: CHANG PO-YA.

Minister of the Financial Supervisory Commission: CHEN YUH-CHANG.

Minister of the Aviation Safety Council: CHANG YU-HERN.

Minister of the National Communications Commission: SU HERNG.

MINISTRIES, COMMISSIONS, ETC.

Office of the President: 122 Chungking South Rd, Zhongzheng District, Taipei 10048; tel. (2) 23113731; fax (2) 23311604; e-mail public@mail.oop.gov.tw; internet www.president.gov.tw.

Ministry of Economic Affairs: 15 Foo Chou St, Taipei 10015; tel. (2) 23212200; fax (2) 23919398; e-mail minister@moea.gov.tw; internet www.moea.gov.tw.

Ministry of Education: 5 Chung Shan South Rd, Zhongzheng District, Taipei 10051; tel. (2) 23566051; fax (2) 23976978; internet www.moe.gov.tw.

Ministry of Finance: 2 Ai Kuo West Rd, Taipei 10066; tel. (2) 23228000; fax (2) 23568774; e-mail mof@mail.mof.gov.tu; internet www.mof.gov.tw.

Ministry of Foreign Affairs: 2 Kaitakeland Blvd, Taipei 10048; tel. (2) 23482999; fax (2) 23805678; e-mail eyes@mofa.gov.tw; internet www.mofa.gov.tw.

Ministry of the Interior: 5–9/F, 5 Syujhou Rd, Taipei 10017; tel. (2) 23565005; fax (2) 23566201; e-mail service@minister.moi.gov.tw; internet www.moi.gov.tw.

Ministry of Justice: 130 Chungking South Rd, Sec. 1, Taipei 10048; tel. (2) 23146871; fax (2) 23896274; internet www.moj.gov.tw.

Ministry of National Defense: 2/F, 164 Po Ai Rd, Taipei 10048; tel. (2) 23116117; fax (2) 23144221; internet www.mnd.gov.tw.

Ministry of Transportation and Communications: 50 Ren Ai Rd, Sec. 1, Zhongzheng District, Taipei 10048; tel. (2) 23492900; fax (2) 23492491; e-mail motceyes@motc.gov.tw; internet www.motc.gov.tw.

Mongolian and Tibetan Affairs Commission: 4/F, 5 Hsu Chou Rd, Sec. 1, Taipei 10055; tel. (2) 23566467; fax (2) 23416186; e-mail mtacserv@mtac.gov.tw; internet www.mtac.gov.tw.

Overseas Compatriot Affairs Commission: 15–17/F, 5 Hsu Chou Rd, Taipei 10055; tel. (2) 23272600; fax (2) 23566323; e-mail ocacinfo@mail.ocac.gov.tw; internet www.ocac.gov.tw.

Directorate-General of Budget, Accounting and Statistics: 1 Chung Hsiao East Rd, Sec. 1, Taipei 10058; tel. (2) 33566500; fax (2) 23825267; e-mail sicbs@dgbas.gov.tw; internet www.dgbas.gov.tw.

Government Information Office: 2 Tientsin St, Taipei 10051; tel. (2) 33568888; fax (2) 23568733; e-mail service@mail.gio.gov.tw; internet www.gio.gov.tw.

Council of Indigenous Peoples: 172 Chungking North Rd, Datong District, Taipei 10357; tel. (2) 25571600; fax (2) 23454323; e-mail minister@apc.gov.tw; internet www.apc.gov.tw.

Council of Agriculture: see under Trade and Industry—Government Agencies.

Atomic Energy Council (AEC): 2–8/F, 80 Cheng Kung Rd, Sec. 1, Yonghe City, Taipei County 23452; tel. (2) 82317919; fax (2) 82317833; e-mail public@aec.gov.tw; internet www.aec.gov.tw.

Central Personnel Administration: 10/F, 2-2 Chinan Rd, Taipei 10051; tel. (2) 23979298; fax (2) 23975505; internet www.cpa.gov.tw.

Consumer Protection Commission: 12 Jihe Rd, Taipei 11166; tel. (2) 28863200; fax (2) 28866646; e-mail tcpc@ms1.hinet.net; internet www.cpc.gov.tw.

Council for Hakka Affairs: 8/F, 3 Songren Rd, Taipei 11010; tel. (2) 87894567; fax (2) 87894620; e-mail src@mail.hakka.gov.tw; internet www.hakka.gov.tw.

Council for Cultural Affairs: 30-1 Beiping East Rd, Zhongzheng District, Taipei 10049; tel. (2) 23434000; fax (2) 23216478; e-mail adm@cca.gov.tw; internet www.cca.gov.tw.

Council for Economic Planning and Development: 3 Baocing Rd, Zhongzheng District, Taipei 10020; tel. (2) 23165300; fax (2) 23700415; internet www.cepd.gov.tw.

Environmental Protection Administration: 83 Chung Hua Rd, Sec. 1, Taipei 10042; tel. (2) 23117722; fax (2) 23115486; e-mail umail@epa.gov.tw; internet www.epa.gov.tw.

Public Construction Commission: 9/F, 3 Songren Rd, Taipei 11010; tel. (2) 87897500; fax (2) 87897800; e-mail secr@mail.pcc.gov.tw; internet www.pcc.gov.tw.

Fair Trade Commission: 12–14/F, 2-2 Chi Nan Rd, Sec. 2, Taipei 10051; tel. (2) 23517588; fax (2) 23974997; e-mail ftcpub@ftc.gov.tw; internet www.ftc.gov.tw.

Department of Health: 36 Ta Cheng St, Datong District, Taipei 10341; tel. (2) 85906666; fax (2) 25502052; internet www.doh.gov.tw.

Council of Labor Affairs: 9/F, 83 Yangping North Rd, Sec. 2, Taipei 10346; tel. (2) 85902866; fax (2) 85902960; internet www.cla.gov.tw.

Mainland Affairs Council: 15/F, 2-2 Chi Nan Rd, Sec. 1, Taipei 10051; tel. (2) 23975589; fax (2) 23975300; e-mail macst@mac.gov.tw; internet www.mac.gov.tw.

National Science Council: 17–22/F, 106 Ho Ping East Rd, Sec. 2, Taipei 10622; tel. (2) 27377992; fax (2) 27377566; e-mail nsc@nsc.gov.tw; internet www.nsc.gov.tw.

National Youth Commission: 14/F, 5 Hsu Chou Rd, Taipei 10055; tel. (2) 23566232; fax (2) 23566307; e-mail nycn@nyc.gov.tw; internet www.nyc.gov.tw.

Research, Development and Evaluation Commission: 6/F, 2-2 Chi Nan Rd, Sec. 1, Taipei 10051; tel. (2) 23419066; fax (2) 23969990; e-mail service@rdec.gov.tw; internet www.rdec.gov.tw.

Sports Affairs Council: 20 Zhu Lun St, Taipei 10481; tel. (2) 87711800; fax (2) 27523600; internet www.sac.gov.tw.

Veterans' Affairs Commission: 222 Chung Hsiao East Rd, Sec. 5, Xinyi District, Taipei 11025; tel. (2) 27571750; fax (2) 27230170; e-mail eyes@mail.vac.gov.tw; internet www.vac.gov.tw.

Financial Supervisory Commission: 18/F, 7 Hsien Ming Blvd, Sec. 2, Panchiao City, Taipei County 22041; tel. (2) 89680899; fax (2) 89681215; e-mail fscey@fscey.gov.tw; internet www.fscey.gov.tw.

Coast Guard Administration: 296 Singlong Rd, Taipei 11698; tel. (2) 22399201; fax (2) 22399258; e-mail master@cga.gov.tw; internet www.cga.gov.tw.

President and Legislature

PRESIDENT

Election, 22 March 2008

Candidate*	Votes	% of votes
Ma Ying-jeou (Kuomintang—KMT)	7,659,014	58.45
Frank C. T. Hsieh (Democratic Progressive Party—DPP)	5,444,949	41.55
Total	13,103,963†	100.00

* The vice-presidential candidates were respectively Vincent V. C. Siew of the KMT and Su Tseng-chang of the DPP.

† Not including invalid or spoiled ballot papers.

LI-FA YUAN
(Legislative Yuan)

President: WANG JIN-PYNG.

Election, 12 January 2008

Party	Seats
Kuomintang (KMT)	81
Democratic Progressive Party (DPP)	27
Non-Partisan Solidarity Union (NPSU)	3
People First Party (PFP)	1
Independents	1
Total	113

Election Commission

Central Election Commission: 10/F, 5 Hsu Chou Rd, Taipei 10055; tel. (2) 23565484; fax (2) 23976898; e-mail cec13@cec.gov.tw; internet www.cec.gov.tw; f. 1980; Chair. and 11–19 commrs nominated by Premier and approved by the President; Chair. is also a member of the Exec. Yuan; Chair. CHANG PO-YA; Sec.-Gen. TENG TIEN-YU.

Political Organizations

At August 2006 a total of 109 parties were registered with the Ministry of the Interior.

Democratic Progressive Party (DPP): 10/F, 30 Beiping East Rd, Taipei 10051; tel. (2) 23929989; fax (2) 23930342; e-mail foreign@dpp.org.tw; internet www.dpp.org.tw; f. 1986; advocates 'self-determination' for the people of Taiwan and UN membership; supports establishment of independent Taiwan following plebiscite; 530,975 mems (2004); Chair. Dr TSAI ING-WEN; Sec.-Gen. SU JIA-CHYUAN.

Green Party Taiwan: 5/F, 13 Chung Hsiao East Rd, Zhongzheng District, Taipei 10049; tel. (2) 23920508; fax (2) 23920512; e-mail contact@greenparty.org.tw; internet www.greenparty.org.tw; f. 1996; est. by breakaway faction of DPP.

Jiann Gwo Party (Taiwan Independence Party—TAIP): 9/F, 15-8 Nanjing East Rd, Sec. 5, Taipei 10564; tel. (2) 22800879; f. 1996; est. by dissident mems of DPP; Chair. HUANG CHIEN-MING; Sec.-Gen. LI SHENG-HSIUNG.

Kuomintang (KMT) (Nationalist Party of China): 232–234 Bade Rd, Sec. 2, Taipei 10492; tel. (2) 87711234; fax (2) 23434561; internet www.kmt.org.tw; f. 1894; aims to supplant communist rule in mainland China; supports democratic, constitutional govt, and advocates the unification of China; aims to promote market economy and equitable distribution of wealth; 1.1m. mems; Chair. MA YING-JEOU; Sec.-Gen. LIAO LIAO-YI.

New Party (NP): 4/F, 65 Guangfu South Rd, Taipei 10563; tel. (2) 27562222; fax (2) 27565750; e-mail webmaster@mail.np.org.tw; internet www.np.org.tw; f. 1993 by dissident KMT legislators (hitherto mems of New Kuomintang Alliance faction); merged with China Social Democratic Party in late 1993; advocates co-operation with the KMT and DPP in negotiations with the People's Republic, maintenance of security in the Taiwan Straits, modernization of the island's defence systems, measures to combat govt corruption, support of small and medium-sized businesses and establishment of a universal social security system; 80,000 mems; Chair. YOK MU-MING.

Non-Partisan Solidarity Union: 3/F, 5–1 Zhenjiang St, Taipei 10051; tel. (2) 23585066; f. 2004; Chair. LIN PIN-KUAN.

People First Party (PFP): 2/F, 63 Chang-an East Rd, Sec. 1, Taipei 10455; tel. (2) 25068555; internet www.pfp.org.tw; f. 2000; advocates the unification of China; seeks economic and cultural interaction between Taiwan and the mainland; Chair. JAMES C. Y. SOONG; Sec.-Gen. CHIN CHIN-SHENG.

Taiwan Solidarity Union (TSU): 7/F, Shaoxing North Rd, Zhongzheng District, Taipei; tel. (2) 23940230; fax (2) 23946616; e-mail service@tsu.org.tw; internet www.tsu.org.tw; f. 2001; est. by breakaway faction of KMT; Chair. HUANG HUN-KUI; Sec.-Gen. LIN CHIH-CHIA.

Taiwanese National Party (TNP): Taipei; f. 2011; advocates self-determination for Taiwan and the holding of a referendum on the issue; Chair. HUANG HUA.

Young China Party (YCP): 12/F, 2 Sinsheng South Rd, Sec. 3, Taipei 10660; tel. (2) 23626715; f. 1923; aims to recover sovereignty over mainland China, safeguard the Constitution and democracy, and foster understanding between Taiwan and the non-communist world; Chair. JEAN JYI-YUAN.

Diplomatic Representation

EMBASSIES IN TAIWAN (REPUBLIC OF CHINA)

Belize: 11/F, 9 Lane 62, Tien Mou West Rd, Taipei 11156; tel. (2) 28760894; fax (2) 28760896; e-mail embelroc@ms41.hinet.net; internet www.embassyofbelize.org.tw; Chargé d'affaires CHERIE NISBET.

Burkina Faso: 6/F, 9-1 Lane 62, Tien Mou West Rd, Taipei 11157; tel. (2) 28733096; fax (2) 28733071; e-mail abftap94@ms17.hinet.net; internet www.ambaburkinataipei.org.tw; Ambassador JACQUES Y. SAWADOGO.

Dominican Republic: 6/F, 9 Lane 62, Tien Mou West Rd, Taipei 11156; tel. (2) 28751357; fax (2) 28752661; e-mail domtaipei@hotmail.com; Ambassador RAFAELA ALBURQUERQUE DE GONZÁLEZ.

El Salvador: 2/F, 9 Lane 62, Tien Mou West Rd, Taipei 11157; tel. (2) 28763606; fax (2) 28763514; e-mail embasal.taipei@msa.hinet.net; Ambassador MARTA CHANG DE TSIEN.

The Gambia: 9/F, 9-1 Lane 62, Tien Mou West Rd, Taipei 11156; tel. (2) 28753911; fax (2) 28752775; e-mail gm.roc@msa.hinet.net; Ambassador Alhaji EBRIMA N. H. JARJOU.

Guatemala: 3/F, 9-1 Lane 62, Tien Mou West Rd, Taipei 11156; tel. (2) 28756952; fax (2) 28740699; e-mail embchina@minrex.gob.gt; Ambassador HÉCTOR IVÁN ESPINOZA FARFÁN.

Haiti: 8/F, 9-1 Lane 62, Tien Mou West Rd, Taipei 11156; tel. (2) 28766718; fax (2) 28766719; e-mail haiti@ms26.hinet.net; Chargé d'affaires MARIO CHOULOUTE.

Holy See: 87 Ai Kuo East Rd, Taipei 10642 (Apostolic Nunciature); tel. (2) 23216847; fax (2) 23911926; e-mail nuntius.taipei@gmail.com; Chargé d'affaires a.i. Mgr PAUL RUSSELL.

Honduras: 9/F, 9 Lane 62, Tien Mou West Rd, Taipei 11156; tel. (2) 28755507; fax (2) 28755726; e-mail honduras@ms9.hinet.net; Ambassador RENÉ FRANCISCO UMAÑA CHINCHILLA.

Marshall Islands: 4/F, 9-1 Lane 62, Tien Mou West Rd, Taipei 11157; tel. (2) 28734884; fax (2) 28734904; e-mail rmiemb.tpe@msa.hinet.net; Ambassador PHILIP K. KABUA.

Nauru: 11/F, 9-1 Lane 62, Tien Mou West Rd, Taipei 11156; tel. (2) 28761950; fax (2) 28761930; Ambassador LUDWIG D. KEKE.

Nicaragua: 3/F, Lane 62, Tien Mou West Rd, Taipei 11156; tel. (2) 28749034; fax (2) 28749080; e-mail icaza@ms13.hinet.net; Ambassador WILLIAM TAPIA.

Palau: 5/F, 9 Lane 62, Tien Mou West Rd, Taipei 11156; tel. (2) 28765415; fax (2) 28760436; e-mail palau.embassy@msa.hinet.net; Ambassador JACKSON HENRY.

Panama: 6/F, 111 Sung Kiang Rd, Taipei 10486; tel. (2) 25099189; fax (2) 25099801; Ambassador LUIS CUCALÓN D'ANELLO.

Paraguay: 7/F, 9-1 Lane 62, Tien Mou West Rd, Taipei 11156; tel. (2) 28736310; fax (2) 28736312; e-mail embapartaiwan@embapartwroc.com.tw; internet www.embapartwroc.com.tw; Ambassador CARLOS MARTÍNEZ RUÍZ DIAZ.

Saint Christopher and Nevis: 5/F, 9-1 Lane 62, Tien Mou West Rd, Taipei 11157; tel. (2) 28733252; fax (2) 28733246; e-mail embskn.tw@msa.hinet.net; Ambassador JASMINE HUGGINS.

São Tomé and Príncipe: 10/F, 9-1 Lane 62, Tien Mou West Rd, Taipei 11156; tel. (2) 28766824; fax (2) 28766984; e-mail stptw@ms69.hinet.net; Ambassador JORGE AMADO.

Solomon Islands: 7/F, 9-1 Lane 62, Tien Mou West Rd, Taipei 11156; tel. (2) 28731168; fax (2) 28735224; e-mail embassy@solomons.org.tw; internet www.solomons.org.tw; Ambassador LAURIE CHAN (designate).

Swaziland: 10/F, 9 Lane 62, Tien Mou West Rd, Taipei 11156; tel. (2) 28725934; fax (2) 28726511; e-mail swazitpi@ms41.hinet.net; Ambassador NJABULISO GWEBU.

Judicial System

Judicial Yuan: 124 Chungking South Rd, Sec. 1, Taipei 10048; tel. (2) 23618577; fax (2) 23898923; e-mail judicial@mail.judicial.gov.tw; internet www.judicial.gov.tw; highest judicial organ; interprets the Constitution and national laws and ordinances; supervises the lower courts; Pres. LAI HAU-MIN; Sec.-Gen. LIN JING-FAN.

Supreme Court: 6 Chang Sha St, Sec. 1, Taipei 10048; tel. (2) 23141160; fax (2) 23114246; e-mail tpsemail@mail.judicial.gov.tw; internet tps.judicial.gov.tw; court of third and final instance for civil and criminal cases; Pres. WU CHII-PIN.

High Court: 124 Chungking South Rd, Sec. 1, Taipei 10048; tel. (2) 23713261; internet tph.judicial.gov.tw; court of second instance for appeals of civil and criminal cases; four branch courts: Taichung, Tainan, Kaohsiung and Hualien.

District Courts: Courts of first instance in civil, criminal and non-contentious cases.

Supreme Administrative Court: 1 Lane 126, Chungking South Rd, Sec. 1, Taipei 10048; tel. (2) 23113691; fax (2) 23111791; e-mail jessie@judicial.gov.tw; internet tpa.judicial.gov.tw; court of final resort in appeals against rulings of the High Administrative Courts and of the Intellectual Property Court; Pres. PENG FENG-ZHI.

High Administrative Courts: Courts of first instance in cases brought against govt agencies; three courts based in Taipei, Taichung and Kaohsiung.

Intellectual Property Court: 3/F, 7 Citizen Rd Banciao, Sec. 2, Taipei; tel. (2) 22726696; e-mail ipc@mail.judicial.gov.tw; Pres. KAO HSIOW-JEN.

Commission on Disciplinary Sanctions Against Functionaries: 3/F, 124 Chungking South Rd, Sec. 1, Taipei 10048; tel. (2) 23119375; fax (2) 23826255; decides on disciplinary measures against public functionaries impeached by the Control Yuan; Chief Commr LIN KUO-HSIEN.

Religion

According to the Ministry of the Interior, in 2004 35% of the population were adherents of Buddhism, 33% of Daoism (Taoism), 3.5% of I-kuan Tao and 2.6% of Christianity.

BUDDHISM

Buddhist Association of Taiwan: Mahayana and Theravada schools; 1,613 group mems and more than 5.4m. adherents; Leader Ven. CHIN-HSIN.

CHRISTIANITY

The Roman Catholic Church

Taiwan comprises one archdiocese, six dioceses and one apostolic administrative area. In December 2007, according to official figures, there were 299,130 adherents.

Bishops' Conference: Chinese Regional Bishops' Conference, 3 Lane 85, Linsen North Rd, Taipei 10443; tel. (2) 23571776; fax (2) 25231078; e-mail celine@catholic.org.tw; internet www.catholic.org.tw; f. 1967; Pres. Most Rev. JOHN HUNG SHAN-CHUAN (Archbishop of Taipei).

Archbishop of Taipei: Most Rev. JOHN HUNG SHAN-CHUAN, Archbishop's House, 94 Loli Rd, Taipei 10668; tel. (2) 27371311; fax (2) 27373710.

The Anglican Communion

Anglicans in Taiwan are adherents of the Protestant Episcopal Church. In 2004 the Church had 1,000 members.

Bishop of Taiwan: Rt Rev. DAVID JUNG-HSIN LAI, 7 Lane 105, Hangchow South Rd, Sec. 1, Taipei 10044; tel. (2) 23411265; fax (2) 23962014; e-mail skhtpe@ms12.hinet.net.

Lutheran Church

Taiwan Lutheran Church: 15 Hang Chow S. Rd, Sec. 2, Taipei 10641; tel. (2) 23519317; fax (2) 23913993; e-mail tlc@mail.twlutheran.org.tw; internet www.twlutheran.org.tw; 18,408 mems; Pastor CHEN ZHIHONG.

Presbyterian Church

Tai-oan Ki-tok Tiu-Lo Kau-Hoe (Presbyterian Church in Taiwan): No. 3, Lane 269, Roosevelt Rd, Sec. 3, Taipei 10647; tel. (2) 23625282; fax (2) 23628096; e-mail pct@mail.pct.org.tw; internet www.pct.org.tw; f. 1865; 224,679 mems (2000); Gen. Sec. Rev. CHANG TE-CHIEN.

DAOISM (TAOISM)

In 2004 there were about 7.6m. adherents. Temples numbered 18,274, and clergy totalled 33,850.

I-KUAN TAO

Introduced to Taiwan in the 1950s, this 'Religion of One Unity' is a modern, syncretic religion, drawn mainly from Confucian, Buddhist and Daoist principles and incorporating ancestor worship. In 2004 there were 3,260 temples. Adherents totalled 810,000.

ISLAM

Leader MOHAMMED NI GUO-AN; 58,000 adherents in 2004.

The Press

In 2010 the number of registered newspapers stood at 2,091. The majority of newspapers are privately owned.

PRINCIPAL DAILIES

Taipei

Apple Daily News: 38, 141 Lane, Xinyi Rd, Taipei 11494; tel. (2) 66013456; fax (2) 66018866; e-mail enquiry@appledaily.com.tw; internet tw.nextmedia.com; jt venture between Hong Kong-based Next Media and several Singapore cos.

The China Post: 8 Fu Shun St, Taipei 10452; tel. (2) 25969971; fax (2) 25957962; e-mail info@mail.chinapost.com.tw; internet www.chinapost.com.tw; f. 1952; morning; English; Publr and Editor JACK HUANG; readership 250,000.

China Times: 132 Da Li St, Taipei 10801; tel. (2) 23087111; fax (2) 23048138; internet www.chinatimes.com; f. 1950; morning; Chinese; Chair. TSAI YAN-MING; Editor-in-Chief WANG MEI-YU; circ. 1.2m.

Commercial Times: 132 Da Li St, Taipei; tel. (2) 66320008; fax (2) 23069456; e-mail service@ctee.com.tw; internet ctee.com.tw; f. 1978; morning; Chinese; Publr PENG CHWEI-MING; Editor-in-Chief SIMON CHENG; circ. 300,000.

Economic Daily News: 369 Datong Rd, Xizhi, Sec. 1, Taipei 22161; tel. (2) 86925588; fax (2) 86925851; internet co.udn.com; f. 1967; morning; Chinese; publ. by United Daily News Group; Chair. ANN WANG.

Liberty Times: 399 Rueiguang Rd, Neihu District, Taipei 11492; tel. (2) 26562828; fax (2) 26561034; e-mail newstips@libertytimes.com.tw; internet www.libertytimes.com.tw; f. 1980; Publr WU A-MING; Editor-in-Chief ROGER CHEN; circ. 682,000 (2009).

Mandarin Daily News: 2 Foo Chou St, Taipei 10078; tel. (2) 23921133; fax (2) 23410203; e-mail feedback@mdnkids.com; internet www.mdnkids.com; f. 1948; children's newspaper; morning; Publr LIN LIANG.

Taipei Times: 14/F, 399 Ruiguang Rd, Neihu District, Taipei 11492; tel. (2) 26561000; fax (2) 26561099; e-mail letters@taipeitimes.com; internet www.taipeitimes.com; f. 1999; English; circ. 700,000 (2007).

Taiwan News: 7/F, 88 Xin Yi Rd, Sec. 2, Taipei 10641; tel. (2) 23517666; fax (2) 23515330; e-mail service@etaiwannews.com; internet www.etaiwannews.com; f. 1949; morning; English; Pres. JACK WONG; Publr LUIS KO.

United Daily News: 369 Datong Rd, Xizhi, Sec. 1, Taipei 22161; tel. (2) 86925588; fax (2) 86925851; e-mail service@udndata.com; internet udn.com; f. 1951; morning; CEO DUNCAN WANG; Editor-in-Chief SUNNY YOU; circ. 1.2m.

Provincial

China Daily News (Southern Edn): 57 Hsi Hwa St, Tainan 70449; tel. (6) 2202691; fax (6) 2201804; f. 1946; morning; Publr C. S. LIU; circ. 670,000.

The Commons Daily: Kaohsiung; tel. (7) 2692121; fax (7) 2692685; e-mail commons911@gmail.com; internet www.thecommonsdaily.tw; f. 1950; fmrly Min Chung Daily News; morning; Executive-in-Chief WANG CHIN-HSIUNG; circ. 148,000.

Keng Sheng Daily News: 36 Wuchuan St, Hualien 97048; tel. (38) 340131; fax (38) 341406; e-mail kengshen@ms6.hinet.net; internet www.ksnews.com.tw; f. 1947; morning; Publr HSIEH LEADER; circ. 50,000.

Taiwan Hsin Wen Daily News: 3 Woo Fu I Rd, Kaohsiung 80252; tel. (7) 2226666; f. 1949; morning; Publr CHANG REI-TE.

Taiwan Times: 32 Kaonan Rd, Renwu Township, Kaohsiung 81453; tel. (7) 3428666; fax (7) 3102828; internet www.twtimes.com.tw; f. 1978; Publr WANG YUH-FA.

SELECTED PERIODICALS

Artist Magazine: 6/F, 147 Chung Ching South Rd, Sec. 1, Taipei 10048; tel. (2) 23866715; fax (2) 23317096; e-mail artvenue@seed.net.tw; f. 1975; monthly; Publr HO CHENG KUANG; circ. 37,600.

Better Life Monthly: 11 Lane 199, Hsin-yih Rd, Sec. 4, Taipei 10685; tel. (2) 27549488; fax (2) 27001516; e-mail bettlife@ms14.hinet.net; f. 1987; Publr JACK S. LIN.

Brain: 12/F, 100 Nanking East Rd, Sec. 2, Taipei 10457; tel. (2) 27132644; fax (2) 25621578; e-mail askbrain@brain.com.tw; internet www.brain.com.tw; f. 1977; media industry; monthly; Publr JOHNSON WU.

Business Next: e-mail service@bxnext.com.tw; internet www.bxnext.com.tw; f. 1999; bi-weekly; circ. 160,000.

Business Weekly: 12/F, 141, Sec. 2, Minsheng East Rd, Taipei 10483; tel. (2) 25056789; fax (2) 27364620; e-mail mailbox@bwnet.com.tw; internet www.businessweekly.com.tw; f. 1987; Publr JIN WEI-TSUN.

Car Magazine: 1/F, 3 Lane 3, Tung Shan St, Taipei 10014; tel. (2) 23218168; fax (2) 23935614; e-mail carguide@ms13.hinet.net; f. 1982; monthly; Publr H. K. LIN; Editor-in-Chief LIN TA-WEI; circ. 85,000.

China Times Weekly: 5/F, 25 Min Chuan East Rd, Sec. 6, Taipei 11494; tel. (2) 27936000; fax (2) 87918589; internet www.chinatimes.com; f. 1978; weekly; Chinese; Publr CHANG KUO-LI.

Commonwealth Monthly: 11/F, 139, Sec. 2, Nanking East Rd, Taipei 10553; tel. (2) 26620332; fax (2) 25082941; e-mail cwadmin@cw.com.tw; internet www.cw.com.tw; f. 1981; monthly; business; Pres. CHARLES H. C. KAO; Publr and Editor DIANE YING; circ. 110,000.

CompoTech Asia: Room 3B, 7 Xinyi Rd, Sec. 5, Taipei; tel. (2) 27201789; e-mail carol_liao@computechasia.com; internet www.compotech.com.tw; f. 1999; monthly; computing; Editor-in-Chief CAROL LIAO.

Cosmopolitan: 5/F, 8 Lane 181, Jiou-Tzung Rd, Taipei 11494; tel. (2) 28797890; fax (2) 287978990; e-mail hwaker@ms13.hinet.net; f. 1992; monthly; Publr MINCHUN CHANG.

Crown Magazine: 50 Alley 120, Tun Hua North Rd, Sec. 4, Taipei; tel. (2) 27168888; fax (2) 25148285; internet www.crown.com.tw; f. 1954; monthly; literature and arts; Publr PING HSIN TAO; Editor CHEN LIH-HWA; circ. 76,000.

Defense Technology Monthly: 6/F, 6 Nanking East Rd, Sec. 5, Taipei 10564; tel. (2) 27669628; fax (2) 27666092; e-mail service@dtm.com.tw; internet www.dtmonline.com; f. 1894; Publr J. D. BIH.

Elle Taiwan: 5/F, 9 Lane 130, Minsheng East Rd, Sec. 3, Taipei 10596; tel. (2) 67706168; fax (2) 87706170; e-mail newmedia@hft.com.tw; internet www.elle.com.tw; f. 1991; monthly; women's magazine; Publr JEAN DE WITT; Editors-in-Chief CINDY HU, DORIS LEE; circ. 50,000.

Evergreen Monthly: 11/F, 2 Pa Teh Rd, Sec. 3, Taipei 10558; tel. (2) 25782321; fax (2) 25786838; f. 1983; health care knowledge; Publr LIANG GUANG-MING; circ. 50,000.

Excellence Magazine: 3/F, 15 Lane 2, Chien Kuo North Rd, Sec. 2, Taipei 10487; tel. (2) 25093578; fax (2) 25173607; f. 1984; monthly; business; Man. LIN HSIN-JYH; Editor-in-Chief LIU JEN; circ. 70,000.

Families Monthly: 11/F, 2 Pa Teh Rd, Sec. 3, Taipei 10558; tel. (2) 25785078; fax (2) 25786838; f. 1976; family life; Editor-in-Chief THELMA KU; circ. 155,000.

Foresight Investment Weekly: 7/F, 52 Nanking East Rd, Sec. 1, Taipei 10450; tel. (2) 25512561; fax (2) 25119596; f. 1980; weekly; Dir and Publr SUN WUN HSIUNG; Editor-in-Chief WU WEN SHIN; circ. 55,000.

Global Views Monthly: 2/F, 1 Lane 93, Sungkiang Rd, Taipei 10455; tel. (2) 25173688; fax (2) 25082941; e-mail gvm@cgvm.com.tw; internet www.gvm.com.tw; f. 1986; Editor-in-Chief TIAO MING-FANG.

Gourmet World: 3/F, 53 Jen-Ai Rd, Sec. 1, Taipei 10052; tel. (2) 23972215; fax (2) 23412184; f. 1992; Publr HSU TANG-JEN.

Harvest Farm Magazine: 14 Wenchow St, Taipei 10648; tel. (2) 23628148; fax (2) 23636724; e-mail h3628148@ms15.hinet.net; internet www.harvest.org.tw; f. 1951; every 2 weeks; CEO LIN SHUE-CHENG; Editor-in-Chief YU SHU-LIEN.

Issues and Studies: A Social Science Quarterly on China, Taiwan and East Asian Affairs: Institute of International Relations, National Chengchi University, 64 Wan Shou Rd, Taipei 11666; tel. (2) 82377377; fax (2) 82377231; e-mail issues@nccu.edu.tw; internet iir.nccu.edu.tw/english_web/e_per.htm; f. 1965; quarterly; English; contemporary Chinese studies and East Asian affairs; Editor YEN CHEN-SHEN.

The Journalist: 16/F, 218 Tun Hua South Rd, Sec. 2, Taipei 10669; tel. (2) 23779977; fax (2) 23775850; f. 1987; weekly; Publr WANG SHIN-CHING.

Ladies Magazine: 11/F, 3, 187 Shin Yi Rd, Sec. 4, Taipei 10681; tel. (2) 27026908; fax (2) 27014090; f. 1978; monthly; Publr CHENG CHIN-SHAN; Editor-in-Chief THERESA LEE; circ. 60,000.

Madame Figaro Taiwan: e-mail service@heritage.com.tw; internet www.figaro.tw; f. 2001; fashion; published by Stone Media.

Management Magazine: 14/F, 248 Nan Jing East Rd, Sec. 3, Taipei County 22103; tel. (2) 86471828; fax (2) 86471466; e-mail frankhung@mail.chinamgt.com; internet www.harment.com; f. 1973; monthly; Chinese; Publr and Editor FRANK L. HUNG; Pres. KATHY T. KUO; circ. 65,000.

Money Monthly: 10/F, 289 Chung Hsiao East Rd, Taipei 10696; tel. (2) 25149822; fax (2) 27154657; f. 1986; monthly; personal financial management; Publr PATRICK SUN; Man. Editor JENNIE SHUE; circ. 55,000.

National Geographic/The Earth: 4/F, 319, Sec. 4, Bade Rd, Taipei 10565; tel. (2) 27485988; fax (2) 27480188.

National Palace Museum Monthly of Chinese Art: 221, Sec. 2, Jishan Rd, Taipei 11143; tel. (2) 28821230; fax (2) 28821507; e-mail wyc@npm.gov.tw; f. 1983; monthly in Chinese; Publr CHOU KUNG-SHIN; circ. 3,500.

Nong Nong Magazine: 11/F, 141, Sec. 2, Minsheng East Rd, Taipei 10483; tel. (2) 2502689; fax (2) 25051989; e-mail group@nongnong.com.tw; f. 1984; monthly; women's interest; Publr ANTHONY TSAI; Editor VIVIAN LIN; circ. 70,000.

PC Home: 4/F, 141, Sec. 2, Minsheng East Rd, Taipei 10483; tel. (2) 25000888; fax (2) 25001920; internet www.pchome.com.tw; f. 1996; monthly; Chair. HUNG-TZE JANG; CEO ARTHUR LEE.

PC Office: 11/F, 8 Tun Hua North Rd, Taipei 10547; tel. (2) 25007779; fax (2) 25007903; internet www.pcoffice.com.tw; f. 1997; monthly; Publr HUNG-TZE JANG.

Reader's Digest (Chinese Edn): 2/F, 2 Minsheng East Rd, Sec. 5, Taipei 10572; tel. (2) 82531198; fax (2) 82531211; internet www.readersdigest.com.tw; monthly; Editor-in-Chief VICTOR FUNG.

Studio Classroom: 10 Lane 62, Ta-Chih St, Taipei 10462; tel. (2) 25338082; fax (2) 25326406; internet www.studioclassroom.com; f. 1962; monthly; English teaching magazine; Publr DORIS BROUGHAM.

Taiwan Journal: 2 Tientsin St, Taipei 10051; tel. (2) 23970180; fax (2) 23568233; e-mail tj@mail.gio.gov.tw; internet taiwanjournal.nat.gov.tw; f. 1964; fmrly Free China Journal; weekly; English; news review; Publr VANESSA YEA-PING SHIH; Editor-in-Chief SUSAN YU; circ. 30,000.

Taiwan Panorama: 5/F, 54 Chung Hsiao East Rd, Sec. 1, Taipei 10049; tel. (2) 23922256; fax (2) 23970655; e-mail service@mail.taiwan-panorama.com; internet www.sinorama.com.tw; f. 1976; fmrly *Sinorama*; monthly; bilingual cultural magazine, with edns in Chinese with Japanese or English; Publr PASUYA WEN-CHIH YAO; Editor-in-Chief LAURA LEE; circ. 70,000.

Taiwan Review: 2 Tientsin St, Taipei 100; tel. (2) 23516419; fax (2) 23510829; e-mail tr@mail.gio.gov.tw; internet taiwanreview.nat.gov.tw; f. 1951; fmrly *Taipei Review*, renamed as above March 2003; monthly; English; illustrated; Publr SU JIN-PIN; Editor-in-Chief CHANG HUI-JHEN.

Time Express: B1/F, 205-1 Beisin Rd, Sec. 3, Sinolian City, Taipei County 23143; tel. (2) 89131717; fax (2) 89132332; e-mail timeex@ccw.com.tw; f. 1973; monthly; Publr RICHARD C. C. HUANG.

Unitas: 10/F, 180 Keelung Rd, Sec. 1, Taipei 11006; tel. (2) 27666759; fax (2) 27491208; e-mail unitas@udngroup.com.tw; monthly; Chinese; literary journal; Publr CHANG PAO-CHING; Editor-in-Chief HSU HUI-CHIH.

Vi Vi Magazine: 7/F, 550 Chung Hsiao East Rd, Sec. 5, Taipei 11081; tel. (2) 27275336; fax (2) 27592031; f. 1984; monthly; women's interest; Pres. TSENG CHING-TANG; circ. 60,000.

Vogue/GQ Conde Nast Interculture: 15/F, 51, Sec. 2, Keelung Rd, Sinyi District, Taipei 11082; tel. (2) 27328899; fax (2) 27390504; e-mail vogueeditor@mail.condenast.com.tw; internet www.vogue.com.tw; f. 1996; monthly; Publr BENTHAM LIU.

Wealth Magazine: 7/F, 52 Nanking East Rd, Sec. 1, Taipei 10444; tel. (2) 25512561; fax (2) 25236933; internet www.wealth.com.tw; f. 1974; monthly; finance; Pres. CHIN-HO HSIEH; Editor PHILIP CHEN; circ. 75,000.

Win Win Weekly: 7/F, 52 Nanking East Rd, Taipei 10444; tel. (2) 25816196; fax (2) 25119596; f. 1996; Publr GIN-HO HSHIE.

Youth Juvenile Monthly: 3/F, 66-1 Chung Cheng South Rd, Sec. 1, Taipei 10045; tel. (2) 23112836; fax (2) 23115368; e-mail customer@

youth.com.tw; internet www.youth.com.tw; f. 1965; Publr LEE CHUNG-GUAI.

NEWS AGENCY

Central News Agency (CNA): 209 Sung Chiang Rd, Taipei 10485; tel. (2) 25058379; fax (2) 25023805; e-mail cnamark@mail.cna.com.tw; internet www.cna.com.tw; f. 1924; news service in Chinese, English and Spanish; feature and photographic services; 25 domestic and 32 overseas bureaux; Pres. SU TZEN-PING; Chair. LIU CHIH-TSUNG.

Publishers

There are more than 8,000 publishing houses in Taiwan. In 2009 a total of 40,575 titles were published.

Art Book Co: 1/F, 18 Lane 283, Roosevelt Rd, Sec. 3, Taipei 10647; tel. (2) 23620578; fax (2) 23623594; e-mail artbook@ms43.hinet.net; Publr HO KUNG SHANG.

Cheng Wen Publishing Co: 3/F, 277 Roosevelt Rd, Sec. 3, Taipei 10647; tel. (2) 23628032; fax (2) 23660806; e-mail book@chengwen.com.tw; internet www.chengwen.com.tw; f. 1965; Publr LARRY C. HUANG.

Children's Publication Co Ltd: 7F-1, 314 Neihu Rd, Sec. 1, Taipei 11444; tel. (2) 87972799; fax (2) 87972700; e-mail nell-012@012book.com.tw; internet www.012book.com.tw; f. 1994.

China Times Publishing Co: 5/F, 240 Hoping West Rd, Sec. 3, Taipei 10803; tel. (2) 23047103; fax (2) 23049302; e-mail jess@readingtimes.com.tw; internet www.readingtimes.com.tw; f. 1975; Pres. MO CHAO-PING.

Chinese Culture University Press: 55 Hua Kang Rd, Yangmingshan, Taipei 11114; tel. (2) 28610511, ext. 17503; fax (2) 28617164; e-mail euca@staff.pccu.edu.tw; internet www2.pccu.edu.tw/cuca/ad3.htm; Publr LEE FU-CHEN.

Cite Publishing Ltd: 2/F, 141 Minsheng East Rd, Sec. 2, Taipei 10482; tel. (2) 25007088; fax (2) 25007579; e-mail regina@hmg.com.tw; internet www.cite.com.tw; f. 1996.

The Commercial Press Ltd: 37 Chungking South Rd, Sec. 1, Taipei 10046; tel. (2) 23713712; fax (2) 23752201; e-mail ecptw@cptw.com.tw; internet www.cptw.com.tw; f. 1897; Chair. SHI JIAMING; Sr Chief Editor JONATHAN LEE.

Commonwealth Publishing Co: 2/F, 1 Lane 93, Sung Chiang Rd, Taipei; tel. (2) 25173688; fax (2) 25173685; e-mail cwpc@cwgv.com.tw; internet www.bookzone.com.tw; f. 1982.

Crown Publishing Group: 50 Lane 120, Tun Hua North Rd, Taipei 10547; tel. (2) 27168888; fax (2) 27133422; e-mail edit3@crown.com.tw; internet www.crown.com.tw; f. 1954; Publr PHILIP PING.

The Eastern Publishing Co Ltd: 4/F, 121 Chungking South Rd, Sec. 1, Taipei 100; tel. (2) 23114514; fax (2) 23317402; e-mail lola@1945.com.tw; f. 1945; Publr CHENG SI-MING.

Elite Publishing Co: 1/F, 33-1 Lane 113, Hsiamen St, Taipei 10048; tel. (2) 23654036; fax (2) 23657047; e-mail elite113@ms12.hinet.net; internet www.elitebooks.com.tw; f. 1975; Publr KO CHING-HWA.

Far East Book Co: 66 Chungking South Rd, Sec. 1, Taipei 10045; tel. (2) 23118740; fax (2) 23114184; e-mail service@mail.fareast.com.tw; internet eng.fareast.com.tw; art, education, history, physics, mathematics, law, literature, dictionaries, textbooks, language tapes, Chinese-English dictionaries; Publr GEORGE C. L. PU.

Global Group Holding Ltd: 3/F, 88 Zhou Zi Rd, Neihu District, Taipei; tel. (2) 27992788; fax (2) 27990909; e-mail readers@gobooks.com.tw; internet www.gobooks.com.tw; Publr CHU PAO-LOUNG; Dir KELLY CHU.

Hsin Yi Foundation: 75 Chungking South Rd, Sec. 2, Taipei 10015; tel. (2) 23913384; fax (2) 23965015; e-mail arni@hsin-yi.org.tw; internet www.hsin-yi.org.tw; f. 1971; children's education and devt; Exec. Dir SING-JU CHANG.

Kwang Hwa Publishing Co: 13/F, 15-1 Hangzhou South Rd, Taipei 10050; tel. (2) 23922256; fax (2) 23970655; e-mail service@mail.taiwan-panorama.com; internet www.sinorama.com.tw; Publr CHENG WEN-TSANG.

Li-Ming Cultural Enterprise Co: 1/F, 49 Chungking South Rd, Sec. 1, Taipei 10045; tel. (2) 23314046; fax (2) 23817230; e-mail king@mail.limingco.com.tw; internet www.limingco.com.tw; f. 1971; Pres. SHEN FANG-SHIN.

Linking Publishing Co Ltd: 561, Sec. 1, Chung Hsiao East Rd, Taipei 10055; tel. (2) 27683708; fax (2) 27567668; e-mail bookcs@udngroup.com; internet www.linkingbooks.com.tw; Publr LIU KUO-JUEI.

Locus Publishing Co: 11/F, 25 Nanking East Rd, Sec. 4, Taipei 10550; tel. (2) 87123898; fax (2) 25453927; e-mail locus@locuspublishing.com; internet www.locuspublishing.com; f. 1996.

San Min Book Co Ltd: 386 Fusing North Rd, Taipei 10476; tel. (2) 25006600; fax (2) 25064000; e-mail editor@sanmin.com.tw; internet www.sanmin.com.tw; f. 1953; literature, history, philosophy, social sciences, dictionaries, art, politics, law; Publr LIU CHEN-CHIANG.

Ta Chien Publishing Co Ltd: 19 Sinheheng Rd, Tainan 70248; tel. (6) 2917489; fax (6) 2921618; e-mail tcpublish@hotmail.com; internet www.tachien.com.tw.

Tung Hua Book Co Ltd: 105 Emei St, Taipei 10844; tel. (2) 23114027; fax (2) 23116615; e-mail service@bookcake.com.tw; internet www.bookcake.com.tw; f. 1965; Publr CHARLES CHOH.

The World Book Co: 6/F, 99 Chungking South Rd, Sec. 1, Taipei 10045; tel. (2) 23113834; fax (2) 23317963; e-mail wbc.ltd@msa.hinet.com; internet www.worldbook.com.tw; f. 1921; literature, textbooks; Chair. YEN FENG-CHANG; Publr YEN ANGELA CHU.

Youth Cultural Enterprise Co Ltd: 3/F, 66-1 Chungking South Rd, Sec. 1, Taipei 10045; tel. (2) 23112836; fax (2) 23115368; e-mail customer@youth.com.tw; internet www.youth.com.tw; f. 1958; Publr LEE CHUNG-KUEI.

Yuan Liou Publishing Co Ltd: 6/F, 81, Sec. 2, Nanchang Rd, Taipei 10084; tel. (2) 23926899; fax (2) 23926658; e-mail ylib@ylib.com; internet www.ylib.com; f. 1975; fiction, non-fiction, children's; Publr WANG JUNG-WEN.

Broadcasting and Communications

TELECOMMUNICATIONS

National Communications Commission: 50 Ren-Ai Rd, Sec. 1, Taipei 10052; tel. (2) 33437377; fax (2) 23433994; f. 2006; telecommunications and broadcasting regulatory authority; Chair. HERNG SU.

Chunghwa Telecommunications Co Ltd: 21 Hsinyi Rd, Sec. 1, Taipei 10048; tel. (2) 23445385; fax (2) 23919166; e-mail chtir@cht.com.tw; internet www.cht.com.tw; f. 1996; previously state-controlled company, privatization completed in 2005; Chair. and CEO SHYUE CHING LU.

Far EasTone Telecom: 468 Ruei Guang Rd, Neihu District, Taipei 11492; tel. (2) 87935000; e-mail ir@fareastone.com.tw; internet www.fareastone.com.tw; mobile tel. services; Pres. JAN NILSSON.

Taiwan Mobile Co Ltd: 18/F, 172–1, Ji-Lung Rd, Sec. 2, Taipei 106; tel. (2) 66062999; fax (2) 66368669; e-mail ir@taiwanmobile.com; internet www.taiwanmobile.com; f. 1998; est. as Pacific Cellular Corpn; merged with Taiwan Tele-Shop in 2005; mobile telephone and internet services; Chair. RICHARD TSAI; Pres. HARVEY CHANG.

BROADCASTING

Radio

In June 2009 there were 172 radio broadcasting corporations in operation.

Broadcasting Corpn of China (BCC): 10/F, 375 Sung Chiang Rd, Taipei 10482; tel. (2) 25019688; fax (2) 25018545; internet www.bcc.com.tw; f. 1928; domestic (5 networks and 1 channel) services; 9 local stations, 131 transmitters; Chair. JAW SHAO-KONG.

Central Broadcasting System (CBS): 55 Pei An Rd, Tachih, Taipei 10464; tel. (2) 28856168; fax (2) 28867088; e-mail rti@rti.org.tw; internet www.cbs.org.tw; f. 1928; national broadcasting system of Taiwan; broadcasts internationally in 13 languages via medium and short wave under the call sign Radio Taiwan International (RTI); CEO KUANG HSIANG-HSIA.

Cheng Sheng Broadcasting Corpn Ltd: 7/F, 66-1 Chungking South Rd, Sec. 1, Taipei 10045; tel. (2) 23617231; fax (2) 23712715; e-mail csbc_server@csbc.com.tw; internet www.csbc.com.tw; f. 1950; 6 stations, 3 relay stations; Chair. GUO RONG-CHANG; Pres. LI YUNG-GUIE.

International Community Radio Taipei (ICRT): 19–5F, 107 Jhongshan Rd, Sec. 1, Sinjhuang, Taipei 24250; tel. (2) 85227766; fax (2) 85227077; internet www.icrt.com.tw; f. 1979; predominantly English-language broadcaster.

Kiss Radio: 34/F, 6 Min Chuan 2 Rd, Kaohsiung 80658; tel. (7) 3365888; fax (7) 3364931; e-mail helena@kiss.com.tw; internet www.kiss.com.tw; Pres. HELENA YUAN.

M-radio Broadcasting Corpn: 8/F, 1-18 Taichung Kang Rd, Sec. 2, Taichung City 40751; tel. (4) 23235656; fax (4) 23231199; e-mail jason@mradio.com.tw; internet www.mradio.com.tw.

UFO Broadcasting Co Ltd: 25/F, 102 Roosevelt Rd, Sec. 2, Taipei 10084; tel. (2) 23636600; fax (2) 23673083; internet www.ufo.net.tw; Pres. CHANG HSIAO-YEN.

Voice of Taipei Broadcasting Co Ltd: 10/F, B Rm, 15-1 Han Chou South Rd, Sec. 1, Taipei 10050; tel. (2) 23957255; fax (2) 23947855; internet www.vot.com.tw; Pres. NITA ING.

Television

China Television Co (CTV): 120 Chung Yang Rd, Nan Kang District, Taipei 11523; tel. (2) 27838308; fax (2) 27896614; e-mail prog@mail.chinatv.com.tw; internet beta.ctv.com.tw; f. 1969; Chinatimes Group; Pres. JIANG FENG-CHE; Chair. CHENG SU-MING.

Chinese Television System (CTS): 100 Kuang Fu South Rd, Taipei 10694; tel. (2) 27510321; fax (2) 27775414; e-mail public@mail.cts.com.tw; internet www.cts.com.tw; f. 1971; Chair. LOUIS CHEN; Pres. LI YUAN.

Formosa Television Co (FTV): 14/F, 30 Pa Teh Rd, Sec. 3, Taipei 10551; tel. (2) 25786686; fax (2) 25798715; internet www.ftv.com.tw; f. 1997; Chair. TIEN TZAI-TING; Pres. CHEN KANG-HSING.

Public Television Service Foundation (PTS): 50 Lane 75, Sec. 3, Kang Ning Rd, Neihu, Taipei 11460; tel. (2) 26338037; fax (2) 26301895; e-mail pub@mail.pts.org.tw; internet www.pts.org.tw; some services merged with Chinese Television System July 2006; Chair. CHENG SHENG-FU; Pres. SYLVIA FENG.

Taiwan Broadcasting System (TBS): ; tel. (2) 26301003; e-mail prg50044@mail.pts.org.tw; internet www.tbs.org.tw; f. 2006, with the merger of CTS and PTS, and six other channels; Chair. Dr LOUIS CHEN.

Taiwan Television Enterprise (TTV): 10 Pa Teh Rd, Sec. 3, Taipei 10502; tel. (2) 27758888; fax (2) 27758957; internet www.ttv.com.tw; f. 1962; Pres. and Chair. HUANG SONG.

Finance

(cap. = capital; dep. = deposits; m. = million; brs = branches; amounts in New Taiwan dollars unless otherwise stated)

BANKING

In December 2010 there were 67 banks operating in Taiwan. In September 2002 the Ministry of Finance announced plans to privatize state banks by 2006, and to sell the Government's stake in commercial banks by 2010.

Central Bank

Central Bank of the Republic of China (Taiwan): 2 Roosevelt Rd, Sec. 1, Taipei 10066; tel. (2) 23936161; fax (2) 23571974; e-mail adminrol@mail.cbc.gov.tw; internet www.cbc.gov.tw; f. 1928; fmrly Central Bank of China; name changed as above in 2007; bank of issue; cap. and res 1,223,386m., dep. 9,515,944m. (Dec. 2009); Gov. PERNG FAI-NAN; Dir-Gen. JAMES YUE.

Domestic Banks

Bank of Taiwan: 120 Chungking South Rd, Sec. 1, Taipei 10036; tel. (2) 23493456; fax (2) 23315840; e-mail botservice@mail.bot.com.tw; internet www.bot.com.tw; f. 1946; subsidiary of govt-owned Taiwan Financial Holdings Co Ltd (f. 2008 by merger of Bank of Taiwan, Land Bank of Taiwan and Export-Import Bank of China); cap. 45,000m., res 183,393.5m., dep. 3,463.2m. (Dec. 2009); Chair. SUSAN CHANG; Pres. CHANG MING-DAW; 162 domestic brs, 6 overseas brs.

Export-Import Bank of the Republic of China (Eximbank): 8/F, 3 Nan Hai Rd, Taipei 100; tel. (2) 23210511; fax (2) 23940630; e-mail eximbank@eximbank.com.tw; internet www.eximbank.com.tw; f. 1979; merged with Bank of Taiwan and Land Bank of Taiwan in Jan. 2008 to form Taiwan Financial Holding Co, but withdrew from parent co in June; cap. 12,000m., res 757.6m., dep. 38,754.7m. (Dec. 2009); Chair. SHENG YEN LEE; Pres. ROBERT CHU; 3 brs.

Land Bank of Taiwan Co Ltd: 46 Kuan Chien Rd, Taipei 10047; tel. (2) 23483456; fax (2) 23757023; e-mail lbot@landbank.com.tw; internet www.landbank.com.tw; f. 1946; subsidiary of govt-owned Taiwan Financial Holdings Co Ltd (f. 2008 by merger between Land Bank of Taiwan, Bank of Taiwan and Export-Import Bank of China); cap. 50,000m., res 49,741.7m., dep. 1,978,737.3m. (Dec. 2009); Chair. YAO-SHING WANG; Pres. LER-MING SU; 147 domestic brs, 3 overseas brs.

Taiwan Co-operative Bank: 77 Kuan Chien Rd, Taipei 10038; tel. (2) 23118811; fax (2) 23752954; e-mail ib02@tcb-bank.com.tw; internet www.tcb-bank.com.tw; f. 1946; acts as central bank for co-operatives, and as major agricultural credit institution; merged with Farmers Bank of China in May 2006; cap. 54,855m., res 47,505.6m., dep. 2,449,277.3m. (Dec. 2009); Chair. LIU DENG-CHENG; Pres. TSAI CHIU-JUNG; 300 brs.

Commercial Banks

Bank of Kaohsiung: 168 Po Ai 2nd Rd, Zuoying Qu, Kaohsiung 81357; tel. (7) 5570535; fax (7) 5580529; e-mail service@mail.bok.com.tw; internet www.bok.com.tw; f. 1982; cap. 5,257.9m., res 4,099.1m., dep. 172,685.8m. (Dec. 2009); Chair. LEI CHUNG-DAR (acting); Pres. WU CHU HUNG; 33 brs.

Bank of Panhsin: 2/F, 18 Cheng Tu St, Ban Chiau City, Taipei County 220; tel. (2) 29629170; fax (2) 29572011; e-mail 0473@bop.com.tw; internet www.bop.com.tw; f. 1997; cap. 9,557m., res –42.2m., dep. 148,207.6m. (Dec. 2009); Chair. LIU PING-HUI; Pres. CHEN AN-HSIUNG; 48 brs.

Bank SinoPac Co Ltd: 6/F, 306 Sec. 2, Bade Rd, Jhongshan District, Taipei 10492; tel. (2) 25082288; fax (2) 81618485; internet www.banksinopac.com.tw; f. 1992; cap. 48,218.4m., res 12,091.2m., dep. 932,244.5m. (Dec. 2009); Chair. CHIU CHENG-HSIUNG; Pres. and CEO DESMOND JIANG; 46 brs, including 2 overseas.

Cathay United Bank: 1/F, 7 Sungren Rd, Taipei, 110; tel. (2) 87226666; fax (2) 87898789; e-mail webservice@cathaybk.com.tw; internet www.cathaybk.com.tw; f. 1974; merged with United World Chinese Commercial Bank in 2003; cap. 52,277m., res 32,180m., dep. 1,392,407.3m. (Dec. 2009); Chair. GREGORY K. H. WANG; Pres. TSU PEI CHEN; 140 domestic brs, 2 overseas brs.

Chang Hwa Commercial Bank Ltd: 57 Chung Shan North Rd, Sec. 2, Taipei 10412; tel. (2) 25362951; fax (2) 25114735; e-mail fi@ms1.chb.com.tw; internet www.chb.com.tw; f. 1905; cap. 62,094.8m., res 15,747.8m., dep. 1,384,276.4m. (Dec. 2009); Chair. JULIUS CHEN; Pres. WILLIAM LIN; 181 brs, 7 overseas.

China Development Industrial Bank: F/3, 125 Nanking East Rd, Sec. 5, Taipei 10504; tel. (2) 27638800; fax (2) 27562144; internet www.cdibank.com; f. 1959; cap. 77,604m., res 56,979.5m., dep. 102,587.7m. (Dec. 2009); Chair. TUNG CHAO-CHIN; Pres. SIMON DZENG; 3 brs.

Chinatrust Commercial Bank: 3 SongShou Rd, Taipei 11051; tel. (2) 27222002; fax (2) 27251499; internet www.chinatrust.com.tw; f. 1966; cap. 75,103.2m., dep. 1,515,712.1m. (Dec. 2009); 100% owned by Chinatrust Financial Holding Co; Chair. CHARLES L. F. LO; Pres. JAMES CHEN; 142 brs.

Cosmos Bank: 5–10/F, 39 Tun Hua South Rd, Sec. 2, Taipei 10681; tel. (2) 27011777; fax (2) 27849848; e-mail ibd@cosmosbank.com.tw; internet www.cosmosbank.com.tw; f. 1992; cap. 16,234m., res 12,992.1m., dep. 120,034.6m. (Dec. 2009); Chair. and Pres. PAUL PO; 66 brs.

Cota Commercial Bank: 32-1, Shih Fu Rd, Taichung 40045; tel. (4) 22245161; fax (4) 22275237; internet www.cotabank.com.tw; f. 1999; cap. 3,431m., dep. 95,737m. (Dec. 2006); Chair. LIAO CHUN-TSE; Pres. CHANG CHIN-TING; 18 brs.

DBS Taiwan: 28/F, 7 Xin Yi Rd, Taipei 101 Tower, Taipei 11049; tel. (2) 81010598; fax (2) 81010599; internet www.dbs.com/tw; f. 2008; Chair KOH BOON HWEE; CEO RICHARD B. STANLEY.

E. Sun Commercial Bank: 13/F, 117 Minsheng East Rd, Sec. 3, Taipei 10546; tel. (2) 21751313; fax (2) 87128613; e-mail wulin@email.esunbank.com.tw; internet www.esunbank.com.tw; f. 1992; cap. 33,624m., res 15,790.8m., dep. 880,750.6m. (Dec. 2009); Chair. GARY TSENG; Pres. DUH WU-LIN; 94 domestic brs, 2 overseas brs.

Entie Commercial Bank: 158 Minsheng East Rd, Sec. 3, Taipei 10596; tel. (2) 27189999; fax (2) 27187843; internet www.entiebank.com.tw; f. 1993; cap. 16,796.7m., res 1,480m., dep. 284,818.6m. (Dec. 2009); Chair. MARK ZOLTAN CHIBA; Pres. and CEO JESSE DING; 53 brs.

Far Eastern International Bank: 27/F, 207 Tun Hua South Rd, Sec. 2, Taipei 10602; tel. (2) 23786868; fax (2) 23779000; e-mail secretarial@feib.com.tw; internet www.feib.com.tw; f. 1992; cap. 19,338m., res 9.3m., dep. 347,336.5m. (Dec. 2009); Chair. HOU CHING-ING; Pres. ELI HONG; 36 brs.

First Commercial Bank: 30 Chungking S Rd, Sec. 1, Taipei 10005; tel. (2) 23481111; fax (2) 23892967; e-mail fcb@mail.firstbank.com.tw; internet www.firstbank.com.tw; f. 1899; cap. 46,490m., res 35,108.4m., dep. 1,821,593m. (Dec. 2009); Chair. TSAI CHING-NAIN; Pres. LIN TZUOO-YAU; 187 domestic brs, 15 overseas brs.

Hua Nan Commercial Bank: 38 Chungking S Rd, Sec. 1, Taipei 10006; tel. (2) 23713111; fax (2) 23316741; e-mail service@ms.hncb.com.tw; internet www.hncb.com.tw; f. 1919; cap. 37,809m., res 39,741.6m., dep. 1,685,521m. (Dec. 2009); Chair. LIN MING-CHEN; Pres. WANG JIUNN-CHIH; 183 brs, 6 overseas.

Hwatai Bank: 246 Chang An E Rd, Sec. 2, Taipei 10492; tel. (2) 27525252; fax (2) 87725177; e-mail callcenter@hwataibank.com.tw; internet www.hwataibank.com.tw; f. 1999; cap. 4,499m., res 1,719m., dep. 73,236m. (Dec. 2004); Chair. M. H. LIN; Pres. THOMAS C. W. LEE; 30 brs.

Industrial Bank of Taiwan: 99 Tiding Blvd, Sec. 2, Taipei; tel. (2) 87527000; fax (2) 27985337; internet www.ibt.com.tw; cap. 23,905m., res 397m., dep. 96,906m. (Dec. 2009); Chair. KENNETH C. M. LO; Pres. HENRY PENG.

Jih Sun International Bank: 85 Nanjing E Rd, Sec. 2, Taipei 10407; tel. (2) 25615888; fax (2) 25217698; e-mail planning@jsun.com; internet www.jihsunbank.com.tw; f. 1992 as Baodao Commercial Bank, assumed present name in Dec. 2001; cap. 12,045.5m., res –91.7m., dep. 178,082.3m. (Dec. 2009); Chair. EDWARD CHEN; Pres. DOLLY YANG; 34 brs.

King's Town Bank: 506 His Men Rd, Sec. 1, Tainan 70051; tel. (6) 2139171; fax (6) 2136885; e-mail president@mail.ktb.com.tw; internet www.ktb.com.tw; fmrly Tainan Business Bank; name changed as above in April 2006; cap. 10,512.3m., res 358.1m., 141,794.2m. (Dec. 2009); Chair. DAI CHENG-ZHI; Pres. J. C. SU.

Mega International Commercial Bank Co Ltd (Megabank): 100 Chi Lin Rd, Sec. 2, Jhongshan District, Taipei 10424; tel. (2) 25632614; fax (2) 25611216; e-mail service@megabank.com.tw; internet www.megabank.com.tw; f. 2006; est. from merger of International Commercial Bank of China and Chiao Tung Bank; cap. 64,109.8m., res 81,044.3m., dep. 1,967,058.7m. (Dec. 2009); Chair. MCKINNEY Y. T. TSAI; Pres. SHIU KUANG-SI; 66 domestic brs, 17 overseas brs.

Shanghai Commercial and Savings Bank: 2 Min Chuan East Rd, Sec. 1, Taipei 10452; tel. (2) 25817111; fax (2) 25318501; e-mail service@scsb.com.tw; internet www.scsb.com.tw; f. 1915; cap. 24,723.3m., dep. 535,954.1m. (Dec. 2009); Chair. H. C. YUNG; Pres. Y. P. CHEN; 61 brs.

Standard Chartered Bank (Taiwan) Ltd: 106 Chung Yang Rd, Hsinchu 300; tel. (3) 5245131; fax (3) 5250977; internet www.standardchartered.com.tw; f. 1948; fmrly Hsinchu International Bank; acquired by Standard Chartered Bank in Oct. 2006; cap. 29,105.7m., res 10,553.1m., dep. 546,251.8m. (Dec. 2009); Pres. and CEO SUNIL KAUSHAL; 86 brs.

Sunny Bank: 88 Shih Pai Rd, Sec. 1, Taipei 11271; tel. (2) 28208166; fax (2) 28233414; internet www.esunnybank.com.tw; f. 1997; absorbed Kao Shin Bank in Nov. 2005; cap. 12,248.5m., res 310.3m., dep. 208,488m. (Dec. 2009); Chair. LIN PENG-LANG; Pres. DING WEI-HAO; 96 brs.

Ta Chong Bank Ltd: 2/F, 2 Xinyi Rd, Sec. 5, Xinyi District, Taipei 11049; tel. (2) 87869888; fax (2) 87869800; e-mail service@tcbank.com.tw; internet www.tcbank.com.tw; f. 1992; cap. 27,293.3m., res –3,872.1m., dep. 343,761.2m. (Dec. 2009); Chair. EDMUND KOH; 52 brs.

Taichung Commercial Bank: 87 Min Chuan Rd, Taichung 40341; tel. (4) 22236021; fax (4) 22240748; e-mail service@ms2.tcbbank.com.tw; internet www.tcbbank.com.tw; f. 1953; cap. 13,719m., res 1,361.4m., dep. 293,210.3m. (Dec. 2009); Chair. HUANG SHIU-NAN; Pres. CHUNG YU-YING; 79 brs.

Taipei Fubon Commercial Bank Co Ltd: 169 Jenai Rd, Sec. 4, Taipei 106; tel. (2) 27716999; fax (2) 66387728; internet www.taipeifubon.com.tw; f. 1969; fmrly City Bank of Taipei; acquired by Fubon Financial Holding in 2002; present name adopted following merger of Taipei Bank and Fubon Commercial Bank in 2005; cap. 47,948.8m., res 28,225.8m., dep. 1,270,093.5m. (Dec. 2009); Chair. DANIEL M. TSAI; Pres. VICTOR KUNG; 125 brs, 3 overseas.

Taishin International Bank: 44 Chung Shan North Rd, Sec. 2, Taipei 104; tel. (2) 25683988; fax (2) 25230539; e-mail pr@taishinbank.com.tw; internet www.taishinbank.com.tw; f. 1992; absorbed Dah An Commercial Bank in Feb. 2002; cap. 49,157.5m., res 3,331.7m., dep. 777,183.8m. (Dec. 2009); Chair. THOMAS T. L. WU; Pres. CHARLES WANG; 24 brs.

Taiwan Business Bank: 30 Tacheng St, Taipei 103; tel. (2) 25597171; fax (2) 25507942; e-mail tbb@mail.tbb.com.tw; internet www.tbb.com.tw; f. 1915; reassumed present name 1976; cap. 38,735.9m., res 1,378m., dep. 1,134,253.7m. (Dec. 2009); Chair. T. C. LO; Pres. LIAO TSAN-CHANG; 128 brs.

Taiwan Shin Kong Commercial Bank: 27–28/F, 66 Chung Hsiao West Rd, Sec. 1, Taipei 100; tel. (2) 23895858; fax (2) 23120164; e-mail service@mail.skbank.com.tw; internet www.skbank.com.tw; f. 2000; cap. 19,577.6m., res 2,125m., dep. 399,499.2m. (Dec. 2009); Chair. PATRICK C. J. LIANG; Gen. Man. LAI JIN-YUAN; 28 brs.

Union Bank of Taiwan: 109 Minsheng East Rd, Sec. 3, Taipei 10544; tel. (2) 27180001; fax (2) 27174093; e-mail 014_0199@email.ubot.com.tw; internet www.ubot.com.tw; f. 1992; cap. 23,188.2m., res –6.3m., dep. 328,887m. (Dec. 2009); Chair. SHIANG-CHANG LEE; Pres. JEFF LIN; 76 brs.

Yuanta Commercial Bank Co Ltd: 66 Tun Hua S Rd, Sec. 1, Taipei 100557; tel. (2) 21736699; fax (2) 23801864; e-mail service@yuanta.com; internet www.yuantabank.com.tw; f. 1992; fmrly Fuhwa Commercial Bank, name changed as above in 2007; cap. 21,500m., res 1,705m., dep. 340,980.2m. (Dec. 2009); Pres. CHIN CHIA-LIN; 88 brs.

There are also a number of Medium Business Banks throughout the country.

Community Financial System

The community financial institutions include both credit co-operatives and credit departments of farmers' and fishermen's associations. These local financial institutions focus upon providing savings and loan services for the community. At the end of 2010 there were 26 credit co-operatives in Taiwan.

Foreign Banks

In December 2010 a total of 28 foreign banks had branches in Taipei.

STOCK EXCHANGE

Under new regulations introduced in 2003, foreign investors were divided into two categories: foreign institutional investors (FINIs) and foreign individual investors (FIDIs). While FIDIs were subject to a US $5m. investment quota, FINIs could benefit from an investment quota with no upper limit. However, some industries continued to impose investment 'ceilings' for foreign investors.

Taiwan Stock Exchange Corpn: 3/F, No. 7, Sec. 5, Xinyi Rd, Taipei 11049; tel. (2) 81013101; fax (2) 81013066; internet www.tse.com.tw; f. 1961; Chair. SCHIVE CHI; Pres. SAMUEL HSU.

Supervisory Body

Securities and Futures Bureau: 85 Hsin Sheng South Rd, Sec. 1, Da-an District, Taipei 106; tel. (2) 87735100; fax (2) 87734143; e-mail sfbmail@sfb.gov.tw; internet www.sfb.gov.tw; Dir-Gen. LEE CHI-HSIEN.

INSURANCE

AIG General Insurance: 16/F, 200 Kee-Lung Rd, Sec. 1, Taipei 110; tel. (2) 37251827; fax (2) 87884338; e-mail aiggeneral@aig.com; internet www.aiggeneral.com.tw.

Allianz President General Insurance Co Ltd: 8/F, 178 Ming Chuan East Rd, Sec. 3, Taipei; tel. (2) 27155888; fax (2) 27176616; e-mail azpl@ms2.seeder.net; internet www.allianz.com.tw; f. 1995; Chair. BRUCE BOWERS.

Bank Taiwan Life Insurance Co Ltd: 6/F, 69 Tun Hua South Rd, Sec. 2, Taipei 10682; tel. (2) 27849151; fax (2) 27052214; internet www.twfhclife.com.tw; f. 1941; life insurance; Dir ZHANG GUOQIN; Gen. Man. FU DENG-HSIEH.

Cathay Life Insurance Co Ltd: 296 Jen Ai Rd, Sec. 4, Taipei 10650; tel. (2) 27551399; fax (2) 27082166; e-mail service@cathaylife.com.tw; internet www.cathaylife.com.tw; f. 1962; Chair. HONG-TU TSAI; Pres. T. K. HUANG.

Central Reinsurance Corpn: 12/F, 53 Nanking East Rd, Sec. 2, Taipei 104; tel. (2) 25115211; fax (2) 25629683; e-mail centralre@centralre.com; internet www.crc.com.tw; f. 1968; Chair. CHENG-TUI YANG; Pres. C. T. JUANG.

China Life Insurance Co Ltd: 5/F, 122 Tun Hua North Rd, Taipei; tel. (2) 27196678; fax (2) 27125966; e-mail services@chinalife.com.tw; internet www.chinalife.com.tw; f. 1963; Chair. CHANG CHING-WANG; Gen. Man. ALAN WANG.

Chung Kuo Insurance Co Ltd: 58 Wucheng St, Sec. 1, Taipei 104; tel. (2) 23812727; fax (2) 23814878; e-mail ckibest@mail.cki.com.tw; internet www.cki.com.tw; f. 1931; Chair. LEON SHEN; Pres. C. Y. LIU.

Far Glory Life Insurance Co Ltd: 18/F, 200 Keelung Rd, Sec. 1, Taipei 110; tel. (2) 27583099; fax (2) 23451635; internet www.fglife.com.tw; f. 1993; Chair. T. S. CHAO; Pres. C. S. TU.

The First Insurance Co Ltd: 54 Chung Hsiao East Rd, Sec. 1, Taipei 100; tel. (2) 23913271; fax (2) 23412864; internet www.firstins.com.tw; f. 1962; Chair. CHENG HANG LEE; Pres. JAMES LAI.

Fubon Insurance Co Ltd: 237 Chien Kuo South Rd, Sec. 1, Da-an District, Taipei 10657; tel. (2) 27067890; fax (2) 27042915; internet www.fubon.com; f. 1961; Chair. DAN CANMING.

Fubon Life Insurance Co Ltd: 14/F, 108 Tun Hua South Rd, Sec. 1, Taipei 105; tel. (2) 87716699; fax (2) 88098889; internet www.fubon.com; f. 1993; Gen. Man. CHENG PENG-YUAN.

Global Life Insurance Co Ltd: 9/F, 50 Chung Hsiao West Rd, Sec. 1, Taipei 10041; tel. (2) 23883399; fax (2) 23887676; e-mail services@globallife.com.tw; internet www.globallife.com.tw; f. 1993; Chair. JOHN TSENG; Pres. LAI YI-MING.

Hontai Life Insurance Co Ltd: 4/F, 156 Minsheng East Rd, Sec. 3, Taipei; tel. (2) 27166888; fax (2) 27166812; e-mail service@hontai.com.tw; internet www.hontai.com.tw; f. 1994; fmrly Hung Fu Life Insurance Co; Chair. DAVID JOU.

Kuo Hua Life Insurance Co Ltd: 277 Song-Ren Rd, Xinyi District, Taipei; tel. (2) 21765166; fax (2) 55519707; internet www.khltw.com; f. 1963; Chair. M. S. HSIA; Pres. CHING JIANG-CHEN.

Mercuries Life Insurance Co Ltd: 6/F, Lane 150, Hsin-Yi North Rd, Sec. 2, Taipei 110; tel. (2) 23455511; fax (2) 23456616; e-mail mmli@mail.mli.com.tw; internet www.mli.com.tw; f. 1993; Chair. HENRY CHEN; Pres. CHUNG-SHIN LU.

MSIG Mingtai Insurance Co Ltd: 1 Jen Ai Rd, Sec. 4, Taipei; tel. (2) 27725678; fax (2) 27726666; internet www.msig-mingtai.com.tw; f. 1961; Chair. LARRY P. C. LIN; Pres. H. T. CHEN.

Nan Shan Life Insurance Co Ltd: 168 Zhuangjing Rd, Xinyi District, Taipei 11049; tel. (2) 87588888; fax (2) 87867087; internet www.nanshanlife.com.tw; f. 1963; Chair. EDMUND TSE; Pres. FRANK CHAN.

Prudential Life Assurance Co Ltd: 10/F, 161 Nanking East Rd, Sec. 5, Taipei; tel. (2) 27678866; fax (2) 27679299; internet www.pcalife.com.tw; f. 1962; Chair. STEPHEN D. JIN.

Shinkong Insurance Co Ltd: 15 Chien Kuo North Rd, Sec. 2, Taipei 104; tel. (2) 25075335; fax (2) 25071645; internet www.skinsurance.com.tw; f. 1963; Chair. ANTHONY T. S. WU; Pres. JUN YU ZHAN.

Shin Kong Life Insurance Co Ltd: 37/F, 66 Chung Hsiao West Rd, Sec. 1, Taipei 100; tel. (2) 23895858; fax (2) 23758688; internet www.skl.com.tw; f. 1963; Chair. EUGENE T. C. WU; Pres. PO TSENG PAN.

Singfor Life Insurance Co Ltd: 8/F, 6 Chung Hsiao West Rd, Sec. 1, Taipei; tel. (2) 23817172; fax (2) 23917176; e-mail sc_lin@singforlife.com.tw; internet www.singforlife.com.tw; f. 1993; Chair. DENG WENCONG; Gen. Man. WEN YEN-CHEN.

South China Insurance Co Ltd: 5/F, 560 Chung Hsiao East Rd, Sec. 4, Xinyi District, Taipei 11071; tel. and fax (2) 27588418; fax (2) 27611069; e-mail ecover@south-china.com.tw; internet www.south-china.com.tw; f. 1963; Chair. JACK E. S. TAI; Pres. KEVIN TU.

Taian Insurance Co Ltd: 59 Kwantsien Rd, Taipei; tel. (2) 23819678; fax (2) 23315332; e-mail eservice@mail.taian.com.tw; internet www.taian.com.tw; f. 1961; Chair. C. H. CHEN; Gen. Man. PATRICK S. LEE.

Taiwan Fire and Marine Insurance Co Ltd: 8–9/F, 49 Kuan Chien Rd, Jungjeng Chiu, Taipei 100; tel. (2) 23821666; fax (2) 23882555; e-mail info@tfmi.com.tw; internet www.tfmi.com.tw; f. 1946; Chair. STEVE LEE; Pres. CHARLES SUNG.

Taiwan Life Insurance Co Ltd: 16–19/F, 17 Hsu Chang St, Taipei; tel. (2) 23116411; fax (2) 23759714; e-mail service1@twlife.com.tw; internet www.twlife.com.tw; f. 1947; Chair. PING-YU CHU; Pres. CHENG-TAO LIN.

Tokio Marine Newa Insurance Co Ltd: 7–12/F, 130 Nanking East Rd, Sec. 3, Taipei 104; tel. (2) 87707777; fax (2) 87891190; internet www.tmnewa.com.tw; f. 1999; Chair. HUANG WEN-CHENG; Pres. CHEN REN-TZE.

Union Insurance Co Ltd: 4/F, 219 Chung Hsiao East Rd, Sec. 4, Taipei; tel. (2) 27765567; fax (2) 27737199; internet www.unionins.com.tw; f. 1963; Chair. S. H. CHIN; Gen. Man. FRANK S. WANG.

Zurich Insurance Taiwan Ltd: 9–12/F, 56 Tun Hua North Rd, Taipei 10551; tel. (2) 27752888; fax (2) 27416004; e-mail webmail.twz@zurich.com; internet www.zurich.com.tw; f. 1961; CEO DANIEL RAYMOND.

INSURANCE ASSOCIATIONS

The Life Insurance Association of the Republic of China (LIAROC) : 5/F, 152 Sung Chiang Rd, Taipei; tel. (2) 25612144; fax (2) 25672844; e-mail liaroc@ms31.hinet.net.tw; internet www.lia-roc.org.tw; f. 1997; est. as Taipei Life Insurance Asscn; Chair. PEN TUI-LAI.

The Non-Life Insurance Association of the Republic of China: 13/F, 125 Nanking East Rd, Sec. 2, Taipei 104; tel. (2) 25071566; fax (2) 25075245; internet www.nlia.org.tw; f. 1949; est. as the Taipei Non-Life Insurance Asscn; Chair. SHIH TSAN-MING.

Trade and Industry

GOVERNMENT AGENCIES

Bureau of Foreign Trade (Ministry of Economic Affairs): 1 Houkow St, Taipei 10066; tel. (2) 23510271; fax (2) 23517080; e-mail boft@trade.gov.tw; internet www.trade.gov.tw; Dir-Gen. CHO SHIH-CHAO.

Council of Agriculture (COA): 37 Nan Hai Rd, Taipei 10014; tel. (2) 23812991; fax (2) 23719233; e-mail coa@mail.coa.gov.tw; internet www.coa.gov.tw; f. 1984; govt agency directly under the Executive Yuan, with ministerial status; a policy-making body in charge of national agriculture, forestry, fisheries, the animal industry and food administration; promotes technology and provides external assistance; Chair. CHEN WU-HSIUNG.

Department of Investment Services (Ministry of Economic Affairs): 8/F, 71 Guancian Rd, Taipei 10047; tel. (2) 23892111; fax (2) 23820497; e-mail generaldois@moea.gov.tw; internet www.dois.moea.gov.tw; f. 1959 to assist investment and planning; Dir-Gen. LING CHIA-YUH.

Industrial Development Bureau (Ministry of Economic Affairs): 41-3 Hsin Yi Rd, Sec. 3, Taipei 10651; tel. (2) 27541255; fax (2) 27030160; e-mail service@moeaidb.gov.tw; internet www.moeaidb.gov.tw; Dir-Gen. DUH TYZZ-JIUN.

CHAMBERS OF COMMERCE

General Chamber of Commerce of the Republic of China: 6/F, 390 Fu Hsing South Rd, Sec. 1, Taipei 10665; tel. (2) 27012671; fax (2) 27555493; e-mail service@roccoc.org.tw; internet www.roccoc.org.tw; f. 1946; 86 group mems, incl. 43 nat. feds of trade asscns, 18 nat. commercial asscns, 22 district export asscns and district chambers of commerce; Chair. CHANG PEN-TSAO; Sec.-Gen. PETER LEE.

Taiwan Chamber of Commerce: 13/F, 168 Sung Chiang Rd, Taipei; tel. (2) 25365455; fax (2) 25211980; e-mail tcoc@tcoc.org.tw; internet www.tcoc.org.tw; f. 1946; 113 mems, comprising 93 provincial trade asscns and 20 local chambers of commerce; Chair. CHANG JONG-WEI.

INDUSTRIAL AND TRADE ASSOCIATIONS

China Productivity Center: 2/F, 79 Hsin Tai 5 Rd, Sec. 1, Hsichih, Taipei County 22101; tel. (2) 26982989; fax (2) 26982976; internet www.cpc.org.tw; f. 1956; management, technology, training, etc.; Pres. CHEN MING-CHANG.

Chinese National Association of Industry and Commerce: 13/F, 390 Fu Hsing South Rd, Sec. 1, Taipei; tel. (2) 27070111; fax (2) 27070977; e-mail service@cnaic.org; internet www.cnaic.org; f. 1975; private, independent, non-profit organization comprising major commercial and industrial firms, financial institutions, business asscns, industrialists and business people; Chair. KENNETH C. M. LO.

Chinese National Federation of Industries (CNFI): 12/F, 390 Fu Hsing South Rd, Sec. 1, Taipei 10665; tel. (2) 27033500; fax (2) 27058317; e-mail cnfi@cnfi.org.tw; internet www.cnfi.org.tw; f. 1948; 152 mem. asscns; Chair. PRESTON W. CHEN; Sec.-Gen. TSAI LIEN-SHENG.

Taiwan External Trade Development Council: 5–7/F, 333 Keelung Rd, Sec. 1, Taipei 11003; tel. (2) 27255200; fax (2) 27576652; e-mail taitra@taitra.org.tw; internet www.taitra.org.tw; trade promotion body; Chair. WANG CHIH-KANG; Pres. and CEO CHAO YUEN-CHUAN.

Taiwan Handicraft Promotion Centre: 1 Hsu Chou Rd, Taipei 10055; tel. (2) 23933655; fax (2) 23937330; e-mail thpc@handicraft.org.tw; internet www.handicraft.org.tw; f. 1957; Pres. J. H. LIN.

Taiwan Robot Industry Development Asscn (Robotics Association Taiwan): Taichung; tel. (4) 23581866; fax (4) 23581566; e-mail service@roboat.org.tw; internet www.roboat.org.tw; f. 2007; industry promotion body; Chair. ZHOU YONG CHOI.

Taiwan Transportation Vehicle Manufacturers Asscn (TTVMA): 9/F, 390, Sec. 1, Fushing South Rd, Da-an District, Taipei 10656; tel. (2) 27051101; fax (2) 27066440; internet www.ttvma.org.tw; f. 1948; 600 mems; Chair. CHEN KUO-RONG.

UTILITIES

Electricity

Taiwan Power Co (Taipower): 242 Roosevelt Rd, Sec. 3, Taipei 10016; tel. (2) 23651234; fax (2) 23650037; e-mail service@taipower.com.tw; internet www.taipower.com.tw; f. 1946; electricity generation; Chair. EDWARD K. M. CHEN; Pres. HAN SHEN LEE.

Gas

The Great Taipei Gas Corpn: 5/F, Lane 11, 35 Kwang Fu North Rd, Taipei 10577; tel. (2) 27684999; fax (2) 27630480; e-mail k2@taipeigas.com.tw; internet www.taipeigas.com.tw; supply of gas and gas equipment; Chair. LI FENG-YAO.

Hsin Kao Gas Co Ltd: 56 Ta-Yi St, Yen Cheng, Kaohsiung; tel. (7) 5315701; fax (7) 5312932; internet www.hkgas.com.tw; Chair. CHEN TIEN-MIAO; Gen. Man. CHEN CHIEN-TONG.

Shin Shin Natural Gas Co Ltd: 100 Yungho Rd, Sec. 1, Yungho, Taipei; tel. (2) 29217811; fax (2) 29282829; e-mail ssngas11@ms67.hinet.net; internet www.shinshingas.com.tw; f. 1971; supplies natural gas to non-industrial users; Chair. CHEN HO-CHIA; Pres. QI KAM-CHEUNG.

Water

Taiwan Water Corpn: 2-1 Shuangshih Rd, Sec. 2, Taichung 40425; tel. (4) 2224191; fax (4) 2224201; e-mail service@mail.water.gov.tw; internet www.water.gov.tw; f. 1974; supplies water throughout Taiwan Province and Kaohsiung City; Chair. HUANG MIN-KON; Pres. CHEN FU-TIEN.

MAJOR COMPANIES

(cap. = capital; res = reserves; m. = million; amounts in New Taiwan dollars unless otherwise stated)

State Enterprises

Aerospace Industrial Development Corpn (AIDC): 111 Lane 68, Fusing North Rd, Taichung 40722; tel. (4) 27070001; fax (4) 22842366; e-mail aidc@ms.aidc.com.tw; internet www.aidc.com.tw; f. 1996; aero parts and products building and repairing, machinery mfrs; sales 10,200m. (2005); Chair. SHUNG YEOU-KUANG; Pres. SHIA YEAU-YI; 3,210 employees.

CPC Corpn, Taiwan: 3 Sung Ren Rd, Xinyi District, Taipei 10010; tel. (2) 87898989; fax (2) 87899000; e-mail ir@cpc.com.tw; internet www.cpc.com.tw; f. 1946; fmrly known as Chinese Petroleum Corpn, Taiwan; natural gas, petroleum products, petrochemical feedstocks; refineries at Kaohsiung, Taoyuan and Talin; cap. and res 312,225.8m. (2007), sales 945,215.2m. (2008); Chair. (vacant); Pres. S. H. CHU; 14,843 employees.

Taiwan Sugar Corpn: 68, East District, Sheng Chaan Rd, Tainan 70176; tel. (6) 3378888; fax (6) 3378500; e-mail tsc01@taisugar.com.tw; internet www.taisugar.com.tw; f. 1964; sugar, edible oils, pork, beverages, snacks, yeast, etc.; also has interests in petroleum, leisure, property and retail; sales 29,745m. (2005); Pres. LIN CHUNG-HONG; Chair. HU MAO-LIN; 4,910 employees.

Selected Private Companies

Cement

Asia Cement Corpn: 30/F, Taipei Metro Tower, 207 Tun Hwa South Rd, Sec. 2, Taipei 10602; tel. (2) 27338000; fax (2) 23785197; e-mail wk.chou@acc.com.tw; internet www.asiacement.com.tw; f. 1957; cement mfr and exporter; cap. 29,857m., revenue 48,080m. (2009); Chair. DOUGLAS TONG HSU; Pres. K. Y. LEE; 5,081 employees.

Taiwan Cement Corpn: 113 Chung Shan North Rd, Sec. 2, Taipei; tel. (2) 25317099; fax (2) 25316650; e-mail ffinance@taiwancement.com; internet www.taiwancement.com; f. 1950; cement mfr and exporter; revenue 20,904m. (2009); Chair. and Pres. KOO CHENG-YUN; 4,714 employees.

Chemicals and Fertilizers

Chi Mei Group: 11–2, 4th St, Rende Township, Tainan County 71702; tel. (6) 62798080; fax (6) 62797713; internet www.chimei.com.tw; f. 1960; mfr of resins and other chemical products, food, hospitality, trading and high-technology manufacturing; Chair. LIN CHIN-SHENG; Man. Dir CHENG LIANG-BIN; 1,500 employees.

China Petrochemical Development Corpn: 10–11/F, 12 Dong Hsing Rd, Taipei 10470; tel. (2) 87878187; fax (2) 23517224; e-mail cpdc@cpdc.com.tw; internet www.cpdc.com.tw; mfr of petroleum-related chemicals and their derivatives; cap. 17,949m., revenue 25,701m. (2009); Chair. HENRY HENG FENG.

Formosa Chemicals and Fibre Corpn: 2/F, 201 Tun-hwa North Rd, Taipei 10508; tel. (2) 27122211; fax (2) 27133229; e-mail management@fcfc.com.tw; internet www.fcfc.com.tw; f. 1965; mfrs of chemicals, pulp, rayon staple, yarns, cloth and nylon filament; cap. US $1,776.6m., revenue US $6,860.1m. (2009); Chair. WANG WENGYUAN; Man. Dir FUYUAN HONG; 4,932 employees.

Formosa Petrochemical Corpn: 4/F, 201 Tun-hwa North Rd, Taipei 10508; tel. (2) 27122211; fax (2) 87128050; e-mail fpccpre@fpcc.com.tw; internet www.fpcc.com.tw; f. 1992; mfrs of naphtha, gasoline, diesel, jet fuel, kerosene, fuel oil and liquefied petroleum gas; cap. US $2,974m., revenue US $19,801.1m. (2009); Chair. WILFRED WANG; 3,959 employees.

Lee Chang Yung Chemical Industry Corpn (LCY Chemical Corpn): 4/F, 83 Bade Rd, Sec. 4, Taipei; tel. (2) 27631611; internet www.lcy.com.tw; f. 1965; solvents mfr; cap. and res 18,723m., sales 35,799m. (2009); Chair. LEE BOWEI.

Taiwan Fertilizer Co Ltd: 88 Nanking East Rd, 6/F, Sec. 2, Chung Shan District, Taipei 10408; tel. (2) 25422231; fax (2) 25634597; e-mail tfc@taifer.com.tw; internet www.taifer.com.tw; f. 1946; privatized in 1999; mfrs of compound fertilizers, urea, ammonium sulphate, calcium super-phosphate, melamine, sulphamic acid, etc.; share cap. 9,800.0m. (2005), revenue 17,124.7m. (2009); Chair. ZHONG RONGJI; 2,292 employees.

Electrical and Computing

Acer Inc: 8/F, 88, Sec. 1, Hsin Tai Wu Rd, Taipei; tel. (2) 26961234; fax (2) 26963535; e-mail stockaffairs@acer.com.tw; internet www.acer.com.tw; f. 1976; personal computers, multi-user systems, computer applications, laser printers, etc.; revenue 573,982.5m. (2009); Chair.and Acting Pres. J. T. WANG; 7,000 employees.

Advanced Semiconductor Engineering Inc: 26 Chin 3 Rd, 811, Nantze Export Processing Zone, Kaohsiung; tel. (7) 3617131; fax (7) 3614546; e-mail ir@aseglobal.com; internet www.asetwn.com.tw; f. 1984; integrated circuit packaging and testing; cap. and res 75,173.4m. (2007), revenue 85,775.3m. (2009); Chair. JASON CHANG CHIEN-SHENG; Pres. RICHARD CHANG HUNG-PENG; 29,538 employees.

Asustek Computer Inc: 15 Li-Te Rd, Peitou, Taipei; tel. (2) 28943447; fax (2) 28926140; e-mail investor@asus.com; internet www.asus.com.tw; f. 1990; mfrs of computer, communications and consumer electronic products; revenue 248,200m. (2009); Chair. JOHNNY SHIH; CEO JERRY SHEN; 8,895 employees.

BenQ Corpn: 16 Jihu Rd, Neihu, Taipei 114; tel. (2) 27278899; fax (2) 27979288; internet www.benq.com; f. 1984; electronic devices incl. digital displays, mobile phones, scanners and keyboards; cap. US $798m., sales $5,040m. (2005); Chair. and CEO K. Y. LEE; Pres. CONWAY LEE; 18,838 employees (global total).

Chung Hwa Picture Tubes Ltd: 1127 Heping Rd, Ta Nan Tsun, Pateh Hsiang, Taoyuan County 33444; tel. (3) 3675151; fax (3) 3667612; e-mail ir@cptt.com.tw; internet www.cptt.com.tw; f. 1971; mfr of electronic components; cap. 94,809m. (2008), revenue 118,500m. (2008); Chair. LIN WEI-SHAN; Pres. LIN SHENG-CHANG; 22,000 employees.

CMC Magnetics Corpn: 15/F, 53, Ming Chuan West Rd, Taipei; tel. (2) 25989890; fax (2) 25973270; e-mail IR@cmcnet.com.tw; internet www.cmcnet.com.tw; f. 1978; mfr of blank CDs for audio, video and CD-ROM uses; revenue 25,701.2m. (2009); Chair. WENG MING-XIAN; Man. Dir YANG YA-XIU; 6,600 employees.

Compal Electronics Inc: 581 Juikuang Rd, Neihu, Taipei; tel. (2) 87978588; fax (2) 26585001; internet www.compal.com; f. 1984; computers and accessories; revenue 675,305.2m. (2009); Chair. XU SHENGXIONG; Man. Dir CHEN RUICONG; 58,025 employees.

Compeq Manufacturing Co Ltd: POB 9-22, 91 Lane 814, Ta Hsin Rd, Shin-chuang Vil., Lu Chu Hsiang, Taoyuan County 33843; tel. (3) 3231111; fax (3) 3138150; e-mail inquiry@compeq.com.tw; internet www.compeq.com.tw; f. 1973; mfr of computers and computer peripherals; cap. and res 12,186.1m., sales 19,144m. (2008); Chair. JIAN WU; Pres. TENGLING LIU; 4,516 employees.

Delta Electronics Inc: 186 Ruey Kuang Rd, Neihu, Taipei 11491; tel. (2) 87972088; fax (2) 87972120; e-mail tse@delta.com.tw; internet www.delta.com.tw; f. 1971; electronic parts, colour monitors, etc.; cap. and res 117,914.7m. (2007), revenue 125,712m. (2009); Chair. BRUCE CHENG; CEO YANSEY HAI; 4,500 employees.

Enlight Corpn: 238 Jungyi Rd, Sec. 2, Dahua Village, Kwei-Shan, Taoyuan County 33378; tel. (3) 3977399; fax (3) 3284056; internet twc.enlightcorp.com; f. 1973; mfr of computer parts and peripherals; revenue 8,756m. (2009); Pres. CHIH MING LIAO; 2,500 employees.

Epistar Corpn: 5 Li-hsin 5th Rd, Science-Based Industrial Park, Hsinchu 300; tel. (3) 5783078; fax (3) 5783080; e-mail rider@epistar.com.tw; internet www.epistar.com.tw; f. 1996; mfrs of high brightness light emitting diode (LED) products; revenue 12,848.8m. (2009); Chair. and Gen. Man. LI BING-JIE; 3,523 employees.

First International Computer Inc: 6/F, 201–04 Tun Hua North Rd, Sungshan District, Taipei; tel. (2) 27174500; fax (2) 27120231; e-mail sobin_chem@fic.com.tw; internet www.fic.com.tw; f. 1980; mfr of consumer electronics; Chair. MING JEN CHIEN; Pres. JOHN VILLEJO; 1,600 employees.

Foxconn Technology Co Ltd: 66-1 Chung-Shan Rd, Tu-Cheng City, Taipei; tel. (2) 22680970; fax (2) 22687176; e-mail ftc@foxconn.com; internet www.foxconntech.com.tw; f. 1974; mfr of computing equipment; revenue 155,058m. (2009); Chair. LIN DONGLIANG; Man. Dir LI HANMING; 54,000 employees.

Gold Circuit Electronics: 113 Shi Yuan Rd, Chung Li Industrial Park, Taoyuan County; tel. (3) 4612541; fax (3) 2506349; e-mail 2c0@gce.com.tw; internet www.gce.com.tw; f. 1981; mfr of circuit boards; revenue 14,277.5m. (2009); Chair. YANG CHANG-JI; CEO CHEN QIU-MING; 4,718 employees.

Hon Hai Precision Industry: 2 Zihyou St, Tu-Cheng City, Taipei 236; tel. (2) 22683466; fax (2) 22686204; e-mail WebAdmin@foxconn.com; internet www.foxconn.com.tw; revenue 1,959,182m. (2009); manufacture and sale of electronic components; Chair. and Gen. Man. GUO TAI-MING.

Inventec Corpn: 66 Hou Kang St, Shih Lin District, Taipei; tel. (2) 28810721; fax (2) 28823605; e-mail iec@inventec.com; internet www.inventec.com.tw; f. 1975; computers and electronic products; cap. and res 36,494.6m. (2007), sales 398,086m. (2009); Chair. LI SHI-QIN; Gen. Man. WANG ZHI-CHENG; 30,077 employees.

Lite-On IT Corpn: 12/F, 392 Ruey Kuang Rd, Neihu, Taipei 114; tel. (2) 87982886; fax (2) 87982825; internet www.liteonit.com.tw; f. 1999; mfr of opto-electronics products; cap. and res 19,749.0m. (2007), revenue 57,514.9m. (2008); Chair. GONGYUAN SONG; Pres. XINGXIAN LIN.

Lite-on Technology Corpn: 22/F, 392 Ruey Kuang Rd, Neihu, Taipei 114; tel. (2) 87982886; fax (2) 87982868; e-mail liteontech.ir@liteon.com; internet www.liteon.com; f. 1980; personal computers, computer peripherals; cap. and res 61,592.8m. (2007), revenue 186,059m. (2009); Chair. RAYMOND SOONG; CEO DAVID LIN; 85,584 employees.

Macronix International Co Ltd: 16 Li-hsin Rd, Science-Based Industrial Park, Hsinchu; tel. (3) 5786688; fax (3) 5632888; e-mail mirandapeng@mxic.com.tw; internet www.macronix.com; f. 1989; mfr of semiconductors; cap. and res 34,091m., revenue 26,838.4m. (2009); Chair. and CEO MIIN WU; Pres. LU CHIH-YUAN; 3,895 employees.

Mitac International Corpn: 200 Wen Hua 2nd Rd, Kwei Shan Hsiang, Taoyuan; tel. (3) 3289000; fax (3) 3280926; e-mail stock@mic.com.tw; internet www.mitac.com; f. 1982; design and manufacture of computers; cap. and res 22,287.1m., revenue 63,369m. (2009); Chair. MATTHEW MIAU; Pres. BILLY HO; 9,622 employees.

Nanya Technology Corporation: Hwa Ya Technology Park 669, Fu Hsing 3rd Rd, Kueishan, Taoyuan 333; tel. 3281688; fax 3960997; internet www.eu.nanya.com/default.aspx; f. 1995; revenue 36,311m. (2008); Chair. CHIA CHAU WU.

Panasonic Taiwan Co Ltd: 579 Yuan Shan Rd, Chung Ho City, Taipei; tel. (2) 22235121; fax (2) 22271266; e-mail webinfo@panasonic.com.tw; internet www.panasonic.com.tw; f. 1962; fmrly Matsushita Electric Co Ltd; home appliances, electronic and consumer products; Chair. M. H. HONG; Pres. AKIHIRO NAKATANI; 4,500 employees.

Philips Electronic Building Elements Industries (Taiwan): 23–30/F, 66 Chung Hsiao West Rd, Section 1, Taipei; internet www.philips.com.tw; f. 1967; mfr of integrated circuits; Chair. Y. C. LO; 2,806 employees.

Philips Electronic Industries (Taiwan) Ltd: Shih Kong Mitsukoshi Bldg, 22–24/F and 27–29/F, Chung Hsiao West Rd, Sec. 1, Taipei; tel. (2) 23887666; fax (2) 25155388; internet www.philips.com.tw; f. 1970; mfr of electronic components; Pres. YI CHIANG LO; 5,267 employees.

ProMOS Technologies Inc: 19 Li-hsin Rd, Hsinchu Science Park, Hsinchu 30078; tel. (3) 5798308; fax (3) 5663300; e-mail promoswebsmaster@promos.com.tw; internet www.promos.com.tw; f. 1996; mfrs of computer memory chips; cap. and res 76,341.4m. (2007), revenue 30,805.6m. (2008); Chair. and Pres. MINLIANG CHEN; 6,800 employees.

Quanta Computer Inc: 211 Wen Hwa 2nd Rd, Kuei Shan Hsiang, Tao Yuan Shien; tel. (3) 3272345; fax (3) 3271511; e-mail qci.ir@quantatw.com; internet www.quantatw.com; f. 1988; mfr of portable personal computers; cap. and res 87,389.9m. (2007), revenue 839,791.3m. (2009); Chair. BARRY LAM; Pres. C. C. LEUNG; 64,719 employees.

Ritek Corpn: 42 Kuang Fu North Rd, Hsinchu Industrial Park, Hsinchu 30316; tel. (3) 5985696; fax (3) 5979963; e-mail personal@ritek.com.tw; internet www.ritek.com.tw; f. 1989; mfr of blank CDs for audio, video and CD-ROM uses; cap. and res 39,548.8m. (2007), revenue 20,449m. (2009); Chair. CHIN TAI YEH; Pres. TSUE GING YEH; 6,000 employees.

Taiwan Semiconductor Manufacturing Co Ltd (TSMC): 25 Li-Hsin Rd, Hsinchu Science Industrial Park, Hsinchu; tel. (3) 5636688; fax (3) 5662051; e-mail invest@tsmc.com.tw; internet www.tsmc.com.tw; f. 1987; mfr of integrated circuits; cap. 314,146.2m., sales 295,742.2m. (2009); Chair. and CEO MORRIS CHANG; Pres. and CEO RICK TSAI; 24,000 employees.

Tatung Co Ltd: 22 Chung Shan North Rd, Sec. 3, Taipei 104; tel. (2) 25925252; fax (2) 25915185; e-mail webmaster@tatung.com.tw; internet www.tatung.com.tw; f. 1918; household electric appliances, audio equipment, computers, telecommunications, wires and cables, heavy electrical apparatus, steel and machinery, material industry, construction and transport equipment; cap. and res 44,243.1m. (2007), sales 30,264m. (2009); Chair. Dr LIN WEI-SHAN; Pres. LIN TING-SHEN; 39,979 employees.

TECO Electric & Machinery Co Ltd: 5/F, 19–9 San Chong Rd, Nan-Kang, Taipei; tel. (2) 26553333; fax (2) 26552212; e-mail ir@teco.com.tw; internet www.teco.com.tw; f. 1956; household appliances, commercial air conditioners, industrial motors and applications; cap. and res 24,050.5m., revenue 22,210.1m. (2009); Chair. C. K. LIU; Pres. SOPHIA CHIU; 9,500 employees.

United Microelectronics Corpn Ltd (UMC): 3 Li-hsin Rd 2, Hsinchu Science Industrial Park, Hsinchu; tel. (3) 5782258; fax (3) 5779392; e-mail foundry@umc.com; internet www.umc.com; f. 1980; semiconductors, microcomputers, communications, etc.; cap. 174,242.7m., revenue 91,389.7m. (2009); Chair. STAN HUNG; CEO SUN SHIH-WEI; 13,051 employees.

Winbond Electronics Corpn: 8 Keya Rd 1, Daya Township, Taichung; tel. (4) 25218168; e-mail InvestorRelation@winbond.com; internet www.winbond.com.tw; f. 1987; design and production of very large-scale integrated circuits; cap. 49,745.9m., revenue 19,532.7m. (2009); Chair. and CEO ARTHUR YU-CHENG CHIAO; Pres. CHAN TUNG-YI; 1,732 employees.

Yageo Corpn: 3/F, 223-1 Pao Chiao Rd, Hsin Tien, Taipei; tel. (2) 29177555; fax (2) 29173789; e-mail ir@yageo.com; internet www.yageo.com.tw; f. 1987; mfr of resistors; cap. and res 31,946.4m. (2007), revenue 22,486m. (2008); Pres. and CEO CHEN TIE-MIN; 7,203 employees.

Engineering

China Motor Corpn: 11/F, 2 Tung Hua South Rd, Sec. 2, Ta-an District, Taipei; tel. (2) 23250000; fax (2) 27082913; e-mail overseas@china-motor.com; internet www.china-motor.com.tw; f. 1969; mfr of motor vehicles; cap. and res 45,651.4m. (2007), revenue 37,469.1m. (2009); Chair. and Pres. KENNETH YEN; 4,332 employees.

Ford Lio Ho Motor Co: 705 Chung Hua Rd, Sec. 1, Chung Li City, Taoyuan; tel. (3) 4553131; fax (3) 4551474; internet www.ford.com.tw; f. 1972; motor vehicles; Chair. WILLIAM CLAY FORD, Jr; Pres. ALBERT LI; 2,700 employees.

Hotai Motor Co Ltd: 8–14/F, 121 Sung Chiang Rd, Chung Shan District, Taipei 10485; tel. (2) 25062121; fax (2) 25041749; e-mail crda@mail.hotaimotor.com.tw; internet www.hotaimotor.com.tw; f. 1947; distributor of Toyota and Hino motor vehicles; cap. and res 19,236.9m. (2007), revenue 72,482.8m. (2009); Chair. SU YANN-HUEI; Pres. JUSTIN SU; 520 employees.

Kuozui Motors Ltd: 11/F 121 Sung Chiang Rd, Taipei; tel. (3) 24529172; fax (3) 24519180; internet www.kuozui.com.tw; f. 1984; mfr of cars and trucks; cap. 3,460m. (2006); Chair. SU YANN-HUEI; 2,880 employees.

Kwang Yang Motor Co Ltd: 35 Wan Hsing St, Sanmin District, Kaohsiung 80794; tel. (7) 3891832; fax (7) 3950021; e-mail service@mail.kymco.com; internet www.kymco.com; f. 1963; mfr of motor cycles; cap. US $177m. (2005); Pres. S. C. WANG; 2,495 employees.

San Yang Industry: 3 Chung Hua Rd, Hukou, Hsinchu County 30352; tel. (3) 5981911; fax (3) 5971981; e-mail omd@sym.com.tw; internet www.sym.com.tw; f. 1954; mfr of cars, motorcycles, etc.; cap. and res 14,498.0m., revenue 34,115.2m. (2007); Chair. S. H. HUANG; Pres. HUANG KUAN-WU; 2,400 employees.

Taiwan Aerospace Corpn (TAC): 17/F, 169 Jen-Ai Rd, Sec. 4, Taipei; tel. (2) 27716681; fax (2) 27716727; f. 1991; mfr of jet aircraft; Chair. JACK SUN; Pres. GEORGE K. LIU.

Yulon Motor Co Ltd: 39–1 Tsuen Po Kong Keng, West Lake San-yi Village, Miaoli County 36743; tel. (3) 7871801; fax (3) 7874790; internet www.yulon-motor.com.tw; f. 1953; mfr of cars and pick-up trucks; cap. and res 56,217.1m. (2007), revenue 48,803.4m. (2009); Chair. VIVIAN W. SHUN-WEN; Pres. YAN KAI-TAI; 7,310 employees.

Food and Drink

Uni-President Enterprises Corpn: 301 Chung Chen Rd, Yan Harng, Yeong Kang Shiang, Tainan Hsien; tel. (6) 2532121; fax (6) 2532661; e-mail public@mail.pec.com.tw; internet www.uni-president.com.tw; f. 1967; noodles, processed foods, soft drinks, etc.; cap. and res 45,094m., revenue 290,196m. (2009); Chair. KAO CHIN-YEN; Pres. JASON C. S. LIN; 6,135 employees.

Ve Wong Corpn: 5/F, 79 Chung Shan North Rd, Sec. 2, Taipei 10448; tel. (2) 25717271; fax (2) 25712920; e-mail tradep@vewong.com.tw; internet www.vewong.com; f. 1959; processed food and drinks; cap. and res 3,260.9m. (2007), revenue 7,073.3m. (2009); Chair. EGAWA TAKETADA; Gen. Man. CHEN GONG-PING; 2,435 employees.

Vedan Enterprise Corpn: POB 9, 65 Hsin An Rd, Shalu, Taichung; tel. (4) 26622111; fax (4) 26626576; e-mail service@mail.vedan.com; internet www.vedan.com.tw; monosodium glutamate, instant noodles, canned foods and biotechnology products; Pres. JENG YANG; 2,000 employees.

Weichuan Foods Corpn: 125 Sung Chiang Rd, Taipei 11058; tel. (2) 25078221; fax (2) 25070623; e-mail service@weichuan.com.tw; internet www.weichuan.com.tw; f. 1953; milk products, monosodium glutamate, canned foods and soy sauce; cap. and res 4,475.4m. (2007), revenue 21,129.4m. (2009); Chair. WEI YING-CHONG; Gen. Man. ZHANG JIAOHUA; 5,449 employees.

Metals

China Steel Corpn: Lin Hai Industrial District, POB 47-29, 1 Chung Kang Rd, Hsiao Kang, Kaohsiung 81233; tel. (7) 8021111; fax (7) 8022511; e-mail f1000@mail.csc.com.tw; internet www.csc.com.tw; f. 1971; steel; state holding reduced to 40.6% in 1999; 16 subsidiaries; cap. 150,926.3m., revenue 251,112.2m. (2009); Chair. J. C. TSOU; Pres. C. H. OU; 9,200 employees.

China Wire & Cable Co Ltd: 54-9, 4/F, Sec. 3, Chung Shang North Rd, Taipei; tel. (2) 25993456; fax (2) 25987766; e-mail acct@cwco.com.tw; internet www.cwco.com.tw; mfr of aluminium doors and windows; cap. and res 3,553.8m. (2007), revenue 3,696.8m. (2009); Chair. CHEN CHIN-CHUN; 593 employees.

First Copper Technology Co Ltd: 170 Chung Cheng 4th Rd, Chien Chin, Kaohsiung; tel. (7) 2814161; fax (7) 2810539; e-mail hg100@hegroup.com.tw; internet www.fcht.com.tw; manufacture and sale of metals and alloys for industrial purposes; cap. 3,590m., revenue 4,587.1m. (2009); Pres. WU HSIEN MING; 283 employees.

Great China Metal Industry Co Ltd: 533 Mingchih Rd, Sec. 3, Taishan County, Taipei 24355; tel. (2) 29015153; fax (2) 29037168; e-mail sales@gcm.com.tw; internet www.gcm.com.tw; mfr of aluminium cans; cap. and res 5,147.2m., revenue 4,833.4m. (2007); Chair. CHIANG CHING-YI; Pres. CHIANG CHENG-SHING; 389 employees.

Tang Eng Iron Works Co Ltd: 4 Yen Hai 2nd Rd, Hsiao Kang, Kaohsiung 81260; tel. (7) 8022811; fax (7) 8010801; internet www.tangeng.com.tw; f. 1940; stainless steel sheets and coils, steel bars, shapes etc., railway rolling stock, buses, general machinery, construction, bridge projects, land development and transport business; cap. and res 7,501.6m., revenue 35,701.7m. (2007); Chair. LIU MIN-ZHONG (acting); Gen. Man. LIANG CHIN-MIN (acting); 797 employees.

Plastics and Glass

China General Plastics Corpn: 7/F, 37 Ji Hu Rd, Neihu District, Taipei 114; tel. (2) 87516888; fax (2) 26599516; e-mail cgpcstk@cgpc.com.tw; internet www.cgpc.com.tw; f. 1964; mfr of PVC products; cap. and res 4,820.7m. (2007), revenue 12,472.7m. (2009); Chair. QUINTIN WU; Gen. Man. ZHOU DE-HUAI; 1,338 employees.

Formosa Plastics Corpn: 39 Chong Shang Rd, Kaohsiung 80049; tel. (7) 3331101; fax (2) 27175287; e-mail formosa@fpc.com.tw; internet www.fpc.com.tw; f. 1958; PVC products, footwear, polyester fibre, etc.; several affiliates; cap. and res 249,300.3m. (2007), revenue 180,074.9m. (2009); Chair. and Pres. C. T. LEE; 5,507 employees.

Nan Ya Plastics Corpn: 35-1, Jongshan 3 Rd, Kaohsiung; tel. (2) 27122211; fax (2) 27178533; e-mail nanya@npc.com.tw; internet www.npc.com.tw; f. 1958; largest affiliate, mfr of plastic products; cap. and res 288,508.1m. (2007), revenue 244,136.3m. (2009); Chair. WU CHIN-JEN; 12,367 employees.

Taiwan Glass Industrial Corpn: 11/F, Taiwan Glass Bldg, 261 Nanking East Rd, Sec. 3, Sungshan District, Taipei 10550; tel. (2) 27130333; fax (2) 27150333; e-mail tgi@taiwanglass.com; internet www.taiwanglass.com; f. 1964; cap. and res 39,675.9m. (2007), revenue 31,689.7m. (2009); Chair. LIN PO-FENG; CEO LIN P.S.; 12,194 employees.

Textiles and Garments

Chung Shing Textile Co Ltd: 463 Hua Cheng Rd, Hsin Chung City, Taipei; tel. (2) 85213322; fax (2) 85210612; e-mail susan@mail.chung-shing.com.tw; internet www.chung-shing.com.tw; f. 1956; textiles and garments; share cap. 9,084.5m., sales 8,633.1m. (2001); Pres. I. S. CHOU; 2,500 employees.

Far Eastern New Century Corpn: 38/F, Taipei Metro Tower, 207 Tun Hua Rd, Sec. 2, Taipei 106; tel. (2) 27338000; fax (2) 27369621; e-mail ir@fenc.com; internet www.fenc.com; f. 1951; fmrly Far Eastern Textile Ltd; name changed as above in 2009; cap. 56,794.9m., revenue 166,973.3m. (2009); polyester staple, polyester filament, texturized yarn, cotton yarn, blended yarn, cotton clothing, shirts, underwear, pyjamas, trousers/suits, bedsheets, etc.; Chair. DOUGLAS TONG HSU; Pres. JOHNNY SHI; 4,445 employees.

Hualon-Teijran: 9/F, 351 Chung Shan Rd, Sec. 2, Taipei; tel. (2) 22266801; fax (2) 22266851; e-mail archives@hualon.com.tw; internet www.hualon.com.tw; f. 1967; mfr of fabrics and yarns; share cap. 24,345.6m., sales 18,668.9m. (2001); Chair. Y. M. WANG; Pres. ZHUANG MING QI; Man. Dir LIANG CHING-HSIUNG; 6,663 employees.

Pou Chen Corpn: 4/F, 78-2, Taichung Kang Rd, Sec. 3, Taichung; tel. (4) 24615678; e-mail ir@pouchen.com; internet www.pouchen.com.tw; mfr of footwear; cap. 35,884.2m., revenue 206,439.8m. (2009); Chair. C. C. TSAI; Exec. Gen. Man. DAVID N. F. TSAI; 332,653 employees.

Shin Kong Synthetic Fibres Corpn: 8/F, 123 Nanking East Rd, Sec. 2, Chung Shan, Taipei; tel. (2) 25071251; fax (2) 25072264; e-mail jnku@shinkong.com.tw; internet www.shinkong.com.tw; f. 1967; mfr of fabrics, yarns and silk; revenue 23,149.5m. (2008); Chair. and CEO DONGSHENG WU; 1,761 employees.

Tai Yuen Textile Co Ltd: 8/F, 2 Tun Hua South Rd, Sec. 2, Taipei 10683; tel. (2) 27552222; fax (2) 77132255; e-mail market@taiyuen.com; internet www.taiyuen.com; f. 1951; yarn, cloth, denim, knitting fabrics, garments and sewing thread; Chair. KENNETH K. T. YEN; Pres. WEI KUNG CHI; 1,939 employees.

Tainan Spinning Co Ltd: 511 Yu Nung Rd, Tung District, Tainan 701; tel. (6) 2376161; fax (6) 2361156; e-mail general@mail.tainanspin.upeg.com.tw; internet www.tainanspin.com.tw; f. 1955; cotton, blended and synthetic yarns, etc.; cap. 14,935.2m., revenue 17,101m. (2009); Chair. CHENG KAO-HUEI; Pres. HOU PO-MING; 1,800 employees.

Miscellaneous

Cheng Loong Corpn: 1 Minsheng Rd, Sec. 1, Panchiao, Taipei Hsien; tel. (2) 22225131; fax (2) 22226110; e-mail clc@mail.clc.com.tw; internet www.clc.com.tw; f. 1959; mfr of paper and paper products; cap. and res 15,945.6m. (2007), revenue 34,191.8m. (2009); Chair. CHENG CHENG-LOONG; 5,472 employees.

Cheng Shin Rubber Industry: 215 Meei-Kong Rd, Ta-Sun Hsiang, Chang-Hwa Hsien; tel. (4) 28525151; fax (4) 28526468; e-mail cst001@ms1.hinet.net; internet www.cst.com.tw; f. 1967; mfr of rubber goods; cap. and res 25,845.8m. (2007), revenue 84,501.5m. (2009); Chair. CHIEH LO; Pres. JUNG HUA CHEN; 15,758 employees.

CSBC Corpn, Taiwan: 3 Chung Kang Rd, Hsiao-kang, Kaohsiung 81234; tel. (7) 8010111; fax (7) 8020805; e-mail 1588@csbcnet.com.tw; internet www.csbcnet.com.tw; f. 1973; fmrly China Shipbuilding Corpn; privatized in 2008; 51% stake sold by Govt through initial public offering; shipbuilding and repairing up to 1m. dwt; machinery mfrs; sales 31,189m. (2009); Chair. CHENG WEN-LON; Pres. TANG TAI-PING; 2,787 employees.

Taiyen Biotech Co Ltd: 297 Chien Kan Rd, Sec. 1, Tainan 702; tel. (6) 2160688; fax (6) 2160999; e-mail service@tybio.com.tw; internet www.tybio.com.tw; f. 1952 as govt-owned Taiwan Salt Works; reorganized as Taiwan Salt Industrial Corpn in 1995; renamed Taiwan Salt Co in 2002; privatized in 2003; current name adopted 2004; mfrs of salt, packaged water, and health and beauty products based on sea-water extracts; cap. and res 9,677.7m., revenue 1,980.1m. (2009); Chair. HUNG HSI-YAO; 550 employees.

Yuen Foong Yu Paper Manufacturing Co Ltd: 4/F, 51 Chung Ching South Rd, Sec. 2, Taipei 10075; tel. (2) 23961166; fax (2) 23966771; e-mail webmaster@yfy.com.tw; internet www.yfy.com.tw; f. 1950; mfr of paper products; cap. 16,037m., revenue 41,800m. (2009); Pres. S. C. HO; 9,454 employees.

TRADE UNIONS

Chinese Federation of Labour: 4/F, 177 Roosevelt Rd, Sec. 3, Taipei 10647; tel. (2) 23660111; fax (2) 23696111; e-mail cfl.labor@msa.hinet.net; internet www.cfl.org.tw; f. 1948; comprises 53 feds of unions representing more than 1m. workers; Pres. CHIEH CHEN.

Principal Federations

Chunghwa Postal Workers' Union: 9/F, 45 Chungking South Rd, Sec. 2, Taipei 10075; tel. (2) 23921380; fax (2) 23563611; e-mail neeko.chang@gmail.com; internet www.cpwu.org.tw; f. 1930; fmrly Chinese Federation of Postal Workers; restructuring completed July 2003; 24,000 mems; Chair. CHIANG TZU-CHEN.

National Chinese Seamen's Union: 8/F, 25 Nanking East Rd, Sec. 3, Taipei 10487; tel. (2) 25150259; fax (2) 25078211; e-mail ncsu.seamen@msa.hinet.net; internet www.ncsu.org.tw; f. 1913; 21,520 mems (June 2005); Pres. SUN ZHEYING.

Taiwan Federation of Labour: 92 Sungann Rd, Sec.1, Taichung 40650; tel. (4) 22309009; fax (2) 22309012; e-mail tpfl@ms39.hinet.net; internet www.tpfl.org.tw; f. 1948; 49 mem. unions and 1,417,816 individual mems; Pres. CHEN JEA; Sec.-Gen. JING-HUNG CHEN.

Taiwan Railway Labor Union: Rm 6044, 6/F, 3 Peiping West Rd, Taipei 10041; tel. (2) 23815226; fax (2) 23896134; e-mail ch.trlu@msa.hinet.net; internet www.trlu.org.tw; f. 1947; 15,579 mems; Pres. CHEN HAN-CHIN.

Transport

RAILWAYS

Taiwan Railway Administration (TRA): 3 Peiping West Rd, Taipei 10041; tel. (2) 23815226; fax (2) 23831367; internet www.railway.gov.tw; f. 1891; public utility under the Ministry of Transportation and Communications; operates both the west line and east line systems, with a route length of 1,101.5 km; Dir-Gen. FRANK FAN.

Taipei Rapid Transit Corpn (TRTC): 7 Lane 48, Zhong Shan North Rd, Sec. 2, Taipei 10448; tel. (2) 25363001; fax (2) 25115003; e-mail email@mail.trtc.com.tw; internet www.trtc.com.tw; f. 1994; 90.5 km (incl. 10.5 km medium-capacity rail) open, with further lines under construction; also operates the Maokong Gondola cable car system; Chair. LIN CHUNG-YIH; Pres. Dr TSAY HUEL-SHENG.

Taiwan High Speed Rail Corpn (THSRC): 3/F, 100 Hsin Yi Rd, Taipei 110; tel. (2) 40666600; fax (2) 66268866; internet www.thsrc.com.tw; f. 1996; operates 345-km high-speed rail link between Taipei and Kaohsiung; Chair. and CEO OU CHIN-DER.

An Airport Rail System linking Taipei with Taiwan Taoyuan International Airport is under construction by the Ministry of Transportation and Communications; this is due for completion in 2012.

ROADS

There were 39,286 km of highways in 2006, most of them asphalt-paved. The Sun Yat-sen Freeway, linking Taipei, Keelung and Kaohsiung, was completed in 1978. Construction of a 505-km Second Freeway, which was to extend to Pingtung, in southern Taiwan, was completed in 2004. The Nantou branch, from the Wufeng system interchange of the Second Freeway to Puli in central Taiwan, with a length of 38 km, was completed in 2008. The 31-km Taipei–Ilan freeway and its 24.1-km extension, from Toucheng to Suao, were completed in 2005.

Directorate-General of Highways: 70 Chung Hsiao West Rd, Sec. 1, Taipei 10041; tel. (2) 23113456; fax (2) 23111644; e-mail thbu10z7@ms1.gsn.gov.tw; internet www.thb.gov.tw; Dir-Gen. WU MEN-FENG.

Kuo-Kuang Motor Transport Co Ltd: 4/F, 17 Hsu Chang St, Taipei 10047; tel. (2) 23810731; fax (2) 23810268; internet www.kingbus.com.tw; f. 2001; operates national bus service; Chair. LEE HONG-SEN.

Taiwan Area National Expressway Engineering Bureau: 1 Lane 1, Hoping East Rd, Sec. 3, Taipei 10669; tel. (2) 27078808; fax (2) 27017818; e-mail neebeyes@taneeb.gov.tw; internet www.taneeb.gov.tw; f. 1990; responsible for planning, design, construction and maintenance of provincial and county highways; Dir-Gen. BANE L. B. CHJOU.

Taiwan Area National Freeway Bureau: 70 Banshanya, Liming Village, Taishan Township, Taipei County 24303; tel. (2) 29096141; fax (2) 29093218; e-mail tanfb1@freeway.gov.tw; internet www.freeway.gov.tw; f. 1970; Dir-Gen. TSENG DAR-JEN.

SHIPPING

Taiwan has seven international ports: Anping, Kaohsiung, Keelung, Taichung, Hualien, Suao and Taipei. In December 2009 the merchant fleet comprised 641 vessels, with a total displacement of 2,636,000 grt. Some of the main shipping companies are as follows:

Evergreen International Storage & Transport Corpn: 899 Ching Kuo Rd, Taoyuan 3305; tel. (3) 3252060; fax (3) 3252059; e-mail mgt@evergreen-eitc.com.tw; internet www.evergreen-eitc.com.tw; Chair. YE JIONG-CHAO.

Evergreen Marine Corpn (Taiwan) Ltd: Evergreen Bldg, 166 Minsheng East Rd, Sec. 2, Taipei 10423; tel. (2) 25057766; fax (2) 25058159; e-mail mgt@evergreen-marine.com; internet www.evergreen-marine.com; f. 1968; world-wide container liner services; Chair. CHANG YUNG-FA; Pres. WANG LONG-SHUNG.

Taiwan Navigation Co Ltd: 2–6/F, 29 Chi Nan Rd, Sec. 2, Taipei 10054; tel. (2) 23927177; fax (2) 23936578; e-mail tnctpe@taiwanline.com.tw; internet www.taiwanline.com.tw; Chair. ZHANG YIYUAN; Pres. SHENGQING WU.

U-Ming Marine Transport Corpn: 29/F, Taipei Metro Tower, 207 Tun Hua South Rd, Sec. 2, Taipei 10602; tel. (2) 27338000; fax (2) 27359900; e-mail uming@metro.feg.com.tw; internet www.uming.com.tw; world-wide transportation services; Chair. TSAI HSIUNG CHAN; Pres. C. K. ONG.

Wan Hai Lines Ltd: 10/F, 136 Sung Chiang Rd, Taipei 10485; tel. (2) 25677961; fax (2) 25216000; e-mail serv@wanhai.com.tw; internet www.wanhai.com.tw; f. 1965; regional container liner services; Chair. C. H. CHEN; Pres. P. T. CHEN.

Yang Ming Marine Transport Corpn (Yang Ming Line): 271 Ming De 1st Rd, Keelung 20646; tel. (2) 24559988; fax (2) 24559958; e-mail tara@yml.com.tw; internet www.yml.com.tw; f. 1972; world-wide container liner services, bulk carrier and supertanker services; Chair. FRANK LU; Pres. ROBERT HO.

CIVIL AVIATION

There are two international airports: Taiwan Taoyuan International Airport (formerly known as Chiang Kai-shek) near Taipei, which opened in 1979, a second passenger terminal and expansion of freight facilities being completed in 2000; and Kaohsiung International Airport, which also offers domestic services. There are 16 domestic airports, three of which offer international charter services.

Civil Aeronautics Administration: 340 Tun Hua North Rd, Taipei 10548; tel. (2) 23496000; fax (2) 23496277; e-mail gencaa@mail.caa.gov.tw; internet www.caa.gov.tw; Dir-Gen. YIN CHEN-PONG.

China Airlines Ltd (CAL): 131 Nanjing East Rd, Sec. 3, Taipei 10410; tel. (2) 27151212; fax (2) 25146004; e-mail ju-reng_chen@email.china-airlines.com; internet www.china-airlines.com; f. 1959; international services to destinations in the Far East, Europe, the Middle East, the USA and Australia; Chair. PHILIP HSING-HSIUNG WEI; Pres. SUN HUANG-HSIANG.

EVA Airways (EVA): Eva Air Bldg, 376 Hsin-nan Rd, Sec. 1, Luchu Township, Taoyuan County 33801; tel. (3) 3515151; fax (3) 3510023; e-mail prd@evaair.com; internet www.evaair.com; f. 1989; subsidiary of Evergreen Group; commenced flights in 1991; services to destinations in Asia, the Middle East, Europe, North America, Australia and New Zealand; Chair. LIN BOU-SHIU; Pres. JENG KUNG-YEUN.

Mandarin Airlines (MDA): 13/F, 134 Minsheng East Rd, Sec. 3, Taipei 10596; tel. (2) 27171188; fax (2) 27170716; e-mail mandarin@mandarin-airlines.com; internet www.mandarin-airlines.com; f. 1991; subsidiary of CAL; merged with Formosa Airlines 1999; domestic and regional services; Chair. HARRIS WANG.

TransAsia Airways (TNA): 9/F, 139 Chengchou Rd, Taipei 10341; tel. (2) 25575767; fax (2) 27913318; e-mail tna@tna.com.tw; internet www.tna.com.tw; f. 1951; fmrly Foshing Airlines; domestic and international services; Chair. LIN MING-SHENG; Gen. Man. CHEN JIA.

UNI Airways Corpn (UIA): 9/F, 100 Chang An East Rd, Sec. 2, Taipei 10491; tel. (2) 25135533; fax (2) 25133202; e-mail communication@uniair.com.tw; internet www.uniair.com.tw; f. 1989; fmrly Makung Airlines; merged with Great China Airlines and Taiwan Airlines 1998; domestic flights and international services (to Bali, Indonesia; Seoul, South Korea; Bangkok, Thailand; and Hanoi, Viet Nam); Chair. SU HOMNG-YIH; Pres. PETER CHEN.

Tourism

The attractions of Taiwan include the island's scenery and cultural heritage. In 2010 visitor arrivals (including Overseas Chinese) were estimated to have increased by 27% to reach almost 5.6m. Revenue from tourism in 2009 reached US $6,816m. The relaxation of official restrictions on the numbers of mainland Chinese visitors has led to a substantial increase in arrivals from the People's Republic.

Tourism Bureau, Ministry of Transportation and Communications: 9/F, 290 Chung Hsiao East Rd, Sec. 4, Taipei 10694; tel. (2) 23491500; fax (2) 27717036; e-mail tbroc@tbroc.gov.tw; internet taiwan.net.tw; f. 1972; Dir-Gen. JANICE LAI.

Taiwan Visitors Association: 5/F, 9 Min Chuan East Rd, Sec. 2, Taipei 10470; tel. (2) 25943261; fax (2) 25943265; internet www.tva.org.tw; f. 1956; promotes domestic and international tourism; Chair. CHANG SHUO LAO.

Defence

As assessed at November 2010, the armed forces totalled an estimated 290,000: army 200,000, navy 45,000 (including 15,000 marines), and air force 45,000. Paramilitary forces totalled 17,000. Reserves numbered 1,657,000. Military service is for 12 months.

Defence Expenditure: Budgeted at NT $297,000m. for 2011.

Chief of the General Staff: Adm. LIN CHEN-YI.

Commander of the Army: Gen. YANG TIEN-HSIAO.

Commander of the Navy: Adm. LONG DONG-XIANG.

Commander of the Air Force: Gen. YEN MING.

Education

Pre-school education is optional, although in 2008/09 a total of 182,049 children were attending kindergarten. In 2009/10 1,519,456 pupils attended primary school, and a total of 1,682,958 pupils were enrolled in secondary (including vocational) education. There are three types of secondary school: junior high, senior high and senior vocational. The net enrolment ratio for children between the ages of six and 14 was 100.2% in 2008. In 2009/10 there were 163 universities, junior colleges and independent colleges. Most of these offer postgraduate facilities. A total of 1,343,603 students were enrolled in higher education in 2009/10. The Government's budgetary expenditure on education in 2008 was NT $492,370.1m.

ELEMENTARY AND SECONDARY EDUCATION

Education is compulsory for only nine years—six years at primary school (between the ages of five and 11 years) and a further three years at junior high school (between the ages of 11 and 14 years).

Senior high schools, which offer a three-year programme, admit junior high school graduates and prepare them for higher education. Vocational schools also offer a three-year programme, and provide training in agriculture, fishery, commerce and industry, etc.

HIGHER AND ADULT EDUCATION

The great majority of higher education courses last four years. Junior colleges provide courses of between two and five years' duration.

In 1987 the nine teachers' junior colleges were upgraded to teachers' colleges. These admit senior secondary graduates for a four-year course. High school teachers are trained at normal universities.

In adult education, the main aim has been to raise the literacy rate and standard of general knowledge. In 2008/09 there were 834 supplementary schools, with a total enrolment of 240,392. Chinese language, general knowledge, arithmetic, music and vocational skills are taught. Radio and television are an important component in the expansion of education. The National Education Radio is supervised by the Ministry of Education to broadcast cultural and educational programmes.

Bibliography

See also the Bibliography of the People's Republic of China

General

Alagappa, Muthiah (Ed.). *Taiwan's Presidential Politics: Democratization and Cross-Strait Relations in the 21st Century*. Armonk, NY, M. E. Sharpe, 2001.

Andrade, Tonio. *How Taiwan Became Chinese: Dutch, Spanish and Han Colonization in the Seventeenth Century*. New York, Columbia University Press, 2007.

Aspalter, Christian. *Democratization and Welfare State Development in Taiwan*. Aldershot, Ashgate, 2002.

Aspalter, Christian, and Kepler, Johannes. *Understanding Modern Taiwan: Essays in Economics, Politics, and Social Policy*. Aldershot, Ashgate, 2001.

Bullard, Monte. *The Soldier and the Citizen—The Role of the Military in Taiwan's Development*. Armonk, NY, M. E. Sharpe, 1997.

Cai, Kevin G. *Cross-Taiwan Straits Relations Since 1979: Policy Adjustment and Institutional Change Across the Straits*. Singapore, World Scientific Publishing, 2011.

Cauquelin, Josiane. *Aborigines of Taiwan—The Puyuma: From Headhunting to the Modern World*. Abingdon, Routledge, 2011.

Chakrabarti, Sreemati, and Sharma, Anita (Eds). *Taiwan Today*. New Delhi, Anthem Press, 2007.

Chang, David, and Williams, Jack. *Taiwan's Environmental Struggle: Toward a Green Silicon Island*. Abingdon, Routledge, 2008.

Chase, Michael S. *Taiwan's Security Policy: External Threats and Domestic Politics*. Boulder, CO, Lynne Rienner Publishers, 2008.

Chi Su. *Taiwan's Relations with Mainland China: A Tail Wagging Two Dogs*. Abingdon, Routledge, 2010.

Chin Ko-Lin. *Heijin: Organized Crime, Business, and Politics in Taiwan*. Armonk, NY, M. E. Sharpe, 2003.

Ching Cheong. *Will Taiwan Break Away: The Rise of Taiwanese Nationalism*. Singapore, World Scientific Publishing, 2001.

Ching, Leo T. S. *Becoming 'Japanese': Colonial Taiwan and the Politics of Identity Formation*. Berkeley, University of California Press, 2001.

Cole, Bernard D. *Taiwan's Security: History and Prospects*. Abingdon, Routledge, 2005.

Copper, John F. *China Diplomacy: The Washington-Taipei-Beijing Triangle*. Boulder, CO, Westview Press, 1993.

Words Across The Taiwan Straits. Lanham, MD, University Press of America, 1995.

Taiwan: Nation-State or Province? Boulder, CO, Westview Press, 1999.

As Taiwan Approaches the New Millennium. Lanham, MD, University Press of America, 2002.

Corcuff, Stephane (Ed.). *Memories of the Future: National Identity Issues and the Search for a New Taiwan*. Armonk, NY, M. E. Sharpe, 2002.

Costa, Meredith A., and Silva, Jeremy P. (Eds). *China, Taiwan & the Evolution of 'One China' Policy*. Hauppage, NY, Nova Science Publishers, 2011.

Crozier, Brian. *The Man Who Lost China: The First Full Biography of Chiang Kai-Shek*. London, Angus and Robertson, 1977.

Damm, Jens, and Schubert, Gunter. *Taiwanese Identity from Domestic, Regional and Global Perspectives*. Munster, Lit Verlag, 2008.

Dell'Orto, Alessandro. *Place and Spirit in Taiwan*. Richmond, Surrey, Curzon Press, 2002.

Edmonds, Martin, and Tsai, Michael (Eds). *Defending Taiwan: The Future Vision of Taiwan's Defence Policy and Military Strategy*. London, RoutledgeCurzon, 2002.

Taiwan's Maritime Security. London, RoutledgeCurzon, 2002.

Taiwan's Security and Air Power. London, RoutledgeCurzon, 2003.

Edmonds, Richard L., and Goldstein, Steven M. (Eds). *Taiwan in the Twentieth Century: A Retrospective*. New York, Cambridge University Press, 2001.

Fell, Dafydd. *Party Politics in Taiwan: Party Change and the Democratic Evolution of Taiwan, 1991–2004*. Abingdon, Routledge, 2005.

Government and Politics in Taiwan. Abingdon, Routledge, 2011.

Fell, Dafydd (Ed.) *Politics of Modern Taiwan*. Abingdon, Routledge, 2008.

Fenby, Jonathan. *Generalissimo: Chiang Kai-shek and the China he Lost*. New York, NY, Free Press, 2003.

Friedman, Edward (Ed.) *China's Rise, Taiwan's Dilemmas and International Peace*. Abingdon, Routledge, 2005.

Garver, John W. *The Sino-American Alliance—Nationalist China and American Cold War Strategy in Asia*. Armonk, NY, M. E. Sharpe, 1997.

Guilloux, Alain. *Taiwan, Humanitarianism and Global Governance*. Abingdon, Routledge, 2009.

Herschensohn, Bruce. *Taiwan: the Threatened Democracy*. Torrance, CA, World Ahead Publishing, 2007.

Herschensohn, Bruce. (Ed.). *Across the Taiwan Strait: Democracy: The Bridge Between Mainland China and Taiwan*. Lanham, MD, Lexington, 2002.

Hickey, Dennis Van Vranken. *Foreign Policy Making in Taiwan: From Principle to Pragmatism*. Abingdon, Routledge, 2006.

Hsiau A-Chin. *Contemporary Taiwanese Cultural Nationalism*. London, Routledge, 2000.

Hsu Long-Hsuen, and Chang Ming-Kai. *History of the Sino-Japanese War*. Chung Wu Publishing Co, 1971.

Hua, Shiping. *Reflections on the Triangular Relations of Beijing-Taipei-Washington Since 1995: Status Quo at the Taiwan Straits?* Basingstoke, Palgrave Macmillan, 2006.

Huang, Junjie. *Taiwan in Transformation, 1895–2005: the Challenge of a New Democracy to an Old Civilization*. New Brunswick, NJ, Transaction Publishers, 2006.

Lan, Pei-Chia. *Global Cinderellas: Migrant Domestics and Newly Rich Employers in Taiwan*. Durham, NC, Duke University Press, 2006.

Lasater, Martin L., Yu, Peter Kien-Hong, Hsu, Kuang-Min, and Lym, Robyn (Eds). *Taiwan's Security in the Post-Deng Xiaoping Era*. London, Frank Cass, 2001.

Lee, Bernice. *The Security Implications of the New Taiwan*. Abingdon, Routledge, 2005.

Lee, David Tawei. *The Making of the Taiwan Relations Act: Twenty Years in Retrospect*. Oxford, Oxford University Press, 2000.

Leng Shao-chuan (Ed.). *Chiang Ching-Kuo's Leadership in the Development of the Republic of China on Taiwan*. Lanham, MD, University Press of America, 1994.

Lo, Chang-fa. *The Legal Culture and System of Taiwan*. Alphen aan den Rijn, Kluwer Law International, 2006.

Manthorpe, Jonathan. *Forbidden Nation: a History of Taiwan*. Basingstoke, Palgrave Macmillan, 2005.

Marsh, Robert M. *The Great Transformation—Social Change in Taipei, Taiwan Since the 1960s*. Armonk, NY, M. E. Sharpe, 1996.

Medeiros, Evan S., Swaine, Michael D., and Yang, Andrew N.D. (Eds). *Assessing the Threat: the Chinese Military and Taiwan's Security*. Washington, DC, Carnegie Endowment for International Peace, 2007.

Ngo, T. W., and Wang, Hong-zen (Eds). *Politics of Difference in Taiwan*. Abingdon, Routledge, 2011.

Rawnsley, Gary D. *Taiwan's Informal Diplomacy and Propaganda*. New York, St Martin's Press, 2000.

Rigger, Shelley. *Politics in Taiwan*. London, Routledge, 1999.

From Opposition to Power: Taiwan's Democratic Progressive Party. Boulder, CO, Lynne Rienner Publishers, 2001.

Taiwan's Rising Rationalism: Generations, Politics, and 'Taiwanese Nationalism'. Washington, DC, East-West Center Washington, 2006.

Why Taiwan Matters: From Small Island to Global Powerhouse. Lanham, MD, Rowman & Littlefield Publishers, 2011.

Roy, Denny. *Taiwan: A Political History*. Ithaca, NY, Cornell University Press, 2003.

Rubinstein, Murray A. (Ed.). *Taiwan: A New History—Expanded Edition*. Armonk, NY, M. E. Sharpe, 2006.

Shambaugh, David (Ed.). *Contemporary Taiwan*. Oxford, Clarendon Press, 1998.

Sheng, Lijun. *China's Dilemma: The Taiwan Issue*. London, I. B. Tauris, 2001.

Cross-Strait Relations Under Chen Shui-bian. Singapore, Institute of Southeast Asian Studies, 2002.

Shlapak, David A., et al. *A Question of Balance—Political Context and Military Aspects of the China–Taiwan Dispute*. Washington, DC, RAND Corpn, 2009.

Su, Chi. *Taiwan's Relations with Mainland China: A Tail Wagging Two Dogs.* New York, Routledge, 2008.

Swaine, Michael. *Taiwan: Foreign and Defense Policymaking 2001.* Santa Monica, CA, Rand, 2001.

Tan, Alexander C., Chan, Steven, and Jillson, Calvin (Eds). *Taiwan's National Security: Dilemmas and Opportunities.* Aldershot, Ashgate, 2001.

Taylor, Jay. *The Generalissimo's Son: Chiang Ching-Kuo and the Revolutions in China and Taiwan.* Cambridge, MA, Harvard University Press, 2000.

Tehpen, Tsai. *Elegy of Sweet Potatoes: Stories of Taiwan's White Terror.* Irvine, CA, Taiwan Publishing Company, 2003.

Teng, Emma Jinhua. *Taiwan's Imagined Geography: Chinese Colonial Travel Writing and Pictures, 1683-1895.* Cambridge, MA, Harvard University Press, 2004.

Tian, John Q. *Government, Business, and the Politics of Interdependence and Conflict across the Taiwan Strait.* Basingstoke, Palgrave Macmillan, 2006.

Tsai, Hui-yu Caroline. *Taiwan in Japan's Empire-Building.* Abingdon, Routledge, 2008.

Tsai, Shih-Shan Henry. *Maritime Taiwan: Historical Encounters with the East and the West.* Armonk, NY, M. E. Sharpe, 2009.

Tsang, Steve. *Peace and Security Across the Taiwan Strait.* Basingstoke, Palgrave Macmillan, 2004.

Tsang, Steve (Ed.). *Political Developments in Taiwan since 1949.* Honolulu, HI, University of Hawaii Press, 1993.

If China Attacks Taiwan: Military Strategy, Politics and Economics. Abingdon, Routledge, 2005.

Tunsjø, Øystein. *US Taiwan Policy: Constructing the Triangle.* Abingdon, Routledge, 2008.

Tucker, Nancy Bernkopf. *United States-Taiwan Relations and the Crisis with China.* Cambridge, MA, Harvard University Press, 2009.

Tubilewicz, Czeslaw. *Taiwan and Post-Communist Europe: Shopping for Allies.* Abingdon, Routledge, 2008.

Wachman, Alan W. *Taiwan: National Identity and Democratization.* Armonk, NY, M. E. Sharpe, 1994.

Why Taiwan?: Geostrategic Rationales for China's Territorial Integrity. Stanford, CA, Stanford University Press, 2007.

Wakeman, Frederic E. *Spymaster: Dai Li and the Chinese Secret Service.* Berkeley, CA, University of California Press, 2003.

Wang, Gabe T. *China and the Taiwan Issue: Incoming War at Taiwan Strait.* Lanham, MD, University Press of America, 2006.

Weller, Robert P. *Discovering Nature: Globalization and Environmental Culture in China and Taiwan.* Cambridge, Cambridge University Press, 2006.

Wong, Joseph. *Healthy Democracies: Welfare Politics in Taiwan and South Korea.* Ithaca, NY, Cornell University Press, 2006.

Zheng, Yongnian, and Wu, Raymond Ray-Kuo (Eds). *Sources of Conflict and Cooperation in the Taiwan Strait.* World Scientific Publishing, 2006.

Economy

Aberbach, Joel D., Dollar, David, and Sokoloff, Kenneth L. (Eds). *The Role of the State in Taiwan's Development.* Armonk, NY, M. E. Sharpe, 1995.

Ash, Robert, Garver, John W., and Prime, Penelope (Eds). *Taiwan's Democracy—Economic and Political Challenges.* Abingdon, Routledge, 2011.

Berger, Suzanne, and Lester, Richard K. (Eds). *Global Taiwan: Building Competitive Strengths in a New International Economy.* Armonk, NY, M. E. Sharpe, 2005.

Champion, Steven R. *The Great Taiwan Bubble: The Rise and Fall of an Emerging Stock Market.* Berkeley, CA, Pacific View Press, 1998.

Chang Chun-yen, Yu Po-lung, and Zhang Junyan (Eds). *Made By Taiwan: Booming in the Information Technology Era.* River Edge, NJ, World Scientific Publishing, 2001.

Chen Fen-Ling. *Working Women and State Policies in Taiwan: A Study in Political Economy.* Basingstoke, Palgrave Macmillan, 2000.

Chow, Peter Y. C., and Bates, Gill (Eds). *Weathering the Storm: Taiwan, Its Neighbours, and the Asian Financial Crisis.* Washington, DC, Brookings Institute Press, 2000.

Chow, Peter Y. C., and Liao, Kuang-sheng (Eds). *Taiwan in the Global Economy: From an Agrarian Economy to an Exporter of High-Tech Products.* New York, Praeger, 2002.

Dwyer, Gerald P. Jnr, Lin Jin-long, Shea Jia-dong and Wu Chung-shu (Eds). *Monetary Policy and Taiwan's Economy.* Northampton, MA, Edward Elgar Publishing, 2002.

Greene, J. Megan. *The Origins of the Developmental State in Taiwan: Science Policy and the Quest for Modernization.* Cambridge, MA, Harvard University Press, 2008.

Greene, J. Megan, and Ash, Robert (Eds). *Taiwan in the 21st Century: Aspects and Limitations of a Development Model.* Abingdon, Routledge, 2007.

Ho Yhi-Min. *Agricultural Development of Taiwan: 1903–1960.* Nashville, TN, Vanderbilt University Press, 1966.

Hsueh Li-Min, Hsu Chen-kuo, and Perkins, Dwight H. (Eds). *Industrialization and the State: The Changing Role of Government in Taiwan's Economy, 1945–1998.* Cambridge, MA, Harvard University Press, 2000.

Jacoby, N. H. *An Evaluation of US Economic Aid to Free China 1951–1965.* New York, Praeger, 1967.

Kuo, Shirley W. Y. *The Taiwan Economy in Transition.* Boulder, CO, Westview Press, 1983.

Kuo, Tai-Chun, and Myers, Ramon H. *Taiwan's Economic Transformation: Leadership, Property Rights and Institutional Change 1949–1965.* Abingdon, Routledge, 2011.

Lee, Joseph S. *The Labour Market and Economic Development of Taiwan.* Cheltenham, Edward Elgar Publishing, 2007.

Lee Teng-hui. *Intersectoral Capital Flows in the Economic Development of Taiwan 1895–1960.* Ithaca, NY, Cornell University Press, 1971.

Lei, Chung Kwok, and Yao, Shujie. *Economic Convergence in Greater China: Mainland China, Hong Kong, Macau and Taiwan.* Abingdon, Routledge, 2011.

Mai, Chao-cheng, and Shih, Chien-sheng (Eds). *Taiwan's Economic Success Since 1980.* Cheltenham, Edward Elgar Publishing, 2001.

Ranis, Gustav, Chu Yun-peng and Hu Sheng-cheng (Eds). *The Political Economy of Taiwan's Development Into the 21st Century.* Cheltenham, Edward Elgar Publishing, 1999.

THAILAND

Physical and Social Geography

HARVEY DEMAINE

The Kingdom of Thailand (formerly Siam) occupies the centre of the South-East Asian mainland, bordered by Myanmar (Burma) to the west, by Laos and Cambodia to the east and by peninsular Malaysia to the south. Its total area is 513,120 sq km (198,117 sq miles). Most of this territory lies to the north of the Bight of Bangkok, and hence well removed from the main shipping routes across the South China Sea between Singapore and Hong Kong, though peninsular Thailand, extending south to the Malaysian border approximately at latitude 6°N, has a coastline of some 960 km facing the Gulf of Thailand, and a somewhat shorter one facing the Andaman Sea. Between these two the peninsula narrows at the isthmus of Kra to a straight-line distance of only 56 km between salt water on both sides.

PHYSICAL AND CLIMATIC ENVIRONMENT

Apart from peninsular Thailand, which (except in the far south) consists of mainly narrow coastal lowlands backed by low and well-wooded mountain ranges, the country comprises four main upland tracts—in the west, north, north-east and south-east—surrounding a large central plain drained by the principal river, the Menam Chao Phraya. Because of its position, while experiencing tropical temperatures throughout its entire area, Thailand receives relatively less rainfall than either Myanmar to the west or most parts of Indo-China to the east. In general, rainfall is highest in the south and south-east, and in the uplands of the west and, to some extent, in the higher hills in the north, but most of the rest of the country, in effect, constitutes a rain-shadow area where the total annual fall is below 1,500 mm.

The western hills are formed by a series of north–south ridges, thickly covered by tropical monsoon forest with much bamboo, and drained by the Kwei Noi and Kwei Yai rivers. Although summit levels here are only of the order of 600 m–900 m, the ridge-and-furrow pattern makes this generally inhospitable country. In the northern uplands, which represent the southernmost portion of the great Yunnan-Shan-Laos plateau, altitudes are higher than in the west, reaching an upper limit of about 1,500 m, and the upland surface is fairly well forested, although the natural cover has clearly deteriorated in many areas as a result of shifting cultivation. However, in the four parallel valleys of the Ping, Wang, Yom and Nan rivers, which flow through these uplands and subsequently converge farther south to form the Chao Phraya, there are relatively broad lowlands with a more open vegetation, now largely cleared for rice cultivation.

The north-eastern plateau, also known as the Khorat plateau, is mostly of much lower altitude than the above two uplands. On its western and southern edges it presents a continuous rim usually exceeding 300 m, and in places much higher than that, but elsewhere it consists of a relatively low and undulating surface, draining eastwards, via the Nam Si and the Nam Mun, to the Mekong, which flows along its entire northern and eastern edge.

In contrast to most of the other uplands, the Khorat plateau is an area of barely adequate rain, which during the dry season presents a barren and desiccated appearance. Since the main rivers flowing across it rise within this same area of low rainfall, Khorat is less favourably placed in respect of irrigation water than the central plain, which, though likewise receiving an annual rainfall of less than 1,500 mm, is well watered by the Chao Phraya system.

Because of its focal position, its fertile alluvial soils and the well-developed system of natural waterways, the central plain forms by far the most important single region within the country; and within this region, the delta, which begins about 190 km from the coast, enjoys all these advantages to a more pronounced extent.

NATURAL RESOURCES

Thailand's main natural resources lie in its agricultural potential, and in particular in the capacity of the central plain (and to a lesser extent the Khorat plateau) to produce a significant surplus of rice. In addition, from the late 1950s substantial areas of upland were opened up for the cultivation of maize, cassava (tapioca), kenaf (upland jute), beans and, subsequently, cotton and pineapple. The more humid and more truly equatorial coastal plains of the southern peninsula of Thailand similarly expanded their production of rubber. Unfortunately, this expansion was very much at the expense of the country's timber resources, which contracted sharply, with the once famous teak of the northern hills now in extremely short supply.

Tin was traditionally the most important mineral extracted, but this was subsequently superseded as an export by gypsum. Various other minerals, including manganese, tungsten, lignite, silver, gold, antimony and iron ore are mined. Phosphate, granite and limestone are also extracted. In addition, massive rock-salt deposits underlie the Khorat plateau. The country's heavy dependence on energy imports began to lessen, following the exploitation of reserves of natural gas in the Gulf of Thailand. Gas reserves were estimated to total some 300,000m. cu m at the end of 2010. Onshore gas discoveries have been made in the Nam Phong area of Khonkaen province, on the north-east plateau. Petroleum deposits were first identified in the north-central plain province of Kamphaengphet. At the end of 2010 total petroleum reserves were estimated at about 400m. barrels.

POPULATION

According to the census of 1 April 2000, the population totalled 60,606,947, increasing to a provisionally estimated total of 65,400,000 at the census of 1 September 2010, the average density in the latter year being 127.5 per sq km. Although average densities decline to between one-quarter and one-half of this in the west and north, the total area of really sparsely populated upland is small. The proportion formed by indigenous minority peoples is low. Apart from a concentration of Muslim Malays in the far south, a smaller number of Cambodians near the eastern borders and some remaining scattered hill peoples (Meo, Lahu, Yao, Lisu, Lawa, Lolo and Kayin or Karen), located mainly in the far north and west, virtually the entire indigenous population belongs to the Thai ethnic group (which also includes the Shan and Lao) and subscribes to Buddhism, predominantly of the Hinayana (Theravada) form. However, the inhabitants of the north-east tend to be closer in speech and custom to the Lao populations on the other side of the Mekong than to those of central Thailand. Excluding the Lao groups, historically the largest minority in Thailand was the ethnic Chinese, most of whom have been assimilated into the Thai culture and become Thai citizens.

Thailand shows only a relatively limited degree of urbanization. The urban scene is totally dominated by the single great complex of Bangkok Metropolis (including Thonburi), which had a population of 6,320,174 at 1 April 2000. According to UN estimates, the population of Bangkok Metropolis had risen to 6,976,000 by mid-2010.

History

RUTH MCVEY

Revised by PATRICK JORY and for this edition by JIRAWAT SAENGTHONG

PREHISTORY AND EARLY PERIOD

Archaeological findings show very ancient civilizations to have existed in what is now Thailand, but the earliest evidence of the Thai people is as part of a population speaking related languages and inhabiting mountainous areas of what is now Yunnan Province in the People's Republic of China. These Thai-speaking groups gradually spread southward into the highland areas of present-day Laos, northern Viet Nam, north-eastern Myanmar (Burma) and northern Thailand, where many preserved their identity as 'hill tribes'. The mountainous terrain in which they lived ensured that their polities remained small and simply organized, but in some river valleys of northern Thailand the development of irrigated rice cultivation led to relatively dense population and complex states controlling water distribution systems. Southward migration of these people brought them to the edge of the great central plain of the Chao Phraya river system; there, in AD 1238, they established the first historical Thai (Siamese) Kingdom of Sukothai.

Sukothai was initially subject to the major mainland power, the Khmer (Cambodian) empire of Angkor, but the growth of its population enabled it to express an increasingly Thai character and finally to assert independence under King Ramkamheng (reigned 1283–c. 1317). He extended the Kingdom's influence against both the Khmers and the Mons to the south and west, establishing Thai power over the central plain and making it a major element in the South-East Asian state system. Ramkamheng was also credited with establishing the standard Thai writing system, which was derived, under Mon and Khmer influence, from Indian scripts, reflecting the great prestige that Indian culture and statecraft had for the ancient civilizations of South-East Asia. The religion of Sukothai was Hinayana (Theravada) Buddhism, which spread initially from Sri Lanka and became the dominant faith of the major population groups of mainland South-East Asia.

The continued southward movement of the Thais on to the central plain brought the establishment in the mid-14th century of a new centre of Siamese power, called Ayudhya, at a point on the Chao Phraya river attainable by sea-going vessels. In 1368 Angkor was conquered and Siam was established as a power with interests in Cambodia. Ayudhya's great King Trailok (reigned 1448–88) pursued the extension against the Burmese to the west, Thai principalities in the north and Malay sultanates in the southern peninsula. He greatly strengthened Siamese state organization, making the first efforts to centralize a bureaucratic structure and ranking system and to codify customary rules into law. None the less, Ayudhya's power was diffuse by modern standards, resting, as in the earliest Thai states, on the ability of a population centre (*muang*), under its lord (*chao muang*), to enforce authority over, and extract tribute from, the rural areas around it. Those who commanded larger resources in population and wealth, usually by virtue of strategic location on a river system that enabled them to control trade, established themselves as overlords; the strongest of these might make himself king. However, the monarch's control remained uncertain, and the borders of the kingdoms shifted according to the central *muang's* ability to exact loyalty from its more distant tributaries.

Ayudhya's position on the central river, near enough to the sea to become involved in the developing trade between Europe and the Far East, gave it a particular advantage in the accumulation of power. The Portuguese, then the dominant European power in South-East Asia, sent a mission to Siam soon after their conquest of Melaka (Malacca) in 1511; thereafter, Ayudhya became increasingly involved in European rivalries until, under King Narai (1657–88), it accepted a French military mission. Narai's death brought a reaction against the involvement with foreigners and inaugurated a long period of isolation. Ayudhya's reduced resources and unstable leadership enabled rising Burmese power to challenge it, and in 1767 the city was laid waste.

EMERGENCE OF A MODERN STATE

On Ayudhya's fall, a new Thai state centre was founded by the Chinese commander Taksin at Thonburi, near the mouth of the Chao Phraya. He was overthrown in 1782 by the house of Chakri, and the capital was transferred across the river to Bangkok. The early Chakri kings were anxious to consolidate Thai power against Burmese and, increasingly, European threats. They pressed the extension of Siamese authority over Laos, western Cambodia and the northern Malay states, and sought to strengthen the central administrative structure and to substitute tax farming for the older tributary system. This concern for increased efficiency received a forceful impetus in 1855, when the Bowring Treaty, imposed by the British, deprived Thai rulers of important income from tolls and monopolies on foreign trade. Under Kings Mongkut (Rama IV, 1851–68) and Chulalongkorn (Rama V, 1868–1910), interest in Western technology and ideas grew rapidly among the royal and noble élite. Chulalongkorn was able to implement a major reorganization of the state, which substituted a modern centralized bureaucracy and fiscal system for the traditional *chao muang* arrangement.

Through its internal reforms and concessions to European interests, Siam was able to maintain formal independence, but it had to concede to France its claims to suzerainty over Laos and western Cambodia, and to the United Kingdom its claims over the Malay states of Kedah, Perlis, Kelantan and Trengganu. In order to placate the Europeans, to improve its expertise, and to finance economic and administrative modernization, Siam sought foreign loans and accepted European and US advisers in important governmental posts. It attempted to prevent any one country from having predominance, but, as the United Kingdom was by far the strongest power in the region, it fell effectively within the British sphere of influence.

However, although Siam suffered under unequal relationships, it prospered with the development of the international rice trade, which provided the major source of finance for the modern Thai state. The extension of rice lands led to a rapid expansion of settlement throughout the central Thai plain. Bangkok developed into a major trading centre, in which (as in colonized South-East Asia) European firms dominated large-scale international activity and Chinese immigrants took roles as shopkeepers, intermediaries and labourers. Central control over Siam's remaining territories was strengthened, but not without alienating people in the north, north-east and south who were still loyal to their customary chiefs. Although unrest was rigorously suppressed in 1902, Bangkok's authority in these regions never penetrated as deeply as in the central plain.

The bureaucracy that was developed to administer the new Siam consisted, in part, of people drawn from the old nobility and partly of commoners recruited through a rapidly expanding modern educational system. Influenced by Western ideas of progress and efficiency, its members soon acquired an ethos that was at variance with the principle of royal absolutism and patronage. In 1912 an attempt by young army officers to overthrow King Wachirawut (Rama VI, 1910–25), in favour of a republic, had already revealed the potential for a rift between royal authority and the new bureaucratic élite. King Wachirawut responded by identifying royalty with the new ideological force of nationalism: 'Nation, Religion, King' became, and remained, the central patriotic slogan. This preserved the royal symbol but not, ultimately, royal power, as tensions between royal and bureaucratic authority culminated over financial stringencies that were imposed by the collapse of the international rice market during the Great Depression of the 1930s. In 1932 a bloodless coup brought to an end the absolute rule of King Prajadhipok (Rama VII, 1925–35).

MILITARY-BUREAUCRATIC RULE, 1932–44

The 'Revolution' of 1932 was led by European-educated radicals of lesser noble rank, Pridi Phanomyang and Maj. (later Marshal) Phibun Songkhram, and by the highest-ranking military officer of commoner background, Col Phahon Phonphayuhasena. The leaders of this faction saw themselves as representing the Thai public interest, but they were very much divided as to what this entailed beyond substituting their own wisdom for that of royalty in managing national affairs. Pridi presented an economic plan that emphasized land nationalization and the abolition of private trade; this probably owed as much to Thai absolutist traditions as to European socialist concepts. However, his programme antagonized the conservative members of the new ruling élite, who had increased their private wealth and financial security with Siam's economic development and the decline in royal prerogatives, and who were no more willing to entrust their welfare to socialism than they were to subject it to the royal whim. They allied with monarchist forces against Pridi, who was denounced as a communist and went into exile.

After a period of instability, a conservative constitutionalist regime was established under Phahon. However, real power lay increasingly with the radical Phibun Songkhram, who brought Pridi back to office; nevertheless, the illegality of communism was confirmed, parties were banned and press censorship was instituted. With little possibility of organizing popular support, civilian politicians could only represent competing factions within the Bangkok élite, and power increasingly rested with the army.

Neither Pridi nor other civilian radicals had tried to mobilize mass support while they had the opportunity, as there seemed to them little possibility that people might be aroused to follow anything but the dictates of local officials and customary chiefs. Thailand's great economic development had taken place without much change in its social structure at the mass level: peasants could plant more rice than previously with little alteration in organization or technology, and profits from the rice trade were such that the State could take its share and still allow the peasants enough to encourage them to produce a surplus. Moreover, the later Chakri kings had identified in peasant smallholders a source of social stability and therefore had limited such landholdings and the possibility of seizing land in payment of debt; this prevented a drastic rural upheaval akin to that experienced by Burma (now Myanmar) during the Great Depression. A certain amount of rural indebtedness and absentee landholding had occurred in the area near Bangkok, largely as a result of real estate investment by members of the capital's élite, but this inspired migration to the city rather than peasant protest.

Nor did there seem to be a basis for urban political mobilization. The only sizeable town was the capital; until the 1970s it surpassed other urban centres in size and importance to such an extent that it was the only place of any political significance. The working class was overwhelmingly Chinese; some of it was radical (indeed, a small communist party was established illegally in the early 1930s), but it was interested in Chinese affairs and had almost no involvement in Thai politics. A few journalists and writers formed a tiny intelligentsia, continuing a tradition of iconoclastic writing that had begun in the late 19th century and reached a high point in the 1920s under Wachirawut, when the King himself took to journalism to set forth his ideas and reply to his critics. However, whatever potential they had for influencing public opinion disappeared with the introduction of the new press laws. The independent middle class was overwhelmingly Chinese, uninterested in Thai intellectual affairs and anxious to avoid the displeasure of the officials on whom depended their chance of trade and their permission to stay in the country. All power and virtually all political participation lay with an élite employed in government service, and most particularly the military part of it. Politics became, in effect, a struggle for office and patronage by the powerful and their associates within the bureaucracy. Whether Thailand's outward form was constitutional or dictatorial, the basic locus of power and the means of exercising it changed little.

This 'bureaucratic polity' was inefficient as an administrative machine, since its members were more involved with internecine power struggles and the maintenance of patronage networks than they were in performing their duties. Conscious of this weakness, which they saw as evidence that Siam was insufficiently modernized, radical Thai leaders made more drastic efforts at renovation. Phibun, who became Prime Minister in 1938, took fascism as his model. He embarked on a militantly anti-Chinese and anti-Western campaign, encouraging a rise of Japanese influence, as a counter to the dominant British, and playing upon popular resentment at the Chinese minority's powerful economic position. Stressing his role as supreme leader and pioneer of a modern society, he changed the country's name from Siam to Thailand in 1939, decreed new words of greeting and imposed modes of dress that he considered modern. He acted ruthlessly against his opponents, encouraged the beginnings of state-sponsored industrialism in order to achieve autarchy in basic military supplies and took an expansionist course aimed at securing, with Japanese aid, the lands that had earlier been lost to the British and French.

In 1940 Thailand attacked Indo-China, then cut off from France by war, and, in a Japanese-sponsored settlement, acquired the Laotian lands west of the Mekong River and the north-western provinces of Cambodia. Japanese troops landed in peninsular Thailand in December 1941, and from there spread south to Malaya. Phibun chose to become Japan's ally, declaring war on the United Kingdom and the USA in January 1942. In 1943 Japan awarded Thailand two of the Shan states that had been incorporated into British Burma and the four states that Siam had been compelled to cede to Malaya.

The fact that Thailand experienced the war as an ally of Japan rather than under its military occupation meant that it underwent far less economic, social and political upheaval than that experienced by the other South-East Asian states. None the less, the war caused considerable privation, and, as it became evident that the Japanese were going to lose, it grew increasingly unpopular. Fortunately, some prominent Thais had always opposed the Japanese alignment, among them the ambassador to the USA, Seni Pramoj. With US help, he established the Free Thai movement, which made contact with Pridi, then regent for King Ananda (Rama VIII, 1935–46, still a child and at school in Switzerland). Pridi established an anti-Japanese resistance which enjoyed some immunity from the Thai authorities. In August 1944 Phibun was formally deposed by the National Assembly, and in September 1945 Seni Pramoj was named Prime Minister.

DEMOCRACY AND TURBULENCE, 1945–57

The initial post-war years brought considerable turmoil, particularly in the life of the capital, as times were hard and inflation rampant. The political system's principal element, the armed forces, had been removed by the failure of the Japanese alliance and by the need to maintain the good graces of the Allies. The civilian leaders were occupied with securing US support against extensive British demands for reparations (the lands that had been gained with Japanese aid were lost). Constitutional democracy was restored and the formation of political parties was permitted, but these groupings represented little more than the personal followers of politicians in the capital. They included the conservative Democrat Party (DP), which included among its adherents Seni Pramoj and his brother Kukrit. The parties were unable to discipline themselves, much less to agree on a common course of policy or to gain control over an increasingly corrupt and demoralized civil service.

In March 1946 Pridi became Prime Minister but, in spite of his long association with Phibun, he was still feared as a socialist by many conservatives. Phibun retained a strong following in the armed forces, which increased as he put himself forward as the spokesman for resentment at civilian corruption and mismanagement. In June the young King Ananda died in mysterious circumstances, and Phibun had a major role in assigning the blame to Pridi, who was forced to resign. In November 1947 the army seized power, in a coup led by Gen. (later Marshal) Phin Choonhavan. He acted on behalf of Phibun, who took power in his own name in April 1948.

One factor that emboldened Phibun was a shift in the international situation. Hitherto, he and the army had been the objects of Allied displeasure but, with the long period of mutual hostility between the USA and the USSR known as the 'Cold War' beginning, Burma apparently near collapse and Indo-China embroiled in revolution, Thailand seemed a possible centre of stability. In February 1949 an attempted coup by Pridi's supporters sent that leader into exile in China, before a bloodless coup by Phibun in November 1951 ended what remained of Thai democracy. The Constitution was abrogated, political parties were banned, radical leaders were imprisoned or executed and dissent was stifled. Thailand embarked upon a new international role as an anti-communist ally of the USA, receiving considerable US military and economic aid, and in 1954 becoming a founding member of the South-East Asian Treaty Organization (SEATO), which established its seat in Bangkok.

Political power in this period rested with a triumvirate composed of Phin, Phibun, and Phin's son-in-law, Gen. Phao Sriyanon, head of the police. Aside from the alliances consolidated by patronage and intermarriage among the country's leading military and bureaucratic families, there were informal (but increasingly close) relations between political powerholders and wealthy local Chinese. In the early days of his post-war rule Phibun had revived some of his economic nationalism and persecution of the Chinese minority, but in the economic boom that accompanied the Korean War (1950–53) the opportunity to profit from Chinese capital and expertise was too great to resist, and increasing numbers of generals joined the boards of directors of Chinese-managed enterprises. The Chinese themselves were becoming more assimilated, but the Thai élite remained overwhelmingly in control of the bureaucracy, through which they extracted tribute and gifts from the politically weak entrepreneurs.

Phibun found it difficult to defend his position against the ambitions of his associates, particularly the new Bangkok army head, Gen. (later Marshal) Sarit Thanarat. He attempted to recoup his position by changing the sources of his support: in 1955, after a trip to Europe and the USA, he restored free speech, allowed the formation of political parties and announced elections for 1957. These took place amid growing turbulence and accusations of corruption; the Government's victory resulted only in it being discredited, so blatantly was the vote manipulated. Sarit, who prudently avoided involvement in the campaign, used the opportunity to seize power, first installing the SEATO Secretary-General, Pote Sarasin, as Prime Minister and finally, in October 1958, assuming the leadership himself.

SARIT AND AUTHORITARIAN DEVELOPMENT, 1958–72

Sarit ended the brief democracy of the election campaign, and urged a restoration of traditional values, including (for the first time since the 1932 Revolution) an appeal for loyalty to the King, Bhumibol Adulyadej (Rama IX, who had succeeded to the throne in 1946). As it was no longer likely that royalty could challenge military rule, Sarit could restore it as a major element in a nationalist appeal for popular support. However, his cultural and political conservatism was accompanied by a conviction that Thailand should open itself to rapid economic modernization. He removed the limits on land-holding and welcomed foreign investment. The time was propitious, as US engagement in the Viet Nam War was creating the conditions for both an economic boom and profitable foreign involvement. Thailand rapidly became a major provider of US military bases and supplies, Bangkok was a rest-and-recreation centre for US troops and Thai troops were serving in the Indo-China campaign.

In the countryside, US-funded road-building for security purposes rapidly increased facilities for communications and transport; peasants became deeply involved in the money economy, moved to towns to seek construction work, or sought to give their children an education that would raise them above peasant status. Both in the cities and the countryside, the traditional social structures were weakening. In the cities the clash of cultures, generations and interests was more obvious, but the contrast was perhaps more serious in the countryside, as hitherto lightly ruled peasants and hill peoples in the distant provinces were confronted with officials who were determined to impose their will in the name of security and development. Rural resentment was encouraged by Chinese, Vietnamese and Pathet Lao aid to rebel groups in the north and north-east, but even in the southern peninsula unrest developed into rebellion. In 1965 a China-based Thai Patriotic Front proclaimed a 'war of national liberation', and by the end of the decade most of the provinces outside the central plain were, to some degree, insecure.

Sarit had died in 1963; he was discovered to have appropriated vast sums of public money, but the scandal was soon forgotten amid nostalgia for his despotic but highly successful rule. His successors, the duumvirate of Gen. Thanom Kittikachorn and Gen. Praphat Charusathien, were less dynamic leaders, although initially they prospered—not only because of the Indo-China War boom but also because of increasing Japanese investment in Thailand. In 1968 they sought to broaden their power base by means of a cautious revival of constitutional democracy. This drew more criticism than they had anticipated, and in November 1971 they again seized full power; by now, however, their authority was severely compromised.

The US Government's decision to withdraw from Viet Nam, following the signing of a peace agreement in January 1973, and to seek a rapprochement with China brought great uncertainty. The economic boom was ending, creating hardship in Bangkok, the population of the capital having been increased by the arrival of rural immigrants. The curtailment of the expansion of education and bureaucratic recruitment owing to lack of finance provoked considerable popular resentment. In rural areas, peasants were turning from rice to more profitable cash crops. In the more distant countryside, revolt was spreading. There was a general weariness of corrupt military rulers. Within the army itself, those outside the Thanom-Praphat faction resented their long separation from lucrative office, while within the faction annoyance grew at the slow rate of promotion and the inability of their leaders to address Thailand's problems.

THE 'DEMOCRATIC REVOLUTION', 1973–76

During 1972 student-led demonstrations began in protest at the regime. Army leaders outside the ruling faction came increasingly to feel that the military should withdraw from direct responsibility for rule, in order not to be identified with the unpopular economic measures any successor government would need to take. In October 1973, when Thanom and Praphat tried to halt the demonstrators by armed action, the army refused to support them. Additionally, King Bhumibol withdrew his support, thus depriving the duumvirate of any legitimacy. The military regime collapsed, and its leaders went into exile.

The upheaval of October 1973 was no more a revolution, in the sense of mass armed action, than had been the Revolution of 1932, but it also represented a new stage in the development of the Thai political system. The demonstrations that brought the downfall of military rule were only the beginning of three turbulent years of political participation. Not only students in the capital, but also those in the new provincial universities, demonstrated for social reform; organized under the National Student Centre of Thailand (NSCT), they presented increasingly radical demands to the Government and worked to organize peasants and labourers against economic exploitation and ill-treatment by officials. The peasants and workers were, in contrast to earlier democratic periods, receptive to urgings for organized action to secure redress: particularly in the central plain, peasants began to form farmers' associations and to send delegations to the capital. Workers in Bangkok's now numerous textile mills began to strike against the low pay and hard working conditions that had attracted international investment to Thai industry. Even the Buddhist monkhood, hitherto apolitical except for a generalized support for established authority, was caught up in the fervour. Younger monks, concerned at social inequality and at the growing secularism and materialism of modern Thai culture, urged the religious to protect the poor from injustice, and aided peasants in pressing their claims.

An interim administration under a university rector, Sanya Thammasak, was appointed by the King. A period of frenetic party formation culminated in elections in January 1975. With great difficulty—as none of the numerous parties had a working parliamentary majority—a coalition Government was formed under Kukrit Pramoj, who had broken with the DP, under his brother Seni, and now headed the Social Action Party (SAP). His administration lasted for less than a year; new elections in April 1976 brought Seni and the DP to power in a centre-right coalition, but this, too, proved unable to formulate, let alone execute, a coherent policy.

The general electoral trend was to the right, while the demands of the petitioners, strikers and demonstrators were increasingly radical. Most workers and peasants were still politically passive and either did not participate in elections or voted as directed by village headmen or district officials. An increasingly conservative trend in voting was accompanied by a disturbing rise in rural insurgency. Thais who had benefited from the recent economic development, and who had hoped for further reform, became alarmed at the gathering disorder and the possibility that economic collapse might endanger their hard-won prosperity. Increasingly, there was not only renewed conservatism in the middle classes, but sympathy for a radical-right response to leftist demands. Rightist mobilization was apparent even among the Buddhist monkhood, where Kittiwutto Bhikku, hitherto noted for his efforts at founding a socially relevant monastic educational system, broke with the Buddhist precept against taking life to announce that the slaying of communists was not a sin.

The parties themselves were poorly organized and still bound largely by ties of personal loyalty and patronage. However, for the first time they were active in the provinces as well as in the capital, and the DP, in particular, had consolidated a national following as the representative of conservative reform. Further to the right were parties composed of leading military and bureaucratic officials, as well as business people; the most important of these was the Chart Thai (Thai Nation) party, which centred on the heirs of the previous Phin-Phao-Phibun military clique. However, these parties were not merely military-bureaucratic factions, as the Thai élite was being drawn increasingly into business endeavours. A growing sector of the major businesses—particularly the banks—was now Thai-owned and confident enough to take an open role in politics. This directed the Thai right wing away from statist solutions; parties confronted economic dilemmas more seriously, while policy differences, as well as personal loyalties, determined the élite coalitions that formed the basis of the right.

Far weaker were the parties of the left. Led by intellectuals and with little popular appeal, they were undermined by the communists, who were pursuing victory by armed action, and by students and other militants who saw extra-parliamentary pressure as the way to achieve reform. From the right they were victimized by a rising trend of counter-revolutionary violence.

As civilian governments showed themselves unable even to keep order, military officers and their civilian allies became increasingly restive. Gen. Krit Siwara, who had become Army Commander-in-Chief just before the downfall of the Thanom-Praphat regime and had gained general acclaim for his refusal to fire upon the students, was unwilling to overthrow a constitutionalist system which he, as well as other moderate conservatives, regarded as the best ultimate guarantee of stability. While he vacillated, military rightists gave funds and encouragement to groups advocating mass action: the Nawaphon movement, of which Kittiwutto was a prominent advocate; the paramilitary Red Gaur squads; and the rural vigilantes of the Village Scout organization. All of these took the late King Wachirawut's motto of 'Nation, Religion, King' as their slogan, and stressed loyalty to the monarch as the basis of Thai nationalism.

REPRESSION AND RESTORATION, 1976–88

Krit's death in April 1976 accelerated the return to military rule, an increasingly popular solution as the urban middle classes came to regard authoritarian government as preferable to paralysis and disorder. A military-dominated National Administrative Reform Council took control, banning political parties, dissolving the National Assembly and establishing a Government headed by a right-wing Supreme Court judge, Thanin Kraivixien. Left-wing activists were arrested; many student leaders fled to the jungle, where they joined the communist forces. Labour unions, left-wing parties and farmers' associations were firmly suppressed, and the already marked level of violence against worker and peasant organizers rose, with officially sanctioned killings. Legally expressed dissent was silenced, but revolutionary protest grew apace.

The harshness of Thanin's regime alienated many who had earlier looked to a military solution, providing the communists with much talent and considerable legitimacy, and did nothing to restore the economy or Thailand's international reputation. Previous repression by the military had been accompanied by killing and imprisonment, but this had involved only a small number of socially obscure or marginal dissidents. This time the repression affected a significant part of the population; moreover, the students who were the chief targets of the action were also the offspring of the ruling élite. In October 1977 the armed forces Commander-in-Chief, Gen. Kriangsak Chomanan, seized power; he restored some elements of democracy by reducing censorship, releasing detainees and permitting the resumption of party activity under arrangements that ensured conservative control of the legislature and important government appointments.

In March 1980, having failed to find economic policies that were both realistic and acceptable to the élite, Kriangsak was replaced as Prime Minister by the Army Commander-in-Chief and Defence Minister, Gen. Prem Tinsulanonda. Prem's regime, like Kriangsak's, was based on a combination of the military and centre-right party politicians. Ultimate power lay with the armed forces, but the political parties played a major role in linking military, civilian, bureaucratic and business interests. The result was a ruling élite too powerful to dislodge but not sufficiently united to govern effectively.

None the less, the evolution of foreign affairs and domestic society combined to reduce the pressures on the Thai polity. Viet Nam's invasion of Cambodia in late 1978 had led to disunity among communist supporters and to a breach between Viet Nam and China, which greatly decreased support for the Thai communist insurgency. Refugees from Laos, Cambodia and Viet Nam burdened Thai facilities, but they also provided testimony against the rigours of communist rule. Thailand found common cause with China as well as the USA in supporting deposed Cambodian leader Pol Pot against the Viet Nam-sponsored Heng Samrin regime. Insurgents in the north and north-east, long accustomed to material support from and refuge in neighbouring Laos, Viet Nam and China, were demoralized by their patrons' quarrel. The students who had joined them were increasingly disillusioned by the rigid insistence of the Communist Party of Thailand's leadership on the outdated Maoist doctrine of protracted rural warfare. The relative liberalism of the post-1977 regimes began to attract them and, following the announcement of an amnesty for dissidents, many of them returned. Later Prem extended the amnesty to the rank and file of the communist insurgency; this resulted in mass defections from the rebellion in late 1982 and early 1983.

These achievements were somewhat marred by lack of success in responding to the consolidation of power by communist regimes in Indo-China. A Thai military operation to dislodge Laotian forces from a disputed border territory ended ingloriously with a truce in March 1988. On the Cambodian border the Thai army showed little ability to respond to Vietnamese incursions, but the Thai Government argued strongly against any compromise on the Cambodian issue by the Association of Southeast Asian Nations (ASEAN), of which it had been an enthusiastic member since that group's founding in 1967.

While maintaining an unyielding stance towards its communist neighbours, the Thai Government quietly restored US military aid projects and training schemes that had been rejected following the 1973 uprising and the defeat of the USA in Viet Nam. In late 1985 US forces began to participate in Thai military exercises on a substantial scale; in April 1986 plans were devised for the establishment of a stockpile of US weapons in Thailand, the first occasion for a US reserve of weapons in a country without US military bases.

Towards the end of the 1970s the discovery of petroleum and natural gas in the Gulf of Thailand helped revive economic optimism. Foreign investors, realizing that Thailand was not after all about to fall to communism, began to move funds into the country. Secondary urban centres began to flourish, challenging the capital's monopoly on political power. The growth of the 1980s differed from that of Sarit's time in that it lacked any clear leadership or ideology. The regimes of Kriangsak and Prem had been reactive rather than dynamic. The Prem Government attempted to remove the army from the political process while safeguarding its interests, an effort that found support in the early 1980s from the Democratic Officers Movement (DOM), whose leaders argued that this was necessary for the sake of national progress, military unity and professionalism. Indeed, the basis of politics appeared to be changing from the previous personalist ties of patron-client relations to alliances based on interest groups and political ideals. Banking, manufacturing and agribusiness interests began to play a significant role in politics; partly because of their participation the parties seemed to acquire more substance, and young army officers began to form groups supporting particular political objectives rather than an individual patron or faction.

The effort to reform the system culminated in constitutional changes, endorsed by the results of the election to the House of Representatives in April 1983, that greatly reduced the power of the appointed Senate and banned the appointment of civil servants (including military officers) to cabinet positions. Such action against entrenched interests did not go unchallenged, both by senior officers aspiring to national leadership and young ones who sought a more dynamic role for the army, and the State in general, in developing the country. In 1981 radical nationalist middle-rank officers had attempted a coup. In 1983 Gen. Arthit Kamlang-ek, Supreme Commander of the Armed Forces and Commander-in-Chief of the Army, formed an alliance with these 'Young Turks' in his attempt to consolidate military support against the constitutional reforms. This culminated in a coup attempt in September 1985, led by Col Manoon Roopkachorn and tacitly supported by senior military officers. Its failure resulted in Arthit's replacement as Supreme Commander of the Armed Forces and Army Commander-in-Chief by Gen. Chavalit Yongchaiyudh, one of Prem's closest advisers and the acknowledged leader of the successful campaign against the communist insurgency.

Chavalit had once been prominent in the DOM, but soon after his elevation he began to voice opinions seemingly more in accordance with the ideas of the 'Young Turks'. He began to urge the transformation of the country's political, economic and social structure by means of a state-led 'revolution'. Increasingly, he appeared as a dynamic alternative to Prem. The latter's administration had been re-endorsed by elections in July 1986, which gave the DP a strong plurality in the House of Representatives. However, the government coalition (comprising the DP, Chart Thai, the SAP and Rassadorn) was highly unstable, and the influence of political parties remained small compared with that of the armed forces. The notable growth of interest-group politics and the middle class meant increased participation, but, often enough, political deadlock as well. During the 1970s and 1980s the King became a pivotal figure in political negotiations, his opinion being sought as a means of breaking the impasse resulting from conflicting interests. Prem, although excellent at the manoeuvring and compromise necessary for political survival, was not able to provide a sense of direction. As a result, what was in many ways a very successful regime was characterized by a high level of popular frustration. Out of this arose the opportunity for a revival of parliamentary government.

PARLIAMENTARY RULE, 1988–91

In July 1988 an election for the House of Representatives was held: it was marred by allegations of malpractice and campaign violence. The results endorsed the existing coalition Government but also revealed a serious decline in the power of the DP, which split, and the growth of the right-wing Chart Thai, which had established itself as the representative of powerful Thai business interests and had spent lavishly on the election campaign. The King asked Prem to continue as Prime Minister, but Prem refused in favour of the leader of Chart Thai, Gen. Chatichai Choonhavan.

The new Prime Minister was not only a retired general but also the son of Phin Choonhavan, founder of the Phin-Phao-Phibun military clique that led Thailand from 1948 to 1957. Nevertheless, his accession was regarded as a major advance towards democracy: for the first time since 1976, an elected leader was in charge of the Government. Chatichai was regarded as a politician rather than as a military man, and he was the main protagonist of Chart Thai's business orientation. The extent of the business community's financial support for Chart Thai's campaign reflected not only appreciation of the party's attitude but also a new respect for the importance of party politics and a departure from reliance on the protection of powerful individuals rather than political organizations. Chatichai's coalition Government comprised Chart Thai, the SAP, the DP, Rassadorn, the United Democratic Party and Muan Chon.

Chatichai initiated reforms that opened Thailand to a major expansion of the business sector, while asserting a concern for the development of poorer regions and securing the passage of the country's first social security law. Chatichai's innovations were particularly notable in foreign affairs. Overcoming considerable bureaucratic and military resistance, he abandoned the previously intransigent Thai stance on the Indo-China question, declaring his ambition to turn Indo-China 'from a battlefield into a market-place'. In November 1988 he succeeded in settling the border dispute with Laos. The Vietnamese withdrawal from Cambodia in September 1989 presented him with an opportunity to stress, against army opposition, a willingness to improve relations with the rest of Indo-China. In December 1988 Chavalit visited Myanmar (formerly Burma), earning the gratitude of its internationally isolated regime.

However, Chatichai's regime began to falter in late 1989. Commerce expanded, but was accompanied by a widespread feeling of unease at Thailand's precipitate capitalist development. The country was experiencing unprecedented prosperity but also witnessing increasing inequality; the promises to aid the poorer regions had not been fulfilled. Public concern mounted over corruption, the high rate of inflation, traffic congestion in Bangkok, pollution and other environmental issues, drug addiction and acquired immunodeficiency syndrome (AIDS). In 1990 a series of no-confidence motions was brought against the Government in the House of Representatives, and Chatichai engaged in increasingly desperate government reorganizations. He attempted to allay military disaffection by giving Chavalit unrestricted responsibility for senior military appointments. Chavalit took advantage of this to allocate important posts to the leaders of the powerful Class 5 Group, based on the 1958 graduates of Chulachomklao Military Academy.

Military Academy class membership had long been an important source of faction and patronage within the army. Previously, Prem and Kriangsak had been careful, as government leaders, to ensure that no one class dominated the military power structure. Chavalit relied for his influence over Class 5 on his generous patronage of it and especially on the presumed personal loyalty of its leader, Gen. Suchinda Kraprayoon, whom he named Deputy Commander-in-Chief of the Army in September 1989. In 1990 Chavalit acted to establish himself as an opposition force within the parliamentary context, resigning from his official posts and forming the New Aspiration Party (NAP) to contest the next elections. His place as Supreme Commander of the Armed Forces was taken by Gen. Sunthorn Kongsompong, who was regarded as favourable to Class 5. The position of Commander-in-Chief of the Army was assumed by Suchinda, whose brother-in-law, Gen. Issarapong Noonpakdi, became his deputy.

RETURN TO MILITARY RULE

Alarmed at this entrenchment of Class 5, the Prime Minister attempted to rally its opponents in the army. On 23 February 1991, however, Chatichai was seized in a bloodless military coup. A National Peace-keeping Council (NPC), headed by Sunthorn, took command of the country. Martial law was declared, the Constitution was suspended and the National Assembly was dissolved.

There was little reaction to the country's 17th coup. The public was too disenchanted with the corruption and unscrupulous capitalism of Chatichai's regime to be willing to defend it. Domestic and international business interests were easily persuaded by the perpetrators of the coup that they intended merely to install a more honest and competent rule of experts. The President of the Federation of Thai Industries, Anand Panyarachun, was appointed Prime Minister. Anand appointed a predominantly civilian interim Cabinet comprising respected technocrats and former ministers. It was declared that an interim National Legislative Assembly would be created to draft a new constitution and prepare for a general election. However, more than one-half of the Assembly consisted of senior military officers (149 of its 292 members). The other members were business executives, bureaucrats and others known for their conservatism and military connections. The new rulers dissolved trade unions in the public sector, announced a new anti-communist campaign and an offensive against crime and corruption, and declared a revival of the uncompromising policy on Cambodia; however, they did not ban political parties, as had occurred following every previous military intervention.

Although parties remained legal, they were in complete disarray. An Assets Examination Committee installed by the new regime identified leaders of the major parties, in particular the former Prime Minister, Chatichai, as possessing 'unusual wealth'. Politicians seeking new allegiance were attracted to the NAP of Chavalit, who had declared himself opposed to the overthrow of parliamentary rule. To offset this, the Class 5 ally, Air Chief Marshal Kaset Rojananin (a member of the NPC), sponsored the Samakkhi Tham party as a channel for supporters of the new regime. In addition, Chart Thai, reportedly in exchange for the abandoning of corruption charges against its major leaders, aligned itself in support of the military regime under a new leader, Air Chief Marshal Somboon Rahong. Class 5 strengthened its control of government, and in August 1991 Suchinda replaced Sunthorn as Supreme Commander of the Armed Forces, appointing Issarapong as Commander-in-Chief of the Army.

In December 1991 the new Constitution, which ensured the protection of conservative, military-bureaucratic interests, was proclaimed. Public opinion endorsed Anand's competent and honest governance, although Thais were increasingly disenchanted with the military's blatant profiting from its control of politics. In March 1992 National Assembly elections were held under the new dispensation. The results provided encouragement for neither the military nor its opponents. By a bare majority, voters returned a weak coalition led by Samakkhi Tham, Chart Thai and the SAP, also including Prachakorn Thai and Rassadorn. None of these presented a credible candidate for Prime Minister, and finally, despite his previous assurances to the contrary, Suchinda assumed the premiership.

Suchinda seemed to have an invincible military-political machine at his disposal. However, his assumption of the premiership compounded civilian unease, and resulted in demonstrations demanding the appointment of an elected Prime Minister. These culminated in a dramatic hunger strike by Maj.-Gen. (retd) Chamlong Srimuang, who had been the highly popular and effective Governor of Bangkok, and was the leader of the Palang Dharma (Righteous Force) party. In May 1992 Suchinda and his chief supporters resorted to violence that led to the deaths of an estimated 100 demonstrators in Bangkok. Royal intervention was required to achieve a settlement. Following the declaration of an amnesty for all 'offenders' in the recent demonstrations, including those responsible for the deaths of protesters, Suchinda submitted his resignation.

THE RE-ESTABLISHMENT OF DEMOCRATIC RULE AND SUBSEQUENT DEVELOPMENTS

The five government coalition parties nominated Somboon Rahong, the leader of Chart Thai, as Prime Minister. However, the fact that Somboon was perceived as having close links with the military leaders led to fears of new unrest, and his appointment was not confirmed. Instead, in June 1992, the King again appointed Anand Panyarachun as Prime Minister. Anand announced that he would organize new elections within four months. The National Assembly approved constitutional amendments reducing the powers of the non-elected Senate and stipulating that the Prime Minister must be an elected member of the Assembly. Anand formed an administration that comprised many of the apolitical individuals whom he had appointed during his previous term of office. At the end of June a 'National Democratic Front' was established by four parties that had opposed the military Government: the DP, the NAP, Palang Dharma and Ekkaparb. In July Chatichai declined the leadership of Chart Thai (offered to him after the resignation of Somboon from that post) and formed a new party, Chart Pattana (National Development).

In August 1992 Anand demoted the military leaders regarded as being responsible for the violent repression of the May demonstrations, and appointed in their place officers who had a reputation as professional soldiers of integrity. The new Commander-in-Chief of the Army, Gen. Wimol Wongwanit, promised that the army would not interfere in politics during his period of command. Anand also reduced military control of state enterprises, appointing civilians instead of military officers to head the national airline, the communications and telephone authorities, and other institutions hitherto regarded as the preserve of the armed forces.

In the general election of September 1992 Thailand's oldest party, the DP, won 79 seats, while Chart Thai took 77 and Chart Pattana 60. With the other parties that belonged to the 'National Democratic Front', the DP was able to form a coalition Government, commanding 185 of the 360 seats in the House of Representatives: Chuan Leekpai, the leader of the DP, became Prime Minister. In order to increase the coalition's narrow majority, the SAP (which had won 22 seats) was also invited to join the coalition, despite having participated in the previous administration.

Major formal shifts in the way Thailand was ruled were not accompanied by clear and consistent changes in public opinion. The underlying reason for the popular rejection of both Chatichai's and Suchinda's regimes was the dismay at blatant corruption and abuse of office. Prime Minister Anand, although he served the military regime and was not himself elected, was perfectly acceptable to public opinion because he was regarded as honest and competent. This public opinion was largely middle class and located in Bangkok, characteristics that no longer reflected the failure of national politics to penetrate the provinces, but rather the urban middle class's growing strength. This could be seen in the importance of business opinion to the acceptance of both the 1991 military coup and Suchinda's downfall. At the same time, those powerful business executives who had access to political decision-makers were reluctant to forgo the advantages of the traditional patronage system, and they found a new source of strength in the rising power of provincial business and political leaders. These relied on relationships of patronage to make profits and to garner votes; money, not principle, was the basis for their loyalties.

On assuming office, Prime Minister Chuan had declared his intention to eradicate corrupt practices and to decentralize government from Bangkok to the provinces. However, although he was regarded as an able and honest politician, his tenure was devoted largely to maintaining the unity of his coalition. There was little business-political support for his reforms, and the decentralization efforts aroused the anger of the still-powerful bureaucracy. Nevertheless, the military appeared to move into the political background. Chavalit indeed served as Minister of the Interior, but this was as much due to the importance of his NAP to the ruling coalition as it was to his continuing influence in military circles.

In June 1993 the position of Chuan's administration was consolidated by its decisive survival of a motion of no confidence in the Cabinet, introduced by Chart Pattana and Chart Thai. In September the SAP announced that it was to merge with four opposition parties, including Chart Pattana, under the leadership of Chatichai, while remaining within the ruling coalition. This appeared to be an attempt to secure the premiership for Chatichai, as the new SAP would command more parliamentary seats than any other member of the coalition. However, the SAP was then expelled from the Government. It was replaced by the Seritham Party, which controlled only eight seats (compared with the 21 of the SAP), bringing the coalition's total representation to 193 seats.

In March 1994 a joint session of the upper and lower houses of the National Assembly was held to consider government proposals to democratize the Constitution, principally by reducing the powers of the appointed Senate and broadening the method by which its members were chosen. The senators, most of whom had been appointed under the Suchinda regime, were understandably reluctant to diminish their powers; together with the opposition parties from the House of Representatives, they defeated the government plan and instead put forward proposals to strengthen the Constitution's authoritarian aspects. A crisis was avoided by the appointment of a joint committee to formulate a compromise reform programme.

In September 1994 Chamlong resumed the leadership of Palang Dharma in party elections. He subsequently persuaded the party executive committee to approve the replacement of all 11 of Palang Dharma's cabinet members. Chamlong's nominations for the cabinet posts, which included Thaksin Shinawatra, a prominent business executive, and Vichit Surapongchai, a former President of the Bangkok Bank, as Minister of Foreign Affairs and Minister of Transport and Communications, respectively, provoked strong protests within the divided party. The protests were led by Prasong Soonsiri, who opposed the selection of non-elected candidates and objected to Chamlong's authoritarian style of leadership. The appointments were confirmed in a cabinet reorganization in late October, when Chamlong was named Deputy Prime Minister.

In December 1994 the NAP withdrew from the ruling coalition over a constitutional amendment providing for the future election of local government representatives, including village headmen. Chavalit voted against the Government in what was widely viewed as an attempt to ingratiate himself with powerful local interests that would control many votes at the next election. The NAP's defection to the opposition left the ruling coalition with a minority of seats in the House of Representatives. Chuan therefore found it necessary to invite Chatichai's Chart Pattana to join the coalition, although this severely compromised the Government's claims to represent honesty and reform.

In January 1995 Chuan finally managed to secure the approval of a joint session of the National Assembly for a series of amendments to the Constitution aimed at expanding the country's democratic base. The reforms included a lowering of the minimum voting age from 20 years to 18, a reduction in the size of the appointed military-dominated Senate to two-thirds that of the elective House of Representatives, equality for women and the prohibition of senators and members of the Government from holding monopolistic concessions with government or state bodies. This last amendment necessitated the resignation of Thaksin as Minister of Foreign Affairs, because of his extensive business interests.

In December 1994 the Minister of Agriculture and Co-operatives, Niphon Phromphan, and his Deputy Minister, Suthep Thaugsuban, had resigned prior to a planned motion of no confidence in the Government, owing to allegations of corruption in connection with a land distribution scheme promoted by Chuan. Following a government investigation, in April 1995 land titles were removed from seven deed-holders, and a senior official was dismissed from the land reform department. However, opposition parties tabled a motion of no confidence in the Government in May, and Chamlong announced that Palang Dharma would not support the coalition in the no-confidence vote. Chuan dissolved the House of Representatives on 19 May and announced an early general election.

The outcome of the election of July 1995 marked the triumph of provincially inclined, money-based politics. Chart Thai secured the largest number of seats (92) in the House of Representatives, not one of them elected by the more sophisticated voters of Bangkok. The party's leader, Banharn Silpa-Archa, became Prime Minister. A self-made businessman and politician from the central Thai province of Suphanburi, he had been one of those leaders accused of being 'unusually rich' by the military junta that seized power in 1991. Banharn headed a seven-party coalition comprising Chart Thai, the NAP, Palang Dharma (led by Thaksin since May), the SAP, Prachakorn Thai, Nam Thai (a business-orientated party formed in 1994 by Amnuay Viravan, a former head of Bangkok Bank) and the Muan Chon party. His Cabinet, unlike that of Chuan, eschewed technocrats in favour of patronage-based politicians. Banharn presented himself as a dynamic leader, willing to ignore legalities and sensitivities in order to achieve progress. He defined his Government's aims much as his predecessor had, as these were issues generally conceded to be urgent. However, Banharn's ability to outperform Chuan was sharply curtailed by the instability of his coalition and by his dependence on serving the interests of provincial patronage. Thus, although resolving Bangkok's infamous traffic congestion was a prime test of effective leadership, he allocated responsibility for the management of traffic in inner Bangkok to Thaksin, and in outer Bangkok to the Prachakorn Thai leader, Samak Sundaravej. Such politicization of decision-making led to much public disillusionment, culminating in August 1995 in an unprecedented criticism of government incompetence by the King.

In an unusual development in September 1995 the Minister of Defence, Chavalit (who was also Deputy Prime Minister), rejected recommendations for promotions by the outgoing Commander-in-Chief of the Army, Wimol, and appointed his own close associate, Gen. Pramon Phalasin, to replace him. This was a set-back to Banharn, but he managed to strengthen his position by the appointment of Gen. Viroj Saengsanit as Supreme Commander of the Armed Forces. Viroj, a Class 5 member and supporter of the 1991 coup, was considered to be unsympathetic to Chavalit. The latter's NAP, with 57 seats, was the third largest party in the legislature and the second largest in the governing coalition. Chavalit had a strong base in the military, and he also endeavoured to increase his support among business interests, by promoting privatization, and among the bureaucracy, by advocating strong central administration.

By early 1996 it was evident that Thailand had replaced weak but relatively honest and competent rule with a weak and patently venal administration. The Banharn Government attempted to regain credibility by pursuing some of the political reform projects it had promised at its inception, and in March the Prime Minister appointed a new Senate that included only 39 military officers, a considerable step towards democratizing that institution. The Government also announced a major programme of investment in education and a plan for financial decentralization, which was intended to promote rural development. However, most of the Government's efforts were blocked by disagreements within the ruling coalition and by the requirements of the all-pervasive patronage system.

In May 1996 the Government confronted a vote of no confidence in which 10 cabinet ministers were accused by the opposition of incompetence and/or corruption. The Government won without difficulty, as it held 233 of the 391 seats in the House of Representatives. None the less, public disillusionment eroded support for the coalition parties. In August Palang Dharma withdrew from the Government, following a cabinet dispute over bribery in the awarding of bank licences. In September Banharn was only able to secure the support of his coalition partners in a scheduled motion of no confidence in his administration by undertaking to resign from the premiership to make way for another candidate. However, the inability of the coalition partners to agree on the appointment of a new Prime Minister led to the dissolution of the House of Representatives.

The general election, which was held in mid-November 1996, was characterized by extensive campaign violence and malpractice on a massive scale. The NAP gained a plurality with 125 (of the total 393) seats secured mostly through patronage politics in the impoverished rural north-east of the country. The DP, which took 123 seats, appealed to more sophisticated voters, winning 29 of Bangkok's 37 seats, thus contributing to the reduction (from 23 at the previous election) of Palang Dharma's representation to only one seat.

The Chavalit Coalition

In November 1996 King Bhumibol formally appointed Chavalit as Prime Minister at the head of a coalition Government, comprising the NAP, Chart Pattana, the SAP, Prachakorn Thai, the Seritham Party and Muan Chon; the coalition commanded a total of 221 seats in the House of Representatives. Besides holding the premiership, Chavalit also retained control of the Ministry of Defence. The position of Minister of the Interior was awarded to Sanoh Thienthong, the former Secretary-General of Chart Thai, in return for Sanoh's support for Chavalit's bid for the premiership prior to the general election and his subsequent defection to Chavalit's NAP. Most other influential ministries were awarded to NAP or Chart Pattana members. Gen. Mongkon Ampornpisit, the Supreme Commander of the Armed Forces, and Gen. Chettha Thanajaro, the Army Commander-in-Chief, were both Chavalit appointees.

As evidence of Chavalit's avowed intention to revive the economy, he allocated the finance portfolio and the deputy premiership with responsibility for economic affairs to Amnuay Viravan, a respected technocrat. However, Chavalit subsequently failed to give Amnuay the necessary support to overcome the obstacles imposed by other coalition members anxious to prevent the implementation of austere fiscal policies. The Government's indecisive handling of the economy contributed to a financial crisis in mid-1997, following a series of sustained offensives against the Thai baht by currency speculators. In June Amnuay resigned and was replaced by the little-known Thanong Bidaya, the President of the Thai Military Bank. In July the Governor of the central bank, Rerngchai Marakanonda, also resigned, citing political interference. The serious deterioration in the economy was reflected in an increase in popular protests; in response, the Government introduced measures in June to restrict media criticism of the authorities and to limit mass protests.

In August 1997 Chavalit and Thanong had an audience with the King to discuss the economic crisis. Chavalit implemented a cabinet reorganization in an attempt to regain public confidence. On the advice of ex-Prime Minister Prem, the former Minister of Finance, Virabongsa Ramangkura, an outspoken critic of the Government's handling of the crisis, was appointed Deputy Prime Minister with responsibility for economic affairs. Thaksin, who had resigned as leader of Palang Dharma, following the party's disastrous performance in the general election, joined the Cabinet as Deputy Prime Minister with responsibility for regional development and trade.

For much of Chavalit's first year in office the major issue on the political agenda was the drafting of a new Constitution by the Constitutional Drafting Assembly, presided over by long-time political activist, Uthai Pimchaichon. The draft Constitution was promoted by its supporters (including the former Prime Minister, Anand Panyarachun) as providing the basis for a truly democratic system of government in Thailand. Many of the provisions sought to address the endemic problems of political corruption and vote-buying that had beset Thai politics for decades. Some of the major amendments contained in the new draft Constitution included the reduction of the number of senators to 200; the introduction of direct elections for the Senate (in place of the system whereby senators were appointed by the Prime Minister); a clause requiring members of the National Assembly who became ministers to resign from the legislature; a requirement that the minimum level of education for a member of the National Assembly be a university degree; a provision that 50,000 eligible voters could initiate investigations into corruption by members of the National Assembly; and restrictions on media censorship by the state. By September 1997 the draft Constitution had gained the support of all opposition parties and most of the print media. However, considerable opposition to the new charter came from within the Chavalit coalition and sections of the Senate. Chavalit himself reneged on his pledge to support the overwhelmingly popular draft, but then finally gave it his endorsement following the application of pressure by both business representatives and the armed forces.

Chavalit ensured his survival of a no-confidence motion tabled by the opposition by scheduling the censure debate prior to the vote on the draft Constitution. If defeated, Chavalit could thus dissolve the National Assembly rather than resign, delaying the vote on the draft Constitution and forcing fresh elections under the existing Constitution. In the event, the Government won the no-confidence vote and the draft Constitution was approved on 27 September 1997. Chavalit was then prohibited by law from dissolving the National Assembly and was allowed 240 days to complete enabling legislation for the new Constitution, prior to a general election (although the King subsequently urged the accelerated completion of the necessary reforms). The new Constitution was promulgated on 11 October.

In October 1997, following the resignation of the Minister of Finance, Thanong Bidaya, Chavalit effected a reorganization of the Cabinet. However, unprecedented media criticism of the Chavalit administration's handling of the worsening economic crisis, as well as opposition to the new Constitution, led in early November to Chavalit's resignation as Prime Minister. In the political manoeuvring that followed, the DP succeeded in persuading 12 members of Prachakorn Thai (later dubbed the 'Cobra faction' by the media) to defect and join the Democrats. With the support of Chart Thai and other minor parties, the DP was able to form a new eight-party coalition commanding the support of 207 members of the 393-member House of Representatives.

The Government of Chuan Leekpai

In November 1997 the leader of the DP, Chuan Leekpai, was appointed Prime Minister. The majority of the important portfolios in the new Cabinet were allocated to DP members. Despite some opposition from within the armed forces, Chuan himself assumed the post of Minister of Defence concurrently with the premiership, thus becoming the first non-military official to occupy the position in recent history. The DP Secretary-General, Sanan Kajornprasart, assumed responsibility for the influential post of Minister of the Interior. The Ministries of Finance and of Commerce were headed by two former bankers, Tarrin Nimmanhaeminda and Supachai Panichpakdi, respectively, while Surin Pitsuwan, also of the DP, became Thailand's first Muslim Minister of Foreign Affairs.

The political agenda in 1998 was dominated by issues relating to the Thai economy. However, the new Government was supported by the media, which perceived in the Chuan administration a more credible team of economic managers. As a consequence of Thailand's co-operation with the IMF, the Chuan Government received considerable international support. In March Chuan visited the USA, where he received strong praise for the Government's handling of the crisis. As the austerity measures began to take effect, numerous factory workers were made redundant. Protesters from farming groups, mostly from the impoverished north-east, regularly rallied outside the National Assembly to criticize the Government's failure to address their problems. Resentment towards the IMF, particularly in relation to the way in which the IMF appeared to be dictating Thailand's economic policy, was increasingly expressed. Despite such pressures, in March the Government easily survived a censure debate led by Chuan's predecessor, Chavalit. Popular support for the Government was demonstrated at the elections to the Bangkok city council, which took place in April, when the DP won 22 of the 60 seats, followed by the non-political supporters of the incumbent Governor, Bhichit Rattakul, who secured 20 seats.

New electoral legislation was approved in May 1998, enabling polls to be held six months subsequently. Despite pressure from the opposition, Chuan stated that elections would not be held until certain economic reforms had been put in place. However, under the new legislation, it appeared likely that 12 of the members of the ruling coalition who had defected from Prachakorn Thai to help form the Government in November 1997 might lose their legal status as legislators, thus placing in jeopardy the Government's parliamentary majority. (The 12 were formally expelled from Prachakorn Thai in October 1998 but continued to form part of the coalition Government.) A new political party, Thai Rak Thai (Thais Love Thais), was formed by the former Deputy Prime Minister, Thaksin Shinawatra, in July 1998.

In August 1998, following a change in the attitude of the Thai press towards Chuan, in an unusual development Queen Sirikit praised Prime Minister Chuan and urged support for the efforts of his Government to stabilize the economy. However, the Government was afflicted by allegations of corruption. In early October Prime Minister Chuan reorganized his Government, bringing the Chart Pattana party into the ruling coalition. The inclusion of Chart Pattana reinforced the Government's majority in the House of Representatives, increasing the number of seats held by the coalition to 257. Five new ministers were appointed to the Cabinet, including the Chart Pattana Secretary-General, Suwat Liptapanlop, who was assigned the industry portfolio. However, many of the most influential portfolios were retained by the DP.

In December 1998 and January 1999 there was intense debate in the National Assembly and in the media concerning 11 'Economic Recovery Bills' introduced by the Government. Ostensibly designed to restore confidence in the economy, the proposed legislation was also intended partly to meet IMF recommendations for its restructuring. Among the most controversial aspects were new bankruptcy laws that would make it much easier for creditors to prosecute debtors defaulting on loans. Another controversial proposal would allow foreigners to hold shares in state enterprises. The Government came under strongest criticism from leading members of the Senate, most notably the upper house's President, Meechai Ruchuphan, who protested that the bills would lead to foreign control of the Thai economy. However, Senate opposition to the bills was not entirely based on nationalistic motives. It was revealed that the proposed legislation would also affect the business interests of a number of influential senators. Despite such opposition, and under considerable pressure from the Government, the bills were eventually approved by the Senate in March 1999.

The Government's standing was further affected in December 1998 when the media uncovered evidence implicating Minister of the Interior Sanan, in a land scandal in Kanchanaburi province. A more damaging issue for the personal reputation of the Prime Minister, who also held the defence portfolio, was the revelation in March that he had countersigned an army recommendation awarding Field Marshal Thanom Kittikachorn an honorary appointment as a Royal Guards officer. Thanom, the military dictator of the 1960s and 1970s, was notorious for his role in the attempt violently to suppress the 1973 pro-democracy demonstrations in Bangkok. Despite considerable pressure from the media for the appointment to be withdrawn, Chuan declined to interfere on the grounds that it was an internal matter for the Armed Forces and that his signature was simply a matter of procedure; however, Thanom subsequently resigned from the position. In April 1999 Chavalit resigned as leader of the NAP, but he was expected to stand for re-election to the post.

In July 1999 intense discord within the SAP concerning the allocation of cabinet positions forced the party to withdraw from the governing coalition. In the ensuing cabinet reorganization Chart Pattana further strengthened its position. Meanwhile, campaigning by Thaksin Shinawatra's party, Thai Rak Thai, intensified in anticipation of an early general election. Speculation that Thai Rak Thai was using financial inducements to recruit members of other parties was confirmed by the senior Democrat ministers, Chamni Sakdiset and Khunying Supatra Massdit, who opened a public debate on the issue, partly as an attempt to prevent support flowing from the DP to Thai Rak Thai. Despite such criticism, the media reported much support for the new party, especially in the northern provinces (Thaksin being a native of Chiang Mai) and in November Chavalit pledged his willingness to support Thai Rak Thai in the forthcoming election in the event of his own NAP performing poorly. By August 1999, with public approval of the Government declining, the Democrats found themselves trying to forestall growing demands from opposition parties and numerous public figures to dissolve the House of Representatives and call fresh elections. A report on the state-owned Krung Thai Bank, which exposed the bank's dubious loan policies and other irregularities, was 'leaked' to the Senate and the press. The report led to criticism of the Government for its handling of the bank, and also resulted in direct allegations of corruption being made against Minister of Finance Tarrin, whose brother, Sirin Nimmanhaeminda, had been the President of Krung Thai Bank until his resignation in January. In March 2000 elections to the new 200-member Senate were held. The elections were contested by more than 1,500 candidates, and a voter participation level of 71.9% was reported. The power of the new Election Commission, which had been established under the 1997 Constitution to oversee the elections, was demonstrated when it disqualified 78 of the 200 winning candidates on the grounds of either vote-buying or fraudulent conduct. The Election Commission subsequently announced that a second round of polling would be held in these 78 constituencies at the end of April 2000, when all but two of the disqualified contestants would be permitted to stand again. A total of 66 senators were duly elected, including more than one-half of those disqualified after the first round of polling. The Election Commission announced that a third round of polling would be held in June to elect senators to the 12 remaining seats, rejecting demands for the dismissal of the allegations of fraud in the interest of political continuity. (While the final results of the elections remained in dispute, none of the declared winners were able to assume their seats as they lacked the necessary quorum, resulting in a backlog of legislation and obliging the outgoing Senate to remain in office in an interim capacity.) In early June the third round of polling was duly held, which resulted in the election of a further eight senators, although voter participation was officially registered at a mere 41.3%. Further allegations of electoral fraud necessitated fourth and fifth rounds of polling in July, both of which attracted voter turn-outs of some 31%. In late July the last of the 200 members of the Senate were finally endorsed, and on 1 August the new Senate was officially sworn in. A significant feature of the composition of the new Senate was the greatly reduced proportion of senators coming from military and bureaucratic backgrounds, and increased numbers from academia, the media and non-governmental organizations (NGOs).

Meanwhile, in March 2000 the DP was set back by the findings of the National Counter Corruption Commission (NCCC; from 2008 the National Anti-Corruption Commission—NACC) following its investigation into Deputy Prime Minister, Minister of the Interior and Secretary-General of the DP, Sanan Kajornprasart, which, in a highly significant decision, indicted Sanan on charges of falsifying his assets statement. Sanan immediately resigned from his ministerial positions and was replaced by Banyat Bantadtan; Sanan's position as Secretary-General of the DP was eventually taken by Anant Anatakul, a former permanent secretary in the Ministry of the Interior, following the former's conviction, in August, of corruption charges by the Constitutional Court, which resulted in a five-year ban from holding political office. Rumours abounded that large numbers of NAP deputies, including the influential Wang Nam Yen faction controlled by Sanoh, were preparing to join Thai Rak Thai. In June the NAP leadership urged the party's deputies to resign from their seats in the House of Representatives in an attempt to force the Government into calling an early election. The controversial strategy revealed the deep divisions within the NAP, with at least 20 NAP legislators refusing to take part in the mass resignation (although almost 100 did resign), including former NAP Secretary-General Chaturon Chaisaeng. However, the NAP's mass defection had little effect on the DP-led coalition, which now confronted a greatly reduced opposition in the House of Representatives. In July a second opposition party, the SAP, also resigned from the House of Representatives.

In November 2000, as support for the Government continued to decline, Prime Minister Chuan Leekpai ended months of speculation by dissolving the legislature and setting a date in January 2001 for an election to the House of Representatives, the first under the 1997 Constitution. Thai Rak Thai had emerged as the DP's major rival, but its leader, Thaksin, had become involved in a major corruption scandal. After a lengthy investigation, in December 2000 Thaksin was indicted by the NCCC on charges that he and his wife had violated assets-disclosure regulations (laid out in the new Constitution) by deliberately concealing shares worth thousands of millions of baht. The NCCC alleged that Thaksin had transferred the shares to his household staff. Refusing to accept the verdict, Thaksin immediately appealed to the 15-member Constitutional Court, another so-called 'independent body', like the NCCC, established under the new Constitution.

The Thai Rak Thai election campaign was characterized by its sophisticated use of the mass media, which portrayed Thai Rak Thai as the party of 'the new generation'. Thaksin was portrayed as a successful business executive who would bring his skills from the corporate world to government, in contrast to Chuan, who was depicted as indecisive and ineffective. Thai Rak Thai also made a series of populist election promises, including: development fund grants of 1m. baht for each of Thailand's 77,000 villages in a bid to stimulate the rural economy; a public health programme whereby Thais would pay just 30 baht for each hospital consultation; and a three-year debt moratorium for Thailand's indebted farmers. The DP's campaign focused on the Government's record of guiding the Thai economy out of the crisis of the late 1990s and its implementation of vital economic reforms, while accusing Thaksin of malpractice.

The result of the election held on 6 January 2001 was an overwhelming victory for Thai Rak Thai. The final outcome (following a second round of elections in a number of constituencies on 29 January as a result of voting irregularities in the earlier poll) gave Thai Rak Thai 248 of the 500 seats in the newly expanded House of Representatives, while the DP secured 128. Chart Thai took 41 seats, the NAP 36, Chart Pattana 29 and the Seritham Party 14.

The Government of Thaksin Shinawatra

Following Thaksin's successful negotiation of a merger between the Seritham Party and Thai Rak Thai, the party became the first in Thai history to hold an absolute majority in the House of Representatives. Further to consolidate its position, Thai Rak Thai chose to form a coalition with Chart Thai and the NAP, thus commanding a total of 339 seats in the legislature. One of the most significant outcomes of the election was the eclipse of a number of long-standing provincial political dynasties, as a result of new electoral rules designed to decrease the influence of smaller parties in the interests of more stable government. Thaksin impressed his dominance on the coalition Government by filling 27 of the 36 cabinet positions with Thai Rak Thai appointees. Given his substantial personal financial assets, his extensive media interests and Thai Rak Thai's dominance of the coalition Government, Thaksin was thus in a more powerful political position than any previous civilian Prime Minister.

From the start, the new Government emphasized its nationalist credentials and distanced itself from the previous administration, which had been widely portrayed in the media as being too accommodating with regard to 'the West'. The new Minister of Foreign Affairs, Surakiart Sathirathai, announced a redirection of Thailand's foreign policy to focus on strengthening economic relations with neighbouring Asian countries, dismissing his predecessor's perceived preoccupation with broader issues of human rights and democracy, which, while winning praise from Western nations, had aggravated numerous governments within ASEAN. In February 2001 Thaksin declared that Thailand must 'cease being a slave to the world' and abandon policies that worked against 'Thai interests'. In another controversial speech in April, Thaksin appeared to indicate that Thailand would be following a more inward-looking, self-sufficient economic policy, and would give more support to 'small and medium enterprise industries'. The Prime Minister also discussed the importance of promoting greater economic integration among Asian countries. Following adverse reports in the Western media, Thaksin later assured the international business community that Thailand would maintain an open economy and continue to welcome foreign investment.

Concerns were expressed about apparent attempts by the Government to limit the powers of a number of the so-called 'independent bodies' established under the 1997 Constitution. Following a decision by the Election Commission (one of the most active of these bodies) to disqualify 10 Senators for alleged violations of electoral laws, the Government mounted a legal challenge to limit the Commission's extensive powers. The NCCC similarly came under pressure from the Government after its investigation into the Thaksin share concealment case. Three members of the NCCC were accused by the Government of violating constitutional regulations, which eventually resulted in the resignation of the leader of the investigation. Thaksin also expressed his intention to review the powers of the Constitutional Court by making amendments to the Constitution. In May 2001, after weeks of tension over interest rate policy, Thaksin dismissed the Governor of the central bank, Chatu Mongol Sonakul, and replaced him with Pridiyathorn Davakula. Concerns were raised about government interference in the independence of the Bank of Thailand. The Thai media were also targeted by the Government, which was accused of attempting to cajole the media into presenting favourable reports.

In early August 2001 months of uncertainty over Thaksin's political future finally ended when the Constitutional Court acquitted him of corruption charges by an eight-to-seven ruling. While the Court's decision received considerable public support, concern was expressed in certain quarters that a number of the judges might have been placed under pressure, or even bribed, into returning a verdict of acquittal. The allegations were sufficiently serious to prompt the Senate to begin an inquiry into the Court's decision.

Thaksin's increasing control over the political process was strengthened in April 2002, when the long-expected merger of the NAP, which had been a major force in Thai politics during the 1990s, with Thai Rak Thai finally took place. However, NAP leader Chavalit retained his post as Minister of Defence and Deputy Prime Minister. Thai Rak Thai's position in the House of Representatives was further consolidated with the defection of Chart Pattana from the opposition to the Government, giving Thai Rak Thai 368 seats, out of a total of 500, with the DP, the next largest party in the House of Representatives, commanding only 129.

Thai Rak Thai's remarkable dominance of the House of Representatives, and Thaksin's often abrasive style of leadership, provoked accusations from the political opposition, sections of the print media, numerous academics and even members of his own party that Thaksin was acting in the manner of a 'dictator'. In a rare public rebuke, King Bhumibol singled out the Prime Minister for criticism in his birthday address of December 2001, warning that Thailand was approaching 'catastrophe' and appealing for increased unity among all politicians. The King's comments led to a sharp decline in the Prime Minister's popularity in the opinion polls and encouraged further criticism in the media. Both the domestic and international media continued to protest against what they perceived to be direct threats to the freedom of the press. To counter what it regarded as inaccurate reporting, the Government initiated the establishment of a new agency intended to implement guidelines to be followed by the state-controlled media. In October 2001 Shin Corporation, the telecommunications conglomerate that Thaksin had founded and in which his family retained a controlling interest, increased its share in Independent Television (ITV), the only non-state-owned television station, from an initial 25% (which it had acquired in 2000), to 77%.

Thai Rak Thai's domination of Thai politics was greatly facilitated by internal divisions within the DP, the most significant opposition party, following veteran leader Chuan Leekpai's announcement that he would stand down from the position in early 2003. Chuan's reluctance to name a clear successor divided the party between supporters of Chuan's talented young protégé Abhisit Vejjajiva, who had been educated at Eton College and Oxford University in the United Kingdom, and the seasoned but uncharismatic deputy from Surat Thani, Banyat Bantadtan. The latter received the crucial support of the DP's powerful former Secretary-General, Sanan Kajornprasart, who was serving a five-year ban from politics on charges of falsifying his assets statement. In April 2003, in a three-way ballot for the leadership joined by outsider Arthit Urairat, Banyat emerged the victor by a narrow margin, with Abhisit assuming the post of Deputy Leader. Pradit Pattaraprasit, a close associate of Sanan, was duly appointed to the important position of Secretary-General. Despite the change in leadership, consistent rumours of party discord and fears of a mass defection in the House of Representatives of DP members to Thai Rak Thai prior to the next election (due in 2005) continued to damage the DP, already disadvantaged in terms of its access to the media. In May a parliamentary no-confidence debate led by the DP against the Government was one of the least effective in recent years. Thai Rak Thai was threatening to overwhelm the DP's power base in the south of the country, where it held every seat apart from those in the predominantly Muslim border provinces. Moreover, the Government's standing in the south, home to most of Thailand's rubber producers, was greatly boosted by its successful rubber-pricing policy.

Thai Rak Thai's political control was increased further by a number of other developments. In October 2002 the Government made new appointments to the Constitutional Court, the body responsible for almost ending Thaksin's political career in the previous year. The Government also attempted to increase its influence over the nominally independent Senate by attempting to bring about the removal of its President, Maj.-Gen. Manoonkrit Roobkajorn, an associate of Sanan Kajornprasart and one of the Government's most outspoken critics. Meanwhile, the Prime Minister sought to avert a division in the ruling coalition by holding negotiations with Chart Pattana with regard to that party's merger with Thai Rak Thai.

In February 2003 the Government commenced its 'war on drugs'. While the country's drugs problem had been recognized as a serious social issue since the mid-1990s, this campaign was unprecedented both in its severity and in the degree of co-ordination among different government agencies. Police departments in each province were required to compile lists of known and suspected drugs-traffickers and drug addicts. The latter were required to undertake rehabilitation programmes, while suspected traffickers were given a period of grace in which they were to promise to abandon the drugs trade or address the consequences. Within days, 'small-time' traffickers were being killed all over the country, either murdered by more important operators in the drugs trade to silence them before police interrogation, or victims of 'extra-judicial killings' carried out by the police, ostensibly in self-defence. Within a few months, more than 2,000 people had died in drugs-related killings. Alarmed by the excessive violence associated with the offensive, the UN High Commissioner for Human Rights, as well as the US Government, publicly criticized the Thai Government's handling of the campaign. In February Thailand's own human rights organization expressed its concern over the killings, and was immediately depicted by the Government as 'unpatriotic'. However, despite the criticism, the campaign received considerable public support. In May, furthermore, the Government announced a new campaign to suppress so-called 'persons with influence', a euphemism used to describe mafia members who wielded significant economic and political power. Lists compiled by the Ministry of the Interior included dealers in drugs and weapons, those involved in illegal gambling and prostitution, and local contractors who used intimidation to win government contracts.

In December 2003, in his annual birthday speech, the King once again chastized the Prime Minister, effectively admonishing him for the manner in which the 'war on drugs' had been conducted and urging the establishment of an investigation into the deaths of almost 3,000 people during the three-month campaign. Tensions with the Palace continued into 2004, and in March the head of one of the King's charities spoke publicly of the monarch's concern over 'integrated' corruption at the highest levels.

A further crisis occurred in the form of an outbreak of avian influenza ('bird flu'). The virus had earlier affected China and Viet Nam, resulting in the deaths (both from the disease itself and from the resultant mass culls) of millions of chickens. The disease had also led to a number of human deaths. The Government initially refused to acknowledge publicly that the disease had entered the country, fearing for the country's important poultry industry. In January 2004, in view of overwhelming evidence, the Government was forced to admit that the virus had indeed reached Thailand and ordered the culling of millions of birds. The country's vital tourism industry was also adversely affected.

However, the most serious crisis for the Thaksin Government was the escalation of violence in the Malay-Muslim majority provinces in the far south of the country, seemingly in response to the Thai Government's increasingly close alignment with the USA from 2003. In October of that year it agreed to a US request that it contribute 450 troops to the Allied occupation force in Iraq. In the same month the Government announced that it had been designated a 'major non-North Atlantic Treaty Organization (NATO) ally' by the USA, a status that would strengthen links between the Thai and US armed forces and give Thailand privileged access to US military intelligence and sophisticated weaponry. Another factor that contributed to the growing unrest in the south was the Government's decision in 2002 to dismantle the military-led southern security council and transfer responsibility for security matters to the police force.

In January 2004, as unrest in the region continued, an assault on the Rajanakharin military camp in Narathiwat province was carried out. Four soldiers were killed in the attack and more than 300 weapons were seized. The Government responded by declaring martial law in all three southern provinces of Pattani, Yala and Narathiwat. However, assaults on police and government buildings and arson attacks on schools increased. In one incident in March, 38 government posts were simultaneously attacked. Killings of police officers, local government officials and villagers occurred on a daily basis. In one incident three Buddhist monks were killed by machete-wielding assailants, signalling a dramatic change in the nature of the violence, since militants had never previously attacked religious targets. Schools were a common focus for the militants. In January, following an attack on two students in Narathiwat province, more than 1,000 state schools in the region were forced to close temporarily, owing to fears for the safety of the students. For their part, local Muslim groups accused the security forces of abducting and murdering villagers. The Government appeared unable to stop the violence and was internally divided as to both its basic causes and responsibility for it. Thaksin initially blamed gangsters, local politicians and drugs traffickers, and categorically denied that the violence was in any way connected to international terrorism. However, public statements made by the military and the Minister of Defence appeared to contradict the Prime Minister. They attributed the violence to separatist groups, which had regrouped in the area.

In mid-March 2004 Thaksin dismissed the Minister of the Interior, the Minister of Defence, the Chief of Police and the Army Commander of the Fourth (southern) Region. In the same month a prominent Muslim human rights lawyer, Somchai Neelaphaijit, who was defending three suspected members of the regional terrorist organization Jemaah Islamiah (JI), disappeared several days after accusing the security forces of using torture on suspected Muslim militants. He was assumed to have been murdered.

In April 2004 militants simultaneously attacked 11 police posts in the three southern provinces. The security forces appeared to have been prepared for the attacks, responding by killing 107 of the attackers and capturing 17. Five security officials died in the fighting. Commandos stormed the ancient, culturally significant Kruese Mosque in Pattani province, killing all 32 militants who had retreated there. National television captured images of the military firing heavy weaponry into the mosque after the occupants refused to surrender. Aware of the damaging symbolism of the attack, the Government immediately ordered the transfer of the officer who had ordered the attack on the mosque. However, subsequent media polls showed overwhelming public support for the extreme measures the Government had taken against the militants.

Meanwhile, another issue that began to gain increasing media attention (despite the constraints within which the media now operated) was the continuing conflict of interest between the Prime Minister's business interests and government policy. Thaksin's Advanced Information Service mobile telephone operating company, which had benefited from government legislation in 2001 limiting foreign ownership in the telecommunications sector, controlled two-thirds of the market by 2003. In February 2004 the Government approved a renegotiation of the operating conditions of ITV, the television station in which the Prime Minister's Shin Corporation had acquired a controlling stake. The licence fee that the station was required to pay to the Government was reduced to a fraction of its former level. Moreover, the station, which had built its reputation on strong and independent news reporting, was permitted to increase the level of entertainment programming it aired during 'prime time' from 30% to 50%. In the months following the announcement of the amended operating conditions, ITV's share price surged by nearly 600%, almost 10 times higher than the average stock market return. Another case involved the deregulation of the low-cost air travel industry, following which Shin Corporation was granted a licence jointly to operate a new budget airline, Air Asia. The venture also benefited from a decision by the Airports Authority of Thailand to reduce the docking fees for the new airline by 50%. Shin Corporation also gained from the Government's new policy of promoting consumer credit by establishing its own credit finance company, Capital OK Co Ltd. Meanwhile, Shin Corporation's satellite services branch, Shin Satellite (Sattel), was granted substantial tax concessions for its new-generation broadband satellite system venture, iPSTAR, among other incentives.

Politically, Thai Rak Thai continued to expand its influence in 2003 and 2004. In November 2003 Korn Dabbaransi, head of Chart Pattana, resigned as party leader and joined Thai Rak Thai, taking with him 15 other Chart Pattana members. In July 2004 there was a mass defection of 23 Chart Thai members who left to join Thai Rak Thai, decimating the membership of Chart Thai. In the same month, after much negotiation, Chart Pattana, led by Suwat Liptapanlop, decided to disband the party, founded in 1992 by Chatichai Choonhavan, and merge with Thai Rak Thai. Meanwhile, the former Secretary-General of the DP, Gen. Sanan Kajornprasart, left the party and established a new grouping, Mahachon.

On 26 December 2004 a huge earthquake off the coast of the Indonesian province of Aceh, measuring 9.0 on the Richter scale, generated a series of powerful tsunamis that devastated coastal regions around the Indian Ocean, causing massive loss of life. In Thailand the worst affected regions were the Andaman coast and the popular resorts of Phuket and Pi Pi; the country's death toll exceeded 5,000, including many foreign holiday-makers. Apart from the great loss of life and destruction of property, the tsunami disaster also resulted in a major set-back for the tourist industry in the south and for the local economy.

Thaksin Shinawatra's Second Term

In the national elections of 6 February 2005 Thai Rak Thai won an overwhelming victory. Of the 500 seats in the House of Representatives, Thai Rak Thai won 377, the DP 96, Chart Thai 25 and Mahachon two. However, the 14 provinces of southern Thailand deviated from the national trend. Of the region's 54 seats, all but two were won by the DP and only one by Thai Rak Thai. The latter party lost the seats that it had previously held in the three border provinces of Pattani, Yala and Narathiwat to the DP. Equally significantly, despite perceptions of popular support in these provinces for separatism, the region recorded an average voter turn-out of more than 70%, which was above the national average. Nevertheless, the DP leader, Banyat Bantadtan, resigned and was replaced by the popular Abhisit Vejjajiva, who promised to make radical reforms to the party.

By far the most serious problem confronting the Government throughout 2004 and 2005 was the rapidly deteriorating security situation in the southern border provinces. In September 2004 a judge in Pattani, who had been involved in trials of suspected militants, was murdered by unidentified gunmen. In early October a student at the Pattani campus of Prince of Songkhla University (PSU) was shot dead by assailants on a motorcycle, close to the university's gates. The killing led to several hundred students withdrawing from their courses at PSU and leaving the university. Repeated attacks and threats against schools and government offices also resulted in unprecedented numbers of requests by teachers and government officials to be transferred out of the region. In late October, at the border town of Tak Bai, Narathiwat province, adjacent to Malaysia's Kelantan state, a crowd gathered around a police station to demand the release of a number of people who had been detained on suspicion of being involved in the ongoing violence. Although reports differed on the events that followed, it appeared that shots were fired into the crowd, killing at least six people. More than 1,300 of the protesters were then arrested. Several hundred of those arrested were loaded onto trucks, which transported the detainees to a holding camp in Pattani, a trip of several hours. Upon arrival, at least 78 of the detainees had died, according to some reports by suffocation. An initial investigation ordered by the Government conceded only that some errors had been made in the handling of the protest, particularly in the transport of the detainees. Prime Minister Thaksin later made a televised statement expressing regret at the deaths, while staunchly defending the security forces' actions. A rare joint sitting of the Senate and House of Representatives also debated the issue. News of the incident prompted widespread domestic and international criticism. In an unusual statement, King Bhumibol asserted that the Government needed to use lenience and to encourage more local participation in dealing with the perpetrators of unrest.

In March 2005 the Prime Minister established a 48-member 'National Reconciliation Council', chaired by former Prime Minister Anand Panyarachun. The Council was composed of academics, social activists, military officers, police and government officials, Muslim clergy (both from Bangkok and the southern region) and local residents. It was charged with issuing independent recommendations to the Government on how best to address the crisis, although these would be non-binding. While some regarded the establishment of the Council as a sign that the Government was genuinely responding to the criticism of its handling of the conflict in the south, others saw it as a public relations exercise designed to divert attention from the Government's uncompromising approach.

In April 2005 bombs exploded simultaneously at Hat Yai International Airport and at a hypermarket and hotel in nearby Songkhla, killing two people and injuring dozens more. Killings by the security forces of *pondok ustaz* (religious school teachers) suspected of links with the militants were countered with revenge killings of Thai Buddhist schoolteachers. In response, the Government acceded to a request to allow government-employed teachers to carry handguns for self-defence. Meanwhile, there were continuing reports of abductions and disappearances of local residents. The case of the disappearance of the prominent Muslim lawyer, Somchai Neelaphaijit, a year earlier (see above) remained unsolved. One of the most audacious attacks to date occurred in July, when approximately 60 militants blew up the electricity generating station in Yala, which caused a major power failure, before carrying out bomb and arson attacks on at least eight targets across the city. Two policemen were killed in the violence and at least 17 people were injured.

A state of emergency in the three southern provinces was immediately declared, and an emergency decree (requiring only cabinet approval) was swiftly approved, giving the Prime Minister wide powers, including an extension of the period in which suspects could be detained without charge to 30 days, as well as the authority to censor news, to conduct searches of houses without warrants, to monitor phones, to prohibit public gatherings and to give immunity from prosecution for the actions of security officials in the region. The decree, and the manner in which it was promulgated, provoked strong criticism from Anand Panyarachun, the National Press Council of Thailand, civil libertarians and pro-democracy activists. The National Human Rights Commission demanded that the decree be withdrawn on the grounds that it violated the Constitution. However, one opinion poll conducted in Bangkok suggested that more than 70% of the public supported the decree. By August 2005 more than 800 people had been reported as having lost their lives in the conflict since the upsurge of violence in January of the previous year.

Amid adverse economic conditions, the hitherto overwhelming political dominance of the Prime Minister and Thai Rak Thai was challenged during the latter half of 2005. In July controversy arose over Thaksin's decision to replace the Auditor-General, Jaruvan Maintaka, who was known to be linked to the Wang Nam Yen faction. Although an acting Auditor-General was appointed in her place, Jaruvan refused to relinquish her position on the grounds that her dismissal had not been approved by the King. In a further, highly unusual, sign of royal dissatisfaction with the Government, the King also withheld approval of a list of Counter Corruption Commissioners submitted to him by the Prime Minister.

Thaksin's control over the media was also challenged. A weekly current affairs television programme, *Muang Thai Rai Sapda* ('This Week in Thailand'), hosted by media tycoon and head of the Manager Media Group Sondhi Limthongkul, became increasingly bold in its revelations of corruption within the Government and the conflicts of interest surrounding the Prime Minister himself. The programme was eventually taken off air under government pressure. Thaksin subsequently filed a lawsuit against Sondhi, suing him for 500m. baht and the Manager Media Group for a further 500m. baht. Legal action was also filed against a journalist working for the *Thai Post* newspaper, Suphinya Klangnarong, who was sued for 1,000m. baht for reporting on an alleged conflict of interest related to the Prime Minister's involvement in his family company, Shin Corporation. Meanwhile, a controversial attempt by a businessman with close links to Thaksin to buy a controlling stake in *Matichon*, one of the country's most respected daily newspapers, eventually failed, following strong public opposition to the deal.

With criticism of Thaksin in the National Assembly and the media effectively muted, the opposition was becoming more active in other forums. A rebel Thai Rak Thai legislator, Pramuan Rotchanaseri, published a widely promoted book, *Royal Power*, which, while ostensibly arguing for the central role of the monarchy in the Thai state, was also widely interpreted as being critical of Thaksin. By October 2005 the rallies that Sondhi was organizing in place of his weekly television programme formed the focal point of public opposition to Thaksin, attracting large crowds, sometimes numbering tens of thousands. During the rallies, Sondhi and other prominent critics of the Government voiced increasingly detailed allegations of corruption. Much of the criticism directed against Thaksin now began to invoke the monarchy. A recurrent theme both at the rallies and in Sondhi's newspaper *The Manager* was Thaksin's perceived lack of respect for the King. He was accused of presiding over a ceremony at the Temple of the Emerald Buddha at the Grand Palace, traditionally the duty of the King, and of attempting to appoint without royal approval a new Supreme Patriarch of the Sangha (Buddhist order) in place of the ailing incumbent.

The perception of a deepening conflict between Thaksin and the King gained further credence following the King's annual birthday speech in December 2005, which appeared to contain criticism of Thaksin's lawsuits against his opponents, as well as of his business interests, and in which the King advised Thaksin's Government to follow his 'self-sufficient economy' theory, first promoted by the monarch almost 10 years previously following the financial crisis of 1997. This criticism was apparently heeded; Thaksin withdrew the lawsuits against Sondhi, Jaruvan Maintaka was reinstated as Auditor-General and government agencies acted to promote the King's self-sufficiency theory with renewed vigour.

The sale in January 2006 of the Shinawatra family's stake in Shin Corporation to Temasek Holdings, the investment wing of the Singaporean Government, for 73,000m. baht (approximately US $1,900m.) precipitated a major political crisis. The sale outraged large sections of the middle class, the media and academics, not only because it had been sold to a foreign company, but also because the sale was tax-free. The deal was heavily criticized at Sondhi's weekly rallies, at which the number of participants had grown significantly. Sondhi had now been joined by the former general and leader of the 1992 pro-democracy demonstrations, Chamlong Srimuang, as well as by a number of academics and union and NGO leaders, to form a loosely based coalition, the People's Alliance for Democracy (PAD). The PAD thus became the focus of demands for Thaksin's resignation. The PAD received support from many groups. Academics came out overwhelmingly against Thaksin, participating in the rallies, signing petitions demanding Thaksin's resignation on the grounds of his alleged lack of 'morality', and contributing articles in the press, which had by now also begun to turn against the Prime Minister. Politicians and prominent businesspeople made appearances at the rallies. Meanwhile, the Privy Council had also begun to assume a more prominent role. Former Prime Minister Prem, now President of the Privy Council and regarded as the King's spokesman, gave numerous speeches criticizing the Government and urging the reintroduction of morality into politics.

In response to this growing political opposition, in February 2006 Thaksin called an early legislative election, to be held in early April. The three main opposition parties—the DP, Chart Thai and Mahachon—immediately announced that they would boycott the election, and reiterated their insistence that Thaksin resign. Meanwhile, the rallies held by Sondhi and the PAD were joined by counter-rallies organized by Thaksin's supporters, which also drew large crowds of many tens of thousands. The PAD, the DP and the other opposition parties, numerous prominent academics, as well as the Press Council and the Law Society of Thailand, appealed in March for the use of Article 7 of the Constitution: for the King to dismiss Thaksin and appoint an interim Prime Minister and Government.

However, as expected, Thai Rak Thai won the legislative election on 2 April 2006 with an adequate, albeit reduced, majority. The party won approximately 16m. votes, almost 60% of the total ballots cast. A notable outcome of the election was Thai Rak Thai's success in Bangkok, hitherto seen as the focus of opposition to Thaksin, where almost one-half of those who voted cast their ballots in support of the ruling party. However, the election produced a constitutional problem in that a number of seats (particularly in the DP's stronghold in southern Thailand) had not returned candidates with the required 20% of the total vote, as a result of the opposition's 'No-vote' campaign. The DP declared that it would also boycott any by-elections held for these seats, thus creating uncertainty as to whether the House of Representatives could be convened by the requisite date (60 days subsequent to the holding of elections).

Following a meeting with the King, Thaksin unexpectedly announced that he would not be forming a new government and would temporarily step down as Prime Minister, appointing Deputy Prime Minister Gen. Chidchai Wannasathit in his place. The Palace's increasingly active intervention in the political crisis was again apparent when later in April 2006 the King summoned the judges of the country's three highest courts—the Supreme Court, the Supreme Administrative Court and the Constitutional Court—to find a resolution to the uncertainty caused by the election. Within two weeks the Constitutional Court had declared the election results void, owing to alleged irregularities in the conduct of the poll. Following this ruling, the Election Commission came under increasing criticism from those who believed that it had been partial to Thai Rak Thai. Lawsuits were filed against all the political parties for infringements of electoral law, which, if successful, would result in the mandatory dissolution of those parties. In May Thaksin resumed his position as interim Prime Minister, arguing that government leadership was needed pending new elections.

The escalating political tension between Thaksin and the Palace was temporarily alleviated in June 2006 by the celebrations held in honour of the 60th anniversary of the King's accession to the throne. In a speech to mark the occasion, the King reiterated the importance of his self-sufficient economy theory. In the same month government offices and the media began a campaign urging the entire country to wear yellow shirts with the slogan 'We Love the King' on Mondays for the remainder of the year as part of the Diamond Jubilee celebrations. In late June Thaksin gave an extraordinary speech to a meeting of senior civil servants in which he referred to a 'charismatic person' who, he claimed, was contravening the Constitution and interfering in the political process without any respect for the rule of law. It was widely believed that the person to whom he referred was the King, the reference remaining implicit because of Thailand's strict *lèse-majesté* law, which prohibited criticism of the monarch. However, any disparaging reference to the monarchy was unprecedented in modern Thai politics. The remarks provoked outrage in the press. Members of the opposition challenged Thaksin to reveal the name of the 'charismatic person', while a group of aristocratic women held a press conference threatening to sue Thaksin for *lèse-majesté*.

Since public discussion of the monarchy's political role was highly circumscribed, owing to the *lèse-majesté* law and constitutional restrictions, there emerged an unusual situation whereby the monarchy was actively involving itself in the political process, yet public discussion of this development was prohibited. Debate in the media was limited and indirect. Although lively and open discussions about the King's political interventions, as well as his enormous business interests, took place on numerous websites, which had become an important forum for political discussion, even these were soon censored. Internet discussion boards containing postings potentially liable to charges of *lèse-majesté* were closed down, and various books and journals criticizing the monarchy were banned. Conversely, the Privy Council repeatedly appealed to all political parties to cease alluding to the King for the purposes of political gain.

In July 2006 the King approved a government request to hold new elections in October, the third legislative poll in less than two years. Meanwhile, in August the three remaining representatives of the Election Commission were imprisoned for four years, following their convictions on charges of improper handling of the by-elections held for those seats that had not produced a clear result in the first round of the poll in April. A number of demonstrators who had protested against their detention were also imprisoned for contempt of court later in that month. The judiciary's unprecedented political activism prompted Thaksin to make another indirect reference to royal interference in the judiciary in a speech in early August.

THE COUP OF 2006 AND SUBSEQUENT EVENTS

On 19 September 2006 a military coup led by the Commander-in-Chief of the Army, Gen. Sonthi Boonyaratglin, ousted the Prime Minister and his Government from power while Thaksin and several other prominent government ministers were in the USA, attending a UN General Assembly meeting in New York. Senior members of the Thai Rak Thai Government were arrested and detained, and others went into hiding. The coup leaders were granted a late-night audience with the King and Queen; President of the Privy Council Prem was also in attendance. An official announcement issued by the military junta following the coup claimed that the action had been taken as a result of divisions in Thai society that threatened to lead to violence, widespread corruption, political domination of independent bodies and repeated insults to the monarchy. The junta, comprising the commanders of the army, navy, air force and police force, called itself (in English) the Council for Democratic Reform under the Constitutional Monarchy. When the coup leaders became concerned about implicating the monarchy in the seizure of power, the English name was changed to the Council for Democratic Reform (CDR), although the Thai name retained the reference to the monarchy. The CDR subsequently announced that an interim Prime Minister would be appointed within two weeks, that a new National Assembly would be selected and that full legislative elections would take place within a year, subsequent to the drafting of a new constitution. In the mean time, martial law was imposed and the military maintained a highly visible presence in Bangkok, with soldiers patrolling the streets and with tanks surrounding Government House. The King issued a royal decree of approval for the creation of the CDR, endorsing the actions of the coup leaders, who had by now banned all meetings of political organizations and imposed strict censorship of the media. The combined effect of the coup leaders' efforts to portray the seizure of power as having received royal approval was that outright criticism of the coup was muted, owing to Thailand's strict laws forbidding criticism of the monarchy.

The coup did not merely remove Thaksin: it set in motion what could be regarded as a minor revolution in government and a reversal of many of the democratic reforms of the previous 15 years. Following its royal endorsement, the CDR carried out a purge of the military, police force and bureaucracy, arresting, transferring or demoting officers in senior positions who were considered loyal to the former Thai Rak Thai Government. On 1 October 2006 the military junta announced the appointment of Gen. Surayud Chulanont, a prominent privy councillor and retired army commander-in-chief, as Thailand's new interim Prime Minister. Besides his close links to the Palace, Surayud was also known to have commanded forces involved in the suppression of pro-democracy demonstrators in May 1992. Having received royal approval, Gen. Surayud was formally sworn in later on the same day and was to remain in office until the holding of legislative elections. A new Interim Constitution—drafted by Meechai Ruchuphan, a conservative lawyer, Prem ally and prominent member of the anti-Thaksin movement, —was promulgated, having been endorsed by the King. Under the terms of the temporary charter, the CDR changed its name to the Council for National Security (CNS), and granted itself substantial powers and responsibilities, including the appointment of a new 250-member legislature in place of the dissolved Senate and House of Representatives. Thaksin, who remained overseas, announced his resignation from Thai Rak Thai, together with more than 100 other party members.

Prime Minister Surayud announced the composition of his interim Cabinet in the following week. Like the Prime Minister himself, this administration was to remain in office until the proposed legislative elections in the latter part of 2007. Most of the cabinet appointees were senior bureaucrats, many regarded as being close to Prem. Among the notable appointments were that of Pridiyathorn Davakula, Governor of the Bank of Thailand, as Deputy Prime Minister and Minister of Finance, and of Kosit Panpiemras, former executive chairman of Bangkok Bank PCL, as Deputy Prime Minister and Minister of Industry. Former army chief of staff Boonrawd Somtas, a Chulachomklao Military Academy classmate of Surayud, was appointed Minister of Defence. Aree Wong-araya, a Muslim and a close associate of the deposed Thaksin, was charged with resolving the ongoing insurgency in Thailand's southern provinces in his new capacity as Minister of the Interior; and Nit Piboonsongkram, who had led the negotiations on Thailand's free trade agreement with the USA, was allocated the foreign affairs portfolio. While there was some mild criticism in the media of the advanced age of many of the ministers, as well as the overwhelmingly bureaucratic composition of the Cabinet, the new administration received the strong support of the King in his birthday speech in early December 2006. The junta also appointed a 'rubber-stamp' National Legislative Assembly (NLA) predominantly composed of military and bureaucratic officials known to be close to Prem and the Palace, as well as a number of individuals who had been active in the anti-Thaksin campaign, including opposition politicians, representatives of Sondhi's Manager Media Group, anti-Thaksin academics and NGOs. Among the appointees from the business community was Jada Wattanasiritham, President and CEO of Siam Commercial Bank, in which the royal family's investment office, the Crown Property Bureau, was the major shareholder (Jada was also the wife of Paiboon Wattanasiritham, appointed by the junta as Minister of Social Development and Human Security and later Deputy Prime Minister). The NLA elected Meechai Ruchuphan as its Speaker. (In 1991 Meechai had attracted controversy by serving as Deputy Prime Minister in the military-installed Government of Anand Panyarachun, and by later drafting the amnesty for the military leaders involved in the killings of pro-democracy demonstrators in May 1992.) In addition, the heads of a number of Thailand's most lucrative state enterprises, including Thai Airways, the Airports Authority of Thailand and the TOT (formerly the Telephone Organization of Thailand), were replaced by members of the junta.

The junta immediately acted to increase the political influence of the military. One of its most controversial measures was to restructure and expand the powers of the Internal Security Operations Command (ISOC), a national security body that had played a major role in the suppression of the communist insurgency in the late 1970s and early 1980s. Coup leader Gen. Sonthi assumed the role of director of the ISOC and gave the organization responsibility for monitoring anti-Government movements (referred to in the media as 'undercurrents') in the rural areas, especially in the north and north-east, which had been the heartland of Thai Rak Thai voter support. In July 2007 the Cabinet sent to the NLA for consideration a draft national security bill, which would formalize the new role that had been given to the ISOC after the coup. Under this proposed legislation, the ISOC would be granted greatly increased powers and funds; it would be headed by the Army Commander-in-Chief, his chief of staff would be in charge of its secretariat, and army regional commanders would head the ISOC's regional branches. In addition, the ISOC would be given authority over other local government agencies in security matters, and would be required only to report to the Prime Minister, with minimal regulation of its powers and the provision of immunity from prosecution for its officials. In effect, the legislation would significantly increase the power of the military for the first time since the pro-democracy movement in 1992.

In the area of economic management the new Government had less success. While the junta had been fortunate in being able to secure the appointment of the respected Pridiyathorn Davakula as Minister of Finance, the regime's anti-foreign, anti-capitalist rhetoric and promotion of the King's so-called self-sufficient economy theory gave conflicting impressions to international markets. In one speech Gen. Sonthi had cited the need to overthrow a 'capitalist dictatorship' as one of the reasons for carrying out the coup. Surayud announced that negotiations regarding free trade agreements would be suspended. The junta's criticism of Singapore's undue influence over Thailand's economy as a result of the controversial Shin Corporation deal also demonstrated a new economic nationalism. In December 2006 the Government was forced to perform an embarrassing reversal after the Bank of Thailand announced that it would impose a 30% reserve requirement for a period of one year on capital brought into Thailand by foreigners. The announcement led to an immediate decrease, in one day, of 15% on Thailand's stock market, prompting the Government to announce that it would exempt certain categories of foreign investment from the requirement. Although the stock market quickly recovered, the perceived indecisiveness of the Government severely damaged its credibility. In February 2007 Somkhit Chatusiphitak, regarded as largely responsible for the Thai Rak Thai Government's economic policy and highly respected internationally, was appointed as an economic adviser; his first duty was to explain to foreign investors the Government's adoption of the King's self-sufficient economy theory as the principal policy. However, Somkhit resigned unexpectedly, after little more than a week, amid media criticism of the Government for appointing a former Thaksin confidant. As rumours spread about internal discord exacerbated by personality clashes and disagreements over policy, Pridiyathorn announced his own resignation. Meanwhile, a growing problem for the Government was the rising value of the baht, which placed increasing pressure on Thailand's exporters.

The junta also acted quickly to exert its control over the media. Interviews given by exiled former Prime Minister Thaksin to international news organizations were banned from Thai television networks, and the satellite and cable services in Thailand of CNN, the British Broadcasting Corporation (BBC) and other global networks that carried the interviews were blocked for the duration of the interview, as were the relevant sections of these networks' websites. The Thai media were publicly warned by the junta not to refer to, or report news about, the former Prime Minister. In May 2007, following their airing of an interview with Thaksin in London, United Kingdom, a number of community radio stations were closed down as part of wider action against approximately 3,000 local stations across the country. The junta also began to take action against websites, where most of the anti-coup discussion was taking place. In April the popular video-clip sharing website YouTube was permanently blocked by the Government after it carried videos maligning the King and his alleged support for military dictatorship. Some of the most popular Thai websites for political debate were either warned, blocked or forced to practise a high degree of self-censorship, in particular on the question of the monarchy's involvement in the coup. A website created by Thaksin was also initially blocked by the Government. The suppression of the manifestation of political opposition on the internet was reinforced in June when the Government signed into law the stringent Computer Crime Act. The new law gave the Government greatly increased control over internet service providers, as well as imposing a maximum prison sentence of five years for anyone found guilty of disseminating material deemed to 'damage national security and cause public alarm' or to 'contradict peace and morality'. Academic criticism of the regime in other forms was also targeted, with various publications being banned. In December 2006 a scandal that appeared in the media involving Surayud's ownership of land and construction of a house in conservation zone forest in Khao Yai national park was rapidly contained.

Meanwhile, an intensive programme of royalist pro-Government propaganda began. The bureaucracy issued a directive that all state employees were to wear yellow shirts every Monday to honour the King's 80th birthday and to demonstrate their loyalty to the throne; this practice was followed by office workers in the private sector, and television presenters and newsreaders also adopted the new uniform. Thai citizens were subsequently encouraged by the state media to wear yellow, if possible, every day of the week for the remainder of the year. Surayud and most of the Cabinet were rarely seen in public without a yellow item of clothing. The Government continued to promote the King's self-sufficient economy theory as the new model for development. The theory supposedly encouraged moderation in economic matters, a problematic concept given the monarchy's own extensive financial interests; however, owing to the strict *lèse-majesté* law, criticism of the theory remained impossible. The Government was also successful in persuading international agencies such as the UN Development Programme, as well as respected individuals in the area of international economics, such as the former Director-General of the World Trade Organization (WTO) and senior member of the DP, Supachai Panichpakdi, and Nobel Prize winner Amartya Sen, to give highly publicized speeches appearing to support the concept. On the other hand, Thaksin and the former Thai Rak Thai party were criticized by the junta almost on a daily basis. Intensive media coverage was given to apparent safety problems at the new Suvarnabhumi International Airport, which were supposedly the result of the corruption of the former regime. On New Year's Eve 2006 a series of bombings occurred in Bangkok, killing three and injuring more than 30. While suspicion fell on Islamist militants involved in the insurgency in the south or on elements of the military itself, Surayud, members of the junta and the Manager Media Group attributed the events to the former Government, a charge that Thaksin vehemently denied.

Some observers had predicted that the overthrow of the Thaksin Government would lead to a reconciliation between the new administration and the insurgents in southern Thailand. In October 2006 Surayud travelled to Pattani and made a forthright apology for the human rights abuses committed under the previous Government. The apology was reported favourably in the international media, which had until then been very critical of the coup and the military regime. The new Government also revived the Southern Border Provinces Administrative Centre and Civilian-Police Military Task Force, which had previously been dissolved under Thaksin. The reformed ISOC was given an increased role in the suppression of the insurgency. However, the violence intensified, and the insurgents began to carry out operations on major targets. Although scarcely reported in the Thai media, the insurgents launched unsuccessful attacks on visits to the south by Princess Sirindhorn, Crown Prince Vajiralongkorn and a close aide to the Queen. In April 2007 the Queen announced that the policy of reconciliation was inadequate and that more force was needed. She herself had already organized weapons-training programmes in the region, in particular for the protection of local teachers, who were among the principal targets of the militants. The junta appeared to respond to the Queen's criticisms and announced that henceforth it would use stronger tactics; but the situation appeared to deteriorate. In one incident a shuttle van travelling from Yala to Songkhla was stopped by militants, and its eight Buddhist passengers were shot dead. The military also began to suffer much heavier casualties as a result of strategies such as roadside bombings.

An important test for the junta was the verdict by the Constitutional Court in the electoral fraud case in which both Thai Rak Thai and the DP had been accused of campaign irregularities in the period prior to the legislative elections of April 2006. The Constitutional Court cleared the royalist DP of all charges, while Thai Rak Thai was found guilty in a unanimous verdict. The Court ordered that Thai Rak Thai be dissolved and 111 of the party's executives be banned for five years from standing for election.

Although Thai Rak Thai, under its new leader, Jaturon Chaisaeng, protested against the Constitutional Court's decision, the dissolution of the party appeared to embolden the Government. In June 2007 the Assets Examination Committee—another body established by the junta following the coup and incorporating many anti-Thaksin appointees (including Jaruvan Maintaka, who had refused to leave her former position as Auditor-General after being dismissed by Thaksin, claiming that she had the King's support—see above)—froze 21 bank accounts belonging to Thaksin and his wife, Pojaman, holding the equivalent of more than US $1,500m. The asset immobilization was regarded as a decisive set-back to Thaksin's ability to fund any anti-Government activities. The ban on political activity was finally removed (although martial law remained in place in 35 provinces). The junta also demanded that Thaksin return to the country to answer charges of corruption, after it had earlier prevented him from returning. Meanwhile, former Thai Rak Thai officials and anti-coup groups began organizing rallies at Sanam Luang in opposition to the Government. The main target of their criticism was Prem, who was portrayed as the principal protagonist in the coup. At one stage, a total of 20,000–30,000 people were attending the weekend rallies. Thaksin's continuing popularity with many Thais was also greatly increased by the announcement in July that he had succeeded in acquiring an English Premier League football team, Manchester City.

An important task for the incoming regime was the drafting of a new constitution to replace that of 1997, which had been abrogated following the coup. In December 2006 a Constitutional Drafting Assembly (CDA) was elected from among the members of a National People's Assembly, which had been appointed by the junta. The Constitution Drafting Committee, comprising members appointed by the CDA and the CNS, was headed by the former CNS Chairman, the elderly Squadron Leader Prasong Soonsiri. Trained by the US Central Intelligence Agency (CIA), Prasong had experience in intelligence operations dating back to the era of the suppression of the communist insurgency in the 1970s–80s. He had once served as secretary to the Prime Minister's office under Prem and was known to be highly favoured by the King. Some months after the coup Prasong revealed to the media that he had played a major role in devising the coup plot, which had begun with a meeting of the heads of the army, navy and air force at the King's palace in the coastal resort of Hua Hin. In contrast to the public hearings and submissions that had been an important element in the drafting that had been conducted in 1997, the drafting of the new Constitution was carried out exclusively by members of the CDA, a task it had completed by July 2007. Copies of the draft were distributed to households throughout the country. Overall, the Constitution was designed with the clear intention of weakening the power of elected politicians, political parties and the Prime Minister, maintaining the power of the monarchy, and greatly increasing the power of the judiciary and 'independent bodies'. One of the most controversial changes was the provision that 74 of the 150 Senators would be appointed by a committee of judges and heads of 'independent bodies'. Another was Article 309, which provided amnesty to those involved in the coup of September 2006. A provision to support the King's self-sufficient economy theory was also included.

Preparations were then made to submit the draft to a referendum, scheduled for August 2007. Vaguely worded legislation was hastily approved by the NLA, prescribing a 10-year prison sentence for those found to be 'influencing or persuading' voters. Sodsri Satayatham, a member of the CDA as well as of the (junta-appointed) Election Commission responsible for overseeing the referendum, publicly stated that any campaigner for the rejection of the draft risked prosecution. Members of the junta implied that if the Constitution were not approved, elections could not be held. Meanwhile, the bureaucracy and the military undertook a public campaign via the media and mass rallies in which participants were asked to wear yellow, in effect encouraging people to vote in favour of the draft. The royalist-leaning DP, Chart Thai and Mahachon parties also gave their support. The remainder of the former Thai Rak Thai party, groups of academics and a number of NGOs ignored the legislation and began a campaign for the draft to be rejected. At the referendum held on 19 August 2007, however, the new Constitution was endorsed, with almost 58% of voters reportedly supporting the draft and 42% rejecting it. Given the difficulties in campaigning, the number of votes against the draft was higher than expected and strongest in the former Thai Rak Thai strongholds of the north and north-east, suggesting the continued popularity of the party among the large rural electorate there. Upon the King's approval, the new Constitution took effect on 24 August.

Following the issuing of a court warrant for his arrest, in August 2007 the CNS finally urged Thaksin to return to Thailand from exile in the United Kingdom to answer corruption charges. In the same month it was announced that elections to the House of Representatives would be held on 23 December—shortly after the King's birthday celebrations. Prasong Soonsiri, one of the protagonists of the coup and Chairman of the CDA, criticized the Government for the timing of the elections and suggested that they be postponed until Thaksin's support base had been more thoroughly reduced. The Government's own concern regarding the elections was indicated by Prime Minister Surayud's declaration that the Government would be unwilling to allow the European Union (EU) to send electoral observers. In September the Government awarded a 4% pay increase to civil servants, who had generally been supportive of the coup.

In order to contest the forthcoming elections, in September 2007 Thaksin supporters regrouped under the People's Power Party (PPP—Palang Prachachon). A veteran conservative politician with impeccable royalist credentials, Samak Sundaravej, was chosen to head the party. To make his loyalties clear to the electorate, Samak publicly declared that he was Thaksin's 'nominee'. The PPP's campaign pledges included an amnesty for the 111 banned Thai Rak Thai politicians and amendments to the new Constitution. Besides the PPP, various other political parties were also established, including Puea Pandin (For the Land) and Matchimathipataya (Neutral Democratic Party), the membership of which included politicians from the dissolved Thai Rak Thai. Campaigning for the elections took place under continuing martial law in 35 provinces (almost one-half of the country), primarily in the former Thai Rak Thai heartland in the north and north-east of the country. The PPP was also subject to frequent threats by the Election Commission that it would disqualify PPP candidates or even recommend the dissolution of the party over alleged violations of the electoral law. In one case, the distribution in areas where the PPP was campaigning of a compact disc, in which Thaksin offered his support to the party, was held to be an electoral offence. Meanwhile, the PPP drew attention to a 'leaked' document signed by the junta leaders and dated 15 September—shortly after the formation of the PPP—which urged the military to undertake a propaganda campaign aimed both at the middle class and ordinary voters to prevent the return of the 'old power', i.e. Thaksin and his followers, via a PPP victory at the elections. The main themes of the propaganda campaign were that Thaksin intended to implement a presidential system, that his 'populist' policies ran counter to the King's theory of economic self-sufficiency, and that the former Prime Minister was using the international media to criticize the monarchy.

In November 2007 the (junta-appointed) NLA adopted the controversial new Internal Security Act, first submitted for its consideration in July, which granted greatly enhanced powers to the ISOC, including authority over the civilian administration and the power to restrict freedom of expression, assembly and movement. Meanwhile, in another sign of the politicization of the judiciary, on 17 December, just days before the elections, the King gave another speech to a group of civilian and military judges. In an indirect reference to Thaksin, he stated that 'someone' was misguidedly taking the country in the wrong direction using trickery and deception, and that it was the judges' responsibility to use the law as a 'weapon' so that the military did not need to stage a coup.

To the dismay of the junta and its supporters, the legislative elections held on 23 December 2007 were yet another triumph for Thaksin's party—this time in its reconstituted form of the PPP. Despite the greatly restricted conditions for campaigning, including martial law, a huge military presence and allegations of electoral irregularities directed at several of its members, the PPP was able to capture 233 of the 480 seats in the House of Representatives. The DP won 164 seats, Chart Thai 34 and Puea Pandin 24. Following protracted negotiations, in January 2008 the PPP was finally able to announce that it had formed a coalition Government with Chart Thai, Puea Pandin and a number of smaller parties. As well as the premiership, Samak, who was known to have good relations with the military, also assumed the important post of Minister of Defence. Other strategic portfolios, such as finance, education, the interior and foreign affairs, were awarded to PPP members.

Following the month-long celebrations of the King's birthday in December 2007, the monarchy remained at the centre of public attention with the announcement of the death of the King's elder sister, Princess Galyani Vadhana, at the beginning of January 2008. The junta-installed Government declared three months of official mourning, during which time the entire civilian bureaucracy was ordered to wear black. Ceremonies in preparation for the Princess's cremation continued throughout the year. Just prior to its official disbandment in January, the CNS recommended a 15% pay rise for the 442 military officers who had participated in the coup of September 2006 (this in addition to a 50% increase in the overall military budget since the coup).

Immediately after it assumed power, the future of the PPP-led Government was in doubt. The Election Commission had already ordered by-elections to be held in a large number of constituencies in which alleged violations of the electoral law had taken place, mostly those won by PPP candidates. In February 2008 the Election Commission voted in favour of disqualifying the Speaker of the House of Representatives, Yongyuth Tiyapairat, PPP deputy for Chiang Rai, from office over alleged vote-buying, and referred the case to the Supreme Court; Yongyuth stood down pending a verdict. Under the provisions of the new Constitution, the case could ultimately result in the dissolution of the PPP, a decision that would be taken by the courts. At the same time, the PPP's coalition partners Chart Thai and Matchimathipataya were also threatened with dissolution for alleged violations of electoral law. In February the 74 appointees to the 150-member Senate were endorsed by the Election Commission, following their selection by a committee consisting of judges and members of junta-appointed committees. Among them were numerous well-known opponents of Thaksin, such as Khamnoon Sitthisamarn, senior editor of Sondhi Limthongkul's Manager Media Group and member of the anti-Thaksin PAD, and Songkram Chuenpibarn, a former member of the CNS.

Following the formation of the PPP-led Government, Thaksin returned to Thailand in late February 2008. His wife, Pojaman Shinawatra, had returned a month earlier, whereupon she was arrested and charged with the evasion of tax related to a land purchase. The PPP reiterated its intention of amending the Constitution, prompting the PAD, which had been dormant during the period of the junta's rule, to resume its demonstrations, this time at the Makhawan Bridge in central Bangkok. The rallies were broadcast nationally via Sondhi's cable television channel Asia Satellite TV (ASTV). The royalist sympathies of the PAD were again clearly on display, with members wearing yellow shirts (symbolic of the King) and blue neckerchiefs (symbolic of the Queen). Sondhi claimed that his own blue neckerchief had been a gift from the Queen, and even declared that the Queen not only approved of the PAD's rallies but had also offered them financial assistance. The PAD's first target was the Minister in the Prime Minister's Office, Chakrapob Penkair, whom the PAD accused of committing *lèse-majesté* in remarks he made during a seminar at the Foreign Correspondents' Club of Thailand (FCCT) in Bangkok in August 2007. After being officially charged with the offence, Chakrapob was forced to resign from the Cabinet at the end of May 2008. A BBC reporter, Jonathan Head, was also charged with *lèse-majesté* over his comments during another seminar at the Club. In July a Thai pro-Thaksin activist, Daranee Charnchoengsilpakul (also known as 'Da Torpedo'), was also arrested and charged with *lèse-majesté* in connection with a speech she had delivered at a pro-Government rally at Sanam Luang. Another activist was similarly charged for not standing when the royal anthem was played in a cinema.

As the focus of anti-Government protest moved to the PAD's rallies, the movement broadened its demands to include the resignation of the entire Government. The PAD raised a new issue, the Thai Government's endorsement of the Cambodian Government's decision to apply to UNESCO for World Heritage status for an 11th-century Khmer temple on the Thai–Cambodian border, Preah Vihear, accusing the Thai Government of 'selling out' the nation. Tensions between Thailand and Cambodia heightened as both countries dispatched hundreds of troops to the disputed border area (see Recent Foreign Relations, below), and the Preah Vihear issue gave rise to one of the main criticisms of the Government at the PAD rallies, with PAD leader Phipop Thongchai accusing Thaksin of co-operating with the Cambodian Prime Minister, Hun Sen, to 'betray the nation'. In July 2008 the Minister of Foreign Affairs, Noppadon Pattama, Thaksin's former lawyer, who was accused by the PAD and the opposition of having ceded Thai sovereignty to Cambodia, was forced to resign to relieve pressure on the Government over the issue. In the same month the PAD, in a reflection of the increasingly radical nature of its demands, proposed a controversial political reform of the House of Representatives, under which 70% of deputies would be appointed and 30% elected.

Meanwhile, attention also focused on the forthcoming court cases involving Thaksin and Pojaman. In late June 2008 three lawyers for Thaksin received six-month prison sentences, having been found guilty of attempting to bribe Supreme Court officials. Thaksin denied any involvement. At the end of July Pojaman and her brother were both convicted of failing to pay tax totalling 546m. baht on a share transaction in 1997 and sentenced to three years' imprisonment. The sentences were longer than many had predicted, increasing speculation that Thaksin might not return to Thailand to answer the charges against him. Pojaman was granted bail, pending an appeal. As rumours began to circulate that Thaksin was planning to seek asylum overseas, discord within the PPP became apparent. On 11 August, the day on which he was due to appear in court, Thaksin issued a statement in which he confirmed that he was seeking political asylum in the United Kingdom, having fled to London with Pojaman. He stated that he had no confidence in the Thai courts, because of interference in the judiciary by his political enemies, and that there had been attempts to assassinate him. He affirmed his loyalty to the monarchy, while urging his supporters to continue their commitment to him. Some political observers regarded his decision to seek asylum as the end of the Thaksin era, suggesting that it might help to end the political divisions of the previous three years.

In the early hours of 26 August 2008 a large group of PAD protesters, armed with golf clubs and knives, stormed and seized control of the National Broadcasting of Thailand (NBT) building; the PAD had accused the television station of being partial towards the Government. The police, apparently acting on information received, were able to detain more than 80 of the PAD demonstrators, who included members of the DP. Most of the remaining protesters left NBT and marched on a number of ministries, before moving to Government House, where they set up camp and demanded the resignation of Samak and his Government and the implementation of the PAD's 'new politics' proposal, whereby 70% of members of the House of Representatives would be appointed. Meanwhile, Samak, unable to enter Government House because of the protesters, established his office at the headquarters of the army. Warrants for the arrest of the PAD leadership on numerous charges, including rebellion, were issued, but the police were prevented from making the arrests by the numerous PAD protesters surrounding Government House. In early September street clashes between supporters of the PAD and of the pro-Government United Front for Democracy against Dictatorship (UDD) left one dead and scores injured. In response, Samak declared a state of emergency in Bangkok.

Also in early September 2008 the Election Commission voted unanimously to recommend the dissolution of the PPP on the grounds of the party's alleged complicity in electoral fraud committed by former Speaker Yongyuth (who had been found guilty of vote-buying by the Supreme Court in July and banned from politics for five years), and referred the case to the Constitutional Court to confirm the decision. On the following day the Government suffered a further reverse when the Minister of Foreign Affairs, Tej Bunnag, who had been transferred from his former position as adviser to the Office of His Majesty's Principal Private Secretary just over a month previously, resigned from his cabinet post. On 9 September the Constitutional Court ruled that Prime Minister Samak had violated the Constitution by accepting payment for his hosting of a television cookery programme, thus forcing him to resign from the premiership. A week later the PPP selected Somchai Wongsawat, a brother-in-law of Thaksin, as the new party leader and Prime Minister.

Somchai became the new target of the PAD, which accused him of being Thaksin's 'nominee' and vowed to oust the new Prime Minister and his Government. In early October 2008 serious clashes broke out near the occupied Government House, as the PAD erected barricades and rolled out razor wire with the intention of blocking road access to the House of Representatives and preventing Somchai from making his inaugural speech. The police were drafted in, and tear gas was used in an attempt to disperse the protesters. At least one demonstrator was killed and hundreds were injured, although it was unclear whether the injuries had been caused by the tear gas or by small 'ping pong' grenades allegedly carried by some of the protesters. A number of policemen were also injured. In a separate incident, an apparent car bomb attack took place outside the offices of Chart Thai, one of the PPP's coalition partners, which killed the vehicle's owner, apparently a PAD supporter. On the following day Queen Sirikit issued an extraordinary public statement declaring that she would donate 100,000 baht towards the medical costs of the injured protesters. The statement appeared to confirm what was already widely suspected: the Queen's support for the PAD. Such sympathy was again demonstrated publicly when in mid-October she and Princess Chulabhorn attended the cremation ceremony of one of the demonstrators. The father of the dead woman reportedly stated that the Queen had thanked him for his daughter's sacrifice to protect the monarchy; furthermore, it was reported that the Queen was concerned for the well-being of all the protesters and that the King had ordered that the family's medical expenses be covered. The clashes exacerbated the divisions in an already polarized society. The pressure on the Government increased as a committee of 30 university presidents urged Prime Minister Somchai to dissolve the legislature and call fresh elections. The clashes also led to the resignation of the Deputy Prime Minister with responsibility for security, Gen. Chavalit Yongchaiyudh, who later appeared to suggest that the only solution to the crisis was a military coup and that the Commander-in-Chief of the Army, Gen. Anupong Paochinda, should not hesitate to take such action. Under considerable pressure himself, Anupong repeatedly denied rumours of an impending coup. Together with the other heads of the Thai armed forces, Anupong appeared on television urging the Government to resign, in order to take responsibility for the violent clashes. In a televised address to the nation, Prime Minister Somchai restated his refusal to resign.

A series of court decisions also went against the Government. The Appeals Court rejected the rebellion charge that had been made against PAD leaders Chamlong Srimuang and Chaiwat Sinsuwong for their seizure of the NBT television station and Government House. Seven other PAD leaders were released on bail, following which they rejoined the protest. Thaksin was sentenced *in absentia* to two years' imprisonment in October 2008, having been found guilty of a corrupt land purchase.

The PAD occupation of Government House continued amid nightly grenade attacks from unidentified assailants, which left a number of protesters killed or injured. With the Government maintaining a firm stance, the PAD intensifed its protests in late November 2008 when it seized control of Suvarnabhumi International Airport, as well as the domestic airport in Bangkok, Don Muang. This action forced the closure of both facilities, causing chaos and stranding an estimated 250,000 foreign visitors. Gen. Anupong urged the dissolution of the House of Representatives and the holding of new elections. Prime Minister Somchai declared a state of emergency. However, the PAD refused to end its protest. The security forces appeared reluctant to move in to dislodge the protesters, apparently fearing injuries to the airport occupants, who included women and children. The crisis was finally resolved in early December when the Constitutional Court once again ruled that the pro-Thaksin PPP, along with its coalition partners Chart Thai and Matchimathipataya, be dissolved and its executives banned from politics for a period of five years. Immediately following the announcement, the PAD agreed to abandon its occupation of the airports.

In the negotiations to form a new government Newin Chidchob, who had been one of the leading power-brokers in the former Thai Rak Thai and PPP Governments and who controlled a number of deputies from the lower north-east region, agreed to take his supporters in the House of Representatives to join a Democrat-led coalition. Amid reports that other members of the legislature had been placed under pressure by the military to join the coalition, the Democrats, having secured a narrow parliamentary majority, were finally able to form a coalition Government, thus returning to power for the first time in eight years.

THE GOVERNMENT OF ABHISIT VEJJAJIVA

On 15 December 2008 Abhisit Vejjajiva, leader of the DP, was appointed Prime Minister. One of the most controversial appointments to the new Cabinet was that of senior diplomat Kasit Piromya as Minister of Foreign Affairs; he had been closely associated with the PAD protests and had participated in the airport occupation.

Soon after taking office the Democrat-led Government instigated new action against websites deemed to be pro-Thaksin or critical of the monarchy. The new Minister of Justice, Democrat Pirapan Salirathavibhaga, announced that his highest priority was to protect the monarchy. He established a 'war room' to monitor websites and (unsuccessfully) urged the extension of the *lèse-majesté* law to outlaw even criticism of the Privy Council. In January 2009 Chulalongkorn University lecturer Giles Ungpakorn (an important figure in Thailand's NGO movement) fled Thailand for the United Kingdom, following his arrest on a charge of *lèse-majesté* arising from a book that he had written in which he was critical of the 2006 coup. A month later Ungpakorn released a statement from exile entitled 'Red Siam', which directly criticized the King and urged the establishment of a republic. In February 2009 an Australian writer who had been imprisoned earlier on *lèse-majesté* charges, Harry Nicolaides, was released after receiving a royal pardon. However, the authorities continued to take action against criticism of the monarchy, actual or perceived. In April Suwicha Thakhor was imprisoned for a minimum of 10 years under the Computer Crimes Act, which had been introduced by the military-supported Government during 2007 to counter the posting on the internet of images deemed offensive to the monarchy. *Lèse-majesté* charges were laid against the entire board of the FCCT in July 2009, for allegedly distributing copies of the speech delivered by Chakrapob Penkair in August 2007 (see above). In August, following a closed trial, Daranee Charnchoengsilpakul was sentenced to 18 years' imprisonment for her speech, delivered in 2008, that was deemed critical of the monarchy (see above). In mid-2009 *The Economist*, a respected news magazine based in the United Kingdom, estimated that 8,300 websites had been blocked for allegedly being critical of the monarchy. Ironically, *The Econo-*

mist itself practised self-censorship in Thailand on several occasions by withdrawing from circulation issues of the weekly publication that dealt with the role of the monarchy in the country's political crisis. A report by a Harvard University institute (USA) concluded that Thailand had become the fifth most rigorous censor of the internet in the world.

The formation of the new Government did little to resolve the deep polarization of Thai society. In January 2009 the pro-Thaksin UDD, led by Weera Musikhaphong, Natthawut Saikuea and Jatuporn Promphan, organized a large rally in Bangkok at which all protesters wore red shirts. Thaksin announced that contrary to his earlier decision to retire from politics he would now fight to defend his reputation and create a 'mature democracy' in Thailand. To counter the Government's near-total control of the television and print media, the UDD—or Red Shirts, as they became popularly known—set up D Station, an internet radio and television station, enabling them to broadcast their rallies and to communicate their message to their supporters. In late March Thaksin took part in a controversial 'phone-in' to a rally of Red Shirts in Chiang Mai, alleging for the first time the direct involvement of Prem in the coup of 2006. He also claimed that Prem and fellow Privy Councillors Gen. Surayud Chulanont (a former Prime Minister) and Chanchai Likhitchitta (a former President of the Supreme Court) had conspired to bring Abhisit and the Democrats to power. As political tensions again increased, in one incident a car carrying Abhisit in the coastal town of Pattaya was attacked by Red Shirt supporters.

From early April 2009 the Red Shirts began a series of mass rallies at Sanam Luang, demanding the resignation of the Privy Councillors accused of involvement in the 2006 coup and of Prime Minister Abhisit himself, and more broadly the overthrow of the élite-dominated 'bureaucratic polity' ('*ammathayathipatai*'). The rallies were supported by Thaksin, who was now residing in Dubai, with nightly televised 'phone-ins', broadcast through many internet sites and community radio stations, in which he appeared to support a popular uprising and the overthrow of the Government. A number of taxi-drivers apparently allied to the Red Shirts closed the streets leading to the Victory Monument traffic intersection, halting traffic throughout Bangkok for several hours before they were persuaded by the Red Shirts' leadership to end the blockade. Also in April 2009 a group of Red Shirts travelled to the site of the East Asia Summit and ASEAN + 3 Summit meetings being held at Pattaya, where they encountered large crowds of blue-shirted government supporters. The latter were reportedly organized and co-ordinated by the Deputy Prime Minister responsible for security, Suthep Thaugsuban, and Newin Chidchob, the de facto leader of the breakaway PPP faction that had joined the Democrat-led Government. Claiming that their peaceful protests had been met with violence by the Blue Shirts, a group of Red Shirts besieged the hotel at which the ASEAN + 3 Summit meeting was being held, forcing its postponement. Meanwhile, in Bangkok another group of Red Shirt protesters attacked a car carrying the Secretary-General of the Prime Minister's Office, Niphon Phromphan, who was known to be closely connected to the Crown Prince. Shortly thereafter Abhisit declared a state of emergency in Bangkok, and troops were ordered to disperse the Red Shirt protesters. The situation erupted into violent riots in various parts of Bangkok, with an unconfirmed number of people killed and scores injured. The leaders of the Red Shirts were arrested and pro-Red Shirt internet sites blocked. Order was restored by the military after several days, and on 24 April the state of emergency decree was rescinded.

The suppression of the Red Shirts' uprising in April 2009 served to consolidate the Democrats' power. Abhisit announced a government campaign to combat the Red Shirts' media network. Other campaigns were mobilized to 'protect the monarchy' and to promote the King's self-sufficient economy theory. The Government appeared to have the strong support of the military, as demonstrated by the former's apparently lenient treatment of the latter with regard to a number of scandals. These included the discovery in the Gulf of Thailand of a submerged container in which more than 100 bodies were found, amid allegations of human rights abuses by the Thai military against Rohingya Muslim refugees who were coming by boat from Myanmar. Meanwhile, in-mid April an assassination attempt was made on Sondhi Limthongkul, leader of the PAD, which had been instrumental in bringing the Democrats to power. While Minister of Foreign Affairs Kasit Piromya implicated Thaksin, Sondhi himself publicly suggested that elements close to the royal family might have been involved. In some public statements Sondhi appeared to suggest that the political reform aims of the PAD and the Red Shirts were not dissimilar, raising speculation about future co-operation between the two groups. Despite the failure of the April uprising, popular support for Thaksin did not appear to have declined. In July celebrations were held for Thaksin's 60th birthday in provinces all around the country, particularly in the north-east and the north. In a televised phone-in programme, Thaksin announced that he was about to open a new global satellite television station to promote Thailand to the world, and that, to mark his birthday, he would offer 6,000 scholarships to underprivileged students. At the same time it was revealed that the Red Shirts were to organize a petition urging a royal pardon for Thaksin. The petition was widely criticized by royalist-leaning academics, senior military officers and 29 department permanent secretaries, who issued a joint critical statement. A rumour circulated in the media that at a meeting of the Privy Council a number of Councillors had also expressed similar opposition to the petition, which was subsequently denied in a statement by the Council. Abhisit announced that such a petition was 'not appropriate' and claimed that it was part of a plot to overthrow the monarchy. Nevertheless, in mid-August the Red Shirts presented the petition, bearing more than 3m. signatures, to a representative of the Palace. In a televised phone-in to a Red Shirt rally at Sanam Luang, Thaksin repeated his loyalty to the monarchy and led the Red Shirts in singing the royal anthem.

The national political crisis diverted attention from the ongoing conflict in the southern border provinces. While the number of incidents had declined substantially since the peak of 2007, violence continued, with regular drive-by shootings and bomb attacks. In January 2009 Amnesty International issued a statement claiming that the Thai security forces had made systematic use of torture on suspected insurgents who had been captured. Amnesty later released another statement condemning attacks by insurgents on civilians. In May a court absolved the military of any wrongdoing related to the Tak Bai incident in 2004, when 78 southern Malay-Muslims had died (see above). In one of the most serious incidents, an attack by gunmen on a mosque in Cho Ai Rong district in Narathiwat province in June 2009 claimed the lives of at least 11 people and injured many others.

In September 2009 the King was admitted to hospital, reportedly suffering from a fever. News of the King's apparently deteriorating condition in the following month led to a 7% decline in the value of the stock market within just two days. Two stockbrokers were subsequently arrested for allegedly posting rumours about the critical state of the King's health on anti-monarchy websites. By the end of the year the King had resumed some of his official duties; however, he remained in hospital more than a year later. The King's hospitalization occurred at a time when Thaksin appeared to be attempting to focus international attention on the role of the monarchy in the country's ongoing political crisis. In an interview with the British newspaper *The Times*, Thaksin claimed that 'circles' close to the Thai monarchy were interfering in Thailand's political and judicial systems, and that reform of the monarchy was urgently needed; Thaksin also expressed staunch support for the unpopular Crown Prince, to whom Thaksin had often been rumoured to be close. The interview was banned from publication in Thailand, but was strongly criticized by members of the Government as an attack on the monarchy—a claim that Thaksin vigorously denied.

In October 2009 former premier Gen. Chavalit Yongchaiyudh announced that he was to join Puea Thai (For Thais)—a pro-Thaksin party founded in 2008—as party Chairman. Following the announcement, Prem issued a statement to the media denouncing Chavalit's actions as tantamount to treachery. Chavalit set about taking a number of actions, both at home and abroad, that were widely held as having been designed to destabilize the Government. In November 2009 he announced a proposal (intended to gain electoral support for Puea Thai in the troubled southern border provinces) by which, if elected, his party would bestow special autonomous status on the region, creating a new administrative unit to be known as Pattani State (*Nakhon Rat Pattani*). (Pattani was the name of the former sultanate that had been dismantled and absorbed into the Thai kingdom two centuries previously.)

In February 2010 the Supreme Court ordered the seizure of US $1,400m. (46,000m. baht) of Thaksin's total assets, frozen following the 2006 coup, after it ruled that the former Prime Minister had concealed his assets and abused his power for personal gain while in office. The amount seized was the difference in the value of Thaksin's assets before and after his tenure as Prime Minister. The fact that only some of his assets were seized was widely perceived as a signal that the state was willing to compromise with the former premier.

In March 2010 Abhisit announced that the Government was to invoke special powers under the Internal Security Act for a two-week period, in advance of a mass rally scheduled to be held by the UDD on 14 March. On 13 March tens of thousands of UDD supporters began to converge in Bangkok. The rally, held as planned on the following day, was one of the largest political demonstrations in Thailand's history; between 100,000 and 150,000 UDD protesters marched through the streets of the capital, before surrounding Government House, whereupon they claimed that Abhisit had come to power illegitimately and demanded that he resign, the House of Representatives be dissolved and fresh elections be held. On 15 March Abhisit stated that the Government had agreed that it could not submit to the demands. On the following day UDD protesters daubed the gates of Government House with blood, donated by the hundreds of UDD supporters, a small number of whom had been allowed to pass through the security cordon around the House, in an indication of the police force's commitment to ensuring a continuation of the peaceful nature of the protests. Thaksin gave frequent nightly addresses, broadcast via satellite, to the protesters who remained encamped outside Government House and pledged to do so until their demands were met. In response, the Government established the Centre for the Resolution of the Emergency Situation (CRES), based at the 11th Infantry Regiment, where Abhisit had taken refuge, and on 28 March Abhisit and the UDD held formal negotiations in an effort to resolve the impasse; however, the talks did not yield an agreement. Abhisit subsequently offered to hold early elections in 2011, but this was rejected by the UDD, which continued to press for the immediate dissolution of the legislature. On 7 April 2010 a group of Red Shirts stormed the parliament building, causing a legislative session to be abandoned; although there were no reports of any violence or injuries, Abhisit declared a state of emergency. Websites deemed to be critical of the monarchy and sympathetic to the Red Shirts were blocked, as was the Red Shirts' satellite television channel, the People Channel, which had broadcast to a wider audience Thaksin's addresses to the protesters.

After weeks of escalating tensions, on the night of 10 April 2010 violent clashes broke out between the security forces, protesters and unidentified armed gunmen (dubbed by the media 'men in black'). Twenty-five people were killed and over 800 injured. Five soldiers were among the dead, over 200 were among those injured, and one-half of all the military vehicles used in the operation to break up the demonstration were seized and destroyed, appearing to suggest the use of considerable force by the UDD protesters or forces aligned with them. The UDD leadership denied charges that they had been involved in any violence, insisting that their protests were non-violent. UDD demands that Abhisit resign to take responsibility for the violence were ignored. Later in April a series of bomb blasts in the capital—at the Sala Daeng mass transit train station, two separate branches of the Bangkok Bank, and the Dusit Thani Hotel (entities regarded as being closely aligned with the Government)—left one dead and 86 injured. The attacks were attributed by the Government to the UDD, which adamantly denied the allegations. However, the public image of the UDD was further damaged when a group of protesters stormed into a hospital located near the main protest site, alleging that the hospital was harbouring security forces.

At the main rally site, by now situated at the Ratchaprasong intersection at the centre of Bangkok's shopping district, UDD leaders appeared to challenge the monarchy by indirectly referring to the monarchy's tacit support for the Democrat-led Government, even while declaring their loyalty to the King. UDD leader Wisa Khanthap reported to the crowd of protesters that the Red Shirts leadership had learned that Abhisit had been informed by Pi Malakul, widely held to be one of the King's closest confidants, that 'the most senior person in the country'—presumably a reference to the King—had strongly advised against the dissolution of the House of Representatives, the UDD's main demand. Some days earlier Gen. Chavalit and former premier Somchai announced that they had requested an audience with the King to urge him to intervene in order to bring an end to the violence; the request was ignored. Meanwhile, the CRES announced that it had uncovered a conspiracy to overthrow the monarchy. A diagram was released to the media showing alleged links between Thaksin, the UDD leadership, politicians associated with Puea Thai and the banned Thai Rak Thai and PPP, and a number of prominent academics, journals, community radio personalities and political activists, both inside the country and overseas.

As tensions grew to breaking point in early May 2010 Abhisit offered the UDD a promise of elections to be held in November in return for an end to the protests. However, a split appeared to have developed within the UDD leadership between those willing to accept a compromise with the Government and those adopting a more rigorous approach. The latter were unwilling to accept Abhisit's offer unless the Government took responsibility for the deaths of UDD protesters in the clashes of 10 April. Meanwhile, one of the most senior UDD figures, Wira Musikapong, withdrew from the grouping's leadership. On 11 May the UDD announced that it would accept the offer of elections in November, but pledged to remain encamped in Bangkok until Deputy Prime Minister Suthep Thaugsuban surrendered himself to the police for his responsibility, as head of security operations at that time, for the fatal clashes of 10 April. On 12 May Abhisit withdrew the offer of an election in November, but stated that reconciliation remained a priority. On the following day Maj.-Gen. Khattiya Sawasdipol, an outspoken supporter of former premier Thaksin and rumoured to be in charge of the UDD's military strategies since mid-March, was shot by a sniper while being interviewed by a US news reporter. He died in hospital several days later.

The shooting of Gen. Khattiya prompted an escalation in the violence, with more than 40 people killed and over 300 injured during 14–18 May 2010. The UDD accused the military of firing on unarmed protesters, while the CRES claimed that the military was targeting only armed 'terrorists'. On 17 May 106 bank accounts of people accused of giving financial support to the UDD protests were frozen. Two days later the military moved in to disperse the UDD protesters from the main rally site at the Ratchaprasong intersection, breaking through the barricades erected around the site in armoured vehicles. Shortly thereafter, from a stage erected within the camp, the UDD leaders announced their decision to surrender, stating that they did not want any more lives to be lost and urging the protesters to return to their homes. While the majority of the protesters heeded this advice, dispersing peacefully from the streets of Bangkok, at least eight people were thought to have died during exchanges of gunfire between retreating protesters and the authorities. A number of UDD leaders were arrested, though some managed to escape. Arson attacks were carried out on 36 buildings around Bangkok, the most serious being the Central World shopping centre, said to be one of the largest in South-East Asia, which was razed to the ground. In a number of provinces in the north and north-east of the country, including Mukdahan, Khon Kaen, Udon Thani and Ubon Ratchathani, provincial administration offices, symbols of central Government and royal authority, were also set alight. The official death toll since the beginning of the protests in March was 91, with a further 1,800 injured. Among the dead were two foreign journalists; a number of other journalists were injured, some of whom claimed that they had been deliberately targeted by the military.

The failure of the UDD protest was followed by extensive arrests of UDD leaders and sympathizers throughout the country. The Government acknowledged that it had detained more than 400 people by the end of June 2010. Human rights organizations reported as many as 100 people missing, while UDD sympathizers accused the Government of secretly ordering extrajudicial killings of UDD organizers in the provinces. Thaksin, along with several members of the UDD leadership, was formally charged with 'terrorism'. (Thaksin was now residing in Montenegro, having been granted citizenship in March.) Universities were ordered to stop students performing political satires and expressing political opinions. There was a renewal of royalist propaganda. In June the Ministry of Justice claimed that it had closed 43,000 websites deemed critical of the monarchy, and that it was in the process of closing down another 3,000. Abhisit announced the creation of an internet security unit called Cyber Scout, which was to assist the Government in monitoring the internet for breaches of national security and criticism of the monarchy. Village headmen were ordered by the Ministry of the Interior to collect signatures pledging an oath of loyalty to the monarchy, and instructed to establish 'monarchy protection' groups. Thaksin stated that the Government's harsh measures against the UDD might lead to a covert guerrilla war, which was interpreted by some as an indirect threat. Some commentators in the media declared that Thailand was already in an undeclared state of civil war. Some of the more extreme members of the UDD were suspected of having fled to Cambodia, where they were said to be awaiting the next phase of the conflict. A reconciliation council was established, chaired by Anand Panyarachun, the former premier and leading royalist figure.

From the end of June 2010 a series of violent incidents occurred in the Bangkok area and in some provinces, especially in the north of the country. The headquarters of the parties in the Democrat-led coalition Government, as well as military camps, the state television station and several public areas, were the targets of a number of bomb and grenade attacks. Although some of the individuals subsequently arrested had links to the UDD, there was no evidence to indicate that the organization itself was behind these attacks. News reports suggested that most of the bombings, which were relatively amateur in nature, had been carried out by rogue individuals driven by anger and a sense of injustice. Although the Government rescinded the state of emergency in five provinces—Kalasin, Nakhon Pathom, Nakhon Sawan, Nan and Si Sa Ket—in early July, it renewed emergency rule for a further three-month period in Bangkok and in 19 other provinces. (By mid-August the Government had rescinded emergency rule in a further nine provinces, and in early October it lifted the decree in a further three provinces, leaving just Bangkok and the neighbouring provinces of Non Thaburi, Pathum Thani and Samut Prakarn still under emergency rule.)

Attempting to assert the legitimacy of its actions, the Government used the state media, as well as the support of other local media, to emphasize the violent actions of the Red Shirts during the events of April and May 2010, and tried to win over public opinion by focusing attention on the arson attacks that had caused damage to parts of Bangkok following the storming of the main UDD rally camp in mid-May. Between June and August the DP comprehensively defeated Puea Thai in local district council elections, city council elections and a by-election in a Bangkok constituency. At the same time anti-Government groups stressed to the public that the civilian killings during April–May constituted the worst incident of political violence in Thailand's modern history. With most of the UDD leaders imprisoned, granted conditional release on bail, or on the run, the new UDD campaigns were co-ordinated by young activists and small factions of the movement. One such example was Sombat Boonngamanong, a prominent UDD member and founding leader of the Red Sunday group, which had held weekly meetings since April in support of the UDD protesters; subsequent to the violent quelling of the protests, Red Sunday continued to hold weekly events, in order to honour the actions of the protesters and to commemorate those who had lost their lives. In mid-September, on the fourth anniversary of the military coup that ousted Thaksin from power, more than 10,000 Red Shirts were reported to have attended a rally at the Ratchaprasong intersection in central Bangkok, during which thousands of red balloons were released and red candles were lit. The event passed off peacefully, and there were no reports of any arrests. Meanwhile, although several cases involving UDD members on charges pertaining to the April–May unrest had been brought to court by the public prosecutor, the Department of Special Investigation (DSI—an investigative agency within the Ministry of Justice charged with handling all UDD protest-related cases) had made slow progress in carrying out investigations into the 91 fatalities officially confirmed to have occurred during the protests. At the end of August Japan's Minister for Foreign Affairs visited Thailand and paid tribute to a Japanese cameraman, employed by the international news agency Reuters. The Minister visited the place at which the cameraman had been fatally shot in April, conveying to the Thai Government Japan's concerns over his death and the repression of the protests. While the Thai authorities and the Abhisit Government continued to incur intense criticism of the perceived brutality of the operation to quell the protests, the uncompromising Gen. Prayuth Chan-ocha, known to be favoured by the Palace, was promoted to Commander-in-Chief of the Army in a military reorganization approved by the King in early September. Allies of Gen. Prayuth and army personnel who had played an important role in dealing with the UDD in the previous two years were also promoted to senior positions.

Meanwhile, the anti-establishment movement continued its campaign, with the Constitutional Court coming under criticism in mid-October 2010, when covertly filmed video footage appearing to reveal the 'leaking' of sensitive information from the Constitutional Court was made public. The video recordings included footage of a clandestine meeting between Pasit Sakdanarong, Secretary to the Constitutional Court President, and Wirat Romyen, a member of the legal team defending the DP in an ongoing trial over the Democrats' alleged misuse of 29m. baht (about US $960,000) in electoral campaign funding prior to the 2005 legislative elections. Following the publication of the footage, Pasit was dismissed. Two further series of controversial video recordings appearing to reveal corruption in the recruitment of court officials and the involvement in vice of certain judges were posted on public websites at the end of October 2010 and in early November. In response to criticism of, and allegations of political interference in, the judicial system, the Constitutional Court filed a defamation suit against an opposition politician as well as three daily newspapers that had published news reports pertaining to the video footage. On 29 November the Constitutional Court dismissed, on a legal technicality, the charges against the DP over the alleged misuse of electoral funds, ruling that the petition had not been properly filed by the prosecution within the specified time frame. About two weeks later the Court dismissed a second charge alleging that the DP had received more than 258m. baht ($8.5m.) in illegal political donations from a private company on similar technical grounds. The dismissals of the two cases against the DP reinforced the already prevalent perception that 'double standards' were being applied, given that Thai Rak Thai and the PPP had both been dissolved in 2007 and 2008, respectively, on account of their involvement in electoral fraud.

At the beginning of December 2010, Thida Thavornseth, formerly a member of the now-defunct Communist Party of Thailand and wife of arrested UDD co-leader Weng Tojirakarn, was appointed chairwoman of the movement on an interim basis, and a new executive committee was appointed. Thida declared that the UDD's priority task was to mount a campaign for the release of all Red Shirts held in police custody. Henceforth, the movement was to embrace a peaceful approach in its political struggle. During the same month the Cabinet finally rescinded the state of emergency in Bangkok and the final three neighbouring provinces, citing the less confrontational approach adopted by the UDD; the CRES, which had been in charge of security operations for the previous eight months, was thus automatically dissolved.

Although there had been signs of an improvement in the political climate, the root causes of Thai political conflict—the abuse of power and the position of the monarchy—had yet to be resolved. An academic forum entitled 'The Monarchy, the Constitution, and Democracy', held by the Nitirat group of legal academics in December 2010 at Thammasat University, marked a major advance in public discussion of the Thai monarchy, which remained strictly governed by *lèse-majesté* legislation. Video footage of the presentations, including discussion of *lèse-majesté* and reform of the monarchy by Somsak Jeamteerasakul, a Thammasat University associate professor, was reproduced, distributed, and sold widely, especially among the Red Shirts. In response to mounting criticism of the monarchy, the Government and the army became increasingly zealous in their roles as its protectors. Among those arrested and charged with *lèse-majesté* in early 2011 were Somsak and Surachai Sae Dan, the leader of the Red Siam group, who was charged in connection with a public speech given during a Red Shirt gathering in December 2010. Reacting to such arrests, an unprecedented number of movements and campaigns were initiated against the *lèse-majesté* law by academics and activists. In mid-March 2011 the Nitirat group announced a series of proposals that included the abolition of *lèse-majesté* legislation, the Privy Council, the daily royalist propaganda bulletin broadcast on national television, and other practices associated with the monarchy that it regarded as undemocratic. The royal family retaliated with an in-depth interview given by Princess Chulabhorn to a popular television programme broadcast in early April; during the interview, the Princess repeatedly emphasized the work undertaken by the monarchy for the Thai people, and spoke of the King's great sorrow and deteriorating health as a result of the political unrest and arson attacks in 2010. The historian Somsak posted two open letters on the internet in response to the Princess's interview, criticizing her for, among other shortcomings, having omitted to mention the deaths of anti-Government protesters during the military operation to quell the unrest. Gen. Prayuth described Somsak as 'a mentally ill academic' who was 'intent on overthrowing the monarchy'. At the end of April 2011 Somsak claimed during a news conference to have received threats from the security authorities, prompting widespread expressions of concern from a large number of international and local intellectuals. Nevertheless, Somsak was arrested again in mid-May on a charge of *lèse-majesté*, which had been filed by the army.

Meanwhile, following the removal of the state of emergency in Bangkok at the end of 2010 and the release of prominent UDD leaders on conditional bail in February 2011, the UDD once again began staging demonstrations periodically in the capital. On 10 April the first anniversary of the clashes between troops and UDD protesters that had claimed 25 lives in 2010 was commemorated with a large gathering held on Ratchadamnoen Avenue. The army was reported to have set up a 'war room' to monitor the situation and all speeches delivered on the rally stage. One of the highlights of the rally was Thida's 'April 10 Declaration', in which she vowed to bring to justice those responsible for the mass killings and to fight against forces trying to interfere with the forthcoming legislative election—in March 2011 the Abhisit Government had announced that parliament would be dissolved by the first week of May in advance of early elections. Other highlights of the rally included a call from Thaksin via video link and the unexpected appearance of Pasit Sakdanarong; during a speech at the rally, Pasit claimed that the President of the Constitutional Court, Chat Chonlaworn, had received a letter and a telephone call from someone seeking to ensure that the DP evade dissolution in the electoral fraud case in 2010 (see above). Two days later, the army filed a *lèse-majesté* complaint on behalf of Gen. Prayuth against UDD leader Jatuporn Prompan and two others for their speeches at the rally. Jatuporn was accused of insulting Princess Chulabhorn by saying that he too would like to be interviewed on television. The DSI also pressed *lèse-majesté* charges against 18 UDD leaders (all of whom were already charged with acts of 'terrorism' and had been freed on bail), on the basis of 'body language' (for example, clapping and cheering) during Jatuporn's speech. Political tensions heightened at the end of April 2011 as the authorities forcibly entered 13 community radio stations in Bangkok and nearby provinces after they were alleged to have aired Jatuporn's rally speech; all but one of the stations were shut down, equipment was seized and three radio station personnel were arrested. At the same time the ISOC had been spearheading the Government's efforts to mobilize the public through various networks and mechanisms, including volunteer groups, co-operation with the army in order to organize concerts across the country, and commandeering 700 community radio stations, to promote patriotism and gratitude for the work of the monarchy.

On 9 May 2011 Abhisit announced the dissolution, approved by the King earlier that day, of the House of Representatives, and called an election for 3 July. Opposition party Puea Thai nominated Yingluck Shinawatra, the younger sister of Thaksin, as its prime ministerial candidate. Although a successful businesswoman, Yingluck had limited political experience and her selection as Puea Thai's candidate was immediately criticized by some members of the ruling DP, who argued that she was merely a 'puppet' of her brother.

Soon after the dissolution of the House of Representatives, the Criminal Court revoked the bail of Jatuporn, who had been named as an electoral candidate for Puea Thai, and fellow UDD leader Nisit Sinthuprai; as a result, both men were imprisoned. Although the military had repeatedly stressed its political neutrality regarding the forthcoming general election, at the end of May 2011 a Puea Thai candidate and supporters were reported to have been intimidated by a special task force established by the Democrat-led Government and commanded by the ISOC, in which the military played a leading role. In mid-June Gen. Prayuth gave an interview on military-owned television channels urging voters to cast their ballots for 'good' parties and 'good' candidates; his comments were widely interpreted as an attempt to discredit Puea Thai. At the same time, the DP found itself being abandoned by some of its former allies. Tensions between the DP and the PAD had been high since late 2010, when the latter had organized protests on the Preah Vihear issue (see Recent Foreign Relations, below). The PAD launched a 'no vote' campaign, which would ultimately damage the Democrats' electoral chances and benefit those of Puea Thai. At the height of the election campaign Chumpol Silpa-archa, leader of Chart Thai Pattana (which had been founded in 2008 by former members of Chart Thai in anticipation of the latter's dissolution, and which formed a coalition with Bhum Jar Thai—another party founded in 2008) strongly criticized Abhisit for making 'disrespectful' comments about smaller coalition parties, and claimed that his party had been placed under pressure by a 'powerful force' to join the coalition during a controversial parliamentary vote in 2008. Both of the main parties ran similar populist campaigns during the early stages. Towards the end of the campaign, with almost all public opinion polls showing Puea Thai in the lead, the DP decided to revise its campaign strategy in order to focus on attributing the violent unrest of 2010 to Thaksin and the UDD.

THE GOVERNMENT OF YINGLUCK SHINAWATRA

Legislative elections were held as planned on 3 July 2011. Puea Thai won a landslide victory, taking 265 seats in the 500-seat House of Representatives (only the second time in Thai history that a single party had secured an absolute majority), while the DP took 159 seats. On the day after the elections Yingluck announced that an agreement had been reached to form a coalition Government consisting of Puea Thai, Chart Thai Pattana, Chart Pattana Puea Paendin Party (which was subsequently renamed Chart Pattana Party, in September), Palang Chon and Mahachon, which would collectively control 299 seats in the House of Representatives. After five tumultuous years of political and social crisis, the election brought to power Thailand's first female Prime Minister and marked another political defeat for the royalist élite and the military establishment. Yingluck's Cabinet, which received royal endorsement on 9 August, reflected Puea Thai's three-pronged strategy of rewarding important patrons, both within the party and in its coalition partners; creating a positive and credible image for the new Government; and avoiding political confrontation with the old establishment. The appointment as Minister of Foreign Affairs of Surapong Towijakchaikul, who had little experience in diplomacy but was related to Thaksin through marriage, understandably elicited strong criticism from the opposition; such criticism primarily focused on the role of the Ministry of Foreign Affairs in the easing or blocking of Thaksin's ability to travel while a fugitive from Thai law. However, the appointment of former Stock Exchange of Thailand President Kittirat Na-Ranong as Deputy Prime Minister and Minister of Commerce and that of former Secretary-General of the Securities and Exchange Commission Thirachai Phuvanatnaranubala as Minister of Finance were better received, on account of the depth of experience and proven records of both men. The appointment of Police Gen. Kowit Wattana as Deputy Prime Minister in charge of Security Affairs and that of Gen. Yutthasak Sasiprapha as Minister of Defence, along with the absence of UDD leaders from the Cabinet, appeared to indicate a desire on the part of the new Prime Minister to be seen as posing no threat to either the military or the monarchy.

RECENT FOREIGN RELATIONS

Thai governments since the mid-1980s, whether military or civilian, had attempted to achieve a *modus vivendi* between established military-bureaucratic élites and the increasingly powerful interests of capitalism. Domestic and international business interests greatly circumscribed the ability of Thailand's rulers to change policy from the *laissez-faire*, export-promoting course upon which the country had embarked. It was not possible, for example, for the military to restore the uncompromising stance on Indo-China that Suchinda's regime had announced on seizing power in 1991. Thai business interests were already too deeply engaged in Laos and keen to penetrate Cambodia, while ASEAN and other countries were increasingly determined to reach an Indo-China settlement. Consequently, the military regime's leaders quietly acceded to Chatichai's vision of Thailand as the capitalist focus for the economically feeble socialist states that surrounded it, and they adopted policies towards Cambodia, Laos and Myanmar that favoured the penetration of Thai interests. Under the democratic regime of Chuan Leekpai, this line was pursued with vigour. In February 1993 Thailand, Viet Nam, Laos and Cambodia signed a joint communiqué that resulted in the establishment of a Bangkok-based commission for developing the Mekong river basin. In October 1993 Thailand was accepted as a full member of the Non-aligned Movement.

Thailand's efforts to establish itself as a patron to its economically weaker neighbours were complicated in Cambodia by the involvement of powerful Thai business and military interests with the communist dissident faction, the Khmers Rouges, a lucrative source of concessions for logging and gem-mining. At the beginning of 1993 Thailand formally closed its borders to trade with the Khmers Rouges, in accordance with UN sanctions. However, unofficial dealings continued, straining Thai relations not only with the UN but also with the USA, which Thailand was otherwise eager to accommodate. In December the Government was deeply embarrassed by the seizure of a large shipment of weapons from a Thai army stockpile, which was evidently on its way to the Khmers Rouges. In January 1994 Chuan became the first Thai Prime Minister to pay an official visit to Cambodia. Thereafter, his Government made increasing efforts to disentangle Thai military and business interests from the Khmers Rouges. In December Chuan issued an order to governors and military commanders of the border provinces to cease their co-operation with Cambodian guerrillas. This was largely successful, and co-operation between the Thai and Cambodian armies on the border increased notably during 1995, although there continued to be clashes between Thai and Cambodian troops as a result of incursions into Thai territory by the latter in pursuit of Khmer Rouge guerrillas. In mid-1996 Thai interests switched to support the breakaway Khmer Rouge faction of Ieng Sary, which controlled the border area on which the gem and timber trade was centred. In the subsequent negotiations between Ieng Sary and the Cambodian Government, Thailand played a major mediating role.

Thailand refused to join in the international boycott of the Myanma military regime, proclaiming instead a policy of 'constructive engagement'. The profitability of this remained considerable, in spite of Myanmar's cancellation of many Thai logging and fishing concessions at the end of 1992. The Myanma military's increasing domination of border areas led to a new influx of refugees into Thailand in 1992–93; Thai authorities accommodated them but took care to prevent their aiding of insurgents. They also acted to reduce possible clashes with the Myanma regime by joint demarcation of the border, and by supporting mediated settlements of Myanmar's ethnic rebellions. At the same time Thai diplomacy within ASEAN successfully secured a more positive approach by the regional organization to Myanmar; Thailand invited the Myanma Minister of Foreign Affairs to attend an ASEAN ministerial meeting in Bangkok in August 1994.

In January and February 1995 about 10,000 members of the Kayin (formerly Karen) National Union (KNU) fled to Thailand, following an assault by Myanma government forces on the rebels' headquarters on the Moei river. Attacks on the refugee camps where the disarmed Kayins were held prompted Thailand to move the refugees to a site 10 km inside Thailand and to warn Myanmar that it would retaliate against border incursions. Bilateral relations deteriorated further in March when Myanmar closed its only land border with Thailand, in retaliation for alleged Thai support for raids in the area by the Mong Tai Army, controlled by the 'opium warlord', Khun Sa. In September Chavalit visited Yangon and assured the Myanma regime that Thailand did not intend to support Khun Sa and his Shan followers.

Thailand achieved mixed results in its efforts to 'open up' its socialist neighbours. Once the countries of what Thai leaders liked to call the 'Greater Mekong Sub-region' had established connections with a range of foreign capitalist interlocutors, they tried to reduce their dependence on Thai patronage. In 1995 Cambodia gave preference to investment from Malaysia and Singapore. Myanmar became less pliable to Thai interests and likewise encouraged investment from Singapore. Relations with Viet Nam were marred by competition over fishing rights in the Gulf of Siam, leading in May 1995 to an armed clash between Thai and Vietnamese naval patrol boats. Even Laos, which normally preferred avoidance to assertion in its international relations, demanded that the headquarters of the Mekong River Commission be removed to Vientiane, and attempted to balance its Thai connections by renewed dealings with China and Viet Nam. None the less, Thailand's political and economic centrality to the mainland South-East Asian area led to increasing international acknowledgement of its regional importance.

Under Chavalit, Thailand's foreign policy included a number of new initiatives. The most important and controversial of these was increased defence links with China. In April 1997 Chavalit led a delegation to Beijing for discussions with the Chinese authorities. While agreements were reached on increasing trade relations between the two countries, media attention focused on China's pledge to strengthen defence links. Chavalit continued Thailand's policy of strengthening bilateral relations with its neighbours by making trips to Viet Nam, Myanmar and Cambodia. On most of these trips the agenda was dominated by security issues. There was continuing instability on Thailand's western border with Myanmar, where tens of thousands of Kayin, Kayinni (formerly Karenni) and Mon refugees had crossed into Thailand as a result of campaigns by the Myanma military against ethnic insurgents. By mid-1997 it was estimated that as many as 100,000 refugees were accommodated in refugee camps inside the Thai border with Myanmar. However, despite the unstable situation on Thailand's border with Myanmar, Thailand's support was a major factor in Myanmar's admission into ASEAN as a full member in July 1997. In Cambodia the fragile alliance between the Co-Prime Ministers, Hun Sen and Prince Ranariddh, broke down in July, with fighting erupting between forces loyal to the two rival leaders. Fierce battles between the two forces extended over Thailand's eastern border with Cambodia, and thousands of refugees fled the fighting and crossed into Thailand. Border issues preoccupied the Armed Forces' Survey Directorate throughout 1997. Negotiations continued with the Laotian and Myanma Governments on disputed border demarcations, while an agreement was reached with Viet Nam regarding its maritime boundaries with Thailand.

Under the Chuan administration, there was a substantial improvement in relations with Malaysia. By April 1998 Chuan and the Malaysian Prime Minister, Mahathir Mohamed, had met an unprecedented five times in as many months to discuss regional and economic issues affecting the two countries. The most important outcome of these discussions was the agreement by Malaysia to end all support for the Muslim separatist movement in the troubled border region of southern Thailand, and to take a more assertive stance in suppressing the activity of known Muslim separatists operating on Malaysian soil. In subsequent months, a number of separatist leaders were apprehended or gave themselves up to the Thai authorities. In April the two Prime Ministers also witnessed the signing of an agreement by the two respective state-owned oil companies of Thailand and Malaysia on the development of gas reserves in the Thai-Malaysian Joint Development Area, once a disputed region between the two countries.

In mid-1998 Thailand's new Minister of Foreign Affairs, Surin Pitsuwan, signalled a change in the country's approach to regional relations within ASEAN. Instead of 'constructive engagement', which effectively meant that ASEAN members were to refrain from commenting on the internal affairs of other member countries, Surin proposed a new policy of 'flexible engagement', in accordance with which ASEAN nations would have the right to discuss the domestic affairs of another member country if those affairs had an impact beyond that country's borders. While Surin's proposal was welcomed by US, European and Australian government officials as a sign of a new political openness in the region, it met with a generally negative response from most other ASEAN members. At the meeting of ASEAN Ministers of Foreign Affairs in the Philippine capital, Manila, in July, the only regional support Thailand received for the 'flexible engagement' concept came from the Philippines, while Indonesia, Malaysia, Myanmar and Viet Nam strongly rejected any modification of ASEAN's long-standing principle of non-interference.

A major issue dominating Thailand's foreign agenda for much of 1998–99 was the impasse over the appointment of the next Director-General of the WTO. The Thai candidate, Deputy Prime Minister and Minister of Commerce Supachai Panichpakdi, who was supported by the majority of Asian nations, was involved in a contest with Michael Moore, the former New Zealand Prime Minister. The issue became one of national pride, and there was intense criticism in the Thai media regarding the apparent support of the USA for Moore. Prime Minister Chuan wrote to US President Bill Clinton to express his wish that the USA remain neutral with regard to the appointment, but the perception remained that the USA was obstructing Supachai's bid for the position. Since the early 1990s, furthermore, Thailand's relations with the USA had been affected by the increasing Asian orientation of the Thai economy, with growing tension over issues such as investment access, US import quotas and intellectual property rights. The impasse at the WTO was finally resolved in July 1999 after Supachai agreed to an Australian proposal for the post to be divided into two consecutive three-year terms, with Supachai taking the second term.

The major foreign affairs issue for the Thai Government in 1999 was its high-profile participation in the UN-organized International Force for East Timor (Interfet). In the intense diplomatic activity that followed the outbreak of militia violence in East Timor (now Timor-Leste—after the referendum on independence held on 30 August), the Thai Government agreed to commit 1,500 troops to the Interfet force. The Thai contingent was the largest of those sent by ASEAN nations (and the second largest after the Australian contribution), and a Thai general, Maj.-Gen. Songkitti Chakrapatr, was appointed Deputy Commander of Interfet. The situation was a very sensitive one for the Thai Government, given that it risked breaking the accepted convention of non-interference in the internal affairs of an ASEAN member state. Prime Minister Chuan and the Minister of Foreign Affairs, Surin Pitsuwan, repeatedly stated that they had agreed to take part in the mission only after being invited to do so by Indonesia's President Habibie, Gen. Wiranto (then Commander-in-Chief of the Indonesian National Defence Forces) and the UN. Within Thailand the Government was accused by the opposition and some sections of the media, especially a number of Thai Muslim news magazines, of pandering to the West and breaking ranks with ASEAN members.

Meanwhile, in Thailand's southern provinces bordering Malaysia, a series of violent incidents occurred in July and August 1999, including the shooting of a policeman, and bombings and arson attacks directed against government property. The Thai authorities attributed the attacks, the first for some time, to a renewed campaign of violence carried out by Muslim separatists. Malaysia promised to co-operate in apprehending anyone suspected of involvement in the attacks who was using Malaysian territory to evade capture by the Thai authorities.

In October 1999 Thai-Myanma relations were strained when a group of heavily armed Myanma students stormed the Myanma embassy in Bangkok, taking hostage all 89 people in the compound, including 13 diplomats. The gunmen demanded that all political prisoners in Myanmar be released, that a dialogue between the military junta and other political parties be opened and that the elected legislature be convened. However, the situation was resolved within 24 hours when the group agreed to release the hostages in exchange for the Thai Government's guarantee of a safe passage by helicopter to the Thai–Myanma border. The Government of Myanmar was quick to express its displeasure at the way in which the crisis had been handled by the Thai Government; it closed the border with Thailand, cancelled fishing concessions and refused to allow Thai fishing vessels into Myanma waters. Relations between the two countries deteriorated further when, in November, the Thai Government began forced repatriations of thousands of illegal Myanma migrant workers. The deterioration in relations between the two countries was eventually halted at the end of November when, following a visit by the Thai Minister of Foreign Affairs, Myanmar agreed to reopen both the common border and its territorial waters to Thai fishing vessels.

The importance that the Thai Government now placed on cordial relations with the junta in Myanmar was evident with the handling of a second hostage crisis in January 2000: 10 armed Myanma rebels from God's Army, an ethnic Kayin faction fighting an armed insurgency against the Myanma Government, took control of a hospital in Ratchaburi Province, close to the Myanmar border, holding more than 500 patients, doctors and nurses hostage. They demanded that the shelling of Kayin positions by the Thai military cease, that medical assistance be given to injured Kayin fighters and that the Thai military withdraw its co-operation with the Myanma forces in suppressing Kayin military activity on the Thai–Myanma border. In contrast to its peaceful resolution of the earlier siege at the Myanma embassy, the Thai Government acted decisively; a team of commandos stormed the hospital in a pre-dawn raid, killing all 10 hostage-takers (according to some hostage reports, after they had already surrendered). The brutal resolution of the incident was praised by the military Government in Myanmar, and many observers viewed the Thai Government's handling of the incident as signalling a broader campaign by the Thai authorities on dissident activity by ethnic Myanma opposition groups operating in Thailand.

Despite the new Thai Rak Thai Government's announcement of a redirection in foreign policy that would focus on strengthening relations with neighbouring countries, relations between Thailand and Myanmar reached a new low point soon after the Thaksin administration took office. In February 2001 thousands of ethnic Shan villagers were forced to cross the border into Thailand, as a result of a renewed campaign by the Myanma Government against Shan insurgents. During the fighting Myanma forces shelled Thai villages in the border region of Chiang Rai province, as well as crossing into Thai territory on a number of occasions in pursuit of the insurgents. The Myanma Government's actions were apparently linked to public accusations by Thai government officials that the Myanma Government was aiding the flow of amphetamines produced in the ethnic Wa-controlled regions into Thailand. (Since the late 1990s amphetamine addiction had come to be regarded in Thailand not only as a serious social issue but also as a problem of national security.) The Myanma regime's official daily newspaper published an unprecedented series of articles highly critical of Thailand, even at one point indirectly criticizing the Thai royal family, which prompted an immediate protest from the Thai Ministry of Foreign Affairs. The rapid deterioration in relations was eventually halted when Prime Minister Thaksin made a long-delayed official visit to Yangon in June.

However, tensions between Thailand and Myanmar persisted, principally because of Thai accusations that the Myanma Government was not doing enough to curb the flow of amphetamines across the border into Thailand, and ongoing Myanma complaints that the Thai military was assisting the ethnic insurgent group, the Shan State Army (SSA), in the Myanma military's campaign against it. In June 2002 a series of articles published in Myanmar on the subject of Thai and Myanma history was deemed to be insulting by the Thai Government. The publication of an article critical of the late 16th-century Thai King Naresuan (who was credited with having recovered the independence of the kingdom of Ayudhya from the Burmese) led to a major diplomatic incident. The Supreme Command of the Thai military lodged an official protest against the article, which it claimed was offensive to the Thai monarchy itself, while radio and television stations, under the control of the Thai military, aired anti-Myanmar programmes. Myanmar responded by closing its border entry points with Thailand. The incident was finally resolved when the Vice-Chairman of the State Peace and Development Council (SPDC), Gen. Maung Aye, delivered a message to the Thai Government promising to prevent the state-controlled media from publishing articles deemed to be insulting to the Thai monarchy.

Relations with Cambodia reached a new low point in February 2003 when rioters in the capital of Phnom-Penh looted and burned down the Thai embassy and a number of Thai businesses. The riots were precipitated by what appeared to have been a fabricated report in the Cambodian press that a Thai television actress had made disparaging remarks about the ancient ruins at Angkor Wat, implying that the site belonged to Thailand. As the rioting continued, Thai nationals were airlifted out of Cambodia. The Thai ambassador, who had escaped from rioters by scaling the wall surrounding the embassy compound, was recalled from Cambodia, diplomatic relations were downgraded and border crossings were closed. The Cambodian Government subsequently made a formal apology to the Thai Government and agreed to pay damages.

For much of the first half of 2003 Thailand's foreign policy was dominated by the US-led invasion of Iraq. Officially, the Thai Government maintained a policy of neutrality, mindful of its military dependence on the USA but also of the sizeable Muslim minority resident in southern Thailand, which was overwhelmingly opposed to the war. Thai public opinion was also generally against the war, while Thailand's predominantly Muslim neighbours, Malaysia and Indonesia, were extremely critical of the USA's actions against Iraq. In June Prime Minister Thaksin flew to the USA to meet President George W. Bush for discussions on counter-terrorism operations. In the aftermath of the devastating bombing of two night-clubs in Bali, Indonesia, in October 2002, which had killed over 200 people, it had been alleged that members of JI, the organization believed to have been responsible for the bombing, might have used Thailand as a base for the planning of the operation. Thaksin's meeting with President Bush coincided with the arrests, in the southern province of Narathiwat, of three suspected JI members, a development that provoked widespread criticism among religious leaders in the largely Muslim provinces of the south.

In September 2003 Thaksin visited Singapore and the Philippines, where he was lauded by the leaders of both countries for his apparently successful economic policies, which had been dubbed 'Thaksinomics'. In October Thailand successfully hosted the Asia-Pacific Economic Co-operation (APEC) summit.

In September 2004 the issue of an extraordinary deal whereby the Thai Government had approved a 4,000m. baht loan by the Export-Import Bank to Myanmar was raised in the House of Representatives. Part of the loan was to be used by a Myanma company, Bagan Cybertech, to purchase broadband satellite telecommunications equipment supplied by Shin Satellite (see above). This loan followed previous loans by the bank to Myanmar for numerous projects, together worth more than 6,000m. baht. However, the deal was cast into uncertainty in October with the arrest on charges of corruption of the Myanma Prime Minister, Khin Nyunt, who had developed close business links with Prime Minister Thaksin (Bagan Cybertech was owned by Khin Nyunt's son).

The increased publicity of Thailand's handling of the violence in the southern provinces resulted in intense international criticism, particularly from Muslim nations, of the Government's human rights record. Although Prime Minister Thaksin repeatedly stated that the unrest was unconnected with religion, the conflict was increasingly represented in religious terms. Following the Tak Bai incident in October 2004 (see above), Mahathir Mohamed, the outspoken former Prime Minister of Malaysia, urged the Thai Government to grant autonomy to the three Muslim majority provinces. This appeal was not supported by his successor, Abdullah Badawi, who reaffirmed Malaysia's commitment to Thailand's territorial sovereignty and willingness to co-operate in combating terrorism. However, the Malaysian legislature later unanimously approved a motion condemning the Thai security forces' suppression of the protest at Tak Bai. Prime Minister Thaksin accused Malaysia of disregarding the existence of terrorist training camps in Kelantan state. The Thai Government criticized Malaysia's unwillingness to extradite Malaysian nationals suspected of involvement in the violence. Prime Minister Thaksin also suggested that some Islamist militants in southern Thailand had been radicalized by Indonesian Muslim extremists while they had been studying in Indonesia.

Thailand's handling of the insurgency in the south continued to put a severe strain on relations with Malaysia. In August 2005 131 Muslim Thai nationals crossed the border from Narathiwat province into Malaysia's Kelantan state, ostensibly as a result of the violence, and requested political asylum. The Malaysian Minister of Foreign Affairs stated that his Government would be willing to allow the group to remain in Malaysia if conditions were unsafe in their home province. The Malaysian Deputy Prime Minister demanded that the Thai Government offer an assurance that the refugees' human rights would be guaranteed before Malaysia would permit their return. The group also received the public support of Mahathir, who had been a harsh critic of the Thai Government's handling of the violence in the south. The Thai Government publicly accused Malaysia of deliberately interfering in Thailand's internal affairs. Protests were staged outside the Malaysian embassy in Bangkok. The Thai Minister of Foreign Affairs, Kantathee Supamongkol, sharply criticized his Malaysian counterpart for comments made by the latter in the Malaysian media, and urged Malaysia to return the refugees, giving his guarantee of their safety once back in Thailand. Kantathee also condemned the Organization of the Islamic Conference for expressing concern about the treatment of Muslims in southern Thailand, and for failing to denounce Islamist militants and their use of religion to 'justify' violence.

The international reaction to the coup of September 2006 was overwhelmingly critical. The US Administration was quick to impose sanctions on Thailand in response to the coup, which it deemed a 'sad development' for Thai democracy. The US sanctions involved a substantial reduction in financial aid for military education and training, peace-keeping operations and counter-terrorism; however, humanitarian funding would not be affected. The United Kingdom, the EU, Australia and New Zealand also issued statements critical of the coup, urging a swift return to democratic rule. A number of Thailand's ASEAN neighbours, in particular Malaysia, Indonesia and the Philippines, released unusually strong statements of concern about the situation in Thailand. International human rights groups including the Asia Human Rights Commission, Human Rights Watch and Amnesty International were also critical.

Prime Minister Surayud's first overseas visits were to Laos and Cambodia. In October 2006 he visited Malaysia, where he held discussions with his Malaysian counterpart, Abdullah Badawi, regarding the violence in Thailand's southern provinces. The Malaysian Government expressed its displeasure a month later when Surayud alleged that the southern insurgents were being funded from within Malaysia. Meanwhile, the new regime's relations with Singapore were decidedly tense. Also in October, the Singapore Government's investment unit, Temasek Holdings, announced that it had appointed one of the Thai Crown Prince's personal counsellors as a 'corporate adviser' to the company in Thailand, in an apparent effort to improve relations with the new regime. In January 2007 the junta was highly critical of a television interview with Thaksin during a visit to Singapore. In retaliation, the Government suspended the Thai-Singapore Civil Service Exchange programme and cancelled a visit by Singapore's Minister for Foreign Affairs.

Despite the return to democratic government following the legislative elections of December 2007, Thailand's foreign policy continued to be overshadowed by the country's internal political problems. The tension afflicted the Ministry of Foreign Affairs, which had to address Thailand's damaged international image following the September 2006 coup and Thaksin's frequent appearances in the international media. In a speech to a gathering of Thai overseas ambassadors and consuls in August 2007, the King made an indirect reference to a lack of national loyalty on the part of some ambassadors (presumably alluding to Thaksin supporters in the ministry) by claiming that some ambassadors were posted overseas and 'after a few days' forgot how to speak Thai and had learned to become 'un-Thai'. Following the formation of the PPP-led Government in January 2008, the importance of the ministry to the Government's political strategy was indicated by the appointment of Thaksin's personal lawyer, Noppadon Pattama, to the position of Minister of Foreign Affairs. Also in that month Surin Pitsuwan, the former Minister of Foreign Affairs and DP deputy, was elected to a four-year term as Secretary-General of ASEAN. In addition, in July Thailand assumed the chairmanship of ASEAN.

In April 2009 the reputation of the Government and the country itself suffered a humiliating set-back when Red Shirt protesters broke through the security cordon and disrupted the East Asia and ASEAN + 3 Summit meetings being held concurrently at Pattaya, leading to the abandonment of the meetings. Visiting heads of state were evacuated from the hotel by helicopter and by boat. The postponed ASEAN Summit was held in Hua Hin in October, with some 36,000 military and police personnel deployed to provide security at the meeting venue. In what was interpreted by some sections of the media as an affront to the Thai Government, the leaders of five member nations—namely Brunei, Cambodia, Indonesia, Malaysia and the Philippines—did not attend the Summit's opening ceremony. Of further embarrassment to the Thai Government were rumours that the Sultan of Brunei had chosen to stay in Thaksin's seaside residence for the duration of the Summit. Meanwhile, in another set-back for Thailand's international reputation, in January 2009 the Thai military was accused of towing boats carrying Rohingya Muslim refugees from Myanmar back out to sea, with little food or water, reportedly leading to the deaths of hundreds of migrants. In a number of cases the refugees were alleged to have been assaulted by Thai soldiers. The military denied the allegations, while Prime Minister Abhisit promised an investigation.

Meanwhile, tension arose between Thailand and Cambodia in July 2008 when the disputed Preah Vihear temple, located on the border between the two countries, was declared a World Heritage Site by UNESCO, and both countries subsequently deployed troops to the area. Although the International Court of Justice (ICJ) had awarded ownership of the temple to Cambodia in a ruling in 1962, sovereignty of the surrounding area remained contentious. Sporadic clashes in late 2008 resulted in injuries and deaths on both sides. Cambodian Prime Minister Hun Sen demanded the withdrawal of Thai troops, and threatened to refer the matter to the ICJ. He later issued an ultimatum stating that he would not hesitate to use force if Thai troops moved to take control of the temple. As the situation on the border deteriorated, the Thai Minister of Foreign Affairs urged Thai nationals to return to their homeland.

Tensions between Thailand and Cambodia were exacerbated by the appointment, in December 2008, of the outspoken Kasit Piromya—who had participated in the occupation by PAD protesters of Bangkok's international airport in November (see above)—as the new Thai Minister of Foreign Affairs, owing to Kasit's forthright criticism of Hun Sen (in one interview he had undiplomatically referred to the Cambodian leader as a 'gangster'). Although the installation of the DP-led coalition Government under the premiership of Abhisit Vejjajiva, together with ongoing bilateral negotiations with regard to the Preah Vihear issue, had appeared to facilitate an amelioration in Thai-Cambodian relations, intermittent border clashes continued. A partial withdrawal of troops from the disputed border area was reported to have begun in August 2009, but minor skirmishes in the disputed area continued to be reported in 2010.

Thai-Cambodian relations suffered yet another set-back in November 2009 when the Cambodian Government appointed Thaksin as an economic adviser. Responding to demands by the Abhisit Government to extradite Thaksin, Hun Sen declared that he would offer Thaksin political asylum and criticized the September 2006 coup that had ousted the former Thai premier. The Thai Government responded to what it denounced as a provocation by recalling its ambassador from Phnom-Penh and the Cambodian authorities withdrew their envoy from Bangkok in a reciprocal gesture. Shortly thereafter bilateral relations worsened even further when Cambodian authorities arrested and later imprisoned a Thai engineer on spying charges. In December 2009, however, he received a royal pardon, which Gen. Chavalit Yongchaiyudh claimed had been secured owing to the intervention of himself and Thaksin. Bilateral relations were further impeded in February 2010, when Hun Sen paid an official visit to the disputed area around the Preah Vihear temple, during which he accused Thailand of planning to invade Cambodia and urged Cambodian troops to continue to protect the country's borders from 'the enemy'. However, in August, following the announcement that Thaksin, citing personal difficulties in fulfilling his role, had resigned from his advisory position in Cambodia, diplomatic relations were immediately restored. The development significantly raised hopes of a rapprochement between the two countries.

Notwithstanding a dispute over accusations by the Thai authorities in early October 2010 that a number of UDD members had received weapons-training in Cambodia, relations between Thailand and Cambodia improved considerably in the latter months of 2010. Following four meetings between Hun Sen and Abhisit, the Cambodian Prime Minister stated in early December that the border dispute had been resolved. The PAD immediately raised the Preah Vihear issue again, and staged protests against the Government's refusal to revoke the Thai-Cambodian memorandum of understanding and the French-delineated map, accusing the Government of causing Thailand to lose territory. Tensions between the two countries were renewed at the end of December when DP parliamentarian Panich Vikitsreth, Veera Somkwamkid (a former leader of the PAD) and five others were arrested in the Thai border province of Sa Kaeo, having allegedly crossed the border and illegally entered a military zone on Cambodian territory. Videos of the arrest anonymously posted on the internet appeared to suggest that the encroachment into Cambodian territory was not accidental. However, members of the PAD gathered outside the Cambodian embassy in Bangkok to demand the release of the group and criticized Thai government officials for accepting the Cambodian authorities' accusation that the group had knowingly encroached upon Cambodian territory. In January 2011 the Phnom-Penh Municipal Court granted bail to five of the detainees, including Panich. However, Veera and his secretary, both of whom were to answer additional charges of espionage, remained in custody, and in early February were sentenced to prison terms of eight and six years, respectively. Under pressure from the PAD, which continued to criticize the Government for its perceived mishandling of the case and intensified its protests by obstructing the road alongside Government House, Abhisit asserted that he had never stated that the Thais were arrested on Cambodian territory.

On 4 February 2011 fierce fighting, including exchanges of artillery and gunfire, broke out at the border near the Preah Vihear temple. During the clashes, which continued for four days, 10 people were killed and thousands of villagers were evacuated. A cease-fire was eventually agreed by the local forces. Immediately after the clashes Hun Sen announced that Cambodia was to ask the ICJ to rule on the border demarcation; however, the Thai Government insisted on bilateral negotiations. Both sides reinforced their troops along the border and periodic clashes continued until March. During the 18th ASEAN Summit meeting in Jakarta, Indonesia, in early April, Thailand, Cambodia and Indonesia agreed to the deployment of Indonesian observers in the disputed border area; however, Thailand later reneged on the agreement and reiterated its insistence on a bilateral resolution to the border conflict. Clashes at the border erupted again. By the end of the month a further 15 people had been killed and 48,200 villagers had been displaced by the violence, until another cease-fire was agreed upon and the border was reopened for trade in early May.

Thailand's relations with Cambodia again deteriorated after the Thai delegation walked out of a summit meeting of the World Heritage committee held in Paris, France, in June 2011, and subsequently announced Thailand's withdrawal from the World Heritage Convention, in protest at the Committee's decision to consider a proposal submitted by Cambodia for the management of the Preah Vihear temple. The decision to withdraw from the Convention, which had been approved by Abhisit, was widely interpreted as part of a government campaign to stoke nationalist sentiment in advance of the legislative election in early July. Following the electoral victory of Puea Thai and the accession to the premiership of Yingluck Shinawatra, the Cambodian Deputy Prime Minister and Minister of Foreign Affairs and International Co-operation, Hor Nam Hong, congratulated the newly elected Government and expressed the hope that the Yingluck administration would 'resolve border issues with Cambodia more positively and peacefully than the previous government'.

Economy

CHRIS DIXON

Revised for this edition by BHANUPONG NIDHIPRABHA

The Thai economy contracted by 2.3% in 2009, its worst performance since 1998 and the sharpest decline in South-East Asia, having entered recession in the first quarter of the year. This followed a significant deceleration in real growth in 2008, to 2.5%, the lowest rate of expansion recorded since 2001. The downturn largely reflected a deterioration in global economic conditions, which led to a sharp reduction in demand for Thai exports and a decline in tourism, but also stemmed from domestic political turmoil and its impact on the confidence of investors and tourists. The economy returned to growth in the last quarter of 2009 and expanded by 7.8% in 2010, as global economic conditions improved, resulting in substantial increases in Thai exports, investment and consumption. Growth slowed to 2.9% in the first half of 2011, primarily owing to a decline in consumer spending and in public investment inflows. However, for the most part, Thailand's broad-based economy has proven to be remarkably resilient under adverse domestic and global conditions.

This resilience has since 2001 been reinforced by a series of governments that have been very much more effective in economic management and policy formulation and implementation than their immediate predecessors. Gross domestic product (GDP) increased by 5.3% in 2002, 7.1% in 2003 and 6.3% in 2004. Growth subsequently slowed to rates of 4.6% in 2005, 5.1% in 2006 and 4.9% in 2007. Thus, comparatively high rates of growth were maintained in 2002–07, despite a series of domestic crises: the December 2004 tsunami disaster; a serious outbreak of avian influenza ('bird flu'); ongoing violence in the south of the country; and, after the September 2006 military coup, political uncertainty (see History). Thailand withstood these events well under difficult international conditions, including sharply rising prices of oil, other raw materials and foodstuffs, and increasing competition from the People's Republic of China for markets and investment. A continuation of the recovery recorded in 2010 would depend largely on continued improvement in economic conditions in Thailand's principal export markets, as well as on the ability of the Puea Thai-led Government of Yingluck Shinawatra, which took office in July 2011, to restore political stability, amid persistent tensions. In addition, there remain some serious long-term structural weaknesses—notably with regard to infrastructure, research and development (R & D), and education and training—and significant issues of regulation, particularly within the financial and corporate sectors (see Structural Problems, below).

Many of these issues were brought into focus by the 1997 regional financial crisis and its aftermath. In 1997 Thai economic growth came to an abrupt halt as a result of major currency and financial crises. In 1997 and 1998, respectively, GDP contracted by 1.4% and 10.5%, industrial output declined by 5.9% and 13.5%, and unemployment rose from 2.2% in February 1997 to 5.3% at the end of 1998. This unprecedented negative growth followed speculative action against the Thai currency, the baht, and the virtual collapse of the financial and property sectors. In August 1997 the depth of the crisis forced the Government to seek assistance from the IMF, and in that month a 'rescue' programme valued at a total of some US $17,200m. was agreed. Conditions attached to this agreement included the rapid enforcement of tight monetary policy and the implementation of major liberalization and privatization programmes, particularly aimed at opening the economy to foreign activity and ownership. The implementation of this programme was accompanied by two years of recession and financial turmoil. By the end of 1999 it was evident that the macroeconomic crisis was over, and Thailand departed from the IMF rescue programme.

The 1997 crisis and its aftermath must be assessed in the context of a remarkable period of growth and structural change. Between 1986 and 1991 Thailand was one of the fastest growing economies in the world. During this period the value of exports grew at an average rate of 30% per year, and GDP at 9.2%. The most striking feature was the expansion of manufacturing. The devaluation and realignment of the baht substantially improved the competitiveness of Thai exports. Thai exporters were remarkably successful in expanding sales in established markets and in penetrating new ones. From 1987 there was a surge of domestic and foreign investment in export-orientated, labour-intensive manufacturing industry. Thailand became a major destination for East Asian investment. Investors were attracted by Thailand's location, stability and low labour costs.

As economic growth accelerated, the Government implemented a wide range of liberalization measures, some of which had originally been advocated during the early 1980s by the World Bank and the IMF. These included the removal of subsidies and marketing restrictions on a wide range of products, simplification of investment promotion procedures, the reduction of tariff levels and a considerable measure of financial liberalization, including the virtual elimination of foreign exchange controls. The furtherance of such measures was an important element in the Seventh (1992–96) and Eighth (1997–2001) National Plans. Under these Plans the Government aimed to reduce its role as the 'principal economic stimulator' by limiting public expenditure and encouraging private investment, and by becoming the 'co-ordinator, adviser and facilitator to the private sector'. To this end, a wide-ranging programme of privatization was announced. However, the programme was subject to considerable debate, opposition and delay. Overall, liberalization accompanied and furthered Thai economic growth, rather than preceding it and playing any significant role in its initiation.

Liberalization from the late 1980s should be viewed in the context of the increased political influence that business interests expected to gain through deregulation and the easing of access to international capital. There was also considerable pressure for liberalization from Thailand's principal trading partners and from international agencies. In addition, tariff reductions and the removal of restrictions on foreign market access and ownership became necessary conditions for membership of the Association of Southeast Asian Nations (ASEAN) Free Trade Area (AFTA) and the World Trade Organization (WTO). Between 1997 and 2000 liberalization was assigned a greater degree of urgency under the IMF programme. The Government of Chuan Leekpai (November 1997 to December 2000) generally followed the IMF programme closely, and was perceived as being in favour of globalization. However, almost every liberalization measure that it proposed resulted in considerable debate and resistance, sometimes accompanied by public demonstrations held with media support. As a result, many measures were either delayed or weakened, and their effectiveness was limited. Reform was thus slow, uneven and far from consistent in its implementation.

Following the election of the Thai Rak Thai-dominated Government of Thaksin Shinawatra in January 2001, economic policy statements became markedly more nationalistic. In the event, however, these statements proved to have little real substance, although there were some significant policy shifts. The Thaksin administration was significantly more interventionist and proactive in managing the economy than its immediate predecessors. There was a consistent commitment to the promotion of economic growth, the elimination of poverty by means of expansionary policies and deficit spending, and a wide range of programmes that sought to address Thailand's major structural and competitive problems. Various attempts were made to stimulate the economy through measures such as tax concessions; low interest rates; loose credit and direction of lending by the state banks and financial institutions; support of small and medium-sized enterprises (SMEs); low-cost public housing construction; and public expenditure in general. Government policies also combined with the changes in the financial sector and the availability of surplus funds to expand consumer credit by a considerable margin. This contributed significantly to the growth of consumption, which was the dominant component of economic growth. As the contribution of consumption showed signs of a decline from 2004, the World Bank perceived that the high level of public spending was becoming the new driving force of growth. This so-called 'Thaksinomics' was also the focus of domestic censure for involving unsustainable levels of public expenditure.

Thaksin won a second term of office with an increased majority in 2005. This second administration appeared to be following similar policies, until it became mired in a protracted political crisis culminating in its removal in September 2006. The military-appointed administration of Surayud Chulanont (2006–07) appeared to distance itself from Thaksin's policies, notably through the announcement of its sufficiency theory of economic management, which centred on 'moderate' consumption, but in general, policies regarding infrastructure, education and training, poverty elimination, and the rural sector remained broadly similar. There were also comparable attempts to stimulate the economy through tax concessions, public expenditure and loans. However, there were some notable and controversial departures, including proposals to limit the privatization of utilities, to constrain foreign ownership further through amendments for the Foreign Business Law (see Investment, below), and to introduce capital controls. In the event, only the last measure was implemented (in May 2006), with the aim of countering the appreciation of the baht and curbing further reductions in Thailand's competitive position. However, capital controls were generally ineffective in these respects and served only to undermine investor confidence, and consequently most were removed in March 2007, with the remainder eliminated a year later. The December 2007 election returned Thailand to democratically elected government. The largest party, the People's Power Party (PPP), which was in many respects a successor to Thaksin's Thai Rak Thai, formed a coalition with five other parties, led by Samak Sundaravej as Prime Minister. In September 2008, however, Samak was forced to resign and replaced by Somchai Wongsawat. Generally, there was considerable continuity of policies under the PPP-led coalition, although some very specific Thaksin programmes, notably the Village Fund, were renewed.

After the Constitutional Court ordered the dissolution of the PPP and two other parties in December 2008, on the grounds of electoral fraud perpetrated during the 2007 election campaign, Somchai was, in turn, forced to leave office. Having secured the support of a significant number of deputies from the dissolved parties, as well as that of several former partners of the PPP, the Democrat Party (DP) formed a new coalition Government with six other parties, headed by Abhisit Vejjajiva. Abhisit's Cabinet was confronted by significant economic difficulties on taking office. The new Prime Minister pledged to continue some of the more populist policies pursued by previous administrations, extending, for example, measures introduced by the PPP-led coalition to reduce utility and transport costs, and swiftly began formulating policies aimed at alleviating the effects of the global recession. A 116,700m. baht economic stimulus plan was announced in January 2009, to provide immediate assistance to impoverished households, the unemployed and small businesses, followed, in September, by a three-year programme of longer-term projects, to be funded by investment of 1,430,000m. baht (see Recent Developments and Prospects, below). In early 2010 the Government confirmed its intention to continue the implementation of this programme, despite an improvement in the economic outlook. Following the election of Puea Thai in July 2011, the incoming administration of Prime Minister Yingluck Shinawatra, Thaksin's younger sister, was expected to resume the populist policies initiated during Thaksin's premiership.

STRUCTURAL PROBLEMS

Since the early 1990s Thai growth has been adversely affected by a number of long-term structural problems. While some of these have been addressed since 2001, notably the limited transport within the Bangkok Metropolitan Region (BMR) and lack of port and air freight facilities, there remain serious deficiencies in roads, railways, water supply and telecommunications (see Communications and Infrastructure, below). Shortages and, in some cases, the high prices of domestically produced materials and components constrained production and accelerated the growth of imports—a problem exacerbated by the limited development of many basic industries. Similarly, the lack of adequate technical training schemes resulted in a serious shortage of skilled labour, which began to restrict the growth of the manufacturing sector. In addition, the quality of secondary and tertiary education is often poor, with a curriculum that is ill suited to the requirements of a modern economy and with low levels of attainment. There is a particular shortage of science and technology graduates. Overall, the limited participation in, and deficiencies of, the education system remain a major barrier to the development of more technology- and skill-intensive production, while Thailand's comparative advantage in labour-intensive manufacturing has been eroded. Since the early 1990s, and more especially since 2001, there have been various government schemes aimed at resolving the skills shortage. The 1997 Constitution guaranteed all children free education until the age of 12 years, and in 1999 the National Education Act set out an ambitious three-year programme of education reform. In addition, during 2001 a Skill Development Act was formulated and a new Skill Development Fund established. The guarantee of 12 years' free education by 2005 was implemented in 2002; this was extended to 14 years in 2004 and to 15 years under the economic stimulus plan announced in January 2009. A World Bank report published in 2006 acknowledged significant increases in secondary education enrolment rates since the late 1980s, but identified a need to implement measures to improve the overall performance of students, to enhance the equitability of access and to increase the share of the education budget allocated to secondary schooling from its current level of 28%. In a further report released in 2010, the World Bank emphasized the need to strengthen links between higher educational institutions and the private sector in order to ensure that graduates have the knowledge and skills demanded by employers, noting the continued shortage of graduates in science and engineering, and recommended granting universities greater autonomy. While it is significant that governments have been addressing the critical issue of education and training, it is also clear that, even if the reforms are effectively implemented, there can be no rapid solution to the skills problem.

In 2008 a joint study by the World Bank and the National Economic and Social Development Board (NESDB) drew attention to the low level of factor productivity growth in Thailand since the mid-1980s and its limited contribution to growth. A similar point was made with respect to the contribution of education and training. According to the study, growth has been driven by increased employment and use of capital. This problem is considered to be particularly acute in the services sector, which accounted for some 42.9% of GDP and around one-third of total employment in 2010—a disturbing situation given the emphasis placed by recent governments on services and the knowledge economy. While there has been no shortage of government initiatives in these areas, the impact on such crucial areas as skills and R & D has hitherto been extremely disappointing.

The growth in the Thai economy has been heavily concentrated in the BMR and its immediate environs, reinforcing the capital's economic dominance: it accounted for 40% of GDP in 2006. According to the 2000 census, 43.3% of the population lived in urban areas—a comparatively low level of urbanization considering the country's per caput GDP—while 12m. (44%) lived in the BMR. Particularly since 1986 there has been a sharp increase in the level of income disparity between the BMR and the rest of the country. In 2006 the official incidence of poverty was 0.5% in the BMR, 3.3% in the Central Region, 5.5% in the South, 12.0% in the North and 16.8% in the North-East. Various programmes have been established with the aim of promoting investment in provincial areas, but these have achieved little success. Congestion and land shortages have begun to extend development into the fringes of the 10 provinces adjacent to the BMR. Similarly, despite the still variable infrastructural provision, there has been considerable expansion along the eastern seaboard region. However, these developments represent the extension of the BMR rather than any dispersal of economic growth.

The 1997 Constitution set out a commitment to significant decentralization of administration, public finance and decision-making. Thus, in 1998 the ability of some 100 urban and municipal authorities to raise funds through taxation and land sales was significantly enhanced. Previously only the Bangkok Metropolitan Administration (BMA) had been empowered to raise significant amounts of funds. Through increased local taxation and the reallocation of central funds, it was intended that by 2006 35% of public funding would be locally controlled. However, there seemed to be considerable reluctance on the part of the Thaksin administration to implement this shift. In addition, the provisions of the 2002 bureaucratic reforms, which subsequently created five new ministries and 35 new departments, appeared to be increasing centralization and state control. Indeed, there were significant delays in the transfer of responsibilities and finance, with only 24.1% of funds locally controlled by 2006. Under the Government of Surayud Chulanont there was a further retreat from financial decentralization, with the suspension of the 35% target and a commitment to maintaining the 2007 level of 25%.

By the early 1990s the concentration of growth in the BMR had created one of the world's most polluted and congested cities. However, since this time there have been significant attempts to establish a comprehensive legal framework for dealing with pollution. While enforcement remains problematic, there have been notable improvements: the fitting of catalytic converters to new cars from 1993, the banning of leaded petrol from 1996, and the revision of limits on exhaust emissions in 1999 have significantly improved the air quality. Thus, by 2002 the World Bank considered Bangkok to have become less polluted than either Manila (the Philippines) or Jakarta (Indonesia). In addition, major transport developments (see Communications and Infrastructure, below) have combined substantially to reduce traffic congestion and related pollution. However, it should be emphasized that Bangkok remains, by any standards, a city where traffic levels and air quality leave much to be desired.

There has been serious, long-term neglect of the rural areas, and shortages of funds, combined with vested interest and unwieldy administration, have limited the impact of programmes directed at such areas as credit, water supply and land reform. In many rural areas there is an acute shortage of land, with much landlessness, illegal forest clearance and cultivation of unsuitable land (including some on watersheds, which are prone to soil erosion). However, there has been increasing official recognition of the environmental consequences of unrestrained development, as witnessed by the creation, in 2002, of a new Ministry of Natural Resources and Environment, but the controls and planning mechanisms remain weak.

The long-term growth of the Thai economy has been associated with a significant decline in the incidence of poverty. The percentage of the population living below the official poverty line declined from 23.0% in 1980 to 18.0% in 1990, and to 11.4% in 1996. In the aftermath of the 1997 financial crisis, the incidence of poverty rose sharply, reaching 21.0% in 2000, before declining with economic recovery to pre-crisis levels by 2004 (11.2%) and to 9.6% in 2006. However, the success in reducing poverty has to be set against an increase in disparities in income. In addition, poverty has become heavily concentrated in rural areas. In 2006 the official incidence was 12.0% in rural areas and 3.6% in urban areas.

Since 2000 there have been some substantive initiatives to address the issue of rural poverty: notably, the Village Fund; the three-year moratorium on the repayment by farmers of loans to the Bank for Agriculture and Agricultural Co-operatives (BAAC); and the establishment of the National Poverty Eradication Centre (NPEC). In October 2004 the NPEC announced a six-year programme aimed at identifying and registering the poor, targeting individual households through 'poverty caravans' of experts and advisers; the Centre set the ambitious—and ultimately unfulfilled—target of eliminating poverty by 2010.

The Village Fund, which was initiated in 2001, granted US $23,000 to each of Thailand's 75,000 villages, to provide credit and working capital for small-scale enterprises. The programme was subsequently expanded to include small-scale loans to villages and groups of villages through the BAAC and the Small and Medium Enterprise Development Bank (SMEDB—see Manufacturing, below). These developments attracted much criticism on the grounds that the funds had either been misused or had failed to reach their target groups. None the less, the Thaksin Government claimed that the Village Fund and the debt moratorium had been of major importance in improving rural living conditions. In this respect, it is perhaps surprising that the administration of Surayud Chulanont effectively relaunched the Village Fund in 2007, albeit with the condition that funds would only be used for 'productive purposes'.

The Tenth National Plan (2007–11) set the target of reducing the incidence of poverty to 4% by 2011. A Centre of Poverty Eradication and Rural Development was established in the Prime Minister's office, intended to monitor and co-ordinate programmes. The Government also allocated 5,000m. baht to the implementation of the Good Living and Happiness Society Strategy, comprising five development plans: the sufficiency economy, aimed at developing skills and the knowledge economy; community development and opportunity creation, to focus on reducing household expenditure through the promotion of the use of organic fertilizers and vegetable production, and on the creation of markets for community products; rehabilitation plans for natural resources; vulnerable people and senior citizens; and basis services, such as health, education and vocational training. These plans were to be formulated and implemented through collaboration between community leaders and local, provincial and central government. However, details of what these plans would mean in practice remained extremely vague.

The recession suffered in 2009 emphasized the Thai economy's overdependence on exports to drive growth and the need to stimulate domestic demand in order to achieve a sustainable recovery in the long term. Exports of goods and services accounted for 76.5% of GDP in 2008 and 68.4% of GDP in 2009.

AGRICULTURE

The contribution of the agricultural sector (including fishing and forestry) to Thai GDP decreased from 40% of GDP in 1980 to a low point of 8.7% in 1993, but subsequently increased, albeit with fluctuations, to 12.4% in 2010. Agriculture's share of export earnings has declined even more markedly, from 60% in 1980 to 8.8% in 2010. Nevertheless, in 2010 the agricultural sector engaged some 38.2% of the employed labour force and directly supported a similar proportion of the population. Having registered growth of 4.2% in 2008, agricultural GDP expanded by only 1.3% in 2009 and declined by 2.2% in 2010, as production of most crops and livestock decreased owing to poor climatic conditions, pest infestations and lower international prices. Most agricultural activity remains small-scale, with low productivity and low levels of household income. In 2006 41.2% of households living below the official poverty line were directly dependent on agriculture.

Thailand is one of only two net food exporters in Asia (the other is Viet Nam). It is the world's largest exporter of rice (a position it attained in 1981), rubber and cassava, and the third largest exporter of sugar. As well as providing a continuing contribution to export earnings and supplying domestic foodstuffs and raw materials, the agricultural sector is the basis of the rapidly expanding agribusiness sector. However, Thailand is becoming a comparatively high-cost producer of agricultural goods, and is losing markets to new low-cost producers. Despite this and other sectoral weaknesses, since the 1997 crisis the agricultural sector has provided an invaluable 'cushion' for a significant proportion of the population, both in terms of its contribution to export earnings and to the economy as whole.

Most Thai agriculture remains unintensive in character, and until about 1990 the sector accommodated increases in production and population by expansion of the area cultivated. Subsequently, expansion of the cultivated area has almost ceased, with the limited clearance for upland and tree crops, often of land that is unsuited to permanent cultivation, being offset by land passing out of cultivation because of salination, declining fertility, erosion and the availability of alternative and more attractive sources of income. Controls over clearance have been generally ineffective, even within forestry reserves. As a result, forest cover declined rapidly, from 54.6% of the country in 1965 to an estimated 12% in 2000. By the late 1980s the expansion of agriculture, weak controls over logging and limited replanting schemes had effectively eliminated the Thai forestry industry.

The long-term expansion has for many crops been associated with stagnant or declining yields. This is largely accounted for by the progressive clearance of less reliable and less fertile land, reinforced by low and uncertain price levels, the high cost of fertilizer, and insecure land tenure. The emergence of land shortages in many areas has resulted in some intensification of production and increasing yields. However, yields and rates of fertilizer application for almost all Thailand's major crops remain among the lowest in Asia. This has been particularly striking in the case of rice. Production remains remarkably extensive in character; the only significant South-East Asian rice-producing country with a lower yield than Thailand is Cambodia. However, output is remarkably resilient, with the serious 2005 drought having had little impact on the crop in that year: at 30.3m. metric tons, according to data published by FAO, the harvest exceeded that achieved in 2004 when generally favourable weather conditions prevailed. Production declined slightly in 2006, to 29.6m. tons, before increasing to 32.1m. tons in 2007. Moderate declines in output, to 31.7m. tons and 31.5m. tons, were recorded in 2008 and 2009, respectively. Rice exports accounted for 2.7% of the total value of exports in 2010.

While rice continues to dominate Thai agriculture, since the early 1960s there has been significant diversification of production. The spread of such crops as maize and cassava brought much land unsuited to rice production into cultivation. Thus, the percentage of land planted with rice contracted from 88% in 1950 to 68% in 1970. These developments were reinforced from the late 1970s by a second phase of diversification, which contributed to the reduction of the rice sector's share of the cultivated area to 52% in 1990 and 50% in 2000. This involved horticulture, aquaculture, tree crops—particularly rubber—and intensive livestock farming. Some of these developments involved substantial capital inputs, and were associated with the emergence of a major agribusiness sector—either through direct control of production or through various contractual arrangements. Particular growth areas for the export market have been frozen chickens, canned fruit (notably pineapples), frozen fruit and vegetables, fresh fruit and vegetables, and cut flowers. In addition, for the domestic market the growth of Western-style supermarkets and the rise of a comparatively wealthy middle class in the BMR have led to the development of packaging and grading of a wide range of produce. This trend has been reinforced by the increased presence of international retailers in the country: for example, the British supermarket chain Tesco, which purchased the Locus chain of shops in 1998.

In the aftermath of the post-1997 recession the Government focused increased attention on the agricultural sector as a principal area for economic growth. Priority was given to the expansion of exports, the creation of employment and the raising of rural incomes, and a series of agricultural development and promotion programmes has been implemented. Particular emphasis has been given to the provision of funding through the Agricultural Sector Programme Loan Scheme and the long-established BAAC. These initiatives have been accompanied by moratoriums on debt repayment and the injection of funds through a series of Village Fund programmes.

Further emphasis on the rural sector has been made under the Tenth National Plan (2007–11) and Good Living and Happiness Society Strategy—notably in respect of community development, the rehabilitation of natural resources, the raising of yields, the improvement of rural infrastructure, the development of trading facilities, the promotion of exports, and related poverty reduction strategies (see Structural Problems, above).

Overall, while increased attention has been devoted to Thailand's rural sector, this does have to be considered in the context of the extent of the problems therein, including doubts regarding the utility of government measures and the limited resources directed at them.

FISHING

Thailand has one of the largest marine fishing sectors in Asia. In 2004 there were 50,000 registered fishing vessels, 17,000 of which were classed as deep-sea trawlers. Most operations are large-scale and are linked to canning and freezing facilities. However, in recent years overfishing has depleted inshore fish stocks. The increase in catches (excluding aquaculture) from 1.7m. metric tons in 1980 to a peak of 3.0m. tons in 2000 resulted from agreements with Oman, India and Bangladesh on the exploration of distant waters, and with Indonesia and Myanmar over joint exploitation of their territorial waters. However, there has been an increasing number of disputes with neighbouring countries; Thai vessels have been excluded from Myanma waters since 1999, and access to Indonesian waters has become increasingly restricted since 2002. As a result, the fish catch declined to 2.7m. tons in 2006, according to FAO—although even this reduced volume provided around 6% of global export earnings. The catch decreased further in subsequent years, delining to 2.3m. tons in 2007, 1.9m. tons in 2008 and 1.7m. tons in 2009. Meanwhile, the problems of the Thai fishing industry were compounded by the devastating tsunami of December 2004, which, in addition to claiming thousands of lives, also seriously damaged vessels, equipment and aquaculture facilities. It was reported that compensation was inadequate and slow to be paid. Further problems have resulted from higher fuel prices associated with increased international prices for petroleum (see Energy, below). In 2005 it was claimed that the combined effects of the tsunami disaster and the increase in fuel prices had forced more than 10,000 trawlers to cease operation, while the incidence of poverty among fishing households increased from 1.8% in 2004 to 5.8% in 2006.

The tsunami disaster also did serious, although short-term, damage to coastal aquaculture, Thailand's most rapidly growing fishing sub-sector since the late 1980s. Output increased from 0.15m. metric tons in 1987 to 0.74m. tons in 2000, and to an estimated 1.37m. tons in 2007, but declined to 1.33m. tons in 2008, before increasing to 1.4m. tons in 2009. Since the mid-1990s Thailand has been the world's largest producer and exporter of prawns and shrimps, accounting for 15.4% of global aquaculture production in 2009. There has been increasing concern over the environmental damage caused by aquaculture, particularly where mangroves are removed to facilitate production. For the Thai market, much fish is still dried, salted, fermented or turned into paste or sauce for preservation. Since the mid-1970s and, more especially, the mid-1980s the development of canning and freezing facilities has greatly expanded the export of seafood, particularly shrimps, prawns and squid. Until the late 1990s the frozen seafood sector expanded extremely rapidly, with the main export markets being Japan, the USA and the European Union (EU). However, expansion slowed as a result of increased competition from lower-cost producers, notably China, India, Indonesia and Viet Nam. In addition, since 1999 there have been increased tariff barriers to markets in the EU and the USA. None the less, in 2003 some 50% of shrimp exports went to the USA. The trade was further threatened by the imposition of an anti-dumping tariff in 2004, upheld in January 2005 by the US International Trade Commission. However, the 6.09% tariff on Thai shrimps was significantly lower than that imposed on its main rivals—China (11.2%) and Viet Nam (25.8%)—and sales to the USA continued to increase. Despite this, Thailand, with the support of India and Japan, filed a case against US anti-dumping measures through the WTO, which ruled in favour of Thailand in 2008. The USA subsequently reduced the general tariff on Thai shrimps to 3.18%, but increased it again in 2009 and 2010, to 4.51% and to 5.34%, respectively. In March 2011 the USA voted to extend the tariff, which had been due to expire later that year, until 2016. In August 2005, meanwhile, the sector received an important boost when an extension of the EU's General System of Preferences—a system of trading arrangements through which the EU offers preferential access to its markets to developing countries—came into effect; the newly expanded system reduced the tariff on Thai shrimps from 12.0% to 4.2%.

MANUFACTURING

Since the early 1980s there has been rapid expansion and diversification of the Thai manufacturing sector. Between 1980 and 2010 the sector increased its share of export earnings, from 28.8% to 88.7%, of GDP, from 21.3% to 35.6%, and of the employed labour force, from 2.0% to 14.1%. This rapid expansion was initially led by the textile and garment sector, from the mid-1980s by electronics and electrical goods, and since the late 1990s by computer accessories and motor vehicle parts.

The electrical goods and electronics sector first emerged during the early 1970s, led by foreign and later by Thai companies producing for the highly protected domestic market. Electronic assembly work for export began during the late 1970s, involving almost exclusively foreign capital. Expansion was rapid after 1986, with heavy investment and relocation of production by companies based particularly in Japan, the Republic of Korea, Taiwan and Singapore. In 1980 the electronics and electrical sector contributed 15.2% of the earnings from manufactured exports; this figure rose to 24.5% in 1991 and to 25.1% in 2002. This rise was accompanied by significant changes in the composition of exports. In 1980 91.0% of manufactured exports were integrated circuits; by 2002, however, these accounted for only 28.1% of the total value of manufactured exports, while computers and computer parts (particularly hard disk drives) accounted for 35.7%, and electrical appliances and machinery for 32.2%. Nevertheless, the extent of skill and technological upgrading remains limited, and the industry is basically a labour-intensive assembly activity. Thailand cannot effectively compete with such lower-cost locations as China, particularly under prevailing conditions of oversupply in the global electronics sector. During 2002 the Taiwan-based company Hana Microelectronics, which had been operating in Thailand since the late 1980s, announced that it was cancelling a planned US $12m.–$15m. expansion of integrated circuit production in the country and transferring all of its operations to the mainland Chinese city of Shanghai. The company cited as reasons for its decision global market conditions and the limited progress made by Thailand over the preceding 10 years in upgrading basic industrial infrastructure. Since 2002, while the hard drive sector has remained buoyant, the contribution of electronics and electrical goods to export earnings from manufactured goods has gradually declined.

Textiles have been a major sector since the 1960s, first for the internal market, and later for export. The expansion of the sector has been closely associated with Japanese investment through partnerships with Thai firms. From 1986 textiles were the largest source of export earnings until they were overtaken by the electronics sector in 1994. The contribution of textiles to total export earnings decreased from 14.6% in 1988 to 4.3% in 2009. Expansion has been impeded by the existence of a surplus in the world textile market and by the imposition of quotas and tariff barriers by the EU and the USA in particular, and by the ending of the Multi-Fibre Arrangement in December 2004. To some extent the loss of established Western markets has been offset by the considerable efforts that have been made to develop new markets in the Middle East, Eastern Europe, Australia and Japan. However, even more so than its electronics industry, Thailand's textile industry is confronting serious competition from lower-cost locations, notably China and Viet Nam. Nevertheless, it was hoped that the free trade agreement signed with Japan in 2007 would give the sector some much-needed stimulus (see Foreign Trade, below).

The textile sector remains heavily dependent on imported raw materials and machinery. Domestic production of cotton is small and of low quality, and 90% of requirements are imported. Similarly, although synthetic fibre production expanded from 239,643 metric tons in 1990 to a peak of 893,859 tons in 2004 (representing more than 95% of the sector's needs), before declining to 601,639 tons by 2009, all the raw materials are imported. Despite the long-term success of textiles, increasing concern has been expressed regarding the large number of outdated plants, ineffective controls on standards, the poor development of dyeing and finishing sections and the shortage of skilled labour. In 2000 less than 25% of the 4m. workers employed in the sector were classed as skilled. During that year the Government began to consider the textile sector a 'problem' industry, and in early 2001 a World Bank project was implemented with the aim of encouraging investment and moves into high-value-added areas of production. However, there is little indication that these initiatives have had any significant impact on the sector's declining competitive position.

In contrast to the diminishing competitiveness of the textile and electronics sectors, Thailand has emerged since the 1997 crisis as a significant source of exports of motor vehicles and, more importantly, vehicle parts. During 2002 Japan's Isuzu Motors Ltd began production in Thailand of trucks for export, and in 2003 another large Japanese automotive manufacturer, Toyota, announced a major expansion of its Samut Prakan plant and the establishment of an R & D centre, the first of its kind in South-East Asia. In addition, Ford, Honda and Thai Yamaha all announced an expansion of the export capacity of their existing plants. These decisions reflected Thailand's established capacity in motor parts, some relaxation of local content rules and the lack of a protected and promoted national car company—in contrast to the example of Proton in Malaysia. By 2008 exports of vehicles and parts accounted for 9.4% of total export earnings. However, there are concerns that Thailand's role as the 'Detroit of Pacific Asia' will be short-lived, owing to the rapid advance of the Chinese economy. The automotive industry suffered from weakened demand in

2009 as a result of the global economic downturn, with the value of Thailand's exports of vehicles and parts declining by 28%. The contribution of vehicles and parts to total export earnings declined to 7.9% in that year.

As the manufacturing sector has expanded, there has been a general increase in the size of manufacturing concerns and a number of very large corporations have emerged—for example, Siam City Cement, which before the 1997 crisis had a controlling interest in more than 40 companies and was the largest manufacturing group in ASEAN. However, the manufacturing sector remained dominated by small-scale operations. In addition, much of the expansion in textiles, garments, and other labour-intensive production has taken place through casual employment, outwork and subcontracting to large numbers of very small workshops—many of these neither registered nor regulated. In 1996 the Ministry of Industry recognized both the importance of the small-scale enterprises and their difficulty in raising capital with the establishment of the Small-Industry Finance Corporation. This was expanded in 2002 into the SMEDB. In 2004 the Ministry of Industry reported that 90% of Thai enterprises were classed as SMEs and were therefore eligible for subsidized loans. Under the economic stimulus plan announced in January 2009, a total of 6,000m. baht was allocated to the SMEDB for the provision of low-interest loans to SMEs, with the aim of mitigating the effects of global recessionary conditions and limiting redundancies. In addition, the SMEDB expanded its range of loans in order to suit different business needs and increased the flexibility of its terms and conditions. The total value of outstanding loans amounted to 56,915m. baht at the end of 2009, a 30.2% increase compared with a year earlier, reflecting the initiatives introduced to assist SMEs experiencing financial difficulties.

In the aftermath of the 1997 crisis there was some restructuring and concentration of production. Between 1997 and 2000 about 20,000 plants closed—16% of the total registered, and most of which were small or medium-sized concerns. In addition, some of the major concerns restructured their operations; the animal feed manufacturer Charoen Pokphand, for example, disposed of a number of domestic and overseas subsidiaries and concentrated on its core agribusiness activities. However, there were few major corporate mergers, reflecting the continuing dominance of family ownership, low levels of capitalization, and cumbersome merger, take-over and bankruptcy procedures. In August 2002, after three years of negotiations, Siam City Cement agreed to merge its two steel concerns with the NTS Steel Group. The resultant Millennium Corporation would therefore control 25% of Thai steel-making capacity. This was by far the largest post-1997 industrial merger, but did not seem to herald the beginning of a major series of mergers, as some observers had predicted.

Following the currency depreciation of 1997, the Thai manufacturing sector regained some of its competitiveness. However, this appeared to be merely a temporary respite, and from the latter part of 2001 there were indications that competitiveness was again declining. Although the problems of low productivity, skills shortages and infrastructural deficiencies were being addressed, Thailand remained unable to compete effectively with other parts of the region for labour- or skills-intensive activities. Concerns have also been expressed regarding the impact of the progressive implementation of AFTA, of various bilateral agreements and of obligations to the WTO. These will in many cases give domestic manufacturers access to cheaper components, raw materials and machinery, but will also open the national market to foreign competition, which may undermine some domestically orientated manufacturing and result in substantial business failures and loss of employment. Of particular concern in this regard are basic industries such as iron and steel products. Since 2001 various productivity and competitiveness enhancing programmes have been announced, notably under the National Competitiveness Committee (established in 2003) and the National Industrial Productivity Master Plan (2007–11). The latter aims to raise the productivity of 13 strategic industries: food, automobiles and parts, electrical appliances and electronics, textiles and garments, iron and steel, machineries, pharmaceuticals, plastics, shoes and leather products, ceramics, software, shipbuilding and repair, and printing. Some 43 industry and six cross-industry projects have been initiated, a significant number aimed at upgrading skills and introducing new technologies. In late 2007, while commenting favourably on the wide range of programmes that recent governments had implemented, the World Bank stressed that progress had been extremely limited.

ENERGY

Thailand has substantial reserves of offshore natural gas, with 13 proven fields in the Gulf of Thailand and rather more limited onshore petroleum reserves in three small fields, the most successful of which is at Kamphaengphet. Gas began to be piped ashore in 1981, and from 1990 production expanded at some 20% per year. By 2010 production had risen to 36,300m. cu m of natural gas, and 334,000 barrels per day of petroleum; in 2009 output of condensate stood at 30.6m. barrels. By 2006 68% of the country's electricity was generated from natural gas. The expansion of oil, gas and, to a much lesser extent, lignite production reduced Thailand's dependence on imported energy from a peak of 90% in 1992 to 60% in 2003, although even this reduced level of imports left the economy vulnerable to increases in international oil prices. Since 1974, however, the impact of such price rises has been mitigated by the Oil Fund (operated by the Energy Fund Administrative Unit) and the imposition of 'ceilings' on domestic price rises for certain grades of fuel. In 2004 international prices for crude petroleum rose by 35% compared with 2003, whereas the increase in the domestic price of diesel, for example, was limited to 18%. Between January 2004 and June 2005 the Oil Fund spent US $2,900m. on subsidizing the domestic price of fuel, which was effectively covered by the Energy Fund Administrative Unit issuing bonds worth $2,800m. However, this level of expenditure was unsustainable, and the intervention ended in July 2005. There has been some slight offsetting of subsequent fuel price rises by a reduction in excise tax.

There are long-term plans to reduce imports through energy-saving campaigns, and through the mass production of bio-fuels. These programmes were given renewed emphasis in 2000 and again in 2007 with the announcement of a target of replacing 10% of gasoline and diesel by 2011. Policy measures include lowering the price of 'gasohol', promoting production through the Board of Investment (BOI), reduced import duties and taxation on 'flexible-fuel' vehicles, and a degree of market liberalization. In addition, since 2002 a series of measures, including tax breaks, have been aimed at promotion of renewable energy. How effective any of these measures will prove to be is debatable, and of more immediate and greater significance appears to be Thailand's increased access to cheap and reliable energy resources in neighbouring countries.

Thailand has been importing electrical power from Laos since 1978; this involves almost the entire 150 MW output of the Nam Ngum plant. In 2000 agreement was reached for the supply of electricity from Laos's largest hydropower plant, Nam Theun 2, which became fully operational in 2010. Under an agreement reached with Laos in December 2007, annual exports of electricity from that country were to increase to 7,000 MW from 2015. Further negotiations are in progress concerning the potential acquisition of additional supplies from Laos and also Cambodia. Moreover, since 2000 the Petroleum Authority of Thailand (PTT) has imported gas from Myanmar's Yadana and Yetagun fields. In 2001 work started on the exploitation, with Malaysia, of the offshore gas reserves of the Joint Development Area. It was envisaged that the project, which entailed the construction of a gas pipeline and an associated separation plant, would give Thailand access to gas that would increase the country's reserves by 40%. Following substantial delays, resulting from protests by local people and environmental groups, the pipeline and separation plant had been completed by 2007. Even more problematic was the exploitation of the substantial offshore gas reserves believed to lie in a 2,600-sq-km area of the 27,000-sq-km overlapping claims area (OCA), sovereignty of which was disputed with Cambodia. Territorial tensions between Thailand and Cambodia were exacerbated from mid-2008 by a renewed dispute over the ownership of the 11th-century Khmer Temple of Preah Vihear (see History) and in mid-2009 by an agreement signed by the Cambodian Government with the French company

Total on petroleum exploration rights in a 2,430-sq-km block in the OCA.

In the energy sector, as with Thai infrastructure as a whole, successive governments have increasingly looked to the private sector to finance developments. During 1996 the Electricity Generating Authority of Thailand (EGAT) reached agreement with two private companies to construct power plants. Additionally, the Ratchaburi Electricity Holding Company, the largest generating plant in the country, was sold in late 2000 following the withdrawal of opposition by the labour unions. However, trade union opposition repeatedly delayed the privatization of the PTT and EGAT. In 2001 the PTT was converted into a limited company (made possible by the 2000 Corporatization Act), and 30% of its shares were subsequently sold. While this raised funds, it left the Government firmly in control of policy and prices, a situation much criticized by foreign investors. It was subsequently announced that a similar approach was to be taken in privatizing EGAT. In March 2006, however, the Supreme Court ruled against the planned flotation.

INVESTMENT

Prior to 1986 foreign direct investment (FDI) in Thailand was relatively small compared with that in other ASEAN countries. In general, Thailand was unattractive to multinational corporations and foreign investors because of poor international communications, uncertainty regarding the country's long-term political stability, and the absence of any significant labour cost advantages. However, between 1986 and 1991 a combination of rising costs elsewhere in the region and a perception of economic and political stability made Thailand one of the most attractive investment locations in Asia, particularly for investors from Japan and the Asian newly industrializing countries (NICs).

Despite the 1997 financial crisis, foreign investment was maintained at a high level until 2001, with net inflows totalling US $18,876m.—an annual average of $3,775m., or 20.1% of gross fixed capital formation. This level of inflow was remarkable, given that during the period 1990–96 inflows totalled only $8,951m.—an annual average of $1,279m., or 4.1% of gross fixed capital formation. Yet for most of this period Thailand was regarded as a 'hot spot' for regional investment, with high levels of economic growth closely related to the level of net inflows. However, much of the incoming FDI during 1998–2001 consisted of the proceeds of mergers and acquisitions (M & A—i.e. the purchase of Thai assets) by foreign companies, rather than 'greenfield' investment (investment in new, or the expansion of existing, Thai assets). Such cross-border M & A (of 10% or more of equity) accounted for 57.6% of inflows over this period, compared with only 12.2% in 1990–96. M & A activity was initially heavily concentrated in the most distressed sectors, notably finance and property, but there were also major acquisitions in retailing and manufacturing. M & A activity was also largely responsible for a shift in the origins of FDI away from Japan and the NICs towards the EU and, to a lesser extent, the USA.

Between 2002 and 2003 there was a sharp decline in overall FDI and an even more marked contraction in M & A, with FDI inflows averaging US $1,449m. (4.5% of gross fixed capital formation), only 10.4% of which came from M & A. However, the decline in M & A should be considered in the context of a general global decline in such activity since 2000, and, in the case of Thailand, the prior acquisition of the most attractive and easily acquired assets. Subsequently, there was a remarkable recovery of FDI, which during 2004–06 averaged $8,178m. (16.6% of gross fixed capital formation), with M & A contributing 23.9%. While the increase in M & A did reflect a major global resurgence of such activity, the M & A in Thailand were heavily concentrated in 2006 and largely accounted for by the $1,900m. sale of 49.6% of the Shin Corporation to the Singapore-based Temasek Holdings. There is evidence that M & A activity in Thailand has become increasingly difficult, with fewer available attractive assets. Net inflows of FDI increased to $11,324m. in 2007, but declined to $8,531m. in 2008 and to $4,976m. in 2009, reflecting the impact of the global recession and investor concerns regarding ongoing political instability in Thailand. Investor confidence, both domestic and foreign, was further undermined in December 2009, when the Supreme Administrative Court upheld the suspension by a lower court of 65 projects at the Map Ta Phut industrial zone for failing to comply fully with requirements regarding environmental and health impact assessments. In September 2010, however, the Court ruled that all but two of the halted projects could resume, after the Government, in an effort to clarify the uncertainties over investment regulations, approved a list (prepared by the National Environment Board) of 11 activities deemed to be harmful to public health, quality of life and the environment. It was hoped that the apparent resolution of this issue would help to restore investor confidence. Moreover, the improved global economic outlook led to a partial recovery in FDI inflows to $5,762m. in 2010, according to the IMF. However, according to the Asian Development Bank (ADB), FDI inflows declined to around $1,400m. in the first half of 2011, from $3,500m. in the corresponding period of 2010.

The higher level of M & A activity from 1998 reflected the rapid liberalization of restrictions on foreign ownership—a condition attached to the 1997 IMF rescue programme. Before the economic crisis the 1972 Alien Business Law governed foreign ownership. This required that every registered business in Thailand should have majority Thai ownership, and prohibited even minority foreign ownership in certain industries. The only exceptions to this were those US-based corporations that were permitted to have 100% foreign ownership under the 1966 Thai-US Treaty of Amity and Co-operation, and companies operating under the BOI promotional programmes (see below).

Following the conclusion of the Thai Government's agreement with the IMF in 1997, immediate action was taken to liberalize foreign ownership. This included the permitting of majority foreign ownership in the troubled financial sector, and in Thai companies operating under the BOI's promotional schemes. These and other ad hoc measures implemented during 1998 and 1999 rapidly opened up the Thai economy and were codified in the Foreign Business Act, which became effective in March 1999 (replacing the 1972 legislation). While most areas became open to majority foreign ownership, foreign participation continued to be limited in some sectors on grounds of national security, cultural considerations, environmental issues, the fact of 'Thai nationals not being ready to compete with foreigners', and other 'special reasons'. These prohibited activities included the media, farming, fishing, real estate, domestic transport, mining, sugar-refining, rice-milling, engineering, architecture services, most construction services, tourism services, low-level wholesaling and retailing, insurance, telecommunications, accountancy, law and some brokerage services. Some foreign control did continue to develop in these areas through the use of Thai nominees and the exercise, in some cases, of majority voting rights with only minority control. While this was illegal under the 1999 legislation, the law does not seem to have been enforced and appears to have been widely ignored. In January 2007, however, the Government approved revisions to the Foreign Business Act that would enforce this provision, redefining foreign ownership to include majority voting rights. Disturbingly for foreign investors, this was to be applied retrospectively in the restricted areas. There was perhaps here an economic nationalist element that had some resonance with the rhetoric of the Thaksin regime.

Even where full foreign access is permitted, there have remained various indirect barriers to foreign purchase. These include continuing restrictions on the direct purchase of real estate, which can sometimes prevent foreign investors from acquiring majority control; anti-trust laws, which can prevent incoming buyers from acquiring a dominant market position following a take-over; and the intricate and demanding legal requirements for mergers. Overall, the country's complex, interlocking family ownership patterns and low levels of capitalization substantially limit the possibilities for hostile take-overs. Since 1959 the BOI has co-ordinated a programme of investment promotion, under which both Thai and foreign firms were issued with 'promotional certificates' that exempted them from restrictions on repatriating profits and capital, and on foreign ownership of land, import duties and taxes on equipment. The certificates were also guarantees against nationalization or competition from state enterprises. From 1982 the promotional programme became more selective: privileges were proportional to the degree to which the firms complied with criteria on employment, the use of Thai raw materials, provincial location and the level of exports. Furthermore, priority was given to the promotion and financing of research into new technology, and particular emphasis was accorded to the development of biotechnology, computer software, solar cells and microwave insulators. Since 1996 the Ministry of Industry has offered incentives additional to those provided by the BOI for firms producing electrical appliances and parts, precision instruments, medical equipment and vehicle parts, packaging, jewellery and processed food. In 2001 a revised incentive programme was announced, which included tax concessions for companies establishing their regional headquarters in Thailand. Incentives have also been modified to encourage more technology- and skills-intensive activities, and from the end of 2008 the BOI planned to end incentives for a wide range of labour-intensive, low-quality and low-technology areas. However, it could be argued that this is merely recognition of Thailand's loss of comparative advantage in such areas. In November 2008, in an attempt to encourage investment during the global economic slowdown, the BOI began offering a range of incentives (including an eight-year exemption from corporate income tax and a 50% reduction in corporate income tax for an additional five years) for projects in six priority sectors: energy saving and alternative energy; high-technology businesses, manufacturing products such as functional fibre, medical equipment and vehicle parts; manufacturers of environmentally friendly materials and products; companies involved in mega-projects; tourism- and real estate-related businesses; and high-technology, agriculture-based manufacturers, producing goods such as sweeteners, dextrin and modified starch. Further incentives were announced in May 2010: for a period of 15 years companies establishing regional headquarters in Thailand would have their corporate tax waived on income from services provided overseas and would be charged a rate of only 10% (rather than 30%) on earnings from domestic services, while expatriates working for such companies would pay a reduced personal income tax rate of 15% for eight years. However, observers warned that the changes were not sufficiently radical given Thailand's political turmoil, which had caused severe disruption to the commercial district in Bangkok, and increasing competition from neighbouring countries, most notably Indonesia and Malaysia.

Since 1972 the BOI has also offered greater incentives to firms locating outside the BMR. In the mid-1980s Thailand was divided into three zones for promotional purposes, generally reflecting levels of development. Both the levels of privileges and the zones themselves were the subject of various minor revisions, and in 1998 the BOI announced the abolition of the whole system, in view of its lack of success in encouraging investment outside the BMR. However, the zones were retained and were further revised in 2000. Zone 1 comprises the BMR and has the lowest level of privileges. Zone 2 comprises the provinces of Ang Thong, Ayutthaya, Chatchoengsai, Chonburi, Kanchanaburi, Nakhon Nayok, Phuket, Ratchaburi, Rayong, Samut Songkhram, Saraburi and Suphanburi; these provinces have all received increased levels of investment and economic activity as a result of the spreading of development from the BMR. Zone 3 contains all the remaining provinces, and has the highest level of privileges. During 2002 further modifications were implemented, particularly with respect to the promotion of industrial estates. However, there is little evidence to suggest that the BOI incentives have resulted in any significant dispersal of investment away from the BMR and its immediate environs. In 2003, in an effort to stimulate manufacturing growth, any impact that the incentives might have had was substantially undermined by the extension to Zone 1 of most of the privileges accorded to Zones 2 and 3. In 2007 the BOI introduced a programme aimed at reviving the economies of the three southernmost provinces (Narathiwat, Pattani and Yala), offering maximum tax incentives and 100% tax deductions for three years for capital investment projects in the area.

Despite streamlining measures and changes in regulations, the BOI has continued to attract criticism for application procedures, bureaucratic delays and the rejection of applications in order to protect influential established producers. Some critics have also viewed the privileges as ineffective in attracting investment. In 2000 the BOI revised the investment privileges, reducing the indirect subsidy element in order to conform to WTO agreements. Tax exemptions were removed for companies that did not export, and the length of corporate tax 'holidays' was reduced. In order fully to comply with WTO obligations, the BOI was subsequently also required to remove regulations regarding levels of exports and the use of domestically produced components and raw materials.

FINANCE AND BANKING

To a considerable extent, the 1997 crisis arose from the rapid liberalization of the financial regime from 1990 without significant development of the system of central regulation. From 1991 virtually all restrictions on foreign exchange and capital movements were removed. Lending rates were liberalized, deposit interest rates (except those for savings) were freed, and a conduit for international capital, the Bangkok International Banking Facility (BIBF), was created in March 1993. The BIBF licensed 32 foreign banks to provide 'offshore' facilities for Thailand, including 12 of the 14 foreign banks already fully licensed to operate branches within the country. This facility in particular, combined with the financial liberalization, gave Thai companies easy access to cheap international funds. The freedom of financial movements, combined with the volatile and ineffectively regulated Stock Exchange of Thailand, the promotion of overseas corporate bond issues, and a currency that was remarkably stable from the early 1980s until 1997, encouraged speculative movements of capital. These movements became increasingly large and erratic, and in 1995 the Bank of Thailand reintroduced some controls. However, these proved of limited effectiveness, and it was clear with the benefit of hindsight that from mid-1996 an extremely unstable financial situation was emerging. The Bank of Thailand, while expressing concern over speculative movements, took no further action to regulate matters. Subsequently, much attention focused on the unsatisfactory nature of the central bank's monitoring and management procedures.

The 1997 financial crisis resulted in the suspension of the activities of 58 of the 91 major financial institutions (42 at the behest of the IMF), of which 56 were subsequently closed and 12 placed under state management. In addition, six banks (Siam City Bank, Bangkok Metropolitan Bank, First Bangkok City Bank, Bangkok Bank of Commerce, Union Bank of Bangkok and Laem Thong Bank) were nationalized, as a result of their inability to recapitalize. These last four were closed, and the assets of the First Bangkok City Bank and the Union Bank of Bangkok were absorbed into the Krung Thai Bank (which was already state-owned before the crisis). Two new state-controlled banks were established to assume control of the assets of the other closed banks and finance companies: BankThai and the Radanasin Bank.

Prior to the 1997 economic crisis, foreign banks had been permitted to open only three branches, one of which was required to be in the provinces, and they were excluded from the purchase of majority ownership of Thai banks. The latter restriction was removed shortly after the economic crisis, permitting the sale of the Radanasin Bank to the Singapore-based United Overseas Bank (UOB) in 1999, the acquisition of the Bank of Asia by the Dutch-based ABN AMRO and the sale of the Thai Danu Bank to the Development Bank of Singapore (DBS). In addition, there were major increases in foreign participation in the Thai Farmers Bank (now the Kasikorn Bank—49.98%), the Bangkok Bank (49%), the Siam Commercial Bank (49%) and the Bank of Ayudhya (40%). While further foreign purchases had been expected, these did not materialize. Potential purchasers were discouraged by the consistently high level of non-performing loans (NPLs) in the sector, which peaked at 47.0% of total lending in May 1999, continued operating difficulties, the failure of the existing foreign banks to expand their market shares, and the large losses that they had recorded. This situation was reflected in the closure during

2001 of the Thai operations of the Sukbank (of Japan), the Dresdner Bank (of Germany) and the Ibducto Bank (of Japan). In the course of 2002 further changes to the banking system took place with the merger of the state-controlled Siam City Bank and the Bangkok Metropolitan Bank, and the privatization of BankThai. In addition, in April of that year the Bank of Thailand issued a restricted licence to the Thanachart Bank, allowing it to issue cheques and to provide overdraft facilities after five years of operation, thereupon effectively turning it into a commercial bank. Further developments took place within the banking sector during 2004. In May ABN AMRO sold its 80.77% holding in the Bank of Asia to Singapore's UOB, which already held a 79% share in UOB Radanasin Bank. It was announced that UOB would merge its two Thai operations, as required under regulations permitting foreign banks to maintain only one representative institution. Additional concentration occurred in September, with a three-way merger of the Thai Military Bank, DBS Thai Danu Bank and the Industrial Finance Corporation of Thailand (IFCT), the two largest shareholders of the new institution being the Ministry of Finance (31.25%) and DBS (16.1%).

Overall, between 1998 and 2004 the structure of the Thai commercial banking sector changed radically. In 1997 there were 15 Thai-owned commercial banks in operation, one of which was state-controlled. By 2005 there were only 11 fully operational banks, three of which were foreign-owned and two under state control. Prior to the crisis, 12 banks had been family-controlled; by 2004 this had been reduced to three—Bangkok Bank, the Thai Farmers Bank and the Bank of Ayudhya—all with much reduced holdings and substantial foreign ownership. However, significant family interests were retained in other banks, notably in two of the banks under majority foreign ownership, where members of the former controlling families remained as chief executive officer.

Meanwhile, the level of NPLs gradually declined, and stood at 5.4% of total loans in June 2009, leaving Thailand's banks in a relatively strong position to withstand the difficulties caused by the global financial crisis that began in the latter part of 2008. Moreover, the banks were generally well capitalized and had little direct exposure to the US 'sub-prime' mortgage market, where the crisis had originated. Indeed, the level of NPLs continued subsequently to decrease, and stood at 3.0% of total loans in June 2011.

While the structure of the banking system has been transformed since 1997, it is important not to exaggerate the extent of foreign control. In 2004 the three banks with majority foreign ownership accounted for only 3.9% of the domestic banking market and 3.8% of the sector's assets. However, foreign influence on the sector has been considerably greater than these figures would suggest. It is apparent that foreign minority holdings have exerted significant influence over policy. Overall, foreign interests are believed to have played an important part in rapid modernization, increasing the accessibility of branches and encouraging the spread of automatic teller machines (ATMs), online banking, and the expansion and diversification of consumer credit. More significantly, the increased foreign presence reinforced the moves by the Ministry of Finance and the Bank of Thailand to introduce international forms of regulation and banking practice. This was particularly evident in the manner in which the pre-crisis debt equity levels, commonly 3:1, have been generally reduced to 1.5:1, compared with the standard Western maximum of 1:1.

Further reform of the banking sector occurred under the Financial Sector Master Plan (FSMP), approved in January 2004. The Plan aimed to transform the country's entire financial sector, fostering competition by placing institutions on a 'level playing field', with new bank licences no longer making a clear distinction between different types of business. The FSMP reduced the number of small finance companies by encouraging mergers. To this end, companies were permitted to apply for full commercial banking status if they merged with at least one other financial institution and had a resultant capital of 5,000m. baht. By the end of 2005 three new commercial banks had been approved on this basis—Tisco Bank, Kiatnakin Bank and ACL Bank. In addition, smaller merged companies (with a minimum capital of 259m. baht) could become retail banks. These offer basic services to SMEs and to low-income customers; two such licences had been issued by January 2006. A second FSMP, aimed at reducing operating costs, promoting competition among institutions, widening access to services and strengthening the infrastructure of the financial sector, was approved by the Cabinet in November 2009 and was to be implemented during 2010–14. Under FSMP II, further mergers were to be encouraged, strong financial institutions would be granted more flexibility in expanding their businesses, foreign banks would be permitted to establish additional branches, and state ownership of banks would be reduced.

In response to the 1997/98 financial crisis, a number of new institutions were established to manage the financial sector's restructuring, most notably the Bank of Thailand's Financial Institutions Development Fund, while a wide range of initiatives was introduced to improve the regulatory situation and increase the supervisory powers of the Bank of Thailand. These developments resulted in some significant improvements in management and regulation, although the financial sector remained highly protected, with minimal foreign participation, thus limiting its contribution to the Thai economy and the extent to which Bangkok could develop as a significant regional financial centre. During 2007 several important measures were consolidated in the Bank of Thailand Act, the Financial Institutions Business Act and the Deposit Insurance Institution Act. Under the Financial Institutions Business Act, which took effect in August 2008, foreign shareholders were permitted to hold a 49% stake in financial institutions, compared with 25% under previous legislation. Foreign ownership between 25% and 49% required prior approval from the Bank of Thailand, which, together with the Minister of Finance, could also authorize an exemption from the 49% limit if deemed necessary to strengthen the stability of an individual institution or of the overall financial system. In mid-2009 the Minister of Finance announced plans to sell the Government's stakes in two small banks, Siam City Bank and ACL Bank, which had been acquired in the aftermath of the 1997/98 financial crisis, declaring his willingness to consider allowing bidders to exceed the 49% limit on foreign shareholdings, in an indication that the new DP-led Government was prepared to encourage increased foreign participation in the Thai economy. During the first half of 2010 majority stakes in Siam City Bank and ACL Bank were acquired by Thanachart Bank (itself 49%-owned by Canada's Bank of Nova Scotia) and Industrial and Commercial Bank of China, respectively.

A Capital Market Development Master Plan was adopted by the Cabinet in November 2009, to be implemented during 2009–13. The Plan outlined eight principal aims: to abolish the monopoly and improve the competitiveness of the Stock Exchange of Thailand; to liberalize the securities business in order to promote market efficiency; to reform the legal framework; to streamline the tax system; to develop a wider range of financial products; to establish a National Savings Fund to provide workers in the informal sector (some 70% of the labour force) with some income after retirement; to foster a culture of savings and investments; and to develop the domestic bond market.

FOREIGN TRADE

In 1980 80.1% of Thailand's export earnings were derived from the primary sector; by 2010 manufactured goods contributed 88.7% of export earnings. This extraordinary change in the composition of Thailand's trade was accompanied between 1986 and 1995 by a remarkable average annual growth rate in export earnings of 18.5%. This expansion came to an abrupt halt in 1996, a result of rising costs, currency realignments and increasing competition from locations with lower costs, particularly China and Viet Nam. Export growth remained extremely depressed and uneven during 1997–2002, averaging only 3.1% per annum. Subsequently, there was a very sharp recovery, with annual growth during 2003–08 averaging 17.5%. While this was a striking recovery, there were some serious concerns regarding its sustainability, and in 2009 exports declined for the first time since 2001, decreasing by 14.0%, owing to reduced global demand resulting from the economic downturn; however, imports declined at an even greater rate, by 25.2%, as domestic demand also weakened, resulting in a record trade surplus. Both exports and imports returned to positive growth in the last quarter of 2009, and expanded by 18.9% and 26.9%, respectively, in 2010, albeit from a low base.

The rapid expansion of the export of manufactured goods was accompanied by increased dependence on US, EU and, later, Japanese markets. However, since 2001 there has been a general shift away from these trading partners. Between 2003 and 2010 their share of exports and imports declined: Japan from 14.2% to 10.5% and 24.1% to 20.75%, respectively; the USA from 17.0% to 10.3% and 9.5% to 5.9%; and the EU from 15.3% to 11.2% and 10.3% to 7.6%. Over the same period China increased its share of Thai exports from 7.1% to 11.0% and of imports from 8.0% to 13.3%. While, particularly since the 1997 crisis, Thailand has made considerable efforts to boost trade with the Middle East and North Africa, increasing that region's share of exports from 3.3% in 1997 to 4.9% in 2010, the Asia-Pacific market has become increasingly important, in 2009 accounting for some 49.5% of exports (compared with 37.4% in 1997). Since 2001 successive administrations have also made efforts to promote exports through the provision of low-cost export credits for SMEs, agreements with other producers—notably with Indonesia and Malaysia over rubber prices—and through negotiating tariff reductions in new and established markets. The latter approach was marked by the negotiation of a variety of bilateral free trade agreements, notably with Australia, Bangladesh, Chile, China, the European Free Trade Association, the EU, India, Japan, the Republic of Korea, Mexico, New Zealand, South Africa and the USA. However, the extent of the advantage for Thailand in these agreements was debatable. The treaty with China, which covered only trade in fruit and vegetables, resulted in considerable protest from Thai farmers, who confronted an influx of cheaper Chinese produce while finding it difficult, because of both costs and health restrictions, to develop markets in that country.

Negotiations with the USA, which began in February 2004, remained highly contentious owing to US demands for full access to such restricted sectors as agriculture and telecommunications. The difficulty in reaching any agreement was further compounded by US accusations of 'dumping' on the part of Thai shrimp exporters (see Fishing, above) and of the failure of the Thai Government to protect US intellectual property rights. In contrast, the visit of Prime Minister Surayud Chulanont to Japan in April 2007 led to the signing of the Japan-Thailand Economic Partnership Agreement. There was some expectation that this agreement would provide a major boost for the textile sector, which was increasingly unable to compete with Chinese and Vietnamese products. In early 2009 the recently appointed Government of Abhisit Vejjajiva expressed hope that free trade negotiations with the USA, which had been suspended since 2006, would resume once the new administrations in both countries had fully settled into office; however, the talks remained in abeyance at mid-2011, and it remained to be seen whether the election of the Puea Thai-led Government in July of that year would lead to a resumption of discussions.

TOURISM

Tourism has been Thailand's largest single source of foreign exchange since 1982. The number of tourist arrivals, including Thai nationals resident abroad, increased from 4.2m. in 1988 to 11.7m. in 2004 and to 14.6m. in 2008. Despite this impressive long-term growth, the sector experienced problems from the early 1990s. Rising prices made Bangkok, Pattaya and Phuket among the most expensive locations in South-East Asia. This was compounded by the adverse publicity attendant on the drugs trade and the sex industry, with its associated treatment of women and children, and by increased competition from other Asia-Pacific tourist centres. In addition, many major tour companies began to avoid Bangkok because of the levels of pollution and congestion, although the capital remained the gateway to the southern coastal locations, despite the increase in direct international flights to provincial centres. The increased pollution of the Gulf of Thailand also had an adverse effect on the coastal resorts. As a result, growth in the number of tourist arrivals occurred principally in the low-spending sector, while the more expensive Bangkok hotels became heavily dependent on business travellers.

The depreciation of the currency during 1997–98 substantially increased Thailand's attraction for tourists. Since 2000, however, the Bali (Indonesia) bombings, the suicide attacks on the USA of September 2001, the conflict in Iraq, violence in southern Thailand, the regional outbreak of Severe Acute Respiratory Syndrome (SARS), avian influenza and the December 2004 tsunami disaster have all had an adverse impact on Thailand's tourism sector. There was a downturn in the number of tourist arrivals from late 2008 and into 2009, a year-on-year decline of 16.1% being recorded in the first half of 2009, as the sector was affected by reduced demand resulting from the recessionary conditions being experienced in much of the world. Another major factor was the persistent domestic political instability, most notably the enforced closure of Bangkok's two airports in November 2008, following their occupation by demonstrators, and the violent protests that prompted the imposition of a two-week state of emergency in the capital in April 2009. In that month the SMEDB announced an initiative to offer tourism operators affected by the economic downturn and political unrest low-interest loans of up to 5m. baht, with no collateral required and flexible conditions in terms of guarantors; a total of 5,000m. baht was allocated to the programme. Nevertheless, arrivals declined to 14.1m. in 2009. Sharp year-on-year increases in tourist arrivals, of 27.9% and 27.8%, were recorded in the last quarter of 2009 and first quarter of 2010, as global economic conditions improved, but a preliminary contraction of 3.6% in the second quarter of 2010 reflected renewed political unrest. The hotel occupancy rate in the Central Region (including Bangkok) notably decreased from 62.8% in the first quarter of 2010 to 35.9% in the second, a much sharper decline than usual. However, following the resumption of relative political stability from June 2010, the industry recovered strongly and arrivals for the year as a whole increased to some 15.9m., while the hotel occupancy rate in the Central Region (including Bangkok) increased to 50.1%; the national hotel occupancy rate increased slightly, from 49.2% in 2009 to 50.2% in 2010.

There has been a general reduction in visitors from North America and from Europe in recent years. However, this decline has been offset, to a very considerable degree, by the arrival of increasing numbers of visitors from the Middle East, India, Japan, Malaysia and China. Since the late 1990s the proportion of tourists from East Asia has been rising, reaching some 52% in 2008.

Despite adverse conditions, the tourism sector has been remarkably resilient. Other than in 2009, only in 2003, with the combination of the US-led military campaign in Iraq and the SARS outbreak, and in 2005, following the tsunami disaster, were serious declines in numbers recorded. In both cases these proved to be extremely brief reversals, and the sector remains successful in identifying new markets and retaining its existing customers. In 2007 55% of arrivals were return visitors.

COMMUNICATIONS AND INFRASTRUCTURE

The rapid growth that the Thai economy experienced from 1986 put extreme pressure on the country's infrastructure. It was apparent that even before this period of accelerated growth there were serious deficiencies in the provision of roads, railways, port facilities, power generation, water supply and telephones. These problems are at their most acute in the BMR and its immediate environs, where the majority of growth has been concentrated. Here, particular problems have centred on the lack of effective water supply and drainage, a road system inadequate in terms of both capacity and connectivity, and a limited and overloaded public transport system.

A rail mass-transit system for Bangkok was proposed as long ago as 1971. In 1993 plans were finalized and contracts awarded for three projects that would together provide 100 km of elevated track. Subsequently, operations were seriously delayed by revisions to the plans and by major disputes with contractors and landowners. In December 1999 the first project, run by the Bangkok Mass Transit System and comprising a 23.5-km elevated railway, began operating, three years behind schedule. This was followed in July 2004 by the 20-km central subway project, the 'Blue Line'. These lines have made a major contribution to mobility within the city, but are far short of a city-wide system. During 2001 the Mass Rapid Transit Authority announced a scheme to extend the central subway project by 13 km. This was superseded in 2004 by a far more ambitious five-year plan to expand the system from 43.7 km to 291 km, at an estimated cost of US $12,000m., which was in turn replaced by a less ambitious $5,500m. project to construct five new lines by 2012. Construction began in 2009 of a 23-km 'Purple Line', from Bang Sue, near the centre of Bangkok, to Bang Yai, north-west of the capital, in Nonthaburi province.

Port facilities at Klongtoey have long been regarded as inadequate. The opening of the new port at Laem Chabang on the eastern seaboard in 1992 provided neither as high nor as rapid a level of relief as had been expected: first, because of the delay in completing links with Bangkok (the road link was completed during 2000, but plans for a high-speed rail link were suspended); and second, owing to inadequate provision of container and handling facilities. The latter problem resulted, from 2002, in the development of new container and cargo facilities at Klongtoey. However, the Government remained committed to diverting traffic to Laem Chabang, and in 2004 it granted a 30-year concession to Hong Kong-based Hutchison Port to build and operate six deep-sea berths. These would increase the container capacity from 3.8m. 20-ft equivalent units (TEUs) to 6m. TEUs.

During the early 1990s increasing congestion at Bangkok's Don Muang Airport, which handled about 35m. passengers annually, led to the construction of a second facility at Nong Ngu Hao, with an eventual capacity of 45m. passengers. The new airport—Suvarnabhumi International—opened in September 2006. Meanwhile, congestion at Don Muang Airport had to some extent been relieved by the upgrading to international status of various facilities, including those at Chiang Mai, Chiang Rai, Hat Yai, Phuket and Surat Thani. Following the opening of Suvarnabhumi International Airport, Don Muang was closed to all commercial operations. In March 2007, however, in response to the emergence of serious defects at Suvarnabhumi, and concerns that its capacity would rapidly be exceeded, Don Muang was reopened for domestic flights. Significant upgrading of Chiang Mai began in 2006, with the aim of creating a major international hub.

There have been considerable improvements in telecommunications since the early 1990s. A major factor in the expansion of provision was the entry of private companies from 1992. The number of fixed telephone lines per 100 persons increased from 4.7 in 1993 to 8.4 in 1999 and to a peak of 10.8 in 2008, before declining slightly to 10.5 in 2009 and further to 10.1 in 2010. This compared unfavourably with Malaysia, which in 2010 had 16.1 fixed lines per 100 persons. The limitations of the Thai telecommunications sector have been particularly apparent in respect of internet connections. While the rate increased from 3.7 users per 100 persons in 2000 to 21.2 in 2010, use continues to be restricted by cost, limited connectivity outside the BMR, a shortage of information technology skills, complex regulations and the lack of Thai-language websites. In 2006 it was reported that the cost of line rental was more than double that in Malaysia and the Philippines.

The telecommunications infrastructure is controlled by two state-owned corporations, TOT (formerly the Telephone Organization of Thailand) and CAT Telecom (established in 2003 from the telecommunications division of the former Communications Authority of Thailand). Considerable vested interests existed within the Thaksin administration and among its supporters, who were opposed to rapid liberalization of the telecommunications sector and increased foreign participation. This delayed the establishment of a National Telecommunications Commission, which was intended to oversee the liberalization of the sector, until 2004. However, plans to privatize TOT and CAT Telecom were abandoned following the coup that ousted Thaksin in September 2006.

Mobile cellular telephone subscriptions increased rapidly, from 2.3m. in 1999 (or 3.8 per 100 persons, compared with 13.1 per 100 in Malaysia) to 69.7m. in 2010 (100.8 per 100 persons, compared with 121.3 per 100 in Malaysia). The sector has been dominated by Shin Corporation, which controls more than 60% of the market through its subsidiary Advanced Info Service. In 2006 the Singapore-based Temasek Holdings purchased a 49.6% stake in Shin Corporation from the family of former Prime Minister Thaksin. The other major operators are Total Access Communications, with some 30% of the market, which is partly owned by the Norwegian company Telenor, and True Corporation, with around 8% of the market.

Since the late 1980s successive governments have increasingly looked to the private sector to finance the development of infrastructure. This view was reinforced by the IMF following the 1997 financial crisis and became the official position—one that was given additional emphasis from 2001 under the Thaksin regime, with its commitment to the use of international funding to support a series of mega-projects. These projects included a 228-km direct road route to China (from Chiang Rai to Kunming in Yunnan Province); an additional Mekong bridge; a regional highway to link Thailand with India via Myanmar; a major national road-building programme; the construction of a new city in Nakorn Nayok; a major house-building programme; and the Kra canal. While the canal project appeared unlikely to proceed, the first stage of the China road link, known as Asia Highway 3, was initiated in 2004 (supported by funding from the ADB). With political crises impeding and then removing the Thaksin Government, many of the mega-projects appeared to have been deferred. However, the second Mekong bridge was opened in December 2006, and the Surayud Chulanont administration announced a major rail-building programme, involving 832 km of double tracking, and expansion of the Bangkok Mass Transit System. Asia Highway 3 was officially inaugurated in 2008, but its full completion required the construction of a bridge between Chiang Khong in Chiang Rai Province and Ban Houayxay in Laos; this project experienced numerous delays and was not expected to be realized until mid-2012. In 2008 the World Bank endorsed the need for significant government investment in such projects, both as a stimulus to the economy and, in the longer term, in order to address Thailand's productivity and competitiveness problems. However, frequent changes of government in that year led to further delays, amid a contraction in public investment and in government spending. None the less, the development of public infrastructure was a major focus of the three-year 'Strong Thailand 2012' programme, which was officially announced in September 2009 by Prime Minister Abhisit Vejjajiva (see Recent Developments and Prospects, below). Some of the first infrastructure projects to be funded under the initiative involved the rehabilitation of rural roads and the construction of the 'Purple Line'.

RECENT DEVELOPMENTS AND PROSPECTS

The economy decelerated in 2006–08 and entered recession in 2009, reflecting the various domestic crises, the slowing of growth in domestic consumption, continuing low levels of domestic investment, more difficult international trading conditions, the rise in international prices for petroleum and the onset of the global financial crisis in late 2008. While the operation of the Oil Fund (see Energy, above) initially moderated the impact of the increased cost of petroleum imports, there was a significant increase in domestic inflation, peaking at a year-on-year rate of 9.2% in July 2008. This caused the Bank of Thailand to raise its main interest rate (to 3.75% by August 2008) and tighten monetary policy. Such policies further reduced the expansion of domestic consumption and private investment. In addition, public investment slowed, principally as a result of delays in implementing and financing infrastructural mega-projects. To a degree, these growth-reducing factors were offset in 2006–07 and much of 2008 by an increase in exports, particularly to China and Australia, and by the resilience of the tourism industry. However, GDP, exports, tourist arrivals, private consumption and investment all contracted in late 2008 and 2009, as a result of the international economic downturn and ongoing domestic political instability. Inflation slowed from August 2008, partly owing to declining international petroleum prices, and in 2009 consumer prices declined by 0.9%. The Bank of Thailand implemented four reductions in its benchmark policy interest rate between December 2008 and April 2009, progressively lowering it to 1.25%.

The Abhisit Government that took office in December 2008 pledged to address the country's economic difficulties. The new administration announced a 116,700m. baht economic stimulus programme in January 2009, which included provisions for low-interest loans to small businesses, a payment of 2,000 baht to workers earning less than 15,000 baht per month, expanded free schooling, and training opportunities for the unemployed. In addition, the Government extended measures to reduce consumer costs for electricity, water, gas and public transport. Also approved were tax reductions worth some 40,000m. baht, targeted particularly at bolstering SMEs, the tourism industry and the property market. More long-term plans were included in the 'Strong Thailand 2012' programme, announced in September 2009, which envisaged investment of some 1,430,000m. baht over a three-year period in a range of projects aimed at, *inter alia*, upgrading public infrastructure, developing tourism and improving health care and education; it was anticipated that some 1.5m. new jobs would be created under the initiative. As a result of this increased government expenditure, the fiscal deficit was projected to widen in 2010/11, leading to a substantial increase in public debt; in the first six months of the fiscal year alone, the deficit rose to 372,000m. baht, an increase of some 44% year-on-year.

A return to year-on-year growth in the last quarter of 2009 was followed by a robust increase in real GDP of 7.8% in 2010, with rising exports, imports, manufacturing output, consumption and investment all reflecting improved global economic conditions, as well as the impact of the Government's stimulus programmes, particularly on domestic demand. In response to the strong performance of the economy in 2010, and in the expectation that inflationary pressures (although currently still low, partly owing to the strength of the baht) would accelerate in 2011, the Bank of Thailand began to tighten monetary policy in mid-2010, raising its benchmark policy interest rate to 1.50% in July 2010 and to 3.50% in August 2011. The NESDB forecast a rise of between 3.5% and 4.0% in GDP in 2011, an inflation rate of between 3.6% and 4.0%, and a current account surplus equivalent to 2.4% of GDP (compared with 4.6% in 2010). With its financial sector comparatively resilient and foreign exchange reserves of US $178,789.37m. in July 2011, the recovery of Thailand's export-dominated economy depended to a large extent on developments in its major markets, notably the USA, Europe and China. Moreover, despite a period of relative calm following a violent end to large-scale anti-Government protests in May 2010, and the subsequent change of Government in June 2011, underlying political tensions persisted at mid-2011, representing a deterrent to prospective tourists, as well as to investors, and therefore a potential threat to a sustained economic recovery. Meanwhile the deteriorating health of King Bhumibol, who had served as a stabilizing force within Thailand's deeply divided society, remained a source of considerable concern.

The draft policy statement of the incoming administration of Prime Minister Yingluck Shinawatra was approved by the Cabinet in mid-August 2011 and was presented to the House of Representatives later in that month; the proposals covered eight main policy areas: urgent policies to be introduced during the first year of office; national security; the economy; social policy and quality of life; natural resources and environment; science and technology, research and innovation; foreign affairs and international commerce; and good governance.

The Yingluck administration proposed restructuring the tax system in order to enhance competitiveness. A reduction in corporate income tax rate, from 30% to 23%, was expected, in line with the anticipated creation of the ASEAN Economic Community (AEC) in 2015. Emphasizing the importance of greater income distribution equality in achieving sustainable economic growth, the Government was to create a long-term base of tax revenue and increase the efficiency of tax collection and non-tariff activities. The Yingluck Government planned to increase the minimum daily wage from 200 baht to 300 baht, a proposal that was welcomed by large corporations but not by SMEs. Similarly, the Government planned to increase the minimum monthly salary of university graduates working in the civil service from 10,050 baht to 15,000 baht. In order to narrow the income inequality gap between rural and urban areas and to raise the standard of living among farmers, the Government proposed the resumption of the paddy price mortgage programme, guaranteeing the price of paddy at 15,000 baht per metric ton and that of jasmine rice at 20,000 baht per ton. Some observers argued that this income policy would lead to a decline in competitiveness as well as encouraging corruption. However, the Government counterclaimed that the poor would benefit from the scheme, and pledged to enhance co-ordination across all government departments in order to combat corruption.

The Government pledged to promote the tourism industry in order to increase the country's revenue from tourism receipts. It also proposed the expansion of agricultural and food businesses in an effort to develop Thailand as a centre both for quality food production and trade and for agricultural futures markets, while the petroleum and alternative energy industry was to be promoted to generate more income and employment.

The Government's proposals for economic restructuring included plans to boost the performance of the agricultural sector, by establishing the National Farmers Council, increasing the efficiency of crop production through research and development, and introducing the registration of farming households, in conjunction with the implementation of a new credit card programme for farmers; under this new scheme, which was to be initiated in November 2011, a total of 3m. credit cards were to be made available to farmers, with use of the cards to be restricted to the purchase of agricultural equipment from a range of co-operatives and stores affiliated with the programme.

The Government's proposals for the industrial sector included reducing production costs for entrepreneurs, and promoting the brand identity and improving the standards of Thai products in order to attract more international recognition. The Government planned to make the transition to more skills- and technology-intensive activities, and to add value to and improve the quality of locally manufactured products. SMEs were to be afforded greater access to financial support. New industrial zones were to be developed, and a previous proposal to construct a land bridge between the Andaman Sea (off the western coast of Thailand) and the Gulf of Thailand (to the south) was to be revived. It was hoped that the new bridge would reduce the cost of transporting energy resources to refineries, thereby rendering Thailand a strategic regional hub for the transportation and storage of oil and gas. In addition, the Government was to accelerate the establishment of new special economic development zones, with an emphasis on border provinces in order to boost trade and investment with neighbouring countries.

Despite continuing political uncertainty and the recession experienced in 2009, Thailand remains essentially economically stable, with generally moderate inflation (notwithstanding the exceptional rise in food and fuel prices in 2008) and a low unemployment rate (0.4% at June 2011). However, its weak competitive position is a cause for concern. The country no longer appears to be regarded as a favourable location for such labour-intensive activities as the manufacture of textiles, footwear, clothing, electronics and electrical goods. In these sectors, Thailand (like many other countries in the region) has found it increasingly difficult to compete with China. There are concerns that Thailand will be caught in a 'middle-income trap'—that is, priced out of the labour-intensive export sectors but unable effectively to make the transition to more skills- and technology-intensive activities. Mindful of the long-term social and economic threats posed by rising income inequality, the Yingluck Government planned to initiate programmes intended to address the issue of poverty and income disparities. Despite disappointing growth of 2.9% in the first six months of 2011, economic performance was expected to strengthen in the second half of the year, with the ADB projecting full-year growth of 4.0%; this was forecast to increase to 4.5% in 2012.

Statistical Survey

Source (unless otherwise stated): National Statistical Office, Thanon Larn Luang, Bangkok 10100; tel. (2) 281-0333; fax (2) 281-3815; e-mail onsoadm@nso.go.th; internet www.nso.go.th.

Area and Population

AREA, POPULATION AND DENSITY

Area (sq km)	513,120*
Population (census results)	
1 April 2000	60,606,947
1 September 2010 (preliminary)	
Males	32,100,000
Females	33,300,000
Total	65,400,000
Density (per sq km) at 2010 census	127.5

* 198,117 sq miles.

POPULATION BY AGE AND SEX

(UN estimates at mid-2011)

	Males	Females	Total
0–14	7,200,176	6,827,010	14,027,186
15–64	24,166,230	25,003,179	49,169,409
65 and over	2,791,062	3,530,902	6,321,964
Total	34,157,468	35,361,091	69,518,559

Note: Estimates not adjusted to take account of preliminary results of 2010 census.

Source: UN, *World Population Prospects: The 2010 Revision*.

REGIONS

(population at 2010 census, preliminary)

	Area (sq km)	Population ('000)	Density (per sq km)
Bangkok	1,568.7	8,200	5,227.3
Central Region	102,336.0	18,100	176.9
Northern Region	169,644.3	11,400	67.2
Northeastern Region	168,855.3	18,800	111.3
Southern Region	70,715.2	8,800	124.4
Total	513,119.5	65,400	127.5

Note: Totals may not be equal to the sum of components, owing to rounding.

PRINCIPAL TOWNS

(population at 2000 census)

Bangkok Metropolis*	6,320,174	Pak Kret	141,788
Samut Prakan	378,694	Si Racha	141,334
Nanthaburi	291,307	Khon Kaen	141,034
Udon Thani	220,493	Nakhon Pathom	120,657
Nakhon Ratchasima	204,391	Nakhon Si Thammarat	118,764
Hat Yai	185,557	Thanya Buri	113,818
Chon Buri	182,641	Surat Thani	111,276
Chiang Mai	167,776	Rayong	106,585
Phra Padaeng	166,828	Ubon Ratchathani	106,552
Lampang	147,812	Khlong Luang	103,282

* Formerly Bangkok and Thonburi.

Mid-2010 ('000 persons, incl. suburbs, UN estimate): Bangkok 6,976 (Source: UN, *World Urbanization Prospects: The 2009 Revision*).

BIRTHS, MARRIAGES AND DEATHS*

	Registered live births		Registered marriages	Registered deaths	
	Number	Rate (per 1,000)	Number	Number	Rate (per 1,000)
2002	782,911	12.5	n.a.	380,364	6.1
2003	742,183	11.8	328,356	384,131	6.1
2004	813,069	13.0	365,721	393,592	6.3
2005	809,485	13.0	345,234	395,374	6.4
2006	793,623	12.7	358,505	391,126	6.2
2007	797,588	12.7	307,910	393,255	6.3
2008	784,256	12.4	318,496	397,327	6.3
2009	765,047	12.1	300,878	393,916	6.2

* Registration is incomplete. According to UN estimates, the average annual rates in 1995–2000: Births 15.6 per 1,000; Deaths 6.1 per 1,000; in 2000–05: Births 14.1 per 1,000; Deaths 6.6 per 1,000; in 2005–10: Births 12.9 per 1,000; Deaths 7.2 per 1,000 (Source: UN, *World Population Prospects: The 2010 Revision*).

Source: partly UN, *Demographic Yearbook*.

Life expectancy (years at birth, WHO estimates): 70 (males 66; females 74) in 2009 (Source: WHO, *World Health Statistics*).

ECONOMICALLY ACTIVE POPULATION*

('000 persons aged 15 years and over, July–September of each year)

	2008	2009	2010
Agriculture, hunting and forestry	15,641	15,477	15,406
Fishing	426	458	339
Mining and quarrying	55	48	33
Manufacturing	5,231	5,301	5,189
Electricity, gas and water	103	106	99
Construction	2,012	2,044	2,083
Wholesale and retail trade; repair of motor vehicles, motorcycles and personal and household goods	5,635	5,872	6,110
Hotels and restaurants	2,353	2,557	2,558
Transport, storage and communications	1,091	1,111	1,048
Financial intermediation	396	372	373
Real estate, renting and business activities	717	743	809
Public administration and defence; compulsory social security	1,303	1,366	1,618
Education	1,098	1,167	1,289
Health and social work	720	715	703
Other community, social and personal service activities	819	786	793
Private households with employed persons	196	224	221
Extra-territorial organizations and bodies	1	3	0
Sub-total	37,798	38,351	38,672
Activities not adequately defined	39	21	20
Total employed	37,837	38,372	38,692
Unemployed	451	456	341
Total labour force	38,288	38,828	39,033

* Excluding the armed forces.

Source: partly ILO.

Health and Welfare

KEY INDICATORS

Total fertility rate (children per woman, 2009)	1.8
Under-5 mortality rate (per 1,000 live births, 2009)	13
HIV/AIDS (% of persons aged 15–49, 2007)	1.4
Physicians (per 1,000 head, 2000)	0.4
Hospital beds (per 1,000 head, 2000)	2.2
Health expenditure (2008): US $ per head (PPP)	328
Health expenditure (2008): % of GDP	4.1
Health expenditure (2008): public (% of total)	74.3
Access to water (% of persons, 2008)	98
Access to sanitation (% of persons, 2008)	96
Total carbon dioxide emissions ('000 metric tons, 2007)	277,284.2
Carbon dioxide emissions per head (metric tons, 2007)	4.1
Human Development Index (2010): ranking	92
Human Development Index (2010): value	0.654

For sources and definitions, see explanatory note on p. vi.

Agriculture

PRINCIPAL CROPS
('000 metric tons)

	2007	2008	2009
Rice, paddy	32,099	31,651	31,463
Maize	3,890	4,249	4,616
Sorghum	57	55	54
Cassava (Manioc, Tapioca)	26,916	25,156	30,088
Sugar cane	64,365	73,502	66,816
Beans, dry	113	110*	103*
Soybeans (Soya beans)	201	187	188
Groundnuts, with shell	114†	112*	132
Coconuts	1,722	1,484	1,381
Oil palm fruit	6,390	9,271	8,162
Cabbages and other brassicas	489	500	511
Tomatoes	175	194	198
Pumpkins, squash, gourds	177	192	195
Cucumbers and gherkins*	173	172	174
Onions, dry*	257	256	258
Garlic	75	86	71
Maize, green	260	269	268
Watermelons*	303	301	304
Bananas	1,929	1,540	1,528
Oranges*	468	414	396
Tangerines, mandarins, clementines, satsumas*	862	763	729
Mangoes, mangosteens and guavas	2,303	2,374	2,470
Pineapples	2,815	2,279	1,895
Papayas	195	201	207
Tobacco, unmanufactured*	66	68	72
Natural rubber	3,022	3,167	3,090

* FAO estimate(s).
† Unofficial figure.

Aggregate production ('000 metric tons, may include official, semi-official or estimated data): Total cereals 36,196 in 2007, 36,107 in 2008, 36,286 in 2009; Total roots and tubers 27,207 in 2007, 25,426 in 2008, 30,400 in 2009; Total vegetables (incl. melons) 3,456 in 2007, 3,445 in 2008, 3,474 in 2009; Total fruits (excl. melons) 10,212 in 2007, 9,041 in 2008, 8,637 in 2009.

Source: FAO.

LIVESTOCK
('000 head, year ending September)

	2007	2008	2009
Horses	6	4	5
Cattle	6,481	6,700	6,700
Buffaloes	1,744	1,699	1,671
Pigs	8,381	7,845	7,481
Sheep	51	44	40
Goats	445	374	384
Chickens	209,105	219,150	228,207
Ducks	16,351	15,931	16,347
Geese and guinea fowl*	270	270	270

* FAO estimates.

Source: FAO.

LIVESTOCK PRODUCTS
('000 metric tons)

	2007	2008	2009
Cattle meat*	197.0	236.2	212.6
Buffalo meat*	68.1	63.8	61.0
Pig meat*	915.0	864.0	755.8
Chicken meat	986.0	1,018.8	1,075.3*
Duck meat*	87.0	89.9	77.4
Cows' milk	729.1	786.2	840.7
Hen eggs*	539.4	562.0	577.0
Other poultry eggs*	330	320	393

* FAO estimate(s).

Source: FAO.

Forestry

ROUNDWOOD REMOVALS
('000 cubic metres, excl. bark, FAO estimates)

	2007	2008	2009
Sawlogs, veneer logs and logs for sleepers	300	300	300
Pulpwood	2,900	2,900	2,900
Other industrial wood	5,500	5,500	5,500
Fuel wood	19,615	19,503	19,398
Total	28,315	28,203	28,098

Source: FAO.

SAWNWOOD PRODUCTION
('000 cubic metres, incl. railway sleepers)

	2003	2004	2005
Coniferous (softwood)*	18	18	18
Broadleaved (hardwood)	270*	2,796†	2,850*
Total*	288	2,814	2,868

* FAO estimate(s).
† Unofficial figure.

2006–09: Production assumed to be unchanged from 2005 (FAO estimates).

Source: FAO.

Fishing

('000 metric tons, live weight)

	2007	2008	2009
Capture	2,305.0	1,873.4	1,741.7
Freshwater fishes	222.2	225.5	242.4
Bigeyes	105.2	32.3	32.2
Sardinellas	97.4	96.5	96.4
Anchovies, etc.	145.6	144.1	144.1
Indian mackerels	136.8	112.6	112.4
Other marine fishes	1,337.4	891.5	888.9
Aquaculture*	1,370.5	1,330.9	1,396.0
Nile tilapia	213.8	217.3	209.0
Catfish (hybrid)	136.6	136.5	136.3
Whiteleg shrimp	508.4	501.4	535.0
Green mussel	228.3	203.2	230.7
Total catch*	3,675.5	3,204.3	3,137.7

* FAO estimates.

Source: FAO.

Mining

(metric tons unless otherwise indicated)

	2007	2008	2009
Lignite ('000 metric tons)	18,239	18,095	20,000*
Crude petroleum ('000 barrels)	48,745	52,805	56,302
Natural gas—gross production (million cu m)	28,778	31,157	30,625
Iron ore—gross weight	1,554,860	2,029,100	1,400,800
Iron ore—metal content*	779,000	855,000	800,000
Zinc ore—metal content	32,921	17,811	34,000*
Tin concentrates—metal content	122	215	153
Manganese ore—metal content	4,550	52,700	50,000*
Tungsten concentrates—metal content	477	617	600*
Tantalum—metal and oxide powder	142	158	50
Silver (kilograms)	7,727	5,465	15,300
Gold (kilograms)	3,401	2,721	5,400
Marble—dimension stone ('000 cu m)	848.8	664.9	760.0*
Granite—dimension stone ('000 cu m)	10.5	10.6	10.0*
Granite—industrial ('000 metric tons)	5,229	5,190	5,000*
Limestone ('000 metric tons)	151,434	142,118	150,200*
Dolomite ('000 metric tons)	1,108.4	1,353.8	1,200.0*
Calcite ('000 metric tons)	672.6	823.7	750.0*
Silica sand ('000 metric tons)	844.1	495.8	500.0*
Ball clay ('000 metric tons)	563.4	1,500.0	1,000.0*
Kaolin—marketable production ('000 metric tons)	518.1	479.4	500.0*
Phosphate rock, crude	3,550	3,675	3,000*
Fluorspar—metallurgical grade ('000 metric tons)	1,820	29,529	20,000*
Feldspar ('000 metric tons)	684.7	670.6	600.0*
Barite ('000 metric tons)	8.6	9.2	9.0*
Perlite	6,400	7,000	7,000*
Gypsum ('000 metric tons)	8,643	8,500	8,500*
Gemstones ('000 carats)	102	32	30*

* Estimate(s).

Source: US Geological Survey.

Industry

SELECTED PRODUCTS

('000 metric tons, unless otherwise indicated)

	2007	2008	2009*
Raw sugar	7,344	8,194	8,747
Beer (million litres)	2,161	2,160	1,837
Spirits (million litres)	551	631	666
Synthetic fibre	674.6	592.7	601.6
Wood pulp	1,037.4	948.5	880.3
Petroleum products (million litres)	49,856	51,216	53,393
Cement	35,668	31,651	31,180
Galvanized iron sheets	247.2	207.5	169.7
Integrated circuits (million units)	14,334	13,758	13,277
Computer monitors ('000 units)	942	705	660
Computer keyboards ('000 units)	931	633	109
Hard disk drives ('000 units)	205,277	246,986	258,271
Printers ('000 units)	17,439	15,693	8,177

* Provisional.

Source: Bank of Thailand, Bangkok.

Finance

CURRENCY AND EXCHANGE RATES

Monetary Units

100 satangs = 1 baht.

Sterling, Dollar and Euro Equivalents (31 May 2011)

£1 sterling = 50.014 baht;
US $1 = 30.306 baht;
€1 = 43.596 baht;
1,000 baht = £19.99 = $33.00 = €22.94.

Average Exchange Rate (baht per US $)

2008 33.313
2009 34.286
2010 31.686

Note: Figures refer to the average mid-point rate of exchange available from commercial banks. In July 1997 the Bank of Thailand began operating a managed 'float' of the baht. In addition, a two-tier market was introduced, creating separate exchange rates for purchasers of baht in domestic markets and those who buy the currency overseas.

GOVERNMENT FINANCE

(central government transactions, non-cash basis, '000 million baht, year ending 30 September)

Summary of Balances

	2006/07	2007/08*	2008/09*
Revenue	1,659.4	1,828.8	1,686.7
Less Expense	1,502.2	1,655.9	1,778.3
Net operating balance	157.2	172.9	–91.7
Less Net acquisition of non-financial assets	145.9	127.7	184.2
Net lending/borrowing	11.2	45.2	–275.8

Revenue

	2006/07	2007/08*	2008/09*
Taxes	1,374.4	1,493.4	1,371.0
Taxes on income, profits and capital gains	614.9	712.7	638.4
Taxes on goods and services	659.7	674.1	645.4
Social contributions	79.8	84.9	82.8
Grants	1.7	2.1	2.2
Other revenue	203.5	248.4	230.7
Total	1,659.4	1,828.8	1,686.7

Expense/Outlays

Expense by economic type	2006/07	2007/08*	2008/09*
Compensation of employees	559.5	584.5	640.6
Use of goods and services	398.6	447.1	548.3
Consumption of fixed capital	38.5	41.1	47.3
Interest	93.3	89.8	97.6
Subsidies	33.6	69.7	42.4
Grants	205.1	216.6	179.0
Social benefits	170.6	184.1	221.5
Other expense	3.0	23.0	1.6
Total	1,502.2	1,655.9	1,778.3

Outlays by functions of government†	2006/07	2007/08*	2008/09*
General public services	304.7	291.0	274.5
Defence	42.9	114.9	150.0
Public order and safety	136.5	109.4	118.4
Economic affairs	398.6	357.9	400.8
Agriculture, forestry and fishing	109.0	99.9	96.5
Fuel and energy	31.8	18.5	27.9
Transport	55.6	66.2	84.8
Environmental protection	4.8	2.5	4.1
Housing and community amenities	10.6	31.3	50.0
Health	185.6	265.4	281.5
Recreation, culture and religion	14.6	21.1	20.4
Education	334.4	371.4	397.8
Social protection	215.7	218.7	265.0
Total	1,648.2	1,783.6	1,962.5

* Preliminary figures.

† Including net acquisition of non-financial assets.

Source: IMF, *Government Finance Statistics Yearbook*.

INTERNATIONAL RESERVES

(US $ million at 31 December)

	2008	2009	2010
Gold (national valuation)	2,347	2,935	4,599
IMF special drawing rights	131	1,523	1,497
Reserve position in IMF	213	361	377
Foreign exchange	108,317	133,599	165,656
Total	111,008	138,418	172,129

Source: IMF, *International Financial Statistics*.

MONEY SUPPLY

('000 million baht at 31 December)

	2008	2009	2010
Currency outside depository corporations	714.8	804.6	895.1
Transferable deposits	288.9	330.6	365.2
Other deposits	8,283.1	8,726.8	9,484.0
Securities other than shares	620.0	715.7	990.0
Broad money	9,906.8	10,577.6	11,734.3

Source: IMF, *International Financial Statistics*.

COST OF LIVING

(Consumer Price Index; base: 2007 = 100)

	2008	2009	2010
Food (incl. non-alcoholic beverages)	111.6	116.5	122.8
Tobacco and alcoholic beverages	102.9	111.7	117.1
Energy	108.0	93.8	102.9
Clothing (incl. footwear)	100.3	98.1	97.1
Housing and furnishing	96.9	95.2	97.1
All items (incl. others)	105.4	104.5	108.0

Source: Bank of Thailand.

NATIONAL ACCOUNTS

(million baht at current prices)

Expenditure on the Gross Domestic Product

	2008	2009*	2010*
Government final consumption expenditure	1,120,842	1,213,928	1,310,027
Private final consumption expenditure	4,999,605	4,993,302	5,429,683
Changes in inventories	152,272	−261,315	121,382
Gross fixed capital formation	2,492,332	2,181,821	2,499,311
Total domestic expenditure	8,765,051	8,127,736	9,360,403
Exports of goods and services	6,941,526	6,180,052	7,203,299
Less Imports of goods and services	6,708,781	5,226,526	6,452,512
Statistical discrepancy	82,670	−39,711	−6,369
GDP in market prices	9,080,466	9,041,551	10,104,821
GDP at constant 1988 prices	4,364,833	4,263,139	4,596,112

Gross Domestic Product by Economic Activity

	2008	2009*	2010*
Agriculture, hunting and forestry	955,710	931,907	1,142,671
Fishing	94,033	104,679	109,136
Mining and quarrying	315,273	306,529	346,631
Manufacturing	3,163,683	3,087,741	3,599,713
Electricity, gas and water	262,027	278,108	296,583
Construction	259,223	246,076	269,273
Wholesale and retail trade; repair of motor vehicles, motorcycles and personal and household goods	1,288,332	1,272,556	1,323,916
Hotels and restaurants	440,173	439,720	479,145
Transport, storage and communications	645,300	647,319	688,136
Financial intermediation	354,619	368,831	410,048
Real estate, renting and business activities	216,681	215,839	228,770
Public administration and defence; compulsory social security	399,094	416,087	441,420
Education	384,444	414,924	435,246
Health and social work	168,839	177,188	185,932
Other community, social and personal service activities	123,353	123,912	138,039
Private households with employed persons	9,682	10,135	10,162
GDP in market prices	9,080,466	9,041,551	10,104,821

* Preliminary figures.

Source: National Economic and Social Development Board, Bangkok.

BALANCE OF PAYMENTS
(US $ million)

	2008	2009	2010
Exports of goods f.o.b.	175,214	150,713	193,533
Imports of goods f.o.b.	–157,829	–118,022	–161,252
Trade balance	17,385	32,691	32,280
Exports of services	33,383	29,940	34,047
Imports of services	–46,263	–37,756	–45,856
Balance on goods and services	4,504	24,876	20,471
Other income received	8,111	5,880	6,026
Other income paid	–15,171	–13,378	–16,604
Balance on goods, services and income	–2,555	17,377	9,893
Current transfers received	5,324	4,972	5,385
Current transfers paid	–558	–488	–582
Current balance	2,211	21,861	14,696
Direct investment abroad	–4,089	–4,114	–5,271
Direct investment from abroad	8,531	4,976	5,762
Portfolio investment assets	395	–8,290	1,371
Portfolio investment liabilities	–2,561	2,343	8,048
Financial derivatives assets	1,385	3,135	170
Financial derivatives liabilities	–2,062	–2,017	–432
Other investment assets	11,927	1,962	–6,076
Other investment liabilities	–1,660	–771	12,348
Net errors and omissions	10,363	5,045	631
Overall balance	24,440	24,131	31,246

Source: IMF, *International Financial Statistics*.

External Trade

PRINCIPAL COMMODITIES
(distribution by SITC, '000 million baht)

Imports c.i.f.	2008	2009	2010
Food	228.5	203.5	226.9
Crude materials (inedible) except fuels	219.9	140.6	180.7
Mineral fuels, lubricants, etc.	1,238.4	855.8	1,010.6
Chemicals and related products	657.0	493.3	640.0
Basic manufactures	1,124.3	762.3	1,060.6
Machinery	1,895.4	1,677.4	2,057.6
Total (incl. others)	5,962.5	4,600.5	5,840.0

Exports f.o.b.	2008	2009	2010
Food	736.0	724.9	757.6
Crude materials (inedible) except fuels	309.3	221.6	352.4
Mineral fuels and lubricants	376.0	264.9	304.4
Chemicals and related products	457.6	424.9	536.2
Basic manufactures	734.8	670.8	753.0
Machinery	2,473.4	2,106.0	2,604.0
Miscellaneous manufactured articles	114.2	194.6	204.4
Total (incl. others)	5,851.4	5,194.6	6,176.3

Source: Bank of Thailand, Bangkok.

PRINCIPAL TRADING PARTNERS
('000 million baht)

Imports c.i.f.	2008	2009	2010
Australia	171.7	130.4	188.7
China, People's Republic	670.3	586.1	775.5
France	49.8	63.9	46.2
Germany	150.0	118.3	148.3
Hong Kong	65.2	59.7	58.2
India	87.3	59.4	72.1
Indonesia	180.3	130.9	181.7
Italy	53.8	49.2	46.8
Japan	1,116.5	860.1	1,211.5
Korea, Republic	228.2	186.8	258.4
Malaysia	323.0	295.3	343.2
Philippines	75.7	61.3	76.0
Russia	95.6	57.0	102.7
Singapore	236.1	197.3	201.9
Switzerland	131.7	85.5	166.5
Taiwan	206.9	165.0	218.2
United Arab Emirates	371.6	229.2	276.0
United Kingdom	60.4	60.7	61.2
USA	380.7	288.6	342.1
Total (incl. others)	5,962.5	4,600.5	5,840.0

Exports f.o.b.	2008	2009	2010
Australia	263.2	292.0	297.1
Belgium	55.8	46.0	47.8
Canada	47.1	42.7	45.1
China, People's Republic	532.3	548.8	678.6
France	62.1	52.7	55.7
Germany	105.3	89.5	104.4
Hong Kong	330.8	323.2	413.8
Indonesia	208.0	158.9	232.9
Italy	65.1	44.9	54.1
Japan	661.6	535.9	645.3
Korea, Republic	121.1	96.1	114.3
Malaysia	325.3	260.9	334.6
Netherlands	137.4	106.5	115.3
Philippines	115.2	102.9	154.9
Singapore	332.4	258.0	285.2
Switzerland	66.0	107.8	129.3
Taiwan	88.8	76.7	102.0
United Arab Emirates	92.2	83.9	90.1
United Kingdom	130.9	110.3	115.7
USA	667.7	567.7	638.8
Viet Nam	165.1	159.2	184.5
Total (incl. others)	5,851.4	5,194.6	6,176.3

Source: Bank of Thailand, Bangkok.

Transport

RAILWAYS
(year ending 30 September)

	2006/07	2007/08	2008/09
Passengers carried ('000)	45,050	47,059	46,978
Passenger-kilometres (million)	8,038	8,225	8,814
Freight carried ('000 metric tons)	11,912	13,541	11,534

2005/06: Freight ton-kilometres (million) 3,508.

ROAD TRAFFIC
('000 motor vehicles in use at 31 December)

	2007	2008	2009
Passenger cars	3,560.2	3,809.1	4,078.5
Buses and trucks	880.5	905.8	926.3
Vans and pick-ups	4,371.5	4,552.3	4,696.9
Motorcycles	15,961.9	16,264.4	16,549.3
Total (incl. others)	25,618.4	26,417.4	27,184.6

SHIPPING

Merchant Fleet
(registered at 31 December)

	2007	2008	2009
Number of vessels	858	879	884
Total displacement ('000 grt)	2,846.9	2,842.4	2,526.1

Source: IHS Fairplay, *World Fleet Statistics*.

International Sea-borne Freight Traffic
(Ports of Bangkok and Laem Chabang, year ending 30 September)

	2004/05	2005/06	2006/07
Goods loaded ('000 metric tons)	21,456	22,401	24,883
Goods unloaded ('000 metric tons)	30,071	32,951	38,024
Vessels entered	7,640	8,975	n.a.

Source: Port Authority of Thailand.

CIVIL AVIATION
(traffic on scheduled services)

	2004	2005	2006
Kilometres flown (million)	223	229	246
Passengers carried ('000)	20,343	18,903	20,102
Passenger-km (million)	51,564	50,809	56,378
Total ton-km (million)	6,579	6,646	7,258

Sources: UN, *Statistical Yearbook*.

2007: Passengers carried ('000) 21,191.7 (Source: World Bank, World Development Indicators database).

2008: Passengers carried ('000) 19,993.1 (Source: World Bank, World Development Indicators database).

Tourism

FOREIGN TOURIST ARRIVALS BY COUNTRY OF RESIDENCE*

Country of origin	2006	2007	2008
Australia	549,547	658,148	693,234
China, People's Republic	949,117	907,117	818,752
France	321,278	373,090	393,013
Germany	516,659	544,495	541,170
Hong Kong	376,636	367,862	334,861
Japan	1,311,987	1,277,638	1,146,633
Korea, Republic	1,092,783	1,083,652	888,344
Malaysia	1,591,328	1,540,080	1,825,379
Singapore	687,160	604,603	570,267
Sweden	306,085	378,387	391,561
Taiwan	475,117	427,474	390,790
United Kingdom	850,685	859,010	822,422
USA	694,258	681,972	663,732
Total (incl. others)	13,821,802	14,464,228	14,536,382

* Includes Thai nationals resident abroad.

Receipts from tourism (US $ million, incl. passenger transport, unless otherwise indicated): 20,623 in 2007; 21,980 in 2008; 15,901 in 2009 (excl. passenger transport, provisional) (Source: World Tourism Organization).

Communications Media

	2008	2009	2010
Telephones ('000 main lines in use)	7,394.3	7,204.9	7,008.9
Mobile cellular telephones ('000 subscribers)	61,837.2	65,952.3	69,683.1
Internet users ('000)	1,792.9	2,295.6	n.a.
Broadband subscribers ('000)	1,792.9	2,295.6	2,672.6

Personal computers: 4,408,000 (66.8 per 1,000 persons) in 2005.

Radio receivers ('000 in use): 13,959 in 1997.

Television receivers ('000 in use): 18,400 in 2001.

Book production (titles, excluding pamphlets): 8,142 in 1996.

Daily newspapers: 35 (with average circulation of 2,766,000 copies) in 1994; 35 (with average circulation of 2,700,000* copies) in 1995; 30 (with average circulation of 3,808,000 copies) in 1996.

Non-daily newspapers: 280 in 1995; 320 in 1996.

* Provisional.

Sources: International Telecommunication Union; UNESCO, *Statistical Yearbook*; UN, *Statistical Yearbook*.

Education

(2005 unless otherwise indicated)

	Institutions	Teachers	Students
Ministry of Education:			
Office of the Permanent Secretary	3,774	123,486	2,296,415
Office of the Basic Education Commission	32,340	420,965	8,697,983
Office of the Higher Education Commission	156	45,824	1,950,892
Office of Vocational Education Commission	408	16,731	615,548
Mahidol Wittayanusorn School	1	63	704
Mahamakut Buddhist University*	8	150	6,436
Mahachulalongkornrajavidyalaya University*	12	373	8,999
Bangkok Metropolitan Education Department	437	13,196	349,063
Royal Thai Police	192	2,082	29,985
Department of Local Administration	520	18,297	400,361
Ministry of Social Development and Human Security	3	38	407
Ministry of Public Health	39	2,971	17,750
Merchant Marine Training Centre	1	220	918
Civil Aviation Training Centre	1	37	1,052
National Bureau of Buddhism	404	3,188	51,414
Fine Arts Department	16	1,423	10,014
Office of Sports and Recreational Development	28	1,857	13,794
Armed Forces	11	1,400	7,476

* Figures for 2004.

Source: Ministry of Education.

Pupil-teacher ratio (primary education, UNESCO estimate): 16.0 in 2007/08 (Source: UNESCO Institute for Statistics).

Adult literacy rate (UNESCO estimates): 94.1% (males 95.9%; females 92.6%) in 2007 (Source: UNESCO Institute for Statistics).

Directory

The Constitution

A new Constitution, approved by referendum earlier in the month, took effect on 24 August 2007. Its provisions include the following:

GENERAL PROVISIONS

Thailand is one indivisible Kingdom, and sovereignty resides in the Thai people. The King as Head of State exercises power through the National Legislative Assembly, the Council of Ministers (Cabinet), the Courts and other institutions in accordance with the rule of law. The human dignity, rights, liberty and equality of the people shall be protected. The Thai people, irrespective of their origin, sex or religion, shall enjoy equal protection under the Constitution. The Constitution is the supreme law of the State. When no provision of the Constitution is applicable to a case, it shall be decided in accordance with constitutional convention.

THE KING

The King shall be enthroned in a position of revered worship and shall not be violated or exposed to any sort of accusation or action. He is a Buddhist and upholder of religions. He holds the position of Head of the Thai Armed Forces. He has the prerogative to create titles and confer decorations. He selects and appoints qualified persons to be the President of the Privy Council and not more than 18 Privy Councillors to constitute the Privy Council. The Privy Council has a duty to render such advice to the King on all matters pertaining to his functions as he may consult. Whenever the King is absent from the Kingdom or unable to perform his functions, he will appoint a Regent. For the purpose of maintaining national public safety or national economic security, or of averting public calamity, the King may issue an Emergency Decree which shall have the force of an Act. The issuance of such Decree shall only be made when the Council of Ministers is of the opinion that it is unavoidable. The King has the prerogative to declare and lift martial law, and to declare war with the approval of the National Assembly.

RIGHTS, LIBERTIES AND DUTIES OF THE THAI PEOPLE

All persons are equal before the law and shall enjoy equal protection under the law. Men and women shall enjoy equal rights. Unjust discrimination against a person on the grounds of origin, race, language, sex, age, physical or health condition, personal status, economic or social standing, religious belief, education or constitutional political views shall not be permitted. A person shall enjoy the rights and liberty in his or her life and person. Torture, brutal acts or punishment by cruel or inhuman means shall not be permitted. A person shall enjoy the liberty of dwelling. A person shall enjoy the liberty of travelling and the liberty of making the choice of his or her residence within the Kingdom. A person's family rights, dignity, reputation or the right of privacy shall be protected. A person shall enjoy the liberty of communication by lawful means. A person shall enjoy full liberty to profess a religion, a religious sect or creed and observe religious precepts or exercise a form of worship in accordance with his or her belief. No person shall be inflicted with a criminal punishment unless he or she has committed an act which the law in force at the time of commission provides to be an offence and imposes punishment. A person shall have the right to an uncomplicated, convenient, quick and thorough access to justice procedure. A person shall enjoy the liberty to express his or her opinion, make speeches, write, print, publicize and make expression by other means. A person shall enjoy an equal right to receive basic education for the duration of not less than 12 years, which shall be provided by the State without charge. A person shall enjoy an equal right to receive standard public health service, and the indigent shall have the right to receive free medical treatment from public health centres of the State. A person shall have the right to gain access to public information in possession of a state agency, state enterprise or local government organization, unless the disclosure of the information shall affect the security of the State, public safety or interests of other persons. A person shall enjoy the liberty to assemble peacefully and without arms, to unite and form an association, a union, league, co-operative, farmers' group, private organization or other group. No person shall exercise the rights and liberties in the Constitution to overthrow the democratic form of government with the King as Head of State or acquire power to rule the country by any means that is not in accordance with the provisions of the Constitution. Every person shall have the duty to uphold the nation, religion, the King and the democratic form of government with the King as Head of State. Every person shall have the duty to exercise his or her right to vote in an election. Failure to vote will result in withdrawal of the right to vote as provided by law. Every person shall have the duty to defend the country, serve in the armed forces, pay taxes and duties, render assistance to the official services, receive education and training, uphold the national arts and culture, and knowledge, and conserve natural resources and environment as provided by law.

THE NATIONAL ASSEMBLY

The National Assembly consists of the House of Representatives and the Senate. It may meet jointly or separately. The President of the House of Representatives is President of the National Assembly. The President of the Senate is Vice-President of the National Assembly. A bill may be proposed only by the Council of Ministers, no fewer than 20 members of the House of Representatives, Courts of statutory agencies, or no fewer than 10,000 eligible voters who sign a petition to propose legislation. A bill approved by the National Assembly is presented by the Prime Minister to the King to be signed within 20 days from the date of receipt, and shall come into force upon its publication in the Government Gazette. If the King refuses his assent, the National Assembly must re-deliberate such bill. If the National Assembly resolves to reaffirm the bill with a two-thirds' majority, the Prime Minister shall present such bill to the King for signature once again. If the King does not sign and return the bill within 30 days, the Prime Minister shall cause the bill to be promulgated as an Act in the Government Gazette as if the King had signed it.

The House of Representatives consists of 480 members, 400 of whom are elected on a constituency basis and 80 of whom are elected on a party-list basis. A person seeking election to the House of Representatives must be of Thai nationality by birth, be not less than 25 years of age, and be a member of any and only one political party for a consecutive period of not less than 90 days, up to the date of applying for candidacy in an election. The term of the House of Representatives is four years from the election day. The King has the prerogative to dissolve the House of Representatives for new election of members of the House, and the day for the new general election must be fixed within 45 days of the promulgation of the Royal Decree. Members of the House may not renounce their party affiliation without resigning their seats. Members of the House of Representatives comprising no less than one-fifth of the existing members have the right to call for a general debate of no confidence in the Prime Minister. The said motion must propose a suitable replacement. For the motion of no confidence to be carried, it must have votes exceeding half the number of the existing members of the House. Members of the House of Representatives comprising not less than one-sixth of the total number have the right to submit a motion for a general debate of no confidence in an individual Minister.

The Senate consists of 150 members, one member from each province, and the remainder to be appointed by a selection committee consisting of the President of the Constitutional Court, the President of the Election Commission, the President of the Ombudsmen, the President of the National Counter Corruption Commission, the President of the Office of Auditor General, the President of the National Human Rights Commission, a judge to be assigned by the general meeting of the Supreme Court of Justice and a judge to be assigned by the Supreme Administrative Court. The Selection Committee shall appoint persons proposed by different organizations, including academia, the public sector, the private sector, occupational groups and other groups. A person seeking election or appointment to the Senate must be of Thai nationality by birth, of not less than 40 years of age, have graduated with not lower than a Bachelor's degree or its equivalent, and must not be the descendants, spouse or ancestors of members of the House of Representatives or persons holding any position in a political party. Senators must not have been members of a political party or members of the House of Representatives for a period of at least five years prior to the date of application or nomination. The term of the Senate is six years from the election day. Upon the expiration of the term of the elected Senate, the King shall issue a Royal Decree calling for a new election of Senators, and the election must be fixed within 30 days.

THE COUNCIL OF MINISTERS

The King appoints the Prime Minister and not more than 35 other Ministers to constitute the Council of Ministers (Cabinet) having the duty to carry out the administration of state affairs on the principle of collective responsibility. The Prime Minister must be appointed by the House of Representatives and must receive the approval of more than half the total number of members of the House. The Prime Minister shall not serve in office for more than eight years. A Minister must be of Thai nationality by birth, of not less than 35 years of age and be a graduate with not lower than a Bachelor's degree or its equivalent.

The National Economic and Social Advisory Council has the duty to give advice and recommendations to the Council of Ministers on economic and social issues and relevant laws. A national economic and social development plan and other plans as provided by law must be approved by the National Economic and Social Development Council prior to their implementation.

THE COURTS

The trial and adjudication of cases are the powers of the courts, which must proceed in accordance with the Constitution and the law and in the name of the King. A judge is free to adjudicate correctly, justly and quickly in accordance with the Constitution and the law. Judges are removed and appointed by the King.

The Constitutional Court consists of the President and eight other judges to be appointed by the King upon advice from the Senate. The President and judges of the Constitutional Court shall hold office for nine years and only for one term.

There are three levels of the Courts of Justice; namely Courts of First Instance, Court of Appeals and the Supreme Court of Justice.

Administrative Courts have the power to try and adjudicate cases of dispute between a state agency, state enterprise, local government organization and state official.

LOCAL GOVERNMENT

The State shall give autonomy to localities in accordance with the principle of self-government according to the will of the people in the locality. A local government shall have powers and duties to provide public services for the benefits of the local people. A local government organization shall have a local assembly and a local administrative committee or local administrators. Members of the local assembly shall be elected. Members of the local administrative committee or local administrators shall be directly elected by the people or approved by the local assembly. Members of a local assembly, local administrative committee or local administrators shall hold office for four years. A member of a local administrative committee or local administrator shall not be a government official holding a permanent position or receiving a salary, or an official or employee of a state agency, state enterprise or local government organization.

AMENDMENT OF THE CONSTITUTION

A motion for amendment must be proposed either by the Council of Ministers or by not less than one-fifth of the total number of members of the House of Representatives or National Assembly, or not less than 50,000 eligible voters. A motion for amendment must be proposed in the form of a draft Constitution Amendment and the National Assembly shall consider it in three readings. Promulgation must be approved by the votes of more than half of the total number of members of both Houses.

The Government

HEAD OF STATE

King: HM King BHUMIBOL ADULYADEJ (King Rama IX—succeeded to the throne June 1946).

PRIVY COUNCIL

The Privy Council comprises a President and not more than 18 Privy Councillors, all of whom are appointed by the King. The Privy Council advises the King on all matters pertaining to his functions.

President: Gen. (retd) PREM TINSULANONDA.

CABINET
(October 2011)

The Cabinet comprises members of the Puea Thai, Chart Thai Pattana, Palang Chon and Chart Pattana Party.

Prime Minister: YINGLUCK SHINAWATRA.

Deputy Prime Minister and Minister of the Interior: YONGYUTH WICHAIDIT.

Deputy Prime Minister and Minister of Commerce: KITTIRAT NA-RANONG.

Deputy Prime Minister and Minister of Tourism and Sports: CHUMPOL SILPA-ARCHA.

Deputy Prime Ministers without Portfolio: Capt. CHALERM YOOBAMRUNG, Police Gen. KOWIT WATTANA.

Ministers in the Prime Minister's Office: SURAWIT KHONSOMBOON, KRISSANA SEEHALAK.

Minister of Defence: Gen. YUTTHASAK SASIPRAPHA.

Minister of Finance: THIRACHAI PHUVANATNARANUBALA.

Minister of Foreign Affairs: SURAPONG TOWIJAKCHAIKUL.

Minister of Information and Communications Technology: Capt. ANUDITH NAKORNTHAP.

Minister of Industry: WANNARAT CHANNUKUL.

Minister of Social Development and Human Security: SANTI PROMPAT.

Minister of Agriculture and Co-operatives: THEERA WONGSAMUT.

Minister of Transport: SUKAMPOL SUWANNATHAT.

Minister of Natural Resources and Environment: PREECHA RENGSOMBOONSUK.

Minister of Energy: PICHAI NARIPTHAPHAN.

Minister of Justice: Police Gen. PRACHA PROMNOK.

Minister of Labour: PADERMCHAI SASOMSAP.

Minister of Culture: SUKUMOL KHUNPLOEM.

Minister of Science and Technology: PLODPRASOP SURASWADI.

Minister of Education: WORAWAT UA-APINYAKUL.

Minister of Public Health: WITTHAYA BURANASIRI.

MINISTRIES

Office of the Prime Minister: Government House, Thanon Phitsanulok, Dusit, Bangkok 10300; tel. (2) 281-4040; fax (2) 282-5131; e-mail opm@opm.go.th; internet www.opm.go.th.

Ministry of Agriculture and Co-operatives: Thanon Ratchadamnoen Nok, Bangkok 10200; tel. (2) 281-5955; fax (2) 282-1425; e-mail webmaster@moac.go.th; internet www.moac.go.th.

Ministry of Commerce: 44/100 Thanon Nonthaburi 1, Amphur Muang, Nonthaburi, Bangkok 11000; tel. (2) 507-7000; fax (2) 547-5210; e-mail webmaster@moc.go.th; internet www.moc.go.th.

Ministry of Culture: 666 Thanon Borommaratchachonnani, Bang Bumru, Bang Plat, Bangkok 10700; tel. (2) 422-8888; e-mail webmaster@m-culture.go.th; internet www.m-culture.go.th.

Ministry of Defence: Thanon Sanam Chai, Bangkok 10200; tel. (2) 222-1121; fax (2) 226-3117; e-mail webmaster@mod.go.th; internet www.mod.go.th.

Ministry of Education: Wang Chankasem, Thanon Ratchadamnoen Nok, Bangkok 10300; tel. (2) 281-9264; fax (2) 281-1753; e-mail website@emisc.moe.go.th; internet www.moe.go.th.

Ministry of Energy: 17 Kasatsuk Bridge, Thanon Rama I, Rong Muang, Pathumwan, Bangkok 10330; tel. (2) 223-3344; fax (2) 222-4495; e-mail moen@energy.go.th; internet www.energy.go.th.

Ministry of Finance: Thanon Rama VI, Samsennai, Phaya Thai, Rajatevi, Bangkok 10400; tel. (2) 273-9021; fax (2) 273-9408; e-mail webmaster-eng@mof.go.th; internet www.mof.go.th.

Ministry of Foreign Affairs: 443 Thanon Sri Ayudhya, Bangkok 10400; tel. (2) 643-5000; fax (2) 643-5102; e-mail information01@mfa.go.th; internet www.mfa.go.th.

Ministry of Industry: Thanon Rama VI, Ratchathewi, Bangkok 10400; tel. (2) 202-3000; fax (2) 202-3048; e-mail pr@industry.go.th; internet www.industry.go.th.

Ministry of Information and Communications Technology: 120 Moo 3, Government Offices, Bldg B, 6th–9th Floors, Thanon Chaengwattana, Thung Song Hong, Laksi, Bangkok 10210; tel. (2) 141-6747; fax (2) 143-8019; e-mail pr@mict.go.th; internet www.mict.go.th.

Ministry of the Interior: Thanon Atsadang, Bangkok 10200; tel. (2) 222-1141; fax (2) 223-8851; e-mail webmaster@moi.go.th; internet www.moi.go.th.

Ministry of Justice: Thanon Chaengwattana, Pakkred, Nonthaburi, Bangkok 11120; tel. (2) 502-8051; fax (2) 502-8059; e-mail webmaster@moj.go.th; internet www.moj.go.th.

Ministry of Labour: Thanon Mitmaitri, Dindaeng, Bangkok 10400; tel. (2) 232-1421; fax (2) 246-1520; e-mail webmaster@mol.go.th; internet www.mol.go.th.

Ministry of Natural Resources and Environment: 92 Phahoyothin Soi 7, Samsen Nai, Phaya Thai, Bangkok 10400; tel. (2) 278-8500; fax (2) 278-8698; e-mail webmaster@mnre.mail.go.th; internet www.mnre.go.th.

Ministry of Public Health: Thanon Tiwanon, Amphur Muang, Nonthaburi 11000; tel. (2) 590-1000; fax (2) 591-8492; e-mail eng-webmaster@health.moph.go.th; internet www.moph.go.th.

Ministry of Science and Technology: 75/47 Thanon Rama VI, Phaya Thai, Bangkok 10400; tel. (2) 333-3700; fax (2) 333-3833; e-mail webmaster@most.go.th; internet www.most.go.th.

Ministry of Social Development and Human Security: 1034 Thanon Krungkasem, Mahanak, Khet Pom Prab Sattruphai, Bangkok 10100; tel. (2) 659-6399; fax 659-6529; e-mail society@m-society.go.th; internet www.m-society.go.th.

Ministry of Tourism and Sports: 4 Ratchadamnoen Nok, Khet Pom Prab Sattruphai, Bangkok 10100; tel. (2) 283-1500; fax (2) 356-0746; e-mail webmaster@mots.go.th; internet www.mots.go.th.

Ministry of Transport: 38 Thanon Ratchadamnoen Nok, Khet Pom Prab Sattruphai, Bangkok 10100; tel. (2) 283-3000; fax (2) 283-3959; e-mail mot@mot.go.th; internet www.mot.go.th.

Legislature

RATHA SAPHA (NATIONAL ASSEMBLY)

Woothi Sapha (Senate)

The Senate consists of 150 members, of whom 76 members are elected to represent each of Thailand's 75 provinces and Bangkok, and the remainder are selected by a committee consisting primarily of judicial officials. Senators thus selected are drawn from lists of nominees made by organizations in various sectors.

Elections to the Senate were held on 2 March 2008.

Speaker of the Senate: Gen. THEERADET MEEPIAN.

Sapha Poothaen Rassadorn (House of Representatives)

Speaker of the House of Representatives and President of the National Assembly: SOMSAK KAITSURANONT.

Election, 3 July 2011

Party	Seats
Puea Thai	265
Democrat Party	159
Bhum Jai Thai	34
Chart Thai Pattana	19
Palang Chon	7
Chart Pattana Puea Pandin	7
Rak Thailand	4
Matubhum Party	2
Rak Santi Party	1
New Democratic Party	1
Mahachon	1
Total	500†

† A total of 375 candidates were elected in multi-member constituencies and the remaining 125 through a party-list system.

Election Commission

Election Commission of Thailand (ECT): 120 Moo 3, Government Offices, Bldg B, 2nd Floor, Thanon Chaengwattana, Thung Song Hong, Laksi, Bangkok 10210; tel. (2) 141-8888; fax (2) 219-3411; e-mail dav@ect.go.th; internet www.ect.go.th; Chair. APHICHART SUKHAGGANOND.

Political Organizations

Bhum Jai Thai (BJT) (Thai Pride Party): Suite 2159, 11 Thanon Phaholyothin, Chatuchak, Bangkok 10900; tel. (2) 940-6999; internet www.bhumjaithai.com; f. 2008; est. by fmr mems of Matchimathipataya (f. 2006) in anticipation of that party's dissolution, in Dec. 2008, by Constitutional Court; merged in Jan. 2009 with Friends of Newin (f. 2008 by NEWIN CHIDCHOB and other defectors from People's Power Party); announced alliance with Chart Thai Pattana for 2011 elections; Leader CHAOVARAT CHANWEERAKUL; Sec. PORNTIWA NAKASAI.

Chart Pattana Party: c/o House of Representatives, Bangkok; f. 2007; est. as Ruam Jai Thai Chart Pattana; renamed Ruam Chart Pattana in 2008; renamed Chart Pattana Puea Pandin Party following merger with Puea Pandin in 2011; present name adopted in Sept. 2011; Leader WANNARAT CHARNNUKUL.

Chart Thai Pattana (Thai Nation Development): 37/157 Moo 11, Sansab, Minburi, Bangkok; f. 2008; est. by fmr mems of Chart Thai (f. 1981) in anticipation of that party's dissolution, in Dec. 2008, by Constitutional Court; right-wing; announced alliance with Bhum Jai Thai in 2011; Leader CHUMPOL SILPA-ARCHA.

Democrat Party (DP) (Prachatipat): 67 Thanon Setsiri, Samsen Nai, Phaya Thai, Bangkok 10400; tel. (2) 270-0036; fax (2) 279-6086; e-mail public@democrat.or.th; internet www.democrat.or.th; f. 1946; liberal; Leader ABHISIT VEJJAJIVA; Sec.-Gen. CHALERMCHAI SRI-ON.

Karn Muang Mai (New Politics Party—NPP): Phra Nakhon Region, Bangkok 10200; tel. (2) 282-9844; fax (2) 282-9850; internet www.npp.or.th; f. 2009; est. by members of the People's Alliance for Democracy (PAD); Leader SOMSAK KOSAISUK; Sec.-Gen. SURIYASAI KATASILA.

Mahachon: 35,37 Soi Nonthaburi 32, Thanon Nonthaburi, Thasai, Muang District, Nonthaburi 11000; tel. (2) 525-48857; fax (2) 525-4887; f. 2004 following split in Democrat Party; Leader SANAN KAJORNPRASART.

Matubhum Party: Benjamas Bldg, 5th Floor, 555 Soi Ruam Chit, Dusit, Bangkok 10300; tel. (2) 715-3870; fax (2) 715-3790; f. 2008; comprises predominantly members of the Muslim Wadah and Pak Nam factions; Leader Gen. SONTHI BOONYARATGLIN.

New Democratic Party: c/o House of Representatives, Bangkok; Leader SUTHIN PICHARN.

Palang Chon (Force of Chon Buri): c/o House of Representatives, Bangkok; internet www.phalangchon.or.th; f. 2011; est. by fmr mems of Bhum Jai Thai; Leader CHAO MANEEWONG.

Pracharaj (Royal People Party): TPI Tower, 18th Floor, 26/56 Thanon Chan Tat Mai, Tungmahamek, Sathorn, Bangkok 10120; f. 2006; est. by breakaway faction of Thai Rak Thai (f. 1998); Leader SNOH THIENTHONG; Sec.-Gen. CHIENGCHUANG KANLAYANAMITH.

Pracha Santi Party: Thanon Amnuay Songkhram, Bangkok; f. 2011; supports formation of a national govt and eradication of corruption; Leader SERI SUWANNAPHANONT.

Puea Thai (For Thais): 626 Soi Jinda Tawil, Thanon Rama IV, Bangrak Mahaprutharam, Bangkok 10500; internet www.ptp.or.th; f. 2008; est. by fmr mems of People's Power Party (f. 2007) in anticipation of that party's dissolution, in Dec. 2008, by Constitutional Court; Chair. CHAVALIT YONGCHAIYUDH; Leader YONGYUTH WICHAIDITH.

Rak Santi Party: c/o House of Representatives, Bangkok; f. 2011; Chair. PURACHAI PIUMSOMBUN; Sec.-Gen. PORNPEN PHETSUKSIRI.

Rak Thailand Party: c/o House of Representatives, Bangkok; f. 2011; Leader CHUWIT KAMOLVISIT; Sec.-Gen. CHAIWAT JUTI KRAIRIKSH.

Social Action Party (SAP) (Kij Sangkhom): 381/28–29 Thanon Mitrapap, Naimuang, Muang, Khon-kaen 40000; tel. and fax (2) 325-2234; f. 1981; disbanded in 2003; revived in mid-2008 by former leader Suwit Khunkitti, following his defection from Puea Pandin; conservative; Sec.-Gen. SUWIT KHUNKITTI.

Other parties that contested the 2011 election included Thai Citizen, Prachathum, Dumrong Thai, Mass Power, Thai Por Pieng, Thai Pen Suk, Thais Is Thai, Thaen Khun Phaendin, Heaven and Earth, The Farmer Network of Thailand, New Politics, Liberal, Chart Samuccee, Bamrungmueang, Kasikorn Thai, Better Life, Palung Sungkom Thai, Thai Party for Thai People, Prachachon Chow Thai, Rakpandin, Civil Peace, New Aspiration, Asamatupoom, Sport Party of Thailand, Parung Chowna Thai, Thai Sangsun, Puen Kaset Thai and Maharatpattana.

Two popular movements, which staged large-scale political rallies and became involved in civil unrest from 2008, emerged in response to the political crises: the **People's Alliance for Democracy (PAD)**, a coalition of groups and individuals, including royalists, opposed to Thaksin Shinawatra, established in 2005 by Sondhi Limthongkul and popularly known as the 'Yellow Shirts' (internet www.padnet.net); and the **United Front for Democracy against Dictatorship (UDD)**, a coalition of broadly pro-Thaksin activists, popularly known as the 'Red Shirts', who rejected the legitimacy of the Government of Abhisit Vejjajiva (internet www.uddthailand.com).

Groupings in armed conflict with the Government include:

Barisan Revolusi Nasional (BRN) (National Revolutionary Front): Yala; f. 1963; was organized into three principal factions—the BRN Congress (its military wing); the BRN Co-ordinate (its political wing); and the BRN Uram (its religious wing)—in the 1980s; Muslim secessionists.

Bersatu (Council of the Muslim People of Pattani): Pattani; f. 1989; umbrella org. incl. the BRN and the PULO; Pattani secessionists.

Gerakan Mujahidin Islam Patani (GMIP): Pattani; f. 1986; dissolved in 1993 following internal disagreement, but re-formed in 1995; seeks the transformation of Pattani into an Islamic state; Leader KARIM KARUBANG.

Patani United Liberation Organization (PULO): f. 1968; subsequently divided into factions; advocates secession of the five southern provinces (Satun, Narathiwat, Yala, Pattani and Songkhla); Pres. ABU YASIR FIKRI.

Runda Kumpulan Kecil (RKK): Yala; f. 2005; splinter group of the BRN Congress; seeks the implementation of an independent Islamic state in Thailand's southern provinces; Leader USTAZ RORHING AHSONG.

Diplomatic Representation

EMBASSIES IN THAILAND

Argentina: 16th Floor, Suite 1601, Glas Haus Bldg, 1 Soi Sukhumvit 25, Wattana, Bangkok 10110; tel. (2) 259-0401; fax (2) 259-0402; e-mail embtail@csloxinfo.com; Ambassador FELIPE FRYDMAN.

Australia: 37 Thanon Sathorn Tai, Bangkok 10120; tel. (2) 344-6300; fax (2) 344-6593; e-mail austembassy.bangkok@dfat.gov.au; internet www.austembassy.or.th; Ambassador JAMES WISE.

Austria: 14 Soi Nandha, off Thanon Sathorn Tai, Soi 1, Bangkok 10120; tel. (2) 303-6257; fax (2) 303-6260; e-mail bangkok-ob@bmeia.gv.at; internet www.aussenministerium.at/botschaft/bangkok; Ambassador Dr JOHANNES PETERLIK.

Bangladesh: 47/8 Ekamai Soi 30, Thanon Sukhumvit 63, Khlong Tan Nua, Wattana, Bangkok 10110; tel. (2) 390-5107; fax (2) 390-5106; e-mail bdootbkk@truemail.co.th; Ambassador KAZI IMTIAZ HOSSAIN.

Belgium: 17th Floor, Sathorn City Tower, 175 Thanon Sathorn Tai, Tungmahamek, Sathorn, Bangkok 10120; tel. (2) 679-5454; fax (2) 679-5467; e-mail bangkok@diplobel.fed.be; internet www.diplomatie.be/bangkok; Ambassador RUDI VEESTRAETEN.

Bhutan: 375/1 Soi Ratchadanivej, Thanon Pracha-Uthit, Huay Kwang, Bangkok 10320; tel. (2) 274-4740; fax (2) 274-4743; e-mail bht_emb_bkk@yahoo.com; Ambassador TSHERING DORJI.

Brazil: 34th Floor, Lumpini Tower, 1168/101 Thanon Rama IV, Tungmahamek, Sathorn, Bangkok 10120; tel. (2) 679-8567; fax (2) 679-8569; e-mail info@brazilembassy.or.th; internet www.brazilembassy.or.th; Ambassador EDGARD TELLES RIBEIRO.

Brunei: 12 Soi Ekamai 2, Thanon Sukhumvit 63, Prakanong Nua, Wattana, Bangkok 10110; tel. (2) 714-7395; fax (2) 714-7382; e-mail bangkok.thailand@mfa.gov.bn; Ambassador Pengiran Dato' Paduka Haji KAMIS BIN Haji TAMIN.

Bulgaria: 83/24 Soi Witthayu 1, Thanon Witthayu, Lumpini, Pathumwan, Bangkok 10330; tel. (2) 627-3872; fax (2) 627-3874; e-mail bulgemth@csloxinfo.com; internet www.mfa.bg/bangkok; Ambassador KAMEN VELICHKOV.

Cambodia: 518/4 Thanon Pracha Uthit, Ramkhamhaeng Soi 39, Wangtonglang, Bangkok 10310; tel. (2) 957-5851; fax (2) 957-5850; e-mail recbkk@cscoms.com; Ambassador YOU AY.

Canada: Abdulrahim Pl., 15th Floor, 990 Thanon Rama IV, Bangrak, Bangkok 10500; tel. (2) 636-0540; fax (2) 636-0566; e-mail bngkk@international.gc.ca; internet www.canadainternational.gc.ca/thailand-thailande; Ambassador RON HOFFMANN.

Chile: 83/17 Witthayu Pl., Soi Witthayu 1, Thanon Witthayu, Lumpini, Pathumwan, Bangkok 10330; tel. (2) 251-9470; fax (2) 2251-9475; e-mail embajada@chile-thai.com; internet www.chile-thai.com; Ambassador ALBERTO YOACHAM.

China, People's Republic: 57 Thanon Ratchadaphisek, Bangkok 10310; tel. (2) 245-7043; fax (2) 246-8247; e-mail chinaemb_th@mfa.gov.cn; internet www.chinaembassy.or.th/eng; Ambassador GUAN MU.

Cuba: Mela Mansion Apt 7AC, 5 Soi Sukhumvit 27, Klongtoey Nua, Wattana, Bangkok 10110; tel. (2) 665-2803; fax (2) 661-6560; e-mail embajada@th.embacuba.cu; internet embacuba.cubaminrex.cu/tailandiaing; Ambassador LÁZARO HERRERA MARTÍNEZ.

Czech Republic: 71/6 Soi Ruamrudi 2, Thanon Ploenchit, Bangkok 10330; tel. (2) 255-3027; fax (2) 253-7637; e-mail bangkok@embassy.mzv.cz; internet www.mfa.cz/bangkok; Ambassador IVAN HOTĚK.

Denmark: 10 Soi Attakarn Prasit, Thanon Sathorn Tai, Bangkok 10120; tel. (2) 343-1100; fax (2) 213-1752; e-mail bkkamb@um.dk; internet www.ambbangkok.um.dk; Ambassador MIKAEL HEMNITI WINTHER.

Egypt: 6 Las Colinas Bldg, 42nd Floor, Sukhumvit 21, Wattana, Bangkok 10110; tel. (2) 661-7184; fax (2) 262-0235; e-mail egyptemb@loxinfo.co.th; Ambassador MOHAMED ASHRAF MOHAMED KAMAL EL-KHOLY.

Finland: Amarin Tower, 16th Floor, 500 Thanon Ploenchit, Bangkok 10330; tel. (2) 250-8801; fax (2) 250-8802; e-mail sanomat.ban@formin.fi; internet www.finland.or.th; Ambassador SIRPA MÄENPÄÄ.

France: 35 Thanon Charoenkrung, Soi 36, Bangkok 10500; tel. (2) 657-5100; fax (2) 657-5111; e-mail ambassade@ambafrance-th.org; internet www.ambafrance-th.org; Ambassador GILDAS LE LIDEC.

Germany: 9 Thanon Sathorn Tai, Bangkok 10120; tel. (2) 287-9000; fax (2) 287-1776; e-mail info@bangkok.diplo.de; internet www.bangkok.diplo.de; Ambassador Dr HANNS HEINRICH SCHUMACHER.

Greece: Unit 25/5-9, 9th Floor, BKI/YWCA Bldg, 25 Thanon Sathorn Tai, Bangkok 10120; tel. (2) 679-1462; fax (2) 679-1463; e-mail gremb.ban@mfa.gr; internet www.mfa.gr/bangkok; Ambassador NIKOLAOS VAMVOUNAKIS.

Holy See: 217/1 Thanon Sathorn Tai, Bangkok 10120 (Apostolic Nunciature); tel. (2) 212-5853; fax (2) 212-0932; e-mail nuntiusth@csloxinfo.com; Apostolic Nuncio Most Rev. GIOVANNI D'ANIELLO (Titular Archbishop of Montemarano).

Hungary: Oak Tower, 20th Floor, President Park Condominium, 95 Sukhumvit Soi 24, Klongtoey, Prakanong, Bangkok 10110; tel. (2) 661-1150; fax (2) 661-1153; e-mail mission.bgk@kum.hu; internet www.mfa.gov.hu/emb/bangkok; Ambassador Dr ANDRAS BALOGH.

India: 46 Soi Prasarnmitr, 23 Thanon Sukhumvit, Bangkok 10110; tel. (2) 258-0300; fax (2) 258-4627; e-mail indiaemb@mozart.inet.co.th; internet indianembassy.gov.in/bangkok; Ambassador PINAK RANJAN CHAKRAVARTY.

Indonesia: 600–602 Thanon Phetchaburi, Ratchathewi, Bangkok 10400; tel. (2) 252-3135; fax (2) 255-1267; e-mail kukbkk@ksc.th.com; internet www.bangkok.deplu.go.id; Ambassador MOHAMMAD HATTA.

Iran: 215 Thanon Sukhumvit, Soi 49, Klongtan Nua, Wattana, Bangkok 10110; tel. (2) 390-0871; fax (2) 390-0867; e-mail info@iranembassy.or.th; internet www.iranembassy.or.th; Ambassador MAJID BIZMARK.

Israel: Ocean Tower II, 25th Floor, 75 Sukhumvit, Soi 19, Thanon Asoke, Bangkok 10110; tel. (2) 204-9200; fax (2) 204-9255; e-mail info@bangkok.mfa.gov.il; internet bangkok.mfa.gov.il; Ambassador ITZHAK SHOHAM.

Italy: 399 Thanon Nang Linchee, Tungmahamek, Yannawa, Bangkok 10120; tel. (2) 285-4090; fax (2) 285-4793; e-mail ambasciata.bangkok@esteri.it; internet www.ambbangkok.esteri.it; Ambassador MICHELANGELO PIPAN.

Japan: 177 Thanon Witthayu, Lumpini, Pathumwan, Bangkok 10330; tel. (2) 207-8500; fax (2) 207-8510; e-mail jis@eoj.or.th; internet www.th.emb-japan.go.jp; Ambassador SEIJI KOJIMA.

Kazakhstan: Suite 4301, 43rd Floor, JTC Bldg, 919/501 Thanon Silom, Bangrak, Bangkok 10500; tel. (2) 234-6365; fax (2) 234-6368; e-mail mail@kazembassythailand.org; internet www.kazembassythailand.org; Chargé d'affaires a.i. AMIR MUSIN.

Kenya: 62 Thonglor Soi 5, Thanon Sukhumvit 55, Klongtan, Wattana, Bangkok 10110; tel. (2) 712-5721; fax (2) 712-5720; Ambassador RICHARD TITUS EKAI.

Korea, Democratic People's Republic: 14 Mooban Suanlaemthong 2, Soi 28, Thanon Pattanakarn, Suan Luang, Bangkok 10250; tel. (2) 319-2686; fax (2) 318-6333; Ambassador AN SONG NAM.

Korea, Republic: 23 Thanon Thiam-Ruammit, Ratchadaphisek, Huay Kwang, Bangkok 10320; tel. (2) 247-7537; fax (2) 247-7535; e-mail koembth@gmail.com; internet tha.mofat.go.kr; Ambassador CHUNG HAE-MOON.

Kuwait: 100/44 Sathorn Nakhon Tower, Level 24A, Thanon Sathorn Nua, Bangrak, Bangkok 10500; tel. (2) 636-6600; fax (2) 636-7360; e-mail kuembasy@inet.co.th; Ambassador HAFEEZ MOHAMMED SALEM AL-AJMI.

Laos: 502/502/1–3 Soi Sahakarnpramoon, Thanon Pracha Uthit, Wangthonglang, Bangkok 10310; tel. (2) 539-6667; fax (2) 539-3827; e-mail sabaidee@bkklaoembassy.com; internet www.bkklaoembassy.com; Ambassador OUAN PHOMMACHACK.

Luxembourg: Q House Lumpini, 17th Floor, Thanon Sathorn Tai, Tungmahamek, Sathorn, Bangkok 10120; tel. (2) 677-7360; fax (2) 677-7364; e-mail bangkok.amb@mae.etat.lu; internet bangkok.mae.lu; Ambassador MARC UNGEHEUER.

Malaysia: 35 Thanon Sathorn Tai, Tungmahamek, Sathorn, Bangkok 10120; tel. (2) 629-6800; fax (2) 679-2208; e-mail malbangkok@kln.gov.my; internet www.kln.gov.my/web/tha_bangkok; Ambassador Dato' HUSNI ZAI BIN YAACOB.

Mexico: 21/60–62 Thai Wah Tower I, 20th Floor, Thanon Sathorn Tai, Sathorn, Bangkok 10120; tel. (2) 285-0995; fax (2) 285-0667; e-mail consular@mexicanembassythailand.com; internet www.sre.gob.mx/tailandia; Ambassador LUIS ARTURO PUENTE ORTEGA.

Mongolia: 100/3, Soi Ekamai 22, 63 Thanon Sukhumvit, Klongtan Nua, Wattana, Bangkok 10110; tel. (2) 381-1400; fax (2) 392-4199; e-mail mongemb@loxinfo.co.th; Ambassador LUVSANDOOGIIN DASHPÜREV.

Morocco: Sathorn City Tower, 12th Floor, 175 Thanon Sathorn Tai, Sathorn, Bangkok 10120; tel. (2) 679-5604; fax (2) 2679-5603; e-mail sifambkk@samarts.com; internet www.moroccoembassybangkok.org; Ambassador EL HASSANE ZAHID.

Myanmar: 132 Thanon Sathorn Nua, Bangkok 10500; tel. (2) 233-2237; fax (2) 236-6898; e-mail myanmarembassybkk@gmail.com; Ambassador AUNG THEIN.

Nepal: 189 Soi 71, Thanon Sukhumvit, Prakanong, Bangkok 10110; tel. (2) 390-2280; fax (2) 381-2406; e-mail nepembkk@asiaaccess.net.th; Ambassador NAVIN PRAKASH JUNG SHAH.

Netherlands: 15 Soi Tonson, Thanon Ploenchit, Lumpini, Pathumwan, Bangkok 10330; tel. (2) 309-5200; fax (2) 309-5205; e-mail ban@minbuza.nl; internet www.mfa.nl/ban; Ambassador TJACO VAN DEN HOUT.

New Zealand: M Thai Tower, 14th Floor, All Seasons Pl., 87 Thanon Witthayu, Lumpini, Pathumwan, Bangkok 10330; tel. (2) 254-2530; fax (2) 253-9045; e-mail nzembbkk@loxinfo.co.th; internet www.nzembassy.com/thailand; Ambassador BEDE GILBERT CORRY.

Nigeria: 412 Thanon Sukhumvit, Soi 71, Prakanong, Wattana, Bangkok 10110; tel. (2) 711-3076; fax (2) 392-6398; e-mail info@embnigeriabkk.com; Ambassador UMARU A. SULAIMAN.

Norway: UBC II Bldg, 18th Floor, 591 Thanon Sukhumvit, Soi 33, Bangkok 10110; tel. (2) 204-6500; fax (2) 262-0218; e-mail emb.bangkok@mfa.no; internet www.emb-norway.or.th; Ambassador KATJA NORDGAARD.

Oman: Saeng Thong Thani Tower, 32nd Floor, 82 Thanon Sathorn Nua, Bangkok 10500; tel. (2) 639-9380; fax (2) 639-9390; e-mail bangkok@mofa.gov.om; Ambassador HAFEEDH SALIM MOHAMED BA-OMAR.

Pakistan: 31 Soi Nana Nua, Thanon Sukhumvit 3, Bangkok 10110; tel. (2) 253-0288; fax (2) 253-0290; e-mail parepbnk@truemail.co.th; internet www.mofa.gov.pk/thailand; Ambassador SOHAIL MAHMOOD.

Panama: 1168/37 Lumpini Tower, 16th Floor, Tungmahamek, Sathorn, Bangkok 10120; tel. (2) 679-7988; fax (2) 679-7991; e-mail embajada@panathai.com; internet www.panathai.com; Ambassador ISAURO RAMON MORA BORRERO.

Peru: Glas Haus Bldg, 16th Floor, 1 Thanon Sukhumvit, Soi 25, Wattana, Bangkok 10110; tel. (2) 260-6243; fax (2) 260-6244; e-mail peru@peruthai.or.th; Ambassador CARLOS MANUEL VELASCO MENDIOLA.

Philippines: 760 Thanon Sukhumvit, cnr Soi 30/1, Klongtan, Klongtoey, Bangkok 10110; tel. (2) 259-0139; fax (2) 259-2809; e-mail inquiry@philembassy-bangkok.net; internet www.philembassy-bangkok.net; Ambassador ANTONIO V. RODRIGUEZ.

Poland: 100/81–82, Vongvanij Bldg B, 25th Floor, Thanon Rama IX, Huay Kwang, Bangkok 10310; tel. (2) 645-0367; fax (2) 645-0365; e-mail ampolbkk@polemb.or.th; internet www.bangkok.polemb.net; Ambassador JERZY BAYER.

Portugal: 26 Bush Lane, Thanon Charoenkrung, Bangkok 10500; tel. (2) 234-2123; fax (2) 238-4275; e-mail portemb@loxinfo.co.th; Ambassador ANTÓNIO FELIX MACHADO DE FARIA E MAYA.

Qatar: Capital Tower, 14th Floor, All Seasons Pl., 87/1 Thanon Witthayu, Lumpini, Pathumwan, Bangkok 10330; tel. (2) 660-1111; fax (2) 660-1122; e-mail info@qatarembassy.or.th; internet www.qatarembassy.or.th; Ambassador JABOER ALI HUSSEIN AL-DOUSARI.

Romania: 20/1 Soi Rajakhru, Phaholyothin Soi 5, Thanon Phaholyothin, Phaya Thai, Bangkok 10400; tel. (2) 617-1551; fax (2) 617-1113; e-mail romembnk@ksc.th.com; Chargé d'affaires a.i. MIHAI SION.

Russia: 78 Thanon Sap, Bangrak, Bangkok 10500; tel. (2) 234-9824; fax (2) 237-8488; e-mail rusembbangkok@rambler.ru; internet www.thailand.mid.ru; Ambassador ALEKSANDR MARIYASOV.

Saudi Arabia: 82 Saengthong Thani Bldg, 23rd & 24th Floors, Thanon Sathorn Nua, Silom, Bangrak, Bangkok 10500; tel. (2) 639-2999; fax (2) 639-2950; Chargé d'affaires NABIL H. H. ASHRI.

Singapore: 129 Thanon Sathorn Tai, Bangkok 10120; tel. (2) 286-2111; fax (2) 286-6966; e-mail singemb_bkk@sgmfa.gov.sg; internet www.mfa.gov.sg/bangkok; Ambassador PETER CHAN.

Slovakia: 25/9-4, BKI/YWCA Bldg, 9th Floor, Thanon Sathorn Tai, Thungmahamek, Bangkok 10120; tel. (2) 677-3445; fax (2) 677-3447; e-mail slovembassy@bangkok.truemail.co.th; Ambassador VASIL PYTEL.

South Africa: M-Thai Tower, Floor 12A, All Seasons Pl., 87 Thanon Witthayu, Pathumwan, Lumpini, Bangkok 10330; tel. (2) 659-2900; fax (2) 685-3500; e-mail saembbkk@loxinfo.co.th; internet www.saembbangkok.com; Ambassador DOUGLAS HARVEY MONRO GIBSON.

Spain: Lake Rajada Office Complex, 23rd Floor, Suite 98–99, 193 Thanon Ratchadaphisek, Klongtoey, Bangkok 10110; tel. (2) 661-8284; fax (2) 661-9220; e-mail emb.bangkok@maec.es; internet www.maec.es/subwebs/embajadas/bangkok; Ambassador DON IGNACIO SAGAZ.

Sri Lanka: Ocean Tower II, 13th Floor, 75/6–7 Sukhumvit, Soi 19, Klongtoey, Wattana, Bangkok 10110; tel. (2) 261-1934; fax (2) 261-1936; e-mail slemb@ksc.th.com; Ambassador JAYARATNA BANDA DISANAYAKA.

Sweden: First Pacific Pl., 20th Floor, 140 Thanon Sukhumvit, Bangkok 10110; tel. (2) 263-7200; fax (2) 263-7260; e-mail ambassaden.bangkok@foreign.ministry.se; internet www.swedenabroad.com/bangkok; Ambassador KLAS MOLIN.

Switzerland: 35 Thanon Witthayu Nua, Lumpini, Pathumwan, Bangkok 10330; tel. (2) 253-0156; fax (2) 255-4481; e-mail ban.vertretung@eda.admin.ch; internet www.eda.admin.ch/bangkok; Ambassador CHRISTINE SCHRANER BURGENER.

Timor-Leste: Thanapoom Tower, 7th Floor, 1550 Thanon Petchaburi, Makasan, Ratchathewi, Bangkok 10400; tel. (2) 654-7501; fax (2) 654-7504; e-mail embdrtl_bkk@yahoo.com; Ambassador JOÃO FREITAS DE CÂMARA.

Turkey: 61/1 Soi Chatsan, Thanon Suthisarn, Huay Kwang, Bangkok 10310; tel. (2) 274-7262; fax (2) 274-7261; e-mail tcturkbe@cscoms.com; Ambassador AHMET OĞUZ ÇELIKKOL.

Ukraine: CRC Tower, 33rd Floor, All Seasons Pl., 87 Thanon Witthayu, Lumpini, Pathumwan, Bangkok 10330; tel. (2) 685-3216; fax (2) 685-3217; e-mail emb_th@mfa.gov.ua; internet www.mfa.gov.ua/thailand; Ambassador MARKIIAN CHUCHUK.

United Arab Emirates: CRC Tower, 29th Floor, All Seasons Pl., 87/2 Thanon Witthayu, Pathumwan, Bangkok 10330; tel. (2) 402-4000; fax (2) 402-4005; Ambassador MUHAMMAD ALI AHMAD OMRAN ASH-SHAMSI.

United Kingdom: 14 Wireless Rd, Lumpini, Pathumwan, Bangkok 10330; tel. (2) 305-8333; fax (2) 255-8619; e-mail info.bangkok@fco.gov.uk; internet ukinthailand.fco.gov.uk; Ambassador ASIF AHMAD.

USA: 95 Thanon Witthayu, Lumpini, Pathumwan, Bangkok 10330; tel. (2) 205-4000; fax (2) 254-1171; e-mail acsbkk@state.gov; internet bangkok.usembassy.gov; Ambassador KRISTIE KENNEY.

Viet Nam: 83/1 Thanon Witthayu, Lumpini, Pathumwan, Bangkok 10330; tel. (2) 251-5836; fax (2) 251-7203; e-mail vnemb.th@mofa.gov.vn; internet www.vietnamembassy-thailand.org; Ambassador NGO DUC THANG.

Judicial System

SUPREME COURT

The Supreme Court (Sarn Dika) is the final court of appeal in all civil, bankruptcy, labour, juvenile and criminal cases. Its quorum consists of three judges. However, the Court occasionally sits in plenary session to determine cases of exceptional importance or where there are reasons for reconsideration or overruling of its own precedents. The quorum, in such cases, is one-half of the total number of judges in the Supreme Court.

President (Chief Justice): SOBCHOK SUKHAROM, 6 Thanon Ratchadamnoen Nai, Bangkok 10200; tel. (2) 221-3161; fax (2) 226-4389; e-mail supremc@judiciary.go.th; internet www.supremecourt.or.th.

Vice-Presidents: PHICHIT KHAMFAENG, THEERARAT PHATTARANWAT, MONGKHOL THAPTHIENG, PANYA SUTHIBODI, WATTANCHAI CHOTICHUTRAKUL, RUNGROJ RUENRENGWONG.

COURT OF APPEALS

The Court of Appeals (Sarn Uthorn) has appellate jurisdiction in all civil, bankruptcy, juvenile and criminal matters. Appeals from all the Courts of First Instance throughout the country, except the central Labour Court, are heard in this Court. Two judges form a quorum.

Chief Justice: KAIT CHATANIBAND, Thanon Ratchadaphisek, Chatuchak, Bangkok 10900.

Deputy Chief Justices: PORNCHAI SMATTAVET, CHATISAK THAMMASAKDI, SOMPOB CHOTIKAVANICH, SOMPHOL SATTAYA-APHITARN.

COURTS OF FIRST INSTANCE

The Courts of First Instance (Sarn Chunton) include the categories of general courts (Civil Courts, Criminal Courts, Provincial Courts and Kwaeng Courts), juvenile and family courts, and specialized courts (Central Labour Court, Central Tax Court, Central Intellectual Property and International Trade Court, Central Bankruptcy Court).

Religion

Buddhism is the predominant religion, professed by more than 95% of Thailand's total population. About 4% of the population are Muslims, being ethnic Malays, mainly in the south. Most of the immigrant Chinese are Confucians. The Christians number about 427,000, mainly in Bangkok and northern Thailand. Brahmins, Hindus and Sikhs number about 85,000.

BUDDHISM

Sangha Supreme Council

The Religious Affairs Dept, Thanon Ratchadamnoen Nok, Bangkok 10300; tel. (2) 281-6080; fax (2) 281-5415.

Governing body of Thailand's 350,000 monks, nuns and novices.

Supreme Patriarch of Thailand: NYANASAMVARA SUVADDHANA.

The Buddhist Association of Thailand: 41 Thanon Phra Aditya, Bangkok 10200; tel. (2) 281-5693; fax (2) 281-9564; f. 1934; under royal patronage; 7,139 mems; Pres. NUTTAPASH INTUPUTI.

CHRISTIANITY

The Roman Catholic Church

For ecclesiastical purposes, Thailand comprises two archdioceses and eight dioceses. At 31 December 2006 there were an estimated 326,978 adherents in the country, representing about 0.5% of the population.

Catholic Bishops' Conference of Thailand

122/11 Soi Naksuwan, Thanon Nonsi, Yannawa, Bangkok 10120; tel. (2) 681-3900; fax (2) 681-5370; e-mail cbct_th@hotmail.com; internet www.cbct.net.

f. 1969; Pres. Rev. LOUIS CHAMNIERN SANTISUKNIRAN (Archbishop of Thare and Nonseng).

Archbishop of Bangkok: Most Rev. FRANCIS XAVIER KRIENGSAK KOVITHAVANIJ, Assumption Cathedral, 51 Thanon Oriental, Charoenkrung 40, Bangrak, Bangkok 10500; tel. (2) 237-5277; fax (2) 237-1033; e-mail webmaster@catholic.or.th; internet www.catholic.or.th.

Archbishop of Tharé and Nonseng: Bishop LOUIS CHAMNIERN SANTISUKNIRAN, POB 6, Amphur Muang, Sakon Nakhon 47000; tel. (42) 711-272; fax (42) 712-023.

The Anglican Communion

Thailand is within the jurisdiction of the Anglican Bishop of Singapore (q.v.).

Other Christian Churches

Baptist Church Foundation (Foreign Mission Board): 90 Soi 2, Thanon Sukhumvit, Bangkok 10110; tel. (2) 252-7078; Mission Admin. TOM WILLIAMS (POB 832, Bangkok 10501).

Church of Christ in Thailand: 328 Thanon Phaya Thai, Phaya Thai, Bangkok 10400; tel. (2) 214-6001; fax (2) 214-6010; e-mail secretary@cct.or.th; internet www.cct.or.th; f. 1934; c. 100,000 communicants; Moderator Rev. Dr BOONRATNA BOAYEN; Gen. Sec. Rev. Dr SINT KIMHACHANDRA.

ISLAM

Office of the Chularajmontri: 100 Soi Prom Pak, Thanon Sukhumvit, Bangkok 10110; Sheikh Al-Islam (Chularajmontri) Haji ASIS PITHAKKHUMPOL.

BAHÁ'Í FAITH

National Spiritual Assembly: 1415 Sriwara Soi 3/4, Ladprao Soi 94, Wangthonglang, Bangkapi, Bangkok 10310; tel. (2) 530-7417; fax (2) 935-6515; e-mail nsa@bahai.or.th; internet www.thai-bahais.org; f. 1964; c. 15,000 mems resident in 76 provinces.

The Press

DAILIES

Thai Language

Baan Muang: 1 Soi Pluem-Manee, Thanon Vibhavadi Rangsit, Bangkok 10900; tel. (2) 513-3101; fax (2) 513-3106; internet www.banmuang.co.th; f. 1972; Editor MANA PRAEBHAND; circ. 200,000.

Daily News: 1/4 Thanon Vibhavadi Rangsit, Laksi, Bangkok 10210; tel. (2) 561-1456; fax (2) 940-9875; internet www.dailynews.co.th; f. 1964; Editor PRACHA HETRAKUL; circ. 800,000.

Khao Sod (Fresh News): 12 Thanon Tethsaban Naruaman, Prachanivate 1, Chatuchak, Bangkok 10900; tel. (2) 580-0021; fax (2) 580-2301; e-mail matisale@matichon.co.th; internet www.matichon.co.th/khaosod; Editor-in-Chief KIATICHAI PONGPANICH; circ. 650,000.

Kom Chad Luek (Sharp, Clear, Deep): 44 Moo 10, Thanon Bangna Trad, Km 4.5, Bang Na, Bangkok 10260; tel. (2) 325-5555; fax (2) 317-2071; internet www.komchadluek.com; Editor ADISAL LIMPRUNGPATAKIT.

Krungthep Turakij Daily: Nation Multimedia Group Public Co Ltd, 44 Moo 10, Thanon Bangna Trad, Bang Na, Prakanong, Bangkok 10260; tel. (2) 317-0042; fax (2) 317-1489; e-mail kteditor@nationgroup.com; internet www.bangkokbiznews.com; f. 1987; Publr and Group Editor SUTHICHAI YOON; Editor DUANGKAMOL CHOTANA; circ. 75,882.

Manager Daily: Baan Phra Atit, 102/1 Thanon Phra Atit, Phra Nakorn, Bangkok; internet www.manager.co.th; f. 1990; Editor KHUNTHONG LORSERIVANICH.

Matichon: 12 Thanon Tethsaban Naruaman, Prachanivate 1, Chatuchak, Bangkok 10900; tel. (2) 580-0021; fax (2) 580-2301; e-mail matisale@matichon.co.th; internet www.matichon.co.th; f. 1977; Man. Editor PRASONG LERTRATANAVISUTH; circ. 550,000.

Naew Na (Frontline): 96 Moo 3, Thanon Vibhavadi Rangsit, Talaat Bang Khen, Bangkok 10210; tel. (2) 973-4250; fax (2) 552-3800; e-mail naewna@naewna.com; internet www.naewna.com; Editor WANCHAI WONGMEECHAI; circ. 200,000.

Post Today: 136 Thanon Na Ranong, Sonthorn Kosa, Klongtoey, Bangkok 10110; tel. (2) 240-3700; fax (2) 671-3147; e-mail nhakranl@posttoday.com; internet www.posttoday.com; f. 2003; business news; Editor NA KAL LAOHAWILAI; circ. 100,000.

Siam Keela (Siam Sport): 66/26–29, Moo 12, Soi Ram Indra 40, Thanon Ram Indra, Klong Kum, Bueng Kum, Bangkok 10230; tel. (2) 508-8000; e-mail webmaster@siamsport.co.th; internet www.siamsport.co.th; f. 1973.

Siam Rath (Siam Nation): 12 Mansion 6, Thanon Ratchadamnoen, Bangkok 10200; tel. (2) 622-1810; fax (2) 224-1982; e-mail siamrath@siamrath.co.th; internet www.siamrath.co.th; f. 1950; Editor CHACHAWAN KHONGUDOM; circ. 120,000.

Thai Post: 1852 Thanon Kasemrat, Klongtoey, Bangkok 10110; tel. (2) 240-2612; fax (2) 249-0295; internet www.thaipost.net; Editor ROJ NGAMMAEN.

Thai Rath: 1 Thanon Vibhavadi Rangsit, Bangkok 10900; tel. (2) 272-1030; fax (2) 272-1324; e-mail feedback@thairath.co.th; internet www.thairath.co.th; f. 1948; Editor SORAWUT WACHARAPHOL; circ. 800,000.

Than Setakij (Economic Base): 222 Than Setakij Bldg, Thanon Vibhavadi Rangsit, Chatuchak, Bangkok 10900; tel. (2) 513-9896; e-mail webmaster@thannews.th.com; internet www.thannews.th.com.

English Language

Bangkok Post: Bangkok Post Bldg, 136 Soi Na Ranong, Klongtoey, Bangkok 10110; tel. (2) 240-3700; fax (2) 240-3665; e-mail bpadmin@bangkokpost.co.th; internet www.bangkokpost.com; f. 1946; morning; Editor-in-Chief PICHAI CHUENSUKSAWADI.

Business Day: Olympia Thai Tower, 22nd Floor, 444 Thanon Ratchadaphisek, Huay Kwang, Bangkok 10310; tel. (2) 512-3579; fax (2) 512-3565; e-mail info@bday.net; internet www.biz-day.com; f. 1994; business news; Man. Editor CHATCHAI YENBAMROONG.

The Nation: 44 Moo 10, Editorial Bldg, 6th Floor, Thanon Bangna Trad, Km 4.5, Bang Na, Phra Khanong, Bangkok 10260; tel. (2) 338-3333; fax (2) 338-3334; e-mail editor@nationgroup.com; internet www.nationmultimedia.com; f. 1971; morning; Publr and Group Editor SUTHICHAI YOON; Editor TULSATHIT TAPTIM; circ. 55,000.

Chinese Language

Sing Sian Yit Pao Daily News: 267 Thanon Charoenkrung, Talad-Noi, Bangkok 10100; tel. (2) 222-6601; fax (2) 225-4663; e-mail info@singsian.com; internet www.singsian.com; f. 1950; Man. Dir NETRA RUTHAIYANONT; Editor TAWEE YODPETCH; circ. 70,000.

Tong Hua Daily News: 877–879 Thanon Charoenkrung, Talad-Noi, Bangkok 10100; tel. (2) 236-9172; fax (2) 238-5286; Editor CHART PAYONITHIKARN; circ. 85,000.

WEEKLIES

Thai Language

Bangkok Weekly: 533–539 Thanon Sri Ayudhya, Bangkok 10400; tel. (2) 245-2546; fax (2) 247-3410; Editor VICHIT ROJANAPRABHA.

Mathichon Weekly Review: 12 Thanon Tethsaban Naruaman, Prachanivate 1, Chatuchak, Bangkok 10900; tel. (2) 580-0021; fax (2) 580-2301; e-mail weekly@matichon.co.th; internet www.matichon.co.th/weekly; Editor RUANGCHAI SABNIRAND; circ. 300,000.

Sakul Thai: 58 Soi 36, Thanon Sukhumvit, Bangkok 10110; tel. (2) 258-5861; fax (2) 258-9130; internet www.sakulthai.com; Editor SANTI SONGSEMSAWAS.

Siam Rath Weekly Review: 12 Mansion 6, Thanon Rajdamnern, Bangkok 10200; Editor PRACHUAB THONGURAI.

English Language

Bangkok Post Weekly Review: U-Chuliang Bldg, 3rd Floor, 968 Thanon Phra Ram Si, Bangkok 10500; tel. (2) 233-8030; fax (2) 238-5430; f. 1989; Editor ANUSSORN THAVISIN; circ. 10,782.

FORTNIGHTLIES

Thai Language

Darathai: 9-9/1 Soi Sri Ak-Sorn, Thanon Chuapleung, Tungmahamek, Sathorn, Bangkok 10120; tel. (2) 249-1576; fax (2) 249-1575; f. 1954; television and entertainment; Editor USA BUKKAVESA; circ. 80,000.

Dichan: 1400 Thai Bldg, Thanon Phra Ram Si, Bangkok; tel. (2) 249-0351; fax (2) 249-9455; e-mail dichan@pacific.co.th; Man. Editor KHUNYING TIPYAVADI PRAMOJ NA AYUDHYA.

Praew: 65/101–103 Thanon Chaiyaphruk, Taling Chan, Bangkok; tel. (2) 422-9999; fax (2) 434-3555; e-mail chantana@amarin.co.th; internet www.praew.com; f. 1979; women and fashion; Editorial Dir SUPAWADEE KOMARADAT; Editor CHANTANA YUTDHANAPHUM; circ. 150,000.

MONTHLIES

Bangkok 30: 98/5–6 Thanon Phra Arthit, Bangkok 10200; tel. (2) 282-5467; fax (2) 280-1302; f. 1986; Thai; business; Publr SONCHAI LIMTHONGKUL; Editor BOONSIRI NAMBOONSRI; circ. 65,000.

Chao Krung: 12 Mansion 6, Thanon Rajdamnern, Bangkok 10200; Thai; Editor NOPPHORN BUNYARIT.

The Dharmachaksu (Dharma-vision): Foundation of Mahamakut Rajavidyalai, 241 Thanon Phra Sumeru, Bangkok 10200; tel. and fax (2) 629-1391; e-mail books@mahamakuta.inet.co.th; internet www.mahamakuta.inet.co.th; f. 1894; Thai; Buddhism and related subjects; Editor SAENG CHANDR-NGAM; circ. 5,000.

Grand Prix: 4/299 Moo 5, Soi Ladplakhao 66, Thanon Ladplakhao, Bangkhen, Bangkok 10220; tel. (2) 971-6450; fax (2) 971-6469; e-mail pinyo@grandprixgroup.com; internet www.grandprixgroup.com/gpi/maggrandprix/grandprix.asp; f. 1970; Editor PINYO SILPASARTDUMRONG; circ. 80,000.

The Investor: Pansak Bldg, 4th Floor, 138/1 Thanon Phetchaburi, Ratchathawi, Bangkok 10400; tel. (2) 282-8166; f. 1968; English language; business, industry, finance and economics; Editor TOS PATUMSEN; circ. 6,000.

Kasikorn: Dept of Agriculture, Catuchak, Bangkok 10900; tel. (2) 561-2825; fax (2) 579-4406; e-mail pannee.v@doa.in.th; internet www.doa.go.th; f. 1928; Thai; agriculture and agricultural research; Editor-in-Chief SOPIDA HE-MAKOM; Editor PANNEE WICHACHOO.

Look: 1/54 Thanon Sukhumvit 30, Pra Khanong, Bangkok 10110; tel. (2) 258-1265; Editor KANOKWAN MILINDAVANIJ.

Look East: 52/38 Soi Saladaeng 2, Silom Condominium, 12th Floor, Thanon Silom, Bangkok 10500; tel. (2) 235-6185; fax (2) 236-6764; f. 1969; English; Editor ASHA SEHGAL; circ. 30,000.

Metro Magazine: 109 Moo 8, 7th Floor, Srithepthai Bldg, Thanon Bangna Trad, Bang Na, Bangkok 10260; tel. (2) 746-7250; fax (2) 746-7266; e-mail mon@bkkmetro.com; internet www.bkkmetro.com; f. 1996; English language; lifestyle, events listings and consumer-oriented articles; Publr and Editor-in-Chief MUNINTRA SAENGSUVIMOL; circ. 35,000.

Motorcycle Magazine: 4/299 Moo 5, Soi Ladplakhao 66, Thanon Ladplakhao, Anusawari, Bangkhan, Bangkok 10220; tel. (2) 522-1731; fax (2) 522-1730; e-mail webmaster@grandprixgroup.com; internet www.grandprixgroup.com; f. 1972; publ. by Grand Prix Int. Co Ltd; Publr PRACHIN EAMLAMNOW; Editor PRAWIT PRAKEENWINCHA; circ. 55,000.

Saen Sanuk: 50 Soi Saeng Chan, Thanon Sukhumvit 42, Bangkok 10110; tel. (2) 392-0052; fax (2) 391-1486; English; travel and tourist attractions in Thailand; Editor SOMTAWIN KONGSAWATKIAT; circ. 85,000.

Sarakadee Magazine: 28-30 Soi Parinayok, Bangkok 10200; tel. (2) 281-6110; fax (2) 282-7003; e-mail admin@sarakadee.com; internet www.sarakadee.com; Thai; events, culture and nature.

Satawa Liang: 689 Thanon Wang Burapa, Bangkok; Thai; Editor THAMRONGSAK SRICHAND.

Villa Wina Magazine: Chalerm Ketr Theatre Bldg, 3rd Floor, Bangkok; Thai; Editor BHONGSAKDI PIAMLAP.

NEWS AGENCY

Thai News Agency (TNA): 63/1 Thanon Phra Rama 9, Huay Kwang, Bangkok 10320; operated by MCOT PCL; news service in Thai and English.

PRESS ASSOCIATIONS

Confederation of Thai Journalists: 299 Thanon Ratchasima, Dusit, Bangkok 10300; tel. (2) 668-9422; fax (2) 668-7505; internet www.ctj.in.th; Pres. CHATRI LIMCHAROON; Sec.-Gen. NATTAYA CHETCHOTIROS.

Press Association of Thailand: 299 Thanon Ratchasima, Dusit, Bangkok 10300; tel. (2) 537-3777; fax (2) 537-3888; e-mail webmaster@thaipressasso.com; internet www.thaipressasso.com; f. 1941; Pres. MANIT LUEPRAPHAI.

Thai Journalists' Association: 538/1 Thanon Samsen, Dusit, Bangkok 10300; tel. (2) 668-9422; fax (2) 668-7505; e-mail reporter@inet.co.th; internet www.tja.or.th; Pres. PRASONG LERTRATANAWISUTE.

There are also regional press organizations and journalists' organizations.

Publishers

Advance Publishing Co Ltd: 1400 Rama IV Shopping Centre, Klongtoey, Bangkok 10110; tel. (2) 249-1824; fax (2) 249-2301; e-mail sirirat@pacific.co.th; Man. PRASERTSAK SIVASAHONG.

Amarin Printing and Publishing Public Co Ltd: 65/101–103 Moo 4, Thanon Chaiyaphruk, Taling Chan, Bangkok 10170; tel. (2) 422-9999; fax (2) 434-3555; e-mail info@amarin.co.th; internet www.amarin.com; f. 1976; general books and magazines; CEO METTA UTAKAPAN.

Bhannakij Trading: 34–42 Thanon Nakornsawan, Wat Sommanas, Bangkok 10100; tel. (2) 282-0282; fax (2) 629-9801; internet www.bhannakij.com; Thai fiction, school textbooks; Man. SOMSAK TECHAKASHEM.

Chalermnit Publishing Co Ltd: 108 Thanon Sukhumvit, Soi 53, Bangkok 10110; tel. (2) 662-6264; fax (2) 662-6265; e-mail chalermnit@hotmail.com; internet www.chalermnit.com; f. 1937; dictionaries, history, literature, guides to Thai language, works on Thailand and South-East Asia; Man. Dir Dr PARICHART JUMSAI.

Prae Pittaya Ltd: POB 914, 716–718 Wangburabha, Bangkok 10200; tel. (2) 221-4283; fax (2) 222-1286; general Thai books; Man. CHIT PRAEPANICH.

Praphansarn: 668–676 Thanon Charansanitwong, Bang Yee Khan, Bang Plat, Bangkok 10700; tel. (2) 435-1671; fax (2) 434-6812; e-mail editer@praphansarn.com; internet www.praphansarn.com; f. 1961; children's, comics, reference books; Man. Dir SUPHOL TAECHATADA.

Ruamsarn (1977): 864 Wangburabha, Thanon Panurangsri, Bangkok 10200; tel. (2) 221-6483; fax (2) 222-2036; f. 1951; fiction and history; Man. PITI TAWEWATANASARN.

Silkworm Books: 6 Thanon Sukkasem, T. Suthep, Muang, Chiang Mai 50200; tel. (53) 226-161; fax (53) 226-643; e-mail info@silkwormbooks.com; internet www.silkwormbooks.com; f. 1991; South-East Asian studies; English language.

Suksapan Panit (Business Organization of Teachers' Institute): 2249 Thanon Ratchasima, Bangkok 10300; tel. (2) 538-3033; e-mail suksapan99@hotmail.com; internet www.suksapan.or.th; f. 1950; general, textbooks, children's, pocket books; Pres. PANOM KAW KAMNERD.

Thai Watana Panich: 1991/129-130 Thanon Sukhumvit 77, Suan-Luang, Bangkok 10250; tel. (2) 320-3271; fax (2) 320-3729; e-mail webmaster@twp.co.th; internet www.twp.co.th; children's, school textbooks; Man. Dir INTIRA BUNNAG.

White Lotus Co Ltd: G.P.O. Box 1141, Bangkok 10501; tel. (3) 823-9883; fax (3) 823-9885; e-mail ande@loxinfo.co.th; internet whitelotusbooks.com; f. 1972; regional interests, incl. art and culture, history, sociology and natural history; Publr DIETHARD ANDE.

PUBLISHERS' ASSOCIATION

Publishers' and Booksellers' Association of Thailand (PUBAT): 83/159 Moo 6, Thanon Ngam Wong Wan, Thung Song Hong, Lak Si, Bangkok 10210; tel. (2) 954-9560; fax (2) 954-9565; e-mail info@pubat.or.th; internet www.pubat.or.th; f. 1960; organizes national book fairs and provides promotional opportunities for publishers; Pres. WORAPAN LOKITSATHAPORN.

Broadcasting and Communications

TELECOMMUNICATIONS

National Telecommunications Commission (NTC): 87 Thanon Phaholyothin, Soi 8, Phayatai, Bangkok 10400; tel. (2) 271-0151; fax (2) 271-3516; e-mail 1200@ntc.or.th; internet www.ntc.or.th; f. 2004; responsible for regulation and administration of telecommunications industry; Chair. Prof. PRASIT PRAPINMONGKOLKARN; Sec.-Gen. TAKORN TANTASITH (acting).

Advanced Info Service Public Co Ltd: 414 Thanon Phaholyothin, Shinawatra Tower I, Phaya Thai, Bangkok 10400; tel. (2) 299-5000; fax (2) 299-5719; e-mail callcenter@ais.co.th; internet www.ais.co.th; mobile telephone network operator providing 3G (third generation) cellular services; Chair. ALLEN LEW KEONG; CEO WICHIAN MEKTRAKARN.

CAT Telecom Public Co Ltd: 99 Thanon Chaengwattana, Moo 3, Laksi, Bangkok 10210-0298; tel. (2) 104-3000; fax (2) 104-3088; e-mail pr@cattelecom.com; internet www.cattelecom.com; f. 2003; est. following division of Communications Authority of Thailand (CAT); originally state-owned; corporatized in 2003; telecommunications and related services; Chair. NATHI PREMRASMI; Pres. JIRAYUT RUNGSRITHONG.

Samart Corpn Public Co Ltd: 99/1 Moo 4, Software Park Bldg, 35th Floor, Thanon Chaengwattana, Pakkred, Nonthaburi, Bangkok 11120; tel. (2) 502-6000; fax (2) 502-6186; e-mail nikhil.a@samartcorp.com; internet www.samartcorp.com; f. 1952; telecommunications installation and distribution; Chair. TONGCHAT HONGLADAROMP; Exec. Chair. and CEO CHAROENRATH VILAILUCK.

Thai Telephone and Telecommunication Public Co Ltd (TT&T): 252/30 Muang Thai Phatra Complex Tower 1, 24th Floor, Thanon Ratchadaphisek, Huay Kwang, Bangkok 10320; tel. (2) 693-2100; fax (2) 693-2124; e-mail icare@ttt.co.th; internet www.ttt.co.th; f. 1992; distributors of telecommunications equipment and services; Chair. SONGRIT KUSOMROSANANAN; Pres. PRACHUAB TANTINONDA.

TOT Public Co Ltd: 89/2 Moo 3, Thanon Chaengwattana, Thung Song Hong, Laksi, Bangkok 10210; tel. (2) 240-0701; e-mail prtot@tot.co.th; internet www.tot.co.th; f. 2002; state-owned; fmrly Telephone Organization of Thailand; name changed to TOT Corpn Public Co Ltd; name changed as above in 2005; telephone operator; de facto regulator; Chair. AREEPONG BHOOCHA-OOM; Pres. VARUT SUWAKORN.

Total Access Communications Public Co Ltd: 319 Chamchuri Sq. Bldg, 22nd–41st Floors, Thanon Phaya Thai, Pathumwan, Bangkok 10330; tel. (2) 202-8000; fax (2) 202-8929; e-mail ir@dtac.co.th; internet www.dtac.co.th; f. 1989; mobile telephone network operator; 41.46% owned by United Communication Industry Public Co Ltd; 29.94% owned by Telenor Asia Pte Ltd; Chair. BOONCHAI BENCHARONGKUL; CEO TORE JOHNSEN.

True Corpn PCL: 18 True Tower, Thanon Ratchadaphisek, Huay Kwang, Bangkok 10310; tel. (2) 643-1111; fax (2) 643-1651; internet www.truecorp.co.th/eng/index.jsp; f. 1990; est. under the name

Telecomasia Corpn PCL; name changed as above in 2004; telecommunications services; Chair. DHANIN CHEARAVANONT; Pres. and CEO SUPHACHAI CHEARAVANONT.

True Move: 18 True Tower, Thanon Ratchadaphisek, Huay Kwang, Bangkok 10310; tel. (2) 647-5000; internet www.truemove.com; f. 2002; fmrly TA Orange Co Ltd; name changed as above in 2005; mobile telephone network operator; Chief Exec. SUPHACHAI CHEARAVANONT.

United Communication Industry Public Co Ltd (UCOM): 333/3 Chai Bldg, 18th Floor, Thanon Vibhavadi Rangsit, Ladyao, Chatuchak, Bangkok 10900; tel. (2) 202-8000; fax (2) 202-8929; e-mail ir.ucom@dtac.co.th; internet www.ucom.co.th; telecommunications service provider; Chair. SRIBHUMI SUKHANETR; Pres. and Chief Exec. BOONCHAI BENCHARONGKUL.

BROADCASTING

Regulatory Authority

Radio and Television Executive Committee (RTEC): Programme, Administration and Law Section, Division of RTEC Works, Government Public Relations Dept, Thanon Ratchadamnoen Klang, Phra Nakhon Region, Bangkok 10200; constituted under Broadcasting and TV Rule 1975, the cttee consists of 17 reps from 14 govt agencies and controls the administrative, legal, technical and programming aspects of broadcasting in Thailand; Dir-Gen. BOWON TECHAINDRA.

Radio

National Broadcasting Services of Thailand (NBT): 236 Thanon Vibhavadi Rangsit, Huay Kwang, Bangkok 10320; tel. (2) 277-8181; fax (2) 277-8182; internet nbt.prd.go.th; f. 1930; govt-controlled; broadcasts educational, entertainment, cultural and news programmes on six national networks; operates more than 150 stations throughout Thailand; external services in French and English commenced in 1938; currently broadcasts in 12 languages; Dir TUENJAI SINTHUVNIK.

Ministry of Education Broadcasting Service: Centre for Innovation and Technology, Ministry of Education, Bangkok; tel. (2) 246-0026; f. 1954; morning programmes for schools (Mon.–Fri.); afternoon and evening programmes for general public (daily); Dir of Centre PISAN SIWAYABRAHM.

Pituksuntirad Radio Stations: stations at Bangkok, Nakorn Ratchasima, Chiang Mai, Pitsanuloke and Songkla; programmes in Thai; Dir-Gen. PAITOON WAIJANYA.

Radio Saranrom: Thanon Ratchadamnoen, POB 2-131, Bangkok 10200; tel. (2) 224-4904; fax (2) 226-1825; internet www.mfa.go.th/web/151.php; f. 1968 as Voice of Free Asia; name changed as above in 1998; operated by the Ministry of Foreign Affairs; broadcasts in Thai; Dir of Broadcasting PAIBOON KUSKUL.

Television

Bangkok Broadcasting & TV Co Ltd (Channel 7): 998/1 Soi Sirimitr, Phaholyothin 18/1, Chatuchak, Bangkok 10900; tel. (2) 610-0777; fax (2) 272-0010; e-mail prdept@ch7.com; internet www.ch7.com; commercial.

Bangkok Entertainment Co Ltd (Channel 3): 3199 Maleenont Tower, Thanon Phra Ram IV, Klong Ton, Klongtoey, Bangkok 10110; tel. (2) 204-3333; fax (2) 204-1384; e-mail info@thaitv3.com; internet www.thaitv3.com; Programme Dir PRAVIT MALEENONT.

MCOT Public Co Ltd: 63/1 Thanon Phra Rama IX, Huay Kuang, Bangkok 10310; tel. (2) 201-6388; fax (2) 245-1855; e-mail ir@mcot.net; internet www.mcot.net; f. 1955; est. as Thai Television Co Ltd; named changed to The Mass Communication Org. of Thailand in 1977; present name adopted 2004; operates Modernine TV (fmrly Channel 9) and a satellite television channel; also operates radio stations and Thai News Agency; Chair. Dr SURAPON NITIKRAIPOJ; Pres. TANAWAT WANSOM.

National Broadcasting Services of Thailand (NBT): internet nbttv.prd.go.th; (see radio); operates TV Channel 11; parent station of eight regional TV networks.

The Royal Thai Army Television HSA-TV (Channel 5): 210 Thanon Phaholyothin, Sanam Pao, Bangkok 10400; tel. (2) 279-2397; fax (2) 271-0930; e-mail webadmin@tv5.co.th; internet www.tv5.co.th; f. 1958; operates channels nation-wide; Dir-Gen. Maj.-Gen. KITTITAT PANECHAPHAN.

Thai Public Broadcasting Service: 1010 Thanon Vibhavadi Rangsit, Chatuchak, Bangkok 10900; tel. (2) 791-1385; fax (2) 791-1383; e-mail people@thaipbs.or.th; internet www.thaipbs.or.th; f. 2008; succeeded the former iTV.

Thai TV Global Network: c/o Royal Thai Army HSA-TV, 210 Thanon Phaholyothin, Phaya Thai, Bangkok 10400; tel. (2) 278-1697; fax (2) 615-2066; e-mail tgn_mail@yahoo.com; internet www.thaitvglobal.com; established with the co-operation of all stations; distributes selected news, information and entertainment programmes from domestic stations for transmission to 170 countries world-wide via six satellite networks; Chair. Maj.-Gen. SOONTHORN SOPHONSIRI.

Finance

(cap. = capital; p.u. = paid up; res = reserves; dep. = deposits; m. = million; brs = branches; amounts in baht)

BANKING

Central Bank

Bank of Thailand: 273 Thanon Samsen, Bangkhunprom, Bangkok 10200; tel. (2) 283-5353; fax (2) 280-0449; e-mail webmaster@bot.or.th; internet www.bot.or.th; f. 1942; bank of issue; cap. 20m., res –74,116.5m., dep. 3,141,445.8m. (Dec. 2009); Gov. PRASARN TRAIRATVORAKUL; 4 brs.

Commercial Banks

Bangkok Bank Public Co Ltd: 333 Thanon Silom, Bangrak, Bangkok 10500; tel. (2) 231-4333; fax (2) 231-4742; e-mail info@bangkokbank.com; internet www.bangkokbank.com; f. 1944; cap. 19,088.4m., res 241,432.7m., dep. 1,342,977.3m. (Dec. 2009); 49% foreign-owned; Chair. KOSIT PANPIEMRAS; Pres. CHARTSIRI SOPHONPANICH; 656 local brs, 22 overseas brs.

Bank of Ayudhya Public Co Ltd: 1222 Thanon Rama III, Bang Phongphang, Yan Nawa, Bangkok 10120; tel. (2) 296-2000; fax (2) 683-1484; e-mail webmaster@krungsri.com; internet www.krungsri.com; f. 1945; cap. 60,741.4m., res 21,074.3m., dep. 569,987.2m. (Dec. 2009); Pres. MARK JOHN ARNOLD; Chair. VERAPHAN TEEPSUWAN; 384 local brs, 3 overseas brs.

CIMB Thai Bank Public Co Ltd: 44 Thanon Langsuan, Lumpini, Pathumwan, Bangkok 10330; tel. (2) 626-7000; fax (2) 573-3333; e-mail cimbthai.carecenter@cimbthai.com; internet www.cimbthai.com; f. 1998; fmrly BankThai Public Co Ltd, name changed as above 2009; cap. 6,674.7m., res 768.5m., dep. 98,583.2m. (Dec. 2009); Chair. CHAKRAMON PHASUKAVANICH; Pres. SUBHAK SIRAWAKSA; 98 brs.

Kasikorn Bank Public Co Ltd: 1 Soi Ratburana 27/1, Thanon Ratburana, Bangkok 10140; tel. (2) 888-8800; fax (2) 888-8882; e-mail info@kasikornbank.com; internet www.kasikornbank.com; f. 1945; fmrly Thai Farmers Bank PCL; name changed as above April 2003; cap. 23,932.6m., res 33,288m., dep. 1,038,818.8m. (Dec. 2009); 48.98% foreign-owned; Chair. BANYONG LAMSAM; Pres. and CEO BANTHOON LAMSAM; 508 local brs, 4 overseas brs.

Kiatnakin Bank Public Co Ltd: Amarin Tower, 11th Floor, 500 Thanon Ploenchit, Pathumwan, Bangkok 10330; tel. (2) 680-3333; fax (2) 256-9933; internet www.kiatnakinbank.com; f. 1971; est. as Kiatnakin Finance and Securities Co Ltd; name changed in 1999 to Kiatnakin Finance Public Co Ltd following separation of its finance and securities businesses; present name adopted 2005; Chair. SUPOL WATTANAVEKIN; Pres. TAWATCHAI SUDTIKITPISAIN; 16 brs.

Krung Thai Bank Public Co Ltd (State Commercial Bank of Thailand): 35 Thanon Sukhumvit, Klongtoey, Bangkok 10110; tel. (2) 255-2222; fax (2) 255-9391; e-mail call@contactcenter.ktb.co.th; internet www.ktb.co.th; f. 1966; cap. 57,604.0m., res 10,429.3m., dep. 1,283,508.6m. (Dec. 2009); taken under the control of the central bank in 1998, pending transfer to private sector; merged with First Bangkok City Bank PCL in 1999; Chair. DUSIT NONTANAKORN; Pres. APISAK TANTIVORAWONG; 719 local brs, 7 overseas brs.

Siam City Bank Public Co Ltd: 1101 Thanon Phetchaburi Tadmai, Bangkok 10400; tel. (2) 208-5000; fax (2) 253-1240; e-mail scibweb@scib.co.th; internet www.scib.co.th; f. 1941; cap. 21,128m., res 6,595m., dep. 348,137.6m. (Dec. 2009); taken under the control of the central bank in Feb. 1998; merged with Bangkok Metropolitan Bank PCL in April 2002; majority stake acquired by Thanachart Bank Public Co in 2010; Chair. BANTERNG TANTIVIT; Pres. and CEO CHAIWAT UTAIWAN; 387 local brs, 1 overseas br.

Siam Commercial Bank Public Co Ltd: 9 Thanon Ratchadaphisek, Ladyao, Chatuchak, Bangkok 10900; tel. (2) 544-1000; fax (2) 937-7754; e-mail investor.relations@scb.co.th; internet www.scb.co.th; f. 1906; cap. 33,991.9m., res 30,686m., dep. 1,008,332.3m. (Dec. 2009); Exec. Chair. Dr VICHIT SURAPHONGCHAI; Pres. KANNIKAR CHALITAPORN; 987 local brs, 3 overseas brs.

Standard Chartered Bank (Thai) Public Co Ltd: 90 Thanon Sathorn Nua, Silom, Bangkok 10500; tel. (2) 724-6327; fax (2) 724-6121; internet www.standardchartered.co.th; f. 1933 as Wang Lee Bank Ltd, renamed 1985; cap. 14,837m., res 9,571.5m., dep. 194,662m. (Dec. 2009); taken under the control of the central bank in July 1999, 75% share sold to Standard Chartered Bank (United Kingdom); name changed to Standard Chartered Nakornthon Bank PCL in 1999; name changed as above in 2005; Chair. KAIKHUSHRU SHIAVAX NORGALWALA; CEO MEE HAR FOO; 67 brs.

Thanachart Bank Public Co Ltd: 1st, 2nd, 14th and 15th Floors, Thonson Bldg, 900 Thanon Phoenchit, Lumpini, Pathumwan, Bangkok 10330; tel. (2) 655-9000; fax (2) 655-9001; e-mail nfs_rb@nfs.co.th; internet www.thanachartbank.co.th; f. 2002; 49% owned by Bank of Nova Scotia—Scotiabank (Canada); cap. 19,346.1m., res 2,684.4m., dep. 291,004m. (Dec. 2009); Chair. BANTERNG TANTIVIT; Man. Dir SUVARNAPHA SUVARNAPRATHIP.

TMB Bank Public Co Ltd: 3000 Thanon Phaholyothin, Chompon, Chatuchak, Bangkok 10900; tel. (2) 299-1111; fax (2) 273-7121; e-mail ir@tmbbank.com; internet www.tmbbank.com; f. 1957; fmrly Thai Military Bank Public Co Ltd; present name adopted 2005; merged with DBS Thai Danu Bank Public Co Ltd and Industrial Finance Corpn of Thailand in 2004; cap. 24,856.6m., res 971.1m., dep. 181,031.4m. (Dec. 2009); Chair. PHILIPPE DAMAS; CEO BOONTUCK WUNGCHAROEN; 431 local brs, 3 overseas brs.

United Overseas Bank (Thai) Public Co Ltd (UOBT): 191 Thanon Sathorn Tai, Bangkok 10120; tel. (2) 343-3000; fax (2) 287-2973; e-mail webmaster@uob.co.th; internet www.uob.co.th; f. 1998 as the result of the merger of Laem Thong Bank Ltd with Radanasin Bank; name changed to UOB Radanasin Bank Public Co Ltd in Nov. 1999; name changed as above in 2005 following merger with Bank of Asia Public Co Ltd; cap. 24,856.6m., res 973.2m., dep. 180,641m. (Dec. 2009); Chair. WEE CHO YAW; Pres. and CEO WONG KIM CHOONG; 154 brs.

Development Banks

Bank for Agriculture and Agricultural Co-operatives (BAAC): 469 Thanon Nakorn Sawan, Dusit, Bangkok 10300; tel. (2) 280-0180; fax (2) 280-0442; e-mail train@baac.or.th; internet www.baac.or.th; f. 1966 to provide credit for agriculture; cap. and res 49,911m., dep. 431,401m. (March 2006); Chair. KORN CHATIKAVANIJ; Pres. LUCK WAJANANAWAT; 491 brs.

Export-Import Bank of Thailand (EXIM Thailand): EXIM Bldg, 1193 Thanon Phaholyothin, Phaya Thai, Bangkok 10400; tel. (2) 271-3700; fax (2) 271-3204; e-mail info@exim.go.th; internet www.exim.go.th; f. 1993; govt-owned; provides financial services to Thai exporters and Thai investors investing locally and abroad; cap. 12,800m., res 2,614m., dep. 18,655.7m. (Dec. 2009); Chair. NARIS CHAIYASOOT; Pres. KANIT SUKONTHAMAN; 9 brs, 7 sub-brs.

Government Housing Bank: 63 Thanon Rama IX, Huay Kwang, Bangkok 10310; tel. (2) 645-9000; fax (2) 246-1789; e-mail crm@ghb.co.th; internet www.ghb.co.th; f. 1953 to provide housing finance; Chair. AREEPONG BHOOCHA-OOM; Pres. WORAVIT CHAILIMPAMONTRI; 120 brs.

Small and Medium Enterprise Development Bank of Thailand: SME Bank Tower, 310 Thanon Phaholyothin, Phaya Thai, Bangkok 10400; tel. (2) 265-3000; fax (2) 265-4000; e-mail sme@smebank.co.th; internet www.smebank.co.th; fmrly Small Industries Finance Office, which became Small Industrial Finance Co Ltd in 1991; present name adopted 2002; Chair. POONNIS SAKUNTANAGA; Pres. SOROS SAKORNVISAVA.

Savings Bank

Government Savings Bank: 470 Thanon Phaholyothin, Phaya Thai, Bangkok 10400; tel. (2) 299-8000; fax (2) 299-8490; e-mail news@gsb.or.th; internet www.gsb.or.th; f. 1913; cap. 0.1m., res –750.7m., dep. 724,704.3m. (Dec. 2008); Chair. VINAI VITTAVASGARNVEJ; Pres. LERSUK CHULADESA; 578 brs.

Bankers' Association

Thai Bankers' Association: Lake Rachada Office Complex, Bldg 2, 4th Floor, 195/5–7 Thanon Ratchadaphisek, Klongtoey, Bangkok 10110; tel. (2) 264-0883; fax (2) 264-0888; e-mail infodesk@tba.or.th; internet www.tba.or.th; f. 1958; Chair. CHARTSIRI SOPHOPANICH.

STOCK EXCHANGE

Stock Exchange of Thailand (SET): The Stock Exchange of Thailand Bldg, 62 Thanon Ratchadaphisek, Klongtoey, Bangkok 10110; tel. (2) 229-2000; fax (2) 654-5649; e-mail contact.tsd@set.or.th; internet www.set.or.th; f. 1975; 27 mems; Pres. CHARAMPORN JOTIKASTHIRA; Chair. SOMPOL KIATPHAIBOOL.

Securities and Exchange Commission: GPF Witthayu Towers, 15th Floor, 93/1 Thanon Witthayu, Lumpini, Pathumwan, Bangkok 10330; tel. (2) 263-6499; fax (2) 256-7711; e-mail info@sec.or.th; internet www.sec.or.th; f. 1992; supervises new share issues and trading in existing shares; chaired by Minister of Finance; Sec.-Gen. VORAPOL SOCATIYANURAK.

INSURANCE

Selected Insurance Companies

Aioi Bangkok Insurance Co Ltd: 22nd Floor, Bangkok Insurance/YWCA Bldg, 25 Thanon Sathorn Tai, Tungmahamek, Sathorn, Bangkok 10120; tel. (2) 620-8000; fax (2) 677-3979; e-mail pr@aioibkkins.co.th; internet www.aioibkkins.co.th; f. 1951; fmrly Wilson Insurance Co Ltd; fire, marine, motor car, general; CEO YOSHIHIKO FUKASAWA; Pres. NOPADOL SANTIPAKORN.

American International Assurance Co Ltd: American International Tower, 181 Thanon Surawongse, Bangrak, Bangkok 10500; tel. (2) 634-8888; fax (2) 236-6452; e-mail th.customer@aia.com; internet www.aia.co.th; f. 1983; ordinary and group life, group and personal accident, credit, life; CEO RON VAN OIJEN.

Ayudhya Insurance Public Co Ltd: 898 Ploenchit Tower, 7th Floor, Thanon Ploenchit, Pathumwan, Bangkok 10300; tel. (2) 263-0335; fax (2) 263-0589; e-mail info@ayud.co.th; internet www.ayud.co.th; non-life; Chair. VERAPHAN TEEPSUWAN; Pres. ROWAN D'ARCY.

Bangkok Insurance Public Co Ltd: Bangkok Insurance Bldg, 25 Thanon Sathorn Tai, Bangkok 10120; tel. (2) 285-8888; fax (2) 610-2100; e-mail corp.comm1@bki.co.th; internet www.bki.co.th; f. 1947; non-life; Chair. and Pres. CHAI SOPHONPANICH.

Bangkok Union Insurance Public Co Ltd: 175–177 Bangkok Union Insurance Bldg, Thanon Surawongse, Bangrak, Bangkok 10500; tel. (2) 233-6920; fax (2) 237-1856; e-mail bui@bui.co.th; internet www.bui.co.th; f. 1929; non-life; Chair. MANU LIEWPAIROT.

China Insurance Co (Siam) Ltd: 36/68–69, 20th Floor, PS Tower, Thanon Asoke, Sukhumvit 21, Bangkok 10110; tel. (2) 259-3718; fax (2) 259-1402; f. 1948; non-life; Chair. JAMES C. CHENG; Man. Dir FANG RONG-CHENG.

Indara Insurance Public Co Ltd: 364/29 Thanon Sri Ayudhya, Ratchathewi, Bangkok 10400; tel. (2) 247-9261; fax (2) 247-9260; e-mail contact@indara.co.th; internet www.indara.co.th; f. 1949; non-life; Chair. PRATIP WONGNIRUND; Man. Dir SUCHART TRISIRIWETAWATTANA.

Mittare Insurance Co Ltd: 295 Thanon Si Phraya, Bangrak, Bangkok 10500; tel. (2) 640-7777; fax (2) 640-7799; internet www.mittare.com; f. 1947; life, fire, marine, health, personal accident, automobile and general; fmrly Thai Prasit Insurance Co Ltd; Chair. SURACHAN CHANSRICHAWLA; Man. Dir SUKHATHEP CHANSRICHAWLA.

Navakij Insurance Public Co Ltd: 90/3–6, 100/50–55 Sathorn Nakorn Tower, Thanon Sathorn Nua, Silom, Bangrak, Bangkok 10500; tel. (2) 664-7777; fax (2) 636-7999; internet www.navakij.co.th; f. 1933; Chair. NIPHON TANGJEERAWONGSA.

Ocean Life Insurance Co Ltd: 170/74–83 Ocean Tower I Bldg, Thanon Ratchadaphisek, Klongtoey, Bangkok 10110; tel. (2) 261-2300; fax (2) 261-3344; e-mail info@ocean.co.th; internet www.ocean.co.th; f. 1949; life; Chair. KIRATI ASSAKUL; Man. Dir DAYANA BUNNAG.

Paiboon Insurance Co Ltd: Thai Life Insurance Bldg, 19th–20th Floors, 123 Thanon Ratchadaphisek, Bangkok 10310; tel. (2) 246-9635; fax (2) 246-9660; f. 1927; non-life; Chair. ANUTHRA ASSAWANONDA; Pres. VANICH CHAIYAWAN.

Prudential Life Assurance (Thailand) Public Co Ltd: Sengthong Thani Tower, 28th, 30th and 31st Floors, 82 Thanon Sathorn Nua, Bangkok 10500; tel. (2) 353-4999; fax (2) 353-4888; e-mail customer.service.ptsl@ibm.net; internet www.prudential.co.th; f. 1983; Chair. BURAPHA ATTHAKON; CEO BINAYAK DUTTA.

Siam Commercial New York Life Insurance Public Co Ltd: 4th Floor, SCB Bldg 1, 1060 Thanon Phetchaburi, SCB Chidlom, Ratchathewi, Bangkok 10400; tel. (2) 655-4000; fax (2) 256-1666; e-mail customerservice@scnyl.com; internet www.scnyl.com; f. 1976; life; Chair. and CEO KHUNYING JADA WATTANASIRITHAM.

Southeast Insurance (2000) Co Ltd (Arkanay Prakan Pai Co Ltd): Southeast Insurance Bldg, Unit 315G, 1–3 Thanon Silom, Bangrak, Bangkok 10500; tel. (2) 631-1331; internet www.seic2000.com; f. 1946; life and non-life; Chair. CHAYUT CHIRALERSPONG; Gen. Man. WICHAI INTARANUKULAKIJ.

Syn Mun Kong Insurance Public Co Ltd: 279 Thanon Srinakarin, Bangkapi, Bangkok 10240; tel. (2) 379-3140; fax (2) 377-5043; e-mail info@smk.co.th; internet www.smk.co.th; f. 1951; fire, marine, automobile and personal accident; Chair. RUENGWIT DUSADEESURAPOJ; Man. Dir RUENGDEJ DUSADEESURAPOJ.

Thai Health Insurance Co Ltd: 31st Floor, RS Tower, 121/89 Thanon Ratchadaphisek, Din-Daeng, Bangkok 10400; tel. (2) 642-3100; fax (2) 642-3130; e-mail care@thaihealth.co.th; internet www.thaihealth.co.th; f. 1979; Chair. APIRAK THAIPATANAGUL; Man. Dir VARANG SRETHBHAKDI.

Thai Insurance Public Co Ltd: 34/3 Soi Lang Suan, Thanon Ploenchit, Lumpini, Pathumwan, Bangkok 10330; tel. (2) 613-0100; fax (2) 652-2870; e-mail tic@thaiins.com; internet www.thaiins.com; f. 1938; non-life; Chair. KAVI ANSVANANDA.

Thai Life Insurance Co Ltd: 123 Thanon Ratchadaphisek, Din-Daeng, Bangkok 10400; tel. (2) 247-0247; fax (2) 246-9946; e-mail thailife@thailife.com; internet www.thailife.com; f. 1942; life; Chair. VANICH CHAIYAWAN; CEO Dr APIRAK THAIPATANAGUL.

ThaiSri Insurance Co Ltd: 126/2 Thanon Krunthonburi, Klongsam, Bangkok 10600; tel. (2) 878-7111; fax (2) 439-4840; e-mail info@

thaisri.com; internet www.thaisri.com; f. 1997; personal accident, automobile, fire, marine; jt venture between Thai Metropole Insurance and Zurich Financial Services Group (Switzerland); Chair. TAWEE BUTSUNTORN; CEO NATEE PANICHEWA.

Viriyah Insurance Co Ltd: RS Tower, 121/7 Thanon Ratchadaphisek, Din-Daeng, Bangkok 10320; tel. (2) 239-1000; fax (2) 641-3580; e-mail info@viriyah.co.th; internet www.viriyah.co.th; f. 1947; Chair. JARE CHUTHARATTANAKUL; Man. Dir SUVAPORN THONGTHEW.

Associations

General Insurance Association: 223 Soi Ruamrudee, Thanon Witthayu, Bangkok 10330; tel. (2) 256-6032; fax (2) 256-6039; e-mail general@thaigia.com; internet www.thaigia.com; Pres. JEERAPHAN ASAWATHANAKUL; Sec.-Gen. ANON VANGVASU; 67 mems.

Thai Life Assurance Association: 36/1 Soi Sapanku, Thanon Rama IV, Tungmahamek, Sathorn, Bangkok 10120; tel. (2) 287-4596; fax (2) 679-7100; e-mail tlaa@tlaa.org; internet www.tlaa.org; Pres. SARA LAMSAM; Sec.-Gen. PHERAPONG UNCHIT; 25 mems.

Trade and Industry

GOVERNMENT AGENCIES

Board of Investment (BOI): 555 Thanon Vibhavadi Rangsit, Chatuchak, Bangkok 10900; tel. (2) 553-8111; fax (2) 553-8222; e-mail head@boi.go.th; internet www.boi.go.th; f. 1958; formed to publicize investment potential and encourage economically and socially beneficial investments and also to provide investment information; chaired by the Prime Minister; Sec.-Gen. ATCHAKA SIBUNRUANG BRIMBLE.

Board of Trade of Thailand: 150/2 Thanon Rajbopit, Bangkok 10200; tel. (2) 622-1860; fax (2) 225-3372; internet www.thaichamber.org; f. 1955; mems: chambers of commerce, trade asscns, state enterprises and co-operative societies (large and medium-sized cos have associate membership); Chair. DUSIT NONTANAKORN.

Financial Sector Restructuring Authority (FSRA): 130–132 Tower 3, Thanon Witthayu, Pathumwan, Bangkok 10330; tel. (2) 263-2620; fax (2) 650-9872; f. 1997 to oversee the restructuring of Thailand's financial system; Chair. KAMOL JUNTIMA; Sec.-Gen. MONTRI CHENVIDAYAKAM.

Forest Industry Organization: 76 Thanon Ratchadamnoen Nok, Bangkok 10100; tel. (2) 282-3243; fax (2) 282-5197; e-mail fio@fio.co.th; internet www.fio.co.th; f. 1947; oversees all aspects of forestry and wood industries; Man. MANOONSAK TONTIWIWATTANA.

Office of the Cane and Sugar Board: Ministry of Industry, 6 Thanon Phra Ram Hok, Bangkok 10400; tel. (2) 202-3075; fax (2) 202-3070; e-mail ocsb0601@ocsb.go.th; internet www.ocsb.go.th; Sec.-Gen. PRASERT TAPANEEYANGKUL.

Rubber Estate Organization: 16 Moo, Nabon Station, Nakhon Si Thammarat Province 80220; tel. (75) 491570; fax (75) 491339; e-mail reothai@reothai.co.th; internet www.reothai.co.th; Man. Dir CHAIROJ THAMMARATTANA (acting).

DEVELOPMENT AGENCIES

National Economic and Social Development Board: 962 Thanon Krung Kasem, Bangkok 10100; tel. (2) 280-4085; fax (2) 281-3938; e-mail pr@nesdb.go.th; internet www.nesdb.go.th; economic and social planning agency; Sec.-Gen. AKHOM TERMPITTHAYAPAISIT.

Royal Development Projects Board: Office of the Prime Minister, Government House, Thanon Nakhon Pathom, Bangkok 10300; tel. (2) 280-6193; e-mail rdpbict.g@rdpb.mail.go.th; internet www.rdpb.go.th; Sec.-Gen. SOMPOL PANMANEE.

CHAMBER OF COMMERCE

Thai Chamber of Commerce (TCC): 150 Thanon Rajbopit, Bangkok 10200; tel. (2) 622-1860; fax (2) 225-3372; e-mail tcc@thaichamber.org; internet www.thaichamber.org; f. 1946; Chair. DUSIT NONTANAKORN.

INDUSTRIAL AND TRADE ASSOCIATIONS

The Federation of Thai Industries: Queen Sirikit National Convention Center, Zone C, 4th Floor, 60 Thanon Ratchadaphisek Tadmai, Klongtoey, Bangkok 10110; tel. (2) 345-1000; fax (2) 345-1296; e-mail information@fti.or.th; internet www.fti.or.th; f. 1987; fmrly The Association of Thai Industries; 4,800 mems; Chair. PAYUNGSAK CHARTSUTHIPOL.

Mining Industry Council of Thailand: Soi 222/2, Thai Chamber of Commerce University, Thanon Vibhavadi Rangsit, Din-Daeng, Bangkok 10400; tel. (2) 275-7684; fax (2) 692-3321; e-mail miningthai@miningthai.org; internet www.miningthai.org; f. 1983; intermediary between govt organizations and private mining enterprises; Chair. YONGYOTH PETCHSUWAN; Sec.-Gen. ORANUCH RAMAKOMUT.

Rice Exporters' Association of Thailand: 37 Soi Ngamdupli, Thanon Phra Rama IV, Tungmahamek, Sathorn, Bangkok 10120; tel. (2) 287-2674; fax (2) 287-2678; e-mail contact@thairiceexporters.or.th; internet www.thairiceexporters.or.th; Pres. KORBSUK IEMSURI; Sec.-Gen. THARNKASEM VANICHJAKVONG.

Sawmills Association: 101 Thanon Amnuaysongkhram, Dusit, Bangkok 10300; tel. (2) 243-4754; fax (2) 243-8629; e-mail info@thaisawmills.com; internet www.thaisawmills.com; Pres. SURASAK IEMDEENGAMLERT.

Thai Coffee Exporters Association: 1302–1306 Thanon Songwad, Samphanthawong, Bangkok 10100; tel. (2) 221-1264; fax (2) 225-1962; e-mail cofexpo@cscoms.com.

Thai Contractors' Association: 2013 Italthail House, 12A Floor, Thanon Petchburi, Huay Kwang, Bangkok 10310; tel. (2) 318-8321; fax (2) 318-8325; e-mail webmaster@tca.or.th; internet www.tca.or.th; f. 1928 under the name The Engineering Association of Siam; name changed to The Engineering Contractors Asscn in 1967 and as above in 1983; Pres. POLPAT KARNASUTA; Sec.-Gen. ANGSURAS AREEKUL.

Thai Diamond Manufacturers Association: 87/139–40, Modern Town Bldg, 18th Floor, Soi Ekamai 3, Thanon Sukhumvit 63, Klong Ton Nua, Wattana, Bangkok 10110; tel. (2) 390-0341; fax (2) 711-4039; e-mail odtcbkk@loxinfo.co.th; internet www.thaidiamonds.org; 11-mem. board; Pres. CHIRAKITTI TANGKATHAC.

Thai Food Processors' Association: Tower 1, Ocean Bldg, 9th Floor, 170/21–22 Thanon Ratchadaphisek Tadmai, Klongtoey, Bangkok 10110; tel. (2) 261-2684; fax (2) 261-2996; e-mail thaifood@thaifood.org; internet www.thaifood.org; Pres. NAT ONSRI.

Thai Lac Association: 57/1 Soi Saphantia, Thanon Sipraya, Mahapreuktaram, Bangrak, Bangkok 10500; tel. (2) 233-4583; fax (2) 633-2913.

Thai Maize and Produce Traders' Association: Sathorn Thani II Bldg, 11th Floor, 92/26–27 Thanon Sathorn Nua, Bangrak, Bangkok 10500; tel. (2) 234-4387; fax (2) 667-0178; e-mail thaimaize@tmpta.org; internet www.thaimaizeandproduce.org; Pres. SUNAN SINGSOMBOON.

Thai Pharmaceutical Manufacturers Association: 188/107 Thanon Charan Sanit Wong, Banchanglaw, Bangkoknoi, Bangkok 10700; tel. (2) 863-5106; fax (2) 863-5108; e-mail tpma@truemail.co.th; internet www.tpma.or.th; f. 1969; Pres. CHERNPORN TENGAMNUAY.

Thai Rice Mills Association: 81–81/1 Trok Rongnamkheng, 24 Thanon Charoenkrung, Talad-Noi, Samphanthawong, Bangkok 10100; internet www.thairicemillers.com; tel. (2) 234-7289; fax (2) 234-7286; Pres. CHANCHAI RAKTHANANON.

Thai Rubber Association: 45–47 Thanon Chotivithayakun 3, Hat Yai, Songkhla 90110; tel. (74) 429-011; fax (74) 429-312; e-mail tra@csloxinfo.com; internet www.thainr.com; f. 1951; est. as Thai Rubber Traders' Asscn; Pres. LUKCHAI KITTIPHOL.

Thai Silk Association: Textile Industry Division, Small Industries Bldg, 5th Floor, Soi Trimitr, Thanon Rama IV, Klongtoey, Bangkok 10110; tel. (2) 712-4328; fax (2) 391-2896; e-mail thsilkas@thaitextile.org; internet www.thaitextile.org/tsa; f. 1962; Pres. BUNTOON WONGSEELASHOTE.

Thai Sugar and Bio-energy Producers' Association: SM Tower, 22nd Floor, 979/56 Thanon Phaholyothin, Phaya Thai, Bangkok 10400; tel. (2) 298-0167; fax (2) 298-0169; e-mail tsma2000@cscoms.com; internet www.thaisugar.org.

Thai Sugar Producers' Association: 8th Floor, Thai Ruam Toon Bldg, 794 Thanon Krung Kasem, Pomprap, Bangkok 10100; tel. (2) 282-0990; fax (2) 281-0342.

Thai Tapioca Trade Association: Sathorn Thani II Bldg, 20th Floor, 92/58 Thanon Sathorn Nua, Silom, Bangkok 10500; tel. (2) 234-4724; fax (2) 236-6084; e-mail ttta@loxinfo.co.th; internet www.ttta-tapioca.org; f. 1963; Pres. SEREE DENWORALAK.

Thai Textile Manufacturing Association: Panjit Tower, 4th Floor, 117/7 Thanon Sukhumvit (22), Soi 55, Klongton Nua, Klongtoey, Bangkok 10110; tel. (2) 392-0753-55; fax (2) 712-5440; e-mail ttma@thaitextile.org; internet www.thaitextile.org/ttma; f. 1960; Pres. PHONGSAK ASSAKUL.

Union Textile Merchants' Association (Thai Textile Merchants' Association): 562 Espreme Bldg, 4th Floor, Thanon Rajchawong, Samphanthawong, Bangkok 10100; tel. (2) 622-6711; fax (2) 622-6714; e-mail tma@thaitextile.org; internet www.thaitextile.org/tma; Chair. SUCHAI PORNSIRIKUL.

UTILITIES

Electricity

Electricity Generating Authority of Thailand (EGAT): 53 Moo 2, Thanon Charan Sanit Wong, Bang Kruai, Nothaburi, Bangkok 11130; tel. (2) 436-0000; fax (2) 436-4723; e-mail correspondence@egat.co.th; internet www.egat.co.th; f. 1969; Gov. SUTHAT PATTAMASIRIWAT.

Electricity Generating Public Co Ltd (EGCO): EGCO Tower, 222 Moo 5, Thanon Vibhavadi Rangsit, Thung Song Hong, Laksi, Bangkok 10210; tel. (2) 998-5999; fax (2) 955-0956; e-mail corp_com@egco.com; internet www.egco.com; subsidiary of EGAT; 59% transferred to the private sector in 1994–96; 14.9% owned by China Light and Power Co (Hong Kong); Chair. PORNCHAI RUJIPRAPA; Pres. VINIT TANGNOI.

The Metropolitan Electricity Authority: 30 Soi Chidlom, Thanon Ploenchit, Lumpini, Pathumwan, Bangkok 10330; tel. (2) 254-9550; fax (2) 251-9586; internet www.mea.or.th; f. 1958; one of the two main power distribution agencies in Thailand; Gov. ARTHORN SINSAWAD.

The Provincial Electricity Authority: 200 Thanon Ngam Wongwan, Chatuchak, Bangkok 10900; tel. (2) 589-0100; fax (2) 589-4850; e-mail webmaster@pea.co.th; internet www.pea.co.th; f. 1960; one of the two main power distribution agencies in Thailand; Gov. ADISORN KIERTICHOKWIWAT.

Water

Metropolitan Waterworks Authority: 400 Thanon Prachachuen, Laksi, Bangkok 10210; tel. (2) 504-0123; fax (2) 503-9493; e-mail mwa1125@mwa.co.th; internet www.mwa.co.th; f. 1967; state-owned; provides water supply systems in Bangkok; Gov. CHAROEN PASSARA.

Provincial Waterworks Authority: 72 Thanon Chaengwattana, Don Muang, Bangkok 10210; tel. (2) 551-1020; fax (2) 552-1547; e-mail pr@pwa.co.th; internet www.pwa.co.th; f. 1979; provides water supply systems except in Bangkok Metropolis; Gov. CHAVALIT SARUN; Chair. SURA-AT THONGNIRAMOL.

MAJOR COMPANIES

(cap. = capital; res = reserves; m. = million; amounts in baht)

Advance Agro Public Co Ltd: 187/3, Moo 1, Thanon Bangna-Trad Km 42, Bang Prakong, Chachoengsao 24180; tel. and fax (38) 538-968; e-mail webmasteraa@DoubleA1991.com; internet www.doubleapaper.com; mfrs of paper; cap. and res 13,307m., sales 18,096m. (2009); Chair. NARONG SRISA-AN.

AGC Flat Glass (Thailand) Public Co Ltd (AGC): 200 Moo 1, Thanon Suksawad, Phra Samut Chedi, Samut Prakan 10290; tel. (2) 815-5000; fax (2) 815-5419; e-mail webmaster@tag.co.th; internet www.agc-flatglass.co.th; f. 1963; fmrly Thai Asahi Glass Public Co Ltd; name change in 2007; subsidiary of Asahi Glass (Japan); mfrs of plain glass; Pres. HIROYUKI ITO; 1,000 employees.

Alucon Public Co Ltd: 500 Moo 1, Soi Sirikam, 72 Thanon Sukhumvit, Tambol Samrong Nua, Amphur Muang-Samutprakarn, Bangkok 10270; tel. (2) 398-0147; fax (2) 398-3455; e-mail alucon@ksc.th.com; internet www.alucon.th.com; f. 1961; mfr of aluminium tubes and containers; cap. and res 2,488.2m., sales 3,504.7m. (2009); Chair. ILSE SCHNEIDER; Man. Dir TAKAAKI TAKEUCHI.

American Standard B&K (Thailand) Public Co Ltd: 1/6 Thanon Paholyothin Km 32, Klongluang, Pathumthani 12120; tel. (2) 901-4455; fax (2) 901-4488; internet www.americanstandard.co.th; f. 1969; mfrs of sanitary ware; Chair. CHALERMBHAND SRIVIKORN; Man. Dir CRAIG MCEACHERN; 1,300 employees.

Asia Fiber Public Co Ltd: Wall Street Tower, 27th Floor, 33/133–136 Thanon Surawong, Bangrak, Bangkok 10500; tel. (2) 632-7071; fax (2) 236-1982; e-mail sales@asiafiber.com; internet www.asiafiber.com; f. 1970; mfrs of nylon filament yarn, nylon textured yarn, filament woven fabrics; cap. and res 960.8m., revenue 1,318.8m. (2010); Chair. PIPAT SIRIKIETSOONG; Pres. CHEN NAMCHAISIRI; 1,421 employees.

Bangchak Petroleum Public Co Ltd: 555/1 Energy Complex, Bldg A, 10th Floor, Thanon Vibhavadi Rangsit, Chatuchak, Bangkok 10900; tel. (2) 140-8999; fax (2) 140-8900; e-mail info@bangchak.co.th; internet www.bangchak.co.th; f. 1984; refining and distribution of petroleum; cap. and res 25,864.7m., revenue 108,681.2m. (2009); Chair. KRAIRIT NILKUHA; Pres. Dr ANUSORN SANGNIMNUAN; 2,753 employees.

Bangkok Agro-Industrial Products Public Co Ltd: C.P. Tower, 313 Thanon Silom, Bangrak, Bangkok 10500; tel. (2) 231-0231; fax (2) 238-1921; mfrs and distributors of animal feedstuffs, animal husbandry, poultry and swine breeding, fruit production; cap. and res 3,405m., sales 4,544m. (2000); subsidiary of Charoen Pokphand Foods Public Co Ltd; Chair. JARAN CHIARAVANONT; Pres. ADIREK SRIPRATAK; 1,650 employees.

Bangkok Expressway Public Co Ltd: 238/7 Thanon Asoke-Dindaeng, Bangkapi, Huay Kwang, Bangkok 10310; tel. (2) 641-4611; fax (2) 641-4610; e-mail webmaster@becl.co.th; internet www.becl.co.th; engaged in the construction and management of Thailand's second stage expressway project; cap. and res 17,581.9m., revenue 7,760m. (2009); Chair. Dr VIRABONGSA RAMANGKURA; Man. Dir PAYAO MARITTANAPORN.

Bangkok Rubber Public Co Ltd: 611/40 Soi Watchan Nai, Bangklo, Bangkloaem, Bangkok 10120; tel. (2) 689-9500; fax (2) 291-1353; e-mail panglobal@pan-group.in.th; internet www.pan-group.com; f. 1974; mfrs of sports shoes and other footwear; revenue 5,754.3m. (2009); Chair. PRASOET CHUNTHIRA; Pres. BOONSONG TONDULYAKUL; 2,369 employees.

Bangkok Steel Industry Public Co Ltd: United Flour Mill Bldg, 5th and 7th Floors, 205 Thanon Rajawongse, Chakkawad, Sampantawongse, Bangkok 10100; tel. (2) 225-0200; fax (2) 222-7497; e-mail info@bangkoksteel.co.th; internet www.bangkoksteel.co.th; f. 1964; mfrs of steel products; Chair. PRASERT TANGTRONGSAKDI; Pres. JARAY BHUMICHITRA; 1,200 employees.

Bangkok Weaving Mills Group Ltd: 879 Thanon Bangkok-Nonthaburi, Bangsue, Bangkok 10800; tel. (2) 586-0901; fax (2) 587-2338; e-mail bwm@bwm-group.com; internet www.bwmgroup.net; f. 1950; mfr of cotton yarn and fabrics; Chair. NANTANA ASSAKUL; 1,900 employees.

Banpu Public Co Ltd: Thanapoom Tower, 26th–28th Floors, 1550 Thanon Phetchaburi Tadmai, Ratchathewi, Bangkok 10400; tel. (2) 694-6600; fax (2) 207-0695; e-mail corp_com@banpu.co.th; internet www.banpu.co.th; mineral mining and power generation; cap. and res 48,429m., revenue 69,071.4m. (2009); Chair. KRIRK-KRAI JIRAPAET; CEO CHANIN VONGKUSOLKIT; 1,126 employees.

Berli Jucker Public Co Ltd: Berli Jucker House, 99 Soi Rubia, 42 Thanon Sukhumvit, Klongtoey, Prakanong, Bangkok 10110; tel. (2) 367-1111; fax (2) 712-2240; e-mail bjc@bjc.co.th; internet www.berlijucker.co.th; f. 1882; engineering; mfr and distribution of consumer, imaging and technical products and packaging; cap. and res 10,350.7m., sales 22,799.2m. (2009); Chair. CHAROEN SIRIVADHANABHAKDI; Pres. and Exec. Dir ASWIN TECHAJAREONVIKUL; 5,700 employees.

Central Pattana Public Co Ltd: 31/F, The Offices at Centralworld, 999/9 Thanon Phra Ram 1, Pathumwan, Bangkok 10330; tel. (2) 264-5555; fax (2) 674-5593; e-mail co.secretary@cpn.co.th; internet www.cpn.co.th; f. 1980; engaged in property investment, development, management and construction; cap. and res 18,673.3m., revenue 15,713.9m. (2009); Chair. SUTHICHAI CHIRATHIVAT; Pres. and CEO KOBCHAI CHIRATHIVAT.

CH Karnchang Public Co Ltd: Viriyathavorn Bldg, 587 Thanon Sutthisarn, Din-Daeng, Bangkok 10400; tel. (2) 277-0460; fax (2) 275-7029; e-mail webmaster@ch-karnchang.co.th; internet www.ch-karnchang.co.th; f. 1972; constructor and sub-contractor, engaged in general construction; cap. and res 5,481m., sales 13,935.1m. (2009); Chair. ASWIN KONGSIRI; Pres. PLEW TRIVISVAVET.

Charoen Pokphand Group: CP Tower, 12th Floor, 313 Thanon Silom, Bangkok 10500; tel. (2) 625-8000; fax (2) 638-2741; e-mail cp@cpthailand.com; internet www.cpthailand.com; f. 1921; operations incl. agribusiness, retail and telecommunications; subsidiaries incl.: Charoen Pokphand Foods PLC, CPF Feeds, Bangkok Produce PLC, Chester Grill Co Ltd, International Pet Food Co Ltd; Chair. DHANIN CHEARAVANONT; Pres. and CEO ADIREK SRIPRATAK; 3,953 employees.

Chevron (Thailand) Ltd: 14–26 Sun Towers B, 123 Thanon Vibhavadi Rangsit, Chatuchak, Bangkok 10900; tel. (2) 612-7000; fax (2) 612-7013; e-mail PGPACaltex@chevron.com; internet www.caltex.co.th; f. 1946; fmrly Caltex (Thailand); distributors of petroleum products; Chief Exec. STEPHEN LONG; 350 employees.

Christiani and Nielsen (Thai) PCL: 451 Thanon La Salle (Sukhumvit 105), Bang Na, Bangkok 10260; tel. (2) 398-0158; fax (2) 398-9860; e-mail cnt@cn-thai.co.th; internet www.cn-thai.co.th; f. 1930; construction and property investment; cap. and res 1,144.2m., revenue 4,375.5m. (2009); Chair. SANTI GRACHANGNETARA; CEO SOMCHAI JONGSILILERD; 451 employees.

Circuit Electronic Industries Public Co Ltd: 45 Moo 12, Rojana Industrial Park, Utahi, Ayutthaya 13210; tel. (3) 522-6280; fax (3) 522-6714; e-mail marketing@cei.co.th; internet www.cei.co.th; f. 1984; mfr of integrated circuits and other electronic components; revenue 608.8m. (2009); Chair. SIVA NGANTHAVEE; Pres. AKAMIN NGANTHAVEE; 1,500 employees.

Delta Electronics (Thailand) Public Co Ltd: 909 Moo 4, Tambon Prakasa, Amphur Muang, Samutprakarn 10280; tel. (2) 709-2800; fax (2) 709-2833; e-mail info@deltathailand.com; internet www.deltathailand.com; f. 1998; design and manufacture of electronic and electrical equipment; cap. and res 17,648m., sales 26,995m. (2009); Chair. JAMES KONG MENG NG; Pres. HENRY HENG-HSIEN HSIEH.

DKSH (Thailand) Ltd: 2535 Thanon Sukhumvit, Bangchak, Prakhanong, Bangkok 10260; tel. (2) 790-8000; fax (2) 332-6101; internet www.dksh.co.th; f. 1906; fmrly Diethelm Trading Co Ltd; retailers of chemicals, consumer products and industrial equipment; sales 102,100m. (2009); Pres. SOMBOON PRASITJUTRAKUL; over 10,000 employees.

Esso (Thailand) Public Co Ltd: 3195/17–29 Thanon Phra Rama IV, Klongtoey, Bangkok 10110; tel. (2) 262-4788; fax (2) 262-4800; e-mail essoIR@exxonmobil.com; internet www.esso.co.th; f. 1965; distributors of petroleum products; cap. and res 24,067.5m., sales 163,230.5m. (2009); Chair. and Man. Dir ROBERT M. COOPER; 1,600 employees.

GFPT Public Co Ltd: GFPT Tower, 312 Thanon Phra Ram II, Bang Mod, Jom Thong, Bangkok 10150; tel. (2) 473-8000; fax (2) 473-8392; e-mail webmaster@gfpt.co.th; internet www.gfpt.co.th; f. 1981; producers of frozen chicken; cap. and res 4,551.7m., sales 11,507.3m. (2009); Chair. PRASIT SIRIMONGKOLKASEM; Man. Dir VIRACH SIRIMONGKOLKASEM; 4,856 employees.

Grammy Entertainment Public Co Ltd: 50 GMM Grammy Place, 21 Thanon Sukhumvit (Asoke), Khlongtoeinuea, Wattana, Bangkok 10110; tel. (2) 669-9000; fax (2) 664-0248; e-mail IR@gmmgrammy.com; internet www.gmmgrammy.com; f. 1983; operators of media businesses, including television and radio; cap. and res 2,483m., sales 8,124.3m. (2009); Chair. PAIBOON DAMRONGCHAITHAM; CEO BOOSABA DAORUENG; 2,000 employees.

Hemaraj Land and Development Public Co Ltd: UM Tower, 18th Floor, 9 Thanon Ramkhamhaeng, Suanluang, Bangkok 10250; tel. (2) 719-9555; fax (2) 719-9546; e-mail marketing@hemaraj.com; internet www.hemaraj.com; engaged in property development; cap. and res 8,458m., sales 2,223m. (2009); Chair. SAWASDI HORRUNGRUANG; Pres. and CEO DAVID NARDONE.

Hino Motor Sales (Thailand) Ltd: 212 Moo 4, Thanon Vibhavadi Rangsit, Talad Bangkhen, Laksi, Bangkok 10210; tel. and fax (2) 900-5000; fax (2) 900-5288; e-mail info@hinothailand.com; internet www.hinothailand.com; f. 1962; distributors of industrial motor vehicles; Chair. KUNIO TOMURA; Pres. TAKEO SAITO; 439 employees.

Honda Automobile (Thailand) Co Ltd: 49 Moo 9, Thanon Rojana, Uthai, Ayutthaya 13210; tel. (3) 533-1000; fax (3) 3533-0974; internet www.honda.co.th; f. 1983; mfrs of motor vehicles; Chair. SAICHIRO FUJIE; Man. Dir NOBUNARI MATSUSHITA.

ICC International Public Co Ltd: 757/10 Soi Pradoo 1, Thanon Sadhupradit, Yannawa, Bangkok 10120; tel. (2) 294-0281; fax (2) 294-3024; e-mail webmaster@icc.co.th; internet www.icc.co.th; distributors of consumer goods; cap. and res 11,803.1m., sales 11,218.8m. (2009); Chair. Dr SOM CHATUSRIPITAK; Pres. Dr BOONKIET CHOKWATANA; 7,091 employees.

IRPC Public Co Ltd: 555/2 Energy Complex Bldg B, 6 Thanon Vibhavadi Rangsit, Chatuchak, Bangkok; tel. (2) 649-7000; fax (2) 649-7001; e-mail contact@irpc.co.th; internet www.irpc.co.th; f. 1978; fmrly Thai Petrochemical Industry (TPI); name changed to above 2006; mfrs of plastics; cap. and res 71,901m., sales 166,036m. (2009); Chair. NORKUN SITTIPHONG; CEO PAILIN CHUCHOTTARWORN.

Italian-Thai Development Public Co Ltd: 2034/132-161 Italthai Tower, Thanon Phetchaburi Tadmai, Bangkapi, Bangkok 10320; tel. (2) 716-1600; fax (2) 716-1488; e-mail cccs@itd.co.th; internet www.itd.co.th; f. 1958; construction; cap. and res 10,648.6m., sales 39,682.9m. (2009); Chair. CHARTACHAI BUNYA-ANANTA; Pres. PREMCHAI KARNASUTA; 23,285 employees.

Jalaprathan Cement Public Co Ltd: 23/124–128 Soi Soonvijai, Thanon Rama 9, Bangkapi, Huay Kwang, Bangkok 10320; tel. (2) 641-5600; fax (2) 641-5682; e-mail A.CallCenter@acc.co.th; internet www.asiacement.co.th; f. 1956; owned by Italcementi Group (Italy); mfrs of cement; cap. and res 998.4m., revenue 1,961.7m. (2009); Chair. Gen. AYUPOON KARNASUTA; Man. Dir RAPEE SUKHAYANGA; 585 employees.

Jasmine International Public Co Ltd: 29th–30th Floors, Moo 4, 200 Thanon Chaengwattana, Pakkred, Nonthaburi, Bangkok 11120; tel. (2) 100-3000; fax (2) 100-3150; e-mail churnkamol.t@jasmine.com; internet www.jasmine.com; mfrs and distributors of telecommunications equipment; cap. and res 5,807.4m., sales 8,370.5m. (2009); Chair. SUDHITHAM CHIRATHIVAT; CEO PETE BODHARAMIK; 1,075 employees.

KGI Securities (Thailand) Public Co: 173 Asia Centre Bldg, 8th-11th Floor, Thanon Sathorn, Thungmahamek, Bangkok 10120; tel. (2) 658-8888; fax (2) 658-8000; e-mail investorrelation@kgi.co.th; internet www.kgieworld.co.th; finance co engaged in securities brokering, dealing and investment advice; cap. and res 4,511m., revenue 1,290m. (2009); 51% owned by a Taiwan-based co; Chair. FOONG HOCK MENG; Pres. WISIT WONGPAISAN.

Loxley Public Co Ltd: 102 Thanon Na Ranong, Klongtoey, Bangkok 10110; tel. (2) 348-8000; fax (2) 348-8001; e-mail info@loxley.co.th; internet www.loxley.co.th; f. 1939; information technology, infrastructure, telecommunications, consumer electronics, consumer products, chemicals, construction materials, environment, media and entertainment; cap. and res 4,598.5m., sales 10,280.2m. (2009); Chair. PAIROTE LAMSAM; Pres. DHONGCHAI LAMSAM.

Luckytex (Thailand) Public Co Ltd: Bubhajit Bldg, 5th Floor, 20 Thanon Sathorn Nua, Silom, Bangrak, Bangkok 10500; tel. (2) 266-6600; fax (2) 238-3957; e-mail visit.h_t@toray.co.th; internet www.toray.co.th; f. 1960; owned by Toray Group; mfrs of spun fabrics and yarn; cap. and res 3,644m., revenue 5,935m. (2009/10); Chair. and Man. Dir YASUO YAMASHITA; 2,424 employees.

Millennium Microtech (Thailand) Co Ltd (MMT): 17/2 Moo 18, Thanon Suwintawong, Tambon Saladang, Amphur Bangnumpriew, Cha Choeng Sao 24000; tel. (38) 845-530; fax (38) 845-597; e-mail SathitTh@m-microtech.com; internet www.m-microtech.com; fmrly Alphatec Semiconductor Packaging Co Ltd; name changed as above 2003; mfr of semiconductors; Pres. and CEO VIC TEE.

Minebea (Thai) Ltd: 19th Floor, Wave Place Bldg, 55 Thanon Witthayu, Lumpini, Pathumwan, Bangkok 10330; tel. (2) 253-4897; fax (2) 253-4537; internet www.minebea.co.th; f. 1984; mfrs of electrical goods and electronic components; Pres. and CEO TAKAYUKI YAMAGISHI; Man. Dir MASAYOSHI YAMANAKA; 31,600 employees.

Osotspa Co Ltd: 348 Thanon Ramkhamhaeng, Huamark, Bangkok 10240; tel. (2) 351-1000; fax (2) 374-7010; e-mail osotspa@osotspa.com; internet www.osotspa.com; f. 1891; mfr of energy drinks; Group Chair. SURAT OSATHANUGRAH; Man. Dir THANA CHAIPRASIT; 3,000 employees.

Padaeng Industry Public Co Ltd: CTI Tower, 26th–27th Floors, 191/18–25 Thanon Ratchadaphisek, Klongtoey, Bangkok 10110; tel. (2) 695-9499; fax (2) 695-9495; e-mail info@padaeng.co.th; internet www.padaeng.co.th; f. 1981; miners and refiners of zinc ingot and zinc alloy; cap. and res 4,469.6m., sales 6,619.4m. (2009); Chair. ARSA SARASIN; Man. Dir ANDRÉ R. VAN DER HEYDEN; 746 employees.

Pakfood Public Co Ltd: 103 Soi Ruammitr, Thanon Nonsee, Yannawa, Bangkok 10120; tel. (2) 295-2001; fax (2) 295-2002; e-mail mkt@pakfood.co.th; internet www.pakfood.co.th; f. 1984; processors and exporters of frozen seafood; cap. and res 967.5m., sales 8,296.7m. (2009); Pres. YONG AREECHAROENLERT; Man. Dir PHANISUAN CHAMNARNWET; 4,194 employees.

Phoenix Pulp and Paper Public Co Ltd: Ocean Tower II, 42nd Floor, Soi Wattana, Thanon Sukhumvit, Klongtoey Nuea, Wattana, Bangkok 10110; tel. (2) 661-7755; fax (2) 665-7231; e-mail mailbox@phoenixpulp.com; internet www.phoenixpulp.com; f. 1975; mfrs of pulp and paper; Chair. CHAOVALIT EKABUT; Man. Dir TERASAK CHAMIKORN; 1,300 employees.

Pranda Jewelry PLC: 333 Soi Rungsang, Thanon Bangna-Trat, Bangna, Bangkok 10260; tel. (2) 361-3311; fax (2) 399-4872; e-mail prapee@pranda.co.th; internet www.pranda.co.th; producers and exporters of jewellery; cap. and res 2,866.3m., sales 3,663.5m. (2009); Chair. PRIDA TIASUWAN; Pres. and Dir PRAPEE SORAKRAIKITIKUL; 6,000 employees.

PTT Chemical Public Co Ltd: Energy Complex Bldg A, 15–18/F, Thanon Vibhavadi Rangsit, Chomphon, Chatuchak, Bangkok 10900; tel. (2) 265-8400; fax (2) 265-8500; e-mail ir@pttchemgroup.com; internet www.pttchem.com; f. 2007; est. from merger of National Petrochemical Public Co Ltd and Thai Olefins Public Co Ltd; producer of olefins and related products; cap. and res 99,264m., revenue 86,029m. (2009); Chair. NONTIGORN KANCHANACHITRA; Pres. and CEO VEERASAK KOSITPAISAL.

PTT Exploration and Production Public Co Ltd (PTTEP): Energy Complex Bldg A, 555/1 Thanon Vibhavadi Rangsit, Chatuchak, Bangkok 10900; tel. (2) 537-4000; fax (2) 537-4444; e-mail cghotline@pttep.com; internet www.pttep.com; f. 1985; petroleum exploration and production; cap. 486,946m., sales 115,548m. (2009); Chair. PRASERT BUNSUMPUN; Pres. and CEO ANON SIRISAENGTAKSIN.

PTT Public Co Ltd: 555 Thanon Vibhavadi Rangsit, Bangkok 10900; tel. (2) 537-2000; fax (2) 537-3499; e-mail corporate@pttplc.com; internet www.pttplc.com; f. 1978; fmrly the Petroleum Authority of Thailand; privatized in 2001; activities relate to the development, exploitation, production and distribution of petroleum and gas; cap. and res 498,090.5m., sales 1,586,174.4m. (2009); Chair. NORKUN SITTHIPHONG; Pres. and CEO PRASERT BUNSUMPUN; 26,500 employees.

Saha Pathanapibul Public Co Ltd: 2156 Thanon Phetchaburi Tadmai, Bangkapi, Huay Kwang, Bangkok 10320; tel. (2) 318-0062; fax (2) 319-1678; e-mail info@sahapat.co.th; internet www.sahapat.co.th; f. 1942; mfr and distributor of soaps, toothpastes, detergents, baby products and food products; cap. and res 6,470.9m., revenue 19,748.3m. (2009); Chair. and Pres. BOONCHAI CHOKWATANA; 1,382 employees.

Saha-Union Public Co Ltd: 1828 Thanon Sukhumvit, Phrakanong, Bangkok 10250; tel. (2) 311-5111; fax (2) 332-5616; e-mail info@sahaunion.com; internet www.sahaunion.co.th; f. 1972; holding co whose subsidiaries produce textiles, plastic and rubber products, garment accessories and footwear; cap. and res 13,482m., revenue

8,617.5m. (2009); Chair. DAMRI DARAKANANDA; Pres. THITIVAT SUEBSAENG; 10,727 employees.

Sahaviriya Steel Industries Public Co Ltd: 2–3/F, Prapawit Bldg, 28/1 Thanon Surasek, Silom, Bangrak, Bangkok 10500; tel. (2) 238-3063; fax (2) 236-8890; e-mail pr-ir@ssi-steel.com; internet www.ssi-steel.com; f. 1990; mfrs of hot-rolled coils; cap. and res 17,755m., sales 33,366m. (2009); Chair. MARUAY PHADOONSIDHI; Pres. and Exec. Dir WIN VIRIYAPRAPAIKIT; 719 employees.

Sanyo Universal Electric Public Co Ltd: 601 Thanon Asoke, 3rd Floor, Din-Daeng, Bangkok 10400; tel. (2) 333-3000; fax (2) 333-3001; f. 1958; mfrs and distributors of electronic equipment and electrical appliances; Chair. PRAMUDE BURANASIRI; 2,130 employees.

Seagate Technology (Thailand) Ltd: Moo 7, 1627 Thanon Theparak, Theparak Muang, Samutprakan 10270; tel. (2) 715-2999; fax (2) 383-5736; e-mail sppsupport@seagate-asia.com; f. 1983; office of US-owned co; mfrs of computer hardware; Man. Dir JIRAPANNEE SUPRATCHYA.

Serm Suk Public Co Ltd (The): Muang Thai Phatra Complex, 27th–28th Floors, 252/35–36 Thanon Ratchadaphisek, Huay Kwang, Bangkok 10310; tel. (2) 693-2255; fax (2) 693-2266; internet www.sermsukplc.com; f. 1952; mfrs and distributors of carbonated soft drinks; sales 19,694m. (2009); Chair. Col PRASIT TANSETTHI; Pres. and CEO SOMCHAI BULSOOK; 9,524 employees.

Sharp Thai Co Ltd: M12/F, Ramaland Bldg, 952 Thanon Phra Ram IV, Suriwong, Bangrak, Bangkok 10500; tel. (2) 638-3500; fax (2) 2638-3900; internet www.sharpthai.co.th; f. 1987; mfrs of kitchen equipment and other electronic household appliances; Co-Chair. CHITTIN SIBUNRUANG, SUPACHAI SUTHIPONGSCHAI; Man. Dir TATSUYA MIYAKI.

Shell Company of Thailand Ltd, The: 10 Thanon Soonthornkosa, Klongtoey, Bangkok 10110; tel. (2) 249-0491; fax (2) 249-8393; e-mail enquiries-th@shell.com; internet www.shell.co.th; distributors of petroleum products; Chair. PISSAWAN ACHANAPORNKUL; 980 employees.

Shin Corporation Public Co Ltd: Shinawatra Tower I, 414 Thanon Paholyothin, Samsennai, Phaya Thai, Bangkok 10400; tel. (2) 299-5050; fax (2) 271-1058; e-mail investor@shincorp.com; internet www.shincorp.com; f. 1983; 49.6% stake owned by Singapore's Temasek Holdings (Pvt) Ltd (a govt holding co) following largest corporate takeover in Thailand's history in Jan. 2006; mfrs and distributors of mobile telephones, pagers and other telecommunications equipment; cap. and res 35,970m., sales 8,533.1m. (2009); Chair. VIRACH APHIMETEETAMRONG; CEO SOMPRASONG BOONYACHAI; 1,620 employees.

Siam Cement Public Co Ltd: 1 Thanon Siam Cement, Bangsue, Bangkok 10800; tel. (2) 586-4444; fax (2) 586-3307; e-mail invest@cementhai.co.th; internet www.siamcement.com; f. 1913; parent company of Siam Cement Group, Thailand's largest industrial group, with subsidiaries manufacturing cement and construction materials, machinery, electrical goods, pulp and paper; cap. and res 104,509m., sales 238,664m. (2009); Chair. CHIRAYU ISARANGKUN NA AYUTHAYA; Pres. KAN TRAKULHOON; 20,000 employees.

Siam City Cement Public Co Ltd (SCCC): 7-12/F, Column Tower, 199 Thanon Ratchadaphisek, Klongtoey, Bangkok 10110; tel. (2) 797-7000; fax (2) 797-7001; e-mail pr@sccc.co.th; internet www.siamcitycement.com; f. 1969; mfrs of cement and ready-mixed concrete; cap. and res 16,372.5m., sales 19,970.6m. (2009); Chair. and Man. Dir PHILIPPE ARTO; 6,200 employees.

Siam Nissan Automobile Co Ltd: Nantawan Bldg, 15/F, 161 Thanon Rajdamri, Lumpini, Pathumwan, Bangkok 10330; tel. (2) 257-4200; fax (2) 257-4210; e-mail info@nissan.co.th; internet www.nissan.co.th; f. 1973; mfrs of motor vehicles; Pres. and CEO CARLOS GHOSN.

Siam Pulp and Paper Public Co Ltd: 1 Thanon Siam Cement, Bangsue, Bangkok 10800; tel. (2) 586-3333; fax (2) 587-0738; e-mail chantimn@cementthai.co.th; mfrs of paper pulp; Chair. CHUMPOL NA LAMLIENG; Man. Dir CHAISAK SAENG-XUTO; 6,121 employees.

Siam Yamaha Co Ltd: 64 Moo 1, Thanon Bangna Trad, Sisa Chorakhe Yai, Bang Saow Tong, Samut Prakarn, Bangkok 10540; tel. (2) 740-8000; fax (2) 740-0977; e-mail yamaha@yamaha-motor.co.th; internet www.yamaha-motor.co.th; f. 1964; mfrs of motor vehicles; Pres. KASEM NARONGDEJ; 3,200 employees.

Singha Corpn Co Ltd: 999 Thanon Samsen, Dusit, Bangkok 10300; tel. (2) 242-4000; fax (2) 669-2089; e-mail pr_relations@boonrawd.co.th; internet www.boonrawd.co.th; f. 1933; fmrly Boon Rawd Brewery Co Ltd; name changed as above in 2006; mfrs of beer and soft drinks; Chair. CHAMNONG BHIROMBHAKDI; Pres. SANTI BHIROMBHAKDI; 2,300 employees.

Srithai Superware Public Co Ltd: Soi 36, 15 Thanon Suksawat, Bangpakok, Rasburana, Bangkok 10140; tel. (2) 427-0088; fax (2) 427-9525; e-mail cs@srithai.co.th; internet www.srithaisuperware.com; f. 1964; mfrs of plastic products and melamine tableware; cap. and res 4,771.3m., total revenue 5,456.5m. (2009); Chair. and Pres. SANAN ANGUBOLKUL; 3,500 employees.

Surapon Foods Public Co Ltd: 247 Moo 6, Thanon Therapak, Therapak, Samutprakan, Bangkok 10270; tel. (2) 385-3038; fax (2) 385-3176; e-mail info@surapon.com; internet www.surapon.com; f. 1977; mfr and exporter of frozen food; cap. and res 1,526.9m., sales 5,373.3m. (2009); Chair. KOSOL CHANTIKUL; CEO SURAPON VONGVADHANAROJ; 1,300 employees.

Tata Steel Thailand Public Co Ltd: Shinawatra Tower 3, 22nd Floor, 1010 Thanon Viphavadi Rangsit, Ladyao, Chatuchak, Bangkok 10900; tel. (2) 949-2949; fax (2) 949-2889; internet www.tatasteelthailand.com; f. 2002; est. following merger between steel-producing facilities of Siam Cement PCL and NTS Steel Group PCL; fmrly Millennium Steel; present name adopted 2006; owned by Tata Steel (India); mfrs of steel rods and bars; Chair. B. MUTHURAMAN; Pres. LAPTAWEE SENAVONGE; 1,080 employees.

Thai Carbon Black Public Co Ltd: Mahatun Plaza, 12th Floor, 888/122–128, Thanon Ploenchit, Lumpini, Pratumwan, Bangkok 10330; tel. (2) 253-6745; fax (2) 254-9031; e-mail tcb.marketing@adityabirla.com; internet www.birlacarbon.com/companies/thai_carbon_black.htm; f. 1978; owned by Birla Carbon (India); chemical products; Head SANJEEV SOOD.

Thai Central Chemical Public Co Ltd: Krungwattana Bldg, 180–184 Thanon Rajawongse, Bangkok 10100; tel. (2) 225-0135; fax (2) 226-1263; e-mail mailbox@thaicentral.co.th; internet www.tcccthai.com; f. 1973; mfrs of chemical fertilizers; cap. and res 3,882.4m., sales 13,995.3m. (2009); Chair. CHIKAHIDE MORI; Pres. and CEO MASATO TAKEI; 940 employees.

Thai Glass Industries Public Co Ltd: 15 Moo 1, Thanon Rajaburana, Bangkok 10140; tel. (2) 427-0060; fax (2) 427-6603; e-mail faxadmin@berlijucker.co.th; internet www.thaiglass.co.th; f. 1951; subsidiary of Berli Jucker PCL; mfrs and distributors of glassware and glass containers; Chair. CHAROEN SIRIWATTANAPHAKDI; 1,634 employees.

Thai Hua Rubber Public Co Ltd: 238/1 Thanon Ratchada Phisek, Huay Kwang, Bangkok 10320; tel. (2) 274-0471; fax (2) 274-0231; e-mail marketing@thaihua.com; internet www.thaihua.com; f. 1985; producer and exporter of rubber products; Chair. SANGOB PANDOKMAI; Pres. and CEO LUCKCHAI KITTIPOL; 1,990 employees.

Thai Oil Public Co Ltd (Thaioil): 555/1, Energy Complex Bldg A, 11th Floor, Thanon Vibhavadi Rangsit, Lardyao, Chatuchak, Bangkok; tel. (2) 229-0000; fax (2) 797-2970; e-mail ir@thaioilgroup.com; internet www.thaioil.co.th; petroleum-refining; cap. and res 66,788.5m., sales 284,123m. (2009); Chair. PICHAI CHUNHAVAJIRA; CEO SURONG BULAKUL; 727 employees.

Thai Plastic and Chemical Public Co Ltd: Rajanakarn Bldg, 14th–15th Floors, 183 Thanon Sathorn Tai, Yannawa, Sathorn, Bangkok 10120; tel. (2) 676-6000; fax (2) 676-6077; e-mail contact_ir@thaiplastic.co.th; internet www.thaiplastic.co.th; f. 1966; mfrs of PVC resins and compounds; cap. and res 12,933.5m., revenue 24,621.8m. (2009); Chair. YOS EUARCHUKIATI; Man. Dir KANET KHAOCHAN; 730 employees.

Thai Rayon Public Co Ltd: Mahatun Plaza, 16th Floor, 888/160-1 Thanon Ploenchit, Lumpini, Pathumwan, Bangkok 10330; tel. (2) 253-6745; fax (2) 2534-3181; e-mail kumaresh.v@adityabirla.com; internet www.thairayon.com; owned by Aditya Birla Group (India); mfrs and distributors of fibre and chemicals; cap. and res 15,321.4m., sales 6,214.4m. (2009); Chair. KUMAR MANGALAM BIRLA; Pres. H. K. AGARWAL; 900 employees.

Thai Union Frozen Products Public Co Ltd: 979/12 M Floor, SM Tower, Thanon Paholyothin, Samsennai, Phaya Thai, Bangkok 10400; tel. (2) 298-0537; fax (2) 298-0548; e-mail chansiri@mail.thaiunion.co.th; internet www.thaiuniongroup.com; f. 1988; manufacture and export of frozen and canned foods; cap. and res 16,331.1m., revenue 68,994.4m. (2009); Chair. KRAISON CHANSIRI; Pres. THIRAPHONG CHANSIRI; 5,140 employees.

Thai Yazaki Corpn Ltd: 25/F, Two Pacific Place Bldg, 142 Thanon Sukhumvit, Klongtoey, Bangkok 10110; tel. (2) 653-2550; fax (2) 653-2617; e-mail tylrecruit@yazaki.co.th; internet www.thaiyazaki.com; f. 1929; subsidiaries incl. Thai Arrow Products Ltd, Thai Metal Processing Co Ltd, Thai Yazaki Electric Wire Co Ltd; mfrs of electrical equipment for motor vehicles; Chair. YAZUMI OISHI; 10,524 employees.

Thaicom Public Co Ltd: 41/103 Thanon Rattanathibet, Moo 8, Nonthaburi 11000; tel. (2) 596-5060; fax (2) 591-0724; e-mail ir@thaicom.net; internet www.thaicom.net; f. 1991; fmrly Shin Satellite Public Co Ltd; operation and administration of satellite projects; cap. and res 15,582.6m., sales 7,188.3m. (2009); Chair. PARON ISRASENA; CEO ARAK CHONLATANON.

Thailand Carpet Manufacturing Co Ltd: 238 Thanon Vipavadee Rangsit, Don Muang, Bangkok 10210; tel. (2) 533-6393; fax (2) 533-6392; e-mail export@royalthai.com; internet www.royalthai.com; f. 1967; mfrs of rugs and carpets; cap. and res 858.7m., revenue

700.5m. (2009); Chair. CHALERMBHAND SRIVIKORN; Man. Dir CHARLIE JANGVIJITKUL.

Thailand Fishery Coldstorage Public Co Ltd: 592 Moo 2, Thanon Thayban, Amphur Muang, Samutprakarn 10280; tel. (2) 387-1171; fax (2) 387-2227; freezers and exporters of shrimps and squids; Chair. and Chief Exec. THAVESAKDI LAOTRAKUL; Pres. and Man. Dir YUWAREE AUKARNJANAWILAI; 885 employees.

Thonburi Automotive Assembly Plant Co Ltd: 62-74 Thanon Ratchadamnoen, Bowon Niwet, Phranakhon, Bangkok 10200; tel. (2) 622-3000; fax (2) 225-2893; internet www.thonburi.com; f. 1960; mfrs of motor vehicles; Man. Dir PARKPIEN WIRIYAPANT.

Tipco Asphalt Public Co Ltd: Tipco Tower, 118/1 Thanon Phra Ram VI, Samsennai, Phaya Thai, Bangkok 10400; tel. (2) 273-6000; fax (2) 279-2541; e-mail investors@tipcoasphalt.com; internet www.tipcoasphalt.com; f. 1979; mfrs of construction materials; cap. and res 2,853m., sales 14,089m. (2009); Chair. ANURAT TIAMTAN; CEO SOMCHIT SERTTHIN; 849 employees.

Toyota Motor Thailand Co Ltd: Moo 1, 186/1 Thanon Old Railway, Samrongtai, Phra Pradaeng, Samutprakarn 10130; tel. (2) 386-1000; fax (2) 384-1891; e-mail pr@toyota.co.th; internet www.toyota.co.th; f. 1962; mfrs and traders of motor vehicles; Chair. PRAMON SUTIVONG; Pres. KYOICHI TANADA; 13,500 employees.

TPI Polene Public Co Ltd: 26/56 Thanon Chan Tadmai, Tungmahamek, Sathorn, Bangkok 10120; tel. (2) 285-5090; fax (2) 213-1035; e-mail tpiplpr@tpipolene.co.th; internet www.tpipolene.co.th; f. 1978; mfrs and distributors of cement and LDPE; cap. and res 53,875.2m., sales 21,860m. (2009); Chair. and Dir VISITH NOIPHAN; CEO PRAYAD LEOPHAIRATANA; 4,500 employees.

Tuntex Textile (Thailand) Co Ltd: 55 Wave Place Bldg, 18th Floor, Room 5, Thanon Wireless, Lumpini, Patumwan, Bangkok 10330; tel. (2) 655-3300; fax (2) 655-3310; e-mail info@tuntextextile.com; internet www.tuntextextile.com; manufacture and distribution of polyester products; Chair. SHAN HUA SHEN; 2,000 employees.

Unicord Public Co Ltd: 404 Thanon Phaya Thai, Wangmai, Patumwan, Bangkok 10330; tel. (2) 216-0200; fax (2) 216-1468; f. 1977; mfrs of canned seafood; largest exporter of canned tuna in Asia; Chair. KAMCHORN SATHIRAKUL; Pres. PORNPHUN KONUNTAKIET; 6,800 employees.

Union Mosaic Industry Public Co Ltd (UMI): Chamnan Phenjati Business Center Bldg, 29th Floor, 65 Thanon Phra Ram IX, Huay Kwang, Bangkok 10310; tel. (2) 248-7007; fax (2) 248-7005; e-mail info@umi-tiles.com; internet www.umi-tiles.com; f. 1973; mfrs of tiles; cap. and res 1,087.9m., revenue 2,352.1m. (2009); Chair. Capt. SERANEE PHENJATI; Pres. PAWEENA LAOWIWATWONG; 1,555 employees.

United Flour Mill Public Co Ltd: UFM Bldg, 9th Floor, 177–179 205 Thanon Rajawong, Sumpuntawong, Bangkok 10100; tel. (2) 226-0680; fax (2) 224-5670; e-mail secretary@ufm.co.th; internet www.ufm.co.th; f. 1961; wheat flour milling; cap. and res 2,333.7m., revenue 4,054.8m. (2009); Chair. SUVIJ SUVARUCHIPHORN; Man. Dir PRACHA RAKSINCHAROENSAK; 288 employees.

Universal Starch Public Co Ltd: Thai Wah Tower, 21st–22nd Floors, 21/63–66 Thanon Sathorn Tai, Bangkok 10120; tel. (2) 285-0040; fax (2) 285-0269; e-mail starch@usc.co.th; internet www.usc.co.th; f. 1947; fmrly Thai Wah Public Co Ltd; mfrs of tapioca products; Chair. PHINYADA VIRIYA; Man. Dir THAWAN PHETLOLIAN; 1,375 employees.

Vanachai Group Public Co Ltd: 2/1 Thanon Pibulsongkram, Bangsue, Bangkok 10800; tel. (2) 585-4900; fax (2) 587-9556; e-mail vanachai@vanachai.com; internet www.vanachai.com; manufacturer of wood-based panels; cap. and res 5,431.4m., sales 7,411.7m. (2009); Chair. SOMPOP SAHAVAT; Man. Dir WANTHANA JAROENNARAWAT.

Vinythai Public Co Ltd: Green Tower, 14th Floor, 3656/41 Thanon Rama IV, Khet Klongtoey, Bangkok 10110; tel. (2) 240-2425; fax (2) 240-1375; e-mail varaiporn.p@vinythai.co.th; internet www.vinythai.co.th; production and distribution of chemicals; cap. and res 14,113.6m., sales 11,845m. (2009); Chair. Dr CHRISTIAN DE SLOOVER; Man. Dir GUENTHER WILHELM NADOLNY; 398 employees.

Wangkanai Group Co Ltd: 889 Thai CC Tower, 28th Floor, Thanon Sathorn Tai, Yannawa, Sathorn, Bankgok 10120; tel. (2) 210-0853; fax (2) 675-8336; e-mail wanginfo@wangkanai.co.th; internet www.wangkanai.co.th; f. 1975 as Wangkanai Sugar Co Ltd; holding co whose subsidiaries manufacture and market raw, refined, white and brown sugar; also conducts research and development work; Man. Dir TEERA NA WANGKANAI.

Wyncoast Industrial Park Public Co Ltd: 105 Moo 3, Thanon Bangna-Trad Km 52, Thakham, Bangpakong, Chachoengsao 24130; tel. (38) 573-161; fax (38) 573-215; e-mail info@wyncoast.com; internet www.wyncoast.com; f. 1985; fmrly Captronic International (Thailand) Public Co Ltd; mfr of computer monitors and printed circuit board assembly; cap. and res 137.5m., revenue 94.2m. (2009); Chair. JAK CHAMIKORN; CEO TIENCHAI DAWANWONG; 2,200 employees.

TRADE UNIONS

Confederation of Thai Labour (CTL): 25/59 Thanon Sukhumvit, Viphavill Village, Tambol Paknam, Amphur Muang, Samutprakarn, Bangkok 10270; tel. (2) 756-5346; fax (2) 755-2165; e-mail ctl_manas@hotmail.com; internet www.ctl.or.th; represents 44 labour unions; Pres. MANAS PHOSORN.

Labour Congress of Thailand (LCT): 420/393–394 Thippavan Village 1, Thanon Teparak, Samrong-Nua, Muang, Samutprakarn, Bangkok 10270; tel. and fax (2) 384-6789; e-mail lct_org@hotmail.com; f. 1978; represents 224 labour unions, four labour federations and approx. 140,000 mems; Pres. CHINCHOTE SAENGSANG; Gen. Sec. SAMAM THOMYA.

National Congress of Private Employees of Thailand (NPET): 142/6 Thanon Phrathoonam Phrakanong, Phrakanong, Klongtoey, Bangkok 10110; tel. and fax (2) 392-9955; represents 31 labour unions; Pres. BANJONG PORNPATTANANIKOM.

National Congress of Thai Labour (NCTL): 1614/876 Samutprakarn Community Housing Project, Sukhumvit Highway Km 30, Tai Baan, Muang, Samutprakarn, Bangkok 10280; tel. (2) 389-5134; fax (2) 385-8975; represents 171 unions; Pres. PANAS THAILUAN.

National Free Labour Union Congress (NFLUC): 277 Moo 3, Thanon Ratburana, Bangkok 10140; tel. (2) 427-6506; fax (2) 428-4543; represents 51 labour unions; Pres. ANUSSAKDI BOONYAPRANAI.

National Labour Congress (NLC): 586/248–250 Moo 2, Mooban City Village, Thanon Sukhumvit, Bang Phu Mai, Mueng, Samutprakarn, Bangkok 10280; tel. and fax (2) 709-9426; represents 41 labour unions; Pres. CHIN THAPPHLI.

Thai Trade Union Congress (TTUC): 420/393–394 Thippavan Village 1, Thanon Teparak, Tambol Samrong-nua, Amphur Muang, Samutprakarn, Bangkok 10270; tel. and fax (2) 384-0438; e-mail thai-tuc@hotmail.com; f. 1983; represents 172 unions; Pres. PANIT CHAROENPHAO.

Thailand Council of Industrial Labour (TCIL): 99 Moo 4, Thanon Sukhaphibarn 2, Khannayao, Bungkum, Bangkok; tel. (2) 517-0022; fax (2) 517-0628; represents 23 labour unions; Pres. TAVEE DEEYING.

Transport

RAILWAYS

Thailand has a railway network of 4,429 km, connecting Bangkok with Chiang Mai, Nong Khai, Ubon Ratchathani, Nam Tok and towns on the isthmus.

State Railway of Thailand: 1 Thanon Rong Muang, Rong Muang, Pathumwan, Bangkok 10330; tel. (2) 220-4567; fax (2) 225-3801; e-mail info@railway.co.th; internet www.railway.co.th; f. 1897; 4,429 km of track in 2007; responsible for licensing a 4,044-km passenger and freight rail system, above ground; Chair. TAWANRAT ORNSIRA; Gov. YUTHANA TUPCHAROEN.

Bangkok Mass Transit System Public Co Ltd: 1000 Thanon Phahonyothin, Chom Phon, Chatuchak, Bangkok 10900; tel. (2) 617-7300; fax (2) 617-7133; e-mail nuduan@bts.co.th; internet www.bts.co.th; f. 1992; responsible for the construction and management of the Skytrain, a two-line, 23.5-km elevated rail system, under the supervision of the Bangkok Metropolitan Area, the initial stage of which was opened in December 1999; Exec. Chair. and CEO KEEREE KANJANAPAS.

Mass Rapid Transit Authority of Thailand (MRTA): 175 Thanon Rama IX, Huay Kwang, Bangkok 10320; tel. (2) 612-2444; fax (2) 612-2436; e-mail pr@mrta.co.th; internet www.mrta.co.th; a 20-km subway system was opened in Bangkok in July 2004; as part of the planned extension of the mass rapid transit system, was charged with the construction of three new lines, totalling 91 km in length: 27-km Blue Line (Hua Lamphong–Bang Khae; Bang Sue–Tha Phra); 24-km Orange Line (Bang Kapi–Bang Bumru); and 40-km Purple Line (Bang Yai–Rat Burana); Chair. SUPOTH SUBLOM; Gov. CHUKIAT PHOTA-YANUVAT.

ROADS

The total length of the road network was an estimated 180,053 km in 2006. A network of toll roads has been introduced in Bangkok in an attempt to alleviate the city's severe congestion problems.

Bangkok Mass Transit Authority (BMTA): 131 Thanon Thiam Ruammit, Huay Kwang, Bangkok 10310; tel. (2) 246-0973; fax (2) 247-2189; e-mail webmaster@bmta.co.th; internet www.bmta.co.th; controls Bangkok's urban transport system; Chair. PIYAPAN CHAMPASUT; Dir and Sec. PINATE PUAPATANAKUL.

Department of Highways: Thanon Sri Ayudhya, Ratchathewi, Bangkok 10400; tel. (2) 354-6668; e-mail webmaster@doh.go.th; internet www.doh.go.th; Dir-Gen. VEERA RUANGSUKSRIWONG.

Department of Land Transport: 1032 Thanon Phaholyothin, Chatuchak, Bangkok 10900; tel. (2) 272-5671; fax (2) 272-5680; e-mail chairat@dlt.go.th; internet www.dlt.go.th; Dir-Gen. CHAIRAT SANGUANSUE.

Department of Rural Roads: 218/1, Thanon Phra Rama VI, Phaya Thai, Bangkok 10400; tel. (2) 299-4591; fax (2) 299-4606; e-mail webmaster@dor.go.th; internet www.dor.go.th; f. 2002; Dir-Gen. VICHARN KUNAKULSAWAS.

Expressway and Rapid Transit Authority of Thailand (ETA): 2380 Thanon Phaholyothin, Senanikhom, Chatuchak, Bangkok 10900; tel. (2) 579-5380; e-mail webmasters@eta.co.th; internet www.eta.co.th; f. 1972; Dir-Gen. PHACHOEN PHAIROJSAK.

SHIPPING

There is an extensive network of canals, providing transport for bulk goods. The port of Bangkok is an important shipping junction for South-East Asia, and consists of 37 berths for conventional and container vessels. At the end of 2009 the Thai merchant fleet (884 vessels) had a combined displacement totalling 2,526,100 grt.

Marine Department: 1278 Thanon Yotha, Talardnoi, Samphanthawong, Bangkok 10100; tel. (2) 233-1311; fax (2) 236-7148; e-mail marine@md.go.th; internet www.md.go.th; Dir-Gen. TAWALYARAT ONSIRA.

Port Authority of Thailand: 444 Thanon Tarua, Klongtoey, Bangkok 10110; tel. (2) 269-3000; fax (2) 249-0885; e-mail info@port.co.th; internet www.port.co.th; 18 berths at Bangkok Port, 12 berths at Laem Chabang Port; originally scheduled for transfer to private sector in 1999, but plans have been repeatedly delayed; Chair. CHALOR KOTCHARAT; Dir-Gen. SUNIDA SAKULRATTANA.

Principal Shipping Companies

Jutha Maritime Public Co Ltd: Mano Tower, 2nd Floor, 153 Soi 39, Thanon Sukhumvit, Wattana, Bangkok 10110; tel. (2) 260-0050; fax (2) 259-9825; e-mail office@jutha.co.th; internet www.jutha.co.th; services between Thailand, Malaysia, Korea, Japan and Viet Nam; Chair. Rear-Adm. CHANO PHENJATI; Man. Dir CHANET PHENJATI.

Precious Shipping Public Co Ltd: Cathay House, 7th Floor, 8/30 Thanon Sathorn Nua, Bangrak, Bangkok 10500; tel. (2) 696-8800; fax (2) 633-8460; e-mail psl@preciousshipping.com; internet www.preciousshipping.com; Chair. Adm. AMNARD CHANDANAMATTHA; Man. Dir HASHIM KHALID MOINUDDIN.

Regional Container Lines Public Co Ltd: Panjathani Tower, 30th Floor, 127/35 Thanon Ratchadaphisek, Chongnonsee Yannawa, Bangkok 10120; tel. (2) 296-1096; fax (2) 296-1098; e-mail rclbkk@rclgroup.com; internet www.rclgroup.com; Chair. KUA PHEK LONG; Pres. SUMATE TANTHUWANIT.

Thai International Maritime Enterprises Ltd: Sarasin Bldg, 5th Floor, 14 Thanon Surasak, Bangkok 10500; tel. (2) 236-8835; services from Bangkok to Japan; Chair. and Man. Dir SUN SUNDISAMRIT.

Thai Maritime Navigation Co Ltd: Manorom Bldg, 15th Floor, 51 Thanon Rama IV, Klongtoey, Bangkok 10110; tel. (2) 672-8690; fax (2) 249-0108; e-mail tmn@tmn.co.th; internet www.tmn.co.th; f. 1940; state-owned; services from Bangkok to Japan, the USA, Europe and ASEAN countries; Chair. NIPHON CHAKSUDUL; Sec.-Gen. SUWAPHAT SUVANNAKIJBORIHAN.

Thai Mercantile Marine Ltd: 599/1 Thanon Chua Phloeng, Klongtoey, Bangkok 10110; tel. (2) 240-2582; fax (2) 249-5656; e-mail tmmbkk@asiaaccess.net.th; f. 1967; services between Japan and Thailand; Chair. SUTHAM TANPHAIBUL; Man. Dir TANAN TANPHAIBUL.

Thoresen Thai Agencies Public Co Ltd: 26/26–27 Orakarn Bldg, 8th Floor, Soi Chidlom, Thanon Ploenchit, Kwang Lumpinee, Khet Pathumwan, Bangkok 10330; tel. (2) 254-8437; fax (2) 655-5631; e-mail tta@thoresen.com; internet www.thoresen.com; shipowner, liner operator, shipping agent (in Thailand and Viet Nam), ship repairs, offshore and diving services; Chair. M. R. CHANDRAM S. CHANDRATAT; Man. Dir M. L. CHANDCHUTHA CHANDRATAT.

Unithai Group: 11th Floor, 25 Alma Link Bldg, Soi Chidlom, Thanon Ploenchit, Pathumwan, Bangkok 10330; tel. (2) 254-8400; fax (2) 254-8424; e-mail paporn.t@unithai.com; internet www.unithai.com; regular containerized/break-bulk services to Europe, Africa and Far East; also bulk shipping/chartering; Chair. SIVAVONG CHANGKASIRI; CEO NARONG BOONYASAQUAN.

CIVIL AVIATION

Bangkok, Chiang Mai, Chiang Rai, Hat Yai, Phuket and Surat Thani airports are of international standard. U-Tapao is an alternative airport. Suvarnabhumi International Airport, a new facility located south-east of Bangkok, opened in September 2006, with an eventual capacity of 45m. passengers a year. Bangkok's former international airport at Don Muang was subsequently reopened to domestic commercial flights.

Airports of Thailand Public Co Ltd (AOT): 333 Thanon Cherdwutagard, Don Muang, Bangkok 10210; tel. (2) 535-1111; fax (2) 535-4061; e-mail aotpr@airportthai.co.th; internet www.airportthai.co.th; f. 1998; develops and manages airports; Chair. PIYAPAN CHAMPASUT; Pres. SERIRAT PRASUTANOND.

Department of Civil Aviation: 71 Soi Ngarmduplee, Thanon Rama IV, Tung Mahamek, Sathorn District, Bangkok 10120; tel. (2) 287-0320; fax (2) 286-3373; e-mail dca@aviation.go.th; internet www.aviation.go.th; f. 1963; Dir-Gen. VUTICHAI SINGHAMANY.

Bangkok Airways: 99 Moo 14, Thanon Vibhavadi Rangsit, Chom Phon, Chatuchak, Bangkok 10900; tel. (2) 270-6699; fax (2) 265-5522; e-mail reservation@bangkokair.com; internet www.bangkokair.com; f. 1968; est. as Sahakol Air; present name adopted 1989; privately owned; scheduled and charter passenger services to 8 domestic and 8 international destinations; Pres. PUTTIPONG PRASARTTONG-OSOTH; CEO Dr PRASERT PRASARTTONG-OSOTH.

Nok Air: 183 Rajanakarn Bldg, 17th Floor, Thanon Sathorn Tai, Yannawa, Bangkok 10120; tel. (2) 627-2000; fax (2) 627-9830; e-mail public.info@thaiairways.co.th; internet www.nokair.com; f. 2004; 39%-owned by Thai Airways International Public Co Ltd; flights to six domestic destinations; CEO PATEE SARASIN.

Nok Mini Airlines: 19/18–19 Royal City Ave, Blk A, Thanon Phra Ram 9, Bangkapi, Huay Kwang, Bangkok 10310; tel. (2) 641-4190; fax (2) 641-4807; e-mail info@sga.aero; internet www.nokmini.com; f. 2002; est. as SGA Airlines; rebranded 2009; scheduled and chartered domestic services; Chair. Capt. THOM SIRISANT; Pres. JAIN CHARNNARONG.

One-Two-Go: UM Tower Bldg, 21st Floor, 9/211 Thanon Ramkhamhaeng, Suanluang, Bangkok 10250; tel. (2) 229-4260; fax (2) 229-4278; e-mail customer_relation@orient-thai.com; internet www.flyorientthai.com; f. 2003; subsidiary of Orient Thai Airlines; low-cost domestic flights; Chair. UDOM TANTIPRASONGCHAI; CEO MANASSANANT TANTIPRASONGCHAI.

Orient Thai Airlines: UM Tower Bldg, 21st Floor, 9/211 Thanon Ramkhamhaeng, Suanluang, Bangkok 10250; tel. (2) 229-4260; fax (2) 229-4278; e-mail customer_relation@orient-thai.com; internet www.flyorientthai.com; f. 1993; est. as Orient Express Air; domestic and international flights; Chair. UDOM TANTIPRASONGCHAI; CEO MANASSANANT TANTIPRASONGCHAI.

Phuket Air: 1168/71, 25th Floor, Lumpini Tower Bldg, Thanon Rama IV, Tungmahamek, Bangkok 10120; tel. (62) 679-8999; fax (62) 285-6480; e-mail info@phuketairlines.com; internet www.phuketairlines.com; f. 1999; international charter services; Pres. VIKROM AISIRI.

Thai AirAsia Co Ltd: Suvarnabhumi Int. Airport, 999 Moo 1, Departure Hall, 4th Floor, Rm T4-B01/01-04, Bangplee, Samutprakarn 10540; internet www.airasia.com; f. 2004; 50% owned by Asia Aviation, 49% owned by Air Asia Sdn Bhd (Malaysia); low-cost domestic flights; Chair. ARAK CHOLTANON; CEO TASSAPON BIJLEVELD.

Thai Airways International Public Co Ltd (THAI): 89 Thanon Vibhavadi Rangsit, Bangkok 10900; tel. (2) 545-3321; fax (2) 545-3322; e-mail public.info@thaiairways.co.th; internet www.thaiair.com; f. 1960; 51% owned by Ministry of Finance; shares listed in July 1991, began trading in July 1992; merged with Thai Airways Co in 1988; domestic services from Bangkok to 20 cities; international services to over 50 destinations in Asia, Australasia, Europe and North America; Chair. AMPON KITTIAMPON; Pres. PIYASVASTI AMRANAND.

Tourism

Thailand is a popular tourist destination, noted for its temples, palaces, beaches and islands. Tourist arrivals were provisionally estimated to total 15.8m. in 2010. Revenue from tourism (including passenger transport) was an estimated US $21,980m. in 2008.

Tourism Authority of Thailand (TAT): 1600 Thanon Phetchaburi Tat Mai, Makkasan, Ratchathewi, Bangkok 10400; tel. (2) 250-5500; fax (2) 250-5511; e-mail center@tat.or.th; internet www.tourismthailand.org; f. 1960; Gov. SURAPHON SVETASRENI.

Tourism Council of Thailand: 16th floor, 1600 Thanon Phetchaburi Tat Mai, Makkasan, Ratchathewi, Bangkok 10400; e-mail info@thailandtourismcouncil.org; internet www.thailandtourismcouncil.org; co-ordinates policy and projects between private sector and govt; membership comprises more than 60 tourism asscns; Pres. PIYAMAN TEJAPAIBUL.

Defence

As assessed at November 2010, the total strength of the armed forces was 305,860: army 190,000 (including an estimated 70,000 conscripts), navy 69,860 (25,849 conscripts), air force an estimated

46,000. Paramilitary forces numbered approximately 113,700, including a National Security Volunteer Corps of 45,000. Military service lasts for two years between the ages of 21 and 30 and is compulsory.

Defence Expenditure: Budget for 2011 was estimated at 170,000m. baht.

Chief of the Defence Forces: Gen. SONGKITTI JAGGABATARA.

Chief of Staff of the Royal Thai Armed Forces: Gen. DAPONG RATANASUWAN.

Commander-in-Chief of the Army: Gen. PRAYUTH CHAN-OCHA.

Commander-in-Chief of the Air Force: Air Chief Marshal ITTHAPORN SUBHAWONG.

Commander-in-Chief of the Navy: Adm. KAMTHORN PHUMPIRUN.

Education

Education in Thailand is free and compulsory for nine years, following the implementation of the Compulsory Education Act of 2003, which extended the period from six years. In 2002 12 years of free basic education was granted to all students throughout the country, and in 2004 this was extended to 14 years, with the two years of pre-primary schooling henceforth also being offered free to all.

There are four types of schools: (i) Government schools established and maintained by government funds; (ii) Local schools, which are usually financed by the Government; however, if they are founded by the people of the district, funds collected from the public may be used in supporting such schools; (iii) Municipal schools, a type of primary school financed and supervised by the municipality; (iv) Private schools set up and owned by private individuals under the provisions of the 1954 Private Schools Act. The National Scheme of Education provides for education on four levels: (i) Pre-School Education (nursery and kindergarten), which is not compulsory; (ii) Primary Education; (iii) Secondary Education; (iv) Higher Education.

Pre-primary education begins at three years and enrolment was equivalent to 80% of the relevant age-group (males 80%, females 80%) in 2007/08. Primary education starts at the age of six and lasts for six years. In 2008/09 enrolment at primary level included 90% (males 91%, females 89%) of the relevant age-group. Secondary education, which also lasts for six years, is divided into two three-year cycles. Enrolment at secondary schools in 2008/09 included 72% (males 68%, females 77%) of students in the relevant age-group. There are numerous public and private universities in Thailand, including 41 Rajabhat Universities (formerly teacher-training colleges) and nine branches of the Rajamangala University of Technology. In 2006 enrolment in tertiary institutions was equivalent to 46% (males 44%, females 47%) of students in the relevant age-group. According to preliminary figures, government expenditure on education amounted to 397,800m. baht (20.2% of total government expenditure) in 2008/09.

Bibliography

General

Askew, Marc. *Bangkok: Place, Practice and Representation.* London, Routledge, 2002.

Connors, Michael Kelly. *Democracy and National Identity in Thailand.* London, RoutledgeCurzon, 2002.

Curran, S. R. *Shifting Boundaries, Transforming Lives—Globalization, Gender and Family Dynamics in Thailand.* Princeton, NJ, Princeton University Press, 2009.

Dearden, Phillip (Ed.). *Environmental Protection and Rural Development in Thailand.* Bangkok, White Lotus, 2002.

Delang, Claudio. *Living at the Edge of Thai Society: The Karen in the Highlands of Northern Thailand.* London, RoutledgeCurzon, 2003.

Fordham, Graham. *A New Look at Thai Aids: Perspectives from the Margin.* New York, NY, Berghahn Books, 2004.

Handley, Paul. *The King Never Smiles: A Biography of Thailand's Bhumibol Adulyadej.* New Haven, CT, Yale University Press, 2006.

Jeffrey, Leslie Ann. *Sex and Borders: Gender, National Identity, and Prostitution Policy in Thailand.* Vancouver, BC, University of British Columbia Press, 2002.

Mackenzie, Rory. *New Buddhist Movements in Thailand: Toward an Understanding of Wat Phra Dhammakaya and Santi Asoke.* Abingdon, Routledge, 2006.

Nguyen, Thang D. *The Thai Challenge: Unity, Stability and Democracy in Times of Uncertainty.* New York, Nova Science Publishers, 2008.

Peleggi, Maurizio. *Thailand: The Worldly Kingdom.* London, Reaktion Books, 2007.

Tanabe, Shigeharu, and Keyes, Charles F. (Eds). *Cultural Crisis and Social Memory: Modernity and Identity in Thailand and Laos.* London, RoutledgeCurzon, 2002.

History

Baker, Christopher, and Phongpaichit, Pasuk. *History of Thailand.* Cambridge, Cambridge University Press, 2005.

Connors, Michael Kelly. *Democracy and National Identity in Thailand.* Copenhagen, Nordic Institute of Asian Studies, 2007.

Fineman, Daniel Mark. *A Special Relationship: The United States and Military Government in Thailand, 1947–1958.* Honolulu, HI, University of Hawaii Press, 1997.

Haberkorn, Tyrell. *Revolution Interrupted: Farmers, Students, Law, and Violence in Northern Thailand.* Madison, WI, University of Wisconsin Press, 2011.

Haseman, John B. *The Thai Resistance Movement During World War II.* Seattle, WA, University of Washington Press, 2002.

Jackson, Peter A. *Buddhadasa: Theravada Buddhism and Modernist Reform in Thailand.* Seattle, WA, University of Washington Press, 2003.

Jayanama, Direk. *Thailand and World War Two.* Chiang Mai, Silkworm Books, 2008.

LeBlanc, Marcel (Ed.). *History of Siam in 1688.* Seattle, WA, University of Washington Press, 2004.

London, Ellen. *Thailand Condensed: 2000 Years of History and Culture.* Singapore, Marshall Cavendish Editions, 2008.

Mead, Kullada Kesboonchoo. *The Rise and Decline of Thai Absolutism.* London, RoutledgeCurzon, 2004.

Montreevat, Sakulrat (Ed.). *Corporate Governance in Thailand.* Singapore, Institute of Southeast Asian Studies, 2006.

Rooney, Dawn F. *Ancient Sukhothai: Thailand's Cultural Heritage.* Bangkok, River Books, 2008.

Terwiel, B. J. *A History of Modern Thailand 1767–1942.* St Lucia, University of Queensland Press, 1983.

Wyatt, David K. *Thailand: A Short History.* New Haven, CT, Yale University Press, 1984.

Economy and Politics

Abuza, Zachary. *A Conspiracy of Silence: the Insurgency in Southern Thailand.* Washington, DC, United States Institute of Peace Press, 2007.

Andrews, Tim, and Siengthai, Sununta (Eds). *The Changing Face of Management in Thailand.* Abingdon, Routledge, 2009.

Arghiros, Daniel. *Democracy, Development and Decentralization in Provincial Thailand.* London, Curzon Press, 2001.

Askew, Marc. *Conspiracy, Politics, and a Disorderly Border: The Struggle to Comprehend Insurgency in Thailand's Deep South.* Washington, DC, East-West Center Washington; Singapore, Institute of Southeast Asian Studies, 2007.

Performing Political Identity: The Democrat Party in Southern Thailand. Chiang Mai, Silkworm Books, 2008.

Baker, Chris, and Phongpaichit, Pasuk (Eds). *Thai Capital: After the 1997 Crisis.* Singapore, Institute of Southeast Asian Studies, 2008.

Barbier, Edward B., and Sathirathai, Suthawan (Eds). *Shrimp Farming and Mangrove Loss in Thailand.* Cheltenham, Edward Elgar Publishing, 2004.

Brown, Andrew. *Labour, Politics and the State in Industrialising Thailand.* London, RoutledgeCurzon, 2003.

Chachavalpongpun, Pavin. *Reinventing Thailand: Thaksin and his Foreign Policy.* Singapore, Institute of Southeast Asian Studies, 2010.

Chalk, Peter. *The Malay Muslim Insurgency in Southern Thailand—Understanding the Conflict's Evolving Dynamic.* Santa Monica, RAND Corpn, 2008.

Chaloemtiarana, Thak. *Thailand: The Politics of Despotic Paternalism.* Ithaca, NY, Southeast Asia Program Publications, Cornell University, 2007.

Connors, Michael. *Contemporary Thailand: Politics, Culture, Rights.* London, Zed Books, 2009.

Dixon, Chris. *The Thai Economy: Uneven Development and Internationalisation.* London, Routledge, 1999.

Doner, Richard F. *The Politics of Uneven Development: Thailand's Economic Growth in Comparative Perspective.* Cambridge, Cambridge University Press, 2009.

Funston, John (Ed.) *Divided Over Thaksin: Thailand's Coup and Problematic Transition.* Singapore, Institute of Southeast Asian Studies, 2009.

Glassman, Jim. *Thailand at the Margins: Internationalization of the State and the Transformation of Labour.* Oxford, Oxford University Press, 2004.

Hewison, Kevin. *The Development of Capital and the Role of the State in Thailand.* New Haven, CT, Yale University Press, 1988.

Power and Politics in Thailand. Manila, Journal of Contemporary Asia Publishers, 1990.

Political Change in Thailand: Democracy and Participation. London and New York, Routledge, 1997.

Hogue, Cavan (Ed.). *Thailand's Economic Recovery.* Singapore, Institute of Southeast Asian Studies, 2005.

Inagawa, Kazuki. *Women and Politics in Thailand: Continuity and Change.* Copenhagen, Nordic Institute of Asian Studies, 2008.

Intarakumnerd, Patarapong, and Lecler, Yveline (Eds). *Sustainability of Thailand's Competitiveness: The Policy Challenges.* Singapore, Institute of Southeast Asian Studies, 2010.

Ivarsson, Soren, and Isager, Lotte (Eds). *Saying the Unsayable: Monarchy and Democracy in Thailand.* Singapore, Institute of Southeast Asian Studies, 2010.

Jonsson, Hjorleifur. *Mien Relations: Mountain People and State Control in Thailand.* Ithaca, NY, Cornell University Press, 2005.

Kiatpongsan, Chaiyakorn. *The EU-Thailand Relations: Tracing the Patterns of New Bilateralism.* Amsterdam, Amsterdam University Press, 2010.

McCargo, Duncan. *Politics and the Press in Thailand: Media Machinations.* London, Routledge, 2000.

McCargo, Duncan (Ed.). *Reforming Thai Politics.* Singapore, Institute of Southeast Asian Studies, 2002.

Rethinking Thailand's Southern Violence. Singapore, Singapore University Press, 2007.

McVey, Ruth T. (Ed.). *Money and Power in Provincial Thailand.* Singapore, Institute of Southeast Asian Studies, 2000.

Montesano, Michael J., and Jory, Patrick (Eds). *Thai South and Malay North: Ethnic Interactions on a Plural Peninsula.* Singapore, Singapore University Press, 2008.

Nishizaki, Yoshinori. *Political Authority and Provincial Identity in Thailand: The Making of Banharn-buri.* Ithaca, NY, Southeast Asia Program Publications, Cornell University, 2011.

Ockey, James. *Making Democracy: Leadership, Class, Gender, and Political Participation in Thailand.* Honolulu, HI, University of Hawaii Press, 2004.

Phatharathananunth, Somchai. *Civil Society and Democratization: Social Movements in Northeast Thailand.* Honolulu, HI, University of Hawaii Press, 2006.

Phongpaichit, Pasuk, and Baker, Chris. *Thailand: Economy and Politics.* Kuala Lumpur, Oxford University Press, 1996.

Thailand's Boom and Bust. Chiang Mai, Silkworm Books, 1998.

Thailand's Crisis. Chiang Mai, Silkworm Books, 2000.

Thaksin: The Business of Politics in Thailand. Copenhagen, Nordic Institute of Asian Studies, 2004.

Phongpaichit, Pasuk, and Piriyarangsan, Sungsidh. *Corruption and Democracy in Thailand.* Chiang Mai, Silkworm Books, 1998.

Pian, Kobkua Suwannathat. *Kings, Country and Constitutions: Thailand's Political Development 1932–2000.* London, Routledge-Curzon, 2002.

Ramstetter, Eric D., and Sjöholm, Fredrik (Eds). *Multinational Corporations in Indonesia and Thailand: Wages, Productivity and Exports.* Basingstoke, Palgrave Macmillan, 2006.

Streckfuss, David. *Truth on Trial in Thailand: Defamation, Treason and Lèse-Majesté.* Abingdon, Routledge, 2009.

Swan, William L. *Japan's Economic Relations with Thailand: the Rise to 'Top Trader'.* Bangkok, White Lotus Press, 2009.

Tomforde, Maren. *The Hmong Mountains: Cultural Spatiality of the Hmong in Northern Thailand.* Münster, Lit, 2006.

Warr, Peter. *Thailand Beyond the Crisis.* London, Routledge, 2002.

Yoshifumi, Tamada. *Myths and Realities: The Democratization of Thai Politics.* Melbourne, Trans Pacific Press, 2008.

Zebioli, Randle C. *Thailand: Economic, Political and Social Issues.* New York, Nova Science Publishers, 2008.

TIMOR-LESTE

(EAST TIMOR)

Physical and Social Geography

PHYSICAL FEATURES AND CLIMATE

The Democratic Republic of Timor-Leste was known as East Timor until its accession to independence in 2002. It is styled Timor Loro Sa'e (Timor of the rising sun) in the principal indigenous language, Tetum. The country occupies the eastern half of the island of Timor, which lies off the north coast of Western Australia and extends between 8° 15' and 10° 30' S and 123° 20' and 127° 10' E. The western half of the island is Indonesian territory. In addition to the eastern half of Timor island, the territory also includes an enclave around Oecusse (Oekussi) Ambeno on the north-west coast of the island, and the islands of Ataúro (Pulo Cambing) and Jaco (Pulo Jako). Timor-Leste occupies an area of 14,609 sq km (5,641 sq miles).

Very irregular, rugged hills and mountains form the core of the island, which is split by a longitudinal series of depressions and by small, discontinuous plateaux. There are many extinct volcanoes. Some good soils have been formed from the older volcanic rock, but the dominant soil consists of soft clay, which does not support heavy vegetation.

Timor's climate is dominated by intense monsoon rain, succeeded by a pronounced dry season. The north coast of the island has a brief rainy season from December to February; the south coast a double rainy season from December to June, with a respite in March. The mountainous spine of the island experiences heavy rains that feed torrential floods. However, every few years the climatic phenomenon known as El Niño is likely to subject the island to serious drought.

POPULATION AND RESOURCES

The indigenous peoples are of mixed origin. The aboriginal population is composed mainly of Melanesians, who probably resulted from the fusion of a basic Papuan stock with immigrant Asian elements. Evidence exists, also, of an Australoid strain. These peoples were displaced from the more favoured areas by subsequent arrivals from Indonesia, while communities of Chinese and other Asians gained control of much of the commerce conducted on the island. In a UN registration process completed in June 2001, the population of East Timor totalled 737,811, about 90% of whom lived in rural areas. More than 250,000 people were displaced by the conflict of 1999. In mid-2001 more than 113,000 remained in refugee camps in neighbouring West Timor. By the end of 2005 most had returned to Timor-Leste, although approximately 28,000 had decided instead to remain permanently in Indonesia. According to the national census conducted on 31 July 2004, the total population had risen to 923,198, increasing to 1,066,409 at the census of 11 July 2010. The population was estimated by the UN at 1,153,835 in mid-2011, when population density reached 79.0 per sq km. The population of the capital, Dili, totalled 234,026 at the census of 2010, in comparison with an estimated 48,731 in mid-2003.

NATURAL RESOURCES

Although onshore mineral deposits are limited, the waters off Timor-Leste's southern coasts contain significant resources. In the 1990s extensive natural gas fields were discovered in and around the Timor Gap zone, and in 2001 petroleum reserves in the area were estimated by some sources to total a potential 500m. barrels. The Timor Sea Arrangement, pertaining to the sharing of petroleum and gas royalties with Australia, was signed in 2002, and in the following year a US company was granted permission to develop the Bayu-Undan liquefied natural gas field in the Timor Sea. Some deposits of high-grade marble remain. Other resources include silver, manganese, gold, copper, chromite and gypsum.

History

ROBERT CRIBB

Revised by GEOFFREY C. GUNN

Only fragments are known of the early history of Timor. The island's name means 'east' and for at least a millennium Timor appears to have remained on the eastern fringe of the Indonesian commercial world, a source of sandalwood for trade to India and China and of slaves for markets in the archipelago. However, Indian and Islamic cultural influences on Timor were meagre, and there is no evidence of literacy or of large-scale state formation before 1600. Rather, it would appear that the island was divided among a fluctuating number of small polities headed by powerful chiefs, later known as *liurai*. Early European accounts report that these polities were grouped into two federations, generally referred to as the Wehale (Belu) and the Sonbai. While the nature of these federations is not clear, they certainly did not constitute co-ordinated political units. Timor's sandalwood attracted Portuguese interest in the mid-16th century, but the Portuguese preferred to establish their bases in the relative security of neighbouring Solor and Larantuka, rather than on the Timor coast itself. During the next century, however, Dominican missionaries converted many *liurai* to Catholicism, and the coastal regions of the island came increasingly under the domination of the so-called Topasses, or 'Black Portuguese'. The Topasses were descendants of Portuguese and other Western and Asian soldiers who married local women; they were rough adventurers who soon established a sphere of influence in western Timor. In the 1640s the Portuguese authorities attempted to assert control over the island by constructing a fort at Kupang at the western end of the island. This fort was no sooner constructed than it was seized in 1653 by the Dutch East Indies Company, which named it Castle Concordia. However, as Topass power grew under the rival de Hornay and da Costa families, the Dutch were unable to expand their power beyond the environs of Kupang. Portuguese influence in the region increased with the arrival of Catholic refugees from Makassar in Sulawesi, which the Dutch had conquered in 1660, but Timor itself remained firmly under the control of the Topasses. Successive Topass leaders received formal appointment as governors of the island from the Governor-General in Goa, and occasionally paid tax or tribute to the Portuguese crown from proceeds of trade in sandalwood, slaves, beeswax, gold and horses. In 1702 the Portuguese shifted their headquarters from Larantuka to Lifau, on the northern coast of west Timor, and appointed outsiders as governors. These governors led a miserable existence, besieged by the Topasses and harassed by the Dominicans, until 1769 when Governor António de Menezes moved his office to what was then the small settlement of Dili, further east along the coast. The Dutch, meanwhile, defeated a Topass attack on Kupang in 1749 and began slowly to expand their hegemony over the western part of the island, although they were never able to subdue the Topass strongholds around Lifau and in the inland region of Noimuti.

For about a century, neither colonial power did any more than continue to exploit the traditional trade of the island. However, from the mid-19th century, the development of modern colonialism and the fear of losing their colonies to newer, more dynamic colonial powers led both the Portuguese and the Dutch to begin to develop the island. The Portuguese began a programme of road-building, which enabled them to exercise closer control both of the *liurai* and of the general population. Coffee plantations were established, and a poll tax was imposed on all Timorese to encourage the growing of cash crops. Eventually, the authority of the *liurai* was formally abolished, although they remained powerful local figures. In 1859 the Portuguese and the Dutch agreed to consolidate their territorial holdings, the Portuguese giving up Larantuka and outposts on other islands in exchange for the establishment of demarcated borders on Timor itself. Under a further treaty, in 1902 the two powers exchanged several small territories in the interior for the sake of a neater border, although the area around Lifau remained as a Portuguese enclave on the north coast, with the name Oecusse (Oekussi). Portugal's interference with the powers of the *liurai* led to a revolt in 1910–12 under Dom Boaventura, but the Timorese were defeated with the assistance of troops sent from Mozambique.

Portugal's cultural influence on East Timor was relatively limited. Although there was an official policy of encouragement of the adoption of Portuguese culture and Catholicism, the colonial authorities were often suspicious of the Catholic Church, and missionaries were banned from the colony for 40 years from 1834. As for general education, the colonial budget was minimal, and few funds were available for schooling. In consequence, even in 1950 adult literacy in East Timor was estimated at less than 5%, while less than 0.5% of the indigenous population was classified as *civilizado*, that is, speaking Portuguese and having an income sufficient to maintain a 'civilized' lifestyle. In addition to the Portuguese administrators, the colonial élite included other Europeans, Chinese and mestizo (mixed race). Portugal declared its neutrality at the start of the Second World War, and apprehension quickly grew in Australia and the Netherlands Indies that the Portuguese authorities in East Timor might accept a Japanese presence in the territory, much as the Vichy French authorities had allowed the Japanese access to French Indo-China. To forestall this possibility, Australia landed troops in Dili in mid-December 1941, despite Portuguese objections. These troops were not numerous enough to resist Japanese landings in mid-February 1942, but they retreated into the interior and undertook highly effective guerrilla warfare until they were evacuated in January 1943. The Japanese occupation appears to have been a very difficult time for the Timorese, partly because of the guerrilla war and Allied and Japanese bombing, and partly because the impoverished territory was cut off from supplies of cloth and other consumer goods.

PRESSURES FOR DECOLONIZATION

By the end of the Second World War in 1945, Portugal's continued tenure of East Timor was by no means assured. Indonesian nationalists considered, and then rejected, the possibility of claiming the territory as a part of the new Indonesian Republic. More seriously, Australia proposed taking over the territory, perhaps with a UN mandate, to ensure that the island could serve as a base for a more effective forward line of defence in the event of another attack from the north. It appeared that Portugal was able to stave off the Australian threat only by negotiating its intention to return to East Timor in exchange for access by the North Atlantic Treaty Organization (NATO) to the Azores, a Portuguese possession strategically located in the North Atlantic. During the 1950s, however, Portugal came under more general pressure to decolonize East Timor. Such pressure even delayed the country's entry into the UN in 1956. In 1951 Portugal declared East Timor, along with its other colonies, to be an overseas province, the subjects of which had the same (limited) political rights as metropolitan Portuguese. However, the UN continued to consider the former colonies as non-self-governing territories. Whereas Portugal's African territories seemed destined for eventual independence, its three small Asian colonies, including East Timor, all appeared likely to be absorbed by their larger neighbours. India occupied Goa in 1961, and in 1968 the People's Republic of China forced Portugal to acknowledge Macao as Chinese territory under Portuguese administration. Indonesian leaders appear to have assumed that East Timor would eventually be absorbed into Indonesia, but until 1968 Indonesia took no action to claim the territory, the Indonesian Government being occupied with the pursuit and consolidation of the archipelago's claim to formerly Dutch West New Guinea. However, Indonesian intelligence forces may have sponsored a brief rebellion in the territory in 1959 and a Government-in-exile shortly afterwards.

In April 1974, however, the future of East Timor was abruptly placed on the international political agenda following a coup by the armed forces in Lisbon, Portugal. The new Portuguese Government removed political restrictions and foreshadowed major political changes, which appeared to include the possibility of independence, with regard to the country's colonies. Within a month, two new Timorese political parties had emerged: the União Democrática Timorense (UDT, Timorese Democratic Union), which was led by plantation owners and senior officials from the Portuguese administration, advocated democratization and eventual independence from Portugal, while the Associação Social Democrática Timorense (Timorese Social Democratic Association), which drew its membership from among younger professionals and intellectuals, argued for a more rapid transition to independence and for more extensive social reforms. A third party, the Associação Popular Democrática Timorense (Apodeti, Timorese Popular Democratic Association), which appears to have been sponsored from the outset by Indonesian intelligence organizations, proposed integration with Indonesia. The UDT was initially the most popular of the parties, but during 1974 it gradually lost support to the Associação Social Democrática Timorense, which adopted an increasingly radical profile. In September 1974 the latter renamed itself Frente Revolucionária do Timor Leste Independente (Fretilin, Revolutionary Front for an Independent East Timor) and claimed to be the sole representative of the East Timorese people.

However, the assumption that East Timor's natural destiny was absorption by Indonesia remained dominant throughout the international community: Portugal was preoccupied with internal political difficulties and with the decolonization of its African colonies, and other international powers had no natural interest in the territory, while the Australian Government believed that East Timor was too small and too poor for independence. In June 1974 the Indonesian Minister of Foreign Affairs formally stated that Indonesia respected East Timor's right to independence and had no intention of taking over the territory. However, the growing popularity and leftward political shift of Fretilin added political weight to the arguments of Indonesian military and intelligence groups already in favour of annexation. Furthermore, less than a decade earlier, the Indonesian military had violently suppressed the Indonesian Communist Party, and in 1974 communist forces in Indo-China were clearly gaining influence. Under these circumstances, the Indonesian military feared that Fretilin would seek to establish a communist regime in East Timor and that such a regime would provide a base for 'subversion' in Indonesia itself. It appears that in about July 1974, therefore, sections of the Indonesian military intelligence initiated what became known as 'Operation Komodo', a broad-based strategy intended to secure the integration of East Timor into Indonesia. This strategy included the provision of funding and logistical assistance for supporters of integration, the promotion of the perception that East Timor was incapable of managing its own independence and the initiation of thinly concealed preparations for armed intervention in the territory.

In January 1975 local Portuguese officials, concerned by Indonesia's shift away from the acceptance of East Timorese independence, persuaded Fretilin and the UDT to form a coalition as the basis for a national transitional government to oversee the territory's passage to independence. From March local elections were held in several areas, most of which were won by Fretilin supporters; the colonial authorities tentatively scheduled the territory's accession to independence for the end of 1976. However, these arrangements had not been ratified by the Portuguese metropolitan Government, which called a conference in Macao in May 1975 to discuss the decolonization of East Timor. Fretilin declined to attend the conference, apparently because its leaders regarded decolonization as a process that should be led from within East Timor itself, rather than by Portugal, and because the movement objected to the inclusion of Apodeti in the negotiations. At about this time, Indonesian intelligence apparently warned UDT leaders that Indonesia would invade East Timor in order to prevent 'communist' Fretilin from coming to power. The UDT responded first by pulling out of the coalition with Fretilin in May and then by staging a coup in Dili on 11 August, with the assistance of the police force. The Portuguese Governor, Col Mário Lemos Pires, was under official instructions not to intervene and subsequently withdrew to the offshore island of Ataúro. However, Fretilin sympathizers in the local army units launched a counter-attack, retaking Dili by 27 August and driving the remaining UDT forces across the border into Indonesian-controlled West Timor by the last week of September. From among the somewhat disorganized collection of East Timorese parties and individuals displaced by Fretilin, Indonesian intelligence then assembled a coalition to demand integration. Meanwhile, Indonesian special forces, disguised as anti-Fretilin guerrillas, began to move into the territory, capturing the border town of Batugade on 8 October. However, difficult terrain and determined resistance by Fretilin forces, who had seized some NATO weaponry from the Portuguese, meant that Indonesian progress was slow. Only in late November, after the fall of the town of Atabae, did Fretilin conclude that Indonesian conquest was likely. On 28 November, in an attempt to galvanize domestic and international support, Fretilin declared East Timor's independence as the Democratic Republic of East Timor, with Francisco Xavier do Amaral as President. Indonesia responded with a naval and airborne attack on Dili on 7 December. The attack took place one day after the departure from Jakarta of the US President, Gerald Ford, who had been on an official visit to Indonesia. The US President and the Secretary of State, Henry Kissinger, were subsequently acknowledged to have given approval to the Indonesian invasion. The operation was officially claimed to have been the work of East Timorese opposed to Fretilin, assisted by Indonesian 'volunteers'; however, the invasion was in fact carried out by regular marines and troops from Indonesia's élite strategic reserve (KOSTRAD). In the period during and after the capture of Dili, Indonesian troops killed several hundred East Timorese civilians suspected of offering resistance or supporting Fretilin, and this pattern was repeated on a smaller scale as the Indonesian troops fanned out across the territory to take other centres. On 17 December Indonesia sponsored a 'provisional Government' of East Timor led by Apodeti and a number of UDT leaders, with Arnaldo dos Reis Araújo as acting Governor. In May 1976 a 'People's Assembly' of 37 specially selected delegates formally petitioned Indonesia for integration, and on 17 July President Suharto of Indonesia formally declared the territory as the country's 27th province.

INDONESIAN RULE AND EAST TIMORESE RESISTANCE

Many observers expected that Indonesia would quickly achieve full control of East Timor and that the East Timorese would soon adjust to the new administration. In the event, however, Fretilin offered effective military resistance to the Indonesian armed forces in the countryside and retained a broad base of support among the East Timorese. Fretilin's initial military success was due to its access to modern weapons from the former Portuguese forces, to the fact that some of its troops had gained previous battle experience in Portugal's African colonies, and to the suitability of the East Timorese terrain for guerrilla warfare. Fretilin's popular support was based principally on the extensive political work carried out by the movement in rural areas since September 1974. In a society deprived of education, Fretilin activists had carried out extensive rural literacy programmes. They had also promoted the development of agricultural and trading co-operatives, which challenged the unpopular economic power of Chinese shopkeepers and wholesalers. At the same time, the activists refrained from suggesting major changes in traditional society and so were able to win the support of many influential *liurai*. Reports on the three months of Fretilin administration in East Timor prior to the Indonesian attack on Dili suggested that Fretilin officials were generally efficient and humane. The contrasting brutality of Indonesian troops during the invasion, moreover, further alienated many East Timorese from the Indonesian cause. However, continuing warfare in the territory, together with Indonesia's resettling of villagers into strategic hamlets between 1977 and 1979, led to a famine in which perhaps 100,000 people died (of an original population of about 650,000). By the end of the resettlement campaign, Indonesia had succeeded in destroying the founding leadership of Fretilin and believed that the territory was under control.

Although the USA and Australia had made it clear that they would not intervene against Indonesia's occupation of East Timor, the UN Security Council approved a resolution on 23 December 1975 urging Indonesia's withdrawal from the territory and East Timorese self-determination. Indonesia refused to co-operate with a visit by the UN Secretary-General's special representative, Winspeare Guicciardi, and the Security Council endorsed a further resolution in April 1976 demanding that Indonesia withdraw from East Timor. However, there was no significant international interest in pursuing the issue to the extent of the imposition of sanctions or other hostile measures. From 1976 to 1982 the UN General Assembly approved annual resolutions affirming the right of the East Timorese to self-determination and independence, while Australia gave *de jure* recognition to Indonesia's annexation of the territory in 1979.

Indonesia's policy in the territory was to suppress the independence movement, while hoping that the slow acculturation of young East Timorese to Indonesian rule would gradually erode the resistance base. Substantial development aid was also allocated to the province, producing a dramatic improvement in communications infrastructure and education. Bahasa Indonesia came to be widely spoken, and by 1993 more than 1,000 East Timorese were studying at Indonesian universities. Many East Timorese sought employment elsewhere in Indonesia, particularly in Bali. In December 1988 Indonesia opened East Timor to foreign tourists, and in April 1990 it disbanded the special military command in the territory. In April 1991 the Indonesian Government announced that only 200 Fretilin guerrillas remained and that the Indonesian security forces would not pursue them because they represented no danger. Throughout this period, however, Indonesian oppression of the East Timorese population continued: both the European Community (EC, now European Union—EU) and the international human rights organization Amnesty International found compelling evidence of widespread killing and systematic torture. Such Indonesian brutality created deep resentment among the East Timorese people, including those of the younger generation who remembered nothing but Indonesian rule. External interests, moreover, came to dominate the province's economy. A military-controlled company obtained an effective monopoly on the coffee crop—the province's main export commodity—while other Indonesian interests dominated the construction and service industries. An indefinite number of Indonesians migrated to the province, and these migrants tended to dominate the administration and to control the lower reaches of the East Timorese economy, so that only a relatively small proportion of the benefits of the province's economic growth reached indigenous East Timorese.

In the mid-1980s resistance re-emerged, led by the Fretilin commander, José Alexandre (subsequently known as Kay Rala) 'Xanana' Gusmão. This resistance encouraged, and was encouraged by, renewed international support for the East Timorese cause. Portugal in particular reasserted its claim—which was supported by the UN—that it was legally the administering power in East Timor, and increasingly used its position in the EC to press the East Timorese case. The former Portuguese colonies in Africa were also sympathetic to East Timor's cause, and the issue remained a persistent source of tension in Indonesia's international relations. In 1990 the Indonesian Minister of Foreign Affairs, Ali Alatas, began discussions with Portugal, through the office of the UN Secretary-General, in the hope of reaching a solution that would allow Indonesia to gain international recognition as the legitimate governing power in East Timor, possibly by finding some special constitutional status for the territory within Indonesia. However, these negotiations were overtaken by political events within East Timor and also within Indonesia itself.

On 12 November 1991 Indonesian security forces at the Santa Cruz cemetery in Dili fired on a demonstration at the funeral of a Fretilin sympathizer, killing between 100 and 180 people. A further 100 witnesses were said to have been summarily executed shortly afterwards. However, foreign news crews had been present, and film of the massacre was smuggled out of the country and widely broadcast. Although the Indonesian armed forces initially claimed that only 19 had died and that the troops involved had been 'provoked' by Fretilin supporters, intense international pressure led President Suharto to establish a separate inquiry, which found that 50 had died and 90 had 'disappeared' in the incident. This rare public criticism of the army led to the court martial and conviction of 10 military personnel and the dismissal of two senior army officers. However, there was widespread criticism of the disparity between the sentences given to protesters and to members of the armed forces.

In November 1992 the resistance suffered a major set-back when Xanana Gusmão was captured near Dili. In May 1993 he was found guilty of rebellion, conspiracy, attempting to establish a separate state and illegal possession of arms, and was condemned to life imprisonment. However, following a plea for clemency, the sentence was commuted to 20 years by Suharto in August. In June 1997 the senior guerrilla leader, David Alex, was apprehended by Indonesian forces and died in a military hospital soon after his capture. The circumstances of his death were highly controversial, with the resistance claiming that Alex had been tortured or poisoned. In March 1998 Konis Santana, the military commander and acting leader of Fretilin, died as the result of an accident; he was subsequently replaced as acting leader by Taur Matan Ruak.

Despite military successes, a senior officer of the Indonesian armed forces acknowledged in early 1994 that Indonesia had failed to win the support of the East Timorese, and suggested that it would take another two generations until Indonesian rule could be accepted. Even this gloomy prognosis was made to seem optimistic by the growing religious dimension of the conflict. The predominantly Catholic East Timorese were deeply offended by incidents such as the mistreatment of nuns, the desecration of a church, and general anti-Catholic remarks by Muslim Indonesian officials, while Indonesians, reluctant to see genuine nationalism behind the Timorese resistance, became increasingly inclined to blame the territory's recalcitrance on Catholic separatism. These issues were complicated by the growing numbers of Muslim Indonesian residents of the province, who sometimes felt targeted by East Timorese demonstrators.

The UN sent a special investigator, Bacre Waly Ndiaye, to report on conditions in East Timor in July 1994; his conclusion that a climate of fear and suspicion dominated the territory subsequently encouraged the UN Secretary-General, Boutros Boutros-Ghali, to organize contact and then talks between Timorese groups for and against integration with Indonesia, in the hope that these discussions might lead to a consensus on the best future for the territory. In December 1998 the UN special envoy, Jamsheed Marker, visited East Timor and held talks with the imprisoned Xanana Gusmão and the acting Bishop of Dili, Carlos Ximenes Belo.

Within the EU, Portugal was the most vociferous in condemning Indonesia and lobbying for a UN-supervised referendum in East Timor; in July 1992 Portugal blocked an economic co-operation treaty between the Association of Southeast Asian Nations (ASEAN) and the EC on these grounds. Portugal also began proceedings against Australia in the International Court of Justice (ICJ), seeking a ruling against the so-called Timor Gap Treaty, concluded between Australia and Indonesia in 1991. The Treaty provided a legal framework for petroleum and gas exploration in the maritime zone between Australia and East Timor, which had not been covered by earlier Indonesian-Australian treaties. Portugal claimed that the agreement infringed upon both Portuguese sovereignty and the East Timorese right to self-determination. (Only Australia was named because Indonesia did not come under the Court's jurisdiction.) In a judgment brought in June 1995, however, the Court ruled that it could not exercise jurisdiction because the central issue was the legality of actions by Indonesia, which had refused to present a case. Formal contact between the Indonesian and Portuguese Governments, especially over the status of Portuguese culture in East Timor, took place in 1995 and 1996, but this was for the most part inconclusive. In January 1996 Portugal began direct satellite television broadcasts to East Timor.

In June 1995, March 1996 and October 1997 All-Inclusive Intra-East Timorese Dialogues (AIETD) were held in Austria under UN auspices. Participants pressed for better protection of human rights in the territory, and in October 1997 adopted the name Loro Sai (Sa'e) for East Timor. On repeated occasions after late 1995 groups of young East Timorese entered foreign embassies in Jakarta to request political asylum; most were allowed to leave Indonesia. International awareness of East Timor was heightened in October 1996 when Bishop Carlos Ximenes Belo and resistance leader José Ramos Horta were jointly awarded the Nobel Peace Prize. The award especially enhanced Ramos Horta's campaign to seek international support for East Timorese self-determination, but there was little diplomatic movement until July 1997 when, with the apparent approval of President Suharto, President Nelson Mandela of South Africa met the imprisoned Xanana Gusmão for informal discussions. However, despite high international hopes and an apparently amicable meeting between Mandela and Suharto on the issue, the Mandela initiative ended without result.

The accession of Bucharuddin Jusuf (B. J.) Habibie to the presidency of Indonesia following the downfall of President Suharto in May 1998 immediately raised expectations that East Timor would be dealt with as part of a more general plan to address problems left by the outgoing regime. Demonstrations against Indonesian rule continued, and the new President publicly suggested both that the territory might be given a new 'special' status within Indonesia and that troops might be withdrawn. However, Xanana Gusmão was not among the numerous political prisoners released by the new regime immediately after the fall of Suharto, and there was initially no indication that Indonesia was prepared to contemplate independence for East Timor. In July speculation that the territory's status might be altered in the near future led thousands of non-East Timorese to flee to neighbouring East Nusa Tenggara province. At the end of the same month the withdrawal from East Timor of hundreds of Indonesian troops began. In early August it was announced that Indonesia and Portugal had agreed to hold discussions on the possibility of 'wide-ranging' autonomy for the province.

On 27 January 1999, however, Indonesia unexpectedly announced that, if East Timor rejected the autonomy programme that was being negotiated, it would consider allowing the province to become independent. Although the Indonesian Government was initially determined that the decision on the future of East Timor should not be reached on the basis of a referendum, it soon agreed to a UN-supervised poll in which all East Timorese would vote on whether to accept the autonomy proposals offered or to opt for independence, and signed an agreement with Portugal to this effect on 5 May, with the poll scheduled to be held on 8 August. Few observers had previously imagined that such a concession would be made, particularly since the Indonesian military was believed to view the relinquishing of East Timor as having dangerous implications for overall national security and as an insult to army prestige. However, the Commander-in-Chief of the Indonesian armed forces, Gen. Wiranto, was reportedly receptive to arguments that the continued garrisoning of East Timor would weaken the army's capacity to maintain order elsewhere in the archipelago; some Muslim leaders were also reported to favour the removal of East Timor's predominantly Catholic population from the Indonesian body politic. A virulent campaign of violence and intimidation waged by a number of anti-independence militia groups based within the territory threatened proceedings and appeared to cast some doubt on the certainty of a vote in favour of independence. The militias were accused of carrying out summary killings, kidnappings, looting, harassment and the forced recruitment of young East Timorese in order to sabotage the poll. Furthermore, it emerged that the Indonesian military itself was supporting, encouraging and training a number of the militias.

The violence continued to escalate throughout April and May 1999. In April anti-independence militia members brutally murdered 57 people in a churchyard in the town of Liquiça; further massacres were reported to have occurred in other areas of the territory, including Dili. Also in April Xanana Gusmão (who in February had been moved from Cipinang prison in Jakarta to serve out the remainder of his 20-year sentence under effective house arrest in the capital) abruptly reversed his previous position on the conflict in response to increasing violence by anti-independence militias and urged guerrilla fighters in Falintil (the military wing of Fretilin) to resume their struggle. The escalating violence in the territory, together with logistical difficulties, led the UN to postpone the referendum to 21 August and then to 30 August. On 18 June the rival pro-independence and integrationist factions signed a peace accord urging a cease-fire and disarmament in advance of the scheduled referendum.

Despite the continuing intimidation and violence, the referendum proceeded on 30 August 1999. About 98.5% of the electorate participated in the poll, which resulted in an overwhelming rejection, by 78.5% of voters, of autonomy proposals and an endorsement of independence for East Timor. However, the announcement of the result precipitated a rapid descent into anarchy. As pro-Jakarta militias embarked upon a campaign of murder and destruction, which many observers believed to be premeditated, hundreds of civilians were killed, thousands were forced to flee their homes, and many buildings were destroyed in arson attacks. Anti-independence activists stormed the residence of the Nobel laureate Bishop Ximenes Belo, evicting at gunpoint some 6,000 refugees who had sought shelter in the compound, and then burned down the home of the bishop. Bishop Ximenes Belo was evacuated to Australia, while Xanana Gusmão took refuge in the British embassy in Jakarta, following his release from house arrest. Thousands of terrified civilians besieged the UN compound in Dili, the premises of other international agencies, churches and police stations in a desperate search for protection from the indiscriminate attacks of the militias.

On 7 September 1999 martial law was declared in the territory, and a curfew was imposed. However, the violence continued unabated, and in mid-September, with international concern rising, the Indonesian Government yielded to pressure and agreed to permit the deployment of a multinational peace-keeping force. Following a visit to Jakarta by the UN High Commissioner for Human Rights, Mary Robinson, the Indonesian President also agreed to the holding of an international inquiry into whether the country's army was responsible for the perpetration of the atrocities. As the massacre of innocent civilians continued, thousands of refugees were airlifted to safety in northern Australia, along with remaining employees of the UN (many local staff members of the UN Mission in East Timor—UNAMET—having been among the victims of the violence). Meanwhile, aid agencies warned that as many as 300,000 East Timorese people risked starvation if humanitarian assistance were not urgently provided: in East Timor itself the number of displaced persons was estimated at 200,000, many of whom were in hiding in the mountains, while a further 100,000 were believed to have been driven into neighbouring West Timor, where their fate was unknown.

The first contingent of several thousand peace-keeping troops, forming the International Force for East Timor (Interfet), landed in the territory on 20 September 1999. Led by Australia, which committed 4,500 troops, the force gradually restored order. Other substantial contributions to the operation were made by the Philippines and Thailand, each of which provided 1,000 soldiers. A week later the Indonesian armed forces formally relinquished responsibility for security to the multinational force. At the end of October, after 24 years as an occupying force, the last Indonesian soldiers left East Timor. Amid scenes of jubilation in Dili, Xanana Gusmão, who had recently returned to his homeland, was able personally to witness the Indonesian commanders' final departure.

UNTAET ADMINISTRATION

On 19 October 1999 the result of the referendum was ratified by the Indonesian legislature, thus permitting East Timor's accession to independence to proceed. Shortly thereafter, on 25 October, the UN Security Council established the UN Transitional Administration in East Timor (UNTAET) as an integrated peace-keeping operation fully responsible for the administration of East Timor during its transition to independence. UNTAET, with an initial mandate extending until 31 January 2001, was to exercise all judicial and executive authority in East Timor, to undertake the establishment and training of a new police force, and to assume responsibility for the co-ordination and provision of humanitarian assistance and emergency rehabilitation; Interfet was scheduled to be replaced as soon as possible by UNTAET's military component. Meanwhile, the UN also began a large-scale emergency humanitarian relief effort. However, the UN administration in East Timor confronted two major areas of difficulty in the months following the referendum. First, in an already poverty-stricken territory, the restoration of basic services after the major destruction of infrastructure during the violence of September 1999 proved to be extremely difficult. Owing to the widespread destruction of houses, many people displaced in the violence were unable to return to their homes. The Indonesian professionals who had provided medical, agricultural, educational and technical services had all fled by the time the UN took control of East Timor, and foreign aid workers were not numerous enough adequately to replace them. In addition, although development aid worth US $523m. had been promised to East Timor by various sources in December 1999, by March 2000 only $22m. had actually been provided. While construction work supplied some employment opportunities, there was little activity in other areas of the economy, and some sources estimated the unemployment rate in the territory to be as high as 80%. Because the Indonesian rupiah (which was itself extremely unstable in the late 1990s) remained the legal currency in the territory, East Timor's economy continued to be adversely affected by fluctuations in the Indonesian economy. Crime rates also increased, but could not be dealt with effectively because of the lack of any proper judicial system and prisons. In May 2000 only 700 of a total 1,610 international police officers promised for the civilian police force (CivPol) established by the UN had been deployed in the territory.

The second major area of difficulty for the UN administration concerned the various conflicts that emerged in East Timorese society following the referendum, as a consequence of the previous 25 years of Indonesian occupation and the violence of 1999. In particular, there were conflicts over the ownership of land that had changed hands as a result of political pressures, and tensions surrounding the issue of whether skilled East Timorese who had co-operated with the Indonesian authorities should be placed in positions of political responsibility in the newly independent East Timor. Although Xanana Gusmão urged the national reconciliation of all East Timorese, tensions were often acute at local level, especially when alleged East Timorese members of pro-Indonesia militia groups returned home. There was considerable discussion over whether the reconciliation of the East Timorese people would be best served by placing militia leaders on trial, by announcing a general amnesty for those involved in the violence, or by installing some form of 'truth and reconciliation commission' as in South Africa.

Following his popularly acclaimed return to Dili in October 1999, Xanana Gusmão met the UNTAET Transitional Administrator, Sérgio Vieira de Mello, in November, and reportedly communicated the concerns of local East Timorese organizations that they were being marginalized by UNTAET officials. In late November he visited Jakarta in order to establish relations with the Indonesian Government, and in early December he visited Australia, where he met with representatives of the Australian Government to discuss the Timor Gap Treaty. A memorandum outlining an agreement temporarily to preserve the provisions of the original Timor Gap Treaty was signed in February 2000 by the Australian Government and East Timor's UN administrators to enable the exploitation of resources in the area to continue; Indonesia had ceased to be party to the original Treaty when it relinquished control of East Timor in October 1999. In May 2000 Australia announced that it was willing to consider the further renegotiation of the Treaty, possibly with a view to conceding rights to a larger share of the area's resources to East Timor.

On 1 December 1999 José Ramos Horta returned to East Timor after 24 years of exile. Ramos Horta, who commanded much popular support, urged the East Timorese people to show forgiveness towards their former oppressors and appealed for reconciliation between Indonesia and East Timor. On 2 December UNTAET established a 15-member National Consultative Council (NCC), comprising representatives of UNTAET itself, the National Council of Timorese Resistance (the nationalist 'umbrella' organization, including Fretilin), the Catholic Church and groups that had formerly supported integration with Indonesia. The NCC's mandate was both to monitor the UNTAET administration and to advise on preparations for full independence. The NCC decided that Portuguese, rather than English, Bahasa Indonesia or the indigenous lingua franca, Tetum, would become the national language. On 23 February 2000 the transfer of command of military operations in East Timor from Interfet to the UNTAET peace-keeping force was completed. The UNTAET force included contingents supplied by Australia, Bangladesh, Brazil, Canada, Fiji, Ireland, Jordan, Kenya, the Republic of Korea, Malaysia, New Zealand, Pakistan, the Philippines and Portugal.

In late January 2000 a panel appointed by the Indonesian Government to investigate human rights abuses in East Timor delivered its report to the Indonesian Attorney-General. The panel reportedly named 24 individuals whom it recommended should be prosecuted for their alleged involvement in violations of human rights in the territory. One of those named was the former Minister of Defence and Security and Commander-in-Chief of the Indonesian armed forces, Gen. Wiranto, who had since been appointed Co-ordinating Minister for Political, Legal and Security Affairs in the Indonesian Government; also named were a number of senior military officers, as well as leaders of the pro-Jakarta militias responsible for the extreme violence perpetrated during the period following the referendum. However, pro-independence leaders in East Timor strongly criticized the report as inadequate. Also in late January the International Commission of Inquiry in East Timor recommended that the UN establish an independent international body to investigate allegations of human rights violations in East Timor, and an international tribunal to deal with the cases of those accused by the investigators. In February the recently appointed President of Indonesia, Abdurrahman Wahid, visited East Timor and publicly apologized for the atrocities committed by the Indonesian armed forces during the Republic's occupation of the territory. In the same month Wahid reaffirmed the commitment of the Indonesian Government to the prosecution of any individuals implicated in the violation of human rights in East Timor and suspended Gen. Wiranto from the Indonesian Government. The UN Secretary-General, Kofi Annan, made an official visit to East Timor in mid-February, during which he pledged that investigations into violations of human rights in the territory would be carried out. The President of Portugal, Dr Jorge Sampaio, also made a three-day official visit to East Timor in that month, during which he expressed the solidarity of the people of Portugal with the East Timorese.

A number of mass graves containing the bodies of suspected victims of the violence perpetrated by the anti-independence militias both before and after the holding of the referendum in August 1999 were discovered in East Timor (including two in the Oecusse enclave) in late 1999 and early 2000. In December 1999 Sonia Picado Sotela, the Chair of the International Commission of Inquiry in East Timor, confirmed that the team of UN investigators had discovered evidence of 'systematic killing'. The UN announced in March 2000 that at least 627 East Timorese had been killed in the violence that followed the referendum, although this estimate was likely to increase as investigations continued. By May approximately 161,000 East Timorese refugees had returned to the territory under official auspices, leaving about 150,000 in 185 camps in Indonesian-controlled West Timor. Although there were fears that these camps were dominated by pro-Indonesia militias who might use them as a base for attacks on East Timor, UNTAET was reluctant to press for the refugees' immediate return because of a lack of facilities to house and feed them. In September the office of the UN High Commissioner for Refugees (UNHCR) temporarily suspended its relief operations in West Timor, following the brutal murder of three of the organization's representatives in the region by pro-Indonesia militia members. During early 2001 the repatriation of refugees resumed, in order to enable people to register to vote in the Constituent Assembly elections scheduled for August. In July the Indonesian authorities formally asked all remaining refugee families to choose between repatriation and resettlement elsewhere in Indonesia. Only 1.1%, representing 1,250 people, chose to return to East Timor. Some observers attributed this figure to intimidation in the camps and to reports of the harassment of returnees in East Timor, but others pointed out that most of those who wished to return had probably already done so.

On 5 April 2000 UNTAET signed an agreement with the Indonesian Government regarding Indonesia's co-operation in efforts to resolve judicial and human rights issues. The agreement allowed for the extradition of Indonesians to East Timor for trial on charges relating to the violence of 1999. However, relations between East Timor and Indonesia remained tense. In July 2000 a 17-member team from the Indonesian Attorney-General's Office visited East Timor to investigate a limited number of cases of human rights violations arising from the violence that occurred in East Timor in 1999. In August 2000 an amendment to Indonesia's Constitution appeared to contradict the assurances previously made to the international community by President Wahid concerning Indonesia's ability to conduct its own independent investigation into atrocities committed in East Timor by members of the country's armed forces. The amendment excluded military personnel from retroactive prosecution and (despite the suggestion of senior Indonesian legislators that the amendment would probably not apply to crimes such as genocide, war crimes and terrorism) was perceived by many international observers as a serious threat to the possibility of the prosecution of members of the Indonesian military believed responsible for recent human rights violations in East Timor. After the murder of the three UNHCR aid workers in West Timor, Indonesia agreed in October to disarm militias still active in its territory, but only a few hundred antiquated weapons were surrendered. In the same month, moreover, Indonesia formally refused to extradite the militia leader, Eurico Guterres, who was accused of playing a leading role in the Liquiça massacre in 1999, promising that he would be tried under Indonesian law. After a three-month trial, in early 2001 Guterres was finally convicted of weapons offences and sentenced to six months' imprisonment. However, in view of the time already spent in custody, he was released after serving only 23 days.

In June 2000 an agreement was reached between UNTAET and East Timorese leaders on the formation of a new transitional coalition Government, in which the two sides were to share political responsibility. The Cabinet of the new transitional Government initially included four East Timorese cabinet ministers: João Carrascalão, President of the UDT, was allocated responsibility for infrastructure; Mari Alkatiri, Secretary-General of Fretilin, was appointed Minister for Economic Affairs; Father Filomeno Jacob was appointed to oversee social affairs; and Ana Pessôa was placed in charge of internal administration. The new Cabinet also included four international representatives. Mariano Lopes da Cruz, an East Timorese national, was appointed as Inspector-General. On 14 July UNTAET approved the establishment of a National

Council—which consisted of 33 East Timorese representatives from the political, religious and private sectors—to advise the new Cabinet. The current NCC was to be dissolved at the first session of the new Council. On 20 October, however, the composition of an expanded, 36-member National Council was announced; the new East Timor National Council was to replace the 15-member NCC, which held its last meeting on that day. On 23 October Xanana Gusmão was elected leader of the new National Council. Earlier in the same month José Ramos Horta was appointed to the Cabinet of the transitional Government as Minister for Foreign Affairs, increasing the number of ministers in the Cabinet to nine.

Both Ramos Horta and Xanana Gusmão stressed their commitment to good relations with Indonesia, downplaying the need to prosecute Indonesian military commanders for their role in the violence and refusing to support the independence movements in the Indonesian provinces of Aceh and Irian Jaya (now Papua). In March 2000 Indonesia agreed to allow a land corridor to link the enclave of Oecusse to the rest of East Timor. In April 2001 East Timor and Indonesia reached an agreement on maintaining border security, and in April 2002 the two sides began a formal border demarcation survey. As interim Minister for Economic Affairs, Mari Alkatiri renegotiated the Timor Gap Treaty with Australia. In July 2001 the two sides reached the Timor Sea Arrangement, under which production from the so-called Joint Petroleum Development Area in the Timor Sea (formal ownership of which was still undecided) was to be divided 90:10 between East Timor and Australia. Although this arrangement appeared to favour East Timor, and was presented as a future economic mainstay for the new country, some observers argued that most of the indirect benefits of the Arrangement would flow to Australia.

On 20 August 2000, meanwhile, Xanana Gusmão retired as the Military Commander of Falintil to concentrate on his political role in the process of guiding East Timor towards full independence in advance of the general election, subsequently scheduled for August 2001. Xanana Gusmão relinquished control of the guerrilla army to his deputy, Taur Matan Ruak. Falintil was formally disbanded on 1 February 2001. Some 650 of its members were recruited into the newly formed East Timor Defence Force (Falintil-ETDF) and given immediate training as regular troops. The first of these trainees graduated in June, and Taur Matan Ruak was sworn in as Brigadier-General and commander of Falintil-ETDF. The remainder of Falintil was demobilized.

Although there was a widespread feeling that only Xanana Gusmão had public support for the future post of President of East Timor, he himself repeatedly declared that he would not be a candidate, and in March 2001 he resigned from the chair of the National Council. In the vote for Gusmão's successor on 9 April, José Ramos Horta (reportedly supported by UNTAET) was defeated by Manuel Carrascalão, who criticized UNTAET for what he described as 'colonialist' practices. In August, after all the newly registered political parties declared Xanana Gusmão to be their preferred candidate and also in response to the encouragement of the international community, he announced that he would in fact contest the presidential election, scheduled for 2002.

In early July 2001 the 16 parties that had registered for the elections agreed on a National Unity Pact, which included a promise of mutual respect during the campaign and to honour the election results. Approximately 380,000 East Timorese were eligible to vote for the 88 members of a Constituent Assembly (13 of them chosen as district representatives, the rest by proportional representation). A transition period began on 15 July: the National Council was dissolved; members of the transitional Cabinet who intended to play a political role resigned from their posts; and formal campaigning began. The Constituent Assembly was to draft a constitution for East Timor and was expected to complete its work before the expiry of the UN mandate on 31 January 2002.

At the election for the Constituent Assembly, conducted on 30 August 2001, Fretilin garnered 57% of the votes cast and secured a total of 55 seats (including 12 of the 13 district seats). Of the remaining 33 seats, the Partido Democrático (PD, Democratic Party) won seven, the Partido Social Democrata Timor Lorosae (PSD, Social Democratic Party of East Timor) six and the Associação Social-Democrata Timorense (ASDT, Timor Social Democratic Association) also six. The composition of the new Cabinet, headed by Mari Alkatiri, was announced in September. Alkatiri, a member of East Timor's small Muslim community, who had lived in exile from 1975 to 1999, retained the portfolio of economic affairs, while José Ramos Horta continued as Minister for Foreign Affairs.

The Constituent Assembly was initially expected to prepare East Timor's Constitution within 90 days, but the final document was not approved until 22 March 2002. The Constitution provided for parliamentary government with a five-year term and with a largely symbolic, but popularly elected, President. A Standing Committee of Parliament was designated to act on behalf of the legislature when it was not in session. The Assembly revived the name Democratic Republic of East Timor, used by the short-lived independent Fretilin Government in late 1975, and declared 28 November 1975 as the date of independence. Although the Constitution provided for an elected parliament of 52–65 members, the 88-member Constituent Assembly declared itself the first National Parliament of the new republic. The Constitution designated Portuguese and Tetum as official languages and permitted East Timorese to hold dual citizenship. It also provided for the separation of church and state.

In January 2002 a Commission for Reception, Truth and Reconciliation (Comissão de Acolhimento, Verdade e Reconciliação—CAVR) was established with a two-year mandate to address the difficult problem of reconciling those responsible for violence in the period from April 1974 to October 1999 with their victims and their victims' families. The aims of the Commission were both to describe, acknowledge and record past human rights abuses along the lines of the post-apartheid South African Truth and Reconciliation Commission, and to devise procedures that would facilitate reconciliation at village level. The CAVR was not empowered to provide amnesties, and serious cases were to be dealt with in the courts. In Jakarta, meanwhile, in March 2002 the former Governor of East Timor, Abílio Soares, was placed on trial, charged with knowingly permitting the mass violence of August–September 1999. In total, 18 senior Indonesian officials were indicted, including three generals. The trial of Maj.-Gen. Tono Suratman, military commander of the province at the time of the violence, began in July 2002. When convicted in August, Abílio Soares received a prison sentence of only three years, provoking international condemnation. Furthermore, the acquittal of the former police chief of East Timor, Timbul Silaen, along with several other officers, prompted human rights groups to demand the UN's intervention in the process.

Xanana Gusmão's overwhelming popularity was confirmed on 14 April 2002, when he was elected President of East Timor with nearly 83% of the votes cast. The only other candidate was Francisco Xavier do Amaral, who had served as President briefly in 1975 and who had declared his candidacy only for the sake of providing an alternative.

East Timor finally achieved independence on 20 May 2002 in a ceremony attended by the UN Secretary-General, Kofi Annan, and the Indonesian President, Megawati Sukarnoputri. From this date the nation officially became known as the Democratic Republic of Timor-Leste. However, the celebrations were marred by the unauthorized arrival of six Indonesian warships in Dili harbour just before the ceremony, ostensibly to guard Megawati. The action was widely seen as an attempt by sections of the Indonesian military to create an incident that would force Megawati to abandon her visit. In the event, however, the warships withdrew peacefully. President Gusmão swore in a new 24-member Cabinet headed by Prime Minister Mari Alkatiri, and the UNTAET administration formally came to an end.

INDEPENDENCE

Independent Timor-Leste confronted several political problems. The ownership of property emerged as a major issue, as confiscation and forced sales in the Indonesian period had often led to several people having rival but legitimate claims to the same property. The issue of law and order was a problem, both because high unemployment encouraged robbery and because demobilized freedom fighters who were not included in the defence force formed a significant social group that readily accused the Government of betraying the ideals of the independence struggle. Tension was also apparent between the older Portuguese-speaking generation of leaders and a younger generation educated under Indonesian rule, for whom English and Bahasa Indonesia were the preferred languages for international communication. Two days of riots occurred in Dili in early December 2002. Supermarkets, shops, hotels and the house of the Prime Minister, Mari Alkatiri, were set on fire, and at least two people were killed when police opened fire on protesting students, before UN troops restored order.

The UN presence remained in Timor-Leste on a reduced scale in the form of the UN Mission of Support in East Timor (UNMISET), headed by a former Indian diplomat, Kamalesh Sharma. UNMISET's mandate, due to last two years only, was to maintain continuity in policing, to pay particular attention to gender and HIV policies and to supervise a continuing military presence of (initially) about 5,000 international troops. Following the Dili riots of December 2002, the UN agreed to keep two peace-keeping battalions near the country's border with Indonesia and to maintain an international police unit for an additional year, although the Timorese authorities began to assume responsibility from the UN for the administration of border controls in August 2003.

Timor-Leste's first political opinion poll, conducted in November 2003, showed that support for the Fretilin Government of Mari Alkatiri had begun to decline. Reports of corruption and ineffectiveness in the management of health, justice and education provided a basis for resentment, which was compounded by the perception that the Government was dominated by a Portuguese-speaking élite that had spent the occupation years outside East Timor. Another poll suggested that 39% of the population felt that they were worse off than under Indonesian rule. Although Alkatiri's insistence on national ownership of Timor-Leste's resources was popular, many of his policies were perceived as a disincentive to the foreign investment needed to create jobs. In addition, there was some disquiet over the Government's handling of revenues from petroleum and gas extraction in the Timor Sea. In June 2005 the Government approved the creation of a Petroleum Fund, which would receive all hydrocarbon revenues and which would form a reserve 'for the benefit of future generations', but Parliament retained the power to disburse these revenues, and there were concerns that Timor-Leste lacked the institutional capacity to prevent their diversion through political patronage. In July a restricted World Bank report warned that increasing corruption within the Government and the public sector threatened Timor-Leste's stability and peace. Many observers noted a sharp personal tension between President Gusmão and Prime Minister Alkatiri. Gusmão fulfilled his election promise to act as a 'watchdog' by accusing parliamentarians of 'irresponsibility' after two sessions of the legislature failed to achieve a quorum and by criticizing the Government for failing to uphold the editorial independence of the state-operated radio and television stations.

The most serious issue confronting the new Government was growing insecurity. Low wages and high levels of unemployment in Dili and other major towns encouraged a culture of street gangs and rising levels of urban crime. Resentful former members of Falintil who had not been integrated into Falintil-ETDF formed the core of many of these gangs. Moreover, a perception that Gusmão loyalists had been given preferential access to the defence force engendered political dissent within the gangs. The new Timor-Leste army, consisting of approximately 1,500 regular soldiers and an additional 1,500 reservists, was deployed in border regions to combat infiltration by former militia from West Timor, but it was soon subject to numerous allegations of arrests without warrant and accusations of assaults of detainees.

In December 2003 the Conselho Popular pela Defesa da República Democrática de Timor Leste (CPD-RDTL, Popular Council for the Defence of the Democratic Republic of East Timor), composed of dissident former guerrillas, launched a minor rebellion against the Government in border regions. Rejecting the use of the Portuguese language and the role of former exiles in government, the organization announced that it would seize power after the UN withdrawal. However, sections of the CPD-RDTL were brutally suppressed in police operations, which aroused renewed fears about potential indiscipline in the police force once UN supervision was removed. Police used tear gas and rubber bullets to disperse a rally of veterans in Dili in July 2004.

Increasingly, the new Timor-Leste police force (Policia Nacional de Timor-Leste—PNTL), numbering 3,400 in 2006, came to be regarded as a political rival of the defence force. Unlike the army, the core of the police force had been recruited largely from the occupation-era police, who were considered to have essential expertise in managing law and order. In September 2003 the UN transferred to the police responsibility for law and order, except in Dili (where the police did not assume responsibility until May 2004). Many observers feared, on the one hand, that the new force was unprepared to carry out its responsibilities after the UN withdrawal scheduled for May 2004, and, on the other, that it was too strong and independent of civilian supervision. During 2003 several East Timorese leaders expressed the hope that some form of UN security presence would remain after the scheduled end of the UN mandate in May 2004. Indeed, subsequent to that date there were growing complaints of brutality and corruption in the police force and of political interference in its operations. The UN Security Council duly extended UNMISET's mandate for a further year, but reduced its presence to 604 officers, while full responsibility for policing and external security in the country was transferred to the Government of Timor-Leste. The UN mission formally ended on 20 May 2005, and the last of the UN peace-keeping troops withdrew in June. The UN retained a presence in the form of the UN Office in Timor-Leste (UNOTIL), the mandate of which was scheduled to expire on 19 May 2006; this was subsequently extended to 20 August.

President Gusmão's authority remained solid, but tension remained over the issue of reconciliation, with Gusmão favouring a general amnesty, while some in Fretilin sought a more punitive approach. In the absence of an amnesty, a UN-sponsored Special Panel for Serious Crimes (SPSC), created in Dili in 2001, continued to indict people for crimes carried out before and just after the independence vote. Some Fretilin leaders were angered in December 2003 when the CAVR held four days of hearings into the events of 1974–76, when a civil war between East Timorese had provided the pretext for the Indonesian invasion and atrocities had been carried out on both sides. The SPSC had charged 391 people by the end of 2004. However, of the 367 people charged by the end of 2003, only 40 had been convicted, while 280 remained free in Indonesia, including at least 32 Indonesian commanders and the former military chief, Gen. Wiranto. Indonesia's own courts, established in response to international pressure, tried only 18 military officers and civilian officials in 2002–03, of whom just six were convicted. These convictions were then overruled by the Indonesian High Court in August 2004. The Court also released former Governor Abílio Soares in November on the grounds that a civilian official should not bear responsibility for the military's handling of public order. In May the Timor-Leste Parliament narrowly adopted a proposal to discuss a general amnesty for all crimes committed prior to 31 March of that year, including the so-called 'serious crimes' perpetrated by Indonesian troops and anti-independence militias in 1999; similar bills had failed to gain approval in 2001 and 2003.

In July 2003 a ruling by Supreme Court judge Claudio Ximenes that the legal system adopted at independence was invalid because it was not derived from previous Portuguese law cast doubt over the whole legal system. Parliament responded in September by approving a law establishing Indonesian, not Portuguese, law as the country's applicable subsidiary legal system, on the grounds that neither courts nor police in Timor-Leste were familiar with Portuguese law. None the less, a critical shortage of judges meant that cases often did not reach the courts until two years after the arrest of suspects. Judicial training programmes in Portugal gradually relieved this problem.

Tension also developed over the place of religion in Timorese society. In April 2005 a two-week rally of about 10,000 people in

Dili urged the Government to maintain compulsory religious education in schools. The Government had planned to make religious education voluntary, in line with the country's secular Constitution. Catholic Church leaders supported the rally, arguing that religious education was needed to curb the growth of secularism. Church leaders also criticized the Government over its policy of accommodation with Indonesia on the trial of the perpetrators of the violence in 1999.

After the election of 2001, the Fretilin Government's public standing was tarnished by growing allegations of corruption and abuse of power. There were persistent rumours that international oil companies had 'paid off' government leaders for drilling rights in the Timor Sea. Prime Minister Alkatiri was accused of having sanctioned the imprisonment of a Malaysian-Chinese UN contractor for failing to show him respect. The Minister for Interior Affairs, Rogerio Lobato, was alleged to have chased and beaten two men whose vehicle had obstructed his while on the road. Journalists expressed misgivings at proposals to make defamation of public officials a criminal offence punishable by three years in prison. The US-based organization Human Rights Watch reported credible accounts of torture in prisons.

Tension escalated sharply when 595 troops, one-third of the national army, mutinied in March 2006. The mutineers were mainly from the west of the country, and they alleged that the Government had ignored their complaints of discrimination by commanders from the east, which was generally regarded as having provided the core of the resistance to Indonesian occupation. President Gusmão had offered to mediate in the dispute, but the Minister of Defence, Roque Rodrigues, and the army Commander-in-Chief, Brig.-Gen. Taur Matan Ruak, dismissed the mutineers while Gusmão was abroad. The mutineers then coalesced under Maj. Alfredo Reinado to demand that the Fretilin Government resign. Fighting broke out in the streets of Dili, involving gangs claiming to be 'eastern' or 'western'. The east–west divide within Timorese society had previously not been regarded as ethnically, politically or socially significant, but rapidly became an all-encompassing framework within which various antagonistic sentiments could be expressed. The 'westerners' stood for a loose coalition of forces opposed to the Government, including conservative Catholics opposed to Alkatiri's secularist policies. It was alleged that senior church figures had approached Ruak in 2005 and 2006 with a view to persuading him to lead a military coup against Alkatiri, and there was evidence that the houses of Fretilin supporters were especially targeted in the violence. In early May 2006 a movement developed within Fretilin in support of the replacement of Alkatiri as party Secretary-General by the Timorese ambassador to the USA and Permanent Representative to the UN, José Luís Guterres, inevitably compromising the authority of the former. However, following an open vote on the leadership at the Fretilin party congress held later that month, Alkatiri was returned to office.

As the Government's authority receded, the civil unrest intensified; armed gangs took over the streets of Dili and looting and the indiscriminate burning of houses became widespread. Documents stored in the Attorney-General's department concerning the 1999 violence were also lost in the looting. About 20 deaths were reported, including the massacre of 12 police officers in late May 2006. By the beginning of June 150,000 people were reported to have fled to refugee camps on the outskirts of the city. The military rebels, meanwhile, set up camp in the hills south of Dili and declared that Alkatiri's resignation was a prerequisite for any reconciliation with the Government.

The breakdown of order in Timor-Leste was of especial concern to Australia, which, shortly prior to the renewal of violence, had argued in favour of decreasing the UN presence resident in Timor-Leste. The Australian Minister for Foreign Affairs, Alexander Downer, received from President Gusmão, Prime Minister Alkatiri and the Speaker of the National Parliament, Francisco Guterres, a written request for Australian assistance before dispatching 1,300 army troops and 700 naval and air force personnel, who arrived in late May 2006. Malaysian and New Zealand troops, as well as Portuguese police officers, also arrived in Dili. The Government formally transferred responsibility for security to the international forces and ordered its own troops to return to their barracks, although many refused to do so.

While Australia presented its actions as a benevolent contribution by a concerned neighbour, many Timorese suspected that the operation was connected with the dispute between the Timorese and Australian Governments over the maritime border issue and the consequent rights to petroleum and gas in the Timor Sea. Comments made by Australian Prime Minister John Howard claiming that Timor-Leste had 'not been well-governed' were regarded by the Timorese as inappropriate interference in the country's internal affairs. The fact that rebel leader Reinado had lived in Australia prior to 1999 and had later been trained at an Australian defence college also added to suspicions.

Publicly, President Gusmão appealed for peace and reconciliation, but it was widely perceived that he was at loggerheads with Alkatiri and was working to find a way of changing the Government. The Prime Minister openly told Gusmão to respect the Constitution, which gave executive power to the Cabinet, rather than to the President. On 30 May 2006, however, Gusmão declared a 30-day state of emergency and assumed responsibility for defence and security, effectively removing all power from Minister for Defence Rodrigues and Minister for Interior Affairs Lobato, both of whom resigned on the following day. Shortly afterwards, Gusmão added the defence portfolio to the duties of Senior Minister for Foreign Affairs José Ramos Horta, and Alcino Barris was appointed as the new Minister for Interior Affairs. Sharp tension persisted within the Government, with Gusmão explicitly urging Alkatiri to resign, while threatening to step down as President if Alkatiri refused. In mid-June Ramos Horta resigned from the Cabinet, insisting that he could no longer work with the Prime Minister. After weeks of mounting pressure, Alkatiri finally resigned on 26 June, acknowledging in a public statement his 'own share of responsibility' for the crisis that had so disrupted the stability of the country. Shortly afterwards, Gusmão appointed Ramos Horta as 'Cabinet Co-ordinator'. In mid-July the President announced that Ramos Horta would serve as Prime Minister until the holding of parliamentary elections, scheduled for August 2007.

The new Government immediately initiated an investigation into claims that, while Prime Minister, Alkatiri had formed a secret militia with a view to consolidating his power base and eliminating his political opponents. In addition, former Minister for Interior Affairs Lobato was charged with illegal arms trading. The new Government also agreed to a renewed role for the UN within Timor-Leste. In August 2006 the UN sent an Independent Special Commission of Inquiry for Timor-Leste to investigate the violence earlier in the year. In the same month UNOTIL's mandate was extended, albeit by only five days, until 25 August. In its place, UN Secretary-General Kofi Annan proposed the creation of a new, extensive UN mission in the country, which he suggested should include a substantial police force.

The violence in Dili, which had been partly suppressed by the international forces, dissipated after Alkatiri's resignation. Ramos Horta offered an amnesty to all rebels who surrendered their weapons. The rebel leader Reinado was arrested in late July 2006, after the expiry of the amnesty, and was charged with multiple offences, including attempted murder, but escaped from prison in August. Australia began to reduce its deployment in Timor-Leste in July, although some 2,000 personnel were projected to remain; Malaysia withdrew its remaining forces in September.

On 25 August 2006 UNOTIL's mandate formally expired, and the UN approved a resolution establishing, with immediate effect, its new mission in Timor-Leste. The stated aims of this UN Integrated Mission in Timor-Leste (UNMIT) included 'consolidating stability, enhancing a culture of democratic governance, and facilitating political dialogue among Timorese stakeholders' in order to help effect a process of national reconciliation and to foster social cohesion. Mandated initially for six months, UNMIT was to play a prominent role in the preparations for the presidential and parliamentary elections due to take place in 2007. (In February 2007 UNMIT's mandate was extended for a further year, to 26 February 2008.)

In October 2006 the UN Independent Special Commission of Inquiry for Timor-Leste released its report on the unrest: among other conclusions, it found that Rodrigues, Lobato and Ruak had unlawfully transferred weapons to civilians and that, although Alkatiri was not necessarily directly implicated in the transfer, he had failed to denounce it. The Commission consequently recommended further investigation into Alkatiri's involvement. Lobato's trial began in January 2007. In March he was found guilty of arming civilians and was sentenced to seven-and-a-half-years' imprisonment. Although stability had been largely restored, outbursts of violence continued, and the ongoing plight of refugees was highlighted by the Australian Minister of Defence, Dr Brendan Nelson, in November 2006; it was estimated that 70,000 internally displaced persons (IDPs) remained in camps. Maj. Reinado continued to elude the security forces, despite the Government's attempts at negotiation, and at the beginning of March 2007 reports of an unsuccessful attempt to capture Reinado prompted protests in Dili.

In February 2007 Prime Minister Ramos Horta declared his candidacy for the forthcoming presidential election. In March President Gusmão indicated his desire to become Prime Minister and announced that he intended to join the Congresso Nacional da Reconstrução de Timor-Leste (CNRT, National Congress for the Reconstruction of Timor-Leste), a new political party, following the expiry of his presidential term. The first stage of the presidential election, held on 9 April, was contested by eight candidates. Francisco Guterres, the President of Fretilin, secured 27.9% of the votes cast, followed by Ramos Horta, who was favoured by Gusmão, with 21.8%, and Fernando de Araújo, President of the PD, with 19.2%. An official appeal against the results, lodged by three of the losing candidates, including de Araújo, on the grounds of alleged widespread manipulation of the vote and other serious irregularities, was dismissed.

As no candidate achieved the requisite overall majority, the two leading contenders proceeded to a second round of voting, which was conducted on 9 May 2007: Ramos Horta received 69.2% of the votes cast. Francisco Guterres duly conceded defeat, promising to support the new President for the sake of the country's development. Unlike the first round, which had been marred by violence and intimidation, the second stage of polling was conducted peacefully with no reports of any serious irregularities. Turn-out was high in both the first and second rounds, at 81.8% and 81.0%, respectively. The election victory of Ramos Horta, who formally took office on 20 May, was attributed to the support of the five non-Fretilin candidates who had been defeated in the first round of voting. Shortly after the inauguration ceremony, one man was killed and several others wounded in clashes in Dili between supporters of rival political parties. Meanwhile, Estanislau Aleixo da Silva, hitherto the Deputy Prime Minister, assumed the role of Prime Minister in an interim capacity. Among the incoming President's priorities were plans for radical reform of the police force and judiciary. He also intended to address the issue of the so-called 'petitioner soldiers' who had mutinied in 2006 in protest at low pay and discrimination (see above). In mid-August Ramos Horta and Reinado held a meeting under the mediation of the Swiss-based Centre for Humanitarian Dialogue. Although Reinado subsequently rejected attempts to initiate further talks aimed at achieving a negotiated settlement, the Government persisted in its efforts to maintain contact with the rebel soldiers.

Legislative elections took place on 30 June 2007, contested by 14 political organizations and alliances. The number of seats in the National Parliament was reduced from 88 to 65. International observers declared their satisfaction with the conduct of the polls, in which 80.5% of the electorate participated. The electoral campaign had been generally peaceful, with the notable exception of the killing of two CNRT supporters in early June and a few minor clashes between rival supporters. Fretilin remained the largest party following the elections, winning 21 seats, although its share of the vote declined to 29% compared with 57% in the 2001 elections. The CNRT came a close second, with 24% of the vote and 18 seats, while an alliance of the ASDT and the PSD took 11 seats and the PD eight. Fretilin's relatively poor performance was attributed to public disillusion with the pace of reform since independence.

As none of the parties had secured sufficient seats to govern alone, on 6 July 2007 the CNRT, the ASDT-PSD alliance and the PD announced their intention to establish a coalition. However, Fretilin insisted on its right, as the largest parliamentary party, to participate in government, initially suggesting that it could form a minority administration and later proposing the creation of a 'government of national unity'. After weeks of deadlock, on 6 August Ramos Horta invited the CNRT-led coalition, dubbed the Parliamentary Majority Alliance (PMA), to form a government. The President's decision was denounced as unconstitutional by Fretilin and prompted violent protests by supporters of the party. Nevertheless, Gusmão was inaugurated as Prime Minister on 8 August; his new Cabinet included José Luís Guterres as Deputy Prime Minister. Gusmão pledged to improve security, to combat corruption and to facilitate the return to their homes of the thousands of refugees who remained in camps following their displacement during the unrest of April–May 2006. Meanwhile, Fernando de Araújo was elected Speaker of the National Parliament at its first session at the end of July 2007.

Forced into opposition, Fretilin persisted in deriding the Gusmão-led PMA Government throughout its first year in office, although it did recognize the legitimacy of the National Parliament, after an initial brief boycott. Meanwhile, the Government had to defend itself against serious charges of corruption and inefficiency. It was also not immune to internal rifts, notably involving the ASDT, which threatened to withdraw from the PMA at the beginning of May 2008. Although this threat was not executed, the President of the ASDT, Xavier do Amoral, nevertheless pledged to work with Fretilin in future elections.

Besides the ongoing security crisis and social problems relating to the resettlement of IDPs, major developments in domestic affairs in mid-2008 included a controversial supplementary budget debate on the question of drawing upon the Petroleum Fund to support vastly expanded expenditure on capital works projects and, amid higher food import costs and very uncertain domestic food security, to subsidize the price of rice for civil servants and veterans. In August the Government also formally inaugurated its National Petroleum Authority, which was vested with responsibility for managing the nation's oil revenues, accruing at an average rate of US $200m. a month. With a total capital of $3,203m. invested in its Petroleum Fund by the end of June, Timor-Leste—one of the poorest countries in Asia—had also, paradoxically, joined the ranks of nations wielding sovereign funds.

Presidential Assassination Attempt of 2008 and Subsequent Events

The fragility of the security situation in Timor-Leste was once again highlighted by the near-fatal shooting of President Ramos Horta on 11 February 2008. Alfredo Reinado and a group of fellow 'petitioners' descended from their hideout in the mountains, undetected by the international security forces charged with the rebel leader's capture, and entered the presidential residence. In the ensuing affray Reinado and a companion were shot dead by a military guard. In turn, the President was seriously wounded by enraged members of Reinado's group. Meanwhile, another party of rebels, led by Gastão Salsinha, mounted an almost simultaneous ambush on Gusmão's car, although the Prime Minister emerged unscathed. Ramos Horta only survived his injuries thanks to expert medical care in Dili and surgery in an Australian hospital. While Reinado's loss was mourned by his many supporters among the 'westerners', his demise obviously offered an opportunity to bring an end to the military mutiny of 2006.

Internationally, the attempt on the life of the Timorese President attracted widespread condemnation. The Australian Government dispatched additional troops and police officers to Timor-Leste and UNMIT's mandate was extended for a further year, but many questions remained to be answered, including whether or not the incident was a coup attempt, an assassination bid or an act of revenge on the part of the rebel leader, piqued at the terms of an amnesty offer. Whatever the case, it was clear that the President and Prime Minister were too trusting in dealing with Reinado through private diplomacy rather than the judicial system.

The hunt by a joint military-police command for Gastão Salsinha and his surviving band of rebels continued until he and 11 others surrendered on 29 April 2008, effectively ending the damaging two-year military rebellion, albeit not dispelling the many conspiracy theories that surrounded the events of 11 February. A 'state of siege' that had been announced following the assassination attempt, imposing curfews across most of the country, was gradually reduced in scope and fully removed on 22 May. Disbanded on 19 June, the controversial joint command was accused of a number of human rights abuses. Meanwhile, by the end of May 709 rebel 'petitioners' had accepted financial compensation to return to civilian life. As the number of returning IDPs increased, 22 camps had been closed by September, including the largest, near the airport—a visible measure of progress achieved in part through offers of 'recovery' or 'integration' funds. Having returned to Dili from recuperation in April, the following month, on the anniversary of independence, Ramos Horta pardoned or commuted the sentences of 94 criminals involved in the violence of 1999 and 2006, including the former Minister for Interior Affairs, Rogerio Lobato, and, particularly controversially, Joni Marques, a militia leader convicted of involvement in the killing of church workers in 1999.

Despite the international financial crisis that developed in the latter part of 2008, Timor-Leste recorded strong economic growth in 2008/09, albeit rising from a low base (see Economy). However, according to some estimates 20% of the country's 1.1m. inhabitants remained unemployed in 2009, one-half of Dili's youth being jobless; more than 50% of the population continued to live below the national poverty line of US $0.88 per day. Timor-Leste was ranked 162nd of 182 countries in the UN Development Programme's *Human Development Report 2009*, making it the poorest nation in the Asia-Pacific region.

The administration of Prime Minister Gusmão continued to defend itself against allegations of corruption by civil society groups and, especially, the Fretilin opposition. Notably, a government plan to purchase heavily polluting power plants from China was challenged in the courts by Fretilin on the grounds that not opening the contract for public tender avoided a mandatory study of the environmental impact of the project. In May 2009 serious allegations of corruption, in respect of the hiring of unqualified friends as foreign advisers, were made against the Minister for Planning and Finance, Emília Pires. In July Fretilin urged Gusmão to resign over allegations that he had awarded a multi-million dollar contract for the import of subsidized rice to a company linked to his daughter. In the same month the country's Ombudsman demanded that the Minister for Justice, Lúcia Lobato, be tried for corruption regarding alleged favours to a friend. The appointment in early February 2010 of Timor-Leste's first-ever anti-corruption commissioner, the lawyer and human rights activist Aderito Soares, went some way towards addressing the complaints of the parliamentary opposition and the international community; however, as Soares himself acknowledged, the elimination of high-level corruption would require a long-term public education campaign.

Meanwhile, fresh confidence that the national security situation had stabilized was confirmed by a number of events. During June and July 2009 the last of a total of 65 camps, established to accommodate IDPs following the unrest of 2006–07, was emptied. Symbolically, at least, this brought a sense of closure to that episode. In May 2009 United Nations Police (UNPol—part of UNMIT) surrendered its authority over the National Police of Timor-Leste (Polícia Nacional de Timor-Leste—PNTL) in Lautem district; it did so again in June and July in the Oecusse and Manatuto districts, respectively. These were important stages in the rebuilding of capacity and confidence in the security sector. Nevertheless, the World Bank cautioned that the country's security forces and civil service remained politicized, which could potentially precipitate a return to instability. In a development reminiscent of previous aid, in mid-2009 UN volunteers began arriving in Timor-Leste to assist with arrangements for local (village) elections, which were successfully held on 9 October. UN observers noted both the determination of the Timorese population to vote and the generally calm conditions under which people were able to cast their ballots. While local councils remained restricted in their remit, it was hoped that the smooth conduct of the polls augured well for the next presidential and legislative elections, due to be held in 2012. Meanwhile, under rare international media attention, the trial began in Dili in mid-July 2009 of 28 defendants on various charges relating to the attack on Ramos Horta and Gusmão in February 2008.

Following the end of the conflict in 1999, Timor-Leste experienced a post-crisis 'baby boom', and the country has continued to record one of the highest birth rates in the world. The population increased at an average annual rate of 3.8% between 2000 and 2008, thereby placing further strains upon the country's social and economic sustainability. Timor-Leste's strong economic growth in 2009/10 was bolstered by continued increases in government expenditure and agricultural productivity. While higher levels of government spending may have helped to secure social cohesion, critics contended that the drawdown from the Petroleum Fund breached the sustainability principle underpinning management of the nation's finite resources. With the notable exceptions of retail trade (an activity increasingly dominated by Timorese-Chinese business networks) and the construction sector, private investment remained limited. Notwithstanding organized activities such as bicycle races and international conferences, visitors to Timor-Leste were few and far between; despite huge potential, the tourism industry languished in a near-dormant state. According to Turismo de Timor-Leste, just 30,000 people visited the country on a tourist visa in 2009.

In a potentially important advance, in December 2009 the National Parliament debated a resolution to implement recommendations issued by the CAVR and the joint Timorese-Indonesian Commission of Truth and Friendship (CTF—see Foreign Relations, below). Just as relations between the Timorese Government and its former colonial power, Indonesia, appeared to be improving, many civil society groups were alarmed by the revelation that an indicted pro-Jakarta militia leader, Marternus Bere, had been released into the custody of the Indonesian embassy in Dili in August 2009 upon the instruction of the Timorese President and Prime Minister—an action that prompted considerable censure from the UN. Bere had been indicted by the UN-supported Serious Crimes Unit in 2003 for his involvement in the massacre of at least 30 East Timorese civilians (and as many as 200, according to some sources) who had been seeking refuge from the militia in a church at Suai, in the south-west of the country, in September 1999.

In January 2010 Ameerah Haq was appointed as the UN Secretary-General's Special Representative in Timor-Leste and head of UNMIT, which continued to implement the progressive transfer of policing responsibility to the PNTL. In an internal security mission in the western part of the country between late 2009 and early 2010, the security forces were deployed to track down an underground 'ninja' movement believed to be linked to dissident elements. However, concerns remained with regard to the effectiveness and integrity of the police force.

A verdict in the trial of those accused of involvement in the February 2008 shooting of President Ramos Horta was delivered in March 2010. The prosecution had sought prison sentences ranging from two to 20 years for the 28 defendants; in the event, four were acquitted, among them Australian national Angelita Pires, reported to have been in a relationship with Alfredo Reinado; 24 were sentenced to prison terms of between nine and 16 years. Gastão Salsinha, who had denied any involvement, insisting that he and his supporters had merely been seeking a meeting with Ramos Horta, was imprisoned for 10 years and eight months on charges of conspiracy and attempted murder. Marcelo Caetano, who had been identified by Ramos Horta as the man who had shot him, was sentenced to 16 years' imprisonment on charges including conspiracy to kill, although the court ruled that he had not fired the bullet that had injured the President. However, the official version of events surrounding the attack was mired in controversy and left many questions unanswered.

Renewed uncertainty concerning the stability of the PMA Government emerged in September 2010, following the resignation of Deputy Prime Minister Mário Viegas Carrascalão, who had been appointed in January 2009 with a mandate to strengthen governance and eradicate corruption. The resignation was provoked by a public rebuke from Gusmão, in which the premier described his deputy, who had latterly been increasingly vociferous in his criticism of the Government's performance, as 'stupid' and 'a liar'. The incident cast doubt on the continued participation of Carrascalão's PSD in the ruling coalition.

With presidential and parliamentary elections scheduled to be held during the first half of 2012, there was considerable speculation over possible candidates during 2011, while political organizations, including some newly formed parties, prepared their electoral strategies. To its credit, Fretilin, which had all along denied the legitimacy of the incumbent PMA Government led by Prime Minister Gusmão, did not seek to destabilize that Government by calling for early elections.

Meanwhile, the Timor-Leste economy continued to expand strongly, primarily owing to further increases in government spending. Private investment also increased, as did the value of the country's Petroleum Fund. However, as President Ramos Horta himself noted, the Government had not demonstrated good leadership in executing the country's state budget for national development, owing to the flawed nature of the procurement process. Similar views were expressed by the parliamentary opposition and by a number of civil society groups. Various civil society groups also criticized the tendering process and apparent lack of environmental safeguards of a new power plant, being constructed near Dili by a Chinese company, which was scheduled to commence operations in late 2011.

In July 2011 an ambitious strategic development plan for the period 2011–30, which had been announced in April 2010, was finally submitted to the National Parliament. Informed by the 2010 national census, the plan set out measures to be undertaken in three major development areas: social capital, infrastructure and the economy. However, elements of the opposition, including Fretilin, protested against the decision-making process, claiming that insufficient time had been allowed to consider and debate the draft before a vote was taken.

By 2011 more than 5,000 corruption cases had been lodged with the prosecutor's office, including claims against government ministers, district administrators and other civil servants. There were high expectations regarding the outcome of two high-profile cases brought before the Dili District Court in 2010–11. These were the linked cases against Minister of Foreign Affairs and Co-operation Zacarias da Costa and Deputy Prime Minister—and Fretilin defector—José Luís Guterres; Guterres was accused of nepotism and abuse of power in appointing his wife as counsel to the Timorese ambassador to the UN in New York, USA, in 2006 and subsequently authorizing a substantial increase in her salary, an arrangement in which da Costa was alleged to have been complicit. Notably, President Ramos-Horta termed the trials a 'test for democracy and law enforcement'. In the event, both da Costa and Guterres were acquitted, in November 2010 and May 2011, respectively, on the grounds of, *inter alia*, insufficient evidence. Although there was no major public challenge to the judicial outcome, critics of the Government alleged that it had interfered in the judicial process.

However, such concerns for due process on the part of the Dili District Court were overshadowed by issues arising from judgments passed down by the now-defunct UN-supported Serious Crimes Unit, which was dissolved in 2005. Although rebutted by Timorese officials, a draft copy of UNDP's *Timor-Leste Human Development Report 2010*, released to the media in January 2011, sternly criticized the Government for its apparent opposition to the pursuit of perpetrators of war crimes and crimes against humanity. Presidential pardons handed down in August 2010 for those convicted of political violence in February 2008 elicited similar expressions of concern from observers. Meanwhile, discussions in the National Parliament on draft laws on reparations and on the establishment of institutions to follow the CAVR and the CTF remained stalled at mid-2011, notwithstanding rhetorical endorsement by Fretilin Secretary-General Mari Alkatiri.

By 2011 Timor-Leste appeared to have decisively progressed beyond the unrest of 2006–07. There had been no major recurrences of violence; improved economic performance, sustained by an expansionary budget, was evident; and cash allocations to resettled IDPs, former military personnel and pensioners had begun to translate into improved livelihoods, at least in urban areas. However, disconcerting questions had been raised by a number of issues, including: the substantial number of missing weapons; disturbing activities by martial arts groups, criminal gangs and unorthodox religious groups; and issues arising from the demobilization of veteran guerrilla fighters. According to the World Bank, at mid-2011 Timor-Leste still confronted major governance challenges. Institutional capacity remained weak within many government ministries, and there had been little strengthening at the district and local levels. The judiciary was in dire need of reform; the human resources base remained very low, and the Government remained highly dependent on foreign advisers and external funding.

FOREIGN RELATIONS

President Gusmão visited Jakarta in July 2002, when he and Indonesian President Megawati announced a plan to promote economic co-operation between the two countries. The two sides also agreed to establish a joint commission to consider Indonesian claims for compensation for assets lost in the territory when it became independent, although Timor-Leste intimated that it might refer to Indonesian exploitation and destruction of property in resisting those claims. Indonesia's claims referred both to infrastructure, such as roads, which it constructed during its rule of the territory, and to the private property of Indonesian citizens abandoned in 1999. The new Government's priority was to ensure good relations with Indonesia, so that issues of trade, border demarcation, militia remnants in West Timor and access to the Oecusse enclave could be resolved easily. Accordingly, Timor-Leste repeatedly assured Indonesia that it did not support the separatist movements in Aceh, Papua and elsewhere. Timorese leaders were also mild in their public criticism of the acquittal of many Indonesian soldiers accused of atrocities in the former East Timor, and of what were seen as light sentences passed on those who were convicted. None the less, there was evidence that Indonesian army elements continued to arm and train militias for incursions across the border from West Timor. At the same time, therefore, the Government of Timor-Leste was keen to consolidate the country's position more firmly in the broader region. It signalled that it would seek membership of ASEAN, although Singapore was reportedly opposed to the entry of another economically weak country into the association. With notable support from Indonesia, Timor-Leste became a participant in the ASEAN Regional Forum (on security issues) in July 2005. In July 2006 Timor-Leste agreed to sign the ASEAN Treaty of Amity and Co-operation, in an initial step towards membership of the Association. It also expressed interest in joining the Pacific Islands Forum. In September 2007 President José Ramos Horta announced that he had established a task force to prepare for Timor-Leste's eventual accession to ASEAN, with a view to securing membership within around five years. Timor-Leste sought good relations with China, which had previously recognized it in 1975 and which was the first country to establish formal diplomatic relations in 2002. Timor-Leste became a member of the UN in September 2002, having previously joined the World Bank, the IMF and the Asian Development Bank (ADB). Relations with China were strengthened in August 2008, prior to the opening ceremony of the Olympic Games in Beijing, when President Ramos Horta joined other world leaders at an official reception hosted by his Chinese counterpart, Hu Jintao, also securing during his visit a pledge from China for the supply of patrol boats. Ramos Horta returned to Timor-Leste via the Philippines, where he sought to promote cultural, political and economic links. Earlier that month, during his journey back from a visit to Portugal, the President travelled on an inaugural commercial flight from Singapore to Dili, a crucial connection for Timor-Leste in terms of boosting both investment and tourism.

In September 2003 Timor-Leste began formal negotiations with Indonesia to demarcate their shared land and maritime borders, including the terms of East Timorese overland access to the Oecusse enclave and provision for border passes to enable residents to visit cross-border markets. Indonesia continued to claim compensation for property abandoned in East Timor in 1999, estimated to be worth €212m., while the Timor-Leste Government argued that accepting such a claim would make Indonesia liable to far greater claims over its actions during the occupation. Indonesia offered to provide military training to Falintil-ETDF, but there was widespread public hostility to this proposal. In December 2003 an Indonesian warship shelled the disputed island of Fatu Sinai (Pulau Batek), off the Oecusse enclave, and in August 2004 Timor-Leste acknowledged Indonesian sovereignty over the island. Smuggling across the border remained a major irritant. In May 2004 the SPSC in Dili finally issued an arrest warrant for Gen. Wiranto, then a candidate for the Indonesian presidency. Both President Gusmão and the Prosecutor-General, Longuinhos Monteiro, described the warrant as a mistake, and stated that the Timor-Leste Government would not enforce it. President Gusmão later met Gen. Wiranto in Bali in a highly publicized reconciliation encounter. In July the two countries reached an agreement demarcating 90% of the land boundary. In April 2005 the Indonesian President, Susilo Bambang Yudhoyono, visited Timor-Leste for the first time since coming to power and signed a final border agreement with President Gusmão. The agreement did not cover Timor-Leste's maritime boundaries with Indonesia. The Indonesian President also visited both the Santa Cruz cemetery, where Indonesian forces had shot more than 100 demonstrators in 1991, and a cemetery for Indonesian troops killed in the initial invasion of 1975–76.

In March 2005 Indonesia agreed to join Timor-Leste in establishing the joint CTF to investigate and report on the violence at the time of the independence referendum. The commission's10 members, appointed in July to serve a two-year term, were evenly divided between Timor-Leste and Indonesia, with its headquarters being established in Bali. To the disappointment of human rights activists, the Commission received no powers to prosecute those responsible for the violence, and was authorized to grant amnesties to those who testified before it. According to President Gusmão, it was time for the two countries to disregard the past and to focus instead on forging stronger bilateral relations. The decision was criticized by international human rights bodies for failing to provide justice on behalf of victims of the 1999 violence. Gusmão expressed much the same view in relation to the detailed report of the CAVR, which had sought to determine the precise extent of death and other loss during the Indonesian occupation. Although the report attributed 180,000 deaths to Indonesian actions and policies, both directly and indirectly, the Timorese Government expressed no interest in prosecuting those who might have been responsible, stating its desire to focus on the future rather than to dwell on the past. The shooting by Timorese border guards of three Indonesian citizens believed to have infiltrated Timorese territory in January 2006 briefly strained relations, but Indonesia did not pursue the issue. The CTF held five sessions of hearings between February and September 2007, before retiring to prepare its recommendations. Prominent figures who appeared before the Commission included Gen. Wiranto, Gusmão and Brig.-Gen. Ruak. In July the UN prohibited its officials from testifying, owing to the decision to grant amnesty to perpetrators of serious crimes, while human rights organizations continued to criticize the process, claiming that insufficient numbers of victims had been summoned to give evidence. Meanwhile, in June, two weeks after taking office as President of Timor-Leste, José Ramos Horta visited Indonesia. Ramos Horta and Indonesian President Yudhoyono reaffirmed their commitment to the CTF, extending its mandate by six months, and emphasized the importance of further improving bilateral relations.

The spirit of reconciliation evident in the domestic administration of justice in Timor-Leste in 2008, exemplified by the pardons granted to prisoners convicted of involvement in the violence of 1999 and 2006 (see above), also took on diplomatic overtones. Although still disavowed by the UN owing to its amnesty provisions, the CTF's report was released in July 2008. While surprisingly blunt in its acknowledgement of institutional crimes committed inside East Timor by the Indonesian military and its militias in 1999, the report failed to name individual perpetrators. Expressing remorse over the events at a meeting held in Bali on 15 July, President Yudhoyono, together with his Timorese counterpart, declared the case closed. Nevertheless, in the opinion of the inhabitants of the Catholic diocese of Dili and of the international human rights community, such closure hardly satisfied the victims. UNMIT also advised the Government not to neglect justice, emphasizing that it would continue to support prosecutions against perpetrators of human rights violations committed in 1999, a UN Serious Crimes Investigation Team having been created in 2007 to examine outstanding cases. It was apparent that the Timorese leadership—the Fretilin opposition included—was adamant in placing close bilateral relations with Indonesia above all other considerations.

Relations with Australia were hindered by disagreement over the maritime boundaries in the Timor Sea. Australia's maritime border with Indonesia in the Timor Sea, settled in 1972, followed the continental shelf and gave a large part of the Sea to Australia. There had been no such agreement with Portugal, and during the Indonesian occupation of East Timor the unregulated space between the territory and Australia was known as the Timor Gap. Although Australia would have preferred to delineate the border following the continental shelf, international law had shifted in such cases to preferring borders drawn along a median line between the two coasts. Pending resolution of this complex issue, Australia and Indonesia had reached an agreement for regulating access to gas resources in the Gap. The agreement created a zone of co-operation (ZOC), the income from which was to be shared by the two countries. This agreement became invalid with East Timor's departure from Indonesia, and the Timorese authorities signalled that they intended to claim the full zone up to the median line, including areas that had been allocated to Australia under the Timor Gap Treaty. The lucrative Greater Sunrise field, which was being exploited by Australia, was within this claimed area. In response, in March 2002 Australia formally withdrew the issue from the jurisdiction of the ICJ and the international tribunal established under the 1982 UN Convention on the Law of the Sea. On 20 May 2002, the day of East Timor's independence, the two countries signed an interim Timor Sea Treaty, which largely preserved the previous arrangement but gave a larger share of revenue to East Timor. In July, however, the new Timor-Leste National Parliament approved a law establishing an Exclusive Economic Zone extending for a circumference of 200 nautical miles, subject to future negotiations with Indonesia and Australia. Timor-Leste based its claim on international law and on its need for income from resources for its own economic development, and sought a rapid permanent settlement of the border issue. Australia and Timor-Leste later signed further agreements for revenue-sharing in the former ZOC (subsequently renamed the Joint Petroleum Development Area—JPDA), but some observers accused Australia of both delaying the formal boundary negotiations and accelerating exploitation of areas that it would almost certainly lose to Timor-Leste under international law. Reserves in the disputed area were estimated to be worth approximately US $8,000m.

Negotiations resumed in September 2003, with Australia being accused of delaying proceedings in order that it might continue to benefit from an inequitable arrangement. In September 2004 the two countries appeared finally to have agreed upon a revenue-sharing arrangement, which over a period of 30 years would afford Timor-Leste $A5,000m. in tax and royalty payments from the natural gas project in the Timor Sea. However, the negotiations again broke down, principally owing to the two countries' failure to agree on the contentious boundary issues. In February 2005 further acrimony ensued when the Australian Government agreed to a mid-point boundary with New Zealand but still refused to consider a similar arrangement with Timor-Leste. Instead, Australia proposed that the decision with Timor-Leste be deferred for up to 100 years while the major petroleum and gas deposits were

political and security-related purposes. However, direct international intervention became necessary again in 2006, following clashes in April and May between demobilized troops and security forces which culminated in widespread violence; the unrest led to numerous deaths, and as many as 150,000 people were displaced as they were forced to flee their homes. In response, some 2,200 foreign peace-keepers were deployed to restore order, and UNOTIL's mandate was extended to August 2006, when it was replaced by the UN Integrated Mission in Timor-Leste (UNMIT). The mandate of UNMIT, extended in each February during 2007–11, encompassed the provision of a variety of political and security-related support services aimed at improving humanitarian and social conditions in Timor-Leste. (See History for further details.)

POST-INDEPENDENCE DEVELOPMENT STRATEGY

At the end of 2001, a Planning Commission was established in Timor-Leste to oversee the preparation of a National Development Plan. The Plan was drafted on the basis of a participatory country-wide consultative process, the findings of which were published in a booklet, entitled *East Timor to 2020: Our Nation, Our Future*, which was distributed to every household in May 2002.

The principal objectives of the National Development Plan were to reduce poverty, promote economic growth, and facilitate human development. It urged a combination of capacity-building measures and co-ordinated efforts to reduce poverty and sector-specific development strategies. To achieve these goals, the Plan proposed a phased approach: in the short term, priority would continue to be given to the building of an appropriate legislative framework and institutional capacities, as well as the further development of infrastructure, education and health; over the longer term, the foundations laid by these efforts were to be built upon to achieve sustainable development funded by the anticipated increase in oil and gas revenues.

The National Development Plan came into operation upon Timor-Leste's independence, and was intended to be implemented on a rolling basis consistent with the country's annual budgets. For this purpose, the formulation of annual action plans and quarterly reporting matrices was initiated with the commencement of the 2002/03 fiscal year, on 1 July 2002. In addition, efforts were made to determine the prioritization and sequencing of the activities envisaged in the Plan through the establishment of 17 Sector Investment Programmes (SIPs) for various socio-economic sectors, and to prepare a 'road map' for its implementation over the following four years. At the same time the Government also began to formulate Timor-Leste's national Millennium Development Goals, based on the objectives established by the world's heads of state at the Millennium Summit held at the UN headquarters in New York, USA, in September 2000. The draft SIPs were finalized and publicly released in 2005. To ensure the availability of the required resources and the effective implementation of the SIPs, joint Sector Working Groups were established by the Government and donors, with relevant NGOs also being consulted.

In a particularly important initiative in the context of implementing the National Development Plan, in 2004 the Government formulated an effective policy and legislative framework for the country's emerging petroleum industry, which covered such issues as production, taxation and revenue management. This initiative, supported by the establishment of an Investment and Export Promotion Agency in mid-2005, aimed to stimulate the development of entrepreneurship in the country, although it was recognized that this would need to be supplemented by a variety of other measures, such as the promulgation of comprehensive legislation dealing with land-ownership, bankruptcy and banking.

The adoption of such economic policy measures suffered a set-back in 2006 as a result of the violence that erupted in April–May. The restoration of political stability and recovery in economic activity in 2007, which was subsequently sustained, despite the assassination attempts on the country's President and Prime Minister in February 2008, allowed further economic measures to be implemented. After the designation of the second half of 2007 as an interim fiscal period, the budgetary year was adjusted to coincide with the calendar year from January 2008 onwards. Meanwhile, in 2007 the Government amended the business-licensing process, reducing the duration of this procedure from 30 days to a maximum of three–five days, and initiated a reform of the education system with the introduction of a nine-year period of mandatory free education. A National Strategic Development Plan for 2011–30 was drafted in 2010, following a series of nation-wide public consultations held during that year. The Plan, which was approved by the National Parliament in July 2011, was an ambitious document, albeit somewhat general in its outlook. Outlining overall strategies for 2011–20, the Plan focused on development in areas such as infrastructure, education and health, and in the industrial and service sectors. Areas of focus for the period 2021–30, as outlined in the Plan, include the improvement of the quality of life for the Timorese population and the promotion of environmental sustainability.

POPULATION AND EMPLOYMENT

The first post-independence population census of Timor-Leste, conducted in July 2004, enumerated a total resident population of 923,198. This exceeded previous estimates of the 2004 population by some 100,000 persons, and was well above the 2001 estimate of 787,000. While much of the difference between the 2001 estimate and the actual figure for 2004 was attributable to the return of refugees who had fled during the post-referendum violence in 1999, the census data also indicated that the fertility rate of 8.3 live births per woman was much higher than the figure of 3–4 live births that had previously been expected. Assuming this figure to be correct, Timor-Leste thus had the highest fertility rate in the world, consistent with an overall annual rate of population growth of about 3%. A Demographic and Health Survey conducted in 2009/10 indicated that the fertility rate had declined to 5.7 births per woman (more than two fewer than in 2003). None the less, in 2010 the UN Population Fund estimated that the population would double within 17 years at the existing annual rate of population growth (some 3.2%). According to the results of a second post-independence census, conducted in July 2010, the population stood at 1,066,409, indicating average annual growth of around 2.4% since the 2004 census. UN estimates put the population at 1,153,835 at mid-2011.

The demographic antecedents of Timor-Leste are less easy to quantify. Estimates prepared during the Portuguese era, which are acknowledged to be unreliable, indicated a total population of 624,564 in 1973. The subsequent civil war and Indonesian military intervention took a heavy toll on the local population. The first formal population census under Indonesian rule, conducted in 1980, thus showed a total population of 555,350. By the time of the next census in 1990 this number had risen to 747,750, and an intercensal survey carried out in 1995 suggested a further increase in the population, to 843,100. The latter figure included a substantial, but unknown, number of non-indigenous people, many of whom left East Timor during the violence following the August 1999 referendum, together with an estimated 250,000–260,000 East Timorese who fled the violence to Indonesian-governed West Timor. These refugees began to return to East Timor once stability had been restored, and almost 205,000 were reported by the office of the UN High Commissioner for Refugees (UNHCR) to have returned by the time of independence, as a result of which at the end of 2002 UNHCR terminated the refugee status of persons who had fled East Timor in 1999. By the end of 2005 the refugee issue had been largely resolved, with approximately 225,000 people having returned to Timor-Leste and a further 28,000 having confirmed their Indonesian citizenship and remained in Indonesia on a permanent basis.

However, by this time the country's demographic pressures had been exacerbated by the impact of the unrest of April–May 2006, and this gave rise to violent clashes between rival groups, which eventually resulted in some 150,000 people leaving their homes and seeking refuge in 65 hastily established camps. Looking after these internally displaced persons (IDPs) and arranging their resettlement subsequently posed a serious challenge for the Government, with as many as 100,000 still needing to be resettled in mid-2008; the last major IDP camp at

Metinaro, near the capital of Dili, was not closed until mid-2009.

Even without the additional problems arising from the political instability and violence, the relatively high rate of population growth in Timor-Leste has serious implications for the country's efforts to overcome poverty. Despite the relatively robust real growth in GDP recorded in 2004 and 2005, estimates by the Asian Development Bank (ADB) indicate that per caput GDP declined from US $467 in 2001 to $338 in 2005. This trend was exacerbated by the economic contraction prompted by the political unrest in 2006, when GDP per head contracted further, to $322, and it was not until 2009, after three years of economic recovery, that GDP per head rose above the level recorded in 2001, to an estimated $529. Government data indicate that per caput income increased to just over $600 in 2010.

Official rates of unemployment in Timor-Leste have remained relatively low since independence. According to the Survey of Living Standards undertaken in 2007, unemployment stood at 6.7%. The Timor-Leste Labour Force Survey 2010 indicated a decline in unemployment to 3.6% in that year, with female unemployment at 4.6% and male unemployment at 3.1%. The overall figure was comparable to the level of unemployment in other countries of the South-East Asian region. However, it is important to note that the definition of 'work' used in the survey included people engaged in as little as one hour of paid or unpaid labour per week, and thus the figures may not provide an accurate portrayal of the true state of unemployment in the country. Furthermore, the survey used additional indicators, such as 'vulnerable employment' and those in 'inactive' employment. The number of people in these categories is much larger. For example, 176,000 people were included within the 'vulnerable employment' category, representing some 70% of the total employed population. Similarly, 50% of the population under the age of 20 were defined as 'inactive'. Recent estimates indicate that 90% of the unemployed are within the 15–24 age group, a factor highlighted in the Government's appraisal in 2010 of progress towards the attainment of the country's Millennium Development Goals (MDGs). Many of the unemployed youth live in Dili, which in recent years has witnessed extremely high levels of immigration of young people.

Around one-quarter of the working population is employed within the public sector, while about 10% (including volunteers not receiving wages) are employed by the non-governmental sector. To address present employment needs, additional jobs will need to be created within the non-oil sector, improvements will be required in skills training, and a system will need to be developed to match existing skills with jobs as they become available. In recent years the Government has implemented programmes providing short-term employment within the infrastructure industry, in areas such as bridge and road construction; however, longer-term, sustainable solutions need to be developed, which will require substantial increases in private sector investment in the agricultural, manufacturing and service sectors.

Until recently, Timor-Leste was one of the poorest countries in the world. In its Human Poverty Index for 2006 (based on data for 2004), the UN Development Programme (UNDP) ranked the country 142nd out of the 177 countries reporting. However, by 2010 its ranking had improved to 120th of the 169 countries reporting, outperforming Laos, Cambodia, and Myanmar (ranked 132nd), as well as most sub-Saharan African countries. However, much of this progress is attributable to increases in per caput income boosted largely by petroleum revenues, and to a lesser extent to the other, non-income areas covered in the HDI. The World Bank estimated that poverty incidence had declined during 2007–09 (from almost 50% to 41% in the latter year), a finding that was corroborated by an assessment of the country's level of human development presented in UNDP's *Timor-Leste Human Development Report 2011*.

ECONOMIC STRUCTURE AND TRENDS

At independence in 2002, Timor-Leste was the poorest country in Asia, with an estimated annual income of US $431 per head. While this figure slightly exceeded the corresponding figure of $424 recorded in 1998, some $400 of it was estimated to have been contributed by foreign donors. The sectoral distribution of GDP has traditionally been very heavily biased towards agriculture, which in 1998–99 accounted for more than 40% of the total, although agriculture's contribution decreased to approximately 25% in 2000–01 as a result of the destruction of the country's productive base in 1999, before recovering in subsequent years. The manufacturing sector is small, but the overall contribution of industry (including mining, construction and utilities) has fluctuated between 15% and 20% in recent years.

As indicated above, the economy contracted sharply in 1999 as a result of the political violence of that year, but it recovered between 2000 and 2001 in response to the financial and technical support received from the international community through UNTAET. However, the subsequent gradual downsizing of the UN presence in Timor-Leste led to a corresponding reduction in economic activity, with the construction, services and financial sectors being particularly badly affected. The negative impact of these developments was exacerbated by a decline in agricultural production owing to unfavourable weather conditions, as a result of which the rate of GDP growth decelerated to 2.4% in 2002. The downturn persisted into 2003, as donor activities continued to slow, with growth of only 0.1% in real terms being recorded in the non-oil component of GDP in that year.

A reversal of this trend began in 2004, with non-oil GDP increasing by 4.2% in 2004 and by 6.2% in 2005. This renewed growth was supported primarily by an increase in agricultural output, which expanded by 6.0% in real terms in 2004 and by 6.3% in 2005. The upward trend in economic growth was interrupted in 2006 by political and social unrest and subsequent dislocations and instability. These events resulted in an extensive and extended disruption of economic activity, caused by the destruction of economic infrastructure, the displacement of the population (including about one-half of the population of the capital and significant numbers from the major agricultural areas), and the interruption of transport and communications. The non-oil economy contracted by 5.8% in 2006, despite a surge in public spending and international aid towards the end of the year. However, the decline in 2006 was followed by a recovery in non-oil GDP growth to 8.4% in 2007 and to 12.8% in 2008, as security was restored and as the Government's rising oil revenues permitted a steady increase in public spending. More moderate growth of 7.5% was recorded in both 2009 and 2010. According to the IMF, the rate of growth was projected to increase to 8.0% by 2012.

Developments in the non-oil economy were supplemented by steady growth in petroleum revenues following the commencement of offshore oil production from the Bayu-Undan field to the south of the country in April 2004, which resulted in a significant rise in overall gross national income. The substantial increase in international prices for petroleum from 2004, and the gradual increase in the number of oilfields coming under production, allowed Timor-Leste to derive significant financial benefits. To prevent this surge in financial resources from undermining the country's economic stability, the Government established a Petroleum Fund, legislation for which was promulgated in August 2005. The Fund began operation in the following month, with the intention of absorbing the country's petroleum revenues and investing them judiciously for the future benefit of the population of Timor-Leste. The initiative was widely acclaimed as embodying the best possible arrangements for the management of oil revenues. While the Petroleum Fund Law of 2005 permits the Government to draw upon its resources for budgetary needs, these withdrawals must be held within sustainable limits, calculated annually as 3% of the sum of the Fund balance and the value of expected petroleum receipts, and known as the Estimated Sustainable Income (ESI). Withdrawing more than this requires the Government to provide Parliament with a detailed explanation as to why such action is in the long-term interests of the country, based on a report certified by an independent auditor. Withdrawals began to exceed the 3% level in 2008–09, in order to fund infrastructure development and subsidize food imports. In June 2010 a budget rectification proposed an increase in expenditure to US $309m. above ESI, and this was implemented during the year. The 2011 budget proposed expenditure at ESI level for 2011, increasing to $418m. above ESI in 2012, and further to $526.1m. above ESI in 2015. Implementation of the Strategic Development Plan for 2011–30 will require expenditure that is more than twice the level of ESI to 2020. In June 2011 the Government submitted to Parliament a bill proposing the removal of many of the controls governing the Petroleum Fund. Under this draft legislation, up to 50% of the value of the Fund would be managed by foreign fund managers for stock market investment. The parliamentary oversight role would be largely abolished and transferred to government ministers. The Fund was to be established as a collateral for debt instruments, and its special status of being separate from state finances was to be removed. The ESI rate was to be increased beyond 3% of the Fund balance, which at July had reached $8,500m.

AGRICULTURE

Although constrained by the country's mountainous terrain, relatively poor soils and a comparatively dry climate, agriculture has traditionally been the mainstay of Timor-Leste's economy, providing employment for approximately 80% of its labour force. One-third of all households in Timor-Leste rely exclusively on subsistence cultivation and most households regularly experience food shortages in any given year. Agriculture currently accounts for only around one-fifth of GDP. The sector's productivity is extremely low, with output per worker less than one-tenth of that in the industry and service sectors. The country historically has produced a variety of food and commercial crops, and also has a history of animal husbandry and fisheries. As with the rest of the economy, the agricultural sector was seriously disrupted by the upheavals that followed the independence referendum in 1999, and a major rehabilitation effort had to be initiated by UNTAET, with financial support from the World Bank and donors, in the following years. This comprised both a rapid-delivery component to facilitate the recovery of agricultural production levels and a number of longer-term measures to ensure the sustained growth of the sector. The programme thus aimed to provide for: the restoration of productive assets to farmers; the community-based repair of rural feeder roads and small irrigation systems; the provision of agricultural credit; the establishment of local radio services to provide information to farmers; and the development of five experimental agricultural service centres managed by private entrepreneurs or NGOs to provide support services to farmers. As a result of such measures, both agriculture and fisheries had recovered to pre-1999 levels by independence in May 2002.

A series of agriculture rehabilitation projects was implemented with World Bank and donor funding between 2001 and 2008, resulting in increases in agricultural productivity and output, and contributing to improvements in food security. Based on World Bank estimates, more than 20,000 rural families received support under these agriculture rehabilitation programmes, while irrigation facilities covering an area of 13,800 ha were rehabilitated, together with 232 km of rural access roads.

In view of the importance of the agricultural sector to the national economy, the post-independence Government gave high priority to its development. Thus, the National Development Plan stated that, 'In the medium term the agricultural sector, more than most, provides opportunities for economic growth, exports, employment and improvements in social welfare throughout East Timor', and projected that, 'By 2020 East Timor will have sustainable, competitive and prosperous agricultural, fisheries and forestry industries that support improved living standards for the nation's people'. To achieve this goal, the Plan provided for the Government, through the newly established Ministry of Agriculture, Forestry and Fisheries, to 'efficiently deliver services to agricultural, fishing and forestry communities in East Timor . . . that support improved productivity, income earning potential and exports and that, therefore, support improved social welfare in the rural areas of the nation'.

The proposals contained in the National Development Plan were developed further in the SIP on agriculture, forestry and fisheries, issued in April 2005. This document set out a number of new policy directions for the development of these sectors. In particular, it emphasized continuing improvements in the productivity of farming systems in upland and dryland areas as a means of enhancing food security. In this respect, it was stressed that government policy towards agriculture would focus on the social functions of agriculture and on supporting subsistence agriculture. In addition, the SIP also defined a very broad range of activities for the Ministry of Agriculture, Forestry and Fisheries, stating that the recently established Ministry would serve as a provider of vital services to farmers within a framework of promoting rural development in general, and as a facilitator and regulator. In the context of this support function, the Ministry established several agricultural high schools, from which the first batch of students graduated with post-secondary degrees in agribusiness in 2008.

These early measures showed impressive results between 2002 and 2005, as the share of the agricultural sector in non-oil GDP increased steadily from 26.6% to 31.8%. However, owing to widespread damage both to the agricultural production base and to marketing infrastructure, as a result of the civil unrest of 2006, agriculture's share in non-oil GDP grew only marginally in that year, to 33.1%, and sector growth declined to just 0.3%, from 6.3% in 2005. Agriculture's contribution to GDP declined to 27.5% in 2007, while the output of the sector contracted by 5.6%, as a result of continuing security problems, drought and locust infestations. According to official data, both output and the area under cultivation of the basic crops, rice and maize, have increased substantially since 2007. Rice output, for example, increased by 73.8% between 2007 and 2009.

Food Crops

The principal food crops grown in Timor-Leste are maize (which is the chief staple of the local population) and rice, although small quantities of other staples such as cassava, sweet potatoes and soybeans are also produced in the country. During Indonesian occupation, emphasis was placed firmly on the cultivation of rice, much of which was exported to Indonesia. Irrigation systems were rehabilitated and extended, particularly in the west of Timor-Leste. The production of food crops was severely disrupted by the unrest of 1999, as a result of which UNTAET estimated that output of both rice and maize declined in 2000 to some 70% of pre-conflict levels. This decrease was caused by a combination of factors, including a reduction in the planted area and dislocation of rural labour owing to the violence linked to the independence ballot, the destruction of irrigation schemes, and the loss of services from government and private sector suppliers. To address these difficulties, UNTAET accorded high priority to supporting a recovery in food crop production and introduced a number of programmes to bring more land under cultivation and to increase yields. These included restitution of farming household assets, rehabilitation of rural feeder roads and irrigation systems, and fertilizer demonstrations.

Although these programmes enabled UNTAET to meet its ambitious target of increasing food production to 80%–120% of 1997 levels by early 2002, the prospects for future expansion were constrained in the short term by the low productivity and high production costs of the food crop sub-sector. By the end of the second agriculture rehabilitation programme in June 2005, Timor-Leste's annual output of rice had increased to 44,000 metric tons, and that of maize to more than 80,000 tons: both thus significantly exceeded the corresponding figures for 1998. Output in 2006 suffered as a result of the renewed political unrest, which caused members of the agricultural population to flee their farms and disrupted market flows. While production of rice was estimated to have recovered to some 40,000 tons in 2007, this amount covered only about one-half of domestic demand. The sharp rise in food prices, especially those of rice, in the first half of 2008 prompted fears of possible food shortages and hunger. The Government responded to the threat of famine by importing large quantities of rice for subsidized resale, placing a severe burden on the budget. These developments strengthened an earlier government decision to place greater emphasis in the future on the promotion of non-rice food staples, on the grounds that rice was not a local food staple before the period of Indonesian rule. Particular priority was to be given to maize in this connection, although the production of other crops such as beans, potatoes, sweet potatoes, cassava and vegetables was also encouraged in order to increase crop diversity and improve nutritional standards. Increased production and productivity in the agricultural sector in 2009 was partly attributed to the use of high-yield seeds and fertilizers. However, a report in mid-2010 by the UN Office for the Coordination of Humanitarian Affairs highlighted the problem of poor storage facilities, with some 30% of maize production believed to be lost annually, mainly to insects and vermin.

Cash Crops and Agricultural Processing

The main commercial crop grown in Timor-Leste is coffee. Compared with the low-value robusta coffees grown throughout the Indonesian archipelago, Timor-Leste produces substantial quantities of higher-value arabica in its loftier elevations. The country's coffee plantations were originally established during the Portuguese colonial era, when they accounted for some 90% of East Timor's export earnings. Production declined sharply in the transitional period of the mid-1970s as a result of the departure of Portuguese agricultural experts and the virtual abandonment of the coffee plantations. This led the Indonesian authorities to initiate a major replanting effort, with more than 1m. arabica and robusta seedlings being planted in the first four years of Indonesian rule. By 1994 annual coffee production had reached almost 8,800 metric tons, although it declined to less than 5,000 tons in 1997–98, as a result of the economic crisis affecting Indonesia and the effects of the drought caused by the weather phenomenon known as *El Niño*. In 1999 coffee production increased to around 10,000 tons, and much of the crop survived the destruction that followed the referendum on independence. After remaining broadly stable in the following years, output declined by about 20% in 2006, owing to the displacement of farmers and the resulting harvest losses caused by the unrest in that year, and by a further 20% in 2007, owing to drought and pest infestations. Despite initial fears that security concerns might also impede the 2008 harvest, production recovered in that year, and subsequently, as political stability was restored and the drought of the previous year receded.

An important feature of the East Timorese coffee industry during the era of Indonesian rule was the controversial marketing system employed by the Indonesian authorities. Soon after the territory was integrated into Indonesia, a monopoly was established over the coffee market by PT Denok, a company associated with the Indonesian military, through the seizure of Portuguese-era coffee plantations and the forced sale of coffee by smallholders to PT Denok at artificially low prices. As a result of pressure from the USA, this monopoly began to disintegrate in the mid-1990s, at which time a new system was put in place linking the Indonesian system of rural co-operatives to the US National Cooperative Business Association (NCBA) and providing local smallholders with significantly higher prices for their output. As a result of this arrangement, which remained in place even after the extensive political changes of 1999, the NCBA accounted for some 25% of the sale of East Timorese coffee. Another major purchaser of East Timorese coffee was the US-based Starbucks Corporation, cited in the media as one of East Timor's principal clients. In 2009 the USA received some 34% of Timor-Leste's coffee exports, followed by Germany (29%) and Portugal (9%).

One serious difficulty suffered by East Timorese coffee producers as a result of the violence of 1999 was that all the 'wet-processing' facilities used for the processing of high-grade arabica coffee were badly damaged and inoperable. As a result, farmers were forced to 'dry-process' their coffee, which then fetched a much lower price. Although the coffee sector consequently did not escape entirely the widespread destruction of 1999, it remained in relatively good condition and was regarded by successive UN missions and the national leadership of Timor-Leste as one of the prime sources of potential export earnings and fiscal revenues.

The coffee industry has benefited from the fact that local trees have never been treated with pesticides or chemicals, thus allowing Timor-Leste coffee to gain organic certification and increasing its value in environmentally conscious Western markets. By the end of 2000 all Timor-Leste's 19 coffee-producing sub-districts had been declared organic zones. This has allowed Timor-Leste to sell its coffee at a premium on international markets and through fair-trade channels. Some estimates suggested that the value of the country's coffee exports could rise to US $50m. per year in the near future, equivalent to almost one-half of its estimated non-oil GDP (of $119m.) in 1999. Official trade statistics issued by the Ministry of Finance indicated that the value of coffee exports rose from less than $8.0m. in 2006 to $12.6m. in 2008, before declining to $8.3m. in 2009. Output of green coffee beans reached 14,000 metric tons in 2009; some 12,500 tons were exported in that year, representing 0.2% of total global supply. Coffee-growing areas increased by 2.4% in 2009.

Apart from coffee, other important cash crops produced in Timor-Leste include cloves, coconuts and cocoa. An additional cash crop is sugar cane, which was introduced during the Indonesian occupation and is currently cultivated primarily by smallholders over an area encompassing some 10,000 ha. Small quantities of candlenut, Manila hemp, black pepper and vanilla are also grown. A variety of fruits are grown, but only in small quantities. Among the most important of these are mango, guava, pineapples, rambutan, peaches, plums and passion fruit. The internal market for these is limited, but there is potential for the drying and exporting of some of them, notably pineapple and mango. Additionally, more juices could be produced locally, rather than importing such items. Moreover, there is potential for the export to Indonesia of additional products, including cashew nuts, vanilla, groundnuts and soybeans; currently, these are only produced in small quantities. In recent years, some cinnamon has been planted, but its potential has not yet been fully assessed. However, possibilities for the marketing of Timorese agricultural products remain limited by high transport costs, the poor condition of the roads, insufficient market information available to farmers, and limited means for food storage and preservation.

As noted above, many of the foods grown in Timor-Leste are sold unprocessed. Considerable value could be added and employment generated by an extension of processing in the cultivation of crops such as coffee and coconut. 'Wet-processing' would improve the quality of coffee beans, and oil could be produced from coconut. Similar improvements could be made in relation to candlenut, which is grown in approximately 50% of the country's districts. There is considerable potential for increased production of bamboo, which is cultivated in many parts of the country, for use in furniture, flooring, textiles and medicines. Although soybeans are grown, the country still imports 85% of its soybean consumption.

Cattle are reared in some areas of Timor-Leste, notably in Viqueque and Covalima, but the quality of the bulls is low and mortality rates are high. If breeding could be more selective and vaccination were more prevalent, then the livestock industry could have a future, since demand for beef in Indonesia is growing, and approximately one-third of Timor-Leste's consumption comes from imported beef. Similarly, pig- and poultry-farming, as well as the production of milk and dairy products, could also be increased, although this would depend on the provision of relevant information to farmers via development schemes, and on improved packaging, transport and refrigeration facilities.

Fishing

The waters around Timor-Leste have rich fisheries resources, which were largely neglected during Portuguese rule. Efforts to develop a viable commercial fishing industry during the Indonesian occupation had some impact, and by the mid-1990s the territory produced more than 2m. metric tons of saltwater fish and 400 tons of freshwater fish per year. However, at the same time, areas of coral were destroyed by the use of explosives in off-shore fishing. Much of the fisheries infrastructure was destroyed in the unrest that followed the 1999 independence referendum, resulting in a significant reduction in the catch. Rehabilitation of the sector with the assistance of a number of programmes administered by NGOs and the UN resulted in a gradual recovery in subsistence fishing and aquaculture, with the result that by 2005 the supply of fish was approaching the level of demand in the main urban areas. With the fishing fleet remaining smaller than it had been in 1999, considerable scope existed for a further expansion of the industry, and the continued development and commercialization of the fisheries industry represented one of the most promising sources of potential additional revenue. Recognizing this potential, the National Development Plan proposed a 50% increase in production and a 25% increase in employment in the industry within five years.

To achieve this objective, in the early years of independence the Government proposed a number of measures, including increased research into the country's offshore fish resources, the training of industry personnel and the development of appropriate marketing networks. Efforts were also made to reach agreements with Timor-Leste's neighbours on the delineation of its maritime boundaries, which would permit the Government more effectively to exploit its exclusive economic zone of some 75,000 sq km. A major step in the development of the fisheries industry was taken in mid-2003 with the completion of an extensive project for the rehabilitation of the Hera fisheries port, about 16 km east of Dili.

More recently, the Government has sought to increase the country's international co-operation in the fisheries sector. In August 2008 Timor-Leste signed a co-operation agreement with the Philippines covering such areas as post-harvest fish-processing and marketing, coastal management and development, marine fisheries conservation, combating illegal, unreported and unregulated fishing practices, and environmental protection. At the same time, the Government also sought the assistance of Australia in controlling illegal fishing in the Timor Sea. In May 2009 it joined with Indonesia, Malaysia, Papua New Guinea, the Philippines and Solomon Islands to launch a 'Coral Triangle Initiative' aimed at managing the region's coastal and marine resources through such measures as the strengthening of marine protected areas, the protection of endangered species and the enhancement of resilience to the adverse impacts of climate change. As stated in UNDP's *Human Development Report 2011*, as well as the provision of more suitable boats and training, investment is also needed in ice factories, transport and the creation of demonstration centres for the use of electronic control systems, cutting, processing, transport and storage. Seaweed farming could also be developed, to foster near-shore herbivore and carnivore fish numbers, creating prawn-, abalone-, crab- and oyster-farming.

Forestry

During the Indonesian occupation, Timor-Leste's forestry sector suffered from unsustainable land management and the extensive clearing of land for agricultural use and fuel wood in the 1980s and 1990s, which resulted in serious deforestation and associated soil degradation and erosion. The dangers of these developments have been recognized by successive Governments since independence, with specific plans for the agriculture, forestry and fisheries sectors requiring that these trends be arrested.

The principal products of Timor-Leste's forestry sector are local timbers such as cendana, eucalyptus, redwood and lontar palm. Teak, although not indigenous to the country, has also been planted extensively over the past 100 years, and especially during the period of Indonesian rule. Sandalwood, which once covered many of the country's mountains and hills, was viewed as another potentially important forestry crop, but required extensive replanting. By 2000 this replanting had already been initiated. In subsequent years, efforts were made to undertake a comprehensive inventory of the country's forestry resources and an analysis of their potential for development. The first stage of the inventory, covering two western districts, was presented at a national workshop in Dili in August 2010. In order to ensure the sustainable exploitation of forestry resources, the National Development Plan proposed the formulation of a Forestry Management Master Plan. The SIP issued in April 2005 provided such a plan, and was supplemented by a Forests Policy and Strategy, including a Community Forests Strategy and the designation of National Parks and Protected Natural Areas. The first National Park, named after the national hero, Nino Konis Santana, was established in 2007 over an area of 123,600 ha, which included 55,600 ha of the offshore Coral Triangle. The Strategic Development Plan for 2011–30 emphasized the need for improvements in forest and watershed management in order to meet the needs of local communities and to contribute to economic growth, while ensuring environmental sustainability for future generations.

As in the fisheries sector, Timor-Leste has sought to increase international co-operation in the forestry sector in recent years. In October 2008 the Government signed a forestry co-operation agreement with Indonesia, which provided, *inter alia*, for the country's forestry officers to receive training from Indonesia. The Government has also entered into a trilateral agreement on forestry co-operation with Brazil and Indonesia, which covers forest restoration, land erosion mitigation, wood product revitalization and tree rejuvenation, as well as the training of forestry officers.

MINING

Onshore Resources

Timor-Leste's main onshore mineral resource is high-grade, high-quality marble. Exploitation of this resource began in the 1980s and 1990s, when marble was employed in the construction of many hotels, office buildings and shopping malls in the Indonesian capital, Jakarta. The vast majority of the marble deposits had been exploited by the mid-1990s. However, some marble deposits remain, in the regions of Manatuto, Manufahi and Viqueque. In addition, the country also has some reserves of silver, manganese, gold, copper, chromite and gypsum.

Offshore Petroleum and Gas

The most notable mineral resources of Timor-Leste are petroleum and natural gas, which are located mainly in the Timor Sea to the south of the country, in the so-called 'Timor Gap' area between Timor-Leste and Australia. In order to be able to proceed with the development of these resources, and despite the uncertainty surrounding the international status of these waters, the Governments of Australia and Indonesia signed a controversial petroleum production revenue-sharing agreement, the Timor Gap Treaty, in 1989. Under Australian pressure, this agreement implicitly demarcated the maritime border between the then Indonesian province of East Timor and Australia not along the median line between the two countries' coastlines, as provided for by the UN Convention on the Law of the Sea (UNCLOS), but at the southern edge of the Timor Trough, an undersea trench lying considerably closer to Timor than to Australia, thereby giving Australia control over the larger share of the offshore petroleum and gas resources in that area. Operationally, the agreement provided for the establishment of a 'zone of co-operation' (ZOCA) in the waters between East Timor and Australia, which was divided into three areas, and decreed that each country had the right to 90% of the petroleum revenues derived from the areas nearest to its own shores, with the other country having the right to the remaining 10%.

The signing of the 1989 agreement resulted in exploration and production concessions being awarded to a number of oil companies. Several of the fields covered by these concessions—the Elang, Kakatua and Kakatua North fields in the south-western corner of ZOCA—entered into production during the period of Indonesian occupation, with the first petroleum being extracted in July 1998. However, the royalties generated by these fields for the contracting states were relatively small, at around US $2m.–$3m. per year, had ceased operation by 2007. Two much larger fields were Bayu-Undan, lying 18 km to the south of the existing fields, and Greater Sunrise, lying partially within the north-eastern corner of ZOCA.

Following the withdrawal of Indonesia from East Timor, the Indonesian Government acknowledged in October 1999 that it no longer retained any jurisdiction over the Timor Gap area. Discussions involving UNTAET, Australia and the East Timorese national leadership were subsequently initiated on the amendment of the Timor Gap Treaty. Following extensive negotiations, provisional arrangements for the sharing of the hydrocarbon resources in the maritime border area between Australia and East Timor were concluded in July 2001, when a new Timor Sea Treaty was initialled by the Australian Government, UNTAET and a representative of the interim Government of East Timor. This agreement covered an area of 75,000 sq km between Timor-Leste and Australia, which became known as the Joint Petroleum Development Area (JPDA). Although the agreement ostensibly assigned 90% of revenues from the area to Timor-Leste and the remainder to Australia, it was widely acknowledged to be far less favourable to Timor-Leste than these figures suggested, owing to a number of complex issues relating to the measurement of petroleum production, the definition of by-products, the taxation of the petroleum production and shipping activities, and the proposed siting of the Timor Sea natural gas processing industry in Darwin, northern Australia, rather than in Timor-Leste.

As this agreement had been negotiated by UNTAET on behalf of Timor-Leste, it needed to be ratified by the country's post-independence Government. After tough negotiations with the Australian Government in the run-up to independence, the Second Transitional Government of East Timor, established after the elections of August 2001, agreed to accept the Timor Sea Treaty, which was duly ratified shortly after the country achieved sovereign independence in May 2002. However, in ratifying the Treaty the Government made it clear that it had done so without prejudice to its maritime claims, and in July 2002 both the National Parliament and the President of the newly independent country stressed their determination to seek a delineation of the maritime boundary between Timor-Leste and Australia midway between the shorelines of the two countries, thereby placing the known Elang, Kakatua, Kakatua North, Bayu-Undan, Laminaria-Corallina and Greater Sunrise oil and gas fields firmly within the territorial waters of Timor-Leste.

In the event, however, the Government of Timor-Leste was forced to accept the original Treaty in March 2003, following prolonged and acrimonious negotiations with the Australian Government, and it made little progress in subsequent negotiating rounds in November 2003 and April 2004. In particular, Australia refused to accept the concept of a midway boundary, having earlier withdrawn from UNCLOS and from the jurisdiction of the International Court of Justice on maritime boundary issues. As a result, Timor-Leste stood to lose control over four-fifths of the Greater Sunrise field to Australia. Not surprisingly, the uncompromising stance of the Australian Government generated great bitterness at all levels in Timor-Leste. (Meanwhile, offshore oil production from the Bayu-Undan field commenced in April 2004; production from the field, which was expected to last until around 2022, had reached 175,000 barrels per day by 2009. Gas from the Bayu-Undan field is transported via pipeline to Darwin.)

The deadlock persisted into 2005, jeopardizing the exploitation of the Greater Sunrise field and giving rise to considerable political opposition to the Australian Government's position even within Australia itself. With little progress being made on the issue of the delineation of the maritime boundary between Timor-Leste and Australia, the two Governments agreed to seek 'creative solutions' to the problem. Such a solution, based on the sharing of oil revenues rather than on the formal demarcation of borders, was finally reached in January 2006 with an agreement to divide the revenues of Greater Sunrise equally between the two countries (compared with an earlier Australian proposal granting Timor-Leste just 18% of the revenues) for a period of 50 years, during which time the issue of the boundary demarcation would be held in abeyance. This agreement was ratified by the Parliaments of Australia and Timor-Leste in early 2007, preparing the way for full commercial exploitation of Greater Sunrise, which was expected to begin in 2015.

From late 2008, however, the development of the Greater Sunrise field suffered a further set-back as a result of disagreements between the Government of Timor-Leste and Woodside Petroleum, the field's operator, on the siting of a liquefaction plant for the natural gas extracted from the field; the latter preferred to locate it in Darwin or to build a floating plant near the field, while the former insisted that it be located on the south coast of Timor-Leste. Following Woodside Petroleum's announcement in April 2010 that it favoured the floating plant option, the Government of Timor-Leste stated that it would not approve any arrangements for the development of Greater Sunrise that did not involve the construction of the liquefaction plant in Timor-Leste, accusing Woodside Petroleum of giving misleading information in its justification of its preference for a floating plant, and noting that as the gas from Bayu-Undan was being processed in Darwin, it was only equitable that Timor-Leste should benefit from hosting the Greater Sunrise plant. In May Woodside attempted to submit its proposed field development plan to Timor-Leste's National Petroleum Authority (Autoridade Nacional do Petróleo—ANP), which had been established in 2008 to regulate petroleum activities in the country, but the Authority reportedly refused to accept it on the grounds that the company had not complied with a requirement to conduct a comparative analysis of all three options. As of mid-2011 a development plan for the Greater Sunrise plant had yet to be agreed, and considerable uncertainty continued to surround the project, with debate continuing to centre on the location of the required gas liquefaction plant. Estimates are very tentative, but Timor-Leste's total income from the project would probably be in the region of US $13,000m., some $4,500m. greater than the value of the country's Petroleum Fund as of July 2011.

Despite the stalemate over the Greater Sunrise project, a number of legal and regulatory measures introduced by the Government to encourage investment in the country's petroleum sector, and to promote its growth and development, had begun to yield benefits from 2008. In March 2008 the Italian oil company ENI announced a discovery at the Kitan oilfield in the JPDA, while Minza, a firm based in Jersey (United Kingdom), which had discovered natural gas at its Chuditch well in the JPDA in 1998, was initiating seismic tests in the area. The planned acquisition of Minza by the Norwegian firm Flex, which specializes in floating liquefaction plants for natural gas, gave rise to expectations that extraction and processing of the Chuditch field could commence as early as 2013. ENI's field development plan for the Kitan oilfield, involving the drilling of three production wells, was approved by the ANP in April 2010; the Timor-Leste Government forecast that it would receive total revenue of US $387m. from Kitan between late 2011, when the field was expected to come on stream, and 2016. In late 2010 ENI began to drill an exploration well in the Cova field, around 100 km from the south-east coast of Timor-Leste, in the country's sovereign area.

Meanwhile, in 2009 the Government announced plans to establish a national oil company in accordance with international best practice, and in May 2009 invited representatives of foreign national oil companies and stakeholders of the country's petroleum sector to a senior-level workshop in Dili to discuss this issue. The company, Timor Gás & Petróleo (Timor GAP), was established in 2011. Efforts have also been made to promote co-operation in the oil and natural gas sector with established producers, including Kuwait and Malaysia, and to develop new markets for the country's products, especially in East Asia.

MANUFACTURING

No manufacturing base of any significance was established in East Timor during the periods of either Portuguese or Indonesian rule, and any enterprises that had been established were destroyed in the violence that followed the referendum in 1999. Thus, manufacturing accounted for only 2.3% of non-oil GDP in 2007, with the bulk of the existing output coming from the weaving of traditional cloth and the production of furniture in relatively small enterprises. A UN study in that year stated that the immediate potential for manufacturing was limited, given the country's shortage of skilled labour, relatively high local living costs and wages, and poor transport links. The report therefore concluded that the nation's best options appeared to be in foreign investment in textiles and footwear.

Since independence, the Timor-Leste Government has recognized the need to develop national processing industries that would add value to local natural resources while generating income and employment opportunities. The Government's SIP for agriculture, forestry and fisheries, published in 2005, made frequent mention of the need to increase the level of local processing of the commodities produced in these sectors, and the SIP on private sector development was concerned primarily with the development of entrepreneurship and the promotion of small and medium-sized enterprises (SMEs) in both processing and trade-related activities. However, progress in achieving such objectives was modest at first, with an estimated average annual growth rate of manufacturing of less than 1% in the initial years after independence, followed by a major contraction of some 25% in 2006 owing to the civil unrest in that year. Since 2007, however, manufacturing has increased in importance, as suggested by the robust growth rates of the non-oil economy, which reached 7.5% in 2010.

There is potential for the further development of craft industries within the rural sector, some of which have expanded in recent years, largely as a result of the increased provision of micro-credit to women. Existing small-scale industries such as brick-making, the production of biomass briquettes (a biofuel substitute for coal and charcoal) and cement production could also be expanded.

INFRASTRUCTURE

Transport and Communications

The transport and communications network established during the period of Portuguese rule was extremely limited, and was intended mainly to enable the colonial administration to achieve its tax-collection objectives and to facilitate the transport of the territory's coffee crop to external markets. The upgrading and expansion of these facilities was a major focus of government policy during the Indonesian occupation, primarily for purposes of military control. Whereas only one paved road, 20 km in length and located in Dili, was built in East Timor during the entire period of Portuguese rule, by the mid-1990s the Indonesian Government had built more than 3,800 km of roads, including 428 km of paved highways, as well as 18 bridges. This was accompanied by a sharp increase in the number of motor vehicles registered, as well as by the establishment of a number of bus routes linking East Timor's towns and villages. Progress was also made by the Indonesian Government in the development of East Timor's air transport infrastructure. In 1981 the construction of Comoro International Airport (subsequently renamed Presidente Nicolau Lobato International Airport) in Dili was completed to complement the airport built at Baucau in the east of the territory.

East Timor's telecommunications system was also upgraded substantially during the Indonesian occupation, with the territory becoming linked with Indonesian telecommunications satellites from the mid-1970s. The transport and communications infrastructure was badly damaged by the events of 1999. The road system fell into particularly serious disrepair, owing to a combination of the impact of the post-referendum violence, the deceleration in repair and maintenance activities caused by the Indonesian economic crisis of 1997–98, and the subsequent wear imposed on the network by the heavy military vehicles of Interfet and the UNTAET peace-keeping force. Similarly, East Timor's ports and airports also suffered serious damage as a result of inadequate maintenance, the destruction of equipment and excessively heavy use in 1999–2000. High priority was therefore given to the restoration of the transport and communications infrastructure; UNTAET launched a wide-ranging emergency rehabilitation programme, followed by a longer-term programme for the sustainable development of the country's infrastructure. By the end of 2000 both the airport and the seaport of Dili had become operational, allowing the restoration of commercial air links via Darwin in Australia and Denpasar in Bali, Indonesia, and the full resumption of commercial shipping. Significant progress was also made in road repairs and maintenance, especially with regard to the major arterial roads needed to ensure access to Timor-Leste's important population centres. With these objectives achieved, UNTAET established comprehensive business plans for the aviation, ports and roads sectors by mid-2001, and also began the reconstruction of public buildings. Increasingly, moreover, it moved its rehabilitation efforts beyond Dili.

Despite the progress made by UNTAET, it was widely acknowledged that much remained to be done, and the National Development Plan drafted by the new Government placed high priority on the restoration and establishment of required physical capabilities and public services. Special emphasis was given to an improvement of the road network, port facilities, and the generation and distribution of power. A five-year road-building programme was announced at the beginning of 2006, and efforts were made to enhance national capacity to expand and manage the country's water supply and sanitation systems. Although the implementation of these projects was affected by the political violence and uncertainty prevailing in Timor-Leste for much of 2006, the subsequent restoration of stability allowed the work to be resumed. The development of the country's infrastructure was identified as the Government's main priority in its budgets for 2009 and 2010. In August 2009, to mark the 10th anniversary of the vote on independence, the Government announced a 'referendum package' of investment, allocating US $70m. for 774 infrastructure projects, including the rehabilitation of roads, the construction of hospitals and schools, and the improvement of sanitation facilities. Infrastructure development remained a priority area in the Strategic Development Plan for 2011–30, and the 2011 budget allocated $599m. for a newly created Infrastructure Fund.

Power

Historically, access to electric power has been very limited in Timor-Leste. As recently as 1985 the proportion of households with electricity totalled only 3.9%. Despite some efforts to improve the situation during the later years of the Indonesian occupation, this ratio had increased only to 20.1% by 1998. The existing infrastructure was seriously damaged by the violence that followed the independence referendum in 1999, necessitating considerable rehabilitation measures in the following years. By mid-2003 this recovery had been largely completed, with the percentage of households with electricity having risen to 20.7%. The total power generation capacity at that time was estimated at some 62.9 GWh, of which 53.3 GWh were located in Dili.

The urgent need for expansion of the power sector has been recognized by post-independence Governments. In September 2004, for example, proposals for this were issued in the form of a master plan for the power sector prepared with the assistance of the ADB. This provided an elaborate framework for meeting the national goal for a comprehensive power supply system nation-wide within 20 years, with the ratio of households having access to an electricity supply scheduled to rise to 80% by 2025. This target was to be achieved on the basis of a number of hydro-based and diesel generation systems, and a gradual interconnection of separate systems into a single grid. In the short term, the plan was to provide for the strengthening of the existing diesel-based system. This was exemplified by the establishment of a new generator in Dili in 2006, which helped to restore a 24-hour supply of electricity to the capital and six hours of electricity per day to all district centres and some sub-districts, and by extensive repairs and renovations at the Dili-based state electricity utility, Electricidade de Timor-Leste, in 2007. A small hydropower plant, with annual production capacity of around 1.5 GWh, was officially opened in Gariuai, near Baucau, in late 2008, while the construction of a much larger 27-MW Ira Lalalo hydropower plant (with anticipated annual production capacity of 189 GWh) and an associated transmission line to Dili and a number of the country's major urban areas is scheduled to be completed by 2012. In February 2009 a Chinese company began to implement a US $400m. project to build three generating stations using heavy fuel oil, and a nation-wide high-voltage distribution system; the first of these plants was being built in the port of Hera, near Dili. In mid-2010 a study commissioned by the Government and conducted by a Portuguese company, Martifer, concluded that there was strong potential in Timor-Leste for the production of energy from renewable sources, particularly from water resources (252 MW) and wind (72 MW). Overall, more than 50 possible projects, with an estimated installed capacity of 451 MW, have been identified. The Government has set a target of more than 50% of the country's electricity being derived from renewable sources by 2020.

SOCIAL DEVELOPMENT

Health

The health care situation in East Timor during the Indonesian occupation was poor, with key indicators of the population's state of health, such as life expectancy and infant mortality rates, showing that the territory lagged far behind most parts of Indonesia. The extensive destruction of the health infrastructure by pro-Indonesia militias in 1999 caused the total breakdown of the health care system. The situation was exacerbated by the complete loss of all health care equipment and medication and by the departure of senior health staff from the central, district and sub-district levels of the health care system as a result of the violence, with a reported 130 of the territory's 160 doctors having left East Timor. Following Indonesia's withdrawal from East Timor in September 1999, immediate humanitarian assistance for health was provided by the International Committee of the Red Cross and various NGOs, supported by several UN agencies and, initially, some Interfet medical staff. Significant efforts subsequently were made to repair the damage inflicted during the period of post-referendum violence, with NGOs playing a particularly important role in this process. By June 2000 some 80 new health facilities had been established, supplemented by a number of mobile clinics. In addition, an operating Interim Health Authority was established in March of that year, while a training programme was initiated for district health officers, and health laboratory services were also developed.

To speed up the recovery of the health services, a wide-ranging Health Sector Rehabilitation and Development Programme was inaugurated in June 2000 by UNTAET, with financial support from the World Bank and a number of bilateral donors. The Programme aimed to restore access to basic health services in the transitional period between the provision of humanitarian relief and the development of the health system, to begin the development of an effective health policy and health system, and to build local administrative capacities to implement and manage the health programme.

By mid-2002 almost 90 community health centres had been established to provide basic services throughout the country. This was accompanied by the establishment of a new medical warehouse to supply medicines and other medical consumables to all districts of East-Timor in February 2002. Moreover, as the construction of community health centres continued, the World Bank reported that, by mid-2003, 85% of the country's children under five years of age had been vaccinated, and that 90% of the population lived within two hours' walking distance of a hospital or clinic. In order to address the shortage of qualified medical personnel, especially in rural areas, in 2005 the Government invited doctors from Cuba to work in Timor-Leste and decided to send Timorese students to that country for medical training.

The National Development Plan continued to allocate high priority to the health sector, which was reaffirmed in the final SIP for this sector, released in 2005. This envisaged the development of a decentralized health care system based on primary and preventive health services. The focus on primary health care services, to be provided at district and sub-district level, appeared entirely justified in view of the findings of a Demographic and Health Survey conducted in 2003, which suggested that Timor-Leste's infant and under-five mortality rates were 60 per 1,000 live births and 83 per 1,000 live births, respectively. These services were to receive considerable funding, with 63% of projected health expenditure (capital and recurrent) until the fiscal year (July–June) 2008/09 to be directed to district health services. A preliminary report on a Demographic and Health Survey conducted in 2009/10 indicated that the efforts to improve primary health care services had resulted in significant reductions in infant mortality and under-five mortality rates since 2003, with the former declining to 44 deaths per 1,000 live births and the latter to 64 deaths per 1,000 live births. Malnutrition rates remained of concern, with 44.8% of children underweight for their age, 15.4% severely so, while the health sector continued to suffer from a shortage of trained health professionals

During the Indonesian occupation and in the early years of independence, Timor-Leste had high maternal mortality rates, with the rate in 2004 standing at 666 deaths per 100,000 live births. There have been substantial improvements in recent years, notably in the numbers of women receiving ante- and post-natal care; consequently, the results of the 2010 national census were expected to show improvements in the maternal mortality rate. Data for 2009 indicate that 86% of women giving birth had at least one ante-natal care visit, compared with a figure of just 42.5% in 2001. However, it should also be noted that only 41.3% of births are attended by trained medical staff (a doctor, nurse or midwife).

According to the Timor-Leste Demographic and Health Survey 2009–10, the country had a high average birth rate of 5.7 births per woman; contraceptive prevalence remained low, at 21% of married women between the ages of 15 and 49 years. According to a health survey conducted in 2008, the incidence of HIV/AIDs was very low, with just 160 recorded cases, mostly within the 15–24 age group.

Education

Following Portuguese neglect, East Timor's education system was developed to some extent during the Indonesian occupation. Prior to the violence of 1999, there were 788 primary schools (including 140 private schools, most of which were administered by the Roman Catholic Church), 114 junior secondary schools, 37 senior secondary schools and 17 vocational and technical schools. At the tertiary level, more than 1,500 East Timorese students were reported to have obtained university scholarships, mainly to the Indonesian universities of Malang, Jakarta and Denpasar. The University of East Timor was established in 1986. However, the rate of illiteracy in East Timor remained high during the period of Indonesian rule, at more than 50% in 1999, and the education provided by the system was often of poor quality, with technical education being particularly weak. Many teachers were inadequately trained and poorly paid, and basic teaching equipment was also in short supply.

The education system was devastated by the extensive post-referendum violence in 1999. Approximately 95% of schools and other educational institutions were destroyed, and a large percentage (perhaps 70%–80%) of senior administrative staff and secondary school teachers was lost from the education system. The rehabilitation of the education system (including the repair of classrooms, the supply of basic teaching and learning resources, and the establishment of a programme of teacher training) was thus a priority concern of UNTAET.

Shortly after assuming control, the transitional administration developed a comprehensive three-stage School System Revitalization Programme (SSRP), with World Bank support, to build upon the voluntary measures already implemented by local communities to revive the school system. The first stage of this programme, comprising an Emergency School Readiness Project, was launched in June 2000 at an estimated cost of US $13.9m. This resulted in the rehabilitation of 2,780 classrooms by mid-2003, together with the provision of much-needed furniture, books and other instructional materials, the building of new schools to replace those that had been irreparably damaged, and the implementation of measures to improve the quality of instruction. Subsequent stages of the SSRP led to further improvements to the school system, enhancing the quality of education and attracting the increased participation of parents, teachers and the broader community in the school improvement process.

At the tertiary level, the University of East Timor was reopened in January 2001, with provision being made for the enrolment of 4,500 students in degree programmes and 3,000 students in bridging courses. In addition, scholarships were provided to some 500 students in 2000 to attend courses at overseas universities. These activities were supplemented by various training programmes for civil servants, administrators, teachers and other professionals. With Portuguese having been restored as one of the country's two official languages, along with the local language, Tetum, these programmes also included Portuguese-language training components, funded largely by Portugal.

The post-independence Timorese Government gave high priority to the strengthening of the education sector, with the National Development Plan setting the goal of easier access to education for all: at least one primary school was to be set up in each village and the quality of teaching was to be improved. With the assistance of UNMISET, the newly established Ministry of Education, Culture, Youth and Sport formulated an educational policy framework and a legislative foundation for the education system, including the drafting of appropriate educational laws and regulations. This was accompanied by an updating of educational plans, the preparation of a variety of project proposals in education-related fields, and the establishment of appropriate monitoring systems.

These early efforts were followed by the formulation of a full-scale SIP for the education sector in 2005, which provided a framework for the achievement of the targets set by the National Development Plan. In particular, the SIP reiterated the need for an appropriate education policy and associated supervision and monitoring systems, including an educational management information system. In addition, it provided for an improvement in the quantity and quality of basic and secondary education through the building of new schools and rehabilitation of existing schools, the upgrading of laboratory and library facilities in secondary schools, and the enhancement of teacher-training facilities, as well as the construction of housing for teachers in remote areas. At the tertiary level, the SIP envisaged the implementation of specific measures to develop the National University of Timor-Leste and the existing 18 private sector institutions offering tertiary education, with the aim of ensuring that the system would provide good-quality courses and meet international accreditation standards. However, recognizing that the achievement of these objectives would take some time, the SIP also envisaged the provision of government support for a robust programme of overseas scholarships for graduate students in specific areas considered vital for national development.

In the first stage of the implementation of these policy measures, a major donor initiative was launched in April 2007, involving a grant of US $12m. from the World Bank and the Australian Government, supplemented by $3.3m. of national resources by the Government of Timor-Leste. The programme, which encompassed the period 2007–12, covered education policy development, resource management skills enhancement, learning materials provision and vocational skills innovation. This was followed in late 2007 by the adoption of an Education Reform Plan introducing nine years of mandatory and free education.

According to government data, the enrolment rate for primary school children increased from 76.6% in 2007 to 86.0% in 2010. In 2009 enrolment at the lower secondary level (for those aged 13–15) stood at 24.7%, while the corresponding rate for the upper secondary level (for those aged 15–17) was just 11.7%. In the initial years after independence, a substantial number of children stopped attending school and either dropped out altogether or subsequently had to repeat years. According to Ministry of Education data, only 56% of students who had commenced their education four years previously still remained in attendance in 2003. However, this situation has subsequently improved, with 88% of students remaining in attendance for four years or more in 2009.

Tetum is used only in the early years of schooling, and the use of Portuguese as the principal language of instruction remains an ongoing problem. Just 8%–12% of the population speak Portuguese, and there is a shortage of appropriate Portuguese-language teaching material; as a result, many teachers resort to Bahasa Indonesia, the pre-independence language of instruction. Although levels of basic literacy have improved substantially since independence, a high proportion of women remain illiterate.

FINANCE

Foreign Aid

The devastation caused by the post-referendum violence left East Timor heavily dependent on external financial assistance for its economic and social reconstruction. The international community responded vigorously to these needs, and a series of senior-level meetings took place between the East Timorese national leadership and donor representatives, the first of which was held in December 1999 in Tokyo. While underlining the donors' commitment to a co-ordinated effort to support the recovery and sustainable development of Timor-Leste, these meetings were intended to monitor the performance of the technical co-operation activities financed by foreign assistance, and to make appropriate adjustments where necessary.

At the first meeting in December 1999, the donors pledged US $523.2m. for a major three-year relief and reconstruction programme for East Timor. These pledges were subsequently supplemented by a variety of other bilateral and multilateral commitments. Although the release of these funds was initially somewhat slow, the rate of disbursement began to accelerate significantly during the latter part of UNTAET's administration, when these foreign funds played a predominant role in driving East Timor's economic recovery. The degree of the country's resulting dependence on external financial support was highlighted by the fact that, of the estimated GDP of $431 per head in 2002, some $400 had been contributed by foreign donors.

To maximize the developmental impact of the externally provided resources, the donor community agreed to co-ordinate their disbursement largely through two trust funds, the Consolidated Fund for East Timor (CFET), administered by UNTAET, and the Trust Fund for East Timor (TFET), administered by the World Bank in partnership with the ADB. The former was intended principally to fund the administrative costs of government and to strengthen the capacity of the Timorese administration-in-waiting, while the latter was intended to finance economic reconstruction and development.

Both the CFET and the TFET were originally scheduled to be phased out by 2003 or 2004, upon completion of the post-crisis rehabilitation and recovery tasks for which they had been established. In recognition of Timor-Leste's short-term funding constraints, the May 2002 donors' meeting in Dili agreed to provide further financial assistance in support of the National Development Plan for at least a few more years until the country's hydrocarbon resources began to generate sufficient revenues. This resulted in the establishment of a series of Transitional Support Programmes (TSPs) by the World Bank in July 2002. Three such programmes were initially envisaged, covering each of the fiscal years between 2002/03 and 2004/05. The period of coverage was subsequently extended by a further two years, despite the earlier-than-anticipated growth in Timor-Leste's petroleum revenues (generated by the rise in international oil prices during 2004–05), because the Government regarded the TSP process as an important means of capacity-building, oversight and donor co-ordination.

The first TSP, covering the 2002/03 fiscal year, was based on a World Bank grant of US $5m., and served as an anchor for a larger multi-donor support programme to the value of $31m. This TSP had four components, encompassing: the establishment of a framework for poverty-reduction planning; the creation of an institutional and legal framework for open democratic governance and an enabling environment for the private sector; measures to ensure the orientation of public spending towards the poor and a strengthening of expenditure management controls; and an improvement of cost recovery in the power sector. The second TSP was based on a World Bank contribution of $4.1m., which attracted approximately $32m. of additional funding from other donors, of which $29m. was channelled through trust funds administered by the World Bank. Becoming operational at a time when the various ministerial and other institutions and agencies of the new Government of Timor-Leste had already been established, this TSP was aimed primarily at supporting the annual action plans of these agencies.

With the implementation of the third TSP in 2004/05 having been supported by rising international prices for oil, which enabled Timor-Leste to finance its budgetary needs for that fiscal year entirely from its own resources, and with the process of institution-strengthening having progressed to a point where the Government was establishing its Petroleum Fund (see above), the Government and its international development partners decided to modify the country's development strategy at the annual donors' meeting in Dili in April 2005. This led to the formulation and adoption of a new three-year Country Assistance Strategy (CAS) covering the financial years 2006–08, under which the World Bank agreed to continue to anchor and co-ordinate donor contributions using the successful TSP model, which was renamed the Consolidation Support Programme (CSP), to emphasize the fact that the transitional phase was now deemed to have been replaced by a more routine developmental phase. In this context, Timor-Leste's donors agreed to provide approximately US $25m. in grants for the first two years of the CAS, which were used principally to support the implementation of the various SIPs finalized by mid-2005. In addition, the CAS was intended to support capacity-building measures for planning and financial management, and to support national efforts in promoting the growth of labour-intensive activities to increase non-oil GDP and create jobs. In response to Timor-Leste's reduced dependence on foreign financial assistance as a result of the increased flow of oil revenues from the mid-2000s, the CSP was discontinued at the end of the CAS period and replaced by direct donor support for the Government's National Priorities Programme, launched in 2008. Timor-Leste received a total of $236.4m. in aid commitments in 2008, $198.8m. of which came from 24 bilateral donors, with the remainder provided by multilateral and UN agencies. The five largest bilateral donors, accounting for 67% of total donor spending, were Australia, Japan, Portugal, the European Union and the USA. In August 2009 the World Bank outlined an Interim Strategy for Timor-Leste, prepared in collaboration with the International Finance Corporation and covering 2010–11, which aimed to support the Government in its efforts to use the country's petroleum revenue to implement policies that maintain stability and create sustained growth in the non-oil sectors of the economy. This Interim Strategy was followed by a full CAS. The increase in petroleum revenues in recent years has enabled the Timor-Leste Government to rely less on donor contributions to finance its budget. Donor contributions as a percentage of the total budget for 2011 stood at just 20%.

Foreign Trade

Timor-Leste's international trade performance from 1999 reflects its development trends. The reconstruction efforts after 1999 prompted a sharp rise in imports of goods, which reached US $262m. by 2001. The subsequent cessation in import-intensive reconstruction activity led to a significant decline in imports to some $123m.–$130m. per year in 2002–06, which was followed by a surge to $200m. in 2007, resulting from a requirement for more imported goods to repair the damage caused by the 2006 unrest, as well as rising commodity prices. Imports rose further in 2008 and 2009, to $310.9m. and $384.9m., respectively. In the initial years imports were funded almost entirely by official transfers, with export earnings falling far below the level of imports, although the situation changed gradually as Timor-Leste's oil revenues began to expand. By contrast, the country's non-oil export revenues have remained modest: having risen from some $4m. in 2000 to a narrow range of $8m.–$9m. in 2003–07, they increased more sharply in 2008, to $12.8m., before declining again to $8.5m. in 2009. Much of this growth was accounted for by exports of coffee (which comprised 97.6% of non-oil export earnings in 2009), with export revenues from other non-oil sources remaining broadly unchanged, at well below $1m.

The growth of oil revenues since 2005 has resulted in a dramatic increase in the surplus on the income account of Timor-Leste's balance of payments, which, combined with services, rose from US $447.0m. in 2006 to $1,068.1m. in 2007 and $1,963.5m. in 2008 (amid high oil prices), before moderating to $1,340.3m. in 2009. This, in turn, has had a remarkable impact on the country's current account balance, which evolved from a deficit of $23m. ($479m. if international assistance flows are disregarded) in 2003 to a surplus of $1,177.2m. in 2007, $2,023.1m. in 2008 and $1,363.2m. in 2009, with further consolidation of the surplus projected. However, as indicated above, only a small proportion of this income is retained for current use, with the bulk being transferred abroad as savings.

Fiscal Policy

As a relatively poor agricultural economy, dependent on coffee as its only significant export commodity, Timor-Leste has historically been unable to cover its financial requirements. During the Indonesian occupation it was reliant on external transfers for approximately 85% of its recurrent and capital expenditure. Following the Indonesian withdrawal, this dependence on external funding was greatly increased as a result of the collapse in domestic revenue-generating capacity and the sharp rise in capital spending required to rebuild the devastated infrastructure. UNTAET therefore placed considerable emphasis on establishing a framework for sustainable public finances and developing the associated financial management systems and human resources. By mid-2000 a Central Fiscal Authority had already been established as the precursor to the Ministry of Finance, which was given the responsibility of developing local capacities in the area of tax administration.

The first consolidated budget for East Timor, covering the 2000/01 fiscal year, proposed total expenditure of US $60.8m. and domestic revenues of $25.1m. The resulting cash deficit of $35.7m. was expected to be fully covered by grants pledged by external donors. The introduction of this budget was accompanied by the adoption of a series of measures relating to tax and user charges intended to generate the required domestic revenues, the achievement of which was also supported by a significant increase in oil revenues from the Timor Gap. At the same time, an institutional framework was created for responsible fiscal management of the economy. The task of executing the budget, including control and monitoring of expenditure, was assigned to a new Treasury agency within the Central Fiscal Authority, which was established to lay the foundations for sound and transparent fiscal management, and which subsequently evolved into a full Ministry of Finance. In addition, the 2000/01 budget provided for the establishment of an Economic Development Agency, to be responsible for business registration and the creation of an appropriate regulatory framework.

The budgets for 2001/02 and 2002/03 followed a broadly similar pattern to that of 2000/01, projecting significant deficits that were expected to be financed in large part from external sources. In fact, however, the 2001/02 budget recorded a modest surplus, which grew exponentially in subsequent years, in response to the growth in oil and gas revenues resulting from the increased extraction of petroleum from Timor-Leste's offshore fields and the rise in international oil prices. Thus, oil and gas revenues increased from US $13.1m. in the 2000/01 fiscal year to $41.4m. in 2003/04, before rising to $265.6m. in 2004/05, well in excess of the budgeted figure of $44.1m. By 2005/06 oil and gas revenues had risen still further, to $481.8m., compared with a budgeted figure of $351m. The effect on the budget was thus a steady rise in the surplus from $1.4m. in 2001/02 to $424.0m., on a cash basis, in 2005/06, despite an increase in budgetary expenditure from $53m. to $93m. over the same period.

The steady rise in Timor-Leste's oil revenues permitted further significant increases in the Government's budget. The budget for 2006/07 provided for a rise in public spending to US $315.5m.; this reflected the need both for increased funding for recovery and rehabilitation measures following the unrest of April 2006 and for a variety of developmental services, especially with a view to promoting employment generation and poverty reduction, in order to reduce the threat of such instability in the future. The interim fiscal period covering the second half of 2007, as the Government shifted its fiscal year to a calendar-year basis from 2008, provided for public expenditure of $108.7m., and the budget for 2008 initially established an expenditure target of $241m., which was subsequently raised to $536m. in the mid-year budget update. However, despite the dramatic easing in the country's resource constraints through the rise in oil- and gas-based revenues, actual public expenditure initially often fell short of budgeted levels—by some $50m. in 2006/07 and by $5m. in the interim fiscal period of the second half of 2007. This implementation shortfall was attributed primarily to inadequate planning and procurement capacities on the part of the relevant government institutions, and gave rise to concerns about the country's ability to achieve its developmental goals at the pace needed to avoid further political unease and unrest, especially in an environment of rising prices, high unemployment, and modest rates of economic growth and job creation.

Budgeted expenditure was intended to be met primarily from the Petroleum Fund, which grew rapidly from US $250m.

at its inception in September 2005 to $8,500m. by mid-2011. Government projections in 2011 forecast an increase in the Fund balance to $14,600m. in 2015 and to $31,700m. in 2035. As its accrued reserves of oil and gas revenues grew, the Government's public expenditure targets became increasingly ambitious, giving rise to fears about the sustainability of its fiscal policy. The expenditure target for the 2009 budget was thus set at $604m., necessitating a withdrawal of $589m. from the Petroleum Fund. Although this figure exceeded the ESI by $181m., it was approved by Parliament on the grounds that it would enable the country to make the necessary investments in its infrastructure, which would serve to stimulate employment creation and yield benefits for future generations. In the event, budgetary expenditure was lower than anticipated in 2009, owing to delays in the implementation of various projects, and a total of only $512m. was withdrawn from the Fund in that year.

The 2010 budget, approved in December 2009, envisaged expenditure of US $660m. and a deficit of $573m., $502m. (equivalent to the ESI) of which was to be financed from the Petroleum Fund. In mid-2010, however, citing the need to accelerate the pace of economic development, particularly through increased expenditure on infrastructure projects, the Government sought, and secured, parliamentary approval of an adjustment to that year's budget, increasing projected expenditure by 27%, to $838m., and the amount to be withdrawn from the Petroleum Fund by 62%, to $811m. (significantly above the ESI). As already noted, the 2011 budget projected expenditure at ESI levels, but in subsequent years expenditure was projected to be above ESI, by $418m. in 2012, and by $526.1m. in 2015. Meanwhile, in September 2009 Parliament approved new legislation concerning the budget and the financial management of the state, which notably enabled the Government for the first time to borrow finance from foreign governments and institutions. The budget for 2010 did not include any such borrowing, as discussions with potential lenders, including the Portuguese and Chinese Governments, had not resulted in any definitive agreements, but the Government did state its intention to seek loans to finance infrastructure projects with an estimated value of some $3,000m. over the medium-to-long term. In 2011 the Government submitted to Parliament a bill proposing amendments to existing petroleum legislation, which would enable the Government to diversify the Petroleum Fund's portfolio, reduce the oversight role of Parliament, use the deposits in the Fund as collateral for debt instruments, and increase the rate of ESI beyond the existing 3%.

With increased oil revenues providing the resources to cover public capital and recurrent expenditure at the levels necessary to sustain economic growth and essential public services, by early 2006 the Government had begun to consider a reform of the national tax system with the aim of removing or sharply reducing non-oil-related taxes and other levies, on the grounds that such a low-tax regime would be conducive to the promotion of both domestic and foreign private investment in the country. This new tax framework, which was reported to have been designed in consultation with, and with the support of, multilateral donor agencies, was submitted to the National Parliament in February 2008 and approved the following June. The framework formed the core of a broader reform programme, incorporating a strengthening of the banking sector, a reform of land ownership and registration procedures, and measures to improve the enforcement of judicial decisions. These proposals were finalized in the Strategic Development Plan for 2011–30.

Money and Banking

The devastation that followed the 1999 independence referendum also took its toll on the financial services sector in East Timor, which suffered an almost total collapse as a result of the withdrawal of Indonesian banks after September 1999. Over the following years, a number of measures were taken to revive and strengthen the banking system. In early 2001 UNTAET established a Central Payments Office, subsequently renamed the Banking and Payments Authority, as a precursor to a central bank; this was charged with the responsibilities of currency management, the making of payments and receipts on behalf of the East Timorese administration, and bank licensing and supervision.

In addition to the Banking and Payments Authority, which acts as a de facto central bank, there were initially only two financial institutions in operation in Timor-Leste—the Australia and New Zealand Banking Group and the Banco Nacional Ultramarino of Portugal—both of which were established in 2000. Their number was increased in the latter half of 2003, with the entry of the Indonesian Bank Mandiri into the market. Prospects for a rapid expansion of the sector remained uncertain, even though several other large foreign banks expressed interest in opening branches in Timor-Leste. In addition, a micro-financing institution, the Instituição de Micro Finanças de Timor-Leste (IMFTL), was established in 2002 under the auspices of a project with TFET-controlled funding and ADB management. Alongside this, micro-finance for the rural sector was also provided by Moris Rasik, an NGO operating a micro-finance programme with a primary focus on poor rural women.

After a slow start, the banking system began to develop rapidly from 2004. Although bank deposits had already risen by the end of 2000 to a level approximately equivalent to those held in September 1999 by the Indonesian banks then operating in East Timor, very little commercial bank credit had been extended, with the exception of loans issued under the TFET-funded small enterprise development project, owing to a lack of adequate collateral. Even by mid-2003, when the volume of bank deposits had increased to US $62m., domestic lending amounted to only $26m., with most of the loans being used for housing. This situation began to improve as the shortage of domestic collateral-based lending opportunities started to ease and the development of the regulatory framework was initiated. The volume of deposits had risen steadily by the end of 2008, to $222.4m., in response to buoyant economic growth, and increased further, to $288.8m., in 2009. By contrast, the volume of loans fell well behind, having risen from $68.6m. at the end of 2004 to $111.0m. at the end of 2009. This slower growth in bank lending was prompted by a combination of factors: political and social instability, inadequate collateral, and the general lack of sophistication of the economy. Banks also experienced sharp growth in the volume of non-performing loans from $3.8m. (5.5% of total loans) at the end of 2004 to $35.6m. (32.1% of total loans) at the end of 2009. In 2008 it was estimated that only about 2% of Timor-Leste's population used banking facilities, the provision of which was heavily concentrated in Dili, with banking services in rural areas being limited to a few rural co-operatives and micro-financing institutions, of which the state-owned IMFTL was the most significant. The limited penetration of the banking industry had serious implications for private sector-led growth in the short-to-medium term.

Consequently, in its Strategic Framework for Rural Development in Timor-Leste covering the period 2010–20, the Government offered a number of suggestions to address financial constraints. One such proposal was the establishment of the National Development Bank, plans for which were approved in early 2011. The new bank was to use both public and private capital to support the establishment of new companies and their functioning. As confirmed in UNDP's *Human Development Report 2011*, the Bank was to focus on supporting SMEs, providing specialized refinancing facilities in co-operation with commercial banks. Subject to parliamentary approval, it may be possible for the Bank's capital base initially to mobilize some resources from the Petroleum Fund. The Bank will channel subsidies from the Government to enterprises in the rural sector. It will also be able to specialize in funding for the extension of agricultural activities, such as the purchase of seeds, machinery, and working capital for developing value chains, and expanding storage facilities. Most importantly, as noted by the UNDP's report, the Bank was also intended to promote and underwrite community-based micro-finance organizations in rural areas.

The lack of a single universally accepted currency posed a problem in the initial years of the transitional administration. Although UNTAET chose the US dollar as East Timor's interim currency in January 2000, three other currencies—the Indonesian rupiah, the Portuguese escudo and the Australian dollar—remained in common use. Despite the US dollar's status as the official currency, its use by the local population was initially hampered by the slow release of budgetary expenditures, the scarcity of low-denomination notes and coins, and the unfamiliarity of the currency. After mid-2001, however, the increased disbursement of TFET funds in particular resulted in an accelerated adoption of the currency, and by mid-2002 the US dollar had begun to circulate widely throughout the country. To facilitate its wider spread and to promote the further monetization of the economy, the Government introduced local coins of 1, 5, 10, 25 and 50 centavos in November 2003. Dollarization thus far has served the country reasonably well and currently there is no obvious alternative. The adoption of an independent monetary policy would be extremely difficult given the absence of a well-functioning financial market and limited administrative capacity.

PROSPECTS

Timor-Leste has made substantial progress since independence. In recent years it has achieved high rates of economic growth and has begun to reduce its high levels of poverty. Since the 2006 crisis, the Government has managed to diminish the impact of pre-existing divisive conflicts within and between the security forces, as well as between various regions. The Strategic Development Plan for 2011–30 outlines strategies intended to address the main economic challenges confronting the country. To ensure that development needs are met, it is essential that the country's petroleum revenues continue to be utilized effectively to promote sustainable development, particularly of the non-oil economy. Revenues will need to be focused specifically on investments in public assets that increase productivity—rather than meeting livelihood needs by the use of cash transfers and subsidies, as has tended to be the case in recent years—and used judiciously, to ensure both that withdrawals do not exceed the capacity to finance rising levels of investment and that the Fund itself is not prejudiced by withdrawals exceeding sustainable income levels. A crucial priority in the coming years will be the promotion and development of the rural sector, and the co-ordination of its development with that of other sectors of the non-oil economy. Off-farm employment may increase in the coming years as a result of the development of eco-tourism, which is currently at an early stage.

As noted in UNDP's *Timor-Leste Human Development Report 2011*, much of the development of the non-oil sector has been government-funded and government-driven. This is likely to continue in the short term, with government expenditure accounting for 60% of non-oil GDP and the private sector for 6% of non-oil GDP. Yet the value added in the non-farm private sector, estimated at almost US $130m., is 20% larger than that of the agriculture and government sectors. Private investment remains low, at 4.6%, and the share of private consumption in non-oil GDP has been declining steadily since 2005. In the medium term, to develop in a sustainable manner, Timor-Leste's non-oil economy can only develop if it attracts investment. Hence a crucial issue for the development of the non-agricultural, non-oil economy is its ability to attract both domestic and foreign investment.

The scale of the problem confronting the development of the non-oil economy is demonstrated by the fact that the private sector currently is able to provide approximately 400 new jobs annually, yet there are around 12,000–15,000 new entrants to the labour market each year. Based on current trends, most young people in the Dili labour market can expect to wait 10 years to reach the employment level of the main economically active population; even then, only about one-half are likely to find employment. The UNDP's report also noted that the majority of off-farm jobs in recent years had been temporary, generated by public expenditure for road construction and other short-term development projects.

Timor-Leste will also be required to address a major demographic challenge. The country has a high rate of population growth, and a huge youthful population, which currently has limited employment prospects. The extent to which Timor-Leste can resolve these problems and continue to improve its levels of human development will in part depend on the success of government efforts to promote inclusive development. This will require strategies for a reduction in recently increasing levels of inequality between the country's economic and political élites and the remainder of the population, and for the promotion of greater participation in decision-making by the Timorese people, notably by accelerating the implementation of a recently developed programme for political decentralization.

Statistical Survey

Area and Population

AREA, POPULATION AND DENSITY

Area (sq km)	14,609*
Population (census results)	
31 July 2004	923,198
11 July 2010	
Males	544,198
Females	522,211
Total	1,066,409
Population (UN estimate at mid-year)†	
2011	1,153,835
Density (per sq km) at mid-2011	79.0

* 5,641 sq miles.

† Source: UN, *World Population Prospects: The 2010 Revision*.

POPULATION BY AGE AND SEX
(UN estimates at mid-2011)

	Males	Females	Total
0–14	270,041	257,784	527,825
15–64	302,023	289,639	591,662
65 and over	16,078	18,270	34,348
Total	588,142	565,693	1,153,835

Source: UN, *World Population Prospects: The 2010 Revision*.

PRINCIPAL TOWNS
(population at 2010 census)

Dili (capital)	234,026	Ermera	33,530
Baucau	46,500	Maliana	25,234

BIRTHS AND DEATHS
(annual averages, UN estimates)

	1995–2000	2000–05	2005–10
Birth rate (per 1,000)	46.1	40.4	39.4
Death rate (per 1,000)	12.9	10.0	8.7

Source: UN, *World Population Prospects: The 2010 Revision*.

Life expectancy (years at birth, WHO estimates): 67 (males 64; females 69) in 2009 (Source: WHO, *World Health Statistics*).

Health and Welfare

KEY INDICATORS

Total fertility rate (children per woman, 2009)	6.4
Under-5 mortality rate (per 1,000 live births, 2009)	56
Physicians (per 1,000 head, 2004)	0.10
Health expenditure (2008): US $ per head	112
Health expenditure (2008): % of GDP	13.9
Health expenditure (2008): public (% of total)	82.9
Access to water (% of persons, 2008)	69
Access to sanitation (% of persons, 2008)	50
Total carbon dioxide emissions ('000 metric tons, 2007)	183.2
Carbon dioxide emissions per head (metric tons, 2007)	0.2
Human development index (2010): ranking	120
Human development index (2010): value	0.502

For sources and definitions, see explanatory note on p. vi.

Agriculture

PRINCIPAL CROPS
('000 metric tons)

	2007	2008	2009
Maize	71.5	100.2	134.7
Cassava (Manioc)	41.2	35.5	37.3
Rice, paddy	60.4	80.3	120.8
Sweet potatoes*	27.3	23.5	24.7
Beans, dry*	7.0	8.0	7.5
Groundnuts, with shell*	5.2	4.4	3.9
Coconuts*	16.6	16.6	16.9
Bananas*	2.7	2.9	3.0
Guavas, mangoes and mangosteens*	5.5	5.6	5.6
Coffee, green	14.0†	14.5*	15.9*

* FAO estimate(s).
† Unofficial figure.

Aggregate production ('000 metric tons, may include official, semi-official or estimated data): Total cereals 131.9 in 2007, 180.4 in 2008, 255.5 in 2009; Total roots and tubers 114.5 in 2007, 98.8 in 2008, 103.7 in 2009; Total vegetables (incl. melons) 20.7 in 2007, 19.7 in 2008, 20.1 in 2009; Total fruits (excl. melons) 11.7 in 2007, 11.9 in 2008, 11.9 in 2009.

Source: FAO.

LIVESTOCK
('000 head)

	2007	2008	2009*
Cattle	142	145	148
Buffaloes	101	102	103
Pigs	373	388	388
Horses*	48	48	48
Goats	135	137	138
Sheep	41	41	42
Chickens*	1,000	1,000	1,000

* FAO estimates.

Source: FAO.

LIVESTOCK PRODUCTS
('000 metric tons, estimates)

	2006	2007	2008
Cattle meat	0.9	0.9	1.0
Pig meat	8.4	8.8	9.1
Chicken meat	1.0	1.0	1.0
Hen eggs	1.2	2.3	2.6

2009: Figures assumed to be unchanged from 2008 (FAO estimates).

Source: FAO.

Fishing

(metric tons, live weight, FAO estimates)

	2007	2008	2009
Total catch	2,944	3,177	3,177

Source: FAO.

Finance

CURRENCY AND EXCHANGE RATES (US currency is used)

Monetary Units
100 cents (centavos) = 1 United States dollar ($).

Sterling and Euro Equivalents (31 May 2011)
£1 sterling = US $1.650;
€1 = $1.439;
US $100 = £60.60 = €69.52.

BUDGET
(US $ million, central government operations, cash basis)

Revenue	2008	2009*	2010†
Domestic revenue	45	60	67
Direct taxes	19	13	16
Indirect taxes	19	30	34
Non-tax revenues and other	6	16	17
Oil and gas revenues	2,399	1,842	2,055
Oil and gas receipts	2,284	1,660	1,816
Interest	115	182	239
Total	2,444	1,902	2,122

Expenditure	2008	2009*	2010†
Recurrent expenditure	358	363	450
Salaries and wages	53	86	96
Goods and services	154	158	161
Transfers	88	94	161
Subsidies to agencies	63	26	40
Capital expenditure and net lending	175	209	175
Total	532	573	625

* Preliminary figures.
† Projections.

Note: Revenue figures exclude receipts from government rice sales.

Source: IMF, *Democratic Republic of Timor-Leste: 2010 Article IV Consultation—Staff Report; Joint World Bank / IMF Debt Sustainability Analysis; Staff Statement; Public Information Notice on the Executive Board Discussion; and Statement by the Executive Director for Timor-Leste* (March 2011).

INTERNATIONAL RESERVES
(US $ million at 31 December)

	2008	2009	2010
IMF special drawing rights	—	12.115	11.901
Reserve position in IMF	0.002	0.002	0.002
Foreign exchange	210.422	237.812	394.286
Total	210.424	249.929	406.188

Source: IMF, *International Financial Statistics*.

MONEY SUPPLY
(US $ million at 31 December)

	2008	2009	2010
Currency outside depository corporations	2.454	2.801	3.374
Transferable deposits	101.837	154.642	138.012
Other deposits	88.367	110.913	153.639
Broad money	192.658	268.356	295.025

Source: IMF, *International Financial Statistics*.

COST OF LIVING
(Consumer Price Index; base: 2005 = 100)

	2008	2009	2010
All items	125.0	125.9	134.4

Source: IMF, *International Financial Statistics*.

NATIONAL ACCOUNTS
(US $ million at current prices)

Expenditure on Non-oil Gross Domestic Product

	2005	2006	2007
Government final consumption expenditure	157.8	175.9	259.0
Private final consumption expenditure	329.5	301.6	352.2
Change in stocks	6.8	6.8	8.2
Gross fixed capital formation	61.9	61.0	103.0
Total domestic non-oil expenditure	556.0	545.3	722.4
Exports of goods and services	38.3	39.4	43.4
Less Imports of goods and services	262.5	258.0	370.3
Non-oil GDP in purchasers' values	331.9	326.8	395.5
Non-oil GDP at constant 2000 prices	331.1	319.8	371.7

Non-oil Gross Domestic Product by Economic Activity

	2005	2006	2007
Agriculture, forestry and fishing	111.3	116.6	124.7
Mining and quarrying (non-oil)	2.9	1.9	2.2
Manufacturing	11.8	8.7	10.2
Electricity, gas and water	5.0	5.0	6.0
Construction	33.4	29.8	44.4
Wholesale and retail trade	24.9	25.4	31.0
Transport and communications	33.8	25.4	31.0
Finance, rents and business services	28.3	28.8	33.6
Public administration and defence	80.5	85.2	112.6
United Nations	18.0	25.6	57.7
Non-oil GDP in purchasers' values	349.9	352.5	453.3

Source: IMF, *Timor-Leste: Selected Issues and Statistical Appendix* (June 2008).

Non-oil GDP in Purchasers' Values (US $ million at current prices): 398.0 in 2007; 499.0 in 2008; 590.0 in 2009 (Source: Asian Development Bank).

BALANCE OF PAYMENTS
(US $ million)

	2007	2008	2009
Exports of goods f.o.b.	6.6	14.1	9.2
Imports of goods f.o.b.	–175.7	–310.9	–384.9
Trade balance	–169.0	–296.9	–375.7
Services and income (net)	1,068.1	1,963.5	1,340.3
Balance on goods, services and income	899.1	1,666.6	964.6
Current transfers (net)	278.1	356.5	398.6
Current balance	1,177.2	2,023.1	1,363.2
Capital account (net)	32.2	17.2	27.3
Direct investment (net)	8.7	39.5	30.4
Portfolio investment (net)	–1,012.1	–2,003.1	–1,325.1
Other investment (net)	–50.6	–94.4	4.2
Net errors and omissions	–8.9	–2.2	–60.5
Overall balance	146.5	–19.9	39.5

Source: Asian Development Bank.

External Trade

SELECTED COMMODITIES
(US $ '000)

Imports c.i.f.	2006*	2008	2009
Meat and edible meat offal	579	3,008	3,919
Dairy and edible products of animal origin	682	2,263	2,662
Cereals	6,516	25,485	35,169
Preparations of cereals, flour, starch or milk; pastry cooks' products	1,609	4,720	4,223
Beverages, spirits and vinegar	1,842	6,749	7,793
Mineral fuels, mineral oils and products of their distillation; bituminous substances; mineral waxes	29,070	71,123	38,040
Boilers, machinery and mechanical appliances; parts thereof	4,512	17,333	22,770
Vehicles, other than railway or tramway rolling stock, and parts thereof	5,830	43,869	58,486
Electrical machinery and equipment and parts thereof; sound recorders and reproducers; televisions, etc.	6,191	17,568	25,198
Pharmaceutical products	1,832	8,100	5,269
Iron or steel articles	1,213	2,304	3,922
Plastics and articles thereof	1,744	2,017	2,643
Total (incl. others)	87,695	258,429	282,595

Exports f.o.b. (excl. oil and gas)	2006*	2008	2009
Coffee	7,999	12,632	8,291
Total (incl. others)	8,455	12,899	8,491

* Comparable data for 2007 were not available.

Re-exports (US $ '000): 52,231 in 2006; 36,307 in 2008; 26,021 in 2009. Note: The significance of re-exports may appear overstated owing to the inclusion of data connected with the outflow of foreign personnel and equipment as peace-keeping operations were scaled down. Note: Comparable data for 2007 were not available.

Source: Ministério do Plano e das Finanças, Dili.

PRINCIPAL TRADING PARTNERS
(US $ '000)

Imports c.i.f.	2006*	2008	2009
Australia	10,951	35,705	47,196
China, People's Republic	2,209	5,363	11,572
Germany	663	2,925	314
Indonesia	37,733	109,840	92,105
Japan	2,183	5,881	7,750
Korea, Republic	98	2,705	1,821
Malaysia	773	11,739	8,052
Portugal	1,946	3,137	9,487
Singapore	17,001	44,112	53,513
Thailand	3,031	5,298	3,346
Viet Nam	4,406	18,099	34,602
Total (incl. others)	87,695	258,429	282,594

Exports f.o.b. (excl. oil and gas)†	2006*	2008	2009
Australia	303	266	250
British Indian Ocean Territory	n.a.	155	142
Canada	n.a.	24	255
Germany	2,042	3,395	2,372
Indonesia	1,146	2,093	412
Japan	119	641	402
Korea, Republic	31	246	106
New Zealand	48	119	86
Portugal	189	808	755
Singapore	642	1,263	289
Taiwan	87	41	33
USA	3,447	3,380	2,873
Total (incl. others)	8,455	12,632	8,491

* Comparable data for 2007 were not available.

† Excluding re-exports (US $ million): 52.2 in 2006; 36.3 in 2008; 26.0 in 2009. Note: The significance of re-exports may appear overstated owing to the inclusion of data connected with the outflow of foreign personnel and equipment as peace-keeping operations were scaled down.

Source: Ministério do Plano e das Finanças, Dili.

SHIPPING

Merchant Fleet
(registered at 31 December)

	2007	2008	2009
Number of vessels	1	1	1
Total displacement ('000 grt)	1,134	1,134	1,134

Source: IHS Fairplay, *World Fleet Statistics*.

Tourism

TOURIST ARRIVALS
('000 foreign visitors, excl. Indonesians, at classified hotels*)

	1996	1997	1998
Total	0.8	1.0	0.3

* Arrivals at non-classified hotels: 204 in 1996; 245 in 1997; 41 in 1998.

Communications Media

	2008	2009	2010
Telephones ('000 main lines in use)	2.4	2.4	2.4
Mobile cellular telephones ('000 subscribers)	125.0	330.0	600.6
Internet users	1,800	2,100	n.a.
Broadband subscribers	100	200	200

Daily newspapers: 2 in 2004.

Non-daily newspapers: 3 in 2004.

Source: UNESCO Institute for Statistics and International Telecommunication Union.

Education

(2008/09 unless otherwise indicated)

	Teachers	Students
Pre-primary*	237	6,987
Primary	7,358	213,783
Lower Secondary†	1,359	33,082
Upper Secondary	1,257†	24,808*
Tertiary	1,196	16,727

* 2004/05.

† 2007/08 estimate(s).

Source: UNESCO Institute for Statistics.

Pupil-teacher ratio (primary education, UNESCO estimate): 29.1 in 2008/09 (Source: UNESCO Institute for Statistics).

Adult literacy rate (UNESCO estimate): 50.6% in 2007 (Source: UNESCO Institute for Statistics).

Directory

The Constitution

The Constitution of the Democratic Republic of East Timor was promulgated by the Constituent Assembly on 22 March 2002 and became effective on 20 May, when the nation formalized its independence. (From this date the country elected to be known by its official name, the Democratic Republic of Timor-Leste.) The main provisions of the Constitution are summarized below:

FUNDAMENTAL PRINCIPLES

The Democratic Republic of East Timor is a democratic, sovereign, independent and unitary state. Its territory comprises the historically defined eastern part of Timor island, the enclave of Oecussi, the island of Ataúro and the islet of Jaco. Oecussi Ambeno and Ataúro shall receive special administrative and economic treatment.

The fundamental objectives of the State include the following: to safeguard national sovereignty; to guarantee fundamental rights and freedoms; to defend political democracy; to promote the building of a society based on social justice; and to guarantee the effective equality of opportunities between women and men.

Sovereignty is vested in the people. The people shall exercise political power through universal, free, equal, direct, secret and periodic suffrage and through other forms stated in the Constitution.

In matters of international relations, the Democratic Republic of East Timor shall establish relations of friendship and co-operation with all other peoples. It shall maintain privileged ties with countries whose official language is Portuguese.

The State shall recognize and respect the different religious denominations, which are free in their organization. Tetum and Portuguese shall be the official languages.

FUNDAMENTAL RIGHTS, DUTIES, LIBERTIES AND GUARANTEES

All citizens are equal before the law and no one shall be discriminated against on grounds of colour, race, marital status, gender, ethnic origin, language, social or economic status, political or ideological convictions, religion, education and physical or mental condition. Women and men shall have the same rights and duties in family, political, economic, social and cultural life. Rights, freedoms and safeguards are upheld by the State and include the following: the right to life; to personal freedom, security and integrity; to habeas corpus; to the inviolability of the home and of correspondence; to freedom of expression and conscience; to freedom of movement, assembly and association; and to participate in political life. Freedom of the press is guaranteed.

Rights and duties of citizens include the following: the right and the duty to work; the right to vote (at over 17 years of age); the right to petition; the right and duty to contribute towards the defence of sovereignty; the freedom to form trade unions and the right to strike; consumer rights; the right to private property; the duty to pay taxes; the right to health and medical care; the right to education and culture.

ORGANIZATION OF POLITICAL POWER

Political power lies with the people. The organs of sovereignty shall be the President of the Republic, the National Parliament, the Government and the Courts. They shall observe the principle of separation and interdependence of powers. There shall be free, direct, secret, personal and regular universal suffrage. No one shall hold political office for life.

PRESIDENT OF THE REPUBLIC

The President of the Republic is the Head of State and the Supreme Commander of the Defence Force. The President symbolizes and guarantees national independence and unity and the effective functioning of democratic institutions. The President of the Republic shall be elected by universal, free, direct, secret and personal suffrage. The candidate who receives more than one-half of the valid votes shall be elected President. Candidates shall be original citizens of the Democratic Republic of East Timor, at least 35 years of age, in possession of his/her full faculties and have been proposed by a minimum of 5,000 voters. The President shall hold office for five years. The President may not be re-elected for a third consecutive term of office.

The duties of the President include the following: to preside over the Supreme Council of Defence and Security and the Council of State; to set dates for elections; to convene extraordinary sessions of the National Parliament; to dissolve the National Parliament; to promulgate laws; to exercise the functions of the Supreme Commander of the Defence Force; to veto laws; to appoint and dismiss the Prime Minister and other government members; to apply to the Supreme Court of Justice; to submit relevant issues of national interest to a referendum; to declare a State of Emergency following the authorization of the National Parliament; to appoint and dismiss diplomatic representatives; to accredit foreign diplomatic representatives; to declare war and make peace with the prior approval of the National Parliament.

COUNCIL OF STATE

The Council of State is the political advisory body of the President of the Republic. It is presided over by the President of the Republic and comprises former Presidents of the Republic who were not removed from office, the Speaker of the National Parliament, the Prime Minister, five citizens elected by the National Parliament and five citizens nominated by the President of the Republic.

NATIONAL PARLIAMENT

The National Parliament represents all Timorese citizens, and shall have a minimum of 52 and a maximum of 65 members, elected by universal, free, direct, equal, secret and personal suffrage for a term of five years. The duties of the National Parliament include the following: to enact legislation; to confer legislative authority on the Government; to approve plans and the Budget and monitor their execution; to ratify international treaties and conventions; to approve revisions of the Constitution; to propose to the President of the Republic that issues of national interest be submitted to a referendum. The legislative term shall comprise five legislative sessions, and each legislative session shall have the duration of one year.

GOVERNMENT

The Government is the supreme organ of public administration and is responsible for the formulation and execution of general policy. It shall comprise the Prime Minister, the Ministers and the Secretaries of State, and may include one or more Deputy Prime Ministers and Deputy Ministers. The Council of Ministers shall comprise the Prime Minister, the Deputy Prime Ministers, if any, and the Ministers. It shall be convened and presided over by the Prime Minister. The Prime Minister shall be appointed by the President of the Republic. Other members of the Government shall be appointed by the President at the proposal of the Prime Minister. The Government shall be responsible to the President and the National Parliament. The Government's programme shall be submitted to the National Parliament for consideration within 30 days of the appointment of the Government.

JUDICIARY

The Courts are independent organs of sovereignty with competence to administer justice. There shall be the Supreme Court of Justice and other courts of law, the High Administrative, Tax and Audit Court, other administrative courts of first instance and military courts. There may also be maritime courts and courts of arbitration.

It is the duty of the Public Prosecutors to represent the State. The Office of the Prosecutor-General shall be the highest authority in public prosecution and shall be presided over by the Prosecutor-General, who is appointed and dismissed by the President of the Republic. The Prosecutor-General shall serve for a term of six years.

ECONOMIC AND FINANCIAL ORGANIZATION

The economic organization of East Timor shall be based on the co-existence of the public, private, co-operative and social sectors of ownership, and on the combination of community forms with free initiative and business management. The State shall promote national investment. The State Budget shall be prepared by the Government and approved by the National Parliament. Its execution shall be monitored by the High Administrative, Tax and Audit Court and by the National Parliament.

NATIONAL DEFENCE AND SECURITY

The East Timor defence force—Falintil-ETDF—is composed exclusively of national citizens and shall be responsible for the provision of military defence to the Democratic Republic of East Timor. There shall be a single system of organization for the whole national territory. Falintil-ETDF shall act as a guarantor of national independence, territorial integrity and the freedom and security of the population against any external threat or aggression. The police shall guarantee the internal security of the citizens.

The Superior Council for Defence and Security is the consultative organ of the President of the Republic on matters relating to defence and security. It shall be presided over by the President of the Republic and shall include a higher number of civilian than military entities.

GUARANTEE AND REVISION OF THE CONSTITUTION

Declaration of unconstitutionality may be requested by: the President of the Republic; the Speaker of the National Parliament; the Prosecutor-General; the Prime Minister; one-fifth of the Members of the National Parliament; the Ombudsman.

Changes to the Constitution shall be approved by a majority of two-thirds of Members of Parliament and the President shall not refuse to promulgate a revision statute.

FINAL AND TRANSITIONAL PROVISIONS

Confirmation, accession and ratification of bilateral and multilateral conventions, treaties, agreements or alliances that took place before the Constitution entered into force shall be decided by the respective bodies concerned; the Democratic Republic of East Timor shall not be bound by any treaty, agreement or alliance not thus ratified. Any acts or contracts concerning natural resources entered into prior to the entry into force of the Constitution and not subsequently confirmed by the competent bodies shall not be recognized.

Indonesian and English shall be working languages, together with the official languages, for as long as is deemed necessary.

Acts committed between 25 April 1974 and 31 December 1999 that can be considered to be crimes of humanity, of genocide or of war shall be liable to criminal proceedings within the national or international courts.

The Government

HEAD OF STATE

President: José Ramos Horta (took office 20 May 2007).

CABINET

(October 2011)

The Government is a coalition of Congresso Nacional da Reconstrução de Timor-Leste (CNRT), Associação Social-Democrata Timorense (ASDT), Partido Democrático (PD), Partido Social Democrata Timor Lorosae (PSD) and Partido Unidade Nacional Democrática da Resistência Timorense (UNDERTIM).

Prime Minister and Minister of Defence and Security: Kay Rala (Xanana) Gusmão.

Deputy Prime Minister: José Luís Guterres.

Minister of State Administration and Territorial Management: Arcângelo Leite Pinto.

Minister of Foreign Affairs and Co-operation: Zacarias Albano da Costa.

Minister of Justice: Maria Lúcia Lobato.

Minister of Health: Nélson Martins.

Minister of Finance: Maria Madalena Emília Pires.

Minister of Education: João Câncio Freitas.

Minister of Economy and Development: JOÃO GONÇALVES.

Minister of Agriculture and Fisheries: MARIANO SABINO LOPES.

Minister of Social Solidarity: MARIA DOMINGAS ALVES.

Minister of Tourism, Trade and Industry: GIL DA COSTA ALVES.

Minister of Infrastructure: PEDRO LAY.

MINISTRIES

Office of the President: Palácio das Cinzas, Caicoli, Dili; tel. 3339011.

Office of the Prime Minister: Palácio do Governo, Av. Presidente Nicolau Lobato, Dili; tel. 7243559; fax 3339503; e-mail mail@primeministerandcabinet.gov.tp; internet www.pm.gov.tp.

Ministry of Agriculture and Fisheries: Edif. 5, Av. Presidente Nicolau Lobato, Dili; tel. 3310418; e-mail agriculture@gov.east-timor.org; internet www.maf.gov.tl.

Ministry of Defence and Security: Palácio do Governo, Edif. 2, 1°, Av. Presidente Nicolau Lobato, Dili; tel. 3331190; e-mail sed-tl@easttimor.minihub.org.

Ministry of Economy and Development: Rua D. Aleixo Corte Real, Edif. Fomento, 2°, Mandarin, Dili; tel. 3339039.

Ministry of Education: Rua de Vila Verde, Dili; tel. 3339654; e-mail education@gov.east-timor.org.

Ministry of Finance: Palácio do Governo, Edif. 5, Av. Presidente Nicolau Lobato, Dili; tel. 3339510; e-mail info@mof.gov.tl; internet www.mof.gov.tl.

Ministry of Foreign Affairs and Co-operation: Av. de Portugal, Praia dos Coqueiros, Dili; tel. 3331234; fax 3339025; e-mail administration@mnec.gov-tl.net.

Ministry of Health: Edif. dos Serviços Centrais do Ministério da Saúde, Rua de Caicoli, POB 374, Dili; tel. 3322467; fax 3325189; e-mail tls_epid@yahoo.com; internet www.moh.gov.tl.

Ministry of Infrastructure: 8 Av. Bispo de Medeiros, Mercado Lama, Dili; tel. 3339355.

Ministry of Justice: Av. Jacinto Candido, Dili; tel. 3331160; e-mail mj@mj.gov.tl; internet www.mj.gov.tl.

Ministry of Social Solidarity: Rua de Caicoli, Dili; tel. 3339582; internet www.mss.gov.tl.

Ministry of State Administration and Territorial Management: Rua Jacinto Candido, Caicoli, Dili; tel. 3339077; e-mail komunikasaun@estatal.gov.tl; internet www.estatal.gov.tl.

Ministry of Tourism, Trade and Industry: Edif. Fomento, Rua Dom Aleixo Corte Real, Mandarin, Dili; tel. 3331202; e-mail mtci.gov.tl@gmail.com; internet www.mtci-timorleste.com.

President and Legislature

PRESIDENT

Presidential Election, First Ballot, 9 April 2007

Candidate	Votes	% of votes
Francisco Guterres (Fretilin)	112,666	27.89
José Ramos Horta (Independent)	88,102	21.81
Fernando de Araújo (PD)	77,459	19.18
Francisco Xavier do Amaral (ASDT)	58,125	14.39
Lucia Maria B. F. Lobato (PSD)	35,789	8.86
Manuel Tilman (KOTA)	16,534	4.09
Avelino Coelho da Silva (PST)	8,338	2.06
João Viegas Carrascalão (UDT)	6,928	1.72
Total	403,941	100.00

Presidential Election, Second Ballot, 9 May 2007

Candidate	Votes	% of votes
José Ramos Horta	285,835	69.18
Francisco Guterres	127,342	30.82
Total	413,177	100.00

NATIONAL PARLIAMENT

A single-chamber Constituent Assembly was elected by popular vote on 30 August 2001. Its 88 members included 75 deputies elected under a national system of proportional representation and one representative from each of Timor-Leste's 13 districts, elected under a 'first-past-the-post' system. Upon independence on 20 May 2002 the Constituent Assembly became the National Parliament; it held its inaugural session on the same day. At the election of June 2007 the number of members was reduced from 88 to 65.

Speaker: FERNANDO DE ARAÚJO.

General Election, 30 June 2007

	Seats
Frente Revolucionária do Timor Leste Independente (Fretilin)	21
Congresso Nacional da Reconstrução de Timor-Leste (CNRT)	18
Associação Social-Democrata Timorense-Partido Social Democrata Timor Lorosae (ASDT-PSD)	11
Partido Democrático (PD)	8
Partido Unidade Nacional (PUN)	3
Aliança Democrática Klibur Oan Timor Asuwain-Partido do Povo de Timor (AD KOTA-PPT)	2
Partido Unidade Nacional Democrática da Resistência Timorense (UNDERTIM)	2
Total	65

Election Commission

National Electoral Commission (CNE): Av. Bispo Medeiros-Kintal, Dili; tel. 3310082; f. 2004; govt body; Chair. Dr FAUSTINO CARDOSO.

Political Organizations

Associação Popular Democrática de Timor Pro Referendo (Apodeti Pro Referendo) (Pro-Referendum Popular Democratic Association of Timor): c/o Frederico Almeida Santos Costa, CNRT Office, Balide, Dili; tel. 3324994; f. 1974; est. as Apodeti; present name adopted Aug. 2000; fmrly supported autonomous integration with Indonesia; Pres. FREDERICO ALMEIDA SANTOS COSTA.

Associação Social-Democrata Timorense (ASDT) (Timor Social Democratic Association): Av. Direitos Humanos Lecidere, Dili; tel. 3983331; f. 2001; Pres. FRANCISCO XAVIER DO AMARAL.

Barisan Rakyat Timor Timur (BRTT) (East Timor People's Front): fmrly supported autonomous integration with Indonesia; Pres. FRANCISCO LOPES DA CRUZ.

Congresso Nacional da Reconstrução de Timor-Leste (CNRT) (National Congress for the Reconstruction of Timor-Leste): Rua Nu Laran, Bairro dos Grilos, Dili; tel. 7358696; internet www.cnrt-timor.org; f. 2007; Pres. KAY RALA 'XANANA' GUSMÃO.

Conselho Popular pela Defesa da República Democrática de Timor Leste (CPD-RDTL) (Popular Council for the Defence of the Democratic Republic of East Timor): opp. the Church, Balide, Dili; tel. 3481462; f. 1999; promotes adoption of 1975 Constitution of Democratic Republic of East Timor; Spokesperson CRISTIANO DA COSTA.

Frente Revolucionária do Timor Leste Independente (Fretilin) (Revolutionary Front for an Independent East Timor): Rua dos Mártires da Pátria, Dili; tel. 3321409; internet fretilin-rdtl.blogspot.com; f. 1974; est. to seek full independence for East Timor; entered into alliance with the UDT in 1986; Pres. VICENTE MAUBOSY.

Klibur Oan Timor Asuwain (KOTA) (Association of Timorese Heroes): Rua dos Mártires da Pátria, Fatuhada, Dili; tel. 3324661; e-mail clementinoamaral@hotmail.com; f. 1974; est. as pro-integration party; supported independence with Timorese traditions; Pres. MANUEL TILMAN.

Partai Democratik Maubere (PDM) (Maubere Democratic Party): Blk B-II, 16 Surikmas Lama Kraik, Fatumeta, Dili; tel. 3184508; e-mail pdm_party@hotmail.com; f. 2000; Pres. PAOLO PINTO.

Partai Liberal (PL) (Liberal Party): Talbessi Sentral, Dili; tel. 3786448; Pres. ARMANDO JOSÉ DOURADO DA SILVA.

Partido Democrata Cristão (PDC) (Christian Democrat Party): Former Escola Cartilha, Rua Quintal Kiik, Bairro Economico, Dili; tel. 3324683; e-mail arlindom@octa4.net.au; f. 2000; Pres. ANTÓNIO XIMENES.

Partido Democrático (PD) (Democratic Party): 1 Rua Democracia, Pantai Kelapa, Dili; tel. 3608421; e-mail flazama@hotmail.com; Pres. FERNANDO DE ARAÚJO.

Partido Nacionalista Timorense (PNT) (Nationalist Party of Timor): Dili; tel. 3323518; internet pnt-timor-leste.planetaclix.pt; Pres. Dr ABÍLIO ARAÚJO.

Partido do Povo de Timor (PPT) (Timorese People's Party): Dili; tel. 3568325; f. 2000; pro-integration; supported presidential candidacy of Kay Rala 'Xanana' Gusmão in 2002 election; Pres. Dr JACOB XAVIER.

Partido Republika National Timor Leste (PARENTIL) (National Republic Party of East Timor): Perumnar Bairopite Bob Madey Ran, Fahan Jalam, Ailobu Laran RTK; tel. 3361393; Pres. FLAVIANO PEREIRA LOPEZ.

Partido Social Democrata Timor Lorosae (PSD) (Social Democrat Party of East Timor): Apdo 312, Correios de Dili, Dili; tel. 3357027; e-mail psdtimor@hotmail.com; f. 2000; Pres. ZACARIAS ALBANO DA COSTA; Sec.-Gen. MARITO MAGONO.

Partido Socialista de Timor (PST) (Socialist Party of Timor): Rua Colegio das Madras, Balide, Dili; tel. 3560246; e-mail kaynaga@hotmail.com; Marxist-Leninist Fretilin splinter group; Pres. AVELINO COELHO DA SILVA.

Partido Trabalhista Timorense (PTT) (Timor Labour Party): 2B Rua Travessa de Befonte, 2 Bairro Formosa, Dili; tel. 3322807; f. 1974; Pres. PAULO FREITAS DA SILVA.

Partido Unidade Nacional (PUN) (United National Party): c/o National Parliament, Dili; f. 2005; Pres. FERNANDA BORGES.

Partido Unidade Nacional Democrática da Resistência Timorense (UNDERTIM): c/o National Parliament, Dili; Pres. CORNELIO GAMA.

União Democrata-Cristão de Timor (UDC/PDC) (Christian Democratic Union of Timor): 62 Rua Almirante Américo Thomás, Mandarin, Dili; tel. 3325042; f. 1998; Pres. VINCENTE DA SILVA GUTERRES.

União Democrática Timorense (UDT) (Timorese Democratic Union): Palapagoa Rua da India, Dili; tel. 3881453; e-mail joaocarrascalao@email.msn.com; internet fitini.net/udttimor; f. 1974; allied itself with Fretilin in 1986; Pres. GILMAN DOS SANTOS; Sec.-Gen. DOMINGOS OLIVEIRA.

Diplomatic Representation

EMBASSIES IN TIMOR-LESTE

Australia: Av. dos Mártires da Pátria, Dili; tel. 3322111; fax 3322247; e-mail austemb_dili@dfat.gov.au; internet www.easttimor.embassy.gov.au; Ambassador MILES ARMITAGE.

Brazil: Av. Governador Serpa Rosa, POB 157, Farol, Dili; tel. 3324203; fax 3324620; e-mail brasdili@mail.timortelecom.tp; Ambassador EDSON MARINHO DUARTE MONTEIRO.

China, People's Republic: Av. Governador Serpa Rosa, POB 131, Farol, Dili; tel. 3325168; fax 3325166; e-mail chinaembassy2002@yahoo.com; internet tl.chineseembassy.org; Ambassador FU YUANCONG.

Indonesia: Farol, Palapaco, POB 207, Dili; tel. 3317107; fax 3323684; e-mail kukridil@hotmail.com; internet www.dili.deplu.go.id; Ambassador EDDY SETIABUDHI.

Japan: Av. de Portugal, Pantai Kelapa, POB 175, Dili; tel. 3323131; fax 3323130; e-mail japan.embassy.in.timor-leste@mofa.go.jp; internet www.timor-leste.emb-japan.go.jp; Ambassador KITAHARA IWAO.

Korea, Republic: Av. de Portugal, Motael, Dili; tel. 3321635; fax 3323636; e-mail koreadili@mofat.go.kr; internet tls.mofat.go.kr; Ambassador SEO KYOUNG-SUK.

Malaysia: Av. de Portugal, Praia dos Coqueiros, Dili; tel. 3321804; fax 3321805; e-mail maldili@kln.gov.my; internet www.kln.gov.my/web/tls_dili; Ambassador NAZARUDIN BIN SALLEH.

New Zealand: Rua Geremias do Amaral, Montael, Dili; tel. 3310087; fax 3324982; e-mail dili@mfat.gov.nz; Ambassador TONY FAUTUA.

Philippines: Av. Governador Serpa Rosa, Farol, Dili; tel. 33310408; fax 3310407; e-mail pe.dili@dfa.gov.ph; Ambassador MARIA H. BUGARIN.

Portugal: Edif. ACAIT, Av. Presidente Nicolau Lobato, Dili; tel. 3312533; fax 3312526; e-mail embaixada.portugal@embpor.tp; internet www.embpor.tp; Ambassador LUÍS MANUEL BARREIRA DE SOUSA.

Thailand: Av. de Portugal, Motael, Dili; tel. 3310609; fax 3322179; e-mail thaidli@mfa.go.th; Ambassador WIWAT KUNTHONTHIEN.

USA: Av. de Portugal, Praia dos Coqueiros, Dili; tel. 3324684; fax 3313206; e-mail ConsDili@state.gov; internet timor-leste.usembassy.gov; Ambassador JUDITH R. FERGIN.

Judicial System

Until independence was granted on 20 May 2002 all legislative and executive authority with respect to the administration of the judiciary in East Timor was vested in the UN Transitional Administration in East Timor (UNTAET). During the transitional period of administration a two-tier court structure was established, consisting of District Courts and a Court of Appeal. The Constitution, promulgated in March 2002, specified that Timor-Leste should have three categories of courts: the Supreme Court of Justice and other law courts; the High Administrative, Tax and Audit Court and other administrative courts of first instance; and military courts. The judiciary would be regulated by the Superior Council of the Judiciary, the function of which would be to oversee the judicial sector and, in particular, to control the appointment, promotion, discipline and dismissal of judges. In July 2003 the Court of Appeal was reconstituted. A new penal code was promulgated in March 2009. At that time a code based on Indonesian law remained in place for civil cases, but it was scheduled for replacement by civil codes based on Portuguese law.

Court of Appeal: Caicoli, Dili; tel. 3331149; e-mail tribunal.recurso@tribunais.tl; internet www.tribunais.tl; Pres. CLAUDIO XIMENES.

District Courts: There are four district courts, located in Dili, Baucau, Oecusse and Suai.

Office of the Prosecutor-General: Dili; Prosecutor-General ANA MARIA PESSÔA PEREIRA DA SILVA PINTO.

Religion

In 2009 it was estimated that about 96.5% of the total population were Roman Catholic.

CHRISTIANITY

The Roman Catholic Church

Timor-Leste comprises the dioceses of Dili and Baucau, directly responsible to the Holy See. In December 2007 there were an estimated 958,383 Roman Catholics.

Bishop of Baucau: Most Rev. BASILIO DO NASCIMENTO, Largo da Catedral, Baucau 88810; tel. 4121209; fax 4121380.

Bishop of Dili: Most Rev. ALBERTO RICARDO DA SILVA, Av. dos Direitos Humanos, Bidau Lecidere, CP 4, Dili 88010; tel. 3324850; fax 3321177.

Bishop of Maliana: Fr NORBERTO DO AMARAL.

Protestant Church

Igreja Protestante iha Timor Lorosa'e (Protestant Church in Timor-Leste): Jl. Raya Comoro, POB 1186, Dili 88110; tel. and fax 3323128; f. 1988; est. as Gereja Kristen Timor Timur (GKTT); adopted present name 2000; Moderator Rev. MOISES A. DA SILVA; 30,000 mems.

The Press

The Constitution promulgated in March 2002 guarantees freedom of the press in Timor-Leste.

Guide Post Magazine: Dili; e-mail advertising@guideposttimor.com; internet www.guideposttimor.com; monthly; Editor LEITH CARROLL.

Lalenok (Mirror): Rua Gov. Celestino da Silva, Farol, Dili; tel. 3321607; e-mail lalenok@hotmail.com; f. 2000; publ. by Kamelin Media Group; Tetum; 3 a week; Dir-Gen. and Chief Editor VIRGÍLIO DA SILVA GUTERRES; Editor JOSÉ MARIA POMPELA; circ. 300.

Lian Maubere: Dili; f. 1999; weekly.

Jornal da República (The Official Gazette of Timor-Leste): Dili; e-mail jornal_republica@mj.gov.tl; internet www.jornal.gov.tl; forum for publication of all govt regulations and directives, acts of national organs or institutions, and other acts of public interest requiring general notification; Portuguese.

Suara Timor Lorosae: STL Park, Surik Mas, Dili; tel. 3322824; fax 3322823; e-mail stl_redaksi@yahoo.com; internet suara-timor-lorosae.com; f. 2000; daily; Editor-in-Chief and Publr SALVADOR J. XIMENES SOARES.

Timor Post: 6 Rua Dom Aleixo Corte-Real, Dili; f. 2000; managed by editors and staff of the fmr Suara Timor Timur; Tetum, English, Portuguese and Bahasa Indonesia; daily; Man. Editor OTELIO OTE; Chief Editor and Dir ADERITO HUGO DA COSTA; circ. 600.

PRESS AGENCY

Timornewsline: Rua Sebastian da Costa, Colmera, Dili; tel. 3324475; e-mail alberico@tlmc.org; internet www.timornewsline.com; operated by Timor-Leste Media Development Center.

PRESS ASSOCIATIONS

Sindicato dos Jornalistas de Timor-Leste (SJTL): Rua Dom Aleixo Corte-Real, Bebora, Dili; tel. 7248549; e-mail sjti@yahoo.com; f. 2001; Pres. RODOLFO DE SOUSA.

Timor Lorosae Journalists' Association (TLJA): Rua de Caicoli, Dili; tel. 3324047; fax 3327505; e-mail ajtl_tlja@hotmail.com; f. 1999; Co-ordinator OTELIO OTE; Pres. VIRGÍLIO DA SILVA GUTERRES.

Broadcasting and Communications

TELECOMMUNICATIONS

In July 2002 the Government granted a consortium led by Portugal Telecom a 15-year concession permitting it to establish and operate Timor-Leste's telecommunications systems. Under the terms of the concession, the consortium agreed to provide every district in Timor-Leste with telecommunications services at the most inexpensive tariffs viable within 15 months. At the expiry of the concession in 2017, the telecommunications system was to be transferred to government control.

Timor-Leste Telecom (TT): Sala No. 7, Hotel Timor, Av. dos Mártires da Pátria, POB 135, Dili; tel. 3303000; fax 3303419; e-mail info@timortelecom.tp; internet www.timortelecom.tp; f. 2002; jt venture mainly operated by Portugal Telecom; provides telecommunications services in Timor-Leste; Chair. RUI PEDRO OLIVEIRA SOARES; CEO Capt. MANUEL AMARO; 114 employees.

BROADCASTING

Following independence, the UN Mission of Support in East Timor (UNMISET) transferred control of public television and radio in Timor-Leste to the new Government. In 2003 a Public Broadcasting Service was established, controlled by an independent board of directors.

Radio

There are 18 radio stations operating in Timor-Leste, including community radio stations for each of the country's 13 districts. In addition to the public service, Radio Timor-Leste, the Roman Catholic Church operates a radio station, Radio Kamanak, while a third populist station, Voz Esperança, broadcasts in Dili. A fourth radio station, Radio Falintil FM, also operates in Dili and in October 2003 the Christian station Voice FM was established. In 2000 the US radio station Voice of America began broadcasting to Timor-Leste seven days a week in English, Portuguese and Bahasa Indonesia.

Radio Timor-Leste (RTL): Rua de Caicoli, Dili; tel. 3321826; e-mail radio@rttl.org; internet www.rttl.org; fmrly Radio UNTAET; name changed as above in 2002; broadcasts mainly in Bahasa Indonesia, but also in English, Portuguese and Tetum, to an estimated 90% of Timor-Leste's population; Man. PAULA RODRIGES.

Television

TV Timor-Leste (TVTL): Rua de Caicoli, Dili; tel. 3321825; e-mail tv@rttl.org; internet www.rttl.org; f. 2000; est. as Televisaun Timor Lorosa'e by UNTAET; adopted present name in May 2002; broadcasts in Tetum and Portuguese; Gen. Man. ANTONIO DIAZ.

Finance

(cap. = capital; res = reserves; dep. = deposits; brs = branches)

BANKING

In February 2001 the East Timor Central Payments Office was officially opened. This was succeeded in November of that year by the Banking and Payments Authority, which was intended to function as a precursor to a central bank. The establishment of the National Development Bank awaited parliamentary approval in 2011.

Banking and Payments Authority (BPA): Av. Bispo Medeiros, POB 59, Dili; tel. 3313712; fax 3313713; e-mail info@bancocentral.tl; internet www.bancocentral.tl; inaugurated Nov. 2001; regulates and supervises Timor-Leste's financial system, formulates and implements payments system policies, provides banking services to Timor-Leste's administration and foreign official institutions, manages fiscal reserves; fmrly Central Payments Office; cap. US $20m., dep. US $191.6m. (June 2009); Chair. and Gen. Man. ABRAÃO F. DE VASCONSELOS; Dep. Gen. Mans MARIA JOSÉ DE JESUS SARMENTO, NUR AINI DJAFAR ALKATIRI.

Instituição de Micro Finanças de Timor-Leste (IMFTL): Av. Martires da Patria, Mandarin, Dili; tel. 3339186; fax 3310444; e-mail smspirito@hotmail.com; f. 2002; microfinance.

Foreign Banks

Australia and New Zealand Banking Group Ltd (ANZ) (Australia): cnr Av. Presidente Nicolau Lobato and Rua Belarmino Lobo, Bidau Lecidere, POB 264, Dili; tel. 3324800; fax 3324822; e-mail easttimor@anz.com; internet www.anz.com/TimorLesteretail and commercial banking services; Gen. Man. CHRIS DURMAN; Group CEO JOHN MCFARLANE.

Banco Nacional Ultramarino (Portugal): Edif. BNU, 12–13 Av. Presidente Nicolau Lobato, Dili; tel. 3323385; fax 3323678; e-mail cgd.timor@cgd.ptwholly owned subsidiary of Caixa Geral de Depósitos, Portugal; Gen. Man. Dr CORREIA PINTO; 9 brs.

PT Bank Mandiri (Persero) (Indonesia): 12 Av. Presidente Nicolau Lobato, Colmera, Dili; tel. 3317777; fax 3317444; e-mail dili_timorleste@bankmandiri.co.id; internet www.bankmandiri.co.id; Group Chair. EDWIN GERUNGAN.

Trade and Industry

GOVERNMENT AGENCIES

Autoridade Nacional do Petróleo—ANP (National Petroleum Authority): Ground Floor, East Wing, Pálacio do Governo, POB 113, Farol, Dili; tel. 3324098; fax 3324082; e-mail info@anp-tl.org; internet www.anp-tl.org; f. 2008; responsible for management of govt petroleum revenues; Pres. GUALDINO DO CARMO DA SILVA.

Direcção Nacional Politica do Recursos Naturais: 1st Floor, Fomento Bldg, Mandarin, POB 171, Dili; tel. and fax 3317143; e-mail amandio_gusmao@yahoo.com.au; internet www.timor-leste.gov.tl/EMRD; Dir AMANDIO GUSMÃO SOARES.

Timor Gás & Petróleo Empresa Pública (Timor GAP EP): Dili; f. 2011; responsible for management of the country's petroleum resources.

TradeInvest Timor-Leste: Memorial Hall, Av. Praia dos Coqueros Farol, Dili 8000; tel. 3331084; fax 3331087; e-mail tradeinvest_tl@yahoo.com; f. 2005; est. to encourage devt of entrepreneurship within Timor-Leste.

UTILITIES

As a result of the civil conflict in 1999, some 13–23 power stations were reported to require repairs ranging from moderate maintenance to almost complete rehabilitation. The rehabilitation of the power sector was funded largely by foreign donors. By July 2003 31 generators had been restored, supplying electricity to Dili, as well as to 12 districts and 33 sub-districts.

Electricidade de Timor-Leste (EDTL): EDTL Bldg, Rua Estrada de Balide, Caicoli, Dili; tel. 3339254; fax 7230095; e-mail virgiliofguterres@hotmail.com; govt dept; responsible for power generation, distribution and financial management of power sector in Timor-Leste; transferred to external management in 2002; Dir VIRGILIO GUTERRES.

CO-OPERATIVES

Cooperativa Café Timor (CCT): 16 Rua Barros Gomes, Dili; tel. 3313139; e-mail boycedjs@gmail.com; f. 2000; est. under the Timor Economic Rehabilitation and Devt Project; produces, markets and distributes organic coffee; also provides information and advisory services for member farmers; Gen. Man. SISTO MONIZ PIEDADE; 21,557 mems.

Cooperativa Fera Nakukun: Rua Vila Guico, Loes, Guico, Maubara; tel. 07358236 (mobile); 100% Timor-owned; fresh food supplier.

MAJOR COMPANIES

Info Timor: Baucau; tel. 7313826; e-mail andrew@infoxchange.net.au; internet www.technology.tl; f. 2006; non-profit org.; ICT training programmes and support; Exec. Dir ANDREW MAHAR.

Kingsbury Capital Partners: Av. de Portugal, Praia dos Coqueiros, POB 142, Dili; tel. 3310823; fax 3310824; e-mail info@kingsburycapital.com; internet kingsburycapital.com; invests in Timorese agriculture, commodities, logistics, construction, security, etc.; Man. Dir MARK CRAMER ROBERTS.

PDL Toll: 2nd Floor, Landmark Plaza Offices, Dili; tel. 3322840; fax 3322833; e-mail contact@pdltoll.com; internet www.pdltoll.com; commercial and military logistics provider; Logistics Man., Timor-Leste ASHWINI JAYKUMAR.

SanCar Group: Rua Bellarmino Lobo, Bidau Licidere, Dili; tel. 3310606; fax 3322517; e-mail sancar@sc-et.com; internet www.sc-et.com; f. 2000; procurement and distribution of vehicles and vehicle parts, generators and generator parts, office equipment, prefabricated buildings, machinery, household goods, etc.

Timor Village Hotels (TVH): Rua Wailaku Rini Loi Hunu, Ossu; tel. 3310616; e-mail villagehotelstl@gmail.com; internet www.tvh.tl; f. 2006; hotel and tourism investor.

Wideform Timor-Leste: Cnr Rua D. Fernando Ave, Governador Alves Aldeia, POB 410, Dili; tel. 3313741; fax 3313001; e-mail dili@wideform.tl; internet www.wideform.com.au; f. 2006; public works, retail, residential, industrial devt and construction; Man. Dir ESTELA FERREIRA.

TRADE UNIONS

Konfederasaun Sindikatu Timor-Leste (KSTL) (Timor Leste Trade Union Confederation): Av. Presidente Nicolao Lobato, Colmera, Dili; tel. 7239824; e-mail kstl.union@gmail.com; f. 2001; represents seven unions, comprising c. 4,700 workers within the press, teaching, nursing, construction, agricultural, maritime and transport sectors; Pres. JOSÉ DA CONCEIÇÃO DA COSTA.

Labour Advocacy Institute of East Timor (LAIFET): Rua Abílio Monteiro Palapaso, Dili; tel. 3317243; Dir DOMINGOS BAPTISTA DE ARAÚJO.

Serikat Buruh Socialis Timor (SBST) (Timor Socialist Workers' Union): Dili; controlled by Partido Socialista de Timor; Dir Dr LUCIANO DA SILVA.

Transport

ROADS

In December 1999 the World Bank reported that some 57% of the country's 1,414 km of paved roads were in poor or damaged condition. Some repair and maintenance work on the road network was carried out in 2005, using funding supplied by external donors. In 2009 the Asian Development Bank (ADB) approved the Road Network Development Sector Project for Timor-Leste: plans included the rehabilitation of 230 km of national roads and the development of a programme of road maintenance.

SHIPPING

Timor-Leste's maritime infrastructure includes ports at Dili, Carabela and Com, smaller wharves at Oecusse (Oekussi) and Liquiça (Likisia), and slip-landing structures in Oecusse, Batugade and Suai. In November 2001, following its reconstruction, the management of the port at Dili was transferred to the Government.

Port Authority of Timor-Leste (APORTIL): Av. de Portugal, Dili; tel. 3317264; f. 2003.

Principal Shipping Companies

Everise Freight Forwarding Inc: 2 Rua Belarmino Lobo, Dili; tel. 3324844; fax 3312856; e-mail everisedili@yahoo.com.

SDV Logistics (East Timor): Av. Presidente Nicolau Lobato, Bairro dos Grilos, POB 398, Dili; tel. 3322818; fax 3324077; e-mail dili@sdv.com; internet www.sdv.com; f. 1999; freight forwarder, shipping agent and customs broker; Man. Dir JÉRÔME PETIT.

CIVIL AVIATION

Timor-Leste has two international airports and eight grass runways. In June 2001 Dili Express Pte was the first Timor-based company to begin international flights, with a service to Singapore. In 2005 Timor-Leste's first national carrier, Kakoak Air, commenced operations. Air North operates regular flights from Australia (Darwin) to Dili.

Civil Aviation Authority (CAA): Dili; tel. 3317110; fax 3317111; e-mail henriques_sabino@yahoo.com; govt authority responsible for overall planning, implementation and operation of aviation services in Timor-Leste; Dir JULIÃO X. CARLOS.

Air Timor: Aeroporto Presidente Nicolau Lobato, POB 888, Dili; tel. 3312777; fax 3312888; e-mail diliadmin@air-timor.com; internet www.air-timor.com; f. 2008; est. as Austasia Airlines; name changed as above in 2010; operates services between Dili and Singapore in collaboration with SilkAir.

Tourism

In 2009, according to Turismo de Timor-Leste, about 30,000 people visited the country on a tourist visa. However, the tourism sector remains relatively undeveloped. The country's first national park, Nino Konis Santana National Park, was established in 2007 and aims to protect a number of endangered species, including 25 endemic birds. The park encompasses more than 123,600 ha, including a marine area of 55,600 ha, which contains a globally important biodiversity of coral and reef fish.

Turismo de Timor-Leste: Apdo 194, Dili; tel. 3310371; fax 3339179; e-mail info@turismotimorleste.com; internet www.turismotimorleste.com; f. 2002; National Dir of Tourism JOSÉ QUINTAS.

Defence

As assessed at November 2010, the East Timor Defence Force (Falintil-ETDF) comprised 1,250 army personnel and a naval element of 82. A total of 404 Australian troops and 80 from New Zealand, as well as various international observers, remained in the country. The mandate of the UN Integrated Mission in Timor-Leste (UNMIT), which superseded the UN Mission of Support in East Timor (UNMISET) in 2006, was extended for a further year in February 2011.

Commander-in-Chief: Brig.-Gen. LERE ANAN TIMUR.

Education

According to UN estimates, the adult literacy rate was 58.6% in 2003. In 2004/05 there were 6,987 pre-primary school students, 177,970 primary school students, 50,014 lower secondary school students and 24,808 upper secondary school students in the country. By 2008/09 the number of students enrolled in primary schools had increased to 213,783 and primary school teachers numbered 7,358. In 2008/09 there were an estimated 16,727 students engaged in tertiary education, principally at the National University of Timor-Leste. The 2008 budget allocated US $45.3m. to education, equivalent to 13.5% of total government expenditure. In 2007 the Government introduced an Education Reform Plan with the aim of providing nine years of free and compulsory education.

Bibliography

See also Indonesia

Aditjondro, George J. *In the Shadow of Mount Ramelau: The Impact of the Occupation of East Timor*. Indonesian Documentation and Information Centre, 1994.

Alatas, Ali. *The Pebble in the Shoe: The Diplomatic Struggle for East Timor*. Jakarta, Aksara Karunia, 2006.

Andersen, Tim. *Aidwatch Background Paper: Main Features of the Timor Sea Agreements*. Aidwatch, Sydney, May 2002.

Asian Development Bank. *Technical Assistance to the Democratic Republic of Timor-Leste for Strengthening Financial Management Capacity*. Manila, 2004.

Trust Fund for East Timor (TFET): Report of the Trustee and Proposed Work Program for May 2005–April 2006. Manila, 2005.

Gender and Nation Building in Timor-Leste. Manila, 2005.

Economic and Social Development Brief. Manila, 2007.

Balint, Ruth. *Troubled Waters: Borders, Boundaries and Possession in the Timor Sea*. St Leonards, NSW, Allen & Unwin, 2006.

Ball, Desmond, and McDonald, Hamish. *Death in Balibo, Lies in Canberra*. St Leonards, NSW, Allen & Unwin, 2000.

Ballard, John R. *Triumph of Self-Determination: Operation Stabilise and United Nations Peacemaking in East Timor*. Westport, CT, Praeger Publishers, 2007.

Binchy, William, et al. (Eds). *Timor-Leste: Challenges for Justice and Human Rights in the Shadow of the Past*. Dublin, Clarus Press, 2009.

Breen, Bob. *Mission Accomplished: East Timor*. St Leonards, NSW, Allen & Unwin, 2001.

Bull, Carolyn. *No Entry Without Strategy: Building the Rule of Law under UN Transitional Administration*. Tokyo, United Nations University Press, 2008.

Cardoso, Luís. *The Crossing: A Story of East Timor*. London, Granta Books, 2000.

Carey, Peter, and Bentley, G. Carter (Eds). *East Timor at the Crossroads: The Forging of a Nation*. Honolulu, HI, University of Hawaii Press, 1995.

Cleary, Paul. *Shakedown: Australia's Grab for Timor Oil*. Crows Nest, NSW, Allen & Unwin, 2007.

Cohen, David. *Indifference and Accountability: The United Nations and the Politics of International Justice in East Timor*. Honolulu, HI, East-West Center, University of Hawaii Press, 2006.

Cotton, James. *East Timor, Australia and Regional Order: Intervention and its Aftermath*. London, RoutledgeCurzon, 2004.

Cristalis, Irena. *Bitter Dawn: East Timor—A People's Story*. London, Zed Press, 2nd edn, 2008.

Da Silva, Estanislau Aleixo. *East Timor Agriculture: Strategic Issues and Policy Directions*. Statement made at the 25th Anniversary Session of the International Fund for Agricultural Development, Rome, 2003.

Downie, Sue, and Kingsbury, Damien (Eds). *The Independence Ballot in East Timor: Report of the Australian Volunteer Observer Group*. Clayton, Vic, Monash Asia Institute, 2001.

Dunn, James. *East Timor: The Balibo Incident in Perspective*. Broadway, NSW, The Australian Centre for Independent Journalism, 1995.

Timor: A People Betrayed. Sydney, ABC Books, 1996.

East Timor: A Rough Passage to Independence. Double Bay, NSW, Longueville Books, 2003.

Durand, Frederic. *East Timor: A Country at the Crossroads of Asia and the Pacific, a Geo-Historical Atlas*. Washington, DC, University of Washington Press, 2006.

Federer, Juan. *The UN in East Timor: Building Timor Leste, a Fragile State*. Darwin, NT, Charles Darwin University Press, 2005.

Fernandes, Clinton. *The Independence of East Timor: Multi-Dimensional Perspectives—Occupation, Resistance, and International Political Activism*. Brighton, Sussex Academic Press, 2011.

Fitzpatrick, Daniel. *Land Claims in East Timor*. Canberra, Asia Pacific Press, 2002.

Fox, James J., and Babo Soares, Dionísio (Eds). *East Timor: Out of the Ashes, the Destruction and Reconstruction of an Emerging State*. Bathurst, NSW, Crawford House, 1999.

Government of Timor-Leste. *Agriculture, Forestry and Fisheries: Priorities and Proposed Sector Investment Program*. Dili, 2005.

Communications: Priorities and Proposed Sector Investment Program. Dili, 2005.

Education and Training: Priorities and Proposed Sector Investment Program. Dili, 2005.

Health Care: Priorities and Proposed Sector Investment Program. Dili, 2005.

Greenlees, Don, and Garran, Robert. *Deliverance: The Inside Story of East Timor's Fight for Freedom*. Crows Nest, NSW, Allen & Unwin, 2002.

Gunn, Geoffrey C. *Wartime Portuguese Timor: The Azores Connection*. Clayton, Vic, Monash University, Centre of Southeast Asian Studies, 1988.

A Critical View of Western Journalism and Scholarship on East Timor. Sydney, Journal of Contemporary Asia Publishers, 1994.

East Timor and the United Nations: The Case for Intervention. Lawrenceville, NJ, Red Sea Press, 1997.

Timor Loro Sae: 500 Years. Macao, Livros do Oriente, 1999.

Gunn, Geoffrey C., and Reyko, Huang (Eds). *New Nation: United Nations Peace Building in East Timor*. Macao, Geoffrey C. Gunn, 2006.

Gusmão, Xanana. *To Resist Is To Win: The Autobiography of Xanana Gusmão*. Richmond, Vic, Aurora Books, 2000.

Hainsworth, Paul, and McCloskey, Stephen (Eds). *The East Timor Question: The Struggle for Independence from Indonesia*. New York, I. B. Tauris, 2000.

Harris, Vandra, and Goldsmith, Andrew (Eds). *Security, Development and Nation-Building in Timor-Leste: A Cross-sectoral Assessment*. Abingdon, Routledge, 2011.

Hill, Hal, and Saldanha, João (Eds). *East Timor and Economic Development*. Singapore, Institute of Southeast Asian Studies, 2001.

East Timor: Development Challenges for the World's Newest Nation. Singapore, Institute of Southeast Asian Studies; and Canberra, Asia Pacific Press, Australian National University, 2001.

Hill, Helen. *Stirrings of Nationalism in East Timor: Fretilin 1974–1978: the Origins, Ideologies and Strategies of a Nationalist Movement*. Otford, NSW, Otford Press, 2002.

Hoadley, J. Stephen. *The Future of Portuguese Timor: Dilemmas and Opportunities*. Singapore, Institute of Southeast Asian Studies, 1975.

Hughes, Caroline. *Dependent Communities: Aid and Politics in Cambodia and East Timor*. Ithaca, NY, Cornell University Press, 2009.

Inbaraj, Sonny. *East Timor: Blood and Tears in Asean*. Chiang Mai, Silkworm Books, 1995.

International Commission of Jurists. *Tragedy in East Timor: Report on the Trials in Dili and Jakarta*. Geneva, 1992.

Report of the Trial of Xanana Gusmão in Dili, East Timor. Geneva, 1993.

International Monetary Fund. *Staff Statement*. Donors' Meeting on East Timor, Dili, 14–15 May 2002.

IMF Executive Board Concludes 2005 Article IV Consultations with the Democratic Republic of Timor-Leste. Public Information Notice No. 05/92, Washington, DC, 2005.

Jardine, Matthew. *East Timor: Genocide in Paradise*. Tucson, AZ, Odonian Press, 1995.

Joint Assessment Mission. *East Timor—Building a Nation: A Framework for Reconstruction and Development*. November 1999.

Agriculture Background Paper.

Health and Education Background Paper.

Macro-Economics Background Paper.

Jolliffe, Jill. *East Timor: Nationalism and Colonialism*. St Lucia, Qld, University of Queensland Press, 1978.

Cover-up: the Inside Story of the Balibo Five. Carlton North, Vic, Scribe, 2001.

Jonsson, Gabriel (Ed.). *East Timor: Nation-building in the 21st Century*. Stockholm, Center for Pacific Asia Studies, Stockholm University, 2003.

Kiernan, Ben. *Genocide and Resistance in Southeast Asia: Documentation, Denial, and Justice in Cambodia and East Timor*. Piscataway, NJ, Transaction Publishers, 2007.

Kim, Insu, and Schwarz, Stephen. *Birth of a Nation: East Timor Gains Independence, Faces Challenges of Economic Management, Poverty Alleviation*. IMF Survey, Volume 31, No. 11, 10 June 2002.

Kingsbury, Damien. *East Timor: The Price of Liberty*. Melbourne, Vic, Palgrave Macmillan, 2009.

Kingsbury, Damien (Ed.). *Guns and Ballot Boxes: East Timor's Vote for Independence*. Melbourne, Vic, Monash Asia Institute, 2000.

Kingsbury, Damien, and Leach, Michael (Eds). *East Timor—Beyond Independence*. Clayton, Vic, Monash Asia Institute Press, 2007.

Kohen, Arnold S. *From the Place of the Dead: The Epic Struggles of Bishop Belo of East Timor*. New York, St Martin's Press, 1999.

Kohen, Arnold, and Taylor, John. *An Act of Genocide: Indonesia's Invasion of East Timor*. London, Tapol, 1979.

Krieger, Heike (Ed.). *East Timor and the International Community: Basic Documents*. Cambridge, Cambridge University Press, 1997.

Leach, Michael. *Nation-building and National Identity in Timor-Leste*. Abingdon, Routledge, 2010.

Leadbetter, Maire. *Negligent Neighbour: New Zealand's Complicity in the Invasion and Occupation of Timor-Leste*. Nelson, C. Potton, 2006.

Lennox, Rowena. *Fighting Spirit of East Timor: The Life of Martinho da Costa Lopes*. Sydney, Pluto Press, 2000.

Marker, Jamsheed. *East Timor: A Memoir for the Negotiations for Independence*. Jefferson, NC, McFarland and Co, 2003.

Martin, Ian. *Self-determination in East Timor: The United Nations, the Ballot, and International Intervention*. Boulder, CO, Lynne Rienner Publishers, 2001.

Martinkus, John. *A Dirty Little War*. Milsons Point, NSW, Random House, 2001.

McDonald, Hamish, et al. *Masters of Terror: Indonesia's Military and Violence in East Timor in 1999*. Canberra, Australian National University, Strategic and Defence Studies Centre, 2002.

Metzner, Joachim K. *Man and Environment in Eastern Timor: A Geoecological Analysis of the Baucau-Viqueque Area as a Possible Basis for Regional Planning*. Canberra, Development Studies Centre, Australian National University, 1997.

Molnar, Andrea Katalin. *Timor Leste: Politics, History, and Culture*. Abingdon, Routledge, 2009.

Mubyarto, et al. *East Timor: The Impact of Integration: An Indonesian Socio-anthropological Study*. Northcote, Vic, Indonesia Resources and Information Program (IRIP), 1991.

Nevins, Joseph. *A Not-So-Distant Horror: Mass Violence in East Timor*. Ithaca, NY, Cornell University Press, 2005.

Nicol, Bill. *Timor: The Stillborn Nation*. Melbourne, Vic, Widescope International, 1978.

Timor: A Nation Reborn. London, Equinox Publishing, 2006.

Nixon, Rod. *Justice and Governance in East Timor: Indigenous Approaches and the 'New Subsistence State'*. Abingdon, Routledge, 2011.

Orentlicher, Diane. *Human Rights in Indonesia and East Timor*. New York, Human Rights Watch, 1988.

Ormeling, Ferdinand Jan. *The Timor Problem: A Geographical Interpretation of an Underdeveloped Island*. Groningen, Wolters, 1955.

Pinto, Constâncio, and Jardine, Matthew. *East Timor's Unfinished Struggle: Inside the Timorese Resistance*. Boston, MA, South End Press, 1997.

Rae, James DeShaw. *Peacebuilding and Transitional Justice in East Timor*. Boulder, CO, Lynne Rienner Publishers, 2009.

Ramos Horta, Arsénio. *The Eyewitness: Bitter Moments in East Timor Jungles*. Singapore, Usaha Quality Printers.

Ramos Horta, José. *Funu: Unfinished Saga of East Timor*. Trenton, NJ, Red Sea Press, 1987.

East Timor and the Region. Singapore, Institute of Southeast Asian Studies, 2001.

Rei, Naldo. *Resistance: A Childhood Fighting for East Timor*. St Lucia, University of Queensland Press, 2008.

Retbøll, Torben (Ed.). *East Timor, Indonesia, and the Western Democracies: A Collection of Documents*. Copenhagen, International Work Group for Indigenous Affairs (IWGIA), 1980.

Robinson, Geoffrey. *If You Leave Us Here, We Will Die: How Genocide Was Stopped in East Timor*. Princeton, NJ, Princeton University Press, 2009.

Roff, Sue Rabbitt. *Timor's Anschluss: Indonesian and Australian Policy in East Timor, 1974–76*. Leviston, NY, Edwin Mellen Press, 1992.

East Timor: A Bibliography, 1970–1993. Canberra, Peace Research Centre, 1994.

Rohland, Klaus. *Opening Remarks*. Donors' Meeting on East Timor, Dili, 14–15 May 2002.

Rothwell, Donald R., and Tsamenyi, Martin (Eds). *The Maritime Dimensions of Independent East Timor*. Wollongong, NSW, Centre for Maritime Policy, University of Wollongong, 2000.

Rowland, Ian. *Timor: including the Islands of Roti and Ndao*. Oxford and Santa Barbara, CA, Clio Press, 1992.

Schlicher, Monika. *Portugal in Ost-Timor: Eine Kritische Untersuchung zur Portugiesischen Kolonialgeschichte in Ost-Timor*. Hamburg, Abera, 1996.

Schulte Nordholt, Henk G. *The Political System of the Atoni of Timor*. The Hague, M. Nijhoff, 1971.

Sherlock, Kevin P. *A Bibliography of Timor: Including East (formerly Portuguese) Timor, West (formerly Dutch) Timor, and the Island of Roti*. Canberra, Australian National University, 1980.

East Timor: Liurais and Chefes de Suco; Indigenous Authorities in 1952. Darwin, NT, 1983.

Sherman, Tom. *Second Report on the Deaths of Australian-based Journalists in East Timor in 1975*. Canberra, Department of Foreign Affairs and Trade, 1999.

Singh, Bilveer. *East Timor, Indonesia, and the World: Myths and Realities*. Kuala Lumpur, ADPR Consult (M), 1996.

Smith, Michael G., and Dee, Moreen. *Peacekeeping in East Timor: The Path to Independence*. Boulder, CO, Lynne Rienner Publishers, 2003.

Smythe, Patrick A. *The Catholic Church and the East Timor Issue*. London, Lit Verlag, 2005.

Sousa Saldanha, João Mariano de. *The Political Economy of East Timor Development*. Jakarta, Pustaka Sinar Harapan, 1994.

Sousa Saldanha, João Mariano de (Ed.). *An Anthology: Essays on the Political Economy of East Timor*. Casuarina, NT, Centre for Southeast Asian Studies, Northern Territory University, 1995.

Stanley, Elizabeth. *Torture, Truth and Justice: The Case of Timor-Leste*. Abingdon, Routledge, 2008.

Stepan, Sasha. *Credibility Gap: Australia and the Timor Gap Treaty*. Canberra, Australian Council for Overseas Aid, 1990.

Subroto, Hendro. *Eyewitness to Integration of East Timor*. Jakarta, Pustaka Sinar Harapan, 1997.

Sugget, Neil. *See the Road Well: Shaping East Timor's Frontier*. Canberra, Research School of Pacific and Asian Studies, Australian National University, 2004.

Suter, Keith. *East Timor and West Irian*. London, Minority Rights Group, 1982.

Sword, Kirsty, and Walsh, Pat (Eds). *'Opening up': Travellers' Impressions of East Timor 1989–1991*. Fitzroy, Vic, Australia East Timor Association, 1991.

Tanter, Richard, Selden, Mark, and Shalom, Stephen R. (Eds). *Bitter Flowers, Sweet Flowers: East Timor, Indonesia, and the World Community*. Lanham, MD, Rowman & Littlefield Publishers, 2001.

Taylor, John G. *East Timor: The Price of Freedom*. New York, Zed Books, 1999.

Tiffen, Rodney. *Diplomatic Deceits: Government, Media and East Timor*. Sydney, University of New South Wales Press, 2001.

Turner, Michele. *Telling East Timor: Personal Testimonies 1942–1992*. Kensington, NSW, New South Wales University Press, 1992.

United Nations. *The United Nations and East Timor: Self-determination through Popular Consultation*. New York, NY, United Nations Department of Public Information, 2004.

Valdivieso, Luís M., et al. *East Timor: Establishing the Foundations of Sound Macroeconomic Management*. Washington, DC, IMF, August 2000.

Way, Wendy (Ed.). *Australia and the Indonesian Incorporation of Portuguese Timor. 1974–1976*. Carlton, Vic, Melbourne University Press, 2000.

Wiarda, Siqueira. *The Portuguese in Southeast Asia: Malacca, Moluccas, East Timor*. Hamburg, Abera Verlag, 1997.

Wise, Amanda. *Exile and Return Among the East Timorese*. Philadelphia, PA, University of Pennsylvania Press, 2006.

World Bank. *Background Paper for Donors' Meeting on East Timor*. Donors' Meeting on East Timor, Dili, 14–15 May 2002.

Background Paper for the Timor-Leste and Development Partners Meeting, 25–26 April 2005. Washington, DC, 2005.

Simplified Implementation Completion Report: Timor-Leste, Second Transition Support Program. Washington, DC, 2005.

VIET NAM

Physical and Social Geography

HARVEY DEMAINE

The Socialist Republic of Viet Nam covers a total area of 331,051.4 sq km (127,819.7 sq miles) and lies along the western shore of the South China Sea, bordered by the People's Republic of China to the north, by Laos to the west and by Cambodia to the south-west. The capital is Hanoi.

PHYSICAL FEATURES AND CLIMATE

The fundamental geographical outlines of the country are determined by the deltas and immediate hinterlands of the Mekong and Songkoi (Red River), which are linked by the mountain backbone and adjacent coastal lowlands of Annam.

Of the two rivers which are thus of major significance in the geography of Viet Nam, the Songkoi, rising, like the Mekong, in south-western China, is much the shorter, and its delta, together with that of a series of lesser rivers, forms a total area of some 14,500 sq km, which is less than one-half that of the great Mekong delta in the south. The north of Viet Nam also includes a much more extensive area of rugged upland, mainly in the north and west, which represents a southward continuation of the Yunnan and adjacent plateaux of south-western China, and forms an inhospitable and sparsely populated divide, some 900–1,500 m above sea-level, between North Viet Nam and northern Laos.

Both the Songkoi and its main right-bank tributary, the Songbo (Black River), flow in parallel north-west/south-east gorges through this upland before their confluence some 100 km above the apex of the delta, while a third main river, the Songma, also follows a parallel course still further to the south, beyond which rises the similarly north-west/south-east inclining Annamite chain or Cordillera. This, in relief if not in structure, constitutes a further prolongation of the massive upland system already described, and extends without a break to within about 150 km of the Mekong delta.

With an average breadth of 150 km, and an extremely rugged and heavily forested surface, at many points exceeding 1,500 m in altitude, the Annamite chain, which lies mainly in southern Viet Nam, provides an effective divide between the Annam coast and the middle Mekong valley of southern Laos and eastern Cambodia. Moreover, from the Porte d'Annam (latitude 18°N) southwards, the chain not only reaches to within a few miles of the coast, but also sends off a series of spurs, which terminate in rocky headlands overlooking the sea. Thus, along the 1,000-km stretch of coast between latitudes 18° and 11°N, the continuity of the coastal plain is repeatedly interrupted and it dwindles to an average width of less than 16 km and often to less than half that figure; but thereafter it broadens out to merge with the vast deltaic plain of the Mekong and its associated natural waterways, the whole forming an almost dead-flat surface covering some 37,800 sq km.

In forming the western hinterland of the South China Sea virtually from the tropic of Cancer to within 9°N of the Equator, Viet Nam might be assumed to be wholly within the zone of the tropical monsoon climate. The greater part of the country does merit such a designation, and the city of Hué, practically at the mid-point of the coastal zone, has a mean monthly temperature range from 20°C in January to 30°C in August, and a total rainfall of 2,600 mm, of which 1,650 mm falls between September and November. However, the Songkoi delta in the north is not strictly tropical in the climatological sense; owing to its exposure to cold northern air during the season of the north-east monsoon, it experiences a recognizable cool season from December to March, and in both January and February the mean monthly temperatures in Hanoi are only 17°C. This fact is of great importance since the cooler weather gives greater effectiveness to the 130 mm–150 mm of rain that fall during these months, and so makes it possible to raise a 'winter' as well as a summer crop of rice in this part of the country.

NATURAL RESOURCES

In terms of agricultural potential, the two river deltas are of major importance. The uplands, until recently, offered far less opportunity for supporting population, not only because of the extremely restricted prospects for rice cultivation but also because of their malarial character. Owing to increasing pressure on land resources in the Tongking delta in particular, great efforts are being made to develop the uplands for cash cropping, although there are suggestions that this may be at the expense of environmental stability. In respect of mineral wealth, on the other hand, the uplands, particularly in the north, contain a wide variety of lesser metallic ores, and also some useful apatite (a source of phosphates). Another important mineral is in the anthracite field of Quang-Yen, immediately to the north-east of the Songkoi delta. Total coal reserves were estimated at 150m. metric tons at the end of 2009. Petroleum is of increasing significance, and Viet Nam has become a major regional exporter. The first deposits were discovered off shore in the north and south of the country. The Bach Ho oilfield, 160 km to the east of Ho Chi Minh City, went into operation in 1986. At the end of 2010 total petroleum reserves were estimated at 4,400m. barrels, and reserves of natural gas totalled an estimated 600,000m. cu m.

POPULATION AND ETHNIC GROUPS

The population of Viet Nam totalled 85,846,997 at the census of 1 April 2009, compared with the 1989 census total of 64,411,713. According to UN estimates, the population stood at 88,791,995 in mid-2011, when the average population density reached 269.2 per sq km. The majority of the population are concentrated within the lowlands. The vast Mekong delta is less densely populated than the Songkoi delta. The higher degree of urbanization has been in southern Viet Nam. In mid-2010 the largest town in Viet Nam was Ho Chi Minh City, in the South, with a population of around 6,167,000, while the largest towns in the North, the capital of Hanoi and its port, Haiphong, had populations of 2,814,000 and 1,970,000, respectively. Following an extension of the boundaries of Hanoi in 2008, which incorporated Ha Tay province and parts of Vinh Phuc and Hoa Binh provinces, the total population of the metropolitan area was estimated at 6.2m. The distribution of population in Viet Nam changed considerably following a vast resettlement programme: 3.5m. people were moved after 1975 and 2.1m. after 1981, mostly to Viet Nam's New Economic Zones or to the Central Highlands.

Vietnamese, who are ethnically related to the southern Chinese, form the majority of the population. There are also significant minority groups, notably the Tai in the North (numbering some 2m.), some 750,000 Hmong and related groups and a number of smaller groups of people in the Central Highlands, usually known as Montagnards and numbering up to 1m. There are perhaps 600,000 Cambodians along Viet Nam's south-western border and a now uncertain number of Chinese, still primarily concentrated in the southern city of Cholon, but much reduced in numbers by migration.

History

JÖRN DOSCH

PRE-COLONIAL HISTORY

The formation of Viet Nam's identity is closely related to the nation's resistance to its huge northern neighbour, China, and to its gradual expansion southwards from the original heartland in the Songkoi (Red River) delta and the north-eastern coastal plain. China ruled Viet Nam for more than 1,000 years, from 112 BC, when the present northern Viet Nam became incorporated into the Chinese Han empire, until AD 939. For the next 900 years Viet Nam's rulers focused on preventing China's attempts to reimpose its power. This led to an increased sense of nationhood and identity *vis-à-vis* China, and proto-nationalism existed in Viet Nam before it emerged in the other countries of South-East Asia. By the time of the Ly dynasty (1010–1225), which was established on the Songkoi delta, the outlines of Vietnamese identity were relatively clear. Unlike other countries in the region (such as Indonesia, Malaysia or the Philippines), Viet Nam was already a clearly defined nation-state before the arrival of the European colonial powers, owing to the existence of an established pre-colonial tradition, a distinct culture and language and the presence of an effective political and economic system.

At the same time Viet Nam remained closely linked with China, both politically and militarily, as a tributary state. The country also absorbed Chinese cultural influences, most prominently Confucianism, upon which Vietnamese family, bureaucratic and social structures and the form of government were modelled. The 15th century was the 'golden age' of Confucian culture in Viet Nam and a period of general stability. In the early 16th century, however, the kingdom began to disintegrate under the pressure of conflict among rival clans, one of which established the Mac dynasty (1527–92). After intermittent civil war in the 16th century, the next 100 years witnessed a more lasting division of Viet Nam between two powerful clans: the Trinh in the north and the Nguyen in central Viet Nam. It was the Nguyen, driven by population pressure, who led the way in a further southward expansion, beginning in about 1658, establishing their control over the greater part of what is now southern Viet Nam.

In the 1770s, however, the Tay Son rebellion cast the entire country into a state of civil war. Although the Tay Son established a new dynasty and defeated a Chinese invasion in 1789, they could not bring greater stability. The last Nguyen survivor recaptured Saigon (now Ho Chi Minh City) and from there went on to conquer the centre and north by 1802. He proclaimed himself Emperor at Hué, with the title Gia Long, and for the first time in its history the present area of Viet Nam was brought under the control of a single ruler. For a brief period Minh Mang (1820–41) extended Vietnamese control to embrace much of Cambodia. However, during the reign of Tu Duc (1847–83), the Vietnamese confronted the challenge of French colonialism.

In 1858–59 a Franco-Spanish fleet attacked Tourane (Da Nang) and then Saigon. Viet Nam's lengthy period of independence ended in 1862, when Emperor Tu Duc, agreeing to French demands, ceded three provinces surrounding Saigon to France (Cochin-China, the southernmost part of Viet Nam). In 1867 the French annexed a further three provinces. A new Franco-Vietnamese treaty, signed in 1874, recognized French possession of all Cochin-China and permitted the French to trade in Tongking (Tonkin). In 1883 the French imposed a treaty of 'protection' on the Vietnamese empire. Two years later, after a border war with China, the French secured Chinese recognition of their protectorate.

FRENCH COLONIAL RULE

By 1885 the whole of Viet Nam was under French colonial rule: Cochin-China, in the south, as a directly administered colony; Tongking and Annam, the north and centre, as protectorates. In 1887 they were united with Cambodia to form the Union Indochinoise, to which Laos was added in 1893. By 1901 the administration of the Union had become an effective central authority with financial control over the whole of Indo-China. Colonialism fundamentally altered the political, social and economic structures of Viet Nam. Although French policy eliminated the emperor and the power of the monarchy, the traditional ruling order was co-opted to serve French colonial rule. By 1900 the authority of Confucian ideology and social institutions, and of the scholar-gentry that had defended the old social order, was rapidly dissipating. In the urban areas French rule was taken for granted and resulted in the emergence of new social classes, including a small industrial working class, which, by the 1920s, was employed in rice mills, the textile industry, mines and plantations. Those Vietnamese who rose under the new bourgeoisie were adjuncts or subordinates of the dominant French capitalists and administrators; the growth of an indigenous bourgeoisie was not possible. In the countryside colonial rule was characterized by the destruction of the traditional equilibrium of village life and by growing hardship for the peasantry owing to a declining portion of land per person, declining rice consumption (as the result of French rice exports of 1m.–2m. metric tons per year) and increasing head taxes. In northern and central Viet Nam (Tongking and Annam) the concept of landownership was unknown before the arrival of the French and access to land was free. Under the colonial administration a new landlord class emerged as village common land was taken over by nobles and rented back to villagers. This process resulted in a new social structure, in which villagers were divided along class lines. In southern Viet Nam (the Mekong delta and Cochin-China generally) new land was auctioned, creating a very different agricultural structure with large landowners—many being absentee landlords, who were educated in France, lived in Saigon and whose interests were closely connected with France—and an overwhelmingly landless peasantry. Peasant rebellions were common.

The fate of the peasants was similar to those throughout South-East Asia under colonialism. The main difference was the arrival of a communist movement that was able to gain the support of the peasantry, as the communists proved to be the most able and adept at championing a new Vietnamese identity. The first major rebellion against colonial rule, known as the Can Vuong (Loyalty to the King) movement, developed in 1885 around the deposed Emperor, Ham Nghi, attracting support from both scholars and peasants. The rebellion was essentially subdued with the capture and exile of Ham Nghi in 1888. Scholar and patriot Phan Dinh Phung continued to lead the resistance until his death in 1895. Although unsuccessful in driving out the French, Can Vuong, with its heroes and patriots, laid an important basis for future Vietnamese independence movements.

Unlike the British colonial regime in India, the French administration refused to tolerate a nation-wide constitutional opposition movement comparable to the Congress Party and, thus, effectively prevented a gradual transition to independence in Indo-China. The colonial regime permitted only limited expression to constitutionalist Vietnamese opposition and harshly suppressed more radical resistance. In these circumstances various communist groups were formed during the 1920s. The Viet Nam Quoc Dan Dang (VNQDD—Viet Nam Nationalist Party) was established in 1927, ideologically based on China's Kuomintang (KMT—Guomindang). However, like similar groups at the time, the VNQDD did not succeed because of its exclusively urban outlook and inability to develop mass mobilization. Furthermore, the party's strategy of gaining independence by coup and assassination did not have the desired impact. An attempt to assassinate the governor-general in 1929 and an attempted military uprising within the French colonial army in 1930 both failed. The Communist Party of Indo-China (CPIC), founded in 1930, initially proved to be more influential when it organized a peasant movement of serious proportions. The movement, generally known as the 'Nghe Tinh Soviets', emerged in mid-1930 in parts of Cochin-China and in Nghe An, Ha Tinh and Annam. It continued until 1931, when it was suppressed with the use of French air power.

Ultimately, the presentation of Marxism-Leninism as an appealing and effective means of recovering Vietnamese independence and the main pillar of nationalism was successful for five reasons. First, the socio-economic and socio-political mobility of the Vietnamese, regarded as only a second or third class in society, was very limited. French and Chinese entrepreneurs and landowners controlled the economy, while French resistance to national independence hindered the development of any political influence by the Vietnamese. Second, the attraction of Marxism in the 1920s was that it provided a scientific explanation of history and a rationalization of superiority and subordination. It denounced inequality and developed a vision of the inevitable victory of the weak. Third, Leninism demonstrated the ability of a vanguard party to accelerate history, enabling the dramatic reordering of society following class analysis based on domestic class forces and international factors. Fourth, Mao Zedong and the people's war in China showed that it was possible to fight a more powerful enemy. Fifth, Communism offered parallels with Confucianism. Similarities between Marxism and Confucianism include the belief in truth and quasi-sacred texts, well-trained élites that indoctrinate the masses, personal ethics and the subordination of the individual to the community.

THE SECOND WORLD WAR AND JAPANESE OCCUPATION

The Second World War would transform the Communist Party's prospects. The capitulation of France to Nazi Germany in June 1940 caught Indo-China by surprise and ended the concept of French military prowess and invincibility. The declining power of France was emphasized by an agreement with Japan in 1940, which allowed Japanese troops to be based in Viet Nam in exchange for recognition of French sovereignty over Indo-China. The war brought increasing economic hardships: taxes and war requisitions became punitive and, by 1943, seizure of rice was causing serious unrest in the countryside, as well as widespread famine in the winter of 1944/45. Politically, the failure of the Japanese forces to impose direct imperial rule over Viet Nam—as Japan did in Burma (now Myanmar) and Indonesia—had two important consequences. A nationalist movement under Japanese tutelage did not come about, as in Burma under Aung San and Indonesia (Netherlands East Indies) under Sukarno; therefore, the Vietnamese communist groups did not have to contend with powerful non-communist nationalist movements. Furthermore, the preservation of French rule by Japan, which amounted to no more than a client role, eroded the legitimacy of French sovereignty. In March 1945 the Japanese forces staged a coup against the French, abolishing the colonial administration. On 11 March Japan declared Viet Nam's independence under its auspices, but chose a leader who was not a prominent nationalist like Aung San or Sukarno, but the Emperor Bao Dai. In the absence of any real contenders for political power, the communist united front organization, the Viet Minh, under the leadership of Ho Chi Minh, who as Nguyen Ai Quoc had played a significant part in founding the CPIC, quickly filled the vacuum left by the surrender of Japan in August 1945. According to the cultural beliefs of many Vietnamese, France had failed to protect Viet Nam from Japan and, consequently, had lost its 'heavenly mandate' to rule.

INDEPENDENCE AND THE FIRST INDO-CHINA WAR

On 2 September 1945 Ho Chi Minh declared an independent Democratic Republic of Viet Nam. The declaration of independence precipitated 30 years of war, with first French and then US involvement. The war started almost immediately, but began in earnest towards the end of 1946, when French forces attacked the Viet Minh in Haiphong in November, provoking a CPIC-led war of resistance against the colonial power. France set about what was essentially a war of reconquest in Indo-China. This decision was embodied by the choice of Gen. Jacques-Philippe Leclerc, liberator of Paris, to head the expeditionary forces to Indo-China. France sought to legitimize military action by presenting it as a war of liberation, with the objective of freeing the Indo-Chinese populations from Japan, from the potentially acquisitive intentions of the British Army, which was overseeing the capitulation of the Japanese troops, or from the influence of China and the USSR. In 1948 the armed confrontation turned into civil war when Bao Dai was chosen again to head a nominally independent Government (based in the old Cochin-China), seen by the majority as a French creation. Ho and the Viet Minh portrayed themselves as the only true representatives of the spirit of resistance against foreign rule. In 1950 the war assumed an international dimension, when France succeeded in portraying the struggle as a fight against communism, in the aftermath of Mao's victory in China and the establishment of the People's Republic, and also the outbreak of war on the Korean peninsula. The US Administration accepted this premise and US military aid began in May 1950, funding 80% of the war in Indo-China by 1953. The USA was increasingly drawn into the conflict, sending advisers and effectively paying for the French war effort.

In the 1940s the CPIC developed a multi-dimensional strategy that held through the French and US wars. The class struggle was subordinated to the nationalist struggle. In the anticipated two phases of revolutionary struggle, the democratic nationalist revolution received priority and, once achieved, would be followed by the socialist revolution. A national united front was established, allied with the traditional class enemies (e.g. patriotic landlords) and with non-communist organizations and groups, such as the Viet Nam Socialist Party, the Democratic Party, Buddhists, hill tribes and students. The Viet Minh established a network of alliances and organizations, which covertly controlled trade unions and other groups that were not overtly political. In 1945 the Viet Minh devised a broad and attractive public programme comprising the establishment of a popular assembly to draft a democratic constitution, the abolition of French taxes, the industrialization and modernization of the agricultural sector, broad social legislation (the five-day week, minimum wages, etc.) and autonomy for ethnic minorities. In military terms, the strategy was influenced by Mao's concept of 'people's war' and dependence on the peasantry and was adapted to the peasant base. The army was divided into three groups: guerrillas (part-time guerrillas but full-time peasants, for those fighting within one or two days' distance of their villages); regional forces (those who agreed to leave their fields for between one and three months per year, were better trained and were involved in major operations); and regular troops (a uniformed, full-time military).

PARTITION OF VIET NAM AND THE US WAR IN INDO-CHINA

The death of Soviet leader Stalin and the signing of a truce in the Korean War in 1953 changed the international climate, leading to a stronger emphasis on diplomacy. On 7 May 1954 the Viet Minh inflicted a humiliating military defeat on the French at Dien Bien Phu, in an inaccessible valley near the border with Laos. At an international conference convened in Geneva, Switzerland, to settle the future of Indo-China, a cease-fire agreement was signed by representatives of the French and Viet Minh high commands on 21 July; an international declaration by 14 governments set forth conditions for an eventual political settlement, emphasizing that, politically, Viet Nam remained one country. Viet Nam's independence was recognized for the first time by the West. In effect, however, two zones were created, administered by the two existing Vietnamese Governments: that of the Democratic Republic in Hanoi and that of the State of Viet Nam in Saigon, with latitude 17°N as the boundary between them, even though the Viet Minh was estimated to control 75% of the country. A period of 300 days was allowed for regrouping, during which time almost 130,000 people moved north, while as many as 900,000 people (mainly Roman Catholics) moved to the South. The Geneva agreements urged the eventual national elections, due by July 1956, to assure the unification of the country. The Democratic Republic of Viet Nam in the North was led by Ho Chi Minh, while the pro-US regime of Ngo Dinh Diem, a deeply anti-French and anti-communist Roman Catholic, ruled in Saigon (1954–63), the capital of the South. Diem repudiated the Geneva declaration and rejected plans to hold elections. In the years that followed he attempted to destroy the Viet Minh (or, as he termed it, Viet Cong) network in the South, curbing hopes of a peaceful reunification. Ho Chi Minh, who regarded nationalism and communism as inseparable, had consented to the Geneva agreements at least partly because he believed that national elections would ensure reunification under communist Viet Minh leadership. Ho's goal of a united Viet Nam was undermined when it became clear that Diem had no intention of merging with the North. In 1959 the Viet Minh decided to pursue a more active political and limited military strategy in the South; in the following year the National Front for the Liberation of South Viet Nam (NLF)—a classic communist united front organization—was formed to unite opposition to, and increase the pressure on, Diem.

In the early 1960s the North Vietnamese provided increasing military support to the NLF. The People's Revolutionary Party—South Viet Nam's communist party, which was controlled by the North—gradually came to dominate the NLF until, ultimately, the two organizations were indistinguishable. To counteract the insurgency, Diem relied on US advisers, weaponry, money and soldiers. US support began in 1954 with 1,000 advisers and military personnel. Despite this support, Diem's own position deteriorated, until US President John F. Kennedy acquiesced in a *coup d'état* against Diem by South Vietnamese generals. The coup, which took place in October 1963, and Diem's concurrent death opened the way for a dozen ineffective and unstable military governments, which were less interested in economic and social reforms than in military victory over the Viet Minh and the North Vietnamese. After Diem's assassination, the conflict increasingly turned into a US war. In August 1964 an alleged attack against US ships by North Vietnamese torpedo boats (the so-called Tongking incident) led to a US Senate resolution (Tongking Resolution) that supported US retaliation and provided the President with full powers to respond. The Senate never actually declared war in Viet Nam, but the Tongking Resolution stated that the President was authorized to 'take all necessary measures to repel any armed attack against the forces of the United States'. President Lyndon B. Johnson interpreted this wording as authorization for full-scale military involvement in Viet Nam. Many years later various reports made clear that the alleged torpedo boat attack had not in fact occurred.

The number of US forces in Viet Nam increased from 23,000 at the beginning of 1965 to more than 500,000 by March 1968; in addition, contingents were sent from the Republic of Korea (South Korea), Australia, the Philippines and Thailand. As a result, the conflict escalated into a war of major proportions, with the communists obliged to send regular North Vietnamese troops to the South and to rely increasingly on aid from the People's Republic of China and the USSR. The USA commenced aerial bombardment of the North in March 1965.

In January 1968 the war reached a critical turning point, when forces of the NLF launched the Tet (Lunar New Year) offensive, a series of surprise attacks throughout South Viet Nam on US positions. During the US response to the offensive, more than 500 civilians died in the massacre at My Lai (in Quang Ngai Province). Thus, although the offensive was a failure militarily, politically it proved to be a remarkable success for the North, because of its visual impact on television within the USA, where the Viet Nam War had become increasingly unpopular. The domestic impact of the Tet offensive led to the announcement by President Johnson at the end of March that he would not seek re-election in November and that the bombing of North Viet Nam would be restricted, in order to start negotiations to end the war with the Vietnamese communists. In 1969 Ho Chi Minh died, and President Richard Nixon began to reduce US ground troops in Viet Nam, as domestic public opposition to the war continued to grow (intensified by revelations such as those about the My Lai massacre, which were published in November). In 1970 Nixon's National Security Advisor, Dr Henry Kissinger, and Le Duc Tho, for the Hanoi Government, started negotiations in Paris, France. In 1971 the Tongking Resolution was repealed, but another two years passed before the USA disengaged from Viet Nam. After the signing of a cease-fire agreement in Paris in January 1973, the US troops' withdrawal was completed by March. However, the remaining terms of the agreement, including provisions for political freedom in the South and the creation of a National Council of Reconciliation and Concord, were virtually ignored during the next two years. Furthermore, the Paris Agreement did not prescribe a withdrawal of the North Vietnamese forces from the South. Nor was there any provision for action by the USA to enforce the agreement, or to end the fighting in neighbouring Cambodia, and in July 1973 the US Congress made any further US military action in Indo-China illegal. An international commission established to supervise the cease-fire was not able to prevent frequent outbreaks of fighting between the two sides, while the North Vietnamese were now free to undertake a final offensive. Following the fall of the entire province of Phuoc Long in January 1975, the pace was accelerated. By the end of March the communists controlled Hué and Da Nang and were advancing southwards along the coast. In April they threatened Saigon. On 30 April the last members of the US embassy and other personnel were evacuated and the communists entered Saigon, which they renamed Ho Chi Minh City. Viet Nam's 30-year war of independence was over. The victorious North rapidly undertook the formal reunification of the country and the Socialist Republic of Viet Nam came into existence on 2 July 1976.

Since 1961 the USA had suffered 45,941 combat deaths and more than 10,000 deaths from other causes in Viet Nam, as well as 150,000 wounded. In the same period, it was estimated, nearly 2m. Vietnamese on both sides had been killed in the war. In retrospect, the question of the reasons for the USA's involvement in Viet Nam is relatively easy to answer (with many details still being debated in the 21st century). President Johnson himself provided the crucial response, when he declared in 1961, 'Viet Nam and Thailand are the immediate and most important spots critical to the US. The basic decision in South-East Asia is here. We must decide whether to help these countries or throw in the towel in the area and pull our defenses back to San Francisco.' Viet Nam was seen solely within the general context of the Cold War (the protracted period of mutual hostility between the USA and the USSR) and more specifically within the US strategy of containment. President Dwight Eisenhower, who came to office in 1953, popularized the image of the 'falling dominos', which, it was feared, would be the fate of South Viet Nam. The cause of the collapsing dominos, according to this view, was transnational communism, which, it was held, had a propensity to expand across state frontiers, consuming all before it. Viet Nam was central to this so-called domino theory. Both Kennedy and Johnson subscribed to this hypothesis, which materialized as a self-fulfilling prophecy. Hence, confronted with the difficult choice of either accepting the impending collapse of South Viet Nam or averting the takeover of the South through direct military intervention, the US Government decided on the latter course of action.

POST-REUNIFICATION

The victory of communist forces in Viet Nam in April 1975 was ranked as one of the most politically significant events of the post-Second World War era in Asia. The speed with which the North finally seized the South, and the almost simultaneous communist victories in Laos and Cambodia, were striking achievements. The achievement was even more phenomenal for having been accomplished despite determined US opposition and for having called into question the very policy of containing communism.

The period from the fall of Saigon in April 1975 to mid-1976 was one of transition. In May 1975 revolutionary committees were created at all levels in the South. The South was recognized as having its own distinct problems, arising from the fact that its 'national democratic' revolution had yet to be completed, whereas the North was already in the stage of 'socialist' revolution. A first priority in the South was to bring the economy under control. Although it was still permissible for small capitalist enterprises to continue operating, the State took measures to control, if not to own, capitalist enterprises left behind by foreign investors. Foreign banks and enterprises were no longer allowed to operate. Former members of the South Vietnamese army and civil service were obliged to undergo 're-education' courses, sometimes in camps where study was combined with labour. More than 300,000 Saigonese officials were sentenced to long-term re-education. In November 1975 a reunification conference was held in Ho Chi Minh City, presided over by Truong Chinh (representing the North) and Pham Hung (representing the South), which formally decided that reunification should take place through elections to be held throughout the country during 1976. Accordingly, a single National Assembly was elected in April and, when it met on 2 July, it declared the inauguration of the Socialist Republic of Viet Nam, with its capital in Hanoi. The Assembly also established a committee to draft a new Constitution. The new Government included some members of the former Provisional Revolutionary Government of South Viet Nam, but it was dominated for the most part by the leaders of the former Democratic Republic and, in effect, of the Political Bureau (Politburo) of the Viet Nam Workers' Party (as the CPIC had been renamed in 1951), which was restyled the Communist Party of Viet Nam (CPV—Dang Cong San Viet Nam) at the Fourth Party Congress in December 1976.

The CPV became the dominant political force in the country. The party's internal structure was similar to that of the Communist Party of the Soviet Union or the Chinese Communist Party. Other important political forces—the Government, the army and the bureaucracy—remained subordinate to it. Like the communist parties in China and Cuba, the CPV had indigenous origins. It was not imposed upon the country by the Red Army, but gained power through a war of national liberation. However, unlike the personality-based regimes of the Democratic People's Republic of Korea (North Korea) and Cuba, for example, the CPV was committed to a system of collective leadership. For almost three decades (from independence in the North in 1954 to the Sixth Party Congress in 1986), the senior leadership of the party remained virtually unchanged: a stability and continuity that distinguished Viet Nam from most other former and surviving communist states, including the USSR and China. According to one estimate, no more than 30 people served on the Politburo between the party's first congress in 1935 and its seventh in 1991. The reasons for this cohesiveness were the circumstances of fighting a revolutionary war of national liberation and the conscious attempt to pursue a collective style of leadership rather than encourage personality cults. From late 1976 the main institutional structures of political power and governance remained intact, government policy being set by the Politburo, the executive of the party. The Politburo continued to be elected by the CPV's Central Committee, which was in turn elected by Party Congresses held, more or less, at five-yearly intervals. The Central Committee party secretariat issued directives to party members and directed government policy on a day-to-day basis, with considerable overlap between party and government. Sectional interests in Vietnamese society were channelled through mass organizations, grouped under the Viet Nam Fatherland Front, which remained subordinate to the party.

Given the tremendous history of military success against powerful external enemies (first France, then the USA), the leadership of the CPV genuinely believed that it could rapidly transform the country to socialism. Originally, reunification was to be gradual, but this concept was abandoned in favour of rapid unification of the two economies. The second mistake was an attempt in 1977 to collectivize the southern economy and act against private trade. The plan rapidly to transform the southern economy was over-ambitious by any standards. The CPV also confronted the challenge of rebuilding the country after 30 years of war. The party had to cope with the doubling of territory and of population. Organizationally, cadres in the South had been almost eliminated. There was also an urgency in providing food, order and employment for the war-weary population.

The hubris of the party leadership precluded any admission that the CPV in its new context was ill-equipped for the task of managing the economy, or that the commitment to the command economy was inappropriate for a small-scale underdeveloped economy ravaged by 30 years of war. Victory had a confirmatory and sanctifying effect on party leadership, preserving and reinforcing the all-encompassing efficacy of the CPV. Later, after the economic decline, the party leadership recognized the extent of its hastiness. As one party official admitted in 1982, 'in the excitement of victory, the scope of which came rather unexpectedly, we rather lost sight of realities. Everything seemed possible and close at hand'.

In the North, once war was over, discipline was relaxed and there was a general sense of anti-climax. People were exhausted and had no motivation left for carrying out the tasks of socialism. In the South, passive resistance to the communists could be observed from the first day, especially from the peasantry. There were two main reasons for peasant resistance to collectivization in the South. First, the USA had belatedly discovered that the support of the peasantry was essential to winning the war. In 1973 a Land to the Tiller Programme was introduced, which eliminated absentee landlords and distributed small plots to peasants. Second, the Saigon Government, which was heavily supported by the USA, had not needed to collect taxes in the countryside and, therefore, many resented the CPV when it started to impose taxes. The economic reality manifested itself in poor harvests, leading to famine in some areas, and the exodus of refugees. The number of refugees reached nearly 1m. in the initial years; many were Chinese, who were the mainstay of the southern economy and usually the highly skilled professionals.

Any political attempts at a peaceful reconstruction of war-ravaged Viet Nam were hindered by Viet Nam's invasion of Cambodia (known as Kampuchea between 1976 and 1989) in December 1978 and January 1979. According to the Vietnamese Government, the intervention was aimed at stopping the genocide in Cambodia and ousting the murderous Khmer Rouge regime under Pol Pot's leadership: both objectives were achieved. However, the West considered the Vietnamese action as an act of international aggression and an attempt to establish Vietnamese hegemony over Indo-China. As a result, both Western states and China severed aid and development assistance to Viet Nam. For Viet Nam's neighbours in South-East Asia, the country became a threat to their security and to regional stability. Viet Nam's prestige was severely damaged and diplomatic isolation threatened. In February 1979 Viet Nam suffered a large-scale Chinese invasion, which further drained its manpower and scarce material resources. The war ended shortly afterwards, but cordial and peaceful relations between the two countries had been lost. Under such circumstances, Viet Nam adopted a 'one-sided tilt' foreign policy (*nhat bien dao*). Viet Nam now completely inclined towards the USSR and the Council for Mutual Economic Assistance (CMEA, or Comecon) for aid and markets. It soon became clear that the aspirations of national liberation and unity would not be realized, partly owing to Viet Nam's international situation. In view of economic collapse and international isolation, the CPV publicly admitted its mistakes at the Fifth Party Congress in 1982.

THE REFORM ERA, 1986–

The first stage of reform began in August 1979, when measures to provide material incentives to producers, while encouraging individual initiative, were introduced in conjunction with the decision to grant greater autonomy to local authorities and production units. Under a new contract system in agriculture, households were allocated land by the collectives. Any output produced above the contracted amount with the collective could be retained and freely sold on the open market. Between 1980 and 1983 the annual average increase in food production was 1m. metric tons, about five times the growth rate of the previous five-year plan. However, these initial measures were only legalizing what was already taking place in practice. Much of the economy was out of the control of the central authorities, and there was a massive parallel market where much of the produce was redirected. A period of reaction against reform (1983–85) was mainly driven by fears among some uncompromising elements of the party about losing control of the economy. Bureaucrats and cadres also resisted reform, as it threatened their vested interests (and continued to do so in the early 21st century). Economic planning was reimposed to make the CPV's control of the South more secure. In this period reformers such as Nguyen Van Linh and former prime minister Vo Van Kiet were removed from the Politburo. Both had been in the South, witnessed the failure of collectivization of the Mekong delta and were pressing strongly for reform.

By 1986 food supplies had decreased sharply, annual price inflation had reached almost 800% and some provinces were nearing starvation. In direct response to the economic decline, the Sixth Party Congress in December 1986 announced the policy of renovation or *doi moi*. The CPV recognized that the socialist system had brought unwelcome results, such as lacklustre production, confusion in distribution and circulation, social difficulties and a crisis of confidence. To reverse the crisis in confidence (which was caused by economic collapse, abuse of power by cadres and corruption) and to recover popular support, the CPV introduced a series of political and economic reforms. The stimulus for change came from below in the form of resistance to party edicts, but the party kept control of the process by taking the initiative and reforming itself.

The Sixth Party Congress represented an important stage in the history of the CPV. The congress initiated a generational change within the party leadership and various political reforms were introduced. The surviving founder members resigned from their positions in the Politburo, Central Committee and the party secretariat. Most of the new intake represented the generation born after the party was founded in 1930. Lower-level party and state officials were more heavily represented. In particular, there was a large influx of provincial party secretaries. This shift signalled the triumph of a new coalition between technocrats and provincial power-holders on which implementation of *doi moi* was to rest. It was this group that could be expected to gain the most from economic policies stressing economic decentralization, local autonomy and greater initiative at the local level. This transformation was epitomized by the return to the Politburo and elevation of Nguyen Van Linh to party General Secretary. However, indicating the party's search for compromise, a conservative, Pham Hung, was elected Prime Minister in 1987 and was succeeded after his death in 1988 by another conservative, Do Muoi.

As a result of this significant shift of power, at the Sixth Party Congress reform measures in six policy areas under the new concept of 'a market-orientated multi-sector commodity economy under state guidance' were introduced: increased independence for state-owned enterprises (SOEs); price liberalization (not administratively but market determined); ownership diversification (encouragement of the private sector); encouragement of foreign direct investment (FDI); top priority given to agriculture (80% of the population lived in rural areas); and separate central banking and commercial banking functions. Within only a few years Viet Nam abolished the neo-Stalinist centrally planned economy that had been introduced in North Viet Nam in 1954 and had been imposed on the South after the country's reunification in 1975.

POLITICAL ADJUSTMENTS AND CHALLENGES

While *doi moi* did not initiate drastic political reforms, adjustments to the mode of governance took place between 1986 and 1989, including the reduction and decentralization of the state administration (by the end of 1989 12 ministries had been dissolved and 43.7% of offices at departmental level closed), the purge of corrupt cadres (citizens were actively invited to complain about and denounce party officials) and an increased role for the National Assembly and local government. Prior to the reforms, the National Assembly had been merely a 'rubber stamp' body, obediently endorsing party decisions, and people's choices during elections were meaningless. In addition, the Central Committee changed its plenum dates to come after the National Assembly session and not before. Therefore, genuine discussion of party proposals and debates was reported throughout the press and in detail. At the local level, the People's Councils were made more independent from People's Committees and a new electoral law permitted more candidates than seats in all but 12 districts. The CPV also launched its own version of Soviet *glasnost* (openness), with the slogan, 'Let the people know, discuss, implement and control', and party and government encouraged an unprecedented degree of critical reporting in the media. In short, political *doi moi* up to 1989 sought to address the problems of bureaucratic centralism and declining popular confidence by structural and procedural changes to every major institution. The reform was initiated and its course controlled by the party.

Until 1989 the pressure to increase the pace and scope of reform grew. However, most senior leaders—even the most radical economic reformers—instinctively opposed any weakening of the party's monopoly on power and its centrality in public affairs. They argued that unchecked demands for 'absolute democracy and openness' would lead to a chaotic and 'anarchic situation'. With the collapse of communism in Eastern Europe, the shift to a less liberal policy was summarized by CPV General Secretary Nguyen Van Linh's statement in March 1989: 'We do not tolerate pluralism. Democracy needs party leadership'. This became even more uncompromising following the Tiananmen Square massacre of pro-democracy demonstrators in the Chinese capital of Beijing. By August Linh had denounced 'bourgeois liberalization, pluralism, political plurality and multi-opposition parties aimed at denying Marxism-Leninism, socialism and the party's leadership'. This was followed by reaffirming the principles of proletarian dictatorship, democratic centralism and the primacy of Marxism-Leninism. Stability was made the highest political priority. Control of the state media was increased, and in March 1990 a turbulent meeting of the Central Committee opted for the more conservative alternative, rejecting democratic reform in general and a multi-party system in particular. Following the death in October 1990 of Le Duc Tho (one of the generation of leaders to have 'retired' in 1986, but who had remained influential), division within the Government on issues of political and economic policy increased. In early 1991, after the publication of articles criticizing government policy and the socialist system, the CPV increased surveillance of dissidents and ordered the media to publish retaliatory articles condemning party critics. Do Muoi replaced Nguyen Van Linh as General Secretary of the CPV in June.

Political *doi moi* regained some momentum in 1992. The National Assembly ratified extensive amendments to the Constitution, whereby the power of the premier and individual ministers would be greatly increased. Like the previous (1980) version, the reformed Constitution emphasized the central role of the CPV; however, it now stipulated that the party must be subject to the law. While affirming adherence to a state-regulated socialist economic system, the new Constitution guaranteed protection for foreign investment in Viet Nam and permitted foreign travel and overseas investment for the Vietnamese. Land remained the property of the State, but the right to long-term leases, which could be inherited or sold, was granted. The National Assembly was given greater power. The Council of State was replaced by a single President as Head of State, who would be responsible for appointing (subject to the approval of the National Assembly) a Prime Minister and senior members of the judiciary, and would command the armed forces (which were now obliged under the Constitution to defend the socialist regime). However, despite the structural reforms, the conservatives retained control of the elections and the progress of reform thereafter.

Viet Nam's National Assembly elections of July 1997 proved to be highly significant. Under a revised electoral law, the National Assembly was expanded from 395 to 450 seats organized in multi-member constituencies, which were contested by a record 663 candidates. The party-controlled pre-selection process was modified to enable more independent (or self-nominated) candidates to stand than previously. The elections resulted in the selection of a younger and better-educated legislature. The number of women and ethnic minority deputies rose markedly, while the number of non-party deputies nearly doubled from 8% to 15% of the total. Significantly, 11 independent candidates qualified to stand, of whom three were elected.

The process of controlled political adjustments continued at the Ninth Party Congress in 2001. The congress ousted CPV General Secretary Le Kha Phieu, who had succeeded Do Muoi in December 1997 and had later been criticized for his mismanagement of the economy, nepotism and misuse of the security services for clandestine surveillance of political rivals. He was replaced by a more moderate candidate, Nong Duc Manh. The party also dismissed some senior advisers and veteran conservatives, and expelled or disciplined thousands of its members for corruption. The campaign against corruption thereafter was accorded the highest priority on the CPV's political agenda. The Government made some modest progress in its efforts to counter corruption, with various high-profile cases (some public) against corrupt government officials, party members and business people.

The 2001 Ninth Party Congress only partly succeeded in conveying the message of political reform. Prior to the Congress, the Government had ordered repressive measures against dissidents, continuing to view organized religion as a threat to its monopoly of power and, in particular, making efforts to suppress the activities of religious leaders who avoided party control. At the same time evangelical Protestant Christianity, the fastest-growing religion in the country, was granted official status and legalized. In the months preceding the Ninth Party Congress an outbreak of mass protests by ethnic minorities in the Central Highlands involved as many as 5,000 members of various ethnic minorities. Unrest related to ethnicity had emerged as a new phenomenon in Viet Nam's modern history and was the result of a decade of quasi-neglect of ethnic minorities. Violence in the Central Highlands intensified in April 2004, when some 10,000 Montagnards (Degars) in Dak Lak and Gia Lai protested against government repression of their religion (many were Christian) and against the confiscation of their land. The Montagnards comprise about a dozen tribes, which are ethnically and culturally distinct from lowland Vietnamese. In the ensuing response from government forces, human rights groups claimed that 10 people had been killed and more than 100 injured; the official toll was two deaths and several injured. However, the Government subsequently began to work towards improving the basic infrastructure in the Central Highlands and towards providing more protection for the rights of minorities. A delegation from the European Union (EU), which visited Dak Lak in November 2008, stated that the province had made 'socio-economic and cultural achievements'. The Government was also working towards greater openness and improved opportunities for political participation by ethnic and religious groups. The election of some representatives from the moderate civic spectrum to the National Assembly in 2002 and the fact that the General Secretary of the CPV, Nong Duc Manh, was a member of an ethnic minority, were regarded as early expressions of a new approach to minorities.

Like all the Party Congresses since 1986, the 10th Party Congress, convened in 2006, again gave mixed indications of the state of political *doi moi* and confirmed the ongoing power struggle between reformists and conservatives. The cautious way in which the Congress was conducted—voting by a show of hands for a list of pre-selected candidates—ensured that the 10th Congress was as formal as the previous ones and offered scant opportunities for reformists. Policy decisions were limited to a few minor adjustments to the post-congress political line: the state-controlled sector was no longer officially to have a predominant role in the economy, and party members would in future be allowed to engage in the private sector. Nong Duc Manh was re-elected as party General Secretary by the newly enlarged, 160-member Central Committee.

As expected, Prime Minister Phan Van Khai and President Tran Duc Luong both resigned from the CPV's Politburo during the 10th Party Congress. In June 2006 the National Assembly appointed Nguyen Minh Triet as President and Nguyen Tan Dung as Prime Minister, both being the sole nominees to their respective posts. The two new leaders were from the more commercialized south of Viet Nam, reflecting the party's shift towards economic reform and global integration. In August 2007 the new National Assembly, which had been elected in May, approved a cabinet reorganization, in which the number of ministers was reduced from 26 to 22. Ten new ministers took office.

Support for reform was not unanimous within the party. Veteran revolutionaries still held considerable influence across Viet Nam's collective leadership. Critics of reform were centred around General Secretary Nong Duc Manh. The rift between the reformist and the conservative camps became particularly visible in the aftermath of the global economic crisis of 2008–09 when the General Secretary's supporters tried to exploit Prime Minister Nguyen Tan Dung's initial difficulties in stabilizing market forces and reducing inflation. The Prime Minister was also attempting to find effective policy responses to counter increasing pollution and congestion, as well as the continuing issue of corruption (see below).

In a further important political development, the influence of the National Assembly in the policy-making process increased. During its third session (May–June 2008), the National Assembly demonstrated its new assertiveness with regard to the Hanoi expansion plan. The plan envisaged expanding the capital to 3.6 times its existing size of 920 sq km by entirely incorporating Ha Tay province and parts of Vinh Phuc and Hoa Binh provinces. Although the National Assembly eventually ratified the plan, several members had criticized its 'poor planning and unclear implementation roadmap'. In June 2010 the National Assembly opposed a major government spending initiative for the first time in its history, blocking an ambitious US $56,000m., 1,630-km high-speed rail link between Hanoi and Ho Chi Minh City, at a time when state finances were coming under close scrutiny in financial markets. Government plans regarding a controversial bauxite project in the Central Highlands and proposals for new nuclear power stations in Ninh Thuan were also topics of keen debate among Assembly members.

However, the legislature's increasingly pro-active approach had yet to be translated into support of pro-democracy reforms. Shortly before the closing of the fourth session in November 2008, the National Assembly rejected a trial plan that would have allowed direct local elections in April 2009. According to the proposal, which had been discussed by National Assembly members and outlined in a detailed assembly paper, citizens in 385 communes nation-wide would have directly elected the chairperson of their people's committee. Comparisons were drawn with the village-level elections introduced by China. In September 2010, however, a local party congress in Viet Nam's third largest city, Danang, directly elected the municipal party leader for the first time, appearing to indicate that Viet Nam was experimenting with the direct election of party leaders, perhaps with a view to implementing the system more widely.

The 11th Party Congress, held in January 2011, consolidated the existing political system and well-established structures and decision-making processes. Nguyen Phu Trong, hitherto Chairman of the National Assembly, was appointed General Secretary of the CPV, replacing Nong Duc Manh who had announced his retirement; Nguyen Sinh Hung was appointed as the new Chairman of the National Assembly. Nguyen Tan Dung was reappointed to the Politburo, preparing the way for his reconfirmation as Prime Minister by the National Assembly later in the year. Dung secured reappointment despite extensive criticism over his handling of Viet Nam's economic difficulties during 2010, as well as a no-confidence vote in the National Assembly following the collapse of state-owned shipbuilding firm Vinashin, which in December 2010 defaulted on debts of US $4,500m. Both the selection of Trong and the reappointment of Dung were widely expected and demonstrated the CPV's preference for stability over sudden change. Nguyen Trong Sang replaced the outgoing Nguyen Minh Triet as party President, who, like Manh, had announced his retirement prior to the Congress. In a largely symbolic vote, the National Assembly duly reconfirmed Dung as Prime Minister in July 2011, as well as approving the appointments of Sang and Trong. The new triumvirate of power, although younger than the outgoing leadership élite, represented continuity, not change. Given that all the principal post-holders were known as pragmatic leaders, no radical alterations to the country's political or economic direction were expected. Both Dung and Sang were market-orientated, and Trong publicly stated that addressing economic problems would be the first order of business. Overall, the political system remained opaque; conflict management took place behind closed doors. Although dissent within the CPV existed, the party had so far succeeded in presenting itself as a united front *vis-à-vis* external audiences.

Elections to the 13th National Assembly (2011–16) took place in May 2011. Of the 500 deputies elected, 333 (two-thirds) were newcomers to the legislature, 122 were female, 78 belonged to an ethnic minority, 62 were under the age of 40 years, 42 were not members of the CPV, and four had nominated themselves for election. Of the 182 candidates nominated by central agencies, all but 15 were elected.

Meanwhile, the issue of corruption and abuse of office remained one of the CPV's most serious problems. In line with frequent similar statements by senior politicians, in his opening speech at the 11th Party Congress in January 2011 outgoing General Secretary Nong Duc Manh identified corruption and wastefulness as the main challenge confronting the party. Party leaders regularly acknowledged that corruption and rampant abuse of power had impeded Viet Nam's progress. Citizen complaints about official corruption, governmental inefficiency and opaque bureaucratic procedures were common. According to the Central Steering Committee for Anti-corruption, in the 12 months to November 2009 a total of 289 corruption cases were prosecuted (an increase of 2.5% year-on-year). In June 2009 Viet Nam ratified the UN Convention against Corruption, which obliged signatories to implement wide-ranging anti-corruption measures, including the criminalization of bribery of domestic or foreign public officials. Although widespread efforts to punish corrupt officials suggested that the Vietnamese Government was committed to tackling corruption, various foreign donors at the annual Consultative Group for Viet Nam held in December 2010 criticized the country's lack of clear progress to this end.

The Vietnamese media continued to play a prominent role in exposing corruption scandals. Since the country lacked civil society groups that might act as 'watchdogs', the exposure of corruption and abuse of office remained largely due to a small number of journalists who worked for newspapers such as *Thanh Nien* and *Tuoi Tre*, which were regarded as progressive. Notable examples included the reporting on the case of Project Management Unit 18, a road-building agency from which officials had embezzled millions of dollars of foreign aid for the purposes of betting on football (soccer) matches. At the same time the Government tried to define the limits of openness. In a firm demonstration of government power that prompted both domestic and international criticism, in October 2008 Nguyen Viet Chien, an investigative journalist of the state-sponsored *Thanh Nien* newspaper, was found guilty of 'abuse of power' and sentenced to two years' imprisonment. A reporter for *Tuoi Tre* newspaper, Nguyen Van Hai, who pleaded guilty to a similar charge relating to forthright coverage of the Unit 18 scandal, received two years' probation without detention. Furthermore, a decree signed by Prime Minister Nguyen Tan Dung in January 2011 increased state control of the online media. The decree set out fines of up to 40m. đông (about US $2,000) for offences including the publishing of information that was 'non-authorized' or not in 'the interests of the people'. The new restrictions seemed specifically to target the country's bloggers, many of whom published under pseudonyms to avoid possible government reprisals.

While the Government remained in control of the entire Vietnamese media, consisting of 600 newspapers and 100 radio and television stations, its ability to control the internet was very limited. Blogs had proliferated in Viet Nam, although most were carefully apolitical. The first prominent exception was Bloc 8406, so named because the group was launched on 8 April 2006. Bloc 8406's 'Manifesto for Freedom and Democracy' urged the restoration of civil liberties, the establishment of opposition political parties, the drafting of a new constitution and democratic elections to the National Assembly. Signatories included religious leaders, former military staff, scholars and writers. Similar blogs on various issues also appeared, but overall did not draw much public attention. Consequently, they did not necessarily provide an accurate representation of wider public opinion. Bloc 8406 ceased to exist, but the movement carried on under different names. In April 2010 a court rejected an appeal from a dissident writer and blogger, Tran Khai Thanh Thuy, who had been sentenced to three-and-a-half years in prison for assault. Well known in dissident circles for advocating the view that the country should adopt a multi-party form of government, Tran Khai Thanh Thuy had also written in support of six pro-democracy activists who had been imprisoned following their conviction in October 2009 for circulating anti-Government propaganda. In January 2010 four other prominent campaigners were sentenced to lengthy prison terms after being convicted of attempting to overthrow the Government. Meanwhile, with the death of veteran campaigner Hoang Minh Chinh in February 2008, the pro-democracy movement lost one of its most prominent activists.

However, in some areas there was further evidence of growing openness. For the first time, in 2006 the Government opened to online public debate the draft Political Report, a comprehensive strategic document, prior to its presentation at the 10th Party Congress. Furthermore, delegates to the Congress were given the responsibility of nominating candidates for the Central Committee, creating the opportunity for the election of new members to the Committee and the Politburo. In 2008 the Government extended the number of religious organizations that enjoyed freedom to practise their faith as long as they did not oppose the Party and existing political structure. Operating licences were granted to 13 additional religious groups, including the Bahá'í faith, the Theravada Buddhist sect, and the Viet Nam Mennonite Church. The Government had recognized more than 100 Protestant Christian groups, licensed more than 1,000 groups and granted land-use certificates to around 30 religious establishments. Even the 2009 update of the Congressional Research Service Report on US-Viet Nam relations, which was traditionally rather critical, concluded that 'most Vietnamese now are able to observe the religion of their choice'. In 2008–09, however, during ongoing disputes between Viet Nam's Catholic community and the Government, hundreds of Catholics protested against the seizure of 14 acres of land by the State. The disputed land had been part of the capital's Thai Ha parish until 1954 when the Communist forces took power from the French in North Viet Nam and seized most church land. The Government refused to discuss the legal aspects of the case advanced by the Catholic Church. Repeated attacks on parishioners and priests, allegedly carried out by gangs with plain-clothed police officers among them, were reported in the Catholic media.

RECENT FOREIGN RELATIONS

Although *doi moi* was primarily directed towards reform and liberalization of the national economy, it had decisive implications for Viet Nam's foreign policy and security outlook. In the mid-1980s the political élite arrived at the conclusion that Viet Nam's foreign affairs, national security and state of the economy were inevitably linked: the de facto international isolation of Viet Nam in the 1970s and 1980s had significantly contributed to the country's deep socio-economic crisis. At the same time, in the view of political leaders, the main security challenges to Viet Nam were not solely the result of aggressive behaviour on the part of foreign powers, but also emanated from the poor state of the economy, with all its consequences, such as poverty and economic degradation. Hence, the success of *doi moi* would largely depend on a radical change in foreign policy. Seen from a different perspective, the Vietnamese Government had to be serious about seizing any opportunity to establish, or re-establish, international links in order to emerge once again as a respected force in the global arena and contribute to the emergence of an international structure favourable to Viet Nam's own development. Between them, multilateral activities on global, inter-regional, regional and sub-regional levels, along with a return to normal bilateral relations with the USA and other powers, were expected to contribute to a secure international environment that would no longer require Viet Nam to use its resources primarily to maintain a strong defence infrastructure.

Politburo Resolution No. 13 of May 1988 outlined a diversified (*da dang hoa*) and 'multilateralized' (*da phuong hoa*) approach in Viet Nam's foreign relations. These guidelines were further developed when the Seventh Party Congress solemnly declared in 1991, 'Viet Nam wishes to befriend all countries in the world community'. The primary objectives of the new foreign policy could be summarized as follows: first, to end the state of economic embargo and diplomatic isolation and to secure a peaceful and stable international environment for 'socialist construction'; second, to boost foreign economic activity, including the attraction of foreign direct investment and official development assistance (ODA), and to increase foreign trade; and, third, to integrate Viet Nam into regional and international organizations.

In the aftermath of the collapse of the USSR and the ending of the Cold War, along with the settlement of the Cambodian conflict in 1991 (Viet Nam withdrew its forces from Cambodia in 1989), the fundamental principles of Vietnamese foreign policy—alliances with the USSR, Eastern Europe, Laos and Cambodia—were broken. Viet Nam then readjusted its foreign policy so decisively that ideological factors appeared to play little or no role in the Government's considerations. Viet Nam restored normal relations with former enemies and, after a short period of readjustment, placed relations with old allies on a new footing. The Eighth Party Congress, in 1996, pressed ahead with intensifying the country's integration into the regional and the global economies. By 2007 Viet Nam had established diplomatic relations with 170 countries and trade links with 224 out of 255 countries and territories. In 1989 Viet Nam had maintained diplomatic relations with just 23 non-communist states. The Government restored normal relations with China in 1991 and with the IMF in 1993. In 1992 Viet Nam became a founding member of the Greater Mekong Subregion (GMS). In 1995 Viet Nam joined the Association of Southeast Asian Nations (ASEAN), establishing official relations with the USA and signing an important framework co-operation agreement with the EU. In January 2007 Viet Nam joined the World Trade Organization (WTO). In October of that year, in one of the country's most important diplomatic achievements, Viet Nam was elected to serve as a non-permanent member of the UN Security Council for 2008–09, a development that allowed it to gain crucial experience on the world stage. The Government had encountered little opposition from other countries to its campaign for a seat on the Council: Viet Nam received 183 of 190 votes. Viet Nam held the rotating presidency of the Security Council in July 2008 and again in October 2009, and had to contend with, *inter alia*, developments in several African countries, sanctions against Iran and North Korea, and the situation in Myanmar (q.v.).

Relations with ASEAN

Viet Nam's relations with ASEAN have been transformed from confrontation through accommodation to membership. Peace in Cambodia removed one obstacle to better relations, and then agreement was reached on the repatriation of refugees from ASEAN countries. In 1992 Viet Nam signed the ASEAN Treaty of Amity and Co-operation (TAC), the organization's code of conduct, and was subsequently granted observer status. In July 1994 Viet Nam became a founding member of the ASEAN Regional Forum (ARF), a mechanism for the informal discussion of security issues in the Asia-Pacific region. In July 1995 Viet Nam was admitted as ASEAN's seventh member and announced its intention to join the ASEAN Free Trade Area (AFTA). Viet Nam attended the first summit meeting for all 10 South-East Asian heads of government in Bangkok, Thailand, in December. In November 1996 ASEAN members successfully supported Viet Nam's application for membership of Asia-Pacific Economic Co-operation (APEC); formal admission took place in November 1998. One month later Viet Nam hosted the sixth summit meeting of the organization's heads of government, followed in July 2001 by the annual series of ASEAN conferences, including the Foreign Ministers' Meeting and the ARF, when Viet Nam held the rotating chairmanship of ASEAN. Viet Nam actively strove for the narrowing of the development gap between the old and new members (the latter being Cambodia, Laos, Myanmar and Viet Nam), with the ultimate goal of committing the wealthier ASEAN members to substantive action. Viet Nam's efforts resulted in the Hanoi Declaration on Narrowing Development Gap for Closer ASEAN Integration, which was signed in July 2001. Viet Nam was also a strong supporter of ASEAN's fundamental principle of non-interference, and obstructed initiatives by Thailand and the Philippines to adopt a more flexible approach. Viet Nam's strong support of non-interference became apparent, for instance, when the Government decided against participation by Vietnamese personnel in the UN Transitional Administration in East Timor (UNTAET), which was established in October 1999. In contrast, Malaysia, the Philippines, Singapore and Thailand contributed to the UN mission.

In October 2003 Prime Minister Phan Van Khai attended the ninth ASEAN summit meeting, in Bali, Indonesia, where the heads of governments signed the second Declaration of ASEAN Concord (Bali Concord II). The agreement envisioned the establishment of an integrated economic, security and socio-cultural community—the ASEAN Economic Community (AEC)—by 2020, although this was subsequently brought forward to 2015. In April 2005 Viet Nam hosted the 11th ASEAN Economic Ministers (AEM) Retreat Meeting, which discussed measures to increase gradually the economic integration of the 10 member countries, in preparation for the planned establishment of the AEC. In November 2007, together with the nine other member states, Viet Nam signed the ASEAN Charter (the Association's new legal and institutional framework) at the 13th ASEAN summit meeting in Singapore. The Charter, which entered into force in December 2008, committed its members, *inter alia*, to democratic principles and the creation of a regional human rights body. Viet Nam initially opposed the inclusion of a human rights mechanism in the Charter, but later agreed to the provision. As the unofficial leader of the 'CLMV' group (Cambodia, Laos, Myanmar and Viet Nam) representing the least developed of the ASEAN countries, Viet Nam hosted a summit meeting of the four countries' respective Prime Ministers in November 2008 in Hanoi. In January 2010 Viet Nam assumed the annually rotating chair of ASEAN, hosting a number of related meetings in Hanoi, including the ARF in July and the 17th ASEAN Summit in October.

Meanwhile, Viet Nam was relatively successful in resolving most of its territorial disputes with neighbouring countries. In September 1992 Viet Nam reached agreement with Malaysia and Thailand on co-operation in the use of the waters of the Gulf of Thailand. As a result of continuing friction between Thai and Vietnamese fishing boats, in April 1996 the two countries agreed to establish a joint commission to resolve the matter. However, in October, a new incident in a series of clashes occurred between Thai fishing trawlers and a Vietnamese naval vessel, in which two Thais were killed. This incident prompted Thailand and Viet Nam to intensify their efforts to reach a *modus vivendi* for the maritime area in which their territorial claims conflicted. Finally, in October 1997 Viet Nam and Thailand reached an agreement to delimit their maritime boundary (continental shelf and exclusive economic zone) in the Gulf of Thailand. This agreement led to joint naval patrols, fishery surveys and petroleum and gas exploration. In 1996 Viet Nam and Malaysia had reached an agreement to develop jointly an area in the Gulf of Thailand where they had overlapping claims not involving a third country. In the same year Viet Nam and the Philippines began discussions on the joint development of their overlapping territorial claims in the South China Sea. In June 2003 Viet Nam and Indonesia signed an agreement on the delimitation of their continental shelf boundary in the contested areas to the north of Indonesia's Natuna islands. The most important development in the return to normal relations between Viet Nam and Cambodia was the signing of a supplementary border treaty in Hanoi in October 2005 to settle the long-standing border dispute. However, the joint demarcation and planting of border markers, originally scheduled to be finalized by 2008, remained ongoing at mid-2011 and was not expected to be completed until 2012.

Relations with China

After centuries of hostilities, which reached their most recent height during the Cold War, Sino-Vietnamese dealings were rapidly transformed into much more cordial relations in the aftermath of Viet Nam's unconditional retreat from Cambodia in 1989 and its constructive role in the process of settling the conflict there. In general terms, Viet Nam's post-1988 'new outlook' in the conduct of its foreign affairs prepared the way for improved relations with China. In November 1991 the two Governments re-established diplomatic links. While political mutual trust, the promotion of economic and trade co-operation, and exchanges in cultural and other fields markedly improved, Sino-Vietnamese affairs were far from trouble-free. In May 1992 Viet Nam made a formal protest against China's unilateral decision to grant a US company petroleum exploration rights in an area in the Gulf of Tongking, which Viet Nam claimed as its own territorial waters. In June discussions took place in Yogyakarta, Indonesia, concerning the sovereignty of the Spratly Islands (Truong Sa). The Spratlys are a collection of mostly barren coral reefs, atolls and sand bars covering an area of some 70,000 sq miles (180,000 sq km). This area is claimed, in whole or in part, by China, Taiwan, Viet Nam, Malaysia, Brunei and the Philippines. The other major area of dispute in the South China Seas concerns the Paracel Islands (Hoang Sa), which are claimed by China and Viet Nam (in 1976 China captured the Paracels from Viet Nam). With the exception of Brunei, all of the disputants maintain a military presence on some of the Spratlys; Viet Nam maintained a military presence on 21 of the islands, China on seven. The controversy itself lay relatively dormant until 1988, when the Chinese and Vietnamese navies clashed at Johnson Reef, sinking several Vietnamese boats and killing more than 70 sailors. Hostilities in the South China Sea have subsequently occurred on a regular basis.

In September 1992 China agreed to discuss land border disputes and the disagreement over the Gulf of Tongking, but ruled out negotiations on the Spratlys. The discussions, which took place in October, failed to achieve significant progress. However, in November–December the Chinese Premier, Li Peng, paid an official visit to Viet Nam (the first by a Chinese head of government since 1971); new accords on economic, scientific and cultural co-operation were concluded, and the two Governments agreed to accelerate the negotiations on disputed territory. The first round of border discussions was duly held in August 1993, and in October the two countries concluded an agreement to avoid the use of force in resolving territorial disputes. However, armed confrontation between Chinese and Vietnamese ships in the disputed waters was only narrowly avoided in April 1994, and in July two Chinese warships blocked access to Vietnamese petroleum-prospecting facilities on one of the Spratly Islands. In September the then Vice-Prime Minister, Phan Van Khai, visited Beijing to discuss the matter, and agreement was reached to continue seeking a negotiated settlement. In the following month China renewed diplomatic protests at Viet Nam's decision to invite foreign oil companies to develop areas of the Gulf of Tongking. These protests occurred immediately prior to a visit to Hanoi in November by the Chinese President and Communist Party General Secretary, Jiang Zemin, the most senior Chinese official to visit Viet Nam since the resumption of normal bilateral relations in late 1991. In early 1995 problems in Sino-Vietnamese relations were exacerbated when it was discovered that the Chinese had occupied Mischief Reef, located in an area of the Spratlys claimed by the Philippines. This was the first such incident involving China in a direct dispute with an ASEAN member, and it served as an opportunity for Viet Nam to demonstrate its solidarity with ASEAN prior to its membership of the Association.

A significant Sino-Vietnamese land border treaty was concluded in December 1999, delineating the 1,300-km land border between northern Viet Nam and southern China and settling more than 100 areas of dispute. The treaty represented an important stage in the improvement of the often-strained relations between the two communist neighbours. The demarcation of the land border was completed in February 2009. Meanwhile, in December 2000, after many sessions of negotiations, the agreement on the demarcation of the Gulf of Tongking was eventually signed, although it took effect only in June 2004, after lengthy negotiations concerning its implementation. There were no contrary claims over the sea border, but its demarcation proved to be an unwieldy process.

The 1992 ASEAN Declaration on the South China Sea, which was also signed by China in 2002, generally eased tensions, but fell short of a legally binding code of conduct. After China and the Philippines signed the August 2004 Joint Marine Seismic Undertaking (JMSU) Agreement to study and identify areas of petroleum and gas exploration in the South China Sea, in March 2005 Viet Nam joined the Philippines and China to sign a new JMSU on conducting joint scientific research in those maritime areas where the Spratlys island chain was disputed. However, clashes and diplomatic sabre-rattling between Viet Nam and China have continued, for example in July 2007, when a Chinese naval vessel fired upon Vietnamese fishing boats in disputed waters, causing one death. Despite strong diplomatic efforts to strengthen Sino-Vietnamese relations, a sense of resentment towards China, emanating from historical legacies, persisted within much of Viet Nam's political élite, as remained the case with a proportion of the wider Vietnamese population. A low point in diplomatic relations was reached in December 2007 when thousands of Vietnamese took to the streets of Hanoi and Ho Chi Minh City to protest against what they viewed as China's incursions into Vietnamese territory in the South China Sea. It was the first public rally in half-a-century in communist Viet Nam. Anti-China protests were renewed in December 2008, but the demonstrations were quickly suppressed by the Vietnamese authorities. In early June 2011 fresh protests against China were held outside the Chinese embassy in Hanoi and also in Ho Chi Minh City as the bilateral maritime dispute escalated, following a number of alleged incursions into Vietnamese territorial waters in the preceding weeks by Chinese vessels in the South China Sea; protests also took place at Chinese embassies in, *inter alia*, the USA, France and Germany. Meanwhile, the Vietnamese Government had lodged an official protest with China owing to that country's alleged violation of Viet Nam's sovereignty. In mid-June Viet Nam conducted live-fire military exercises in the South China Sea, as it accused the Chinese Government of raising tensions in the region. Both China and Viet Nam were, at mid-2011, engaged in the building of more structures, including armed bunkers, on some of the islands that they occupied. Viet Nam also followed the Chinese example of using archaeological evidence to strengthen its sovereignty claims, in addition to reference to the 1982 UN Convention on the Law of the Sea.

The USA was also drawn into the dispute, seemingly taking the side of Viet Nam and ASEAN. In July 2010 the ARF meeting in Hanoi was attended by US Secretary of State Hillary Clinton and the Chinese Minister of Foreign Affairs, Yang Jiechi. Despite Chinese efforts to keep the South China Sea off the agenda, at the urging of Viet Nam and other ASEAN members, Clinton addressed the matter directly, stating that the USA had 'a national interest' in seeing a resolution to the dispute and was in favour of 'a collaborative diplomatic process by all claimants for resolving the various territorial disputes without coercion'. These remarks outraged China, which was strategically opposed to a 'collaborative' settlement with ASEAN members, preferring bilateral talks where it could be the dominant negotiator. Yang went so far as to describe Clinton's remarks 'an attack on China'. Joint US-Vietnamese naval exercises in the South China Sea and other signs of Viet Nam's deepening relations with the USA in August 2010 (see below) did little to appease Chinese irritation. In response to the escalating Sino-Vietnamese tensions in mid-2011, the US Administration urged restraint on all sides and the holding of urgent talks to find a diplomatic resolution to the territorial dispute.

Relations with the USA

Relations between Viet Nam and the USA remained in part an exception to the general improvement in relations with the outside world during 1991–94, owing to the ongoing problem of the more than 2,600 US servicemen listed as 'missing in action' (MIA) during the Viet Nam War. In 1986 and 1987 agreements were reached for Vietnamese co-operation in the search for missing servicemen, in return for a promise of humanitarian aid from the USA. The Vietnamese Government also agreed in principle to permit the emigration to the USA of former re-education camp detainees and their families, subject to assurances that they would not engage in 'anti-Vietnamese' activities. Between November 1988 and January 1989 the remains of 86 soldiers were returned to the US Government. In October 1990 the Vietnamese Minister of Foreign Affairs, Nguyen Co Thach, met leading US officials in Washington, DC (the first visit by a senior Vietnamese official to the US capital in 15 years) to discuss the UN peace plan for Cambodia and the possible release of information concerning the MIA. The meeting represented a significant initiative towards the establishment of diplomatic relations between the two countries. In early 1991 a US representative was stationed in Hanoi to supervise inquiries into the MIA, the first official US presence in Viet Nam since 1975. In December of the same year the USA ended restrictions on US citizens travelling to Viet Nam.

In February 1994 President Bill Clinton announced the removal of the US economic embargo against Viet Nam. He expressed the hope that this would encourage the Vietnamese to give further assistance in the investigations of the MIA (the number of whom was now believed to be about 1,600). In May Viet Nam and the USA agreed to open liaison offices in their respective capitals; the USA opened its office in Hanoi in February 1995. The restoration of full diplomatic relations was finally announced by President Clinton on 11 July, and in the following month the new US embassy was inaugurated in Hanoi.

In March 1998 Viet Nam's co-operation with the USA on a resettlement programme for Vietnamese 'boat people' in camps in South-East Asia resulted in President Clinton's decision to waive the Jackson-Vanik Amendment to the 1974 Trade Act. This amendment prohibited the USA from trading with, or providing investment funds to, countries that did not permit free emigration. As a result of the waiver, the Overseas Private Investment Corporation (OPIC) and the Export-Import Bank were permitted to commence operations in Viet Nam. (OPIC provided special insurance cover for US firms doing business in Viet Nam, while the Export-Import Bank provided loans to US companies to assist their exports to Viet Nam.)

In February 1999 President Clinton affirmed that Viet Nam was 'fully co-operating in good faith' in all areas of bilateral relations in which the USA itself sought progress (particularly in the area of joint searches for the remains of the MIA). Viet Nam also intensified its co-operation with the USA on immigration issues in 1999: following some initial difficulties, the Vietnamese Government gave permission for refugees in overseas camps to return to Viet Nam for processing, in preparation for emigration to the USA under the Resettlement of Vietnamese Returnees Programme, and also expedited the processing of former re-education camp detainees. Improved Vietnamese co-operation in these areas led to President Clinton's agreement to the second waiver of the Jackson-Vanik Amendment, as a consequence of which US export promotion and investment support programmes were permitted to recommence.

The US Secretary of Defense, William Cohen, travelled to Viet Nam in April 2000. Although the visit represented progress in improving bilateral military links, the Vietnamese Government appeared reluctant to support Cohen's suggestion that Viet Nam and the USA were potential allies against 'growing hegemony' in the region and to allow port visits by US naval vessels. In July the newly appointed Minister of Trade, Vu Khoan, travelled to Washington, DC, and, as expected, the long-awaited bilateral trade agreement with the USA was finally signed. Viet Nam was accorded normal trade relations (NTR) status (formerly known as most favoured nation—MFN—trading status), effectively lowering tariff rates on exports from 40% to 3%. Both the US Congress and the Vietnamese National Assembly delayed ratification of the bilateral trade agreement for domestic political reasons. The US Congress finally ratified the agreement in August 2001, and the National Assembly endorsed it in November. The agreement prepared the way for Vietnamese membership of the WTO, which Viet Nam joined after various delays in January 2007. President Bill Clinton visited Viet Nam in November 2000, the first visit by a US President to the unified Viet Nam. Clinton's official reception was austere and there was little ceremony surrounding the visit, but he was generally welcomed by the public.

Viet Nam responded cautiously to the US Government's announcement of a 'war on terror', following the attacks against New York and Washington, DC, on 11 September 2001. While condemning the terrorist acts against the USA and supporting UN and ASEAN resolutions, Viet Nam was highly critical of the use of military force in Afghanistan. Nevertheless, Viet Nam granted US military aircraft overflight rights to Vietnamese territory. An alleged conspiracy by terrorists linked to the al-Qa'ida organization to attack US naval vessels in Singapore prompted the US Commander-in-Chief of Pacific Forces, Adm. Dennis Blair, to make the issue of port access to Cam Ranh Bay a priority. The Vietnamese Government had rejected initial requests from both the USA and China for access to the former Russian (previously Soviet) base, but had not refused to permit port visits.

Bilateral relations reached a temporary low point in 2003, when Viet Nam was antagonized by various measures adopted by the US Congress, which it perceived to constitute blatant interference in its internal affairs. These included the Viet Nam Freedom of Information Bill and the Viet Nam Human Rights Bill, which sought to reduce non-humanitarian aid. The Vietnamese Government openly condemned the US-led campaign to oust the regime of Saddam Hussain in Iraq in early 2003 and expressed sympathy for the Iraqi people, while urging the UN to take a lead with regard to events in the country.

Relations between Viet Nam and the USA strengthened from 2003. Most significantly, US Secretary of Defense Donald Rumsfeld hosted his Vietnamese counterpart, Pham Van Tra, in November, the first visit by a Vietnamese military chief since the end of the Viet Nam War in 1975. While no agreements were signed on military co-operation, Viet Nam urged the USA to do more to help the 2m. Vietnamese suffering as a result of exposure to Agent Orange, a herbicide used by the US military during the Viet Nam War. The USA requested rights to make port visits to Cam Ranh Bay, but Viet Nam, sensitive to reactions from China, resisted this; however, the first port visit by a US naval ship, USS *Vandegrift*, took place in Ho Chi Minh City in November 2003.

In April 2005 Prime Minister Phan Van Khai visited the USA, the first such trip by a senior Vietnamese communist leader. Arriving in Viet Nam for the first time to attend the APEC summit meeting hosted by Viet Nam in November 2006, US President George W. Bush gave his full support to the host's WTO membership application. President Bush set aside ongoing disputes with Viet Nam on human rights, religious freedom and democracy; thus, he decided to exclude Viet Nam from the US list of countries of particular concern (CPCs—states that were deemed to have 'engaged in or tolerated particularly severe violations of religious freedom') shortly before his trip. A state visit by the recently appointed Vietnamese President, Nguyen Minh Triet, in June 2007 was seen as representing a new improvement in the bilateral relationship, with the two countries now regarding each other as important economic partners, as demonstrated by their signature of a Trade and Investment Framework Agreement (TIFA). The TIFA had been negotiated under President Bush's Enterprise for ASEAN Initiative, which was aimed at strengthening US economic relations with South-East Asia. Bilateral relations further improved following the inauguration of President Barack Obama in January 2009. In the same year Viet Nam became the USA's second largest supplier of clothing, behind only China. Bilateral trade between the USA and Viet Nam totalled US $18,577m. in 2010 and was mainly driven by Vietnamese exports to the USA. The latter's trade deficit stood at $ 11,558m.

In August 2010 the US Department of Defense and the Vietnamese Ministry of National Defence held the first round of annual senior-level discussion, known as the Defense Policy Dialogue. In the same month several US media outlets reported that the USA was conducting negotiations with Viet Nam with a view to reaching an agreement that would allow Viet Nam to purchase nuclear fuel, as well as US nuclear technology and reactors. Significantly, the agreement would also allow Viet Nam to enrich its own uranium to produce fuel for its power reactors, subject to monitoring by the International Atomic Energy Agency. The talks were widely interpreted as a sign that the Obama Administration was engaged in a strategy of countering Chinese influence throughout the Asian region. In a further demonstration of closer bilateral links, also in August, the USA sent the aircraft carrier *USS George Washington* to Viet Nam to mark the 15th anniversary of the normalization of relations between the two countries, and inaugural joint US-Vietnamese naval exercises were held in the South China Sea.

However, issues pertaining to the Viet Nam War and Viet Nam's human rights record continue to threaten the relationship. Although Viet Nam was removed from the US Department of State's list of CPCs in November 2006 (see above), the USA and Viet Nam continued to conduct a twice-yearly human rights dialogue, in which the US representatives raised questions on religious freedom and democratic reforms in Viet Nam. Driven by what some US policy-makers regarded as a breach of Viet Nam's undertaking to embrace reforms towards greater political freedom and substantial improvements in human rights when it joined the WTO, the US House of Representatives approved binding legislation in September 2007. This linked US foreign aid to Viet Nam to its human rights record while serving the purpose of promoting the 'development of freedom, human rights, and the rule of law' in the country. Vietnamese Americans, a growing political force in the USA, were trying to persuade US legislators to exert greater pressure on Viet Nam to improve human rights. During a visit to Hanoi in July 2010, US Secretary of State Hillary Clinton publicly pressed Viet Nam to open further its political system, amid concerns regarding the Government's suppression of democracy activists and its restrictions on the use of the internet.

Other Relations

Viet Nam has been a leading recipient of Western and Japanese overseas development assistance (ODA) in the region in absolute terms. The total value of ODA pledged between 1993 and 2009 totalled US $42,500m. ODA commitments steadily increased, from $1,800m. for 1994 to $8,060m. for 2010. However, total pledges for 2011 declined slightly to $7,900m. There has been a disparity of about 40% between commitments and actual disbursements, and Viet Nam has received around 3% of its gross domestic product in grants and concessional loans. By 2011 there were 51 donors (28 bilateral and 23 multilateral) operating regularly in Viet Nam. For 2010 Japan was the largest bilateral donor (pledging $1,640m.), followed by France, the United Kingdom and Germany. The largest multilateral donor in the same year was the World Bank, which committed $2,500m., followed by the Asian Development Bank, which pledged $1,480m. The Vietnamese Government effectively utilized international assistance for its domestic policy agenda, primarily to strengthen its reform programme, particularly in the areas of poverty reduction and improvement of the infrastructure. Together with Ghana, Viet Nam was identified as a 'star performer' in efforts to reach the UN's Millennium Development Goals (MDGs), according to a report published in 2010 by a British research centre, the Overseas Development Institute. Similarly, a study published in the same year by the UN Economic and Social Commission for Asia and the Pacific concluded that Viet Nam had assumed the lead within the Asia-Pacific region in terms of the number of MDGs that had been achieved ahead of schedule.

The year 2010 marked the 20th anniversary of diplomatic relations between Viet Nam and the EU. The Viet Nam-EU Framework Co-operation Agreement was signed in July 1995, and the Delegation of the European Commission to Viet Nam was officially opened in 1996. Viet Nams relations with the EU rapidly and significantly improved from 2002, when the two signed a co-operation strategy for the 2002–06. The sum of €304m. was allocated for development co-operation with Viet Nam during 2007–13 (€160m. for 2007–10 and €144m. for 2011–13). By 2005, meanwhile, the EU had become Viet Nam's second largest trading partner, with the value of bilateral trade having quadrupled over the previous decade; two-way trade reached US $12,000m. in 2010. In October 2004 the EU became Viet Nam's first major partner to conclude bilateral WTO market access negotiations, in an agreement that gave considerable impetus to the country's WTO accession process, and the EU supported Viet Nam's (ultimately successful) bid for non-permanent membership of the UN Security Council for the 2008–09 term. Also in October 2004, Viet Nam hosted the fifth summit of the Asia-Europe Meeting; the most important result was the admission of the 10 new EU member states, as well as Cambodia, Laos and (controversially) Myanmar, to the most important multilateral dialogue forum in relations between the two continents. The strengthening of Viet Nam's relations with the EU was underlined in March 2005 when National Assembly Chairman Nguyen Van An visited various European states at the invitation of the European Parliament. In October 2007 Vietnamese Prime Minister Nguyen Tan Dung made an official visit to France. The two countries signed 11 agreements, including one on the purchase by Viet Nam of Airbus aircraft and one on the promotion of Vietnamese exports (mainly garments and seafood) to France and other EU markets. In the same month, during the 117th Assembly of the Inter-Parliamentary Union (IPU) in Geneva, a representative of Viet Nam was elected to serve a four-year term on the 17-member Executive Committee in recognition of the country's active contribution to the IPU's development. Discussions between Viet Nam and the European Commission regarding a Viet Nam-EU Free Trade Agreement were initiated in March 2010; however, as of mid-2011 no tangible progress had been made, owing to the parties' divergent views on the scope and depth of the proposed trade liberalization.

Economy

SUIWAH LEUNG

INTRODUCTION

By 2008 Viet Nam had formally attained the status of a middle-income country, with annual per caput income in excess of US $1,000 and with the percentage of the population living on less than $1 per day having declined from 60% to less than 12%. This remarkable transformation from a very poor country to middle-income status took place within a span of less than 25 years, starting from the initiation of economic reform under the slogan of *doi moi* (renovation) in 1986. The process of transformation took place alongside (and arguably resulted from) two other important developments: the move from a closed to an open economy and the transition from a centrally planned to a market economy.

Although *doi moi* officially began in 1986, the opening of the Vietnamese economy to international trade and investment flows did not effectively occur until 1989 when the USSR and the Council for Mutual Economic Assistance (CMEA, or Comecon) disintegrated. Throughout the 1990s gross domestic product (GDP) grew at an average annual rate of between 7% and 8%, albeit from a very low base. Per caput GDP at that time was less than US $200. Growth during this decade came mainly from the creation of markets for agricultural produce and agricultural land. Being able to sell their produce at market prices enabled farmers to identify what to produce and to use fertilizers to improve crop yield. At the same time, availability of titles in the form of 'land-use rights' and the ability to lease these rights for 50 years gave farmers the incentive to invest in dams and other capital equipment. Agricultural production rose rapidly as a result, and by 1997 Viet Nam had gone from being a rice importer less than eight years previously to becoming the world's second largest exporter of rice.

The expansion of international trade was accompanied by growth of foreign direct investment (FDI). Between 1990 and 1997 FDI increased at an average annual rate of about 43%, although this was from a very low base. However, the trade and investment regimes at the time were so orientated towards the state sector that by 1996 around 99% of FDI was in the form of joint ventures with state-owned enterprises (SOEs). Continued profitability for the foreign partners was limited, and registered FDI into Viet Nam had begun declining by 1996, one year prior to the onset of the Asian financial crisis in 1997.

The Asian financial crisis was a stark warning for Viet Nam. Just prior to the emergence of the regional crisis in Thailand in July 1997, Viet Nam experienced a mini-crisis of its own, involving letters of credit issued by state-owned commercial banks (SOCBs) on behalf of SOEs. Tight domestic credit conditions in 1996 opened up an interest rate differential (of around 0.8%) between the Vietnamese dông and the US dollar. The pegged exchange rate at the time gave rise to the belief that the Vietnamese Government was willing and able to defend the dông against any depreciation. It thus became profitable for enterprises to borrow in US dollars. Prior to 1996, informal arrangements existed for some SOEs to obtain trade credit from their suppliers. In 1996 SOEs were able to obtain these trade credits by the SOCBs issuing letters of credit. From the point of view of the banking sector, this amounted to the SOCBs borrowing from foreign creditors on behalf of the SOEs. The amount of foreign borrowing through this channel rose rapidly, because demand was driven by the aforementioned interest differential. Supply was also encouraged by the fact that these borrowings were guaranteed by the SOCBs (and hence by the Vietnamese Government). A proportion of the funds was channelled into unprofitable uses. Some SOEs invested in real estate, causing a sharp rise in asset prices, which faltered during 1995–97. Others used the imported inputs in products for which markets had declined. In the event, by early 1997 an estimated 40% of the letters of credit (equivalent to 3% of GDP at the time) became bad debts. Some SOCBs were not able to meet the guarantees. The subsequent rescue of these SOCBs by the State Bank of Viet Nam (SBV) reduced the country's international reserves to five weeks' worth of imports and resulted in Viet Nam's sovereign debt credit rating being downgraded. Strict administrative controls over the SOCBs and over imports averted disaster, but economic growth did not recover to pre-crisis levels until 2005.

By the turn of the new millennium, it had become clear to the Vietnamese leadership that the gross policy bias towards the state sector was no longer tenable. In order to generate 1.6m. new jobs each year to achieve social stability and an improvement in living standards, the potential of the domestic private sector had to be released and allowed to develop. There thus ensued a second phase of economic reforms.

The first Enterprises Law was enacted in 2001. Prior to this, all domestic private enterprises, however small, were required to have a licence, which in some cases needed to be renewed every month or every quarter. Quite apart from the strong discouragement to private sector activities, this licensing system provided the basis for widespread low-level corruption. The 2001 Enterprises Law abolished the requirements for hundreds of different business licences. Registered businesses grew rapidly, at a rate of some 30%, although this figure inevitably involved some double-counting, as a number of unlicensed businesses would already have been in existence prior to the abolition of licensing. Nevertheless, the rapid growth was indisputable.

Domestic private sector growth was accompanied by an increase in some non-traditional agricultural exports. Throughout the 1990s rice dominated agricultural exports. Between 1999/2000 and 2005/06, however, the dominance of rice was steadily eroded as export values declined while non-traditional exports such as coffee, rubber and, more importantly, processed foods increased in importance. Fish and fish products featured prominently in processed foods exports, rising from around 17% of primary exports in 1992/93 to 33% in 1999/2000 and further to 43% in 2005/06. Such growth had implications for poverty reduction (see below).

Towards the latter half of the 1990s and into the new millennium, exports of traditional labour-intensive manufactured products (apparel, footwear and furniture) expanded rapidly, with their share in total non-oil exports increasing from around 12% in 1991 to more than 58% in 2006. However, Viet Nam's participation in the manufacture and assembly of the parts and components trade, within regional production networks, did not take place until further domestic reforms were instituted.

These reforms were embodied in the enactment in 2006 of a second Enterprises Law and of the Unified Investment Law. The reforms allowed, at least in principle, the equal treatment of domestic and international investors, and of state-owned and privately owned enterprises. Furthermore, they opened the way for foreign firms to have majority shareholdings in domestic enterprises. This last development was important for Viet Nam's participation in the parts and components trade (principally in electronics), as foreign firms in these production networks were no longer interested in joint ventures with domestic firms to explore 'greenfield' enterprises. Instead, foreign firms in these production networks needed to have substantial control over their domestic counterparts in order to ensure quality control as well as timeliness of delivery. Mergers and acquisitions thus became the modus operandi for foreign investments into emerging market economies.

In addition to regulatory reforms during this period, the costs of doing business in Vietnamese cities were also significantly lowered and became competitive with other countries in the region. Although wages in Hanoi and Ho Chi Minh City had for a long time been very competitive with other cities in the region, the cost of international telephone calls, container transport, electricity and the rental of office space, as well as of residential accommodation for expatriate staff, were high in comparison with other cities in the region. By 2006 all the other costs except rental expenses had declined substantially to become very competitive. Combined with a relatively literate, young and disciplined work-force, aided by political stability, this rendered Viet Nam very attractive to foreign investors. Following a sharp decline in 1996/97 and a period of subdued growth during the first half of the 2000s, FDI increased by 22.8% in 2006.

Accession to the World Trade Organization (WTO) in January 2007, and the approval by the US Congress in the previous month of legislation permitting 'permanent normal trade relations' with Viet Nam, further entrenched the country's domestic reforms and reflected the Government's commitment to continue transforming Viet Nam into a fully functioning market economy. FDI increased to US $6,500m. (equivalent to 9.4% of GDP) in 2007, and rose further to $9,600m. (10.6% of GDP) in 2008.

Not only were foreign investors taking notice of the favourable conditions in Viet Nam, but also Vietnamese workers abroad were sending home record remittances. During 2000–05 remittances from abroad through banking and other formal channels accounted for between 4% and 6% of GDP per year. From 2006, however, remittances rose to around 9% of GDP. According to the IMF, the portfolio (or investment) motive was significant in these remittances; such a view is supported by the fact that remittances were positively correlated with the country's economic conditions, the investment climate and the relaxation of the regulatory environment from the late 1990s.

With a pegged exchange rate and inadequate monetary constraints, such strong capital inflows brought about a rapid increase in money supply. Credit grew by almost 50% in 2007, leading to 'bubbles' in the real estate and share markets. House prices rose by 11% in 2007 and by 21% in 2008. The stock market oscillated between 2007 and 2008, with the index increasing 10-fold in 2007, before declining by 67% in 2008. The 'overheating' of the economy was accompanied by an increase in the annual rate of inflation, which reached 28% in the second quarter of 2008. This marked the beginning of a period of macroeconomic turbulence. Meanwhile, political support for large state-owned conglomerates (with interests in the banking sector) continued to complicate macroeconomic management as well as compounding the effects of the economy's inefficient use of capital.

STRUCTURAL CHANGES

Like all the rapidly industrializing countries in Asia, such as the People's Republic of China, Indonesia and Thailand, as a relative newcomer to this process Viet Nam has experienced significant structural changes in its economy. The contribution of agriculture to GDP halved between 1989 and 2009, declining from 42.1% of GDP to 20.9%. However, compared with Thailand (where agriculture's share of GDP stood at 11.6% in 2009) and countries such as China and Indonesia, for example, the agricultural sector remains very important in Viet Nam, with three-quarters of its population residing in rural areas. As productivity increases in agriculture reach their limits, continuous growth can come only from the amalgamation of small farms so that large machinery such as tractors can be employed. This stage coincides with the relocation of much of the rural population to cities as has been happening in China, resulting in rapid infrastructure development and strong demand for mineral resources. At the end of the first decade of the 21st century, therefore, urbanization had yet to occur on a large scale in Viet Nam.

However, the industrial sector has increased in importance in Viet Nam, its contribution to GDP almost doubling from 22.9% in 1989 to 40.2% in 2009. This is still somewhat lower than in China, Indonesia and Thailand, where the respective figures are well over 40% (reaching 49.1% in Indonesia). In particular, the manufacturing sector's contribution to Vietnamese GDP in 2009, at 20.1%, was significantly lower than the corresponding figures for China and Thailand, both of which were around 34%. This probably reflects Viet Nam's status as a late entrant to the global supply chain of parts and components manufacture and assembly (principally, but not exclusively, in electronics), which has accounted for a significant proportion of the Chinese economy since the early 1990s. Within the Vietnamese manufacturing industry, food-processing and textiles and garments comprise approximately one-half of the value added.

The share of services in the economy has remained relatively stable, standing at 35.0% of GDP in 1989 and at 38.8% in 2009. However, this aggregate figure could conceal some significant changes: for example, a shift from unskilled labour and domestic services to more highly skilled services, as indicated by the rapid growth in Viet Nam's banking sector, the stock market, real estate and tourism since 2007.

While the stock market and the real estate sector have exhibited significant volatility in recent years, Viet Nam has significant potential for growth in its tourism sector, with 2,000 miles of coastline, diverse scenery and an interesting history and culture. Although Viet Nam attracted a record 5.05m. tourist arrivals in 2010, this remained low in relation to the size of the resident population, which totalled 85.8m. at the 2009 census. Cumbersome and expensive visa requirements, along with inadequate marketing, present significant challenges for the Vietnamese tourism industry. Although the Government has seemed reluctant to address the visa issue on the grounds of security concerns, it appears prepared to be more pro-active in destination marketing, emphasizing the many attractions of the country, in addition to cultural interests, in an attempt to increase the number of visitors to the country.

Given the export-orientated growth strategy espoused by the Vietnamese Government, exports could obviously be expected to drive much of the change in economic structure. Prior to the instigation of *doi moi* in 1986, the bulk of exports (principally of agricultural commodities and oil) went to the former USSR. After the opening up of the economy to international trade and foreign investment, oil exports reached a high point in 1992, owing to production from the White Tiger oilfield, in the Cuu Long basin of the South China Sea, while rice production and rice exports grew rapidly as a result of reforms in the agricultural sector. In addition to rice, Viet Nam moved into other forms of commodity exports such as coffee and rubber. At 2008 Viet Nam was estimated to have captured around 8.3% of the global coffee market and 4.2% of the world market in rubber.

According to Business Monitor International estimates, crude petroleum production reached 400,000 barrels per day (b/d) in 2010 and was projected to decline to 325,000 b/d by 2019. Oil consumption was set to increase, with growth ranging from 5.0% to 7.0% per year over this period; the country was projected to be using 625,000 b/d by 2019. Hence, Viet Nam is likely to continue as a net oil importer for the remainder of this decade. Gas production, in contrast, was expected to rise from an estimated 9,100m. cu m in 2010 to 34,000m. cu m in 2019. With domestic demand growing at a lower rate, there is potential for Viet Nam to become a net exporter of gas before 2019.

From 1990 Viet Nam took advantage of global growth in exports of processed food, in particular processed seafood. Immigration, increases in travel and changes in consumer tastes in the developed world created the demand conditions for imported processed food, while improvements in processing methods and refrigeration technology enabled this demand to be met from developing countries. Exports of processed seafood from Viet Nam increased at an annual rate of around 15%, while other manufactured exports (notably footwear, garments and furniture) all recorded annual growth rates in excess of 20%. Between 1990 and 2010, therefore, total non-oil exports from Viet Nam expanded at an average annual rate of 19.1%, almost twice as fast as the average annual rate of developing countries (9.5%), and accounting for much of the growth in the manufacturing sector.

However, despite rapid growth rates, export growth came from a low base so that the share of Viet Nam's share of the global non-oil export market stood at only around 0.3% in 2008, while its share in the global processed seafood market was estimated at around 5%. The corresponding figure for garments was 2.6%, footwear 5.9% and furniture 2.0%, according to data from the General Statistics Office of Viet Nam (GSO) and the IMF. There is, therefore, significant capacity for continued growth.

Furthermore, being a latecomer to the region's parts and components manufacture and assembly of electronics, the share of Viet Nam in the world electronics market in 2008 was only around 0.3%, suggesting that there were significant opportunities for much greater growth and diversification in manufacturing. Reforms throughout the first decade of this century (including the Enterprises Law 2001, the New Enterprises Law 2006, the Unified Investments Law 2006 and accession to the WTO in 2007) reversed the former controls over the domestic private sector. This release of the potential of private enterprise, together with reductions in the costs of doing business, greatly improved Viet Nam's competitiveness in the Asian region, resulting in an rapid increase in FDI inflows. A significant proportion of these inflows were aimed at utilizing Viet Nam's low-cost labour in the manufacture and assembly of components in electronic equipment. The South Korean-based company Samsung, for instance, began producing mobile phones in Viet Nam in 2009, with an initial investment of US $700m. and employing around 2,300 workers. Intel Corporation, the world's largest semiconductor producer, established an assembly and testing plant in Ho Chi Minh City in 2010, with an investment of $1,000m. and a projected staff of 4,000 workers. The mobile phone company Nokia planned to start operations in Viet Nam in 2012, with an initial investment of $200m. This certainly bears out the experience of Singapore, Thailand and the Philippines, where there has been evidence of 'herd mentality' in the choice of sites by electronic multinational companies; once one site has been selected by a major producer, others tend to follow. Provided that the Vietnamese Government can deliver greater macroeconomic stability and a continued tolerance of domestic private enterprise, then the future for growth in the manufacturing and export of electronic components in Viet Nam should be highly favourable. However, in order to generate greater internal values for Vietnamese firms and to move up the value chain in production networks, significantly higher levels of investment in education and health, as well as greater incentives for innovations in products and processes, will be needed if Viet Nam is to escape from the 'middle-income trap' (see below).

POVERTY REDUCTION AND SOCIO-ECONOMIC DEVELOPMENT

As mentioned above, Viet Nam's record of economic development since the initiation of *doi moi* has been impressive. Within two decades, not only has the average income increased four-fold in nominal terms (or three-fold in purchasing power adjusted terms), the percentage of the population living on less than US $1 per day has declined from more than 60% to less than 12%. Using a different definition of poverty by measuring the costs of a consumption basket of food and non-food items, the GSO estimated that the incidence of poverty decreased from 58.1% in 1993 to 37.4% in 1998, 28.9% in 2002 and 19.5% in 2004, while the incidence of food poverty (defined as the inability to afford to consume 2,100 daily calories per person) declined from 24.9% in 1993 to 15.0% in 1998, 10.9% in 2002 and 7.4% in 2004.

The rapid rate of poverty reduction in the 1990s is widely attributed to land reforms in 1988 and again in 1993. With the decollectivization of farming in 1988, agricultural co-operatives were dismantled, and all agricultural lands (approximately 4m. ha) had to be divided among the rural households that were assigned land use rights (in effect, leaseholds) for an initial period of 15 years. The equitable manner in which these initial allocations of land use rights were assigned was crucial to poverty reduction, as agricultural land was effectively the only income-producing asset for the three-quarters of the population that made its living from farming at the time. There was no evidence to suggest that land allocation was unduly influenced by connections with the local cadres. An important factor was that reformers in the central Government were fully aware of the dangers of 'capture' by the local cadres in charge of land allocations, and hence it formed close alliances with the local farmers, who were deeply concerned about the inefficiency of collective farming. For a limited time, the central Government actively promoted farmers' organizations and used the press to expose complaints about corruption at the local level. Furthermore, while distribution of land according to educational attainments would, in theory, have further increased productivity, as educated farmers could be expected to provide better inputs of labour and management, in practice education was already fairly equitably distributed in Viet Nam under the communist regime. Hence, the marginal loss in efficiency of production was perhaps more than offset by the equitable distribution of land; the final result was growth with a significant reduction in poverty.

The second phase of land reform was initiated in 1993, when leaseholds on agricultural land were extended to 20 years for annual cropland and to 50 years for perennial cropland. Furthermore, farmers were allowed to rent out and mortgage their land, and to transfer their land use rights, including transfer by inheritance. This gave significant incentives for some farmers to expand their holdings, and to invest in dams and other means of improving the productivity of their land. However, this could also have created a class of landless poor. The fact that poverty reduction occurred equally among the landed and landless poor meant that the latter were able to take up employment opportunities created by growth in commercial crops such as coffee, rubber and fisheries. Also, the greater rate of urbanization among the rural poor at that time suggests that they were taking up jobs in the labour-intensive manufacturing that was being established in the cities. In general, even after the creation of the rural land market, very large landholdings did not emerge in Viet Nam to the extent witnessed in other countries. Perhaps the history of suppressing large landlords in the 1950s still resonated in Viet Nam and prevented the extremes of large rural landlords and the landless poor.

It was to be expected that, in comparison with the pace of the 1990s, the speed of poverty reduction would gradually decelerate in the new millennium. None the less, poverty declined by an annual average of 2.98 percentage points between 1998 and 2004, compared with a reduction of 4.14 percentage points during 1993–97. The pro-poor nature of Viet Nam's economic growth is indicated by the fact that 5.9% growth in per caput income was associated with a 7.0% reduction in poverty. This reflected the Government's commitment to equality and social inclusion, as shown in the Comprehensive Poverty Reduction and Growth Strategy (CPRGS), within which most of the foreign aid programmes were co-ordinated throughout much of the 2000s.

There is an increasing urban–rural divide, with urban poverty estimated at 3.6% in 2004 and rural poverty at 25.0%. Poverty is also strongly related to ethnicity. The rate of poverty among the Kinh and Chinese was estimated at about 13.5%, compared with a corresponding rate of more than 60% among the ethnic minorities. Food poverty among the Kinh and Chinese was virtually non-existent (at 3.5%), while the comparable rate among ethnic minorities was estimated to be more than one-third. Three-quarters of Viet Nam's ethnic minorities live in the country's northern mountainous regions or the Central Highlands. The rate of poverty has declined among the minorities living in the Mekong Delta, whereas the reverse is the case with the minorities in the Central Highlands. Population growth in the upland regions puts pressure on the environment and forestry, and this is compounded by lack of expertise and of access to social services, creating a downward poverty spiral.

School enrolment levels for ethnic minorities living in the Central Highlands and the northern mountainous region have remained low in absolute levels, although overall primary school enrolment levels among ethnic minorities nation-wide have been rising. The gap between ethnic minorities and the Kinh and Chinese population is more significant at secondary school level, where language and cultural barriers, together with a lack of infrastructure, quality teachers and suitable curriculum, are prominent. The Asian Development Bank (ADB) estimated in 2001 that in the Central Highlands up to 50% of the teachers were not fully trained, while the isolated nature of these areas limits access to public services and economic opportunities.

Approximately 23% of ethnic minority children in these areas were underweight for their age, according to 2002 data, while infant and child mortality rates were significantly higher among these groups. Coffee has been introduced in the Central Highlands as a cash crop, but the fluctuations in world coffee prices have increased the uncertainty in the livelihoods of the people living there. Furthermore, it seems that coffee crops have supported the livelihoods of the Kinh rather than the ethnic minorities. Recent initiatives have included the assignment parts of the native forests to individual household ownership and management. However, without proper skills in forest management and easy access to markets, private ownership by households per se will not be sufficient to lift these ethnic minority people out of poverty in a sustainable manner. It is clear that economic growth alone will not be enough to combat this type of regional poverty.

Female enrolment levels in secondary schooling and vocational training in remain lower than the corresponding levels among the male population. Vietnamese women also have more limited access to productive assets such as land, credit and knowledge. Female-headed households have lower average expenditure levels than male-headed households, and female representation in public life remains comparatively low. As confirmed in a report issued by the ADB in early 2006, women were estimated to account for only about 26% of public servants and about 18% of those classified as professionals. Despite rapid economic growth and increases in average incomes, the gender gap remains significant in Viet Nam.

Finally, migrants into the cities constitute the majority of the urban poor. While rapid growth of the private sector (both foreign and domestic) has led to the creation of jobs for many migrants, there is a proportion for whom such employment could be either unattainable or, indeed, unsuitable. Female migrants with little education and/or a limited skills set could be particularly vulnerable to exploitation, in the form of very low wages or other abuses. HIV/AIDS is usually more prevalent among this group. Children of migrants tend to lack educational opportunities as some provinces do not allow children of unregistered residents to attend local public schools. Health insurance availability is another issue among unregistered residents in some provinces.

Several national target programmes have been implemented in addition to the CPRGS. A significant shortcoming of these programmes is a lack of proper evaluation and assessment so that the actual outcomes of these programmes remain unknown and, perhaps more importantly, opportunities to learn from past mistakes are squandered. It is clear that quality public institutions capable of designing and delivering social services (including anti-poverty measures) will be needed in order to reduce the residual entrenched poverty in Viet Nam. Nevertheless, Viet Nam's impressive record of pro-poor growth since the 1990s has resulted in favourable socio-economic development and contributed to strong fundamentals that will, it is hoped, support future economic development.

As for Viet Nam's socio-economic indicators, life expectancy at birth in 2009 was estimated by WHO at around 72 years. Viet Nam's infant mortality rate among children under the age of five was 24 per 1,000 live births in 2009. These indicators are considerably more favourable than those found in neighbouring Cambodia, Laos and Myanmar. According to UN population projections, Viet Nam's population is at the more youthful and productive end of the spectrum, having recovered from the disastrous effects of the Viet Nam War. The median age in Viet Nam was estimated at around 25 years in 2005, and this was projected to increase to about 34 years by 2025, and further to 42 years by 2050. Indeed, in 2005 Viet Nam entered the so-called 'demographic window', a situation in which the proportion of the population of working age is dominant. The ratio of children and the elderly to adults of working age (i.e. the total dependency ratio) is expected to decline (to 44.15%) until 2025, before rising again (to 57.23%) by 2050. Hence, by the middle of this century Viet Nam can expect to have approximately two working age adults to each dependant. By way of comparison, China entered its demographic window in 1990, after which very rapid economic growth ensued.

Viet Nam's relatively favourable demographic window currently means that it can expect increases in labour supply, and in aggregate savings and investment, which are positive signs for continued economic growth. Indeed, in view of the very high costs of pensions and health care associated with an ageing population (not to mention the time needed to put in place superannuation and health care policies), sustained growth of some 8%–9% annually appears necessary. The imperative of continued rapid growth into the next two decades makes it all the more essential that Viet Nam overcomes its current macroeconomic challenges and addresses vulnerabilities relating to its financial sector as soon as possible. Otherwise, once inflationary expectations became entrenched, the costs in terms of growth forgone would be much higher.

FINANCIAL SECTOR DEVELOPMENTS

Developments in Viet Nam's financial sector have implications for its short-term macroeconomic stability as well as its longer-term efficiency and growth. It is also important to bear in mind that the penetration rate of Viet Nam's banks and other institutions in the formal market is estimated to be only about 10% of Vietnamese businesses and households; hence, informal finance obviously plays a significant role, particularly in rural areas. This section examines the impact of recent developments in the formal sector on informal finance in Viet Nam.

The three major market-orientated reforms in Viet Nam's formal financial sector have been: the deregulation of domestic interest rates (on both dông- and foreign currency-denominated deposits and loans) during the period 1996–2002; the decision in May 2005 to restructure the country's five SOCBs with a view to privatizing them by 2010 (although at mid-2011 only two—namely the Joint Stock Commercial Bank for Foreign Trade of Viet Nam (Vietcombank) and Vietnam Joint Stock Commercial Bank for Industry and Trade (VietinBank)—had successfully sold shares to private investors; see below); and the opening of the sector to wholly foreign-owned banks, in accordance with Viet Nam's commitment to the WTO, in 2007. Meanwhile, Viet Nam operates a pegged exchange rate regime supported by capital controls.

Viet Nam's formal financial sector has expanded and diversified rapidly in recent years. Bank deposits and loans, as a percentage of GDP, doubled from around 45% in 2002 to more than 90% in 2007. Between 2006 and 2007 bank deposits and loans increased from around 75% of GDP to over 90% of GDP, indicating the beginnings of a credit boom, and there was evidence of increased provision of a wider range of financial services as the economy developed and more households and businesses began to engage with the formal banking sector. The local share market capitalization grew from less than 1% of GDP in 2002 to around 6% in 2005, to 23% in 2006 and further to a remarkable 43% of GDP in 2007, before declining to 15% in 2008 as a result of the onset of the global economic crisis. The bond market and pension and insurance funds have been established in the new millennium, but remain underdeveloped by regional standards.

According to the SBV, at mid-2011 Viet Nam had four major SOCBs and one minor SOCB, 37 joint stock banks, 48 foreign bank branches, five joint venture banks, and one policy bank, namely the Vietnam Bank for Social Policies (VBSP—formerly the Vietnam Bank for the Poor). The SOCBs still comprise more than one-half of Viet Nam's market, both in terms of deposits and loans, although their dominance was significantly reduced from 70%–80% in 2001 to 50%–60% in 2007. The SOEs have traditionally relied on borrowings from the SOCBs and, following the Asian financial crisis of 1997/98, the SOCBs were heavily laden with the non-performing loans of the SOEs. Concerted efforts were made in 2005 to improve the non-performing loans situation of the SOCBs and to recapitalize them with a view to their privatization in subsequent years. Formal policy lending by the SOCBs was also halted, and other policy banks were established for this purpose.

However, in reality, the SOCBs continued to favour lending to SOEs for a number of reasons: first, the assets of the SOCBs are considered state assets, the loss of which in Viet Nam is considered a capital offence, and thus loan officers tend to prefer lending to SOEs (transferring state assets from one state entity to another) rather than take the risk of lending to the private sector; second, the private sector still has difficulties of access to urban land use rights to be utilized as collateral for loans, while SOEs generally do not have such problems; and third, SOCBs are not allowed to lend to businesses with a track record of less than two years, supposedly for prudential regulatory reasons. This effectively prevents the provision of credit to start-up companies, which are often the entities most in need of financing.

It is, therefore, difficult to envisage significant changes in the loan portfolios of SOCBs, even if the majority of them were to be privatized, except perhaps if the fear of capital punishment being imposed on bank loan officers was removed or at least diminished. As it is, there appears to be little competition among the SOCBs, with their deposit and loan rates moving in tandem and their business strategies showing little variation. As mentioned above, the market shares of SOCBs have been declining since they were forced by the Government to rationalize their non-performing loans, and the spare capacity has been taken up by the joint stock banks.

In principle, growth of joint stock banks should be a good sign for the domestic private sector, as traditionally the majority of their lending has been provided to households and private businesses. However, in reality, a lax regulatory environment meant that within a very short space of time 11 rural credit institutions were given banking licences in urban areas where demand for credit was growing rapidly. This resulted in credit growth reaching almost 95% in 2007. Funds were invested in the speculative real estate and share markets, resulting in 'overheating', with inflation reaching 28% in the first quarter of 2008. The subsequent monetary tightening brought about the inevitable collapse, with share prices declining by more than 60%.

In addition to granting bank licences to the rural credit institutions, the SBV also came under pressure to grant licences to a number of entities effectively owned and controlled by large SOEs, which saw the rapid expansion of the financial sector as a way of making quick speculative profits as well as providing yet another conduit (in addition to SOCBs) for channelling the country's savings to the large SOEs. Both of these developments resulted in rapid growth of the joint stock banks and of credit conditions. This weakened Viet Nam's banking sector and added to the vulnerabilities of the macroeconomy (see below).

By mid-2011 five foreign banks had entered the market as wholly foreign-owned subsidies since Viet Nam's accession to the WTO in January 2007. They have taken market share away from the SOCBs and put further pressure on the latter to be privatized, a process that to date has been slow. Only around 10% each of Vietcombank and VietinBank had been sold by mid-2011. In the case of Vietcombank, the SBV officially held 90.72% of the shares, with the remainder divided between domestic shareholders (6.36%) and foreign shareholders (2.93%). The Government was listed as holding 89.23% of shares in VietinBank, with 6.97% held by the domestic private sector, 2.41% by the bank's trade union and only 1.39% by foreign investors.

Viet Nam has two regulated stock markets, one in Ho Chi Minh City and the other in Hanoi. The market capitalization in 2008 was 15% of GDP, having decreased from around 43% at the height of the market in 2007. The two stock markets are highly speculative. In 2007 20 companies formed the bulk of the listing on the markets, with price-earning (P/E) ratios of around 73, compared with average P/E ratios of between 10 and 20 in other South-East Asian markets. The State Securities Commission of Vietnam (SSC), a division within the Ministry of Finance, is formally responsible for the regulation and supervision of the two markets under the Securities Law (2007), supported by the amended Investment Law (2006) and the revised Enterprises Law (2006). As with many other commercial laws in Viet Nam (for example, the Bankruptcy Law), the actual impact depends on the operational effectiveness of the associated courts and judiciary. What is clear is that transparency and disclosures on the part of the listed companies are currently poor, and there is an urgent need for the Securities Law and associated public institutions to work effectively in the context of Vietnamese society.

Viet Nam's bond market (as measured by the ratio of outstanding bonds to GDP) more than doubled from about 7% of GDP in 2003 to around 15% in 2008. However, this is still very small compared with a regional average of around 63% of GDP. Furthermore, the market is fragmented because of significant management issues. First, Vietnamese government borrowings are sourced domestically and internationally in roughly the same proportions. However, there is not, and never has been, any agency that manages the total debt, resulting in small issues of varying maturities, thereby rendering it difficult for the development of criteria for government bonds against which other types of debt could be benchmarked. Second, there has been no co-ordination between government borrowing requirements and cash management. To use government cash flows efficiently, shorter-term treasury bills (shorter than the existing 364 days) would be needed, and these would have to be co-ordinated with the bills issued by the SBV itself. Third, there are no clear guidelines for the management of private sector borrowing, with the result that only a few large SOEs have been able to raise funds from abroad, with the implicit understanding that these would be guaranteed by the Government.

These issues have been recognized and were to have been addressed through the process of a Public Debt Law. However, resolving these issues in practice would require significant co-operation among a number of public agencies, including the Ministry of Finance, the SSC, the General Department of Taxation and the SBV. Meanwhile, these structural weaknesses add to the challenges of macroeconomic stabilization in the short term, as well as limiting potential sources of finance for Vietnamese industries in the longer term (see below).

Insurance and pension funds in Viet Nam are currently very small and underdeveloped. A major issue hampering their development is the lack of high-yielding, good-quality, long-term investments in the Vietnamese currency. The problems with the Government and the private sector bond market discussed above are a case in point. Until the prudential regulatory framework succeeds in achieving increased transparency and improved corporate governance of Viet Nam's listed companies, the lack of reputable longer-term investments increases the chances of speculative short-term asset 'bubbles' and hampers the efficient use of capital, leading to sub-optimal growth in the longer term.

In theory, financial institutions in the formal sector have lower borrowing costs than those in the informal sector, owing to the former's established reputation in the market. On the other hand, they have higher costs arising from the monitoring of borrowers because lenders in the informal market tend to have more intimate knowledge of their borrowers. Therefore, a welfare-enhancing solution would be for institutions in the formal market to lend funds, sourced at lower cost, to entities in the informal market for them, in turn, to lend to borrowers. In this way, borrowers would benefit from the lower borrowing cost of formal lenders and the lower monitoring costs of the informal lenders. However, there is reason to believe that developments in Viet Nam's formal financial market have had a negative impact on its informal financial sector, rather than resulted in co-operation with it.

Much of the formal market in competition with informal finance occurs in two institutions: the Vietnam Bank for Agriculture and Rural Development (VBARD—one of Viet Nam's five SOCBs) and the VBSP. The smaller joint stock banks do not appear to be major protagonists in this field, as suggested by their desire to move out of the countryside to urban areas from 2007. The VBARD lends on commercial terms, requires collateral on most loans, and can be expected to deal with relatively large businesses in the rural areas. By contrast, the VBSP (formerly the Vietnam Bank for the Poor, founded in 1995) was established specifically for policy lending and is exempt from regulations governing SOCBs as well as those governing microfinance institutions. It sources its funds variously from the state budget, taxes on SOCB deposits, and borrowings from the SBV and the State Treasury, as well as from the Vietnam Postal Service Savings Company, which makes use of post offices around the country to tap savings in rural areas for policy and other lending. The VBSP lends directly to small businesses and to poor households through savings and credit groups in the microfinance model. It is therefore in direct competition with informal lenders. However, as the VBSP is not operating under competitive market pressures, it would not be surprising if it did not attempt to co-operate with lenders in the informal market. Indeed, a World Bank study published in 2008 found no signs of any particular co-operation with lenders in the informal sector. This is unfortunate as increased linkages in the supply of credit between the formal and informal markets could help overall monetary and stabilization policies, as the latter's impact is mainly on the formal market, with repercussions for the informal sector. This is becoming particularly relevant as macroeconomic challenges threaten to undermine continued rapid growth in the coming decade.

MACROECONOMIC TURBULENCE (2008–)

Since a period of hyperinflation in 1986–88, during which inflation reached 600% and food shortages were widespread, Viet Nam's macroeconomy remained under control, with inflation kept mostly within single digits, until 2007. This allowed the authorities to pursue pro-growth policies, with poverty reduction and continuous improvement in living standards crucial to the perceived legitimacy of one-party communist rule. This stability was abruptly ended in the first quarter of 2008 when inflation increased to 28%. Concerns about the viability of the domestic banking sector and Viet Nam's external position were also heightened. In other words, in the first half of 2008, before the collapse of the US-based financial services company Lehman Brothers in September of that year and the onset of the global financial crisis, Viet Nam was at risk of a banking and currency crisis.

The origins of this episode can be found in the euphoria created by Viet Nam's hosting of the Asia-Pacific Economic Cooperation (APEC) forum in 2006, followed by its accession to the WTO in January 2007. With Viet Nam's international profile raised by these two events, foreign capital inflows increased from around 5%–6% of GDP to 25% of GDP in 2007. Remittances from Vietnamese resident abroad also increased, to around 9% of GDP in 2007, from about 6.0%–6.5% in earlier years. With an exchange rate pegged predominantly to the US dollar, the SBV intervened actively in the foreign exchange market, buying US dollars and selling dông, in order to prevent the latter from appreciating. International reserves rose by US $10,000m. in 12 months to reach $21,100m. by the end of 2007. In a fully functioning market economy with well-established bond markets, such a sudden increase in liquidity could have been addressed by the central bank's sale of its stock of government bonds through open-market operations, in order to absorb the excess liquidity. However, owing to the grossly underdeveloped nature of Viet Nam's bond market, the challenge of dealing with such large inflows of capital was overwhelming.

Credit growth among the joint stock banks reached almost 95% in 2007, with significant proportions of the loans being provided to the large SOEs and being invested in the then rising real estate and stock markets. Therefore, a loss of control over the money supply and SOE spending, compounded by a failure to supervise the joint stock banks, resulted in a significant 'overheating' of the economy in 2008. Inflation was approaching 30%, and the current account deficit reached 11.5% of GDP in that year.

Not surprisingly, market sentiment turned negative and capital began to leave the country, resulting in a net outflow of about US $2,000m. by the second quarter of 2008. Government action eventually helped to stabilize the macroeconomic situation. The measures implemented were largely of an administrative nature, including the SBV's raising of reserve requirements and reduction of credit limits of banks on the one hand, and the Ministry of Finance restricting SOEs' spending to 'core' spending. The policy interest rate was raised, and the dông outside the official market (that is, the dông in the parallel or 'grey' market) depreciated to some 15% below the official rate.

These administrative measures appeared to have been effective, at least in the short term, and by September 2008 inflationary pressures were easing and the dông in the parallel market was trading closer to the official bands. Declining global oil and fuel prices, as a result of reduced activity owing to the global financial crisis, also helped to ease the pressure. However, this episode of instability exposed the vulnerabilities of the Vietnamese economy, including the grossly underdeveloped debt market, the prudential laxity of the SBV vis-à-vis the joint stock banks and of the Ministry of Finance vis-à-vis the SOEs. The delayed response to this crisis also reflected a lack of professional competence on the part of these crucial macroeconomic institutions, concealing a fundamental lack of political will to reform the large SOEs. Although Viet Nam had formally reached the status of a middle-income country, the Government was seemingly unable to manage the economy in a market-friendly manner and in the increasingly globalized context in which the country found itself.

Nevertheless, in response to the onset of the global financial crisis in September 2008, Viet Nam's reprieve from a banking and currency crisis encouraged the Government to act to sustain growth in view of expected declines in export demand. Initial action took the form of reversing the tight monetary policy and reducing the policy interest rate from 14.0% to 8.5%, while simultaneously decreasing the reserve requirement on dông deposits from 11% to 6%. A US $960m. programme of fiscal stimulus measures was announced in December 2008, which included additional monetary easing: for example, a further reduction in the policy interest rate to 7%, a four-percentage-point interest rate subsidy on domestic currency loans, and another decrease in the reserve requirement to 3%.

The stimulus programme had the unfortunate impact of renewing the pressure on the dông throughout 2009. The pressure did not emanate from the outflow of short-term foreign capital, most of which had left the country by mid-2008, nor did it come from the balance of payments deficit, which, although unusually large at some 10% of GDP, was easily covered by FDI and foreign aid inflows. Significantly, the pressure was due to very large, unidentified 'errors and omissions', which were equivalent to more than 13% of GDP. Experience of financial crises in general, and of the 1997/98 Asian financial crisis in particular, indicate that this type of unidentified outflow tends to be associated with capital flight by residents, in the form of gold and US dollar holdings outside the banking system. This observation is supported by a flurry of activity in the domestic gold market. Indeed, the so-called 'dollar shortage' at the time was, in fact, indicative of an unwillingness on the part of Vietnamese individuals and enterprises to retain dông holdings. With the SBV intervening strongly to prevent the dông from depreciating, international reserves declined by 30% in the first nine months of 2009, from US $23,000m. to $16,000m.

Uncertainties associated with the global financial crisis certainly played a part in the increased awareness of risk on the part of the Vietnamese public. In addition, perception of the weaknesses associated with the balance of payments and international reserves position was renewed and perhaps intensified through the recent experience of Viet Nam's mini-crisis in the first half of 2008. In the event, the dông depreciated by 6.5% on the parallel market in October–November 2009, and the Government was forced to implement a second series of stabilization policy measures. In late November the Government announced that all stimulus measures, including the interest rate subsidy, would expire on schedule, and the SBV was told to begin tightening monetary policy again. The dông was devalued by 5.5%, and temporary stability was restored as the exchange rate on the parallel market again moved back to within the official band. Furthermore, by mid-2010 it had become clear that Viet Nam, with a growth rate of 5.3% in 2009, while lagging behind China and India, had withstood the global financial crisis better than most other member countries of the Association of Southeast Asian Nations (ASEAN).

Despite this, market perception was still poor. Confusion on the part of market participants and domestic investors regarding the oscillations in government policy was understandable. This was compounded by the failure to make publicly available important information such as the level of international reserves. Market uncertainties were not helped either by the proximity of the exchange rate to the lower levels of the official band, and the inflation rate and the current account balance being close to 'safety thresholds'. There was clearly an urgent need for significantly better management of monetary and fiscal policy and improved communication to the market of policy stances. All this required the modernization of macroeconomic institutions.

Viet Nam was ranked 68th for overall global competitiveness in the Global Competitiveness Report for 2007/08 published by the World Economic Forum (WEF), but declined to 70th position in 2008/09 and further to 75th in 2009/10. Concerns over macroeconomic management appeared to be a major factor in this decline. Viet Nam's ranking for macroeconomic stability declined from 51st in 2007/08 to 112th place in 2009/10. Its overall ranking improved to 59th in 2010/11, but slipped back to 65th in the 2011/12 report.

The market's concern about macroeconomic management was vindicated in that, as soon as there were some signs of a return to stability in the second quarter of 2010, the Government began sending clear signals to the SBV to lower interest rates again in order to promote growth. This time, the SBV left policy rates unchanged, but it did ease liquidity in order to bring down the overnight interbank interest rate.

Throughout 2010 market sentiment moved against the dông. In addition to the aforementioned weaknesses on the external front, increasing commodity prices resulting from the very high demand for food and minerals from the emerging market economies (principally China) again put pressure on inflation. Furthermore, worries about European sovereign debt led to a focus on the state of the Vietnamese Government's public finances—in particular, the contingent liabilities associated with the borrowings of the large SOEs. All this culminated in the near-bankruptcy and US $600m. debt default of Vinashin, a huge shipbuilding, real estate and financial conglomerate, in late 2010. So politically charged was this development that the personal standing of Prime Minister Nguyen Tan Dung within the Communist Party of Viet Nam was called into question. The macroeconomic instability of recent years did seem to have caught the attention of the policymakers. Action was taken shortly after the Party Congress in January 2011, beginning with a large devaluation of the dông (by 9% of the central rate, plus a reduction of the band around the central rate from 3% to 1%). This was followed three weeks later by a new resolution (Resolution 11) intended to shift the focus away from economic growth towards macroeconomic stabilization. This was to be done by tightening monetary policy, reducing fiscal spending, continuing with reform of the SOEs and developing social security nets.

The initial consequence of the large devaluation (the fourth in the 18 months) was a further weakening of the dông, as expectation of a spiral of inflation/devaluation led to further capital flight into gold and US dollars. Subsequent administrative edicts to ban the trading of gold and dollars in the open market, while emphasizing the determination of the Government, could have served to drive such activities underground. However, raising the policy interest rate on four separate occasions over a four-month period, increasing it from 9% to 14%, as well as reducing the target credit growth to below 20% per year, did have some impact, and the parallel exchange rate began trading at close to the official band. Nevertheless, the challenge was far from over, as evidenced by yet another interest rate increase (to 15%) in the last week of May 2011. However, this was reversed in early July, with the interest rate being reduced to 14%, resulting once again in the sending of mixed signals to the market. Viet Nam has one of the highest credit to GDP ratios in the region (its stock of credit being equivalent to more than 120% of its GDP). In view of the possibility of the inflation rate reaching 20% in 2011 (driven partly by increases in the administered prices of fuel and utilities), it would take greater and more sustained efforts to curb inflationary pressures. A clear mandate from the Government to the SBV to attain certain targeted levels of inflation and international reserves would be helpful.

In the fiscal area, it was reported that public investment was to be reduced by 7.4% in 2011, but guidance was badly needed on a trajectory of future government spending that would be consistent with macroeconomic stability. Furthermore, the important Ministries of Finance and of Planning and Investment need to be free from political interference to conduct proper cost-benefit analysis of public investment projects, and to eliminate those that are uneconomical and wasteful, even if they are supported by powerful political interests.

With regard to the SOEs, the Ministry of Finance has attempted to set quotas for their foreign borrowings and to require them to seek approvals from the SBV in individual cases. This was no doubt a reaction to the Vinashin debacle. Any increase in public oversight and improved governance of the large state-owned conglomerates is a move in the right direction, but the authority and operational independence of the SBV will be tested.

As for the development of social security nets, little progress had been made by 2011, and it is clear that significant challenges will need to be addresses if tangible results are to be achieved. For instance, Viet Nam has various forms of health insurance schemes, but there is evidence that sick people have a much greater incentive (and are allowed) to join these schemes than healthy members of the population. This is known as 'adverse selection', and unless these issues of design are addressed the Government's aim of universal health insurance coverage will remain unattainable. Even if adverse selection is addressed, considerable government financial resources will be needed, rendering it imperative that the Ministry of Finance be able effectively and efficiently to harness and manage government revenue and spending.

THE ISSUE OF THE 'MIDDLE-INCOME TRAP'

Even if the challenges of macroeconomic stability are adequately met, rapid long-term growth through industrialization is not necessarily assured. So far, Viet Nam's industrialization and development have depended significantly on the opening of the economy to international trade and investment on the one hand, and the release of the potential of the domestic private sector on the other. As noted above, the second phase of economic reforms in the new millennium has enabled Vietnamese companies to reach the lower rung of regional production networks (electronic components assembly), and has encouraged foreign firms such as Samsung and Nokia to to begin operations in the country. However, this bottom rung relies principally on low wage costs and would not generate the income growth necessary to propel Viet Nam from middle-income to higher-income status.

If the experience of other Asian countries is to serve as an example, the next stage would be for Vietnamese firms to manufacture those parts and components, but essentially under contract to foreign firms. This would allow for the transfer of some technology from the foreign firms, as well as ensuring proper quality control and enabling the development of supporting industries within Viet Nam. This development has essentially brought Malaysia and Thailand to their present stage of economic development: solid middle-income countries that are unable to break through the 'glass ceiling', unable to follow the examples of Taiwan and South Korea where firms have been able successfully to create their own brand name products to become multinationals in their own right, establishing their own investments in other countries of the very dynamic Asian region.

Latecomers to the industrialization process such as Viet Nam are required to address a number of additional challenges in developing effective and sustainable policies for their industries. First, they are locked into international integration (such as with the WTO) early in the process so that they are not able to give any overt protection to their industries in the early stages of industrialization. Second, their own private sectors are very underdeveloped so that they lack the industrial complexes of Japan, the *chaebol* (conglomerates) of South Korea, or the Chinese or Indian merchant networks. Third, they typically have weak public institutions and administrative capabilities. Consequently, they are unable to initiate effective policies to support their private firms, such as industrial clustering as has been the case in Singapore; in that country the Government worked with domestic companies to retain skills and knowledge passed on by foreign investors, in order to improve overall productivity, as well as to rise up the value chain of distribution, marketing, product design and research and development. Perhaps it was in reaction to these challenges that the Vietnamese Government erroneously allowed the large SOEs to develop into conglomerates under the slogan of having a 'market economy with socialist orientation'.

However, as noted above, the forays of large industrial SOEs into the financial sector (in the establishment of new joint stock banks) have the unfortunate result of destabilizing the banking sector and the macroeconomic environment as well as adding to real estate 'bubbles'. The contingent liability for the Government associated with the foreign borrowings of these state-owned conglomerates is a risk that Viet Nam can ill afford. The near-collapse of Vinashin in late 2010 was a clear indication that industrial policy along the lines of huge state-owned conglomerates is not the way forward for Viet Nam.

In addition to the three challenges for latecomers to the industrialization process, Viet Nam appears to be unusual among Asian countries in its large dependence on FDI. Of course, newly industrializing economies lack domestic savings and hence are reliant on foreign savings (in the form of FDI) to fund the industrialization and development process. However, in the context of regional industrialization, Viet Nam is notable for its reliance on FDI. In the two decades since the initiation of *doi moi*, FDI as a percentage of Viet Nam's annual GDP has averaged almost 6%.

Despite such a high level of dependence on FDI, there is evidence of significant inefficiency in the use of capital in Viet Nam. The incremental capital-output ratio (ICOR), defined as the increase in capital needed to generate an extra unit of output, has steadily increased in recent years, with sizeable rises during 2007–09. The slowing of growth as a result of the global financial crisis and Viet Nam's macroeconomic turbulence could have accounted for these increases. The huge expansion of credit, which inevitably led to poor loan assessment and lending practices, compounded the problem of low-performing investments. Even so, in the early to mid-1990s Viet Nam's ICOR was relatively low while the contribution of total factor productivity was high. This indicates that growth during this period was as a result of increased productivity (compared with the years of central planning) with relatively little use of capital. As Viet Nam's ICOR has increased in recent years, the contribution of total factor productivity to growth has declined and the contribution of capital to growth has increased, indicating that growth was predominantly driven by investment and capital was used inefficiently, for which there are several reasons.

First, Viet Nam's grossly underdeveloped capital markets not only create difficulties in macroeconomic management in the short run, but also mean that capital is poorly allocated in the longer term. Indeed, inefficient utilization of capital is a corollary of poorly functioning capital markets. Second, although the SOEs' share in industrial production declined from 50% to 25% between 1995 and 2008, they still commanded more than one-half of the country's funds available for investment in the latter year. As a result of their ability to access land as collateral, SOEs still have privileged access to finance from the SOCBs, despite the cessation of formal policy lending. Furthermore, the move of the large SOEs into the financial sector in 2007–08 has provided an additional conduit through which investment funds are channelled into the state sector, and it is well known that the SOEs in capital-intensive industries are generally inefficient in their use of capital. Third, public investment decisions seem to be made with the minimum of professionalism. Cost-benefit analyses are apparently present in public investment documentations, but the cost and revenue projections are often not realistic, with politics dominating economics in these decisions. For example, it seems obviously inefficient for Viet Nam to have as many as 20 seaports along its coastline; nor does it make sense to have a high-speed passenger train linking Hanoi and Ho Chi Minh City when the rail freight system is badly in need of repair. Poor public investment decisions are of particular concern as Viet Nam's infrastructure has not kept pace with rapid growth, despite having invested around 10% of GDP for the best part of a decade. The ADB estimates that infrastructure investment would need to increase to 11%–12% of GDP in order for Viet Nam to achieve its goal of becoming an industrialized economy by 2020. Thus, investment in physical infrastructure need to be as efficient as possible, as does public investment more generally; wasteful public investment projects divert funds away from investment in health and education, which is essential for developing the necessary human capital to enable Vietnamese firms to move up the value chain in the global supply networks.

In view of the difficulties experienced by Malaysia and Thailand in implementing their respective industrial policies, it remains unclear as to which model of industrial development is the most appropriate for Viet Nam. However, from the viewpoint of short-term macroeconomic management, longer-term industrial development, and development of social policies, it seems evident that the building of strong public institutions with effective administrative capability should form the focus of Viet Nam's economic reforms over the coming decade.

PUBLIC INSTITUTIONS

State Bank of Viet Nam

The experience of other ASEAN countries suggests that the quality of the central bank is of great significance during times of macroeconomic turbulence. The SBV has yet to become a truly modern central bank, and the macroeconomic turbulence since 2008 has revealed the central bank to be slow in initiating policy changes, poor in communicating such changes to the market and weak in its role as prudential supervisor of the banking sector. Furthermore, although in a formal sense the SBV has been found to be comparable to its regional counterparts in terms of legal and political independence, independence in an operational sense remains seriously lacking. This is not surprising as monetary policy formulation requires technical ability to forecast economic trends and experience to judge the timing of policy instruments. In other words, these tasks require a core of well-trained and experienced economists, particularly those working in policy research and formulation. The SBV has begun a serious programme of upgrading its staff through education in Western universities, and this constraint could be resolved within a matter of years.

The conflict of interest between the SBV as owner and as supervisor of the SOCBs needs to be resolved. The SBV needs to be extricated from the boards of the SOCBs, and shares in the latter sold to foreign banks, as has happened in China. The remaining shares in these commercial banks owned by the State should then be transferred to the State Capital Investment Corporation (SCIC), which is tasked with managing the State's capital in a profitable manner. In this way, the SBV can exercise prudential supervision over the commercial banking sector without being compromised.

In accordance with its WTO obligations, Viet Nam has opened up to wholly foreign-owned banking subsidiaries, and by mid-2011 there were five such banking subsidiaries in the market. It is crucial that the SBV be the sole supervisor of banks in Viet Nam and to be seen as such by the supervising authorities of the foreign banks in their countries of domicile. Close liaison between the SBV and foreign supervisory agencies is also necessary: an incident involving a foreign subsidiary could be relatively minor as far as the headquarter country is concerned, but could generate systemic risks in Viet Nam. Whether the foreign subsidiary should be rescued, and by whom, becomes an important issue. In this regard, the relationship between the SBV and other financial supervising authorities in Viet Nam (such as the National Financial Supervision Committee) needs to be clarified.

Ministry of Finance

Viet Nam scored 14 out of 100 in the 2010 Open Budget Index (published by the International Budget Partnership) which, although an improvement on 2 out of 100 in 2006, was a disappointing result. This index is not surprising given the myriad of different and incompatible management and accounting systems being used within the Ministry of Finance. Hence, fiscal plans are often based on unreliable data, resulting in wide variations between planned targets and actual outcomes. Given that Viet Nam is already highly dependent on foreign capital inflows to fund its significant current account deficit, the experience of South Korea's Ministry of Strategy and Finance is instructive. In the 1990s this Ministry failed to consolidate the balance sheets of South Korean banking subsidiaries operating abroad; as a result, it under-reported South Korea's total external liabilities because these subsidiaries were taking deposits in foreign countries. As Viet Nam now operates in an increasingly globalized financial market, the reform of its Ministry of Finance's internal accounting and management system would appear to be a priority in maintaining the confidence of investors.

The need for the development of an effective government bond market has been examined above. Private sector bonds, as well as securities, are very important funding channels for Vietnamese firms to move up the value chain and enable the country to escape the 'middle-income trap'. Currently, the private bond market is grossly underdeveloped, while the stock markets are highly speculative. This indicates that the regulatory functions of the SSC need to be strengthened within the Ministry of Finance.

Public Access to Quality Data

Public institutions, defined more broadly, include the publication of reliable data on the economy and the country more generally. Important data such as the country's level of international reserves should be made publicly available so as to inform market participants and help anchor expectations. Furthermore, the adoption of international standards of accounting and auditing, including the definition of non-performing loans in banks as well as definitions in the financial accounts of private sector companies, would help to improve transparency and accountability, resulting in greater public confidence in public and private institutions. As Viet Nam rises through the ranks of a middle-income country, significantly better communication between the market and the State will be necessary in order to minimize speculation and concentrate the country's efforts in productive endeavours.

Public Administration Reform

Unlike the situation in many other developing countries, the number of people employed in Viet Nam's civil service, at around 500,000, is not very substantial in relation to the size of the population. In principle, therefore, it should not be too difficult to increase public sector salaries in order to attract better-qualified staff, while ensuring that costs are kept within affordable limits.

However, in practice, there are at least two problems. First, by an historical legacy many civil servants have been provided with housing as part of their remuneration. A concerted effort has been made to find a monetary equivalent for such salary 'packages', with the intention that the civil servants could then rent their apartments back from the Government. One issue has been the lack of strata titles to those apartments occupied by civil servants. The legal and practical aspects of this have yet to be resolved. Second, civil service salaries in Viet Nam are unusually low and are regarded as more of a retainer than as full compensation. Civil servants are expected to earn additional pay through working in projects, funded either by foreign aid or by domestic development budgets. While this custom means that well-qualified specialists have no difficulty in earning a great deal of extra money, ordinary civil servants are very poorly paid and this creates an environment in which low-level corruption has thrived.

These issues need to be resolved and public administration reform must be accelerated if Viet Nam is to develop strong public institutions that will enable the country to continue rapid economic development, to address remaining areas poverty and to move successfully beyond the 'middle-income trap'.

CONCLUSION

Viet Nam's spectacular transition from being a poor developing country to middle-income status within the space of a quarter of a century has been accompanied by the transformation from a centrally planned and closed economy to a more market-orientated, open economy. Rapid economic growth has also been accompanied by a significant reduction in poverty, leaving the country with strong socio-economic and demographic advantages for continued growth in the coming decades.

However, this positive image has been marred, at least in the short term, by the macroeconomic turbulence that began to emerge in 2008 and continued in mid-2011. In the longer term, inefficiencies in the use of capital need to be addressed. Failure to meet this challenge could result in Viet Nam remaining mired in the lower end of the middle-income range, unable to realize its full potential as indicated by its fundamentally favourable attributes.

The strengthening of public institutions, beginning with the SBV and the Ministry of Finance, could be an effective way of meeting Viet Nam's current development challenges. Effective macroeconomic institutions capable of formulating appropriate fiscal and monetary policies, and of communicating the Government's policy stance to the market would help to restore investor confidence in the short term and assist in the development of workable financial markets, resulting in the longer term in efficient capital use. This could then be followed by the consolidation of institutions in charge of the formulation and delivery of social policies and alleviation of the poverty that remains entrenched in some part of the country. Political will and leadership will certainly be needed in the coming years to embark on this third phase of economic reform in order to realize Viet Nam's goal of attaining the status of a modern industrialized economy by 2020.

Statistical Survey

Sources (unless otherwise stated): General Statistics Office of Viet Nam, 2 Hoang Van Thu, Ba Dinh District, Hanoi; tel. (4) 7332997; e-mail banbientap@gso.gov.vn; internet www.gso.gov.vn; Communist Party of Viet Nam, 1 Hoang Van Thu, Hanoi; e-mail cpv@hn.vnn.vn; internet www.cpv.org.vn.

Area and Population

AREA, POPULATION AND DENSITY

Area (sq km)	331,051*
Population (census results)	
1 April 1999	76,323,173
1 April 2009	
Males	42,413,143
Females	43,433,854
Total	85,846,997
Population (UN estimates at mid-year)†	
2010	87,848,445
2011	88,791,995
Density (per sq km) at mid-2011	268.2

* 127,819 sq miles.

† Source: UN, *World Population Prospects: The 2010 Revision*.

POPULATION BY AGE AND SEX

(UN estimates at mid-2011)

	Males	Females	Total
0–14	10,548,698	10,069,314	20,618,012
15–64	31,143,912	31,676,460	62,820,372
65 and over	2,212,890	3,140,721	5,353,611
Total	43,905,500	44,886,495	88,791,995

Source: UN, *World Population Prospects: The 2010 Revision*.

ADMINISTRATIVE DIVISIONS

(2009 census)

	Area (sq km)	Population ('000)	Density (per sq km)
Red River Delta	21,063.1	19,584.3	930
Hanoi	3,344.6	6,451.9	1,929
Vinh Phuc	1,231.8	999.8	812
Bac Ninh	822.7	1,024.5	1,245
Quang Ninh	6,099.0	1,145.0	188
Hai Duong	1,650.2	1,705.1	1,033
Haiphong	1,522.1	1,837.2	1,207
Hung Yen	923.5	1,127.9	1,221
Thai Binh	1,567.4	1,781.8	1,137
Ha Nam	860.2	784.1	912
Nam Dinh	1,652.5	1,828.1	1,106
Ninh Binh	1,389.1	899.0	647
North East	57,893.9	8,331.4	144
Ha Giang	7,945.8	724.5	91
Cao Bang	6,724.6	507.2	75
Bac Kan	4,859.4	293.8	60
Tuyen Quang	5,870.4	724.8	123
Lao Cai	6,383.9	614.6	96
Yen Bai	6,899.5	740.4	107
Thai Nguyen	3,526.2	1,123.1	319
Lang Son	8,323.8	732.5	88
Bac Giang	3,827.8	1,554.1	406
Phu Tho	3,532.5	1,316.4	373
North West	37,444.8	2,722.1	73
Dien Bien	9,562.9	490.3	51
Lai Chau	9,112.3	370.5	41
Son La	14,174.4	1,076.1	76
Hoa Binh	4,595.2	785.2	171
North Central Coast	51,524.6	10,070.2	195
Thanh Hoa	11,133.4	3,400.6	305
Nghe An	16,490.7	2,912.0	177
Ha Tinh	6,025.6	1,227.0	204
Quand Binh	8,065.3	844.9	105
Quang Tri	4,747.0	598.3	126
Thua Thien-Hué	5,062.6	1,087.4	215
South Central Coast	33,192.3	7,032.8	212
Da Nang	1,283.4	887.4	691
Quang Nam	10,438.4	1,422.3	136
Quang Ngai	5,152.7	1,216.8	236
Binh Dinh	6,039.6	1,486.5	246
Phu Yen	5,060.6	862.2	170
Khanh Hoa	5,217.6	1,157.6	222
Central Highlands	54,640.6	5,115.1	94
Kon Tum	9,690.5	430.1	44
Gia Lai	15,536.9	1,274.4	82
Dak Lak	13,125.4	1,733.6	132
Dak Nong	6,515.6	489.4	75
Lam Dong	9,772.2	1,187.6	122
South East	34,773.5	15,799.5	454
Ninh Thuan	3,358.0	565.0	168
Binh Thuan	7,810.4	1,167.0	149
Binh Phuoc	6,874.4	873.6	127
Tay Ninh	4,049.2	1,066.5	263
Binh Duong	2,695.2	1,481.6	550
Dong Nai	5,903.4	2,486.2	421
Ba Ria-Vung Tau	1,987.4	996.7	502
Ho Chi Minh City	2,095.5	7,162.9	3,418
Mekong River Delta	40,518.5	17,191.4	424

—continued	Area (sq km)	Population ('000)	Density (per sq km)
Long An	4,493.8	1,436.1	320
Tien Giang	2,484.2	1,672.3	673
Ben Tre	2,360.2	1,255.9	532
Tra Vinh	2,295.1	1,003.0	437
Vinh Long	1,479.1	1,024.7	693
Dong Thap	3,375.4	1,666.5	494
An Giang	3,536.8	2,142.7	606
Kien Giang	6,346.3	1,688.2	266
Can Tho	1,401.6	1,188.4	848
Hau Giang	1,601.1	757.3	473
Soc Trang	3,311.8	1,292.9	390
Bac Lieu	2,501.5	856.5	342
Ca Mau	5,331.6	1,206.9	226
Total	331,051.4	85,847.0	259

PRINCIPAL TOWNS
(excl. suburbs, estimated population at mid-1992)

Ho Chi Minh City (formerly Saigon)	3,015,743*	Nam Dinh	171,699
Hanoi (capital)	1,073,760	Qui Nhon	163,385
Haiphong	783,133	Vung Tau	145,145
Da Nang	382,674	Rach Gia	141,132
Buon Ma Thuot	282,095	Long Xuyen	132,681
Nha Trang	221,331	Thai Nguyen	127,643
Hué	219,149	Hong Gai	127,484
Can Tho	215,587	Vinh	112,455
Cam Pha	209,086		

* Including Cholon.

Source: UN, *Demographic Yearbook*.

Mid-2010 (incl. suburbs, '000 persons, UN estimates): Ho Chi Minh City 6,167; Hanoi 2,814 (refers to urban population in city districts); Haiphong 1,970 (Source: UN, *World Urbanization Prospects: The 2009 Revision*).

BIRTHS AND DEATHS
(annual averages, UN estimates)

	1995–2000	2000–05	2005–10
Birth rate (per 1,000)	19.0	17.2	17.2
Death rate (per 1,000)	5.8	5.3	5.2

Source: UN, *World Population Prospects: The 2010 Revision*.

Life expectancy (years at birth, WHO estimates): 72 (males 70; females 74) in 2009 (Source: WHO, *World Health Statistics*).

EMPLOYMENT
('000 persons aged 15 years and over, averages at mid-year)

	2007	2008	2009*
Agriculture, hunting and forestry	22,696.6	22,705.5	23,022.0
Fishing	1,672.8	1,742.2	1,766.5
Mining and quarrying	406.8	446.0	477.4
Manufacturing	6,103.0	6,523.1	6,851.2
Power and utilities	201.6	232.3	262.6
Construction	2,320.9	2,476.4	2,692.8
Wholesale and retail trade; repair of motor vehicles, motor cycles and personal and household goods	4,984.1	5,131.5	5,285.2
Hotels and restaurants	766.6	793.7	811.6
Transport, storage and communications	1,146.6	1,167.0	1,207.9
Financial intermediation	197.7	210.3	219.6
Scientific activities and technology	25.3	25.7	26.7
Real estate, renting and business activities	203.4	240.2	267.4
Public administration and defence; compulsory social security	1,688.2	1,771.9	1,819.0
Education and training	1,277.8	1,338.7	1,370.2
Health and social work	361.9	381.9	391.5
Recreational, cultural and sporting activities	128.5	128.7	128.9
Activities of the Communist Party and of membership organizations	181.7	210.3	205.3
Community, social and personal service activities and private households with employed persons	844.5	935.4	937.6
Total employed	45,208.0	46,460.8	47,743.6

* Preliminary figures.

Unemployed (million persons): 1.0 in 2006; 0.9 in 2007; 1.1 in 2008 (Source: Asian Development Bank).

Health and Welfare

KEY INDICATORS

Total fertility rate (children per woman, 2009)	2.0
Under-5 mortality rate (per 1,000 live births, 2009)	24
HIV/AIDS (% of persons aged 15–49, 2007)	0.5
Physicians (per 1,000 head, 2002)	0.6
Hospital beds (per 1,000 head, 2005)	2.6
Health expenditure (2008): US $ per head (PPP)	201
Health expenditure (2008): % of GDP	7.2
Health expenditure (2008): public (% of total)	38.5
Access to water (% of persons, 2008)	94
Access to sanitation (% of persons, 2008)	75
Total carbon dioxide emissions ('000 metric tons, 2007)	111,286.7
Carbon dioxide emissions per head (metric tons, 2007)	1.3
Human Development Index (2007): ranking	116
Human Development Index (2007): value	0.725

For sources and definitions, see explanatory note on p. vi.

Agriculture

PRINCIPAL CROPS
('000 metric tons)

	2007	2008	2009
Rice, paddy	35,943	38,725	38,896
Maize	4,303	4,531	4,382
Potatoes*	437	486	443
Sweet potatoes	1,438	1,326	1,208
Cassava (Manioc)	8,193	9,396	8,557
Sugar cane	17,397	16,128	15,246
Beans, dry*	197	224	210
Cashew nuts, with shell	1,250	1,234	958
Soybeans (Soya beans)	276	269	214
Groundnuts, with shell	510	530	525
Coconuts	1,035	1,095	1,129
Cabbages and other brassicas*	723	744	752

—continued	2007	2008	2009
Onions, dry*	276	295	324
Watermelons*	426	461	526
Bananas*	1,355	1,455	1,532
Oranges*	615	544	600
Guavas, mangoes and mangosteens*	414	424	540
Pineapples	519	483	460
Coffee, green†	1,251	1,067	1,176
Tea	164	174	186
Tobacco, unmanufactured	32	29	39
Natural rubber	606	660	724

* FAO estimates.
† Unofficial figures.

Aggregate production ('000 metric tons, may include official, semi-official or estimated data): Total cereals 40,248 in 2007, 43,258 in 2008, 43,279 in 2009; Total roots and tubers 10,067 in 2007, 11,208 in 2008, 10,207 in 2009; Total vegetables (incl. melons) 8,036 in 2007, 7,750 in 2008, 7,963 in 2009; Total fruits (excl. melons) 5,689 in 2007, 5,669 in 2008, 5,959 in 2009.

Source: FAO.

LIVESTOCK
('000 head, year ending September)

	2007	2008	2009
Horses	103.5	121.0	102.2
Cattle	6,724.7	6,337.7	6,103.3
Buffaloes	2,996.4	2,897.7	2,886.6
Pigs	26,560.7	26,701.6	27,627.7
Goats	1,777.6	1,483.5	1,375.1
Chickens	158,200	173,110	196,140
Ducks	67,800	75,190	84,060

Source: FAO.

LIVESTOCK PRODUCTS
('000 metric tons)

	2007	2008	2009
Cattle meat	206.1	226.7	257.8
Buffalo meat*	109.7	106.0	105.6
Pig meat	2,662.7	2,782.7	2,908.5
Chicken meat	358.8	448.2	518.3
Duck meat*	81.6	82.0	80.6
Cows' milk	234.4	262.2	278.2
Buffaloes' milk*	33.0	32.0	33.2
Hen eggs*	223	247	309
Silk-worm cocoons*	3.4	2.6	2.2

* FAO estimates.

Source: FAO.

Forestry

ROUNDWOOD REMOVALS
('000 cubic metres, excl. bark)

	2006	2007	2008
Sawlogs, veneer logs and logs for sleepers*	2,200	2,150	2,450
Pulpwood	1,291	1,920	2,500
Other industrial wood	1,380	1,380	900
Fuel wood*	26,151	22,000	22,000
Total*	31,022	27,450	27,850

* FAO estimates.

2009: Production assumed to be unchanged from 2008 (FAO estimates).

Source: FAO.

SAWNWOOD PRODUCTION
('000 cubic metres, incl. railway sleepers)

	2007	2008	2009
Total (all broadleaved)	4,500	5,000	5,000

Source: FAO.

Fishing

('000 metric tons, live weight)

	2007	2008	2009
Capture*	2,020.4	2,087.5	2,243.1
Freshwater fishes	133.6	129.9	133.4
Marine fishes	1,385.5	1,420.8	1,513.0
Prawns and shrimps	111.4	113.3	138.7
Cephalopods	211.6	227.7	246.5
Aquaculture*	2,085.4	2,462.4	2,556.2
Freshwater fishes*	1,530.3	1,467.3	1,325.5
Giant tiger prawns	170.0*	324.6	316.0
Marine molluscs	170.5*	170.0*	165.0
Total catch*	4,105.8	4,549.9	4,799.3

* FAO estimate(s).

Note: Figures exclude aquatic plants ('000 metric tons, all aquaculture): 38 in 2007; 36 in 2008; 34 in 2009.

Source: FAO.

Mining

('000 metric tons unless otherwise indicated)

	2007	2008	2009
Crude petroleum ('000 barrels)	116,741	109,291	119,528
Natural gas (million cubic metres)*	7,080	7,499	8,010
Coal (anthracite)	42,483	39,777	43,715
Chromium ore—gross weight	103.8	55.9	37.1
Ilmenite—gross weight†	643	693	687
Gold (kilograms)†	3,000	3,000	3,000
Kaolin†	650	650	650
Barite (metric tons)	90,000	80,000	70,000
Phosphate rock:			
gross weight	1,523	2,101	1,896
P_2O_5 content†	460	630	570
Salt (unrefined)	857	717	718

* Gross production.
† Estimates.

Source: US Geological Survey.

Industry

SELECTED PRODUCTS
('000 metric tons unless otherwise indicated)

	2008	2009	2010*
Raw sugar	1,611.0	1,509.0	1,423.0
Beer (million litres)	1,847.2	2,007.5	2,377.2
Cigarettes ('000 million packets)	4.4	4.8	5.0
Fabrics (million metres)	1,076.4	1,187.3	1,219.6
Chemical fertilizers	2,459.4	2,359.9	2,573.9
Insecticides	65.4	75.4	82.2
Soap	452.4	537.2	567.2
Cement	40,009	48,800	55,800
Crude steel	5,001	6,500	7,900
Paint	200.5	254.4	292.6
Footwear (million pairs)	169.2	187.7	203.7
Ready-made clothes (million pieces)	2,045.0	2,641.6	3,024.6

* Preliminary figures.

Electric energy (million kWh): 64,147 in 2007; 72,100 in 2008; 80,700 in 2009 (Source: Asian Development Bank).

Finance

CURRENCY AND EXCHANGE RATES

Monetary Units
100 xu = 1 new dông.

Sterling, Dollar and Euro Equivalents (31 March 2011)
£1 sterling = 33,315.3 dông;
US $1 = 20,703.0 dông;
€1 = 29,412.8 dông;
100,000 new dông = £3.00 = $4.83 = €3.40.

Average Exchange Rate (new dông per US $)

2008	16,302.3
2009	17,065.1
2010	18,612.9

Note: The new dông, equivalent to 10 former dông, was introduced in September 1985.

BUDGET
('000,000 million dông)

Revenue (incl. grants)	2005	2006	2007*
Tax revenue	166.2	210.3	231.4
Corporate income tax	71.7	100.8	99.0
Individual income tax	4.2	5.2	6.1
Tax on the transfer of properties	2.8	3.4	3.8
Value-added tax (VAT)	45.7	54.8	78.9
Excises	15.7	17.1	17.1
Taxes on international trade	23.6	26.3	23.8
Other taxes	2.3	2.8	2.7
Non-tax and capital revenue	48.5	50.3	47.5
Fees and charges	21.0	23.1	23.1
Income from natural resources	21.9	20.2	19.9
Capital revenues	0.9	1.5	0.8
Grants	2.3	3.6	3.0
Total	217.1	264.2	281.9

Expenditure (cash basis)†	2005	2006	2007*
Current expenditure	155.0	181.5	221.3
General administrative services	16.8	19.0	24.8
Economic services	12.8	15.0	16.3
Social services	77.3	91.4	97.3
Education	29.1	33.8	38.1
Health	10.7	12.7	14.7
Social subsidies	23.6	28.7	26.8
Other services (incl. defence)	13.8	16.3	17.8
Interest on public debt	7.0	8.9	11.7
Capital expenditure	72.0	86.1	99.5
Total	226.9	267.6	320.7

* Forecasts.

† Excluding off-budget investment expenditure ('000,000 million dông): 39.4 in 2005; 33.7 in 2006; 39.4 in 2007 (forecast).

Source: IMF, *Vietnam: Statistical Appendix* (December 2007).

2007 ('000 billion dông, revised): *Revenue:* Tax revenue 269 (Oil revenues 79, Non-oil tax revenues 190); Non-tax and capital revenues 53; Total 322 (excl. grants 6). *Expenditure:* Government expenditure 336; Other expenditure 14; Total 350 (Source: IMF, *Vietnam: 2010 Article IV Consultation—Staff Report and Public Information Notice*—September 2010).

2008 ('000 billion dông, estimates): *Revenue:* Tax revenue 368 (Oil revenues 90, Non-oil tax revenues 278); Non-tax and capital revenues 53; Total 421 (excl. grants 9). *Expenditure:* Government expenditure 410; Other expenditure 33; Total 443 (Source: IMF, *Vietnam: 2010 Article IV Consultation—Staff Report and Public Information Notice*—September 2010).

2009 ('000 billion dông, budgeted figures): *Revenue:* Tax revenue 345 (Oil revenues 64, Non-oil tax revenues 282); Non-tax and capital revenues 40; Total 385 (excl. grants 5). *Expenditure:* Government expenditure 456; Other expenditure 74; Total 529 (Source: IMF, *Vietnam: 2010 Article IV Consultation—Staff Report and Public Information Notice*—September 2010).

INTERNATIONAL RESERVES
(US $ million at 31 December)

	2008	2009	2010
Gold (market valuation)	285.7	356.1	459.6
IMF special drawing rights	8.2	419.7	412.5
Foreign exchange	23,882.0	16,027.4	12,054.1
Total	24,175.9	16,803.2	12,926.2

Source: IMF, *International Financial Statistics*.

MONEY SUPPLY
('000 million dông at 31 December)

	2008	2009	2010
Currency outside banks	236,848	293,225	337,949
Demand deposits at banks	196,470	271,988	287,503
Total money	433,318	565,213	625,451

Source: IMF, *International Financial Statistics*.

COST OF LIVING
(Consumer Price Index; base: previous year = 100)

	2008	2009	2010
Food	136.6	108.7	110.7
Beverages and tobacco	110.8	109.6	108.2
Clothing (incl. footwear)	110.3	108.9	106.9
Household goods	109.1	108.5	105.4
Housing and construction	120.5	103.5	114.7
Transport and communications	116.0	n.a.	n.a.
Education	104.2	105.7	110.4
All items (incl. others)	123.0	106.9	109.2

NATIONAL ACCOUNTS
('000 million dông at current prices)

Expenditure on the Gross Domestic Product

	2007	2008	2009
Government final consumption expenditure	69,247	90,904	104,540
Private final consumption expenditure	740,615	1,000,972	1,102,279
Increase in stocks	55,598	75,759	59,800
Gross fixed capital formation	437,702	513,987	572,526
Total domestic expenditure	1,303,162	1,681,622	1,839,144
Exports of goods and services	879,461	1,157,178	1,132,688
Less Imports of goods and services	1,060,763	1,383,006	1,304,350
Sub-total	1,121,860	1,455,794	1,667,481
Statistical discrepancy	21,855	29,243	–9,092
GDP in purchasers' values	1,143,715	1,485,038	1,658,389
GDP at constant 1994 prices	461,344	490,459	516,568

Gross Domestic Product by Economic Activity

	2007	2008	2009
Agriculture, forestry and fishing	232,586	329,886	346,786
Mining and quarrying	111,700	146,607	165,310
Manufacturing	243,142	302,136	333,166
Electricity, gas and water	39,869	47,169	58,592
Construction	79,712	95,696	110,255
Trade	156,442	212,139	244,933
Transport, storage and communications	51,118	66,359	72,412
Finance	20,756	27,215	31,617
Public administration	94,578	113,856	128,904
Other community, social and personal services	113,812	143,975	166,414
Total	1,143,715	1,485,038	1,658,389

Source: Asian Development Bank.

BALANCE OF PAYMENTS
(US $ million)

	2007	2008	2009
Exports of goods f.o.b.	48,561	62,685	57,096
Imports of goods f.o.b.	–58,999	–75,467	–65,402
Trade balance	–10,438	–12,782	–8,306
Exports of services	6,030	7,041	5,656
Imports of services	–6,785	–7,956	–6,886
Balance on goods and services	–11,193	–13,697	–9,536
Other income received	1,166	1,357	753
Other income paid	–3,356	–5,758	–3,781
Balance on goods, services and income	–13,383	–18,098	–12,564
Current transfers (net)	6,430	7,311	6,448
Current balance	–6,953	–10,787	–6,116
Direct investment abroad	–184	–300	–700
Direct investment from abroad	6,700	9,579	7,600
Portfolio investment (net)	6,243	–578	128
Other investment assets	2,623	677	–305
Other investment liabilities	2,348	2,963	5,146
Net errors and omissions	–565	–1,080	–13,509
Overall balance	10,212	474	–7,756

Source: IMF, *International Financial Statistics*.

External Trade

SELECTED COMMODITIES
(distribution by SITC, US $ million)

Imports c.i.f.	2006	2007	2008
Food and live animals	2,299	3,280	4,525
Beverages and tobacco	145	183	269
Crude materials (inedible) except fuels	2,084	2,741	4,006
Mineral fuels, etc.	6,699	8,744	12,330
Animal and vegetable fats, and oils	254	473	636
Chemicals and related products	6,317	8,369	10,298
Basic manufactures	12,164	17,062	20,113
Machinery and transport equipment	10,806	17,860	22,425
Miscellaneous manufactured goods	2,244	2,737	3,384
Total (incl. others)	44,891	62,765	80,714

Exports f.o.b.	2006	2007	2008
Food and live animals	7,509	9,192	12,164
Crude materials (inedible) except fuels	1,845	2,200	2,492
Mineral fuels, etc.	9,709	10,061	12,751
Basic manufactures	2,926	3,976	6,398
Machinery and transport equipment	4,195	5,601	7,368
Total (incl. others)	39,826	48,561	62,685

2009: Total imports 69,949; Total exports 57,096.

2010 (preliminary): Total imports 84,801; Total exports 72,192.

PRINCIPAL TRADING PARTNERS
(US $ million)

Imports c.i.f.	2007	2008	2009
China, People's Republic	12,710.0	15,652.1	13,198.5
Hong Kong	1,950.7	2,633.3	3,564.7
Japan	6,188.9	n.a.	7,170.2
Korea, Republic	5,340.4	7,066.3	6,241.4
Malaysia	2,289.9	2,596.1	2,161.3
Singapore	7,613.7	9,392.5	7,689.0
Thailand	3,744.2	4,905.6	5,132.7
USA	1,700.5	2,635.3	3,418.4
Total (incl. others)	62,764.7	80,713.8	79,896.9

Exports f.o.b.	2007	2008	2009
Australia	3,802.2	4,225.2	2,447.6
China, People's Republic	3,646.1	4,535.7	4,039.9
Germany	1,854.9	2,073.4	2,359.6
Japan	6,090.0	8,537.9	6,326.5
Korea, Republic	1,243.4	1,784.4	1,576.1
Malaysia	1,555.0	1,955.3	1,706.8
Philippines	965.1	1,824.7	1,739.9
Singapore	2,234.4	2,659.7	2,062.3
USA	10,104.5	11,868.5	11,853.0
Total (incl. others)	48,561.4	62,685.1	55,400.5

Note: Data reflect the IMF's direction of trade methodology and, as a result, the totals may not be equal to those presented for trade in commodities.

Source: Asian Development Bank.

Transport

RAILWAYS
(traffic)

	2008	2009	2010*
Passengers carried (million)	11.3	11.1	11.6
Passenger-km ('000 million)	4.6	4.1	4.5
Freight carried (million metric tons)	8.5	8.1	8.0
Freight ton-km ('000 million)	4.2	3.9	4.0

* Preliminary figures.

ROAD TRAFFIC

	2008	2009	2010*
Passengers carried (million)	1,629.0	1,761.0	2,011.1
Passenger-km ('000 million)	54.2	61.5	69.2
Freight carried (million metric tons)	455.9	513.6	585.0
Freight ton-km ('000 million)	28.0	31.6	36.3

* Preliminary figures.

Commercial vehicles ('000 in use): 49.4 in 1998; 57.8 in 1999; 69.9 in 2000 (Source: UN, *Statistical Yearbook*).

INLAND WATERWAYS

	2008	2009	2010*
Passengers carried (million)	143.0	151.3	157.5
Passenger-km ('000 million)	3.2	3.0	3.2
Freight carried (million metric tons)	133.0	137.7	144.3
Freight ton-km ('000 million)	24.9	31.2	31.5

* Preliminary figures.

SHIPPING

Merchant Fleet
(registered at 31 December)

	2007	2008	2009
Number of vessels	1,235	1,312	1,415
Total displacement ('000 grt)	2,529.6	2,993.1	3,451.1

Source: IHS Fairplay, *World Fleet Statistics*.

International Sea-Borne Shipping
(freight traffic)

	2008	2009	2010*
Freight carried (million metric tons)	55.7	55.8	64.7
Freight ton-km ('000 million)	115.6	132.1	146.6

* Preliminary figures.

CIVIL AVIATION
(traffic on scheduled services)

	2006	2007	2008
Domestic:			
Passengers carried ('000)	4,313.5	5,478.4	6,820.9
Passenger-km (million)	3,551.9	4,685.6	5,541.0
Freight carried ('000 metric tons)	73.2	86.5	83.7
Freight ton-km (million)	81.2	94.7	88.3
International:			
Passengers carried ('000)	3,132.0	3,419.2	3,379.1
Passenger-km (million)	9,264.7	9,996.0	10,611.3
Freight carried ('000 metric tons)	47.6	43.1	47.7
Freight ton-km (million)	188.2	185.2	207.3

Tourism

TOURIST ARRIVALS BY COUNTRY OF RESIDENCE

Country	2006	2007	2008
Australia	172,519	227,300	234,760
Cambodia	154,956	150,655	n.a.
China, People's Republic	516,286	558,719	650,055
France	132,304	182,501	182,048
Japan	383,896	411,557	392,999
Korea, Republic	421,741	475,535	449,237
Laos	33,980	31,374	n.a.
Malaysia	105,558	145,535	174,008
Singapore	104,947	127,040	158,405
Taiwan	274,663	314,026	303,527
Thailand	123,804	160,747	183,142
United Kingdom	84,264	105,918	n.a.
USA	385,654	412,301	417,198
Total (incl. others)	3,583,486	4,171,564	4,253,740

2009: Australia 218,461; China, People's Republic 527,610; France 174,525; Japan 359,231; Korea, Republic 362,115; Malaysia 166,284; Taiwan 271,643; Thailand 152,633; USA 403,930; Total (incl. others) 3,772,359.

2010: Australia 278,155; China, People's Republic 905,360; France 199,351; Japan 442,089; Korea, Republic 495,902; Malaysia 211,337; Taiwan 334,007; Thailand 222,839; USA 430,993; Total (incl. others) 5,049,855.

Source: Viet Nam National Administration of Tourism.

Tourism receipts (US $ million, excl. passenger transport): 3,750 in 2007; 3,930 in 2008; 3,050 in 2009 (Source: World Tourism Organization).

Communications Media

	2008	2009	2010
Telephones ('000 main lines in use)	14,767.6	17,427.4	16,400.0
Mobile cellular telephones ('000 subscribers)	74,872.3	98,224.0	154,000.0
Internet subscribers ('000)	6,700.0	n.a.	n.a.
Broadband subscribers ('000)	1,092.3	3,214.2	3,631.4

Personal computers: 8,118,000 (96.5 per 1,000 persons) in 2006.

Radio receivers ('000 in use): 8,200 in 1997.

Television receivers ('000 in use): 14,750 in 2000.

Book production: 11,455 titles (166,500,000 copies) in 2001.

Daily newspapers: 5 (with estimated circulation of 450,000 copies) in 1999.

Non-daily newspapers: 80 in 2004.

Sources: partly International Telecommunication Union; UN, *Statistical Yearbook*; UNESCO, *Statistical Yearbook*.

Education

(2010/11, preliminary)

	Institutions	Teachers ('000)	Students (million)
Pre-primary	12,678	157.3	3.0
Primary	15,242	359.7	6.9
Lower secondary	10,132	313.1	5.0
Upper secondary	2,289	147.6	2.8
Universities and colleges	414	71.5	2.0

Pupil-teacher ratio (primary education, UNESCO estimate): 19.5 in 2008/09 (Source: UNESCO Institute for Statistics).

Adult literacy rate (UNESCO estimates): 92.8% (males 95.2%; females 90.5%) in 2009 (Source: UNESCO Institute for Statistics).

Directory

The Constitution

On 15 April 1992 the National Assembly adopted a new Constitution, a revised version of that adopted in December 1980 (which in turn replaced the 1959 Constitution of the Democratic Republic of Viet Nam). The National Assembly approved amendments to 24 articles of the Constitution on 12 December 2001. The main provisions of the Constitution (which originally entered into force after elections in July 1992) are summarized as follows:

POLITICAL SYSTEM

All state power belongs to the people. The Communist Party of Viet Nam is a leading force of the state and society. All party organizations operate within the framework of the Constitution and the law. The people exercise power through the National Assembly and the People's Councils.

ECONOMIC SYSTEM

The State develops a multi-sectoral economy, in accordance with a market mechanism based on state management and socialist orientations. All lands are under state management. The State allots land to organizations and individuals for use on a stabilized and long-term basis: they may transfer the right to the use of land allotted to them. Individuals may establish businesses with no restrictions on size or means of production, and the State shall encourage foreign investment. Legal property of individuals and organizations, and business enterprises with foreign invested capital, shall not be subjected to nationalization.

THE NATIONAL ASSEMBLY

The National Assembly is the people's highest representative agency, and the highest organ of state power, exercising its supreme right of supervision over all operations of the State. It elects the President and Vice-President, the Prime Minister and senior judicial officers, and ratifies the Prime Minister's proposals for appointing members of the Government. It decides the country's socio-economic development plans, national financial and monetary policies, and foreign policy. The term of each legislature is five years. The National Assembly Standing Committee supervises the enforcement of laws and the activities of the Government. Amendments to the Constitution may only be made by a majority vote of at least two-thirds of the Assembly's members.

THE PRESIDENT OF THE STATE

The President, as Head of State, represents Viet Nam in domestic and foreign affairs. The President is elected by the National Assembly from among its deputies, and is responsible to the National Assembly. The President's term of office is the same as that of the National Assembly. He or she is Commander-in-Chief of the people's armed forces, and chairs the National Defence and Security Council. The President asks the National Assembly to appoint or dismiss the Vice-President, the Prime Minister, the Chief Justice of the Supreme People's Court and the Chief Procurator of the Supreme People's

Organ of Control. According to resolutions of the National Assembly or of its Standing Committee, the President appoints or dismisses members of the Government, and declares war or a state of emergency.

THE GOVERNMENT

The Government comprises the Prime Minister, the Vice-Prime Ministers, ministers and other members. Apart from the Prime Minister, ministers do not have to be members of the National Assembly. The Prime Minister is responsible to the National Assembly, and the term of office of any Government is the same as that of the National Assembly, which ratifies the appointment or dismissal of members of the Government.

LOCAL GOVERNMENT

The country is divided into provinces and municipalities, which are subordinate to the central Government; municipalities are divided into districts, precincts and cities, and districts are divided into villages and townships. People's Councils are elected by the local people.

JUDICIAL SYSTEM

The judicial system comprises the Supreme People's Court, local People's Courts, military tribunals and other courts. The term of office of the presiding judge of the Supreme People's Court corresponds to the term of the National Assembly, and he or she is responsible to the National Assembly. The Supreme People's Organ of Control ensures the observance of the law and exercises the right of public prosecution. Its Chief Procurator is responsible to the National Assembly. There are local People's Organs of Control and Military Organs of Control.

The Government

HEAD OF STATE

President: Truong Tan Sang (appointment approved by the 12th National Assembly on 25 July 2011).

Vice-President: Nguyen Thi Doan.

CABINET
(October 2011)

The Cabinet is formed by Dang Cong San Viet Nam (the Communist Party of Viet Nam).

Prime Minister: Nguyen Tan Dung.

Deputy Prime Ministers: Nguyen Thien Nhan, Hoang Trung Hai, Nguyen Xuan Phuc, Vu Van Ninh.

Minister of Foreign Affairs: Pham Binh Minh.

Minister of National Defence: Gen. Phung Quang Thanh.

Minister of Public Security: Tran Dai Quang.

Minister of Justice: Ha Hung Cuong.

Minister of Finance: Vuong Dinh Hue.

Minister of Labour, War Invalids and Social Affairs: Pham Thi Hai Chuyen.

Minister of Health: Nguyen Thi Kim Tien.

Minister of Education and Training: Pham Vu Luan.

Minister of Culture, Sports and Tourism: Hoang Tuan Anh.

Minister of Construction: Trinh Dinh Dung.

Minister of Transport: Dinh La Thang.

Minister of Home Affairs: Nguyen Thai Binh.

Minister of Agriculture and Rural Development: Cao Duc Phat.

Minister of Industry and Trade: Vu Huy Hoang.

Minister of Planning and Investment: Bui Quang Vinh.

Minister of Science and Technology: Nguyen Quan.

Minister of Natural Resources and the Environment: Nguyen Minh Quang.

Minister of Information and Communications: Nguyen Bac Son.

Chief Government Inspector: Hyunh Phong Tranh.

Minister, Chairman of the Committee for Ethnic Minority Affairs: Giang Seo Phu.

Minister, Chairman of the Government Office: Vu Duc Dam.

MINISTRIES AND COMMITTEES

Ministry of Agriculture and Rural Development: 2 Ngoc Ha, Ba Dinh District, Hanoi; tel. (4) 38468161; fax (4) 38454319; e-mail webmaster@agroviet.gov.vn; internet www.agroviet.gov.vn.

Ministry of Construction: 37 Le Dai Hanh, Hai Ba Trung District, Hanoi; tel. (4) 39760271; fax (4) 39762153; e-mail vanphong@moc.gov.vn; internet www.moc.gov.vn.

Ministry of Culture, Sports and Tourism: 51–53 Ngo Quyen, Hoan Kiem District, Hanoi; tel. (4) 39439915; fax (4) 39439009; e-mail phongthongtin@cinet.gov.vn; internet www.cinet.gov.vn.

Ministry of Education and Training: 49 Dai Co Viet, Hai Ba Trung District, Hanoi; tel. (4) 38692397; fax (4) 38694085; e-mail bogddt@moet.edu.vn; internet www.moet.gov.vn.

Ministry of Finance: 28 Tran Hung Dao, Hoan Kiem District, Hanoi; tel. (4) 22202828; fax (4) 22208091; e-mail support@mof.gov.vn; internet www.mof.gov.vn.

Ministry of Foreign Affairs: 1 Ton That Dam, Ba Dinh District, Hanoi; tel. (4) 37992000; fax (4) 38231872; e-mail banbientap@mofa.gov.vn; internet www.mofa.gov.vn.

Ministry of Health: 138A Giang Vo, Ba Dinh District, Hanoi; tel. (4) 62732273; fax (4) 38464051; e-mail byt@moh.gov.vn; internet www.moh.gov.vn.

Ministry of Home Affairs: 37A Nguyen Binh Khiem, Hai Ba Trung District, Hanoi; tel. (4) 39764116; fax (4) 39781005; e-mail websitemaster@moha.gov.vn; internet www.moha.gov.vn.

Ministry of Industry and Trade: 54 Hai Ba Trung, Hoan Kiem District, Hanoi; tel. (4) 22202222; fax (4) 22202525; e-mail bbt@moit.gov.vn; internet www.moit.gov.vn.

Ministry of Information and Communications: 18 Nguyen Du, Hanoi; tel. (4) 39435602; fax (4) 38263477; e-mail otonghop@mic.gov.vn; internet mic.gov.vn.

Ministry of Justice: 60 Tran Phu, Ba Dinh District, Hanoi; tel. (4) 37332802; fax (4) 38431431; e-mail banbientap@moj.gov.vn; internet www.moj.gov.vn.

Ministry of Labour, War Invalids and Social Affairs: 12 Ngo Quyen, Hoan Kiem District, Hanoi; tel. (4) 38248913; fax (4) 38248036; e-mail lasic@molisa.gov.vn; internet www.molisa.gov.vn.

Ministry of National Defence: 7 Nguyen Tri Phuong, Ba Dinh District, Hanoi; tel. (69) 534223; fax (69) 532090.

Ministry of Natural Resources and the Environment: 83 Nguyen Chi Thanh, Dong Da District, Hanoi; tel. (4) 38343911; fax (4) 37736892; e-mail baotainguyenmoitruong@gmail.com; internet www.monre.gov.vn.

Ministry of Planning and Investment: 6B Hoang Dieu, Ba Dinh District, Hanoi; tel. (4) 38433360; fax (80) 48473; e-mail banbientap@mpi.gov.vn; internet www.mpi.gov.vn.

Ministry of Public Security: 44 Yet Kieu, Hoan Kiem District, Hanoi; tel. (4) 38226602; fax (4) 39420223.

Ministry of Science and Technology: 39 Tran Hung Dao, Hoan Kiem District, Hanoi; tel. (4) 39437056; fax (4) 39439733; e-mail bbt@most.gov.vn; internet www.most.gov.vn.

Ministry of Transport: 80 Tran Hung Dao, Hoan Kiem District, Hanoi; tel. (4) 39424015; fax (4) 39423291; e-mail vpmot@mt.gov.vn; internet www.mt.gov.vn.

Committee for Ethnic Minority Affairs: 80 Phan Dinh Phung, Ba Dinh District, Hanoi; tel. (4) 38431876; fax (4) 38230235; e-mail banbientap@cema.gov.vn; internet www.cema.gov.vn.

Government Inspection Committee: 220 Doi Can, Ba Dinh District, Hanoi; tel. (80) 43490; fax (80) 48493; e-mail ttcp@thanhtra.gov.vn; internet www.thanhtra.gov.vn.

NATIONAL DEFENCE AND SECURITY COUNCIL

President: Nguyen Minh Triet.

Vice-President: Nguyen Tan Dung.

Members: Nguyen Phu Trong, Pham Gia Khiem, Phung Quang Thanh, Le Hong Anh.

Legislature

QUOC HOI
(National Assembly)

Elections for the 13th National Assembly were held on 22 May 2011. More than 90% of the new Assembly's 500 legislators were reported to be members of the Communist Party. Of these, people from ethnic minority groups won 78 seats and women 122 seats. Also elected were 42 non-party candidates, including four independents.

Standing Committee

Chairman: Nguyen Sinh Hung.

Vice-Chairmen: Uong Chu Luu, Nguyen Thi Kim Ngan, Tong Thi Phong, Huynh Ngoc Son.

Political Organizations

COMMUNIST PARTY

Dang Cong San Viet Nam (Communist Party of Viet Nam—CPV): 1A Hung Vuong, Hanoi; e-mail dangcongsan@cpv.org.vn; internet www.cpv.org.vn; f. 1976; ruling party; fmrly the Viet Nam Workers' Party (f. 1951 as the successor to the Communist Party of Indo-China, f. 1930); Cen. Cttee of 175 full mems and 25 alternate mems elected at 11th National Congress held in Jan. 2011; 14-mem. Politburo and four-mem. Secretariat elected (see below); 3.6m. mems; Gen. Sec. of Cen. Cttee NGUYEN PHU TRONG.

Political Bureau (Politburo)

Members: LE HONG ANH, NGO VAN DU, NGUYEN TAN DUNG, LE THANH HAI, NGUYEN SINH HUNG, DINH THE HUYNH, PHAM QUANG NGHI, TONG THI PHONG, NGUYEN XUAN PHUC, TRAN DAI QUANG, TO HUY RUA, TRUONG TAN SANG, Gen. PHUNG QUANG THANH, NGUYEN PHU TRONG.

Secretariat

Members: TRUONG HOA BINH, HA THI KHIET, NGO XUAN LICH, NGUYEN THI KIM NGAN.

OTHER POLITICAL ORGANIZATIONS

Ho Chi Minh Communist Youth Union: 62 Ba Trieu, Hanoi; tel. (4) 62631874; fax (4) 62631875; e-mail vanphongtwd@doantn.vn; internet doanthanhnien.vn; f. 1931; 4m. mems; First Sec. VO VAN THUONG.

People's Action Party (PAP): POB 4752, San Jose, CA 95150-4752, USA; e-mail dang@ndhd.net; internet www.dndhd.org; Chair. NGUYEN SI BINH.

Viet Nam Fatherland Front: 46 Trang Thi, Hanoi; tel. (4) 9287401; e-mail ubmttqvn@mattran.org.vn; internet www.mattran.org.vn; f. 1930; replaced the Lien Viet (Viet Nam National League), the successor to Viet Nam Doc Lap Dong Minh Hoi (Revolutionary League for the Independence of Viet Nam) or Viet Minh; in 1977 the original org. merged with the National Front for the Liberation of South Viet Nam and the Alliance of National, Democratic and Peace Forces in South Viet Nam to form a single front; 200-mem. Cen. Cttee; Pres. Presidium of Cen. Cttee HUYNH DAM; Gen. Sec. NONG DUC MANH.

Vietnam Women's Union (VWU): 39 Hang Chuoi, Hanoi; tel. (4) 9713436; fax (4) 9713143; internet hoilhpn.org.vn; f. 1930; 13m. mems; Pres. NGUYEN THI THANH HOA.

Diplomatic Representation

EMBASSIES IN VIET NAM

Algeria: 13 Phan Chu Trinh, Hanoi; tel. (4) 38253865; fax (4) 38260830; e-mail ambalghanoi@ambalgvn.org.vn; internet www.ambalgvn.org.vn; Ambassador CHÉRIF CHIKHI.

Argentina: Office Tower, 8th Floor, Daeha Business Centre, 360 Kim Ma, Ba Dinh District, Hanoi; tel. (4) 38315262; fax (4) 38315577; e-mail eviet@mrecic.gov.ar; internet www.eviet.mrecic.gob.ar; Ambassador ALBERTO J. KAMINKER.

Australia: 8 Dao Tan, Ba Dinh District, Hanoi; tel. (4) 37740100; fax (4) 37740111; e-mail austemb@fpt.vn; internet www.vietnam.embassy.gov.au; Ambassador ALLASTER COX.

Austria: Prime Centre, 8th Floor, 53 Quang Trung, Hai Ba Trung District, Hanoi; tel. (4) 39433050; fax (4) 39433055; e-mail hanoi-ob@bmeia.gv.at; internet www.bmeia.gv.at/botschaft/hanoi; Ambassador Dr GEORG HEINDL.

Bangladesh: Vuon Dao Compound, Villa D6B-05, 675 Lac Long Quan, Tay Ho District, Hanoi; tel. (4) 37716625; fax (4) 37716628; e-mail bdoothn@netnam.org.vn; internet www.bangladeshembassy.vn; Ambassador SUPRADIP CHAKMA.

Belarus: 52 Tay Ho, Tay Ho District, Hanoi; tel. (4) 38290494; fax (4) 37197125; e-mail vietnam@belembassy.org; internet www.vietnam.belembassy.org; Ambassador VALERIY E. SADOKHO.

Belgium: Hanoi Towers, 9th Floor, 49 Hai Ba Trung, Hanoi; tel. (4) 39346179; fax (4) 39346183; e-mail Pub.Hanoi@diplobel.fed.be; internet www.diplomatie.be/hanoi; Ambassador BRUNO ANGELET.

Brazil: Villa D6-07, 14 Thuy Khue, Tay Ho District, Hanoi; tel. (4) 38430817; fax (4) 38432542; e-mail vetbrem@vnn.vn; internet hanoi.itamaraty.gov.br; Ambassador JOÃO DE MENDONÇA LIMA NETO.

Brunei: Villa 8 & 9, 44/8 Van Bao, Van Phuc Diplomatic Quarter, Ba Dinh District, Hanoi; tel. (4) 7262001; fax (4) 7262010; e-mail bruemviet@hn.vnn.vn; Ambassador Dato Paduka Haji MAHADI BIN WASLI.

Bulgaria: Van Phuc Quarter, 5 Nui Truc, Hanoi; tel. (4) 38452908; fax (4) 38460856; e-mail bgremb@fpt.vn; internet www.mfa.bg/bg/22; Chargé d'affaires VLADIMIR MOSKOV.

Cambodia: 71A Tran Hung Dao, Hanoi; tel. (4) 8253788; fax (4) 9423225; e-mail arch@fpt.vn; Ambassador HUL PHANY.

Canada: 31 Hung Vuong, Hanoi; tel. (4) 37345000; fax (4) 37345049; e-mail hanoi@international.gc.ca; internet www.canadainternational.gc.ca/vietnam; Ambassador DEBORAH CHATSIS.

Chile: Villa C8–D8, 14 Thuy Khue, Tay Ho District, Hanoi; tel. (4) 39351147; fax (4) 38430762; e-mail embajada1@chile.org.vn; internet chileabroad.gov.cl/vietnam; Ambassador FERNANDO URRUTIA.

China, People's Republic: 46 Hoang Dieu, Hanoi; tel. (4) 38453736; fax (4) 38232826; e-mail eossc@hn.vnn.vn; internet vn.chineseembassy.org; Ambassador KONG XUANYOU.

Cuba: 65A Ly Thuong Kiet, Hanoi; tel. (4) 9424775; fax (4) 9422426; e-mail embacuba@fpt.vn; internet embacuba.cubaminrex.cu/vietnam; Ambassador FREDESMÁN TURRÓ GONZÁLEZ.

Czech Republic: 13 Chu Van An, Hanoi; tel. (4) 38454131; fax (4) 38233996; e-mail hanoi@embassy.mzv.cz; internet www.mfa.cz/hanoi; Ambassador MICHAL KRÁL.

Denmark: 19 Dien Bien Phu, Hanoi; tel. (4) 38231888; fax (4) 38231999; e-mail hanamb@um.dk; internet www.ambhanoi.um.dk; Ambassador JOHN NIELSEN.

Egypt: 63 To Ngoc Van, Quang An, Tay Ho District, Hanoi; tel. (4) 8294999; fax (4) 8294997; e-mail arabegypt@ftp.vn; Ambassador MUHAMMAD R. K. EL-TAIFY.

Finland: Central Bldg, 6th Floor, Suite 63, 31 Hai Ba Trung, Hanoi; tel. (4) 38266788; fax (4) 38266766; e-mail sanomat.han@formin.fi; internet www.finland.org.vn; Ambassador KIMMO LÄHDEVIRTA.

France: 57 Tran Hung Dao, Hanoi; tel. (4) 39445700; fax (4) 39445717; e-mail ambafrance.hanoi@diplomatie.gouv.fr; internet www.ambafrance-vn.org; Ambassador JEAN-FRANÇOIS GIRAULT.

Germany: 29 Tran Phu, Hanoi; tel. (4) 38453836; fax (4) 38453838; e-mail info@hanoi.diplo.de; internet www.hanoi.diplo.de; Ambassador KLAUS WUNDERLICH.

Hungary: Daeha Business Centre, 12th Floor, 360 Kim Ma, Ba Dinh District, Hanoi; tel. (4) 37715714; fax (4) 37715716; e-mail mission.hoi@kum.hu; internet www.mfa.gov.hu/kulkepviselet/vn; Ambassador LÁSZLÓ VIZI.

India: 58–60 Tran Hung Dao, Hanoi; tel. (4) 38244990; fax (4) 38244998; e-mail embassyindia@fpt.vn; internet www.indembassy.com.vn; Ambassador RANJIT RAE.

Indonesia: 50 Ngo Quyen, Hanoi; tel. (4) 38253353; fax (4) 38259274; e-mail komhan@hn.vnn.vn; internet www.deplu.go.id/hanoi; Ambassador (vacant).

Iran: 54 Tran Phu, Ba Dinh District, Hanoi; tel. (4) 8232068; fax (4) 8232120; e-mail embiri@fpt.vn; internet www.iranembassy.org.vn; Ambassador JAVAD GHAVAM SHAHIDI.

Iraq: 66 Tran Hung Dao, Hanoi; tel. (4) 39424141; fax (4) 39424055; e-mail hanemb@iraqmfamail.com; internet www.mofamission.gov.iq/vnm; Ambassador FARIS ABD AL-KARIM ZAARAWI.

Ireland: Vincom City Towers, 8th Floor, 191 Ba Trieu, Hai Ba Trung District, Hanoi; tel. (4) 39743291; fax (4) 39743295; e-mail irishembassyhanoi@dfanet.ie; internet www.embassyofireland.vn; Ambassador DAMIEN COLE.

Israel: 68 Nguyen Thai Hoc, Dong Da, Hanoi; tel. (4) 38433140; fax (4) 38435760; e-mail info@hanoi.mfa.gov.il; internet hanoi.mfa.gov.il; Ambassador AMNON EFRAT.

Italy: 9 Le Phung Hieu, Hoan Kiem District, Hanoi; tel. (4) 38256256; fax (4) 38267602; e-mail ambasciata.hanoi@esteri.it; internet www.ambhanoi.esteri.it; Ambassador LORENZO ANGELONI.

Japan: 27 Lieu Giai, Ba Dinh District, Hanoi; tel. (4) 38463000; fax (4) 38463043; e-mail soumuhan@vnn.vn; internet www.vn.emb-japan.go.jp; Ambassador YASUAKI TANIZAKI.

Korea, Democratic People's Republic: 25 Cao Ba Quat, Hanoi; tel. (4) 8453008; fax (4) 8231221; e-mail emb.dprk@hn.vnn.vn; Ambassador KIM CHANG IL.

Korea, Republic: Daeha Business Centre, 4th Floor, 360 Kim Ma, Ba Dinh District, Hanoi; tel. (4) 38315111; fax (4) 38315117; e-mail koreambviet@mofat.go.kr; internet hanquocngaynay.com; Ambassador HA CHAN-HO.

Kuwait: Hanoi; tel. (4) 9330609; fax (4) 9330611; e-mail hanoi@mofa.gov.kw; Ambassador HAMAD SALEH AL-JUTAILI.

Laos: 22 Tran Binh Trong, Hai Ba Trung, Hanoi; tel. (4) 9424576; fax (4) 8228414; internet www.embalaohanoi.gov.la; Ambassador SOMPHONE SICHALENNE.

Libya: A3 Van Phuc Residential Quarter, Kim Ma, Hanoi; tel. (4) 8453379; fax (4) 8454977; e-mail libpbha@yahoo.com; Secretary SALEM ALI SALEM DANNAH.

Malaysia: 43–45 Dien Bien Phu, Ba Dinh District, Hanoi; tel. (4) 37343836; fax (4) 37343832; e-mail malhanoi@kln.gov.my; internet www.kln.gov.my/web/vnm_hanoi; Ambassador Datuk AZMIL MOHD ZABIDI.

Mexico: 14 Thuy Khue, T-11, Hanoi; tel. (4) 38470948; fax (4) 38470949; e-mail embvietnam@sre.gob.mx; internet www.sre.gob.mx/vietnam; Ambassador GILBERTO LIMON ENRIQUEZ.

Mongolia: Villa 6, Van Phuc Diplomatic Quarter, Hanoi; tel. (4) 38453009; fax (4) 38454954; e-mail mongembhanoi@vnn.vn; Ambassador PALAMYN SÜNDEV.

Morocco: 9 Chu Van, Ba Dinh District, Hanoi; tel. (4) 37345586; fax (4) 37345589; e-mail embassymorocco.hanoi@fpt.vn; Ambassador EL HOUCINE FARDANI.

Myanmar: 298A Kim Ma, Hanoi; tel. (4) 38453369; fax (4) 38452404; e-mail mevhan@fpt.vn; Ambassador (vacant).

Netherlands: Daeha Office Tower, 6th Floor, 360 Kim Ma, Ba Dinh District, Hanoi; tel. (4) 38315650; fax (4) 38315655; e-mail han@minbuza.nl; internet www.netherlands-embassy.org.vn; Ambassador JOZEF WILLEM SCHEFFERS.

New Zealand: Level 5, 63 Ly Thai To, Hanoi; tel. (4) 38241481; fax (4) 38241480; e-mail nzembhan@fpt.vn; internet www.nzembassy.com/viet-nam; Ambassador HEATHER RIDDELL.

Norway: Vincom City Towers, Blk B, 10th Floor, 191 Ba Trieu, Hanoi; tel. (4) 39742930; fax (4) 39743301; e-mail emb.hanoi@mfa.no; internet www.norway.org.vn; Ambassador STÅLE TORSTEIN RISA.

Pakistan: 44/2 Van Bao, Van Phuc Diplomatic Quarter, Hanoi; tel. (4) 37262251; fax (4) 37262253; e-mail parepvietnam@yahoo.com; internet www.mofa.gov.pk/vietnam; Ambassador SHAHID M. G. KIANI.

Panama: 17F, 191 Ba Trieu, Hai Ba Trung, Hanoi; tel. (4) 9365213; Ambassador EDUARDO ANTONIO YOUNG VIRZI.

Philippines: 27B Tran Hung Dao, Hanoi; tel. (4) 39437873; fax (4) 39435760; e-mail hnpe2000@gmail.com; internet www.hanoipe.org; Ambassador JERRIL G. SANTOS.

Poland: 3 Chua Mot Cot, Hanoi; tel. (4) 38452027; fax (4) 38236914; e-mail hanoi.amb.sekretariat@msz.gov.pl; internet www.hanoi.polemb.net; Ambassador ROMAN IWASZKIEWICZ.

Romania: 5 Le Hong Phong, Hanoi; tel. (4) 38452014; fax (4) 38430922; e-mail romambhan@fpt.vn; Ambassador DUMITRU OLARU.

Russia: 191 La Thanh, Hanoi; tel. (4) 38336991; fax (4) 38336995; e-mail moscow.vietnam@hn.vnn.vn; internet www.vietnam.mid.ru; Ambassador ANDREI GRIGORIEVICH KOVTUN.

Saudi Arabia: Regus Hanoi Opera House, 2nd Floor, 63 Ly Thai To, Hoan Kiem District, Hanoi; tel. (4) 39366722; fax (4) 39367401; Ambassador SALAH AHMAD SARHAN.

Singapore: 41–43 Tran Phu, Hanoi; tel. (4) 38489168; fax (4) 38489178; e-mail singemb_han@sgmfa.gov.sg; internet www.mfa.gov.sg/hanoi; Ambassador SIMON WONG WIE KUEN.

South Africa: Central Bldg, 3rd Floor, 31 Hai Ba Trung, Hanoi; tel. (4) 9362000; fax (4) 9361991; e-mail admin.hanoi@foreign.gov.za; Ambassador RATUBATSI SUPER MOLOI.

Spain: Daeha Business Centre, 15th Floor, 360 Kim Ma, Ba Dinh District, Hanoi; tel. (4) 37715207; fax (4) 37715206; e-mail embajadaesp@vnn.vn; internet www.maec.es/subwebs/embajadas/hanoi; Ambassador FERNANDO CURCIO RUIGÓMEZ.

Sri Lanka: 55B Tran Phu, Ba Dinh District, Hanoi; tel. (4) 37341894; fax (4) 37341897; e-mail slembvn@fpt.vn; internet www.slembvn.org; Ambassador KALAHE GAMAGE IVAN AMARASINGHE.

Switzerland: 44B Ly Thuong Kiet, Central Office Bldg, 15th Floor, Hanoi; tel. (4) 39346589; fax (4) 39346591; e-mail han.vertretung@eda.admin.ch; internet www.eda.admin.ch/hanoi; Ambassador ANDREJ MOTYL.

Thailand: 63–65 Hoang Dieu, Hanoi; tel. (4) 38235092; fax (4) 38235088; e-mail thaiemhn@netnam.org.vn; Ambassador ANUSON CHIVANNO.

Turkey: 4 Da Tuong, Hoan Kiem District, Hanoi; tel. (4) 38222460; fax (4) 38222458; e-mail turkeyhn@fpt.vn; internet hanoi.emb.mfa.gov.tr; Ambassador AHMED AKIF OKTAY.

Ukraine: 6B Le Hong Phong, Ba Dinh District, Hanoi; tel. (4) 37344484; fax (4) 37344497; e-mail emb_vn@mfa.gov.ua; internet www.mfa.gov.ua/vietnam; Ambassador OLEKSIY SHOVKOPLIAS.

United Arab Emirates: 44/3 Van Bao, Van Phuc Diplomatic Quarter, Ba Dinh District, Hanoi; tel. (4) 37264545; fax (4) 37262020; e-mail feedback@uaeembassy.vn; internet uaeembassy.vn; Ambassador Sheikh AHMED ALI AL-MUALLA.

United Kingdom: Central Bldg, 4th Floor, 31 Hai Ba Trung, Hanoi; tel. (4) 39360500; fax (4) 39360561; e-mail behanoi02@vnn.vn; internet ukinvietnam.fco.gov.uk; Ambassador Dr ANTHONY STOKES.

USA: Rose Garden Tower, 3rd Floor, 170 Ngoc Khanh, Hanoi; tel. (4) 38505000; fax (4) 38505120; e-mail hanoiac@state.gov; internet vietnam.usembassy.gov; Ambassador DAVID SHEAR.

Venezuela: 368 Lac Long Quan, Tay Ho District, Hanoi; tel. (4) 7588891; fax (4) 7588893; e-mail embavenezhanoi@yahoo.com; Ambassador JORGE JOSÉ RONDÓN UZCÁTEGUI.

Judicial System

The Supreme People's Court in Hanoi is the highest court and exercises civil and criminal jurisdiction over all lower courts. The Supreme Court may also conduct trials of the first instance in certain cases. There are People's Courts in each province and city which exercise jurisdiction in the first and second instance. Military courts hear cases involving members of the People's Army and cases involving national security. In 1993 legislation was adopted on the establishment of economic courts to consider business disputes. The observance of the law by ministries, government offices and all citizens is the concern of the People's Organs of Control, under a Supreme People's Organ of Control. The Chief Justice of the Supreme People's Court and the Chief Procurator of the Supreme People's Organ of Control are elected by the National Assembly, on the recommendation of the President.

Chief Justice of the Supreme People's Court: TRUONG HOA BINH, 48 Ly Thuong Kiet, Hanoi.

Chief Procurator of the Supreme People's Organ of Control: TRAN QUOC VUONG.

Religion

Traditional Vietnamese religion included elements of Indian and all three Chinese religions: Mahayana Buddhism, Daoism and Confucianism. Its most widespread feature was the cult of ancestors, practised in individual households and clan temples. Various Buddhist sects belong to the 'new' religions of Caodaism and Hoa Hao. The Protestant and Roman Catholic Churches are also represented. In 2007 operating licences were granted to several additional religious groups, including the Mennonite Church, the Baptist Church and the Bahá'í faith.

BUDDHISM

In the North a Buddhist organization, grouping Buddhists loyal to the Democratic Republic of Viet Nam, was established in 1954. In the South the United Buddhist Church was formed in 1964, incorporating several disparate groups, including the 'militant' An-Quang group (mainly natives of central Viet Nam), the group of Thich Tam Chau (mainly northern emigrés in Saigon) and the southern Buddhists of the Xa Loi temple. In 1982 most of the Buddhist sects were amalgamated into the state-approved Viet Nam Buddhist Church (which comes under the authority of the Viet Nam Fatherland Front). The number of adherents was estimated at 10m. in 2005, approximately 12% of the total population. The Unified Buddhist Church of Viet Nam is an anti-Government organization.

Viet Nam Buddhist Church: e-mail trisu@phattuvietnam.net; internet www.phattuvietnam.net; Pres. Exec. Council Most Ven. THICH TRI TINH; Gen. Sec. THICH MING CHAU.

Unified Buddhist Church of Viet Nam: Leader Patriarch THICH QUANG DO.

CAODAISM

Formally inaugurated in 1926, this is a syncretic religion based on spiritualist seances with a predominantly ethical content, but sometimes with political overtones. There are 13 different sects, of which the most politically involved (1940–75) was that of Tay Ninh. Another sect, the Tien Thien, was represented in the National Liberation Front from its inception. There were an estimated 2.4m. adherents in 2005, resident mainly in the South.

Leader: Cardinal THAI HUU THANH.

CHRISTIANITY

In 2005 the number of Christian adherents represented an estimated 7.2% of the total population.

The Roman Catholic Church

The Roman Catholic Church has been active in Viet Nam since the 17th century, and since 1933 has been led mainly by Vietnamese priests. Many Roman Catholics moved from North to South Viet Nam in 1954–55, but some remained in the North. The total number of adherents was estimated at 6,089,223 in December 2007, representing 6.9% of the population. For ecclesiastical purposes, Viet Nam comprises three archdioceses and 23 dioceses.

Bishops' Conference

Conférence Episcopale du Viet Nam, 22 Tran Phu, Khank Hoa, Nha Trang; tel. (58) 822842; fax (58) 815494; e-mail vptk.hdgm@gmail.com.

f. 1980; Pres. Most Rev. PIERRE NGUYEN VAN NHON (Bishop of Da Lat).

Archbishop of Hanoi: Most Rev. PIERRE NGUYEN VAN NHON, Archevêché, 40 Pho Nha Chung, Hanoi; tel. (4) 8254424; fax (4) 9285073; e-mail ttgmhn@hn.vnn.vn.

Archbishop of Ho Chi Minh City: Cardinal JEAN-BAPTISTE PHAM MINH MÂN, Archevêché, 180 Nguyen Dinh Chieu, Ho Chi Minh City 3; tel. (8) 9303828; fax (8) 9300598.

Archbishop of Hué: Most Rev. ETIENNE NGUYEN NHU THE, Archevêché, 37 Phan Dinh Phung, Hué; tel. (54) 824937; fax (54) 833656; e-mail tgmhue@dng.vnn.vn.

Committee for Solidarity of Patriotic Vietnamese Catholics: 59 Trang Thi, Hanoi; Pres. Rev. VUONG DINH AI.

The Protestant Church

Introduced in 1920 with 500 adherents; the total number was estimated at 500,000 in 2005.

HOA HAO

A new manifestation of an older religion called Buu Son Ky Huong, the Hoa Hao sect was founded by Nguyen Phu So in 1939. There were an estimated 1.6m. adherents in 2005.

ISLAM

The number of Muslims was estimated at 65,000 in 2005.

The Press

The Ministry of Information and Communication supervises the activities of newspapers, news agencies and periodicals.

DAILIES

Hanoi

Le Courrier du Viet Nam: 33 Le Thanh Tong, Hanoi; tel. (4) 38252096; fax (4) 38258368; e-mail courrier@vnagency.com.vn; internet lecourrier.vnagency.com.vn; French; publ. by the Viet Nam News Agency; Editor-in-Chief HOANG LAN HUONG.

Dan Tri (Intellectual People's Standard): 2/48 Giang Vo, Dong Da District, Hanoi; tel. (4) 37366491; fax (4) 37366490; e-mail dantri@dantri.com.vn; internet www.dantri.com.vn; f. 1982, fmrly known as *Tin Tuc* (News); publ. by the Viet Nam News Agency; afternoon; Vietnamese; Editor-in-Chief HUY HOAN PHAM.

Hanoi Moi (New Hanoi): 44 Le Thai To, Hoan Kiem District, Hanoi; tel. (4) 38253067; fax (4) 39287445; e-mail webmaster@hanoimoi.com.vn; internet www.hanoimoi.com.vn; f. 1976; organ of Hanoi Cttee of the Communist Party of Viet Nam; Editor HO QUANG LOI; circ. 35,000.

Lao Dong (Labour): 52B Nguyen Thi Dinh, Trung Hoa, Cau Giay, Hanoi; tel. (4) 35562295; fax (4) 35562275; e-mail webmaster@laodong.com.vn; internet www.laodong.com.vn; f. 1929; organ of the Viet Nam General Confederation of Labour; Editor-in-Chief VUONG VAN VIET; circ. 80,000.

Nhan Dan (The People): 71 Hang Trong, Hoan Kiem District, Hanoi; tel. (4) 38254231; fax (4) 38255593; e-mail toasoan@nhandan.org.vn; internet www.nhandan.org.vn; f. 1946; official organ of the Communist Party of Viet Nam; Editor-in-Chief THUAN HUU; circ. 220,000.

Nong Nghiep Viet Nam (Viet Nam Agriculture): 1059 Hongha, Hoan Kiem, Hanoi; tel. (4) 38256492; fax (4) 38252923; e-mail baonnvn@hn.vnn.vn; internet www.nongnghiep.vn; f. 1987; fmrly a weekly publ; Editor-in-Chief LE NAM SON.

Quan Doi Nhan Dan (People's Army): 7 Phan Dinh Phung, Hanoi; tel. (4) 37471748; fax (4) 37474913; e-mail dientubqd@gmail.com; internet www.qdnd.vn; f. 1950; organ of the armed forces; Editor NGUYEN LE PHUC; circ. 80,000.

Thanh Nien: 248 Cong Quynh, District 1, Ho Chi Minh City; tel. (8) 39255738; fax (8) 39255901; e-mail admin@thanhniennews.com; internet www.thanhniennews.com; f. 1986; flagship publication of the Viet Nam National Youth Federation; Chief Editor NGUYEN QUANG THONG.

Viet Nam Economic Times: 96 Hoang Quoc Viet, Cau Giay District, Hanoi; tel. (4) 37552060; fax (4) 37552046; e-mail editor@vneconomy.vn; internet vneconomy.vn; f. 1994; in Vietnamese (with monthly edn in English); Editor-in-Chief Prof. DAO NGUYEN CAT; Dep. Editor-in-Chief NGUYEN THI VAN ANH; circ 38,900.

Viet Nam News: 11 Tran Hung Dao, Hanoi; tel. (4) 39332316; fax (4) 39332311; e-mail vnnews@vnagency.com.vn; internet vietnamnews.vnanet.vn; f. 1991; English; publ. by the Viet Nam News Agency; Editor-in-Chief TRAN MAI HUONG; circ. 60,000.

Ho Chi Minh City

Sai Gon Giai Phong (Liberated Saigon): 399 Hong Bang, Ward 14, District 5, Ho Chi Minh City; tel. (8) 39294092; fax (8) 39294083; e-mail sggponline@sggp.org.vn; internet www.sggp.org.vn; f. 1975; organ of Ho Chi Minh City Cttee of the Communist Party of Viet Nam; Editor-in-Chief TRAN THE TUYEN; circ. 100,000.

Saigon Times: 35 Nam Ky Khoi Nghia, District 1, Ho Chi Minh City; tel. (8) 38295936; fax (8) 38294294; e-mail sgt@thesaigontimes.vn; internet www.thesaigontimes.vn; f. 1991; Vietnamese and English; business issues; Editor-in-Chief TRAN THI NGOC HUE.

PERIODICALS

Dai Doan Ket (Great Unity): 66 Ba Trieu, Hanoi; tel. (4) 38228303; fax 38228547; e-mail toasoan@baodaidoanket.com.vn; internet www.daidoanket.vn; f. 1977; weekly; organ of the Viet Nam Fatherland Front; Editor DINH DUC LAP.

Dau Tu: 47 Quan Thanh, Ba Dinh, Hanoi; tel. (4) 38450537; fax (4) 38235281; e-mail baodautu.vn@gmail.com; internet baodautu.vn/portal/public/vir/trangchu; 3 a week; business newspaper publ. in Vietnamese; Editor-in-Chief Dr NGUYEN ANH TUAN; circ. 40,000.

Dau Tu Chung Khoan: 47 Quan Thanh, Ba Dinh, Hanoi; tel. (4) 98450537; fax (4) 38430969; e-mail tinnhanhchungkhoan@vir.com.vn; internet www.tinnhanhchungkhoan.vn; weekly; stock market news publ. in Vietnamese; Editor-in-Chief Dr NGUYEN ANH TUAN; circ. 50,000.

Giao Duc Thoi Dai (People's Teacher): 29B Ngo Quyen, Hoan Kiem District, Hanoi; tel. (4) 39369800; fax (4) 39345611; e-mail gdtddientu@gmail.com; internet www.gdtd.vn; f. 1959; weekly; organ of the Ministry of Education and Training; Chief Editor Dr NGUYEN DANH BINH.

Giao Thong-Van Tai (Communications and Transport): 1 Nha Tho, Hoan Kiem, Hanoi; tel. (4) 9286763; fax (4) 8255387; e-mail toasoan@giaothongvantai.com.vn; internet giaothongvantai.com.vn; f. 1962; weekly (Thur.); organ of Ministry of Transport; Editor NGUYEN VAN LUU; circ. 30,000.

Hoa Hoc Tro (Pupils' Flowers): 5 Hoa Ma, Hanoi; tel. (4) 8211065; internet www.hoahoctro.vn; weekly; Chief Editor NGUYEN HUY LOC; circ. 150,000.

Khoa Hoc Ky Thuat Kinh Te The Gioi (World Science, Technology and Economy): 5 Ly Thuong Kiet, Hanoi; tel. (4) 8252931; f. 1982; weekly.

Khoa Hoc va Doi Song (Science and Life): 70 Tran Hung Dao, Hanoi; tel. (4) 8253427; f. 1959; weekly; Editor-in-Chief TRAN CU; circ. 30,000.

Nghe Thuat Dien Anh (Cinematography): 65 Tran Hung Dao, Hanoi; tel. (4) 8262473; f. 1984; fortnightly; Editor DANG NHAT MINH.

Nguoi Cong Giao Viet Nam (Vietnamese Catholic): 59 Trang Thi, Hanoi; tel. (4) 8256242; f. 1984; weekly; organ of the Cttee for Solidarity of Patriotic Vietnamese Catholics; Editor-in-Chief SO CHI.

Nguoi Dai Bieu Nhan Dan (People's Deputy): 35 Ngo Quyen, Hanoi; tel. (4) 08046231; fax (4) 08046659; e-mail ndbnd@hn.vnn.vn; f. 1988; bi-weekly; disseminates resolutions of the National Assembly and People's Council; Editor-in-Chief HO ANH TAI (acting); circ. 2m.

Nguoi Hanoi (The Hanoian): 19 Hang Buom, Hanoi; tel. (4) 8255662; f. 1984; Editor VU QUAN PHUONG.

Nha Bao Va Cong Luan (The Journalist and Public Opinion): 59 Ly Thai To, Hanoi; tel. (4) 8253609; fax (4) 8250797; f. 1985; monthly review; organ of the Viet Nam Journalists' Asscn; Editor-in-Chief PHAN DUOC TOAN; circ. 40,000.

Outlook: 11 Tran Hung Dao, Hanoi; tel. (4) 8222884; fax (4) 9424908; e-mail vnnews@vnagency.com.vn; internet vietnamnews.vnanet.com.vn; f. 2002; monthly news magazine; Editor-in-Chief TRAN MAI HUONG; circ. 6,000.

Phu Nu (Woman): Vietnam Women's Union, International Relations Dept, 39 Hang Chuoi, Hanoi; e-mail VWUnion@netnam.org.vn; f. 1997; fortnightly; women's magazine; circ. 100,000.

Phu Nu Thu Do (Capital Women): 72 Quan Su, Hanoi; tel. (4) 8247228; fax (4) 8223989; f. 1987; weekly; magazine of the Hanoi Women's Union; Editor-in-Chief MAI THUC.

Phu Nu Viet Nam (Vietnamese Women): 39 Hang Chuoi, Hanoi; tel. (4) 8253500; weekly; magazine of the Vietnam Women's Union; Editor-in-Chief PHUONG MINH.

Suc Khoe Va Doi Song (Health and Life): 138A Giang Vo, Ba Dinh District, Hanoi; tel. (4) 38461684; fax (4) 38443144; e-mail tranyenchau@gmail.com; internet suckhoedoisong.vn; f. 1961; weekly; published by the Ministry of Health; Editor-in-Chief TRAN SI TUAN; circ. 45,000.

Tap Chi Cong San (Communist Review): 28 Tran Binh Trong Thanh, Hanoi; tel. (4) 9429753; fax (4) 9429754; e-mail baodientu@tccs.org.vn; internet www.tapchicongsan.org.vn; f. 1955 as *Hoc Tap*; fortnightly; political and theoretical organ of the Communist Party of Viet Nam; Editor-in-Chief Dr VU VAN PHUC; circ. 50,000.

Tap Chi Nghiên Cuu Van Hoc (Literature Research Magazine): 20 Ly Thai To, Hanoi; tel. (4) 8252895; e-mail tcvapmail@vnn.vn; monthly; published by the Institute of Literature; Editor-in-Chief PHAN TRONG THUONG.

Tap Chi San Khau (Theatre Magazine): 51 Tran Hung Dao, Hanoi; tel. (4) 9434423; fax (4) 9434293; e-mail trongkhoi@hn.vnn.vn; f. 1973; monthly; Editor NGO THAO.

Tap Chi Tac Pham Van Hoc: 65 Nguyen Du, Hanoi; tel. (4) 8252442; f. 1987; monthly; organ of the Viet Nam Writers' Asscn; Editor-in-Chief NGUYEN DINH THI; circ. 15,000.

Tap Chi Tu Tuong Van Hoa (Ideology and Culture Review): Hanoi; f. 1990; organ of the Central Committee Department of Ideology and Culture; Editor PHAM HUY VAN.

The Thao Van Hoa (Sports and Culture): 5 Ly Thuong Kiet, Hanoi; tel. (4) 8267043; fax (4) 8264901; f. 1982; weekly; Editor-in-Chief NGUYEN HUU VINH; circ. 100,000.

The Thao Viet Nam (Viet Nam Sports): 5 Trinh Hoai Duc, Hanoi; tel. (4) 35625457; fax (4) 35625455; e-mail baottvn@yahoo.com; internet www.thethaovietnam.com.vn; f. 1968; weekly; Editor HOANG DUR.

Thieu Nhi Dan Toc (The Ethnic Young): 5 Hoa Ma, Hanoi; tel. (4) 9317133; bi-monthly; Editor PHAM THANH LONG; circ. 60,000.

Thieu Nien Tien Phong (Young Pioneers): 5 Hoa Ma, Hanoi; tel. (4) 39713133; fax (4) 38215710; e-mail toasoan@thieunien.vn; internet www.thieunien.vn; 3 a week; Editor VU QUANG VINH; circ. 210,000.

Thoi Bao Kinh Te Viet Nam: 175 Nguyen Thai Hoc, Hanoi; tel. (4) 8452411; fax (4) 8432755; f. 1993; 2 a week; Editor-in-Chief PAVEF DAONGUYENCAT; circ. 37,000.

Thoi Trang Tre (New Fashion): 12 Ho Xuan Huong, Hanoi; tel. (4) 8254032; fax (4) 8226002; f. 1993; monthly; Editor VU QUANG VINH; circ. 80,000.

Thuong Mai (Commerce): 100 Lo Duc, Hanoi; tel. (4) 8263150; f. 1990; weekly; organ of the Ministry of Industry and Trade; Editor TRAN NAM VINH.

Tien Phong (Vanguard): 15 Ho Xuan Huong, Hanoi; tel. (4) 8264031; fax (4) 8225032; f. 1953; four a week; organ of the Ho Chi Minh Communist Youth Union and of the Forum of Vietnamese Youth; Editor DUONG XUAN NAM; circ. 165,000.

Van Hoa (Culture and Arts): 26 Dien Bien Phu, Hanoi; tel. (4) 8257781; f. 1957; fortnightly; Editor PHI VAN TUONG.

Van Nghe (Arts and Letters): 17 Tran Quoc Toan, Hanoi; tel. (4) 8264430; f. 1949; weekly; organ of the Vietnamese Writers' Union; Editor HUU THINH; circ. 40,000.

Van Nghe Quan Doi (Army Literature and Arts): 4 Ly Nam De, Hanoi; tel. (4) 8254370; f. 1957; monthly; Editor NGUYEN TRI HUAN; circ. 50,000.

Viet Nam Business Forum: 9 Dao Duy Anh, 4th Floor, Dong Da District, Hanoi; tel. (4) 35743985; fax (4) 35743063; e-mail vbfhn@hn.vnn.vn; internet vibforum.vcci.com.vn; f. 1995; weekly magazine in English; publ. by the Viet Nam Chamber of Commerce and Industry; Editor-in-Chief DOAN DUY KHUONG.

Viet Nam Courier: 5 Ly Thuong Kiet, Hanoi; tel. (4) 8261847; fax (4) 8242317; weekly; English; publ. by the Viet Nam News Agency; Editor-in-Chief NGUYEN DUC GIAP.

Viet Nam Cultural Window: 46 Tran Hung Dao, Hanoi; tel. (4) 38253841; fax (4) 38269578; e-mail vncw@hn.vnn.vn; f. 1998; every 2 months; English; Dir TRAN DOAN LAM.

Viet Nam Investment Review (VIR): 47 Quan Thanh, Ba Dinh, Hanoi; tel. (4) 38450537; fax (4) 38457937; e-mail vir.hn@vir.com.vn; internet www.vir.com.vn; f. 1990; weekly; business newspaper publ. in English; Editor-in-Chief Dr NGUYEN ANH TUAN; circ 40,000.

Vietnam Pictorial: 11 Tran Hung Dao, Hanoi; tel. (4) 39332303; fax (4) 39332291; e-mail vietnamvnp@gmail.com; f. 1954; monthly online, in Vietnamese, English, French, Chinese, Japanese, Spanish and Russian; fmrly Viet Nam Review; Editor-in-Chief NGUYEN THANG; circ. 138,000.

Viet Nam Renovation: Hanoi; f. 1994; quarterly magazine on reform of the agricultural sector; in Vietnamese, Chinese and English.

Viet Nam Social Sciences: 27 Tran Xuan Soan, Hanoi; tel. (4) 9784578; fax (4) 9783869; e-mail 21.6.tapchikhxh@fpt.vn; f. 1984; every 2 months; publ. in English and Vietnamese; organ of Viet Nam Social Academy; Editor-in-Chief Dr LE DINH CUC.

Vietnamese Studies: 46 Tran Hung Dao, Hanoi; tel. (4) 38253841; fax (4) 38269578; e-mail thegioi@hn.vnn.vn; internet www.thegioipublishers.com.vn; f. 1964; quarterly; English and French edns; Dir and Chief Editor Dr TRAN DOAN LÂM.

NEWS AGENCY

Viet Nam News Agency (VNA): 79 Ly Thuong Kiet, Hoan Kiem District, Hanoi; tel. (4) 38255443; fax (4) 38252984; e-mail btk@vnanet.vn; internet www.vnanet.vn; f. 1945; mem. of Organization of Asian and Pacific News Agencies; Gen. Dir TRAN MAI HUONG.

PRESS ASSOCIATION

Viet Nam Journalists' Association (VJA): 59 Ly Thai To, Hanoi; tel. (4) 39386270; fax (4) 38250797; e-mail hnbvietnam@gmail.com; internet www.vja.org.vn; f. 1950; asscn of editors, reporters and photographers working in the press, radio, television and news agencies; 17,000 mems (2008); Pres. NGUYEN CHU NHAC; Vice-Pres. HA MINH HUE.

Publishers

Am Nhac Dia Hat (Music) Publishing House: 61 Ly Thai To, Hoan Kiem District, Hanoi; tel. (4) 8256208; f. 1986; produces cassettes, videocassettes, books and printed music; Dir PHAM DUC LOC.

Cong An Nhan Dan (People's Public Security) Publishing House: 167 Mai Hac De, Hai Ba Trung District, Hanoi; tel. (4) 8260910; f. 1981; cultural and artistic information, public order and security; Dir PHAM VAN THAM.

Giao Thong Van Tai (Communications and Transport) Publishing House: 80B Tran Hung Dao, Hanoi; tel. (4) 39423346; fax (4) 38224784; e-mail nxbgtvt@fpt.vn; f. 1983; managed by the Ministry of Transport; 350 titles annually; Dir LE TU GIANG.

Khoa Hoc Va Ky Thuat (Science and Technology) Publishing House: 70 Tran Hung Dao, Hanoi; tel. (4) 39423172; fax (4) 8220658; e-mail nxbkhkt@hn.vnn.vn; internet www.nxbkhkt.com.vn; f. 1960; scientific and technical works, guide books, dictionaries, popular and management books; Dir PHAM VAN DIEN.

Khoa Hoc Xa Hoi (Social Sciences) Publishing House: 61 Phan Chu Trinh, Hanoi; tel. (4) 8255428; f. 1967; managed by the Institute of Social Science; Dir Dr NGUYEN DUC ZIEU.

Kim Dong Publishing House: 55 Quang Trung, Hanoi; tel. (4) 39434730; fax (4) 38229085; e-mail kimdong@hn.vnn.vn; internet www.nxbkimdong.com.vn; f. 1957; children's; managed by the Ho Chi Minh Communist Youth Union; Dir PHAM QUANG VINH; Dir PHAM QUANG VINH.

Lao Dong (Labour) Publishing House: 54 Giang Vo, Hanoi; tel. (4) 8515380; f. 1945; translations and political works; managed by the Viet Nam Gen. Confed. of Labour; Dir LE THANH TONG.

My Thuat (Fine Arts) Publishing House: 44B Hamlong, Hanoi; tel. (4) 39449076; fax (4) 39436133; e-mail ngandangminh@yahoo.com.vn; f. 1987; managed by the Plastic Arts Workers' Asscn; Dir NGAN DANG THI BICH.

Nha Xuat Ban Giao Duc (Education) Publishing House: 81 Tran Hung Dao, Hanoi; tel. (4) 38220801; fax (4) 39422010; e-mail vanphong@nxbgd.vn; internet www.nxbgd.vn; f. 1957; managed by the Ministry of Education and Training; Dir NGO TRAN AI; Editor-in-Chief NGUYEN QUY THAO.

Nha Xuat Ban Hoi Nha Van (Writers' Association) Publishing House: 65 Nguyen Du, Hoan Kiem District, Hanoi; tel. and fax (4) 8222135; f. 1957; managed by the Vietnamese Writers' Asscn; Editor-in-Chief NGO VAN PHU.

Nong Nghiep (Agriculture) Publishing House: DH 14, Phuong Mai Ward, Dong Da District, Hanoi; tel. (4) 8523887; f. 1976; managed by the Ministry of Agriculture and Rural Devt; Dir DUONG QUANG DIEU.

Phu Nu (Women) Publishing House: 16 Alexandre De Rhodes, Hanoi; tel. (4) 8294459; f. 1957; managed by the Vietnamese Women's Union; Dir TRAN THU HUONG.

Quan Doi Nhan Dan (People's Army) Publishing House: 25 Ly Nam De, Hanoi; tel. (4) 8255766; managed by the Ministry of National Defence; Dir DOAN CHUONG.

San Khau (Theatre) Publishing House: 51 Tran Hung Dao, Hanoi; tel. (4) 8264423; f. 1986; managed by the Stage Artists' Asscn; Dir NGO THE NGOC.

Su That (Truth) Publishing House: 24 Quang Trung, Hanoi; tel. (4) 8252008; fax (4) 8251881; f. 1945; Marxist-Leninist classics, politics and philosophy; managed by the Communist Party of Viet Nam; Dir TRAN NHAM.

Thanh Nien (Youth) Publishing House: 270 Nguyen Dinh Chieu, District 3, Hanoi; tel. and fax (4) 8222612; f. 1954; managed by the Ho Chi Minh Communist Youth Union; Dir BUI VAN NGOI.

The Duc The Thao (Physical Education and Sports) Publishing House: 7 Trinh Hoai Duc, Hanoi; tel. (4) 8256155; f. 1974; managed by the Ministry of Culture, Sports and Tourism; Dir NGUYEN HIEU.

The Gioi Publishers: 46 Tran Hung Dao, Hanoi; tel. (4) 38253841; fax (4) 38269578; e-mail thegioi@hn.vnn.vn; internet www.thegioipublishers.com.vn; f. 1957; foreign language publs; managed by the Ministry of Culture, Sports and Tourism; Dir and Chief Editor Dr TRAN DOAN LÂM.

Thong Ke (Statistics) Publishing House: 86–98 Thuy Khe, Hanoi; tel. (4) 38471483; fax (4) 38473714; e-mail nxbthongke@hn.vnn.vn; internet www.nxbthongke.com.vn; f. 1980; managed by the Gen. Statistics Office; Dir TRAN HUU THUC.

Van Hoa (Culture) Publishing House: 43 Lo Duc, Hanoi; tel. (4) 8253517; f. 1971; managed by the Ministry of Culture, Sports and Tourism; Dir QUANG HUY.

Van Hoc (Literature) Publishing House: 19 Nguyen Truong To, Ba Dinh, Hanoi; tel. (4) 8294783; fax (4) 8294781; f. 1948; managed by the Ministry of Culture, Sports and Tourism; Dir NGUYEN VAN CU.

Xay Dung (Building) Publishing House: 37 Le Dai Hanh, Hanoi; tel. (4) 8268271; fax (4) 8215369; f. 1976; managed by the Ministry of Construction; Dir NGUYEN LUONG BICH.

Y Hoc (Medicine) Publishing House: 4 Le Thanh Ton, Phan Chu Trinh, Hoan Kiem District, Hanoi; tel. (4) 8255281; e-mail xuatbanyhoc@netnam.vn; managed by the Ministry of Health; Dir HOANG TRONG QUANG.

PUBLISHERS' ASSOCIATION

Viet Nam Publishers' Association (Hoi Xuat Ban Viet Nam): Lo 2, B15, My Dinh 1, Tu Liem District, Hanoi; tel. and fax (4) 62872645; e-mail thuytp1803@gmail.com; Pres. NGUYEN KIEM.

Broadcasting and Communications

TELECOMMUNICATIONS

Directorate General for Posts and Telecommunications (DGPT): Department of Science-Technology and International Cooperation, 18 Nguyen Du, Hanoi; tel. (4) 8226580; fax (4) 8226590; industry regulator; Sec.-Gen. Dr MAI LIEM TRUC.

Board of the Technical and Economic Programme on Information Technology: 39 Tran Hung Dao, Hanoi; e-mail nyenet@itnet.gov.vn; Gen. Dir Dr DO VAN LOC.

Electricity of Viet Nam Telecommunications Co (EVN Telecom): 30A, Pham Hong Thai, Ba Dinh District, Hanoi; tel. (4) 22232323; fax (4) 22286868; internet www.evntelecom.com; provides fixed and cellular telephone services, as well as broadband internet services.

Hanoi Telecommunications Co (Hanoi Telecom): 2 Chua Boc, Dong Da District, Hanoi; tel. (3) 35729833; fax (4) 35729834; e-mail info@hanoitelecom.com; internet www.hanoitelecom.com; f. 2005; cellular telephone service provider; Chair. PHAM NGOC LANG.

Saigon Post and Telecommunications Service Corpn: 199 Dien Bien Phu, Binh Thanh District, Ho Chi Minh City; tel. (8) 54040608; fax (8) 54040609; e-mail info@spt.vn; internet www.spt.vn; f. 1995; partially state-owned; nation-wide post and telecommunications services; Chair. TRAN THI NGOC BINH; Pres. PHAM NGOC TUAN.

Viet Nam Military Electronics and Telecommunications Corpn (Viettel): 1 Giang Van Minh, Ba Dinh District, Hanoi; tel. (4) 62556789; fax (4) 62996789; e-mail gopy@viettel.com.vn; internet www.viettel.com.vn; f. 1998; offers range of post and telecommunication services, including cellular, 3G, telephone and broadband internet services; CEO TONG VIET TRUNG.

Viet Nam Posts and Telecommunications Corpn (VNPT): VNPT Bldg, 57 Huynh Thuc Khang, Dong Da District, Hanoi; tel. (3) 35775104; fax (3) 37741093; e-mail vnpt_website@vnpt.com.vn; internet www.vnpt.com.vn; f. 1995; state-owned communications co; Chair. PHAM LONG TRAN; Pres. and CEO VU TUAN HUNG.

Viet Nam Mobile Telecommunication Services Co (MobiFone): Lot VP1, Yen Hoa Ward, Cau Giay District, Hanoi; tel. (4) 37831733; e-mail webmaster@mobifone.com.vn; internet www.mobifone.com.vn; f. 1993; mobile cellular telephone service provider; Dir PHAM NGOC MINH.

Viet Nam Telecommunication Services Co (VinaPhone): 1 Nam Thanh Cong, Lot A, Dong Da District, Hanoi; tel. (4) 8358816; fax (4) 7731745; internet www.vinaphone.com.vn; f. 1996; provides mobile cellular telephone services; Man. Dir LAM HOANG VINH.

Vietnam Power Telecommunications Co (VP Telecom): Hanoi; f. 2004; cellular telephone service provider.

RADIO

Voice of Viet Nam (VOV): 58 Quan Su, Hanoi; tel. (4) 39344231; fax (4) 39344230; e-mail toasoan@vovnews.vn; internet www.vov.org.vn; f. 1945; four domestic channels in Vietnamese; two foreign service channels in English, Japanese, French, Khmer, Laotian, Spanish, Thai, Cantonese, Mandarin, Indonesian, Vietnamese and Russian; Dir-Gen. Dr VU VAN HIEN.

TELEVISION

Viet Nam Television (VTV): 43 Nguyen Chi Thanh, Hanoi; tel. (4) 8354992; fax (4) 8350882; e-mail webmaster@vtv.org.vn; internet www.vtv.org.vn; television was introduced in South Viet Nam in 1966 and in North Viet Nam in 1970; broadcasts from Hanoi (via satellite) to the whole country, the Asia region, Western Europe and North America; Vietnamese, French, English; Dir-Gen. Dr VU VAN HIEN.

Vietnam Multimedia Corpn (Vietnam Television Corpn—VTC): 8 Duong Tam Trinh, Hanoi; e-mail vtcvod@vtc.vn; internet www.vtc.com.vn; controlled by the Ministry of Information and Communication; Dir TAN THAI MINH.

Finance

(cap. = capital; res = reserves; dep. = deposits; m. = million; brs = branches; amounts in new dông unless otherwise indicated)

BANKING

In 2010 the Vietnamese banking system comprised five state-owned commercial banks, one policy bank, five joint-venture banks, 48 foreign bank branches, 37 joint-stock commercial banks and 1,016 local credit funds, supervised by the Central People's Credit Fund. The Vietnam Bank for the Poor, established in 1995, was renamed the Vietnam Bank for Social Policies in 2003. It provides subsidized credit. From March 2006 foreign banks were for the first time allowed to offer a full range of banking services.

Central Bank

State Bank of Viet Nam: 49 Ly Thai To, Hanoi; tel. (4) 39343327; fax (4) 39349569; e-mail webmaster@sbv.gov.vn; internet www.sbv.gov.vn; f. 1951; central bank of issue; provides a national network of banking services and supervises the operation of the state banking system; Gov. NGUYEN VAN BINH; 61 brs and sub-brs.

State Banks

Bank for Investment and Development of Vietnam (BIDV): BIDV Tower, 35 Hang Voi, Hoan Kiem District, Hanoi; tel. (4) 22205544; fax (4) 22200399; e-mail bidv@hn.vnn.vn; internet www.bidv.com.vn; cap. 10,498,568m., res 5,651,721m., dep. 220,150,826m. (Dec. 2009); Chair. TRAN BAC HA; Gen. Dir TRAN ANH TUAN.

Housing Bank of Mekong Delta (MHB): 9 Vo Van Tan, District 3, Ho Chi Minh City; tel. (8) 39302501; fax (8) 39302506; e-mail webmaster@mhb.com.vn; internet www.mhb.com.vn; f. 1997; cap. 823,394m., res 337,948m., dep. 30,000,745m. (Dec. 2009); Chair. HUYNH NAM DUNG.

Joint Stock Commercial Bank for Foreign Trade of Viet Nam (Vietcombank): 198 Tran Quang Khai, Hanoi; tel. (4) 9343137; fax (4) 8269067; e-mail webmaster@vietcombank.com.vn; internet www.vietcombank.com.vn; f. 1963; authorized to deal in foreign currencies and all other international banking business; undergoing equitization in mid-2005; cap. 12,146,020m., res 1,460,250m., dep. 230,485,478m. (Dec. 2009); Chair. NGUYEN HOA BINH; Dir-Gen. NGUYEN PHUOC THANH; 23 brs.

Vietnam Bank for Agriculture and Rural Development (VBARD): 2 Lang Ha, Ba Dinh District, Hanoi; tel. (4) 8313717; fax (4) 8313719; e-mail webmaster@agribank.com.vn; internet www.agribank.com.vn; f. 1988; cap. 11,283,171m., res 7,418,666m., dep. 376,625,401m. (Dec. 2009); Chair. NGUYEN THE BINH; Gen. Dir PHAM THANH TAN; 2,200 brs.

Vietnam Joint Stock Commercial Bank for Industry and Trade (VietinBank): 108 Tran Hung Dao, Hanoi; tel. (4) 39421030; fax (4) 39421032; internet www.vietinbank.vn; f. 1987; fmrly Industrial and Commercial Bank of Viet Nam (Incombank); authorized to receive personal savings, extend loans, issue stocks and invest in export-orientated cos and jt ventures with foreign interests; cap. 11,252,973m., res 482,829m., dep. 172,347,747m. (Dec. 2009); Chair. PHAM HUY HUNG; Gen. Dir PHAM XUAN LAP; 150 brs.

Joint-Stock and Other Banks

Asia Commercial Bank: 442 Nguyen Thi Minh Khai, District 3, Ho Chi Minh City; tel. (8) 39290999; fax (8) 38343269; e-mail acb@acb

.com.vn; internet www.acb.com.vn; f. 1993; Chair. TRAN XUAN GIA; Pres. LY XUAN HAI.

CBD (Codo Rural Share Commercial Bank): Co Do, Thoi Dong, O Mon, Can Tho Province; tel. (71) 61642; Dir TRAN NGOC HA.

DS Bank (Dongthap Commercial Joint-Stock Bank): 48 Rad 30/4, Cao Lanh Town, Dong Thap Province; tel. (67) 51441; fax (67) 51878; Dir HOANG VAN TU.

Ficombank (Denhat Joint-Stock Commercial Bank): 715 Tran Hung Dao, Ward 1, District 5, Ho Chi Minh City; tel. (8) 39237128; fax (8) 39234314; internet www.ficombank.com.vn; CEO NGUYEN NGOC THINH.

Indovina Bank Ltd: 46–50 Pham Hong Thai, District 1, Ho Chi Minh City; tel. (8) 38224995; fax (8) 38230131; e-mail support@indovinabank.com.vn; internet www.indovinabank.com.vn; f. 1990; jt venture of Cathay United Bank (Taiwan) and VietinBank; also has brs in Hanoi, Haiphong, Binh Duong, Can Tho and Dong Nai; cap. US $25m., res $3.4m., dep. $151m. (Dec. 2004); Chair. ROGER MING HSIEN LEE; Gen. Dir JAN YEI-FONG; 9 brs.

Maritime Commercial Joint Stock Bank: 88 Lang Ha, Dong Da District, Hanoi; tel. (4) 37718989; fax (4) 37718899; e-mail msb@msb.com.vn; internet www.msb.com.vn; f. 1991; cap. 3,000,000m., res 370,752m., dep. 54,314,306m. (Dec. 2009); Chair. LE THI LIEN; Gen. Dir TRAN ANH TUAN; 9 brs.

Phuong Nam Commercial Joint-Stock Bank (Southern Bank): 279 Ly Thuong Kiet, District 11, Ho Chi Minh City; tel. (8) 38663890; fax (8) 38663891; e-mail icsc@southernbank.com.vn; internet www.southernbank.com.vn; f. 1993; cap. 2,949,318m., dep. 31,758,689m. (Dec. 2009); Chair. MACH THIEU DUC.

Sacombank (Saigon Thuong Tin Commercial Joint-Stock Bank): 266–268 Nam Ky Khoi Nghia, Ward 8, District 3, Ho Chi Minh City; tel. (8) 39320420; fax (8) 39320424; e-mail info@sacombank.com.vn; internet www.sacombank.com.vn; f. 1991; became the first bank to list on the Securities Trading Centre in July 2006; cap. 8,078,178m., res 2,210,823m., dep. 83,943,435m. (Dec. 2009); Chair. DANG VAN THANH; CEO TRAN XUAN HUY.

Saigon Bank for Industry and Trade: 2C Pho Duc Chinh, District 1, Ho Chi Minh City; tel. (8) 39143183; fax (8) 39143193; e-mail webadmin@saigonbank.com.vn; internet www.saigonbank.com.vn; cap. 1,500,715m., res 223,928.1m., dep. 9,096,920.7m. (Dec. 2009); specializes in trade and industry activities; Chair. NGUYEN PHUC MINH; Dir-Gen. TRAN THI VIET ANH; 32 brs.

Shinhanvina Bank: 100 Nguyen Thi Minh Khai, Ward 6, District 3, Ho Chi Minh City; tel. (8) 38291581; fax (8) 38211648; internet www.shinhanvina.com.vn; f. 1993; jt venture between Vietcombank and Korea First Bank; fmrly known as Chohung Vina Bank; cap. US $30.0m., res $3.3m., dep. $181.5m. (Dec. 2007); Chair. PHU THAI VU; CEO CHOI HEUNG YEON.

Southeast Asia Commercial Joint Stock Bank (SeABank): 25 Tran Hung Dao, Hoan Kiem, Hanoi; tel. (4) 39448688; fax (4) 39448689; e-mail seabank@seabank.com.vn; internet www.seabank.com.vn; f. 1994; cap. 5,068,600m., res 141,552m., dep. 24,646,214m. (Dec. 2009); Chair. NGUYEN THI NGA.

VID Public Bank: Prime Bldg Centre, 7th Floor, 53 Quang Trung, Hanoi; tel. (4) 9438999; fax (4) 9439005; e-mail vidservice@vnn.vn; internet www.vidpublicbank.com.vn; f. 1992; jt venture between Bank for Investment and Devt of Viet Nam and Public Bank Bhd (Malaysia); commercial bank; cap. US $20m. (2001); Chair. TRAN ANH TUAN (acting); Gen. Dir KONG CHEE FIRE; 7 brs.

Vietnam Export-Import Commercial Joint-Stock Bank (Vietnam Eximbank): 7 Le Thi Hong Gam, District 1, Ho Chi Minh City; tel. (8) 38210055; fax (8) 38296063; e-mail website@eximbank.com.vn; internet www.eximbank.com.vn; f. 1989; est. as Vietnam Export Import Bank; present name adopted 1992; authorized to undertake banking transactions for the production and processing of export products and export-import operations; cap. 12,526,947m., res 377,856m., dep. 49,517,147m. (Dec. 2009); Chair. LE HUNG DUNG; Dir-Gen. TRUONG VAN PHUOC; 124 brs and offices.

Viet Nam Technological and Commercial Joint-Stock Bank (Techcombank): 70–72 Ba Trieu, Hoan Kiem District, Hanoi; tel. (4) 39446368; fax (4) 39446362; internet www.techcombank.com.vn; cap. 5,400,417m., res 525,719m., dep. 84,104,081m. (Dec. 2009); Chair. HO HUNG ANH; Gen. Dir NGUYEN DUC VINH.

VinaSiam Bank: 2 Pho Duc Chinh, District 1, Ho Chi Minh City; tel. (8) 38210630; fax (8) 38210585; e-mail vsb@vsb.com.vn; internet www.vinasiambank.com; f. 1995; jt venture between Bank for Agriculture and Rural Devt, Siam Commercial Bank (Thailand) and Charoen Pokphand Group (Thailand); cap. US $20.0m., res. $1.1m., dep. $37.2m. (Dec. 2005); Chair. LE VAN SO; Gen. Man. VIROJ THANAPITAK.

VP Bank (Viet Nam Commercial Joint-Stock Bank for Private Enterprises): 8 Le Thai To, Hoan Kiem District, Hanoi; tel. (4) 39288869; fax (4) 39288867; internet www.vpb.com.vn; cap. 2,117,474m., res 301,046m., dep. 23,974,394m. (Dec. 2009); Chair. NGO CHI DUNG; Gen. Dir NGUYEN HUNG.

STOCK EXCHANGES

Hanoi Stock Exchange (HNX): 81 Tran Hung Dao, Hoan Kiem, Hanoi; tel. (4) 39360750; fax (4) 39347818; e-mail marketinfo@hnx.vn; internet www.hnx.vn; f. 2005; est. as Hanoi Securities Trading Centre; renamed as above 2009; 382 listed stocks (May 2011); CEO TRAN VAN DZUNG.

Ho Chi Minh Stock Exchange: 45–47 Ben Chuong Duong, District 1, Ho Chi Minh City; tel. (8) 38217713; fax (8) 38217452; internet www.hsx.vn; f. 2000; fmrly Securities Trading Centre; name changed as above in 2007; Chair. NGUYEN DOAN HUNG.

Supervisory Body

State Securities Commission: 164 Tran Quang Khai, Hanoi; tel. (4) 39340750; fax (4) 39340739; e-mail banbientap@ssc.gov.vn; internet www.ssc.gov.vn; f. 1997; responsible for developing the capital markets, incl. the establishment of a stock exchange; 13 mems; Chair. BANG VU.

INSURANCE

In September 2006 there were 22 insurance companies operating in the country.

Aon Vietnam Ltd: Suites 1403–07, 14th Floor, Vietcombank Tower, 198 Tran Quang Khai, Hoan Kiem District, Hanoi; tel. (4) 38260832; fax (4) 38243983; e-mail vu_my_lan@aon-asia.com; internet www.aon.com/vietnam; f. 1993; fmrly Inchibrok Insurance; Man. Dir VU MY LAN.

Bao Long (Nha Rong Joint-Stock Insurance Co): 185 Dien Bien Phu, Dakao Ward, District 1, Ho Chi Minh City; tel. (8) 8239219; fax (8) 8239223; internet www.nharonginsurance.com; Dir TRAN VAN BINH.

Bao Minh Insurance Co (Ho Chi Minh City Insurance Co): 26 Ton That Dam, District 1, Ho Chi Minh City; tel. (8) 38294180; fax (8) 38294185; e-mail baominh@baominh.com.vn; internet www.baominh.com.vn; f. 1994; non-life; Chair. and CEO VINH DUC TRAN; Gen. Dir LE VAN THANH.

Baoviet (Viet Nam Insurance Co): 35 Hai Ba Trung, Hoan Kiem District, Hanoi; tel. (4) 38262774; fax (4) 38257188; e-mail bvvn@baoviet.com.vn; internet www.baoviet.com.vn/bvvn.asp; f. 1965; property and casualty, personal accident, liability and life insurance; total assets 8,817,000m. dông (2004); Chair. LE QUANG BINH; CEO TRAN TRONG PHUC.

Dai-ichi Life Insurance Co of Vietnam Ltd: 3rd Floor, Saigon Riverside Office Center, 2A–4A, Ton Duc Thang, District 1, Ho Chi Minh City; tel. (8) 38291919; fax (8) 38293131; e-mail info@dai-ichi-life.com.vn; internet www.dai-ichi-life.com.vn; f. 2007; Chair. and CEO TAKASHI FUJII.

Manulife (Vietnam) Ltd: Manulife Plaza, 75 Hoang Van Thai, Tan Phu Ward, District 7, Ho Chi Minh City; tel. (8) 54166888; fax (8) 54161818; e-mail manulifevn_info@manulife.com; internet www.manulife.com.vn; f. 1999; fmrly Chinfon-Manulife Life Insurance Co Ltd; first wholly foreign-owned life insurance co to operate in Viet Nam; Gen. Dir CARL GUSTINI.

Petrolimex Joint-Stock Insurance Co (PJICO Insurance): 532 Lang Ha, Dong Da District, Hanoi; tel. (4) 37760867; fax (4) 37760868; e-mail pjico@petrolimex.com.vn; internet www.pjico.com.vn; f. 1995; non-life insurance; Chair. NGUYEN VAN TIEN; Gen. Dir NGUYEN ANH DUNG.

PetroVietnam Insurance Joint Stock Corpn (PVI): 154 Nguyen Thai Hoc, Ba Dinh District, Hanoi; tel. (4) 37335588; fax (4) 37336284; e-mail contact@pvi.com.vn; internet www.pvi.com.vn; f. 1996; non-life insurance; Chair. NGUYEN ANH TUAN; Gen. Dir BUI VAN THUAN.

Viet Nam International Assurance Co (VIA): Sun Red River Bldg, 6th Floor, 23 Phan Chu Trinh, Hoan Kiem District, Hanoi; tel. (4) 39330704; fax (4) 39330706; e-mail hn@via.com.vn; internet www.via.com.vn; f. 1996; jt-venture co, 51% owned by Baoviet, 49% owned by Tokio Marine and Nichido Fire Insurance Co (Japan); non-life insurance and reinsurance for foreign cos; Marketing Man. VU THI KIM CHI.

INSURANCE ASSOCIATION

Association of Vietnamese Insurers: 8th Floor, 141 Le Duan, Hanoi; tel. (4) 39412063; fax (4) 39422601; internet www.avi.org.vn; Chair. TRINH QUANG TUYEN.

Trade and Industry

GOVERNMENT AGENCIES

State Financial and Monetary Council (SFMC): f. 1998; established to supervise, review and resolve matters relating to national financial and monetary policy.

Vietrade (Viet Nam Trade Promotion Agency): 20 Ly Thuong Kiet, Ba Dinh District, Hanoi; tel. (4) 39347628; fax (4) 39344260; e-mail vietrade@vietrade.gov.vn; internet www.vietrade.gov.vn; part of the Ministry of Industry and Trade; responsible for state management, co-ordination and implementation of trade and trade-related investment promotion and development activities; Dir-Gen. DO THANG HAI.

Vinacontrol (The Viet Nam Superintendence and Inspection Joint Stock Co): 54 Tran Nhan Tong, Hanoi; tel. (4) 39433840; fax (4) 39433844; e-mail vinacontrolvn@hn.vnn.vn; internet www.vinacontrol.com.vn; f. 1957; brs in all main Vietnamese ports and trade centres; controls quality and volume of exports and imports and transit of goods, and conducts inspections, sampling and testing of deliveries and production processes; price, assets and enterprise valuation, marine survey, damage survey, claim settling and adjustment; Chair. BUI DUY CHINH; Gen. Dir MAI TIEN DUNG; 600 employees.

CHAMBER OF COMMERCE

VCCI (Viet Nam Chamber of Commerce and Industry): 9 Dao Duy Anh, 4th Floor, Hanoi; tel. (4) 35742022; fax (4) 35742020; e-mail webmaster@vcci.com.vn; internet www.vcci.com.vn; f. 1963; offices throughout Viet Nam; promotes business and investment between foreign and Vietnamese cos; organizes exhibitions, provides information etc.; represents foreign applicants for patents and trade mark registration; helps domestic and foreign businesses to settle disputes by negotiation or arbitration; Pres. and Chair. Dr VU TIEN LOC; Sec.-Gen. PHAM GIA TUC; assoc. orgs: Viet Nam Int. Arbitration Centre, Viet Nam General Average Adjustment Cttee, Advisory Bd.

Viet Nam International Arbitration Centre (VIAC): 9 Dao Duy Anh, 6th Floor, Dong Da District, Hanoi; tel. (4) 35744001; fax (4) 35743001; e-mail viac-vcci@hn.vnn.vn; internet www.viac.org.vn; f. 1993; adjudicates in disputes concerning both domestic and international economic relations.

INDUSTRIAL AND TRADE ORGANIZATIONS

Agrex Saigon (Agricultural Products and Foodstuffs Export Co): 58 Vo Van Tan, District 3, Ho Chi Minh City; tel. (8) 39303186; fax (8) 38725194; e-mail tt-agr@hcm.fpt.vn; internet www.agrexsaigon.com.vn; f. 1976; exports agricultural produce, coffee, frozen foods and aquatic products; imports agricultural and industrial materials, machinery and equipment, and consumer goods; Gen. Dir LE THI MY LINH; 1,200 employees.

Agrimex (Viet Nam National Agricultural Products Corpn): 173 Hai Ba Trung, District 3, Ho Chi Minh City; tel. (8) 8241049; fax (8) 8291349; e-mail agrimex@hcm.fpt.vn; f. 1956; imports and exports agricultural products; Gen. Dir NGUYEN BACH TUYET.

Airimex (General Civil Aviation Import-Export and Forwarding Co): 414 Nguyen Van Cu, Gia Lam, Long Bien District, Hanoi; tel. (4) 38271939; fax (4) 38271925; e-mail contact@airimex.vn; internet www.airimex.vn; f. 1989; imports and exports aircraft, spare parts and accessories for aircraft and air communications; Gen. Dir PHAM DOA HONG.

An Giang Afiex Co (An Giang Agriculture and Foods Import and Export Co): 25/40 Tran Hung Dao, Long Xuyen Town, An Giang Province; tel. (76) 932985; fax (76) 932981; e-mail xnknstpagg@hcm.vnn.vn; internet www.afiex-seafood.com.vn; f. 1992; mfr and sale of agricultural products, also beverages; Dir PHAM VAN BAY.

Artexport–Vietnam (Viet Nam Handicrafts and Art Articles Export-Import Joint Stock Co): 2A Pham Su Manh, Hanoi; tel. (4) 38266576; fax (4) 38259275; e-mail ducquantri@artexport.com.vn; internet www.artexport.com.vn; f. 1964; deals in craft products and art articles; Gen. Dir DO VAN KHOI.

B12 Petroleum Co: Cai Lan, Bay Chay Sub-District, Ha Long City, Quang Ninh Province; tel. (33) 846360; fax (33) 846349; internet www.b12petroleum.com.vn; distribution of petroleum products; Dir VU NGOC HAI.

Barotex (Viet Nam Investment and Trading Joint Stock Co): 100 Thai Thinh, Dong Da District, Hanoi; tel. (4) 38573428; fax (4) 38573036; e-mail info@barotex.com.vn; internet www.barotex.com.vn; f. 1971; specializes in art and handicrafts made from natural materials, sports shoes, ceramic and lacquer wares, gifts and other housewares, fibres, agricultural and forest products; Gen. Dir TA QUOC TOAN.

Bim Son Cement Co: Badinh, Bimson Town, Thanh Hoa Province; tel. (37) 3824242; fax (37) 3824046; e-mail ktkh_bs@yahoo.com; internet www.ximangbimson.com.vn; mfr of cement; Dir NGUYEN NHU KHUE.

Binh Tay Import-Export Joint Stock Co (BITEX): 110–112 Hau Giang, District 6, Ho Chi Minh City; tel. (8) 9604325; fax (8) 9602478; e-mail bitexvn@bitexvn.com; trade in miscellaneous goods; Dir NGUYEN VAN THIEN.

Centrimex (Viet Nam National General Import-Export Corpn): 247 Giang Vo, Dong Da District, Hanoi; tel. (58) 8512986; fax (58) 8512974; e-mail centrimexhn@fpt.vn; internet www.centrimexhn.com.vn; f. 1986; exports and imports goods for five provinces in the south-central region of Viet Nam; Gen. Dir HOANG DINH DUNG.

Coalimex (Vinacomin Coal Import-Export Joint Stock Co): 47 Quang Trung, Hanoi; tel. (4) 9423166; fax (4) 9422350; e-mail coalimex@fpt.vn; internet www.coalimex.com.vn; f. 1982; exports coal, imports mining machinery and equipment; Gen. Dir PHAM HONG KHANH.

Cocenex (Central Production Import-Export Corpn): 80 Hang Gai, Hanoi; tel. (4) 8254535; fax (4) 8294306; f. 1988; Gen. Dir BUI THI THU HUONG.

Coffee Supply, Processing and Materials Co: 38B Nguyen Bieu, Nha Trang City, Khanh Hoa Province; tel. (58) 21176; coffee mfr.

Cokyvina (Post and Telecommunication Equipment Import-Export Service Corpn): 178 Trieu Viet Vuong, Hai Ba Trung, Hanoi; tel. (4) 39781323; fax (4) 39782368; e-mail info@cokyvina.com.vn; internet www.cokyvina.com.vn; f. 1987; imports and exports telecom equipment, provides technical advice on related subjects, undertakes authorized imports, jt ventures, jt co-ordination and co-operation on investment with foreign and domestic economic orgs; Dir NGUYEN KIM KY.

Constrexim (Viet Nam Construction Investment and Export-Import Holdings Corpn): 39 Nguyen Dinh Chieu, Hai Ba Trung, Hanoi; tel. (4) 2812000; fax (4) 7820176; e-mail constrexim@fpt.vn; internet www.constrexim.com.vn; f. 1982; exports and imports building materials, equipment and machinery; undertakes construction projects in Viet Nam and abroad, and production of building materials with foreign partners; also involved in investment promotion and project management, real estate development, and human resources development and training; Gen. Dir DO MANH VU.

Culturimex (State Enterprise for the Export and Import of Works of Art and other Cultural Commodities): 22B Hai Ba Trung, Hanoi; tel. (4) 8252226; fax (4) 8259224; e-mail namson@fpt.vn; f. 1988; exports cultural items and imports materials for the cultural industry; Gen. Dir NGUYEN LAI.

Dau Tieng Rubber Corpn: Dau Tieng Townlet, Dau Tieng District, Binh Duong Province; tel. (650) 561847; fax (650) 561488; e-mail vanphong@caosudautieng.com.vn; internet www.caosudautieng.com.vn; f. 1981; planting, processing and export of natural rubber; Man. Dir LE VAN KHOA.

Epco Ltd (Export Import and Tourism Co Ltd): 1 Nyuyen Thuong Hien, District 3, Ho Chi Minh City; tel. (8) 8324392; fax (8) 8324744; f. 1986; processes seafood; tourism and hotel business; Gen. Dir NGUYEN LOC RI.

Foodcosa (Food Co Ho Chi Min City): 57 Nguyen Thi Minh Khai, District 1, Ho Chi Minh City; tel. (8) 39309184; fax (8) 39304552; e-mail info@foodcosa.vn; internet www.foodcosa.vn; mfr and distributor of food products (rice, instant noodles, porridge, sauces, biscuits); Dir NGO VAN TAN; 3,500 employees.

Forexco Quang Nam (Quang Nam Forest Products Export Joint Stock Co): Xa Dien Ngoc, Dien Ban District, Quangnam Province; tel. (510) 3944073; fax (510) 3843619; e-mail forexcoqnam@dng.vnn.vn; internet forexco.com.vn; f. 1986; mfr and exporter of furniture and other wood products; Gen. Dir PHAM PHU THONG.

Garmex Saigon (Saigon Garment Manufacturing Import-Export Co): 236/7 Nguyen Van Luong, Ward 17, Go Vap District, Ho Chi Minh City; tel. (8) 39844822; fax (8) 39844746; e-mail gmsg@hcm.fpt.vn; internet www.garmexsaigon-gmc.com; f. 1993; garment production and export; Pres. LE QUANG HUNG; Man. Dir NGUYEN AN.

Genecofov (General Co of Foods and Services): 64 Ba Huyen Thanh Quan, District 3, Ho Chi Minh City; tel. (8) 9325366; fax (8) 9325428; e-mail gecofov@hcm.fpt.vn; f. 1956; import and export of food products, handicrafts and ceramics, garage services, vehicle trading; under the Ministry of Trade; Dir TO VAN PHAT.

Generalexim (Viet Nam National General Export-Import Corpn): 46 Ngo Quyen, Hoan Kiem, Hanoi; tel. (4) 38264009; fax (4) 38259894; e-mail gexim@generalexim.com.vn; internet www.generalexim.com.vn; f. 1981; export and import on behalf of production and trading organizations, also garment processing for export and manufacture of toys; Gen. Dir HOANG TUAN KHAI.

Generalimex (General II Import-Export Joint Stock Co): 212/1 Nguyen Trai, District 1, Ho Chi Minh City; tel. (8) 62907517; fax (8) 62907518; e-mail generalimex@generalimex.com.vn; internet www.generalimex.com.vn; exports of agricultural products and spices, imports of machinery, vehicles, chemicals and fertilizers; Gen. Dir NGUYEN VAN HOANG.

Haprosimex (Hanoi General Production and Import-Export Company): Km 11, National Highway 1A, Van Dien, Hanoi; tel. (4) 8618341; fax (4) 8615390; e-mail business@hapro.com.vn; internet www.hapro.com.vn; specializes in handicrafts, textiles, clothing and agricultural and forestry products; Gen. Dir NGUYEN MINH TUAN.

Hatien 1 Cement Joint Stock Co: 360 Ben Chuong Dong, P. Cau Kho, District 1, Ho Chi Minh City; tel. (8) 38368363; fax (8) 38361278; e-mail hatien1@hatien1.com.vn; internet www.hatien1.com.vn; mfr of cement; Dir NGUYEN NGOC ANH.

Hatien Cement Co No 2: Kien Luong Town, Ha Tien, Kien Giang Province; tel. (77) 53004; fax (77) 53005; e-mail xmht2@vnn.vn; internet www.xmht2.com; mfr of cement; Dir NGUYEN MANH.

Haugiang Petrolimex (Haugiang Petrol and Oil Co): 21 Cach Mang Thang 8, Can Tho City, Can Tho Province; tel. (71) 21657; fax (71) 12746; distributor of fuel; Dir TRINH MANG THANG.

Hoang Thach Cement Co: Minh Tan Hamlet, Kinh Mon, Hai Durong; tel. (32) 3821092; fax (32) 3821098; e-mail contact@ximanghoangthach.com; internet www.ximanghoangthach.com.vn; sale of construction materials; Dir NGOC BINH DAO.

Intimex Import-Export Corpn: 96 Tran Hung Dao, Hanoi; tel. (4) 39423529; fax (4) 39424250; e-mail intimex@hn.vnn.vn; internet www.intimexco.com; f. 1979; exports mainly agricultural products and processed items; imports mainly consumer goods, motorcycles and raw materials, machinery and equipment for the construction industry; Chair. NGUYEN THI NGA; Gen. Dir HOANG HOANG HANH.

Lefaso (Viet Nam Leather and Footwear Asscn): 160 Hoang Hoa Tham, Tay Ho, Hanoi; tel. (4) 37281560; fax (4) 37281561; e-mail hhdg@hn.vnn.vn; internet www.lefaso.org.vn; f. 1990 to promote external trade relations, to provide technical support and technological training and to disseminate market information; Chair. NGUYEN DUC THUAN; Gen. Sec. NGUYEN THI TONG.

Machinoimport (Viet Nam Machinery and Spare Parts Co): 8 Trang Thi, Hoan Kiem, Hanoi; tel. (4) 8253703; fax (4) 8254050; e-mail machinokhdt@hn.vnn.vn; internet www.machinoimport.com.vn; f. 1956 as Vietnam National Machinery Export-Import Corpn; reorganized in 2003; controlled by Ministry of Industry and Trade; imports and exports machinery, spare parts and tools; consultancy, investment, jt-venture, and manufacturing services; comprises 12 cos; Chair. NGUYEN TRAN DAT; Gen. Dir TRAN DUC TRUONG.

Marine Supply (Marine Technical Materials Import-Export and Supplies): 276A Da Nang, Ngo Quyen, Haiphong; tel. (31) 847308; fax (31) 845159; f. 1985; imports and exports technical materials for marine transportation industry; Dir PHAN TRANG CHAN.

Mecanimex (Viet Nam National Mechanical Products Export-Import Co): 37 Trang Thi, Hoan Kiem District, Hanoi; tel. (4) 8257459; fax (4) 9349904; e-mail mecahn@fpt.vn; internet mecanimex.com.vn; exports and imports mechanical products and hand tools; Gen. Dir TRAN BAO GIOC.

Nafobird (Viet Nam Forest and Native Birds, Animals and Ornamental Plants Export-Import Enterprises): 64 Truong Dinh, District 3, Ho Chi Minh City; tel. (8) 8290211; fax (8) 8293735; f. 1987; exports native birds, animals and plants, and imports materials for forestry; Dir VO HA AN.

Naforimex (Hanoi Forest Products Export-Import and Production Corpn): 19 Ba Trieu, Hoan Kiem District, Hanoi; tel. (4) 8261255; fax (4) 8259264; e-mail naforimexhanoi@fpt.vn; f. 1960; imports chemicals, machinery and spare parts for the forestry industry and water supply network; exports oils, forest products, gum benzoin and resin; CEO NGUYEN BA HUNG.

Nitagrex (Ninh Thuan Agricultural Products Import-Export Co): 158 Bac Ai, Do Vinh Ward, Phan Rang Thap Cham, Ninh Thuan Province; tel. (68) 888779; fax (68) 888842; e-mail nitagrex@hcm.vnn.vn; internet www.nitagrex.com.vn; f. 1999; production and export of agricultural products; import of consumer goods, transport vehicles and agricultural materials and equipment; Gen. Dir DAO VAN CHAN.

Packexport (Viet Nam National Packaging Technology and Import-Export Co): 31 Hang Thung, Hanoi; tel. (4) 8262792; fax (4) 8269227; e-mail packexport-vn@vnn.vn; f. 1976; manufactures packaging for domestic and export demand, and imports materials for the packaging industry; Gen. Dir TRINH LE KIEU.

Petec Trading and Investment Corpn: 194 Nam Ky Khoi Nghia, District 3, Ho Chi Minh City; tel. (8) 39303633; fax (8) 39305686; e-mail petectonghop@hcm.vnn.vn; internet www.petec.com.vn; f. 1981; imports equipment and technology for oil drilling, exploration and oil production; exports crude petroleum, rice, coffee and agricultural products; invests in silk, coffee, financial and transport sectors; Chair. and CEO NGUYEN MINH TRUC.

Petrol and Oil Co (Zone 1): Duc Gliang Town, Gia Lam, Hanoi; tel. (4) 8271400; fax (4) 8272432; sales of oil and gas; Dir PHAN VAN DU.

Petrolimex (Viet Nam National Petroleum Corpn): 1 Kham Thien, Dong Da District, Hanoi; tel. (4) 38512603; fax (4) 38519203; e-mail xttm@petrolimex.com.vn; internet www.petrolimex.com.vn; f. 1956; import, export and distribution of petroleum products and liquefied petroleum gas; Chair. NGUYEN THANH SON; Dir-Gen. BUI NGOC BAO.

Petrolimex Saigon Petroleum Co (Zone 2): 15 Le Duan, District 1, Ho Chi Minh City; tel. (8) 8292081; fax (8) 8222082; sales of petroleum products; Dir TRAN VAN THANG.

Petrovietnam (The Viet Nam Oil and Gas Corpn): 18 Lang Ha, Ba Dinh, Hanoi; tel. (4) 38252526; fax (4) 38265942; e-mail info@pvn.vn; internet www.petrovietnam.com.vn; f. 1975; exploration and production of petroleum and gas; Chair. DINH LA THANG; Pres. and CEO PHUNG DINH THUC.

Saigon Beer Alcohol Beverage Corpn (Sabeco): 6 Hai Ba Trung, Ben Nghe District, Ho Chi Minh City; tel. (8) 38294083; fax (8) 38296856; e-mail biasaigon@sabeco.com.vn; internet www.sabeco.com.vn; producer of beer; Pres. NGUYEN ANH DZUNG.

Seaco (Sundries Electric Appliances Co): 64 Pho Duc Chinh, District 1, Ho Chi Minh City; tel. (8) 8210961; fax (8) 8210974; deals in miscellaneous electrical goods; Dir MAI MINH CUONG.

Seaprodex Hanoi (Hanoi Sea Products Export-Import Co): 20 Lang Ha, Dong Da, Hanoi; tel. (4) 38345678; fax (4) 38354125; e-mail seahn@seaprodexhanoi.com.vn; internet www.seaprodexhanoi.com.vn; Dir LE CONG DUC.

Seaprodex Saigon (Ho Chi Minh City Sea Products Import-Export Corpn): 87 Ham Nghi, District 1, Ho Chi Minh City; tel. (8) 38214186; fax (8) 39142236; e-mail info@seaprodexsg.com; internet www.seaprodexsg.com; f. 1978; exports frozen and processed sea products; imports machinery and materials for fishing and processing; Gen. Dir NGUYEN DUY DUNG.

SJC (Saigon Jewellery Co): 115 Nguyen Cong Tru, District 1, Ho Chi Minh City; tel. (8) 39144056; fax (8) 39144057; e-mail info@sjc.com.vn; internet www.sjc.com.vn; f. 1998; manufacturing, processing and trading of gold, gemstones, silver and jewellery; Man. Dir NGUYEN THANH LONG.

Technimex JSC (Technology Import-Export Joint Stock Company): 70 Tran Hung Dao, Hoan Kiem District, Hanoi; tel. (4) 7519423; fax (4) 3778220; e-mail technimex@hn.vnn.vn; internet www.technimexvn.com; f. 1982 under the name Viet Nam Technology Import-Export Corpn; name changed as above in 2001; exports and imports machines, equipment, instruments, etc.; Dir NGUYEN HUY BINH.

Technoimport (Viet Nam National Complete Equipment and Technics Import-Export Corpn): 16–18 Trang Thi, Hanoi; tel. (4) 38254974; fax (4) 38254059; e-mail technohn@netnam.vn; internet technoimport.vn; f. 1959; imports and exports equipment, machinery, transport equipment, spare parts, materials and various consumer commodities; exports products by co-investment and jt-venture enterprises; provides consulting services for trade and investment, transport and forwarding services; acts as import-export brokering and trading agents; Gen. Dir VU CHU HIEN.

Terraprodex (Corpn for Processing and Export-Import of Rare Earth and Other Specialities): 35 Dien Bien Phu, Hanoi; tel. (4) 8232010; fax (4) 8256446; f. 1989; processing and export of rare earth products and other minerals; Dir TRAN DUC HIEP.

Thanglong Minerals and Metals Co Ltd: 127 Khuat Duy Tien, Hanoi; tel. (4) 35535218; fax (4) 35532669; e-mail thanglong@thanglongcastiron.com; internet www.thanglongcastiron.com; fmrly Viet Nam National Minerals Export Import Corpn; exports cast iron products; imports pig iron and crude steel; Gen. Dir LE THI MINH.

Tocontap Saigon (Saigon Sundries Export-Import Joint Stock Co): 35 Le Quy Don, District 3, Ho Chi Minh City; tel. (8) 39325687; fax (8) 39325963; e-mail info@tocontapsaigon.com; internet www.tocontapsaigon.com; f. 1956; imports and exports apparel, agricultural products, art and handicrafts and sundries; Gen. Dir LE THI THANH HUONG.

Tracimexco (Transport Investment Co-operation and Import-Export Corpn): 22 Phan Dinh Giot, Ward 2, Tan Binh District, Ho Chi Minh City; tel. (8) 8442247; fax (8) 8445240; e-mail tralico@hn.vnn.vn; internet www.tracimexco.com.vn; fmrly Vietranscimex; exports and imports specialized equipment and materials for transportation and communication; Gen. Dir PHAM QUANG VINH.

Vama (Viet Nam Automobile Manufacturers' Association): Viglacera Bldg, 8th Floor, Me Tri Ward, Tu Liem District, Hanoi; tel. (4) 35536893; fax (4) 35536841; e-mail vama.office@gmail.com; internet www.vama.org.vn; f. 2000; 18 mems; Chair. AKITO TACHIBANA.

Vasep (Viet Nam Asscn of Seafood Exporters and Producers): Lot 218A, 6 An Kanh, An Phu Ward, District 2, Ho Chi Minh City; tel. (8) 62810432; fax (8) 62810450; e-mail vasep@fpt.vn; internet www.vasep.com.vn; f. 1998; exports seafood products; provides essential market information to Viet Nam's seafood industry; organizes and implements activities designed to develop and promote the industry; Chair. TRAN THIEN HAI.

Vegetexco (Viet Nam National Vegetables and Fruit Export-Import Corpn): 2 Pham Ngoc Thach, Dong Da District, Hanoi; tel. (4) 5744592; fax (4) 8523926; e-mail vegetexcovn@fpt.vn; internet www.vegetexcovn.com.vn; f. 1971; exports fresh and processed vegetables and fruit, spices and flowers, and other agricultural products; imports vegetable seeds and processing materials; Gen. Dir LE VAN ANH.

Vicem (Viet Nam Cement Industry Corpn—Vinacement): 228 Le Duan, Dong Da District, Hanoi; tel. (4) 8512425; fax (4) 8512778; e-mail banbt@vinacement.com.vn; internet www.vicem.vn; f. 1980; manufactures and exports cement and clinker; Chair. LE VAN CHUNG; Gen. Dir NGUYEN NGOC ANH.

Viet Nam Dairy Products JS Company (VINAMILK): 10 Tan Trao, Ward Tan Phu, District 7, Ho Chi Minh City; tel. (8) 54155555; fax (8) 54161226; e-mail vinamilk@vinamilk.com.vn; internet www.vinamilk.com.vn; f. 1976; producer of dairy products; Dir MAI KIEU LIEN.

Vietnam Rubber Group: 236 Nam Ky Khoi Nghia, District 3, Ho Chi Minh City; tel. (8) 9327857; fax (8) 9327341; merged with Rubexim (rubber export-import corpn) in 1991; fmrly known as GERUCO; manages and controls the Vietnamese rubber industry, including the planting, processing and trading of natural rubber and rubber wood products; also imports chemicals, machinery and spare parts for the industry; Chair. TRAN NGOC THANH; Dir-Gen. LE QUANG THUNG.

Vietrans (Viet Nam National Foreign Trade Forwarding and Warehousing Corpn): 13 Ly Nam De, Hoan Kiem District, Hanoi; tel. (4) 38457417; fax (4) 38455829; e-mail info@vietrans.com.vn; internet vietrans.com.vn; f. 1970; agent for forwarding and transport of exports and imports, diplomatic cargoes and other goods, warehousing, shipping and insurance; Gen. Dir THAI DUY LONG.

Viettronimex (Viet Nam Electronics Import-Export Corpn): 74–76 Nguyen Hue, District 1, Ho Chi Minh City; tel. (8) 8298201; fax (8) 8294873; e-mail vtr@hcm.vnn.vn; internet viettronimex.com.vn; f. 1981; imports and exports electronic goods; Dir NGUYEN HUU THINH.

Vigecam (Viet Nam General Corpn of Agricultural Materials): 16 Ngo Tat To, Dong Da District, Hanoi; tel. and fax (4) 37478890; e-mail info@vigecam.vn; internet www.vigecam.vn; exports and imports agricultural products; Gen. Dir TRAN VAN KANH.

Viglacera (Viet Nam Glass and Ceramics Corpn): 16–17 Viglacera Bldg, 1 Thang Long, Ward Me Tri, Tu Liem, Hanoi; tel. (4) 5536660; fax (4) 5536671; e-mail vgc@hn.vnn.vn; internet www.viglacera.com.vn; f. 1974; mfr of building materials; Gen. Dir NGUYEN ANH TUAN.

Vimedimex II (Vimedimex Medi-Pharma Joint Stock Co): 602/45D Dien Bien Phu, Ward 22, Binh Thanh District, Ho Chi Minh City; tel. (8) 38990164; fax (8) 38990165; e-mail info@vietpharm.com.vn; internet www.vietpharm.com.vn; f. 1984; exports and imports medicinal and pharmaceutical materials and products, medical instruments; Gen. Dir NGUYEN TIEN HUNG.

Vimico (Viet Nam National Minerals Corpn): 562 Nguyen Van Cu, Gia Lam District, Hanoi; tel. (8) 8770010; fax (8) 8770006; e-mail vimico@hn.vnn.vn; internet www.vimicovn.com; Chair. VU XUAN KHOAT; Gen. Dir NGO VAN TROI.

Vinacafe (Viet Nam National Coffee Import-Export Corpn): 211–213 Tran Huy Lieu, Ward 8, Phu Nuan District, Ho Chi Minh City; tel. (8) 54495514; fax (8) 54495513; e-mail vinacafe@hn.vnn.vn; internet www.vinacafe.com.vn; f. 1995; state-owned; exports coffee, and imports equipment and chemicals for coffee production; Chair. Dr DOAN DINH THIEM.

Vinachem (Viet Nam National Chemical Corpn): 1A Trang Tien, Hoan Kiem District, Hanoi; tel. (4) 38240551; fax (4) 38252995; e-mail info@vinachem.com.vn; internet www.vinachem.com.vn; f. 1969; production, import and export of chemicals and fertilizers; Chair. NGUYEN QUOC TUAN; Pres. and CEO NGUYEN DINH KHANG.

Vinachimex (Viet Nam National Chemicals Import-Export Corpn): 4 Pham Ngu Lao, Hanoi; tel. (4) 8256377; fax (4) 8257727; f. 1969; exports and imports chemical products, minerals, rubber, fertilizers, machinery and spare parts; Dir NGUYEN VAN SON.

Vinacomin (Viet Nam National Coal-Mineral Industries Group): 226 Le Duan, Dong Da District, Hanoi; tel. (4) 5180141; fax (4) 8510724; e-mail info@vinacomin.vn; internet www.vinacomin.vn; f. 2005; est. following merger of Vietnam Coal Corpn and Vietnam Minerals Corpn; subsidiaries include Vinacomin Port Co; coal and bauxite mining, shipbuilding, automobile manufacturing, tourism, financing, and power generation in thermal power plants; Gen. Dir TRAN XUAN HOA.

Vinafilm (Viet Nam Film Import, Export and Film Service Corpn): 73 Nguyen Trai, Dong Da District, Hanoi; tel. (4) 8244566; f. 1987; export and import of films and videotapes; film distribution; organization of film shows and participation of Vietnamese films in international film festivals; Gen. Man. NGO MANH LAN.

Vinafimex (Viet Nam National Agricultural Produce and Foodstuffs Import and Export Corpn): 58 Ly Thai To, Hanoi; tel. (4) 8255768; fax (4) 8255476; e-mail fime@hn.vnn.vn; internet www.vinafimex.com.vn; f. 1984; exports cashews, peanuts, coffee, rubber and other agricultural products, and garments; imports malt, fertilizer, insecticide, seeds, machinery and equipment, etc.; Pres. NGUYEN TOAN THANG; Gen. Dir NGUYEN VAN THANG.

Vinafood Hanoi (Hanoi Food Import-Export Co): 6 Ngo Quyen, Hoan Kiem District, Hanoi; tel. (4) 8256771; fax (4) 8258528; f. 1988; exports rice, maize, tapioca; imports fertilizers, insecticides, wheat and wheat flour; Dir NGUYEN DUC HY.

Vinalivesco (Vietnam National Livestock Corpn): 519 Minh Khai, Hai Ba Trung District, Hanoi; tel. (4) 38621814; fax (4) 38623645; e-mail vilico@vilico.vn; internet vilico.vn; f. 1996; imports and exports animal and poultry products, animal feeds and other agro-products, and foodstuffs; Gen. Dir NGUYEN VAN KHAC.

Vinapimex (Viet Nam Paper Corpn): 25A Ly Thuong Kiet, Hanoi; tel. (4) 8260143; fax (4) 8260381; f. 1995; production and marketing of paper; Pres. and CEO VO SY DONG.

Vinaplast (Viet Nam Plastics Corpn): 92–94 Ly Tu Trong, District 1, Ho Chi Minh City; tel. (8) 39453301; fax (8) 39453298; e-mail vinaplast@vinaplast.com.vn; internet www.vinaplast.com.vn; f. 1976; import and export of products for plastic processing industry; production and trade of plastic products; Gen. Dir NGUYEN KHAC LONG.

Vinasteel (Viet Nam National Steel Corpn): D2 Ton That Tung, Dong Da District, Hanoi; tel. (4) 8525537; fax (4) 8262657; distributor of metal products; Dir NGO HUY PHAN.

Vinataba (Viet Nam National Tobacco Corpn): 25A Ly Thuong Kiet, Hoan Kiem District, Hanoi; tel. (4) 8265778; fax (4) 8265777; internet www.vinataba.com.vn; mfr of tobacco products; Chair. NGUYEN THAI SINH; Gen. Dir NGUYEN NAM HAI.

Vinatea (Viet Nam National Tea Development Investment and Export-Import Co): 92 Vo Thi Sau, Hanoi; tel. (4) 6226990; fax (4) 6226991; e-mail info@vinatea.com.vn; internet www.vinatea.com.vn; exports tea, imports tea-processing materials; Gen. Dir NGUYEN THIEN TOAN.

Vinatex (Viet Nam National Textile and Garment Corpn): 25 Ba Trieu, Hoan Kiem District, Hanoi; tel. (4) 38257700; fax (4) 38262269; e-mail vinatexhn@vinatex.com.vn; internet www.vinatex.com; f. 1995; imports raw material, textile and sewing machinery, spare parts, accessories, dyestuffs; exports textiles, ready-made garments, carpets, jute, silk; Gen. Dir VU DUC GIANG.

Vitas (Viet Nam Tea Association): 92 Vo Thu Sau, Hai Ba Trung District, Hanoi; tel. (4) 36250908; fax (4) 36251801; e-mail vitas@fpt.vn; internet www.vitas.org.vn; f. 1988; promotes the trading and marketing of tea products; offers advice and information, both to the Govt and to farmers, regarding development schemes and policies; Chair. and Pres. NGUYEN VAN THU.

Vocarimex (National Co for Vegetable Oils, Aromas, and Cosmetics of Viet Nam): 58 Nguyen Binh Khiem, District 1, Ho Chi Minh City; tel. (8) 8294513; fax (8) 8290586; e-mail vocar@hcm.vnn.vn; internet www.vocarimex.com; f. 1976; producing and trading vegetable oils, oil-based products and special industry machinery; packaging; operating port facilities; Gen. Dir DO NGOC KAI.

Xunhasaba (Viet Nam State Corpn for Export and Import of Books, Periodicals and other Cultural Commodities): 32 Hai Ba Trung, Hanoi; tel. (4) 38262989; fax (4) 38252860; e-mail xunhasaba@hn.vnn.vn; internet www.xunhasaba.com.vn; f. 1957; exports and imports books, periodicals, postage stamps, greetings cards, calendars and paintings; Dir HA TRIEU KIEN.

UTILITIES

Electricity

Electricity of Viet Nam (EVN): 18 Tran Nguyen Han, Hanoi; tel. (4) 8249508; fax (4) 8249461; e-mail vp@evn.com.vn; internet www.evn.com.vn; produces, transmits and distributes electrical power; Chair. DAO VAN HUNG; Pres. and CEO PHAM LE TANH.

Power Co No 1 (PC1): 20 Tran Nguyen Han, Hoan Kiem, Hanoi; tel. (4) 8255074; fax (4) 8244033; e-mail anhdn@pc1.com.vn; manages the generation, transmission and distribution of electrical power in northern Viet Nam; Dir DO VAN LOC.

Power Co No 3 (PC3): 315 Trung Nu Vuong, Hai Chau District, Da Nang; tel. (511) 621028; fax (511) 625071; f. 1975; manages the generation, transmission and distribution of electrical power in central Viet Nam; Gen. Dir TA CANH.

Southern Power Corpn (EVN SPC): 72 Hai Ba Trung, District 1, Ho Chi Minh City; tel. (8) 22200350; fax (8) 22200352; fmrly Power Co No 2; reorg. and renamed as above in early 2010; manages the distribution of electrical power in southern Viet Nam; Gen. Dir NGUYEN THANH DUY.

Water

Hanoi Water Business Co: 44 Yen Phu, Hanoi; tel. (4) 8293179; fax (4) 8294069; f. 1954; responsible for the supply of water to Hanoi and its five urban and two suburban districts; Dir-Gen. NHU HAI NGUYEN.

Saigon Water Corpn (SAWACO): 1 Cong Truong Quoc Te, District 3, Ho Chi Minh City; tel. (8) 38291974; fax (8) 38241644; e-mail hcmcwater@hcm.vnn.vn; f. 1966; manages the water services and water construction works of Ho Chi Minh City; Gen. Dir DINH PHU TRAN.

CO-OPERATIVES

Viet Nam Co-operative Alliance (VCA): 77 Nguyen Thai Hoc, Ba Dinh District, Hanoi; tel. (4) 8431689; fax (4) 8431883; e-mail admin@vca.org.vn; internet www.vca.org.vn; f. 1993; fmrly Viet Nam Co-operatives Council; Pres. DAO XUAN CAN.

TRADE UNIONS

Tong Lien doan Lao dong Viet Nam (Vietnam General Confederation of Labour): 82 Tran Hung Dao, POB 627, Hanoi; tel. (4) 9421794; fax (4) 9423781; e-mail doingoaitld@hn.vnn.vn; internet www.congdoanvn.org.vn; f. 1929; merged in 1976 with the South Viet Nam Trade Union Fed. for Liberation; 6m. mems; 20 affiliated unions; Pres. DANG NGOC TUNG; Vice-Pres. NGUYEN HOA BINH.

Cong Doan Nong Nghiep Cong Nghiep Thu Pham Viet Nam (Viet Nam Agriculture and Food Industry Trade Union): Hanoi; f. 1987; 550,000 mems.

National Union of Building Workers: 12 Cua Dong, Hoan Kiem, Hanoi; tel. (4) 38253781; fax (4) 38281407; e-mail cdxdvn12@gmail.com; f. 1957; Pres. NGUYEN VAN BINH.

Vietnam National Union of Industrial Workers: 54 Hai Ba Trung, Hanoi; tel. (4) 9344426; fax (4) 8245306; f. 1997; Pres. VU TIEN SAU.

Vietnam National Union of Post and Telecoms Workers: 30 Hang Chuoi, Hai Ba Trung, Hanoi; tel. (4) 9713514; fax (4) 9720236; f. 1947; Chair. HOANG HUY LOAT.

Transport

RAILWAYS

Plans to construct a new rail link between Hanoi and Ho Chi Minh City, which would reduce the journey time from 29 hours to less than 10 hours, were postponed in mid-2010, owing to concerns over the cost. In 2008 construction commenced of a metro system in Ho Chi Minh City. The 19.7-km route was due for completion in 2014.

Duong Sat Viet Nam (DSVN) (Viet Nam Railways): 118 Le Duan, Hanoi; tel. (4) 8220537; fax (4) 9422866; e-mail dsvn@vr.com.vn; internet www.vr.com.vn; 2,600 km of main lines (1996); lines in operation are: Hanoi–Ho Chi Minh City (1,726 km), Hanoi–Haiphong (102 km), Hanoi–Dong Dang (167 km), Hanoi–Lao Cai (296 km), Hanoi–Thai Nguyen (75 km), Thai Nguyen–Kep–Bai Chay (106 km); Chair. and Gen. Dir Dr NGUYEN HUU BANG.

ROADS

In 2007 there were an estimated 160,089 km of roads, of which 13,554 km were highways and 31,575 km were secondary roads. In 2006 an upgrade of National Highway No. 2, linking An Giang province in Viet Nam to Takeo province in Cambodia, was completed. In the following year the Government announced plans to upgrade the section of National Highway No. 1 in the central province of Thua Thien-Hué; construction was scheduled for completion in 2010.

SHIPPING

The principal port facilities are at Haiphong, Da Nang and Ho Chi Minh City. At the end of 2009 the Vietnamese merchant fleet (1,415 vessels) had a combined displacement totalling 3,451,100 grt.

Transport and Chartering Corpn (Vietfracht): 74 Nguyen Du, Hai Ba Trung, Hanoi; tel. (4) 38228915; fax (4) 39423679; e-mail vfhan@vietfracht.com.vn; internet www.vietfracht.com.vn; f. 1963; ship broking, chartering, ship management, shipping agency, international freight forwarding; logistic and consultancy services, import-export services; Pres. TRAN VAN QUY; Gen. Dir NGO XUAN HONG.

Viet Nam National Shipping Lines (Vinalines): Ocean Park Bldg, 1 Dao Duy Anh, Phuong Mai Quarter, Dang Da District, Hanoi; tel. (4) 35770825; fax (4) 35770850; e-mail vnl@vinalines.com.vn; internet www.vinalines.com.vn; f. 1996; 27 subsidiaries and 36 associated companies; import and export of maritime materials and equipment, shipping agency and repair, construction, hotels, tourism, warehousing and logistics services; Chair. DUONG CHI DUNG.

Viet Nam Ocean Shipping Agency Corporation (VOSA Corpn): Unit 801, Harbour View Tower, 35 Nguyen Hue, District 1, Ho Chi Minh City; tel. (8) 39141490; fax (8) 39140423; e-mail vosagroup@hcm.vnn.vn; internet www.vosagroup.com; f. 1957; fmrly the Viet Nam Ocean Shipping Agency; controlled by Vinalines; in charge of merchant shipping; arranges ship repairs, salvage, passenger services, air and sea freight forwarding services; offices throughout Viet Nam; Dir-Gen. VU XUAN TRUNG.

Viet Nam Ocean Shipping Joint Stock Co (VOSCO) (Cong Ty Van Tai Duong Bien Viet Nam): 215 Tran Quoc Toan, Ngo Quyen District, Haiphong; tel. (31) 3731090; fax (31) 3731007; e-mail pid@vosco.vn; drycargo@vosco.vn; internet www.vosco.com.vn; controlled by the Viet Nam General Dept of Marine Transport; Gen. Dir BUI VIET HOAI.

Viet Nam Sea Transport and Chartering Co (Vitranschart): 428 Nguyen Tat Thanh, Ward 18, District 4, Ho Chi Minh City; tel. (8) 39404271; fax (8) 39404711; e-mail vtc-hcm@vitranschart.com.vn; internet www.vitranschart.com.vn; Dir VO PHUNG LONG.

Viet Nam Shipbuilding Industry Group (Vinashin): 172 Ngo Quyen, Hanoi; tel. (4) 37711212; fax (4) 37711535; e-mail contact@vinashin.com.vn; internet www.vinashin.com.vn; f. 1972; shipbuilding and ship repair, marine transport and trade services; Chair. NGUYEN HONG TRUONG; Gen. Dir TRUONG VAN TUYEN.

CIVIL AVIATION

Viet Nam's principal airports are Tan Son Nhat International Airport (located 6 km north of Ho Chi Minh City) and Noi Bai International Airport (Hanoi), which handle both overseas and domestic traffic. By 2010 the Government aimed to expand the annual capacity of Tan Son Nhat to 30m. passengers and 1m. metric tons of freight. A third international airport is located at Da Nang, and an international terminal was inaugurated at Can Tho in January 2011, following the upgrading of that airport's facilities. In 2004 plans were announced for the construction of a new international airport at Long Thang, in Dong Nai province; work on the project was expected to commence in 2011. The airport, with a projected passenger capacity of 20m. a year, was to have four runways and four terminals, the first of which were scheduled to become operational in 2015. As of late 2006 there were 20 domestic airports in Viet Nam, including Ca Mau, Con Son, Chu Lai and Nha Trang.

Jetstar Pacific Airlines: 112 Hong Ha, Tan Binh District, Ho Chi Minh City; tel. (8) 38450092; fax (8) 38450085; internet www.jetstar.com/vn/vi/index.aspx; f. 1991; fmrly Pacific Airlines; present name adopted 2008; 70% owned by Viet Nam's State Capital Investment Corpn and 27% owned by Qantas (Australia); operates low-cost domestic flights; Chair. LE SONG LAI.

Viet Nam Airlines: 200 Nguyen Son, Long Bien District, Hanoi; tel. (4) 38320320; fax (4) 38722375; internet www.vietnamairlines.com; fmrly the Gen. Civil Aviation Admin. of Viet Nam, then Hang Khong Viet Nam; privatization plans mooted; operates domestic passenger services from Hanoi and from Ho Chi Minh City to the principal Vietnamese cities, and international services to 18 countries; Pres. and CEO PHAM NGOC MINH; Chair. NGUYEN SY HUNG.

Tourism

Tourist arrivals increased from 3.8m. in 2009 to 5.0m. in 2010. Of these, the largest proportion in 2010 was from the People's Republic of China (18%); other important sources of visitors include the Republic of Korea, Japan and the USA. Revenue from tourism totalled US $3,926m. in 2008.

Viet Nam National Administration of Tourism (VNAT): 80 Quan Su, Hanoi; tel. (4) 39423998; fax (4) 39424115; e-mail titc@vietnamtourism.gov.vn; internet www.vietnamtourism.com; f. 1960; Chair. NGUYEN VAN TUAN.

Hanoi Tourism Service Co (HANOI TOSERCO): 273 Kim Ma, Hanoi; tel. (4) 7262626; fax (4) 7262571; e-mail hanoitoserco@hn.vnn.vn; internet www.tosercohanoi.com; f. 1988; manages the devt of tourism, hotels and restaurants in the capital, and other services incl. staff training; Dir TRAN TIEN HUNG.

Tong Cong ty Du lich Sai Gon (Saigon Tourist Holding Co): 23 Le Loi, District 1, Ho Chi Minh City; tel. (8) 8225887; fax (8) 8291026; e-mail saigontourist@sgtourist.com.vn; internet www.saigon-tourist.com; f. 1975; holding co controlling 11 tour operators, 56 hotels, 10 resorts and 24 restaurants; Gen. Dir NGUYEN HUU THO.

Defence

As assessed at November 2010, the total strength of the armed forces was an estimated 482,000: army 412,000; navy 40,000; air force 30,000. Men are subject to a two-year minimum term of compulsory military service between 18 and 35 years of age. Paramilitary forces number in excess of 5m. and include the urban People's Self Defence Force and the rural People's Militia. Border defence troops number an estimated 40,000.

Defence Expenditure: Budgeted at US $2,410m. for 2010.

Commander-in-Chief of the Armed Forces: NGUYEN MINH TRIET.

Chief of General Staff (Army): DO BA TY.

Commander of the Navy: Vice-Adm. NGUYEN VAN HIEN.

Education

Primary education, which is compulsory, begins at six years of age and lasts for five years. Secondary education, beginning at the age of 11, lasts for up to seven years, comprising a first cycle of four years and a second cycle of three years. n 2004/05 enrolment in primary schools included 87.7% of children in the relevant age-group, while enrolment in secondary schools included 69.3% of children in the relevant age-group. According to preliminary official figures in 2010/11 a total of 3.0m. pupils attended pre-primary institutions, at which 157,300 teachers were employed. In the same year, a total of 6.9m. pupils attended primary schools, at which 359,700 teachers were employed; and 7.8m. students were enrolled in secondary level institutions, at which 460,700 teachers were employed. In 1989 Viet Nam's first private college since 1954, Thang Long College, was opened in Hanoi to cater for university students. In 1999/2000 total enrolment at tertiary level was equivalent to 9.7% of students in the relevant age-group (males 11.2%; females 8.1%). In 2010/11, according to preliminary official figures, 2m. students were enrolled within a total of some 414 universities and colleges, at which 71,500 teachers were employed. Of total planned budgetary expenditure by the central Government in 2007, 38,100,000m. dông (11.9% of total expenditure) was allocated to education.

Bibliography

See also Cambodia and Laos

Alpert, William T. (Ed.). *The Vietnamese Economy and its Transformation to an Open Market System.* New York, M. E. Sharpe, 2004.

Anderson, David L. *The Vietnam War.* Basingstoke, Palgrave Macmillan, 2005.

Ang Cheng Guan. *The Vietnam War from the Other Side.* London, RoutledgeCurzon, 2002.

Ending the Vietnam War: The Vietnamese Communists' Perspective. London, RoutledgeCurzon, 2003.

Southeast Asia and the Vietnam War. Abingdon, Routledge, 2011.

Balme, Stephanie, and Sidel, Mark (Eds). *Vietnam's New Order: International Perspectives on the State and Reform in Vietnam.* Basingstoke, Palgrave Macmillan, 2007.

Beresford, Melanie, and Angie Ngoc Tran (Eds). *Reaching for the Dream: Challenges of Sustainable Development in Vietnam.* Copenhagen, Nordic Institute of Asian Studies, 2003.

Binh Tran Nam and Chi Do Pham (Eds). *The Vietnamese Economy.* London, RoutledgeCurzon, 2002.

Boothroyd, Peter, and Pham Xuan Nam (Eds). *Socio-Economic Renovation in Vietnam—The Origin, Evolution and Impact of Doi Moi.* Singapore, Institute of Southeast Asian Studies, 2000.

Brocheux, Pierre. *The Mekong Delta: Ecology, Economy, and Revolution, 1860–1960.* New York, Cambridge University Press, 2008.

Chan, Anita (Ed.). *Labour in Vietnam.* Singapore, Institute of Southeast Asian Studies, 2011.

Corfield, Justin. *The History of Vietnam.* Westport, CT, Greenwood Press, 2008.

Dang, Chat V., Ho, Hien V., and Vo, Nghia M. *The Women of Vietnam.* Denver, CO, Outskirts Press, 2008.

Decaro, Peter A. *Rhetoric of Revolt: Ho Chi Minh's Discourse for Revolution.* Westport, CT, Praeger Publishers, 2002.

Dien, Khong. *Population and Ethno-Demography in Vietnam.* Washington, DC, University of Washington Press, 2003.

Dollar, David, Glewwe, Paul, and Agrawal, Nisha (Eds). *Economic Growth, Poverty, and Household Welfare in Vietnam.* Washington, DC, World Bank, 2004.

Elliott, David W. P. *The Vietnamese War: Revolution Social Change in the Mekong Delta, 1930–1975.* Armonk, NY, M. E. Sharpe, 2007.

Eucker, Dennis. *Towards Good Governance in the Coastal Zone of Vietnam.* München, VMD Verlag, 2008.

Faure, Guy, and Schwab, Laurent. *Japan–Vietnam: A Relation under Influences.* Singapore, NUS Press, 2008.

Fforde, Adam. *Vietnamese State Industry and the Political Economy of Commercial Renaissance: Dragon's Tooth or Curate's Egg?* Oxford, Chandos, 2007.

Fitzgerald, Frances. *Fire in the Lake: The Vietnamese and the Americans in Vietnam.* London, Little, Brown, 2002.

Gainsborough, Martin. *Changing Political Economy of Vietnam: The Case of Ho Chi Minh City.* London, RoutledgeCurzon, 2002.

Vietnam: Rethinking the State. London, Zed Books, 2010.

Giebel, Christoph. *Imagined Ancestries of Vietnamese Communism: Ton Duc Thang and the Politics of History and Memory.* Seattle, WA, University of Washington Press, 2004.

Gittinger, Ted, and Gardner, Lloyd C. (Eds). *Search for Peace in Vietnam, 1964–68.* College Station, TX, Texas A & M University Press, 2004.

Griffiths, Philip Jones. *Agent Orange: Collateral Damage in Vietnam.* London, Trolley, 2003.

Gubry, Patrick. *The Vietnamese City in Transition.* Singapore, Institute of Southeast Asian Studies, 2009.

Halberstam, David. *The Making of a Quagmire: America and Vietnam during the Kennedy Era.* Lanham, MD, Rowman and Littlefield, 2007.

Hardy, Andrew. *Red Hills: Migrants and the State in the Highlands of Vietnam.* Honolulu, HI, University of Hawaii Press, 2002.

Hayton, Bill. *Vietnam: Rising Dragon.* New Haven, CT, Yale University Press, 2011.

Hock, David Koh Wee. *Wards of Hanoi.* Singapore, Institute of Southeast Asian Studies, 2006.

Jeffries, Ian. *Vietnam: A Guide to Economic and Political Developments.* Abingdon, Routledge, 2006.

Contemporary Vietnam: A Guide to Economic and Political Developments.

Karnow, Stanley. *Vietnam, A History.* Hawthorn, Vic, Penguin Books, Revised edn, 1997.

Kerkvliet, Benedict J. Tria. *The Power of Everyday Politics: How Vietnamese Peasants Transformed National Policy.* Singapore, Institute of Southeast Asian Studies, 2005.

Kerkvliet, Benedict, Heng, Russell, and Hock, David Koh Wee (Eds). *Getting Organized in Vietnam: Moving in and Around the Socialist State.* Singapore, Institute of Southeast Asian Studies, 2003.

Kerkvliet, Benedict, and Marr, David G. *Beyond Hanoi: Local Government in Vietnam.* Singapore, Institute of Southeast Asian Studies, 2004.

Kim, Annette Miae. *Learning to be Capitalists: Entrepreneurs in Vietnam's Transition Economy.* New York, Oxford University Press, 2008.

Kovstead, Jens, Rand, John, and Tarp, Finn. *From Monobank to Commercial Banking: Financial Sector Reforms in Vietnam.* Singapore, Institute of Southeast Asian Studies, 2005.

Lamb, David. *Vietnam, Now: A Reporter Returns.* New York, PublicAffairs, 2003.

Langguth, A. J. *Our Vietnam: The War 1954–1975.* New York, Simon and Schuster, 2002.

Le Manh Hung. *The Impact of World War II on the Economy of Vietnam, 1939–45.* Singapore, Times Academic Press, 2004.

Logevall, Frederik. *Choosing War: the Lost Chance for Peace and the Escalation of War in Vietnam.* Berkeley, CA, University of California Press, 2001.

London, Jonathan D. *Education in Vietnam.* Singapore, Institute of Southeast Asian Studies, 2011.

Lucius, Casey. *Vietnam's Political Process: How Education Shapes Political Decision-Making.* Abingdon, Routledge, 2009.

Luibrand, Annette. *Transition in Vietnam: Impact of the Rural Reform Process on an Ethnic Minority.* Frankfurt, Peter Lang, 2002.

Luong, Hy Van (Ed.). *Postwar Vietnam: Dynamics of a Transforming Society.* Singapore, Institute of Southeast Asian Studies, 2003.

McCargo, Duncan. *Rethinking Vietnam.* London, RoutledgeCurzon, 2004.

McHale, Shawn Frederick. *Print and Power: Buddhism, Confucianism and Communism in the Making of Modern Vietnam.* Honolulu, HI, University of Hawaii Press, 2003.

McKelvey, Robert S. *A Gift of Barbed Wire: America's Allies Abandoned in South Vietnam.* Seattle, WA, University of Washington Press, 2002.

Mai, Pham Hoang. *Foreign Direct Investment and Development in Vietnam: Policy Implications.* Singapore, Institute of Southeast Asian Studies, 2003.

Malarney, Shaun. *Culture, Ritual and Revolution in Vietnam.* London, RoutledgeCurzon, 2002.

Maraniss, David. *They Marched into Sunlight: War and Peace, Vietnam and America October 1967.* Pymble, NSW, Simon and Schuster Australia, 2003.

Masina, Pietro. *Vietnam's Development Strategies.* Abingdon, Routledge, 2006.

Neale, Jonathan. *The American War.* London, Bookmarks Publications, 2001.

Nghia M. Vo. *The Bamboo Gulag: Political Imprisonment in Communist Vietnam.* Jefferson, NC, McFarland and Co, 2003.

Nguyen Long Thanh Nam. *Hoa Hao Buddhism in the Course of Vietnam's History.* Hauppauge, NY, Nova Science Publishers, 2004.

O'Rourke, Dara. *Community-Driven Regulation: Balancing Development and the Environment in Vietnam.* Cambridge, MA, MIT Press, 2004.

Pelley, Patricia M. *Postcolonial Vietnam.* Durham, NC, Duke University Press, 2002.

Pham Hoang Mai. *Foreign Direct Investment and Development in Vietnam: Policy Implications.* Singapore, Institute of Southeast Asian Studies, 2003.

Phan Cam. *Vietnam: Economic, Political and Social Issues.* Hauppauge, NY, Nova Science Publishers, 2008.

Quinn-Judge, Sophie. *Ho Chi Minh: the Missing Years.* Berkeley, CA, University of California Press, 2002.

Ramsay, Jacob. *Mandarins and Martyrs: the Church and the Nguyen Dynasty in Early Nineteenth-Century Vietnam.* Stanford, CA, Stanford University Press, 2008.

Ravallion, Martin, and van de Walle, Dominique. *Land in Transition: Reform and Poverty in Rural Vietnam.* Basingstoke, Palgrave Macmillan, 2008.

Salemink, Oscar. *The Ethnography of Vietnam's Central Highlanders.* London, RoutledgeCurzon, 2002.

SarDesai, D. R. *Vietnam: Past and Present.* Boulder, CO, Westview Press, 4th edn, 2005.

Schoenl, William (Ed.). *New Perspectives on the Vietnam War: Our Allies' Views.* Lanham, MD, University Press of America, 2002.

Sidel, Mark. *Law and Society in Vietnam: the Transition from Socialism in Comparative Perspective.* Cambridge, Cambridge University Press, 2008.

The Constitution of Vietnam: A Contextual Analysis. Oxford, Hart Publishing, 2009.

Smith, Ralph B. *Viet Nam and the West.* London, Heinemann Educational, 1968.

An International History of the Vietnam War: Vol. 1—Revolution versus Containment, 1955–1961; Vol. 2—The Struggle for South-east Asia, 1961–65; Vol. 3—Making of a United War, 1965–66. London, Macmillan, 1983, 1985, 1990.

Smith, T. O. *Britain and the Origins of the Vietnam War: UK Policy in Indo-China, 1943-50.* Basingstoke, Palgrave Macmillan, 2007.

Statler, Kathryn C. *Replacing France: The Origins of American Intervention in Vietnam.* Lexington, KY, University Press of Kentucky, 2007.

Sterling, Eleanor Jane, Hurley, Martha Maud, and Le Duc Minh. *Vietnam: A Natural History.* New Haven, CT, Yale University Press, 2006.

Taylor, Philip. *Cham Muslims of the Mekong Delta: Place and Mobility in the Cosmopolitan Periphery.* Honolulu, HI, University of Hawaii Press, 2007.

Goddess on the Rise: Pilgrimage and Popular Religion in Vietnam. Honolulu, HI, University of Hawaii Press, 2004.

Modernity and Re-enchantment: Religion in Post-Revolutionary Vietnam. Lanham, MD, Lexington Books, 2008.

Taylor, Philip (Ed.). *Social Inequality in Vietnam and the Challenges to Reform.* Singapore, Institute of Southeast Asian Studies, 2005.

Minorities at Large: New Approaches to Minority Ethnicity in Vietnam. Singapore, Institute of Southeast Asian Studies, 2011.

Thomas, Mandy, and Drummond, Lisa (Eds). *Consuming Urban Culture in Contemporary Vietnam.* London, RoutledgeCurzon, 2003.

Werner, Jayne. *Gender, Household and State in Post-Revolutionary Vietnam.* Abingdon, Routledge, 2008.

Wiest, Andrew. *The Vietnam War 1956–1975.* London, Routledge-Curzon, 2003.

Vietnam's Forgotten Army: Heroism and Betrayal in the ARVN. New York, New York University Press, 2008.

New Perspectives on the Vietnam War. Abingdon, Routledge, 2009.

Willbanks, James H. *Abandoning Vietnam: How America Left and South Vietnam Lost its War.* Lawrence, KS, University Press of Kansas, 2004.

The Tet Offensive: A Concise History. New York, Columbia University Press, 2008.

Windrow, Martin. *The Last Valley: Dien Bien Phu and the French Defeat in Vietnam.* London, Weidenfeld and Nicolson, 2004.

Womack, Brantly. *China and Vietnam: The Politics of Asymmetry.* New York, Cambridge University Press, 2009.

PART THREE
Regional Information

REGIONAL ORGANIZATIONS

THE UNITED NATIONS

Address: United Nations, New York, NY 10017, USA.

Telephone: (212) 963-1234; **fax:** (212) 963-4879; **internet:** www.un.org.

The United Nations (UN) was founded on 24 October 1945. The organization, which has 193 member states, aims to maintain international peace and security and to develop international co-operation in addressing economic, social, cultural and humanitarian problems. The principal organs of the UN are the General Assembly, the Security Council, the Economic and Social Council, the International Court of Justice and the Secretariat. The General Assembly, which meets for three months each year, comprises representatives of all UN member states. The Security Council investigates disputes between member countries, and may recommend ways and means of peaceful settlement: it comprises five permanent members (the People's Republic of China, France, Russia, the United Kingdom and the USA) and 10 other members elected by the General Assembly for a two-year period. The Economic and Social Council comprises representatives of 54 member states, elected by the General Assembly for a three-year period: it promotes co-operation on economic, social, cultural and humanitarian matters, acting as a central policy-making body and co-ordinating the activities of the UN's specialized agencies. The International Court of Justice comprises 15 judges of different nationalities, elected for nine-year terms by the General Assembly and the Security Council: it adjudicates in legal disputes between UN member states.

Secretary-General: BAN KI-MOON (Republic of Korea) (2007–15).

MEMBER STATES IN THE FAR EAST AND AUSTRALASIA

(with assessments for percentage contributions to UN budget for 2010–12, and year of admission)

Australia	1.933	1945
Brunei	0.028	1984
Cambodia	0.003	1955
China, People's Republic*	3.189	1945
Fiji	0.004	1970
Indonesia	0.238	1950
Japan	12.530	1956
Kiribati	0.001	1999
Korea, Democratic People's Republic	0.007	1991
Korea, Republic	2.260	1991
Laos	0.001	1955
Malaysia	0.253	1957
Marshall Islands	0.001	1991
Micronesia, Federated States	0.001	1991
Mongolia	0.002	1961
Myanmar	0.006	1948
Nauru	0.001	1999
New Zealand	0.273	1945
Palau	0.001	1994
Papua New Guinea	0.002	1975
Philippines	0.090	1945
Samoa	0.001	1976
Singapore	0.335	1965
Solomon Islands	0.001	1978
Thailand	0.209	1946
Timor-Leste	0.001	2002
Tonga	0.001	1999
Tuvalu	0.001	2000
Vanuatu	0.001	1981
Viet Nam	0.033	1977

* From 1945 to 1971 the Chinese seat was occupied by the Republic of China (confined to Taiwan since 1949).

Sovereign Country not in the United Nations

Republic of China (Taiwan)

Diplomatic Representation

PERMANENT MISSIONS TO THE UNITED NATIONS

(October 2011)

Australia: 150 East 42nd St, 33rd Floor, New York, NY 10017; tel. (212) 351-6600; fax (212) 351-6610; e-mail australia@un.int; internet www.unny.mission.gov.au; Permanent Representative GARY QUINLAN.

Brunei: 771 United Nations Plaza, New York, NY 10017; tel. (212) 697-3465; fax (212) 697-9889; e-mail info@bruneimission-ny.org; Permanent Representative LATIF BIN TUAH.

Cambodia: 327 East 58th St, New York, NY 10022; tel. (212) 336-0777; fax (212) 759-7672; e-mail cambodia@un.int; internet www.un.int/cambodia; Permanent Representative SEA KOSAL.

China, People's Republic: 350 East 35th St, New York, NY 10016; tel. (212) 655-6100; fax (212) 634-7626; e-mail chinamission_un@fmprc.gov.cn; internet www.china-un.org; Permanent Representative LI BAODONG.

Fiji: 630 Third Ave, 7th Floor, New York, NY 10017; tel. (212) 687-4130; fax (212) 687-3963; e-mail fiji@un.int; internet www.fijiprun.org; Permanent Representative PETER THOMSON.

Indonesia: 325 East 38th St, New York, NY 10016; tel. (212) 972-8333; fax (212) 972-9780; e-mail ptri@indonesiamission-ny.org; internet www.indonesiamission-ny.org; Permanent Representative HASAN KLEIB.

Japan: 866 United Nations Plaza, 2nd Floor, New York, NY 10017; tel. (212) 223-4300; fax (212) 751-1966; e-mail japan.mission@un-japan.org; internet www.un.int/japan; Permanent Representative TSUNEO NISHIDA.

Korea, Democratic People's Republic: 820 Second Ave, 13th Floor, New York, NY 10017; tel. (212) 972-3105; fax (212) 972-3154; e-mail dpr.korea@verizon.net; Permanent Representative SIN SON HO.

Korea, Republic: 335 East 45th St, New York, NY 10017; tel. (212) 439-4000; fax (212) 986-1083; e-mail korea@un.int; internet www.un.int/korea; Permanent Representative KIM SOOK.

Laos: 317 East 51st St, New York, NY 10022; tel. (212) 832-2734; fax (212) 750-0039; e-mail lao@un.int; internet www.un.int/lao; Permanent Representative KANIKA PHOMMACHANH.

Malaysia: 313 East 43rd St, New York, NY 10017; tel. (212) 986-6310; fax (212) 490-8576; e-mail malnyun@kln.gov.my; internet www.un.int/malaysia; Permanent Representative HANIFF HUSSEIN.

Marshall Islands: 800 Second Ave, 18th Floor, New York, NY 10017; tel. (212) 983-3040; fax (212) 983-3202; e-mail marshallislands@un.int; internet marshallislands.un.int; Permanent Representative PHILLIP H. MULLER.

Micronesia, Federated States: 820 Second Ave, Suite 17A, New York, NY 10017; tel. (212) 697-8370; fax (212) 697-8295; e-mail fsmun@fsmgov.org; internet www.fsmgov.org/fsmun; Permanent Representative MASAO NAKAYAMA, JANE JIMMY CHIGIYAL (designate).

Mongolia: 6 East 77th St, New York, NY 10075; tel. (212) 737-3874; fax (212) 861-9464; e-mail mongolia@un.int; internet www.un.int/mongolia; Permanent Representative OCHIR ENKHTSETSEG.

Myanmar: 10 East 77th St, New York, NY 10075; tel. (212) 744-1271; fax (212) 744-1290; e-mail myanmar@un.int; Permanent Representative U THAN SWE.

Nauru: 800 Second Ave, Suite 400A, New York, NY 10017; tel. (212) 937-0074; fax (212) 937-0079; e-mail nauru@un.int; internet www.un.int/nauru; Permanent Representative MARLENE INEMWIN MOSES.

New Zealand: 600 Third Ave, 14th Floor, New York, NY 10016; tel. (212) 826-1960; fax (212) 758-0827; e-mail nzmissionny@earthlink.net; internet www.nzmissionny.org; Permanent Representative JIM MCLAY.

Palau: 866 United Nations Plaza, Suite 575, New York, NY 10017; tel. (212) 813-0310; fax (212) 813-0317; e-mail mission@palauun.org; internet www.palauun.org; Permanent Representative STUART BECK.

Papua New Guinea: 201 East 42nd St, Suite 405, New York, NY 10017; tel. (212) 557-5001; fax (212) 557-5009; e-mail pngmission@pngun.org; Permanent Representative ROBERT GUBA AISI.

Philippines: 556 Fifth Ave, 5th Floor, New York, NY 10036; tel. (212) 764-1300; fax (212) 840-8602; e-mail newyorkpm@gmail.com; internet www.un.int/philippines; Permanent Representative LIBRAN N. CABACTULAN.

Samoa: 800 Second Ave, Suite 400J, New York, NY 10017; tel. (212) 599-6196; fax (212) 599-0797; e-mail samoa@un.int; Permanent Representative ALI'IOAIGA FETURI ELISAIA.

Singapore: 231 East 51st St, New York, NY 10022; tel. (212) 826-0840; fax (212) 826-2964; e-mail singapore@un.int; internet www.mfa.gov.sg/newyork; Permanent Representative ALBERT CHUA.

Solomon Islands: 800 Second Ave, Suite 400L, New York, NY 10017; tel. (212) 599-6193; fax (212) 661-8925; e-mail simun@foreignaffairs-solomons.org; Permanent Representative COLIN D. BECK.

Thailand: 351 East 52nd St, New York, NY 10022; tel. (212) 754-2230; fax (212) 754-2535; e-mail thailand@un.int; Permanent Representative NORACHIT SINHASENI.

Timor-Leste: 866 Second Ave, Suite 441, New York, NY 10017; tel. (212) 759-3675; fax (212) 759-4196; e-mail timor-leste@un.int; internet www.un.int/timor-leste; Permanent Representative SOFIA MESQÍTA BORGES.

Tonga: 250 East 51st St, New York, NY 10022; tel. (917) 369-1025; fax (917) 369-1024; e-mail tongaunmission@aol.com; Permanent Representative SONATANE TU'AKINAMOLAHI TAUMOEPEAU-TUPOU.

Tuvalu: 800 Second Ave, Suite 400D, New York, NY 10017; tel. (212) 490-0534; fax (212) 808-4975; e-mail tuvalu@onecommonwealth.org; Permanent Representative AFELEE F. PITA.

Vanuatu: 800 Second Ave, Suite 400B, New York, NY 10017; tel. (212) 661-4303; fax (212) 661-5544; e-mail vanunmis@aol.com; Permanent Representative (vacant).

Viet Nam: 866 United Nations Plaza, Suite 435, New York, NY 10017; tel. (212) 644-0594; fax (212) 644-5732; e-mail info@vietnam-un.org; internet www.vietnam-un.org; Permanent Representative LE HOAI TRUNG.

OBSERVERS

Intergovernmental organizations, etc., active in the region that participate in the sessions and the work of the UN General Assembly as Observers, maintaining permanent offices at the UN.

Asian-African Legal Consultative Organization: 188 East 76th St, Apt 26B, New York, NY 10021; tel. (917) 623-2861; fax (206) 426-5442; e-mail aalco@un.int; Permanent Observer ROY LEE.

Commonwealth Secretariat: 800 Second Ave, 4th Floor, New York, NY 10017; tel. (212) 599-6190; fax (212) 808-4975; e-mail comsec@thecommonwealth.org.

International Committee of the Red Cross: 801 Second Ave, 18th Floor, New York, NY 10017; tel. (212) 599-6021; fax (212) 599-6009; e-mail newyork.nyc@icrc.org; Head of Delegation WALTER A. FÜLLEMANN.

International Criminal Police Organization: One United Nations Plaza, Rm 2610, New York, NY 10017; tel. (917) 367-3463; fax (917) 367-3476; e-mail a.torbet@interpol.int; Special Representative a.i. MICHAEL OLMSTED, WILLIAM J. S. ELLIOTT (Canada) (designate, from Nov. 2011).

International Development Law Organization: 336 East 45th St, New York, NY 10017; tel. (212) 867-9707; fax (212) 867-9717; e-mail pcivili@idlo.int; Permanent Observer PATRIZIO M. CIVILI.

International Institute for Democracy and Electoral Assistance: 336 East 45th St, 14th Floor, New York, NY 10017; tel. (212) 286-1084; fax (212) 286-0260; e-mail unobserver@idea.int; Permanent Observer MASSIMO TOMMASOLI.

International Olympic Committee: 708 Third Ave, 6th Floor, New York, NY 10017; tel. (212) 209-3952; fax (212) 209-7100; e-mail IOC-UNObserver@olympic.org; Permanent Observer MARIO PESCANTE.

International Trade Union Confederation: 211 East 43rd St, Suite 710, New York, NY 10017, USA; tel. (212) 370-0180; fax (212) 370-0188; e-mail unoffice@ituc-csi.org; Perm. Rep. GEMMA ADABA.

Inter-Parliamentary Union: 220 East 42nd St, Suite 3002, New York, NY 10017; tel. (212) 557-5880; fax (212) 557-3954; e-mail ny-office@mail.ipu.org; Permanent Observer ANDA FILIP.

IUCN (International Union for Conservation of Nature): 801 Second Ave, 13th Floor, New York, NY 10017; tel. (212) 286-1076; fax (212) 286-1079; e-mail iucn@un.int; Permanent Observer NARINDER KAKAR (India).

Organization of Islamic Cooperation: 320 East 51st St, New York, NY 10022; tel. (212) 883-0140; fax (212) 883-0143; e-mail oicny@un.int; internet www.oicun.org; Permanent Observer UFUK GOKCEN.

Partners in Population and Development: 336 East 45th St, 14th Floor, New York, NY 10017; tel. (212) 286-1082; fax (212) 286-0260; e-mail srao@ppdsec.org; Permanent Observer SETHURAMIAH L.N. RAO.

University for Peace: 801 Second Ave, 13th Floor, New York, NY 10017; tel. (212) 286-1076; fax (212) 286-1079; e-mail nyinfo@upeace.org; Permanent Observer NARINDER KAKAR (India).

The African, Caribbean and Pacific Group of States, Association of Southeast Asian Nations, Conference on Interaction and Confidence-building Measures in Asia, Economic Cooperation Organization, Islamic Development Bank, Pacific Islands Forum and the Shanghai Cooperation Organization are among several intergovernmental organizations that have a standing invitation to participate as observers but do not maintain permanent offices at the UN.

United Nations Information Centres/Services

Australia: Level 1, 7 National Circuit, Barton, ACT 2600; tel. (2) 6270-9200; fax (2) 6273-8206; e-mail unic.canberra@unic.org; internet www.un.org.au; also covers Fiji, Kiribati, Nauru, New Zealand, Samoa, Tonga, Tuvalu and Vanuatu.

Indonesia: Gedung Surya, 14th Floor, 9 Jalan M. H. Thamrin Kavling, Jakarta 10350; tel. (21) 3983-1011; fax (21) 3983-1014; e-mail unic-jakarta@unic-jakarta.org; internet www.unic-jakarta.org.

Japan: UNU Bldg, 8th Floor, 53–70 Jingumae 5-chome, Shibuya-ku, Tokyo 150 0001; tel. (3) 5467-4451; fax (3) 5467-4455; e-mail unic@untokyo.jp; internet www.unic.or.jp.

Myanmar: 6 Natmauk Rd, Tamwe P.O., Yangon; tel. (1) 546933; fax (1) 542634; e-mail unic.myanmar@undp.org; internet yangon.unic.org.

Philippines: POB 7285 ADC (DAPO), 1300 Domestic Rd, Pasay City, Metro Manila; tel. (2) 338-5520; fax (2) 338-0177; e-mail unic.manila@unic.org; internet www.unicmanila.org; also covers Papua New Guinea and Solomon Islands.

Thailand: ESCAP, United Nations Bldg, Rajadamnern Nok Ave, Bangkok 10200; tel. (2) 288-1234; fax (2) 288-1000; e-mail unisbkk.unescap@un.org; internet www.unescap.org/unis; also covers Cambodia, Laos, Malaysia, Singapore and Viet Nam.

Economic and Social Commission for Asia and the Pacific—ESCAP

Address: United Nations Bldg, Rajadamnern Nok Ave, Bangkok 10200, Thailand.

Telephone: (2) 288-1234; **fax:** (2) 288-1000; **e-mail:** unisbkk .unescap@un.org; **internet:** www.unescap.org.

The Commission was founded in 1947, at first to assist in post-war reconstruction, and subsequently to encourage the economic and social development of Asia and the Far East; it was originally known as the Economic Commission for Asia and the Far East (ECAFE). The title ESCAP, which replaced ECAFE, was adopted after a reorganization in 1974. ESCAP's main objectives are to promote inclusive and sustainable economic and social development in Asia and the Pacific, and to help member countries to achieve internationally agreed development goals.

MEMBERS

Afghanistan	Korea, Democratic People's Republic	Philippines
Armenia	Korea, Republic	Russia
Australia	Kyrgyzstan	Samoa
Azerbaijan	Laos	Singapore
Bangladesh	Malaysia	Solomon Islands
Bhutan	The Maldives	Sri Lanka
Brunei	Marshall Islands	Tajikistan
Cambodia	Micronesia, Federated States	Thailand
China, People's Republic	Mongolia	Timor-Leste
Fiji	Myanmar	Tonga
France	Nauru	Turkey
Georgia	Nepal	Turkmenistan
India	Netherlands	Tuvalu
Indonesia	New Zealand	United Kingdom
Iran	Pakistan	USA
Japan	Palau	Uzbekistan
Kazakhstan	Papua New Guinea	Vanuatu
Kiribati		Viet Nam

ASSOCIATE MEMBERS

American Samoa	Hong Kong	Northern Mariana Islands
Cook Islands	Macao	
French Polynesia	New Caledonia	
Guam	Niue	

Organization

(October 2011)

COMMISSION

The main legislative organ of ESCAP is the Commission, which meets annually at ministerial level to examine the region's problems, to review progress, to establish priorities and to decide upon the recommendations of the Executive Secretary or the subsidiary bodies of the Commission. It reports to the UN Economic and Social Council (ECOSOC). Ministerial and intergovernmental conferences on specific issues may be held on an ad hoc basis with the approval of the Commission, although no more than one ministerial conference and five intergovernmental conferences may be held during one year.

COMMITTEES AND SPECIAL BODIES

The following Committees and Special Bodies advise the Commission with regard to their specialized areas and help to oversee the work of the Secretariat. They meet every two years, while any sub-committees meet in the intervening years.

Committee on Macroeconomic Policy, Poverty Reduction and Inclusive Development;

Committee on Trade and Investment;

Committee on Transport;

Committee on Environment and Development;

Committee on Information and Communications Technology;

Committee on Disaster Risk Reduction;

Committee on Social Development;

Committee on Statistics;

Special Body on Least Developed and Landlocked Developing Countries;

Special Body on Pacific Island Developing Countries.

In addition, an Advisory Committee of permanent representatives and other representatives designated by members of the Commission functions as an advisory body; it generally meets every month.

SECRETARIAT

The Secretariat operates under the guidance of the Commission and its subsidiary bodies. It consists of the Office of the Executive Secretary and two servicing divisions, covering administration and programme management, in addition to the following substantive divisions: Environment and Development; Information and Communications Technology and Disaster Risk Reduction; Macroeconomic Policy and Development; Social Development; Statistics; Trade and Investment; and Transport.

Executive Secretary: Noeleen Heyzer (Singapore).

SUB-REGIONAL OFFICES

ESCAP Pacific Operations Centre (EPOC): Private Mail Bag, Suva, Fiji; tel. 3319669; fax 3319671; e-mail epoc@un.org; internet www.unescap.org/epoc; f. 1984, relocated to Fiji 2005; responsible for ESCAP's sub-programme on Development of Pacific Island Countries and Territories; assists Pacific island governments in forming and implementing national sustainable development strategies, particularly poverty reduction programmes that create access to services by socially vulnerable groups; conducts research, promotes regional co-operation and knowledge-sharing, and provides advisory services, training and pilot projects; Dir Iosefa Maiava (Samoa).

Sub-Regional Office for East and North-East Asia: Meet-you-all Tower, 17th Floor, Techno Park, 7-50 Songdo-dong, Yeonsu-gu, Incheon, Republic of Korea; tel. (32) 458-6601; fax (32) 458-6699; e-mail vanlaere@un.org; f. 2010; covers activities in the People's Republic of China, Japan, the Democratic People's Republic of Korea, the Republic of Korea, Mongolia and Russia; Dir Peter Van Laere (Samoa).

In May 2011 an agreement was signed to be establish a Sub-Regional Office for North and Central Asia, in Almatı, Kazakhstan. An office to serve South and South-West Asia, was also scheduled to be established during that year, in New Delhi, India.

Activities

ESCAP acts as a UN regional centre, providing the only intergovernmental forum that includes the whole of Asia and the Pacific, and executing a wide range of development programmes through technical assistance, advisory services to governments, research, training and information. In May 2002, having considered the recommendations of an intergovernmental review meeting held in March, ESCAP determined to implement a restructuring of its structures and thematic priorities. Three main thematic programmes were identified: poverty reduction; managing globalization; and emerging social issues. In May 2007 the Commission, meeting in Almatı, Kazakhstan, commemorated the 60th anniversary of ESCAP and reaffirmed its central role in fostering regional and sub-regional co-operation. In April 2008 the Commission approved a new conference structure and requested a reorganization of the Secretariat in order to reflect the new structure and programme of work for the two years 2010–11. The meeting of the Commission in May 2011 was held on the theme 'Beyond the crises: long-term perspectives on social protection and development in Asia and the Pacific'.

Social Development: ESCAP's Social Development Division, formerly the Emerging Social Issues Division, comprises three sections: Social Protection and Social Justice; Social Policy and Population; and Gender Equality and Empowerment. The Division's main objective is to assess and respond to regional trends and challenges in social development, and to help member countries to build more inclusive societies, through social and financial policies and measures promoting social protection, social inclusion, gender equality and development. The Social Protection and Social Justice Section aims to strengthen the capacity of public and non-government institutions to address the problems of marginalized social groups and to promote initiatives to provide income to the poor. The Gender Equality and Empowerment Section promotes the advancement of women by helping to improve their access to education, economic resources, information and communication technologies and decision-making; it is also committed to combating violence against women, including trafficking. The Social Policy and Population Section focuses on issues concerning ageing, youth, disability, migration and population. Activities include providing technical assistance to national population programmes, promoting the rights of people with disabilities, supporting improvement of access to social services by poor people, and helping governments to form policies that take into account the increasing proportion of older people in the population. ESCAP chairs the UN Interagency Group on Youth, which was established to promote implementation of the World Programme of Action on Youth, UN Millennium Development Goals (MDGs) relating to young people, and events concerning the International Year of Youth (2010–11).

The Division implements global and regional mandates, such as the Programme of Action of the World Summit for Social Development and the Jakarta Plan of Action on Human Resources Development. The Biwako Millennium Framework for Action towards an Inclusive, Barrier-free and Rights-based Society for Persons with Disabilities in Asia and the Pacific was adopted by ESCAP as a regional guideline underpinning the Asian and Pacific Decade of Disabled Persons (2003–12). In 1998 ESCAP initiated a programme of assistance in establishing a regional network of Social Development Management Information Systems (SOMIS). ESCAP collaborated with other agencies towards the adoption, in November 2001, of a Regional Platform on Sustainable Development for Asia and the Pacific. The Commission undertook regional preparations for the World Summit on Sustainable Development, which was held in Johannesburg, South Africa, in August–September 2002. In following up the summit ESCAP undertook to develop a biodiversity park, which was officially inaugurated in Rawalpindi, Pakistan, in January 2005. The Commission also prepares specific publications relating to population and implements the Programme of Action of the International Conference on Population and Development. The Secretariat co-ordinates the Asia-Pacific Population Information Network (POPIN). The fifth Asia and Pacific Population Conference, sponsored by ESCAP, was held in Bangkok, Thailand, in December 2002. Expert group meetings to assess implementation of the Plan of Action on Population and Poverty adopted at the Conference were held in November 2005 and in February 2009. In September 2004 ESCAP convened a senior-level intergovernmental meeting on the regional review and implementation of the Beijing Platform for Action (Beijing + 10), relating to gender equality. A further intergovernmental review meeting, Beijing + 15, was hosted by ESCAP in November 2009. In October 2010 ESCAP established an Asia-Pacific Regional Advisory Group on Women, Peace and Security, which aimed to promote the effective implementation throughout the region of UN Security Council Resolution 1325 relating to the impact of conflict on women and girls and their role in peace-building. The 67th Commission, meeting in Bangkok, in May 2011, pledged commitment to protecting the poor and vulnerable sectors of the region's population from the aftershocks of economic and natural crises.

Following the massive earthquake and consequent devastating sea movements (tsunami), that occurred in late December 2004 in the Indian Ocean, ESCAP assisted other UN and international agencies with an initial emergency response and undertook early reviews of the impact of the event. In January 2005 the Executive Secretary appointed a Task Force on Tsunami Disaster Management to assist countries to address issues relating to natural disaster management, and to raise those issues at a regional level. The chairman of the Task Force was also appointed co-chair of an Inter-Agency Regional Task Force on Tsunami Relief and Rehabilitation that was established at a heads of agency meeting, convened by ESCAP later in that month, with particular responsibility to exchange information relating to rehabilitation and reconstruction in the aftermath of the tsunami disaster and to more general capacity-building on disaster preparedness. At the end of January a ministerial meeting, in Phuket, Thailand, approved the establishment of a regional tsunami early-warning system. ESCAP administers the voluntary, multi-donor Tsunami Regional Trust Fund, which was inaugurated in late 2005 to support reconstruction and national and regional efforts to establish the early-warning system. In March 2011 ESCAP and the Government of Thailand, the founding donor of the Fund, signed an agreement to expand the mandate of the Fund and rename it as the Multi-Donor Trust Fund for Tsunami, Disaster and Climate Preparedness in Indian Ocean and Southeast Asian Countries.

Environment and Development: ESCAP is concerned to strengthen national capabilities to achieve environmentally sound and sustainable development by integrating economic concerns, such as the sustainable management of natural resources, into economic planning and policies. The Environment and Development Division comprises sections on Energy Security, Environment and Development Policy, and Water Security. Activities include the promotion of integrated water resources development and management, including water quality and conservation and a reduction in water-related natural disasters; strengthening the formulation of policies in the sustainable development of land and mineral resources; and the consideration of energy resource options, such as rural energy supply, energy conservation and the planning of power networks. The Division administers a North-East Asia Subregional Programme for Environmental Co-operation (NEASPEC). Through the Division ESCAP prepares a report entitled 'State of the Environment in Asia and the Pacific' which is published at five-yearly intervals. ESCAP helps to organize a ministerial conference on environment and development, also convened every five years. In March 2005 ministers meeting in Seoul, Republic of Korea, adopted a Regional Implementation Plan for Sustainable Development in Asia and the Pacific (2006–10) and a Seoul Initiative on Environmentally Sustainable Economic Growth. The Division supports efforts to co-ordinate and monitor implementation of these initiatives. In particular, it received a mandate to work on issues related to climate change caused by global warming: it collates information, conducts regional seminars on adapting to climate change, and provides training in clean technology and guidance on reduction of harmful gas emissions. In March 2008 ESCAP organized an inaugural meeting of the Asia-Pacific Regional Platform on Climate Change and Development. In the following month ESCAP organized the first Asia-Pacific Mayors' Forum on Environmentally Sustainable Urban Infrastructure Development, convened in Ulsan, Republic of Korea. In June 2011 ESCAP hosted an Asia-Pacific Urban Forum, in Bangkok, which was convened on the theme 'Cities of opportunity: Partnerships for an inclusive and sustainable future'. In late September 2011 an expert group meeting on sustainable energy development in Asia and the Pacific, organized by ESCAP, UNDP, UNIDO and FAO, focused on the need for developing national policies in the region aimed at ensuring universal access to clean and efficient energy services, as a means of advancing poverty reduction and improving health and well-being.

In May 2010 the 66th Commission, convened in Incheon, Republic of Korea, adopted a Declaration urging countries to strengthen and adopt 'green growth' strategies, in order to support recovery from the global economic and financial crisis and to achieve sustainable economic and social development. The sixth ministerial conference on environment and development, convened in Astana, Kazakhstan, in September–October, adopted a Ministerial Declaration on Green Growth, committing member countries to promoting environmentally sustainable economic growth and development. The conference also adopted a Regional Implementation Plan for Sustainable Development in Asia and the Pacific, covering the period 2011–15, and a Green Bridge Initiative to promote environmental partnerships and co-operation between Europe and Asia.

Information and Communications Technology and Disaster Risk Reduction : ESCAP's Information and Communications Technology (ICT) and Disaster Risk Reduction Division comprises the following sections: ICT and Development; Disaster Risk Reduction; and Space Technology Applications. The Division aims to strengthen capacity for access to and the application of ICT and space technology, in order to enhance socio-economic development and maximize the benefits of globalization. It supports the development of cross-sectoral policies and strategies, and also supports regional co-operation aimed at sharing knowledge between advanced and developing economies and in areas such as cyber-crime and information security. In May 2005 the Commission approved the establishment, in the Republic of Korea, of the Asian and Pacific Training Centre for ICT for Development (APCICT); APCICT was inaugurated in June 2006 (see below). In June 2005 the Division convened a senior-level meeting of experts to consider technical issues relating to disaster management and mitigation in Asia and the Pacific. The Division organized several conferences in preparation for the second phase of the World Summit on the Information Society (WSIS), which took place in November 2005, and co-ordinates regional activities aimed at achieving WSIS targets for the widespread use of ICT by 2015. It helps members to include space technology in their development planning, for example the use of satellites in meteorology, disaster prevention, remote sensing and distance learning. In August 2007 the Division hosted an international meeting on the use of space technology to combat avian influenza and other infectious diseases. A meeting of national policymakers on disaster management was convened in March 2008 to discuss access to satellite information as a means of predicting and managing natural disasters. The Division's policy with relation to disaster risk reduction is guided by the Hyogo Framework for Action, covering the period 2005–15, which was adopted by the World Conference on Disaster Reduction, held in Kobe, Hyogo, Japan, in January 2005. The accompanying Declaration, adopted by the Conference, emphasized the need to develop and strengthen regional strategies and operational mechanisms in order to ensure rapid and effective disaster response. A new Committee on Disaster Risk Reduction convened for an inaugural session in March 2009; participants agreed to strengthen information and knowledge-sharing in relation to risk reduction. During 2010 ESCAP worked with the International Strategy for Disaster Reduction to produce an 'Asia and Pacific Disaster Report', which was published in October.

Microeconomic Policy and Development: The work of the Division, formerly the Poverty and Development Division, is undertaken by the following sections: Development Policy, and Microeconomic Policy and Analysis. The Division aims to increase the understanding of the economic and social development situation in the region, with particular attention given to the attainment of the MDGs, sustainable economic growth, poverty alleviation, the integration of environmental concerns into macroeconomic decisions and policy-making processes, and enhancing the position of the region's disadvantaged economies, including those Central Asian countries undergoing transition from a centrally-planned economy to a market economy. The Division is responsible for the provision of technical assistance, and the production of relevant documents and publications. It publishes the *Economic and Social Survey of Asia and the Pacific*. The 63rd Commission, meeting in Almatı, Kazakhstan, in May 2007, endorsed a regional plan, developed by ESCAP, UNDP and the Asian Development Bank, to help poorer member countries to achieve the MDGs. Assistance was to be provided in the following areas: knowledge and capacity-building; expertise; resources; advocacy; and regional co-operation in delivering public goods (including infrastructure and energy security). The Commission also approved a resolution urging greater investment in health care in all member countries. In 2009 the Microeconomic Policy and Development Division co-ordinated the preparation of a joint report of all five UN Regional Commissions, entitled *The Global Economic and Financial Crisis: Regional Impacts, Responses and Solutions*, which was published in May. In February 2010 a regional report on achieving the MDGs acknowledged the impact of the crisis and highlighted the need to strengthen social protection throughout the region.

Statistics: ESCAP's Statistics Division provides training and advice in priority areas, including national accounts statistics, poverty indicators, gender statistics, population censuses and surveys, and the strengthening and management of statistical systems. It supports co-ordination throughout the region of the development, implementation and revision of selected international statistical standards, and, in particular, co-ordinates the International Comparison Programme (ICP) for Asia and the Pacific (part of a global ICP initiative). The Division disseminates comparable socio-economic statistics, with increased use of the electronic media, promotes the use of modern technology in the public sector and trains senior-level officials in the effective management of ICT. Training is provided by the Statistical Institute for Asia and the Pacific (see below).

Trade and Investment: ESCAP aims to help members to benefit from globalization by increasing global and regional flows of trade and investment. Its Trade and Investment Division provides technical assistance and advisory services. It aims to enhance institutional capacity-building; gives special emphasis to the needs of least-developed, land-locked and island developing countries, and to Central Asian countries that are in transition to a market economy, in accelerating their industrial and technological advancement, promoting their exports, and furthering their integration into the region's economy; supports the development of electronic commerce and other information technologies in the region; and promotes the intra-regional and inter-subregional exchange of trade, investment and technology through the strengthening of institutional support services such as regional information networks.

The Division functions as the secretariat of the Asia-Pacific Trade Agreement (APTA), concluded in 1975 to promote regional trade through mutually agreed concessions by the participating states (in 2011 they comprised Bangladesh, People's Republic of China, India, Republic of Korea, Laos and Sri Lanka; accession proceedings for Mongolia were ongoing). Since 2004 the Division has organized an annual Asia-Pacific Business Forum, involving representatives of governments, the private sector and civil society. It operates the Asia-Pacific Trade and Investment Agreements Database, the Trade and Transport Facilitation Online Database and an online Directory of Trade and Investment-Related Organizations, and publishes the 'Asia-Pacific Trade and Investment Review' twice a year. The Division acts as the Secretariat of the Asia-Pacific Research and Training Network on Trade (ARTNeT), established in 2004, which aims to enhance the region's research capacity. ESCAP, with the World Trade Organization (WTO), implements a technical assistance programme, helping member states to implement WTO agreements and to participate in ongoing multilateral trade negotiations. In March 2009 ESCAP launched the UN Network of Experts for Paperless Trade in Asia and the Pacific (UN NExT).

Transport: ESCAP's Transport Division aims to improve the regional movement of goods and people, and to assist member states to manage and to benefit from globalization. The Division has three sections: Transport Infrastructure; Transport Facilitation and Logistics; and Transport Policy and Development (incorporating a sub-programme on Tourism). One of the Division's principal tasks is the implementation of the Asian Land Transport Infrastructure Development (ALTID) programme, initiated in 1992. ALTID projects include the development of the Trans-Asian Railway and of the Asian Highway road network. Other activities are aimed at improving the planning process in developing infrastructure facilities and services, in accordance with the Regional Action Programme of the New Delhi Action Plan on Infrastructure Development in Asia and the Pacific (which was adopted at a ministerial conference held in October 1996), and at enhancing private sector involvement in national infrastructure development through financing, management, operations and risk-sharing. The Division aims to reduce the adverse environmental impact of the provision of infrastructure facilities and to promote more equitable and easier access to social amenities. A Ministerial Conference on Infrastructure Development was organized by ESCAP in November 2001 (see below). An Intergovernmental Agreement on the Asian Highway Network (adopted in 2003, identifying some 141,000 km of roads in 32 countries) came into effect in July 2005. The first meeting of a working group on the highway network, which was to convene twice a year, was held in December. By November 2007 about 10,000 km of the highway network had been upgraded to meet the minimum standards set by the Agreement, and in that month an Asian Highway Investment Forum was convened by ESCAP to finance the improvements still required on a further 12,000 km of the network. In November 2005 ESCAP organized an intergovernmental meeting to conclude a draft agreement on the establishment of a Trans-Asian Railway Network. The intergovernmental accord was adopted in April 2006, and entered into force in June 2009, at which time it had received 22 signatures and been ratified by eight member states. The network was to comprise some 114,000 km of rail routes over 28 countries. The first meeting of a working group on the Trans-Asian Railway Network was held in December, in Bangkok, Thailand. In 2004 ESCAP and the UN Economic Commission for Europe (ECE) initiated a project for developing Euro-Asian transport linkages, aiming to identify and overcome the principal obstacles (physical and otherwise) along the main transport routes linking Asia and Europe. In November 2003 ESCAP approved a new initiative, the Asia-Pacific Network for Transport and Logistics Education and Research (ANTLER), to comprise education, training and research centres throughout the region. In November 2006 the Ministerial Conference on Transport, held in Busan, Republic of Korea, adopted the Busan Declaration, which outlined a long-term development strategy for regional transport and identified investment priorities. The meeting also adopted a Ministerial Declaration on Road Safety which pledged to implement safety measures to save some 600,000 lives in the region in the period 2007–15. In April 2008 the ESCAP Commission determined to establish a Forum of Asian Ministers of Transport to provide strategic guidance for the development of efficient, reliable and cost-effective transport services throughout the region. The inaugural meeting of the Forum was held in December 2009, in Bangkok, Thailand.

ESCAP's tourism concerns include the development of human resources, improved policy planning for tourism development, greater investment in the industry, and minimizing the environmental impact of tourism. A Plan of Action for Sustainable Tourism in the Asia and Pacific Region (1999–2005) was adopted in April 1999, and a second phase of the Plan was to cover the period 2006–12. A Network of Asia-Pacific Education and Training Institutes in Tourism, established in 1997, comprised 261 institutes and organizations in 2011.

CO-OPERATION WITH OTHER ORGANIZATIONS

ESCAP works with other UN agencies and non-UN international organizations, non-governmental organizations, academic institutions and the private sector; such co-operation includes joint planning of programmes, preparation of studies and reports, participating in meetings, and sharing information and technical expertise. In July 1993 a memorandum of understanding (MOU) was signed by ESCAP and the Asian Development Bank, outlining priority areas of co-operation between the two organizations. These were: regional and sub-regional co-operation; issues concerning the least-developed, land-locked and island developing member countries; poverty alleviation; women in development; population; human resource development; the environment and natural resource management; statistics and data bases; economic analysis; transport and communications; and industrial restructuring and privatization. The two organizations were to co-operate in organizing workshops, seminars and conferences, in implementing joint projects, and in exchanging information and data on a regular basis. A new MOU between the two organizations was signed in May 2004 with an emphasis on achieving poverty reduction throughout the region. In 2001 ESCAP, with the Bank and UNDP, established a regional partnership to promote the MDGs (see above); a joint regional report on implementation of the goals was prepared by the partnership and published in June 2005 prior to a global review, conducted at the UN General Assembly in September, and a further regional review was published in 2007. In May 2007 ESCAP endorsed a regional plan developed by the partnership with the aim of addressing regional challenges (in particular those faced by poorer countries) to the achievement of the MDGs. The UN Special Programme for the Economies of Central Asia (SPECA), begun in 1998, is implemented jointly by ESCAP and ECE (see below). In May

2007 ESCAP signed an MOU with ECE and the Eurasian Economic Community to strengthen co-operation in sustainable development, in support of the MDGs. In the following month ESCAP signed an MOU with the International Organization for Migration (IOM) to provide for greater co-operation and co-ordination on international migration issues. In September 2008 ESCAP and the IOM organized an Asia-Pacific high-level meeting on international migration and development.

REGIONAL INSTITUTIONS

Asian and Pacific Centre for Agricultural Engineering and Machinery (APCAEM): A-7/F, China International Science and Technology Convention Centre, 12 Yumin Rd, Chaoyang District, Beijing 100029, People's Republic of China; tel. (10) 8225-3581; fax (10) 8225-3584; e-mail info@unapcaem.org; internet www.unapcaem.org; f. 1977 as Regional Network for Agricultural Engineering and Machinery, elevated to regional centre in 2002; aims to reduce poverty by enhancing environmentally sustainable agriculture and food production, and applying 'green' and modern agro-technology for the well-being of producers and consumers; work programmes comprise agricultural engineering, food chain management, and agro-enterprise development and trade; undertakes research, training, technical assistance and the exchange of information. Active mems: Bangladesh, People's Republic of China, Fiji, India, Indonesia, Iran, Democratic People's Republic of Korea, Republic of Korea, Mongolia, Nepal, Pakistan, Philippines, Sri Lanka, Thailand, Viet Nam; Dir LeRoy Hollenbeck; publ. *APCAEM Policy Brief* (quarterly).

Asian and Pacific Centre for Transfer of Technology: APCTT Bldg, POB 4575, C-2 Qutab Institutional Area, New Delhi 110 016, India; tel. (11) 26966509; fax (11) 26856274; e-mail postmaster@apctt.org; internet www.apctt.org; f. 1977 to assist countries of the ESCAP region by strengthening their capacity to develop, transfer and adopt technologies relevant to the region, and to identify and promote regional technology development and transfer; operates Business Asia Network (www.business-asia.net) to promote technology-based co-operation, particularly between small and medium-sized enterprises; Dir Dr Krishnamurthy Ramanathan; publs *Asia Pacific Tech Monitor*, *VATIS Updates on Biotechnology*, *Food Processing*, *Ozone Layer Protection*, *Non-Conventional Energy*, and *Waste Management* (each every 2 months).

Asian and Pacific Training Centre for ICT for Development (APCICT): Bonbudong, 3rd Floor Songdo Techno Park, 7-50 Songdo-dong, Yeonsu-gu, Incheon City, Republic of Korea; tel. 245-1700; fax 245-7712; e-mail info@unapcict.org; internet www.unapcict.org; f. 2006 to provide training to ICT policy-makers and professionals, advisory services and analytical studies, to promote best practices in the field of ICT, and to contribute to narrowing the digital divide in the region; developed an Academy of ICT Essentials for Government Leaders, a virtual Academy, and an e-Collaborative hub; Dir Hyuen-Suk Rhee.

Centre for Alleviation of Poverty through Secondary Crops' Development in Asia and the Pacific (CAPSA): Jalan Merdeka 145, Bogor 16111, Indonesia; tel. (251) 343277; fax (251) 336290; e-mail capsa@uncapsa.org; internet www.uncapsa.org; f. 1981 as CGPRT Centre, current name adopted April 2004; initiates and promotes socio-economic and policy research, training, dissemination of information and advisory services to enhance the living conditions of rural poor populations reliant on secondary crop agriculture; Dir Dr Katinka Weinberger (Germany); publs *CAPSA Flash* (monthly), *Palawija News* (3 a year), working paper series, monograph series and statistical profiles.

Statistical Institute for Asia and the Pacific (SIAP): JETRO-IDE Building, 2–2 Wakaba 3-chome, Mihama-ku, Chiba-shi, Chiba 2618787, Japan; tel. (43) 2999782; fax (43) 2999780; e-mail staff@unsiap.or.jp; internet www.unsiap.or.jp; f. 1970 as Asian Statistical Institute, present name 1977; became a subsidiary body of ESCAP in 1995; trains government statisticians at the Institute and in various co-operating countries in Asia and the Pacific; prepares teaching materials, assists in the development of training on official statistics in national and sub-regional centres; Dir Davaasuren Chultemjamts (Mongolia); publ. *SIAP Newsletter* (annually).

ASSOCIATED BODIES

ESCAP/WMO Typhoon Committee: Av. de 5 de Outubro, Coloane, Macao, SAR, People's Republic of China; tel. 88010531; fax 88010530; e-mail info@typhooncommittee.org; internet www.typhooncommittee.org; f. 1968; an intergovernmental body sponsored by ESCAP and the World Meteorological Organization for mitigation of typhoon damage; aims to establish efficient typhoon and flood warning systems through improved meteorological and telecommunication facilities; promotes disaster preparedness, trains personnel and co-ordinates research. The committee's programme is supported from national resources and also by UNDP and other international and bilateral assistance. Mems: Cambodia, People's Republic of China, Hong Kong, Japan, Democratic People's Republic of Korea, Republic of Korea, Laos, Macao, Malaysia, Philippines, Singapore, Thailand, USA, Viet Nam; Sec. Olavo Rasquinho.

WMO/ESCAP Panel on Tropical Cyclones: Technical Support Unit (TSU), c/o Pakistan Meteorological Dept, POB 1214, H-8/2, Islamabad, Pakistan; tel. (51) 9257314; fax (51) 4432588; e-mail tsupmd@hotmail.com; internet www.tsuptc-wmo.org; f. 1972 to mitigate damage caused by tropical cyclones in the Bay of Bengal and the Arabian Sea. Mems: Bangladesh, India, the Maldives, Myanmar, Oman, Pakistan, Sri Lanka, Thailand; TSU Co-ordinator Dr Qamar-uz-Zaman Chaudhry.

Finance

For the two-year period 2010–11 ESCAP's programme budget, an appropriation from the UN budget, was US $93.9m. The regular budget is supplemented annually by funds from various sources for technical assistance.

Publications

Annual Report.

Asia-Pacific Development Journal (2 a year).

Asia-Pacific in Figures (annually).

Asia-Pacific Population Journal (3 a year).

Asia-Pacific Trade and Investment Review (2 a year).

Asia and Pacific Disaster Report.

Bulletin on Asia-Pacific Perspectives (annually).

Economic and Social Survey of Asia and the Pacific (annually).

Environment and Sustainable Development News (quarterly).

ESCAP Energy News (2 a year).

ESCAP Human Resources Development Newsletter (2 a year).

ESCAP Population Data Sheet (annually).

ESCAP Tourism Review (annually).

Foreign Trade Statistics of Asia and the Pacific (every 2 years).

Key Economic Developments and Prospects in the Asia-Pacific Region (annually).

Population Headliners (several a year).

Poverty Alleviation Initiatives (quarterly).

Socio-Economic Policy Brief (several a year).

State of the Environment in Asia and the Pacific (every 5 years).

Statistical Indicators for Asia and the Pacific (quarterly).

Statistical Newsletter (quarterly).

Statistical Yearbook for Asia and the Pacific.

Technical Co-operation Yearbook.

Trade and Investment Information Bulletin (monthly).

Transport and Communications Bulletin for Asia and the Pacific (annually).

Water Resources Journal (annually).

Manuals; country and trade profiles; commodity prices; statistics; Atlas of Mineral Resources of the ESCAP Region (country by country).

United Nations Children's Fund—UNICEF

Address: 3 United Nations Plaza, New York, NY 10017, USA.

Telephone: (212) 326-7000; **fax:** (212) 887-7465; **e-mail:** info@unicef.org; **internet:** www.unicef.org.

UNICEF was established in 1946 by the UN General Assembly as the UN International Children's Emergency Fund, to meet the emergency needs of children in post-war Europe. In 1950 its mandate was expanded to respond to the needs of children in developing countries. In 1953 the General Assembly decided that UNICEF should become a permanent branch of the UN system, with an emphasis on programmes giving long-term benefits to children everywhere, particularly those in developing countries. In 1965 UNICEF was awarded the Nobel Peace Prize.

Organization

(October 2011)

EXECUTIVE BOARD

The Executive Board, as the governing body of UNICEF, comprises 36 member governments from all regions, elected in rotation for a three-year term by ECOSOC. The Board establishes policy, reviews programmes and approves expenditure. It reports to the General Assembly through ECOSOC.

SECRETARIAT

The Executive Director of UNICEF is appointed by the UN Secretary-General in consultation with the Executive Board. The administration of UNICEF and the appointment and direction of staff are the responsibility of the Executive Director, under policy directives laid down by the Executive Board, and under a broad authority delegated to the Executive Director by the Secretary-General. In 2009 there were more than 9,800 UNICEF staff positions, of which about 85% were in field offices.

Executive Director: Anthony Lake (USA).

UNICEF OFFICES

Japan: UNU Headquarters Bldg, 8th Floor, 53–70, Jingumae 5-chome, Shibuya-ku, Tokyo 150-0001, Japan; tel. (3) 5467-4431; fax (3) 5467-4437; e-mail tokyo@unicef.org; internet www.unicef.or.jp.

Regional Office for East Asia and the Pacific: POB 2-154, Bangkok 10200, Thailand; tel. (2) 2805931; fax (2) 2803563; e-mail eapro@unicef.org; internet www.unicef.org/eapro/.

UNICEF Innocenti Research Centre: Piazza SS. Annunziata 12, 50122 Florence, Italy; tel. (055) 20330; fax (055) 2033220; e-mail info@unicef-irc.org; internet www.unicef-irc.org; f. 1988; undertakes research in two thematic areas: Social and economic policies and children; and Child protection and implementation of international standards for children; Dir Gordon Alexander.

UNICEF Supply Division: UNICEF Plads, Freeport 2100, Copenhagen, Denmark; tel. 35-27-35-27; fax 35-26-94-21; e-mail supply@unicef.org; internet www.unicef.org/supply; responsible for overseeing UNICEF's global procurement and logistics operations.

NATIONAL COMMITTEES

UNICEF is supported by 36 National Committees, mostly in industrialized countries, whose volunteer members raise money through various specific campaigns and activities, including the sale of greetings cards and collection of foreign coins. The Committees also undertake advocacy and awareness campaigns on a number of issues and provide an important link with the general public.

Activities

UNICEF is dedicated to the well-being of children, adolescents and women and works for the realization and protection of their rights within the frameworks of the Convention on the Rights of the Child, which was adopted by the UN General Assembly in 1989, and by 2011 was almost universally ratified, and of the Convention on the Elimination of All Forms of Discrimination Against Women, adopted by the UN General Assembly in 1979. Promoting the full implementation of the Conventions, UNICEF aims to ensure that children worldwide are given the best possible start in life and attain a good level of basic education, and that adolescents are given every opportunity to develop their capabilities and participate successfully in society. The Fund also continues to provide relief and rehabilitation assistance in emergencies. Through its extensive field network in more than 150 developing countries and territories, UNICEF undertakes, in co-ordination with governments, local communities and other aid organizations, programmes in health, nutrition, education, water and sanitation, the environment, gender issues and development, and other fields of importance to children. Emphasis is placed on low-cost, community-based programmes. UNICEF programmes are increasingly focused on supporting children and women during critical periods of their life, when intervention can make a lasting difference. Since the 1950s UNICEF has engaged the services of prominent individuals as Goodwill Ambassadors and Advocates, who can use their status to attract attention to particular causes and support UNICEF's objectives.

The principal themes of UNICEF's medium-term strategic plan for the period 2006–11 are: young child survival and development; basic education and gender equality (including the Fund's continued leadership of the UN Girls' Education Initiative, see below); HIV/AIDS and children (including participation in the Joint UN Programme on HIV/AIDS—UNAIDS—see below); child protection from violence, exploitation and abuse; and policy advocacy and partnerships for children's rights. These priority areas are guided by the relevant UN Millennium Development Goals (MDGs) adopted by world leaders in 2000, and by the 'A World Fit for Children' declaration and plan of action endorsed by the UN General Assembly Special Session on Children in 2002. The 'A World Fit for Children' declaration reaffirmed commitment to the agenda of the 1990 World Summit for Children. The plan of action resolved to work towards the attainment by 2015 of 21 new goals and targets supporting the MDGs in the areas of education, health and the protection of children; these included: a reduction of mortality rates for infants and children under five by two-thirds; a reduction of maternal mortality rates by three-quarters; a reduction by one-third in the rate of severe malnutrition among children under the age of five; and enrolment in primary education by 90% of children. UNICEF issues regular reports that monitor progress in achieving the MDGs. The ninth in the series, entitled *Progress for Children: Achieving the MDGs with Equity (No. 9)*, was published in September 2010. The final agreement of a summit convened in that month on progress towards achieving the MDGs placed particular emphasis on children's rights.

UNICEF estimates that more than 500,000 women die every year during pregnancy or childbirth, largely because of inadequate maternal healthcare, and nearly 4m. newborns die within 28 days of birth. For every maternal death, approximately 30 further women suffer permanent injuries or chronic disabilities as a result of complications during pregnancy or childbirth. Under the Global Partnership for Maternal, Newborn and Child Health, UNICEF works with WHO, UNFPA and other partners in countries with high maternal mortality to improve maternal health and prevent maternal and newborn death through the integration of a continuum of home, community, outreach and facility-based care, embracing every stage of maternal, newborn and child health. UNICEF and partners work with governments and policy-makers to ensure that ante-natal and obstetric care is a priority in national health plans. UNICEF's recent activities in this area have included support for obstetric facilities and training in, and advocacy of, women's health issues, such as ending child marriage, eliminating female genital mutilation/cutting (FGM/C), and preventing malaria and promoting the uptake of tetanus toxoid vaccinations and iron and folic acid supplements among pregnant women.

YOUNG CHILD SURVIVAL AND DEVELOPMENT

In 2010 UNICEF allocated some 50% of total programme assistance to young child survival and development. In 2009 UNICEF estimated that around 8.1m. children under five years of age died (compared with some 20m. child mortalities in 1960 and some 13m. in 1990)—mainly in developing countries (three-quarters occurring in the People's Republic of China, the Democratic Republic of the Congo, India, Nigeria, and Pakistan), and the majority from largely preventable causes. UNICEF has worked with WHO and other partners to increase global immunization coverage against the following six diseases: measles, poliomyelitis, tuberculosis, diphtheria, whooping cough and tetanus. In 2003 UNICEF, WHO, the World Bank and other partners established a new Child Survival Partnership, which acts as a forum for the promotion of co-ordinated action in support of efforts to save children's lives in 68 targeted developing countries. UNICEF, WHO, the World Bank and the UN Population Division established an Inter-agency Group for Child Mortality Estimation (IGME) in 2004, to advance work on monitoring progress towards meeting the MDG on reducing child mortality. In September 2005 UNICEF, WHO and other partners launched the Partnership for Maternal, Newborn and Child Health, which aimed to accelerate progress towards the attainment of the MDGs to reduce child and maternal mortality. In 2000 UNICEF, WHO, the World Bank and a number of public- and private-sector partners launched the Global

Alliance for Vaccines and Immunization (GAVI), subsequently renamed the GAVI Alliance, which aims to protect children of all nationalities and socio-economic groups against vaccine-preventable diseases. GAVI's strategy includes improving access to sustainable immunization services, expanding the use of existing vaccines, accelerating the development and introduction of new vaccines and technologies and promoting immunization coverage as a focus of international development efforts. In 2006 UNICEF, WHO and other partners launched the Global Immunization Vision and Strategy (GIVS), a global 10-year framework, covering 2006–15, aimed at reducing deaths due to vaccine-preventable diseases by at least two-thirds compared to 2000 levels, by 2015; and increasing national vaccination coverage levels to at least 90%. (In 2009 the global child vaccination coverage rate was estimated at 82%.) From 2006 a Global Immunization Meeting was convened annually by UNICEF, WHO and GAVI Alliance partners; the fifth Meeting, held in February 2010, addressed issues including means of improving routine vaccination and supporting accelerated disease control initiatives; the introduction of new vaccines; and vaccine supply, including the status of pandemic influenza vaccines.

UNICEF works to improve safe water supply, sanitation and hygiene, and thereby reduce the risk of diarrhoea and other water-borne diseases. In partnership with other organizations the Fund supports initiatives to make schools in more than 90 developing countries safer through school-based water, sanitation and hygiene programmes. UNICEF places great emphasis on increasing the testing and protection of drinking water at its source as well as in the home. UNICEF, the World Bank and other partners participate in the Global Public-Private Partnership for Handwashing with Soap, which was established in 2001 with the aim of empowering communities in developing countries to prevent diarrhoea and respiratory infections through the promotion of the practice of thorough hand-washing with soap. In 2006 UNICEF and partners established the Global Task Force on Water and Sanitation with the aim of providing all children with access to safe water, and accelerating progress towards MDG targets on safe drinking water and basic sanitation.

UNICEF-assisted programmes for the control of diarrhoeal diseases promote the low-cost manufacture and distribution of pre-packaged salts or home-made solutions. The use of 'oral rehydration therapy' has risen significantly in recent years, and is believed to prevent more than 1m. child deaths annually. During 1990–2000 diarrhoea-related deaths were reduced by one-half. UNICEF also promotes the need to improve sanitation and access to safe water supplies in developing nations in order to reduce the risk of diarrhoea and other water-borne diseases (see 20/20 initiative, below). To control acute respiratory infections, another leading cause of death in children under five in developing countries, UNICEF works with WHO in training health workers to diagnose and treat the associated diseases. At the UN General Assembly Special Session on Children, in 2002, goals were set to reduce measles deaths by 50%. Expanded efforts by UNICEF, WHO and other partners led to a reduction in world-wide measles deaths by 78% between 2000 and 2008. Around 1m. children die from malaria every year, mainly in sub-Saharan Africa. In October 1998 UNICEF, together with WHO, UNDP and the World Bank, inaugurated a new global campaign, Roll Back Malaria, to fight the disease. UNICEF is actively engaged in developing innovative and effective ways to distribute highly-subsidized insecticide-treated mosquito nets at local level, thereby increasing the proportion of children and pregnant women who use them.

According to UNICEF estimates, around 25% of children under five years of age are underweight, while each year malnutrition contributes to more than one-third of the child deaths in that age group and leaves millions of others with physical and mental disabilities. UNICEF supports national efforts to reduce malnutrition, for example, fortifying staple foods with micronutrients, widening women's access to education, improving the nutritional status of pregnant women, strengthening household food security and basic health services, providing food supplies in emergencies, and promoting sound childcare and feeding practices. Since 1991 more than 19,000 hospitals in about 130 countries have been designated 'baby-friendly', having implemented a set of UNICEF and WHO recommendations entitled '10 steps to successful breast-feeding'.

The results of integrated approaches to child health, such as the Accelerated Child Survival and Development (ACSD) strategy and community-based Integrated Management of Childhood Illnesses (IMCI) programme, have demonstrated new potential to reduce child mortality. The ACSD strategy, implemented by UNICEF since 2002, is an intensive combination of life-saving interventions including the promotion of antenatal care, vaccination and breast-feeding, volunteer health-worker follow-up of newborns, and the distribution of insecticide-treated mosquito nets. Focused in 97 high-mortality districts in 11 mainly West African countries, ACSD has reached around 16m. people, including 2.8m. children under the age of five.

BASIC EDUCATION AND GENDER EQUALITY

In 2010 UNICEF allocated some 20% of total programme assistance to basic education and gender equality. UNICEF considers education to be a fundamental human right, and works to ensure all children receive equal access to quality education. UNICEF participated in and fully supports the objectives and framework for action adopted by the World Education Forum in Dakar, Senegal, in April 2000, including the Education for All initiative. UNICEF was assigned formal responsibility within the initiative for education in emergencies, early childhood care and technical and policy support. UNICEF leads and acts as the secretariat of the United Nations Girls' Education Initiative (UNGEI), which aims to increase the enrolment of girls in primary schools in more than 100 countries. It is estimated that more than 100m. school-age children world-wide, of whom more than one-half are girls, remain deprived of basic education. In May 2010 UNGEI convened the first ever international conference on 'Engendering Empowerment: Education and Equality' ('E4'), in Dakar, Senegal. The E4 conference unanimously adopted the Dakar Declaration on Accelerating Girls' Education and Gender Equality, in which it urged that increased focus should be placed on accelerating access to education for the most socially deprived girls, deemed to be the most disadvantaged group in education.

UNICEF advocates the implementation of the Child Friendly School model, designed to facilitate the delivery of safe, quality education. UNICEF, in partnership with UNESCO, has developed an Essential Learning Package to support countries to reduce disparities in the provision of basic education. The initiative was implemented for the first time by Burkina Faso in 2003, and has since been adopted by a further 11 countries in West and Central Africa.

Major 'back-to-school' campaigns and enrolment drives were launched in countries struck by the December 2004 Indian Ocean tsunamis; within three months of the disaster 90% of affected children had returned to school. Similar campaigns have been undertaken in countries emerging from civil conflict, for example Kyrgyzstan, Somalia and South Sudan, and include advocacy efforts as well as the distribution of essential educational supplies, often in the form of specially designed 'school-in-a-box' kits.

HIV/AIDS AND CHILDREN

In 2010 UNICEF allocated some 5% of total programme assistance to combating HIV/AIDS. UNICEF is concerned at the danger posed by HIV/AIDS to the realization of children's rights and aims to provide expertise, support, logistical co-ordination and innovation towards ending the epidemic and limiting its impact on children and their mothers. At the end of 2009 it was estimated that 2.5m. children under the age of 15 were living with HIV/AIDS world-wide. During that year some 370,000 children under the age of 15 were estimated to have been newly infected with HIV, while 260,000 died as a result of AIDS and AIDS-related illnesses. Some 16.6m. children world-wide have lost one or both parents to AIDS since the start of the pandemic, and as a result of HIV/AIDS many children have suffered poverty, homelessness, discrimination, and loss of education and other life opportunities. UNICEF's priorities in this area include prevention of infection among young people (through, for example, support for education programmes and dissemination of information through the media), reduction in mother-to-child transmission, care and protection of orphans and other vulnerable children, and care and support for children, young people and parents living with HIV/AIDS. UNICEF works closely in this field with governments and co-operates with other UN agencies in the Joint UN Programme on HIV/AIDS (UNAIDS), which became operational on 1 January 1996. Young people aged 15–24 are reported to account for around 45% of new HIV infections world-wide. In July 2002 UNICEF, UNAIDS and WHO jointly produced a study entitled *Young People and HIV/AIDS: Opportunity in Crisis*, examining young people's sexual behaviour patterns and knowledge of HIV/AIDS. UNICEF advocates Life Skills-Based Education as a means of empowering young people to cope with challenging situations and of encouraging them to adopt healthy patterns of behaviour. In July 2004 UNICEF and other partners produced a *Framework for the Protection, Care and Support of Orphans and Vulnerable Children Living in a World with HIV and AIDS*. In October 2005 UNICEF launched Unite for Children, Unite against AIDS, a campaign that was to provide a platform for child-focused advocacy aimed at reversing the spread of HIV/AIDS amongst children, adolescents and young people; and to provide a child-focused framework for national programmes based on the following four pillars (known as the 'Four Ps'): the prevention of mother-to-child HIV transmission, improved provision of paediatric treatment, prevention of infection among adolescents and young people, and protection and support of children affected by HIV/AIDS. In December 2009 UNICEF issued its fourth *Children and AIDS: A Stocktaking Report*, detailing ongoing progress and challenges. In October 2010 UNICEF issued its first Mother-Baby Pack, containing drugs to prevent mother-to-child transmission of HIV in the poorest households.

At December 2009 it was estimated that some 8,000 children aged between 0–14 were living with HIV/AIDS in East Asia, and that 3,100 children under 15 in the Pacific region were infected with the virus.

CHILD PROTECTION FROM VIOLENCE, EXPLOITATION AND ABUSE

In 2010 UNICEF allocated some 9% of total programme assistance to child protection activities. UNICEF is actively involved in global-level partnerships for child protection, including the Inter-Agency Co-ordination Panel on Juvenile Justice; the Inter-Agency Working Group on Unaccompanied and Separated Children; the Donors' Working Group on Female FGM/C (see above); the Better Care Network; the Study on Violence Against Children; the Inter-Agency Standing Committee (IASC) Task Force on Protection from Sexual Exploitation and Abuse in Humanitarian Crises; and the IASC Task Force on Mental Health and Psychological Support in Emergency Settings.

UNICEF estimates that the births of around 48m. children annually (about 36% of all births) are not registered, and that some 63% of births occuring in South Asia, and 55% of births in sub-Saharan Africa, are unregistered. UNICEF promotes universal registration in order to prevent the abuse of children without proof of age and nationality, for example through trafficking, forced labour, early marriage and military recruitment.

UNICEF estimates that some 158m. children aged from five–14 are engaged in child labour, while around 1.2m. children world-wide are trafficked each year. The Fund, which vigorously opposes the exploitation of children as a violation of their basic human rights, works with the ILO and other partners to promote an end to exploitative and hazardous child labour, and supports special projects to provide education, counselling and care in developing countries. UNICEF co-sponsored and actively participated in the Third Congress Against Commercial Sexual Exploitation of Children, held in Rio de Janeiro, Brazil, in November 2008.

More than 250,000 children are involved in armed conflicts as soldiers, porters and forced labourers. UNICEF encourages ratification of the Optional Protocol to the Convention on the Rights of the Child on the involvement of children in armed conflict, which was adopted by the General Assembly in May 2000 and entered into force in February 2002, and bans the compulsory recruitment of combatants below the age of 18. The Fund also urges states to make unequivocal statements endorsing 18 as the minimum age of voluntary recruitment to the armed forces. UNICEF, with Save the Children, co-chairs the Steering Group of the Paris Principles, which aims to support the implementation of a series of 'Commitments', first endorsed in 2007, to end the recruitment of children, support the release of children from the armed forces and facilitate their reintegration into civilian life. By the end of 2010 95 countries had voluntarily signed up to the Paris Commitments. It is estimated that landmines kill and maim between 8,000 and 10,000 children every year. UNICEF supports mine awareness campaigns, and promotes the full ratification of the Convention on the Prohibition of the Use, Stockpiling, Production and Transfer of Anti-Personnel Mines and on their Destruction, which was adopted in December 1997 and entered into force in March 1999. By October 2011 the Convention had been ratified by 156 countries.

POLICY AND ADVOCACY AND PARTNERSHIPS FOR CHILDREN'S RIGHTS

In 2010 UNICEF allocated some 11% of total programme assistance to policy and advocacy and partnerships for children's rights. UNICEF's annual publication *The State of the World's Children* includes social and economic data relevant to the well-being of children. In 1995 UNICEF developed its Multiple Indicator Cluster Survey (MICS) method of data collection, which is used as a main tool in measuring progress towards the achievement of the UN MDGs.

Since 2005 young people from the Group of Eight (G8) nations (Canada, France, Germany, Italy, Japan, Russia, the United Kingdom and the USA) and selected emerging countries (Brazil, People's Republic of China, Egypt, India, Mexico and South Africa in 2009) have participated in a Junior 8 (J8) summit, which is organized with support from UNICEF on the fringes of the annual G8 summit. The J8 summits address issues including education, energy, climate change, HIV/AIDS, the global financial crisis, and tolerance. The fifth J8 summit meeting took place in L'Aquila, Italy, in July 2009. In June 2010 the first ever G(irls)20 summit was convened in Toronto, Canada, immediately prior to a summit of G20 leaders; the participants represented the G20 countries, and, in addition, a young female representative of the African Union was invited to attend.

UNICEF aims to break the cycle of poverty by advocating for the provision of increased development aid to developing countries, and aims to help poor countries obtain debt relief and to ensure access to basic social services. UNICEF was the leading agency in promoting the 20/20 initiative, which was endorsed at the World Summit for Social Development, held in Copenhagen, Denmark, in March 1995. The initiative encouraged the governments of developing and donor countries to allocate at least 20% of their domestic budgets and official development aid to healthcare, primary education, and low-cost safe water and sanitation.

Through this focus area, UNICEF seeks to work with partners to strengthen capacities to design and implement cross-sectoral social and economic policies, child-focused legislative measures and budgetary allocations that enable countries to meet their obligations under the Convention on the Rights of the Child and the Convention on the Elimination of All Forms of Discrimination against Women. UNICEF has identified the following priority areas of support to 'upstream' policy work: child poverty and disparities; social budgeting; decentralization; social security and social protection; holistic legislative reform for the two Conventions; and the impact of migration on children.

HUMANITARIAN RESPONSE

UNICEF provides emergency relief assistance to children and young people affected by conflict, natural disasters and food crises. In situations of violence and social disintegration the Fund provides support in the areas of education, health, mine-awareness and psychosocial assistance, and helps to demobilize and rehabilitate child soldiers. In 2010 funding requirements for humanitarian activities amounted to US $1,153.7m., of which the largest allocation, $172.0m., was for Sudan, and $122.5m. for the Democratic Republic of the Congo.

In 1999 UNICEF adopted a Peace and Security Agenda to help guide international efforts in this field. Emergency education assistance includes the provision of 'Edukits' in refugee camps and the reconstruction of school buildings. In the area of health the Fund co-operates with WHO to arrange 'days of tranquillity' in order to facilitate the immunization of children in conflict zones. Psychosocial assistance activities include special programmes to support traumatized children and help unaccompanied children to be reunited with parents or extended families.

During 2005–07 the Fund assisted an estimated 6m. children, young people and women in areas affected by the devastating December 2004 Indian Ocean tsunamis. UNICEF's relief and recovery efforts included the immunization of some 1.2m. children against measles, the supply of essential drugs and Vitamin A supplements to more than 3m. children, as well as the provision of water and basic sanitation to help prevent disease outbreaks. UNICEF and partners have trained more than 56,000 health personnel, provided key supplies and equipment to more than 7,000 health facilities and to around 2m. children, developed child protection policies, and constructed or rehabilitated 107 schools, 59 health facilities, 28 child centres, and water facilities to serve some 700,000 people.

In the mid-2000s UNICEF country offices prepared contingency plans for a possible future avian influenza pandemic among humans, with a particular focus on children, as part of the inter-agency response to the threat.

Since 1998 UNICEF's humanitarian response has been structured within a framework of identified Core Commitments for Children in Humanitarian Action (CCCs). Revised CCCs were issued in April 2010 to reflect new humanitarian structures and best practices. The revised CCCs incorporated UNICEF's commitment to working in partnership with international organizations, national authorities and civil society in order to strengthen risk reduction, disaster preparedness and response, and early recovery. During 2005 the UN's Inter-Agency Standing Committee (IASC), concerned with co-ordinating the international response to humanitarian disasters, developed a concept of organizing agency assistance to IDPs through the institutionalization of a 'Cluster Approach', comprising 11 core areas of activity. UNICEF is the lead agency for the clusters on Education (jointly with Save The Children); Nutrition; and Water, Sanitation and Hygiene. In addition, it leads the Gender-based Violence Area of Responsibility sub-cluster (jointly with UNFPA) and the Child Protection Area of Responsibility sub-cluster within the Protection Cluster.

Finance

UNICEF is funded by voluntary contributions from governments and non-governmental and private sector sources. UNICEF's income is divided into contributions for 'regular resources' (used for country programmes of co-operation approved by the Executive Board, programme support, and management and administration costs) and contributions for 'other resources' (for special purposes, including expanding the outreach of country programmes of co-operation, and ensuring capacity to deliver critical assistance to women and children, for example during humanitarian crises). UNICEF's total income in 2010 was US $3,682m., of which $2,083m. (57%) was from governments, $1,188m. (32%) from the private sector and non-governmental organizations, and $356m. (10%) from inter-organizational arrangements. UNICEF's total expenditure in 2009 was $3,355m.

In 2010 some 53% of the Fund's total programme expenditure was allocated to activities in Africa south of the Sahara, 26% to activities in Asia, 9% to Latin America and the Caribbean, 4% to the Middle East and North Africa, 3% to Central and Eastern Europe and the CIS, and 5% to interregional projects.

Publications

Progress for Children (in English, French and Spanish).

The State of the World's Children (annually, in Arabic, English, French, Russian and Spanish and about 30 other national languages).

UNICEF Annual Report (in English, French and Spanish).

UNICEF at a Glance (in English, French and Spanish).

UNICEF Humanitarian Action Report (annually).

Reports and studies; series on children and women; nutrition; education; children's rights; children in wars and disasters; working children; water, sanitation and the environment; analyses of the situation of children and women in individual developing countries.

United Nations Development Programme—UNDP

Address: One United Nations Plaza, New York, NY 10017, USA.

Telephone: (212) 906-5300; **fax:** (212) 906-5364; **e-mail:** hq@undp.org; **internet:** www.undp.org.

The Programme was established in 1965 by the UN General Assembly. Its central mission is to help countries to eradicate poverty and achieve a sustainable level of human development, an approach to economic growth that encompasses individual well-being and choice, equitable distribution of the benefits of development, and conservation of the environment. UNDP advocates for a more inclusive global economy. UNDP co-ordinates global and national efforts to achieve the UN Millennium Development Goals.

Organization

(October 2011)

UNDP is responsible to the UN General Assembly, to which it reports through ECOSOC.

EXECUTIVE BOARD

The Executive Board is responsible for providing intergovernmental support to, and supervision of, the activities of UNDP and the UN Population Fund (UNFPA). It comprises 36 members: eight from Africa, seven from Asia and the Pacific, four from eastern Europe, five from Latin America and the Caribbean and 12 from western Europe and other countries. Members serve a three-year term.

SECRETARIAT

Offices and divisions at the Secretariat include: an Operations Support Group; Offices of the United Nations Development Group, the Human Development Report, Development Studies, Audit and Performance Review, Evaluation, and Communications; and Bureaux for Crisis Prevention and Recovery, Resources and Strategic Partnerships, Development Policy, and Management. Five regional bureaux, all headed by an assistant administrator, cover: Africa; Asia and the Pacific; the Arab states; Latin America and the Caribbean; and Europe and the Commonwealth of Independent States. UNDP's Administrator (the third most senior UN official, after the Secretary-General and the Deputy Secretary-General) is in charge of strategic policy and overall co-ordination of UN development activities (including the chairing of the UN Development Group), while the Associate Administrator supervises the operations and management of UNDP programmes.

Administrator: HELEN CLARK (New Zealand).

Associate Administrator: REBECA GRYNSPAN (Costa Rica).

Assistant Administrator and Director, Regional Bureau for Asia and the Pacific: AJAY CHHIBBER (India).

COUNTRY OFFICES

In almost every country receiving UNDP assistance there is an office, headed by the UNDP Resident Representative, who usually also serves as the UN Resident Co-ordinator, responsible for the co-ordination of all UN technical assistance and development activities in that country, so as to ensure the most effective use of UN and international aid resources.

OFFICES OF UN RESIDENT CO-ORDINATORS IN THE FAR EAST AND AUSTRALASIA

Cambodia: 53 rue Pasteur, Boeung Keng Kang, POB 877, Phnom-Penh; tel. (23) 216167; fax (23) 216257; e-mail registry.kh@undp.org; internet www.un.org.kh/undp; Resident Co-ordinator DOUGLAS BRODERICK.

China, People's Republic: 2 Liangmahe Nan Lu, 100600 Beijing; tel. (10) 85320800; fax (10) 85320900; e-mail registry.cn@undp.org; internet www.undp.org.cn; Resident Co-ordinator RENATA LOK-DESSALLIEN.

Fiji: Level 8, Kadavu House, 414 Victoria Parade, Suva; tel. 331-2500; fax 330-1718; e-mail registry.fj@undp.org; internet www.undp.org.fj; Resident Co-ordinator KNUT OSTBY; also covers French Polynesia, Kiribati, Marshall Islands, Federated States of Micronesia, Nauru, New Caledonia, Palau, Solomon Islands, Tonga, Tuvalu, Vanuatu and Wallis and Futuna.

Indonesia: POB 2338, 14 Jalan M. H. Thamrin Kav 3, Jakarta 10250; tel. (21) 314-1308; e-mail registry.id@undp.org; internet www.undp.or.id; Resident Co-ordinator EL-MOSTAFA BENLAMLIH.

Korea, Democratic People's Republic: Resident Co-ordinator JEROME SAUVAGE (acting).

Korea, Republic: 201 Sa-ok Bldg, Hannam Tower, 730 Hannam-2 dong, Yongsan-gu, Seoul; tel. 790-9562; fax 749-1417; e-mail registry.kr@undp.org; internet www.undp.or.kr; Resident Co-ordinator (vacant).

Laos: POB 345, Lane Xang Ave, Vientiane; tel. (21) 267777; fax (21) 264939; e-mail registry.la@undp.org; internet www.undplao.org; Resident Co-ordinator MINH PHAM.

Malaysia: Wisma UN, Block C, Kompleks Pejabat Damansara, Jalan Dungun, Damansara Heights, 50490 Kuala Lumpur; tel. (3) 2095-9122; fax (3) 2095-2870; e-mail registry.my@undp.org; internet www.undp.org.my; Resident Co-ordinator KAMAL MALHOTRA; also covers Brunei and Singapore.

Mongolia: POB 49/1009, Ulan Bator; tel. (11) 327585; fax (11) 326221; e-mail registry.mn@undp.org; internet www.undp.mn; Resident Co-ordinator SEZIN SINANOGLU.

Myanmar: POB 650, No. 6 Natmauk Rd, Tamwe Township, Yangon 11211; tel. (1) 542911; fax (1) 545634; e-mail registry.mm@undp.org; internet www.mm.undp.org; Resident Co-ordinator RAMESH SHRESTHA.

Papua New Guinea: POB 1041, Port Moresby; tel. 3212877; fax 3211224; e-mail registry.pg@undp.org; internet www.undp.org.pg; Resident Co-ordinator DAVID MCLACHLAN-KARR.

Philippines: POB 7285, Domestic Airport, Post Office Locker Box, 1300 Domestic Rd, Pasay City; tel. (2) 9010100; fax (2) 9010200; e-mail registry.ph@undp.org; internet www.undp.org.ph; Resident Co-ordinator JACQUELINE BADCOCK.

Samoa: Lauofo Meti's Bldg, Four Corners, Matautu-uta, Private Mail Bag, Apia; tel. 23670; fax 23555; e-mail registry.ws@undp.org; internet www.undp.org.ws; Resident Co-ordinator NILEEMA NOBLE; also covers Cook Islands, Niue and Tokelau.

Thailand: GPO Box 618, Bangkok 10501; tel. (2) 2881234; fax (2) 2800556; e-mail registry.th@undp.org; internet www.undp.or.th; Resident Co-ordinator REBECCA HANSEN; also covers Hong Kong.

Timor-Leste: Caicoli St 14, Dili; tel. 3312481; fax 3313534; e-mail registry.tp@undp.org; internet www.tl.undp.org; Resident/Humanitarian Co-ordinator FINN RESKE-NIELSEN.

Viet Nam: 25–29 Phan Bôi Chau, Hanoi; tel. (4) 9421495; fax (4) 94233004; e-mail registry.vn.undp.org; internet www.undp.org.vn; Resident Co-ordinator EAMONN MURPHY.

Activities

UNDP describes itself as the UN's global development network, advocating for change and connecting countries to knowledge, experience and resources to help people build a better life. In 2011 UNDP was active in 166 countries. It provides advisory and support services to governments and UN teams with the aim of advancing sustainable human development and building national development capabilities. Assistance is mostly non-monetary, comprising the provision of experts' services, consultancies, equipment and training for local workers. Developing countries themselves contribute significantly to the total project costs in terms of personnel, facilities, equipment and supplies. UNDP also supports programme countries in attracting aid and utilizing it efficiently.

From the mid-1990s UNDP assumed a more active co-ordinating role within the UN system. In 1997 the UNDP Administrator was appointed to chair the UN Development Group (UNDG), which was established as part of a series of structural reform measures initiated by the UN Secretary-General, with the aim of preventing duplication and strengthening collaboration between all UN agencies, programmes and funds concerned with development. The UNDG promotes coherent policy at country level through the system of UN Resident Co-ordinators (see above), the Common Country Assessment mechanism (CCA, a process for evaluating national development needs), and the UN Development Assistance Framework (UNDAF, for planning and co-ordination development operations at country level, based on the CCA).

During the late 1990s UNDP undertook an extensive internal process of reform, which placed increased emphasis on its activities in the field and on performance and accountability. In 2001 UNDP established a series of Thematic Trust Funds to enable increased support of priority programme activities. In accordance with the more results-oriented approach developed under the reform process UNDP introduced a new Multi-Year Funding Framework (MYFF), which outlined the country-driven goals around which funding was to be mobilized, integrating programme objectives, resources, budget and outcomes. The MYFF was to provide the basis for the Administrator's Business Plans for the same duration and enables policy coherence in the implementation of programmes at country, regional and global levels. A Results-Oriented Annual Report (ROAR) was produced for the first time in 2000 from data compiled by country offices and regional programmes. New measures were introduced in 2006 to improve UNDP's management accountability, internal auditing, evaluation and procurement procedures.

In accordance with the third phase of the MYFF, covering 2008–11, UNDP adopted a Strategic Plan that focused on the following five areas: democratic governance; poverty reduction; energy and the environment; crisis prevention and recovery; and combating HIV/AIDS. Other important 'cross-cutting' themes, to be incorporated throughout the programme areas, included gender equality and the empowerment of women, information and communication technologies, and human rights. The 2008–11 Strategic Plan emphasized UNDP's 'overarching' contribution to achieving sustainable human development through capacity development strategies, to be integrated into all areas of activity. (The UNDP Capacity Development Group, established in 2002 within the Bureau for Development Policy, organizes UNDP capacity development support at local and national level.) Other objectives identified by the 2008–11 Plan included strengthening national ownership of development projects and promoting and facilitating South-South co-operation.

MILLENNIUM DEVELOPMENT GOALS

UNDP, through its leadership of the UNDG and management of the Resident Co-ordinator system, has a co-ordinating function as the focus of UN system-wide efforts to achieve the so-called Millennium Development Goals (MDGs), pledged by UN member governments attending a summit meeting of the UN General Assembly in September 2000. The objectives were to establish a defined agenda to reduce poverty and improve the quality of lives of millions of people and to serve as a framework for measuring development. There are eight MDGs, as follows, for which one or more specific targets have been identified:

i) to eradicate extreme poverty and hunger, with the aim of reducing by 50% (compared with the 1990 figure) the number of people with an income of less than US $1 a day and those suffering from hunger by 2015, and to achieve full and productive employment and decent work for all, including women and young people;

ii) to achieve universal primary education by 2015;

iii) to promote gender equality and empower women, in particular to eliminate gender disparities in primary and secondary education by 2005 and at all levels by 2015;

iv) to reduce child mortality, with a target reduction of two-thirds in the mortality rate among children under five by 2015 (compared with the 1990 level);

v) to improve maternal health, specifically to reduce by 75% the numbers of women dying in childbirth and to achieve universal access to reproductive health by 2015 (compared with the 1990 level);

vi) to combat HIV/AIDS, malaria and other diseases, with targets to have halted and begun to reverse the incidence of HIV/AIDS, malaria and other major diseases by 2015 and to achieve universal access to treatment for HIV/AIDS for all those who need it by 2010;

vii) to ensure environmental sustainability, including targets to integrate the principles of sustainable development into country policies and programmes, to reduce by 50% (compared with the 1990 level) the number of people without access to safe drinking water by 2015, and to achieve significant improvement in the lives of at least 100m. slum dwellers by 2020;

viii) to develop a global partnership for development, including an open, rule-based, non-discriminatory trading and financial system, and efforts to deal with international debt, to address the needs of least developed countries and landlocked and small island developing states, to provide access to affordable, essential drugs in developing countries, and to make available the benefits of new technologies.

UNDP plays a leading role in efforts to integrate the MDGs into all aspects of UN activities at country level and to ensure that the MDGs are incorporated into national development strategies. The Programme supports efforts by countries, as well as regions and sub-regions, to report on progress towards achievement of the goals, and on specific social, economic and environmental indicators, through the formulation of MDG reports. These form the basis of a global report, issued annually by the UN Secretary-General since mid-2002. UNDP also works to raise awareness of the MDGs and to support advocacy efforts at all levels, for example through regional publicity campaigns, target-specific publications and the Millennium Campaign to generate support for the goals in developing and developed countries. UNDP provides administrative and technical support to the Millennium Project, an independent advisory body established by the UN Secretary-General in 2002 to develop a practical action plan to achieve the MDGs. Financial support of the Project is channelled through a Millennium Trust Fund, administered by UNDP. In January 2005 the Millennium Project presented its report, based on extensive research conducted by teams of experts, which included recommendations for the international system to support country level development efforts and identified a series of 'Quick Wins' to bring conclusive benefit to millions of people in the short-term. International commitment to achieve the MDGs by 2015 was reiterated at a World Summit, convened in September 2005. In December 2006 UNDP and the Spanish Government concluded an agreement on the establishment of the MDG Achievement Fund (MDG-F), which aims to support the acceleration of progress towards the achievement of the MDGs and to enhance co-operation at country level between UN development partners. UNDP and the UN Department of Economic and Social Affairs are lead agencies in co-ordinating the work of the Millennium Development Goals Gap Task Force, which was established by the UN Secretary-General in May 2007 to track, systematically and at both international and country level, existing international commitments in the areas of official development assistance, market access, debt relief, access to essential medicines and technology. In November the UN, in partnership with two major US companies, launched an online MDG Monitor (www.mdgmonitor.org) to track progress and to support organizations working to achieve the goals.

UNDP, ESCAP and the Asian Development Bank established a regional partnership in 2001 to promote the MDGs. In June 2005 the partnership published a joint regional report on the implementation of the goals. A roadmap developed by the partnership with the aim of addressing regional challenges to the achievement of the MDGs was endorsed by regional governments in May 2007. In March of that year UNDP, ESCAP and the Asian Development Bank sponsored an East and Southeast Asia Millennium Development Goal Forum, convened in Hanoi, Viet Nam, with the aim of developing a specialized sub-regional action plan for promoting the MDGs. In September 2010 the three agencies jointly published a report entitled *Paths to 2015: MDG Priorities in Asia and the Pacific*.

DEMOCRATIC GOVERNANCE

UNDP supports national efforts to ensure efficient and accountable governance, to improve the quality of democratic processes, and to build effective relations between the state, the private sector and civil society, which are essential to achieving sustainable development. As in other practice areas, UNDP assistance includes policy advice and technical support, capacity-building of institutions and individuals, advocacy and public information and communication, the promotion and brokering of dialogue, and knowledge networking and sharing of good practices.

UNDP works to strengthen parliaments and other legislative bodies as institutions of democratic participation. It assists with constitutional reviews and reform, training of parliamentary staff, and capacity-building of political parties and civil organizations as part of this objective. UNDP undertakes missions to help prepare for and ensure the conduct of free and fair elections. It helps to build the long-term capacity of electoral institutions and practices within a country, for example by assisting with voter registration, the establishment of electoral commissions, providing observers to verify that elections are free and fair, projects to educate voters, and training journalists to provide impartial election coverage.

Within its justice sector programme UNDP undertakes a variety of projects to improve access to justice, in particular for the poor and disadvantaged, and to promote judicial independence, legal reform and understanding of the legal system. UNDP also works to promote access to information, the integration of human rights issues into activities concerned with sustainable human development, and support for the international human rights system.

Since 1997 UNDP has been mandated to assist developing countries to fight corruption and improve accountability, transparency and integrity (ATI). It has worked to establish national and international partnerships in support of its anti-corruption efforts and used its role as a broker of knowledge and experience to uphold ATI principles at all levels of public financial management and governance. UNDP publishes case studies of its anti-corruption efforts and assists governments to conduct self-assessments of their public financial management systems.

In March 2002 a UNDP Governance Centre was inaugurated in Oslo, Norway, to enhance the role of UNDP in support of democratic governance and to assist countries to implement democratic reforms in order to achieve the MDGs. In 2011 the Centre's areas of focus were: access to information and e-governance; access to justice and rule of law; anti-corruption; civic engagement; electoral systems and processes; human rights; local governance; parliamentary development; public administration; and women's empowerment. The Democratic Governance Network (DGP-Net) allows discussion and the sharing of information. In 2007 UNDP also helped to establish the iKnow Politics Network, which aims to help women become involved in politics.

In July 2008 UNDP initiated a new Multi-Donor Programme in Indonesia to support the process of preparing for a legislative election that was held in April 2009. During 2008 UNDP provided technical and policy assistance in support of the developing democratic framework in Papua New Guinea.

Within the democratic governance practice area UNDP supports more than 300 projects at international, country and city levels designed to improve conditions for the urban poor, in particular through improvement in urban governance. The Local Initiative Facility for Urban Environment (LIFE) undertakes small-scale projects in low-income communities, in collaboration with local authorities, the private sector and community-based groups, and promotes a participatory approach to local governance. UNDP also works closely with the UN Capital Development Fund to implement projects in support of decentralized governance, which it has recognized as a key element to achieving sustainable development goals.

UNDP aims to ensure that, rather than creating an ever-widening 'digital divide', ongoing rapid advancements in information and communications technology (ICT) are harnessed by poorer countries to accelerate progress in achieving sustainable human development. UNDP advises governments on ICT policy, promotes digital entrepreneurship in programme countries and works with private sector partners to provide reliable and affordable communications networks. The Bureau for Development Policy operates the Information and Communication Technologies for Development Programme, which aims to establish technology access centres in developing countries. A Sustainable Development Networking Programme focuses on expanding internet connectivity in poorer countries through building national capacities and supporting local internet sites. UNDP has used mobile internet units to train people even in isolated rural areas. In 1999 UNDP, in collaboration with an international communications company, Cisco Systems, and other partners, launched NetAid, an internet-based forum (accessible at www.netaid.org) for mobilizing and co-ordinating fundraising and other activities aimed at alleviating poverty and promoting sustainable human development in the developing world. With Cisco Systems and other partners, UNDP has worked to establish academies of information technology to support training and capacity-building in developing countries. UNDP and the World Bank jointly host the secretariat of the Digital Opportunity Task Force, a partnership between industrialized and developing countries, business and non-governmental organizations (NGOs) that was established in 2000. UNDP is a partner in the Global Digital Technology Initiative, launched in 2002 to strengthen the role of ICT in achieving the development goals of developing countries. In January 2004 UNDP and Microsoft Corporation announced an agreement to develop jointly ICT projects aimed at assisting developing countries to achieve the MDGs.

During 2011–14 UNDP was implementing several projects, jointly with FAO, in the Democratic Republic of Korea, which were aimed at improving seed production and harvests.

POVERTY REDUCTION

UNDP's activities to facilitate poverty eradication include support for capacity-building programmes and initiatives to generate sustainable livelihoods, for example by improving access to credit, land and technologies, and the promotion of strategies to improve education and health provision for the poorest elements of populations (especially women and girls). UNDP aims to help governments to reassess their development priorities and to design initiatives for sustainable human development. In 1996, following the World Summit for Social Development, which was held in Copenhagen, Denmark, in March 1995, UNDP launched the Poverty Strategies Initiative (PSI) to strengthen national capacities to assess and monitor the extent of poverty and to combat the problem. All PSI projects were to involve representatives of governments, the private sector, social organizations and research institutions in policy debate and formulation. Following the introduction, in 1999, by the World Bank and IMF of Poverty Reduction Strategy Papers (PRSPs), UNDP has helped governments to draft these documents, and, since 2001, has linked the papers to efforts to achieve and monitor progress towards the MDGs. In early 2004 UNDP inaugurated the International Poverty Centre, in Brasília, Brazil, which fosters the capacity of countries to formulate and implement poverty reduction strategies and encourages South-South co-operation in all relevant areas of research and decision-making. In particular, the Centre aims to assist countries to meet MDGs through research into and implementation of pro-poor policies that encourage social protection and human development, and through the monitoring of poverty and inequality. UNDP's Secretariat hosts the Special Unit for South-South Co-operation (SU/SSC), which was established by the United Nations General Assembly in 1978.

UNDP country offices support the formulation of national human development reports (NHDRs), which aim to facilitate activities such as policy-making, the allocation of resources, and monitoring progress towards poverty eradication and sustainable development. In addition, the preparation of Advisory Notes and Country Co-operation Frameworks by UNDP officials helps to highlight country-specific aspects of poverty eradication and national strategic priorities. In January 1998 the Executive Board adopted eight guiding principles relating to sustainable human development that were to be implemented by all country offices, in order to ensure a focus to UNDP activities. Since 1990 UNDP has published an annual *Human Development Report*, incorporating a Human Development Index, which ranks countries in terms of human development, using three key indicators: life expectancy, adult literacy and basic income required for a decent standard of living. UNDP's 2011 *Human Development Report*, to be published in November, was to focus on the need to address in tandem the urgent global challenges of achieving sustainibility and equity, and identified policies at global and national level to advance progress. In 1997 a Human Poverty Index and a Gender-related Development Index, which assesses gender equality on the basis of life expectancy, education and income, were introduced into the Report for the first time. Jointly with the International Labour Organization (ILO) UNDP operates a Programme on Employment for Poverty Reduction, which undertakes analysis and studies, and supports countries in improving their employment strategies. Microstart, a UNDP scheme to support private sector and community-based initiatives in generating employment opportunities, has been in operation since 1997.

UNDP is committed to ensuring that the process of economic and financial globalization, including national and global trade, debt and capital flow policies, incorporates human development concerns. It aimed to ensure that the Doha Development Round of World Trade Organization (WTO) negotiations should achieve an expansion of trade opportunities and economic growth to less developed countries. With the UN Conference on Trade and Development (UNCTAD), UNDP manages a Global Programme on Globalization, Liberalization and Sustainable Human Development, which aims to support greater integration of developing countries into the global economy. UNDP manages a Trust Fund for the Integrated Framework for Trade-related Technical Assistance to Least Developed Countries, which was inaugurated in 1997 by UNDP, the IMF, the International Trade Centre, UNCTAD, the World Bank and the WTO.

UNDP's Asia Pacific Trade and Investment Initiative, based in Colombo, Sri Lanka, produces technical support documents on different aspects of trade and investment to assist regional governments in forming their policies.

In 2011 UNDP issued a report on human development in Europe and the CIS entitled *Beyond Transition Towards Inclusive Societies*, providing an overview of social exclusion in the region.

In 1996 UNDP initiated a process of collaboration between city authorities world-wide to promote implementation of the commitments made at the 1995 Copenhagen summit for social development and to help to combat aspects of poverty and other urban problems, such as poor housing, transport, the management of waste disposal, water supply and sanitation. The World Alliance of Cities Against Poverty was formally launched in October 1997, in the context of the International Decade for the Eradication of Poverty. The seventh global Forum of the Alliance (convened every two years) took place in February 2010.

UNDP sponsors the International Day for the Eradication of Poverty, held annually on 17 October.

ENVIRONMENT AND ENERGY

UNDP plays a role in developing the agenda for international co-operation on environmental and energy issues, focusing on the relationship between energy policies, environmental protection, poverty and development. UNDP promotes development practices that are environmentally sustainable, for example through the formulation and implementation of Poverty Reduction Strategies and National Strategies for Sustainable Development. Together with the UN Environment Programme (UNEP) and the World Bank, UNDP is an implementing agency of the Global Environment Facility (GEF), which was established in 1991 to finance international co-operation in projects to benefit the environment.

UNDP recognizes that desertification and land degradation are major causes of rural poverty and promotes sustainable land management, drought preparedness and reform of land tenure as means of addressing the problem. It also aims to reduce poverty caused by land degradation through implementation of environmental conventions at a national and international level. In 2002 UNDP inaugurated an Integrated Drylands Development Programme which aimed to ensure that the needs of people living in arid regions are met and considered at a local and national level. The Drylands Development Centre implements the programme in 19 African, Arab and West Asian countries. UNDP is also concerned with sustainable management of forestries, fisheries and agriculture. Its Biodiversity Global Programme assists developing countries and communities to integrate issues relating to sustainable practices and biodiversity into national and global practices. Since 1992 UNDP has administered a Small Grants Programme, funded by the GEF, to support community-based initiatives concerned with biodiversity conservation, prevention of land degradation and the elimination of persistent organic pollutants. The Equator Initiative was inaugurated in 2002 as a partnership between UNDP, representatives of governments, civil society and businesses, with the aim of reducing poverty in communities along the equatorial belt by fostering local partnerships, harnessing local knowledge and promoting conservation and sustainable practices.

In 2006 UNDP inaugurated a new multi-partner initiative, Mangroves for the Future, to promote investment in coastal ecosystem conservation, in particular in those countries affected by the December 2004 tsunami, in order to support sustainable development. The project was to focus on mangrove swamps, which formerly provided a natural protection against flooding, but which have been cleared in order to provide land for rice-growing, fish-farming or shrimp-farming. In April 2008 a regional technical review forum of the initiative was convened, in Ahungalla, Sri Lanka, to assess programmes of work and national strategies.

In December 2005 UNDP (in collaboration with Fortis, a private sector provider of financial services) launched the MDG Carbon Facility, whereby developing countries that undertake projects to reduce emissions of carbon dioxide, methane and other gases responsible for global warming may sell their 'carbon credits' to finance further MDG projects. The first projects under the MDG Carbon Facility were inaugurated in February 2008, in Uzbekistan, the former Yugoslav republic of Macedonia, Yemen and Rwanda.

UNDP supports efforts to promote international co-operation in the management of chemicals. It was actively involved in the development of a Strategic Approach to International Chemicals Management which was adopted by representatives of 100 governments at an international conference convened in Dubai, UAE, in February 2006.

UNDP works to ensure the effective governance of freshwater and aquatic resources, and promotes co-operation in transboundary water management. It works closely with other agencies to promote safe sanitation, ocean and coastal management, and community water supplies. In 1996 UNDP, with the World Bank and the Swedish International Development Agency, established a Global Water Partnership to promote and implement water resources management. UNDP, with the GEF, supports an extensive range of projects which incorporate development and ecological requirements in the sustainable management of international waters. These include the Global Mercury Project, a project for improved municipal waste-water management in coastal cities of the African, Caribbean and Pacific states, a Global Ballast Water Management Programme and an International Waters Learning Exchange and Resources Network.

UNDP projects concerned with protecting international waters in Asia and the Pacific include environmental management of the seas of East Asia, Pacific Islands oceanic fisheries, the Tumen River and the Yellow Sea Large Marine Ecosystem.

CRISIS PREVENTION AND RECOVERY

UNDP is not primarily a relief organization, but collaborates with other UN agencies in countries in crisis and with special circumstances to promote relief and development efforts, in order to secure the foundations for sustainable human development and thereby increase national capabilities to prevent or mitigate future crises. In particular, UNDP is concerned to achieve reconciliation, reintegration and reconstruction in affected countries, as well as to support emergency interventions and management and delivery of programme aid. It aims to facilitate the transition from relief to longer-term recovery and rehabilitation. Special development initiatives in post-conflict countries include the demobilization of former combatants and destruction of illicit small armaments, rehabilitation of communities for the sustainable reintegration of returning populations and the restoration and strengthening of democratic institutions. UNDP is seeking to incorporate conflict prevention into its development strategies. It has established a mine action unit within its Bureau for Crisis Prevention and Recovery in order to strengthen national and local de-mining capabilities including surveying, mapping and clearance of anti-personnel landmines. It also works to increase awareness of the harm done to civilians by cluster munitions, and participated in the negotiations that culminated in May 2008 with the adoption of an international Convention on Cluster Munitions, which in February 2010 received its 30th ratification, enabling its entry into force on 1 August. UNDP also works closely with UNICEF to raise awareness and implement risk reduction education programmes, and manages global partnership projects concerned with training, legislation and the socio-economic impact of anti-personnel devices. In 2005 UNDP adopted an '8-Point Agenda' aimed at improving the security of women and girls in conflict situations and promoting their participation in post-crisis recovery processes. In late 2006 UNDP began to administer the newly established Peacebuilding Fund, the purpose of which is to strengthen essential services to maintain peace in countries that have undergone conflict. During 2008 UNDP developed a new global programme aimed at strengthening the rule of law in conflict and post-conflict countries; the programme placed particular focus on women's access to justice, institution-building and transitional justice.

In 2006 UNDP launched an Immediate Crisis Response programme (known as 'SURGE') aimed at strengthening its capacity to respond quickly and effectively in the recovery phase following a conflict or natural disaster. Under the programme Immediate Crisis Response Advisors—UNDP staff with special expertise in at least one of 12 identified areas, including early recovery, operational support and resource mobilization—are swiftly deployed, in a 'SURGETeam', to UNDP country offices dealing with crises. In 2008 Immediate Crisis Response Advisors were deployed to northern Cameroon (in February) in response to a sudden influx of Chadian refugees; to Chad (also in February) to review the destruction of the local UNDP office in a period of violent unrest; to Myanmar (May) to assess the aftermath of Cyclone Nargis; and to Haiti (September) following a series of hurricanes there. In January 2009 a SURGETeam was deployed to assess the situation in Gaza, in view of the onset in December 2008 of an intense period of conflict. Following the earthquake that devastated Haiti in January 2010 a SURGETeam, comprising four experts on operations, recovery and security, was deployed immediately to assess the operational requirements of UNDP's office there; subsequently 24 SURGE advisers developed a SURGE work plan for the country.

UNDP is the focal point within the UN system for strengthening national capacities for natural disaster reduction (prevention, preparedness and mitigation relating to natural, environmental and technological hazards). UNDP's Bureau of Crisis Prevention and Recovery, in conjunction with the Office for the Co-ordination of Humanitarian Affairs and the secretariat of the International Strategy for Disaster Reduction, oversees the system-wide Capacity for Disaster Reduction Initiative (CADRI), which was inaugurated in 2007, superseding the former United Nations Disaster Management Training Programme. In February 2004 UNDP introduced a Disaster Risk Index that enabled vulnerability and risk to be measured and compared between countries and demonstrated the correspondence between human development and death rates following natural disasters. UNDP was actively involved in preparations for the second World Conference on Disaster Reduction, which was held in Kobe, Japan, in January 2005. Following the Kobe Conference UNDP initiated a new Global Risk Identification Programme. During 2005 the Inter-Agency Standing Committee, concerned with co-ordinating the international response to humanitarian disasters, developed a concept of providing assistance through a 'cluster' approach, comprising core areas of activity (see OCHA). UNDP was designated the lead agency for the Early Recovery cluster, linking the immediate needs following a disaster with medium- and long-term recovery efforts.

In November 2005, in response to the devastating Indian Ocean tsunami of December 2004, UNDP launched a Regional Programme on Capacity-building for Sustainable Recovery and Risk Reduction. The Programme aims, in co-operation with UNDP country offices and disaster management agencies in India, Indonesia, the Maldives, Sri Lanka and Thailand, to provide technical assistance to tsunami-affected countries and to support the development of early warning systems. In March 2011, immediately following the earthquake and tsunami that devastated northeastern coastal areas of Japan at that time, some 108,000 people in coastal areas of the Albay region of the Philippines were evacuated—as a precautionary measure—under a UNDP-supported tsunami warning system in that country.

HIV/AIDS

UNDP regards the HIV/AIDS pandemic as a major challenge to development, and advocates making HIV/AIDS a focus of national planning and national poverty reduction strategies; supports decentralized action against HIV/AIDS at community level; helps to strengthen national capacities at all levels to combat the disease; and aims to link support for prevention activities, education and treatment with broader development planning and responses. UNDP places a particular focus on combating the spread of HIV/AIDS through the promotion of women's rights. UNDP is a co-sponsor, jointly with the World Health Organization (WHO) and other UN bodies, of the Joint UN Programme on HIV/AIDS (UNAIDS), which became operational on 1 January 1996. UNAIDS co-ordinates UNDP's HIV and Development Programme. UNDP works in partnership with the Global Fund to Fight HIV/AIDS, Tuberculosis and Malaria, in particular to support the local principal recipient of grant financing and to help to manage fund projects.

UNDP administers a global programme concerned with intellectual property and access to HIV/AIDS drugs, to promote wider and cheaper access to antiretroviral drugs, in accordance with the agreement on Trade-Related Aspects of Intellectual Property Rights (TRIPS), amended by the WTO in 2005 to allow countries without a pharmaceutical manufacturing capability to import generic copies of patented medicines.

UNDP's Regional HIV and Development Programme for South and North East Asia, the second phase of which was entitled REACH beyond Borders, promotes an integrated approach to containing the spread and impact of HIV/AIDS in the region. It aims to build partnerships and enhanced co-operation between governments and organizations at national and regional levels, and highlights specific issues, for example the vulnerability of mobile populations and reducing discrimination against people affected by HIV/AIDS.

Finance

UNDP and its various funds and programmes are financed by the voluntary contributions of members of the UN and the Programme's participating agencies, cost-sharing by recipient governments and third-party donors. In 2008 UNDP's gross regular (core) income was US $1,100m., and total non-core contributions amounted to $3,700m. Of total provisional programme expenditure of $4,096m. in 2008, some 34.9% was allocated to fostering democratic governance; 30.6% to achieving the MDGs and reducing human poverty; 16.0% to supporting crisis prevention and recovery; and 9.9% to managing energy and the environment for sustainable development. Some 28% of provisional total programme expenditure was allocated to Latin America and the Caribbean; 22% to Asia and the Pacific; 21% to Africa; 12% to the Arab states; and 8% to Europe and the CIS. For the period 2008–11 total voluntary contributions were projected at $20,600m., of which $5,300m. constituted regular (core) resources, $5,000m. bilateral donor contributions, $5,500m. contributions from multilateral partners, and $4,800m. cost-sharing by recipient governments.

Publications

Annual Report of the Administrator.

Choices (quarterly).

Human Development Report (annually).

Poverty Report (annually).

Results-Oriented Annual Report.

Associated Funds and Programmes

UNDP is the central funding, planning and co-ordinating body for technical co-operation within the UN system. A number of associated funds and programmes, financed separately by means of voluntary contributions, provide specific services through the UNDP network. UNDP manages a trust fund to promote economic and technical co-operation among developing countries.

GLOBAL ENVIRONMENT FACILITY (GEF)

The GEF, which is managed jointly by UNDP, the World Bank (which hosts its secretariat) and UNEP, began operations in 1991 and was restructured in 1994. Its aim is to support projects in the six thematic areas of: climate change, the conservation of biological diversity, the protection of international waters, reducing the depletion of the ozone layer in the atmosphere, arresting land degradation and addressing the issue of persistent organic pollutants. Capacity-building to allow countries to meet their obligations under international environmental agreements, and adaptation to climate change, are priority cross-cutting components of these projects. The GEF acts as the financial mechanism for the Convention on Biological Diversity and the UN Framework Convention on Climate Change. UNDP is responsible for capacity-building, targeted research, pre-investment activities and technical assistance. UNDP also administers the Small Grants Programme of the GEF, which supports community-based activities by local NGOs, and the Country Dialogue Workshop Programme, which promotes dialogue on national priorities with regard to the GEF. In October 2010 donor countries pledged US $4,350m. for the fifth periodic replenishment of GEF funds (GEF-5), covering the period 2011–14.

The GEF administers a regional project on the prevention and management of marine pollution in East Asian seas and a South Pacific Biodiversity Programme.

Chair. and CEO: MONIQUE BARBUT (France).

Executive Co-ordinator of UNDP-GEF Unit: YANNICK GLEMAREC; 304 East 45th St, 9th Floor, New York, NY 10017, USA; fax (212) 906-6998; e-mail gefinfo@undp.org; internet www.undp.org/gef/.

MDG ACHIEVEMENT FUND (MDG-F)

The Fund, established in accordance with an agreement concluded in December 2006 between UNDP and the Spanish Government, and with funding from the Spanish Government of nearly €528m. to cover the period 2007–10, aims to support the acceleration of progress towards the achievement of the MDGs and to advance country-level co-operation between UN development partners. The Fund operates through the UN development system and focuses mainly on financing collaborative UN activities addressing multi-dimensional development challenges. By 2011 some 128 programmes were under way in 49 countries, in the thematic areas of children and nutrition; climate change; conflict prevention; culture and development; economic governance; gender equality and women's empowerment; and youth employment.

Director of MDG-F Secretariat: SOPHIE DE CAEN (Canada); MDG-F Secretariat, c/o UNDP, One United Nations Plaza, New York, NY 10017, USA; tel. (212) 906-6180; fax (212) 906-5364; e-mail pb.mdgf.secretariat@undp.org; internet www.mdgfund.org.

MONTREAL PROTOCOL

Through its Montreal Protocol/Chemicals Unit UNDP collaborates with public and private partners in developing countries to assist them in eliminating the use of ozone-depleting substances (ODS), in accordance with the Montreal Protocol to the Vienna Convention for the Protection of the Ozone Layer, through the design, monitoring and evaluation of ODS phase-out projects and programmes. In particular, UNDP provides technical assistance and training, national capacity-building and demonstration projects and technology transfer investment projects.

SPECIAL UNIT FOR SOUTH-SOUTH CO-OPERATION (SU/SSC)

The SU/SSC, established in 1978 by the UN General Assembly and hosted by UNDP, aims to co-ordinate and support South-South co-operation in the political, economic, social, environmental and technical areas, and to support 'triangular' collaboration on a UN system-wide and global basis. The Special Unit organizes the annual UN Day for South-South Co-operation (December 19), and manages the UN Trust Fund for South-South Co-operation (UNFSC) and the Perez-Guerrero Trust Fund for Economic and Technical Co-operation among Developing Countries (PGTF), as well as undertaking programmes financed by UNDP.

Director: YIPING ZHOU (People's Republic of China); 304 East 45th St, 12th Floor, New York, NY 11017, USA; tel. (212) 906-6944; fax (212) 906-6352; e-mail ssc.info@undp.org; internet ssc.undp.org.

UNDP DRYLANDS DEVELOPMENT CENTRE (DDC)

The Centre, based in Nairobi, Kenya, was established in February 2002, superseding the former UN Office to Combat Desertification and Drought (UNSO). (UNSO had been established following the conclusion, in October 1994, of the UN Convention to Combat Desertification in Those Countries Experiencing Serious Drought and/or Desertification, Particularly in Africa; in turn, UNSO had replaced the former UN Sudano-Sahelian Office.) The DDC was to focus on the following areas: ensuring that national development planning takes account of the needs of dryland communities, particularly in poverty reduction strategies; helping countries to cope with the effects of climate variability, especially drought, and to prepare for future climate change; and addressing local issues affecting the utilization of resources.

Officer-in-Charge: ELIE KODSIE; UN Gigiri Compound, United Nations Ave, POB 30552, 00100 Nairobi, Kenya; tel. (20) 7624640; fax (20) 7624648; e-mail ddc@undp.org; internet www.undp.org/drylands.

UNDP-UNEP POVERTY-ENVIRONMENT INITIATIVE (UNPEI)

UNPEI, inaugurated in February 2007, supports countries in developing their capacity to launch and maintain programmes that mainstream poverty-environment linkages into national development planning processes, such as MDG achievement strategies and PRSPs. In May 2007 UNDP and UNEP launched the Poverty-Environment Facility (UNPEF) to co-ordinate, and raise funds in support of, UNPEI.

Officer-in-Charge: DAVID SMITH; UN Gigiri Compound, United Nations Avenue, POB 30552, 00100, Nairobi, Kenya; e-mail facility.unpei@unpei.org; internet www.unpei.org.

UNITED NATIONS CAPITAL DEVELOPMENT FUND (UNCDF)

The Fund was established in 1966 and became fully operational in 1974. It invests in poor communities in least developed countries (LDCs) through local governance projects and microfinance operations, with the aim of increasing such communities' access to essential local infrastructure and services and thereby improving their productive capacities and self-reliance. UNCDF encourages participation by local people and local governments in the planning, implementation and monitoring of projects. The Fund aims to promote the interests of women in community projects and to enhance their earning capacities. A Special Unit for Microfinance (SUM), established in 1997 as a joint UNDP/UNCDF operation, was fully integrated into UNCDF in 1999. UNCDF/SUM helps to develop financial services for poor communities and supports UNDP's MicroStart initiative. UNCDF hosts the UN high-level Advisors Group on Inclusive Financial Sectors, established in respect of recommendations made during the 2005 International Year of Microcredit. In November 2008 UNCDF launched MicroLead, a US $26m. fund that was to provide loans to leading microfinance institutions and other financial service providers (MFIs/FSPs) in developing countries; MicroLead was also to focus on the provision of early support to countries in post-conflict situations. In 2010 UNCDF had a programme portfolio with a value of around $200m., in support of initiatives ongoing in 38 LDCs.

Executive Secretary: DAVID MORRISON (Canada); Two United Nations Plaza, 26th Floor, New York, NY 10017, USA; fax (212) 906-6479; e-mail info@uncdf.org; internet www.uncdf.org.

UNITED NATIONS VOLUNTEERS (UNV)

The United Nations Volunteers is an important source of middle-level skills for the UN development system supplied at modest cost, particularly in the least developed countries (LDCs). Volunteers expand the scope of UNDP project activities by supplementing the work of international and host-country experts and by extending the influence of projects to local community levels. UNV also supports technical co-operation within and among the developing countries by encouraging volunteers from the countries themselves and by forming regional exchange teams comprising such volunteers. UNV is involved in areas such as peace-building, elections, human rights, humanitarian relief and community-based environmental programmes, in addition to development activities.

The UN International Short-term Advisory Resources (UNISTAR) Programme, which is the private sector development arm of UNV, has increasingly focused its attention on countries in the process of economic transition. Since 1994 UNV has administered UNDP's Transfer of Knowledge Through Expatriate Nationals (TOKTEN) programme, which was initiated in 1977 to enable specialists and professionals from developing countries to contribute to development efforts in their countries of origin through short-term technical assignments. In March 2000 UNV established an Online Volunteering Service to connect development organizations and volunteers using the internet; in 2010,127 online volunteers made their skills available through the Online Volunteering Service.

During 2010 some 7,765 national and international UNVs were deployed in 132 countries, on 7,960 assignments; some 1,147 UNV assignments were undertaken in Asia and the Pacific in that year.

Executive Co-ordinator: FLAVIA PANSIERI (Italy); POB 260111, 53153 Bonn, Germany; tel. (228) 8152000; fax (228) 8152001; e-mail information@unvolunteers.org; internet www.unv.org.

United Nations Environment Programme—UNEP

Address: POB 30552, Nairobi 00100, Kenya.

Telephone: (20) 621234; **fax:** (20) 623927; **e-mail:** unepinfo@unep.org; **internet:** www.unep.org.

The United Nations Environment Programme was established in 1972 by the UN General Assembly, following recommendations of the 1972 UN Conference on the Human Environment, in Stockholm, Sweden, to encourage international co-operation in matters relating to the human environment.

Organization

(October 2011)

GOVERNING COUNCIL

The main functions of the Governing Council (which meets every two years in ordinary sessions, with special sessions taking place in the alternate years) are to promote international co-operation in the field of the environment and to provide general policy guidance for the direction and co-ordination of environmental programmes within the UN system. It comprises representatives of 58 states, elected by the UN General Assembly, for four-year terms, on a regional basis. The Global Ministerial Environment Forum (first convened in 2000) meets annually as part of the Governing Council's regular and special sessions. The Governing Council is assisted in its work by a Committee of Permanent Representatives.

SECRETARIAT

Offices and divisions at UNEP headquarters include the Offices of the Executive Director and Deputy Executive Director; the Secretariat for Governing Bodies; Offices for Evaluation and Oversight, Programme Co-ordination and Management, and Resource Mobilization; and divisions of communications and public information, early warning and assessment, environmental policy implementation, technology, industry and economics, regional co-operation and representation, environmental law and conventions, and Global Environment Facility co-ordination.

F**Executive Director:** ACHIM STEINER (Germany).

Deputy Executive Director: AMINA MOHAMED (Kenya).

REGIONAL OFFICES

UNEP maintains six regional offices. These work to initiate and promote UNEP objectives and to ensure that all programme formulation and delivery meets the specific needs of countries and regions. They also provide a focal point for building national, sub-regional and regional partnership and enhancing local participation in UNEP initiatives. A co-ordination office has been established at headquarters to promote regional policy integration, to co-ordinate programme planning, and to provide necessary services to the regional offices.

Asia and the Pacific: United Nations Bldg, 2nd Floor, Rajadamnern Nok Ave, Bangkok 10200, Thailand; tel. (2) 288-1870; fax (2) 280-3829; e-mail uneproap@un.org; internet www.unep.org/roap.

UNEP Beijing Office: 2 Liangmahe Nalu, Beijing 100600, People's Republic of China; tel. (10) 8532-0921 (ext. 219); fax (10) 6532-2567; e-mail unep@public.un.org.cn.

OTHER OFFICES

Convention on International Trade in Endangered Species of Wild Fauna and Flora (CITES): 15 chemin des Anémones, 1219 Châtelaine, Geneva, Switzerland; tel. 229178139; fax 227973417; e-mail info@cites.org; internet www.cites.org; Sec.-Gen. JOHN SCANLON (Australia).

Global Programme of Action for the Protection of the Marine Environment from Land-based Activities: GPA Co-ordination Unit, UNEP, POB 30552, 00100 Nairobi, Kenya; tel. (20) 7621206; fax (20) 7624249; internet www.gpa.unep.org.

Regional Co-ordinating Unit for East Asian Seas: UN Bldg, 2nd Floor, Rajadamnern Nok Ave, Bangkok 10200, Thailand; tel. (2) 288-1860; fax (2) 281-2428; e-mail kleesuwan.unescap@un.org; internet www.cobsea.org; Co-ordinator Dr ELLIK ADLER.

Secretariat of the Basel Convention: CP 356, 13–15 chemin des Anémones, 1219 Châtelaine, Geneva, Switzerland; tel. 229178218; fax 227973454; e-mail sbc@unep.ch; internet www.basel.int; Exec. Sec. KATHERINA KUMMER PEIRY.

Secretariat of the Multilateral Fund for the Implementation of the Montreal Protocol: 1800 McGill College Ave, 27th Floor, Montréal, QC, Canada H3A 3J6; tel. (514) 282-1122; fax (514) 282-0068; e-mail secretariat@unmfs.org; internet www.multilateralfund.org; Chief Officer MARIA NOLAN.

UNEP/CMS (Convention on the Conservation of Migratory Species of Wild Animals) Secretariat: Hermann-Ehlers-Str. 10, 53113 Bonn, Germany; tel. (228) 8152402; fax (228) 8152449; e-mail secretariat@cms.int; internet www.cms.int; Exec. Sec. ELIZABETH MARUMA MREMA.

UNEP Chemicals: International Environment House, 11–13 chemin des Anémones, 1219 Châtelaine, Geneva, Switzerland; tel. 229178192; fax 227973460; e-mail chemicals@unep.ch; internet www.chem.unep.ch; Head TIM KASTEN.

UNEP Division of Technology, Industry and Economics: 15 rue de Milan, 75441 Paris, Cedex 09, France; tel. 1-44-37-14-50; fax 1-44-37-14-74; e-mail unep.tie@unep.fr; internet www.unep.fr; Dir SILVIE LEMMET (France).

UNEP International Environmental Technology Centre (IETC): 2–110 Ryokuchi koen, Tsurumi-ku, Osaka 538-0036, Japan; tel. (6) 6915-4581; fax (6) 6915-0304; e-mail ietc@unep.or.jp; internet www.unep.or.jp; Dir PER BAKKEN.

UNEP Ozone Secretariat: POB 30552, Nairobi, Kenya; tel. (20) 762-3851; fax (20) 762-4691; e-mail ozoneinfo@unep.org; internet ozone.unep.org; Exec. Sec. MARCO GONZÁLEZ (Costa Rica).

UNEP-SCBD (Convention on Biological Diversity—Secretariat): 413 St Jacques St, Suite 800, Montréal, QC, Canada H2Y 1N9; tel. (514) 288-2220; fax (514) 288-6588; e-mail secretariat@cbd.int; internet www.cbd.int; Exec. Sec. AHMED DJOGHLAF (Algeria).

UNEP Secretariat for the UN Scientific Committee on the Effects of Atomic Radiation: Vienna International Centre, Wagramerstrasse 5, POB 500, 1400 Vienna, Austria; tel. (1) 26060-4330; fax (1) 26060-5902; e-mail malcolm.crick@unscear.org; internet www.unscear.org; Sec. Dr MALCOLM CRICK.

Activities

UNEP represents a voice for the environment within the UN system. It is an advocate, educator, catalyst and facilitator, promoting the wise use of the planet's natural assets for sustainable development. It aims to maintain a constant watch on the changing state of the environment; to analyse the trends; to assess the problems using a wide range of data and techniques; and to undertake or support projects leading to environmentally sound development. It plays a catalytic and co-ordinating role within and beyond the UN system. Many UNEP projects are implemented in co-operation with other UN agencies, particularly UNDP, the World Bank group, FAO, UNESCO and WHO. About 45 intergovernmental organizations outside the UN system and 60 international non-governmental organizations (NGOs) have official observer status on UNEP's Governing Council, and, through the Environment Liaison Centre in Nairobi, UNEP is linked to more than 6,000 non-governmental bodies concerned with the environment. UNEP also sponsors international conferences, programmes, plans and agreements regarding all aspects of the environment.

In February 1997 the Governing Council, at its 19th session, adopted a ministerial declaration (the Nairobi Declaration) on UNEP's future role and mandate, which recognized the organization as the principal UN body working in the field of the environment and as the leading global environmental authority, setting and overseeing the international environmental agenda. In June a special session of the UN General Assembly, referred to as 'Rio + 5', was convened to review the state of the environment and progress achieved in implementing the objectives of the UN Conference on Environment and Development (UNCED—known as the Earth Summit), that had been held in Rio de Janeiro, Brazil, in June 1992. UNCED had adopted Agenda 21 (a programme of activities to promote sustainable development in the 21st century) and the 'Rio + 5' meeting adopted a Programme for Further Implementation of Agenda 21 in order to intensify efforts in areas such as energy, freshwater resources and technology transfer. The meeting confirmed UNEP's essential role in advancing the Programme and as a global authority promoting a coherent legal and political approach to the environmental challenges of sustainable development. An extensive process of restructuring and realignment of functions was subsequently initiated by UNEP, and a new organizational structure reflecting the decisions of the Nairobi Declaration was implemented during 1999. UNEP played a leading role in preparing for the World Summit on Sustainable Development (WSSD), held in August–September 2002 in Johannesburg, South Africa, to assess strategies for strengthening the implementation of Agenda 21. Governments participating in the conference adopted the Johannesburg Declaration and WSSD Plan of Implementation, in which they strongly reaffirmed commitment to the principles underlying Agenda 21 and also pledged support to all internationally agreed development goals, including the UN Millennium Development Goals adopted by governments attending a summit meeting of the UN General Assembly in September 2000. Participating governments made concrete commitments to attaining several specific objectives in the areas of water, energy, health, agriculture and fisheries, and biodiversity. These included a reduction by one-half in the proportion of people world-wide lacking access to clean water or good sanitation by 2015, the restocking of depleted fisheries by 2015, a reduction in the ongoing loss in biodiversity by 2010, and the production and utilization of chemicals without causing harm to human beings and the environment by 2020. Participants determined to increase usage of renewable energy sources and to develop integrated water resources management and water efficiency plans. A large number of partnerships between governments, private sector interests and civil society groups were announced at the conference. The UN Conference on Sustainable Development (UNCSD) (also known as Earth Summit 2012 and as 'Rio + 20') was scheduled to be convened in May 2012, once again in Rio de Janeiro.

In May 2000 UNEP's first annual Global Ministerial Environment Forum (GMEF), was held in Malmö, Sweden, attended by environment ministers and other government delegates from more than 130 countries. Participants reviewed policy issues in the field of the environment and addressed issues such as the impact on the environment of population growth, the depletion of earth's natural resources, climate change and the need for fresh water supplies. The Forum issued the Malmö Declaration, which identified the effective implementation of international agreements on environmental matters at national level as the most pressing challenge for policy-makers. The Declaration emphasized the importance of mobilizing domestic and international resources and urged increased co-operation from civil society and the private sector in achieving sustainable development. The GMEF was subsequently convened annually.

EARLY WARNING AND ASSESSMENT

The Nairobi Declaration resolved that the strengthening of UNEP's information, monitoring and assessment capabilities was a crucial element of the organization's restructuring, in order to help establish priorities for international, national and regional action, and to ensure the efficient and accurate dissemination of information on emerging environmental trends and emergencies.

UNEP's Division of Early Warning and Assessment analyses the world environment, provides early warning information and assesses global and regional trends. It provides governments with data and helps them to use environmental information for decision-making and planning.

UNEP's Global Environment Outlook (GEO) process of environmental analysis and assessment, launched in 1995, is supported by an extensive network of collaborating centres. The fourth 'umbrella' report on the GEO process (*GEO-4*) was issued in October 2007, identifying climate change, land degradation and loss of biodiversity as the world's greatest environmental challenges. *GEO-5* was to be available online from May 2012. In recent years regional and national GEO reports have been issued focusing on Africa, the Andean region, the Atlantic and Indian oceans, Brazil, the Caucasus, Latin America and the Caribbean, North America, and the Pacific; and the following thematic GEO reports have been produced: *The Global Deserts Outlook* (2006) and *The Global Outlook for Ice and*

Snow (2007). Various GEO technical reports have also been published.

In 1998 UNEP and the World Meteorological Organization (WMO) established the Intergovernmental Panel on Climate Change (IPCC, see below), as an objective source of scientific information about the warming of the earth's atmosphere. UNEP's Global International Waters Assessment (GIWA) considers all aspects of the world's water-related issues, in particular problems of shared transboundary waters, and of future sustainable management of water resources. UNEP is also a sponsoring agency of the Joint Group of Experts on the Scientific Aspects of Marine Environmental Pollution and contributes to the preparation of reports on the state of the marine environment and on the impact of land-based activities on that environment. In November 1995 UNEP published a Global Biodiversity Assessment, which was the first comprehensive study of biological resources throughout the world. The UNEP-World Conservation Monitoring Centre (UNEP-WCMC), established in June 2000 in Cambridge, United Kingdom, manages and interprets data concerning biodiversity and ecosystems, and makes the results available to governments and businesses. In October 2008 UNEP-WCMC, in partnership with the IUCN, launched a new online database of the world's national parks and protected areas; detailed images of more than 100,000 sites could be viewed on the site. In 2007 the Centre undertook the 2010 Biodiversity Indicators Programme, with the aim of supporting decision-making by governments so as to reduce the threat of extinction facing vulnerable species. UNEP is a partner in the International Coral Reef Action Network—ICRAN, which was established in 2000 to monitor, manage and protect coral reefs world-wide. In June 2001 UNEP launched the Millennium Ecosystem Assessment, which was completed in March 2005. Other major assessments undertaken include the International Assessment of Agricultural Science and Technology for Development; the Solar and Wind Energy Resource Assessment; the Regionally Based Assessment of Persistent Toxic Substances; the Land Degradation Assessment in Drylands; and the Global Methodology for Mapping Human Impacts on the Biosphere (GLOBIO) project.

In June 2010 delegates from 85 countries, meeting in Busan, Republic of Korea, at the third conference addressing the creation of a new Intergovernmental Science-Policy Platform on Biodiversity and Ecosystem Services (IPBES), adopted the Busan Outcome Document finalizing details of the establishment of the IPBES. The Platform, inaugurated in December 2010, following approval of the Outcome Document by the UN General Assembly, was to undertake, periodically, assessments, based on current scientific literature, of biodiversity and ecosystem outputs beneficial to humans, including timber, fresh water, fish and climatic stability. The first plenary session of IPBES was convened in October 2011.

UNEP's environmental information network includes the UNEP-INFOTERRA programme, which facilitates the exchange of environmental information through an extensive network of national 'focal points' (national environmental information centres, usually located in the relevant government ministry or agency). By October 2011 177 countries were participating in the network, whereby UNEP promotes public access to environmental information, as well as participation in environmental concerns. UNEP's information, monitoring and assessment structures also serve to enhance early-warning capabilities and to provide accurate information during an environmental emergency.

In September 2008 the UN Reduced Emissions from Deforestation and Forest Degradation (UN-REDD) Programme, a collaboration between UNEP, UNDP and FAO, was launched. Through a trust fund, established in July 2008, UN-REDD aimed to enable donors to pool resources to promote a transformation of forest resource use patterns. In August 2011 UN-REDD endorsed a Global Programme Framework covering 2011–15.

ENVIRONMENTAL LAW AND CONVENTIONS

UNEP promotes international environmental legislation and the development of policy tools and guidelines in order to achieve the sustainable management of the world environment. It helps governments to implement multilateral environmental agreements, and to report on their results. At a national level it assists governments to develop and implement appropriate environmental instruments and aims to co-ordinate policy initiatives. Training in various aspects of environmental law and its applications is provided. The eighth Global Training Programme on Environmental Law and Policy was conducted by UNEP in November 2007, with participants from 62 countries; regional training programmes are also offered. UNEP supports the development of new legal, economic and other policy instruments to improve the effectiveness of existing environmental agreements. It updates a register of international environmental treaties, and publishes handbooks on negotiating and enforcing environmental law. It acts as the secretariat for a number of regional and global environmental conventions (see list above).

UNEP worked in collaboration with WMO to formulate the 1992 UN Framework Convention on Climate Change (UNFCCC), with the aim of reducing the emission of gases that have a warming effect on the atmosphere (known as greenhouse gases). (See Secretariat of the UN Framework Convention on Climate Change, below.)

In late June 2009 the first meeting was convened, in Belgrade, Serbia, of a new Consultative Group of Ministers and High-level Representatives on International Environment Governance; the meeting reviewed UNEP's role and stressed the linkages between sustainable environmental policies and development. From end-June–early July five successive UNEP Executive Directors and other prominent environmentalists met, in Glion, Switzerland, to discuss means of bringing about change in the functioning of the world economy to prioritize a sustainable approach to using and preserving the environment for the benefit of long-term human welfare.

UNEP was instrumental in the drafting of a Convention on Biological Diversity (CBD) to preserve the immense variety of plant and animal species, in particular those threatened with extinction. The Convention entered into force at the end of 1993; by October 2011 192 states and the European Union (EU) were parties to the CBD. The CBD's Cartagena Protocol on Biosafety (so called as it had been addressed at an extraordinary session of parties to the CBD convened in Cartagena, Colombia, in February 1999) was adopted at a meeting of parties to the CBD in January 2000, and entered into force in September 2003; by October 2011 the Protocol had been ratified by 160 states parties and the EU. The Protocol regulates the transboundary movement and use of living modified organisms resulting from biotechnology, in order to reduce any potential adverse effects on biodiversity and human health. It establishes an Advanced Informed Agreement procedure to govern the import of such organisms. In January 2002 UNEP launched a major project aimed at supporting developing countries with assessing the potential health and environmental risks and benefits of genetically modified (GM) crops, in preparation for the Protocol's entry into force. In February the parties to the CBD and other partners convened a conference on ways in which the traditional knowledge and practices of local communities could be preserved and used to conserve highly threatened species and ecosystems. The sixth conference of parties to the CBD, held in April 2002, adopted detailed voluntary guidelines concerning access to genetic resources and sharing the benefits attained from such resources with the countries and local communities where they originate; a global work programme on forests; and a set of guiding principles for combating alien invasive species. In October 2010 the 10th conference of the parties to the CBD, meeting in Nagoya, Japan, approved the Nagoya-Kuala Lumpur Supplementary Protocol to the CBD, with a view to establishing an international regime on access and benefit sharing (ABS) of genetic resources, alongside a strategic 10-year plan with targets and timetables to combat loss of the planet's nature-based resources. The Supplementary Protocol was opened for signature in March 2011. The UN Decade on Biodiversity was being celebrated during 2011–20. UNEP supports co-operation for biodiversity assessment and management in selected developing regions and for the development of strategies for the conservation and sustainable exploitation of individual threatened species (e.g. the Global Tiger Action Plan). It also provides assistance for the preparation of individual country studies and strategies to strengthen national biodiversity management and research. UNEP administers the Convention on International Trade in Endangered Species of Wild Flora and Fauna (CITES), which entered into force in 1975 and comprised 175 states parties at October 2011. CITES has special programmes on the protection of elephants, falcons, great apes, hawksbill turtles, sturgeons, tropical timber (jointly with the International Tropical Timber Organization), and bigleaf mahogany. Meeting in St Petersburg, Russia, in November 2010, at the International Tiger Forum, the heads of UNODC, the Convention on International Trade in Endangered Species of Wild Fauna and Flora (CITES), the World Customs Organization, INTERPOL and the World Bank jointly approved the establishment of a new International Consortium on Combating Wildlife Crime (ICCWC), with the aim of combating the poaching of wild animals and illegal trade in wild animals and wild animal products.

In December 1996 the Lusaka Agreement on Co-operative Enforcement Operations Directed at Illegal Trade in Wild Flora and Fauna entered into force, having been concluded under UNEP auspices in order to strengthen the implementation of the CBD and CITES in Eastern and Central Africa. UNEP and UNESCO jointly co-sponsor the Great Apes Survival Project (GRASP), which was launched in May 2001. GRASP supports, in 23 'great ape range states' (of which 21 are in Africa and two—Indonesia and Malaysia—in South-East Asia), the conservation of gorillas, chimpanzees, orang-utans and bonobos. GRASP's first intergovernmental meeting, held in Kinshasa, Democratic Republic of the Congo in September 2005, was attended by representatives of governments of great ape habitat states, donor and other interested states, international organizations, NGOs, and private-sector and academic interests. The meeting adopted a Global Strategy for the Survival of Great Apes, and the Kinshasa Declaration pledging commitment and action towards achieving this goal. GRASP, CITES and the World

Association of Zoos and Aquariums jointly declared 2009 the Year of the Gorilla. In June 2009 160 government representatives participating in a conference to mark the Year of the Gorilla, convened in Frankfurt, Germany, issued the Frankfurt Declaration to Call for Better Protection of Gorillas.

A CITES Tiger Enforcement Task Force met for the first time in New Delhi, India, in April 2001; all trade in tigers and tiger parts is prohibited under CITES.

The Convention on the Conservation of Migratory Species of Wild Animals (CMS, also referred to as the Bonn Convention), concluded under UNEP auspices in 1979, aims to conserve migratory avian, marine and terrestrial species throughout the range of their migration. The secretariat of the CMS is hosted by UNEP. At October 2011 there were 116 states parties to the Convention. A number of agreements and memoranda of understanding (MOU) concerning conservation have been concluded under the CMS. An Agreement on the Conservation of Albatrosses and Petrels (ACAP) was concluded, under CMS auspices, in 2001 and entered into force in 2004. It is envisaged that the scope of ACAP, currently covering only the Southern Hemisphere, will be extended to include species from the Northern Hemisphere. MOU cover, *inter alia*: the Marine Turtles and their Habitats of the Indian Ocean and South-East Asia, Cetaceans and their Habitats of the Pacific Island Region, and Dugongs and their Habitats.

In October 1994 87 countries, meeting under UN auspices, signed a Convention to Combat Desertification (see UNDP Drylands Development Centre), which aimed to provide a legal framework to counter the degradation of arid regions. An estimated 75% of all drylands have suffered some land degradation, affecting approximately 1,000m. people in 110 countries. UNEP continues to support the implementation of the Convention, as part of its efforts to protect land resources. UNEP also aims to improve the assessment of dryland degradation and desertification in co-operation with governments and other international bodies, as well as identifying the causes of degradation and measures to overcome these.

UNEP is the principal UN agency for promoting environmentally sustainable water management. It regards the unsustainable use of water as one of the most urgent environmental issues, and estimates that two-thirds of the world's population will suffer chronic water shortages by 2025, owing to rising demand for drinking water as a result of growing populations, decreasing quality of water because of pollution, and increasing requirements of industries and agriculture. In 2000 UNEP adopted a new water policy and strategy, comprising assessment, management and co-ordination components. The Global International Waters Assessment (see above) is the primary framework for the assessment component. The management component includes the Global Programme of Action (GPA) for the Protection of the Marine Environment from Land-based Activities (adopted in November 1995), which focuses on the effects of pollution on freshwater resources, marine biodiversity and the coastal ecosystems of small island developing states. UNEP promotes international co-operation in the management of river basins and coastal areas and for the development of tools and guidelines to achieve the sustainable management of freshwater and coastal resources. In 2007 UNEP initiated a South-South Co-operation programme on technology and capacity-building for the management of water resources. UNEP provides scientific, technical and administrative support to facilitate the implementation and co-ordination of 14 regional seas conventions and 13 regional plans of action. UNEP's Regional Seas Programme aims to protect marine and coastal ecosystems, particularly by helping governments to put relevant legislation into practice.

UNEP administers the Basel Convention on the Control of Transboundary Movements of Hazardous Wastes and their Disposal, which entered into force in 1992 with the aim of preventing the uncontrolled movement and disposal of toxic and other hazardous wastes, particularly the illegal dumping of waste in developing countries by companies from industrialized countries. At October 2011 175 countries and the EU were parties to the Convention.

In 1996 UNEP, in collaboration with FAO, began to work towards promoting and formulating a legally binding international convention on prior informed consent (PIC) for hazardous chemicals and pesticides in international trade, extending a voluntary PIC procedure of information exchange undertaken by more than 100 governments since 1991. The Convention was adopted at a conference held in Rotterdam, Netherlands, in September 1998, and entered into force in February 2004. It aims to reduce risks to human health and the environment by restricting the production, export and use of hazardous substances and enhancing information exchange procedures. UNEP played a leading role in formulating a multilateral agreement to reduce and ultimately eliminate the manufacture and use of Persistent Organic Pollutants (POPs), which are considered to be a major global environmental hazard. The Stockholm Convention on POPs, targeting 12 particularly hazardous pollutants, was adopted by 127 countries in May 2001 and entered into force in May 2004. In May 2009 the fourth conference of parties to the Stockholm Convention agreed on a list of nine further POPs; these were incorporated into the Convention in an amendment that entered into force in August 2010.

In February 2009 140 governments agreed, under the auspices of UNEP, to launch negotiations on the development of an international treaty to combat toxic mercury emissions world-wide. The first session of the intergovernmental negotiating committee on preparing the proposed treaty was convened in June 2010, in Stockholm, Sweden. The second session was held January 2011, in Chiba, Japan, and a third was to take place in late October 2011. Pending the adoption of the planned treaty (envisaged for 2013) it was agreed that a voluntary Global Mercury Partnership would address mercury pollution.

UNEP was the principal agency in formulating the 1987 Montreal Protocol to the Vienna Convention for the Protection of the Ozone Layer (1985), which provided for a 50% reduction in the production of chlorofluorocarbons (CFCs) by 2000. An amendment to the Protocol was adopted in 1990, which required complete cessation of the production of CFCs by 2000 in industrialized countries and by 2010 in developing countries. The Copenhagen Amendment, adopted in 1992, stipulated the phasing out of production of hydrochlorofluorocarbons (HCFCs) by 2030 in developed countries and by 2040 in developing nations. Subsequent amendments aimed to introduce a licensing system for all controlled substances, and imposed stricter controls on the import and export of HCFCs, and on the production and consumption of bromochloromethane (Halon-1011, an industrial solvent and fire extinguisher). In September 2007 the states parties to the Vienna Convention agreed to advance the deadline for the elimination of HCFCs: production and consumption were to be frozen by 2013, and were to be phased out in developed countries by 2020 and in developing countries by 2030. A Multilateral Fund for the Implementation of the Montreal Protocol was established in June 1990 to promote the use of suitable technologies and the transfer of technologies to developing countries. UNEP, UNDP, the World Bank and UNIDO are the sponsors of the Fund, which by 2011 had approved financing for more than 6,700 projects and activities in 145 developing countries at a cost of more than US $2,600m. The Fund's total budget for 2009–11 was $490m. In September 2009, following ratification by Timor-Leste, the Montreal Protocol, with 196 states parties, became the first agreement on the global environment to attain universal ratification.

GLOBAL ENVIRONMENT FACILITY

UNEP, together with UNDP and the World Bank, is an implementing agency of the Global Environment Facility (GEF), established in 1991 to help developing countries, and those undergoing economic transition, to meet the costs of projects that benefit the environment in six specific areas: biological diversity, climate change, international waters, depletion of the ozone layer, land degradation and persistent organic pollutants. Important cross-cutting components of these projects include capacity-building to allow countries to meet their obligations under international environmental agreements (described above), and adaptation to climate change. During 1991–2011 some 522 projects were approved by the GEF to be implemented by UNEP, with a total value amounting to US $1,646m. UNEP services the Scientific and Technical Advisory Panel, which provides expert advice on GEF programmes and operational strategies.

TECHNOLOGY, INDUSTRY AND ECONOMICS

UNEP's Division of Technology, Industry and Economics encourages governments and the private sector to develop and adopt policies and practices that are cleaner and safer, make efficient use of natural resources, incorporate environmental costs, ensure the environmentally sound management of chemicals, and reduce pollution and risks to human health and the environment. In collaboration with other organizations UNEP works to formulate international guidelines and agreements to address these issues. UNEP also promotes the transfer of appropriate technologies and organizes conferences and training workshops to provide sustainable production practices. Relevant information is disseminated through the International Cleaner Production Information Clearing House. By October 2011 UNEP, together with UNIDO, had established 47 National Cleaner Production Centres in developing and transition countries to promote a preventive approach to industrial pollution control. In October 1998 UNEP adopted an International Declaration on Cleaner Production, with a commitment to implement cleaner and more sustainable production methods and to monitor results. In 1997 UNEP and the Coalition for Environmentally Responsible Economies initiated the Global Reporting Initiative, which, with participation by corporations, business associations and other organizations, develops guidelines for voluntary reporting by companies on their economic, environmental and social performance. In April 2002 UNEP launched the 'Life Cycle Initiative', which evaluates the impact of products over their entire life cycle (from manufacture to disposal) and aims to assist governments, businesses and other consumers with adopting environmentally sound policies and practice, in view of the upward trend in global consumption patterns. UNEP Finance Initiatives (FI) is a programme encouraging banks, insurance companies and other financial institutions to invest in an environmentally responsible way: an annual FI Global Roundtable meeting is held, together with regional meetings. In April 2007 UNEP hosted the first annual Business for Environment (B4E) meeting, on corporate environmental responsibility, in Singapore; the 2012 meeting was to be held in April, in Berlin, Germany. During 2007 UNEP's Programme on Sustainable Consumption and Production established an International Panel for Sustainable Resource Management (comprising experts whose initial subjects of study were to be the environmental risks of biofuels and of metal recycling), and initiated forums for businesses and NGOs in this field.

In October 2008, in response to the global economic, fuel and food crises that escalated during that year, UNEP launched the *Green Economy Initiative (GEI)*, also known as the 'Global Green New Deal', which aimed to mobilize and refocus the global economy towards investments in clean technologies and the natural infrastructure (for example the infrastructures of forests and soils), with a view to, simultaneously, combating climate change and promoting employment. The UNEP Executive Director stated that the global crises were in part related to a broad market failure that promoted speculation while precipitating escalating losses of natural capital and nature-based assets, compounded by an over-reliance on finite, often subsidized fossil fuels. The GEI, which was initially to be operational for a two-year period, was to have three key dimensions: the compilation of the *Green Economy* report, to provide an analysis of how public policy might support markets in accelerating the transition towards a low-carbon green economy; the Green Jobs Initiative, a partnership launched by UNEP, the ILO and the International Trade Union Confederation in 2007 (and joined in 2008 by the International Organisation of Employers); and the Economics of Ecosystems and Biodiversity (TEEB) partnership project, focusing on valuation issues. In February 2009 UNEP issued a report, entitled *The Environmental Food Crisis: Environment's Role in Averting Future Food Crises*, that urged a transformation in the way that food is produced, handled and disposed of, in order to feed the world's growing population and protect the environment; at that time the UNEP Executive Director emphasized the need for a 'Green revolution in a Green Economy'.

In 1994 UNEP inaugurated the International Environmental Technology Centre (IETC), based in Osaka, Japan. The Centre promotes and implements environmentally sound technologies for disaster prevention and post-disaster reconstruction; sustainable production and consumption; and water and sanitation (in particular waste-water management and more efficient use of rainwater).

The Division's Chemicals branch was established to promote the sound management of hazardous substances, central to which has been the International Register of Potentially Toxic Chemicals (IRPTC). UNEP aims to facilitate access to data on chemicals and hazardous wastes, in order to assess and control health and environmental risks, by using the IRPTC as a clearing house facility of relevant information and by publishing information and technical reports on the impact of the use of chemicals. UNEP provides technical support for implementing the Convention on Persistent Organic Pollutants (see above), encouraging the use of alternative pesticides, and monitoring the emission of pollutants through the burning of waste. UNEP administers the Strategic Approach to International Chemicals Management, adopted by the International Conference on Chemicals in 2006. With UNDP, UNEP helps governments to integrate sound management of chemicals into their development planning.

Pollutant Release and Transfer Registers (PRTRs), for collecting and disseminating data on toxic emissions, are in effect in Japan and the Republic of Korea.

The Division's OzonAction branch promotes information exchange, training and technological awareness, helping governments and industry in developing countries to undertake measures towards the cost-effective phasing-out of ozone-depleting substances (see under Environmental Law and Conventions, above).

UNEP also encourages the development of alternative and renewable sources of energy, as part of its efforts to mitigate climate change. To achieve this, UNEP has created the Global Network on Energy for Sustainable Development, linking 20 centres of excellence in industrialized and developing countries to conduct research and exchange information on environmentally sound energy technology resources. UNEP's Rural Energy Enterprise Development (REED) initiative helps the private sector to develop affordable 'clean' energy technologies, such as solar crop-drying and water-heating, wind-powered water pumps and efficient cooking stoves. UNEP is a member of the Global Bioenergy Partnership initiated by the G8 group of industrialized countries to support the sustainable use of biofuels. Through its Sustainable Transport Programme UNEP promotes the use of renewable fuels and the integration of environmental factors into transport planning, while the Sustainable Buildings and Construction Initiative promotes energy efficiency in the construction industry. In conjunction with UN-Habitat, UNDP, the World Bank and other organizations and institutions, UNEP promotes environmental concerns in urban planning and management through the Sustainable Cities Programme, and projects concerned with waste management, urban pollution and the impact of transportation systems.

To counter the problems caused by the rapid growth of cities in the Asia-Pacific region, UNEP's Prevention Approach–Urban Environment project promotes sustainable transport and eco-friendly buildings. In July 2007 UNEP established a partnership with the Bangkok Metropolitan Authority, Thailand, providing technical assistance for reducing the city's carbon emissions.

During 2007 UNEP (with WMO and WTO) convened a second International Conference on Climate Change and Tourism, together with two meetings on sustainable tourism development and a conference on global eco-tourism.

In January 2011 UNEP and the World Tourism Organization launched the Global Partnership for Sustainable Tourism, also comprising other UN agencies, OECD, 18 governments, and other partners, with the aim of guiding policy and developing projects in the area of sustainable tourism, providing a global platform for discussion, and facilitating progress towards a green economy.

In June 2009 UNEP and WTO jointly issued a report entitled *Trade and Climate Change*, reviewing the intersections between trade and climate change from the perspectives of: the science of climate change; economics; multilateral efforts to combat climate change; and the effects on trade of national climate change policies. During that month UNEP welcomed OECD's 'Green Growth' declaration, which urged the adoption of targeted policy instruments to promote green investment, and emphasized commitment to the realization of an ambitious and comprehensive post-2012 global climate agreement.

REGIONAL CO-OPERATION AND REPRESENTATION

UNEP maintains six regional offices. These work to initiate and promote UNEP objectives and to ensure that all programme formulation and delivery meets the specific needs of countries and regions. They also provide a focal point for building national, sub-regional and regional partnerships and enhancing local participation in UNEP initiatives. UNEP's Division of Regional Co-operation promotes regional policy integration, co-ordinates programme planning, and provides necessary services to the regional offices. UNEP provides administrative support to several regional conventions, and organizes regional conferences and training programmes.

COMMUNICATIONS AND PUBLIC INFORMATION

UNEP's public education campaigns and outreach programmes promote community involvement in environmental issues. Further communication of environmental concerns is undertaken through coverage in the press, broadcasting and electronic media, publications (see below), an information centre service and special promotional events, including World Environment Day (celebrated on 5 June; slogan in 2011: 'Forests: Nature at your Service'), the Focus on your World photography competition, and the awarding of the annual Sasakawa Prize (to recognize distinguished service to the environment by individuals and groups) and of the Champions of the Earth awards (for outstanding environmental leaders from each of UNEP's six regions). An annual Global Civil Society Forum (preceded by regional consultative meetings) is held in association with UNEP's Governing Council meetings. From April 2007 UNEP undertook a two-year programme on strengthening trade unions' participation in environmental processes. UNEP's Tunza programme for children and young people includes conferences, online discussions and publications. UNEP co-operates with the International Olympic Committee, the Commonwealth Games organizing body and international federations for football, athletics and other sports to encourage 'carbon neutral' sporting events and to use sport as a means of outreach. UNEP's Billion Tree Campaign, initiated in February 2007, initially encouraged governments, community organizations and individuals to plant 1,000m. trees before the end of the year, and exceeded that target; by October 2011 some 11,960m. trees had been planted under the continuing campaign.

Finance

The projected budget approved by the Governing Council for UNEP's activities during 2010–11 totalled US $493.9m. UNEP is allocated a contribution from the regular budget of the United Nations, and derives most of its finances from voluntary contributions to the Environment Fund and to trust funds.

Publications

Annual Report.

CBTF (Capacity Building Task Force on Trade, Environment and Development) Newsletter.

DEWA/GRID Europe Quarterly Bulletin. E+ (Energy, Climate and Sustainable Development).

The Environment and Poverty Times.

Global 500.

Great Apes Survival Project Newsletter.

IETC (International Environmental Technology Centre) Insight.

Life Cycle Initiatives Newsletter.

Our Planet (quarterly).

Planet in Peril: Atlas of Current Threats to People and the Environment.

ROA (Regional Office for Africa) News (2 a year).

Tourism Focus (2 a year).

RRC.AP (Regional Resource Centre for Asia and the Pacific) Newsletter.

Sustainable Consumption Newsletter.

Tunza (quarterly magazine for children and young people).

UNEP Chemicals Newsletter.

UNEP Year Book.

World Atlas of Biodiversity.

World Atlas of Coral Reefs.

World Atlas of Desertification.

Studies, reports (including the *Global Environment Outlook* series), legal texts, technical guidelines, etc.

Associated Bodies

Intergovernmental Panel on Climate Change (IPCC): established in 1988 by WMO and UNEP; comprises some 3,000 scientists as well as other experts and representatives of all UN member governments. Approximately every five years the IPCC assesses all available scientific, technical and socio-economic information on anthropogenic climate change. The IPCC provides, on request, scientific, technical and socio-economic advice to the Conference of the Parties to the UN Framework Convention on Climate Change (UNFCCC) and to its subsidiary bodies, and compiles reports on specialized topics, such as *Aviation and the Global Atmosphere* and *Regional Impacts of Climate Change.* The IPCC informs and guides, but does not prescribe, policy. In December 1995 the IPCC presented evidence to 120 governments, demonstrating 'a discernible human influence on global climate'. In 2001 the Panel issued its *Third Assessment Report,* in which it confirmed this finding and presented new and strengthened evidence attributing most global climate warming over the past 50 years to human activities. The IPCC's *Fourth Assessment Report*, the final instalment of which was issued in November 2007, concluded that increases in global average air and ocean temperatures, widespread melting of snow and ice, and the rising global average sea level, demonstrate that the warming of the climate system is unequivocal; that observational evidence from all continents and most oceans indicates that many natural systems are being affected by regional climate changes; that a global assessment of data since 1970 has shown that it is likely that anthropogenic warming has had a discernable influence on many physical and biological systems; and that other effects of regional climate changes are emerging. The *Fourth Assessment Report* was awarded a share of the Nobel Peace Prize for 2007. In January 2010 the IPCC accepted criticism that an assertion in the 2007 *Report*, concerning the rate at which Himalayan glaciers were melting, was exaggerated, and in February 2010 the Panel agreed that the *Report* had overstated the proportion of the Netherlands below sea level. In late February it was announced that an independent board of scientists would be appointed to review the work of the IPCC. The *Fifth Assessment Report* of the IPCC was to be published in 2014. In May 2011 a meeting of delegates from IPCC member states determined that a 13-member executive committee, under the leadership of the IPCC Chairman, should be established to supervise the day-to-day operations of the Panel and to consider matters requiring urgent action.

Chair.: RAJENDRA K. PACHAURI (India).

Secretariat of the UN Framework Convention on Climate Change (UNFCCC): Haus Carstanjen, Martin-Luther-King-Strasse 8, 53175 Bonn, Germany; tel. (228) 815-1000; fax (228) 815-1999; e-mail secretariat@unfccc.int; internet unfccc.int; WMO and UNEP worked together to formulate the Convention, in response to the first report of the IPCC, issued in August 1990, which predicted an increase in the concentration of 'greenhouse' gases (i.e. carbon dioxide and other gases that have a warming effect on the atmosphere) owing to human activity. The UNFCCC was signed in May 1992 and formally adopted at the UN Conference on Environment and Development, held in June. It entered into force in March 1994. It committed countries to submitting reports on measures being taken to reduce the emission of greenhouse gases and recommended stabilizing these emissions at 1990 levels by 2000; however, this was not legally binding. In July 1996, at the second session of the Conference of the Parties (COP) of the Convention, representatives of developed countries declared their willingness to commit to legally binding objectives for emission limitations in a specified timetable. Multilateral negotiations ensued to formulate a mandatory treaty on greenhouse gas emissions. At the third COP, held in Kyoto, Japan, in December 1997, 38 industrial nations endorsed mandatory reductions of combined emissions of the six major gases by an average of 5.2% during the five-year period 2008–12, to pre-1990 levels. The so-called Kyoto Protocol was to enter into force on being ratified by at least 55 countries party to the UNFCCC, including industrialized countries with combined emissions of carbon dioxide in 1990 accounting for at least 55% of the total global greenhouse gas emissions by developed nations. Many of the Protocol's operational details, however, remained to be determined. The fourth COP, convened in Buenos Aires, Argentina, in November 1998, adopted a plan of action to promote implementation of the UNFCCC and to finalize the operational details of the Kyoto Protocol. These included the Clean Development Mechanism, by which industrialized countries may obtain credits towards achieving their reduction targets by assisting developing countries to implement emission-reducing measures, and a system of trading emission quotas. The fifth COP, held in Bonn, Germany, in October–November 1999, and the first session of the sixth COP, convened in The Hague, Netherlands, in November 2000, failed to reach agreement on the implementation of the Buenos Aires plan of action, owing to a lack of consensus on several technical matters, including the formulation of an effective mechanism for ascertaining compliance under the Kyoto Protocol, and adequately defining a provision of the Protocol under which industrialized countries may obtain credits towards achieving their reduction targets in respect of the absorption of emissions resulting from activities in the so-called land-use, land-use change and forestry (LULUCF) sector. Further, informal, talks were held in Ottawa, Canada, in early December. Agreement on implementing the Buenos Aires action plan was finally achieved at the second session of the sixth COP, held in Bonn in July 2001. The seventh COP, convened in Marrakech, Morocco, in October–November, formally adopted the decisions reached in July, and elected 15 members to the Executive Board of the Clean Development Mechanism. The eighth COP, convened in New Delhi, India, in October–November 2002, issued the Delhi Declaration, urging states parties that had not done so already to ratify the Kyoto Protocol, and urging the integration of climate change objectives in key areas into national sustainable development strategies. In March the USA (the most prolific national producer of harmful gas emissions) announced that it would not ratify the Kyoto Protocol. A major advance achieved at the ninth COP was agreement on the modalities and scope for carbon-absorbing forest management projects in the Clean Development Mechanism. The Kyoto Protocol eventually entered into force on 16 February 2005, 90 days after its ratification by Russia. Negotiations commenced in May 2007 on establishing an international agreement to succeed the Kyoto Protocol after its expiry in 2012. Participants in COP 13, convened in Bali, Indonesia, in December 2007, adopted the Bali Roadmap, detailing a two-year process leading to the planned conclusion of the schedule of negotiations in December 2009. Further rounds of talks were held during 2008 in Bangkok, Thailand (March–April); Bonn (June); and in Accra, Ghana (August). The UN Climate Change Conference (COP 14), convened in Poznań, Poland, in December 2008, finalized the Kyoto Protocol's Adaptation Fund, which was to finance projects and programmes in developing signatory states that were particularly vulnerable to the adverse effects of climate change. Addressing the Conference, the UN Secretary-General urged the advancement of a 'Green New Deal', to address simultaneously the ongoing global climate and economic crises. COP 15 was held, concurrently with the fifth meeting of parties to the Kyoto Protocol, in Copenhagen, Denmark, in December 2009. Heads of state and government and other delegates attending the Conference approved the Copenhagen Accord, which determined that international co-operative action should be taken, in the context of sustainable development, to reduce global greenhouse gas emissions so as to hold the ongoing increase in global temperature below 2°C. It was agreed that enhanced efforts should be undertaken to reduce vulnerability to climate change in developing countries, with special reference to least developed countries, small island states and Africa. Developed countries agreed to pursue the achievement by 2020 of strengthened carbon emissions targets, while developing nations were to implement actions to slow down growth in emissions. The need to reduce deforestation and forest degradation, and thereby enhance removals of greenhouse gas emissions, was emphasized by the Accord. A new Copenhagen Green Climate Fund was inaugurated to support climate change mitigation actions in developing countries, and a Technology Mechanism was also established, with the aim of accelerating technology development and transfer in support of climate change adaptation and mitigation activities. COP 16, convened, concurrently with the sixth meeting of parties to the Kyoto Protocol, in Cancun, Mexico, in November–December 2010, adopted the several decisions (the 'Cancun Agreements'), which included mandating the establishment of a Cancun Adaptation Framework and associated Adaptation Committee, and approving a work programme which was to consider approaches to environmental damage linked to unavoidable impacts of climate change in vulnerable countries, as well as addressing forms of adaptation action, such as: strengthening the resilience of ecological systems; undertaking impact, vulnerability and adaptation assessments; engaging the participation of vulnerable communities in ongoing processes; and valuing traditional indigenous knowledge alongside the best available science. COP 17 was to be held in Durban, South Africa, during November–December 2011. By October 2011 the Kyoto Protocol had received ratifications from 192 states and the European Community, including ratifications by industrialized nations with combined responsibility for 63.7% of greenhouse gas emissions by developed nations in 1990 (although excluding participation by the USA).

Executive Secretary: CHRISTIANA FIGUERES (Costa Rica).

United Nations High Commissioner for Refugees—UNHCR

Address: CP 2500, 1211 Geneva 2 dépôt, Switzerland.

Telephone: 227398111; **fax:** 227397312; **e-mail:** unhcr@unhcr.org; **internet:** www.unhcr.org.

The Office of the High Commissioner was established in 1951 to provide international protection for refugees and to seek durable solutions to their problems. In 1981 UNHCR was awarded the Nobel Peace Prize.

OFFICE IN THE FAR EAST AND AUSTRALASIA

Regional Office for Australia, New Zealand, Papua New Guinea and the South Pacific: 3 Lyons Place, Lyons, ACT 2606, Australia; tel. (2) 6260-3411; fax (2) 6260-3477; e-mail aulca@unhcr.org; internet www.unhcr.org.au.

Organization

(October 2011)

HIGH COMMISSIONER

The High Commissioner is elected by the United Nations General Assembly on the nomination of the Secretary-General, and is responsible to the General Assembly and to the UN Economic and Social Council (ECOSOC).

High Commissioner: ANTÓNIO MANUEL DE OLIVEIRA GUTERRES (Portugal).

Deputy High Commissioner: L. CRAIG JOHNSTONE (USA).

EXECUTIVE COMMITTEE

The Executive Committee of the High Commissioner's Programme (ExCom), established by ECOSOC, gives the High Commissioner policy directives in respect of material assistance programmes and advice in the field of international protection. In addition, it oversees UNHCR's general policies and use of funds. ExCom, which comprises representatives of 66 states, both members and non-members of the UN, meets once a year.

ADMINISTRATION

Headquarters, based in Geneva, Switzerland, include the Executive Office, comprising the offices of the High Commissioner, the Deputy High Commissioner and the two Assistant High Commissioners (for Operations and Protection). The Inspector General, the Director of the UNHCR liaison office in New York, and the Director of the Ethics Office (established in 2008) report directly to the High Commissioner. The principal administrative Divisions cover: International Protection; Programme and Support Management; Emergency Security and Supply; Financial and Administrative Management; Human Resources Management; External Relations; and Information Systems and Telecommunications. A UNHCR Global Service Centre, based in Budapest, Hungary, was inaugurated in 2008 to provide administrative support to the Headquarters. There are five regional bureaux covering Africa, Asia and the Pacific, Europe, the Americas, and North Africa and the Middle East. In 2011 UNHCR employed around 7,190 regular staff, of whom more than 6,488 were working in the field. At that time there were 396 UNHCR offices in 123 countries.

All UNHCR personnel are required to sign, and all interns, contracted staff and staff from partner organizations are required to acknowledge, a Code of Conduct, to which is appended the UN Secretary-General's bulletin on special measures for protection from sexual exploitation and sexual abuse. The post of Senior Adviser to the High Commissioner on Gender Issues, within the Executive Office, was established in 2004.

Activities

The competence of the High Commissioner extends to any person who, owing to well-founded fear of being persecuted for reasons of race, religion, nationality or political opinion, is outside the country of his or her nationality and is unable or, owing to such fear or for reasons other than personal convenience, remains unwilling to accept the protection of that country; or who, not having a nationality and being outside the country of his or her former habitual residence, is unable or, owing to such fear or for reasons other than personal convenience, is unwilling to return to it. This competence may be extended, by resolutions of the UN General Assembly and decisions of ExCom, to cover certain other 'persons of concern', in addition to refugees meeting these criteria. Refugees who are assisted by other UN agencies, or who have the same rights or obligations as nationals of their country of residence, are outside the mandate of UNHCR.

In recent years there has been a significant shift in UNHCR's focus of activities. Increasingly UNHCR has been called upon to support people who have been displaced within their own country (i.e. with similar needs to those of refugees but who have not crossed an international border) or those threatened with displacement as a result of armed conflict. In addition, greater support has been given to refugees who have returned to their country of origin, to assist their reintegration, and UNHCR is working to enable local communities to support the returnees, frequently through the implementation of Quick Impact Projects (QIPs). In 2004 UNHCR led the formulation of a UN system-wide Strategic Plan for internally displaced persons (IDPs). During 2005 the UN's Inter-Agency Standing Committee (IASC), concerned with co-ordinating the international response to humanitarian disasters, developed a concept of organizing agency assistance to IDPs through the institutionalization of a 'Cluster Approach', currently comprising 11 core areas of activity (see OCHA). UNHCR is the lead agency for the clusters on Camp Co-ordination and Management (in conflict situations; the International Organization for Migration leads that cluster in natural disaster situations), Emergency Shelter, and (jointly with OHCHR and UNICEF) Protection.

In the mid-2000s UNHCR widened its scope from its (mandate to protect and assist people fleeing persecution and violence) in response to the enormous impact of two devastating natural disasters. Following the series of tidal waves (tsunamis), emanating from an earthquake in the Indian Ocean, that devastated coastal regions in 14 countries in South and South-East Asia and East Africa in December 2004, UNHCR requested emergency funding totalling US $77m. in support of a 12-month relief operation to provide shelter, non-food relief supplies and logistical support for survivors in Aceh, Indonesia (close to the epicentre of the earthquake), Sri Lanka and Somalia. This was part of a pan-UN inter-agency appeal for $1,100m. In October 2005 UNHCR provided an immediate response to support survivors of the South Asian earthquake that struck northern Pakistan and bordering areas of India and Afghanistan. In May 2008 UNHCR donated tents to provide shelter for some 55,000 people following a devastating earthquake in Sichuan province, People's Republic of China.

UNHCR has been increasingly concerned with the problem of statelessness, where people have no legal nationality, and promotes new accessions to the 1954 Convention Relating to the Status of Stateless Persons and the 1964 Convention on the Reduction of Statelessness. UNHCR maintains that a significant proportion of the global stateless population has not hitherto been systematically identified. In October 2006 ExCom urged member states to share with UNHCR data on stateless persons and on persons with undetermined nationality.

In July 2006 UNHCR issued a '10 Point Plan of Action on Refugee Protection and Mixed Migration' (*10 Point Plan*), a framework document detailing 10 principal areas in which UNHCR might make an impact in supporting member states with the development of comprehensive migration strategies. The 10 areas covered by the Plan were as follows: co-operation among key players; data collection and analysis; protection-sensitive entry systems; reception arrangements; mechanisms for profiling and referral; differentiated processes and procedures; solutions for refugees; addressing secondary movements; return of non-refugees and alternative migration options; and information strategy. A revised version of the *10 Point Plan* was published in January 2007. Addressing the annual meeting of ExCom in October 2007 the High Commissioner, while emphasizing that UNHCR was not mandated to manage migration, urged a concerted international effort to raise awareness and comprehension of the broad patterns (including the scale, complexity, and causes—such as poverty and the pursuit of improved living standards) of global displacement and migration. In order to fulfil UNHCR's mandate to support refugees and others in need of protection within ongoing mass movements of people, he urged better recognition of the mixed nature of many 21st century population flows, often comprising both economic migrants and refugees, asylum seekers and victims of trafficking who required detection and support. It was also acknowledged that conflict and persecution—the traditional reasons for flight—were being increasingly compounded by factors such as environmental degradation and the detrimental effects of climate change. A Dialogue on Protection Challenges, convened by the High Commissioner in December 2007, agreed that the *10 Point Plan* should be elaborated further. Regional activities based on the Plan have been focused on Central America, Western Africa, Eastern Africa and Southern Asia; and on countries along the Eastern and South-Eastern borders of European Union member states.

In 2009 UNHCR launched the first annual Global Needs Assessment (GNA), with the aim of mapping comprehensively the situation and needs of populations of concern falling under the mandate of the Office. The GNA was to represent a blueprint for planning and decision-making for UNHCR, populations of concern, governments and other partners. In 2008 a pilot GNA, undertaken in eight countries, revealed significant unmet protection needs including in education, food security and nutrition, distribution of non-food items, health, access to clean water and sanitation, shelter, and prevention of sexual violence.

At December 2010 the total global population of concern to UNHCR, based on provisional figures, amounted to 33.9m. At that time the refugee population world-wide totalled 10.5m. UNHCR was also concerned with some 197,626 recently returned refugees, 14.7m. IDPs, 2.9m. returned IDPs, 3.5m. stateless persons, and 837,478 asylum seekers. UNHCR maintains an online statistical population database.

In 2011 UNHCR reported that in 2010 358,800 applications for asylum were made in industrialized countries, compared with 620,000 in 2011.

World Refugee Day, sponsored by UNHCR, is held annually on 20 June.

INTERNATIONAL PROTECTION

As laid down in the Statute of the Office, UNHCR's primary function is to extend international protection to refugees and its second function is to seek durable solutions to their problems. In the exercise of its mandate UNHCR seeks to ensure that refugees and asylum seekers are protected against *refoulement* (forcible return), that they receive asylum, and that they are treated according to internationally recognized standards. UNHCR pursues these objectives by a variety of means that include promoting the conclusion and ratification by states of international conventions for the protection of refugees. UNHCR promotes the adoption of liberal practices of asylum by states, so that refugees and asylum seekers are granted admission, at least on a temporary basis.

The most comprehensive instrument concerning refugees that has been elaborated at the international level is the 1951 United Nations Convention relating to the Status of Refugees. This Convention, the scope of which was extended by a Protocol adopted in 1967, defines the rights and duties of refugees and contains provisions dealing with a variety of matters which affect the day-to-day lives of refugees. The application of the Convention and its Protocol is supervised by UNHCR. Important provisions for the treatment of refugees are also contained in a number of instruments adopted at the regional level. These include the 1969 Convention Governing the Specific Aspects of Refugee Problems adopted by the Organization of African Unity (now the African Union—AU) member states in 1969, the European Agreement on the Abolition of Visas for Refugees, and the 1969 American Convention on Human Rights. In October 2009 AU member states adopted the AU Convention for the Protection and Assistance of IDPs in Africa, the first legally binding international treaty providing legal protection and support to internally displaced populations.

UNHCR has actively encouraged states to accede to the 1951 United Nations Refugee Convention and the 1967 Protocol: 147 states had acceded to either or both of these basic refugee instruments by May 2011. An increasing number of states have also adopted domestic legislation and/or administrative measures to implement the international instruments, particularly in the field of procedures for the determination of refugee status. UNHCR has sought to address the specific needs of refugee women and children, and has also attempted to deal with the problem of military attacks on refugee camps, by adopting and encouraging the acceptance of a set of principles to ensure the safety of refugees. In recent years it has formulated a strategy designed to address the fundamental causes of refugee flows. In 2001, in response to widespread concern about perceived high numbers of asylum seekers and large-scale international economic migration and human trafficking, UNHCR initiated a series of Global Consultations on International Protection with the signatories to the 1951 Convention and 1967 Protocol, and other interested parties, with a view to strengthening both the application and scope of international refugee legislation. A consultation of 156 Governments, convened in Geneva, in December 2001, reaffirmed commitment to the central role played by the Convention and Protocol. The final consultation, held in May 2002, focused on durable solutions and the protection of refugee women and children. Subsequently, based on the findings of the Global Consultations process, UNHCR developed an Agenda on Protection with six main objectives: strengthening the implementation of the 1951 Convention and 1967 Protocol; the protection of refugees within broader migration movements; more equitable sharing of burdens and responsibilities and building of capacities to receive and protect refugees; addressing more effectively security-related concerns; increasing efforts to find durable solutions; and meeting the protection needs of refugee women and children. The Agenda was endorsed by ExCom in October 2002. In September of that year the High Commissioner for Refugees launched the *Convention Plus* initiative, which aimed to address contemporary global asylum issues by developing, on the basis of the Agenda on Protection, international agreements and measures to supplement the 1951 Convention and 1967 Protocol.

UNHCR is one of the 10 co-sponsors of UNAIDS.

ASSISTANCE ACTIVITIES

The first phase of an assistance operation uses UNHCR's capacity of emergency response. This enables UNHCR to address the immediate needs of refugees at short notice, for example, by employing specially trained emergency teams and maintaining stockpiles of basic equipment, medical aid and materials. A significant proportion of UNHCR expenditure is allocated to the next phase of an operation, providing 'care and maintenance' in stable refugee circumstances. This assistance can take various forms, including the provision of food, shelter, medical care and essential supplies. Also covered in many instances are basic services, including education and counselling.

As far as possible, assistance is geared towards the identification and implementation of durable solutions to refugee problems—this being the second statutory responsibility of UNHCR. Such solutions generally take one of three forms: voluntary repatriation, local integration or resettlement in another country. Where voluntary repatriation, increasingly the preferred solution, is feasible, the Office assists refugees to overcome obstacles preventing their return to their country of origin. This may be done through negotiations with governments involved, or by providing funds either for the physical movement of refugees or for the rehabilitation of returnees once back in their own country. UNHCR supports the implementation of the Guidance Note on Durable Solutions for Displaced Persons, adopted in 2004 by the UN Development Group.

When voluntary repatriation is not an option, efforts are made to assist refugees to integrate locally and to become self-supporting in their countries of asylum. This may be done either by granting loans to refugees, or by assisting them, through vocational training or in other ways, to learn a skill and to establish themselves in gainful occupations. One major form of assistance to help refugees re-establish themselves outside camps is the provision of housing. In cases where resettlement through emigration is the only viable solution to a refugee problem, UNHCR negotiates with governments in an endeavour to obtain suitable resettlement opportunities, to encourage liberalization of admission criteria and to draw up special immigration schemes. During 2009 an estimated 84,000 refugees were resettled under UNHCR auspices.

In the 1990s UNHCR consolidated efforts to integrate certain priorities into its programme planning and implementation, as a standard discipline in all phases of assistance. The considerations include awareness of specific problems confronting refugee women, the needs of refugee children, the environmental impact of refugee programmes and long-term development objectives. In an effort to improve the effectiveness of its programmes, UNHCR has initiated a process of delegating authority, as well as responsibility for operational budgets, to its regional and field representatives, increasing flexibility and accountability. A Policy Development and Evaluation Service reviews systematically UNHCR's operational effectiveness.

EAST ASIA AND THE PACIFIC

In June 1989 an international conference was convened by UNHCR in Geneva to discuss the ongoing problem of refugees and displaced persons in and from the Indo-Chinese peninsula. The participants adopted the Comprehensive Plan of Action for Indo-Chinese Refugees (CPA), which provided for the 'screening' of all Vietnamese arrivals in the region to determine their refugee status, the resettlement of 'genuine' refugees and the repatriation (described as voluntary 'in the first instance') of those deemed to be economic migrants. A steering committee of the international conference met regularly to supervise the plan. In March 1996 UNHCR confirmed that it was to terminate funding for the refugee camps (except those in Hong Kong) at the end of June to coincide with the formal conclusion of the CPA; however, it pledged to support transitional arrangements regarding the completion of the repatriation process and maintenance of the remaining Vietnamese 'non-refugees' during the post-CPA phase-out period, as well as to continue its support for the reintegration and monitoring of returning nationals in Viet Nam and Laos. The prospect of forcible repatriation provoked rioting and violent protests in many camps throughout the region. By mid-1996 more than 88,000 Vietnamese and 22,000 Laotians had returned to their countries of origin under the framework of the CPA, with Malaysia and Singapore having completed the repatriation process. In late July the Philippines Government agreed to permit the remaining camp residents to settle permanently in that country. In September the remaining Vietnamese refugees detained on the island of Galang, in Indonesia, were repatriated, and in February 1997 the last camp for Vietnamese refugees in Thailand was formally closed. In mid-June of that year the main Vietnamese detention camp in Hong Kong was closed. However, the scheduled repatriation of all remaining Vietnamese before the transfer of sovereignty of the territory to the People's Republic of China (PRC) at the end of June was not achieved. In early 1998 the Hong Kong authorities formally terminated the policy of granting a port of first asylum to Vietnamese 'boat people'. In February 2000 UNHCR, which had proposed the integration of the remaining Vietnamese as a final durable solution to the situation, welcomed a decision by the Hong Kong authorities to offer permanent residency status to the occupants of the last remaining Vietnamese detention camp (totalling 973 refugees and 435 'non-refugees'). By the end of May, when the camp was closed, more than 200 Vietnamese had failed to apply for residency. At 31 December 2010 there were an estimated further 300,897 Vietnamese refugees in mainland PRC. In 1995, in accordance with an agreement concluded with the PRC Government, UNHCR initiated a programme to redirect its local assistance to promote long-term self-sufficiency in the poorest settlements, including support for revolving-fund rural credit schemes. UNHCR favours the local integration of the majority of the Vietnamese refugee population in the PRC as a durable solution to the situation.

During 2011 UNHCR was advocating for the accession of the Hong Kong Special Administrative Region—which attracts mixed inflows of refugees, asylum seekers and economic migrants—to the 1951 United Nations Convention relating to the Status of Refugees (of which the PRC is a signatory).

The conclusion of a political settlement of the conflict in Cambodia in October 1991 made possible the eventual repatriation of some 370,000 Cambodian refugees and displaced persons by April 1993. Meanwhile, however, thousands of ethnic Vietnamese (of whom there were estimated to be 200,000 in Cambodia) fled to Viet Nam, as a result of violence perpetrated against them by Cambodian armed groups. In March 1994 25,000 supporters of the Khmers Rouges in Cambodia fled across the border into Thailand, following advances by government forces. The refugees were immediately repatriated by the Thai armed forces into Khmer Rouge territory, which was inaccessible to aid agencies. In July 1997 armed conflict between opposing political forces in northern Cambodia resulted in large-scale population movement. A voluntary repatriation programme was initiated in October, and in late March 1999 UNHCR announced that the last Cambodian refugees had left camps in Thailand, the majority having been repatriated to north-western Cambodia. A UNHCR programme was initiated to monitor the welfare of returnees and assist in their reintegration; this was terminated at the end of 2000. In January 2002 UNHCR signed an agreement with the Governments of Viet Nam and Cambodia for the safe repatriation of an estimated 1,000 Montagnards who had fled from the Central Highland provinces of Viet Nam during 2001. UNHCR was to be permitted unlimited access to the region to assist and monitor the return process. In March 2002, however, UNHCR withdrew from the agreement owing to alleged intimidation of refugees and UN staff. In January 2005 UNHCR, Cambodia and Viet Nam signed a memorandum of understanding providing for the preservation of asylum space in Cambodia for Montagnard asylum seekers and establishing mechanisms for the implementation of solutions to their plight; consequently, during 2005–10 UNHCR worked to facilitate solutions for Montagnards still sheltering in Cambodia. In December 2010 the Cambodian authorities ordered the closure of the UNHCR refugee centre for Montagnards in Phnom Penh, subsequently agreeing an extension until February 2011, by which time solutions had been found for most of the Montagnard community. During 2008 UNHCR undertook two monitoring visits to assess the well-being of 315 Montagnards who had recently returned to their native Central Highlands; a number of micro-projects were implemented in the education sector at that time, jointly by UNHCR and the Viet Nam authorities, to facilitate their reintegration.

From April 1991 increasing numbers of Rohingya Muslims in Myanmar fled into Bangladesh to escape brutality and killings perpetrated by the Myanma armed forces. UNHCR launched an international appeal for financial aid for the refugees, at the request of Bangladesh, and collaborated with other UN agencies in providing humanitarian assistance. UNHCR refused to participate in a programme of repatriation of the Myanma refugees agreed by Myanmar and Bangladesh, on the grounds that no safe environment existed for them to return to. In May 1993 a memorandum of understanding between UNHCR and Bangladesh was signed, whereby UNHCR would be able to monitor the repatriation process and ensure that people were returning of their own free will. In November a memorandum of understanding, signed with the Myanma Government, secured UNHCR access to the returnees. The first refugees returned to Myanmar with UNHCR assistance at the end of April 1994. They and all subsequent returnees were provided with a small amount of cash, housing grants and two months' food rations, and were supported by several small-scale reintegration projects. Attempts by UNHCR to find a local solution for those unwilling to return to Myanmar have been met with resistance by the Bangladeshi Government. By the end of December 2010 an estimated 29,226 Myanma refugees were continuing to receive basic UNHCR care in in camps in Bangladesh. During 2010 UNHCR made progress in improving camp conditions, with a particular focus on the areas of nutrition, reproductive health, infrastructure and skills training. The Office also addressed malnutrition in the camps through the provision of feeding programmes for infants. In 2011 UNHCR also aimed to improve the conditions, mainly through community-based support, of an estimated 200,000 unregistered Myanma refugees living outside its camps in Bangladesh.

In the early 1990s members of ethnic minorities in Myanmar attempted to flee attacks by government troops into Thailand; however, the Thai Government refused to recognize them as refugees or to offer them humanitarian assistance. In December 1997 Thailand and Myanmar agreed to commence 'screening' the refugees to determine those who had fled persecution and those who were economic migrants. Screening activities were suspended during 2001–04. In February 2004 the Myanma Government granted UNHCR access to areas along the Myanmar-Thailand border, thereby potentially enabling the large-scale voluntary repatriation of the Myanma (mainly Karen/Kayin) refugee population remaining in camps there. The Myanma Government requested that UNHCR should plan for the return and reintegration of IDPs as well as refugees. UNHCR, however, decided to postpone repatriation and reintegration operations pending the conclusion of an internationally acceptable peace agreement between the Myanma authorities and militants that would secure the safety of returnees. A large-scale process to resettle Myanma refugees from Thailand to third countries commenced in that year. From 2009 UNHCR aimed to upgrade its activities in the Rakhine region of northern Myanmar, covering health, education, water and sanitation, agriculture, and infrastructure improvement, to assist the reintegration of Muslim returnees to the area, as well as stateless residents (numbering around 750,000 in 2010). From late 2008 there were significant outflows of Muslims from Rakhine towards Malaysia, as well as to Indonesia and Thailand; UNHCR has worked with regional governments for the adoption of a collective approach to addressing the situation. UNHCR assisted 10,823 Myanma refugees with resettlement in 2010, reducing the numbers still sheltering in (nine) border camps to 95,718 at the end of that year. At 31 December 2010 there were some 76,120 Myanma refugees in Malaysia (all UNHCR-assisted), of whom 21,104 arrived during that year.

UNHCR has sought access, so far unsuccessfully, to Laotian Hmong would-be asylum seekers sheltering since 2005 in temporary shelters in Thailand, whom the Thai authorities classify as illegal migrants. During 2005–10 some 7,500 Lao-Hmong were forcibly returned from Thailand to Laos, including some 4,000 who were returned en masse in December 2009.

In 2008 Thailand was the focus of a pilot project for UNHCR's Global Needs Assessment (formally inaugurated in 2009, see above). In view of the project's findings, UNHCR aimed to enhance its efforts to improve protection and to facilitate durable solutions for refugees in that country.

In April 1999, following the announcement by the Indonesian Government, in January, that it would consider a form of autonomy or independence for East Timor, some 26,000 Indonesian settlers left their homes as a result of clashes between opposing groups and uncertainty regarding the future of the territory. The popular referendum on the issue, conducted at the end of August, and the resulting victory for the independence movement, provoked a violent reaction by pro-integration militia. UNHCR, along with other international personnel, was forced to evacuate the territory in early September. At that time there were reports of forced mass deportations of East Timorese to West Timor, while a large number of others fled their homes into remote mountainous areas of East Timor. In mid-September UNHCR staff visited West Timor to review the state of refugee camps, allegedly under the control of militia, and to persuade the authorities to permit access for humanitarian personnel. It was estimated that 250,000–260,000 East Timorese had fled to West Timor, of whom some 230,000 were registered in 28 camps at the end of September. At that time there were also an estimated 190,000–300,000 people displaced within East Timor, although the International Committee of the Red Cross estimated that a total of 800,000 people, or some 94% of the population, had been displaced, or deported, during the crisis. The arrival of multinational troops, from 20 September, helped to stabilize the region and enable the safe receipt and distribution of food supplies, prompting several thousands to return from hiding. Most homes, however, along with almost all other buildings in the capital, Dili, had been destroyed. In early October UNHCR, together with the International Organization for Migration, initiated a repatriation programme for the refugees in West Timor. However, despite an undertaking by the Indonesian Government in mid-October that it would ensure the safety of all refugees and international personnel, persistent intimidation by anti-independence militia impeded the registration and repatriation processes. UNHCR initially aimed to complete the repatriation programme by mid-2001, prior to the staging of elections to a Constituent Assembly by the UN Transitional Administration in East Timor (UNTAET, which assumed full authority over the territory in February 2000). However, in September 2000 UNHCR suspended its activities in West Timor, following the murder by militiamen there of three of its personnel. A UN Security Council resolution, adopted soon afterwards, deplored this incident and strongly urged the Indonesian authorities to disable the militia and to guarantee the future security of all refugees and humanitarian personnel. In mid-September UNTAET and the Indonesian Government signed a Memorandum of Understanding on co-operation in resolving the refugee crisis. However, despite a subsequent operation by the Indonesian security forces to disarm the militia, intimidation of East Timorese refugees reportedly persisted, and UNHCR did not redeploy personnel to West Timor. The Office did, however, liaise with other humanitarian organizations to facilitate continuing voluntary repatriations, which have been encouraged by the Indonesian authorities. UNHCR's operation in East Timor aimed to promote the safe voluntary repatriation of refugees, monitor returnees, support their reintegration through the implementation of QIPs, pursue efforts towards sustainable development and the rehabilitation of communities, and promote reconciliation and respect for human rights. In mid-May East Timor (now Timor-Leste) achieved independence. At that time almost 205,000 East Timorese refugees were reported to have returned since October 1999. UNHCR and the newly elected administration co-operated to encourage further repatriation, as well as to assist with Timor-Leste's accession to the international instruments of protection and with the development of new national refugee protection legislation. On 31 December 2002 UNHCR terminated the refugee status of people who fled East Timor in 1999. The Indonesian Government granted Indonesian citizenship in 2006 to unreturned East Timorese (whose numbers included former militants); many, however, remained unsettled, continuing to live in camps, with poor conditions, near the Timor-Leste border. During 2011 UNHCR was assisting the Indonesian Government with efforts to prepare for accession to the 1951 Convention relating to the Status of Refugees and its 1967 Protocol.

Renewed violent unrest in Timor-Leste that erupted in April 2006 resulted in significant new population displacement within the country, and, at the end of that year, more than 155,200 Timorese IDPs were of concern to UNHCR. During May–August 2006 the Office provided immediate relief to the newly uprooted IDPs, in the form of non-food items such as tents, and was subsequently involved in IDP protection and reconciliation activities.

UNHCR endeavours to facilitate safe passage to the Republic of Korea for people who have fled from the Democratic People's Republic of Korea to the PRC and other countries in the region.

CO-OPERATION WITH OTHER ORGANIZATIONS

UNHCR works closely with other UN agencies, intergovernmental organizations and non-governmental organizations (NGOs) to increase the scope and effectiveness of its operations. Within the UN system UNHCR co-operates, principally, with the WFP in the distribution of food aid, UNICEF and WHO in the provision of family welfare and child immunization programmes, OCHA in the delivery of emergency humanitarian relief, UNDP in development-related activities and the preparation of guidelines for the continuum of emergency assistance to development programmes, and the Office of the UN High Commissioner for Human Rights. UNHCR also has close working relationships with the International Committee of the Red Cross and the International Organization for Migration. UNHCR planned to engage with more than 470 NGOs during 2010–11.

TRAINING

UNHCR organizes training programmes and workshops to enhance the capabilities of field workers and non-UNHCR staff, in the following areas: the identification and registration of refugees; people-orientated planning; resettlement procedures and policies; emergency response and management; security awareness; stress management; and the dissemination of information through the electronic media.

Finance

The United Nations' regular budget finances a proportion of UNHCR's administrative expenditure. The majority of UNHCR's programme expenditure (about 98%) is funded by voluntary contributions, mainly from governments. The Private Sector and Public Affairs Service aims to increase funding from non-governmental donor sources, for example by developing partnerships with foundations and corporations. Following approval of the Unified Annual Programme Budget any subsequently identified requirements are managed in the form of Supplementary Programmes, financed by separate appeals. UNHCR's projected funding requirements for 2011 totalled US $3,320.0m.

Publications

Global Trends (annually).

Refugees (quarterly, in English, French, German, Italian, Japanese and Spanish).

Refugee Resettlement: An International Handbook to Guide Reception and Integration.

Refugee Survey Quarterly.

Refworld (annually).

Sexual and Gender-based Violence Against Refugees, Returnees and Displaced Persons: Guidelines for Prevention and Response.

The State of the World's Refugees (every 2 years).

Statistical Yearbook (annually).

UNHCR Handbook for Emergencies.

Press releases, reports.

Statistics

PERSONS OF CONCERN TO UNHCR IN THE FAR EAST AND AUSTRALASIA

('000 persons, at 31 December 2010*)

Host country	Refugees	Asylum seekers	Returned refugees	Others of concern†
Australia	21.8	3.8	—	—
China, People's Rep.	301.0	0.1	0.0	—
Malaysia	81.5	11.3	—	120.0
Myanmar	—	—	—	859.4
Thailand	96.7	10.3	—	542.5

* Figures are provided mostly by governments, based on their own records and methods of estimations. Countries with fewer than 10,000 persons of concern to UNHCR are not listed.

† Mainly internally displaced persons (IDPs), recently-returned IDPs or stateless persons.

United Nations Peace-keeping

Address: Department of Peace-keeping Operations, Room S-3727-B, United Nations, New York, NY 10017, USA.

Telephone: (212) 963-8077; **fax:** (212) 963-9222; **internet:** www.un.org/Depts/dpko/.

United Nations peace-keeping operations have been conceived as instruments of conflict control. The UN has used these operations in various conflicts, with the consent of the parties involved, to maintain international peace and security, without prejudice to the positions or claims of parties, in order to facilitate the search for political settlements through peaceful means such as mediation and the good offices of the UN Secretary-General. Each operation is established with a specific mandate, which requires periodic review by the UN Security Council. In 1988 the United Nations Peace-keeping Forces were awarded the Nobel Peace Prize.

United Nations peace-keeping operations fall into two categories: peace-keeping forces and observer missions. Peace-keeping forces are composed of contingents of military and civilian personnel, made available by member states. These forces assist in preventing the recurrence of fighting, restoring and maintaining peace, and promoting a return to normal conditions. To this end, peace-keeping forces are authorized as necessary to undertake negotiations, persuasion, observation and fact-finding. They conduct patrols and interpose physically between the opposing parties. Peace-keeping forces are permitted to use their weapons only in self-defence.

Military observer missions are composed of officers (usually unarmed), who are made available, on the Secretary-General's request, by member states. A mission's function is to observe and report to the Secretary-General (who, in turn, informs the Security Council) on the maintenance of a cease-fire, to investigate violations and to do what it can to improve the situation. Peace-keeping forces and observer missions must at all times maintain complete impartiality and avoid any action that might affect the claims or positions of the parties.

The UN's peace-keeping forces and observer missions are financed in most cases by assessed contributions from member states of the organization. In recent years a significant expansion in the UN's peace-keeping activities has been accompanied by a perpetual financial crisis within the organization, as a result of the increased financial burden and some member states' delaying payment. At 31 July 2011 outstanding assessed contributions to the peace-keeping budget amounted to some US $3,910m.

By October 2011 the UN had deployed a total of 66 peace-keeping operations, of which 13 were authorized in the period 1948–88 and 53 since 1988. At 30 September 2011 114 countries were contributing some 97,675 uniformed personnel to the (15) ongoing operations, of whom 81,260 were peace-keeping troops, 14,307 police and 2,108 military observers.

UNITED NATIONS INTEGRATED MISSION IN TIMOR-LESTE—UNMIT

Address: Dili, Timor-Leste.

Telephone: 3301400; **fax:** 3304410; **internet:** www.unmit.org.

Special Representative of the UN Secretary-General and Head of Office: AMEERAH HAQ (Bangladesh).

Police Commissioner: LUIS MIGUEL CARRILHO (Portugal).

Establishment and Mandate: In succession to the UN Mission in Support of East Timor (UNMISET), the UN Transitional Administration in East Timor (UNTAET) and the UN Office in Timor-Leste (UNOTIL), UNMIT was established by UN Security Council Resolution 1704 in August 2006 to support the Timor-Leste authorities with consolidating stability, promoting democratic governance and facilitating the process of national reconciliation. The mission was to co-operate with the Australian-led International Stabilization Force (ISF, also comprising troops from Malaysia, New Zealand and Portugal), which had been deployed to Timor-Leste in late May 2006 to secure key installations following an eruption of violent unrest in the previous month. The mission was authorized to assist with all aspects of the staging of the 2007 presidential and legislative elections, with restoring and maintaining public security, and with the promotion of human rights and justice.

Activities: In January 2007 UNMIT signed a trilateral agreement with the Timorese authorities and Australian Government to enhance co-ordination of all security-related activities. During the first half of 2007 the UNMIT police presence was expanded to provide full support to the Timorese national police and ISF in facilitating public security during the electoral process. In May UNMIT reported that the presidential election, conducted in April–May, had been 'free and fair'. Parliamentary elections were conducted in late June, and in early August the Special Representative of the UN Secretary-General (SRSG) welcomed the establishment of a new coalition Government. The inauguration of the new Government, however, prompted renewed violent unrest in several districts of the country. Consequently, during August, UNMIT convened a meeting of representatives of national political groupings to address means of calming the unrest, and also offered practical assistance to the Timorese authorities towards restoring security and delivering humanitarian aid to those affected by the violence. In November a delegation of the UN Security Council visited the country. In February 2008 the UN condemned violent attacks against the Prime Minister and President in Timor-Leste. In that month, in extending UNMIT's mandate by one year, the Security Council requested that UNMIT continue to assist the Government to enhance the effectiveness of the judiciary, to review and reform the security sector, to co-ordinate donor co-operation for institutional capacity-building, and to assist in the formulation of poverty reduction and economic growth strategies. In June UNMIT confirmed that it was to assist the Timor-Leste authorities to undertake a comprehensive review of its security sector. In August the mission published a second report on the human rights situation in Timor-Leste, focusing on access to justice and the security sector. The mission's mandate was extended by a further 12-month period in February 2009. In March the Prime Minister and the SRSG announced that there was to be a gradual resumption of responsibilities for police operations by the national police force, the Policia Nacional de Timor-Leste (PNTL), contingent on the outcome of a joint assessment process. The first transfer of primary responsibility for policing from UNMIT to the PNTL was officially conducted in Lautém district in May 2009, and in September the PNTL assumed responsibility for the national police training centre, in Dili. In February 2010 the UN Security Council endorsed a recommendation of the Secretary-General to reconfigure the UNMIT police component, including its drawdown, in accordance with the phased transfer of policing responsibilities to the PNTL. In January a technical assessment mission was sent to Timor-Leste to make recommendations to the UN Secretary-General concerning UNMIT's role during 2010–12. By 2011 UNMIT had transferred responsibility to the PNTL for policing in 10 districts and six units, as well as the Immigration Department, the Border Patrol Unit and the Interpol office. In February 2011 the UN Security Council, extending the mission's mandate by a further 12-month period, recognised the need for a continued UN police presence in the country in order to support further constitutional development, PNTL capacity building and preparations for presidential and parliamentary elections, scheduled to be conducted in 2012.

Operational Strength: At 30 September 2011 UNMIT comprised 1,191 police officers and 33 military liaison officers; it was assisted by 203 UN Volunteers and (at 31 July) by a team of 398 international and 894 local civilian staff.

Finance: The General Assembly apportioned US $196.1m. to finance the operation during the period 1 July 2011–30 June 2012.

World Food Programme—WFP

Address: Via Cesare Giulio Viola 68, Parco dei Medici, 00148 Rome, Italy.

Telephone: (06) 65131; **fax:** (06) 6513-2840; **e-mail:** wfpinfo@wfp.org; **internet:** www.wfp.org.

WFP, the principal food assistance organization of the United Nations, became operational in 1963. It aims to alleviate acute hunger by providing emergency relief following natural or man-made humanitarian disasters, and supplies food assistance to people in developing countries to eradicate chronic undernourishment, to support social development and to promote self-reliant communities.

Organization

(October 2011)

EXECUTIVE BOARD

The governing body of WFP is the Executive Board, comprising 36 members, 18 of whom are elected by the UN Economic and Social Council (ECOSOC) and 18 by the Council of the Food and Agriculture Organization (FAO). The Board meets four times each year at WFP headquarters.

SECRETARIAT

WFP's Executive Director is appointed jointly by the UN Secretary-General and the Director-General of FAO and is responsible for the management and administration of the Programme. In 2008 there were 10,200 staff members, of whom 91% were working in the field. WFP administers some 87 country offices, in order to provide operational, financial and management support at a more local level, and maintains six regional bureaux, located in Bangkok, Thailand (for Asia), Cairo, Egypt (for the Middle East, Central Asia and Eastern Europe), Panama City, Panama (for Latin America and the Caribbean), Johannesburg, South Africa (for Southern Africa), Kampala, Uganda (for Central and Eastern Africa), and Dakar, Senegal (for West Africa).

Executive Director: JOSETTE SHEERAN (USA).

Activities

WFP is the only multilateral organization with a mandate to use food assistance as a resource. It is the second largest source of assistance in the UN, after the World Bank group, in terms of actual transfers of resources, and the largest source of grant aid in the UN system. WFP handles more than one-third of the world's food assistance. WFP is also the largest contributor to South–South trade within the UN system, through the purchase of food and services from developing countries (at least three-quarters of the food purchased by the Programme originates in developing countries). WFP's mission is to provide food assistance to save lives in refugee and other emergency situations, to improve the nutrition and quality of life of vulnerable groups and to help to develop assets and promote the self-reliance of poor families and communities. WFP aims to focus its efforts on the world's poorest countries and to provide at least 90% of its total assistance to those designated as 'low-income food-deficit'. At the World Food Summit, held in November 1996, WFP endorsed the commitment to reduce by 50% the number of undernourished people, no later than 2015. During 2010 WFP food assistance, distributed through development projects, emergency operations (EMOPs) and protracted relief and recovery operations (PRROs), benefited some 109.2m. people, including 89m. women and children, and 15.4m. IDPs, in 75 countries. Total food deliveries in 2010 amounted to 4.6m. metric tons.

WFP rations comprise basic food items (staple foods such as wheat flour or rice; pulses such as lentils and chickpeas; vegetable oil fortified with vitamins A and D; sugar; and iodized salt). Where possible basic rations are complemented with special products designed to improve the nutritional intake of beneficiaries. These include fortified blended foods, principally 'Corn Soya Blend', containing important micronutrients; ready-to-use foods, principally peanut-based pastes enriched with vitamins and minerals trademarked as 'Plumpy Doz' and 'Supplementary Plumpy', which are better suited to meeting the nutritional needs of young and moderately malnourished children; high energy biscuits, distributed in the first phases of emergencies when cooking facilities may be scarce; micronutrient powder ('sprinkles'), which can be used to fortify home cooking; and compressed food bars, given out during disaster relief operations when the distribution and preparation of local food is not possible. The Programme's food donations must meet internationally agreed standards applicable to trade in food products. In May 2003 WFP's Executive Board approved a policy on donations of genetically modified (GM) foods and other foods derived from biotechnology, determining that the Programme would continue to accept donations of GM/biotech food and that, when distributing it, relevant national standards would be respected. It is WFP policy to buy food as near to where it is needed as possible, with a view to saving on transport costs and helping to sustain local economies. From 2008 targeted cash and voucher schemes started to be implemented, as a possible alternative to food rations (see below). During 2011 WFP and several corporate partners started to implement pilot schemes in targeted areas in Bangladesh and Indonesia under a new Project Laser Beam (PLB) initiative, aimed at addressing child malnutrition.

WFP aims to address the causes of chronic malnourishment, which it identifies as poverty and lack of opportunity. It emphasizes the role played by women (who are most likely to sow, reap, harvest and cook household food) in combating hunger, and endeavours to address the specific nutritional needs of women, to increase their access to food and development resources, and to promote girls' education. WFP estimates that females represent four-fifths of people engaged in farming in Africa and three-fifths of people engaged in farming in Asia, and that globally women are the sole breadwinners in one-third of households. Increasingly WFP distributes food assistance through women, believing that vulnerable children are more likely to be reached in this way. In September 2011 WFP and UN Women announced an agreement to provide income generating opportunities for women in rural areas. The Programme also focuses resources on supporting the nutrition and food security of households and communities affected by HIV/AIDS, and on promoting food security as a means of mitigating extreme poverty and vulnerability and thereby combating the spread and impact of HIV/AIDS. In February 2003 WFP and the Joint UN Programme on HIV/AIDS (UNAIDS) concluded an agreement to address jointly the relationship between HIV/AIDS, regional food shortages and chronic hunger, with a particular focus on Africa, Southeast Asia and the Caribbean. In October of that year WFP became a co-sponsor of UNAIDS. WFP also urges the development of new food assistance strategies as a means of redressing global inequalities and thereby combating the threat of conflict and international terrorism.

WFP is a participant in the High Level Task Force (HLTF) on the Global Food Security Crisis, which was established by the UN Secretary-General in April 2008, with the aim of addressing the global impact of soaring levels of food and commodity prices, and of formulating a comprehensive framework for action. WFP participated in the High-Level Conference on World Food Security and the Challenges of Climate Change and Bioenergy that was convened by FAO in June. At that time WFP determined to allocate some US $1,200m. in extra-budgetary funds to alleviate hunger in the worst-affected countries. In January 2009 the HLTF participated in a follow-up high-level meeting convened in Madrid, Spain, and attended also by 62 government ministers and representatives from 126 countries. The meeting agreed to initiate a consultation process with regard to the establishment of a Global Partnership for Agriculture, Food Security and Nutrition. WFP participated in a World Summit on Food Security, organized by FAO, in Rome, in November 2009, with the aim of securing greater coherence in the global governance of food security and setting a 'new world food order'.

In June 2008 WFP's Executive Board approved a four-year strategic plan, covering the period 2008–11, that shifted the focus of WFP's activities from the supply of food aid to the supply of food assistance, and aimed to provide a new institutional framework to support vulnerable populations affected by the ongoing global food crisis and by possible future effects of global climate change. The five principal objectives of the 2008–11 plan were: saving lives and protecting livelihoods in emergencies; preparing for emergencies; restoring and rebuilding lives after emergencies; reducing chronic hunger and undernutrition everywhere; and strengthening the capacity of countries to reduce hunger. The plan emphasized prevention of hunger through early warning systems and analysis; local purchase of food; the maintenance of efficient and effective emergency response systems; and the use of focused cash and voucher programmes (including electronic vouchers) to ensure the accessibility to vulnerable people in urban environments of food that was locally available but, owing to the high level of market prices and increasing unemployment, beyond their financial means. It was envisaged that the cash and voucher approach would reduce the cost to WFP of transporting and storing food supplies, and would also benefit local economies (both being long-term WFP policy objectives). Some 2.9m. people were assisted through cash and voucher programmes during 2010.

WFP has developed a range of mechanisms to enhance its preparedness for emergency situations (such as conflict, drought and other natural disasters) and to improve its capacity for responding effectively to crises as they arise. Through its Vulnerability Analysis and Mapping (VAM) project, WFP aims to identify potentially vulnerable groups by providing information on food security and the capacity of different groups for coping with shortages, and to enhance emergency contingency-planning and long-term assistance objectives. VAM produces food security analysis reports, guidelines, reference documents and maps. In 2009 VAM field units were operational in 43 countries world-wide. The key elements of WFP's emergency response capacity are its strategic stores of food and logistics equipment (drawn from 'stocks afloat': ships loaded with WFP food supplies that can be re-routed to assist in crisis situations; development project stocks redesignated as emergency project contingency reserves; and in-country borrowing from national food reserves enabled by bilateral agreements); stand-by arrangements to enable the rapid deployment of personnel, communications and other essential equipment; and the Augmented Logistics Intervention Team for Emergencies (ALITE), which undertakes capacity assessments and contingency-planning. When engaging in a crisis WFP dispatches an emergency preparedness team to quantify the amount and type of food assistance required, and to identify the beneficiaries of and the timescale and logistics (e.g. means of transportation; location of humanitarian corridors, if necessary; and designated food distribution sites, such as refugee camps, other emergency shelters and therapeutic feeding centres) underpinning the ensuing EMOP. Once the EMOP has been drafted, WFP launches an appeal to the international donor community for funds and assistance to enable its implementation. WFP special operations are short-term logistics and infrastructure projects that are undertaken to facilitate the movement of food aid, regardless of whether the food is provided by the Agency itself. Special operations typically complement EMOPs or longer rehabilitation projects.

During 2000 WFP led efforts, undertaken with other UN humanitarian agencies, for the design and application of local UN Joint Logistics Centre facilities, which aimed to co-ordinate resources in an emergency situation. In 2001 a UN Humanitarian Response Depot was opened in Brindisi, Italy, under the direction of WFP experts, for the storage of essential rapid response equipment. In that year the Programme published a set of guidelines on contingency planning. Since 2003 WFP has been mandated to provide aviation transport services to the wider humanitarian community. During 2005 the UN's Inter-Agency Standing Committee (IASC), concerned with co-ordinating the international response to humanitarian disasters, developed a concept of organizing agency assistance to IDPs through the institutionalization of a 'Cluster Approach', currently comprising 11 core areas of activity. WFP was designated the lead agency for the clusters on Emergency Telecommunications (jointly with OCHA and UNICEF) and Logistics. During January 2008–June 2009 WFP implemented a special operation to improve country-specific communications services in order to enhance country-level cluster capacities. A review of the humanitarian cluster approach, undertaken during 2010, concluded that a new cluster on Food Security should be established. The new cluster, established accordingly in 2011, is led jointly by WFP and FAO, and aims to combine expertise in food aid and agricultural assistance in order to boost food security and to improve the resilience of food-insecure disaster-affected communities.

WFP aims to link its relief and development activities to provide a continuum between short-term relief and longer-term rehabilitation and development. In order to achieve this objective, WFP aims to promote capacity-building elements within relief operations, e.g. training, income-generating activities and environmental protection measures; and to integrate elements that strengthen disaster mitigation into development projects, including soil conservation, reafforestation, irrigation infrastructure, and transport construction and rehabilitation. In all its projects WFP aims to assist the most vulnerable groups (such as nursing mothers and children) and to ensure that beneficiaries have an adequate and balanced diet. Through its development activities, WFP aims to alleviate poverty in developing countries by promoting self-reliant families and communities. No individual country is permitted to receive more than 10% of the Programme's available development resources. WFP's Food-for-Assets development operations pay workers living in poverty with food in return for participation in self-help schemes and labour-intensive projects, with the aim of enabling vulnerable households and communities to focus time and resources on investing in lasting assets with which to raise themselves out of poverty (rather than on day-to-day survival). Food-for-Assets projects provide training in new techniques for achieving improved food security (such as training in new agricultural skills or in the establishment of home gardening businesses); and include, for example, building new irrigation or terracing infrastructures; soil and water conservation activities; and allocating food rations to villagers to enable them to devote time to building schools and clinics. In areas undermined by conflict WFP offers food assistance as an incentive for former combatants to put down their weapons and learn new skills. WFP focuses on providing good nutrition for the *first 1,000 days of life*, from the womb to two years of age, in order to lay the foundations for a healthy childhood and adulthood. WFP's *1,000 days plus* approach supports children over the age of two through school feeding activities, which aim to expand educational opportunities for poor children (given that it is difficult for children to concentrate on studies without adequate food and nutrition, and that food-insecure households frequently have to choose between educating their children or making them work to help the family to survive), and to improve the quality of the teaching environment. During 2010 school feeding projects benefited 21.1m. children. As an incentive to promote the education of vulnerable children, including orphans and children with HIV/AIDS, and to encourage families to send their daughters to school, WFP also implements 'take-home ration' projects, under which it provides basic food items to certain households, usually including sacks of rice and cans of cooking oil. WFP's Purchase for Progress (P4P) programme, launched in September 2008, expands the Programme's long-term 'local procurement' policy, enabling smallholder and low-income farmers in developing countries to supply food to WFP's global assistance operations. Under P4P farmers are taught techniques and provided with tools to enable them to compete competitively in the market-place. P4P also aims to identify and test specific successful local practices that could be replicated to benefit small-scale farmers on a wider scale. During 2008–13 P4P initiatives were being piloted in 21 countries, in Africa, Latin America and Asia. By 2011 WFP had established links under P4P with 630 farmers' organizations representing 800,000 farmers world-wide.

Since 1999 WFP has been implementing PRROs, where the emphasis is on fostering stability, rehabilitation and long-term development for victims of natural disasters, displaced persons and refugees. PRROs are introduced no later than 18 months after the initial EMOP and last no more than three years. When undertaken in collaboration with UNHCR and other international agencies, WFP has responsibility for mobilizing basic food commodities and for related transport, handling and storage costs.

In 2009 WFP operational expenditure in Asia amounted to US $763.4m. (19.2% of total operational expenditure in that year), including $650.8m. for emergency relief operations, $27.0m. for special operations, and $77.3m. for agricultural, rural and human resource development projects. During 2008–13 WFP's new P4P programme (see above) was being piloted in Afghanistan and Laos.

The food situation in the Democratic People's Republic of Korea (DPRK) has required substantial levels of emergency food supplies in recent years, owing to natural disasters and consistently poor harvests. During 1995–99 an estimated 1.5m.–3.5m. people died of starvation in the DPRK. In August 2005 the DPRK Government requested WFP to shift its focus from emergency relief to development activities and consequently, in February 2006, WFP approved a US $102.2m. PRRO for the DPRK, covering the period 1 April 2006–31 March 2008, which followed on from 10 successive emergency operations that had hitherto achieved some progress in reducing rates of malnutrition in that country. The two-year PRRO aimed to provide 150,000 metric tons of food aid to 1.9m. people, and to support the Government's strategy to achieve long-term food security. The operation provided for the distribution to young children and women of child-bearing age of vitamin- and mineral-enriched domestically produced foods, and for the allocation of cereal rations to under-employed communities with a view to enabling them to build and rehabilitate agricultural and other community assets. A short-term emergency operation to assist 215,000 people affected by floods that struck the DPRK in August 2007 was implemented during August–November of that year. In June 2008 a WFP/FAO Rapid Food Security Assessment of the DPRK found that access to food had deteriorated significantly since 2007, particularly for urban households in areas of low industrial activity, who had been severely affected by rising food and fuel prices, reductions in food rationing and decreasing rates of employment. WFP subsequently approved a $503.6m. EMOP covering the period 1 September 2008–30 November 2009 (later extended to June 2010), which aimed to target assistance at food-insecure populations through mother and child nutrition activities; food assistance to schools, elderly people and other vulnerable groups; and food for community development activities. WFP stated that comprehensive interventions were required to improve agricultural production in the DPRK, and that, conditions permitting, humanitarian assistance would be reduced following the expiry of the emergency operation and the long-term development approach pursued under the 2006–08 PRRO would be resumed. Accordingly, in June 2010, a new PRRO was approved, covering the two-year period until June 2012, which was to target 157,047 metric tons of nutrition support at women and children, at a total cost to WFP of $96m. In view of worsening food insecurity caused by high rainfall in 2010 and a harsh winter over 2010–11, the DPRK Government made a formal appeal to WFP in January 2011 requesting emergency food assistance. WFP, FAO and UNICEF conducted an inter-agency rapid food security assessment of the country during February–March. WFP initiated an EMOP covering 1 April 2011–31 March 2012, which aimed to support some 3.5m. vulnerable people (mainly women and children), incorporating and expanding activities launched under the PRRO initiated in June 2010. The PRRO was suspended, to be renewed following the completion of the EMOP.

A PRRO to improve the food security, nutrition status and livelihoods of vulnerable populations in Myanmar (targeting 2.0m. individuals), at a cost of US $121.8m., was being implemented during the three-year period 1 January 2010–31 December 2012. In late September 2007 WFP urged the Myanmar authorities to ease restrictions on the movement of food supplies that had been imposed owing to unrest in that country, as these were inhibiting WFP's implementation of its relief activities; assurances were reportedly received from the Myanmar regime at the end of that month that WFP would be permitted to undertake its scheduled food deliveries. In October WFP urged the Myanmar authorities to pursue critical social and economic reforms aimed at reducing poverty and hunger in that country, stating that international humanitarian assistance could not meet all the requirements of the Myanma population. An EMOP was undertaken during May–November 2008 to provide food assistance to 750,000 people in Myanmar, in response to the devastation caused by Cyclone Nargis in early May to domestic food stocks, livestock, crops, shrimp farms, fishing ponds, fish hatcheries, fishing boats and other food production assets.

An EMOP to provide food assistance to 1.6m. people whose livelihoods had been affected by long-term conflict in Mindanao, Philippines, was implemented over the period 1 June 2008–31 May 2009. From late September 2009 a series of typhoons resulted in extensive flooding in the Philippines, causing serious damage in the capital city, Manila, and in Luzon, the country's main rice-producing region. In response, WFP launched a US $57m. relief operation, which targeted assistance at more than 1m. people. Owing to further heavy rains, flooding and landslides in 2010–11 the operation was extended. In October 2011 WFP provided immediate food assistance (including High Energy Biscuits) to communities in northern Luzon whose lands were flooded by Typhoon Nesat. During 1 July 2010–31 December 2011 WFP was implementing a development programme in Laos aimed at addressing malnutrition in mothers and children; and development programmes supporting primary education in remote areas, and assisting food-insecure households were also under way in 2011. In June 2011 WFP approved a country programme for Cambodia covering the period 2011–16, aimed at improving food security. In September 2008 a PRRO was approved to assist on average 255,600 vulnerable people in Timor-Leste per year over the two-year period 1 September 2008–31 August 2010; this was subsequently extended until August 2011.

Finance

The Programme is funded by voluntary contributions from donor countries, intergovernmental bodies such as the European Commission, and the private sector. Contributions are made in the form of commodities, finance and services (particularly shipping). Commitments to the International Emergency Food Reserve (IEFR), from which WFP provides the majority of its food supplies, and to the Immediate Response Account of the IEFR (IRA), are also made on a voluntary basis by donors. WFP's operational expenditures in 2010 amounted to some US $4,000.3m. Contributions by donors in that year totalled $3,810.3m.

Publications

Annual Report.

Food and Nutrition Handbook.

School Feeding Handbook.

World Hunger Series.

Food and Agriculture Organization of the United Nations—FAO

Address: Viale delle Terme di Caracalla, 00100 Rome, Italy.

Telephone: (06) 5705-1; **fax:** (06) 5705-3152; **e-mail:** fao-hq@fao.org; **internet:** www.fao.org.

FAO, the first specialized agency of the UN to be founded after the Second World War, aims to alleviate malnutrition and hunger, and serves as a co-ordinating agency for development programmes in the whole range of food and agriculture, including forestry and fisheries. It helps developing countries to promote educational and training facilities and to create appropriate institutions.

Organization

(October 2011)

CONFERENCE

The governing body is the FAO Conference of member nations. It meets every two years, formulates policy, determines the organization's programme and budget on a biennial basis, and elects new members. It also elects the Director-General of the Secretariat and the Independent Chairman of the Council. Regional conferences are also held each year.

COUNCIL

The FAO Council is composed of representatives of 49 member nations, elected by the Conference for rotating three-year terms. It is the interim governing body of FAO between sessions of the Conference. There are eight main Governing Committees of the Council: the Finance and Programme Committees, and the Committees on Commodity Problems, Fisheries, Agriculture, Forestry, World Food Security, and Constitutional and Legal Matters.

SECRETARIAT

There are some 3,600 FAO staff, of whom about one-half are based at headquarters. FAO maintains five regional offices (see below), nine sub-regional offices, five liaison offices (in Yokohama, Japan; Washington, DC, USA, liaison with North America; Geneva, Switzerland and New York, USA, with the UN; and Brussels, Belgium, with the European Union), and some 74 country offices. Work is undertaken by the following departments: Agriculture and Consumer Protection; Economic and Social Development; Fisheries and Aquaculture; Forestry; Human, Financial and Physical Resources; Knowledge and Communication; Natural Resource Management and Environment; and Technical Co-operation.

Director-General: Jacques Diouf (Senegal) (until 31 December 2011), Dr José Graziano da Silva (Brazil) (designate).

REGIONAL OFFICES

Asia and the Pacific: Maliwan Mansion, 39 Phra Atit Rd, Bangkok 10200, Thailand; tel. (2) 697-4000; fax (2) 697-4445; e-mail fao-rap@fao.org; internet www.fao.org/world/regional/rap; Regional Rep. Hiroyuki Konuma.

Sub-regional Office for the Pacific Islands: Private Mail Bag, Apia, Samoa; tel. 22127; fax 22126; e-mail fao-sapa@fao.org; internet www.fao.org/world/subRegional/SAPA/default_en.htm; Sub-regional Rep. Vili Fuavao.

Activities

FAO aims to raise levels of nutrition and standards of living by improving the production and distribution of food and other commodities derived from farms, fisheries and forests. FAO's ultimate objective is the achievement of world food security, 'Food for All'. The organization provides technical information, advice and assistance by disseminating information; acting as a neutral forum for discussion of food and agricultural issues; advising governments on policy and planning; and developing capacity directly in the field.

In November 1996 FAO hosted the World Food Summit, which was held in Rome and was attended by heads of state and senior government representatives of 186 countries. Participants approved the Rome Declaration on World Food Security and the World Food Summit Plan of Action, with the aim of halving the number of people afflicted by undernutrition, then estimated to total 828m. worldwide, by no later than 2015. A review conference to assess progress in achieving the goals of the summit, entitled World Food Summit: Five Years Later, held in June 2002, reaffirmed commitment to this objective, which is also incorporated into the UN Millennium Development Goals (MDGs). During that month FAO announced the formulation of a global 'Anti-Hunger Programme', which aimed to promote investment in the agricultural sector and rural development, with a particular focus on small-scale farmers, and to enhance food access for those most in need, for example through the provision of school meals, schemes to feed pregnant and nursing mothers and food-for-work programmes. FAO hosts the UN System Network on Rural Development and Food Security, comprising some 20 UN bodies, which was established in 1997 as an inter-agency mechanism to follow-up the World Food Summits.

In November 1999 the FAO Conference approved a long-term Strategic Framework for the period 2000–15, which emphasized national and international co-operation in pursuing the goals of the 1996 World Food Summit. The Framework promoted interdisciplinarity and partnership, and defined three main global objectives: constant access by all people to sufficient, nutritionally adequate and safe food to ensure that levels of undernourishment were reduced by 50% by 2015 (see above); the continued contribution of sustainable agriculture and rural development to economic and social progress and well-being; and the conservation, improvement and sustainable use of natural resources. It identified five corporate strategies (each supported by several strategic objectives), covering the following areas: reducing food insecurity and rural poverty; ensuring enabling policy and regulatory frameworks for food, agriculture, fisheries and forestry; creating sustainable increases in the supply and availability of agricultural, fisheries and forestry products; conserving and enhancing sustainable use of the natural resource base; and generating knowledge. In October 2007 the report of an Independent External Evaluation (IEE) into the role and functions of FAO recommended that the organization elaborate a plan for reform to ensure its continued efficiency and effectiveness. In November 2008 a Special Conference of member countries approved a three-year Immediate Plan of Action to reform the governance and management of the organization based on the recommendations of the IEE.

In December 2007 FAO inaugurated an Initiative on Soaring Food Prices (ISFP) to help to boost food production in low-income developing countries and improve access to food and agricultural supplies in the short term, with a view to countering an escalation since 2006 in commodity prices. (During 2006–08 the Food Price Index maintained by FAO recorded that international prices for many basic food commodities had increased by around 60%, and the FAO Cereal Price Index, covering the prices of principal food staples such as wheat, rice and maize, recorded a doubling in the international price of grains over that period.) In April 2008 the UN Secretary-General appointed FAO's Director-General as Vice-Chairman of a High Level Task Force (HLTF) on the Global Food Security Crisis, which aimed to address the impact of the ongoing soaring levels of food and fuel prices and formulate a comprehensive framework for action. In June FAO hosted a High Level Conference on World Food Security and the Challenges of Climate Change and Bioenergy. The meeting adopted a Declaration on Food Security, urging the international donor community to increase its support to developing countries and countries with economies in transition. The Declaration also noted an urgent need to develop the agricultural sectors and expand food production in such countries and for increased investment in rural development, agriculture and agribusiness. In January 2009 a follow-up high level meeting was convened in Madrid, Spain, and attended by 62 government ministers and representatives from 126 countries. The meeting agreed to initiate a consultation process with regard to the establishment of a Global Partnership for Agriculture, Food Security and Nutrition to strengthen international co-ordination and governance for food security. FAO's long-standing Committee on World Food Security (CFS) underwent reform in 2009; henceforth the Committee was to be a central component of the new Global Partnership, and was to influence hunger elimination programmes at global, regional and national level, taking into account that food security relates not just to agriculture but also to economic access to food, adequate nutrition, social safety nets and human rights.

In May 2009 the European Union donated €106m. to FAO, to support farmers and improve food security in 10 developing countries in Africa, Asia and the Caribbean that were particularly badly affected by the recently emerged global food crisis. Addressing the World Grain Forum, convened in St Petersburg, Russia, in June 2009, the FAO Director-General demanded a more effective and coherent global governance system to ensure future world food security, and urged that a larger proportion of development aid should be allocated to agriculture, to enable developing countries to invest in rural infrastructures. During June it was estimated that, in 2009, the number of people world-wide suffering chronic, daily hunger had risen to an unprecedented 1,020m., of whom an estimated 642m. were in Asia and the Pacific; 265m. in sub-Saharan Africa; 53m. in Latin America and the Caribbean; and 42m. in the Middle East and North Africa. Around 15m. people resident in developed countries were estimated at that time to be afflicted by chronic hunger. The *OECD-FAO Agricultural Outlook 2009–18*, issued in June 2009, found the global agriculture sector to be showing more resilience to the ongoing world-wide economic crisis than other sectors, owing to the status of food as a basic human necessity. However, the report warned that the state of the agriculture sector could become more fragile if the ongoing global downturn were to worsen. In July the FAO Director-General welcomed the L'Aquila Joint Statement on Global Food Security (promoting sustainable agricultural development), and the Food Security Initiative with commitments of US $20,000m., that were approved in that month by G8 leaders.

In mid-October 2009 a high-level forum of experts was convened by FAO to discuss policy on the theme 'How to Feed the World in 2050'. In November 2009 FAO organized a World Summit on Food Security, in Rome, with the aim of achieving greater coherence in the global governance of food security and setting a 'new world food order'. Leaders attending the Summit issued a declaration in which they adopted a number of strategic objectives, including: ensuring urgent action towards achieving World Food Summit objectives/the UN MDG relating to reducing undernutrition; promoting the new Global Partnership for Agriculture, Food Security and Nutrition and fully committing to reform of the CFS; reversing the decline in national and international funding for agriculture, food security and rural development in developing countries, and encouraging new investment to increase sustainable agricultural production; reducing poverty and working towards achieving food security and access to 'Food for All'; and confronting proactively the challenges posed by climate change to food security. The Summit determined to base its pursuit of these strategic objectives on the following *Five Rome Principles for Sustainable Global Food Security*: (i) investment in country-owned plans aimed at channelling resources to efficient results-based programmes and partnerships; (ii) fostering strategic co-ordination at national, regional and global level to improve governance, promote better allocation of resources, avoid duplication of efforts and identify response gaps; (iii) striving for a comprehensive twin-track approach to food security comprising direct action to combat hunger in the most vulnerable, and also medium- and long-term sustainable agricultural, food security, nutrition and rural development programmes to eliminate the root causes of hunger and poverty, including through the progressive realization of the right to adequate food; (iv) ensuring a strong role for the multilateral system by sustained improvements in efficiency, responsiveness, co-ordination and effectiveness of multilateral institutions; and (v) ensuring sustained and substantial commitment by all partners to investment in agriculture and food security and nutrition, with provision of necessary resources in a timely and reliable fashion, aimed at multi-year plans and programmes.

With other UN agencies, FAO attended the Summit of the World's Regions on Food Insecurity, held in Dakar, Senegal, in January 2010. The summit urged that global governance of food security should integrate players on every level, and expressed support for the developing Global Partnership for Agriculture, Food Security and Nutrition.

In February 2011 the FAO Food Price Index recorded the highest levels of global food prices since 1990, with prices having risen in each consecutive month during July 2010–February 2011 (and having, in December 2010, exceeded the previous peak reached during mid-2008). The Cereal Price Index also recorded in February 2011 the highest price levels since mid-2008. FAO maintains, additionally, a Dairy Price Index, an Oils/Fats Price Index, a Meat Price Index and a Sugar Price Index.

World Food Day, commemorating the foundation of FAO, is held annually on 16 October. In May 2010 FAO launched an online petition entitled the *1billionhungry project*, with the aim of raising awareness of the plight of people world-wide suffering from chronic hunger.

AGRICULTURE AND CONSUMER PROTECTION

FAO's overall objective is to lead international efforts to counter hunger and to improve levels of nutrition. Within this context FAO is concerned to improve crop and grassland productivity and to develop sustainable agricultural systems to provide for enhanced food security and economic development. It provides member countries with technical advice for plant improvement, the application of plant biotechnology, the development of integrated production systems and rational grassland management. There are groups concerned with the main field cereal crops, i.e. rice, maize and wheat, which *inter alia* identify means of enhancing production, collect and analyse relevant data and promote collaboration between research institutions, government bodies and other farm management organizations. In 1985 and 1990 FAO's International Rice Commission endorsed the use of hybrid rice, which had been developed in the People's Republic of China, as a means of meeting growing demand for the crop, in particular in the Far East, and has subsequently assisted member countries to acquire the necessary technology and training to develop hybrid rice production. In Africa FAO has collaborated with the West African Rice Development Association to promote and facilitate the use of new rice varieties and crop management practices. FAO actively promotes the concept of Conservation Agriculture, which aims to minimize the need for mechanical soil tillage or additional farming resources and to reduce soil degradation and erosion.

FAO is also concerned with the development and diversification of horticultural and industrial crops, for example oil seeds, fibres and medicinal plants. FAO collects and disseminates data regarding crop trials and new technologies. It has developed an information processing site, Ecocrop, to help farmers identify appropriate crops and environmental requirements. FAO works to protect and support the sustainable development of grasslands and pasture, which contribute to the livelihoods of an estimated 800m. people world-wide.

FAO's plant protection service incorporates a range of programmes concerned with the control of pests and the use of pesticides. In February 2001 FAO warned that some 30% of pesticides sold in developing countries did not meet internationally accepted quality standards. In November 2002 FAO adopted a revised International Code of Conduct on the Distribution and Use of Pesticides (first adopted in 1985) to reduce the inappropriate distribution and use of pesticides and other toxic compounds, particularly in developing countries. In September 1998 a new legally binding treaty on trade in hazardous chemicals and pesticides was adopted at an international conference held in Rotterdam, Netherlands. The so-called Rotterdam Convention required that hazardous chemicals and pesticides banned or severely restricted in at least two countries should not be exported unless explicitly agreed by the importing country. It also identified certain pesticide formulations as too dangerous to be used by farmers in developing countries, and incorporated an obligation that countries halt national production of those hazardous compounds. The treaty entered into force in February 2004. FAO was co-operating with UNEP to provide an interim secretariat for the Convention. FAO has promoted the use of Integrated Pest Management (IPM) initiatives to encourage the use, at local level, of safer and more effective methods of pest control, such as biological control methods and natural predators.

FAO hosts the secretariat of the International Plant Protection Convention (first adopted in 1951, revised in 1997) which aims to prevent the spread of plant pests and to promote effective control measures. The secretariat helps to define phytosanitary standards, promote the exchange of information and extend technical assistance to contracting parties (177 at October 2011).

FAO is concerned with the conservation and sustainable use of plant and animal genetic resources. It works with regional and international associations to develop seed networks, to encourage the use of improved seed production systems, to elaborate quality control and certification mechanisms and to co-ordinate seed security activities, in particular in areas prone to natural or man-made disasters. FAO has developed a World Information and Early Warning System (WIEWS) to gather and disseminate information concerning plant genetic resources for food and agriculture and to undertake periodic assessments of the state of those resources. FAO is also developing, as part of the WIEWS, a Seed Information Service to extend information to member states on seeds, planting and new technologies. In June 1996 representatives of more than 150 governments convened in Leipzig, Germany, at an International Technical Conference organized by FAO to consider the use and conservation of plant genetic resources as an essential means of enhancing food security. The meeting adopted a Global Plan of Action, which included measures to strengthen the development of plant varieties and to promote the use and availability of local varieties and locally adapted crops to farmers, in particular following a natural disaster, war or civil conflict. In November 2001 the FAO Conference adopted the International Treaty on Plant Genetic Resources for Food and Agriculture (also referred to as the Seed Treaty), with the aim of providing a framework to ensure access to plant genetic resources and to related knowledge, technologies, and—through the Treaty's Benefit-sharing Fund (BSF)—funding. The Seed Treaty entered into force in June 2004, having received the required number of ratifications, and, by October 2011, had 127 states parties. The BSF assists poor farmers in developing countries with conserving, and also adapting to climate change, their most important food crops; in 2011 the Fund was supporting 11 high-impact projects for small-scale farmers in four regions. It was hoped that international donors would raise US $116m. for the BSF by 2014. By end-2010 some 1,750 gene banks had been established world-wide, storing more than 7m. plant samples.

FAO's Animal Production and Health Division is concerned with the control and management of major animal diseases, and, in recent years, with safeguarding humans from livestock diseases. Other programmes are concerned with the contribution of livestock to poverty alleviation, the efficient use of natural resources in livestock production, the management of animal genetic resources, promoting the exchange of information and mapping the distribution of livestock around the world. In 2001 FAO established a Pro-Poor Livestock Policy Initiative to support the formulation and implementation of livestock-related policies to improve the livelihood and nutrition of the world's rural poor, with an initial focus on the Andean region, the Horn of Africa, West Africa, South Asia and the Mekong.

The Emergency Prevention System for Transboundary Animal and Plant Pests and Diseases (EMPRES) was established in 1994 to strengthen FAO's activities in the prevention, early warning, control and, where possible, eradication of pests and highly contagious livestock diseases (which the system categorizes as epidemic diseases of strategic importance, such as rinderpest or foot-and-mouth; diseases requiring tactical attention at international or regional level, e.g. Rift Valley fever; and emerging diseases, e.g. bovine spongiform encephalopathy—BSE). EMPRES has a desert locust component, and has published guidelines on all aspects of desert locust monitoring. FAO assumed responsibility for technical leadership and co-ordination of the Global Rinderpest Eradication Programme (GREP), which had the objective of eliminating that disease by 2011; in June 2011 the FAO Conference adopted a resolution declaring global freedom from rinderpest. In November 1997 FAO initiated a Programme Against African Trypanosomiasis, which aimed to counter the disease affecting cattle in almost one-third of Africa. In November 2004 FAO established a specialized Emergency Centre for Transboundary Animal Disease Operations (ECTAD) to enhance FAO's role in assisting member states to combat animal disease outbreaks and in co-ordinating international efforts to research, monitor and control transboundary disease crises. In May 2004 FAO and the World Organisation for Animal Health (OIE) signed an agreement to clarify their respective areas of competence and improve co-operation, in response to an increase in contagious transboundary animal diseases (such as foot-and-mouth disease and avian influenza, see below). The two bodies agreed to establish a global framework on the control of transboundary animal diseases, entailing improved international collaboration and circulation of information. In early 2006 FAO, OIE and the World Health Organization (WHO) agreed on the establishment of a Global Early Warning and Response System for Major Animal Diseases, including Zoonoses (GLEWS), in order to strengthen their joint capacity to detect, monitor and respond to animal disease threats. In October 2006 FAO inaugurated a new Crisis Management Centre (CMC) to co-ordinate (in close co-operation with OIE) the organization's response to outbreaks of H5N1 and other major emergencies related to animal or food health.

In September 2004 FAO and WHO declared an ongoing epidemic in certain east Asian countries of the H5N1 strain of highly pathogenic avian influenza (HPAI) to be a 'crisis of global importance': the disease was spreading rapidly through bird populations and was also transmitting to human populations through contact with diseased birds (mainly poultry). In that month FAO published *Recommendations for the Prevention, Control and Eradication of Highly Pathogenic Avian Influenza in Asia*. In April 2005 FAO and OIE established an international network of laboratories and scientists (OFFLU) to exchange data and provide expert technical advice on avian influenza. In the following month FAO, with WHO and OIE, launched a global strategy for the progressive control of the disease. In November a conference on Avian Influenza and Human Pandemic Influenza, jointly organized by FAO, WHO and OIE and the World Bank, issued a plan of action identifying a number of responses, including: supporting the development of integrated national plans for H5N1 containment and human pandemic influenza preparedness and response; assisting countries with the aggressive control of H5N1 and with establishing a more detailed understanding of the role of wild birds in virus transmission; nominating rapid response teams of experts to support epidemiological field investigations; expanding national and regional capacity in surveillance, diagnosis, and alert and response systems; expanding the network of influenza laboratories; establishing multi-country networks for the control or prevention of animal transboundary diseases; expanding the global antiviral stockpile; strengthening veterinary infrastructures; and mapping a global strategy and work plan for co-ordinating antiviral and influenza vaccine research and development. In June 2006 FAO and OIE convened a scientific conference on the spread of H5N1 that advocated as a basis for H5N1 management early detection of the disease in wild birds, improved biosecurity and hygiene in the poultry trade, rapid response to disease outbreaks, and the establishment of a global tracking and monitoring facility involving participation by all relevant organizations, as well as by scientific centres, farmers' groupings, bird-watchers and hunters, and wildlife and wild bird habitat conservation bodies. The conference also urged investment in telemetry/satellite technology to improve tracking capabilities. International conference and pledging meetings on the disease were convened in Washington, DC, USA, in October 2005, Beijing, People's Republic of China (PRC), in January 2006, Bamako, Mali, in December and in New Delhi, India, in December 2007. In August 2008 a new strain of HPAI not previously recorded in sub-Saharan Africa was detected in Nigeria. In October the sixth international ministerial conference on avian influenza was convened in Sharm el-Sheikh, Egypt. FAO, with WHO, UNICEF, OIE, the World Bank and the UN System Influenza Co-ordinator, presented a new strategic framework, within the concept of 'One World, One Health',

to improve understanding and co-operation with respect to emerging infectious diseases, to strengthen animal and public health surveillance and to enhance response mechanisms. During 2003–end-June 2011 outbreaks of H5N1 were recorded in 63 countries and territories, the most recent newly infected country being Bhutan, with cases reported in free-range chickens in Chhukha district in February 2010.

In April 2009, in response to a major outbreak in humans of the swine influenza variant pandemic (H1N1) 2009, the FAO Crisis Management Centre mobilized a team of experts to increase animal disease surveillance and maintain response readiness to protect the global pig sector from infection with the emerging virus. In early May FAO, OIE, WHO and WTO together issued a statement stressing that pork products handled in accordance with hygienic practices could not be deemed a source of infection

In December 1992 FAO, with WHO, organized an International Conference on Nutrition, which approved a World Declaration on Nutrition and a Plan of Action, aimed at promoting efforts to combat malnutrition as a development priority. Since the conference, more than 100 countries have formulated national plans of action for nutrition, many of which were based on existing development plans such as comprehensive food security initiatives, national poverty alleviation programmes and action plans to attain the targets set by the World Summit for Children in September 1990. FAO promotes other efforts, at household and community level, to improve nutrition and food security, for example a programme to support home gardens. It aims to assist the identification of food-insecure and vulnerable populations, both through its *State of Food Insecurity in the World* reports and taking a lead role in the development of Food Insecurity and Vulnerability Information and Mapping Systems (FIVIMS), a recommendation of the World Food Summit. In 1999 FAO signed a memorandum of understanding with UNAIDS on strengthening co-operation to combat the threat posed by the HIV/AIDS epidemic to food security, nutrition and rural livelihoods. FAO is committed to incorporating HIV/AIDS into food security and livelihood projects, to strengthening community care and to highlighting the importance of nutrition in the care of those living with HIV/AIDS.

FAO is committed to promoting food quality and safety in all different stages of food production and processing. It supports the development of integrated food control systems by member states, which incorporate aspects of food control management, inspection, risk analysis and quality assurance. The joint FAO/WHO Codex Alimentarius Commission, established in 1962, aims to protect the health of consumers, ensure fair trade practices and promote the co-ordination of food standards activities at an international level. In January 2001 a joint team of FAO and WHO experts issued a report concerning the allergenicity of foods derived from biotechnology (i.e. genetically modified—GM—foods). In July the Codex Alimentarius Commission agreed the first global principles for assessing the safety of GM foods, and approved a series of maximum levels of environmental contaminants in food. In June 2004 FAO published guidelines for assessing possible risks posed to plants by living modified organisms (LMOs). In July 2001 the Codex Alimentarius Commission adopted guidelines on organic livestock production, covering organic breeding methods, the elimination of growth hormones and certain chemicals in veterinary medicines, and the use of good quality organic feed with no meat or bone meal content. In January 2003 FAO organized a technical consultation on biological risk management in food and agriculture which recognized the need for a more integrated approach to so-called biosecurity, i.e. the prevention, control and management of risks to animal, human and plant life and health. FAO has subsequently developed a *Toolkit*, which was published in 2007, to help countries to develop and implement national biosecurity systems and to enhance biosecurity capacity.

FAO aims to assist member states to enhance the efficiency, competitiveness and profitability of their agricultural and food enterprises. FAO extends assistance in training, capacity-building and the formulation of agribusiness development strategies. It promotes the development of effective 'value chains' connecting primary producers with consumers and supports other linkages within the agribusiness industry. Similarly, FAO aims to strengthen marketing systems, links between producers and retailers and training in agricultural marketing, and works to improve the regulatory framework for agricultural marketing. FAO promotes the use of new machinery and technologies to increase agricultural production and extends a range of services to support mechanization, including training, maintenance, testing and the promotion of labour saving technologies. Other programmes are focused on farm management, post-harvest management, food and non-food processing, rural finance, and rural infrastructure. FAO helps reduce immediate post-harvest losses, with the introduction of improved processing methods and storage systems. FAO participates in PhAction, a forum of 12 agencies that was established in 1999 to promote post-harvest research and the development of effective post-harvest services and infrastructure.

FAO's Joint Division with the International Atomic Energy Agency (IAEA) is concerned with the use of nuclear techniques in food and agriculture. It co-ordinates research projects, provides scientific and technical support to technical co-operation projects and administers training courses. A joint laboratory in Seibersdorf, Austria, is concerned with testing biotechnologies and in developing non-toxic fertilizers (especially those that are locally available) and improved strains of food crops (especially from indigenous varieties). In the area of animal production and health, the Joint Division has developed progesterone-measuring and disease diagnostic kits. Other sub-programmes of the Joint Division are concerned with soil and water, plant breeding and nutrition, insect pest control and food and environmental protection.

In March 2011, in view of the severe damage suffered by the Fukushima Daiichi nuclear plant in Japan following an earthquake and tsunami, FAO, the IAEA and WHO issued a joint statement on food safety issues in the aftermath of the emergency, emphasizing their commitment to mobilizing knowledge and expertise in support of the Japanese authorities.

NATURAL RESOURCES MANAGEMENT AND ENVIRONMENT

FAO is committed to promoting the responsible and sustainable management of natural resources and other activities to protect the environment. FAO assists member states to mitigate the impact of climate change on agriculture, to adapt and enhance the resilience of agricultural systems to climate change, and to promote practices to reduce the emission of greenhouse gases from the agricultural sector. In recent years FAO has strengthened its work in the area of using natural biomass resources as fuel, both at grassroots level and industrial processing of cash crops. In 2006 FAO established the International Bioenergy Platform to serve as a focal point for research, data collection, capacity-building and strategy formulation by local, regional and international bodies concerned with bioenergy. FAO also serves as the secretariat for the Global Bioenergy Partnership, which was inaugurated in May 2006 to facilitate the collaboration between governments, international agencies and representatives of the private sector and civil society in the sustainable development of bioenergy.

FAO aims to enhance the sustainability of land and water systems, and as a result to secure agricultural productivity, through the improved tenure, management, development and conservation of those natural resources. The organization promotes equitable access to land and water resources and supports integrated land and water management, including river basin management and improved irrigation systems. FAO has developed AQUASTAT as a global information system concerned with water and agricultural issues, comprising databases, country and regional profiles, surveys and maps. AquaCrop, CropWat and ClimWat are further productivity models and databases which have been developed to help to assess crop requirements and potential yields. Since 2003 FAO has participated in UN Water, an inter-agency initiative to co-ordinate existing approaches to water-related issues. In December 2008 FAO organized a Ministerial Conference on Water for Agriculture and Energy in Africa: 'the Challenges of Climate Change', in Sirte, Libya, which was attended by representatives of 48 African member countries and other representatives of international, regional and civil organizations.

Within the FAO's Natural Resources Management and Environment Department is a Research and Extension Division, which provides advisory and technical services to support national capacity-building, research, communication and education activities. It maintains several databases which support and facilitate the dissemination of information, for example relating to proven transferable technologies and biotechnologies in use in developing countries. The Division advises countries on communication strategies to strengthen agricultural and rural development, and has actively supported the use of rural radio. FAO is the UN lead agency of an initiative, 'Education for Rural People', which aims to improve the quality of and access to basic education for people living in rural areas and to raise awareness of the issue as an essential element of achieving the MDGs. The Research and Extension Division hosts the secretariat of the Global Forum on Agricultural Research, which was established in October 1996 as a collaboration of research centres, non-governmental and private sector organizations and development agencies. The Forum aims to strengthen research and promote knowledge partnerships concerned with the alleviation of poverty, the increase in food security and the sustainable use of natural resources. The Division also hosts the secretariat of the Science Council of the Consultative Group on International Agricultural Research (CGIAR), which, specifically, aims to enhance and promote the quality, relevance and impact of science within the network of CGIAR research centres and to mobilize global scientific expertise.

In September 2009 FAO published, jointly with the Centre for Indigenous People's Nutrition and Environment (CINE—based in

McGill University, Montreal, Canada) a report entitled *Indigenous People's Food Systems: The Many Dimensions of Culture, Diversity and Environment for Nutrition and Health*, which aimed to demonstrate the wealth of knowledge on nutrition retained within indigenous communities world-wide.

FISHERIES AND AQUACULTURE

FAO aims to facilitate and secure the long-term sustainable development of fisheries and aquaculture, in both inland and marine waters, and to promote its contribution to world food security. In March 1995 a ministerial meeting of fisheries adopted the Rome Consensus on World Fisheries, which identified a need for immediate action to eliminate overfishing and to rebuild and enhance depleting fish stocks. In November the FAO Conference adopted a Code of Conduct for Responsible Fishing, which incorporated many global fisheries and aquaculture issues (including fisheries resource conservation and development, fish catches, seafood and fish processing, commercialization, trade and research) to promote the sustainable development of the sector. In February 1999 the FAO Committee on Fisheries adopted new international measures, within the framework of the Code of Conduct, in order to reduce over-exploitation of the world's fish resources, as well as plans of action for the conservation and management of sharks and the reduction in the incidental catch of seabirds in longline fisheries. The voluntary measures were endorsed at a ministerial meeting, held in March and attended by representatives of some 126 countries, which issued a declaration to promote the implementation of the Code of Conduct and to achieve sustainable management of fisheries and aquaculture. In March 2001 FAO adopted an international plan of action to address the continuing problem of so-called illegal, unreported and unregulated fishing (IUU). In that year FAO estimated that about one-half of major marine fish stocks were fully exploited, one-quarter under-exploited, at least 15% over-exploited, and 10% depleted or recovering from depletion. IUU was estimated to account for up to 30% of total catches in certain fisheries. In October FAO and the Icelandic Government jointly organized the Reykjavík Conference on Responsible Fisheries in the Marine Ecosystem, which adopted a declaration on pursuing responsible and sustainable fishing activities in the context of ecosystem-based fisheries management (EBFM). EBFM involves determining the boundaries of individual marine ecosystems, and maintaining or rebuilding the habitats and biodiversity of each of these so that all species will be supported at levels of maximum production. In March 2005 FAO's Committee of Fisheries adopted voluntary guidelines for the so-called eco-labelling and certification of fish and fish products, i.e. based on information regarding capture management and the sustainable use of resources. In March 2007 the Committee agreed to initiate a process of negotiating an internationally-binding agreement to deny port access to fishing vessels involved in IUU activities; the eventual 'Agreement on Port State Measures to Prevent, Deter and Eliminate Illegal, Unreported and Unregulated Fishing' was endorsed by the Conference in November 2009.

FAO undertakes extensive monitoring, publishing every two years *The State of World Fisheries and Aquaculture*, and collates and maintains relevant databases. It formulates country and regional profiles and has developed a specific information network for the fisheries sector, GLOBEFISH, which gathers and disseminates information regarding market trends, tariffs and other industry issues. FAO aims to extend technical support to member states with regard to the management and conservation of aquatic resources, and other measures to improve the utilization and trade of products, including the reduction of post-harvest losses, preservation marketing and quality assurance. FAO promotes aquaculture (which contributes almost one-third of annual global fish landings) as a valuable source of animal protein and income-generating activity for rural communities. It has undertaken to develop an ecosystem approach to aquaculture (EAA) and works to integrate aquaculture with agricultural and irrigation systems. In February 2000 FAO and the Network of Aquaculture Centres in Asia and the Pacific (NACA) jointly convened a Conference on Aquaculture in the Third Millennium, which was held in Bangkok, Thailand, and attended by participants representing more than 200 governmental and non-governmental organizations. The Conference debated global trends in aquaculture and future policy measures to ensure the sustainable development of the sector. It adopted the Bangkok Declaration and Strategy for Aquaculture Beyond 2000.

FORESTRY

FAO is committed to the sustainable management of trees, forests and forestry resources. It aims to address the critical balance of ensuring the conservation of forests and forestry resources while maximising their potential to contribute to food security and social and economic development. In March 2009 the Committee on Forestry approved a new 10-year FAO Strategic Plan for Forestry, replacing a previous strategic plan initiated in 1999. The new plan, which was 'dynamic' and was to be updated regularly, covered the social, economic and environmental aspects of forestry. The first World Forest Week was held in March 2009 and the second in October 2010. 2011 was declared the International Year of Forests by the UN General Assembly.

FAO assists member countries to formulate, implement and monitor national forestry programmes, and encourages the participation of all stakeholders in developing plans for the sustainable management of tree and forest resources. FAO also helps to implement national assessments of those programmes and of other forestry activities. At a global level FAO undertakes surveillance of the state of the world's forests and publishes a report every two years. A separate 'Forest Resources Assessment' is published every five years, the latest (for 2010) was initiated in March 2008. FAO is committed to collecting and disseminating accurate information and data on forests. It maintains the Forestry Information System (FORIS) to make relevant information and forest-related databases widely accessible.

FAO is a member of the Collaborative Partnership on Forests, which was established in April 2004 on the recommendation of the UN's Economic and Social Council. FAO organizes a World Forestry Congress, generally held every six years; the 13th Congress was convened in Buenos Aires, Argentina, in October 2009.

ECONOMIC AND SOCIAL DEVELOPMENT

FAO provides a focal point for economic research and policy analysis relating to food security and sustainable development. It produces studies and reports on agricultural development, the impact of development programmes and projects, and the world food situation, as well as on commodity prices, trade and medium-term projections. It supports the development of methodologies and guidelines to improve research into food and agriculture and the integration of wider concepts, such as social welfare, environmental factors and nutrition, into research projects. In November 2004 the FAO Council adopted a set of voluntary Right to Food Guidelines, and established a dedicated administrative unit, that aimed to 'support the progressive realization of the right to adequate food in the context of national food security' by providing practical guidance to countries in support of their efforts to achieve the 1996 World Food Summit commitment and UN MDG relating to hunger reduction. FAO's Statistical Division assembles, analyses and disseminates statistical data on world food and agriculture and aims to ensure the consistency, broad coverage and quality of available data. The Division advises member countries on enhancing their statistical capabilities. It maintains FAOSTAT as a core database of statistical information relating to nutrition, fisheries, forestry, food production, land use, population etc. In 2004 FAO developed a new statistical framework to provide for the organization and integration of statistical data and metadata from sources within a particular country. CountrySTAT was piloted in Kenya, Kyrgyzstan and Ghana in 2005 and in 15 more developing countries in 2006/07. FAO's internet-based interactive World Agricultural Information Centre (WAICENT) offers access to agricultural publications, technical documentation, codes of conduct, data, statistics and multimedia resources. FAO compiles and co-ordinates an extensive range of international databases on agriculture, fisheries, forestry, food and statistics, the most important of these being AGRIS (the International Information System for the Agricultural Sciences and Technology) and CARIS (the Current Agricultural Research Information System). In June 2000 FAO organized a high-level Consultation on Agricultural Information Management (COAIM), which aimed to increase access to and use of agricultural information by policy-makers and others. The second COAIM was held in September 2002 and the third meeting was convened in June 2007.

FAO's Global Information and Early Warning System (GIEWS), which become operational in 1975, maintains a database on and monitors the crop and food outlook at global, regional, national and sub-national levels in order to detect emerging food supply difficulties and disasters and to ensure rapid intervention in countries experiencing food supply shortages. It publishes regular reports on the weather conditions and crop prospects in sub-Saharan Africa and in the Sahel region, issues special alerts which describe the situation in countries or sub-regions experiencing food difficulties, and recommends an appropriate international response. FAO has also supported the development and implementation of Food Insecurity and Vulnerability Information and Mapping Systems (FIVIMS) and hosts the secretariat of the inter-agency working group on development of the FIVIMS. In October 2007 FAO inaugurated an online Global Forum on Food Security and Nutrition, to contribute to the compilation and dissemination of information relating to food security and nutrition throughout the world. In December 2008 a regular report issued by GIEWS identified 33 countries as being in crisis and requiring external assistance, of which 20 were in Africa, 10 in Asia and the Near East and three in Latin America and the Caribbean. All countries were identified as lacking the resources to deal with critical problems of food insecurity, including many severely affected by the high cost of food and fuel. The publication *Crop Prospects and Food*

Situation reviews the global situation, and provides regional updates and a special focus on countries experiencing food crises and requiring external assistance, on a quarterly basis. *Food Outlook*, issued in June and November, analyses developments in global food and animal feed markets.

In November 2010 GIEWS issued a special report on the food production situation in the Democratic People's Republic of Korea (DPRK), based on the findings of an FAO/WFP Crop and Food Supply Evaluation Mission conducted in September–October. In February and March 2011 GIEWS issued special reports on the People's Republic of China and Laos, respectively.

TECHNICAL CO-OPERATION

The Technical Co-operation Department has responsibility for FAO's operational activities, including policy development assistance to member countries; the mobilization of resources; investment support; field operations; emergency operations and rehabilitation; and the Technical Co-operation Programme.

FAO provides policy advice to support the formulation, implementation and evaluation of agriculture, rural development and food security strategies in member countries. It administers a project to assist developing countries to strengthen their technical negotiating skills, in respect to agricultural trade issues. FAO also aims to co-ordinate and facilitate the mobilization of extrabudgetary funds from donors and governments for particular projects. It administers a range of trust funds, including a Trust Fund for Food Security and Food Safety, established in 2002 to generate resources for projects to combat hunger, and the Government Co-operative Programme. FAO's Investment Centre, established in 1964, aims to promote greater external investment in agriculture and rural development by assisting member countries to formulate effective and sustainable projects and programmes. The Centre collaborates with international financing institutions and bilateral donors in the preparation of projects, and administers cost-sharing arrangements, with, typically, FAO funding 40% of a project. The Centre is a co-chair (with the German Government) of the Global Donor Platform for Rural Development, which was established in 2004, comprising multilateral, donor and international agencies, development banks and research institutions, to improve the co-ordination and effectiveness of rural development assistance.

FAO's Technical Co-operation Programme, which was inaugurated in 1976, provides technical expertise and funding for small-scale projects to address specific issues within a country's agriculture, fisheries or forestry sectors. An Associate Professional Officers programme co-ordinates the sponsorship and placement of young professionals to gain experience working in an aspect of rural or agricultural development.

FAO's Special Programme for Food Security (SPFS), initiated in 1994, assists low-income countries with a food deficit to increase food production and productivity as rapidly as possible, primarily through the widespread adoption by farmers of improved production technologies, with emphasis on areas of high potential. Within the SPFS framework are national and regional food security initiatives, all of which aim towards the MDG objective of reducing the incidence of hunger by 50% by 2015. The SPFS is operational in more than 100 countries. The Programme promotes South-South co-operation to improve food security and the exchange of knowledge and experience. Some 39 bilateral co-operation agreements are in force, for example, between Gabon and the People's Republic of China, Egypt and Cameroon, and Viet Nam and Benin. In 2011 some 70 countries were categorized formally as 'low-income food-deficit'.

FAO organizes an annual series of fund-raising events, 'TeleFood', some of which are broadcast on television and the internet, in order to raise public awareness of the problems of hunger and malnutrition. Since its inception in 1997 public donations to TeleFood have exceeded some US $28m. (2011), financing more than 2,700 'grass-roots' projects in 130 countries. The projects have provided tools, seeds and other essential supplies directly to small-scale farmers, and have been especially aimed at helping women.

The Technical Co-operation Division co-ordinates FAO's emergency operations, concerned with all aspects of disaster and risk prevention, mitigation, reduction and emergency relief and rehabilitation, with a particular emphasis on food security and rural populations. FAO works with governments to develop and implement disaster prevention policies and practices. It aims to strengthen the capacity of local institutions to manage and mitigate risk and provides technical assistance to improve access to land for displaced populations in countries following conflict or a natural disaster. Other disaster prevention and reduction efforts include dissemination of information from the various early-warning systems and support for adaptation to climate variability and change, for example by the use of drought-resistant crops or the adoption of conservation agriculture techniques. Following an emergency FAO works with governments and other development and humanitarian partners to assess the immediate and longer-term agriculture and food security needs of the affected population. It has developed an Integrated Food Security and Humanitarian Phase Classification Scheme to determine the appropriate response to a disaster situation. Emergency co-ordination units may be established to manage the local response to an emergency and to facilitate and co-ordinate the delivery of inter-agency assistance. In order to rehabilitate agricultural production following a natural or man-made disaster FAO provides emergency seed, tools, other materials and technical and training assistance. During 2005 the UN's Inter-Agency Standing Committee, concerned with co-ordinating the international response to humanitarian disasters, developed a concept of providing assistance through a 'cluster' approach, comprising core areas of activity. FAO was designated the lead agency for the then Agriculture cluster. A review of the humanitarian cluster approach, undertaken during 2010, concluded that a new cluster on Food Security should be established, replacing the Agriculture cluster. The new cluster, established accordingly in 2011, is led jointly by FAO and WFP, and aims to combine expertise in agricultural assistance and food aid in order to boost food security and to improve the resilience of food-insecure disaster-affected communities. FAO also contributes the agricultural relief and rehabilitation component of the UN's Consolidated Appeals Process (CAP), which aims to co-ordinate and enhance the effectiveness of the international community's response to an emergency; in November 2010 FAO appealed for US $240.3m. in funding under the 2011 CAP process. In April 2004 FAO established a Special Fund for Emergency and Rehabilitation Activities to enable it to respond promptly to a humanitarian crisis before making an emergency appeal for additional resources.

During 2008–mid-2011 projects (providing fertilizers, seeds and other support necessary to ensure the success of harvests) were undertaken in more than 90 countries under the framework of the Initiative on Soaring Food Prices (see above); some US $314m. in project funding was provided by the EU Food Facility, while other projects (to the value of $37m.) were implemented through FAO's Technical Co-operation Programme.

In 2011 FAO was undertaking a regional support initative aimed at alleviating the impact of volatile food prices on the most acutely affected vulnerable farming populations in Asia. The FAO has implemented a Regional Programme for Food Security in the DPRK since 1998. In 2011 technical co-operation projects were being undertaken in the DPRK aimed at improving the production and processing of sweet sorghum for food, sugar, biofuel and fodder, in reclaimed land, seasonal wetlands, and arid regions; and aimed at supporting improvement in walnut production; capacity-building in seed production, and juvenile rearing of ark shell and sea urchins; and providing emergency assistance for the early detection, response and control of foot-and-mouth disease outbreaks. During 2011–14 FAO was jointly implementing several projects in the DPRK with UNDP, aimed at improving seed production and harvests.

FAO Statutory Bodies

(based at the Rome headquarters, unless otherwise indicated)

Animal Production and Health Commission for Asia and the Pacific: c/o FAO Regional Office, Maliwan Mansion, 39 Phra Atit Rd, Bangkok 10200, Thailand; f. 1975 to support national and regional livestock production and research; 17 member states.

Asia and Pacific Commission on Agricultural Statistics: c/o FAO Regional Office, Maliwan Mansion, 39 Phra Atit Rd, Bangkok 10200, Thailand; e-mail rap-statistics.fao.org; internet www.faorap-apcas.org; f. 1963; reviews recent developments in agricultural statistical systems, provides a platform for the exchange of ideas relating to the state of food and agricultural statistics in the region; senior officials responsible for the development of agricultural statistics from 25 member states.

Asia and Pacific Plant Protection Commission: c/o FAO Regional Office, Maliwan Mansion, Phra Atit Rd, Bangkok 10200, Thailand; f. 1956 (new title 1983) to strengthen international co-operation in plant protection to prevent the introduction and spread of destructive plant diseases and pests; 25 member states.

Asia-Pacific Fishery Commission: c/o FAO Regional Office, Maliwan Mansion, 39 Phra Atit Rd, Bangkok 10200, Thailand; f. 1948 to develop fisheries, encourage and co-ordinate research, disseminate information, recommend projects to governments, propose standards in technique and management measures; 20 member states.

Asia-Pacific Forestry Commission: internet www.apfcweb.org; f. 1949 to advise on the formulation of forest policy, and review and co-ordinate its implementation throughout the region; to exchange information and advise on technical problems; 29 member states.

Codex Alimentarius Commission (Joint FAO/WHO Food Standards Programme): e-mail codex@fao.org; internet www.codexalimentarius.net; f. 1962 to make proposals for the co-ordination of all international food standards work and to publish a code of international food standards; Trust Fund to support participation by least-developed countries was inaugurated in 2003; there are numerous specialized Codex committees, e.g. for food labelling, hygiene, additives and contaminants, pesticide and veterinary residues, milk and milk products, and processed fruits and vegetables; and an intergovernmental task force on antimicrobial resistance; 184 member states and the European Union (at October 2011).

International Rice Commission: internet www.fao.org/ag/AGP/AGPC/doc/field/commrice/welcome.htm; f. 1949 to promote national and international action on production, conservation, distribution and consumption of rice, except matters relating to international trade; supports the International Task Force on Hybrid Rice, the Working Group on Advanced Rice Breeding in Latin America and the Caribbean, the Inter-regional Collaborative Research Network on Rice in the Mediterranean Climate Areas, and the Technical Co-operation Network on Wetland Development and Management/Inland Valley Swamps; 60 member states.

Finance

FAO's Regular Programme, which is financed by contributions from member governments, covers the cost of FAO's Secretariat, its Technical Co-operation Programme (TCP) and part of the cost of several special action programmes. The regular budget for the two-year period 2010–11 totalled US $1,000m. Much of FAO's technical assistance programme and emergency (including rehabilitation) support activities are funded from extra-budgetary sources, predominantly by trust funds that come mainly from donor countries and international financing institutions; voluntary donor contributions to FAO were projected at around $1,200m. in 2010–11.

Publications

Commodity Review and Outlook (annually).
Crop Prospects and Food Situation (5/6 a year).
Ethical Issues in Food and Agriculture.
FAO Statistical Yearbook (annually).
FAOSTAT Statistical Database (online).
Food Outlook (2 a year).
Food Safety and Quality Update (monthly; electronic bulletin).
Forest Resources Assessment.
The State of Agricultural Commodity Markets (every 2 years).
The State of Food and Agriculture (annually).
The State of Food Insecurity in the World (annually).
The State of World Fisheries and Aquaculture (every 2 years).
The State of the World's Forests (every 2 years).
Unasylva (quarterly).
Yearbook of Fishery Statistics.
Yearbook of Forest Products.
Commodity reviews; studies, manuals. A complete catalogue of publications is available at www.fao.org/icatalog/inter-e.htm.

International Atomic Energy Agency—IAEA

Address: POB 100, Wagramerstrasse 5, 1400 Vienna, Austria.
Telephone: (1) 26000; **fax:** (1) 26007; **e-mail:** official.mail@iaea.org; **internet:** www.iaea.org.

The International Atomic Energy Agency (IAEA) is an intergovernmental organization, established in 1957 in accordance with a decision of the General Assembly of the United Nations. Although it is autonomous, the IAEA is administratively a member of the United Nations, and reports on its activities once a year to the UN General Assembly. Its main objectives are to enlarge the contribution of atomic energy to peace, health and prosperity throughout the world and to ensure, so far as it is able, that assistance provided by it or at its request or under its supervision or control is not used in such a way as to further any military purpose. The 2005 Nobel Peace Prize was awarded, in two equal parts, to the IAEA and to the Agency's Director-General.

Organization
(October 2011)

GENERAL CONFERENCE

The Conference, comprising representatives of all member states, convenes each year for general debate on the Agency's policy, budget and programme. It elects members to the Board of Governors, and approves the appointment of the Director-General; it admits new member states.

BOARD OF GOVERNORS

The Board of Governors consists of 35 member states elected by the General Conference. It is the principal policy-making body of the Agency and is responsible to the General Conference. Under its own authority, the Board approves all safeguards agreements, important projects and safety standards.

SECRETARIAT

The Secretariat, comprising 2,338 staff at 31 December 2010, is headed by the Director-General, who is assisted by six Deputy Directors-General. The Secretariat is divided into six departments: Technical Co-operation; Nuclear Energy; Nuclear Safety and Security; Nuclear Sciences and Applications; Safeguards; and Management. A Standing Advisory Group on Safeguards Implementation advises the Director-General on technical aspects of safeguards.

Director-General: YUKIYA AMANO (Japan).

Activities

In recent years the IAEA has implemented several reforms of its management structure and operations. The three pillars supporting the Agency's activities are: technology (assisting research on and practical application of atomic energy for peaceful uses), safety, and verification (ensuring that special fissionable and other materials, services, equipment and information made available by the Agency or at its request or under its supervision are not used for any non-peaceful purpose).

TECHNICAL CO-OPERATION AND TRAINING

The IAEA provides assistance in the form of experts, training and equipment to technical co-operation projects and applications worldwide, with an emphasis on radiation protection and safety-related activities. Training is provided to scientists, and experts and lecturers are assigned to provide specialized help on specific nuclear applications. The IAEA supported the foundation in September 2003 of the World Nuclear University, comprising a world-wide network of institutions that aim to strengthen international co-operation in promoting the safe use of nuclear power in energy production, and in the application of nuclear science and technology in areas including sustainable agriculture and nutrition, medicine, fresh water resources management and environmental protection.

FOOD AND AGRICULTURE

In co-operation with FAO, the Agency conducts programmes of applied research on the use of radiation and isotopes in fields including: efficiency in the use of water and fertilizers; improvement of food crops by induced mutations; eradication or control of destructive insects by the introduction of sterilized insects (radiation-based Sterile Insect Technique); improvement of livestock nutrition and health; studies on improving efficacy and reducing residues of pesticides, and increasing utilization of agricultural wastes; and food preservation by irradiation. The programmes are implemented by the Joint FAO/IAEA Division of Nuclear Techniques in Food and Agriculture and by the FAO/IAEA Agriculture and Biotechnology Laboratory, based at the IAEA's laboratory complex in Seibersdorf, Austria. A Training and Reference Centre for Food and Pesticide Control, based at Seibersdorf, supports the implementation of national legislation and trade agreements ensuring the quality and safety of food products in international trade. The Agency's Marine Environment Laboratory (IAEA-MEL), in Monaco, studies radionuclides and other ocean pollutants.

LIFE SCIENCES

In co-operation with the World Health Organization (WHO), the IAEA promotes the use of nuclear techniques in medicine, biology and health-related environmental research, provides training, and conducts research on techniques for improving the accuracy of radiation dosimetry.

The IAEA/WHO Network of Secondary Standard Dosimetry Laboratories (SSDLs) comprises 81 laboratories in 62 member states. The Agency's Dosimetry Laboratory in Seibersdorf performs dose inter-comparisons for both SSDLs and radiotherapy centres. The IAEA undertakes maintenance plans for nuclear laboratories; national programmes of quality control for nuclear medicine instruments; quality control of radioimmunoassay techniques; radiation sterilization of medical supplies; and improvement of cancer therapy through the IAEA Programme of Action for Cancer Therapy (PACT), inaugurated in 2004, and through which Agency works with WHO and other partners. In May 2009 the IAEA and WHO launched a new Joint Programme on Cancer Control, aimed at enhancing efforts to fight cancer in the developing world.

PHYSICAL AND CHEMICAL SCIENCES

The Agency's programme in physical sciences includes industrial applications of isotopes and radiation technology; application of nuclear techniques to mineral exploration and exploitation; radiopharmaceuticals; and hydrology, involving the use of isotope techniques for assessment of water resources. Nuclear data services are provided, and training is given for nuclear scientists from developing countries. The Physics, Chemistry and Instrumentation Laboratory at Seibersdorf supports the Agency's research in human health, industry, water resources and environment. The Abdus Salam International Centre for Theoretical Physics, based in Trieste, Italy, operates in accordance with a tripartite agreement in force between the IAEA, UNESCO and the Italian Government.

NUCLEAR POWER

In 2011 there were 442 nuclear power plants in operation and 65 reactors under construction world-wide. Nuclear power accounts for about 13% of total electrical energy generated globally. The IAEA helps developing member states to introduce nuclear-powered electricity-generating plants through assistance with planning, feasibility studies, surveys of manpower and infrastructure, and safety measures. The Agency also assesses life extension and decommissioning strategies for ageing nuclear power plants. It publishes books on numerous aspects of nuclear power, and provides training courses on safety in nuclear power plants and other topics. An energy data bank collects and disseminates information on nuclear technology, and a power-reactor information system monitors the technical performance of nuclear power plants. There is increasing interest in the use of nuclear reactors for seawater desalination and radiation hydrology techniques to provide potable water. In July 1992 the EC, Japan, Russia and the USA signed an agreement to co-operate in the engineering design of an International Thermonuclear Experimental Reactor (ITER); the People's Republic of China (PRC), Republic of Korea and India subsequently also joined the process. The project aims to demonstrate the scientific and technological feasibility of fusion energy, with the aim of providing a source of clean, abundant energy in the 21st century. In June 2005 the states participating in ITER agreed that the installation should be constructed in Cadarache, France, and in November 2006 an ITER Agreement was concluded, establishing, upon its entry into force in October 2007, a formal ITER organization, with responsibility for constructing, operating and decommissioning ITER. It was envisaged that ITER would enter fully into operation by 2026. In May 2001 the International Project on Innovative Nuclear Reactors and Fuel Cycles (INPRO) was inaugurated. INPRO, which has 28 members, aims to promote nuclear energy as a means of meeting future sustainable energy requirements and to facilitate the exchange of information by member states to advance innovations in nuclear technology. The IAEA is a permanent observer at the Generation IV International Forum (GIF), which was inaugurated in 2000 and aims to establish a number of international collaborative nuclear research and development agreements. In 2010 the IAEA established an Integrated Nuclear Infrastructure Group (ING), which aimed to integrate information from disparate databases to enable more effective planning; to offer training in the use of planning tools; to provide legislative assistance; to provide guidance on ensuring self-assessment capabilities among governmental and operating organizations; and to organize education and training materials. An advisory Technical Working Group on Nuclear Power Infrastructure was also initiated during 2010.

RADIOACTIVE WASTE MANAGEMENT

The Agency provides practical help to member states in the management of radioactive waste. The Waste Management Advisory Programme (WAMAP) was established in 1987, and undertakes advisory missions in member states. A code of practice to prevent the illegal dumping of radioactive waste was drafted in 1989, and another on the international transboundary movement of waste was drafted in 1990. A ban on the dumping of radioactive waste at sea came into effect in 1994, under the Convention on the Prevention of Marine Pollution by Dumping of Wastes and Other Matters. The IAEA was to determine radioactive levels, for purposes of the Convention, and provide assistance to countries for the safe disposal of radioactive wastes. A new category of radioactive waste—very low level waste (VLLW)—was introduced in the early 2000s. A VLLW repository, at Morvilliers, France, became fully operational in 2004. The Agency has issued modal regulations for the air, sea and land transportation of all radioactive materials.

In September 1997 the IAEA adopted a Joint Convention on the Safety of Spent Fuel Management and on the Safety of Radioactive Waste Management. The first internationally binding legal device to address such issues, the Convention was to ensure the safe storage and disposal of nuclear and radioactive waste, during both the construction and operation of a nuclear power plant, as well as following its closure. The Convention entered into force in June 2001, and had been ratified by 62 parties at October 2011.

NUCLEAR SAFETY

The IAEA's nuclear safety programme encourages international co-operation in the exchange of information, promoting implementation of its safety standards and providing advisory safety services. It includes the IAEA International Nuclear Event Scale (INES), which measures the severity of nuclear events, incidents and accidents; the Incident Reporting System; an emergency preparedness programme (which maintains an Emergency Response Centre, located in Vienna, Austria); operational safety review teams; the International Nuclear Safety Group (INSAG); the Radiation Protection Advisory Team; and a safety research co-ordination programme. The safety review teams provide member states with advice on achieving and maintaining a high level of safety in the operation of nuclear power plants, while research programmes establish risk criteria for the nuclear fuel cycle and identify cost-effective means to reduce risks in energy systems. A new version of the INES, issued in July 2008, incorporated revisions aimed at providing more detailed ratings of activities including human exposure to sources of radiation and the transportation of radioactive materials.

The nuclear safety programme promotes a global safety regime, which aims to ensure the protection of people and the environment from the effects of ionizing radiation and the minimization of the likelihood of potential nuclear accidents, etc. Through the Commission on Safety Standards (which has sub-committees on nuclear safety standards, radiation safety standards, transport safety standards and waste safety standards) the programme establishes IAEA safety standards and provides for their application. In September 2006 the IAEA published a new primary safety standard, the Fundamental Safety Principles, representing a unified philosophy of nuclear safety and protection that was to provide the conceptual basis for the Agency's entire safety standards agenda. The IAEA's *Safety Glossary Terminology Used in Nuclear Safety and Radiation Protection* is updated regularly. In 2010 IAEA established a Global Safety Assessment (G-SAN), facilitating collaboration between experts world-wide with the aim of harmonizing nuclear safety.

The Convention on the Physical Protection of Nuclear Material was signed in 1980, and committed contracting states to ensuring the protection of nuclear material during transportation within their territory or on board their ships or aircraft. In July 2005 delegates from 89 states party adopted a number of amendments aimed at strengthening the Convention.

Following a serious accident at the Chernobyl nuclear power plant in Ukraine (then part of the USSR) in April 1986, two conventions were formulated by the IAEA and entered into force in October. The first, the Convention on Early Notification of a Nuclear Accident, commits parties to provide information about nuclear accidents with possible transboundary effects at the earliest opportunity (it had 111 parties by October 2011); and the second, the Convention on Assistance in the Case of a Nuclear Accident or Radiological Emergency, commits parties to endeavour to provide assistance in the event of a nuclear accident or radiological emergency (this had 105 parties by October 2011). During 1990 the IAEA organized an assessment of the consequences of the Chernobyl accident, undertaken by an international team of experts, who reported to an international conference on the effects of the accident, convened at the IAEA headquarters in Vienna in May 1991. In February 1993 INSAG published an updated report on the Chernobyl incident, which emphasized the role of design factors in the accident, and the need to implement safety measures in the RBMK-type reactor. In March 1994 an IAEA expert mission visited Chernobyl and reported continuing serious deficiencies in safety at the defunct reactor and the units remaining in operation. An international conference reviewing the radiological consequences of the accident, 10 years after the event, was held in April 1996, co-sponsored by the IAEA, WHO and the European

Commission. The last of the Chernobyl plant's three operating units was officially closed in December 2000. During the 2000s the IAEA was offering a wide range of assistance with the decommissioning of Chernobyl. In April 2009 the IAEA, UNDP, UNICEF and WHO launched the International Chernobyl Research and Information Network (ICRIN), a three-year initiative, costing US $2.5m., which aimed to provide up-to-date scientific information and sound practical advice to communities in areas of Ukraine, Belarus and Russia that remained affected by the Chernobyl accident. In November 2008 the IAEA and other UN agencies approved a UN Action Plan on Chernobyl to 2016, which had been developed by UNDP, and was envisaged as a framework for the regeneration of these areas.

An International Convention on Nuclear Safety was adopted at an IAEA conference in June 1994. The Convention applies to land-based civil nuclear power plants: adherents commit themselves to fundamental principles of safety, and maintain legislative frameworks governing nuclear safety. The Convention entered into force in October 1996 and had been ratified by 74 states by October 2011.

In September 1997 more than 80 member states adopted a protocol to revise the 1963 Vienna Convention on Civil Liability for Nuclear Damage, fixing the minimum limit of liability for the operator of a nuclear reactor at 300m. Special Drawing Rights (SDRs, the accounting units of the IMF) in the event of an accident. The amended protocol also extended the length of time during which claims may be brought for loss of life or injury. It entered into force in October 2003. The International Expert Group on Nuclear Liability (INLEX) was established in the same year. A Convention on Supplementary Compensation for Nuclear Damage established a further compensatory fund to provide for the payment of damages following an accident; contributions to the Fund were to be calculated on the basis of the nuclear capacity of each member state. The Convention had four contracting states by October 2011.

In July 1996 the IAEA co-ordinated a study on the radiological situation at the Mururoa and Fangatauta atolls, following the French nuclear test programmes in the South Pacific. Results published in May 1998 concluded that there was no radiological health risk and that neither remedial action nor continued environmental monitoring was necessary.

The IAEA is developing a training course on measurement methods and risk analysis relating to the presence of depleted uranium (which can be used in ammunition) in post-conflict areas. In November 2000 IAEA specialists participated in a fact-finding mission organized by UNEP in Kosovo and Metohija, which aimed to assess the environmental and health consequences of the use of depleted uranium in ammunition by NATO during its 1999 aerial offensive against the then Federal Republic of Yugoslavia. (A report on the situation was published by UNEP in March 2001.) In June 2003 the Agency published the results of an assessment undertaken in 2002 of the possible long-term radiological impact of depleted uranium residues, derived from the 1991 Gulf War, at several locations in Kuwait; it determined that the residues did not pose a health threat to local populations.

In May 2001 the IAEA convened an international conference to address the protection of nuclear material and radioactive sources from illegal trafficking. In September, in view of the perpetration of major terrorist attacks against targets in the USA during that month, the IAEA General Conference addressed the potential for nuclear-related terrorism. It adopted a resolution that emphasized the importance of the physical protection of nuclear material in preventing its illicit use or the sabotage of nuclear facilities and nuclear materials. Three main potential threats were identified: the acquisition by a terrorist group of a nuclear weapon; acquisition of nuclear material to construct a nuclear weapon or cause a radiological hazard; and violent acts against nuclear facilities to cause a radiological hazard. In March 2002 the Board of Governors approved in principle an action plan to improve global protection against acts of terrorism involving nuclear and other radioactive materials. The plan addressed the physical protection of nuclear materials and facilities; the detection of malicious activities involving radioactive materials; strengthening national control systems; the security of radioactive sources; evaluation of security and safety at nuclear facilities; emergency response to malicious acts or threats involving radioactive materials; ensuring adherence to international guidelines and agreements; and improvement of programme co-ordination and information management. It was estimated that the Agency's upgraded nuclear security activities would require significant additional annual funding. In March 2003 the IAEA organized an International Conference on Security of Radioactive Sources, held in Vienna. In April 2005 the UN General Assembly adopted the International Convention for the Suppression of Acts of Nuclear Terrorism. The Convention, which opened for signature in September of that year and entered into force in July 2007, established a definition of acts of nuclear terrorism and urged signatory states to co-operate in the prevention of terrorist attacks by sharing information and providing mutual assistance with criminal investigations and extradition proceedings. Under the provisions of the Convention it was required that any seized nuclear or radiological material should be held in accordance with IAEA safeguards. By the end of 2010 a total of 1,980 incidents had been reported to the Illicit Trafficking Database (ITDB) since its creation in 1995; of the 147 incidents that were reported to have occurred during 2010, 13 involved illegal possession of and attempts to sell nuclear material or radioactive sources; 22 involved reported theft or loss; and 111 concerned discoveries of uncontrolled material, unauthorized disposals, and inadvertent unauthorized shipments and storage. The ITDB had 107 participant states in that year.

In June 2004 the Board of Governors approved an international action plan on the decommissioning of nuclear facilities; the plan was revised in 2007. In September 2007 the IAEA launched a Network of Centres of Excellence for Decommissioning. In 2011 the Agency was managing four ongoing international projects related to safe decommissioning.

In October 2008 the IAEA inaugurated the International Seismic Safety Centre (ISSC) within the Agency's Department of Safety and Security. The ISSC was to serve as a focal point for avoiding and mitigating the consequences of extreme seismic events on nuclear installations world-wide, and was to be supported by a committee of high-level experts in the following areas: geology and tectonics; seismology; seismic hazard; geotechnical engineering; structural engineering; equipment; and seismic risk. In August 2007, and January–February and December 2008, the IAEA sent missions to visit the Kashiwazaki-Kariwa nuclear power plant in Japan, in order to learn about the effects on that facility of an earthquake that struck it in July 2007, and to identify and recommend future precautions. In March 2011, in the aftermath of the severe earthquake and tsunami flooding that had struck and severely damaged Fukushima Daiichi nuclear power plant, the Japanese authorities requested IAEA support in monitoring the effects of the ensuing release of radiation on the environment and on human health. Accordingly, the IAEA dispatched radiation monitoring teams to Japan to provide assistance to local experts, with a particular focus on: worker radiation protection, food safety, marine and soil science, and Boiling Water Reactor (BWR) technology. In partnership with WMO, the IAEA also provided weather forecast updates as part of its immediate emergency response. In late March the IAEA, FAO and WHO issued a joint statement on food safety issues following the Fukushima nuclear emergency, emphasizing their commitment to mobilizing knowledge and expertise in support of the Japanese authorities. During late May–early June 2011 an IAEA team comprising 20 international experts visited Japan to assess the ongoing state of nuclear safety in that country.

In June 2011, in view of the Fukushima Daiichi accident, the IAEA Ministerial Conference on Nuclear Safety adopted a Ministerial Declaration which formed the basis of the first IAEA Action Plan for Nuclear Safety. The Plan, which was unanimously endorsed in September 2011 by the 55th General Conference, emphasized greater transparency in nuclear safety matters and the improvement of safety regimes, including the strengthening of peer reviews, emergency and response mechanisms, and national regulatory bodies. Safety standards were to be reviewed and an assessment of the vulnerabilities of nuclear power plants was to be undertaken.

DISSEMINATION OF INFORMATION

The International Nuclear Information System (INIS), which was established in 1970, provides a computerized indexing and abstracting service. Information on the peaceful uses of atomic energy is collected by member states and international organizations and sent to the IAEA for processing and dissemination (see list of publications below). The IAEA also co-operates with FAO in an information system for agriculture (AGRIS) and with the World Federation of Nuclear Medicine and Biology, and the non-profit Cochrane Collaboration, in maintaining an electronic database of best practice in nuclear medicine. The IAEA Nuclear Data Section provides cost-free data centre services and co-operates with other national and regional nuclear and atomic data centres in the systematic world-wide collection, compilation, dissemination and exchange of nuclear reaction data, nuclear structure and decay data, and atomic and molecular data for fusion.

SAFEGUARDS

The Treaty on the Non-Proliferation of Nuclear Weapons (known also as the Non-Proliferation Treaty or NPT), which entered into force in 1970, requires each 'non-nuclear-weapon state' (one which had not manufactured and exploded a nuclear weapon or other nuclear explosive device prior to 1 January 1967) which is a party to the Treaty to conclude a safeguards agreement with the IAEA. Under such an agreement, the state undertakes to accept IAEA safeguards on all nuclear material in all its peaceful nuclear activities for the purpose of verifying that such material is not diverted to nuclear weapons or other nuclear explosive devices. In May 1995 the Review and Extension Conference of parties to the NPT agreed to extend the NPT indefinitely, and reaffirmed support for the IAEA's role in verification and the transfer of peaceful nuclear technologies. At the next review conference, held in April–May 2000, the five 'nuclear-weapon states'—the PRC, France, Russia, the United Kingdom and the USA—issued a joint statement pledging their commitment to the ultimate goal of complete nuclear disarmament under effective international controls. A further review conference was convened in May 2005. The 2010 review conference, held in May of that year, unanimously adopted an outcome document containing a 22-point action plan aimed at advancing nuclear disarmament, non-proliferation and the peaceful uses of nuclear energy over the following five years. The Conference also proposed that a regional conference should be convened to address means of eliminating nuclear and other weapons of mass destruction in the Middle East; resolved that the nuclear-weapon states should commit to further efforts to reduce and ultimately eliminate all types of nuclear weapons, including through unilateral, bilateral, regional and multilateral measures, with specific emphasis on the early entry into force and full implementation of the Treaty on Measures for the Further Reduction and Limitation of Strategic Offensive Arms (known as the New START Treaty), signed by the Presidents of Russia and the USA in April 2010; and determined that the Conference on Disarmament should immediately establish a subsidiary body to address nuclear disarmament within the context of an agreed and comprehensive programme of work. The Conference noted a five-point proposal of the UN Secretary-General for nuclear disarmament, including consideration of negotiations on a convention on nuclear weapons, and recognized the interests of non-nuclear-weapon states in constraining nuclear-weapon states' development of nuclear weapons. At October 2011 185 non-nuclear-weapon states and the five nuclear-weapon states were parties to the NPT. A number of non-nuclear-weapon states, however, had not complied, within the prescribed time-limit, with their obligations under the Treaty regarding the conclusion of the relevant safeguards agreement with the Agency.

The five nuclear-weapon states have concluded safeguards agreements with the Agency that permit the application of IAEA safeguards to all their nuclear activities, excluding those with 'direct national significance'. A Comprehensive Nuclear Test Ban Treaty (CTBT) was opened for signature in September 1996, having been adopted by the UN General Assembly. The Treaty was to enter into international law upon ratification by all 44 nations with known nuclear capabilities. A separate verification organization was to be established, based in Vienna. A Preparatory Commission for the treaty organization became operational in 1997. By October 2011 182 countries had signed the CTBT and 155 had ratified it, including 35 of the 44 states with known nuclear capabilities. However, the US Senate rejected ratification of the CTBT in October 1999. The May 2010 NPT review conference determined that all nuclear-weapon states should undertake to ratify the CTBT, and emphasized that, pending the entry into force of the CTBT, all states should refrain from conducting test explosions of nuclear weapons.

Several regional nuclear weapons treaties require their member states to conclude comprehensive safeguards agreements with the IAEA, including the Treaty for the Prohibition of Nuclear Weapons in Latin America (Tlatelolco Treaty, with 33 states party at October 2011); the South Pacific Nuclear-Free Zone Treaty (Rarotonga Treaty, 13 states party at October 2011); the Treaty in the South-East Asia Nuclear-Weapon Free Zone (Treaty of Bangkok, adopted in 1995, 10 states party at October 2011); and the African Nuclear-Weapon Free Zone Treaty (Pelindaba Treaty, adopted in 1996, with 30 states party at October 2011). In September 2006 experts from Kazakhstan, Kyrgyzstan, Tajikistan, Turkmenistan and Uzbekistan adopted a treaty on establishing a Central Asian Nuclear Weapon Free Zone (CANWFZ); all five states subsequently ratified the treaty. At the end of 2010 IAEA safeguards agreements were in force with 175 states, covering 674 nuclear facilities. During that year the Agency conducted 1,983 inspections. Expenditure on the Safeguards Regular Budget for 2010 was €116.1m., and extra-budgetary programme expenditure amounted to €18.2m. The IAEA maintains an imagery database of nuclear sites, and is installing digital surveillance systems (including unattended and remote monitoring capabilities) to replace obsolete analogue systems.

In June 1995 the Board of Governors approved measures to strengthen the safeguards system, including allowing inspection teams greater access to suspected nuclear sites and to information on nuclear activities in member states, reducing the notice time for inspections by removing visa requirements for inspectors and using environmental monitoring (i.e. soil, water and air samples) to test for signs of radioactivity. In April 1996 the IAEA initiated a programme to prevent and combat illicit trafficking of nuclear weapons, and in May 1998 the IAEA and the World Customs Organization signed a Memorandum of Understanding to enhance co-operation in the prevention of illicit nuclear trafficking. In May 1997 the Board of Governors adopted a model additional protocol approving measures to strengthen safeguards further, in order to ensure the compliance of non-nuclear-weapon states with IAEA commitments. The new protocol compelled member states to provide inspection teams with improved access to information concerning existing and planned nuclear activities, and to allow access to locations other than known nuclear sites within that country's territory. By December 2010 104 states had ratified additional protocols to their safeguards agreements.

The IAEA's Safeguards Analytical Laboratory (at the Seibersdorf complex) analyses nuclear fuel-cycle samples collected by IAEA safeguards inspectors.

In April 1992 the Democratic People's Republic of Korea (DPRK) ratified a safeguards agreement with the IAEA. In late 1992 and early 1993, however, the IAEA unsuccessfully requested access to two non-declared sites in the DPRK, where it was suspected that material capable of being used for the manufacture of nuclear weapons was stored. In March 1993 the DPRK announced its intention of withdrawing from the NPT: it suspended its withdrawal in June, but continued to refuse full access to its nuclear facilities for IAEA inspectors. In May 1994 the DPRK began to refuel an experimental nuclear power reactor at Yongbyon, but refused to allow the IAEA to analyse the spent fuel rods in order to ascertain whether plutonium had been obtained from the reactor for possible military use. In June the IAEA Board of Governors halted IAEA technical assistance to the DPRK (except medical assistance) because of continuous violation of the NPT safeguards agreements. In the same month the DPRK withdrew from the IAEA (though not from the NPT); however, it allowed IAEA inspectors to remain at the Yongbyon site to conduct safeguards activities. In October the Governments of the DPRK and the USA concluded an agreement whereby the former agreed to halt construction of two new nuclear reactors, on condition that it received international aid for the construction of two 'light water' reactors (which could not produce materials for the manufacture of nuclear weapons). The DPRK also agreed to allow IAEA inspections of all its nuclear sites, but only after the installation of one of the light water reactors had been completed (entailing a significant time lapse). In November IAEA inspectors visited the DPRK to initiate verification of the suspension of the country's nuclear programme, in accordance with the agreement concluded in the previous month. From 1995 the IAEA pursued technical discussions with the DPRK authorities as part of the Agency's efforts to achieve the full compliance of the DPRK with the IAEA safeguards agreement. By the end of 1999 the canning of spent fuel rods from the Yongbyon nuclear power reactor was completed. However, little overall progress had been achieved, owing to the obstruction of inspectors by the authorities in that country, including their refusal to provide samples for analysis. The IAEA was unable to verify the suspension of the nuclear programme and declared that the DPRK continued to be in non-compliance with its NPT safeguards agreement. In accordance with a decision of the General Conference in September 2001, IAEA inspectors subsequently resumed a continuous presence in the DPRK. The DPRK authorities permitted low-level inspections of the Yongbyon site by an IAEA technical team in January and May 2002. It was envisaged at that time that the new 'light water' reactors would become operational by 2008. However, in December 2002, following repeated requests by the IAEA that the DPRK verify the accuracy of reports that it was implementing an undeclared uranium enrichment programme, the DPRK authorities disabled IAEA safeguards surveillance equipment placed at three facilities in Yongbyon and took measures to restart reprocessing capabilities at the site, requesting the immediate withdrawal of the Agency's inspectors. (The inspectors were withdrawn at the end of the month.) In early January 2003 the IAEA Board of Governors adopted a resolution deploring the DPRK's non-co-operation and urging its immediate and full compliance with the Agency. Shortly afterwards, however, the DPRK announced its withdrawal from the NPT, while stating that it would limit its nuclear activities to peaceful purposes. In February the IAEA found the DPRK to be in further non-compliance with its safeguards agreement, and condemned the reported successful reactivation of the Yongbyon reactor. In August a series of six-party talks on the situation was launched, involving the DPRK, the PRC, Japan, the Republic of Korea, Russia and the USA, under the auspices of the PRC Government. In September 2004 the General Conference adopted a resolution that urged the DPRK to dismantle promptly and completely any nuclear weapons programme and to recognize the verification role of the Agency, while strongly encouraging the ongoing diplomatic efforts to achieve a peaceful outcome. In February 2005 the DPRK suspended its participation in the six-party talks, and asserted that it had developed nuclear weapons as a measure of self-defence. The talks resumed during July–September, when the six parties signed a joint statement, in which the DPRK determined to resume its adherence to the NPT and Agency safeguards, and consequently to halt its development of nuclear weapons; the USA and the Republic of Korea affirmed that no US nuclear weapons were deployed on the Korean Peninsula; the five other parties recognized the DPRK's right to use nuclear energy for peaceful purposes, and agreed to consider at a later date the provision of a light water reactor to that country; and all parties undertook to promote co-operation in security and economic affairs. A timetable for future progress was to be established at the next phase of the six-party talks, the first session of which convened briefly in early

November; the DPRK, however, subsequently announced that it would only resume the talks pending the release by the USA of recently-frozen DPRK financial assets. In July 2006 the UN Security Council condemned a recent ballistic missile test by the DPRK, noting the potential of such missiles to be used for delivering nuclear, chemical or biological payloads, and urged the DPRK to return immediately to the six-party talks without precondition and work towards the implementation of the September 2005 joint statement. In early 2006 October the IAEA Director-General expressed serious concern in response to an announcement by the DPRK that it had conducted a nuclear test. In mid-October the Security Council adopted Resolution 1718, demanding that the DPRK suspend all activities related to its ballistic missile programme, abandon all nuclear weapons and existing nuclear programmes, abandon all other existing weapons of mass destruction and ballistic missile programmes in a complete, verifiable and irreversible manner, and return to the six-party talks. The Council also imposed sanctions against the DPRK.

The six-party talks were resumed in February 2007, and resulted in an ad hoc agreement by all the participants that the DPRK would shut down and seal—for the purpose of eventual abandonment—the Yongbyon facility, and would invite back IAEA personnel to conduct all necessary monitoring and verifications; that the DPRK would discuss with the other parties a list of all its nuclear programmes; that the DPRK and the USA would enter into negotiations aimed at resolving pending bilateral issues and moving toward full diplomatic relations; that the USA would initiate the process of removing the designation of the DPRK as a state-sponsor of terrorism; that the DPRK and Japan would start negotiations aimed at normalizing their relations; and that the parties would agree to co-operate in security and economic affairs (as detailed under the September 2005 joint statement). In the latter regard, the parties agreed to the provision of emergency energy assistance to the DPRK. In mid-July 2007 an IAEA team visited the DPRK and verified the shutdown of the Yongbyon facility. Upon the resumption of the six-party talks in late September, the participants adopted an agreement wherein the DPRK resolved to disable permanently its nuclear facilities.

In early June 2008 the IAEA Director-General asserted that, as long as the legal status of the DPRK's accession to the NPT remained unclear, the safeguards responsibilities of the Agency towards the DPRK were also uncertain. Later in June the DPRK released to the PRC, the chair of the six-party talks, documents outlining its capabilities in the areas of nuclear power and nuclear weapons. In the following month the participants in the next round of six-party talks agreed that a verification regime should be established, that the disablement of the DPRK's Yongbyon nuclear facilities should be completed, and that assistance equivalent to 1m. tons of heavy fuel oil should be delivered to the DPRK. In August the DPRK authorities announced their intention to reactivate the Yongbyon facility in reaction to the refusal, hitherto, of the USA to remove the DPRK from its terrorism blacklist despite the declaration of the DPRK's nuclear capabilities released in June. In late September the IAEA reported that all Agency seals and surveillance equipment had been removed from Yongbyon, and that the DPRK authorities would no longer sanction visits by IAEA inspectors to the reprocessing facility. In mid-October, shortly after the conclusion of an agreement between the DPRK and USA on a series of measures aimed at verifying the DPRK's denuclearization, and the US Government's subsequent removal of the DPRK from its terrorism blacklist, the DPRK authorities permitted the return of IAEA inspectors to Yongbyon. A round of the six-party talks convened in December failed to reach agreement on the formulation of a verification protocol, which was to be based on the verification measures agreed in October.

In mid-April 2009 a long-range rocket test conducted by the DPRK, in violation of UN Security Council Resolution 1718 (see above), was unanimously condemned by the Council. The DPRK responded by announcing its withdrawal from the six-party talks; withdrawing from the ad hoc agreement concerning the Yongbyon facility reached in February 2007; stating its intention to restart the Yongbyon facility; and ceasing, with immediate effect, all co-operation with the IAEA. Accordingly, IAEA inspectors removed all seals and surveillance equipment from the Yongbyon complex and departed the country. A further nuclear test conducted by the DPRK in late May 2009 was deplored by the Security Council, which strengthened the sanctions regime against that country, in June, and demanded that it rejoin the NPT. Reporting to the Board of Governors in June and September the IAEA Director-General urged all concerned parties to continue to work through diplomatic channels for a comprehensive solution that would bring the DPRK back to the NPT and address that country's security concerns and humanitarian, economic and political requirements. In September 2011 the 55th IAEA Conference expressed concern at reports of the construction of a new uranium enrichment facility and light water reactor in the DPRK.

NUCLEAR FUEL CYCLE

The Agency promotes the exchange of information between member states on technical, safety, environmental, and economic aspects of nuclear fuel cycle technology, including uranium prospecting and the treatment and disposal of radioactive waste; it provides assistance to member states in the planning, implementation and operation of nuclear fuel cycle facilities and assists in the development of advanced nuclear fuel cycle technology. The Agency operates a number of databases and a simulation system related to the nuclear fuel cycle through its Integrated Nuclear Fuel Cycle Information System (iNFCIS). Every two years, in collaboration with OECD, the Agency prepares estimates of world uranium resources, demand and production.

Finance

The Agency is financed by regular and voluntary contributions from member states. Expenditure approved under the regular budget for 2010 amounted to some €315m., while the target for voluntary contributions to finance the IAEA technical co-operation programme in that year was €85m.

Publications

Annual Report.

Atoms for Peace.

Fundamental Safety Principles.

IAEA Bulletin (quarterly).

IAEA Newsbriefs (every 2 months).

IAEA Safety Glossary Terminology Used in Nuclear Safety and Radiation Protection.

IAEA Yearbook.

INIS Atomindex (bibliography, 2 a month).

INIS Reference Series.

INSAG Series.

Legal Series.

Meetings on Atomic Energy (quarterly).

The Nuclear Fuel Cycle Information System: A Directory of Nuclear Fuel Cycle Facilities.

Nuclear Fusion (monthly).

Nuclear Safety Review (annually).

Nuclear Technology Review (annually).

Panel Proceedings Series.

Publications Catalogue (annually).

Safety Series.

Technical Directories.

Technical Reports Series.

International Bank for Reconstruction and Development—IBRD (World Bank)

Address: 1818 H St, NW, Washington, DC 20433, USA.

Telephone: (202) 473-1000; **fax:** (202) 477-6391; **e-mail:** pic@worldbank.org; **internet:** www.worldbank.org.

The IBRD was established in December 1945. Initially it was concerned with post-war reconstruction in Europe; since then its aim has been to assist the economic development of member nations by making loans where private capital is not available on reasonable terms to finance productive investments. Loans are made either directly to governments, or to private enterprises with the guarantee of their governments. The World Bank, as it is commonly known, comprises the IBRD and the International Development Association (IDA). The affiliated group of institutions, comprising the IBRD, IDA, the International Finance Corporation (IFC), the Multilateral Investment Guarantee Agency (MIGA) and the International Centre for Settlement of Investment Disputes (ICSID, see below), is referred to as the World Bank Group.

Organization

(October 2011)

Officers and staff of the IBRD serve concurrently as officers and staff in IDA. The World Bank has offices in New York, Brussels, Paris (for Europe), Frankfurt, London, Geneva and Tokyo, as well as in more than 100 countries of operation. Country Directors are located in some 30 country offices.

BOARD OF GOVERNORS

The Board of Governors consists of one Governor appointed by each member nation. Typically, a Governor is the country's finance minister, central bank governor, or a minister or an official of comparable rank. The Board normally meets once a year.

EXECUTIVE DIRECTORS

The general operations of the Bank are conducted by a Board of 25 Executive Directors. Five Directors are appointed by the five members having the largest number of shares of capital stock, and the rest are elected by the Governors representing the other members. The President of the Bank is Chairman of the Board.

PRINCIPAL OFFICERS

The principal officers of the Bank are the President of the Bank, three Managing Directors, two Senior Vice-Presidents and 25 Vice-Presidents.

President and Chairman of Executive Directors: ROBERT B. ZOELLICK (USA).

Vice-President, East Asia and Pacific: PAMELA COX (USA).

Activities

The World Bank's primary objectives are the achievement of sustainable economic growth and the reduction of poverty in developing countries. In the context of stimulating economic growth the Bank promotes both private sector development and human resource development and has attempted to respond to the growing demands by developing countries for assistance in these areas. In September 2001 the Bank announced that it was to become a full partner in implementing the UN Millennium Development Goals (MDGs), and was to make them central to its development agenda. The objectives, which were approved by governments attending a special session of the UN General Assembly in September 2000, represented a new international consensus to achieve determined poverty reduction targets. The Bank was closely involved in preparations for the International Conference on Financing for Development, which was held in Monterrey, Mexico, in March 2002. The meeting adopted the Monterrey Consensus, which outlined measures to support national development efforts and to achieve the MDGs. During 2002/03 the Bank, with the IMF, undertook to develop a monitoring framework to review progress in the MDG agenda. The first *Global Monitoring Report* was issued by the Bank and the IMF in April 2004.

In October 2007 the Bank's President defined the following six strategic themes as priorities for Bank development activities: the poorest countries; fragile and post-conflict states; middle-income countries; global public goods; the Arab world; and knowledge and learning. In May 2008 the Bank established a Global Food Crisis Response Programme (GFRP, see below) to assist developing countries affected by the escalating cost of food production. In December the Bank resolved to establish a new facility to accelerate the provision of funds, through IDA, for developing countries affected by the global decline in economic and financial market conditions. The Bank participated in the meeting of heads of state and government of the Group of 20 (G20) leading economies, that was held in Washington, DC, USA, in November 2008 to address the global economic situation, and pursued close collaboration with other multinational organizations, in particular the IMF and OECD, to analyse the impact of the ongoing economic instability. In January 2009 the Bank's President proposed the establishment of a Vulnerability Fund to support essential investment projects in developing countries, to be financed by developed economies appropriating 0.7% of their economic stimulus measures to the Fund. During early 2009 the Bank elaborated its operational response to the global economic crisis. Three operational platforms were devised to address the areas identified as priority themes, i.e. protecting the most vulnerable against the effects of the crisis; maintaining long-term infrastructure investment programmes; and sustaining the potential for private sector-led economic growth and employment creation. Consequently, a new Vulnerability Financing Facility was established, incorporating the GFRP and a new Rapid Social Response Programme, to extend immediate assistance to the poorest groups in affected low- and middle-income countries. Infrastructure investment was to be supported through a new Infrastructure Recovery and Assets Platform, which was mandated to release funds to secure existing infrastructure projects and to finance new initiatives in support of longer-term economic development. Private sector support for infrastructure projects, bank recapitalization, microfinance, and trade financing was to be led by IFC.

The Bank's efforts to reduce poverty include the compilation of country-specific assessments and the formulation of country assistance strategies (CASs) to review and guide the Bank's country programmes. In 1998/99 the Bank's Executive Directors endorsed a Comprehensive Development Framework (CDF) to effect a new approach to development assistance based on partnerships and country responsibility, with an emphasis on the interdependence of the social, structural, human, governmental, economic and environmental elements of development. The CDF, which aimed to enhance the overall effectiveness of development assistance, was formulated after a series of consultative meetings organized by the Bank and attended by representatives of governments, donor agencies, financial institutions, non-governmental organizations, the private sector and academics. In December 1999 the Bank introduced a new approach to implement the principles of the CDF, as part of its strategy to enhance the debt relief scheme for heavily indebted poor countries (HIPCs, see below). Applicant countries were requested to formulate, in consultation with external partners and other stakeholders, a results-oriented national strategy to reduce poverty, to be presented in the form of a Poverty Reduction Strategy Paper (PRSP). In cases where there might be some delay in issuing a full PRSP, it was permissible for a country to submit a less detailed 'interim' PRSP (I-PRSP) in order to secure the preliminary qualification for debt relief. The approach also requires the publication of annual progress reports. In 2001 the Bank introduced a new Poverty Reduction Support Credit to help low-income countries to implement the policy and institutional reforms outlined in their PRSP. Increasingly, PRSPs have been considered by the international community to be the appropriate country-level framework to assess progress towards achieving the MDGs.

FINANCIAL OPERATIONS

IBRD capital is derived from members' subscriptions to capital shares, the calculation of which is based on their quotas in the IMF. At 30 June 2010 the total subscribed capital of the IBRD was US $189,943m., of which the paid-in portion was $11,492m. (6.1%); the remainder is subject to call if required. Most of the IBRD's lendable funds come from its borrowing, on commercial terms, in world capital markets, and also from its retained earnings and the flow of repayments on its loans. IBRD loans carry a variable interest rate, rather than a rate fixed at the time of borrowing.

IBRD loans usually have a 'grace period' of five years and are repayable over 15 years or fewer. Loans are made to governments, or must be guaranteed by the government concerned, and are normally made for projects likely to offer a commercially viable rate of return. In 1980 the World Bank introduced structural adjustment lending, which (instead of financing specific projects) supports programmes and changes necessary to modify the structure of an economy so that it can restore or maintain its growth and viability in its balance of payments over the medium term.

The IBRD and IDA together made 354 new lending and investment commitments totalling US $58,747.1m. during the year ending 30 June 2010, compared with 302 (amounting to $46,906.0m.) in the previous year. During 2009/10 the IBRD alone approved commitments totalling $44,197.4m. (compared with $32,910.8m. in the previous year). During 2009/10 IBRD lending amounting to $5,864.7m. (13% of the total) was allocated to projects in East Asia and the Pacific and $6,688.7m. (15%) to South Asia. Total disbursements by the IBRD in the year ending 30 June 2010 amounted to $28,854m.

In September 1996 the World Bank/IMF Development Committee endorsed a joint initiative to assist HIPCs to reduce their debt burden to a sustainable level, in order to make more resources available for poverty reduction and economic growth. A new Trust Fund was established by the World Bank in November to finance the initiative. The Fund, consisting of an initial allocation of US $500m. from the IBRD surplus and other contributions from multilateral creditors, was to be administered by IDA. In early 1999 the World Bank and IMF initiated a comprehensive review of the HIPC initiative. In June the G8 countries, meeting in Cologne, Germany, agreed to increase contributions to the HIPC Trust Fund and to cancel substantial amounts of outstanding debt, and proposed more flexible terms for eligibility. In September the Bank and IMF reached an agreement on an enhanced HIPC scheme, with further revenue to be generated through the revaluation of a percentage of IMF gold reserves. It was agreed that, in order to qualify for debt relief and additional concessional lending, countries were to formulate a PRSP, and should demonstrate prudent financial management in the implementation of the strategy for at least one year. Those countries still deemed to have an unsustainable level of debt at the pivotal 'decision point' of the process were to qualify for assistance. In the majority of cases a sustainable level of debt was targeted at 150% of the net present value (NPV) of the debt in relation to total annual exports (compared with 200%–250% under the original HIPC scheme). Other countries with a lower debt-to-export ratio were to be eligible for assistance under the initiative, providing that their export earnings were at least 30% of GDP (lowered from 40%) and government revenue at least 15% of GDP (reduced from 20%). In September 2005 the Bank and IMF endorsed a proposal of the G8 to cancel all debt owed by countries that had reached their completion point, under a new Multilateral Debt Relief Initiative. By March 2011 32 countries had reached completion point and a further four had reached decision point of the process.

There are three HIPCs in the Far East and Australasia region: Laos, Myanmar and Viet Nam.

During 2000/01 the World Bank strengthened its efforts to counter the problem of HIV and AIDS in developing countries. In November 2001 the Bank appointed its first Global HIV/AIDS Adviser. The Bank has undertaken research into the long-term effects of HIV/AIDS, and hosts the Global HIV/AIDS Monitoring and Evaluation Support Team of UNAIDS. A new regional strategy to address HIV/AIDS in East Asia and the Pacific was published in mid-2004. In November the Bank launched an AIDS Media Center to improve access to information regarding HIV/AIDS, in particular to journalists in developing countries. In July 2006 the Bank began to implement initiatives within the framework of an AIDS Strategy and Action Plan (ASAP) on behalf of UNAIDS.

In March 2007 the Board of Executive Directors approved an action plan to develop further its Clean Energy for Development Investment Framework, which had been formulated in response to a request by the G8 heads of state, meeting in Gleneagles, United Kingdom, in July 2005. The action plan focused on efforts to improve access to clean energy, in particular in sub-Saharan Africa; to accelerate the transition to low carbon-emission development; and to support adaptation to climate change. In October 2008 the Bank Group endorsed a new Strategic Framework on Development and Climate Change, which aimed to guide the Bank in supporting the efforts of developing countries to achieving growth and reducing poverty, while recognizing the operational challenges of climate change. In June 2010 the Bank appointed a Special Envoy to lead the Bank's representation in international discussions on climate change.

TECHNICAL ASSISTANCE AND ADVISORY SERVICES

In addition to providing financial services, the Bank also undertakes analytical and advisory services, and supports learning and capacity-building, in particular through the World Bank Institute (see below), the Staff Exchange Programme and knowledge-sharing initiatives. The Bank has supported efforts, such as the Global Development Gateway, to disseminate information on development issues and programmes, and, since 1988, has organized the Annual Bank Conference on Development Economics (ABCDE) to provide a forum for the exchange and discussion of development-related ideas and research. In September 1995 the Bank initiated the Information for Development Programme (InfoDev) with the aim of fostering partnerships between governments, multilateral institutions and private-sector experts in order to promote reform and investment in developing countries through improved access to information technology.

The provision of technical assistance to member countries has become a major component of World Bank activities. The economic and sector work (ESW) undertaken by the Bank is the vehicle for considerable technical assistance and often forms the basis of CASs and other strategic or advisory reports. In addition, project loans and credits may include funds earmarked specifically for feasibility studies, resource surveys, management or planning advice, and training. The World Bank Institute has become one of the most important of the Bank's activities in technical assistance. It provides training in national economic management and project analysis for government officials at the middle and upper levels of responsibility. It also runs overseas courses aiming to build up local training capability, and administers a graduate scholarship programme.

Technical assistance (usually reimbursable) is also extended to countries that do not need Bank financial support, e.g. for training and transfer of technology. The Bank encourages the use of local consultants to assist with projects and stimulate institutional capability.

The Project Preparation Facility (PPF) was established in 1975 to provide cash advances to prepare projects that may be financed by the Bank. In 1992 the Bank established an Institutional Development Fund (IDF), which became operational on 1 July; the purpose of the Fund was to provide rapid, small-scale financial assistance, to a maximum value of US $500,000, for capacity-building proposals. In 2002 the IDF was reoriented to focus on good governance, in particular financial accountability and system reforms.

ECONOMIC RESEARCH AND STUDIES

In the 1990s the World Bank's research, conducted by its own research staff, was increasingly concerned with providing information to reinforce the Bank's expanding advisory role to developing countries and to improve policy in the Bank's borrowing countries. The principal areas of current research focus on issues such as maintaining sustainable growth while protecting the environment and the poorest sectors of society, encouraging the development of the private sector, and reducing and decentralizing government activities.

The Bank chairs the Consultative Group on International Agricultural Research (CGIAR), which was founded in 1971 to raise financial support for international agricultural research work for improving crops and animal production in developing countries; it supports 15 research centres.

CO-OPERATION WITH OTHER ORGANIZATIONS

The World Bank co-operates with other international partners with the aim of improving the impact of development efforts. It collaborates with the IMF in implementing the HIPC scheme and the two agencies work closely to achieve a common approach to development initiatives. The Bank has established strong working relationships with many other UN bodies, in particular through a mutual commitment to poverty reduction objectives. In May 2000 the Bank signed a joint statement of co-operation with OECD. The Bank holds regular consultations with other multilateral development banks and with the European Union with respect to development issues. The Bank-NGO Committee provides an annual forum for discussion with non-governmental organizations (NGOs). Strengthening co-operation with external partners was a fundamental element of the Comprehensive Development Framework, which was adopted in 1998/99 (see above). In 2001/02 a Partnership Approval and Tracking System was implemented to provide information on the Bank's regional and global partnerships. In June 2007 the World Bank and the UN Office on Drugs and Crime launched a joint Stolen Asset Recovery (StAR) initiative, as part of the Bank's new Governance and Anti-Corruption (GAC) strategy. In April 2009 the G20 recommended that StAR review and propose mechanisms to strengthen international co-operation relating to asset recovery. The first global forum on stolen asset recovery and development was convened by StAR in June 2010.

In 1997 the Bank, in partnership with the IMF, UNCTAD, UNDP, the World Trade Organization (WTO) and the International Trade Commission, established an Integrated Framework for Trade-related Assistance to Least Developed Countries, at the request of the WTO, to assist those countries to integrate into the global trading system and improve basic trading capabilities. Also in 1997 a Partnerships Group was established to strengthen the Bank's work with development institutions, representatives of civil society and the private sector. The Group established a new Development Grant Facility, which became operational in October, to support partnership initiatives and to co-ordinate all of the Bank's grant-making activities. The Bank establishes trust funds, open to contributions from member countries and multilateral organizations, NGOs, and private sector institutions, in order to support development partnerships. By 30 June 2010 the Bank had a portfolio of 1,070 active trust funds, with assets of almost US $26,000m.

In June 1995 the World Bank joined other international donors (including regional development banks, other UN bodies, Canada, France, the Netherlands and the USA) in establishing a Consultative Group to Assist the Poorest (CGAP), which was to channel funds to the most needy through grass-roots agencies. An initial credit of approximately US $200m. was committed by the donors. The Bank manages the CGAP Secretariat, which is responsible for the administration of external funding and for the evaluation and approval of project financing. The CGAP provides technical assistance, training and strategic advice to microfinance institutions and other relevant bodies. As an implementing agency of the Global Environment Facility (GEF) the Bank assists countries to prepare and supervise GEF projects relating to biological diversity, climate change and other environmental protection measures. It is an example of a partnership in action which addresses a global agenda, complementing Bank country assistance activities. Other funds administered by the Bank include the Global Program to Eradicate Poliomyelitis, launched during the financial year 2002/03, the Least Developed Countries Fund for Climate Change, established in September 2002, an Education for All Fast-Track Initiative Catalytic Trust Fund, established in 2003/04, a Carbon Finance Assistance Trust Fund, established in 2004/05, and a Trust Fund for Anti-Money Laundering and Combating Financing of Terrorism for Asia-Pacific and for Central America and the Caribbean, established in 2005/06. In 2006/07 the Bank established a Global Facility for Disaster Reduction and Recovery. In September 2007 the Bank's Executive Directors approved a Carbon Partnership Facility and a Forest Carbon Partnership Facility to support its climate change activities. In December 2010 the Bank inaugurated a Partnership for Market Readiness, with initial pledged contributions of US $20m., to support developing countries to use carbon market and emissions trading mechanisms. In May 2008 the Bank inaugurated the Global Food Crisis Response Programme (GFRP) to provide financial support, with resources of some $1,200m., to help meet the immediate needs of countries affected by the escalating cost of food production and by food shortages. Grants and loans were to be allocated on the basis of rapid needs assessments, conducted by the Bank with the FAO, the WFP and IFAD. As part of the facility a Multi-Donor Trust Fund was established to facilitate co-ordination among donors and to leverage financial support for the rapid delivery of seeds and fertilizer to small-scale farmers. In April 2009 the Bank increased the resources available under the GFRP to $2,000m. By April 2010 $1,170m. had been approved under the GFRP for initiatives in 35 countries, of which $884m. had been disbursed.

In March 1998 the Bank helped to organize the first Asia Development Forum, which convened some 300 representatives of government, the private sector and academia to discuss the region's prospects for economic recovery. A second Forum was held in June 2000, in Singapore, and the third, organized by the Bank with the Asian Development Bank, the ADB Institute, and ESCAP to enhance further development capacity, was convened in June 2001, in Bangkok, Thailand. A fourth Forum was held in Seoul, Republic of Korea, in November 2002, on the theme of trade and poverty.

The Bank is a lead organization in providing reconstruction assistance following natural disasters or conflicts, usually in collaboration with other UN agencies or international organizations, and through special trust funds. The Bank is a trustee, with the Asian Development Bank, of the Trust Fund for East Timor, which was established in December 1999, with donations of some US $147m., to channel support for reconstruction projects and preparations for independence and the post-independence period. The Bank hosts, every six months, a Timor-Leste and Development Partners Meeting. In response to the extreme financial difficulties that confronted several Asian economies in 1997/98 the Bank established a Special Financial Operations Unit to help to alleviate the consequences of the crisis in all affected countries. The Bank pledged some $16,000m., in addition to its regular lending programme, to lessen the social consequences of the crisis by protecting social services and strengthening social security and other public funding for the poor and disadvantaged, mainly in Thailand and Indonesia. The Bank also helped to formulate programmes to strengthen legal and institutional frameworks and to restructure the financial services sector and corporate governance. In June 1998 a Japan Social Development Fund, with resources amounting to some $93m., was established by the Japanese Government to fund social programmes to assist the poorest communities affected by the financial crisis and other grass-roots capacity-building activities. In April the Bank agreed to administer a new $40m. Asian Financial Crisis Response Trust Fund, which had been established at the second Asia-Europe Meeting to provide support in 70 activities in seven countries, mainly relating to corporate and banking sector reforms, at a total cost of some $43.8m. A second phase of the so-called ASEM Trust Fund became operational in March 2001, focusing on social welfare and safety nets, and financing and corporate restructuring. Contributions to the Fund were expected to total more than $38m. At the end of 2004 the Bank responded immediately to assist countries affected by a massive earthquake and subsequent tsunami which devastated many coastal areas of some 14 countries in the Indian Ocean. Bank staff undertook assessments and other efforts to accelerate recovery planning, mobilize financial support and help to co-ordinate relief and recovery efforts in affected regions. Some $672m. was allocated by the Bank, mainly in grants to be directed to Indonesia, Sri Lanka and the Maldives, for the first phase of reconstruction efforts. In February 2005 the Bank opened an office in Aceh Province, Indonesia, which was closest to the epicentre of the earthquake. By the end of June the Bank had committed some $837.5m. to tsunami recovery programmes in India, Indonesia, the Maldives and Sri Lanka, in particular to repair damaged services, to assist the reconstruction of housing and to restore livelihoods. The Bank administers a Multi-Donor Trust Fund for Aceh and North Sumatra that was established by the Indonesian Government to manage some $550m. in pledged aid. In May the Fund approved four projects, with funding of $250m., concerned with housing, land rights and community facilities. The Japan Social Development Fund was to finance projects to support affected communities and vulnerable groups in southern Thailand. In September the Bank hosted a meeting of the Global Consortium on Tsunami Recovery, convened by former US President Clinton, comprising the Bank President, heads of other UN agencies and international organizations and representatives of the affected countries. The Consortium endorsed a plan of action to deliver and construct improved transitional shelters. By 30 September 2009 $685.2m. had been pledged for the Multi-Donor Trust Fund, of which some $399m. had been disbursed.

The Bank has worked with FAO, WHO and the World Organisation of Animal Health (OIE) to develop strategies to monitor, contain and eradicate the spread of highly pathogenic avian influenza. In September 2005 the Bank organized a meeting of leading experts on the issue and in November it co-sponsored, with FAO, WHO and OIE, an international partners' conference, focusing on control of the disease and preparedness planning for any future related influenza pandemic in humans. In January 2006 the Bank's Board of Directors approved the establishment of a funding programme (the Global Program for Avian Influenza Control and Human Pandemic Preparedness and Response—GPAI), with resources of up to US $500m., to assist countries to combat the disease. Later in that month the Bank co-sponsored, with the European Commission and the People's Republic of China, an International Ministerial Pledging Conference on Avian and Human Pandemic Influenza (AHI), convened in Beijing. Participants pledged some $1,900m. to fund disease control and pandemic preparedness activities at global, regional and country levels. Commitments to the AHI facility amounted to $126m. at January 2009. In June the Bank approved an additional $500m. to expand the GPAI in order to fund emergency operations required to prevent and control outbreaks of the new swine influenza variant pandemic (H1N1).

The Bank conducts co-financing and aid co-ordination projects with official aid agencies, export credit institutions, and commercial banks to leverage additional concessional funds for recipient countries. During the year ending 30 June 2010 79 Bank projects leveraged US $10,800m. in co-financing.

EVALUATION

The Independent Evaluation Group is an independent unit within the World Bank. It conducts Country Assistance Evaluations to assess the development effectiveness of a Bank country programme, and studies and publishes the results of projects after a loan has been fully disbursed, so as to identify problems and possible improvements in future activities. In addition, the department reviews the Bank's global programmes and produces the *Annual Review of Development Effectiveness*. In 1996 a Quality Assurance Group was established to monitor the effectiveness of the Bank's operations and performance. In March 2009 the Bank published an Action Plan on Aid Effectiveness, based on the Accra Agenda for Action that had been adopted in September 2008 during the Third High Level Forum on Aid Effectiveness, held in Ghana.

In September 1993 the Bank established an independent Inspection Panel, consistent with the Bank's objective of improving project implementation and accountability. The Panel, which became operational in September 1994, was to conduct independent investigations and report on complaints from local people concerning the design, appraisal and implementation of development projects supported by the Bank. By the end of 2010 the Panel had received 71 formal requests for inspection.

IBRD INSTITUTIONS

World Bank Institute (WBI): founded in March 1999 by merger of the Bank's Learning and Leadership Centre, previously responsible for internal staff training, and the Economic Development Institute (EDI), which had been established in 1955 to train government officials concerned with development programmes and policies. The new Institute aimed to emphasize the Bank's priority areas through the provision of training courses and seminars relating to poverty, crisis response, good governance and anti-corruption strategies. The Institute supports a Global Knowledge Partnership, which was established in 1997 to promote alliances between governments, companies, other agencies and organizations committed to applying information and communication technologies for development purposes. Under the EDI a World Links for Development programme was also initiated to connect schools in developing countries with partner establishments in industrialized nations via the internet. In 1999 the WBI expanded its programmes through distance learning, a Global Development Network, and use of new technologies. A new initiative, Global Development Learning Network (GDLN), aimed to expand access to information and learning opportunities through the internet, video conferences and organized exchanges. By early 2010 the GDLN comprised more than 120 recognized global institutions, or Affiliates, in some 80 countries. At that time the WBI had also established 60 formal partnership arrangements with learning centres and public, private and non-governmental organizations to support joint capacity building programmes; many other informal partnerships were also in place. During 2009/10 new South-South Learning Middle-income country (MIC)–OECD Knowledge Exchange facilities were to be established. In July 2009 the Institute began implementing a renewal strategy to refocus its work on the following key development areas: fragile and conflict-affected states; the global economic crisis; governance; climate change; health systems; public-private partnerships in infrastructure; and sustainable urban development; Vice-Pres. SANJAY PRADHAN (India); publs *Annual Report*, *Development Outreach* (quarterly), other books, working papers, case studies.

International Centre for Settlement of Investment Disputes (ICSID): founded in 1966 under the Convention of the Settlement of Investment Disputes between States and Nationals of Other States. The Convention was designed to encourage the growth of private foreign investment for economic development, by creating the possibility, always subject to the consent of both parties, for a Contracting State and a foreign investor who is a national of another Contracting State to settle any legal dispute that might arise out of such an investment by conciliation and/or arbitration before an impartial, international forum. The governing body of the Centre is its Administrative Council, composed of one representative of each Contracting State, all of whom have equal voting power. The President of the World Bank is (*ex officio*) the non-voting Chairman of the Administrative Council. At August 2011 356 cases had been registered with the Centre, of which 227 had been concluded and 129 were pending consideration. At that time 147 countries had signed and ratified the Convention to become ICSID Contracting States; Sec.-Gen. MEG KINNEAR (Canada).

Publications

Abstracts of Current Studies: The World Bank Research Program (annually).
African Development Indicators (annually).
Annual Report on Operations Evaluation.
Annual Report on Portfolio Performance.
Annual Review of Development Effectiveness.
Doing Business (annually).
Global Commodity Markets (quarterly).
Global Development Finance (annually).
Global Economic Prospects (annually).
ICSID Annual Report.
ICSID Review—Foreign Investment Law Journal (2 a year).
Joint BIS-IMF-OECD-World Bank Statistics on External Debt (quarterly).
News from ICSID (2 a year).
Poverty Reduction and the World Bank (annually).
Poverty Reduction Strategies Newsletter (quarterly).
Research News (quarterly).
Staff Working Papers.
The World Bank and the Environment (annually).
World Bank Annual Report.
World Bank Atlas (annually).
World Bank Economic Review (3 a year).
World Bank Research Observer.
World Development Indicators (annually).
World Development Report (annually).

Statistics

IBRD LOANS APPROVED IN THE FAR EAST AND AUSTRALASIA, 1 JULY 2009–30 JUNE 2010
(US $ million)

Country	Purpose	Amount
China, People's Republic	Ningbo new countryside development	50.0
	China Wuhan second urban transport specific investment loan	100.0
	Shandong ecological afforestation	60.0
	Jilin agricultural product safety and quality	100.0
	Ningxia highway investment	250.0
	Anhui medium cities urban transport	100.0
	Henan ecological livestock initiative	80.0
	Liaoning and Shandong technical and vocational education and training	40.0
	Nanning urban environment	100.0
	Chongqing urban rural integration	84.0
	Sustainable development in poor rural areas	100.0
	Taiyuan urban transport	150.0
	Xinjiang Turpan Basin water conservation	100.0
	Second energy efficiency financing financial intermediary loan	100.0
Indonesia	Urban water supply and sanitation	23.6
	Health professional education quality	77.8
	Sixth development policy loan	750.0
	Third infrastructure development policy loan	250.0
	Third national programme for community empowerment in rural areas specific investment loan	785.0
	Third national programme for community empowerment in urban areas sector investment loan	150.0
	Climate change development policy loan	200.0
	Java-Bali power sector restructuring and strengthening (additional financing)	30.0
	'Knowledge improvement for transparency and accountability' (additional financing)	500.0
	Local government and decentralization	220.0
Philippines	Social welfare and development reform	405.0
	Food crisis response (additional financing)	250.0
	Autonomous region in Muslim Mindanão social fund	30.0
Thailand	Highways management (additional financing)	79.3
Viet Nam	First power sector reform development policy loan*	200.0
	First public investment reform development policy loan	500.0

* Joint IBRD/IDA project.
Source: World Bank, *Annual Report 2010*.

International Development Association—IDA

Address: 1818 H Street, NW, Washington, DC 20433, USA.

Telephone: (202) 473-1000; **fax:** (202) 477-6391; **internet:** www.worldbank.org/ida.

The International Development Association began operations in November 1960. Affiliated to the IBRD, IDA advances capital to the poorer developing member countries on more flexible terms than those offered by the IBRD.

Organization

(October 2011)

Officers and staff of the IBRD serve concurrently as officers and staff of IDA.

President and Chairman of Executive Directors: ROBERT B. ZOELLICK (USA).

Activities

IDA assistance is aimed at the poorer developing countries (i.e. those with an annual GNP per capita of less than US $1,165 were to qualify for assistance in 2010/11) in order to support their poverty reduction strategies. Under IDA lending conditions, credits can be extended to countries whose balance of payments could not sustain the burden of repayment required for IBRD loans. Terms are more favourable than those provided by the IBRD; credits are for a period of 35 or 40 years, with a 'grace period' of 10 years, and carry no interest charges. In 2011 79 countries were eligible for IDA assistance, including several small-island economies with a GNP per head greater than $1,165, but which would otherwise have little or no access to Bank funds, and 16 so-called 'blend borrowers' which are entitled to borrow from both IDA and the IBRD.

IDA's total development resources, consisting of members' subscriptions and supplementary resources (additional subscriptions and contributions), are replenished periodically by contributions from the more affluent member countries. In December 2007 an agreement was concluded to replenish IDA resources by some US $41,600m., for the period 1 July 2008–30 June 2011, of which $25,100m. was pledged by 45 donor countries. In March 2010 negotiations on the 16th replenishment of IDA funds (IDA16) commenced, in Paris, France. Participants determined that overarching theme of IDA16 should be achieving development results, and the following areas of focus be 'special themes': gender; climate change; fragile and conflicted affected states; and crisis response. Replenishment meetings were subsequently held in Bamako, Mali, in June, and in Washington, DC, USA, in October. An agreement was concluded in December, at a meeting convened in Brussels, Belgium. The IDA16 replenishment amounted to $49,300m., to cover the period 1 July 2011–30 June 2014, of which $26,400m. was committed by 51 donor countries.

During the year ending 30 June 2010 new IDA commitments amounted to US $14,550m. for 190 projects, compared with $14,041m. for 176 projects in the previous year. Of total IDA assistance during 2010/11 $7,179m. (49%) was for Africa and $4,645m. (32%) for South Asia. In that financial year some 37% of lending was for infrastructure projects (including energy and mining, transportation, water sanitation and flood protection, and information and communications and technologies sectors), 29% for social sector projects, and 18% for law, justice and public administration. In August 2010 the World Bank determined to reallocate some $900m. of IDA funding of planned and ongoing projects in order to support emergency relief and reconstruction activities in areas of Pakistan damaged by extensive flooding.

In December 2008 the Bank's Board of Executive Directors approved a new IDA facility, the Financial Crisis Response Fast Track Facility, to accelerate the provision of up to US $2,000m. of IDA15 resources to help the poorest countries to counter the impact of the global economic and financial crisis. The first operations approved under the Facility, in February 2009, were for Armenia (amounting to $35m.) and the Democratic Republic of Congo ($100m.) in support of employment creation and infrastructure development initiatives and meeting the costs of essential services. In December the Board of Executive Directors approved a pilot Crisis Response Window to deploy an additional $1,300m. of IDA funds to support the poorest countries affected by the economic crisis until the end of the IDA15 period (30 June 2011). The new facility was proposed during a mid-term review of IDA15, held in November, with the aim of assisting those countries to maintain spending on sectors critical to achieving the Millennium Development Goals. Permanent funding for the Crisis Response Window, which additionally was to assist low-income countries manage the impact of natural disasters, was agreed as part of the IDA16 replenishment accord in December 2010. In mid-2011 $250m. was allocated from the Crisis Response Window to provide relief and longer-term rehabilitation assistance to areas of the Horn of Africa affected by a severe drought. In September the World Bank announced that $30m. of those funds were to be disbursed through UNHCR in order to improve basic facilities in settlements occupied by persons displaced as a result of the drought.

IDA administers a Trust Fund, which was established in November 1996 as part of a World Bank/IMF initiative to assist heavily indebted poor countries (HIPCs). In September 2005 the World Bank's Development Committee and the International Monetary and Financial Committee of the IMF endorsed a proposal of the Group of Eight (G8) industrialized countries to cancel the remaining multilateral debt owed by HIPCs that had reached their completion point under the scheme (see IBRD). In December IDA convened a meeting of donor countries to discuss funding to uphold its financial capability upon its contribution to the so-called Multilateral Debt Relief Initiative (MDRI). IDA's participation in the scheme was approved by the Board of Executive Directors in March 2006 and entered into effect on 1 July. During IDA15 US $6,300m. was allocated to the provision of debt relief under the MDRI, $1,700m. under the HIPC initiative and a further $1,100m. to finance arrears clearance operations. At 30 June 2010 total debt relief to be provided by IDA was estimated at $51,400m. in nominal value terms, of which $35,500m. was for the MDRI.

Publication

Annual Report.

Statistics

IDA CREDITS APPROVED IN THE FAR EAST AND AUSTRALASIA, 1 JULY 2009–30 JUNE 2010
(US $ million)

Country	Purpose	Amount
Cambodia	Smallholder agriculture and social protection support	5.0
Laos	Fifth poverty reduction support grant	20.0
	Capacity building in the hydropower and mining sectors	8.0
	Lao environment and social grant (additional financing)	3.0
	Rural electrification phase II	20.0
	Second education development grant (additional financing)	15.5
	Road sector investment	27.8
	Lao uplands food security improvement	10.0
	Sixth poverty reduction support grant	20.0
Mongolia	Index-based livestock insurance (additional financing)	10.0
	Energy sector (additional financing)	12.0
	Multi-sectoral technical assistance credit	12.0

Country—*continued*	Purpose	Amount
Papua New Guinea	'Productive partnerships in agriculture'	25.0
Samoa	Second health sector management programme support credit (additional financing)	3.0
	Economic crisis recovery support	20.0
Solomon Islands	Telecommunications and ICT development	3.3
	Rapid employment emergency recovery grant	3.2
Timor-Leste	Education sector (additional financing)	5.0
Viet Nam	Local development investment funds	190.0
	Viet Nam urban upgrading (additional financing)	160.0
	Livestock competitiveness and food safety	65.3
	Central North region health support	65.0
	First power sector reform development policy credit*	111.8
	Ho Chi Minh City environmental sanitation (additional financing)	90.0
	Red river delta rural water supply and sanitation (additional financing)	65.3
	Second northern mountains poverty reduction specific investment credit	150.0
	Natural disaster risk management (additional financing)	75.0
	System efficiency improvement, equitization and renewables (additional financing)	26.5
	New model university specific investment credit	180.4
	Ninth poverty reduction support credit	150.0
	Project preparation technical assistance facility	100.0

* Joint IBRD/IDA project.
Source: World Bank, *Annual Report 2010*.

International Finance Corporation—IFC

Address: 2121 Pennsylvania Ave, NW, Washington, DC 20433, USA.

Telephone: (202) 473-3800; **fax:** (202) 974-4384; **e-mail:** information@ifc.org; **internet:** www.ifc.org.

IFC was founded in 1956 as a member of the World Bank Group to stimulate economic growth in developing countries by financing private sector investments, mobilizing capital in international financial markets, and providing technical assistance and advice to governments and businesses.

Organization

(October 2011)

IFC is a separate legal entity in the World Bank Group. Executive Directors of the World Bank also serve as Directors of IFC. The President of the World Bank is *ex officio* Chairman of the IFC Board of Directors, which has appointed him President of IFC. Subject to his overall supervision, the day-to-day operations of IFC are conducted by its staff under the direction of the Executive Vice-President. The senior management team includes 10 Vice-Presidents responsible for regional and thematic groupings. At the end of June 2010 IFC had 3,354 staff members, of whom 54% were based in field offices in 86 countries.

PRINCIPAL OFFICERS

President: ROBERT B. ZOELLICK (USA).

Executive Vice-President: LARS THUNELL (Sweden).

Vice-President, Asia Pacific: KARIN FINKELSTON (USA).

Director, Tokyo Office: HIDEAKI SUZUKI (Japan).

OFFICES IN THE FAR EAST AND AUSTRALASIA

Regional headquarters: One Pacific Place, 14th Floor, 88 Queensway, Admiralty, Hong Kong, SAR, People's Republic of China; tel. 25098100; fax 25099363; e-mail spimenta@ifc.org; Dir SERGIO PIMENTA.

Australia: Level 18, CML Bldg, 14 Martin Pl., Sydney, NSW 2000, GPO Box 1612, Sydney, NSW 2000; tel. (2) 9235-6519; fax (2) 9235-6595; e-mail gmurray@ifc.org; Regional Man. GAVIN MURRAY.

Cambodia: 70 Norodom Blvd, Sangkat Chaktomuk, Phnom Penh; tel. (23) 210922; fax (23) 215157; e-mail cschneider@ifc.org; Resident Rep. CHARLES SCHNEIDER.

China, People's Republic (Chengdu): Hongda International Plaza, 10th Floor, 2 Xianan Rd, Chengdu, Sichan Province 610041; tel. (28) 65522836; fax (28) 86767362; e-mail jlai1@ifc.org; Head JINCHANG LAI.

China, People's Republic (Beijing): China World Tower 2, 15th Floor, China World Trade Center, 1 Jian Guo Men Wai Ave, Beijing 100004; tel. (10) 58603000; fax (10) 58603100; e-mail hcho@ifc.org; Country Man. HYUN-CHAN CHO.

Indonesia: Stock Exchange Bldg, Tower II, 9th Floor, Jalan Jenderal Sudirman Kav. 52–53, 12190 Jakarta; tel. (21) 2994-8001; fax (21) 2994-8002; e-mail asack@ifc.org; Country Man. ADAM SACK.

Japan: Fukoku Seimei Bldg, 10th Floor, 2-2-2, Uchisaiwai-cho, Tokyo 100-0011; tel. (3) 3597-6657; fax (3) 3597-6698; e-mail hsuzuki1@ifc.org; Dir HIDEAKI SUZUKI.

Laos: 90 Phonexay Rd, POB 9690, Vientiane; tel. (21) 450017; fax (21) 450020; e-mail achatzinikolaou@ifc.org; Country Co-ordinator AIMILIOS CHATZINIKOLAOU.

Mongolia: MONNIS Tower, 7th Floor, 15 Chingis Ave, Ulan Bator; tel. (11) 312694; fax (11) 312696; e-mail abornstein@ifc.org; Resident Rep. ADAM BORNSTEIN.

Papua New Guinea: Deloitte Tower, Level 13, Douglas St, Port Moresby; tel. 3217111; fax 3217730; e-mail cblacklock@ifc.org; Resident Rep. CAROLYN BLACKLOCK.

Philippines (Davao City): Landco Corporate Center, J. P. Laurel Ave, Bajada, Davao City, Philippines; tel. (82) 2286682; fax (82) 2286670; e-mail ctaylor1@ifc.org.

Philippines (Manila): Tower One, 11th Floor, Ayala Triangle, Ayala Ave, Makati City 1226; tel. (2) 8487333; fax (2) 8487339; e-mail jang@ifc.org; Resident Rep. JESSE ANG.

Thailand: Siam Tower, 30th Floor, 989 Rama I Rd, Bangkok 10330; tel. (2) 2686-8300; fax (2) 2686-8379; e-mail sandrews2@ifc.org; Regional Man. SIMON ANDREWS.

Timor-Leste: Rua Dos Direitos Humanos, Dili; tel. 3324649; fax 3321178; e-mail mday@ifc.org; Resident Rep. MILISSA DAY.

Viet Nam (Hanoi): 63 Ly Thai To, 7th Floor, Hoan Kiem, Hanoi; tel. (4) 39342282; fax (4) 39342289; e-mail sandrews2@ifc.org; Regional Man. SIMON ANDREWS.

Viet Nam (Ho Chi Minh): Somerset Chancellor Bldg, 3rd Floor, 21–23 Nguyen Thi Minh Khai St, District 1, Ho Chi Minh City, Viet Nam; tel. (8) 38235266; fax (8) 38235271; e-mail sandrews2@ifc.org; Regional Man. SIMON ANDREWS.

Activities

IFC aims to promote economic development in developing member countries by assisting the growth of private enterprise and effective capital markets. It finances private sector projects, through loans, the purchase of equity, quasi-equity products, and risk management services, and assists governments to create conditions that stimulate the flow of domestic and foreign private savings and investment. IFC may provide finance for a project that is partly state-owned, provided that there is participation by the private sector and that the project is operated on a commercial basis. IFC also mobilizes additional resources from other financial institutions, in particular through syndicated loans, thus providing access to international capital markets. IFC provides a range of advisory services to help to improve the investment climate in developing countries and offers technical assistance to private enterprises and governments. In 2008 IFC formulated a policy document to help to increase its impact in the three-year period 2009–11. The IFC Road Map identified five strategic 'pillars' as priority areas of activity: strengthening the focus on frontier markets (i.e. the lowest-income countries or regions of middle-income countries, those affected by conflict, or underdeveloped industrial sectors); building long-term partnerships with emerging 'players' in developing countries; addressing climate change and securing environmental and social sustainability; promoting private sector growth in infrastructure, health and education; and developing local financial markets. From late 2008 IFC's overriding concern was to respond effectively to the difficulties facing member countries affected by the global economic and financial crisis and to maintain a sustainable level of development. In particular it aimed to preserve and create employment opportunities, to support supply chains for local businesses, and to provide credit.

To be eligible for financing projects must be profitable for investors, as well as financially and economically viable; must benefit the economy of the country concerned; and must comply with IFC's environmental and social guidelines. IFC aims to promote best corporate governance and management methods and sustainable business practices, and encourages partnerships between governments, non-governmental organizations and community groups. In 2001/02 IFC developed a Sustainability Framework to help to assess the longer-term economic, environmental and social impact of projects. The first Sustainability Review was published in mid-2002. In 2002/03 IFC assisted 10 international banks to draft a voluntary set of guidelines (the Equator Principles), based on IFC's environmental, social and safeguard monitoring policies, to be applied to their global project finance activities. In September 2009 IFC initiated a Performance Standards Review Process to define new standards to be applied within the Equator Principles framework. At January 2011 70 financial institutions had signed up to the Equator Principles.

In November 2004 IFC announced the establishment of a Global Trade Finance Programme (GTFP), with initial funding of some US $500m., which aimed to support small-scale importers and exporters in emerging markets, and to facilitate South–South trade in goods and services, by providing guarantees for trade transactions, as well as extending technical assistance and training to local financial institutions. Additional funding of $500m. was approved in January 2007, and in October 2008, by which time there were 147 confirming banks from 70 countries participating in the initiative and 126 issuing banks in 66 countries. In December, as part of a set of measures to support the global economy, the Board of Directors approved an expansion of the GTFP, doubling its funding to $3,000m. Other initiatives included the establishment of an Infrastructure Crisis Facility to provide investment for existing projects affected by a lack of private funding, and a new Bank Capitalization Fund (to be financed, up to $3,000m., with the Japan Bank for International Cooperation) to provide investment and advisory services to banks in emerging markets. In May 2009 IFC established an Asset Management Company, as a wholly owned subsidiary, to administer the Capitalization Fund. In February of that year IFC inaugurated a Microfinance Enhancement Facility, with a German development bank, to extend credit to microfinancing institutions and to support lending to low-income borrowers, with funds of up to $500m. IFC committed $1,000m. in funds to a new Global Trade Liquidity Program (GTLP), which was inaugurated by the World Bank Group in April, with the aim of mobilizing support of up to $50,000m. in trade transactions through financing extended by governments, other development banks and the private sector. In October IFC established a Debt and Asset Recovery Program to help to restore stability and growth by facilitating loan restructuring for businesses and by investing in funds targeting distressed assets and companies. IFC pledged to contribute $1,550m. to the Program over a three-year period, and aimed to mobilize resources through partnerships with other international financial institutions and private sector companies.

IFC's authorized capital is US $2,450m. At 30 June 2010 paid-in capital was $2,369m. The World Bank was originally the principal source of borrowed funds, but IFC also borrows from private capital markets. IFC's net income amounted to $1,756m. (after a $200m. grant transfer to IDA), compared with –$151m. in 2008/09 (after a $450m. transfer to IDA). In December 2008 the Board of Directors approved a Sovereign Funds Initiative to enable IFC to raise and manage commercial capital from sovereign funds. In July 2010 the Board of Directors recommended a special capital increase of $130m., to raise authorized capital to $2,580m. The increase required the approval of the Board of Governors.

In the year ending 30 June 2010 project financing approved by IFC amounted to US $18,041m. for 528 projects in 103 countries (compared with $14,509 for 447 projects in the previous year). Of the total approved in 2009/10, $12,664m. was for IFC's own account, while $5,388m. was in the form of loan syndications and parallel loans, underwriting of securities issues and investment funds and funds mobilized by the IFC Asset Management Company. Generally, IFC limits its financing to less than 25% of the total cost of a project, but may take up to a 35% stake in a venture (although never as a majority shareholder). Disbursements for IFC's account amounted to $6,793m. in 2009/10 (compared with $5,640m. in the previous year).

Since the economic crisis in east Asia in the late 1990s IFC focused its activities in East Asia and the Pacific on restructuring and strengthening corporate and financial sectors in market economies and promoting the development of market institutions in transition economies. IFC's other priority areas in the region have been to finance and advise small and medium-sized enterprises (SMEs), to support private participation in infrastructure and social services, to improve access to finance and develop alternative financial institutions, and promote sustainability. In assessing the impact on the region of the global financial and economic crisis, IFC identified the following areas as potential sources of growth: urban development, agribusiness, and domestic consumption. In August 2010 IFC inaugurated a four-year Pacific Microfinance Initiative which aimed to improve access to basic financial services, in particular for women, rural households, and enterprises in Papua New Guinea, Timor-Leste, and the Pacific Islands. During the financial year 2009/10 IFC approved total financing of US $1,547m. for 57 projects in East Asia and the Pacific (compared with $1,197m. for 45 projects in the previous year).

IFC's Advisory Services are a major part of the organization's involvement with member countries to support the development of private enterprises and efforts to generate funding, as well as to enhance private sector participation in developing infrastructure. Advisory services cover the following five main areas of expertise: the business enabling environment (i.e improving the investment climate in a country); access to financing (including developing financing institutions, improving financial infrastructure and strengthening regulatory frameworks); infrastructure (mainly encouraging private sector participation); environment and social sustainability; and corporate advice (in particular in support of small and medium-sized enterprises—SMEs). In December 2008 the Board of Directors determined to provide additional funding to IFC advisory services in order to strengthen the capacity of financial institutions and governments to respond to the crisis in the global financial markets. At 30 June 2010 there were 736 active Advisory Service projects with a value of US $854m. Total expenditure on Advisory Services during that year amounted to $268m. IFC manages, jointly financed with the World Bank and MIGA, the Foreign Investment Advisory Service (FIAS), which provides technical assistance and advice on promoting foreign investment and strengthening the country's investment framework at the request of governments. Under the Technical Assistance Trust Funds Program (TATF), established in 1988, IFC manages resources contributed by various governments and agencies to provide finance for feasibility studies, project identification studies and other types of technical assistance relating to project preparation. In 2004 a Grassroots Business Initiative was established, with external donor funding, to support businesses that provide economic opportunities for disadvantaged communities in Africa, Latin America, and South and Southeast Asia. Since 2002 IFC has administered an online SME Toolkit to enhance the accessibility of business training and advice. By 2010 the service was available in 16 languages.

Since 2004 IFC has presented an annual Client Leadership Award to a chosen corporate client who more represents IFC values in innovation, operational excellence and corporate governance.

Publications

Annual Report.

Doing Business (annually).

Emerging Stock Markets Factbook (annually).

Lessons of Experience (series).

Outcomes (quarterly).

Results on the Ground (series).

Review of Small Businesses (annually).

Sustainability Report (annually).

Other handbooks, discussion papers, technical documents, policy toolkits, public policy journals.

Multilateral Investment Guarantee Agency—MIGA

Address: 1818 H Street, NW, Washington, DC 20433, USA.

Telephone: (202) 473-6163; **fax:** (202) 522-2630; **internet:** www.miga.org.

MIGA was founded in 1988 as an affiliate of the World Bank. Its mandate is to encourage the flow of foreign direct investment to, and among, developing member countries, through the provision of political risk insurance and investment marketing services to foreign investors and host governments, respectively.

Organization

(October 2011)

MIGA is legally and financially separate from the World Bank. It is supervised by a Council of Governors (comprising one Governor and one Alternate of each member country) and an elected Board of Directors (of no less than 12 members).

President: ROBERT B. ZOELLICK (USA).

Executive Vice-President: IZUMI KOBAYASHI (Japan).

Activities

The convention establishing MIGA took effect in April 1988. Authorized capital was US $1,082m., although the convention provided for an increase of capital stock upon the admission of new members. In April 1998 the Board of Directors approved an increase in MIGA's capital base. A grant of $150m. was transferred from the IBRD as part of the package, while the capital increase (totalling $700m. callable capital and $150m. paid-in capital) was approved by MIGA's Council of Governors in April 1999. A three-year subscription period then commenced, covering the period April 1999–March 2002 (later extended to March 2003). At 30 June 2010 110 countries had subscribed $749.9m. of the general capital increase. At that time total subscriptions to the capital stock amounted to $1,912.8m., of which $364.9m. was paid-in.

MIGA guarantees eligible investments against losses resulting from non-commercial risks, under four main categories:

(i) transfer risk resulting from host government restrictions on currency conversion and transfer;

(ii) risk of loss resulting from legislative or administrative actions of the host government;

(iii) repudiation by the host government of contracts with investors in cases in which the investor has no access to a competent forum;

(iv) the risk of armed conflict and civil unrest.

Before guaranteeing any investment, MIGA must ensure that it is commercially viable, contributes to the development process and is not harmful to the environment. During the fiscal year 1998/99 MIGA and IFC appointed the first Compliance Advisor and Ombudsman to consider the concerns of local communities directly affected by MIGA- or IFC-sponsored projects. In February 1999 the Board of Directors approved an increase in the amount of political risk insurance available for each project, from US $75m. to $200m. In April 2009 the Board of Directors approved modifications to MIGA's policies and operational regulations in order to enhance operational flexibility and efficiency, in particular in the poorest countries and those affected by conflict. In November 2010 the Council of Governors approved amendments to MIGA's convention (the first since 1988) to broaden the eligibility for investment projects and to enhance the effectiveness of MIGA's development impact.

During the year ending 30 June 2010 MIGA issued 28 investment insurance contracts for 19 projects with a value of US $1,500m. (compared with 30 contracts amounting to $1,400m. in the previous year). Since 1990 the total investment guarantees issued amounted to some $22,400m., through 980 contracts in support of 616 projects.

MIGA works with local insurers, export credit agencies, development finance institutions and other organizations to promote insurance in a country, to ensure a level of consistency among insurers and to support capacity-building within the insurance industry. MIGA also offers investment marketing services to help to promote foreign investment in developing countries and in transitional economies, and to disseminate information on investment opportunities. In early 2007 MIGA's technical assistance services were amalgamated into the Foreign Advisory Investment Service (FIAS, see IFC), of which MIGA became a lead partner, along with IFC and the World Bank.

In October 1995 MIGA established a new network on investment opportunities, which connected investment promotion agencies (IPAs) throughout the world on an electronic information network. The so-called IPA*net* aimed to encourage further investments among developing countries, to provide access to comprehensive information on investment laws and conditions and to strengthen links between governmental, business and financial associations and investors. A new version of IPA*net* was launched in 1997 (and can be accessed at www.ipanet.net). In June 1998 MIGA initiated a new internet-based facility, 'PrivatizationLink', to provide information on investment opportunities resulting from the privatization of industries in developing economies. In October 2000 a specialized facility within the service was established to facilitate investment in Russia (russia.privatizationlink.com). During 2000/01 an office was established in Paris, France, to promote and co-ordinate European investment in developing countries, in particular in Africa and Eastern Europe. In March 2002 MIGA opened a regional office, based in Johannesburg, South Africa. In September a new regional office was inaugurated in Singapore, in order to facilitate foreign investment in Asia. A Regional Director for Asia and the Pacific was appointed, for the first time, in August 2010 to head a new Asian Hub, operating from offices in Singapore, Hong Kong SAR and the People's Republic of China.

In April 2002 MIGA launched a new service, 'FDIXchange', to provide potential investors, advisors and financial institutions with up-to-date market analysis and information on foreign direct investment opportunities in emerging economies. An FDIXchange Investor Information Development Programme was launched in January 2003. In January 2004 a new online FDI Promotion Centre became available (www.fdipromotion.com) to facilitate information exchange and knowledge-sharing among investment promotion professionals, in particular in developing countries. During 2003/04 MIGA established a new fund, the Invest-in-Development Facility, to enhance the role of foreign investment in attaining the Millennium Development Goals. In 2005/06 MIGA supported for the first time a project aimed at selling carbon credits gained by reducing greenhouse gas emissions; it provided US $2m. in guarantee coverage to the El Salvador-based initiative. A new internet service, relating to political risk management and insurance, was launched during 2006/07 (www.pri-center.com).

Publications

Annual Report.

MIGA News (online newsletter; every 2 months).

World Investment and Political Risk (annually).

Other guides, brochures and regional briefs.

International Fund for Agricultural Development—IFAD

Address: Via Paolo di Dono 44, 00142 Rome, Italy.

Telephone: (06) 54591; **fax:** (06) 5043463; **e-mail:** ifad@ifad.org; **internet:** www.ifad.org.

IFAD was established in 1977, following a decision by the 1974 UN World Food Conference, with a mandate to combat hunger and eradicate poverty on a sustainable basis in the low-income, food-deficit regions of the world. Funding operations began in January 1978.

Organization

(October 2011)

GOVERNING COUNCIL

Each member state is represented in the Governing Council (the Fund's highest authority) by a Governor and an Alternate. Sessions are held annually with special sessions as required. The Governing Council elects the President of the Fund (who also chairs the Executive Board) by a two-thirds majority for a four-year term. The President is eligible for re-election.

EXECUTIVE BOARD

Consists of 18 members and 18 alternates, elected by the Governing Council, who serve for three years. The Executive Board is responsible for the conduct and general operation of IFAD and approves loans and grants for projects; it holds three regular sessions each year. An independent Office of Evaluation reports directly to the Board.

The governance structure of the Fund is based on the classification of members. Membership of the Executive Board is distributed as follows: eight List A countries (i.e. industrialized donor countries), four List B (petroleum-exporting developing donor countries), and six List C (recipient developing countries), divided equally among the three Sub-List C categories (i.e. for Africa, Europe, Asia and the Pacific, and Latin America and the Caribbean).

President and Chairman of Executive Board: Kanayo F. Nwanze (Nigeria).

Vice-President: Yukiko Omura (Japan).

Activities

IFAD provides financing primarily for projects designed to improve food production systems in developing member states and to strengthen related policies, services and institutions. In allocating resources IFAD is guided by: the need to increase food production in the poorest food-deficit countries; the potential for increasing food production in other developing countries; and the importance of improving the nutrition, health and education of the poorest people in developing countries, i.e. small-scale farmers, artisanal fishermen, nomadic pastoralists, indigenous populations, rural women, and the rural landless. All projects emphasize the participation of beneficiaries in development initiatives, both at the local and national level. Issues relating to gender and household food security are incorporated into all aspects of its activities. IFAD is committed to achieving the Millennium Development Goals (MDGs), pledged by governments attending a special session of the UN General Assembly in September 2000, and, in particular, the objective to reduce by 50% the proportion of people living in extreme poverty by 2015. In 2001 the Fund introduced new measures to improve monitoring and impact evaluation, in particular to assess its contribution to achieving the MDGs.

In May 2011 the Executive Board adopted IFAD's Strategic Framework for 2011–15, in which it reiterated its commitment to improving rural food security and nutrition, and enabling the rural poor to overcome their poverty. The 2011–15 Strategic Framework was underpinned by five strategic objectives: developing a natural resource and economic asset base for poor rural communities, with improved resilience to climate change, environmental degradation and market transformation; facilitating access for the rural poor to services aimed at reducing poverty, improving nutrition, raising incomes and building resilience in a changing environment; supporting the rural poor in managing profitable, sustainable and resilient farm and non-farm enterprises and benefiting from decent employment opportunities; enabling the rural poor to influence policies and institutions that affect their livelihoods; and enabling institutional and policy environments that support agricultural production and the related non-farm activities.

IFAD is a participant in the High Level Task Force (HLTF) on the Global Food Security Crisis, which was established by the UN Secretary-General in April 2008 and aims to address the impact of soaring global levels of food and fuel prices and to formulate a comprehensive framework for action. In June IFAD participated in the High-Level Conference on World Food Security and the Challenges of Climate Change and Bioenergy, convened by FAO in Rome, Italy. The meeting adopted a Declaration on Food Security, which noted an urgent need to develop the agricultural sectors and expand food production in developing countries and countries with economies in transition, and for increased investment in rural development, agriculture and agribusiness. In January 2009 the HLTF participated in a follow-up high level meeting convened in Madrid, Spain, which agreed to initiate a consultation process with regard to the establishment of a Global Partnership for Agriculture, Food Security and Nutrition.

IFAD is a leading repository of knowledge, resources and expertise in the field of rural hunger and poverty alleviation. In 2001 it renewed its commitment to becoming a global knowledge institution for rural poverty-related issues. Through its technical assistance grants, IFAD aims to promote research and capacity-building in the agricultural sector, as well as the development of technologies to increase production and alleviate rural poverty. In recent years IFAD has been increasingly involved in promoting the use of communication technology to facilitate the exchange of information and experience among rural communities, specialized institutions and organizations, and IFAD-sponsored projects. Within the strategic context of knowledge management, IFAD has supported initiatives to establish regional electronic networks, such as Electronic Networking for Rural Asia/Pacific (ENRAP, conducted over three phases during the period 1998–2010), and FIDAMERICA in Latin America and the Caribbean (conducted over four phases during 1995–2009), as well as to develop other lines of communication between organizations, local agents and the rural poor.

IFAD is empowered to make both loans and grants. Loans are available on highly concessionary, hardened, intermediate and ordinary terms. Highly concessionary loans carry no interest but have an annual service charge of 0.75% and a repayment period of 40 years; loans approved on hardened terms carry no interest charge, have an annual service charge of 0.75%, and are repaid over 20 years; intermediate loans are subject to a variable interest charge, equivalent to 50% of the interest rate charged on World Bank loans, and are repaid over 20 years; and ordinary loans carry a variable interest charge equal to that levied by the World Bank, and are repaid over 15–18 years. New Debt Sustainability Framework (DSF) grant financing was introduced in 2007 in place of highly concessional loans for heavily indebted poor countries (HIPCs). In 2010 highly concessionary loans represented some 66.3% of total lending in that year, DSF grants 18.8%, intermediate loans 3.4%, and ordinary loans 9.7%. Research and technical assistance grants are awarded to projects focusing on research and training, and for project preparation and development. In order to increase the impact of its lending resources on food production, the Fund seeks as much as possible to attract other external donors and beneficiary governments as cofinanciers of its projects. In 2010 external cofinancing accounted for some 28.5% of all project funding, while domestic contributions, i.e. from recipient governments and other local sources, accounted for 38.2%.

The IFAD Indigenous Peoples Assistance Facility was created in 2007 to fund microprojects that aim to build upon the knowledge and natural resources of indigenous communities and organizations. In September 2010, the Executive Board approved the establishment of a new Spanish Food Security Cofinancing Facility Trust Fund (the 'Spanish Trust Fund'), which was to be used to provide loans to IFAD borrower nations. On 31 December 2010 the Spanish Government provided, on a loan basis, €285.5m. to the Spanish Trust Fund.

In November 2006 IFAD was granted access to the core resources of the HIPC Trust Fund, administered by the World Bank, to assist in financing the outstanding debt relief on post-completion point countries participating in the HIPC debt relief initiative (see under IBRD). By 31 December 2010 35 of 38 eligible countries had passed their decision points, thereby qualifying for HIPC debt relief assistance from IFAD, and 31 countries had reached completion point, thereby qualifying for full and irrevocable debt reduction.

IFAD's development projects usually include a number of components, such as infrastructure (e.g. improvement of water supplies, small-scale irrigation and road construction); input supply (e.g. improved seeds, fertilizers and pesticides); institutional support (e.g. research, training and extension services); and producer incentives (e.g. pricing and marketing improvements). IFAD also attempts to enable the landless to acquire income-generating assets: by increasing the provision of credit for the rural poor, it seeks to free them from dependence on the capital market and to generate productive activities.

In addition to its regular efforts to identify projects and programmes, IFAD organizes special programming missions to certain selected countries to undertake a comprehensive review of the constraints affecting the rural poor, and to help countries to design strategies for the removal of these constraints. In general, projects based on the recommendations of these missions tend to focus on institutional improvements at the national and local level to direct inputs and services to small farmers and the landless rural poor. Monitoring and evaluation missions are also sent to check the progress of projects and to assess the impact of poverty reduction efforts.

The Fund supports projects that are concerned with environmental conservation, in an effort to alleviate poverty that results from the deterioration of natural resources. In addition, it extends environmental assessment grants to review the environmental consequences of projects under preparation. Since 1997 IFAD has administered the Global Mechanism of the 1996 Convention to Combat Desertification in those Countries Experiencing Drought and Desertification, particularly in Africa. The Mechanism mobilizes and channels resources for the implementation of the Convention (having supported, by September 2011, action programmes in 29 countries) and IFAD is its largest financial contributor. IFAD is an executing agency of the Global Environmental Facility, specializing in the area of combating rural poverty and environmental degradation.

During 2010 IFAD approved lending for nine operations in Asia and the Pacific, involving loans amounting to US $194.2m. (or 24.1% of the total committed in that year). Under a Field Presence Pilot Programme, approved by the Executive Board in 2003 in order to strengthen project implementation, policy dialogue, partnership building and knowledge management, IFAD established field presences in the following countries: the People's Republic of China (also covering the Democratic People's Republic of Korea and Mongolia), India and Viet Nam. At end-2010 58 programmes and projects were ongoing in 18 countries in the region.

During 1998 the Executive Board endorsed a policy framework for the Fund's provision of assistance in post-conflict situations, with the aim of achieving a continuum from emergency relief to a secure basis from which to pursue sustainable development. In July 2001 IFAD and UNAIDS signed a memorandum of understanding on developing a co-operation agreement.

During the late 1990s IFAD established several partnerships within the agribusiness sector, with a view to improving performance at project level, broadening access to capital markets, and encouraging the advancement of new technologies. Since 1996 it has chaired the Support Group of the Global Forum on Agricultural Research (GFAR), which facilitates dialogue between research centres and institutions, farmers' organizations, non-governmental bodies, the private sector and donors. In October 2001 IFAD became a co-sponsor of the Consultative Group on International Agricultural Research (CGIAR). In 2006 IFAD reviewed the work of the International Alliance against Hunger, which was established in 2004 to enhance co-ordination among international agencies and non-governmental organizations concerned with agriculture and rural development, and national alliances against hunger. In November 2009 IFAD and the Islamic Development Bank concluded a US $1,500m. framework cofinancing agreement for jointly financing priority projects during 2010–12 in many of the 52 countries that had membership of both organizations.

Finance

In accordance with the Articles of Agreement establishing IFAD, the Governing Council periodically undertakes a review of the adequacy of resources available to the Fund and may request members to make additional contributions. A target of US $1,200m. was set for the eighth replenishment of IFAD funds, covering the period 2010–12. The provisional budget for administrative expenses for 2011 amounted to $140.1m., while some $15.9m. was budgeted in that year to the Fund's capital budget.

Publications

Annual Report.
IFAD Update (2 a year).
Rural Poverty Report.
Staff Working Papers (series).

Statistics

PROJECTS IN EAST ASIA AND THE PACIFIC APPROVED IN 2010

Country	Purpose	Loan amount (SDR m.*)
Papua New Guinea	Productive partnerships in agriculture	9.2
Solomon Islands	Rural development programme	2.6
Viet Nam	Sustainable economic empowerment of ethnic minorities in Dak Nong	12.8

* The average value of the SDR—Special Drawing Right—in 2010 was US $1.52571.

International Monetary Fund—IMF

Address: 700 19th St, NW, Washington, DC 20431, USA.

Telephone: (202) 623-7000; **fax:** (202) 623-4661; **e-mail:** publicaffairs@imf.org; **internet:** www.imf.org.

The IMF was established at the same time as the World Bank in December 1945, to promote international monetary co-operation, to facilitate the expansion and balanced growth of international trade and to promote stability in foreign exchange.

Organization

(October 2011)

Managing Director: CHRISTINE LAGARDE (France).

First Deputy Managing Director: DAVID LIPTON (USA).

Deputy Managing Directors: NAOYUKI SHINOHARA (Japan), NEMAT SHAFIK (Egypt/United Kingdom/USA), MIN ZHU (People's Republic of China).

Director, Asia and Pacific Department: ANOOP SINGH (India).

BOARD OF GOVERNORS

The highest authority of the Fund is exercised by the Board of Governors, on which each member country is represented by a Governor and an Alternate Governor. The Board normally meets annually. The voting power of each country is related to its quota in the Fund. An International Monetary and Financial Committee (IMFC, formerly the Interim Committee) advises and reports to the Board on matters relating to the management and adaptation of the international monetary and financial system, sudden disturbances that might threaten the system and proposals to amend the Articles of Agreement.

BOARD OF EXECUTIVE DIRECTORS

The 24-member Board of Executive Directors is responsible for the day-to-day operations of the Fund. The USA, United Kingdom, Germany, France and Japan each appoint one Executive Director. There is also one Executive Director from the People's Republic of China, Russia and Saudi Arabia, while the remainder are elected by groups of the remaining countries.

REGIONAL REPRESENTATION

There is a network of regional offices and Resident Representatives in more than 90 member countries. In addition, special information and liaison offices are located in Tokyo, Japan (for Asia and the Pacific), in New York, USA (for the United Nations), and in Europe (Paris, France; Geneva, Switzerland; Belgium, Brussels; and Warsaw, Poland, for Central Europe and the Baltic states).

Regional Office for Asia and the Pacific: 21F Fukoku Seimei Bldg, 2-2-2, Uchisaiwai-cho, Chiyodu-ku, Tokyo 100, Japan; tel. (3) 3597-6700; fax (3) 3597-6705; f. 1997; Dir SHOGO ISHII (Japan).

Activities

The purposes of the IMF, as defined in the Articles of Agreement, are:

(i) To promote international monetary co-operation through a permanent institution which provides the machinery for consultation and collaboration on monetary problems;

(ii) To facilitate the expansion and balanced growth of international trade, and to contribute thereby to the promotion and maintenance of high levels of employment and real income and to the development of members' productive resources;

(iii) To promote exchange stability, to maintain orderly exchange arrangements among members, and to avoid competitive exchange depreciation;

(iv) To assist in the establishment of a multilateral system of payments in respect of current transactions between members and in the elimination of foreign exchange restrictions which hamper the growth of trade;

(v) To give confidence to members by making the general resources of the Fund temporarily available to them, under adequate safeguards, thus providing them with the opportunity to correct maladjustments in their balance of payments, without resorting to measures destructive of national or international prosperity;

(vi) In accordance with the above, to shorten the duration of and lessen the degree of disequilibrium in the international balances of payments of members.

In joining the Fund, each country agrees to co-operate with the above objectives. In accordance with its objective of facilitating the expansion of international trade, the IMF encourages its members to accept the obligations of Article VIII, Sections two, three and four, of the Articles of Agreement. Members that accept Article VIII undertake to refrain from imposing restrictions on the making of payments and transfers for current international transactions and from engaging in discriminatory currency arrangements or multiple currency practices without IMF approval. At the end of 2010 some 90% of members had accepted Article VIII status.

In 2000/01 the Fund established an International Capital Markets Department to improve its understanding of financial markets and a separate Consultative Group on capital markets to serve as a forum for regular dialogue between the Fund and representatives of the private sector. In mid-2006 the International Capital Markets Department was merged with the Monetary and Financial Systems Department to create the Monetary and Capital Markets Department, with the intention of strengthening surveillance of global financial transactions and monetary arrangements. In June 2008 the Managing Director presented a new Work Programme, comprising the following four immediate priorities for the Fund: to enable member countries to deal with the current crises of reduced economic growth and escalating food and fuel prices, including efforts by the Fund to strengthen surveillance activities; to review the Fund's lending instruments; to implement new organizational tools and working practices; and to advance further the Fund's governance agenda.

The deceleration of economic growth in the world's major economies in 2007 and 2008 and the sharp decline in global financial market conditions, in particular in the second half of 2008, focused international attention on the adequacy of the governance of the international financial system and of regulatory and supervisory frameworks. The IMF aimed to provide appropriate and rapid financial and technical assistance to low-income and emerging economies most affected by the crisis and to support a co-ordinated, multinational recovery effort. The Fund worked closely with the Group of 20 (G20) leading economies to produce an Action Plan, in November 2008, concerned with strengthening regulation, transparency and integrity in financial markets and reform of the international financial system. In March 2009 the IMF released a study on the 'Impact of the Financial Crisis on Low-income Countries', and in that month convened, with the Government of Tanzania, a high-level conference, held in Dar es Salaam, to consider the effects of the global financial situation on African countries, as well as areas for future partnership and growth. Later in that month the Executive Board approved a series of reforms to enhance the effectiveness of the Fund's lending framework, including new conditionality criteria, a new flexible credit facility and increased access limits (see below).

In April 2009 a meeting of G20 heads of state and government, convened in London, United Kingdom, determined to make available substantial additional resources through the IMF and other multinational development institutions in order to strengthen global financial liquidity and support economic recovery. There was a commitment to extend US $250,000m. to the IMF in immediate bilateral financial contributions (which would be incorporated into an expanded New Arrangements to Borrow facility) and to support a general allocation of special drawing rights (SDRs), amounting to a further $250,000m. It was agreed that additional resources from sales of IMF gold were to be used to provide $6,000m. in concessional financing for the poorest countries over the next two to three years. The G20 meeting also resolved to implement several major reforms to strengthen the regulation and supervision of the international financial system, which envisaged the IMF collaborating closely with a new Financial Stability Board. In September G20 heads of state and government endorsed a Mutual Assessment Programme, which aimed to achieve sustainable and balanced growth, with the IMF providing analysis and technical assistance. In 2011 the IMF was undertaking a review of its mandate and role in the 'post-crisis' global economy. Short-term priorities included advising countries on moving beyond the policies they implemented during the crisis; reviewing the Fund's mandate in surveillance and lending, and investigating ways of improving the stability of the international monetary system; strengthening macro-financial and cross-country analyses, including early warning exercises; and studying ways to make policy frameworks more resilient to crises.

In August 2009 the Fund's Board of Governors approved the new general allocation of SDRs, amounting to SDR 161,200m., which became available to all members, in proportion to their existing quotas, from 28 August. A further SDR 21,400m, (equivalent to US $33,000m.) became available on 9 September under a special allocation provided for by the Fourth Amendment to the Articles of Agreement, which entered into force in the previous month having been ratified by members holding 85% of the total voting power.

In September 2011 the IMF joined other international financial institutions active in the Middle East and North Africa region to endorse the so-called Deauville Partnership, established by the G8 in May to support political and economic reforms being undertaken by several countries, notably Egypt, Jordan, Morocco and Tunisia. The Fund was committed to supporting those countries to maintain economic and financial stability, and to promote inclusive growth.

QUOTAS

MEMBERSHIP AND QUOTAS IN THE FAR EAST AND AUSTRALASIA

(million SDR*)

Country	October 2011
Australia	3,236.4
Brunei	215.2
Cambodia	87.5
China, People's Republic	9,525.9
Fiji	70.3
Indonesia	2,079.3
Japan	15,628.5
Kiribati	5.6
Korea, Republic	3,366.4
Laos	52.9
Malaysia	1,773.9
Marshall Islands	3.5
Micronesia, Federated States	5.1
Mongolia	51.1
Myanmar	258.4
New Zealand	894.6
Palau	3.1
Papua New Guinea	131.6
Philippines	1,019.3
Samoa	11.6
Singapore	1,408.0
Solomon Islands	10.4
Timor-Leste	8.2
Thailand	1,440.5
Tonga	6.9
Tuvalu	1.8
Vanuatu	17.0
Viet Nam	460.7

* The Special Drawing Right (SDR) was introduced in 1970 as a substitute for gold in international payments, and was intended eventually to become the principal reserve asset in the international monetary system. Its value (which was US $1.57201 at 18 October 2011, and averaged $1.52571 in 2010) is based on basket of international currencies comprising the US dollar, Japanese yen, euro and pound sterling. Each member is assigned a quota related to its national income, monetary reserves, trade balance and other economic indicators; the quota approximately determines a member's voting power and the amount of foreign exchange it may purchase from the Fund. A member's subscription is equal to its quota. Quotas are reviewed at intervals of not more than five years, to take into account the state of the world economy and members' different rates of development. In September 2006 the Board of Governors adopted a resolution on Quota and Voice Reform in the IMF, representing a two-year reform package aimed at improving the alignment of the quota shares of member states to represent more accurately their relative positions in the global economy and also to enhance the participation and influence of low-income countries. An immediate ad hoc quota increase was approved for the People's Republic of China, the Republic of Korea, Mexico and Turkey. In December 2010 the Board of Governors concluded the 14th General Review, with an agreement to increase quotas by 100%, to realign quota shares to ensure greater representation of emerging economies and to preserve the basic votes share of low-

income countries. The reforms required approval by member states constituting 85% of total quotas in order to enter into effect. A Quota and Voice Reform agreement, concluded in March 2008 to increase quotas by a total of SDR 20,800m. for 54 member countries, entered into effect in March 2011. As at October total quotas in the Fund amounted to SDR 237,953.4m.

RESOURCES

Members' subscriptions form the basic resource of the IMF. They are supplemented by borrowing. Under the General Arrangements to Borrow (GAB), established in 1962, the Group of Ten industrialized nations (G10—Belgium, Canada, France, Germany, Italy, Japan, the Netherlands, Sweden, the United Kingdom and the USA) and Switzerland (which became a member of the IMF in May 1992 but which had been a full participant in the GAB from April 1984) undertake to lend the Fund as much as SDR 17,000m. in their own currencies to assist in fulfilling the balance of payments requirements of any member of the group, or in response to requests to the Fund from countries with balance of payments problems that could threaten the stability of the international monetary system. In 1983 the Fund entered into an agreement with Saudi Arabia, in association with the GAB, making available SDR 1,500m., and other borrowing arrangements were completed in 1984 with the Bank for International Settlements, the Saudi Arabian Monetary Agency, Belgium and Japan, making available a further SDR 6,000m. In 1986 another borrowing arrangement with Japan made available SDR 3,000m. In May 1996 GAB participants concluded an agreement in principle to expand the resources available for borrowing to SDR 34,000m., by securing the support of 25 countries with the financial capacity to support the international monetary system. The so-called New Arrangements to Borrow (NAB) was approved by the Executive Board in January 1997. It was to enter into force, for an initial five-year period, as soon as the five largest potential creditors participating in NAB had approved the initiative and the total credit arrangement of participants endorsing the scheme had reached at least SDR 28,900m. While the GAB credit arrangement was to remain in effect, the NAB was expected to be the first facility to be activated in the event of the Fund's requiring supplementary resources. In July 1998 the GAB was activated for the first time in more than 20 years in order to provide funds of up to US $6,300m. in support of an IMF emergency assistance package for Russia (the first time the GAB had been used for a non-participant). The NAB became effective in November, and was used for the first time as part of an extensive programme of support for Brazil, which was adopted by the IMF in early December. (In March 1999, however, the activation was cancelled.) In November 2002 NAB participants approved Chile's Central Bank as the 26th participant. In November 2008 the Executive Board initiated an assessment of IMF resource requirements and options for supplementing resources in view of an exceptional increase in demand for IMF assistance. In February 2009 the Board approved the terms of a borrowing agreement with the Government of Japan to extend some SDR 67,000m. (some $100,000m.) in supplemental funding, for an initial one-year period. In April G20 heads of state and government resolved to expand the NAB facility, to incorporate all G20 economies, in order to increase its resources by up to SDR 367,500m. ($500,000m.). The G20 summit meeting held in September confirmed that it had contributed the additional resources to the NAB. In April 2010 the IMF's Executive Board approved the expansion and enlargement of NAB borrowing arrangements; these came into effect in March 2011, having completed the ratification process. At that time 13 new countries had committed to participating in the NAB.

FINANCIAL ASSISTANCE

The Fund makes resources available to eligible members on an essentially short-term and revolving basis to provide members with temporary assistance to contribute to the solution of their payments problems. Before making a purchase, a member must show that its balance of payments or reserve position makes the purchase necessary. Apart from this requirement, reserve tranche purchases (i.e. purchases that do not bring the Fund's holdings of the member's currency to a level above its quota) are permitted unconditionally. Exchange transactions within the Fund take the form of members' purchases (i.e. drawings) from the Fund of the currencies of other members for the equivalent amounts of their own currencies.

With further purchases, however, the Fund's policy of conditionality means that a recipient country must agree to adjust its economic policies, as stipulated by the IMF. All requests other than for use of the reserve tranche are examined by the Executive Board to determine whether the proposed use would be consistent with the Fund's policies, and a member must discuss its proposed adjustment programme (including fiscal, monetary, exchange and trade policies) with IMF staff. New guidelines on conditionality, which, *inter alia*, aimed to promote national ownership of policy reforms and to introduce specific criteria for the implementation of conditions given different states' circumstances, were approved by the Executive Board in September 2002. In March 2009 the Executive Board approved reforms to modernize the Fund's conditionality policy, including greater use of pre-set qualification criteria and monitoring structural policy implementation by programme review (rather than by structural performance criteria).

Purchases outside the reserve tranche are made in four credit tranches, each equivalent to 25% of the member's quota; a member must reverse the transaction by repurchasing its own currency (with SDRs or currencies specified by the Fund) within a specified time. A credit tranche purchase is usually made under a 'Stand-by Arrangement' with the Fund, or under the Extended Fund Facility. A Stand-by Arrangement is normally of one or two years' duration, and the amount is made available in instalments, subject to the member's observance of 'performance criteria'; repurchases must be made within three-and-a-quarter to five years. An Extended Arrangement is normally of three years' duration, and the member must submit detailed economic programmes and progress reports for each year; repurchases must be made within four-and-a-half to 10 years. In October 1994 the Executive Board approved an increase in members' access to IMF resources, on the basis of a recommendation by the then Interim Committee. The annual access limit under IMF regular tranche drawings, Stand-by Arrangements and Extended Fund Facility credits was increased from 68% to 100% of a member's quota, with the cumulative access limit set at 300%. In March 2009 the Executive Board agreed to double access limits for non-concessional loans to 200% and 600% of a member's quota for annual and cumulative access respectively. In 2009/10 regular funding arrangements approved (and augmented) amounted to SDR 74,175m. (compared with SDR 66,736m. in the previous financial year and SDR 1,333m. in 2007/08).

In addition, special-purpose arrangements have been introduced, all of which are subject to the member's co-operation with the Fund to find an appropriate solution to its difficulties. In December 1997 the Executive Board established a new Supplemental Reserve Facility (SRF) to provide short-term assistance to members experiencing exceptional balance of payments difficulties resulting from a sudden loss of market confidence. The SRF was activated immediately to provide SDR 9,950m. to the Republic of Korea, as part of a Stand-by Arrangement amounting to SDR 15,550m. (at that time the largest amount ever committed by the Fund). In March 2009 the Executive Board decided to terminate the SRF.

In October 1995 the Interim Committee of the Board of Governors endorsed recent decisions of the Executive Board to strengthen IMF financial support to members requiring exceptional assistance. An Emergency Financing Mechanism was established to enable the IMF to respond swiftly to potential or actual financial crises, while additional funds were made available for short-term currency stabilization. The Mechanism was activated for the first time in July 1997, in response to a request by the Philippines Government to reinforce the country's international reserves, and was subsequently used during that year to assist Thailand, Indonesia and the Republic of Korea. It was used in 2001 to accelerate lending to Turkey. In September 2008 the Mechanism was activated to facilitate approval of a Stand-by Arrangement amounting to SDR 477.1m. for Georgia, which urgently needed to contain its fiscal deficit and undertake rehabilitation measures following a conflict with Russia in the previous month. In November the Board approved a Stand-by Arrangement of SDR 5,169m., under the Emergency Financing Mechanism procedures, to support an economic stabilization programme in Pakistan, one for Ukraine, amounting to SDR 11,000m., and another of SDR 10,538m. for Hungary, which constituted 1,015% of its quota, to counter exceptional pressures on that country's banking sector and the Government's economic programme. An arrangement for Latvia, amounting to SDR 1,522m., was approved in the following month. In May 2010 the Board endorsed a three-year Stand-by Arrangement for Greece amounting to SDR 26,400m., accounting for some 2,400% of that country's new quota (under the 2008 quota reform). The Arrangement was approved under the Emergency Financing Mechanism, as part of a joint financial assistance package with the euro area countries, which aimed to alleviate Greece's sovereign debt crisis and to support an economic recovery and reform programme. In July 2011 the Fund completed a fourth review of the country's economic performance under the Stand-by Arrangement, enabling a further disbursement of SDR 2,900m. At that time total Fund disbursements under the Arrangement amounted to SDR 15,600m.

In October 2008 the Executive Board approved a new Short-Term Liquidity Facility (SLF) to extend exceptional funds (up to 500% of quotas) to emerging economies affected by the turmoil in international financial markets and economic deceleration in advanced economies. Eligibility for lending under the new Facility was to be based on a country's record of strong macroeconomic policies and having a sustainable level of debt. In March 2009 the Executive Board decided to replace the SLF with a Flexible Credit Line (FCL) facility, which, similarly, was to provide credit to countries with strong economic foundations, but was also to be primarily considered as precautionary. In addition, it was to have a longer repayment period (of up to five years) and have no access 'cap'. The first arrangement under the FCL was approved in April for Mexico, making available funds of up to SDR 31,528m. for a one-year period. Three FCL arrangements, amounting to SDR 52,184m., were approved in 2009/10, accounting for more than 70% of Fund lending commitments in that year.

In January 2006 a new Exogenous Shocks Facility (ESF) was established to provide concessional assistance to economies adversely affected by events deemed to be beyond government control, for example commodity price changes, natural disasters, or conflicts in neighbouring countries that disrupt trade. Loans under the ESF were to be offered on the same terms as those of the Poverty Reduction and Growth Facility (PRGF) for low-income countries without a PRGF in place. In September 2008 modifications to the ESF were approved, including a new rapid-access component (to provide up to 25% of a country's quota) and a high-access component (to provide up to 75% of quota). These came into effect in late November.

In January 2010 the Fund introduced new concessional facilities for low-income countries as part of broader reforms to enhance flexibility of lending and to focus support closer to specific national requirements. The three new facilities aimed to support country-owned programmes to achieve macroeconomic positions consistent with sustainable poverty reduction and economic growth. They carried zero interest rate, although this was to be reviewed every two years. An Extended Credit Facility (ECF) succeeded the existing PRGF to provide medium-term balance of payments assistance to low-income members. ECF loans were to be repayable over 10 years, with a five-and-a-half-year grace period. A Standby Credit Facility (SCF) replaced the high-access component of the Exogenous Shocks Facility (see above) in order to provide short-term balance of payments financial assistance, including on a precautionary basis. SCF loans were to be repayable over eight years, with a grace period of four years. A new Rapid Credit Facility was to provide rapid financial assistance to members requiring urgent balance of payments assistance, under a range of circumstances. Loans were repayable over 10 years, with a five-and-a-half-year grace period.

In May 2001 the Executive Board decided to provide a subsidized loan rate for emergency post-conflict assistance for PRGF-eligible countries, in order to facilitate the rehabilitation of their economies and to improve their eligibility for further IMF concessionary arrangements. In January 2005 the Executive Board decided to extend the subsidized rate for natural disasters.

During 2009/10 the IMF approved nine new Stand-by Arrangements amounting to SDR 19,825m. (compared with 14 Arrangements totalling some SDR 34,249m. in the previous year). In 2009/10 two new EFF arrangements, amounting to SDR 205m., and 11 ECF/ESF arrangements, amounting to SDR 1,961m., were approved. During 2009/10 members' purchases from the general resources account amounted to SDR 21,087m., compared with SDR 16,363m. in the previous year. Outstanding IMF credit at 30 April 2010 totalled SDR 46,349m., compared with SDR 24,625m. in the previous year.

IMF participates in an initiative to provide exceptional assistance to heavily indebted poor countries (HIPCs), in order to help them to achieve a sustainable level of debt management. The initiative was formally approved at the September 1996 meeting of the Interim Committee, having received the support of the 'Paris Club' of official creditors, which agreed to increase the relief on official debt from 67% to 80%. In all 41 HIPCs were identified, of which 33 were in sub-Saharan Africa. Resources for the HIPC initiative were channelled through the PRGF Trust. In early 1999 the IMF and the World Bank initiated a comprehensive review of the HIPC scheme, in order to consider modifications of the initiative and to strengthen the link between debt relief and poverty reduction. A consensus emerged among the financial institutions and leading industrialized nations to enhance the scheme, in order to make it available to more countries, and to accelerate the process of providing debt relief. In September the IMF Board of Governors expressed its commitment to undertaking an off-market transaction of a percentage of the Fund's gold reserves (i.e. a sale, at market prices, to central banks of member countries with repayment obligations to the Fund, which were then to be made in gold), as part of the funding arrangements of the enhanced HIPC scheme; this was undertaken during the period December 1999–April 2000. Under the enhanced initiative it was agreed that countries seeking debt relief should first formulate, and successfully implement for at least one year, a national poverty reduction strategy (see above). In May 2000 Uganda became the first country to qualify for full debt relief under the enhanced scheme. In September 2005 the IMF and the World Bank endorsed a proposal of the Group of Eight (G8) nations to achieve the cancellation by the IMF, IDA and the African Development Bank of 100% of debt claims on countries that had reached completion point under the HIPC initiative, in order to help them to achieve their Millennium Development Goals. The debt cancellation was to be undertaken within the framework of a Multilateral Debt Relief Initiative (MDRI). The IMF's Executive Board determined, additionally, to extend MDRI debt relief to all countries with an annual per caput GDP of US $380, to be financed by IMF's own resources. Other financing was to be made from existing bilateral contributions to the PRGF Trust Subsidy Account. In December the Executive Board gave final approval to the first group of countries assessed as eligible for 100% debt relief under the MDRI, including 17 countries that had reached completion point at that time, as well as Cambodia and Tajikistan. The initiative became effective in January 2006 once the final consent of the 43 contributors to the PRGF Trust Subsidy Account had been received. By March 2011 a further 15 countries had qualified for MDRI relief. At March 2010 the IMF had committed some $6,500m. in debt relief under the HIPC initiative, of a total of $75,600m. pledged for the initiative (in 2009 net present value terms). In June 2010 the Executive Board approved the establishment of a Post-Catastrophe Debt Relief Trust (PCDR Trust) to provide balance of payments assistance to low-income members following an exceptional natural disaster.

SURVEILLANCE

Under its Articles of Agreement, the Fund is mandated to oversee the effective functioning of the international monetary system. Accordingly, the Fund aims to exercise firm surveillance over the exchange rate policies of member states and to assess whether a country's economic situation and policies are consistent with the objectives of sustainable development and domestic and external stability. The Fund's main tools of surveillance are regular, bilateral consultations with member countries conducted in accordance with Article IV of the Articles of Agreement, which cover fiscal and monetary policies, balance of payments and external debt developments, as well as policies that affect the economic performance of a country, such as the labour market, social and environmental issues and good governance, and aspects of the country's capital accounts, and finance and banking sectors. In April 1997 the Executive Board agreed to the voluntary issue of Press Information Notices (PINs) following each member's Article IV consultation, to those member countries wishing to make public the Fund's views. Other background papers providing information on and analysis of economic developments in individual countries continued to be made available. The Executive Board monitors global economic developments and discusses policy implications from a multilateral perspective, based partly on World Economic Outlook reports and Global Financial Stability Reports. In addition, the IMF studies the regional implications of global developments and policies pursued under regional fiscal arrangements. The Fund's medium-term strategy, initiated in 2006, determined to strengthen its surveillance policies to reflect new challenges of globalization for international financial and macroeconomic stability. In June 2007 the Executive Board approved a Decision on Bilateral Surveillance to update and clarify principles for a member's exchange rate policies and to define best practice for the Fund's bilateral surveillance activities. In October 2008 the Board adopted a Statement of Surveillance Priorities, based on a series of economic and operational policy objectives, for the period 2008–11. The need to enhance surveillance and economic transparency was a priority throughout 2009 as the Fund assessed the global economic and financial crisis and its own role in future crisis prevention. In September 2010 the Executive Board decided that regular financial stability assessments, within the Financial Sector Assessment Programme framework (see below), were to be a mandatory exercise for 25 jurisdictions considered to have systemically important financial sectors.

In April 1996 the IMF established the Special Data Dissemination Standard (SDDS), which was intended to improve access to reliable economic statistical information for member countries that have, or are seeking, access to international capital markets. In March 1999 the IMF undertook to strengthen the Standard by the introduction of a new reserves data template. By September 2009 64 countries had subscribed to the Standard. The financial crisis in Asia, which became apparent in mid-1997, focused attention on the importance of IMF surveillance of the economies and financial policies of member states and prompted the Fund further to enhance the effectiveness of its surveillance through the development of international standards in order to maintain fiscal transparency. In December 1997 the Executive Board approved a new General Data Dissemination System (GDDS), to encourage all member countries to improve the production and dissemination of core economic data. The operational phase of the GDDS commenced in May 2000. ByOctober 2011 102 countries were participating in the GDDS. The Fund maintains a Dissemination Standards Bulletin Board, which aims to ensure that information on SDDS subscribing countries is widely available.

In April 1998 the then Interim Committee adopted a voluntary Code of Good Practices on Fiscal Transparency: Declaration of Principles, which aimed to increase the quality and promptness of official reports on economic indicators, and in September 1999 it adopted a Code of Good Practices on Transparency in Monetary and Financial Policies: Declaration of Principles. The IMF and World Bank jointly established a Financial Sector Assessment Programme (FSAP) in May 1999, initially as a pilot project, which aimed to promote greater global financial security through the preparation of confidential detailed evaluations of the financial sectors of individual countries. In September 2009 the IMF and World Bank determined to enhance the FSAP's surveillance effectiveness with new features, for example introducing a risk assessment matrix, targeting it more closely to country needs, and improving its cross-country analysis and perspective. As part of the FSAP Fund staff may conclude a Financial System Stability Assessment (FSSA), addressing issues relating to macroeconomic stability and the strength of a country's financial system. A separate component of the FSAP are Reports on the Observance of Standards and Codes (ROSCs), which are compiled after an assessment of a country's implementation and observance of internationally recognized financial standards.

TECHNICAL ASSISTANCE

Technical assistance is provided by special missions or resident representatives who advise members on every aspect of economic management, while more specialized assistance is provided by the IMF's various departments. In 2000/01 the IMFC determined that technical assistance should be central to the IMF's work in crisis prevention and management, in capacity-building for low-income countries, and in restoring macroeconomic stability in countries following a financial crisis. Technical assistance activities subsequently underwent a process of review and reorganization to align them more closely with IMF policy priorities and other initiatives.

Since 1993 the IMF has delivered some technical assistance, aimed at strengthening local capacity in economic and financial management, through regional centres. The first, established in that year, was a Pacific Financial Technical Assistance Center, located in Fiji. A Caribbean Regional Technical Assistance Centre (CARTAC), located in Barbados, began operations in November 2001. In October 2002 an East African Regional Technical Assistance Centre (East AFRITAC), based in Dar es Salaam, Tanzania, was inaugurated and a second AFRITAC was opened in Bamako, Mali, in May 2003, to cover the West African region. In October 2004 a new technical assistance centre for the Middle East (METAC) was inaugurated, based in Beirut, Lebanon. A regional technical assistance centre for Central Africa, located in Libreville, Gabon, was inaugurated in 2006/07. The fourth AFRITAC, located in Port Louis, Mauritius serving Southern Africa and the Indian Ocean, was inaugurated in October 2011. A Regional Technical Assistance Centre for Central America, Panama and the Dominican Republic (CAPTAC-DR), was inaugurated in June 2009, in Guatemala City, Guatemala. In September 2002 the IMF signed a memorandum of understanding with the African Capacity Building Foundation to strengthen collaboration, in particular within the context of a new IMF Africa Capacity-Building Initiative.

The IMF Institute, which was established in 1964, trains officials from member countries in macroeconomic management, financial analysis and policy, balance of payments methodology and public finance. The IMF Institute also co-operates with other established regional training centres and institutes in order to refine its delivery of technical assistance and training services. The IMF is a co-sponsor, with the Austrian authorities, the EBRD, OECD and WTO, of the Joint Vienna Institute, which was opened in the Austrian capital in October 1992 and which trains officials from former centrally-planned economies in various aspects of economic management and public administration. In May 1998 an IMF-Singapore Regional Training Institute (an affiliate of the IMF Institute) was inaugurated, in collaboration with the Singaporean Government, in order to provide training for officials from the Asia-Pacific region. In January 1999 the IMF, in co-operation with the African Development Bank and the World Bank, announced the establishment of a Joint Africa Institute, in Abidjan, Côte d'Ivoire, which was to offer training to officials from African countries. (It relocated to Tunis, Tunisia, in 2003.) Also in 1999 a Joint Regional Training Programme, administered with the Arab Monetary Fund, was established in the United Arab Emirates. During 2000/01 the Institute established a new joint training programme for government officials of the People's Republic of China, based in Dalian, Liaoning Province. A Joint Regional Training Centre for Latin America became operational in Brasília, Brazil, in 2001. In July 2006 a Joint India-IMF Training Programme was inaugurated in Pune, India.

Publications

Annual Report.

Balance of Payments Statistics Yearbook.

Civil Society Newsletter (quarterly).

Direction of Trade Statistics (quarterly and annually).

Emerging Markets Financing (quarterly).

F & D—Finance and Development (quarterly).

Financial Statements of the IMF (quarterly).

Global Financial Stability Report (2 a year).

Global Monitoring Report (annually, with the World Bank).

Government Finance Statistics Yearbook.

Handbook on Securities Statistics (published jointly by IMF, BIS and the European Central Bank).

IMF Commodity Prices (monthly).

IMF Financial Activities (weekly, online).

IMF in Focus (annually).

IMF Research Bulletin (quarterly).

IMF Survey (monthly, and online).

International Financial Statistics (monthly and annually).

Joint BIS-IMF-OECD-World Bank Statistics on External Debt (quarterly).

Quarterly Report on the Assessments of Standards and Codes.

Staff Papers (quarterly).

World Economic Outlook (2 a year).

Other country reports, regional outlooks, economic and financial surveys, occasional papers, pamphlets, books.

United Nations Educational, Scientific and Cultural Organization—UNESCO

Address: 7 place de Fontenoy, 75352 Paris 07 SP, France.

Telephone: 1-45-68-10-00; **fax:** 1-45-67-16-90; **e-mail:** bpi@unesco.org; **internet:** www.unesco.org.

UNESCO was established in 1946 'for the purpose of advancing, through the educational, scientific and cultural relations of the peoples of the world, the objectives of international peace and the common welfare of mankind'.

Organization

(October 2011)

GENERAL CONFERENCE

The supreme governing body of the Organization, the Conference meets in ordinary session once in two years and is composed of representatives of the member states. It determines policies, approves work programmes and budgets and elects members of the Executive Board.

EXECUTIVE BOARD

The Board, comprising 58 members, prepares the programme to be submitted to the Conference and supervises its execution; it meets twice a year.

SECRETARIAT

The organization is headed by a Director-General, appointed for a four-year term. There are Assistant Directors-General for the main thematic sectors, i.e education, natural sciences, social and human sciences, culture, and communication and information, as well as for the support sectors of external relations and co-operation and of administration.

Director-General: IRINA BOKOVA (Bulgaria).

CO-OPERATING BODIES

In accordance with UNESCO's constitution, national Commissions have been set up in most member states. These help to integrate work within the member states and the work of UNESCO. Most member states also have their own permanent delegations to UNESCO. UNESCO aims to develop partnerships with cities and local authorities.

FIELD CO-ORDINATION

UNESCO maintains a network of offices to support a more decentralized approach to its activities and enhance their implementation at field level. Cluster offices provide the main structure of the field co-ordination network. These cover a group of countries and help to co-ordinate between member states and with other UN and partner agencies operating in the area. In 2010 there were 27 cluster offices covering 148 states. In addition 21 national offices serve a single country, including those in post-conflict situations or economic transition and the nine most highly populated countries. The regional bureaux (see below) provide specialized support at a national level.

REGIONAL BUREAUX

Regional Bureau for Education in Asia and the Pacific: POB 967, Bangkok 10110, Thailand; tel. (2) 391-0577; fax (2) 391-0866; e-mail bangkok@unescobkk.org; internet www.unescobkk.org; Dir GWANG-JO KIM.

Regional Science Bureau for Asia and the Pacific: UNESCO Office, Jalan Galuh II 5, Kebayoran Baru, Jakarta 12110, Indonesia; tel. (21) 7399818; fax (21) 72796489; e-mail jakarta@unesco.org; internet www.unesco.or.id; Dir HUBERT J. GIJZEN.

Activities

In the implementation of all its activities UNESCO aims to contribute to achieving the UN Internationally Agreed Development Goals, and the UN Millennium Development Goal (MDG) of halving levels of extreme poverty by 2015, as well as other MDGs concerned with education and sustainable development. UNESCO was the lead agency for the International Decade for a Culture of Peace and Non-violence for the Children of the World (2001–10). In November 2007 the General Conference approved a medium-term strategy to guide UNESCO during the period 2008–13. UNESCO's central mission as defined under the strategy was to contribute to building peace, the alleviation of poverty, sustainable development and intercultural dialogue through its core programme sectors (Education; Natural Sciences; Social and Human Sciences; Culture; and Communication and Information). The strategy identified five 'overarching objectives' for UNESCO in 2008–13, within this programme framework: Attaining quality education for all; Mobilizing scientific knowledge and science policy for sustainable development; Addressing emerging ethical challenges; Promoting cultural diversity and intercultural dialogue; and Building inclusive knowledge societies through information and communication.

EDUCATION

UNESCO recognizes education as an essential human right, and an overarching objective for 2008–13 was to attain quality education for all. Through its work programme UNESCO is committed to achieving the MDGs of eliminating gender disparity at all levels of education and attaining universal primary education in all countries by 2015. The focus of many of UNESCO's education initiatives are the nine most highly-populated developing countries (Bangladesh, Brazil, the People's Republic of China (PRC), Egypt, India, Indonesia, Mexico, Nigeria and Pakistan), known collectively as the E-9 ('Education-9') countries.

UNESCO leads and co-ordinates global efforts in support of 'Education for All' (EFA), which was adopted as a guiding principle of UNESCO's contribution to development following a world conference, convened in March 1990. In April 2000 several UN agencies, including UNESCO and UNICEF, and other partners sponsored the World Education Forum, held in Dakar, Senegal, to assess international progress in achieving the goal of Education for All and to adopt a strategy for further action (the 'Dakar Framework'), with the aim of ensuring universal basic education by 2015. The Dakar Framework, incorporating six specific goals, emphasized the role of improved access to education in the reduction of poverty and in diminishing inequalities within and between societies. UNESCO was appointed as the lead agency in the implementation of the Framework, focusing on co-ordination, advocacy, mobilization of resources, and information-sharing at international, regional and national levels. It was to oversee national policy reforms, with a particular focus on the integration of EFA objectives into national education plans. An EFA Global Action Plan was formulated in 2006 to reinvigorate efforts to achieve EFA objectives and, in particular, to provide a framework for international co-operation and better definition of the roles of international partners and of UNESCO in leading the initiative. UNESCO's medium-term strategy for 2008–13 committed the organization to strengthening its role in co-ordinating EFA efforts at global and national levels, promoting monitoring and capacity-building activities to support implementation of EFA objectives, and facilitating mobilization of increased resources for EFA programmes and strategies (for example through the EFA-Fast Track Initiative, launched in 2002 to accelerate technical and financial support to low-income countries).

UNESCO advocates 'Literacy for All' as a key component of Education for All, regarding literacy as essential to basic education and to social and human development. UNESCO is the lead agency of the UN Literacy Decade (2003–12), which aims to formulate an international plan of action to raise literacy standards throughout the world and to assist policy-makers to integrate literacy standards and goals into national education programmes. The Literacy Initiative for Empowerment (LIFE) was developed as an element of the Literacy Decade to accelerate efforts in some 35 countries where illiteracy is a critical challenge to development. UNESCO is also the co-ordinating agency for the UN Decade of Education for Sustainable Development (2005–14), through which it aims to establish a global framework for action and strengthen the capacity of education systems to incorporate the concepts of sustainable development into education programmes. The April 2000 World Education Forum recognized the global HIV/AIDS pandemic to be a significant challenge to the attainment of Education for All. UNESCO, as a co-sponsor of UNAIDS, takes an active role in promoting formal and non-formal preventive health education. Through a Global Initiative on HIV/AIDS and Education (EDUCAIDS) UNESCO aims to develop comprehensive responses to HIV/AIDS rooted in the education sector, with a particular focus on vulnerable children and young people. An initiative covering the 10-year period 2006–15, the Teacher Training Initiative in sub-Saharan Africa, aims to address the shortage of teachers in that region (owing to HIV/AIDS, armed conflict and other causes) and to improve the quality of teaching.

A key priority area of UNESCO's education programme is to foster quality education for all, through formal and non-formal educational opportunities. It assists members to improve the quality of education provision through curricula content, school management and teacher training. UNESCO aims to expand access to education at all levels and to work to achieve gender equality. In particular, UNESCO aims to strengthen capacity-building and education in natural, social and human sciences and promote the use of new technologies in teaching and learning processes.

The Associated Schools Project (ASPnet—comprising more than 9,000 institutions in 180 countries in 2011) has, since 1953, promoted the principles of peace, human rights, democracy and international co-operation through education. It provides a forum for dialogue and for promoting best practices. At tertiary level UNESCO chairs a University Twinning and Networking (UNITWIN) initiative, which was established in 1992 to establish links between higher education institutions and to foster research, training and programme development. A complementary initiative, Academics Across Borders, was inaugurated in November 2005 to strengthen communication and the sharing of knowledge and expertise among higher education professionals. In October 2002 UNESCO organized the first Global Forum on International Quality Assurance, Accreditation and the Recognition of Qualifications to establish international standards and promote capacity-building for the sustainable development of higher education systems.

Within the UN system UNESCO is responsible for providing technical assistance and educational services in the context of emergency situations. This includes establishing temporary schools, providing education for refugees and displaced persons, as well as assistance for the rehabilitation of national education systems. In Palestine, UNESCO collaborates with UNRWA to assist with the training of teachers, educational planning and rehabilitation of schools. In February 2010 UNESCO agreed to form an International Co-ordination Committee in support of Haitian culture, in view of the devastation caused by an earthquake that had struck that country in January, causing 230,000 fatalities and the destruction of local infrastructure and architecture.

In February 2010 a high-level meeting on Education for All, comprising ministers of education and international co-operation, and representatives from international and regional organizations, civil society and the private sector, was held to assess the impact on education of the ongoing global economic crisis, and to consider related challenges connected to social marginalization.

NATURAL SCIENCES

The World Summit on Sustainable Development, held in August–September 2002, recognised the essential role of science (including mathematics, engineering and technology) as a foundation for achieving the MDGs of eradicating extreme poverty and ensuring environmental sustainability. UNESCO aims to promote this function within the UN system and to assist member states to utilize and foster the benefits of scientific and technical knowledge. A key objective for the medium-term strategy (2008–13) was to mobilize science knowledge and policy for sustainable development. Throughout the natural science programme priority was to be placed on Africa, least developed countries and small island developing states. The Local and Indigenous Knowledge System (LINKS) initiative aims to strengthen dialogue among traditional knowledge holders, natural and social scientists and decision-makers to enhance the conservation of biodiversity, in all disciplines, and to secure an active and equitable role for local communities in the governance of resources.

In November 1999 the General Conference endorsed a Declaration on Science and the Use of Scientific Knowledge and an agenda for action, which had been adopted at the World Conference on Science, held in June–July 1999, in Budapest, Hungary. By leveraging scientific knowledge, and global, regional and country level science networks, UNESCO aims to support sustainable development and the sound management of natural resources. It also advises governments on approaches to natural resource management, in particular the collection of scientific data, documenting and disseminating good practices and integrating social and cultural aspects into management structures and policies. UNESCO's Man and the Biosphere Programme supports a world-wide network of biosphere reserves (comprising 564 biosphere reserves in 109 countries in 2011), which aim to promote environmental conservation and research, education and training in biodiversity and problems of land use (including the fertility of tropical soils and the cultivation of sacred sites). The third World Congress of Biosphere Reserves, held in Madrid, Spain, in February 2008, adopted the Madrid Action Plan, which aimed to promote biosphere reserves as the main internationally-designated areas dedicated to sustainable development. UNESCO also supports a Global Network of National Geoparks (77 in 20 countries in 2011) which was inaugurated in 2004 to promote collaboration among managed areas of geological significance to exchange knowledge and expertise and raise awareness of the benefits of protecting those environments. In April 2010 UNESCO organized the fourth International Geoparks Conference.

UNESCO promotes and supports international scientific partnerships to monitor, assess and report on the state of Earth systems. With the World Meteorological Organization and the International Council of Science, UNESCO sponsors the World Climate Research Programme, which was established in 1980 to determine the predictability of climate and the effect of human activity on climate. UNESCO hosts the secretariat of the World Water Assessment Programme (WWAP), which prepares the periodic *World Water Development Report*. UNESCO is actively involved in the 10-year project, agreed by more than 60 governments in February 2005, to develop a Global Earth Observation System of Systems (GEOSS). The project aims to link existing and planned observation systems in order to provide for greater understanding of the earth's processes and dissemination of detailed data, for example predicting health epidemics or weather phenomena or concerning the management of ecosystems and natural resources. UNESCO's Intergovernmental Oceanographic Commission serves as the Secretariat of the Global Ocean Observing System. The International Geoscience Programme, undertaken jointly with the International Union of Geological Sciences (IUGS), facilitates the exchange of knowledge and methodology among scientists concerned with geological processes and aims to raise awareness of the links between geoscience and sustainable socio-economic development. The IUGS and UNESCO jointly initiated the International Year of Planet Earth (2008).

UNESCO is committed to contributing to international efforts to enhance disaster preparedness and mitigation. Through education UNESCO aims to reduce the vulnerability of poorer communities to disasters and improve disaster management at local and national levels. It also co-ordinates efforts at an international level to establish monitoring networks and early-warning systems to mitigate natural disasters, in particular in developing tsunami early-warning systems in Africa, the Caribbean, the South Pacific, the Mediterranean Sea and the North East Atlantic similar to those already established for the Indian and Pacific oceans. Other regional partnerships and knowledge networks were to be developed to strengthen capacity-building and the dissemination of information and good practices relating to risk awareness and mitigation and disaster management. Disaster education and awareness were to be incorporated as key elements in the UN Decade of Education for Sustainable Development (see above). UNESCO is also the lead agency for the International Flood Initiative, which was inaugurated in January 2005 at the World Conference on Disaster Reduction, held in Kobe, Japan. The Initiative aims to promote an integrated approach to flood management in order to minimize the damage and loss of life caused by floods, mainly with a focus on research, training, promoting good governance and providing technical assistance. The fifth International Conference on Flood Management was convened in Tsukuba, Japan, in September 2011.

A priority of the natural science programme has been to promote policies and strengthen human and institutional capacities in science, technology and innovation. At all levels of education UNESCO aims to enhance teaching quality and content in areas of science and technology and, at regional and sub-regional level, to strengthen co-operation mechanisms and policy networks in training and research. With the International Council of Scientific Unions and the Third World Academy of Sciences, UNESCO operates a short-term fellowship programme in the basic sciences and an exchange programme of visiting lecturers.

UNESCO is the lead agency of the New Partnership for Africa's Development (NEPAD) Science and Technology Cluster and the NEPAD Action Plan for the Environment.

SOCIAL AND HUMAN SCIENCES

UNESCO is mandated to contribute to the world-wide development of the social and human sciences and philosophy, which it regards as of great importance in policy-making and maintaining ethical vigilance. The structure of UNESCO's Social and Human Sciences programme takes into account both an ethical and standard-setting dimension, and research, policy-making, action in the field and future-oriented activities. One of UNESCO's so-called overarching objectives in the period 2008–13 was to address emerging ethical challenges.

A priority area of UNESCO's work programme on Social and Human Sciences has been to promote principles, practices and ethical norms relevant for scientific and technological development. The programme fosters international co-operation and dialogue on emerging issues, as well as raising awareness and promoting the sharing of knowledge at regional and national levels. UNESCO supports the activities of the International Bioethics Committee (IBC—a group of 36 specialists who meet under UNESCO auspices) and the Intergovernmental Bioethics Committee, and hosts the secretariat of the 18-member World Commission on the Ethics of Scientific Knowledge and Technology (COMEST), established in 1999, which aims to serve as a forum for the exchange of information and ideas and to promote dialogue between scientific communities, decision-makers and the public.

The priority Ethics of science and technology element aims to promote intergovernmental discussion and co-operation; to conduct explorative studies on possible UNESCO action on environmental ethics and developing a code of conduct for scientists; to enhance public awareness; to make available teaching expertise and create regional networks of experts; to promote the development of international and national databases on ethical issues; to identify ethical issues related to emerging technologies; to follow up relevant declarations, including the Universal Declaration on the Human Genome and Human Rights (see below); and to support the Global Ethics Observatory, an online world-wide database of information on applied bioethics and other applied science- and technology-related areas (including environmental ethics) that was launched in December 2005 by the IBC.

UNESCO itself provides an interdisciplinary, multicultural and pluralistic forum for reflection on issues relating to the ethical dimension of scientific advances, and promotes the application of international guidelines. In May 1997 the IBC approved a draft version of a Universal Declaration on the Human Genome and Human Rights, in an attempt to provide ethical guidelines for developments in human genetics. The Declaration, which identified some 100,000 hereditary genes as 'common heritage', was adopted by the UNESCO General Conference in November and committed states to promoting the dissemination of relevant scientific knowledge and co-operating in genome research. In October 2003 the General Conference adopted an International Declaration on Human Genetic Data, establishing standards for scientists working in that field, and in October 2005 the General Conference adopted the Universal Declaration on Bioethics and Human Rights. At all levels UNESCO aims to raise awareness and foster debate about the ethical implications of scientific and technological developments and promote exchange of experiences and knowledge between governments and research bodies.

UNESCO recognizes that globalization has a broad and significant impact on societies. It is committed to countering negative trends of social transformation by strengthening the links between research and policy formulation by national and local authorities, in particular concerning poverty eradication. In that respect, UNESCO promotes the concept that freedom from poverty is a fundamental human right. In 1994 UNESCO initiated an international social science research programme, the Management of Social Transformations (MOST), to promote capacity-building in social planning at all levels of decision-making. In 2003 the Executive Board approved a continuation of the programme but with a revised strategic objective of strengthening links between research, policy and practice. In 2008–13 UNESCO aimed to promote new collaborative social science research programmes and to support capacity-building in developing countries.

UNESCO aims to monitor emerging social or ethical issues and, through its associated offices and institutes, formulate preventative action to ensure they have minimal impact on the attainment of UNESCO's objectives. As a specific challenge UNESCO is committed to promoting the International Convention against Doping in Sport, which entered into force in 2007. UNESCO also focuses on the educational and cultural dimensions of physical education and sport and their capacity to preserve and improve health.

Fundamental to UNESCO's mission is the rejection of all forms of discrimination. It disseminates information aimed at combating racial prejudice, works to improve the status of women and their access to education, promotes equality between men and women, and raises awareness of discrimination against people affected by HIV/AIDS, in particular among young people. In 2004 UNESCO inaugurated an initiative to enable city authorities to share experiences and collaborate in efforts to counter racism, discrimination, xenophobia and exclusion. As well as the International Coalition of Cities against Racism, regional coalitions were to be formed with more defined programmes of action. A Coalition of Cities against Discrimination in Asia and the Pacific (APCaRD) was inaugurated in Bangkok, Thailand, in August 2006. An International Youth Clearing House and Information Service (INFOYOUTH) aims to increase and consolidate the information available on the situation of young people in society, and to heighten awareness of their needs, aspirations and potential among public and private decision-makers. Supporting efforts to facilitate dialogue among different cultures and societies and promoting opportunities for reflection and consideration of philosophy and human rights, for example the celebration of World Philosophy Day, are also among UNESCO's fundamental aims.

CULTURE

In undertaking efforts to preserve the world's cultural and natural heritage UNESCO has attempted to emphasize the link between culture and development. In December 1992 UNESCO established the World Commission on Culture and Development, to strengthen links between culture and development and to prepare a report on the issue. The first World Conference on Culture and Development was held in June 1999, in Havana, Cuba. In November 2001 the General Conference adopted the UNESCO Universal Declaration on Cultural Diversity, which affirmed the importance of intercultural dialogue in establishing a climate of peace. UNESCO's medium-term strategy for 2008–13 recognized the need for a more integrated approach to cultural heritage as an area requiring conservation and development and one offering prospects for dialogue, social cohesion and shared knowledge.

UNESCO aims to promote cultural diversity through the safeguarding of heritage and enhancement of cultural expressions. In January 2002 UNESCO inaugurated the Global Alliance on Cultural Diversity, to promote partnerships between governments, non-governmental bodies and the private sector with a view to supporting cultural diversity through the strengthening of cultural industries and the prevention of cultural piracy. In October 2005 the General Conference approved an International Convention on the Protection of the Diversity of Cultural Expressions. It entered into force in March 2007 and the first session of the intergovernmental committee servicing the Convention was convened in Ottawa, Canada, in December.

UNESCO's World Heritage Programme, inaugurated in 1978, aims to protect historic sites and natural landmarks of outstanding universal significance, in accordance with the 1972 UNESCO Convention Concerning the Protection of the World Cultural and Natural Heritage, by providing financial aid for restoration, technical assistance, training and management planning. The medium-term strategy for 2008–13 acknowledged that new global threats may affect natural and cultural heritage. It also reinforced the concept that conservation of sites contributes to social cohesion. During mid-2011–mid-2012 the 'World Heritage List' comprised 936 sites globally, of which 725 had cultural significance, 183 were natural landmarks, and 28 were of 'mixed' importance. UNESCO also maintains a list of 'World Heritage in Danger', comprising 35 sites during mid-2011–mid-2012. UNESCO participated in the successful campaign to safeguard the Buddhist temple at Borobudur, Indonesia (1973–83). The organization is assisting in the preservation of numerous historical and natural sites in the Far East and Australasia region, including the Great Barrier Reef (Australia), the Great Wall of China and the Imperial tombs of the Ming and Qing dynasties (PRC), the Himeji Castle (Japan), Sukhothai (Thailand) and Luang Prabang (Laos).

UNESCO supports the safeguarding of humanity's non-material 'intangible' heritage, including oral traditions, music, dance and medicine. An Endangered Languages Programme was initiated in 1993. By 2010 the Programme estimated that, of some 6,700 languages spoken world-wide, about one-half were endangered. It works to raise awareness of the issue, for example through publication of the *Atlas of the World's Languages in Danger of Disappearing,* to strengthen local and national capacities to safeguard and document languages, and administers a Register of Good Practices in Language Preservation. In October 2003 the UNESCO General Conference adopted a Convention for the Safeguarding of Intangible Cultural Heritage, which provided for the establishment of an intergovernmental committee and for participating states to formulate national inventories of intangible heritage. The Convention entered into force in April 2006 and the intergovernmental committee convened its inaugural session in November. The second session was held in Tokyo, Japan, in September 2007. A Representative List of the Intangible Cultural Heritage of Humanity, inaugurated in November 2008, comprised, at October 2011, 213 elements ('masterpieces of the oral and intangible heritage of humanity') deemed to be of outstanding value; these included: Chinese calligraphy; falconry; several dances, such as the tango, which originated in Argentina and Uruguay, and the dances of the Ainu in Japan; the chant of the Sybil on Majorca, Spain; and the Ifa Divination System (Nigeria). The related List of Intangible Cultural Heritage in Need of Urgent Safeguarding comprised 16 elements in October 2011. UNESCO's culture programme also aims to safeguard movable cultural heritage and to support and develop museums as a means of preserving heritage and making it accessible to society as a whole.

In November 2001 the General Conference authorized the formulation of a Declaration against the Intentional Destruction of Cultural Heritage. In addition, the Conference adopted the Convention on the Protection of the Underwater Cultural Heritage, covering the protection from commercial exploitation of shipwrecks, submerged historical sites, etc., situated in the territorial waters of signatory states. UNESCO also administers the 1954 Hague Convention on the Protection of Cultural Property in the Event of Armed Conflict and the 1970 Convention on the Means of Prohibiting and Preventing the Illicit Import, Export and Transfer of Ownership of Cultural Property. In 1992 a World Heritage Centre was established to enable rapid mobilization of international technical assistance for the preservation of cultural sites. Through the World Heritage Information Network (WHIN), a world-wide network of more than 800 information providers, UNESCO promotes global awareness and information exchange.

UNESCO aims to support the development of creative industries and or creative expression. Through a variety of projects UNESCO promotes art education, supports the rights of artists, and encourages crafts, design, digital art and performance arts. In October 2004 UNESCO launched a Creative Cities Network to facilitate public and private sector partnerships, international links, and recognition of a city's unique expertise. In 2011 the following cities were participating in the Network: Aswan (Egypt), Icheon (Republic of Korea), Kanazawa (Japan) and Santa Fe (Mexico) (UNESCO Cities of Craft and Folk Art); Berlin (Germany), Buenos Aires (Argentina), Graz (Austria), Montreal (Canada), Nagoya and Kobe (Japan), Seoul (Republic of Korea), Shanghai and Shenzhen (PRC), Saint-Étienne (France) (UNESCO Cities of Design); Chengdu (PRC), Östersund (Sweden), Popayan (Colombia) (UNESCO Cities of Gastronomy); Dublin (Republic of Ireland), Edinburgh (United Kingdom), Iowa City (USA), Melbourne (Australia), Reykjavik (Iceland) (UNESCO Cities of Literature); Bologna (Italy), Ghent (Belgium), Glasgow (United Kingdom), Seville (Spain) (UNESCO Cities of Music); Bradford (United Kingdom), Sydney (Australia) (UNESCO Cities of Film); and Lyon (France) (UNESCO City of Media Arts). UNESCO is active in preparing and encouraging the enforcement of international legislation on copyright, raising awareness on the need for copyright protection to uphold cultural diversity, and is contributing to the international debate on digital copyright issues and piracy.

Within its ambition of ensuring cultural diversity, UNESCO recognizes the role of culture as a means of promoting peace and dialogue. Several projects have been formulated within a broader concept of Roads of Dialogue. In Central Asia a project on intercultural dialogue follows on from an earlier multi-disciplinary study of the ancient Silk Roads trading routes linking Asia and Europe, which illustrated many examples of common heritage. Other projects include a study of the movement of peoples and cultures during the slave trade, a Mediterranean Programme, the Caucasus Project and the Arabia Plan, which aims to promote world-wide knowledge and understanding of Arab culture. UNESCO has overseen an extensive programme of work to formulate histories of humanity and regions, focused on ideas, civilizations and the evolution of societies and cultures. These have included the *General History of Africa, History of Civilizations of Central Asia,* and *History of Humanity*. UNESCO endeavoured to consider and implement the findings of the Alliance of Civilizations, a high-level group convened by the UN Secretary-General that published a report in November 2006.

UNESCO was designated as the lead UN agency for organizing the International Year for the Rapprochement of Cultures (2010). In February 2010, at the time of the launch of the International Year, the UNESCO Director-General established a High Panel on Peace and Dialogue among Cultures, which was to provide guidance on means of advancing tolerance, reconciliation and balance within societies world-wide.

COMMUNICATION AND INFORMATION

UNESCO regards information, communication and knowledge as being at the core of human progress and well-being. The Organization advocates the concept of knowledge societies, based on the principles of freedom of expression, universal access to information and knowledge, promotion of cultural diversity, and equal access to quality education. In 2008–13 it determined to consolidate and implement this concept, in accordance with the Declaration of Principles and Plan of Action adopted by the World Summit on the Information Society (WSIS) in November 2005.

A key strategic objective of building inclusive knowledge societies was to be through enhancing universal access to communication and information. At national and global levels UNESCO promotes the rights of freedom of expression and of access to information. It promotes the free flow and broad diffusion of information, knowledge, data and best practices, through the development of communications infrastructures, the elimination of impediments to freedom of expression, and the development of independent and pluralistic media, including through the provision of advisory services on media legislation, particularly in post-conflict countries and in countries in transition. UNESCO recognizes that the so-called global 'digital divide', in addition to other developmental differences between countries, generates exclusion and marginalization, and that increased participation in the democratic process can be attained through strengthening national communication and information capacities. UNESCO promotes policies and mechanisms that enhance provision for marginalized and disadvantaged groups to benefit from information and community opportunities. Activities at local and national level include developing effective 'infostructures', such as libraries and archives and strengthening low-cost community media and information access points, for example through the establishment of Community Multimedia Centres (CMCs). Many of UNESCO's principles and objectives in this area are pursued through the Information for All Programme, which entered into force in 2001. It is administered by an intergovernmental council, the secretariat of which is provided by UNESCO. UNESCO also established, in 1982, the International Programme for the Development of Communication (IPDC), which aims to promote and develop independent and pluralistic media in developing countries, for example by the establishment or modernization of news agencies and newspapers and training media professionals, the promotion of the right to information, and through efforts to harness informatics for development purposes and strengthen member states' capacities in this field. In March 2011 the IPDC approved funding for 93 new media development projects in developing and emerging countries worldwide.

UNESCO supports cultural and linguistic diversity in information sources to reinforce the principle of universal access. It aims to raise awareness of the issue of equitable access and diversity, encourage good practices and develop policies to strengthen cultural diversity in all media. In 2002 UNESCO established Initiative B@bel as a multidisciplinary programme to promote linguistic diversity, with the aim of enhancing access of under-represented groups to information sources as well as protecting underused minority languages. In December 2009 UNESCO and the Internet Corporation for Assigned Names and Numbers (ICANN) signed a joint agreement which aimed to promote the use of multilingual domain names using non-Latin script, with a view to promoting linguistic diversity. UNESCO's Programme for Creative Content supports the development of and access to diverse content in both the electronic and audiovisual media. The Memory of the World project, established in 1992, aims to preserve in digital form, and thereby to promote wide access to, the world's documentary heritage. Documentary material includes stone tablets, celluloid, parchment and audio recordings. By October 2011 245 inscriptions had been included on the project's register; three inscriptions originated from international organizations: the Archives of the ICRC's former International Prisoners of War Agency, 1914–23, submitted by the ICRC, and inscribed in 2007; the League of Nations Archives, 1919–46, submitted by the UN Geneva Office, and inscribed in 2009; and the UNRWA Photo and Film Archives of Palestinian Refugees' Documentary Heritage, submitted by UNRWA, and also inscribed in 2009. UNESCO also supports other efforts to preserve and disseminate digital archives and, in 2003, adopted a Charter for the Preservation of Digital Heritage. In April 2009 UNESCO launched the internet based World Digital Library, accessible at www.wdl.org, which aims to display primary documents (including texts, charts and illustrations), and authoritative explanations, relating to the accumulated knowledge of a broad spectrum of human cultures.

UNESCO promotes freedom of expression, of the press and independence of the media as fundamental human rights and the basis of democracy. It aims to assist member states to formulate policies and legal frameworks to uphold independent and pluralistic media and infostructures and to enhance the capacities of public service broadcasting institutions. In regions affected by conflict UNESCO supports efforts to establish and maintain an independent media service and to use it as a means of consolidating peace. UNESCO also aims to develop media and information systems to respond to and mitigate the impact of disaster situations, and to integrate these objectives into wider UN peace-building or reconstruction initiatives. UNESCO is the co-ordinating agency for 'World Press Freedom Day', which is held annually on 3 May. The theme for 2011 was '21st Century Media: New Frontiers, New Barriers'. It also awards an annual World Press Freedom Prize. UNESCO maintains an Observatory on the Information Society, which provides up-to-date information on the development of new ICTs, analyses major trends, and aims to raise awareness of related ethical, legal and societal issues. UNESCO promotes the upholding of human rights in the use of cyberspace. In 1997 it organized the first International Congress on Ethical, Legal and Societal Aspects of Digital Information ('INFOethics').

UNESCO promotes the application of information and communication technology for sustainable development. In particular it supports efforts to improve teaching and learning processes through electronic media and to develop innovative literacy and education initiatives, such as the ICT-Enhanced Learning (ICTEL) project. UNESCO also aims to enhance understanding and use of new technologies and support training and ongoing learning opportunities for librarians, archivists and other information providers.

Finance

UNESCO's activities are funded through a regular budget provided by contributions from member states and extrabudgetary funds from other sources, particularly UNDP, the World Bank, regional banks and other bilateral Funds-in-Trust arrangements. UNESCO co-operates with many other UN agencies and international non-governmental organizations.

UNESCO's Regular Programme budget for the two years 2010–11 was US $653m.

Publications

(mostly in English, French and Spanish editions; Arabic, Chinese and Russian versions are also available in many cases)

Atlas of the World's Languages in Danger of Disappearing (online).
Copyright Bulletin (quarterly).
Encyclopedia of Life Support Systems (online).
Education for All Global Monitoring Report.
International Review of Education (quarterly).
International Social Science Journal (quarterly).
Museum International (quarterly).
Nature and Resources (quarterly).
The New Courier (quarterly).
Prospects (quarterly review on education).
UNESCO Sources (monthly).
UNESCO Statistical Yearbook.
World Communication Report.
World Educational Report (every 2 years).
World Heritage Review (quarterly).
World Information Report.
World Science Report (every 2 years).
Books, databases, video and radio documentaries, statistics, scientific maps and atlases.

Specialized Institutes and Centres

Abdus Salam International Centre for Theoretical Physics: Strada Costiera 11, 34151 Trieste, Italy; tel. (040) 2240111; fax (040) 224163; e-mail sci_info@ictp.it; internet www.ictp.it; f. 1964; promotes and enables advanced study and research in physics and mathematical sciences; organizes and sponsors training opportunities, in particular for scientists from developing countries; aims to provide an international forum for the exchange of information and ideas; operates under a tripartite agreement between UNESCO, IAEA and the Italian Government; Dir FERNANDO QUEVEDO (Guatemala).

International Bureau of Education (IBE): POB 199, 1211 Geneva 20, Switzerland; tel. 229177800; fax 229177801; e-mail doc .centre@ibe.unesco.org; internet www.ibe.unesco.org; f. 1925, became an intergovernmental organization in 1929 and was incorporated into UNESCO in 1969; the Council of the IBE is composed of representatives of 28 member states of UNESCO, designated by the General Conference; the Bureau's fundamental mission is to deal with matters concerning educational content, methods, and teaching/learning strategies; an International Conference on Education is held periodically; Dir CLEMENTINA ACEDO (Venezuela); publs *Prospects* (quarterly review), *Educational Innovation* (newsletter), educational practices series, monographs, other reference works.

UNESCO Institute for Information Technologies in Education: 117292 Moscow, ul. Kedrova 8, Russia; tel. (495) 129-29-90; fax (495) 129-12-25; e-mail info@iite.ru; internet www.iite.ru; the Institute aims to formulate policies regarding the development of, and to support and monitor the use of, information and communication technologies in education; it conducts research and organizes training programmes; Chair Prof. BERNARD CORNU.

UNESCO Institute for Life-long Learning: Feldbrunnenstr. 58, 20148 Hamburg, Germany; tel. (40) 448-0410; fax (40) 410-7723; e-mail uil@unesco.org; internet www.unesco.org/uil/index.htm; f. 1951, as the Institute for Education; a research, training, information, documentation and publishing centre, with a particular focus on adult basic and further education and adult literacy; Dir ADAMA OUANE (Mali).

UNESCO Institute for Statistics: CP 6128, Succursale Centre-Ville, Montréal, QC, H3C 3J7, Canada; tel. (514) 343-6880; fax (514) 343-6882; e-mail uis@unesco.org; internet www.uis.unesco.org; f. 2001; collects and analyses national statistics on education, science, technology, culture and communications; Dir HENDRIK VAN DER POL (Netherlands).

UNESCO Institute for Water Education: Westvest 7, 2611 AX Delft, Netherlands; tel. (15) 2151-715; fax (15) 2122-921; e-mail info@unesco-ihe.org; internet www.unesco-ihe.org; f. 2003; activities include education, training and research; and co-ordination of a global network of water sector organizations; advisory and policy-making functions; setting international standards for postgraduate education programmes; and professional training in the water sector; Rector ANDRÁS SZÖLLÖSI-NAGY.

UNESCO International Centre for Technical and Vocational Education and Training: UN Campus, Hermann-Ehlers-Str. 10, 53113 Bonn, Germany; tel. (228) 8150-100; fax (228) 8150-199; e-mail info@unevoc.unesco.org; internet www.unevoc.unesco.org; f. 2002; promotes high-quality lifelong technical and vocational education in UNESCO's member states, with a particular focus on young people, girls and women, and the disadvantaged; Head SHYAMAL MAJUMDAR (India).

UNESCO International Institute for Educational Planning (IIEP): 7–9 rue Eugène Delacroix, 75116 Paris, France; tel. 1-45-03-77-00; fax 1-40-72-83-66; e-mail info@iiep.unesco.org; internet www.unesco.org/iiep; f. 1963; serves as a world centre for advanced training and research in educational planning; aims to help all member states of UNESCO in their social and economic development efforts, by enlarging the fund of knowledge about educational planning and the supply of competent experts in this field; legally and administratively a part of UNESCO, the Institute is autonomous, and its policies and programme are controlled by its own Governing Board, under special statutes voted by the General Conference of UNESCO; a satellite office of the IIEP is based in Buenos Aires, Argentina; Dir KHALIL MAHSHI (Jordan).

World Health Organization—WHO

Address: Ave Appia 20, 1211 Geneva 27, Switzerland.

Telephone: 227912111; **fax:** 227913111; **e-mail:** info@who.int; **internet:** www.who.int.

WHO, established in 1948, is the lead agency within the UN system concerned with the protection and improvement of public health.

Organization

(October 2011)

WORLD HEALTH ASSEMBLY

The Assembly meets in Geneva, once a year. It is responsible for policy-making and the biennial programme and budget; appoints the Director-General; admits new members; and reviews budget contributions.

EXECUTIVE BOARD

The Board is composed of 34 health experts designated by a member state that has been elected by the World Health Assembly to serve on the Board; each expert serves for three years. The Board meets at least twice a year to review the Director-General's programme, which it forwards to the Assembly with any recommendations that seem necessary. It advises on questions referred to it by the Assembly and is responsible for putting into effect the decisions and policies of the Assembly. It is also empowered to take emergency measures in case of epidemics or disasters.

Chairman: RAHHAL EL-MAKKAOUI (Morocco).

SECRETARIAT

Director-General: Dr MARGARET CHAN (People's Republic of China).

Deputy Director-General: Dr ANARFI ASAMOA-BAAH (Ghana).

Assistant Directors-General: ALA ALWAN (Iraq) (Non-communicable Diseases and Mental Health), Dr BRUCE AYLWARD (Canada), FLAVIA BUSTREO (Italy) (Family and Community Health), Dr CARISSA F. ETIENNE (Dominica) (Health Systems and Services), KEIJI FUKUDA (Health Security and Environment), MOHAMED ABDI JAMA (Somalia) (General Management), MARIE-PAULE KIENY (France) (Innovation, Information, Evidence and Research), HIROKI NAKATANI (Japan) (HIV/AIDS, TB, Malaria and Neglected Tropical Diseases).

PRINCIPAL OFFICES

Each of WHO's six geographical regions has its own organization, consisting of a regional committee representing relevant member states and associate members, and a regional office staffed by experts in various fields of health.

South-East Asia Office: World Health House, Indraprastha Estate, Mahatma Gandhi Rd, New Delhi 110002, India; tel. (11) 23370804; fax (11) 23379507; e-mail registry@searo.who.int; internet www.searo.who.int; Dir Dr SAMLEE PLIANBANGCHANG.

Western Pacific Office: POB 2932, Manila 1000, Philippines; tel. (2) 5288001; fax (2) 5211036; e-mail pio@wpro.who.int; internet www.wpro.who.int; Dir Dr SHIN YOUNG SOO (Republic of Korea).

WHO Centre for Health Development: I. H. D. Centre Bldg, 9th Floor, 5–1, 1-chome, Wakinohama-Kaigandori, Chuo-ku, Kobe, Japan; tel. (78) 230-3100; fax (78) 230-3178; e-mail wkc@wkc.who.int; internet www.who.or.jp; f. 1995 to address health development issues; Dir Dr JACOB KUMARESAN (India).

WHO Lyon Office for National Epidemic Preparedness and Response: 58 ave Debourg, 69007 Lyon, France; tel. 4-72-71-64-70; fax 4-72-71-64-71; e-mail oms@lyon.who.int; internet www.who.int/ihr/lyon/en/index.html; supports global capacity-building for detection of and response to epidemics of infectious diseases; provides bridging role between WHO headquarters, the regional offices and ongoing activities in the field; Dir Dr GUÉNAËL RODIER.

Activities

WHO's objective is stated in its constitution as 'the attainment by all peoples of the highest possible level of health'. 'Health' is defined as 'a state of complete physical, mental and social well-being and not merely the absence of disease and infirmity'.

WHO has developed a series of international classifications, including the *International Statistical Classification of Disease and Related Health Problems (ICD)*, providing an etiological framework of health conditions, and currently in its 10th edition; and the complementary *International Classification of Functioning, Disability and Health (ICF)*, which describes how people live with their conditions.

WHO acts as the central authority directing international health work, and establishes relations with professional groups and government health authorities on that basis.

It provides, on request from member states, technical and policy assistance in support of programmes to promote health, prevent and control health problems, control or eradicate disease, train health workers best suited to local needs and strengthen national health systems. Aid is provided in emergencies and natural disasters.

A global programme of collaborative research and exchange of scientific information is carried out in co-operation with about 1,200 national institutions. Particular stress is laid on the widespread communicable diseases of the tropics, and the countries directly concerned are assisted in developing their research capabilities.

It keeps diseases and other health problems under constant surveillance, promotes the exchange of prompt and accurate information and of notification of outbreaks of diseases, and administers the International Health Regulations (the most recently revised version of which entered into force in June 2007). It sets standards for the quality control of drugs, vaccines and other substances affecting health. It formulates health regulations for international travel.

It collects and disseminates health data and carries out statistical analyses and comparative studies in such diseases as cancer, heart disease and mental illness.

It receives reports on drugs observed to have shown adverse reactions in any country, and transmits the information to other member states.

It promotes improved environmental conditions, including housing, sanitation and working conditions. All available information on effects on human health of the pollutants in the environment is critically reviewed and published.

Co-operation among scientists and professional groups is encouraged. The organization negotiates and sustains national and global partnerships. It may propose international conventions and agreements, and develops and promotes international norms and standards. The organization promotes the development and testing of new technologies, tools and guidelines. It assists in developing an informed public opinion on matters of health.

WHO's first global strategy for pursuing 'Health for all' was adopted in May 1981 by the 34th World Health Assembly. The objective of 'Health for all' was identified as the attainment by all citizens of the world of a level of health that would permit them to lead a socially and economically productive life, requiring fair distribution of available resources, universal access to essential health care, and the promotion of preventive health care. In May 1998 the 51st World Health Assembly renewed the initiative, adopting a global strategy in support of 'Health for all in the 21st century', to be effected through regional and national health policies. The new framework was to build on the primary health care approach of the initial strategy, but aimed to strengthen the emphasis on quality of life, equity in health and access to health services. The following have been identified as minimum requirements of 'Health for all':

Safe water in the home or within 15 minutes' walking distance, and adequate sanitary facilities in the home or immediate vicinity;

Immunization against diphtheria, pertussis (whooping cough), tetanus, poliomyelitis, measles and tuberculosis;

Local health care, including availability of essential drugs, within one hour's travel;

Trained personnel to attend childbirth, and to care for pregnant mothers and children up to at least one year old.

In the implementation of all its activities WHO aims to contribute to achieving by 2015 the UN Millennium Development Goals (MDGs) that were agreed by the September 2000 UN Millennium Summit. WHO has particular responsibility for the MDGs of: reducing child mortality, with a target reduction of two-thirds in the mortality rate among children under five; improving maternal health, with a specific goal of reducing by 75% the numbers of women dying in childbirth; and combating HIV/AIDS, malaria and other diseases. In addition, it directly supports the following Millennium 'targets': halving the proportion of people suffering from malnutrition; halving the proportion of people without sustainable access to safe drinking water and basic sanitation; and providing access, in co-operation with pharmaceutical companies, to affordable, essential drugs in developing countries. Furthermore, WHO reports on 17 health-related MDG indicators; co-ordinates, jointly with the World Bank, the High-Level Forum on the Health MDGs, comprising government ministers, senior officials from developing countries, and representatives of bilateral and multilateral agencies, foundations, regional organizations and global partnerships; and undertakes technical and normative work in support of national and regional efforts to reach the MDGs.

The Eleventh General Programme of Work, for the period 2006–15, defined a policy framework for pursuing the principal objectives of building healthy populations and combating ill health. The Programme took into account: increasing understanding of the social, economic, political and cultural factors involved in achieving better health and the role played by better health in poverty reduction; the increasing complexity of health systems; the importance of safeguarding health as a component of humanitarian action; and the need for greater co-ordination among development organizations. It incorporated four interrelated strategic directions: lessening excess mortality, morbidity and disability, especially in poor and marginalized populations; promoting healthy lifestyles and reducing risk factors to human health arising from environmental, economic, social and behavioural causes; developing equitable and financially fair health systems; and establishing an enabling policy and an institutional environment for the health sector and promoting an effective health dimension to social, economic, environmental and development policy. WHO is the sponsoring agency for the Health Workforce Decade (2006–15).

In its work WHO adheres to a six-point agenda covering: promoting development; fostering health security; strengthening health systems; harnessing research, information and evidence; enhancing partnerships; and improving performance.

During 2005 the UN's Inter-Agency Standing Committee (IASC), concerned with co-ordinating the international response to humanitarian disasters, developed a concept of organizing agency assistance to IDPs through the institutionalization of a 'Cluster Approach', comprising 11 core areas of activity. WHO was designated the lead agency for the cluster on Health.

COMMUNICABLE DISEASES

WHO identifies infectious and parasitic communicable diseases as a major obstacle to social and economic progress, particularly in developing countries, where, in addition to disabilities and loss of productivity and household earnings, they cause nearly one-half of all deaths. Emerging and re-emerging diseases, those likely to cause epidemics, increasing incidence of zoonoses (diseases or infections passed from vertebrate animals to humans by means of parasites, viruses, bacteria or unconventional agents), attributable to factors such as environmental changes and changes in farming practices, outbreaks of unknown etiology, and the undermining of some drug therapies by the spread of antimicrobial resistance, are main areas of concern. In recent years WHO has noted the global spread of communicable diseases through international travel, voluntary human migration and involuntary population displacement.

WHO's Communicable Diseases group works to reduce the impact of infectious diseases world-wide through surveillance and response; prevention, control and eradication strategies; and research and product development. The group seeks to identify new technologies and tools, and to foster national development through strengthening health services and the better use of existing tools. It aims to strengthen global monitoring of important communicable disease problems. The group advocates a functional approach to disease control. It aims to create consensus and consolidate partnerships around targeted diseases and collaborates with other groups at all stages to provide an integrated response. In 2000 WHO and several partner institutions in epidemic surveillance established the Global Outbreak Alert and Response Network (GOARN). Through the Network WHO aims to maintain constant vigilance regarding outbreaks of disease and to link world-wide expertise to provide an immediate response capability. From March 2003 WHO, through the Network, was co-ordinating the international investigation into the global spread of Severe Acute Respiratory Syndrome (SARS), a previously unknown atypical pneumonia. From the end of that year WHO was monitoring the spread through several Asian countries of the virus H5N1 (a rapidly mutating strain of zoonotic highly pathogenic avian influenza—HPAI) that was transmitting to human populations through contact with diseased birds, mainly poultry. It was feared that H5N1 would mutate into a form transmissable from human to human. In March 2005 WHO issued a *Global Influenza Preparedness Plan*, and urged all countries to develop national influenza pandemic preparedness plans and to stockpile antiviral drugs. In May, in co-operation with FAO and the World Organisation for Animal Health (OIE), WHO launched a Global Strategy for the Progressive Control of Highly Pathogenic Avian Influenza. A conference on Avian Influenza and Human Pandemic Influenza that was jointly organized by WHO, FAO, OIE and the World Bank in November 2005 issued a plan of action identifying a number of responses, including: supporting the development of integrated national plans for H5N1 containment and human pandemic influenza preparedness and response; assisting countries with the aggressive control of H5N1 and with establishing a more detailed understanding of the role of wild birds in virus transmission; nominating rapid response teams of experts to support epidemiological field investigations; expanding national and regional capacity in surveillance, diagnosis, and alert and response systems; expanding the network of influenza laboratories; establishing multi-country networks for the control or prevention of animal transboundary diseases; expanding the global antiviral stockpile; strengthening veterinary infrastructures; and mapping a global strategy and work plan for co-ordinating antiviral and influenza vaccine research and development. An International Pledging Conference on Avian and Human Influenza, convened in January 2006 in Beijing, People's Republic of China (PRC), and co-sponsored by the World Bank, European Commission and PRC Government, in co-operation with WHO, FAO and OIE, requested a minimum of US $1,200m. in funding towards combating the spread of the virus. By 9 August 2011 a total of 564 human cases of H5N1 had been laboratory confirmed, in Azerbaijan, Bangladesh, Cambodia, PRC, Djibouti, Egypt, Indonesia, Iraq, Laos, Myanmar, Nigeria, Pakistan, Thailand, Turkey and Viet Nam, resulting in 330 deaths. Cases in poultry had become endemic in parts of Asia and Africa, and outbreaks in poultry had also occurred in some European and Middle Eastern countries.

In April 2009 GOARN sent experts to Mexico to work with health authorities there in response to an outbreak of confirmed human cases of a new variant of swine influenza A(H1N1) that had not previously been detected in animals or humans. In late April, by which time cases of the virus had been reported in the USA and

Canada, the Director-General of WHO declared a 'public health emergency of international concern'. All countries were instructed to activate their national influenza pandemic preparedness plans (see above). At the end of April the level of pandemic alert was declared to be at phase five of a six-phase (phase six being the most severe) warning system that had been newly revised earlier in the year. Phase five is characterized by human-to-human transmission of a new virus into at least two countries in one WHO region. On 11 June WHO declared a global pandemic (phase six on the warning scale, characterized by human-to-human transmission in two or more WHO regions). The status and development of pandemic influenza vaccines was the focus of an advisory meeting of immunization experts held at the WHO headquarters in late October. In June 2010 the WHO Director-General refuted allegations, levelled by a British medical journal and by the Parliamentary Assembly of the Council of Europe, regarding the severity of pandemic (H1N1) 2009 and the possibility that the Organization had, in declaring the pandemic, used advisers with a vested commercial interest in promoting pharmaceutical industry profitability. In August 2010 the WHO Director-General declared that transmission of the new H1N1 virus had entered a post-pandemic phase.

One of WHO's major achievements was the eradication of smallpox. Following a massive international campaign of vaccination and surveillance (begun in 1958 and intensified in 1967), the last case was detected in 1977 and the eradication of the disease was declared in 1980. In May 1996 the World Health Assembly resolved that, pending a final endorsement, all remaining stocks of the variola virus (which causes smallpox) were to be destroyed on 30 June 1999, although 500,000 doses of smallpox vaccine were to remain, along with a supply of the smallpox vaccine seed virus, in order to ensure that a further supply of the vaccine could be made available if required. In May 1999, however, the Assembly authorized a temporary retention of stocks of the virus until 2002. In late 2001, in response to fears that illegally held virus stocks could be used in acts of biological terrorism (see below), WHO reassembled a team of technical experts on smallpox. In January 2002 the Executive Board determined that stocks of the virus should continue to be retained, to enable research into more effective treatments and vaccines. World Health Assemblies (most recently in May 2011) have affirmed that remaining the remaining stock of variola virus should be destroyed following the completion of the ongoing research. The state of variola virus research was to be reviewed in 2014, by the 67th World Health Assembly, which was to discuss nominating a deadline for the destruction of the remaining virus stocks.

In 1988 the World Health Assembly launched the Global Polio Eradication Initiative (GPEI), which aimed, initially, to eradicate poliomyelitis by the end of 2000; this target was subsequently extended to 2013 (see below). Co-ordinated periods of Supplementary Immunization Activity (SIA, facilitated in conflict zones by the negotiation of so-called 'days of tranquillity'), including National Immunization Days (NIDs), Sub-National Immunization Days (SNIDs), mop-up campaigns, VitA campaigns (Vitamin A is administered in order to reduce nutritional deficiencies in children and thereby boost their immunity), and Follow up/Catch up campaigns, have been employed in combating the disease, alongside the strengthening of routine immunization services. Since the inauguration of the GPEI WHO has declared the following regions 'polio-free': the Americas (1994); Western Pacific (2000); and Europe (2002). Furthermore, type 2 wild poliovirus has been eradicated globally (since 1999), although a type 2 circulating vaccine-derived poliovirus (cVDPV) was reported to be active in northern Nigeria during 2006–early 2010. In January 2004 ministers of health of affected countries, and global partners, meeting under the auspices of WHO and UNICEF, adopted the Geneva Declaration on the Eradication of Poliomyelitis, in which they made a commitment to accelerate the drive towards eradication of the disease, by improving the scope of vaccination programmes. Significant progress in eradication of the virus was reported in Asia during that year. In sub-Saharan Africa, however, an outbreak originating in northern Nigeria in mid-2003—caused by a temporary cessation of vaccination activities in response to local opposition to the vaccination programme—had spread, by mid-2004, to 10 previously polio-free countries. These included Côte d'Ivoire and Sudan, where ongoing civil unrest and population displacements impeded control efforts. During 2004–05 some 23 African governments, including those of the affected West and Central African countries, organized, with support from the African Union, a number of co-ordinated mass vaccination drives, which resulted in the vaccination of about 100m. children. By mid-2005 the sub-regional epidemic was declared over; it was estimated that since mid-2003 it had resulted in the paralysis of nearly 200 children. In Nigeria itself, however, the number of confirmed wild poliovirus cases had by 2006 escalated to 1,122 from 202 in 2002. In February 2007 the GPEI launched an intensified eradication effort aimed at identifying and addressing the outstanding operational, technical and financial barriers to eradication. The May 2008 World Health Assembly adopted a resolution urging all remaining polio-affected member states to ensure the vaccination of every child during each SIA. By the end of 2008, having received independent advice that the intensified eradication effort initiated in 2007 had demonstrated that the remaining challenges to eradication were surmountable, the GPEI endorsed a strategic plan covering the period 2009–13 (replacing a previous plan for 2004–08), with the aim of achieving the interruption of type 1 wild poliovirus transmission in India, and the cessation of all prolonged outbreaks in Africa by the end of 2009; the interruption of all poliovirus transmission in Afghanistan, India and Pakistan, of type 1 wild poliovirus transmission in Nigeria, and of all wild poliovirus transmission elsewhere in Africa, by end-2010; the interruption of type 3 wild poliovirus transmission in Nigeria by end-2011; and the eradication of new cVDPVs within six months of detection by end-2013. During 2009, however, polio outbreaks, which were subsequently eradicated, occurred in 10 of 15 previously polio-free countries in Africa. In June 2010 a new strategic plan, covering 2010–12, was launched, incorporating the following targets: cessation in mid-2010 of all polio outbreaks with onset in 2009; cessation by end-2010 of all re-established wild poliovirus transmission; cessation by end-2011 of all transmission in at least two of the four countries designated at that time as polio-endemic (i.e. Afghanistan, India, Nigeria, and Pakistan); and the cessation by end-2012 of all transmission. Some 1,292 polio cases were confirmed world-wide in 2010, of which 232 were in the four polio-endemic countries (Nigeria, 21 cases; India, 42 cases; Pakistan, 144 cases; and Afghanistan, 25 cases), and 1,060 cases were recorded in non-endemic countries. (In 1988 35,000 cases had been confirmed in 125 countries, with the actual number of cases estimated at around 350,000.)

WHO is committed to the elimination of leprosy (the reduction of the prevalence of leprosy to less than one case per 10,000 population). The use of a highly effective combination of three drugs (known as multi-drug therapy—MDT) resulted in a reduction in the number of leprosy cases world-wide from 10m.–12m. in 1988 to 213,036 registered cases in January 2010. In 2008 some 249,007 cases were detected in 121 countries. The number of countries having more than one case of leprosy per 10,000 had declined to four by January 2007 (Brazil, Democratic Republic of the Congo, Mozambique and Nepal), compared with 122 in 1985. The country with the highest prevalence of leprosy cases in 2007 was Brazil (3.21 per 10,000 population) and the country with the highest number of cases was India (139,252). The Global Alliance for the Elimination of Leprosy was launched in November 1999 by WHO, in collaboration with governments of affected countries and several private partners, including a major pharmaceutical company, to support the eradication of the disease through the provision of free MDT treatment; WHO has supplied free MDT treatment to leprosy patients in endemic countries since 1995. In June 2005 WHO adopted a Strategic Plan for Further Reducing the Leprosy Burden and Sustaining Leprosy Control Activities, covering the period 2006–10 and following on from a previous strategic plan for 2000–05. In 1998 WHO launched the Global Buruli Ulcer Initiative, which aimed to co-ordinate control of and research into Buruli ulcer, another mycobacterial disease. In July of that year the Director-General of WHO and representatives of more than 20 countries, meeting in Yamoussoukro, Côte d'Ivoire, signed a declaration on the control of Buruli ulcer. In May 2004 the World Health Assembly adopted a resolution urging improved research into, and detection and treatment of, Buruli ulcer.

The Special Programme for Research and Training in Tropical Diseases, established in 1975 and sponsored jointly by WHO, UNDP and the World Bank, as well as by contributions from donor countries, involves a world-wide network of some 5,000 scientists working on the development and application of vaccines, new drugs, diagnostic kits and preventive measures, and applied field research on practical community issues affecting the target diseases.

The objective of providing immunization for all children by 1990 was adopted by the World Health Assembly in 1977. Six diseases (measles, whooping cough, tetanus, poliomyelitis, tuberculosis and diphtheria) became the target of the Expanded Programme on Immunization (EPI), in which WHO, UNICEF and many other organizations collaborated. As a result of massive international and national efforts, the global immunization coverage increased from 20% in the early 1980s to the targeted rate of 80% by the end of 1990. In 2006 WHO, UNICEF and other partners launched the Global Immunization Vision and Strategy (GIVS), a global 10-year framework, covering 2006–15, aimed at reducing deaths due to vaccine-preventable diseases by at least two-thirds compared to 2000 levels, by 2015; and increasing national vaccination coverage levels to at least 90%. In 2009 the global child vaccination coverage rate was estimated at 82%.

In June 2000 WHO released a report entitled 'Overcoming Antimicrobial Resistance', in which it warned that the misuse of antibiotics could render some common infectious illnesses unresponsive to treatment. At that time WHO issued guidelines which aimed to mitigate the risks associated with the use of antimicrobials in livestock reared for human consumption.

HIV/AIDS, TB, MALARIA AND NEGLECTED DISEASES

Combating the human immunodeficiency virus/acquired immunodeficiency syndrome (HIV/AIDS), tuberculosis (TB) and malaria are organization-wide priorities and, as such, are supported not only by their own areas of work but also by activities undertaken in other areas. TB is the principal cause of death for people infected with the HIV virus and an estimated one-third of people living with HIV/AIDS globally are co-infected with TB. In July 2000 a meeting of the Group of Seven industrialized nations and Russia, convened in Genoa, Italy, announced the formation of a new Global Fund to Fight AIDS, TB and Malaria (as previously proposed by the UN Secretary-General and recommended by the World Health Assembly).

The HIV/AIDS epidemic represents a major threat to human well-being and socio-economic progress. Some 95% of those known to be infected with HIV/AIDS live in developing countries, and AIDS-related illnesses are the leading cause of death in sub-Saharan Africa. It is estimated that more than 25m. people world-wide died of AIDS during 1981–2008. WHO supports governments in developing effective health sector responses to the HIV/AIDS epidemic through enhancing their planning and managerial capabilities, implementation capacity, and health systems resources. The Joint UN Programme on HIV/AIDS (UNAIDS) became operational on 1 January 1996, sponsored by WHO and other UN agencies; the UNAIDS secretariat is based at WHO headquarters. Sufferers of HIV/AIDS in developing countries have often failed to receive advanced antiretroviral (ARV) treatments that are widely available in industrialized countries, owing to their high cost. In May 2000 the World Health Assembly adopted a resolution urging WHO member states to improve access to the prevention and treatment of HIV-related illnesses and to increase the availability and affordability of drugs. A WHO-UNAIDS HIV Vaccine Initiative was launched in that year. In June 2001 governments participating in a special session of the UN General Assembly on HIV/AIDS adopted a Declaration of Commitment on HIV/AIDS. WHO, with UNAIDS, UNICEF, UNFPA, the World Bank, and major pharmaceutical companies, participates in the 'Accelerating Access' initiative, which aims to expand access to care, support and ARVs for people with HIV/AIDS. In March 2002, under its 'Access to Quality HIV/AIDS Drugs and Diagnostics' programme, WHO published a comprehensive list of HIV-related medicines deemed to meet standards recommended by the Organization. In April WHO issued the first treatment guidelines for HIV/AIDS cases in poor communities, and endorsed the inclusion of HIV/AIDS drugs in its *Model List of Essential Medicines* (see below) in order to encourage their wider availability. The secretariat of the International HIV Treatment Access Coalition, founded in December of that year by governments, non-governmental organizations, donors and others to facilitate access to ARVs for people in low- and middle-income countries, is based at WHO headquarters. In September 2006, Brazil, Chile, France, Norway and the United Kingdom launched UNITAID, an international drug purchase facility aiming to provide sustained, strategic market intervention, with a view to reducing the cost of medicines for priority diseases and increasing the supply of drugs and diagnostics. In July 2008, UNITAID created the Medicines Patent Pool; the Pool, a separate entity, was to focus on increasing access to HIV medicines in developing countries. The Pool is funded by UNITAID, under a five-year arrangement. By the end of 2009 an estimated 5.2m. people in developing and middle-income countries were receiving appropriate HIV treatment, compared with 4m. at end-2008. In May 2011 the 64th World Health Assembly adopted a new Global Health Sector Strategy on HIV/AIDS, covering 2011–15, which aimed to promote greater innovation in HIV prevention, diagnosis, treatment, and the improvement of care services to facilitate universal access to care for HIV patients. WHO supports the following *Three Ones* principles, endorsed in April 2004 by a high-level meeting organized by UNAIDS, the United Kingdom and the USA, with the aim of strengthening national responses to the HIV/AIDS pandemic: for every country there should be one agreed national HIV/AIDS action framework; one national AIDS co-ordinating authority; and one agreed monitoring and evaluation system.

At December 2009 an estimated 4.1m. people in South and South-East Asia and 770,000 people in East Asia were reported to have HIV/AIDS, with an estimated 352.000 newly infected during the year. There are serious HIV/AIDS epidemics in Indonesia and Thailand, while the People's Republic of China has serious localized epidemics in certain provinces and autonomous regions, including Guangxi, Sichuan, Xinjiang and Yannan.

In 1995 WHO established a Global Tuberculosis Programme to address the challenges of the TB epidemic, which had been declared a global emergency by the Organization in 1993. According to WHO estimates, one-third of the world's population carries the TB bacillus. In 2009 this generated 9.4m. new active cases (1.1m. in people co-infected with HIV), and killed 1.7m. people (0.4m. of whom were also HIV-positive). Some 22 high-burden countries account for four-fifths of global TB cases. The largest concentration of TB cases is in South-East Asia. WHO provides technical support to all member countries, with special attention given to those with high TB prevalence, to establish effective national tuberculosis control programmes. WHO's strategy for TB control includes the use of the expanded DOTS (direct observation treatment, short-course) regime, involving the following five tenets: sustained political commitment to increase human and financial resources and to make TB control in endemic countries a nation-wide activity and an integral part of the national health system; access to quality-assured TB sputum microscopy; standardized short-course chemotherapy for all cases of TB under proper case-management conditions; uninterrupted supply of quality-assured drugs; and maintaining a recording and reporting system to enable outcome assessment. Simultaneously, WHO is encouraging research with the aim of further advancing DOTS, developing new tools for prevention, diagnosis and treatment, and containing new threats (such as the HIV/TB co-epidemic). Inadequate control of DOTS in some areas, leading to partial and inconsistent treatments, has resulted in the development of drug-resistant and, often, incurable strains of TB. The incidence of so-called Multidrug Resistant TB (MDR-TB) strains, that are unresponsive to at least two of the four most commonly used anti-TB drugs, has risen in recent years, and WHO estimates that about four-fifths are 'super strains', resistant to at least three of the main anti-TB drugs; an estimated 3.3% of new TB cases were reported to be MDR in 2009. MDR-TB cases occur most frequently in Eastern Europe, Central Asia, the People's Republic of China, and India; it was reported in 2010 that in certain areas of the former Soviet Union up to 28% of all new TB cases were MDR. WHO has developed DOTS-Plus, a specialized strategy for controlling the spread of MDR-TB in areas of high prevalence. By August 2010 59 countries had reported at least one case of Extensive Drug Resistant TB (XDR-TB), defined as MDR-TB plus resistance to additional drugs. XDR-TB is believed to be most prevalent in Eastern Europe and Asia. In 2007 WHO launched the Global MDR/XDR Response Plan, which aimed to expand diagnosis and treatment to cover, by 2015, some 85% of TB patients with MDR-TB.

The 'Stop TB' partnership, launched by WHO in 1999, in partnership with the World Bank, the US Government and a coalition of non-governmental organizations, co-ordinates the Global Plan to Stop TB, which represents a 'roadmap' for TB control covering the period 2006–15. The Global Plan aims to facilitate the achievement of the MDG of halting and beginning to reverse by 2015 the incidence of TB by means of access to quality diagnosis and treatment for all; to supply ARVs to 3m. TB patients co-infected with HIV; to treat nearly 1m. people for MDR-TB (this target was subsequently altered by the 2007 Global MDR/XDR Response Plan, see above); to develop a new anti-TB drug and a new vaccine; and to develop rapid and inexpensive diagnostic tests at the point of care. A second phase of the Global Plan, launched in late 2010 and covering 2011–15, updated the Plan to take account of actual progress achieved since its instigation in 2006. The Global TB Drug Facility, launched by 'Stop TB' in 2001, aims to increase access to high-quality anti-TB drugs for sufferers in developing countries. In 2007 'Stop TB' endorsed the establishment of a new Global Laboratory Initiative with the aim of expanding laboratory capacity.

In December 2010 WHO endorsed a new rapid nucleic acid amplification test (NAAT) that provided an accurate diagnosis of TB in around 100 minutes; it was envisaged that NAAT, by eliminating the current wait of up to three months for a TB diagnosis, would greatly enhance management of the disease and patient care.

In October 1998 WHO, jointly with UNICEF, the World Bank and UNDP, formally launched the Roll Back Malaria (RBM) programme. The disease acutely affects at least 350m.–500m. people, and kills an estimated 1m. people, every year. Some 90% of all malaria cases occur in sub-Saharan Africa. It is estimated that the disease directly causes 18% of all child deaths in that region. The global RBM Partnership, linking governments, development agencies, and other parties, aims to mobilize resources and support for controlling malaria. The RBM Partnership Global Strategic Plan for the period 2005–15, adopted in November 2005, lists steps required to intensify malaria control interventions with a view to attaining targets set by the Partnership for 2010 and 2015 (the former targets include: ensuring the protection of 80% of people at risk from malaria and the diagnosis and treatment within one day of 80% of malaria patients, and reducing the global malaria burden by one-half compared with 2000 levels; and the latter: achieving a 75% reduction in malaria morbidity and mortality over levels at 2005). WHO recommends a number of guidelines for malaria control, focusing on the need for prompt, effective antimalarial treatment, and the issue of drug resistance; vector control, including the use of insecticide-treated bednets; malaria in pregnancy; malaria epidemics; and monitoring and evaluation activities. WHO, with several private and public sector partners, supports the development of more effective anti-malaria drugs and vaccines through the 'Medicines for Malaria' venture.

Joint UN Programme on HIV/AIDS (UNAIDS): 20 ave Appia, 1211 Geneva 27, Switzerland; tel. 227913666; fax 227914187; e-mail communications@unaids.org; internet www.unaids.org; established in 1996 to lead, strengthen and support an expanded response to the global HIV/AIDS pandemic; activities focus on prevention, care and support, reducing vulnerability to infection, and alleviating the socioeconomic and human effects of HIV/AIDS; launched the Global Coalition on Women and AIDS in Feb. 2004; guided by UN Security Council Resolution 1308, focusing on the possible impact of AIDS on social instability and emergency situations, and the potential impact of HIV on the health of international peace-keeping personnel; by the UN Millennium Development Goals adopted in Sept. 2000; by the Declaration of Commitment on HIV/AIDS agreed in June 2001 by the first-ever Special Session of the UN General Assembly on HIV/AIDS, which acknowledged the AIDS epidemic as a 'global emergency'; and the Political Declaration on HIV/AIDS, adopted by the June 2006 UN General Assembly High Level Meeting on AIDS; launched the Global Coalition on Women and AIDS in Feb. 2004; co-sponsors: WHO, UNICEF, UNDP, UNFPA, UNODC, the ILO, UNESCO, the World Bank, WFP, UNHCR; Exec. Dir MICHEL SIDIBÉ (Mali).

NON-COMMUNICABLE DISEASES AND MENTAL HEALTH

The Non-communicable Diseases (NCDs) and Mental Health group comprises departments for the surveillance, prevention and management of uninfectious diseases, and departments for health promotion, disability, injury prevention and rehabilitation, substance abuse and mental health. Surveillance, prevention and management of NCDs, tobacco, and mental health are organization-wide priorities.

Addressing the social and environmental determinants of health is a main priority of WHO. Tobacco use, unhealthy diet and physical inactivity are regarded as common, preventable risk factors for the four most prominent NCDs: cardiovascular diseases, cancer, chronic respiratory disease and diabetes. It is estimated that the four main NCDs are collectively responsible for an estimated 35m. deaths—60% of all deaths—globally each year, and that up to 80% of cases of heart disease, stroke and type 2 diabetes, and more than one-third of cancers, could be prevented by eliminating shared risk factors, the main ones being: tobacco use, unhealthy diet, physical inactivity and harmful use of alcohol. WHO envisages that the disease burden and mortality from these diseases will continue to increase, most rapidly in Africa and the Eastern Mediterranean, and that the highest number of deaths will occur in the Western Pacific region and in South-East Asia. WHO aims to monitor the global epidemiological situation of NCDs, to co-ordinate multinational research activities concerned with prevention and care, and to analyse determining factors such as gender and poverty. The 53rd World Health Assembly, convened in May 2000, endorsed a Global Strategy for the Prevention and Control of NCDs. In May 2008 the 61st World Health Assembly endorsed a new Action Plan for 2008–13 for the Global Strategy for the Prevention and Control of NCDs, based on the vision of the 2000 Global Strategy. The Action Plan aimed to provide a roadmap establishing and strengthening initiatives on the surveillance, prevention and management of NCDs, and emphasized the need to invest in NCD prevention as part of sustainable socio-economic development planning.

The sixth Global Conference on Health Promotion, convened jointly by WHO and the Thai Government, in Bangkok, Thailand, in August 2005, adopted the Bangkok Charter for Health Promotion in a Globalized World, which identified ongoing key challenges, actions and commitments.

In May 2004 the World Health Assembly endorsed a Global Strategy on Diet, Physical Activity and Health; it is estimated that more than 1,000m. adults world-wide are overweight, and that, of these, some 300m. are clinically obese. WHO has studied obesity-related issues in co-operation with the International Association for the Study of Obesity (IASO). The International Task Force on Obesity, affiliated to the IASO, aims to encourage the development of new policies for managing obesity. WHO and FAO jointly commissioned an expert report on the relationship of diet, nutrition and physical activity to chronic diseases, which was published in March 2003.

In co-operation with the IASO WHO has studied obesity-related issues affecting countries in Asia and the Pacific. In October 2001 the first Asia-Oceania Conference on Obesity was convened in Japan under the auspices of IASO; a second conference was held in Kuala Lumpur, Malaysia, in September 2003, a third in Taipei, Taiwan, in March 2005; and a fourth in Seoul, Republic of Korea, in February 2007. The fifth conference was held in Mumbai, India, in February 2009.

WHO's programmes for diabetes mellitus, chronic rheumatic diseases and asthma assist with the development of national initiatives, based upon goals and targets for the improvement of early detection, care and reduction of long-term complications. WHO's cardiovascular diseases programme aims to prevent and control the major cardiovascular diseases, which are responsible for more than 14m. deaths each year. It is estimated that one-third of these deaths could have been prevented with existing scientific knowledge. The programme on cancer control is concerned with the prevention of cancer, improving its detection and cure, and ensuring care of all cancer patients in need. In May 2004 the World Health Assembly adopted a resolution on cancer prevention and control, recognizing an increase in global cancer cases, particularly in developing countries, and stressing that many cases and related deaths could be prevented. The resolution included a number of recommendations for the improvement of national cancer control programmes. In May 2009 WHO and the IAEA launched a Joint Programme on Cancer Control, aimed at enhancing efforts to fight cancer in the developing world. WHO is a co-sponsor of the Global Day Against Pain, which is held annually on 11 October. The Global Day highlights the need for improved pain management and palliative care for sufferers of diseases such as cancer and AIDS, with a particular focus on patients living in low-income countries with minimal access to opioid analgesics, and urges recognition of access to pain relief as a basic human right.

The WHO Human Genetics Programme manages genetic approaches for the prevention and control of common hereditary diseases and of those with a genetic predisposition representing a major health factor. The Programme also concentrates on the further development of genetic approaches suitable for incorporation into health care systems, as well as developing a network of international collaborating programmes.

WHO works to assess the impact of injuries, violence and sensory impairments on health, and formulates guidelines and protocols for the prevention and management of mental problems. The health promotion division promotes decentralized and community-based health programmes and is concerned with developing new approaches to population ageing and encouraging healthy lifestyles and self-care. It also seeks to relieve the negative impact of social changes such as urbanization, migration and changes in family structure upon health. WHO advocates a multi-sectoral approach—involving public health, legal and educational systems—to the prevention of injuries, which represent 16% of the global burden of disease. It aims to support governments in developing suitable strategies to prevent and mitigate the consequences of violence, unintentional injury and disability. Several health promotion projects have been undertaken, in collaboration between WHO regional and country offices and other relevant organizations, including: the Global School Health Initiative, to bridge the sectors of health and education and to promote the health of school-age children; the Global Strategy for Occupational Health, to promote the health of the working population and the control of occupational health risks; Community-based Rehabilitation, aimed at providing a more enabling environment for people with disabilities; and a communication strategy to provide training and support for health communications personnel and initiatives. In 2000 WHO, UNESCO, the World Bank and UNICEF adopted the joint Focusing Resources for Effective School Health (FRESH Start) approach to promoting life skills among adolescents.

WHO supports the UN Convention, and its Optional Protocol, on the Rights of Persons with Disabilities, which came into force in May 2008, and seeks to address challenges that prevent the full participation of people with disabilities in the social, economic and cultural lives of their communities and societies; at that time the WHO Director-General appointed a Taskforce on Disability to ensure that WHO was reflecting the provisions of the Convention overall as an organization and in its programme of work.

In February 1999 WHO initiated a new programme, 'Vision 2020: the Right to Sight', which aimed to eliminate avoidable blindness (estimated to be as much as 80% of all cases) by 2020. Blindness was otherwise predicted to increase by as much as twofold, owing to the increased longevity of the global population.

The Tobacco or Health Programme aims to reduce the use of tobacco, by educating tobacco-users and preventing young people from adopting the habit. In 1996 WHO published its first report on the tobacco situation world-wide. According to WHO, about one-third of the world's population aged over 15 years smoke tobacco, which causes approximately 3.5m. deaths each year (through lung cancer, heart disease, chronic bronchitis and other effects). In 1998 the 'Tobacco Free Initiative', a major global anti-smoking campaign, was established. In May 1999 the World Health Assembly endorsed the formulation of a Framework Convention on Tobacco Control (FCTC) to help to combat the increase in tobacco use (although a number of tobacco growers expressed concerns about the effect of the convention on their livelihoods). The FCTC entered into force in February 2005. The greatest increase in tobacco use is forecast to occur in developing countries. In 2008 WHO published a comprehensive analysis of global tobacco use and control, the *WHO Report on the Global Tobacco Epidemic*, which designated abuse of tobacco as one of the principal global threats to health, and predicted that during the latter part of the 21st century the vast majority of tobacco-related deaths would occur in developing countries. The Report identified and condemned a global tobacco industry strategy to target young people and adults in the developing world, and it detailed six key proven strategies, collectively known as the 'MPOWER package', that were aimed at combating global tobacco use: monitoring tobacco use and implementing prevention policies; protecting people from tobacco smoke; offering support to people to enable them to give up tobacco use; warning about the dangers of tobacco; enforcing bans on tobacco advertising, promotion and sponsorship; and raising taxes on tobacco. The MPOWER package provided a roadmap to support countries in building on their obligations under the FCTC. The FCTC obligates its states parties to require 'health warnings describing the harmful effects of tobacco use' to appear on packs of tobacco and their outside packaging, and recommends the use of warnings that contain pictures. WHO provides technical and other assistance to countries to support them in meeting this obligation through the Tobacco Free Initiative. WHO encourages governments to adopt tobacco health warnings meeting the agreed criteria for maximum effectiveness in convincing consumers not to smoke: these appear on both the front and back of a cigarette pack, should cover more than half of the pack, and should contain pictures.

WHO's Mental Health and Substance Abuse department was established in 2000 from the merger of formerly separate departments to reflect the many common approaches in managing mental health and substance use disorders.

WHO defines mental health as a 'state of well-being in which every individual realizes his or her own potential, can cope with the normal stresses of life, can work productively and fruitfully, and is able to make a contribution to her or his community'. WHO's Mental Health programme is concerned with mental health problems that include unipolar and bipolar affective disorders, psychosis, epilepsy, dementia, Parkinson's disease, multiple sclerosis, drug and alcohol dependency, and neuropsychiatric disorders such as post-traumatic stress disorder, obsessive compulsive disorder and panic disorder. Although, overall, physical health has improved, mental, behavioural and social health problems are increasing, owing to extended life expectancy and improved child mortality rates, and factors such as war and poverty. WHO aims to address mental problems by increasing awareness of mental health issues and promoting improved mental health services and primary care. In October 2008 WHO launched the so-called mental health Gap Action Programme (mhGAP), which aimed to improve services addressing mental, neurological and substance use disorders, with a special focus on low and middle income countries. It was envisaged that, with proper care, psychosocial assistance and medication, many millions of patients in developing countries could be treated for depression, schizophrenia, and epilepsy; prevented from attempting suicide; and encouraged to begin to lead normal lives. A main focus of mhGAP concerns forging strategic partnerships to enhance countries' capacity to combat stigma commonly associated with mental illness, reduce the burden of mental disorders, and promote mental health. WHO is a joint partner in the Global Campaign against Epilepsy: Out of the Shadows, which aims to advance understanding, treatment, services and prevention of epilepsy world-wide.

The Substance Abuse programme addresses the misuse of all psychoactive substances, irrespective of legal status and including alcohol. WHO provides technical support to assist countries in formulating policies with regard to the prevention and reduction of the health and social effects of psychoactive substance abuse, and undertakes epidemiological surveillance and risk assessment, advocacy and the dissemination of information, strengthening national and regional prevention and health promotion techniques and strategies, the development of cost-effective treatment and rehabilitation approaches, and also encompasses regulatory activities as required under the international drugs-control treaties in force. In May 2010 WHO endorsed a new global strategy to reduce the harmful use of alcohol; this promoted measures including taxation on alcohol, minimizing outlets selling alcohol, raising age limits for those buying alcohol, and the employment of effective measures to deter people from driving while under the influence of alcohol.

In June 2010 WHO launched the Global Network of Age-Friendly Cities, as part of a broader response to the ageing of populations world-wide. The Network was to support cities in creating urban environments that would enable older people to remain active and healthy.

FAMILY AND COMMUNITY HEALTH

WHO's Family and Community Health group addresses the following areas of work: child and adolescent health, research and programme development in reproductive health, making pregnancy safer and men's and women's health. Making pregnancy safer is an organization-wide priority. The group's aim is to improve access to sustainable health care for all by strengthening health systems and fostering individual, family and community development. Activities include newborn care; child health, including promoting and protecting the health and development of the child through such approaches as promotion of breast-feeding and use of the mother-baby package, as well as care of the sick child, including diarrhoeal and acute respiratory disease control, and support to women and children in difficult circumstances; the promotion of safe motherhood and maternal health; adolescent health, including the promotion and development of young people and the prevention of specific health problems; women, health and development, including addressing issues of gender, sexual violence, and harmful traditional practices; and human reproduction, including research related to contraceptive technologies and effective methods. In addition, WHO aims to provide technical leadership and co-ordination on reproductive health and to support countries in their efforts to ensure that people: experience healthy sexual development and maturation; have the capacity for healthy, equitable and responsible relationships; can achieve their reproductive intentions safely and healthily; avoid illnesses, diseases and injury related to sexuality and reproduction; and receive appropriate counselling, care and rehabilitation for diseases and conditions related to sexuality and reproduction.

In September 1997 WHO, in collaboration with UNICEF, formally launched a programme advocating the Integrated Management of Childhood Illness (IMCI). IMCI recognizes that pneumonia, diarrhoea, measles, malaria and malnutrition cause some 70% of the approximately 11m. childhood deaths each year, and recommends screening sick children for all five conditions, to obtain a more accurate diagnosis than may be achieved from the results of a single assessment. WHO's Division of Diarrhoeal and Acute Respiratory Disease Control encourages national programmes aimed at reducing childhood deaths as a result of diarrhoea, particularly through the use of oral rehydration therapy and preventive measures. The Division is also seeking to reduce deaths from pneumonia in infants through the use of a simple case-management strategy involving the recognition of danger signs and treatment with an appropriate antibiotic.

In March 1996 WHO's Centre for Health Development opened at Kobe, Japan. The Centre researches health developments and other determinants to strengthen policy decision-making within the health sector.

SUSTAINABLE DEVELOPMENT AND HEALTHY ENVIRONMENTS

The Sustainable Development and Healthy Environments group focuses on the following areas of work: health in sustainable development; nutrition; health and environment; food safety; and emergency preparedness and response. Food safety is an organization-wide priority.

WHO promotes recognition of good health status as one of the most important assets of the poor. The Sustainable Development and Healthy Environment group seeks to monitor the advantages and disadvantages for health, nutrition, environment and development arising from the process of globalization (i.e. increased global flows of capital, goods and services, people, and knowledge); to integrate the issue of health into poverty reduction programmes; and to promote human rights and equality. Adequate and safe food and nutrition is a priority programme area. WHO collaborates with FAO, WFP, UNICEF and other UN agencies in pursuing its objectives relating to nutrition and food safety. It has been estimated that 780m. people world-wide cannot meet basic needs for energy and protein, more than 2,000m. people lack essential vitamins and minerals, and that 170m. children are malnourished. In December 1992 WHO and FAO hosted an international conference on nutrition, at which a World Declaration and Plan of Action on Nutrition was adopted to make the fight against malnutrition a development priority. Following the conference, WHO promoted the elaboration and implementation of national plans of action on nutrition. WHO aims to support the enhancement of member states' capabilities in dealing with their nutrition situations, and addressing scientific issues related to preventing, managing and monitoring protein-energy malnutrition; micronutrient malnutrition, including iodine deficiency disorders, vitamin A deficiency, and nutritional anaemia; and diet-related conditions and NCDs such as obesity (increasingly affecting children, adolescents and adults, mainly in industrialized countries), cancer and heart disease. In 1990 the World Health Assembly resolved to eliminate iodine deficiency (believed to cause mental retardation); a strategy of universal salt iodization was launched in 1993. In collaboration with other international agencies, WHO is implementing a comprehensive strategy for promoting appropriate infant, young child and maternal nutrition, and for dealing effectively with nutritional emergencies in large populations. Areas of emphasis include promoting healthcare practices that enhance successful breast-feeding; appropriate complementary feeding; refining the use and interpretation of body measurements for assessing nutritional status; relevant information, education and training; and action to give effect to the International Code of Marketing of Breast-milk Substitutes. The food safety programme aims to protect human health against risks associated with biological and chemical contaminants and additives in food. With FAO, WHO establishes food standards (through the work of the Codex Alimentarius Commission and its subsidiary committees) and evaluates food additives, pesticide residues and other contaminants and their implications for health. The programme provides expert advice on such issues as food-borne pathogens (e.g. listeria), production methods (e.g. aquaculture) and food biotechnology (e.g. genetic modification). In July 2001 the Codex Alimentarius Commission adopted the first global principles for assessing the safety of genetically modified (GM) foods. In March 2002 an intergovernmental task force established by the Commission finalized 'principles for the risk analysis of foods derived from biotechnology', which were to provide a framework for assessing the safety of GM foods and plants. In the following month WHO and FAO announced a joint review of their food standards operations. In February 2003 the FAO/WHO Project and Fund for Enhanced Participation in Codex was launched to support the participation of poorer countries in the Commission's activities.

WHO's programme area on environmental health undertakes a wide range of initiatives to tackle the increasing threats to health and well-being from a changing environment, especially in relation to air pollution, water quality, sanitation, protection against radiation, management of hazardous waste, chemical safety and housing hygiene. In 2008 it was estimated that some 1,200m. people worldwide had no access to clean drinking water, while a further 2,600m. people are denied suitable sanitation systems. WHO helped launch the Water Supply and Sanitation Council in 1990 and regularly updates its *Guidelines for Drinking Water Quality*. In rural areas the emphasis continues to be on the provision and maintenance of safe and sufficient water supplies and adequate sanitation, the health aspects of rural housing, vector control in water resource management, and the safe use of agrochemicals. In urban areas assistance is provided to identify local environmental health priorities and to improve municipal governments' ability to deal with environmental conditions and health problems in an integrated manner; promotion of the 'Healthy City' approach is a major component of the programme. Other programme activities include environmental health information development and management, human resources development, environmental health planning methods, research and work on problems relating to global environment change, such as UV-radiation. The WHO Global Strategy for Health and Environment, developed in response to the WHO Commission on Health and Environment which reported to the UN Conference on Environment and Development in June 1992, provides the framework for programme activities. In May 2008 the 61st World Health Assembly adopted a resolution urging member states to take action to address the impact of climate change on human health.

Through its International EMF Project WHO is compiling a comprehensive assessment of the potential adverse effects on human health deriving from exposure to electromagnetic fields (EMF). In May 2011 the International Agency for Research on Cancer, an agency of WHO, classified radiofrequency EMF as possibly carcinogenic to humans, on the basis of an increased risk for glioma (malignant brain cancer) associated with the use of wireless phones.

WHO's work in the promotion of chemical safety is undertaken in collaboration with the ILO and UNEP through the International Programme on Chemical Safety (IPCS), the Central Unit for which is located in WHO. The Programme provides internationally evaluated scientific information on chemicals, promotes the use of such information in national programmes, assists member states in establishment of their own chemical safety measures and programmes, and helps them strengthen their capabilities in chemical emergency preparedness and response and in chemical risk reduction. In 1995 an Inter-organization Programme for the Social Management of Chemicals was established by UNEP, the ILO, FAO, WHO, UNIDO and OECD, in order to strengthen international co-operation in the field of chemical safety. In 1998 WHO led an international assessment of the health risk from bendocine disruptors (chemicals which disrupt hormonal activities).

Since the major terrorist attacks perpetrated against targets in the USA in September 2001, WHO has focused renewed attention on the potential malevolent use of bacteria (such as bacillus anthracis, which causes anthrax), viruses (for example, the variola virus, causing smallpox) or toxins, or of chemical agents, in acts of biological or chemical terrorism. In September 2001 WHO issued draft guidelines entitled 'Health Aspects of Biological and Chemical Weapons'.

Within the UN system, WHO's Department of Emergency and Humanitarian Action co-ordinates the international response to emergencies and natural disasters in the health field, in close co-operation with other agencies and within the framework set out by the UN's Office for the Co-ordination of Humanitarian Affairs. In this context, WHO provides expert advice on epidemiological surveillance, control of communicable diseases, public health information and health emergency training. Its emergency preparedness activities include co-ordination, policy-making and planning, awareness-building, technical advice, training, publication of standards and guidelines, and research. Its emergency relief activities include organizational support, the provision of emergency drugs and supplies and conducting technical emergency assessment missions. The Division's objective is to strengthen the national capacity of member states to reduce the adverse health consequences of disasters. In responding to emergency situations, WHO always tries to develop projects and activities that will assist the national authorities concerned in rebuilding or strengthening their own capacity to handle the impact of such situations. Under the UN's inter-agency Consolidated Appeals Process (CAP) for 2011, launched in November 2010, WHO appealed for US $162.5m. to fund its emergency humanitarian operations.

WHO's emergency response to a severe earthquake in the Pacific Ocean, measuring 9.0 on the international Richter scale, and a tsunami, that in mid-March 2011 devastated northeastern coastal areas of Japan and destroyed part of the Fukushima Daiichi nuclear plant, included collating available technical guidelines on nuclear issues; developing plans to address potential nuclear-related human health needs that might arise from the incident; making available funds for initiating training and planning to address related psychosocial issues; and issuing information on food safety. In late March 2011 WHO, FAO and the IAEA issued a joint statement on food safety issues in the aftermath of the Fukushima nuclear emergency, emphasizing their commitment to mobilizing knowledge and expertise in support of the Japanese authorities.

HEALTH TECHNOLOGY AND PHARMACEUTICALS

WHO's Health Technology and Pharmaceuticals group, made up of the departments of essential drugs and other medicines, vaccines and other biologicals, and blood safety and clinical technology, covers the following areas of work: essential medicines—access, quality and rational use; immunization and vaccine development; and world-wide co-operation on blood safety and clinical technology. Blood safety and clinical technology are an organization-wide priority.

In January 1999 the Executive Board adopted a resolution on WHO's Revised Drug Strategy which placed emphasis on the inequalities of access to pharmaceuticals, and also covered specific aspects of drugs policy, quality assurance, drug promotion, drug donation, independent drug information and rational drug use. Plans of action involving co-operation with member states and other international organizations were to be developed to monitor and analyse the pharmaceutical and public health implications of international agreements, including trade agreements. In April 2001 experts from WHO and the World Trade Organization participated in a workshop to address ways of lowering the cost of medicines in less developed countries. In the following month the World Health Assembly adopted a resolution urging member states to promote equitable access to essential drugs, noting that this was denied to about one-third of the world's population. WHO participates with other partners in the 'Accelerating Access' initiative, which aims to expand access to antiretroviral drugs for people with HIV/AIDS (see above).

WHO reports that 2m. children die each year of diseases for which common vaccines exist. In September 1991 the Children's Vaccine Initiative (CVI) was launched, jointly sponsored by the Rockefeller Foundation, UNDP, UNICEF, the World Bank and WHO, to facilitate the development and provision of children's vaccines. The CVI has as its ultimate goal the development of a single oral immunization shortly after birth that will protect against all major childhood diseases. An International Vaccine Institute was established in Seoul, Republic of Korea, as part of the CVI, to provide scientific and technical services for the production of vaccines for developing countries. The first edition of a comprehensive survey, entitled *State of the World's Vaccines and Immunization*, was published by WHO, jointly with UNICEF, in 1996; a revised edition of the survey was issued in 2003. In 1999 WHO, UNICEF, the World Bank and a number of public and private sector partners formed the Global Alliance for Vaccines and Immunization (GAVI), which aimed to expand the provision of existing vaccines and to accelerate the development and introduction of new vaccines and technologies, with the ultimate goal of protecting children of all nations and from all socio-economic backgrounds against vaccine-preventable diseases.

WHO supports states in ensuring access to safe blood, blood products, transfusions, injections, and healthcare technologies.

INFORMATION, EVIDENCE AND RESEARCH

The Information, Evidence and Research group addresses the following areas of work: evidence for health policy; health information management and dissemination; and research policy and promotion and organization of health systems. Through the generation and dissemination of evidence the Information, Evidence and Research group aims to assist policy-makers assess health needs, choose intervention strategies, design policy and monitor performance, and thereby improve the performance of national health systems. The group also supports international and national dialogue on health policy.

WHO co-ordinates the Health InterNetwork Access to Research Initiative (HINARI), which was launched in July 2001 to enable relevant authorities in developing countries to access biomedical journals through the internet at no or greatly reduced cost, in order to improve the world-wide circulation of scientific information; by 2011 more than 7,500 information resources were being made available to health institutions in 105 countries.

Finance

WHO's regular budget is provided by assessment of member states and associate members. An additional fund for specific projects is provided by voluntary contributions from members and other sources, including UNDP and UNFPA.

A regular budget of US $5,382.7m. was proposed for the two years 2010–11, of which some 11.6%, or $627.0m., was provisionally allocated to South-East Asia and 6.7% ($358.5m.) to the Western Pacific.

Publications

Bulletin of WHO (monthly).

Eastern Mediterranean Health Journal (annually).

International Classification of Functioning, Disability and Health—ICF.

International Pharmacopoeia.

International Statistical Classification of Disease and Related Health Problems.

International Travel and Health.

Model List of Essential Medicines (every two years).

Pan-American Journal of Public Health (annually).

3 By 5 Progress Report.

Toxicological Evaluation of Certain Veterinary Drug Residues in Food (annually).

Weekly Epidemiological Record (in English and French, paper and electronic versions available).

WHO Drug Information (quarterly).

WHO Global Atlas of Traditional, Complementary and Alternative Medicine.

WHO Model Formulary.

WHO Report on the Global Tobacco Epidemic.

World Health Report (annually, in English, French and Spanish).

World Cancer Report.

World Malaria Report (with UNICEF).

Zoonoses and Communicable Diseases Common to Man and Animals.

Technical report series; catalogues of specific scientific, technical and medical fields available.

Other UN Organizations Active in the Region

OFFICE FOR THE CO-ORDINATION OF HUMANITARIAN AFFAIRS—OCHA

Address: United Nations Plaza, New York, NY 10017, USA.

Telephone: (212) 963-1234; **fax:** (212) 963-1312; **e-mail:** ochany@un.org; **internet:** ochaonline.un.org.

The Office was established in January 1998 as part of the UN Secretariat, with a mandate to co-ordinate international humanitarian assistance and to provide policy and other advice on humanitarian issues. It administers the Humanitarian Early Warning System, as well as Integrated Regional Information Networks (IRIN), to monitor the situation in different countries, and a Disaster Response System. A complementary service, Reliefweb, which was launched in 1996, monitors crises and publishes information on the internet. The UN Emergency Relief Co-ordinator presides over an Inter-Agency Task Force on Disaster Reduction (IATF/DR), which comprises 25 UN, international, regional and civil society organizations and is the principal body within the UN system responsible for developing disaster reduction policy.

Under-Secretary-General for Humanitarian Affairs and Emergency Relief Co-ordinator: VALERIE AMOS (United Kingdom).

UN WOMEN—UNITED NATIONS ENTITY FOR GENDER EQUALITY AND THE EMPOWERMENT OF WOMEN

Address: 304 East 45th St, 15th Floor, New York, NY 10017, USA.

Telephone: (212) 906-6400; **fax:** (212) 906-6705; **internet:** www.unwomen.org.

UN Women was established by the UN General Assembly in July 2010 in order to strengthen the UN's capacity to promote gender equality, the empowerment of women, and the elimination of discrimination against women and girls. It commenced operations on 1 January 2011, incorporating the functions of the Office of the Special Adviser on Gender Issues and Advancement of Women, the Division for the Advancement of Women of the Secretariat, the United Nations Development Fund for Women (UNIFEM) and the International Research and Training Institute for the Advancement of Women (INSTRAW).

Executive Director and Under-Secretary-General: MICHELLE BACHELET (Chile).

UNITED NATIONS OFFICE ON DRUGS AND CRIME—UNODC

Address: Vienna International Centre, POB 500, 1400 Vienna, Austria.

Telephone: (1) 26060-0; **fax:** (1) 26060-5866; **e-mail:** unodc@unodc.org; **internet:** www.unodc.org.

The Office was established in November 1997 (as the UN Office of Drug Control and Crime Prevention) to strengthen the UN's integrated approach to issues relating to drug control, crime prevention and international terrorism. It comprises two principal components: the United Nations Drug Programme and the Crime Programme.

Executive Director: YURI FEDOTOV (Russia).

OFFICE OF THE UNITED NATIONS HIGH COMMISSIONER FOR HUMAN RIGHTS—OHCHR

Address: Palais Wilson, 52 rue de Paquis, 1201 Geneva, Switzerland.

Telephone: 229179290; **fax:** 229179022; **e-mail:** infodesk@ohchr.org; **internet:** www.ohchr.org.

The Office is a body of the UN Secretariat and is the focal point for UN human-rights activities. Since September 1997 it has incorporated the Centre for Human Rights. The High Commissioner is the UN official with principal responsibility for UN human rights activities.

High Commissioner: NAVANETHEM PILLAY (South Africa).

UNITED NATIONS HUMAN SETTLEMENTS PROGRAMME—UN-HABITAT

Address: POB 30030, Nairobi, Kenya.

Telephone: (20) 621234; **fax:** (20) 624266; **e-mail:** infohabitat@unhabitat.org; **internet:** www.unhabitat.org.

UN-Habitat was established, as the United Nations Centre for Human Settlements, in October 1978 to service the intergovernmental Commission on Human Settlements. It became a full UN programme on 1 January 2002, serving as the focus for human settlements activities in the UN system.

Executive Director: JOAN CLOS (Spain).

Regional Office for Asia and the Pacific: ACROS Fukuoka Building, 8th Floor 1-1-1 Tenjin, Chuo-ku Fukuoka 810, Japan; tel. (92) 724-7121; fax (92) 724-7124; e-mail habitat.fukuoka@unhabitat.org; internet www.fukuoka.unhabitat.org.

UNITED NATIONS CONFERENCE ON TRADE AND DEVELOPMENT—UNCTAD

Address: Palais des Nations, 1211 Geneva 10, Switzerland.

Telephone: 229171234; **fax:** 229070043; **e-mail:** info@unctad.org; **internet:** www.unctad.org.

UNCTAD was established in 1964. It is the principal organ of the UN General Assembly concerned with trade and development, and is the focal point within the UN system for integrated activities relating to trade, finance, technology, investment and sustainable development. It aims to maximize the trade and development opportunities of developing countries, in particular least-developed countries, and to assist them to adapt to the increasing globalization and liberalization of the world economy. UNCTAD undertakes consensus-building activities, research and policy analysis and technical co-operation.

Secretary-General: Dr SUPACHAI PANITCHPAKDI (Thailand).

UNITED NATIONS POPULATION FUND—UNFPA

Address: 605 Third Ave, New York, NY 10158, USA.

Telephone: (212) 297-5000; **fax:** (212) 370-0201; **e-mail:** hq@unfpa.org; **internet:** www.unfpa.org.

Created in 1967 as the Trust Fund for Population Activities, the UN Fund for Population Activities (UNFPA) was established as a Fund of the UN General Assembly in 1972 and was made a subsidiary organ of the UN General Assembly in 1979, with the UNDP Governing Council (now the Executive Board) designated as its governing body. In 1987 UNFPA's name was changed to the United Nations Population Fund (retaining the same acronym).

Executive Director: BABATUNDE OSOTIMEHIN (Nigeria).

Regional Office for Asia and the Pacific: UN Service Bldg, 4th Floor, Rajdamnern Nok Ave, Bangkok 10200, Thailand; tel. (2) 280-3320; fax (2) 280-2715; e-mail apd@unfpa.org; sub-regional offices are located in Kathmandu, Nepal, and in Suva, Fiji (serving the Pacific).tion)

UN Specialized Agencies

INTERNATIONAL CIVIL AVIATION ORGANIZATION—ICAO

Address: 999 University St, Montréal, QC H3C 5H7, Canada.

Telephone: (514) 954-8219; **fax:** (514) 954-6077; **e-mail:** icaohq@icao.org; **internet:** www.icao.int.

ICAO was founded in 1947, on the basis of the Convention on International Civil Aviation, signed in Chicago, in 1944, to develop the techniques of international air navigation and to help in the planning and improvement of international air transport.

Secretary-General: RAYMOND BENJAMIN (France).

Asia and Pacific Office: 252/1 Vibhavadi Rangsit Rd, Chatuchak, Bangkok 10900, Thailand; tel. (2) 537-8189; fax (2) 537-8199; e-mail icao_apac@bangkok.icao.int; internet www.bangkok.icao.int.

INTERNATIONAL LABOUR ORGANIZATION—ILO

Address: 4 route des Morillons, 1211 Geneva 22, Switzerland.

Telephone: 227996111; **fax:** 227988685; **e-mail:** ilo@ilo.org; **internet:** www.ilo.org.

ILO was founded in 1919 to work for social justice as a basis for lasting peace. It carries out this mandate by promoting decent living standards, satisfactory conditions of work and pay and adequate employment opportunities. Methods of action include the creation of international labour standards; the provision of technical co-operation services; and training, education, research and publishing activities to advance ILO objectives.

Director-General: JUAN O. SOMAVÍA (Chile).

Regional Office for Asia and the Pacific: POB 2-349, Bangkok 10200, Thailand; tel. (2) 288-1234; fax (2) 288-1735; e-mail bangkok@ilo.org; internet www.ilo.org/asia.

INTERNATIONAL MARITIME ORGANIZATION—IMO

Address: 4 Albert Embankment, London, SE1 7SR, United Kingdom.

Telephone: (20) 7735-7611; **fax:** (20) 7587-3210; **e-mail:** info@imo.org; **internet:** www.imo.org.

The Inter-Governmental Maritime Consultative Organization (IMCO) began operations in 1959, as a specialized agency of the UN to facilitate co-operation among governments on technical matters affecting international shipping. Its main aims are to improve the safety of international shipping, and to control pollution caused by ships. IMCO became IMO in 1982.

Secretary-General: EFTHIMIOS MITROPOULOS (Greece) (until 31 Dec. 2011), KOJI SEKIMIZU (Japan) (designate).

INTERNATIONAL TELECOMMUNICATION UNION—ITU

Address: Place des Nations, 1211 Geneva 20, Switzerland.

Telephone: 227305111; **fax:** 227337256; **e-mail:** itumail@itu.int; **internet:** www.itu.int.

Founded in 1865, ITU became a specialized agency of the UN in 1947. It acts to encourage world co-operation for the improvement and use of telecommunications, to promote technical development, to harmonize national policies in the field, and to promote the extension of telecommunications throughout the world. ITU helped to organize the World Summit on the Information Society, held, in two phases, in 2003 and 2005, and supports follow-up initiatives. ITU assumed responsibility for issues relating to cybersecurity.

Secretary-General: HAMADOUN TOURÉ (Mali).

UNITED NATIONS INDUSTRIAL DEVELOPMENT ORGANIZATION—UNIDO

Address: Vienna International Centre, POB 300, 1400 Vienna, Austria.

Telephone: (1) 260260; **fax:** (1) 2692669; **e-mail:** unido@unido.org; **internet:** www.unido.org.

UNIDO began operations in 1967 and became a specialized agency in 1985. Its objectives are to promote sustainable and socially equitable industrial development in developing countries and in countries with economies in transition. It aims to assist such countries to integrate fully into global economic system by mobilizing knowledge, skills, information and technology to promote productive employment, competitive economies and sound environment.

Director-General: KANDEH YUMKELLA (Sierra Leone).

UNIVERSAL POSTAL UNION—UPU

Address: Weltpoststr., 3000 Bern 15, Switzerland.

Telephone: 313503111; **fax:** 313503110; **e-mail:** info@upu.int; **internet:** www.upu.int.

The General Postal Union was founded by the Treaty of Berne (1874), beginning operations in July 1875. Three years later its name was changed to the Universal Postal Union. In 1948 UPU became a specialized agency of the UN. It aims to develop and unify the international postal service, to study problems and to provide training.

Director-General: EDOUARD DAYAN (France).

WORLD INTELLECTUAL PROPERTY ORGANIZATION—WIPO

Address: 34 chemin des Colombettes, 1211 Geneva 20, Switzerland.

Telephone: 223389111; **fax:** 227335428; **e-mail:** wipo.mail@wipo.int; **internet:** www.wipo.int.

WIPO was established in 1970. It became a specialized agency of the UN in 1974 concerned with the protection of intellectual property (e.g. industrial and technical patents and literary copyrights) throughout the world. WIPO formulates and administers treaties embodying international norms and standards of intellectual property, establishes model laws, and facilitates applications for the protection of inventions, trademarks etc. WIPO provides legal and technical assistance to developing countries and countries with economies in transition and advises countries on obligations under the World Trade Organization's agreement on Trade-Related Aspects of Intellectual Property Rights (TRIPS).

Director-General: FRANCIS GURRY (Australia).

WORLD METEOROLOGICAL ORGANIZATION—WMO

Address: 7 bis, ave de la Paix, 1211 Geneva 2, Switzerland.

Telephone: 227308111; **fax:** 227308181; **e-mail:** wmo@wmo.int; **internet:** www.wmo.int.

WMO was established in 1950 and was recognized as a Specialized Agency of the UN in 1951, aiming to improve the exchange of information in the fields of meteorology, climatology, operational hydrology and related fields, as well as their applications. WMO jointly implements, with UNEP, the UN Framework Convention on Climate Change. In June 2011 the 16th World Meteorological Congress endorsed a new Global Framework for Climate Services.

Secretary-General: MICHEL JARRAUD (France).

WORLD TOURISM ORGANIZATION—UNWTO

Address: Capitán Haya 42, 28020 Madrid, Spain.

Telephone: (91) 5678100; **fax:** (91) 5713733; **e-mail:** omt@world-tourism.org; **internet:** www.world-tourism.org.

The World Tourism Organization was established in 1975 and was recognized as a Specialized Agency of the UN in December 2003. It works to promote and develop sustainable tourism, in particular in support of socio-economic growth in developing countries.

Secretary-General: TALEB RIFAI (Jordan).

SPECIAL HIGH LEVEL APPOINTMENT OF THE UN SECRETARY-GENERAL

Special Envoy for HIV/AIDS in Asia and in the Pacific: NAFIS SADIK (Pakistan).

Affiliated Body

EXTRAORDINARY CHAMBERS IN THE COURTS OF CAMBODIA—ECCC

Address: National Rd 4, Chaom Chau Commune, Dangkao District, POB 71, Phnom-Penh, Cambodia.

Telephone: (23) 219824; **fax:** (23) 219841; **e-mail:** info@eccc.gov.kh; **internet:** www.eccc.gov.kh. Formally established as the Extraordinary Chambers in the Courts of Cambodia for the Prosecution of Crimes Committed during the Period of Democratic Kampuchea, the ECCC was inaugurated in July 2006 on the basis of an agreement concluded in June 2003 between the Cambodian Government and the UN. The ECCC is mandated to prosecute senior leaders of the former Khmer Rouge regime for serious contraventions of Cambodian and international law—including crimes against humanity, genocide and war crimes—committed during the period 17 April 1975–6 January 1979. The ECCC is a hybrid Cambodian tribunal with international participation, combining Cambodian and international judges and personnel. It applies international standards and acts independently of the Cambodian Government and the UN. The ECCC comprises a Pre-Trial Chamber, Trial Chamber and Supreme Court Chamber; an Office of the Co-Prosecutors; an Office of the Co-Investigating Judges; a Defence Support section; a Victims' Unit; and an Office of Administration. The UN Assistance to the Khmer Rouge Trials (UNAKRT) provides technical assistance to the ECCC. Victims may file complaints before the ECCC, and may apply to become Civil Parties to the proceedings. By October 2011 some 3,866 people had been admitted as Civil Parties in Case 002 (ongoing, see below). In February 2009 the ECCC initiated proceedings ('Case 001') against its first defendent, Kaing Guek Eav (also known as 'Duch'), who had been charged under international law with crimes against humanity and grave breaches of the Geneva Conventions, and under Cambodian national law with homicide and torture offences, in relation to his former role under the Khmer Rouge regime as director of Tuol Sleng prison, where at least 15,000 prisoners had been tortured and executed. The presentation of evidence in the Kaing Guek Eav case was concluded in September 2009, closing statements were made in November. In July 2010 Kaing Guek Eav was found guilty and sentenced to 35 years of imprisonment; an appeal in that case commenced in March 2011. In September 2010 four other senior figures in the Khmer Rouge regime (Nuon Chea, formerly the Deputy Secretary of the Party of Democratic Kampuchea; Ieng Sary, formerly Minister of Foreign Affairs; Khieu Samphan, formerly President of the State Presidium; and Ieng Thirith, formerly Minister of Social Affairs and Action) were indicted on charges of crimes against humanity, grave breaches of the Geneva Conventions, genocide, and offences under the Cambodian criminal code ('Case 002'). In January 2011 the Pre-Trial Chamber ordered the case to be sent for trial. In September 2011 the Trial Chamber ordered the division of Case 002 into a series of smaller trials, which were to be tried and adjudicated separately. The first trial was to focus on the forced movement of population and related charges of crimes against humanity. In September 2009 the International Prosecutor, submitting to investigating judges a confidential list of the names of five additional suspects, requested a formal judicial investigation into two further cases ('Case 003' and 'Case 004', the subject matter of which also remained confidential). In October 2011 the then International Co-Investigating Judge resigned, citing attempted interference by government officials in the investigation into Cases 003 and 004.

National Co-Prosecutor: CHEA LEANG (Cambodia).

International Co-Prosecutor: ANDREW T. CAYLEY (United Kingdom).

National Co-Investigating Judge: YOU BUNLENG (Cambodia).

International Co-Investigating Judge: (vacant).

ASIA-PACIFIC ECONOMIC COOPERATION—APEC

Address: 35 Heng Mui Keng Terrace, Singapore 119616.

Telephone: 68919600; **fax:** 68919690; **e-mail:** info@apec.org; **internet:** www.apec.org.

The Asia-Pacific Economic Cooperation (APEC) was initiated in November 1989, in Canberra, Australia, as an informal consultative forum. Its aim is to promote multilateral economic co-operation on issues of trade and investment.

MEMBERS

Australia	Japan	Philippines
Brunei	Korea, Republic	Russia
Canada	Malaysia	Singapore
Chile	Mexico	Taiwan*
China, People's Republic	New Zealand	Thailand
Hong Kong	Papua New Guinea	USA
Indonesia	Peru	Viet Nam

* Admitted as Chinese Taipei.

Note: APEC has three official observers: the Association of Southeast Asian Nations (ASEAN) Secretariat; the Pacific Economic Co-operation Council; and the Pacific Islands Forum Secretariat. Observers may participate in APEC meetings and have full access to all related documents and information.

Organization

(October 2011)

ECONOMIC LEADERS' MEETINGS

The first meeting of APEC heads of government was convened in November 1993, in Seattle, Washington, USA. Subsequently, each annual meeting of APEC ministers of foreign affairs and of economic affairs has been followed by an informal gathering of the leaders of the APEC economies, at which the policy objectives of the grouping are discussed and defined. The 17th Economic Leaders' Meeting was convened in November 2010, in Yokohama, Japan; the 18th was to be held in Honolulu, Hawaii, in November 2011.

MINISTERIAL MEETINGS

APEC ministers of foreign affairs and ministers of economic affairs meet annually. These meetings are hosted by the APEC Chair, which rotates each year, although it was agreed, in 1989, that alternate Ministerial Meetings were to be convened in an ASEAN member country. A Senior Officials' Meeting (SOM) convenes regularly between Ministerial Meetings to co-ordinate and administer the budgets and work programmes of APEC's committees and working groups. Other meetings of ministers are held on a regular basis to enhance co-operation in specific areas.

SECRETARIAT

In 1992 the Ministerial Meeting, held in Bangkok, Thailand, agreed to establish a permanent secretariat to support APEC activities. The Secretariat became operational in February 1993. In accordance with a decision of the 2007 Leaders' Meeting, from 1 January 2010 an Executive Director with a three-year fixed term of office was appointed (hitherto the Executive Director had served a one-year term). A Policy Support Unit was established within the Secretariat in 2008.

Executive Director: MUHAMAD NOOR YACOB (Malaysia).

COMMITTEES

Budget and Management Committee (BMC): f. 1993 as Budget and Administrative Committee, present name adopted 1998; advises APEC senior officials on budgetary, administrative and managerial issues. The Committee reviews the operational budgets of APEC committees and groups, evaluates their effectiveness and conducts assessments of group projects. In 2005 the APEC Support Fund (ASF) was established under the auspices of the BMC, with the aim of supporting capacity-building programmes for developing economies; subsidiary funds of the ASF have been established relating to human security and avian influenza.

Committee on Trade and Investment (CTI): f. 1993 on the basis of a Declaration signed by ministers meeting in Seattle, Washington,

USA, in order to facilitate the expansion of trade and the development of a liberalized environment for investment among member countries; undertakes initiatives to improve the flow of goods, services and technology in the region. Supports Industry Dialogues to promote collaboration between public and private sector representatives in the following areas of activity: Automotive; Chemical; Non-ferrous Metal; and Life Sciences Innovation. An Investment Experts' Group was established in 1994, initially to develop non-binding investment principles. In May 1997 an APEC Tariff Database was inaugurated, with sponsorship from the private sector. A Market Access Group was established in 1998 to administer CTI activities concerned with non-tariff measures. In 2001 the CTI finalized a set of nine non-binding Principles on Trade Facilitation, which aimed to help eliminate procedural and administrative impediments to trade and to increase trading opportunities. A Trade Facilitation Action Plan (TFAP) was approved in 2002. By 2005 a strategy was adopted to systematize transparency standards. TFAP II, which aimed reduce trade transaction costs by 5% during 2007–10, was endorsed by the APEC ministers responsible for trade in July 2007 and by APEC leaders in September; an assessment of achievements made under TFAP II was under way in 2011. In 2007 the Electronic Commerce Steering Group, established in 1999, became aligned to the CTI. An Investment Facilitation Action Plan (IFAP) was undertaken during 2008–10, with the aim of assisting investment flows into the region. The most recent (seventh) edition of the official *Guide to the Investment Regimes of the APEC Member Economies* was published in January 2011.

Economic Committee (EC): f. 1994 following an agreement, in November, to transform the existing ad hoc group on economic trends and issues into a formal committee; aims to enhance APEC's capacity to analyse economic trends and to research and report on issues affecting economic and technical co-operation in the region. In addition, the Committee is considering the environmental and development implications of expanding population and economic growth. During 2007–10 the EC implemented a work plan on the implementation of the Leaders' Agenda to Implement Structural Reform (LAISR, agreed in November 2004 by the 12th Economic Leaders' Meeting, see below).

SOM Steering Committee on ECOTECH (SCE): f. 1998 to assist the SOM with the co-ordination of APEC's economic and technical co-operation programme (ECOTECH); reconstituted in 2006, with an enhanced mandate to undertake greater co-ordination and oversee project proposals of the working groups; monitors and evaluates project implementation and also identifies initiatives designed to strengthen economic and technical co-operation in infrastructure.

ADVISORY COUNCIL

APEC Business Advisory Council (ABAC): Philamlife Tower, 43rd Floor, 8767 Paseo de Roxas, Makati City, 1226 Metro Manila, Philippines; tel. (2) 8454564; fax (2) 8454832; e-mail abacsec@pfgc.ph; internet www.abaconline.org; an agreement to establish ABAC, comprising up to three senior representatives of the private sector from each APEC member economy, was concluded at the Ministerial Meeting held in November 1995. ABAC is mandated to advise member states on the implementation of APEC's Action Agenda and on other business matters, and to provide business-related information to APEC fora. ABAC meets three or four times each year and holds an annual CEO Summit alongside the annual APEC Economic Leaders' Meeting; Exec. Dir ALEX PARLE (USA) (2011).

Activities

APEC is focused on furthering objectives in three key areas, or 'pillars': trade and investment liberalization; business facilitation; and economic and technical co-operation. It was initiated in 1989 as a forum for informal discussion between the then six ASEAN members and their six dialogue partners in the Pacific, and, in particular, to promote trade liberalization in the Uruguay Round of negotiations, which were being conducted under the General Agreement on Tariffs and Trade (GATT). The Seoul Declaration, adopted by ministers meeting in the Republic of Korea in November 1991, defined the objectives of APEC.

ASEAN countries were initially reluctant to support any more formal structure of the forum, or to admit new members, owing to concerns that it would undermine ASEAN's standing as a regional grouping and be dominated by powerful non-ASEAN economies. In August 1991 it was agreed to extend membership to the People's Republic of China (PRC), Hong Kong and Taiwan (subject to conditions imposed by the PRC, including that a Taiwanese official of no higher than vice-ministerial level should attend the annual meeting of ministers of foreign affairs). Mexico and Papua New Guinea acceded to the organization in November 1993, and Chile joined in November 1994. The summit meeting held in November 1997 agreed that Peru, Russia and Viet Nam should be admitted to APEC at the 1998 meeting, but imposed a 10-year moratorium on further expansion of the grouping.

In September 1992 APEC ministers agreed to establish a permanent secretariat. In addition, the meeting created an 11-member non-governmental Eminent Persons Group (EPG), which was to assess trade patterns within the region and propose measures to promote co-operation. At the Ministerial Meeting in Seattle, Washington, USA, in November 1993, members agreed on a framework for expanding trade and investment among member countries, and to establish a permanent committee (the CTI, see above) to pursue these objectives.

In August 1994 the EPG proposed the following timetable for the liberalization of all trade across the Asia-Pacific region: negotiations for the elimination of trade barriers were to commence in 2000 and be completed within 10 years in developed countries, 15 years in newly industrialized economies and by 2020 in developing countries. Trade concessions could then be extended on a reciprocal basis to non-members in order to encourage world-wide trade liberalization, rather than isolate APEC as a unique trading bloc. In November 1994 the meeting of APEC heads of government adopted the Bogor Declaration of Common Resolve, which endorsed the EPG's timetable for free and open trade and investment in the region by the year 2020. Other issues incorporated into the Declaration included the implementation of GATT commitments in full and strengthening the multilateral trading system through the forthcoming establishment of the World Trade Organization (WTO), intensifying development co-operation in the Asia-Pacific region and expanding and accelerating trade and investment programmes. In November 1995 the Ministerial Meeting decided to dismantle the EPG, and to establish the APEC Business Advisory Council (ABAC), consisting of private sector representatives.

Meeting in Osaka, Japan, in November 1995, APEC heads of government adopted the Osaka Action Agenda as a framework to achieve the commitments of the Bogor Declaration. Part One of the Agenda identified action areas for the liberalization of trade and investment and the facilitation of business, for example, customs procedures, rules of origin and non-tariff barriers. It incorporated agreements that the process was to be comprehensive, consistent with WTO commitments, comparable among all APEC economies and non-discriminatory. Each member economy was to ensure the transparency of its laws, regulations and procedures affecting the flow of goods, services and capital among APEC economies and to refrain from implementing any trade protection measures. A second part of the Agenda was to provide a framework for further economic and technical co-operation between APEC members in areas such as energy, transport, infrastructure, SMEs and agricultural technology. In order to resolve a disagreement concerning the inclusion of agricultural products in the trade liberalization process, a provision for flexibility was incorporated into the Agenda, taking into account diverse circumstances and different levels of development in APEC member economies. Liberalization measures were to be implemented from January 1997 (i.e. three years earlier than previously agreed). A Trade and Investment Liberalization and Facilitation Special Account was established to finance projects in support of the implementation of the Osaka Action Agenda. Each member economy was to prepare an Individual Action Plan (IAP) on efforts to achieve the trade liberalization measures, that were to be reviewed annually.

In November 1996 the Economic Leaders' Meeting, held in Subic Bay, Philippines, approved the Manila Action Plan for APEC (MAPA), which incorporated the IAPs and other collective measures aimed at achieving the trade liberalization and co-operation objectives of the Bogor Declaration, as well as the joint activities specified in the second part of the Osaka Agenda. Heads of government also endorsed a US proposal to eliminate tariffs and other barriers to trade in information technology products by 2000 and determined to support efforts to conclude an agreement to this effect at the forthcoming WTO conference; however, they insisted on the provision of an element of flexibility in achieving trade liberalization in this sector.

The 1997 Economic Leaders' Meeting, held in Vancouver, Canada, in November, was dominated by concern at the financial instability that had affected several Asian economies during that year. The final declaration of the summit meeting endorsed a framework of measures that had been agreed by APEC deputy ministers of finance and central bank governors at an emergency meeting convened in the previous week in Manila, the Philippines (the so-called Manila Framework for Enhanced Asian Regional Cooperation to Promote Financial Stability). The meeting, attended by representatives of the IMF, the World Bank and the Asian Development Bank, committed all member economies receiving IMF assistance to undertake specified economic and financial reforms, and supported the establishment of a separate Asian funding facility to supplement international financial assistance (although this was later rejected by the IMF). APEC ministers of finance and governors of central banks were urged to accelerate efforts for the development of the region's financial and capital markets and to liberalize capital flows in the region. Measures were to include strengthening financial market supervision and clearing and settlement infrastructure, the reform of pension systems, and promoting co-operation among export credit agencies and financing institutions. The principal item on the Vancouver summit agenda was an initiative to enhance trade liberalization, which, the grouping insisted, should not be undermined by the financial instability in Asia. The following 15 economic sectors were identified for 'early voluntary sectoral liberalization' ('EVSL'): environmental goods and services; fish and fish products; forest products; medical equipment and instruments; toys; energy; chemicals; gems and jewellery; telecommunications; oilseeds and oilseed products; food; natural and synthetic rubber; fertilizers; automobiles; and civil aircraft. The implementation of EVSL was to encompass market opening, trade facilitation, and economic and technical co-operation activities.

In May 1998 APEC finance ministers met in Canada to consider the ongoing financial and economic crisis in Asia and to review progress in implementing efforts to alleviate the difficulties experienced by several member economies. The ministers agreed to pursue activities in the following three priority areas: capital market development, capital account liberalization and strengthening financial systems (including corporate governance). The region's economic difficulties remained the principal topic of discussion at the Economic Leaders' Meeting held in Kuala Lumpur, Malaysia, in November. A final declaration reiterated their commitment to co-operation in pursuit of sustainable economic recovery and growth, in particular through the restructuring of financial and corporate sectors, promoting and facilitating private sector capital flows, and efforts to strengthen the global financial system. The meeting endorsed a proposal by ABAC to establish a partnership for equitable growth, with the aim of enhancing business involvement in APEC's programme of economic and technical co-operation. Other initiatives approved included an Agenda of APEC Science and Technology Industry Cooperation into the 21st Century (for which the PRC announced it was to establish a special fund), and an Action Programme on Skills and Development in APEC. Japan's persisting opposition to a reduction of tariffs in the fish and forestry sectors prevented the conclusion of tariff negotiations under the EVSL scheme, and it was therefore agreed that responsibility for managing the tariff reduction element of the initiative should be transferred to the WTO.

In September 1999 political dialogue regarding civil conflict in East Timor (now Timor-Leste) dominated the start of the annual meetings of the grouping, held in Auckland, New Zealand, although the issue remained separate from the official agenda. The Economic Leaders' Meeting considered measures to sustain the economic recovery in Asia and endorsed the APEC Principles to Enhance Competition and Regulatory Reform (for example, transparency, accountability, non-discrimination) as a framework to strengthen APEC markets and to enable further integration and implementation of the IAPs. Also under discussion was the forthcoming round of multilateral trade negotiations, to be initiated by the WTO. The heads of government proposed the objective of completing a single package of trade agreements within three years and endorsed the abolition of export subsidies for agricultural products. The meeting determined to support the efforts of the PRC, Russia, Taiwan and Viet Nam to accede to WTO membership. An APEC Business Travel Card scheme, to facilitate business travel within the region, was inaugurated in 1999, having been launched on a trial basis in 1997. By 2011 more than 80,000 individuals were registered under the scheme, in which 19 economies were participating fully.

The Economic Leaders' Meeting for 2000, held in Brunei in November, urged that an agenda for the now-stalled round of multilateral trade negotiations should be formulated without further delay. The meeting endorsed a plan of action to promote the utilization of advances in information and communications technologies in member economies, for the benefit of all citizens. It adopted the aim of tripling the number of people in the region with access to the internet by 2005, and determined to co-operate with business and education sector interests to attract investment and expertise in the pursuit of this goal. A proposal that the Democratic People's Republic of Korea be permitted to participate in APEC working groups was approved at the meeting.

The 2001 Economic Leaders' Meeting, held in October, in Shanghai, PRC, condemned the terrorist attacks against targets in the USA of the previous month and resolved to take action to combat the threat of international terrorism. The heads of government declared terrorism to be a direct challenge to APEC's vision of free, open and prosperous economies, and concluded that the threat made the continuing move to free trade, with its aim of bolstering economies, increasing prosperity and encouraging integration, even more of a priority. Leaders emphasized the importance of sharing the benefits of globalization, and adopted the Shanghai Accord, which identified development goals for APEC during its second decade and clarified measures for achieving the Bogor goals within the agreed timetable. A process of IAP Peer Reviews was initiated. (By late 2005 the process had been concluded for each member economy.) The meeting also outlined the e-APEC Strategy developed by the e-APEC Task Force established after the Brunei Economic Leaders' meeting. Considering issues of entrepreneurship, structural and regulatory reform, competition, intellectual property rights and information security, the strategy aimed to facilitate technological development in the region. Finally, the meeting adopted a strategy document relating to infectious diseases in the Asia Pacific region, which aimed to promote a co-ordinated response to combating HIV/AIDS and other contagious diseases.

In September 2002 a meeting of APEC ministers of finance was held in Los Cabos, Mexico. Ministers discussed the importance of efforts to combat money-laundering and the financing of terrorism. The meeting also focused on ways to strengthen global and regional economic growth, to advance fiscal and financial reforms and to improve the allocation of domestic savings for economic development. The theme of the 2002 Economic Leaders' Meeting, held in the following month in Los Cabos, was 'Expanding the Benefits of Cooperation for Economic Growth and Development—Implementing the Vision'. The meeting issued a statement on the implementation of APEC standards of transparency in trade and investment liberalization and facilitation. Leaders also issued a statement on fighting terrorism and promoting growth. In February the first conference to promote the Secure Trade in the APEC Region (STAR) initiative was convened in Bangkok, Thailand, and attended by representatives of all APEC member economies as well as senior officers of private sector companies and relevant international organizations. The second STAR conference was held in Viña del Mar, Chile, in March 2004; the third in Incheon, Republic of Korea, in February 2005; the fourth in Hanoi, Viet Nam, in February 2006; the fifth in Sydney, Australia, in June 2007; the sixth in Lima, Peru, in August 2008; the seventh in Singapore, in July 2009; and the eighth in Washington, DC, USA, in September 2011.

The 2003 Economic Leaders' Meeting, convened in October, in Bangkok, Thailand, considered means of advancing the WTO's stalled Doha round of trade negotiations, emphasizing the central importance of its development dimension, and noted progress made hitherto in facilitating intra-APEC trade. The meeting also addressed regional security issues, reiterating the Community's commitment to ensuring the resilience of APEC economies against the threat of terrorism. The Leaders adopted the Bangkok Declaration on Partnership for the Future, which identified the following areas as priority concerns for the group: the promotion of trade and investment liberalization; enhancing human security; and helping people and societies to benefit from globalization. The Bangkok meeting also issued a statement on health security, which expressed APEC's determination to strengthen infrastructure for the detection and prevention of infectious diseases, as well as the surveillance of other threats to public health, and to ensure a co-ordinated response to public health emergencies, with particular concern to the outbreak, earlier in the year, of Severe Acute Respiratory Syndrome (SARS).

The 12th Economic Leaders' Meeting was held in Santiago, Chile, in November 2004, on the theme 'One Community, Our Future'. The meeting reaffirmed the grouping's commitment to the Doha Development Agenda, and endorsed the package of agreements concluded by the WTO in July. The meeting approved a Santiago Initiative for Expanded Trade in APEC, to promote further trade and investment liberalization in the region and advance trade facilitation measures. Other areas discussed were human security, HIV/AIDS and other emerging infectious diseases, and energy security. Efforts to combat corruption and promote good governance included a Santiago Commitment to Fight Corruption and Ensure Transparency, the APEC Course of Action on Fighting Corruption and Ensuring Transparency, and a Leaders' Agenda to Implement Structural Reform (LAISR). LAISR covers the following five policy areas: regulatory reform, competition policy, public sector governance, corporate governance, and strengthening economic and legal infrastructure.

In September 2005 APEC finance ministers, meeting in Jeju, Republic of Korea, discussed two main issues: the increased importance of capital flows among member economies, particularly those from worker remittances; and the challenge presented by the region's ageing population. The meeting resolved to promote capital account liberalization and to develop resilient and efficient capital markets. It also adopted the 'Jeju Declaration on Enhancing Regional Cooperation against the Challenges of Population Ageing', in which it acknowledged the urgency of such domestic reforms such as creating sustainable pension systems, providing an increased range of savings products and improving financial literacy. In November 2005 the 13th Economic Leaders' Meeting endorsed a Busan Roadmap to the Bogor Goals, based on an assessment of action plans, which outlined key priorities and frameworks. Particular focus was drawn to support for the multilateral trading system, efforts to promote high quality regional trade agreements and free trade agreements, and strengthened collective and individual action plans. It also incorporated a Busan Business Agenda and commitments to a strategic approach to capacity building and to a pathfinder approach to promoting trade and investment in the region, through work on areas such as intellectual property rights, anti-corruption, secure trade and trade facilitation.

The 14th Economic Leaders' Meeting, held in Hanoi, Viet Nam, in November 2006 on the theme 'Towards One Dynamic Community for Sustainable Development and Prosperity', reaffirmed support for the stalled negotiations on the WTO's Doha Development Agenda; adopted the Hanoi Action Plan on the implementation of the Busan Roadmap (endorsed by the 2005 Leaders' Meeting); endorsed the APEC Action Plan on Prevention and Response to Avian and Influenza Pandemics; and expressed strong concern at the nuclear test conducted by the Democratic Republic of Korea in October.

The participants at the 15th Economic Leaders' Meeting, convened in Sydney, Australia, in September 2007, on the theme 'Strengthening our Community, Building a Sustainable Future', adopted a Declaration on Climate Change, Energy Security and Clean Development, wherein they acknowledged the need to ensure energy supplies to support regional economic growth while also preserving the quality of the environment. The Declaration incorporated an Action Agenda and agreements to establish an Asia-Pacific Network for Energy Technology and an Asia-Pacific Network for Sustainable Forest Management and Rehabilitation. The Economic Leaders also issued a statement once again affirming the need successfully to resolve the stalled WTO Doha Development Round; endorsed a report on means of further promoting Asia-Pacific economic integration; agreed to examine the options and prospects for the development of a Free Trade Area of the Asia-Pacific (FTAAP); welcomed efforts by the Economic Committee to enhance the implementation of the LAISR; endorsed the second Trade Facilitation Action Plan, which aimed to achieve a 5% reduction in business and trade transaction costs by 2010; determined to continue to strengthen the protection and enforcement of intellectual property rights in the region; and approved the Anti-corruption Principles for the Public and Private Sectors, and related codes of conduct, that had been adopted in June 2007 by the Anti-corruption and Transparency Experts' Task Force and endorsed by the September 2007 Ministerial Meeting.

The 16th Economic Leaders' Meeting, held in November 2008, in Lima, Peru, under the theme 'A New Commitment to Asia-Pacific Development', addressed the implications for the region of the then deteriorating global economic situation. The APEC Leaders urged the promotion of good Corporate Social Responsibility (CSR) practices in the region; commended the progress made hitherto in examining the prospects for establishing the proposed FTAAP; and urged ministers of finance to examine more fully means of optimizing linkages between private infrastructure finance and economic growth and development. Expressing deep concern at the impact on the region of volatile global food prices, and at food shortages in some developing economies, the meeting determined to support the regional implementation of the Comprehensive Framework for Action of the UN Task Force on the Global Food Security Crisis, and to increase technical co-operation and capacity-building measures aimed at fostering the growth of the agricultural sector.

Convened in November 2009, in Singapore, the 17th Economic Leaders' Meeting expressed support for the goals of the G-20 'Framework for Strong, Sustainable and Balanced Growth' (adopted in September), and adopted a Declaration on a New Growth Paradigm for a Connected Asia-Pacific in the 21st Century, aimed at navigating a future post-global economic crisis landscape; reaffirming commitment to addressing issues related to the threat of climate change; and welcoming the implementation of a peer review of energy efficiency in APEC economies.

The first APEC Ministerial Meeting on Food Security, held in October 2010, in Niigata, Japan, endorsed a new APEC Action Plan on Food Security. In November the 18th Economic Leaders' Meeting, held in Yokohama, Japan, adopted the APEC Leaders' Growth Strategy, representing a comprehensive long-term framework for promoting high-quality growth in the region. The Growth Strategy included an action plan, which was to outline work towards progress in the areas of structural reform; human resource and entrepreneurship development; human security; green growth; and the development of a knowledge-based economy. Progress in the implementation of the Growth Strategy was to be reviewed in 2015. The November 2010 Leaders' Meeting also endorsed a report and issued an assessment on the state of progress towards achieving the Bogor Goals,. Leaders reaffirmed strong commitment to pursuing the proposed FTAAP and towards achieving a successful conclusion to the Doha Development Agenda, while determining to refrain from adopting protectionist measures until 2014. In May 2011 APEC and the World Bank concluded a Memorandum of Understanding on strengthening collaboration on food safety in the Asia-Pacific region.

SPECIAL TASK GROUPS

These may be established by the Senior Officials' Meeting to identify issues and make recommendations on areas for consideration by the grouping.

Anti-corruption and Transparency Experts' Task Force (ACT): the Ministerial Meeting, held in Santiago, Chile, in November 2004, endorsed the establishment of the ACT to implement an APEC Course of Action on Fighting Corruption and Ensuring Transparency. Activities to be undertaken included the promotion of ratification and implementation of the UN Convention against Corruption, strengthening measures to prevent and combat corruption and to sanction public officials found guilty of corruption, the promotion of public-private partnerships and enhancing co-operation within the region to combat problems of corruption. An APEC Anti-Counterfeiting and Piracy Initiative was launched in mid-2005. In June 2007 the ACT approved a Code of Conduct for Business, in collaboration with ABAC, a set of Conduct Principles for Public Officials, and Anti-corruption Principles for the Public and Private Sectors. In February 2010 the ACT endorsed the final result of a project entitled 'Stocktaking of Bilateral and Regional Arrangements on Anti-corruption Matters Between/Among APEC Member Economies'. An ACT Workshop on Successful Training Techniques for Implementing the Principles of Conduct for Public Officials was held in September 2010, in Sendai, Japan.

Counter Terrorism Task Force (CTTF): established in February 2003 to co-ordinate implementation of the Leaders' Statement on Fighting Terrorism and Promoting Growth, which had been adopted in October 2002. It was subsequently mandated to implement all other APEC initiatives to enhance human security. The CTTF assists member economies to identify and assess counter-terrorism needs and co-ordinates individual Counter Terrorism Action Plans, which identify measures required and the level of implementation achieved to secure trade.

Gender Focal Point Network: in 1996 an SOM Ad Hoc Advisory Group on Gender Integration was established, which worked until 2002 to implement a Framework for the Integration of Women in APEC and to recommend efforts to further gender integration. In October 2002 ministers meeting in Los Cabos, Mexico, endorsed the establishment of the Gender Focal Point Network to pursue this work programme. The Network reports regularly to the SOM and convenes an annual meeting: the eighth meeting was convened in Saitama, Japan, in September 2010. The Network maintains a *Gender Experts List* and a *Register of Best Practices on Gender Integration*. The Network is compiling a gender and trade database.

Mining Task Force (MTF): the first meeting of the MTF was convened in May 2008, in Arequipa, Peru. The Task Force was to provide a unified, cohesive mining, minerals and metals forum for APEC member economies. Its ongoing work programme includes undertaking a study on means of attracting investment to the regional mining sector, with a particular focus on investment; the regulatory framework; and the availability of skilled workforces. A Conference on Sustainable Development of the Mining Sector in the APEC Region was held in July 2009, in Singapore.

WORKING GROUPS

APEC's structure of working groups aims to promote practical and technical co-operation in specific areas, and to help implement individual and collective action plans in response to the directives of the Economic Leaders and meetings of relevant ministers.

Agricultural Technical Co-operation (ATCWG): formally established as an APEC expert's group in 1996, and incorporated into the system of working groups in 2000. The ATCWG aims to enhance the role of agriculture in the economic growth of the region and to promote co-operation in the following areas: conservation and utilization of plant and animal genetic resources; research, development and extension of agricultural biotechnology; processing, marketing, distribution and consumption of agricultural products; plant and animal quarantine and pest management; development of an agricultural finance system; sustainable agriculture; and agricultural technology transfer and training. The ATCWG has primary responsibility for undertaking recommendations connected with the implementation of the APEC Food System, which aims to improve the efficiency of food production, supply and trade within member economies. The ATCWG has conducted projects on human resource development in post-harvest technology and on capacity-building, safety assessment and communication in biotechnology. A high-level policy dialogue on agricultural biotechnology was initiated in 2002. Following the outbreak of so-called avian flu and its impact on the region's poultry industry, in 2004 it was agreed that the ATCWG would develop the enhanced biosecurity planning and surveillance capacity considered by APEC's member economies as being essential to protect the region's agricultural sector from the effects of future outbreaks of disease. A quarantine regulators' seminar on Implementing Harmonised Arrangements for Ensuring Effective Quarantine Treatments, and an APEC Workshop on Avian Influenza Risks in the Live Bird Market System, were organized in 2008; and in August 2009 a symposium on the Approach of Organic Agriculture: New Markets, Food Security and a Clean Environment was held. In April 2010 a Report on Developing and Applying a Traceability

System in Agriculture Production and Trade was issued. The ATCWG contributed to the development of the APEC Action Plan on Food Security, which was endorsed by the October 2010 APEC Ministerial Meeting on Food Security.

Emergency Preparedness (EPWG): established in March 2005, as a special task force, in response to the devastating natural disaster that had occurred in the Indian Ocean in late December 2004; upgraded to a working group in 2010. The EPWG is mandated to co-ordinate efforts throughout APEC to enhance disaster management capacity-building, to strengthen public awareness regarding natural disaster preparedness, prevention and survival, and to compile best practices. An APEC Senior Disaster Management Co-ordinator Seminar, convened in Cairns, Australia, in August 2007, and comprising representatives of APEC member economies and of international humanitarian organizations, determined to support the development of a three- to five-year emergency preparedness strategic plan. The fourth APEC Emergency Management CEOs' Forum was held in January 2010, in Kobe, Japan.

Energy (EWG): APEC ministers responsible for energy convened for the first time in August 1996 to discuss major energy challenges confronting the region. The main objectives of the EWG, established in 1990, are: the enhancement of regional energy security and improvement of the fuel supply market for the power sector; the development and implementation of programmes of work promoting the adoption of environmentally sound energy technologies and promoting private sector investment in regional power infrastructure; the development of energy efficiency guidelines; and the standardization of testing facilities and results. The EWG is supported by five expert groups, on: clean fossil energy, efficiency and conservation, energy data and analysis, new and renewable energy technologies, and minerals and energy exploration and development; and by two task forces, on: renewable energy and energy efficiency financing, and biofuels. In March 1999 the EWG resolved to establish a business network to improve relations and communications with the private sector. The first meeting of the network took place in April. In May 2000 APEC energy ministers meeting in San Diego, California, USA, launched the APEC 21st Century Renewable Energy Initiative, which aimed to encourage co-operation in and advance the utilization of renewable energy technologies, envisaging the establishment of a Private Sector Renewable Energy Forum. In June 2003 APEC energy ministers agreed on a framework to implement APEC's Energy Security Initiative. The first meeting of ministers responsible for mining was convened in Santiago, Chile, in June 2004. In 2004, amid challenges to energy security and unusually high oil prices, the EWG was instructed by APEC Economic Leaders to accelerate the implementation of the Energy Security Initiative, a strategy aimed at responding to temporary supply disruptions and at addressing the broader challenges facing the region's energy supply by means of longer-term policy. In October 2005 APEC ministers responsible for energy convened in Gyeongju, Republic of Korea, to address the theme 'Securing APEC's Energy Future: Responding to Today's Challenges for Energy Supply and Demand'. Meeting in May 2007 in Darwin, Australia, under the theme 'Achieving Energy Security and Sustainable Development through Efficiency, Conservation and Diversity', energy ministers directed the EWG to formulate a voluntary Energy Peer Review Mechanism. The ministers welcomed the work of the Asia-Pacific Partnership on Clean Development and Climate, launched in January 2006 by Australia, PRC, India, Japan, Republic of Korea and the USA. In June 2010 energy ministers gathered, in Fukui, Japan, under the theme 'Low Carbon Path to Energy Security'. Pursuant to the Osaka Action Agenda adopted by APEC Economic Leaders in 1995, the Asia Pacific Energy Research Centre (APERC) was established in July 1996 in Tokyo, Japan; APERC's mandate and programmes focus on energy sector development in APEC member states. APERC maintains a comprehensive regional Energy Database.

Fisheries (FWG): aims to maximize the economic benefits and sustainability of fisheries resources for all APEC members. Recent concerns include food safety, the quality of fish products and resource management. In 1996 the FWG initiated a four-year study on trade and investment liberalization in the sector, in the areas of tariffs, non-tariff barriers and investment measures and subsidies. In 1997 the FWG organized two technical workshops on seafood inspection systems, and conducted a workshop addressing destructive fishing techniques. The first APEC Aquaculture Forum, which considered the sustainable development of aquaculture in the region and the development of new markets for APEC fish products, was held in Taipei, Taiwan, in June 1998. In May 1999 new guidelines were adopted to encourage the participation of the private sector in the activities of the FWG. The FWG's first business forum was convened in July 2000. In April 2002 the first ocean-related ministerial meeting, held in Seoul, Republic of Korea, adopted the Seoul Oceans Declaration, detailing recommendations on marine environmental protection and integrated coastal management. In September 2005 the second ocean-related ministerial meeting took place in Bali, Indonesia, at which the Bali Plan of Action (BPA) 'Towards Healthy Oceans and Coasts for the Sustainable Growth and Prosperity of the Asia Pacific Community' was adopted. Meeting in Sanctuary Cove, Gold Coast, Australia, in April 2007, APEC member economies considered future priority activities in support of the Bali Plan of Action, covering areas such as illegal, unreported and unregulated (IUU) fishing and monitoring, control and surveillance (MCS) measures. A stocktake of the BPA was concluded during 2008. In June 2010 a meeting of fisheries ministers, held in Lima, Peru, adopted a strategic plan for the FWG covering 2010–12.

Health: in October 2003 a Health Task Force (HTF) was established, on an ad hoc basis, to implement health-related activities as directed by APEC leaders, ministers and senior officials, including a Health Safety Initiative, and to address health issues perceived as potential threats to the region's economy, trade and security, in particular emerging infectious diseases. The HTF convened for the first time in Taiwan, in April 2004. It was responsible for enhancing APEC's work on preventing, preparing for and mitigating the effects of highly pathogenic avian influenza (avian flu) and any future related human influenza pandemic. APEC organized an intergovernmental meeting on Avian and Pandemic Influenza Preparedness and Response, convened in Brisbane, Australia, in October 2005. In May 2006 a Ministerial Meeting on Avian and Influenza Pandemics, held in Da Nang, Viet Nam, endorsed an APEC Action Plan on the Prevention of and Response to Avian and Influenza Pandemics. In June 2007 APEC ministers of health, meeting in Sydney, Australia, determined to reconstitute the HTF as the Health Working Group. The Group convened for its first official meeting in February 2008. Meeting in June 2010, the HWG identified the following priority areas: enhancing preparedness for combating vector-borne diseases, including avian and human pandemic influenza, and HIV/AIDS; capacity-building in the areas of health promotion and prevention of lifestyle-related diseases; improving health outcomes through advances in health information technologies; and strengthening health systems in each member economy.

Human Resources Development (HRD): established in 1990; comprises three networks: the Capacity Building Network, with a focus on human capacity-building, including management and technical skills development and corporate governance; the Education Network, promoting effective learning systems and supporting the role of education in advancing individual, social and economic development; and the Labour and Social Protection Network, concerned with promoting social integration through the strengthening of labour markets, the development of labour market information and policy, and improvements in working conditions and social safety net frameworks. The HRD undertakes activities through these networks to implement ministerial and leaders' directives. A voluntary network of APEC study centres links higher education and research institutions in member economies. Private sector participation in the HRD has been strengthened by the establishment of a network of APEC senior executives responsible for human resources management. Recent initiatives have included a cyber-education co-operation project, a workshop on advanced risk management, training on the prevention and resolution of employment and labour disputes, and an educators' exchange programme on the use of information technology in education. The 5th APEC HRD ministerial meeting was convened in September 2010, in Beijng, PRC.

Industrial Science and Technology (ISTWG): aims to contribute to sustainable development in the region, improve the availability of information, enhance human resources development in the sector, improve the business climate, promote policy dialogue and review and facilitate networks and partnerships. Accordingly, the ISTWG has helped to establish an APEC Virtual Centre for Environmental Technology Exchange in Japan; a Science and Technology Industrial Parks Network; an International Molecular Biology Network for the APEC Region; an APEC Centre for Technology Foresight, based in Thailand; and the APEC Science and Technology Web, an online database. During 1997 and 1998 the ISTWG formulated an APEC Action Framework on Emerging Infectious Diseases and developed an Emerging Infections Network (EINet), based at the University of Washington, Seattle, USA. In March 2004 the fourth meeting of science ministers was held in Christchurch, New Zealand, the first since 1998. ISTWG work plan for 2010–12 outlined the following goals: enhanced economic growth, trade and investment opportunities, and sustainable development; improved quality of life and a cleaner environment; a safe and secure society; human resource capacity building; enhanced international science and technology networks; improved interconnection between research and innovation; and strengthened technological co-operation.

Marine Resource Conservation (MRCWG): promotes initiatives within APEC to protect the marine environment and its resources. An APEC Action Plan for Sustainability of the Marine Environment was adopted by ministers responsible for the environment, meeting in June 1997. The Plan aimed to promote regional co-operation, an integrated approach to coastal management, the prevention, reduction and control of marine pollution, and sustainable development. Strategies to encourage private sector participation in promoting the sustainable management of marine resources were endorsed by the MRCWG in June 2000. Four main themes were identified for the Action Plan in the 21st century: balancing coastal development and resource protection; ensuring sustainable fisheries and aquaculture; understanding and observing the oceans and seas; and promoting economic and technical co-operation in oceans management. The Seoul Oceans Declaration, endorsed in April 2002 (see above), established the direction of the MRCWG's future activities. A new strategic framework for the Group was adopted in May 2004, at a meeting held in Puerto Varas, Chile. In October the third integrated Oceans Management Forum took place on Easter Island, Chile. The MRCWG contributed to the policy directions outlined in the Bali Plan of Action, which was adopted by the APEC ocean-related ministerial meeting convened in Bali, Indonesia, in September 2005 (see under Fisheries). Prior to the third APEC Oceans-related Ministerial Meeting, convened in Paracas, Peru, in October 2010, the MRCWG organized preparatory work in the following areas: marine debris; oceans and climate change; capacity-building; food security and food safety; and ecosystem-based management. The October 2010 meeting adopted the Paracas Declaration on Healthy Oceans and Fisheries Management Towards Food Security, focusing on sustainable development and protection of the marine environment; impact of climate change on the oceans; promotion of free and open trade and investment; and the role of oceans in food security.

Small and Medium Enterprises (SMEWG): established in 1995, as the Ad Hoc Policy Level Group on Small and Medium Enterprises (SMEs), with a temporary mandate to oversee all APEC activities relating to SMEs. It supported the establishment of an APEC Centre for Technical Exchange and Training for Small and Medium Enterprises, which was inaugurated at Los Baños, near Manila, the Philippines, in September 1996. A five-year action plan for SMEs was endorsed in 1998. The group was redesignated as a working group, with permanent status, in 2000. In August 2002 the SMEWG's action plan was revised to include an evaluation framework to assist APEC and member economies in identifying and analysing policy issues. In the same month a sub-group specializing in micro-enterprises was established. The first APEC Incubator Forum was held in July–August 2003, in Taiwan, to promote new businesses and support their early development. During 2003 the SMEWG undertook efforts to develop a special e-APEC Strategy for SMEs. In 2004 the APEC SME Coordination Framework was finalized. The 12th APEC SME ministerial meeting, held in Daegu, Republic of Korea, in September 2005, adopted the 'Daegu Initiative on SME Innovation Action Plan', which provided a framework for member economies to create economic and policy environments more suitable to SME innovation. In 2006 the 'APEC Private Sector Development Agenda' was launched. The sixth APEC SME Technology Conference and Fair was convened in June–July 2010, in Fuzhou, PRC.

Telecommunications and Information (TEL): incorporates three steering groups concerned with different aspects of the development and liberalization of the sector—Liberalization; ICT development; and Security and prosperity. Activities are guided by directives of ministers responsible for telecommunications, who first met in 1995, in the Republic of Korea, and adopted a Seoul Declaration on Asia Pacific Information Infrastructure (APII). The second ministerial meeting, held in Gold Coast, Australia, in September 1996, adopted more detailed proposals for liberalization of the sector in member economies. In June 1998 ministers, meeting in Singapore, agreed to remove technical barriers to trade in telecommunications equipment (although Chile and New Zealand declined to sign up to the arrangement). At their fourth meeting, convened in May 2000 in Cancún, Mexico, telecommunications ministers approved a programme of action that included measures to bridge the 'digital divide' between developed and developing member economies, and adopted the APEC Principles on International Charging Arrangements for Internet Services and the APEC Principles of Interconnection. The fifth ministerial meeting, held in May 2002, issued a Statement on the Security of Information and Communications Infrastructures; a compendium of IT security standards has been disseminated in support of the Statement. A Mutual Recognition Arrangement Task Force (MRATF) (under the Liberalization steering group) implements a mutual recognition arrangement for conformity assessment of telecommunications equipment. An APEC Digital Prosperity Checklist is under development, with the aim of promoting ICT as a means of fuelling economic growth; the first and second seminars on the implementation of the Checklist were conducted, respectively, in July 2009 and March 2010. An Asia-Pacific Information Infrastructure (APII) Testbed Network Project, which aimed to facilitate researchers' and engineers' work and to promote the use of new generation internet, and a Stock-Take on Regulatory Convergence are also ongoing.

Tourism (TWG): established in 1991, with the aim of promoting the long-term sustainability of the tourism industry, in both environmental and social terms. The TWG administers a Tourism Information Network and an APEC International Centre for Sustainable Tourism. The first meeting of APEC ministers of tourism, held in the Republic of Korea in July 2000, adopted the Seoul Declaration on the APEC Tourism Charter. The TWG's work plan is based on four policy goals inherent in the Seoul Declaration, namely: the removal of impediments to tourism business and investment; increased mobility of visitors and increased demand for tourism goods and services; sustainable management of tourism; and enhanced recognition of tourism as a vehicle for economic and social development. At a meeting of the TWG in April 2001, APEC and the Pacific Asia Travel Association (PATA) adopted a Code for Sustainable Tourism. The Code is designed for adoption and implementation by a variety of tourism companies and government agencies. It urges members to conserve the natural environment, ecosystems and biodiversity; respect local traditions and cultures; conserve energy; reduce pollution and waste; and ensure that regular environmental audits are carried out. In 2004 the TWG published a report on Best Practices in Safety and Security to Safeguard Tourism against Terrorism. In October 2004 the 'Patagonia Declaration on Tourism in the APEC region' was endorsed at the third tourism ministers' meeting in Punta Arenas, Chile. The Declaration set out a strategic plan to ensure the viability of the regional tourism industry by measuring sustainability, safety and security and developing niche projects such as sports and health tourism. The fourth meeting of tourism ministers, held in Hoi An, Viet Nam, in October 2006, adopted the 'Hoi An Declaration on Tourism', which aimed to promote co-operation in developing sustainable tourism and investment in the region, with a focus on the following areas: encouragement of private sector participation in a new APEC Tourism and Investment Forum, and the promotion of the APEC Tourism Fair, both of which were to be held on the sidelines of tourism sector ministerial meetings; and liberalization of the air routes between the cultural heritage sites of APEC member states. In April 2008 tourism ministers, meeting in Lima, Peru, adopted the 'Pachacamac Declaration on Responsible Tourism'. The TWG recognizes tourism as a vehicle of social development, as well as an economic force. The sixth meeting of APEC tourism ministers was convened in Nara, Japan, in September 2010.

Transportation (TPTWG): undertakes initiatives to enhance the efficiency and safety of the regional transportation system, in order to facilitate the development of trade. The TPTWG focuses on three main areas: improving the competitiveness of the transportation industry; promoting a safe and environmentally sound regional transportation system; and human resources development, including training, research and education. The TPTWG has published surveys, directories and manuals on all types of transportation systems, and has compiled an inventory on regional co-operation on oil spills preparedness and response arrangements. A Road Transportation Harmonization Project aims to provide the basis for common standards in the automotive industry in the Asia-Pacific region. The TPTWG has established an internet database on ports and the internet-based Virtual Centre for Transportation Research, Development and Education. It plans to develop a regional action plan on the implementation of Global Navigation Satellite Systems, in consultation with the relevant international bodies. A Special Task Force was established by the TPTWG in 2003 to assist member economies to implement a new International Ship and Port Facility Security Code, sponsored by the International Maritime Organization, which entered into force on 1 July 2004. In April 2004 an Aviation Safety Experts' Group met for the first time since 2000. In July 2004 the fourth meeting of APEC ministers of transport directed the TPTWG to prepare a strategy document to strengthen its activities in transport liberalization and facilitation. A Seminar on Post Tsunami Reconstruction and Functions of Ports Safety was held in 2005. The fifth APEC Transportation ministerial meeting was held in Adelaide, Australia, in March 2007; the sixth, convened in Manila, Philippines, in April 2009, issued a joint ministerial statement detailing the following future focus areas for the TPTWG: liberalization and facilitation of transport services; seamless transportation services; aviation safety and security; land transport and mass transit safety and security; maritime safety and security; sustainable transport; industry involvement; and information sharing. The seventh meeting of APEC transport ministers, convened in September 2011, in San Francisco, USA, pledged increased efforts towards greener, more energy-efficient co-operation.

Publications

ABAC Report to APEC Leaders (annually).
APEC at a Glance (annually).
APEC Business Travel Handbook.
APEC Economic Outlook (annually).
APEC Economic Policy Report.
APEC Energy Handbook (annually).
APEC Energy Statistics (annually).
APEC Outcomes and Outlook
Guide to the Investment Regimes of the APEC Member Economies (every three years).
Key APEC Documents (annually).
Towards Knowledge-based Economies in APEC
Trade and Investment Liberalization in APEC
Working group reports, regional directories, other irregular surveys.

ASIAN DEVELOPMENT BANK—ADB

Address: 6 ADB Ave, Mandaluyong City, 0401 Metro Manila, Philippines; POB 789, 0980 Manila, Philippines.

Telephone: (2) 6324444; **fax:** (2) 6362444; **e-mail:** information@adb.org; **internet:** www.adb.org.

The ADB commenced operations in December 1966. The Bank's principal functions are to provide loans and equity investments for the economic and social advancement of its developing member countries, to give technical assistance for the preparation and implementation of development projects and programmes and advisory services, to promote investment of public and private capital for development purposes, and to respond to requests from developing member countries for assistance in the co-ordination of their development policies and plans.

MEMBERS

There are 48 member countries and territories within the ESCAP region and 19 others (see list of subscriptions below).

Organization

(October 2011)

BOARD OF GOVERNORS

All powers of the Bank are vested in the Board, which may delegate its powers to the Board of Directors except in such matters as admission of new members, changes in the Bank's authorized capital stock, election of Directors and President, and amendment of the Charter. One Governor and one Alternate Governor are appointed by each member country. The Board meets at least once a year. The 44th meeting was held in Ha Noi, Viet Nam, in May 2011; the 44th meeting was scheduled to be convened in Manila, Philippines, in May 2012.

BOARD OF DIRECTORS

The Board of Directors is responsible for general direction of operations and exercises all powers delegated by the Board of Governors, which elects it. Of the 12 Directors, eight represent constituency groups of member countries within the ESCAP region (with about 65% of the voting power) and four represent the rest of the member countries. Each Director serves for two years and may be re-elected.

Three specialized committees (the Audit Committee, the Budget Review Committee and the Inspection Committee), each comprising six members, assist the Board of Directors in exercising its authority with regard to supervising the Bank's financial statements, approving the administrative budget, and reviewing and approving policy documents and assistance operations.

The President of the Bank, though not a Director, is Chairman of the Board.

Chairman of Board of Directors and President: HARUHIKO KURODA (Japan).

Vice-Presidents: URSULA SCHÄFER-PREUSS (Germany), ZHAO XIAOYU (People's Republic of China), BINDU LOHANI (Nepal), STEPHEN P. GROFF (USA), LAKSHMI VENKATACHALAM (India).

ADMINISTRATION

The Bank had 2,833 staff, from 59 countries, at 31 December 2010.

Five regional departments cover Central and West Asia, East Asia, the Pacific, South Asia, and South-East Asia. Other departments and offices include Anticorruption and Integrity, Central Operations Services, Cofinancing Operations, Economics and Research, Private Sector Operations, Regional and Sustainable Development, Risk Management, Strategy and Policy, as well as other administrative units.

There are Bank Resident Missions in Afghanistan, Armenia, Azerbaijan, Bangladesh, Cambodia, the People's Republic of China, Georgia, India, Indonesia, Kazakhstan, Kyrgyzstan, Laos, Mongolia, Nepal, Pakistan, Papua New Guinea, Sri Lanka, Tajikistan, Thailand, Turkey, Uzbekistan and Viet Nam, all of which report to the head of the regional department. In addition, the Bank maintains a Country Office in the Philippines, a Special Liaison Office in Timor-Leste, a Pacific Liaison and Co-ordination Office in Sydney, Australia, and a South Pacific Sub-Regional Mission, based in Fiji. Representative Offices are located in Tokyo, Japan, Frankfurt am Main, Germany (for Europe), and Washington, DC, USA (for North America).

INSTITUTE

ADB Institute (ADBI): Kasumigaseki Bldg, 8th Floor, 2–5 Kasumigaseki 3-chome, Chiyoda-ku, Tokyo 100-6008, Japan; tel. (3) 3593-5500; fax (3) 3593-5571; e-mail info@adbi.org; internet www.adbi.org; f. 1997 as a subsidiary body of the ADB to research and analyse long-term development issues and to disseminate development practices through training and other capacity-building activities; Dean Dr MASAHIRO KAWAI (Japan).

FINANCIAL STRUCTURE

The Bank's ordinary capital resources (which are used for loans to the more advanced developing member countries) are held and used entirely separately from its Special Funds resources (see below). In May 2009 the Board of Governors approved a fifth General Capital Increase (GCI V), increasing the Bank's resources by some 200% to US $165,000m.

At 31 December 2010 the position of subscriptions to the capital stock was as follows: authorized US $163,843m.; subscribed $143,950m.

The Bank also borrows funds from the world capital markets. Total borrowings during 2010 amounted to US $14,940m. (compared with $10,359m. in 2009). At 31 December 2010 total outstanding debt amounted to $51,822m.

In July 1986 the Bank abolished the system of fixed lending rates, under which ordinary operations loans had carried interest rates fixed at the time of loan commitment for the entire life of the loan. Under the new system the lending rate is adjusted every six months, to take into account changing conditions in international financial markets.

Activities

Loans by the ADB are usually aimed at specific projects. In responding to requests from member governments for loans, the Bank's staff assesses the financial and economic viability of projects and the way in which they fit into the economic framework and priorities of development of the country concerned. In 1985 the Bank decided to expand its assistance to the private sector, hitherto comprising loans to development finance institutions, under government guarantee, for lending to small and medium-sized enterprises; a programme was formulated for direct financial assistance, in the form of equity and loans without government guarantee, to private enterprises. During the early 1990s the Bank aimed to expand its role as project financier by providing assistance for policy formulation and review and promoting regional co-operation, while placing greater emphasis on individual country requirements. During that period the Bank also introduced a commitment to assess development projects for their impact on the local population and to avoid all involuntary resettlement where possible and established a formal procedure for grievances, under which the Board may authorize an inspection of a project by an independent panel of experts, at the request of the affected community or group. The currency instability and ensuing financial crises affecting many Asian economies in 1997/98 prompted the Bank to reflect on its role in the region. The Bank resolved to strengthen its activities as a broad-based development institution, rather than solely as a project financier, through lending policies, dialogue, co-financing and technical assistance.

In November 1999 the Board of Directors approved a new overall strategy objective of poverty reduction, which was to be the principal consideration for all future Bank activities. The strategy incorporated key aims of supporting sustainable, grass-roots based economic growth, social development and good governance. During 2000 the Bank began to refocus its country strategies, projects and lending targets to complement the poverty reduction strategy. In addition, it initiated a process of consultation to formulate a long-term strategic framework, based on the target of reducing by 50% the incidence of extreme poverty by 2015, one of the so-called Millennium Development Goals (MDGs) identified by the UN General Assembly. The framework, establishing the operational priorities and principles for reducing poverty, was approved in March 2001. A review of the strategy, initiated at the end of 2003, concluded that more comprehensive, results-oriented monitoring and evaluation be put in place. It also recommended a closer alignment of Bank operations with national poverty reduction strategies and determined to include capacity development as a new overall thematic priority for the Bank, in addition to environmental sustainability, gender and development, private sector development and regional co-operation. In mid-2004 the Bank initiated a separate reform agenda to incorporate the strategy approach 'Managing for development results' throughout the organization. In April 2005 a Regional Monitoring Unit was replaced by an Office of Regional Economic Integration, which aimed to promote economic co-operation and integration among developing member countries and to contribute to economic growth throughout the whole region. In July 2006 the Bank adopted a strategy to promote regional co-operation and integration in order to combat poverty through collective regional and cross-border activities.

In June 2006 the Bank convened a panel of eminent persons to assess the Bank's future role within the region. The report of the panel, submitted in March 2007, prompted further wide-ranging consultations. In April 2008 the Bank published a new long-term strategic framework to cover the period 2008–20 ('Strategy 2020'), replacing the previous 2001–15 strategic framework, in recognition of the unprecedented economic growth of recent years and its associated challenges, including the effect on natural resources, inadequate infrastructure to support economic advances, and widening disparities both within and between developing member countries. The Bank determined to refocus its activities onto three critical agendas: inclusive economic growth; environmentally sustainable growth; and regional integration. It determined to initiate a process of restructuring its operations into five core areas of specialization: infrastructure; environment, including climate change; regional co-operation and integration; financial sector development; and education. Some 80% of Bank lending was to be allocated to these five areas by 2012. Under the strategy the Bank resolved to act as an agent of change, stimulating economic growth and widening development assistance, for example by supporting the private sector with more risk guarantees, investment and other financial instruments, placing greater emphasis on good governance, promoting gender equality and improving accessibility to and distribution of its knowledge services. It also committed to expanding its partnerships with other organizations, including with the private sector and other private institutions. The strategy was endorsed at the annual meeting of the Board of Governors, convened in Madrid, Spain, in May 2008.

In September 2008 the Bank organized a high level conference, attended by representatives of multilateral institutions, credit rating agencies, regulatory and supervisory bodies and banks to discuss and exchange ideas on measures to strengthen the region's financial markets and contain the global financial instability evident at that time. In March 2009 the Bank hosted a South Asia Forum on the Impact of the Global Economic and Financial Crisis, as the first of a proposed series of sub-regional conferences. At the end of that month the Bank expanded its Trade Finance Facilitation Program (TFFP, inaugurated in 2004) to support the private sector by increasing its exposure limit to guarantee trade transactions from US $150m. to $1,000m. In May 2009 the Board of Governors approved a general capital increase of some 200% to enable the Bank to extend the lending required to assist countries affected by the global economic downturn, as well as to support the longer-term development objectives of Strategy 2020. In June 2009 the Board of Directors approved a new Countercyclical Support Facility, with resources of $3,000m., to extend short-term, fast-disbursing loans to help developing member countries to counter the effects of the global financial crisis. Countries eligible for the funds were required to formulate a countercyclical development programme, to include plans for investment in public infrastructure or social safety net initiatives. The Board approved an additional $400m, to be made available through the Asian Development Fund (ADF), for countries with no access to the Bank's ordinary capital resources.

In 2010 the Bank's total financing operations amounted to US $17,514m, compared with $19,156m. in the previous year. Of the total amount approved in 2010, $11,463m. was for 118 loans, of which loans from ordinary capital resources totalled $9,250m., while loans from the ADF amounted to $2,213m. In 2010 the Bank approved 40 grants amounting to US $982m. financed mainly by the ADF, as well as by other Special Funds (see below) and bilateral and multilateral sources. It also approved funding of $176m. for 243 technical assistance projects, $243m. for eight equity investments, and $982m. in guarantees for five projects. During 2010 $3,669m. of the total financing approved came from cofinancing partners, for 155 investment and technical assistance projects, compared with $3,418m. in 2009.

An Operations Evaluation Office prepares reports on completed projects, in order to assess achievements and problems. In April 2000 the Bank announced that some new loans would be denominated in local currencies, in order to ease the repayment burden on recipient economies.

The Bank co-operates with other international organizations active in the region, particularly the World Bank, the IMF, UNDP and APEC, and participates in meetings of aid donors for developing member countries. In May 2001 the Bank and UNDP signed a memorandum of understanding (MOU) on strategic partnership, in order to strengthen co-operation in the reduction of poverty, for example the preparation of common country assessments and a common database on poverty and other social indicators. Also in 2001 the Bank signed an MOU with the World Bank on administrative arrangements for co-operation, providing a framework for closer co-operation and more efficient use of resources. In May 2004 the Bank signed a revised MOU with ESCAP to enhance co-operation activities to achieve the MDGs. In early 2002 the Bank worked with the World Bank and UNDP to assess the preliminary needs of the interim administration in Afghanistan, in preparation for an International Conference on Reconstruction Assistance to Afghanistan, held in January, in Tokyo, Japan. The Bank pledged to work with its member governments to provide highly concessional grants and loans of some US $500m. over two-and-a-half years, with a particular focus on road reconstruction, basic education, and agricultural irrigation rehabilitation. In June 2008, at an international donors' conference held in Paris, France, the Bank pledged up to $1,300m. to finance infrastructure projects in Afghanistan in the coming five years. A new policy concerning co-operation with non-governmental organizations (NGOs) was approved by the Bank in 1998. The Bank administers an NGO Center to provide advice and support to NGOs on involvement in country strategies and development programmes.

In June 2004 the Bank approved a new policy to provide rehabilitation and reconstruction assistance following disasters or other emergencies. The policy also aimed to assist developing member countries with prevention, preparation and mitigation of the impact of future disasters. At the end of December the Bank announced assistance amounting to US $325m. to finance immediate reconstruction and rehabilitation efforts in Indonesia, the Maldives and Sri Lanka, which had been severely damaged by the tsunami that had spread throughout the Indian Ocean as a result of a massive earthquake that had occurred close to the west coast of Sumatra, Indonesia. Of the total amount $150m. was to be drawn as new lending commitments from the ADF. Teams of Bank experts undertook to identify priority operations and initiated efforts, in co-operation with governments and other partner organizations, to prepare for more comprehensive reconstruction activities. In accordance with the 2004 policy initiative, an interdepartmental task force was established to co-ordinate the Bank's response to the disaster. In January 2005, at a Special ASEAN Leaders' Meeting, held in Jakarta, Indonesia, the Bank pledged assistance amounting to $500m.; later in that month the Bank announced its intention to establish a $600m. Multi-donor Asian Tsunami Fund to accelerate the provision of reconstruction and technical assistance to countries most affected by the disaster. In March 2006 the Bank hosted a high-level co-ordination meeting on rehabilitation and reconstruction assistance to tsunami-affected countries. In October the Bank, with representatives of the World Bank, undertook an immediate preliminary damage and needs assessment following a massive earthquake in north-western Pakistan, which also affected remote parts of Afghanistan and India. The report identified relief and reconstruction requirements totalling some $5,200m. The Bank made an initial contribution of $80m. to a Special Fund (see below) and also pledged concessional support of up to $1,000m. for rehabilitation and reconstruction efforts in the affected areas. In August 2010 the Bank announced that it was to extend up to $2,000m. in emergency rehabilitation and reconstruction assistance to Pakistan, large areas of which had been severely damaged by flooding. The Bank agreed to undertake, jointly with the World Bank, a damage and needs assessment to determine priority areas of action.

The Bank has actively supported regional, sub-regional and national initiatives to enhance economic development and promote economic co-operation within the region. The Bank is the main co-ordinator and financier of a Greater Mekong Sub-region (GMS) programme, initiated in 1992 to strengthen co-operation between Cambodia, the People's Republic of China (PRC), Laos, Myanmar, Thailand and Viet Nam. Projects undertaken have included transport and other infrastructure links, energy projects and communicable disease control. The first meeting of GMS heads of state was convened in Phnom-Penh, Cambodia, in November 2002. A second summit was held in Kunming, PRC, in July 2005, and a third summit in Vientiane, Laos, in March 2008, on the theme 'Enhancing Competitiveness through Greater Connectivity'. In June a GMS Economic Corridors Forum was held, in Kunming, PRC, to accelerate development of economic corridors in the sub-region. A second Forum was convened in Phnom-Penh, Cambodia, in September 2009. Other sub-regional initiatives supported by the Bank include the Central Asian Regional Economic Co-operation (CAREC) initiative, the South Asia Sub-regional Economic Cooperation (SASEC) initiative, the Indonesia, Malaysia, Thailand Growth Triangle (IMT-GT), and the Brunei, Indonesia, Malaysia, Philippines East ASEAN Growth Area (BIMP-EAGA).

SPECIAL FUNDS

The Bank is authorized to establish and administer Special Funds. The Asian Development Fund (ADF) was established in 1974 in order to provide a systematic mechanism for mobilizing and administering resources for the Bank to lend on concessionary terms to the least-developed member countries. In 1998 the Bank revised the terms of ADF. Since 1 January 1999 all new project loans are repayable within 32 years, including an eight-year grace period, while quick-disbursing programme loans have a 24-year maturity, also including an eight-year grace period. The previous annual service charge was redesignated as an interest charge, including a portion to cover administrative expenses. The new interest charges on all loans are 1%–1.5% per annum. In May 2008 30 donor countries pledged US $4,200m. towards the ninth replenishment of ADF resources (ADF X), which totalled $11,300m. to provide resources for the four-year period 2009–12. The total amount included replenishment of the Technical Assistance Special Fund (TASF—see below). During 2010 ADF loans approved amounted to $2,212.3m.

The Bank provides technical assistance grants from its TASF. A fourth replenishment of its resources was approved in August 2008 for the period 2009–12. By the end of 2010 the Fund's total resources amounted to US $1,759.7m. During 2010 $147.1m. was approved under the TASF project preparation, advisory and capacity development activities. The Japan Special Fund (JSF) was established in 1988 to provide finance for technical assistance by means of grants, in both the public and private sectors. The JSF aims to help developing member countries restructure their economies, enhance the opportunities for attracting new investment, and recycle funds. The Japanese Government had committed a total of 112,900m. yen (equivalent to some $973.7m.) to the JSF by the end of 2010. The Bank administers the ADB Institute Special Fund, which was established to finance the ADB Institute's operations. By 31 December 2010 cumulative commitments to the Special Fund amounted to 18,645m. yen and A$0.5m. (or $166.2m.).

In February 2005 the Bank established the Asian Tsunami Fund, with funds of US $600m., to accelerate the provision of reconstruction and technical assistance to countries most affected by the natural disaster that had affected several countries in the region in December 2004. At the end of 2010 the Fund's uncommitted resources amounted to $2.6m., of total resources amounting to $586.9m. The Pakistan Earthquake Fund was established in November 2005, with a commitment from the Bank of $80m., to help to deliver emergency grant financing and technical assistance required for immediate rehabilitation and reconstruction efforts following the massive earthquake that had occurred in October. At the end of 2010 the Fund's total resources amounted to some $145.2m., of which $3.9m. was uncommitted. In February 2007 the Bank established, with an initial $40.0m., the Regional Co-operation and Integration Fund to fund co-operation and integration activities. By the end of 2010 the Fund's total resources amounted to $53.0m., of which $10.4m. was uncommitted. In April 2008 the Bank established a Climate Change Fund, with an initial contribution of $40.0m. By 31 December 2010 total resources amounted to $51.0m., of which $19.1m. was uncommitted. In April 2009 the Bank's Board of Directors approved the establishment of an Asia Pacific Disaster Response Fund (APDRF) to extend rapid assistance to developing countries following a natural disaster. Some $40.0m. from the Asian Tsunami Fund was transferred to inaugurate the APDRF, which was mandated to provide grants of up to $3.0m. to fund immediate humanitarian relief operations. The APDRF was used in late September to provide assistance for more than 300,000 families in the Philippines affected by extensive flooding and damage to infrastructure caused by a tropical storm. In the following month the Bank approved $1.0m. from the Fund to support emergency efforts in Samoa, following an earthquake and tsunami. In August 2010 $3.0m. was approved under the APDRF to extend immediate emergency assistance following devastating flooding in Pakistan. At that time the Bank established a special flood reconstruction fund to administer donor contributions for relief and rehabilitation efforts in Pakistan.

TRUST FUNDS

The Bank also manages and administers several trust funds and other bilateral donor arrangements. The Japanese Government funds the Japan Scholarship Program, under which 2,696 scholarships had been awarded to recipients from 35 member countries between 1988 and 2010. In May 2000 the Japan Fund for Poverty Reduction was established, with an initial contribution of 10,000m. yen (approximately US $92.6m.) by the Japanese Government, to support ADB-financed poverty reduction and social development activities. During 2010 the Fund's mandate was expanded to provide for technical assistance grants. By the end of 2010 cumulative resources available to the Fund totalled $445.8m. In March 2004 a Japan Fund for Public Policy Training was established, with an initial contribution by the Japanese Government, to enhance capacity-building for public policy management in developing member countries.

The majority of grant funds in support of the Bank's technical assistance activities are provided by bilateral donors under channel financing arrangements (CFAs), the first of which was negotiated in 1980. CFAs may also be processed as a thematic financing tool, for example concerned with renewable energy, water or poverty reduction, enabling more than one donor to contribute. A Co-operation Fund for Regional Trade and Financial Security Initiative was established in July 2004, with contributions by Australia, Japan and the USA, to support efforts to combat money laundering and the financing of terrorism. Other financing partnerships facilities may also be established to mobilize additional financing and investment by development partners. In November 2006 the Bank approved the establishment of an Asia Pacific Carbon Fund (within the framework of a Carbon Market Initiative) to finance clean energy projects in developing member countries. To complement this Fund a new Future Carbon Fund was established, in July 2008, to provide resources for projects beyond 2012 (when the Kyoto Protocol regulating trade in carbon credits was due to expire). In December 2006 the Bank established a Water Financing Partnership Facility to help to achieve the objectives of its Water Financing Program. In April 2007 a Clean Energy Financing Partnership Facility (CEFPF) was established, further to provide investment in clean energy projects for developing member countries. An Asian Clean Energy Fund and an Investment Climate Facilitation Fund were established in 2008 within the framework of the CEFPF. A separate Carbon Capture and Storage Fund was established, under the CEFPF, with funding from the Australian Government, in July 2009. In November the Bank, with funding from the United Kingdom, initiated a five-year strategic partnership to combat poverty in India. In the following month the Bank established a multi-donor Urban Financing Partnership Facility. In November 2010 the Board of Directors approved the establishment of an Afghanistan Infrastructure Trust Fund, to be administered by the Bank, to finance and co-ordinate donor funding for infrastructure projects in that country.

In April 2010 the Board of Directors agreed to allocate US $130m. to a new Credit Guarantee and Investment Facility, established by ASEAN + 3 governments, with a further capital contribution of some $570m., in order to secure longer-term financing for local businesses and to support the development of Asian bond markets.

Finance

Internal administrative expenses totalled US $430.6m. in 2010 and were budgeted at $496.4m. for 2011.

Publications

ADB Business Opportunities (monthly).

ADB Institute Newsletter.

ADB Review (monthly).

Annual Report.

Asia Bond Monitor (quarterly).

Asia Capital Markets Monitor (annually).

Asia Economic Monitor (2 a year).

Asian Development Outlook (annually; an *Update* published annually).

Asian Development Review (2 a year).

Basic Statistics (annually).

Development Asia (2 a year).

Key Indicators for Asia and the Pacific (annually).

Law and Policy Reform Bulletin (annually).

Sustainability Report.

Studies and technical assistance reports, information brochures, guidelines, sample bidding documents, staff papers.

Statistics

SUBSCRIPTIONS AND VOTING POWER
(31 December 2010)

Country	Voting power (% of total)	Subscribed capital (% of total)
Regional:		
Afghanistan	0.329	0.038
Armenia	0.570	0.339
Australia	5.555	6.571
Azerbaijan	0.703	0.505
Bangladesh	1.226	1.160
Bhutan	0.304	0.007
Brunei	0.405	0.133
Cambodia	0.343	0.056
China, People's Republic	6.153	7.318
Cook Islands	0.301	0.003
Fiji	0.360	0.077
Georgia	0.609	0.388
Hong Kong	0.793	0.618
India	6.050	7.190
Indonesia	5.246	6.185
Japan	14.477	17.723
Kazakhstan	1.031	0.916
Kiribati	0.302	0.005
Korea, Republic	4.875	5.721
Kyrgyzstan	0.570	0.340
Laos	0.311	0.016
Malaysia	2.772	3.092
The Maldives	0.302	0.005
Marshall Islands	0.301	0.003
Micronesia, Federated States	0.300	0.002
Mongolia	0.312	0.017
Myanmar	0.793	0.618
Nauru	0.302	0.005
Nepal	0.432	0.167
New Zealand	1.694	1.744
Pakistan	2.278	2.474
Palau	0.301	0.004
Papua New Guinea	0.384	0.107
Philippines	2.463	2.706
Samoa	0.299	0.001
Singapore	0.402	0.129
Solomon Islands	0.305	0.008
Sri Lanka	0.825	0.659
Taiwan	1.288	1.237
Tajikistan	0.559	0.325
Thailand	1.535	1.546
Timor-Leste	0.307	0.011
Tonga	0.302	0.005
Turkmenistan	0.529	0.288
Tuvalu	0.299	0.001
Uzbekistan	0.910	0.765
Vanuatu	0.305	0.008
Viet Nam	0.402	0.129
Sub-total	71.417	71.361
Non-regional:		
Austria	0.608	0.386
Belgium	0.608	0.386
Canada	5.051	5.940
Denmark	0.608	0.386
Finland	0.608	0.386
France	2.413	2.643
Germany	4.229	4.913
Ireland	0.402	0.129
Italy	1.940	2.052
Luxembourg	0.608	0.386
Netherlands	1.230	1.165
Norway	0.608	0.386
Portugal	0.402	0.129
Spain	0.608	0.386
Sweden	0.608	0.386
Switzerland	0.475	0.221
Turkey	0.402	0.129
United Kingdom	2.154	2.319
USA	5.025	5.908
Sub-total	29.583	28.639
Total	100.000	100.000

LOAN APPROVALS BY SECTOR

Sector	2010 Amount (US $ million)	2010 %	1968–2010 Amount
Agriculture and natural resources	613.9	5.4	19,624.2
Education	70.0	0.6	6,178.8
Energy	2,454.0	21.4	32,857.4
Finance	1,263.4	11.0	20,337.7
Health and social protection	177.0	1.5	3,832.9
Industry and trade	—	—	4,588.0
Public sector management	894.5	7.9	13,980.3
Transport and information and communication technology (ICT)	3,831.1	33.4	41,141.2
Water supply and other municipal infrastructure and services	607.0	5.3	14,060.8
Multi-sector	1,551.4	13.5	10,414.8
Total	11,462.3	100.0	167,116.2

APPROVALS BY COUNTRY, 2010
(US $ million)

Country	Ordinary Capital loans	ADF loans	Total approvals*
Afghanistan	—	—	362.4
Armenia	210.0	—	210.0
Azerbaijan	27.0	—	438.0
Bangladesh	800.0	449.0	2,967.5
Bhutan	—	—	30.4
Brunei	—	—	0.8
Cambodia	—	95.0	203.2
China, People's Republic	1,577.5	—	1,947.9
Cook Islands	—	—	0.3
Georgia	338.0	85.0	596.4
India	2,119.6	—	2,395.2
Indonesia	785.0	—	901.6
Kazakhstan	606.0	—	674.7
Kiribati	—	12.0	32.8
Kyrgyzstan	—	88.2	168.8
Laos	—	151.6	211.9
Maldives	—	—	0.7
Marshall Islands	—	9.5	11.7
Mongolia	—	48.0	110.4
Nepal	—	154.9	301.2
Pakistan	378.8	270.0	1,094.0
Palau	12.6	3.4	16.0
Papua New Guinea	40.9	29.4	77.5
Philippines	600.0	—	708.0
Samoa	—	16.0	16.0
Solomon Islands	—	—	78.6
Sri Lanka	350.0	107.2	507.1
Tajikistan	—	—	122.8
Thailand	504.3	—	509.1
Timor-Leste	—	—	1.8
Tonga	—	—	0.5
Turkmenistan	—	—	0.4
Uzbekistan	390.0	265.0	957.4
Vanuatu	—	—	0.5
Viet Nam	510.0	580.0	1,246.5
Total	9,249.7	2,212.6	17,513.5

* Includes guarantees, equity investments, grants, technical assistance financing and co-financing.

Source: Asian Development Bank, *Annual Report 2010*.

ASSOCIATION OF SOUTHEAST ASIAN NATIONS—ASEAN

Address: 70A Jalan Sisingamangaraja, POB 2072, Jakarta 12110, Indonesia.

Telephone: (21) 7262991; **fax:** (21) 7398234; **e-mail:** public@aseansec.org; **internet:** www.aseansec.org.

ASEAN was established in August 1967 in Bangkok, Thailand, to accelerate economic progress and to increase the stability of the South-East Asian region. In November 2007 its 10 members signed an ASEAN Charter, which, after ratification by all member states, was formally to accord the grouping the legal status of an intergovernmental organization. The Charter entered into force on 15 December 2008.

MEMBERS

Brunei	Malaysia	Singapore
Cambodia	Myanmar	Thailand
Indonesia	Philippines	Viet Nam
Laos		

Organization

(October 2011)

SUMMIT MEETING

The summit meeting is the highest authority of ASEAN, bringing together the heads of state or government of member countries. The first meeting was held in Bali, Indonesia, in February 1976. The new ASEAN Charter specified that summit meetings were to be convened at least twice a year, hosted by the member state holding the Chairmanship of the organization (a position that rotates on an annual basis). The 18th summit meeting was held in Jakarta, Indonesia, in May 2011.

ASEAN CO-ORDINATING COUNCIL

The inaugural meeting of the Council was convened in December 2008, upon the entering into force of the new ASEAN Charter. Comprising the ministers of foreign affairs of member states, the Council was to meet at least twice a year to assist in the preparation of summit meetings, to monitor the implementation of agreements and summit meeting decisions and to co-ordinate ASEAN policies and activities.

ASEAN COMMUNITY COUNCILS

Three new Community Councils were established within the framework of the ASEAN Charter in order to pursue the objectives of the different pillars of the grouping and to enhance regional integration and co-operation. The ASEAN Political-Security Community Council, the ASEAN Economic Community Council and the ASEAN Socio-Cultural Community Council each were to meet at least twice a year, chaired by the appropriate government minister of the country holding ASEAN Chairmanship. Each Council was to oversee a structure of Sectoral Ministerial Bodies, many of which had established mandates as ministerial meetings, councils or specialized bodies.

COMMITTEE OF PERMANENT REPRESENTATIVES

The Committee, according to the new Charter, was to comprise a Permanent Representative appointed, at ambassadorial level, by each member state. Its functions were to include supporting the work of ASEAN bodies, liaising with the Secretary-General, and facilitating ASEAN co-operation with external partners.

SECRETARIATS

A permanent secretariat was established in Jakarta, Indonesia, in 1976 to form a central co-ordinating body. The Secretariat comprises the Office of the Secretary-General and Bureaux relating to Economic Integration and Finance, External Relations and Co-ordination, and Resources Development. The Secretary-General holds office for a five-year term and is assisted by four Deputy Secretaries-General, increased from two in accordance with the new ASEAN Charter. Two were to remain as nominated positions, rotating among member countries for a non-renewable term of three years; the two new positions of Deputy Secretary-General were to be openly recruited on a renewable three-year term. Each member country is required to maintain an ASEAN National Secretariat to co-ordinate implementation of ASEAN decisions at the national level and to raise awareness of the organization and its activities within that country. In July 2009 the first ASEAN Secretariat Policy Forum was convened with the aim of promoting public debate on the activities of the Secretariat.

ASEAN Committees in Third Countries (composed of heads of diplomatic missions) may be established to promote ASEAN's interests and to support the conduct of relations with other countries and international organizations.

Secretary-General: Dr SURIN PITSUWAN (Thailand).

Deputy Secretary-General, for the ASEAN Political Security Community: SAYAKANE SISOUVONG (Laos).

Deputy Secretary-General, for the ASEAN Economic Community: SUNDRAM PUSHPANATHAN (Singapore).

Deputy Secretary-General, for the ASEAN Socio-Cultural Community: MISRAN KARMAIN (Malaysia).

Deputy Secretary-General, for Community and Corporate Affairs: BAGAS HAPSORO (Indonesia).

Activities

ASEAN was established in 1967 with the signing of the ASEAN Declaration, otherwise known as the Bangkok Declaration, by the ministers of foreign affairs of Indonesia, Malaysia, the Philippines, Singapore and Thailand. In February 1976 the first ASEAN summit meeting adopted the Treaty of Amity and Co-operation in South-East Asia and the Declaration of ASEAN Concord. Brunei joined the organization in January 1984, shortly after attaining independence. Viet Nam was admitted as the seventh member of ASEAN in July 1995. Laos and Myanmar joined in July 1997 and Cambodia was formally admitted in April 1999, fulfilling the organization's ambition to incorporate all 10 countries in the sub-region.

In December 1997 ASEAN heads of government agreed upon a series of commitments to determine the development of the grouping into the 21st century. The so-called Vision 2020 envisaged ASEAN as 'a concert of Southeast Asian nations, outward looking, living in peace, stability and prosperity, bonded together in partnership in dynamic development and in a community of caring societies'. In October 2003 ASEAN leaders adopted a declaration known as 'Bali Concord II', which committed signatory states to the creation of an ASEAN Economic Community, an ASEAN Security Community and an ASEAN Socio-Cultural Community. In December 2005 heads of state determined to establish a High Level Task Force to formulate a new ASEAN Charter. The finalized document, codifying the principles and purposes of the grouping and according it the legal status of an intergovernmental organization, was signed in November 2007 by ASEAN heads of government attending the 13th summit meeting, convened in Singapore. In July 2008 the ASEAN Ministerial Meeting of ministers of foreign affairs reaffirmed their commitment to ratifying the Charter by the 14th summit meeting, scheduled to be held in Bangkok, Thailand, in December. Early in that month, however, the summit meeting was postponed, owing to political instability in Thailand. None the less, the Charter entered into force on 15 December, having been ratified by each member state. The occasion was commemorated at a Special ASEAN Foreign Ministers' Meeting, convened at the Secretariat, which consequently became the inaugural meeting of the new ASEAN Co-ordinating Council.

In March 2009, at the end of the reconvened 14th summit meeting, held in Cha-am and Hua Hin, Thailand, ASEAN heads of state and government signed the Cha-am Hua Hin Declaration on the Roadmap for an ASEAN Community (2009–15), comprising Blueprints on ASEAN Political Security, Economic, and Socio-cultural Communities as well as a second Initiative for ASEAN Integration Work Plan. The meeting also issued a Statement on the Global Economic and Financial Crisis, which emphasised the need for co-ordinated policies and joint actions to restore financial stability and to safeguard economic growth in the region.

In October 2010 ASEAN heads of state, meeting in Hanoi, Viet Nam, adopted a Master Plan on ASEAN Connectivity, which identified priority projects to enhance communications and community-building in three dimensions: physical, institutional and people-to-people.

TRADE AND ECONOMIC CO-OPERATION

In January 1992 heads of government, meeting in Singapore, signed an agreement to create an ASEAN Free Trade Area (AFTA) by 2008. In accordance with the agreement, a common effective preferential tariff (CEPT) scheme came into effect in January 1993. The CEPT covered all manufactured products, including capital goods, and processed agricultural products (which together accounted for two-thirds of intra-ASEAN trade), but was to exclude unprocessed agricultural products. Tariffs were to be reduced to a maximum of 20% within a period of five to eight years and to 0%–5% during the subsequent seven to 10 years. Fifteen categories were designated for accelerated tariff reduction. In October 1993 ASEAN trade ministers agreed to modify the CEPT, with only Malaysia and Singapore having adhered to the original tariff reduction schedule. The new AFTA programme, under which all member countries except Brunei were scheduled to begin tariff reductions from 1 January 1994, substantially enlarged the number of products to be included in the tariff reduction process (i.e. on the so-called 'inclusion list') and reduced the list of products eligible for protection. In September 1994 ASEAN ministers of economic affairs agreed to accelerate the implementation of AFTA, advancing the deadline for its entry into operation from 2008 to 1 January 2003. Tariffs were to be reduced to 0%–5% within seven to 10 years, or within five to eight years for products designated for accelerated tariff cuts. In July 1995, Viet Nam was admitted as a member of ASEAN and was granted until 2006 to implement the AFTA trade agreements. In December 1995 heads of government, at a meeting convened in Bangkok, Thailand, agreed to extend liberalization to certain service industries, including banking, telecommunications and tourism. In July 1997 Laos and Myanmar became members of ASEAN and were granted a 10-year period, from 1 January 1998, to comply with the AFTA schedule.

In December 1998, meeting in Hanoi, Viet Nam, heads of government approved a Statement on Bold Measures, detailing ASEAN's strategies to deal with the economic crisis that had prevailed in the region since late 1997. These included incentives to attract investors, for example a three-year exemption on corporate taxation, accelerated implementation of the ASEAN Investment Area (AIA, see below), and advancing the AFTA deadline, for the original six members, to 2002, with some 85% of products to be covered by the arrangements by 2000, and 90% by 2001. It was envisaged that the elimination of tariffs would be achieved by 2015, by the original six members, or by 2018, by the new members. The Hanoi Plan of Action, which was also adopted at the meeting as a framework for the development of the organization over the period 1999–2004, incorporated a series of measures aimed at strengthening macroeconomic and financial co-operation and enhancing economic integration. In April 1999 Cambodia, on being admitted as a full member of ASEAN, signed an agreement to implement the tariff reduction programme over a 10-year period, commencing 1 January 2000. Cambodia also signed a declaration endorsing the commitments of the 1998 Statement on Bold Measures. In May 2000 Malaysia was granted a special exemption to postpone implementing tariff reductions on motor vehicles for two years from 1 January 2003. In November 2000 a protocol was approved permitting further temporary exclusion of products from the CEPT scheme for countries experiencing economic difficulties. On 1 January 2002 AFTA was formally realized among the original six signatories (Brunei, Indonesia, Malaysia, the Philippines, Singapore and Thailand), which had achieved the objective of reducing to less than 5% trade restrictions on 96.24% of products on the inclusion list. By 1 January 2005 tariffs on just under 99% of products on the 2005 CEPT inclusion list had been reduced to the 0%–5% range among the original six signatory countries, with the average tariff standing at 1.93%. With regard to Cambodia, Laos, Myanmar and Viet Nam, some 81% of products fell within the 0%–5% range. On 1 August 2008 comprehensive revised CEPT rules of origin came into effect.

To complement AFTA in facilitating intra-ASEAN trade, member countries committed to the removal of non-tariff barriers (such as quotas), the harmonization of standards and conformance measures, and the simplification and harmonization of customs procedures. In June 1996 the Working Group on Customs Procedures completed a draft legal framework for regional co-operation, designed to simplify and harmonize customs procedures, legislation and product classification. The agreement was signed in March 1997 at the inaugural meeting of ASEAN finance ministers. (Laos and Myanmar signed the customs agreement in July and Cambodia assented to it in April 1999.) In 2001 ASEAN finalized its system of harmonized tariff nomenclature, implementation of which commenced in the following year. In November the summit meeting determined to extend ASEAN tariff preferences to ASEAN's newer members from January 2002, under the ASEAN Integration System of Preferences (AISP), thus allowing Cambodia, Laos, Myanmar and Viet Nam tariff-free access to the more developed ASEAN markets earlier than the previously agreed target date of 2010. In April 2002 ASEAN ministers of economic affairs signed an agreement to facilitate intra-regional trade in electrical and electronic equipment by providing for the mutual recognition of standards (for example, testing and certification). The agreement was also intended to lower the costs of trade in those goods, thereby helping to maintain competitiveness.

In November 2000 heads of government endorsed an Initiative for ASEAN Integration (IAI), which aimed to reduce economic disparities within the region through effective co-operation. In July 2002 the AMM endorsed an IAI Work Plan, which focused on the following priority areas: human resources development; infrastructure; information and communications technology (ICT); and regional economic integration. The Plan was to be implemented over the six-year period 2002–08. Much of the funding for the Initiative came from ASEAN's external partners, including Australia, India, Japan, Norway and the Republic of Korea. A second IAI Work Plan, covering the period 2009–15, was adopted by ASEAN heads of state and government in March 2009.

The Bali Concord II, adopted in October 2003, affirmed commitment to existing ASEAN economic co-operation frameworks, including the Hanoi Plan of Action (and any subsequently agreed regional plans of action) and the IAI, and outlined plans for the creation, by 2020, of an integrated ASEAN Economic Community (AEC), entailing: the harmonization of customs procedures and technical regulations by the end of 2004; the removal of non-tariff trade barriers and the establishment of a network of free trade zones by 2005; and the progressive withdrawal of capital controls and strengthening of intellectual property rights. An ASEAN legal unit was to be established to strengthen and enhance existing dispute settlement systems. (A Protocol on Enhanced Dispute Settlement Mechanism was signed in November 2004.) The free movement of professional and skilled workers would be facilitated by standardizing professional requirements and simplifying visa procedures, with the adoption of a single ASEAN visa requirement envisaged by 2005. In 2004 ASEAN economic and trade ministers worked closely, in co-operation with the private sector, to produce a roadmap for the integration of 11 sectors identified as priority areas in the AEC plan of action. In July the ASEAN Ministerial Meeting reviewed progress in preparing the Vientiane Action Programme (VAP), the proposed successor to the Hanoi Plan of Action. In November the 10th meeting of ASEAN heads of state, held in Vientiane, Laos, endorsed the VAP with commitments to deepen regional integration and narrow the development gap within the grouping. An ASEAN Development Fund was to be established to support the implementation of the VAP and other action programmes. The leaders adopted two plans of action (concerning security and socio-cultural affairs) to further the implementation of the Bali Concord II regarding the establishment of a three-pillared ASEAN Community, which included the AEC. An ASEAN Framework Agreement for Integration of the Priority Sectors and its Protocols was also signed. Import duties (on 85% of products) were to be eliminated by 2007 for the original members (including Brunei) and by 2012 for newer member states in 11 sectors, accounting for more than 50% of intra-ASEAN trade in 2003. A Blueprint and Strategic Schedule for realizing the AEC by 2015 was approved by ASEAN ministers of economic affairs in August 2007 and was signed by ASEAN heads of state, meeting in November. During 2008 ASEAN developed a 'scorecard' mechanism to track the implementation of the Blueprint by member countries. The first AEC Scorecard was published in April 2010, which demonstrated that 73% of the targets set by the Blueprint had been achieved. In March 2009 heads of state agreed that the new Roadmap for an ASEAN Community should replace the VAP. In May 2010 an ASEAN Trade in Goods Agreement entered into force, which aimed to consolidate all trade commitments and tariff liberalisation schedules.

In November 1999 an informal meeting of leaders of ASEAN countries, the People's Republic of China, Japan and the Republic of Korea (designating themselves 'ASEAN + 3') issued a Joint Statement on East Asian Co-operation, in which they agreed to strengthen regional unity, and addressed the long-term possibility of establishing an East Asian common market and currency. In July 2000 ASEAN + 3 ministers of foreign affairs convened an inaugural formal summit in Bangkok, Thailand, and in October ASEAN + 3 economic affairs ministers agreed to hold their hitherto twice-yearly informal meetings on an institutionalized basis. In November an informal meeting of ASEAN + 3 leaders approved further co-operation in various sectors and initiated a feasibility study into a proposal to establish a regional free trade area. In May 2001 ASEAN + 3 ministers of economic affairs endorsed a series of projects for co-operation in ICT, environment, small and medium-sized enterprises, Mekong Basin development, and harmonization of standards. In July 2002 ASEAN + 3 ministers of foreign affairs declared their support for other regional initiatives, namely an Asia Co-operation Dialogue, which was initiated by the Thai Government in June, and an Initiative for Development in East Asia (IDEA), which had been announced by the Japanese Government in January. An IDEA ministerial meeting was convened in Tokyo, in August. ASEAN + 3 ministers of labour convened in May 2003. In September the sixth consultation between ASEAN + 3 ministers of economic affairs was held, at which several new projects were endorsed, including two on e-commerce. During 2004 an ASEAN + 3 Unit was established in the ASEAN Secretariat. In November the ASEAN summit meeting agreed to convene a meeting of an East Asia grouping, to be developed in parallel with the ASEAN + 3 framework.

In October 2008 ASEAN heads of state held a special meeting, in Beijing, People's Republic of China, to consider the impact on the region of the deceleration of growth in the world's most developed economies and the ongoing instability of global financial markets. The meeting was followed by a specially convened ASEAN + 3 summit to discuss further regional co-operation to counter the impact of the crisis. In April 2010 ASEAN heads of state, convened in Hanoi, Viet Nam, adopted an ASEAN Strategy for Economic Recovery and Development to ensure sustainable recovery from the global financial and economic crisis. Leaders determined to strengthen efforts to enhance financial monitoring and surveillance, to foster infrastructure and sustainable development and to achieve regional economic integration. The Strategy determined to pursue the ASEAN Connectivity Initiative, which had been approved at the 15th summit in October 2009, as well as efforts to develop a Master Plan on ASEAN Connectivity.

In August 2010 an inaugural meeting of ministers of economic affairs of Cambodia, Laos, Myanmar and Viet Nam (the so-called 'CLMV' countries) was convened, in Da Nang, Viet Nam, further to strengthen intra-economic and trade relations. In particular, the meeting considered measures to enhance trade promotion and to narrow the development gap between the CLMV countries and other countries in the region.

FINANCE AND INVESTMENT

In 1987 heads of government agreed to accelerate regional financial co-operation, to support intra-ASEAN trade and investment. They adopted measures to increase the role of ASEAN currencies in regional trade, to assist negotiations on the avoidance of double taxation, and to improve the efficiency of tax and customs administrators. An ASEAN Reinsurance Corporation was established in 1988, with initial authorized capital of US $10m. Other measures to attract greater financial resource flows in the region, including an ASEAN Plan of Action for the Promotion of Foreign Direct Investment and Intra-ASEAN Investment, were implemented during 1996.

In February 1997 ASEAN central bank governors agreed to strengthen efforts to combat currency speculation through the established network of foreign exchange repurchase agreements. However, from mid-1997 several Asian currencies were undermined by speculative activities. Subsequent unsuccessful attempts to support the foreign-exchange rates contributed to a collapse in the value of financial markets in some countries and to a reversal of the region's economic growth, at least in the short term, while governments undertook macroeconomic structural reforms. In December ASEAN ministers of finance, meeting in Malaysia, agreed to liberalize markets for financial services and to strengthen surveillance of member country economies, to help prevent further deterioration of the regional economy. The ministers also endorsed a proposal for the establishment of an Asian funding facility to provide emergency assistance in support of international credit and structural reform programmes.

In October 1998 ministers of economic affairs, meeting in Manila, the Philippines, signed a Framework Agreement on an ASEAN Investment Area (AIA), which was to provide for equal treatment of domestic and other ASEAN direct investment proposals within the grouping by 2010, and of all foreign investors by 2020. The meeting also confirmed that the proposed ASEAN Surveillance Process (ASP), to monitor the economic stability and financial systems of member states, would be implemented with immediate effect, and would require the voluntary submission of economic information by all members to a monitoring committee, to be based in Jakarta, Indonesia. The ASP and the Framework Agreement on the AIA were incorporated into the Hanoi Plan of Action, adopted by heads of state in December 1998. The summit meeting also resolved to accelerate reforms, particularly in the banking and financial sectors, in order to strengthen the region's economies, and to promote the liberalization of the financial services sector. In March 1999 ASEAN ministers of trade and industry, meeting in Phuket, Thailand, as the AIA Council, agreed to open their manufacturing, agriculture, fisheries, forestry and mining industries to foreign investment. Investment restrictions affecting those industries were to be eliminated by 2003 in most cases, although Laos and Viet Nam were granted until 2010. In addition, ministers adopted a number of measures to encourage investment in the region, including access to three-year corporate income tax exemptions, and tax allowances of 30% for investors. The AIA agreement formally entered into force in June 1999, having been ratified by all member countries. In September 2001 ministers agreed to accelerate the full realization of the AIA for non-ASEAN investors in manufacturing, agriculture, forestry, fishing and mining sectors. The date for full implementation was advanced to 2010 for the original six ASEAN members and to 2015 for the newer members. In August 2007 the AIA Council determined to revise the Framework Agreement on the AIA in order to implement a more comprehensive investment arrangement in support of the establishment of the AEC.

In May 2000, ASEAN + 3 ministers of economic affairs, meeting in Chiang Mai, Thailand, proposed the establishment of an enhanced currency swap mechanism, enabling countries to draw on liquidity support to defend their economies during balance of payments difficulties or speculative currency attacks and to prevent future financial crises. The so-called Chiang Mai Initiative Multilateralisation (CMIM) on currency swap arrangements was formally approved by ASEAN + 3 finance ministers in May 2001. In August 2003 ASEAN + 3 finance ministers agreed to establish a Finance Co-operation Fund, to be administered by the ASEAN Secretariat; the Fund was to support ongoing economic reviews relating to projects such as the CMIM. An Asian Bond Markets Initiative (ABMI) was launched by ASEAN + 3 countries in 2003 to develop local-currency denominated bond markets. In February 2009 ministers of finance of ASEAN + 3 countries convened a special meeting, in Phuket, Thailand, to consider the impact on the region of the global economic and financial crisis, and issued an Action Plan to Restore Economic and Financial Stability of the Asian Region. Ministers agreed to expand the CMIM (from US $80m. to $120m.) and to establish an independent regional surveillance unit to strengthen economic monitoring. The CMIM entered into force in March 2010. In May ASEAN + 3 finance ministers, convened in Tashkent, Uzbekistan, announced the launch, within the ABMI framework, of a Credit Guarantee and Investment Facility, with an initial capital of $700m., as a trust fund of the Asian Development Bank. Ministers also acknowledged that agreement had been reached on the establishment, in Singapore, of an ASEAN + 3 Macroeconomic Research Office, to monitor and analyse regional economies and to support the effectiveness of the CMIM. The Office was inaugurated in April 2011.

POLITICS AND SECURITY

In 1971 ASEAN members endorsed a declaration envisaging the establishment of a Zone of Peace, Freedom and Neutrality (ZOPFAN) in the South-East Asian region. This objective was incorporated in the Declaration of ASEAN Concord, which was adopted at the first summit meeting of the organization, held in Bali, Indonesia, in February 1976. Heads of state also signed a Treaty of Amity and Co-operation, establishing principles of mutual respect for the independence and sovereignty of all nations, non-interference in the internal affairs of one another and settlement of disputes by peaceful means. The Treaty was amended in December 1987 by a protocol providing for the accession of Papua New Guinea and other non-member countries in the region. In January 1992 ASEAN leaders agreed that there should be greater co-operation on security matters within the grouping, and that ASEAN's post-ministerial conferences (PMCs) should be used as a forum for discussion of questions relating to security with dialogue partners and other countries. In July 1992 Viet Nam and Laos signed ASEAN's Treaty of Amity and Co-operation. Cambodia acceded to the Treaty in January 1995 and Myanmar signed it in July.

In December 1995 ASEAN heads of government, meeting in Bangkok, Thailand, signed a treaty establishing a South-East Asia Nuclear-Weapon Free Zone (SEANWFZ). The treaty was also signed by Cambodia, Myanmar and Laos. It was extended to cover the offshore economic exclusion zones of each country. On ratification by all parties, the treaty was to prohibit the manufacture or storage of nuclear weapons within the region. Individual signatories were to decide whether to allow port visits or transportation of nuclear weapons by foreign powers through territorial waters. The treaty entered into force in March 1997. ASEAN senior officials were mandated to oversee implementation of the treaty, pending the establishment of a permanent monitoring committee. In July 1999 the People's Republic of China and India agreed to observe the terms of the SEANWFZ.

In July 1992 the ASEAN Ministerial Meeting issued a statement calling for a peaceful resolution of the dispute concerning the strategically significant Spratly Islands in the South China Sea, which are claimed, wholly or partly, by the People's Republic of China, Viet Nam, Taiwan, Brunei, Malaysia and the Philippines. In 1999 ASEAN established a special committee to formulate a code of conduct for the South China Sea to be observed by all claimants to the Spratly Islands. In November 2002 ASEAN and China's foreign ministers adopted a Declaration on the Conduct (DOC) of Parties in the South China Sea, agreeing to promote a peaceful environment and durable solutions for the area, to resolve territorial disputes by peaceful means, to refrain from undertaking activities that would aggravate existing tensions (such as settling unpopulated islands and reefs), and to initiate a regular dialogue of defence officials. In December 2004 in Kuala Lumpur, Malaysia, at the first senior officials' meeting between ASEAN and China on the implementation of the DOC, it was agreed to adopt the Terms of Reference of the newly established joint working group as a step towards enhancing security and stability in the South China Sea.

In July 1997 ASEAN ministers of foreign affairs reiterated their commitment to the principle of non-interference in the internal affairs of other countries. However, the group's efforts in negotiating a political settlement to the internal conflict in Cambodia marked a significant shift in diplomatic policy towards one of 'constructive intervention', which had been proposed by Malaysia's Deputy Prime

Minister in recognition of the increasing interdependence of the region. At the Ministerial Meeting in July 1998 Thailand's Minister of Foreign Affairs, supported by his Philippine counterpart, proposed that the grouping formally adopt a policy of 'flexible engagement'. The proposal, based partly on concerns that the continued restrictions imposed by the Myanma authorities on dissident political activists was damaging ASEAN relations with its dialogue partners, was to provide for the discussion of the affairs of other member states when they have an impact on neighbouring countries. While rejecting the proposal, other ASEAN ministers agreed to pursue a more limited version, referred to as 'enhanced interaction', and to maintain open dialogue within the grouping. In September 1999 the unrest prompted by the popular referendum on the future of East Timor (now Timor-Leste) and the resulting humanitarian crisis highlighted the unwillingness of some ASEAN member states to intervene in other member countries and undermined the political unity of the grouping. A compromise agreement, enabling countries to act on an individual basis rather than as representatives of ASEAN, was formulated prior to an emergency meeting of ministers of foreign affairs, held during the APEC meetings in Auckland, New Zealand. Malaysia, the Philippines, Singapore and Thailand declared their support for the establishment of a multinational force to restore peace in East Timor and committed troops to participate in the Australian-led operation. At their informal summit in November 1999 heads of state approved the establishment of an ASEAN Troika, which was to be constituted as an ad hoc body comprising the foreign ministers of the Association's current, previous and future chairmanship with a view to providing a rapid response mechanism in the event of a regional crisis.

On 12 September 2001 ASEAN issued a ministerial statement on international terrorism, condemning the attacks of the previous day in the USA and urging greater international co-operation to counter terrorism. The seventh summit meeting in November issued a Declaration on a Joint Action to Combat Terrorism. This condemned the September attacks, stated that terrorism was a direct challenge to ASEAN's aims, and affirmed the grouping's commitment to strong measures to counter terrorism. The summit encouraged member countries to sign (or ratify) the International Convention for the Suppression of the Financing of Terrorism, to strengthen national mechanisms against terrorism, and to work to deepen co-operation, particularly in the area of intelligence exchange; international conventions to combat terrorism would be studied to see if they could be integrated into the ASEAN structure, while the possibility of developing a regional anti-terrorism convention was discussed. The summit noted the need to strengthen security co-operation to restore investor confidence. In its Declaration and other notes, the summit explicitly rejected any attempt to link terrorism with religion or race, and expressed concern for the suffering of innocent Afghanis during the US military action against the Taliban authorities in Afghanistan. The summit's final Declaration was worded so as to avoid any mention of the US action, to which Muslim ASEAN states such as Malaysia and Indonesia were strongly opposed. In November 2002 the eighth summit meeting adopted a Declaration on Terrorism, reiterating and strengthening the measures announced in the previous year. (See, also, Transnational Crime, below.)

The ASEAN Charter that entered into force in December 2008 envisaged the establishment of a new ASEAN human rights body. It was to extend, for the first time within the grouping, a formal structure for the promotion and protection of human rights and fundamental freedoms. In July 2009 the ASEAN Ministerial Meeting of ministers of foreign affairs adopted the terms of reference of the body, which had been drafted by a High Level Panel. It was to be established as the ASEAN Intergovernmental Commission on Human Rights (AICHR) and composed of a national expert representative from each member state. At the same meeting, ASEAN ministers urged the authorities in Myanmar to release all political detainees, including the main opposition leader Aung San Suu Kyi, in order to enable them to participate freely in elections scheduled to be conducted in 2010. In August 2009 Thailand, acting in its capacity as the ASEAN Chair, expressed deep disappointment at the sentencing of Aung San Suu Kyi for allegedly breaching the terms of her house arrest. The inaugural meeting of the AICHR was held at the ASEAN Secretariat in March–April 2010. The Commission considered the formulation of rules of procedure, the development of a five-year work plan and priority activities for 2010/11.

In May 2011 ASEAN heads of state, meeting in Jakarta, Indonesia, urged foreign ministers to elaborate plans to establish an ASEAN Institute for Peace and Reconciliation.

ASEAN Regional Forum (ARF): In July 1993 the meeting of ASEAN ministers of foreign affairs sanctioned the establishment of a forum to discuss and promote co-operation on security issues within the region, and, in particular, to ensure the involvement of the People's Republic of China in regional dialogue. The ARF was informally initiated during that year's PMC, comprising the ASEAN countries, its dialogue partners (at that time Australia, Canada, the EC, Japan, the Republic of Korea, New Zealand and the USA), and the People's Republic of China, Laos, Papua New Guinea, Russia and Viet Nam. The first formal meeting of the ARF was conducted in July 1994, following the Ministerial Meeting held in Bangkok, Thailand, and it was agreed that the ARF would be convened on an annual basis. The 1995 meeting, held in Brunei, in August, attempted to define a framework for the future of the Forum. It was perceived as evolving through three stages: the promotion of confidence-building (including disaster relief and peace-keeping activities); the development of preventive diplomacy; and the elaboration of approaches to conflict. The third ARF, convened in July 1996, which was attended for the first time by India and Myanmar, agreed a set of criteria and guiding principles for the future expansion of the grouping. In particular, it was decided that the ARF would only admit as participants countries that had a direct influence on the peace and security of the East Asia and Pacific region. The ARF held in July 1997 reviewed progress made in developing the first two 'tracks' of the ARF process, through the structure of inter-sessional working groups and meetings. The Forum's consideration of security issues in the region was dominated by concern at the political situation in Cambodia; support was expressed for ASEAN mediation to restore stability within that country. Mongolia was admitted into the ARF at its meeting in July 1998. India rejected a proposal that Pakistan attend the meeting to discuss issues relating to both countries' testing of nuclear weapons. The meeting ultimately condemned the testing of nuclear weapons in the region, but declined to criticize specifically India and Pakistan. In July 1999 the ARF warned the Democratic People's Republic of Korea (DPRK) not to conduct any further testing of missiles over the Pacific. At the seventh meeting of the ARF, convened in Bangkok, in July 2000, the DPRK was admitted to the Forum. The meeting considered the positive effects and challenges of globalization, including the possibilities for greater economic interdependence and for a growth in transnational crime. The eighth ARF meeting in July 2001 in Hanoi, Viet Nam, pursued these themes, and also discussed the widening development gap between nations. The meeting agreed to enhance the role of the ARF Chairman, enabling him to issue statements on behalf of ARF participants and to organize events during the year. The ninth ARF meeting, held in Bandar Seri Begawan, Brunei, in July 2002, assessed regional and international security developments, and issued a statement of individual and collective intent to prevent any financing of terrorism. The statement included commitments by participants to freeze the assets of suspected individuals or groups, to implement international financial standards and to enhance co-operation and the exchange of information. In October the Chairman, on behalf of all ARF participants, condemned the terrorist bomb attacks committed against tourist targets in Bali, Indonesia. Pakistan joined the ARF in July 2004. In November the first ARF Security Policy Conference was held in Beijing, People's Republic of China. The Conference recommended developing various aspects of bilateral and multilateral co-operation, including with regard to non-traditional security threats. Timor-Leste and Bangladesh became participants in the ARF in July 2005. In July 2006 the ARF issued statements on 'co-operation in fighting cyber attacks and terrorist misuse of cyber space' and on disaster management and emergency responses, which determined to formulate guidelines for enhanced co-operation in humanitarian operations. In January 2007 an ARF maritime security shore exercise was conducted, in Singapore. In March the first ARF Defense Ministers Retreat was convened, in Bali. The 14th ARF, held in Manila, Philippines, in July, approved the establishment of a 'Friends of the Chair' mechanism, comprising three ministers, to promote preventive diplomacy and respond rapidly to political crises. In July 2008 the 15th ARF determined further to strengthen co-operation in natural disaster preparedness and relief operations and resolved to organize training in those areas and a disaster relief exercise. At that time the DPRK acceded to ASEAN's Treaty of Amity and Co-operation. The USA acceded to the Treaty in July 2009; Canada and Turkey acceded to the Treaty in July 2010. In July 2009, the ARF marked its 15th anniversary by adopting a Vision Statement for the period up to 2020. It reaffirmed its commitment to 'building a region of peace, friendship and prosperity' and proposed measures to strengthen the ARF and to develop security-based partnerships. In the following 12-month period inter-sessional meetings of the ARF were held on disaster relief, maritime security, confidence-building measures and preventive diplomacy, counter-terrorism and transnational crime, and non-proliferation and disarmament. The 17th meeting of the ARF, convened in Hanoi, in July 2010, adopted a Plan of Action to implement the Vision Statement 2020. The meeting also discussed security in the South China Sea, preparations for a general election in Myanmar and efforts to achieve the denuclearisation of the Korean Peninsula.

Since 2000 the ARF has published the *Annual Security Outlook*, to which participating countries submit assessments of the security prospects in the region.

In October 2010 the first so-called ASEAN Defence Ministers' Meeting (ADMM) Plus was held, in Hanoi, incorporating ASEAN ministers and their counterparts from eight dialogue partner countries, i.e. Australia, People's Republic of China, Japan, Republic of

Korea, New Zealand, Russia and the USA. The new body was intended to complement the work of the ARF.

TRANSNATIONAL CRIME

In June 1999 the first ministerial meeting to consider issues relating to transnational crime was convened. Regular meetings of senior officials and ministers were subsequently held. The third ministerial meeting, in October 2001, considered initiatives to combat transnational crime, which was defined as including terrorism, trafficking in drugs, arms and people, money-laundering, cyber-crime, piracy and economic crime. In May 2002 ministers responsible for transnational crime issues convened a Special Ministerial Meeting on Terrorism, in Kuala Lumpur, Malaysia. The meeting approved a work programme to implement a plan of action to combat transnational crime, including information exchange, the development of legal arrangements for extradition, prosecution and seizure, the enhancement of co-operation in law enforcement, and the development of regional security training programmes. In a separate initiative Indonesia, Malaysia and the Philippines signed an agreement on information exchange and the establishment of communication procedures. Cambodia acceded to the agreement in July. In November 2004 ASEAN leaders adopted an ASEAN Declaration against Trafficking in Persons, Particularly Women and Children, which aimed to strengthen co-operation to prevent and combat trafficking, through, *inter alia*, the establishment of a new regional focal network, information-sharing procedures and standardized immigration controls. In late May 2011 ASEAN leaders issued a joint statement on enhancing co-operation against trafficking in persons in South East Asia. The Plan of Action of the ASEAN Security Community (envisaged by the Bali Concord II—see above) had as its five key areas: political development; shaping and sharing of norms; conflict prevention; conflict resolution; and post-conflict peace building. In November 2004 eight member countries, namely Brunei, Cambodia, Indonesia, Malaysia, Laos, the Philippines, Singapore and Viet Nam, signed a Treaty on Mutual Legal Assistance in Criminal Matters in Kuala Lumpur, Malaysia.

In January 2007 ASEAN leaders, meeting in Cebu, the Philippines, signed an ASEAN Convention on Counter Terrorism. The Convention entered into force in late May 2011, having received the required ratification by six member states: Brunei, Cambodia, the Philippines, Singapore, Thailand and Viet Nam.

INDUSTRY

The ASEAN-Chambers of Commerce and Industry (CCI) aims to enhance ASEAN economic and industrial co-operation and the participation in these activities of the private sector. In March 1996 a permanent ASEAN-CCI secretariat became operational at the ASEAN Secretariat. The first AIA Council-Business Sector Forum was convened in September 2001, with the aim of developing alliances between the public and private sectors. An ASEAN Business Advisory Council held its inaugural meeting in April 2003.

The ASEAN Industrial Co-operation (AICO) scheme, initiated in 1996, encourages companies in the ASEAN region to undertake joint manufacturing activities. Products derived from an AICO arrangement benefit immediately from a preferential tariff rate of 0%–5%. The AICO scheme superseded the ASEAN industrial joint venture scheme, established in 1983. The attractiveness of the scheme was expected slowly to diminish as ASEAN moves towards the full implementation of the CEPT scheme. ASEAN has initiated studies of new methods of industrial co-operation within the grouping, with the aim of achieving further integration. In April 2004 ASEAN economic ministers signed a Protocol to Amend the Basic Agreement on the AICO Scheme, which aimed to maintain its relevance. As from 1 January 2005 the tariff rate for Brunei, Cambodia, Indonesia, Laos, Malaysia and Singapore was 0%; for the Philippines 0%–1%, for Thailand 0%–3% and for Myanmar and Viet Nam 0%–5%.

The ASEAN Consultative Committee on Standards and Quality (ACCSQ) aims to promote the understanding and implementation of quality concepts, considered to be important in strengthening the economic development of a member state and in helping to eliminate trade barriers. ACCSQ comprises three working groups: standards and information; conformance and assessment; and testing and calibration. A Standards and Quality Bulletin is published regularly to disseminate information and promote transparency on standards, technical regulations and conformity assessment procedures. In September 1994 an ad hoc Working Group on Intellectual Property (IP) Co-operation was established, with a mandate to formulate a framework agreement on intellectual property co-operation and to strengthen ASEAN activities in intellectual property protection. An ASEAN Intellectual Property Right (IPR) Action Plan 2004–10 aimed, *inter alia,* to accelerate IP asset creation and to develop and harmonize regional mechanisms for IPR registration, protection and enforcement.

In 1988 the ASEAN Fund was established, with capital of US $150m., to provide finance for portfolio investments in ASEAN countries, in particular for small and medium-sized enterprises (SMEs). The Hanoi Plan of Action, which was adopted by ASEAN heads of state in December 1998, incorporated a series of initiatives to enhance the development of SMEs, including training and technical assistance, co-operation activities and greater access to information. In September 2004 ASEAN economic ministers approved an ASEAN Policy Blueprint for SME Development 2004–14, first proposed by a working group in 2001, which comprised strategic work programmes and policy measures for the development of SMEs in the region. The first meeting of a new ASEAM SME Advisory Board was held in Singapore, in June 2011.

In January 2007 senior officials concluded a five-year ASEAN plan of action to support the development and implementation of national occupational safety and health frameworks. In May 2010 ASEAN ministers responsible for labour adopted a Work Programme for the period 2010–15, which aimed to support the realisation of the ASEAN Community and further the objectives of achieving adequate social protection for all workers in the region and fostering productive employment.

FOOD, AGRICULTURE AND FORESTRY

In October 1983 a ministerial agreement on fisheries co-operation was concluded, providing for the joint management of fish resources, the sharing of technology, and co-operation in marketing. In July 1994 a Conference on Fisheries Management and Development Strategies in the ASEAN region resolved to enhance fish production through the introduction of new technologies, aquaculture development, improvements of product quality and greater involvement by the private sector. In June 2011 the ministerial session of the ASEAN-Southeast Asian Fisheries Development Center Conference on Sustainable Fisheries for Sustainable Development adopted a resolution on Sustainable Fisheries for Food Security for the ASEAN Region Towards 2020, to be implemented through individual and collective efforts among member states.

Co-operation in forestry is focused on joint projects, funded by ASEAN's dialogue partners, which include a Forest Tree Seed Centre, an Institute of Forest Management and the ASEAN Timber Technology Centre. In 2005 an Ad Hoc Experts Working Group on International Forest Policy Processes was created, to support the development of ASEAN joint positions and approaches on regional and international forest issues. An ASEAN Social Forestry Network was also established in that year. In November 2007 ASEAN ministers responsible for forestry issued a statement on strengthening forest law enforcement and governance.

There is an established ASEAN programme of training and study exchanges for farm workers, agricultural experts and members of agricultural co-operatives. Other areas of co-operation aim to enhance food security and the international competitiveness of ASEAN food, agriculture and forestry products, to promote the sustainable use and conservation of natural resources, to encourage greater involvement by the private sector in the food and agricultural industry, and to strengthen joint approaches on international and regional issues. An ASEAN Task Force has been formed to harmonize regulations on agricultural products derived from biotechnology. In December 1998 heads of state determined to establish an ASEAN Food Security Information Service to enhance the capacity of member states to forecast and manage food supplies. In 1999 agriculture ministers endorsed guidelines on assessing risk from genetically modified organisms (GMOs) in agriculture, to ensure a common approach. In 2001 work was undertaken to increase public and professional awareness of GMO issues, through workshops and studies. In October ASEAN + 3 agriculture and forestry ministers met for the first time, and discussed issues of poverty alleviation, food security, agricultural research and human resource development. An East Asia Emergency Rice Reserve (enhancing the original emergency rice reserve scheme, established in 1979) was initiated by ASEAN + 3 ministers in 2003 as a pilot project. In October 2004 ministers of agriculture and forestry, meeting in Yangon, Myanmar, endorsed a Strategic Plan of Action on ASEAN Co-operation in Food, Agriculture and Forestry 2005–10. The ministers also approved certain regional food standards, endorsed the establishment of an ASEAN Animal Health Trust Fund, and resolved to establish a Task Force to co-ordinate regional co-operation for the control and eradication of highly pathogenic avian influenza (HPAI). A Regional Strategy for the Progressive Control and Eradication of HPAI, covering the period 2008–10, was endorsed at a meeting of ASEAN ministers of agriculture and forestry held in November 2007. The meeting also determined to establish an ASEAN Network on Aquatic Animal Health Centres to strengthen diagnostic and certification measures of live aquatic animals within the region. In October 2010 ASEAN ministers of agriculture and forestry endorsed a 'Roadmap Towards an HPAI-Free ASEAN Community by 2020', as a strategic framework to address avian influenza and other transboundary and zoonotic diseases of significant priority to the region.

In February–March 2009 ASEAN heads of state, meeting in Cha-am and Hua Hin, Thailand, adopted an Integrated Food Security Framework and a Strategic Plan of Action on Food Security in the

ASEAN Region. An ASEAN-FAO Regional Conference on Food Security was held in Bangkok, Thailand, in May. In October 2010 ministers endorsed the transformation of the ASEAN Plus Three Emergency Rice Reserve into a permanent scheme for meeting emergency food requirements and improving food security.

MINERALS AND ENERGY

The ASEAN Centre for Energy (ACE), based in Jakarta, Indonesia, provides an energy information network, promotes the establishment of interconnecting energy structures among ASEAN member countries, supports the development of renewable energy resources and encourages co-operation in energy efficiency and conservation. An ASEAN energy business forum is held annually and attended by representatives of the energy industry in the private and public sectors. In November 1999 a Trans-ASEAN Gas Pipeline Task Force was established and in April 2000 an ASEAN Interconnection Masterplan Study Working Group was established to formulate a study on the power grid. In July 2002 ASEAN ministers of energy signed a memorandum of understanding (MOU) to implement the pipeline project, involving seven interconnections. In early 2005 the Trans-Thai-Malaysia Gas Pipeline became operational. In June 2004 the first meeting of ASEAN + 3 energy ministers was also convened in June 2004. Later in that year a permanent Secretariat of the heads of ASEAN Power Utilities/Authorities was established on a three-year rotation basis. An MOU on the regional power grid initiative was signed by ministers of energy, meeting in August 2007. In July 2009 ministers of energy adopted an ASEAN Plan of Action for Energy Cooperation (APAEC) 2010–15.

A Framework of Co-operation in Minerals was adopted by an ASEAN working group of experts in August 1993. The group has also developed a programme of action for ASEAN co-operation in the development and utilization of industrial minerals, to promote the exploration and development of mineral resources, the transfer of mining technology and expertise, and the participation of the private sector in industrial mineral production. The programme of action is implemented by an ASEAN Regional Development Centre for Mineral Resources, which also conducts workshops and training programmes relating to the sector. An ASEAN Minerals Co-operation Action Plan for 2005–10 aimed to attract investment in the sector while also promoting environmentally and socially sustainable practices. In August 2005 ASEAN ministers responsible for minerals held an inaugural meeting, in Kuching, Malaysia. A second meeting was convened, in October 2008, in Manila, the Philippines.

TRANSPORT

ASEAN objectives for the transport sector include developing multimodal transport, harmonizing road transport laws and regulations, improving air space management and developing ASEAN legislation for the carriage of dangerous goods and waste by land and sea. In September 1999 ASEAN ministers of transport and communications adopted a programme of action for development of the sector in 1999–2004. By September 2001, under the action programme, a harmonized road route numbering system had been completed, a road safety implementation work plan agreed, and two pilot courses, on port management and traffic engineering and safety, had been adopted. A Framework Agreement on Facilitation of Goods in Transit entered into force in October 2000. In September 2002 ASEAN transport ministers signed Protocol 9 on Dangerous Goods, one of the implementing protocols under the framework agreement, which provided for the simplification of procedures for the transportation of dangerous goods within the region using internationally accepted rules and guidelines. In November 2004 the ASEAN Transport Action Plan 2005–10 was adopted. A roadmap to support the development of an integrated and competitive maritime transport sector in the ASEAN region was signed by ministers of transport in November 2007. At the same time an agreement to strengthen co-operation in maritime cargo and passenger transport was signed with the People's Republic of China. The November 2008 meeting of ministers of transport concluded an ASEAN Framework Agreement on the Facilitation of Inter-State Transport. In November 2010 ASEAN ministers of transport adopted a successor Transport Action Plan, for the period 2011–15, which incorporated measures to support the realisation of the AEC by 2015 and the regional transport priorities of the Master Plan on ASEAN Connectivity.

In October 2001 ministers approved the third package of commitments for the air and transport sectors under the ASEAN framework agreement on services (according to which member countries were to liberalize the selling and marketing of air and maritime transport services). A protocol to implement the fourth package of commitments was signed by ministers in November 2004. In September 2002 ASEAN senior transport officials signed the MOU on air freight services, which represented the first stage in full liberalization of air freight services in the region. As one of the priority sectors within the ASEAN Framework Agreement for Integration of the Priority Sectors and its Protocols, air travel in the region was to be fully integrated by 2010. The Action Plan for ASEAN Air Transport Integration and Liberalisation 2005–15 was adopted in November 2004. The Master Plan for ASEAN Connectivity, adopted by heads of state in October 2010, incorporated objectives for the development and implementation of an ASEAN Single Aviation Market, as well as an ASEAN Single Shipping Market, by 2015.

TELECOMMUNICATIONS

ASEAN aims to achieve interoperability and interconnectivity in the telecommunications sector. In November 2000 ASEAN heads of government approved an e-ASEAN Framework Agreement to promote and co-ordinate e-commerce and internet utilization. The Agreement incorporated commitments to develop and strengthen ASEAN's information infrastructure, in order to provide for universal and affordable access to communications services. Tariff reduction on information and communication technology (ICT) products was to be accelerated, with the aim of eliminating all tariffs in the sector by 2010. In July 2001 the first meeting of ASEAN ministers responsible for telecommunications (TELMIN) was held, in Kuala Lumpur, Malaysia, during which a Ministerial Understanding on ASEAN co-operation in telecommunications and ICT was signed. In September ASEAN ministers of economic affairs approved a list of ICT products eligible for the elimination of duties under the e-ASEAN Framework Agreement. This was to take place in three annual tranches, commencing in 2003 for the six original members of ASEAN and in 2008 for the newer member countries. During 2001 ASEAN continued to develop a reference framework for e-commerce legislation. In September 2003 the third ASEAN telecommunications ministerial meeting adopted a declaration incorporating commitments to harness ASEAN technological advances, create digital opportunities and enhance ASEAN's competitiveness in the field of ICT. The ministers also endorsed initiatives to enhance cybersecurity, including the establishment of computer emergency response teams in each member state. In August 2004 an ASEAN ICT Fund was established to accelerate implementation of the grouping's ICT objectives. At the fifth meeting of telecommunications ministers, held in Hanoi, Viet Nam, in September 2005, the Hanoi Agenda on Promoting Online Services and Applications was adopted. 'ASEANconnect', a web portal collating all essential information and data regarding ICT activities and initiatives within ASEAN, was also launched. In August 2007 ASEAN telecommunications ministers, convened in Siem Reap, Cambodia, endorsed a commitment to enhance universal access of ICT services within ASEAN, in particular to extend the benefits of ICT to rural communities and remote areas. At the same time ministers met their counterparts from the People's Republic of China, Japan and the Republic of Korea to strengthen co-operation in ICT issues. An ASEAN Connectivity Initiative, approved by ASEAN heads of state in October 2009, envisaged greater investment and targets for co-operation in ICT, as well as transport, energy and cross-border movement of goods and people. A Master Plan on ASEAN Connectivity was adopted by heads of state meeting in Hanoi, in October 2010. In January 2011 ASEAN telecommunications ministers adopted an ASEAN ICT Masterplan 2015 ('AIM2015').

SCIENCE AND TECHNOLOGY

ASEAN's Committee on Science and Technology (COST) supports co-operation in food science and technology, meteorology and geophysics, microelectronics and ICT, biotechnology, non-conventional energy research, materials science and technology, space technology applications, science and technology infrastructure and resources development, and marine science. There is an ASEAN Science Fund, used to finance policy studies in science and technology and to support information exchange and dissemination.

The Hanoi Plan of Action, adopted in December 1998, envisaged a series of measures aimed at promoting development in the fields of science and technology, including the establishment of networks of science and technology centres of excellence and academic institutions, the creation of a technology scan mechanism, the promotion of public and private sector co-operation in scientific and technological (particularly ICT) activities, and an increase in research on strategic technologies. In September 2001 the ASEAN Ministerial Meeting on Science and Technology, convened for its first meeting since 1998, approved a new framework for implementation of ASEAN's Plan of Action on Science and Technology during the period 2001–04. The Plan aimed to help less developed member countries become competitive in the sector and integrate into regional co-operation activities. In September 2003 ASEAN and the People's Republic of China inaugurated a Network of East Asian Think-tanks to promote scientific and technological exchange. In November 2004 a Ministerial Meeting on Science and Technology decided to establish an ASEAN Virtual Institute of Science and Technology with the aim of developing science and technology human resources in the region. In August 2006 an informal Ministerial Meeting on Science and Technology endorsed in principle a Plan of Action on Science and Technology for 2007–11. The document envisaged ASEAN-COST focusing work on the following areas of activity: environment and disaster management; new and renewable energy; open source software system; and food safety and security.

ENVIRONMENT

An ASEAN Agreement on the Conservation of Nature and Natural Resources was signed in July 1985. In April 1994 a ministerial meeting on the environment approved long-term objectives on environmental quality and standards for the ASEAN region, aiming to enhance joint action in addressing environmental concerns. At the same time, ministers adopted standards for air quality and river water to be achieved by all ASEAN member countries by 2010. In June 1995 ministers agreed to co-operate to counter the problems of transboundary pollution. An ASEAN Regional Centre for Biodiversity Conservation (ARCBC) was established in February 1999.

In December 1997 ASEAN heads of state endorsed a Regional Haze Action Plan to address the environmental problems resulting from forest fires, which had afflicted several countries in the region throughout that year. A Haze Technical Task Force undertook to implement the plan, with assistance from the UN Environment Programme. Sub-regional fire-fighting arrangement working groups for Sumatra and Borneo were established in April 1998 and in May the Task Force organized a regional workshop to strengthen ASEAN capacity to prevent and alleviate the haze caused by the extensive fires. A pilot project of aerial surveillance of the areas in the region most at risk of forest fires was initiated in July. In December heads of government resolved to establish an ASEAN Regional Research and Training Centre for Land and Forest Fire Management. In March 2002 members of the working groups on sub-regional fire-fighting arrangements for Sumatra and Borneo agreed to intensify early warning efforts and surveillance activities in order to reduce the risks of forest fires. In June ASEAN ministers of the environment signed an Agreement on Transboundary Haze Pollution, which was intended to provide a legal basis for the Regional Haze Action Plan. The Agreement, which entered into force in November 2003, required member countries to co-operate in the prevention and mitigation of haze pollution, for example, by responding to requests for information by other states and facilitating the transit of personnel and equipment in case of disaster. The Agreement also provided for the establishment of an ASEAN Co-ordination Centre for Transboundary Haze Pollution Control. The first conference of parties to the Agreement was held in November 2004. An ASEAN Specialized Meteorological Centre (ASMC) based in Singapore, plays a primary role in long-range climatological forecasting, early detection and monitoring of fires and haze. In August 2005, guided by the ASEAN Agreement on Transboundary Haze Pollution, member countries activated bilateral and regional mechanisms to exchange information and mobilize resources to deal with severe fires in Sumatra (Indonesia), peninsular Malaysia and southern Thailand. In September 2007 ASEAN ministers agreed to establish a sub-regional Technical Working Group to focus on addressing land and forest fires in the northern part of the region.

In May 2001 environment ministers launched the ASEAN Environment Education Action Plan (AEEAP), with the aim of promoting public awareness of environmental and sustainable development issues. In November 2003 ASEAN + 3 ministers of environment agreed to prioritize environmental activities in the following areas: environmentally sustainable cities; global environmental issues; land and forest fires and transboundary haze pollution; coastal and marine environment; sustainable forest management; freshwater resources; public awareness and environmental education; promotion of green technologies and cleaner production; and sustainable development monitoring and reporting. The Vientiane Action Plan (see above) incorporated objectives for environmental and natural resource management for the period 2004–10. In September 2005 the ASEAN Centre for Biodiversity, funded jointly by ASEAN and the EU, was inaugurated in La Union, near Manila, the Philippines. In that month ministers of the environment approved an ASEAN Strategic Plan of Action on Water Resources Management. The ASEAN summit meeting convened in November 2007 was held on the theme of 'energy, environment, climate change, and sustainable development'. A final Declaration on Environmental Sustainability incorporated specific commitments to strengthen environmental protection management, to respond to climate change and to work towards the conservation and sustainable management of natural resources. A Special Ministerial Meeting on the environment was held in Hua Hin, Thailand, in September 2009. The meeting reviewed ongoing programmes and approved the establishment of an ASEAN Working Group on Climate Change. In the following month ASEAN environment ministers endorsed the terms of reference of an ASEAN Climate Change Initiative and adopted a Singapore Resolution on Environmental Sustainability and Climate Change, recognising the need for closer co-operation in responding to climate change. In April 2010 ASEAN heads of state, meeting in Hanoi, Viet Nam, adopted a Leaders' Statement on Joint Response to Climate Change, which reaffirmed ASEAN's commitment to securing a new legally binding agreement on carbon emissions and to strengthening ASEAN efforts to counter and respond to climate change.

SOCIAL WELFARE AND DEVELOPMENT

ASEAN is concerned with a range of social issues including youth development, the role of women, health and nutrition, education and labour affairs. In December 1993 ASEAN ministers responsible for social affairs adopted a Plan of Action for Children, which provided a framework for regional co-operation for the survival, protection and development of children in member countries. ASEAN supports efforts to combat drug abuse and illegal drugs-trafficking. It aims to promote education and drug-awareness campaigns throughout the region, and administers a project to strengthen the training of personnel involved in combating drug abuse. In July 1998 ASEAN ministers of foreign affairs signed a Joint Declaration for a Drug-Free ASEAN, which envisaged greater co-operation among member states, in particular in information exchange, educational resources and legal procedures, in order to eliminate the illicit production, processing and trafficking of narcotic substances by 2020. (This deadline was subsequently advanced to 2015.)

In December 1998 ASEAN leaders approved a series of measures aimed at mitigating the social impact of the financial and economic crises that had affected many countries in the region. Plans of Action were formulated on issues of rural development and poverty eradication, while Social Safety Nets, which aimed to protect the most vulnerable members of society, were approved. The summit meeting emphasized the need to promote job generation as a key element of strategies for economic recovery and growth. In November 2001 the leaders meeting considered the widening development gap between ASEAN members and concluded that bridging this gap was a priority. The meeting approved an Initiative for ASEAN Integration Work Plan, which identified infrastructure development, human resource development, access to ICT and the promotion of regional economic integration as priority areas of activity, in particular to assist the newer signatory states, i.e. Cambodia, Laos, Myanmar and Viet Nam. The Plan of Action for the ASEAN Socio-Cultural Community (envisaged in the Bali Concord II—see above) was adopted by ASEAN leaders in November 2004. The first ASEAN + 3 Ministerial Meeting for social welfare and development was convened in Bangkok, Thailand, in December, at which it was agreed that the three key areas of co-operation were to be: the promotion of a community of caring societies in the region; developing policies and programmes to address the issue of ageing; and addressing human resource development in the social sector. In July 2005 it was agreed to establish an ASEAN Development Fund, to which each member country would make an initial contribution of US $1m. In November 2006 ASEAN senior officials adopted a Strategic Framework and Plan of Action for Social Welfare, Family and Children for the period 2007–10. The sixth ASEAN Ministerial Meeting for social welfare and development was convened in Hanoi, Viet Nam, in December 2007. It focused on 'mainstreaming persons with disability in development' and discussed overcoming the development gap between member countries as an essential element of an integrated ASEAN community. An ASEAN Commission on the Promotion and Protection of the Rights of Women and Children was inaugurated in April 2010.

The seventh ASEAN summit meeting, held in November 2001, declared work on combating HIV and AIDS to be a priority. The second phase of a work programme to combat AIDS and provide help for sufferers was endorsed at the meeting. Heads of government expressed their readiness to commit the necessary resources for prevention and care, and to attempt to obtain access to cheaper drugs. An ASEAN task force on AIDS has been operational since March 1993. An ASEAN Co-operation Forum on HIV/AIDS was held in February 2003, in Bangkok. An East Asia and Pacific Consultation on Children and AIDS was convened in March 2006 and identified nine urgent actions to respond to children affected by HIV/AIDS. In April 2003 a Special ASEAN Leaders' Meeting on Severe Acute Respiratory Syndrome (SARS) endorsed the recommendations of ministers of health, who convened in special session a few days previously, and agreed to establish an ad hoc ministerial-level Joint Task Force to follow-up and monitor implementation of those decisions. Co-operation measures approved included public information and education campaigns, health and immigration control procedures, and the establishment of an early-warning system on emerging infectious diseases. In June 2006 ASEAN ministers responsible for health adopted a declaration entitled 'ASEAN Unity in Health Emergencies'. In June 2008 ASEAN inaugurated an internet-based information centre on emerging infectious diseases in the ASEAN + 3 countries to exchange data relating to infection outbreaks and surveillance. In May 2009 ASEAN +3 ministers of health convened a Special Meeting on Influenza A(H1N1), a new strain of swine flu that had recently emerged as a serious threat to humans. The meeting agreed to strengthen surveillance and effective responses; to implement national pandemic preparedness plans; and to ensure effective public communication. It urged regional co-operation to promote surveillance and the transfer of technology, in relation to the production of vaccines. An International Ministerial Conference on Animal and Pandemic Influenza was convened in Hanoi, Viet Nam, in April 2010. The meeting commended the efforts to counter infectious diseases, but noted the continued threat of highly pathogenic avian influenza (HPAI—see above).

In October 2004 ASEAN ministers approved a new framework action plan on rural development and poverty eradication, covering the period 2004–10, to address priorities including the different levels of development among member countries and issues concerning globalization and social protection. In January 2007 the fifth ASEAN Ministerial Meeting on rural development and poverty eradication, convened in Bangkok, focused on community empowerment as a means of addressing rural poverty.

In January 1992 the ASEAN summit meeting resolved to establish an ASEAN University Network (AUN) to hasten the development of a regional identity. A draft AUN Charter and Agreement were adopted in 1995. The Network aims to strengthen co-operation within the grouping, develop academic and professional human resources and transmit information and knowledge. The 17 universities linked by the Network carry out collaborative studies and research programmes. Three more universities became members of the AUN in November 2006. At the seventh ASEAN summit in November 2001 heads of government agreed to establish the first ASEAN University, in Malaysia. In August 2005 it was agreed to convene a regular ASEAN Ministerial Meeting on education; the first meeting was held in March 2006. In March 2007 education ministers determined to restart an ASEAN Student Exchange Programme.

In January 2007 ASEAN heads of government signed a Declaration on the Protection and Promotion of the Rights of Migrant Workers, which mandated countries to promote fair and appropriate employment protection, payment of wages, and adequate access to decent working and living conditions for migrant workers. A Committee on the Implementation of the ASEAN Declaration held its inaugural meeting in September 2008.

DISASTER MANAGEMENT

An ASEAN Committee on Disaster Management was established in early 2003 and worked to formulate a framework for co-operation in disaster management and emergency response. In January 2005 a Special ASEAN Leaders' Meeting was convened in Jakarta, Indonesia, to consider the needs of countries affected by an earthquake and devastating tsunami that had occurred in the Indian Ocean in late December 2004. The meeting, which was also attended by the UN Secretary-General, the President of the World Bank and other senior envoys of donor countries and international organizations, adopted a Declaration on Action to Strengthen Emergency Relief, Rehabilitation, Reconstruction and Prevention on the Aftermath of Earthquake and Tsunami Disaster. In July 2005 an ASEAN Agreement on Disaster Management and Emergency Response was signed in Vientiane, Laos. The Agreement stated as its objective the provision of mechanisms that would effectively reduce the loss of life and damage to the social, economic and environmental assets of the region and the response to disaster emergencies through concerted national efforts and increased regional and international co-operation. By October 2009 the Agreement had been ratified by each member state and it entered into force in December. In May ASEAN, with the World Bank and UN International Strategy for Disaster Reduction, announced a new co-operation programme to strengthen disaster reduction, including reducing vulnerability to natural hazards, and disaster management in South-East Asia. In October ASEAN established a Co-operation Fund for Emergency Relief to co-ordinate humanitarian assistance to communities affected by tropical storm damage and severe flooding in Cambodia, Laos, the Philippines and Viet Nam, and by two major earthquakes in western Sumatra, Indonesia, in late September. ASEAN also mobilized emergency rapid assessment teams to review the situation in the worst-hit areas.

In May 2008 ASEAN dispatched an emergency rapid assessment team to Myanmar to view the large-scale devastation in the Yangon and Ayeyarwady delta divisions of that country caused by tropical cyclone 'Nargis'. A Special ASEAN Foreign Ministers Meeting, convened in Singapore later in the month, agreed to establish an ASEAN Humanitarian Task Force (AHTF) and co-ordinating mechanism to facilitate the delivery and distribution of international humanitarian assistance. At that time ASEAN, with the UN, organized an international pledging conference, in Yangon, which was attended by representatives of 51 countries. The conference endorsed the establishment of a Tripartite Core Group (TCG), comprising ASEAN, the UN and the Government of Myanmar, as a mechanism to co-ordinate humanitarian relief and rehabilitation efforts. In June the TCG organized, with support from the Asian Development Bank and the World Bank, a Post-Nargis Joint Assessment to monitor the situation in the worst-affected areas and to identify the immediate needs of the local populations. The report of the joint assessment was published in the following month. In February 2009 the TCG initiated a Post-Nargis Recovery and Preparedness Plan to provide a framework for rehabilitation of the Ayeyarwady delta in the three-year period 2009–11. The first meeting of a TCG Recovery Forum was held in October 2009, in Yangon, to discuss policy and strategic issues relating to the recovery process. At the meeting the TCG determined to convene a Post-Nargis Assistance Conference in order to generate US $103m. to fund outstanding humanitarian requirements. In early 2010 the latest TCG review estimated that 100,000 households were still vulnerable owing to lack of shelter assistance. AHTF operations were formally terminated on 31 July 2010.

In March 2011 ASEAN member states extended immediate financial and practical support to Japan, in order to assist recovery efforts in the north of the country which had been devastated by an earthquake and tsunami. Some 700 personnel were diverted from a large-scale disaster emergency exercise, being co-hosted by Japan and Indonesia, to support the rescue and recovery efforts.

TOURISM

National tourist organizations from ASEAN countries meet regularly to assist in co-ordinating the region's tourist industry, and a Tourism Forum is held annually to promote the sector. (In January 2011 the Forum was held in Phnom-Penh, Cambodia.) The first formal meeting of ASEAN ministers of tourism was held in January 1998, in Cebu, the Philippines. The meeting adopted a Plan of Action on ASEAN Co-operation in Tourism, which aimed to promote intra-ASEAN travel, greater investment in the sector, joint marketing of the region as a single tourist destination and environmentally sustainable tourism. In January 1999 the second meeting of ASEAN ministers of tourism agreed to appoint country co-ordinators to implement various initiatives, including the designation of 2002 as 'Visit ASEAN Millennium Year'; research to promote the region as a tourist destination in the 21st century, and to develop a cruise ship industry; and the establishment of a network of ASEAN Tourism Training Centres to develop new skills and technologies in the tourist industry. The third meeting of tourism ministers, held in Bangkok, Thailand, in January 2000, agreed to reformulate the Visit ASEAN Millennium Year initiative as a long-term Visit ASEAN programme. This was formally launched in January 2001. The first phase of the programme promoted brand awareness through an intense marketing effort; the second phase, initiated at the fifth meeting of tourism ministers, held in Yogyakarta, Indonesia, in January 2002, was to direct campaigns towards end-consumers. Ministers urged member states to abolish all fiscal and non-fiscal travel barriers to encourage tourism, including intra-ASEAN travel. Tourism ministers from the ASEAN + 3 countries attended the meeting for the first time. In November the eighth summit of heads of state adopted a framework agreement on ASEAN co-operation in tourism, aimed at facilitating domestic and intra-regional travel. ASEAN national tourism organizations signed an implementation plan for the agreement in May 2003, when they also announced a Declaration on Tourism Safety and Security. In January 2011 ASEAN ministers of tourism approved a new ASEAN Tourism Strategic Plan for the period 2011–15. The Plan envisaged promoting the region as a single tourist destination, developing a set of ASEAN tourism standards with a certification process, and enabling visitors to travel throughout the region with a single visa.

CULTURE AND INFORMATION

Regular workshops and festivals are held in visual and performing arts, youth music, radio, television and films, and print and interpersonal media. In addition, ASEAN administers a News Exchange and provides support for the training of editors, journalists and information officers. In 2000 ASEAN adopted new cultural strategies, with the aim of raising awareness of the grouping's objectives and achievements, both regionally and internationally. The strategies included: producing ASEAN cultural and historical educational materials; promoting cultural exchanges; and achieving greater exposure of ASEAN cultural activities and issues in the mass media. An ASEAN Youth Camp was held for the first time in that year, and subsequently has been organized on an annual basis. ASEAN ministers responsible for culture and arts (AMCA) met for the first time in October 2003. The fourth ministerial meeting was convened, with their ministerial counterparts from the ASEAN + 3 countries, in Clark, Angelus City (Pampanga province), the Philippines, in March 2010. The fourth ASEAN Festival of Arts was held concurrently, on the theme 'The Best of ASEAN', while Clark was named as the first ASEAN City of Culture.

In July 1997 ASEAN ministers of foreign affairs endorsed the establishment of an ASEAN Foundation to promote awareness of the organization and greater participation in its activities; this was inaugurated in July 1998 and is based at the ASEAN secretariat building (www.aseanfoundation.org).

EXTERNAL RELATIONS

ASEAN's external relations have been pursued through a dialogue system, initially with the objective of promoting co-operation in economic areas with key trading partners. The system has been expanded in recent years to encompass regional security concerns and co-operation in other areas, such as the environment. The ARF (see above) emerged from the dialogue system, and more recently the formalized discussions of ASEAN with the People's Republic of China, Japan and the Republic of Korea (ASEAN + 3) has evolved as a separate process with its own strategic agenda. In February 2000 a meeting of ASEAN heads of state and the Secretary-General of the United Nations (UN) took place in Bangkok, Thailand. (A second ASEAN-UN summit was held in September 2005, in New York, USA, and a third was convened in October 2010, in Hanoi, Viet Nam.) In December 2006 the UN General Assembly granted ASEAN permanent observer status at its meetings.

In December 2005 the first East Asia Summit (EAS) meeting was convened, following the ASEAN leaders' meeting in Kuala Lumpur, Malaysia. It was attended by ASEAN member countries, the People's Republic of China, Japan, the Republic of Korea (the '+ 3' countries), India, Australia and New Zealand; Russia participated as an observer. The meeting agreed to pursue co-operation in areas of common interest and determined to meet annually. It concluded a Declaration on Avian Influenza Prevention, Control and Response. At the second EAS meeting, held in Cebu, the Philippines, in January 2007, a Declaration on East Asian Energy Security was adopted. An inaugural meeting of East Asian ministers of energy was convened in August. The third summit meeting was convened in Singapore, in November; it issued the Singapore Declaration on Climate Change, Energy and the Environment and held discussions on issues of mutual concern. The fourth EAS, scheduled to be held in Bangkok, in December 2008, was postponed owing to civil unrest, and was again deferred, in April 2009, owing to violent anti-government demonstrations at a new venue in Pattaya, Thailand. A statement by EAS heads of state, issued in June, declared their support for efforts to counter the global economic and financial crisis, including measures agreed by the G20, completion of the WTO's Doha Round, and a Comprehensive Economic Partnership in East Asia Initiative.

European Union: In March 1980 a co-operation agreement was signed between ASEAN and the European Community (EC, as the EU was known prior to its restructuring on 1 November 1993), which provided for the strengthening of existing trade links and increased co-operation in the scientific and agricultural spheres. A Joint Co-operation Committee met in November (and annually thereafter). An ASEAN-EC Business Council was launched in December 1983 to promote private sector co-operation. The first meeting of ministers of economic affairs from ASEAN and EC member countries took place in October 1985. In December 1990 the Community adopted new guidelines on development co-operation, with an increase in assistance to Asia, and a change in the type of aid given to ASEAN members, emphasizing training, science and technology and venture capital, rather than assistance for rural development. In October 1992 the EC and ASEAN agreed to promote further trade between the regions, as well as bilateral investment, and made a joint declaration in support of human rights. An EU-ASEAN Junior Managers Exchange Programme was initiated in November 1996, as part of efforts to promote co-operation and understanding between the industrial and business sectors in both regions. In December 2000 an ASEAN-EU Ministerial Meeting was held in Vientiane, Laos. Both sides agreed to pursue dialogue and co-operation and issued a joint declaration that accorded support for the efforts of the UN Secretary-General's special envoy towards restoring political dialogue in Myanmar. Myanmar agreed to permit an EU delegation to visit the country and political opposition leaders in early 2001. In September the Joint Co-operation Committee, meeting for the first time since 1999, resolved to strengthen policy dialogue, in particular in areas fostering regional integration. An ASEAN-EU Business Network was established in Brussels, Belgium, in 2001, to develop political and commercial contacts between the two sides. An ASEAN-EU Business Summit meeting was convened for the first time in May 2011, in Jakarta, Indonesia.

In May 1995 ASEAN and EU senior officials endorsed an initiative to strengthen relations between the two economic regions within the framework of an Asia-Europe Meeting of heads of government (ASEM). The first ASEM was convened in Bangkok, Thailand, in March 1996, at which leaders approved a new Asia-Europe Partnership for Greater Growth. The second ASEM summit meeting, held in April 1998, focused heavily on economic concerns. In February 1997 ministers of foreign affairs of countries participating in ASEM met in Singapore. Despite ongoing differences regarding human rights issues, in particular concerning ASEAN's granting of full membership status to Myanmar and the situation in East Timor (which precluded the conclusion of a new co-operation agreement), the Ministerial Meeting issued a final joint declaration, committing both sides to strengthening co-operation and dialogue on economic, international and bilateral trade, security and social issues. The third ASEM summit meeting was convened in Seoul, Korea in October 2000. At the 14th ASEAN-EU Ministerial Meeting, held in Brussels, in January 2003, delegates adopted an ASEAN-EU Joint Declaration on Co-operation to Combat Terrorism. An ASEM seminar on combating terrorism was held in Beijing, People's Republic of China, in October. In February 2003 the EU awarded €4.5m. under the ASEAN-EU Programme on Regional Integration Support (APRIS) to enhance progress towards establishing AFTA. (The first phase of the APRIS programme was concluded in September 2006, and a second three-year phase, APRIS II, was initiated in November with a commitment by the EU of €7.2m.) In April 2003 the EU proposed the creation of a regional framework, the Trans-Regional EU-ASEAN Trade Initiative (TREATI), to address mutual trade facilitation, investment and regulatory issues. It was suggested that the framework might eventually result in a preferential trade agreement. In January 2004 a joint statement was issued announcing a roadmap for implementing the TREATI and an EU-ASEAN work plan for that year. The fifth ASEM meeting of heads of state and government was held in Hanoi, Viet Nam, in October, attended for the first time by the 10 new members of the EU and by Cambodia, Laos, and Myanmar. At the session of the Joint Co-operation Committee held in February 2005, in Jakarta, Indonesia, it was announced that the European Commission's communication entitled 'A New Partnership with Southeast Asia', issued in July 2003, would form the basis for the development of the EU's relations with ASEAN, along with Bali Concord II and the VAP. Under the new partnership, the TREATI would represent the framework for dialogue on trade and economic issues, whereas the READI (Regional EC ASEAN Dialogue Instrument) would be the focus for non-trade issues. The sixth ASEM, convened in Helsinki, Finland, in September 2006, on the theme '10 Years of ASEM: Global Challenges and Joint Responses', was attended for the first time by the ASEAN Secretariat, Bulgaria, India, Mongolia, Pakistan and Romania. The participants adopted a Declaration on Climate Change, aimed at promoting efforts to reach consensus in international climate negotiations, and the Helsinki Declaration on the Future of ASEM, detailing guidelines and practical recommendations for developing future ASEM co-operation. A Declaration on an Enhanced Partnership was endorsed in March 2007 and a plan of action to pursue strengthened co-operation was adopted at an ASEAN-EU summit meeting held in November. The seventh ASEM summit, convened in Beijing, People's Republic of China, in October 2008, issued a Declaration on Sustainable Development, focusing on the MDGs, climate change and energy security, and social cohesion. In May 2009 ASEAN and EU ministers of foreign affairs signed a declaration committing both sides to completing EU accession to the Treaty of Amity and Co-operation as a priority. The 18th ASEAN-EU Ministerial Meeting was held in Madrid, Spain, in May 2010, on the theme of 'Partners in Regional Integration'. The eighth ASEM summit took place in October, in Brussels. During the meeting Australia, New Zealand and Russia acceded to the grouping. The ninth ASEM summit was to be convened in Japan, in November 2012.

People's Republic of China: Efforts to develop consultative relations between ASEAN and the People's Republic of China were initiated in 1993. Joint Committees on economic and trade co-operation and on scientific and technological co-operation were subsequently established. The first formal consultations between senior officials of the two sides were held in April 1995. In July 1996, in spite of ASEAN's continued concern at China's territorial claims to the Spratly Islands in the South China Sea, China was admitted to the PMC as a full dialogue partner. In February 1997 a Joint Co-operation Committee was established to co-ordinate the China-ASEAN dialogue and all aspects of relations between the two sides. Relations were further strengthened by the decision to form a joint business council to promote bilateral trade and investment. China participated in the informal summit meeting held in December, at the end of which both sides issued a joint statement affirming their commitment to resolving regional disputes through peaceful means. China was a participant in the first official ASEAN + 3 meeting of foreign ministers, which was convened in July 2000. An ASEAN-China Experts Group was established in November, to consider future economic co-operation and free trade opportunities. The Group held its first meeting in April 2001 and proposed a framework agreement on economic co-operation and the establishment of an ASEAN-China free trade area within 10 years (with differential treatment and flexibility for newer ASEAN members). Both proposals were endorsed at the seventh ASEAN summit meeting in November 2001. In November 2002 an agreement on economic co-operation was concluded by the ASEAN member states and China. The Framework Agreement on Comprehensive Economic Co-operation between ASEAN and China entered into force in July 2003, and envisaged the establishment of an ASEAN-China Free Trade Area (ACFTA) by 2010 (with the target for the newer member countries being 2015). The Agreement provided for strengthened co-operation in key areas including agriculture, information and telecommunications, and human resources development. It was also agreed to implement the consensus of the Special ASEAN-China Leaders' Meeting on SARS, held in April 2003, and to set up an ASEAN + 1 special fund for health co-operation. In October China acceded to the

Treaty on Amity and Co-operation and signed a joint declaration with ASEAN on Strategic Partnership for Peace and Prosperity on strengthening co-operation in politics, economy, social affairs, security and regional and international issues. It was also agreed to continue consultations on China's accession to the SEANWFZ and to expedite the implementation of the Joint Statement on Co-operation in the Field of Non-Traditional Security Issues and the Declaration on the Conduct of Parties in the South China Sea. In November 2004 ASEAN and China signed the Agreement on Trade in Goods and the Agreement on Dispute Settlement Mechanism of the Framework Agreement on Comprehensive Economic Co-operation, to be implemented from 1 July 2005. A Plan of Action to Implement ASEAN-China Joint Declaration on Strengthening Strategic Partnership for Peace and Prosperity was also adopted by both parties at that time. In August 2005 ASEAN signed an MOU with China on cultural co-operation. An ASEAN-China Agreement on Trade in Services was signed in January 2007, within the Framework Agreement on Comprehensive Economic Co-operation, and entered into force on 1 July. The final component of the Framework Agreement, an ASEAN-China Investment Agreement, was signed in August 2009. Accordingly, ACFTA entered fully into effect on 1 January 2010. In November 2007 the ASEAN-China summit resolved that the environment should be included as a priority area for future co-operation and endorsed agreements concluded earlier in that month to strengthen co-operation in aviation and maritime transport. An ASEAN-China Environmental Co-operation Centre was formally inaugurated in Beijing, in May 2011. It was announced in October 2011 that China was to establish a mission to ASEAN during 2012.

Japan: The first meeting between the two sides at ministerial level was held in October 1992. At this meeting, and subsequently, ASEAN requested Japan to increase its investment in member countries and to make Japanese markets more accessible to ASEAN products, in order to reduce the trade deficit with Japan. Since 1993 ASEAN-Japanese development and cultural co-operation has expanded under schemes including the Inter-ASEAN Technical Exchange Programme, the Japan-ASEAN Co-operation Promotion Programme and the ASEAN-Japan Friendship Programme. In December 1997 Japan, attending the informal summit meeting in Malaysia, agreed to improve market access for ASEAN products and to provide training opportunities for more than 20,000 young people in order to help develop local economies. In December 1998 ASEAN heads of government welcomed a Japanese initiative to allocate US $30,000m. to promote economic recovery in the region. In mid-2000 a new Japan-ASEAN General Exchange Fund (JAGEF) was established to promote and facilitate the transfer of technology, investment and personnel. In November 1999 Japan, with the People's Republic of China and the Republic of Korea, attending an informal summit meeting of ASEAN, agreed to strengthen economic and political co-operation with the ASEAN countries, to enhance political and security dialogue, and to implement joint infrastructure and social projects. Japan participated in the first official ASEAN + 3 meeting of foreign ministers, which was convened in July 2000. In recent years Japan has provided ICT support to ASEAN countries, and has offered assistance in environmental and health matters and for educational training and human resource development (particularly in engineering). In October 2003 ASEAN and Japan signed a Framework for Comprehensive Partnership. In December Japan concluded a joint action plan with ASEAN with provisions on reinforcing economic integration within ASEAN and enhancing competitiveness, and on addressing terrorism, piracy and other transnational issues. A joint declaration was also issued on starting discussions on the possibility of establishing an ASEAN-Japan FTA by 2012 (with the newer ASEAN countries participating from 2017). Negotiations on a Comprehensive Economic Partnership Agreement were initiated in April 2005 and concluded in November 2007. The accord was signed in April 2008 and entered into force on 1 December. In July 2004 Japan acceded to the Treaty on Amity and Co-operation. In November the ASEAN-Japan summit meeting adopted the ASEAN-Japan Joint Declaration for Co-operation in the Fight Against International Terrorism. In July 2008 ASEAN concluded a formal partnership agreement with the new Japan International Co-operation Agency, with the aim of working together to strengthen ASEAN integration and development. In April 2011 a Special ASEAN-Japan Ministerial Meeting was convened, in Jakarta, Indonesia, to reaffirm mutual support, in particular in respect to Japan's recovery from a massive earthquake in the previous month.

Australia and New Zealand: In 1999 ASEAN and Australia undertook to establish the ASEAN-Australia Development Co-operation Programme (AADCP), to replace an economic co-operation programme that had begun in 1974. In August 2002 the two sides signed a formal MOU on the AADCP. It was to comprise three core elements, with assistance amounting to $A45m.: a Program Stream, to address medium-term issues of economic integration and competitiveness; a Regional Partnerships Scheme for smaller collaborative activities; and the establishment of a Regional Economic Policy Support Facility within the ASEAN Secretariat. In July 2009 ASEAN and Australia signed an MOU on implementation of a second phase of the AADCP.

In September 2001 ASEAN ministers of economic affairs signed a Framework for Closer Economic Partnership (CEP) with their counterparts from Australia and New Zealand (the Closer Economic Relations—CER—countries), and agreed to establish a Business Council to involve the business communities of all countries in the CEP. In November 2004 a Commemorative Summit, marking 30 years of dialogue between the nations, took place between ASEAN leaders and those of Australia and New Zealand at which it was agreed to launch negotiations on a free trade agreement. In July 2005 New Zealand signed ASEAN's Treaty of Amity and Co-operation; Australia acceded to the Treaty in December. In August 2007 the Australian and ASEAN ministers of foreign affairs signed a Joint Declaration on a Comprehensive Partnership, and in November they agreed upon a plan of action to implement the accord. An agreement establishing an ASEAN–Australia–New Zealand free trade area was negotiated during 2008 and signed in Cha-am/Hua Hin, Thailand, in February 2009. An ASEAN-New Zealand Joint Declaration on Comprehensive Partnership for the period 2010-2015 was signed by ministers of foreign affairs of both sides in July 2010.

South Asia: In July 1993 both India and Pakistan were accepted as sectoral partners, providing for their participation in ASEAN meetings in sectors such as trade, transport and communications and tourism. An ASEAN-India Business Council was established, and met for the first time, in New Delhi, in February 1995. In December 1995 the ASEAN summit meeting agreed to enhance India's status to that of a full dialogue partner; India was formally admitted to the PMC in July 1996. At a meeting of the ASEAN-India Working Group in March 2001 the two sides agreed to pursue co-operation in new areas, such as health and pharmaceuticals, social security and rural development. The fourth meeting of the ASEAN-India Joint Co-operation Committee in January 2002 agreed to strengthen co-operation in these areas and others, including technology. The first ASEAN-India consultation between ministers of economic affairs, which took place in September, resulted in the adoption as a long-term objective, of the ASEAN-India Regional Trade and Investment Area. The first ASEAN-India summit at the level of heads of state was held in Phnom-Penh, Cambodia, in November. In October 2003 India acceded to the Treaty of Amity and Co-operation and signed a joint Framework Agreement on Comprehensive Economic Co-operation, which was to enter into effect in July 2004. The objectives of the Agreement included: strengthening and enhancing economic, trade and investment co-operation; liberalizing and promoting trade in goods and services; and facilitating economic integration within ASEAN. It was also agreed that negotiations would begin on establishing an ASEAN-India Regional Trade and Investment Area (RTIA), including a free trade area, for Brunei, Indonesia, Malaysia, Singapore and Thailand. A Partnership for Peace, Progress and Shared Prosperity was signed at the third ASEAN-India summit, held in November 2004. At the sixth summit meeting, held in November 2007, it was noted that annual bilateral ASEAN-India trade had reached US $20,000m. ASEAN-India agreements on trade in goods and on a dispute settlement mechanism were concluded in August 2008. The agreement on trade in goods was signed by both sides in August 2009, enabling the RTIA to enter into force on 1 January 2010.

An ASEAN-Pakistan Joint Business Council met for the first time in February 2000. In early 2001 both sides agreed to co-operate in projects relating to new and renewable energy resources, ICT, agricultural research and transport and communications. Pakistan acceded to the Treaty on Amity and Co-operation in July 2004. In January 2007 Timor-Leste acceded to the Treaty; Sri Lanka and Bangladesh acceded in August.

Republic of Korea: In July 1991 the Republic of Korea was accepted as a 'dialogue partner' in ASEAN, and in December a joint ASEAN-Korea Chamber of Commerce was established. The Republic of Korea participated in ASEAN's informal summit meetings in December 1997 and November 1999 (see above), and took part in the first official ASEAN + 3 meeting of foreign ministers, convened in July 2000. The Republic of Korea's assistance in the field of ICT has become particularly valuable in recent years. In March 2001, in a sign of developing co-operation, ASEAN and the Republic of Korea exchanged views on political and security issues in the region for the first time. The Republic of Korea acceded to the Treaty on Amity and Co-operation in November 2004. In that month an ASEAN-Korea summit meeting agreed to initiate negotiations on the establishment of a free trade area between the two sides. The Framework Agreement on Comprehensive Economic Co-operation, providing for the establishment of an ASEAN-Korea Free Trade Area, was signed in December 2005, eliminating tariffs on some 80% of products, with effect from 1 January 2010. In May 2006 governments of both sides (excluding Thailand, owing to a dispute concerning trade in rice) signed an Agreement on Trade in Goods. An ASEAN–Korea agreement on trade in services entered into force in May 2009. An ASEAN-Korea Investment Agreement was signed in June.

Russia: In March 2000 the first ASEAN-Russia business forum opened in Kuala Lumpur, Malaysia. In July 2004 ASEAN and Russia signed a Joint Declaration to Combat International Terrorism, while in November Russia acceded to the Treaty of Amity and Co-operation. The first ASEAN-Russia summit meeting was held in December 2005. The leaders agreed on a comprehensive programme of action to promote co-operation between both sides in the period 2005–15. This included commitments to co-operate in areas including counter-terrorism, human resources development, finance and economic activities and science and technology. In July 2008 both sides adopted a roadmap to further implementation of the comprehensive programme of action.

USA and Canada: In 1990 ASEAN and the USA established an ASEAN-US Joint Working Group, the purpose of which was to review ASEAN's economic relations with the USA and to identify measures by which economic links could be strengthened. In recent years, dialogue has increasingly focused on political and security issues. In August 2002 ASEAN ministers of foreign affairs met with their US counterpart, and signed a Joint Declaration for Co-operation to Combat International Terrorism. At the same time, the USA announced the ASEAN Co-operation Plan, which was to include activities in the fields of ICT, agricultural biotechnology, health, disaster response and training for the ASEAN Secretariat. In July 2009 the USA signed ASEAN's Treaty of Amity and Co-operation. The first official ASEAN meeting with the US President took place in November, in Singapore. Both sides resolved to enhance collaboration and to establish an ASEAN-US Eminent Persons Group. A second ASEAN-US leaders' meeting was held in September 2010.

ASEAN-Canadian co-operation projects include fisheries technology, the telecommunications industry, use of solar energy, and a forest seed centre. A Working Group on the Revitalization of ASEAN-Canada relations met in February 1999. At a meeting in Bangkok, Thailand, in July 2000, the two sides agreed to explore less formal avenues for project implementation. A Work Plan for ASEAN-Canada Co-operation 2007–10 was adopted in August 2007.

Indo-China: In June 1996 ministers of ASEAN countries, and of the People's Republic of China, Cambodia, Laos and Myanmar adopted a framework for ASEAN-Mekong Basin Development Co-operation. The initiative aimed to strengthen the region's cohesiveness, with greater co-operation on issues such as drugs-trafficking, labour migration and terrorism, and to facilitate the process of future expansion of ASEAN. Groups of experts and senior officials were to be convened to consider funding issues and proposals to link the two regions, including a gas pipeline network, rail links and the establishment of a common time zone. In December 1996 the working group on rail links appointed a team of consultants to conduct a feasibility study of the proposals. The completed study was presented at the second ministerial conference on ASEAN-Mekong Basin Development Co-operation, convened in Hanoi, Viet Nam, in July 2000. At the November 2001 summit China pledged US $5m. to assist with navigation along the upper stretches of the Mekong River, while other means by which China could increase its investment in the Mekong Basin area were considered. At the meeting the Republic of Korea was invited to become a core member of the grouping. Other growth regions sponsored by ASEAN include the Brunei, Indonesia, Malaysia, Philippines, East ASEAN Growth Area (BIMP-EAGA), the Indonesia, Malaysia, Singapore Growth Triangle (IMS-GT), and the West-East Corridor within the Mekong Basin Development initiative.

Gulf States: In June 2009 ASEAN ministers of foreign affairs held an inaugural meeting with their counterpart from the Co-operation Council for the Arab States of the Gulf (GCC). The meeting, convened in Manama, Bahrain, adopted a GCC-ASEAN Joint Vision as a framework for future co-operation between the two groupings. A second meeting, held in Singapore, in May–June 2010, approved an ASEAN–GCC Action Plan, which identified specific measures for closer co-operation to be undertaken in the two-year period 2010–12.

Publications

Annual Report.

Annual Security Report.

ASEAN Investment Report (annually).

ASEAN State of the Environment Report (1st report: 1997; 2nd report: 2000; 3rd report: 2006; 4th report: 2009).

Business ASEAN (quarterly).

ASEAN Updates.

Public Information Series, briefing papers, documents series, educational materials.

THE COMMONWEALTH

Address: Commonwealth Secretariat, Marlborough House, Pall Mall, London, SW1Y 5HX, United Kingdom.

Telephone: (20) 7747-6500; **fax:** (20) 7930-0827; **e-mail:** info@commonwealth.int; **internet:** www.thecommonwealth.org.

The Commonwealth is a voluntary association of 53 independent states (at October 2011), comprising about one-quarter of the world's population. It includes the United Kingdom and most of its former dependencies, and former dependencies of Australia and New Zealand (themselves Commonwealth countries). All Commonwealth countries accept Queen Elizabeth II as the symbol of the free association of the independent member nations and as such the Head of the Commonwealth.

MEMBERS IN THE FAR EAST AND AUSTRALASIA

Australia	Tonga	Tuvalu
Kiribati	Fiji*	Samoa
Nauru	Malaysia	Vanuatu
Papua New Guinea	New Zealand	
	Solomon Islands	

* In October 1987 Fiji's membership was declared to have lapsed (following the proclamation of a republic there). It was readmitted in October 1997, but was suspended from participation in meetings of the Commonwealth in June 2000. Fiji was formally readmitted to Commonwealth meetings in December 2001 following the staging of free and fair legislative elections in August–September. However, following a military coup in December 2006, Fiji was once again suspended from participation in meetings of the Commonwealth, and, in September 2009, Fiji's Commonwealth membership was fully suspended. In June 2011 Nauru was reinstated as a full member of the Commonwealth, having been classed as a 'member in arrears' from 2003.

TERRITORIES AND OTHER DEPENDENCIES

Australia	New Zealand	United Kingdom
Christmas Island	Cook Islands	Pitcairn Islands
Cocos (Keeling) Islands	Niue	
Coral Sea Islands Territory	Tokelau	
Norfolk Island		

Organization

(October 2011)

The Commonwealth is not a federation: there is no central government nor are there any rigid contractual obligations such as bind members of the United Nations.

The Commonwealth has no written constitution but its members subscribe to the ideals of the Declaration of Commonwealth Principles unanimously approved by a meeting of heads of government in Singapore in 1971. Members also approved the Gleneagles Agreement concerning apartheid in sport (1977); the Lusaka Declaration on Racism and Racial Prejudice (1979); the Melbourne Declaration on relations between developed and developing countries (1981); the New Delhi Statement on Economic Action (1983); the Goa Declaration on International Security (1983); the Nassau Declaration on World Order (1985); the Commonwealth Accord on Southern Africa (1985); the Vancouver Declaration on World Trade (1987); the Okanagan Statement and Programme of Action on Southern Africa (1987); the Langkawi Declaration on the Environment (1989); the Kuala Lumpur Statement on Southern Africa (1989); the Harare Commonwealth Declaration (1991); the Ottawa Declaration on Women and Structural Adjustment (1991); the Limassol Statement on the Uruguay Round of multilateral trade negotiations (1993); the

Millbrook Commonwealth Action Programme on the Harare Declaration (1995); the Edinburgh Commonwealth Economic Declaration (1997); the Fancourt Commonwealth Declaration on Globalization and People-centred Development (1999); the Coolum Declaration on the Commonwealth in the 21st Century: Continuity and Renewal (2002); the Aso Rock Commonwealth Declaration and Statement on Multilateral Trade (2003); the Malta Commonwealth Declaration on Networking for Development (2005); the Munyonyo Statement on Respect and Understanding (2007); the Marlborough House Statement on Reform of International Institutions (2008); and the Commonwealth Climate Change Declaration (2009).

MEETINGS OF HEADS OF GOVERNMENT

Commonwealth Heads of Government Meetings (CHOGMs) are private and informal and operate not by voting but by consensus. The emphasis is on consultation and exchange of views for co-operation. A communiqué is issued at the end of every meeting. Meetings are normally held every two years in different capitals in the Commonwealth. The 2009 meeting was held in Trinidad and Tobago, in November. The 2011 meeting was held in Perth, Australia, at the end of October.

OTHER CONSULTATIONS

The Commonwealth Ministerial Action Group on the Harare Declaration (CMAG) was formed in 1995 to support democracy in member countries (see Activities, below). It comprises a group of nine ministers of foreign affairs, with rotating membership. In November 2009 the membership of CMAG was reconstituted for the ensuing two-year period, to comprise the ministers responsible for foreign affairs of Australia, Bangladesh, Ghana, Jamaica, Maldives, Namibia, New Zealand, Vanuatu and Trinidad and Tobago.

Since 1959 Commonwealth finance ministers have met in the week prior to the annual meetings of the IMF and the World Bank. Ministers responsible for civil society, education, the environment, foreign affairs, gender issues, health, law, tourism and youth also hold regular meetings.

Senior officials—cabinet secretaries, permanent secretaries to heads of government and others—meet regularly in the year between meetings of heads of government to provide continuity and to exchange views on various developments.

COMMONWEALTH SECRETARIAT

The Secretariat, established by Commonwealth heads of government in 1965, operates as an intergovernmental organization at the service of all Commonwealth countries. It organizes consultations between governments and runs programmes of co-operation. Meetings of heads of government, ministers and senior officials decide these programmes and provide overall direction. A Board of Governors, on which all eligible member governments are represented, meets annually to review the Secretariat's work and approve its budget. The Board is supported by an Executive Committee which convenes four times a year to monitor implementation of the Secretariat's work programme. The Secretariat is headed by a secretary-general, elected by heads of government.

In 2002 the Secretariat was restructured, with a view to strengthening the effectiveness of the organization to meet the priorities determined by the meeting of heads of government held in Coolum, Australia, in March 2002. Under the reorganization the number of deputy secretaries-general was reduced from three to two. Certain work divisions were amalgamated, while new units or sections, concerned with youth affairs, human rights and good offices, were created to strengthen further activities in those fields. Accordingly, the Secretariat's divisional structure is as follows: Legal and constitutional affairs; Political affairs; Corporate services; Communications and public affairs; Strategic planning and evaluation; Economic affairs; Governance and institutional development; Social transformation programmes; Youth affairs (from 2004); and Special advisory services. (Details of some of the divisions are given under Activities, below.) In addition there are units responsible for human rights and project management and referrals, and an Office of the Secretary-General.

The Secretariat's strategic plan for 2008/09–2011/12, approved by the Board of Governors in May 2008, set out two main, long-term objectives for the Commonwealth. The first, 'Peace and Democracy', was to support member countries in preventing or resolving conflicts, to strengthen democracy and the rule of law, and to achieve greater respect for human rights. The second, 'Pro-Poor Growth and Sustainable Development', was to support policies for economic growth and sustainable development, particularly for the benefit of the poorest people, in member countries. Four programmes were to facilitate the pursuit of the first objective: Good Offices for Peace; Democracy and Consensus Building; Rule of Law; and Human Rights. The second objective was to be pursued through the following four programmes: Public Sector Development; Economic Development; Environmentally Sustainable Development; and Human Development.

Secretary-General: KAMALESH SHARMA (India).

Deputy Secretaries-General: MMASEKGOA MASIRE-MWAMBA (Botswana), RANSFORD SMITH (Jamaica).

Assistant Secretary-General for Corporate Affairs: STEPHEN CUTTS (United Kingdom).

Activities

PROMOTING DEMOCRACY, HUMAN RIGHTS AND DEVELOPMENT

In October 1991 heads of government, meeting in Harare, Zimbabwe, issued the Harare Commonwealth Declaration, in which they reaffirmed their commitment to the Commonwealth Principles declared in 1971, and stressed the need to promote sustainable development and the alleviation of poverty. The Declaration placed emphasis on the promotion of democracy and respect for human rights and resolved to strengthen the Commonwealth's capacity to assist countries in entrenching democratic practices. In November 1995 Commonwealth heads of government, convened in New Zealand, formulated and adopted the Millbrook Commonwealth Action Programme on the Harare Declaration, to promote adherence by member countries to the fundamental principles of democracy and human rights (as proclaimed in the 1991 Declaration). The Programme incorporated a framework of measures to be pursued in support of democratic processes and institutions, and actions to be taken in response to violations of the Harare Declaration principles, in particular the unlawful removal of a democratically elected government. A Commonwealth Ministerial Action Group on the Harare Declaration (CMAG) was to be established to implement this process and to assist the member country involved to comply with the Harare principles. On the basis of this Programme, the leaders suspended Nigeria from the Commonwealth with immediate effect, following the execution by that country's military Government of nine environmental and human rights protesters and a series of other violations of human rights. The meeting determined to expel Nigeria from the Commonwealth if no 'demonstrable progress' had been made towards the establishment of a democratic authority by the time of the next summit meeting. In addition, the Programme formulated measures to promote sustainable development in member countries, which was considered to be an important element in sustaining democracy, and to facilitate consensus-building within the international community.

In December 1995 CMAG convened for its inaugural meeting in London, United Kingdom, and considered efforts to restore democratic government in the three Commonwealth countries then under military regimes, i.e. The Gambia, Nigeria and Sierra Leone. At the second meeting of the Group, in April 1996, ministers commended the conduct of presidential and parliamentary elections in Sierra Leone and the announcement by The Gambia's military leaders that there would be a transition to civilian rule. In June a three-member CMAG delegation visited The Gambia to reaffirm Commonwealth support of the transition process in that country and to identify possible areas of further Commonwealth assistance. In August the Gambian authorities issued a decree removing the ban on political activities and parties, although shortly afterwards they prohibited certain parties and candidates involved in political life prior to the military take-over from contesting the elections. CMAG recommended that in such circumstances no Commonwealth observers should be sent to either the presidential or parliamentary elections, which were held in September 1996 and January 1997 respectively. Following the restoration of a civilian Government in early 1997, CMAG requested the Commonwealth Secretary-General to extend technical assistance to The Gambia in order to consolidate the democratic transition process. In April 1996 it was noted that the human rights situation in Nigeria had continued to deteriorate. CMAG, having pursued unsuccessful efforts to initiate dialogue with the Nigerian authorities, outlined a series of punitive and restrictive measures (including visa restrictions on members of the administration, a cessation of sporting contacts and an embargo on the export of armaments) that it would recommend for collective Commonwealth action in order to exert further pressure for reform in Nigeria. Following a meeting of a senior delegation of the Nigerian Government and CMAG in June, the Group agreed to postpone the implementation of the sanctions, pending progress on the dialogue. (Canada, however, determined, unilaterally, to impose the measures with immediate effect; the United Kingdom did so in accordance with a decision of the European Union to implement limited sanctions against Nigeria.) A proposed CMAG mission to Nigeria was postponed from August until November, owing to restrictions imposed by the military authorities on access to political detainees and other civilian activists in that country. In October 1997 Commonwealth heads of government endorsed CMAG's recommendation that the imposition of sanctions against Nigeria be held in abeyance, pending the scheduled completion of a transition programme towards democracy by October 1998. In October 1998 CMAG, convened for its 10th formal meeting, acknowledged Gen. Abdulsalam Abubakar's efforts towards restoring a democratic government and recommended that member states begin to remove sanctions against Nigeria and that it resume participation in certain Commonwealth activities. The Commonwealth Secretary-General subsequently announced a programme of technical assistance to support Nigeria in the planning and conduct of democratic elections. Staff teams from the Commonwealth Secretariat observed local government, and state and governorship elections, held in December and in January 1999, respectively. A Commonwealth Observer Group was also dispatched to Nigeria to monitor preparations and conduct of legislative and presidential elections, held in February. While the Group reported several irregularities in the conduct of the polling, it confirmed that, in general, the conditions had existed for free and fair elections and that the elections were a legitimate basis for the transition of power to a democratic, civilian government. In April CMAG voted to readmit Nigeria to full membership on 29 May, upon the installation of the new civilian administration.

In July 1997 the Group CMAG reiterated the Commonwealth Secretary-General's condemnation of a military coup in Sierra Leone in May, and decided that the country's participation in meetings of the Commonwealth should be suspended pending the restoration of a democratic government. In March 1998 CMAG commended the efforts of the Economic Community of West African States (ECOWAS) in restoring the democratically elected Government of President Ahmed Tejan Kabbah in Sierra Leone, and agreed to remove all restrictions on Sierra Leone's participation in Commonwealth activities. Later in that month, a representative mission of CMAG visited Sierra Leone to express its support for Kabbah's administration and to consider the country's needs in its process of reconstruction. At the CMAG meeting held in October members agreed that Sierra Leone should no longer be considered under the Group's mandate; however, they urged the Secretary-General to continue to assist that country in the process of national reconciliation and to facilitate negotiations with opposition forces to ensure a lasting cease-fire. A Special Envoy of the Secretary-General was appointed to co-operate with the UN, ECOWAS and the Organization of African Union (OAU, now African Union—AU) in monitoring the implementation of the Sierra Leone peace process, and the Commonwealth supported the rebuilding of the Sierra Leone police force. In September 2001 CMAG recommended that Sierra Leone be removed from its remit, but that the Secretary-General should continue to monitor developments there.

In 1999 the Commonwealth Secretary-General appointed a Special Envoy to broker an agreement in order to end a civil dispute in Honiara, Solomon Islands. An accord was signed in June, and it was envisaged that the Commonwealth would monitor its implementation. In October a Commonwealth Multinational Police Peace Monitoring Group was stationed in Solomon Islands; this was renamed the Commonwealth Multinational Police Assistance Group in February 2000. Following further internal unrest, however, the Group was disbanded. In June CMAG determined to send a new mission to Solomon Islands in order to facilitate negotiations between the opposing parties, to convey the Commonwealth's concern and to offer assistance. The Commonwealth welcomed the peace accord concluded in Solomon Islands in October, and extended its support to the International Peace Monitoring Team that was established to oversee implementation of the peace accords. CMAG welcomed the conduct of parliamentary elections held in Solomon Islands in December 2001. CMAG removed Solomon Islands from its agenda in December 2003 but was to continue to receive reports from the Secretary-General on future developments.

In mid-October 1999 a special meeting of CMAG was convened to consider the overthrow of the democratically elected Government of Pakistan in a military coup. The meeting condemned the action as a violation of Commonwealth principles and urged the new authorities to declare a timetable for the return to democratic rule. CMAG also resolved to send a four-member delegation to discuss this future course of action with the military regime. Pakistan was suspended from participation in meetings of the Commonwealth with immediate effect. The suspension, pending the restoration of a democratic government, was endorsed by heads of government, meeting in November, who requested that CMAG keep the situation in Pakistan under review.

In November 1999 heads of government also agreed to establish a new ministerial group on Guyana and to reconvene a ministerial committee on Belize, in order to facilitate dialogue in ongoing territorial disputes with neighbouring countries.

In June 2000, following the overthrow in May of the Fijian Government by a group of armed civilians, and the subsequent illegal detention of members of the elected administration, CMAG suspended Fiji's participation in meetings of the Commonwealth pending the restoration of democratic rule. In September, upon the request of CMAG, the Secretary-General appointed a Special Envoy to support efforts towards political dialogue and a return to democratic rule in Fiji. The Special Envoy undertook his first visit in December. In December 2001, following the staging of democratic legislative elections in August–September, Fiji was readmitted to Commonwealth meetings on the recommendation of CMAG. Fiji was removed from CMAG's agenda in May 2004, although the Group determined to continue to note developments there, as judgments were still pending in the Fiji Supreme Court on unresolved matters concerning the democratic process. In December 2006, following the overthrow of the Fijian Government by the military, an extraordinary meeting of CMAG determined that Fiji should once again be suspended from meetings of the Commonwealth, pending the reinstatement of democratic governance. In September 2007 the Group urged the Fijian authorities to hold a democratic general election by March 2009 and determined to keep the situation in that country under review; the March 2009 election deadline was not, however, met by the Fijian authorities. CMAG expressed support at the March meeting for ongoing political dialogue in Fiji, jointly mediated by the Commonwealth and the UN. In April the Commonwealth Secretary-General condemned the unconstitutional conduct of the Fijian authorities in abrogating the Constitution, dismissing the judiciary and announcing that democratic elections were to be postponed to 2014, following a judgment by Fiji's Court of Appeal declaring the appointment of the current interim government to be unlawful and urging the prompt restoration of democracy. Meeting at the end of July, CMAG demanded that the Fijian regime reactivate by 1 September 2009 the Commonwealth- and UN-mediated political dialogue process, leading to the staging of elections no later than October 2010. At the beginning of September 2009 the Commonwealth Secretary-General announced that the Fijian regime had not acted to meet CMAG's demands and that Fiji's Commonwealth membership was consequently fully suspended with immediate effect. Meeting in September 2010 and April 2011 CMAG reiterated its concern at the situation in Fiji and maintained the suspension of Fiji's Commonwealth membership.

In March 2001 CMAG resolved to send a ministerial mission to Zimbabwe, in order to relay to the government the Commonwealth's concerns at the ongoing violence and abuses of human rights in that country, as well as to discuss the conduct of parliamentary elections and extend technical assistance. The mission was rejected by the Zimbabwe Government, which queried the basis for CMAG's intervention in the affairs of an elected administration. In September, under the auspices of a group of Commonwealth foreign ministers partly derived from CMAG, the Zimbabwe Government signed the Abuja Agreement, which provided for the cessation of illegal occupations of white-owned farms and the resumption of the rule of law, in return for financial assistance to support the ongoing process of land reform in that country. In January 2002 CMAG expressed strong concern at the continuing violence and political intimidation in Zimbabwe. The summit of Commonwealth heads of government convened in early March (see below) also expressed concern at the situation in Zimbabwe, and, having decided on the principle that CMAG should be permitted to engage with any member Government deemed to be in breach of the organization's core values, mandated a Commonwealth Chairperson's Committee on Zimbabwe to determine appropriate action should an impending presidential election (scheduled to be held during that month) be found not to have been conducted freely and fairly. Following the publication by a Commonwealth observer team of an unfavourable report on the conduct of the election, the Committee decided to suspend Zimbabwe from meetings of the Commonwealth for one year. In March 2003 the Committee concluded that the suspension should remain in force pending consideration by the next summit of heads of government.

In March 2002, meeting in Coolum, near Brisbane, Australia, Commonwealth heads of government adopted the Coolum Declaration on the Commonwealth in the 21st Century: Continuity and Renewal, which reiterated commitment to the organization's principles and values. Leaders at the meeting condemned all forms of terrorism and endorsed a Plan of Action for combating international terrorism, establishing a Commonwealth Committee on Terrorism, convened at ministerial level, to oversee the implementation of the Plan. The leaders welcomed the Millennium Development Goals (MDGs) adopted by the UN General Assembly; requested the Secretary-General to constitute an expert group on implementing the objectives of the Fancourt Commonwealth Declaration on Globalization and People-Centred Development (see Economic Co-operation, below); pledged continued support for small states; and urged renewed efforts to combat the spread of HIV/AIDS. They also endorsed a Commonwealth Local Government Good Practice Scheme, to be managed by the Commonwealth Local Government Forum (established in 1995). The heads of government adopted a report on the future of the Commonwealth drafted by the High Level Review Group. The document recommended strengthening the Commonwealth's role in conflict prevention and resolution and support of democratic practices; enhancing the 'good offices' role of the Secretary-General; better promoting member states' economic and development needs; strengthening the organization's role in facilitating member states' access to international assistance; and promoting increased access to modern information and communications technologies. The meeting expanded CMAG's mandate to enable the Group to consider action against serious violations of the Commonwealth's core values perpetrated by elected administrations (such as that in Zimbabwe, see above) as well as by military regimes.

A Commonwealth team of observers dispatched to monitor legislative and provincial elections that were held in Pakistan, in October 2002, found them to have been well-organized and conducted in a largely transparent manner. The team made several recommendations on institutional and procedural issues. CMAG subsequently expressed concern over the promulgation of new legislation in Pakistan following the imposition earlier in the year of a number of extra-constitutional measures. CMAG determined that Pakistan should continue to be suspended from meetings of the Commonwealth, pending a review of the role and functioning of its democratic institutions. Pakistan's progress in establishing democratic institutions was welcomed by a meeting of CMAG in May 2003.

In November 2002 a Commonwealth Expert Group on Papua New Guinea, established in the previous month to review the electoral process in that country (in view of unsatisfactory legislative elections that were conducted there in July), made several recommendations aimed at enhancing the future management of the electoral process.

In December 2003 the meeting of heads of government, held in Abuja, Nigeria, resolved to maintain the suspension of Pakistan and Zimbabwe from participation in Commonwealth meetings. President Mugabe of Zimbabwe responded by announcing his country's immediate withdrawal from the Commonwealth and alleging a pro-Western bias within the grouping. Support for Zimbabwe's position was declared by a number of members, including South Africa, Mozambique, Namibia and Zambia. A Commonwealth committee, consisting of six heads of government, was established to monitor the situation in Zimbabwe.

In concluding the 2003 meeting heads of government issued the Aso Rock Commonwealth Declaration, which emphasized their commitment to strengthening development and democracy, and incorporated clear objectives in support of these goals. Priority areas identified included efforts to eradicate poverty and attain the MDGs, to strengthen democratic institutions, empower women, promote the involvement of civil society, combat corruption and recover assets (for which a working group was to be established), facilitate finance for development, address the spread of HIV/AIDS and other diseases, combat illicit trafficking in human beings, and promote education. The leaders also adopted a separate statement on multilateral trade, in particular in support of the stalled Doha Round of World Trade Organization negotiations.

In response to the earthquake and tsunami that devastated coastal areas of several Indian Ocean countries in late December 2004, the Commonwealth Secretary-General appealed for assistance from Commonwealth Governments for the mobilization of emergency humanitarian relief. In early January 2005 the Secretariat dispatched a Disaster Relief Co-ordinator to the Maldives to assess the needs of that country and to co-ordinate ongoing relief and rehabilitation activities, and later in that month the Secretariat sent emergency medical doctors from other member states to the Maldives. In mid-January, meeting during the fifth Summit of the Alliance of Small Island States, in Port Louis, Mauritius, the Secretaries-General of the Commonwealth, the Caribbean Community and Common Market (CARICOM), the Pacific Islands Forum and the Indian Ocean Commission determined to take collective action to strengthen the disaster-preparedness and response capacities of their member countries in the Caribbean, Pacific and Indian Ocean areas.

In May 2004 Pakistan was readmitted to the Commonwealth. However, CMAG urged the prompt separation of the military and civilian offices held by the President Musharraf, deeming this arrangement to be undemocratic. In February 2005 CMAG expressed serious concern that Musharraf had failed to relinquish the role of chief of army staff. Noting President Musharraf's own undertaking not to continue as chief of army staff beyond 2007, the Group stated its view that the two offices should not be combined in one person beyond the end (in that year) of the current presidential term. In November 2005, following Musharraf's re-election as President of Pakistan in early October, CMAG condemned the recent abrogation of Pakistan's Constitution and the institution there of a non-constitutional state of emergency; expressed grave concern at the recent dismissal of the Chief Justice and several other members of the judiciary and their placement under house arrest, and at other actions taken against lawyers, opposition politicians and civil society leaders, and at the suspension of all private media broadcasts and restrictions on the press; and noted with alarm a recent legislation that retrospectively gave military courts the right to try civilians on charges of 'anti-national activities'. While welcoming an announcement by President Musharraf that parliamentary elections would be staged in early 2008, CMAG maintained that such elections would only be credible if the state of emergency were revoked and constitutional rights restored. CMAG also noted with concern that Musharraf continued to retain the role of chief of army staff. The Group urged the Government of Pakistan to fulfil its obligations in accordance with Commonwealth principles through the implementation of the following measures: immediate repeal of the state of emergency, immediate release of political party leaders, lawyers, journalists and other activists detained under the state of emergency, and full restoration of the Constitution and of the independence of the judiciary; and for President Musharraf to relinquish his role as chief of army staff. Meeting on 22 November CMAG noted that these measures had not been implemented, as a consequence of which Pakistan was once again suspended from the Councils of the Commonwealth 'pending restoration of democracy and rule of law in the country'. President Musharraf relinquished his command of the Pakistan military at the end of November and the state of emergency was lifted in the following month. Meeting in May 2008 CMAG commended the transition to a democratically elected government in Pakistan, though it urged reform of the electoral system, and welcomed recent positive actions made by the Pakistan regime, including the relaxation of restrictions on the media and the release of political detainees. CMAG concluded that Pakistan should be readmitted to meetings of the Councils of the Commonwealth, and requested the Secretary-General to continue to provide technical assistance to the Pakistan Government towards strengthening the country's democratic institutions and processes.

The 2007 meeting of Commonwealth heads of government, convened in Kampala, Uganda, in November, issued the Munyonyo Statement on Respect and Understanding, which commended the work of the Commonwealth Commission on Respect and Understanding (established in 2005) and endorsed its recently published report entitled *Civil Paths to Peace* aimed at building tolerance and understanding of diversity.

In November 2009 Commonwealth heads of government, meeting in Trinidad and Tobago, welcomed recent progress in the discussion of border disputes between Belize and Guatemala, and between Guyana and Venezuela. They expressed support for negotiations on the reunification of Cyprus, initiated in 2008, and welcomed the recent agreement on power-sharing in Zimbabwe. They urged the renewal of commitment to the non-proliferation of nuclear weapons at the next Non-Proliferation Treaty review conference (convened in May 2010), and the negotiation of a comprehensive Arms Trade Treaty (on conventional weapons) at a conference to be held in 2012. Heads of government also urged the conclusion of a UN treaty on international terrorism and discussed combating piracy and human trafficking. In July 2010, in view of a decision of the 2009 heads of government meeting, a new Commonwealth Eminent Persons Group (EPG) was inaugurated, with a mandate to make recommendations on means of strengthening the organization; the EPG presented a report to the October 2011 heads of government meeting in which it recommended the appointment of a Commonwealth Commissioner for Democracy, Rule of Law and Human Rights. During June 2010 the Commonwealth Secretariat hosted the first Small States Biennial Conference.

Political Affairs Division: assists consultation among member governments on international and Commonwealth matters of common interest. In association with host governments, it organizes the meetings of heads of government and senior officials. The Division services committees and special groups set up by heads of government dealing with political matters. The Secretariat has observer status at the United Nations, and the Division manages a joint office in New York to enable small states, which would otherwise be unable to afford facilities there, to maintain a presence at the United Nations. The Division monitors political developments in the Commonwealth and international progress in such matters as disarmament and the Law of the Sea. It also undertakes research on matters of common interest to member governments, and reports back to them. The Division is involved in diplomatic training and consular co-operation.

In 1990 Commonwealth heads of government mandated the Division to support the promotion of democracy by monitoring the preparations for and conduct of parliamentary, presidential or other elections in member countries at the request of national governments. Commonwealth observer groups were dispatched to observe legislative and presidential elections in Uganda in February 2011; legislative and presidential elections in Nigeria in April; and presidential elections in Seychelles in May of that year.

Under the reorganization of the Secretariat in 2002 a Good Offices Section was established within the Division to strengthen and support the activities of the Secretary-General in addressing political conflict in member states and in assisting countries to adhere to the principles of the Harare Declaration. The Secretary-General's good offices may involve discreet 'behind the scenes' diplomacy to prevent or resolve conflict and assist other international efforts to promote political stability.

Human Rights Unit: undertakes activities in support of the Commonwealth's commitment to the promotion and protection of fundamental human rights. It develops programmes, publishes human rights materials, co-operates with other organizations working in the field of human rights, in particular within the UN system, advises the Secretary-General, and organizes seminars and meetings of experts; it provides training for police forces, magistrates and government officials in awareness of human rights. The Unit aims to integrate human rights standards within all divisions of the Secretariat.

Legal and Constitutional Affairs Division: promotes and facilitates co-operation and the exchange of information among member governments on legal matters and assists in combating financial and organized crime, in particular transborder criminal activities. It administers, jointly with the Commonwealth of Learning (see below), a distance training programme for legislative draftsmen and assists governments to reform national laws to meet the obligations of international conventions. The Division organizes the triennial meeting of ministers, Attorneys General and senior ministry officials concerned with the legal systems in Commonwealth countries. It has also initiated four Commonwealth schemes for co-operation on extradition, the protection of material cultural heritage, mutual assistance in criminal matters and the transfer of convicted offenders within the Commonwealth. It liaises with the Commonwealth Magistrates' and Judges' Association, the Commonwealth Legal Education Association, the Commonwealth Lawyers' Association (with which it helps to prepare the triennial Commonwealth Law Conference for the practising profession), the Commonwealth Association of Legislative Counsel, and with other international non-governmental organizations. The Division provides in-house legal advice for the Secretariat. The Commonwealth Law Bulletin, published four times a year, reports on legal developments in and beyond the Commonwealth. The Commonwealth Human Rights Law Digest (three a year) contains details of decisions relating to human rights cases from across the Commonwealth.

ECONOMIC AND ENVIRONMENTAL CO-OPERATION

In May 1998 the Commonwealth Secretary-General appealed to the Group of Eight industrialized nations (G8) to accelerate and expand the initiative to ease the debt burden of the most heavily indebted poor countries (HIPCs—see World Bank and IMF). In October Commonwealth finance ministers reiterated their appeal to international financial institutions to accelerate the HIPC initiative. The meeting also issued a Commonwealth Statement on the global economic crisis and endorsed proposals to help to counter the difficulties experienced by several countries. These measures included a mechanism to enable countries to suspend payments on all short-term financial obligations at a time of emergency without defaulting, assistance to governments to attract private capital and to manage capital market volatility, and the development of international codes of conduct regarding financial and monetary policies and corporate governance. In March 1999 the Commonwealth Secretariat hosted a joint IMF-World Bank conference to review the HIPC scheme and initiate a process of reform. In November Commonwealth heads of government, meeting in South Africa, declared their support for measures undertaken by the World Bank and IMF to enhance the HIPC initiative. At the end of an informal retreat the leaders adopted the Fancourt Commonwealth Declaration on Globalization and People-Centred Development, which emphasized the need for a more equitable spread of wealth generated by the process of globalization, and expressed a renewed commitment to the elimination of all forms of discrimination, the promotion of people-centred development and capacity-building, and efforts to ensure that developing countries benefit from future multilateral trade liberalization measures. In June 2002 the Commonwealth Secretary-General urged more generous funding of the HIPC initiative. Meetings of ministers of finance from Commonwealth member countries participating in the HIPC initiative are convened twice a year, as the Commonwealth Ministerial Debt Sustainability Forum. The Secretariat aims to assist HIPCs and other small economies through its Debt Recording and Management System (DRMS), which was first used in 1985 and updated in 2002; in July 2010 Liberia became the 60th country to join the System. In July 2005 the Commonwealth Secretary-General welcomed an initiative of the G8 to eliminate the debt of those HIPCs that had reached their completion point in the process, in addition to a commitment substantially to increase aid to Africa.

In February 1998 the Commonwealth Secretariat hosted a meeting of intergovernmental organizations to promote co-operation between small island states and the formulation of a unified policy approach to international fora. A second meeting was convened in March 2001, where discussions focused on the forthcoming WTO ministerial meeting and OECD's Harmful Tax Competition Initiative. In September 2000 Commonwealth finance ministers, meeting in Malta, reviewed the OECD initiative and agreed that the measures, affecting many member countries with offshore financial centres, should not be imposed on governments. The ministers mandated the involvement of the Commonwealth Secretariat in efforts to resolve the dispute; a joint working group was subsequently established by the Secretariat with the OECD. In April 2002 a meeting on international co-operation in the financial services sector, attended by representatives of international and regional organizations, donors and senior officials from Commonwealth countries, was held under Commonwealth auspices in Saint Lucia. In September 2005 Commonwealth finance ministers, meeting in Barbados, considered new guidelines for Public Financial Management Reform.

In November 2005 Commonwealth heads of government issued the Malta Declaration on Networking the Commonwealth for Development, expressing their commitment to making available to all the benefits of new technologies and to using information technology networks to enhance the effectiveness of the Commonwealth in supporting development. The meeting endorsed a new Commonwealth Action Programme for the Digital Divide and approved the establishment of a special fund to enable implementation of the programme's objectives. Accordingly a Commonwealth Connects programme was established in August 2006 to develop partnerships and help to strengthen the use of and access to information technology in all Commonwealth countries. The 2005 Heads of Government Meeting also issued the Valletta Statement on Multilateral Trade, emphasizing their concerns that the Doha Round of WTO negotiations proceed steadily, on a development-oriented agenda, to a successful conclusion and reiterating their objectives of achieving a rules-based and equitable international trading system. A separate statement drew attention to the specific needs and challenges of small states and urged continued financial and technical support, in particular for those affected by natural disasters.

The Commonwealth Climate Change Action Plan, adopted by heads of government in November 2007, acknowledged that climate change posed a serious threat to the very existence of some small island states within the Commonwealth, and to the low-lying coastal areas of others. It offered unqualified support for the UN Framework Convention on Climate Change, and recognized the need to overcome technical, economic and policy-making barriers to reducing carbon emissions, to using renewable energy, and to increasing energy efficiency. The Plan undertook to assist developing member states in international negotiations on climate change; to support improved land use management, including the use of forest resources; to investigate the 'carbon footprint' of agricultural exports from member countries; to increase support for the management of natural disasters in member countries; and to provide technical assistance to help least developed members and small states to assess the implications of climate change and adapt accordingly. A high-level meeting on climate finance, convened in London, in January 2011, determined to establish a working group to advance climate-related Commonwealth initiatives; and to integrate work on climate-related finance mechanisms into the next (2012–16) strategic plan.

In June 2008 the Commonwealth issued the Marlborough House Statement on Reform of International Institutions, declaring that ongoing global financial turbulence and soaring food and fuel prices highlighted the poor responsiveness of some international organizations mandated to promote economic stability, and determining to identify underlying principles and actions required to reform the international system. In November 2009 heads of government reiterated the need for reform in the UN system, demanding greater representation for developing countries in international economic decision-making, with particular reference to the IMF and the World Bank. They expressed concern that many Commonwealth countries were falling behind the MDG targets, and resolved to strengthen existing networks of co-operation: in particular, they undertook to take measures to improve the quality of data used in policy-making, and to strengthen the links between research and policy-making. A new Commonwealth Partnership Platform Portal was to provide practical support for sharing ideas and best practices. Heads of government also undertook to promote investment in science, technology and innovation.

Economic Affairs Division: organizes and services the annual meetings of Commonwealth ministers of finance and the ministerial group on small states and assists in servicing the biennial meetings of heads of government and periodic meetings of environment ministers. It engages in research and analysis on economic issues of interest to member governments and organizes seminars and conferences of government officials and experts. The Division actively supports developing Commonwealth countries to participate in the Doha Round of multilateral trade negotiations and is assisting the ACP group of countries to negotiate economic partnership agreements with the European Union. It continues to help developing countries to strengthen their links with international capital markets and foreign investors. The Division also services groups of experts on economic affairs that have been commissioned by governments to report on, among other things, protectionism; obstacles to the North-South negotiating process; reform of the international financial and trading system; the debt crisis; management of technological change; the impact of change on the development process; environmental issues; women and structural adjustment; and youth unemployment. A separate section within the Division addresses the

specific needs of small states and provides technical assistance. The work of the section covers a range of issues including trade, vulnerability, environment, politics and economics. In 2000 a Commonwealth Secretariat/World Bank Joint Task Force on Small States finalized a report entitled *Small States: Meeting Challenges in the Global Economy*. A review of the report was issued in 2005. In June 2010 the first Commonwealth Biennial Small States Conference was convened, in London, comprising representatives of small states from the Africa, Asia-Pacific and Caribbean regions. In January 2011 a new Commonwealth Small States Office was inaugurated in Geneva, Switzerland; the Office was to provide subsidized office space for the Geneva-based diplomatic missions of Commonwealth small states, and business facilities for both diplomatic personnel and visiting delegations from small member states. The Economic Affairs Division also co-ordinates the Secretariat's environmental work and manages the Iwokrama International Centre for Rainforest Conservation and Development.

The Division supported the establishment of a Commonwealth Private Investment Initiative (CPII) to mobilize capital, on a regional basis, for investment in newly privatized companies and in small and medium-sized businesses in the private sector. The first regional fund under the CPII, the Commonwealth Africa Investment Fund (Comafin), was operational during the period July 1996–end-December 2006, and made 19 investments (of which three were subsequently written off) to assist businesses across nine sectors in seven countries in sub-Saharan Africa. A Pan-Commonwealth Africa Partners Fund was launched in 2002, which aimed to help existing businesses expand to become regional or pan-African in scope. In August 1997 an investment fund for the Pacific Islands (known as the Kula Fund) was launched, with an initial capital of US $15.0m.; a successor fund (Kula Fund II), with financing of some $20m., was launched in October 2005, with the aim of injecting capital into the smaller Pacific Island countries. A $200m. South Asia Regional Fund (SARF) was established at the heads of government meeting in October 1997. In October 1998 the Tiona Fund for the Commonwealth Caribbean was inaugurated, at a meeting of Commonwealth finance ministers; this was subsequently absorbed into the Caribbean Investment Fund (established in 1993 by member states of CARICOM).

SOCIAL WELFARE

Social Transformation Programmes Division: consists of three sections concerned with education, gender and health.

The **Education Section** arranges specialist seminars, workshops and co-operative projects, and commissions studies in areas identified by ministers of education, whose meetings it also services. Its areas of work include improving the quality of and access to basic education; strengthening science, technology and mathematics education in formal and non-formal areas of education; improving the quality of management in institutions of higher learning and basic education; improving the performance of teachers; strengthening examination assessment systems; and promoting the movement of students between Commonwealth countries. The Section also promotes the elimination of gender disparities in education, support for education in difficult circumstances, such as areas affected by conflict or natural disasters, and mitigating the impact of HIV and AIDS on education. It attempts to address the problems of scale particular to smaller member countries, and encourages collaboration between governments, the private sector and other non-governmental organizations.

The **Gender Affairs Section** is responsible for the implementation of the Commonwealth Plan of Action for Gender Equality, covering the period 2005–15, which succeeded the Commonwealth Plan of Action on Gender and Development (adopted in 1995 and updated in 2000). The Plan of Action supports efforts towards achieving the MDGs, and the objectives of gender equality adopted by the 1995 Beijing Declaration and Platform for Action and the follow-up Beijing + 5 review conference, held in 2000, and Beijing + 10 in 2005. Gender equality, poverty eradication, promotion of human rights, and strengthening democracy are recognized as intrinsically inter-related, and the Plan has a particular focus on the advancement of gender mainstreaming in the following areas: democracy, peace and conflict; human rights and law; poverty eradication and economic empowerment; and HIV/AIDS.

The **Health Section** organizes ministerial, technical and expert group meetings and workshops, to promote co-operation on health matters, and the exchange of health information and expertise. The Section commissions relevant studies and provides professional and technical advice to member countries and to the Secretariat. It also supports the work of regional health organizations and promotes health for all people in Commonwealth countries.

The **Youth Affairs Division**, reporting directly to a Deputy Secretary-General, was established within the Secretariat in 2002. The unit acquired divisional status in 2004.

The Division administers the Commonwealth Youth Programme (CYP), which was initiated in 1973 to promote the involvement of young people in the economic and social development of their countries. The CYP, funded through separate voluntary contributions from governments, was awarded a budget of £2.8m. for 2009/10. The Programme's activities are in three areas: Youth Enterprise and Sustainable Livelihoods; Governance, Development and Youth Networks; and Youth Work Education and Training. Regional centres are located in Zambia (for Africa), India (for Asia), Guyana (for the Caribbean), and Solomon Islands (for the Pacific). The Programme administers a Youth Study Fellowship scheme, a Youth Project Fund, a Youth Exchange Programme (in the Caribbean), and a Youth Development Awards Scheme. It also holds conferences and seminars, carries out research and disseminates information. The CYP Diploma in Youth Development Work is offered by partner institutions in 45 countries, primarily through distance education. The Commonwealth Youth Credit Initiative, initiated in 1995, provides funds and advice for young entrepreneurs setting up small businesses. A Plan of Action for Youth Empowerment, covering the period 2007–15, was approved by the sixth meeting of Commonwealth ministers responsible for youth affairs, held in Nassau, Bahamas, in May 2006. The first Commonwealth Youth Games was held in Edinburgh, United Kingdom in 2000, and has been convened every four years since. The seventh Commonwealth Youth Forum was convened in Trinidad and Tobago, in November 2009.

TECHNICAL ASSISTANCE

Commonwealth Fund for Technical Co-operation (CFTC): f. 1971 to facilitate the exchange of skills between member countries and to promote economic and social development; it is administered by the Commonwealth Secretariat and financed by voluntary subscriptions from member governments. The CFTC responds to requests from member governments for technical assistance, such as the provision of experts for short- or medium-term projects, advice on economic or legal matters, and training programmes. Public sector development, allowing member states to build on their capacities, is the principal element in CFTC activities. This includes assistance for improvement of supervision and combating corruption; improving economic management, for example by advising on exports and investment promotion; strengthening democratic institutions, such as electoral commissions; and improvement of education and health policies. The CFTC also administers the Langkawi awards for the study of environmental issues, which is funded by the Canadian Government; the CFTC budget for 2009/10 amounted to £29.2m, supplemented by external resources through partnerships.

CFTC activities are mainly implemented by the following divisions:

Governance and Institutional Development Division: strengthens good governance in member countries, through advice, training and other expertise in order to build capacity in national public institutions. The Division administers the Commonwealth Service Abroad Programme (CSAP), which is funded by the CFTC. The Programme extends short-term technical assistance through highly qualified volunteers. The main objectives of the scheme are to provide expertise, training and exposure to new technologies and practices, to promote technology transfers and sharing of experiences and knowledge, and to support community workshops and other local activities.

Special Advisory Services Division: provides advice and technical assistance in four principal areas: debt management; economic and legal services; enterprise and agriculture; and trade.

Finance

The Secretariat's budget for 2009/10 amounted to £15.0m. Member governments meet the cost of the Secretariat through subscriptions on a scale related to income and population.

Publications

Advisory (annual newsletter of the Special Advisory Services Division).

Global (electronic magazine).

Commonwealth News (weekly e-mail newsletter).

Report of the Commonwealth Secretary-General (every 2 years).

Numerous reports, studies and papers (catalogue available).

Commonwealth Organizations

(in the United Kingdom, unless otherwise stated)

The two principal intergovernmental organizations established by Commonwealth member states, apart from the Commonwealth Secretariat itself, are the Commonwealth Foundation and the Commonwealth of Learning. In 2011 there were nearly 90 other professional or advocacy organizations bearing the Commonwealth's name and associated with or accredited to the Commonwealth, a selection of which are listed below.

PRINCIPAL INTERGOVERNMENTAL ORGANIZATIONS

Commonwealth Foundation: Marlborough House, Pall Mall, London, SW1Y 5HY; tel. (20) 7930-3783; fax (20) 7839-8157; e-mail geninfo@commonwealth.int; internet www.commonwealthfoundation.com; f. 1966; intergovernmental body promoting people-to-people interaction, and collaboration within the non-governmental sector of the Commonwealth; supports non-governmental organizations, professional associations and Commonwealth arts and culture; awards an annual Commonwealth Writers' Prize; funds are provided by Commonwealth govts; Chair. SIMONE DE COMARMOND (Seychelles); Dir Dr MARK COLLINS (United Kingdom); publ. *Commonwealth People* (quarterly).

Commonwealth of Learning (COL): 1055 West Hastings St, Suite 1200, Vancouver, BC V6E 2E9, Canada; tel. (604) 775-8200; fax (604) 775-8210; e-mail info@col.org; internet www.col.org; f. 1987 by Commonwealth Heads of Government to promote the devt and sharing of distance education and open learning resources, including materials, expertise and technologies, throughout the Commonwealth and in other countries; implements and assists with national and regional educational programmes; acts as consultant to international agencies and national governments; conducts seminars and studies on specific educational needs; core financing for COL is provided by Commonwealth governments on a voluntary basis; COL had a budget of C $11.2m. for the two-year period 2009–10; Pres. and CEO Sir JOHN DANIEL (Canada/UK); publs *Connections, EdTech News*.

The following represents a selection of other Commonwealth organizations:

ADMINISTRATION AND PLANNING

Commonwealth Association for Public Administration and Management (CAPAM): 1075 Bay St, Suite 402, Toronto, ON M5S 2B1, Canada; tel. (416) 920-3337; fax (416) 920-6574; e-mail capam@capam.org; internet www.capam.org; f. 1994; aims to promote sound management of the public sector in Commonwealth countries and to assist those countries undergoing political or financial reforms; an international awards programme to reward innovation within the public sector was introduced in 1997, and is awarded every 2 years; more than 1,200 individual mems and 80 institutional memberships in some 80 countries; Pres. GERALDINE FRASER-MOLEKETI (South Africa); Exec. Dir and CEO DAVID WAUNG.

Commonwealth Association of Planners: c/o Royal Town Planning Institute in Scotland, 18 Atholl Crescent, Edinburgh, EH3 8HQ; tel. (131) 229-9628; fax (131) 229-9332; e-mail annette.odonnell@rtpi.org.uk; internet www.commonwealth-planners.org; aims to develop urban and regional planning in Commonwealth countries, to meet the challenges of urbanization and the sustainable development of human settlements.

Commonwealth Local Government Forum: 16A Northumberland Ave, London, WC2N 5AP; tel. (20) 7389-1490; fax (20) 7389-1499; e-mail info@clgf.org.uk; works to promote democratic local government in Commonwealth countries, and to encourage good practice through conferences, programmes, research and the provision of information; regional offices in Fiji, India and South Africa.

AGRICULTURE AND FORESTRY

Commonwealth Forestry Association: Crib, Dinchope, Craven Arms, Shropshire, SY7 9JJ; tel. (1588) 672868; fax (870) 0116645; e-mail cfa@cfa-international.org; internet www.cfa-international.org; f. 1921; produces, collects and circulates information relating to world forestry and promotes good management, use and conservation of forests and forest lands throughout the world; mems: 1,200; Pres. DAVID BILLS (Australia/UK); publs *International Forestry Review* (quarterly), *Commonwealth Forestry News* (quarterly), *Commonwealth Forestry Handbook* (irregular).

Royal Agricultural Society of the Commonwealth: Ingliston House, Royal Highland Centre, Edinburgh, EH28 8NB; tel. (131) 335-6200; fax (131) 335 6229; e-mail rasc@commagshow.org; internet www.commagshow.org; f. 1957 to promote development of agricultural shows and good farming practice, in order to improve incomes and food production in Commonwealth countries.

Standing Committee on Commonwealth Forestry: Forestry Commission, 231 Corstorphine Rd, Edinburgh, EH12 7AT; tel. (131) 314-6137; fax (131) 316-4344; e-mail libby.jones@forestry.gsi.gov.uk; internet www.cfc2010.org; f. 1923 to provide continuity between Confs, and to provide a forum for discussion on any forestry matters of common interest to mem. govts which may be brought to the Cttee's notice by any mem. country or organization; 54 mems; June 2010 Conference: Edinburgh, United Kingdom; Sec. LIBBY JONES; publ. *Newsletter* (quarterly).

BUSINESS

Commonwealth Business Council: 18 Pall Mall, London, SW1Y 5LU; tel. (20) 7024-8200; fax (20) 7024-8201; e-mail info@cbcglobal.org; internet www.cbcglobal.org; f. 1997 by the Commonwealth Heads of Government Meeting to promote co-operation between governments and the private sector in support of trade, investment and development; the Council aims to identify and promote investment opportunities, in particular in Commonwealth developing countries, to support countries and local businesses to work within the context of globalization, to promote capacity-building and the exchange of skills and knowledge (in particular through its Information Communication Technologies for Development programme), and to encourage co-operation among Commonwealth members; promotes good governance; supports the process of multilateral trade negotiations and other liberalization of trade and services; represents the private sector at government level; Dir-Gen. and CEO Dr MOHAN KAUL.

COMMONWEALTH STUDIES

Institute of Commonwealth Studies: South Block, 2nd Floor, Senate House, Malet Street, London, WC1E 7HU; tel. (20) 7862-8844; fax (20) 7862-8813; e-mail ics@sas.ac.uk; internet commonwealth.sas.ac.uk/; f. 1949 to promote advanced study of the Commonwealth; provides a library and meeting place for postgraduate students and academic staff engaged in research in this field; offers postgraduate teaching; Dir Prof. PHILIP MURPHY; publs *Annual Report*, *Collected Seminar Papers*, *Newsletter*, *Theses in Progress in Commonwealth Studies*.

EDUCATION AND CULTURE

Association of Commonwealth Universities (ACU): Woburn House, 20-24 Tavistock Sq., London, WC1H 9HF; tel. (20) 7380-6700; fax (20) 7387-2655; e-mail info@acu.ac.uk; internet www.acu.ac.uk; f. 1913; promotes international co-operation and understanding; provides assistance with staff and student mobility and development programmes; researches and disseminates information about universities and relevant policy issues; organizes major meetings of Commonwealth universities and their representatives; acts as a liaison office and information centre; administers scholarship and fellowship schemes; operates a policy research unit; mems: c. 500 universities in 36 Commonwealth countries or regions; Sec.-Gen. Prof. JOHN TARRANT; publs include *Yearly Review*, *Commonwealth Universities Yearbook*, *ACU Bulletin* (quarterly), *Who's Who of Executive Heads: Vice-Chancellors, Presidents, Principals and Rectors*, *International Awards*, student information papers (study abroad series).

Commonwealth Association of Museums: R.R.1, De Winton, Alberta, T0L 0X0, Canada; tel. and fax (403) 938-3190; e-mail rvinel@fclc.com; internet www.maltwood.uvic.ca/cam; f. 1985; professional asscn working for the improvement of museums throughout the Commonwealth; encourages links between museums and assists professional development and training through distance learning, workshops and seminars; general assembly held every three or four years; c. 700 mems in 32 Commonwealth countries; Pres. Prof. LOIS IRVINE.

Commonwealth Association of Science, Technology and Mathematics Educators (CASTME): c/o Dr Egan, Faculty of Education, University of Winchester, SO22 4NR; e-mail Bridget.Egan@winchester.ac.uk; internet www.castme.org; f. 1974; special emphasis is given to the social significance of education in these subjects; organizes an Awards Scheme to promote effective teaching and learning in these subjects, and biennial regional seminars; Chair. BRIDGET EGAN; publ. *CASTME Journal* (3 a year).

Commonwealth Council for Educational Administration and Management: Suite 161, Private Bag X9, Melville 2109, Johannesburg, South Africa; tel. (18) 302200; fax (866) 312639; e-mail zandileK@mgsl.co.za; internet www.cceam.org; f. 1970; aims to foster quality in professional development and links among educational administrators; holds nat. and regional confs, as well as visits and seminars; mems: 24 affiliated groups representing 3,000 persons; Pres. ZANDILE KUNENE; publ. *International Studies in Educational Administration* (2 a year).

Commonwealth Education Trust: New Zealand House, 80 Haymarket, London, SW1Y 4TQ; tel. (20) 7024-9822; fax (20) 7024-9833; e-mail info@cet1886.org; internet www.cet1886.org; f. 2007 as the

successor trust to the Commonwealth Institute; funds the Centre of Commonwealth Education, established in 2004 as part of Cambridge University; supports the Lifestyle of Our Kids (LOOK) project initiated in 2005 by the Commonwealth Institute (Australia); Chief Exec. JUDY CURRY.

League for the Exchange of Commonwealth Teachers: 7 Lion Yard, Tremadoc Rd, London, SW4 7NQ; tel. (870) 7702636; fax (870) 7702637; e-mail info@lect.org.uk; internet www.lect.org.uk; f. 1901; promotes educational exchanges between teachers throughout the Commonwealth; Dir ANNA TOMLINSON; publ. *Annual Review*.

HEALTH AND WELFARE

Commonwealth Medical Trust (COMMAT): BMA House, Tavistock Sq., London, WC1H 9JP; tel. (20) 7272-8492; fax (1689) 890609; e-mail office@commat.org; internet www.commat.org; f. 1962 (as the Commonwealth Medical Association) for the exchange of information; provision of tech. co-operation and advice; formulation and maintenance of a code of ethics; promotes the Right to Health; liaison with WHO and other UN agencies on health issues; meetings of its Council are held every three years; mems: medical asscns in Commonwealth countries; Dir MARIANNE HASLEGRAVE.

Commonwealth Nurses' Federation: c/o Royal College of Nursing, 20 Cavendish Sq., London, W1G 0RN; tel. (20) 7647-3593; fax (20) 7647-3413; e-mail jill@commonwealthnurses.org; internet www.commonwealthnurses.org; f. 1973 to link national nursing and midwifery asscns in Commonwealth countries; aims to influence health policy, develop nursing networks, improve nursing education and standards, and strengthen leadership; Exec. Sec. JILL ILIFFE.

Commonwealth Organization for Social Work: Melbourne, Australia; tel. (3) 9489-3774; e-mail cosw@aasw.asn.au; internet www.sasw.org.sg/cosw; promotes communication and collaboration between social workers in Commonwealth countries; provides network for information and sharing of expertise.

Commonwealth Pharmacists Association: 1 Lambeth High St, London, SE1 7JN; tel. (20) 7572-2364; fax (20) 7572-2508; e-mail admin@commonwealthpharmacy.org; internet www.commonwealthpharmacy.org; f. 1970 (as the Commonwealth Pharmaceutical Association) to promote the interests of pharmaceutical sciences and the profession of pharmacy in the Commonwealth; to maintain high professional standards, encourage links between members and the creation of nat. asscns; and to facilitate the dissemination of information; holds confs (every four years) and regional meetings; mems: pharmaceutical asscns from over 40 Commonwealth countries; Pres. IVAN KOTZÉ; publ. *Quarterly Newsletter*.

Commonwealth Society for the Deaf (Sound Seekers): 34 Buckingham Palace Rd, London, SW1W 0RE; tel. (20) 7233-5700; fax (20) 7233-5800; e-mail sound.seekers@btinternet.com; internet www.sound-seekers.org.uk; f. 1959; undertakes initiatives to establish audiology services in developing Commonwealth countries, including mobile clinics to provide outreach services; aims to educate local communities in aural hygiene and the prevention of ear infection and deafness; provides audiological equipment and organizes the training of audiological maintenance technicians; conducts research into the causes and prevention of deafness; Chief Exec. GARY WILLIAMS; publ. *Annual Report*.

Royal Commonwealth Ex-Services League: Haig House, 199 Borough High St, London, SE1 1AA; tel. (20) 3207-2413; fax (20) 3207-2115; e-mail mgordon-roe@commonwealthveterans.org.uk; internet www.commonwealthveterans.org.uk; links the ex-service orgs in the Commonwealth, assists ex-servicemen of the Crown who are resident abroad; holds conferences every 4 years; 56 mem. orgs in 48 countries; Grand Pres. HRH The Duke of EDINBURGH; publ. *Annual Report*.

Sightsavers (Royal Commonwealth Society for the Blind): Grosvenor Hall, Bolnore Rd, Haywards Heath, West Sussex, RH16 4BX; tel. (1444) 446600; fax (1444) 446688; e-mail info@sightsavers.org; internet www.sightsavers.org; f. 1950 to prevent blindness and restore sight in developing countries, and to provide education and community-based training for incurably blind people; operates in collaboration with local partners in some 30 developing countries, with high priority given to training local staff; Chair. Lord NIGEL CRISP; Chief Exec. Dr CAROLINE HARPER; publ. *Sight Savers News*.

INFORMATION AND THE MEDIA

Commonwealth Broadcasting Association: 17 Fleet St, London, EC4Y 1AA; tel. (20) 7583-5550; fax (20) 7583-5549; e-mail cba@cba.org.uk; internet www.cba.org.uk; f. 1945; gen. confs are held every two years (2010: Johannesburg, South Africa); mems: c. 100 in more than 50 countries; Pres. ABUBAKAR JIJIWA; Sec.-Gen. ELIZABETH SMITH; publs *Commonwealth Broadcaster* (quarterly), *Commonwealth Broadcaster Directory* (annually).

Commonwealth Journalists Association: c/o Canadian Newspaper Association, 890 Yonge St, Suite 200, Toronto, ON M4W 3P4, Canada; tel. (416) 575-5377; fax (416) 923-7206; e-mail cantleyb@commonwealthjournalists.com; internet www.commonwealthjournalists.com; f. 1978 to promote co-operation between journalists in Commonwealth countries, organize training facilities and confs, and foster understanding among Commonwealth peoples; Exec. Dir BRYAN CANTLEY; publ. *Newsletter* (3 a year).

CPU Media Trust (Association of Commonwealth Newspapers, News Agencies and Periodicals): e-mail webform@cpu.org.uk; internet www.cpu.org.uk; f. 2008 as a 'virtual' organization charged with carrying on the aims of the Commonwealth the Commonwealth Press Union (CPU, f. 1950, terminated 2008); promotes the welfare of the Commonwealth press; Chair. GUY BLACK.

LAW

Commonwealth Lawyers' Association: c/o Institute of Advanced Legal Studies, 17 Russell Sq., London, WC1B 5DR; tel. (20) 7862-8824; fax (20) 7862-8816; e-mail cla@sas.ac.uk; internet www.commonwealthlawyers.com; f. 1983 (fmrly the Commonwealth Legal Bureau); seeks to maintain and promote the rule of law throughout the Commonwealth, by ensuring that the people of the Commonwealth are served by an independent and efficient legal profession; upholds professional standards and promotes the availability of legal services; organizes the biannual Commonwealth Law Conference; Sec.-Gen. CLAIRE MARTIN; publs *The Commonwealth Lawyer*, *Clarion*.

Commonwealth Legal Advisory Service: c/o British Institute of International and Comparative Law, Charles Clore House, 17 Russell Sq., London, WC1B 5DR; tel. (20) 7862-5151; fax (20) 7862-5152; e-mail info@biicl.org; internet www.biicl.org; f. 1962; financed by the British Institute and by contributions from Commonwealth govts; provides research facilities for Commonwealth govts and law reform commissions; Chair. Rt Hon. Lord BROWNE-WILKINSON; publ. *New Memoranda* series.

Commonwealth Legal Education Association: c/o Legal and Constitutional Affairs Division, Commonwealth Secretariat, Marlborough House, Pall Mall, London, SW1Y 5HX; tel. (20) 7747-6415; fax (20) 7004-3649; e-mail clea@commonwealth.int; internet www.clea-web.com; f. 1971 to promote contacts and exchanges and to provide information regarding legal education; Gen. Sec. SELINA GOULBOURNE; publ. *Commonwealth Legal Education Association Newsletter* (3 a year).

Commonwealth Magistrates' and Judges' Association: Uganda House, 58–59 Trafalgar Sq., London, WC2N 5DX; tel. (20) 7976-1007; fax (20) 7976-2394; e-mail info@cmja.org; internet www.cmja.org; f. 1970 to advance the administration of the law by promoting the independence of the judiciary, to further education in law and crime prevention and to disseminate information; confs and study tours; corporate membership for asscns of the judiciary or courts of limited jurisdiction; assoc. membership for individuals; Pres. Hon. Mrs Justice NORMA WADE-MILLER; Exec. Vice-Pres. Sir PHILIP BAILHACHE; publs *Commonwealth Judicial Journal* (2 a year), *CMJA News*.

PARLIAMENTARY AFFAIRS

Commonwealth Parliamentary Association: Westminster House, Suite 700, 7 Millbank, London, SW1P 3JA; tel. (20) 7799-1460; fax (20) 7222-6073; e-mail hq.sec@cpahq.org; internet www.cpahq.org; f. 1911 to promote understanding and co-operation between Commonwealth parliamentarians; organization: Exec. Cttee of 35 MPs responsible to annual Gen. Assembly; 176 brs in national, state, provincial and territorial parliaments and legislatures throughout the Commonwealth; holds annual Commonwealth Parliamentary Confs and seminars; also regional confs and seminars; Sec.-Gen. Dr WILLIAM F. SHIJA; publ. *The Parliamentarian* (quarterly).

SCIENCE AND TECHNOLOGY

Commonwealth Association of Architects: POB 508, Edgware, Middx, HA8 9XZ; tel. and fax (20) 8951-0550; e-mail info@comarchitect.org; internet comarchitect.org; f. 1964; an asscn of 38 socs of architects in various Commonwealth countries; objectives: to facilitate the reciprocal recognition of professional qualifications; to provide a clearing house for information on architectural practice; and to encourage collaboration. Plenary confs every three years; regional confs are also held; Exec. Dir TONY GODWIN; publs *Handbook, Objectives and Procedures: CAA Schools Visiting Boards, Architectural Education in the Commonwealth* (annotated bibliography of research), *CAA Newsnet* (2 a year), a survey and list of schools of architecture.

Commonwealth Engineers' Council: c/o Institution of Civil Engineers, 1 Great George St, London, SW1P 3AA; tel. (20) 7665-2005; fax (20) 7223-1806; e-mail neil.bailey@ice.org.uk; internet www.ice.org.uk/cec; f. 1946; links and represents engineering institutions across the Commonwealth, providing them with an opportunity to exchange views on collaboration and mutual support; holds international and regional conferences and workshops; mems: 45 institutions in 44 countries; Pres. TOM FOULKES; Sec.-Gen. NEIL BAILEY.

Commonwealth Telecommunications Organization: 26–28 Hammersmith Grove, London, W6 7BA; tel. (870) 7777697; fax (870) 0345626; e-mail info@cto.int; internet www.cto.int; f. 1967 as an international development partnership between Commonwealth and non-Commonwealth governments, business and civil society organizations; aims to help to bridge the digital divide and to achieve social and economic development by delivering to developing countries knowledge-sharing programmes in the use of information and communication technologies in the specific areas of telecommunications, IT, broadcasting and the internet; CEO Dr EKWOW SPIO-GARBRAH; publs *CTO Update* (quarterly), *Annual Report*, *Research Reports*.

Conference of Commonwealth Meteorologists: c/o International Branch, Meteorological Office, FitzRoy Rd, Exeter, EX1 3PB; tel. (1392) 886435; fax (1392) 885681; e-mail commonwealth@metoffice.gov.uk; internet internet www.commonwealthmet.org; links national meteorological and hydrological services in Commonwealth countries; conferences held every four years.

SPORT AND YOUTH

Commonwealth Games Federation: 2nd Floor, 138 Piccadilly, London, W1J 7NR; tel. (20) 7491-8801; fax (20) 7409-7803; e-mail info@thecgf.com; internet www.thecgf.com; the Games were first held in 1930 and are now held every four years; participation is limited to competitors representing the mem. countries of the Commonwealth; 2010 games: New Delhi, India, in October; 2014 games: Glasgow, United Kingdom; mems: 72 affiliated bodies; Pres. MICHAEL FENNELL; CEO MICHAEL HOOPER.

Commonwealth Youth Exchange Council: 7 Lion Yard, Tremadoc Rd, London, SW4 7NQ; tel. (20) 7498-6151; fax (20) 7622-4365; e-mail mail@cyec.org.uk; internet www.cyec.org.uk; f. 1970; promotes contact between groups of young people of the United Kingdom and other Commonwealth countries by means of educational exchange visits, provides information for organizers and allocates grants; provides host governments with technical assistance for delivery of the Commonwealth Youth Forum, held every two years (2009: Trinidad and Tobago); mems: 222 orgs, 134 local authorities, 88 voluntary bodies; Chief Exec. V. S. G. CRAGGS; publs *Contact* (handbook), *Exchange* (newsletter), *Final Communiqués* (of the Commonwealth Youth Forums), *Safety and Welfare* (guidelines for Commonwealth Youth Exchange groups).

RELATIONS WITHIN THE COMMONWEALTH

Commonwealth Countries League: 37 Priory Ave, Sudbury, Middx, HA0 2SB; tel. (20) 8248- 3275; e-mail rennie158@btinternet.com; internet www.ccl-int.org; f. 1925; aims to secure equality of liberties, status and opportunities between women and men and to promote friendship and mutual understanding throughout the Commonwealth; promotes women's political and social education and links together women's organizations in most countries of the Commonwealth; an education sponsorship scheme was established in 1967 to finance the secondary education of bright but needy girls in their own Commonwealth countries; the CCL Education Fund was sponsoring more than 243 girls throughout the Commonwealth (2010); Exec. Chair. MARJORIE RENNIE; publs *News Update* (3 a year), *Annual Report*.

Commonwealth War Graves Commission: 2 Marlow Rd, Maidenhead, Berks, SL6 7DX; tel. (1628) 634221; fax (1628) 771208; internet www.cwgc.org; casualty and cemetery enquiries; e-mail casualty.enq@cwgc.org; f. 1917 (as Imperial War Graves Commission); responsible for the commemoration in perpetuity of the 1.7m. members of the Commonwealth Forces who died during the wars of 1914–18 and 1939–45; provides for the marking and maintenance of war graves and memorials at some 23,000 locations in 150 countries; mems: Australia, Canada, India, New Zealand, South Africa, United Kingdom; Pres. HRH The Duke of KENT; Dir-Gen. ALAN PATEMAN-JONES.

Council of Commonwealth Societies: c/o Royal Commonwealth Society, 25 Northumberland Ave, London, WC2N 5AP; tel. (20) 7766-9200; fax (20) 7930-9705; e-mail ccs@rcsint.org; internet www.rcsint.org/day; f. 1947; provides a forum for the exchange of information regarding activities of mem. orgs which promote understanding among countries of the Commonwealth; co-ordinates the distribution of the Commonwealth Day message by Queen Elizabeth, organizes the observance of and promotes Commonwealth Day, and produces educational materials relating to the occasion; seeks to raise the profile of the Commonwealth; mems: 30 official and unofficial Commonwealth orgs; Chair. Lord ALAN WATSON; Sec. ALICE KAWOWA.

Royal Commonwealth Society: 25 Northumberland Ave, London, WC2N 5AP; tel. (20) 7766-9200; fax (20) 7930-9705; e-mail info@thercs.org; internet www.thercs.org; f. 1868; to promote international understanding of the Commonwealth and its people; organizes meetings and seminars on topical issues, projects for young people, a youth leadership programme, and cultural and social events; Chair. Baroness PRASHAR; Dir Dr DANNY SRISKANDARAJAH; publs *RCS Exchange* (3 a year), conference reports.

Royal Over-Seas League: Over-Seas House, Park Place, St James's St, London, SW1A 1LR; tel. (20) 7408-0214; fax (20) 7499-6738; e-mail info@rosl.org.uk; internet www.rosl.org.uk; f. 1910 to promote friendship and understanding in the Commonwealth; clubhouses in London and Edinburgh; membership is open to all British subjects and Commonwealth citizens; Dir-Gen. ROBERT F. NEWELL; publ. *Overseas* (quarterly).

Victoria League for Commonwealth Friendship: 55 Leinster Sq., London, W2 4PW; tel. (20) 7243-2633; fax (20) 7229-2994; e-mail victorialeaguehq@btconnect.com; internet www.victorialeague.co.uk; f. 1901; aims to further personal friendship among Commonwealth peoples and to provide hospitality for visitors; maintains Student House, providing accommodation for students from Commonwealth countries; has brs elsewhere in the UK and abroad; Chair. LYN D. HOPKINS; Gen. Sec. JOHN M. W. ALLAN; publ. *Annual Report*.

EUROPEAN UNION—EU

Presidency of the Council of the European Union: Poland (July–December 2011); Denmark (January–June 2012); Cyprus (July–December 2012).

President of the European Council: HERMAN VAN ROMPUY (Belgium).

High Representative of the Union for Foreign Affairs and Security Policy: CATHERINE ASHTON (United Kingdom).

Far East and Australasia

Relations between the EU and the Association of Southeast Asian Nations (ASEAN) are based on the Co-operation Agreement of 1980. Under this agreement, joint committee meetings are held approximately every 18 months. There are also regular ministerial meetings and post-ministerial conferences. In addition, the EU is a member of the ASEAN Regional Forum (ARF), a security grouping designed to promote peace and stability, established in 1994. In December of that year the European Council endorsed a new strategy for Asia, which recognized the region's increasing economic and political importance and pledged to strengthen bilateral and regional dialogue. In May 1995 ASEAN and EU senior officials endorsed an initiative to convene an Asia-Europe Meeting of heads of government (ASEM). The first ASEM summit was held in March 1996 in Bangkok, Thailand. It was agreed to launch an Asia-Europe Partnership for Greater Growth, in order to expand trade, investment and technology transfer. An Asia-Business Forum was to be formed, as well as an Asia-Europe Foundation in Singapore to promote educational and cultural exchanges. The second ASEM summit, convened in the United Kingdom in April 1998, was dominated by economic and financial concerns, and both sides' declared intention to prevent a return to protectionist trading policies. The meeting established an ASEM Trust Fund, under the auspices of the World Bank, to alleviate the social impact of financial crisis. Other initiatives adopted by ASEM were an Asia-Europe Co-operation Framework (AECF) to co-ordinate political, economic and financial co-operation, a Trade Facilitation Action Plan, and an Investment Promotion Action Plan, which incorporated a new Investment Experts Group. ASEM heads of government convened for the third time in Seoul, Republic of Korea, in October 2000. The meeting established a new AECF, identifying ASEM's principles and priorities for the next 10 years. ASEM IV took place in Copenhagen, Denmark, in September 2002. At the same time, the first EU-Korea summit was held; discussion centred on a reduction in customs barriers and aid to shipbuilding. ASEM V took place in Hanoi, Viet Nam, in October 2004; at the meeting regional developments in Europe and Asia, including the recent EU enlargement and the human rights situation in Myanmar, were addressed. ASEM VI, convened in Helsinki, Finland, in September 2006, addressed the theme '10 Years of ASEM: Global Challenges and Joint Responses'. The participants adopted a Declaration on Climate Change, aimed at promoting efforts to reach consensus in international climate negotiations, and the Helsinki Declaration on the Future of ASEM, detailing practical recommendations for developing future ASEM co-operation. ASEM VII was held in Beijing, the People's Republic of China (PRC), in October 2008. The meeting had the theme 'Vision and Action: Towards a Win-Win Solution', focusing on advancing dialogue regarding mutually beneficial co-operation on economic and social and cultural issues, and on sustainable development. The meeting resulted in the Beijing Declaration on Sustainable Development, which recognized the challenges posed to sustainable development by increasing global population, environmental degradation, depletion of resources, and deteriorating ecological 'carrying' capacity, and included provisions reaffirming commitment to internationally agreed targets underpinning co-operation for sustainable development, urging a comprehensive strategy to address the effects of rising food prices, and reaffirming that the issue of climate change should be dealt with within the framework of sustainable development. The eighth ASEM summit meeting took place in Brussels, Belgium, in October 2010.

A trade agreement was signed with the PRC in 1978 and renewed in May 1985. In June 1989, following the violent repression of the Chinese pro-democracy movement by the PRC Government, the EC imposed economic sanctions and an embargo on arms sales to that country. In October 1990 it was decided that relations with the PRC should be 'progressively normalized'. The EU has supported the PRC's increased involvement in the international community and, in particular, supported its application for membership of the WTO. The first EU-PRC meeting of heads of government was convened in April 1998. In November the President of the Commission made an official visit to the PRC and urged that country to remove trade restrictions imposed on European products. In the same month the EU and Hong Kong signed a co-operation agreement to combat drugs-trafficking and copyright piracy. A bilateral trade agreement between the EU and the PRC was concluded in May 2000, removing a major barrier to the PRC's accession to the WTO; this was approved in November 2001. A third EU-PRC summit meeting was held in Beijing in October 2000. At the fourth summit, convened in September 2001, the two sides agreed to strengthen and widen political dialogue and to continue discussions on human rights issues. In March 2002 the European Commission approved a strategy document setting out a framework for co-operation between the EU and the PRC over the period 2002–06, and in September the fifth EU-PRC summit discussed trade relations and future co-operation on illegal immigrants and tourism. At the sixth EU-PRC summit, held in Beijing in October 2003, two agreements were signed establishing a new dialogue on industrial policy and confirming the PRC's participation in the 'Galileo' project; in addition, a memorandum of understanding (MOU) was initialled, paving the way for Chinese tourist groups to travel to the EU more easily. At the seventh EU-PRC summit, which took place in The Hague, the Netherlands, in December 2004, the two sides further strengthened their maturing strategic partnership. The EU raised the topics of human rights and the fight against illegal migration, and discussions also focused on economic issues, including the Doha Development Round, textiles and other trade concerns. In addition, a number of international issues, including the situation in the Democratic People's Republic of Korea (DPRK) and Myanmar, featured in the talks. A joint declaration was signed on nuclear non-proliferation and arms control, and agreements were also concluded on customs co-operation, and science and technology. The eighth summit, held in Beijing in September 2005, marked the 30th anniversary of the establishment of EU-PRC diplomatic relations. During the meeting, the establishment of an EU-PRC partnership on climate change was confirmed. The two sides also agreed to move towards early negotiations on a new framework agreement, and two MOUs were signed on labour, employment and social affairs and on the initiation of a dialogue on energy and transport strategies. The ninth EU-PRC summit, convened in September 2006, agreed that negotiations should be initiated on concluding a comprehensive Partnership and Co-operation Agreement (PCA) and on updating the 1985 trade and economic co-operation agreement. In October 2006, in a strategy communication, the Commission set forth details of a new agenda for EU-PRC relations, the priorities of which included support for the PRC's transition towards greater openness and political pluralism and co-operation on climate change. In a separate policy paper, the Commission detailed a new strategy for expanding EU-PRC relations in the areas of trade and investment. Negotiations for a comprehensive PCA were launched in January 2007, and were ongoing in 2010. The 10th EU-PRC summit took place in Beijing in November 2007. At the meeting, heads of state and of government witnessed the signature of a €500m. framework loan from the European Investment Bank to support efforts to tackle climate change. In addition, the Chinese side urged the EU to lift the arms embargo imposed against the PRC, and both sides agreed to increase co-operation in order to facilitate the holding of the 2008 Summer Olympic Games in Beijing. In January 2009 the PRC and EU adopted nine agreements aimed at strengthening joint co-operation. Convened in Prague, Czech Republic, in May, the 11th EU-PRC summit addressed issues including the ongoing global financial and economic crisis and climate change. At the 12th EU-PRC summit, held in Nanjing in November, the two sides agreed to make efforts to facilitate the further implementation of the EU-China Joint Declaration on Climate Change, and agreed to strengthen the existing Partnership on Climate Change. The 13th EU-PRC summit took place in Brussels in October 2010, at which it was decided to designate 2011 as the EU-China Year of Youth.

A framework agreement on trade and co-operation between the EU and the Republic of Korea was signed in 1996 and entered into force in April 2001. In October 1997 the EU and the Republic of Korea signed an agreement regarding a reciprocal opening of markets for telecommunications equipment, following a protracted dispute, which had led the EU to lodge a complaint with the WTO. In September 1997, however, the Commission submitted a further complaint to the WTO, accusing the Republic of Korea of tax discrimination against European spirits exporters. In September 1998 the WTO ruled against the Republic of Korea, which, after losing a subsequent appeal, amended its legislation on the taxation of alcohol. In September 2006 an agreement was concluded on the Republic of Korea's participation in the EU's 'Galileo' programme. In May 2007 the EU and the Republic of Korea commenced negotiations towards the adoption of a free trade agreement, and an agreement was initialled in October 2009. The deal, which provided for the elimination of almost all duties in the agricultural and industrial sectors, was signed formally at an EU-Republic of Korea summit meeting in October 2010. The agreement was approved by the European Parliament in February 2011, with the addition of a clause ensuring that new Korean legislation on carbon-dioxide limits from cars would not damage the interests of European car-makers; the free trade agreement was to enter into force in July. Meanwhile, in June 2008 negotiations began, aimed at updating the mutual framework agreement. In May 2010 the EU and the Republic of Korea signed a new framework agreement on bilateral relations. In September 1997 the EU joined the Korean Peninsula Energy Development Organization, an initiative founded in 1995 to increase nuclear safety and reduce the risk of nuclear proliferation from the energy programme of the DPRK. In September 1999, for the first time, ministerial-level discussions took place between the EU and the DPRK at the UN General Assembly. In May 2001 the EU announced that it was to establish diplomatic relations with the DPRK to facilitate the Union's efforts in support of reconciliation in the Korean Peninsula and, in particular, in support of economic reform and the easing of the acute food and health problems in the DPRK. In October 2002 the EU expressed its deep concern after the DPRK admitted that it had conducted a clandestine nuclear weapons programme, in serious breach of the country's international non-proliferation commitments. In the following month the EU stated that failure to resolve the nuclear issue would jeopardize the future development of EU-DPRK relations. In response to the DPRK's announcement in October 2006 that it had conducted a nuclear test, the EU strongly condemned the 'provocative' action and urged the DPRK to abandon its nuclear programme. In April 2009 the EU strongly condemned the DPRK for launching a rocket in contravention of relevant UN Security Council resolutions. In December 2010 the Council reinforced sanctions in place against a number of individuals and entities in the DPRK.

In June 1992 the EC signed trade and co-operation agreements with Mongolia and Macao, with respect for democracy and human rights forming the basis of envisaged co-operation. The 10th EU-Mongolia joint committee, held in Brussels in September 2007, focused on political and economic issues, and concluded that negotiations would be initiated on a PCA. An agreement on aviation was also reached, as a result of which legal certainty was to be restored to 11 air-service agreements between Mongolia and individual EU member states. The 13th EU-Macao joint committee met in Brussels in December. A co-operation accord was formally signed with Viet Nam in July 1995, under which the EU agreed to increase quotas for Vietnamese textiles products, to support the country's efforts to join the WTO and to provide aid for environmental and public management projects. The agreement entered into force in June 1996. A permanent EU mission to Viet Nam was established in February 1996. In October 2004 the EU and Viet Nam concluded a bilateral agreement on market access in preparation for Viet Nam's accession to the WTO, which took place in January 2007. In addition, an agreement signed in December 2004 lifted all EU quantitative restrictions for Vietnamese textiles with effect from 1 January 2005. In May 2007 the EU and Viet Nam commenced negotiations on a new PCA, to replace that of 1995. Non-preferential co-operation agreements were signed with Laos and Cambodia in April 1997. The agreement with Laos (which emphasized development assistance and economic co-operation) entered into force on 1 December; the agreement with Cambodia was postponed owing to adverse political developments in that country. The EU concluded a textiles agreement with Laos, which provisionally entered into force in December 1998; as a result of the agreement, exports of textiles to the EU from Laos increased significantly. In 1998 the EU provided financial assistance to support preparations for a general election in Cambodia, and dispatched observers to monitor the election, which was held in July. The EU co-operation agreement with Cambodia entered into force in November 1999. EU-Cambodia relations were further enhanced with the opening of an EU delegation in Phnom-Penh in early 2002 and a Cambodian embassy in Brussels in late 2004. In September 1999 the EU briefly imposed an arms embargo against Indonesia, which was at that time refusing to permit the deployment of an international peace-keeping force in East Timor (now Timor-Leste). In April 2005 the EU extended preferential trade conditions to Indonesia, which meant that the country would benefit from lower customs duties in certain sectors. From September of that year the EU, together with contributing countries from ASEAN, as well as Norway and Switzerland, deployed a monitoring mission in the Indonesian province of Aceh to supervise the implementation of a peace agreement between the Government of Indonesia and the separatist Gerakan Aceh Merdeka (Free Aceh Movement). Having achieved its aims, the mission was concluded in December 2006. In November 2009 an EU-Indonesia PCA was signed.

In October 1996 the EU imposed strict limits on entry visas for Myanma officials, because of Myanmar's refusal to allow the Commission to send a mission to the country to investigate allegations of forced labour. In March 1997 EU ministers of foreign affairs agreed to revoke Myanmar's special trade privileges under the Generalized System of Preferences (GSP). The EU has successively extended its ban on arms exports to Myanmar and its prohibition on the issuing of visas. In April 2003 a new 'Common Position' was adopted by the EU, which consolidated and extended the scope of existing sanctions against Myanmar and strengthened the arms embargo; EU sanctions were further extended in April 2004 in view of the military regime's failure to make any significant progress in normalizing the administration of the country and addressing the EU's concerns with regard to human rights. EU foreign ministers agreed to Myanmar's participation in ASEM V in October at a level below head of government. Following the summit, however, the EU revised the Common Position, further broadening sanctions against Myanmar, as the military regime had failed to comply with certain demands, including the release from house arrest of the opposition leader Aung San Suu Kyi. The Common Position was renewed in April 2006, November 2007, and April 2009. In August 2009 an amended Common Position was adopted, extending sanctions to the Myanmar judiciary, following proceedings against Aung San Suu Kyi related to alleged violation of the terms of her house arrest. In November 2010 Catherine Ashton, High Representative of the Union for Foreign Affairs and Security Policy and Vice-President of the Commission, urged the Government of Myanmar to initiate negotiations that included Aung San Suu Kyi, following her release from house arrest, to bring about national reconciliation.

The EU's long-term assistance strategy for Timor-Leste has focused on stabilization and dialogue, combating poverty, and humanitarian support. Under the EU country strategy for Timor-Leste during 2008–13, rural development was to be strengthened, with a view to achieving sustained poverty reduction and food security, and the health sector and capacity building were to be supported.

Textiles exports by Asian countries have caused concern in the EU, owing to the depressed state of its textiles industry. In 1982 bilateral negotiations were held under the former Multi-Fibre Arrangement (MFA, see WTO) with Asian producers, notably Hong Kong, the Republic of Korea and Macao. Agreements were eventually reached involving reductions in clothing quotas and 'anti-surge' clauses to prevent flooding of European markets. In 1986 new bilateral negotiations were held and agreements were reached with the principal Asian textiles exporters, for the period 1987–91 (later extended to December 1993, when the 'Uruguay Round' of GATT negotiations was finally concluded): in most cases a slight increase in quotas was permitted. Under the conclusions of the Uruguay Round, the MFA was replaced by an Agreement on Textiles and Clothing (ATC), which provided for the progressive elimination of the quotas that existed under the MFA during 1994–2004. In January 1995 bilateral textiles agreements, signed by the EU with India, Pakistan and the PRC, specified certain trade liberalization measures to be undertaken, including an increase of the PRC's silk export quota. In May 2005 the EU imposed limits on textiles imports from the PRC, in response to a dramatic increase in PRC clothing exports since the expiry of the ATC on 1 January. In June the EU and the PRC Government agreed import quotas on 10 clothing and textiles categories until 2008, but by August several of the quotas for 2005 had already been breached. In September the dispute was resolved when it was agreed that one-half of the estimated 80m. Chinese garments that had been impounded at European ports would be released and the remainder counted against the quotas for 2006. Also in September 2005 a report published by the high-level group on textiles and clothing—established by the Commission in 2003—sought, *inter alia*, to chart the likely development of the sectors up to 2020. With regard to the quota-free environment for textiles and clothing that had been introduced at the beginning of 2005, the report noted that a Commission statement released in mid-2006 had indicated that the disruptive impact of liberalization of Chinese textiles exports to the EU had been confined to a fairly restricted range of product categories. None the less, the PRC's share of exports to the EU of products in the liberalized categories had risen markedly, to the detriment of traditional EU suppliers. Overall, however, only a modest increase in EU imports of textiles and clothing (in both the liberalized categories and in total) had occurred. The statement noted, too, that the PRC was becoming a key growth market for exports of textiles and clothing from the EU. In October 2007 the European Commission agreed not to renew quotas on textiles from the PRC, but instead to introduce a system of monitoring imports.

Numerous discussions have been held since 1981 on the EU's increasing trade deficit with Japan, and on the failure of the Japanese market to accept more European exports. In July 1991 the heads of government of Japan and of the EC signed a joint declaration on closer co-operation in both economic and political matters. The European office of the EU-Japan Industrial Co-operation Centre was opened in Brussels in June 1996; the Centre, which was established in 1987 as a joint venture between the Japanese Government and the European Commission, sought to increase industrial co-operation between the EU and Japan. In October 1996 the WTO upheld a long-standing complaint brought by the EU that Japanese taxes on alcoholic spirits discriminated against certain European products. In January 1998 an EU-Japan summit meeting was held, followed by a meeting at ministerial level in October. Subsequent summits (the 19th was held in Brussels in April 2011) have aimed to strengthen dialogue.

Regular consultations are held with Australia at ministerial and senior official level. In January 1996 the Commission proposed a framework agreement to formalize the EU's trade and political relationship with that country. In September, however, after the Australian Government had objected to the human rights clause contained in all EU international agreements, negotiations were suspended. In June 1997 a joint declaration was signed, committing both sides to greater political, cultural and economic co-operation. In 2001 a National Europe Centre, based at the Australian National University in Canberra, was established jointly by the EU and the University to consolidate EU-Australia relations. The EU-Australia ministerial consultations convened in Melbourne, Australia, in April 2003, adopted a five-year Agenda for Co-operation. In October 2008 ministers of foreign affairs from the EU and Australia, meeting in Paris, France, adopted a Partnership Framework, outlining future co-operation in the areas of: foreign policy and security issues; trade; relations with Asia and the Pacific; environment; and science, technology and education. The Partnership Framework was updated at a meeting of ministers of foreign affairs held in Stockholm, Sweden, in October 2009. In March 1997 New Zealand took a case relating to import duties to the WTO, which later ruled against the EU. A joint declaration detailing areas of co-operation and establishing a consultative framework to facilitate the development of these was signed in May 1999. Mutual recognition agreements were also signed with Australia and New Zealand in 1999, with the aim of facilitating bilateral trade in industrial products. In March 2004 a European Commission Delegation was inaugurated in Wellington, New Zealand. In September 2007 a new joint declaration on relations and co-operation was adopted by the EU and New Zealand, replacing the 1999 joint declaration and 2004 action plan.

The last European Commission Humanitarian Aid Office (ECHO) programmes in Indonesia, in support of those affected by the 2004 tsunami, were completed in June 2007. During 2010 assistance granted to the region through ECHO totalled €48.8m., and included €17.25m. in humanitarian and food aid to Myanmar and Thailand.

African, Caribbean and Pacific (ACP) Countries

In June 2000, meeting in Cotonou, Benin, heads of state and of government of the EU and African, Caribbean and Pacific (ACP) countries concluded a new 20-year partnership accord between the EU and ACP states. The EU-ACP Partnership Agreement, known as the Cotonou Agreement, entered into force on 1 April 2003 (although many of its provisions had been applicable for a transitional period since August 2000), following ratification by the then 15 EU member states and more than the requisite two-thirds of the ACP countries. Previously, the principal means of co-operation between the Community and developing countries were the Lomé Conventions. The First Lomé Convention (Lomé I), which was concluded at Lomé, Togo, in February 1975 and came into force on 1 April 1976, replaced the Yaoundé Conventions and the Arusha Agreement. Lomé I was designed to provide a new framework of co-operation, taking into account the varying needs of developing ACP countries. The Second Lomé Convention entered into force on 1 January 1981 and the Third Lomé Convention on 1 March 1985 (trade provisions) and 1 May 1986 (aid). The Fourth Lomé Convention, which had a 10-year commitment period, was signed in December 1989: its trade provisions entered into force on 1 March 1990, and the remainder entered into force in September 1991.

The Cotonou Agreement was to cover a 20-year period from 2000 and was subject to revision every five years. A financial protocol was attached to the Agreement, which indicated the funds available to the ACP through the European Development Fund (EDF), the main instrument for Community aid for development co-operation in ACP countries. The ninth EDF, covering the initial five-year period from March 2000, provided a total budget of €13,500m., of which €1,300m. was allocated to regional co-operation and €2,200m. was for the new investment facility for the development of the private sector. In addition, uncommitted balances from previous EDFs amounted to a further €2,500m. The new Agreement envisaged a more participatory approach with more effective political co-operation to encourage good governance and democracy, increased flexibility in the provision of aid to reward performance, and a new framework for economic and trade co-operation. Its objectives were to alleviate poverty, contribute to sustainable development and integrate the ACP economies into the global economy. Negotiations to revise the Cotonou Agreement were initiated in May 2004 and concluded in February 2005. The political dimension of the Agreement was broadly strengthened and a reference to co-operation in counter-terrorism and the prevention of the proliferation of weapons of mass destruction was included. The revised Cotonou Agreement was signed on 24 June 2005.

Under the provisions of the new accord, the EU was to finalize free trade arrangements (replacing the previous non-reciprocal trade preferences) with the most-developed ACP countries during 2000–08; these would be structured around a system of six regional free trade zones, and would be designed to ensure full compatibility with World Trade Organization (WTO) provisions. Once in force, the agreements would be subject to revision every five years. The first general stage of negotiations for the Economic Partnership Agreements (EPAs), involving discussions with all ACP countries regarding common procedures, began in September 2002. The regional phase of EPA negotiations to establish a new framework for trade and investment commenced in October 2003. Negotiations had been scheduled for completion in mid-2007 to allow for ratification by 2008, when the WTO exception for existing arrangements expired. However, the negotiation period was subsequently extended. By November 2010 36 ACP states had signed full or interim EPAs, covering the liberalization of goods and agricultural products. The EPAs attracted some criticism for their focus on trade liberalization and their perceived failure to recognize the widespread poverty of ACP countries.

In March 2010 negotiations were concluded on the second revision of the Cotonou Agreement, which sought to take into account various factors, including the increasing importance of enhanced regional co-operation and a more inclusive partnership in ACP countries; the need for security; efforts to meet the Millennium Development Goals; the new trade relationship developed following the expiry of trade preferences at the end of 2007; and the need to ensure the effectiveness and coherence of international aid efforts. The second revised Cotonou Agreement was formally signed in Ouagadougou, Burkina Faso, in June 2010, and entered into effect, on a provisional basis, at the beginning of November.

Meanwhile, the EU had launched an initiative to allow free access to the products of the least-developed ACP nations by 2005. Stabex and Sysmin, instruments under the Lomé Conventions designed to stabilize export prices for agricultural and mining commodities, respectively, were replaced by a system called FLEX, introduced in 2000, to compensate ACP countries for short-term fluctuations in export earnings. In February 2001 the EU agreed to phase out trade barriers on imports of everything but military weapons from the world's 48 least-developed countries, 39 of which were in the ACP group. Duties on sugar, rice, bananas and some other products were to remain until 2009 (these were withdrawn from October of that year). In May 2001 the EU announced that it would cancel all outstanding debts arising from its trade accords with former colonies of member states.

One major new programme set up on behalf of the ACP countries and financed by the EDF was Pro€Invest, which was launched in 2002, with funding of €110m. over a seven-year period. In October 2003 the Commission proposed to incorporate the EDF into the EU budget (it had previously been a fund outside the EU budget, to which the EU member states made direct voluntary contributions). The cost-sharing formula for the 25 member states would automatically apply, obviating the need for negotiations about contributions for the 10th EDF. The Commission proposal was endorsed by the European Parliament in April 2004. Despite the fears of ACP countries that the enlargement of the EU could jeopardize funding, the 10th EDF was agreed in December 2005 by the European Council and provided funds of €22,682m. for 2008–13.

On 1 July 1993 the EC introduced a regime to allow the preferential import into the Community of bananas from former French and British colonies in the Caribbean. This was designed to protect the banana industries of ACP countries from the availability of cheaper bananas, produced by countries in Latin America. Latin American and later US producers brought a series of complaints before the WTO, claiming that the EU banana import regime was in contravention of free trade principles. The WTO upheld their complaints on each occasion leading to adjustments of the complex quota and tariffs systems in place. Following the WTO authorization of punitive US trade sanctions, in April 2001 the EU reached agreement with the USA and Ecuador on a new banana regime. Under the new accord, the EU was granted the so-called Cotonou waiver, which allowed it to maintain preferential access for ACP banana exports, in return for the adoption of a new tariff-only system for bananas from Latin American countries from 1 January 2006. The Latin American producers were guaranteed total market access under the agreement and were permitted to seek arbitration if dissatisfied with the EU's proposed tariff levels. Following the WTO rejection of EU proposals for tariff levels of €230 and €187 per metric ton (in comparison with existing rates of €75 for a quota of 2.2m. tons and €680 thereafter), in November 2005 the EU announced that a tariff of €176, with a duty-free quota of 775,000 metric tons for ACP producers, would be implemented on 1 January 2006. In late 2006 Ecuador initiated a challenge to the EU's proposals at the WTO. Twelve other countries subsequently initiated third-party challenges to the proposals at the WTO, in support of the challenge by Ecuador. In April 2008 the WTO upheld the challenge by Ecuador, and ordered the EU to align its tariffs with WTO regulations. In December 2009 representatives from the EU and Latin American countries initialled the EU-Latin America Bananas Agreement, which aimed to end the dispute. Under the Agreement, which made no provision for import quotas, the EU was gradually to reduce its import tariff on bananas from Latin American countries, from €176 per metric ton to €114 per ton by 2017. The EU also pledged to mobilize up to €200m. to support the main ACP banana-exporting countries in adjusting to the anticipated increase in market competition from Latin America. (ACP countries would continue to benefit from duty- and quota-free access to EU markets.) For their part, Latin American banana-producing countries undertook not to demand further tariff reductions; and to withdraw several related cases against the EU that were pending at the WTO. In response to the Agreement, the US authorities determined to settle ongoing parallel complaints lodged with the WTO against the EU relating to bananas.

Following a WTO ruling at the request of Brazil, Australia and Thailand in 2005 that the EU's subsidized exports of sugar breached legal limits, reform of the EU's sugar regime was required by May 2006. Previously, the EU purchased fixed quotas of sugar from ACP producers at two or three times the world price, the same price that it paid to sugar growers in the EU. In November 2005 the EU agreed to reform the sugar industry through a phased reduction of its prices for white sugar of 36% by 2009 (which was still twice the market price in 2005). Compensation to EU producers amounted to €6,300m. over the four years beginning in January 2006, but compensation to ACP producers was worth just €40m. in 2006. Development campaigners and impoverished ACP countries, notably Jamaica and Guyana, condemned the plans.

In May 2003 Timor-Leste joined the ACP and the ACP-EC Council of Ministers approved its accession to the ACP-EC Partnership Agreement. Cuba, which had been admitted to the ACP in December 2000, was granted observer status. Cuba withdrew its application to join the Cotonou Agreement in July 2003.

ORGANIZATION OF ISLAMIC COOPERATION—OIC

Address: Medina Rd, Sary St, POB 178, Jeddah 21411, Saudi Arabia.

Telephone: (2) 690-0001; **fax:** (2) 275-1953; **e-mail:** info@oic-oci.org; **internet:** www.oic-oci.org.

The Organization was formally established, as the Organization of the Islamic Conference, at the first conference of Muslim heads of state convened at Rabat, Morocco, in September 1969; the first conference of Muslim foreign ministers, held in Jeddah in March 1970, established the General Secretariat; the latter became operational in May 1971. In June 2011 the 38th ministerial conference agreed to change the name of the Organization, with immediate effect, to the Organization of Islamic Cooperation (abbreviated, as hitherto, to OIC).

MEMBERS

Afghanistan	Indonesia	Qatar
Albania	Iran	Saudi Arabia
Algeria	Iraq	Senegal
Azerbaijan	Jordan	Sierra Leone
Bahrain	Kazakhstan	Somalia
Bangladesh	Kuwait	Sudan
Benin	Kyrgyzstan	Suriname
Brunei	Lebanon	Syria
Burkina Faso	Libya	Tajikistan
Cameroon	Malaysia	Togo
Chad	Maldives	Tunisia
Comoros	Mali	Turkey
Côte d'Ivoire	Mauritania	Turkmenistan
Djibouti	Morocco	Uganda
Egypt	Mozambique	United Arab Emirates
Gabon	Niger	Uzbekistan
The Gambia	Nigeria	Yemen
Guinea	Oman	
Guinea-Bissau	Pakistan	
Guyana	Palestine	

Note: Observer status has been granted to Bosnia and Herzegovina, the Central African Republic, Russia, Thailand, the Muslim community of the 'Turkish Republic of Northern Cyprus', the Moro National Liberation Front (MNLF) of the southern Philippines, the UN, the African Union, the Non-Aligned Movement, the League of Arab States, the Economic Cooperation Organization, the Union of the Arab Maghreb and the Cooperation Council for the Arab States of the Gulf. The revised OIC Charter, endorsed in March 2008, made future applications for OIC membership and observer status conditional upon Muslim demographic majority and membership of the UN.

Organization

(October 2011)

SUMMIT CONFERENCES

The supreme body of the Organization is the Conference of Heads of State, which met in 1969 at Rabat, Morocco, in 1974 at Lahore, Pakistan, and in January 1981 at Mecca, Saudi Arabia, when it was decided that summit conferences would normally be held every three years in future. An extraordinary summit conference was convened in Doha, Qatar, in March 2003, to consider the situation in Iraq. A further extraordinary conference, held in December 2005, in Mecca, determined to restructure the OIC. The 12th ordinary Conference was to be held in Cairo, Egypt, in 2011. The summit conference troika comprises member countries equally representing the OIC's African, Arab and Asian membership.

CONFERENCE OF MINISTERS OF FOREIGN AFFAIRS

Conferences take place annually, to consider the means of implementing the general policy of the Organization, although they may also be convened for extraordinary sessions. The ministerial conference troika comprises member countries equally representing the OIC's African, Arab and Asian membership.

SECRETARIAT

The executive organ of the organization, headed by a Secretary-General (who is elected by the Conference of Ministers of Foreign Affairs for a five-year term, renewable only once) and four Assistant Secretaries-General (similarly appointed).

Secretary-General: Prof. Dr Ekmeleddin Ihsanoglu (Turkey).

At the summit conference in January 1981 it was decided that an International Islamic Court of Justice should be established to adjudicate in disputes between Muslim countries. Experts met in January 1983 to draw up a constitution for the court; however, by 2011 it was not yet in operation.

EXECUTIVE COMMITTEE

The third extraordinary conference of the OIC, convened in Mecca, Saudi Arabia, in December 2005, mandated the establishment of the Executive Committee, comprising the summit conference and ministerial conference troikas, the OIC host country, and the OIC Secretariat, as a mechanism for following up resolutions of the Conference.

STANDING COMMITTEES

Al-Quds Committee: f. 1975 to implement the resolutions of the Islamic Conference on the status of Jerusalem (Al-Quds); it meets at the level of foreign ministers; maintains the Al-Quds Fund; Chair. King Muhammad VI of Morocco.

Standing Committee for Economic and Commercial Co-operation (COMCEC): f. 1981; Chair. Abdullah Gül (Pres. of Turkey).

Standing Committee for Information and Cultural Affairs (COMIAC): f. 1981; Chair. Abdoulaye Wade (Pres. of Senegal).

Standing Committee for Scientific and Technological Co-operation (COMSTECH): f. 1981; Chair. Asif Ali Zardari (Pres. of Pakistan).

Other committees comprise the Islamic Peace Committee, the Permanent Finance Committee, the Committee of Islamic Solidarity with the Peoples of the Sahel, the Eight-Member Committee on the Situation of Muslims in the Philippines, the Six-Member Committee on Palestine, the Committee on UN reform, and the ad hoc Committee on Afghanistan. In addition, there is an Islamic Commission for Economic, Cultural and Social Affairs, and there are OIC contact groups on Bosnia and Herzegovina, Iraq, Kosovo, Jammu and Kashmir, Sierra Leone, and Somalia. A Commission of Eminent Persons was inaugurated in 2005.

Activities

The Organization's aims, as proclaimed in the Charter (adopted in 1972, with revisions endorsed in 1990 and 2008), are:

(i) To promote Islamic solidarity among member states;

(ii) To consolidate co-operation among member states in the economic, social, cultural, scientific and other vital fields, and to arrange consultations among member states belonging to international organizations;

(iii) To endeavour to eliminate racial segregation and discrimination and to eradicate colonialism in all its forms;

(iv) To take necessary measures to support international peace and security founded on justice;

(v) To co-ordinate all efforts for the safeguard of the Holy Places and support of the struggle of the people of Palestine, and help them to regain their rights and liberate their land;

(vi) To strengthen the struggle of all Muslim people with a view to safeguarding their dignity, independence and national rights;

(vii) To create a suitable atmosphere for the promotion of co-operation and understanding among member states and other countries.

The first summit conference of Islamic leaders (representing 24 states) took place in 1969 following the burning of the al-Aqsa Mosque in Jerusalem. At this conference it was decided that Islamic governments should 'consult together with a view to promoting close co-operation and mutual assistance in the economic, scientific, cultural and spiritual fields, inspired by the immortal teachings of Islam'. Thereafter the foreign ministers of the countries concerned met annually, and adopted the Charter of the Organization of the Islamic Conference in 1972.

At the second Islamic summit conference (Lahore, Pakistan, 1974), the Islamic Solidarity Fund was established, together with a committee of representatives that later evolved into the Islamic Commission for Economic, Cultural and Social Affairs. Subsequently, numerous other subsidiary bodies have been set up (see below).

ECONOMIC CO-OPERATION

A general agreement for economic, technical and commercial co-operation came into force in 1981, providing for the establishment of joint investment projects and trade co-ordination. This was followed by an agreement on promotion, protection and guarantee of investments among member states. A plan of action to strengthen economic co-operation was adopted at the third Islamic summit conference in 1981, aiming to promote collective self-reliance and the development of joint ventures in all sectors. The fifth summit conference, held in 1987, approved proposals for joint development of modern technology, and for improving scientific and technical skills in the less developed Islamic countries. In 1994 the 1981 plan of action was revised to place greater emphasis on private sector participation in its implementation. In October 2003 a meeting of COMCEC endorsed measures aimed at accelerating the hitherto slow implementation of the plan of action. A new 10-year plan of action for fostering member states' development and strengthening economic and trade co-operation was launched in December 2005.

In 1991 22 OIC member states signed a Framework Agreement on a Trade Preferential System among the OIC Member States (TPS-OIC); this entered into force in 2003, following the requisite ratification by more than 10 member states, and was envisaged as representing the first step towards the eventual establishment of an Islamic common market. A Trade Negotiating Committee (TNC) was established following the entry into force of the Framework Agreement. The first round of trade negotiations on the establishment of the TPS-OIC, concerning finalizing tariff-reduction modalities and an implementation schedule for the Agreement, was held during April 2004–April 2005, and resulted in the conclusion of a Protocol on the Preferential Tariff Scheme for TPS-OIC (PRETAS). In November 2006, at the launch of the second round of negotiations, ministers adopted a roadmap towards establishing the TPS-OIC; the second round of negotiations ended in September 2007 with the adoption of rules of origin for the TPS-OIC. PRETAS entered into force in February 2010.

In March 2008 the summit adopted a five-year Special Programme for the Development of Africa, covering the period 2008–12, which aimed to promote the economic development of OIC African member states and to support these countries in achieving the UN Millennium Development Goals.

The first OIC Anti-Corruption and Enhancing Integrity Forum was convened in August 2006 in Kuala Lumpur, Malaysia. The 13th Trade Fair of the OIC member states was staged in Sharjah, Saudi Arabia, in April 2011. The seventh World Islamic Economic Forum was convened in Astana, Kazakhstan, in June 2011. In November 2009 a COMCEC Business Forum was held, in Istanbul, Turkey.

CULTURAL AND TECHNICAL CO-OPERATION

The Organization supports education in Muslim communities throughout the world, and was instrumental in the establishment of Islamic universities in Niger and Uganda. It organizes seminars on various aspects of Islam, and encourages dialogue with the other monotheistic religions. Support is given to publications on Islam both in Muslim and Western countries. In June 1999 an OIC Parliamentary Union was inaugurated; its founding conference was convened in Tehran, Iran.

The OIC organizes meetings at ministerial level to consider aspects of information policy and new technologies. An OIC Digital Solidarity Fund was inaugurated in May 2005. Participation by OIC member states in the Fund was promoted at the 11th OIC summit meeting in March 2008, and the meeting also requested each member state to establish a board to monitor national implementation of the Tunis Declaration on the Information Society, adopted by the November 2005 second phase of the World Summit on the Information Society. The first OIC Conference on Women was held in November 2006, on the theme 'The role of women in the development of OIC member states'. In January 2009 the OIC and the League of Arab States signed an agreement providing for the strengthening of co-operation and co-ordination in the areas of politics, media, the economy, and in the social and scientific spheres. In August 2011 the OIC organized a Decorative Arts and Calligraphy Exhibition, at its headquarters in Jeddah.

HUMANITARIAN ASSISTANCE

Assistance is given to Muslim communities affected by wars and natural disasters, in co-operation with UN organizations, particularly UNCHR. The OIC has established trust funds to assist vulnerable people in Afghanistan, Bosnia and Herzegovina, and Sierra Leone. Humanitarian assistance provided by OIC member states has included aid to the Muslim population affected by the conflict in Chechnya; to victims of conflict in Darfur, southern Sudan; to Indonesia following the tsunami disaster in December 2004; and to Pakistan following the major earthquake there in October 2005. In October 2009 an OIC humanitarian mission was sent to support survivors of the earthquake that struck Padang, Indonesia, at the end of September. In mid-August 2010, at the request of the Pakistan Government, the OIC organized an emergency meeting to review the ongoing humanitarian relief operation supporting survivors of the severe floods that had devastated northern and central areas of Pakistan during that month (seriously adversely affecting at least 15m. people, of whom 8m. were believed to be at high risk of contracting waterborne diseases, and including 2m. people who had been displaced from their homes). By the end of August OIC member countries had pledged US $1,000m. in support of the flood-affected communities. It was announced at that time that an OIC Emergency Fund for Natural Disasters would be established, to assist survivors of any natural disaster occurring in future in a Muslim country. The countries of the Sahel region (Burkina Faso, Cape Verde, Chad, The Gambia, Guinea, Guinea-Bissau, Mali, Mauritania, Niger and Senegal) receive particular attention as victims of drought.

In March 2008 the OIC launched a humanitarian support operation for Palestinians in Gaza; an initial 'assistance caravan' transported medical supplies and equipment to the area. An expanded extraordinary meeting of the Executive Committee, convened, at the level of ministers of foreign affairs, in January 2009 to address the ongoing intensive bombardment of the Gaza Strip that was initiated by Israeli forces in late December 2008 with the stated aim of ending rocket attacks launched by Hamas and other militant groups on Israeli targets, requested the OIC Secretariat to co-ordinate with member states' civil society organizations to provide urgent humanitarian relief to the Palestinian people. OIC convoys of humanitarian aid, including medical supplies, food and clothing, were subsequently dispatched to Gaza.

In August 2011 OIC governments pledged US $350m. in aid to combat famine in Somalia, where some 3.7m. people were reported at that time to be at risk of starvation. The OIC Secretary-General urged donor nations to help to rehabilitate Somalia's infrastructure and agricultural production with a view to improving the long-term prospects for food security. In early October 2011 the OIC convened a conference on the theme 'Water for Life in Somalia', with participation by 32 non-governmental humanitarian relief agencies; the conference adopted a declaration pledging to drill 682 boreholes in 11 provinces of Somalia, with a view to alleviating the acute shortage of water that had contributed to the famine.

The first conference of Islamic humanitarian organizations was convened by the OIC in March 2008, and a second conference, bringing together 32 organizations, took place in April 2009. The third conference of Islamic humanitarian organizations, held in March 2010, established a working group to draft a plan aimed at strengthening co-operation between the OIC and other humanitarian organizations active in Afghanistan, Gaza, Darfur, Iraq, Niger, Somalia, and Sudan; and also approved the formation of a joint commission which was to study the structure and mechanism of co-operation and co-ordination between humanitarian organizations. The fourth conference was convened in June 2011, with the theme 'Civil Society Organizations in the Muslim World: Responsibilities and Roles'.

POLITICAL CO-OPERATION

The OIC gives support to member countries in maintaining or regaining political stability. During early 2011, for example, it participated in International Contact Groups on Afghanistan and Libya, co-operating with the UN and other international organizations and national governments in supporting efforts to restore constitutional rule in those countries. Delegations of the OIC acted as observers in legislative elections in Bosnia and Herzegovina, and in Kyrgyzstan, in October 2010. In April 2009 an intergovernmental group of experts met to discuss the formation of an OIC Independent Human Rights Commission. In June 2011 OIC foreign ministers adopted the Astana Declaration on Peace, Co-operation and Development, in which they recognized emerging challenges presented by unfolding significant political developments in the Middle East and North Africa (the so-called 'Arab Spring') and appealed for engagement in constructive dialogue towards peaceful solutions. The Declaration expressed grave concern at the ongoing conflict in Libya, and at the humanitarian consequences thereof. The foreign ministers also adopted the OIC Action Plan for Cooperation with Central Asia, which aimed to establish centres of excellence with a view to encouraging scientific innovation; and to promote job training and public-private partnership; to promote a reduction in the incidence of HIV/AIDS, polio, malaria and TB in the region; to build cultural understanding; and to combat trafficking in human beings and in illegal drugs.

Israel/Palestine: Since its inception the OIC has called for the vacation of Arab territories by Israel, recognition of the rights of Palestinians and of the Palestine Liberation Organization (PLO) as their sole legitimate representative, and the restoration of Jerusalem to Arab rule. The 1981 summit conference called for a *jihad* (holy war—though not necessarily in a military sense) 'for the liberation of Jerusalem and the occupied territories'; this was to include an

Islamic economic boycott of Israel. In 1982 Islamic ministers of foreign affairs decided to establish Islamic offices for boycotting Israel and for military co-operation with the PLO. The 1984 summit conference agreed to reinstate Egypt (suspended following the peace treaty signed with Israel in 1979) as a member of the OIC, although the resolution was opposed by seven states. In December 1991, at the sixth summit conference, disagreement arose between the PLO and the majority of other OIC members when a proposal was adopted to cease the OIC's support for the PLO's *jihad* in the Arab territories occupied by Israel, in an attempt to further the Middle East peace negotiations. In December 1995 the OIC Conference of Ministers of Foreign Affairs declared that Palestine and the establishment of fully autonomous Palestinian control of Jerusalem were issues of central importance for the Muslim world. The Conference urged the removal of all aspects of occupation and the cessation of the construction of Israeli settlements in the occupied territories. In December 1996 OIC ministers of foreign affairs urged the international community to apply pressure on Israel in order to ensure its implementation of the terms of the Middle East peace process. In March 1997, at an extraordinary summit held in Pakistan, OIC heads of state and of government reiterated the organization's objective of increasing international pressure on Israel to ensure the full implementation of the peace process. In June the OIC condemned the decision by the US House of Representatives to recognize Jerusalem as the Israeli capital. The Secretary-General of the OIC issued a statement rejecting the US decision as counter to the role of the USA as sponsor of the Middle East peace plan. In March 1998 OIC ministers of foreign affairs urged all states to end the process of restoring normal trading and diplomatic relations with Israel pending that country's withdrawal from the occupied territories and acceptance of an independent Palestinian state. In view of the significant deterioration in relations between Israel and the Palestinian (National) Authority (PA) during late 2000, in December of that year the ninth summit conference of heads of state and of government, held in Doha, Qatar, issued a Declaration pledging solidarity with the Palestinian cause and accusing the Israeli authorities of implementing large-scale systematic violations of human rights against Palestinians. In May 2001 the OIC convened an emergency meeting, following an escalation of Israeli–Palestinian violence. The meeting resolved to halt all diplomatic and political contacts with the Israeli Government, while restrictions remained in force against Palestinian-controlled territories. In August the Secretary-General condemned Israel's seizure of several Palestinian institutions in East Jerusalem and aerial attacks against Palestinian settlements. The OIC initiated senior level diplomatic efforts to convene a meeting of the UN Security Council in order to discuss the situation. In April 2002 OIC ministers of foreign affairs strongly condemned Israel's ongoing military intervention in areas controlled by the PA, and in June they repeated demands for the international community to exert pressure on Israel to withdraw from all Palestinian-controlled territories and for the establishment of an independent Palestinian state. They endorsed the peace plan for the region that had been adopted by the summit meeting of the League of Arab States in March. In May 2004 the Secretary-General of the OIC condemned the ongoing destruction of Palestinian homes by Israeli forces, and consequent population displacement, particularly in Rafah, Gaza. He urged international organizations to condemn Israel's actions and appealed to the UN Security Council to intervene promptly in the situation and to compel Israel to respect international law. An observer mission dispatched by the OIC to monitor presidential elections held in the Palestinian territories in early January 2005, at the request of the PA, was rejected by Israel. In August 2006 the OIC convened a meeting of humanitarian bodies in Istanbul, Turkey, to address means of collecting donations for and delivering assistance to victims of the ongoing crises in Lebanon and the Palestinian territories. Shortly afterwards a meeting of the newly formed Executive Committee, held in Kuala Lumpur, Malaysia, agreed to form a Contact Group for Lebanon, to be co-ordinated by Malaysia. The summit meeting held in March 2008 welcomed recent contacts between the Israeli and Palestinian leaders. In early January 2009 an expanded extraordinary meeting of the Executive Committee, at the level of ministers of foreign affairs, convened to address the ongoing intensive bombardment of the Gaza Strip that was initiated by Israeli forces in late December 2008 with the stated aim of ending rocket attacks launched by Hamas and other militant groups on Israeli targets. The meeting strongly condemned the Israeli attacks and ensuing destruction and loss of civilian life, and requested the OIC Secretariat to co-ordinate with member states' civil society organizations to provide urgent humanitarian relief to the Palestinian people. In March 2009, while visiting the affected area, the OIC Secretary-General urged the reconciliation of the different Palestinian political factions. In October the OIC Secretary-General strongly condemned recent raids by Israeli special forces on the al-Aqsa Mosque in Jerusalem. An extraordinary meeting of the Executive Committee held at the beginning of November issued a final communiqué condemning Israeli violations of al-Aqsa and rejecting Israeli attempts to change the status of Jerusalem (Al-Quds) and consider it the united capital of Israel. The meeting urged the UN Security Council to address the Israeli actions.

In June 2010 an expanded extraordinary ministerial meeting of the Executive Committee condemned the attack by Israeli security forces, at the end of May, against a flotilla of vessels carrying humanitarian aid to Gaza, which had resulted in nine civilian deaths and caused injuries to at least 40 people. The OIC rejected a UN-commissioned report on the flotilla incident, released in September 2011, which—while concluding that the Israeli army had used 'excessive and unreasonable' force—also found the Israeli naval blockade of Gaza to have been imposed as a 'legitimate security measure' to prevent weapons from reaching Gaza by sea, and found that the flotilla had acted recklessly in attempting to breach the naval blockade. The OIC Secretary-General supported efforts to bring the issue of the blockade of Gaza before competent international legal authorities. In late September the OIC Secretary-General condemned a decision by Israel to build 1,100 new housing units in occupied East Jerusalem. During that month the OIC expressed support for the formal request by the Executive President of the Palestinian Authority for Palestine's admission to the UN, and recognition of its independent statehood.

Iraq: In August 1990 a majority of OIC member states' ministers of foreign affairs condemned Iraq's recent invasion of Kuwait, and demanded the withdrawal of Iraqi forces. In August 1991 the Conference of Ministers of Foreign Affairs obstructed Iraq's attempt to propose a resolution demanding the repeal of economic sanctions against the country. The sixth summit conference, held in Senegal in December, reflected the divisions in the Arab world that resulted from Iraq's invasion of Kuwait and the ensuing war. Twelve heads of state did not attend, reportedly to register protest at the presence of Jordan and the PLO at the conference, both of which had given support to Iraq. In December 1994 OIC heads of state supported the decision by Iraq to recognize Kuwait, but advocated that Iraq comply with all UN Security Council decisions. In December 1996 OIC ministers of foreign affairs demanded that Iraq fulfil its obligations for the establishment of security, peace and stability in the region. In early 1998 the OIC appealed for an end to the threat of US-led military action against Iraq arising from a dispute regarding access granted to international weapons inspectors. The crisis was averted by an agreement concluded between the Iraqi authorities and the UN Secretary-General in February. In March OIC ministers of foreign affairs, meeting in Doha, Qatar, requested an end to the international sanctions against Iraq. In December the OIC appealed for a diplomatic solution to the tensions arising from Iraq's withdrawal of co-operation with UN weapons inspectors, and criticized subsequent military air-strikes, led by the USA, as having been conducted without renewed UN authority. An extraordinary summit conference of Islamic leaders convened in Doha, in early March 2003, to consider the ongoing Iraq crisis, welcomed the Saddam Hussain regime's acceptance of UN Security Council Resolution 1441 and consequent co-operation with UN weapons inspectors, and emphatically rejected any military strike against Iraq or threat to the security of any other Islamic state. The conference also urged progress towards the elimination of all weapons of mass destruction in the Middle East, including those held by Israel. In mid-May 2004 the OIC Secretary-General urged combat forces in Iraq to respect the inviolability of that country's holy places. In December 2005 he appealed to the people of Iraq to participate peacefully in the legislative elections that took place later in that month. In October 2006 a meeting of Iraqi Islamic scholars from all denominations issued a declaration on the Iraqi situation, in which they urged unity between different Islamic factions in that country. During 2008–10 the OIC Secretary-General repeatedly appealed for an end to sectarian strife in Iraq, and in October 2008 he condemned the persecution of Christians in northern Iraq.

Bosnia and Herzegovina and Kosovo: In August 1992 the UN General Assembly approved a non-binding resolution, introduced by the OIC, that requested the UN Security Council to take increased action, including the use of force, in order to defend the non-Serbian population of Bosnia and Herzegovina (some 43% of Bosnians being Muslims) from Serbian aggression, and to restore its 'territorial integrity'. The OIC Conference of Ministers of Foreign Affairs, which was held in December, demanded anew that the UN Security Council take all necessary measures against Serbia and Montenegro, including military intervention, in order to protect the Bosnian Muslims. A special ministerial meeting on Bosnia and Herzegovina was held in July 1993, at which seven OIC countries committed themselves to making available up to 17,000 troops to serve in the UN Protection Force in the former Yugoslavia (UNPROFOR). The meeting also decided to dispatch immediately a ministerial mission to persuade influential governments to support the OIC's demands for the removal of the arms embargo on Bosnian Muslims and the convening of a restructured international conference to bring about a political solution to the conflict. In December 1994 OIC heads of state, convened in Morocco, proclaimed that the UN arms embargo on Bosnia and Herzegovina could not be applied to the Muslim authorities of that Republic. The Conference also resolved to review economic relations between OIC member states and any country that supported Serbian activities. An aid fund was established, to which member states were requested to contribute between US $500,000 and $5m., in order to provide further humanitarian and economic assistance to Bosnian Muslims. In July 1995 the OIC contact group on Bosnia and Herzegovina (at that time comprising Egypt, Iran, Malaysia, Morocco, Pakistan, Saudi Arabia, Senegal and Turkey), meeting in Geneva, Switzerland, declared the UN arms embargo against Bosnia and Herzegovina to be 'invalid'. Several Governments subsequently announced their willingness officially to supply weapons and other military assistance to the Bosnian Muslim forces. In September a meeting of all OIC ministers of defence and foreign affairs endorsed the establishment of an 'assistance mobilization group' which was to supply military, economic, legal and other assistance to Bosnia and Herzegovina. In a joint declaration the ministers also demanded the return of all territory seized by Bosnian Serb forces, the continued NATO bombing of Serb military targets, and that the city of Sarajevo be preserved under a Muslim-led Bosnian Government. In November the OIC Secretary-General endorsed the peace accord for the former Yugoslavia, which was concluded, in Dayton, USA, by leaders of all the conflicting factions, and reaffirmed the commitment of Islamic states to participate in efforts to implement the accord. In the following month the OIC Conference of Ministers of Foreign Affairs, convened in Conakry, Guinea, requested the full support of the international community to reconstruct Bosnia and Herzegovina through humanitarian aid as well as economic and technical co-operation. In December 1996 the ministers reaffirmed the importance of ensuring that the provisions of the Dayton Peace Agreement for the former Yugoslavia were fully implemented. In early April 1999 ministers of foreign affairs of the countries comprising OIC's contact group met to consider the crisis in Kosovo. The meeting condemned Serbian atrocities being committed against the local Albanian population and urged the provision of international assistance for the thousands of people displaced by the conflict. The group resolved to establish a committee to co-ordinate relief aid provided by member states. The ministers also expressed their willingness to help to formulate a peaceful settlement and to participate in any subsequent implementation force. In May 2009 the OIC passed a resolution welcoming progress made following Kosovo's declaration of independence in February 2008; official recognition of Kosovo's independence was, however, to be decided by each member state on an individual basis.

Kashmir: A report by an OIC fact-finding mission, which in February 1993 visited Azad Kashmir while investigating allegations of repression of the largely Muslim population of the Indian state of Jammu and Kashmir by the Indian armed forces, was presented to the 1993 Conference of Ministers of Foreign Affairs. The meeting urged member states to take the necessary measures to persuade India to cease the 'massive human rights violations' in Jammu and Kashmir and to allow the Indian Kashmiris to 'exercise their inalienable right to self-determination'. In September 1994 ministers of foreign affairs, meeting in Islamabad, Pakistan, agreed to establish a contact group on Jammu and Kashmir, which was to provide a mechanism for promoting international awareness of the situation in that region and for seeking a peaceful solution to the dispute. In December OIC heads of state approved a resolution condemning reported human rights abuses by Indian security forces in Kashmir. In June 2002 the OIC Secretary-General expressed his concern at the escalation of tensions between Pakistan and India regarding Kashmir. He urged both sides to withdraw their troops and to refrain from the use of force. In June 2004 the Secretary-General welcomed progress achieved by a round of expert-level talks on nuclear confidence-building measures conducted during that month by India and Pakistan. In August 2008 the Secretary-General condemned the 'excessive and unwarranted use of force' following the suppression of protests over the regional government's transfer of forest land to a Hindu shrine in a predominantly Muslim area of Kashmir. An OIC special envoy for Kashmir was nominated in October 2009.

Afghanistan: In July 1994 the OIC Secretary-General visited Afghanistan and proposed the establishment of a preparatory mechanism to promote national reconciliation in that country. In mid-1995 Saudi Arabia, acting as a representative of the OIC, pursued a peace initiative for Afghanistan and issued an invitation for leaders of the different factions to hold negotiations in Jeddah. In April 1998 the OIC, jointly with the UN, sponsored new peace negotiations between the main disputing factions in Afghanistan, which were conducted in Islamabad, Pakistan. In early May, however, the talks collapsed and were postponed indefinitely. In September the Secretaries-General of the OIC and the UN agreed to establish a joint mission to counter the deteriorating security situation along the Afghan–Iranian border, following the large-scale deployment of Taliban troops in the region and consequent military manoeuvres by the Iranian authorities. In early March 2000 the OIC mediated contacts between the parties to the conflict in Afghanistan, with a view to reviving peace negotiations. Talks, held under OIC auspices, ensued in May. Both the elected Government of Afghanistan and its opponents, the Taliban, sent delegations to the OIC summit conference, held in Doha, Qatar. The summit determined that Afghanistan's official participation in the OIC, suspended in 1996, should not yet be reinstated. In early 2001 a senior-level delegation from the OIC visited Afghanistan in an attempt to prevent further destruction of ancient statues by Taliban supporters. In October 2001 OIC ministers of foreign affairs established a fund to assist Afghan civilians, following US-led military attacks on targets in Afghanistan. In mid-2010 the OIC determined to appoint a permanent representative for Afghanistan, to be based in an OIC office in Kabul, the Afghan capital. The OIC Kabul office was inaugurated in January 2011. In March 2011 the OIC Secretary-General, addressing the International Contact Group on Afghanistan, stressed OIC support for the High Peace Council, established in Afghanistan in 2010 as a platform for dialogue between the Afghan administration and the Taliban, and stated the willingness of the Organization to contribute to peace in that country.

Combating Terrorism: In December 1994 OIC heads of state adopted a Code of Conduct for Combating International Terrorism, in an attempt to control Muslim extremist groups. The code commits states to ensuring that militant groups do not use their territory for planning or executing terrorist activity against other states, in addition to states refraining from direct support or participation in acts of terrorism. An OIC Convention on Combating International Terrorism was adopted in 1998. In September 2001 the OIC Secretary-General strongly condemned major terrorist attacks perpetrated against targets in the USA. Soon afterwards the US authorities rejected a proposal by the Taliban regime that an OIC observer mission be deployed to monitor the activities of the Saudi Arabian-born exiled militant Islamist fundamentalist leader Osama bin Laden, who was accused by the US Government of having co-ordinated the attacks from alleged terrorist bases in the Taliban-administered area of Afghanistan. An extraordinary meeting of OIC ministers of foreign affairs, convened in early October, in Doha, Qatar, to consider the implications of the terrorist atrocities, condemned the attacks and declared its support for combating all manifestations of terrorism within the framework of a proposed collective initiative co-ordinated under the auspices of the UN. The meeting, which did not pronounce directly on the recently-initiated US-led military retaliation against targets in Afghanistan, urged that no Arab or Muslim state should be targeted under the pretext of eliminating terrorism. In February 2002 the Secretary-General expressed concern at statements of the US administration describing Iran and Iraq (as well as the Democratic People's Republic of Korea) as belonging to an 'axis of evil' involved in international terrorism and the development of weapons of mass destruction. In early April OIC ministers of foreign affairs convened an extraordinary session on terrorism, in Kuala Lumpur, Malaysia. The meeting issued the Kuala Lumpur Declaration, which reiterated member states' collective resolve to combat terrorism, recalling the organization's 1994 code of conduct and 1998 convention to this effect; condemned attempts to associate terrorist activities with Islam or any other particular creed, civilization or nationality, and rejected attempts to associate Islamic states or the Palestinian struggle with terrorism; rejected the implementation of international action against any Muslim state on the pretext of combating terrorism; urged the organization of a global conference on international terrorism; and urged an examination of the root causes of international terrorism. The meeting adopted a plan of action on addressing the issues raised in the declaration. Its implementation was to be co-ordinated by a 13-member committee on international terrorism. Member states were encouraged to sign and ratify the Convention on Combating International Terrorism in order to accelerate its implementation. In June 2002 ministers of foreign affairs issued a declaration reiterating the OIC call for an international conference to be convened, under UN auspices, in order clearly to define terrorism and to agree on the international procedures and mechanisms for combating terrorism through the UN. In May 2003 the 30th session of the Conference of Ministers of Foreign Affairs, entitled 'Unity and Dignity', issued the Tehran Declaration, in which it resolved to combat terrorism and to contribute to preserving peace and security in Islamic countries. The Declaration also pledged its full support for the Palestinian cause and rejected the labelling as 'terrorist' of those Muslim states deemed to be resisting foreign aggression and occupation.

Supporting Muslim Minorities and Combating Anti-Islamic Feeling: In December 1995 OIC ministers of foreign affairs determined that an intergovernmental group of experts should be established to address the situation of minority Muslim communities residing in non-OIC states. The OIC committee of experts responsible for formulating a plan of action for safeguarding the rights of Muslim communities and minorities met for the first time in 1998. In June 2001 the OIC condemned attacks and ongoing discrimination against the Muslim community in Myanmar. In October 2005 the OIC Secretary-General expressed concern at the treatment of Muslims in the southern provinces of Thailand. The first tripartite meeting between the OIC, the Government of the Philippines and Muslim separatists based in the southern Philippines took place in November 2007, and in April 2009 the OIC Secretary-General announced the appointment of an OIC special envoy to assist in negotiating a peaceful solution to the conflict in the southern Philippines.

In January 2006 the OIC strongly condemned the publication in a Norwegian newspaper of a series of caricatures of the Prophet Muhammad that had originally appeared in a Danish publication in September 2005 and had caused considerable offence to many Muslims. An Islamic Observatory on Islamophobia was established in September 2006; in April 2011 the Observatory released its fourth annual report on Islamophobia. In December 2007 the OIC organized the first International Conference on Islamophobia, aimed at addressing concerns that alleged instances of defamation of Islam appeared to be increasing world-wide (particularly in Europe). Responding to a reported rise in anti-Islamic attacks in western nations, OIC leaders denounced stereotyping and discrimination, and urged the promotion of Islam by Islamic states as a 'moderate, peaceful and tolerant religion'. In June 2011 the OIC Secretary-General issued a statement strongly condemning 'attacks on Islam and insult and vilification of the Prophet Muhummad and his wives' by the right-wing Dutch politician Geert Wilders.

Reform of the OIC: In March 1997, at an extraordinary meeting of heads of state and of government, held in Islamabad, Pakistan, an Islamabad Declaration was adopted, which pledged to increase co-operation between members of the OIC. In November 2000 OIC heads of state attended the ninth summit conference, held in Doha, Qatar, and issued the Doha Declaration, which reaffirmed commitment to the OIC Charter and undertook to modernize the organization. The 10th OIC summit meeting, held in October 2003, in Putrajaya, Malaysia, issued the Putrajaya Declaration, in which Islamic leaders resolved to enhance Islamic states' role and influence in international affairs. The leaders adopted a plan of action that entailed: reviewing and strengthening OIC positions on international issues; enhancing dialogue among Muslim thinkers and policy-makers through relevant OIC insitutions; promoting constructive dialogue with other cultures and civilizations; completing an ongoing review of the structure and efficacy of the OIC Secretariat; establishing a working group to address means of enhancing the role of Islamic education; promoting among member states the development of science and technology, discussion of ecological issues, and the role of information communication technology in development; improving mechanisms to assist member states in post-conflict situations; and advancing trade and investment through data-sharing and encouraging access to markets for products from poorer member states. In January 2005 the inaugural meeting of an OIC Commission of Eminent Persons was convened in Putrajaya. The Commission was mandated to make recommendations in the following areas: the preparation of a strategy and plan of action enabling the Islamic community to meet the challenges of the 21st century; the preparation of a comprehensive plan for promoting enlightened moderation, both within Islamic societies and universally; and the preparation of proposals for the future reform and restructuring of the OIC system. In December the third extraordinary OIC summit, convened in Mecca, Saudi Arabia, adopted a Ten-Year Programme of Action to Meet the Challenges Facing the Ummah (the Islamic world) in the 21st Century, a related Mecca Declaration and a report by the Commission of Eminent Persons. The summit determined to restructure the OIC, and mandated the establishment of an Executive Committee, comprising the summit conference and ministerial conference troikas (equally reflecting the African, Arab and Asian member states), the OIC host country, and the OIC Secretariat, to implement Conference resolutions.

The 11th OIC heads of state summit meeting, held in Dakar, Senegal, in March 2008, endorsed a revised OIC Charter.

Finance

The OIC's activities are financed by mandatory contributions from member states.

Subsidiary Organs

Islamic Centre for the Development of Trade: Complexe Commercial des Habous, ave des FAR, BP 13545, Casablanca, Morocco; tel. (522) 314974; fax (522) 310110; e-mail icdt@icdt-oic.org; internet www.icdt-oic.org; f. 1983 to encourage regular commercial contacts, harmonize policies and promote investments among OIC mems; Dir-Gen. ALLAL RACHDI; publs *Tijaris: International and Inter-Islamic Trade Magazine* (bi-monthly), *Inter-Islamic Trade Report* (annually).

Islamic Jurisprudence (Fiqh) Academy: POB 13917, Jeddah, Saudi Arabia; tel. (2) 667-1664; fax (2) 667-0873; internet www.fiqhacademy.org.sa; f. 1982; Gen. Sec. MAULANA KHALID SAIFULLAH RAHMANI.

Islamic Solidarity Fund: c/o OIC Secretariat, POB 178, Jeddah 21411, Saudi Arabia; tel. (2) 680-0800; fax (2) 687-3568; f. 1974 to meet the needs of Islamic communities by providing emergency aid and the finance to build mosques, Islamic centres, hospitals, schools and universities; Exec. Dir IBRAHIM BIN ABDALLA AL-HUZEIM.

Islamic University in Uganda: POB 2555, Mbale, Uganda; tel. (35) 2512100; fax (45) 433502; e-mail info@iuiu.ac.ug; internet www.iuiu.ac.ug/; f. 1988 to meet the educational needs of Muslim populations in English-speaking African countries; second campus in Kampala; mainly financed by OIC; Rector Dr AHMAD KAWESA SENGENDO.

Islamic University of Niger: BP 11507, Niamey, Niger; tel. 20-72-39-03; fax 20-73-37-96; e-mail unislam@intnet.ne; internet www.universite_say.ne/; f. 1984; provides courses of study in *Shari'a* (Islamic law) and Arabic language and literature; also offers courses in pedagogy and teacher training; receives grants from Islamic Solidarity Fund and contributions from OIC member states; Rector Prof. ABDELJAOUAD SEKKAT.

Islamic University of Technology (IUT): Board Bazar, Gazipur 1704, Dhaka, Bangladesh; tel. (2) 9291250; fax (2) 9291260; e-mail vc@iut-dhaka.edu; internet www.iutoic-dhaka.edu; f. 1981 as the Islamic Centre for Technical and Vocational Training and Resources, named changed to Islamic Institute of Technology in 1994, current name adopted in 2001; aims to develop human resources in OIC mem. states, with special reference to engineering, technology, and technical education; 145 staff and 800 students; library of 30,450 vols; Vice-Chancellor Prof. Dr M. IMTIAZ HOSSAIN; publs *Journal of Engineering and Technology* (2 a year), *News Bulletin* (annually), *News Letter* (6 a year), annual calendar and announcement for admission, reports, human resources development series.

Research Centre for Islamic History, Art and Culture (IRCICA): POB 24, Beşiktaş 34354, İstanbul, Turkey; tel. (212) 2591742; fax (212) 2584365; e-mail ircica@ircica.org; internet www.ircica.org; f. 1980; library of 60,000 vols; Dir-Gen. Prof. Dr HALIT EREN; publs *Newsletter* (3 a year), monographical studies.

Statistical, Economic and Social Research and Training Centre for Islamic Countries (SESRIC) : Attar Sokak No. 4, GOP 06700, Ankara, Turkey; tel. (312) 4686172; fax (312) 4673458; e-mail oicankara@sesric.org; internet www.sesric.org; became operational in 1978; has a three-fold mandate: to collate, process and disseminate socio-economic statistics and information on, and for the utilization of, its member countries; to study and assess economic and social developments in member countries with the aim of helping to generate proposals for advancing co-operation; and to organize training programmes in selected areas; the Centre also acts as a focal point for technical co-operation activities between the OIC system and related UN agencies; and prepares economic and social reports and background documentation for OIC meetings; Dir-Gen. Dr SAVAS ALPAY; publs *Annual Economic Report on the OIC Countries*, *Journal of Economic Cooperation and Development* (quarterly), *Economic Cooperation and Development Review* (semi-annually), *InfoReport* (quarterly), *Statistical Yearbook* (annually), *Basic Facts and Figures on OIC Member Countries* (annually).

Specialized Institutions

International Islamic News Agency (IINA): King Khalid Palace, Madinah Rd, POB 5054, Jeddah 21422, Saudi Arabia; tel. (2) 665-8561; fax (2) 665-9358; e-mail iina@islamicnews.org; internet www.iina.me/english; f. 1972; distributes news and reports daily on events in the Islamic world, in Arabic, English and French; Dir-Gen. ERDEM KOK.

Islamic Educational, Scientific and Cultural Organization (ISESCO): BP 2275 Rabat 10104, Morocco; tel. (37) 772433; fax (37) 772058; e-mail cid@isesco.org.ma; internet www.isesco.org.ma; f. 1982; Dir-Gen. Dr ABDULAZIZ BIN OTHMAN ALTWAIJRI; publs *ISESCO Newsletter* (quarterly), *Islam Today* (2 a year), *ISESCO Triennial*.

Islamic States Broadcasting Union (ISBU): POB 6351, Jeddah 21442, Saudi Arabia; tel. (2) 672-1121; fax (2) 672-2600; e-mail isbo@isbo.org; internet www.isboo.org; f. 1975; Sec.-Gen. Dr MOHAMED AHMED SOBAIHI.

Affiliated Institutions

International Association of Islamic Banks (IAIB): King Abdulaziz St, Queen's Bldg, 23rd Floor, Al-Balad Dist, POB 9707, Jeddah

21423, Saudi Arabia; tel. (2) 651-6900; fax (2) 651-6552; f. 1977 to link financial institutions operating on Islamic banking principles; activities include training and research; mems: 192 banks and other financial institutions in 34 countries.

Islamic Chamber of Commerce and Industry: POB 3831, Clifton, Karachi 75600, Pakistan; tel. (21) 5874910; fax (21) 5870765; e-mail icci@icci-oic.org; internet www.iccionline.net/en/icci-en/index.aspx; f. 1979 to promote trade and industry among member states; comprises nat. chambers or feds of chambers of commerce and industry; Sec.-Gen. Dr MOSTAFA HODIEB.

Islamic Committee for the International Crescent: POB 17434, Benghazi, Libya; tel. (61) 9095824; fax (61) 9095823; e-mail info@icic-oic.org; internet www.icic-oic.org; f. 1979 to attempt to alleviate the suffering caused by natural disasters and war; Pres. ALI MAHMOUD BUHEDMA.

Islamic Solidarity Sports Federation: POB 5844, Riyadh 11442, Saudi Arabia; tel. (1) 480-9253; fax (1) 482-2145; e-mail issf@awalnet.net.sa; f. 1981; Sec.-Gen. Dr MOHAMMAD SALEH QAZDAR.

Organization of Islamic Capitals and Cities (OICC): POB 13621, Jeddah 21414, Saudi Arabia; tel. (2) 698-1953; fax (2) 698-1053; e-mail webmaster@oicc.org; internet www.oicc.org; f. 1980; aims to preserve the identity and the heritage of Islamic capitals and cities; to achieve and enhance sustainable development in member capitals and cities; to establish and develop comprehensive urban norms, systems and plans to serve the growth and prosperity of Islamic capitals and cities and to enhance their cultural, environmental, urban, economic and social conditions; to advance municipal services and facilities in the member capitals and cities; to support member cities' capacity-building programmes; and to consolidate fellowship and co-ordinate the scope of co-operation between members; comprises 147 capitals and cities as active members, eight observer members and 16 associate members, in Asia, Africa, Europe and South America; Sec.-Gen. OMAR KADI.

Organization of the Islamic Shipowners' Association: POB 14900, Jeddah 21434, Saudi Arabia; tel. (2) 663-7882; fax (2) 660-4920; e-mail mail@oisaonline.com; internet www.oisaonline.com; f. 1981 to promote co-operation among maritime cos in Islamic countries; in 1998 mems approved the establishment of a new commercial venture, the Bakkah Shipping Company, to enhance sea transport in the region; Sec.-Gen. Dr ABDULLATIF A. SULTAN.

World Federation of Arab-Islamic Schools: 2 Wadi el-Nile St, Maadi, Cairo, Egypt; tel. (2) 358-3278; internet www.wfais.org; f. 1976; supports Arab-Islamic schools world-wide and encourages co-operation between the institutions; promotes the dissemination of the Arabic language and Islamic culture; supports the training of personnel.

PACIFIC COMMUNITY

Address: BP D5, 98848 Nouméa Cédex, New Caledonia.

Telephone: 26-20-00; **fax:** 26-38-18; **e-mail:** spc@spc.int; **internet:** www.spc.int.

In February 1947 the Governments of Australia, France, the Netherlands, New Zealand, the United Kingdom, and the USA signed the Canberra Agreement establishing the South Pacific Commission, which came into effect in July 1948. (The Netherlands withdrew from the Commission in 1962, when it ceased to administer the former colony of Dutch New Guinea, now Papua, formerly known as Irian Jaya, part of Indonesia.) In October 1997 the 37th South Pacific Conference, convened in Canberra, Australia, agreed to rename the organization the Pacific Community, with effect from 6 February 1998. The Secretariat of the Pacific Community (SPC) services the Community, and provides research, technical advice, training and assistance in economic, social and cultural development to 22 countries and territories of the Pacific region. It serves a population of about 6.8m., scattered over some 30m. sq km, more than 98% of which is sea.

MEMBERS

American Samoa
Australia
Cook Islands
Fiji
France
French Polynesia
Guam
Kiribati
Marshall Islands
Federated States of Micronesia
Nauru
New Caledonia
New Zealand
Niue
Northern Mariana Islands
Palau
Papua New Guinea
Pitcairn Islands
Samoa
Solomon Islands
Tokelau
Tonga
Tuvalu
USA
Vanuatu
Wallis and Futuna Islands

Organization

(October 2011)

CONFERENCE OF THE PACIFIC COMMUNITY

The Conference is the governing body of the Community (replacing the former South Pacific Conference) and is composed of representatives of all member countries and territories. The main responsibilities of the Conference, which meets every two years, are to appoint the Director-General, to determine major national or regional policy issues in the areas of competence of the organization and to note changes to the Financial and Staff Regulations approved by the Committee of Representatives of Governments and Administrations (CRGA). The sixth Conference of the Pacific Community was convened in October 2009 in Nuku'alofa, Tonga; the seventh Conference was scheduled to be held in Majuro, Marshall Islands, in November 2011.

COMMITTEE OF REPRESENTATIVES OF GOVERNMENTS AND ADMINISTRATIONS (CRGA)

The CRGA comprises representatives of all member states and territories, having equal voting rights. It meets annually to consider the work programme evaluation conducted by the Secretariat and to discuss any changes proposed by the Secretariat in the context of regional priorities; to consider and approve any policy issues for the organization presented by the Secretariat or by member countries and territories; to consider applicants and make recommendations for the post of Director-General; to approve the administrative and work programme budgets; to approve amendments to the Financial and Staff Regulations; and to conduct annual performance evaluations of the Director-General.

SECRETARIAT

The Secretariat of the Pacific Community (SPC) is headed by a Director-General, a Senior Deputy Director-General and a Deputy Director-General, based in Suva, Fiji. In October 2009 the CRGA approved a reorganization which was completed by January 2011 and included the transfer to SPC of activities from the Pacific Islands Applied Geoscience Commission (SOPAC), with a view to making SPC the lead co-ordinating agency for the Pacific regional energy sector. The reorganization provided for Secretariat divisions of Applied Geoscience and Technology; Economic Development; Land Resources; Fisheries, Aquaculture and Marine Ecosystems; Public Health; and Social Resources; and for the merger into the SPC of the South Pacific Board for Educational Assessment (SPBEA), initially as a stand-alone programme. The Secretariat provides information services, including library facilities, publications, translation and computer services.

Director-General: Dr JIMMIE RODGERS (Solomon Islands).

Deputy Directors-General: FEKITAMOELOA KATOA 'UTOIKAMANU (Tonga), RICHARD MANN (Germany).

North Pacific Regional Office: POB 2299, Botanical Garden 2, Kolonia, Pohnpei, Federated States of Micronesia; tel. 320-7523; fax 320-5854; e-mail amenay@spc.int.

Suva Regional Office: Private Mail Bag, Suva, Fiji; tel. 3370733; fax 3370021; e-mail spcsuva@spc.org.fj.

Activities

SPC provides, on request of its member countries, technical assistance, advisory services, information and clearing-house services aimed at developing the technical, professional, scientific, research, planning and management capabilities of the regional population. SPC also conducts regional conferences and technical meetings, as well as training courses, workshops and seminars at the regional or country level. It provides small grants-in-aid and awards to meet specific requests and needs of members. In November 1996 the Conference agreed to establish a specific Small Islands States (SIS) fund to provide technical services, training and other relevant activities. The Pacific Community oversees the maritime programme and telecommunications policy activities of the Pacific Islands Forum Secretariat.

The 1999 Conference, held in Tahiti in December, adopted the 'Déclaration de Tahiti Nui', a mandate that detailed the operational policies and mechanisms of the Pacific Community, taking into account operational changes not covered by the founding Canberra Agreement. The Declaration was regarded as a 'living document' that would be periodically revised to record subsequent modifications of operational policy.

SPC has signed memoranda of understanding with the World Health Organization (WHO), the Forum Fisheries Agency, the South Pacific Regional Environment Programme (SPREP), and several other partners. The organization participates in meetings of the Council of Regional Organizations in the Pacific (CROP). Representatives of SPC and SPREP have in recent years convened periodic meetings to develop regional technical co-operation and harmonization of work programmes.

SPC aims to develop joint country strategies with each of the Pacific Community's member countries and territories, detailing the full scope of its assistance over a defined period.

APPLIED GEOSCIENCE AND TECHNOLOGY

The reorganization of SPC implemented during 2010 provided for the core work programme of SOPAC (see above) to be absorbed into SPC as a new Applied Geoscience and Technology Division. The Division has responsibility for ensuring the productive regional utilization of earth sciences (geology, geophysics, oceanography and hydrology), and comprises the following three technical work programmes: ocean and islands; water and sanitation; and disaster reduction.

ECONOMIC DEVELOPMENT

The Economic Development Division (EDD) has the following four pillars: programmes in the areas of Transport, Energy, Infrastructure and Information and Communications Technology (ICT). An inaugural Regional Meeting of Ministers for Energy, ICT and Transport was held in April 2011, on the theme of 'strategic engagement for economic development'.

The Transport Programme comprises the work of the former Regional Maritime Programme (RMP—amalgamated into the main Transport Programme in mid-2011), as well as research and advisory services relating to specific capacity in aviation, and research into transport research. The RMP's principal areas of focus were to advise member governments on maritime issues; the provision of technical capacity support; and training in the areas of maritime administration, institutions, ports, shipping and seafaring. In 2002 the RMP launched the model Pacific Islands Maritime Legislation and Regulations as a framework for the development of national maritime legislation. The RMP's priorities during 2006–10 were: supporting Pacific Islands and territories (PICTs) in retaining/gaining status on the International Maritime Organization's 'white list' of nations deemed to be implementing fully the International Convention on Standards of Training, Certification and Watchkeeping for Seafarers; supporting further regional compliance with the international security regime; and advancing regional professional peer networks. Since 2006 the Transport programme has provided the secretariat of the Pacific Maritime Transport Alliance. The inaugural regional meeting of ministers responsible for maritime transport was convened in April 2007. In April 2011 SPEC transport ministers adopted a Framework for Action on Transport Services (FATS) to support all PICTs to provide regular, safe and affordable air and sea transport services

The Energy Programme comprises related activities transferred from SOPAC (see above), including its advisory functions and activities relating to petroleum data and information. The Programme co-ordinates and leads work on: energy policy, planning, legislation and regulation; petroleum, including procurement, transport, storage and pricing mechanisms; renewable energy production; energy efficiency and conservation; and support for the Pacific Power Association and other relevant bodies regarding to power generation and electric utilities. In April 2011 ministers responsible for energy adopted a Framework for Action on Energy Security in the Pacific (FAESP) and an implementation plan.

The Pacific ICT Outreach (PICTO) Programme, established in January 2010, implements the 'Framework for Action on ICT for Development in the Pacific', endorsed in June 2010 by ministers responsible for ICT; and takes into account initiatives such as the Pacific Regional Infrastructure facility; to implement the Pacific Plan Digital Strategy; to take over work on ICT policy and regulations hitherto undertaken by the Pacific Islands Forum Secretariat; to continue ongoing SPC work relating to submarine cable and satellite communication technology; and to support the ongoing Oceania 'one laptop per child' (OLPC) initiative. In October SPC launched the e-Pacific Island Countries (e-PIC), an online portal providing access to information including country profiles; downloadable documents relating to policy, legal and regulatory matters, publications, news and research materials; a regional forum; and a register of ICT professionals and policy makers. In April 2011 SPC hosted a Pacific ICT Ministerial Forum, and signed an agreement with the International Telecommunications Union to enhance co-operation between the two organizations and facilitate the implementation of ICT and cyber protection programmes throughout the region. A Pacific Regional Workshop on Cybercrime, was held in Nukúalofa, Tonga, in May.

With other regional partners, including the Pacific Islands Forum and Asian Development Bank, the SPC supported the Pacific Conference on the Human Face of the Global Economic Crisis, hosted by the Vanuatu Government in February 2010, in Port Vila.

LAND RESOURCES

The Land Resources Division (LRD) comprises three major programmes: the sustainable management of integrated forest and agriculture systems programme; the biosecurity and trade support programme; and the food security and health programme. In September 2008 ministers of agriculture and forestry of Pacific Island countries, convened in Apia, Samoa, approved a second LRD strategic plan, following on from a first strategic plan that had been implemented during 2005–08. The second plan, covering the period 2009–12, emphasized three primary objectives: strengthened regional food and nutritional security (identified in view of recently soaring global food prices); integrated and sustainable agriculture and forestry resource management and development; and improved biosecurity and increased trade in agriculture and forestry products. The LRD has increasingly decentralized the delivery of its services, which are co-ordinated at the country level by personnel within national agricultural systems. The LRD aims to develop the capacity of PICTs in initiatives such as policy analysis and advice, and support for agricultural science and technology. SPC hosts the Centre for Pacific Crops and Trees (CePaCT, known prior to 2007 as the Regional Germplasm Centre), which assists PICTs in efforts to conserve and access regional genetic resources. In 2001 the Pacific Community endorsed the Pacific Agricultural Plant Genetic Resources Network (PAPGREN), which is implemented by the LRD and other partners. The Pacific Animal Health Information System (PAHIS) provides data on regional livestock numbers and the regional status of animal diseases, and the Pacific Islands Pest List Database provides a register of regional agriculture, forestry and environmental pests. In 2003 an EU-funded Development of Sustainable Agriculture in the Pacific (DSAP) project was initiated to assist 10 member countries to implement sustainable agriculture measures and to improve food production and security. A further six Pacific countries joined the programme in 2004. The LRD co-ordinates the development of organic agriculture in the Pacific region. In 2008 it adopted the Pacific Organic Standard, and it supports the Pacific Organic and Ethical Trade Community (POETCom), which was launched in 2009 to replace a previous Regional Organic Task Force (established in 2006). In December 2009 a POETCom technical experts' group met to finalize a farmers' version of the Pacific Organic Standard. IFAD and the International Federation of Organic Agricultural Movement (IFOAM) contributed to the development of the Pacific Regional Organic Strategic Plan for 2009–13. In late September 2009 SPC organized a meeting of heads of forestry agencies in the Pacific, on the theme 'Forests, Climate Change and Markets'. In October 2010 a multi-agency Food Secure Pacific (FSP) working group, established in 2008 by SPC, Pacific Islands Forum Secretariat, FAO, UNICEF and WHO, began implementing a new Framework for Action on Food Security in the Pacific, which had been endorsed by a Pacific Food Summit, convened in April 2010, in Port Vila, Vanuatu.

FISHERIES, AQUACULTURE AND MARINE ECOSYSTEMS

The Fisheries, Aquaculture and Marine Ecosystems (FAME) Division aims to support and co-ordinate the sustainable development and management of inshore fisheries resources in the region, to undertake scientific research in order to provide member governments with relevant information for the sustainable development and management of tuna and billfish resources in and adjacent to the South Pacific region, and to provide data and analytical services to national fisheries departments. The principal programmes under FAME are the Coastal Fisheries Programme (CFP) and the Oceanic Fisheries Programme (OFP). The development and advisory activities of the CFP are focused within the near territorial and archipelagic waters of the PICTs. The CFP is divided into the following sections: the Reef Fisheries Observatory; sustainable fisheries development; fisheries management; fisheries training; and aqualculture. SPC administers the Pacific Island Aquaculture Network, a forum for promoting regional aquaculture development. During 2007 a Pacific Regional Aquatic Biosecurity Initiative was initiated. In contrast to the CFP, the OFP focuses it activities within 200-mile exclusive economic zones and surrounding waters, and is mandated to equip PICTs with the necessary scientific information and advice for rationally managing and exploiting the regional resources of tuna, billfish and related species. The OFP consists of the following three sections: statistics and monitoring; tuna ecology and biology; and stock assessment and modelling. The statistics and monitoring section maintains a database of industrial tuna fisheries in the region. The OFP contributed research and statistical information for the formulation of the Convention for the Conservation and Management of Highly Migratory Fish Stocks in the Western and Central Pacific, which entered into force in June 2004 and aims to establish a regime for the sustainable management of tuna reserves. In March 2002 SPC and European Commission launched a Pacific Regional Oceanic and Coastal Fisheries Project (PROCFISH). The oceanic component of the project aimed to assist the OFP with advancing knowledge of tuna fisheries ecosystems, while the coastal element was to produce the first comparative regional baseline assessment of reef fisheries. A workshop on the ecosystem approach to management of coastal fisheries in PICTs was convened in March–April 2009 jointly by the Pacific Community and FAO. The theme of the fifth Pacific Community Conference, convened in November 2007, was 'The future of Pacific fisheries'; a set of recommendations on managing the regional fisheries was endorsed by the Conference.

SPC hosts the Pacific Office of the WorldFish Center (the International Centre for Living Aquatic Resources Management—ICLARM); SPC and the WorldFish Center have jointly implemented a number of projects. SPC also hosts the Co-ordination Unit of the Coral Reef Initiative for the South Pacific (CRISP), which was launched in January 2005 to address the protection and management of the region's coral reefs.

PUBLIC HEALTH

The Public Health Division aims to implement health promotion programmes; to assist regional authorities to strengthen health information systems and to promote the use of new technology for health information development and disease control; to promote efficient health services management; and to help all Pacific Islanders to attain a level of health and quality of life that will enable them to contribute to the development of their communities. The three main areas of focus of the Public Health Division are: noncommunicable diseases (such as heart disease, cerebrovascular disease and diabetes, which are prevalent in parts of the region); communicable diseases (such as HIV/AIDS, other sexually tranmitted infections—STIs, TB, and vector-borne diseases such as malaria and dengue fever); and public health policy. A Healthy Pacific Lifestyle section aims to assist member countries to improve and sustain health, in particular through advice on nutrition, physical activity and the damaging effects of alcohol and tobacco. The Public Health Surveillance and Communicable Disease Control section is the focal point of the Pacific Public Health Surveillance Network (PPHSN), a regional framework established in 1996 jointly by SPC and WHO, with the aim of sustainably advancing regional public health surveillance and response. SPC operates a project (mainly funded by Australia and New Zealand), to prevent AIDS and STIs among young people through peer education and awareness. SPC is the lead regional agency for co-ordinating and monitoring the implementation of the Pacific Regional Strategy on HIV/AIDS and other STIs, endorsed by both the Community and the Pacific Islands Forum, and covering the period 2009–13. In March 2007 the Pacific Community launched the Oceania Society for Sexual Health and HIV Medicine, a new Pacific network aimed at ensuring access to best practice prevention, treatment, care and support services in the area of sexual health and HIV/AIDS. SPC and WHO jointly organize regular meetings aimed at strengthening TB control in the region. In February 2006 SPC established a Pacific Regional Infection Control Network, based in Fiji, to improve communication and access to expert technical advice on all aspects of infectious diseases and control. During 2006 SPC, in partnership with FAO, WHO and the World Organisation for Animal Health, established the Pacific Regional Influenza Pandemic Preparedness Project (PRIPPP), with the aim of supporting the PICTs in elaborating plans to prepare for outbreaks of avian influenza or other rapidly contagious diseases. A Pacific Community Pandemic Task Force, established under the PRIPPP and comprising human and animal health experts from Pacific governments and international and regional organizations, met for the first time in March 2007 at the Pacific Community headquarters. In July 2009 Pacific ministers of health met to discuss issues including the development of strategies to control and prevent escalating diseases in the region, and the impact on regional nutrition and health of reduced household incomes in view of the global economic crisis. A Pacific Non-communicable Disease (NCD) Forum, held in Nadi, Fiji, in August, agreed recommendations on action to address the increasing regional prevalence of NCDs (also referred to as 'lifestyle diseases'). In June 2011 SPC, with WHO, organised the ninth meeting of Pacific Island ministers of health, at which it was acknowledged that the escalation in incidence of NCDs remained a priority for all regional governments.

SOCIAL RESOURCES

The Social Resources Division comprises the Human Development Programme (HDP), the Regional Media Centre, the Pacific Regional Rights Resource Team, and the Statistics and Demography Programmes.

The HDP focuses on the areas of gender; youth; culture; and community education. The HDP's Pacific Women's Bureau (PWB) aims to promote the social, economic and cultural advancement of women in the region by assisting governments and regional organizations to include women in the development planning process. The PWB also provides technical and advisory services, advocacy and management support training to groups concerned with women in development and gender and development, and administers the Pacific Women's Information Network (PACWIN). A new adviser for gender equality was appointed in September 2008. The SPC hosted the 11th Triennial Conference of Pacific Women, at its Nouméa, New Caledonia headquarters, in August 2010. The Pacific Youth Bureau (PYB) co-ordinates the implementation of the Pacific Youth Strategy (PYS), which is updated at five-yearly intervals, most recently to cover the period 2011–15, and aims to develop opportunities for young people to play an active role in society. The PYB provides non-formal education and support for youth, community workers and young adults in community development subjects and provides grants to help young people find employment. It also advises and assists the Pacific Youth Council in promoting a regional youth identity. At the first Pacific Youth Festival, held in Tahiti in July 2006, a Pacific Youth Charter was formulated, to be incorporated into the PYS. A Pacific Youth Mapping Exercise (PYME) was undertaken in 2007, with the aim of establishing a complete picture of youth programmes being implemented across the region. The second Pacific Youth Festival, held in Suva, Fiji, in July 2009, included discussions on the following issues: promoting healthy living; Pacific identity; adaptation to climate change; and governance, peace and security. In September 2011 the Community published a *State of Pacific Youth Report*, which had been prepared with the Pacific Office of the UN Children's Fund.

The HDP works to preserve and promote the cultural heritage of the Pacific Islands. The Programme assists with the training of librarians, archivists and researchers and promotes instruction in local languages, history and art at schools in the PICTs. SPC acts as the secretariat of the Council of Pacific Arts, which organizes the Festival of Pacific Arts on a four-yearly basis. The 10th Festival was staged in July–August 2008, in American Samoa, and the 11th was to be held in 2012, in Solomon Islands. In March 2010 representatives of cultural interests from PICTs met to consider means of strengthening the profile of Pacific culture, including developing a regional cultural strategy, incorporating culture into educational programmes, establishing partnerships at national, regional and international level, and accessing funding for cultural projects. In November 2006 the HDP published *Guidelines for developing national legislation for the protection of traditional knowledge and expressions of culture*, with the aim of protecting indigenous Pacific knowledge and cultures. The SPC regional office in Fiji administers a Community Education Training Centre (CETC), which conducts a seven-month training course for up to 40 women community workers annually, with the objective of training women in methods of community development so that they can help others to achieve better living conditions for island families and communities.

The Pacific Regional Rights Resource Team provides training, technical support, and policy and advocacy services specifically tailored towards the Pacific region.

The Regional Media Centre provides training, technical assistance and production materials in all areas of the media for member countries and territories, community work programmes, donor projects and regional non-governmental organizations. The Centre comprises a radio broadcast unit, a graphic design and publication unit and a TV and video unit.

The Statistics Programme assists governments and administrations in the region to provide effective and efficient national statistical services through the provision of training activities, a statistical information service and other advisory services. A Regional Meeting of Heads of Statistics facilitates the integration and co-ordination of statistical services throughout the region, while the Pacific Regional Information System (PRISM), initiated by the National Statistics Office of the Pacific Islands and developed with British funding, provides statistical information about member countries and territories. The first regional meeting concerned with cultural statistics was convened in May 2011.

The Demography Programme provides technical support in population, demographic and development issues to member governments, other SPC programmes, and organizations active in the region. The Programme aims to assist governments effectively to analyse data and utilize it into the formulation of national development policies and programmes. The Programme organizes national workshops in population and development planning, provides short-term professional attachments, undertakes demographic research and analysis, and disseminates information.

SOUTH PACIFIC BOARD FOR EDUCATIONAL ASSESSMENT

Under the 2010 reorganization of SPC, the South Pacific Board for Educational Assessment (SPBEA, established in 1980 to develop procedures for assessing national and regional secondary education certificates) merged into the Community, in January 2010, initially as a stand-alone programme.

Finance

SPC's 2009 budget totalled US $64m., to be funded jointly by Community member states and international donors.

Annual Report.
Fisheries Newsletter (quarterly).
Pacific Aids Alert Bulletin (quarterly).
Pacific Island NCDs.
Pacific Island Nutrition (quarterly).
Regional Tuna Bulletin (quarterly).
Report of the Conference of the Pacific Community.
Women's Newsletter (quarterly).
Technical publications, statistical bulletins, advisory leaflets and reports.

PACIFIC ISLANDS FORUM

Address: Private Mail Bag, Suva, Fiji.

Telephone: 3312600; **fax:** 3301102; **e-mail:** info@forumsec.org.fj; **internet:** www.forumsec.org.

The Pacific Islands Forum (which in October 2000 changed its name from South Pacific Forum, in order to reflect the expansion of its membership since its establishment) was founded as the gathering of Heads of Government of the independent and self-governing states of the South Pacific; the first annual Forum meeting was held on 5 August 1971, in Wellington, New Zealand. The Pacific Islands Forum Secretariat was established (as the South Pacific Bureau for Economic Co-operation—SPEC) by an agreement signed on 17 April 1973, at the third Forum meeting, in Apia, Western Samoa (now Samoa). SPEC was redesignated as the South Pacific Forum Secretariat in 1988, and the present name was adopted in October 2000. The Secretariat aims to enhance the economic and social well-being of the Pacific Islands peoples, in support of the efforts of national governments. In October 2005 the 36th Forum adopted an Agreement Establishing the Pacific Islands Forum, which aimed to formalize the grouping's status as a full intergovernmental organization.

Australia	Niue
Cook Islands	Palau
Fiji*	Papua New Guinea
Kiribati	Samoa
Marshall Islands	Solomon Islands
Federated States of Micronesia	Tonga
Nauru	Tuvalu
New Zealand	Vanuatu

* In May 2009 Fiji was suspended from participation in the Forum.

Note: French Polynesia and New Caledonia were admitted to the Forum as associate members in 2006. The Asian Development Bank, the Commonwealth, the UN, Timor-Leste, Tokelau, Wallis and Futuna, the Western and Central Pacific Fisheries Commission, and the World Bank are observers. In September 2011 the 42nd Forum offered observer status to the ACP Group.

Organization

(October 2011)

FORUM OFFICIALS COMMITTEE

The Forum Officials Committee is the Secretariat's executive board, overseeing its activities. It comprises representatives and senior officials from all member countries. It meets twice a year, immediately before the meetings of the Pacific Islands Forum and at the end of the year, to discuss in detail the Secretariat's work programme and annual budget.

FORUM MEETING

Each annual leaders' Forum is chaired by the Head of Government of the country hosting the meeting, who remains as Forum Chairperson until the next Forum. The Forum has no written constitution or international agreement governing its activities nor any formal rules relating to its purpose, membership or conduct of meeting. Decisions are always reached by consensus, it never having been found necessary or desirable to vote formally on issues. In October 1994 the Forum was granted observer status by the General Assembly of the United Nations. The 42nd Forum was convened in Auckland, New Zealand, in September 2011.

DIALOGUE PLENARY MEETING

From 1989–2006 each annual Pacific Islands Forum meeting was followed by individual dialogues with representatives of selected countries considered to have a long-term interest in the region. A review of the post-Forum dialogues, undertaken in August 2006, recommended that the individual dialogues should be replaced by a new single Post-Forum Dialogue Plenary Meeting, to enable structured communication at ministerial level between Forum and Dialogue countries; and that 'core' dialogue partners, with a special engagement in and commitment to the region, should be identified. The findings of the review were approved in October 2006 by the 37th Forum meeting, and the new post-Forum dialogue structure was initiated following the 38th Forum. In 2011 Canada, the People's Republic of China, France, India, Indonesia, Italy, Japan, the Republic of Korea, Malaysia, Philippines, Thailand, the United Kingdom, the USA, and the European Union (EU) had dialogue partner status. A separate post-Forum session is convened between the Republic of China (Taiwan) and six of the Forum member states. In August 2010 leaders attending the 41st Forum determined to establish a review process to reassess the status of Post-Forum Dialogue partners; it was announce in September 2011 that implementation would begin during 2012.

SECRETARIAT

The Secretariat acts as the administrative arm of the Forum. It is headed by a Secretary-General, assisted by two Deputy Secretaries-General, and has a staff of some 70 people drawn from the member countries. The Secretariat comprises the following four Divisions: Corporate Services; Development and Economic Policy; Trade and Investment; and Political, International and Legal Affairs. The Secretariat's Pacific Plan Office services the Pacific Plan Action Committee and supports the overall implementation of the Pacific Plan. A Pacific ACP/EU Co-operation unit assists member states and regional organizations with submitting projects to the EU. A Smaller Island States (SIS) unit was established within the Secretariat in 2006. The Secretariat chairs the Council of Regional Organizations in the Pacific (CROP), an ad hoc committee comprising the heads of 11 regional organizations, which aims to discuss and co-ordinate the policies and work programmes of the various agencies in order to avoid duplication of or omissions in their services to member countries.

Secretary-General: TUILOMA NERONI SLADE (Samoa).

Deputy Secretary-General (Strategic Partnership and Co-ordination): FELETI PENITALA TEO (Tuvalu).

Deputy Secretary-General (Economic Governance and Security: ANDIE FONG TOY (New Zealand).

Activities

The Pacific Islands Forum provides an opportunity for informal discussions to be held on a wide range of common issues and problems and meets annually or when issues require urgent attention.

The Pacific Islands Forum Secretariat organizes Forum-related events, implements decisions by the Leaders, facilitates the delivery of development assistance to member states, and undertakes the political and legal mandates of Forum meetings.

In August 2003 regional leaders attending the 34th Forum, held in Auckland, New Zealand, determined that a review of the activities of the Forum and its Secretariat should be undertaken, and established an Eminent Persons Group to initiate that process.

In February 2007 a Regional Institutional Framework (RIF) Taskforce, comprising representatives of the member states of the Council of Regional Organizations in the Pacific agencies, convened for the first time, under Secretariat auspices. The RIF Taskforce was mandated by the October 2006 Forum to develop an appropriate institutional framework for supporting the implementation of the Pacific Plan. It was envisaged that the Pacific regional institutions would be reorganized under the following three 'pillars': a political and general policy institution; an activity sector-focused technical institution; and academic/training organizations. Lourdes Pangelinan, a former Director-General of the Pacific Community, was given responsibility for overseeing the development of the RIF.

In December 2008 the Forum Officials Committee approved a Forum corporate plan, covering the period 2008–12, and focusing on the following strategic areas: economic governance; political governance and security; regional co-ordination; and corporate services.

PACIFIC PLAN

In April 2004 a Special Leaders' Retreat convened in Auckland, New Zealand, in order to consider the future activities and direction of the Forum, mandated the development of a new 'Pacific Plan on Strengthening Regional Co-operation and Integration' as a means of addressing the challenges confronting the Pacific Island states. Consequently a Pacific Plan Task Force, managed by the Forum Secretary-General in consultation with a core leaders' group, undertook work to formulate the document. The finalized Pacific Plan, which was endorsed by the October 2005 Forum, incorporates development initiatives that are focused around the four 'pillars' of economic growth, sustainable development, good governance, and regional security and partnerships. It also recognizes the specific needs of SIS. The Pacific Plan is regarded as a 'living document', which can be amended and updated continuously to accommodate emerging priorities. The Pacific Plan Action Committee (PPAC), comprising representatives of the Forum member states and chaired by the Forum Chairperson, has met regularly since January 2006. Regional organizations, working in partnership with national governments and other partners, are responsible for co-ordinating the implementation of—and compiling reports on—many of the specific Pacific Plan initiatives, some 30 of which were designated for 'immediate implementation' during 2006–08. The 37th Forum leaders' meeting in October 2006 adopted the Nadi Decisions on the Pacific Plan, prioritizing several key commitments in the four pillar areas; these were consequently incorporated into the ('living') Plan during 2007. In October 2007 the 38th Forum adopted a further set of key commitments, the Vava'U Decisions on the Pacific Plan. More key commitments and priority areas, to advance the Pacific Plan over the period 2010–12, were adopted by the 40th Forum, in August 2009. The five main themes of the Plan during 2010–12 were: fostering economic development and promoting opportunities for broad-based growth; improving the livelihoods and the wellbeing of the Pacific peoples; addressing the impacts of climate change; achieving stronger national development through better governance; and ensuring improved social, political and legal conditions to enable future stability, safety and security.

POLITICAL AND SOCIAL AFFAIRS AND REGIONAL SECURITY

The Political, International and Legal Affairs Division of the Secretariat organizes and services the meetings of the Forum, disseminates its views, administers the Forum's observer office at the United Nations, and aims to strengthen relations with other regional and international organizations, in particular APEC and ASEAN. The Division's other main concern is to promote regional co-operation in law enforcement and legal affairs, and it provides technical support for the drafting of legal documents and for law enforcement capacity-building.

In recent years the Forum Secretariat has been concerned with assessing the legislative reforms and other commitments needed to ensure implementation of the 1992 Honiara Declaration on Law Enforcement Co-operation. The Secretariat assists member countries to ratify and implement the 1988 UN Convention against Illicit Trafficking in Narcotic Drugs and Psychotropic Substances. At the end of 2001 a conference of Forum immigration ministers expressed concern at rising levels of human-trafficking and illegal immigration in the region, and recommended that member states become parties to the 2000 UN Convention Against Transnational Organized Crime. A Pacific Transnational Crime Co-ordination Centre was established in Suva, Fiji, in 2004, to enhance and gather law enforcement intelligence. In September 2006 the Forum, in co-operation with the USA and the UN Global Programme Against Money Laundering (administered by the UN Office on Drugs and Crime), launched the Pacific Anti-Money Laundering Programme (PALP). PALP provides technical assistance to member states for the development of their national anti-money laundering and counter-terrorism financing regimes, in accordance with the Pacific Plan's development priority of regional security. Under the Pacific Plan, the Forum Secretariat requested the establishment of a Pacific Islands Regional Security Technical Co-operation Unit to support legislative efforts regarding, *inter alia*, transnational organized crime, counter-terrorism and financial intelligence.

The South Pacific Nuclear-Free Zone Treaty (Treaty of Rarotonga), prohibiting the acquisition, stationing or testing of nuclear weapons in the region, came into effect in December 1986, following ratification by eight states. The USSR signed the protocols to the treaty (whereby states possessing nuclear weapons agree not to use or threaten to use nuclear explosive devices against any non-nuclear party to the Treaty) in December 1987 and ratified them in April 1988; the People's Republic of China did likewise in December 1987 and October 1988 respectively. In July 1993 the Forum petitioned the USA, the United Kingdom and France, asking them to reconsider their past refusal to sign the Treaty in the light of the end of the 'Cold War'. In July 1995, following the decision of the French Government to resume testing of nuclear weapons in French Polynesia, members of the Forum resolved to increase diplomatic pressure on the three Governments to sign the Treaty. In October the United Kingdom, the USA and France announced their intention to accede to the Treaty, by mid-1996. Following France's decision, announced in January 1996, to end the programme four months earlier than scheduled, representatives of the Governments of the three countries signed the Treaty in March. In view of its resumption of nuclear testing in 1995–96, France's 'dialogue partner' status was suspended by the Forum Government during October 1995–September 1996.

Since 2001 the Forum has sent election observer groups to monitor elections taking place in member states, and, since 2004, joint election observer missions have been undertaken with the Commonwealth. During 2010 election observer teams were dispatched to observe parliamentary elections held in Nauru (in April), in Solomon Islands (August), and in the Cook Islands (November).

In September 2008 the first Pacific Islands-EU troika ministerial meeting was convened, in Brussels, Belgium, under a new Forum-EU enhanced political dialogue framework, which was to cover areas including regional security and governance, development co-operation, economic stability and growth, the environment and trade.

In October 2000 leaders attending the 31st Forum, convened in Tarawa, Kiribati, adopted the Biketawa Declaration, which outlined a mechanism for responding to any security crises that might occur in the region, while also urging members to undertake efforts to address the fundamental causes of potential instability. In August 2003 regional leaders convened at the 34th Forum commended the swift response by member countries and territories in deploying a Regional Assistance Mission in Solomon Islands (RAMSI), which had been approved by Forum ministers of foreign affairs at a meeting held in Sydney, Australia, in June, in accordance with the Biketawa Declaration; RAMSI was still operative in 2011. In May 2009 a Solomon Islands Government (SIG)-RAMSI Partnership Framework was endorsed by the Forum and by the Solomon Islands authorities. In January 2009 Forum heads of state and government convened a Special Leaders' Retreat, in Port Moresby, Papua New Guinea, to consider the political situation in Fiji. The meeting resolved to suspend Fiji from the Forum if no date for democratic elections had been set by the interim authorities in that country by 1 May. Fiji's suspension was confirmed in May.

The 33rd Forum, held in Suva, Fiji, in August 2002, adopted the Nasonini Declaration on Regional Security, which recognized the need for immediate and sustained regional action to combat international terrorism and transnational crime, in view of the perceived increased threat to global and regional security following the major terrorist attacks perpetrated against targets in the USA in September 2001.

In August 2003 regional leaders attending the 34th Forum adopted a set of Forum Principles of Good Leadership, establishing key requirements for good governance, including respect for law and the system of government, and respect for cultural values, customs and traditions, and for freedom of religion.

In August 2004 the 35th Forum approved an HIV/AIDS Regional Strategy and requested its implementation with immediate effect. In October 2005 the 36th Forum welcomed the development of a Pacific Regional Influenza Pandemic Preparedness Project, which covered the period 1 July 2006–30 June 2010.

In December 2009 the Forum Secretariat and the World Intellectual Property Organization launched a Traditional Knowledge Action Plan for Forum Island Countries, which sought to protect Pacific traditional knowledge from misuse without compensation to its owners.

In August 2010 the 41st Forum welcomed the outcome of the Pacific Conference on the Human Face of the Global Economic Crisis, which had been convened in February of that year, with participation by policy-makers and civil society and private-sector delegates from 16 Pacific Island countries, as well as development partners and representatives of UN agencies and regional organizations, including the Forum Secretariat.

In October 2010 a multi-agency Food Secure Pacific (FSP) working group, established in 2008 by the Forum Secretariat, the Secretariat of the Pacific Community, FAO, UNICEF and WHO, began implementing a new Framework for Action on Food Security in the Pacific, which had been endorsed by a Pacific Food Summit, convened in April 2010, in Port Vila, Vanuatu.

TRADE, ECONOMIC CO-OPERATION AND SUSTAINABLE DEVELOPMENT

The Secretariat's Trade and Investment Division extends advice and technical assistance to member countries in policy, development, export marketing, and information dissemination. Trade policy activities are mainly concerned with improving private sector policies, for example investment promotion, assisting integration into the world economy (including the provision of information and technical assistance to member states on WTO-related matters and supporting Pacific Island ACP states with preparations for negotiations on trade partnership with the EU under the Cotonou Agreement), and the development of businesses. During 2004–09 the Secretariat was supported in these activities through PACREIP (see below). The Secretariat aims to assist both island governments and private sector companies to enhance their capacity in the development and exploitation of export markets, product identification and product development. A regional trade and investment database is being developed. The Secretariat co-ordinates the activities of the regional trade offices located in Australia, New Zealand and Japan (see below). A representative trade office in Beijing, People's Republic of China, opened in January 2002. A Forum office was opened in Geneva, Switzerland, in 2004 to represent member countries at the WTO. In April 2005 the Pacific Islands Private Sector Organisation (PIPSO), representing regional private sector interests, was established. The PIPSO Secretariat, hosted by the Forum Secretariat, was inaugurated in April 2007. In August of that year PIPSO organized the first Pacific Islands Business Forum, convened in Nadi, Fiji.

In 1981 the South Pacific Regional Trade and Economic Co-operation Agreement (SPARTECA) came into force. SPARTECA aimed to redress the trade deficit of the Pacific Island countries with Australia and New Zealand. It is a non-reciprocal trade agreement under which Australia and New Zealand offer duty-free and unrestricted access or concessional access for specified products originating from the developing island member countries of the Forum. In 1985 Australia agreed to further liberalization of trade by abolishing (from the beginning of 1987) duties and quotas on all Pacific products except steel, cars, sugar, footwear and garments. In August 1994 New Zealand expanded its import criteria under the agreement by reducing the rule of origin requirement for garment products from 50% to 45% of local content. In response to requests from Fiji, Australia agreed to widen its interpretation of the agreement by accepting as being of local content manufactured products that consist of goods and components of 50% Australian content. A new Fiji/Australia Trade and Economic Relations Agreement (AFTERA) was concluded in March 1999 to complement SPARTECA and compensate for certain trade benefits that were in the process of being withdrawn.

In July 1997 the inaugural meeting of Forum economy ministers was convened in Cairns, Australia. It formulated an Action Plan to encourage the flow of foreign investment into the region by committing members to economic reforms, good governance and the implementation of multilateral trade and tariff policies.

Two major regional trade accords signed by Forum heads of state in August 2001 entered into force in April 2003 and October 2002, respectively: the Pacific Island Countries Trade Agreement (PICTA), providing for the establishment of a Pacific Island free trade area (FTA); and the related Pacific Agreement on Closer Economic Relations (PACER), incorporating trade and economic co-operation measures and envisaging the phased establishment of a regional single market comprising the PICTA FTA and Australia and New Zealand. The FTA was to be implemented over a period of eight years for developing member countries and 10 years for SIS and least developed countries. It was envisaged that negotiations on free trade agreements between Pacific Island states and Australia and New Zealand, with a view to establishing the larger regional single market envisaged by PACER, would commence within eight years of PICTA's entry into force. SPARTECA (see above) would remain operative pending the establishment of the larger single market, into which it would be subsumed. Under the provisions of PACER, Australia and New Zealand were to provide technical and financial assistance to PICTA signatory states in pursuing the objectives of PACER. In August 2003 regional leaders attending the 34th Forum agreed, in principle, that the USA and France should become parties to both PICTA and PACER. In September 2004 Forum trade officials adopted a Regional Trade Facilitation Programme (RTFP), within the framework of PACER, which included measures concerned with customs procedures, quarantine, standards and other activities to harmonize and facilitate trade between Pacific Island states and Australia and New Zealand, as well as with other international trading partners. It was announced in August 2007 that a review of the RTFP was to be undertaken. In March 2008 negotiations commenced on expanding PICTA to include provisions for trade in services as well as trade in goods; the sixth round of negotiations was convened in August 2011. In August 2009 leaders attending the 40th Forum agreed a recommendation from Forum ministers of trade that negotiations on a new regional trade and economic integration agreement, to be known as PACER-Plus, should commence forthwith. The participants in the PACER-Plus negotiations (which were ongoing in 2011) are Australia, the Cook Islands, Kiribati, the Marshall Islands, the Federated States of Micronesia, Nauru, New Zealand, Niue, Palau, Papua New Guinea, Samoa, the Solomon Islands, Tonga, Tuvalu and Vanuatu. A meeting of Forum ministers of trade, convened in April 2010, proposed that a shared 10-year strategy for trade and investment promotion should be developed, for consideration by the Forum trade ministers during 2011. The April 2010 meeting established a new umbrella body, Pacific Islands Trade and Invest, to cover and develop a co-ordinated corporate strategy for the former Pacific Islands Trade and Investment Commissions, based in Auckland, New Zealand and Sydney, Australia; and trade offices in Beijing, People's Republic of China and Tokyo, Japan.

In April 2001 the Secretariat convened a meeting of seven member island states—the Cook Islands, the Marshall Islands, Nauru, Niue, Samoa, Tonga and Vanuatu—as well as representatives from Australia and New Zealand, to address the regional implications of the OECD's Harmful Tax Competition Initiative. (OECD had identified the Cook Islands, the Marshall Islands, Nauru and Niue as so-called 'tax havens' lacking financial transparency and had demanded that they impose stricter legislation to address the incidence of international money-laundering on their territories.) The meeting requested the OECD to engage in conciliatory negotiations with the listed Pacific Island states. The August 2001 Forum reiterated this stance, proclaiming the sovereign right of nations to establish individual tax regimes, and supporting the development of a new co-operative framework to address financial transparency concerns. In December the Secretariat hosted a workshop for officials from nine member states concerned with combating financial crime. The workshop was attended and sponsored by several partner organizations and bodies, including the IMF.

The Development and Economic Policy Division of the Secretariat aims to co-ordinate and promote co-operation in development activities and programmes throughout the region. The Division administers a Short Term Advisory Service, which provides consultancy services to help member countries meet economic development priorities, and a Fellowship Scheme to provide practical training in a range of technical and income-generating activities. A Small Island Development Fund aims to assist the economic development of the SIS sub-group of member countries (see below) through project financing. A separate fellowship has also been established to provide training to the Kanak population of New Caledonia, to assist in their social, economic and political development. In 2004 the Secretariat formulated a Pacific Regional Assistance to Nauru (PRAN) initiative, that had been endorsed by Forum leaders in August; PRAN was terminated following a decision of the August 2009 Forum meeting. The Division aims to assist regional organizations to identify development priorities and to provide advice to national governments on economic analysis, planning and structural reforms.

The Secretariat services the Pacific Group Council of ACP states receiving assistance from the EU, and in 1993 a joint unit was established within the Secretariat headquarters to assist Pacific ACP countries and regional organizations in submitting projects to the EU for funding. The Pacific Regional Economic Integration Programme (PACREIP), launched in February 2004 as the largest programme under EU-Pacific co-operation, and covering the period 2004–09, focused on building the capacity of the Pacific ACP states to advance regional economic integration through the implementation of PICTA, to negotiate effectively at the WTO, and to conduct negotiations on the conclusion of an EU-Pacific Economic Co-operation Agreement (EPA). A draft EPA was published in August 2007. The first ever special dialogue between the EU and the PIF was convened in Nuku'alofa, Tonga, in October 2007, determined to launch an enhanced EU–Forum dialogue to enable future structured partnership. In November 2008 the Forum and the EU approved a Pacific Regional Strategy Paper (RSP) and Regional Indicative Programme (RIP), representing the framework for co-operation between the Pacific ACP States and European Commission over the period 2008–13.

In October 1999 heads of state and government attending the 30th Forum, held in Koror, Palau, adopted a Forum Vision for the Pacific Information Economy, which recognized the importance of information technology infrastructure for the region's economic and social development and the possibilities for enhanced co-operation in investment, job creation, education, training and cultural exchange. In October 2000 the 31st Forum endorsed a proposal to establish a Regional Financial Information Sharing Facility and national financial intelligence units.

ENVIRONMENT

The Forum actively promotes the development of effective international legislation to reduce emissions by industrialized countries of so-called 'greenhouse gases'. Such gases contribute to the warming of the earth's atmosphere (the 'greenhouse effect') and to related increases in global sea levels, and have therefore been regarded as a major threat to low-lying islands in the region. The Secretariat has played an active role in supporting regional participation at meetings of the Conference of the Parties to the UN Framework Convention on Climate Change (UNFCCC), and helps to co-ordinate Forum policy on the environment. With support from the Australian Government, it administers a network of stations to monitor sea levels and climate change throughout the Pacific region. The 29th Forum, held in Pohnpei, Federated States of Micronesia, in August 1998, adopted a Statement on Climate Change, which urged all countries to ratify and implement the gas emission reductions agreed upon by UN member states in December 1997 (the so-called Kyoto Protocol of the UNFCCC), and emphasized the Forum's commitment to further measures for verifying and enforcing emission limitation. In October 2005 the 36th Forum approved the Pacific Islands Framework for Action on Climate Change 2006–15, and noted the need to implement national action plans to address climate change issues. In October 2007 leaders attending the 38th Forum reiterated deep concern over the economic, social and environmental impact of climate change, noting the recent findings of the IPCC's *Fourth Assessment Report* and the importance of negotiating a comprehensive international framework to tackle climate change after the expiry of the Kyoto Protocol in 2012. A mid-term review of the Pacific Islands Framework for Action on Climate Change was undertaken in 2010.

In September 1995 the 26th Forum, held in Madang, Papua New Guinea, endorsed a draft Code of Conduct on the management and monitoring of indigenous forest resources in selected South Pacific countries, which had been initiated at the 25th Forum; however, while the six countries concerned committed themselves to implementing the Code through national legislation, its signing was deferred, owing to an initial unwillingness on the part of Papua New Guinea and Solomon Islands.

In August 2002 regional leaders attending the 33rd Forum approved a Pacific Island Regional Ocean Policy, which aimed to ensure the future sustainable use of the ocean and its resources by Pacific Island communities and external partners. A Declaration on Deep Sea Bottom Trawling to Protect Biodiversity on the High Seas was adopted in October 2005 by the 36th Forum. In October 2007 leaders attending the 38th Forum urged increased efforts among Forum members to foster a long-term strategic approach to ensuring the effective management of fish stocks, with a particular focus on tuna, and adopted a related Declaration on Pacific Fisheries Resources. In August 2010 the 41st Forum endorsed both a new Regional Monitoring Control and Surveillance Strategy, adopted by Forum ministers responsible for fisheries in July, as the overarching framework to support regional fisheries management, and also endorsed a new Framework for a Pacific Oceanscape, aimed at ensuring the long-term, co-operative sustainable development, management and conservation of the Pacific.

In September 1995 the 26th Forum adopted the Waigani Convention, banning the import into the region of all radioactive and other hazardous wastes, and providing controls for the transboundary movement and management of these wastes. Forum leaders have frequently reiterated protests against the shipment of radioactive materials through the region.

In January 2005, meeting on the fringes of the fifth Summit of the Alliance of Small Island States, in Port Louis, Mauritius, the Secretaries-General of the Pacific Islands Forum Secretariat, the Commonwealth, CARICOM, and the Indian Ocean Commission determined to take collective action to strengthen the disaster preparedness and response capacities of their member countries in the Pacific, Caribbean and Indian Ocean areas. In October 2005 the 36th Forum endorsed the Pacific Regional Framework for Action for Building the Resilience of Nations and Communities to Disasters during 2005–15.

In August 2008 the 39th Forum endorsed the Niue Declaration on Climate Change, which urged international partners to undertake immediate and effective measures to reduce emissions, to use cleaner fuels, and to increase use of renewable energy sources, and directed the Forum Secretariat to work with relevant agencies and member countries and territories in support of a number of commitments, including examining the potential for regional climate change insurance arrangements, and advancing regional expertise in the development and deployment of adaptation technologies. In November 2008 the EU and the Forum Secretariat adopted a joint declaration on co-operating in combating the challenges posed by climate change. The 40th Forum, in August 2009, adopted the Pacific Leaders Call for Action on Climate Change.

TRANSPORT

The Forum established the Pacific Forum Line and the Association of South Pacific Airlines (see below), as part of its efforts to promote co-operation in regional transport. On 1 January 1997 the work of the Forum Maritime Programme, which included assistance for regional maritime training and for the development of regional maritime administrations and legislation, was transferred to the regional office of the South Pacific Commission (renamed the Pacific Community from February 1998) at Suva. Telecommunications policy activities were also transferred to the then South Pacific Commission at the start of 1997. In May 1998 ministers responsible for aviation in member states approved a new regional civil aviation policy, which envisaged liberalization of air services, common safety and security standards and provisions for shared revenue.

In August 2004 the 35th Forum adopted a set of Principles on Regional Transport Services, based on the results of a study requested by the 34th Forum, 'to improve the efficiency, effectiveness and sustainability of air and shipping services'.

The Pacific Islands Air Services Agreement (PIASA) was opened for signature in August 2003, and entered into effect in October 2007, having been ratified by six Pacific Island countries. In August 2004 the Pacific Islands Civil Aviation and Security Treaty (PICASST) was opened for signature, and, in June 2005 PICASST entered into force, establishing a Port Vila, Vanuatu-based Pacific Aviation Security Office. In accordance with the Principles on Regional Transport Services, which were adopted by Forum Leaders in August 2004, the Secretariat was to support efforts to enhance air and shipping services, as well as develop a regional digital strategy.

SMALLER ISLAND STATES

In 1990 the Cook Islands, Kiribati, Nauru, Niue and Tuvalu, amongst the Forum's smallest island member states, formed the Forum SIS economic sub-group, which convenes an annual summit meeting to address their specific smaller island concerns. These include, in particular, economic disadvantages resulting from a poor resource base, absence of a skilled work-force and lack of involvement in world markets. Small island member states have also been particularly concerned about the phenomenon of global warming and its potentially damaging effects on the region. In September 1997 the Marshall Islands was admitted as the sixth member of SIS, and Palau was subsequently admitted as the seventh member. In February 1998 senior Forum officials, for the first time, met with representatives of the Caribbean Community and the Indian Ocean Commission, as well as other major international organizations, to discuss means to enhance consideration and promotion of the interests of small island states. An SIS unit, established within the Forum Secretariat in 2006, aims to enable high-profile representation of the SIS perspective, particularly in the development of the Pacific Plan, and to enable the small island member states to benefit fully from the implementation of the Plan. In August 2010 the 41st Forum welcomed the outcome of a Pacific High Level Dialogue (convened in February of that year) on the five-year review conference of the 2005 Mauritius Strategy for the further Implementation of the 1994 Barbados Programme of Action for the Sustainable Development of SIS, which was convened in September 2010.

Recent Meetings of the Pacific Islands Forum

Leaders attending the 36th Forum, convened in Papua New Guinea in October 2005, endorsed the newly formulated Pacific Plan, and adopted an Agreement Establishing the Pacific Islands Forum, which aimed to formalize the grouping's status as a full intergovernmental organization. Leaders also approved the Pacific Islands Framework for Action on Climate Change 2006–15 and endorsed the Pacific Regional Framework for Action for Building the Resilience of Nations and Communities to Disasters during 2005–15. The 36th Forum urged the adoption of national and regional avian influenza preparedness measures and considered a proposal to establish a Pacific Health Fund to address issues such as avian influenza, HIV/AIDS, malaria, and non-communicable diseases.

The 37th Forum, held in Nadi, Fiji in October 2006, approved the Nadi Decisions, a series of key commitments aimed at advancing the implementation of the Pacific Plan in the Plan's four 'pillars' of economic growth, sustainable development, good governance, and regional security and partnerships. Leaders attending the 37th Forum also determined that a taskforce should be established to develop a new regional institutional framework for its member states. In addition they adopted a Declaration on Deep Sea Bottom Trawling to Protect Biodiversity on the High Seas; welcomed the development of the Pacific Regional Influenza Pandemic Preparedness Project; agreed to establish a task force to review RAMSI; and determined to develop a Regional Co-operation for Counter-Terrorism Assistance and Response model.

The 38th Forum, convened in Nuku'alofa, Tonga, in October 2007, noted that considerable progress had been achieved in the implementation of initiatives across all four of the pillars of the Pacific Plan and agreed on several key commitments (the Vava'U Decisions) in order to move the Plan forwards. Leaders attending the Forum adopted a Declaration on Pacific Fisheries Resources; and noted the importance of negotiating a comprehensive post-2012 framework to tackle climate change. Leaders commended the work of RAMSI, and noted that a consultative mechanism between the Government of Solomon Islands, RAMSI and the Pacific Islands Forum had been established, and also the findings of the task force on RAMSI. They also noted the continuing work of the Pacific Regional Assistance to Nauru initiative.

The 39th Forum, held in Alofi, Niue, in August 2008, welcomed an expression of interest by Japan in co-operating with RAMSI; agreed to extend the Pacific Regional Assistance to Nauru initiative; welcomed the new Pacific Region Infrastructure Facility initiated by the World Bank, Asian Development Bank and Governments of Australia and New Zealand; and appointed a new Secretary-General of the Forum Secretariat. The Forum endorsed the Niue Declaration on Climate Change (see above).

Leaders attending the 40th Forum, convened in Cairns, Australia, in August 2009, adopted the Pacific Leaders Call for Action on Climate Change, designating climate change as the greatest ongoing regional challenge; endorsed the Cairns Compact on Strengthening Development Co-ordination in the Pacific, aimed at improving regional economic and development progress despite the ongoing global economic crisis; and agreed several key commitments and priority areas to advance the Pacific Plan over the period 2010–13. Leaders agreed that negotiations on a new regional trade and economic integration agreement (PACER-Plus) should commence forthwith, and welcomed a decision of Forum ministers of trade to establish the position of Office of the Chief Trade Adviser (OCTA).

The 41st Forum, which took place in Port Vila, Vanuatu, in August 2010, endorsed the Port Vila Declaration on Accelerating Progress on the Achievement of the UN Millennium Development Goals; endorsed a new Regional Monitoring Control and Surveillance Strategy for fisheries (see above); stated strong support for the Pacific Regional Strategy on Disability covering 2010–15, which had been approved by Forum disability ministers in October 2009; endorsed a Framework for Action on Energy Security in the Pacific; and endorsed the Framework for a Pacific Oceanscape (see above).

In early September 2011 the 42nd Forum, held in Auckland, New Zealand, endorsed the Waiheke Declaration on Sustainable Economic Development—recognizing the importance of focusing regional efforts on sectors such as tourism, fisheries and agriculture, in which there is comparative advantage; and a Forum Leaders' Statement on Non-Communicable Diseases (NCDs). Leaders emphasized maximizing the economic benefit from fisheries, expressed concern at the effect of illegal, unreported and unregulated fishing, and stressed the importance of transport links and secure access to energy. The leaders recalled the Honiara Communiqué on the Pacific NCD Crisis, issued by regional health ministers in June 2011, which highlighted the impact of a rapid increase in NCDs in the region (the estimated cause of three-quarters of adult deaths). Leaders undertook to support the Marshall Islands in raising the profile of the issue of international contaminants at international fora.

Finance

The Governments of Australia and New Zealand each contribute some one-third of the annual budget and the remaining amount is shared by the other member Governments. Extra-budgetary funding is contributed mainly by Australia, New Zealand, Japan, the EU and France. The Forum's 2010 budget amounted to $F43.5m. Following a decision of the 36th Forum a Pacific Fund was established to support the implementation of the Pacific Plan, under the management of the Pacific Plan Action Committee.

Publications

Annual Report.
Forum News (quarterly).
Forum Trends.
Forum Secretariat Directory of Aid Agencies.
Pacific Plan Progress Report.
South Pacific Trade Directory.
SPARTECA (guide for Pacific island exporters).
Reports of meetings; profiles of Forum member countries.

Overseas Agencies and Affiliated Organizations

Association of South Pacific Airlines (ASPA): POB 9817, Nadi Airport, Nadi, Fiji; tel. 6723526; fax 6720196; e-mail georgefaktaufon@aspa.aero; internet aspa.aero/index.php; f. 1979 at a meeting of airlines in the South Pacific, convened to promote co-operation among the member airlines for the development of regular, safe and economical commercial aviation within, to and from the South Pacific; mems: 16 regional airlines, two associates; Sec.-Gen. George E. Faktaufon.

Forum Fisheries Agency (FFA): POB 629, Honiara, Solomon Islands; tel. (677) 21124; fax (677) 23995; e-mail info@ffa.int; internet www.ffa.int; f. 1979 to promote co-operation in fisheries among coastal states in the region; collects and disseminates information and advice on the living marine resources of the region, including the management, exploitation and development of these resources; provides assistance in the areas of law (treaty negotiations, drafting legislation, and co-ordinating surveillance and enforcement), fisheries development, research, economics, computers, and information management; the FFA was closely involved in the legal process relating to the establishment of a Western and Central Pacific Fisheries Commission, which was inaugurated in 2004; implements a Vessel Monitoring System, to provide automated data collection and analysis of fishing vessel activities throughout the region; on behalf of its 16 member countries, the FFA administers a multilateral fisheries treaty, under which vessels from the USA operate in the region, in exchange for an annual payment; the FFA is implementing the FFA Strategic Plan 2005–20, detailing the medium-term direction of the Agency; Dir Su'a N. F. Tanielu; publs *FFA News Digest* (every two months), *FFA Reports*, *MCS Newsletter* (quarterly), *Tuna Market Newsletter* (monthly).

Pacific Forum Line: POB 105-612, Auckland 1143, New Zealand; tel. (9) 356-2333; fax (9) 356-2330; e-mail info@pflnz.co.nz; internet www.pflnz.co.nz; f. 1977 as a joint venture by South Pacific countries, to provide shipping services to meet the special requirements of the region; operates three container vessels; conducts shipping agency services in Australia, Fiji, New Zealand and Samoa, and stevedoring in Samoa; CEO Sean Bolt.

Pacific Islands Centre (PIC): Meiji University, 1-1 Kanda-Surugadai, Chiyoda-ku, Tokyo 101-8301, Japan; tel. (3) 3296-4545; e-mail info@pic.or.jp; internet www.pic.or.jp; f. 1996 to promote and to facilitate trade, investment and tourism among Forum members and Japan; Dir K. Sohma.

Pacific Islands Forum Trade Office: 5-1-3-1 Tayuan Diplomatic Compound, 1 Xin Dong Lu, Chaoyang District, Beijing 100600, People's Republic of China; tel. (10) 6532-6622; fax (10) 6532-6360; e-mail answers@pifto.org.cn; internet www.pifto.org.cn; f. 2001.

Pacific Islands Private Sector Organization (PIPSO): c/o Pacific Islands Forum Secretariat, Private Mail Bag, Suva, Fiji; tel. 3312600; fax 3301102; e-mail info@pipso.org.fj; internet www.pipso.org; f. 2005 to represent regional private sector interests; organizes Pacific Islands Business Forum; CEO Mereia Volavola.

Pacific Islands Trade and Invest (Sydney): Level 11, 171 Clarence St, Sydney, NSW 20010, Australia; tel. (2) 9290-2133; fax (2) 9299-2151; e-mail info@pitic.org.au; internet www.pitic.org.au; f. 1979 as Pacific Islands Trade and Investment Commission (Sydney), current name adopted 2010; assists Pacific Island Governments and business communities to identify market opportunities in Australia and promotes investment in the Pacific Island countries; Trade Commr Caleb Jarvis; Investment Promotion Man. Patrick Martin.

Pacific Islands Trade and Invest (New Zealand): POB 109-395, 5 Short St, Level 3, Newmarket, Auckland, New Zealand; tel. (9) 5295165; fax (9) 5231284; e-mail info@pitic.org.nz; internet www.pitic.org.nz; f. 1988 as Pacific Islands Trade and Investment Commission (New Zealand), current name adopted 2010; Trade Commr Adam Denniss; Senior Investment Man. Manuel Valdez.

OTHER REGIONAL ORGANIZATIONS

Agriculture, Food, Forestry and Fisheries

(for organizations concerned with agricultural commodities, see Commodities)

AVRDC—the World Vegetable Center: AVRDC—the World Vegetable Center: ; POB 42, Shanhua, Tainan 74199, Taiwan; tel. (6) 5837801; fax (6) 5830009; e-mail info@worldveg.org; internet www.avrdc.org; f. 1971 as the Asian Vegetable Research and Development Center; aims to enhance the nutritional well-being and raise the incomes of the poor in rural and urban areas of developing countries, through improved varieties and methods of vegetable production, marketing and distribution; runs an experimental farm, laboratories, gene-bank, greenhouses, quarantine house, insectarium, library and weather station; provides training for research and production specialists in tropical vegetables; exchanges and disseminates vegetable germplasm through regional centres in the developing world; serves as a clearing-house for vegetable research information; and undertakes scientific publishing; a Regional Center for Africa was opened in Arusha, Tanzania, in 1992; mems: Australia, France, Germany, Japan, Republic of Korea, Philippines, Taiwan, Thailand, USA; Dir-Gen. Dr Dyno Keatinge; publs *Annual Report*, *Technical Bulletin*, *Proceedings*, *Centerpoint* (quarterly).

CAB International (CABI): Nosworthy Way, Wallingford, Oxon, OX10 8DE, United Kingdom; tel. (1491) 832111; fax (1491) 829292; e-mail corporate@cabi.org; internet www.cabi.org; f. 1929 as the Imperial Agricultural Bureaux (later Commonwealth Agricultural Bureaux), current name adopted in 1985; aims to improve human welfare world-wide through the generation, dissemination and application of scientific knowledge in support of sustainable development; places particular emphasis on sustainable agriculture, forestry, human health and the management of natural resources, with priority given to the needs of developing countries; a separate microbiology centre, in Egham, Surrey (UK), undertakes research, consultancy, training, capacity-building and institutional development measures in sustainable pest management, biosystematics and molecular biology, ecological applications and environmental and industrial microbiology; compiles and publishes extensive information (in a variety of print and electronic forms) on aspects of agriculture, forestry, veterinary medicine, the environment and natural resources, and Third World rural development; maintains regional centres in the People's Republic of China, India, Kenya, Malaysia, Pakistan, Switzerland, Trinidad and Tobago, and the USA; mems: 45 countries and territories; Chair. John Ripley (United Kingdom); CEO Dr Trevor Nicholls (United Kingdom).

Commission for the Conservation of Southern Bluefin Tuna: Unit 1, J.A.A. House, 19 Napier Close, Deakin, Canberra, ACT 2600, Australia; tel. (2) 6282-8396; fax (2) 6282-8407; e-mail sec@ccsbt.org; internet www.ccsbt.org; f. 1994 when the Convention for the Conservation of Southern Bluefin Tuna (signed in May 1993) entered into force; aims to promote sustainable management and conservation of the southern bluefin tuna; holds an annual meeting and annual scientific meeting; collates relevant research, scientific information and data; encourages non-member countries and bodies to co-operate in the conservation and optimum utilization of Southern Bluefin Tuna through accession to the Convention or adherence to the Commission's management arrangements; mems: Australia, Japan, Republic of Korea, New Zealand; co-operating non-mems: Philippines, South Africa, European Community; Exec. Sec. Robert Kennedy.

Indian Ocean Tuna Commission (IOTC): POB 1011, Victoria, Mahé, Seychelles; tel. 225494; fax 224364; e-mail iotc.secretary@iotc.org; internet www.iotc.org; f. 1996 as a regional fisheries organization with a mandate for the conservation and management of tuna and tuna-like species in the Indian Ocean; mems: Australia, Belize, People's Republic of China, the Comoros, European Union, Eritrea, France, Guinea, India, Indonesia, Iran, Japan, Kenya, Republic of Korea, Madagascar, Malaysia, Mauritius, Oman, Pakistan, Philippines, Seychelles, Sudan, Sri Lanka, Tanzania, Thailand, United Kingdom, Vanuatu; co-operating non-contracting parties: Indonesia, Senegal, South Africa; Exec. Sec. Alejandro Anganuzzi (Argentina).

Inter-American Tropical Tuna Commission (IATTC): 8604 La Jolla Shores Drive, La Jolla, CA 92037-1508, USA; tel. (858) 546-7100; fax (858) 546-7133; e-mail info@iattc.org; internet www.iattc.org; f. 1950; administers two programmes, the Tuna-Billfish Programme and the Tuna-Dolphin Programme. The principal responsibilities of the Tuna-Billfish Programme are: to study the biology of the tunas and related species of the eastern Pacific Ocean to estimate the effects of fishing and natural factors on their abundance; to recommend appropriate conservation measures in order to maintain stocks at levels which will afford maximum sustainable catches; and to collect information on compliance with Commission resolutions. The principal functions of the Tuna-Dolphin Programme are: to monitor the abundance of dolphins and their mortality incidental to purse-seine fishing in the eastern Pacific Ocean; to study the causes of mortality of dolphins during fishing operations and promote the use of fishing techniques and equipment that minimize these mortalities; to study the effects of different fishing methods on the various fish and other animals of the pelagic ecosystem; and to provide a secretariat for the International Dolphin Conservation Programme; mems: Colombia, Costa Rica, Ecuador, El Salvador, France, Guatemala, Japan, Mexico, Nicaragua, Panama, Peru, Republic of Korea, Spain, USA, Vanuatu, Venezuela; co-operating non-contracting parties: Belize, Canada, China, Cook Islands, European Union and Chinese Taipei (Taiwan); Dir Guillermo A. Compeán; publs *Bulletin* (irregular), *Annual Report*, *Fishery Status Report*, *Stock Assessment Report* (annually), *Special Report* (irregular).

International Crops Research Institute for the Semi-Arid Tropics (ICRISAT): Patancheru, Andhra Pradesh 502 324, India; tel. (40) 30713071; fax (40) 30713074; e-mail icrisat@cgiar.org; internet www.icrisat.org; f. 1972 to promote the genetic improvement of crops and for research on the management of resources in the world's semi-arid tropics, with the aim of reducing poverty and protecting the environment; research covers all physical and socio-economic aspects of improving farming systems on unirrigated land; maintains regional centres in Nairobi, Kenya (for eastern and southern Africa) and in Niamey, Niger (for western and central Africa); Dir-Gen. Dr William D. Dar (Philippines); publs *ICRISAT Report* (annually), *Journal of Semi-Arid Tropical Agricultural Research* (2 a year), information and research bulletins.

International Food Policy Research Institute (IFPRI): 2033 K St, NW, Washington, DC 20006, USA; tel. (202) 862-5600; fax (202) 467-4439; e-mail ifpri@cgiar.org; internet www.ifpri.org; f. 1975; co-operates with academic and other institutions in further research; develops policies for cutting hunger and malnutrition; committed to increasing public awareness of food policies; Dir-Gen. Shenggen Fan (People's Republic of China).

International Service for National Agricultural Research (ISNAR): IFPRI, ISNAR Division, ILRI, POB 5689, Addis Ababa, Ethiopia; tel. (11) 646-3215; fax (11) 646-2927; e-mail ifpri-addisababa@cgiar.org; fmrly based in The Hague, Netherlands, the ISNAR Program relocated to Addis Ababa in 2004, under the governance of IFPRI; Dir Dr Wilberforce Kisamba-Mugerwa.

International Rice Research Institute (IRRI): Los Baños, Laguna, DAPO Box 7777, Metro Manila, Philippines; tel. (2) 5805600; fax (2) 5805699; e-mail irri@cgiar.org; internet www.irri.org; f. 1960; conducts research on rice, with the aim of developing technologies of environmental, social and economic benefit; works to enhance national rice research systems and offers training; operates Riceworld, a museum and learning centre about rice; maintains a library of technical rice literature; organizes international conferences and workshops (3rd International Rice Congress held in Hanoi, Viet Nam, in November 2010); Dir-Gen. Dr Robert S. Zeigler; publs *Rice Literature Update*, *Rice Today* (quarterly), *Hotline*, *Facts about IRRI*, *News about Rice and People*, *International Rice Research Notes*.

International Whaling Commission (IWC): The Red House, 135 Station Rd, Impington, Cambridge, CB24 9NP, United Kingdom; tel. (1223) 233971; fax (1223) 232876; e-mail secretariat@iwcoffice.com; internet www.iwcoffice.org; f. 1946 under the International Convention for the Regulation of Whaling, for the conservation of world whale stocks; reviews the regulations covering whaling operations; encourages research; collects, analyses and disseminates statistical and other information on whaling. A ban on commercial whaling was passed by the Commission in July 1982, to take effect three years subsequently (in some cases, a phased reduction of commercial operations was not completed until 1988). A revised whale-management procedure was adopted in 1992, to be implemented after the development of a complete whale management scheme; mems: 88 countries; Sec. Dr NICOLA GRANDY; publs *Annual Report*, *Journal of Cetacean Research and Management*.

Network of Aquaculture Centres in Asia and the Pacific (NACA): POB 1040, Kasetsart University Post Office, Bangkok 10903, Thailand; tel. (2) 561-1728; fax (2) 561-1727; e-mail sena.desilva@enaca.org; internet www.enaca.org; f. 1990; promotes the development of aquaculture in the Asia and Pacific region through development planning, interdisciplinary research, regional training and information; mems: Australia, Bangladesh, Cambodia, People's Republic of China, Hong Kong SAR, India, Indonesia, Iran, Democratic People's Republic of Korea, Malaysia, Myanmar, Nepal, Pakistan, Philippines, Sri Lanka, Thailand and Viet Nam; Dir-Gen. SENA S. DE SILVA; publs *NACA Newsletter* (quarterly), *Aquaculture Asia* (quarterly).

North Pacific Anadromous Fish Commission: 889 W. Pender St, Suite 502, Vancouver, BC V6C 3B2, Canada; tel. (604) 775-5550; fax (604) 775-5577; e-mail secretariat@npafc.org; internet www.npafc.org; f. 1993; mems: Canada, Japan, Republic of Korea, Russia, USA; Exec. Dir VLADIMIR FEDORENKO; publs *Annual Report*, *Newsletter* (2 a year), *Statistical Yearbook*, *Scientific Bulletin*, *Technical Report*.

South Pacific Regional Fisheries Management Organization: Interim Secretariat, L4, ASB Bank House, POB 3797, Wellington 6140, New Zealand; tel. (4) 499-9889; fax (4) 473-9579; e-mail interim.secretariat@southpacificrfmo.org; internet www.southpacificrfmo.org; international negotiations on the establishment of a South Pacific regional fisheries management body commenced in 2005, led by New Zealand, Australia and Chile; the negotiations were concluded at the 8th international meeting on the establishment of the org., held in Auckland, New Zealand, in Nov. 2009 and the Convention was adopted unanimously; Chair. BILL MANSFIELD; Exec. Sec. Dr ROBIN ALLEN.

Western and Central Pacific Fisheries Commission: Kaselehie St, POB 2356, Kolonia, Pohnpei State 96941, Federated States of Micronesia; tel. 3201992; fax 3201108; e-mail wcpfc@wcpfc.int; internet www.wcpfc.int; f. 2004 under the Convention for the Conservation and Management of Highly Migratory Fish Stocks in the Western and Central Pacific, which entered into force in June of that year, six months after the deposit of the 13th ratification; inaugural session convened in December, in Pohnpei, Federated States of Micronesia; mems: 31 countries and the European Community; Exec. Dir GLENN HURRY; publs *Secretariat Quarterly Report*, *Newsletter*.

WorldFish Center (International Centre for Living Aquatic Resources Management—ICLARM): Jalan Batu Maung, Batu Maung, 11960 Bayan Lepas, Penang, Malaysia; POB 500, GPO, 10670 Penang; tel. (4) 626-1606; fax (4) 626-5530; e-mail worldfishcenter@cgiar.org; internet www.worldfishcenter.org; f. 1973; became a mem. of the Consultative Group on International Agricultural Research (CGIAR) in 1992; aims to contribute to food security and poverty eradication in developing countries through the sustainable development and use of living aquatic resources; carries out research and promotes partnerships; Dir-Gen. Dr STEPHEN J. HALL.

World Organisation of Animal Health: 12 rue de Prony, 75017 Paris, France; tel. 1-44-15-18-88; fax 1-42-67-09-87; e-mail oie@oie.int; internet www.oie.int; f. 1924 as Office International des Epizooties (OIE); objectives include promoting international transparency of animal diseases; collecting, analysing and disseminating scientific veterinary information; providing expertise and promoting international co-operation in the control of animal diseases; promoting veterinary services; providing new scientific guidelines on animal production, food safety and animal welfare; launched in May 2005, jointly with FAO and WHO, a Global Strategy for the Progressive Control of Highly Pathogenic Avian Influenza (H5N1), and, in partnership with other organizations, has convened conferences on avian influenza; experts in a network of 156 collaborating centres and reference laboratories; mems: 177; Dir-Gen. BERNARD VALLAT; publs *Disease Information* (weekly), *World Animal Health* (annually), *Scientific and Technical Review* (3 a year), other manuals, codes, etc.

Arts and Culture

Organization of World Heritage Cities: 15 rue Saint-Nicolas, Québec, QC G1K 1M8, Canada; tel. (418) 692-0000; fax (418) 692-5558; e-mail secretariat@ovpm.org; internet www.ovpm.org; f. 1993 to assist cities inscribed on the UNESCO World Heritage List to implement the Convention concerning the Protection of the World Cultural and Natural Heritage (1972); promotes co-operation between city authorities, in particular in the management and sustainable development of historic sites; holds an annual General Assembly, comprising the mayors of member cities; mems: 227 cities world-wide; Sec.-Gen. DENIS RICARD; publ. *OWHC Newsletter* (2 a year, in English, French and Spanish).

Royal Asiatic Society of Great Britain and Ireland: 14 Stephenson Way, London, NW1 2HD, United Kingdom; tel. (20) 7388-4539; fax (20) 7391-9429; e-mail info@royalasiaticsociety.org; internet www.royalasiaticsociety.org; f. 1823 for the study of history and cultures of the East; mems: c. 700, branch societies in Asia; Pres. Prof. GORDON JOHNSON; Dir ALISON OHTA; publ. *Journal* (3 a year).

Commodities

Asian and Pacific Coconut Community (APCC): 3rd Floor, Lina Bldg, Jalan H. R. Rasuna Said Kav. B7, Kuningan, Jakarta 12920, Indonesia; POB 1343, Jakarta 10013; tel. (21) 5221712; fax (21) 5221714; e-mail apcc@indo.net.id; internet www.apccsec.org; f. 1969 to promote and co-ordinate all activities of the coconut industry, to achieve higher production and better processing, marketing and research; organizes annual Coconut Technical Meeting (COCOTECH); mems: Fiji, India, Indonesia, Kiribati, Malaysia, Marshall Islands, Federated States of Micronesia, Papua New Guinea, Philippines, Samoa, Solomon Islands, Sri Lanka, Thailand, Vanuatu, Viet Nam; Exec. Dir ROMULO N. ARANCON, Jr ; publs *Cocomunity* (monthly), *CORD* (2 a year), *CocoInfo International* (2 a year), *Coconut Statistical Yearbook*, guidelines and other ad hoc publications.

Association of Natural Rubber Producing Countries (ANRPC): Bangunan Getah Asli, 148 Jalan Ampang, 7th Floor, 50450 Kuala Lumpur, Malaysia; tel. (3) 2611900; fax (3) 2613014; e-mail anrpc.secretariat@gmail.com; internet www.anrpc.org; f. 1970 to co-ordinate the production and marketing of natural rubber, to promote technical co-operation among members and to bring about fair and stable prices for natural rubber; holds seminars, meetings and training courses on technical and statistical subjects; a joint regional marketing system has been agreed in principle; mems: Cambodia, People's Republic of China, India, Indonesia, Malaysia, Papua New Guinea, Philippines, Singapore, Sri Lanka, Thailand, Viet Nam; Sec.-Gen. Dr KAMARUL BAHARAIN BIN BASIR; publs *NR Trends & Statistics* (monthly), *Qtrly NR Market Review, Market and Industry Update*.

Gas Exporting Countries Forum: POB 3212, 'Q' Blding, 6th Floor, Majlis Al Taawon St, Doha, Qatar; tel. 449-1654; fax 449-1651; e-mail gecfsg@gmail.com; internet www.gecforum.org; f. 2001 to represent and promote the mutual interests of gas exporting countries; aims to increase the level of co-ordination among member countries and to promote dialogue between gas producers and consumers; a ministerial meeting is convened annually; the 7th ministerial meeting, convened in Moscow, Russia, in Dec. 2008, agreed on a charter and a permanent structure for the grouping; mems: Algeria, Bolivia, Egypt, Equatorial Guinea, Iran, Libya, Nigeria, Qatar, Russia, Trinidad and Tobago, Venezuela; observers: Kazakhstan, Netherlands, Norway.

International Coffee Organization (ICO): 22 Berners St, London, W1T 3DD, United Kingdom; tel. (20) 7612-0600; fax (20) 7612-0630; e-mail info@ico.org; internet www.ico.org; f. 1963 under the International Coffee Agreement, 1962, which was renegotiated in 1968, 1976, 1983, 1994 (extended in 1999), 2001 and 2007; aims to improve international co-operation and provide a forum for intergovernmental consultations on coffee matters; to facilitate international trade in coffee by the collection, analysis and dissemination of statistics; to act as a centre for the collection, exchange and publication of coffee information; to promote studies in the field of coffee; and to encourage an increase in coffee consumption; mems: 33 exporting countries and six importing countries, plus the European Union; Chair. of Council EWALD WERMUTH (Netherlands); Exec. Dir JOSÉ SETTE (Brazil).

International Cotton Advisory Committee (ICAC): 1629 K St, NW, Suite 702, Washington, DC 20006-1636, USA; tel. (202) 463-6660; fax (202) 463-6950; e-mail secretariat@icac.org; internet www.icac.org; f. 1939 to observe developments in world cotton; to collect and disseminate statistics; to suggest measures for the furtherance of international collaboration in maintaining and developing a sound world cotton economy; and to provide a forum for international discussions on cotton prices; mems: 44 countries; Exec. Dir Dr TERRY TOWNSEND (USA); publs *Cotton This Week!* (internet/e-mail only), *Cotton This Month*, *Cotton: Review of the World Situation* (every 2 months), *Cotton: World Statistics* (annually), *The ICAC Recorder*, *World Textile Demand* (annually), other surveys, studies, trade analyses and technical publications.

International Energy Forum (IEF): POB 94736, Diplomatic Quarter, Riyadh-11614, Saudi Arabia; tel. (1) 4810022; fax (1) 4810055; e-mail info@ief.org; internet www.ief.org; f. 1991; annual gathering of ministers responsible for energy affairs from states accounting for about 90% of global oil and gas supply and demand; the IEF is an intergovernmental arrangement aimed at promoting dialogue on global energy matters among its membership; the annual IEF is preceded by a meeting of the International Business Energy Forum (IEBF), comprising energy ministers and CEOs of leading energy companies; 13th IEF and 5th IEBF: March 2012, Kuwait; 87 mem. states, including the mems of OPEC and the International Energy Agency; Sec.-Gen. NOÉ VAN HULST (until 31 December 2011), ALDO FLORES-QUIROGA (designate).

International Grains Council (IGC): 1 Canada Sq., Canary Wharf, London, E14 5AE, United Kingdom; tel. (20) 7513-1122; fax (20) 7513-0630; e-mail igc@igc.int; internet www.igc.int; f. 1949 as International Wheat Council, present name adopted in 1995; responsible for the administration of the International Grains Agreement, 1995, comprising the Grains Trade Convention (GTC) and the Food Aid Convention (FAC, under which donors pledge specified minimum annual amounts of food aid for developing countries in the form of grain and other eligible products); aims to further international co-operation in all aspects of trade in grains, to promote international trade in grains, and to achieve a free flow of this trade, particularly in developing member countries; seeks to contribute to the stability of the international grain market; acts as a forum for consultations between members; provides comprehensive information on the international grain market (with effect from 1 July 2009 the definition of 'grain' was extended to include rice); mems: 26 countries and the EU; Exec. Dir ETSUO KITAHARA; publs *World Grain Statistics* (annually), *Wheat and Coarse Grain Shipments* (annually), *Report for the Fiscal Year* (annually), *Grain Market Report* (monthly), *IGC Grain Market Indicators* (weekly), *Rice Market Bulletin* (weekly).

International Jute Study Group (IJSG): 145 Monipuriparu, Tejgaon, Dhaka 1215, Bangladesh; POB 6073, Gulshan, Dhaka; tel. (2) 9125581; fax (2) 9125248; e-mail info@jute.org; internet www.jute.org; f. 2002 as successor to International Jute Organization (f. 1984 in accordance with an agreement made by 48 producing and consuming countries in 1982, under the auspices of UNCTAD); aims to improve the jute economy and the quality of jute and jute products through research and development projects and market promotion; Sec.-Gen BHUPENDRA SINGH (India).

International Organization of Spice Trading Associations (IOSTA): c/o American Spice Trade Association, 2025 M St, NW, Suite 800, Washington, DC 20036, USA; tel. (202) 367-1127; fax (202) 367-2127; e-mail info@astaspice.org; internet www.astaspice.org; f. 1999; mems: 8 national and regional spice orgs.

International Pepper Community (IPC): 4th Floor, Lina Bldg, Jalan H. R. Rasuna Said, Kav. B7, Kuningan, Jakarta 12920, Indonesia; tel. (21) 5224902; fax (21) 5224905; e-mail io@ipcnet.org; internet www.ipcnet.org; f. 1972 for promoting, co-ordinating and harmonizing all activities relating to the pepper economy; mems: Brazil, India, Indonesia, Malaysia, Federated States of Micronesia, Papua New Guinea, Sri Lanka, Thailand; publs *Pepper Statistical Yearbook*, *International Pepper News Bulletin* (quarterly), *Directory of Pepper Exporters*, *Directory of Pepper Importers*, *Weekly Prices Bulletin*, *Pepper Market Review*.

International Rubber Study Group: 111 North Bridge Rd, 23-06 Peninsula Plaza, Singapore 179098; tel. 68372411; fax 63394369; e-mail irsg@rubberstudy.com; internet www.rubberstudy.com; f. 1944 to provide a forum for the discussion of problems affecting synthetic and natural rubber and to provide statistical and other general information on rubber; mems: 16 governments and the EU; Sec.-Gen. Dr STEPHEN V. EVANS; publs *Rubber Statistical Bulletin* (every 2 months), *Rubber Industry Report* (every 2 months), *Proceedings of International Rubber Forums* (annually), *World Rubber Statistics Handbook*, *Key Rubber Indicators*, *Rubber Statistics Yearbook*, *Outlook for Elastomers* (annually).

International Sugar Organization: 1 Canada Sq., Canary Wharf, London, E14 5AA, United Kingdom; tel. (20) 7513-1144; fax (20) 7513-1146; e-mail exdir@isosugar.org; internet www.isosugar.org; administers the International Sugar Agreement (1992), with the objectives of stimulating co-operation, facilitating trade and encouraging demand; aims to improve conditions in the sugar market through debate, analysis and studies; serves as a forum for discussion; holds annual seminars and workshops; sponsors projects from developing countries; mems: 84 countries producing some 83% of total world sugar; Exec. Dir Dr PETER BARON; publs *Sugar Year Book*, *Monthly Statistical Bulletin*, *Market Report and Press Summary*, *Quarterly Market Outlook*, seminar proceedings.

International Tea Committee Ltd (ITC): 1 Carlton House Terrace, London, SW1Y 5DB, United Kingdom; tel. (20) 7839-5090; e-mail info@inttea.com; internet www.inttea.com; f. 1933 to administer the International Tea Agreement; now serves as a statistical and information centre; in 1979 membership was extended to include consuming countries; producer mems: national tea boards or asscns in Bangladesh, People's Republic of China, India, Indonesia, Kenya, Malawi, Sri Lanka and Tanzania; consumer mems: United Kingdom Tea Asscn, Tea Asscn of the USA Inc., Irish Tea Trade Asscn, Netherland Coffee Roasters and Tea Packers' Asscn, and the Tea Asscn of Canada; assoc. mems: Netherlands and UK ministries of agriculture, and national tea boards/asscns in 8 producing and 2 consuming countries; Chief Exec. MANUJA PEIRIS; publs *Annual Bulletin of Statistics*, *Monthly Statistical Summary*.

International Tobacco Growers' Association (ITGA): Av. Gen. Humberto Delgado 30-A, 6001-081 Castelo Branco, Portugal; tel. (272) 325901; fax (272) 325906; e-mail itga@tobaccoleaf.org; internet www.tobaccoleaf.org; f. 1984 to provide a forum for the exchange of views and information of interest to tobacco producers; holds annual meeting; mems: 23 countries producing over 80% of the world's internationally traded tobacco; Chief Exec. ANTÓNIO ABRUNHOSA (Portugal); publs *Tobacco Courier* (quarterly), *Tobacco Briefing*.

International Tropical Timber Organization (ITTO): International Organizations Center, 5th Floor, Pacifico-Yokohama, 1-1-1, Minato-Mirai, Nishi-ku, Yokohama 220-0012, Japan; tel. (45) 223-1110; fax (45) 223-1111; e-mail itto@itto.or.jp; internet www.itto.int; f. 1985 under the International Tropical Timber Agreement (1983); a new treaty, ITTA 1994, came into force in 1997; provides a forum for consultation and co-operation between countries that produce and consume tropical timber, and is dedicated to the sustainable development and conservation of tropical forests; facilitates progress towards 'Objective 2000', which aims to move as rapidly as possible towards achieving exports of tropical timber and timber products from sustainably managed resources; encourages, through policy and project work, forest management, conservation and restoration, the further processing of tropical timber in producing countries, and the gathering and analysis of market intelligence and economic information; mems: 33 producing and 26 consuming countries and the EU; Exec. Dir EMMANUEL ZE MEKA (Cameroon); publs *Annual Review and Assessment of the World Timber Situation*, *Tropical Timber Market Information Service* (every 2 weeks), *Tropical Forest Update* (quarterly).

Organization of the Petroleum Exporting Countries (OPEC): 1010 Vienna, Helferstorferstrasse 17; tel. (1) 211-12-279; fax (1) 214-98-27; e-mail prid@opec.org; internet www.opec.org; f. 1960 to unify and co-ordinate members' petroleum policies and to safeguard their interests generally; holds regular conferences of member countries to set reference prices and production levels; conducts research in energy studies, economics and finance; provides data services and news services covering petroleum and energy issues; mems: Algeria, Angola, Iran, Iraq, Kuwait, Libya, Nigeria, Qatar, Saudi Arabia, United Arab Emirates, Venezuela; Sec.-Gen. ABDULLA SALEM EL-BADRI (Libya); publs *Annual Report*, *Annual Statistical Bulletin*, *OPEC Bulletin* (10 year), *OPEC Review* (quarterly), *Monthly Oil Market Report*, *World Oil Outlook* (annually).

Development and Economic Co-operation

Afro-Asian Rural Development Organization (AARDO): No. 2, State Guest Houses Complex, Chanakyapuri, New Delhi 110 021, India; tel. (11) 24100475; fax (11) 24672045; e-mail aardohq@nde.vsnl.net.in; internet www.aardo.org; f. 1962 to act as a catalyst for the co-operative restructuring of rural life in Africa and Asia and to explore opportunities for the co-ordination of efforts to promote rural welfare and to eradicate hunger, thirst, disease, illiteracy and poverty; carries out collaborative research on development issues; organizes training; encourages the exchange of information; holds international conferences and seminars; awards 150 individual training fellowships at nine institutes in Egypt, India, Japan, the Republic of Korea, Malaysia and Taiwan; mems: 15 African countries, 14 Asian countries, 1 African associate; Sec.-Gen. ABDALLA YAHIA ADAM (Sudan); publs *Afro-Asian Journal of Rural Development* (2 a year), *Annual Report*, *AARDO Newsletter* (2 a year).

Asian and Pacific Development Centre: Pesiaran Duta, POB 12224, 50770 Kuala Lumpur, Malaysia; tel. (3) 6511088; fax (3) 6510316; internet www.apdc.org; f. 1980; undertakes research and training, acts as clearing-house for information on development and offers consultancy services, in co-operation with national institutions; current programme includes assistance regarding the implementation of national development strategies; the Centre aims to promote economic co-operation among developing countries of the region for their mutual benefit; mems: 19 countries and 2 associate members; CEO Dr FRANKLIN P. KIM; publs *Annual Report*, *Newsletter* (2 a year), *Asia-Pacific Development Monitor* (quarterly), studies, reports, monographs.

Asia-Pacific Mountain Network (APMN): c/o International Centre for Integrated Mountain Development, GPO Box 3226, Khumaltar, Lalitpur, Nepal; tel. (1) 5003222; fax (1) 5003299;

e-mail apmn@mtnforum.org; internet www.icimod.org/apmn; f. 1995; forum for the production and dissemination of information on sustainable mountain development, reducing the risk of mountain disasters, economic development, the elimination of poverty, and cultural heritage; mems: about 2,000.

Association of Development Financing Institutions in Asia and the Pacific (ADFIAP): Skyland Plaza, 2nd Floor, Sen. Gil J. Puyat Ave, Makati City, Metro Manila, 1200 Philippines; tel. (2) 8161672; fax (2) 8176498; e-mail info@adfiap.org; internet www.adfiap.org; f. 1976 to promote the interests and economic development of the respective countries of its member institutions, through development financing; mems: 113 institutions in 42 countries; Chair. NAWANG GYETSE (Samoa); Sec.-Gen. OCTAVIO B. PERALTA; publs *Asian Banking Digest*, *Journal of Development Finance* (2 a year), *ADFIAP Newsletter*, *ADFIAP Accompli*, *DevTrade Finance*.

Central Asia Regional Economic Co-operation (CAREC): CAREC Unit, ADB, POB 789, 0980 Manila, Philippines; tel. (2) 6326368; fax (2) 6362387; internet www.adb.org/Carec; f. 1997; a sub-regional alliance supported by several multilateral institutions (Asian Development Bank, European Bank for Reconstruction and Development, International Monetary Fund, Islamic Development Bank, United Nations Development Programme, and World Bank) to promote economic co-operation and development; supports projects in the following priority areas: transport, energy, trade policy, trade facilitation; a Cross-Border Transport Agreement was signed by Kyrgyzstan and Tajikistan in Oct. 2010 (an agreement for Afghanistan to accede to the Agreement was concluded in Aug. 2011); mems: Afghanistan, Azerbaijan, Kazakhstan, Kyrgyzstan, Mongolia, Tajikistan, Uzbekistan, Xinjiang Uygur Autonomous Region (of the People's Republic of China).

Centre on Integrated Rural Development for Asia and the Pacific (CIRDAP): Chameli House, 17 Topkhana Rd; GPO Box 2883, Dhaka 1000, Bangladesh; tel. (2) 9558751; fax (2) 9562035; e-mail infocom@cirdap.org; internet www.cirdap.org.sg; f. 1979 to support integrated rural development; promotes regional co-operation; mems: Afghanistan, Bangladesh, Fiji, India, Indonesia, Iran, Laos, Malaysia, Myanmar, Nepal, Pakistan, Philippines, Sri Lanka, Thailand, Viet Nam; Dir DURGA PRASAD PAUDYAL.

Colombo Plan: POB 596, 31 Wijerama Rd, Colombo 7, Sri Lanka; tel. (11) 2684188; fax (11) 2684386; e-mail info@colombo-plan.org; internet www.colombo-plan.org; f. 1950, as the Colombo Plan for Co-operative Economic and Social Development in Asia and the Pacific, by seven Commonwealth countries, to encourage economic and social development in that region, based on principles of partnership and collective effort; the Plan comprises four training programmes: the Drug Advisory Programme, to enhance the capabilities of officials, in government and non-governmental organizations, involved in drug abuse prevention and control; the Programme for Public Administration, to develop human capital in the public sector; the Programme for Private Sector Development, which implements skill development programmes in the area of small and medium-sized enterprises and related issues; and the Staff College for Technician Education (see below); all training programmes are voluntarily funded, while administrative costs of the organization are shared equally by all member countries; developing countries are encouraged to become donors and to participate in economic and technical co-operation activities; mems: 26 countries; Sec.-Gen. ADAM MANIKU (Maldives); publs *Annual Report*, *Colombo Plan Focus* (quarterly), *Consultative Committee Proceedings and Conclusions* (every 2 years).

Colombo Plan Staff College for Technician Education: blk C, DepEd Complex, Meralco Ave, Pasig City 1600, Metro Manila, Philippines; tel. (2) 6310991; fax (2) 6310996; e-mail cpsc@cpsctech.org; internet www.cpsctech.org; f. 1973 with the support of member governments of the Colombo Plan; aims to enhance the development of technician education systems in developing mem. countries; Dir MOHAMMAD NAIM BIN YAAKUB (Malaysia); publ. *CPSC Quarterly*.

Council of Regional Organizations in the Pacific (CROP): c/o Private Mail Bag, Suva, Fiji; tel. 3312600; fax 3305573; f. 1988 as South Pacific Organizations' Co-ordinating Committee; renamed 1999; aims to co-ordinate work programmes in the region and improve the efficiency of aid resources; holds annual meetings; chairmanship alternates between the participating organizations; first meeting of subcommittee on information technologies convened in 1998; mems: Pacific Islands Development Programme, Secretariat of the Pacific Community (SPC), Pacific Islands Applied Geoscience Commission, Pacific Islands Forum Secretariat, Secretariat of the Pacific Regional Environment Programme, Pacific Islands Forum Fisheries Agency, the South Pacific Tourism Organization (southpacific.travel), the Fiji School of Medicine, the South Pacific Board for Educational Assessment, the Pacific Power Association, and the University of the South Pacific.

Developing Eight (D-8): Maya Aka Center, Buyukdere Cad. 100–102, Esentepe, 34390, Istanbul, Turkey; tel. (212) 3561823; fax (212) 3561829; e-mail secretariat@developing8.org; internet www.developing8.org; inaugurated at a meeting of heads of state in June 1997; aims to foster economic co-operation between member states and to strengthen the role of developing countries in the global economy; project areas include trade and industry, agriculture, human resources, telecommunications, rural development, finance (including banking and privatization), energy, environment, and health; sixth Summit meeting: convened in Kuala Lumpur, Malaysia, July 2008; mems: Bangladesh, Egypt, Indonesia, Iran, Malaysia, Nigeria, Pakistan, Turkey; Sec.-Gen. Dr WIDI PRATIKTO (Indonesia).

Foundation for the Peoples of the South Pacific, International (FSPI): GPO Box 18006, Victoria Cnr Bldg, Suva, Fiji; tel. 3312250; fax 3312298; e-mail admin@fspi.org.fj; internet www.fspi.org.fj; f. 1965; provides training and technical assistance for self-help community development groups and co-operatives; implements long-term programmes in sustainable forestry and agriculture, the environment, education, nutrition, women in development, child survival, and fisheries; mems: non-governmental affiliates operating in Australia, Fiji, Kiribati, Papua New Guinea, Samoa, Solomon Islands, Tonga, Tuvalu, United Kingdom, USA, Vanuatu; Exec. Dir REX S. HOROI; publs *Annual Report*, *News* (quarterly), technical reports (e.g. on intermediate technology, nutrition, teaching aids).

Group of 15 (G15): G15 Technical Support Facility, 1 route des Morillons, CP 2100, 1218 Grand Saconnex, Geneva, Switzerland; tel. 227916701; fax 227916169; e-mail tsf@g15.org; internet www.g15.org; f. 1989 by 15 developing nations during the 9th summit of the Non-Aligned Movement; retains its original name although current membership totals 17; convenes biennial summits to address the global economic and political situation and to promote economic development through South-South co-operation and North-South dialogue; mems: Algeria, Argentina, Brazil, Chile, Egypt, India, Indonesia, Iran, Jamaica, Kenya, Malaysia, Mexico, Nigeria, Senegal, Sri Lanka, Venezuela, Zimbabwe; Head of Office AUDU A. KADIRI.

Group of 77 (G77): c/o UN Headquarters, Rm NL-2077, New York, NY 10017, USA; tel. (212) 963-0192; fax (212) 963-1753; e-mail secretariat@g77.org; internet www.g77.org; f. 1964 by the 77 signatory states of the 'Joint Declaration of the Seventy-Seven Countries' (the G77 retains its original name, owing to its historic significance, although its membership has expanded since inception); first ministerial meeting, held in Algiers, Algeria, in Oct. 1967, adopted the Charter of Algiers as a basis for G77 co-operation; subsequently G77 Chapters were established with liaison offices in Geneva (UNCTAD), Nairobi (UNEP), Paris (UNESCO), Rome (FAO/IFAD), Vienna (UNIDO), and the Group of 24 (G24) in Washington, DC (IMF and World Bank); as the largest intergovernmental organization of developing states in the United Nations the G77 aims to enable developing nations to articulate and promote their collective economic interests and to improve their negotiating capacity with regard to global economic issues within the United Nations system; in Sept. 2006 G77 ministers of foreign affairs, and the People's Republic of China, endorsed the establishment of a new Consortium on Science, Technology and Innovation for the South (COSTIS); a chairperson, who also acts as spokesperson, co-ordinates the G77's activities in each Chapter; the chairmanship rotates on a regional basis between Africa, Asia, and Latin America and the Caribbean; the supreme decision-making body of the G77 is the South Summit, normally convened at five-yearly intervals (2005: Doha, Qatar; the third Summit was scheduled to be convened in Africa, in 2011); the annual meeting of G77 ministers of foreign affairs is convened at the start (in September) of the regular session of the UN General Assembly; periodic sectoral ministerial meetings are organized in preparation for UNCTAD sessions and prior to the UNIDO and UNESCO General Conferences, and with the aim of promoting South-South co-operation; other special ministerial meetings are also convened from time to time; the first G77 Ministerial Forum on Water Resources was convened in February 2009, in Muscat, Oman; mems: 131 developing countries.

International Centre for Integrated Mountain Development (ICIMOD): 4/80 Jawalakhel, Lalitpur, GPO Box 3226, Kathmandu, Nepal; tel. (1) 5003222; fax (1) 5003299; e-mail info@icimod.org; internet www.icimod.org; f. 1983; an autonomous organization sponsored by regional member countries and by the governments of Nepal, Germany, Switzerland, Austria, Netherlands and Denmark, to help promote an economically and environmentally sound ecosystem and to improve the living standards of the population in the Hindu Kush-Himalaya; aims to serve as a focal point for multi-disciplinary documentation, training and applied research, and as a consultative centre in scientific and practical matters pertaining to mountain development; participating countries: Afghanistan, Bangladesh, Bhutan, People's Republic of China, India, Myanmar, Nepal, Pakistan; Dir-Gen. ANDREAS SCHILD (Switzerland).

Mekong River Commission (MRC): POB 6101, Unit 18 Ban Sithane Neua, Sikhottabong District, Vientiane, Laos 01000; tel.

(21) 263263; fax (21) 263264; e-mail mrcs@mrcmekong.org; internet www.mrcmekong.org; f. 1995 as successor to the Committee for Co-ordination of Investigations of the Lower Mekong Basin ('Mekong Committee' f. 1957); aims to promote and co-ordinate the sustainable development and use of the water and related resources of the Mekong River Basin for navigational and non-navigational purposes, in order to assist the social and economic development of member states and preserve the ecological balance of the basin; provides scientific information and policy advice; supports the implementation of strategic programmes and activities; organizes an annual donor consultative group meeting; maintains regular dialogue with Myanmar and the People's Republic of China; the first meeting of heads of government was convened in Hua Hin, Thailand, in April 2010; mems: Cambodia, Laos, Thailand, Viet Nam; CEO JEREMY BIRD; publs *Annual Report*, *Catch and Culture* (3 a year), *Mekong News* (quarterly).

OPEC Fund for International Development: Postfach 995, 1010 Vienna, Austria; tel. (1) 515-64-0; fax (1) 513-92-38; e-mail info@ofid.org; internet www.ofid.org; f. 1976 by mem. countries of OPEC, to provide financial co-operation and assistance in support of social and economic development in low-income countries, and to promote co-operation between OPEC countries and other developing states; in 2010 new approvals amounted to US $1,374.3m; Dir-Gen. SULEIMAN J. AL-HERBISH (Saudi Arabia); publs *Annual Report*, *OPEC Fund Newsletter* (3 a year).

Pacific Basin Economic Council (PBEC): Unit 1202 ING Tower, 308 Des Voeux Road Central, Hong Kong SAR; tel. 2815-6550; fax 2545-0499; e-mail info@pbec.org; internet www.pbec.org; f. 1967; an asscn of business representatives aiming to promote business opportunities in the region, in order to enhance overall economic development; advises governments and serves as a liaison between business leaders and government officials; encourages business relationships and co-operation among members; holds business symposia; mems: 20 economies (Australia, Canada, Chile, People's Republic of China, Colombia, Ecuador, Hong Kong, Indonesia, Japan, Republic of Korea, Malaysia, Mexico, New Zealand, Peru, Philippines, Russia, Singapore, Taiwan, Thailand, USA); Chair. WARREN K. K. LUKE; publs *PBEC Update* (quarterly), *Executive Summary* (annual conference report).

Pacific Economic Cooperation Council (PECC): 29 Heng Mui Keng Terrace, Singapore 119620; tel. 67379822; fax 67379824; e-mail info@pecc.org; internet www.pecc.org; f. 1980; an independent, policy-orientated organization of senior research, government and business representatives from 26 economies in the Asia-Pacific region; aims to foster economic development in the region by providing a forum for discussion and co-operation in a wide range of economic areas; PECC is an official observer to APEC; holds a General Meeting annually; mems: Australia, Brunei, Canada, Chile, the People's Republic of China, Colombia, Ecuador, Hong Kong, Indonesia, Japan, the Republic of Korea, Malaysia, Mexico, Mongolia, New Zealand, Peru, Philippines, Singapore, Taiwan, Thailand, USA, Viet Nam and the Pacific Islands Forum; assoc. mem.: France (Pacific Territories); Sec.-Gen. EDUARDO PEDROSA; publs *Issues PECC* (quarterly), *Pacific Economic Outlook* (annually), *Pacific Food Outlook* (annually).

Pacific Islands Development Program: East-West Centre, 1601 East-West Rd, Honolulu, HI 96848-1601, USA; tel. (808) 944-7745; fax (808) 944-7670; e-mail pidp@eastwestcenter.org; f. 1980; promotes regional development by means of education, research and training; serves as the secretariat of the Pacific Islands Conference of Leaders; mems: 22 Pacific islands; Dir Dr SITIVENI HALAPUA; publ. *Pacific Islands Report*.

Pacific Trade and Development Forum (PAFTAD): PAFTAD International Secr., John Crawford Bldg, Asia Pacific School of Economics and Government, Australian National University, Canberra, ACT 0200, Australia; tel. (2) 6125-3780; fax (2) 6125-0767; e-mail paftad.sec@anu.edu.au; internet www.paftad.org; f. 1968; holds annual conference for discussion of regional trade policy issues by senior economists and experts; Exec. Officer LUKE HURST.

Partners in Population and Development (PPD): IPH Bldg, 2nd Floor, Mohakhali, Dhaka 1212, Bangladesh; tel. (2) 988-1882; fax (2) 882-9387; e-mail partners@ppdsec.org; internet www.partners-popdev.org; f. 1994; aims to implement the decisions of the International Conference on Population and Development, held in Cairo, Egypt in 1994, in order to expand and improve South-South collaboration in the fields of family planning and reproductive health; administers a Visionary Leadership Programme, a Global Leadership Programme, and other training and technical advisory services; mems: 24 developing countries; Exec. Dir HARRY S. JOOSEERY.

Trans-Pacific Strategic Economic Partnership Agreement (P4): c/o Ministry of Foreign Affairs and Trade, Private Bag 1890, Wellington, New Zealand; tel. (4) 439-8446; f. 2006 upon entry into force of agreement signed by the four founding mems; eliminated some 90% of tariffs on trade between mems; negotiations on financial services and investment commenced in March 2008; negotiations on an expanded partnership agreement, to include Australia, Malaysia, Peru, the USA and Viet Nam, commenced in March 2010; mems: Brunei, Chile, New Zealand, Singapore.

US-Pacific Island Nations Joint Commercial Commission: c/o Pacific Islands Development Program, 1601 East-West Rd, Honolulu, HI 96848, USA; tel. (808) 944-7721; fax (808) 944-7670; e-mail kroekers@eastwestcenter.org; internet pidp.eastwestcenter.org/jcc; f. 1993 to promote mutually beneficial commercial and economic relations between the independent Pacific island nations and the USA; mems: Cook Islands, Fiji, Kiribati, Marshall Islands, Federated States of Micronesia, Nauru, Niue, Papua New Guinea, Samoa, Solomon Islands, Tonga, Tuvalu, USA and Vanuatu.

World Economic Forum: 91–93 route de la Capite, 1223 Cologny/Geneva, Switzerland; tel. 228691212; fax 227862744; e-mail contact@weforum.org; internet www.weforum.org; f. 1971; the Forum comprises commercial interests gathered on a non-partisan basis, under the stewardship of the Swiss Government, with the aim of improving society through economic development; convenes an annual meeting in Davos, Switzerland; organizes the following programmes: Technology Pioneers; Women Leaders; and Young Global Leaders; and aims to mobilize the resources of the global business community in the implementation of the following initiatives: the Global Health Initiative; the Disaster Relief Network; the West-Islamic World Dialogue; and the G20/International Monetary Reform Project; the Forum is governed by a guiding Foundation Board; an advisory International Business Council; and an administrative Managing Board; regular mems: representatives of 1,000 leading commercial companies world-wide; selected mem. companies taking a leading role in the movement's activities are known as 'partners'; Chair. KLAUS SCHWAB.

Economics and Finance

Asian Clearing Union (ACU): 207/1 Pasdaran Ave, POB 15875-7177, 16646 Tehran, Iran; tel. (21) 22842076; fax (21) 22847677; e-mail acusecret@cbi.ir; internet www.asianclearingunion.org; f. 1974; provides a facility to settle payments, on a multilateral basis, for international transactions among participating central banks, thereby contributing to the expansion of trade and economic activity among ESCAP countries; the Central Bank of Iran is the agent for the Union; units of account are, with effect from 1 January 2009, denominated as the ACU dollar and the ACU euro; mems: central banks of Bangladesh, Bhutan, India, Iran, Myanmar, Nepal, Pakistan, Sri Lanka; Sec.-Gen. LIDA BORHAN-AZAD; publs *Annual Report*, *Monthly Newsletter*.

Asian Reinsurance Corporation: 17th Floor, Tower B, Chamnan Phenjati Business Center, 65 Rama 9 Rd, Huaykwang, Bangkok 10320, Thailand; tel. (2) 245-2169; fax (2) 248-1377; e-mail asianre@asianrecorp.com; internet www.asianrecorp.com; f. 1979 under ESCAP auspices; aims to operate as a professional reinsurer serving the needs of the Asia Pacific region; also aims to provide technical assistance to national insurance markets; cap. (auth.) US $100m., (subscribed and p.u.) $30.2m. (Dec. 2010); mems: Afghanistan, Bangladesh, Bhutan, People's Republic of China, India, Iran, Republic of Korea, Philippines, Sri Lanka, Thailand; Pres. and CEO S. A. KUMAR.

Association of Asian Confederations of Credit Unions (AACCU): 24 Soi 60 Ramkanheang Rd, Bangkapi, Bangkok 10240, Thailand; tel. (2) 374-3170; fax (2) 374-5321; e-mail accu@aaccu.coop; internet www.aaccu.asia; links and promotes credit unions and co-operatives in Asia, provides research facilities and training programmes; mems: in credit union leagues and federations in 24 Asian countries; CEO RANJITH HETTIARACHCHI (Thailand); publs *ACCU News* (every 3 months), *Annual Report*, *ACCU Directory*.

Bank for International Settlements (BIS): Centralbahnplatz 2, 4002 Basel, Switzerland; tel. 612808080; fax 612809100; e-mail email@bis.org; internet www.bis.org; f. pursuant to the Hague Agreements of 1930 to promote co-operation among national central banks and to provide additional facilities for international financial operations; provides the secretariat for the Basel Committee on Banking Supervision and the Financial Stability Board; representative offices in Hong Kong SAR, and Mexico; mems: central banks in 55 countries; Chair. CHRISTIAN NOYER (France); Gen. Man. JAIME CARUANA (Spain); publs *Annual Report*, *Quarterly Review: International Banking and Financial Market Developments*, *The BIS Consolidated International Banking Statistics* (every 6 months), *Joint BIS-IMF-OECD-World Bank Statistics on External Debt* (quarterly), *Regular OTC Derivatives Market Statistics* (every 6 months), *Central Bank Survey of Foreign Exchange and Derivatives Market Activity* (every 3 years).

Equator Principles Association: e-mail secretariat@equator-principles.com; f. July 2010; aims to administer and develop further the Equator Principles, first adopted in 2003, with the support of the International Finance Corporation, as a set of industry standards for the management of environmental and social risk in project financing; a Strategic Review conference was convened in Beijing, People's Republic of China, in Dec. 2010; 70 signed-up Equator Principles Financial Institutions (EPFIs).

Financial Action Task Force (FATF) (Groupe d'action financière—GAFI): 2 rue André-Pascal, 75775 Paris Cédex 16, France; tel. 1-45-24-79-45; fax 1-44-30-61-37; e-mail contact@fatf-gafi.org; internet www.fatf-gafi.org; f. 1989, on the recommendation of the Group of Seven industrialized nations (G7), to develop and promote policies to combat money laundering and the financing of terrorism; formulated a set of recommendations (40+9) for countries world-wide to implement; established partnerships with regional task forces in the Caribbean, Asia-Pacific, Central Asia, Europe, East and South Africa, the Middle East and North Africa and South America; mems: 34 state jurisdictions, the European Commission, and the Cooperation Council for the Arab States of the Gulf; observers: India, Basel Committee on Banking Supervision, Eurasian Group (EAG) on combating money laundering and financing of terrorism; Pres. GIANCARLO DEL BUFALO (Italy); Exec. Sec. RICK MCDONELL; publs *Annual Report*, *e-Bulletin*.

Financial Stability Board: c/o BIS, Centralbahnplatz 2, 4002 Basel, Switzerland; tel. 612808298; fax 612809100; e-mail fsb@bis.org; internet www.financialstabilityboard.org; f. 1999 as the Financial Stability Forum, name changed in April 2009; brings together senior representatives of national financial authorities, international financial institutions, international regulatory and supervisory groupings and committees of central bank experts and the European Central Bank; aims to promote international financial stability and strengthen the functioning of the financial markets; in March 2009 agreed to expand its membership to include all Group of 20 (G20) economies, as well as Spain and the European Commission; in April 2009 the meeting of G20 heads of state and government determined to re-establish the then Forum as the Financial Stability Board, strengthen its institutional structure (to include a plenary body, a steering committee and three standing committees concerned with Vulnerabilities Assessment; Supervisory and Regulatory Co-operation; and Standards Implementation) and expand its mandate to enhance its effectiveness as an international mechanism to promote financial stability; the Board was to strengthen its collaboration with the International Monetary Fund, and conduct joint 'early warning exercises'; in December 2009 the Board initiated a peer review of implementation of the Principles and Standards for Sound Compensation Practices; in Nov. 2010 determined to establish six FSB regional consultative groups; Chair. MARIO DRAGHI (until 31 Oct. 2011).

Group of Seven (G7): f. 1975 as an informal framework of co-operation; despite the formation in 1998 of the Group of Eight (G8), incorporating Russia, and the inclusion of Russia in all G8 sectoral areas from 2003, the Group of Seven major industrialized countries (G7) remains a forum for regular discussion (at the level of ministers of finance and central bank governors) of developments in the global economy and of economic policy; the IMF Managing Director is normally invited to participate in G7 meetings; mems: ministers of finance and central bank governors of Canada, France, Germany, Italy, Japan, United Kingdom and the USA; European Union representation.

Group of 20 (G20): internet www.g20.org; f. Sept. 1999 as an informal deliberative forum of finance ministers and central bank governors representing both industrialized and 'systemically important' emerging market nations; aims to strengthen the international financial architecture and to foster sustainable economic growth and development; in 2004 participating countries adopted the G20 Accord for Sustained Growth and stated a commitment to high standards of transparency and fiscal governance; the IMF Managing Director and IBRD President participate in G20 annual meetings; an extraordinary Summit on Financial Markets and the World Economy was convened in Washington, DC, USA, in November 2008, attended by heads of state or government of G20 member economies; a second summit meeting, held in London, United Kingdom, in April 2009, issued as its final communiqué a *Global Plan for Recovery and Reform* outlining commitments to restore economic confidence, growth and jobs, to strengthen financial supervision and regulation, to reform and strengthen global financial institutions, to promote global trade and investment and to ensure a fair and sustainable economic recovery; detailed declarations were also issued on measures agreed to deliver substantial resources (of some US $850,000m.) through international financial institutions and on reforms to be implemented in order to strengthen the financial system; as a follow-up to the London summit, G20 heads of state met in Pittsburgh, USA, in September 2009; the meeting adopted a *Framework for Strong, Sustainable, and Balanced Growth* and resolved to expand the role of the G20 to be at the centre of future international economic policymaking; summit meetings were held in June 2010, in Canada (at the G8 summit), and in Seoul, Republic of Korea, in November; the sixth G20 summit was scheduled to be held in Cannes, France, in November 2011; mems: Argentina, Australia, Brazil, Canada, People's Republic of China, France, Germany, India, Indonesia, Italy, Japan, Republic of Korea, Mexico, Russia, Saudi Arabia, South Africa, Turkey, United Kingdom, USA and the European Union; observers: the Netherlands, Spain.

Insurance Institute for Asia and the Pacific: Zapote Rd, Alabang, Metro Manila, Philippines; tel. (2) 8420691; fax (2) 8420692; e-mail education@iiap.com.ph; internet www.iiap.com/ph; f. 1974 to provide insurance management training and conduct research in subjects connected with the insurance industry; Chair. MELECIO C. MALLILLIN; publ. *IIAP Journal* (quarterly).

Inter-American Development Bank: 1300 New York Ave, NW, Washington, DC 20577, USA; tel. (202) 623-1000; fax (202) 623-3096; e-mail pic@iadb.org; internet www.iadb.org; f. 1959 to promote the individual and collective development of Latin American and Caribbean countries through the financing of economic and social development projects and the provision of technical assistance; mems: 48 countries, incl. People's Rep. of China, Japan and Rep. of Korea; Pres. LUIS ALBERTO MORENO (Colombia); publs *Annual Report* (in English, French, Spanish and Portuguese), *Equidad* (quarterly), *IDBamérica* (monthly, in English and Spanish), other reports, newsletters, economic reviews.

Intergovernmental Group of 24 (G24) on International Monetary Affairs and Development: 700 19th St, NW, Rm 3-600 Washington, DC 20431, USA; tel. (202) 623-6101; fax (202) 623-6000; e-mail G24@G24.org; internet www.g24.org/; f. 1971; aims to co-ordinate the position of developing countries on monetary and development finance issues; operates at the political level of ministers of finance and governors of central banks, and also at the level of government officials; mems (Africa): Algeria, Côte d'Ivoire, DRC, Egypt, Ethiopia, Gabon, Ghana, Nigeria, South Africa; (Latin America and the Caribbean): Argentina, Brazil, Colombia, Guatemala, Mexico, Peru, Trinidad and Tobago and Venezuela; (Asia and the Middle East): India, Iran, Lebanon, Pakistan, Philippines, Sri Lanka and Syrian Arab Republic; the People's Republic of China has the status of special invitee at G24 meetings; G77 participant states may attend G24 meetings as observers.

Islamic Financial Services Board: POB 10591, 50714 Kuala Lumpur, Malaysia; tel. (3) 26984248; fax (3) 26984280; e-mail ifsb_sec@ifsb.org; internet www.ifsb.org; f. 2002; aims to formulate standards and guiding principles for regulatory and supervisory agencies working within the Islamic financial services industry; mems: 29 full mems (incl. Islamic Development Bank), 23 associate mems (incl. Asian Development Bank, the Bank for International Settlements, the IMF and the World Bank), and 139 observer mems; Sec.-Gen. JASEEM AHMED.

Education

Asian Institute of Technology (AIT): POB 4, Klong Luang, Pathumthani 12120, Thailand; tel. (2) 516-0144; fax (2) 516-2126; e-mail president@ait.ac.th; internet www.ait.ac.th; f. 1959; Master's, Doctor's and Diploma programmes are offered in four schools: Advanced Technologies, Civil Engineering, Environment, Resources and Development, and Management; specialized training is provided by the Center for Library and Information Resources (CLAIR), the Continuing Education Center, the Center for Language and Educational Technology, the Regional Computer Center, the AIT Center in Viet Nam (based in Hanoi) and the Swiss-AIT-Viet Nam Management Development Program (in Ho Chi Minh City); other research and outpost centres are the Asian Center for Engineering Computations and Software, the Asian Center for Research on Remote Sensing, the Regional Environmental Management Center, the Asian Center for Soil Improvement and Geosynthetics and the Urban Environmental Outreach Center; there are four specialized information centres (on ferro-cement, geotechnical engineering, renewable energy resources, environmental sanitation) under CLAIR; the Management of Technology Information Center conducts short-term courses in the management of technology and international business; Pres. Prof. SAID IRANDOUST; Dir ARJUNAPERMAL SUBBIAH; publs *AIT Annual Report*, *Annual Report on Research and Activities*, *AIT Review* (3 a year), *Prospectus*, other specialized publs.

Asian South Pacific Bureau of Adult Education (ASPBAE): c/o MAAPL, Eucharistic Congress Bldg No. 3, 9th Floor, 5 Convent St, Colaba, Mumbai 400 039, India; tel. (22) 22021391; fax (22) 22832217; e-mail aspbae@vsnl.com; internet www.aspbae.org; f. 1964 to assist non-formal education and adult literacy; organizes training courses and seminars; provides material and advice relating to adult education; mems in 31 countries and territories; Sec.-Gen. MARIA-LOURDES ALMAZAN-KHAN; publ. *ASPBAE News* (3 a year).

Association of South-East Asian Institutions of Higher Learning (ASAIHL): Secretariat, Rm 113, Jamjuree 1 Bldg, Chulalongkorn University, Phyathai Rd, Bangkok 10330, Thailand; tel. (2) 251-6966; fax (2) 253-7909; e-mail ninnat.o@chula.ac.th; internet www.seameo.org/asaihl; f. 1956 to promote the economic, cultural and social welfare of the people of South-East Asia by means of educational co-operation and research programmes; and to cultivate a sense of regional identity and interdependence; collects and disseminates information, organizes discussions; mems: 170 university institutions in 20 countries; Pres. Prof. Mai Trong Nhuan; Sec.-Gen. Dr Ninnat Olanvoravuth; publs *Newsletter*, *Handbook* (every 3 years).

International Union for Oriental and Asian Studies: c/o Közraktar u. 12a 11/2, 1093 Budapest, Hungary; f. 1951 by the 22nd International Congress of Orientalists under the auspices of UNESCO, to promote contacts between orientalists throughout the world, and to organize congresses, research and publications; mems: in 24 countries; Sec.-Gen. Prof. György Hazai.

Southeast Asian Ministers of Education Organization (SEAMEO): M. L. Pin Malakul Bldg, 920 Sukhumvit Rd, Bangkok 10110, Thailand; tel. (2) 391-0144; fax (2) 381-2587; e-mail secretariat@seameo.org; internet www.seameo.org; f. 1965 to promote co-operation among the Southeast Asian nations through projects in education, science and culture; SEAMEO has 19 regional centres including: BIOTROP for tropical biology, in Bogor, Indonesia; INNOTECH for educational innovation and technology, in Philippines; SEAMOLEC, an open-learning centre, in Indonesia; RECSAM for education in science and mathematics, in Penang, Malaysia; RELC for languages, in Singapore; RIHED for higher education development, in Bangkok, Thailand; SEARCA for graduate study and research in agriculture, in Los Baños, Philippines; SPAFA for archaeology and fine arts, in Bangkok, Thailand; TROPMED for tropical medicine and public health, with regional centres in Indonesia, Malaysia, Philippines and Thailand and a central office in Bangkok; VOCTECH for vocational and technical education; QITEPs, regional centres for quality improvement of teachers and education personnel, for language, based in Jakarta, Indonesia, for mathematics, in Yogyakarta, Indonesia, and for science, in Bandung, Indonesia; RETRAC, a training centre, in Ho Chi Minh City, Viet Nam; and the SEAMEO Regional Centre for History and Tradition (CHAT) in Yangon, Myanmar; mems: Brunei, Cambodia, Indonesia, Laos, Malaysia, Philippines, Singapore, Thailand, Timor-Leste and Viet Nam; assoc. mems: Australia, Canada, France, Germany, Netherlands, New Zealand, Norway and Spain; Dir Dato' Dr Ahamad bin Sipon (Malaysia); publs *Annual Report*, *SEAMEO Education Agenda*.

University of the South Pacific: University of the South Pacific, Laucala Campus, Suva, Fiji; tel. 3231000; fax 3231551; e-mail chandra_r@usp.ac.fj; internet www.usp.ac.fj; f. 1968; comprises three main campuses (in Fiji, Samoa and Vanuatu), 11 regional campuses and three faculties (arts and law; business and economics; and science, technology and environment); mems: Cook Islands, Fiji, Kiribati, Marshall Islands, Nauru, Niue, Samoa, Solomon Islands, Tokelau, Tonga, Tuvalu, Vanuatu; Vice-Chancellor Rajesh Chandra; publs *USP Annual Report*, *USP Beat* (monthly), *USP Calendar* (annually), *Oceanian Wave* (quarterly).

Environmental Conservation

Commission for the Conservation of Antarctic Marine Living Resources (CCAMLR) : POB 213, North Hobart, Tasmania 7002, Australia; tel. (3) 6210-1111; fax (3) 6224-8744; e-mail ccamlr@ccamlr.org; internet www.ccamlr.org; established under the 1982 Convention on the Conservation of Antarctic Marine Living Resources to manage marine resources in the Antarctic region; Exec. Sec. Denzil G. M. Miller.

Consortium for Ocean Leadership: 1201 New York Ave, NW, Suite 420, Washington, DC 20005, USA; tel. (202) 232-3900; fax (202) 462-8754; e-mail info@oceanleadership.org; internet www.oceanleadership.org; f. 2007, following the merger of the Consortium for Oceanographic Research and Education (CORE, f. 1999) and the Joint Oceanographic Institutions (JOI); aims to promote, support and advance the science of oceanography; Pres. Robert B. Gagosian.

Global Coral Reef Monitoring Network: POB 772, Townsville MC 4810, Australia; tel. (7) 4721-2699; fax (7) 4772-2808; e-mail clive.wilkinson@rrrc.org.au; internet www.gcrmn.org; f. 1994, as an operating unit of the International Coral Reef Initiative; active in more than 80 countries; aims include improving the management and sustainable conservation of coral reefs, strengthening links between regional organizations and ecological and socioeconomic monitoring networks, and disseminating information to assist the formulation of conservation plans; Global Co-ordinator Dr Clive Wilkinson (Australia); publ. *Status of Coral Reefs of the World*.

International Coral Reef Initiative: 27 rue Oudinot, 75007 Paris, France; internet www.icriforum.org; f. 1994 at the first Conference of the Parties of the Convention on Biological Diversity; a partnership of governments, non-governmental organizations, scientific bodies and the private sector; aims to highlight the degradation of coral reefs and provide a focus for action to ensure the sustainable management and conservation of these and related marine ecosystems; in 1995 issued a Call to Action and a Framework for Action; the Secretariat rotates among members (2009–11, France); Co-Chair. Jean-Pierre Thébault (France), Faalavaau Perina Sila (Samoa).

International Renewable Energy Agency: C67 Office Bldg, Khalidiyah (32nd) St, POB 236, Abu Dhabi, United Arab Emirates; internet www.irena.org; f. 2009 at a conference held in Bonn, Germany; aims to promote the development and application of renewable sources of energy; to act as a forum for the exchange of information and technology transfer; and to organize training seminars and other educational activities; inaugural Assembly convened in April 2011; mems: 148 signatory countries and the European Union; Dir-Gen. Adnan Amin (Kenya).

IUCN—International Union for Conservation of Nature: 28 rue Mauverney, 1196 Gland, Switzerland; tel. 229990000; fax 229990002; e-mail press@iucn.org; internet www.iucn.org; f. 1948, as the International Union for Conservation of Nature and Natural Resources; supports partnerships and practical field activities to promote the conservation of natural resources, to secure the conservation of biological diversity as an essential foundation for the future; to ensure wise use of the earth's natural resources in an equitable and sustainable way; and to guide the development of human communities towards ways of life in enduring harmony with other components of the biosphere, developing programmes to protect and sustain the most important and threatened species and eco-systems and assisting governments to devise and carry out national conservation strategies; incorporates the Species Survival Commission (SSC), a science-based network of volunteer experts aiming to ensure conservation of present levels of biodiversity; compiles annually updated Red List of Threatened Species, comprising in 2011 some 59,508 species, of which 19,265 were threatened with extinction; maintains a conservation library and documentation centre and units for monitoring traffic in wildlife; mems: more than 1,000 states, government agencies, non-governmental organizations and affiliates in some 140 countries; Pres. Ashok Khosla (India); Dir-Gen. Julia Marton-Lefèvre (USA); publs *World Conservation Strategy*, *Caring for the Earth*, *Red List of Threatened Plants*, *Red List of Threatened Species*, *United Nations List of National Parks and Protected Areas*, *World Conservation* (quarterly), *IUCN Today*.

Permanent Commission of the South Pacific (Comisión Permanente del Pacífico Sur): Av. Carlos Julio Arosemena, Km 3 Edificio Inmaral, Guayaquil, Ecuador; e-mail cpps_pse@cpps-int.org; internet www.cpps-int.org; f. 1952 to consolidate the presence of the zonal coastal states; Sec.-Gen. Héctor Soldi Soldi (Peru).

Secretariat of the Antarctic Treaty: Av. Leandro Alem 884, piso 4, C1001AAQ Buenos Aires, Argentina; tel. (11) 5169-1500; fax (11) 5169-1513; e-mail secret@ats.aq; internet www.ats.aq; f. 2004 to administer the Antarctic Treaty (signed in 1959); has developed an Electronic Information Exchange System; organizes annual Consultative Meeting (2011: Buenos Aires, Argentina, June–July); mems: 49 states party to the Treaty; Exec. Sec. Manfred Reinke.

Secretariat of the Pacific Regional Environment Programme (SPREP): POB 240, Apia, Samoa; tel. 21929; fax 20231; e-mail sprep@sprep.org; internet www.sprep.org; f. 1978 by the South Pacific Commission (where it was based, now Pacific Community), the South Pacific (now Pacific Islands) Forum, ESCAP and UNEP; formally established as an independent institution in 1993; SPREP's mandate is to promote co-operation in the Pacific islands region and to provide assistance in order to protect and improve the environment and to ensure sustainable development for present and future generations; SPREP operates two programmes: Island Ecosystems and Pacific Futures; in March 2010 letters of agreement were signed relating to the transfer and integration to SPREP from the Pacific Islands Applied Geoscience Commission of the following functions: the Pacific Islands Global Ocean Observing System (PI-GOOS); the Islands Climate Update (ICU); the Climate and Meteorological Databases (CMD); and climate change-associated energy activities; mems: 21 Pacific islands, Australia, France, New Zealand, USA; Dir David Sheppard (Australia).

World Association of Zoos and Aquariums (WAZA): IUCN Conservation Centre, 28 rue Mauverney, 1196 Gland, Switzerland; tel. 229990790; fax 229990791; e-mail secretariat@waza.org; internet www.waza.org; f. 1946, current name adopted 2000; aims to provide leadership and support for zoos and aquariums and to promote biodiversity, environmental education, and global sustainability; adopted WAZA Code of Ethics and Animal Welfare, and a Consensus Document on Responsible Reproductive Management, in 2003; in 2005 WAZA launched a World Zoo and Aquarium Conservation Strategy, adopted Research Guidelines, and participated for the first time in Conferences of the Parties to the Ramsar Convention and the Convention of Migratory Species; mems: leading zoos and aquariums and related regional and national asscn; affiliate conservation orgs; Pres. MARK PENNING; Exec. Dir GERALD DICK.

World Rainforest Movement (WRM): Maldonado 1858, Montevideo 11200, Uruguay; tel. (2) 4132989; fax (2) 4100985; e-mail wrm@wrm.org.uy; internet www.wrm.org.uy; f. 1986; aims to secure the lands and livelihoods of rainforest peoples and supports their efforts to defend rainforests from activities including commercial logging, mining, the construction of dams, the development of plantations, and shrimp farming; issued the Penang Declaration in 1989 setting out the shared vision of an alternative model of rainforest development based on securing the lands and livelihoods of forest inhabitants; released in 1998 the Montevideo Declaration, campaigning against large-scale monocrop plantations, for example of pulpwood, oil palm and rubber; and issued the Mount Tamalpais Declaration in 2000, urging governments not to include tree plantations as carbon sinks in international action against climate change; publ. *WRM Bulletin* (monthly).

WWF International: 27 ave du Mont-Blanc, 1196 Gland, Switzerland; tel. 223649111; fax 223648836; e-mail info@wwfint.org; internet www.panda.org; f. 1961 (as World Wildlife Fund), name changed to World Wide Fund for Nature in 1986, current nomenclature adopted 2001; aims to stop the degradation of natural environments, conserve bio-diversity, ensure the sustainable use of renewable resources, and promote the reduction of both pollution and wasteful consumption; addresses six priority issues: forests, freshwater, marine, species, climate change, and toxics; has identified, and focuses its activities in, 200 'ecoregions' (the 'Global 200'), believed to contain the best part of the world's remaining biological diversity; actively supports and operates conservation programmes in more than 90 countries; mems: 54 offices, 5 associate orgs, c. 5m. individual mems world-wide; Pres. YOLANDA KAKABADSE (Ecuador); Dir-Gen. JAMES P. LEAPE; publs *Annual Report*, *Living Planet Report*.

Government and Politics

Afro-Asian Peoples' Solidarity Organization (AAPSO): 89 Abdel Aziz Al-Saoud St, POB 11559-61 Manial El-Roda, Cairo, Egypt; tel. (2) 3636081; fax (2) 3637361; e-mail aapso@idsc.net.eg; f. 1958; acts among and for the peoples of Africa and Asia in their struggle for genuine independence, sovereignty, socio-economic development, peace and disarmament; mems: national committees and affiliated organizations in 66 countries and territories, assoc. mems in 15 European countries; Sec.-Gen. NOURI ABDEL RAZZAK HUSSEIN (Iraq); publs *Solidarity Bulletin* (monthly), *Socio-Economic Development* (3 a year).

Alliance of Small Island States (AOSIS): c/o 800 Second Ave, Suite 400K, New York, NY 10017, USA; tel. (212) 599-0301; fax (212) 599-1540; e-mail grenada@un.int; internet www.sidsnet.org/aosis; f. 1990 as an ad hoc intergovernmental grouping to focus on the special problems of small islands and low-lying coastal developing states; mems: 43 island nations; Chair. Dr DESSIMA WILLIAMS (Grenada) (until 31 Dec. 2011); Chair. MARLENE MOSES (Nauru) (from 1 Jan. 2012); publ. *Small Islands, Big Issues*.

ANZUS: c/o Dept of Foreign Affairs and Trade, R. G. Casey Bldg, John McEwen Crescent, Barton, ACT 0221, Australia; tel. (2) 6261-1111; fax (2) 6271-3111; internet www.dfat.gov.au; the ANZUS Security Treaty was signed in 1951 by Australia, New Zealand and the USA, and ratified in 1952 to co-ordinate partners' efforts for collective defence for the preservation of peace and security in the Pacific area, through the exchange of technical information and strategic intelligence, and a programme of exercises, exchanges and visits. In 1984 New Zealand refused to allow visits by US naval vessels that were either nuclear-propelled or potentially nuclear-armed, and this led to the cancellation of joint ANZUS military exercises: in 1986 the USA formally announced the suspension of its security commitment to New Zealand under ANZUS. Instead of the annual ANZUS Council meetings, bilateral talks were subsequently held every year between Australia and the USA. ANZUS continued to govern security relations between Australia and the USA, and between Australia and New Zealand; security relations between New Zealand and the USA were the only aspect of the treaty to be suspended. Senior-level contacts between New Zealand and the USA resumed in 1994. The Australian Govt invoked the ANZUS Security Treaty for the first time following the international terrorist attacks against targets in the USA that were perpetrated in September 2001.

Association of North East Asia Regional Governments (NEAR): Pohang, Gyeongsangbuk-do, Republic of Korea; tel. (54) 223-2318; fax (54) 223-2309; e-mail jaykim51@yahoo.co.kr; internet www.neargov.org; f. 1996 to promote co-operation among local governments in support of sub-regional economic development; mems: 69 local govts in six countries (People's Republic of China, Japan, Mongolia, Democratic People's Republic of Korea, Republic of Korea, Russia; Sec.-Gen. KIM JAE HYO.

Association of Pacific Islands Legislatures (APIL): Carl Rose Bldg, Suite 207, 181 E. Marine Corps Drive, Hagatna, Guam; tel. (671) 477-2719; fax (671) 473-3004; e-mail apil@guam.net; internet www.apilpacific.com; f. 1981 to provide a permanent structure of mutual assistance for representatives of the people of the Pacific Islands; comprises legislative representatives from 12 Pacific Island Govts; Sec.-Gen. ALIK J. ALIK (Marshall Islands).

Club of Madrid: Calle Goya 5-7, Pasaje 2A, 28001 Madrid, Spain; tel. (91) 1548230; fax (91) 1548240; e-mail clubmadrid@clubmadrid.org; internet www.clubmadrid.org; f. 2001, following Conference on Democratic Transition and Consolidation; forum of former Presidents and Prime Ministers; aims to strengthen democratic values and leadership; maintains office in Brussels, Belgium; Sec.-Gen. FERNANDO PERPIÑÁ (Spain).

Comunidade dos Países de Língua Portuguesa (CPLP) (Community of Portuguese-Speaking Countries): rua S. Caetano 32, 1200-829 Lisbon, Portugal; tel. (21) 392-8560; fax (21) 392-8588; e-mail comunicacao@cplp.org; internet www.cplp.org; f. 1996; aims to produce close political, economic, diplomatic and cultural links between Portuguese-speaking countries and to strengthen the influence of the Lusophone Commonwealth within the international community; dispatched an observer mission to oversee presidential elections held in Timor-Leste in May 2007; mems: Angola, Brazil, Cape Verde, Guinea-Bissau, Mozambique, Portugal, São Tomé and Príncipe, Timor-Leste; associate observers: Equatorial Guinea, Mauritius, Senegal; Exec. Sec. DOMINGOS SIMÕES PEREIRA (Guinea-Bissau).

Conference on Interaction and Confidence-building Measures in Asia: 050000, Almatı, Aiteke Bi 65, Kazakhstan; tel. (727) 272-01-08; fax (727) 272-40-96; e-mail s-cica@s-cica.kz; internet www.s-cica.org; f. 1999 at first meeting of 16 Asian ministers for foreign affairs, convened in Almatı; aims to provide a structure to enhance co-operation, with the objectives of promoting peace, security and stability throughout the region; first meeting of heads of state held in June 2002, adopted the Almatı Act; activities focused on a catalogue of confidence-building measures grouped into five areas: economic dimension; environmental dimension; human dimension; fight against new challenges and threats; and military-political dimension; mems: Afghanistan, Azerbaijan, People's Republic of China, Egypt, India, Iran, Israel, Jordan, Kazakhstan, Republic of Korea, Kyrgyzstan, Mongolia, Pakistan, Palestine, Russia, Tajikistan, Thailand, Turkey, United Arab Emirates, Uzbekistan; observers: Indonesia, Japan, Malaysia, Qatar, Viet Nam, Ukraine, USA and the UN, OSCE and League of Arab States; Exec. Dir DULAT BAKISHEV.

Eastern Regional Organization for Public Administration (EROPA): National College of Public Administration, Univ. of the Philippines, Diliman, Quezon City 1101, Philippines; tel. and fax (2) 9297789; e-mail eropa.secretariat@gmail.com; internet www.eropa.org.ph; f. 1960 to promote regional co-operation in improving knowledge, systems and practices of governmental administration, to help accelerate economic and social development; organizes regional conferences, seminars, special studies, surveys and training programmes; accredited, in 2000, as an online regional centre of the UN Public Administration Network for the Asia and Pacific region; there are three regional centres: Training Centre (New Delhi), Local Government Centre (Tokyo), Development Management Centre (Seoul); mems: 11 countries, 74 groups, 394 individuals; Sec.-Gen. ORLANDO S. MERCADO (Philippines); publs *EROPA Bulletin* (quarterly), *Asian Review of Public Administration* (2 a year).

Group of Eight (G8): an informal meeting of developed nations, originally comprising France, Germany, Italy, Japan, United Kingdom and the USA, first convened in Nov. 1975, at Rambouillet, France, at the level of heads of state and government; Canada became a permanent participant in 1976, forming the Group of Seven major industrialized countries—G7; from 1991 Russia was invited to participate in the then G7 summit outside the formal framework of co-operation; from 1994 Russia contributed more fully to the G7 political dialogue and from 1997 Russia became a participant in nearly all of the summit process scheduled meetings, excepting those related to finance and the global economy; from 1998 the name of the co-operation framework was changed to Group of Eight—G8, and since 2003 Russia has participated fully in all scheduled summit meetings, including those on the global economy; the European Union is also represented at G8 meetings, although it may not chair fora; G8 heads of government and the President of the European Commission and President of the European Council convene an annual summit meeting, the chairmanship and venue of which are rotated in the following order: France, USA, United Kingdom, Russia, Germany, Japan, Italy, Canada (July 2009: L'Aquila, Italy; June 2010: Huntsville, Ontario, Canada); G8 summit meetings address and seek consensus, published in a final declaration, on social and economic issues confronting the international community;

the following ('+8') nations: Australia, Brazil, People's Republic of China, India, Indonesia, Mexico, Republic of Korea and South Africa were guest participants at the June 2008 G8 summit; G8 sectoral ministerial meetings (covering areas such as energy, environment, finance and foreign affairs) are held on the fringes of the annual summit, and further G8 sectoral ministerial meetings are convened through the year; mems: Canada, France, Germany, Italy, Japan, Russia, United Kingdom and the USA; European Union representation.

International Institute for Democracy and Electoral Assistance (IDEA): Strömsborg, 103 34 Stockholm, Sweden; tel. (8) 698-3700; fax (8) 20-2422; e-mail info@idea.int; internet www.idea.int; f. 1995; aims to promote sustainable democracy in new and established democracies; works with practitioners and institutions promoting democracy in Africa, Asia, Arab states and Latin America; 25 mem. states; Sec.-Gen. VIDAR HELGESEN (Norway).

Inter-Parliamentary Union (IPU): 5 chemin du Pommier, CP 330, 1218 Le Grand-Saconnex/Geneva, Switzerland; tel. 229194150; fax 229194160; e-mail postbox@mail.ipu.org; internet www.ipu.org; f. 1889 to promote peace, co-operation and representative democracy by providing a forum for multilateral political debate between representatives of national parliaments; mems: national parliaments of 155 sovereign states; 9 assoc. mems; Sec.-Gen. ANDERS B. JOHNSSON (Sweden); publs *Chronicle of Parliamentary Elections* (annually), *The World of Parliaments* (quarterly), *World Directory of Parliaments* (annually).

Melanesian Spearhead Group (MSG): MSG Secretariat, Port Vila, Vanuatu; tel. 27750; fax 27832; f. 1986 to promote political and cultural co-operation among the Melanesian peoples; supports independence process in New Caledonia; first Melanesian arts festival held in 1991; in July 1993 a free-trade agreement was signed, awarding each member country most-favoured nation status for all trade; heads of state or of government meet every two years; regular meetings of Group trade and economic officials are also held; a permanent constitution was adopted by the Group in March 2007; mems: Fiji, Papua New Guinea, Solomon Islands, Vanuatu; Front de Libération Nationale Kanake Socialiste (New Caledonia); Exec. Dir RIVA RAVUSIRO.

Non-aligned Movement (NAM): c/o Permanent Representative of Cuba to the UN, 315 Lexington Ave, New York, NY 10016; tel. (212) 689-7215; fax (212) 779-1697; e-mail cuba@un.int; internet www.canada.cubanoal.cu; f. 1961 by a meeting of 25 heads of state, with the aim of linking countries that had refused to adhere to the main East/West military and political blocs; co-ordination bureau established in 1973; works for the establishment of a new international economic order, and especially for better terms for countries producing raw materials; maintains special funds for agricultural development, improvement of food production and the financing of buffer stocks; South Commission promotes co-operation between developing countries; seeks changes in the United Nations to give developing countries greater decision-making power; holds summit conference every three years; a 50th anniversary conference was convened in Bali, Indonesia, in May 2011; mems: 118 countries.

Shanghai Cooperation Organization (SCO): 41 Liangmaqiao Rd, Chaoyang District, Beijing, People's Republic of China; tel. (10) 65329806; fax (10) 65329808; e-mail sco@sectsco.org; internet www.sectsco.org; f. 2001, replacing the Shanghai Five (f. 1996 to address border disputes); aims to achieve security through mutual co-operation: promotes economic co-operation and measures to eliminate terrorism and drugs-trafficking; agreement on combating terrorism signed June 2001; a Convention on the Fight against Terrorism, Separatism and Extremism signed June 2002; Treaty on Long-term Good Neighbourliness, Friendship and Co-operation was signed August 2007; maintains an SCO anti-terrorism centre in Tashkent, Uzbekistan; holds annual summit meeting (June 2011: Astana, Kazakhstan); mems: People's Republic of China, Kazakhstan, Kyrgyzstan, Russia, Tajikistan and Uzbekistan; Sec.-Gen. MURATBEK IMANALIEV (Kyrgyzstan).

Industrial and Professional Relations

International Federation of Business and Professional Women (BPW International): POB 568, Horsham RH13 9ZP, United Kingdom; tel. (1403) 739343; fax (1403) 734432; e-mail presidents.office@bpw-international.org; internet www.bpw-international.org; f. 1930 to promote interests of business and professional women and secure combined action by such women; mems: national federations, associate clubs and individual associates, totalling more than 100,000 mems in over 100 countries; Pres. ELIZABETH BENHAM (USA); Exec. Sec. Dr JEAN MURRAY (Australia); publ. *BPW News International* (every 2 months).

International Trade Union Confederation-Asian Pacific (ITUC-AP): One Marina Blvd, NTUC Centre, 9th Floor, Singapore 018989; tel. 63273590; fax 63273576; e-mail gs@ituc-ap.org; internet www.ituc-ap.org; f. 2007 by merger of ICFTU-APRO (f. 1951) and Brotherhood of Asian Trade Unionists (f. 1963); mems: 68 affiliate organizations in 29 countries; Pres. G. RAJASEKARAN (Malaysia); Gen. Sec. NORIYUKI SUZUKI (Japan); publs *Asian and Pacific Labour* (monthly), *ICFTU-APRO Labour Flash* (2 a week).

Law

Asian-African Legal Consultative Organization (AALCO): 29-C, Rizal Marg, Diplomatic Enclave, Chanakyapuri, New Delhi 110057, India; tel. (11) 24197000; fax (11) 26117640; e-mail mail@aalco.int; internet www.aalco.int; f. 1956 to consider legal problems referred to it by member countries and to serve as a forum for Afro-Asian co-operation in international law, including international trade law, and economic relations; provides background material for conferences, prepares standard/model contract forms suited to the needs of the region; promotes arbitration as a means of settling international commercial disputes; trains officers of member states; has permanent UN observer status; has established four International Commercial Arbitration Centres in Kuala Lumpur, Malaysia, Cairo, Egypt, Lagos, Nigeria and Tehran, Iran; mems: 47 countries; Sec.-Gen. Prof. Dr RAHMAT BIN MOHAMAD (Malaysia).

International Association of Chiefs of Police (IACP): 515 North Washington St, Alexandria, VA, 22314, USA; tel. (703) 836-6767; fax (703) 836-4543; e-mail rosenblatt@theiacp.org; internet www.theiacp.org; f. 1893 to advance the science and art of police services; Pres. MARK A. MARSHALL; Exec. Dir DANIEL N. ROSENBLATT.

International Criminal Police Organization (INTERPOL): 200 quai Charles de Gaulle, 69006 Lyon, France; tel. 4-72-44-70-00; fax 4-72-44-71-63; e-mail info@interpol.int; internet www.interpol.int; f. 1923, reconstituted 1946; aims to promote and ensure mutual assistance between police forces in different countries; co-ordinates activities of police authorities of member states in international affairs; works to establish and develop institutions with the aim of preventing transnational crimes; centralizes records and information on international criminals; operates a global police communications network linking all member countries; holds General Assembly annually; mems: 188 countries; Sec.-Gen. RONALD K. NOBLE (USA); publ. *Annual Report*.

International Development Law Organization (IDLO): Viale Vaticano, 106 00165 Rome, Italy; tel. (06) 40403200; fax (06) 404032327; e-mail idlo@idlo.int; internet www.idlo.int; f. 1983; aims to promote the rule of law and good governance in developing countries, transition economies and nations emerging from conflict and to assist countries to establish effective infrastructure to achieve sustainable economic growth, security and access to justice; activities include Policy Dialogues, Technical Assistance, Global Network of Alumni and Partners, Training Programs, Research and Publications; maintains Regional Offices in Cairo, Egypt, covering Arabic-speaking countries and in Sydney, Australia, covering the Asia Pacific area; also operates Project Offices in Afghanistan, Indonesia, Sudan and Kyrgyzstan; mems: 22 mems (21 states and OPEC Fund for International Development); Dir-Gen. ANTONIO BADINI (Italy).

Law Association for Asia and the Pacific (LAWASIA): LAWASIA Secretariat, GPO Box 980, Brisbane, Qld 4001, Australia; tel. (7) 3222-5888; fax (7) 3222-5850; e-mail lawasia@lawasia.asn.au; internet www.lawasia.asn.au; f. 1966; provides an international, professional network for lawyers to update, reform and develop law within the region; comprises six Sections and 21 Standing Committees in Business Law and General Practice areas, which organize speciality conferences; also holds an annual conference (2011: Seoul, Republic of Korea, in Oct.); mems: national orgs in 23 countries; 1,500 mems in 55 countries; CEO JANET NEVILLE; publs *Directory* (annually), *Journal* (annually), *LAWASIA Update* (3 a year).

Medicine and Health

Asia Pacific Academy of Ophthalmology (APAO): c/o Dept of Ophthalmology and Visual Sciences, Chinese University of Hong Kong, 3/F 147 K Argyle St, Kowloon, Hong Kong, SAR; tel. 27623171; fax 27159490; e-mail secretariat@apaophth.org; internet www.apaophth.org; f. 1956; holds Congress annually since 2006 (previously every two years); mems: 17 mem. orgs; Pres. FRANK MARTIN; Sec.-Gen. DENNIS LAM.

Asia Pacific Dental Federation (APDF): c/o 242 Tanjong Katong Rd, Singapore 437030; tel. 6345-3125; fax 6344-2116; e-mail droliver@singnet.com.sg; internet www.apdfederation.com; f. 1955 to establish closer relationships among dental asscns in Asian and Pacific countries and to encourage research on dental health in the region; administers the International College of Continuing Dental Education (ICCDE); holds congress every year; mems: 26 national dental asscns; Sec.-Gen. Dr OLIVER HENNEDIGE.

Council for International Organizations of Medical Sciences (CIOMS): c/o WHO, ave Appia, 1211 Geneva 27, Switzerland; tel. 227913413; fax 227914286; e-mail cioms@who.int; internet www.cioms.ch; f. 1949 to serve the scientific interests of the international biomedical community; aims to facilitate and promote activities in biomedical sciences; runs long-term programmes on bioethics, health policy, ethics and values, drug development and use, and the international nomenclature of diseases; maintains collaborative relations with the UN; holds a general assembly every three years; mems: 66 orgs; Pres. Prof. MICHEL B. VALLOTTON; Sec.-Gen. Dr GUNILLA SJÖLIN-FORSBERG; publs *Bioethics and Health Policy' Reports on Drug Development and Use*, *Proceedings of CIOMS Conferences*, *International Nomenclature of Diseases*.

Global Fund to Fight AIDS, TB and Malaria: 6–8 chemin Blandonnet, 1214 Vernier-Geneva, Switzerland; tel. 587911700; fax 587911701; e-mail info@theglobalfund.org; internet www.theglobalfund.org; f. 2000 as a partnership between governments, civil society, private sector interests, UN bodies (including WHO, UNAIDS, the IBRD and UNDP), and other agencies to raise resources for combating AIDS, TB and malaria; the Fund supports but does not implement assistance programmes; US $11,700m. was pledged by international donors at a conference convened in Oct. 2010 to replenish the Fund during 2011–13; by Oct. 2011 the Fund had approved $21,700m. towards programmes supporting prevention and treatment in 150 countries; at 2009 the cumulative allocation of grant funding by region was as follows: Africa (57%), the Middle East and North Africa and South Asia (14%), East Asia and the Pacific (14%), Eastern Europe and Central Asia (8%), and Latin America and the Caribbean (8%); while the approximate distribution by health sector was: HIV/AIDS (61%), malaria (25%), and TB (14%); Exec. Dir Dr MICHEL KAZATCHKINE (France).

International Association for the Study of Obesity (IASO): 28 Portland Pl., London, W1B 1LY, United Kingdom; tel. (20) 7467-9610; fax (20) 7636-9258; e-mail enquiries@iaso.org; internet www.iaso.org; f. 1986; supports research into the prevention and management of obesity throughout the world and disseminates information regarding disease and accompanying health and social issues; incorporates the International Obesity Task Force; international congress every four years (2010: Stockholm, Sweden); mems: 52 asscns representing 56 countries; Exec. Dir CHRISTINE TRIMMER.

Pan-Pacific Surgical Association: 1212 Punahou St, Suite 3506, Honolulu, HI 96826, Hawaii, USA; tel. (808) 941-1010; fax (808) 951-7004; e-mail ppsa.info@panpacificsurgical.org; internet www.panpacificsurgical.org; f. 1929 to bring together surgeons to exchange scientific knowledge relating to surgery and medicine, and to promote the improvement and standardization of hospitals and their services and facilities; congresses are held every two years; mems: 2,716 regular, associate and senior mems from 44 countries; Pres. Dr JEROME C. GOLDSTEIN.

World Medical Association (WMA): 13 chemin du Levant, CIB-Bâtiment A, 01210 Ferney-Voltaire, France; tel. 4-50-40-75-75; fax 4-50-40-59-37; e-mail wma@wma.net; internet www.wma.net; f. 1947 to achieve the highest international standards in all aspects of medical education and practice, to promote closer ties among doctors and national medical asscns by personal contact and all other means, to study problems confronting the medical profession, and to present its views to appropriate bodies; holds an annual General Assembly; mems: 83 national medical asscns; Pres. Dr WONCHAT SUBHACHATURAS (Thailand); Sec.-Gen. Dr OTMAR KLOIBER (Germany); publ. *The World Medical Journal* (quarterly).

Posts and Telecommunications

Asia-Pacific Telecommunity (APT): No. 12/49, Soi 5, Chaengwattana Rd, Thungsonghong, Bangkok 10210, Thailand; tel. (2) 573-0044; fax (2) 573-7479; e-mail aptmail@apt.int; internet www.aptsec.org; f. 1979 to cover all matters relating to telecommunications in the region; serves as the focal organization for ICT in the Asia-Pacific region; contributes, through its various programmes and activities, to the growth of the ICT sector in the region and assists members in their preparation for global telecommunications conferences, as well as promoting regional harmonization for such events; mems: Afghanistan, Australia, Bangladesh, Bhutan, Brunei, People's Republic of China, Fiji, India, Indonesia, Iran, Japan, Democratic Republic of Korea, Republic of Korea, Laos, Malaysia, Maldives, Marshall Islands, Federated States of Micronesia, Mongolia, Myanmar, Nauru, Nepal, New Zealand, Pakistan, Palau, Papua New Guinea, Philippines, Samoa, Singapore, Sri Lanka, Thailand, Tonga, Viet Nam; assoc. mems: Republic of China, Cook Islands, Hong Kong, Macao, Niue; 101 affiliated mems; Sec.-Gen. TOSHIYUKI YAMADA.

Asian-Pacific Postal Union (APPU): APPU Bureau, POB 1, Laksi Post Office, 111 Chaeng Wattana Rd, Bangkok 10210, Thailand; tel. (2) 573-7282; fax (2) 573-1161; e-mail admin@appu-bureau.org; internet www.appu-bureau.org; f. 1962 to extend, facilitate and improve the postal relations between the member countries and to promote co-operation in the field of postal services; holds Congress every five years (2009: Auckland, New Zealand); mems: postal administrations in 32 countries; Dir SOMCHAI REOPANICHKUL; publs *Annual Report*, *Exchange Program of Postal Officials*, *APPU Newsletter*.

International Multinational Partnership against Cyber Threats (IMPACT): Jalan IMPACT, 63000 Cyberjaya, Malaysia; tel. (3) 83132020; fax (3) 83192020; e-mail contactus@impact-alliance.org; internet www.impact-alliance.org; f. 2006 as a global public-private partnership; aims to promote collaboration in order strengthen the capability of the international community and individual partner countries to prevent, defend against and respond to cyber threats; incorporates a Global Response Centre, a Centre for Policy and International Co-operation, a Centre for Training and Skills Development, and a Centre for Security Assurance and Research; signed a Memorandum of Understanding with the ITU in Sept. 2008 to administer the Global Cyber Agenda; Chair. MOHD NOOR AMIN.

Pacific Islands Telecommunications Association (PITA): Level 8, Dominion House, Edward St, Suva, Fiji; tel. 3311638; fax 3308750; e-mail pita@connect.com.fj; internet www.pita.org.fj; represents the interests in the area of telecommunications of Pacific region small island nations; mems: telecommunication entities in the Pacific region; Pres. IVAN FONG; Man. FRED CHRISTOPHER.

Pacific Telecommunications Council (PTC): 914 Coolidge St, Honolulu, HI 96826-3085, USA; tel. (808) 941-3789; fax (808) 944-4874; e-mail info@ptc.org; internet www.ptc.org; f. 1978 to facilitate the adoption of telecommunications and advanced information technologies throughout the Asia-Pacific region.; enables the exchange of ideas and commerce through its annual conference each January; mems: 3,000 mem. representatives from more than 60 countries; Pres. JOHN HIBBARD (USA); CEO SHARON NAKAMA.

Press, Radio and Television

Asia-Pacific Broadcasting Union (ABU): POB 1164, Lorong Maarof, 59000 Kuala Lumpur, Malaysia; tel. (3) 22823592; fax (3) 22844382; e-mail info@abu.org.my; internet www.abu.org.my; f. 1964 to foster and co-ordinate the development of broadcasting in the Asia-Pacific area, to develop means of establishing closer collaboration and co-operation among broadcasting orgs, and to serve the professional needs of broadcasters in Asia and the Pacific; holds annual General Assembly; mems: more than 200 in 57 countries and territories; Pres. IBRAHIM YAHAYA (acting); Sec.-Gen. JAVAD MOTTAGHI (Iran); publs *ABU News* (every 2 months), *ABU Technical Review* (every 2 months).

Confederation of ASEAN Journalists: Gedung Dewan Pers, 4th Floor, 34 Jalan Kebon Sirih, Jakarta 10110, Indonesia; tel. (21) 3453131; fax (21) 3453175; e-mail aseanjour@cbn.net.id; internet www.cajnet.org; f. 1975; holds General Assembly every two years, Press Convention, workshops; mems: journalists' asscns in Brunei, Indonesia, Laos, Malaysia, Philippines, Singapore, Thailand and Viet Nam; observers: journalists' asscns in Cambodia and Myanmar; Perm. Sec. MUHAMMAD SAIFUL HADI; publs *The ASEAN Journalist* (quarterly), *CAJ Yearbook*.

Organization of Asia-Pacific News Agencies (OANA): c/o Bernama News Agency, 38 Jalan 1/65A, 50400 Kuala Lumpur, Malaysia; tel. (3) 26939933; fax (3) 26981102; internet www.oananews.org; f. 1961 to promote co-operation in professional matters and mutual exchange of news, features, etc. among the news agencies of Asia and the Pacific via the Asia-Pacific News Network (ANN); 14th General Assembly: Istanbul, Turkey, Nov. 2010; mems: 43 news agencies in 34 countries; Pres. KEMAL ÖZTÜRK (Turkey); Sec.-Gen. SAIFUL HADI.

Pacific Islands News Association (PINA): 46 Gordon St, PMB, Suva, Fiji; tel. 3303623; fax 3317055; e-mail pina@connect.com.fj; internet www.pina.com.fj; f. 1991; regional press asscn; defends freedom of information and expression, promotes professional co-operation, provides training and education; mems: media orgs in 23 countries and territories; Pres. MOSES STEVENS.

Pasifika Media Association (PasiMA): Apia, Samoa; internet www.pacific-media.org; f. 2010; Chair. SAVEA SANO MALIFA.

World Catholic Association for Communication (SIGNIS): 310 rue Royale, 1210 Brussels, Belgium; tel. (2) 734-97-08; fax (2) 734-70-18; e-mail sg@signis.net; internet www.signis.net; f. 2001; brings together professionals working in radio, television, cinema, video, media education, internet, and new technology; Sec.-Gen. ALVITO DE SOUZA.

Religion

Bahá'í International Community: Bahá'í World Centre, POB 155, 31001 Haifa, Israel; tel. (4) 8358394; fax (4) 8313312; e-mail opi@bwc.org; internet www.bahai.org; f. 1844; promotes and applies the principles of the Bahá'í Faith, i.e. the abandonment of all forms of prejudice, the equality of women and men, recognition of the oneness of religion, the elimination of extremes of poverty and wealth, the realization of universal education and recognition that true religion is in harmony with reason and the pursuit of scientific knowledge, in order to contribute to the development of a peaceful, just, and sustainable society, and the resolution of the challenges currently facing humanity; Baha'is undertake to strengthen the moral and spiritual character of communities, for example by conducting classes that address the development of children and channel the energies of young people, and initiating study groups that enable people of varied backgrounds to explore the application of the Bahá'í teachings to their individual and collective lives; in some communities there is an annual election of a local council to administer affairs at that level; at the national level, there elected governing councils; the head of the Baha'i Faith is the Universal House of Justice, a body of nine members elected by the 186 National Spiritual Assemblies; more than 5 m., living in more than 100,000 localities; 186 national governing councils; Sec.-Gen. ALBERT LINCOLN (USA); publs *Bahá'í World News Service* (online), *One Country* (quarterly, in 6 languages).

Christian Conference of Asia (CCA): c/o Payap Univ. Muang, Chiang Mai 50000, Thailand; tel. (53) 243906; fax (53) 247303; e-mail cca@cca.org.hk; internet www.cca.org.hk; f. 1957 (present name adopted 1973) to promote co-operation and joint study in matters of common concern among the Churches of the region and to encourage interaction with other regional Conferences and the World Council of Churches; mems: nearly 100 national churches, and 17 national councils in 21 countries; Gen. Sec. HENRIETTE HUTABARAT LEBANG (Indonesia); publ. *CCA News* (quarterly), *CTC Bulletin* (occasional).

Muslim World League (MWL) (Rabitat al-Alam al-Islami): POB 537, Makkah, Saudi Arabia; tel. (2) 5600919; fax (2) 5601319; e-mail mymwlsite@hotmail.com; internet www.muslimworldleague.org; f. 1962; aims to advance Islamic unity and solidarity, and to promote world peace and respect for human rights; provides financial assistance for education, medical care and relief work; has 45 offices throughout the world; Sec.-Gen. Prof. Dr ABDULLAH BIN ABDUL MOHSIN AL-TURKI; publs *Al-Aalam al Islami* (weekly, Arabic), *Dawat al-Haq* (monthly, Arabic), *Muslim World League Journal* (monthly, English), *Muslim World League Journal* (quarterly, Arabic).

Pacific Conference of Churches: POB 208, 4 Thurston St, Suva, Fiji; tel. 3311277; fax 3303205; e-mail pacific@pcc.org.fj; internet www.pcc.org.fj; f. 1961; organizes assembly every five years, as well as regular workshops, meetings and training seminars throughout the region; mems: 36 churches and councils; Moderator Bishop APIMELEKI QILIHO; Gen. Sec. FE'ILOAKITAU TEVI.

World Council of Churches (WCC): 150 route de Ferney, Postfach 2100, 1211 Geneva 2, Switzerland; tel. 227916111; fax 227910361; e-mail info@wcc-coe.org; internet www.wcc-coe.org; f. 1948 to promote co-operation between Christian Churches and to prepare for a clearer manifestation of the unity of the Church; activities are grouped under the following programmes: The WCC and the ecumenical movement in the 21st century; Unity, mission, evangelism and spirituality; Public witness: addressing power, affirming peace; Justice, *diakonia* and responsibility for creation; Education and ecumenical formation; and Inter-religious dialogue and co-operation; mems: 349 Churches in more than 110 countries; Gen. Sec. Dr OLAV FYKSE TVEIT (Norway); publs *Current Dialogue* (2 a year), *Ecumenical News International* (weekly), *Ecumenical Review* (quarterly), *International Review of Mission* (quarterly), *WCC News* (quarterly), *WCC Yearbook*.

World Fellowship of Buddhists: 616 Benjasiri Pk, Soi Medhinivet off Soi Sukhumvit 24, Bangkok 10110, Thailand; tel. (2) 661-1284; fax (2) 661-0555; e-mail wfb_hq@truemail.co.th; internet www.wfb-hq.org; f. 1950 to promote strict observance and practice of the teachings of the Buddha; holds General Conference every two years; 164 regional centres in 38 countries; Pres. PHAN WANNAMETHEE; Sec.-Gen. PHALLOP THAIARRY; publs *WFB Journal* (quarterly), *WFB Review* (quarterly), *WFB Newsletter* (monthly), documents, booklets.

World Hindu Federation: POB 20418, Kathmandu, Nepal; tel. (1) 470182; fax (1) 470131; e-mail whfintl@wlink.com.np; internet www.worldhindufederation; f. 1981 to promote and preserve Hindu philosophy and culture and to protect the rights of Hindus, particularly the right to worship; executive board meets annually; mems: in 45 countries and territories; Int. Pres. HEM BAHADUR KARKI; Sec.-Gen. Dr BINOD RAJBHANDARI (Nepal); publ. *Vishwa Hindu* (monthly).

World Union of Catholic Women's Organisations: 37 rue Notre-Dame-des-Champs, 75006 Paris, France; tel. 1-45-44-27-65; fax 1-42-84-04-80; e-mail wucwosecgen@gmail.com; internet www.wucwo.org; f. 1910 to promote and co-ordinate the contribution of Catholic women in international life, in social, civic, cultural and religious matters; General Assembly held every four or five years (2010: Jerusalem, Israel, in Oct.); mems: some 100 orgs representing 5m. women; Pres. MARIA GIOVANNA RUGGIERI (Italy); Sec.-Gen. LILIANE STEVENSON; publ. *Women's Voice* (quarterly, in 4 languages).

Science

Co-ordinating Committee for Geoscience Programmes in East and Southeast Asia (CCOP): CCOP Building, 75/10 Rama VI Rd, Phayathai, Ratchathewi, Bangkok 10400, Thailand; tel. (2) 644-5468; fax (2) 644-5429; e-mail ccopts@ccop.or.th; internet www.ccop.or.th; f. 1966 as a regional intergovernmental organization, to promote and co-ordinate geoscientific programmes concerning the exploration of mineral and hydrocarbon resources and environmentally sound coastal zone management in the offshore and coastal areas of member nations; fmrly the Co-ordinating Committee for Coastal and Offshore Geoscience Programmes in East and Southeast Asia, current name adopted in 2002; works in partnership with developed nations which have provided geologists and geophysicists as technical advisers; receives aid from co-operating countries, and other sources; mems: Cambodia, People's Republic of China, Indonesia, Japan, Republic of Korea, Malaysia, Papua New Guinea, Philippines, Singapore, Thailand, Viet Nam; Chair. Steering Cttee Dato' YUNUS ABDUL RAZAK (Malaysia); Dir Technical Secretariat Dr HE QINGCHENG (People's Republic of China); publs *CCOP Newsletter* (quarterly), *CCOP Geo-Resources E-News*, *Technical Bulletin*, *Technical Publication*, *CCOP Map Series*, *Proceedings of Annual Session*, digital dataset/CD-ROM series, other technical reports.

Federation of Asian Scientific Academies and Societies (FASAS): c/o Australian Academy of Science, POB 783, Canberra ACT 2601, Australia; tel. (2) 6201-9456; fax (2) 6201-9494; e-mail fasas@science.org.au; internet www.fasas.org.au; f. 1984 to stimulate regional co-operation and promote national and regional self-reliance in science and technology, by organizing meetings, training and research programmes and encouraging the exchange of scientists and of scientific information; mems: 16 national scientific academies and societies from Afghanistan, Australia, Bangladesh, People's Republic of China, India, Republic of Korea, Malaysia, Nepal, New Zealand, Pakistan, Philippines, Singapore, Sri Lanka, Thailand; Pres. Tan Sri Datuk Dr OMAR ABDUL RAHMAN (Malaysia); Sec. Dato' IR LEE YEE CHEONG (Malaysia).

International Association for Earthquake Engineering: Kenchiku-kaikan Bldg, 3rd Floor, 5-26-20, Shiba, Minato-ku, Tokyo 108-0014, Japan; tel. (3) 3453-1281; fax (3) 3453-0428; e-mail secretary@iaee.or.jp; internet www.iaee.or.jp; f. 1963 to promote international co-operation among scientists and engineers in the field of earthquake engineering through exchange of knowledge, ideas and results of research and practical experience; mems: national cttees in 49 countries; Pres. Prof. POLAT GÜLKAN (Turkey); Sec.-Gen. MANABU YOSHIMURA (Japan).

International Council for Science (ICSU): 5 rue Auguste Vacquerie 75116 Paris, France; tel. 1-45-25-03-29; fax 1-42-88-94-31; e-mail secretariat@icsu.org; internet www.icsu.org; f. 1919 as International Research Council; present name adopted 1931; new statutes adopted 1996; incorporates national scientific bodies and International Scientific Unions, as well as more than 20 Interdisciplinary Bodies (international scientific networks established to address specific areas of investigation); through its global network co-ordinates interdisciplinary research to address major issues of relevance to both science and society; advocates for freedom in the conduct of science, promotes equitable access to scientific data and information, and facilitates science education and capacity-building; General Assembly of representatives of national and scientific members meets every three years to formulate policy. Interdisciplinary Bodies and Joint Initiatives: Scientific Committee on Problems of the Environment (SCOPE); Committee on Space Research (COSPAR); International Polar Year (IPY); Scientific Committee on Antarctic Research (SCAR); Scientific Committee on Oceanic Research (SCOR); Scientific Committee on Solar-Terrestrial Physics (SCOSTEP); Integrated Research on Disaster Risk (IRDR); Programme on Ecosystem Change and Society (PECS); DIVERSITAS; International Geosphere-Biosphere Programme (IGBP); International Human Dimensions Programme on Global Environmental Change (IHDP); World Climate Research Programme (WCRP); Global Climate Observing System (GCOS); Global Ocean Observing System (GOOS); Global Terrestrial Observing System (GTOS); Committee on Data for Science and Technology (CODATA); International Network for the Availability of Scientific Publications (INASP); Scientific Committee on Frequency Allocations for Radio Astronomy and Space Science (IUCAF); World Data System (WDS); mems: 119 national mems from 139 countries, 30 International Scientific Unions; Pres. CATHERINE BRÉCHIGNAC (France); Exec. Dir DELIANG CHEN (Sweden); publs *Insight* (quarterly), *Annual Report*.

Pacific Science Association: 1525 Bernice St, Honolulu, HI 96817, USA; tel. (808) 848-4124; fax (808) 847-8252; e-mail info@pacificscience.org; internet www.pacificscience.org; f. 1920; a regional non-governmental organization that seeks to advance science, technology, and sustainable development in and of the Asia-Pacific region, by actively promoting interdisciplinary and international research and collaboration; sponsors Pacific Science Congresses and Inter-Congresses and scientific working groups and facilitates research initiatives on critical emerging issues for the region; 11th Inter-Congress: Tahiti, French Polynesia, 2009; 22nd Congress: Kuala Lumpur, Malaysia, June 2011; mems: institutional representatives from 35 areas, scientific societies, individual scientists; Pres. Prof. NANCY D. LEWIS (USA); Sec-Gen. MAKOTO TSUCHIYA (Japan); publs *Pacific Science* (quarterly), *Information Bulletin* (2 a year).

Social Sciences

Eastern Regional Organisation for Planning and Housing: Ministry of Housing and Local Government, Aras 4, BlockB (North), Pusat Bandar Damansara, Kuala Lumpur, Malaysia; tel. (3) 20925217; fax (3) 20924217; e-mail secretariat@earoph.info; internet www.earoph.info; f. 1956 to promote and co-ordinate the study and practice of housing and regional town and country planning; maintains offices in Japan, India and Indonesia; mems: 57 orgs and 213 individuals in 28 countries; Pres. MICHAEL HARBISON (Australia); Sec.-Gen. NORLIZA HASHIM (Malaysia); publs *EAROPH News and Notes* (monthly), *Town and Country Planning* (bibliography).

International Peace Institute: 777 United Nations Plaza, New York, NY 10017-3521, USA; tel. (212) 687-4300; fax (212) 983-8246; e-mail ipi@ipinst.org; internet www.ipacademy.org; f. 1970 (as the International Peace Academy) to promote the prevention and settlement of armed conflicts between and within states through policy research and development; educates government officials in the procedures needed for conflict resolution, peace-keeping, mediation and negotiation, through international training seminars and publications; off-the-record meetings are also conducted to gain complete understanding of a specific conflict; Chair. RITA E. HAUSER; Pres. TERJE ROD-LARSEN.

Social Welfare and Human Rights

Global Migration Group: UNDP Bureau for Development Policy, 304 East, 45th St, 10th Floor, New York, NY 10017, USA; tel. (212) 906-5001; internet www.globalmigrationgroup.org; f. 2003, as the Geneva Migration Group; renamed as above in 2006; mems: ILO, IOM, UNCTAD, UNDP, United Nations Department of Economic and Social Affairs (UNDESA), UNFPA, OHCHR, UNHCR, UNODC, and the World Bank; holds regular meetings to discuss issues relating to int. migration, chaired by mem. orgs on a six-month rotational basis.

International Federation of Red Cross and Red Crescent Societies: 17 chemin des Crêts, Petit-Saconnex, CP 372, 1211 Geneva 19, Switzerland; tel. 227304222; fax 227330395; e-mail secretariat@ifrc.org; internet www.ifrc.org; f. 1919 to prevent and alleviate human suffering and to promote humanitarian activities by national Red Cross and Red Crescent societies; conducts relief operations for refugees and victims of disasters, co-ordinates relief supplies and assists in disaster prevention; Pres. TADATERU KONOÉ (Japan); Sec.-Gen. BEKELE GELETA (Canada/Ethiopia); publs *Annual Report*, *Red Cross Red Crescent* (quarterly), *Weekly News*, *World Disasters Report*, *Emergency Appeal*.

International Organization for Migration (IOM): 17 route des Morillons, CP 71, 1211 Geneva 19, Switzerland; tel. 227179111; fax 227986150; e-mail info@iom.int; internet www.iom.int; f. 1951 as Intergovernmental Committee for Migration; name changed in 1989; a non-political and humanitarian organization, activities include the handling of orderly, planned migration to meet the needs of emigration and immigration countries and the processing and movement of refugees, displaced persons etc. in need of international migration services; mems: 120 states; observer status is held by 20 states and 71 intergovernmental and non-governmental organizations; Dir-Gen. WILLIAM LACY SWING (USA); publs include *International Migration* (quarterly), *Migration* (quarterly, in English, French and Spanish), *World Migration Report* (every 2 years, in English).

Médecins sans frontières (MSF): 78 rue de Lausanne, CP 116, 1211 Geneva 21, Switzerland; tel. 228498400; fax 228498404; internet www.msf.org; f. 1971; independent medical humanitarian org. composed of physicians and other members of the medical profession; aims to provide medical assistance to victims of war and natural disasters; operates longer-term programmes of nutrition, immunization, sanitation, public health, and rehabilitation of hospitals and dispensaries; awarded the Nobel Peace Prize in 1999; mems: national sections in 21 countries in Europe, Asia and North America; Pres. Dr UNNI KRISHNAN KARUNAKARA; Sec.-Gen. KRIS TORGESON; publ. *Activity Report* (annually).

Pan-Pacific and South East Asia Women's Association (PPSEAWA): POB 119, Nuku'alofa, Tonga; tel. 24003; fax 41404; e-mail info@ppseawa.org; internet www.ppseawa.org; f. 1928 to foster better understanding and friendship among women in the region, and to promote co-operation for the study and improvement of social conditions; holds international conference every three years (2010: Bali, Indonesia, in May); mems: 22 national member orgs; Pres. Dr VIOPAPA ANNANDALE; publ. *PPSEAWA Bulletin* (2 a year).

World Social Forum (WSF): Support Office: Rua General Jardim 660, 7° andar, São Paulo, Brazil 01223-010; tel. (11) 3258-8914; fax (11) 3258-8469; e-mail fsminfo@forumsocialmundial.org.br; internet www.forumsocialmundial.org.br; f. 2001 as an annual global meeting of civil society bodies; a Charter of Principles was adopted in June 2002; the WSF is a permanent global process which aims to pursue alternatives to neo-liberal policies and commercial globalization; its objectives include the development and promotion of democratic international systems and institutions serving social justice, equality and the sovereignty of peoples, based on respect for the universal human rights of citizens of all nations and for the environment; the 10th (2011) WSF was held in Dakar, Senegal, in February; an International Council, comprising more than 150 civil society orgs and commissions, guides the Forum and considers general political questions and methodology; the Support Office in São Paulo, Brazil, provides administrative assistance to the Forum process, to the International Council and to the specific organizing committees for each biannual event; mems: civil society orgs and movements world-wide.

Sport and Recreations

Badminton World Federation: Batu 3, 1/2 Jalan Cheras, 56000 Kuala Lumpur, Malaysia; tel. (3) 92837155; fax (3) 92847155; e-mail bwf@bwfbadminton.org; internet www.internationalbadminton.org; f. 1934, as International Badminton Federation, to oversee the sport of badminton world-wide; mems: affiliated national orgs in 164 countries and territories; Pres. Dr KANG YOUNG JOONG; Chief Operating Officer THOMAS LUND; publs *World Badminton* (available online), *Statute Book* (annually).

International Federation of Association Football (Fédération internationale de football association—FIFA): FIFA-Str. 20, POB 8044, Zürich, Switzerland; tel. 432227777; fax 432227878; e-mail media@fifa.org; internet www.fifa.com; f. 1904 to promote the game of association football and foster friendly relations among players and national asscns; to control football and uphold the laws of the game as laid down by the International Football Association Board; to prevent discrimination of any kind between players; and to provide arbitration in disputes between national asscns; organizes World Cup competition every four years (2014: Brazil; the FIFA Executive Committee—comprising the Federation's President, eight vice-presidents and 15 members—meets at least twice a year; in late May 2011 FIFA provisionally suspended, with immediate effect, one of the Federation's vice-presidents and a member of the Executive Committee in relation to alleged violations of the Federation's code of ethics relating to the election to the FIFA presidency held on 1 June 2011; mems: 208 national asscns, 6 continental confederations; Pres. JOSEPH (SEPP) BLATTER (Switzerland); Gen. Sec. JÉRÔME VALCKE (France); publs *FIFA News* (monthly), *FIFA Magazine* (every 2 months) (both in English, French, German and Spanish), *FIFA Directory* (annually), *Laws of the Game* (annually), *Competitions' Regulations* and *Technical Reports* (before and after FIFA competitions).

International Go Federation (Fédération internationale d'escrime—FIE): 4th Floor, Nihon Ki-in Kaikan, 7-2 Gobancho, Chiyoda-ku, Tokyo 102-0076, Japan; tel. (3) 3288-8727; fax (3) 3239-0899; e-mail igf@nihonkiin.or.jp; internet www.intergofed.org; f. 1982; promotes the sport of Go; organizes World Amateur Go Championships; mems: 71 national federations; Pres. CHANG ZHENMING (People's Republic of China); Sec.-Gen. YUKI SHIGENO (Japan); publ. *Ranka* (quarterly).

International Kung Fu Federation: 1073 Baku, 529 Block, Metbuat Ave, Azerbaijan; tel. (12) 470-14-65; e-mail office@internationalkungfu.com; internet www.internationalkungfu.com; f. 2003; governing authority of national and international kung fu and taichi organizations world-wide; established internationally recognized rules and regulations and promotes regional and world championships; Pres. DAVUD MAHMUDZADEH (Azerbaijan).

International Rugby Board: Huguenot House, 35-38 St Stephen's Green, Dublin 2, Ireland; tel. (1) 240-9200; fax (1) 240-9201; e-mail irb@irb.com; internet www.irb.com; f. 1886; serves as the world governing and law-making body for the game of rugby union; supports education and development of the game and promotes it through regional and world tournaments; since 1987 has organized a Rugby World Cup every four years (2011: New Zealand); holds General Assembly every two years; mems: 97 national unions as full mems, 20 assoc. mems and 6 regional asscns; Chair. BERNARD LAPASSET; CEO MIKE MILLER.

Olympic Council of Asia: POB 6706, Hawalli, 32042 Kuwait City, Kuwait; tel. 25734972; fax 25734973; e-mail info@ocasia.org; internet www.ocasia.org; f. 1982; organizes Asian Games and Asian Winter Games (held every four years), and Asian Indoor Games and Asian Beach Games (held every two years); mems: 45 national Olympic committees; Dir-Gen. HUSAIN A. H. Z. AL-MUSALLAM.

Technology

World Association of Industrial and Technological Research Organizations (WAITRO): c/o SIRIM Berhad, 1 Persiaran Dato' Menteri, Section 2, POB 7035, 40911 Shah Alam, Malaysia; tel. 55446635; fax 55446735; e-mail info@waitro.sirim.my; internet www.waitro.org; f. 1970 by the UN Industrial Development Organization to organize co-operation in industrial and technological research; provides financial assistance for training and joint activities; arranges international seminars; facilitates the exchange of information; mems: 168 research institutes in 77 countries; Pres. Dr DIETER R. FUCHS (Germany); Sec.-Gen. Dr ROHANI HASHIM; publ. *WAITRO News* (quarterly).

Tourism

Pacific Asia Travel Association (PATA): Unit B1, 28th Floor, Siam Tower, 989 Rama 1 Rd, Pratumwan, Bangkok 10330, Thailand; tel. (2) 658-2000; fax (2) 658-2010; e-mail patabkk@pata.org; internet www.pata.org; f. 1951; aims to enhance the growth, value and quality of Pacific Asia travel and tourism for the benefit of PATA members; holds annual conference and travel fair; divisional offices in Germany (Frankfurt), Australia (Sydney), USA (Oakland, CA) and the People's Republic of China (Beijing); mems: more than 1,200 governments, carriers, tour operators, travel agents and hotels; Chair. HIRAN COORAY (Sri Lanka); CEO MARTIN CRAIGS (United Kingdom/Ireland) (from 31 Oct. 2011); publs *PATA Compass* (every 2 months), *Statistical Report* (quarterly), *Forecasts Book*, research reports, directories, newsletters.

South Pacific Tourism Organization: POB 13119, Suva, Fiji; tel. 3304177; fax 3301995; e-mail tourism@spto.org; internet www.south-pacific.travel; fmrly the Tourism Council of the South Pacific; also known as south-pacific.travel; aims to foster regional co-operation in the development, marketing and promotion of tourism in the island nations of the South Pacific; receives EU funding and undertakes sustainable activities; mems: 13 govts in the South Pacific, more than 200 private sector members in 25 countries world-wide; CEO ILISONI VUIDREKETI (Fiji); publ. *Weekly Newsletter*.

Trade and Industry

Asian Productivity Organization: Hirakawacho Daiichi Seimei Bldg 2F, 1-2-10 Hirakawa-cho, Chiyoda-ku, Tokyo 102–0093, Japan; tel. (3) 5226-3920; fax (3) 5226-3950; e-mail apo@apo-tokyo.org; internet www.apo-tokyo.org; f. 1961 as non-political, non-profit-making, non-discriminatory regional intergovernmental organization with the aim of contributing to the socio-economic development of Asia and the Pacific through productivity promotion; activities cover industry, agriculture and service sectors, with the primary focus on human resources development; five key areas are incorporated into its activities: knowledge management, green productivity, strengthening small and medium enterprises, integrated community development and development of national productivity organizations; serves its members as a think tank, catalyst, regional adviser, institution builder and clearing house; mems: 20 countries; Sec.-Gen. RYUICHIRO YAMAZAKI (Japan); publs *APO News* (monthly), *Annual Report*, *APO Productivity Databook*, *Eco-products Directory*, other books and monographs.

Cairns Group: (no permanent secretariat); e-mail agriculture.negotiations@dfat.gov.au; internet www.cairnsgroup.org; f. 1986 by major agricultural exporting countries; aims to bring about reforms in international agricultural trade, including reductions in export subsidies, in barriers to access and in internal support measures; represents members' interests in WTO negotiations; mems: Argentina, Australia, Bolivia, Brazil, Canada, Chile, Colombia, Costa Rica, Guatemala, Indonesia, Malaysia, New Zealand, Pakistan, Paraguay, Peru, Philippines, South Africa, Thailand, Uruguay; Chair. Dr CRAIG EMERSON (Australia).

Confederation of Asia-Pacific Chambers of Commerce and Industry (CACCI): 13th Floor, 3 Sungshou Rd, Taipei 110, Taiwan; tel. (2) 27255663; fax (2) 27255665; e-mail cacci@ttn.net; internet www.cacci.org.tw; f. 1966; holds biennial conferences to examine regional co-operation, and an annual Council meeting; liaises with governments to promote laws conducive to regional co-operation; serves as a centre for compiling and disseminating trade and business information; encourages contacts between businesses; conducts training and research; mems: 29 national chambers of commerce and industry from the region, also affiliate and special mems; Pres. BENEDICTO V. YUJUICO; Dir-Gen. Dr WEBSTER KIANG; publs *CACCI Profile* (monthly), *CACCI Journal of Commerce and Industry* (2 a year).

International Co-operative Alliance (ICA): Regional Office for Asia and Pacific: 9 Aradhana Enclave, Ring Rd, Sector 13, R.K. Puram, New Delhi 110 066, India; tel. (11) 26888250; fax (11) 2688-8067; e-mail info@icaroap.coop; internet www.icaroap.coop; f. 1960; promotes economic relations and encourages technical assistance among the national co-operative movements; represents the ICA in other regional forums; holds courses, seminars and conferences, and maintains the Co-operative Information Resource Centre (holding more than 20,000 volumes); administers the ICA Domus Trust (f. 1988) which, *inter alia*, supports the propagation of co-operative principles, publication of material for the study and teaching of co-operation, education and training activities and the promotion of collaboration between co-operatives and the state; mem. orgs: 60 in 22 countries of the region; Pres. LI CHUNSHENG; publs *Annual Report*, *Asia and Pacific Co-op News*, *Co-op Dialogue*, *Review of International Co-operation*.

Pacific Power Association: Private Mail Bag, Suva, Fiji; tel. 3306022; fax 3302038; e-mail ppa@ppa.org.fj; internet www.ppa.org.fj; f. 1992 to facilitate co-operation and development of regional power utilities; represents the Pacific Islands' power sector at international meetings; mems: 25 power utilities throughout the region; mems: in 18 countries; Exec. Dir TONY NEIL; publ. *Pacific Power* (quarterly).

South East Asia Iron and Steel Institute: POB 7094, 40702 Shah Alam, Selangor Darul Ehson, Malaysia; tel. (3) 55191102; fax (3) 55191159; e-mail seaisi@seaisi.org; internet www.seaisi.org; f. 1971 to further the development of the iron and steel industry in the region, encourage regional co-operation, provide advisory services and a forum for the exchange of knowledge, establish training programmes, promote standardization, collate statistics and issue publications; mems: more than 800 in 40 countries; Chair. FAZWAR BUJANG; Sec.-Gen. TAN AH YONG; publs *SEAISI Quarterly Journal*, *SEAISI Directory* (annually), *Iron and Steel Statistics* (annually, for each member country), *SEASI Quarterly Journal*, *Newsletter* (monthly), country reports.

World Customs Organization (WCO): 30 rue du Marché, 1210 Brussels, Belgium; tel. (2) 209-92-11; fax (2) 209-92-62; e-mail information@wcoomd.org; internet www.wcoomd.org; f. 1952 as Customs Co-operation Council (CCC); aims to enhance the effectiveness and efficiency of customs administrations by building capacity for more effective border enforcement, better application of international trade regulations, enhanced measures to protect society, and increased revenue security; signed a memorandum of understanding with the Asian Development Bank in May 2010; mems: customs administrations of 176 countries; Sec.-Gen. KUNIO MIKURIYA (Japan); publ. *WCO News* (3 a year).

Transport

Association of Asia Pacific Airlines: Kompleks Antarabangsa, 9th Floor, Jalan Sultan Ismail, 50250 Kuala Lumpur, Malaysia; tel. (3) 21455600; fax (3) 21452500; e-mail info@aapa.org.my; internet www.aapairlines.org; f. 1966 as Orient Airlines Asscn; present name adopted in 1997; as the trade association of the region's airlines, the AAPA aims to represent their interests and to provide a forum for all members to exchange information and views on matters of common concern; maintains international representation in Brussels, Belgium, and in Washington, DC, USA; mems: 17 scheduled international airlines (carrying approx. one-fifth of global passenger traffic and one-third of global cargo traffic); Dir-Gen. ANDREW J. HERDMAN; publs *Annual Report*, *Annual Statistical Report*, *Asia Pacific Perspectives*, *Orient Aviation* (10 a year).

Youth and Students

Asian Students Association: 2 Jordan Rd, Kowloon, Hong Kong; tel. 23880515; fax 27825535; e-mail asasec@netvigator.com; internet www.asianstudents.blogspot.com/; f. 1969; aims to promote students' solidarity in struggling for democracy, self-determination, peace, justice and liberation; conducts campaigns, training of activists, and workshops on human rights and other issues of importance; there are Student Commissions for Peace, Education and Human Rights; mems: 40 national or regional student unions in 25 countries and territories; publs *Movement News* (monthly), *ASA News* (quarterly).

WFUNA Youth: c/o WFUNA, 1 United Nations Plaza, Room DC1-1177, New York, NY 10017, USA; tel. (212) 963-5610; fax (212) 963-0447; e-mail info@wfuna-youth.net; internet www.wfuna-youth.org; f. 1948 by the World Federation of United Nations Associations (WFUNA) as the International Youth and Student Movement for the United Nations (ISMUN), independent since 1949; an international non-governmental organization of students and young people dedicated especially to supporting the principles embodied in the United Nations Charter and Universal Declaration of Human Rights; encourages constructive action in building economic, social and cultural equality and in working for national independence, social justice and human rights on a world-wide scale; maintains regional offices in Austria, France, Ghana, Panama and the USA; mems: asscns in over 100 mem. states of the UN.

World Alliance of Young Men's Christian Associations: 12 Clos. Belmont, 1208 Geneva, Switzerland; tel. 228495100; fax 228495110; e-mail office@ymca.int; internet www.ymca.int; f. 1855; organizes World Council every four years (2010: Hong Kong, SAR); mems: federation of YMCAs in 124 countries with a membership of over 45m.; Pres. KEN COLLOTON (USA); Sec.-Gen. Rev. JOHAN VILHELM ELTVIK (Norway); publ. *YMCA World* (quarterly).

World Scout Bureau/Asia-Pacific Region: POB 4050, MCPO 1280, Makati City, Metro Manila, Philippines; tel. (2) 8180984; fax (2) 8190093; e-mail asia-pacific@scout.org; internet www.scout.org/asia-pacific; f. 1956 to further the Scout Movement in the Asia-Pacific region by promoting the spirit of brotherhood, unity of purpose, co-operation and mutual assistance amongst Scout organizations within the region; conducts training courses, seminars, workshops, youth forums, jamborees and conferences; mems: over 19m. Scouts in 23 countries; Regional Dir ABDULLAH RASHEED; publs *Asia-Pacific Scouting Newsletter* (monthly), *Regional Director's Report*, *APRiN-BOX* (electronic publ.).

MAJOR COMMODITIES OF ASIA AND THE PACIFIC

Note: For each of the commodities in this section, there is a statistical table relating to recent levels of production. Each production table shows estimates of output for the world and for the countries covered by this volume. In addition, the table lists the main producing countries of the Far East and Australasia and, for comparison, the leading producers from outside the region. Unless otherwise specified, pricing information is in US dollars.

ALUMINIUM AND BAUXITE

Aluminium (known as aluminum in the USA and, generally, Canada) is the second most abundant metallic element in the earth's crust after silicon, comprising about 8% of the total. However, it is much less widely used than steel, despite having about the same strength and only half the weight. Aluminium has important applications as a metal because of its lightness, ease of fabrication and other desirable properties. Other products of alumina (aluminium oxide trihydrate, into which bauxite, the commonest aluminium ore, is refined) are materials in refractories, abrasives, glass manufacture, other ceramic products, catalysts and absorbers. Alumina hydrates are used for the production of aluminium chemicals, fire retardant in carpet-backing, and industrial fillers in plastics and related products.

The major markets for aluminium are in transportation, packaging, building and construction, electrical and other machinery and equipment, and consumer durables. Transportation was estimated to have accounted for about one-third, and containers and packaging for about 26%, of all US aluminium end-use in 2009, for example. Although the production of aluminium is energy-intensive, its light weight results in a net saving, particularly in the transportation industry, where the use of the metal as a substitute for steel, in particular in the manufacture of road motor vehicles and components, is well established. Aluminium is valued by the aerospace industry for its weight-saving characteristics and for its low cost relative to alternative materials. Aluminium-lithium alloys command considerable potential for use in this sector, although the traditional dominance of aluminium in the aerospace industry has been challenged since the 1990s by 'composites' such as carbonepoxy, a fusion of carbon fibres and hardened resins, the lightness and durability of which can exceed that of many aluminium alloys.

Bauxite is the principal aluminium ore. Nepheline syenite, kaolin, shale, anorthosite and alunite are all potential alternative sources of alumina, but these are not currently economic to process. Of all bauxite mined, approximately 85% is converted to alumina (Al_2O_3) for the production of aluminium metal. The developing countries, in which at least 70% of known bauxite reserves are located, supply some 60% of the ore required. According to the US Geological Survey (USGS), 32% of potential world bauxite resources lie in Africa, 23% in Oceania, 21% in Latin America and the Caribbean, and 18% in Asia. Total world bauxite production in 2010 was estimated at 210,000 metric tons by the USGS, compared with 199,000 tons in 2009. Australia was by far the largest producer, providing 70,000 tons, or one-third, of the 2010 total, followed by the People's Republic of China (19%), Brazil (15%), India (9%), Guinea (8%) and Jamaica (4%).

The industry is structured in three stages: bauxite mining, alumina refining, and smelting. While the high degree of 'vertical integration' (i.e. the control of successive stages of production) in the industry means that a significant proportion of trade in bauxite and alumina is in the form of intra-company transfers, and the increasing tendency to site alumina refineries near to bauxite deposits has resulted in a shrinking bauxite trade, there is a growing free market in alumina, serving the needs of the increasing number of independent (i.e. non-integrated) smelters.

The alumina is separated from the ore by the Bayer process. After mining, bauxite is fed direct to process if mine-run material is adequate (as in Jamaica), or else it is crushed and beneficiated. Where the ore 'as mined' presents handling problems, or weight reduction is desirable, it may be dried prior to shipment.

At the alumina plant the ore is slurried with spent-liquor direct, if the soft Caribbean type is used, or, in the case of other types, it is ball-milled to reduce it to a size that will facilitate the extraction of the alumina. The bauxite slurry is then digested with caustic soda to extract the alumina from the ore while leaving the impurities as an insoluble residue. The digest conditions depend on the aluminium minerals in the ore and the impurities. The liquor, with the dissolved alumina, is then separated from the insoluble impurities by combinations of sedimentation, decantation and filtration, and the residue washed to minimize the soda losses. The clarified liquor is concentrated and the alumina precipitated by seeding with hydrate. The precipitated alumina is then filtered, washed and calcined to produce alumina. The ratio of bauxite to alumina is approximately 1.95:1.

The smelting of the aluminium is generally by electrolysis in molten cryolite. Owing to the high consumption of electricity by this process, alumina is usually smelted in areas where low-cost electricity is available. However, most of the electricity now used in primary smelting in the Western world is generated by hydroelectricity—a renewable energy source.

The recycling of aluminium is economically, as well as environmentally, desirable, as the process uses only 5% of the electricity required to produce a similar quantity of primary aluminium. Aluminium recycled from scrap accounted for approximately one-third of the total annual world output of primary aluminium in 2008, according to the International Aluminium Institute (IAI), which also reckoned that three-quarters of the aluminium produced since the 19th century was still in use. With the added impetus of environmental concerns, considerable growth occurred world-wide in the recycling of used beverage cans (UBC) during the 1990s and 2000s. The IAI reckoned that in 2007 some 69% of UBC globally were being collected for recycling, making this the world's most recycled container (the industry was aiming for a recycling rate of 75% by 2015).

At the end of the 20th century world markets for finished and semi-finished aluminium products were dominated by six Western producers—Alcan (Canada), Alcoa, Reynolds, Kaiser (all USA), Pechiney (France) and algroup (formerly Alusuisse, of Switzerland). From 2000 the picture began to change dramatically, through mergers and the emergence of new international players from Russia and China. In mid-2000 Alcoa merged with Reynolds. In October Alcan took over algroup; a tripartite merger proposal from the previous year, which had also included Pechiney, was effectively achieved in 2003. Concerns regarding the safeguarding of competition were met by divestment of some of the new group's rolled aluminium assets into a new group, Novelis, in 2005; two years later Novelis was bought by India's Hindalco, which thus became the world's largest aluminium rolling company and one of Asia's biggest producers of primary aluminium. Meanwhile, in 2002, after the purchase of Germany's VAW, Norway's Norsk Hydro became the world's third largest integrated aluminium concern. (Hydro separated out its fertilizer business in 2005 and its petroleum and gas concerns, through a merger with Norway's Statoil, in 2007.) The level of dominance of the six major Western producers was already being challenged by a significant geographical shift in the location of alumina and aluminium production to countries where cheap power is available, such as Australia, Brazil, Norway, Canada and Venezuela. In the Persian (Arabian) Gulf, Bahrain and Dubai (United Arab Emirates), with the advantage of low energy costs, also produce primary aluminium. From the mid-1990s Russia emerged as a significant force in the world aluminium market, and in 2000 the country's principal producers, together with a number of plants located in other former Soviet states, joined together to form the Russian Aluminium Co (RUSAL). In March 2007 United Company RUSAL was formed by RUSAL's merger with Russia's second largest aluminium producer, Siberian-Urals Aluminium Company (SUAL), and the alumina assets of Switzerland's Glencore International AG. At mid-2009 United Company RUSAL claimed to be the world's largest aluminium company, accounting for almost 12% of world output of primary aluminium and 15% of global alumina production. In late 2007 the multinational mining concern Rio Tinto purchased Canada's Alcan Inc.—like United Company RUSAL, Rio Tinto Alcan, as the Rio Tinto division formed by the purchase was named (administratively, still based in Canada, although the aluminium and bauxite subdivision is based in Australia), also claims to be the world's biggest aluminium company. In February 2008 China's principal aluminium producer, Aluminium Corpn of China (Chinalco), and the USA's Alcoa jointly purchased a 12% stake in Rio Tinto in a move that was perceived as intended to obstruct an attempt by the Anglo-Australian company BHP Billiton, the world's largest mining company (and the sixth largest primary aluminium producer), to take over Rio Tinto. In June 2009 Rio Tinto ended moves towards greater integration with Chinalco (or, more specifically, its listed subsidiary, Chalco) amid some recriminations.

In 2010, according to USGS estimates, world output of primary aluminium totalled 41.4m. metric tons—compared with some 37.3m. tons in 2009, when eastern Asia accounted for 35.2% of the global total (34.6% by China alone, but with some production in Indonesia and a little in Japan), with an additional 5.9% in Oceania (mainly Australia, but also New Zealand). North America provided 12.8% of world production in that year, Europe 12.1%, Russia and the other Soviet successor states 11.7%, the Middle East and North Africa 7.6%, Latin America (mainly Brazil, but also Venezuela and some in Argentina) 6.8%, sub-Saharan Africa (South Africa, Mozambique, Cameroon and some in Nigeria) 3.9% and South Asia (India) 3.8%. In 2010 the USGS estimated that China alone provided 40.6% of estimated world primary aluminium production, followed by Russia (9.3%), Canada (7.1%), Australia (4.7%), the USA (4.2%) and Brazil (3.7%).

China displaced the USA as the most significant country for the international aluminium industry in the 2000s, accounting for about one-third of both consumption and production globally by 2009. The USA was for many years the world's principal producing country, but in 2001 US output of primary aluminium was surpassed by that of Russia and China. From 2002 Canadian production also exceeded that of the USA. In 2010 production of primary aluminium by China was estimated to be some 10 times that by the USA.

China was, therefore, by far the world's leading producer of primary aluminium in 2010, accounting for 41% of global output. Annual production capacity has increased rapidly, reaching an estimated 19.0m. tons by the end of 2009, having increased by almost 27% in one year alone, although it then fell back to 18.4m. tons by the end of 2010. Estimated actual output of primary aluminium, however, dipped in 2009, from 13.2m. tons to 12.9m. tons, owing to global economic conditions, but increased to 16.8m. tons in 2010. The increase in production through the mid-2000s had occurred despite government attempts to check the rapid growth of the sector by limiting support for expansion projects, funnelling imports of raw materials and, in 2008, even eliminating preferential power prices. Most primary aluminium production in China is based on imported bauxite and alumina, and the influence of Chinese demand on world markets for these commodities has increased tremendously as its aluminium sector has been developed. However, the country was also the world's largest producer of bauxite after Australia, with an estimated output of some 40m. tons (19% of global production) in 2010. Nevertheless, China imported about 45% of its total alumina requirement in 2004 and 34% (6.9m. tons) in 2006, although domestic production was expected to meet demand in 2010. Alumina production more than tripled between 2004 and 2008, recording annual increases of some 60% in 2006 and 42% in 2007. The high price of alumina in the mid-2000s, which fuelled the increase in production capacity, and power shortages in the second half of the decade were restraints on the rapid expansion of the aluminium sector—aluminium smelting reportedly accounted for 4.5% of national electricity consumption in the late 2000s. Global recession, however, accounted for the 2009 contraction in primary aluminium production (and the 2010 contraction in capacity), as China is an important exporter. According to the World Bureau of Metal Statistics (WBMS), China was also the key driver of aluminium consumption, representing 32.1% of the global total, with domestic consumption of aluminium in 2007 totalling some 12.1m. tons, compared with 6.0m. tons in 2004. This was substantially less than domestic output, as China retained its status as a net exporter of aluminium and aluminium alloys that it first achieved in 2002. Consumption was projected to account for 34.8% of the global total in 2008, with domestic consumption reaching 14.1m. tons. In 2001 Chalco, a subsidiary of Chinalco, was listed on the Hong Kong and New York, USA, stock markets (it is also listed in Shanghai). Chinalco had a 9.3% stake in Rio Tinto, which it wished to increase to 18.5% in 2009, but the multinational instead sought other investment.

Japan is a leading importer of primary (unwrought) aluminium, to meet domestic requirements for which it is almost entirely dependent on foreign suppliers. Japan's consumption of primary aluminium was steady in the mid-2000s, according to WBMS data, with 2.3m. tons recorded in each year in 2004–07. In 2006, according to the US Geological Survey (USGS), imports (comprising both ingots and alloys) increased by 2.0%, compared with 2005, to total some 3.0m. metric tons (1.9m. tons of aluminium ingots, 1.1m. tons of aluminium alloys). According to industry estimates, in 2006 about 50% of primary aluminium imported by Japan was supplied by smelter projects (including in Australia, Brazil, Canada, Indonesia, Mozambique, New Zealand and Venezuela) in which Japanese companies were substantial investors. However, Russia, in whose aluminium sector Japanese companies had no equity interest, was the principal supplier of aluminium and aluminium alloy (23.5%) in 2005, followed by Australia (19.4%) and China (11.9%). Japan was reported to have imported primary aluminium from more than 50 countries in 2006. Japanese exports of primary aluminium amounted to about 24,314 tons (5,363 tons of aluminium ingots, 18,951 tons of aluminium alloys) in 2006, with a value of US $73.1m., according to the USGS. Thailand was the principal market for Japanese aluminium ingots in 2005, absorbing 72.8% of the total exported, while the Republic of Korea (South Korea) was the destination for 21.2% of Japanese exports of aluminium alloys. Japan is entirely reliant upon imports of bauxite for the production of alumina and aluminium hydrate, and is therefore a key importer in the market. Australia (44.7%), Indonesia (37.3%) and India (13.4%) were the main suppliers of bauxite in 2005. Much of the alumina and aluminium hydrate produced in Japan is destined for export (production is primarily by Nippon Light Metal Co Ltd, in the Shizuoka prefecture), but the USGS reported similar levels of production in 2008 and 2009, although recession was restricting world-wide demand, and primary production of the metal fell by 37% (secondary production fell by 26%) in 2009.

South Korea relies entirely on imports for supplies of primary aluminium. In 2008 it received shipments totalling almost 1.1m. tons (773,833 tons of primary aluminium ingots, 311,206 tons of primary aluminium alloys), although this represented a continuing small decline, of 0.9%, compared with the previous year. China and Russia were the principal suppliers in that year, providing, respectively, 38.4% and 24.2% of the total, followed by Australia (19.5%). The country's scrap imports of aluminium and its alloys increased by 7.6% in 2008 (following 23.9% increase in 2007), to 0.5m. tons. Domestic demand for primary aluminium declined by 4.0% in 2006, 6.3% in 2007 and 10.8% in 2008.

Australia is by far the world's largest producer and exporter of bauxite and alumina, as well as the fourth largest producer of raw aluminium (having overtaken the USA in 2009, according to the USGS). The country accounted for about 33% of the world's estimated bauxite production in 2010 and for some 26% of estimated global output of alumina in 2009. Australia's bauxite mines were restrained by recession in the major world economies from the greater growth that had been previously anticipated, and output fell from 62.4m. metric tons in 2007 to 61.4m. tons in 2008, although it recovered to some 65.2m. tons in 2009 and more strongly to an estimated 70.0m. tons in 2010. The country's alumina refineries include the huge Worsley facility in Western Australia, reported to be probably the lowest-cost refinery in the world. Expansion of the Worsley plant, increasing its annual capacity from 1.7m. tons to 3.1m. tons (so making it the world's largest alumina refinery at that time), was completed in 2000. A further expansion in capacity, to 4.6m. tons, was reported at mid-year to be scheduled for completion by October 2011. In 2009 the largest capacity refinery in Australia was Alcoa's Pinjarra plant (4.2m. tons), also in Western Australia, followed by Rio Tinto Alcan's Gladstone refinery (with 20% owned by RUSAL—3.9m. tons) in Queensland and its Gove refinery (3.8m. tons) in the Northern Territory. At the beginning of the decade Alcoa owned 56% of the Worsley refinery, but the company was required to dispose of this interest, among several assets, as a precondition imposed by competition authorities for its merger with Reynolds (see above); BHP Billiton now has an 86% share in the operating company of the refinery, with Japan Alumina Associates (Australia) Pty Ltd owning 10%. Capacity expansion to 4.6m. tons annually is planned by the second half of 2011. Australia's output of alumina increased steadily through the mid-2000s, reaching 17.7m. tons in 2005, then rising to 18.8m. tons by 2007 and 19.3m. tons in 2008, and exceeding 20m. tons in 2009. Although Chinese demand (which had helped fuel the expansion of Australian refinery capacity) for alumina was expected to slacken as its domestic production increased, bauxite demand was likely only to continue to increase. Australia has extensive bauxite deposits in Western Australia, the Northern Territory and Queensland. Owing to the easy availability of bauxite and alumina (Australia's bauxite reserves, estimated at 5,400m. tons in 2010, account for 19% of the world's identified economic reserves), and of low-cost power (vast coal resources), the country provides a desirable location for aluminium smelters. In 2010 Australia's output of primary aluminium was reckoned to be steady at 2.0m. tons. In 2009 the smelters with the largest capacity were both majority owned by Rio Tinto Alcan—Boyne Island, in Queensland, and Tomago, in New South Wales—which also owned a smaller smelter at Bell Bay in Tasmania, while the third largest smelter was Alcoa of Australia's Portland plant in Victoria; Alcoa also owned and operated another smelter at Point Henry, Victoria; Hydro, which had a minority stake in the Tomago smelter, had a small smelter near Newcastle, New South Wales. Rio Tinto Alcan and Alcoa dominated the bauxite resources and alumina refineries (sometimes with other companies having a stake), while BHP Billiton was the third player. In 2009 Australia's exports of aluminium alone (ores and concentrates, unwrought or the metal and articles thereof) generated revenue of US $10,463m., representing 6.8% of total earnings from merchandise exports.

New Zealand has a single aluminium smelter, commissioned in 1971, at Tiwai Point, near Invercargill, South Island. The plant is operated by a subsidiary of Rio Tinto Alcan. Expansions of the smelter had taken annual capacity to 350,000 metric tons of primary aluminium at the end of 2009. The refinery had been concentrating on high-purity aluminium for some years, for competitive reasons and given its resource of cheap hydroelectric power. Raw material for the Tiwai Point smelter is imported mainly from Rio Tinto's alumina refinery in Queensland, Australia. Approximately 86% of primary aluminium production in 2007 was exported to Japan and other Asian countries.

Indonesia is the location of the sole aluminium smelter in South-East Asia—operated by PT Indonesia Asahan Aluminium (Inalum) at Kuala Tanjung. At the end of 2009 the smelter's annual capacity was 250,000 metric tons. In some years the facility's output of metal can be hampered by a shortage of water to supply its dedicated hydroelectric power plant. A Japanese consortium, Nippon Asahan Aluminium Co Ltd, operates the company (until 2013) and holds a 59% stake in the smelter, while the remaining equity belongs to the Government. The Inalum smelter, which is fed with alumina imported from Australia, exports 60% of its output to China and Japan, while the remainder is consumed locally. In mid-2010 it was announced that Aneka Tambang (Antam) would acquire a stake in Inalum and acquire control of the company when the Japanese consortium's contract came to an end in 2013. Feasibility studies pertaining to the development of an alumina project in Tayan, West Kalimantan (Borneo), were completed in 2004—however, Antam only began commercial mining at its bauxite mine in Tayan in 2009 and, in 2010, announced that it and its minority Japanese partner would begin construction of a chemical-grade alumina plant early the following year, with commercial production expected in 2014. Initial annual production of 300,000 tons of alumina was expected. India's National Aluminium Corpn (NALCO), meanwhile, planned a 500,000-ton smelter project in Indonesia, using Indian bauxite and local coal. Originally planned for South Sumatra, NALCO and its United Arab Emirates investment partners decided that accompanying infrastructure could be completed more quickly in coal-rich East Kalimantan. Construction of the smelter and captive power plant was expected to begin in late 2011.

The bauxite reserves located in Viet Nam's central highlands have been assessed as the third largest such resource in the world, representing, possibly, some 8% of economic reserves (actual bauxite production in 2010 remained at an estimated 30,000 metric tons). The country's first bauxite and aluminium complex began production at Ran Thai in 2006, although cost and power issues caused smelting plans to be postponed. A second complex, at Lam Dong in the central highlands, was agreed with a subsidiary of Chalco in 2008 and came into production in January 2011. The lead official agency for the bauxite and aluminium industry is the Viet Nam National Coal-Mineral Industries Group (Vinacomin), which has a number of projects scheduled to come into operation after 2010, including the construction of three 300,000-ton aluminium smelters, at Binh Thuan and Quang Ninh, as well as Lam Dong. Vinacomin was also responsible for implementing the development plans for bauxite resources in Thai Nguyen, which emphasized the production of high-quality alumina. Other alumina refineries were planned. By 2025 the Government planned to invest US $15,600m. in the national bauxite and aluminium industry, and Chinese companies were particularly interested in adding to that process.

Production of Bauxite
(crude ore, '000 metric tons)

	2008	2009*
World total (excl. USA)	211,000	199,000
Far East and Australasia	103,866	106,741
Leading regional producers		
Australia	61,389	65,231
China, People's Repub.*	35,000	40,000
Indonesia	1,152	1,200
Other leading producers		
Brazil	28,098	28,200
Guinea†	18,400	15,600
India	21,210	16,000
Jamaica†	14,363	7,817
Kazakhstan	5,160	5,130
Russia*	5,675	5,775
Suriname	5,200	4,000
Venezuela	5,500*	2,500

* Estimated production.
† Dried equivalent of crude ore.

Source: US Geological Survey.

In 2006 the average settlement price for aluminium (unalloyed primary ingots, high grade—minimum 99.7% purity) traded on the London Metal Exchange (LME) was, at US $2,567 per metric ton, 35.2% higher than in 2005 (cash price). During the year the metal traded within a range of $2,267–$3,275 per ton. Generally, stocks of aluminium held by the LME rose in the first half of 2006, reaching 710,075 tons at the end of January and 779,100 tons at the end of March. At the end of June inventories totalled 760,900 tons. In the second half of the year, however, stocks declined steadily in September–November, before rising in December to total 698,425 tons. Key market influences in 2006 were increased Chinese consumption and the renewed interest of investment funds in aluminium, in combination with restructuring in European and US aluminium.

In 2007 the average price of aluminium traded on the LME increased by 2.8%, compared with the previous year, to US $2,639 per metric ton. During 2007 aluminium traded within a range of $2,317–$2,953 per ton. Prices fluctuated throughout the year, but, generally, were lower in the second half of the year than in the first. Chinese consumption remained a key market influence in 2007. In January–May, according to analysts, Chinese utilization rose by 47%, while consumption world-wide in the same period grew at a substantially lower rate of 10.5%. LME inventories of aluminium rose steadily in January–May, totalling 833,525 tons at the end of that period. In June, however, they declined to 823,625 tons. By the end of September stocks had risen to 937,400 tons, but they fell in October, to 918,250 tons at the end of that month. At the end of 2007 LME stocks of aluminium totalled 929,450 tons.

In 2008 the average LME price for aluminium per metric ton was US $2,573, part of a dramatic escalation in commodity prices until the onset of global economic anxieties in the second half of the year. By July 2008 the monthly average price of aluminium traded on the LME had soared to a record $3,380 per ton. Stocks of the metal held by the LME, meanwhile, had risen to more than 1.1m. tons by the end of May, compared with 956,475 tons at the end of January. The general trend in the prices of base metals was downward, but aluminium prices were supported by a continued decline in the value of the US dollar and by concern about possible shortages. However, weak demand in the West and the generally weak economic context world-wide caused the average monthly aluminium price to collapse, falling below $1,800 per ton by February 2009.

In 2009 the average LME aluminium price was US $1,665 per metric ton. In the first quarter an average price of only $1,360 per ton was recorded, but there was some recovery thereafter. Although demand in the USA, Japan and Europe remained weak, and stocks continued to increase, aluminium prices rose later in 2009 because there were expectations of recovering demand, as well as a resurgence in Chinese growth. There was a realization that many of the stocks were committed, aluminium production had lessened, and car-makers had returned to the market. In July prices exceeded $1,800 per ton for the first time since the previous November, and they then spiked beyond $2,000 per ton: the average quarterly price for October–December was $2,003 per ton. LME stocks were put at 4.6m. tons in July 2009, having doubled since the end of 2008.

In 2010 the average price for aluminium on the LME was US $2,173 per metric ton. After early rises at the beginning of the year, the average price fell back into February before beginning to recover in the latter part of that month. Prices peaked in April, with a monthly average of $2,317 per ton, and then in October, at $2,347 per ton. The lowest prices were in June, which recorded a monthly average price of $1,931 per ton. Prices were rising into 2011. LME stocks were put at just above 4.4m. tons in mid-August 2010.

In the first seven months of 2011 the average price for aluminium on the LME was US $2,552 per metric ton. Average monthly prices rose steadily at the beginning of the year, to peak at $2,678 per ton in April, but then fell back slowly. The average monthly price in July was $2,525 per ton. LME stocks were put at 4.6m. tons in mid-June, and were expected to remain above 4.0m. tons at the end of the year.

The IAI, based in London, United Kingdom, is a global forum of producers of aluminium dedicated to the development and wider use of the metal. In 2011 the IAI had 27 member companies, representing every part of the world, including Russia and China, and responsible for more than 80% of global primary aluminium production and a significant proportion of the world's secondary output.

CASSAVA (Manioc, Tapioca, Yuca) (*Manihot esculenta*)

Cassava is a perennial woody shrub, up to 5 m in height, which is cultivated mainly for its enlarged, starch-rich roots, although the young shoots and leaves of the plant are also edible. The plant can be harvested at any time from seven months to three years after planting. A native of Central and South America, cassava is now one of the most important food plants in all parts of the tropics (except at the highest altitudes), having a wide range of adaptation for rainfall (500–8,000 mm per year). Cassava is also well adapted to low-fertility soils, and grows where other crops will not. It is produced mainly on marginal agricultural land, with virtually no input of fertilizers, fungicides or insecticides.

The varieties of the plant fall into two broad groups, bitter and sweet cassava, formerly classed as two separate species, *M. utilissima* and *M. dulcis* or *aipi*. The roots of the sweet variety are usually boiled and then eaten. The roots of the bitter variety are either soaked, pounded and fermented to make a paste, or dried, as in the case of 'gaplek' in Indonesia, or given an additional roasting to produce 'gari'. They can also be made into starch, from which a high-fructose syrup may be derived, and flour, or dried and pelletized as animal feed.

The cassava plant contains two toxic substances, linamarin and lotaustralin, in its edible roots and leaves which release the poison cyanide, or hydrocyanic acid, when plant tissues are damaged. Sweet varieties of cassava produce as little as 20 mg of acid per kg of fresh roots, whereas bitter varieties may produce more than 1,000 mg per kg. Although traditional methods of food preparation are effective in reducing cyanogenic content to harmless levels, if roots of bitter varieties are under-processed and the diet lacks protein and iodine (as occurs during famines and wars), cyanide poisoning can cause fatalities. Despite the disadvantages of the two toxins, some farmers prefer to cultivate the bitter varieties, possibly because the cyanide helps to protect the plant from potential pests, and possibly because the texture of certain food products made from bitter varieties is preferred to that of sweet cassavas.

Cassava is the most productive source of carbohydrates, and produces more calories per unit of land than any single cereal crop. Cassava is a staple source of carbohydrates and forms an essential part of the diet throughout tropical areas. Although the nutrient content of the roots consists almost entirely of starch, the leaves are high in vitamins, minerals and protein. A plot of cassava may be left unattended in the ground for two years after maturity without deterioration of the roots, and the plant is resistant to prolonged drought, so the crop is valued as a famine reserve. The roots are highly perishable after harvest and, if not consumed immediately, must be processed into flour, starch, pellets, etc.

While the area under cassava has expanded considerably in recent years, there is increasing concern that the rapid expansion of cassava root planting may threaten the fertility of the soil and subsequently other crops. Under cropping systems where no fertilizer is used, cassava is the last crop in the succession because of its particular adaptability to infertile soils and its high nutrient use-efficiency in yield terms (although there is now evidence to suggest that cassava yields increase with the use of fertilizer). Soil fertility is not threatened by cassava itself, but rather by the cultivation systems that employ it without fertilizer use.

Production of Cassava
('000 metric tons)

	2008	2009
World total	233,359	233,796
Far East	67,241	71,719
Oceania	222	169
Leading regional producers		
Cambodia	3,676	3,497*
China, People's Repub.†	4,409	4,506
Indonesia	21,593	22,039
Thailand	25,156	30,088
Viet Nam	9,396	8,557
Other leading producers		
Angola	10,057	12,828
Brazil	26,703	24,404
Congo, Dem. Repub.	15,014	15,000*
Ghana	11,351	12,231
India	9,056	9,623
Mozambique†	5,410	5,672
Nigeria	44,582	36,804
Tanzania	5,392	5,916
Uganda	5,072	5,179

* Unofficial figure.
† FAO estimates.

Source: FAO.

Some interest has been shown in the utilization of cassava as an industrial raw material as well as a food crop: cassava is a potential source of ethyl alcohol (ethanol), a substitute for petroleum. 'Alcogas' (a blend of cassava alcohol and petrol) can be mixed with petrol to provide motor fuel, while the high-protein residue from its production can be used for animal feed. The possibility of utilizing cassava leaves and stems (which represent about 50% of the plant and are normally discarded as cattle-feed concentrates) has also received scientific attention.

Thailand and Brazil vie for second place, after Nigeria, as the world's largest grower of cassava, but Thailand is clearly the world's leading exporter of aggregate dry cassava products (tapioca), accounting in 2008, for instance, for about 69% of shipments of dried cassava world-wide (compared with 80% in 2002) and about 91% of shipments of cassava starch (88% in 2002). In 2008 world exports of dried cassava amounted to 1.3m. metric tons (of which 91% were from South-East Asia), and of cassava starch to 4.2m. tons (94% from South-East Asia). Used in the preparation of animal feed, in combination with a protein source, cassava provides a cheap substitute for cereals such as barley and maize. In 2008 the main importers of cassava products (according to FAO) were the People's Republic of China and the member states of the European Union (EU—especially the Netherlands and Spain). Regionally, Indonesia and the Republic of Korea (South Korea) were other major importers. From 1994 the Government of Thailand offered cassava growers incentives to plant alternative crops. From 2001 developing countries in the Far East represented the major market for cassava. In the latter half of the 2000s Thailand was the world's second largest producer, according to FAO figures, in 2007 and in 2009, output reaching 30.1m. tons in the latter year.

In 2000 the average price of hard cassava pellets (f.o.b. Bangkok, Thailand) was US $55 per metric ton. In 2001 an average price of $59 per ton was recorded, and in 2002 the average price rose to $66 per ton. Further increases, to, respectively, $71.9 per ton and $78 per ton, were recorded in 2003 and 2004. An average price of $111 per ton was recorded in 2005, followed by an average of $109 in 2006. In January–April 2007 the average price of hard cassava pellets of Thai origin was $113 per ton. In 1999 the average international price of cassava (tapioca) starch (f.o.b. Bangkok) was $181 per ton, the lowest price since 1993. This price declined further throughout 2000, to an average of $157.4 per ton. In 2001 an average price of $173.8 per ton was recorded, and in 2002 the average price increased to $184.6 per ton. After falling to $172.7 per ton in 2003, the average international price of cassava starch recovered to $188.2 per ton in 2004. A substantial increase, of more than one-third, to $252 per ton, was recorded in the Bangkok price of cassava starch in 2005, but the price decreased slightly in 2006, to $221.7 per ton. The average price of cassava starch of Thai origin rose by some 13% in 2007, to $250.5 per ton, and more dramatically into 2008, even surpassing $400 per ton for a time. The FAO put the average price for 2008 as a whole at $383.6 per ton, dragged down by the collapse in commodity prices later in the year, which continued into 2009 and held that annual average to $281.3 per ton. In January–October the average cassava starch price had reached $496.0 per ton, and the trend was rising. According to the listing of weekly export prices (f.o.b. Bangkok) by the Thai Tapioca Starch Association, tapioca starch prices had risen steadily through 2007, from $245 per metric ton to $355 per ton, continuing to rise into 2008, to peak at $440 per ton. Some authorities have argued that the general commodity price rise, and its reversal later in 2008, with the international financial crisis and the onset of recession, had obscured the general crisis in food supplies, particularly in the developing world. Certainly, the pressure on prices seemed to be upward from 2009. The weekly price at the start of the year was $280 per ton and, although it dipped to $240 per ton for much of February, it then rose steadily, to end the year at $395 per ton, continuing the upward trend into 2010. The cassava starch price then reached a peak for 2010 in the week beginning 10 August, at $630 per metric ton. The surge in food commodity prices came amid fears of inflation arising from economic stimulus spending in the developed world and, for cassava in particular, because of a fall in Thailand's crop, as a result of a bug infestation from 2009, as well as adverse weather conditions. In 2010 average weekly prices for cassava starch had fallen to $545 per ton in mid-October, but then rose again to stabilize at $580 per ton in December and into the first week of January 2011. The price then fell, though no lower than $560 per ton, before rising back to $590 per ton from the end of March to the beginning of May, after another fall stabilizing through July, but fluctuating downwards again in August, ending the month on $440 per ton, the lowest price since March 2010.

COAL

Coal is a mineral of organic origin, formed from the remains of vegetation over millions of years. There are several grades: anthracite, the hardest coal with the highest proportion of carbon, which burns smoke-free; bituminous and sub-bituminous coal, used for industrial power: some is made into coke when the volatile matter is driven off by heating; and lignite or brown coal, the lowest grade and nearest to the peat stage. Anthracite and bituminous coal are classed as 'hard' coal; premium hard coal is known as coking coal, usually used in steel manufacture, while other hard coals, used in power generation, are known as steam or thermal coal. Coal gas is made from brown coal, but is not widely used for energy except in the republics of the former USSR.

Geographically, coal is one of the most evenly distributed of the fossil fuels. According to the World Energy Council, of estimated world proven reserves of 860,938m. metric tons at the end of 2010 (comprising 404,762m. tons of anthracite and bituminous coal and 456,176m. tons of sub-bituminous coal and lignite), about 35% were located in Europe (including Turkey) and Eurasia (i.e. Russia and the other former Soviet states—26%), some 28% in North America (excluding Mexico), 24% in the Far East and Australasia, 7% in South Asia and less than 2% in Latin America and the Caribbean. The leading countries at the end of 2010 were the USA (28% of the world total), Russia (18%), the People's Republic of China (13%), Australia (9%), India (7%), Germany (5%), Ukraine (4%), Kazakhstan (4%) and South Africa (4%). Most countries possess reserves both of hard coal and of sub-bituminous coal and lignite. However, Russia, for instance, has mainly lower-grade resources (69%), while India's reserves are 93% anthracite or bituminous coal and South Africa's entirely so. Among smaller producers, too, the imbalance can be pronounced: Pakistan, Thailand and the Republic of Korea (South Korea) have almost entirely sub-bituminous and lignite reserves, while Japan and Viet Nam the higher grade, harder coal.

During 1981–2010 annual world production of coal almost doubled, from 3,831m. metric tons to an estimated 7,273m. tons (figures cited by BP). Total coal production rose steadily from 1999, up 57% 11 years later. (In 2010 the World Coal Association had global output of brown coal or lignite at an estimated 1,042m. tons—the main producers being Germany and Indonesia—or 17% the level of hard coal production.) High levels of output and demand were maintained owing to the use of hard coal world-wide as the primary fuel for electricity generation. Environmentalists have, however, increasingly cited the large-scale use of fossil fuels as a prime causative factor in 'acid rain' pollution and the warming of the global atmosphere by accretions of carbon gases: in the 2000s the development of 'carbon capture and storage' technology was being encouraged to neutralize this impact. Globally, in 2009 coal accounted for 30% of primary energy supply and 42% of electricity generation; coal is also vital in steel production, 13% of coal production being used by the steel industry, and 60% of steel production depended on coal (World Coal Association).

As the greater part of coal output is consumed within the producing country, only a relatively small proportion of coal production enters world trade. According to the World Coal Association, in 2010 an estimated 676m. metric tons of steam coal (for power generation) was traded internationally, together with about 262m. tons of coking coal (for use in metallurgical industries). The world's leading exporter in 2010 was Australia, mainly (52%) because of coking coal; Indonesia, the largest steam coal exporter, came second overall, followed by Russia, while Japan, China. South Korea, India, Taiwan and Germany were the leading importers. About 87% of total world consumption of coal was both mined and used in the same producing countries (2010 estimate—i.e. production that did not enter international trade), mainly the USA and China, but also India. In 2010, according to BP and in terms of oil equivalent, China was estimated to have accounted for 48% of world coal production and for 48% of world consumption. In common with other producing countries, China was highly dependent on coal for electricity generation (79%—other examples, according to World Coal Association figures for 2008 and 2009, include South Africa 93%, Australia 76%, India 69% and the USA 45%).

The main change in the global pattern of coal consumption between 1980 and 2010 was the near halving of (Western) European consumption and the dramatic increase in consumption in the Asia-Pacific region, most notably in China and India, but also in the 'tiger' economies such as South Korea, or even Japan. In 2010 Asia-Pacific accounted for 67% of world consumption (oil equivalent), North America 15% and the European Union (EU) 8%. In the Asia-Pacific region, the largest consumer was China (72% of the regional total and almost one-half the world total), while South Asia (mainly India) accounted for 12% of Asia-Pacific (8% globally) and Japan 5% (3%).

China, with identified reserves of 114,500m. metric tons (including sub-bituminous coal and lignite) at the end of 2010, is the world's largest producer of hard coal (in 2010 Chinese production was equivalent to 51% of world consumption). About 75% of these deposits are located in the north and north-west regions, notably the Xinjiang Uygur and Inner Mongolia (Nei Monggol) Autonomous Regions and in Shanxi province. Shanxi, hitherto the largest producer in China, consolidated its coal-mining industry from 2006, closing smaller mines, and, as a consequence, output fell (although still accounting for one-fifth of national production) and Inner Mongolia, which had increased coal output by 37%, became the leading provincial producer. Inner Mongolian coal, although likely to remain produced in greater volume, has a higher ash content and lower heating content than Shanxi coal. Shaanxi and Henan provinces are next in importance. Only about 7% of China's proven reserves of anthracite and bituminous coal can be surface-mined, however. In 1992 the Government began to implement a comprehensive restructuring of the coal industry, in which uneconomic and dangerous mines were closed, the industry's labour force was reduced and controls on the selling prices of coal were abolished. The reorganization continued to the end of the century. As a result, China's annual production of coal (including brown coal) decreased from a peak of 1,397m. tons in 1996 to 1,250 in 1998 and 1,280m. tons in 1999. During the latter year about 31,000 small mines (some of them operating illegally) were closed, leaving fewer than 38,000 functioning at the end of 1999. The programme continued in 2000, when a further 18,900 coal mines were scheduled for closure. Greater demand stimulated coal production throughout the first decade of the 21st century, reaching 3,240m. tons by 2010, up from 2,973m. tons in 2009, 2,802m. tons in 2008, 2,692m. tons in 2007 and 2,529m. tons in 2006. Mine safety remained a major problem into the 2000s. Efforts by the Government to reduce the number of injuries and deaths in the mining industry have included the creation of the State Administration of Coal Mine Safety Supervision and the State Administration of Safety in Production Supervision. The Government was also reported to have sought more vigorously to enforce safety regulations in the coal-mining sector by closing mines for safety violations. Conditions in the mines have improved markedly since the 1990s, in particular in the larger ones, with facilities operated by more prestigious firms observed to be functioning at a standard comparable to international competitors. Traditionally China exported only a very small proportion of its coal. However, the greater efficiency and improved competitiveness of the Chinese coal industry achieved since the 1990s at the same time led to a substantial increase in foreign sales—in particular to Japan, the South Korea and Taiwan, whose markets were formerly generally dominated by Australia—and China is now a major participant in the international coal trade. In 2008, according to the World Coal Association, Chinese exports totalled an estimated 47m. tons (43m. tons of steam coal and 4m. tons of coking coal), compared with 63m. tons (59m. tons of steam coal and 4m. tons of coking coal) in 2007. China was the world's seventh largest coal exporter in 2008 (after Australia, Indonesia, Russia, Colombia, the USA and South Africa), as well as the sixth largest importer (after Japan, South Korea, Taiwan, India and Germany), but dropped out of the top eight by 2010. Continued increased demand in China, and reduced demand world-wide, owing to the effects of the global financial crisis, meant that in 2009 and 2010 China was estimated to be the world's second largest importer, after Japan (73% of imports consisted of steam coal in the latter year). About one-half of China's coal consumption is accounted for by power plants, while two-thirds of the country's electricity production comes from coal. Government refusal to increase electricity prices in line with increasing coal prices from the mid-2000s impacted severely on domestic power companies, and contributed to the pressure to approve negotiated contracts after 2009, for which year coal producers and power companies failed to agree a price for steam coal ('planned coal'). Another problem had been that the sharp difference between contract prices available domestically and internationally (see below) apparently encouraged producers to increase shipments abroad rather than supply internal demand at reduced profit. According to the US Geological Survey, in 2009 China became a net importer of coal.

From the 1990s, because of the relative low cost of coal, China pushed forward with efforts to convert coal into feasible substitutes for petroleum and gas. In early 2008 China reportedly possessed 20 coal-gasification plants, which provided the chemical industry with source material for the manufacture of plastics, pharmaceuticals and other products previously derived from natural gas. Additional projects were either planned or under development. Furthermore, continuing increases in prices for petroleum during 2007–08 prompted a renewed interest in processing liquid fuels (such as gasoline and diesel) from coal. The Chinese firm Shenhua Energy was scheduled to commence production of coal-derived liquids in 2008, following the inauguration of its first processing unit in Inner Mongolia. There were, however, concerns relating to the environmental impact of coal conversion projects, which emit large quantities of carbon dioxide.

Production of Coal*
(million metric tons)

	2009	2010
World total	6,880.8	7,273.3
Far East and Australasia†	3,771.6	4,110.3
Leading regional producers		
Australia	413.2	423.9
China, People's Repub.	2,973.0	3,240.0
Indonesia	256.2	305.9
Thailand	17.8	17.9
Viet Nam	45.0	44.1
Other leading producers		
Germany	183.7	182.3
India	556.0	569.9
Kazakhstan	100.9	110.8
Poland	135.2	133.2
Russia	301.3	316.9
South Africa	250.6	253.8
USA	975.2	984.6

* Commercial solid fuels only, comprising bituminous coal and anthracite (hard coal), and lignite and brown (sub-bituminous) coal.

† Asia-Pacific excluding India and Pakistan.

Source: BP, *Statistical Review of World Energy 2011*.

Australia is also an important coal producer in the region, having overtaken the USA in 1986 as the world's leading coal exporter: it accounted in 2010 for about 21% of world trade in steam coal and 59% of world trade in coking coal (32% of all coal traded internationally). Although at the end of 2010 Australia possessed only 9% of the world's coal reserves, it has become a major exporter because of comparatively low domestic demand for coal (which supplied about 42.6% of domestic primary energy in 2009), and the mineral's location in unpopulated areas that are inexpensive to mine. According to the World Coal Association, about 84% of Australia's coal output was exported in 2010, with Japan being the primary market, mainly for use in its steel industry. Coal is Australia's principal export commodity, and in 2010 coal exports (coal, coke and briquettes) were valued at some $A38,572m. (representing 19% of the country's total export earnings). In the 2000s China emerged as a significant competitor to Australia in world markets for steam coal, although Indonesia became the largest exporter in the second half of the decade—an estimated 160m. tons in 2010, compared with Australia's 143m. tons—while China's increasing domestic demand saw it drop lower down the rankings by the end of the decade. High prices for metallurgical coals after the mid-2000s in particular were reported to have prompted an unparalleled surge of investment in mines and mining infrastructure in Australia's coalproducing areas. In Queensland and New South Wales, for example, various port and railway development projects were reported to have been initiated. It was reported in 2006 that 12 metallurgical coal-mining expansions were under way in Queensland, and six in New South Wales. However, limited capacity at Australian ports (particularly Newcastle, New South Wales) caused severe delays to coal shipments, and precipitated increases in contract prices for hard coking coal (see below) as well as affecting exports. The international mining group Xstrata subsequently requested that planned expansions be either postponed or slowed down until the appropriate infrastructure was in place to handle the additional output. Such problems encouraged investment in infrastructure, the Queensland Government, for instance, planning an expansion in the coal-exporting capacity of the rail and port facilities to 200m. tons per year in 2008 and 242m. tons per year by 2010, while the New South Wales Government increased the coal royalty tax to 1.5% in 2008, in order to fund infrastructure development. However, the catastrophic flooding of late 2010 and early 2011 severely disrupted coal infrastructure and transport links, with a probable effect on output.

By the 2000s Indonesia had emerged as a significant regional producer and exporter of coal; its total reserves were estimated at 5,529m. metric tons at the end of 2010. These reserves are in part formed by a sort with an exceptionally low content of sulphur and ash, the causative factors in air pollution resulting from coal combustion. Output of this coal, which has attracted interest in the USA, Japan, Spain and the Nordic countries, totalled 2m. tons in 1991, and subsequently increased to 91.9m. tons by 2001. Total Indonesian coal production continued to expand in subsequent years, reaching 193.8m. tons in 2006, 216.9m. tons in 2007, 240.2m. tons in 2008, 256.2m. tons in 2009 and 305.9m. tons in 2010—in which year it contributed 4.2% of the world's total coal output. In 2010 Indonesia was the world's largest exporter of steam coal, exporting some 160m. tons in that year. Increasing exploitation of coal resources has been accompanied by considerable interest, and investment, from foreign companies. Meanwhile, plans to develop coal-fired power plants in Indonesia—if followed through to completion—were expected significantly to increase domestic consumption. Indonesia was also an important exporter of coking coal, although sales abroad fell to only 2m. tons in 2010. The major markets for Indonesian coal are Japan, South Korea, Taiwan, Hong Kong and the Philippines.

The world's leading coal importer is Japan, which is seeking to reduce its dependence on petroleum in the generation of energy. In 2010 Japan imported around 187m. tons of coal (69% steam coal), accounting for 20% of the world trade. In 2009, however, coal accounted for only about 23% of Japan's total primary energy supply. The exploitation of Japan's proven coal reserves, estimated to total only 350m. metric tons at 31 December 2010, has proved too expensive for domestic supplies to be able to compete with much cheaper imported coal. The country's coal industry has been in decline since the mid-1980s, with uneconomic mines closing, despite government provisions of subsidies and 'guidelines' seeking to persuade the steel industry to purchase domestic coal at prices far above those on the international market. Despite an increase of around 18% in coal production in 2006, to reach 1.4m. tons, output had reached a low of 1.1m. tons in 2005, compared with 17.7m. tons in 1981. Production remained at 1.4m. tons in 2007, but fell back to 1.2m. in 2008, 1.3m. tons in 2009 and 0.9m. tons in 2010.

The world's third coal importer is South Korea, displaced from second place by China from 2009. South Korea bought 119m. tons from abroad in 2010 (76% steam coal). Annual domestic production averaged some 2.8m. tons in 2005–09, down from 3.6m. tons in the early 2000s and almost 4.5m. tons in the late 1990s; it was down to 2.1m. tons in 2010. Production had been at a peak of 24.3m. tons per year in 1986–88.

At the end of 2010 Viet Nam's exploitable reserves of high-quality anthracite and bituminous coal totalled 150m. metric tons. In the late 1990s the country emerged as a leading supplier of anthracite to the Japanese steel industry and to Western European countries, where its low ash, nitrogen, phosphorous and sulphur content facilitate compliance with measures being implemented to protect the environment. Coal exports increased from some 12m. tons in 2004 to more than 32m. tons by 2007, only to fall back to some 19m. tons in 2008. Although production continued to increase (consistently in 2000–09, from 11.6m. tons to 45.0m. tons), anxieties about reserve diminution encouraged the authorities to limit exports. In 2010 production declined for the first time since 1999, to 44.1m. tons. Rising electricity consumption meant that government officials reckoned Viet Nam would need to start depending on coal imports by 2015. The mining, distribution and export of coal is undertaken mainly by the state-controlled Viet Nam National Coal Corpn (Vinacoal).

As noted above, only a relatively small proportion of the total amount of coal produced world-wide enters world trade. In the international market for coking coal Australia accounts for more than one-half of all exports (59% in 2010); and in that for thermal coal, for about one-fifth of all exports (21%). Japan is the destination of about 40% of Australia's coal exports (2008/09)—once more than 60%—and, as a result, Australian exporters negotiate prices direct with Japanese users. Economic conditions world-wide from late 2008 put downward pressure on prices, but also impelled the Australian producers to press for quarterly rather than annual contract prices, paralleling developments in the iron ore market. The Japanese steel mills were still hoping for a return to annual contracts in 2010, helped by other international suppliers continuing to offer annual contracts, but Australian exports dominate the world trade and the trend seemed to be set towards quarterly pricing. Prices rose in 2010 and into 2011, in particular given the disruptions to production from serious flooding in Queensland in December 2010–January 2011. BHP Billiton-Mitsubishi Alliance (BMA) is Australia's largest coal producer and exporter, and the largest supplier of the seaborne coking coal market in the world. Contract prices for thermal and semi-soft metallurgical coals generally follow similar trends to coking coal, although there is some diversion. This market was also dominated by the same major Australian producers, such as BMA, Rio Tinto and Xstrata Coal.

According to industry data, annual average import prices (c.i.f.) for both coking and steam coal in the Japanese market declined fairly steadily during the course of the 1990s. In 2000 the average price for coking coal was US $39.69 per metric ton, while the price of imported steam or thermal coal averaged $34.58 per ton in that year. In 2001 prices began to recover, although the two price scales sometimes varied in their fortunes. Both average Japanese import prices rose substantially in 2004, to be followed in 2005 by an increase of 47%, to $89.33 per ton, for coking coal and 23%, to $62.90 per ton, for steam coal. The increases in 2006 were far smaller, coking coal going to $93.46 per ton and steam coal to $63.04 per ton. The average price of Japanese imported coking coal declined in 2007, to $88.24 per ton, but steam coal reached an average price of $69.86 per ton in 2007. Both markets saw dramatic price increases in 2008, before world-wide recession bit, with the average import price for coking coal more than doubling, up by 102% to $179.03 per ton, and steam coal up by 76%, to $122.81. Prices fell dramatically at the end of 2008 and into 2009, given the economic uncertainties globally, but a strong recovery later in the year meant that the average for 2009 was only slightly down on the previous year's price, at $167.82 per ton. Coking coal prices performed particularly strongly, but average import prices for steam coal into Japan also recovered well in 2009, to end with an average for the year only down to $110.11 per ton. The downward trend continued into 2010, the average prices for the year being $158.95 per ton of coking coal and $105.19 per ton of steam coal. World Bank figures (Australian thermal coal—f.o.b., piers at Newcastle/Port Kemble) indicated rising average prices into the first quarter of 2011: $71.84 per ton in 2009; $98.97 per ton in 2010; and $123.85 per ton in January–July 2011; the July monthly average was down to $120.00 per ton.

COCOA (*Theobroma cacao*)

The cocoa or cacao tree, which can be up to 14 m tall, originated in the tropical forests of South America. The first known cocoa plantations were in southern Mexico around AD 600, although the crop may have been cultivated for some centuries earlier. Cocoa first came to Europe in the 16th century, after Spanish explorers had found the beans being used in Mexico as a form of primitive currency as well as the basis of a beverage. The Spanish and Portuguese introduced cocoa into Africa—on the islands of Fernando Póo (now Bioko), in Equatorial Guinea, and São Tomé and

Príncipe—at the beginning of the 19th century. At the end of the century the tree was established on the African mainland, first in Ghana and then in other West African countries. In the Asia-Pacific region, Criollo cocoa was introduced to Indonesia in 1560, but its cultivation remained confined to the island of Java. In the late 19th century, after the failure of the coffee crop on Java in 1880 had given impetus to the adoption of cocoa by farmers, the exposure of Criollo stock to Forastero cocoa led to the development of a robust Trinitario variant producing the so-called Java A bean. Elsewhere, Trinitario cocoa (originally from Trinidad) was first planted in Sri Lanka in 1834 and was subsequently taken from there to Singapore, Fiji and Samoa.

Cocoa is now widely grown in the tropics, usually at altitudes of less than 300 m above sea-level, where it needs a fairly high rainfall and good soil. The cocoa tree has a much shallower tap root than, for example, the coffee bush, making cocoa more vulnerable to dry weather. Cocoa trees can take up to four years from planting before producing sufficient fruit for harvesting. They may live to 80 years or more, although the fully productive period is usually about 20 years. The tree is highly vulnerable to pests and diseases, and it is also very sensitive to climatic changes. Its fruit is a large pod, about 15 cm–25 cm in length, which at maturity is yellow in some varieties and red in others. The ripe pods are cut from the tree, where they grow directly out of the trunk and branches. When opened, cocoa pods disclose a mass of seeds (beans) surrounded by white mucilage. After harvesting, the beans and mucilage are scooped out and fermented. Fermentation lasts several days, allowing the flavour to develop. The mature fermented beans, dull red in colour, are then dried, ready to be bagged as raw cocoa which may be further processed or exported.

Cultivated cocoa trees may be broadly divided into three groups. Most cocoas belong to the Amazonian Forastero group, which now accounts for more than 80% of world cocoa production. It includes the Amelonado variety, suitable for chocolate manufacturing. Criollo cocoa is not widely grown, and is used only for luxury confectionery. The third group is Trinitario, which comprises about 15% of world output and is cultivated mainly in Central America and the northern regions of South America.

The cocoa production chain is extremely labour-intensive: the International Cocoa Organization (ICCO) estimated that in the 2000s some 3m. smallholders accounted for 90% of global cocoa output. Large-scale plantations are found only in Brazil and Indonesia. The cocoa-processing industry, meanwhile, is highly concentrated. In the few years up to 2010 the ICCO reckoned that the three major companies (Archer Daniels Midland, Barry Callebaut and Cargill) processed about 40% of global cocoa production. Most cocoa-processing takes place in importing countries, mainly in the USA and the Netherlands. The processes include shelling, roasting and grinding the beans. The primary product of grinding is chocolate liquor, a part of which is sold directly to chocolate-manufacturers; the remainder is then processed further, in order to extract a fat—cocoa butter—and chocolate powder. Almost half of each bean after shelling consists of cocoa butter. Cocoa powder for use as a beverage is largely fat-free. Cocoa is a mildly stimulating drink, because of its caffeine content, and, unlike coffee and tea, is highly nutritious.

The most important use of cocoa is in the manufacture of chocolate, of which it is the main ingredient. About 90% of all cocoa produced is used in chocolate-making, for which extra cocoa butter is added, as well as other substances such as sugar—and milk in the case of milk chocolate. Proposals that were initially announced in December 1993 (and subsequently amended in November 1997) by the consumer countries of the European Union (EU), permitting chocolate-manufacturers in member states to add as much as 5% vegetable fats to cocoa solids and cocoa fats in the manufacture of chocolate products, have been perceived by producers as potentially damaging to the world cocoa trade. In 1998 it was estimated that the implementation of this plan could reduce world demand for cocoa beans by 130,000–200,000 metric tons annually. In July 1999, despite protests from Belgium, which, with France, Germany, Greece, Italy, Luxembourg, the Netherlands and Spain, prohibits the manufacture or import of chocolate containing non-cocoa-butter vegetable fats, the European Commission cleared the way to the abolition of this restriction throughout the EU countries, which took effect in June 2000. The implementation of the new regulations by all member states ensued in 2003. The implementation of the new regulations took effect in May 2000. Producers identified another, potentially more damaging, threat when, in March 2007, the US Chocolate Manufacturers Association, following a similar request at the end of 2006 by the Grocery Manufacturers of America, began to lobby the US Food and Drug Administration (FDA) to change the legal definition of chocolate, in order to allow them to substitute at will vegetable fats and oils for cocoa butter in products labelled as chocolate. In response, the FDA initiated a public consultation. Meanwhile, an EU study that evaluated the new regulations, published in June 2006, found that the rate of growth of net cocoa imports had increased to an annual 3.5% by 2005, despite a saturated chocolate-product market. The study attributed this growth mainly to an increase in consumer demand for products with a high cocoa content. According to a report published by the International Cocoa Organization (ICCO) in June 2008, changes in consumption behaviour had had a significant impact on demand for cocoa beans in terms of both quality and quantity. Between 2001/02 and 2006/07 world cocoa consumption expanded at an average annual rate of 3.8%. In 2006/07 consumption increased by 2.5%, compared with the previous season. A significant part of the increase resulted from higher consumption in Europe (where it rose by 21%), where consumers were increasingly inclined to purchase organic, fine-flavour and high cocoa-content products. In particular, the growing demand for products with a high cocoa content was influenced by research findings on the beneficial health properties of cocoa, and led in turn to increased demand for cocoa beans of superior quality—which command higher prices. In the same year global consumption of dark chocolate was estimated to constitute 5%–10% of the total consumption of chocolate bars, with the highest share (20%) in continental Europe, particularly in the Netherlands, France, Belgium and Switzerland. Consumption of dark chocolate in the USA increased by an average annual rate of 9% between 2001 and 2005. In addition, concerns about food safety and environmental issues prompted an increase in demand for organic chocolate, the share of which in global production was, however, still estimated at less than 0.5% of output world-wide in 2005. According to the ICCO, such changes in the pattern of consumption were primarily of benefit to the economies of those countries recognized by the International Cocoa Council as exporters of premium cocoa (including Indonesia and Papua New Guinea—also Colombia, Costa Rica, Dominica, the Dominican Republic, Ecuador, Grenada, Jamaica, Madagascar, Peru, Saint Lucia, São Tomé and Príncipe, Trinidad and Tobago, and Venezuela). At the same time as the expansion of existing, saturated markets, increased consumption in emerging and newly industrialized countries, in particular Russia and Asian countries, sustained demand for bulk cocoa. However, premium chocolate manufacturers proved less resilient during the world-wide economic recession beginning in late 2008 than the mass-market producers.

A combination of growing consumer concerns about poverty in less developed countries and a more organized fair-trade movement established steady growth in sales of fair-trade products from the early 1990s. Sales of cocoa labelled 'fair trade' increased from 700 metric tons in 1996 to 5,657 tons in 2005, equivalent to annual growth of 23%, although at the end of that period the share of fair-trade cocoa was still estimated to represent less than 0.2% of global production. In 2005 83% of sales of fair-trade cocoa world-wide were distributed among only six countries: the United Kingdom (40%), Germany and France (13% each), Austria, Italy and Switzerland (6% each).

Global consumption of chocolate products is dominated by the EU and North America, which generally account for at least three-quarters of cocoa imports from developing countries. The principal cocoa-bean importing countries in 2008 were the Netherlands (with 680,942 tons, representing about 22% of the total), Malaysia (398,253 tons—unofficial estimate), the USA (355,751 tons) and Germany (334,033 tons); the EU in total accounted for 55% of imports world-wide.

In 2009, according to FAO, the most important producing area in the world was Africa, which accounted for 65% of total output, followed by South-East Asia and Oceania, at 22%, and Latin America and the Caribbean, at 13%. In 2008 Africa accounted for two thirds of foreign sales of cocoa beans world-wide, by volume, South-East Asia and Oceania 17% and Latin America and the Caribbean 5% (the balance includes re-exports). According to ICCO figures, the largest single producer of cocoa beans in 2010/11, despite problems earlier in the decade, remained Côte d'Ivoire, with a forecast 1.30m. metric tons (up from 1.24m. tons in 2009/10), followed by Ghana with 960,000 tons (up from 632,000 tons), Indonesia with 510,000 tons (down from 550,000 tons), Nigeria with 240,000 tons (235,000 tons), Cameroon with 215,000 tons (205,000 tons), Brazil with 198,000 tons (161,000 tons) and Ecuador with 140,000 tons (144,000 tons). World output of cocoa beans, according to FAO, was 4.00m. tons in 2007, 4.23m. tons in 2008 and 4.08m. tons in 2009. ICCO figures for production tend to be lower: world production was put at 3.62m. tons of cocoa beans in 2008/09, 3.63m. tons in 2009/10 and a projected 4.03m. tons in 2010/11. Since two-fifths of the processing (grinding) of cocoa beans does not take place in the country of origin, the Netherlands is the world leader, accounting for 13.6% of the world total of 3.68m. tons in 2009/10, followed by Côte d'Ivoire (10.9%), the USA (10.4%), Germany (9.8%), Malaysia (8.1%), Brazil (6.1%) and Ghana (5.8%). Overall, Europe accounted for 41% of grindings, the Americas 22%, Asia and Oceania 19% and Africa 18%. Global consumption of chocolate products is dominated by the EU (53%); and by Northern America (26%).

Production of Cocoa Beans
('000 metric tons)

	2008	2009
World total	4,234	4,082
Far East	827	824
Oceania	57	56
Leading regional producers		
Indonesia	793	800*
Malaysia	28	18
Papua New Guinea†	52	51
Other leading producers		
Brazil	202	218
Cameroon†	188	226
Côte d'Ivoire†	1,382	1,222
Ghana†	729	662
Nigeria	367	370*

* FAO estimate.
† Unofficial figures.

Source: FAO.

In Indonesia, as noted above, the cultivation of cocoa began in the second half of the 16th century, but for many years remained confined to Java and to northern Sumatra where, according to the ICCO, cocoa plantations covered some 6,500 ha prior to the Second World War. Indonesian output at that time amounted to about 2,000 metric tons annually, but increased gradually as cultivation commenced on Sulawesi (Celebes) and Kalimantan (Borneo). In 1975 a national programme to expand smallholder cultivation of cocoa was initiated that involved the extensive distribution of seedlings of the Upper Amazon Interclonal Hybrid cocoa variety. By 1980, according to FAO, cocoa was being harvested from some 19,355 ha in Indonesia; by 1989 the area under the crop had risen to more than 135,000 ha, while 10 years later it was estimated to be up to 1m. ha (similarly, in 2009, according to FAO estimates). Output rose accordingly, from some 10,000 tons in 1980 to almost 111,000 tons in 1989, thus having increased by an annual average rate of more than 30% in 1980–89. In 1997 Indonesia overtook Ghana as the world's second largest producer of cocoa beans after Côte d'Ivoire, which was still the case in 2009, although it has not retained that rank in every subsequent year (relinquishing it most recently in 2004–05). Annual output rose in each year of the 2000s until 2007, when it fell back slightly, averaging more than 670,000 tons in 2003–07. It is likely that production would have risen still further had it not been for infestation by the cocoa pod borer, *Conopomorpha cramerella*, a pest that by the late 1990s reportedly beset up to one-fifth of all Indonesian cocoa. By means of cultural control (regular, thorough harvesting with machetes), biological control (through the black (cocoa) ant *Dolichoderus thoracicus* and the parasitoid wasp *Trichogrammatoidea bactrae fumata*), and behavioural control (trapping the adult moths into which the cocoa pod borer beetle develops using sex pheromones) infestations have been contained, but the cocoa pod borer nevertheless remains the single greatest constraint on the expansion of Indonesian cocoa production. A 2000s threat to the black ant, from the invasive yellow crazy ant (*Anoplolepis gracilipes*), could be countered, it was realized at the end of the decade, by the native Sulawesi toad (*Ingerophrynus celebensis*). Production recovered in 2008 and 2009, to reach an estimated 800,000 tons of beans in the latter year. The cultivation of cocoa in Indonesia was still dominated by smallholders, who accounted for more than 75% of the total area under cocoa at the beginning of the 2000s. Plantations, both government-owned and private, accounted for the remainder.

Malaysia is the second most important producer of cocoa in the region, after Indonesia, with output there totalling some 35,000 metric tons in 2007. However, production fell back to just below 28,000 tons in 2008 and only 18,152 tons in 2009. As in Indonesia, output of cocoa expanded considerably in the 1980s, in response to government incentives. From some 35,000 tons in 1980, output increased to a peak of 247,000 tons in 1990, while the area under cocoa reached a record 398,950 ha in 1991. In the 1990s, however, as a consequence of the depressed international price of cocoa and the superior profitability of alternative crops, such as oil palm, both output of and area under cocoa declined precipitously. In 2004 Malaysian cocoa production, at 33,400 tons, and the area under cultivation, at 33,313 ha, were less than they were prior to the expansion programme of the 1980s. Malaysian exports of cocoa fell consequently. In 1988, at some 190,000 tons, they were more than three times greater than Indonesia's foreign sales of cocoa. In 2004, however, Malaysia's exports of cocoa had dwindled to a low point of just 6,815 tons. Local annual cocoa-processing capacity was estimated at 100,000 tons in the mid-2000s, much of which now had to be supplied by imports. In the early 2000s, according to the Cocoa Producers' Alliance (COPAL—see below), the Government's second National Master Plan and its third National Agricultural Policy both included among their objectives the revival of cocoa production. Exports recovered steadily in 2005–07, reaching 17,821 tons in the last year (a similar trend was recorded for cocoa butter exports).

Cocoa is an important cash crop for Papua New Guinea, where the sales of cocoa beans contributed an estimated 3.4% of the country's export revenue in 2007, according to the Asian Development Bank. Papua New Guinea accounts for the overwhelming bulk of Oceania's output of cocoa, with estimated production of 51,000 metric tons in 2009, down on the record 51,500 tons of the year before—infestations by the cocoa pod borer beetle were discovered in Papuan crops in 2006, affecting output for a time. Elsewhere in the region, modest producers of cocoa include the Philippines, whose declining annual output fell to between 6,000 and 5,000 tons in 2002–09, and some of the island territories of the Pacific, notably Solomon Islands (a record 4,671 tons in 2009) and Vanuatu (however, production of 1,314 tons in 2006 fell to 738 tons by 2008 and, according to FAO figures, only 102 tons in 2009).

World prices for cocoa are highly sensitive to changes in supply and demand, making its market position volatile. Negotiations to secure international agreement on stabilizing the cocoa industry began in 1956. Full-scale cocoa conferences, under UN auspices, were held in 1963, 1966 and 1967, but all proved abortive. A major difficulty was the failure to agree on a fixed minimum price. In 1972 the fourth UN Cocoa Conference took place in Geneva, Switzerland, and resulted in the first International Cocoa Agreement (ICCA), adopted by 52 countries, although the USA, the world's principal cocoa importer at that time, did not participate. The ICCA took formal effect in October 1973. It operated for three quota years and provided for an export quota system for producing countries, a fixed price range for cocoa beans and a buffer stock to support the agreed prices. In accordance with the ICCA, the ICCO, based in London, United Kingdom, was established in 1973. In October 2010 the membership of the 2001 ICCA (see below) comprised 44 countries (15 exporting members, 29 importing members), representing about 85% of world cocoa production and some 60% of world cocoa consumption. The EU is also an intergovernmental party to the 2001 Agreement—its 27 members, together with Russia and Switzerland, comprise the importing membership. However, the USA, a leading importer of cocoa, is not a member, nor is Indonesia, which is now the third largest producer in the world. The governing body of the ICCO is the International Cocoa Council (ICC), established to supervise implementation of the ICCA. It is planned to relocate the ICCO to Abidjan, Côte d'Ivoire.

A second ICCA operated during 1979–81. It was followed by an extended agreement, which was in force in 1981–87. A fourth ICCA took effect in 1987. During the period of these ICCAs, the effective operation of cocoa price stabilization mechanisms was frequently impeded by a number of factors, principally by crop and stock surpluses, which continued to overshadow the cocoa market in the early 1990s. In addition, the achievement of ICCA objectives was affected by the divergent views of producers and consumers, led by Côte d'Ivoire (for the producers) and by the USA (for the consumers) as to appropriate minimum price levels. Disagreements also developed over the allocation of members' export quotas and the conduct of price support measures by means of the buffer stock (which ceased to operate during 1983–88), and subsequently over the disposal of unspent buffer stock funds. The effectiveness of financial operations under the fourth ICCA was severely curtailed by the accumulation of arrears of individual members' levy payments, notably by Côte d'Ivoire and Brazil. The fourth ICCA was extended for a two-year period from October 1990, although the suspension of the economic clauses relating to price support operations rendered the agreement ineffective in terms of exerting any influence over cocoa market prices.

Preliminary discussions on a fifth ICCA, again held under UN auspices, ended without agreement in May 1992, when consumer members, while agreeing to extend the fourth ICCA for a further year (until October 1993), refused to accept producers' proposals for the creation of an export quota system as a means of stabilizing prices, on the grounds that such arrangements would not impose sufficient limits on total production to restore equilibrium between demand and supply. Additionally, no agreement was reached on the disposition of cocoa buffer stocks, then totalling 240,000 metric tons. In March 1993 ICCO delegates abandoned efforts to formulate arrangements whereby prices would be stabilized by means of a stock-withholding scheme. At a further negotiating conference in July, however, terms were finally agreed for a new ICCA, to take effect from October, subject to its ratification by at least five exporting countries (accounting for at least 80% of total world exports) and by importing countries (representing at least 60% of total imports). Unlike previous commodity agreements sponsored by the UN, the fifth ICCA aimed to achieve stable prices by regulating supplies and promoting consumption, rather than through the operation of buffer stocks and export quotas.

The fifth ICCA, operating until September 1998, entered into effect in February 1994. Under the new agreement, buffer stocks totalling 233,000 metric tons that had accrued from the previous ICCA were to be released on the market at the rate of 51,000 tons annually over a maximum period of four-and-a-half years, beginning in the 1993/94 crop season. At a meeting of the ICCO, held in October 1994, it was agreed that, following the completion of the stocks reduction programme, the extent of stocks held should be limited to the equivalent of three months' consumption. ICCO members also assented to a voluntary reduction in output of 75,000 tons annually, beginning in 1993/94 and terminating in 1998/99. Further measures to achieve a closer balance of production and consumption, under which the level of cocoa stocks would be maintained at 34% of world grindings during the 1996/97 crop year, were introduced by the ICCO in September 1996. The ICCA was subsequently extended until September 2001. In April 2000 the ICCO agreed to implement measures to remedy low levels of world prices (see below), which were to centre on the elimination of sub-grade cocoa in world trade: these cocoas were viewed by the ICCO as partly responsible for the downward trend in prices. In mid-July Côte d'Ivoire, Ghana, Nigeria and Cameroon disclosed that they had agreed to destroy a minimum of 250,000 tons of cocoa at the beginning of the 2000/01 crop season, with a view to assisting prices to recover and to 'improving the quality of cocoa' entering world markets.

A sixth ICCA was negotiated, under the auspices of the UN, in February 2001. Like its predecessor, the sixth ICCA aimed to achieve stable prices through the regulation of supplies and the promotion of consumption. The agreement took provisional effect on 1 October 2003, for an initial five-year period; it was twice extended for two years, latterly from 1 October 2010. In December, in accordance with its provisions, the ICC established a Consultative Board on the World Cocoa Economy, a private sector board with a mandate to 'contribute to the development of a sustainable cocoa economy; identify threats to supply and demand and propose action to meet the challenges; facilitate the exchange of information on production, consumption and stocks; and advise on other cocoa-related matters within the scope of the Agreement'. In November 2005, on its ratification by the Dominican Republic, the sixth ICCA entered definitively into force (this was the first time that an ICCA had ever entered definitively into force). The agreement was to remain open to new signatories until 2010.

A seventh ICCA was signed in Geneva, Switzerland, on the last day of the UN Cocoa Conference of 21–25 June 2010. It was to be opened for signature on 1 October for two years (in March 2010 the ICC had agreed to extend the existing ICCA between the same dates). On 6 July 2011 Costa Rica became the third signatory to the document, following Switzerland and the EU. Previous agreements had been for five years, with extensions possible. The new document built on the strengths of the 2001 Agreement, improving product quality and co-operation between exporters and importers, emphasizing improved incomes for farmers and other producer benefits and aiming for sustainability in the cocoa economies. The 2010 Agreement, unlike the previous five-year accords, was to be in effect for 10 years, provisionally from 1 October 2012, with the possibility of two four-year extensions, recognizing the perceived success of the current regime. Officials also expressed hopes that Indonesia might accede to the new treaty.

International prices for cocoa were generally very low until the early 2000s. In 1998 the average of the ICCO's daily prices (based on selected quotations from the London and New York markets) was US $1,676 per metric ton, its highest level since 1982, but in 1999 it slumped to $1,140 per ton (a fall of 32.0%). In 2000 the average of the ICCO's daily prices again declined steeply, falling well below that recorded in 1992—$1,099.5 per ton—to only $888 per ton, a reduction of some 22%. (The average ICCO quotation ranged between $942 per ton in June 2000 and $801 per ton in November, the lowest monthly average since March 1973.) Prices recovered somewhat in 2001, but, even so, the ICCO's daily quotation averaged only $1,089 per ton in that year, the second lowest average price recorded since 1972. In 2002, however, the average price rebounded by almost 63%, compared with the previous year, to reach $1,778 per ton. In 2003 the ICCO's average daily price fell slightly, by 1.3%, to $1,755 per ton. A more substantial decline, of 11.8%, was recorded in 2004, when the ICCO's daily quotation averaged $1,548 per ton. In 2005 the average quotation fell marginally, by 0.6%, compared with the previous year, to $1,538 per ton. The ICCO's average daily price rose by 3.5% in 2006, to $1,592 per ton. The average daily price increased substantially, by 22.6%, to $1,952 per ton in 2007, and again, by 32.0%, to $2,577 per ton in 2008. Global economic concerns, which had depressed cocoa quotations in the second half of 2008 and had affected all commodity prices, were pronounced into the first half of 2009, despite continued expectation of a production deficit. Nevertheless, the average price for 2009 was $2,889 per ton, the price having risen considerably later in the year (the final quarter average was $3,418 per ton). After a monthly peak of $3,525 per ton in January 2010, prices fell back somewhat from earlier heights and fluctuated downwards, in particular from September, but still recorded an average of $3,133 per ton over the year. In the first seven months of 2011 the average cocoa price was $3,203 per ton, owing to a strong rise at the beginning of the year (to peak at a monthly average of $3,472 per ton in February) and a recovery in July, when the monthly average of the ICCO daily price in July was $3,167 per ton. Assurance of sufficient supply to meet demand had eased the price by the middle of 2011 but, in the longer term, fears remained of a cocoa deficit, despite the expected beginnings of recovery in Côte d'Ivoire's production.

COPAL, with headquarters in Lagos, Nigeria, had 10 members in 2011, including Malaysia. COPAL was formed in 1962 with the aim of preventing excessive price fluctuations by regulating the supply of cocoa. Members of COPAL currently account for about three-quarters of world cocoa production. COPAL has acted in concert with successive ICCAs.

The principal centres for cocoa-trading in the industrialized countries are the London Cocoa Terminal Market, in the United Kingdom, and the New York Coffee, Sugar and Cocoa Exchange, in the USA.

COCONUT (*Cocos nucifera*)

The coconut palm is a tropical tree, up to 25 m tall, with a slender trunk surmounted by a feathery crown of leaves. The geographical origins of the tree are thought to be in the Asia-Pacific region. Its presence in most coastal areas and on many islands in the tropics is largely due to man, who introduced it to West Africa and the Americas. The tree's fruits first appear after about six years, though the palm may not reach full bearing until it is about 20 years old. It may continue fruiting for a further 60 years. (Hybrid varieties have advanced the time of initial fruiting from the sixth to the fourth year, and the onset of full bearing from the 20th to the 10th year.) The fruits, green at first but turning yellow as they ripen, are often left to fall naturally, but, as many are then over-ripe, harvesting by hand is widely practised.

Coconut, the most important of all cultivated palms, is frequently a smallholder crop, found mainly in small plots around houses and in gardens, although in the Philippines the average coconut farm covers 4–7 ha in area. The plant's fruit, fronds and wood provide many thousands of families with a cash income as well as basic necessities such as food, drink, fuel and shelter. The palms grow with little or no attention where conditions are favourable. More than 80 varieties are known, divided broadly into tall palms, produced by cross-pollination, and dwarf palms, which are self-pollinating. The sap of the coconut palm itself can be evaporated to produce sugar or fermented to make an alcoholic drink known as 'toddy'. This may be distilled to produce a spirit called 'arrack'.

Production of Coconuts
('000 metric tons)

	2008	2009
World total	61,483	61,708
Far East	38,745	41,022
Oceania	2,452	2,380
Leading regional producers		
Indonesia	19,500*	21,566†
Malaysia	455	460
Papua New Guinea	910*	930†
Philippines	15,320	15,668
Thailand	1,484	1,381
Viet Nam	1,095	1,129
Other leading producers		
Brazil	2,759	1,973
India	10,894	10,148
Mexico†	1,246	1,005
Sri Lanka	2,211	2,099

* Unofficial figure.
† FAO estimate(s).

Source: FAO.

Coconut oil is a rich source of medium-chain triglycerides (MCT), whose applications in medical nutrition include infant milk formulas and foods for persons unable to digest and assimilate fats. Its other food applications include use as a flavouring and also as an ingredient to prolong the shelf life of certain food products.

All parts of the fruit have their uses. Beneath the outer skin is a thick layer of fibrous husk. The fibres can be combed out to produce coir (from the Malay word *kayar*, which means 'cord'), a material used for making ropes, coconut matting, brushes, mattresses and upholstery (see below). Inside the husk is the nut—what people in temperate areas think of as a 'coconut' since the whole fruit is not usually imported. The nut has a hard shell, inside which is a thin white fleshy layer of edible 'meat'. The nut's hollow interior is partially filled with a liquid, called 'coconut water', which is gradually absorbed as the fruit ripens. This 'water' is a refreshing and nutritious drink when taken from a young nut (7–8 months), while that from more mature nuts can be prepared as a soft drink and is also used in the production of yeast, alcohol, wine and vinegar. So-called coconut milk is the white, creamy extract obtained after pressing freshly grated coconut 'meat'. Coconut flour, a by-product of 'coconut milk', is a useful nutritional source of dietary fibre. The shells are mainly utilized as fuel, but small quantities are used to make containers, ornaments, ladles and buttons, and pulverized shells can be used as filler in plastics moulding, plywood and mosquito coil repellents. Raw coconut shell is a more efficient fuel after it has been carbonized into charcoal, and, on further processing, can be converted into the still more efficient activated carbon, which finds a market in highly industrialized countries concerned with pollution control.

After harvesting, the fruits are split open, the husk is removed and the nuts are usually broken open. The 'meat' is sometimes eaten directly or used to prepare desiccated coconut, widely used in the bakery and confectionery trades. However, by far the most important economic product of the plant is obtained by drying the 'meat' into copra, either in the sun or in a kiln which may be heated by burning the coconut shells. The dried copra is the source of coconut oil, used mainly in the manufacture of soap, detergent and cosmetics, and also as a cooking oil and in margarine production. As technology advances, more uses for coconut oil are being developed. Experiments have shown that it can be converted into diesel fuel, and a programme of conversion might alleviate the financial burden on countries that are heavily dependent on petroleum imports. The residue left after the extraction of oil from copra is a valuable oilcake for feeding livestock, particularly dairy cattle.

Coconuts are usually processed into copra near where they are grown. Other processing is often done elsewhere. By far the most valuable international trade in coconuts and their products is in coconut oil. Globally, exports of coconut oil were worth US $2,373m. in 2008, according to FAO—exports of desiccated coconut were valued at only 16% of that total, coconuts 6%, cake of copra 5%, copra 3% and coir only 1%. The Philippines is the world's largest exporter of coconut products, and about one-third of its population is directly or indirectly dependent on the coconut sector for a livelihood. South Asia has a hugely important internal market. The largest exporters of unprocessed coconuts were Viet Nam and Indonesia, followed by Sri Lanka and Thailand, then the Dominican Republic, Côte d'Ivoire and India (FAO, 2008); the largest importer is the People's Republic of China.

Good copra has an oil content of about 64%. Most extraction is done in the coconut-growing and copra-processing countries, although there is a substantial trade in copra to countries that extract the oil themselves. In 1992 the Philippines was overtaken by Papua New Guinea as the largest exporter of copra. However, the reduced role of the Philippines as a copra exporter was attributable to increased levels of crushings of its copra into crude coconut oil for export. In 2002 Papua New Guinea was in turn overtaken as the largest exporter of copra by Indonesia. In 2008, however, Indonesian exports fell to 26,110 metric tons (from 46,919 tons in the previous year), while sales abroad in Oceania surged, by 31% to an estimated 28,000 tons from the Solomon Islands and by a dramatic 169% to 32,100 tons from Papua New Guinea, the latter accounting for 24% of world-wide exports of copra in that year. South-East Asia as a whole therefore only sold 21% of the copra exported in 2008 and Oceania, notably Papua New Guinea, the Solomon Islands and Vanuatu, 48%. South Asia provided 20% of world exports of copra in 2008, and Sri Lanka alone almost 10%, although in that year a dramatic rise in Indian exports, to 13,578 tons (compared with 1,671 tons in 2007) put that country on a 10% share of the world trade, slightly ahead of Sri Lanka. However, in value terms, Sri Lanka's exports of copra continued to earn more per unit: in 2008 and, according to FAO, with sales worth US $13.7m., Sri Lanka accounted for 22% of the value of the world's exports of copra, followed by India (20%), Solomon Islands (18%) and Papua New Guinea (16%). Much of the copra exported from Indonesia and Oceania went to feed the extraction industries of the Philippines and Malaysia, making them the largest importers (of the volume of world imports in 2008, 52% and 12%, respectively—the latter down from 19% in 2007). Japan, once the main importer of copra, virtually ceased any imports in 2003. Germany, meanwhile, in the mid-1990s accounted, on average, for about 20%–25% of all copra imports. However, as the European single market took effect, that share declined in the 2000s, and the country's European Union (EU) partner Belgium became more important. Germany and Belgium's partners within the EU constitute a major market for copra, coconut oil, desiccated coconut and copra meal. Meanwhile, Pakistan and Bangladesh had become important copra importers, a surge in purchases during 2008 pushing the latter ahead of Pakistan and just behind Malaysia, in volume terms. In 2008, according to FAO, the most spent on copra imports was by the Philippines (an estimated US $35.0m.—of a global total of $64.5m.), followed by Pakistan and Bangladesh ($10.9m. and $4.8m., respectively, of a South Asian total of $17.2m.), Malaysia ($4.7m.), China ($1.6m.) and Nepal ($1.5m.). The value of German imports, meanwhile, fell from $3.2m. tons in 2007 to just $15,000 in 2008, according to FAO figures. The principal exporters of cake of copra are the Philippines and Indonesia, while the principal importer by far was the Republic of Korea (South Korea), which accounted for 76% of all imports in 2008, followed more distantly by Viet Nam and then the EU and India.

Production of Coconut (Copra) Oil
('000 metric tons, USDA estimates)

	2009/10	2010/11
World total	3,615	3,676
Far East and Oceania	2,895	2,956
Leading regional producers		
Indonesia	968	968
Malaysia	31	32
Papua New Guinea	63	63
Philippines	1,630	1,690
Thailand	46	46
Viet Nam	153	153
Other leading producers		
Côte d'Ivoire	28	28
India	447	447
Mexico	145	145
Mozambique	25	25
Sri Lanka	38	38
Tanzania	21	21

Source: US Department of Agriculture (USDA).

Coconut oil has encountered competition from the development of more productive annual oilseed crops, such as soybeans and rapeseed in the northern hemisphere, and from oil palm in the tropics. Up to 7 metric tons of oil per ha can be produced from oil palm, compared with a maximum of 3.25 tons from coconuts. The necessity for the production of copra prior to the extraction of oil has further eroded the competitiveness of coconuts in the world market for vegetable oils. In 2008 the Philippines accounted for about 42% of world exports of coconut oil by volume (valued at $905.9m.) and Indonesia for 32% ($769.1m.); in terms of the volume of trade, South-East Asia therefore accounted for 81% of exports world-wide, the EU for 12%, Oceania 4% and South Asia less than 0.1%. The EU is the main importer of coconut oil (42% of export tonnage globally—$1,096.1m., of $2,705.4m.), then North America (excluding Mexico) 24%, East Asia 13%, South-East Asia 9% and South Asia just over 1%. In terms of individual countries, the USA is the main importer, taking 24% of total world imports by volume ($642.3m. in 2008), followed by the Netherlands (15%), Germany (10%), Malaysia (7%), China (7%) and Russia (6%); South Asia spent just $33.7m. on imports in 2008 (India $18.8m. and Pakistan $9.2m.).

The Philippines is the world's largest exporter of coconut products, and about one-third of the country's population is directly or indirectly dependent on the coconut sector for a livelihood. In 1979 the Philippine Government agreed to the operation of a monopoly of the coconut industry by a group of private producers who controlled 80% of the country's coconut-milling capacity and accounted for more than 50% of coconut exports. The monopoly was dismantled in 1985, and the export of coconut products was opened to private enterprises. At that time 10 coconut trading co-operatives were established, with the government-controlled United Coconut Planters Bank as the common majority shareholder. This has, however, given rise to criticism that the abolition of the former monopoly was more apparent than real, and coconut farmers proved reluctant to conduct business with the new trading firms. Government financial support for replanting of the crop ceased in 1986. In 2009 coconuts were harvested from 3.4m. ha in the Philippines. The coconut sector was severely damaged by a series of powerful typhoons that swept across the southern Philippines in late 2006. The UN estimated that some 85,000 ha of arable land dedicated to the cultivation of coconut palm was affected. Recovery in the sector was expected to be a lengthy process, as new plantings would need a number of years to mature before producing fruit. The Philippine Coconut Authority (PCA) stated in August 2007 that programmes were under way to aid recovery and to reach a target production of 3m. tons by 2010. However, the PCA warned in September 2007 that productivity in the coconut industry could be significantly reduced within three years, with more than 130,000 fruit-bearing trees being affected by an infestation of coconut leaf beetle (*Brontispa longissima*). In March 2009 the PCA announced that all 1.6m. affected trees had been treated and that the infestation was under control. According to FAO figures, production figures dipped slightly in 2007, to 14.85m. metric tons (from 14.96m. tons in 2006), but then recovered, to 15.32m. tons in 2008 and a preliminary 15.67m. tons in 2009.

International promotion of biodegradable products during the late 1990s generated a revival of demand for coir products, of which India is the largest producer (52% of global production) and exporter, principally to markets in the EU and the USA, which in 2004 were together estimated to have accounted for 87% of world imports of mats, matting and rugs, etc., made from coir. China was overwhelmingly the main market for raw coir. In 2009 South Asia accounted for 64% of (brown) coir fibre production, of a total of 1.1m. metric tons, followed by South-East Asia 32% and Africa 4%. In fact, FAO only lists eight producers of coir, the largest being India (507,400 tons), followed by Viet Nam (282,000 tons), Sri Lanka (191,200 tons), Thailand (50,000 tons) and Ghana (39,400 tons)—also, Malaysia, Bangladesh and Côte d'Ivoire. Indian exports of coir products totalled some 107,996 tons in 2007 (41% of the world total), but only 14,558 tons (13%) in 2008, meaning that it was exceeded not only by the hitherto second exporter, Viet Nam, with 67,953 tons (59%) but by Indonesia as well, with 16,691 tons (15%); the exports of Sri Lanka amounted to about 185,356 tons in 2005, but production was severely affected by the great tsunami at the end of that year, and the effect on exports fed through until none was recorded for 2008. Indonesia and the Philippines, each of whose coconut output exceeds that of India, were both deficient in facilities for coir production, although Indonesia increased its capacity significantly from 2006. The largest importer, by far, was China, which took 97% of all coir imports worldwide.

Commodity prices for coconuts, copra and coir are not widely available, but the coconut oil price provides an indication of the markets, the Philippines price for the European market being the most important. According to the World Bank, the average import price of coconut oil of Philippine/Indonesian origin (bulk, c.i.f., Rotterdam) rose to US $661 per metric ton by 2004, but in 2005 it eased somewhat, to $617 per ton, while a further decline produced an average price of $607 per ton for 2006. The effects of the 2006 typhoon season in the Philippines caused a contraction in the supply of raw coconut, with an associated increase in the monthly price of coconut oil throughout 2007. The average price for the year was $919 per ton, rising to a record $1,224 for 2008 (with a monthly peak of $1,551 in June). A significant decline in prices from October 2008, in common with other commodities, owing to fears about the global recession, meant that the Rotterdam quotation for imported Philippine coconut oil averaged only $725 per ton over 2009 (reaching as low as $625 for March). Historically, however, prices remained high, recovering strongly in 2010 and rising into the first months of 2011. The average price for 2010 was $1,124 per ton, while for January–July 2011 it was $1,982 per ton. Average monthly prices had doubled between October 2009 ($706 per ton) and October 2010 ($1,412 per ton), with the rate of increase accelerating thereafter, to reach a peak of $2,256 per ton in February 2011. Prices fell back from those heights in March, but remained strong in the next two months, before beginning to decline (by 21% between May and July), to reach $1,663 per ton in July.

The Asian and Pacific Coconut Community, with headquarters in Jakarta, Indonesia, was established in 1969. At 2011 its 17 members (and one associate member) accounted for more than 90% of world coconut output and exports of coconut products.

COFFEE (*Coffea*)

The coffee plant is an evergreen shrub or small tree, generally 5–10 m in height, indigenous to Asia and tropical Africa. Wild trees grow to 10 m, but cultivated shrubs are usually pruned to a maximum of 3 m. The dried seeds (beans) are roasted, ground and brewed in hot water to provide one of the most popular of the world's non-alcoholic beverages. Coffee is drunk in every country in the world, and its consumers comprise an estimated one-third of the world's population. Although it has little nutrient value, coffee acts as a mild stimulant, owing to the presence of caffeine, an alkaloid also present in tea and cocoa.

There are about 40 species of *Coffea*, most of which grow wild in the eastern hemisphere. The species of economic importance are *C. arabica* (native to Ethiopia), which in the mid-2000s accounted for about 60%–65% of world production, and *C. canephora* (the source of Robusta coffee), which accounted for almost all of the remainder. Arabica coffee is more aromatic, but Robusta, as the name implies, is a stronger plant. Coffee grows in the tropical belt, between 20°N and 20°S, and from sea-level to as high as 2,000 m above. The optimum growing conditions are found at 1,250–1,500 m above sea-level, with an average temperature of around 17°C and an average annual rainfall of 1,000–1,750 mm. Trees begin bearing fruit three to five years after planting, depending upon the variety, and give their maximum yield (up to 5 kg of fruit per year) from the sixth to the 15th year. Few shrubs remain profitable beyond 30 years.

Arabica coffee trees are grown mostly in the American tropics and supply the largest quantity and the best quality of coffee beans. In Africa and Asia Arabica coffee is vulnerable in lowland areas to a serious leaf disease, and consequently cultivation has been concentrated on highland areas. Some highland Arabicas, such as those grown in Kenya, have a reputation for high quality.

The Robusta coffee tree, grown mainly in East and West Africa, and in the Far East, has larger leaves than Arabica, but the beans are generally smaller and of lower quality and, consequently, fetch a lower price. However, Robusta coffee has a higher yield than Arabica as the trees are more resistant to disease. and it can be grown at lower elevations—from 500–1,500 m above sea level—than Arabicas. Robusta is also more suitable for the production of soluble ('instant') coffee, and is favoured by multinational roasters and manufacturers of instant coffee on account of its low cost. In the mid-2000s four main roasting companies (Kraft, Nestlé, Procter & Gamble and Sara Lee) purchased more than 50% of global Robusta coffee output. Soluble coffee accounts for more than one-fifth of world coffee consumption. About 60% of African coffee is of the Robusta variety.

Each coffee berry, green at first but red when ripe, usually contains two beans (white in Arabica, light brown in Robusta) which are the commercial product of the plant. To produce the best quality Arabica beans—known in the trade as 'mild' coffee—the berries are opened by a pulping machine and the beans fermented briefly in water before being dried and hulled into green coffee. Much of the crop is exported in green form. Robusta beans are generally prepared by dry-hulling. Roasting and grinding are usually undertaken in the importing countries, for economic reasons and because roasted beans rapidly lose their freshness when exposed to air.

Apart from beans, coffee produces a few minor by-products. When the coffee beans have been removed from the fruit, what remains is a wet mass of pulp and, at a later stage, the dry material of the 'hull' or fibrous sleeve that protects the beans. Coffee pulp is used as cattle feed, the fermented pulp makes a good fertilizer, and coffee bean oil is an ingredient in soaps, paints and polishes.

Production of Green Coffee Beans
('000 bags, each of 60 kg, local marketing years)

	2009/10	2010/11
World total	123,216	133,308
Far East and Oceania*	31,472	29,358
Regional producers		
Indonesia	11,380	8,856
Papua New Guinea	1,038	867
Philippines	13	383
Thailand	794	752
Timor-Leste	47	64
Viet Nam	18,200	18,500
Other leading producers		
Brazil	39,470	48,096
Colombia	8,098	9,200
Ethiopia	6,931	7,450
Guatemala	3,835	3,950
Honduras	3,575	3,830
India	4,950	4,983
Mexico	4,200	4,000
Peru	3,286	4,000
Uganda	2,797	2,800

* Regional total excludes Laos (not a member of the ICO).

Source: International Coffee Organization.

More than one-half of the world's coffee is produced on smallholdings of less than 5 ha. In many producing countries, and especially in Africa, coffee is almost entirely an export crop, with little domestic consumption. Green coffee accounts for some 96% of all the coffee that is exported, with soluble and roasted coffee comprising the balance. Tariffs on green/raw coffee are usually low or non-existent, but those applied to soluble coffee may be as high as 30%. The USA is the largest single importer, although its volume of coffee purchases was overtaken in 1975 by the combined imports of the (then) nine countries of the European Community (EC, now the European Union—EU, with 27 members).

After petroleum, coffee is the major raw material in world trade, and it is the single most valuable agricultural export of the tropics. Of the estimated total world crop of coffee beans in 2010/11, Latin American and Caribbean countries accounted for 60.5% (Brazil alone contributed 36.9% of the world total). Africa, which formerly ranked second, was overtaken in 1992/93 by Asian producers. In 2010/11 African producers accounted for 13.3% of the estimated world coffee crop, compared with 22.0% for countries in the Far East of Asia and Oceania. India harvested a further 3.6% of the world coffee crop in the same year; the only other producer in South Asia was Sri Lanka, a non-member of the International Coffee Organization—ICO. (The above shares have been calculated on the basis of data released by the ICO. Non-members of the ICO accounted for 0.4% of the world coffee crop in 2010/11.) The largest single producer after Brazil is Viet Nam (13.9% of world production), followed by a resurgent Colombia (6.9%) and Indonesia (6.4%). Forecasts for 2011/12 reckoned on a lower harvest, primarily because it was the lower yield year in the biennial Arabica cycle for the important Brazilian crop.

Viet Nam has emerged, in a very short period of time, as a major producer and exporter of coffee. According to FAO, in 1980 coffee was grown on only 10,800 ha in Viet Nam. By 1994 the area cultivated had been increased almost tenfold, to 106,300 ha, while the yield obtained per hectare rose from 0.7 metric tons to 1.6 tons. The increase in the area cultivated took place in the context of a programme of economic reform that, with regard to the agricultural sector, emphasized the expansion of cash crop production. The area under coffee increased by more than three-quarters between 1999 and 2000. In 2009, according to FAO figures, coffee was harvested from 504,100 ha in Viet Nam, compared with about 473,500 ha in 2001 (the highest and lowest figures of the 2000s hitherto). Most of the coffee cultivated in Viet Nam is Robusta, but since the mid-2000s a programme has been under way to expand the area of Arabica plantations in the country's central highlands—where optimal growing conditions exist, notably in Lam Dong province. However, in 2008/09 98% of Vietnamese coffee production was Robusta. Coffee has been officially identified as one of 18 key export commodities on which the promotion of Viet Nam's foreign trade should focus. Since the late 1990s Viet Nam has overtaken Indonesia as the world's largest exporter of Robustas, and Colombia as the world's second largest exporter—after Brazil—of all coffees. In 2010/11, according to data from the ICO, Viet Nam's exports of all coffees, assessed at a high 17.16m. 60-kg bags (a little over 1.0m. metric tons), accounted for 16.4% of the provisional total world-wide. Exports are mainly to North American and European destinations, including the USA, Germany, the United Kingdom, Italy and Switzerland. According to the Asian Development Bank (ADB), in 2007 the value of Viet Nam's exports of coffee amounted to US $1,911m., accounting for 4.2% of Viet Nam's estimated total export earnings. Viet Nam was accused of having contributed, by rapidly expanding its output, to the glut of supplies available for export that plunged coffee production into a world-wide crisis in 2001 (see below). Viet Nam responded in that year by implementing fully the stock-retention initiative launched by the Association of Coffee Producing Countries (see below) to limit exports. In recent years, the inferior quality of Viet Nam's Robusta exports—many lots of which were rejected at European ports in 2006/07—has limited the depressive impact of Viet Nam's increasing exports on world coffee prices.

Until the 1999/2000 crop year, when it was overtaken by Viet Nam, Indonesia was the largest producer of coffee in the Far East and Australasia, and the world's largest producer of Robusta. Production, mainly of Robusta varieties, had by the late 1990s risen approximately threefold since the late 1960s, although it continued to be based on smallholdings rather than large estates. In 1999/2000 output of all coffees (Indonesia also produces high quality Arabicas) amounted to about 376,000 metric tons. Production fluctuated upwards, to as high as 549,540 tons in 2005/06. In the next year production declined once more, to 448,980 tons, but then rose steadily thereafter, to reach a record estimated 682,800 tons in 2009/10, falling back to 531,360 tons in 2010/11. In the 2000s (calendar years) Indonesian exports of coffee fell below 300,000 tons only in 2002, 2003 and 2007; exports reached 404,646 tons in 2005, but then fell back, to as low as 248,965 tons in 2007, before recovering strongly, to a record 474,436 tons in 2009; exports in 2010 amounted to 329,349 tons. Indonesia generally exports as green coffee about 70% of its total production, but the importance of the commodity in the country's total foreign trade has declined as that of petroleum and manufactured goods has risen. In 2007, according to the ADB, exports of coffee contributed less than 1% of Indonesia's total export earnings. In that year, according to FAO, the principal markets for Indonesian coffee were the USA, Germany, Japan and Italy.

Papua New Guinea ranked as the third largest producer of coffee in the Far East and Australasia in 2008/09, after Viet Nam and Indonesia (the country was the largest regional Arabica producer, after Indonesia). In the 2007/08 crop year output was assessed at about 58,080 metric tons, compared with some 48,420 tons in 2006/07 and 76,080 tons in 2005/06; in 2008/09 total production amounted to 61,680 tons (of which Arabica accounted for about 96% of all coffee cultivated) and, despite early estimates of a lower total in 2009/10, the harvest rose slightly, to 62,280 tons. In 2010/11 coffee production declined sharply to 52,020 tons. Production, initially based on large estates, but subsequently dominated by smallholdings, began to expand in the early 1950s. Papua New Guinea exports peaked at some 71,978 tons in 2005 (the year of a record harvest of 76,080 tons), but they declined very substantially in 2006, to only about 50,928 tons. Exports recovered slightly in 2007, to some 54,525, and more strongly in 2008, to some 65,755 tons. Exports in 2009 amounted to 61,618 tons, and in 2010 to 55,760 tons. In 2007, according to ADB figures, exports of coffee accounted for about 2.9% of Papua New Guinea's total export earnings.

Thailand was the next largest regional producer, on an estimated 45,120 metric tons, in 2010/11, followed by the Philippines, on an estimated 22,980 tons. The latest regional ICO member, Timor-Leste, produced 3,840 tons in 2010/11. The French Pacific territory of New Caledonia, which is not a member of the ICO, produces a negligible amount of coffee. Another producing non-member in the Far East and Australasia region is Laos; the ICO put total non-member production world-wide (Equatorial Guinea, Guyana, Laos, Sierra Leone, Sri Lanka and Trinidad and Tobago) at 26,760 tons in 2010/11.

Effective international attempts to stabilize coffee prices began in 1954, when a number of producing countries made a short-term agreement to fix export quotas. After three such agreements, a five-year International Coffee Agreement (ICA), covering both producers and consumers and introducing a quota system, was signed in 1962. This led to the establishment in 1963 of the ICO, with its headquarters in London, United Kingdom. In 2007 the International Coffee Council, the highest authority of the ICO, comprised 77 members (45 exporting countries and 32 importing countries). Successive ICAs took effect in 1968, 1976, and 1983. The system of export quotas to stabilize prices was eventually abandoned in July 1989. In October 1993 the USA withdrew from the ICO (it did not rejoin it until 2005), which was increasingly perceived at that time to have been eclipsed by the Association of Coffee Producing Countries (ACPC—see below). In 1994 the ICO agreed provisions for a new ICA, again with primarily consultative and administrative functions, to operate for a five-year period, until September 1999. In November of that year it was agreed to extend this limited ICA until September 2001. A successor ICA took effect provisionally in October 2001, and definitively in May 2005. By May 2007 the new ICA had been endorsed by 74 of the International Coffee Council's 77 members. Among the principal objectives of the 2001 ICA were the promotion of international co-operation with regard to coffee, and the provision of a forum for consultations, both intergovernmental and with the private sector, with the aim of achieving a reasonable balance between world supply and demand in order to guarantee adequate supplies of coffee at fair prices for consumers, and markets for coffee at remunerative prices for producers. A seventh ICA, agreed between the 77 members of the ICC, was formally adopted in September 2007. The new agreement reiterated the objectives contained in the sixth ICA, emphasizing the need to support the advancement of a sustainable coffee economy to benefit small-scale farmers. It established in particular a Consultative Forum of Coffee Sector Finance that was to facilitate access to financial and market information in the coffee sector, and a Promotion and Market Development Committee that was to co-ordinate information campaigns, research and studies. At June 2011 the ICO consisted of 32 exporting members and eight importing members (including the EU, which consists of 27 countries).

During each ICA up to and including the one implemented in 1994, contention arose regarding the allocation of members' export quotas, the operation of price support mechanisms, and, most importantly, illicit sales by some members of surplus stocks to non-members of the ICO (notably to the USSR and to countries in Eastern Europe and the Middle East). These 'leaks' of low-price coffee, often at less than one-half of the official ICA rate, also found their way to consumer members of the ICO through free ports, depressing the general market price and making it more difficult for exporters to fulfil their quotas. The issue of coffee export quotas had become further complicated in the 1980s, as consumers in the main importing market, the USA, and, to a lesser extent, in the EC came to prefer the milder Arabica coffees grown in Central America to the Robustas exported by Brazil and the main African producers. Disagreements over a new system of quota allocations, taking account of coffee by variety, had the effect of undermining efforts in 1989 to preserve the economic provisions of the ICA, pending the negotiation of a new agreement. The ensuing deadlock between consumers and producers, as well as among the producers themselves, led in July to the collapse of the quota system and the suspension of the economic provisions of the ICA. The administrative clauses of the agreement, however, continued to operate and were subsequently extended until October 1993, pending an eventual settlement of the quota issue and the entry into force of a successor ICA.

In September 1993 the Latin American producers announced the formation of an Association of Coffee Producing Countries (ACPC) to implement an export-withholding, or coffee retention, plan. In the following month the Inter-African Coffee Organization (IACO), whose membership includes Côte d'Ivoire, Kenya and Uganda, agreed to join the Latin American producers in a new plan to withhold 20% of output whenever market prices fell below an agreed limit. With the participation of Asian producers, a 28-member ACPC was formally established. (Angola and Zaire, now the Democratic Republic of the Congo, were subsequently admitted to membership.) With headquarters in London, its signatory member countries numbered 28 in 2001, 14 of which were ratified. Production by the 14 ratified members in 1999/2000 accounted for 61.4% of coffee output world-wide.

The ACPC coffee-retention plan came into operation in October 1993 and gradually generated improved prices; by April 1994 market quotations for all grades and origins of coffee had achieved their highest levels since 1989. Ultimately, however, in spite of this initial success, the ACPC was unable—even with the support of non-members—to bring about lasting price stability by pursuing coffee/export-retention strategy. In September 2001 the ICO daily composite indicator price reached a nadir unseen for decades, averaging 41.17 US cents per lb—the average for the whole year was 45.59 cents per lb, compared with an average of 64.24 cents per lb for the whole of 2000, itself the lowest annual average since 1973. In October 2001 the ACPC announced that it would dissolve itself in January 2002. The Association's relevance had been increasingly compromised by the failure of some of its members to comply with the retention plan in operation at that time, and by some members' inability to pay operating contributions to the group owing to the depressed state of the world market for coffee. Meanwhile, in May 2001 the collapse in the price of coffee had been described as the most serious crisis in a global commodity market since the 1930s, with prices at their lowest level ever in real terms. The collapse of the market was regarded, fundamentally, as the result of an ongoing increase in world production at twice the rate of growth in consumption, this over-supply having led to an overwhelming accumulation of stocks. In this connection, some observers highlighted the role of Viet Nam, which had substantially increased its production and exports of coffee in recent years (see above): by 2000 Viet Nam had overtaken Indonesia to become the world's leading supplier of Robusta coffee, and had surpassed Colombia as the second largest coffee-producing country overall.

In early July 2001 the price of the Robusta coffee contract for September delivery fell below US $540 per metric ton, marking a record 30-year 'low'. At about the same time the ICO recorded its lowest composite price ever. Despite a recovery beginning in October, the average composite price recorded by the ICO for 2001 was 29% lower than the average composite price recorded in 2000. In 2001 coffee prices were at their lowest level since 1973 in nominal terms, and at a record low level in real terms. Although prices began to recover slowly, the low returns for producers in the early 2000s created what was sometimes called the 'coffee crisis'. In 2005 the average composite price recorded by the ICO, at 89.36 US cents per lb, was 43.8% higher than in 2004, with the price of Robustas recovering strongly. In its review of the 2004/05 crop year the ICO noted that the crisis in the coffee economy of exporting countries had abated somewhat. The ICO composite indicator price continued its steady recovery through the mid-2000s, regaining the levels of the mid-1990s by 2008: 95.75 cents per lb in 2006, 107.68 cents per lb in 2007 and 124.25 cents per lb in 2008.

In common with other commodities, coffee prices were stronger in the first half of 2008, before economic uncertainties set in, although the ICO also attributed the upward trend in its composite average price to a 4% reduction in coffee supply in the second half of 2007, when exports from both Kenya—which consist exclusively of Arabicas—and Uganda were affected by social and political unrest in Kenya. According to the ICO, the composite average price for February 2008, at 138.82 US cents per lb, was the highest since June 1997, but the year ended with an average price of only 103.07 cents per lb in December. The annual average ICO composite price for 2009 was 115.67 cents per lb, indicating a gradual if erratic recovery of prices through the year, after the lows of late 2008. That the 2009 average price had not fallen by more than 6.9% on the previous year's price was largely a result of the strength of the Arabica price—the annual average price for Colombian Mild Arabicas increased by 24.0% and Other Mild Arabicas by 2.9% (the 2009 average price for Robustas fell by a massive 29.2%, and the price for Brazilian Natural Arabicas by 8.9%, on 2008). The Colombian Mild price remained particularly strong into 2010, and the Robusta price stabilized, so that the monthly averages for the ICO composite price, from December 2009, consistently remained above the levels seen since October 2008. Prices surged in July 2010, for all the four main coffee groups, driven by tight supplies and the efforts of major producers to replenish stocks, and that general trend continued into 2011. The average monthly composite price in February 2011 (216.03 cents per lb) was three-quarters as much again as one year previously (123.37 cents per lb—the lowest such figure for 2010), and the rise continued, although the ICO implemented a change in the criteria for its pricing from March, so data are not strictly comparable. The average July 2011 price (daily weighted average) for Colombian Milds was 285.21 cents per lb (up 26.5% on the 2010 average), for Other Milds 268.02 cents per lb (36.8%), Brazilian Naturals 245.69 cents per lb (59.9%) and Robustas 112.73 cents per lb (43.2%), giving an ICO composite price of 210.36 cents per lb (42.9% higher than the average for 2010).

GOLD

Gold minerals commonly occur in quartz, and are also found in alluvial deposits and in rich thin underground veins. In South Africa gold occurs in sheets of low-grade ore (reefs) which may be at great depths below ground level. Gold is associated with silver, which is the commonest by-product of gold-mining. Uranium oxide is another valuable by-product, particularly in the case of South Africa. Depending upon its associations, gold is separated by cyaniding, or else is concentrated and smelted.

Gold, silver and platinum are customarily measured in troy weight. A troy pound (now obsolete) contains 12 ounces, each of 480 grains. One troy oz is equal to 31.1 grams (1 kg = 32.15 troy oz), compared with the avoirdupois oz of 28.3 grams.

In modern times the principal function of gold has been as bullion in reserve for bank notes issued. Since the early 1970s, however, the USA has actively sought to 'demonetize' gold and so make it simply another commodity. This objective was later adopted by the IMF, which has attempted to end the position that gold occupied for many years in the international monetary system (see below).

For more than 100 years South Africa was the world's leading gold producer. In 2007, however, when the country accounted for 10.9% of world output, and for 52.8% of that mined in Africa, it relinquished primacy to the People's Republic of China, where output had been rising steadily since 1999. China's position was confirmed in 2008 (when it accounted for 12.1% of world and 38.1% of Far East and Australasian production), in which year the USA also exceeded South African production. In 2009 South Africa was just ahead of the USA, but behind Australia. The next year China remained the largest gold producer, accounting for 13.0% of global production, followed by Australia (9.7%) and, just ahead of South Africa, Russia (both the latter accounting for 7.6%). Also in 2010 East and South-East Asia accounted for 21.6% of world mine production, and Oceania (including Papua New Guinea) 11.8%. Despite a recovery in African output, the continent (with 19.6% of world output) remained in third place among the largest gold-producing regions for a third successive year, behind Latin America's 20.1%. From the mid-1980s the South African gold industry was adversely affected by the rising costs of extracting generally declining grades of ore from ageing and increasingly marginal (low-return) mines. Additionally, the level of world gold prices was not sufficiently high to stimulate the active exploration and development of new mines. Output accordingly fell markedly from the mid-1990s. The relative decline of South Africa's position in world gold markets was accompanied by substantial increases in output as new capacity was brought into production in, notably, Australia, Brazil, Canada, China, Indonesia, Papua New Guinea, Peru, Russia and the USA. Following the dissolution of the USSR in 1991, the successor states, especially Russia (which had accounted for about two-thirds of Soviet output) and Uzbekistan (which contains what is reputedly the world's largest open-cast gold mine), assumed an increasingly significant role in international gold trading, particularly following the abolition in 1997 of Russia's state monopoly on gold purchases. However, the rate of advance of the gold-mining sector was inhibited by a number of adverse short-term factors (including unpaid debts, shortages of mining equipment, transport difficulties and sharp rises in the cost of electric power), and by the longer-term problem of depletion of reserves. From the late 1990s, however, there was a considerable increase in foreign financial participation in the development of gold deposits in Russia, as well as in Uzbekistan, Kazakhstan, Kyrgyzstan and Armenia. In 2001–05, according to the US Geological Survey (USGS), foreign companies controlled 15%–18% of Russia's production of gold. In 2010 the former Soviet states provided 12% of world mined gold production.

In the mid-19th century, in order to check the emigration of Australians attracted to California, USA, by reports of gold discoveries there, the Government of New South Wales introduced the payment of rewards for gold discovered locally, which accordingly became known as 'payable' gold. The first such discovery was reportedly rewarded in 1851. Gold has since been found and is now mined in every state and territory of Australia, but it is the state of Western Australia, in particular mining operations in the area around Kalgoorlie, that accounts for the bulk of output—62% of the total in 2008 (down from 70% in 2003), but 68% in 2009, according to the USGS. An estimated 14% of the world's economic gold reserves were located in Australia in 2010, where they are exploited principally by open pit mining. According to figures from Gold Fields Mineral Services Ltd (GFMS), in 2003, with output of 283.4 metric tons, Australia overtook the USA as the world's second largest producer of gold, after South Africa. In 2004, however, a decline in output of about 9%, to 258.1 tons, relegated Australia to the rank of third largest producer, after South Africa and the USA. The decline in output in 2004 to its lowest level since 1995 was attributed to mine closures and to heavy rainfall in some producing areas in February and March. In 2005, however, at 262.9 tons, Australia's production once again outstripped that of the USA and was second in world terms only to that of South Africa. Increased output in 2005 reflected in large part the beginning of operations at Newcrest's new Telfer mine. In 2006 mining operations were adversely affected by a combination of severe weather conditions—in Western Australia—and technical difficulties. Scheduled lower-grade mining and the closure of two mines also contributed to the decline in Australian gold production, which fell to its lowest level—247.1 tons—since 1992. For the first time, outranked not only by South Africa and the USA but also by China, Australia was relegated to the position of fourth largest producer. Although the level of gold production declined further in 2007, to 246.3 tons, Australia was third in the ranking of gold producing nations, behind China (the new market leader) and South Africa. The Australian decline in production continued in 2008, with lower output at the main working mines, as well as closures of a number of smaller mines, with only 215.2 tons of gold being extracted. Australia was thus relegated to the position of fourth largest producer in that year, after China, the USA and South Africa. In 2009, however, a recovery in mined production, and the continuing contraction in South African and US output, put Australia's 223.5 tons behind only that of China, which position it preserved in 2010, with 260.9 tons. In 2010 the value of Australia's exports of unwrought and semi-manufactured gold, at US $12,816m., represented 6.2% of the value of all of the country's merchandise exports.

Liberalization has transformed the gold sector of China in the 2000s. Until 2002 the country's gold market was state-controlled, with the Government requiring all producers to sell all of their output to the central People's Bank of China (PBC) at non-market prices. The inauguration of the Shanghai Gold Exchange in 2002 and the new role of the PBC as an exclusively monetary bank, together with the removal of other advantages and subsidies, reportedly reflected the decision of the Government to reduce the status of gold as a national asset. In 2006, when production increased to 247.2 metric tons, China overtook Australia as the world's third largest producer (compared with 172.2 tons at the beginning of the decade). (The 8% increase in 2006—the seventh consecutive increase in annual output—also included a re-evaluation of the country's informal production.) Since 2002 foreign companies have been permitted to invest in Chinese mining, although national interests retain control of refining activities in the country. As noted above, China overtook South Africa to become the world's leading gold producer in 2007. An increase of 13.5%, to 280.5 tons, was recorded in Chinese gold output in 2007. In 2007 China additionally increased its share of the global retail gold sector, replacing the USA as the second largest market (after India) in terms of sales volume following an increased demand of some 26%. By the end of the decade, China was firmly established behind India as the world's second largest market for demand in fabricated gold, in 2009 also becoming the second largest bar hoarder (after India). Mined gold production again rose in 2008, 2009 and 2010, to reach 350.9 tons; in 2010 China accounted for 13% of world production.

In 2004 Indonesia's output of gold fell heavily, by more than 30%, to 114.2 metric tons, compared with 163.7 tons in 2003. Production was reported to have declined as a result of pit wall failures in late 2003 at the Grasberg copper-gold mine—the largest gold-producing mine in the world—that restricted access to high-grade gold ores until mid-2004. In 2005, thanks to a successful programme of repairs at Grasberg, national output recovered to 166.6 tons. In 2006, however, production fell sharply again, by 29.5%, to only 116.3 tons. This substantial fall was attributed mainly to scheduled mining of lower-grade ore at Grasberg. Production recovered in 2007, rising by 26.1%, to 146.6 tons. Most of Indonesia's output of gold is as a by-product of copper mining at the Grasberg and Batu Hijau mines, with 55% of the country's total gold production coming from the Grasberg mine in 2007. Annual output at Grasberg is normally about 100 tons, but the level fluctuated considerably after 2002, more than halving in 2008 alone (having fallen by 55% compared with 2007, to 36 tons), owing to mine sequencing problems and the failure of a pit wall. Indonesian production in 2008 thus fell below 100 tons for the first time in more than a decade, to 94.7 tons. However, output recovered strongly in 2009, reaching 160.4 tons and making the country the world's seventh largest producer of gold, as repeated in 2010. Healthy output from the Batu Hijau mine in 2010 did not offset the loss from Grasberg (45% of Indonesian mined gold) as lower grades were mined; the total for the year was down to 136.6 tons.

Production of Gold Ore
(metric tons, gold content)

	2009	2010
World total	2,589.5	2,688.9
Far East*	572.3	580.6
Oceania†	308.8	345.8
Leading regional producers		
Australia	223.5	260.9
China, People's Repub.	324.0	350.9
Indonesia	160.4	136.6
Papua New Guinea	70.6	70.5
Philippines	37.0	40.8
Mongolia	14.1	13.9
New Zealand	13.4	12.2
Other leading producers		
Argentina	48.8	63.5
Brazil	64.6	68.3
Canada	96.0	92.2
Ghana	90.3	92.4
Mexico	62.4	69.9
Peru	182.4	162.0
Russia	205.2	203.4
South Africa	219.8	203.3
USA	221.4	233.9
Uzbekistan	70.5	71.0

* Asia, excluding India, Papua New Guinea, Saudi Arabia and Turkey.

† Including Papua New Guinea.

Source: Gold Fields Mineral Services Ltd.

In the Philippines, in the first half of the 2000s, annual gold production was between 31 and 35 metric tons, at its highest in 2000 (34.7 tons) and its lowest in 2004 (31.7 tons). From 2005, when new legislation permitted greater foreign investment through unrestricted ownership of mines, beginning to reverse the decline in production in the formal sector, gold output increased, reaching a peak of 38.8 tons in 2007. However, there was a general falling-off of output in 2008, particularly among small-scale miners, which reduced production to 35.6 tons. Output recovered to 37.0 tons in 2009 and reached a new record of 40.8 tons in 2010.

There was substantial development of the gold sector of Mongolia from around the mid-1990s, when the Government began to privatize the mining sector; the number of companies engaged in the production of gold had increased to more than 100 by the end of the decade. However, many companies were operating placer (i.e. alluvial) deposits, which were almost depleted in the early 2000s. In 2004 a number of mines became operational. In particular, output was boosted by more than 70%, to 19.2 metric tons, by the inauguration of commercial operations at the open pit Boroo gold mine, which is located north of Ulan Bator, and which in that year contributed 40% of Mongolia's total gold output. The mine's operator, Boroo Gold Co, is a subsidiary of Centerra Gold Inc. of Canada. Mongolia's gold production amounted to 18.4 tons in 2005 and 18.9 tons in 2006. Although production had been expected to increase substantially in the following years, output declined to 18.4 tons in 2007 amid concerns that a new minerals law enacted the previous year, stipulating reduced tax incentives, increased licence fees and the establishment of customs tariffs, could undermine foreign investors' confidence; the trend was confirmed by further contractions in output in 2008, to 16.5 tons, in 2009, to 14.1 tons, and in 2010, to 13.9 tons. Domestic demand for gold was reported to be mainly from the jewellery sector, some 90% of the output of which was exported to China.

Japan produced 8.3 metric tons of gold in both 2004 and 2005, 8.9 tons per year in 2006 and 2007, but just 6.9 tons in 2008, the lowest level of the 2000s; production was 7.7 tons in 2009, and 8.5 tons in 2010. Sumitomo Metal Mining is the main Japanese producer, operating mines in the Hishikari area of Kagoshima prefecture on Kyushu Island. In 2006 the company also began to operate the Pogo gold mine in Alaska (USA) through a wholly owned subsidiary, Sumitomo Metal Mining America Inc. The Japanese market for gold is generally characterized by high demand for hoarding, or private investment. Output in the Democratic People's Republic of Korea (North Korea) reportedly totalled 6.3 tons in each year in 2003–10. Thailand's output of gold fell to 3.3 tons in 2007 and 2.5 tons in 2008, compared with a peak of 5.5 tons in 2002. The country's Chatree mine, in Pinchit province, which is operated by Akara Mining Ltd (a subsidiary of Australia's Kingsgate Consolidated Ltd) using modern mining and processing technology, is one of the world's lowest-cost gold mines. In 2006 Tongkah Harbour PLC began commercial gold production in Loei province. An improvement in processing of Chatree ores helped boost the country's production to 5.4 tons in 2009, more than doubling the figure for the previous year, but output fell back to 4.2 tons in 2010. Thailand, like Japan, is an important market for hoarding. Output of gold in Malaysia declined in the second half of the 2000s, from a peak of 5.7 tons in 2005 to as low as 3.8 tons per year in 2008, before recovering to 4.2 tons in 2009 and 5.2 tons in 2010. Most of Malaysia's gold is produced at the Penjom mine in the state of Pahang, supplemented by a number of small-scale operations and by some output of gold as a by-product of tin-mining. Penjom mine is owned by Avocet Mining PLC of the United Kingdom, whose exploration activities in the Penjom area are ongoing. Otherwise, few companies have shown any interest in exploring for gold in Malaysia. Output of gold by Laos reached 6.7 tons in 2005, compared with just 0.2 tons annually in the early 2000s. However, there was some decline in production, to 6.5 tons, in 2006, followed by a more substantial decline, to 4.5 tons, in 2007; output was 4.7 tons in 2008, 5.4 tons in 2009 and 5.9 tons in 2010. Gold-mining takes place mainly at the Sepon mine (operated by Oxiana Ltd of Australia). Pan Australian Resources also produced gold in Laos. The gold sector and mining generally in Laos remain relatively undeveloped, and there is believed to be strong potential for the discovery of new deposits. In 2008 Laotian exports of gold (including re-exports) accounted for about 7.3% of total revenue from exports. In Viet Nam output of gold reached 2.7 tons per year in 2007 and 2008, compared with 2.5 tons in 2006, rising to 3.1 tons in 2009 and 3.5 tons in 2010. Deposits of gold in Viet Nam were reportedly the focus of exploration by a number of foreign companies from the mid-2000s. Viet Nam represents East Asia's second most important market for gold for private investment, after Japan.

After Australia, Papua New Guinea is Oceania's largest gold producer. Alluvial gold was first discovered in significant quantities in the country during the late 19th century. Alluvial operations were subsequently superseded by hard-rock mining operations, of which those at the Porgera mine in Enga province in the country's highlands, operated by Placer Dome, are today the most important. Output of gold in Papua New Guinea fell to 70.9 metric tons in

2005, compared with a 2000s peak of 76.1 tons in 2004. The decline in production was attributed to a structural failure in one of the Porgera mine's pit walls, and to a landslide at Lihir, the country's second largest mine. In 2006 structural repairs at Porgera were largely accountable for a further decline in Papua New Guinea's gold production, which fell to its lowest level for nine years—61.7 tons—a level that was maintained in 2007 only because Lihir Gold's Lihir Island mine achieved record production over the year. National production rose to 70.3 tons in 2008, with Lihir again achieving record production (24 tons), Porgera recovering from power supply problems in the previous year, and a new mine being opened by Allied Gold at Simberi in February. The Hidden Valley project poured its first gold in June 2009. Part of operations in Morobe province by a joint venture of Harmony of South Africa with Australia's Newcrest, Hidden Valley was expected to produce more than 250,000 oz of gold per year over a 14-year period, with peak annual output of 275,000 oz. National gold production reached 70.6 tons in 2009 and stayed stable at 70.5 tons in 2010, as the newer sources of output offset declines at more established mines. In 2010 exports of unwrought and semi-manufactured gold accounted for 41% of the total value of Papua New Guinea's merchandise exports, according to the Bank of Papua New Guinea—the increase in the contribution of gold sales abroad to total exports was attributed to the high commodity price available on international markets.

Elsewhere in Oceania, New Zealand's output of gold dipped to 9.3 metric tons in 2003, but rose thereafter, to an annual 10.6 tons in 2005–07, then 13.4 tons in 2008 and in 2009, before falling to 12.2 tons in 2010. The country's largest mine is the open-cut Macraes operation, north of Dunedin in East Otago (South Island), and the second largest is the open-cut Martha Hill mine, south-east of Auckland (North Island). There are also many smaller operators—some 50 small-scale gold mines were reportedly in operation in New Zealand in 2003. The considerable production increase in 2008 was attributable to both new mines and boosted output in established ventures. In 2003, according to the USGS, unrefined gold was Fiji's second most important export commodity, contributing 6%–7% of all revenue from foreign sales. At 2.9 tons in 2005, Fiji's annual production of gold was lower than 3 tons for the first time since 1991; in 2004 output had amounted to 4.0 tons. Production almost halved in 2006 and virtually ceased in 2007, but the only mine was reopened in 2008, achieving production of 1.1 tons in the rest of the year. The Vatukoula mine on the island of Viti Levu was the sole producer of gold in Fiji. The operator, Emperor Mines Ltd, was reportedly confronted by a number of operational difficulties in 2005. Production fell by one-half, to 1.5 tons, in 2006. At the end of that year the company announced that the mine was economically unviable, and began to implement a 'care and maintenance' programme; as a consequence, output was just 0.1 tons in 2007. However, the mine, now owned by Vatukoula Gold Mines PLC, reopened in 2008, and production of 1.1 tons was achieved in that year, with 2.1 tons in the next. Gold exports, meanwhile, recovered from being worth less than US $2m. in 2007 to some $150m. in 2008, or 1.8% of the country's total exports. Solomon Islands reportedly produced about 100 kg of gold in each year in 2001–10. The country's Gold Ridge mine, operated by Delta Gold Ltd of Australia, was forced to close in 2000 owing to civil unrest, and the small quantities of gold subsequently obtained have been from primitive panning and sluicing operations. Australian Solomons Gold Ltd became responsible for re-establishing mining infrastructure at Gold Ridge from 2005, but in 2010 was formally taken over by Australia-based Allied Gold. which planned a $A150m. redevelopment of the mine, with production planned to recommence in 2011.

World supply of gold in 2010 was characterized by strong mine production (up 3.8%, to 2,689 metric tons, with gains across all regions for the first time since 1988), a fall of 2.9% on scrap (down to 1,645 tons, from the record of the previous year, so still the second highest ever) and net official sales shifting from the supply side to the demand side (last seen in 1988). Mine production accounted for 62% of the gold supply in 2010 and scrap for 38%. Demand, meanwhile, recorded a slight rise as greater jewellery offtake and net official purchases offset de-hedging and the fall in world investment (this latter was mainly because demand had been so strong in 2009). Investment demand was the principal driver of the gold price in 2010, as economic problems in Europe and then fears about inflation in the USA drove investors to the traditional haven of gold. As a general rule, when fears of recession recede, gold prices are likely to fall. Despite high prices, jewellery still accounted for one-half of end-use gold consumption in 2010, according to the *Gold Survey 2011* of Gold Fields Mineral Services Ltd, and identifiable investment for 38% (the main component was physical bar investment, which surged by 66% to a new record of 880 tons, mainly because of buying in India and China). Electronics was the most important industrial use of gold (8% of global end-use in 2010).

As a portable real asset which is easily convertible into cash, gold is widely esteemed as a store of value. Another distinguishing feature of gold is that new production in any one year is very small in relation to existing stocks. Much of the world's gold is in private bullion stocks, held for investment purposes, or is hoarded as a 'hedge' against inflation. Private investment stocks of gold throughout the world have been estimated at 15,000–20,000 metric tons, much of it held in East Asia and India.

During the 19th century gold was increasingly adopted as a monetary standard, with prices set by governments. In 1919 the Bank of England allowed some South African gold to be traded in London, United Kingdom, 'at the best price obtainable'. The market was suspended in 1925–31, when sterling returned to a limited form of the gold standard, and again in 1939–54. In 1934 the official price of gold was fixed at US $35 per troy oz, and, by international agreement, all transactions in gold had to take place within narrow margins around that price. In 1960 the official gold price came under pressure from market demand. As a result, an international gold 'pool' was established in 1961 at the initiative of the USA. This 'pool' was originally a consortium of leading central banks with the object of restraining the London price of gold in case of excessive demand. It later widened into an arrangement by which eight central banks agreed that all purchases and sales of gold should be handled by the Bank of England. However, growing private demand for gold continued to exert pressure on the official price, and the gold 'pool' was ended in 1968 in favour of a two-tier price system. Central banks continued to operate the official price of $35 per troy oz, but private markets were permitted to deal freely in gold. However, the free-market price did not rise significantly above the official price.

In August 1971 the USA announced that it would cease dealing freely in gold to maintain exchange rates for the dollar within previously agreed margins. This 'floating' of the dollar against other major currencies continued until December, when it was agreed to raise the official gold price to US $38 per oz. Gold prices on the free market rose to $70 per oz in August 1972. In February 1973 the US dollar was devalued by a further 10%, the official gold price rising to $42.22 per oz. Thereafter the free-market price rose even higher, reaching $127 per oz in June 1973. In November it was announced that the two-tier system would be terminated, and from 1974 governments were permitted to value their official gold stocks at market prices.

In 1969 the IMF introduced a new unit for international monetary dealings, the special drawing right (SDR), with a value of US $1.00, and the first allocation of SDRs was made on 1 January 1971. The SDR was linked to gold at an exchange rate of SDR 35 per troy oz. When the US dollar was devalued in December 1971, the SDR retained its gold value and a new parity with the US dollar was established. A further adjustment was made following the second dollar devaluation, in February 1973, and in July 1974 the direct link between the SDR and the US dollar was ended and the SDR was valued in terms of a weighted 'basket' of national currencies. At the same time the official gold price of SDR 35 per troy oz was retained as the IMF's basis for valuing official reserves.

In 1976 the membership of the IMF agreed on proposals for far-reaching changes in the international monetary system. These reforms, which were implemented on a gradual basis during 1977–81, included a reduction in the role of gold in the international system and the abolition of the official price of gold. A principal objective of the IMF plan was achieved in April 1978, when central banks were able to buy and sell gold at market prices. The physical quantity of reserve gold held by the IMF and member countries' central banks as national reserves has subsequently fallen (see below). The USA still maintains the largest national stock of gold, although the volume of its reserves has been substantially reduced in recent years. At the end of 1949 US gold reserves were 701.8m. oz, but since the beginning of the 1980s the level has been in the range of 261.4m.–264.6m. oz. At the end of 2009 the total gold reserves held by members of the IMF, excluding international financial organizations and countries not reporting, amounted to 970.64m. oz (30,741 metric tons), of which the USA had 26.5% and Germany 11.1%.

In June 1996 the Group of Seven (G7) major industrialized countries considered proposals by the United Kingdom and the USA whereby the IMF would release for sale US $5,000m.–$6,000m. of its $40,000m. gold reserves to finance debt-relief for the world's poorest countries, principally in Africa. The plan, which was opposed by Germany on the grounds that it could prompt demands for similar gold sales by its central bank, remained the subject of discussion within the IMF during 1997. In early 1999 the G7 endorsed a revised proposal whereby the IMF would sell about 10% of its holdings of gold to provide debt-relief for 36 of the world's poorest countries. Under the plan, the proceeds of the IMF disposals would be invested and the resulting revenue used to amortize IMF loans to the designated countries. However, in response to concerns that these disposals by the IMF and central banks would depress world gold prices further and seriously affect gold-producing countries, the IMF announced in September that the operation was to be restricted at the time to 'off-market' sales to members having repayment obligations. Between December 1999 and April 2000 13m. oz of gold were 'sold' to Brazil and Mexico at prevailing market prices, and the profit on the sales was placed in special accounts designated for debt-relief. Brazil and Mexico then immediately returned the same gold to the IMF, at the same price that they had paid for it, in order to settle debt repayments falling due.

During 1996 substantial amounts of gold bullion, jointly exceeding 500 metric tons, were sold by the central banks of Belgium and the Netherlands, and the Swiss National Bank announced its intention to allocate part of its gold reserves to fund a new humanitarian foundation. In July 1997 the Reserve Bank of Australia announced that it had disposed of more than two-thirds of its bullion holdings (reducing its reserves from 247 tons to 80 tons) over the previous six months. In October a Swiss government advisory group recommended the sale of more than one-half of Switzerland's gold reserves, and in December the Government of Argentina disclosed that it had sold the bulk of its gold reserves during a seven-month period earlier in the year. During 1997 loans to the market of official stocks of gold were carried out by the central banks of Germany, the Netherlands and Switzerland, and in March 1998 Belgium's central bank disposed of one-half of its gold reserves. In April 1999 the Government of Switzerland implemented constitutional changes that removed the requirement for gold to support the national currency. In May the British Government announced that it intended to reduce its gold reserves by 415 tons, to 300 tons, over several years, including the offering for sale of 125 tons in the year to March 2000. The initial disposal, of 25 tons, followed in July 1999, and the second auction of British gold reserves, again offering 25 tons, took place in September. In response to concerns that the official sector's unco-ordinated gold sales were depressing gold prices, later that month the European Central Bank (ECB), in a joint statement with the central banks of Switzerland and 13 members of the European Union (Sweden, the United Kingdom and the 11 countries then in the euro zone), announced a five-year moratorium on new sales of gold held in official reserves. Total gold reserves held by the 15 signatory banks totalled 16,336 metric tons, accounting for around 48% of global gold reserves. The agreement—referred to as the Central Bank Gold Agreement (CBGA) and also known as the Washington Agreement on gold—allowed impending sales that had already been decided to proceed, although total sales were not to exceed 400 tons per year over the five-year period. The announcement also stated that gold would remain an important element of global monetary reserves. The European agreement was generally welcomed for removing uncertainty from the gold market, although the permitted rate of sales (400 tons per year) was more than 100% greater than the average net sales by the signatory countries in 1989–98. In March 2004 the renewal of the CBGA was announced, to cover the five-year period from September 2004 to September 2009, without the United Kingdom but with Greece as a new signatory. The second CBGA ended the moratorium on sales not already decided, and annual sales quotas were raised to 500 tons in order to take into account the consolidation of the price of gold that had occurred. Slovenia became a signatory of the second CBGA in December 2006, immediately prior to its adoption of the euro as its currency. Cyprus and Malta likewise became CBGA signatories on adopting the euro in January 2008, as did Slovakia in January 2009. The third CBGA entered effect at the end of September 2009, with the same signatories as those to the second agreement. Under the new CBGA, covering the five-year period to 2014, the cap on annual sales was again reduced to 400 tons (with the signatories noting that the intention of the IMF to sell 403 tons of gold could be accommodated within the overall quotas). At the end of 2010 gold reserves held by the CBGA signatories amounted to 12,268 tons.

The unit of dealing in international gold markets is the 'good delivery' gold bar, weighing about 400 oz (12.5 kg). The principal centres for gold trading are London, Hong Kong and Zürich, Switzerland. The dominant markets for gold futures (buying and selling for future delivery) are the New York Commodity Exchange (COMEX) in the USA and the Tokyo Commodity Exchange (TOCOM) in Japan. Futures trading on the Shanghai Gold Exchange, established in China in 2002, is anticipated.

Gold Prices on the London Bullion Market
(afternoon 'fixes', US $ per troy oz)

	Average	Highest	Lowest
2000	279.10	312.70 (7 Feb.)	263.80 (27 Oct.)
2008	871.96	1,011.25 (17 March)	712.50 (24 Oct.)
2009	972.35	1,212.50 (2 Dec.)	810.00 (15 Jan.)
2010	1,224.52	1,421.00 (9 Nov.)	1,058.00 (5 Feb.)

A small group of dealers meets twice on each working day (morning and afternoon) to 'fix' the price of gold in the London Bullion Market, and the table above is based on the second of these daily 'fixes'. During any trading day, however, prices may fluctuate above or below these levels. In 1999 the average London gold price was only US $278.6 per oz—5.3% below the 1998 average and the lowest annual level, in nominal terms, since 1978. In real terms (i.e. taking inflation into account), the average price of gold in 1999, measured in US dollars, was the lowest since 1972. In 2000 a slightly higher average price—in nominal terms—of $279.1 (£187.04) was recorded for gold traded on the London market. In 2001, at $271.0 per oz, the average price, even in nominal terms, was the lowest recorded since 1978, and 3% lower than the average price registered in 2000. In 2002, at $309.7 (£206.1) per oz, the average London gold price was 14% higher than the average price recorded in 2001. However, although this was, in percentage terms, the greatest year-on-year increase since 1987, and the greatest increase within a single year since 1979, commentators noted that, in real terms, the average price of gold in 2002 was at its lowest level since 1972. In 2003 the average price of gold, at $363.3 (£222.2) per oz, was 17.3% higher than the average price recorded in 2002, the year-on-year increase thus overtaking that recorded in 2002 as the highest since 1987. Price volatility subsided during 2004 and the first half of 2005, while the average price rose—particularly influenced towards the end of 2005 by global economic and inflation anxieties prompted by the increase in petroleum prices.

In 2006 the average London price of gold, expressed in US dollars, increased dramatically, by 35.8%, to US $603.8 per oz. In nominal terms the average price was at its highest level since the $614.5 registered in 1980, while in real terms it was the highest price recorded since 1989. During 2006 the London afternoon gold fix ranged between $524.75 (January) per oz and $725.0 per oz (May). The highest fix represented a 26-year record in nominal terms and an 18-year 'high' in real terms. Price volatility, at 24%, was also exceptional, reaching its highest level for 26 years and almost double that recorded for 2005. The intra-year gain, however, was more modest: at 19.2% it was just below the rise recorded in 2005. Analysts noted that comparable increases in the price of gold were registered in other currencies. None the less, the rise in the average price was significantly higher when expressed in terms of the South African rand and the Japanese yen, in which average year-on-year increases of, respectively, 43% and 45% were recorded. Intra-year increases in prices were also more accented when expressed in terms of the rand (32%) and the yen (16%), while the intra-year rise expressed in euros—5%—was considerably lower. According to analysts, strong investment demand combined with reduced above-ground supply—derived mainly from diminishing official sales—underpinned the sharp increase in the first five months of the year. Analysts also noted that the decline in the value of the US dollar had contributed to a change in the attitude of official financial institutions towards gold in recent years. For the first time since the mid-1990s countries outside the CBGA group emerged as net buyers of the metal, while the ECB announced that the sales quota for the second CBGA was unlikely to be reached. The fall in June 2006 in the price of gold was largely fuelled by speculative selling in response to concerns about the sustainability of prices, while rumours concerning undeclared sales contributed to depress the price of gold in September–October. Russia's announcement, in September, that it planned to raise its gold reserves, and the Chinese central bank's comments on the need to diversify its reserves, contributed to the recovery in the price of gold in the final quarter of the year.

In 2007, expressed in US dollars, the average London price of gold rose by 15%, to a record US $695.39 per oz—some 13% higher than the nominal average price of $614.50 recorded in 1980. In real terms, the average price recorded in 2007 was the highest since 1988, although less than half of that registered in 1980. During 2007 the London afternoon gold fix ranged between $841.1 per oz (November) and $608.4 per oz (January). Price volatility, at 16%, was considerably lower than the level recorded in 2006, while the intra-year gain, at 30.3%, was substantially higher. Analysts noted that, expressed in terms of the euro, the Australian dollar, the Turkish lira and the Indian rupee, the increase in the price of gold was far more subdued than when expressed in US dollars, while in terms of the Japanese yen and the Indonesian rupiah increases comparable with those recorded in terms of the US dollar occurred. In terms of the South African rand, the increase in the price of gold was more marked. In terms of other currencies generally, the intra-year gain in the price of gold was lower than that recorded in terms of the US dollar—only in terms of the Indonesian rupiah was the intra-year gain, at 36.2%, higher. Analysts identified a surge in investor demand for gold towards the end of the year as the key factor behind the increase in the London price in 2007: the price of gold rose by almost $170 per oz in September–November. At the same time, however, it was noted that a solid base for such a surge had been established earlier by strong demand from the jewellery fabrication sector and a relatively low level of supply from scrap.

In 2008 the average London gold price reached a new record level of US $871.96 per oz, as well as reaching a new record daily high of $1,011.25 per oz in March (although, in real terms, these records still did not exceeding 1980 prices). The year-on-year increase in the average annual gold price was 25.4%, but the intra-year rise (i.e. the difference between prices at the beginning of the year and at the end) was a much more modest 2.7%, although prices in other currencies recorded larger increases, particularly those of producer countries. The South African rand price rose by 46.0% year-on-year and 41.1% intra-year in 2008. Prices in Japanese yen, particularly, and Chinese yuan recorded intra-year declines. The year was noteworthy for the extreme price volatility (32% on the London price for the year, with 45% in the final quarter of the year), with the March high followed by further price spikes in July, September and December. In common with other commodities, gold experienced soaring prices in the first quarter of the year, followed by falls with the onset of apprehension about global economic recession. Prices fell most dramatically from July into September, recovered strongly and then collapsed into October, followed by a resurgence at the end of the year. The typical alignment of the gold price with petroleum prices was less apparent from October 2008, as the financial crisis prompted many investors to seek refuge in gold.

In 2009 the average annual gold price rose for the eighth consecutive year, despite a weak start, and in the final quarter prices surged to new heights. The average price year-on-year increased by 11.5%, but the intra-year rise was a strong 24.4%. Price volatility, however, was down. Non-US dollar prices tended to show stronger gains year-on-year (except for the yen and, to a lesser extent, the yuan), but intra-year changes were generally less varied, the notable exceptions being in terms of the Australian and South African currencies, which recorded small devaluations in the average gold price. Prices were driven up mainly by investment (which, if broadly defined, exceeded jewellery demand for the first time since 1980), including net official purchases of gold, although jewellery demand recovered into 2010. The new nominal record price over 2009 was US $972.35 per oz, the daily high also reaching a new nominal record on 3 December (morning fix basis), at $1,218.25 per oz. The prices underwent a short, sharp correction at the end of the year, continuing into 2010—falling to $1,058 per oz in early February—then stabilizing around $1,100 per oz before rising again (reaching a new daily record on 21 June—morning fix—at $1,259.50 per oz), falling back and then edging up again into September. According to the World Bank, the average London gold price for the first seven months of 2010 was $1,158 per oz.

In 2010 the average annual gold price rose for the ninth consecutive year, growth that continued into 2011 as recovering demand atypically combined with economic uncertainty pushed the price to new records. The average price year-on-year increased by a strong 25.9%, while the intra-year rise was much the same at 25.3%, indicating the remorseless nature of the rise, in particular from February 2010. Price volatility was restrained. Non-US dollar prices tended to show weaker gains, in particular among producers, certainly year-on-year (except for the euro), but also intra-year (except for not only the euro price but the Turkish and Russian currencies). The euro prices were driven up by the eurozone's sovereign debt problems. The new nominal record price over 2010 was US $1,224.52 per oz, the daily high also reaching a new nominal record on 7 December (morning fix basis), at $1,426.00 per oz. The gold price continued to climb in 2011, rising through successive nominal records and reaching over $1,800.00 per oz in August (peaking for the first eight months of the year at $1,886 per oz on 23 August, morning fix); the lowest price of January–August 2011 was on 28 January ($1,316.00 per oz, morning fix). According to the World Bank, the average London gold price for the first seven months of 2011 was $1,464 per oz.

The World Gold Council (WGC), founded in 1987, is an international association of gold-producing companies which aims to promote gold as a financial asset and to increase demand for the metal. The WGC, based in London, had 22 corporate members in 2011, and a number of associate members.

GROUNDNUT (Peanut, Monkey Nut, Earth Nut) (*Arachis hypogaea*)

This is not a true nut, although the underground pod, which contains the kernels, forms a more or less dry shell at maturity. The plant is a low-growing annual herb introduced from South America.

Each groundnut pod contains between two and four kernels, enclosed in a reddish skin. The kernels are very nutritious because of their high content of both protein (about 30%) and oil (40%–50%). In tropical countries the crop is grown partly for domestic consumption and partly for export. Whole nuts of selected large dessert types, with the skin removed, are eaten raw or roasted. Peanut butter is made by removing the skin and germ and grinding the roasted nuts. The most important commercial use of groundnuts is the extraction of oil. Groundnut oil is used as a cooking and salad oil, as an ingredient in margarine and, in the case of lower-quality oil, in soap manufacture. According to the US Department of Agriculture (USDA), the world's most produced vegetable oils are palm oil and soybean oil, then rapeseed oil and sunflowerseed oil, and distantly followed by palm kernel oil, cottonseed oil and groundnut oil (then coconut oil and olive oil). Consumption followed a similar pattern, but in terms of world exports palm oil was by far the most important vegetable oil, with groundnut oil eighth of the nine listed by USDA in 2009/10. Oilseed production, however, in volume terms, is dominated by soybean, followed by rapeseed, cottonseed and groundnut, then sunflowerseed, palm kernel and copra.

An oilcake, used in animal feed, is manufactured from the groundnut residue left after oil extraction. However, trade in this groundnut meal is limited by health laws in some countries, as groundnuts can be contaminated by a mould that generates toxic and carcinogenic metabolites, the most common and most dangerous of which is aflatoxin B_1. The European Union (EU) bans imports for use as animal feed of oilcake and meal which contain more than 0.03 mg of aflatoxin per kg. The meal can be treated with ammonia, which both eliminates the aflatoxin and enriches the cake. Groundnut shells, which are usually incinerated or simply discarded as waste, can be converted into a low-cost organic fertilizer, which has been produced since the early 1970s.

Production of Groundnuts
(in shell, '000 metric tons)

	2008	2009
World total	37,651	36,457
Far East	17,182	17,685
Oceania	25	25
Leading regional producers		
China, People's Repub.	14,341	14,765
Indonesia	774	778
Myanmar	1,305	1,362
Thailand	112*	132†
Viet Nam	530	525
Other leading producers		
Argentina	625	605
Chad	403	413*
Ghana	470	485
India	7,168	5,510
Nigeria	2,873	2,969
Senegal	731	1,033
Sudan	716	942
USA	2,342	1,673

* FAO estimate.
† Provisional figure.

Source: FAO.

Since the late 20th century more than 90% of the world's groundnut output has come from developing countries. According to USDA, world output of groundnut peaked at 33.2m. metric tons in 2005/06, before falling back to 31.0m. in the following year, then rising to a new high of 34.8m. tons by 2008/09. USDA figures put production at 33.4m. tons in 2009/10 and 35.8m. tons in 2010/11, predicting a slightly lower 34.3m. tons for the following year. In 2010/11 the Far East and Australasia accounted for 52% of world groundnut production (East Asia alone 44% and South-East Asia 8%). USDA put the world's largest individual producer of groundnut as the People's Republic of China (almost 44% of the world total in 2010/11), followed by India (17%), the USA (5%) and Nigeria (4%). In that year Argentina and China were the world's leading exporters of edible (shelled) groundnut, each with 27% of total world exports, respectively, followed by India, the USA, Nicaragua, Brazil, the EU and Viet Nam. The EU was the world's largest importer (38% of the world total), followed by Indonesia, Mexico, Russia, Canada and Japan. In terms of consumption (including for processing), the world's largest domestic markets for groundnut were China (42% of global consumption in 2010/11), India (16%), the USA (5%), Nigeria (4%), Indonesia (4%) and Myanmar (3%). Production was similar: each year in 1997–2006, according to FAO, China was the world's leading exporter of edible (shelled) groundnuts. In 2005 China's foreign sales of groundnuts totalled an estimated 363,435 metric tons, while those of the USA, which earlier in the decade had generally been its nearest rival in this trade, amounted to an estimated 124,668 tons. However, Chinese exports fell by 36% in 2006, by 13% in 2007 and then by a further 18%, to 167,054 tons, in 2008 (still representing 14% of worldwide international sales). As a result, in 2007 India became the world's leading exporter of groundnuts, a position it consolidated in 2008, with 293,128 tons sold (25% of global exports). In 2003, for the first time since 1997, foreign sales of groundnuts by India had overtaken those of the USA, doing so again from 2005. Recovering sales volumes by Argentina, which had been the world's second largest exporter in 2000, took its exports past the USA's again in 2006 and 2007, but in 2008 exports contracted by one-fifth to only 12% of world exports. Resurgent US exports, therefore, accounting for 18% of global foreign sales, meant that the country took second place among the world's leading exporters in 2008.

Meanwhile, in 2000 the average import price of edible groundnuts at Rotterdam (Netherlands—c.i.f., any origin, US runner, 40%–50% shelled basis) rose slightly, from US $836 per metric ton in 1999 to $838 per ton. The import price declined slightly in 2001, and more substantially in 2002, to $751 per ton. From late 2002 the import price at Rotterdam rose steeply, in March 2003 achieving an average price of $1,000 per ton, and the monthly average remained at, or very close to, that level until July, when it fell slightly. For the whole of 2003 an average price of $976 per ton was recorded. A slight decline in the average annual price was recorded in 2004, and a more substantial one in 2003 (to $888 per ton), followed, in 2006, by an increase of 2%, to $906 per ton. Like that of the oil, the average import price of groundnuts at Rotterdam rose very considerably in 2007, by 40%, to $1,268 per ton for the year. The rate of increase stabilized towards the end of the year, steadying, on a monthly basis, at $1,700 per ton in December 2007 and in January 2008, dipping in February, then steadying again at $1,795 per ton (March–May), before rising to a peak of $1,850 per ton in July. Prices then began to decline, although an average Rotterdam price of $1,644 per ton was recorded for the whole of 2008. By December the price had fallen to $1,282 per ton, and the decline continued into 2009, to a low point of $1,108 per ton in March. The average import price then recovered, variably, but stabilized up at $1,1602 per ton for most of the second half of the year, but rising in December and the first two months of the following year—the average Rotterdam import price for groundnuts for the whole of 2009 was $1,160 per ton. After dipping for March–April, average monthly import prices for groundnuts tended upwards, giving an average price at Rotterdam for 2010 of $1,279 per ton. The average price for January–June 2011 was some $1,732 per ton, no monthly price falls having been recorded since March the previous year; the average monthly price for June was $1,923 per ton.

In 2010/11, according to USDA estimates, world output of groundnut oil was 5.2m. metric tons, 46% from East Asia (overwhelmingly China) and 4% from South-East Asia. The region contributed little to world exports (dominated by Argentina), but from the second half of the 2000s East Asia at least began to figure in the import of groundnut oil—the sub-region purchased a record 38% of world imports in 2010/11. The major producing countries world-wide in that year were estimated to be China (2.4m. tons) and India (1.4m. tons). The only other significant regional producer of groundnut oil, apart from China, was Myanmar, for which USDA calculated output at 173,000 tons in 2010/11, followed by Indonesia (21,000), Thailand (8,000 tons) and Viet Nam (7,000 tons).

Prices for groundnut oil have generally been more volatile than those for groundnuts in the 2000s. The average import price of groundnut oil at the port of Rotterdam, Netherlands, reached its lowest annual average in 2001, at US $680 per metric ton. In 2002 the average price rose slightly, to $687 per ton. From late 2002 the average import price of groundnut oil at Rotterdam rose precipitously, averaging $718 per ton, $771 per ton and $845 per ton, respectively, in the final three months of the year. In March 2003 an average price of $1,195 per ton was recorded, and in July this rose further, to $1,397 per ton. For the whole of 2003 an average price of $1,243 per ton was recorded. One factor influencing these sharp increases was anticipation of sharply reduced production of groundnuts in 2002/03 as a consequence of weather-related damage to crops in Argentina, India, Senegal and the USA. Additionally, from the final quarter of 2003 the price of groundnut oil was supported by higher demand for, and lower supply of, soybeans world-wide. In 2004 the average import price of groundnut oil at Rotterdam eased somewhat, to $1,161 per ton, and in 2005 it was $1,060 per ton. The average import price fell considerably, by about 9%, to $970 per ton in 2006. This decline was succeeded, in 2007, by a dramatic increase, of almost 40%, in the average import price at Rotterdam, to about $1,352 per ton. In the first half of 2008 and into the third quarter the average import price of groundnut oil continued to rise steadily, from $1,861 per ton in January, to $2,328 per ton in April–June, and $2,417 per ton in the third quarter. Over the year the average import price was $2,105 per ton—in common with other international commodity prices, groundnut oil prices had begun to slide steeply from October with the onset of the global financial crisis. The Rotterdam average import price then fell steadily each month up to September 2009, when it reached $1,120 per ton, although the rate of decline since May had slowed. The average price for October was a little higher, but then fell back to $1,116 per ton in November, before beginning a steadier recovery into the first quarter of the next year. The average import price for groundnut oil over the whole of 2009, therefore, was only $1,184 per ton, but this recovered to $1,404 per ton over 2010. Prices had fallen after reaching a peak in March 2010, but rose steadily after July, continuing the trend into 2011. The average import price for groundnut oil for January–July 2011 was $1,825 per ton, but the average monthly price in Rotterdam was $2,120 per ton by July.

MAIZE (Indian Corn, Mealies) (*Zea mays*)

Maize is one of the world's three principal cereal crops, with wheat and rice. Originally from America, maize has been dispersed to many parts of the world. The main varieties are dent maize (which has large, soft, flat grains) and flint maize (which has round, hard grains). Dent maize is the predominant type world-wide. Maize may be white or yellow (there is little nutritional difference), but the former is often preferred for human consumption. Maize is an annual crop, planted from seed, which matures within three to five months. It requires a warm climate and ample water supplies during the growing season. Genetically modified varieties of maize, with improved resistance against pests, are now being developed, particularly in the USA, and also in Argentina and the People's Republic of China. Ecological and consumer concerns are, however, placing in question the further commercialization of genetically modified varieties.

Maize is an important foodstuff in parts of Far East Asia, such as Indonesia, the Philippines and southern China, where the climate precludes the extensive cultivation of wheat. It tends, however, to be replaced by wheat in diets as disposable incomes rise; maize consumption per head has been declining in most of the developing countries. In some countries the grain is ground into a meal, mixed with water, and boiled to produce a gruel or porridge. In other areas it is made into (unleavened) corn bread or breakfast cereals. Maize is also the source of an oil, which is used in cooking.

The high starch content of maize makes it highly suitable as a compound feed ingredient, especially for pigs and poultry. Animal feed is the main use of maize in the USA, Europe and Japan, and large quantities are now also used for feed in developing countries in Far East Asia, Latin America and, to some extent, in North Africa. Maize also has a variety of industrial uses, including the preparation of ethyl alcohol (ethanol), which may be added to petrol to produce a blended motor fuel. In addition, maize is a source of dextrose and fructose, which can be used as artificial sweeteners, many times sweeter than sugar. The amounts used for these purposes depend, critically, on prices relative to petroleum, sugar and other potential raw materials. Maize cobs, previously discarded as a waste product, may be used as feedstock to produce various chemicals (such as acetic acid and formic acid).

Since 2000 global production has averaged about 670m. metric tons annually. From 2006 the world maize crop grew steadily, to reach a record 827m. tons in 2008, before falling back slightly to 819m. tons in 2009 (FAO figures). The USA is by far the largest producer, with annual harvests of, on average, about 270m. tons in 2000–07; the 2006 harvest of 270m. tons increasing to 331m. tons in 2007, before contracting to 307m. tons in 2008, and then rising to 333m. tons in 2009. (In years of drought or excessive heat, however, US output can fall significantly: in 1995, for example, the maize crop totalled only 188m. tons.) In the crop year 2010/11 US output accounted for 38% of global maize production, according to the US Department of Agriculture (USDA). China, whose maize output has been expanding rapidly, is the second largest producer—its harvest averaged about 133m. tons annually in 2000–08, reaching a height of 166m. tons in the final year of that series, but falling slightly in 2009 to 164m. tons (FAO figures). China's production, however, is mainly destined for the domestic market, whereas US output makes the country the world's largest exporter by far (a low 50% of global exports in 2010/11). Argentina (16% in 2010/11) and Brazil (12%) follow, with Ukraine emerging in a clear fourth place since 2008/09 (7% in 2010/11); some forecasts for 2011/12 even had Ukraine displacing Brazil as the world's third largest exporter.

The world's principal maize importer is Japan. However, the volume of Japanese imports remained stable through the 2000s, as the domestic livestock industry was rationalized to compete with imported meat. Japanese imports of maize totalled about 15.5m. metric tons in 2010/11. Rapidly growing livestock industries elsewhere in eastern Asia made the region the major world market for maize, although in terms of individual countries Mexico sometimes challenges the Republic of Korea (South Korea) for the title of second largest importer: each buying 8.0m. tons in 2010/11). Feed users in South Korea are willing to substitute other grains for maize, particularly feed wheat, when prices are attractive, so that maize imports are variable. The European Union (EU) together imported 7.3m. tons in 2010/11, but the next largest single importer had become Egypt, which purchased 5.4m. tons of maize from abroad in 2010/11.

East Asia accounts for about one-fifth of world maize production (21.0% in 2010/11, according to USDA) and South-East Asia up to a further one-20th (3.3% in 2010/11). The major producer in the region is China. Assisted by the expanded use of hybrid varieties, China's annual maize harvest increased by more than 50% in the 1980s, enabling the country to become, for a few seasons, a significant exporter of maize, until the rapid growth in domestic feed requirements drew level with supplies in the mid-1990s. New efforts to stimulate production, including higher support prices, resulted in a record crop of 128m. tons in 1996, and the accumulation of substantial maize stocks, which enabled supplies to be maintained without recourse to imports, following a smaller harvest in 1997. Output recovered to a new record level of 133m. tons in 1998, but it declined to 128m. tons in 1999 and to only 106m. tons in 2000. By 2004, at 130m. tons, production approached the record level reached in 1998. In 2005 that record was surpassed, with production recorded at about 139m. tons. Despite the growth in maize production, the rate of consumption has meant that the supply in China has remained tight. In order to meet domestic demand, China's Ministry of Agriculture set a target for maize production of more than 150m. tons by 2010, although this level was exceeded throughout the second half of the decade, peaking at 166m. tons in 2008/09, before falling back to 158m. tons in 2009/10. A new record of 173m. tons of harvested maize was reached in 2010/11, with USDA forecasting a small increase in the following year, to 178m. tons.

Production of Maize
('000 metric tons)

	2008	2009
World total	826,718	818,823
Far East	202,446	202,720
Oceania	609	629
Leading regional producers		
China, People's Repub.	166,032	164,108
Indonesia	16,324	17,630
Philippines	6,928	7,034
Thailand	4,249	4,616
Viet Nam	4,531	4,382
Other leading producers		
Argentina	22,017	13,121
Brazil	58,933	51,232
Canada	10,592	9,561
France	15,819	15,288
India	19,730	16,680
Mexico	24,320	20,143
South Africa	12,700	12,050
Ukraine	11,447	10,486
USA	307,142	333,011

Source: FAO.

In Indonesia maize is a secondary crop, usually planted in the dry season after the main rice crop. The high cost of seed and other inputs deters farmers from planting hybrid varieties, although the Government is encouraging the expansion of maize output to meet the country's rapidly growing requirements for animal feed, otherwise required to be covered by imports. Annual production rose steadily in the first half of the 2000s, from 5.9m. metric tons in 2000/01 to 7.2m. tons in 2004/05, before falling back the following year, and then resuming its rise, reaching 8.7m. tons in 2008/09; production declined to 6.9m. tons in 2009/10 and 6.8m. tons in 2010/11, but was expected to increase back to 8.1m. tons the following year. About one-half of the Philippine crop (which first rose above 5.0m. tons in the five years up to 2004/05) consists of white flint maize, used for human consumption. Feed use (for pigs and poultry) is increasing rapidly. Production rose in the second half of the decade, peaking at 7.3m. tons in 2007/08, but falling to 6.2m. tons by 2009/10, although 7.3m. tons were harvested in the next year and a similar if slightly less level forecast for 2011/12. Maize was formerly an important export crop in Thailand, but the areas under maize declined sharply in the late 1980s because of the greater profitability of other crops, such as sugar cane. By the mid-1990s Thailand had to resort to imports in most years to satisfy its domestic feed requirements. Production fluctuated around 4.0m. tons annually in the 2000s, recording 4.0m. tons in 2010/11—compared with 5.0m. tons in Viet Nam, which since 2006/07 had exceeded Thailand's production every year but 2008/09.

Export prices of maize are mainly influenced by the level of supplies in the USA, and the intensity of competition between the exporting countries. Record quotations were achieved in April 1996, when the price of US No. 2 Yellow Corn (f.o.b. Gulf ports) reached US $210 per metric ton. The quotation subsequently declined, however. In each of the five years in 2000–04 an increase in the quotation was recorded, the average price rising to $88.4 per ton in 2000, $89.6 per ton in 2001, $99.2 per ton in 2002, $105.2 per ton in 2003 and $111.7 per ton in 2004. In 2005, however, the average export price declined to $98.5 per ton. The price rose substantially in 2006, to $122.1 per ton, not least reflecting the impact of increasing demand for ethanol. Prices continued to increase in 2007, to $162.7 per metric ton, rising to $223.1 in 2008, as global stocks fell to a 24-year low at the end of the 2007/08 crop year, despite a 9.5% increase in global production and a 24% increase in US output. The global recession that had gained momentum by the end of 2008 restrained prices in 2009, so that the average US No. 2 Yellow Corn price for the year fell to $165.5. In 2010 the price rose to an annual average of $185.9 per ton, although this relatively modest increase disguises the surge in the price in the last quarter of the year and into 2011. The average for the first seven months of 2011 was $298.1, as food commodity prices soared world-wide. The average monthly price in June was $310.6 per ton and in July $300.8 per ton, which was higher, atypically, than the price for the lower protein class of wheat (Soft Red Winter), prompting some Asian countries to substitute it for maize as feed. The price inversion was caused by restricted US maize supplies being accompanied by high domestic demand in the world's leading producer, while wheat exports from the Black Sea area had recovered. High corn prices were likely to encourage further planting in Argentina and Brazil for 2011/12. Maize and grain prices were also generally projected to increase in line with the expanding market for ethanol, which is closely linked to the price of petroleum. New energy legislation in 2007, in both the EU and the USA, stipulated the greater use of biofuels for motor vehicles. According to the World Bank, the share of global maize production used for ethanol increased from 2.5% in 2000 to 11.0% in 2007, and the trend remained evident thereafter. However, maize-based ethanol production remained a heavily subsidized industry in the USA, and it remained a costly and relatively inefficient substitute for its sugar-based equivalent (see below). Critics remained sceptical regarding the long-term prospects for the industry, especially as sugar-based ethanol was already being produced more cheaply in Latin America.

NICKEL

Nickel is a silvery, malleable metal occurring in various types of ores, the most important being sulphide ores and laterite ores. Sulphide ores are generally mined by underground methods, while laterites are usually mined by open-cast methods. Nickel in sulphide ores is often found in conjunction with copper, cobalt and platinum-group metals; in laterites it is often found with iron, chromium and cobalt. The sulphide ore is subjected to crushing and grinding, with final treatment by the flotation method. The resulting concentrate is roasted and smelted in furnaces to remove the bulk of the sulphur, leaving a matte of nickel and copper. The nickel and copper can then be separated from each other by a variety of processes and sent to an electrolytic refinery. The primary product of processing laterites is ferronickel; a few ferronickel operations also produce limited amounts of matte by the deliberate addition of pyrite or sulphur to the ore at the drying stage. Nickel production is an energy-intensive operation, and the cost of energy to the industry has risen steeply in recent years. Since the late 1990s several laterite nickel producers have found that some ores (notably, those from Western Australia and Goro, New Caledonia) are more suitable for processing through high-pressure acid leaching. The world's land-based reserves of nickel ore in 2010 were estimated by the US Geological Survey (USGS) at 76m. metric tons on an elemental basis, of which about 40% were in sulphide deposits and 60% in laterite ores. The distinction is significant, as sulphide ores are cheaper to process. According to USGS estimates, the largest proportion of nickel reserves is in Australia (32% of the world total), followed by Brazil (11%), New Caledonia (9%), Russia (8%), Cuba (7%), Indonesia (5%), Canada (5%) and South Africa (5%). In 2008 Asia accounted for 54% of nickel demand, the People's Republic of China alone accounting for 25% (compared with 4% 10 years earlier).

Nickel is used in a wide range of alloys, where it imparts corrosion resistance and high-temperature strength. Its most important use is in steel production, and the majority of high-tensile steels contain nickel. On a world-wide basis, the stainless steel industry accounts for about 65% of nickel consumption. Nickel continues to be a significant constituent of much military equipment. Alloys containing a high proportion of nickel are used in power and chemical plants. The metal also has high-temperature applications, such as gas turbines, and rocket engines for the aerospace industry.

Extensive deposits of ferromanganese nodules—also containing nickel, copper and cobalt—are known to exist on the floor of the world's oceans. A conservative estimate assesses world nodule reserves at 290m. metric tons of nickel, 240m. tons of cobalt and 6,000m. tons of manganese. However, quite apart from the question of rights of recovery tortuously negotiated at the UN Conference on the Law of the Sea, experts believe that the extraction of metals from the nodules is unlikely to be commercially practicable for many years.

Until 2005 the nickel industry was dominated in Western countries by the four companies that, historically, were the largest producers—International Nickel (Inco), Falconbridge (both of Canada), Western Mining (of Australia) and the French-controlled Société Le Nickel (SLN). In recent years, however, a series of acquisitions and mergers has realigned somewhat the distribution of the corporate ownership of nickel production. In 2005 BHP Billiton PLC of the United Kingdom took control of Western Mining. BHP Billiton subsequently established Nickel West to manage the nickel assets acquired in the takeover. In 2006 Xstrata PLC, a Swiss-based mining group, took over Falconbridge—subsequently renamed Xstrata Nickel—and in 2007 Brazil's Companhia Vale do Rio Doce (CVRD) completed its acquisition of Inco (now Vale Inco), which had traditionally met almost one-third of the major industrial countries' nickel requirements. In 2006 Norilsk Nickel of Russia was the world's single largest producer, followed by what became Vale Inco and, in third position, BHP Billiton. In 2007 Norilsk Nickel bought the nickel interests of LionOre of Canada, acquiring a number of new mines and, for example, becoming the second largest nickel producer in Australia. In 2008 PT Aneka Tambang (PT Antam) of Indonesia displaced BHP Billiton as the world's third largest nickel-producing company, owing to its satisfaction of Chinese demand.

The major nickel-producing countries in the Asia-Pacific region are Indonesia, the Philippines, Australia and the French Pacific territory of New Caledonia. In 2010, according to USGS estimates, Indonesia was the world's second largest mined nickel producer for a second successive year (15% of the world total). Russia, accounting for 17% of world production, remained the leading nickel miner. Indonesia's main nickel-producing companies are government-controlled PT Antam and PT International Nickel Indonesia (PT Inco), a Vale Inco subsidiary. The main nickel centres are on Sulawesi (Celebes), at Pomalaa in South-East Sulawesi province and at Soroako in South Sulawesi province, although development also took place in the Maluku (Moluccas) archipelago in the 2000s, on and around the large island of Halmahera in North Maluku, where resources were estimated to amount to 155m. metric tons, at a grade of 1.45%. Indonesian mine output rose, dramatically, from about 140,000 tons in 2006 to 229,000 tons in 2007. Although production fell back to 192,600 tons in 2008, it rose again in 2009, to 202,800 tons, and in 2010, to an estimated 232,000 tons; the country remained by far the largest nickel producer in the Asia-Pacific region.

Mined nickel output by the Philippines increased rapidly as new sources came into production from 2005: up by 143% in 2006, 41% in 2007, 88% in 2008, 70% in 2009 and an estimated 13% in 2010, to reach some 156,000 metric tons. In 2009, therefore, the Philippines matched Canada as the world's fourth largest producer of mined nickel, while in 2010 both countries exceeded Australia, and the Philippines edged ahead of Canada, to become the world's third largest and Asia-Pacific's second largest mine producer. Output and sales abroad, in particular to China, continued to increase into 2011. In 2010 the USGS put the nickel reserves of the Philippines at an estimated 1.1m. tons (metal content).

In 2010 Australia was the world's fifth largest producer of the mined metal, after Russia, Indonesia, the Philippines and Canada. The country was the world's second largest producer in 2004. Australia's ore production began to fall in late 2008, as smaller mines in particular were closed or put into 'care and maintenance', reflecting world economic conditions; mined output (ores and concentrates) therefore fell from a 2008 peak of 199,200 metric tons (12% of world output) to an estimated 139,000 tons by 2010 (9%). Almost all nickel projects are in the state of Western Australia, although BHP Billiton transports some ore to its nickel/cobalt refinery at Yabulu, Queensland. Inflationary pressures in Australia, together with shortages of both material and skilled workers, caused the capital costs of projects to increase, and fears of cheaper foreign competition were particularly realized by the development of Canada's Voisey's Bay project. (Due to be completed by 2018, it began producing concentrates in 2005, and by 2008 had helped put Canadian production up to 16% of world output, just behind Russia's 17%—the Canadian share fell back, but was still an estimated 10% in 2010.) According to estimates by the Australian Bureau of Agricultural and Resource Economics, the value of Australia's exports of nickel ores and concentrates and of intermediate products of nickel increased by some 160%, to $A9,024m., in the year ending June 2007, representing 6.5% of the total value of merchandise exports (compared with 2.7% in 2005/06).

New Caledonia, which has the unique status of a collectivité *sui generis* within the French Republic, possesses the world's largest identified deposits of nickel-bearing laterite, accounting for some 25% of global reserves. In 2010 New Caledonia was estimated to be the world's sixth largest producer of nickel in terms of mine output, accounting for 9% of the global total (output, at a record 138,000 metric tons, was up almost one-half as much again on the previous year, as a result of the entry into production of the new Goro mine). Production had also been affected by cyclone damage and then by decreasing world demand during economic recession in 2008–09. The territory's dominant production company is SLN, 60% of which belongs to the French government-controlled mining conglomerate Eramet, 30% to Société Territoriale Calédonienne de Participation Industrielle (STCPI—representing the interests of the three provinces of New Caledonia) and 10% to Nishin Steel of Japan. The company exploits deposits of nickel-bearing ores at five mining centres, all on La Grande Terre, New Caledonia's main island. Mining at a sixth SLN site—the Etoile du Nord deposit, also on La Grande Terre—has been contracted to an independent company, Société Minière Georges Montagnat. Ore from these mines is sent for processing in the company's smelter at Doniambo, near Nouméa, in the south of the island. Eramet is the world's leading company producing ferronickel (in 2008 New Caledonia itself was the world's second largest producer of ferronickel after Japan), and SLN's Doniambo smelter is the largest ferronickel plant in the world, with annual production capacity (as of mid-2009) of 60,000 tons.

Products from the Doniambo plant are destined for export, while much of the ore production of the other mining companies on New Caledonia tends to go abroad for smelting—in 2007 40% of foreign sales of ore went to Japan, 31% to China and 29% to Australia. Ferronickel exports that year went mainly to the European Union (EU—33%), Taiwan (24%) and Japan (24%), and nickel matte exports to France. Foreign sales of ferronickel, nickel matte and nickel ore contribute almost the entirety of New Caledonia's export earnings—91.0% of the total in 2009 (58% of those export sales are accounted for by ferronickel). During the late 1990s more than one-half of the nickel ore from the country's mines was exported without further processing, and there has been strong local support for proposals to construct additional smelting facilities. However, New Caledonia's heavy dependence on the nickel industry has resulted in periods of economic recession, and since the mid-1980s mining operations have been intermittently overshadowed by political and social unrest. (New Caledonia's overall production of nickel ore decreased by 8.0% in 2006, as a consequence of labour unrest at two of the SLN mining sites and a general strike at the end of the year.) During the 1980s and 1990s a major issue in discussions concerning the political future of New Caledonia was the extent of participation by the indigenous Melanesian people (Kanaks) in the territory's development, including in its major industry. The Société Minière du Sud-Pacifique (SMSP), controlled by Kanak interests, is the most important of the independent nickel-mining companies in New Caledonia. During negotiations regarding increased autonomy for the territory local representatives sought an expansion of indigenous involvement in the nickel sector. Political and financial negotiations in the late 1990s, into 2000, had a profound effect on the structure of New Caledonia's nickel industry, resulting in both the acquisition of the Koniambo site in the Kanak-dominated north by SMSP (which planned to develop the deposits and build a smelter in a venture with Falconbridge of Canada) and the formation of the local STCPI stake in SLN. Despite some delays and doubts about Falconbridge's commitment to the Koniambo project, as well as various legal challenges, preparation work began in 2005, with construction beginning on the mine works and the smelter in February 2007, the same year in which Xstrata PLC of Switzerland acquired the former Falconbridge assets in New Caledonia. The project was scheduled to open in 2011 and to reach full capacity by 2013. Meanwhile, another major development project got under way at Goro, in the south of the main island, in the early 2000s. The majority shareholder in the Goro project, which was to exploit nickel-cobalt deposits estimated at some 195m. metric tons of ore, averaging 1.48% nickel, using new pressure acid leaching and solvent extraction technologies, was Inco (Vale Inco from 2006). Local activism, particularly concerned about the environmental and social impacts, again involved delay, legal manoeuvres and rising capital costs. The opening of the development was expected during 2009, although it was delayed by a serious industrial accident involving a spill of sulphuric acid, but the first nickel was still actually produced in 2010. The Goro facility was expected to become one of the world's main nickel laterite mines by the time it reached full production capacity of 60,000 tons of ore per year in 2013. In 2006 SMSP established a joint venture for the mining and refining of nickel with (South Korean) Pohang Iron & Steel Co (POSCO); the latter was to invest US $352m. in the construction of a nickel refinery with a capacity of 30,000 metric tons in the Gwabgyangme free economic zone. Construction was scheduled to begin in 2008. The third major nickel company in New Caledonia has been the Société des Mines de la Tontouta (SMT).

Production of Nickel Ore
(nickel content, '000 metric tons)

	2008	2009
World total*	1,560	1,400
Far East*	345	420
Oceania	302	258
Leading regional producers		
Australia	199	165
China, People's Repub.*	72	79
Indonesia	193	203
New Caledonia	103	93
Philippines	81	137
Other leading producers		
Brazil	67	67†
Canada	260	137
Colombia	77	72
Cuba	67	65*
Russia	267	262

2010 (nickel content, 000 metric tons)*: *Leading regional producers:*Australia 139; China, People's Repub. 77; Indonesia 232; New Caledonia 138; Philippines 156. *Other leading producers:* Canada 155; Colombia 70; Russia 265; World total (incl. others) 1,550.

* Estimated or provisional figure(s). World and Far East totals are rounded.

† Preliminary figure.

Source: US Geological Survey.

In 2009 China's steel industry overtook that of the EU as the largest consumer of nickel. Chinese consumption had increased dramatically since the late 1990s, rising from 66,800 metric tons in 2000 to 472,000 tons by 2009. According to the USGS, the EU used 174,000 tons in 2009 and Japan 79,900 tons, putting it in third place internationally; the International Nickel Study Group had the EU accounting for 24% of primary nickel usage in that year. In 2005 Chinese consumption of nickel had overtaken that of Japan for the first time (Chinese consumption had outstripped that of the USA in 2003). The Chinese stainless steel industry, the output of which increased dramatically in 1999–2005, accounts for about 46% of the country's primary nickel demand. China remained unchallenged as the world's leading consumer of nickel in 2010. The Republic of Korea (South Korea) and Taiwan, regionally, and the countries of the former USSR and the USA are also important consumers; of the EU countries, Germany is especially important.

In April 1979 dealing in nickel began on the London Metal Exchange (LME), despite opposition from the major producers, who feared that speculative free-market trading would increase volatility in prices. These fears have proved to be justified, and since the late 1970s nickel-producers have been operating in a highly cyclical trading environment, with wide and unpredictable fluctuations on the free market. However, the amount of nickel traded in this way is still relatively small. Producers typically obtain about 20 US cents per lb more for nickel that they supply than for metal that is traded on the LME. This arrangement, however, has been affected since 1991 by significant sales of nickel cathodes by Russia's Norilsk Nickel, which is the world's largest producer of nickel.

In 2003 the average monthly price of nickel traded on the LME ranged between US $7,910 per metric ton (April) and $14,613 per ton (December). Daily prices ranged between $7,210 and $16,670 per ton. For the whole of 2003 the average 'spot' price of nickel in London was $9,640 per ton, an increase of about 42% on the average price recorded in 2002. At 31 December 2003 the LME's holdings of nickel had risen to 24,072 tons. In 2004 the average price of nickel traded on the Exchange rose by about 44%, to $13,852 per ton. Daily prices ranged between $10,530 and $17,770 per ton in 2004. By the end of 2004 stocks of nickel held by the LME had declined to 20,898 tons. In 2005 the price of nickel traded on the LME rose by about 6.4%, to an average of $14,733 per ton. During 2005 the London price of nickel ranged between $11,500 and $17,750 per ton. By the end of December stocks of nickel held by the Exchange had risen to 36,042 tons, compared with only 7,032 tons at the end of June. In 2006 the average price of nickel increased very substantially, by 65%, to an average of $24,287 per ton. During that year monthly prices ranged between $13,505 and $35,455 per ton. This price increase was supported by a corresponding decline in stocks of nickel, from 37,152 tons in January to 6,594 tons in December. The sharp increase in the price of nickel traded on the LME was sustained in the first five months of 2007, when the average monthly price rose by 42%, from $36,111 per ton in January, to a record level of $52,179 per ton in May. In June, however, the average monthly price of nickel declined to $41,719 per ton, at which time inventories reached 8,856 tons—an extremely low level relative to historical trends, but equivalent to an 11.9% increase on stocks the previous month. LME holdings continued to accumulate during the remaining months of 2007, owing to slackening demand from steel manufacturers who decided to reduce purchases and allow prices to stabilize. Nickel prices, unlike the prices of most other commodities, which peaked in the second or third quarter of 2008, generally declined throughout that year, reaching a low of $9,678 per ton in December. Prices began to recover during 2009, with the average LME cash price for nickel again touching $20,000 per ton in August. Stocks grew during the period of falling prices in 2008 and, from the end of the year particularly, given the world-wide economic recession, reaching new heights: LME holdings had reached 78,000 tons by the beginning of 2009 and first exceeded 100,000 tons in March, generally remaining at that level thereafter. LME stocks were above 120,000 tons more than 18 months later, in October 2010, but were under pressure from June 2011, soon falling below the 100,000-ton level (stocks were just above 99,000 tons in the first week of September). According to the World Bank, citing the LME settlement price (nickel cathodes, minimum 99.8% purity), the average price for 2007 was US $37,230 per ton, falling to $21,111 per ton for 2008 (owing to the financial crisis in the second half of the year and the onset of global recession) and only $14,655 per ton in 2009 (a firm rebound, given the $10,471 per ton price in the first quarter of 2009). There was a strong recovery in prices through 2009 and into the following year. Prices slackened from June 2010, but surged up strongly towards the end of the year, giving an annual average of $21,809 per ton and, on the strength of the same continuing momentum, an average price of $25,360 per ton in January–July 2011. Monthly nickel prices had peaked at $28,252 per ton in February, declining slowly thereafter until June; the price briefly rose in July, but by August it was $21,845 per ton, as doubts about steel demand in an uncertain global economic situation, as well as the prospect of a nickel production surplus, exerted downward pressure.

OIL PALM (*Elaeis guineensis*)

This tree, which is native to West Africa, is widely cultivated, mainly on plantations, in the Far East and Australasia. The palm fruit is a red colour, about the size of a big plum, and grows in large clusters that can contain hundreds of fruit and usually weigh 40–50 kg. The entire fruit is of use commercially; palm oil is made from its pulp, and palm kernel oil from the seed. Palm oil is a versatile product, and, because of its very low acid content (4%–5%), is almost all used in food. It is used in margarine and other edible fats; as a 'shortener' for pastry and biscuits; as an ingredient in ice cream and in chocolate; and in the manufacture of soaps and detergents. Palm kernel oil, which is similar to coconut oil, is also used for making soaps and fats. The sap from the stems of the tree is used to make palm wine, an intoxicating beverage. Most processing is done near where the oil palms are harvested, so the production figures cited tend to be for palm oil and for palm kernels, the latter giving an indication of the number of fruit harvested—for every 100 kg of palm fruit bunches, 22 kg of palm oil and 1.6 kg of palm kernel oil can typically be produced.

Palm oil can be produced virtually throughout the year once the palms have reached oil-bearing age, which takes about five years. The palms continue to bear oil for 30 years or more and the yield far exceeds that of any other oil plant, with 1 ha of oil palms producing as much oil as 6 ha of groundnuts or 10–12 ha of soybeans. However, it is an intensive crop, needing considerable investment and skilled labour.

During the 1980s palm oil accounted for more than 15% of world production of vegetable oils (second only to soybean oil), owing mainly to a substantial expansion in Malaysian output. Largely driven by high levels of demand in Asia, especially in the People's Republic of China, palm oil production increased considerably, to account for almost one-third of world vegetable oils (33% in 2010/11, according to the US Department of Agriculture—USDA, compared with 28% soybean oil and 16% rapeseed oil). In world markets for vegetable oils, the dominance of palm oil was even more marked: in 2010/11 palm oil accounted for 61% of all exports of vegetable oils globally. In that year the equivalent of 77% of palm oil production world-wide entered international markets. The main producers of palm oil are, overwhelmingly, Indonesia and Malaysia, which accounted, respectively, for almost 50% and for 38% of world output in 2010/11, followed by Thailand (3%) and Nigeria (2%). Indonesia replaced Malaysia as the world's leading individual producer in 2005/06, while in the following year Thailand definitively replaced Nigeria in third place; Columbia was forecast to displace Nigeria as the world's fourth largest producer in 2011/12. Indonesia and Malaysia likewise dominate export markets, with Papua New Guinea and Benin being in distant third and fourth places. The principal consumers are India (15% of world domestic consumption in 2010/11) and Indonesia (13%), the latter surpassing China (13%) for the first time in that year, followed by the countries of the European Union (EU), Malaysia, Pakistan, Thailand, Nigeria and Bangladesh.

In 2009, according to FAO, world output of palm fruit totalled 210.3m. metric tons and of palm oil 45.1m. tons. According to USDA, steadily increasing palm oil production had taken world output to 44.0m. tons in 2008/09, 45.9m. tons in 2009/10 and an estimated 47.7m. tons in 2010/11, meaning that world production had about doubled in 10 years; a further rise was forecast for 2011/12, to 50.3m. tons. South-East Asia was the main producing area. In 2010/11 the region produced 43.0m. tons of palm oil, or 90% of the global total. Oceania produced a further 0.5m. tons of palm oil, or 1% of the world's total.

Traditionally, the leading producer and exporter of palm oil is Malaysia, although from 2005/06 the country found its output of palm oil exceeded by that of Indonesia. However, Malaysia remained the principal exporter until 2008/09. The country easily remained the world's second largest producer and exporter of palm oil in 2009/10 and 2010/11, with output in the latter year at 37.8% of the global total and exports at 42.5%. More than four-fifths of the country's production is exported (86% in 2010/11), and in 2009 earnings from palm oil exports represented 6.6% of Malaysia's total export revenue. The most important markets for Malaysian palm oil are India, the EU, the USA, Japan and Pakistan. According to USDA, Malaysian production of palm oil exceeded 15.0m. metric tons from the mid-2000s, rising 15% to 17.6m. tons in 2007/08, then falling to 17.3m. tons, before increasing again in 2009/10, to a new record of 17.8m. tons, and in 2010/11, to 18.0m. tons. A further production increase was forecast for 2011/12. In May 2000 a new statutory body, the Malaysian Palm Oil Board (absorbing the Palm Oil Registration and Licensing Authority—PORLA, through which the Malaysian Government had encouraged the industry since 1977), became operational.

In Indonesia, which had become the world's largest producer and exporter of palm oil by the end of the first decade of the 21st century, the area under oil palm expanded rapidly into the 2000s. While in 1990 approximately 715,000 ha were harvested, in 2009 FAO estimated that about 5.0m. ha were harvested. In the early 1990s, when about 100,000–150,000 ha per year were being brought under oil palm cultivation, production of palm oil was forecast to reach 4.9m. metric tons annually by 2000. In the event, this target was achieved in 1996. Output increased steadily thereafter, according to USDA, doubling between 2000/01 and 2006/07, with 16.6m. tons in the latter year. The country produced 18.0m. tons of palm oil in 2007/08, 20.5m. tons in 2008/09, 22.0m. tons in 2009/10 and 23.6m. tons in 2010/11, with a further increase forecast for the following year. In 2010/11 Indonesia accounted for almost one-half of world production (the country was expected to exceed one-half of production in 2011/12) and 47.1% of world exports. In 2010 Indonesia derived 8.5% of its total export revenue from sales of palm oil and its fraction.

From the 1990s oil palm cultivation was encouraged in Papua New Guinea. According to FAO, by 2008 and 2009 Papua New Guinea's output of palm oil was almost triple the level of production in 1990. USDA figures put production as low as 316,000 metric tons in 2002/03, but then rising steadily to some 500,000 tons in 2010/11, with a further increase expected in 2011/12. Most production was exported, making the country one of the world's most important exporters (the third largest, with a 1.4% share of global export markets. Oil palm cultivation is long established in neighbouring Solomon Islands, but at less than one-10th the level in Papua New Guinea (an estimated 190,000 tons in 2009, according to FAO). Thailand is the region's largest producer-exporter after Papua New Guinea and, in production terms, is third in the world (1.3m. tons in 2010/11). The Philippines is also a minor producer, but only occasionally an exporter, like China

Production of Palm Fruit
('000 metric tons)

	2008	2009
World total	207,837	210,327
Far East	178,405	180,190
Oceania	1,870	1,920
Leading regional producers		
China, People's Repub.*	668	670
Indonesia*	85,000	86,000
Malaysia*	83,000	84,842
Papua New Guinea*	1,700	1,730
Thailand	9,271	8,162
Other leading producers		
Colombia*	3,200	3,200
Ecuador*	2,100	2,100
Ghana	1,897	2,104
Nigeria*	8,500	8,500

* FAO estimates.

Source: FAO.

Production of Palm Oil
('000 metric tons)

	2008	2009
World total	43,428	45,084
Far East	38,251	39,745
Oceania	504	510
Leading regional producers		
China, People's Repub.*	225	230
Indonesia†	18,910	20,550
Malaysia	17,734	17,565
Papua New Guinea†	465	470
Thailand†	1,300	1,310
Other leading producers		
Colombia†	778	802
Côte d'Ivoire†	290	325
Ecuador*	309	321
Honduras†	273	290
Nigeria*	1,330	1,380

* FAO estimates.
† Unofficial figures.

Source: FAO.

Internationally, palm oil is faced with sustained competition from the other major edible lauric oils—soybean, rapeseed and sunflower oils—and these markets are subject to a complex and changing interaction of production, stocks and trade. Two main distinguishing features have traditionally characterized palm oil relative to its competitors: a very high trade-to-production ratio—far greater than that of comparable crops; and the geographical concentration of both production and trade, for both of which Indonesia and Malaysia account for approximately 90%. Palm oil has enjoyed a long-term price advantage over its principal competitor, soybean oil, that has enabled it to achieve a very high degree of market penetration. It was only from the end of the 20th century—since, roughly, 1999—that the prices recorded for palm oil consistently exceeded the long-term trend, reflecting new demand for feedstocks for biodiesel production. Even so, palm oil is the lowest-priced vegetable oil and it is, in the opinion of many market analysts, the most competitive biodiesel feedstock. However, its utilization for this purpose has remained very low compared, in particular, with rapeseed oil, which enjoys a high level of subsidization in the member states of the EU, where it is the principal biodiesel feedstock. The average import price (c.i.f. North West Europe) of Malaysian crude palm oil (5% bulk) recovered from a 2000s low in 2001 until 2004, but then declined by about one-10th in 2005, to US $422.1 per metric ton, before recovering to $478.3 per ton in 2006. The average annual price then almost doubled in two years, reaching $780 per ton in 2007 and $948 per ton in 2008. The average monthly price of palm oil rose above $800 per ton in June 2007 (it had been rising steadily since September 2006), and thereafter increased in each subsequent month of 2007, until November, with an average only slightly down in December, at $950 per ton. The upward trend continued until March 2008, when the average monthly price peaked at $1,249 per ton. The palm oil import price then remained fairly stable until June but, as the financial crisis and fears of world-wide recession made their impact on commodities, the price then sank to as low as $488 per ton by November (a fall of 60% since June). There was a slow recovery in the price until May 2009, but even thereafter the prices did not fall back to the level of the first quarter, giving an average palm oil import price over the year of $683 per ton. Steadily rising prices from September 2009 until March 2010, and generally stable thereafter, meant that the average price for 2010 was $901 per ton. The average price in January–July 2011 was $1,183 per ton, the rising trend since June 2010 peaking in February 2011 at $1,292 per ton over the month, and falling to $1,088 per ton in July.

PETROLEUM

Crude oils, from which petroleum fuel is derived, consist essentially of a wide range of hydrocarbon molecules which are separated by distillation in the refining process. Refined oil is treated in different ways to make the different varieties of fuel. More than four-fifths of total world oil supplies are used as fuel for the production of energy in the form of power or heating.

Petroleum, together with its associated mineral fuel, natural gas, is extracted both from onshore and offshore wells in many areas of the world. World-wide, demand for this commodity totalled an estimated 87.4m. barrels per day (b/d) in 2010, a rise of about 3.1% compared with the previous year. The world's 'published proven' reserves of petroleum and natural gas liquids at 31 December 2010 were estimated to total 188,788m. metric tons, equivalent to about 1,383,207m. barrels (1 metric ton is equivalent to approximately 7.3 barrels, each of 42 US gallons or 34.97 imperial gallons, i.e. 159 litres). The dominant producing region is the Middle East, whose proven reserves in December 2010 accounted for 53.9% of known world deposits of crude petroleum and natural gas liquids. The Middle East accounted for 30.3% of estimated world output in 2010. The combined proven reserves of Australia, Brunei, the People's Republic of China, Indonesia, Malaysia, Thailand and Viet Nam amounted to 4,606m. tons (2.4% of the world total) at the end of 2010, in which year those countries accounted for 8.8% of estimated world production.

From storage tanks at the oilfield wellhead, crude petroleum is conveyed, frequently by pumping for long distances through large pipelines, to coastal depots where it is either treated in a refinery or delivered into bulk storage tanks for subsequent shipment for refining overseas. In addition to pipeline transportation of crude petroleum and refined products, natural (petroleum) gas is, in some areas, also transported through networks of pipelines. Crude petroleum varies considerably in colour and viscosity, and these variations are a determinant both of price and of end-use after refining.

In the refining process, crude petroleum is heated until vaporized. The vapours are then separately condensed, according to their molecular properties, passed through airless steel tubes and pumped into the lower section of a high, cylindrical tower, as a hot mixture of vapours and liquid. The heavy unvaporized liquid flows out at the base of the tower as a 'residue' from which is obtained heavy fuel and bitumen. The vapours passing upwards then undergo a series of condensation processes that produce 'distillates', which form the basis of the various petroleum products.

The most important of these products is fuel oil, composed of heavy distillates and residues, which is used to produce heating and power for industrial purposes. Products in the kerosene group have a wide number of applications, ranging from heating fuels to the powering of aviation gas turbine engines. Gasoline (petrol) products fuel internal combustion engines (used mainly in road motor vehicles), and naphtha, a gasoline distillate, is a commercial solvent that can also be processed as a feedstock. Propane and butane, the main liquefied petroleum gases, have a wide range of industrial applications and are also used for domestic heating and cooking.

Indonesia, China and Malaysia are the major petroleum exporters in the Far East and Australasia, and Indonesia is a leading exporter of liquefied natural gas (LNG). China and Japan are, respectively, the world's second and third largest consumers of petroleum—Chinese consumption overtook that of Japan for the first time in 2002. Australia, the Republic of Korea, Singapore, Taiwan and Thailand are also major consumers of petroleum.

Within the region generally, there has been a rising level of exploration activity by international petroleum companies in recent years. Joint ventures have increasingly been sought by countries committed to policies of state control and central economic planning. These countries include not only China and Viet Nam, but also Myanmar and Cambodia.

Production of Crude Petroleum
('000 metric tons, including natural gas liquids)

	2009	2010
World total	3,831,017	3,913,652
Far East and Oceania*	331,132	346,936
Leading regional producers		
Australia	21,899	23,843
Brunei	8,191	8,394
China, People's Repub.	189,490	203,000
Indonesia	47,936	47,801
Malaysia	33,129	32,118
Thailand	13,690	13,820
Viet Nam	16,797	17,960
Other leading producers		
Algeria	77,922	77,667
Angola	87,440	90,742
Brazil	100,355	105,716
Canada	156,116	162,776
India	35,399	38,880
Iran	201,481	203,325
Iraq	119,775	120,445
Kazakhstan	78,214	81,647
Kuwait	121,688	122,465
Libya	77,084	77,461
Mexico	147,471	146,280
Nigeria	99,143	115,209
Norway	108,796	98,562
Qatar	57,868	65,685
Russia	494,247	505,130
Saudi Arabia	464,720	467,772
United Arab Emirates	126,306	130,788
United Kingdom	68,198	62,973
USA	328,648	339,106
Venezuela	124,822	126,581

* Figures are the sums of output by the leading regional producers only.

Source: BP, *Statistical Review of World Energy 2011*.

Australia's proven reserves of petroleum were estimated at 446m. metric tons at 31 December 2010. Production in that year was estimated to have totalled 23.8m. tons, compared with peak output of 35.3m. tons in 2000. Exploration activity has increased in recent years—boosted, notably, by tax concessions applied by the Government to frontier blocks opened in 2004–08—as there is growing concern at the rising insufficiency of domestic supply as oilfields mature and demand rises. According to government data, Australia's dependency on imported petroleum was expected to reach about 80% by around 2010. It was hoped, however, that new projects (mainly undertaken by the domestic companies Woodside, Santos and BHP Billiton), currently in their early stages of operation or planned for the near future, would go some way towards compensating for the loss of output from mature fields. A more distant prospect is the exploitation of the country's reserves of shale oil, whose feasibility has been explored sporadically. According to the US Geological Survey (USGS), in 2009 crude petroleum and its refined products remained Australia's main imported mineral and fuel commodity. Imports of crude petroleum in 2010 totalled US $14,576m. (representing 7.7% of total imports and 56.2% of total imports of mineral fuels). According to the Energy Information Administration (EIA) of the US Department of Energy, of the 954,000 b/d of crude oil that Australia consumed in 2009, 40% was imported. Analysts have commented that Australia's dependence on petroleum imports will continue to rise as consumption increases and domestic production declines.

Malaysia's proven reserves of petroleum totalled 759m. metric tons at the end of 2010. Production, which has remained fairly steady since 1998, was estimated to have amounted to 32.1m. tons in 2010, compared with 33.1m. tons in 2009. Over half of Malaysia's oil production comes from the Tapis field in the Malay Basin off shore. Production in Malaysia peaked in 2004 at 862,000 b/d. All petroleum production and exploration activities fall under the control of the state oil and gas operator Petronas. The participation of foreign and private companies is only possible via production-sharing contract (PSC) with Petronas. Virtually all domestic output is from offshore oilfields, and since 2002 exploration by Petronas and PSC signatories has been focused mainly on deep-water fields off shore. The entry into production of seven new fields in 2008 raised the number of producing oilfields in the country to 68. In early 2009 Brunei and Malaysia were reported to have resolved a territorial dispute that had impeded the exploration of petroleum reserves off Borneo since 2003. Petronas and the Government of Brunei agreed in September 2010 to develop two blocks off the coast of Borneo. A production-sharing agreement lasting for 40 years for Block CA1 was signed, while an agreement on Block CA2 was also expected to be concluded. Malaysia consumes most of its production. Exports in 2009 amounted to 157,000 b/d, according to the EIA. However, consumption continues to rise steadily while production declines. Before the country becomes a net importer of petroleum, the Government is committed to enhancing production at existing fields and developing new fields off the coast of Sarawak and Sabah. The Gumusat/Kapat project, located off shore of Sabah, was expected to be producing 150,000 b/d by 2012. According to Oil and Gas Journal, Malaysia's refining capacity at the country's six facilities was some 515,000 b/d at January 2010—sufficient to meet most domestic demand for refined products. Most domestic output is exported to Japan, Thailand, the Republic of Korea and Singapore, with net foreign sales amounting to some 157,000 b/d in 2009.

Thailand's oil reserves have been boosted by small new discoveries off shore, in the Gulf of Thailand, in recent years, and were estimated at 52m. metric tons in December 2010. The country's consumption rose steadily in 2001–05, despite greater use of natural gas for electricity generation and an ethanol-substitution programme for motor fuel. Oil consumption subsequently declined in each year in 2006–08. However, consumption increased by 1.8% in 2009 and was estimated to have risen slightly, by 1.4%, to 50.2m. tons, in 2010.

In 2010 Viet Nam's proven reserves of petroleum amounted to 595m. metric tons. Output rose steadily in 1998–2004, but thereafter declined in each year in 2005–08. In 2009 production was estimated to have risen by 7.1%, to 16.8m. tons. In 2010 production rose by a further 6.9%, to 18.0m. tons. As of 2007 production derived from the Bach Ho (White Tiger), Rang Dong (Dawn), Rong, Ruby, Su Tu Den (Black Lion) and Su Tu Trang (White Lion) oilfields, located in the Cuu Long basin; the Bungwa Kekwa oilfield, located in the Malay-Tho Chu basin; and the Dia Ho oilfield, located in the Nam Con Son basin. A further four fields—Ca Ngu Vang, Phuong Dong, Song Doc and Su Tu Vang—became operational in 2008. Foreign companies active in exploration for and production of petroleum in Viet Nam in 2007 included Talisman Energy Inc. (Canada), Petronas Carigali Sdn. Bhd. (Malaysia), PTT Exploration and Production Public Co Ltd (Thailand), SOCO International PLC (United Kingdom), Nippon Oil Corpn (Japan), ConocoPhillips Co (USA), SK Energy Co Ltd (Republic of Korea), Geopetrol S. A. (France) and Japan Oil, Gas and Metals National Corpn (Japan). Agreements governing refining and exploration activities—including exploration by the state-owned national oil company, PetroVietnam, in the Orinoco Basin—were reportedly concluded between PetroVietnam and Petróleos de Venezuela in 2008. In 2009, according to the USGS, Viet Nam's exports of crude petroleum amounted to 98.3m. barrels, representing a decline of 2.8% compared with the previous year. The decline in exports was attributed to the commissioning that year of the country's first refinery, at Dung Quat. In 2008 the construction of a second refinery, Nghi Son, in the province of Thanh Hoa, began as part of the Nghi Son petrochemical refinery project. The refinery, with anticipated annual capacity of 10m. tons, was scheduled to become operational in 2013. Kuwait Petroleum International, one of the shareholders in Nghi Son, is reportedly committed to supplying all of the crude the refinery will process. Together, the refineries at Dung Quat and Nghi Son will have sufficient capacity to meet some two-thirds of Viet Nam's domestic demand for fuel and petroleum products. Plans to construct a third refinery—Long Song—as part of another petroleum complex project, in Ba Ria-Vung Tau province, were also announced in 2008. The Long Song facility, with annual capacity of 10m. tons, was, like Nghi Son, scheduled to commence operations in 2013. Viet Nam has asserted exploration claims over a large area of the South China Sea, but these are disputed by China, the Philippines, Indonesia, Brunei, Malaysia and Taiwan. In mid-2007, in view of Viet Nam's and China's competing claims, BP abandoned an exploration project located between Viet Nam and the Spratly Islands.

China has also pursued a dispute with Japan over the sovereignty of the Diaoyu (Senkaku) group of eight uninhabited islands in the East China Sea, which are believed to lie in an area of offshore production potential. In mid-2008 China and Japan agreed jointly to develop the Chunxiao/Shirakaba and Longjing/Asurao oilfields, but the agreement collapsed in 2009 after China claimed sovereignty over the fields. The Republic of Korea and the Democratic People's Republic of Korea are also involved in disputes with China over the demarcation of exploration rights in the Yellow Sea continental shelf.

Since overtaking Japan as the world's second largest consumer of petroleum after the USA in 2002, China has retained this position, and by an increasing margin: in 2010 the country's consumption, at an estimated 428.6m. metric tons (some 9.1m. b/d), was more than double that of Japan, where demand for oil has fallen steadily since 2003 owing to economic stagnation. China's production of crude petroleum in 2010 amounted to an estimated 203m. tons. In 2009, according to the EIA, China's net oil imports totalled an estimated 4.3m. b/d, making the country the world's second largest net importer of oil after the USA. According to data cited by the EIA, Chinese demand for crude oil will rise to 9.6m. b/d in 2011, and will, by the end of that year, have accounted for more than one-third of estimated growth in global demand for oil in non-member countries of the Organisation for Economic Co-operation and Development (OECD) in 2009–11. Growth in Chinese demand for oil now exerts the strongest influence on international markets for crude petroleum and petroleum products. China has been a net importer of petroleum since 1993, and domestic production is orientated primarily towards meeting domestic consumption. The Daqing oilfield, in Heilongjiang Province, contributed the largest share of output in 2009, but production there is declining owing to natural depletion. SINOPEC's Shengli oilfield, where output is likewise waning, was the country's second most productive field in 2009. Chinese production capacity is currently, by and large, located onshore, and the development of offshore reserves—in which the participation of foreign companies has been permitted—is a focus of government energy strategy. Recent exploration activity has reportedly been concentrated on offshore areas in the Bohai Sea and the South China Sea, and on onshore fields in Xinjiang, Sichuan, Gansu and Inner Mongolia (Nei Monggol) provinces. Foreign oil companies involved in offshore exploration and production activities in 2008 included Royal Dutch/Shell, Chevron, BP, Husky Energy, Anadarko and ENI. Realizing that its dependence on imports is likely to increase, China's oil companies (in particular China National Petroleum Corpn—see below—which held oil assets in 27 countries in mid-2011) have purchased interests in various foreign exploration and production projects. In mid-2009, according to the EIA, China was pursuing (through its huge reserves of foreign exchange) a policy of accelerated global acquisitions and oil-industry financing projects in order to profit from relatively low asset values—a consequence of the global economic downturn. Loans-for-oil agreements had reportedly recently been concluded at that time with Brazil, Kazakhstan, Russia and Venezuela. The EIA indicated that so-called equity oil output increased from 140,000 b/d in 2000 to 900,000 b/d in 2008, representing about 23% of total production in the latter year. Most overseas oil production was handled by CNPC, which, in late 2010, was planning to expand overseas production to some 4m. b/d by 2020. According to data cited by the EIA, China's imports of crude petroleum amounted to 4m. b/d in 2009, of which Middle Eastern countries (in particular Saudi Arabia) were the source of about 50% and African countries (especially Angola) the source of about 30%. Asian-Pacific countries supplied about 5% of China's petroleum imports in 2009. Exports of crude petroleum were reported to have totalled some 0.5m. b/d in 2009. Imports of the principal petroleum products amounted to about 0.7m. b/d in 2009, while the corresponding figure for exports was some 0.5m. b/d. In 2006, as part of the first transnational pipeline initiative in which China has participated, deliveries of Kazakh and Russian oil to the country commenced via the Sino–Kazakh pipeline, a CNPC-KazMunaiGaz (KMG) joint venture that originates in Kazakhstan. A project to expand the pipeline was expected to be completed in 2011—doubling the pipeline's capacity from its initial 200,000 b/d—in order to allow Russian crude oil from Western Siberia to flow through it. In late 2010 it was reported that KMG had allowed CNPC equity in upstream petroleum in exchange for loans to fund downstream projects. Meanwhile, Russia's Eastern Siberia–Pacific Ocean (ESPO) pipeline project was also to allow China to source crude imports from Russia's Far East. In early 2009 China concluded loans-for-oil agreements with Russian companies, providing for the delivery of 300,000 b/d of crude from the end of 2010, for a 20-year period. China has also concluded an agreement with Myanmar for the construction of a pipeline bypassing the Strait of Malacca, at a cost of some US $2,900m. China's recoverable petroleum reserves were estimated to total 2,020m. tons at 31 December 2010.

China's oil sector has been substantially reformed since the mid-1990s, in particular the companies that operate in it. Two, the China National Petroleum Corpn (CNPC) and the China Petroleum and Chemical Corpn (SINOPEC), have been granted control of most of the country's state-owned petroleum and gas assets. CNPC (via a subsidiary, PetroChina), SINOPEC and the China National Offshore Oil Corpn (CNOOC) all raised capital in the early 2000s by selling minority stakes for purchase via the New York and Hong Kong stock exchanges. Several of the major multinational oil companies, which are obliged to find Chinese partners before they can begin to operate in Chinese markets, invested substantially in these share offerings. In 2003 a State Energy Administration was established to regulate China's oil and other energy industries. The Government launched the National Energy Administration (NEA) in July 2008 as the country's principal regulatory body for energy. In 2004 the construction, in phases, of a national strategic petroleum reserve (SPR) commenced. In 2009 all of China's first-phase SPR projects were reported to be active, providing reserve capacity of at least 102m. barrels. At mid-2010 second-phase SPR projects with total designed capacity of 169m. barrels were reportedly under way. At that time sites were also reportedly being selected for third-phase projects, which were to add another 169m. barrels of reserve capacity by 2020. On completion of the third-phase projects, China's SPR would be equivalent to 100 days' consumption of imported petroleum. Analysts have estimated that by 2015, of the 500m. barrels of petroleum that China could be storing, more than 60% will be owned by SINOPEC and CNPC. Excluding the SPR, China had capacity to store some 300m. barrels of petroleum in mid-2010.

In 1989 the Governments of Australia and Indonesia established a 'zone of co-operation' in an area of the Timor Sea known as the 'Timor Gap', to allow petroleum exploration and development to proceed, on a profit-sharing basis, in a disputed maritime area covering 62,000 sq km. This agreement was unsuccessfully challenged at the International Court of Justice by Portugal, acting on behalf of the people of its former colony of East Timor. Indonesia, which, with reserve depletion, became a net importer of oil in 2004, is actively promoting exploration for new reserves in remote areas of its eastern archipelago. In 1999 it was estimated that total reserves in the 'zone of co-operation' exceeded 100m. barrels of petroleum. Following the vote for independence in East Timor, the UN, as the body responsible for a transitional administration there, signed a treaty with Australia in February 2000 to extend the terms of the 1989 agreement. Timor-Leste, as East Timor became, hopes that an eventual petroleum sector will provide as much as 50% of its gross domestic product and 85%–90% of government revenues and foreign exchange. In Indonesia, meanwhile, it is intended that production from a number of major new petroleum projects, either planned or under way, will, in the short term at least, arrest the decline in the country's output, which fell in each year in 2001–07. In 2008 production rose to 49.0m. metric tons, compared with 47.5m. tons in 2007. However, output was estimated to have fallen again in 2009, to 47.9m. tons, and (slightly) in 2010, to 47.8m. tons. In 2000 output had amounted to 71.5m. tons. Indonesia withdrew from the Organization of the Petroleum Exporting Countries (OPEC), which it had joined in 1962, from January 2009, as a consequence of falling production. The Cepu block, located in East and Central Java, is one of the country's few remaining undeveloped oilfields. In 2006 ExxonMobil and state-owned PT PERTAMINA concluded a joint operation agreement for the Cepu field, where production began in 2009. According to the EIA, at May 2011 reserves were estimated at 600m. barrels, with peak production expected to reach 165,000 b/d by 2014. At January 2010 only one area (Banyu Urip) of the field was producing, and its production levels had reached just 18,000 b/d. At the end of 2003 PERTAMINA lost its monopoly on domestic production, and in mid-2004 its monopoly on the distribution of petroleum products was also terminated. This liberalization has—in theory at least, since actual progress has been slow—increased the scope for participation in the Indonesian petroleum industries by foreign companies, which already play a substantial role in parts of the sector. PERTAMINA became a limited liability company in 2003, and is scheduled for eventual privatization. As of 2009, Indonesia's refinery capacity amounted to about 992,745 b/d, distributed among eight facilities.

In 1991 the Government of Cambodia invited foreign tenders for 26 onshore and offshore blocks, and further exploration concessions were granted in the following year. In 1994 foreign capital was sought for the exploration of three additional offshore blocks and for 19 onshore blocks along the Ton Le Sap lake area and along the Mekong river, and 10 additional blocks were made available in 1996. In 2005 the US-based Chevron (which had been granted an exploration concession in 2002) estimated that between 400m. and 500m. barrels of recoverable petroleum were situated in an offshore oilfield demarcated as Block A. In 2008 Chevron Overseas Petroleum (Cambodia) Ltd announced plans to commence production from Block A in 2009. In addition to Chevron (55%), Mitsui & Co. Ltd (30%) and GS Caltex Corpn of the Republic of Korea (15%) were reported also to hold stakes in the Block A project. According to the USGS, the Government of Cambodia granted Chevron an extension to the original exploration period, until the third quarter of 2010, in exchange for the company's agreement to drill the three exploration wells. In late 2009 Chevron requested approval—still pending as of early 2010—to sub-contract the exploration of Block A. The arrangement would entail the company operating and owning 30% of the block. As of the end of 2009, the development of all blocks—with the exception of Block A—was suspended until maritime boundary disputes with Thailand had been resolved. In 2007 Petrotech of China announced the discovery of a substantial deposit in Block D (also located off shore), with preliminary estimates placing recoverable reserves at some 227m. barrels.

In 2002, according to Myanmar Oil and Gas Enterprise, Myanmar's total recoverable reserves (both onshore and offshore) of petroleum amounted to some 3,200m. barrels. In that year foreign companies from the Bahamas, China, Cyprus, Indonesia and the United Kingdom were reported to be active in the exploitation of the country's inland oilfields. The operation of the Yadana gas pipeline in Myanmar by French-based Total, together with Chevron and Thailand's PTTP, has aroused considerable controversy in view of international opposition to the military junta that governs the country. In particular, human rights campaigners have alleged that forced labour has been employed in the construction and maintenance of the pipeline, and that revenues from its operation—estimated to have totalled US $5,000m.—have to a large extent enabled the military regime to withstand the impact of international sanctions imposed against it. In 2009, according to the USGS, production of crude petroleum amounted to 6.9m. barrels, complemented by output of about 4.1m. barrels of refinery products.

During the period 2000–10 petroleum consumption in the Asia-Pacific region (including Australia, China, the (Chinese) Special Administrative Region of Hong Kong, Indonesia, Japan, Malaysia, Philippines, Singapore, the Republic of Korea, Taiwan and Thailand) increased by an annual average of 2.5%. Singapore, which itself has no petroleum reserves, is one of the world's leading refining centres, with a capacity of more than 1m. b/d. The Republic of Korea, Indonesia and Thailand have been expanding their refinery capacity to enable them to export refined products. Japan has been increasing its primary refining capacity, in an effort to reduce its reliance on imports. In pursuit of the same aim, Viet Nam's first refinery commenced operations in 2009 (see above), and two further refineries were scheduled to be producing in 2013. The construction of a second facility commenced in 2008.

In 1993 the People's Republic of China became, for the first time in 30 years, a net importer of crude petroleum and petroleum products. China's petroleum import requirements have subsequently increased, and have been forecast by the EIA to rise as high as 10.9m. b/d (net) by 2025. According to Oil and Gas Journal, China's crude petroleum refining capacity totalled 6.4m. b/d at the beginning of 2009, divided among 53 facilities. CNPC and SINOPEC together reportedly controlled about 85% of the country's refining facilities. CNOOC was reported to have commissioned its first refinery in early 2009. As of mid-2009 the national oil companies of Kuwait, Russia, Saudi Arabia, Qatar and Venezuela were reported to be participating in joint ventures with Chinese companies for the construction of new refining facilities. The NEA aimed to raise China's refining capacity to 8.8m. b/d by 2011. According the EIA, crude petroleum distillation capacity in 2009 was 6.45m. b/d. PetroChina has also begun to acquire stakes in other countries' refining facilities, notably in Japan and Singapore.

International petroleum prices are strongly influenced by OPEC, founded in 1960 to co-ordinate the production and marketing policies of those countries whose main source of export earnings is petroleum. OPEC had 12 members in 2011—the withdrawal of Indonesia, hitherto the sole participant in the Far East and Australasia (and now a net importer of petroleum), having taken effect at the beginning of 2009.

Price History of the OPEC 'Basket' of Crude Oils
(US $ per barrel)

	Average	Highest month(s)	Lowest month(s)
2000	27.60	31.48 (Sept.)	22.93 (April)
2001	23.12	26.10 (June)	17.53 (Dec.)
2002	24.36	28.39 (Dec.)	18.33 (Jan.)
2003	28.10	31.54 (Feb.)	25.34 (April)
2004	36.05	45.37 (Oct.)	29.56 (Feb.)
2005	50.54	57.88 (Sept.)	40.24 (Jan.)
2006	61.08	68.89 (July)	54.97 (Oct.)
2007	69.08	88.84 (Nov.)	50.79 (Jan.)
2008	94.45	131.22 (July)	38.60 (Dec.)
2009	61.06	76.29 (Nov.)	41.41 (Feb.)
2010	77.45	88.56 (Dec.)	72.51 (July)

Source: OPEC, *Annual Reports*.

In August 2010 the average price of the OPEC reference 'basket' (ORB) of crude oils was US $74.15 per barrel, 2.3%—or $1.64—higher than that recorded in July. The price of Brent increased by $1.43, compared with the previous month, to average $77.07 per barrel for August. The average price of West Texas Intermediate (WTI) also increased—by $0.51—to reach $76.62 per barrel. Prices showed strong growth at the beginning of the month (to just under $79 per barrel) in response to the strength of share markets worldwide, the weakness of the US dollar and positive economic data from the USA. However, it dropped to below $70 per barrel when poor macroeconomic data for countries of the Organisation for Economic Co-operation and Development (OECD) were announced, before recovering some ground by the end of the month. Regionally, the performance of crudes was generally in line with price movements overall: the Middle East crudes showed signs of weakening demand (especially in Asia) after a strong start to the month; African crudes began the month at a premium, boosted by Indian purchases, before faltering as a result of higher supplies. Meanwhile, there were concerns that demand in OECD countries would fall as government stimulus packages came to an end. Usually, China offsets any fall in demand, but the Chinese Government was thought to be considering slowing down its economy, thus dampening the country's oil demand.

The average price of the ORB in September 2010 was US $74.63 per barrel, $0.48 higher than the average of the previous month and the highest average for five months. The price of Brent rose by 0.9% compared with that of August, to reach $77.80 per barrel. WTI was down $1.48 compared with August, to $75.14 per barrel. The month saw a general upward trend in the ORB as a result of improved macroeconomic indicators globally. Reflecting the summer heat and a gradually recovering global economy, consumption levels remained stable. However, heavy seasonal flooding in India (a rapidly developing market for diesel specifically) disrupted transport and slowed the growth in diesel consumption to its lowest level there in almost 18 months. By the second week in October the ORB had moved past $80 per barrel, this strengthening attributed to further improvements in macroeconomic data and a weakened US dollar.

In October 2010 the average price of the ORB reached US $79.86 per barrel, $5.23 (7.0%) higher than the previous month's average. The price of Brent increased by $4.95 (6.3%) compared with the price in September, to reach $82.75 per barrel. WTI also showed strong growth during the month, increasing by $6.75 (8.9%) over the same period and averaging $81.89 per barrel for the month. Analysts attributed the strong growth to continued improvement in macroeconomic sentiment (projected growth in the global economy was revised upwards, according to OPEC's monthly report, to 4.1%, for 2010), which was itself driven by expansion in the manufacturing sector of OECD. African crudes showed relatively weak growth in October as a result of lower demand in Europe—strikes disrupted refineries and ports in France for a number of weeks—with the analysis being that the negative effects of refinery outages were offset by surpluses in product inventories. Middle East crudes contributed to higher ORB prices as they continued to meet high Asian demand. Notably, sales of Chinese passenger cars increased in October by 27% compared with the same month one year earlier. Latin American crudes also saw significant increases in October: the price of Ecuador's Oriente crude grew by 8.1%, the largest price movement in the 'basket' for the month. Better than expected global demand in the third quarter was attributed to the effects of various national economic stimulus plans, which led to higher consumption levels. The price of the ORB continued to increase, reaching $85.27 in the second week of November.

In November 2010 the average price of the ORB increased by US $2.97, or 3.7%, compared with the average price in October, to reach $82.83 per barrel. The price of the ORB stayed above $80 per barrel for the entire month. The price of Brent crude increased by $2.58, or 3.1%, to $85.33 per barrel. The price of WTI also showed a significant increase, of $2.19, or 2.7%: its average for November was $84.08 per barrel. The global economic recovery continued to drive growth in demand. Asian demand in particular remained positive as naphtha and middle distillate cracks from the Middle East increased steeply ahead of peak Asian demand for winter. Meanwhile, it was announced that supplies of Russian ESPO (Eastern Siberia–Pacific Ocean) crude via the Asian port of Kozmino would decrease by some 9%. The news strengthened the position of Middle Eastern crudes in the first few weeks of December, when the ORB price overall increased to $87.92 per barrel. Latin American crudes fared worse in November because of lower demand from US refineries. Angolan Girassol, on the other hand, benefited from disruptions in Nigerian production to record its largest differential (6.9%) in more than a year-and-a-half. Oil demand in Europe finally showed signs of growth, as winter necessitated the purchase of greater quantities of fuel and heating oil. However, consumption of transport fuel in the region continued to be sluggish.

Crude oil prices continued to surge in December 2010, when the average price of the ORB reached US $88.56 per barrel—$5.73 (6.9%) higher than the average price for November. This was the highest average since September 2008. Compared to the previous year, the price of the ORB increased by 26.8% in 2010, averaging $77.45 per barrel over the year. The price of Brent averaged $91.53 per barrel in December, an increase of $6.20 (7.3%) compared with the average in November. The average price of WTI reached $89.15, which showed an increase of $5.07 (6.0%) over the same period. High prices were driven by improved global macroeconomic expectations and the early onset of colder winters in the northern hemisphere, which led to declining supplies of crude oil above the average for the time of year. The sustained increases in prices were in spite of weak demand for transport fuel, with heating oil in particular driving demand. In

December all crudes across regions remained positive, with African light grades, Basrah Light, Arab Light and Ecuadorean Oriente all gaining 7.2% in value. Meanwhile, growth in oil demand in Latin America (tracking above that of the Middle East) was driven by Brazil, where growth in gasoline consumption was expected to reach some 18% over 2010. Consumption in China continued to increase at very high rates: diesel consumption grew by 16.4% year on year, while sales of passenger cars in the country grew by 33% in 2010 compared with the previous year. By mid-January 2011 the price of the ORB had increased to $94.04 per barrel.

In January 2011 the average price of the ORB reached US $92.83 per barrel, representing a month-on-month increase of $4.27 (4.8%)—the sixth consecutive rise. The average price of Brent crude was $96.35 per barrel, or $4.82 (5.3%) greater than the average price of the previous month. WTI showed only a slight increase in its average price over the same period—$0.34 (0.4%)—to $89.49 per barrel. The growth in prices slowed in January (compared with December 2010), but remained high as cold weather continued to drive demand for heating oil, as did strong industrial output in the USA and China—as a result of stimulus plans and government incentives, respectively. Latin American crudes (Venezuelan Merey and Ecuadorean Oriente) increased significantly in response to strong demand from US refineries on the west coast. This was as a result of the temporary shut-down of the Trans-Alaska Pipeline. However, demand weakened once the pipeline had been repaired and was once again transporting Alaskan crude. Meanwhile, increased seasonal travel in the USA resulted in increased gasoline consumption (by 2%) in January.

The average price of the ORB in February 2011 was US $100.29 per barrel, which was $7.46 (8.0%) more than the average for January. When the price moved past $100 per barrel, on 21 February, it was the first time it had done so since September 2008. The price of Brent crude also increased in February, by $7.41 (7.7%), to an average of $103.76 per barrel. However, the price of WTI showed a very slight drop compared with that for January—$0.09, or 0.1%—averaging $89.40 per barrel for the month. The overall increase in prices was attributed to unrest in the Middle East and North Africa regions, which led to concerns of sustained disruption in the production and export of crude in the affected countries; and consequently to fears of supply shortages. Analysts pointed in particular at disruptions to European refineries supplied with North African crude. Demand remained high in February, as cold weather lingered. It was expected to ease in the second quarter—particularly if prices remained high—when consumption generally dips, before picking up once again in the third quarter in anticipation of the agricultural season.

The price of the ORB and its contributing crudes continued to surge in March 2011, averaging US $109.84 per barrel for the month, which represented an increase of $9.55 (9.5%) compared with the average price in February. The average price of Brent was also significantly higher than it was in the month before ($10.84, or 10.4%), reaching $114.60 per barrel. Meanwhile, the price of WTI increased in March—by $13.59, or 15.2%, to average $102.99 per barrel—following a slight decline in February. In fact, all 'basket' components showed very strong growth in March. The price of Ecuador's Oriente increased by close to $15 (16.5%) over the period. High prices were driven once more by unrest in Libya (and elsewhere in the Middle East and North Africa), where production had fallen by close to 80% on normal levels. What crude was being produced in Libya was being consumed locally. Some OPEC member countries increased their output in response, which helped to offset any supply problems. Furthermore, following the earthquake, tsunami and nuclear accident in Japan, consumption in that country declined initially, allaying to a large extent concerns regarding oil supply; but Japan was already seeking larger inflows of crude in the aftermath in order to meet refinery demand. Indeed, reconstruction in Japan would require exceedingly high levels of energy. High demand was maintained during March, as positive economic data came out of the USA (including lower levels of joblessness and improved activity in the manufacturing sector). In the second week of April the average price of the ORB continued to increase rapidly, reaching $120.30 per barrel.

In April 2011, at an increase of US $8.25 (7.5%), to $118.09 per barrel, the ORB was as high as it had been since the financial crisis began in Western economies in 2008. The average price of Brent also increased significantly (by $9.12, or 8.0%), to $123.72 per barrel, as did the average price of WTI—to $109.89 per barrel, representing a 6.7% rise on the average price in March. The weakness of the US dollar was considered by analysts to have contributed to the higher prices overall. Little change was noted in the global economy compared with March. The prices of all component oils in the 'basket' increased in April, with African grades—especially Brent—showing very strong growth: Algeria's Saharan blend showed the biggest increase ($10.62, or 9.2%). African crudes benefited from the ongoing unrest in Libya, stepping in to fill the gap created by that country's severe lack of oil exports. The price of the ORB appeared to move into a higher range (between $116 and $121 per barrel) in the first few days of May, but then a very large sell-off of commodities—including oil—caused prices to decline precipitously: on 5 May alone the price of Brent crude fell by $10 per barrel. In the context of a stronger US dollar and the release of weaker than expected macroeconomic data, the price of the ORB fell for six consecutive days, losing $16.50 over that time.

Following nine consecutive months of increases, the average price of the ORB fell in May 2011, by US $8.15 (6.9%), to $109.94 per barrel. The average price of Brent crude declined, by $8.62 (7.0%), to $115.10 per barrel. WTI decreased, by $8.70 (7.9%), to $101.19 per barrel. Declines across the 'basket' were attributed to a global slow-down in manufacturing and to high levels of unemployment. None the less, prices were still significantly higher than they had been a year earlier. African grades were more than 50% up compared with the same month in 2010, while Ecuadorean Oriente had risen by 52%. Concerns over debt situations in OECD countries became more relevant as stimulus plans came to an end and fiscal consolidation began. It was also unclear when the reconstruction in Japan (following the earthquake, tsunami and nuclear accident earlier in the year) would boost consumption and encourage higher prices. However, power shortages were expected in China later in the year, with the use of diesel generators likely to strengthen demand in the short term. News that US shale oil production had been revised upwards supported the overall belief that supply levels were higher than had been anticipated earlier in the year. However, the ORB price remained around $110 per barrel as a result of the unrest (and consequent supply risk) in the Middle East and North Africa.

The average price of the ORB continued to decline in June 2011, though at a slower rate than in the previous month. The 'basket' averaged US $109.04 per barrel, representing a fall of $0.90 (0.8%) compared with the price in May. The average price of Brent also decreased, by $1.06 (0.9%), to $114.04 per barrel, while WTI's price in June declined by a more substantial $4.98 (4.9%), averaging $96.21 per barrel for the month. The weaker position of crudes was attributed to the decision by the International Energy Agency (IEA) to release oil from its emergency reserves; lower average prices in June were also blamed on reduced macroeconomic confidence. Debt levels and persistently high unemployment in key Western markets continued to place a risk on the global economic recovery. None the less, oil demand remained robust: increases were recorded in China, India, the Middle East and Latin America. Meanwhile, losses were recorded across the 'basket'. Ecuadorean Oriente and Venezuelan Merey showed the largest declines, of 5.5% and 1.5% respectively. Prices of Latin American grades of crude were most affected in June as a result of weaker markets for its heavy-sour grades within Latin America. Despite the impact on oil production of unrest in Libya, African crudes also declined. Demand in Europe was once again down over the course of June, a consequence, analysts considered, of ongoing debt problems in Greece, Ireland and Portugal. Amid further volatility, and in the context of weaker manufacturing data, the price of the ORB reached $111.35 on 11 July.

Following two months of decline, the average price of the ORB recovered in July 2011, as markets stabilized and the US dollar weakened, to reach US $111.62 per barrel—an increase of $2.58 (2.4%) compared with June. The average Brent price likewise increased during July, by $2.85 (2.5%), to $116.89 per barrel. The average price of WTI was $97.14, $0.93 (1%) higher than in June. The price range for the month narrowed, reflecting a more stable environment. Data reflected a spur in Japanese demand, as reconstruction plans (finalized in July) necessitated increased imports of oil. Meanwhile, high unemployment, high gasoline prices and a slowing of the economy weakened US demand for oil. Demand in Europe was also down, although not as markedly as in the previous two months. Consumption in the Netherlands, Spain and France was particularly subdued as consumers were deterred by high transport fuel prices. Rapidly developing economies—especially China and India—helped to offset lower demand elsewhere, but overall demand was down over the course of July. Prices of the ORB fell sharply once again in early August, as concerns regarding euro zone debt undermined macroeconomic confidence. On 8 August the ORB price stood at $102.37 per barrel.

In August 2011 the average price of the ORB fell by US $5.30 (4.7%), compared with that for July, to $106.32. This was the largest decline in percentage terms since May 2010. The average price of Brent crude also fell, by $6.42 (5.5%), to $110.46. The largest decline compared with July was recorded by WTI, the average price of which fell by $10.84 (11.2%), to $86.30. Prices fell sharply at the beginning of the month as a result of continued concerns regarding credit and the US economy—GDP data in the first half of 2011 were more disappointing than expected—but recovered later in the month following supply disruptions in the North Sea and the US Gulf, the latter as a result of seasonal storms. All components within the ORB declined in August, with African grades recording the most significant losses. The rebound in prices towards the end of the month was partly offset by expectations that Libya would resume production in the near future. Lower demand in the USA had been reported in 2011—in June a year-on-year decline in consumption of 1.3% was registered—attributed to higher fuel prices and improved vehicle fuel efficiency. China showed a year-on-year growth in consumption of 2.3% in July—despite the Government's having ended its programme of vehicle incentives, which led to a downward revision in gasoline consumption for the third quarter of 2011. Demand in Brazil was better than expected in the same month.

RICE (*Oryza sativa*)

Rice is the staple food in most of the countries of monsoon Asia, and almost 90% of the total world area under rice lies within the region (89% in 2008, according to FAO). The greatest area lies in South Asia (39% of the world total) and South-East Asia (29%), while the People's Republic of China (19%) contains the bulk of the eastern Asia total. Rice is the main food crop because it is well suited to Asian climatic conditions, producing high yields of a nutritious grain where other cereal crops will not readily grow. Wet rice cultivation is typically associated with the alluvial lowlands of monsoon Asia, but rice will tolerate a wide range of geographic, climatic and ecological conditions and is even grown under upland cultivation.

There are two cultivated species of rice, *Oryza sativa* and *O. glaberrima* or African rice. *O. sativa*, which is native to tropical Asia, is widely grown in tropical and semi-tropical areas, while the cultivation of *O. glaberrima* is limited to the high rainfall zone of West Africa. In Asia and Africa unmilled rice is referred to as 'paddy', but 'rough' rice is the common appellation in the West. After removal of the outer husk, it is called 'brown' rice. After the grain is milled to remove the bran layers, it is described as 'milled' rice. As it loses 30%–40% of its weight in the milling process, most rice is traded in the milled form, to minimize shipping expenses.

Rice is an annual grass belonging to the same family as (and having many similar characteristics to) small grains such as wheat, oats, rye and barley. It is principally the semi-aquatic nature of rice that distinguishes it from other grain species, and this is an important factor in determining its place of origin, its dominant role in monsoon Asia and its extension to other environments. Rice varieties may broadly be classified into two main groups: the long-grain indica and japonica. (There is also an intermediate or javanica type, cultivated in parts of Indonesia, which is now more generally known as tropical japonica.) However, many rice varieties currently being grown are improved crosses of indica and the short-grain sticky japonica rices. The indica group, prevalent in South and South-East Asia, and covering a high proportion of the total rice area of Asia, has been associated with low yields and primitive production techniques. The japonica types (which predominate in East Asia), while not inherently more productive than the indica types, are more responsive to natural and artificial fertilizers and give higher average yields.

Production of Paddy Rice
('000 metric tons)

	2008	2009
World total	689,140	685,240
Far East	406,717	413,701
Oceania	206	287
Leading regional producers		
China, People's Repub.	193,354	196,681
Indonesia	60,251	64,399
Japan	11,029	10,593*
Myanmar	32,573	32,682
Philippines	16,816	16,266
Thailand	31,651	31,463
Viet Nam	38,725	38,896
Other leading producers		
Bangladesh	46,742	47,724
Brazil	12,062	12,652
India	148,770	133,700
Pakistan	10,428	10,325
USA	9,241	9,972

* Unofficial figure.

Source: FAO.

Underlying the low average rice yields in South-East Asia (including Laos, Cambodia, Viet Nam and Thailand), compared with those in East Asia (China, Korea and Japan), are the lack of modern varieties adapted to local conditions, and the shortage of associated technology, including fertilizers and pesticides, and of adequate and timely supplies of water. Thailand and India have the poorest yields among the major rice-producing countries. Conventional rice varieties respond to increased fertilizer usage by producing more leaf and stalk, instead of grain, causing the plant to lodge (fall over) and decreasing net yields.

During the 1960s the International Rice Research Institute (IRRI), based in the Philippines, developed a series of stiff-stemmed, semi-dwarf varieties, bearing upright leaves, that respond positively to high rates of fertilizer application and other improved cultural practices. These improved varieties may yield as much as 10 metric tons of paddy rice per ha, while old varieties may yield less than 1 ton per ha. Most of the newly developed varieties are resistant to insect pests, diseases and some soil problems, although much work remains to be done in the selection of resistant varieties. Agronomists at the IRRI, and in national programmes, are continually developing varieties that will tolerate drought, flood, deep water and suboptimum temperatures, and high-yielding varieties (HYVs) which are designed for areas without costly irrigation or where water is scarce. Farmers cultivating these varieties may expect a reduced risk of crop failures, and are more likely to invest in other production inputs. In the late 1990s the IRRI was developing new HYVs that, it believed, could increase harvest yields by 20%–30% by the 2000s. Hybrid rice technology developed by the IRRI has clearly demonstrated yields that are 1–1.5 tons per ha higher than modern inbred varieties commonly cultivated in such countries as the Philippines and Viet Nam. In 2003, according to the IRRI, the area under rice hybrids increased to 600,000 ha in Viet Nam and to 100,000 ha in the Philippines. Indonesia was reported to have also begun to commercialize this technology on, initially, some 5,000 ha. The IRRI assessed in 2010 that annual world rice production would have to advance by 8m.–10m. metric tons in order to keep pace with current rates of population growth. Furthermore, water crises were increasingly seen as a threat, rice-growing countries being likely to be most affected by the progression of climate change: by 2035 up to 20m. ha of land under rice could be afflicted by water scarcity. The IRRI has developed varieties better able to cope with both drought and submergence, and it also seeks to add essential minerals and vitamins to the strains.

The People's Republic of China developed its own high-yielding semi-dwarf rice varieties in the late 1950s, and these were widely disseminated in the country by the mid-1960s, prior to the release of the first IRRI varieties. Of interest has been the development in Hunan province of a true hybrid rice that increases yields by as much as 20%. In 1999 it was reported that a new HYV, which could increase yields by 30%, had been developed in China. In 2001, according to the IRRI, hybrid varieties were planted on about 16m. ha throughout China, approximately one-half of the total area planted to rough rice. A major limitation of the hybrids (apart from the high cost of seed production) is their rather long maturation period, which limits their suitability for intensive cropping patterns. In 2005 it was reported that the use of a genetically modified (GM), high-yielding 'super rice' variety had been promoted in 12 of China's provinces. In mid-2006, according to FAO, the Government remained undecided as to whether to release GM rice varieties to farmers for free cultivation. To do so would possibly endanger China's access to markets that did not allow GM rice varieties to be imported. However, at the end of 2009 it was reported that the Government was prepared to approve GM rice for commercial planting, pending scientific tests, within a few years—to enable a 50m.-metric-ton increase in rice production by 2020. Although China was exporting more than 1m. metric tons of rice annually in the late 1980s, shortcomings in the country's internal transport structure necessitated imports, mainly from Thailand, of more than 200,000 tons per year. Chinese production declined considerably after 1998, when serious floods reduced output by more than 2m. tons. More significant than the occasional adverse growing conditions that affect Chinese production, however, was a process of agricultural reform which, according to FAO, caused the contraction of, in particular, early and late Chinese rice crops. FAO forecast that China's output of rice in 2008 would remain at a similar level to that of 2007—some 187m. tons—owing to adverse climatic conditions in the latter part of 2007 and major earthquakes that affected Sichuan province (a region that usually accounts for 7% of China's total rice output) in May 2008. However, secondary crops in the latter part of 2008, in China as elsewhere in mainland Asia, yielded better than expected production, according to FAO, amounting to 193m. tons, and Chinese output rose further, to 197m. tons, in 2009 (preliminary figures). The US Department of Agriculture (USDA) had Chinese milled rice production rising steadily, from about 130m. tons in 2007/08 to 137m. tons by 2010/11, with 138m. tons forecast for 2011/12.

Thailand became the world's leading rice exporter in 1981, and rice has remained the country's principal agricultural export commodity, accounting for 3.5% of its export income (including re-exports) in 2008, according to the Bank of Thailand. Owing to the depressed state of the world rice market from the early 1980s and the achievement of self-sufficiency by a number of Asian countries, Thailand increased its exports of rice largely at the expense of the USA. However, the decision by the USA to include rice in its Food Security Act, which came into operation in 1986 (making US-grown rice eligible for subsidized export credits), significantly affected the level of foreign sales by Asian rice producers by undercutting the price of their exports. During the late 1980s, however, Thailand substantially expanded sales of its high-quality rice to the European Community (now the European Union—EU), Russia, South Africa, Saudi Arabia and Iran. Thailand's dominance in the world rice market has come under increasing pressure, and in 2009 exports dipped to some 8.6m. metric tons, although in 2010 they recovered to some 10.m. tons (31% of the world market, according to USDA); export levels were expected to be maintained in 2011, but to fall thereafter. Thai exports remained comfortably ahead of Viet Nam's 6.4m. tons in 2010, and of the 3.5m. tons exported by India, the 3.2m. tons by the USA and the 2.8m. tons by Pakistan (the last down from 4.0m. tons one year earlier). Indian exports had fallen as low as 2.1m. tons in 2009, from 6.3m. tons two years before, but were expected to remain at about the 2010 level into 2012—more was unlikely while the country's non-basmati rice export ban remained in place. Cambodia, Uruguay, Myanmar and Brazil all exported more rice than China in 2010, which was also matched by Argentina in that year.

Viet Nam's harvests were greatly stimulated by the Government's willingness—a shift in the late 20th century—to grant long-term land tenure to farmers. In 1989 Viet Nam became the world's third largest rice exporter, after Thailand and the USA, and in that year sales by Viet Nam of low-grade rice at prices substantially below those of Thai exporters prompted the Thai Government to introduce a programme of domestic rice subsidies. Vietnamese exports of (milled, paddy) rice, which totalled 1.6m. metric tons in 1990, advanced to almost 2m. tons in 1992. In 1995 Viet Nam's exports of about 2m. tons positioned the country as the world's fourth largest exporter of rice, after the USA, India and Thailand. In 1996 exports of rice provided 16.7% of Viet Nam's foreign revenue, and in 1997 the country became, after Thailand, the second largest exporter of rice. In early 1998, however, the Vietnamese Government imposed temporary controls on rice export volumes in order to maintain the security of domestic supplies. Nevertheless, foreign sales of rice increased steadily during 1998–99, reaching a record level of 4.5m. tons in the latter year (by which time Viet Nam had replaced India as the second largest supplier of the global market). Rice exports contributed 8.9% of the country's total export earnings in 1999. In 2000, however, Viet Nam's exports of milled rice declined by more than 20%, to only 3.5m. tons. Exports recovered somewhat in 2001, reaching 3.7m. tons, but then fell to 3.2m. tons in 2002. Viet Nam gradually increased the volume of rice allocated to foreign buyers in the years thereafter, and a new record of 5.3m. tons was realized in 2005. According to USDA, rice exports stabilized between 4.5m. tons and 4.7m. tons during 2006–2008, although a spike in rice sales by India displaced Viet Nam from second place in the international rice trade in one year (2007/08). Despite increased price volatility and subsequent export restrictions (see above), USDA reported that Viet Nam exported almost 6m. tons of rice in 2008/09, almost 7m. in 2009/10 and more than 6m. in 2010/11, with similar levels reported for 2011/12. In the medium and long term, increasing competition for land from property and business interests—whose influence has risen *vis-à-vis* rapid industrialization—was thought likely to diminish the total area appropriated for rice cultivation. In 2007 foreign sales of rice contributed 3.1% of the value of total exports.

Exports of rice, in the late 20th century, constituted a key component of the economy of Myanmar, accounting for 10.9% of export revenue in 1995/96. In 1998/99, however, this proportion fell to only 2.4%. According to official sources, the total area under paddy rice in 2003/04 was 6.5m. ha (including about 56,000 on which hybrid rice varieties were cultivated), compared with about 6m. ha in 1997/98. Rice was harvested from 8.0m. ha in 2009, according to FAO. Production advanced strongly during the 1990s, largely as a result of the increased use of HYVs. However, export growth was inhibited by the relatively low quality of Myanmar's rice in relation to that of competitors such as Thailand, and to the enforced curtailment of exports by the Government in order to avert domestic shortages. Myanmar's exports of (milled paddy) rice totalled only 28,000 tons in 1997, but fluctuated to as high as 939,000 tons by 2001. In 2002 the volume of rice shipped by Myanmar fell back to about 790,000 tons, but exports were estimated to have fallen precipitously thereafter, to only 182,000 tons by 2004. Foreign sales of rice stabilized in 2004, at some 180,000 tons, before resuming their decline. Exports fell by 40% in 2006, to only 71,180 tons, while 2007 export levels were only 2% those of the previous year, at 1,624 tons. Cyclone Nargis, which swept across Myanmar in March 2008, destroyed a sizeable portion of the rice crop and damaged cultivation areas (particularly in the Ayeyarwady (Irrawaddy) Delta region, where many rice paddies suffered exposure to salt water). As a consequence, the 2008/09 planting season was expected to be delayed significantly and, although the country exported 1.1m. tons of milled rice in that year (USDA estimate), this fell to 0.4m. tons in the following year, although 0.8m. tons were sold abroad in 2010/11.

Indonesia, the region's third largest rice producer, improved production only slowly through the 2000s, to some 54m. metric tons per year in the mid-2000s. Production then increased to 57m. tons in 2007, then 60m. tons in 2008 and 64m. tons in 2009, when, according to FAO, rice was harvested from 12.9m. ha. USDA recorded a 5% dip in milled rice production in 2009/10, from a peak of 38.3m. tons the year before, and a 2% increase to 37.1m. tons in 2010/11, with stable production expected into 2012. Indonesia had achieved self-sufficiency in rice during 1984–93. However, Indonesia's rice imports, principally from Thailand and Viet Nam, rose from only about 10,000 tons in 1997 to about 2.9m. tons in 1998. Imports were subject to greater volatility thereafter as the authorities sought to supplement rice shortages in the event of adverse weather and, more generally, in response to rising domestic consumption. For example, almost 1.0m. tons of milled rice was purchased in 2002, compared with some 287,000 tons in 2001 and 829,000 tons in 2003. According to FAO, Indonesia bought around 320,000 tons of rice on the world market in 2004. In an effort to curb the import bill, the Government imposed restrictions on foreign purchases in 2005; rice imports totalled only 122,637 tons in that year. The Indonesian Government set a target of growth in production of 2m. tons in 2007, with a further 5% growth in each subsequent year under its Rice Production Increase Programme (RPIP). To aid this development, a new three-year agreement was signed with the IRRI in March 2007 focusing on three main areas: supporting the RPIP; collaborative research; and development of human resources in the sector. Meanwhile, rice imports increased to 306,680 tons in 2006 and 1.0m. tons in 2007. USDA reported minimal rice exports in the late 2000s and into 2011.

By the end of the 20th century Australia had emerged as a significant exporter of rice, especially to Japan, although its trade is on a much smaller scale than the major exporters of the Far East. Australia's annual exports averaged more than 600,000 tons in 1995–2001, but, owing to the effects of drought, rice sales abroad fell to only about 129,000 tons in 2002 and 100,000 tons in 2003. FAO put Australian exports at little more than 22,000 tons of milled rice in 2004, and shipments recovered only slowly in 2005, to 34,000 tons. Rice exports in 2006 amounted to 285,603 tons in 2006, but fell back to 171,777 tons in 2007. USDA, estimating figures for milled rice, put Australian exports rising from only 17,000 metric tons in 2008/09 (only 35% of the level in the previous year) to 350,000 tons in 2010/11, with a further rise forecast for 2011/12.

Thailand became the world's leading rice exporter in 1981, and in 2010/11 it exported 10m. tons, followed by Viet Nam, the USA, Pakistan, India and Cambodia. Myanmar was the next most important exporter regionally in that year, ahead of China. The world's principal importers were Indonesia, Nigeria, Iran and Bangladesh, followed by the EU and Iraq, then Saudi Arabia, Malaysia and the Philippines.

The average export price of Thai milled white rice ('Thai 100% B second grade', f.o.b. Bangkok) strengthened steadily from 2002, when it had fallen to was US $177.4 per metric ton, to reach $290.5 per ton by 2005. A further increase, of only 7% (compared with the previous year's 19% rise), to $311.2 per ton, was recorded in 2006. At $334.5 per ton, the average export price of Thai milled white rice was 7.5% higher in 2007 than in 2006. From September 2007 the average monthly price rose remorselessly, from $332.8 per ton to an unprecedented peak of $962.6 per ton in May 2008—a price that was 150% higher than that recorded in January. Market observers placed the extraordinarily high levels to which international prices of rice rose in the first half of 2008 in the context of a rising trend in the prices of basic food commodities—in particular wheat, soya, maize, rape and palm oil—that had been apparent for two years, prompted to a large extent by the inability, owing to such factors as accelerated urbanization and crop losses attributed to climate change, of supply to keep pace with increasing demand for food that proceeded from a generally higher standard of living in developing countries—especially in Asia. A high level of speculative investment in agricultural commodities also contributed, because they had come to be viewed as a refuge from rising inflation and the weakness of the US dollar (for a three-month period in the first half of 2008 rice reportedly became the agricultural 'market of choice' for speculative funds). Additionally, despite rising world production, high prices for rice stemmed from export curbs or other restrictions imposed by some major rice-exporting countries—including China, India, Egypt and Viet Nam—as part of attempts to restrain domestic consumer price inflation, or to placate social unrest, as in the Philippines or Thailand. Such policies—with some countries reducing exports and others increasing imports—are of particular significance because of the small proportion of world rice production that enters world trade. Given the continuation of such restrictions, notably in India, rice prices remained firm after the general commodity price correction in the second half of 2008. The annual average price of Thai milled white rice in 2008 was more than double that in 2007, and although it had fallen back to $582.0 by December, this remained much higher than prices in the early months of 2008. Such levels were maintained, with the annual average price for 2009 being $583.5 per ton, ranging between a monthly low of $534.6 per ton (October) and a high of $637.0 per ton (March). The year ended with the average December price for Thai rice being up at $618.0 per ton, only for a decline to set in during the first half of 2010, the average monthly price falling steadily until July, when it reached $465.8 per ton. Prices recovered somewhat in August, with some quotations stabilizing and Vietnamese prices responding to government attempts to stimulate them. The overall annual average of Thai milled white rice (100% B second grade) in 2010 was $520.0 per ton, and in January–July 2011 the average was $528.9 per ton. In 2010 and 2011 record consumption was matched by record production, but increased purchases from Bangladesh and Indonesia in the latter year drove up the need for exports. Such demand was expected to slacken in 2012, although falling exports from Thailand would probably be offset by India, Pakistan and Egypt. Internationally, there was still a determined rebuilding of stocks, which kept prices high historically, if not compared with some recent years. From the end of 2009 average monthly prices fell steadily until July 2010 ($465.8 per ton), then rose progressively to the end of the year, reaching $563.8 per ton in December. After a dip in prices at the beginning of 2011, they then rose to give a monthly average of $554.3 per ton in February, but had fallen to $500.3 per ton in May. By mid-August the average price was up to some $567.0 per ton, because in June the Thai Government had promised a return to its official rice purchasing scheme, which was likely to drive up prices of Thai rice and, therefore, international rice prices.

RUBBER (*Hevea brasiliensis*)

Rubber cultivation is suited to both estate and smallholder methods of farming, but productivity on rubber estates is greater as it is the estates that have pioneered both the development of cultivation techniques and the improvement of the clones, or selected high-yield strains. These may either be planted as seedlings or propagated by grafting on to seedlings of ordinary trees (root stock) and planted out subsequently.

Of total estimated world production of 10.4m. metric tons of natural rubber in 2010 (up by 7% on the previous year, according to the International Rubber Study Group—IRSG), Asian countries accounted for 95%. The principal Asian producers are Thailand, Indonesia, Malaysia, India, Viet Nam, the People's Republic of China, the Philippines and Sri Lanka. Other important producers world-wide are Nigeria, Brazil and Côte d'Ivoire. In terms of export revenue for producers, rubber is of particular significance to Thailand (responsible for 68% of all natural rubber entering international trade in 2008, according to FAO) and Malaysia (6%).

Natural rubber can be produced from plants other than *Hevea*. One of these is guayule, a desert shrub found in Mexico and the south-western USA. Commercial rubber production from guayule has been undertaken at various times, notably during periods of restricted supplies of *Hevea*. Research into the development and commercialization of guayule as a source of natural rubber in the USA has received new impetus from the discovery that its latex does not contain the allergens found in *Hevea* latex.

In 2010, according to the IRSG, natural rubber accounted for some 44% of world consumption of new rubber, the remainder being met by petroleum-based synthetic rubber. Almost three-quarters of total rubber output, both natural and synthetic, is used in motor vehicles, particularly tyres, which themselves account for more than 50% of natural rubber demand and 70% of synthetic rubber demand. Epoxidized natural rubber (ENR), which is natural rubber treated with peracids (which are made by treating acetic acid with hydrogen peroxide and formic acid) to enhance its ability to resist stress, was developed in the United Kingdom and Malaysia as an alternative to synthetic rubber for use in the manufacture of car tyres.

The IRSG assessed that in 2010 world consumption of natural and synthetic rubber increased by 15.6%, to 24.8m. metric tons, after two years of decline, owing to world recession since late 2008, in particular in the automobile industry. Consumption of natural rubber in 2010 decreased by 15.5%, compared with 2009, to 10.8m. tons, according to the same source, while that of synthetic rubber rose by about 14.4%, to some 14.2m. tons. Global stocks of rubber were only 3.1m. tons at the end of 2008, rising to 3.3m. tons by the end of 2009 and 3.5m. tons by the end of 2010.

In 1975 the Association of Natural Rubber Producing Countries (ANRPC), whose members (now Cambodia, China, India, Indonesia, Malaysia, Papua New Guinea, Philippines, Singapore, Sri Lanka, Thailand and Viet Nam) accounted for some 92% of world natural rubber output in 2010, initiated plans to establish a buffer stock of natural rubber and to 'rationalize' supplies by keeping surplus stocks off the market. The operation of the buffer stock and the supply rationalization scheme was to be entrusted to an International Natural Rubber Council (INRC), which was established in 1978. Action to implement this plan was deferred, however, in the hope that discussions under the auspices of the UN Conference on Trade and Development (UNCTAD) would result in a more broadly based price stabilization agreement involving both producers and consumers. In 1979 the UNCTAD conference of 55 countries reached accord on the terms of an International Natural Rubber Agreement (INRA), which became fully operational in 1982, administered by an International Natural Rubber Organization (INRO), with headquarters in Kuala Lumpur, Malaysia.

The first INRA (which, with two extensions, remained in force until January 1989, when a successor agreement, operating on similar principles, took effect) provided for an adjustable price range (quoted in combined Malaysian/Singaporean dollars and cents), maintained by means of a buffer stock. In January 1993 negotiations began, under the auspices of INRO, to seek the formulation of a new agreement, to take effect at the expiry of the current INRA in December 1993. By mid-1993, however, wide areas of disagreement over the operation of pricing provisions of a third INRA remained unresolved. In November, after producers agreed to a 5% reduction in reference prices for buffer stock operations, the INRC decided to resume negotiations for a third INRA and to extend the current agreement by one year. These negotiations, which continued during 1994, resulted in the adoption, in February 1995, of a third INRA, to take effect from late December, on expiry of the current agreement. Subsequent delays in full ratification arrangement caused INRA provisions technically to lapse, although the INRO secretariat continued to exercise administrative functions, and meant that the third INRA did not enter into force until March 1997. The new agreement again provided for a guaranteed reference price, maintained by means of a buffer stock, the reference price being subject to review every 12 months. The duration of the agreement was four years, with the option of two extensions of one year each. The effective operation of successive INRAs was attributable, in large part, to each agreement's acceptance by virtually all producing and consuming countries. However, only about 40% of all rubber consumed is natural rubber, and INRA provisions did not cover trading in synthetic rubber.

Production of Natural Rubber
('000 metric tons, dry weight)

	2008	2009
World total	10,573	10,221
Far East	8,858	8,554
Oceania	8	8
Leading regional producers		
China, People's Repub.	548	619
Indonesia	2,922	2,790*
Malaysia	1,072	857
Philippines	411	391
Thailand	3,167	3,090
Viet Nam	660	724
Other leading producers		
Brazil	121	127
Côte d'Ivoire*	116	114
Guatemala*	89	93
India	864	821†
Liberia†	85	60
Nigeria*	110	145
Sri Lanka	129	136

* FAO estimate(s).
† Unofficial figure(s).

Source: FAO.

In June 1992 the membership of ANRPC announced that it was to seek the creation of a single, centralized open market, probably to be based in Singapore, as a means of counteracting the large volume of private transactions between smallholder groups and consumers (estimated to represent more than 70% of the world's natural rubber trade), which the ANRPC blamed for depressed price levels. During 1993 Indonesia, Malaysia and Thailand expressed dissatisfaction with the operational record of INRO, which, they stated, had failed to ensure adequate financial returns on rubber sales.

The persistence of depressed market conditions for natural rubber (see below) intensified the discontent of these producers with the operation of the third INRA, particularly in relation to the price support and buffer stock arrangements as operated by INRO. Criticism was led by Malaysia and Thailand, which, during July and August 1998, indicated that they were actively considering withdrawal from INRO, on the grounds that the guaranteed intervention price provided by the INRA was too low, and that buffer stock increases were insufficient to counteract falling prices. It was reported that Thailand and Malaysia, together with Indonesia, intended forming a producers' organization that would implement voluntary supply restriction arrangements, independent of INRO, under which production of natural rubber would be limited to 20% below world demand. The possibility was also discussed of forming a new regional rubber exchange, and of a co-ordinated marketing system to reduce competition among producers. In October 1998 Malaysia gave the requisite 12 months' notice of withdrawal from INRO. Although Indonesia subsequently affirmed its intention to remain in the organization, Thailand announced in March 1999 that it would terminate its membership with effect from March 2000. The withdrawal of Thailand deprived INRO of about 40% of the total financial contributions that it received from producer members. Meanwhile, the Government of Thailand indicated that it was formulating a plan to restructure its national rubber sector, with a view to doubling export revenue from this source during the period 2000–04. The plan included a price intervention mechanism, which was to be financed in part from the retrieval of the rubber stocks held by INRO, the value of which in early 1999 was estimated at US $65m.

In April 1999 INRO met in Kuala Lumpur, Malaysia, but was unable to persuade Malaysia and Thailand to reconsider their decision to withdraw, and in August Sri Lanka announced that it too would terminate its membership, leaving only Indonesia, Nigeria and Côte d'Ivoire as producer members: at that time INRO had also grouped 16 importing members, including the European Union (EU), the USA and Japan. Following a further meeting in September, INRO announced that it was to disband with effect from October. It was subsequently announced that all INRO-owned rubber (a stockpile estimated at 138,000 metric tons) would be sold by mid-2001. In the mean time, Thailand and Malaysia announced that they were to co-ordinate their operations in purchasing rubber direct from growers. It was also intended to harmonize the two countries' stock disposals, and to maintain a minimum market price. Efforts to include Indonesia in this agreement were, however, unsuccessful.

Thailand, the world's leading producer and exporter of natural rubber, carried out the replanting of more than 50% of its rubber-producing areas during 1961–93. During 1971–2000 Thailand's annual production of rubber increased at an average annual rate of 6.7%. Thailand attained successive record levels of output in each year in 2000–04. Production fell slightly in 2005, before recovering in 2006, to 3.1m. metric tons, but falling slightly in 2007, to 3.0m. tons. Higher prices for rubber from 2003 combined with the advantages gained from the replanting programme to boost output from that year. The emphasis on high-yielding stock resulted in a substantial improvement in the general quality of latex output, which increased Thailand's competitiveness in the production of motor vehicle tyres and led to the rapid expansion of Thailand's rubber goods industry. In 2008, according to FAO, Thailand's exports of natural rubber totalled some 836,404 tons (equivalent to 26% of production in that year), in decline since the 947,755 tons of 2006 (the highest volume of the 2000s). Given the increase in commodity prices until the first half of 2008, that year's export earnings were the highest of the decade, at US $1,388m., according to FAO. In 2001 2.1% of Thailand's total export earnings were derived from exports of natural rubber. During the late 1990s the Government implemented pilot schemes to extend the cultivation of rubber into the eastern and north-eastern regions of the country. As in Malaysia (see below), most rubber production in Thailand is carried out by smallholder farmers. Rubber manufacturers in Thailand expressed concern regarding the future of the industry in mid-2007, as a combination of falling rubber prices, strong competition and a strong baht resulted in a decline in competitiveness. Smaller operators among the country's approximately 140 manufacturers were reported to be most at risk. While global demand for rubber was expected to increase to reflect population trends, the switch in demand in many sectors towards synthetic rubber, owing to its lower cost, was perceived to represent a further threat to Thai manufacturers. Furthermore, the onset of global recession following the financial crisis in the second half of 2008 depressed demand from much of the world, and from the motor industry in particular. In 2009, despite a fall of 2% on record production of the year before, Thailand still produced 30% of the world's natural rubber. Preliminary IRSG figures for 2011 indicated that world rubber production, consumption and trade was continuing the recovery seen in 2010.

Since 1995 Malaysia has produced, on average, about 1m. metric tons of natural rubber annually, representing approximately 11%–18% of world output, although in 2009 production was down by one-fifth on the previous year and one-third on the peak year of 2006, and provided only 8% of world output. Owing to the low international price of rubber, and a consequent acceleration in the conversion of rubber land to other crops, output generally declined in the late 1990s and early 2000s, falling to a low point of about 770,000 tons in 1999. However, production was estimated to have recovered to about 1.2m. tons in 2004, compared with about 990,000 tons in 2003. Increased output in 2003 and 2004 was reported to have resulted from a shift in the relative advantage of rubber *vis-à-vis* other crops, especially palm oil, that prompted smallholders to revive their tapping activities. Production was put at 1.3m. tons in 2006, 1.2m. 2007, 1.1m. tons in 2008 and 0.9m. tons in 2009. Estate production declined from the 1960s, owing to a change in emphasis from rubber to oil palm and cocoa. Instead, smallholders became and remain the principal producers of rubber, as the large estates expanded the cultivation of these alternative crops, which usually guaranteed a substantially higher return than that from rubber. As a result of government encouragement (in the form of tax incentives and higher replanting grants), average smallholder yields rose to 700–800 kg per ha, and smallholders now account for about 70% of Malaysian rubber production (about 82% of the area planted with rubber is the property of smallholders). In 1999 the total area under rubber cultivation was estimated to be 1.5m. ha, of which 85% was located in Peninsular Malaysia. (In 2009, according to FAO estimates, rubber was harvested from 1.2m. ha in Malaysia.) In recent years Malaysia's exports have accounted for a falling share of about 5%–19% of the world rubber trade, according to FAO. Export volumes fell steadily in the 2000s, except in 2006 when record production pushed sales abroad up slightly, and by 2008 Malaysia exported only some 44,599 tons of natural rubber, compared with 91,803 tons in 2000. However, the value of exports, at least in nominal terms, remained high and stable in 2006–08, at just above US $130m. annually. In 2001 exports of natural rubber latex, natural rubber and gums accounted for less than 1% of Malaysia's total export earnings.

In Indonesia, once the world's main source of natural rubber, production in 2005, at an estimated 2.1m. metric tons, was at approximately the same level as in 2004. According to FAO, output increased to 2.6m. tons, 2.8m. tons and 2.9m. tons in 2006, 2007 and 2008, respectively. Production fell back to 2.8m. tons in 2009, but Indonesia was still firmly the world's second largest producer of rubber, after Thailand (accounting for 27% of global production). As domestic markets and manufacturing capacity have increased, the country has become less significant in international markets. Nevertheless, as in Malaysia and Thailand, output was boosted by the higher prices obtainable for rubber on world markets from 2003. According to FAO, Indonesia's exports of natural rubber ranged from 9,095 tons in 2000 to 8,547 tons in 2008, with a low of 4,014 tons in 2005 and a high of 12,526 tons in 2003. Viet Nam's output of natural rubber increased rapidly from the late 1990s. In 2009 FAO put the total at 723,700 tons, compared with 124,700 tons in 1995. Increased demand for natural rubber from Asian countries, in particular from China, was one of the factors that boosted the price of the commodity on world markets in 2003 and 2004. In China output rose from some 481,571 tons in 2000 to an estimated 588,380 tons in 2007; production fell to 547,861 tons in 2008, but then rose to 618,866 tons in 2009. China became the world's leading importer of natural rubber in 2003.

Ribbed smoked sheets (RSS) are the principal source of reference for rubber prices in commodity markets. Since 2003 the price of rubber on international markets, which had fallen to historically low levels in (approximately) 1997–2002, has recovered substantially as a result of booming Asian demand, in particular from manufacturers of tyres and other rubber products in China. In 2003, according to FAO, the average price of RSS3-grade rubber in Thailand was 44,500 baht per metric ton (about US $1,070 per ton), an increase of 36% compared with the average price recorded in 2002, and of 77% compared with that recorded in 2001. Similar increases in the price of rubber occurred on other major markets, including London, United Kingdom, and Tokyo, Japan—the world's largest market for trading rubber futures contracts. The price of RSS3 in Thailand rose to 55,900 baht per ton in June 2004, but thereafter declined in response to increased output of rubber world-wide—a consequence of the higher prices obtainable—and a reduction in Chinese demand. None the less, the average price of RSS3-grade rubber in Thailand in August was about 52,000 baht per ton, some 16% higher than in August 2003. Demand for natural rubber has also benefited from the steep rise in the international price of petroleum, especially since early 2004, as petroleum is the raw material used to produce synthetic rubber. In August 2003–August 2004 the US Gulf 'spot' price for butadiene, the main petrochemical base for synthetic rubber, increased by about 40%, to some US $227 per ton. According to the IRSG, the price for natural rubber averaged US $2,113 per ton in 2006, increasing to $2,321 per ton in 2007; a rise of 9.8%. In common with other commodities, the price of rubber reached a peak in the third quarter of 2008 (averaging $3,159 per ton), giving a 17.6% rise in the annual average price for 2008 of $2,729 per ton. The natural rubber price then fell back to $1,516 per ton in the first quarter of 2009, before recovering to $1,683 per ton in the second quarter. The price of synthetic rubber (US export value), meanwhile, increased from $1,710 per ton in terms of export values in 2006 to $2,012 per ton in 2007. In 2008 the average price over the year increased, likewise, to $2,511 per ton (having reached a third quarter peak of $2,879 per ton), but it continued to decline into the second quarter of 2009, achieving $1,582 per ton, before recovering. Over 2009 as a whole the synthetic rubber price was $1,936 per ton, the rise in prices continuing into 2010 and reaching $2,617 per ton in the third quarter, resuming strong increases by the end of the year and into the first half of 2011; the average price of synthetic rubber for 2010 as a whole was, therefore, $2,505 per ton, but had reached $3,337 per ton in the second quarter of 2011. The natural rubber price, meanwhile, exhibited an even stronger rise: the World Bank cites prices (nearby contracts) in Singapore for Asian rubber, RSS3 grade, and reported an average annual price of $2,586 per metric ton for 2008, falling to $1,921 per ton for 2009, but then rising strongly into 2010, averaging $3,654 per ton over the year, and the first few months of 2011, averaging $5,405 per ton in January–July. Quarterly prices for natural rubber had reached $5,732 per ton in January–March 2011, but by May prices were falling; the average monthly price for July was still $4,732 per ton.

The IRSG is an intergovernmental body which was established in 1944 to provide a forum for the discussion of problems affecting the production and consumption of, and trade in, both natural and synthetic rubber. In 2011 the contributing members of the IRSG were 17 in number, including the European Commission (and Japan, Malaysia, Singapore and Thailand). In 2003 IRSG members collectively accounted for about 52% of all natural and synthetic rubber consumed world-wide, and for 74% of global natural rubber and 65% of global synthetic rubber production. The Group's secretariat, which moved from London to Singapore in July 2008, regularly publishes current statistical information on rubber production, consumption and trade. Issues of global supply and demand in the rubber industry are considered at the annual World Rubber Summit; this took place in 2011 in Singapore in July (the which in 2011 was scheduled to take place in April in Abidjan, Côte d'Ivoire; however, owing to political unrest in that country, the meeting was moved to Singapore, in July 2011, where a revised IRSG constitution was agreed and where it was decided that the next three World Rubber Summits would also be held in the city state.

SOYBEANS

The soybean plant (*Glycine max* or *G. soya*) is a legume, a member of the pea family (*Fabaceae*). Like other legumes it is able to collect its own nitrogen from the air and release it into the soil. The soybean has accordingly played an important role in the maintenance of soil fertility under traditional crop rotation regimes. Owing to the plant's sensitivity to light, it has been possible to optimize cultivation through the selection of varieties adapted, according to the length of their crop durations, to geographical differences in daylight hours. It is the breeding of such varieties that has allowed successful cultivation to extend from northern, temperate zones, where the soybean originated, to, for example, subtropical and tropical regions of the USA and South America. In North America, the main area of cultivation, soybeans are generally planted in the late spring. The plant flowers in the summer, producing 60–80 pods from which two to four pea-sized beans are harvested in the autumn.

Cultivation of the soybean plant is thought to have originated more than 5,000 years ago in northern China, and to have spread southwards from there to Korea, Japan and throughout South-East Asia. In the regions of its origin and early dissemination the soybean has for centuries been a primary source of protein for human consumption. However, it was not until the mid-20th century that soybeans began to be traded internationally to a significant degree.

During the Second World War, and into the 1950s and 1960s, US soybean production was greatly expanded, with the aim of substituting domestically produced soybean oil for imported oils and fats. Thereafter, the protein-rich meal, which is a by-product of crushing for oil, was used to boost livestock production in the USA. Until recently, the soybean had for long been the most important source of vegetable oil world-wide. Today, however, the oil palm rivals it as the most important source, production of palm oil superseding soybean oil definitively in 2004 (FAO figures). Soybean meal, meanwhile, accounts for about 70% of the world's supply of protein-rich animal feedstuffs. The meal (also known as cake), almost all of which is used for livestock feed, is the most valuable product obtained from processing, generally accounting for 50%–75% of total value, depending on the difference in the prices of meal and oil. Furthermore, in addition to the traditional foods derived from soy for human consumption, the plant's derivatives are widely employed in processed foods marketed in Europe and North America. Among many industrial applications, the soybean also provides a raw material for the manufacture of ink, soap, paint and a fuel for diesel engines. It remains uncertain, however, to what extent demand will increase for soybeans as a biofuel feedstock, since, under production and trading regimes as of the beginning of 2009, especially in the European Union (EU), the economic viability of many other crop-derived feedstocks was superior to that of soybeans.

The USA has dominated world production of soybeans since the 1950s, when US output overtook that of the People's Republic of China. In 2010/11, according to the US Department of Agriculture (USDA), US production amounted to some 90.6m. metric tons, equivalent to 34.3% of total world output of some 263.9m. tons. Earlier in the decade, US output in 2005/06 was about 84m. tons (38% of the global total), in 2006/07 87m. tons (37%), in 2007/08 only 73m. tons (33%), in 2008/09 81m. tons (38%) and in 2009/10 91m. tons (35%). Thus, despite generally improving harvests, the USA's share of world production has been in decline since the 1970s, when the country was regularly the source of more than two-thirds of global output. Soybeans are also grown in Canada—in 2010/11, with output totalling about 4.3m. tons, Canada ranked as the world's seventh largest producer.

One of the reasons for the decline in the USA's share of world soybean production has been the very substantial increases in the output of Latin America and the Caribbean, which since 2002 (with the exception of 2004, when North America—the USA and Canada—regained primacy) has ranked as the world's largest producer region, even in 2008/09, when most countries in the region experienced a dip in harvest levels. In 2010/11 Latin America and the Caribbean accounted for one-half (52%) of the world total. Brazil is the largest producer in the region, and the second largest world-wide, with a second year of strongly recovering output, to 75.5m. metric tons in 2010/11 (USDA). Production by Argentina, the world's third largest grower, amounted to about 49.0m. tons in 2010/11, while Paraguay, with output of about 8.3m. tons, is the other major producer among Latin American and Caribbean countries. Brazil, Argentina and Paraguay accounted for almost 98% of the regional soybean harvest. According to FAO, the next largest producer is Bolivia, with estimated output of soybeans amounting to some 1.5m. tons in 2009 (compared with some 57.3m. tons in Brazil). China and India complement the list of major world producers, with estimated output, respectively, of about 15.1m. metric tons and some 9.6m. metric tons in 2010/11, according to USDA. The Chinese harvest was recovering from a dip in the previous yea, while Indian output fell after an unexpected increase in the harvest in the previous year.

In the Far East and Australasia China is the leading producer of soybeans. According to USDA, Chinese output of soybeans was expected to total about 15m. metric tons in 2010/11—about 6% of global production—compared with some 16m. in the mid-2000s. Elsewhere in the region, Indonesia (650,000 tons in 2010/11) was the next largest producer, followed by Viet Nam (297,000 tons), Japan (220,000 tons), Myanmar (200,000 tons), Thailand (180,000 tons), the Democratic People's Republic of Korea (North Korea—160,000 tons) and the Republic of Korea (South Korea—105,000).

Production of Soybeans
('000 metric tons, USDA estimates)

	2009/10	2010/11
World total	260,838	263,948
Leading regional producer		
China, People's Repub.	14,980	15,100
Other major producers		
Argentina	54,500	49,000
Brazil	69,000	75,500
Canada	3,507	4,345
India	9,700	9,600
Paraguay	7,200	8,300
USA	91,417	90,610

Source: US Department of Agriculture (USDA).

The pattern of production of soybean meal is similar to that of unprocessed soybeans, except that the USA, hitherto the dominant world producer, was edged out of the leading position in 2009/10 by China, the output of which USDA put at 43.6m. metric tons by 2010/11, or 25% of total world production of 176.0m. tons. The USA produced output of 35.9m. tons (20% of world production) in that year. On a regional basis, however, world output is dominated by Latin America and the Caribbean—99% of the regional total is accounted for by Argentina, Brazil and, to a lesser extent, Mexico; the aggregated production of those three countries provided 34% of world output in 2010/11. Brazil and Argentina vie to be the main regional producer; Argentina has tended to produce more soybean meal in recent years, except—barely—in 2008/09. With output of about 10.1m. tons, the 27 member states of the EU ranked as the world's fifth largest producer of soybean meal in 2010/11. India was the remaining major producer in that crop year, with production of some 7.5m. tons.

China, obviously is the largest regional producer of soybean meal. Steadily rising production was expected to reach 45.0m. metric tons in 2011/12 by USDA, accounting for 26% of output world-wide. The only other regional producers of any significance lag far behind, Japan producing 1.7m. tons of soybean meal in 2010/11 (compared with China's 43.6m. tons), Taiwan 1.7m. tons, Thailand 1.4m. tons, South Korea 729,000 tons, Viet Nam 315,000 and Malaysia 307,000 tons.

Production of Soybean Meal
('000 metric tons, USDA estimates)

	2009/10	2010/11
World total	165,280	176,023
Leading regional producer		
China, People's Repub.	38,644	43,639
Other major producers		
Argentina	26,624	29,880
Brazil	26,120	27,900
European Union	9,880	10,018
India	5,985	7,500
Mexico	2,825	2,853
USA	37,836	35,932

Source: US Department of Agriculture (USDA).

As with soybean meal, in 2009/10, in the following year as a producer of soybean oil China displaced the USA as the world leader, according to USDA figures. In 2010/11 China produced 9.9m. metric tons of soybean oil, or 24% of world production amounting to about 41.6m. tons; the USA produced 8.6m. tons in that crop year. On a regional basis, Latin America—again, Argentina, Brazil and Mexico providing 99% of the total—dominates world output, the aggregated production of the three countries (the third, fourth and seventh largest producers) totalling about 14.9m. tons in 2010/11, equivalent to some 36% of output world-wide in that year. The members states of the EU occupied fifth position, with total output amounting to some 2.3m. tons. India complemented the list of major producers of soybean oil in 2010/11, with production totalling about 1.7m. tons.

China is by far the leading producer of soybean oil in the Far East and Australasia, the next largest producer, Japan, providing little more than 4% of the Chinese total. In 2010/11 China's output was 9.9m. metric tons, and Japan's 419,000 tons, followed by Taiwan's 400,000 tons, Thailand on 321,000 tons and South Korea on 168,000 tons.

Production of Soybean Oil
('000 metric tons, USDA estimates)

	2009/10	2010/11
World total	38,893	41,644
Leading regional producer		
China, People's Repub.	8,726	9,857
Other major producers		
Argentina	6,476	7,320
Brazil	6,470	6,910
European Union	2,280	2,315
India	1,340	1,690
USA	8,897	8,634

Source: US Department of Agriculture (USDA).

Soybeans are by far the most important oilseed in international trade. In 2010/11, according to USDA, soybean imports, totalling about 89m. metric tons, accounted for some 86% of all world oilseed imports (including, additionally, those of copra, cottonseed, palm kernels, groundnuts, rapeseed and sunflowerseed), totalling about 103m. tons, while exports of soybeans, at some 91m. tons, were equivalent to about 86% of world exports of oilseeds amounting to 107m. tons. Rapeseed, which ranks as the second largest oilseed in international trade (and of increasing significance in the second half of the 2000s, until a significant decline from 2009/10), accounted for less than 10% of all oilseeds imported and exported (down from 13% two years before). China was the principal importer of soybeans in 2010/11, receiving shipments totalling almost 51m. tons, or about 51% of total world imports, followed by the member states of the EU (16%), Japan (6%) and Mexico (5%). Taiwan, Turkey, Thailand, Indonesia, Egypt and the Republic of Korea (South Korea) are other leading importers. The USA is the leading exporter of soybeans, with foreign sales totalling some 42m. tons in 2010/11—equivalent to about 39% of world exports. On a regional basis, Latin America ranks as the leading world exporter of soybeans, with the aggregated exports of Brazil, Argentina and Paraguay accounting for 43% of global exports in 2010/11. Brazil ranked as the world's second largest exporter country in 2010/11, with foreign sales totalling some 30m. tons, followed by Canada (10m. tons), Argentina (9m. tons), Paraguay (6m. tons) and Ukraine (3m. tons).

Soybean meal is the leading protein meal in international trade, accounting for 77% of all world exports of protein meal in 2010/11, according to USDA. In comparison, exports of palm kernel meal—the second most widely traded protein meal—accounted for almost 6% of total world exports of protein meal in that year. International trade in soybean meal has increased steadily since the 1970s. Latin America is the leading exporting region, Argentina and Brazil between them accounting for about 72% of world exports totalling 43m. metric tons in 2010/11, according to USDA. Within the region, Argentina overtook Brazil as the leading exporter in the late 1990s. In 2010/11 Argentina exported almost 29m. tons and Brazil 14m. tons. The USA ranked as the world's third largest exporter of soybean meal in 2010/11, with foreign sales by weight totalling about 8m. tons—some 14% of total world exports—followed by India (7%), then Paraguay (2%). In 2010/11 the member states of the EU accounted for by far the largest share—40%—of world imports of soybean meal totalling about 58m. tons. Most other significant importers of soybean meal—Indonesia, Thailand, Viet Nam, Japan, South Korea, the Philippines and Malaysia—were located in South-East and East Asia, with their aggregated imports accounting for some 26% of the world total. The exceptions were Iran, in sixth place among major importers of soybean meal in 2010/11 (3% of the world total, just ahead of South Korea), and Mexico (3%, just ahead of Malaysia).

Although soybeans dominate international trade in unprocessed oilseeds, and soybean meal that in protein meals, trade in vegetable oils is increasingly dominated by palm oil. In 2010/11, according to USDA, palm oil accounted for about 33% of vegetable oil production (soybean oil 28%); however, palm oil contributed 61% of world exports of vegetable oils (including, additionally, coconut, cottonseed, olive, palm kernel, groundnut, rapeseed—canola, soybean and sunflowerseed oils) totalling about 61m. metric tons, and for some 63% of vegetable oil imports—amounting to about 57m. tons—worldwide. Soybean oil, which costs about one-fifth more than palm oil to produce, ranks second, accounting for 16% of world vegetable oil exports and about 16% of world vegetable oil imports in 2010/11. In that year Argentina ranked as the world's leading exporter of soybean oil, its foreign sales, at 5m. tons (still down from almost 6m. tons in 2006/07, but up on the 4m. tons of the previous year), accounting for one-half of world exports totalling some 10m. tons. The combined exports of Argentina, Brazil, Paraguay and Bolivia represented about 72% of world exports of soybean oil in 2010/11, far greater than those of any other region or trading bloc; the USA was the third largest exporter, supplying more than 1m. tons. China was the world's leading importer of soybean oil in 2010/11, accounting for 17% of world imports totalling some 9m. tons, but this was considerably down on the 28% of two years previously. China was followed by the member states of the EU (10%) and India (10%). Iran imported some 5% of the world total, followed by Algeria (5%) and Morocco (4%). Among the next four top importing countries were two Latin American countries, Peru and Venezuela, with Egypt and Bangladesh dovetailed between. According to some forecasts, it is anticipated that demand, supply and trade in vegetable oil might increase substantially. Owing to the complexity of the calculations involved, increasing demand for biofuels has not always been factored into medium-term predictions. Soybean oil has hitherto accounted for only a small proportion—relative to, above all, rapeseed oil and sunflowerseed oil—of biodiesel derived from vegetable oil, and, under current production and trading conditions, in terms of economic viability trails palm oil and rapeseed oil, as well as other crops (e.g. sugar and cassava) that can be used as biodiesel feedstocks.

As there are relatively few major producers of soybeans worldwide, and as soybeans are the most important oilseed in world trade, US policy has influenced not only the world market for soybeans, but also the markets for the eight major competing oilseeds—rapeseed, sunflowerseed, cottonseed, groundnuts, flaxseed, copra, palm and palm kernels. Moreover, with regard to unprocessed soybeans, US influence has been reinforced by the fact that international trade has historically been comparatively free of tariffs and other restrictions on imports. (Tariffs applied to protect the oilseed-processing industries of importing countries, however, have typically been fixed at about twice the rate applied to the unprocessed commodity.) Since the mid-1970s, however, the USA's dominance of the international soybean market has steadily declined, in spite of growth in both production and export volume. Above all, this has been due to the rapid expansion in production and exports by Argentina and Brazil, whose individual exports of soybean meal and soybean oil have both overtaken those of the USA. Lower-cost production of soybeans in Argentina and Brazil has given those countries a considerable competitive advantage in international markets.

The leading role of the USA in the production and export of soybeans means that US prices are the most accurate and readily available guide to the international market. According to USDA, the US farm price for soybeans averaged US $205 per metric ton in 2005/06 (October–September), rising to $254 per ton in 2006/07. (A decade earlier, in 1996/97, the US farm price averaged $274 per ton.) In the 2007/08 crop year the average price rose steeply, to $414 per ton for the whole year, but ranging between $307 per ton in October 2007, at the beginning of the year, and a peak of $489 per ton in July 2008. The average price in 2008/09 was only $368 per ton, falling to a monthly low of $330 per ton three months into the year (December 2008), and maintaining the best prices in May–August 2009 (including a June high point of $419 per ton). The average price in 2009/10, at $354 per ton, was lower than in the previous year, though steady at below-average level in February–June 2010. Higher prices from the second half of the calendar year meant that the 2010/11 crop year (or at least its first 10 months) saw an uninterrupted monthly rise from an average of $375 per ton in October, already a higher price than in any month of the previous crop year, to a preliminary figure of $492 per ton in July. The October–July average US farm price for 2010/11 was $451 per ton.

Fluctuations in prices for soybean products tend to follow variations in the price of unprocessed beans, with an additional vulnerability to market conditions for alternatives, especially in the case of soybean oil. In 2005/06 (October–September) the average US wholesale price for soybean meal (48% protein) was US $192 per metric ton, rising to $226 per ton in 2006/07 and $370 per ton in 2007/08. The price did not fall back as much in 2008/09 as it did for unprocessed soybeans, averaging $365 per ton, but this concealed monthly fluctuations between $287 per ton in October and $461 per ton in June. In 2009/10 the average US wholesale price fell to $343 per ton, ranging between $306 per ton in March 2010 and $368 per ton in December. Between September (the last month of the 2009/10 crop year) and January 2011, the average monthly price rose (to peak at $406 per ton), before falling back to $370 per ton by April, although that was still above the start of the year ($355 per ton in October 2010). By July the US wholesale price for soybean meal had risen back to a preliminary monthly average of $382 per ton, to give a $381 price for the first 10 months of 2010/11. In 2004/05 the quotation (f.o.b.) for Brazilian soybean meal (45%–46%) protein at Rio Grande was $172 per ton, its lowest point in the century. The representative Brazilian quotation rose to $337 by 2007/08, before falling back to $333 per ton in 2008/09 and $327 per ton in 2009/10. In October 2010–July 2011 an average price of $385 per ton was recorded at Rio Grande, the quotation ranging between $380 per ton (October) and $408 per ton (February). The price of Argentinian soybean meal pellets (f.o.b.) at Buenos Aires had risen to an average $299 in 2007/08, before falling back to $290 per ton in 2008/09. In 2009/10 the average representative Argentinian quotation was $311 per ton (the only one of the four major price quotations to record a rise on the previous year), soybean meal having traded within a range of $239–$365 per ton in that year. In 2005/06 the average import price (f.o.b., ex-mill) of soybean meal recorded at Hamburg, Germany, was $215 per ton. In 2007/08, this had reached $469 per ton, but the average fell back to $401 per ton in 2008/09 and $391 per ton in 2009/10. In October 2010–July 2011 the average import price recorded at Hamburg rose to $421 per ton, having traded between $395 per ton (June) and $447 per ton (February) in that period.

According to USDA, the average US price of soybean oil (wholesale tank, crude) was US $516 per metric ton in 2005/06 (October–September). In 2006/07 the average US price increased to $684 per ton, and in 2007/08 it increased dramatically to $1,147 per ton, before falling back to $709 per ton in 2008/09. In 2009/10 a recovery in the US price for soybean oil saw it average $793 per ton, ranging between $731 per ton in October 2009 and $864 per ton in September 2010, the last month of the marketing year. The average price for the first 10 months of the 2010/11 crop year was $1,166 per ton, ranging between $970 per in October 2010 and $1,249 per ton in April 2011; the preliminary average price for July was $1,216 per ton. Similar annual fluctuations were observed in the other main price quotations. The representative Brazilian quotation (f.o.b. bulk rate) for soybean oil averaged $1,190 per ton by 2007/08, then $740 per ton in 2008/09 and $848 per ton in 2009/10. In the first 10 months of 2010/11 the average Brazilian quotation increased further to $1,207 per ton. In 2007/08 the representative quotation (f.o.b.) for soybean oil of Argentine origin averaged $1,191, before falling back to $741 per ton in 2008/09 and then recovering to $829 per ton in 2009/10 and $1,207 per ton in October 2010–July 2011. At Rotterdam, Netherlands, an average import price (Dutch f.o.b., ex-mill) of $1,327 per ton was registered for soybean oil in 2007/08, before it fell back to $826 per ton in 2008/09. The average Rotterdam quotation for 2009/10 was $924 per ton, and in October 2010–July 2011 it ranged from $1,157 per ton in the first month of the crop year, up to $1,374 per ton in January 2011, then $1,337 in July (preliminary figure).

SUGAR

Sugar is a sweet crystalline substance which may be derived from the juices of various plants. Chemically, the basis of sugar is sucrose, one of a group of soluble carbohydrates which are important sources of energy in the human diet. It can be obtained from trees, including the maple and certain palms, but virtually all manufactured sugar is derived from two plants, sugar beet (*Beta vulgaris*) and sugar cane, a giant perennial grass of the genus *Saccharum*.

Production of Sugar Cane
('000 metric tons)

	2008	2009
World total	1,728,944	1,661,251
Far East	279,242	259,245
Oceania	35,265	33,869
Leading regional producers		
Australia	32,621	31,457
China, People's Repub.	124,918	116,251
Fiji	2,321	2,089
Indonesia*	26,000	26,500
Myanmar†	9,000	8,500
Philippines	26,601	22,933
Thailand	73,502	66,816
Viet Nam	16,128	15,246
Other leading producers		
Argentina†	29,950	29,950
Brazil	645,300	671,395
Colombia†	38,500	38,500
India	348,188	285,029
Mexico	51,107	49,493
Pakistan	63,920	50,045
USA	25,041	27,456

* Unofficial figures.
† FAO estimates.

Source: FAO.

Sugar cane, found in tropical areas, grows to a height of up to 5 m. The plant is native to Polynesia, but its distribution is now widespread. It is not necessary to plant cane every season as, if the root of the plant is left in the ground, it will grow again in the following year. This practice, known as 'ratooning', may be continued for as long as three years, after which yields begin to decline. Cane is ready for cutting 12–24 months after planting, depending on local conditions. More than half of the world's sugar cane is still cut by hand, but rising costs are hastening the change to mechanical harvesting. The cane is cut as close as possible to the ground, and the top leaves, which may be used as cattle fodder, are removed.

After cutting, the cane is loaded by hand or by machine into trucks or trailers and towed directly to a factory for processing. Sugar cane deteriorates rapidly after it has been cut and should be processed as soon as possible. At the factory the cane passes first through shredding knives or crushing rollers, which break up the hard rind and expose the inner fibre, and then to squeezing rollers, where the crushed cane is subjected to high pressure and sprayed with water. The resulting juice is heated, and lime is added for clarification and the removal of impurities. The clean juice is then concentrated in evaporators. This thickened juice is next boiled in steam-heated vacuum pans until a mixture or 'massecuite' of sugar crystals and 'mother syrup' is produced. The massecuite is then spun in centrifugal machines to separate the sugar crystals (raw cane sugar) from the residual syrup (cane molasses).

After the milling of sugar, the cane has dry fibrous remnants known as bagasse, which is usually burned as fuel in sugar mills. Bagasse can also be pulped and used for making fibreboard, particle board and most grades of paper. As the costs of imported wood pulp have risen, cane-growing regions have turned increasingly to the manufacture of paper from bagasse. In view of rising energy costs, some countries (such as Cuba) have encouraged the use of bagasse as fuel for electricity production in order to conserve foreign exchange expended on imports of petroleum. Another by-product, cachaza, has been utilized as an animal feed.

Production of Centrifugal Sugar
(raw value, '000 metric tons)

	2009/10	2010/11*
World total†	153,678	160,948
Far East and Australasia	29,303	30,427
Leading regional producers		
Australia	4,700	3,800
China, People's Repub.	11,429	11,303
Indonesia	1,910	1,770
Philippines	2,000	2,200
Thailand	6,930	9,160
Other leading producers		
Argentina	2,230	2,010
Brazil	36,400	38,150
Colombia	2,294	2,200
European Union (EU)	16,687	15,091
Guatemala	2,340	2,259
India	20,637	26,650
Mexico	5,115	5,550
Pakistan	3,420	3,920
Russia	3,444	3,980
South Africa	2,265	1,975
Turkey	2,531	2,275
USA	7,234	7,213

* Preliminary figures.
† Including beet sugar production ('000 metric tons): 33,406 in 2009/10 (China 652, EU 16,400, Pakistan 20, Russia 3,444, USA 4,150); 31,526 in 2010/11 (China 863, EU 14,800, Pakistan 20, Russia 2,980, USA 4,355).

Source: US Department of Agriculture.

The production of beet sugar follows the same process as sugar from sugar cane, except that the juice is extracted by osmotic diffusion. Its manufacture produces white sugar crystals that do not require further refining. In most producing countries it is consumed domestically, and a fall in the production of beet sugar by the European Union (EU), which only accounted for little more than one-20th of total world sugar output in 2009, has meant that it has become a net importer of white refined sugar. Beet sugar accounted for only 12% of estimated world production in 2009, according to FAO. The production data in the first table, therefore, is for sugar cane, covering all crops harvested, except crops grown explicitly for feed. The second table covers the production of raw sugar by the centrifugal process (including beet sugar). While global output of non-centrifugal sugar (i.e. produced from sugar cane which has not undergone centrifugation) is not insignificant, it tends to be destined for domestic consumption. The main producer of non-centrifugal sugar is India, but countries such as Brazil and Colombia are also significant producers.

Most of the world's output of raw cane sugar is sent to refineries outside the country of origin, unless the sugar is for local consumption. Thailand, Australia and the People's Republic of China are among the few cane-producers in the region that export part of their output as refined sugar. The refining process further purifies the sugar crystals and eventually results in finished products of various grades, such as granulated, icing or castor sugar. The ratio of refined to raw sugar is usually about 0.9:1.

As well as providing sugar, quantities of cane are grown in some countries for seed, feed, fresh consumption, the manufacture of alcohol and other uses. Molasses may be used as cattle feed or fermented to produce alcoholic beverages for human consumption, such as rum, a distilled spirit manufactured in Caribbean countries. Sugar cane juice may be used to produce ethyl alcohol (ethanol). This chemical can be utilized, either exclusively or mixed with petroleum derivatives, as a fuel for motor vehicles. The steep rise in the price of petroleum after 1973 made the large-scale conversion of sugar cane into ethanol economically attractive (particularly to developing countries), especially as sugar, unlike petroleum, is a renewable source of energy. Several countries developed ethanol production by this means in order to reduce petroleum imports and to support cane growers. Ethanol-based fuel, a type of biofuel that generates fewer harmful exhaust hydrocarbons than petroleum-based fuel, may be known as 'gasohol', 'alcogas', 'green petrol' or, as in Brazil, simply as alcohol. Brazil was the pioneer in this field, establishing in 1975, in the wake of the first global oil crisis, the largest ethanol-based fuel production programme—PROALCOOL—in the world. Public subsidies and tax concessions encouraged farmers to plant more sugar cane, investors to construct more distilleries, and designers to blueprint cars fuelled exclusively by ethanol. By the early 1980s almost every new car sold in Brazil was fuelled exclusively by ethanol. In the 1990s, however, a shortage of ethanol, in conjunction with lower world petroleum prices and the Government's withdrawal of ethanol subsidies, resulted in a sharp fall in Brazil's output of such vehicles. Research to improve efficiency in ethanol production continued none the less, so that by the time petroleum prices reached new heights, in the mid-2000s, the production cost of ethanol had been reduced by two-thirds. Most Brazilian filling stations now offer as vehicle fuels, in addition to gasoline (petrol), a choice of pure ethanol or a blend of gasoline and 20% ethanol. By 2010 more than 90% of new cars sold in the country were so-called 'flex-fuel' models (first introduced in 2003), and by 2011 flex-fuel vehicles were expected to account for almost 50% of the light vehicles fleet. Moreover, Brazil was becoming a significant exporter of ethanol, as interest in biofuel increased world-wide—in 2007 Brazil exported 20% of its production, accounting for almost one-half of world exports. Although Asian attempts to establish 'gasohol' proved less successful (e.g. in the Philippines and Papua New Guinea), other Latin American countries were encouraged by free trade agreements with the USA, where the Energy Independence and Security Act of 2007 requires the greater use of biofuel. The EU also adopted similar legislation in 2007. Global output of ethanol (including ethanol derived from crops other than sugar, such as maize) had already increased by 70% in 2000–06, from 30,000m. litres to 51,000m. litres, while production in 2010 was expected to reach some 103,000m. litres—equivalent to 2% of world petroleum consumption. Since 2006 the USA had been the largest producer of ethanol (48% in 2010), followed by Brazil (38%). Sugar cane cultivation is projected to expand in line with ethanol production, as it is the most cost-effective feedstock for biofuel production, and as demand is expected to increase by 80% between 2010 and 2015.

By the mid-2000s the promotion of biofuels was becoming increasingly controversial. In April 2008 a report compiled by the World Bank argued that the drive for biofuels by the US and European governments had been the most important factor responsible for the rapid increase in the prices of internationally traded food commodities since 2002. In the same month a UN report warned that unchecked expansion of the production of biofuel jeopardized food security in developing countries, not only by raising food prices, but also by making 'substantial demands on the world's land and water resources at a time when demand for both food and forest products is also rising rapidly'. The UN urged governments to put in place regulations to manage the growth of the biofuel industry.

From the last part of the 20th century sugar encountered increased competition from other sweeteners, including maize-based products, such as isoglucose (a form of high-fructose corn syrup or HFCS), and chemical additives, such as saccharine, aspartame (APM) and xylitol. Consumption of HFCS in the USA was equivalent to about 42% of the country's sugar consumption in the late 1980s, while in Japan and the Republic of Korea (South Korea). HFCS accounted for 19% and 25%, respectively, of domestic sweetener use. APM was the most widely used high-intensity artificial sweetener in the early 1990s, its market dominance then came under challenge from sucralose, which is about 600 times as sweet as sugar (compared with 200–300 times for other intense sweeteners) and is more resistant to chemical deterioration than APM. In 1998 the US Government approved the domestic marketing of sucralose, the only artificial sweetener made from sugar. Sucralose was stated to avoid many of the taste problems associated with other artificial sweeteners. From the late 1980s research was conducted in the USA to formulate means of synthesizing thaumatin, a substance derived from the fruit of the West African katemfe plant, *Thaumatococcus daniellii*, which is about 2,500 times as sweet as sugar. As of 2005, the use of thaumatin had been approved in the EU, Israel and Japan, while in the USA its use as a flavouring agent had been endorsed. By 2011 sugar use was rising because of health concerns about other sweeteners—for example, sugar producers attempted to preserve this advantage in the US courts by preventing the Corn Refiners Association from renaming HFCS 'corn sugar'.

Production of sugar cane is dominated by Latin America and the Caribbean, which grow about one-half of the world total: 54% in 2009, according to FAO (South America 47%, Central America 6% and Caribbean less than 2%). South Asia grew 21% of the world's sugar cane, eastern Asia and Oceania 18%, and Africa 6%. The area under sugar cane cultivation in the whole of Latin America and the Caribbean more than doubled in 40 years. The area from which sugar cane was harvested went from 4.6m. ha in 1968 to 11.7m. ha in 2009 (FAO), as part of an attempt to satisfy greater domestic consumption and to diversify from predominant industries (such as coffee and cocoa), but this figure conceals important sub-regional variations. In Central America the area harvested increased by 76% between 1968 and 2009, to 1.2m. ha, meaning that in importance to sugar production it displaced the Caribbean, where the area harvested fell by 59% over the same period. In South America, however, the area harvested for sugar cane increased almost fourfold between 1968 and 2009, from 2.4m. ha to 9.9m. ha. Moreover, South America enjoyed productive yields, whereas the Caribbean yield was the lowest in the world. In 2009 South America, followed by Oceania, had the highest average yields. Latin America and the Caribbean also dominate world trade in sugar. According to the US Department of Agriculture (USDA), exports of (centrifugal) sugar from Latin American and Caribbean countries contributed 60% of total world sales abroad in 2009/10, compared with 20% from (eastern and southern) Asia and Oceania, notably Thailand and Australia (major producers such as India and China being net importers). The main importing region was also Asia and Oceania (40% in 2009/10, mainly India and Indonesia), followed by the Middle East (18%), Africa (excluding Egypt—14%), Europe (Eastern Europe—mainly Russia—7%; and Western Europe—mainly the EU—6%) and the USA and Canada (8%).

The major sugar producers in East and South-East Asia and Oceania are China, Thailand, Australia, the Philippines and Indonesia. Of these, China and Indonesia were net importers rather than net exporters in 2010/11, according to USDA. Thailand was the world's leading sugar exporter after Brazil, followed by Australia. Indonesia, China, Malaysia, South Korea and Japan, followed by Taiwan, Viet Nam, Singapore and New Zealand, were the region's main importers. Indonesia, following unsuccessful efforts to achieve self-sufficiency in sugar, became one of the main buyers of Indian sugar, but then relied on other sources. Indonesia's total imports were estimated at about 3.0m. metric tons (raw value) in 2010/11. Thailand, after seeking a reduction in sugar production to encourage a change-over to other crops, promoted a controlled expansion of sugar production. However, sugar exports (both raw and refined) accounted for less than 1% of Thailand's export revenue in 2001. Thailand's exports of sugar (raw value) totalled an estimated 6.9m. tons in 2010/11, up from 4.9m. tons the year before, according to USDA, compared with some 2.7m. tons in 2002/03. In the case of Australia, sugar is the most important export crop after wheat. The export trade accounts for about three-quarters of the country's annual raw sugar production. Sugar (including sugar preparations and honey) accounted for 1.5% of Australian export earnings in 1997/98. In 1998/99 and 1999/2000, however, the contribution of sugar to total export revenues was only 0.2%. Australian exports of sugar declined from 4.2m. tons in 2005/06 to 3.5m. tons by 2008/09, although they increased slightly in 2009/10, to 3.6m. tons; exports fell back to 2.8m. tons in 2010/11. The sugar industry in the Philippines was, for many years, an important source of foreign exchange earnings. Since 1983, however, the country's output of raw sugar has reflected depressed price levels and curbs on production, exemplified by the export total of just 202,000 tons in 2010/11. Viet Nam reduced its dependence on sugar imports to the extent that foreign purchases were estimated at only about 4,500 tons in 2004, compared with more than 150,000 tons in 1995. However, according to USDA, by 2009/10 Viet Nam's imports of sugar had risen to 450,000 tons, although they fell back to 250,000 tons the following year.

The first International Sugar Agreement (ISA) was negotiated in 1958, and its economic provisions operated until 1961. A second ISA did not come into operation until 1969. It included quota arrangements and associated provisions for regulating the price of sugar traded on the open market, and established the International Sugar Organization (ISO) to administer the agreement. However, the USA and the six original members of the European Community (EC, now the EU) did not participate in the ISA, and, following its expiry in 1974, it was replaced by a purely administrative interim agreement; this remained operational until the finalization of a third ISA, which took effect in 1978. The new agreement's implementation was supervised by an International Sugar Council (ISC), which was empowered to establish price ranges for sugar-trading and to operate a system of quotas and special sugar stocks. Owing to the reluctance of the USA and EC countries (which were not a party to the agreement) to accept export controls, the ISO ultimately lost most of its power to regulate the market, and since 1984 the activities of the organization have been restricted to compiling statistics and providing a forum for discussion between producers and consumers. Subsequent ISAs, without effective regulatory powers, have been in operation since 1985. The USA withdrew from the ISO in 1992, following a disagreement over the formulation of members' financial contributions.

In tandem with world output of cane and beet sugars, stock levels (of centrifugal sugar) are an important factor in determining the prices at which sugar is traded internationally. These stocks, which were at relatively low levels in the late 1980s, increased significantly in the 1990s, although not, according to USDA data, in each successive trading year (September–August). In 2005/06, when world production of sugar amounted to about 145m. tons and world consumption to some 144m. tons, world sugar stocks fell for a third consecutive year, to about 31m. tons. In 2006/07, when world production of sugar totalled 164m. tons and world consumption 151m. tons, world sugar stocks increased to some 40m. tons. World stocks of sugar increased to 41m. tons in 2007/08, in which year world production amounted to 166m. tons and consumption to 155m. tons. In 2008/09, on the basis of the decline in world production to 144m. tons and reasonably steady consumption at 154m. tons, USDA assessed that stocks fell sharply, to 28m. tons. In 2009/10, with an increase in world production to 154m. tons and steady consumption of 156m. tons, USDA had stocks strengthening slightly to 29m. tons, but the forecast for 2011/12 was for stocks to end the year just below 29m. tons (on production of 168m. tons and consumption of 162m. tons).

After reasonably steady sugar prices during 2005 (the average ISA daily price for the year was 9.90 US cents per lb), in 2006 they displayed a high level of volatility. Overall, the average ISA daily price rose by 49%, to 14.75 cents per lb, in 2006. The highest average monthly price was 18.05 cents per lb in February; the lowest—11.65 cents per lb—was recorded in December. In 2007 prices declined by 32%, compared with 2006, to 10.07 cents per lb. The lowest average monthly price, 9.38 cents per lb, was recorded in June, and the highest, 11.01 cents per lb, in January. This decline in prices was largely attributed to continued substantial excess of supply, and was exacerbated by the weakness of the US dollar. According to the ISO, prices in real terms were too low to cover production costs. However, the relative weakness of sugar prices, compared with those of other agricultural commodities, subsequently spurred speculative investment, and sugar prices recovered in 2008 to peak at 14.51 cents per lb in August. The average ISA daily price was 12.79 cents per lb for that year, rising to 18.00 cents per lb in 2009, because of the basic underlying deficit in the world sugar market and because of the impact of high petroleum prices on demand for ethanol. Average monthly prices in 2009 recorded a steady increase until September, rising from 12.49 cents per lb in January and staying above 22.00 cents per lb at the end of the year. A jump back up in December, to 23.23 cents per lb, marked the start of a speculative rise in the price in the course of January 2010, with an average of 26.46 cents per lb over the month, a 30-year high. After a small decline in February prices fell considerably, recording a 43% decline by May, as the markets adjusted to better-than-expected production in India and Brazil. Prices rose steadily from June, with their general level being sustained by the production shortfall, and reached a new 30-year monthly peak in January 2011 of 29.61 cents per lb. The price slipped in February and then decline steadily, to 26% below the January peak by May (22 cents per lb). Crops in Brazil and Thailand had been unexpectedly bountiful, and India too seemed likely to export sugar.

The World Bank records three sugar prices, to reflect the major markets. The world price that it quotes is the ISA daily price for raw sugar (f.o.b., stowed at greater Caribbean ports), but using different measurements to the prices cited above: the average price for 2008 was 28.21 US cents per kg, for 2009 it was 40.00 cents per kg, for 2010 it was 46.93 cents per kg, and for the first seven months of 2011 the average was 58.28 cents per kg. The rising prices into February meant that the average ISA daily price for the first quarter of the year reached 62.70 cents per kg, but the average monthly price by June was 48.39 cents per kg, albeit recovering to 62.21 cents per kg by July. The US price, under nearby futures contract (c.i.f.), recorded similar but more pronounced fluctuations: 46.86 cents per kg in 2008, 54.88 cents per kg in 2009, 79.25 cents per kg in 2010 and 83.45 cents per kg in January–July 2011. An average US price of 86.56 cents per kg in the first quarter of 2011 fell in the second quarter; but had recovered somewhat from the low monthly price of 78.18 cents per kg in May to 83.62 cents per kg by July. The increasingly anachronistic EU negotiated import price for raw, unpackaged sugar from ACP countries under the Lomé Conventions (c.i.f., European ports) recorded a decline from an annual average of 69.69 cents per kg in 2008 to 52.44 cents per kg in 2009 and 44.18 cents per kg in 2010, but rose slightly to 45.97 cents per kg in January–July 2011; the price had recovered since June 2010, rising steadily into the second quarter of 2011 (47.02 cents per kg) and remaining stable at that sort of level into July (46.67 cents per kg).

Based on data for 2009, the 86 members of the ISO (then including Australia, Fiji, South Korea, the Philippines and Viet Nam) together contributed 83% of world sugar production and 95% of world exports of sugar; ISO members additionally accounted for 69% of global sugar consumption and 47% of world imports. At mid-2011 the ISO had 87 members, Indonesia having joined in May of that year. The ISO is based in London, United Kingdom.

TEA (*Camellia sinensis*)

Tea is a beverage made by infusing in boiling water the dried young leaves and unopened leaf-buds of the tea plant, an evergreen shrub or small tree. Black and green tea are the most common finished products. The former accounts for the bulk of the world's supply and is associated with machine manufacture and plantation cultivation, which guarantees an adequate supply of leaf to the factory. The latter, produced mainly in the People's Republic of China and Japan, is grown mostly on smallholdings, and much of it is consumed locally. There are two main varieties of tea, the China and the Assam, although hybrids may be obtained, such as Darjeeling. In this survey, wherever possible, data on production and trade relate to made tea, i.e. dry, manufactured tea. Where figures have been reported in terms of green (unmanufactured) leaf, appropriate allowances have been made to convert the reported amounts to the approximate equivalent weight of made tea.

Total recorded tea exports by producing countries achieved successive records in each of the years 1983–90. World exports (excluding transactions between former Soviet republics) declined in 1991 and 1992, but then fluctuated until volumes began to increase again from 1995, reaching a new record in 1998, then easing in 1999, before recording successive records in 2000–02 (1,436,678 metric tons in 2002). Exports fell to 1,391,800 tons in 2003, but in the following five years foreign sales of tea world-wide increased to successive new record levels, 1,578,568 tons in 2006, 1,578,963 tons in 2007 and 1,653,062 tons in 2008. Foreign sales of tea world-wide were estimated to have contracted in 2009, by 4.4%, to 1,580,102 tons, but they recovered strongly to a new record of 1,728,812 tons in 2010. The major exporting countries in 2010 were Kenya, China, Sri Lanka and India; an estimated 43% of tea production world-wide was exported. Global production of tea reached an unprecedented level in 1998 (3,026,340 tons), with record crops in all of the major producing countries (India, China, Sri Lanka and Kenya). From 2000 world output increased steadily every year up to and including 2010, exceeding 3m. tons of tea for a second time in 2001. Production almost reached 3.5m. in 2005, continuing to increase and rising to 4,162,327 tons in 2010, a rise of 5.9% on the previous year. China, meanwhile, achieved successive years of record production throughout the 2000s (consistently over 1996–2010, in fact, exceeding 1m. tons for the first time in 2006), with national records in Sri Lanka in 2000, 2002, 2005, 2008 and 2010; in Kenya in 2001, 2004, 2007 and 2010; and in India each year of 2004–07. In 2010 China and India's joint tea output accounted for an estimated 59% of global production—China's output represented 35% of production world-wide, while that of India accounted for 23%. Despite expectations of an interruption in the growth of global production in 2009, by 2010 the tea harvest world-wide was still growing. In 2009 Sri Lanka's tea production reached its lowest level in the 2000s, but Kenya's worst expectations were not realized. Both countries performed strongly in 2010, recording record production, the Sri Lankan harvest up by 14.4% on the previous year and Kenya's up by a massive 27.0%.

Indian production continued to decline (down 1.3% on the previous year).

Almost all of the world's green tea is produced in East and South-East Asia (99% in 2010), mainly in China (81%). Japan is the next largest producer, most of its output being green tea, followed by Viet Nam, where 48% of production was green tea in 2010. Indonesia is the next most significant producer, followed by Taiwan, at one-half that level, but green tea is a minority part of total tea output in the former country, whereas it consists almost of the entirety of Taiwanese production. The People's Republic of China is the largest exporter of green tea, sales abroad reaching the record level of 234,167 metric tons in 2010 (79% of world-wide exports). The next largest exporter of green tea, Viet Nam, sold an estimated 35,000 tons (12% of world-wide exports) abroad in 2010, and Indonesia 11,403 tons (4%). India and Sri Lanka are the next largest exporters, then, back in the region, Japan.

Production of Made Tea
('000 metric tons)

	2009	2010
World total*	3,932.0	4,162.3
Far East*	1,784.4	1,791.9
Oceania*	8.4	8.5
Leading regional producers		
China, People's Repub.[1]	1,358.6	1,475.1
Indonesia*[2]	136.5	129.2
Japan*[3]	93.1	93.0
Myanmar*	18.7	19.0
Taiwan[4]	16.8	17.5
Viet Nam*[5]	154.0	157.0
Other leading producers		
Argentina*[6]	90.0	90.0
Bangladesh[7]	60.0	59.3*
India*[8]	979.0	966.4
Kenya	314.2	399.0
Malawi	52.6	51.6
Sri Lanka[9]	289.8	331.4
Turkey*	153.0	148.0
Uganda	51.0	56.5

* Provisional.
[1] Mainly green tea (1,046,382 tons in 2010).
[2] Including green tea (about 33,000 tons in 2010).
[3] Almost all green tea (92,500 tons in 2010).
[4] Crude tea—almost all green tea (17,100 tons in 2010).
[5] Including green tea (about 76,000 tons in 2010).
[6] Twelve months beginning 1 May of year stated.
[7] Including green tea (about 260 tons in 2010).
[8] Including green tea (about 10,600 tons in 2010).
[9] Including green tea (3,285 tons in 2010).

Source: International Tea Committee, *Annual Bulletin of Statistics 2011*.

From 2009 China became Asia's largest tea exporter overall, but globally was exceeded still by Kenya. During the 1960s India and Sri Lanka together exported more than two-thirds of all the tea sold by producing countries, but their joint foreign sales gradually declined during the 1970s, until they came to constitute less than one-half of world exports (by 2010 the proportion was put at 28%). Over the years Sri Lankan sales came to exceed those of India by a comfortable margin (Indian exports have been far exceeded by those of Sri Lanka throughout the 2000s—and, indeed, by those of China). From 1990 until 1995, when it was displaced by Kenya, Sri Lanka ranked as the main exporting country. Exports by Sri Lanka again took primacy in 1997, when Kenya's tea sales declined sharply. Sri Lanka remained the principal tea exporter until 2003. In 2004 and 2005, however, Kenya again overtook Sri Lanka as the main tea exporting country. In 2004 Kenya's shipments rose sharply, by about 24% compared with 2003, and in 2005 the country's foreign sales rose by a further 5%. In 2006, albeit by a small margin, Sri Lanka regained the rank of principal exporting country, Kenyan sales having declined by 10%. Kenya's foreign sales recovered strongly in 2007 and 2008, however, propelling the country into the first place among tea exporters world-wide. The country retained that place in 2009, despite a 10.7% contraction in exports, and a surge in exports in 2010 took its total to 441,021 metric tons, or 26% of the world total, China accounted for just over 17%, with Sri Lanka on 17% and India on 11%. Kenya's exports in 2010 were equivalent to 90% of the combined foreign sales of India and Sri Lanka. Exports by India have been surpassed by those of China (whose sales include a large proportion of green tea) in every year since 1996; in 2009 China became Asia's largest tea exporter for the first time in centuries. A newer challenge to the four principal exporters has come from Viet Nam, which became the world's fifth largest seller of tea on the international market in 2000–09, increasing its exports every year except 2003 and 2005 to reach a peak of 110,929 tons in 2007; however, in 2008 exports declined to some 95,000 tons, only rising to some 98,000 tons in 2010 (6% of total global exports), barely above the 87,101 of the next largest exporter, Indonesia. Argentina, meanwhile, increased its exports by 48% to an estimated 102,323 tons in 2010, exceeding both Asian countries and becoming the world's fifth largest exporter for the first time.

For many years the United Kingdom was the largest single importer of tea. However, the country's annual consumption of tea per person, which amounted to 4.55 kg in 1958, had declined to 2.44 kg by 1997–99. In 1999–2001 an average of 2.27 kg per head of tea was consumed in the United Kingdom, but by 2003–05 it had declined to 2.12 kg, only to recover somewhat in 2004–06, to 2.17 kg. A similar trend was observed in other developed countries, although it is not so clear in the Republic of Ireland, the world's largest consumer of tea per caput in the early 2000s. Annual consumption per person advanced from 3.17 kg in 1994–96 to 3.23 kg in 1995–97, before evidencing a decline to 2.78 kg by 1997–99. In 1999–2001, however, average annual Irish consumption per head had risen to 2.71 kg, and in 2000–02 a further increase, to 2.75 kg, was recorded. In 2001–03 average annual consumption of tea per person in Ireland rose sharply, to 2.96 kg. Average annual consumption per person resumed its decline in 2003–05; at 2.79 kg during this period, it remained above the levels recorded in 1996–2002, but fell to 2.35 kg in 2004–06. In 2005–07 the level of tea consumption in the United Kingdom remained stable (at 2.17 kg per head), while it fell in Ireland (2.16 kg per head), meaning that the United Kingdom displaced its neighbour as Europe's largest consumer of tea per head. Their positions were reversed in 2006–08, when Irish consumption was 2.17 kg per head, compared with the United Kingdom's 2.11 kg per head, and this situation was consolidated in 2007–09, with Ireland up to 2.23 kg per head and the United Kingdom down to 2.07 kg per head. In 2006–08 Ireland had also became the world's leading tea-drinking nation, with the United Kingdom in third place, after Kuwait (2.21 kg per head). Kuwait was first in 2007–09, with 2.46 kg per head consumption, ahead of Ireland and the United Kingdom, which were followed, in turn, by Qatar and Turkey. In 2008–10 Kuwait remained the world's leading tea-drinking nation (2.86 kg per head), followed by Ireland (2.31 kg per head), Turkey (2.02 kg), Afghanistan (2.01 kg) and the United Kingdom (1.97 kg). From the late 1980s consumption and imports expanded significantly in developing countries (notably in countries of the Middle East) and, particularly, in the USSR, which in 1989 overtook the United Kingdom as the world's principal tea importer. However, internal factors following the break-up of the USSR in 1991 caused a sharp decline in tea imports by its successor republics; as a result, the United Kingdom regained its position as the leading tea importer in 1992. In 1993 the former Soviet republics (whose own tea production had fallen sharply) once more displaced the United Kingdom as the major importer, but in 1994 the United Kingdom was again the principal importing country. Since 1995, however, imports by the former USSR have exceeded those of the United Kingdom by a substantial and, generally, increasing margin. In 2010 Russia alone imported an estimated 174,620 metric tons of tea, accounting for 11% of the world market, followed in that year for the first time by the USA, with 126,836 tons (8%), then Pakistan, with 120,345 tons (7%), just ahead of the United Kingdom, with 119,178 tons (7%), and Egypt, with 93,000 tons (6%). Other major importers of tea in 2010 were Dubai (United Arab Emirates), Afghanistan, Morocco and Iran.

Much of the tea traded internationally is sold by auction, principally in the exporting countries. Until declining volumes brought about their termination in June 1998 (Kenya having withdrawn in 1997, and a number of other exporters, including Sri Lanka and Malawi, having established their own auctions), the weekly London auctions in the United Kingdom had formed the centre of the international tea trade. At the London auctions, five categories of tea were offered for sale: 'low medium' (based on a medium Malawi tea), 'medium' (based on a medium Assam and Kenyan tea), 'good medium' (representing an above-average East African tea), 'good' (referring to teas of above-average standard) and (from April 1994) 'best available'. At the end of June 1998, with the prospect of a record Kenyan crop, the quotation for 'medium' tea at the final London auction was £980 per ton. Based on country of origin, the highest-priced tea at London auctions during 1989–94 was that from Rwanda, which realized an average of £1,613 per ton in the latter year. The quantity of tea sold at these auctions declined from 43,658 tons in 1990 to 11,208 tons in 1997.

The China National Native Produce and Animal By-Products Import and Export Corpn is the sole exporter of tea produced in that country. Of the other exporting countries in the region, only Indonesia has established a noteworthy tea auction. Even so, the quantity of tea traded annually at the Jakarta auction is very small in comparison with that traded at its main African (Mombasa, Kenya) and South Asian (Colombo, Sri Lanka) counterparts. It does, however, frequently surpass the quantity traded annually at the smaller Indian auctions. Total annual sales at the Jakarta auction amounted to 42,357 metric tons in 2007, compared with 35,227 tons in 2006 and

36,971 tons in 2005. Sales fell slightly in 2008, to 40,538 tons, and again in 2009, to 39,372 tons, and in 2010, to 38,499 tons. The average price per metric ton of tea sold at the Jakarta auction in 2010 was steady at US $1,817, compared with US $1,825 in 2009, $1,509 in 2008, $1,329 in 2007, $1,340 in 2006 and $1,037 in 2005.

An International Tea Agreement (ITA), signed in 1933 by the governments of India, Ceylon (now Sri Lanka) and the Netherlands East Indies (now Indonesia), established the International Tea Committee (ITC), based in London, United Kingdom, as an administrative body. Although ITA operations ceased after 1955, the ITC has continued to function as a statistical and information centre. In 2011 there were eight producer/exporter members (the tea boards or associations of Bangladesh, India, Indonesia, Kenya, Malawi, Sri Lanka and Tanzania, and the China Chamber of Commerce for the Import and Export of Foodstuffs, Native Produce and Animal By-Products), five consumer members, 22 associate members and 35 corporate members.

In 1969 the FAO Consultative Committee on Tea (renamed Intergovernmental Group on Tea in 1970) was formed, and an exporters' group, meeting under this committee's auspices, set voluntary export quotas in an attempt to avert an overall long-term decline in the real price of tea. This succeeded in raising prices for two years, but collapsed subsequently as (mainly) African countries—Kenya in particular—opposed efforts to restrict their rapidly increasing production. The regulation of tea prices is further complicated by the perishability of tea, which impedes the effective operation of a buffer stock. India, while opposing the revival of a formal ITA to regulate supplies and prices, has advocated greater co-operation between producers to regulate the market.

TIN

The world's known tin reserves, estimated by the US Geological Survey (USGS) to total 5.2m. metric tons in 2010, are located mainly in the equatorial zones of Asia and Africa, in central South America and in Australia. Cassiterite is the only economically important tin-bearing mineral, and it is generally associated with tungsten, silver and tantalum minerals. There is a clear association of cassiterite with igneous rocks of granitic composition, and 'primary' cassiterite deposits occur as disseminations, or in veins and fissures in or around granites. If the primary deposits are eroded, as by rivers, cassiterite may be concentrated and deposited in 'secondary', sedimentary deposits. These secondary deposits form the bulk of the world's tin reserves. The ore is treated, generally by gravity method or flotation, to produce concentrates prior to smelting.

Tin owes its special place in industry to its unique combination of properties: low melting point, the ability to form alloys with most other metals, resistance to corrosion, non-toxicity and good appearance. Its main uses are in tinplate (about 40% of world tin consumption), in alloys (tin-lead solder, bronze, brass, pewter, bearing and type metal), and in chemical compounds (in paints, plastics, medicines, coatings and as fungicides and insecticides). Since the late 1990s a number of possible new applications for tin have been under study: these included its use in fire-retardant chemicals, and as an environmentally preferable substitute for cadmium in zinc alloy anti-corrosion coatings on steel.

Production of Tin Concentrates
(tin content, metric tons)

	2008	2009*
World total	257,000	260,000
Far East and Australasia	172,677	178,772
Regional producers		
Australia	1,783	1,400
China, People's Repub.*	110,000	115,000
Indonesia	53,228	55,000
Malaysia	2,605	2,380
Viet Nam*	3,500	3,500
Other leading producers		
Bolivia	17,320	19,273
Brazil	13,000	13,000
Congo, Dem. Repub.*	11,800	9,400
Peru	39,037	37,053
Russia*	1,500	1,200

* Estimated production.

Source: US Geological Survey.

According to the USGS, the People's Republic of China (44% of estimated global production in 2010) and Indonesia (23%) each produced more tin than Latin America until towards the end of the first decade of the 21st century, even though the region includes the world's next two largest producers and its sixth largest. In 2010, in line with revised figures for the previous two years, the three major Latin American producers between them had exceeded Indonesia's mine production, providing 25% of the world total. China and Indonesia are the world's leading tin smelters, accounting for 40% and 22% of metal production, respectively, in 2009. In all, the Far East and Australasia provided 72% of mined tin and 75% of smelted tin in 2009. Traditionally, South-East Asian countries were the most important mined tin producers, but since the 1970s tin has sharply declined in importance as an export commodity in Malaysia and Thailand, previously among the region's main producers (in Thailand the metal provided 12.9% of the country's export earnings in 1967, while in Malaysia sales of tin accounted for 23% of total exports in 1965). The depressed level of world tin prices from late 1985 effectively marginalized Thailand's mining activity, although it remains an important smelting industry, and accelerated the industry's decline in Malaysia, although the country possesses substantial resources of tin and remained a leading world centre for tin smelting. Major mining operations ended in 1993, although in 1998 the Malaysian Government took action to encourage the reactivation of dormant mines. Most tin production in South-East Asia comes from gravel-pump mines and dredges, working alluvial deposits, although there are underground and open-cast mines working hard-rock deposits. Output in minor producers, such as Myanmar and Laos, is exported in concentrate form for smelting abroad, sometimes regionally. Thailand and Malaysia smelt almost all their own production (and import additional ore), as does Indonesia, but on a far larger scale, as the country is now South-East Asia's largest producer. An independent tin smelter is in operation in Singapore.

In 2002 the Indonesian Government imposed a ban on the export of tin and tin concentrates as part of an attempt to prevent smuggling of the metal into Singapore, where a higher price was obtainable for tin ore. Measures to curb illegal tin mining and smelting in Indonesia in 2007 led to significant price increases for the metal, and continuing measures, into 2009 and 2010, further disrupted the Indonesian tin industry. The country remained the world's second largest producer of tin, however, and, owing to decreased exports from China, in 2007 Indonesia became the world's leading tin exporter. In 2010, according to USGS estimates, the country possessed 15% of world tin reserves, the second largest; in that year mined production increased to an estimated 60,000 metric tons (metal content). Indonesia produced some 30% of the world's refined tin in 2009. The industry is concentrated on the tin-rich islands of Bangka and Belitung (incidentally, the latter island's name is the origin of the Billiton in BHP Billiton, the Australian mining company).

Most Australian production was traditionally based in Tasmania and Western Australia. The low-cost Renison Bell mine in Tasmania, which is operated by Metals X Ltd, is the larger of Australia's two principal tin mines, the other being the alluvial Ardlethan mine in New South Wales, operated by Marlborough Resources. Metals X also integrated the Mt Bischoff tin mine, located close to Renison but idle since 1921, to provide an ore feed to the Renison tin-concentrating works while improvements, expected to be completed by 2011, were made at Renison Bell. Metals X, through its Bluestone subsidiary, also operated the Collingwood tin mine in Queensland, which significantly increased Australian tin production upon opening in 2007, but which was placed in 'care and maintenance' in 2008, mining there having proved more problematic than expected. Australia's tin concentrate is sent to Malaysia and Thailand for smelting, although there is also a smelter in Western Australia, at the site of the Greenbushes tantalum/tin mine. Australian mined output was estimated to increase by more than two-fifths in 2010.

China is, by far, the world's largest tin (primary metal) producer. China's output of tin ore rose by about 4% in 1998, to 70,100 metric tons, and again in 1999, by 14.3%, to 80,100 tons. In 2000 production increased for a third consecutive year, this time by 24.1%, reaching 99,400 tons. In 2001, however, output declined by 4.4%, to 95,000 tons. Production fell very heavily, by about 35%, to 62,000 tons in 2002, but the decline in production was reported to have been reversed in 2003, when output rose by about 65% to an estimated 102,000 tons. Output was estimated at 110,000 tons in 2004. The falls in production in 2001 and 2002 were attributed to the Government's closure of illegal tin-mining (and smelting) operations in Hunan and Yunnan provinces and in Guangxi Zhuang Autonomous Region, following flooding at a tin mine in Nandan (Guangxi) in 2001 in which 81 miners were killed. The recovery in production was more than sustained in the mid-2000s, with output reaching 126,000 tons in 2005 and 2006 and 146,000 tons in 2007. However, in 2008 production fell to 110,000 tons, which fed through to a fall in smelter production, although mined output recovered to an estimated 115,000 tons in both 2009 and 2010. From a low of 62,000 tons in 2002, China's output of tin metal was estimated to have recovered to 98,000 tons in 2003 and to 115,000 tons in 2004. The figure in 2005 showed a further increase, to 122,000 tons, in 2006 to 132,000 tons and in 2007 to 149,000 tons, before falling to 129,000 tons in 2008. Smelter production was expected to recover in 2009. In 2004, according to USGS, China's exports of tin (unwrought) amounted to 32,032 tons, and those of tin alloys to 6,993 tons, compared, respectively, with 31,285 tons and 9,896 tons in 2003. Exports of tin (unwrought) declined in 2005, to 22,928 tons, while foreign sales of tin alloys totalled 4,085 tons, representing a 41.6% reduction on the previous year. Exports of unwrought tin and its alloys declined even further in 2006, to 21,526 tons. In 2006 the Government announced that tin export quotas (for tin and tin products, including alloys, forgings and tin metals) would be reduced by 30% to just 37,000 tons, in 2007. In 2007 exports of unwrought tin and its alloys amounted to 23,582 tons. Increased domestic demand was cited as the reason for the reduction in exports over the mid-2000s and, in 2007, China lost its place as the world's leading tin exporter. Imports of tin concentrates amounted to 7,485 tons in 2005, compared with 8,912 tons in 2004 and just 2,739 tons in 2003. In the first six months of 2008 China's exports of unwrought tin and its alloys declined significantly, by some 98% compared with the same period a year earlier. The decrease was due to a new export duty, which had entered effect at the beginning of the year, intended to encourage suppliers to fulfil the demand for tin in the domestic chemicals and electronics industries. Consumption of primary tin in China, according to the World Bureau of Metal Statistics, has increased consistently in recent years. In 2004 consumption was 92,900 tons, representing 27.6% of the global total. By 2007 consumption of 125,000 tons was recorded, and forecasts for 2008 suggested that China would account for 35.8% of world primary tin consumption.

Over the period 1956–85 much of the world's tin production and trade was covered by successive international agreements, administered by the International Tin Council (ITC), based in London, United Kingdom. The aim of each successive International Tin Agreement (ITA), of which there were six, was to stabilize prices within an agreed range by using a buffer stock to regulate the supply of tin. The buffer stock was financed by producing countries, with voluntary contributions by some consuming countries. 'Floor' and 'ceiling' prices were fixed, and market operations conducted by a buffer stock manager who intervened, as necessary, to maintain prices within these agreed limits. For added protection, the ITA provided for the imposition of export controls if the 'floor' price was being threatened. The ITA was effectively terminated in October 1985, when the ITC's buffer stock manager informed the London Metal Exchange (LME) that he no longer had the funds with which to support the tin market. The factors underlying the collapse of the ITA included its limited membership (Bolivia and the USA, leading producing and consuming countries, were not signatories) and the accumulation of tin stocks which resulted from the widespread circumvention of producers' quota limits. The LME responded by suspending trading in tin, leaving the ITC owing more than £500m. to some 36 banks, tin smelters and metals traders. The crisis was eventually resolved in March 1990, when a financial settlement of £182.5m. was agreed between the ITC and its creditors. The ITC was itself dissolved in July. Transactions in tin contracts were resumed on the LME in 1989

These events lent new significance to the activities of the Association of Tin Producing Countries (ATPC), founded in 1983 by Malaysia, Indonesia and Thailand and later joined by Bolivia, Nigeria, Australia and Zaire (now the Democratic Republic of the Congo—DRC). Immediately prior to the withdrawal of Australia and Thailand at the end of 1996 (see below), members of the ATPC, which is based in Kuala Lumpur, Malaysia, accounted for about two-thirds of world mine production. The ATPC, which was intended to operate as a complement to the ITC and not in competition with it, introduced export quotas for tin for the year from 1 March 1987. Brazil and China agreed to co-operate with the ATPC in implementing these supply restrictions, which were renegotiated to cover succeeding years, with the aim of raising prices and reducing the level of surplus stocks. The ATPC membership also took stringent measures to control smuggling. Brazil and China (jointly accounting for more than one-third of world tin production) both initially held observer status at the ATPC. (China became a full member in 1994, but at the time Brazil remained as an observer—together with Peru and Viet Nam.) China and Brazil agreed to participate in the export quota arrangements, for which the ATPC had no formal powers of enforcement.

The ATPC members' combined export quota was fixed at 95,849 metric tons for 1991, and was reduced to 87,091 tons for 1992. However, the substantial level of world tin stocks, combined with depressed demand, led to mine closures and reductions in output, with the result that members' exports in 1991 were below quota entitlements. The progressive depletion of stock levels led to a forecast by the ATPC, in May 1992, that export quotas would be removed in 1994 if these disposals continued at their current rate. The ATPC had previously set a target level for stocks of 20,000 tons, representing about six weeks of world tin consumption. Projections that world demand for tin would remain at about 160,000 tons annually, together with continued optimism about the rate of stock disposals, led the ATPC to increase its members' 1993 export quota to 89,700 tons. The persistence, however, of high levels of annual tin exports by China (estimated to have totalled 30,000 tons in 1993 and 1994, compared with its ATPC quota of 20,000 tons), together with sales of surplus defence stocks of tin by the US Government, necessitated a reduction of the quota to 78,000 tons for 1994. In late 1993 prices had fallen to a 20-year 'low' and world tin stocks were estimated at 38,000–40,000 tons, owing partly to the non-observance of quota limits by Brazil and China, as well as to increased production by non-ATPC members. World tin stocks resumed their rise in early 1994, reaching 48,000 tons in June. However, the effects of reduced output, from both ATPC and non-ATPC producing countries, helped to reduce stock levels to 41,000 tons at the end of December. In 1995 exports by ATPC members exceeded the agreed voluntary quotas by 10%, and in May 1996, when world tin stocks were estimated to have been reduced to 20,000 tons, the ATPC suspended its quota arrangements. Shortly before the annual meeting of the ATPC was convened in September, Australia and Thailand announced their withdrawal from the organization, on the grounds that its activities had ceased to be effective in maintaining price levels favourable to tin-producers. Although China and Indonesia indicated that they would continue to support the ATPC, together with Bolivia, Malaysia and Nigeria (Zaire had ceased to be an active producer of tin), the termination of its quota arrangements in 1996, together with the continuing recovery in the tin market, indicated that its future role would be that of a forum for tin-producers and consumers. Malaysia, Australia and Indonesia left the ATPC in 1997, and Brazil became a full member in 1998. In June 1999, when the organization's headquarters were moved from Kuala Lumpur to Rio de Janeiro, Brazil, the membership comprised Brazil, Bolivia, China, the DRC and Nigeria.

After consumption, and prices, of tin suffered something of a decline in the early 2000s, demand for tin world-wide was estimated to have increased by about 7% in 2003, and provisional figures indicated a similar level of growth in 2004, when output surged in response to the growth that had occurred in the previous year. The price of tin in London (i.e. the average quotation for tin for immediate delivery traded on the LME) increased by almost 75% in 2004—a larger increase than that recorded for any other metal traded on the LME—to an average of US $8,513 per metric ton, and stocks of tin held by the Exchange declined precipitously. In 2005 the average price of tin traded on the LME declined by 13.4%, relative to the previous year, to $7,370 per ton. In mid-2005 the market for tin was characterized by uncommonly low stocks—LME inventories totalled only 3,855 tons at the end of June—but, by the end of the year, LME stocks had recovered to 16,725 tons. This recovery reflected the return of tin markets to surplus, a consequence of a surge in Indonesian production, among other factors. The average price of tin traded on the LME increased by 18.9% in 2006, to $8,763 per ton. During 2006 the price of tin traded in London ranged between $6,595 and $11,900 per ton. The average price of tin traded on the LME rose in each month in January–May 2007. In May an average price of $14,148 per ton was recorded, but in June the average price fell to $14,107 per ton. The average price rose, by 4.5%, to $14,747 per ton in July, when speculative funds were reported to have exerted a strong influence on the tin market. On the final day of July the 'spot' or cash price for tin in London rose to a record 'high' of $16,480 per ton. Concern about the level of future supplies from Bolivia, China and Indonesia were cited by analysts as the key drivers of the rise in the price of tin and, with rising demand in China and Europe, far outweighed data indicating weak demand for tin in the USA and Japan. The price of tin traded on the LME continued to rise in the second half of 2007, peaking at an average price of $16,692 per ton in November. For the whole of 2007 an average price of tin traded on the LME of $14,536 per ton was recorded, an increase (in nominal terms) of 65.9%. In January–May 2008 the price of tin traded in London rose steeply, from an average of $16,337 per ton in January to $24,214 per ton in May. The average price recorded in May represented an all-time 'high', and, on a daily basis, the 'spot' price of $25,000 per ton recorded on 15 May was also a record. According to analysts, a key factor behind the rise in the price of tin in early 2008 were data confirming China's evolution from a tin exporter to a net importer of the metal, including tin concentrates. Prices declined dramatically in the final quarter of 2008, owing to the onset of global recession, but average prices for the year remained higher than in 2007. According to the World Bank (based on the LME settlement price), the average price of refined tin in the final quarter of 2008 was $13,100 per ton, restraining the average price for the whole of 2008 to $18,510 per ton. In the first quarter of 2009 the price fell further, to an average of $11,030 per ton, but by the second quarter prices were recovering, following strong demand in China and supply problems in Indonesia. Prices rose fairly steadily thereafter into the first months of 2011, as global economic recovery, notably in China, set in, averaging $13,570 per ton for 2009 as a whole and $20,410 per ton for 2010. The average London tin price for the first seven months of 2011 was $29,080 per ton, the monthly averages having peaked in April at $32,363 per ton. The monthly price fell to $25,520 per ton on average in June, but rose to $27,400 per ton in July, following the end of the restraint on production from heavy rains in Indonesia.

The success, after 1985, of the ATPC in restoring orderly conditions in tin trading (partly by the voluntary quotas and partly by working towards the reduction of tin stockpiles) unofficially established it as the effective successor to the ITC as the international co-ordinating body for tin interests. The International Tin Study Group, comprising 36 producing and consuming countries, was established by the ATPC in 1989 to assume the informational functions of the ITC. In 1991 the secretariat of the United Nations Conference on Trade and Development assumed responsibility for the publication of statistical information on the international tin market. The International Tin Research Institute, founded in 1932 and based in London, United Kingdom, promotes scientific research and technical development in the production and use of tin.

TOBACCO (*Nicotiana tabacum*)

Tobacco originated in South America and was used in rituals and ceremonials or as a medicine; it was smoked and chewed for centuries before its introduction into Europe, the Middle East, Africa and South Asia in the 16th century. The generic name *Nicotiana* denotes the presence of the alkaloid nicotine in its leaves. The most important species in commercial tobacco cultivation is *N. tabacum*. Another species, *N. rustica*, is widely grown, but on a smaller scale, to yield cured leaf for snuff or simple cigarettes and cigars.

In 2009, according to FAO, tobacco was harvested from about 3.9m. ha world-wide. Commercially grown tobacco (from *N. tabacum*) can be divided into four major types—flue-cured, air-cured (including burley, cigar, light and dark), fire-cured and sun-cured (including oriental)—depending on the procedures used to dry or 'cure' the leaves. Each system imparts specific chemical and smoking characteristics to the cured leaf, although these may also be affected by other factors, such as the type of soil on which the crop is grown, the type and quantity of fertilizer applied to the crop, the cultivar used, the spacing of the crop in the field and the number of leaves left at topping (the removal of the terminal growing point). Each type is used, separately or in combination, in specific products (e.g. flue-cured in Virginia cigarettes). All types are grown in Asia.

As in other major producing areas, local research organizations in Asia have developed new cultivars with specific, desirable chemical characteristics, disease-resistance properties and improved yields. Almost all tobacco production in the Far East is from smallholdings; there is no cultivation of the crop on estates, as is common with tea. Emphasis has been placed on improving yields by the selection of cultivars, by the increased use of fertilizers and by the elimination or reduction of crop loss (through use of crop chemicals) and on reducing requirements for hand labour through the mechanization of land preparation and the use of crop chemicals. Harvesting continues to be entirely a manual operation, as the size of farmers' holdings and the cost of harvesting devices (now commonly used in the USA and Canada) preclude such development in Asia. The flue-curing process requires energy in the form of oil, gas, coal or wood. To ensure that supplies of wood are continuously renewed, the tobacco industry in several countries encourages the planting of trees.

The principal type of tobacco cultivated by Asian farmers is flue-cured. Of the countries producing this tobacco in the Far East, the most important are the People's Republic of China, Japan and the Koreas. China is the world's principal producer, as well as the largest consumer, of tobacco, and, while most of its output is still retained for local use, exports expanded by an annual average rate of about 14% in 1990–2005, totalling 167,822 metric tons in the latter year and, after an 11% dip, 168,836 tons in 2007; tobacco exports exceeded the 2004 peak in 2008, however, reaching a record (198,829 tons. In 2002 China supplanted the USA as the world's second largest exporter of unmanufactured tobacco, after Brazil. The USA regained second place in 2006 and 2007, while in the same years India pushed China into the position of the world's fourth largest exporter of tobacco; the USA fell to fourth place in 2008. Production in China in the 2000s benefited from significant changes in the organization of, and in the methods of cultivation that are practised in, tobacco-growing areas. The tobacco sector is also a significant domestic employer: according to the International Tobacco Growers' Association (ITGA—see below), about 16m. people were engaged in tobacco-growing in China in the late 1990s.

Production of Unmanufactured Tobacco
('000 metric tons)

	2008	2009
World total	6,691	7,193
Far East	3,374	3,632
Oceania	4	5
Leading regional producers		
China, People's Repub.	2,840	3,068
Indonesia	170	181*
Japan	39	37
Korea, Dem. People's Repub.*	74	80
Korea, Repub.*	39	42
Laos†	33	26
Philippines	32	36
Thailand*	68	72
Viet Nam	29	39
Other leading producers		
Argentina*	158	159
Brazil	851	863
India	490	620
Italy*	121	119
Malawi	160	208
Pakistan	108	105
Turkey	93	85
USA	363	373
Zimbabwe*	82	96

* FAO estimate(s).
† Unofficial estimates.

Source: FAO.

The only significant regional producers of burley tobacco are Indonesia, Japan (for domestic consumption) and the Koreas (for domestic consumption and for export), although Thailand is increasing its output of this type. Production of dark air-cured tobacco is limited mainly to China and Indonesia. Asia is not a significant producer of fire-cured and oriental tobaccos.

Japan is unable to produce sufficient flue-cured tobacco for domestic consumption, owing mainly to pressure on the availability of land, and thus relies on substantial and increasing imports. Japanese exports increased in the mid-2000s, and averaged more than 6,200 metric tons per year in 2003–08. Korean flue-cured is now accepted on international markets. In both Thailand and the Koreas domestic requirements are likely to maintain pressure on production. The level of exports from these countries has stabilized (sales by the Democratic People's Republic of Korea—North Korea—have fallen very substantially since 1998), and this position is unlikely to be reversed despite the increased supplies of flue-cured tobacco now available on international markets from Brazil, Malawi and Zimbabwe, although the price competitiveness of Korean flue-cured does not enhance its export prospects. Annual exports from Thailand in the 2000s, up to 2008, averaged just over 32,000 tons, and from the Republic of Korea (South Korea) almost 3,600 tons.

Of the other tobacco-producing countries in the Far East, Indonesia is a significant producer and exporter of cigar tobaccos, yet still requires imported flue-cured tobacco to sustain its domestic market, although increasing quantities of domestic flue-cured are being grown on Sulawesi (Celebes), Bali and Lombok in the Lesser Sunda Islands (Nusa Tenggara). Domestic tobacco production is increasing in Malaysia, under the aegis of the National Tobacco Board. The Philippines produces both flue-cured and air-cured tobacco acceptable to world markets.

Growing conditions in New Zealand and Australia are wholly dissimilar to those in other countries in the Asia-Pacific region, and neither country is a significant producer in world terms. However, both countries contain large tobacco holdings, and mechanization is considerable. Problems related to the cultivation of the crop, such as the occurrence of blue mould in Australia, are unique. Domestic production, mainly flue-cured, is encouraged through government legislation stipulating a minimum quantity of such tobacco to be incorporated into tobacco products that are marketed in Australia and New Zealand.

About two-fifths of world tobacco production are traded internationally. Until 1993, when it was overtaken by Brazil, the USA was the world's principal tobacco-exporting country. Since 1993 Brazil has consolidated its position as the world's leading exporter of tobacco, largely at the expense of the USA and Zimbabwe. Brazil's share of global exports of unmanufactured tobacco increased in volume from 13% in 1993 to about one-quarter in the mid-2000s (26% in 2008). According to the UN Conference on Trade and Development, tobacco prices soon recovered from the commodity slump of late 2008 and early 2009, when the average price for unmanufactured tobacco (US import unit value) over August 2008 to July 2009 was US $3,988 per metric ton. The average annual price for 2008 as a whole was $3,589 per ton; in 2009 it was $4,239 per ton, and in 2010 $3,251 per ton. Prices rose through 2009 and into 2010, peaking at $4,466 per ton in January 2010, before falling back to $4,180 per ton in April. One year later the monthly average peaked again, at $4,577 per ton in April 2011, having risen sharply over the previous two months, as commodity prices world-wide rose; the US import unit value was $4,390 per ton in June and July.

According to FAO, world tobacco demand is expected to increase until 2010 due to population and income growth—albeit at lower rates than in the past—despite the progress of anti-smoking measures in developed countries. While the share of developed countries in world tobacco consumption is projected to fall to 29% (compared with 34% in 1998), more tobacco will be smoked in developing countries, where consumption is expected to increase by an average annual rate of 1.7%, to about 5m. metric tons. A substantial part of the increase in demand is projected to be in the Far East, particularly in China, whose share of world-wide tobacco consumption is expected to remain around 37% in 2010.

The ITGA, with headquarters in Castelo Branco, Portugal, was formed in 1984 by growers' groups in Argentina, Brazil, Canada, Malawi, the USA and Zimbabwe. In 2011 its members numbered 22 countries, including China and Malaysia. ITGA members account for more than 80% of the world's internationally traded tobacco. The Association provides a forum for the exchange of information among tobacco producers, conducts research and publishes studies on tobacco issues.

WHEAT (*Triticum*)

The most common species of wheat, *Triticum vulgare*, includes hard, semi-hard and soft varieties which have different milling characteristics but which, in general, are suitable for bread-making. Another species, *T. durum*, is grown mainly in semi-arid areas, including regions bordering the Mediterranean Sea. This wheat is very hard and is suitable for the manufacture of semolina, the basic ingredient of pasta and couscous. A third species, spelt (*T. spelta*), is also included in production figures for wheat. It is grown in very small quantities in parts of Europe and is used mainly as animal feed.

Although a most adaptable crop, wheat does not thrive in hot and humid climates, and it requires timely applications of water (either through rainfall or irrigation). Wheat is an important crop in most countries in Asia north of the Tropic of Cancer, wherever the terrain is favourable and sufficient water is available. The most concentrated producing areas in the Asia-Pacific region are to be found in Pakistan, northern India and eastern parts of the People's Republic of China.

World wheat production declined during the 1990s, albeit only marginally, at an average rate of less than 0.1% a year. The fall was largely due to the sharp decline in agricultural output in the former USSR, excluding which the trend in world production growth has been upward. Wheat production is highly variable from year to year. Part of the variation is attributable to weather conditions, particularly rainfall, in the main producing areas, but national policies on support for producers have also been a major influence. In the 1990s several major wheat-producing countries, including leading exporters, pursued policies of market deregulation and began to remove the links between producers' support and the financial returns from particular commodities. This encouraged farmers in these countries more readily to switch between crops according to expected relative market returns. After 1996, for example, when wheat was in short supply on world markets, output was stimulated in many growing areas, and a record 613m. metric tons was harvested in 1997. Production then declined, to some 586m. tons by 2000, only increasing again in 2001, to about 590m. tons. Wheat production world-wide fell sharply, to some 560m. tons by 2003. Output recovered to a new record level of 632m. tons in 2004, but lapsed to 627m. tons in 2005 and to 603m. tons in 2006. FAO figures suggested a small recovery in output in 2007, to 613m. tons, then a dramatic increase of 12% in 2008, to another new record of 683m. tons, with a smaller rise in 2009, to 686m. tons. At August 2011 US Department of Agriculture (USDA) figures, which use local marketing years, put total world production in 2006/07 at 596m. tons, rising to 612m. tons in 2007/08, a record 683m. tons in 2008/09 and 684m. tons in 2009/10, before declining to 648m. tons in 2010/11; a recovery to 662m. tons was forecast for 2011/12. The largest producer of wheat in the world is the European Union (EU—21% of the world total in 2010/11), followed by East Asia (18%) and South Asia (18%). The countries of the former USSR (12%) normally constitute the world's third wheat-producing region, but drought and fires during 2010 reduced the Russian harvest by almost one-third; in 2010/11 North America too outperformed the former USSR. By far the largest individual wheat producers internationally in 2010/11 were the People's Republic of China (18%), which accounted for most of the East Asian production, India (12%), the USA (9%) and, still, Russia (6%).

World consumption, which has, in the long term, been increasing at a similar rate to production, varies much less from year to year than the wheat harvest. Wheat food use has been expanding at the expense of rice: its growth is associated with rising consumer incomes and an increasing number of fast-food outlets. Substantial amounts of wheat are used for animal feed in Europe and, when prices are favourable, in North America. Substantial quantities were also used for feed in the 1980s in the what was then the USSR, but this volume decreased sharply in response to the diminution in livestock numbers. Some wheat is used for feed in Japan, while the Republic of Korea (South Korea) imports wheat for feed when prices are low in comparison with those of coarse grains such as sorghum and maize (corn). According to USDA, domestic consumption of wheat was highest in the EU until 2010/11, when East Asia just exceeded it for the first time (both on 19% of the world total of 654m. metric tons), followed by South Asia (18%). Most of the countries in such regions are also producers.

Wheat is the principal cereal in international trade. FAO, in its latest available figures, assessed international trade in wheat at about 133m. metric tons in 2007, the fourth successive year of increase, with a dip to 131m. tons in 2008. USDA figures had world trade in wheat, flour and products peaking in 2008/09, before falling back in 2009/10, with a further decline in 2010/11, largely owing to global economic problems and high prices dampening consumption; a small recovery was expected in 2011/12. The downward tendency was emphasized by government policies—to counter high prices, for instance—such as the decision by the Government of India in 2009 to restrict wheat exports. In 2010 the drought in Russia further restricted supplies to the world market. The largest importing region, by far, was the Middle East and North Africa (32% of world imports in 2010/11), followed by South-East Asia (13%), sub-Saharan Africa (all African states except the five Mediterranean littoral countries—11%), East Asia (11%) and South America (10%). According to USDA data, amounts exported in 2004/05–2007/08 ranged between 109m. metric tons and 117m. tons annually, rising in the following year to 143m. tons, before falling to 134m. tons in 2009/10 and 131m. tons in 2010/11. The main exporter in 2009/10 was still the USA (18% of the world total), whose share had declined from about 30% of the total in the first half of the 1990s to about 24% in 2005/06. However, in 2010/11 dramatically increased US exports, up by almost one-half, and the collapse in Russian exports (to 4m. tons, from 19m. tons the previous year), led to a surge in the US share of world exports back up to 27%. Other major exporters are the EU, Australia, Canada, Kazakhstan, Ukraine and, usually, Russia. EU imports had declined substantially since the early 2000s, owing to the introduction of a system of import quotas designed to curb purchases of cheap Ukrainian and Russian wheat. Developed countries were formerly the principal consumers of wheat, but the role of developing countries as importers has been steadily increasing and they now regularly account for approximately two-thirds of world imports.

Wheat production in East Asia has increased at a considerably faster rate than that of output in the world as a whole. In the mid-1970s the region's harvest averaged about 47m. metric tons per year, or approximately 12% of the world total, but by the late 1990s it averaged 116m. tons (approximately one-fifth of the total). This growth was attributable, in large part, to an accelerated rate of expansion of wheat output in China, brought about by extensive irrigation, better supplies of fertilizers and, perhaps most influential of all, the introduction of cash incentives to farmers. Local abundance gave rise to storage problems in some areas in the mid-1980s, and, as a result, some producers lost interest in wheat and converted to cultivation of cash crops. However, the subsequent introduction of stricter marketing regulations, higher prices payable to wheat producers and more abundant fertilizer supplies led to a resumption of growth. By the mid-1990s China, with annual output averaging about 105m. tons, was by far the world's leading wheat-producing country—which status it has retained despite a substantial decline in output since 1997 (when production was more than 120m. tons) to, on average, 90.6m. tons annually in 2000–09. According to FAO, however, production had recovered steadily from 2004, to reach 112.5m. tons by 2008 and 115.1m. tons in 2009 (accounting for 16.8% of the world total). East Asia as a whole accounted for 17.0% of global production in 2009, and Oceania (mainly Australia) for a further 3.2%. After China, the next largest wheat producer in East Asia is Japan (674,200 tons in 2009, or less than 1% of the Chinese total). Mongolia is an increasingly important wheat producer, recovering strongly from a low point of 73,419 tons in 2005 and almost doubling in 2008, to 209,830 tons; FAO figures for 2009 put Mongolian wheat production at 388,122 tons, which compared favourably with a still declining Japanese total. The Koreas also produce some wheat. South-East Asia is not a significant grower of wheat, most of the region's production accounted for by Myanmar (an estimated 179,000 tons in 2009), with a notional 1,081 tons imputed for Thailand.

Australia is one of the world's major wheat-exporting countries, and in the year to June 2006 sales of wheat earned the country $A3,213m., representing 2.1% of total merchandise export earnings that year. Production varies considerably from year to year, however. The incidence of drought in the main producing areas is a major determinant (the 1994 wheat crop was reduced by 45% as a result of drought conditions), but plantings also reflect world market conditions, as Australian wheat-farming receives no government subsidies. In 2002, for instance, output fell drastically, by more than one-half the level of the previous two years, to only 10m. tons, as a consequence of drought in all of Australia's main wheat-growing regions. Production recovered strongly in 2003, to 26.1m. tons, but fell to 21.9m. tons in 2004. Output in 2005 was 25.2m. tons. However, output was again significantly reduced in 2006, according to FAO data, to just 10.8m. tons, largely because of adverse weather conditions. Production improved somewhat in 2007, but only to around 13.6m. tons, because of damage caused to much of the country's

harvest by hot winds. In 2008 production was back up to 21.4m. tons, while 2009 recorded 21.7m. tons. In 2010/11, according to USDA figures, Australia had risen to be the world's third most important wheat exporter, after the USA and the EU, not only because of increased output but because of poor harvests in Canada, owing to adverse weather, and Russia, owing to drought and fires; in 2011/12 Australia was even expected to exceed EU wheat production. The only other country in the Pacific area with significant wheat production is New Zealand, which is usually self-sufficient in this cereal. Production had fallen from above 300,000 tons each year in the first half of the decade to 261,798 tons in 2006, but then rose steadily to reach 403,464 tons in 2009. New Caledonia produces a negligible amount of wheat: an estimated and declining eight tons in 2009.

East Asia has long been one of the world's principal wheat-importing regions. Imports rose considerably during the 1980s, but reduced purchases by China caused a temporary reverse in the early 1990s. Japan has been a major importer since the 1960s. Its imports, of between 5m. and 6m. metric tons annually, represent an important element of stability in the world wheat trade. Despite the scale of its own production, China is frequently a major wheat importer. However, following purchases of 12.5m. tons in 1995/96, its imports thereafter averaged only about 2m. tons annually, owing to large harvests, abundant stocks and a slower rate of growth in wheat consumption. In 2004/05, however, Chinese wheat imports rose to about 6.7m. tons, despite higher domestic production. USDA reported that Chinese imports declined in 2007/08 to just 49,000 tons, owing to higher domestic output and comparatively slow growth in domestic consumption, and were higher but remained negligible in both the year before and the year after. However, in 2009/10 wheat imports amounted to some 1.4m. tons, falling back to 0.9m. tons in 2010/11, with a similar level expected the following year. South Korea also buys varying amounts of wheat. Its basic food needs account for more than 2m. metric tons annually, but it also purchases additional amounts, of up to 4m. tons, for animal feed if the price is competitive with maize and other feed grains. For this reason, against the regional trend, Korean imports of low-grade wheat were forecast to rise to some 4.6m. tons in 2008/09, in order to compensate for a regional shortage of maize, but the onset of global recession dampened demand and exports amounted to some 3.4m. tons. However, imports reached 4.5m. tons in 2009/10 and 4.8m. tons in 2010/11, although they were expected to fall back marginally in 2011/12

Several countries in the region, notably in South-East Asia, grow no wheat, such as Indonesia, Malaysia and the Philippines, and have become major importers, Indonesia first among them (6.6m. metric tons in 2010/11).

Production of Wheat
('000 metric tons, including spelt)

	2008	2009
World total*	683,070	685,614
Far East*	113,911	116,538
Oceania*	21,764	22,059
Leading regional producers		
Australia	21,420	21,656
China, People's Repub.	112,463	115,115
Other leading producers		
Canada	28,611	26,848
France	39,006	38,332
Germany	25,989	25,190
India	78,570	80,680
Pakistan	20,959	24,033
Russia	63,765	61,740
Ukraine	25,885	20,886
USA	68,016	60,314

* Including estimated data.

Source: FAO.

The export price (f.o.b. Gulf ports) of US No. 2 Hard Red Winter, one of the most widely-traded wheat varieties, averaged US $119 per metric ton in 2000, rising to $151 per ton by 2002. Prices fluctuated thereafter, the average price falling in 2005 to $158 per ton. In 2006 the average price jumped to $200 per ton, and thereafter the price continued to rise substantially, reaching $264 per ton in 2007 to $345 per ton in 2008. Average monthly prices in 2008 attained a record $482 per ton in March, in line with other international commodity prices, but had fallen as low as $235 per ton by December. In 2009 the average export price of US No. 2 Hard Winter wheat was $236 per ton, ranging between a high of $270 in June and a low of $201 in September. The average price in 2010 was $241 per ton. Prices fell as low as $183 per ton by June (the lowest monthly price in more than four years, since March 2006), but jumped to $304 per ton by September, forced up by anxiety about the drought in Russia and other countries of the former USSR, notably Kazakhstan and Ukraine—in particular given the devastating fires in central Russia in the intense summer heat of that year. Average prices for US No. 2 Hard Red Winter rose above $300 per ton by the end of 2010 ($320 per ton in December) and had remained so at mid-August 2011. Although Black Sea exports from Russia, Kazakhstan and Ukraine had returned to the market in 2011, helping keep prices below the monthly average peak of $362 per ton in February, prices remained above $320 per ton into August, despite dipping to the low point of the year in July, at $308 per ton. The average price for January–July 2010 was $342 per ton.

From 1949 nearly all world trade in wheat was conducted under the auspices of successive international agreements, administered by the International Wheat Council (IWC) in London, United Kingdom. The early agreements involved regulatory price controls and supply and purchase obligations, but such provisions became inoperable in more competitive market conditions, and were abandoned in 1972. The IWC subsequently concentrated on providing detailed market assessments to its members and encouraging them to confer on matters of mutual concern. A new Grains Trade Convention, which entered into force in July 1995, allows for improvements in the provision of information on all grains to members of what had become the International Grains Council (IGC—the successor to the IWC), and enhances opportunities for consultations. In mid-2011 the IGC consisted of 26 members, including the member states of the EU (which are counted as a single member). Membership in East Asia and Oceania comprises Australia, Japan and the Republic of Korea.

Since 1967 a series of Food Aid Conventions (FACs), linked to the successive Wheat and Grains Trade Conventions, have ensured continuity of supplies of food aid in the form of cereals to needy countries. Under the latest FAC, negotiated in 1999, the 22 donor countries (including the member states of the EU) have pledged to supply a minimum of some 5m. metric tons of food aid annually to developing countries, with priority being given to least developed countries and other low-income food-importing countries. Aid is to be provided mostly in the form of cereals, and all aid given to least developed countries is to be in the form of grants. The FAC seeks to improve the effectiveness, and increase the impact, of food aid by improved monitoring and consultative procedures. In mid-2004 FAC members undertook a renegotiation of the 1999 FAC in order 'to strengthen its capacity to meet identified needs when food aid is the appropriate response'. However, it was decided that this renegotiation should await the conclusion of discussions on trade-related food aid issues in agriculture negotiations at the World Trade Organization. In the mean time, the FAC, 1999, was extended for two years from July 2005; further, one-year extensions were agreed in mid-2007, mid-2008, mid-2009 and mid-2010. In December 2010 formal negotiations on the future of the FAC commenced, and in May 2011 the FAC was again extended, until 30 June 2012, to give the discussions a fair chance of fruition.

ACKNOWLEDGEMENTS

We gratefully acknowledge the assistance of the following organizations in the preparation of this section: US Department of Agriculture (USDA); International Aluminium Institute; International Cocoa Organization; International Coffee Organization; International Monetary Fund; International Rice Research Institute; International Rubber Study Group; International Tea Committee; International Tobacco Growers' Association; Food and Agriculture Organization of the UN (FAO); US Geological Survey, US Department of the Interior; US Department of Energy; World Bureau of Metal Statistics; World Coal Institute.

CALENDARS AND TIME RECKONING

The Islamic Calendar

The Islamic era dates from 16 July 622, which was the beginning of the Arab year in which the *Hijra* ('flight' or migration) of the Prophet Muhammad (the founder of Islam), from Mecca to Medina (in modern Saudi Arabia), took place. The Islamic or *Hijri* Calendar is lunar, each year having 354 or 355 days, the extra day being intercalated 11 times every 30 years. Accordingly, the beginning of the *Hijri* year occurs earlier in the Gregorian Calendar by a few days each year. Dates are reckoned in terms of the *anno Hegirae* (AH) or year of the Hegira (*Hijra*). The Islamic year AH 1432 began on 7 December 2010.

The year is divided into the following months:

1. Muharram	30 days	7. Rajab	30 days
2. Safar	29 days	8. Shaaban	29 days
3. Rabia I	30 days	9. Ramadan	30 days
4. Rabia II	29 days	10. Shawwal	29 days
5. Jumada I	30 days	11. Dhu'l-Qa'da	30 days
6. Jumada II	29 days	12. Dhu'l-Hijja	29 or 30 days

The *Hijri* Calendar is used for religious purposes throughout the Islamic world.

PRINCIPAL ISLAMIC FESTIVALS

New Year: 1st Muharram. The first 10 days of the year are regarded as holy, especially the 10th.

Ashoura: 10th Muharram. Celebrates the first meeting of Adam and Eve after leaving Paradise, also the ending of the Flood and the death of Husain, grandson of the Prophet Muhammad. The feast is celebrated with fairs and processions.

Mouloud (Birth of Muhammad): 12th Rabia I.

Leilat al-Meiraj (Ascension of Muhammad): 27th Rajab.

Ramadan (Month of Fasting).

Id al-Fitr (The Small Feast): Three days beginning 1st Shawwal. This celebration follows the constraint of the Ramadan fast.

Id al-Adha (The Great Feast, Feast of the Sacrifice): Four days beginning on 10th Dhu'l-Hijja. The principal Islamic festival, commemorating Abraham's sacrifice and coinciding with the pilgrimage to Mecca. Celebrated by the sacrifice of a sheep, by feasting and by donations to the poor.

Islamic Year	1431	1432	1433
New Year	18 Dec. 2009	7 Dec. 2010	26 Nov. 2011
Ashoura	27 Dec. 2009	16 Dec. 2010	5 Dec. 2011
Mouloud	26 Feb. 2009	15 Feb. 2011	4 Feb. 2012
Leilat al-Meiraj	8 July 2010	28 June 2011	16 June 2012
Ramadan begins	11 Aug. 2010	31 July 2011	19 July 2012
Id al-Fitr	10 Sept. 2010	30 Aug. 2011	18 Aug. 2012
Id al-Adha	16 Nov. 2010	6 Nov. 2011	25 Sept. 2012

Note: Local determinations may vary by one day from those given here.

THE CHINESE CALENDAR

China has both lunar and solar systems of dividing the year. The lunar calendar contains 12 months of 29 or 30 days, and in each period of 19 years seven intercalary months are inserted at appropriate intervals. In order not to disturb the 12-month cycle, each of these extra months bears the same title as that which preceded it. The intercalary months may not be introduced after the first, 11th or 12th month of any year.

The solar year, which is used by the agrarian community of China, begins regularly on 5 February of the Gregorian calendar, and is divided into 24 sections of 14, 15 or 16 days. This calendar is not upset by the discrepant cycle of the moon, and is therefore suitable for the regulation of agriculture.

Until the revolution of 1911, years were named according to a 60-year cycle, made up of 10 stems (*Ban*) and 12 branches (*Ji*). Each year of the cycle has a composite name composed of a different combination of stem and branch. Similar 60-year cycles of year-names have been in use in Thailand and Japan at various times and are still used in Hong Kong, Malaysia and Singapore.

Since 1911 years have been dated from the revolution as Years of the Republic; AD 2012 is the 101st year of the republican era. The Republic of China has been confined to Taiwan since 1949. In the People's Republic of China the Gregorian system is used.

Japan has used the Gregorian system since 1873, but a National Calendar has also been introduced, derived from the traditional date of accession of the first emperor, Zinmu, in 660 BC. The year AD 2012 corresponds to 2671 of this era.

BUDDHIST CALENDARS

The Buddhist era (BE) is attributed to the death of Gautama Buddha, historically dated at about 483 BC. The era in use is dated, in fact, from 544 BC, making the year 2012 of the Christian era equal to 2555 of the Buddhist era.

In South-East Asia there is widespread use of a lunar year of 354 days, with months of alternately 29 or 30 days, and with extra (intercalary) months approximately every third year. Under this system, New Year may fall in either April or March. In Myanmar (formerly Burma), New Year is regularly on 13 April. The Burmese era, the *Khaccapancha*, is ascribed to the ruler Popa Sawrahan, and begins in AD 638. The year 2012 of the Gregorian Calendar is equivalent to 1374 BE.

Thailand used the Burmese calendar until 1889, when a new civil era was introduced, commemorating the centenary of the first king of Bangkok. Since 1909 a calendar based on the year 543 BC (traditionally the year of Gautama Buddha's attainment of nirvana) has been in official use. The months have been adapted to correspond with those of the Gregorian Calendar, and New Year is celebrated on 1 January. In this calendar, called the *Pra Putta Sakarat*, AD 2012 is equivalent to 2555.

FESTIVALS

The principal festivals in the Buddhist calendars are the New Year and the spring and autumn equinox, and local festivals connected with important pagodas.

STANDARD TIME

The following table gives the standard time adopted in the various countries and territories covered in this book, in relation to Greenwich Mean Time (GMT).

Standard Time

The following table gives the standard time adopted in the various countries and territories covered in this book, in relation to Greenwich Mean Time (GMT).

$+6\frac{1}{2}$	+7	+8	+9	$+9\frac{1}{2}$
Cocos (Keeling Is)	Cambodia	Australia (Western Australia)	Timor-Leste (fmrly East Timor)	Australia (Northern Territory, South Australia)
Myanmar (fmrly Burma)	Christmas Island	Brunei	Indonesia (Maluku/ Moluccas, Papua)	
	Indonesia (Sumatra, Java, Madura, West and Central Kalimantan)	China, People's Republic	Japan	
	Laos	Hong Kong	Korea	
	Mongolia (western)	Indonesia (Bali, East and South Kalimantan, West Timor, Celebes/ Sulawesi)	Mongolia (eastern)	
	Thailand	Macao	Palau	
	Viet Nam	Malaysia		
		Mongolia (central)		
		Philippines		
		Singapore		
		Taiwan		

+10	+11	$+11\frac{1}{2}$	+12	$+12\frac{3}{4}$
Australia (the ACT, NSW, Queensland, Tasmania, Victoria)	Federated States of Micronesia (eastern)	Norfolk Island	Fiji	New Zealand (Chatham Is)
Guam	New Caledonia		Kiribati (excl. Millennium (fmrly Caroline) Island)	
Northern Mariana Is	Solomon Is		Marshall Is	
Federated States of Micronesia (western)	Vanuatu		Nauru	
Papua New Guinea (excl. North Solomons Province)			New Zealand	
			Tuvalu	
			Wallis and Futuna Is	
			Wake Island	

+13	–11	–10	–8	
Kiribati (Millennium (fmrly Caroline) Island)	American Samoa	Cook Is	Pitcairn Is	
Samoa (from 31 Dec. 2011)	Midway Island	French Polynesia (except Gambier Is and Marquesas Is)		
Tokelau (from 31 Dec. 2011)	Niue			
Tonga				

RESEARCH INSTITUTES

ASSOCIATIONS AND INSTITUTIONS STUDYING THE FAR EAST AND AUSTRALASIA*

AUSTRALIA

Asia Institute: Level 2, Sidney Myer Asia Centre, cnr Swanston St and Monash Rd, University of Melbourne, Vic 3010; tel. (3) 8344-5554; fax (3) 9349-4870; e-mail j.forsyth@unimelb.edu.au; internet www.asiainstitute.unimelb.edu.au; conducts research, and undergraduate and postgraduate study programmes, on the languages, culture, politics, history, and religious traditions of Asia and of the Islamic world; Dir Prof. KEE POOKONG.

Asia Research Centre on Social, Political and Economic Change: Murdoch University, Murdoch, WA 6150; tel. (8) 9360-2263; fax (8) 9360-6381; e-mail arc@murdoch.edu.au; internet www.arc.murdoch.edu.au; f. 1991; provides analysis of contemporary East and South-East Asia; Dir Prof. GARRY RODAN.

Asian Economics Centre: Dept of Economics, Economics and Commerce Bldg, University of Melbourne, Vic 3010; tel. (3) 8344-5035; fax (3) 8344-6899; e-mail d.maclaren@unimelb.edu.au; internet www.economics.unimelb.edu.au/AsianEcoCentre/home.shtml; fmrly Asian Business Centre; Dir Assoc. Prof. DONALD MACLAREN.

Asian Studies Program, La Trobe University: Melbourne, Vic 3086; tel. (3) 9479-2844; fax (3) 9479-1478; internet www.latrobe.edu.au/humanities/areas-of-study/asian-studies; f. 1994; Exec. Dean TIM MURRAY.

Australia-Japan Research Centre: Crawford School of Economics and Government, Australian National University, Canberra, ACT 0200; tel. (2) 6125-0168; fax (2) 6125-0767; e-mail ajrc@anu.edu.au; internet www.crawford.anu.edu.au; f. 1980; Exec. Dir Prof. JENNY CORBETT; publs include *Asia Pacific Economic Papers* (monthly), *APEC Economies Newsletter* (monthly).

The Australian Centre: The University of Melbourne, 137 Barry St, Carlton, Vic 3053; tel. (3) 8344-4154; fax (3) 9347-7731; e-mail arts-austcentre@unimelb.edu.au; internet www.australian.unimelb.edu.au; f. 1989; research, teaching and outreach programmes; Dir Dr SARA WILLS.

Australian Institute of Aboriginal and Torres Strait Islander Studies (AIATSIS): GPOB 553, Canberra 2601, ACT; tel. (2) 6246-1111; fax (2) 6261-4285; e-mail executive@aiatsis.gov.au; internet www.aiatsis.gov.au; research, publishing and outreach programmes; film, photographs, video and audio recordings collections, and the world's largest collections of printed and other resource materials for Indigenous studies; publs of the Aboriginal Studies Press, publishing br. of AIATSIS, incl. *Australian Aboriginal Studies Journal* (2 a year), books and monographs; Principal RUSSELL TAYLOR.

Australian Institute of International Affairs: 32 Thesiger Court, Deakin, ACT 2600; tel. (2) 6282-2133; fax (2) 6285-2334; e-mail ceo@aiia.asn.au; internet www.aiia.asn.au; f. 1933; 1,300 mems; Nat. Pres. CLIVE HILDEBRAND; Nat. Exec. Dir MELISSA H. CONLEY-TYLER; publs *The Australian Journal of International Affairs* (quarterly), *Australia in World Affairs* (book series, every 5 years).

The Australian Public Intellectual Network (API Network): Director, Institute for Media, Creative Arts and Technologies, Murdoch University, WA 6152; tel. (8) 9360-2170; e-mail orders@api-network.com; internet api-network.com; f. 1997; maintains a free, scholarly communications network for researchers in the field of Australian studies; not-for-profit publr of Australian scholarly titles; Dir Prof. RICHARD NILE; publs *Journal of Australian Studies*, *Australian Cultural History*, and books series.

Centre for Aboriginal Studies: Curtin University of Technology, GPOB U 1987, Perth 6845, WA; tel. (8) 9266-7091; fax (8) 9266-2888; e-mail cas.enquiries@curtin.edu.au; internet karda.curtin.edu.au/home/index.cfm; f. 1983; teaching, student support and services, publishing; promotes participation of Aboriginal and Torres Strait Islander people in tertiary studies; publs include books and monographs; Dir ANITA LEE HONG.

Centre for Asian Studies, University of Adelaide: University of Adelaide, Ligertwood Bldg, Adelaide, SA 5005; tel. (8) 8303-5815; fax (8) 8303-4388; e-mail asian.studies@adelaide.edu.au; internet www.hss.adelaide.edu.au/asian/; specializes in China, Japan and Korea; Dir Prof. MOBO CHANG FAN GAO.

Centre for Australian Indigenous Studies (CAIS): POB 55, Monash University, Clayton 3800, Vic; tel. (3) 9905-4200; fax (3) 9902-0321; e-mail cais@arts.monash.edu.au; internet arts.monash.edu.au/cais/; f. 1964; teaching and research; Dir Prof. LYNETTE RUSSELL.

Centre for International Economic Studies: University of Adelaide, Adelaide, SA 5005; tel. (8) 8303-5672; fax (8) 8223-1460; e-mail cies@adelaide.edu.au; internet www.adelaide.edu.au/cies; f. 1989; conducts theoretical and policy-orientated research with particular reference to the Asia-Pacific region; Dir Prof. CHRISTOPHER FINDLAY; publs include monographs.

Centre for Japanese Economic Studies: Dept of Economics, Macquarie University, Sydney, NSW 2109; tel. (2) 9850-7444; fax (2) 9850-8586; e-mail helen.boneham@mq.edu.au; internet www.econ.mq.edu.au/cjes; f. 1991; Dean Prof. MARK GABBOTT; publs include working papers.

Contemporary China Centre: Dept of Political and Social Change, College of Asia and the Pacific, Australian National University, Canberra, ACT 0200; tel. (2) 6125-4790; fax (2) 6125-9047; e-mail ccc@anu.edu.au; internet www.rspas.anu.edu.au/ccc; f. 1970; analyses post-1949 China; Dir Prof. JONATHAN UNGER; publs include *The China Journal*, *Contemporary China Books*.

Griffith Asia Institute: Rm 1.41, Business 1 Bldg (N50), Griffith University, 170 Kessels Rd, Nathan, Qld 4111; tel. (7) 3875-3730; fax (7) 3875-3731; e-mail gai@griffith.edu.au; internet www.griffith.edu.au/business/griffith-asia-institute; f. 1978; fmrly the Centre for the Study of Australia-Asia Relations; conducts research relating to Asian migration to Australia, security in the Asia-Pacific region, Asian perceptions of Australia and Australian-Asian economic relations; Dir Prof. ANDREW O'NEIL.

Korea Australasia Research Centre: University of New South Wales, Sydney, NSW 2052; tel. (2) 9385-4466; fax (2) 9385-5622; e-mail karec@unsw.edu.au; internet www.karec.unsw.edu.au; f. 2000; non-profit research institute; conducts and supports Korean studies in Australia, New Zealand and South-East Asia; Dir Assoc. Prof. CHUNG-SOK SUH.

Monash Asia Institute: POB 197, Caulfield East, Vic 3145; tel. (3) 9903-5043; fax (3) 9905-5370; e-mail mai.enquiries@adm.monash.edu.au; internet www.monash.edu.au/mai; f. 1992; incorporates National Centre for South Asian Studies, Japanese Studies Centre, Malaysian Studies Centre, Asia Pacific Health and Nutrition Centre and Centre of Southeast Asian Studies; Dir Prof. MARIKA VICZIANY.

National Centre for Australian Studies (NCAS): POB 197, Caulfield Campus, Monash University, Caulfield East, Vic 3145; tel. (3) 9903-4038; fax (3) 9903-4225; e-mail australian.studies@arts.monash.edu.au; internet arts.monash.edu.au/ncas; f. 1988; Dir BRUCE SCATES.

National Thai Studies Centre: Faculty of Asian Studies, Australian National University, Canberra, ACT 0200; tel. (2) 6125-4661; fax (2) 6125-0745; e-mail ntsc@anu.edu.au; internet www.anu.edu.au/thaionline; f. 1991; Chair. ANNETTE ELLIS; Exec. Dir Prof. PETER WARR; publs include Thai language teaching materials, *Thailand Update Series*.

Research Institute for Asia and the Pacific (RIAP): Rm 205, Old Teachers' College A22, University of Sydney, NSW 2006; tel. (2) 9351-8547; fax (2) 9351-8562; e-mail riap.reception@usyd.edu.au; internet www.riap.usyd.edu.au; research on human resource development, information technology, media, the environment, public administration, regional security and managing systems that underpin institutional capacity; Dir Assoc. Prof. ROBYN MCCONCHIE.

Research School of Asia and the Pacific: Australian National University, Canberra, ACT 0200; tel. (2) 6125-2221; fax (2) 6257-1893; e-mail enquiries.asiapacific@anu.edu.au; internet asiapacific.anu.edu.au/researchschool; publs include *The China Journal*, *Bulletin of Indonesian Economic Studies*, *Pacific Economic Bulletin*, *East Asian History*, *Journal of Pacific History*, *Chinese Southern Diaspora Studies* and monograph series; Dean Prof. ANDREW MACINTYRE.

School of Asian Languages and Studies, University of Tasmania: Private Bag 91, Hobart, Tasmania 7001; tel. (3) 6226-2342; fax (3) 6226-7813; e-mail SALS.Admin@utas.edu.au; internet www.utas.edu.au/sals; f. 1990; fmrly Asia Centre; offers courses in Asian Studies, Chinese, Indonesian and Japanese; Head of School Assoc. Prof. PAM ALLEN.

School of Languages and Cultures, University of Sydney: Brennan MacCallum A18, University of Sydney, NSW 2006; tel. (2)

*See also Regional Organizations

9351-2869; fax (2) 9351-2319; e-mail arts.slcadmin@sydney.edu.au; internet sydney.edu.au/arts/slc; f. 1991; includes the depts of Asian Studies, Chinese Studies, Japanese and Korean Studies, Indian Subcontinental and Buddhist Studies, and Southeast Asian Studies; Head Prof. JEFFREY RIEGEL.

AUSTRIA

Afro-Asiatisches Institut in Wien (Afro-Asian Institute in Vienna): 1090 Vienna, Türkenstrasse 3; tel. (1) 3105145-311; fax (1) 3105145-312; e-mail office@aai-wien.at; internet www.aai-wien.at; f. 1959; religious and cultural exchanges between Austria and African and Asian countries; assistance to students from Africa and Asia; public relations, lectures, seminars; Rector Dr RAINER PORSTNER; Gen. Man. NIKOLAUS HEGER.

Institut für Ostasienwissenschaften der Universität Wien: 1090 Vienna, Spitalgasse 2-4; tel. (1) 4277-43801; fax (1) 4277-9438; e-mail ostasien@univie.ac.at; internet www.univie.ac.at/ostasien; f. 1965; Japanese, Chinese and Korean studies; Dir Dr SEPP LINHART; publ. *Institutsbericht* (annually).

BELGIUM

Egmont—Institut Royal des Relations Internationales: 69 rue de Namur, 1000 Brussels; tel. (2) 223-4114; fax (2) 223-4116; e-mail info@egmontinstitute.be; internet www.egmontinstitute.be; f. 1947; research in international relations, economics, law and politics; specialized library containing 700 vols and 50 periodicals; archives; holds lectures and conferences; Pres. Viscount E. DAVIGNON; Dir-Gen. MARC TRENTESEAU; publ. *Studia Diplomatica* (every 3 months).

European Institute for Asian Studies (EIAS): EIAS asbl, 67 rue de la Loi, 1040 Brussels; tel. (2) 230-8122; fax (2) 230-5402; e-mail eias@eias.org; internet www.eias.org; Chair. Prof. Dr LUDO CUYVERS; Gen. Sec. and Acting Dir DICK GUPWELL.

Institut Orientaliste: Faculté de Philosophie, Arts et Lettres, Université Catholique de Louvain, Collège Erasme, 1348 Louvain-la-Neuve; tel. (10) 474958; fax (10) 479169; e-mail ori@glor.ucl.ac.be; internet www.fltr.ucl.ac.be/FLTR/GLOR/ORI; f. 1936; Pres. Prof. CHRISTOPHE VIELLE; publs *Le Muséon* (2 a year), *Bibliothèque du Muséon, Publications de l'Institut Orientaliste de Louvain (PIOL), Corpus Scriptorum Christianorum Orientalium (CSCO)*.

BRAZIL

Centro de Estudos Afro-Asiáticos (CEAA): Praça Pio X 7, 10° andar, 20040-020, Rio de Janeiro, RJ; tel. (21) 2233-9294; fax (21) 3518-2798; e-mail ceaa@candidomendes.edu.br; internet www.candidomendes.br/ceaa; f. 1973; Deputy Dir BELUCE BELLUCCI; publ. *Estudos Afro-Asiáticos*.

BRUNEI

Academy of Brunei Studies: Universiti Brunei Darussalam, Jalan Tungku Link, Gadong, Bandar Seri Begawan BE 1410; tel. and fax 2249518; e-mail abs@apd.ubd.edu.bn; internet www.ubd.edu.bn/academic/faculty/apb; f. 1990; research on wide variety of subjects relating to Bruneian life, including its history, economic development, language, religion, literature, geography and education; Dir Dr Haji ABU BAKAR BIN Haji SARIFUDDIN.

CAMBODIA

Cambodia Development Resource Institute (CDRI): BP 622, 56 rue 315, Khan Tuol Kok, Phnom-Penh; tel. (23) 883603; fax (23) 880734; e-mail cdrimail@online.com.kh; internet www.cdri.org.kh; f. 1990; research into socio-economic issues of importance to Cambodia and the region; Exec. Dir LARRY STRANGE.

Center for Khmer Studies (CKS): BP 9380, Wat Damnak, Siem Reap; tel. (63) 964385; fax (63) 963035; e-mail center@khmerstudies.org; internet www.khmerstudies.org; f. 1999; promotes research, teaching and public service in the social sciences, arts and humanities; Dir Dr PHILIPPE PEYCAM.

Economic Institute of Cambodia: BP 1008, Suite 234, Phnom Penh Center, Sangkat Tonle Bassac, Phnom-Penh; tel. (23) 987941; fax (23) 224626; e-mail eic@eicambodia.org; internet www.eicambodia.org; f. 2003; Dir SOK HACH.

CANADA

Asian Pacific Research and Resource Centre: 1401 Dunton Tower, 1125 Colonel By Dr., Ottawa, ON K1S 5B6; tel. (613) 520-6655; fax (613) 520-2889; e-mail international_affairs@carleton.ca; internet www.carleton.ca/npsia/research_centres/aprrc.html; f. 1989; conducts research in commerce and investment in the Asia-Pacific region; Dir Prof. FEN HAMPSON; publs monographs, working papers.

Canadian Council for International Co-operation: Suite 200, 450 Rideau St, Ottawa, ON K1N 5Z4; tel. (613) 241-7007; fax (613) 241-5302; e-mail info@ccic.ca; internet www.ccic.ca; f. 1968; information and training centre for international development and forum for voluntary agencies; 100 mems; Pres. and CEO GERRY BARR; publs include newsletter and directory of NGOs working overseas.

Canadian International Council (CIC): Rm 210, 45 Willcocks St, Toronto, ON M5S 1C7; tel. (416) 946-7209; fax (416) 946-7319; e-mail mailbox@canadianinternationalcouncil.org; internet www.canadianinternationalcouncil.org; f. 1928; research in international relations; library containing 8,000 vols; Chair. JIM BALSILLIE; Pres. DOUGLAS GOOLD; publs *International Journal* (quarterly), *Annual Report*, *Strategic Datalink*.

Centre for Developing-Area Studies: McGill University, Peterson Hall, 3460 McTavish St, Montréal, QC H3A 1X9; tel. (514) 398-3507; fax (514) 398-8432; e-mail adm.cdas@mcgill.ca; internet www.mcgill.ca/cdas; Dir Dr PHILIP OXHORN; publs *Discussion Paper Series*.

Department of Asian Studies, University of British Columbia: UBC Asian Centre 1871 West Mall, Vancouver, BC V6T 1Z2; tel. (604) 822-0019; fax (604) 822-8937; e-mail astudies@interchange.ubc.ca; internet www.asia.ubc.ca; f. 1961; instruction and research in East, South and South-East Asia; Head Dr ROSS KING.

Institute of Asian Research: University of British Columbia, C. K. Choi Bldg, 1855 West Mall, Vancouver, BC V6T 1Z2; tel. (604) 822-4688; fax (604) 822-5207; e-mail iar@interchange.ubc.ca; internet www.iar.ubc.ca; f. 1978; Dir MASAO NAKAMURA (acting); publs *Asia Pacific Report* (2 a year), *Pacific Affairs* (quarterly), research papers.

International Development Research Centre: POB 8500, Ottawa ON K1G 3H9; tel. (613) 236-6163; fax (613) 563-2476; e-mail info@idrc.ca; internet www.idrc.ca; f. 1970; est. as a public corpn to support scientific research aimed at helping communities in the developing world to find solutions to social, environmental and economic problems; regional offices incl. Singapore and India; Pres. DAVID M. MALONE; publs *IDRC Bulletin* (online magazine) and books.

PEOPLE'S REPUBLIC OF CHINA

China Centre for International Studies (CCIS): 22 Xianmen Dajie, POB 1744, Beijing 100017; tel. (10) 63097083; fax (10) 63095802; f. 1982; conducts research on international relations and problems; organizes academic exchanges; Dir-Gen. LI LUYE.

China-Europe International Business School (CEIBS): 699 Hong Feng Lu, Shanghai 201206; tel. (21) 28905888; fax (21) 28905108; e-mail info@mail.ceibs.edu.cn; internet www.ceibs.edu; Exec. Pres. Dr ALBERT BENNETT; Dean ROLF D. CREMER.

China Institute of Contemporary International Relations (CICIR): 2A Wanshousi, Haidian, Beijing 100081; tel. (10) 88547553; fax (10) 68418641; e-mail admin@cicir.ac.cn; internet www.cicir.ac.cn; f. 1980; research on international development and peace issues; Pres. CUI LIRU; publ. *Contemporary International Relations* (monthly).

China Institute for International Strategic Studies: 3 Toutiao, Tajichang, Beijing 100005; internet www.ciis.org.cn; Pres. MA ZHENGANG.

Chinese Academy of Social Sciences: 5 Jianguomen Nei Da Jie, Beijing 100732; tel. (10) 65137744; fax (10) 65138154; internet bic.cass.cn/English; f. 1977; Pres. HU SHENG; Sec.-Gen. GUO YONGCAI; comprises more than 40 research institutes and centres and one graduate school.

Chinese People's Institute of Foreign Affairs: 71 Nanchizi Jie, Beijing 100006; tel. (10) 65131824; e-mail cpifa@public.bta.net.cn; Pres. MEI ZHAORONG; Sec.-Gen. XU SHAOHAI.

Institute of Asia-Pacific Studies, Chinese Academy of Social Sciences: 3 Zhang Zizhong Lu, Beijing 100007; tel. (10) 64063042; fax (10) 64063041; e-mail aprccass@public3.bta.net.cn; f. 1988; theoretical and policy-orientated research in economic, political, social and cultural studies; Dir ZHANG YUNLING.

Institute of Asian-Pacific Studies, Shanghai Academy of Social Sciences: 7/622 Huai Hai Zhong Lu, Shanghai 200020; tel. (21) 63271170; fax (21) 63270004; e-mail jmzhou@fudan.ihep.ac.cn; internet english.sass.org.cn; f. 1990; Dir Dr ZHOU JIANMING.

Institute for Southeast Asian Studies, Jinan University: 601 Huang Pu Da Dao Xi Rd, Guangzhou 510630; tel. (20) 85220292; fax (20) 85226122; e-mail tzhangzj@jnu.edu.cn; internet dny.jnu.edu.cn; f. 1960; Dir Dr ZHENJIANG ZHANG.

Institute of World Economy: Fudan University, 220 Handan Lu, Shanghai 200433; tel. (21) 65492222; fax (21) 65491875; Dirs Prof. WU YIKANG, MA XOXIANG.

International Business Research Institute: University of International Business and Economics, Hui Xin Dong Jie, He Ping Jie N., Beijing 100029; tel. (10) 64225522; fax (10) 64212022; Dir Prof. TENG DEXIANG.

International Trade Research Institute: 17 Hubei Lu, Qingdao, Shandong; tel. and fax (531) 6270179; f. 1980; conducts research on developments in international commerce and economics; Dir CHEN CHINGCHANG; publs *International Economic and Trade Information, Shandong Foreign Trade*.

Research Institute for International Economic Co-operation (RIIEC): 28 An Wai Dong Hou Xiang, Beijing; tel. (10) 64212106; fax (10) 64212175; f. 1980; Dir YANG JINBO; publ. *International Economic Co-operation*.

Research Institute of International Politics: Beijing University, 1 Loudouqiao, Haidian, Beijing 100871; tel. (10) 62554002; fax (10) 62564095; Dir LIANG SHOUDE.

Shanghai Institute of International Issues (SIIS): 1 Alley, 845 Ju Lu, Shanghai 200040; tel. (21) 62471148; fax (21) 62472272; f. 1960; Dir CHEN PEIYAO; publs *Survey of International Affairs* (annually), *Guoji Zhanwang* (2 a month), papers, monographs.

Shanghai University of Finance and Economics, Asian Economic Research Institute: 777 Guoding Lu, Shanghai 200433; tel. and fax (21) 65361955; f. 1993; Chair. YI JUANQIU.

Taiwan Economy Research Institute: Nankai University, Balitai, Tianjin 200071; tel. (22) 63358825; fax (22) 63344853; Dir Prof. BAO JUEMIN.

West Asian and African Studies Institute: Chinese Academy of Social Sciences, 3 Zhangzhizhong Rd, Beijing 100007; e-mail iwaas@public.fhnet.cn.net; f. 1961; Dir-Gen. Prof. YANG GUANG.

CROATIA

Institute for International Relations (IMO): 10000 Zagreb, POB 303, ul. Ljudevita Farkaša Vukotinovića 2/II; tel. (1) 4877460; fax (1) 4828361; e-mail ured@irmo.hr; internet www.imo.hr; f. 1963; affiliated to the University of Zagreb and the Ministry of Science and Technology; public, non-profit, scientific policy research org; Dir Prof. Dr MLADEN STANIČIĆ; publs include *Croatian International Relations Review* (quarterly), *Culturelink* (3 a year).

CZECH REPUBLIC

Czech Society for Eastern Studies: c/o Oriental Institute, Academy of Sciences, Pod vodárenskou věží 4, 182 08 Prague 8; tel. (2) 66052483; fax (2) 86581897; e-mail aror@orient.cas.cz; f. 1958; 71 mems; Pres. LŮBICA OBUCHOVÁ.

Orientální ústav AV ČR (Oriental Institute of the Academy of Sciences of the Czech Republic): Pod vodárenskou věží 4, 182 08 Prague 8; tel. (2) 66053111; fax (2) 86581897; e-mail orient@orient.cas.cz; internet www.orient.cas.cz; f. 1922; research on languages, social and economic aspects, etc. of Asia and Africa; Chinese library of 66,177 vols, general library of more than 190,000 vols; Dir Dr STANISLAVA VAVROUŠKOVÁ; publs *Archiv orientální* (quarterly), *Nový Orient* (quarterly).

DENMARK

Asia Research Centre: Copenhagen Business School, Dalgas Have 15, DK-2000, Frederiksberg; tel. 38-15-34-09; e-mail arc@cbs.dk; internet www.cbs.dk/arc; f. 1995; research areas include China, Japan and South-East Asia; Dir Prof. KJELD ERIK BRØDSGAARD.

Nordic Institute of Asian Studies (NIAS): Leifsgade 33, 2300 Copenhagen S; tel. 35-32-95-00; fax 35-32-95-49; e-mail sec@nias.ku.dk; internet www.nias.ku.dk; f. 1967; known until 1988 as the Scandinavian Institute of Asian Studies; non-profit org. funded through Nordic Council of Ministers; research and documentation centre for the study of modern Asian societies and cultures from the perspective of the humanities and social sciences, with a multi-disciplinary profile; library of 35,000 vols and 500 periodicals; Chair. of Bd Dr LARS BILLE; Dir Dr GEIR HELGESEN; publs include *NIASnytt / Asia Insights* (3 a year), monographs, anthologies and research reports.

FIJI

School of Governance and Development Studies (SGDS): University of the South Pacific, Private Bag, Laucala Bay Campus, Suva; tel. 3232764; fax 3231524; e-mail governance@usp.ac.fj; internet www.usp.ac.fj/index.php?id=piasdg; f. 2003; fmrly Pacific Institute of Advanced Studies in Development and Governance; administers Development Studies Programme and Governance Programme, promoting research into issues of the islands of the Pacific; Dir Prof. GRAHAM HASSALL.

FINLAND

Aasian ja Afrikan kielten ja kulttuurien laitos (Institute for Asian and African Studies): POB 59 (Unioninkatu 38B), University of Helsinki, 00014 Helsinki; tel. (9) 191-22224; fax (9) 191-22094; e-mail maria.colliander@helsinki.fi; internet www.helsinki.fi/hum/aakkl; f. 1974; teaching and research of the languages and cultures of Asia, Africa and the Middle East; Dir Prof. KLAUS KARTTUNEN.

Suomen Itämainen Seura (Finnish Oriental Society): c/o Dept of World Cultures, POB 59, University of Helsinki, 00014 Helsinki; tel. (9) 191-22224; fax (9) 191-22094; e-mail saana.svard@helsinki.fi; internet www.suomenitamainenseura.org; f. 1917; Pres. Prof. TAPANI HARVIAINEN; Sec. SAANA SVÄRD; publs *Studia Orientalia* (English, French and German, irregular); occasional papers series (Finnish and Swedish, irregular).

The Bank of Finland Institute for Economies in Transition (BOFIT): Snellmaninaukio 1, POB 160, 00100 Helsinki; tel. (10) 831-2268; fax (10) 831-2294; e-mail bofit@bof.fi; internet www.bof.fi/bofit; f. 1991 as the Unit for Eastern European Economies; name changed as above 1998; monitors macroeconomic performance and financial markets in China; Dir Dr PEKKA SUTELA; publs *BOFIT China Review* (quarterly), *BOFIT Weekly*.

World Institute for Development Economics Research of the United Nations University (UNU-WIDER): Katajanokanlaituri 6B, 00160 Helsinki; tel. (9) 615-9911; fax (9) 615-99333; e-mail wider@wider.unu.edu; internet www.wider.unu.edu; f. 1984; research and training centre of the UNU (Japan); publs include *WIDER Discussion Papers, Policy Briefs, Research Papers, Annual Lectures, WIDER Angle* (newsletter).

FRANCE

Institut National des Langues et Civilisations Orientales: 2 rue de Lille, 75343 Paris Cedex 07; tel. 1-70-23-26-00; fax 1-70-23-26-99; internet www.inalco.fr; courses in 93 languages; research; information centre; organizes international exchanges; specializes in international relations; Pres. JACQUES LEGRAND; publs research serials, textbooks, translations, etc.

Musée National des Arts Asiatiques Guimet: 6 place d'Iéna, 75116 Paris; tel. 1-56-52-53-00; fax 1-56-52-53-54; internet www.museeguimet.fr; f. 1889; library of 100,000 vols; art, archaeology, religions, literature and music of India, Central Asia, Tibet, Pakistan, Viet Nam, China, Korea, Japan, Cambodia, Thailand, Laos, Myanmar (fmrly Burma) and Indonesia; Dir JEAN-FRANÇOIS JARRIGE; Librarian F. MACOUIN; publs *Annales du Musée Guimet, Arts Asiatiques*.

Société Asiatique: 3 rue Mazarine, 75006 Paris; tel. and fax 1-44-27-18-04; internet www.aibl.fr/fr/asie/present.html; f. 1829; library of 100,000 vols; 750 mems; Pres. DANIEL GIMARET; publs *Journal Asiatique* (2 a year), *Nouveaux Cahiers*.

Unité Formation et Recherche (UFR) Langues et Civilisations de l'Asie Orientale (UFR LCAO): Université Denis-Diderot, Batiment C, 4ème étage, Case 7009, 16 rue Marguerite Duras, 75205 Paris Cedex 13; tel. 1-44-27-57-81; fax 1-44-27-78-98; f. 1971; Dir ERIC GUERASSIMOFF.

FRENCH POLYNESIA

Te Fare Tauhiti Nui—Maison de la culture: 646 Blvd Pomaré, BP 1709, Papeete; tel. 544544; fax 428569; e-mail tauhiti@mail.pf; internet www.maisondelaculture.pf; f. 1980; promotes culture locally and abroad; sponsors many public and private cultural events; library of 9,500 vols, children's library of 7,000 vols; Dir GEORGES ESTALL.

GERMANY

AAI-Abteilung für Sprache und Kultur Japans, Universität Hamburg: 20146 Hamburg, Edmund-Siemers-Allee 1, Ostflügel; tel. (40) 42838-2670; fax (40) 42838-6200; e-mail japanologie@uni-hamburg.de; internet www.uni-hamburg.de/japanologie; f. 1914; research into Japanese studies; 44,500 vols; Dir Prof. Dr JÖRG B. QUENZER; publs include *Oriens Extremus, Nachrichten, Kagami* and monograph series *MOAG*.

China-Institut: Johann Wolfgang Goethe-Universität, 60054 Frankfurt am Main, Senckenberganlage 31; e-mail B.Sude@em.uni-frankfurt.de; Dir Prof. Dr DOROTHEA WIPPERMANN.

Deutsche Gesellschaft für Asienkunde eV (German Association for Asian Studies): 20148 Hamburg, Rothenbaumchaussee 32; tel. (40) 445891; fax (40) 4107945; e-mail post@asienkunde.de; internet www.asienkunde.de; f. 1967; promotion and co-ordination of contemporary Asian research; 800 mems; Pres. Dr CHRISTIAN P. HAUSWEDELL; publs *ASIEN: The German Journal on Contemporary Asia, Wirtschaft und Kultur* (quarterly).

Deutsche Gesellschaft für Auswärtige Politik eV (German Society for Foreign Affairs): Rauchstr. 17/18, 10787 Berlin; tel. (30) 2542310; fax (30) 25423116; e-mail info@dgap.org; internet www.dgap.org; f. 1955; promotes research on problems of international politics; library of 79,500 vols; 2,300 mems; Pres. Dr AREND OETKER; Exec. Vice-Pres. FRITJOF VON NORDENSKJÖLD; Dir Research

Inst. Prof. Dr EBERHARD SANDSCHNEIDER; publs *Internationale Politik* (monthly), *Die Internationale Politik* (annually).

Deutsche Morgenländische Gesellschaft eV (DMG) (German Oriental Society): Orientalisches Seminar, Islamwissenschaft/Turkologie, 79085 Freiburg/Brsg., Werthmannplatz 3; tel. (761) 2033159; fax (761) 2033152; e-mail Jens.Peter.Laut@orient.uni-freiburg.de; internet www.dmg-web.de; f. 1845; sponsors research and holds meetings and lectures in the field of Oriental studies; 650 mems; Sec. Prof. Dr JENS PETER LAUT; publs include *Zeitschrift, Abhandlungen für die Kunde des Morgenlandes*.

Forschungsinstitut für Wirtschaftliche Entwicklungen im Pazifikraum eV (Asia-Pacific Economic Research Institute): University of Duisburg-Essen, Campus Duisburg, 47048 Duisburg, Lotharstrasse 65; tel. (203) 3794114; fax (203) 3794157; e-mail guenter.heiduk@uni-due.de; internet www.uni-due.de/fip/fip_eng.htm; f. 1985; research on economic developments in the Pacific region; Dirs Prof. Dr GÜNTER HEIDUK, Prof. Dr WERNER PASCHA, Prof. Dr MARKUS TAUBE.

GIGA Institut für Asien-Studien (German Institute of Global and Area Studies): 20148 Hamburg, Rothenbaumchaussee 32; tel. (40) 4288740; fax (40) 4107945; e-mail ias@giga-hamburg.de; internet www.giga-hamburg.de/ias; f. 1956; research into political, economic and social aspects of contemporary South, South-East and East Asia; Dir Dr PATRICK KÖLLNER (acting); publs *Journal of Current Chinese Affairs—China aktuell* (quarterly), *Journal of Current Southeast Asian Affairs* (quarterly), *Korea Yearbook—Politics, Economy and Society* (annually).

Museum für Islamische Kunst (Islamic Art and Antiquities): Staatliche Museen zu Berlin Preussischer Kulturbesitz, 10178 Berlin, Bodestrasse 1–3; tel. (30) 20905400; fax (30) 20905402; e-mail isl@smb.spk-berlin.de; internet www.smb.spk-berlin.de/isl; f. 1904; Dir Dr STEFAN WEBER.

HONG KONG

Asia-Pacific Financial Markets Research Centre: City University of Hong Kong, 83 Tat Chee Ave, Kowloon; tel. 27887940; fax 27888806; internet www.cityu.edu.hk/ref/index.htm; f. 1983; research into financial markets in the Asia-Pacific region; Dir Prof. RICHARD HO; publ. *Technical Reports* (monthly).

The Asia-Pacific Institute of Business: Chinese University of Hong Kong, Li Dak Sum Bldg, 2nd Floor, Shatin, New Territories; tel. 26097428; fax 26035136; e-mail apib@cuhk.edu.hk; f. 1990; provides research, consultancy and educational courses on business and economic issues concerning Hong Kong and the Asia-Pacific region; Exec. Dir Prof. LESLIE YOUNG; publ. *The Hong Kong Securities Industry*.

Hong Kong Institute of Asia-Pacific Studies: Chinese University of Hong Kong, Esther Lee Bldg, Shatin, New Territories; tel. 26096740; fax 26035215; e-mail hkiaps@cuhk.edu.hk; internet www.cuhk.edu.hk/hkiaps/homepage.htm; f. 1990; Dir Prof. FANNY CHEUNG; publs occasional papers, research monographs, seminar series.

Institute of Chinese Studies: The Chinese University of Hong Kong, Shatin, New Territories; tel. 26097394; fax 26035149; e-mail ics@cuhk.edu.hk; internet www.cuhk.edu.hk/ics; f. 1967; comprises Art Museum, Research Center for Translation, Center for Chinese Archaeology and Art, T. T. Ng Chinese Language Research Center, Research Center for Contemporary Chinese Culture and Research Centre for Chinese Ancient Texts; Dir Prof. JENNY FONG SUK SO; publs include *ICS Journal* (2 a year), *Renditions* (2 a year), *The Chinese Language Newsletter* (quarterly) and *Twenty-First Century* (every 2 months).

Southeast Asia Research Centre: City University of Hong Kong, 7/F, Block 2, To Yuen Bldg, 31 To Yuen St, Kowloon; tel. 34426302; e-mail w.case@cityu.edu.hk; internet www.cityu.edu.hk/searc; Dir Prof. WILLIAM CASE.

HUNGARY

Magyar Tudományos Akadémia Világgazdasági Kutató Intézete (Institute for World Economics of the Hungarian Academy of Sciences): 1014 Budapest, Országház u. 30; tel. (1) 224-6760; fax (1) 224-6761; e-mail vki@vki.hu; internet www.vki.hu; f. 1967; library of 103,000 vols; Dir ANDRAS INOTAI; publs *Working Papers* (c. 15 a year, in English), *Kihívások* (10–15 a year, in Hungarian), *Muhelytanulmányok* (10–15 a year, in Hungarian).

INDIA

Centre for Development Studies: Prasanth Nagar Rd, Ulloor, Trivandrum 695 011; tel. (471) 2448412; fax (471) 2442482; e-mail somannair@cds.ac.in; internet www.cds.edu; f. 1971; promotes interdisciplinary research and academic instruction in disciplines relevant to development issues; library of 125,000 vols; Dir Dr PULAPRE BALAKRISHNAN; Chief Librarian V. SRIRAM; publs include *Kerala Studies Series* and monographs and public lecture series.

Centre for South, Central, South-East Asian and South-West Pacific Studies: Jawaharlal Nehru University, New Mehrauli Rd, New Delhi 110 067; tel. (11) 26704388; fax (11) 26741435; e-mail sahadevan@mail.jnu.ac.in; internet www.jnu.ac.in/main.asp?sendval=cscseaswpsAboutus; Chair. Prof. P. SAHADEVAN.

Indian Society for Afro-Asian Studies: 297 Saraswati Kunj, Indraprastha Extension, Mother Dairy Rd, New Delhi 110 092; tel. (11) 22248246; fax (11) 22425698; e-mail isaas@giasdl01; f. 1980; research and promotion of co-operation among African and Asian countries; Pres. LALIT BHASIN; Gen. Sec. Dr DARAMPAL; publs monographs, papers.

Indira Gandhi Institute of Development Research (IGIDR): Gen. A. K. Vaidya Marg, Goregaon (E), Mumbai 400 065; tel. (22) 28400919; fax (22) 28402752; internet www.igidr.ac.in; f. 1986; Dir Prof. S. MAHENDRA DEV; publs books and monographs.

Institute of Economic Growth: University Enclave, Delhi 110 007; tel. (11) 27667101; fax (11) 27667410; e-mail diroffice@iegindia.org; internet www.iegindia.org; f. 1958; research into the problems of social and economic development of South and South-East Asia; major research themes include: macroeconomic analysis and policy; globalization and trade; industry and development; agriculture and rural development; environmental and natural resource economics; population and human resource development; social change and social structure; health economics and policy; labour and welfare; and library and documentation services; Dir Prof. BINA AGARWAL; publs include *Monthly Monitor*, *Contributions to Indian Sociology: Occasional Studies* (irregular).

Namgyal Institute of Tibetology: Deorali, Gangtok, Sikkim 737 101; e-mail info@tibetology.net; internet www.tibetology.net; f. 1958; research centre for study of Mahayana (Northern Buddhism) and Himalayan cultures; library of Tibetan literature (canonical of all sects and secular) in MSS and xylographs; museum of icons and art objects; Pres. BALMIKI PRASAD SINGH (Gov. of Sikkim); Dir TASHI DENSAPA; publs include *Bulletin of Tibetology* (publ. suspended in 2004) and publs in Tibetan, Sanskrit and English.

Nava Nalanda Mahavihara (Nalanda University): PO Nalanda, Bihar 803 111; tel. (6112) 281672; fax (6112) 281505; e-mail nnmdirector@sify.com; internet navanalandamahavihara.org; f. 1951; under Ministry of Culture; postgraduate studies and research in Pali, Buddhist studies, ancient Indian and Asian history and philosophy, Tibetan, Sanskrit, Chinese and Japanese; library of 50,000 vols; Dir Dr RAVINDRA PANTH; publs include *Nava Nalanda Mahavihara Research* (annually).

New Asia Forum, Research and Information System for Developing Countries: Zone IV-B, 4th Floor, India Habitat Centre, Lodhi Rd, New Delhi 110 003; tel. (11) 24682177; fax (11) 24682173; e-mail dgoffice@ris.org.in; internet www.newasiaforum.org; trade and development issues; Dir-Gen. Dr BISWAJIT DHAR; publs include *South Asia Development and Cooperation Reports* (every 2 years), *World Trade and Development Reports* (every 2 years), *South Asia Economic Journal* (2 a year), *Asian Biotechnology and Development Review* (3 a year), *New Asia Monitor* (quarterly).

INDONESIA

Centre for Social and Cultural Studies: Indonesian Institute of Sciences, Gedung Widya Graha Lt. 11, Jalan Jenderal Gatot Subroto, POB 4492, Jakarta 12044; tel. (21) 511542; fax (21) 5701232.

Centre for Strategic and International Studies (CSIS): Jakarta Post Bldg, 3rd Floor, Jalan Palmerah Barat No. 142–143, Jakarta 10270; tel. (21) 53654601; fax (21) 53654607; e-mail csis@csis.or.id; internet www.csis.or.id; f. 1971; undertakes policy-orientated studies in international and domestic matters in collaboration with the industrial, commercial, political, legal and journalistic communities of Indonesia; interdisciplinary research projects; Exec. Dir RIZAL SUKMA; publs include *The Indonesian Quarterly*, *Analisis CSIS* (4 a year).

Indonesian Institute of World Affairs: c/o Universitas Indonesia, Salemba Raya 4, Jakarta; tel. (21) 882955; Chair. Prof. SUPOMO; Sec. SUDJATMOKO.

Institute for Regional Economic Research: Universitas Andalas, Kampus Limau Manis, Padang 26163, West Sumatra; tel. (751) 71389; fax (751) 71085; Dir SYAHRUDDIN.

Perpustakaan Nasional RI (National Library of Indonesia): Jalan Salemba Raya, No. 28A, Jakarta Pusat 10430; tel. (21) 3101411; fax (21) 3103554; internet www.pnri.go.id; f. 1989; 844,480 vols, 25,000 maps, 10,857 microfilms and microfiches, 10,000 MSS; Dir MASTINI HARDJOPRAKOSO; publs include *National Bibliography*.

Pusat Bahasa (National Centre for Language): Jalan Daksinapati Barat IV, POB 2625, Rawamangun, Jakarta 13220; tel. and fax (21) 4706678; f. 1975; attached to the Ministry of National Education; language policy and planning, research on language teaching and

literature; library of 20,000 titles; Dir Dr DENDY SUGONO; Librarian AGNES SANTI; publs include *Informasi Pustaka Kebahasaan* (quarterly), *Bahasa dan Susastra dalam Guntingan* (monthly).

IRAN

Asia Institute: University of Shiraz, Shiraz; tel. (71) 32111; Dir Dr Y. M. NAVABI; publs *Bulletin*, monographs.

Institute for Political and International Studies: Shaheed Bahonar Ave, Shaheed Aghaii St, POB 19395-1793, Tajrish, Tehran; tel. (21) 2571010; fax (21) 270964; e-mail Mousavi@ipis.ir; internet www.ipis.ir/English; f. 1983; research and information on international relations, economics, law and Islamic studies; library of 22,000 vols; Dir Dr SEYED RASOUL MOUSAVI; publs include *Iranian Journal of International Affairs* (quarterly).

ISRAEL

Harry S. Truman Research Institute for the Advancement of Peace: The Hebrew University of Jerusalem, Mt Scopus, Jerusalem 91905; tel. (2) 5882300; fax (2) 5828076; e-mail truman@savion.huji.ac.il; internet www.truman.huji.ac.il; f. 1965; conducts and sponsors social science and historical research, organizes conferences and publs works on many regions, including Asia; Academic Dir Prof. STEVEN KAPLAN.

Institute of Asian and African Studies: The Hebrew University of Jerusalem, Mt Scopus, Jerusalem 91905; tel. (2) 5883659; fax (2) 5883658; e-mail AsiaAfrica@h2.hum.cc.huji.ac.il; internet asiafrica.huji.ac.il; f. 1926 as Institute of Oriental Studies; provides degree and postgraduate courses, covering history, social sciences and languages, in Chinese, Japanese, Korean, Tibetan and South Asian studies; Dir Prof. MEIR BAR-ASHER; Sec. YEHUDIT MAGEN.

ITALY

The Bologna Center of the Paul H. Nitze School of Advanced International Studies of the Johns Hopkins University (SAIS): Via Belmeloro 11, 40126 Bologna; tel. (051) 2917811; fax (051) 228505; e-mail Registrar@jhubc.it; internet www.jhubc.it; f. 1955; graduate studies in international affairs and economics; Dir KENNETH H. KELLER; publs *Bologna Center Catalogue*, *EuroSAIS* (alumni newsletter), occasional papers series.

Institute of East Asian Economic and Social Studies (ISESAO): Università Commerciale Luigi Bocconi, Via G. Roentgen 1, Milan; tel. (02) 58363317; fax (02) 58363309; e-mail isesao@unibocconi.it; internet www.isesao.unibocconi.it; Dir Prof. CARLO FILIPPINI.

Istituto Affari Internazionali (IAI): Palazzo Rondinini, Via Angelo Brunetti 9, 00186 Rome; tel. (06) 3224360; fax (06) 3224363; e-mail iai@iai.it; internet www.iai.it; f. 1965; research on European integration, international political economy, Mediterranean and Middle East, defence and security, transatlantic relations; Pres. STEFANO SILVESTRI; Dir ETTORE GRECO; publs include *The International Spectator* (English, quarterly), *La politica estera dell'Italia* (Italian, annually), *IAI Quaderni* (English and Italian, 6 a year), working papers and monographs.

Istituto Italiano per l'Africa e l'Oriente (ISIAO): Via Ulisse. Aldrovandi 16, 00197 Rome; tel. (06) 328551; fax (06) 3225348; e-mail info@isiao.it; internet www.isiao.it; f. 1995; Pres. Prof. GHERARDO GNOLI; publs include *Africa* (quarterly), *Cina* (annually), *East and West* (quarterly), *Il Giappone* (annually).

Istituto per gli Studi di Politica Internazionale (ISPI) (Institute for the Study of International Politics): Palazzo Clerici, Via Clerici 5, 20121 Milan; tel. (02) 8633131; fax (02) 8692055; e-mail ispi.segreteria@ispionline.it; internet www.ispionline.it/it/index; f. 1933 for the promotion of the study and knowledge of all problems concerning international relations; seminars at postgraduate level; library of 100,000 vols; Dir PAOLO MAGRI; publs *ISPI Relazioni Internazionali* (quarterly), papers (20 a year).

Università degli Studi l'Orientale (Oriental University of Naples): Maurizio Taddei Library, Dept of Asian Studies, Piazza San Domenico Maggiore 12, 80134 Naples; tel. (081) 5522468; fax (081) 5522468; e-mail bibsa@unior.it; internet www.unior.it; f. 1732; library of 230,000 vols, 2,000 periodical titles; Head Prof. FRANCESCO SFERRA; publs include 4 series (*Maior, Minor, Serie Tre* and *Baluchistan Monograph Series*), *Annali* and *Ming Qing Yanjiu*.

JAPAN

Ajia Daigaku (Institute for Asian Studies): Asia University, 5-24-10 Sakai, Musashino-shi, Tokyo 180-8629; tel. (422) 54-3111; fax (422) 36-1083; e-mail kkbinfo@asia-u.ac.jp; internet www.asia-u.ac.jp/english/main/asian.htm; f. 1973; Dir S. SAITO; publs *Journal* (annually), *Bulletin of Institute for Asian Studies* (quarterly).

Ajia Seikei Gakkai (Japan Association for Asian Studies): Tokyo; f. 1953; 1,040 mems; Pres. TOSHIO WATANABE; publ. *Aziya Kenkyu* (quarterly).

The Center for Southeast Asian Studies: 46 Shimoadachicho, Yoshida, Sakyo-ku, Kyoto 606-8501; tel. (75) 753-7300; fax (75) 753-7350; f. 1963; attached to Kyoto Univ; Dir HIROMU MAEDA SHIMIZU; publs include *Southeast Asian Studies* (quarterly), monographs (English and Japanese, irregular).

Centre for Asian and Pacific Studies: Seikei University, 3-3-1, Kichijoji-Kitamachi, Musashino-shi, Tokyo 180-8633; tel. (422) 37-3549; fax (422) 37-3866; e-mail caps@jim.seikei.ac.jp; internet www.seikei.ac.jp/university/caps; f. 1981; conducts and finances research on modernization, industrialization and structural changes in the Asia-Pacific region; publs include *Review of Asian and Pacific Studies*.

The Economic Research Institute for Northeast Asia (ERINA): 13th Floor, Bandaijima Bldg, Bandaijima 5-1, Chuo-ku, Niigata 950-0078; tel. (25) 290-5545; fax (25) 249-7550; internet www.erina.or.jp; f. 1993.

The International Centre for the Study of East Asian Development: 11-4 Otemachi, Kokurakita, Kitakyushu, 803-0814; tel. (93) 583-6202; fax (93) 583-6576; e-mail office@icsead.or.jp; internet www.icsead.or.jp; Dir HIDEHIKO TANIMURA.

Nihon Boeki Shinkokiko Ajia Keizai Kenkyusho (Institute of Developing Economies, Japan External Trade Organization—IDE–JETRO): 3-2-2 Wakaba, Mihama-ku, Chiba-shi, Chiba 261-8545; tel. (43) 299-9536; fax (43) 299-9726; e-mail info@ide.go.jp; internet www.ide.go.jp; Ajia Keizai Kenkyusho est. 1960, merged with JETRO 1998; independent administrative institution; research on economic and related subjects in Asia and other developing areas; aims to promote economic co-operation and to improve trade relations between Japan and the developing countries; 247 mems; Chair. YASUO HAYASHI; library of 576,604 vols; publs include *Ajia Keizai* (Japanese, monthly), *Ajiken Warudo Torendo* (World Trends, Japanese, monthly), *The Developing Economies* (English, quarterly), occasional papers series (English, irregular).

Nihon Keizai Kenkyu Senta (Japan Center for Economic Research): Nikkei Kayabacho Bldg, 2-6-1 Nihonbashi Kayabacho, Chuo-ku, Tokyo 103-0025; tel. (3) 3639-2801; fax (3) 3639-2839; internet www.jcer.or.jp; f. 1963; 370 corporate and 300 individual mems; library of 37,000 vols and 2,000 titles; Chair. YUTAKA KOSAI; Pres. NAOHIRI YASHIRO; publs *Nihon Keizai Kenkyu Senta Kaiho* (bi-monthly), *Nihon Keizai Kenkyu* (annually), *Economic Foreaast Series*, *International Conference Series*.

Nihon Kokusai Mondai Kenkyusho (The Japan Institute of International Affairs): 3-2-5 Kasumigaseki Chiyodaku, Tokyo; tel. (3) 3503-7261; fax (3) 3503-7292; internet www.jiia.or.jp; f. 1959; Chair. YOSHIZANE IWASA; Pres. YOSHIJI NOGAMI; publs include *Kokusai Mondai* (International Affairs, monthly), *Japan Review of International Affairs* (4 a year), newsletters, books and monographs.

Nomura Research Institute (NRI): Marunouchi Kitaguchi Bldg, 1-6-5 Marunouchi, Chiyoda-ku, Tokyo 100-0005; internet www.nri.co.jp; f. 1965; research into Japanese and international economic and security issues; Chair. and Pres. AKIHISA FUJINUMA; publ. *NRI Policy Research*.

Research Institute for the Study of Languages and Cultures of Asia and Africa (ILCAA): Tokyo University of Foreign Studies, Asahicho 3-11-1, Fuchu, Tokyo 183-8534; tel. (42) 330-5592; fax (42) 330-5599; e-mail director@aa.tufs.ac.jp; internet www.aa.tufs.ac.jp; f. 1964; library of 65,445 vols; Dir HIROHIDE KURIHARA; publs *Journal of Asian and African Studies* (2 a year), *Newsletter* (3 a year).

Tōhō Gakkai (Institute of Eastern Culture): 2-4-1 Nishi-Kanda, Chiyoda-ku, Tokyo 101-0065; tel. (3) 3262-7221; fax (3) 3262-7227; e-mail iec@tohogakkai.com; internet www.tohogakkai.com; f. 1947; 1,550 mems; Chair. Prof. YOSHIO TOGAWA; Sec.-Gen. HIDEO KWAGUCHI; publs include *Acta Asiatica*, *Tōhōgaku*, *Transactions of the International Conference of Eastern Studies*.

Tokyo Daigaku Toyo Bunka Kenkyujo (Institute for Advanced Studies on Asia, University of Tokyo): 7-3-1 Hongo, Bunkyo-ku, Tokyo 113-0033; tel. (3) 5841-5830; fax (3) 5841-5898; internet ioc.u-tokyo.ac.jp; f. 1941; Dir MASASHI HANEDA; publs *Tōyō bunka kenkyūjo kiyō* (2 a year), *Tōyō bunka* (annually).

Toyo Bunko (Modern Chinese Studies): Honkomagome 2-28-21 Bunkyo-ku, Tokyo 113-0021; tel. (3) 3942-0121; f. 1962; collection on modern China; Asian studies library of 870,000 vols; publ. *Kindai Chugoku Kenkyu Iho* (annually).

United Nations Centre for Regional Development: Nagono 1-47-1, Nakamura-ku, Nagoya 450-0001; tel. (52) 561-9377; fax (52) 561-9375; e-mail rep@uncrd.or.jp; internet www.uncrd.or.jp; f. 1971; undertakes training, research, consultation and information exchange on regional development issues affecting developing countries; Dir KAZUNOBU ONOGAWA; publs *Regional Development Dialogue* (2 a year), *Regional Development Studies* (annually).

REPUBLIC OF KOREA

Asiatic Research Center: Korea University, Anam-dong, 5, ga-1, Sungbuk-gu, Seoul; tel. (2) 3290-1600; fax (2) 923-4661; e-mail arcku@korea.ac.kr; f. 1957; Dir CHOI JANG-JIP; publ. *Journal of Asiatic Studies*.

Dankook University Institute of Oriental Studies (DIOS): 8 Hannam-dong, Yeongsan-gu, Seoul 140-714; tel. (2) 709-2234; fax (2) 798-3010; f. 1970; library of 40,000 vols; Dir Prof. KIM SANG-BAI; publs include journal and newsletter.

Ilmin International Relations Institute: Korea University, Anam-dong, Seongbuk-gu, Seoul; e-mail ksunghan@chol.com; Dir Prof. HAN KIM-SUNG.

Institute of Economic Research, Korea University: 1, 5-ga, Anam-dong, Sungbuk-gu, Seoul 136-701; tel. (2) 3290-2200; fax (2) 926-3601; e-mail eghwang@kuccnx.korea.ac.kr; f. 1957; Dir Prof. EUI-GAK HWANG.

Institute of Economic Research, Seoul National University: Sinlim-dong, Kwanak-gu, Seoul 151-742; tel. (2) 877-1629; fax (2) 926-3601; f. 1961.

Institute for Far Eastern Studies: Kyungnam University, 28-42 Samchung-dong, Chongno-gu, Seoul 110-230; tel. (2) 3700-0700; fax (2) 3700-0707; e-mail ifes@kyungnam.ac.kr; internet ifes.kyungnam .ac.kr; f. 1972; Dir SU HOON-LEE; publs monographs, 3 journals (on international and regional studies, 4 a year).

Institute of Korean Studies: Yonsei University, 134 Shinchon-dong, Sudaemun-gu, Seoul 120-749; tel. (2) 361-3502; fax (2) 365-0937; f. 1948; Dir NAM KI SHIM; publ. *Dong Bang Hak Chi* (quarterly).

Korea Development Institute: POB 113, Cheongryang, Seoul 130-012; tel. (2) 958-4114; fax (2) 961-5092; e-mail kdi-guide@ kdiux.kdi.re.kr; internet www.kdiux.kdi.re.kr; f. 1971; conducts research in order to help maintain high economic growth and price stability; library of 120,000 vols; Pres. LEE JIN-SOON; publs *KDI Economic Outlook* (quarterly), *KDI Journal and Economic Policy* (quarterly).

Korea Institute for Economics and Technology (KIET): POB 205, Cheongryang, Seoul; tel. (2) 962-6211; fax (2) 963-8540; f. 1982.

Research Institute of Asian Economics: Haeyoung Bldg, Rm 304, 148 Anguk-dong, Chongno-gu, Seoul; tel. (2) 738-1875; fax (2) 720-2367; Pres. SHIN TAE-WHAN.

Research Institute of Oriental Culture: Sung Kyun Kwan University, 53, 3-ga, Myung Ryun-dong, Chongno-gu, Seoul 110-745; Dir WOO-SUNG LEE.

Royal Asiatic Society, Korea Branch: Korean Christian Bldg, Rm 611, POB 255, Seoul 100-602; tel. (2) 763-9483; fax (2) 766-3796; e-mail raskb@kornet.net; internet www.raskb.com; f. 1900 to promote an interest in Korean arts, customs, history and literature; Gen. Man. SUE J. BAE.

Samsung Economic Research Institute (SERI): 7th–8th Floors, Hanil Group Bldg, 191 Hangangro, 2-ga, Yeongsan-gu, Seoul; tel. (2) 3780-8000; fax (2) 3780-8289; e-mail homemst@seri21.org; internet seriecon.seri-samsung.org; f. 1986; Pres. CHUNG KI YOUNG.

MACAO

Centre of Macao Studies: University of Macao, University Hill, Taipa, POB 3001.

Macao Development Strategy Research Centre: Edif. da Associação Comercial Chinesa, 19/F, Rua de Xangai 175; tel. 28780124; fax 28780565; e-mail cpedm@macau.ctm.net; internet www.cpedm .com; f. 1997.

Macau Ricci Institute: Ave Cons. Ferreira d'Almeida, 95-E; tel. 28532536; fax 28568274; e-mail info@riccimac.org; internet www .riccimac.org; f. 1999; Dir ARTUR WARDEGA; publs *Macau Ricci Institute Studies*, *Chinese Cross Currents* (quarterly).

MALAYSIA

Asian and Pacific Development Centre: Persiaran Duta, POB 12224, 50770 Kuala Lumpur; tel. (3) 6511088; fax (3) 6510316; e-mail info@apdc.po.my; f. 1980; Dir Dr HARKA GURUNG; publs annual report, newsletter, and monographs.

Dewan Bahasa dan Pustaka (Institute of Language and Literature, Malaysia): POB 10803, 50926 Kuala Lumpur; tel. (3) 21481011; fax (3) 21444460; internet www.dbp.gov.my; f. 1956 to develop and enrich the Malay language; to develop literary talent particularly in Malay; to print, publish or promote publication in Malay and other languages; to standardize spelling and pronunciation and devise appropriate technical terms in Malay; Chair. Datuk JOHAN BIN JAAFAR; Dir-Gen. Dato' Haji TERMUZI BIN ABDUL AZIZ; publs include magazines, textbooks, higher learning books and general books.

Pusat Dokumentasi Melayu DBP (Malay Documentation Centre): ; tel. (3) 2481011 ext. 201; fax (3) 2442081; 120,000 vols, 3,000 periodicals, audio-visual materials, special collection on Malay language and literature; Chief Librarian ROHANI RUSTAM; publs *Mutiara Pustaka* (annually), subject bibliography (occasional).

Institute for Development Studies (Sabah): Block C, Suite 7 CFO1, 7th Floor, Karamunsing Complex, 88300 Kota Kinabalu, Sabah; tel. (88) 246166; fax (88) 234707; e-mail info@ids.org.my; internet www.ids.org.my; Dir HASNOL AYUB; publs include *Borneo Review* (2 a year).

Institute of Malaysian and International Studies (IKMAS): Universiti Kebangsaan Malaysia, 43600 Bangi, Selangor; tel. (3) 8293205; fax (3) 8261022; e-mail ikmas@ukm.my; f. 1995; Dir Prof. Dr THAM SIEW YEAN.

Institute of Strategic and International Studies (ISIS): 1, Pesiaran Sultan Salahuddin, POB 12424, 50778 Kuala Lumpur; tel. (3) 2939366; fax (3) 2913210; e-mail jawhar@isis.po.my; internet www.isis.org.my/isis; f. 1983; undertakes studies in strategic and policy issues directly relevant to national interests and public welfare; Dir-Gen. Dato' MOHAMED JAWHAR HASSAN.

Malaysian Branch of the Royal Asiatic Society: 4B, 2nd Floor, Jalan Kemuja, Bangsar, 59000 Kuala Lumpur; tel. (3) 22835345; fax (3) 22822458; e-mail mbras@tm.net.my; f. 1877; 886 mems; Pres. Tun MOHAMMED HANIF BIN OMAR; Hon. Sec. Datuk Haji BURHANUDDIN BIN AHMAD TAJUDIN; publs include *Journal* (2 a year), monographs, reprints.

Malaysian Institute of Economic Research (MIER): 9th Floor, Menara Dayabumi, Jalan Sultan Hishamuddin, 50050 Kuala Lumpur; tel. (3) 22730214; fax (3) 22730197; e-mail ariff@mier.po.my; internet www.mier.org.my; f. 1985; conducts policy- and business-orientated research; Exec. Dir MOHAMMED ARIFF.

South East Asian Central Bank—Research and Training Centre: Lorong University A, 59100 Kuala Lumpur; tel. (3) 7568622; fax (3) 7574616; f. 1972; research into financial and economic affairs; publs include *Economic Survey of the SEACEN Countries*.

MEXICO

Asociación Latinoamericana de Estudios de Asia y Africa (Latin American Assen for Asian and African Studies): El Colegio de México, Camino al Ajusco 20, Pedregal de Santa Teresa, CP 10740, Magdalena Contreras, México DF; tel. (55) 5449-3021; fax (55) 5645-4584; e-mail aalada@colmex.mx; internet ceaa.colmex.mx/aladaa; f. 1976; 450 mems; promotes African and Asian studies in Latin America; Sec.-Gen. Prof. LUIS MESA DELMONTE; publs newsletters and proceedings.

Centro de Estudios de Asia y África (Centre for Asian and African Studies): El Colegio de México, Camino al Ajusco 20, Pedregal de Sta Teresa, México DF 10740; tel. (55) 5449-3000; e-mail bprecia@colmex .mx; internet ceaa.colmex.mx/nuevositioceaa/; f. 1964; part of El Colegio de México; Dir BENJAMÍN PRECIADO SOLÍS; publ. *Estudios de Asia y África* (quarterly).

MONGOLIA

Centre of Strategic Studies: POB 870, Ulan Bator; tel. (11) 353034; f. 1990; research into national and international security and strategy, with emphasis on North-East Asia; Dir S. DZORIG; publs include *Security and Development Issues* (2 a year).

Institute of Oriental and International Studies: Academy of Sciences, Ulan Bator; fax (11) 322613; Dir Dr TS. BATBAYAR; publs *East-West* (in Mongolian, with summaries and contents in English, quarterly), *Mongolian Journal of International Affairs* (in English, annually).

MYANMAR

(formerly Burma)

Burma Research Society: Universities' Central Library, University PO, Yangon; f. 1910 to promote cultural and scientific studies and research relating to Myanmar and neighbouring countries; 1,040 mems; Pres. U HTIN GYI; Hon. Sec. Dr SHEIN; publ. *Journal* (2 a year).

Institute of Economics (Yangon): Pyay Rd, University Estate, Kamayut Township, 11041 Yangon; tel. (1) 32433; e-mail iey@ mptmail.net.mm; f. 1964; library of 100,000 vols; Rector Dr KAN ZAW.

NEPAL

Centre for Nepal and Asian Studies (CNAS): Tribhuvan University, POB 3757, Kirtipur, Kathmandu; tel. (1) 4332078; fax (1) 4331184; e-mail info@cnastu.org.np; internet www.cnastu.org.np; f. 1972; conducts political and social research both in Nepalese and Asian contexts; Exec. Dir Prof. YAGYA PRASAD ADHIKARI; publs include *Contributions to Nepalese Studies* (2 a year), monographs, bibliographies, occasional papers.

United Nations Regional Centre for Peace and Disarmament in Asia and the Pacific (UNRCPD): POB 107, Kathmandu; tel. (1) 5010257; fax (1) 5010223; e-mail info@unrcpd.org.np; internet www.unrcpd.org.np; f. 1988; promotes dialogue in disarmament and regional security-related matters; Dir TAIJIRO KIMURA.

NETHERLANDS

International Institute for Asian Studies (IIAS): POB 9515, 2300 RA Leiden; tel. (71) 5272227; fax (71) 5274162; e-mail iias@let.leidenuniv.nl; internet www.iias.nl; based in Leiden and Amsterdam; post-doctoral research centre; Dir Prof. MAX SPARREBOOM; publ. *IIAS Newsletter*.

Koninklijk Instituut voor Taal-, Land- en Volkenkunde (KITLV) (Royal Netherlands Institute of Southeast Asian and Caribbean Studies): Reuvens-plaats 2, POB 9515, 2300 RA Leiden; tel. (71) 5272295; fax (71) 5272638; e-mail kitlv@kitlv.nl; internet www.kitlv.nl; f. 1851 to collect and catalogue books and other documents, to carry out and support research, and to publish books and journals on South-East Asia (especially Indonesia), the Pacific area and the Caribbean region (in particular Suriname and the Netherlands Antilles); 2,044 mems; library of 280,000 titles; Pres. Prof. P. J. M. NAS; Dir Prof. G. J. OOSTINDIE; publs include *Bijdragen* (quarterly), *New West Indian Guide* (quarterly), *Verhandelingen*, *Bibliotheca Indonesica*, *Working Papers Series*, *Volkenkunde* (quarterly), bibliographies, translations.

NEW CALEDONIA

Société des Etudes Mélanésiennes: Musée Neo-Calédonien, BP 2393, Nouméa; tel. 27-23-42; fax 28-41-43; f. 1938; anthropology; publ. *Etudes Mélanésiennes* (annually).

NEW ZEALAND

Macmillan Brown Centre for Pacific Studies: University of Canterbury, PB 4800, Christchurch 8004; tel. (3) 364-2957; fax (3) 364-2002; e-mail mbcps@canterbury.ac.nz; internet www.pacs.canterbury.ac.nz; f. 1988; researches and teaches on the history, society and culture of the peoples of the Pacific; Chair. Prof. ERIC PAWSON; Dir Prof. KAREN NERO; publs include a Working Paper Series and Occasional Paper Series.

New Zealand Asia Institute: University of Auckland, PB 92019, Auckland; tel. (9) 373-7599; fax (9) 308-2312; e-mail x.chen@auckland.ac.nz; internet www.auckland.ac.nz/nzai; f. 1995; consists of China Studies Centre, Japan Studies Centre, Korean Studies Centre and Southeast Asian Studies Centre; Programme Officer Dr XIN CHEN; publs include *NZAI Regional Analysis Series* (occasional) and *NZAI Annual Report*.

New Zealand Geographical Society: c/o School of Geography, Geology and Environmental Science, University of Auckland, PB 92019; tel. (9) 373-7599, ext. 88464; fax (9) 373-7434; e-mail nzgs@auckland.ac.nz; internet www.nzgs.co.nz; f. 1944; 6 brs; Pres. Prof. MICHAEL CROZIER; Sec. MARIA BOROVNIK; publs include *New Zealand Geographer* (3 a year).

New Zealand Institute of Economic Research: POB 3479, Wellington 6140; tel. (4) 4721-880; fax (4) 4721-211; e-mail econ@nzier.org.nz; internet www.nzier.org.nz; f. 1958; independent non-profit making organization; research into NZ economic development; quarterly forecast of the national economy and annual medium-term industry outlook; quarterly survey of business opinion; economic investigations on contract basis; Chief Exec. JEAN-PIERRE DE RAAD; Chair. MICHAEL WALLS; publs *Quarterly Predictions*, *Quarterly Survey of Business Opinion*, research monographs, discussion papers.

New Zealand Institute of International Affairs: c/o Victoria University of Wellington, POB 600, Wellington 6140; tel. (4) 463-5356; fax (4) 463-5437; e-mail nziia@vuw.ac.nz; internet www.vuw.ac.nz/nziia; f. 1934 to examine international questions, particularly in relation to Asia and the South Pacific; Pres. RUSSELL MARSHALL; Dir BRIAN LYNCH; publ. *New Zealand International Review* (6 a year), books.

Pacific Cooperation Foundation: 660 Great South Rd, Central Park Business Centre, Bldg 10, Level 3, Ellerslie, POB 74084, Greenland, Auckland; tel. (9) 969-1494; fax (9) 969-1495; e-mail info@pcf.org.nz; internet www.pcf.org.nz; f. 2002; independent trust; focuses on political, economic, social and devt issues in the Pacific region; CEO MEG POUTASI.

Polynesian Society: c/o Maori Studies Dept, University of Auckland, PB 92019, Auckland 1; e-mail jps@auckland.ac.nz; internet www.arts.auckland.ac.nz/departments/index.cfm?p=9144; f. 1892 to promote the study of the anthropology, ethnology, philology, history and antiquities of the New Zealand Maori and other Pacific Island peoples; library; 900 mems; Pres. Dame JOAN METGE; publs *Memoirs*, *Journal* (quarterly), *Maori Monographs*, *Maori Texts*.

PAKISTAN

Islamic Research Academy: D-35, Block 5, Federal 'B' Area, Karachi 75950; tel. (21) 6349840; fax (21) 6361040; e-mail info@irak.pk; internet www.irak.pk; f. 1963; includes reference library, books in Urdu, Arabic, English, rare edns of classical Islamic literature, archive of periodicals; Dir SAYYED SHAHID HASHMI; publs *Maarif Feature Service* (fortnightly).

Islamic Research Institute: International Islamic University, POB 1035, Islamabad 44000; tel. (51) 228128; fax (51) 2250821; e-mail ziansari@gmail.com; internet my.iiu.edu.pk/Institutes/IslamicResearchInstitute/tabid/207/Default.aspx; f. 1960 to conduct and co-ordinate research in Islamic studies; organizes seminars, conferences, etc; library of 75,000 vols, 1,300 microfilms and microfiches, 258 MSS; 170 cassettes; Dir-Gen. Dr ZAFAR ISHAQ ANSARI; publs include *Al-Dirasat al-Islamiyyah* (Arabic, quarterly), *Islamic Studies* (English, quarterly), *Fikr-o-Nazar* (Urdu, quarterly), monographs.

Pakistan Institute of International Affairs: Aiwan-e-Sadar Rd, POB 1447, Karachi 74200; tel. (21) 5682891; fax (21) 5686069; e-mail info@piia.org.pk; internet www.piia.org.pk; f. 1947 to promote interest and research in international affairs; library of over 32,400 vols; over 500 mems; Chair. FATEHYAB ALI KHAN; Sec. Dr QAZI SHAKIL AHMAD (acting); publs *Pakistan Horizon* (quarterly), books and monographs.

PAPUA NEW GUINEA

Institute of National Affairs: POB 1530, Port Moresby; tel. 3211045; fax 3217223; e-mail inapng@daltron.com.pg; internet www.inapng.com; f. 1978; owned by mems; mems include about 80 PNG and PNG-based businesses, chambers and councils; Council Pres. PHIL FRANKLIN; Exec. Dir PAUL BARKER; publs discussion and working papers.

National Research Institute of Papua New Guinea: POB 5854, Boroko; tel. 3260300; fax 3260213; e-mail nri@global.net.pg; internet www.nri.org.pg; f. 1989 by amalgamation of Institute of Applied Social and Economic Research, Institute of Papua New Guinea Studies and Education Research Unit; promotion of research into social, legal, military, political, economic, educational, environmental and cultural issues in PNG; library of 13,000 vols; Dir Dr THOMAS WEBSTER; publs *Monographs*, *Discussion Papers*, *Bibliography*, *Post Courier Index* (annually), special and educational reports, etc.

THE PHILIPPINES

Asian Center: University of the Philippines, Diliman, Quezon City, Metro Manila 1101; tel. and fax (2) 9270909; e-mail asianctr@up.edu.ph; internet ac.upd.edu.ph; f. 1955 as Institute of Asian Studies; Dean Dr AILEEN BAVIERA; publs include *Asian Studies Journal* (2 a year), monographs, occasional papers and books.

Asia-Pacific Peace Research Association: 41 Rajah Matanda, Project 4, Quezon City, Metro Manila 1109; tel. (2) 9139255; fax (2) 9136435; e-mail appra@csi.com.ph; Sec.-Gen. MARY SOLEDAD PERPIÑAN.

Center for Pacific Rim Studies: University of Asia and the Pacific, Pearl Drive, Ortigas Center, Pasig City 1600; tel. and fax (2) 6370912; fax (2) 6370912; e-mail mcrapisora@uap.edu.ph; f. 1967; fmrly Center for Research and Communication; name change and university status 1995; Dept Chair. MARIA CONCEPCION RAPISORA.

Cultural Center of the Philippines: CCP Complex, Roxas Blvd, Pasay City, Metro Manila; tel. (2) 8321125; fax (2) 8323683; e-mail ccp@culturalcenter.gov.ph; internet www.culturalcenter.gov.ph; f. 1966 to preserve, develop and promote Philippine arts and culture; Pres. and Artistic Dir NESTOR O. JARDIN.

Institute of Philippine Culture: Ateneo de Manila University, Frank Lynch Hall, Social Development Complex, Loyola Heights Campus, Quezon City, POB 154, Metro Manila 1099; tel. (2) 4266001; fax (2) 4266067; e-mail ipc@admu.edu.ph; internet www.ipc-ateneo.org/; f. 1960; conducts research into rural and urban poverty, agrarian reform, irrigation, community health, coastal resources, forestry and women's affairs; assists development agencies; trains agency personnel and local communities in the use of research methodologies; library of 3,166 vols, 4,070 reprints and vertical file databank; Dir Dr CZARINA. SALOMA-AKPEDONU; publs include *IPC Papers*, *IPC Monograph Series*, *IPC Final Reports*, *IPC Reprints* (all irregular).

Research Institute for Mindanao Culture: Xavier University, Ateneo de Cagayan, POB 24, Cagayan de Oro City 9000; tel. (8822) 8574817; fax (8822) 723228; e-mail rimcu@xu.edu.ph; internet rimcu.elizaga.net; f. 1957 to study and assist the development of north Mindanao, the Philippines in general and their peoples; Dir ISAIAS

SEALZA; publs *Bahandi* (annually), *RIMCU Updates* (quarterly), periodicals.

Research Institute for Politics and Economics: Polytechnic University of the Philippines, Anonas St, Santa Mesa, Manila; tel. (2) 616775; fax (2) 7161143; Dir Prof. DANILO CUETO.

POLAND

Institute of Developing Countries: University of Warsaw, ul. Karowa 20, 00-324 Warsaw; tel. (22) 55-23-237; fax (22) 55-23-227; e-mail ikr@uw.edu.pl; internet www.ikr.uw.edu.pl; f. 1962; undergraduate and postgraduate studies; interdisciplinary research on developing countries; Dir Prof. MIROSŁAWA CZERNY.

Institute of Oriental Studies: 00-927 Warsaw, ul. Krakowskie Przedmieście 26/28; tel. (22) 55-20-349; e-mail dyrekcja@orient.uw.edu.pl; internet www.orient.uw.edu.pl/~pto; f. 1922; Pres. Prof. JOLANTA SIERAKOWSKA-DYNDO; Sec. MARIA KOZŁOWSKA; publ. *Przegląd Wschodni*.

Komitet Nauk Orientalistycznych PAN (Committee for Oriental Studies of the Polish Academy of Sciences): 00-927 Warsaw, ul. Krakowskie Przedmieście 26/28; tel. (22) 8285577; internet kno.pan.pl; f. 1952; Asian and African studies, particularly social sciences; Pres. Prof. Dr MAREK MEJOR; publs *Rocznik Orientalistyczny* (2 a year), series *Prace orientalistyczne* (irregular).

PORTUGAL

Museu Etnográfico da Sociedade de Geografia de Lisboa (Ethnographical Museum): Rua Portas de Santo Antão 100, 1100 Lisbon; tel. (1) 3425068; fax (1) 3464553; e-mail soc.geografia.lisboa@clix.pt; f. 1875; native arts, arms, clothing, musical instruments, statues of navigators and historians, relics of voyages of discovery, scientific instruments; Dir Prof. JOÃO PEREIRA NETO; Curator Dr MANUEL CANTINHO.

RUSSIA

Institute of Far Eastern Studies: Russian Academy of Sciences, 117218 Moscow, pr. Nakhimovsky 32; tel. (495) 124-08-35; fax (495) 310-70-56; e-mail ifes@cemi.rssi.ru; f. 1966; Dir Prof. MIKHAIL L. TITARENKO; publs include *Far Eastern Affairs* (6 a year).**Centre for Japanese Studies:** Russian Academy of Sciences, 117218 Moscow, pr. Nakhimovsky 32; tel. (495) 124-08-35; fax (495) 310-70-56; e-mail ifes@cemi.rssi.ru; f. 1922; part of the Institute of Far Eastern Studies; Chair. Dr VIKTOR N. PAVLYATENKO.

Moscow State Institute of International Relations: 119454 Moscow, Vernadskogo pr. 76; tel. (495) 434-91-58; fax (495) 434-90-66; internet www.mgimo.ru; f. 1944; library of 920,000 vols; Rector ANATOLII V. TORKUNOV; publ. *Moscow Journal of International Law*.

SINGAPORE

Asia Research Institute (ARI): 469 A Tower Block, 10-01 Bukit Timah Rd, National University of Singapore, Bukit Timah Campus, Singapore 259770; tel. 65163810; fax 67791428; e-mail arisec@nus.edu.sg; internet www.ari.nus.edu.sg; f. 2001 to provide a focus for multi-disciplinary research on the Asian region; Dir LILY KONG; publs *Asian Population Studies* (3 a year), working paper series, newsletter, annual report.

Asian Mass Communication Research and Information Centre (AMIC): Singapore; tel. 6251506; fax 62534535; e-mail amicline@singnet.com.sg; internet sunsite.nus.edu.sg/amic/; f. 1971; library of 13,000 books, periodicals and conference papers; Sec.-Gen. VIJAY MENON; publs *ACMB* (6 a year), *Asian Journal of Communication* (2 a year), *Media Asia* (quarterly).

The China Society: 47 Hill St, 06-06, Singapore 179365; e-mail chinasociety_sec@singnet.com.sg; f. 1948 to promote the study of Chinese culture; 106 mems; Pres. SIMON K. C. HU; publ. *Journal of the China Society*.

East Asian Institute, National University of Singapore (EAI): 469 A Bukit Timah Rd, Tower Block, No. 06-01, Singapore 259770; tel. 65163715; fax 67793409; e-mail eaiyd@nus.edu.sg; internet www.nus.edu.sg/NUSinfo/EAI; f. 1997 to promote the study of China's political, economic and social development; Dir Prof. DALI YANG.

Institute of Policy Studies: Lee Kuan Yew School of Public Policy, National University of Singapore, House 5, 1C Cluny Rd, Singapore 259599; tel. 65168388; fax 67770700; e-mail ips@nus.edu.sg; internet www.spp.nus.edu.sg/ips; Dir JANADAS DEVAN.

Institute of Southeast Asian Studies: 30 Heng Mui Keng Terrace, Pasir Panjang, Singapore 119614; tel. 68712401; fax 67756184; e-mail admin@iseas.edu.sg; internet www.iseas.edu.sg; f. 1968 for the promotion of research into the problems of economic development, stability and security and political and social change in South-East Asia; library of 300,000 vols; Dir K. KESAVAPANY; publs *Southeast Asian Affairs* (annually), *Regional Outlook* (annually), *Contemporary Southeast Asia* (3 a year), *SOJOURN, Journal of Social Issues in Southeast Asia* (2 a year), *ASEAN Economic Bulletin* (3 a year).

Singapore Institute of International Affairs: 2 Nassim Rd, Singapore 258370; tel. 67349600; fax 67336217; e-mail research@siiaonline.org; f. 1961; organizes seminars, lectures and conferences; 390 mems; Chair. SIMON TAY; Dir Dr YEO LAY HWEE.

SOLOMON ISLANDS

Solomon Islands National Museum and Cultural Centre: POB 313, Honiara; tel. 24896; e-mail loafoa@yahoo.com; research into all aspects of Solomons culture; Dir LAWRENCE FOANAOTA.

SOUTH AFRICA

Centre for Chinese Studies: University of Stellenbosch, Admin A, Rm 1082, Ryneveld St, Stellenbosch 7600; tel. (21) 8082840; fax (21) 8082841; e-mail ccsinfo@sun.ac.za; internet www.ccs.org.za; Dir Dr MARTYN DAVIES.

SPAIN

Centro de Estudios de Asia Oriental (Centre for East Asian Studies): Universidad Autónoma, Campus de Cantoblanco, 28049 Madrid; tel. (91) 4974695; fax (91) 4975278; e-mail ceao@uam.es; internet www.uam.es/ceao; f. 1992; promotes research relating to the economy, society and culture of East Asian countries, with particular emphasis on China and Japan; Dir TACIANA FISAC; publs include *Boletín* (annually).

SWEDEN

Centre for East and Southeast Asian Studies, Lund University: Box 792, 220 07, Lund; tel. (46) 222-30-40; fax (46) 222-30-41; e-mail info@ace.lu.se; internet www.ace.lu.se; f. 1997; Dir Prof. ROGER GREATREX; publ. *Working Papers in Contemporary Asian Studies*.

Centrum för Stillahavsasienstudier (Centre for Pacific Asia Studies): 106 91 Stockholm; tel. (8) 162897; fax (8) 168810; e-mail cpas@orient.su.se; internet www.cpas.su.se; f. 1984; attached to Stockholm University; Dir Dr MASAKO IKEGAMI.

European Institute of Japanese Studies (EIJS): Stockholm School of Economics, Box 6501, 113 83 Stockholm; tel. (8) 736-93-64; fax (8) 31-30-17; e-mail asia@hhs.se; f. 1992; Dir Prof. MAGNUS BLOMSTRÖM; publs papers, monographs, reports.

SWITZERLAND

Centre for Asian Studies (CEA): Graduate Institute of International and Development Studies, 20 rue Rothschild, 1202 Geneva 21; tel. (22) 9085820; fax (22) 9084401; e-mail mariejo.duc@graduateinstitute.ch; internet graduateinstitute.ch/cas; f. 1971; Dir PHILIPPE BURRIN; publs books, research reports, occasional papers, articles and newsletters.

Schweizerische Asiengesellschaft (Swiss Asia Society): c/o Ostasiatisches Seminar, Universität Zürich, Zürichbergstrasse 4, 8032 Zürich; tel. (1) 634-3181; fax (1) 634-4921; e-mail office@oas.uzh.ch; internet www.sagw.ch/dt/Mitglieder/outer.aspzid=40; f. 1939; 185 mems; Pres. Prof. Dr V. RUDOLPH; publs *Asiatische Studien / Etudes Asiatiques* (quarterly), *Schweizer Asiatische Studien / Etudes Asiatiques Suisses* (series).

Schweizerisches Institut für Auslandforschung (Swiss Institute of International Studies): Seilergraben 49, 8001 Zürich; tel. (44) 212-1313; fax (44) 212-7854; e-mail siafcd@pw.unizh.ch; internet www.siaf.ch; Dir Prof. DIETER RULOFF; publ. *Sozialwissenschaftliche Studien* (annually).

TAIWAN

Academia Historica: 406 Sec. 2, Pei Yi Rd, Hsintien, Taipei; tel. (2) 22171535; fax (2) 22171640; contains national archives, library, documents; engaged in preparing history of China since 1894; Pres. CHU SHAO-HWA.

Asia and World Institute (AWI): 10th Floor, 102 Kuang Fu South Rd, Taipei; f. 1976; research into international relations, and North American, Asian and Pacific, and European affairs; Dir Dr PHILLIP M. CHEN; publs *AWI Digest*, *AWI Lecture and Essay Series*, *AWI Monograph Series*.

Chia Hsin Foundation: 96 Chung Shan Rd, North, Sec. 2, Taipei 10449; tel. (2) 25231461; fax (2) 25231204; f. 1963 for the promotion of culture in Taiwan; operates nationally in the fields of the arts, social studies, science and medicine, law and education, through research projects, courses, conferences, etc.; Chair. Dr YEN CHEN-HSING; Sec. TSENG WU-HSIONG.

Chung-hua Institution for Economic Research: 75 Chang Hsing St, Taipei 106; tel. (2) 27356006; fax (2) 27356035; e-mail chung-hua@cier.edu.tw; internet www.cier.edu.tw; Pres. MAI CHAO-CHENG.

Graduate Institute of International Business: National Taiwan University, 1 Roosevelt Rd, Sec. 4, Taipei; tel. (2) 23638399; e-mail yljaw@mba.ntu.edu.tw; Dir YI-LONG JAW.

Institute of Economics, Academia Sinica: Nankang, Taipei 11529; tel. (2) 27822791; fax (2) 27853946; e-mail service@ieas.econ.sinica.edu.tw; internet www.sinica.edu.tw/econ; f. 1970; Pres. Dr LEE YUAN-TSEH.

Institute of International Relations: 64 Wan Shou Rd, Wenshan District, Taipei 116; tel. (2) 82377277; fax (2) 29382133; e-mail dschen@cc.nccu.edu.tw; internet www.iir.nccu.edu.tw; f. 1953; research on international relations and mainland Chinese affairs; Dir TUAN Y. CHENG; publs *Mainland China Studies* (monthly), *Montai to Kenkyu* (in Japanese, every 2 months).

Taiwan Institute of Economic Research (TIER): 7th Floor, 16-8 Tehwei St, Taipei; tel. (2) 5865000; fax (2) 5860997; internet www.tier.org.tw; f. 1976.

Taiwan Research Institute (TRI): 29/F, 27 Jungjeng East Rd, Sec. 2, Danshuei, Taipei 251; tel. (2) 88095688; e-mail admin@tri.org.tw; internet www.tri.org.tw; f. 1994; Pres. WU TSAI-YI; publ. *Finance Forum Series*.

THAILAND

Asian Institute of Technology (AIT): POB 4, Klong Luang, Pathumthani 12120; tel. (2) 516-0110; fax (2) 516-2126; e-mail jlarmand@ait.ac.th; internet www.ait.ac.th; f. 1959; Pres. Prof. SAID IRANDOUST; publs *AIT Annual Report*, *Annual Report on Research and Activities*, *AIT Review* (3 a year), *Prospectus*, other specialized publs.

Institute of Asian Studies (IAS): 7th Floor, Prajadhipok-Rambhai Barni Bldg, Chulalongkorn University, Thanon Phyathai, Bangkok 10330; tel. (2) 251-5199; fax (2) 255-1124; e-mail ias@chula.ac.th; f. 1967; promotion of interdisciplinary Asian studies; Dir Dr SUPANG CHANTAVANICH; publs monographs, journals.

Institute of East Asian Studies: Thammasat University, Rangsit Campus, Pathum Thani 12121; tel. (2) 564-5000; fax (2) 564-4777; e-mail ieas@tu.ac.th; internet www.asia.tu.ac.th; f. 1984; Dir Assoc. Prof. YUPHA KLANGSUWAN.

Siam Society: 131 Soi 21 (Asoke), Thanon Asokemontri, Bangkok 10110; tel. (2) 661-6470; fax (2) 258-3491; e-mail info@siam-society.org; internet www.siam-society.org; f. 1904 to promote interest and research in art, science and cultural affairs of Thailand and neighbouring countries; library of 35,000 vols; Pres. ATHUECK ASVANUND; Hon. Sec. BARENT SPRINGSTED; publs include journals and *The Natural History Bulletin*.

Thailand Development Research Institute (TDRI): 565 Ramkhamhaeng 39 (Thepleela 1), Bangkapi, Bangkok 10310; tel. (2) 718-5460; fax (2) 718-5461; e-mail publications@tdri.or.th; internet www.info.tdri.or.th; f. 1984; independent policy research on Thailand's economic and social development issues; Pres. Dr NIPON POAPONGSAKORN.

TIMOR-LESTE

Timor Institute of Development Studies (TIDS): Rua Maucocomate, Becora, POB 181, Dili; tel. and fax 3323889; e-mail admin@tids-et.org; internet www.tids-et.org; f. 1997; fmrly East Timor Study Group (ETSG); promotes research and teachings in democracy and social change, economics and management, and agriculture and applied technology; Exec. Dir Dr JOÃO M. SALDANHA; publ. *Observer* (every 2 months).

UNITED KINGDOM

Asia Research Centre: London School of Economics and Political Science, Houghton St, London, WC2A 2AE; tel. (20) 7955-7388; fax (20) 7107-5285; e-mail arc@lse.ac.uk; internet www.lse.ac.uk/collections/asiaResearchCentre; f. 1995; conducts social science research on Asia; Dir Dr ATHAR HUSSAIN.

Asian and African Studies (British Library): 96 Euston Rd, London, NW1 2DB; tel. (20) 7412-7873; fax (20) 7412-7641; e-mail apac-enquiries@bl.uk; internet www.bl.uk/reshelp/bldept/apac/apacoll/apac.html; f. 1801; fmrly Asia, Pacific and Africa Collections; c. 900,000 printed books in Asian and African languages, more than 120,000 vols of periodicals and newspapers, c. 65,000 manuscripts, extensive collection of scholarship in European languages; other resources incl. sound recordings, maps and sheet music; Head SUSAN WHITFIELD; publs catalogues of the collections.

British Association for Chinese Studies: e-mail secretary@bacsuk.org.uk; internet www.bacsuk.org.uk; f. 1976; provides forum for academics and others in the field; holds annual conference; Pres. TIM WRIGHT; publs *Newsletter* (2 a year), *Annual Bulletin*.

Centre for Applied South Asian Studies (CASAS): c/o Roger Ballard, Red Croft, Howard St, Stalybridge, SK15 3ER; tel. and fax (161) 303-1709; e-mail roger@casas.org.uk; internet www.casas.org.uk; promotes research into the social, cultural, and religious dimensions of the South Asian presence in the United Kingdom.

Centre for Asia-Pacific Studies, Nottingham Trent University: School of Arts and Humanities, Nottingham Trent University, Clifton Lane, Nottingham, NG11 8NS; tel. (115) 848-3175; fax (115) 848-6319; e-mail roy.smith@ntu.ac.uk; internet www.ntu.ac.uk/HUM/; Dir Dr ROY SMITH.

Centre for East Asian Studies, University of Bristol: University of Bristol, 8 Woodland Rd, Bristol, BS8 1TN; tel. (117) 954-5577; fax (117) 954-6604; e-mail ceas-admin@bristol.ac.uk; internet www.bris.ac.uk/ceas; Dir Prof. KA HO MOK.

Contemporary China Institute: School of Oriental and African Studies, University of London, Thornhaugh St, Russell Sq., London, WC1H 0XG; tel. (20) 7898-4736; f. 1968; publs *Research Notes and Studies* (short monographs) and CCI/Oxford University Press series.

Department of East Asian Studies, University of Leeds: Leeds, LS2 9JT; tel. (113) 343-3460; fax (113) 343-6741; e-mail east@leeds.ac.uk; internet leeds.wreac.org; Head of Dept Prof. JOERN DOSCH.

East Asian Section, Asian Department, Victoria and Albert Museum: South Kensington, London, SW7 2RL; tel. (20) 7942-2244; fax (20) 7942-2252; e-mail asia.enquiries@vam.ac.uk; internet www.vam.ac.uk; f. 1970; perm. displays and exhbns of art from China, Japan and Korea; lectures and research; Keeper, Asian Dept BETH MCKILLOP.

Faculty of Oriental Studies: University of Oxford, Pusey Lane, Oxford, OX1 2LE; tel. (1865) 278200; fax (1865) 278190; e-mail orient@orinst.ox.ac.uk; internet www.orinst.ox.ac.uk; f. 1960; comprises Oriental Institute and Institute for Chinese Studies; Sec. ELIZABETH CULL.

Institute of Asia-Pacific Studies, University of Nottingham: School of Politics, University Park, Nottingham, NG7 2RD; tel. (115) 951-4862; fax (115) 951-4859; e-mail gary.rawnsley@nottingham.ac.uk; internet www.nottingham.ac.uk/iaps; Dir Dr GARY RAWNSLEY.

Institute of Commonwealth Studies: 2nd Floor, South Block, Senate House, Malet St, London WC1E 7HU; tel. (20) 7862-8844; fax (20) 7862-8813; e-mail ics@sas.ac.uk; internet www.commonwealth.sas.ac.uk; f. 1949 to promote advanced study of the Commonwealth; provides a library and meeting place for postgraduate student and academic staff engaged in research on this field; offers postgraduate teaching; Dir PHILIP MURPHY; publs *Annual Report*, *Collected Seminar Papers*, *Newsletter*, *Theses in Progress in Commonwealth Studies*.

Institute of Development Studies at the University of Sussex: Brighton, Sussex, BN1 9RE; tel. (1273) 606261; fax (1273) 621202; e-mail ids@ids.ac.uk; internet www.ids.ac.uk/ids; f. 1966; research, teaching and communications on international development; Dir LAWRENCE HADDAD; publs include *IDS Bulletin* (quarterly), *IDS Discussion Papers*, *Annual Report*, *Research Reports*.

International Institute for Strategic Studies (IISS): Arundel House, 13–15 Arundel St, Temple Place, London, WC2R 3DX; tel. (20) 7379-7676; fax (20) 7836-3108; internet www.iiss.org; f. 1958; conducts research and analysis, and provides a forum for contacts on military and political developments relevant to the prospects, course and consequences of conflict world-wide; c. 2,500 individual mems and 400 corporate and institutional mems; Chair. Prof. FRANÇOIS HEISBOURG; Dir-Gen. and Chief Exec. Dr JOHN CHIPMAN; publs include *The Military Balance* (annually), *Strategic Survey* (annually), *Strategic Comments* (10 a year), *Survival: Global Politics and Strategy* (every 2 months), *Adelphi Papers* (monograph series).

Mongolia and Inner Asia Studies Unit (MIASU): The Mond Bldg, Free School Lane, Cambridge CB2 3RF; tel. (1223) 334690; fax (1223) 767280; e-mail admin@innerasiaresearch.org; internet innerasiaresearch.org; f. 1986; Dir Prof. CAROLINE HUMPHREY; publs *Journal* (2 a year) and the Inner Asia Series.

Nissan Institute of Japanese Studies, University of Oxford: 27 Winchester Rd, Oxford, OX2 6NA; tel. (1865) 274570; fax (1865) 274574; e-mail secretary@nissan.ox.ac.uk; internet www.nissan.ox.ac.uk; f. 1981; devoted to the study of modern Japan; Dir Dr I. J. NEARY; publs *Nissan Institute / Routledge Japanese Studies* series, *Nissan Occasional Papers* series.

The Oriental Ceramic Society: POB 517, Cambridge, CB21 5BE; tel. and fax (1223) 881328; e-mail ocslondon@btinternet.com; internet ocs-london.com; f. 1921 to increase knowledge and appreciation of South-East Asian ceramics and other arts; registered charity; Pres. SHELAGH VAINKE; Administrator MARY PAINTER.

Overseas Development Institute: Costain House, 111 Westminster Bridge Rd, London, SE1 7JD; tel. (20) 7922-0300; fax (20) 7922-0399; e-mail odi@odi.org.uk; internet www.odi.org.uk; f. 1960 as a research centre and forum for the discussion of development issues; publishes its research findings in books and working papers; library of over 15,000 vols; Chair. Baroness JAY; Dir ALISON EVANS; publs include *Development Policy Review*, *Disasters: The Journal of Disaster Studies and Management*.

Progressio (CIIR): Unit 5, Canonbury Yard, 190A New North Rd, London, N1 7BJ; tel. (20) 7354-0883; fax (20) 7359-0017; e-mail enquiries@progressio.org.uk; internet www.progressio.org.uk; f. 1940; fmrly the Catholic Institute for International Relations; information and research on developing countries; recruits professionals for development projects overseas; Exec. Dir CHRISTINE ALLEN.

Royal Asiatic Society of Great Britain and Ireland: 14 Stephenson Way, London, NW1 2HD; tel. (20) 7388-4539; fax (20) 7391-9429; e-mail info@royalasiaticsociety.org; internet www.royalasiaticsociety.org; f. 1823 for the study of the history, sociology, institutions, customs, languages and art of Asia; c. 800 mems; c. 700 subscribing libraries; affiliated societies in various Asian cities; library of 80,000 vols and MSS, paintings, drawings, photographs, coins; Pres. Prof. GORDON JOHNSON; Dir ALISON OHTA; publs *Journal* and monographs.

Royal Commonwealth Society: 25 Northumberland Ave, London, WC2N 5AP; tel. (20) 7766-9231; fax (20) 7930-9705; e-mail info@thercs.org; internet www.thercs.org; f. 1868; est. to promote international understanding of the Commonwealth and its people; organizes meetings and seminars on topical issues, and cultural and social events; library housed by Cambridge University Library; Chair. Baroness PRASHAR; Dir DANNY SRISKANDARAJAH; publs *Annual Report*, *Newsletter* (3 a year), conference reports.

Royal Institute of International Affairs: Chatham House, 10 St James's Sq., London, SW1Y 4LE; tel. (20) 7957-5700; fax (20) 7957-5710; e-mail contact@chathamhouse.org; internet www.chathamhouse.org; f. 1920 to facilitate the scientific study of international questions; c. 3,000 mems; Chair. Dr DEANNE JULIUS; Dir ROBIN NIBLETT; publs include *International Affairs* (6 a year), *The World Today* (monthly), *Chatham House Papers*, *Annual Report*, etc.

Royal Society for Asian Affairs: 2 Belgrave Sq., London, SW1X 8PJ; tel. (20) 7235-5122; e-mail info@rsaa.org.uk; internet www.rsaa.org.uk; f. 1901; 1,200 mems; library of c. 6,500 vols; Pres. Lord DENMAN; Chair. Sir DAVID JOHN; Sec. NEIL PORTER; publ. *Journal* (3 a year).

St Antony's College Asian Studies Centre: 62 Woodstock Rd, Oxford, OX2 6JF; tel. and fax (1865) 274559; e-mail asian@sant.ox.ac.uk; internet www.sant.ox.ac.uk/asian; f. 1954; devoted to the comparative study of modern Asia; Dir Dr RACHEL MURPHY.

School of Development Studies, University of East Anglia: Norwich, NR4 7TJ; tel. (1603) 592329; fax (1603) 451999; e-mail dev.general@uea.ac.uk; internet www.uea.ac.uk/dev; f. 1970; teaching, research and advisory work; Head Dr STEVE RUSSELL; publ. *Reports and Policy Papers*.

School of East Asian Studies (SEAS), University of Sheffield: Floor 5, Arts Tower, Western Bank, Sheffield, S10 2TN; tel. (114) 222-8400; fax (114) 222-8432; e-mail SEAS@sheffield.ac.uk; internet www.shef.ac.uk/seas; Japanese, Korean and Chinese studies; Chair. Prof. TIMOTHY WRIGHT.

School of Oriental and African Studies (SOAS): University of London, Thornhaugh St, Russell Sq., London, WC1H 0XG; tel. (20) 7898-4016; fax (20) 7898-4019; e-mail study@soas.ac.uk; internet www.soas.ac.uk; f. 1916; centre for the study of Asia, Africa and the Middle East; includes Centre of Chinese Studies, Centre of South Asian Studies, Centre of South East Asian Studies, Centre of Korean Studies, Japan Research Centre, Contemporary China Institute, Centre for the Study of Japanese Religion, Centre for the Study of the Literature of Asia and Africa, Centre of East Asian Law; Dir Prof. PAUL WEBLEY; publs include *The Bulletin*, *China Quarterly*.

School of Oriental and African Studies Library: University of London, Thornhaugh St, Russell Sq., London, WC1H 0XG; tel. (20) 7898-4163; fax (20) 7898-4159; e-mail libenquiry@soas.ac.uk; internet www.soas.ac.uk/library; f. 1916; c. 1,500,000 vols and pamphlets; 4,700 current periodicals, 54,000 maps, 7,000 microforms, 2,000 DVDs and videos, 2,800 manuscripts and private papers collections, extensive missionary archives; all covering Asian and African languages, literatures, philosophy, religions, history, law, cultural anthropology, art and archaeology, music, film and media studies, gender studies, development studies, economics, politics and finance; Dir JOHN ROBINSON.

UNITED STATES OF AMERICA

American Oriental Society: Near East Division, Hatcher Graduate Library, University of Michigan, Ann Arbor, MI 48109-1205; tel. (734) 647-4760; fax (734) 763-6743; e-mail jrodgers@umich.edu; internet www.umich/edu/~aos; f. 1842; 1,400 mems; library of 23,000 vols; Pres. ROBERT JOE CUTTER; Sec.-Treas. JONATHAN RODGERS; publs *Journal of the American Oriental Society* (quarterly), *AOS Monograph Series* (irregular).

The Asia Foundation: POB 193223, San Francisco, CA 94119; tel. (415) 982-4640; fax (415) 392-8863; e-mail info@asiafound.org; internet www.asiafoundation.org; br. in Washington, DC, and 17 offices throughout Asia; private, non-profit NGO; f. 1951; library of 3,370 vols; supports programmes in Asia that help improve governance, law and civil society, women's empowerment; economic reform and development, and international relations; collaborates with private and public partners to support leadership and institutional development, exchanges, and policy research; Pres. DAVID D. ARNOLD; publ. *Annual Report*.

Asia-Pacific Center for Security Studies: 2058 Maluhia Rd, Honolulu, HI 96815; tel. (808) 971-8900; fax (808) 971-8999; e-mail pao@apcss.org; internet www.apcss.org; f. 1995; Pres. H. C. STACKPOLE.

Asia Society: 725 Park Ave, New York, NY 10021; tel. (212) 288-6400; fax (212) 517-8315; e-mail webmaster@asiasoc.org; internet www.asiasociety.org; f. 1956; carries out educational and cultural programmes to increase awareness of the arts, history and contemporary affairs of Asia; regional brs in Washington, DC, Houston, Los Angeles, San Francisco, Hong Kong, Manila, Melbourne and Shanghai; 8,000 mems; Pres. VISHAKA DESAI; publs *Archives of Asian Art*, exhibition catalogues, contemporary affairs publications.

Asian Art Museum of San Francisco/Chong-Moon Lee Center for Asian Art and Culture: 200 Larkin St, San Francisco, CA 94102; tel. (415) 581-3500; fax (415) 861-4700; e-mail pr@asianart.org; internet www.asianart.org; f. 1966; museum and centre of research and publication on outstanding collections representing the countries and cultures of Asia; holds over 17,000 Asian works of art spanning 6,000 years of history; library of 40,000 vols; Dir JAY XU.

Asian Cultural Council: 6 West 48th St, 12th Floor, New York, NY 10036-1802; tel. (212) 843-0403; fax (212) 843-0343; e-mail acc@accny.org; internet www.asianculturalcouncil.org; f. 1980; supports cultural exchanges in the visual and performing arts between the USA and Asia; publicly supported; Dir JENNIFER GOODALE.

Association for Asian Studies (AAS): 825 Victors Way, Suite 310, Ann Arbor, MI 48108; tel. (734) 665-2490; fax (734) 665-3801; internet www.asian-studies.org; f. 1941; Exec. Dir MICHAEL PASCHAL; publs include *Asian Studies Newsletter* (quarterly), *Journal of Asian Studies* (quarterly), *Education About Asia* (3 a year) and monographs.

The Brookings Institution: 1775 Massachusetts Ave, NW, Washington, DC 20036-2188; tel. (202) 797-6000; fax (202) 797-6004; e-mail communications@brookings.edu; internet www.brookings.edu; f. 1916; research, education and publishing in economics, govt, and foreign policy; maintains Social Science Computation Center; education division, Center for Public Policy Education, organizes conferences and seminars; 50 resident scholars; library of c. 85,000 vols; Pres. STROBE TALBOTT; publs *Annual Report*, *The Brookings Review* (quarterly), *Brookings Papers on Economic Activity* (3 a year), *Brookings Papers on Education Policy* (annually), *Brookings/Wharton Papers on Financial Policy* (annually).

Center for Asia Pacific Policy: RAND, 1776 Main St, Santa Monica, CA 90407-2138; tel. (703) 413-1100 ext. 5338; fax (703) 413-8111; e-mail Mcnaugher_Thomas_L@rand.org; internet www.rand.org/nsrd/capp; Dir TOM MCNAUGHER (acting).

Center for Chinese Studies, University of Michigan: Suite 4668 SSWB, 1080 South University, Ann Arbor, MI 48109-1106; tel. (734) 764-6308; fax (734) 764-5540; e-mail chinese.studies@umich.edu; internet www.ii.umich.edu/ccs; f. 1961; library of more than 610,000 vols, reels of microfilm and sheets of microfiches; Dir MARY GALLAGHER; publs include *Michigan Monographs in Chinese Studies*.

Center for East Asian Studies, Stanford University: 100 Encina Commons, 615 Crothers Way, Stanford University, Stanford, CA 94305-6023; tel. (650) 723-3363; fax (650) 725-3350; e-mail cfsun@stanford.edu; internet ceas.stanford.edu; f. 1973; Dir Prof. CHAOFEN SUN.

Center on Japanese Economy and Business: Columbia University, Business School, 321 Uris Hall, MC 5968, 3022 Broadway, New York, NY 10027-6902; tel. (212) 854-3976; fax (212) 678-6958; e-mail htp1@columbia.edu; internet www.columbia.edu/cu/business/japan; Dir HUGH PATRICK.

Center for Japanese Studies, University of Michigan: 1080 South University, Suite 4640, Ann Arbor, MI 48109-1106; tel. (734) 764-6307; fax (734) 936-2948; e-mail umcjs@umich.edu; internet www.ii.umich.edu/cjs; f. 1947; library of 685,725 vols, 43,564 reels of microfilm, 32,243 microfiche, 2,332 CD-ROMs, 2,467 current serial titles and 79 newspapers; Dir KEN ITO; publs *Michigan Classics in Japanese Studies*, *Michigan Papers in Japanese Studies*, *Michigan Monograph Series in Japanese Studies*, etc.

Center for Pacific Islands Studies: School of Pacific and Asian Studies, University of Hawaii at Mānoa, Moore Hall 215, 1890 East–West Rd, Honolulu, HI 96822; tel. (808) 956-7700; fax (808) 956-7053; e-mail cpis@hawaii.edu; internet www.hawaii.edu/cpis; f. 1950; Dir TERENCE WESLEY-SMITH; publ. *The Contemporary Pacific* (2 a year).

Center for the Pacific Rim: University of San Francisco, 2130 Fulton St, CA 94117-1080; tel. (415) 422-6357; fax (415) 422-5933; e-mail pacrim@usfca.edu; internet www.pacificrim.usfca.edu; f. 1988; Exec. Dir KEN KOPP (acting).

Center for Southeast Asian Studies, University of Michigan: 1080 South University, Suite 3603, Ann Arbor, MI 48109-1106; tel. (734) 764-0352; fax (734) 936-0996; e-mail cseas@umich.edu; internet www.ii.umich.edu/cseas; f. 1961; constituent unit of the College of Literature, Science and the Arts; governed by an exec. cttee; Dir JUDITH BECKER; Dir (Southeast Asia Business Program, Business School) ALLEN HICKEN (tel. (734) 764-0352); publs *Michigan Papers on South and Southeast Asia*, *Michigan Studies of South and Southeast Asia*, *Michigan Studies in Buddhist Literature* (occasional papers), *CSEAS Newsletter* (2 a year).

Columbia University East Asian Weatherhead Institute: Mail Code 3333, Columbia University, 420 West 118th St, New York, NY 10027; tel. (212) 854-2592; fax (212) 749-1497; e-mail eaiinfo@columbia.edu; internet www.columbia.edu/weai; f. 1949; Dir XIAOBO LU.

Cornell University East Asia Program (EAP): 140 Uris Hall, Ithaca, NY 14853-7601; tel. (607) 255-6222; fax (607) 255-1388; e-mail cueap@cornell.edu; internet www.einaudi.cornell.edu/eastasia; f. 1950 for the development of instruction and research on East Asia; library of 460,000 vols; 180 graduate students; Dir Prof. JOHN B. WHITMAN; publ. *Cornell East Asia Series (CEAS)*.

Cornell University Southeast Asia Language and Area Center: 180 Uris Hall, Ithaca, NY 14853-7601; tel. (607) 255-2378; fax (607) 254-5000; e-mail seap@cornell.edu; internet www.einaudi.cornell.edu/SoutheastAsia; f. 1950 for the development of instruction and research on South-East Asia; library of 212,060 vols, 19,950 periodicals and 841 newspapers; Dir Prof. THAK CHALOEMTIARANA.

Council on Foreign Relations, Inc: 58 East 68th St, New York, NY 10065; tel. (212) 434-9400; fax (212) 434-9800; e-mail corporate@cfr.org; internet www.cfr.org; f. 1921; over 4,500 mems; Pres. RICHARD N. HAASS; publs include *Foreign Affairs* (every 2 months).

East-West Center—Center for Cultural and Technical Interchange between East and West, Inc: 1601 East-West Rd, Honolulu, HI 96848; tel. (808) 944-7111; fax (808) 944-7376; e-mail ewcinfo@EastWestCenter.org; internet www.eastwestcenter.org; f. 1960 by Congress to promote better relations and understanding among the nations and peoples of Asia, the Pacific and the USA through co-operative study, training and research; conducts multidisciplinary programmes on environmental policy, population, resources, development, journalism and Pacific Islands development; provides awards and grants to scholars, journalists, graduate students, and managers to participate in the Center's studies; Pres. Dr CHARLES MORRISON.

Freer Gallery of Art and Arthur M. Sackler Gallery: 1050 Independence Ave, SW, Washington, DC 20013-7012; tel. (202) 633-1000; fax (202) 357-4911; e-mail publicaffairsasia@si.edu; internet www.asia.si.edu; f. 1906, opened 1923; conducts research on the major collections of Asian and late 19th and early 20th century American art, gift of the late Charles L. Freer; art collection of 37,000 objects; library of 55,000 vols, 75,000 slides; Dir Dr JULIAN RABY; publs include *Artibus Asiae*, *Ars Orientalis*.

Henry M. Jackson School of International Studies: 400 Thomson Hall, University of Washington, Seattle, WA 98195; tel. (206) 543-4370; fax (206) 685-0668; e-mail jsis@uw.edu; internet jsis.washington.edu; Dir REŞAT KASABA.

The Jamestown Foundation: 1111 16th St NW, Washington, DC 20036; tel. (202) 483-8888; fax (202) 483-8337; internet www.jamestown.org; f. 1984; Pres. GLEN E. HOWARD; publs include *Terrorism Monitor*.

John King Fairbank Center for Chinese Studies (Harvard University): 1730 Cambridge St, Cambridge, MA 02138; tel. (617) 495-4046; fax (617) 495-9976; internet www.fas.harvard.edu/~fairbank; Dir Prof. WILLIAM C. KIRBY; publs include *Papers on Chinese History*, *Harvard Studies on Taiwan*, etc.

The Mongolia Society: 322 Goodbody Hall, Indiana University, 1011 E Third St, Bloomington, IN 47405-7005; tel. (812) 855-4078; fax (812) 855-7500; e-mail monsoc@indiana.edu; internet www.indiana.edu/~mongsoc; f. 1961 to promote the study of Mongolia, its history, language and culture; sponsors and helps to support Mongolian panels, exhibits and lectures; Pres. Dr ALICIA J. CAMPI; publs include *Mongolian Studies: Journal of the Mongolia Society*, *Mongol Survey* (newsletter), *Special Papers* (in Mongolian classical script) and *Occasional Papers* (translation series); dictionaries.

National Bureau of Asian Research (NBR): 1414 NE 42nd St, Suite 300, Seattle, WA 98105; tel. (206) 632-7370; fax (206) 632-7487; e-mail nbr@nbr.org; internet www.nbr.org; conducts research on policy-related issues in East, Central and South Asia and Russia; Pres. RICHARD J. ELLINGS; publs include NBR book series, *NBR Analysis*, *NBR Special Reports*, *Asia Policy*, *Strategic Asia*.

Princeton Institute for International and Regional Studies: Princeton University, Aaron Burr Hall, Princeton, NJ 08544; tel. (609) 258-7497; fax (609) 258-3988; e-mail piirs@princeton.edu; internet www.princeton.edu/piirs; f. 2003; international and regional studies; Dir MARK BEISSINGER; publs include *World Politics* (quarterly), monographs.

Princeton University, East Asian Studies Department: Princeton, NJ 08544; tel. (609) 452-5905; e-mail collcutt@princeton.edu; internet www.princeton.edu/~eastasia; Chair. MARTIN COLLCUTT.

St John's University Institute of Asian Studies: 8000 Utopia Parkway, Jamaica, NY 11439; tel. (718) 990-2000; fax (718) 990-1881; e-mail webmaster@stjohns.edu; Dir Dr JOHN LIN.

School of International and Public Affairs: Columbia University, 420 West 118th St, New York, NY 10027; tel. (212) 854-4604; internet www.sipa.columbia.edu; Dean JOHN COATSWORTH; publs *SIPA News* (2 a year), *Journal of International Affairs* (2 a year).

School of Pacific and Asian Studies: University of Hawaii at Mānoa, Moore Hall 315, 1890 East-West Rd, Honolulu, HI 96822; tel. (808) 956-8543; fax (808) 956-6345; e-mail jingco@hawaii.edu; internet manoa.hawaii.edu/spas; administers Centers for Chinese, Hawaiian, Japanese, Korean, Pacific Islands, Philippine, South Asian, South-East Asian and Buddhist Studies; Dean EDWARD SHULTZ.

Seton Hall University Department of Asian Studies: South Orange, NJ 07079; tel. (973) 761-9464; fax (973) 761-9596; library of 40,000 vols; Chair. EDWIN LEUNG.

The Sigur Center for Asian Studies: George Washington University, 1957 E St, NW, Suite 503, Washington, DC 20052; tel. (202) 994-5886; fax (202) 994-6096; e-mail gsigur@gwu.edu; internet www.gwu.edu/~sigur.

University of Arizona Department of East Asian Studies: Tucson, AZ 85721; tel. (520) 621-7505; e-mail vancet@u.arizona.edu; internet www.arizona.edu/~EAS; Head Dr TIMOTHY VANCE.

University of California at Berkeley, Department of East Asian Languages and Cultures: 3413 Dwinelle Hall, Berkeley, CA 94720-2230; tel. (510) 642-3480; fax (510) 642-6031; e-mail ealang@berkeley.edu; internet www.ealc.berkeley.edu; Head of Dept Prof. ALAN TANSMAN.

University of California Department of South and Southeast Asian Studies: 7233 Dwinelle Hall, Berkeley, CA 94720-2540; tel. (510) 642-4564; fax (510) 643-2959; e-mail pennyedwards@berkeley.edu; internet sseas.berkeley.edu; Chair. PENNY EDWARDS.

University of Illinois Center for East Asian and Pacific Studies: 910 S Fifth St, Champaign, IL 61801; tel. (217) 333-7273; fax (217) 244-5729; f. 1965; Dir GEORGE T. YU.

University of Kansas Center for East Asian Studies: Bailey Hall, 1440 Jayhawk Blvd, Rm 202, Lawrence, KS 66045-7574; tel. (785) 864-3849; fax (785) 864-5034; e-mail ceas@ku.edu; internet www.ceas.ku.edu; Dir Dr ELAINE GERBERT; publs research and reference series.

University of Pittsburgh Department of East Asian Languages and Literatures: 702 Old Engineering Hall, Pittsburgh, PA 15260; tel. (412) 624-5568; fax (412) 624-3458; e-mail hnara@pitt.edu; internet www.pitt.edu/~deall; Chair. HIROSHI NARA.

University of Southern California East Asian Studies Center: 823 West 34th St, CLH 101, Los Angeles, CA 90089-0127; tel. (213) 740-2991; fax (213) 740-8409; e-mail easc@usc.edu; internet www.usc.edu/easc; f. 1975; Dir STANLEY ROSEN.

Walter H. Shorenstein Asia/Pacific Research Center: Stanford University, Encina Hall, Rm E301, 616 Serra St, Stanford, CA 94305-6055; tel. (650) 723-9741; fax (650) 723-6530; e-mail asia-pacific-research-center@stanford.edu; internet aparc.stanford.edu; Dir Prof. GI-WOOK SHIN.

Yale University Southeast Asia Studies: Yale University, POB 208206, New Haven, CT 06520-8206; tel. (203) 432-3431; fax (203) 432-3432; e-mail seas@yale.edu; internet www.yale.edu/seas; library of 260,000 vols; Chair. J. JOSEPH ERRINGTON; Librarian RICHARD RICHIE; publs *The Vietnam Forum*, *Lac Viet* series, *Southeast Asia Monograph* series.

VIET NAM

Institute of Economics: Commission for Social Sciences, 27 Tran Xuan Soan St, Hanoi; tel. (4) 254774; fax (4) 259071; f. 1960; library of 8,000 vols; publs *Economic Studies Review* (2 a year), *Nghien Cuu Kinh Te* (2 a year).

SELECT BIBLIOGRAPHY—BOOKS

See also bibliographies at end of relevant chapters and for the Pacific Islands in Part Two.

Abbott, Jason P. *Developmentalism and Dependency in Southeast Asia: The Case of the Automotive Industry*. London, RoutledgeCurzon, 2002.

Abuza, Zachary. *Militant Islam in Southeast Asia: Crucible of Terror*. Boulder, CO, Lynne Rienner Publishers, 2003.

Acharya, Amitav. *Constructing a Security Community in Southeast Asia—ASEAN and the Problem of Regional Order*. London, Routledge, 2nd Edn, 2009.

The Quest for Identity: International Relations of South-East Asia. Oxford, Oxford University Press, 2001.

Whose Ideas Matter?: Agency and Power in Asian Regionalism. Singapore, Institute of Southeast Asian Studies, 2010.

The Making of Southeast Asia: International Relations of a Region. Ithaca, NY, Cornell University Press, 2011.

Adelman, Howard (Ed.). *Protracted Displacement in Asia: No Place to Call Home*. Aldershot, Ashgate, 2009.

Ahrari, Ehsan, Wirsing, Robert G. (Eds). *Fixing Fractured Nations: The Challenge of Ethnic Separatism in Asia-Pacific*. Basingstoke, Palgrave Macmillan, 2010.

Akaha, Tsuneo, and Vassilieva, Anna (Eds). *Crossing National Borders: International Migration Issues in Northeast Asia*. Tokyo, United Nations University Press, 2006.

Akami, Tomoko. *Internationalizing the Pacific*. London, Routledge, 2002.

Akhand, Hafiz, and Gupta, Kanhaya. *Economic Development in Pacific Asia*. Abingdon, Routledge, 2006.

Alatas, Ali. *A Voice for Peace*. Singapore, Institute of Southeast Asian Studies, 2001.

Aldrich, Richard J., Rawnsley, Gary D., and Rawnsley, Ming-Yeh T. (Eds). *The Clandestine Cold War in Asia, 1945–65*. Ilford, Frank Cass, 2000.

Aljunied, Syed Muhd Khairudin. *Colonialism, Violence and Muslims in Southeast Asia: The Maria Hertogh Controversy and Its Aftermath*. Abingdon, Routledge, 2009.

Amer, Ramses, and Ganesan, Narayanan (Eds). *International Relations in Southeast Asia: Between Bilateralism and Multilateralism*. Singapore, Institute of Southeast Asian Studies, 2010.

Ananta, Aris, and Arifin, Evi Nurvidya (Eds). *International Migration in Southeast Asia*. Singapore, Institute of Southeast Asian Studies, 2004.

Andersson, Martin, and Gunnarsson, Christer. *Development and Structural Change in Asia-Pacific: Globalising Miracles or the End of a Model?* London, RoutledgeCurzon, 2003.

Andrews, Tim, Baldwin, Bryan J., and Chompusri, Nartnalin. *The Changing Face of Multinationals in South East Asia*. London, Routledge, 2002.

Antons, Christoph (Ed.). *Law and Development in East and South-East Asia*. Richmond, Curzon Press, 2001.

Ariff, Mohamed, and Khalid, Ahmed M. *Liberalization and Growth in Asia: 21st Century Challenges*. Cheltenham, Edward Elgar Publishing, 2005.

Armstrong, Charles K., Kotkin, Stephen, Rozman, Gilbert, and Kim, Samuel S. (Eds). *Korea at the Center: Dynamics of Regionalism in Northeast Asia*. Armonk, NY, M. E. Sharpe, 2005.

Asian Development Bank. *The Economics of Climate Change in Southeast Asia: A Regional Review*. Manila, Asian Development Bank, 2009.

The Global Economic Crisis: Challenges for Developing Asia and ADB's Response. Manila, Asian Development Bank, 2009.

Arrighi, Giovanni, Takeshi, Hamashita, and Selden, Mark (Eds). *The Resurgence of East Asia*. London, RoutledgeCurzon, 2003.

Athukorala, Prema-chandra, Manning, Chris, and Wickramasekara, Piyasiri. *Growth, Employment and Migration in Southeast Asia—Structural Change in the Greater Mekong Countries*. Cheltenham, Edward Elgar Publishing, 2000.

Athukorala, Prema-chandra (Ed.). *The Rise of Asia: Trade and Investment in Global Perspective*. Abingdon, Routledge, 2011.

Atkins, William. *The Politics of Southeast Asia's New Media*. Richmond, Curzon Press, 2001.

Aung-Thwin, Michael Arthur, and Hall, Kenneth (Eds). *New Perspectives on the History and Historiography of Southeast Asia: Continuing Explorations*. Abingdon, Routledge, 2011.

Backman, Michael. *Asian Eclipse: Exposing the Dark Side of Business in Asia (Revised Edn)*. Singapore, John Wiley & Sons, 2001.

Bagshaw, Dale, and Porter, Elisabeth. *Mediation in the Asia-Pacific Region: Transforming Conflicts and Building Peace*. Abingdon, Routledge, 2009.

Bahramitash, Roksana. *Liberation from Liberalization: Gender and Globalization in South East Asia*. London, Zed Books, 2005.

Bales, Kevin. *Disposable People: New Slavery in the Global Economy*. Berkeley, CA, University of California Press, 2000.

Balisacan, Arsenio (Ed.). *Agricultural and Rural Development in Asia: Ideas, Paradigms, and Policies Three Decades After*. Singapore, Institute of Southeast Asian Studies, 2006.

Balisacan, Arsenio, and Nobuhiko Fuwa (Eds). *Reasserting the Rural Development Agenda: Lessons Learned and Emerging Challenges in Asia*. Singapore, Institute of Southeast Asian Studies, 2007.

Barr, Michael D. *Cultural Politics and Asian Values—The Tepid War*. London, RoutledgeCurzon, 2002.

Bayly, Christopher, and Harper, Tim. *Forgotten Wars: Freedom and Revolution in Southeast Asia*. Cambridge, Belknap Press of Harvard University Press, 2007.

Beer, Lawrence W. *Human Rights Constitutionalism in Japan and Asia: the Writings of Lawrence E. Beer*. Folkestone, Global Oriental, 2008.

Beeson, Mark. *Reconfiguring East Asia—Regional Institutions and Organizations after the Crisis*. London, RoutledgeCurzon, 2002.

Institutions of the Asia-Pacific: ASEAN, APEC and Beyond. Abingdon, Routledge, 2008.

Beeson, Mark (Ed.). *Contemporary South East Asia: Regional Dynamics, National Differences*. New York, Palgrave Macmillan, 2004.

Beeson, Mark, and Bellamy, Alex J. (Eds). *Securing Southeast Asia: the Politics of Security Sector Reform*. New York, Routledge, 2nd Edn, 2009.

Bell, Daniel. *Why Western Democracy Won't Work in East Asia*. Princeton, NJ, Princeton University Press, 2006.

Beyond Liberal Democracy: Political Thinking for an East Asian Context. Princeton, NJ, Princeton University Press, 2006.

Beng, Ooi Kee, and Ming, Ding Choo (Eds). *Continent, Coast, Ocean: the Dynamics of Regionalism in Eastern Asia*. Singapore, Institute of Southeast Asian Studies, 2008.

Benson, John, and Ying Zhu (Eds). *Unemployment in Asia: Organizational and Institutional Relationships*. Abingdon, Routledge, 2005.

Bercovitch, Jacob, Kwei-Bo Huang, and Chung-Chian Teng (Eds). *Conflict Management, Security and Intervention in East Asia*. Abingdon, Routledge, 2007.

Bercovitch, Jacob, and DeRouen Jr, Karl, et al. *Unraveling Internal Conflicts in East Asia and the Pacific: Incidence, Consequences, and Resolution*. Lanham, MD, Lexington Books, 2011.

Bergquist, Karin Bo (Ed.). *Images of Asia: Cultural Perspectives on a Changing Asia*. Honolulu, HI, University of Hawaii Press, 2004.

Bernholz, Peter (Ed.). *Political Competition, Innovation and Growth in the History of Asian Civilizations*. Cheltenham, Edward Elgar Publishing, 2004.

Bert, Wayne. *The United States, China and Southeast Asian Security: A Changing of the Guard?* New York, Palgrave Macmillan, 2003.

Binton, Mary C. (Ed.). *Women's Working Lives in East Asia*. Stanford, CA, Stanford University Press, 2001.

Bishop, Ryan, Phillips, John, and Yeo Wei Wei. *Postcolonial Urbanism: The Southeast Asia Supplement*. New York, Routledge, 2003.

Bisley, Nick. *Building Asia's Security*. Abingdon, Routledge, 2010.

Blench, Roger, Sagart, Laurent, and Sanchez-Mazas, Alicia (Eds). *The Peopling of East Asia*. Abingdon, Routledge, 2005.

Boomgaard, Peter, and Brown, Ian (Eds). *Weathering the Storm: The Economies of Southeast Asia in the 1930s Depression*. Singapore, Institute of Southeast Asian Studies, 2000.

Booth, Anne, and Ash, Robert (Eds). *The Economies of Asia 1945–1998.* London, Routledge, 1999.

Booth, Anne. *Colonial Legacies: Economic and Social Development in East and Southeast Asia.* Honolulu, HI, University of Hawaii Press, 2007.

Borrus, Michael, Ernst, Dieter, and Haggard, Stephan (Eds). *International Production Networks in Asia—Rivalry or Riches.* London, Routledge, 2000.

Borthwick, Mark. *Pacific Century: the Emergence of Modern Pacific Asia.* Boulder, CO, Westview Press, 2007.

Boudreau, Vincent. *Resisting Dictatorship: Repression and Protest in Southeast Asia.* Cambridge, Cambridge University Press, 2nd Edn, 2009.

Bromley, Michael, and Romano, Angela (Eds). *Journalism and Democracy in Asia.* Abingdon, Routledge, 2005.

Brown, R. A. *The Rise of the Corporate Economy in Southeast Asia.* Abingdon, Routledge, 2006.

Brunner, Hans-Peter, and Allen, Peter M. *Productivity, Competitiveness and Incomes in Asia: An Evolutionary Theory of International Trade.* Cheltenham, Edward Elgar Publishing, 2005.

Buadaeng, Kwanchewan, Leepreecha, Prasit, and McCaskill, Don (Eds). *Challenging the Limits: Indigenous Peoples of the Mekong Region.* Chiang Mai, Mekong Press, 2008.

Bubandt, Nils Ole, and van Beek, Martijn (Eds). *Varieties of Secularism in Asia: Anthropological Explorations of Religion, Politics and the Spiritual.* Abingdon, Routledge, 2011.

Buckley, Roger. *The United States in the Asia-Pacific since 1945.* Cambridge, Cambridge University Press, 2002.

Butcher, John G. *The Closing of the Frontier: A History of the Marine Fisheries of Southeast Asia, c. 1850–2000.* Singapore, Institute of Southeast Asian Studies, 2004.

Byrnes, Michael. *Australia and the Asia Game: The Politics of Business and Economics in Asia.* St Leonards, NSW, Allen & Unwin, 2nd Edn, 2006.

Caballero-Anthony, Mely. *Regional Security in Southeast Asia: Beyond the ASEAN Way.* Singapore, Institute of Southeast Asian Studies, 2005.

Cady, Linell E., and Simon, Sheldon W. (Eds). *Religion and Conflict in South and Southeast Asia.* Abingdon, Routledge, 2006.

Callahan, William A. *Cultural Governance and Resistance in Pacific Asia.* Abingdon, Routledge, 2006.

Camilleri, Joseph A. *States, Markets and Civil Society in Asia Pacific.* The Political Economy of the Asia-Pacific Region, Vol. I, Cheltenham, Edward Elgar Publishing, 2000.

Regionalism in the New Asia-Pacific Order. The Political Economy of the Asia-Pacific Region, Vol. II, Cheltenham, Edward Elgar Publishing, 2003.

Caouette, Dominique, and Turner, Sarah. *Agrarian Angst and Rural Resistance in Contemporary Southeast Asia.* Abingdon, Routledge, 2009.

Capie, David, and Evans, Paul. *The Asia-Pacific Security Lexicon.* Singapore, Institute of Southeast Asian Studies, 2002.

Carney, Richard (Ed.). *Lessons from the Asian Financial Crisis.* Abingdon, Routledge, 2011.

Carter, Connie, and Harding, Andrew (Eds). *Special Economic Zones in Asian Market Economies.* Abingdon, Routledge, 2010.

Case, William. *Politics in Southeast Asia—Democracy or Less.* London, RoutledgeCurzon, 2002.

Comparing Politics in Southeast Asia. London, Sage Publications, 2003.

Contemporary Authoritarianism in Southeast Asia. Abingdon, Routledge, 2009.

Chaisse, Julien, and Gugler, Philippe (Eds). *Expansion of Trade and FDI in Asia: Strategic and Policy Challenges.* Abingdon, Routledge, 2011.

Chan, Angelique, Jones, Gavin, and Paulin, Tay-Straughan (Eds). *Ultra-low Fertility in Pacific Asia: Trends, Causes and Policy Dilemmas.* Abingdon, Routledge, 2008.

Chan Chak-Kwan, and Ngok, Kinglun (Eds). *Welfare Reform in East Asia: Towards Workfare.* Abingdon, Routledge, 2011.

Chan Kwok-bun. *Chinese Identities, Ethnicity and Cosmopolitanism.* Abingdon, Routledge, 2005.

Migration, Ethnic Relations and Chinese Business. Abingdon, Routledge, 2005.

Chang Ching-Cheng, Mendelsohn, Robert, and Shaw, Daigee. *Global Warming and the Asian Pacific.* Cheltenham, Edward Elgar Publishing, 2003.

Chang Sea-Jin (Ed.). *Business Groups in East Asia: Financial Crisis, Restructuring, and New Growth.* Oxford, Oxford University Press, 2006.

Chaturvedi, Sachin, and Rao, S. R. (Eds). *Biotechnology and Development: Challenges and Opportunities for Asia.* Singapore, Institute of Southeast Asian Studies, 2004.

Cheema, G. Shabbir, and Popovsk, Vesselin (Eds). *Building Trust in Government: Innovations in Governance Reform in Asia.* Tokyo, United Nations University Press, 2010.

Chen Wen and Liao Shaolian. *China-ASEAN Trade Relations: A Discussion on Complementarity and Competition.* Singapore, Institute of Southeast Asian Studies, 2005.

Chern, Wen S., Carter, Colin A., and Shei Shun-yi (Eds). *Food Security in Asia: Economics and Policies.* Cheltenham, Edward Elgar Publishing, 2000.

Cheung, Anthony, and Scott, Ian. *Governance and Public Sector Reform in Asia—Paradigm Shift or Business as Usual?* London, RoutledgeCurzon, 2002.

Cheung, Anthony, Newman, Joanna, and Haggith, Toby (Eds). *Public Service Reform in East Asia: Reform Issues and Challenges in Japan, Korea, Singapore and Hong Kong.* Hong Kong, Chinese University Press, 2006.

Chia Lin Sien (Ed.). *Southeast Asia Transformed: A Geography of Change.* Singapore, Institute of Southeast Asian Studies, 2003.

Chia Lin Sien, Goh, Mark, and Tongzon, Jose. *Southeast Asian Regional Port Development: A Comparative Analysis.* Singapore, Institute of Southeast Asian Studies, 2003.

Chia Siow Yue and Lim, Jamus Jerome (Eds). *Information Technology in Asia: New Development in Paradigms.* Singapore, Institute of Southeast Asian Studies, 2002.

Chirathivat, Suthiphand, Claassen, Emil-Maria, and Schroeder, Jürgen (Eds). *East Asia's Monetary Future.* Cheltenham, Edward Elgar, 2004.

Choi, Jungug. *Governments and Markets in East Asia: The Politics of Economic Crises.* Abingdon, Routledge, 2006.

Chong, Terence (Ed.). *Globalization and its Counter-Forces in Southeast Asia.* Singapore, Institute of Southeast Asian Studies, 2008.

Chong Yah Lim. *Southeast Asia: The Long Road Ahead.* Singapore, World Scientific Publishing, 2002.

Chou, Cynthia, and Houben, Vincent (Eds). *Southeast Asian Studies: Debates and New Directions.* Singapore, Institute of Southeast Asian Studies, 2006.

Chow, Peter C. Y. (Ed.). *Economic Integration, Democratization and National Security in East Asia.* Cheltenham, Edward Elgar Publishing, 2007.

Chowdhury, Anis, and Islam, Iyanatul (Eds). *Beyond the Asian Crisis—Pathways to Sustainable Growth.* Cheltenham, Edward Elgar Publishing, 2001.

Handbook on the Northeast and Southeast Asian Economies. Cheltenham, Edward Elgar Publishing, 2007.

Christie, Clive J. *A Modern History of Southeast Asia: Decolonization, Nationalism and Separatism.* Singapore, Institute of Southeast Asian Studies, 1996.

Christie, Kenneth, and Roy, Denny. *The Politics of Human Rights in East Asia.* London, Pluto Press, 2001.

Chu Yin-Wah and Wong Siu-Lun (Eds). *East Asia's New Democracies: Deepening, Reversal, Non-liberal Alternatives.* Abingdon, Routledge, 2010.

Chu Yun-Peng and Hill, Hal (Eds). *The Social Impact of the Asian Financial Crisis.* Cheltenham, Edward Elgar Publishing, 2001.

The East Asian High-Tech Drive. Cheltenham, Edward Elgar Publishing, 2006.

Chufrin, Gennady. *East Asia: Between Regionalism and Globalism.* Singapore, Institute of Southeast Asian Studies, 2006.

Chufrin, Gennady, and Hong, Mark (Eds). *Russia-ASEAN Relations: New Directions.* Singapore, Institute of Southeast Asian Studies, 2008.

Church, Peter. *A Short History of South-East Asia.* Singapore, John Wiley & Sons, 2005.

Ciorciari, John D. *The Limits of Alignment: Southeast Asia and the Great Powers Since 1975.* Washington, DC, Georgetown University Press, 2010.

Clad, James, McDonald, Sean M., and Vaughn, Bruce (Eds). *The Borderlands of Southeast Asia: Geopolitics, Terrorism, and Globalization.* Washington, DC, National Defense University Press, 2011.

Coclanis, Peter A. *Time's Arrow, Time's Cycle: Globalization in Southeast Asia over la Longue Durée.* Singapore, Institute of Southeast Asian Studies, 2006.

Collins, Alan. *The Security Dilemmas of Southeast Asia.* Singapore, Institute of Southeast Asian Studies, 2001.

Security and Southeast Asia: Domestic, Regional and Global Issues. Boulder, CO, Lynne Rienner Publishers, 2003.

Connors, Michael, Dosch, Jörn, and Davison, Remy. *The New Global Politics of the Asia Pacific.* Abingdon, Routledge, 2nd Edn 2011.

Conroy, F. Hilary, Conroy, Francis, and Quinn-Judge, Sophie. *West Across the Pacific: the American Involvement in East Asia from 1898 to the Vietnam War.* Youngstown, NY, Cambria Press, 2008.

Cooney, Sean, Lindsey, Tim, and Zhu Ying (Eds). *Law and Labour Market Regulation in South East Asia.* London, Routledge, 2002.

Cotterell, Arthur. *Western Power in Asia: Its Slow Rise and Swift Fall, 1415-1999.* Singapore, John Wiley & Sons, 2009.

Crump, Thomas. *Asia Pacific: A History of Empire and Conflict.* London, Hambledon Continuum, 2008.

Curley, Melissa, and Thomas, Nicholas (Eds). *Advancing East Asian Regionalism.* Abingdon, Routledge, 2006.

Curley, Melissa, and Wong Siu-lun (Eds). *Migration and Securitisation in Southeast Asia.* Abingdon, Routledge, 2007.

Dahles, Heidi, and van den Muijzenberg, Otto (Eds). *Capital and Knowledge in Asia: Changing Power Relations.* London, RoutledgeCurzon, 2003.

Dalton, Russell J., and Doh Chull Shin (Eds). *Citizens, Democracy, and Markets around the Pacific Rim.* Oxford, Oxford University Press, 2006.

Dalton, Russell J., Doh Chull Shin, and Yu-han Chu (Eds). *Party Politics in East Asia: Citizens, Elections, and Democratic Development.* Boulder, CO, Lynne Rienner Publishers, 2008.

Daquila, Teofilo C. *The Transformation of Southeast Asian Economies.* Hauppage, NY, Nova Science Publishers, 2007.

Dator, Jim, Pratt, Dick, and Yongseok Seo (Eds). *Fairness, Globalization, and Public Institutions: East Asia and Beyond.* Honolulu, HI, University of Hawaii Press, 2006.

Davidson, P. J. *ASEAN: The Evolving Legal Framework for Economic Co-Operation.* Singapore, Times Academic Press, 2003.

Davies, Gloria, and Nyland, Chris (Eds.). *Globalization in the Asian Region.* Cheltenham, Edward Elgar Publishing, 2004.

Davies, Sara. *Legitimising Rejection: International Refugee Law in Southeast Asia.* Leiden, Martinus Nijhoff Publishers, 2008.

Davis, Malcolm R. *Military Transformation in East Asia.* Abingdon, Routledge, 2006.

De Brouwer, Gordon, and Yunjong Wang. *Financial Governance in East Asia.* London, RoutledgeCurzon, 2003.

De Jonge, Huub, and Kaptein, Nico. *Transcending Borders: Arabs, Politics, Trade and Islam in Southeast Asia.* Singapore, Institute of Southeast Asian Studies, 2004.

Dee, Philippa (Ed.). *Institutions for Economic Reform in Asia.* Abingdon, Routledge, 2009.

Dent, Christopher M. *East Asian Regionalism.* Abingdon, Routledge, 2008.

Dent, Christopher M., and Huang, David W. F. (Eds). *Northeast Asian Regionalism—Lessons from the European Experience.* London, RoutledgeCurzon, 2002.

Derichs, Claudia (Ed.). *Power of Ideas: Intellectual Input and Political Change in East and Southeast Asia.* Honolulu, HI, University of Hawaii Press, 2005.

Devereux, Michael, Lane, Philip, Park Cyn-Young, and Wei Shang-Jin (Eds). *The Dynamics of Asian Financial Integration: Facts and Analytics.* Abingdon, Routledge, 2011.

DeWitt, David B. *Globalization, Development and Security in Southeast Asia: The International Political Economy of New Regionalisms.* Burlington, VT, Ashgate Publishing Company, 2003.

Dick, Howard, and Rimmer, Peter J. *The City in Southeast Asia: Patterns, Processes and Policy.* Honolulu, HI, University of Hawaii Press, 2008.

Dieter, Heribert (Ed.). *The Evolution of Regionalism in Asia: Economic and Security Issues.* Abingdon, Routledge, 2011.

Donald, Stephanie Hemelryk, Anderson, Theresa, and Spry, Damien. *Youth, Society and Mobile Media in Asia.* Abingdon, Routledge, 2009.

Dosch, Jörn. *The Changing Dynamics of Southeast Asian Politics.* Boulder, CO, Lynne Rienner Publishers, 2007.

Drysdale, Peter (Ed.). *Reform and Recovery in East Asia.* London, Routledge, 2000.

The New Economy in East Asia and the Pacific. London, Routledge, 2003.

Drysdale, Peter, and Terada, Takashi (Eds). *Asia-Pacific Economic Co-operation.* Abingdon, Routledge, 2006.

DuBois, Thomas David (Ed.). *Casting Faiths: Imperialism and the Transformation of Religion in East and Southeast Asia.* Singapore: Palgrave Macmillan, 2009.

Duncan, Christopher (Ed.). *Civilising the Margins: Southeast Asian Government Policies for the Development of Minorities.* Ithaca, NY, Cornell University Press, 2004.

Dupont, Alan. *East Asia Imperilled: Transnational Challenges to Security.* Cambridge, Cambridge University Press, 2001.

Eaton, Peter. *Land Tenure, Conservation and Development in Southeast Asia.* Abingdon, Routledge, 2005.

Edmonds, Christopher M. (Ed.). *Reducing Poverty in Asia: Emerging Issues in Growth, Targeting and Measurement.* Cheltenham, Edward Elgar Publishing, 2003.

Elmhirst, Becky, and Saptari, Ratner (Eds). *Labour in Southeast Asia—Local Processes in a Globalised World.* London, Routledge, 2nd Edn, 2004.

Emmers, Ralf. *Cooperative Security and the Balance of Power in ASEAN and the ARF.* London, RoutledgeCurzon, 2003.

Engelbert, Thomas, and Kubitscheck, Hans Dieter (Eds). *Ethnic Minorities and Politics in Southeast Asia.* New York, Peter Lang, 2004.

Fahn, James David. *A Land on Fire: The Environmental Consequences of the Southeast Asian Boom.* Boulder, CO, Westview Press, 2003.

Fealy, Greg, and Hooker, Virginia (Eds). *Voices of Islam in Southeast Asia: A Contemporary Sourcebook.* Singapore, Institute of Southeast Asian Studies, 2006.

Federspiel, Howard M. *Sultans, Shamans, and Saints: Islam and Muslims in Southeast Asia.* Honolulu, HI, University of Hawaii, 2007.

Feinberg, Richard E. (Ed.). *APEC as an Institution: Multilateral Governance in the Asia-Pacific.* Singapore, Institute of Southeast Asian Studies, 2003.

Feinberg, Richard E., and Zhao Ye (Eds). *Assessing APEC's Progress: Trade, Ecotech, and Institutions.* Singapore, Institute of Southeast Asian Studies, 2001.

Ferguson, Kathy, and Mironesco, Monique (Eds). *Gender and Globalization in Asia and the Pacific: Method, Practice, Theory.* Honolulu, University of Hawaii Press, 2008.

Findlay, Christopher, and Soesastro, Hadi (Eds). *Reshaping the Asia Pacific Economic Order.* Abingdon, Routledge, 2005.

Flynn, Dennis O., Frost, Lionel, and Latham, A. J. H. (Eds). *Pacific Centuries—Pacific and Pacific Rim Economic History since the 16th Century.* London, Routledge, 1998.

Forrest, Ray, and Mok, Joshua Ka Ho (Eds). *Changing Governance and Public Policy in East Asia.* Abingdon, Routledge, 2011.

François, Joseph, Rana, Pradumm B., and Wignajara, Ganeshan (Eds). *Pan-Asian Integration.* Basingstoke, Palgrave Macmillan, 2009.

Fraschini, Angela, Bernardi, Luigi, and Shome, Parthasarathi. *Tax Systems and Tax Reforms in South and East Asia.* Abingdon, Routledge, 2006.

Freeman, Nick (Ed.). *Financing Southeast Asia's Economic Development.* Singapore, Institute of Southeast Asian Studies, 2003.

Freeman, Nick, and Bartels, Frank (Eds). *The Future of Foreign Investment in Southeast Asia.* London, RoutledgeCurzon, 2003.

Frey, Marc, Pruessen, Ronald W., and Tai Yong Tan (Eds). *The Transformation of Southeast Asia: International Perspectives on Decolonization.* Armonk, NY, M. E. Sharpe, 2003.

Frost, Ellen L. *Asia's New Regionalism.* Boulder, CO, Lynne Rienner Publishers, 2008.

Fu Tsu-Tan, Huang, Cliff J., and Lovell, C. A. Knox (Eds). *Productivity and Economic Performance in the Asia-Pacific Region.* Cheltenham, Edward Elgar Publishing, 2002.

Fujita, Masahisa, Kuroiwa, Ikuo, and Kumagai, Satoru. *The Economics of East Asian Integration: A Comprehensive Introduction to Regional Issues.* Cheltenham, Edward Elgar Publishing, 2011.

Funston, John (Ed.). *Government & Politics in Southeast Asia.* Singapore, Institute of Southeast Asian Studies, 2002.

Ganguly, Rajat, and Macduff, Ian. *Ethnic Conflict and Secessionism in South and Southeast Asia: Causes, Dynamics, Solutions.* London, Sage Publications, 2003.

Gillespie, John, and Peerenboom, Randall (Eds). *Regulation in Asia—Pushing Back on Globalization.* Abingdon, Routledge, 2009.

Gilson, Julie. *Asia Meets Europe.* Cheltenham, Edward Elgar Publishing, 2002.

Glassman, Jim. *Bounding the Mekong: The Asian Development Bank, China, and Thailand.* Honolulu, HI, University of Hawaii Press, 2010.

Glover, Ian, and Bellwood, Peter. *South East Asia: An Archaeological History*. London, RoutledgeCurzon, 2003.

Goenka, Aditya, and Henley, David (Eds). *Southeast Asia's Credit Revolution: from Moneylenders to Microfinance*. Abingdon, Routledge, 2009.

Goh, Robbie B. H. *Christianity in Southeast Asia*. Singapore, Institute of Southeast Asian Studies, 2005.

Goldman, Emily O., and Mahnken, Thomas G. (Eds). *Information Revolution in Military Affairs in Asia*. Basingstoke, Palgrave Macmillan, 2004.

Goldman, Merle, and Gordon, Andrew (Eds). *Historical Perspectives on Contemporary East Asia*. Cambridge, MA, Harvard University Press, 2000.

Gomez, Edmund. *Political Business in East Asia*. London, Routledge, 2001.

Gosling, David. *Religion and Ecology in India and Southeast Asia*. London, Routledge, 2001.

Gourevitch, Peter A. (Ed.). *The Pacific Region: Challenges to Policy and Theory*. Newbury Park, CA, Sage Publications, 1989.

Gray, Sidney J., Purcell, William R., and McGaughey, Sara L. (Eds). *Asia-Pacific Issues in International Business*. Cheltenham, Edward Elgar Publishing, 2001.

Greenough, Paul R., and Lowenhaupt Tsing, Anna (Eds). *Nature in the Global South: Environmental Projects in South and Southeast Asia*. Durham, NC, Duke University Press, 2003.

Guan, Lee Hock (Ed.). *Ageing in Southeast and East Asia: Family, Social Protection and Policy*. Singapore, Institute of Southeast Asian Studies, 2008.

Guan, Lee Hock, and Suryadinata, Lee (Eds). *Language, Nation and Development in Southeast Asia*. Singapore, Institute of Southeast Asian Studies, 2008.

Gupta, Avijit. *The Physical Geography of Southeast Asia*. Oxford, Oxford University Press, 2005.

Haacke, Jürgen. *ASEAN's Diplomatic and Security Culture—Origins, Developments and Prospects*. London, RoutledgeCurzon, 2002.

Hack, Karl, and Rettig, Tobias (Eds). *Colonial Armies in South-East Asia*. Abingdon, Routledge, 2006.

Hafez, Mohammed Zakirul. *Dimensions of Regional Trade Integration in Southeast Asia*. New York, Transnational Publishers, 2005.

Haggard, Stephan. *The Political Economy of the Asian Financial Crisis*. Washington, DC, Institute for International Economics, 2000.

Hall, D. G. E. *A History of South-East Asia*. Basingstoke, Macmillan Press, 1981.

Hamada, Koichi, Reszat, Beate, and Volz, Ulrich (Eds). *Towards Monetary and Financial Integration in East Asia*. Cheltenham, Edward Elgar Publishing, 2009.

Hamashita, Takeshi. *China, East Asia and the Global Economy: Regional and Historical Perspectives*. Abingdon, Routledge, 2008.

Hamayaka, Shintaro. *Asian Regionalism and Japan: The Politics of Membership in Regional Diplomatic, Financial and Trade Groups*. Abingdon, Routledge, 2011.

Hamilton-Hart, Natasha. *Asian States, Asian Bankers: Central Banking in Southeast Asia*. Ithaca, NY, Cornell University Press, 2002.

Harris, Paul G. *Global Warming and East Asia: The Domestic and International Politics of Climate Change*. London, RoutledgeCurzon, 2003.

Harrison, Brian. *South-East Asia: A Short History*. London, Macmillan Press, and New York, St Martin's Press, 2nd Edn, 1964.

Harvie, Charles, Kimura, F. and Lee, H. *New East Asian Regionalism: Causes, Progress and Country Perspectives*. Cheltenham, Edward Elgar Publishing, 2006.

Harvie, Charles, and Lee Boon-Chye. *Globalisation and SMEs in East Asia*. Cheltenham, Edward Elgar Publishing, 2002.

The Role of SMEs in National Economies in East Asia. Cheltenham, Edward Elgar Publishing, 2002.

Hassall, Graham, and Saunders, Cheryl. *Asia-Pacific Constitutional Systems*. Cambridge, Cambridge University Press, 2006.

Hastings, Justin V. *No Man's Land: Globalization, Territory, and Clandestine Groups in Southeast Asia*. Ithaca, NY, Cornell University Press, 2010.

Hawkins, John N., Hershock, Peter D., and Mason, Mark (Eds). *Changing Education: Leadership, Innovation and Development in a Globalizing Asia Pacific*. London, Springer, 2008.

Henders, Susan J. (Ed.). *Democratization and Identity: Regimes and Ethnicity in East and Southeast Asia (Global Encounters)*. Lanham, MD, Lexington Books, 2003.

Henderson, Jeffrey. *The Political Economy of East Asian Development*. Abingdon, Routledge, 2009.

East Asian Transformation: On the Political Economy of Dynamism, Governance and Crisis. Abingdon, Routledge, 2011.

Heng, Russell Hiang Khng (Ed.). *Media Fortunes, Changing Times: ASEAN States in Transition*. Singapore, Institute of Southeast Asian Studies, 2002.

Heng, Russell Hiang Khng, and Sen, Rahul (Eds). *Regional Outlook: Southeast Asia 2005–2006*. Singapore, Institute of Southeast Asian Studies, 2005.

Heng, Toh Mun, and Kuroiwa, Ikuo. *Production Networks and Industrial Clusters: Integrating Economies in Southeast Asia*. Singapore, Institute of Southeast Asian Studies, 2008.

Hersh, Jacques. *The USA and the Rise of East Asia since 1945*. New York, St Martin's Press, 1995.

Heryanto, Ariel, and Mandal, Sumit K. (Eds). *Challenging Authoritarianism in Southeast Asia: Comparing Indonesia and Malaysia*. London, RoutledgeCurzon, 2003.

Hew, Denis (Ed.). *Roadmap to an ASEAN Economic Community*. Singapore, Institute of Southeast Asian Studies, 2005.

Hew, Denis, and Loi Wee Nee (Eds). *Entrepreneurship and SMEs in Southeast Asia*. Singapore, Institute of Southeast Asian Studies, 2004.

Hewison, Kevin, and Robison, Richard (Eds). *East Asia and the Trials of Neo-Liberalism*. Abingdon, Routledge, 2005.

Hill, Hal (Ed.). *The Economic Development of Southeast Asia*. Cheltenham, Edward Elgar Publishing, 2002.

Hill, Ronald. *Southeast Asia: People, Land and Economy*. St Leonards, NSW, Allen & Unwin, 2002.

Hirono, Ryokichi (Ed.). *Asian Development Experience Vol. 3: Regional Co-operation in Asia*. Singapore, Institute of Southeast Asian Studies, 2003.

Ho, Alfred Kuo-liang. *The Far East in World Trade: Developments and Growth since 1945*. New York, F. A. Praeger, 1967.

Ho Khai Leong (Ed.). *Reforming Corporate Governance in Southeast Asia: Economics, Politics, and Regulations*. Singapore, Institute of Southeast Asian Studies, 2005.

ASEAN-Korea Relations: Security, Trade and Community Building. Singapore, Institute of Southeast Asian Studies, 2006.

Connecting and Distancing: Southeast Asia and China. Singapore, Institute of Southeast Asian Studies, 2009.

Ho Khai Leong, and Ku, Samuel C. Y. (Eds). *China and Southeast Asia: Global Changes and Regional Challenges*. Singapore, Institute of Southeast Asian Studies, 2005.

Hoadley, Stephen, and Rüland, Jürgen (Eds). *Asian Security Reassessed*. Singapore, Institute of Southeast Asian Studies, 2006.

Hoare, James E., and Pares, Susan. *A Political and Economic Dictionary of East Asia*. Abingdon, Routledge, 2005.

Holcombe, Charles. *A History of East Asia: From the Origins of Civilization to the Twenty-First Century*. Cambridge, Cambridge University Press, 2010.

Hollingsworth, David Anthony. *The Rise, the Fall, and the Recovery of Southeast Asia's Minidragons: How Can Their History be Lessons We Shall Learn During the Twenty-First Century and Beyond?* Lanham, MD, Lexington Books, 2007.

Hook, Glenn D. *Japan and the Emerging Asia-Pacific Order*. Abingdon, Routledge, 2006.

Hooker, M. Barry (Ed.). *Law and the Chinese in Southeast Asia*. Singapore, Institute of Southeast Asian Studies, 2002.

Hooker, Virginia, and Saikal, Amin (Eds). *Islamic Perspectives on the New Millennium*. Singapore, Institute of Southeast Asian Studies, 2004.

Horowitz, Shale, and Heo, Uk (Eds). *The Political Economy of International Financial Crisis—Interest Groups, Ideologies and Institutions*. Singapore, Institute of Southeast Asian Studies, 2001.

Hotta, Eri. *Pan-Asianism and Japan's War 1931–1945*. New York, Palgrave Macmillan, 2008.

Hu Teh-Wei and Hsieh Chee-Ruey (Eds). *The Economics of Health Care in Asia-Pacific Countries*. Cheltenham, Edward Elgar Publishing, 2002.

Huang, Xiaoming. *Politics in Pacific Asia*. Singapore, Palgrave Macmillan, 2009.

Hutanuwatr, Pracha, and Manivannan, Ramu (Eds). *The Asian Future. Dialogues for Change Vols 1 & 2*. London, Zed Books, 2004.

Hutchison, Jane, and Brown, Andrew (Eds). *Organising Labour in Globalising Asia*. London, Routledge, 2001.

Ikeo, Aiko. (Ed.). *Economic Development in Twentieth-Century East Asia—The International Context*. London, Routledge, 1996.

Inomata, Satoshi (Eds). *Asia Beyond The Global Economic Crisis—The Transmission Mechanism of Financial Shocks*. Cheltenham, Edward Elgar Publishing, 2011.

Islam, Iyanatul, and Hossain, Moazzem (Eds). *Globalisation and the Asia-Pacific: Contested Perspectives and Diverse Experiences.* Cheltenham, Edward Elgar Publishing, 2005.

Islam, Nurul. *Reducing Rural Poverty in Asia.* Binghamton, NY, Haworth Press, 2005.

Ito, Takatoshi. *A Basket Currency for Asia.* Abingdon, Routledge, 2006.

Ito, Takatoshi, and Rose, Andrew K. *The Economic Consequences of Demographic Change in East Asia.* National Bureau of Economic Research, East Asia Seminar on Economics, Vol. 19, Chicago, IL, Chicago University Press, 2010.

Iwanaga, Kazuki. *Women's Political Participation and Representation in Asia: Obstacles and Challenges.* Copenhagen, NIAS Press, 2008.

Janowski, Monica, and Kerlogue, Fiona (Eds). *Kinship and Food in South East Asia.* Copenhagen, Nordic Institute of Asian Studies, 2007.

Johnson, Derek, and Valencia, Mark (Eds). *Piracy in Asia: Status, Issues, and Responses.* Singapore, Institute of Southeast Asian Studies, 2004.

Jomo, K. S. (Ed.). *Tigers in Trouble: Financial Governance, Liberalisation and Crises in East Asia.* London, Zed Books, 1999.

Manufacturing Competitiveness in Asia. London, Routledge Curzon, 2003.

Southeast Asian Paper Tigers? London, RoutledgeCurzon, 2003.

After the Storm: Crisis, Recovery and Sustaining Development in Four Asian Economies. Honolulu, HI, University of Hawaii Press, 2004.

Jomo, K. S., and Folk, Brian C. *Ethnic Business: Chinese Capitalism in Southeast Asia.* London, Routledge, 2003.

Jones, Anthony, and Kim, Byung-Kook (Eds). *Power and Security in Northeast Asia: Shifting Strategies.* Boulder, CO, Lynne Rienner Publishers, 2007.

Jones, David Martin (Ed.). *Globalisation and the New Terror: The Asia Pacific Dimension.* Cheltenham, Edward Elgar Publishing, 2004.

Jones, David Martin, and Smith, M. L. R. *ASEAN and East Asian International Relations.* Cheltenham, Edward Elgar Publishing, 2006.

Kane, John, and Wong, Benjamin (Eds). *Dissident Democrats: The Challenge of Democratic Leadership in Asia.* Singapore, Palgrave Macmillan, 2008.

Kapur, Ashok. *Regional Security Structures in Asia.* London, RoutledgeCurzon, 2002.

Katzenstein, Peter J., and Takashi, Shiraishi (Eds). *Beyond Japan: The Dynamics of East Asian Regionalism.* Ithaca, NY, Cornell University Press, 2006.

Kaup, Katherine Palmer (Ed.). *Understanding Contemporary Asia Pacific.* Boulder, CO, Lynne Rienner Publishers, 2007.

Kawai, Masahiro, and Wignaraj, Ganeshan (Eds). *Asia's Free Trade Agreements: How is Business Responding?* Cheltenham, Edward Elgar Publishing, 2010.

Keat Gin Ooi (Ed.). *Southeast Asia: A Historical Encyclopaedia, From Angkor Wat to Timor.* Oxford, ABC Clio, 2004.

Kesavapany, K. and Lim, Hank. *APEC at 20: Recall, Reflect, Remake.* Singapore, Institute of Southeast Asian Studies, 2009.

Khan, Haider A. *Global Markets and Financial Crises in Asia: Towards a Theory for the 21st Century.* Basingstoke, Palgrave Macmillan, 2004.

Khan, Ilyas. *Underdogs in Overdrive: 10 Insanely Great Ideas For the Asian Techno-preneur.* Singapore, John Wiley & Sons, 2001.

Kidd, John B., and Richter, Frank-Jürgen. *Infrastructure and Productivity in Asia: Political, Financial, Physical and Intellectual Underpinnings.* Basingstoke, Palgrave Macmillan, 2005.

Kiernan, Ben. *Genocide and Resistance in Southeast Asia: Documentation, Denial and Justice in Cambodia and East Timor.* New Jersey, Transaction Publishers, 2008.

Kingsbury, Damien. *South-East Asia—A Political Profile.* Oxford, Oxford University Press, 2nd Edn, 2005.

Kingsbury, Damien (Ed.). *Violence in Between: Conflict and Security in Archipelagic Southeast Asia.* Singapore, Institute of Southeast Asian Studies, 2006.

Kinnvall, Catarina, and Jonsson, Kristina. *Globalization and Democratization in Asia—The Construction of Identity.* London, RoutledgeCurzon, 2002.

Kohama, Hirhisa (Ed.). *Asian Development Experience Vol. 1: External Factors for Asian Development.* Singapore, Institute of Southeast Asian Studies, 2003.

Kohsaka, Akira (Ed.). *Infrastructure Development in the Asia Pacific Region.* Abingdon, Routledge, 2005.

Kratoska, Paul H. (Ed.). *South East Asia.* London, Routledge, 2001.

Kreinin, Mordechai E., and Plummer, Michael G. (Eds). *Economic Integration and Asia—The Dynamics of Regionalism in Europe, North America and the Asia-Pacific.* Cheltenham, Edward Elgar Publishing, 2001.

Kuhonta, Erik Martinez, Slater, Dan, and Vu Tuong (Eds). *Southeast Asia in Political Science: Theory, Region and Qualitative Analysis.* Stanford, CA, Stanford University Press, 2008.

Kumar, Nagesh. *Towards an Asian Economic Community: Vision of a New Asia.* Singapore, Institute of Southeast Asian Studies, 2005.

Lafond, Renald, and Sinha, Chaitali (Eds). *E-Commerce in the Asian Context: Selected Case Studies.* Singapore, Institute of Southeast Asian Studies, 2005.

Latham, A. J. H., and Kawakatsu, Heita (Eds). *Asia-Pacific Dynamism 1550–2000.* London, Routledge, 2000.

Lawson, Stephanie. *Europe and the Asia-Pacific.* London, Routledge, 2002.

Leaman, Oliver (Ed.). *Encyclopedia of Asian Philosophy.* London, Routledge, 2000.

Lee, Chung H. *Financial Liberalization and the Economic Crisis in Asia.* London, RoutledgeCurzon, 2002.

Lee, Grace, and Warner, Malcolm. *The Political Economy of the SARS Epidemic: the Impact on Human Resources in East Asia.* Abingdon, Routledge, 2008.

Lee Hock Guan (Ed.). *Civil Society in Southeast Asia.* Singapore, Institute of Southeast Asian Studies, 2004.

Leifer, Michael. *Dictionary of the Modern Politics of South-east Asia.* London, Routledge, 2000.

Asian Nationalism. London, Routledge, 2000.

Selected Works on Southeast Asia. Singapore, Institute of Southeast Asian Studies, 2005.

Leung, Suiwah, Bingham, Ben, and Davies, Matt (Eds). *Globalization and Development in the Mekong Economies.* Cheltenham, Edward Elgar Publishing, 2010.

Lim, Robyn. *The Geopolitics of East Asia.* London, RoutledgeCurzon, 2003.

Liu Fu-kuo and Régnier, Philippe (Eds). *Regionalism in East Asia.* London, RoutledgeCurzon, 2002.

Lovell, David W. (Ed.). *Asia-Pacific Security: Policy Challenges.* Singapore, Institute of Southeast Asian Studies, 2003.

Low, Linda. *ASEAN Economic Co-operation and Challenges.* Singapore, Institute of Southeast Asian Studies, 2004.

Lowe, Peter. *Contending with Nationalism and Communism: British Policy Towards South-East Asia, 1945–65.* Basingstoke, Palgrave Macmillan, 2009.

Lugg, Amy, and Hong, Mark. *Energy Issues in the Asia-Pacific Region.* Singapore, Institute of Southeast Asian Studies, 2010.

Lukauskas, Arvid J., and Rivera-Batiz, Francisco L. *The Political Economy of the East Asian Crisis and its Aftermath—Tigers in Distress.* Cheltenham, Edward Elgar Publishing, 2001.

Lumsdaine, David Halloran. *Evangelical Christianity and Democracy in Asia.* New York, Oxford University Press, 2008.

MacIntyre, Andrew (Ed.). *Business and Government in Industrialising Asia.* St Leonards, NSW, Allen & Unwin, 2nd Edn, 2001.

Maddison, Angus, Rao, Prasada D. S., and Shepherd, William (Eds). *The Asian Economies in the Twentieth Century.* Cheltenham, Edward Elgar Publishing, 2002.

Mahadevan, Renuka. *The Economics of Productivity in Asia and Australia.* Cheltenham, Edward Elgar Publishing, 2004.

Mah-Hui, Michael Lim and Lim Chin. *Nowhere to Hide: The Great Financial Crisis and Challenges for Asia.* Singapore, Institute of Southeast Asian Studies, 2010.

Mallet, Victor. *The Trouble with Tigers: The Rise and Fall of Southeast Asia.* London, HarperCollins, 1999.

Manning, Robert A. *The Asian Energy Factor: Myths and Dilemmas of Energy, Security and the Pacific Future.* Hampshire, Palgrave, 2001.

Marsh, Ian. *Democratisation, Governance and Regionalism in East and Southeast Asia: A Comparative Study.* Abingdon, Routledge, 2006.

Masuyama, Seiichi, and Vandenbrink, Donna (Eds). *Towards a Knowledge-Based Economy: East Asia's Changing Industrial Geography.* Singapore, Institute of Southeast Asian Studies, 2003.

Masuyama, Seiichi, Vandenbrink, Donna, and Hew, Denis (Eds). *The Development of Capital for East Asia's Economic Future.* Singapore, Institute of Southeast Asian Studies, 2005.

McCargo, Duncan. *Media and Politics in Pacific Asia*. London, Routledge, 2002.

McDougall, Derek. *Asia Pacific in World Politics*. Boulder, CO, Lynne Rienner Publishers, 2006.

McGregor, Andrew. *Southeast Asian Development*. Abingdon, Routledge, 2008.

McKinnon, Ronald I. *Exchange Rates Under the East Asian Dollar Standard: Living with Conflicted Virtue*. Cambridge, MA, MIT Press, 2005.

McLeod, Ross H., and Garnaut, Ross (Eds). *East Asia in Crisis—From Being a Miracle to Needing One?* London, Routledge, 1998.

McNally, Christopher A., and Morrison, Charles E. (Eds). *Asia Pacific Security Outlook: 2002*. Washington, DC, Brookings Institution, 2002.

McTurnan Kahin, George. *Southeast Asia: A Testament*. London, RoutledgeCurzon, 2002.

Means, Gordon P. *Political Islam in Southeast Asia*. Boulder, CO, Lynne Rienner Publishers, 2009.

Medalla, Erlinda (Ed.). *Competition Policy in East Asia*. Abingdon, Routledge, 2005.

Meek, V. Lynn, and Suwanwela, Charas (Eds). *Higher Education, Research and Knowledge in the Asia-Pacific Region*. Basingstoke, Palgrave Macmillan, 2007.

Meyer, Karl, and Brysac, Shareen. *Tournament of Shadows: The Great Game and the Race for Empire in Asia*. London, Little, Brown, 2001.

Midgley, James, and Tang Kwong-Leung (Eds). *Social Policy and Poverty in East Asia—The Role of Social Security*. Abingdon, Routledge, 2009.

Milhaupt, Curtis, Kon-Sik Kim, and Kanda, Hideki (Eds). *Transforming Corporate Governance in East Asia*. Abingdon, Routledge, 2008.

Miller, Michelle Ann (Ed.). *Ethnic and Racial Minorities in Asia: Inclusion or Exclusion?* Abingdon, Routledge, 2011.

Milner, Anthony. *Region, Security and the Return of History*. Singapore, Institute of Southeast Asian Studies, 2003.

The Malays. Singapore, John Wiley & Sons, 2008.

Min Gyo Koo. *Island Disputes and Maritime Regime Building in East Asia*. New York, Springer, 2009.

Miranti, Riyana, and Hew, Denis (Eds). *APEC in the 21st Century*. Singapore, Institute of Southeast Asian Studies, 2004.

Mok, Joshua Ka Ho. *Education Reform and Education Policy in East Asia*. Abingdon, Routledge, 2005.

Moller, Jorgen Orstrom. *How Asia Can Shape the World: From the Era of Plenty to the Era of Scarcities*. Singapore, Institute of Southeast Asian Studies, 2010.

Monfries, John (Ed.). *Different Societies, Shared Futures: Australia, Indonesia and the Region*. Singapore, Institute of Southeast Asian Studies, 2006.

Montes, Manuel F., and Popov, Vladimir V. *The Asian Crisis Turns Global*. Singapore, Institute of Southeast Asian Studies, 1999.

Montesano, Michael J., and Lee Poh Onn (Eds). *Regional Outlook: Southeast Asia 2011–2012*. Singapore, Institute of Southeast Asian Studies, 2011.

Morrison, Charles E., and Perdosa, Eduardo (Eds). *An APEC Trade Agenda? The Political Economy of a Free Trade Area of the Asia Pacific*. Singapore, Institute of Southeast Asian Studies, 2008.

Munataka, Naoko. *Transforming East Asia: The Evolution of Regional Economic Integration*. Washington, DC, Brookings Institution, 2005.

Murphey, Rhoads. *East Asia: A New History*. London, Longman, 2006.

Nakagawa, Junki (Ed.). *Multilateralism and Regionalism in Global Economic Governance: Trade, Investment and Finance*. Abingdon, Routledge, 2011.

Nakamura, Mitsuo, Siddique, Sharon, and Bajunid, Omar Farouk (Eds). *Islam and Civil Society in Southeast Asia*. Singapore, Institute of Southeast Asian Studies, 2001.

Narine, Shaun. *Explaining ASEAN: Regionalism in Southeast Asia*. Boulder, CO, Lynne Rienner Publishers, 2002.

Nathan, K. S., and Kamali, Mohammad Hashim (Eds). *Islam in Southeast Asia: Political, Social and Strategic Challenges for the 21st Century*. Singapore, Institute of Southeast Asian Studies, 2005.

Naya, Seiji, and Plummer, Michael G. *The Economics of the Enterprise for ASEAN Initiative*. Singapore, Institute of Southeast Asian Studies, 2005.

Neary, Ian. *Human Rights in Japan, South Korea and Taiwan*. London, RoutledgeCurzon, 2006.

Neher, Clark. *Southeast Asia in the New International Era*. Boulder, CO, Westview Press, 2002.

Nesadurai, Helen, and Djiwandono, J. Soedradjad (Eds). *Southeast Asia in the Global Economy: Securing Competitiveness and Social Protection*. Singapore, Institute of Southeast Asian Studies, 2009.

Nevins, Joseph, and Peluso, Nancy Lee (Eds). *Taking Southeast Asia to Market: Commodities Nature and People in the Neoliberal Age*. Ithaca, NY, Cornell University Press, 2008.

Odgaard, Liselotte. *The Balance of Power in Asia-Pacific Security: US-China Policies on Regional Order*. Abingdon, Routledge, 2006.

O'Reilly, Dougald J. W. *Early Civilizations of Southeast Asia*. Lanham, MD, AltaMira Press, 2007.

Osborne, Milton. *Southeast Asia—An Introductory History*. St Leonards, NSW, Allen & Unwin, 10th Edn, 2010.

Owen, Norman G. (Ed.). *The Emergence of Modern Southeast Asia: A New History*. Honolulu, HI, University of Hawaii Press, 2005.

Park, Jehoon, Pempel T. J., and Kim Heungchong (Eds)a. *Regionalism, Economic Integration And Security In Asia: A Political Economy Approach*. Cheltenham, Edward Elgar Publishing, 2011.

Park, Yung Chul. *Economic Liberalization and Integration in East Asia: A Post-Crisis Paradigm*. Oxford, Oxford University Press, 2006.

Park, Yung Chul, Ito, Takatoshi, and Wang, Yunjong (Eds). *A New Financial Market Structure for East Asia*. Cheltenham, Edward Elgar Publishing, 2005.

Paul, Erik. *Obstacles to Democratization in Southeast Asia: A Study of the Nation State, Regional and Global Order*. Basingstoke, Palgrave Macmillan, 2010.

Pempel, T. J. (Ed.). *The Politics of the Asian Economic Crisis*. Ithaca, NY, Cornell University Press, 1999.

Remapping East Asia: The Construction of a Region. Ithaca, NY, Cornell University Press, 2004.

Peou, Sorpong. *The ASEAN Regional Forum and Post-Cold War IR Theories—A Case for Constructive Realism?* Singapore, Institute of Southeast Asian Studies, 1999.

Percival, Bronson. *The Dragon Looks South: China and Southeast Asia in the New Century*. Westport, CT, Praeger Security International, 2007.

Petri, Peter A. (Ed.). *Regional Co-operation and Asian Recovery*. Singapore, Institute of Southeast Asian Studies, 2000.

Inclusive, Balanced, Sustained Growth in the Asia-Pacific. Singapore, Institute of Southeast Asian Studies, 2010.

Phillips, David R., and Chan, Alfred C. M. (Eds). *Ageing and Long-term Care: National Policies in the Asia-Pacific*. Singapore, Institute of Southeast Asian Studies, 2003.

Piper, Nicola, and Uhlin, Anders. *Transnational Activism in Asia*. London, Routledge, 2003.

Plummer, Michael G. *The Global Economic Crisis and Its Implications for Asian Economic Cooperation*. Washington, DC, East-West Center, 2010.

Plummer, Michael G., and Chia Siow Yue(Eds). *Realizing the ASEAN Economic Community: A Comprehensive Assessment*. Singapore, Institute of Southeast Asian Studies, 2009.

Prasad, Eswar, Kawai, Masahiro (Eds). *Asian Perspectives on Financial Sector Reforms and Regulation*. Washington, DC, Brookings Institution Press, 2011.

Preston, P. W., and Gilson, Julie (Eds). *The European Union and East Asia—Inter-Regional Linkages in a Changing Global System*. Cheltenham, Edward Elgar Publishing, 2001.

Pye, Lucien W., and Pye, Mary W. *Asian Power and Politics: The Cultural Dimensions of Authority*. Cambridge, MA, Harvard University Press, 2006.

Ravenhill, John. *APEC and the Construction of Pacific Rim Regionalism*. Cambridge, Cambridge University Press, 2002.

Ravi, Srilata, Rutten, Mario, and Goh, Beng-Lan (Eds). *Asia in Europe, Europe in Asia*. Singapore, Institute of Southeast Asian Studies, 2004.

Reilly, Benjamin. *Democracy and Diversity: Political Engineering in the Asia-Pacific*. Oxford, Oxford University Press, 2008.

Rettig, Tobias, and Hack, Karl (Eds). *Colonial Armies in Southeast Asia*. Abingdon, Routledge, 2005.

Rich, Roland. *Pacific Asia in Quest of Democracy*. Boulder, CO, Lynne Rienner Publishers, 2007.

Ricklefs, M. C., et al. *A New History of Southeast Asia*. Basingstoke, Palgrave Macmillan, 2010.

Ries, Philippe. *The Asian Storm—Asia's Economic Crisis Examined*. Tokyo, Tuttle Publishing, 2001.

Rigg, Jonathan. *Southeast Asia—The Human Landscape of Modernization and Development*. London, Routledge, 2002.

Robertson, Justin. *US-Asia Economic Relations.* Abingdon, Routledge, 2008.

Robles, Alfredo C. *The Political Economy of Interregional Relations: ASEAN and the EU (The International Political Economy of New Regionalisms Series),* Burlington, VT, Ashgate, 2004.

Rock, Michael T. *Pollution Control in East Asia: Lessons from Newly Industrializing Economies.* Singapore, Institute of Southeast Asian Studies, 2002.

Rodan, Garry. *Transparency and Authoritarian Rule in Southeast Asia: Singapore and Malaysia.* London, RoutledgeCurzon, 2004.

Rodan, Garry, and Hewison, Kevin (Eds). *Neoliberalism and Conflict in Asia After 9/11.* Abingdon, Routledge, 2005.

Rodan, Garry, Hewison, Kevin, and Robison, Richard (Eds). *The Political Economy of South-East Asia: Conflict, Crises and Change.* Oxford, Oxford University Press, 2001.

Political Economy of South-East Asia: Markets, Power and Contestation. New York, Oxford University Press, 2006.

Rondinelli, Dennis A., and Heffron, John M. (Eds). *Globalization and Change in Asia.* Boulder, CO, Lynne Rienner Publishers, 2007.

Rudd, Kevin. *Building on ASEAN's Success: Towards an Asia Pacific Community.* Singapore, Institute of Southeast Asian Studies, 2009.

Rüland, Jürgen, Jürgenmeyer, Clemens, Nelson, Michael H., and Ziegenhain, Patrick. *Parliaments and Political Change in Asia.* Singapore, Institute of Southeast Asian Studies, 2005.

Rüland, Jürgen, Manske, Eva, and Draguhn, Werner (Eds). *Asia-Pacific Economic Cooperation (APEC)—The First Decade.* London, RoutledgeCurzon, 2002.

Rutton, Mario. *Rural Capitalists in Asia—A Comparative Analysis on India, Indonesia and Malaysia.* Richmond, Curzon Press, 2001.

Sakhuja, Vijay. *Asian Maritime Power in the 21st Century—Strategic Transactions: China, India and Southeast Asia.* Singapore, Institute of Southeast Asian Studies, 2011.

Sally, Razeen. *Southeast Asia in the WTO.* Singapore, Institute of Southeast Asian Studies, 2004.

Saravanamuttu, Johan. *Islam and Politics in Southeast Asia.* Abingdon, Routledge, 2009.

SarDesai, D. R. *Southeast Asia.* Basingstoke, Macmillan Press, 1997.

Southeast Asia: Past and Present. Boulder, CO, Westview Press, 2003.

Southeast Asian History: Essential Readings. Boulder, CO, Westview Press, 2006.

Satyanath, Shanker. *Globalization, Politics, and Financial Turmoil: Asia's Banking Crisis.* Cambridge, Cambridge University Press, 2005.

Saw Swee-Hock, Sheng Lijun, and Chin Kin Wah (Eds). *ASEAN-China Relations: Realities and Prospects.* Singapore, Institute of Southeast Asian Studies, 2005.

Saw Swee-Hock (Ed.). *Managing Economic Crisis in Southeast Asia.* Singapore, Institute of Southeast Asian Studies, 2011.

Saw Swee-Hock and Wong, John (Eds). *Managing Economic Crisis in East Asia.* Singapore, Institute of Southeast Asian Studies, 2010.

Schafferer, Christian. *Election Campaigning in East and Southeast Asia: Globalization of Political Marketing.* Burlington, VT, Ashgate Publishing, 2006.

See Seng Tan and Acharya, Amitav (Eds). *Asia-Pacific Security Cooperation: National Interests and Regional Order.* Armonk, NY, M. E. Sharpe, 2004.

Sen, Rahul. *Free Trade Agreements in Southeast Asia.* Singapore, Institute of Southeast Asian Studies, 2004.

Sen, Rahul (Ed.). *Regional Economic Integration: Case for a Regional Export Credit Agency for Asia.* Singapore, Institute of Southeast Asian Studies, 2005.

Severino, Rodolfo C. *ASEAN and Regionalism.* Singapore, Institute of Southeast Asian Studies, 2005.

Southeast Asia in Search of an ASEAN Community. Singapore, Institute of Southeast Asian Studies, 2006.

The ASEAN Regional Forum. Singapore, Institute of Southeast Asian Studies, 2009.

Sharma, Kishor (Ed.). *Trade Policy, Growth and Poverty in Asian Developing Countries.* London, Routledge, 2003.

Shaw, Daigee, and Liu, Bih Jane. *The Impact Of The Economic Crisis On East Asia: Policy Responses from Four Economies.* Cheltenham, Edward Elgar Publishing, 2011.

Shimomura, Yasutami (Ed.). *Asian Development Experience Vol. 2: The Role of Governance in Asia.* Singapore, Institute of Southeast Asian Studies, 2003.

Sidel, John. *The Islamist Threat in Southeast Asia: a Reassessment.* Singapore, Institute of Southeast Asian Studies, 2007.

Simon, Sheldon W., and Goh, Evelyn (Eds). *China, the United States and South-East Asia: Contending Perspectives on Politics, Security and Economics.* Abingdon, Routledge, 2007.

Singh, Daljit. *Terrorism in South and Southeast Asia in the Coming Decade.* Singapore, Institute of Southeast Asian Studies, 2009.

By Design or Accident: Reflections on Asian Security. Singapore, Institute of Southeast Asian Studies, 2010.

Singh, Daljit, and Salazar, Lorraine C. (Eds). *Southeast Asian Affairs 2006.* Singapore, Institute of Southeast Asian Studies, 2006.

Singh, Shalini (Ed.). *Domestic Tourism in Asia: Diversity and Divergence.* Singapore, Institute of Southeast Asian Studies, 2011.

Sjöholm, Fredrik, and Tongzon, José (Eds). *Institutional Change in Southeast Asia.* Abingdon, Routledge, 2005.

Slater, Dan. *Ordering Power: Contentious Politics and Authoritarian Leviathans in Southeast Asia.* New York, Cambridge University Press, 2010.

Smith, Anthony L. (Ed.). *Southeast Asia and New Zealand: A History of Regional and Bilateral Relations.* Singapore, Institute of Southeast Asian Studies, 2005.

Smith, Heather (Ed.). *The Economic Development of Northeast Asia.* Cheltenham, Edward Elgar Publishing, 2002.

Smith, Paul J. *Terrorism and Violence in Southeast Asia.* Armonk, NY, M. E. Sharpe, 2004.

Smith, R. B. *Changing Visions of East Asia, 1943–93: Transformations and Continuities.* Abingdon, Routledge, 2006.

Communist Indochina. Abingdon, Routledge, 2008.

Pre-communist Indochina. Abingdon, Routledge, 2008.

Snitwongse, Kusuma, and Thompson, Scott (Eds). *Ethnic Conflict in Southeast Asia.* Singapore, Institute of Southeast Asian Studies, 2005.

Solidum, Estrella D. *Politics of ASEAN: An Introduction to Southeast Asian Regionalism.* Singapore, Times Academic Press, 2003.

Spivak, Gayatri Chakravorty. *Other Asias.* Singapore, John Wiley & Sons, 2007.

Steinberg, David Joel (Ed.). *In Search of Southeast Asia—A Modern History (Revised Edn).* Honolulu, HI, University of Hawaii Press, 1987.

St John, Ronald Bruce. *Revolution, Reform and Regionalism in Southeast Asia: Cambodia, Laos and Vietnam.* Abingdon, Routledge, 2009.

Stokhof, Wim, van der Velde, Paul, and Yeo Lay Hwee (Eds). *The Eurasian Space: Far More Than Two Continents.* Singapore, Institute of Southeast Asian Studies, 2004.

Stoler, Andrew, Redden, Jim, and Jackson, Lee Ann (Eds). *Trade and Poverty Reduction in the Asia-Pacific Region: Case Studies and Lessons from Low-income Communities.* Cambridge University Press, 2009.

Stubbs, Richard. *Rethinking Asia's Economic Miracle: The Political Economy of War, Prosperity and Crisis.* Basingstoke, Palgrave Macmillan, 2005.

Sudo, Sueo. *The International Relations of Japan and Southeast Asia—Forging a New Regionalism.* London, Routledge, 2001.

Evolution of ASEAN-Japanese Relations. Singapore, Institute of Southeast Asian Studies, 2005.

Suh, J. J., Katzenstein, Peter J., and Carlson, Allen (Eds). *Rethinking Security in East Asia: Identity, Power, and Efficiency.* Stanford, CA, Stanford University Press, 2004.

Suryadinata, Leo (Ed.). *Nationalism and Globalization: East and West.* Singapore, Institute of Southeast Asian Studies, 2000.

Ethnic Relations and Nation-Building in Southeast Asia. Singapore, Institute of Southeast Asian Studies, 2004.

Southeast Asia's Chinese Businesses in an Era of Globalization: Coping with the Rise of China. Singapore, Institute of Southeast Asian Studies, 2006.

Tan, Andrew T. H. *A Handbook of Terrorism and Insurgency in Southeast Asia.* Cheltenham, Edward Elgar Publishing, 2007.

Taplin, Ruth, and Nowak, Alojzy Z. (Eds). *Intellectual Property, Innovation and Management in Emerging Economies.* Abingdon, Routledge, 2010.

Tarling, Nicholas. *Nations and States in South East Asia.* Cambridge, Cambridge University Press, 1998.

Imperialism in South East Asia. London, Routledge, 2001.

South-East Asia: A Modern History. Oxford, Oxford University Press, 2001.

Nationalism in Southeast Asia. London, Routledge, 2004.

Regionalism in Southeast Asia: To Foster the Political Will. Abingdon, Routledge, 2006.

Southeast Asia and the Great Powers. Abingdon, Routledge, 2009.

Tarling, Nicholas (Ed.). *The Cambridge History of Southeast Asia* (2 vols). Cambridge, Cambridge University Press, 1993.

Corruption and Good Governance in Asia. Abingdon, Routledge, 2nd Edn, 2009.

Taylor, Brendan. *American Sanctions in the Asia-Pacific.* Abingdon, Routledge, 2008.

Than, Mya (Ed.). *ASEAN Beyond the Regional Crisis: Challenges and Initiatives.* Singapore, Institute for Southeast Asian Studies, 2001.

Timmer, Marcel. *The Dynamics of Asian Manufacturing—A Comparative Perspective in the Late Twentieth Century.* Cheltenham, Edward Elgar Publishing, 2000.

Tongzon, Jose L. *The Economies of Southeast Asia—Before and After the Crisis.* Cheltenham, Edward Elgar Publishing, 2002.

Tonts, Matthew, and Siddique, M. A. (Eds). *Globalisation, Agriculture and Development: Perspectives from the Asia-Pacific.* Cheltenham, Edward Elgar Publishing, 2011.

Tow, William T. *Asia-Pacific Strategic Relations: Seeking Convergent Security.* Cambridge, Cambridge University Press, 2002.

Tran Van Hoa (Ed.). *The Asia Recovery—Issues and Aspects of Development, Growth, Trade and Investment.* Cheltenham, Edward Elgar Publishing, 2001.

Competition Policy and Global Competitiveness in Major Asian Economies. Cheltenham, Edward Elgar Publishing, 2003.

Tran Van Hoa and Harvie, Charles. *New Asian Regionalism: Responses to Globalisation and Crises.* New York, Palgrave Macmillan, 2004.

Regional Trade Agreements in Asia. Cheltenham, Edward Elgar Publishing, 2007.

Urata, Shujiro, and Aggarwal, Vinod (Eds). *Bilateral Trade Agreements in the Asia-Pacific: Origins, Evolution, and Implications.* Abingdon, Routledge, 2005.

Urata, Shujiro, Chia Siow Yue and Kimura, Fukunari (Eds). *Multinationals and Economic Growth in East Asia: Foreign Direct Investment, Corporate Strategies and National Economic Development.* Abingdon, Routledge, 2006.

Vicziany, Marika (Ed.). *Controlling Arms and Terror in the Asia Pacific: After Bali and Baghdad.* Cheltenham, Edward Elgar Publishing, 2006.

Vicziany, Marika, Wright-Neville, David, and Lentini, Pete (Eds). *Regional Security in the Asia-Pacific: 9/11 and After.* Cheltenham, Edward Elgar Publishing, 2004.

Wah, Francis Loh Kok, and Öjendal, Joakim (Eds). *Southeast Asian Responses to Globalization: Restructuring Governance and Deepening Democracy.* Singapore, Institute of Southeast Asian Studies, 2005.

Wallace, Ben. *The Changing Village Environment in Southeast Asia.* Abingdon, Routledge, 2005.

Walter, Andrew. *Governing Finance: East Asia's Adoption of International Standards.* Ithaca, NY, Cornell University Press, 2008.

Wang Gungwu. *The Chinese Overseas: From Earthbound China to the Quest for Autonomy.* Cambridge, MA, Harvard University Press, 2000.

Nation-Building: Five Southeast Asian Histories. Singapore, Institute of Southeast Asian Studies, 2005.

Wang, Zhengxu. *Democratization in Confucian East Asia: Citizen Politics in China, Japan, Singapore, South Korea, Taiwan and Vietnam.* New York, Cambria Press, 2008.

Warner, Malcolm. *Culture and Management in Asia.* London, RoutledgeCurzon, 2003.

Weatherbee, Donald E., and Emmers, Ralf. *International Relations in Southeast Asia: The Struggle for Autonomy.* Lanham, MD, Rowman & Littlefield Publishers, 2005.

Weber, Maria. *Reforming Economic Systems in Asia—A Comparative Analysis of China, Japan, South Korea, Malaysia and Thailand.* Cheltenham, Edward Elgar Publishing, 2001.

Wee, C. J. W. L. *Local Cultures and the 'New Asia': The State, Culture, and Capitalism in Southeast Asia.* Singapore, Institute of Southeast Asian Studies, 2002.

Wee, Vivienne (Ed.). *Political Fragmentation in Southeast Asia: Alternative Nations in the Making.* Abingdon, Routledge, 2006.

Weeks, Donna. *The East Asian Security Community.* Abingdon, Routledge, 2009.

Weightman, Barbara A. *Dragons and Tigers: A Geography of South, East and Southeast Asia.* Singapore, John Wiley & Sons, 3rd Edn, 2011.

Weiss, John (Ed.). *Poverty Targeting in Asia.* Manila, Asian Development Bank Institute and Cheltenham, Edward Elgar Publishing, 2005.

Poverty Strategies in Asia: A Growth Plus Approach. Manila, Asian Development Bank Institute and Cheltenham, Edward Elgar Publishing, 2006.

Weiss, Julian (Ed.). *Tigers' Roar—Asia's Recovery and its Impact.* Armonk, NY, M. E. Sharpe, 2001.

Weller, Robert P. (Ed.). *Civil Life, Globalization and Political Change in Asia: Organizing Between Family and State.* Abingdon, Routledge, 2005.

Whiting, Amanda, and Evans, Carolyn (Eds). *Mixed Blessings: Laws, Religions and Women's Rights in the Asia-Pacific Region.* Leiden, Brill, 2006.

Williams, Brad, and Newman, Andrew (Eds). *Japan, Australia and Asia-Pacific Security.* Abingdon, Routledge, 2006.

Winter, Tim, Teo, Peggy, and T. C. Chang (Eds). *Asia on Tour: Exploring the Rise of Asian Tourism.* London, Routledge, 2008.

Woo, Jongseok. *Security Challenges and Military Politics in East Asia: From State Building to Post-Democratization.* New York, Continuum, 2011.

Wu Yanrui. *The Macroeconomics of East Asian Growth.* Cheltenham, Edward Elgar Publishing, 2002.

Yahuda, Michael. *The International Politics of the Asia-Pacific.* Abingdon, Routledge, 3rd Edn, 2011.

Yamazawa, Ippei. *Economic Integration in the Asia Pacific Region.* London, Routledge, 2000.

(Ed.). *Asia Pacific Economic Cooperation (APEC)—Challenges and Tasks for the Twenty-first Century.* London, Routledge, 2000.

Asia-Pacific Economic Cooperation: New Agenda in Its Third Decade. Singapore, Institute of Southeast Asian Studies, 2011.

Yegar, Moshe. *Between Integration and Secession: The Muslim Communities of the Southern Philippines, Southern Thailand, and Western Burma/Myanmar.* Lanham, MD, Lexington Books, 2002.

Yen, Ching-hwang. *The Chinese in Southeast Asia and Beyond.* NJ, World Scientific Publishing, 2008.

Yen, Denis Hew Wei (Ed.). *Brick by Brick: the Building of an ASEAN Economic Community.* Singapore, Asia Pacific Press, 2008.

Yeoh, Brenda S. A., Teo, Peggy, and Huang, Shirlena (Eds). *Gender Politics in the Asia-Pacific Region.* London, Routledge, 2002.

Yeung, Henry Wai-Chung (Ed.). *Handbook of Research on Asian Business.* Cheltenham, Edward Elgar Publishing, 2006.

Young, Adam. *Contemporary Maritime Piracy in Southeast Asia: History, Causes and Remedies.* Singapore, Institute of Southeast Asian Studies, 2008.

Young, Soogil, Choi, Dosoung, Seade, Jesus, and Shirai, Sayuri. *Competition among Financial Centres in Asia-Pacific: Prospects, Benefits, Risks and Policy Challenges.* Singapore, Institute of Southeast Asian Studies, 2009.

Yueh, Linda. *The Future of Asian Trade and Growth: Economic Development with the Emergence of China.* Abingdon, Routledge, 2009.

Zhal, Fan (Ed.). *From Growth to Convergence: Asia's Next Two Decades.* Basingstoke, Palgrave Macmillan, 2009.

Zhang Yumei. *Pacific Asia.* London, Routledge, 2002.

SELECT BIBLIOGRAPHY—PERIODICALS

Acta Asiatica: Bulletin of the Institute of Eastern Culture (Tōhō Gakkai), 2-4-1 Nishi-Kanda, Chiyoda-ku, Tokyo 101-0065 Japan; tel. (3) 3262-7221; fax (3) 3262-7227; e-mail iec@tohogakkai.com; internet www.tohogakkai.com; f. 1961; in English; 2 a year.

Archaeology in Oceania: 116 Darlington Rd, University of Sydney, NSW 2006, Australia; tel. (2) 9351-2666; fax (2) 9351-7488; e-mail arts.oceania@usyd.edu.au; internet www.arts.usyd.edu.au/publications/oceania; f. 1966; archaeology and physical anthropology; available online from 2007; 3 a year; Editor J. Peter White.

Archiv orientální: Journal of African and Asian Studies of the Oriental Institute of the Czech Academy of Sciences, Pod vodárenskou věží 4, 182 08 Prague 8, Czech Republic; tel. (2) 6605-2483; fax (2) 8658-1897; e-mail aror@orient.cas.cz; internet aror.orient.cas.cz; f. 1929; book reviews and notes; contributions in English, French and German; quarterly; Editor Dr Stanislava Vavroušková.

Artibus Asiae: Museum Rietberg Zürich, Gablerstr. 15, 8002 Zürich, Switzerland; tel. (1) 2063131; fax (1) 2063132; e-mail artibus.asiae@zuerich.ch; internet www.artibusasiae.com; in co-operation with the Arthur M. Sackler Gallery, Smithsonian Institution, Washington, DC, USA; f. 1925; Asian art and archaeology; illustrated; 2 a year; Editor-in-Chief Prof. Dr Amy McNair.

Arts of Asia: 803-6 Kowloon Centre, 29–39 Ashley Rd, Kowloon, Hong Kong; tel. 23762228; fax 23763713; e-mail info@artsofasianet.com; internet www.artsofasianet.com; f. 1971; 6 a year; Publr and Editor Tuyet Nguyet.

Arts Asiatiques: Musée National des Arts Asiatiques Guimet, 6 Place d'Iéna, 75116 Paris, France; tel. 1-55-73-31-77; e-mail arts.asiatiques@efeo.net; internet www.museeguimet.fr; f. 1924; annually.

ASEAN Briefing: GPO Box 10874, Hong Kong; fax (USA) (708) 570-7421; politics and economics; monthly.

ASEAN Economic Bulletin—A Journal of Asian and Pacific Economic Affairs: Institute of Southeast Asian Studies, 30 Heng Mui Keng Terrace, Pasir Panjang, Singapore 119614; tel. 67780955; fax 67756259; e-mail publish@iseas.edu.sg; internet www.bookshop.iseas.edu.sg; f. 1968; economic issues in the Asia-Pacific region; Dir K. Kesavapany; Man. Editor Triena Ong.

Asia Pacific Business Review: 4 Park Sq., Milton Park, Abingdon, Oxon, OX14 4RN, United Kingdom; tel. (20) 7017-6000; fax (20) 7017-6336; e-mail tf.enquiries@tandf.co.uk; internet www.tandf.co.uk/journals; 4 a year; Editors Chris Rowley, Malcolm Warner.

Asia Pacific Consensus Forecasts: Consensus Economics Inc, 53 Upper Brook St, London, W1K 2LT, United Kingdom; tel. (20) 7491-3211; fax (20) 7409-2331; internet www.consensuseconomics.com; monthly; Editor Suyin Kan.

Asia Pacific Journal of Education: 4 Park Sq., Milton Park, Abingdon, Oxon, OX14 4RN, United Kingdom; tel. (20) 7017-6000; fax (20) 7017-6336; e-mail journals.orders@tandf.co.uk; internet www.tandf.co.uk/journals; publ. on behalf of the National Institute of Education, Singapore; 4 a year; Exec. Editors Jason Tan, David Hogan.

Asia Pacific Journal of Tourism Research: 4 Park Sq., Milton Park, Abingdon, Oxon, OX14 4RN, United Kingdom; tel. (20) 7017-6000; fax (20) 7017-6336; e-mail tf.enquiries@tandf.co.uk; internet www.tandf.co.uk/journals; official journal of the Asia Pacific Tourism Asscn; 4 a year; Editor-in-Chief Kaye Chon.

Asia-Pacific Review: 4 Park Sq., Milton Park, Abingdon, Oxon, OX14 4RN, United Kingdom; tel. (20) 7017-6000; fax (20) 7017-6336; e-mail tf.enquiries@tandf.co.uk; internet www.tandf.co.uk/journals; f. 1994; 2 a year; Editor Terri Nii.

Asia Pacific Viewpoint: Institute of Geography, Victoria University of Wellington, Box 600, Wellington, New Zealand; tel. (4) 472-1000, ext. 5029; fax (4) 495-5127; e-mail apv@vuw.ac.nz; internet www.blackwellpublishing.com; f. 1996 (to replace *Pacific Viewpoint*); 3 a year; Man. Editor Dr Warwick E. Murray.

Asiamoney: Euromoney Institutional Investor (Jersey) Ltd, 5/F Printing House, 6 Duddell St, Central, Hong Kong; tel. 29128081; fax (20) 28656225; e-mail richard.morrow@asiamoney.com; internet www.asiamoney.com; monthly; Editor Richard Morrow.

Asian Affairs: Journal of the Royal Society for Asian Affairs, 2 Belgrave Sq., London, SW1X 8PJ, United Kingdom; tel. (20) 7235-5122; fax (20) 7259-6771; e-mail info@rsaa.org.uk; internet www.rsaa.org.uk; covers economic, cultural and political matters relating to the Near and Middle East, Central Asia, South and South-East Asia, and the Far East; 3 a year; Editor Barney Smith.

Asian Ethnicity: 4 Park Sq., Milton Park, Abingdon, Oxon, OX14 4RN, United Kingdom; tel. (20) 7017-6000; fax (20) 7017-6336; e-mail journals.orders@tandf.co.uk; internet www.tandf.co.uk/journals; f. 2000; 3 a year; Editor-in-Chief Prof. Chih-yu Shih.

Asian Journal of Communication: 4 Park Sq., Milton Park, Abingdon, Oxon, OX14 4RN, United Kingdom; tel. (20) 7017-6000; fax (20) 7017-6336; e-mail tf.enquiries@tandf.co.uk; internet www.tandf.co.uk/journals/rajc; f. 1990; issues related to communications; 6 a year; Editor Kuan-hsing Chen.

Asian Journal of Political Science: 4 Park Sq., Milton Park, Abingdon, Oxon, OX14 4RN, United Kingdom; tel. (20) 7017-6000; fax (20) 7017-6336; e-mail journals.orders@tandf.co.uk; internet www.tandf.co.uk/journals; sponsored by the Department of Political Science, National University of Singapore; 3 a year; Editor M. Shamsul Haque.

Asian-Pacific Economic Literature: Crawford School of Economics and Government, Australian National University, Canberra, ACT 0200, Australia; tel. (2) 6125-0407; fax (2) 6125-8448; e-mail apel@anu.edu.au; abstracting and survey journal; 2 a year; Editor Prof. Ron Duncan.

Asian Perspective: Institute for Far Eastern Studies, Kyungnam University, 28–42 Samchung-dong, Chongno-ku, Seoul 110-230, Republic of Korea; tel. (2) 3700-0725; fax (2) 3700-0707; e-mail ifes@kyungnam.ac.kr; internet www.ifes.kyungnam.ac.kr; f. 1977; regional and international affairs; 4 a year; Editor-in-Chief Melvin Gurtov.

Asian Population Studies: 4 Park Sq., Milton Park, Abingdon, Oxon, OX14 4RN, United Kingdom; tel. (20) 7017-6000; fax (20) 7017-6336; e-mail ariaps@nus.edu.sg; internet www.tandf.co.uk/journals; f. 2005; Asia Research Institute, National University of Singapore; 3 a year; Editor Prof. Gavin Jones (National University of Singapore).

Asian Profile: POB 1211, Metrotown Regional Post Office, Burnaby, BC V5H 4J8, Canada; tel. (604) 8211321; fax (604) 2760813; e-mail info@asianresearchservice.com; internet www.asianresearchservice.com; f. 1973; multi-disciplinary study of Asian affairs; 6 a year; Editor Nelson Leung.

Asian Security: 4 Park Sq., Milton Park, Abingdon, Oxon, OX14 4RN, United Kingdom; tel. (20) 7017-6000; fax (20) 7017-6336; e-mail enquiry@tandf.co.uk; internet www.tandf.co.uk/journals; f. 2005; 3 a year; Editors Devin T. Hagerty, Michael R. Chambers, Amy L. Freedman.

Asian Studies: Asian Center, University of the Philippines, Diliman, Quezon City, Metro Manila 1101, Philippines; tel. (2) 9261841; fax (2) 9261821; e-mail asiancenter@ac.upd.edu.ph; annually.

Asian Studies Review: Asian Studies Association, Australian National University, Canberra, ACT 0200, Australia; e-mail asr_admin@anu.edu.au; internet asaa.asn.au/publications/asr.php; journal; 4 a year; Editor Assoc. Prof. Peter Jackson.

Asian Survey: Institute of East Asian Studies, University of California, Rm 419, 2223 Fulton St, Berkeley, CA 94720-2318, USA; tel. (510) 643-4117; fax (510) 643-7062; e-mail asiansurvey@berkeley.edu; f. 1961; every 2 months; Editor Lowell Dittmer.

Asiatische Studien / Etudes Asiatiques: Peter Lang AG, Internationaler Verlag der Wissenschaften, Hochfeldstrasse 32, CH-3012 Bern, Switzerland; tel. (31) 306-1717; fax (31) 306-1727; e-mail info@peterlang.com; internet www.peterlang.com; journal of the Swiss Asia Society; Editor R. H. Gassmann; Euelstrasse 76, 8408 Winterthur, Switzerland; tel. (1) 634-3181; fax (1) 634-4921; e-mail asiengesellschaft@oas.uzh.ch; internet www.sagw.ch/asiengesellschaft; 4 a year.

ASIEN (The German Journal on Contemporary Asia): Deutsche Gesellschaft für Asienkunde eV (German Association for Asian Studies), Rothenbaumchaussee 32, 20148 Hamburg, Germany; tel. (40) 445891; fax (40) 4107945; e-mail post@asienkunde.de; internet www.asienkunde.de; f. 1981; quarterly; Editor Günter Schucher.

Australian Aboriginal Studies Journal: Aboriginal Studies Press, AIATSIS, GPOB 553, Canberra 2601, ACT; tel. (2) 6246-1183; fax (2) 6261-4288; e-mail asp@aiatsis.gov.au; internet www.aiatsis.gov.au/asj/asj.html; 2 a year; Editor Dr Cressida Fforde.

Australian Geographer: Geographical Society of New South Wales Inc, POB 162, Ryde, NSW 1680, Australia; tel. (2) 9807-3586; fax (2) 9807-3589; e-mail geog@idx.com.au; internet www.gsnsw.org.au; f. 1928; 3 a year; Editors Assoc. Prof. JAMES FORREST, Dr GEOFF HUMPHREYS, Dr PAULINE MCGUIRK.

Australian Historical Studies: 4 Park Sq., Milton Park, Abingdon, Oxon, OX14 4RN, United Kingdom ; tel. (20) 7017-6000; fax (20) 7017-6336; e-mail ahs-history@unimelb.edu.au; histories of Australia, New Zealand and the Pacific region; 3 a year; Editors Prof. STUART MACINTYRE, Assoc. Prof. SHURLEE SWAIN.

Australian Journal of International Affairs: Stephen House, 32 Thesiger Court, Deakin, ACT 2600, Australia; tel. (2) 6282-2133; fax (2) 6285-2334; e-mail ceo@aiia.asn.au; internet www.aiia.asn.au; f. 1947; 5 a year; Editor Prof. ANDREW O'NEIL (e-mail andrew.oneil@-flinders.edu.au).

Australian Journal of Politics and History: Wiley-Blackwell, 155 Cremorne St, Richmond, Vic 3121, Australia; e-mail iward@mailbox .uq.edu.au; f. 1955; Australia and modern Europe; 3 a year; Editors IAN WARD, ANDREW BONNELL.

BCA China Analyst: 1002 Sherbrooke St West, Suite 1600, Montréal, QC H3A 3L6, Canada; tel. (514) 499-9706; fax (514) 499-9709; e-mail circ@bcapub.com; trends in economic conditions, assessment of investment opportunities and risks in North and South-East Asia; monthly; Chair. and Editor-in-Chief J. ANTHONY BOECKH.

Beijing Review: 24 Baiwanzhuang Lu, Beijing 100037, People's Republic of China; tel. (10) 68996252; fax (10) 68326628; e-mail contact@bjreview.com.cn; internet www.bjreview.com.cn; f. 1958; current affairs; in English, French, Spanish, German and Japanese; weekly; Editor-in-Chief LII HAIBO.

Beiträge zur Japanologie: Institut für Ostasienwissenschaften der Universität Wien, Japanologie, AAKH-Campus, Hof 2, Spitalgasse 2–4, 1090 Vienna, Austria; tel. (1) 4277-43801; fax (1) 4277-9438; e-mail japanologie.ostasien@univie.ac.at; internet www.univie.ac .at/Japanologie; regular; Editor Dr SEPP LINHART.

BIISS Journal: Bangladesh Institute of International & Strategic Studies (BIISS), 1/46 Old Elephant Rd, Eskaton, Dhaka 1000, Bangladesh; tel. (2) 8312609; fax (2) 8312625; e-mail dgbiiss@biiss .org; internet biiss.org; f. 1978; quarterly; Chief Editor Maj.-Gen. GOLAM MOHAMMAD.

BOFIT Weekly: Bank of Finland, 3rd Floor, POB 160, FIN-00101, Helsinki, Finland; tel. (10) 831-2268; fax (10) 831-2294; e-mail bofit@ bof.fi; internet www.bof.fi/bofit; f. 2001; economic news incl. China; in English; available online; Editor SEIJA LAINELA.

Boletín del Centro de Estudios de Asia Oriental: Universidad Autónoma de Madrid, 28049 Madrid, Spain; tel. (91) 397-4112; fax (91) 397-4123; e-mail asociación.orientalistas@uam.es; annually.

Bulletin de l'Ecole Française d'Extrême-Orient (BEFEO): Ecole Française d'Extrême-Orient, 22 ave du Président Wilson, 75116 Paris, France; tel. 1-53-70-18-60; fax 1-53-70-87-60; internet www .efeo.fr; f. 1901; annually.

Bulletin of Indonesian Economic Studies: Arndt-Corden Dept of Economics, Crawford School, College of Asia and the Pacific, Australian National University, Canberra, ACT 0200, Australia; tel. (2) 6125-2370; fax (2) 6125-3700; e-mail tf.enquiries@tandf.co.uk; internet www.tandf.co.uk/journals/cbie; f. 1965; predominantly Indonesian economy, but also law, govt and politics, demography, environment, education and health; 3 a year; Editor ROSS H. MCLEOD.

Bulletin of the School of Oriental and African Studies: School of Oriental and African Studies, University of London, Thornhaugh St, Russell Sq., London, WC1H 0XG, United Kingdom; tel. (20) 7898-4064; fax (20) 7898-4849; e-mail bulletin@soas.ac.uk; internet www .soas.ac.uk; publ. by Cambridge University Press for the School of Oriental and African Studies, University of London; f. 1917; 3 a year; Editor Dr ULRICH PAGEL.

Business News IndoChina: POB 9794, Hong Kong; tel. 28800307; fax 28561184; provides independent information about business in Viet Nam, Cambodia, Laos and Myanmar; Publr JOHN COPE.

China Economic Journal: 4 Park Sq., Milton Park, Abingdon, Oxon, OX14 4RN, United Kingdom; tel. (20) 7017-6000; fax (20) 7017-6336; e-mail tf.enquiries@tandf.co.uk; internet www.tandf.co.uk/journals; 3 a year; Editor FENG LU.

China Economic Quarterly: Dragonomics Advisory Services, 6A Hilltop Plaza, 49 Hollywood Rd Central, Hong Kong; tel. 28698363; fax 28698131; e-mail editorial@dragonomics.net; internet www.dragonomics.net; f. 1997; quarterly; analysis of the Chinese economy for business professionals, diplomats and academics; Man. Editor ARTHUR KROEBER.

The China Journal: Contemporary China Centre, Dept of Political and Social Change, College of Asia and the Pacific, Australian National University, Canberra, ACT 0200, Australia; tel. (2) 6125-4790; fax (2) 6125-9047; e-mail ccc@anu.edu.au; f. 1979; 2 a year; Editors ANDREW KIPNIS, LUIGI TOMBA.

China and North East Asia Monitor: Senator House, 85 Queen Victoria St, London, EC4V 4AB, United Kingdom; tel. (20) 7248-0468; fax (20) 7248-0467; e-mail subs@businessmonitor.com; internet www.asiamonitor.com; Publrs RICHARD LONDESBOROUGH, JONATHAN FEROZE.

The China Quarterly: School of Oriental and African Studies, University of London, Thornhaugh St, Russell Sq., London, WC1H 0XG, United Kingdom; tel. (20) 7898-4063; fax (20) 7898-4849; e-mail chinaq@soas.ac.uk; internet www.journals.cambridge.org/jid_CQY; f. 1960; all aspects of 20th century China, including Taiwan and the overseas Chinese; quarterly; Editor JULIA STRAUSS.

China Watch: Orbis Publications LLC, 1924 47th St NW, Washington, DC 20007, USA; tel. (202) 298-7936; fax (202) 298-7938; e-mail orbis@orbischina.com; internet www.orbischina.com; politics, business and economy; monthly; Editor DEREK SCISSORS.

Chinese Cross Currents: Macau Ricci Institute, Av. Cons. Ferreira d'Almeida 95E, Macao; tel. 28532536; fax 28568274; e-mail currents@ riccimac.org; internet www.riccimac.org; f. 2004; quarterly; in Chinese and English; Editor YVES CAMUS.

The Chinese Economy: M. E. Sharpe Inc, 80 Business Park Drive, Armonk, NY 10504, USA; tel. (914) 273-1800; fax (914) 273-2106; e-mail custserve@mesharpe.com; internet www.mesharpe.com; f. 1967; translations from Chinese economics journals and official party publications; 6 a year; Editor HUNG GAY FUNG.

Chinese Education and Society: M. E. Sharpe Inc, 80 Business Park Drive, Armonk, NY 10504, USA; tel. (914) 273-1800; fax (914) 273-2106; e-mail custserv@mesharpe.com; internet www.mesharpe.com; f. 1968; translations from Chinese sources; surveys and information about the Chinese educational system; every 2 months; Editors STANLEY ROSEN, GERARD A. POSTIGLIONE.

Chinese Journal of Communication: 4 Park Sq., Milton Park, Abingdon, Oxon, OX14 4RN, United Kingdom; tel. (20) 7017-6000; fax (20) 7017-6336; e-mail tf.enquiries@tandf.co.uk; internet www .tandf.co.uk/journals/rcjc; f. 2008; Chinese communications studies; quarterly; Editor HAO XIAOMING.

The Chinese Journal of International Politics: Oxford University Press, Great Clarendon St, Oxford, United Kingdom, OX2 6DP; tel. (1865) 353907; fax (1865) 353485; e-mail jnls.cust.serv@ oxfordjournals.org; internet www.oxfordjournals.org; f. 2006; analysis of Chinese foreign policy and regional relations; Editor-in-Chief YAN XUETONG.

Chinese Law and Government: M. E. Sharpe Inc, 80 Business Park Drive, Armonk, NY 10504, USA; tel. (914) 273-1800; fax (914) 273-2106; e-mail custserv@mesharpe.com; internet www.mesharpe.com; f. 1968; translations of Chinese scholarly works and political policy documents; every 2 months; Editor JAMES TONG.

Chinese Sociology and Anthropology: M. E. Sharpe Inc, 80 Business Park Drive, Armonk, NY 10504, USA; tel. (914) 273-1800; fax (914) 273-2106; e-mail custserv@mesharpe.com; internet www.mesharpe .com; f. 1968; translations of contemporary studies of social issues; quarterly; Editors GREGORY GULDIN, ZHOU DAMING.

Chinese Studies in History: M. E. Sharpe Inc, 80 Business Park Drive, Armonk, NY 10504, USA; tel. (914) 273-1800; fax (914) 273-2106; e-mail custserv@mesharpe.com; internet www.mesharpe.com; f. 1967; translations of articles; quarterly; Editor QINGJIA EDWARD WANG.

CHINOPERL Papers: The Conference on Chinese Oral and Performing Literature, c/o Prof. Wenwei Du, Box 120, Vassar College, Poughkeepsie, NY 12603, USA; tel. (845) 437-7502; fax (914) 437-7833; e-mail wedu@vassar.edu; f. 1969; Chinese oral and performing literature; annually; Pres. WENWEI DU.

Cina: Istituto Italiano per l'Africa e l'Oriente, Via Ulisse Aldrovandi 16, 00197 Rome, Italy; fax (06) 328558; f. 1956; art, science and thought in contemporary China; annually; Editor Prof. LIONELLO LANCIOTTI.

Comparative Sociology: Brill, POB 9000, 2300 PA, Leiden, Netherlands; tel. (71) 5353500; fax (71) 5317532; e-mail cs@brill.nl; internet www.brill.nl; f. 2002; 6 a year; Editor DAVID SCIULLI.

Contemporary Chinese Thought: M. E. Sharpe Inc, 80 Business Park Drive, Armonk, NY 10504, USA; tel. (914) 273-1800; fax (914) 273-2106; e-mail custserv@mesharpe.com; internet www.mesharpe.com; f. 1969; translations of articles from Chinese sources; quarterly; Editor CARINE DEFOORT.

The Contemporary Pacific: Center for Pacific Islands Studies, University of Hawaii at Manoa, 1890 East West Rd, 215 Moore Hall, Honolulu, HI 96822, USA.

Contemporary Southeast Asia—A Journal of International and Strategic Issues: Institute of Southeast Asian Studies, 30 Heng Mui Keng Terrace, Pasir Panjang, Singapore 119614; tel. 68702447; fax 67756259; e-mail pubsunit@iseas.edu.sg; internet bookshop.iseas.edu.sg; 3 a year; Chair. K. KESAVAPANY; Editor IAN STOREY.

The Copenhagen Journal of Asian Studies: Asia Research Centre, Copenhagen Business School, Dalgas Have 15, DK-2000 Frederiksberg, Denmark ; tel. 38-15-34-09; e-mail cjas@cbs.dk; internet www.cjas.dk; f. 1987; 2 a year; Editor KJELD ERIK BRØDSGAARD.

Critical Asian Studies: 4 Park Sq., Milton Park, Abingdon, Oxon, OX14 4RN, United Kingdom; tel. (20) 7017-6000; fax (20) 7017-6336; e-mail journals.orders@tandf.co.uk; internet www.tandf.co.uk/journals; f. 1969; 4 a year; Man. Editor Dr THOMAS P. FENTON.

The Developing Economies: Nihon Boeki Shinkokiko Ajia Keizai Kenkyusho (Institute of Developing Economies, Japan External Trade Organization), 3-2-2 Wakaba, Mihama-ku, Chiba-shi, Chiba 261-8545, Japan; tel. (43) 299-9500; fax (43) 299-9726; e-mail journal@ide.go.jp; internet www.ide.go.jp/English/Publish/Periodicals/De; f. 1962; in English; quarterly; Editor SHUJIRO URATA.

Development Bulletin: Development Studies Network, Research School of Social Sciences, Australian National University, Canberra, ACT 0200, Australia; tel. (2) 6125-2466; fax (2) 6125-9785; e-mail devnetwork@anu.edu.au; internet devnet.anu.edu.au; development issues in the Pacific and South-East Asia; quarterly; Dir PAMELA THOMAS.

Development and Socio-Economic Progress: Afro-Asian People's Solidarity Organization, 89 Abdel Aziz Al-Saoud St, POB 11559, El Malek El Saleh, Cairo, Egypt; tel. (2) 3636081; fax (2) 3637361; e-mail aapso@idsc.net.eg; 3 a year; Exec. Editor E. A. VIDYASKERA; Editor-in-Chief NOURI ABDEL RAZZAK HUSSEIN.

Dong Bang Hak Chi (The Journal of Korean Studies): Institute of Korean Studies, Yonsei University, Seodaemun-gu, Seoul 120-749, Republic of Korea; tel. (2) 2123-3502; fax (2) 365-0937; f. 1948; in Korean; quarterly; Dir SUL SUNG GYUNG.

East and West: Istituto Italiano per l'Africa e l'Oriente, Via Ulisse Aldrovandi 16, 00197 Rome, Italy; fax (6) 3225348; internet www.isiao.it; f. 1950; in English; quarterly; Editor GHERARDO GNOLI.

East Asian Review: Institute for East Asian Studies, 508-143 Jungnung 2-dong, Sungbuk-gu, Seoul 136-851, Republic of Korea; tel. (2) 917-4976; fax (2) 919-5360; e-mail eastasia@ieas.or.kr; internet www.ieas.or.kr; f. 1978; quarterly; Editor KIM HYEONG-KI.

Economic Record: Economics M251, University of Western Australia, 35 Stirling Highway, Crawley, WA 6009, Australia; tel. (8) 6488-2924; fax (8) 6488-1035; e-mail Paul.Miller@uwa.edu.au; f. 1925; journal of Economic Soc. of Australia; quarterly; Editor Prof. PAUL MILLER; circ. 3,500.

Estudios de Asia y Africa: Centre for Asian and African Studies, El Colegio de México, Camino al Ajusco 20, Pedregal de Sta Teresa, México DF 10740, Mexico; tel. (5) 5449-3000, ext. 3116; fax (5) 5645-0464; e-mail rcornejo@colmex.mx; f. 1966; quarterly; Chief Editor ROMER CORNEJO.

Harvard Journal of Asiatic Studies: Harvard-Yenching Institute, 2 Divinity Ave, Cambridge, MA 02138, USA; tel. (617) 495-2758; fax (617) 495-7798; e-mail jfhsmith@fas.harvard.edu; internet www.hjas.org; f. 1936; 2 a year; Editor JOANNA HANDLIN SMITH.

Hitotsubashi Journal of Arts and Sciences: Japan Publication Trading Co Ltd, POB 5030, Tokyo International, Tokyo 100-3191, Japan; fax (3) 3292-0410; e-mail serials@jptco.co.jp; f. 1960; annually; Editors KATSUMI HASHINAWA, HAJIME MACHIDA.

Hitotsubashi Journal of Economics: Japan Publication Trading Co Ltd, POB 5030, Tokyo International, Tokyo 100-3191, Japan; fax (3) 3292-0410; e-mail serials@jptco.co.jp; f. 1960; 2 a year; Editors N. ABE, J. ISHIKAWA, T. IWAISAKO, M. SATO.

Hong Kong Law Journal: Faculty of Law, The University of Hong Kong, Hong Kong; tel. 28592939; fax 25463475; e-mail hklj@hku.hk; internet www.hklj.com; f. 1971; 3 a year; Editor RICK GLOFCHESKI.

Indonesia and the Malay World: 4 Park Sq., Milton Park, Abingdon, Oxon, OX14 4RN, United Kingdom; tel. (20) 7017-6000; fax (20) 7017-6336; e-mail tf.enquiries@tandf.co.uk; internet www.tandf.co.uk/journals/cimw; f. 1973; languages, literature, art, archaeology, history, religion, anthropology, performing arts, cinema and tourism of the region of maritime South-East Asia; 3 a year; Man. Editors PAULINE KHNG, Dr BEN MURTAGH.

The Indonesian Quarterly: Centre for Strategic and International Studies, Jalan Tanah Abang III/23-27, Jakarta 10160, Indonesia; tel. (21) 5365-4601; fax (21) 5365-4607; e-mail csis@csis.or.id; internet www.csis.or.id; f. 1972; Editor HADI SOESASTRO.

Inter-Asia Cultural Studies: 4 Park Sq., Milton Park, Abingdon, Oxon, OX14 4RN, United Kingdom; tel. (20) 7017-6000; fax (20) 7017-6336; e-mail journals.orders@tandf.co.uk; internet www.tandf.co.uk/journals/riac; f. 2000; 4 a year; Editors CHEN KUAN-HSING, CHUA BENG-HUAT.

International Journal (IJ): 45 Willcocks St, Box 210, Toronto, ON M5S 1C7, Canada; tel. (416) 977-9000; fax (416) 946-7319; e-mail ij@canadianinternationalcouncil.org; internet www.internationaljournal.ca; f. 1946; quarterly; Man. Editor RIMA BERNS-MCGOWN; Co-Editors DAVID G. HAGLUND, JOSEPH T. JOCKEL.

International Journal of Asian Studies (IJAS): Cambridge University Press, The Edinburgh Bldg, Shaftesbury Rd, Cambridge, CB2 8RU, United Kingdom; tel. (1223) 326070; fax (1223) 325150; e-mail journals@cambridge.org; internet journals.cambridge.org/asi; f. 2004; 2 a year; Editor-in-Chief Dr TAKESHI HAMESHITA.

Internationales Asienforum: Arnold-Bergstraesser-Institut, Windausstr. 16, 79110 Freiburg, Germany; tel. (761) 888780; fax (761) 8887878; e-mail abifr@abi.uni-freiburg.de; internet www.arnold-bergstraesser.de; f. 1970; political and socio-economic developments, Asian studies; 4 or 2 double editions a year.

Japan Forum: 4 Park Sq., Milton Park, Abingdon, Oxon, OX14 4RN, United Kingdom; tel. (20) 7017-6000; fax (20) 7017-6336; e-mail tf.enquiries@tandf.co.uk; internet www.tandf.co.uk/journals/rjfo; f. 1989; Japanese archaeology, language, literature, philosophy, culture, history, economics, politics, international relations and law; quarterly; Sr Editor ANGUS LOCKYER.

Japan Quarterly: Asahi Shimbun Publishing Co, 5-3-2 Tsukiji, Chuo-ku, Tokyo 104-8011, Japan; tel. (3) 5541-8699; fax (3) 5541-8700; e-mail jpnqtrly@mx.asahi-np.co.jp; f. 1954; in English; quarterly; Editor-in-Chief TAKENOBU ETSUO.

Japanese Annual of International Law: The International Law Association of Japan, Kenkyushitsu, Faculty of Law, University of Tokyo, 3-1 Hongo 7-chome, Bunkyo-ku, Tokyo 113, Japan; f. 1957; Editors-in-Chief Prof. SOJI YAMAMOTO, AKIRA KOTERA.

The Japanese Economy: M. E. Sharpe Inc, 80 Business Park Drive, Armonk, NY 10504, USA; tel. (914) 273-1800; fax (914) 273-2106; e-mail custserv@mesharpe.com; internet www.mesharpe.com; f. 1972; examines the practical implications of current economic policies; est. to create dialogue among economists, political scientists and other professionals; translations from Japanese sources; 4 a year; Editor DAVID J. FLATH.

Japanese Studies: 4 Park Sq., Milton Park, Abingdon, Oxon, OX14 4RN, United Kingdom; tel. (20) 7017-6000; fax (20) 7017-6336; e-mail tf.enquiries@tandf.co.uk; internet www.tandf.co.uk/journals/cjst; f. 1981; multidisciplinary post-war politics and society, international relations, environmental issues, business and economics, literature, history, legal system, gender studies, Japanese media, film and popular culture, and Japanese language teaching; 3 a year; Editor JUDITH SNODGRASS.

Journal of the American Oriental Society: American Oriental Society, Hatcher Graduate Library, University of Michigan, Ann Arbor, MI 48109-1205, USA; tel. (734) 647-4760; f. 1842; quarterly; Editor-in-Chief STEPHANIE JAMISON, University of California, Los Angeles, CA 90095-1540, USA.

Journal of the Asia Pacific Economy: 4 Park Sq., Milton Park, Abingdon, Oxon, OX14 4RN, United Kingdom; tel. (20) 7017-6000; fax (20) 7017-6336; e-mail tf.enquiries@tandf.co.uk; internet www.tandf.co.uk/journals/rjap; f. 1996; economic, historical, political, social and cultural aspects of the economies of the Asia Pacific region; quarterly; Man. Editor Prof. DAVID LIM.

Journal of Asian History: Harrassowitz Verlag, 65174 Wiesbaden, Germany; tel. (611) 530901; fax (611) 530999; e-mail service@harrassowitz.de; internet www.harrassowitz.de; f. 1967; in English, French, German, Russian; 2 a year; Editor DENIS SINOR, Goodbody Hall, Indiana University, Bloomington, IN 47405, USA; tel. (812) 855-0959; fax (812) 855-7500; e-mail sinord@indiana.edu.

Journal of Asian Public Policy: 4 Park Sq., Milton Park, Abingdon, Oxon, OX14 4RN, United Kingdom; tel. (20) 7017-6000; fax (20) 7017-6336; e-mail tf.enquiries@tandf.co.ukjournals.orders@tandf.co.uk; internet www.tandf.co.uk/journals; 3 a year; Editors KA HO MOK, IAN HOLLIDAY, RAY FORREST.

Journal of Asian Studies: JAS Editorial Office, c/o Prof. Jeffrey N. Wasserstrom, Dept of History, 546 Murray Krieger Hall, University of California, Irvine, CA 92697, USA; tel. (949) 824-6521; fax (949) 824-2865; e-mail jas@journalofasianstudies.org; internet www.asian-studies.org; f. 1941; selected articles on history, arts, social sciences, philosophy and contemporary issues; extensive book reviews; in English; quarterly; Editor Prof. JEFFREY N. WASSERSTROM.

Journal Asiatique: La Société Asiatique, 3 rue Mazarine, 75006 Paris, France; tel. and fax 1-44-41-43-14; f. 1822; covers all phases of Oriental research; 2 a year; Editor ANNA SCHERRER-SCHAUB.

Journal of Australian Studies: University of Queensland Press, POB 6042, St Lucia, Qld 4067, Australia; tel. (7) 3365-2452; fax (7) 3365-1988; e-mail rosiec@uqp.uq.edu.au; internet www.uqp.uq.edu.au; 4 a year; Editors MELISSA HARPER, MARTIN CROTTY.

Journal of Chinese Economic and Business Studies: 4 Park Sq., Milton Park, Abingdon, Oxon, OX14 4RN, United Kingdom; tel. (20) 7017-6000; fax (20) 7017-6336; e-mail tf.enquiries@tandf.co.uk; internet www.tandf.co.uk/journals; f. 2003; official journal of the Chinese Economic Asscn; 3 a year; Editor-in-Chief XIAMING LIU.

Journal of Chinese Philosophy: Blackwell Publishing Co, POB 11071, Honolulu, HI 96828, USA; f. 1974; quarterly; Editor CHENG CHUNG-YING.

Journal of Contemporary Asia: 4 Park Sq., Milton Park, Abingdon, Oxon, OX14 4RN, United Kingdom; tel. (20) 7017-6000; fax (20) 7017-6336; e-mail tf.enquiries@tandf.co.uk; internet www.tandf.co.uk/journals; f. 1970; social, political and economic affairs; in English; quarterly; Editors PETER LIMQUECO, KEVIN HEWISON.

Journal of Contemporary China: 4 Park Sq., Milton Park, Abingdon, Oxon, OX14 4RN, United Kingdom; tel. (20) 7017-6000; fax (20) 7017-6336; e-mail tf.enquiries@tandf.co.uk; internet www.tandf.co.uk/journals/cjcc; f. 1992; Chinese economics, political science, law, culture, literature, business, history, international relations, sociology and other social sciences and humanities; 5 a year; Editor SUISHENG ZHAO.

Journal of the Economic and Social History of the Orient: Brill Academic Publishing, POB 9000, 2300 PA Leiden, Netherlands; tel. (71) 5353500; fax (71) 5317532; internet www.brill.nl; f. 1957; in English, French and German; 4 a year; Editor-in-Chief JOS GOMMANS, Dept of South and Central Asian Studies, Kern Inst., POB 9515, 2300 RA Leiden; email jesho@let.leidenuniv.nl.

Journal of the Hong Kong Branch of the Royal Asiatic Society: GPO Box 3864, Hong Kong; tel. and fax 28137500; e-mail membership@royalasiaticsociety.org.hk; internet www.royalasiaticsociety.org.hk; f. 1960; Hong Kong and South China studies, especially pre-1946 local history, ethnography, etc; annually; Hon. Editor PETER CUNICH; Pres. ROBERT NIELD.

Journal of International and Area Studies: Institute of International Affairs, Graduate School of International Studies, Seoul National University, 56-1 Shinrim-dong San, Gwanak-ku, Seoul 151-742, Republic of Korea; tel. (2) 880-8975; fax (2) 874-7368; internet iia.snu.ac.kr; international affairs, including Korean studies; 2 a year; Editor Prof. KIM CHONG-SUP.

Journal of Islamic Studies: Oxford Centre for Islamic Studies, George St, Oxford, OX1 2AR, United Kingdom; tel. (1865) 278730; fax (1865) 248942; e-mail islamic.studies@oxcis.ac.uk; internet jis.oxfordjournals.org; all aspects of Islam; 3 a year; Editor Dr FARHAN AHMAD NIZAMI.

Journal of Japanese Studies: Society for Japanese Studies, University of Washington, Box 353650, Seattle, WA 98195-3650, USA; tel. (206) 543-9302; fax (206) 685-0668; e-mail jjs@uw.edu; internet depts.washington.edu/jjs; f. 1974; 2 a year; Co-Editors MARIE ANCHORDOGUY, KEVIN M. DOAK.

Journal of the Malaysian Branch of the Royal Asiatic Society: 4B, 2nd Floor, Jalan Kemuja, Bangsar, 59000 Kuala Lumpur, Malaysia; tel. (3) 22835345; fax (3) 22822458; e-mail mbras@tm.net.my; f. 1877; 2 a year; Hon. Editor Dr CHEAH BOON KHENG.

Journal of the Oriental Society of Australia (JOSA): c/o Hon. Sec., Oriental Society of Australia, Room 544, Brennan MacCallum A18, School of Languages and Cultures, University of Sydney, Sydney, NSW 2006, Australia; tel. (2) 9351-4716; fax (2) 9351-2319; e-mail susan.wiles@uni.sydney.edu.au; internet sydney.edu.au/arts/publications/JOSA/journals.htm; f. 1961; annually; Editor SUE WILES.

Journal of Oriental Studies: Dept of Chinese, University of Hong Kong, Pokfulam Rd, Hong Kong; tel. 28597923; fax 28581334; e-mail joshkusu@hkucc.hku.hk; internet www.hku.hk/chinese/jos; 2 a year; Chief Editor Prof. C. Y. SIN.

Journal of Pacific History: Australian National University, Canberra, ACT 0200, Australia; tel. (2) 6125-3145; fax (2) 6125-5525; e-mail tf.enquiries@tandf.co.uk; internet www.tandf.co.uk/journals/cjph; f. 1966; 3 a year; Exec. Editor VICKI LUKER.

Journal of the Pacific Society: Pacific Society, 2-6-4 Kinakawacho, Chiyoda-ku, Tokyo, Japan.

Journal of the Polynesian Society: c/o Dept of Maori Studies, University of Auckland, PB 92019, Auckland, New Zealand; tel. (9) 373-7999 ext. 87463; fax (9) 373-7409; e-mail jps@auckland.ac.nz; internet www.arts.auckland.ac.nz/ant/jps/polsoc.html; f. 1892; study of the peoples of the Pacific area; quarterly; Editor JUDITH HUNTSMAN; circ. 1,000.

Journal of the Royal Asiatic Society of Great Britain and Ireland: 14 Stephenson Way, London, NW1 2HD, United Kingdom; tel. (20) 7388-4539; fax (20) 7391-9429; e-mail info@royalasiaticsociety.org; internet www.royalasiaticsociety.org; f. 1823; covers all aspects of oriental research; 4 a year; Editor Dr SARAH ANSARI.

Journal of the Siam Society: 131 Soi 21 (Asoke), Thanon Asokemontri, Bangkok 10110, Thailand; tel. (2) 661-6470; fax (2) 258-3491; e-mail info@siam-society.org; internet www.siam-society.org; f. 1904; most articles in English; also in Thai, French and German; at least 1 a year; Hon. Editor Dr CHRISTOPHER J. BAKER.

Journal of Southeast Asian Studies: Dept of History, National University of Singapore, 11 Arts Link, Singapore 117570; tel. 65166670; fax 67742528; e-mail hisjseas@nus.edu.sg; f. 1970; 3 a year; Editor MUN CHEONG YONG.

Jurnal Undang-Undang/Journal of Malaysian and Comparative Law: c/o Faculty of Law, University of Malaya, 50603 Kuala Lumpur, Malaysia; tel. (3) 79676511; fax (3) 79573239; e-mail jmcl@um.edu.my; internet www.um.edu.my/law/jmcl.htm; f. 1974; in English and Malay; annually; Gen. Editor Assoc. Prof. Dr CHIU MEI YONG.

Kansai University Review of Business: Kansai University, Suita, Osaka, Japan; annually; Editor TOSHIAKI KAMEI.

Kansai University Review of Economics: Kansai University, Suita, Osaka, Japan; annually; Editor YASUO MURATA.

Keio Economic Studies: Keio Economic Society, 2-15-45 Mita, Minato-ku, Tokyo 108-8345, Japan; tel. (3) 3453-4511; fax (3) 5427-1578; f. 1963; 1 a year; Editor Prof. COLIN MCKENZIE.

Korea Observer: The Institute of Korean Studies, CPO Box 3410, Seoul 100-634, Republic of Korea; tel. (2) 569-5574; fax (2) 564-1190; f. 1968; quarterly; Editor EUN HO LEE.

Kyoto University Economic Review: Faculty of Economics, Kyoto University, Sakyo-ku, Kyoto, Japan; f. 1926; 2 a year.

LAWASIA: Law Association for Asia & the Pacific, GPOB 980, Brisbane, Qld 4001, Australia; tel. (7) 3222-5888; fax (7) 3222-5850; e-mail lawasia@lawasia.asn.au; internet www.lawasia.asn.au; f. 1966; legal issues related to Asia and the Pacific; annually; Editors Dr CRAIG FORREST, Dr ANTHONY CASSIMATIS.

Melanesian Law Journal: Faculty of Law, University of Papua New Guinea, POB 317, University 134, NCD, Papua New Guinea; tel. 3267516; fax 3267187; e-mail Law.Publications@upng.ac.pg; f. 1971; annually; Editor G. LINGE.

Modern Asian Studies: Cambridge University Press, The Edinburgh Bldg, Shaftesbury Rd, Cambridge, CB2 8RU, United Kingdom; tel. (1223) 326070; e-mail modernasianstudies@cambridge.org; internet www.journals.cambridge.org/ASS; f. 1967; quarterly; Editor Dr JOYA CHATTERJI.

Modern China: Sage Publications Inc, 2455 Teller Rd, Newbury Park, CA 91320, USA; tel. (805) 499-0721; fax (805) 499-0871; e-mail huang@history.ucla.edu; f. 1975; history and social sciences; quarterly; Editor PHILIP C. C. HUANG.

Mongolian Studies: The Mongolia Society, 322 Goodbody Hall, Indiana University, 1011 E 3rd St, Bloomington, IN 47405-7005, USA; tel. (812) 855-4078; fax (812) 855-7500; e-mail monsoc@indiana.edu; internet www.mongoliasociety.org; f. 1974; Mongolia and Inner Asia of all periods; Journal Editor Dr ALICIA CAMPI.

Monumenta Nipponica: Sophia University, 7-1 Kioi-cho, Chiyoda-ku, Tokyo 102-8554, Japan; tel. (3) 3238-3544; fax (3) 3238-3835; e-mail mnoffice@sophia.ac.jp; internet monumenta.cc.sophia.ac.jp; f. 1938; studies in Japanese culture; quarterly; Editor KATE WILDMAN NAKAI.

Monumenta Serica: Arnold-Janssen-Strasse 20, 53757 St Augustin, Germany; tel. (2241) 237431; fax (2241) 237486; e-mail institut@monumenta-serica.de; internet www.monumenta-serica.de; f. 1935; journal of oriental studies; articles and book reviews on traditional Chinese culture; annually; Editor ROMAN MALEK.

Le Muséon: Université Catholique de Louvain, Institut Orientaliste, place Blaise-Pascal 1, B-1348 Louvain-la-Neuve, Belgium; tel. (10) 473793; fax (10) 472001; e-mail lemuseon@uclouvain.be; internet www.fltr.ucl.ac.be/FLTR/GLOR/ORI/LeMuseon.htm; f. 1881; oriental studies; 2 double vols a year; Pres. Prof. B. COULIE; Editor Prof. A. SCHMIDT.

Oceania: 116 Darlington Rd, University of Sydney, Sydney, NSW 2006, Australia; tel. (2) 9351-2666; fax (2) 9351-7488; e-mail arts.oceania@sydney.edu.au; internet www.arts.usyd.edu.au/publications/oceania/oceania1.htm; f. 1930; anthropology; 3 vols a year; Editors Dr NEIL MACLEAN, Dr JADRAN MIMICA.

Oriens Extremus: Zeitschrift für Sprache, Kunst und Kultur des Länder des Fernen Ostens, Harrassowitz Verlag, 65174 Wiesbaden, Germany; tel. (611) 530901; fax (611) 530999; e-mail verlag@harrassowitz.de; f. 1954; in German and English; annually; Editor BERND EBERSTEIN.

Pacific Affairs: Ste. 376-1855 West Mall, Vancouver, BC V6T 1Z2, Canada; tel. (604) 822-4534; fax (604) 822-9452; e-mail enquiry@pacificaffairs.ubc.ca; internet www.pacificaffairs.ubc.ca; f. 1928; current political, economic, social and diplomatic issues of the Asia-Pacific region; research articles, book reviews; quarterly; Editor Dr LYNN HYUNG-GU; Man. Editor CAROLYN GRANT.

Pacific Connection: Pacific Cooperation Foundation, 660 Great South Rd, Central Park Business Centre, Bldg 10, Level 3, Ellerslie, POB 74084, Greenland, Auckland, New Zealand; tel. (9) 969-1494; fax (9) 969-1495; e-mail info@pcf.org.nz; internet www.pcf.org.nz; political, economic, social and development issues in the Pacific region; 2 a year; CEO MARKERITA POUTASI.

Pacific Economic Bulletin: Crawford School, The Australian National University, Canberra, ACT 0200, Australia; tel. (2) 6125-8258; fax (2) 6125-8448; e-mail peb@anu.edu.au; internet peb.anu.edu.au; f. 1986; 3 a year; Editors RON DUNCAN, MAREE TAIT.

Pacific Historical Review: 487 Cramer Hall, Portland State University, Portland, OR 97207-0751, USA; tel. (503) 725-8230; fax (503)

L

M

N

O

P

R

S

T

U

Index of Territories